Collins



Collins COBUILD

# Inglés/Español Diccionario Para Estudiantes Latinoamericanos:

English/Spanish Student's Dictionary of American English

HEINLE
CENGAGE Learning™

Australia • Brazil • Japan • Korea • Mexico • Singapore • Spain • United Kingdom • United States

HEINLE
CENGAGE Learning™

Collins | COBUILD

**Collins COBUILD Inglés/Español Diccionario Para Estudiantes Latinoamericanos:**
**English/Spanish Student's Dictionary of American English**

**Heinle**
President: Dennis Hogan
Editorial Director: Joe Dougherty
Publisher: Sherrise Roehr
Development Editor: Katherine Carroll
Director of Global Marketing: Ian Martin
Executive Marketing Manager: Jim McDonough
Product Marketing Manager: Katie Kelley
Director of Content and Media Production: Michael Burggren
Content Project Manager: Dawn Marie Elwell
Asset Development Coordinator: Noah Vincelette
Sr. Frontlist Buyer: Mary Beth Hennebury
Editors: Grant Barrett, Catherine Weller
Front and End Matter Typeset: Parkwood Composition Service, Inc.
Illustration and Photography: See pgs 1280-1282
Cover Layout: Linda Beaupre



**Heinle**
25 Thomson Place
Boston, MA 02210
USA

Cengage Learning products are represented in Canada by Nelson Education, Ltd.

Visit Heinle online at **elt.heinle.com**

Visit our corporate website at **www.cengage.com**

**Collins COBUILD**
Founding Editor-in-Chief: John Sinclair
Publisher: Elaine Higgleton
Project Manager: James Flockhart
For the English text
Contributors: Sandra Anderson, Carol Braham, Katharine Coates, Rosalind Combley, Robert Grossmith, Penny Hands, Lucy Hollingworth, Alison Macaulay, Enid Pearsons, Elizabeth Potter, Laura Wedgeworth
For the Spanish Text
Project Co-ordinator and Consultant: Patrick Goldsmith
Contributors: Liliana Andrade Llanas
Guillermina del Carmen Cuevas Mesa
Magdalena Palencia Castro
Mario Alfonso Zamudio Vega
Computing Support by Thomas Callan
Typeset by Wordcraft



**Harper Collins Publishers**
Westerhill Road
Bishopbriggs
Glasgow
G64 2QT
Great Britain

**www.collins.co.uk**



Library of Congress Control Number: 2007904769

Book
ISBN 13: 978-1-4240-1961-8
ISBN 10: 1-4240-1961-3
CD-ROM
ISBN 13: 978-1-4240-1960-1
ISBN 10: 1-4240-1960-5
Book + CD-ROM
ISBN 13: 978-1-4240-1962-5
ISBN 10: 1-4240-1962-1

Printed in China
1 2 3 4 5 6 7 13 12 11 10 09 08

# Contents

Acknowledgements

The publishers would like to acknowledge the following for their invaluable contribution to the original COBUILD concept:

John Sinclair
Patrick Hanks
Gwyneth Fox
Richard Thomas

Stephen Bullion, Jeremy Clear, Rosalind Combley, Susan Hunston, Ramesh Krishnamurthy, Rosamund Moon, Elizabeth Potter

Jane Bradbury, Joanna Channell, Alice Deignan, Andrew Delahunty, Sheila Dignen, Gill Francis, Helen Liebeck, Elizabeth Manning, Carole Murphy, Michael Murphy, Jonathan Payne, Elaine Pollard, Christina Rammell, Penny Stock, John Todd, Jenny Watson, Laura Wedgeworth, John Williams

We would like to acknowledge the assistance of the many hundreds of individuals and companies who have kindly given permission for copyright material to be used in the Bank of English™. The written sources include many national and regional newspapers in Britain and overseas; magazines and periodical publishers; and book publishers in Britain, the United States and Australia. Extensive spoken data has been provided by radio and television broadcasting companies; research workers at many universities and other institutions; and numerous individual contributors. We are grateful to them all.

---

Consultant
Paul Nation

Reviewers—USA
Lorenza Lara
Denver Public Schools
Denver, Colorado

Jeanette E. Page
Kennett School District
Kennett Square, Pennsylvania

Linda Skroback-Heisler
Clark County School District
Las Vegas, Nevada

John Sullivan
ELL East Region Coordinator
East Region Center
Las Vegas, Nevada

Katia Valdeos
Hernando High School
Brooksville, Florida

Reviewers—International
Hugh Walter Acuña-Barié
Language Link American English
Buenos Aires, Argentina

Calvin L. Bailey
Language Link American English
Buenos Aires, Argentina

Monica Imirtzian
Instituto Susini
Buenos Aires, Argentina

Silvana Kuskunov
Saint George's College North
Buenos Aires, Argentina

# John Sinclair

## Founding Editor-in-Chief, Collins COBUILD Dictionaries

## 1933-2007

John Sinclair was Professor of Modern English Language at the University of Birmingham for most of his career; he was an outstanding scholar, one of the very first modern corpus linguists, and one of the most open-minded and original thinkers in the field. The COBUILD project in lexical computing, funded by Collins, revolutionized lexicography in the 1980s, and resulted in the creation of the largest corpus of English language texts in the world.

Professor Sinclair personally oversaw the creation of this very first electronic corpus, and was instrumental in developing the tools needed to analyze the data. Having corpus data allowed Professor Sinclair and his team to find out how people really use the English language, and to develop new ways of structuring dictionary entries. Frequency information, for example, allowed him to rank senses by importance and usefulness to the learner (thus the most common meaning should be put first); and the corpus highlights collocates (the words which go together), information which had only been sketchily covered in previous dictionaries. Under his guidance, his team also developed a full-sentence defining style, which not only gave the user the sense of a word, but showed that word in grammatical context.

When the first *Collins COBUILD Dictionary of English* was published in 1987, it revolutionized dictionaries for learners, completely changed approaches to dictionary-writing, and led to a new generation of corpus-driven dictionaries and reference materials for English language learners.

Professor Sinclair worked on the Collins COBUILD range of titles until his retirement, when he moved to Florence, Italy and became president of the Tuscan Word Centre, an association devoted to promoting the scientific study of language. He remained interested in dictionaries until his death, and the Collins COBUILD range of dictionaries remains a testament to his revolutionary approach to lexicography and English language learning. Professor Sinclair will be sorely missed by everyone who had the great pleasure of working with him.

# Benefits of Semibilingual Dictionary

Collins COBUILD and Heinle are pleased to offer a new type of dictionary for learners of English. The *Collins COBUILD Inglés/Español Diccionario Para Estudiantes Latinoamericanos: English/Spanish Student's Dictionary of American English* is a semibilingual dictionary designed for intermediate level learners of English.

- This semibilingual dictionary includes all the features of a COBUILD monolingual dictionary, such as full sentence definitions and corpus-based examples.
- Additionally, for learners who feel they would benefit from access to Spanish translations, they are included for all definitions, senses, and examples.
- The Spanish translations are presented within the same entry as the English text but in italic and underlined for easy reference.
- Spanish translations are included to complement the English material and provide additional support to the learner when they encounter a difficult word or expression.
- The index lists the translations found in the dictionary and directs the learner, in Spanish, to the relevant English entry.

Thus users have all the information on meaning and usage typically found in COBUILD dictionaries, but with plenty of support in Spanish.

# Guide to Key Features

Through a collaborative initiative, Collins COBUILD and Heinle are co-publishing a dynamic new line of learners dictionaries offering unparalleled pedagogy and learner resources.

The *Collins COBUILD Inglés/Español Diccionario Para Estudiantes Latinoamericanos: English/Spanish Student's Dictionary of American English* is specially designed for Spanish speaking learners of English who need the extra support of their native language. This bilingual learner's dictionary provides Spanish translations for all definitions, senses, and examples to complement the English material and to provide additional support to the learner when they encounter a difficult word or expression.

With innovations such as Definitions*PLUS* and vocabulary builders, the *Collins COBUILD Inglés/Español Diccionario Para Estudiantes Latinoamericanos: English/Spanish Student's Dictionary of American English* transforms the learner's dictionary from an occasional reference into the ultimate resource and must-have dictionary for language learners. The definitions have been created using a controlled vocabulary, and each definition has been reviewed by a team of classroom teachers to ensure that they are appropriate for learners at the intermediate level.

## Definitions*PLUS*

- **Collocations:** Each definition is written using the high-frequency words native speakers naturally use with the target word.
- **Grammar:** Each definition includes naturally occurring grammatical patterns to improve accurate language use.
- **Natural English:** Each definition is a model of how to use the language appropriately.

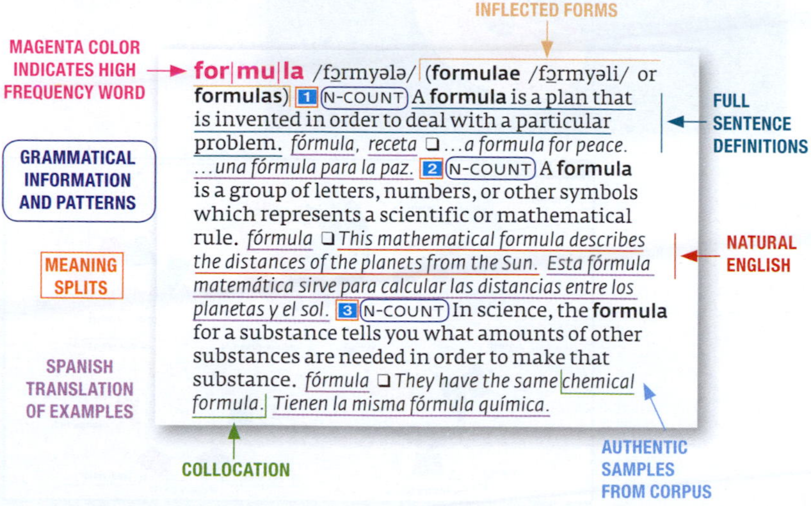
INFLECTED FORMS
MAGENTA COLOR INDICATES HIGH FREQUENCY WORD
GRAMMATICAL INFORMATION AND PATTERNS
MEANING SPLITS
SPANISH TRANSLATION OF EXAMPLES
for|mu|la /fɔrmyələ/ (formulae /fɔrmyəli/ or formulas) 1 N-COUNT A formula is a plan that is invented in order to deal with a particular problem. fórmula, receta ❑ ...a formula for peace. ...una fórmula para la paz. 2 N-COUNT A formula is a group of letters, numbers, or other symbols which represents a scientific or mathematical rule. fórmula ❑ This mathematical formula describes the distances of the planets from the Sun. Esta fórmula matemática sirve para calcular las distancias entre los planetas y el sol. 3 N-COUNT In science, the formula for a substance tells you what amounts of other substances are needed in order to make that substance. fórmula ❑ They have the same chemical formula. Tienen la misma fórmula química.
FULL SENTENCE DEFINITIONS
NATURAL ENGLISH
COLLOCATION
AUTHENTIC SAMPLES FROM CORPUS

BANK of ENGLISH

The Bank of English™ is the original and the most current computerized corpus of authentic American English. This robust research tool was used to create each definition with language appropriate for intermediate level learners. All sample sentences are drawn from the rich selection that the corpus offers which also allows for level appropriate sentences.

### Vocabulary Builders

Over 2,400 pedagogical features encourage curiosity and exploration, which in turn builds the learner's bank of active and passive vocabulary knowledge. The "Vocabulary Builders" outlined here enhance vocabulary acquisition, increase language fluency, and improve accurate communication. They provide the learner with a greater depth and breadth of knowledge of the English language. The *Collins COBUILD Inglés/Español Diccionario Para Estudiantes Latinoamericanos: English/Spanish Student's Dictionary of American English* offers a level of content and an overall learning experience unmatched in other dictionaries.

**"Picture Dictionary" boxes** illustrate vocabulary and concepts. The words are chosen for their usefulness in an academic setting, frequently showing a concept or process that benefits from a visual presentation.

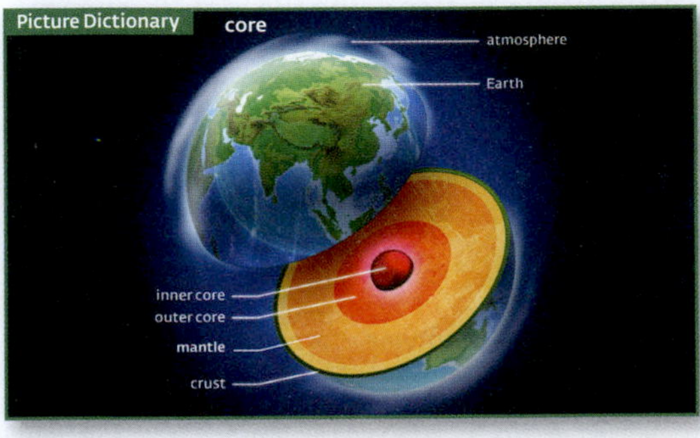


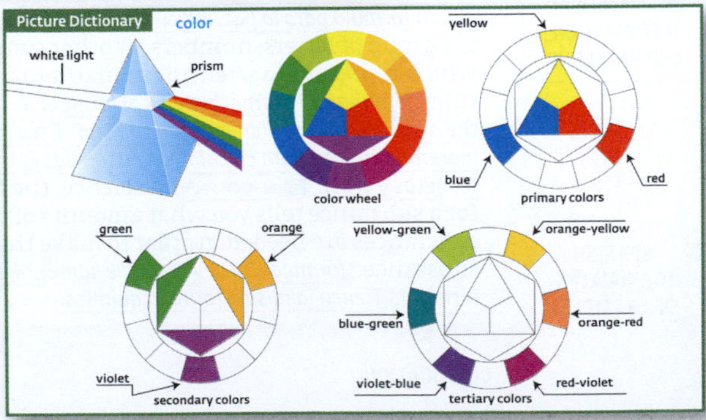

**"Word Webs"** present topic-related vocabulary through encyclopedia-like readings combined with stunning art, creating opportunities for deeper understanding of the language and concepts. All key words in bold are defined in the dictionary. Upon looking up one word, learners discover other related words that draw them further into the dictionary and the language. The more sustained time learners spend exploring words, the greater and richer their language acquisition is. The "Word Webs" encourage language exploration.

**Word Web** spice

While studying the use of **spices** in cooking, scientists found that many spices can help prevent disease. Bacteria can grow quickly on food and cause serious illnesses in humans. The researchers found that many spices kill bacteria. For example, **garlic**, **onion**, allspice, and oregano kill almost all common **germs**. **Cinnamon**, tarragon, cumin, and **chili peppers** also stop about 75% of bacteria. And even common, everyday **black pepper** kills about 25% of all germs. The scientists also found that food is connected to climate. **Spicy** food is common in hot climates. **Bland** food is common in cold climates.

**Word Web** wave

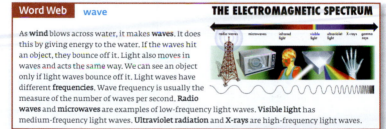

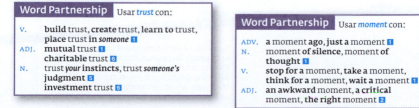

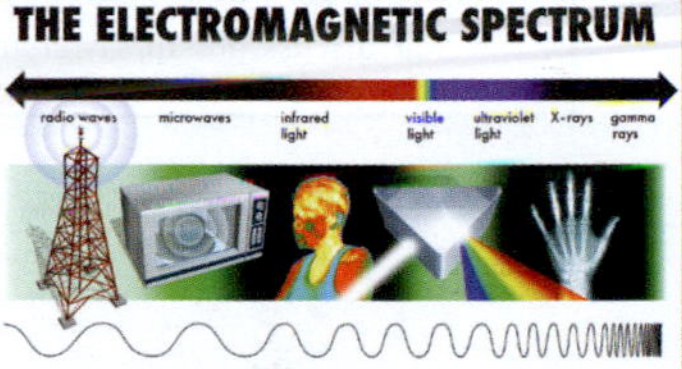


As **wind** blows across water, it makes **waves**. It does this by giving energy to the water. If the waves hit an object, they bounce off it. Light also moves in waves and acts the same way. We can see an object only if light waves bounce off it. Light waves have different **frequencies**. Wave frequency is usually the measure of the number of waves per second. **Radio waves** and **microwaves** are examples of low-frequency light waves. **Visible light** has medium-frequency light waves. **Ultraviolet radiation** and **X-rays** are high-frequency light waves.

Chosen based on frequency in the Bank of English™, **"Word Partnerships"** show high-frequency word patterns, giving the complete collocation with the headword in place to clearly demonstrate use. The numbers refer the student to the correct meaning within the definition of the word that collocates with the headword.

**Word Partnership** Usar *trust* con:

V. **build** trust, **create** trust, **learn to** trust, **place** trust **in** ***someone*** 1
ADJ. **mutual** trust 1
**charitable** trust 6
N. trust ***your*** **instincts**, trust ***someone's*** **judgment** 5
**investment** trust 6

**Word Partnership** Usar *moment* con:

ADV. a moment **ago**, **just a** moment 1
N. moment **of silence**, moment **of thought** 1
V. **stop for a** moment, **take a** moment, **think for a** moment, **wait a** moment 1
ADJ. **an awkward** moment, **a critical** moment, **the right** moment 2

**"Word Links"** exponentially increase language awareness by showing how words are built in English, something that will be useful for learners in all areas of academic work as well as in daily communication. Focusing on prefixes, suffixes, and word roots, each "Word Link" provides a simple definition of the building block and then gives three examples of it used in a word. Providing three examples encourages learners to look up these words to further solidify understanding.

> **Word Link** *port ≈ carrying : export, import, portable*

> **Word Link** *geo ≈ earth : geography, geology, geothermal energy*

**"Thesaurus"** entries offer both synonyms and antonyms for high frequency words. An extra focus on synonyms offers learners an excellent way to expand vocabulary knowledge and usage by directing them to other words they can research in the dictionary. The numbers refer the student to the correct meaning within the definition of the headword.

> **Thesaurus** *talk* Ver también:
>
> N. argument, conversation, dialogue, discussion, interview, negotiation; (*ant.*) silence 1
>
> V. chat, discuss, gossip, say, share, speak, tell; (*ant.*) listen 1

> **Thesaurus** *difficult* Ver también:
>
> ADJ. challenging, demanding, hard, tough; (*ant.*) easy, simple, uncomplicated 1 disagreeable, irritable; (*ant.*) accommodating, cooperative 2

**"Usage"** notes highlight explain shades of meaning, clarify cultural references, and highlight important grammatical information.

> **Usage** **less** and **fewer**
>
> *Less* is used to describe general amounts (or noncount nouns). *Less snow fell in December than in January*. *Fewer* is used to describe amounts of countable items. *Maria is working fewer hours this semester*.

> **Usage** **one** and **you**
>
> Sometimes *one* is used to refer to any person or to people in general, but it sounds formal: *One has to be smart about buying a computer*. In everyday English, use *you* instead of *one*: *You should only call 911 in an emergency*.

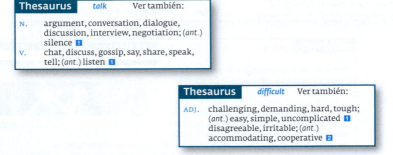

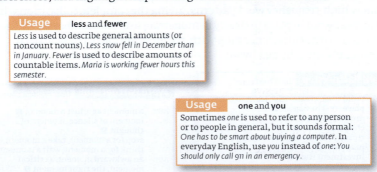

## CD-ROM

A valuable enhancement to the learning experience, the *Collins COBUILD Inglés/Español Diccionario Para Estudiantes Latinoamericanos: English/Spanish Student's Dictionary of American English* CD-ROM offers learners a fast and simple way to explore words and their meanings while working on a computer.

- **Search** definitions, sample sentences, word webs, and picture dictionary boxes.
- **"PopUp" Dictionary**: Find the definition of a word while working in any computer application.
- **Audio pronunciation with record and playback** provides pronunciation practice.
- **"My Dictionary"** allows learners to create a personalized tool by adding their own words, definitions, and sample sentences.
- **Bookmarks** allow learners to save and organize vocabulary. There are 105 bookmark folders already created with topic related vocabulary to act as a springboard for vocabulary learning.

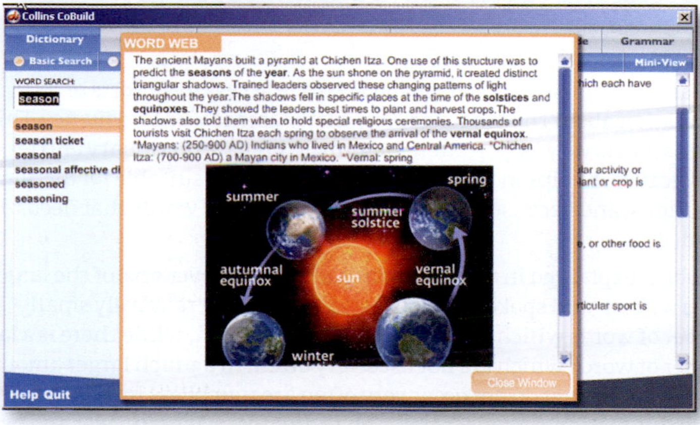


By using the resources found in this volume, learners will discover that the *Collins COBUILD Inglés/Español Diccionario Para Estudiantes Latinoamericanos: English/Spanish Student's Dictionary of American English* is something that they want to delve into and spend time exploring, not just something to flip through for a quick answer. As they investigate options for words that will best serve their individual communicative needs at any given point, learners will find more opportunities for learning than they have ever seen in a traditional reference tool. This will become their ultimate resource and partner in their language learning journey.

# Introduction

A dictionary is probably the single most important reference book that a student of English can buy. The *Collins COBUILD Inglés/Español Diccionario Para Estudiantes Latinoamericanos: English/Spanish Student's Dictionary of American English* is a new type of dictionary. It is especially designed for Latin American students who already have a good working knowledge of English, but who may not be entirely comfortable using a monolingual English dictionary. All the features of a monolingual dictionary are included, with Spanish translations provided for all senses, examples, and explanatory terms. The dictionary also includes an index which lists alphabetically the translations found in the dictionary and which directs you to the relevant English entry through the medium of Spanish.

Like all COBUILD dictionaries, the *Collins COBUILD Inglés/Español Diccionario Para Estudiantes Latinoamericanos: English/Spanish Student's Dictionary of American English* is based on a huge database of text, both written and spoken, called The Bank of English™. At this printing, The Bank of English™ contains over 650 million words, and it is the basis of all the statements that COBUILD makes about the language. It allows the dictionary editors to study the way the language works, and shows the patterns and systems of the English language.

The Bank of English™ gives fast and accurate access to all sorts of information about the language. One major area is word frequency. This information is very important in helping to prepare dictionary entries, both because it helps in the choice of words that are suitable for dictionary definitions, and because it provides a sensible list of words that need to be included.

The words explained in this dictionary account for over 90% of the language that is written and spoken. That is because there is a relatively small number of words which are used over and over again, while there is a large number of words which are not used very often. In a much larger amount of text, the words that do not occur very often are much less important. That is why this dictionary concentrates on the words that occur over and over again, and why the entries represent the language that students really do need to know and to use.

One of the main aims of a learner's dictionary is to provide information about those words that the user already "knows," as well as to provide information that the user does not know. Many words have several uses and meanings, and we do not really "know" a word until we are familiar with its full range of meaning and grammatical behavior.

The entries contain a detailed account of the main uses and meanings of each word. Each of the forms is listed at the start of each entry, along with information about alternative spellings, if any exist. Explanations are written in full sentences, and show typical grammatical behavior.

The explanations also give a clear description of meaning. And of course, the thousands of examples are taken directly from The Bank of English™, showing typical patterns of use and grammatical structure. The information in this dictionary has been carefully chosen in order to allow the dictionary user to be a confident language user. It will enable students to write better English as well as understand English better.

The *Collins COBUILD Inglés/Español Diccionario Para Estudiantes Latinoamericanos: English/Spanish Student's Dictionary of American English* is printed in full color, which helps the entries to stand out on the page. Over 3,000 of the most frequently used English words in the dictionary are clearly shown by having the headword highlighted in magenta. These have been identified by using the frequency information in The Bank of English™.

Entries which are very long or complex are treated differently to make it easier to find exactly what you are looking for. A menu shows the sections the entry is divided into, and how they are ordered, so that you can immediately go to the correct section to find the meaning you want. For example, **hand** is divided into two sections, showing its noun and verb uses. The entry for **fire** has three sections showing different groups of meaning.

There are a number of language notes which supplement the information already provided in the dictionary entries. In many cases, these language notes draw together information that helps to clarify the differences that exist between some items.

# Guide to the Dictionary Entries

### Entries and Letter Index

The main text of the dictionary is made up of entries from A to Z. An **entry** is a complete explanation of a word and all its meanings. For example, the first entries on page 63 are *babble, babe,* and *baby.* Entries are shown under the letter that they begin with. A **letter index** at the side of each page shows you the complete alphabet and highlights the first letter of all the entries on that page. On left-hand pages, the alphabet is shown in capital letters, and on right-hand pages, it is shown in small letters.

### Guide Words

At the top of every page you will see a word. This is called a **guide word.** On left-hand pages, the guide word is the same as the first complete entry on that page. For example, on page 2 the first complete entry is *abiotic* and this is the guide word at the top of the page. On right-hand pages the guide word is the same as the last entry that begins on that page. On page 3, for example, the guide word is *absorb* because that is the last entry which begins on the page.

### Entry Order

Entries are ordered alphabetically and spaces, hyphens, apostrophes, and accents do not make any difference to this. For example, *up-to-date* comes after *upsurge* and before *uptown*, and *baby carriage* comes after *baby* and before *babysit*. In the same way, abbreviations and entries beginning with capital letters are treated like ordinary words, so *DVD* comes after *duty* and before *DVD burner*, and *April* comes between *apricot* and *apron*.

## Headwords and Superheadwords

Every entry begins with a **headword**, starting at the left-hand edge of the column. Most of the headwords are printed in blue. Words which are closely related in meaning to the headword are also printed in blue, with a black circle before them. For example, on page 1 of the main text, *abandoned* appears as part of the entry for *abandon*.

Some entries are very long or have very different meanings. These entries are called **superheadwords.** They are divided into numbered sections, with a menu at the beginning of the entry to guide you to the correct section for the meaning you are looking for. For example, *ahead* on page 21 is divided into two sections; section 1 is adverb uses and section 2 is preposition uses.

## Inflected Forms and Alternative Spellings

**Inflected forms** are the different grammatical forms that a word can have. Different forms are shown after the pronunciation. Verbs are shown with the 3rd person singular, the *-ing* form, the past tense, and, where it is different from the past tense, the past participle. Adjectives and adverbs are shown with their comparative forms and nouns are shown with their plural forms. Where a noun does not change its form in the plural, this information is also given. Where there are alternative spellings for the headword, these are given in blue before the pronunciation.

## Definitions, Meanings, and Set Structures

**Definitions** are written in full sentences using simple words and show the common ways in which the headword is used. When there is more than one **meaning**, the different meanings are numbered. If a word or expression is used to show approval or disapproval, this information is also given in the definition.

Many words are used in particular grammatical patterns. The definitions show you these important patterns by highlighting these **set structures** in **bold** (black) print.

For example, if you look at the entry for the verb *agree* on page 20, you can see that the preposition *with* is also bold to show that it is used with this verb.

## Examples

The **examples** follow the definitions and are written in *italics*. They are all examples of real language taken from the Bank of English™. They show how the word or phrase is generally used, and give more information about the grammatical patterns in which it is most often used.

## Grammatical Labels

Before a definition, there is a **grammatical label**. These labels are explained on pages xviii–xxiv. Where a word has more than one meaning, there is a grammatical label at the beginning of each numbered meaning.

## Style and Usage

Some words are used by particular groups of people or in particular contexts. This is shown in the dictionary by a label in square brackets and in small capitals after the definition.

### Style labels:

[BUSINESS]: used mainly when talking about the field of business, e.g. *asset*

[COMPUTING]: used mainly when talking about the field of computing, e.g. *chat room*

[DIALECT]: used in some dialects of English, e.g. *howdy*

[FORMAL]: used mainly in official situations such as politics and business, e.g. *allege*

[INFORMAL]: used mainly in informal situations, conversations, and personal letters, e.g. *pal*

[LEGAL]: used mainly in legal documents, in law courts, and by the police in official situations, e.g. *accused*

[LITERARY]: used mainly in novels, poetry, and other forms of literature, e.g. *maiden*

[MEDICAL]: used mainly in medical texts, and by doctors in official situations, e.g. *clinical*

[SPOKEN]: used mainly in speech rather than in writing, e.g. *pardon*

[TECHNICAL]: used mainly when talking or writing about specialist subjects, such as science or music, e.g. *biotechnology*

[WRITTEN]: used mainly in writing rather than in speech, e.g. *advertisement*

# Pronunciation

The suggested pronunciations in this dictionary use the principle that "if you pronounce it like this, most people will understand you." They are based on the most widely taught accent of American English, General American.

The system of showing pronunciations developed from original work by Dr. David Brazil for the *Collins COBUILD English Language Dictionary*. The symbols used in the dictionary are adapted from those of the International Phonetic Alphabet (IPA).

## IPA Symbols

| Vowel | Sounds | Consonant | Sounds |
|---|---|---|---|
| ɑ | calm, ah | b | bed, rub |
| æ | act, mass | d | done, red |
| aɪ | dive, cry | f | fit, if |
| aʊ | out, down | g | good, dog |
| ɛ | met, lend, pen | h | hat, horse |
| eɪ | say, weight | j | yellow, you |
| ɪ | fit, win | k | king, pick |
| i | seem, me | l | lip, bill |
| ɒ | lot, spot | ᵊl | handle, panel |
| oʊ | note, coat | m | mat, ram |
| ɔ | claw, more | n | not, tin |
| ɔɪ | boy, joint | ᵊn | hidden, written |
| ʊ | could, stood | p | pay, lip |
| u | you, use | r | run, read |
| ʌ | fund, must | s | soon, bus |
| ə | *the first vowel in* **a**bout | t | talk, bet |
| i | *the second vowel in* ver**y** | v | van, love |
| u | the *second vowel* in act**u**al | w | win, wool |
| | | x | loch |
| | | z | zoo, buzz |
| | | ʃ | ship, wish |
| | | ʒ | measure, leisure |
| | | ŋ | sing, working |
| | | tʃ | cheap, witch |
| | | θ | thin, myth |
| | | ð | then, bathe |
| | | dʒ | joy, bridge |

## Stress

Stress is shown by underlining the vowel in the stressed syllable:

**two** /tu/

**result** /rɪzʌlt/

**disappointing** /dɪsəpɔɪntɪŋ/

When a word is spoken in isolation, stress falls on the syllables which have vowels which are underlined. If there is one syllable underlined, it will have primary stress.

"TWO"

"reSULT"

If two syllables are underlined, the first will have secondary stress, and the second will have primary stress:

"DISapPOINTing"

A few words are shown with three underlined syllables, for example "disqualification" /dɪskwɒlɪfɪkeɪʃᵊn/. In this case, the third underlined syllable will have primary stress, while the secondary stress may be on the first or second syllable:

"DISqualifiCAtion" or "disQUALifiCAtion"

GenAm usually prefers "dis-", while RP tends to prefer "DIS-".

In the case of compound words, where the pronunciation of each part is given separately, the stress pattern is shown by underlining the headword: "air-conditioned", "first-class", but "cake pan".

## Stressed syllables

When words are used in context, the way in which they are pronounced depends upon the information units that are constructed by the speaker. For example, a speaker could say:

1 "the reSULT was disapPOINTing"

2 "it was a DISappointing reSULT"

3 "it was VERy disappointing inDEED"

In (3), neither of the two underlined syllables in disappointing /dɪsəpɔɪntɪŋ/ receives either primary or secondary stress. This shows that it is not possible for a dictionary to predict whether a particular syllable will be stressed in context.

It should be noted, however, that in the case of adjectives with two stressed syllables, the second syllable often loses its stress when it is used before a noun:

"a FIRST-class SEAT"

"AIR-conditioned TRAINS"

Two things should be noted about the marked syllables:

1 They can take primary or secondary stress in a way that is not shared by the other syllables.

2 Whether they are stressed or not, the vowel must be pronounced distinctly; it cannot be weakened to /ə/, /ɪ/ , or /ʊ/.

These features are shared by most of the one-syllable words in English, which are therefore transcribed in this dictionary as stressed syllables:

**two** /tu̲/

**inn** /ɪ̲n/

**tree** /tri̲/

### Unstressed syllables

It is an important characteristic of English that vowels in unstressed syllables tend not to be pronounced clearly. Many unstressed syllables contain the vowel /ə/, a neutral vowel which is not found in stressed syllables. The vowels /ɪ/ , or /ʊ/. which are relatively neutral in quality, are also common in unstressed syllables.

Single-syllable grammatical words such as "shall" and "at" are often pronounced with a weak vowel such as /ə/. However, some of them are pronounced with a more distinct vowel under certain circumstances, for example when they occur at the end of a sentence. This distinct pronunciation is generally referred to as the strong form, and is given in this dictionary after the word STRONG.

**shall** /ʃəl, STRONG ʃæl/

**at** /ət, STRONG æt/

## Grammatical Labels Used in the Dictionary

Nearly all the words that are explained in this dictionary have grammar information given about them. For each word or meaning, its word class is shown in capital letters, just before the definition. Examples of word classes are N-COUNT, VERB, PRON and ADV.

The sections below contain further information about each word class.

### Verbs

A verb is a word which is used to say what someone or something does or what happens to them, or to give information about them.

### V-I

An **intransitive verb** is one which takes an indirect object or no object, e.g.:

bake: *I love to* *__bake__*.

### V-T

A **transitive verb** is one which takes a direct object, e.g.:

mail: *He mailed me the contract.*

### V-T/V-I

Some verbs may be **transitive** or **intransitive** depending on how they are used, e.g.:

open: *He opened the window.* (transitive) *The flower opened.* (intransitive)

### V-T PASSIVE

**V-T PASSIVE** means **passive verb.** A passive verb is a verb that is formed using a form of *be* followed by the past participle of the main verb. Passive verbs focus on the person or thing that is affected by the action, e.g.:

born: *She was born in Milan on April 29, 1923.*

### PHR-VERB

**PHR-VERB** means **phrasal verb.** A phrasal verb is a combination of a verb and an adverb (e.g. *catch up*) or a verb and a preposition (e.g., *call for*), which together have a particular meaning. Some phrasal verbs have both an adverb and a preposition (for example *add up to*).

catch up: *I stopped and waited for her to catch up.*

call off: *He called off the trip.*

add up to: *Profits can add up to millions of dollars.*

### V-LINK

**V-LINK** means **link verb.** A **link verb** is a verb such as *be*, *feel*, or *seem*. These verbs connect the subject of a sentence to a complement. Most link verbs do not occur in the passive, e.g.:

be: *The sky was black.*

feel: *It feels good to finish a piece of work.*

seem: *The thunder seemed quite close.*

### V-RECIP

**V-RECIP** means **reciprocal verb.** A reciprocal verb describes a process in which two or more people, groups, or things do the same thing to each other, or take part in the same action or event. Reciprocal verbs are used where the subject is both people, e.g. *Fred and Sally met*. The people can also be referred to separately, e.g. *Fred met Sally. Fred argued with Sally.* These patterns are reciprocal because they also mean that *Sally met Fred* and *Sally argued with Fred.* Many reciprocal verbs can also be used in a way that is not reciprocal. For example, *Fred and Sally spoke* is reciprocal, but *Fred spoke to Sally* is not reciprocal (because it does not mean that Sally also spoke to Fred).

### V-RECIP-PASSIVE

**V-RECIP-PASSIVE** means **passive reciprocal verb.** A passive reciprocal verb behaves like both a passive verb and a reciprocal verb, e.g. *I don't think Susan and I will be reconciled.*

### MODAL

A **modal** is a **modal verb** such as *may*, *must*, or *would*. A **modal** is used before the infinitive form of a verb, e.g., *I must go home now.* In questions, it comes before the subject, e.g., *May we come in?* In negatives, it comes before the negative word, e.g., *She wouldn't say where she bought her shoes.* It does not inflect, for example, it does not take an *-s* in the third person singular, e.g. *I can take care of myself.*

## Nouns

### N-COUNT

**N-COUNT** means a **count noun.** Count nouns refer to things which can be counted, and they have both the singular and plural forms. When a count noun is used in the singular, it must normally have a word such as *a*, *an*, *the*, or *her* in front of it, e.g.:

head: *She turned her head away from him.*

room: *A minute later he left the room.*

### N-UNCOUNT

**N-UNCOUNT** means an **uncount noun.** Uncount nouns refer to things that are not normally counted or which we do not think of as individual items. Uncount nouns do not have a plural form, and are used with a singular verb, e.g.:

help: *He shouted for help.*

rain: *We got very wet in the rain.*

bread: *She bought a loaf of bread.*

### N-VAR

**N-VAR** means a **variable noun.** Variable nouns are uncount when they refer to something in general, and count nouns when they refer to a particular instance of something, e.g.:

night: *The rain continued all night.*

*Night finally fell.*

Other variable nouns refer to substances. They are uncount when they refer to a mass of the substance, and count nouns when they refer to types or brands, e.g.:

coffee: *Would you like some coffee?*

*We had a coffee.*

### N-SING

**N-SING** means a **singular noun.** A singular noun is always singular and must have a word such as *a*, *an*, *the*, or *my* in front of it, e.g.:

sun: *The sun was now high in the sky.*

fault: *The accident was my fault.*

### N-PLURAL

**N-PLURAL** means a **plural noun.** A plural noun is always plural and is used with plural verbs, e.g.:

clothes: *Moira went upstairs to change her clothes.*

feelings: *I'm sorry if I hurt your feelings.*

### N-TITLE

**N-TITLE** means a noun that is used to refer to someone who has a particular role or position. Titles come before the name of the person and begin with a capital letter, e.g. *President Bush, Queen Elizabeth.*

### N-VOC

**N-VOC** means a **vocative noun.** A vocative noun is a noun that is used when speaking directly to someone or writing to them, e.g.:

darling: *Thank you, darling.*

dear: *Are you feeling better, dear?*

### N-PROPER

**N-PROPER** means a **proper noun.** A proper noun refers to one person, place, thing, or institution, and begins with a capital letter, e.g.:

Earth: *The space shuttle Atlantis returned safely to Earth today.*

Pentagon: *There was a news conference at the Pentagon.*

## Other Word Classes

### ADJ

**ADJ** means an **adjective.** An adjective is a word which is used to tell you more about a person or thing, such as its appearance, color, size, or other qualities, e.g.:

angry: *An angry crowd gathered.*

wet: *He dried his wet hair.*

white: *He had nice white teeth.*

### ADV

**ADV** means an **adverb.** An adverb is a word that gives more information about when, how, or where something happens, e.g.:

tomorrow: *Bye, see you tomorrow.*

slowly: *He spoke slowly and clearly.*

home: *She wanted to go home.*

### AUX

**AUX** means an **auxiliary verb.** An auxiliary verb is used with another verb to add particular meanings to that verb, for example, to form the continuous or the passive, or to form negatives and questions. The verbs *be, do, get* and *have* are used as auxiliary verbs in some meanings, e.g.:

be: *She didn't always think carefully about what she was doing.*

do: *They don't want to work.*

have: *Alex has already gone.*

get: *A pane of glass got broken.*

### COLOR

A **color** word refers to a color. It is like an adjective, e.g. *the blue sky . . . The sky was blue,* and also like a noun, e.g. *She was dressed in red. . . . several shades of yellow.*

### CONJ

**CONJ** means a **conjunction.** Conjunctions are words such as *and, but, although,* or *since,* which are used to link two words or two clauses in a sentence, e.g.:

although: *They all play basketball, although on different teams.*

but: *I'm sorry, but it's true.*

since: *So much has changed since I was a teenager.*

### CONVENTION

A **convention** is a word or fixed phrase which is used in conversation, for example when greeting someone, apologizing, or replying. Examples of conventions are *hello, sorry,* and *I'm afraid,* e.g.:

hello: *Hello, Trish. How are you?*

I'm afraid: *We don't have anything like that, I'm afraid.*

### DET

**DET** means a **determiner.** A determiner is a word such as *a, the, my,* or *every* which is used at the beginning of a noun group, e.g.:

an: *One way of making friends is to go to an evening class.*

the: *Daily walks are the best exercise.*

every: *Every room has a window facing the ocean.*

### EXCLAM

**EXCLAM** means an **exclamation.** An exclamation is a word or phrase which is spoken suddenly or loudly in order to express a strong emotion, e.g.:

oh: *"Oh!" Kenny said. "Has everyone gone?"*

why: *Why hello, Tom.*

### FRACTION

A **fraction** is used in numbers, e.g. *five and a half, two and two thirds;* before *of* and a noun group, e.g. *half of the money, a third of the children, an eighth of a gallon;* after *in* or *into,* e.g. *in half, into thirds.* A fraction is also used like a count noun, e.g. *two halves, the first quarter of the year.*

### QUANT

**QUANT** means a **quantifier.** A quantifier is a word or phrase like *plenty* or *a lot* which allowed you to say in a general way how many there are of something, or how much there is of something. Quantifiers are often followed by *of*, e.g.:

all: *This problem affects all of us.*

enough: *They had enough cash for a one-way ticket.*

whole: *We spent the whole summer in Italy.*

### QUANT-NEG

**QUANT-NEG** is a **negative quantifier.** These are words like *neither,* e.g.:

neither: *Neither of us felt like going out.*

### NEG

**NEG** means **negative.** This is used to describe *not*, which is used to make negative statements and questions. Please see the entry for *not.*

### NUM

**NUM** means **number,** e.g.:

eighteen: *He worked for them for eighteen years.*

billion: *. . . 3 billion dollars.*

### ORD

**ORD** means **ordinal.** An ordinal is a number that is used like an adjective or an adverb, e.g.:

hundredth: *The bank's hundredth anniversary is in December.*

first: *January is the first month of the year.*

## PHRASE

A **phrase** is a group of words which have a particular meaning when they are used together. This meaning is not always understandable from the separate parts, e.g.:

change hands: *The company has changed hands many times.*

sit tight: *Sit tight, I'll be right back.*

## PREDET

**PREDET** means a **predeterminer.** A predeterminer is a word such as *all* or *half* which can come before a determiner, e.g.:

all: *She's worked all her life.*

half: *We waited half an hour for the bus.*

## PREP

**PREP** means a **preposition.** A preposition is a word such as *by*, *with*, or *from* which is always followed by a noun group or the *-ing* form of a verb, e.g.:

near: *He stood near the door.*

of: *She is a young woman of twenty-six.*

## PRON

**PRON** means a **pronoun.** A pronoun is used to refer to someone or something that has already been mentioned or whose identity is already known, e.g.:

she: *When Ann arrived home she found Brian watching TV.*

they: *She said goodbye to the children as they left for school.*

this: *I have seen many movies, but never one like this.*

## PRON-NEG

**PRON-NEG** means a negative pronoun such as *neither*, e.g.:

neither: *Neither noticed him leave the room.*

Some meanings in entries have more than one word class. For example:

officer 2: N-COUNT; N-VOC

This means that *officer* is both a count noun and a vocative noun for meaning 2.

*The officer saw no sign of a break-in.*

*Officer Montoya was the first on the scene.*

## Irregular Verbs

| Infinitive | Past Tense | Past Participle |
|---|---|---|
| **arise** | arose | arisen |
| **be** | was, were | been |
| **beat** | beat | beaten |
| **become** | became | become |
| **begin** | began | begun |
| **bend** | bent | bent |
| **bet** | bet | bet |
| **bind** | bound | bound |
| **bite** | bit | bitten |
| **bleed** | bled | bled |
| **blow** | blew | blown |
| **break** | broke | broken |
| **bring** | brought | brought |
| **build** | built | built |
| **burn** | burned *or* burnt | burned *or* burnt |
| **burst** | burst | burst |
| **buy** | bought | bought |
| **can** | could | – |
| **cast** | cast | cast |
| **catch** | caught | caught |
| **choose** | chose | chosen |
| **cling** | clung | clung |
| **come** | came | come |
| **cost** | cost *or* costed | cost *or* costed |
| **creep** | crept | crept |
| **cut** | cut | cut |
| **deal** | dealt | dealt |
| **dig** | dug | dug |
| **dive** | dived *or* dove | dived |
| **do** | did | done |
| **draw** | drew | drawn |
| **dream** | dreamed *or* dreamt | dreamed *or* dreamt |
| **drink** | drank | drunk |
| **drive** | drove | driven |
| **eat** | ate | eaten |
| **fall** | fell | fallen |
| **feed** | fed | fed |
| **feel** | felt | felt |
| **fight** | fought | fought |
| **find** | found | found |
| **fly** | flew | flown |
| **forbid** | forbade | forbidden |
| **forget** | forgot | forgotten |

| | | |
|---|---|---|
| **freeze** | froze | frozen |
| **get** | got | gotten, got |
| **give** | gave | given |
| **go** | went | gone |
| **grind** | ground | ground |
| **grow** | grew | grown |
| **hang** | hung *or* hanged | hung *or* hanged |
| **have** | had | had |
| **hear** | heard | heard |
| **hide** | hid | hidden |
| **hit** | hit | hit |
| **hold** | held | held |
| **hurt** | hurt | hurt |
| **keep** | kept | kept |
| **kneel** | kneeled *or* knelt | kneeled *or* knelt |
| **know** | knew | known |
| **lay** | laid | laid |
| **lead** | led | led |
| **lean** | leaned | leaned |
| **leap** | leaped *or* leapt | leaped *or* leapt |
| **learn** | learned | learned |
| **leave** | left | left |
| **lend** | lent | lent |
| **let** | let | let |
| **lie** | lay | lain |
| **light** | lit *or* lighted | lit *or* lighted |
| **lose** | lost | lost |
| **make** | made | made |
| **may** | might | – |
| **mean** | meant | meant |
| **meet** | met | met |
| **pay** | paid | paid |
| **put** | put | put |
| **quit** | quit | quit |
| **read** | read | read |
| **rid** | rid | rid |
| **ride** | rode | ridden |
| **ring** | rang | rung |
| **rise** | rose | risen |
| **run** | ran | run |
| **say** | said | said |
| **see** | saw | seen |
| **seek** | sought | sought |
| **sell** | sold | sold |
| **send** | sent | sent |
| **set** | set | set |

| | | |
|---|---|---|
| **shake** | shook | shaken |
| **shed** | shed | shed |
| **shine** | shined *or* shone | shined *or* shone |
| **shoe** | shod | shod |
| **shoot** | shot | shot |
| **show** | showed | shown |
| **shrink** | shrank | shrunk |
| **shut** | shut | shut |
| **sing** | sang | sung |
| **sink** | sank | sunk |
| **sit** | sat | sat |
| **sleep** | slept | slept |
| **slide** | slid | slid |
| **smell** | smelled | smelled |
| **speak** | spoke | spoken |
| **speed** | sped *or* speeded | sped *or* speeded |
| **spell** | spelled *or* spelt | spelled *or* spelt |
| **spend** | spent | spent |
| **spill** | spilled *or* spilt | spilled *or* spilt |
| **spit** | spit *or* spat | spit, *or* spat |
| **spoil** | spoiled *or* spoilt | spoiled *or* spoilt |
| **spread** | spread | spread |
| **spring** | sprang | sprung |
| **stand** | stood | stood |
| **steal** | stole | stolen |
| **stick** | stuck | stuck |
| **sting** | stung | stung |
| **stink** | stank | stunk |
| **strike** | struck | struck *or* stricken |
| **swear** | swore | sworn |
| **sweep** | swept | swept |
| **swell** | swelled | swollen |
| **swim** | swam | swum |
| **swing** | swung | swung |
| **take** | took | taken |
| **teach** | taught | taught |
| **tear** | tore | torn |
| **tell** | told | told |
| **think** | thought | thought |
| **throw** | threw | thrown |
| **wake** | woke *or* waked | woken *or* waked |
| **wear** | wore | worn |
| **weep** | wept | wept |
| **win** | won | won |
| **wind** | wound | wound |
| **write** | wrote | written |

# Activity Guide Contents

# Activity Guide

## 1. USING YOUR BRAIN

| Word Web Activities<br>Choosing the Right Definition | Word Link Activities<br>Practice with Pragmatics |
|---|---|

1. **Word Web Activities**

   Use the Word Web feature entitled *brain* to answer the following questions about the brain.

   a. Which part tells you it's time to eat? ________________

   b. Which part helps you learn to speak? ________________

   c. Which part makes sure you stand up straight? ________________

   d. Which part controls your heartbeat? ________________

   e. Which part is wrapped around the outside of the brain? ________________

2. **Choosing the Right Definition**

   Study the numbered definitions for *brain*. Then write the number of the definition that relates to each sentence below.

   a. _____ Angela mastered the new computer program in one day. She has some brain!

   b. _____ Some studies show that people with larger brains are more intelligent than people with smaller brains.

   c. _____ They say that Martin is the brains behind the success of the company.

   d. _____ If you'll just use your brain, you'll make the right decision.

   e. _____ In proportion to the size of its body, the elephant's brain is very small.

3. **Word Link Activities**

a. The definition of *brain* says that it "enables you to think." The prefix in the word *enable* is ____________________.

b. Find the Word Link for this prefix. What does the prefix mean? ____________________

c. What two other words with this prefix do you find?

____________________ ____________________

Guess what each word means. Then check your answers by looking up the words.

4. **Practice with Pragmatics**

Study the information about the fourth meaning of the definition of *brain*. Read the four sentences below. Write *Yes* if the sentence uses the term appropriately, and *No* if the usage is inappropriate.

a. ______ I think Anna was the brains behind the kids' plan to skip school on Friday.

b. ______ History states that Einstein was the brains behind the discovery of the theory of relativity.

c. ______ The president said that the governor was the brains behind the economic recovery in her state.

d. ______ I supplied the money, but Mike was the brains behind the surprise party.

**ANSWER KEY:**

1. **a.** medulla oblongata; **b.** cerebrum; **c.** cerebellum; **d.** medulla oblongata; **e.** cerebrum
2. **a.** 3, **b.** 1, **c.** 4; **d.** 2; **e.** 1
3. **a.** en; **b.** making or putting; **c.** enact, endanger
4. **a.** Yes; **b.** No; **c.** No; **d.** Yes

## 2. GOING IN CIRCLES

| Grammar Activities<br>Picture Dictionary Activities | Word Link Activities |
|---|---|

1. **Grammar Activities**

Many different words are based on the word *circle*. Write the part of speech of each underlined word—noun, verb, or adjective. Use your dictionary to check your answers.

- **a.** The moon was perfectly circular last night. ______
- **b.** The students arranged the chairs in a circle. ______
- **c.** Vitamin E improves the circulation of the blood. ______
- **d.** Airplanes sometimes circle several times before landing. ______
- **e.** Please open the window so the air can circulate. ______
- **f.** What is the circulation of *The Times*? ______
- **g.** Did the teacher circle your mistakes? ______
- **h.** I like circular eyeglasses, not square ones. ______

2. **Picture Dictionary Activities—A**

- **a.** How many other shapes can you think of besides the circle? Write your list below.

  ______

  Look at the Picture Dictionary feature *shapes* and check your answers.
- **b.** Which two shapes most closely resemble the circle?

  ______ ______

3. **Picture Dictionary Activities—B**

Look at the Picture Dictionary feature entitled *area*. Pay special attention to how to find the area of a circle.

- **a.** What do you call the distance from the center of the circle to the outside edge? ______
- **b.** What do you call the line that runs around the outside of the circle? ______
- **c.** What do you call the line that runs across the circle from one side to the other? ______
- **d.** What is the formula for finding the area of a circle? ______
- **e.** If a circle has a radius of 3 inches, what is its area? Use $\pi = 3.14$. ______

4. **Word Link Activities**

a. The first four letters of the word *circle* form a Word Link. What is that link? __________

b. Look up the words *circle*, *circuit*, and, *circulate*. Notice the Word Link *circ* in those words. Write each word below.

Then look it up in the dictionary and identify it as *verb*, *noun*, or *both*.

______________________, _________________
(word) (part of speech)

______________________, _________________
(word) (part of speech)

______________________, _________________
(word) (part of speech)

c. Complete each sentence below with the correct word from item b.

1. Blood ____________ around the body.
2. A ____________ is a shape with all points the same distance from the center.
3. A tree fell on the power lines and broke the electrical ____________.

**ANSWER KEY:**

1. **a.** adjective; **b.** noun; **c.** noun; d. verb; **e.** verb; **f.** noun; **g.** verb; **h.** adjective
2. **a.** Answers will vary; **b.** ellipse, oval
3. **a.** radius; **b.** circumference; **c.** diameter; **d.** $\pi r^2$; **e.** 28.26 inches
4. **a.** circ; **b.** circle, both; circuit, noun; circulate, verb; **c1.** circulate; **c2.** circle; **c3.** circuit

## 3. TRANSPORTATION

| | |
|---|---|
| Choosing the Right Definition<br>Word Web Activities | Dictionary Research<br>Word Link Activities |

1. **Choosing the Right Definition**

Study the numbered definitions for *transportation*. Then write the number of the definition that relates to each sentence below.

a. ______ The transportation of nuclear waste through large cities can be dangerous.

b. ______ Using mass transportation helps the environment.

c. ______ Many schools provide transportation for children in the form of school buses.

d. ______ Subways provide rapid transportation.

e. ______ Bad weather slows down most forms of transportation.

2. **Word Web Activities—A**

Use the Word Web feature entitled *transportation* to answer the following questions.

What are the three names for underground transportation systems?

s________________ m________________ t________________

3. **Word Web Activities—B**

Use the Word Web feature entitled *ship* to answer the following questions.

Look up these words in the dictionary to check your answers.

a. What do you call things other than people that are carried on ships? ________________

b. What do you call the place where a ship stops? ________________

c. What do you call the person who steers a large ship? ________________

d. What do you call the place where a plane can land on a large ship? ________________

4. **Dictionary Research**

a. Reread the definition of *transportation*. Write your own definition of the word *goods* as it is used in the definition.

______________________________________________

b. Look up the word *goods* in the dictionary and complete these sentences.

*Goods* are things that people make and then later __________.

*Goods* are things that people __________ and can move from one place to another.

5. **Word Link Activities**

The first five letters of the word *transportation* form a Word Link.

a. What is the Word Link? __________

b. What does the Word Link *trans* mean? __________

c. Look up the words *transfer*, *transition*, and *translate*. Notice the Word Link *trans* in those words. Read the definitions.

d. Complete each sentence below with the correct word from item c. Check your answers by looking up each word in the dictionary.

1. I don't know how to read Chinese. Can you __________ this letter for me?
2. After the president of the college left, there was a period of __________ before a new one was appointed.
3. You'll have to take two buses to get there. You can __________ from the 101 to the 145 at Main Street.

**ANSWER KEY:**

1. **a.** 3, **b.** 2, **c.** 1; **d.** 2; **e.** 3
2. subway, metro, tube
3. **a.** cargo; **b.**port; **c.** captain; **d.** (flight) deck
4. **a.** Answers will vary; **b.** sell; own or make
5. **a.** trans; **b.** across; **d1.** translate; **d2.** transition; **d3.** transfer

## 4. TRIAL BY JURY

| | |
|---|---|
| Dictionary Research<br>Word Web Activities<br>Word Partnership Activities | Word Link Activities<br>Choosing the Right Definition |

1. **Dictionary Research**

   Study the first numbered definition for *trial*. Think about the meaning of the four words listed below. Then match each word with the correct definition below. Look up these words in the dictionary if you are not sure.

   _____ **a.** judge
   _____ **b.** guilty
   _____ **c.** jury
   _____ **d.** evidence

   **1.** something you see that causes you to believe something is true
   **2.** a person who decides how a law is applied
   **3.** responsible for a crime
   **4.** group of people who decide if a person is guilty or not

2. **Word Web Activities**

   Study the Word Web feature entitled *trial*. Then use bold words from this Word Web feature to complete the following sentences. Look up any words you aren't sure of.

   **a.** The defendant will get a trial by _________.
   **b.** The defendant may or may not _________ guilty.
   **c.** The person who accused the defendant is the _________.
   **d.** The _________ will tell what they know about the crime.
   **e.** The words the witnesses say is called their _________.
   **f.** In the end, the jury will deliver a _________.

3. **Word Partnership Activities**

Study the Word Partnership feature for *jury*. Pay special attention to the phrases below. Then match each phrase with the correct definition. Look up the words in the dictionary if you are not sure.

_____ **a.** jury convicts
_____ **b.** hung jury
_____ **c.** jury duty

**1.** a jury that can't agree on a verdict
**2.** a jury finds someone guilty
**3.** a citizen's obligation to serve on a jury

4. **Word Link Activities**

Study the Word Link feature for the words *illegal*, *illegitimate*, and *illiterate*. Read the definitions.

**a.** What is the meaning of the Word Link *il*? __________

Which of these words (*illegal, illegitimate, illiterate*) names or describes the following? Read the definitions again if you are not sure.

**b.** a person who is unable to read __________
**c.** something that is not considered right __________
**d.** something that is against the law __________

5. **Choosing the Right Definition**

Study the definition of *trial*. Then write the number of the definition that relates to each sentence below.

**a.** _____ Elena learned to bake bread by trial and error.
**b.** _____ You should give aspirin a trial before you ask for anything stronger.
**c.** _____ The murderer's trial lasted for six weeks.
**d.** _____ The boss gave me a three-week trial to see if I could handle the responsibilities.

**ANSWER KEY:**

1. **a.** 2; **b.** 3; **c.** 4; **d.** 1
2. **a.** jury; **b.** plead; **c.** plaintiff; **d.** witnesses; **e.** testimony; **f.** verdict
3. **a.** 2; **b.** 1; **c.** 3
4. **a.** not; **b.** illiterate; **c.** illegitimate; **d.** illegal
5. **a.** 3; **b.** 2; **c.** 1; **d.** 2

## 5. ORCHESTRA

| Word Web Activities<br>Word Partnership Activities | Word Link Activities<br>Choosing the Right Definition |
|---|---|

**1. Word Web Activities**

Study the information in the Word Web feature entitled *orchestra*. Then answer the questions below. Write T for *true* or F for *false*.

_____ **a.** A symphony orchestra usually has more than 100 players.
_____ **b.** The largest section of the orchestra is the string section.
_____ **c.** The double bass plays in the string section.
_____ **d.** The brass section needs to play very loud.
_____ **e.** The timpani is part of the brass section.

**2. Word Partnership Activities**

The job of a symphony orchestra is to *perform* for the public. Look up the word *perform* in the dictionary.

**a.** Write the number of the definition that applies to music. ______________

Study the Word Partnership feature for *perform*. Then complete the four sentences below using the word *perform* before or after one of these words or phrases: *tasks, able to, miracles, well*. Use each of these words or phrases one time.

**b.** Some people believe holy people can ______________ ______________.
**c.** The violinist felt ill and was not ______________ ______________.
**d.** The new truck ______________ ______________ on the icy roads.
**e.** Doctors believe the brains of adults and children ______________ ______________ in different ways.

3. **Word Link Activities**

Look up *symphony* and read the Word Links *sym* and *phon*.

**d.** What does *sym* mean? ______________

**e.** What does *phon* mean? ______________

**f.** So *symphony* means to make ______________ ______________.

4. **Choosing the Right Definition**

Reread the Word Web feature for *orchestra*. Several of the bold words in this feature have multiple meanings.

Study the numbered definitions for *composition*. Then write the number of the definition that relates to each sentence below.

_____ **a.** The composition of furniture in the store window was very attractive.

_____ **b.** Have you written any new compositions lately?

Study the numbered definitions for *instrument*. Then write the number of the definition that relates to each sentence below.

_____ **c.** The piano is my favorite instrument.

_____ **d.** The dentist placed the instruments on the shelf.

**ANSWER KEY:**

1. **a.** F; **b.** T; **c.** T; **d.** F; **e.** F
2. **a.** 2; **b.** perform miracles; **c.** able to perform; **d.** performed well; **e.** perform tasks
3. **a.** together; **b.** sound; **c.** sound together
4. **a.** 1; **b.** 2 or 3; **c.** 2; **d.** 1

## 6. COOKING

| | |
|---|---|
| Word Web Activities<br>Picture Dictionary Activities | Thesaurus Activities<br>Grammar Activities<br>Dictionary Research |

### 1. Word Web Activities

As you complete this activity, look up any words you aren't sure of.

Read the definitions for *cook* and *cooking*. Then use the Word Web feature entitled *cooking* to answer the following questions.

**a.** Which bold word means the opposite of *tough*? ________

**b.** Which bold word means *absorb food into your body*? ________

Now use the Word Web feature entitled *spice* to answer the following questions.

**c.** Which spice is the least effective in killing germs? ________

**d.** What kind of food do people in cold climates usually like? ________

Now use the Word Web feature entitled *pan* to answer the following questions.

**e.** Cooking pans are very heavy when made of what material? ________

**f.** Copper pans are usually covered with a thin layer of what metal? ________

### 2. Picture Dictionary Activities—A

Look at the Picture Dictionary feature for *cook*. Then complete the sentences correctly.

**a.** If you want to make tea, you have to ________ the water.

**b.** You need an oven if you want to ________, ________, or ________ food.

**c.** When you put food in a wire container with boiling water under it, you ________ the food.

**d.** When you make a slice of bread brown by cooking it you ________ it.

**e.** When you cook food in an oven very close to the flame, you ________ it.

### 3. Picture Dictionary Activities—B

Look at the Picture Dictionary feature for *egg*. Then answer the questions below. Look up any words you aren't sure of. Write T for *true* or F for *false*.

_____ **a.** The scrambled eggs have peppers in them.

_____ **b.** The hard-boiled egg has a round yolk.

_____ **c.** The fried egg is in a frying pan.

4. **Thesaurus Activities**

Find the Thesaurus feature with the word *cook*. Then complete the sentences using words from the feature. Look up any words you aren't sure of.

a. A __________ works in a restaurant.

b. Yeast is the ingredient that ________ bread rise.

c. If the meal is cooked but it has gotten cold, you might __________ __________ the food.

d. Busy people tend to eat meals that are simple to __________.

5. **Grammar Activities**

Write the part of speech of each underlined word—noun or verb.

a. I don't like <u>cooking</u> vegetables. __________

b. My sister's <u>cooking</u> is fantastic. __________

c. Which do you prefer <u>cooking</u> or baking? __________

d. On Sunday I <u>cooked</u> dinner for my family. __________

e. My husband is a very good <u>cook</u>. __________

6. **Dictionary Research**

Look at other words and phrases that follow the word *cook* in the dictionary.

a. Which one describes a collection of recipes? __________

b. Which one describes something you eat? __________

c. Which one describes how someone plans to do something? __________

d. Which one describes cooking outside? __________

**ANSWER KEY:**

1. **a.** tender; **b.** digest; **c.** black pepper; **d.** bland; **e.** cast iron; **f.** tin
2. **a.** boil; **b.** roast, bake, broil; **c.**steam; **d.** toast; **e.** broil
3. **a.** F; **b.** T; **c.** T
4. **a.** chef; **b.** makes; **c.** heat up; **d.** prepare
5. **a.** verb; **b.** noun; **c.** verb; **d.** verb; **e.** noun
6. **a.** cookbook; **b.** cookie; **c.** cook up; **d.**cookout

## 7. ENERGY

| | |
|---|---|
| Choosing the Right Definition<br>Word Web Activities | Word Link Activities<br>Grammar Activities |

### 1. Choosing the Right Definition

Study the numbered definitions for *energy*. Then write the number of the definition that relates to each sentence below.

**a.** ______ She's putting all her energies into her school work.
**b.** ______ My children have more energy than I do.
**c.** ______ One problem with nuclear energy is that it produces radioactive waste.
**d.** ______ You should put more energy into your homework.
**e.** ______ Which energy source do you think is the cleanest?
**f.** ______ Conserve your energy. Go to bed early.

### 2. Word Web Activities

Use the Word Web feature entitled *energy* to answer the following questions. Answer each question with one of the bold words in the Word Web feature.

**a.** What kind of power plants were built in the 1970s? ____________
**b.** What kind of gas is still used for home heating? ____________
**c.** What was the primary energy source for American settlers? ____________
**d.** What was the source of electrical power in the early 1900s? ____________

### 3. Word Link Activities

Look up the words below to find the Word Link in the word. Write the Word Link.

**a.** hydraulic ______
**b.** hands-free ______
**c.** electricity ______
**d.** complicate ______
**e.** seller ______

Match the Word Link with the correct definition.

| Word Link | Definition |
|---|---|
| ______ **f.** hydr | **1.** without |
| ______ **g.** free | **2.** cause to be |
| ______ **h.** electr | **3.** one who acts as |
| ______ **i.** ate | **4.** water |
| ______ **j.** er | **5.** electric |

Now look back at the Word Web feature for *energy*. Write the three words from this feature that are formed from these Word Links.

**k.** g_________ **l.** h_________ **m.** e_________

4. **Grammar Activities**

Review the dictionary entry for *energy* and *energetic*. Then complete each sentence with the correct form of a word starting with the letters *energ-*. Identify the part of speech of each word you use—noun, verb, adjective, or adverb.

| | Part of Speech |
|---|---|
| **a.** Celia is very _________ today. | _________ |
| **b.** I don't know what happened to all my _________. I'm really tired. | _________ |
| **c.** David washed the car _________. | _________ |

**ANSWER KEY:**

1. **a.** 2; **b.** 1; **c.** 3; **d.** 2; **e.** 3; **f.** 1
2. **a.** nuclear; **b.** natural; **c.** wood; **d.** coal
3. **a.** hydr; **b.** free; **c.** electr; **d.** ate; **e.** er; **f.** 4; **g.** 1; **h.** 5; **i.** 2; **j.** 3; **k.** generate; **l.** hydroelectric; **m.** electrical , electricity
4. **a.** energetic, adjective; **c.** energy, noun; **d.** energetically, adverb

## 8. SEEDS AND PLANTS

| Choosing the Right Definition<br>Picture Dictionary Activities | Dictionary Research<br>Word Link Activities |
|---|---|

### 1. Choosing the Right Definition

Study the numbered definitions for *plant*. Then write the number of the definition that relates to each sentence below.

_____ **a.** The child shouted "No" and planted her feet firmly on the ground.

_____ **b.** I brought a plant as a housewarming present.

_____ **c.** My brother works in a power plant in Milwaukee.

Study the definition of *seed*. Then write the number of the definition that relates to each sentence below.

_____ **d.** I bought a package of flower seeds to plant in the garden.

_____ **e.** I didn't have all the details worked out, but I did have the seed of an idea.

### 2. Picture Dictionary Activities

Use the Picture Dictionary feature entitled *plants* to answer the following questions. Look up the meaning of any words you don't know.

**a.** What tree loses its leaves? _____________________

**b.** What tree is always green? _____________________

### 3. Dictionary Research

Study the first three numbered definitions for *plant*. Think about the meaning of the four words listed below. Then match each word with the correct definition. Look up these words in the dictionary if you are not sure.

_____ **a.** root

_____ **b.** exotic

_____ **c.** produce

_____ **d.** stem

1. very unusual
2. the long thin part of a plant that is above ground
3. the part of a plant that is underground
4. to make something

4. **Word Link Activities**

a. Some plants are *annual* plants. These plants bloom for only one year or season. Notice the root word *ann* in the word *annual*. Look up *annual* and find the Word Link. What does *ann* mean ? ___________

b. What other words with the root *ann* do you find?

___________________________ ___________________________

c. Which word in item b. above means a particular amount each year? ___________

d. Which word in item b. above means something you celebrate every year? ___________

**ANSWER KEY:**

1. **a.** 6; **b.** 1; **c.** 4; **d.** 1; **e.** 2
2. **a.** deciduous; **b.** evergreen
3. **a.** 3; **b.** 1; **c.** 4; **d.** 2
4. **a.** year; **b.** anniversary, per annum; **c.** per annum; **d.** anniversary

## 9. STARS AND ASTRONOMERS

| Word Web Activities<br>Choosing the Right Definition | Word Partnership Activities<br>Thesaurus Activities<br>Word Link Activities |
|---|---|

### 1. Word Web Activities

Use the Word Web feature entitled *star* to answer the following questions. Look up each word in the dictionary to check your answers.

**a.** What is a group of stars called? a ________

**b.** What do people call the idea that the stars control our lives? ________

**c.** What is the scientific study of the stars called? ________

**d.** Which star is used to guide ships on the sea? the ________

Use the Word Web feature entitled *astronomer* to answer this question:

**e.** Galileo was an astronomer who thought that the center of the universe was the ________.

### 2. Choosing the Right Definition

Study the six numbered definitions for *star*. Then write the number of the definition that relates to each sentence below.

**a.** _____ Eric is starring in a new TV comedy called *Just for You*.

**b.** _____ It was cloudy last night, and we couldn't see any stars.

**c.** _____ Madonna is my favorite singing star.

**d.** _____ The flag of the United States has 50 stars on it.

### 3. Word Partnership Activities

Reread the Word Web feature for *star*. Find the word *object* in the second sentence. Look up the word *object* in the dictionary and read the definitions.

**a.** The first meaning of *object* is *something that has a fixed* ________ or ________.

**b.** The second meaning of *object* is ________ or ________.

Study the Word Partnership feature for the word *object*. Then complete the four sentences below using the word *object* and one of these words: *foreign, inanimate, moving, solid*. Use each of these words one time. Look up any words you aren't sure of.

**c.** Dogs are not usually interested in an ________ ________.

**d.** We watched as the magician passed a ________ ________ through a mirror.

**e.** A fast-________ ________ has a high speed.

**f.** If a child swallows a ________ ________ call a doctor for advice.

4. **Thesaurus Activities**

Reread the Word Web feature entitled *astronomer*. Notice the word *study* in the second sentence of the feature. A synonym for *study* is *observe*. Look up *observe* in the dictionary and study the Thesaurus feature that accompanies it. Which of the words in the box goes with each sentence below?

| notice | watch | study |
|---|---|---|

**a.** I'll show you how to do it observe me. ________

**b.** I checked the level of the water every hour, but I didn't observe any change. ________

**c.** Jane Goodall would observe the chimps carefully for hours without moving. ________

5. **Word Link Activities**

The first four letters of the word *astronomer* form a Word Link. Look at the information in the Word Link for *astro*.

**a.** What does the Word Link *astro* mean? ________

**b.** What are the three Word Links for *astro*?

________ ________ ________

**c.** Complete each sentence below with the correct word from item b. Check your answers by looking up each word in the dictionary.

1. This symbol (*) is called the ________.
2. You need a telescope to study ________.
3. You have to know how to fly a plane before you can study to become an ________.

**d.** Reread the Word Web feature for *star*. Find the word *astrology*. It contains two Word Links. You have studied the Word Link *astro*. Now look up *geology* and find the Word Link *logy*.

1. What does *logy* mean? ________
2. So the literal meaning of *astrology* is the ________ of ________.

**ANSWER KEY:**

1. **a.** constellation; **b.** astrology; **c.** astronomy; **d.** North Star; **e.** Sun
2. **a.** 4; **b.** 1; **c.** 3; **d.** 2
3. **a.** shape, form; **b.** aim, purpose; **c.** inanimate object; **d.** solid object; **e.** moving object; **f.** foreign object
4. **a.** watch; **b.** notice; **c.** study
5. **a.** star; **b.** asterisk, astronaut, astronomy; **c1.** asterisk; **c2.** astronomy; **c3.** astronaut; **d1.** study of; **d2.** study, stars

## 10. FOOD

| | |
|---|---|
| Word Web Activities<br>Thesaurus Activities<br>Picture Dictionary Activities | Choosing the Right Definition<br>Dictionary Research |

1. **Word Web Activities**

   Study the information in the Word Web feature entitled *food*. Then answer the questions below. Write T for *true* or F for *false*.

   _____ **a.** Snakes are herbivores.

   _____ **b.** Mice are predators.

   _____ **c.** Green plants store energy from the sun.

2. **Thesaurus Activities**

   The Word Web feature for *food* says that a hawk is a *top predator*. Look at the Thesaurus feature for the word *top*. Then complete the sentences using words from the feature. Look up any words you aren't sure of.

   **a.** The adjective meaning for top is _________.

   **b.** Which adjective best describes the hawk's position as a top predator? _________

   **c.** Which two noun meanings describe the top of a mountain? _________ and _________.

3. **Picture Dictionary Activities**

   Look at the Picture Dictionary feature for *dessert*. Then answer the questions below. Look up any words you aren't familiar with.

   **a.** Which three desserts don't have to be cooked? _________, _________ and _________

   **b.** Which two desserts are usually very cold? _________ and _________

   **c.** Which dessert is always brown? _________

   **d.** Which dessert is made mostly of eggs? _________

   **e.** Which dessert is made mostly of a white grain? _________

## 4. Choosing the Right Definition

The word *feed* is related to the word *food*. Look up the word *feed* and study the numbered definitions. Then write the number of the definition that relates to each sentence below.

a. ______ My mother always feeds the children dinner early on Friday nights.

b. ______ The squirrels in our yard like to feed on the seed we leave for the birds.

c. ______ Newborn babies usually feed every three hours.

d. ______ We collected money to feed the hurricane victims in Louisiana.

## 5. Dictionary Research

a. Look up the word *nutrient*. Write your own definition of the word *nutrient* as it is used in the definition.

______________________________________________

b. Use the definiton of *nutrients* to complete this sentence.
*Nutrients* are things that help plants and animals __________ .

**ANSWER KEY:**

1. **a.** F; **b.** F; **c.** T
2. **a.** best; **b.** best; **c.** peak, summit
3. **a.** ice cream, sundae, fruit salad; **b.** ice cream, sundae; **c.** brownie; **d.** custard; **e.** rice pudding
4. **a.** 1; **b.** 3; **c.** 4; **d.** 2
5. **a.** Answers will vary; **b.** grow

## 11. ART

| Word Web Activities<br>Thesaurus Activities | Word Link Activities<br>Choosing the Right Definition |
|---|---|

### 1. Word Web Activities

Use the Word Web feature entitled *art* to answer the following questions.

**a.** What inspired the term "Impressionist"? a painting by ________

**b.** In what part of the world did Impressionism start? in ________

**c.** What did the Impressionists usually paint? ________

**d.** What elements did they emphasize in their paintings? ________ and color

**e.** The art of what country influenced the Impressionists? ________

### 2. Thesaurus Activities

The Word Web feature for *art* says that the Impressionists were interested in light and color. Find the Thesaurus feature with the word *light*. Then complete the sentences using words from the feature. Look up any words you aren't sure of.

**a.** The noun meanings for *light* are ________, ________, ________, and ________.

**b.** Which noun meaning best describes the soft light of a fire when there are no flames? ________

**c.** Which noun meaning describes the happiness on a person's face? ________

**d.** Which adjective describes a room with a lot of windows facing south? ________

### 3. Word Link Activities

Review the Word Web feature for *art* noting the words *realistic* and *depiction*. Look up the words below and study the Word Links. Then answer the questions.

Look up *reality, realize, really*

**a.** What does the Word Link *real* mean? ________

**b.** Which word in this link means "to make something happen"? ________

**c.** Which word in this link means "actually"? ________

Look up *artist*, *chemist*, *pianist*

**d.** What does *ist* mean? ____________

**e.** Which word in this word link means someone who produces works of art? ____________

**f.** Which word describes someone who studies chemistry? ____________

**4. Choosing the Right Definition**

The Word Web feature for *art* says that the Impressionists stopped painting in their *studios*. Study the numbered definitions for *studio*. Then write the number of the definition that relates to each sentence below.

**a.** _____ The TV show originated in a studio in New York City.

**b.** _____ The photographer has a large studio with large windows.

**ANSWER KEY:**

1. **a.** Monet; **b.** Europe; **c.** landscapes; **d.** light; **e.** Japan
2. **a.** brightness, glow, radiance, shine; **b.** glow; **c.** radiance/glow; **d.** sunny
3. **a.** actual; **b.** realize; **c.** really; **d.** one who practices; **e.** artist; **f.** pharmacist
4. **a.** 2; **b.** 1

## 12. TELEVISION

| | |
|---|---|
| Word Web Activities<br>Thesaurus Activities<br>Word Link Activities | Choosing the Right Definition<br>Grammar Activities |

### 1. Word Web Activities

Use the Word Web feature entitled *television* to answer the following questions. Look up any words you don't know in the dictionary.

**a.** What kind of tube was used in old-fashioned televisions? ____________

**b.** What are the tiny dots of light on a TV screen called? ____________

**c.** What are the three sources of TV signals?

____________, ____________ and ____________

### 2. Thesaurus Activities

The Word Web feature for *television* says that high-definition televisions have a very *clear image*.

**a.** Read the dictionary definition for *clear*. *Clear* is used to describe a TV picture that is easy to ________.

Find the Thesaurus feature for *clear*. Then complete the sentence using words from the feature. Look up any words you aren't sure of.

**b.** These words describe something that is easy to understand.

________ ________ ________

Read the dictionary definition for *picture*. Then study the Thesaurus feature for this word and answer the questions below.

**c.** Which synonym for the word *picture* applies to a television picture?

________

**d.** Look at the verb meanings of *picture* in the Thesaurus entry. They describe a picture that exists only in a person's ________.

### 3. Word Link Activities

Television

**a.** Look up the Word Link for *tele*. What does *tele* mean? ________

**b.** Look up the word *visible*. Read the Word Link above *visible*. What does the prefix *vis* mean? ________

**c.** So television is something that lets you ________ things at a ________.

## 4. Choosing the Right Definition

Reread the Word Web feature for *television*. Pay special attention to the words *screen* and *station*. Then look up these words in the dictionary. Study the numbered definitions for *screen*. Then write the number of the definition that relates to each sentence below.

_____ **a.** At the movies a tall person sat in front of me and it was hard to see the screen.

_____ **b.** Blood samples are screened in a laboratory.

Study the numbered definitions for *station*. Then write the number of the definition that relates to each sentence below.

_____ **c.** We live only three blocks from the subway station.

_____ **d.** Which station is showing the soccer game tonight?

## 5. Grammar Activities

The Word Web feature says that cathode ray tubes are used to *produce* a television picture. Many different words are based on the word *produce*. Write the part of speech of each underlined word—noun, verb, adjective, or adverb. Use your dictionary to check your answers.

**a.** I always buy my produce from the fruit market on the corner. _____

**b.** There are so many new products on the market, I don't know which to buy. _____

**c.** A lot of movie production takes place on the streets of New York. _____

**d.** I am the most productive early in the morning. _____

**e.** The thief produced a gun from his pocket. _____

**ANSWER KEY:**

1. **a.** cathode ray; **b.** pixels; **c.** ground stations, satellites, cables
2. **a.** see; **b.** obvious, plain, straightforward; **c.** image; **d.** mind
3. **a.** distance; **b.** seeing; **c.** see, distance
4. **a.** 1; **b.** 6; **c.** 1; **d.** 3
5. **a.** noun; **b.** noun; **c.** noun; **d.** adjective; **e.** verb

## 13. MONEY

| | |
|---|---|
| Word Web Activities<br>Word Partnership Activities<br>Thesaurus Activities | Choosing the Right Definition<br>Dictionary Research |

1. **Word Web Activities**

Use the Word Web feature entitled *money* to answer the following questions.

a. Which word in the feature means the same as *trade*? ________

b. What form of ocean life was used as money at one time? ________

c. Were the first coins round? ________

d. What country had the first circular coins? ________

e. Which two metals were used by the Lydians to make coins? ________ and ________

2. **Word Partnership Activities**

Look up the word *buy* in the dictionary.

a. What is the past tense of the verb *buy*? ________

b. Which meaning of *buy* is found in this sentence?
*I bought myself a few minutes to think of the answer to the question.*
sense number ________

Study the Word Partnership feature for *buy*. Then complete the four sentences below using the word *buy* before or after one of these words or phrases: *online, and sell, tickets, afford to*. Use each of these items once.

c. I can't ________ ________ a flat screen TV. I don't have enough money.

d. If you ________ ________ stocks at the right time, you can get rich.

e. Is it safe to ________ ________?

f. Let's ________ ________ to the concert.

3. **Thesaurus Activities**

Find the Thesaurus feature with the word *money*. Then complete the sentences using words from the feature. Look up any words you aren't sure of.

a. A single ________ is now in use in all European Union countries.

b. I never use ________. I prefer to pay by credit card or check.

c. I don't have the amount of ________ I need to start my own business.

d. The group decided to raise ________ to help people with AIDS.

e. The discovery of oil brought great ________ to the Middle East.

4. **Choosing the Right Definition**

Study the numbered definitions for *bill*. Then write the number of the definition that relates to each sentence below.

_____ **a.** My electric bill this month was over $100.

_____ **b.** He handed me three crisp dollar bills.

_____ **c.** The mechanic billed us for some work he didn't do.

_____ **d.** Congress passed a bill that prohibited smoking in hospitals.

5. **Dictionary Research**

The Word Web feature for *money* says that the Lydians *minted* three types of coins. Look up the word *mint* in the dictionary.

| | Meaning number |
|---|---|
| **a.** Which numbered meaning of *mint* is used in the Word Web feature? | _____ |
| **b.** Which meaning names an herb people cook with? | _____ |
| **c.** Which meaning names a type of candy? | _____ |
| **d.** Which meaning tells where money is manufactured? | _____ |

**ANSWER KEY:**

1. **a.** barter; **b.** cowrie shells; **c.** no; **d.** China; **e.** gold, silver
2. **a.** bought; **b.** 2; **c.** afford to, buy; **d.** buy, and sell; **e.** buy, online; **f.** buy, tickets
3. **a.** currency; **b.** cash; **c.** capital; **d.** funds; **e.** wealth
4. **a.**1; **b.** 3; **c.** 2; **d.** 4
5. **a.** 4; **b.** 1; **c.** 2; **d.** 3

## 14. POLLUTION AND THE GREENHOUSE EFFECT

| Word Web Activities<br>Word Partnership Activities<br>Word Link Activities | Choosing the Right Definition<br>Dictionary Research |
|---|---|

### 1. Word Web Activities

Use the Word Web feature entitled *pollution* to answer the following questions. Look up any words you aren't sure of.

**a.** *Smog* is a combination of smoke and __________.

**b.** Factories in the Midwest cause __________ that falls in the East.

**c.** A substance used to kill insects is called a __________.

Use the Word Web feature entitled *the greenhouse effect* to answer these questions.

**d.** Energy that comes from the sun is called __________ radiation.

**e.** Gasoline is an example of a __________ fuel.

### 2. Word Partnership Activities

Notice how the word *cause* is used in the Word Web features for *pollution* and *the greenhouse effect*. Next study the Word Partnership feature for *cause*. Use the correct Word Partnership phrase to complete each sentence below. If necessary, look up new words in the dictionary.

**a.** Scientists are looking for answers. They want to _______________ of global warming.

**b.** My cold isn't serious at all. There's no _______________.

**c.** They want to know why their dog died. The vet is looking for the _______________.

### 3. Word Link Activities

**a.** The prefix in the word *explode* is __________.

**b.** Find the Word Link at the entry for *explode*. What does the prefix mean? _______________ _______________ _______________

Which of the words in the *ex* Word Link means the same as the following? Look up the words in the dictionary if you are not sure.

**c.** to leave __________

**d.** to break into many pieces __________

**e.** to go beyond __________

4. **Choosing the Right Definition**

The Word Web feature for *the greenhouse effect* mentions carbon dioxide and other *gases*. Study the numbered definitions for *gas*. Then write the number of the definition that relates to each sentence below.

_____ a. I need to put some gas in the car before we leave this afternoon.
_____ b. The soldiers were gassed by a small group of enemy troops.
_____ c. Our new stove uses gas instead of electricity.
_____ d. Cigarette smoke contains poisonous gases.
_____ e. Oxygen is a gas that plants give off.

5. **Dictionary Research**

The Word Web feature for *greenhouse effect* says that global average *temperature* has risen over the past 100 years. Search the Word Webs to find the answers to the following questions about temperature.

| | Word Web | Question | Answer |
|---|---|---|---|
| a. | thermometer | On the Fahrenheit scale water boils at _________. | _______ |
| b. | climate | In the last 100 years, the earth's temperature has increased by _________. | _______ |
| c. | wind | Air flows from one place to another because of the _________ in temperature from one area to another. | _______ |
| d. | cooking | Heating food to a high temperature kills _________. | _______ |

**ANSWER KEY:**

1. **a.** fog; **b.** acid rain; **c.** pesticide; **d.** solar; **e.** fossil
2. **a.** determine the cause; **b.** cause for concern; **c.** cause of death
3. **a.** ex; **b.** away, from, out; **c.** exit; **d.** explode; **e.** exceed
4. **a.** 3; **b.** 4; **c.** 1; **d.** 2; **e.** 1
5. **a.** 212 degrees; **b.** about 1° Fahrenheit; **c.** difference; **d.** bacteria

# 15. BRIDGES AND DAMS

| Word Web Activities<br>Thesaurus Activities | Grammar Activities<br>Word Partnership Activities |
|---|---|

## 1. Word Web Activities

Study the Word Web feature for *bridge*. Then match each number below with the correct description.

1. The height in feet of the Akashi Kaikyo Bridge _____
2. When the Brooklyn Bridge was built _____
3. The length of the Evergreen Point Floating Bridge _____
4. How many vehicles cross the Brooklyn Bridge every day _____
5. The strength of an earthquake that the Akashi Kaikyo Bridge can withstand _____
6. The length of the Akashi Kaikyo Bridge _____

a. over 1 mile
b. 1883
c. 120,000
d. 1,000
e. 8.5
f. 12,828 feet

Study the Word Web feature for *dam*. Then answer the questions below. Write T for *true* or F for *false*.

_____ g. The world's first dam was built near Memphis, Egypt.
_____ h. The world's first dam prevented flooding.
_____ i. Hydroelectric dams provide 20% of the world's electricity.
_____ j. The Itapu Dam took 10 years to build.

## 2. Thesaurus Activities

The Word Web feature for *dam* states that dams sometimes damage valuable forest *lands*. Find the Thesaurus feature with the word *land*. Then complete the sentences below using words from the feature. Look up any words you aren't sure of.

a. Someday I will return to the _________ of my birth.
b. Harry doesn't own a house, but he does own some _________ _________ outside of town.
c. We weren't sure when the plane would _________.
d. Do you live in a safe _________ ?

3. **Grammar Activities**

The Word Web feature for *dam* describes the world's longest *suspension* bridge. Study the list of words that are formed from the root word *suspend*. Write the part of speech of each underlined word—noun, verb, or adjective. Use your dictionary to check your answers.

**a.** I drove over a large rock and damaged the car's suspension. ________

**b.** The airline suspends flights during storms. ________

**c.** I use suspenders instead of a belt. ________

**d.** I couldn't stand the suspense, so I asked the teacher what my grade was. ________

4. **Word Partnership Activities**

Study the Word Partnership feature for *build*. Use one of the phrases in this feature to complete each sentence below. If necessary, look up new words in these phrases in the dictionary.

**a.** Leo works out at the gym and has a very ____________.

**b.** Many female ballet dancers have a ________________.

**c.** The government will ____________ to connect all the major cities in the country.

**d.** Tax revenue often helps to ___________ and ____________.

**ANSWER KEY:**

1. **a.** 3; **b.** 2; **c.** 4; **d.** 1; **e.** 5; **f.** 6; **g.** T; **h.** F; **i.** T; **j.** F
2. **a.** country; **b.** real estate; **c.** arrive, touch down; **d.** area
3. **a.** noun; **b.** verb; **c.** noun; **d.** noun
4. **a.** athletic/strong build; **b.** slender build; **c.** build roads; **d.** build bridges, build schools

## 16. CLONE

| Word Web Activities<br>Thesaurus Activities | Word Link Activities<br>Choosing the Right Definition |
|---|---|

1. **Word Web Activities**
   Use the Word Web feature entitled *clone* to answer the following questions. Answer each question with one of the bold words in the Word Web feature. Look up any words you aren't sure of.
   **a.** Maria and her sister are _________.
   **b.** I need to give them a _________ of my driver's license.
   **c.** The girls look like _________ , but they were born a year apart.
   **d.** Each _________ in your body contains DNA.
   **e.** Scientists use _________ to create new types of plants.

2. **Thesaurus Activities**
   Find the Thesaurus feature for the word *natural*. Then complete the sentences using words from the feature. Look up any words you aren't sure of.
   **a.** It is _________ for new students to be a little nervous at first.
   **b.** This doesn't look like _________ leather to me. I think it's plastic.
   **c.** Please accept my _________ apology for what I said.
   **d.** Farm-grown strawberries are good, but _________ strawberries are better.

3. **Word Link Activities**

Find the word *identical* in the Word Web feature for *clone*. Look up *identical*. Study the Word Link feature for the root *ident*.

**a.** What does the Word Link *ident* mean? ____________

Write the word in this Word Link that matches each definition below. Look up the words in the dictionary if you are not sure.

**b.** your passport or driver's license ______

**c.** exactly the same ______

**d.** unknown or nameless ______

Find the word *donor* in the Word Web feature for *clone*. Look up *donor*. Study the Word Link feature for the root *don*.

**e.** What does the Word Link *don* mean? ____________

Write the word in this Word Link that matches each definition below. Look up the words in the dictionary if you are not sure.

**f.** to forgive someone ______

**g.** someone who gives something away ______

**h.** to give money or goods to an organization ______

4. **Choosing the Right Definition**

Scientists produce clones by *genetic engineering*. Study the numbered definitions for *engineer*. Then write the number of the definition that relates to each sentence below.

____ **a.** The building engineer repaired the water heater.

____ **b.** My "accidental" meeting with Rosa was actually engineered by her sister.

____ **c.** A famous civil engineer designed that bridge.

____ **d.** They engineered the car in such a way that it would get good gas mileage.

**ANSWER KEY:**

1. **a.** identical; **b.** copy; **c.** twins; **d.** cell; **e.** genetic engineering
2. **a.** normal; **b.** genuine; **c.** sincere; **d.** wild
3. **a.** same; **b.** identification; **c.** identical; **d.** unidentified; **e.** giving; **f.** pardon; **g.** donor; **h.** donate
4. **a.** 2; **b.** 4; **c.** 1; **d.**3

# Aa



**a** /ə, STRONG eɪ/ also **an** /ən, STRONG æn/

> **A** or **an** is the indefinite article. It is used at the beginning of noun groups that refer to only one person or thing. The form **an** is used in front of words that begin with vowel sounds.

**1** DET You use **a** or **an** when you are referring to someone or something for the first time or when people may not know which particular person or thing you are talking about. un, una ❑ *A waiter entered with a glass and a bottle of water.* *Un mesero entró con una botella y un vaso de agua.* ❑ *He started eating an apple.* *Comenzó a comerse una manzana.* **2** DET You use **a** or **an** when you are referring to any person or thing of a particular type and do not want to be specific. un, una ❑ *You should leave it to an expert.* *Deberías dejárselo a un experto.* ❑ *Bring a sleeping bag.* *Trae una bolsa de dormir.* **3** DET You use **a** or **an** in front of a noun when that noun is followed by words that describe it more fully. un, una ❑ *They shared a love of music.* *Compartían un amor por la música.* **4** DET You use **a** or **an** instead of the number "one" in front of some numbers or measurements. un, una ❑ *...a hundred miles.* *...cien millas* **5** DET You use **a** or **an** in expressions such as **eight hours a day** to express a rate or ratio. por ❑ *Prices start at $13.95 a yard for cotton.* *Los precios del algodón van desde 13.95 dólares por yarda.*

**AB** /eɪ bi/ N-UNCOUNT A piece of music or a poem that has an **AB** form or structure consists of two separate parts. *dos partes*

**ABA** /eɪ bi eɪ/ N-UNCOUNT A piece of music or a poem that has an **ABA** form or structure consists of three separate parts. The second part contrasts with the first part, and the third part repeats the first part in a different form. *tres partes*

**aban|don** /əbændən/ (**abandons, abandoning, abandoned**) **1** V-T If you **abandon** a place, thing, or person, you leave the place, thing, or person permanently or for a long time, especially when you should not do so. *abandonar* ❑ *He claimed that his parents had abandoned him.* *Afirmó que sus padres lo habían abandonado.* ● **aban|doned** ADJ *abandonado* ❑ *...a network of abandoned tunnels.* *...una red de túneles abandonados.* ● **aban|don|ment** N-UNCOUNT *abandono* ❑ *...her father's abandonment of her.* *...el abandono por parte de su padre.* **2** V-T If you **abandon** an activity or piece of work, you stop doing it before it is finished. *suspender* ❑ *The authorities have abandoned any attempt to distribute food.* *Las autoridades han suspendido cualquier intento de distribuir comida.* ● **aban|don|ment** N-UNCOUNT *suspensión* ❑ *Rain forced the abandonment of the game.* *La lluvia obligó la suspensión del juego.* **3** V-T If you **abandon** an idea or way of thinking, you stop having that idea or thinking in that way. *renunciar* ❑ *She abandoned the idea of going to nursing school.* *Renunció a la idea de ir a la escuela de enfermería.* **4** N-UNCOUNT If you do something **with abandon,** you behave in a wild, uncontrolled way. *desenfreno* ❑ *He lived life with reckless abandon.* *Vivía de una manera desenfrenada.*

| **Thesaurus** | *abandon* | Ver también: |
|---|---|---|
| V. | desert, leave, quit; (*ant.*) stay **1** | |
| | break off, give up, quit, stop; (*ant.*) continue **2** | |

**ab|bey** /æbi/ (**abbeys**) N-COUNT An **abbey** is a church with buildings attached to it in which monks or nuns live or used to live. *abadía*

**ab|bre|vi|ate** /əbriviеɪt/ (**abbreviates, abbreviating, abbreviated**) V-T If you **abbreviate** something, especially a word or a piece of writing, you make it shorter. *abreviar* ❑ *"Compact disc" is often abbreviated to "CD."* *"Disco compacto" se abrevia "CD", por sus siglas en inglés.*

**ab|bre|via|tion** /əbriviеɪʃᵊn/ (**abbreviations**) N-COUNT An **abbreviation** is a short form of a word or phrase, made by leaving out some of the letters or by using only the first letter of each word. *abreviatura* ❑ *The abbreviation for Kansas is KS.* *La abreviatura de Kansas es KS.*

**ABC's** also **ABCs** /eɪ bi siz/ **1** N-PLURAL The **ABC's of** a subject or activity are the parts of it that you have to learn first because they are the most important and basic. *ABC* ❑ *...the ABC's of cooking.* *...el ABC de la cocina.* **2** N-PLURAL Children who have learned their **ABC's** have learned to recognize, write, or say the alphabet. *abecedario* [INFORMAL]

**ab|do|men** /æbdəmən/ (**abdomens**) N-COUNT Your **abdomen** is the part of your body below your chest where your stomach is. *abdomen* [FORMAL] ❑ *The pain in my abdomen grew worse.* *El dolor en mi abdomen aumentaba.* ● **ab|domi|nal** /æbdɒmɪnᵊl/ ADJ *abdominal* [FORMAL] ❑ *...the abdominal muscles.* *...los músculos abdominales.*

→ see **insect**

**abil|ity** /əbɪlɪti/ (**abilities**) N-VAR Your **ability** is the quality or skill that you have which makes it possible for you to do something. *habilidad* ❑ *Her drama teacher spotted her acting ability.* *Su maestra de teatro detectó su habilidad dramática.* ❑ *His mother had strong musical abilities.* *Su mamá tenía grandes habilidades musicales.*

| **Thesaurus** | *ability* | Ver también: |
|---|---|---|
| N. | capability, competence, craft, knack, skill, technique | |

A

**Word Partnership** Usar *ability* con:

V. ability **to handle, have the** ability, **lack the** ability
N. **lack of** ability
ADJ. **natural** ability

**abiot|ic** /eɪbaɪɒtɪk/ ADJ **Abiotic** factors in the environment are things such as the climate and the quality of the soil, which affect the ability of organisms to survive. *abiótico* [TECHNICAL]

**able** /eɪbᵊl/ (**abler** /eɪblər/ (**ablest**) **1** PHRASE If you **are able to** do something, you have skills or qualities which make it possible for you to do it. *ser capaz de* ❑ *The 10-year-old child should be able to prepare a simple meal. Un niño de 10 años debería ser capaz de preparar una comida sencilla.* ❑ *The company says they're able to keep prices low. La compañía dice que son capaces de mantener los precios bajos.* **2** PHRASE If you **are able to** do something, you have enough freedom, power, time, or money to do it. *poder* ❑ *You'll be able to read in peace. Podrás leer en paz.* ❑ *Are you able to help me or not? ¿Puedes ayudarme o no?* **3** ADJ Someone who is **able** is very intelligent or very good at doing something. *hábil* ❑ *Mr. Nicholas was one of the most able men in the industry. El señor Nicholas era uno de los hombres más hábiles en la industria.* ● **ably** /eɪbli/ ADV *hábilmente* ❑ *He was ably assisted by Robert James. Era hábilmente asistido por Robert James.*

**Usage** **be able to** and **could**

*Could* is used to refer to ability in the past: *When I was younger I could swim very fast.* When referring to single events in the past, use *be able to* instead: *I was able to finish my essay last night.* In negative sentences or when referring to things that happened frequently or over a period of time, you can use either *be able to* or *could*: *I wasn't able to/couldn't finish my essay last night. When you were in college could you usually/were you usually able to get your work done on time?*

**ab|nor|mal** /æbnɔrmᵊl/ ADJ Someone or something that is **abnormal** is unusual, especially in a way that is troublesome. *anómalo* ❑ *...an abnormal heartbeat. ...un latido anómalo.* ● **ab|nor|mal|ly** ADV *anormalmente* ❑ *...abnormally high ocean temperatures. ...temperaturas oceánicas anormalmente altas.*

**aboard** /əbɔrd/ PREP If you are **aboard** a ship or plane, you are on it or in it. *a bordo* ❑ *He's invited us aboard his boat. Nos invitó a subir a bordo.* ● **Aboard** is also an adverb. *a bordo* ❑ *It took two hours to get all the people aboard. Tomó dos horas subir a toda la gente a bordo.*

**abol|ish** /əbɒlɪʃ/ (**abolishes, abolishing, abolished**) V-T If someone in authority **abolishes** a system or practice, they put an end to it. *abolir* ❑ *The committee voted Thursday to abolish the death penalty. El comité votó el jueves para abolir la pena de muerte.* ● **abo|li|tion** /æbəlɪʃᵊn/ N-UNCOUNT *abolición* ❑ *I support the total abolition of slavery. Apoyo la abolición total de la esclavitud.*

**Thesaurus** *abolish* Ver también:

V. eliminate, end; (*ant.*) continue

**abor|tion** /əbɔrʃᵊn/ (**abortions**) N-VAR If a woman has an **abortion**, she ends her pregnancy deliberately so that the baby is not born alive. *aborto* ❑ *This drug is not used as a method of abortion in the U.S. Este medicamento no se utiliza como método para el aborto en los EE.UU.*

**about** /əbaʊt/ **1** PREP You use **about** to introduce who or what something relates to or concerns. *sobre, acerca de* ❑ *She knew a lot about food. Sabía mucho sobre comida* ❑ *He never complains about his wife. Nunca se queja de su esposa.* **2** PREP When you say that there is a particular quality **about** someone or something, you mean that they have this quality. *en* ❑ *There was something special about her. Había algo de especial en ella.* ❑ *There was a warmth and passion about him you never knew. Había en él una calidez y una pasión que tú nunca conociste.* **3** ADV **About** is used in front of a number to show that the number is not exact. *alrededor de* ❑ *The child is about eight years old. El niño tiene alrededor de cuatro años.* ❑ *The rate of inflation is about 2.7 percent. La tasa de inflación es de alrededor del 2.7 por ciento.* **4** ADJ If you are **about to** do something, you are going to do it very soon. *a punto de* ❑ *I think he's about to leave. Creo que está a punto de salir.* ❑ *Visas are about to be abolished. Están a punto de abolir las visas.* **5** **how about** → see **how** **6** **just about** → see **just** **7** **what about** → see **what**

**Usage** **about to**

*About to* is used to say that something is going to happen very soon without specifying exactly when. A time expression is not necessary and should be avoided: *The concert is about to start.* means that it is imminent; *The concert starts in five minutes.* tells us exactly when.

**above** /əbʌv/ **1** PREP If one thing is **above** another one, it is directly over it or higher than it. *sobre* ❑ *He lifted his hands above his head. Levantó sus manos sobre su cabeza.* ❑ *Apartment 46 was a quiet apartment, unlike the one above it. El departamento 46 era tranquilo, al contrario del que estaba sobre él.* ● **Above** is also an adverb. *de lo alto* ❑ *A long scream sounded from somewhere above. Se oyó un gran grito de lo alto.* ❑ *...a picture of the new house as seen from above. ...un cuadro de la casa nueva vista desde lo alto.* **2** PREP If an amount or measurement is **above** a particular level, it is greater than that level. *arriba de* ❑ *The temperature rose to just above 40 degrees. La temperatura subió justo arriba de los 40 grados.* ❑ *Victoria Falls has had above average levels of rainfall this year. Este año, las Cascadas Victoria han tenido niveles de lluvia más arriba de los normales.* ● **Above** is also an adverb. *arriba* ❑ *Banks have been charging 25 percent and above for loans. Los bancos han estado cobrando arriba de 25 por ciento por préstamos.* **3** PREP If someone is **above** you, they are in a higher social position than you or in a position of authority over you. *arriba de* ❑ *You have people above you making decisions. Tienes gente arriba de ti tomando decisiones.* ● **Above** is also an adverb. *arriba* ❑ *The policemen were acting on orders from above. Los policías actuaban de acuerdo a las órdenes de arriba.* **4** PREP If someone thinks they are **above** something, they act as if they are too good or important for it. *por encima de* ❑ *He thought he was above failure. Pensaba que estaba*

*por encima del fracaso.* **5** PREP If someone is **above** criticism or suspicion, they cannot be criticized or suspected because of their good qualities or their position. *por encima de* ❑ *He was a respected academic and above suspicion. Era un respetado académico que estaba por encima de toda sospecha.* **6** ADV In writing, you use **above** to refer to something that has already been mentioned or discussed. *lo anterior* ❑ *Several conclusions could be drawn from the results described above. Por lo anterior, podríamos llegar a varias conclusiones.* • **Above** is also a noun. *los anteriores* ❑ *For additional information, contact any of the above. Para más información, contacte a cualquiera de los anteriores.* • **Above** is also an adjective. *anterior* ❑ *For a copy of their brochure, write to the above address. Para obtener copia del folleto, escriba a la dirección anterior.* **7** **over and above** → see **over**
→ see **location**

**abra|sion** N-UNCOUNT **Abrasion** is the gradual wearing away of the surface of rock as a result of other rock or sand particles rubbing against it. *abrasión*

**abroad** /əbr<u>ɔ</u>d/ ADV If you go **abroad,** you go to a foreign country. *al extranjero, en el extranjero* ❑ *I would love to go abroad this year. Me encantaría ir al extranjero este año.* ❑ *The owner of the house is abroad. El dueño de la casa está en el extranjero.*

**ab|rupt** /əbr<u>ʌ</u>pt/ **1** ADJ An **abrupt** change or action is very sudden, often in a way that is unpleasant. *abrupto* ❑ *His career came to an abrupt end in 1998. Su carrera tuvo un abrupto final en 1998.* • **ab|rupt|ly** ADV *abruptamente* ❑ *He stopped abruptly and looked my way. Se detuvo abruptamente y volteó hacia donde yo estaba.* **2** ADJ Someone who is **abrupt** speaks or acts in a rude, unfriendly way. *brusco, cortante* ❑ *His voice was abrupt. Habló en tono cortante.* • **ab|rupt|ly** ADV *abruptamente* ❑ *"Good night, then," she said abruptly. —Entonces buenas noches —dijo abruptamente.*

**ab|sence** /æbsᵊns/ (**absences**) **1** N-VAR Someone's **absence** from a place is the fact that they are not there. *ausencia* ❑ *A letter arrived for me in my absence. Me llegó una carta en mi ausencia.* **2** N-SING The **absence** of something from a place is the fact that it is not there or does not exist. *a falta de* ❑ *She told the child that in the absence of his father, he was the head of the family. Le dijo al niño que a falta de su padre, él era el jefe de la familia.*

**ab|sent** /æbsᵊnt/ **1** ADJ If someone or something is **absent from** a place or situation, they are not there. *faltar* ❑ *He has been absent from his desk for two weeks. Ha faltado a su trabajo desde hace dos semanas.* ❑ *The pictures, too, were absent from the walls. También faltaban los cuadros de las paredes.* **2** ADJ If someone appears **absent,** they are not paying attention. *ausente* ❑ *"Nothing," Rosie said in an absent way. —Nada —dijo Rosie de manera ausente.* • **ab|sent|ly** ADV *de manera ausente* ❑ *He nodded absently. Asintió de manera ausente.*

**ab|sen|tee** /æbsᵊnt<u>i</u>/ (**absentees**) **1** N-COUNT An **absentee** is a person who should be in a particular place but who is not there. *ausente* ❑ *Two of the absentees had good reasons for being away. Dos de los ausentes tuvieron buenas razones para irse.* **2** ADJ In elections in the United States, if you vote by **absentee** ballot or if you are an **absentee** voter, you vote in advance because you will be unable to go to the polling place. ❑ *He voted by absentee ballot. Ejerció su voto de ausencia.*
→ see **election**

**absent-m<u>i</u>nded** ADJ Someone who is **absent-minded** forgets things or does not pay attention to what they are doing. *distraído* ❑ *In his later life he became even more absent-minded. Con la edad, se volvió incluso más distraído.* • **absent-mindedly** ADV *distraídamente* ❑ *Elliot absent-mindedly scratched his head. Elliot se rascó distraídamente la cabeza.*

**ab|so|lute** /æbsəl<u>u</u>t/ (**absolutes**) **1** ADJ **Absolute** means total and complete. *absoluto* ❑ *It's not really suitable for absolute beginners. No es muy apropiado para absolutos principiantes.* ❑ *...absolute proof. ...prueba absoluta.* **2** ADJ **Absolute** rules and principles are believed to be true or right in all situations. *absoluto* ❑ *There are no absolute rules. No hay reglas absolutas.* **3** N-COUNT An **absolute** is a rule or principle that is believed to be true or right in all situations. *absoluto* ❑ *This is one of the few absolutes in U.S. law. Éste es uno de los pocos absolutos en la ley de EE.UU.*

**ab|so|lute da|ting** N-UNCOUNT In archeology, **absolute dating** is a method of estimating the age of something such as a building or tool by examining its physical or chemical properties. *datación absoluta*

**ab|so|lute|ly** /æbsəl<u>u</u>tli/ **1** ADV **Absolutely** means totally and completely. *absolutamente* ❑ *Joan is absolutely right. Joan tiene absolutamente toda la razón.* **2** ADV **Absolutely** is an emphatic way of saying yes or of agreeing with someone. **Absolutely not** is an emphatic way of saying no or of disagreeing with someone. *definitivamente* ❑ *"It's worrying though, isn't it?" —"Absolutely." —Sin embargo es preocupante, ¿no? —Definitivamente.*

**ab|so|lute mag|ni|tude** (**absolute magnitudes**) N-COUNT The **absolute magnitude** of a star or galaxy is a measure of its actual brightness, after its distance from the Earth has been taken into account. *magnitud absoluta* [TECHNICAL]

**ab|so|lute va<u>l</u>ue** (**absolute values**) N-COUNT In mathematics, the **absolute value** of a number is the difference between that number and zero. The absolute value of -4 is 4, and the absolute value of +4 is 4. *valor absoluto*

**ab|so|lute zero** N-UNCOUNT **Absolute zero** is a theoretical temperature that is thought to be the lowest possible temperature. *cero absoluto*

**ab|sorb** /əbs<u>ɔ</u>rb, -z<u>ɔ</u>rb/ (**absorbs, absorbing, absorbed**) **1** V-T To **absorb** a substance means to soak it up or take it in. *absorber* ❑ *Cook the rice until it absorbs the water. Cocine el arroz hasta que absorba el agua.* • **ab|sorp|tion** /əbs<u>ɔ</u>rpʃᵊn, -z<u>ɔ</u>rp-/ N-UNCOUNT *absorción* ❑ *The heat of the water helps the absorption of the oil through the skin. El calor del agua ayuda a la absorción del aceite por la piel.* **2** V-T If a group **is absorbed into** a larger group, it becomes part of the larger group. *integrarse* ❑ *In 1662, the New Haven colony was absorbed into Connecticut. En 1662, la colonia de New Haven se integró a Connecticut.* • **ab|sorp|tion** N-UNCOUNT *integración* ❑ *...the absorption of the old East Germany into the new republic ...la integración de la antigua Alemania del Este a la nueva república.* **3** V-T If something **absorbs** a force or shock, it reduces its effect. *absorber* ❑ *...shoes that absorb the impact of running. ...zapatos que absorben el impacto al correr.* **4** V-T If you **absorb** information, you learn and understand it. *asimilar* ❑ *Often he only absorbs half the information in the instruction manual. A menudo sólo asimila la mitad de la información del manual de instrucciones.* **5** V-T If something **absorbs** you, it interests you a lot and takes up all your attention and energy. *absorber* ❑ *Her new career absorbed her completely. Su nueva carrera la absorbía completamente.*

**ab|stract** /æbstrækt/ (**abstracts**) **1** ADJ An **abstract** idea or way of thinking is based on general ideas rather than on real things and events. *abstracto* ❑ *...starting with a few abstract ideas. ...comenzando por algunas ideas abstractas* **2** ADJ **Abstract** art makes use of shapes and patterns rather than showing people or things. *abstracto* ❑ *...a modern abstract painting. ...una moderna pintura abstracta* **3** N-COUNT An **abstract** is an abstract work of art. *pintura abstracta* ❑ *His abstracts are held in many collections. Sus pinturas abstractas están en muchas colecciones.* **4** PHRASE When you talk or think about something **in the abstract,** you talk or think about it in a general way, rather than considering particular things or events. *en teoría* ❑ *Money was something she only thought about in the abstract. El dinero era algo en lo que ella sólo pensaba en teoría.*

**ab|surd** /æbsɜrd, -zɜrd/ ADJ If you say that something is **absurd,** you are criticizing it because you think that it is ridiculous or that it does not make sense. *absurdo* ❑ *That's absurd. Eso es absurdo.* ❑ *It's absurd to suggest that they knew what was going on but did nothing. Es absurdo sugerir que ellas sabían lo que estaba pasando pero no hicieron nada.* • **The absurd** is something that is absurd. *absurdo* [FORMAL] ❑ *She has a strong sense of the absurd. Tiene un alto sentido del absurdo.* • **ab|surd|ly** ADV *absurdamente* ❑ *Prices were still absurdly low. Los precios eran todavía absurdamente bajos.* • **ab|surd|ity** /æbsɜrdɪti, -zɜrd-/ N-VAR (**absurdities**) *lo absurdo* ❑ *...the absurdity of the situation. ...lo absurdo de la situación.*

| **Thesaurus** | *absurd* | Ver también: |
|---|---|---|
| ADJ. | crazy, foolish | |

**abun|dant** /əbʌndənt/ ADJ Something that is **abundant** is present in large quantities. *abundante* ❑ *...an abundant supply of food. ...una abundante provisión de comida.*

**abuse** (**abuses, abusing, abused**)

> The noun is pronounced /əbyus/. The verb is pronounced /əbyuz/.

**1** N-VAR **Abuse** of someone or something is cruel and violent treatment of them. *abuso* ❑ *...child abuse. ...abuso infantil.* ❑ *...victims of physical abuse. ...víctimas de abuso físico.* **2** N-UNCOUNT **Abuse** is extremely rude and insulting things that people say when they are angry. *insultos* ❑ *I shouted abuse as the car drove off. Grité insultos mientras el coche se alejaba.* **3** N-VAR **Abuse** of something is the use of it in a wrong way or for a bad purpose. *abuso* ❑ *...the abuse of power. ...el abuso de poder.* **4** V-T If someone **is abused,** they are treated cruelly and violently. *abusar de* ❑ *The film is about her daughter, who was abused as a child. La película trata de su hija, quien fue abusada de niña.* ❑ *A person who abuses animals is likely to be violent with people. Una persona que abusa de los animales puede llegar a ser violenta con las personas.* **5** V-T You can say that someone **is abused** if extremely rude and insulting things are said to them. *abusar de* ❑ *He said that he was verbally abused by other soldiers. Dijo que había sido abusado verbalmente por los otros soldados.* **6** V-T If you **abuse** something, you use it in a wrong way or for a bad purpose. *abusar de* ❑ *The rich and powerful sometimes abuse their position. Los ricos y poderosos a veces abusan de su posición.*

| **Thesaurus** | *abuse* | Ver también: |
|---|---|---|
| N. | damage, harm, injury, violation **1** | |
| | blame, injury, insult; (*ant.*) compliment **2** | |
| V. | damage, harm, injure, mistreat; (*ant.*) care for, protect, respect **4** | |
| | insult, offend, pick on, put down; (*ant.*) compliment, flatter, praise **5** | |

**abu|sive** /əbyusɪv/ **1** ADJ Someone who is **abusive** behaves in a cruel and violent way toward other people. *abusivo* ❑ *He was violent and abusive toward Ben's mother. Fue violento y abusivo con la mamá de Ben.* **2** ADJ **Abusive** language is extremely rude and insulting. *grosero* ❑ *I did not use any bad or abusive language. No utilicé ni malas palabras ni lenguaje grosero.*

**abys|sal plain** /əbɪsəl pleɪn/ (**abyssal plains**) N-COUNT An **abyssal plain** is a wide, flat area at the bottom of an ocean. *plano abisal*

**a/c** also **A/C** /eɪ si/ N-UNCOUNT **a/c** is an abbreviation for **air-conditioning.** *A/C, aire acondicionado* ❑ *Keep your windows closed and the a/c on high. Mantenga las ventanas cerradas y el aire acondicionado encendido al máximo.* ❑ *60 Motel Units. All Units A/C, Heat, Cable TV. 60 unidades de motel. Todas las unidades con A/C, calefacción y tv de cable.*

**aca|dem|ic** /ækədɛmɪk/ (**academics**) **1** ADJ **Academic** means relating to the work done in schools, colleges, and universities, especially work that involves studying and reasoning rather than practical or technical skills. *académico* ❑ *Their academic standards are high. Sus estándares académicos son altos.* ❑ *...the start of the academic year. ...el comienzo del año académico.* • **aca|dem|ical|ly** ADV *académicamente* ❑ *He is academically gifted. Es académicamente dotado.* **2** N-COUNT An **academic** is a member of a university or college who teaches or does research. *académico* ❑ *...a group of academics. ...un grupo de académicos.*

**acad|emy** /əkædəmi/ (**academies**) **1** N-COUNT **Academy** is sometimes used in the names of schools and colleges, especially those specializing in particular subjects or skills, or private high schools in the United States. *Academia* ❑ *He is an English teacher at the Seattle Academy for Arts and Sciences. Es maestro de inglés en la Academia de Artes y Ciencias de Seattle.* **2** N-COUNT **Academy** appears in the names of some societies formed to improve or maintain standards in a particular field. *Academia* ❑ *...the National Academy of Sciences. ...la Academia Nacional de Ciencias.*

**ac|cel|er|ate** /æksɛləreɪt/ (**accelerates,**

**accelerating, accelerated)** 1 V-T/V-I If the process or rate of something **accelerates** or if something **accelerates** it, it gets faster and faster. *acelerar* ❑ *Growth will accelerate to 2.9 percent next year. El crecimiento se acelerará a 2.9 por ciento el año próximo.* ● **ac|cel|era|tion** /æksɛləreɪʃᵊn/ N-UNCOUNT *aceleración* ❑ *...the acceleration of knowledge this century. ...la aceleración del conocimiento en este siglo.* 2 V-I When a moving vehicle **accelerates,** it goes faster and faster. *acelerar* ❑ *Suddenly the car accelerated. De pronto, el auto aceleró.* ● **ac|cel|era|tion** N-UNCOUNT *aceleración* ❑ *Acceleration to 60 mph takes just 5.7 seconds. La aceleración llega a las 60 millas por hora en solo 5.7 segundos.*

**ac|cel|era|tion** /æksɛləreɪʃᵊn/ 1 N-UNCOUNT **Acceleration** is the rate at which the speed of an object increases. *aceleración* [TECHNICAL] 2 → see also **accelerate**
→ see **motion**

**ac|cel|era|tor** /æksɛləreɪtər/ (**accelerators**) N-COUNT The **accelerator** in a car or other vehicle is the pedal that you press with your foot in order to make the vehicle go faster. *acelerador* ❑ *He took his foot off the accelerator. Quitó el pie del acelerador.*

**ac|cent** /æksɛnt/ (**accents**) 1 N-COUNT Someone who speaks with a particular **accent** pronounces the words of a language in a distinctive way that shows which country, region, or background they come from. *acento* ❑ *He had a slight southern accent. Tenía un ligero acento sureño.* 2 N-COUNT An **accent** is a short line or other mark which is written above certain letters in some languages and which indicates the way those letters are pronounced. *acento* ❑ *Some languages use accents to change the sound of a letter. Algunos idiomas hacen uso de acentos para cambiar el sonido de una letra.*

**Word Partnership** Usar *accent* con:

| | |
|---|---|
| ADJ. | **American/French** accent, **regional** accent, **thick** accent 1 |
| V. | **do an** accent, **have an** accent 1 **put the** accent **on** 2 |

**ac|cept** /æksɛpt/ (**accepts, accepting, accepted**) 1 V-T/V-I If you **accept** something that you have been offered, you say yes to it or agree to take it. *aceptar* ❑ *She accepted his offer of marriage. Aceptó su propuesta de matrimonio.* ❑ *All those invited to next week's peace conference have accepted. Todos los invitados a la conferencia de paz de la próxima semana han aceptado venir.* ● **ac|cept|ance** /æksɛptəns/ N-UNCOUNT *aceptación* ❑ *...his acceptance speech for the Nobel Peace Prize. ...su discurso de aceptación del Premio Nobel de la Paz* 2 V-T If you **accept** an idea, statement, or fact, you believe that it is true or valid. *aceptar* ❑ *I accept that I cannot be perfect. Acepto que no soy perfecto.* ❑ *I don't think they will accept that view. No creo que acepten esa visión.* ● **ac|cept|ance** N-UNCOUNT *aceptación* ❑ *The theory is gaining acceptance. La teoría está ganando aceptación.* 3 V-T If you **accept** an unpleasant fact or situation, you get used to it or recognize that it is necessary or cannot be changed. *aceptar* ❑ *People often accept noise as part of city life. La gente normalmente acepta el ruido como parte de la vida citadina.* ● **ac|cept|ance** N-UNCOUNT *aceptación* ❑ *...his acceptance of pain. ...su aceptación del dolor.* 4 V-T If an organization or group **accepts** you, you are allowed to join the organization or become part of the group. *aceptar* ❑ *We do not accept all-male groups. No aceptamos grupos enteramente varoniles.* ❑ *Some men find it difficult to accept a woman as a business partner. A algunos hombres les cuesta trabajo aceptar a una mujer como socia en los negocios.* ● **ac|cept|ance** N-UNCOUNT *aprobación* ❑ *...his acceptance into American society. ...su aprobación dentro de la sociedad americana* 5 V-T If you **accept** the responsibility or blame for something, you recognize that you are responsible for it. *aceptar* ❑ *The company cannot accept responsibility for loss or damage. La compañía no puede aceptar responsabilidades por pérdida o daños.* 6 → see also **accepted**

**Usage** **accept** and **except**

*Accept* and *except* sound similar but have different meanings. *Accept* means "to receive." *Monique accepted her diploma. Except* means "other than." *Everyone in the class knew the answer except John.*

**Thesaurus** *accept* Ver también:

| | |
|---|---|
| V. | receive, take; (*ant.*) refuse, reject 1<br>acknowledge, agree to, recognize; (*ant.*) object, oppose, refuse 2<br>endure, live with; (*ant.*) disallow, reject 3 |

**Word Link** ***able* ≈ *able to be* : *acceptable, incurable, portable***

**ac|cept|able** /æksɛptəbᵊl/ 1 ADJ **Acceptable** activities and situations are those that most people approve of or consider to be normal. *aceptable, admisible* ❑ *This is not acceptable behavior. Esta conducta no es aceptable.* ● **ac|cept|abil|ity** /æksɛptəbɪlɪti/ N-UNCOUNT *aceptabilidad* ❑ *...public acceptability of the plan. ...aceptabilidad pública del problema.* ● **ac|cept|ably** ADV *de forma aceptable* ❑ *The aim of discipline is to teach children to behave acceptably. El fin de la disciplina es enseñar a los niños a comportarse de manera aceptable.* 2 ADJ If something is **acceptable,** it is good enough or fairly good. *aceptable* ❑ *On the far side of the street was a restaurant that looked acceptable. Del otro lado de la calle, había un restaurante que se veía aceptable.*

**ac|cept|ed** /æksɛptɪd/ 1 ADJ **Accepted** ideas are agreed by most people to be correct or reasonable. *aceptado* ❑ *It was not a widely accepted idea. La idea no fue muy bien aceptada.* 2 → see also **accept**

**ac|cess** /æksɛs/ (**accesses, accessing, accessed**) 1 N-UNCOUNT If you have **access to** a building or other place, you are able or allowed to go into it. *acceso, entrada, paso* ❑ *The general public does not have access to the White House. El público en general no tiene acceso a la Casa Blanca.* 2 N-UNCOUNT If you have **access to** something such as information or equipment, you have the opportunity or right to see it or use it. *acceso* ❑ *Patients have access to their medical records. Los pacientes tienen acceso a su*

A

*historia clínica.* **3** N-UNCOUNT If you have **access to** a person, you have the opportunity or right to see them or meet them. *acceso* ❑ *He was not allowed access to a lawyer. No le permitieron consultar a un abogado.* **4** V-T If you **access** something, especially information held on a computer, you succeed in finding or obtaining it. *entrar en, tener acceso a, acceder a* ❑ *The software allows parents to see which sites their children have accessed. El programa permite que los padres sepan qué sitios visitan sus hijos.*

**ac|ces|sible** /æksɛsɪbᵊl/ **1** ADJ If a place or building is **accessible to** people, it is easy for them to reach it or get into it. *accesible, asequible* ❑ *The center is easily accessible to the general public. El centro es de fácil acceso para el público en general.* • **ac|ces|sibil|ity** /æksɛsɪbɪlɪti/ N-UNCOUNT *accesibilidad* ❑ *...the easy accessibility of the area. ...el fácil acceso al área.* **2** ADJ If something is **accessible to** people, they can easily use it or obtain it. *accesible, asequible* ❑ *The computer system is accessible to all our workers. El sistema de cómputo está a disposición de todos nuestros trabajadores.* • **ac|ces|sibil|ity** N-UNCOUNT *accesibilidad* ❑ *...growing public concern about the cost, quality, and accessibility of health care. ...creciente preocupación del público por el costo, la calidad y la accesibilidad de los servicios de salud.*
→ see **disability**

**ac|ces|so|ry** /æksɛsəri/ (**accessories**) **1** N-COUNT **Accessories** are items of equipment that are not usually essential, but can be used with or added to something else in order to make it more efficient, useful, or decorative. *accesorio* ❑ *...bathroom accessories. ...accesorios de baño.* **2** N-COUNT **Accessories** are articles such as belts and scarves which you wear or carry but which are not part of your main clothing. *accesorios* ❑ *...handbags, scarves and other accessories. ...bolsas de mano, mascadas y otros accesorios.* **3** N-COUNT An **accessory to** a crime is someone who helps the person who commits it, or knew it was being committed but did not tell the police. *cómplice* [LEGAL] ❑ *The fact that you have that key could make you an accessory to murder. El hecho de que usted tenga esa llave, podría convertirlo en cómplice de asesinato.*

**ac|ci|dent** /æksɪdənt/ (**accidents**) **1** N-COUNT An **accident** happens when a vehicle hits a person, an object, or another vehicle, causing injury or damage. *accidente* ❑ *She had a serious car accident last week. La semana pasada tuvo un serio accidente automovilístico.* **2** N-COUNT If someone has an **accident,** something unpleasant happens to them that was not intended, sometimes causing injury or death. *accidente* ❑ *5,000 people die every year because of accidents in the home. Cinco mil personas mueren anualmente por accidentes en el hogar.* **3** PHRASE If something happens **by accident,** it happens completely by chance. *por accidente, accidentalmente, sin querer* ❑ *She discovered the problem by accident during a visit to a nearby school. Descubrió el problema accidentalmente, en una visita a la escuela del vecindario.*

**Word Partnership** Usar *accident* con:

| | |
|---|---|
| N. | **car** accident **1** |
| | **the cause of an** accident **1** **2** |
| ADJ. | **bad** accident, **a tragic** accident **1** **2** |
| V. | **cause an** accident, **insure against** accident, **killed in the** accident, **report** an accident **1** **2** |
| PREP. | **without** accident **2** |
| | **by** accident **3** |

**ac|ci|den|tal** /æksɪdɛntᵊl/ ADJ An **accidental** event happens by chance or as the result of an accident, and is not intended. *accidental, por accidente* ❑ *...the accidental death of his younger brother. ...la muerte accidental de su hermano menor.* • **ac|ci|den|tal|ly** /æksɪdɛntli/ ADV *accidentalmente* ❑ *Names were accidentally removed from computer disks. Los nombres se borraron accidentalmente de discos de computadoras.*

**Word Link** *claim, clam ≈ shouting : acclaim, clamor, exclaim*

**ac|claim** /əkleɪm/ (**acclaims, acclaiming, acclaimed**) **1** V-T If someone or something **is acclaimed,** they are praised enthusiastically. *aclamar, aplaudir, vitorear* [FORMAL] ❑ *The restaurant has been widely acclaimed for its excellent French food. El restaurante se ha hecho famoso por su excelente comida francesa.* ❑ *He was acclaimed as America's greatest filmmaker. Lo aclamaron como el más grande cineasta estadounidense.* • **ac|claimed** ADJ *aplaudido, aclamado* ❑ *She has published six highly acclaimed novels. Ha publicado seis novelas muy aplaudidas.* **2** N-UNCOUNT **Acclaim** is public praise for someone or something. *aplauso, ovación, aclamación* [FORMAL] ❑ *Angela Bassett has won acclaim for her excellent performance. Angela Bassett se ha ganado el aplauso por sus excelentes interpretaciones.*

**ac|cli|mate** /æklɪmeɪt, əklaɪmɪt/ (**acclimates, acclimating, acclimated**) also **ac|cli|ma|tize** /əklaɪmətaɪz/ V-T/V-I When you **acclimate** or **are acclimated to** a new situation, place, or climate, you become used to it. *aclimatar(se), adaptar(se)* ❑ *I help them acclimate to living in the U.S. Los ayudo a adaptarse a vivir en los Estados Unidos.* ❑ *I hadn't had any time to acclimate myself. No había tenido tiempo de aclimatarme.* • **ac|cli|ma|tion** /æklɪmeɪʃən/ N-UNCOUNT *aclimatación* ❑ *...acclimation to physical exercise. ...adaptación al ejercicio físico.*

**ac|com|mo|date** /əkɒmədeɪt/ (**accommodates, accommodating, accommodated**) **1** V-T If a building or space can **accommodate** someone or something, it has enough room for them. *tener cabida, albergar, dar cabida* ❑ *The school was not big enough to accommodate all the children. La escuela no era suficientemente grande como para dar cabida a todos los niños.* **2** V-T To **accommodate** someone means to provide them with a place to live or stay. *alojar, hospedar* ❑ *The hotel can accommodate up to seventy-five people. En el hotel se pueden alojar setenta y cinco personas.*

**ac|com|mo|da|tion** /əkɒmədeɪʃᵊn/ (**accommodations**) N-VAR **Accommodations** are buildings or rooms where people live or stay. *alojamiento, hospedaje, instalaciones* ❑ *The government will provide accommodations for up to three thousand* homeless people. El gobierno proporcionará alojamiento para un máximo de tres mil personas sin hogar.

**ac|com|pa|ny** /əkʌmpəni/ (**accompanies, accompanying, accompanied**) **1** V-T If you **accompany** someone, you go somewhere with them. acompañar [FORMAL] ❑ *Ken agreed to accompany me on a trip to Africa.* Ken aceptó acompañarme en un viaje a África. ❑ *She was accompanied by her younger brother.* La acompañó su hermano menor. **2** V-T If one thing **accompanies** another, the two things happen or exist at the same time. acompañar [FORMAL] ❑ *Stress accompanies change of any sort.* El estrés va de la mano con todo tipo de cambios. **3** V-T If you **accompany** a singer or a musician, you play one part of a piece of music while they sing or play the main tune. acompañar ❑ *Eddie Higgins accompanies her on all the songs on her new CD.* Eddie Higgins la acompaña en todas las canciones de su nuevo CD.

**ac|com|plish** /əkɒmplɪʃ/ (**accomplishes, accomplishing, accomplished**) V-T If you **accomplish** something, you succeed in doing it. lograr, conseguir, llevar a cabo ❑ *If we all work together, I think we can accomplish our goal.* Si trabajamos en conjunto, creo que lograremos nuestro objetivo. ● **ac|com|plish|ment** /əkɒmplɪʃmənt/ N-UNCOUNT logro, consumación, realización ❑ *...the accomplishment of his highly important mission.* ...el logro de su importantísima misión.

| Thesaurus | *accomplish* | Ver también: |
|---|---|---|
| V. | achieve, complete, gain, realize, succeed | |

**ac|com|plished** /əkɒmplɪʃt/ ADJ If someone is **accomplished** at something, they are very good at it. consumado [FORMAL] ❑ *He is an accomplished painter.* Es un pintor de gran talento.

**ac|com|plish|ment** /əkɒmplɪʃmənt/ (**accomplishments**) **1** N-COUNT An **accomplishment** is something unusual or special that has been done or achieved. logro ❑ *This is the proudest accomplishment of my life.* Es el mayor logro de mi vida. **2** → see also **accomplish**

| Word Link | *cor ≈ with : accord, correspond, escort* |
|---|---|

**ac|cord** /əkɔrd/ (**accords, according, accorded**) **1** N-COUNT An **accord** between countries or groups of people is a formal agreement; for example, to end a war. acuerdo, convenio, arreglo ❑ *...the 1991 peace accords.* ...los acuerdos de paz de 1991. **2** V-T If you **are accorded** a particular kind of treatment, people act toward you or treat you in that way. conceder, otorgar, conferir [FORMAL] ❑ *He was accorded the very highest status.* Le concedieron el estatus más elevado. ❑ *The government accorded him the rank of Colonel.* El gobierno le confirió el rango de coronel. **3** → see also **according to** **4** PHRASE If something happens **of its own accord**, it seems to happen by itself, without anyone making it happen. por sí solo ❑ *In many cases the disease will clear up of its own accord.* En muchos casos la enfermedad desaparece espontáneamente. **5** PHRASE If you do something **of your own accord**, you do it because you want to, without being asked or forced. voluntariamente ❑ *He left his job of his own accord.* Abandonó el empleo de motu proprio.

**ac|cord|ing|ly** /əkɔrdɪŋli/ ADV You use **accordingly** to say that one thing happens as a result of another. en la debida forma ❑ *It is a difficult job and we should pay them accordingly.* Es un trabajo difícil y debemos pagar como corresponde.

**ac|cord|ing to** **1** PHRASE If something is true **according to** a particular person, book, or other source of information, that is where the information comes from. de acuerdo con ❑ *The van raced away, according to police reports.* Según los reportes de la policía, la camioneta se fugó. **2** PHRASE If something is done **according to** a particular set of principles, these principles are used as a basis for the way it is done. según ❑ *They played the game according to the rules.* Jugaron de acuerdo con las reglas. **3** PHRASE If something happens **according to plan,** it happens in exactly the way that it was intended to happen. conforme a ❑ *Everything is going according to plan.* Todo está saliendo según el plan.

**ac|count** /əkaʊnt/ (**accounts, accounting, accounted**) **1** N-COUNT If you have an **account** with a bank, you leave your money there and take some out when you need it. cuenta ❑ *Some banks make it difficult to open an account.* En algunos bancos es difícil abrir una cuenta. **2** N-COUNT In business, a regular customer of a company can be referred to as an **account.** cuenta [BUSINESS] ❑ *Already Transamerica has two major accounts.* Transamerica ya tiene dos cuentas importantes. **3** N-COUNT **Accounts** are detailed records of all the money that a person or business receives and spends. cuentas [BUSINESS] ❑ *He kept detailed accounts.* Llevaba cuentas detalladas. **4** N-COUNT An **account** is a written or spoken report of something that has happened. informe, explicación ❑ *He gave a detailed account of what happened.* Dio una detallada explicación de lo que sucedió. **5** → see also **accounting, checking account** **6** PHRASE If you tell someone not to do something **on your account,** you mean that they should do it only if they want to, and not because they think it will please you. por cuenta propia [SPOKEN] ❑ *Don't leave on my account.* No lo hagas por mí. **7** PHRASE If you say that something should **on no account** be done, you are emphasizing that it should not be done under any circumstances. de ninguna manera ❑ *On no account should the liquid boil.* El líquido no debe hervir por ningún motivo. **8** PHRASE If you **take** something **into account,** or **take account of** something, you consider it when you are thinking about a situation or deciding what to do. considerar, tomar en consideración ❑ *You have to take everyone into account before making a decision.* Tienes que tomar en cuenta a todos antes de tomar una decisión.
→ see **history**

▸ **account for** **1** PHR-VERB If a particular thing **accounts for** a part of something, that part consists of that thing, or is used or produced by it. representar, constituir ❑ *Computers account for 5% of the country's electricity use.* Las computadoras constituyen el 5% del uso de la electricidad en el país. **2** PHR-VERB If you can **account for** something, you can explain it or give the necessary information about it. explicar ❑ *How do you account for these differences?* ¿Cómo explicas estas diferencias?

**ac|count|able** /əkaʊntəbᵊl/ ADJ If you are

A

**accountable for** something that you do, you are responsible for it. responsable ante ❑ *We are accountable to taxpayers.* *Somos responsables ante quienes pagan impuestos.* • **ac|count|abil|ity** /əkaʊntəbɪlɪti/ N-UNCOUNT responsabilidad ❑ *There's too much waste and too little accountability.* *Es demasiado desperdicio y muy poca responsabilidad.*

**ac|count|ant** /əkaʊntənt/ (**accountants**) N-COUNT An **accountant** is a person whose job is to keep financial accounts. contador o contadora

**ac|count|ing** /əkaʊntɪŋ/ N-UNCOUNT **Accounting** is the theory or practice of keeping financial accounts. contabilidad

**ac|cu|mu|late** /əkyuːmyəleɪt/ (**accumulates, accumulating, accumulated**) V-T/V-I When you **accumulate** things or when they **accumulate,** they collect or are gathered over a period of time. acumular(se), amontonar(se), atesorar ❑ *He accumulated $42,000 in 6 years.* *Acumuló 42,000 dólares en 6 años.* • **ac|cu|mu|la|tion** /əkyuːmyəleɪʃən/ N-VAR (**accumulations**) acumulación ❑ *...the accumulation of wealth.* *...la acumulación de la riqueza.*

| Word Link | *ate ≈ filled with : accurate, considerate, desperate* |
|---|---|

**ac|cu|rate** /ækyərɪt/ **1** ADJ **Accurate** information, measurements, and statistics are correct to a very detailed level. exacto, preciso, fiel ❑ *This is the most accurate description of the killer we have.* *Ésta es la descripción más exacta que tenemos del asesino.* • **ac|cu|ra|cy** N-UNCOUNT exactitud, precisión, fidelidad ❑ *...the accuracy of weather reports.* *...la exactitud de los reportes climatológicos.* • **ac|cu|rate|ly** ADV exactamente, precisamente ❑ *He described it quite accurately.* *Lo describió con bastante precisión.* **2** ADJ A person, device, or machine that is **accurate** is able to perform a task without making a mistake. exacto, preciso ❑ *We require grammar and spelling to be accurate.* *Exigimos correcta gramática y ortografía.* • **ac|cu|ra|cy** N-UNCOUNT exactitud, corrección ❑ *We edit letters for length and accuracy.* *Modificamos las cartas en cuanto a extensión y exactitud.* • **ac|cu|rate|ly** ADV exactamente, precisamente ❑ *He hit the golf ball powerfully and accurately.* *Le dio con fuerza y precisión a la pelota de golf.*

| Thesaurus | *accurate* | Ver también: |
|---|---|---|
| ADJ. | right, true; (*ant.*) inaccurate **1** | |
| | correct, precise, rigorous **2** | |

**ac|cu|sa|tion** /ækyuzeɪʃən/ (**accusations**) N-VAR If you make an **accusation** against someone, you criticize them or express the belief that they have done something wrong. acusación ❑ *...an accusation of murder.* *...un cargo por asesinato.*

**ac|cuse** /əkyuːz/ (**accuses, accusing, accused**) **1** V-T If you **accuse** someone **of** something, you say that you believe they did something wrong or dishonest. acusar, culpar, incriminar ❑ *They accused her of lying.* *La acusaron de haber mentido.* ❑ *Her assistant was accused of theft by the police.* *La policía acusó de robo a su asistente.* **2** → see also **accused**

| Thesaurus | *accuse* | Ver también: |
|---|---|---|
| V. | blame, charge, implicate | |

**ac|cused** /əkyuːzd/ (**accused**) N-COUNT **The accused** refers to a person or a group of people charged with a crime or on trial for it. acusado o acusada [LEGAL] ❑ *The accused is a high school senior.* *El acusado está terminando el bachillerato.*

**ace** /eɪs/ (**aces**) **1** N-COUNT An **ace** is a playing card with a single symbol on it. as ❑ *...the ace of hearts.* *...el as de corazones.* **2** N-COUNT If you describe someone such as a sports player as an **ace,** you mean that they are very good at what they do. as ❑ *...former tennis ace John McEnroe.* *...el ex campeón de tenis, John McEnroe.* • **Ace** is also an adjective. prominente ❑ *...ace film producer Lawrence Woolsey.* *...Lawrence Woolsey, destacado productor cinematográfico.* **3** N-COUNT In tennis, an **ace** is a serve which is so fast that the other player cannot return the ball. as ❑ *Agassi served three aces in the final set of the tennis match.* *Agassi puso tres servicios as en el último set del partido.*

**ache** /eɪk/ (**aches, aching, ached**) **1** V-I If you **ache** or a part of your body **aches,** you feel a steady, fairly strong pain. doler ❑ *Her head was hurting and she ached all over.* *Se lastimó la cabeza y le dolía todo el cuerpo.* ❑ *My leg still aches when I sit down.* *La pierna todavía me duele cuando me siento.* **2** N-COUNT An **ache** is a steady, fairly strong pain in a part of your body. dolor ❑ *She had an ache in the knee she hurt last year.* *Tenía un dolor en la rodilla que se lastimó el año pasado.* **3** → see also **headache, heartache**

| Thesaurus | *ache* | Ver también: |
|---|---|---|
| V. | throb **1** | |
| N. | hurt, pain, pang **2** | |

**achieve** /ətʃiːv/ (**achieves, achieving, achieved**) V-T If you **achieve** a particular aim or effect, you succeed in doing it or causing it to happen, usually after a lot of effort. lograr, conseguir ❑ *He worked hard to achieve his goals.* *Trabajó duro para alcanzar sus metas.*

| Thesaurus | *achieve* | Ver también: |
|---|---|---|
| V. | accomplish, bring about; (*ant.*) fail, lose, miss | |

**achieve|ment** /ətʃiːvmənt/ (**achievements**) **1** N-COUNT An **achievement** is something that someone has succeeded in doing, especially after a lot of effort. logro, éxito, triunfo ❑ *It was a great achievement to reach this agreement so quickly.* *Fue un gran éxito llegar a este acuerdo tan rápidamente.* **2** N-UNCOUNT **Achievement** is the process of achieving something. logro, consecución ❑ *Only the achievement of these goals will bring peace.* *Sólo el logro de esos objetivos traerá paz.*

**achoo** /ɑtʃuː/ **Achoo** is used, especially in writing, to represent the sound that you make when you sneeze. achú ❑ *"Achoo!" she sneezed. And then, "Achoo!" she sneezed again.* *—¡Achú! —estornudó. Y después —¡achú! —volvió a estornudar.*

**acid** /æsɪd/ (**acids**) **1** N-VAR An **acid** is a chemical substance, usually a liquid, which contains hydrogen and can react with other substances to form salts. Some acids burn or dissolve other substances that they come into contact with. ácido ❑ *...citric acid.* *...ácido cítrico.* **2** ADJ An **acid** substance contains acid.

*ácido* ❑ *These plants must have an acid soil. Estas plantas necesitan un suelo ácido.* • **acid|ity** /əsɪdɪti/ N-UNCOUNT *acidez* ❑ *...the acidity of rainwater. ...la acidez del agua de lluvia.*

**acid rain** also **acid precipitation** N-UNCOUNT **Acid rain** is rain polluted by acid that has been released into the atmosphere from factories and other industrial processes. Acid rain is harmful to the environment. *lluvia ácida*
→ see **pollution**

**ac|knowl|edge** /æknɒlɪdʒ/ (**acknowledges, acknowledging, acknowledged**) **1** V-T If you **acknowledge** a fact or a situation, you accept or admit that it is true or that it exists. *admitir, reconocer* [FORMAL] ❑ *He acknowledged that he was wrong. Aceptó que estaba equivocado.* ❑ *At last, the government has acknowledged the problem. Por fin el gobierno ha reconocido el problema.* **2** V-T If you **acknowledge** a message or letter, you write to the person who sent it in order to say that you have received it. *acusar recibo de, responder a* ❑ *The army sent me a postcard acknowledging my request. El ejército me mandó un acuse de recibo de mi solicitud.* **3** V-T If you **acknowledge** someone, for example, by moving your head or smiling, you show that you have seen and recognized them. *reconocer* ❑ *He saw her but refused to acknowledge her. Él la vio, pero no quiso reconocerla.*

**ac|knowl|edg|ment** /æknɒlɪdʒmənt/ (**acknowledgments**) also **acknowledgement** **1** N-SING An **acknowledgment** is a statement or action which recognizes that something exists or is true. *reconocimiento* ❑ *It's an acknowledgment that there is a problem. Es una confirmación de que el problema existe.* **2** N-PLURAL The **acknowledgments** in a book are the section in which the author thanks all the people who have helped him or her. *agradecimientos* ❑ *...two whole pages of acknowledgments. ...dos páginas enteras de agradecimientos.*

**acne** /ækni/ N-UNCOUNT If someone has **acne,** they have a skin condition which causes a lot of pimples on their face and neck. *acné, barros* ❑ *...a new treatment for mild to severe acne. ...un nuevo tratamiento para el acné de ligero a grave.*

**acous|tic** /əkustɪk/ (**acoustics**) **1** ADJ An **acoustic** guitar or other instrument is one whose sound is produced without any electrical equipment. *acústico* **2** N-PLURAL The **acoustics** of a space are the structural features which determine how well you can hear music or speech in it. *acústica* ❑ *The theater's acoustics are very clear. La acústica del teatro es muy buena.* **3** N-UNCOUNT **Acoustics** is the scientific study of sound. *acústica* ❑ *...his work in acoustics. ...su trabajo en el campo de la acústica.*
→ see **string**

**ac|quaint|ance** /əkweɪntəns/ (**acquaintances**) **1** N-COUNT An **acquaintance** is someone who you have met, but don't know well. *conocido o conocida* ❑ *He spoke to the owner, an old acquaintance of his. Habló con el propietario, un viejo conocido.* **2** N-VAR If you have an **acquaintance with** someone, you have met them and you know them. *conocimiento* ❑ *The author talks about his personal acquaintance with Picasso. El autor habla de su relación personal con Picasso.*

**ac|quire** /əkwaɪər/ (**acquires, acquiring, acquired**) **1** V-T If you **acquire** something, you obtain it. *adquirir, obtener* [FORMAL] ❑ *Recently, I acquired two new printers. Recientemente conseguí dos impresoras nuevas.* **2** V-T If you **acquire** a skill or a habit, you learn it or develop it. *adquirir* ❑ *I've never acquired a taste for coffee. Nunca me ha gustado el café.*

**ac|qui|si|tion** /ækwɪzɪʃən/ (**acquisitions**) **1** N-VAR If a company or business person makes an **acquisition,** they buy another company or part of a company. *adquisición* [BUSINESS] ❑ *...AT&T's acquisition of TCI. ...la adquisición de TCI por AT&T.* **2** N-COUNT If you make an **acquisition,** you buy or obtain something, often to add to things that you already have. *adquisición, compra* ❑ *Her acquisition of a computer music program helped her to start writing music. Como compró un programa de computadora para hacer música, pudo empezar a componer.* **3** N-UNCOUNT The **acquisition** of a skill or a particular type of knowledge is the process of learning it or developing it. *adquisición* ❑ *...language acquisition. ...adquisición de una lengua.*

**ac|quit** /əkwɪt/ (**acquits, acquitting, acquitted**) V-T If someone **is acquitted of** a crime in a court of law, they are formally declared not to have committed the crime. *absolver, exculpar* ❑ *Mr. Castorina was acquitted of attempted murder. El Sr. Castorina fue exonerado de intento de asesinato.*

**acre** /eɪkər/ (**acres**) N-COUNT An **acre** is an area of land measuring 4,840 square yards or 4,047 square meters. *acre* ❑ *The property has two acres of land. La propiedad incluye dos acres de tierras.*

**ac|ro|nym** /ækrənɪm/ (**acronyms**) N-COUNT An **acronym** is a word composed of the first letters of the words in a phrase, especially when this is used as a name. An example of an acronym is NATO which is made up of the first letters of the "North Atlantic Treaty Organization." *acrónimo, sigla*

**across** /əkrɔs/

> In addition to the uses shown below, **across** is used in phrasal verbs such as "come across," "get across," and "put across."

**1** PREP If someone or something goes **across** a place or a boundary, they go from one side of it to the other. *a través* ❑ *She walked across the floor and sat down. Atravesó la pista de baile y se sentó.* ❑ *He watched Karl run across the street. Vio a Karl atravesar corriendo la calle.* • **Across** is also an adverb. *de un lado a otro* ❑ *Richard stood up and walked across to the window. Richard se puso de pie y atravesó hacia la ventana.* **2** PREP If something is situated or stretched **across** something else, it is situated or stretched from one side of it to the other. *a través* ❑ *...the bridge across Lake Washington. ...el puente que cruza el lago Washington.* ❑ *He wrote his name across the bill. Escribió su nombre encima de la cuenta.* • **Across** is also an adverb. *a través* ❑ *Cut across using scissors. Córtalo en diagonal con las tijeras.* **3** PREP When something happens **across** a place or organization, it happens equally everywhere within it. *de un lado a otro* ❑ *The movie opens across the country on December 11. La película se estrena el 11 de diciembre en todo el país.* **4** ADV If you look **across** at a place, person, or thing, you look toward them.

A

*hacia* ❑ *He looked across at his sleeping wife.* *Miró hacia su mujer, que dormía.* **5** ADV **Across** is used in measurements to show the width of something. *de ancho* ❑ *This plate measures 14 inches across.* *Esta placa mide 14 pulgadas de ancho.*

**act** /ækt/ (**acts, acting, acted**) **1** V-I When you **act,** you do something for a particular purpose. *actuar, tomar medidas, comportarse* ❑ *The police acted to stop the riot.* *La policía hizo lo necesario para acallar la revuelta.* **2** V-I If someone **acts** in a particular way, they behave in that way. *comportarse* ❑ *...youths who were acting suspiciously.* *...jóvenes que actuaban de manera sospechosa.* ❑ *He acted as if he hadn't heard any of it.* *Se comportó como si no hubiera oído nada al respecto.* **3** V-I If someone or something **acts as** a particular thing, they have that role or function. *hacer las veces de* ❑ *He acted as the ship's doctor.* *Fungía como médico del barco.* **4** V-I If someone **acts** in a particular way, they pretend to be something that they are not. *comportarse, actuar* ❑ *He acted surprised when I talked about Japan.* *Se hizo el sorprendido cuando le hablé de Japón.* **5** V-I If you **act** in a play or film, you have a part in it. *actuar* ❑ *He acted in many films, including "Reds."* *Trabajó en muchas películas, incluso en "Reds".* **6** N-COUNT An **act** is a single thing that someone does. *hecho, acción, acto* [FORMAL] ❑ *As a child I loved the act of writing.* *De niño me encantaba escribir.* **7** N-COUNT An **Act** is a law passed by the government. *ley, decreto* ❑ *...an Act of Congress.* *...un decreto del congreso.* **8** N-COUNT An **act** in a play, opera, or ballet is one of the main parts into which it is divided. *acto* ❑ *Act II contained a really funny scene.* *En el segundo acto había una escena muy divertida.* **9** N-COUNT An **act** in a show is a short performance which is one of several in the show. *acto* ❑ *This year many bands are playing, as well as comedy acts.* *Este año tocan muchas bandas, y también hay números de comedia.* **10** N-SING If you say that someone's behavior is an **act,** you mean that it does not express their real feelings. *fingir* ❑ *His anger was real. It wasn't an act.* *Su enojo era real, no estaba haciendo teatro.*

**act|ing** /æktɪŋ/ **1** N-UNCOUNT **Acting** is the activity or profession of performing in plays or films. *actuación* ❑ *I'd like to do a little acting some day.* *Algún día quisiera dedicarme un poco a la actuación.* **2** ADJ You use **acting** before the title of a job to indicate that someone is doing that job temporarily. *suplente, interino* ❑ *...the new acting president.* *...el nuevo presidente en funciones.*

**act|ing area** (**acting areas**) N-COUNT In a theater, the **acting areas** are the different parts of the stage such as the front or back of the stage. *zona de actores*

**ac|tion** /ækʃᵊn/ (**actions**) **1** N-UNCOUNT **Action** is doing something for a particular purpose. *acción, medida* ❑ *The government is taking emergency action.* *El gobierno está tomando medidas de emergencia.* **2** N-UNCOUNT The fighting which takes place in a war can be referred to as **action.** *acción* ❑ *Our leaders have generally supported military action if it proves necessary.* *En general, nuestros líderes han apoyado las medidas militares cuando han sido necesarias.* **3** N-COUNT An **action** is something that you do on a particular occasion. *acción, medida* ❑ *Peter had a reason for his action.* *Peter tenía una razón para tomar esas medidas.* **4** N-SING In physics, **action** is the force that is applied to an object. *acción* **5** N-UNCOUNT The **action** of a chemical is the way that it works, or the effect that it has. *acción* **6** PHRASE If someone or something is **out of action,** they are injured or damaged and cannot work or be used. *fuera de circulación* ❑ *He's been out of action for 16 months with a knee injury.* *Ha estado 16 meses sin jugar por una lesión de rodilla.* **7** PHRASE If you **put** an idea or policy **into action,** you begin to use it or cause it to operate. *poner en práctica* ❑ *Agnes decided to put her plan into action.* *Agnes decidió ejecutar su plan.*
→ see **genre, motion**

| Word Partnership | Usar *action* con: |
|---|---|
| N. | **course of** action, **plan of** action **1** |
| V. | **take** action **1** |
| ADJ. | **disciplinary** action **1** |
| | **military** action **2** |

**ac|ti|vate** /æktɪveɪt/ (**activates, activating, activated**) V-T If a device or process **is activated,** something causes it to start working. *activar* ❑ *Video cameras can be activated by movement.* *El movimiento puede activar las videocámaras.*

**ac|ti|va|tion en|er|gy** N-SING In chemistry and biology, the **activation energy** is the minimum amount of energy that is needed in order for a chemical reaction to occur. *energía de activación*

**ac|tive** /æktɪv/ **1** ADJ Someone who is **active** moves around a lot or does a lot of things. *activo* ❑ *With three active little kids, there was plenty to keep me busy.* *Con tres niños activos, siempre tenía cosas que hacer.* **2** ADJ If someone is **active** in an organization or cause, they do things for it rather than just giving it their support. *activo* ❑ *We should play an active role in politics.* *Deberíamos jugar un papel activo en la política.* ● **ac|tive|ly** ADV *activamente* ❑ *They are actively involved in job training.* *Toman parte activa en la capacitación laboral.* **3** ADJ **Active** is used to emphasize that someone is taking action in order to achieve something, rather than just waiting for it to happen. *activo* ❑ *Companies need to take active steps to increase exports.* *Las compañías necesitan tomar medidas activas para aumentar las exportaciones.* ● **ac|tive|ly** ADV *activamente* ❑ *Many adults are actively looking for work.* *Muchos adultos buscan empleo activamente.* **4** ADJ An **active** volcano has erupted recently or is expected to erupt soon. *activo* ❑ *...lava from an active volcano.* *...lava de un volcán activo.*

| Word Partnership | Usar *active* con: |
|---|---|
| ADV. | **politically** active **2** |
| N. | active **role** **2** |

**ac|tive du|ty** N-UNCOUNT Someone who is on **active duty** is taking part in a war as a member of the armed forces. *servicio activo*

**ac|tive so|lar heat|ing** N-UNCOUNT **Active solar heating** is a method of heating a building by using solar collectors and pipes to distribute energy from the sun throughout the building. *calentamiento solar activo*

**ac|tive trans|port** N-UNCOUNT In biology, **active transport** is the movement of chemicals and other substances through the membranes of cells, which requires the cells to use energy. *transporte activo*

**ac|tive voice** N-SING In grammar, *the* **active voice** means the forms of a verb which are used when the subject of the sentence refers to a person or thing that does something. For example, in "I saw her yesterday," the verb is in the active voice. *voz activa*

**ac|tiv|ist** /æktɪvɪst/ (**activists**) N-COUNT An **activist** is a person who works to bring about political or social changes. *activista* ❑ *...animal rights activists. ...activistas de los derechos de los animales.*

**ac|tiv|ity** /æktɪvɪti/ (**activities**) **1** N-UNCOUNT **Activity** is a situation in which a lot of things are happening. *actividad* ❑ *Children are supposed to get 60 minutes of physical activity every day. Se supone que los niños necesitan 60 minutos diarios de actividad física.* **2** N-COUNT An **activity** is something that you spend time doing. *actividad* ❑ *Activities for small children and adults. Actividades para niños y adultos.* **3** N-PLURAL The **activities** of a group are the things that they do in order to achieve their aims. *actividades* ❑ *...criminal activities. ...actividades criminales.*

**ac|tor** /æktər/ (**actors**) N-COUNT An **actor** is someone whose job is acting in plays or movies. "Actor" in the singular usually refers to a man, but some women who act prefer to be called "actors" rather than "actresses." *actor o actriz* ❑ *His father was an actor. Su padre fue actor.*

→ see **drama, theater**

**ac|tor's po|si|tion** (**actor's positions** or **actors' positions**) N-COUNT In the theater, an **actor's position** is the position that an actor occupies in relation to the audience, for example facing toward the audience or facing away from the audience. *posición del actor*

**ac|tress** /æktrɪs/ (**actresses**) N-COUNT An **actress** is a woman whose job is acting in plays or movies. *actriz* ❑ *She's a really good actress. Es muy buena actriz.*

**ac|tual** /æktʃuəl/ **1** ADJ You use **actual** to emphasize that you are referring to something real or genuine. *real* ❑ *The stories in this book are based on actual people. Las historias de este libro se basan en personas reales.* **2** ADJ You use **actual** to contrast the important aspect of something with a less important aspect. *en realidad, en sí* ❑ *The movie lasts 100 minutes, but the actual story is 90 minutes. La película dura 100 minutos, pero la historia en sí dura 90 minutos.*

**ac|tu|al|ly** /æktʃuəli/ **1** ADV You use **actually** to indicate that a situation exists or that it is true. *de hecho, hasta* ❑ *One afternoon I actually fell asleep for a few minutes. Una tarde, hasta me quedé dormido unos minutos.* **2** ADV You use **actually** when you are correcting or contradicting someone, or to introduce a new topic into a conversation. *de hecho* ❑ *No, I'm not a student. I'm a doctor, actually. No, no soy estudiante. De hecho, soy doctor.* ❑ *Actually, that's not quite right. De hecho, eso no está bien.*

**acute** /əkyut/ **1** ADJ An **acute** situation or feeling is very severe or intense. *agudo* ❑ *He was in acute pain. Tenía un dolor agudo.* • **acute|ly** ADV *sumamente* ❑ *People were acutely interested in what we did. La gente estaba sumamente interesada en lo que hicimos.* **2** ADJ If a person's or animal's senses are **acute,** they are sensitive and powerful. *agudo* ❑ *When she lost her sight, her other senses grew more acute. Cuando perdió la vista, sus demás sentidos se hicieron más agudos.* • **acute|ly** ADV *plenamente* ❑ *He was acutely aware of the smell. Estaba plenamente consciente del olor.* **3** ADJ An **acute** angle is less than 90°. Compare **obtuse** angle. *agudo*

**ad** /æd/ (**ads**) N-COUNT An **ad** is an advertisement. *anuncio* [INFORMAL] ❑ *...a "help wanted" ad. ...un anuncio solicitando ayuda.*

**AD** /eɪ di/ You use **AD** in dates to indicate the number of years or centuries that have passed since the year in which Jesus Christ is believed to have been born. Compare **BC.** *dC.* ❑ *The building dates from 600 AD. El edificio data de 600 dC.*

**ad agen|cy** (**ad agencies**) N-COUNT An **ad agency** is a company whose business is to create advertisements for other companies or organizations. *agencia de publicidad*

**a|dapt** /ədæpt/ (**adapts, adapting, adapted**) **1** V-I If you **adapt to** a new situation, you change your ideas or behavior in order to deal with it. *adaptar* ❑ *The world will be different in the future, and we will have to adapt to the change. En el futuro el mundo será diferente, y nos tendremos que adaptar al cambio.* **2** V-T If you **adapt** something, you change it to make it suitable for a new purpose or situation. *adaptar* ❑ *They adapted the library for use as an office. Adaptaron la biblioteca para usarla como oficina.* ❑ *She'll adapt the rooms to her needs. Adaptará las habitaciones a sus necesidades.* **3** → see also **adapted**

**Usage** **adapt** and **adopt**

*Adapt* and *adopt* sound similar and have similar meanings, but be careful not to confuse them. When you *adapt* something, you change it to make it fit your purpose: *Gilberto tried to adapt the recipe to cook a fish instead of a chicken—what a mistake!* When you *adopt* something, you use it unchanged: *Lucas adopted his boss's technique for dealing with rude customers—he ignored them!*

**Thesaurus** *adapt* Ver también:

V. acclimate, adjust, conform **1**
modify, revise **2**

**ad|ap|ta|tion** /ædæpteɪʃᵊn/ (**adaptations**) **1** N-COUNT An **adaptation** of a book or play is a film or a television program that is based on it. *adaptación* ❑ *...his screen adaptation of Shakespeare's "Henry the Fifth." ...su adaptación a la pantalla de "Henry V" de Shakespeare.* **2** N-UNCOUNT **Adaptation** is the act of changing something to make it suitable for a new purpose or situation. *adaptación* ❑ *Most living creatures are capable of adaptation. La mayoría de los seres vivos son capaces de adaptarse.*

**ad cam|paign** (**ad campaigns**) N-COUNT An **ad campaign** is a planned series of advertisements. *campaña publicitaria* ❑ *...a $50 million government ad campaign. ...una campaña publicitaria del gobierno de $50 millones.*

**add** /æd/ (**adds, adding, added**) **1** V-T If you **add** one thing **to** another, you put it with the

A

other thing, to complete or improve it. *agregar, añadir* ❑ *Add the grated cheese to the sauce. Agrega el queso rallado a la salsa.* ❑ *Vinegar is added to improve the flavor. Se le agrega vinagre para mejorar el sabor.* **2** V-T If you **add** numbers or amounts **together**, you calculate their total. *sumar* ❑ *If there is more than one number, add these together. Si hay más de un número, súmalos.* **3** V-I If one thing **adds to** another, it makes the other thing greater in degree or amount. *agregar* ❑ *The cosy look of the fireplace adds to the room. La apariencia acogedora de la chimenea le agrega calor al cuarto.* • **add|ed** ADJ *más, mayor* ❑ *For added protection choose lipsticks with a sunscreen. Para mayor protección, elige un lápiz labial con protector solar.* **4** V-T To **add** a particular quality **to** something means to cause it to have that quality. *añadir* ❑ *The generous amount of garlic adds flavor. Una cantidad generosa de ajo le añade sabor.* **5** V-T If you **add** something when you are speaking, you say something more. *agregar* ❑ *"He's very angry," Mr. Smith added. —Está muy enojado —agregó Mr. Smith.* **6** V-I If you can **add,** you are able to calculate the total of numbers or amounts. *sumar* ❑ *Many seven-year-olds cannot add properly. Muchos niños de siete años no pueden sumar correctamente.*
→ see **fraction**

▸**add in** PHR-VERB If you **add in** something, you include it as a part of something else. *agregar, añadir* ❑ *Once the vegetables start to cook add in a couple of tablespoons of water. Una vez que las verduras se empiezan a cocer, agrega dos cucharadas de agua.*

▸**add on** **1** PHR-VERB If you **add on** an extra amount or item to a list or total, you include it. *agregar* ❑ *Many tour operators add on extra charges. Muchos operadores turísticos agregan cargos adicionales.* **2** PHR-VERB If you **add on,** you increase the size of a house or other building by constructing one or more extra rooms. *agregar* ❑ *We've added on two bedrooms and a bathroom. Agregamos dos recámaras y un baño.*

▸**add up** **1** PHR-VERB If you **add up** numbers or amounts, or if you **add** them **up,** you calculate their total. *sumar* ❑ *Add up the total of those six games. Suma el total de esos seis juegos.* ❑ *We just added all the numbers up. Sumamos todos los números, nada más.* **2** PHR-VERB If facts or events do not **add up,** they make you confused about a situation because they do not seem to be consistent. If something that someone has said or done **adds up,** it is reasonable and sensible. *cuadrar* ❑ *His story did not add up. Su historia no cuadraba.* **3** PHR-VERB If small amounts of something **add up,** they gradually increase. *acumularse* ❑ *Even small savings, 5 cents here or 10 cents there, can add up. Hasta pequeños ahorros, 5 centavos aquí o 10 centavos allá, se acumulan.*

▸**add up to** PHR-VERB If amounts **add up to** a particular total, they result in that total when they are put together. *ascender a* ❑ *Profits can add up to millions of dollars. Las ganancias pueden ascender a millones de dólares.*

| **Thesaurus** | *add* | Ver también: |
|---|---|---|
| v. | put on, throw in **1** | |
| | calculate, tally, total; (*ant.*) reduce, subtract **2** | |
| | augment, increase; (*ant.*) lessen, reduce **3** | |

**ad|dict** /ædɪkt/ (**addicts**) **1** N-COUNT An **addict** is someone who cannot stop doing something harmful or dangerous, such as taking harmful drugs. *adicto o adicta* ❑ *...a drug addict. ...un adicto a las drogas.* **2** N-COUNT You can say that someone is an **addict** when they like a particular activity very much. *adicto o adicta* ❑ *She is a TV addict. Es adicta a la televisión.*

**ad|dict|ed** /ədɪktɪd/ **1** ADJ Someone who is **addicted to** a harmful drug cannot stop taking it. *adicto* ❑ *Many of the women are addicted to heroin and cocaine. Muchas de estas mujeres son adictas a la heroína y la cocaína.* **2** ADJ If someone is **addicted to** something, they like it very much. *adicto* ❑ *She had become addicted to golf. Se volvió adicta al golf.*

**ad|dic|tion** /ədɪkʃᵊn/ (**addictions**) **1** N-VAR **Addiction** is the condition of being addicted to drugs. *adicción* ❑ *She helped him fight his drug addiction. Lo ayudó a combatir su adicción a las drogas.* **2** N-VAR An **addiction to** something is a very strong desire or need for it. *adicción* ❑ *...his addiction to winning. ...su adicción a ganar.*

**ad|dic|tive** /ədɪktɪv/ **1** ADJ If a drug is **addictive,** people who take it cannot stop taking it. *adictivo* ❑ *Cigarettes are highly addictive. Los cigarros son sumamente adictivos.* **2** ADJ Something that is **addictive** is so enjoyable that it makes you want to do it or have it a lot. *adictivo* ❑ *...an addictive cream-cheese icing. ...un fondant de queso crema adictivo.*

**ad|di|tion** /ədɪʃᵊn/ (**additions**) **1** PHRASE You use **in addition** when you want to mention another item connected with the subject you are discussing. *además* ❑ *He had nine children in addition to his son Steve. Tuvo nueve niños además de su hijo Steve.* **2** N-COUNT An **addition to** something is a thing which is added to it. *adición* ❑ *This is a fine book; a fine addition to the series. Éste es un magnífico libro; una magnífica adición a la serie.* • **ad|di|tion|al** /ədɪʃənᵊl/ ADJ *adicional* ❑ *Add the garlic and cook for an additional three minutes. Agregue el ajo y deje cocer tres minutos adicionales.* **3** N-COUNT An **addition** is a new room or building which is added to an existing building or group of buildings. *anexo* ❑ *They spent $20,000 on building an addition to their kitchen. Se gastaron $20,000 en construir un anexo a su cocina.* **4** N-UNCOUNT **Addition** is the process of calculating the total of two or more numbers. *suma, adición* ❑ *...simple addition and subtraction problems. ...problemas sencillos de sumas y restas.*
→ see **mathematics**

**ad|di|tive** /ædɪtɪv/ (**additives**) **1** N-COUNT An **additive** is a substance which is added to foods in order to improve them or to make them last longer. *aditivo* ❑ *...food additives. aditivos alimenticios* **2** ADJ **Additive** sculpture is sculpture that is created by adding material such as clay or wax until the sculpture is complete. *escultura aditiva*

**ad|dress** (**addresses, addressing, addressed**)

> The noun is pronounced /ədrɛs/ or /ædrɛs/. The verb is pronounced /ədrɛs/.

**1** N-COUNT Your **address** is the number of the house or apartment and the name of the street and the town where you live or work. *dirección* ❑ *The address is 2025 M Street, NW, Washington, DC, 20036. La dirección es 2025 M Street, NW, Washington, DC, 20036.* **2** N-COUNT The **address** of a website is its location on the Internet, for example, http://elt.heinle.com. *dirección* [COMPUTING] ❑ *Full details, including the website address, are at the bottom of this page.* *Todos los detalles, incluyendo la dirección del sitio web, se encuentran al final de esta página.* **3** V-T If a letter, envelope, or parcel **is addressed to** you, your name and address have been written on it. *dirigir* ❑ *One of the letters was addressed to her.* *Una de las cartas estaba dirigida a ella.* **4** V-T If you **address** a group of people, you give a speech to them. *dirigirse a* ❑ *He addressed the crowd of 17,000 people.* *Se dirigió a una multitud de 17,000 personas.* • **Address** is also a noun. *discurso* ❑ ...*an address to the American people.* ...*un discurso a los estadounidenses.*

**Thesaurus** *address* Ver también:

N. lecture, speech, talk **4**

**Word Partnership** Usar *address* con:

N. **name and** address, **street** address **1**
address **remarks to** **4**
ADJ. **permanent** address **1**
**inaugural** address, **public** address **4**

**ad|enine** /ædᵊnin, -nɪn/ (**adenines**) N-VAR **Adenine** is an organic molecule that forms an important part of the structure of DNA. *adenina* [TECHNICAL]

**ad|equate** /ædɪkwɪt/ ADJ If something is **adequate,** there is enough of it or it is good enough to be used or accepted. *adecuado* ❑ *One in four people worldwide do not have adequate homes.* *Una de cada cuatro personas en el mundo no tiene un hogar adecuado.* • **ad|equa|cy** /ædɪkwəsi/ N-UNCOUNT *aceptabilidad* ❑ ...*the adequacy of their work.* ...*la aceptabilidad de su trabajo.* • **ad|equate|ly** ADV *suficientemente, de forma adecuada* ❑ *Many students are not adequately prepared for higher education.* *Muchos estudiantes no están suficientemente preparados para la educación superior.*

**ad|he|sive** /ædhisɪv/ (**adhesives**) **1** N-VAR An **adhesive** is a substance such as glue, which is used to make things stick firmly together. *adhesivo, pegamento* ❑ *Glue the mirror in with a strong adhesive.* *Pega el espejo con un adhesivo fuerte.* **2** ADJ An **adhesive** substance is able to stick firmly to something else. *adhesivo* ❑ ...*adhesive tape.* ...*cinta adhesiva.*

**ad ho|mi|nem** /æd hɒmɪnɛm, -nəm/ ADJ; ADV In logic, an **ad hominem** argument is an argument which attacks the motives or character of the person presenting a claim rather than the claim itself. *ad hominem*

**ad|jec|tive** /ædʒɪktɪv/ (**adjectives**) N-COUNT An **adjective** is a word such as "big," "dead," or "financial" that describes a person or thing, or gives extra information about them. Adjectives usually come before nouns or after linking verbs. *adjetivo*

**ad|jec|tive phrase** (**adjective phrases**) N-COUNT An **adjective phrase** or **adjectival phrase** is a group of words based on an adjective, such as "very nice" or "interested in football." An adjective phrase can also consist simply of an adjective. *frase adjetival*

**ad|just** /ədʒʌst/ (**adjusts, adjusting, adjusted**) **1** V-T/V-I When you **adjust to** a new situation, you get used to it by changing your behavior or your ideas. *adaptarse* ❑ *We have been preparing our fighters to adjust themselves to civil society.* *Hemos preparado a nuestros luchadores para que se adapten a la sociedad civil.* ❑ *She has adjusted to the idea of being a mother very well.* *Se ha adaptado muy bien a la idea de ser madre.* • **ad|just|ment** /ədʒʌstmənt/ N-COUNT (**adjustments**) *cambio* ❑ *He will have to make adjustments to his thinking.* *Tendrá que hacer algunos cambios a sus ideas.* **2** V-T If you **adjust** something, you change it so that it is more effective or appropriate. *ajustar* ❑ *The company adjusted gas prices once a year.* *La compañía ajustó los precios del gas una vez al año.* • **ad|just|ment** N-COUNT *ajuste* ❑ ...*a new monthly cost adjustment.* ...*un nuevo ajuste a los costos mensuales.* **3** V-T If you **adjust** something such as your clothing or a machine, you correct or alter its position or setting. *arreglar* ❑ *Liz adjusted her mirror and then moved the car out of its parking space.* *Liz arregló el espejo y después movió el carro del lugar de estacionamiento.* • **ad|just|ment** N-COUNT *arreglo* ❑ ...*a large workshop for repairs and adjustments.* ...*un taller grande para arreglos y reparaciones.*

**Thesaurus** *adjustable* Ver también:

ADJ. adaptable; (*ant.*) fixed

**ad|min|is|ter** /ædmɪnɪstər/ (**administers, administering, administered**) **1** V-T If someone **administers** something such as a country, the law, or a test, they take responsibility for organizing and supervising it. *administrar* ❑ *Who will administer these accounts and what will it cost?* *¿Quién va a administrar estas cuentas y cuánto va a costar?* **2** V-T If a doctor or a nurse **administers** a drug, they give it to a patient. *administrar* [FORMAL] ❑ *The tests will focus on how to administer the drug safely.* *Las pruebas se enfocarán a cómo administrar la droga de manera segura.*

**ad|min|is|tra|tion** /ædmɪnɪstreɪʃᵊn/ (**administrations**) **1** N-UNCOUNT **Administration** is the range of activities connected with organizing and supervising the way that an organization or institution functions. *administración* ❑ *We spend too much time on administration.* *Le dedicamos mucho tiempo a la administración.* **2** N-SING **The administration** of a company or institution is the group of people who organize and supervise it. *administración* ❑ *The administration wants to increase spending.* *La administración quiere aumentar los gastos.* **3** N-COUNT You can refer to a country's government as **the administration**; used especially in the United States. *administración* ❑ ...*the Bush administration.* ...*la administración de Bush.*

**ad|min|is|tra|tive** /ædmɪnɪstreɪtɪv/ ADJ **Administrative** work involves organizing and supervising an organization or institution. *administrativo* ❑ ...*administrative costs.* ...*costos administrativos.*

**ad|min|is|tra|tor** /ædmɪnɪstreɪtər/ (**administrators**) N-COUNT An **administrator** is a person whose job involves helping to organize and supervise the way that an organization or institution functions. *administrador o*

A

administradora ❑ Students and parents met with school administrators. Los alumnos y sus padres tuvieron una junta con los administradores de la escuela.

**ad|mi|rable** /ædmɪrəbᵊl/ ADJ An **admirable** quality or action is one that deserves to be praised and admired. *admirable* ❑ *She did an admirable job of holding their attention. Hizo un trabajo admirable para mantener su atención.* ● **ad|mi|rably** /ædmɪrəbli/ ADV *admirablemente, de forma admirable* ❑ *Peter dealt admirably with the questions. Peter contestó de manera admirable las preguntas.*

**ad|mi|ral** /ædmərəl/ (**admirals**) N-COUNT; N-TITLE An **admiral** is a very senior officer who commands a navy. *almirante* ❑ *...Admiral Hodges. ...el almirante Hodges.*

**ad|mi|ra|tion** /ædmɪreɪʃᵊn/ N-UNCOUNT **Admiration** is a feeling of great liking and respect. *admiración* ❑ *I have the greatest admiration for him. Siento una gran admiración por él.*

**ad|mire** /ədmaɪər/ (**admires, admiring, admired**) 1 V-T If you **admire** someone or something, you like and respect them. *admirar* ❑ *I admired her when I first met her and I still think she's marvelous. La admiro desde que la conocí y todavía pienso que es maravillosa.* ● **ad|mir|er** N-COUNT (**admirers**) *admirador, admiradora* ❑ *He was an admirer of her grandfather's paintings. Era un admirador de las pinturas de su abuelo.* 2 V-T If you **admire** someone or something, you look at them with pleasure. *admirar* ❑ *We took time to stop and admire the view. Nos dimos tiempo de detenernos y admirar la vista.*

| Thesaurus | *admire* | Ver también: |
|---|---|---|
| V. | adore, esteem, honor, look up to, respect 1 | |

**ad|mis|sion** /ædmɪʃᵊn/ (**admissions**) 1 N-VAR **Admission** is permission given to a person to enter a place, or permission given to a country to enter an organization. **Admission** is also the act of entering a place. *admisión* ❑ *Yesterday was the anniversary of Bosnia's admission to the United Nations. Ayer fue el aniversario de la admisión de Bosnia a las Naciones Unidas.* 2 N-VAR An **admission** is a statement that something bad, unpleasant, or embarrassing is true. *admisión, reconocimiento* ❑ *By his own admission, he is not playing well. Reconoció que no está jugando bien.* 3 N-UNCOUNT **Admission** at a park, museum, or other place is the amount of money that you pay to enter it. *entrada, admisión* ❑ *Gates open at 10:30 a.m. and admission is free. Las puertas abren a las 10:30 a.m. y la entrada es gratuita.* ● **Admission** is also used before a noun. *de admisión* ❑ *The admission price is $8 for adults. El precio de admisión es de $8 para adultos.*
→ see **hospital**

**ad|mit** /ædmɪt/ (**admits, admitting, admitted**) 1 V-T/V-I If you **admit** that something bad, unpleasant, or embarrassing is true, you agree, often unwillingly, that it is true. *admitir* ❑ *I am willing to admit that I make mistakes. Estoy dispuesto a admitir que cometo errores.* ❑ *They didn't admit to doing anything wrong. No admitieron haber hecho algo malo.* ❑ *None of these people will admit responsibility. Ninguna de estas personas va a admitir su responsabilidad.* 2 V-T If someone **is admitted to** a hospital, they are taken into the hospital for treatment. *admitir* ❑ *She was admitted to the hospital with a very high temperature. Fue admitida en el hospital con temperatura muy alta.* 3 V-T If someone **is admitted to** a place or organization, they are allowed to enter it or join it. *admitir* ❑ *She was admitted to law school. Fue admitida en la escuela de leyes.* ❑ *Security officers refused to admit him or his wife. Los oficiales de seguridad se negaron a admitirlo a él o a su esposa.*

| Word Partnership | Usar *admit* con: |
|---|---|
| V. | **ashamed to** admit, **be the first to** admit, **must** admit, **willing to** admit 1 |
| N. | admit **defeat** 1 |
| CONJ. | admit **that** 1 |

**ado|les|cent** /ædᵊlɛsᵊnt/ (**adolescents**) ADJ **Adolescent** is used to describe young people who are no longer children but who have not yet become adults. *adolescente* ❑ *...an adolescent boy. ...un adolescente.* ● An **adolescent** is an adolescent boy or girl. *adolescente* ❑ *Adolescents are happiest with small groups of close friends. Los adolescentes son más felices con pequeños grupos de amigos cercanos.* ● **ado|les|cence** /ædᵊlɛsᵊns/ N-UNCOUNT *adolescencia* ❑ *...the early part of my life from childhood through adolescence. ...la primera parte de mi vida desde la infancia hasta la adolescencia.*
→ see **age, child**

| Word Link | *opt ≈ choosing : adopt, option, optional* |
|---|---|

**adopt** /ədɒpt/ (**adopts, adopting, adopted**) 1 V-T If you **adopt** a new attitude, plan, or way of behaving, you begin to have it. *adoptar* ❑ *Students should adopt a more positive attitude to the environment. Los alumnos deberían adoptar una actitud más positiva hacia el ambiente.* ● **adop|tion** /ədɒpʃᵊn/ N-UNCOUNT *adopción* ❑ *The meeting ended with the adoption of a plan of action. La reunión terminó con la adopción de un plan de acción.* 2 V-T/V-I If you **adopt** someone else's child, you take it into your own family and make it legally your son or daughter. *adoptar* ❑ *There are hundreds of people who want to adopt a child. Hay cientos de personas que quieren adoptar un niño.* ● **adop|tion** N-VAR (**adoptions**) *adopción* ❑ *They gave their babies up for adoption. Dieron a sus bebés en adopción.* 3 → see also **adapt**

| Thesaurus | *adopt* | Ver también: |
|---|---|---|
| V. | approve, endorse, support; (*ant.*) refuse, reject 1<br>care for, raise, take in 2 | |

**adore** /ədɔr/ (**adores, adoring, adored**) 1 V-T If you **adore** someone, you feel great love and admiration for them. *adorar* ❑ *She adored her parents and would do anything to please them. Adoraba a sus padres y habría hecho cualquier cosa por complacerlos.* ● **ado|ra|tion** /ædɔreɪʃᵊn/ N-UNCOUNT *adoración* ❑ *The adoration of his fans has helped him. La adoración de sus fans lo ha ayudado.* 2 V-T If you **adore** something, you like it very much. *adorar* [INFORMAL] ❑ *Robyn adores university life. Robyn adora la vida universitaria.*
→ see **emotion**

**adult** /ədʌlt/ (**adults**) 1 N-COUNT An **adult** is a

mature, fully developed person or animal. *adulto* ❑ *Becoming a father meant that he was now an adult. Convertirse en padre significó que ahora era un adulto.* ❑ *...a pair of adult birds. ...dos pájaros adultos.* 2 ADJ **Adult** means relating to the time when you are an adult, or typical of adult people. *adulto* ❑ *I've lived most of my adult life in Arizona. He vivido casi toda mi vida de adulto en Arizona.*
→ see **age**

| **Thesaurus** | *adult* | Ver también: |
|---|---|---|
| N. | grown-up, man, woman 1 | |

**ad|vance** /ædvæns/ (**advances, advancing, advanced**) 1 V-I To **advance** means to move forward, often in order to attack someone. *avanzar* ❑ *Soldiers are advancing on the capital. Los soldados están avanzando hacia la capital.* ❑ *The water is advancing at a rate of between 8 and 10 inches a day. El agua está avanzando a una velocidad de entre 20 y 25 centímetros por día.* 2 V-I To **advance** means to make progress, especially in your knowledge of something. *avanzar* ❑ *Science advanced greatly in the last 100 years. La ciencia ha avanzado enormemente en los últimos 100 años.* 3 → see also **advanced** 4 V-T If you **advance** someone a sum of money, you lend it to them, or pay it to them earlier than arranged. *anticipar* ❑ *I advanced him some money, which he repaid on our way home. Le anticipé dinero, y me lo devolvió cuando íbamos camino a casa.* 5 V-T To **advance** an event, or the time or date of an event, means to bring it forward to an earlier time or date. *anticipar, adelantar* ❑ *A poor diet may advance the aging process. Una mala dieta puede adelantar el proceso de envejecimiento.* 6 N-COUNT An **advance** is money lent or paid to someone before they would normally receive it. *anticipo* ❑ *She was paid a $100,000 advance for her next two novels. Recibió un anticipo de $100,000 por sus próximas dos novelas.* 7 N-VAR An **advance** is a forward movement of people or vehicles, usually as part of a military operation. *avance* ❑ *Hitler's army began its advance on Moscow in June 1941. El ejército de Hitler comenzó su avance sobre Moscú en junio de 1941.* 8 N-VAR An **advance** in a particular subject or activity is progress in understanding it or in doing it well. *avance, progreso* ❑ *...advances in medicine and public health. ...los avances en la medicina y la salud pública.* 9 ADJ **Advance** booking, notice, or warning is done or given before an event happens. *previo, anticipado* ❑ *You must give 30 days' advance notice. Debes dar un aviso con 30 días de anticipación.* 10 PHRASE If you do something **in advance**, you do it before a particular date or event. *con anticipación* ❑ *The theater sells tickets in advance. El teatro vende boletos con anticipación.*

**ad|vanced** /ædvænst/ 1 ADJ An **advanced** system, method, or design is modern and has been developed from an earlier version of the same thing. *avanzado* ❑ *...one of the most advanced phones available. ...uno de los teléfonos más avanzados disponibles.* 2 ADJ A country that is **advanced** has reached a high level of industrial or technological development. *desarrollado* ❑ *...advanced countries like the United States. ...países desarrollados como los Estados Unidos.* 3 ADJ An **advanced** student has already learned the basic facts of a subject and is doing more difficult work. *avanzado* ❑ *This course is for advanced students only. Este curso es únicamente para alumnos avanzados.*

| **Thesaurus** | *advanced* | Ver también: |
|---|---|---|
| ADJ. | cutting-edge, foremost, latest 1<br>sophisticated 2 | |

**ad|van|tage** /ædvæntɪdʒ/ (**advantages**) 1 N-COUNT An **advantage** is something that puts you in a better position than other people. *ventaja* ❑ *They think that going to a private school will give them an advantage in getting into college. Piensan que el asistir a una escuela privada les dará ventaja para ingresar a la universidad.* 2 N-COUNT An **advantage** is a way in which one thing is better than another. *ventaja* ❑ *The advantage of home-grown oranges is their great flavor. La ventaja de las naranjas cultivadas en casa es su gran sabor.* 3 N-UNCOUNT **Advantage** is the state of being in a better position than others who are competing against you. *superioridad* ❑ *We were in a position of advantage before this game. Estábamos en una posición de superioridad hasta antes de este partido.* 4 PHRASE If you **take advantage of** something, you make good use of it while you can. *aprovechar* ❑ *I'm going to take advantage of this trip to go shopping. Voy a aprovechar este viaje para ir de compras.* 5 PHRASE If someone **takes advantage of** you, they treat you unfairly for their own benefit, especially when you are trying to be kind or to help them. *aprovecharse de* ❑ *She took advantage of him even after they were divorced. Ella se aprovechó de él aún después del divorcio.* 6 PHRASE If you use or turn something **to your advantage**, you use it in order to benefit from it. *para el provecho de uno* ❑ *He could turn any situation to his advantage. Podía sacar provecho de cualquier situación.*

| **Word Partnership** | Usar *advantage* con: |
|---|---|
| ADJ. | **competitive** advantage, **unfair** advantage 1 |
| V. | **have an** advantage 1<br>**take** advantage **of** ***something*** 4<br>**use to** ***someone's*** advantage 6 |

**ad|ven|ture** /ædvɛntʃər/ (**adventures**) N-VAR An **adventure** is a series of events that is unusual, exciting, and perhaps dangerous. *aventura* ❑ *I set off for a new adventure in Alaska. Me embarqué hacia una nueva aventura en Alaska.* ❑ *...a spirit of adventure. ...un espíritu de aventura.* • **ad|ven|tur|er** N-COUNT (**adventurers**) *aventurero o aventurera* ❑ *...American adventurer Steve Fossett. ...el aventurero americano Steve Fossett.*

| **Word Link** | *verb ≈ word : adverb, proverb, verbal* |
|---|---|

**ad|verb** /ædvɜrb/ (**adverbs**) N-COUNT An **adverb** is a word such as "slowly," "now," "very," "politically," or "happily" which adds information about an action, event, or situation. *adverbio*

**ad|verb phrase** (**adverb phrases**) N-COUNT An **adverb phrase** or **adverbial phrase** is a group of words based on an adverb, such as "very slowly" or "fortunately for us." An adverb phrase can also consist simply of an adverb. *frase adverbial*

**ad|verse** /ædvɜrs/ ADJ **Adverse** decisions, conditions, or effects are unfavorable to you.

A

adverso ❑ *There may be adverse effects as a result of this treatment.* *Puede haber efectos adversos como resultado de este tratamiento.* ● **ad|verse|ly** ADV adversamente ❑ *The change didn't adversely affect him.* *El cambio no lo afectó adversamente.*

**ad|ver|tise** /ædvərtaɪz/ (**advertises, advertising, advertised**) **1** V-T/V-I If you **advertise** something such as a product, an event, or a job, you tell people about it in newspapers, on television, or on posters. anunciar ❑ *They are advertising houses for sale.* *Están anunciando casas en venta.* ❑ *We advertise on radio stations* *Nos anunciamos en estaciones de radio.* **2** V-I If you **advertise for** someone to do something for you, for example, to work for you or share your accommodation, you announce it in a newspaper, on television, or on a bulletin board. anunciar ❑ *We advertised in a local newspaper.* *Nos anunciamos en el diario local.* ● **ad|ver|tis|er** N-COUNT (**advertisers**) anunciante ❑ *...television advertisers.* *...anunciantes televisivos.* **3** → see also **advertising**

**ad|ver|tise|ment** /ædvərtaɪzmənt/ (**advertisements**) N-COUNT An **advertisement** is an announcement in a newspaper, on television, or on a poster about something such as a product, event, or job. anuncio [WRITTEN] ❑ *Miss Parrish placed an advertisement in the local newspaper.* *La señorita Parrish colocó un anuncio en el diario local.*

**ad|ver|tis|ing** /ædvərtaɪzɪŋ/ N-UNCOUNT **Advertising** is the activity of creating advertisements and making sure people see them. publicidad ❑ *I work in advertising.* *Trabajo en publicidad.*

**ad|vice** /ædvaɪs/ N-UNCOUNT If you give someone **advice,** you tell them what you think they should do in a particular situation. consejo ❑ *I'll give you some advice that will change your life.* *Te daré un consejo que cambiará tu vida.* ❑ *Take my advice and stay away from him!* *¡Toma mi consejo y mantente alejado de él!*

**Usage** advice and advise

Be careful not to confuse *advice* and *advise*. *Advice* is a noun, and the *c* is pronounced like the *ss* in *less*; *advise* is a verb, and the *s* is pronounced like the *z* in *size*: *Quang advised Tuyet not to give people advice!*

**Thesaurus** *advice* Ver también:

N. counsel, encouragement, guidance, help, information; (*ant.*) input, opinion, recommendation, suggestion

**Word Partnership** Usar *advice* con:

PREP. **against** advice
V. **ask for** advice, **give** advice, **need some** advice, **take** advice
ADJ. **bad/good** advice, **expert** advice

**ad|vice col|umn** (**advice columns**) N-COUNT In a newspaper or magazine, the **advice column** contains letters from readers about their personal problems, and advice on what to do about them. consultorio sentimental

**ad|vice col|umn|ist** (**advice columnists**) N-COUNT An **advice columnist** is a person who writes a column in a newspaper or magazine in which they reply to readers who have written to them for advice on their personal problems. consejero o consejera sentimental

**ad|vise** /ædvaɪz/ (**advises, advising, advised**) **1** V-T If you **advise** someone **to** do something, you tell them what you think they should do. aconsejar ❑ *The minister advised him to leave as soon as possible.* *El ministro le aconsejó retirarse lo antes posible.* ❑ *I would strongly advise against it.* *Le aconsejo que de ninguna manera lo haga.* **2** V-T If an expert **advises** people **on** a particular subject, he or she gives them help and information on that subject. aconsejar ❑ *...an officer who advises students on money matters.* *...un funcionario que aconseja a los estudiantes en materia de dinero.* **3** → see also **advice**

**ad|vis|er** /ædvaɪzər/ (**advisers**) also **advisor** N-COUNT An **adviser** is an expert whose job is to give advice to another person or to a group of people. consejero o consejera ❑ *The president and his advisers spent the day in meetings.* *El presidente y sus consejeros pasaron el día en reuniones.*

**Word Link** *ory ≈ relating to : advisory, contradictory, sensory*

**ad|vi|so|ry** /ædvaɪzəri/ (**advisories**) **1** N-COUNT An **advisory** is an official announcement or report that warns people about bad weather, diseases, or other dangers or problems. advertencia ❑ *...public health advisories.* *...advertencias de salubridad pública.* **2** ADJ An **advisory** group regularly gives suggestions and help to people or organizations, especially about a particular subject or area of activity. consultivo [FORMAL] ❑ *...an advisory group on oil and gas.* *...un cuerpo consultivo en materia de gas y petróleo.*

**Word Link** *voc ≈ speaking : advocate, vocabulary, vocal*

**ad|vo|cate** (**advocates, advocating, advocated**)

The verb is pronounced /ædvəkeɪt/. The noun is pronounced /ædvəkɪt/.

**1** V-T If you **advocate** a particular action or plan, you recommend it publicly. promocionar, abogar por [FORMAL] ❑ *He advocates improvements to the bus service.* *Aboga por mejoras en el servicio de autobús.* **2** N-COUNT An **advocate of** a particular action or plan is someone who recommends it publicly. defensor o defensora [FORMAL] ❑ *He was a great advocate of checking other people's work.* *Defendía la posición de revisar el trabajo de otros.* **3** N-COUNT An **advocate** for a particular group is a person who works for the interests of that group. defensor o defensora ❑ *...advocates for the homeless.* *...defensores de los desamparados.* **4** N-COUNT An **advocate** is a lawyer who speaks in favor of someone or defends them in a court of law. abogado o abogada [LEGAL]

**Word Link** *aer ≈ air : aerial, aerobics, aerophone*

**aer|ial** /ɛəriəl/ (**aerials**) ADJ **Aerial** means from an airplane. aéreo ❑ *The aerial attacks may continue for weeks more.* *Los ataques aéreos podrían continuar por semanas.* ❑ *...an aerial photograph.* *...una fotografía aérea.*

**aer|ial per|spec|tive** (**aerial perspectives**) N-VAR In a painting or drawing, **aerial perspective**

is a method of representing more distant objects by using lighter or duller colors. perspectiva aérea

**Word Link** *aer ≈ air : aerial, aerobics, aerophone*

**aero|bics** /ɛəroʊbɪks/ N-UNCOUNT **Aerobics** is a form of exercise which increases the amount of oxygen in your blood, and strengthens your heart and lungs. The verb that follows **aerobics** may be either singular or plural. *aerobics* ❑ *...an aerobics class. ...una clase de aerobics.*

**aero|phone** /ɛərəfoʊn/ (**aerophones**) N-COUNT An **aerophone** is a musical instrument such as a trumpet or flute which produces sound by causing the air to vibrate. *aerófono*

**aes|thet|ic** /ɛsθɛtɪk/ also **esthetic** ADJ **Aesthetic** is used to talk about beauty or art, and people's appreciation of beautiful things. *estética* ❑ *We chose the products for their aesthetic appeal. Escogimos los productos por su atractivo estético.* ● **aes|theti|cal|ly** /ɛsθɛtɪkli/ ADV *estéticamente* ❑ *...an aesthetically pleasing product. ...un producto estéticamente agradable.*

**aes|thet|ic cri|teria** N-PLURAL **Aesthetic criteria** are standards that are used in making judgments about the artistic value of a work of art. *criterios estéticos*

**aes|thet|ics** /ɛsθɛtɪks/ also **esthetics** N-UNCOUNT **Aesthetics** is a branch of philosophy concerned with the study of the idea of beauty. *estética*

**af|fair** /əfɛər/ (**affairs**) **1** N-SING You can refer to an event as **an affair** when you are talking about it in a general way. *asunto* ❑ *He has handled the whole affair badly. Manejó mal todo el asunto.* **2** N-COUNT If two people who are not married to each other have an **affair**, they have a sexual relationship. *amorío* ❑ *He was having an affair with the woman next door. Tenía un amorío con la vecina.* **3** N-PLURAL You can use **affairs** to refer to all the important facts or activities that are connected with a particular subject. *asuntos* ❑ *He does not want to interfere in the affairs of another country. No desea interferir en los asuntos de otro país.* **4** → see also **current affairs** **5** N-PLURAL Your **affairs** are all the matters connected with your life that you consider to be private. *asuntos* ❑ *He was unable to make important decisions or handle his affairs. Era incapaz de tomar decisiones importantes y manejar sus asuntos.*

**af|fect** /əfɛkt/ (**affects, affecting, affected**) **1** V-T If something **affects** a person or thing, it influences them or causes them to change in some way. *afectar* ❑ *This problem affects all of us. Este problema nos afecta a todos.* ❑ *We were close to the area affected by the earthquake. Estábamos cerca del área afectada por el terremoto.* **2** V-T If a disease **affects** you it makes you ill. *afectar* ❑ *Arthritis is a disease which affects people all over the world. La artritis es una enfermedad que afecta a personas en todo el mundo.* **3** → see also **effect**

**af|fec|tion** /əfɛkʃᵊn/ (**affections**) **1** N-UNCOUNT If you regard someone or something with **affection**, you are fond of them. *afecto* ❑ *She thought of him with affection. Lo recordaba con afecto.* **2** N-PLURAL Your **affections** are your feelings of love or fondness for someone. *sentimientos de afecto* ❑ *Caroline is the object of his affections. A la que quiere es a Caroline.*
→ see **love**

**af|fili|ate** (**affiliates, affiliating, affiliated**)

The noun is pronounced /əfɪliɪt/. The verb is pronounced /əfɪlieɪt/.

**1** N-COUNT An **affiliate** is an organization which is officially connected with another, larger organization or is a member of it. *filial, compañía afiliada* [FORMAL] ❑ *The World Chess Federation has affiliates in around 120 countries. La Federación Mundial de Ajedrez tiene filiales en alrededor de 120 países.* **2** V-I If an organization **affiliates with** another larger organization, it forms a close connection with the larger organization or becomes a member of it. *afiliarse con* [FORMAL] ❑ *Local parent groups are welcome to affiliate with us. Las asociaciones de padres de familia de la localidad son bienvenidas a afiliarse con nosotros.* ● **af|filia|tion** /əfɪlieɪʃᵊn/ N-VAR (**affiliations**) *afiliación* [FORMAL] ❑ *They had no affiliation with any other group. No estaban afiliados a ningún otro grupo.* **3** V-I If a professional person such as a lawyer or doctor **affiliates with** an organization, they become officially connected with that organization. *asociarse con* [FORMAL] ❑ *He wanted to affiliate with a U.S. firm because he needed "expert advice." Deseaba asociarse con un bufete estadounidense porque requería de "consejos expertos".*

**Word Link** *firm ≈ making strong : affirm, confirm, firm*

**af|firm** /əfɜrm/ (**affirms, affirming, affirmed**) **1** V-T If you **affirm** that something is true, you state firmly and publicly that it is true. *afirmar* [FORMAL] ❑ *The newspaper report affirmed that the story was true. En la nota del diario se afirmaba que la historia es cierta.* ● **af|fir|ma|tion** /æfərmeɪʃᵊn/ N-VAR (**affirmations**) *afirmación* ❑ *...an affirmation of support. ...una afirmación de su apoyo.* **2** V-T If an event **affirms** something, it shows that it is true or exists. *afirmar* [FORMAL] ❑ *Everything I did seemed to affirm that opinion. Todo lo que hacía parecía afirmar aquella opinión.* ● **af|fir|ma|tion** N-UNCOUNT; N-SING *afirmación* ❑ *Maguire's performance is an affirmation of his talent. La actuación de Maguire es una afirmación de su talento.*

**af|firma|tive ac|tion** N-UNCOUNT **Affirmative action** is the policy of giving jobs and other opportunities to members of groups such as racial minorities or women who might not otherwise have them. *acción afirmativa*

**af|fix** /æfɪks/ (**affixes**) N-COUNT An **affix** is a letter or group of letters, for example, "un-" or "-y," which is added to either the beginning or the end of a word to form a different word with a different meaning. For example, "un-" is added to "kind" to form "unkind." Compare **prefix** and **suffix**. *afijo*

**af|ford** /əfɔrd/ (**affords, affording, afforded**) **1** V-T If you **can afford** something, you have enough money to pay for it. *darse el lujo de* ❑ *Some people can't even afford a new refrigerator. Algunas personas ni siquiera se pueden dar el lujo de comprar un refrigerador nuevo.* **2** V-T If you cannot **afford to** do something or allow it to happen, you must not do it or must prevent it from happening because it

A

would be harmful or embarrassing to you. *darse el lujo de* ❑ *We can't afford to wait. No podemos darnos el lujo de esperar.*

**Word Partnership** Usar *afford* con:

V. afford **to buy/pay** 1
**can/could** afford,
**can't/couldn't** afford 1 2
afford **to lose** 2
ADJ. **able/unable to** afford 1 2

**af|ford|able** /əfɔrdəbəl/ ADJ If something is **affordable,** most people have enough money to buy it. *accesible (económicamente)* ❑ *...affordable housing. ...casas a un precio accesible.* ● **af|ford|abil|ity** /əfɔrdəbɪlɪti/ N-UNCOUNT *viabilidad (financiera)* ❑ *Affordability is a problem for students going to college. La viabilidad financiera es un problema que enfrentan los alumnos que van a la universidad.*

**afloat** /əfloʊt/ 1 ADV If someone or something is **afloat,** they remain partly above the surface of water and do not sink. *a flote* ❑ *They tried to keep the ship afloat. Trataron de mantener el barco a flote.* 2 ADV If a person, business, or country stays **afloat** or is kept **afloat,** they have just enough money to pay their debts and continue operating. *solvente, sin deudas* [BUSINESS] ❑ *Many businesses are finding it hard to stay afloat. Muchos negocios encuentran que es muy difícil mantenerse a flote.*

**afraid** /əfreɪd/ 1 ADJ If you are **afraid of** someone or **afraid to** do something, you are frightened because you think that something very unpleasant is going to happen to you. *tener miedo* ❑ *She was not at all afraid. Ella no tenía nada de miedo.* ❑ *I was afraid of the other boys. Yo les tenía miedo a los otros muchachos.* 2 ADJ If you are **afraid for** someone else, you are worried that something horrible is going to happen to them. *preocupado* ❑ *She's afraid for her family in Somalia. Ella está preocupada por su familia en Somalia.* 3 ADJ If you are **afraid** that something unpleasant will happen, you are worried that it may happen. *tener miedo* ❑ *I was afraid that nobody would believe me. Tenía miedo de que nadie me creyera.* 4 PHRASE If you want to apologize to someone or to disagree with them in a polite way, you can say **I'm afraid.** *me temo* [SPOKEN] ❑ *We don't have anything like that, I'm afraid. Me temo que no tenemos ese tipo de cosas.*

**Thesaurus** *afraid* Ver también:

ADJ. alarmed, fearful, frightened, petrified, scared, terrified 1
worried 3

**Af|ri|can** /æfrɪkən/ (**Africans**) 1 ADJ **African** means belonging or relating to the continent of Africa, or to its countries or people. *africano* ❑ *...the African continent. ...el continente africano.* ❑ *...traditional African culture. ...la cultura tradicional africana.* 2 ADJ **African** is used to describe someone who comes from Africa. *africano* ❑ *...African women. ...mujeres africanas* ● An **African** is someone who is African. *africano o africana* ❑ *Fish is an important part of the diet of many Africans. El pescado forma una parte importante en la dieta de muchos africanos.*

**African-American** (**African-Americans**) N-COUNT **African-Americans** are people living in the United States who are descended from families that originally came from Africa. *afroamericano o afroamericana* ❑ *Today African-Americans are 12 percent of the population. Los afroamericanos constituyen el 12 por ciento de la población.* ● **African-American** is also an adjective. *afroamericano* ❑ *She is the daughter of an African-American father and an East Indian mother. Ella es hija de un padre afroamericano y una madre asiática.*

**African-Caribbean** (**African-Caribbeans**) ADJ **African-Caribbean** refers to people from the Caribbean whose ancestors came from Africa. *afrocaribeño* ❑ *...modern African-Caribbean culture. ...la cultura afrocaribeña moderna.* ● An **African-Caribbean** is someone who is African-Caribbean. *afrocaribeño o afrocaribeña*

**af|ter** /æftər/

In addition to the uses shown below, **after** is used in phrasal verbs such as "look after," and "take after."

1 PREP If something happens or is done **after** a particular date or event, it happens or is done during the period of time that follows that date or event. *después de, tras* ❑ *He died after a long illness. Murió tras una larga enfermedad.* ❑ *After breakfast Amy took a taxi to the station. Después de desayunar, Amy tomó un taxi a la estación.* ● **After** is also a conjunction. *después (puede usarse como conjunción o palabra introductoria)* ❑ *After Don told me this, he spoke of his mother. Después de que me hubo dicho aquello, Don habló sobre su madre.* 2 PREP If you go **after** someone, you follow or chase them. *tras* ❑ *Alice said to Gina, "Why don't you go after him, he's your son." Alice le dijo a Gina: -Es tu hijo, ¿por qué no vas tras él?* 3 PREP If you are **after** something, you are trying to get it. *en busca de* ❑ *They were after the money. Iban en busca del dinero.* 4 PREP If you call or shout **after** someone, you call or shout at them as they move away from you. *No se usa en el español.* ❑ *"Come back!" he called after me. —¡Regresa! —me gritó.* 5 PREP You use **after** in order to give the most important aspect of something when comparing it with another aspect. *después de* ❑ *After Germany, America is Britain's second-biggest customer. Después de Alemania, Estados Unidos es el comprador más importante de productos británicos.* 6 PREP To be named **after** someone means to be given the same name as them. *llamado como, llamado en honor a* ❑ *He wanted Virginia to name the baby after him. Deseaba que Virginia llamara al bebé como él.* 7 PREP **After** is used when telling the time. If it is, for example, **ten after six,** the time is ten minutes past six. *después, pasadas* 8 CONVENTION If you say **"after you"** to someone, you are being polite and allowing them to go in front of you or through a doorway before you do. *pase usted, adelante* 9 **after all** → see **all** 3

**after|math** /æftərmæθ/ N-SING **The aftermath of** an important event, especially a harmful one, is the situation that results from it. *consecuencia, secuela* ❑ *The team worked closely together in the aftermath of the fire. El equipo trabajó de forma unida en el periodo subsiguiente al fuego.*

**after|noon** /æftərnun/ (**afternoons**) N-VAR The **afternoon** is the part of each day that begins at lunchtime and ends at about six o'clock. *tarde*

❑ *He's arriving in the afternoon.* *Llegará en la tarde.* ❑ *He stayed in his room all afternoon.* *Estuvo en su cuarto toda la tarde.*
→ see **time**

**after|ward** /æftərwərd/ also **afterwards** ADV If you do something or if something happens **afterward,** you do it or it happens after a particular event or time that has already been mentioned. *después* ❑ *Shortly afterward, the police arrived.* *La policía llegó poco después.*

**again** /əgɛn, əgeɪn/ **1** ADV You use **again** to indicate that something happens a second time, or after it has already happened before. *de nuevo, otra vez, de nueva cuenta* ❑ *He kissed her again.* *La besó de nuevo.* ❑ *Again there was a short silence.* *Otra vez hubo un silencio corto.* **2** ADV You use **again** to indicate that something is now in a particular state or place that it used to be in. *de nuevo* ❑ *He opened his case, took out a folder, then closed it again.* *Abrió su portafolios, sacó un folder y lo cerró de nuevo.* **3** PHRASE You can use **again and again** or **time and again** to emphasize that something happens many times. *una y otra vez* ❑ *He would go over his work again and again until he thought it was right.* *Repasaba su trabajo una y otra vez hasta que se aseguraba de que estaba bien.* **4** **now and again** → see **now**

**against** /əgɛnst, əgeɪnst/

> In addition to the uses shown below, **against** is used in phrasal verbs such as "come up against," "guard against," and "hold against."

**1** PREP If one thing is leaning or pressing **against** another, it is touching it. *en, sobre* ❑ *She leaned against him.* *Ella se recargó en él.* ❑ *The rain was beating against the window panes.* *La lluvia golpeaba en los vidrios de las ventanas.* **2** PREP If you are **against** something such as a plan, policy, or system, you think it is wrong, bad, or stupid. *contra, en contra de* ❑ *He was against the war.* *Estaba en contra de la guerra.* ● **Against** is also an adverb. *en contra* ❑ *66 percent were in favor of the decision and 34 against.* *66 por ciento votó a favor y 34 por ciento en contra.* **3** PREP If you compete **against** someone in a game, you try to beat them. *contra* ❑ *This is the first of two games against Denver.* *Éste es el primero de dos juegos contra Denver.* **4** PREP If you take action **against** someone or something, you try to harm them. *contra* ❑ *Security forces are still using violence against opponents of the government.* *Las fuerzas de seguridad aún están haciendo uso de violencia contra los opositores al gobierno.* **5** PREP If you do something **against** someone's wishes, advice, or orders, you do not do what they want you to do or tell you to do. *contra, a pesar de* ❑ *Against medical advice, she left the hospital.* *Dejó el hospital a pesar del consejo del médico.* **6** PREP If you do something in order to protect yourself **against** something unpleasant or harmful, you do something that will make its effects on you less serious if it happens. *contra* ❑ *Any business needs insurance against fire, flood, and breakage.* *Los negocios necesitan asegurarse contra incendio, inundación y descomposturas.* **7** PREP If something is **against** the law or **against** the rules, there is a law or a rule which says that you must not do it. *contra* ❑ *It is against the law to help others kill themselves.* *Es contra la ley ayudar a otros a cometer suicidio.* **8** PREP The odds **against** something happening are the chances or odds that it will not happen. *en contra de* ❑ *The odds against him surviving are very great.* *Las probabilidades en contra de que sobreviva son enormes.* ● **Against** is also an adverb. *en contra* ❑ *What were the odds against?* *¿Cuál era la probabilidad en contra?*

**age** /eɪdʒ/ (**ages, aging** or **ageing, aged**) **1** N-VAR Your **age** is the number of years that you have lived. *edad* ❑ *She has a nephew who is ten years of age.* *Tiene un sobrino de 10 años [de edad].* ❑ *Demi left school at the age of 16.* *Demi dejó la escuela a los [a la edad de] 16 años.* **2** N-UNCOUNT **Age** is the state of being old or the process of becoming older. *los años, el paso del tiempo* ❑ *He has grown wiser with age.* *Se ha vuelto más sabio con los años.* **3** V-T/V-I When someone **ages,** or when something **ages** them, they seem much older and less strong or less alert. *envejecer* ❑ *Both parents said they have aged in the past six months.* *Ambos padres dijeron haber envejecido en los últimos seis meses.* ❑ *Worry had aged him.* *La preocupación lo había hecho envejecer.* ● **aging** N-UNCOUNT *envejecimiento* ❑ *He isn't showing any signs of aging.* *No muestra señales de envejecimiento.* **4** N-COUNT An **age** is a period in history. *edad, época, era* ❑ *...the age of silent films.* *...la era del cine mudo.* **5** → see also **aged, middle age**
→ see Picture Dictionary: **age**

**aged**

> Pronounced /eɪdʒd/ for meaning **1**, and /eɪdʒɪd/ for meanings **2** and **3**.

**1** ADJ You use **aged** followed by a number to say how old someone is. *tener (edad), de (edad)* ❑ *Alan has two children, aged eleven and nine.* *Alan tiene dos niños de once y nueve.* **2** ADJ **Aged** means very old. *anciano, viejo* ❑ *She has an aged parent who can be very difficult.* *Tiene un padre anciano que puede ser de muy difícil trato.* **3** N-PLURAL You can refer to all people who are very old as **the aged.** *los ancianos* ❑ *...daycare centers and homes for the aged.* *...centros de atención diurna y hogares para ancianos.* **4** → see also **middle-aged**

**agen|cy** /eɪdʒənsi/ (**agencies**) **1** N-COUNT An **agency** is a business that provides a service on behalf of other businesses. *agencia* [BUSINESS] ❑ *...an advertising agency.* *...una agencia publicitaria.* **2** → see also **ad agency** **3** N-COUNT An **agency** is a government organization responsible for a certain area of administration. *entidad* ❑ *...local, state and federal agencies.* *...entidades locales, estatales y federales.*

**agen|da** /ədʒɛndə/ (**agendas**) **1** N-COUNT You can refer to the political issues that are important at a particular time as an **agenda.** *plan* ❑ *...the president's education agenda.* *...el plan educativo del presidente.* **2** N-COUNT An **agenda** is a list of the items that have to be discussed at a meeting. *orden del día* ❑ *...an item on Monday's meeting agenda.* *...un inciso en el orden del día de la junta del lunes.*

**Word Partnership** Usar ***agenda*** con:

| | |
|---|---|
| ADJ. | **domestic/legislative/political** agenda, **hidden** agenda **1** |
| PREP. | **on the** agenda **2** |
| V. | **set the** agenda **2** |

A

## Picture Dictionary age

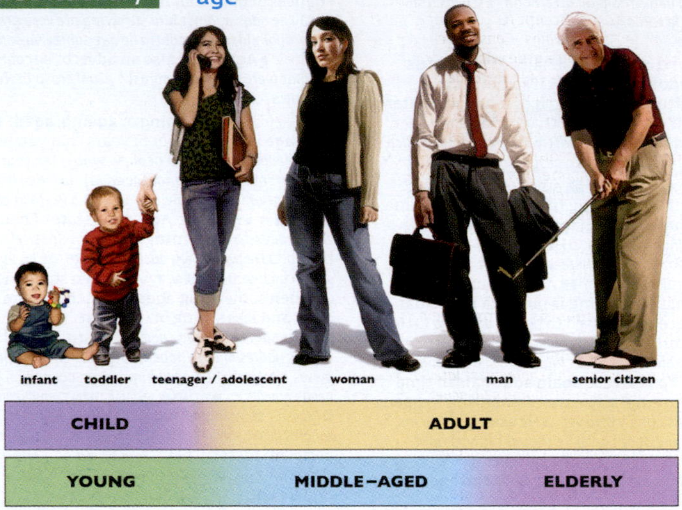


**agent** /eɪdʒənt/ (**agents**) **1** N-COUNT An **agent** is a person who arranges work or business for someone else or does business on their behalf. *representante, agente* [BUSINESS] ❑ *You are buying direct, not through an agent. La compra es directa, no a través de un representante.* **2** N-COUNT An **agent** is a person who works for a country's secret service. *espía* ❑ *...world-famous secret agent James Bond. ...el mundialmente famoso espía James Bond.* **3** N-COUNT A chemical that has a particular effect or is used for a particular purpose can be referred to as a particular kind of **agent**. *agente* ❑ *...the bleaching agent in flour. ...el agente blanqueador en la harina.*
→ see **concert**

**ag|gres|sion** /əgrɛʃᵊn/ N-UNCOUNT **Aggression** is violent and attacking behavior. *agresión* ❑ *They are using aggression and violence against their neighbours. Están usando agresión y violencia contra sus vecinos.*
→ see **anger**

**Word Partnership** Usar *aggression* con:

| | |
|---|---|
| N. | **act of** aggression |
| PREP. | aggression **against** |
| ADJ. | **military** aggression, **physical** aggression |

**ag|gres|sive** /əgrɛsɪv/ **1** ADJ An **aggressive** person or animal behaves angrily or violently toward other people. *agresivo* ❑ *Some children are much more aggressive than others. Algunos niños son mucho más agresivos que otros.* ● **ag|gres|sive|ly** ADV *agresivamente* ❑ *They'll react aggressively. Reaccionarán agresivamente.* **2** ADJ People who are **aggressive** in their work or other activities behave in a forceful way because they are very eager to succeed. *agresivo* ❑ *He was an aggressive manager. Era un gerente agresivo.* ● **ag|gres|sive|ly** ADV *agresivamente* ❑ *They want to play aggressively and do what is necessary to be successful. Quieren activar agresivamente y hacer lo que sea necesario para ser exitosos.*

**ag|ile** /ædʒᵊl/ **1** ADJ Someone who is **agile** can move quickly and easily. *ágil* ❑ *At 20 years old he was not as agile as he is now. Cuando tenía 20 años de edad no era tan ágil como ahora.* ● **agil|ity** /ədʒɪlɪti/ N-UNCOUNT *agilidad* ❑ *She was surprised at his agility. Su agilidad la sorprendió.* **2** ADJ If you have an **agile** mind, you think quickly and intelligently. *ágil* ❑ *She had a very agile mind. Tenía una mente muy ágil.* ● **agil|ity** N-UNCOUNT *agilidad* ❑ *His mental agility has never been in doubt. Su agilidad mental nunca ha estado en duda.*

**ago** /əgoʊ/ ADV You use **ago** when you are referring to past time. For example, if something happened one year **ago**, it is one year since it happened. If it happened a long time **ago**, it is a long time since it happened. *hace* ❑ *I got your letter a few days ago. Recibí tu carta hace unos días.*

**ago|ny** /ægəni/ (**agonies**) N-VAR **Agony** is great physical or mental pain. *agonía* ❑ *He tried to move but screamed in agony. Trató de moverse pero soltó un grito de agonía.*

**agree** /əgri/ (**agrees, agreeing, agreed**) **1** V-RECIP If people **agree with** each other about something, they have the same opinion about it or say that they have the same opinion. *estar de acuerdo* ❑ *Both have agreed on the need for money. Ambos están de acuerdo en la necesidad de tener dinero.* ❑ *Do we agree there's a problem? ¿Estamos de acuerdo en que eso es un problema?* ❑ *I agree with you. Estoy de acuerdo contigo.* ❑ *"It's a shame."—"It is. I agree." -Es una pena. -Lo es. Estoy de acuerdo.* ❑ *I agree with every word you've just said. Estoy de acuerdo con todo lo que has dicho.* **2** V-RECIP If people **agree on** something, they all decide to accept or do something. *convenir en* ❑ *They agreed on a price of $85,000. Convinieron en*

a

*que el precio fuera $85,000.* **3** V-T/V-I If you **agree to** do something, you say that you will do it. If you **agree to** a proposal, you accept it. *consentir en* ❑ *He agreed to pay me for the drawings. Consintió en pagarme por los dibujos.* **4** V-I If you **agree with** an action or suggestion, you approve of it. *estar de acuerdo* ❑ *Most people agreed with what we did. La mayoría estaba de acuerdo con lo que hicimos.* **5** V-RECIP If one account of an event or one set of figures **agrees with** another, the two accounts or sets of figures are the same or are consistent with each other. *concordar* ❑ *His second statement agrees with mine. Su segunda aseveración concuerda con la mía.*

**Word Link** *ment ≈ state, condition : agreement, management, movement*

**agree|ment** /əgriːmənt/ (**agreements**) **1** N-COUNT An **agreement** is a formal decision about future action that is made by two or more countries, groups, or people. *acuerdo, convenio* ❑ *Government officials reached agreement late Sunday. Los funcionarios del gobierno llegaron a un acuerdo el domingo, ya tarde.* **2** N-UNCOUNT **Agreement** with someone means having the same opinion as they have. *acuerdo, coincidencia* ❑ *The doctors were in agreement. Los doctores estaban de acuerdo.* PHRASE • If you are **in agreement with** someone, you have the same opinion as they have. *de acuerdo con* ❑ *We are all in agreement with her. Todos coincidimos con ella.*

**Word Partnership** Usar *agreement* con:

N. **peace** agreement, **terms of an** agreement, **trade** agreement **1**
V. **enter into an** agreement, **sign an** agreement **1**
**reach** agreement **2**

**ag|ri|cul|ture** /ægrɪkʌltʃər/ N-UNCOUNT **Agriculture** is farming and the methods that are used to raise and take care of crops and animals. *agricultura, agronomía* ❑ *Governments must invest more in agriculture and farmers. Los gobiernos deben invertir más en la agricultura y los agricultores.*
• **ag|ri|cul|tur|al** /ægrɪkʌltʃərəl/ ADJ *agrícola* ❑ *...agricultural land. ...tierras agrícolas.*
→ see **farm, grassland, industry**

**ahead**
❶ ADVERB USES
❷ PREPOSITION USES

❶ **ahead** /əhɛd/

In addition to the uses shown below, **ahead** is used in phrasal verbs such as "get ahead," "go ahead," and "press ahead."

**1** ADV Something that is **ahead** is in front of you. If you look **ahead,** you look directly in front of you. *adelante, delante* ❑ *Brett looked straight ahead. Brett miró directamente al frente.* ❑ *The road ahead was now blocked solid. Adelante, el camino estaba totalmente bloqueado.* **2** ADV If you are **ahead** in your work or achievements, you have made more progress than you expected to and are performing well. *adelantado* ❑ *He wanted a good job, a home, and a chance to get ahead. Quería un buen trabajo, una casa y la oportunidad de avanzar.* **3** ADV If a person or a team is **ahead** in a competition, they are winning. *adelante* ❑ *Australia was ahead throughout the game. Australia llevó la delantera durante todo el juego.* **4** ADV **Ahead** means in the future. *venidero* ❑ *A much bigger battle is ahead for the president. Al presidente le espera una lucha aún más intensa.* **5** ADV If you go **ahead,** or if you go on **ahead,** you go in front of someone who is going to the same place so that you arrive there some time before they do. *adelante* ❑ *I went ahead and waited with Sean. Me adelanté y esperé con Sean.*

**Word Partnership** Usar *ahead* con:

ADV. **straight** ahead ❶ **1**
ahead **of schedule/time** ❶ **2**
**in the days/months/years** ahead ❶ **4**
V. **lie** ahead, **look** ahead ❶ **1** **4**
**get** ahead ❶ **2**
**go** ahead ❶ **5**

❷ **ahead of** **1** PHRASE If someone is **ahead of** you, they are in front of you. *adelante de* ❑ *I saw a man thirty yards ahead of me. Vi a un hombre unos diez metros adelante de mí.* **2** PHRASE If an event or period of time lies **ahead of** you, it is going to happen or take place soon or in the future. *delante de* ❑ *Heather was thinking about the future that lay ahead of her. Heather pensaba en el futuro que tenía por delante.* **3** PHRASE If something happens **ahead of** schedule or **ahead of** time, it happens earlier than was planned. *antes de* ❑ *We were a week ahead of schedule. Íbamos una semana adelantados.* **4** PHRASE If someone is **ahead of** someone else, they have made more progress and are more advanced in what they are doing. *adelante de* ❑ *Henry was ahead of the others in most subjects. Henry se les había adelantado a los demás en muchas materias.* **5** **one step ahead of** someone or something → see **step** **6** **ahead of** your **time** → see **time**

**ahold** /əhoʊld/ **1** PHRASE If you **get ahold of** someone or something, you manage to contact, find, or get them. *encontrar a, conseguir a, ponerse en contacto con* [INFORMAL] ❑ *I tried to get ahold of my cousin Joan. Traté de ponerme en contacto con mi prima Joan.* **2** PHRASE If you **get ahold of yourself,** you force yourself to become calm and sensible after a shock or in a difficult situation. *controlarse* [INFORMAL] ❑ *I'm going to have to get ahold of myself. Voy a tener que controlarme.*

**aid** /eɪd/ (**aids, aiding, aided**) **1** N-UNCOUNT **Aid** is money, equipment, or services that are provided for people, countries, or organizations who need them but cannot provide them for themselves. *ayuda, apoyo, auxilio* ❑ *They have promised billions of dollars in aid. Han prometido miles de millones de dólares de ayuda.* **2** V-T To **aid** a country, organization, or person means to provide them with money, equipment, or services that they need. *ayudar, apoyar* ❑ *...a $1 billion fund to aid storm victims. ...un fondo de mil millones de dólares para apoyar a las víctimas de la tormenta.* **3** V-T To **aid** someone means to help or assist them. *ayudar, apoyar* [WRITTEN] ❑ *He is doing what he can to aid his friend. Está haciendo lo posible por ayudar a su amigo.* • **Aid** is also a noun. *ayuda, apoyo* ❑ *He fell into the water and shouted for aid. Se cayó al agua y gritó pidiendo ayuda.* **4** V-T/V-I If something **aids** a process, it makes it easier or

A

more likely to happen. *facilitar* ❑ *The design of the pages might aid the reader's understanding. El diseño de las páginas ayudaría al lector a entender.* ❑ *...a medicine that will aid in the treatment of cancer. ...una medicina que favorece el tratamiento del cáncer.* **5** N-COUNT An **aid** is an object, device, or technique that makes something easier to do. *ayuda, auxiliar* ❑ *The book is a valuable aid to teachers of literature. El libro es una valiosa ayuda para los maestros de literatura.* **6** → see also **first aid** **7** PHRASE If you **come** or **go to** someone's **aid,** you try to help them when they are in danger or difficulty. *ir/venir en auxilio* ❑ *Dr. Fox went to the aid of the dying man. El Dr. Fox fue a auxiliar al hombre agonizante.*

**aide** /eɪd/ (**aides**) **1** N-COUNT An **aide** is an assistant to someone who has an important job, especially in government or in the armed forces. *asistente o asistenta* ❑ *An aide to the president described the meeting as very useful. Un asistente del presidente describió a la reunión como muy útil.* **2** → see also **teacher's aide**

**AIDS** /eɪdz/ N-UNCOUNT **AIDS** is a disease that destroys the natural system of protection that the body has against other diseases. **AIDS** is an abbreviation for **acquired immune deficiency syndrome.** *SIDA, síndrome de inmunodeficiencia adquirida* ❑ *...people suffering from AIDS. ...personas aquejadas por el SIDA.*

**Word Partnership** Usar *AIDS* con:

| | |
|---|---|
| N. | AIDS **activists**, AIDS **epidemic**, AIDS **patient**, AIDS **research**, **spread of** AIDS, AIDS **victims** |
| V. | **infected with** AIDS |

**aim** /eɪm/ (**aims, aiming, aimed**) **1** V-T/V-I If you **aim for** something or **aim to** do something, you plan or hope to achieve it. *aspirar a* ❑ *He is aiming for the 100 meter world record. Aspira al récord mundial de los 100 metros planos.* ❑ *The appeal aims to raise money for children with special needs. El objetivo del llamado es reunir dinero para los niños con necesidades especiales.* **2** V-T If you **aim to** do something, you decide or want to do it. *querer, proponerse* [INFORMAL] ❑ *I aim to please. Quiero ser agradable.* **3** V-T If your actions or remarks **are aimed at** a particular person or group, you intend that the person or group should notice them and be influenced by them. *apuntar* ❑ *Most of their advertisements are aimed at women. Gran parte de su publicidad está dirigida a las mujeres.* **4** V-T If you **aim** a weapon or object **at** something or someone, you point it toward them before firing or throwing it. *apuntar* ❑ *He was aiming the rifle at Wright. Apuntaba a Wright con el rifle.* **5** N-COUNT The **aim** of something that you do is the purpose for which you do it or the result that it is intended to achieve. *objeto, meta* ❑ *The aim of the event is to bring parents and children together. El objetivo del evento es reunir a padres e hijos.* **6** V-T If an action or plan **is aimed at** achieving something, it is intended or planned to achieve it. *dirigir, enfocar* ❑ *The plan is aimed at reaching an agreement. El plan tiende a lograr un acuerdo.* **7** N-SING Your **aim** is your skill or action in pointing a weapon or other object at its target. *puntería* ❑ *His aim was good. Tenía buena puntería.* **8** PHRASE When you **take aim,** you point a weapon or object at someone or something. *apuntar* ❑ *She saw a man with a shotgun taking aim. Vio a un hombre que apuntaba con un arma de fuego.*

**air** /ɛər/ (**airs, airing, aired**) **1** N-UNCOUNT **Air** is the mixture of gases that forms the earth's atmosphere and that we breathe. *aire* ❑ *Keith opened the window and leaned out into the cold air. Keith abrió la ventana y sacó la cabeza al aire frío.* **2** N-UNCOUNT **Air** is used to refer to travel in aircraft. *en avión* ❑ *Air travel will continue to grow at about 6% per year. Los viajes en avión seguirán incrementándose al 6% anual.* **3** N-SING **The air** is the space around things or above the ground. *aire* ❑ *He was waving his arms in the air. Agitaba los brazos en el aire.* **4** V-T If a broadcasting company **airs** a television or radio program, they show it on television or broadcast it on the radio. *transmitir, emitir* ❑ *Tonight PBS will air a documentary called "Democracy In Action." Hoy en la noche PBS transmitirá un documental llamado "Democracia en acción".* ● **air|ing** N-SING *transmisión* ❑ *...the airing of a new television commercial. ...la transmisión de un nuevo comercial de televisión.* **5** V-T If you **air** a room or building, you let fresh air into it. *airear, ventilar* ❑ *One day a week her mother cleaned and aired each room. Su madre limpiaba y ventilaba las recámaras un día a la semana.* **6** PHRASE If you do something to **clear the air,** you do it in order to resolve any problems or disagreements that there might be. *despejar el ambiente* ❑ *...a meeting to clear the air and agree on the facts. ...una reunión para aclarar las cosas y llegar a acuerdos.* **7** PHRASE If someone is **on the air,** they are broadcasting on radio or television. If a program is **on the air,** it is being broadcast on radio or television. If it is **off the air,** it is not being broadcast. *transmitir* ❑ *We go on the air at 11:30 a.m. Salimos al aire a las 11.30 am.*
→ see Word Web: **air**
→ see **erosion, respiratory system, wind**

**air|borne** /ɛərbɔrn/ ADJ **Airborne** means flying in the air or coming from the air. *aerotransportado, transportado por aire, aéreo, en el aire* ❑ *The pilot did manage to get airborne. El piloto logró arreglárselas para despegar.*

**air-conditioned** ADJ If a room or vehicle is **air-conditioned,** the air in it is kept cool and dry by means of a special machine. *con aire acondicionado* ❑ *...air-conditioned trains. ...trenes con aire acondicionado.*

**air-condition|ing** N-UNCOUNT **Air-conditioning** is a method of providing buildings and vehicles with cool dry air. *aire acondicionado, acondicionamiento del aire*

**air|craft** /ɛərkræft/ (**aircraft**) N-COUNT An **aircraft** is a vehicle that can fly, for example, an airplane or a helicopter. *avión, aeronave* ❑ *The aircraft landed safely. El avión aterrizó sin problemas.*
→ see **fly, ship**

**air force** (**air forces**) N-COUNT An **air force** is the part of a country's armed forces that is concerned with fighting in the air. *fuerza aérea* ❑ *...the United States Air Force. ...la Fuerza Aérea de los Estados Unidos.*

**air|lift** /ɛərlɪft/ (**airlifts, airlifting, airlifted**) **1** N-COUNT An **airlift** is an operation to move people, troops, or goods by air, especially in a war

a

**Word Web** air

The **air** we breathe has seventeen different **gases**. It is made up mostly of **nitrogen**, not **oxygen**. Recently, human activities have changed the balance in the earth's **atmosphere**. The widespread burning of coal and oil increases the levels of **carbon dioxide** gas. Scientists believe this air **pollution** may cause **global warming**. Certain chemicals used in air conditioners, farming, and manufacturing are the problem. With less protection from the sun, the air temperature rises and makes the earth warmer. This leads to harmful effects on people, farming, animals, and the natural environment.

**Composition of Air**

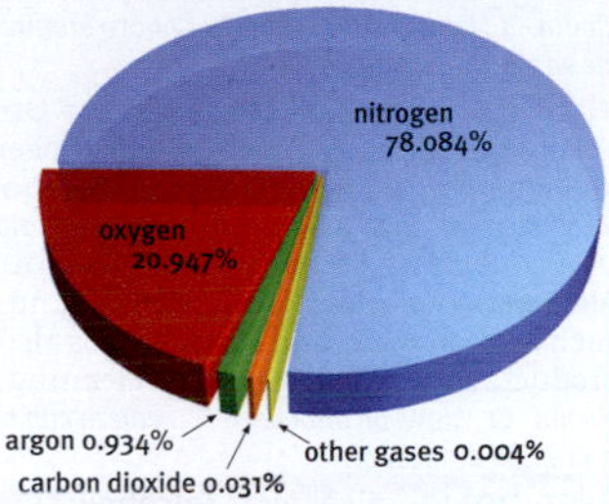


or when land routes are closed. *puente aéreo* ❑ *...an airlift of food, medicines, and blankets. ...un puente aéreo de alimentos, medicinas y cobertores.* **2** V-T If people, troops, or goods **are airlifted** somewhere, they are carried by air, especially in a war or when land routes are closed. *transportar por aire* ❑ *The injured were airlifted to a hospital in Dayton. Los heridos fueron llevados por aire a un hospital de Dayton.*

**air|line** /ɛərlaɪn/ (**airlines**) N-COUNT An **airline** is a company that provides regular services carrying people or goods in airplanes. *línea aérea, aerolínea* ❑ *...the world's largest airline. ...la aerolínea más grande del mundo.*

**air mass** (**air masses**) N-COUNT An **air mass** is a large area of air that has the same temperature and amount of moisture throughout. *masa de aire*

**air|plane** /ɛərpleɪn/ (**airplanes**) N-COUNT An **airplane** is a vehicle with wings and one or more engines that enable it to fly through the air. *avión, aeroplano*
→ see **fly**

**air|port** /ɛərpɔrt/ (**airports**) N-COUNT An **airport** is a place where planes land and take off, and that has buildings and facilities for passengers. *puerto aéreo, aeropuerto* ❑ *Heathrow Airport is the busiest international airport in the world. El Aeropuerto Heathrow es el aeropuerto internacional más concurrido del mundo.*

**air pres|sure** N-UNCOUNT **Air pressure** is a measure of the force with which air presses against a surface. *presión del aire*

**air sac** (**air sacs**) N-UNCOUNT An **air sac** is a very small, round structure in the lungs of some animals that helps them to breathe. *bolsa de aire*

**air|space** /ɛərspeɪs/ also **air space** N-UNCOUNT A country's **airspace** is the part of the sky that is over that country and is considered to belong to it. *espacio aéreo* ❑ *Forty minutes later, they left Colombian airspace. Cuarenta minutos después abandonaron el espacio aéreo colombiano.*

**aisle** /aɪl/ (**aisles**) N-COUNT An **aisle** is a long narrow gap that people can walk along between rows of seats in a public building such as a church or between rows of shelves in a store. *corredor, pasillo* ❑ *...the frozen food aisle. ...el pasillo de los alimentos congelados.*

**à la mode** /ɑ ləmoʊd/ also **a la mode** ADJ A dessert **à la mode** is served with ice cream. *à la mode, a la moda* ❑ *...apple pie à la mode. ...pay de manzana con helado.* • **À la mode** is also used as an adverb. *à la mode, a la moda* ❑ *...served à la mode with vanilla ice cream. ...se sirve a la moda, con helado de vainilla.*

**alarm** /əlɑrm/ (**alarms, alarming, alarmed**) **1** N-UNCOUNT **Alarm** is a feeling of fear or anxiety that something unpleasant or dangerous might happen. *gran preocupación* ❑ *She greeted the news with alarm. Se preocupó mucho con las noticias.* **2** V-T If something **alarms** you, it makes you afraid or anxious that something unpleasant or dangerous might happen. *preocupar, alarmar* ❑ *I don't know what alarmed him. No sé por qué se alarmó.* • **alarmed** ADJ *alarmado, muy preocupado* ❑ *They should not be alarmed by the press reports. No deben alarmarse por los informes de prensa.* • **alarm|ing** ADJ *alarmante, preocupante* ❑ *The disease has spread at an alarming rate. La enfermedad se ha difundido con velocidad alarmante.* • **alarm|ing|ly** ADV *de manera alarmante* ❑ *...the alarmingly high rate of heart disease. ...la alarmante elevación del porcentaje de enfermedades cardíacas.* **3** N-COUNT An **alarm** is an automatic device that warns you of danger, for example, by ringing a bell. *alarma* ❑ *He heard the alarm go off. Oyó que se encendía la alarma.* **4** N-COUNT An **alarm** is the same as an **alarm clock**. *despertador, reloj despertador* ❑ *Dad set the alarm for eight the next day. Papá puso el despertador para que sonara a las ocho del día siguiente.* **5** → see also **false alarm**

**Word Partnership** Usar *alarm* con:

| | |
|---|---|
| V. | **cause** alarm **1** |
| | **set** the alarm **3** **4** |
| N. | alarm **system** **3** |

**alarm clock** (**alarm clocks**) N-COUNT An **alarm clock** is a clock that you can set to make a noise so that it wakes you up at a particular time. *despertador, reloj despertador* ❑ *I set my alarm clock for 4:30. Puse mi despertador a las 4:30.*

**al|be|it** /ɔlbiɪt/ ADV You use **albeit** to introduce a fact or comment that reduces the force or significance of what you have just said. *aunque, no obstante, bien que* [FORMAL] ❑ *It was just another work day, albeit a quieter one. Fue un día más de trabajo, si bien muy tranquilo.*

**al|bum** /ælbəm/ (**albums**) **1** N-COUNT An **album** is a collection of songs that is available on a CD, record, or cassette. *álbum* ❑ *Chris has a large collection of albums. Chris tiene una enorme colección de discos.* ❑ *Oasis released their new album on July 1. Oasis sacó su nuevo disco el 1 de julio.* **2** N-COUNT An

A

**album** is a book in which you keep things such as photographs or stamps that you have collected. *álbum* ❑ *Theresa showed me her photo album. Theresa me enseñó su álbum de fotos.*

**al|co|hol** /ælkəhɔl/ **1** N-UNCOUNT Drinks that can make people drunk, such as beer, wine, and whiskey, can be referred to as **alcohol.** *bebida alcóholica, alcohol* ❑ *Do either of you drink alcohol? ¿Alguno de ustedes bebe alcohol?* **2** N-UNCOUNT **Alcohol** is a colorless liquid that is found in drinks such as beer, wine, and whiskey. It is also used in products such as perfumes and cleaning fluids. *alcohol* ❑ *...low-alcohol beer. ...cerveza con bajo contenido de alcohol.*

**al|co|hol|ic** /ælkəhɔlɪk/ (**alcoholics**) **1** N-COUNT An **alcoholic** is someone who cannot stop drinking alcohol, even when this is making them ill. *alcohólico o alcohólica, enfermo alcohólico o enferma alcohólica* ❑ *He admitted that he is an alcoholic. Aceptó que es alcohólico.* ● **al|co|hol|ism** /ælkəhɒlɪzəm/ N-UNCOUNT *alcoholismo* ❑ *She was treated for alcoholism. Estaba en tratamiento para el alcoholismo.* **2** ADJ **Alcoholic** drinks are drinks that contain alcohol. *alcohólico* ❑ *Wine and beer are alcoholic drinks. El vino y la cerveza son bebidas alcohólicas.*

**alert** /əlɜrt/ (**alerts, alerting, alerted**) **1** ADJ If you are **alert,** you are paying full attention to things around you and are able to deal with anything that might happen. *atento, alerta, vigilante* ❑ *We all have to stay alert. Todos tenemos que estar prevenidos.* ● **alert|ness** N-UNCOUNT *estado de alerta* ❑ *Coffee may increase alertness. El café puede incrementar el estado de alerta.* **2** ADJ If you are **alert to** something, you are fully aware of it. *alerta, prevenido* ❑ *He is alert to the danger. Está alerta ante el peligro.* **3** N-COUNT An **alert** is a situation in which people prepare themselves for something dangerous that might happen soon. *sobre aviso, estado de alerta* ❑ *...last week's storm alert. ...la alerta por la tormenta de la semana pasada.* **4** V-T If you **alert** someone **to** a situation, especially a dangerous or unpleasant situation, you tell them about it. *alertar, poner sobre aviso* ❑ *He wanted to alert people to the danger. Quería poner a la gente sobre aviso del peligro.* **5** PHRASE When soldiers, police or other authorities are **on alert** they are ready to deal with anything that may happens. *sobre aviso, en guardia* ❑ *Health officials have put hospitals on alert. Los funcionarios de sanidad han dado la alerta a los hospitales.*

**al|gae** /ældʒi/ N-PLURAL **Algae** are plants with no stems or leaves that grow in water or on damp surfaces. *alga* ❑ *...an effort to control algae in Green Lake. ...un esfuerzo para controlar las algas en el lago Green.*

**al|ge|bra** /ældʒɪbrə/ N-UNCOUNT **Algebra** is a type of mathematics in which letters are used to represent possible quantities. *álgebra*
→ see **mathematics**

**al|go|rithm** /ælgərɪðəm/ (**algorithms**) N-COUNT An **algorithm** is a series of mathematical steps, especially in a computer program, which will give you the answer to a particular kind of problem or question. *algoritmo*

**al|ien** /eɪliən/ (**aliens**) **1** ADJ **Alien** means belonging to a different country, race, or group, usually one you do not like or are frightened of. *extranjero, ajeno* [FORMAL] ❑ *The group sings about growing up in an alien culture. El grupo canta sobre crecer en una cultura extraña.* **2** ADJ If something is **alien to** you or **to** your normal feelings or behavior, it is not the way you would normally feel or behave. *ajeno* [FORMAL] ❑ *Such behavior is alien to most people. Ese comportamiento es ajeno a la mayoría de la gente.* **3** N-COUNT An **alien** is someone who is not a legal citizen of the country in which they live. *extranjero o extranjera* [LEGAL] ❑ *He's an illegal alien. Es un inmigrante ilegal.* **4** N-COUNT In science fiction, an **alien** is a creature from outer space. *extraterrestre, alienígena* ❑ *...aliens from another planet. ...alienígenas de otro planeta.* **5** N-COUNT An **alien** is a plant or an animal that lives in a different geographical area from the place where it originally lived. *ajeno* [TECHNICAL]

**al|ien|ate** /eɪliəneɪt/ (**alienates, alienating, alienated**) **1** V-T If you **alienate** someone, you make them become unfriendly or unsympathetic toward you. *alejar(se), distanciar(se)* ❑ *We do not want to alienate anybody. No queremos distanciarnos de nadie.* **2** V-T To **alienate** a person **from** someone or something that they are normally linked with means to cause them to be emotionally or intellectually separated from them. *alejar* ❑ *His second wife, Alice, alienated him from his two boys. Alice, su segunda esposa, lo alejó de sus dos hijos.* ● **alienated** ADJ *alejado, distanciado* ❑ *Most of these students feel alienated from their parents. Casi todos estos estudiantes se sienten alejados de sus padres.* ● **alienation** N-UNCOUNT *alejamiento, distanciamiento, marginación* ❑ *...her sense of alienation from the world. ...su sentido de alejamiento del mundo.*

**align|ment** /əlaɪnmənt/ N-UNCOUNT The **alignment** of a person's body is the relationship between the position of their spine and their feet when they are standing or sitting. *alineación*

| Word Link | like ≈ similar : alike, likewise, unlike |
|---|---|

**alike** /əlaɪk/ **1** ADJ If two or more things are **alike,** they are similar in some way. *igual, semejante* ❑ *We looked very alike. Nos parecíamos mucho.* **2** ADV **Alike** means in a similar way. *del mismo modo* ❑ *They even dressed alike. Incluso se vestían igual.*

| Thesaurus | *alike* | Ver también: |
|---|---|---|
| ADJ. | comparable, equal, equivalent, matching, parallel, similar; (*ant.*) different **1** | |

**A-list** ADJ An **A-list** celebrity is a celebrity who is very famous. *lista de personajes importantes* ❑ *...an A-list Hollywood actress. ...una actriz de Hollywood incluida en la lista de los actores más importantes.*

**alive** /əlaɪv/ **1** ADJ If people or animals are **alive,** they are not dead. *vivo* ❑ *She does not know if he is alive or dead. No sabe si él está vivo o muerto.* **2** ADJ If you say that someone seems **alive,** you mean that they seem to be very lively and to enjoy everything that they do. *activo, enérgico, animado* ❑ *She seemed more alive and looked forward to getting up in the morning. Parecía estar más animada y tenía ganas de levantarse por la mañana.* **3** ADJ If an activity, organization, or situation is **alive,** it continues to exist or function. *vigente, en uso* ❑ *The big factories are trying to stay alive by cutting costs. Las grandes fábricas tratan de seguir funcionando reduciendo sus* *costos.* **4** ADJ If a place is **alive with** something, there are a lot of people or things there and it seems busy or exciting. *animado* ❑ *The river was alive with birds.* *El río estaba lleno de aves.* **5** PHRASE If people, places, or events **come alive,** they start to be lively again after a quiet period. *cobrar vida* ❑ *John's voice came alive and his eyes shone.* *La voz de John se animó y sus ojos brillaron.*

**Word Partnership** Usar *alive* con:

ADJ. **dead** or alive **1**
ADV. alive **and well** **1**
**still** alive **1** **3**
V. **found** alive, **keep** *someone/something* alive **1**
**stay** alive **1** **3**
**feel** alive **1** **5**
**come** alive **5**

**al|ka|li met|al** (**alkali metals**) N-COUNT **Alkali metals** are a group of metallic elements that includes sodium and potassium. *metal alcalino* [TECHNICAL]

**alkaline-earth met|al** (**alkaline-earth metals**) also **alkaline earth** N-COUNT **Alkaline-earth metals** are a group of metallic elements that includes calcium and strontium. *metal de tierra alcalina* [TECHNICAL]

**all**
1 EVERYTHING, THE WHOLE OF SOMETHING
2 EMPHASIS
3 OTHER PHRASES

**1 all** /ɔl/ **1** PREDET You use **all** to indicate that you are referring to the whole of a particular group or thing or to everyone or everything of a particular kind. *todo* ❑ *...the restaurant that Hugh and all his friends go to.* *...el restaurante al que van Hugh y todos sus amigos.* ● **All** is also a determiner. *todo* ❑ *There is storage space in all bedrooms.* *Hay espacio para guardar en todas las recámaras.* ❑ *He loved all literature.* *Le encantaba toda la literatura.* ● **All** is also a quantifier. *todo* ❑ *He threw away all of his letters.* *Se deshizo de todas sus cartas.* **2** DET You use **all** to refer to the whole of a particular period of time. *todo, completo* ❑ *He watched TV all day.* *Vio la tele todo el día.* ● **All** is also a predeterminer. *todo* ❑ *She's worked all her life.* *Ha trabajado toda su vida.* **3** PRON You use **all** to refer to a situation or to life in general. *todo* ❑ *All is silent on the island now.* *Ahora todo es silencio en la isla.* **4** PHRASE **In all** means in total. *en total* ❑ *There was a $5,000 first prize and 30 prizes in all.* *Había un primer premio de 5,000 dólares y 30 premios en total.* **5** PHRASE You use **all in all** to introduce a summary or general statement. *en general* ❑ *We both thought that all in all it wasn't a bad idea.* *Ambos pensábamos que en general no era mala idea.*

**Usage** **all**

As a determiner or quantifier, *all* can often be followed by *of* with no change in meaning: *All (of) her friends are here. Please put all (of) the paper back in the drawer.* *Of* is required after *all* when a pronoun follows: *Harry took all of us to the movies.*

**2 all** /ɔl/ **1** ADV You use **all** to emphasize the extent to which something happens or is true. *énfasis* ❑ *I ran away and left her all alone.* *Corrí y la dejé completamente sola.* ❑ *...universities all around the world.* *...universidades de todo el mundo.* **2** ADV **All** is used in structures such as **all the more** or **all the better** to mean even more or even better than before. *énfasis superlativo* ❑ *The fact that it's hard to get there makes it all the more exciting.* *El hecho de que sea difícil llegar ahí lo hace aún más emocionante.* **3** PHRASE You say **above all** to indicate that the thing you are mentioning is the most important point. *ante todo* ❑ *Above all, chairs should be comfortable.* *Primero que nada, las sillas deben ser cómodas.* **4** PHRASE You use **at all** at the end of a clause to give emphasis in negative statements, conditional clauses, and questions. *en absoluto* ❑ *Richard never really liked him at all.* *A Richard realmente nunca le gustó nada.* **5** PHRASE You use **of all** to emphasize the words "first" or "last," or a superlative adjective or adverb. *antes que nada* ❑ *First of all, answer these questions.* *Primero que nada, responde estas preguntas.*

**3 all** /ɔl/ **1** ADV You use **all** when you are talking about an equal score in a game. For example, if the score is three **all,** both players or teams have three points. *iguales* **2** PHRASE You use **after all** when introducing a statement that supports or helps explain something you have just said. *al fin y al cabo* ❑ *I thought you might know somebody. After all, you live here.* *Pensé que conocerías a alguien, después de todo, aquí vives.* **3** PHRASE You use **after all** when you are saying that something that you thought might not be true is in fact true. *después de todo* ❑ *There may be a way out after all.* *Podría haber una forma de salir, después de todo.* **4** PHRASE You use **for all** to indicate that the thing mentioned does not affect or contradict the truth of what you are saying. *con todo* ❑ *For all its faults, the movie instantly became a classic.* *Con todo y sus defectos, la película se convirtió inmediatamente en un clásico.*

**all-around** **1** ADJ An **all-around** person is good at a lot of different skills, academic subjects, or sports. *completo* ❑ *He is a great all-around player.* *Es un jugador muy versátil* **2** ADJ **All-around** means doing or relating to all aspects of a job or activity. *completo* ❑ *She has a great all-around game.* *El juego de ella es muy completo.*

**al|le|ga|tion** /ælɪgeɪʃᵊn/ (**allegations**) N-COUNT An **allegation** is a statement saying that someone has done something wrong. *acusación, imputación* ❑ *The company denied the allegations.* *La compañía negó todas las imputaciones.*

**al|lege** /əlɛdʒ/ (**alleges, alleging, alleged**) V-T If you **allege that** something bad is true, you say it but do not prove it. *sostener, pretender* [FORMAL] ❑ *They alleged that the murder resulted from a quarrel between the two men.* *Afirmaban que el asesinato era el resultado de una riña entre los dos hombres.* ❑ *The accused is alleged to have killed a man.* *Alegaban que el acusado había matado a un hombre.* ● **al|leg|ed|ly** /əlɛdʒɪdli/ ADV *supuestamente* ❑ *His van allegedly hit them as they were crossing the street.* *Según se dice, los atropelló con su camioneta cuando cruzaban la calle.*

**al|le|giance** /əlidʒᵊns/ (**allegiances**) N-VAR Your **allegiance** is your support for and loyalty to a particular group, person, or belief. *lealtad, fidelidad*

❑ *My allegiance to Kendall was very strong. Mi lealtad para con Kendall era muy grande.*

**al|lele** /əlil/ (**alleles**) N-COUNT **Alleles** are different forms of a particular gene within an organism. *alelo* [TECHNICAL]

**al|ler|gic** /əlɜrdʒɪk/ **1** ADJ If you are **allergic to** something, you become ill or get a rash when you eat it, smell it, or touch it. *alérgico* ❑ *I'm allergic to cats. Soy alérgico a los gatos.* **2** ADJ If you have an **allergic** reaction to something, you become ill or get a rash when you eat it, smell it, or touch it. *alérgico* ❑ *He had an allergic reaction to oranges. Tuvo una reacción alérgica a la naranja.*
→ see **peanut**

**al|ler|gy** /ælərdʒi/ (**allergies**) N-VAR If you have a particular **allergy,** you become ill or get a rash when you eat, smell, or touch something that does not normally make people ill. *alergia* ❑ *He has an allergy to nuts. Es alérgico a las nueces.*

**al|ley** /æli/ (**alleys**) N-COUNT An **alley** is a narrow passage or street with buildings or walls on both sides. *callejón*

**al|li|ance** /əlaɪəns/ (**alliances**) **1** N-COUNT An **alliance** is a group of countries or political parties that are formally united and working together because they have similar aims. *alianza* ❑ *The two parties formed an alliance. Los dos partidos formaron una alianza.* **2** N-COUNT An **alliance** is a relationship in which two countries, political parties, or organizations work together for some purpose. *alianza* ❑ *...Britain's alliance with the United States. ...la alianza de Gran Bretaña con Estados Unidos.*

**al|lied** /əlaɪd/ **1** ADJ **Allied** countries, troops, or political parties are united by a political or military agreement. *aliado* ❑ *...forces from three allied nations. ...las fuerzas de las tres naciones aliadas.* **2** ADJ If one thing or group is **allied to** another, it is related to it because the two things have particular qualities or characteristics in common. *relacionado* ❑ *...books on subjects allied to health, beauty and fitness. ...libros sobre temas relacionados con la salud, la belleza o la condición física.*

**al|li|ga|tor** /ælɪgeɪtər/ (**alligators**) N-COUNT An **alligator** is a large reptile with short legs, a long tail, and very powerful jaws. *caimán* ❑ *Do not feed the alligators. Prohibido alimentar a los caimanes.*

alligator

**all-in-one** **1** ADJ **All-in-one** means having several different parts or several different functions. *todo en uno* ❑ *...an all-in-one printer that's also a scanner, fax, and copier. ...una impresora todo en uno que también es escáner, fax y copiadora.* **2** → see also **one**

**al|lit|era|tion** /əlɪtəreɪʃən/ (**alliterations**) N-VAR **Alliteration** is the use in speech or writing of several words close together that all begin with the same letter or sound. *aliteración* [TECHNICAL]

**al|lo|cate** /æləkeɪt/ (**allocates, allocating, allocated**) V-T If one item or share of something **is allocated to** a particular person or **for** a particular purpose, it is given to that person or used for that purpose. *asignar* ❑ *Tickets will be allocated to those who apply first. Los boletos serán asignados a quienes los soliciten primero.* ❑ *Our plan is to allocate one member of staff to handle appointments. Nuestro plan es asignar a un miembro de la dirección para que maneje las citas.*
• **al|lo|ca|tion** /æləkeɪʃᵊn/ N-UNCOUNT ❑ *...the allocation of land for new homes. ...la asignación de tierras para nuevas viviendas.*

**all-over** ADJ You can use **all-over** to describe something that covers an entire surface. *Todo, completo, integral* ❑ *They got great all-over suntans. Lograron un bronceado completo.*

**al|low** /əlaʊ/ (**allows, allowing, allowed**) **1** V-T If someone **is allowed to** do something, it is all right for them to do it. *permitir* ❑ *The children are allowed to watch TV after school. A los niños se les permite ver la televisión después de la escuela.* **2** V-T If you **are allowed** something, you are given permission to have it or are given it. *permitir* ❑ *Gifts like chocolates or flowers are allowed. Los obsequios como chocolates o flores están permitidos.* **3** V-T If you **allow** something **to** happen, you do not prevent it. *permitir* ❑ *He won't allow himself to fail. No se permitirá fracasar.* **4** V-T If one thing **allows** another thing **to** happen, the first thing creates the opportunity for the second thing to happen. *permitir* ❑ *A period of rest will allow me to become stronger. Un tiempo de descanso me permitirá fortalecerme.* **5** V-T If you **allow** a particular length of time or a particular amount of something **for** a particular purpose, you include it in your planning. *considerar* ❑ *Please allow 28 days for delivery. Por favor, considere 28 días para la entrega.*
▸ **allow for** PHR-VERB If you **allow for** certain problems or expenses, you include some extra time or money in your planning so that you can deal with them if they occur. *tomar en consideración* ❑ *They allowed for a public meeting. Tomaron en consideración una reunión pública.*

| **Thesaurus** | *allow* | Ver también: |
|---|---|---|
| v. | approve, consent, tolerate; (*ant.*) disallow, forbid, prohibit, prevent **3**<br>let **4** | |

**al|low|ance** /əlaʊəns/ (**allowances**) **1** N-COUNT An **allowance** is money that is given regularly to someone. *mensualidad* ❑ *She gets an allowance for taking care of Amy. Recibe una mensualidad por cuidar de Amy.* **2** N-COUNT A child's **allowance** is money that is given to him or her every week or every month by his or her parents. *mesada* ❑ *When you give kids an allowance make sure they save some of it. Cuando les des su mesada a los muchachos, asegúrate de que ahorren una parte.* **3** PHRASE If you **make allowances for** something, you take it into account in your decisions, plans, or actions. *tomar en consideración* ❑ *She tried to make allowances for his age. Ella trató de tomar en consideración la edad de él.* **4** PHRASE If you **make allowances for** someone, you accept behavior from them that you would not normally accept, because of a problem that they have. *indulgente* ❑ *He's tired so I'll make allowances for him. Está cansado, así que seré indulgente con él.*

**al|loy** /ælɔɪ/ (**alloys**) N-VAR An **alloy** is a metal that is made by mixing two or more types of metal together. *aleación*

**all-points bul|letin** (**all-points bulletins**)

N-COUNT An **all-points bulletin** is a message sent by a police force to all its officers. The abbreviation **APB** is also used. boletín general ❑ *An all-points bulletin gave out their names and addresses.* *Sus nombres y domicilios aparecieron en un boletín general de la policía.*

**all right** 1 ADJ If you say that someone or something is **all right**, you mean that they are satisfactory or acceptable. bien, adecuado ❑ *I'll do that if it's all right with you.* *Lo haré si te parece bien.* ● **All right** is also used before a noun. bueno [INFORMAL] ❑ *He's an all right kind of guy really.* *Es realmente un buen tipo.* 2 ADJ If someone or something is **all right**, they are well or safe. bien ❑ *Are you all right?* *¿Estás bien?* 3 CONVENTION You say "**all right**" when you are agreeing to something. estar bien ❑ *"I think you should go now." —"All right."* *—Creo que ya deberías irte.—Está bien.*

**all-time** ADJ You use **all-time** when you are comparing all the things of a particular type that there have ever been. For example, if you say that something is the **all-time** best, you mean that it is the best thing of its type that there has ever been. de todos los tiempos, sin precedentes ❑ *It's one of my all-time favorite movies.* *Es una de mis películas preferidas de todos los tiempos.*

**al|lu|vial fan** also **alluvial cone** /əluviəl fæn/ (**alluvial fans**) N-COUNT An **alluvial fan** is material such as sand and gravel, shaped like a fan, that is deposited on the land by a fast-flowing river. abanico aluvial [TECHNICAL]

**al|lu|vium** /əluviəm/ N-UNCOUNT **Alluvium** is soil or rock that has been deposited by a river. aluvión [TECHNICAL]

**ally** (**allies, allying, allied**)

> The noun is pronounced /ælaɪ/. The verb is pronounced /əlaɪ/.

1 N-COUNT A country's **ally** is another country that has an agreement to support it, especially in war. aliado o aliada ❑ *...the Western allies.* *...los aliados de Occidente.* 2 N-COUNT If you describe someone as your **ally**, you mean that they help and support you, especially when other people are opposing you. aliado ❑ *He is a close ally of the president.* *Es un aliado cercano del presidente.* 3 V-T If you **ally yourself with** someone or something, you give your support to them. aliarse ❑ *He allied himself with his father-in-law.* *Se alió con su suegro.* 4 → see also **allied**

> **Word Link** *most ≈ superlative degree : almost, mostly, utmost*

**al|most** /ɔlmoʊst/ ADV **Almost** means very nearly but not completely. casi ❑ *We have been married for almost three years.* *Llevamos casados casi tres años.* ❑ *He caught Spanish flu, which almost killed him.* *Se contagió la gripe española, que casi lo mata.*

> **Usage** almost and most
>
> Be sure to use *almost*, not *most*, before such words as *all*, *any*, *anyone*, *every*, and *everyone*: *Almost all people like chocolate. Almost anyone can learn to ride a bike. Strangely, almost every student in the class is left-handed.*

> **Thesaurus** *almost* Ver también:
>
> ADV. about, most, practically, virtually

**alone** /əloʊn/ 1 ADJ When you are **alone**, you are not with any other people. solo ❑ *She wanted to be alone.* *Quería estar sola.* ● **Alone** is also an adverb. solo ❑ *He lived alone in this house for almost five years.* *Vivió solo en esa casa durante casi cinco años.* 2 ADJ If one person is **alone with** another person, or if two or more people are **alone**, they are together, without anyone else present. solo, a solas ❑ *He wanted to be alone with her.* *Quería estar a solas con ella.* ❑ *We were alone together.* *Estábamos solos.* 3 ADJ If you say that you are **alone** or feel **alone**, you mean that nobody who is with you, or nobody at all, cares about you. solo ❑ *She had never felt so alone.* *Nunca se había sentido tan sola.* 4 ADV You say that one person or thing **alone** does something when you are emphasizing that only one person or thing is involved. sólo ❑ *You alone should decide what is right for you.* *Sólo tú debes decidir lo que está bien para ti.* 5 ADV When someone does something **alone**, they do it without help from other people. solo ❑ *Bringing up a child alone is very difficult.* *Criar solo a un hijo es muy difícil.* 6 to **leave** someone or something **alone** → see **leave** 7 **let alone** → see **let**

> **Thesaurus** *alone* Ver también:
>
> ADJ. solitary; (*ant.*) crowded, together 1

**along** /əlɔŋ/

> In addition to the uses shown below, **along** is used in phrasal verbs such as "go along with," "play along," and "string along."

1 PREP If you move or look **along** something such as a road, you move or look toward one end of it. a lo largo de ❑ *Pedro walked along the street.* *Pedro caminó a lo largo de la calle.* 2 PREP If something is situated **along** a road, river, aisle or hallway, it is situated in it or beside it. a lo largo ❑ *There were traffic jams all along the roads.* *Había embotellamientos de tráfico a todo lo largo de las carreteras.* 3 ADV When someone or something moves **along**, they keep moving in a particular direction. avanzar ❑ *He was talking as they walked along.* *Iba hablando mientras avanzaban.* 4 ADV If you say that something is going **along** in a particular way, you mean that it is progressing in that way. avanzar ❑ *The discussions are moving along very slowly.* *Las discusiones avanzan muy lentamente.* 5 ADV If you take someone or something **along** when you go somewhere, you take them with you. consigo (con variantes de persona) ❑ *Bring along your friends and family.* *Lleva a tus amigos y tu familia contigo.* 6 ADV If someone or something is coming **along** or is sent **along**, they are coming or being sent to a particular place. ❑ *He's coming along to help me.* *Viene para ayudarme.* 7 PHRASE You use **along with** to mention someone or something else that is also involved in an action or situation. junto con ❑ *She escaped from the fire along with her two children.* *Escapó al fuego junto con sus dos hijos.* 8 PHRASE If something has been true or been present **all along**, it has been true or been present throughout a period of time. todo el tiempo ❑ *I was right all along.* *Yo tuve la razón todo el tiempo.*

A

**along|side** /əlɔŋsaɪd/ **1** PREP If one thing is **alongside** another thing, the first thing is next to the second. *al lado de* ❑ *He crossed the street and walked alongside Central Park. Cruzó la calle y caminó al lado de Central Park.* ● **Alongside** is also an adverb. *junto a* ❑ *He waited several minutes for a car to pull up alongside. Esperó varios minutos que un carro se detuviera junto a él.* **2** PREP If you work **alongside** other people, you all work together in the same place. *junto con, codo con codo* ❑ *He worked alongside Frank and Mark and they became friends. Trabajaba junto con Frank y Mark y se hicieron amigos.*

**aloud** /əlaʊd/ ADV When you speak, read, or laugh **aloud,** you speak or laugh so that other people can hear you. *alto, en voz alta* ❑ *When we were children, our father read aloud to us. Cuando éramos niños, nuestro padre nos leía en voz alta.*

**al|pha|bet** /ælfəbɛt, -bɪt/ (**alphabets**) N-COUNT An **alphabet** is a set of letters usually presented in a fixed order which is used for writing the words of a language. *alfabeto* ❑ *The modern Russian alphabet has 31 letters. El alfabeto ruso moderno consta de 31 letras.*

**al|pha|beti|cal** /ælfəbɛtɪkᵊl/ ADJ **Alphabetical** means arranged according to the normal order of the letters in the alphabet. *alfabético* ❑ *The books are arranged in alphabetical order. Los libros están dispuestos en orden alfabético.*

**al|pha|bet|ic prin|ci|ple** N-SING *The* **alphabetic principle** is the idea that each of the letters of an alphabet represents a particular sound in the language. *principio alfabético*

**al|pha par|ti|cle** /ælfəpɑrtɪkᵊl/ (**alpha particles**) N-COUNT **Alpha particles** are subatomic particles that are emitted by radioactive substances such as uranium and radium. *partícula alfa*

**al|ready** /ɔlrɛdi/ **1** ADV You use **already** to show that something has happened, or that something had happened before the moment you are referring to. Some speakers use **already** with the simple past tense of the verb instead of a perfect tense. *ya* ❑ *They've spent nearly a billion dollars on it already. Ya han gastado casi mil millones de dólares en eso.* ❑ *She says she already told the neighbors not to come over for a couple of days. Dice que ya les dijo a los vecinos que no vinieran por un par de días.* **2** ADV You use **already** to show that a situation exists at this present moment or that it exists at an earlier time than expected. You use **already** after the verb "be" or an auxiliary verb, or before a verb if there is no auxiliary. When you want to add emphasis, you can put **already** at the beginning of a sentence. *ya* ❑ *He was already rich. Él ya era rico.* ❑ *Already, she is thinking ahead. Ya está pensando por adelantado.*

> **Usage** **already** and **all ready**
>
> It's easy to confuse *already* and *all ready*. *Already* means "before now" : *Have you finished eating already? Akiko had already heard the good news. All ready* means "completely prepared" : *Jacob is all ready to leave, but Michelle still has to get dressed.*

**also** /ɔlsoʊ/ **1** ADV You can use **also** to give more information about a person or thing. *también* ❑ *The book also includes an index of all U.S. presidents. El libro también incluye un índice de todos los presidentes de EE.UU.* ❑ *We've got a big table and also some stools and benches. Tenemos una mesa grande y también algunos taburetes y bancos.* **2** ADV You can use **also** to indicate that something you have just said about one person or thing is true of another person or thing. *también* ❑ *I was surprised but also thankful that people remembered us. Estaba sorprendido y también agradecido de que la gente nos recordara.*

> **Thesaurus** *also* Ver también:
>
> ADV. additionally, and, furthermore, likewise; (*ant.*) plus, still, too **1**

**al|ter** /ɔltər/ (**alters, altering, altered**) V-T/V-I If something **alters** or if you **alter** it, it changes. *alterar* ❑ *World War II altered American life in many ways. La segunda guerra mundial alteró la vida estadunidense en muchos sentidos.* ● **al|tera|tion** /ɔltəreɪʃᵊn/ N-VAR (**alterations**) *cambio, modificación, arreglo* ❑ *...clothing alterations. ...se arregla ropa.*

**al|ter|nate** (**alternates, alternating, alternated**)

> The verb is pronounced /ɔltərneɪt/. The adjective and noun are pronounced /ɔltɜrnɪt/.

**1** V-RECIP When you **alternate** two things, you keep using one then the other. When one thing **alternates with** another, the first regularly occurs after the other. *alternar* ❑ *Rain alternated with wet snow. La lluvia alternaba con las nevadas.* ❑ *Starting with the onions, alternate meat and onions until they are all used. Empezando por las cebollas, alterne la carne y las cebollas hasta que no quede más.* **2** ADJ **Alternate** actions, events, or processes regularly occur after each other. *alterno* ❑ *...alternate bands of color. ...bandas de color alternas.* ● **al|ter|nate|ly** ADV *alternativamente* ❑ *He lived alternately in New York and Seattle. Vivía alternadamente en Nueva York y Seattle.* **3** ADJ If something happens on **alternate** days, it happens on one day, then happens on every second day after that. In the same way, something can happen in **alternate** weeks, years, or other periods of time. *alterno* ❑ *Jim went skiing in alternate years. Jim iba a esquiar un año sí y otro no.* **4** ADJ You use **alternate** to describe a plan, idea, or system which is different from the one already in operation and can be used instead of it. *alternativo* ❑ *His group was forced to turn back and take an alternate route. Su grupo se vio obligado a retroceder y tomar un camino alternativo.* **5** N-COUNT An **alternate** is a person or thing that replaces another, and can act or be used instead of them. *suplente* ❑ *...a jury of twelve jurors and two alternates. ...un jurado de doce miembros y dos suplentes.* **6** → see also **alternative**

**al|ter|na|tive** /ɔltɜrnətɪv/ (**alternatives**) **1** N-COUNT If one thing is an **alternative to** another, the first can be found, used, or done instead of the second. *alternativa* ❑ *The new treatment may provide an alternative to painkillers. El nuevo tratamiento puede ser una alternativa a los calmantes.* **2** ADJ An **alternative** plan or offer is different from the one that you already have, and can be done or used instead. *alternativo* ❑ *Alternative methods of travel were available. Formas de viaje alternativas cuando las haya disponibles.* **3** ADJ **Alternative** is used to describe something that is different from the usual things of its kind, or the usual ways of doing something. *alternativo* ❑ *...alternative health care. ...asistencia médica alternativa.*

a

**al|ter|na|tive|ly** /ɔltɜrnətɪvli/ ADV You use **alternatively** to introduce a suggestion or to mention something different from what has just been stated. *alternativamente* ❑ *Hotels are not too expensive. Alternatively you could stay in an apartment. Los hoteles no son demasiado caros. Alternativamente, se puede alojar en un departamento.*

**Usage** **alternatively** and **alternately**
*Alternatively* and *alternately* are often confused. *Alternatively* is used to talk about a choice between different things: *Sheila might go to the beach tomorrow; alternatively, she could go to the museum. Alternately* is used to talk about things that regularly occur after each other: *The traffic light was alternately green, yellow, and red. The days have been alternately sunny and rainy.*

**al|though** /ɔlðoʊ/ **1** CONJ You use **although** to introduce a statement that contrasts with something else that you are saying. *aunque* ❑ *Their system worked, although no one knew how. Su sistema funcionaba, aunque nadie sabía cómo.* ❑ *Although I was only six, I can remember seeing it on TV. Aunque apenas tenía seis años, recuerdo haberlo visto en la televisión.* **2** CONJ You use **although** to introduce clauses that modify what is being said or give further information. *aunque* ❑ *They all play basketball, although on different teams. Todos juegan básquetbol, aunque en diferentes equipos.*

**Thesaurus** *although* Ver también:
PREP. despite **1** **2**
CONJ. despite, though, while **1** **2**

**al|ti|tude** /æltɪtud/ (**altitudes**) N-VAR If something is at a particular **altitude**, it is at that height above sea level. *altitud* ❑ *The aircraft reached an altitude of about 39,000 feet. El avión alcanzó una altitud de aproximadamente 12,000 metros.*

**al|to|geth|er** /ɔltəgɛðər/ **1** ADV You use **altogether** to emphasize that something has stopped, been done, or finished completely. *totalmente* ❑ *Babies should stay out of the sun altogether. Los bebés deben estar totalmente protegidos contra el sol.* **2** ADV You use **altogether** in front of an adjective or adverb to emphasize a quality that someone or something has. *totalmente* ❑ *That's an altogether different story. Es una historia totalmente diferente.* **3** ADV If several amounts add up to a particular amount **altogether**, that amount is their total. *en total* ❑ *There were eleven of us altogether. Éramos once en total.*

**Usage** **altogether** and **all together**
*Altogether* and *all together* are easily confused. *Altogether* means "in all" : *Altogether, I saw four movies at the film festival last week. All together* means "together in a group" : *It was the first time we were all together in four years and it meant a lot to me.*

**al|to|stra|tus** /æltoʊstreɪtəs, -stræt-/ (**altostrati**) N-VAR **Altostratus** is a type of thick gray cloud that forms at intermediate altitudes. *altoestrato* [TECHNICAL]
→ see **cloud**

**al|tri|cial** /æltrɪʃəl/ ADJ An **altricial** chick is a young bird that is weak and blind when it is born and is dependent on its parents for food and care. *altricial* [TECHNICAL]

**alum** /əlʌm/ (**alums**) N-COUNT An **alum** is the same as an **alumnus**. *estudiante, alumno o alumna* [INFORMAL] ❑ *...a University of Chicago alum. ...un estudiante de la Universidad de Chicago.*

**alu|mi|num** /əluminəm/ N-UNCOUNT **Aluminum** is a lightweight metal used, for example, for making cooking equipment and aircraft parts. *aluminio* ❑ *...aluminum cans. ...latas de aluminio.*

**alum|nus** /əlʌmnəs/ (**alumni** /əlʌmnaɪ/) N-COUNT The **alumni** of a school, college, or university are the people who used to be students there. *alumno*

**al|veo|lus** /ælviələs/ (**alveoli**) N-COUNT **Alveoli** are hollow structures in the lungs of mammals, which carry oxygen to the bloodstream. *alveolo* [TECHNICAL]

**al|ways** /ɔlweɪz/ **1** ADV If you **always** do something, you do it whenever a particular situation occurs. If you **always** did something, you did it whenever a particular situation occurred. *siempre* ❑ *She's always late for everything. Siempre llega tarde para todo.* ❑ *Always lock your door. Cierra siempre la puerta con llave.* **2** ADV If you **always** do particular thing, you do it all the time, continuously. *siempre* ❑ *They always talked sports together. Siempre hablaban de deportes cuando estaban juntos.* **3** ADV You use **always** in expressions such as **can always** or **could always** when you are making suggestions or suggesting an alternative approach or method. *siempre* ❑ *If you don't know, you can always ask me. Si no sabes, siempre puedes preguntarme.*

**Thesaurus** *always* Ver también:
ADV. consistently, constantly, continuously, endlessly, repeatedly; (*ant.*) never, rarely **1** **2**

**am** /əm, STRONG æm/ **Am** is the first person singular of the present tense of **be. Am** is often shortened to **'m** in spoken English. The negative forms are "I am not" and "I'm not." In questions and tags in spoken English, these are usually changed to "aren't I." *primera persona del singular del presente de* ***be***.

**AM** /eɪ ɛm/ **AM** is a method of transmitting radio waves that can be used to broadcast sound. **AM** is an abbreviation for 'amplitude modulation.' *A.M., amplitud modulada*

**a.m.** /eɪ ɛm/ **a.m.** after a number indicates that the number refers to a particular time between midnight and noon. *a.m., antes meridiano* ❑ *The program starts at 9 a.m. El programa empieza a las 9 a.m.*

**ama|teur** /æmətʃər, -tʃʊər/ (**amateurs**) N-COUNT An **amateur** is someone who does something as a hobby and not as a job. *aficionado o aficionada* ❑ *Jerry is an amateur who dances because he likes it. Jerry es un aficionado que baila porque le gusta.* ❑ *...amateur runners. ...corredores aficionados.*

**amaze** /əmeɪz/ (**amazes, amazing, amazed**) V-T/V-I If something **amazes** you, it surprises

A

you very much. *asombrar* ❑ *He amazed us by his knowledge of Colorado history. Nos asombró por su conocimiento de la historia de Colorado.* ❑ *14-year-old Michelle Wie continued to amaze. La joven Michelle Wie, de 14 años de edad, siguió asombrando a todos.* • **amazed** ADJ *asombrado, perplejo* ❑ *I was amazed at how difficult it was. Me asombró lo difícil que era.*

**Word Partnership** Usar *amaze* con:

V. **continue to** amaze, **never cease to** amaze
N. amaze **your friends**

**amaz|ing** /əmeɪzɪŋ/ ADJ You say that something is **amazing** when it is very surprising and makes you feel pleasure, approval, or wonder. *increíble* ❑ *It's amazing what we can remember if we try. Es increíble lo que podemos recordar cuando nos esforzamos.* • **amaz|ing|ly** ADV *Increíblemente.* ❑ *She was an amazingly good cook. Era una cocinera increíblemente buena.*

**Thesaurus** *amazing* Ver también:

ADJ. astonishing, astounding, extraordinary, incredible; (*ant.*) stunning, wonderful

**am|bas|sa|dor** /æmbæsədər/ (**ambassadors**) N-COUNT An **ambassador** is an important official who lives in a foreign country and represents his or her own country's interests there. *embajador o embajadora* ❑ *...the ambassador to Poland. ...el embajador en Polonia.*

**am|bigu|ous** /æmbɪgyuəs/ ADJ If you describe something as **ambiguous,** you mean that it is unclear or confusing because it can be understood in more than one way. *ambiguo* ❑ *This agreement is very ambiguous. Este acuerdo es muy ambiguo.* • **am|bigu|ous|ly** ADV *Ambiguamente, con ambigüedad.* ❑ *...an ambiguously worded statement. ...una declaración expresada con ambigüedad.*

**am|bi|tion** /æmbɪʃᵊn/ (**ambitions**) **1** N-COUNT If you have an **ambition to** do or achieve something, you want very much to do it or achieve it. *ambición* ❑ *His ambition is to sail around the world. Su ambición es navegar alrededor del mundo.* **2** N-UNCOUNT **Ambition** is the desire to be successful, rich, or powerful. *ambición* ❑ *Even when I was young I never had any ambition. Ni siquiera cuando era joven tuve alguna ambición.*

**am|bi|tious** /æmbɪʃəs/ **1** ADJ Someone who is **ambitious** has a strong desire to be successful, rich, or powerful. *ambicioso* ❑ *Chris is very ambitious. Chris es muy ambicioso.* **2** ADJ An **ambitious** idea or plan is on a large scale and needs a lot of work to be carried out successfully. *ambicioso* ❑ *He has ambitious plans for the firm. Tiene planes ambiciosos para la empresa.*

**am|bu|lance** /æmbyələns/ (**ambulances**) N-COUNT An **ambulance** is a vehicle for taking people to and from a hospital. *ambulancia*

**am|bush** /æmbʊʃ/ (**ambushes, ambushing, ambushed**) **1** V-T If a group of people **ambush** their enemies, they attack them after hiding and waiting for them. *emboscar* ❑ *Gunmen ambushed and killed 10 soldiers. Unos terroristas emboscaron y mataron a 10 soldados.* **2** N-VAR An **ambush** is an attack on someone by people who have been hiding and waiting for them. *emboscada* ❑ *Three civilians were killed in an ambush. Tres civiles murieron en una emboscada.*

**amend** /əmɛnd/ (**amends, amending, amended**) **1** V-T If you **amend** something that has been written such as a law, or something that is said, you change it in order to improve it or make it more accurate. *enmendar* ❑ *The governor tried to amend the law. El gobernador trató de enmendar la ley.* **2** PHRASE If you **make amends** when you have harmed someone, you show that you are sorry by doing something to please them. *dar satisfacciones* ❑ *He wanted to make amends for his mistakes. Quería dar satisfacciones por sus errores.*

**amend|ment** /əmɛndmənt/ (**amendments**) N-VAR An **amendment** is a section that is added to a law or rule in order to change it. *enmienda* ❑ *...an amendment to the defense bill. ...una enmienda al proyecto de ley de defensa.*

**amen|ity** /əmɛnɪti/ (**amenities**) N-COUNT **Amenities** are things such as shopping centers or sports facilities that are provided for people's convenience, enjoyment, or comfort. *atractivo* ❑ *Amenities include a heated swimming pool. Los atractivos incluyen una alberca de agua caliente.*
→ see **hotel**

**Ameri|can** /əmɛrɪkən/ (**Americans**) **1** ADJ **American** means belonging to or coming from the United States of America. *estadounidense, americano* ❑ *...the American ambassador at the United Nations. ...el embajador estadounidense ante la Organización de las Naciones Unidas.* ❑ *...American television and movies. ...la televisión y el cine estadounidenses.* **2** → see also **Latin American** • An **American** is someone who is American. *estadounidense* ❑ *He's an American living in Canada. Es un estadounidense que vive en Canadá.*

**Ameri|cas** /əmɛrɪkəz/ N-PLURAL People sometimes refer to North America, Central America, and South America collectively as **the Americas.** *Continente Americano, Américas* ❑ *...music of the Americas. ...música de las Américas.*

**Amish** /ɑmɪʃ/ **1** N-PLURAL **The Amish** are members of a Protestant group who have a strict and simple way of life. *amish* ❑ *Many Amish are moving to other regions. Muchos amish se están mudando a otras regiones.* **2** ADJ **Amish** means relating to the Amish people or their religion. *amish* ❑ *...an Amish community. ...una comunidad amish.*

**am|mu|ni|tion** /æmyʊnɪʃᵊn/ **1** N-UNCOUNT **Ammunition** is bullets and rockets that are made to be fired from weapons. *munición, bala, cartucho* ❑ *He had only seven rounds of ammunition. Sólo tenía siete balas.* **2** N-UNCOUNT You can describe information that you can use against someone in an argument or discussion as **ammunition.** *arma* ❑ *The data in the study might be used as ammunition. Los datos del estudio pueden usarse como armas.*

**am|nes|ty** /æmnɪsti/ (**amnesties**) **1** N-VAR An **amnesty** is an official pardon granted to a group of prisoners by the state. *amnistía* ❑ *...an amnesty for political prisoners. ...una amnistía para los presos políticos.* **2** N-COUNT An **amnesty** is a period of time during which people can admit to a crime

a

or give up weapons without being punished. *amnistía* ❑ *The government announced an immediate amnesty.* *El gobierno anunció una amnistía inmediata.*

**am|ni|on** /æmniɒn, -ən/ (**amnions**) N-COUNT The **amnion** is a thin covering that surrounds and protects an embryo in reptiles, birds, and mammals. *amnios* [TECHNICAL]

**amoe|ba** /əmibə/ (**amoebae** /əmibi/ or **amoebas**) N-COUNT An **amoeba** is the smallest kind of living creature. Amoebae consist of only one cell, and are found in water or soil. *amiba*

**among** /əmʌŋ/ **1** PREP Someone or something that is **among** a group of things or people is surrounded by them. *entre* ❑ *...teenagers sitting among adults.* *...los adolescentes sentados entre los adultos.* ❑ *They walked among the crowds.* *Caminaron entre las multitudes.* **2** PREP If someone or something is **among** a group, they are a member of that group and share its characteristics. *entre* ❑ *A young girl was among the injured.* *Entre los heridos había una joven.* **3** PREP If something happens **among** a group of people, it happens within the whole of that group or between the members of that group. *entre* ❑ *We discussed it among ourselves.* *Lo discutimos entre nosotros.* **4** PREP If something such as a feeling, opinion, or situation exists **among** a group of people, most of them have it or experience it. *entre* ❑ *There is concern among parents about teaching standards.* *Hay preocupación entre los padres sobre la calidad de la enseñanza.* **5** PREP If something is shared **among** a number of people, some of it is given to all of them. *entre* ❑ *The money will be shared among family members.* *El dinero se repartirá entre los miembros de la familia.* **6** → see also **between**

**amount** /əmaʊnt/ (**amounts, amounting, amounted**) **1** N-VAR The **amount of** something is how much there is, or how much you have, need, or get. *cantidad* ❑ *He needs that amount of money to live.* *Necesita esa cantidad de dinero para vivir.* ❑ *I still do a certain amount of work for them.* *Todavía hago cierta cantidad de trabajo para ellos.* **2** V-I If something **amounts to** a particular total, all the parts of it add up to that total. *sumar* ❑ *The payment amounted to $42 billion.* *El pago sumó 42,000 millones de dólares.*

▸**amount to** PHR-VERB If you say that one thing **amounts to** something else, you consider the first thing to be the same as the second thing. *equivaler* ❑ *The proposal amounts to less money for us.* *La propuesta equivale a menos dinero para nosotros.*

> **Usage** **amount** and **number**
>
> *Number* is used to talk about how many there are of something: *Madhu was surprised at the large number of students in the class.* *Amount* is used to talk about how much there is of something: *There is only a small amount of water in the glass.*

**am|per|sand** /æmpərsænd/ (**ampersands**) N-COUNT An **ampersand** is the sign &, used to represent the word "and." *et (del latín, en uso en español, también se representa con el signo &)*

**am|phib|ian** /æmfɪbiən/ (**amphibians**) N-COUNT **Amphibians** are animals such as frogs and toads that can live both on land and in water. *anfibio*
→ see Word Web: **amphibian**

**am|phi|thea|ter** /æmfiθiətər/ (**amphitheaters**) N-COUNT An **amphitheater** is a large open area surrounded by rows of seats sloping upward. Amphitheaters were built mainly in Greek and Roman times for the performance of plays. *anfiteatro*

**am|ple** /æmpᵊl/ (**ampler, amplest**) ADJ If there is an **ample** amount of something, there is enough of it and usually some extra. *abundante, mucho* ❑ *There'll be ample opportunity to relax.* *Habrá muchas oportunidades para relajarse.* ● **am|ply** ADV *ampliamente* ❑ *He has amply shown his ability.* *Ha demostrado ampliamente su habilidad.*

**am|pli|tude** /æmplɪtud/ (**amplitudes**) N-VAR In physics, the **amplitude** of a sound wave or electrical signal is its strength. *amplitud* [TECHNICAL]
→ see **sound**

**amu** /eɪ ɛm yu/ (**amu**) **amu** is an abbreviation for **atomic mass unit.** *unidad de masa atómica.*

**amuse** /əmyuz/ (**amuses, amusing, amused**) **1** V-T If something **amuses** you, it makes you want to laugh or smile. *divertir* ❑ *The thought amused him.* *La idea lo divirtió.* **2** V-T If you **amuse yourself**, you do something in order to pass the time and not become bored. *entretenerse* ❑ *I wrote the story for children and to amuse myself.* *Escribí el cuento para los niños y para entretenerme.* **3** → see also **amusing**

**amused** /əmyuzd/ ADJ If you are **amused by** something, it makes you want to laugh or smile. *divertido* ❑ *Sara was amused by his jokes.* *Sus bromas divertían a Sara.*

**amuse|ment** /əmyuzmənt/ (**amusements**) **1** N-UNCOUNT **Amusement** is the feeling that you have when you think that something is funny or amusing. *diversión* ❑ *Tom watched them with amusement.* *Tom los observaba divertido.* **2** N-UNCOUNT **Amusement** is the pleasure that you get from being entertained or from doing something interesting. *diversión* ❑ *I fell, much to everyone's amusement.* *Me caí, y a todos les hizo gracia.* **3** N-COUNT **Amusements** are ways of passing the time pleasantly. *diversión* ❑ *People did not have many amusements to choose from.* *La gente no tenía muchas diversiones de dónde escoger.* **4** N-PLURAL **Amusements** are games, rides, and other things that you can enjoy, for example, at an amusement park or resort. *juegos* ❑ *...a place full of swings and amusements.* *...un lugar con muchos columpios y juegos.*

**amuse|ment park** (**amusement parks**) N-COUNT An **amusement park** is a place where people pay to ride on various machines for pleasure or try to win prizes in games. *parque de diversiones*

**amus|ing** /əmyuzɪŋ/ ADJ Someone or something that is **amusing** makes you laugh or smile. *divertido, entretenido* ❑ *He had a great sense of humor and could be very amusing.* *Tenía un gran sentido del humor y podía ser muy divertido.* ● **amus|ing|ly** ADV *de manera muy divertida* ❑ *The article was very amusingly written.* *El tono del artículo era muy divertido.*

**an** /ən, STRONG æn/ DET **An** is used instead of "a" in front of words that begin with vowel sounds. *un, uno*

A

## Word Web amphibian

**Amphibians** were the first four-legged animals to develop **lungs**. They were the dominant animal on Earth for nearly 75 million years. Amphibians lay eggs in water. The **larvae** use **gills** to breathe. During **metamorphosis**, the larvae begin to breathe with lungs and move onto land. **Frogs** follow this cycle, going from egg to **tadpole** to adult. Amphibians have **permeable** skin. They are extremely sensitive to changes in their **environment**. This makes them a bellwether **species**. Scientists use the disappearance of amphibians as an early warning sign of damage to the local **ecology**.

## Usage a and an with the letter h

Before a word beginning with *h*: *a* is used if the *h* is pronounced and the first syllable is stressed at all: *Paul has a hidden agenda. That is a harmonica. I'm staying at a hotel. A* or *an* is used if the *h* is pronounced by the speaker: *This is a/an historic moment. He is making a/an habitual mistake.* (If *an* is used, the *h* isn't pronounced.) *An* is used if the *h* is never pronounced: *It is an honor to meet you.*

## Word Link *a, an ≈ not, without : anaerobic, anesthetic, asymmetry*

**an|aero|bic** /ænəroʊbɪk/ ADJ **Anaerobic** creatures or processes do not need oxygen in order to function or survive. *anaeróbico*

**ana|log** /ænəlɔg/ also **analogue** 1 ADJ **Analog** technology involves measuring, storing, or recording information by using physical quantities such as voltage. *análogo, analógico* ❑ *...the change from analog to digital television. ...el cambio de la televisión analógica a la digital.* 2 ADJ An **analog** watch or clock shows what it is measuring with a pointer on a dial rather than with a number display. Compare **digital**. *análogo*
→ see **time**

**analo|gous** /ənæləgəs/ ADJ **Analogous** colors are colors that are similar or related to one another such as yellow and green. *semejante*

## Word Partnership Usar *analogy* con:

PREP. analogy **between**
V. **draw an** analogy, **make an** analogy
ADJ. **false** analogy

**analy|sis** /ənælɪsɪs/ (**analyses** /ənælɪsiz/) 1 N-VAR **Analysis** is the process of considering something carefully or using statistical methods in order to understand it or explain it. *análisis* ❑ *...a careful analysis of the situation. ...un análisis cuidadoso de la situación.* 2 N-VAR **Analysis** is the scientific process of examining something in order to find out what it consists of. *análisis* ❑ *They collect blood samples for analysis. Obtienen muestras de sangre para analizarlas.*

**ana|lyst** /ænəlɪst/ (**analysts**) 1 N-COUNT An **analyst** is a person whose job is to analyze a subject and give opinions about it. *analista* ❑ *...a political analyst. ...un analista político.* 2 N-COUNT An **analyst** is someone who examines and treats people who have emotional problems. *psicoanalista* ❑ *My analyst helped me to feel better about myself. Mi psicoanalista me ayudó a sentirme mejor conmigo mismo.*

**ana|lyze** /ænəlaɪz/ (**analyzes, analyzing, analyzed**) V-T If you **analyze** something, you consider it carefully in order to fully understand it or to find out what it consists of. *analizar* ❑ *We need more time to analyze the decision. Necesitamos más tiempo para analizar la decisión.* ❑ *They haven't* *analyzed those samples yet.* *Todavía no han analizado esas muestras.*

**Thesaurus** *analyze* Ver también:
v. consider, examine, inspect

**ana|phase** /ænəfeɪz/ N-UNCOUNT **Anaphase** is a stage in the process of cell division that takes place within animals and plants. *anafase* [TECHNICAL]

**anato|my** /ənætəmi/ N-UNCOUNT **Anatomy** is the study of the structure of the bodies of people or animals. *anatomía* ❑ *...a course in anatomy.* *...un curso de anatomía* • **ana|tomi|cal** /ænətɒmɪkᵊl/ ADJ *anatómico* ❑ *...anatomical differences between insects.* *...las diferencias anatómicas entre los insectos.*
→ see **medicine**

**an|ces|tor** /ænsɛstər/ (**ancestors**) N-COUNT Your **ancestors** are the people from whom you are descended. *antepasado o antepasada* ❑ *Our daily lives are so different from those of our ancestors.* *Nuestra vida cotidiana es muy diferente a la de nuestros antepasados.* • **an|ces|tral** /ænsɛstrəl/ ADJ *ancestral* ❑ *...the family's ancestral home.* *...la casa ancestral de la familia.*

**an|chor** /æŋkər/ (**anchors, anchoring, anchored**) **1** N-COUNT An **anchor** is a heavy hooked object that is dropped from a boat into the water at the end of a chain in order to make the boat stay in one place. *ancla* **2** V-T/V-I When a boat **anchors** or when you **anchor** it, its anchor is dropped into the water in order to make it stay in one place. *anclar* ❑ *The boat anchored off the island.* *El barco ancló frente a la isla.* **3** V-T If an object **is anchored** somewhere, it is fixed to something to prevent it moving from that place. *fijar* ❑ *The roots anchor the plant in the earth.* *Las raíces fijan la planta al suelo.* **4** V-T The person who **anchors** a television or radio program, especially a news program. *presentador o presentadora*

anchor

**an|cient** /eɪnʃənt/ ADJ **Ancient** means very old, or having existed for a long time. *antiguo* ❑ *...ancient Jewish traditions.* *...las antiguas tradiciones judías.*
→ see **history**

**and** /ənd, STRONG ænd/ **1** CONJ You use **and** to link two or more words, groups, or clauses. *y* ❑ *She and Simon have already gone.* *Ella y Simon ya se fueron.* ❑ *I'm 53 and I'm very happy.* *Tengo 53 años y soy muy feliz.* **2** CONJ You use **and** to link two words or phrases that are the same in order to emphasize the degree of something, or to suggest that something continues or increases over a period of time. *y* ❑ *Learning becomes more and more difficult as we get older.* *Aprender es más y más difícil a medida que se envejece.* ❑ *We talked for hours and hours.* *Hablamos durante horas y horas.* **3** CONJ You use **and** to link two statements about events when one of the events follows the other. *y* ❑ *I waved goodbye and went down the steps.* *Hice un ademán de despedida y descendí por los peldaños.* **4** CONJ You use **and** to link two statements when the second statement continues the point that has been made in the first statement. *y* ❑ *You can only really tell the effects of the disease over a long time, and five years isn't long enough.* *Sólo es posible identificar los efectos de la enfermedad después de mucho tiempo, y cinco años no es mucho.* ❑ *"He used to be so handsome." —"And now?"* *—Solía ser tan bien parecido. —¿Y ahora?* **5** CONJ You use **and** to indicate that two numbers are to be added together. *y* ❑ *What does two and two make?* *¿Cuánto suman dos y dos?*

**an|ec|do|tal script|ing** N-UNCOUNT **Anecdotal scripting** is a method of recording and organizing information about a text such as a play or novel by writing notes in the margins of the text. *glosa, nota al margen* [TECHNICAL]

**an|ec|dote** /ænɪkdoʊt/ (**anecdotes**) N-VAR An **anecdote** is a short, amusing account of something that has happened. *anécdota* ❑ *Pete told them an anecdote about their mother.* *Pete les contó una anécdota sobre su madre.*

**anemia** /əni̲miə/ N-UNCOUNT **Anemia** is a medical condition in which there are too few red cells in your blood, causing you to feel tired and look pale. *anemia* ❑ *She suffered from anemia.* *Padecía anemia.*

**anemic** /əni̲mɪk/ ADJ Someone who is **anemic** suffers from anemia. *anémico* ❑ *Tests showed that she was anemic.* *Los análisis mostraron que estaba anémica.*

**an|emom|eter** /ænɪmɒmɪtər/ (**anemometers**) N-COUNT An **anemometer** is an instrument that is used to measure wind speeds. *anemómetro*

**an|es|thesi|olo|gist** /ænɪsθizi̲ɒlədʒɪst/ (**anesthesiologists**) N-COUNT An **anesthesiologist** is a doctor who specializes in giving anaesthetics to patients. *anestesista, anestesiólogo o anestesióloga*

**Word Link** *a, an ≈ not, without : anaerobic, anesthetic, asymmetry*

**an|es|thet|ic** /ænɪsθɛtɪk/ (**anesthetics**) N-VAR **Anesthetic** is a substance that doctors use to stop you feeling pain during an operation, either in the whole of your body when you are unconscious, or in a part of your body when you are awake. *anestesia* ❑ *The operation was carried out under a general anesthetic.* *La operación se llevó a cabo con anestesia general.*

**an|gel** /eɪndʒᵊl/ (**angels**) **1** N-COUNT **Angels** are spiritual beings that some people believe are God's servants in heaven. *ángel* ❑ *My daughter believes in angels.* *Mi hija cree en los ángeles.* **2** N-COUNT If you describe someone as an **angel,** you mean that they seem to be very kind and good. *ángel* ❑ *Thank you so much, you're an angel.* *Muchas gracias; eres un ángel.*

**an|ger** /æŋgər/ (**angers, angering, angered**) **1** N-UNCOUNT **Anger** is the strong emotion that you feel when you think that someone has behaved in an unfair, cruel, or unacceptable way. *ira, enfado* ❑ *He cried with anger.* *Lloró con ira.* **2** V-T If something **angers** you, it makes you feel angry. *enfurecer* ❑ *The decision angered some Californians.* *La decisión enfureció a algunos californianos.*
→ see Word Web: **anger**
→ see **emotion**

A

## Word Web anger

**Anger** can be a positive thing. Until we feel anger, we may not know how **upset** we are about a situation. Anger can give us a sense of our own power. Showing someone how **annoyed** we are with them may lead them to change. Anger also helps us to let go of **tension** in **frustrating** situations. This allows us to move on with our lives. But anger has its downside. It's hard to think clearly when we're **furious**. We may use bad judgment. **Rage** can also keep us from seeing the truth about ourselves. And when anger turns into **aggression**, people get hurt.

**an|ger man|age|ment** N-UNCOUNT **Anger management** is a set of guidelines that are designed to help people control their anger. *control de la ira* ❑ *...anger management courses. ...cursos para el control de la ira.*

**an|gio|sperm** /ændʒiəspɜrm/ (**angiosperms**) N-COUNT An **angiosperm** is a plant that produces seeds within its flowers. *angiosperma* [TECHNICAL]

**an|gle** /æŋgᵊl/ (**angles**) **1** N-COUNT An angle is the difference in direction between two lines or surfaces. Angles are measured in degrees. *ángulo* ❑ *...a 30 degree angle. ...un ángulo de 30 grados.* **2** → see also **right angle** **3** N-COUNT An **angle** is the direction from which you look at something. *ángulo* ❑ *From this angle, he looks young. Desde este ángulo, parece joven.* **4** N-COUNT You can refer to a way of presenting something or thinking about it as a particular **angle**. *ángulo* ❑ *He was considering the idea from all angles. Estaba considerando la idea desde todos los ángulos.* **5** PHRASE If something is **at an angle,** it is leaning in a particular direction so that it is not straight, horizontal, or vertical. *en ángulo* ❑ *An iron bar stuck out at an angle. Una barra de hierro sobresalía en ángulo.* → see **mathematics**

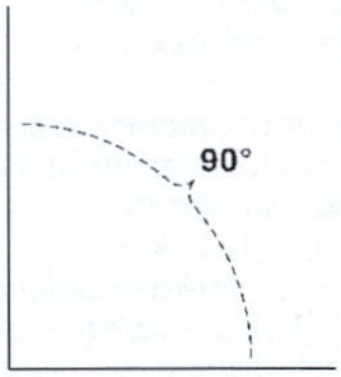


angle

**an|glo|phone** /æŋgləfoʊn/ (**anglophones**) **1** ADJ **Anglophone** communities are English-speaking communities in areas where more than one language is commonly spoken. *anglófono, anglohablante* ❑ *...anglophone Canadians. ...los canadienses anglófonos.* **2** N-COUNT **Anglophones** are people whose native language is English or who speak English because they live in a country where English is one of the official languages. *anglófono o anglófona, anglohablante*

**an|gry** /æŋgri/ (**angrier, angriest**) ADJ When you are **angry,** you feel strong dislike or impatience about something. *enojado, airado* ❑ *Are you angry with me for some reason? ¿Estás enojado conmigo por algo?* ❑ *I was angry about the rumors. Estaba enojado por los rumores.* ❑ *An angry crowd gathered. Se reunió una multitud airada.* ● **an|gri|ly** /æŋgrɪli/ ADV *airadamente, con enojo* ❑ *"Do you know what this means?" she said angrily. —¿Sabes qué significa esto?—dijo airadamente (con enojo).*

**Thesaurus** *angry* Ver también:

ADJ. bitter, enraged, mad; (*ant.*) content, happy, pleased

**an|guish** /æŋgwɪʃ/ N-UNCOUNT **Anguish** is great mental suffering or physical pain. *angustia* ❑ *Mark looked at him in anguish. Mark lo miró con angustia.*

**Word Link** *anim ≈ alive, mind : animal, animation, unanimous*

**ani|mal** /ænɪmᵊl/ (**animals**) **1** N-COUNT An **animal** is a living creature such as a dog, lion, or rabbit, rather than a bird, fish, insect, or human being. *animal, bestia* ❑ *He was attacked by wild animals. Lo atacaron unas bestias salvajes.* **2** N-COUNT Any living creature, including a human being, can be referred to as an **animal.** *animal* → see **earth, pet**

**Word Partnership** Usar *animal* con:

N. animal **kingdom** **1**
**cruelty to** animals, animal **hide**, animal **noises**, **plant and** animal, animal **shelter** **1** **2**

ADJ. **domestic** animal, **stuffed** animal, **wild** animal **1** **2**

**Ani|ma|lia** /ænɪmeɪlyə, -liə/ N-PLURAL All the animals, birds, and insects in the world can be referred to together as **Animalia.** *reino animal* [TECHNICAL]

**ani|ma|tion** /ænɪmeɪʃᵊn/ N-UNCOUNT **Animation** is the process of making films in which drawings or puppets appear to move. *animación* ❑ *...computer animation. ...animación por computadora.* → see Word Web: **animation**

**ani|ma|tor** /ænɪmeɪtər/ (**animators**) N-COUNT An **animator** is a person who makes films by means of animation. *animador o animadora* → see **animation**

**an|kle** /æŋkᵊl/ (**ankles**) N-COUNT Your **ankle** is the joint where your foot joins your leg. *tobillo* ❑ *John twisted his ankle badly. John se torció mucho el tobillo.* → see **body, foot**

**Word Link** *ann ≈ year : anniversary, annual, perannum*

**an|ni|ver|sa|ry** /ænɪvɜrsəri/ (**anniversaries**) N-COUNT An **anniversary** is a date that is

a

**Word Web** animation

TV **cartoons** are one of the most popular forms of **animation**. Each **episode**, or show, begins with a storyline. Once the **script** is final, cartoonists make up storyboards. The director uses them to plan how the **artists** will **illustrate** the episode. First the illustrators **draw** some **sketches**. Next they draw a few important **frames** for each **scene**. **Animators** turn these into moving storyboards. This form of the cartoon looks unfinished. The producers then look at the storyboard and suggest changes. After they make these changes, the artists fill in the missing frames. This makes the movements of the characters look smooth and natural.

remembered or celebrated because a special event happened on that date in a previous year. *aniversario* ❑ *...their fiftieth wedding anniversary. ...su quincuagésimo aniversario de bodas.*

**an|no|ta|ted bib|li|og|ra|phy** (**annotated bibliographies**) N-COUNT An **annotated bibliography** is a list of books or articles on a particular subject that contains additional comments such as a summary of each book or article. *bibliografía anotada*

**Word Link** *nounce ≈ repoting : announce, denounce, pronounce*

**an|nounce** /ənaʊns/ (**announces, announcing, announced**) **1** V-T If you **announce** something, you tell people about it publicly or officially. *anunciar* ❑ *He will announce tonight that he is resigning from office. Esta noche va a anunciar que renunciará al cargo.* ❑ *She was planning to announce her engagement. Estaba planeando anunciar su compromiso.* **2** V-T If you **announce** a piece of news or an intention, you say it loudly and clearly, so that everyone you are with can hear it. *anunciar* ❑ *Peter announced that he was not going to university. Peter anunció que no iría a la universidad.*

**Thesaurus** *announce* Ver también:

V. advertise, make public, reveal; (*ant.*) withhold **1**
declare **1** **2**

**an|nounce|ment** /ənaʊnsmənt/ (**announcements**) **1** N-COUNT An **announcement** is a public statement that gives information about something that has happened or that will happen. *declaración* ❑ *She made her announcement after talks with the president. Hizo su declaración después de hablar con el presidente.* **2** N-SING The **announcement of** something that has happened is the act of telling people about it. *anuncio* ❑ *...the announcement of their engagement. ...el anuncio de su compromiso.*

**Word Partnership** Usar *announcement* con:

ADJ. **formal** announcement, **official** announcement, **public** announcement, **surprise** announcement **1** **2**
V. **make an** announcement **1** **2**

**an|noy** /ənɔɪ/ (**annoys, annoying, annoyed**) **1** V-T If someone or something **annoys** you, it makes you fairly angry and impatient. *molestar* ❑ *Rosie said she didn't mean to annoy anyone. Rosie afirmó que no tenía la intención de molestar a nadie.* ❑ *It annoyed me that she believed him. Me molestó que le creyera.* **2** → see also **annoyed, annoying**

**an|noy|ance** /ənɔɪəns/ N-UNCOUNT **Annoyance** is the feeling that you get when someone makes you feel fairly angry or impatient. *molestia* ❑ *To her annoyance he did not go away. Le molestó que no se fuera.*

**an|noyed** /ənɔɪd/ **1** ADJ If you are **annoyed**, you are fairly angry about something. *irritado, enojado* ❑ *She was annoyed that Sasha was there. Estaba enojada porque Sasha estaba ahí.* **2** → see also **annoy**
→ see **anger**

**an|noy|ing** /ənɔɪɪŋ/ **1** ADJ Someone or something that is **annoying** makes you feel fairly angry and impatient. *irritante* ❑ *It's very annoying when this happens. Es muy irritante cuando pasa esto.* **2** → see also **annoy**

**Word Link** *ann ≈ year : anniversary, annual, perannum*

**an|nual** /ænyuəl/ **1** ADJ **Annual** events happen once every year. *anual* ❑ *They held their annual meeting May 20. Sostuvieron su reunión anual el 20 de mayo.* ● **an|nual|ly** ADV *anualmente* ❑ *The prize is awarded annually. El premio se otorga anualmente.* **2** ADJ **Annual** quantities or rates relate to a period of one year. *anual* ❑ *The company has annual sales of about $80 million. La empresa tiene ventas anuales de aproximadamente 80 millones de dólares.* ● **an|nual|ly** ADV *anualmente* ❑ *El Salvador produces 100,000 tons of copper annually. El Salvador produce 100,000 toneladas de cobre anualmente.*

**an|nual ring** (**annual rings**) N-COUNT An **annual ring** is the layer of wood that forms during a single year in a plant such as a tree. Annual rings can be used to measure the age of plants. *anillo anual*

**an|nu|lar eclipse** /ænyələr ɪklɪps/ (**annular eclipses**) N-COUNT An **annular eclipse** is a solar eclipse in which the edge of the sun can be seen around the moon. *eclipse anular* [TECHNICAL]

**anony|mous** /ənɒnɪməs/ ADJ If you remain **anonymous** when you do something, you do not let people know that you were the person who did it. *anónimo* ❑ *You can remain anonymous if you wish. Puedes permanecer anónimo, si lo deseas.* ● **ano|nym|ity** /ænɒnɪmɪti/ N-UNCOUNT *anonimato* ❑ *Both mother and daughter have requested anonymity. Tanto la madre como la hija solicitaron permanecer en el anonimato.* ● **anony|mous|ly** ADV *anónimamente* ❑ *The*

A

*photographs were sent anonymously to the magazine's offices.* *Las fotografías fueron enviadas anónimamente a las oficinas de la revista.*

**an|oth|er** /ənʌðər/ **1** DET **Another** thing or person means an additional thing or person of the same type as one that already exists. *otro* ❑ *We're going to have another baby.* *Vamos a tener otro hijo.* • **Another** is also a pronoun. *otro* ❑ *He said one thing and did another.* *Dijo una cosa pero hizo otra.* **2** DET You use **another** when you want to emphasize that an additional thing or person is different from one that already exists. *otro* ❑ *I think he's going to deal with this problem another day.* *Creo que va a abordar el problema otro día.* • **Another** is also a pronoun. *otro* ❑ *I don't believe that one person can read another's mind.* *No creo que alguien pueda leer la mente de otro.* **3** PRON You use **one another** to indicate that each member of a group does something to or for the other members. *uno al otro* ❑ *...women learning to help themselves and one another.* *...las mujeres que aprenden a ayudarse a sí mismas y una a otra.* **4** PHRASE If you talk about **one** thing **after another**, you are referring to a series of repeated or continuous events. *una cosa tras otra* ❑ *They faced one difficulty after another.* *Enfrentaron una dificultad tras otra.*

**Word Partnership** Usar *another* con:

ADV. **yet** another **1**
N. another **chance**, another **day**, another **one** **1**
another **man/woman**, another **thing** **2**
V. **tell one from** another **2**
PRON. **one** another **3**

**an|swer** /ænsər/ (**answers, answering, answered**) **1** V-T/V-I When you **answer** someone who has asked you something, you say something back to them. *contestar* ❑ *Just answer the question.* *Sólo contesta la pregunta.* ❑ *I asked him but he didn't answer.* *Le pregunté, pero no me contestó.* ❑ *Williams answered that he didn't know.* *Williams contestó que no sabía.* **2** V-T/V-I If you **answer** a letter or advertisement, you write to the person who wrote it. *contestar* ❑ *I wrote to him but he didn't answer.* *Le escribí pero no contestó.* **3** V-T/V-I When you **answer** the telephone, you pick it up when it rings. When you **answer** the door, you open it when you hear a knock or the bell. *contestar* ❑ *Why didn't you answer when I called?* *¿Por qué no contestaste cuando llamé?* • **Answer** is also a noun. *respuesta* ❑ *I knocked at the front door and there was no answer.* *Llamé a la puerta del frente, pero nadie respondió.* **4** V-T When you **answer** a question in a test or quiz, you write or say something in an attempt to give the facts that are asked for. *contestar* ❑ *Always read an exam through at least once before you start to answer any questions.* *Siempre lee todo el examen antes de empezar a contestar las preguntas.* **5** N-COUNT An **answer** is something that you say or write when you answer someone. *respuesta* ❑ *Without waiting for an answer, he turned and went in through the door.* *Sin esperar respuesta, se volvió y entró por la puerta.* ❑ *I wrote to him but I never had an answer back.* *Le escribí, pero nunca tuve respuesta.* **6** N-COUNT An **answer to** a problem is a solution to it. *respuesta* ❑ *There are no easy answers to this problem.* *No hay respuestas fáciles a ese problema.* **7** N-COUNT An **answer to** a question in a test or quiz is what someone writes or says in an attempt to give the facts that are asked for. *respuesta* ❑ *Simply marking an answer wrong will not help the student to get future questions correct.* *El marcar como incorrecta una respuesta, no ayudará al estudiante a contestar correctamente en el futuro.*
→ see Picture Dictionary: **answer**

▸ **answer for** PHR-VERB If you have to **answer for** something bad or wrong you have done, you are punished for it. *responder por* ❑ *He must be made to answer for his crime.* *Debe hacérsele responder por su crimen.*

**Thesaurus** *answer* Ver también:

V. reply, respond **1** **2**

**Word Partnership** Usar *answer* con:

V. **refuse to** answer **1** **2**
**have an** answer, **wait for an** answer **5** **6**
**find the** answer **6**
N. answer **a question** **1** **4**
answer **the door/telephone** **3**
DET. **no** answer **3**
ADJ. **correct/right** answer, **straight** answer, **wrong** answer **7**

**an|swer|ing ma|chine** (**answering machines**) N-COUNT An **answering machine** is a device which records telephone messages. *contestador automático*

**ant** /ænt/ (**ants**) **1** N-COUNT **Ants** are small crawling insects that live in large groups. *hormiga* **2** → see also **aunt**
→ see **insect**

**ante|ced|ent** /æntɪsidᵊnt/ (**antecedents**) N-COUNT In grammar, an **antecedent** is a word, phrase, or clause to which a pronoun that occurs later in the sentence refers. For example, in the sentence "Mary tried but she failed," "Mary" is the antecedent of "she." *antecedente*

**an|ten|na** /æntɛnə/ (**antennae** /æntɛni/ or **antennas**)

**Antennas** is the usual plural form for meaning **2**.

**1** N-COUNT The **antennae** of something such as an insect are the two long, thin parts attached to its head that it uses to feel things with. *antena* **2** N-COUNT An **antenna** is a device that sends and receives television or radio signals. *antena*
→ see **insect**

**an|them** /ænθəm/ (**anthems**) N-COUNT An **anthem** is a song that is used to represent a particular nation, society, or group and that is sung on special occasions. *himno* ❑ *The band played the national anthem.* *La banda tocó el himno nacional.*

**an|ther** /ænθər/ (**anthers**) N-COUNT The **anther** is the male part of a flower, which produces pollen. *antera* [TECHNICAL]

**an|thro|pol|ogy** /ænθrəpɒlədʒi/ N-UNCOUNT **Anthropology** is the scientific study of people, society, and culture. *antropología*
• **an|thro|polo|gist** *antropólogo o antropóloga* N-COUNT (**anthropologists**) ❑ *...an anthropologist who worked in the South Pacific.* *...un antropólogo que trabajó en el Pacífico del Sur.* → see **evolution**

## Picture Dictionary answer

**Check**
Check the correct answer.
"Small" is a/an ___.
✓ noun
___ adjective
___ verb

**Choose**
Choose the correct answer.
b Q: Is he a waiter?
A: Yes, he ___.
a. am
b. is
c. are

**Circle**
Circle the best answer.
She isn't tall. She's
( thin / short / little ).

**Cross out**
Cross out the word that doesn't belong.
chicken
dog
table
cow

**Match**
Match the words that go together.
savings — dispenser
cash — guard
security — account

**Fill in the circle**
Fill in the oval.
Ann ___ with her family.
○ live
○ living
● lives

**Fill in the blank**
Fill in the blank.
Q: Have you met Bill?
A: Yes, I have.

**Underline**
Underline the adjectives.
The young woman was talking with a tall man.

**Unscramble**
Unscramble the words.
(been / you / where / have)
Where have you been?

**Word Link** *anti ≈ against : antibiotic, antibody, antiseptic*

**Word Link** *otic ≈ afecting, causing : antibiotic, exotic, patriotic*

**an|ti|bi|ot|ic** /æntibaɪɒtɪk, æntaɪ-/ (**antibiotics**) N-COUNT **Antibiotics** are medical drugs used to kill bacteria and treat infections. *antibiótico* ❑ *Your doctor may prescribe antibiotics.* *Su médico puede prescribir antibióticos.*
→ see **medicine**

**anti|body** /æntibɒdi, æntaɪ-/ (**antibodies**) N-COUNT **Antibodies** are substances that your body produces in order to fight diseases. *anticuerpo* ❑ *Your body produces antibodies to fight disease.* *Su cuerpo produce anticuerpos para combatir las enfermedades.*

**an|tici|pate** /æntɪsɪpeɪt/ (**anticipates, anticipating, anticipated**) **1** V-T If you **anticipate** an event, you realize in advance that it may happen and you are prepared for it. *prever* ❑ *We couldn't have anticipated the result of our campaign.* *No podíamos haber previsto el resultado de nuestra campaña.* ❑ *It is anticipated that 192 jobs will be lost.* *Se prevé que se perderán 192 puestos de trabajo.* **2** V-T If you **anticipate** a question, request, or need, you do what is necessary or required before the question, request, or need occurs. *anticipar, predecir* ❑ *Jeff anticipated my next question.* *Jeff se anticipó a mi siguiente pregunta.*

**anti|cline** /æntɪklaɪn/ (**anticlines**) N-COUNT An **anticline** is a rock formation in which layers of rock are folded so that they resemble an arch. *anticlinal* [TECHNICAL]

**an|ti|per|spi|rant** /æntipɜrspɪrənt, æntaɪ-/ (**antiperspirants**) N-VAR **Antiperspirant** is a substance that you can use on your body, especially under your arms, to prevent or reduce sweating. *antitranspirante, desodorante* ADJ ❑ *...an antiperspirant for sensitive skins.* *...un antitranspirante para pieles sensibles.*

**an|tique** /æntik/ (**antiques**) N-COUNT An **antique** is an old object such as a piece of china or furniture that is valuable because of its beauty or rarity. *antigüedad* ❑ *...a genuine antique.* *...una antigüedad genuina.*

**anti|sep|tic** /æntəsɛptɪk/ (**antiseptics**) N-VAR **Antiseptic** is a substance that kills germs and harmful bacteria. *antiséptico* ❑ *She washed the cut with antiseptic.* *Lavó la herida con un antiséptico.*
→ see **medicine**

**anti-virus** also **antivirus** ADJ **Anti-virus** software is software that protects a computer against viruses. *antivirus*

**anxi|ety** /æŋzaɪɪti/ (**anxieties**) N-VAR **Anxiety** is a feeling of nervousness or worry. *ansiedad* ❑ *Her voice was full of anxiety.* *Su voz se oía llena de ansiedad.*

**anx|ious** /æŋkʃəs/ **1** ADJ If you are **anxious to** do something or **anxious that** something should happen, you very much want to do it or very much want it to happen. *ansioso* ❑ *He is anxious to go back to work.* *Está ansioso por volver al trabajo.* ❑ *I'm anxious that we succeed.* *Estoy ansioso de que tengamos éxito.* **2** ADJ If you are **anxious**, you are nervous or worried about something. *preocupado, nervioso* ❑ *She became very anxious.* *Se preocupó mucho.* • **anx|ious|ly** ADV *ansiosamente* ❑ *They are waiting anxiously for news.* *Esperan ansiosamente las noticias.*

A

**any** /ɛni/ **1** DET You use **any** in statements with negative meaning to indicate that no thing or person of a particular type exists, is present, or is involved in a situation. ninguno ❑ *I'm not making any promises.* No haré ninguna promesa. ❑ *We are doing this all without any support.* Hacemos esto sin ningún apoyo. ❑ *It is too early to say what effect, if any, there will be.* Es demasiado pronto para decir qué efecto tendrá, si lo hay. ● **Any** is also a quantifier. ninguno ❑ *You don't know any of my friends.* No conoces a ninguno de mis amigos. ● **Any** is also a pronoun. nada ❑ *The children needed new clothes and Kim couldn't afford any.* Los niños necesitaban ropa nueva, pero Kim no pudo comprarles nada. **2** DET You use **any** in questions and conditional clauses to ask whether there is some of a particular thing or some of a particular group of people, or to suggest that there might be. algún ❑ *Do you speak any foreign languages?* ¿Habla algún idioma extranjero? ● **Any** is also a quantifier. algo ❑ *Do you use any of the following?* ¿Usa algo de lo siguiente? ● **Any** is also a pronoun. alguno ❑ *I'll be happy to answer questions if there are any.* Tendré mucho gusto en contestar preguntas, si tienen alguna. **3** DET You use **any** in positive statements when you are referring to someone or something of a particular kind that might exist, occur, or be involved in a situation, when their exact identity or nature is not important. cualquier ❑ *He admired any person who did their job well.* Admiraba a cualquier persona que hiciera bien su trabajo. ● **Any** is also a quantifier. cualquier ❑ *I'm prepared to take any advice.* Estoy dispuesto a aceptar cualquier consejo. ● **Any** is also a pronoun. ninguno ❑ *We looked at several programs but didn't find any that were good enough.* Revisamos varios programas, pero no encontramos ninguno que fuese lo suficientemente bueno. **4** ADV You can also use **any** to emphasize a comparative adjective or adverb in a negative statement. en absoluto ❑ *I can't see things getting any easier.* No veo que las cosas se faciliten en absoluto. **5** PHRASE If something does not happen or is not true **any longer,** it has stopped happening or is no longer true. ya no, ya no...más (tiempo) ❑ *I couldn't keep the tears hidden any longer.* Ya no pude ocultar las lágrimas. **6** **any old** → see **old** **7** **at any rate** → see **rate**

**any|body** /ɛnibɒdi, -bʌdi/ PRON **Anybody** means the same as **anyone.** cualquiera

**any|how** /ɛnihaʊ/ ADV **Anyhow** means the same as **anyway.** de cualquier modo, en cualquier forma

**any|more** /ɛnimɔr/ also **any more** ADV If something does not happen or is not true **anymore,** it has stopped happening or is no longer true. ya no ❑ *I don't ride my motorbike much anymore.* Ya no manejo mi motocicleta casi nunca. ❑ *I couldn't trust him anymore.* Ya no podía confiar en él.

> **Usage** **anymore** and **any more**
>
> *Anymore* and *any more* are different. *Anymore* means "from now on": *Jacqueline doesn't wear glasses anymore, so she won't have to worry anymore about losing them. Any more* means "an additional quantity of something": *Please don't give me any more cookies—I don't have any more room in my stomach!*

**any|one** /ɛniwʌn/

> The form **anybody** is also used.

**1** PRON You use **anyone** or **anybody** in negative statements to indicate in a general way that nobody is present or involved in an action. nadie ❑ *I won't tell anyone I saw you here.* No le diré a nadie que te vi aquí. ❑ *You needn't talk to anyone if you don't want to.* No necesitas hablar con nadie si no quieres. **2** PRON You use **anyone** or **anybody** in questions and conditional clauses to ask or talk about whether someone is present or doing something. alguien ❑ *Why would anyone want that job?* ¿Por qué querría alguien ese trabajo? ❑ *If anybody wants me, I'll be in my office.* Estaré en mi oficina, por si alguien me busca. **3** PRON You use **anyone** or **anybody** before words that indicate the kind of person you are talking about. aquellos ❑ *It's not a job for anyone who is slow with numbers.* No es un trabajo para aquellos que sean malos con las matemáticas. **4** PRON You use **anyone** or **anybody** to refer to a person when you are emphasizing that it could be any person out of a very large number of people. cualquiera ❑ *Anyone could do what I'm doing.* Cualquiera puede hacer lo que yo hago.

> **Usage** **anyone** and **any one**
>
> *Anyone* and *any one* are different. *Anyone* can refer to an unspecified person: *Does anyone know the answer? Any one* refers to an unspecified individual person or thing in a group: *Any one of the players is capable of winning. All those desserts look good—please give me any one with strawberries on it.*

**any|place** /ɛnipleɪs/ ADV **Anyplace** means the same as **anywhere.** lugar alguno, algún lugar [INFORMAL] ❑ *She didn't have anyplace to go.* No tenía lugar alguno a dónde ir.

**any|thing** /ɛniθɪŋ/ **1** PRON You use **anything** in negative statements to indicate in a general way that nothing is present or that an action or event does not or cannot happen. nada ❑ *We can't do anything.* No podemos hacer nada. ❑ *She couldn't see or hear anything at all.* Ella no podía ver ni escuchar nada en absoluto. **2** PRON You use **anything** in questions and conditional clauses to ask or talk about whether something is present or happening. algo ❑ *What happened, is anything wrong?* ¿Qué pasó, algo anda mal? ❑ *Did you find anything?* ¿Encontraste algo? **3** PRON You can use **anything** before words that indicate the kind of thing you are talking about. cualquier ❑ *More than anything else, he wanted to become a teacher.* Más que cualquier cosa, él quería ser maestro. ❑ *Anything that's cheap this year will be even cheaper next year.* Cualquier cosa que sea barata este año lo será más al siguiente. **4** PRON You use **anything** to emphasize a possible thing, event, or situation, when you are saying that it could be any one of a very large number of things. lo que sea ❑ *He is young and ready for anything.* Él es joven y está listo para lo que sea. **5** PRON You use **anything** in expressions such as **anything near, anything close to** and **anything like** to emphasize a statement that you are making. algo como, algo parecido a ❑ *This is the only way he can live anything near a normal life.* Este es el único modo en que puede vivir algo parecido a una vida normal.

**any|time** /ɛnitaɪm/ ADV You use **anytime** to mean a point in time that is not fixed or set. en cualquier momento, en cuanto ❑ *The college admits students anytime during the year.* *El colegio acepta estudiantes en cualquier momento durante el año.* ❑ *He can leave anytime he wants.* *Se puede ir en cuanto lo desee.*

**any|way** /ɛniweɪ/

The form **anyhow** is also used.

**1** ADV You use **anyway** or **anyhow** to indicate that a statement explains or supports a previous point. de cualquier modo, no importa ❑ *I'm sure David told you. Anyway, everyone knows that he owes money.* *Estoy seguro de que David te lo dijo. De cualquier modo, todos saben que él tiene deudas.* **2** ADV You use **anyway** or **anyhow** to suggest that a statement is true or relevant in spite of other things that have been said. de todos modos ❑ *I don't know why I went there, but anyway I did.* *No sé por qué fui, pero de todos modos lo hice.* **3** ADV You use **anyway** or **anyhow** to correct or modify a statement. claro ❑ *Mary Ann doesn't want to have children. Not right now, anyway.* *Mary Ann no quiere tener hijos. No por ahora, claro.* **4** ADV You use **anyway** or **anyhow** to change the topic or return to a previous topic. en todo caso ❑ *I found Z in the last book with W, X, and Y. Which is understandable. Anyway, I took it back to my room.* *Encontré la Z en el último libro con W, X y Y, lo cual es comprensible. En todo caso, lo tomé y regresé a mi cuarto.*

**Usage** **anyway** and **any way**

Be sure to use *anyway* and *any way* correctly. *Anyway* can mean "in any situation, no matter what": *It's raining, but let's go for a walk anyway.* *Any way* means "by any method": *It's not far to Tom's house, so we can walk, drive, or ride our bikes—any way you want.*

**any|where** /ɛniwɛər/ **1** ADV You use **anywhere** in negative statements, questions and conditional clauses to refer to a place without saying exactly where you mean. algún lado, ningún lugar ❑ *Did you try to get help from anywhere?* *¿Intentaste obtener ayuda en algún lado?* ❑ *I haven't got anywhere to live.* *No tengo ningún lugar dónde vivir.* **2** ADV You use **anywhere** in positive statements to emphasize an expression that refers to a place or area. en cualquiera lugar ❑ *He'll meet you anywhere you want.* *Se reunirá contigo donde quieras.* **3** ADV When you do not want to be exact, you use **anywhere** to refer to a particular range of things. desde ❑ *His shoes cost anywhere from $200 up.* *Sus zapatos cuestan de $200 para arriba.*

**apart**
❶ POSITIONS AND STATES
❷ INDICATING EXCEPTIONS AND FOCUSING

**❶ apart** /əpɑrt/

In addition to the uses shown below, **apart** is used in phrasal verbs such as "grow apart" and "take apart."

**1** ADV When people or things are **apart**, they are some distance from each other. alejado ❑ *He was standing a bit apart from the rest of us.* *Estaba de pie un poco alejado de nosotros.* ❑ *Ray and his sister lived just 25 miles apart.* *Ray y su hermana vivían a sólo 25 millas de distancia.* **2** ADV If two people are **apart**, they are no longer living together or spending time together. separado ❑ *It was the first time Jane and I had been apart for more than a few days.* *Era la primera vez que Jane y yo estábamos separados por más de unos días.* **3** ADV If you take something **apart**, you separate it into the pieces that it is made of. If it comes or falls **apart**, its parts separate from each other. desarmar, desbaratar ❑ *When the clock stopped he took it apart, found what was wrong, and put it together again.* *Desarmó el reloj cuando éste se detuvo, averiguó qué andaba mal, y lo volvió a armar.*

**Word Partnership** Usar *apart* con:

| | |
|---|---|
| ADV. | **far** apart ❶ **1** |
| N. | **miles** apart ❶ **1** |
| V. | **take** apart ❶ **3** |

**❷ apart** /əpɑrt/ **1** PHRASE **Apart from** means the same as **aside from.** además de **2** ADV You use **apart** when you are making an exception to a general statement. salvo por ❑ *The room was empty apart from one man sitting beside the fire.* *El cuarto estaba vacío salvo por un hombre sentado junto al fuego.*

**apart|heid** /əpɑrthaɪt/ N-UNCOUNT **Apartheid** was a political system in South Africa in which people were divided into racial groups and kept apart by law. apartheid, segregación racial ❑ *...the struggle against apartheid.* *...la lucha contra la segregación racial.*

**apart|ment** /əpɑrtmənt/ (**apartments**) N-COUNT An **apartment** is a separate set of rooms for living in, in a house or a building with other apartments. departamento ❑ *Christina has her own apartment.* *Cristina tiene su propio departamento.*
→ see **city**

**apart|ment build|ing** (**apartment buildings**) also **apartment house** N-COUNT An **apartment building** or **apartment house** is a tall building which contains different apartments on different floors. edificio de departamentos ❑ *They live in a Manhattan apartment house.* *Viven en un edificio de departamentos en Manhattan.*

**apart|ment com|plex** (**apartment complexes**) N-COUNT An **apartment complex** is a group of buildings that contain apartments and are managed by the same company. multifamiliar, desarrollo habitacional ❑ *...a 10-story apartment complex.* *...un desarrollo habitacional compuesto por edificios de 10 plantas.*

**ape** /eɪp/ (**apes, aping, aped**) **1** N-COUNT **Apes** are chimpanzees, gorillas, and other animals in the same family. mono, primate, simio ❑ *...chimpanzees and other apes.* *...chimpancés y otros monos.* **2** V-T If you **ape** someone's speech or behavior, you imitate it. imitar ❑ *People began to ape European customs.* *Las personas comenzaron a imitar las costumbres europeas.*
→ see **primate**

ape

A

**aphe|li|on** /əfiliən, -liən, æphil-/ (**aphelia**) N-SING The **aphelion** of a planet is the point in its orbit at which it is furthest from the sun. *afelio* [TECHNICAL]

**aphid** /eɪfɪd, æf-/ (**aphids**) N-COUNT **Aphids** are very small insects that live on plants and suck their juices. *afídido, áfido*
→ see **herbivore**

**apolo|gize** /əpɒlədʒaɪz/ (**apologizes, apologizing, apologized**) V-I When you **apologize to** someone, you say that you are sorry that you have hurt them or caused trouble for them. You can say **"I apologize"** as a formal or polite way of saying sorry. *disculparse, ofrecer una disculpa* ❑ *I apologize for being late. Me disculpo por llegar tarde.* ❑ *He apologized to everyone. Le ofreció disculpas a todos.*

**Word Link** *log ≈ reason, speech : apology, dialogue, logic*

**apol|ogy** /əpɒlədʒi/ (**apologies**) N-VAR An **apology** is something that you say or write in order to tell someone that you are sorry that you have hurt them or caused trouble for them. *disculpa* ❑ *I didn't get an apology. No obtuve una disculpa.* ❑ *We received a letter of apology. Recibimos una carta de disculpa.*

**Word Partnership** Usar *apology* con:

| | |
|---|---|
| V. | **demand an** apology, **make an** apology, **owe *someone* an** apology |
| ADJ. | **formal/public** apology |
| N. | **letter of** apology |

**apos|tro|phe** /əpɒstrəfi/ (**apostrophes**) N-COUNT An **apostrophe** is the mark ' when it is written to indicate that one or more letters have been left out of a word, as in "isn't" and "we'll." It is also added to nouns to form possessives, as in "Mike's car." *apóstrofo*
→ see **punctuation**

**ap|pall** also **ap|pal** /əpɔl/ (**appalls, appalling, appalled**) V-T If something **appalls** you, it shocks you because it seems so bad or unpleasant. *espantar* ❑ *His rudeness appalled me. Su grosería me espantó.* ❑ *We are appalled by the news. Nos parece espantosa la noticia.*

**ap|pal|ling** /əpɔlɪŋ/ **1** ADJ Something that is **appalling** is so bad that it shocks you. *espantoso* ❑ *They have been living under the most appalling conditions. Han estado viviendo en las condiciones más espantosas.* ● **ap|pal|ling|ly** ADV *espantosamente* ❑ *...an appallingly bad speech. ...un discurso simplemente espantoso.* **2** → see also **appall**

**ap|par|ent** /əpærənt/ **1** ADJ An **apparent** situation, quality, or feeling seems to exist, although you cannot be certain that it does exist. *aparente* ❑ *I was worried by our apparent lack of progress. Estaba preocupado por nuestra aparente falta de progreso.* **2** ADJ If something is **apparent,** it is clear and obvious. *patente* ❑ *It's apparent that standards have improved. Es patente que los estándares han mejorado.*

**ap|par|ent|ly** /əpærəntli/ ADV You use **apparently** to refer to something that seems to be true, although you are not sure whether it is or not. *aparentemente* ❑ *Apparently the girls are not at all amused. Aparentemente las niñas no lo encuentran en absoluto divertido.*

**ap|par|ent mag|ni|tude** (**apparent magnitudes**) N-COUNT The **apparent magnitude** of a star or galaxy is a measure of how bright it appears to an observer on Earth. *magnitud aparente*

**ap|peal** /əpil/ (**appeals, appealing, appealed**) **1** V-I If you **appeal to** someone **to** do something, you make a serious and urgent request to them. *hacer un llamamiento a* ❑ *Police appealed to the public for help. La policía hizo un llamamiento al público pidiendo ayuda.* ❑ *The country's prime minister appealed for calm. El primer ministro del país hizo un llamamiento a la calma.* **2** V-T If you **appeal** a decision **to** someone in authority, you formally ask them to change it. *apelar* ❑ *We intend to appeal the verdict. Nuestra intención es apelar el veredicto.* **3** V-I If something **appeals to** you, you find it attractive or interesting. *atraer* ❑ *The idea appealed to him. La idea le atraía.* **4** N-COUNT An **appeal** is a serious and urgent request. *súplica* ❑ *...an appeal for help. ...una súplica de ayuda.* **5** N-VAR An **appeal** is a formal request for a decision to be changed. *apelación* ❑ *They took their appeal to the Supreme Court. Llevaron su apelación a la Suprema Corte.* **6** N-UNCOUNT The **appeal** of something is a quality that people find attractive or interesting. *encanto* ❑ *...tiny dolls with great appeal to young girls. ...pequeñas muñecas que son un encanto para las niñas.*

**Word Partnership** Usar *appeal* con:

| | |
|---|---|
| PREP. | appeal **to *someone*** 1 3 5<br>appeal **to a court**, appeal **for *something*** 2 |
| V. | **make an** appeal 4 5<br>appeal **a case/decision** 5 |

**ap|peals court** (**appeals courts**) N-COUNT An **appeals court** is the same as an **appellate court.** *corte de apelaciones*

**ap|peal to author|ity** (**appeals to authority**) N-VAR In logic, an **appeal to authority** is a type of argument in which someone tries to support their view by referring to an expert on the subject who shares their view. *argumento de autoridad*

**ap|peal to emo|tion** (**appeals to emotion**) N-VAR In logic, an **appeal to emotion** is a type of argument in which someone tries to support their view by using emotional language that is intended to arouse feelings such as excitement, anger or hatred. *argumento emocional*

**ap|peal to pa|thos** (**appeals to pathos**) also **appeal to pity** N-VAR In logic, an **appeal to pathos** is a type of argument in which someone tries to support their view by using language that is intended to arouse feelings of pity or mercy. *argumento emocional*

**ap|peal to rea|son** (**appeals to reason**) N-VAR In logic, an **appeal to reason** is a type of argument in which someone tries to support their view by showing that it is based on good reasoning. *argumento racional*

**ap|pear** /əpɪər/ (**appears, appearing, appeared**) **1** V-LINK If you say that something **appears to** be the way you describe it, you are reporting what you believe or what you have been told, though you cannot be sure it is true. *parecer* ❑ *The aircraft appears to have crashed. El avión parece haberse estrellado.* **2** V-LINK If someone or something **appears to** have a particular quality or characteristic, they give the impression of having that quality or characteristic. *parecer* ❑ *She appeared more confident than she felt. Parecía tener más confianza de la que en verdad sentía.* ❑ *There appeared to be a problem with the baby's breathing... Parecía haber un problema con la respiración del bebé...* **3** V-I When someone or something **appears,** it becomes possible to see them or obtain them. *aparecer* ❑ *A woman appeared at the far end of the street. Una mujer apareció al final de la calle.* ❑ *...small white flowers which appear in early summer. ...pequeñas flores blancas que aparecen al principio del verano.* **4** V-I When someone **appears in** something such as a play, a show, or a television program, they take part in it. *aparecer* ❑ *Jill Bennett appeared in several of Osborne's plays. Jill Bennett apareció en varias de las obras de Osborne.* **5** V-I When someone **appears before** a court of law or **before** an official committee, they go there in order to answer questions or to give information as a witness. *comparecer* ❑ *They will appear in federal court today. Hoy comparecerán en la corte federal.*

**Thesaurus** *appear* Ver también:
V. seem **1**
look like, resemble, seem **2**
arrive, show up, turn up; (*ant.*) disappear, vanish **3**

**ap|pear|ance** /əpɪərəns/ (**appearances**) **1** N-COUNT When someone makes an **appearance** at a public event or in a broadcast, they take part in it. *aparición* ❑ *It was the president's second public appearance. Fue la segunda aparición en público del presidente.* **2** N-SING Someone's or something's **appearance** is the way that they look. *apariencia* ❑ *She used to care a lot about her appearance. A ella solía importarle mucho su apariencia.* **3** N-SING The **appearance of** someone or something in a place is the fact of their arriving or becoming visible there. *aparición* ❑ *...the welcome appearance of Uncle John. ...la bienvenida aparición del tío John.* ❑ *Flowering plants were making their first appearance. Las plantas con flores estaban haciendo su primera aparición en el mundo.*

**Word Partnership** Usar *appearance* con:
N. **court** appearance **1**
V. **make an** appearance **1 3**
**change *your*** appearance **2**
ADJ. **public** appearance, **sudden** appearance **1 3**
**physical** appearance **2**

**ap|pel|late court** /əpɛlɪt kɔrt/ (**appellate courts**) N-COUNT In the United States, an **appellate court** is a special court where people who have been convicted of a crime can appeal against their conviction. *tribunal de apelaciones* ❑ *An appellate court overturned his conviction. Un tribunal de apelaciones declaró inválido el resultado de su primer juicio.*

**ap|pen|dix** /əpɛndɪks/ (**appendixes**)

The plural form **appendices** /əpɛndɪsiːz/ is usually used for meaning **2**.

**1** N-COUNT Your **appendix** is a small closed tube inside your body that is attached to your digestive system. *apéndice* ❑ *...a burst appendix. ...el apéndice reventado.* **2** N-COUNT An **appendix to** a book is extra information that is placed after the end of the main text. *apéndice* ❑ *...an appendix to the main document. ...un apéndice al documento principal.*

**ap|pe|tite** /æpɪtaɪt/ (**appetites**) **1** N-VAR Your **appetite** is your desire to eat. *apetito* ❑ *He has a healthy appetite. Tiene buen apetito.* **2** N-COUNT Someone's **appetite for** something is their strong desire for it. *apetito* ❑ *...his appetite for success. ...su apetito por triunfar.*

**ap|plaud** /əplɔd/ (**applauds, applauding, applauded**) **1** V-T/V-I When a group of people **applaud,** they clap their hands in order to show approval, for example, when they have enjoyed a play or concert. *aplaudir* ❑ *The audience laughed and applauded. El público rió y aplaudió.* ❑ *We applauded him for his bravery. Lo felicitamos por su valentía* **2** V-T When an attitude or action **is applauded,** people praise it. *aplaudir* ❑ *He should be applauded for his courage. Deberíamos aplaudir su coraje.* ❑ *We applaud her determination. Aplaudimos su determinación.*

**ap|plause** /əplɔz/ N-UNCOUNT **Applause** is the noise made by a group of people clapping their hands to show approval. *aplauso* ❑ *...a round of applause. ...una ronda de aplausos.*

**ap|ple** /æpᵊl/ (**apples**) N-VAR An **apple** is a round fruit with smooth skin and firm white flesh. *manzana* ❑ *I want an apple. Quiero una manzana.* ❑ *...the finest apples in the world. ...las mejores manzanas del mundo.*
→ see **fruit**

**ap|pli|ance** /əplaɪəns/ (**appliances**) N-COUNT An **appliance** is a device or machine in your home that you use to do a job such as cleaning or cooking. *electrodoméstico, aparato* [FORMAL] ❑ *This shop sells all sorts of appliances—refrigerators, heaters, stoves and washing machines. Esta tienda vende toda clase de electrodomésticos: refrigeradores, calentadores, estufas y lavadoras.*

**ap|pli|cant** /æplɪkənt/ (**applicants**) N-COUNT An **applicant for** something such as a job or a college is someone who makes a formal written request to be considered for it. *aspirante* ❑ *We've had many applicants for these positions. Hemos tenido muchos aspirantes a esos puestos.*

**ap|pli|ca|tion** /æplɪkeɪʃᵊn/ (**applications**) **1** N-COUNT An **application for** something such as a job or membership of an organization is a formal written request for it. *solicitud* ❑ *We are unable to accept your application. Nos vemos imposibilitados de aceptar su solicitud.* **2** N-COUNT In computing, an **application** is a piece of software designed to carry out a particular task. *aplicación* ❑ *...a software application that is accessed via the Internet. ...una aplicación de software al que se accede por el Internet.* **3** N-VAR The **application of** a rule or piece of knowledge is the use of it in a particular situation. *aplicación* ❑ *...the practical application of the theory. ...la aplicación práctica de la teoría.*

A

**Word Partnership** Usar *application* con:

V. **accept/reject an** application, **file/submit an** application, **fill out an** application 1
N. **college** application, application **form**, **grant/loan** application, **job** application, **membership** application 1
application **software** 2
ADJ. **practical** application 3

**ap|ply** /əplaɪ/ (**applies, applying, applied**) 1 V-T/V-I If you **apply for** something such as a job or membership of an organization, you write a letter or fill out a form in order to ask formally for it. solicitar ❑ *I am applying for jobs.* *Estoy solicitando empleo.* ❑ *They applied to join the organization.* *Solicitaron unirse a la organización.* 2 V-T If you **apply yourself to** something or **apply** your mind **to** something, you concentrate hard on it. *dedicarse a* ❑ *He has applied himself to this task with great energy.* *Él se ha dedicado a esta tarea con mucha energía.* 3 V-I If something such as a rule or a remark **applies to** a person or a situation, it is relevant to them. ❑ *The rule does not apply to them.* 4 V-T If you **apply** something such as a rule, system, or skill, you use it in a situation or activity. *hacer uso de, aplicar* ❑ *We are applying technology to reduce costs.* *Estamos haciendo uso de la tecnología para reducir costos.* 5 V-T If you **apply** something **to** a surface, you put it on or rub it into the surface. *aplicar* ❑ *Apply direct pressure to the wound.* *Aplique presión directamente sobre la herida.*
→ see **makeup**

**Word Partnership** Usar *apply* con:

PREP. apply **for admission**, apply **for a job** 1
N. **laws/restrictions/rules** apply 3
apply **makeup**, apply **pressure** 5

**ap|point** /əpɔɪnt/ (**appoints, appointing, appointed**) V-T If you **appoint** someone **to** a job or official position, you formally choose them for it. *nombrar, designar* ❑ *Mr. Putin appointed him to the job in 2000.* *El Sr. Putin lo designó para ocupar el puesto en 2000.* ❑ *The bank appointed Kenneth Conley as manager of its office in Aurora.* *El banco nombró a Kenneth Conley como el gerente de su oficina en Aurora.*
• **ap|point|ment** N-UNCOUNT *nombramiento, designación* ❑ *...his appointment to the position of manager.* *...su nombramiento en la posición de gerente.*

**ap|point|ment** /əpɔɪntmənt/ (**appointments**) 1 N-COUNT An **appointment** is a job or position of responsibility. *nombramiento, designación* ❑ *I decided to accept the appointment as music director.* *Decidí aceptar el nombramiento como gerente.* 2 N-COUNT If you have an **appointment with** someone, you have arranged to see them at a particular time, usually in connection with their work or for a serious purpose. *cita con* ❑ *She has an appointment with her doctor.* *Ella tiene una cita con el doctor.* 3 PHRASE If something can be done **by appointment,** people can arrange in advance to do it at a particular time. *previa cita* ❑ *Groups are welcome by appointment only.* *Se reciben grupos únicamente previa cita.* 4 → see also **appoint**

**Thesaurus** *appointment* Ver también:

N. date, engagement, meeting 2

**ap|posi|tive** /əpɒzɪtɪv/ (**appositives**) ADJ In grammar, an **appositive** word or phrase is a word or phrase that modifies the meaning of the noun that comes before it. For example, in the sentence "My son David got married," "David" is appositive. *en aposición* • **Appositive** is also a noun. *aposición*

**ap|prais|al** /əpreɪzᵊl/ (**appraisals**) 1 N-VAR If you make an **appraisal of** something, you consider it carefully and form an opinion about it. *evaluación* ❑ *We need a calm appraisal of the situation.* *Necesitamos una evaluación calmada de la situación.* 2 N-COUNT An **appraisal** is a judgment that someone makes about how much money something such as a house or a company is worth. *avalúo* ❑ *We may need to get a new appraisal of the property.* *Podríamos necesitar un nuevo avalúo de la propiedad.*

**ap|pre|ci|ate** /əpriʃieɪt/ (**appreciates, appreciating, appreciated**) 1 V-T If you **appreciate** something, you like it because you recognize its good qualities. *apreciar* ❑ *Anyone can appreciate our music.* *Cualquiera puede apreciar nuestra música.* • **ap|pre|cia|tion** /əpriʃieɪʃᵊn/ N-SING *apreciación* ❑ *...children's appreciation of art.* *...la apreciación de los niños del arte.* 2 V-T If you **appreciate** a situation or problem, you understand it and know what it involves. *reconocer, alcanzar a reconocer* ❑ *I don't think we appreciated how much time it would take.* *Creo que no alcanzamos a reconocer cuánto tiempo nos llevaría.* • **ap|pre|cia|tion** N-SING *reconocimiento* ❑ *...an appreciation of each patient's needs.* *...tener en cuenta las necesidades de cada paciente.* 3 V-T If you **appreciate** something that someone has done for you or is going to do for you, you are grateful for it. *agradecer* ❑ *Peter helped me when I most needed it. I'll always appreciate that.* *Peter me ayudó cuando más lo necesitaba. Siempre le estaré agradecido por ello.* • **ap|pre|cia|tion** N-SING *agradecimiento* ❑ *He expressed his appreciation for their help.* *Expresó su agradecimiento por su auyda.* 4 V-I If something that you own **appreciates** over a period of time, its value increases. *subir de precio* ❑ *People feel their houses will appreciate in value.* *Las personas sienten que sus casas subirán de precio.* • **ap|pre|cia|tion** N-UNCOUNT *aumento de precio* ❑ *You have to take appreciation of the property into account.* *Tienes que tomar en cuenta el aumento de precio de la propiedad.*

**ap|proach** /əproʊtʃ/ (**approaches, approaching, approached**) 1 V-T/V-I When you **approach** something, you get closer to it. *acercarse a* ❑ *He approached the front door.* *Se acercó a la puerta principal.* ❑ *When I approached, they grew silent.* *Cuando me acerqué a ellos, guardaron silencio.* • **Approach** is also a noun. *acercamiento* ❑ *At their approach the little boy ran away and hid.* *Como se acercaron, el niño corrió a esconderse.* 2 V-T If you **approach** someone **about** something, you speak to them about it for the first time, often making an offer or request. *hacer propuestas a* ❑ *Robinson first approached him about the job in late September.* *Robinson le hizo la primera propuesta acerca del empleo en septiembre.* ❑ He approached me about the job. Me hizo una propuesta acerca del empleo. • **Approach** is also a noun. propuesta ❑ *There have already been approaches from buyers.* Ya ha habido propuestas de parte de compradores. **3** V-T When you **approach** a task, problem, or situation in a particular way, you deal with it or think about it in that way. abordar ❑ *The bank has approached the situation in a practical way.* El banco ha abordado la situación de forma práctica. **4** V-I As a future time or event **approaches,** it gradually gets nearer as time passes. acercar ❑ *As autumn approached, the plants and colors in the garden changed.* A medida que se acercaba el otoño, las plantas y los colores del jardín cambiaron. • **Approach** is also a noun. cercanía ❑ *...the approach of Christmas.* ...la cercanía de la Navidad. **5** V-T As you **approach** a future time or event, time passes so that you get gradually nearer to it. acercar ❑ *We are approaching the end of the year.* Nos acercamos al final del año. **6** V-T If something **approaches** a particular level or state, it almost reaches that level or state. acercar ❑ *...speeds approaching 200mph.* ...velocidades cercanas a las 200 millas por hora. **7** N-COUNT An **approach to** a place is a road, path, or other route that leads to it. acceso ❑ *Two men stood on the approach to the bridge.* Dos hombres estaban de pie en el acceso al puente. **8** N-COUNT Your **approach to** a task, problem, or situation is the way you deal with it or think about it. enfoque, camino ❑ *There are two approaches: spend less money or find a new job.* Hay dos caminos: gastar menos dinero o encontrar un trabajo nuevo.

| **Thesaurus** | *approach* Ver también: |
|---|---|
| V. | close in, near; (*ant.*) go away, leave **1** |
| N. | attitude, method, technique **8** |

**ap|pro|pri|ate** /əproʊpriɪt/ ADJ Something that is **appropriate** is suitable or acceptable for a particular situation. adecuado ❑ *Is it appropriate that they pay for it?* ¿Es adecuado que paguen por ello? ❑ *Wear clothes appropriate to the job.* Usa ropa adecuada para el trabajo. • **ap|pro|pri|ate|ly** ADV adecuadamente ❑ *Behave appropriately and ask intelligent questions.* Compórtate adecuadamente y haz preguntas inteligentes.

| **Thesaurus** | *appropriate* Ver también: |
|---|---|
| ADJ. | correct, fitting, relevant, right; (*ant.*) improper, inappropriate, incorrect |

**ap|prov|al** /əpruvᵊl/ **1** N-UNCOUNT If you get someone's **approval for** something that you ask for or suggest, they agree to it. aprobación ❑ *The chairman gave his approval for an investigation.* El director dio su aprobación para iniciar una investigación. **2** N-UNCOUNT If someone or something has your **approval,** you like and admire them. aprobación ❑ *She wanted her father's approval.* Quería obtener la aprobación de su padre.

**ap|prove** /əpruv/ (**approves, approving, approved**) **1** V-I If you **approve of** someone or something, you like them or think they are good. dar su aprobación ❑ *My father approves of you.* Mi padre te da su aprobación. **2** V-T If someone in a position of authority **approves** a plan or idea, they formally agree to it and say that it can happen. aprobar ❑ *The directors have approved the change.* Los directores han aprobado el cambio.

**ap|proved** /əpruvd/ ADJ An **approved** method or course of action is officially accepted as appropriate in a particular situation. probado ❑ *There is an approved method of dealing with these things.* Hay un método probado para lidiar con estas cosas.

**ap|proxi|mate** (**approximates, approximating, approximated**)

> The adjective is pronounced /əprɒksɪmət/. The verb is pronounced /əprɒksɪmeɪt/.

**1** ADJ An **approximate** number, time, or position is close to the correct number, time, or position, but is not exact. aproximado ❑ *What is its approximate age?* ¿Cuál es su edad aproximada? • **ap|proxi|mate|ly** ADV aproximadamente ❑ *They've spent approximately $150 million.* Han gastado aproximadamente 150 millones de dólares. **2** V-T If something **approximates** something else, it is similar to it but is not exactly the same. parecer, aproximar ❑ *The test approximates the students' daily math program.* Este examen se parece al programa diario de matemáticas de los alumnos.

**apri|cot** /æprɪkɒt, eɪp-/ (**apricots**) N-VAR An **apricot** is a small, soft, round fruit with yellowish-orange flesh and a large seed inside. albaricoque, chabacano ❑ *...12 oz. fresh apricots.* ...340 gramos de chabacanos

**April** /eɪprɪl/ (**Aprils**) N-VAR **April** is the fourth month of the year in the Western calendar. abril ❑ *I'm getting married in April.* Me caso en abril.

**apron** /eɪprən/ (**aprons**) N-COUNT An **apron** is a piece of clothing that you put on over the front of your normal clothes and tie around your waist, especially when you are cooking, in order to prevent your clothes from getting dirty. delantal

**apt** /æpt/ **1** ADJ An **apt** remark, description, or choice is especially suitable. adecuado, apropiado ❑ *"Happy" is an apt description of Maggie.* Una descripción adecuada de Maggie es "feliz". • **apt|ly** ADV adecuadamente, apropiadamente ❑ *...the aptly named town of Oceanside.* ...la ciudad llamada, apropiadamente, Oceanside. **2** ADJ If someone is **apt to** do something, they often do it and so it is likely that they will do it again. propenso ❑ *She was apt to raise her voice.* Tenía la propensión a alzar la voz.

**aqui|fer** /ækwɪfər/ (**aquifers**) N-COUNT In geology, an **aquifer** is an area of rock underneath the surface of the earth which absorbs and holds water. acuífero [TECHNICAL]

**arach|nid** /əræknɪd/ (**arachnids**) N-COUNT **Arachnids** are a group of small insects such as spiders and scorpions that have eight legs and no antennae. arácnido [TECHNICAL]

**ar|bi|trary** /ɑrbɪtrɛri/ ADJ An **arbitrary** action, rule, or decision is not based on any principle, plan, or system. It often seems unfair because of this. arbitrario ❑ *This arbitrary arrangement often fails to work.* Este arreglo arbitrario suele fracasar. • **ar|bi|trari|ly** /ɑrbɪtrɛərɪli/ ADV arbitrariamente, al azar ❑ *The victims were not chosen arbitrarily.* Las víctimas no fueron seleccionadas al azar.

**ar|bi|trary col|or** (**arbitrary colors**) N-VAR An artist who uses **arbitrary colors** paints things in colors that do not naturally belong to the object being painted, for example a blue horse, in order to express their feelings about the object. colores caprichosos

A

**arch** /ɑrtʃ/ (**arches, arching, arched**) **1** N-COUNT An **arch** is a structure that is curved at the top and is supported on either side by a pillar, post, or wall. arco ❑ *The bridge is 65 feet at the top of the main arch.* *El puente tiene 19.80 metros de altura en la parte superior del arco principal.* **2** → see also **arched** **3** V-T/V-I If you **arch** a part of your body such as your back or if it **arches,** you bend it so that it forms a curve. arquear ❑ *Don't arch your back.* *No arquees la espalda.*
→ see **architecture, foot**

**Ar|chae|bac|te|ria** /ɑrkibæktɪəriə/ N-PLURAL **Archaebacteria** are a type of bacteria that can live in extreme environments such as volcanoes. arquebacteria [TECHNICAL]

**ar|che|ol|ogy** /ɑrkiɒlədʒi/ N-UNCOUNT **Archeology** is the study of the past by examining the remains of things such as buildings, tools, and other objects. arqueología • **ar|cheo|logi|cal** /ɑrkiəlɒdʒɪkəl/ ADJ arqueológico ❑ *...one of the region's most important archeological sites.* *...uno de los sitios arqueológicos más importantes de la región.* • **ar|che|olo|gist** /ɑrkiɒlədʒɪst/ N-COUNT (**archeologists**) arqueólogo o arqueóloga ❑ *The archeologists found a house built around 300 BC.* *Los arqueólogos descubrieron una casa construida en el siglo III AC.*
→ see **history**

**ar|che|typ|al criti|cism** N-UNCOUNT **Archetypal criticism** is a type of literary criticism that interprets a literary work by emphasizing its use of archetypes such as ancient myths and symbols. crítica arquetípica [TECHNICAL]

**ar|che|type** /ɑrkɪtaɪp/ (**archetypes**) N-COUNT An **archetype** is something that is considered to be a perfect or typical example of a particular kind of person or thing, because it has all their most important characteristics. arquetipo [FORMAL] ❑ *He is the archetype of the successful businessman.* *Es el arquetipo del hombre de negocios exitoso.* • **ar|che|typ|al** /ɑrkɪtaɪpəl/ ADJ arquetípico [FORMAL] ❑ *...the archetypal American middle-class family.* *...la familia arquetípica de la clase media estadounidense.*
→ see **myth**

**Archimedes' prin|ci|ple** /ɑrkɪmidiz prɪnsɪpəl/ N-UNCOUNT **Archimedes' principle** is a law of physics which states that, when an object is in a fluid such as water, its apparent loss of weight is equal to the weight of the fluid that the object has displaced. principio de Arquímedes

**archi|tect** /ɑrkɪtɛkt/ (**architects**) **1** N-COUNT An **architect** is a person who designs buildings. arquitecto o arquitecta **2** N-COUNT The **architect of** an idea, event, or institution is the person who invented it or made it happen. artífice ❑ *Robert Moses was the architect of New York State's highway system.* *Robert Moses fue el artífice del sistema de carreteras del estado de Nueva York.*

**archi|tec|ture** /ɑrkɪtɛktʃər/ **1** N-UNCOUNT **Architecture** is the art of planning, designing, and constructing buildings. arquitectura ❑ *He studied architecture in Rome.* *Estudió arquitectura en Roma.* • **archi|tec|tur|al** /ɑrkɪtɛktʃərəl/ ADJ arquitectónico ❑ *...architectural drawings.* *...dibujos arquitectónicos.* • **archi|tec|tur|al|ly** ADV desde el punto de vista arquitectónico ❑ *The old city center is architecturally rich.* *El centro antiguo de la ciudad es rico desde el punto de vista arquitectónico.* **2** N-UNCOUNT The **architecture** of a building is the style in which it is designed and constructed. arquitectura ❑ *...modern architecture.* *...arquitectura moderna.*
→ see Word Web: **architecture**

**ar|chive** /ɑrkaɪv/ (**archives**) N-COUNT **Archives** are a collection of documents and records that contain historical information. archivo ❑ *...the State Library's archives.* *...los archivos de la Biblioteca Estatal.*

**are** /ər, STRONG ɑr/ **Are** is the plural and the second person singular of the present tense of the verb **be. Are** is often shortened to **-'re** after

**Word Web** architecture

The Colosseum (sometimes spelled Coliseum) in Rome is a great **architectural** success of the ancient world. This amphitheater, built in the first century BC, could hold 50,000 people. It was used for animal fights, human executions, and staged battles. The oval shape allowed people to be closer to the action. It also prevented participants from hiding in the corners. The **arches** are an important part of the **building.** They are an example of a Roman improvement to the simple arch. Each arch is supported by a **keystone** in the top center. The **design** of the Colosseum has influenced the design of thousands of other public places. Many modern day sports stadiums are the same shape.

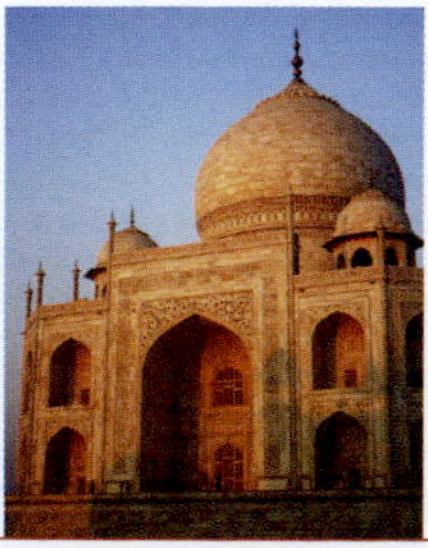

Picture Dictionary area

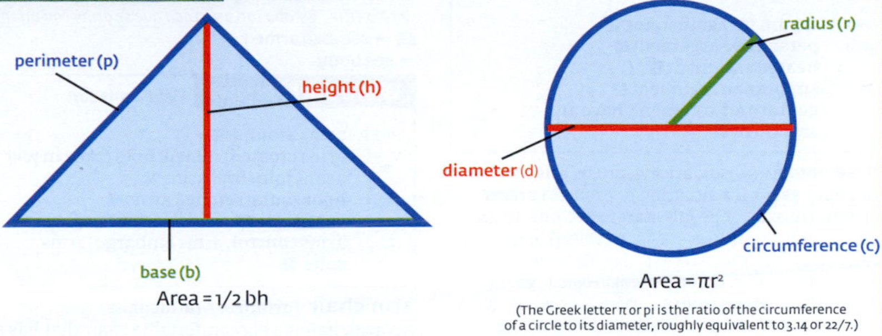


pronouns in spoken English. *segunda persona del singular y primera, segunda y tercera personas del plural del presente de* ***be***

**area** /ɛəriə/ (**areas**) **1** N-COUNT An **area** is a particular part of a town, a country, a region, or the world. *área* ❑ *There are 11,000 people living in the area.* *En el área viven 11,000 personas.* **2** N-COUNT A particular **area** is a piece of land or part of a building that is used for a particular activity. *área* ❑ *...a picnic area.* *...un área para días de campo.* **3** N-COUNT You can use **area** to refer to a particular subject or topic, or to a particular part of a larger, more general situation or activity. *área* ❑ *...the area of child care.* *...el área de cuidados infantiles.* **4** N-VAR The **area** of a surface such as a piece of land is the amount of flat space or ground that it covers, measured in square units. *área* ❑ *The islands cover a total area of 400 square miles.* *Las islas comprenden un área total de 1,036 kilómetros cuadrados.* **5** → see also **gray area**
→ see Picture Dictionary: **area**

**Word Partnership** Usar *area* con:

N. **downtown** area, **tourist** area **1**
ADJ. **local** area, **metropolitan** area, **remote** area, **rural/suburban/urban** area, **surrounding** area **1**
**residential** area, **restricted** area **2**
PREP. **throughout the** area **1** **2**
area **of expertise** **3**

**area code** (**area codes**) N-COUNT The **area code** for a particular city or region is the series of numbers that you have to dial before someone's personal number if you are making a telephone call to that place from a different area. *código de zona* ❑ *The area code for western Pennsylvania is 412.* *El código de zona del oeste de Pensilvania es el 412.*

**arena** /ərinə/ (**arenas**) **1** N-COUNT An **arena** is a place where sports, entertainments, and other public events take place. *estadio* ❑ *...the largest indoor sports arena in the world.* *...el mayor estadio deportivo cubierto del mundo.* **2** N-COUNT You can refer to a field of activity, especially one where there is a lot of conflict or action, as an **arena** of a particular kind. *palestra* ❑ *He entered the political arena in 1987.* *Ingresó a la palestra política en 1987.*

**aren't** /ɑrnt, ɑrənt/ **1** **Aren't** is the usual spoken form of "are not." *forma hablado usual de* ***are not***. **2** **Aren't** is the form of "am not" that is used in questions or tags in spoken English. *Muletilla equivalente a "¿No es cierto?", "¿Verdad?" o, simplemente, "¿No?".*

**arête** /əreɪt/ (**arêtes**) N-COUNT An **arête** is a thin ridge of rock separating two valleys in mountainous regions. *arista, cresta, cresta peñascosa*

**ar|gue** /ɑrgyu/ (**argues, arguing, argued**) **1** V-RECIP If you **argue with** someone, you disagree with them about something, often angrily. *discutir* ❑ *He was arguing with his wife about their daughter.* *Estaba discutiendo con su esposa respecto a su hija.* ❑ *They are arguing over details.* *Están discutiendo por detalles.* **2** V-T If you **argue that** something is true, you state it and give the reasons why you think it is true. *argumentar* ❑ *They are arguing that the money belongs to them.* *Argumentan que el dinero es suyo.* **3** V-I If you **argue for** something, you say why you agree with it, in order to persuade people that it is right. If you **argue against** something, you say why you disagree with it, in order to persuade people that it is wrong. *argumentar* ❑ *He argued against having the meeting.* *Expuso sus argumentos en contra de la reunión.*

**Thesaurus** *argue* Ver también:

V. bicker, disagree, dispute, fight, quarrel; (*ant.*) agree **1**
claim **2**

**ar|gu|ment** /ɑrgyəmənt/ (**arguments**) **1** N-VAR An **argument** is a statement or set of statements that you use in order to try to convince people that your opinion about something is correct. *argumento, razón* ❑ *There's a strong argument for lowering the price.* *Hay razones de mucho peso para reducir el precio.* **2** N-COUNT An **argument** is a conversation in which people disagree with each other angrily or noisily. *discusión* ❑ *Annie had an argument with one of the other girls.* *Annie tuvo una discusión con una de las otras muchachas.*

A

**Word Partnership** Usar *argument* con:

PREP. argument **against/for** 1
ADJ. **persuasive** argument 1
**heated** argument 2
V. **support an** argument 1
**get into an** argument, **have an** argument 2

**arise** /əraɪz/ (**arises, arising, arose, arisen** /ərɪzən/) 1 V-I If a situation or problem **arises,** it begins to exist or people start to become aware of it. presentarse ❑ *When the opportunity finally arose, thousands of workers left.* *Cuando se presentó la oportunidad, miles de obreros se marcharon.* 2 V-I If something **arises from** a particular situation, or **arises out of** it, it is created or caused by the situation. surgir ❑ *The idea arose from discussions held last year.* *La idea surgió de las discusiones sostenidas el año pasado.*

**arith|me|tic** /ərɪθmɪtɪk/ N-UNCOUNT **Arithmetic** is the part of mathematics that is concerned with the addition, subtraction, multiplication, and division of numbers. aritmética ❑ *...teaching the basics of reading, writing and arithmetic.* *...enseña lectura, escritura y aritmética básicas.*
→ see **mathematics**

**ar|ith|met|ic se|quence** /ærɪθmɛtɪk sikwəns/ (**arithmetic sequences**) also **arithmetic progression** N-COUNT An **arithmetic sequence** is a series of numbers in which each number differs from the one before it by the same amount, for example the sequence 3, 6, 9, 12. progresión aritmética

**arm** /ɑrm/ (**arms, arming, armed**) 1 N-COUNT Your **arms** are the two parts of your body between your shoulders and your hands. brazo ❑ *She stretched her arms out.* *Estiró los brazos.* 2 N-COUNT The **arm** of a chair is the part on which you rest your arm when you are sitting down. brazo ❑ *Mack held the arms of the chair.* *Mack sujetó los brazos del sillón.* 3 N-COUNT The **arm** of a piece of clothing is the part of it that covers your arm. manga ❑ *The coat was short in the arms.* *El abrigo tenía las mangas cortas.* 4 N-PLURAL **Arms** are weapons, especially bombs and guns. armas ❑ *Soldiers searched their house for illegal arms.* *Los soldados registraron su casa en busca de armas ilegales.* 5 V-T If you **arm** someone with a weapon, you provide them with a weapon. armar ❑ *She was so frightened that she armed herself with a rifle.* *Estaba tan asustada que se armó con un rifle.* 6 → see also **armed**
→ see **body**

**Word Partnership** Usar *arms* con:

PREP. arms **around** 1
V. arms **crossed/folded; hold/take in** *your* arms, **join/link** arms 1
ADJ. **open/outstretched** arms 1
V. **bear** arms 4
N. arms **control**, arms **embargo**, arms **sales** 4

**arm|chair** /ɑrmtʃɛər/ (**armchairs**) N-COUNT An **armchair** is a big comfortable chair that has a support on each side for your arms. sillón ❑ *She was sitting in an armchair.* *Estaba sentada en un sillón.*

**armed** /ɑrmd/ 1 ADJ Someone who is **armed** is carrying a weapon, usually a gun. armado ❑ *City police said the man was armed with a gun.* *La policía de la ciudad afirmó que estaba armado con una pistola.* ❑ *...armed guards.* *...guardias armados.* 2 ADJ An **armed** attack or conflict involves people fighting with guns or carrying weapons. armado ❑ *They were found guilty of armed robbery.* *Los declararon culpables de robo a mano armada.* 3 → see also **arm**
→ see **war**

**armed forces** N-PLURAL The **armed forces** or the **armed services** of a country are its military forces, usually the army, navy, marines, and air force. fuerzas armadas ❑ *...members of the armed forces.* *...miembros de las fuerzas armadas.*

**ar|mor** /ɑrmər/ 1 N-UNCOUNT In former times, **armor** was special metal clothing that soldiers wore for protection in battle. armadura ❑ *...knights in armor.* *...caballeros con armadura.* 2 N-UNCOUNT **Armor** is a hard, usually metal, covering that protects a vehicle against attack. blindaje ❑ *...armor-piercing bullets.* *...balas perforantes.*
→ see **army**

**ar|mored** /ɑrmərd/ ADJ **Armored** vehicles are equipped with a hard metal covering in order to protect them from gunfire and other missiles. blindado ❑ *More than forty armored vehicles have gone into the area.* *Más de cuarenta vehículos blindados han ido al área.*

**Word Web** army

The first Roman **army** was a poorly organized **militia band**. Its members had no **weapons** such as **swords** or **spears**. Things changed after the Etruscans, an advanced society from west-central Italy, **conquered** Rome. Then the Roman army became more powerful. They learned how to **deploy** their **troops** to **fight** better in **battles**. By the first century BC, the Roman army learned the importance of protective equipment. They started using bronze **helmets**, **armor**, and wooden **shields**. They fought many **military campaigns** and won many **wars**.

**arm|pit** /ɑrmpɪt/ (**armpits**) N-COUNT Your **armpits** are the areas of your body under your arms where your arms join your shoulders. *axila, sobaco* ❑ *I shave my armpits every couple of days. Me rasuro las axilas cada tercer día.*

**army** /ɑrmi/ (**armies**) **1** N-COUNT An **army** is a large organized group of people who are armed and trained to fight on land in a war. Most armies are organized and controlled by governments. *ejército* ❑ *Perkins joined the Army in 1990. Perkins se alistó en el ejército en 1990.* **2** N-COUNT An **army of** people, animals, or things is a large number of them, especially when they are regarded as a force of some kind. *ejército* ❑ *...an army of volunteers. ...un ejército de voluntarios.*
→ see Word Web: **army**

**aro|ma** /əroʊmə/ (**aromas**) N-COUNT An **aroma** is a strong, pleasant smell. *aroma* ❑ *...the wonderful aroma of fresh bread. ...el maravilloso aroma del pan recién horneado.*

**arose** /əroʊz/ **Arose** is the past tense of **arise**. *Pasado de* ***arise***

**around** /əraʊnd/

> **Around** is an adverb and a preposition. **Around** is often used with verbs of movement, such as "walk" and "drive," and also in phrasal verbs such as "get around" and "turn around."

**1** PREP To be positioned **around** a place or object means to surround it or be on all sides of it. To move **around** a place means to go along its edge, back to your starting point. *alrededor* ❑ *She looked at the papers around her. Miró los papeles a su alrededor.* ❑ *She wore her hair down around her shoulders. Llevaba el pelo sobre los hombros.* ● **Around** is also an adverb. *alrededor* ❑ *...a village with hills all around. ...un pueblo rodeado de colinas., ...un pueblo con colinas alrededor.* ❑ *They celebrated their win by running around on the football field. Celebraron su triunfo corriendo alrededor del campo de fútbol.* **2** PREP If you move **around** a corner or obstacle, you move to the other side of it. If you look **around** a corner or obstacle, you look to see what is on the other side. *a la vuelta* ❑ *The photographer stopped taking pictures and hurried around the corner. El fotógrafo dejó de tomar fotografías y dio vuelta a la esquina apresuradamente.* **3** PREP You use **around** to say that something happens in different parts of a place or area. *en, en todo* ❑ *Police say ten people have died in violence around the country. La policía dice que la violencia ha causado diez muertes en el país.* ● **Around** is also an adverb. *por todas partes* ❑ *Why are you following me around? ¿Por qué me andas siguiendo?* **4** ADV If you move things **around,** you move them so that they are in different places. *de un lado a otro* ❑ *She moved things around so the table was underneath the window. Movió las cosas de un lado a otro y la mesa quedó bajo la ventana.* **5** ADV If someone or something is **around,** they exist or are present in a place. *por aquí* ❑ *You haven't seen my wife anywhere around, have you? No has visto a mi esposa por aquí, ¿o sí?* **6** ADV **Around** means approximately. *aproximadamente* ❑ *My salary was around $45,000. Mi salario era de aproximadamente 45,000 dólares.* ● **Around** is also a preposition. *alrededor* ❑ *We're leaving around May 15. Nos vamos alrededor del 15 de mayo.* **7** **the other way around** → see **way**

**arouse** /əraʊz/ (**arouses, arousing, aroused**) V-T If something **arouses** a particular reaction or feeling in you, it causes you to have that reaction or feeling. *despertar, suscitar* ❑ *The smell of frying bacon aroused his hunger. El olor del tocino friéndose le despertó el apetito.*

**ar|range** /əreɪndʒ/ (**arranges, arranging, arranged**) **1** V-T If you **arrange** an event or meeting, you make plans for it to happen. *concertar, quedar en, encargarse de* ❑ *She arranged an appointment for Friday afternoon. Concertó una cita para el viernes por la tarde.* ❑ *I've arranged to see him Thursday. Quedé que lo vería el jueves.* ❑ *I will arrange for someone to take you around. Me encargaré de que alguien te acompañe.* **2** V-T If you **arrange** things somewhere, you place them in a particular position, usually in order to make them look attractive or neat. *arreglar* ❑ *She enjoys arranging dried flowers. Disfruta haciendo arreglos de flores secas.*

**ar|range|ment** /əreɪndʒmənt/ (**arrangements**) **1** N-COUNT **Arrangements** are plans and preparations that you make so that something can happen. *preparativo* ❑ *They're working on final arrangements for the meeting. Están haciendo los preparativos finales para la reunión.* **2** N-COUNT An **arrangement** of things, for example, flowers or furniture, is a group of them displayed in a particular way. *arreglo* ❑ *...flower arrangements. ...arreglos florales.*

**ar|ray** /əreɪ/ (**arrays**) N-COUNT An **array of** different things or people is a large number or wide range of them. *despliegue, selección* ❑ *...a wide array of products. ...una gran selección de productos.*

**ar|rest** /ərɛst/ (**arrests, arresting, arrested**) **1** V-T If the police **arrest** you, they take charge of you and take you to a police station, because they believe you may have committed a crime. *detener, arrestar* ❑ *Police arrested five young men in connection with the attacks. La policía detuvo a cinco jóvenes en relación con los ataques.* ● **Arrest** is also a noun. *detención, arresto* ❑ *Police later made two arrests. Más tarde, la policía hizo dos arrestos.* **2** → see also **house arrest**

**ar|ri|val** /əraɪvᵊl/ (**arrivals**) **1** N-VAR When a person or vehicle arrives at a place, you can refer to their **arrival**. *llegada* ❑ *...the day after his arrival in Wichita. ...el día posterior a su llegada a Wichita.* **2** N-SING When something is brought to you or becomes available, you can refer to its **arrival.** *llegada* ❑ *I read the newspaper while I was waiting for the arrival of orange juice and coffee. Leí el periódico mientras esperaba que me sirvieran el jugo de naranja y el café.* **3** N-COUNT You can refer to someone who has just arrived at a place as a new **arrival.** *recién llegado o recién llegada* ❑ *Many of the new arrivals are skilled professionals. Muchos de los recién llegados son profesionales calificados.*

**ar|rive** /əraɪv/ (**arrives, arriving, arrived**) **1** V-I When a person or vehicle **arrives** at a place, they come to it from somewhere else. *llegar* ❑ *Their train arrived on time. Su tren llegó a tiempo.* **2** V-I When something **arrives,** it is brought to you or becomes available. *estar* ❑ *The movie will finally arrive in the stores this month. La película estará finalmente en las tiendas este mes.* **3** V-I When you **arrive at** something such as a decision, you decide something after thinking about it or discussing it.

tomar ❑ *John was unable to arrive at a decision.* *John fue incapaz de tomar una decisión.*

| Thesaurus | *arrive* | Ver también: |
|---|---|---|
| v. | enter, land, pull in, reach; (*ant.*) depart **1** | |

**ar|ro|gant** /ærəgənt/ ADJ Someone who is **arrogant** behaves in a proud, unpleasant way toward other people because they believe that they are more important than others. *arrogante* ❑ *He was so arrogant.* *Era tan arrogante.* ❑ *That sounds arrogant, doesn't it?* *Suena arrogante, ¿verdad?* ● **ar|ro|gance** N-UNCOUNT *arrogancia* ❑ *...the arrogance of powerful people.* *...la arrogancia de los poderosos.* ● **ar|ro|gant|ly** ADV *con arrogancia* ❑ *The doctor arrogantly dismissed their cry for help.* *El médico desestimó con arrogancia su llamado de auxilio.*

**ar|row** /æroʊ/ (**arrows**) **1** N-COUNT An **arrow** is a long thin weapon that is sharp and pointed at one end. An arrow is shot from a bow. *flecha* ❑ *They were armed with bows and arrows.* *Iban armados con arcos y flechas.* **2** N-COUNT An **arrow** is a written or printed sign that points in a particular direction to indicate where something is. *flecha* ❑ *The arrow pointed down.* *La flecha apuntaba hacia abajo.*

**ar|son** /ɑrsᵊn/ N-UNCOUNT **Arson** is the crime of deliberately setting fire to a building or vehicle. *incendio provocado* ❑ *The wooden building burned to the ground in an arson attack on January 4.* *El edificio de madera quedó reducido a cenizas por un incendio provocado el 4 de enero.*

**art** /ɑrt/ (**arts**) **1** N-UNCOUNT **Art** consists of paintings, sculpture, and other pictures or objects that are created for people to look at. *arte* ❑ *...modern American art.* *...arte moderno estadounidense.* **2** N-UNCOUNT **Art** is the activity or educational subject that consists of creating paintings, sculptures, and other pictures or objects for people to look at. *arte* ❑ *...art classes.* *...clases de arte.* ❑ *...Savannah College of Art and Design.* *...Escuela de Arte y Diseño de Savannah.* **3** N-PLURAL **The arts** are activities such as music, painting, literature, film, and dance. *las bellas artes* ❑ *...people working in the arts.* *...gente que trabaja en las artes.* **4** N-PLURAL At a university or college, **arts** are subjects such as history, literature, or languages in contrast to scientific subjects. *letras* ❑ *...arts and social science graduates.* *...licenciados en letras y ciencias sociales.* **5** N-COUNT If you describe an activity as an **art**, you mean that it requires skill and that people learn to do it by instinct or experience, rather than by learning facts or rules. *arte* ❑ *...the art of acting.* *...el arte de la actuación.* **6** → see also **martial art, state-of-the-art**
→ see Word Web: **art**
→ see **culture**

**art criti|cism** N-UNCOUNT **Art criticism** is the study and evaluation of the visual arts, especially painting. *crítica de arte*

**art el|ement** (**art elements**) N-COUNT **Art elements** are the basic parts that a painting or drawing consists of, such as lines, colors and shapes. *elemento artístico*

**ar|tery** /ɑrtəri/ (**arteries**) N-COUNT **Arteries** are the tubes in your body that carry blood from your heart to the rest of your body. Compare **vein**. *arteria* ❑ *...patients suffering from blocked arteries.* *...pacientes que sufren de arterias obstruidas.*
→ see **cardiovascular system**

**ar|te|sian spring** /ɑrtiʒən sprɪŋ/ (**artesian springs**) N-COUNT An **artesian spring** is a place where water rises naturally through holes or cracks in the ground. *pozo artesiano, aguas artesianas*

**ar|thri|tis** /ɑrθraɪtɪs/ N-UNCOUNT **Arthritis** is a medical condition in which the joints in your body are swollen and painful. *artritis* ❑ *I have a touch of arthritis in the wrist.* *Tengo un poco de artritis en la muñeca.* ● **ar|thrit|ic** /ɑrθrɪtɪk/ ADJ *artrítico* ❑ *...arthritic hands.* *...manos afectadas por la artritis.*

**ar|ti|choke** /ɑrtɪtʃoʊk/ (**artichokes**) N-VAR **Artichokes** or **globe artichokes** are round green vegetables that have fleshy leaves arranged like the petals of a flower. *alcachofa*

| Word Link | *cle ≈ small : article, follicle, particle* |
|---|---|

**ar|ti|cle** /ɑrtɪkᵊl/ (**articles**) **1** N-COUNT An **article** is a piece of writing that is published in a newspaper or magazine. *artículo* ❑ *...a newspaper article.* *...un artículo periodístico.* **2** N-COUNT You can refer to objects as **articles** of some kind. *artículo, prenda* ❑ *...articles of clothing.* *...prendas de vestir.* ❑ *He removed all articles of value.* *Removió todos los artículos de valor.* **3** N-COUNT An **article** of a formal agreement or document is a section of it that deals with a particular point. *artículo* ❑ *...Article 50 of the UN charter.* *...el Artículo 50 de la Carta de las Naciones Unidas.*

**Word Web** art

The Impressionist movement in **painting** began in Europe during the second half of the 19th century. The Impressionists no longer used traditional **realistic depictions** of people and objects painted in **studios**. They often painted **landscapes**, with more light and color in their **interpretations** of everyday life. Among these painters were French artists Paul Cézanne, Pierre Renoir, and Claude Monet. The word "Impressionist" comes from the name of a Monet painting, "Impression, Sunrise." Japanese prints also had an effect on the Impressionist movement. The Impressionists liked the use of contrasting dark and bright colors found in these prints.

**ar|ticu|late** (**articulates, articulating, articulated**)

The adjective is pronounced /ɑrtɪkyəlɪt/. The verb is pronounced /ɑrtɪkyəleɪt/.

**1** ADJ If you describe someone as **articulate,** you mean that they are able to express their thoughts and ideas easily and well. *elocuente* ❑ *She is an articulate young woman. Es una joven que se expresa muy bien.* **2** V-T When you **articulate** your ideas or feelings, you express them clearly in words. *expresarse con claridad* [FORMAL] ❑ *She articulated her views. Expresó sus opiniones con claridad.*

**ar|ticu|la|tion** /ɑrtɪkyəleɪʃᵊn/ N-UNCOUNT **Articulation** is the action of producing a sound or word clearly, in speech or music. *articulación* [FORMAL]

**ar|ti|fact** /ɑrtɪfækt/ (**artifacts**) N-COUNT An **artifact** is an ornament, tool, or other object that is made by a human being, especially one that is historically or culturally interesting. *objeto* ❑ *They repair broken religious artifacts. Reparan objetos religiosos rotos.*
→ see **history**

**Word Link** *fact, fic ≈ making : artificial, factor, manufacture*

**ar|ti|fi|cial** /ɑrtɪfɪʃᵊl/ **1** ADJ **Artificial** objects, materials, or processes do not occur naturally and are created by human beings. *artificial* ❑ *The city has many small lakes, natural and artificial. La ciudad tiene muchos lagos pequeños, naturales y artificiales.* ❑ *...a diet free from artificial additives. ...un régimen alimenticio libre de aditivos artificiales.* ● **ar|ti|fi|cial|ly** ADV *artificialmente* ❑ *...artificially sweetened lemonade. ...limonada edulcorada artificialmente.* **2** ADJ An **artificial** state or situation exists only because someone has created it, and therefore often seems unnatural or unnecessary. *afectado, forzado* ❑ *...a fixed, artificial smile. ...una sonrisa afectada, petrificada.* ● **ar|ti|fi|cial|ly** ADV *artificialmente* ❑ *...artificially low prices. ...precios artificialmente bajos.*

**Thesaurus** *artificial* Ver también:
ADJ. manmade, manufactured, synthetic, unnatural; (*ant.*) natural **1** **2**

**ar|ti|fi|cial light** (**artificial lights**) N-VAR **Artificial light** is light from a source such as an electric light or a gas lamp rather than from the sun. *luz artificial*

**ar|til|lery** /ɑrtɪləri/ **1** N-UNCOUNT **Artillery** consists of large, powerful guns that are transported on wheels. *artillería* ❑ *...tanks and heavy artillery. ...tanques y artillería pesada.* **2** N-SING **The artillery** is the section of an army that is trained to use large, powerful guns. *artillería* ❑ *From 1935 to 1937 he was in the artillery. De 1935 a 1937 estuvo en la artillería.*

**Word Link** *ist ≈ one who practices : artist, chemist, pianist*

**art|ist** /ɑrtɪst/ (**artists**) **1** N-COUNT An **artist** is someone who draws, paints or produces other works of art. *artista* ❑ *Each poster is signed by the artist. Cada cartel está firmado por el artista.* ❑ *She considers herself a serious artist. Se considera una artista seria.* **2** N-COUNT An **artist** is a performer such as a musician, actor, or dancer. *artista* ❑ *...a popular artist who has sold millions of records. ...un artista popular que ha vendido millones de discos.*
→ see **animation**

**ar|tis|tic** /ɑrtɪstɪk/ **1** ADJ Someone who is **artistic** is good at drawing or painting, or arranging things in a beautiful way. *artístico* ❑ *The boys are sensitive and artistic. Los niños son sensibles y tienen dotes artísticas.* **2** ADJ **Artistic** means relating to art or artists. *artístico* ❑ *He's the artistic director of the Montreal Opera. Es el director artístico de la Ópera de Montreal.* ● **ar|tis|ti|cal|ly** /ɑrtɪstɪkli/ ADV *con dotes artísticas* ❑ *...artistically gifted children. ...niños con dotes artísticas.*

**as**
❶ CONJUNCTION AND PREPOSITION USES
❷ USED WITH OTHER PREPOSITIONS AND CONJUNCTIONS

❶ **as** /əz, STRONG æz/ **1** CONJ If one thing happens **as** something else happens, it happens at the same time. *cuando, al hacer algo* ❑ *We shut the door behind us as we entered. Cerramos la puerta tras nosotros al entrar.* **2** CONJ You use **as** to say how something happens or is done. *como* ❑ *Today, as usual, he was wearing a suit. Hoy, como de costumbre, llevaba un traje.* **3** CONJ You can use **as** to mean "because." *porque* ❑ *This is important as it sets the mood for the rest of the day. Esto es importante, porque establece el humor para el resto del día.* **4** PHRASE You use **as...as** when you are comparing things, or emphasizing how large or small something is. *tan...como, hasta* ❑ *This was not as easy as we imagined. No fue tan fácil como imaginamos.* ❑ *She gets as many as eight thousand letters a month. Recibe hasta ocho mil cartas al mes.* ● **As** is also a conjunction. *tan...como* ❑ *Being a mother isn't as bad as I thought at first! ¡Ser madre no es tan malo como creí al principio!* **5** PREP You use **as** when you are indicating what someone or something is or is thought to be. *como* ❑ *The news came as a complete surprise. La noticia fue una verdadera sorpresa.* **6** PREP You use **as** in expressions like **as a result** and **as a consequence** to indicate how two situations or events are linked to each other. *como* ❑ *She was unable to walk as a result of her injuries. Como resultado de sus heridas, no podía caminar.* **7** **as ever** → see **ever** **8** **as a matter of fact** → see **fact** **9** **as follows** → see **follow** **10** **as long as** → see **long** **11** **as opposed to** → see **opposed** **12** **as regards** → see **regard** **13** **as soon as** → see **soon** **14** **as such** → see **such** **15** **as well** → see **well** **16** **as well as** → see **well**

❷ **as** /əz, STRONG æz/ **1** PHRASE You use **as for** and **as to** in order to introduce a slightly different subject. *en cuanto a* ❑ *I don't know why he shouted at me. And as for going back there, certainly I would never go back. No sé por qué me gritó. En cuanto a volver allá, nunca volvería, sin duda alguna.* **2** PHRASE You use **as to** to indicate what something refers to. *respecto a* ❑ *They should make decisions as to whether the student needs more help. Deben tomar decisiones respecto a si el estudiante necesita más ayuda.* **3** PHRASE If you say that something will happen **as of** a particular

A

date or time, you mean that it will happen from that time on. *a partir de* ❑ *The store will be open as of January the 1st. La tienda abrirá a partir del 1 de enero.* **4** PHRASE You use **as if** and **as though** when you are giving a possible explanation for something or saying that something appears to be the case when it is not. *como si* ❑ *Anne stopped, as if she didn't know what to say next. Anne calló, como si no supiera qué otra cosa decir.*

**asexu|al re|pro|duc|tion** N-UNCOUNT **Asexual reproduction** is a form of reproduction that involves no sexual activity. *reproducción asexual*

**ash** /æʃ/ (**ashes**) **1** N-VAR **Ash** is the gray or black powdery substance that is left after something is burned. You can also refer to this substance as **ashes.** *ceniza* ❑ *...a cloud of ash. ...una nube de ceniza.* **2** N-VAR An **ash** is a tree that has smooth gray bark and loses its leaves in winter. *fresno* ● **Ash** is the wood from this tree. *fresno* ❑ *The chairs are made from ash. Las sillas están hechas de fresno.*
→ see **fire, glass, volcano**

**ashamed** /əʃeɪmd/ ADJ If you are **ashamed** of someone or something, you feel embarrassed or guilty because of them. *avergonzado* ❑ *I was ashamed of myself. Me avergonzaba de mí mismo.* ❑ *She was ashamed that she looked so messy. Se avergonzaba de verse tan desarreglada.*

**Asian** /eɪʒᵊn/ (**Asians**) ADJ Someone or something that is **Asian** comes from or is associated with Asia, for example China, Korea, Thailand, Japan, or Vietnam. *asiático* ❑ *...Asian music. ...música asiática.* ● An **Asian** is a person who comes from or is associated with a country or region in Asia. *asiático o asiática* ❑ *Many of the shops were run by Asians. Muchas de las tiendas tenían dueños asiáticos.*

**aside** /əsaɪd/

> In addition to the uses shown below, **aside** is used in phrasal verbs such as "cast aside," "stand aside," and "step aside."

**1** ADV If you move something **aside,** you move it to one side of you. *a un lado* ❑ *Sarah closed the book and laid it aside. Sarah cerró el libro y lo puso a un lado.* **2** ADV If you take or draw someone **aside,** you take them a little way away from a group of people in order to talk to them in private. *a un lado, aparte* ❑ *I took him aside and discussed it with him. Lo llevé aparte y hablé con él.* **3** ADV If you move **aside,** you get out of someone's way. *a un lado* ❑ *She stepped aside to let them pass. Se hizo a un lado para dejarlos pasar.* **4** PHRASE You use **aside from** when you are making an exception to a general statement. *con excepción de, salvo por* ❑ *The room was empty aside from one man seated beside the fire. El cuarto estaba vacío, con excepción del hombre sentado al lado de la chimenea.* **5** PHRASE You use **aside from** to indicate that you are aware of one aspect of a situation, but that you are going to focus on another aspect. *aparte de, además de* ❑ *Aside from the bruises, there were no other injuries. Aparte de los moretones, no hubo otras lesiones.*

**ask** /æsk/ (**asks, asking, asked**) **1** V-T/V-I If you **ask** someone something, you say something to them in the form of a question because you want to know the answer. *preguntar* ❑ *"How is Frank?" he asked. —¿Cómo está Frank?—preguntó.* ❑ *I asked him his name. Le pregunté su nombre.* ❑ *She asked me if I'd enjoyed my dinner. Me preguntó si había disfrutado mi cena.* ❑ *All you have to do is ask. Lo único que tienes que hacer es preguntar.* **2** V-T If you **ask** someone **to** do something, you tell them that you want them to do it. *pedir* ❑ *We had to ask him to leave. Tuvimos que pedirle que se fuera.* **3** V-T If you **ask to** do something, you tell someone that you want to do it. *pedir, solicitar* ❑ *I asked to see the director. Pedí ver al director.* **4** V-I If you **ask for** something, you say that you would like it. *pedir* ❑ *She asked for my address, which I didn't want to give her. Me pidió mi dirección, pero no quise dársela.* **5** V-I If you **ask for** someone, you say that you would like to speak to them. *preguntar por* ❑ *There's a man at the gate asking for you. Hay alguien allá afuera que pregunta por ti.* **6** V-T If you **ask** someone's permission, opinion, or forgiveness, you try to obtain it. *pedir* ❑ *He asked permission to leave. Pidió permiso para retirarse.* **7** V-T If you **ask** someone **to** an event or place, you invite them to go there. *invitar* ❑ *I asked Juan to the party. Invité a Juan a la fiesta.* **8** PHRASE You can say **"if you ask me"** to emphasize that you are stating your personal opinion. *si me preguntas a mí, si quieres saber* ❑ *He was nuts, if you ask me. Estaba loco, si me preguntas a mí.*

**Thesaurus** *ask* Ver también:

| | |
|---|---|
| V. | demand, interrogate, question, quiz; (*ant.*) answer, reply, respond **1** |
| | beg, plead, request; (*ant.*) command, insist **6** |

**Word Partnership** Usar *ask* con:

| | |
|---|---|
| ADJ. | **afraid to** ask **1** |
| V. | **come to** ask, **have to** ask **1** |
| DET. | ask **how/what/when/where/who/why** **1** |
| CONJ. | ask **if/whether** **1** |
| PREP. | ask **about** **1** |
| | ask **to** **2** **3** **7** |
| | ask **for** **4** **5** |
| N. | ask **a question** **1** |
| | ask **for help** **4** |
| | ask **forgiveness**, ask ***someone's* opinion**, ask **permission** **6** |

**asleep** /əslip/ **1** ADJ Someone who is **asleep** is sleeping. *dormido* ❑ *My daughter was asleep on the sofa. Mi hija estaba dormida en el sillón.* **2** PHRASE When you **fall asleep,** you start sleeping. *quedarse dormido* ❑ *Sam soon fell asleep. Sam pronto se quedó dormido.* **3** PHRASE Someone who is **fast asleep** or **sound asleep** is sleeping deeply. *profundamente dormido* ❑ *They were both fast asleep in their beds. Los dos estaban profundamente dormidos en sus camas.*
→ see **sleep**

**as|para|gus** /əspærəgəs/ N-UNCOUNT **Asparagus** is a vegetable that is long and green and has small shoots at one end. *espárrago*
→ see **vegetable**

**as|pect** /æspɛkt/ (**aspects**) **1** N-COUNT An **aspect** of something is one of the parts of its character or nature. *aspecto* ❑ *Climate and weather affect every aspect of our lives. Las condiciones climáticas afectan cada aspecto de nuestras vidas.* ❑ *He was interested in all aspects of the work here. Le interesaban todos los aspectos del trabajo aquí.* **2** N-COUNT The

**aspect** of a building or window is the direction in which it faces. *vista* [FORMAL] ❑ *The house had a southwest aspect.* *La casa estaba orientada al suroeste.*

| **Word Link** | *spir ≈ breath : aspiration, inspire, respiratory* |
|---|---|

**as|pi|ra|tion** /æspɪreɪʃᵊn/ (**aspirations**) N-VAR Someone's **aspirations** are their desire to achieve things. *aspiración* ❑ *The girl had aspirations to a movie career.* *La chica tenía aspiraciones de hacer carrera en el cine.*

**as|pi|rin** /æspərɪn, -prɪn/ (**aspirins**)

The form **aspirin** can also be used for the plural.

N-VAR **Aspirin** is a mild drug that reduces pain and fever. *aspirina*

**as|sas|si|nate** /əsæsɪneɪt/ (**assassinates, assassinating, assassinated**) V-T When someone important **is assassinated,** they are murdered as a political act. *asesinar* ❑ *Robert Kennedy was assassinated in 1968.* *Robert Kennedy fue asesinado en 1968.* • **as|sas|si|na|tion** /əsæsɪneɪʃᵊn/ (**assassinations**) N-VAR *asesinato* ❑ *She wants an investigation into the assassination of her husband.* *Quiere que se investigue el asesinato de su esposo.* ❑ *He lives in fear of assassination.* *Vive con el temor de que lo asesinen.*

**as|sault** /əsɔlt/ (**assaults, assaulting, assaulted**) **1** N-COUNT An **assault** by an army is a strong attack made against an enemy. *asalto* ❑ *They are making a new assault.* *Están llevando a cabo un nuevo asalto.* **2** N-VAR An **assault on** a person is a physical attack on them. *agresión, asalto* ❑ *...a series of assaults in the university area.* *...una serie de agresiones en terrenos de la universidad.* **3** V-T To **assault** someone means to physically attack them. *agredir, atacar* ❑ *The gang assaulted him with iron bars.* *La pandilla lo atacó con tubos.*

**as|sem|blage** /əsɛmblɪdʒ/ (**assemblages**) N-COUNT An **assemblage** is a piece of sculpture that combines a number of different objects. *montaje*

**as|sem|ble** /əsɛmbᵊl/ (**assembles, assembling, assembled**) **1** V-T/V-I When people **assemble** or when someone **assembles** them, they come together in a group. *reunirse* ❑ *There was nowhere for students to assemble between classes.* *No había ningún lugar para que los estudiantes se reunieran entre las clases.* **2** V-T To **assemble** something means to collect it together or to fit the different parts of it together. *armar* ❑ *Workers were assembling airplanes.* *Los trabajadores estaban armando aviones.*

**as|sem|bly** /əsɛmbli/ (**assemblies**) **1** N-COUNT An **assembly** is a group of people gathered together for a particular purpose. *asamblea* ❑ *He waited until complete quiet settled on the assembly.* *Esperó hasta que hubo completo silencio en la asamblea.* **2** N-UNCOUNT The **assembly** of a machine, device, or object is the process of fitting its different parts together. *ensamblaje* ❑ *...final assembly of the cars.* *...el ensamblaje final de los carros.*
→ see **industry**

**as|sem|bly line** (**assembly lines**) N-COUNT An **assembly line** is an arrangement of workers and machines in a factory, where each worker deals with only one part of a product. The product passes from one worker to another until it is finished. *línea de ensamblaje/montaje/armado*

**as|sert** /əsɜrt/ (**asserts, asserting, asserted**) **1** V-T If you **assert** a fact or belief, you state it firmly. *afirmar* [FORMAL] ❑ *He asserted that he had a right to go anywhere.* *Afirmó que tenía el derecho de ir a donde fuera.* ❑ *He asserted his innocence.* *Afirmó que era inocente.* • **as|ser|tion** /əsɜrʃᵊn/ N-VAR (**assertions**) *afirmación* ❑ *There is nothing to support these assertions.* *No hay nada que respalde estas afirmaciones.* **2** V-T If you **assert yourself** or **assert** your authority, you speak and act in a forceful way. *hacer(se) valer, imponerse, infundir respeto* ❑ *He's speaking up and asserting himself.* *Está hablando con firmeza e imponiéndose.* • **as|ser|tion** N-UNCOUNT *afirmación* ❑ *The decision is an assertion of his authority.* *La decisión es una afirmación de su autoridad.*

**as|ser|tive** /əsɜrtɪv/ ADJ Someone who is **assertive** states their needs and opinions clearly, so that people take notice. *asertivo, confiado, agresivo* ❑ *I learned to be more assertive.* *Aprendí a ser más agresivo* • **as|ser|tive|ness** N-UNCOUNT *asertividad* ❑ *...assertiveness training.* *...capacitación en asertividad.*

**as|sess** /əsɛs/ (**assesses, assessing, assessed**) V-T When you **assess** a person, thing, or situation, you consider them in order to make a judgment about them. *evaluar* ❑ *I looked around and assessed the situation.* *Miré alrededor y evalué la situación.* ❑ *The doctor is assessing whether she is well enough to travel.* *El doctor está evaluando si ella está en condiciones de viajar.* • **as|sess|ment** N-VAR (**assessments**) *evaluación* ❑ *...the assessment of senior managers.* *...la evaluación de los gerentes superiores.*

**as|set** /æsɛt/ (**assets**) **1** N-COUNT An **asset** is something or someone that is considered useful or helps a person or organization to be successful. *bien* ❑ *He is a great asset to the company.* *Es un empleado muy valioso para la compañía.* **2** N-PLURAL The **assets** of a company or a person are all the things that they own. *activos* [BUSINESS] ❑ *In 1989 the group had assets of $3.5 billion.* *En 1989 el grupo tenía activos por 3,500 millones de dólares.*

**as|sign** /əsaɪn/ (**assigns, assigning, assigned**) **1** V-T If you **assign** a piece of work **to** someone, you give them the work to do. *asignar* ❑ *I assign a topic to the children for them to write about.* *Les asigno un tema a los niños para que escriban sobre él.* ❑ *The teacher will assign them homework.* *El profesor les asignará su tarea.* **2** V-T If someone **is assigned to** a particular place, group, or person, they are sent to work there. *asignar a* ❑ *He was assigned to head office.* *Se le asignó a la oficina principal.* ❑ *Did you choose Russia or were you assigned there?* *¿Usted escogió Rusia o ahí le asignaron?*

**as|sign|ment** /əsaɪnmənt/ (**assignments**) N-COUNT An **assignment** is a task or piece of work that you are given to do, especially as part of your job or studies. *tarea, trabajo* ❑ *...written assignments and practical tests.* *...trabajos escritos y pruebas prácticas.*

| **Thesaurus** | *assignment* | Ver también: |
|---|---|---|
| N. | chore, duty, job, task | |

**as|simi|late** /əsɪmɪleɪt/ (**assimilates, assimilating, assimilated**) **1** V-T/V-I When people

A

such as immigrants **assimilate into** a community or when that community **assimilates** them, they become an accepted part of it. *integrar(se)* ❑ *School should help assimilate immigrants. La escuela debería ayudar a integrar a los inmigrantes.* ● **as|simi|la|tion** /əsɪmɪleɪʃᵊn/ N-UNCOUNT *integración* ❑ *...the assimilation of minority groups. ...la integración de los grupos minoritarios.* **2** V-T If you **assimilate** new ideas, customs, or techniques, you learn them or adopt them. *asimilar, adoptar* ❑ *You need to relax and assimilate the changes in your life. Necesitas tranquilizarte y asimilar los cambios en tu vida.* ● **as|simi|la|tion** N-UNCOUNT *asimilación* ❑ *...assimilation of knowledge. ...la asimilación de conocimiento.*

→ see **culture**

**as|sist** /əsɪst/ (**assists, assisting, assisted**) V-T/V-I If someone or something **assists** you, they help you. *ayudar, asistir* ❑ *The family decided to assist me with my work. La familia decidió ayudarme con mi trabajo.* ❑ *Please do all you can to assist us in this work. Por favor, haz todo lo posible por ayudarnos con este trabajo.* ❑ *They assisted with serving meals. Ayudaban sirviendo comidas.*

**as|sis|tance** /əsɪstəns/ **1** N-UNCOUNT If you give someone **assistance,** you help them. *ayuda, asistencia* ❑ *We greatly welcome any assistance. Con gusto aceptamos cualquier ayuda.* **2** PHRASE Someone or something that **is of assistance** to you is helpful or useful to you. *ser de ayuda, ser útil* ❑ *Can I be of any assistance? ¿Puedo ayudarte en algo?*

**Word Partnership** Usar *assistance* con:

| | |
|---|---|
| ADJ. | **emergency** assistance, **financial** assistance, **medical** assistance, **technical** assistance **1** |
| V. | **need/require** assistance, **provide** assistance **1** |

**as|sis|tant** /əsɪstənt/ (**assistants**) **1** ADJ **Assistant** is used in front of titles or jobs to indicate a slightly lower rank. For example, an assistant director is one rank lower than a director in an organization. *asistente* ❑ *...the assistant secretary of defense. ...el subsecretario de defensa.* **2** N-COUNT Someone's **assistant** is a person who helps them in their work. *asistente* ❑ *Kalan called his assistant, Hashim, to take over while he went out. Kalan llamó a su asistente, Hashim, para que se hiciera cargo mientras él no estuviera.* **3** N-COUNT An **assistant** is a person who works in a store selling things to customers. *dependiente* ❑ *The assistant took the book and checked the price. El dependiente tomó el libro y revisó el precio.*

**as|sis|tant pro|fes|sor** (**assistant professors**) N-COUNT; N-TITLE An **assistant professor** is a college teacher who ranks above an instructor but below an associate professor. *profesor asistente o profesora asistente* ❑ *...an assistant professor of mathematics. ...un profesor asistente de matemáticas.* ❑ *...Assistant Professor Rob Nideffer. ...el profesor asistente Rob Nideffer.*

**as|sis|ted liv|ing** N-UNCOUNT **Assisted living** is a type of housing specially designed for people who need help in their everyday lives, but who do not need specialist nursing care. In **assisted living facilities**, residents live in independent rooms or apartments, but receive help with day-to-day activities, for example bathing, dressing, preparing meals, and taking their medicines. *hogar de convalecencia* ❑ *One million elderly Americans live in assisted living facilities. Un millón de ancianos estadounidenses viven en hogares de convalecencia.* ❑ *Now she's in assisted living, and her niece and nephew are helping with her affairs. Ahora vive en un hogar de convalecencia y sus sobrinos la ayudan con sus asuntos.*

**Word Link** ***soci ≈ companion : associate, social, sociology***

**as|so|ci|ate** (**associates, associating, associated**)

The verb is pronounced /əsoʊʃieɪt, -sieɪt/. The noun and adjective are pronounced /əsoʊʃiɪt, -siɪt/.

**1** V-T If you **associate** someone or something **with** another thing, the two are connected in your mind. *asociar con* ❑ *Some people associate thinness with happiness. Algunas personas asocian la delgadez con la felicidad.* **2** V-T If you **are associated with** a particular organization, cause, or point of view, or if you **associate yourself with** it, you support it publicly. *asociar(se) con* ❑ *We're associated with the U.S. Airways group. Estamos asociados con el grupo US Airways.* **3** V-I If you say that someone **is associating with** another person or group of people, you mean they are spending a lot of time in the company of people you do not approve of. *juntarse con* ❑ *I think she's associating with a bad crowd. Creo que anda en malas compañías.* **4** N-COUNT Your **associates** are the people you are closely connected with, especially at work. *colega* ❑ *...business associates. ...asociados de negocios.*

**as|so|ci|ate de|gree** (**associate degrees**) N-COUNT An **associate degree** is a college degree that is awarded to a student who has completed a two-year course of study. *diploma técnico de dos años* ❑ *She has an associate degree in food management. Tiene un diplomado en administración de alimentos.*

**as|so|ci|ate pro|fes|sor** (**associate professors**) N-COUNT; N-TITLE An **associate professor** is a college teacher who ranks above an assistant professor but below a professor. *profesor adjunto o profesora adjunta* ❑ *...an associate professor of psychiatry. ...un profesor adjunto de psiquiatría.* ❑ *...Associate Professor Saifi Karibash. ...el Profesor Adjunto Saifi Karibash.*

**as|so|cia|tion** /əsoʊʃieɪʃᵊn, -sieɪ-/ (**associations**) **1** N-COUNT An **association** is an official group of people who have the same job, aim, or interest. *asociación* ❑ *...the National Basketball Association. ...la Asociación Nacional de Basquetbol.* **2** N-COUNT Your **association with** a person or a thing such as an organization is the connection that you have with them. *relación con* ❑ *...the company's association with retailer J.C. Penney. ...la relación de la compañía con el proveedor J.C. Penney.* **3** N-COUNT If something has particular **associations** for you, it is connected in your mind with a particular memory, idea, or feeling. *asociación* ❑ *He has lots of things which have happy associations for him. Tiene muchas cosas que le traen recuerdos felices.* **4** PHRASE If you do something **in association with** someone else, you do it together.

a

*junto con, en asociación con* ❑ *The book was published in association with the Walden Woods Project. Se publicó el libro en coedición con el Walden Woods Project.*

**as|sort|ment** /əsɔ̲rtmənt/ (**assortments**) N-COUNT An **assortment** is a group of similar things that are of different sizes or colors or have different qualities. *colección* ❑ *...an assortment of books. ...una colección de libros.*

**Word Link** *sume ≈ taking : assume, consume, presume*

**as|sume** /əsu̲m/ (**assumes, assuming, assumed**) **1** V-T If you **assume that** something is true, you suppose that it is true, sometimes wrongly. *suponer* ❑ *I assume the eggs will be fresh. Supongo que los huevos estarán frescos.* ❑ *Men are assumed to be stronger than women. Se supone que los hombres son más fuertes que las mujeres.* **2** V-T If someone **assumes** power or responsibility, they take power or responsibility. *asumir* ❑ *Mr. Cross will assume the role of CEO. El señor Cross asumirá el cargo de director general.* **3** V-T If you **assume** a particular expression or way of behaving, you start to look or behave in this way. *adoptar* ❑ *He assumed an air of calm. Adoptó una apariencia de tranquilidad.*

**Word Partnership** Usar *assume* con:

V. **let's** assume ***that***, **tend to** assume **1**
ADV. assume **so** **1**
**automatically** assume **1** **2**
N. assume **the worst** **1**
assume **control/power**, assume **responsibility**, assume **a role** **2**

**as|sum|ing** /əsu̲mɪŋ/ CONJ You use **assuming** or **assuming that** when you are considering a possible situation or event, so that you can think about the consequences. *tomar en cuenta* ❑ *"Assuming you're right," he said, "there's not much I can do about it, is there?" —Suponiendo que tengas razón —le dijo—, no puedo hacer gran cosa al respecto, ¿verdad?*

**Word Link** *sumpt ≈ taking : assumption, consumption, resumption*

**as|sump|tion** /əsʌ̲mpʃᵊn/ (**assumptions**) N-COUNT If you make an **assumption that** something is true or will happen, you suppose that it is true or will happen, often wrongly. *suposición* ❑ *You are making an assumption that I agree with you. Estás suponiendo que estoy de acuerdo contigo.*

**as|sur|ance** /əʃʊ̲ərəns/ (**assurances**) **1** N-VAR If you give someone an **assurance that** something is true or will happen, you say that it is definitely true or will definitely happen, in order to make them feel less worried. *garantía* ❑ *I gave him an assurance that it wouldn't happen again. Le aseguré que no volvería a suceder.* **2** N-UNCOUNT If you do something **with assurance,** you do it with a feeling of confidence and certainty. *con certeza* ❑ *Masur led the orchestra with assurance. Masur dirigió la orquesta con seguridad.*

**as|sure** /əʃʊ̲ər/ (**assures, assuring, assured**) **1** V-T If you **assure** someone **that** something is true or will happen, you tell them that it is definitely true or will definitely happen, often in order to make them less worried. *asegurar* ❑ *He assured me that there was nothing wrong. Me aseguró que todo estaba bien.* ❑ *"Are you sure it's safe?" she asked anxiously. "It couldn't be safer," Max assured her. —¿Estás seguro de que no hay peligro? —preguntó con inquietud. —No tienes nada de qué preocuparte —le aseguró Max.* **2** → see also **assured** **3** V-T To **assure** someone **of** something means to make certain that they will get it. *asegurar* ❑ *His performance yesterday assured him of a medal. Su actuación de ayer le aseguró una medalla.*

**as|sured** /əʃʊ̲ərd/ ADJ Someone who is **assured** is very confident and relaxed. *confiado* ❑ *He gave an assured performance. Mostró un gran aplomo en su actuación.*

**Word Link** *aster, astro ≈ star : asterisk, astronaut, astronomy*

**as|ter|isk** /æ̲stərɪsk/ (**asterisks**) N-COUNT An **asterisk** is the sign. *asterisco*

**as|ter|oid** /æ̲stərɔɪd/ (**asteroids**) N-COUNT An **asteroid** is one of the very small planets that move around the sun between Mars and Jupiter. *asteroide*

**as|ter|oid belt** (**asteroid belts**) N-COUNT *The* **asteroid belt** is the region of the solar system between Mars and Jupiter where most asteroids occur. *cinturón de asteroides*

**as|theno|sphere** /æsθɛ̲nəsfɪər/ N-SING *The* **asthenosphere** is the region of the Earth which lies between approximately 70 and 120 miles below the surface. *astenósfera, astenosfera* [TECHNICAL]

**asth|ma** /æ̲zmə/ N-UNCOUNT **Asthma** is a lung condition that causes difficulty in breathing. *asma*

**astig|ma|tism** /əstɪ̲gmətɪzəm/ N-UNCOUNT If someone has **astigmatism,** the front of their eye has a slightly irregular shape, so they cannot see properly. *astigmatismo*
→ see **eye**

**aston|ish** /əstɒ̲nɪʃ/ (**astonishes, astonishing, astonished**) V-T If something or someone **astonishes** you, they surprise you very much. *asombrar* ❑ *My news will astonish you. Las nuevas que traigo te van a asombrar.* • **aston|ished** ADJ *asombrado, estupefacto, helado* ❑ *They were astonished to find the driver was a six-year-old boy. Se quedaron helados al saber que el conductor era un niño de seis años.*

**aston|ish|ing** /əstɒ̲nɪʃɪŋ/ ADJ Something that is **astonishing** is very surprising. *sorprendente* ❑ *...an astonishing display of strength. ...una sorprendente muestra de fortaleza.* • **aston|ish|ing|ly** ADV *sorprendentemente, asombrosamente, increíblemente* ❑ *Andrea was an astonishingly beautiful young woman. Andrea era una joven asombrosamente bella.*

**as|trol|ogy** /əstrɒ̲lədʒi/ N-UNCOUNT **Astrology** is the study of the movements of the planets, sun, moon, and stars in the belief that these movements can have an influence on people's lives. *astrología* • **as|trolo|ger** N-COUNT (**astrologers**) *astrólogo o astróloga* ❑ *He went to see an astrologer. Fue a ver a un astrólogo.*

A

**Word Link** *aster, astro ≈ star : asterisk, astronaut, astronomy*

astronaut

**as|tro|naut** /æstrənɔt/ (**astronauts**) N-COUNT An **astronaut** is a person who is trained for traveling in a spacecraft. *astronauta*

**as|tro|nomi|cal unit** (**astronomical units**) N-COUNT An **astronomical unit** is a unit of distance used in astronomy that is equal to the average distance between the Earth and the sun. The abbreviation *AU* is also used. *unidad astronómica*

**as|trono|my** /əstrɒnəmi/ N-UNCOUNT **Astronomy** is the scientific study of the stars, planets, and other natural objects in space. *astronomía* • **as|trono|mer** N-COUNT (**astronomers**) *astrónomo o astrónoma* ❑ *...an amateur astronomer. ...un astrónomo aficionado.*
→ see Word Web: **astronomer**
→ see **galaxy, star, telescope**

**A-student** (**A-students**) also **A student** N-COUNT An **A-student** is a student who regularly receives the highest grades for his or her work. *estudiante de puros dieces, sobresaliente* ❑ *...good, hard-working A students. ...estudiantes buenos, trabajadores y de puros dieces.*

**asy|lum** /əsaɪləm/ (**asylums**) N-UNCOUNT If a government gives a person from another country **asylum**, they allow them to stay, usually because they are unable to return home safely for political reasons. *asilo* ❑ *He applied for asylum in 1987. Solicitó asilo en 1987.*

**asym|met|ri|cal** /eɪsɪmɛtrɪkəl/ ADJ Something that is **asymmetrical** has two sides or halves that are different in shape, size, or style. *asimétrico*

**Word Link** *a, an ≈ not, without : anaerobic, anesthetic, asymmetry*

**asym|me|try** /eɪsɪmətri/ (**asymmetries**) N-VAR **Asymmetry** is the appearance that something has when its two sides or halves are different in shape, size, or style. *asimetría*

**as|ymp|tote** /æsɪmtoʊt, -ɪmp-/ (**asymptotes**) N-COUNT An **asymptote** is a straight line to which a curved line approaches closer and closer as one moves along it. *asíntota* [TECHNICAL]

**at** /ət, STRONG æt/

In addition to the uses shown below, **at** is used after some verbs, nouns, and adjectives to introduce extra information. **At** is also used in phrasal verbs such as "get at" and "play at."

**1** PREP You use **at** to say where something happens or is situated. *en* ❑ *He will be at the airport to meet her. Estará en el aeropuerto para recibirla.* ❑ *I didn't like being alone at home. No me gustaba estar solo en casa.* ❑ *They agreed to meet at a restaurant. Quedaron en verse en un restaurante.* **2** PREP You use **at** to say when something happens. *a la, a las/los, al* ❑ *The funeral will be this afternoon at 3:00. El funeral será a las 3 de la tarde.* ❑ *Zachary started playing violin at age 4. Zachary empezó a tocar el violín a los 4 años.* **3** PREP You use **at** to express a rate, frequency, level, or price. *a* ❑ *I drove back down the highway at normal speed. Manejé de regreso por la autopista a velocidad normal.* ❑ *Hair grows at a rate of about 1 centimeter a month. El cabello crece a un promedio mensual de 1 centímetro.* **4** PREP If you look **at** someone or something, you look toward them. If you direct an object or a comment **at** someone, you direct it toward them. *hacia, a* ❑ *He looked at Michael and laughed. Miró a Michael y se rió.* **5** PREP If you are working **at** something, you are dealing with it. If you are aiming **at** something, you are trying to achieve it. *en* ❑ *She has worked hard at her marriage. Se ha esforzado mucho en su matrimonio.* **6** PREP If something is done **at** your invitation or request, it is done as a result of it. *a* ❑ *She closed the window at his request. Cerró la ventana a petición suya.* **7** PREP You use **at** to say that someone or something is in a particular state or condition. *en* ❑ *The two nations are living at peace with each other. Los dos países viven en paz mutua.* **8** PREP You use **at** to say how something is being done. *al* ❑ *We'll pick three winners at random from correct entries. Escogeremos tres ganadores al azar de entre las respuestas correctas.* **9** PREP You use **at** to indicate an activity or task when saying how well someone does it. *en* ❑ *I'm good at my work. Soy bueno en mi trabajo.* **10** PREP You use **at** to indicate what someone is reacting

**Word Web** astronomer

The Italian **astronomer** Galileo Galilei did not invent the telescope. However, he was the first person to use it to study **celestial** bodies. He recorded his findings. What Galileo saw through the telescope supported the theory that the **planet** Earth is not the center of the universe. This theory was written by the Polish astronomer Nicolaus Copernicus in 1530. Copernicus said that all of the planets in the solar system revolve around the **sun**. In 1609, Galileo used a telescope to see the **craters** on Earth's **moon**. He also discovered the four largest **satellites** of the planet Jupiter. These four bodies are called the Galilean moons.

to. *por* ❑ *Elena was annoyed at having to wait so long. Elena estaba molesta por tener que esperar tanto.* **11 at all** → see **all**

**ate** /eɪt/ **Ate** is the past tense of **eat**. *pasado de eat.*

**ath|lete** /æθlit/ (**athletes**) N-COUNT An **athlete** is a person who does any kind of physical sports, exercise, or games, especially in competitions. *atleta* ❑ *Jesse Owens was one of the greatest athletes of the twentieth century. Jesse Owens fue uno de los mejores atletas del siglo veinte.*

**ath|let|ic** /æθlɛtɪk/ **1** ADJ **Athletic** means relating to athletes and athletics. *atlético* ❑ *He comes from an athletic family. Viene de una familia de atletas.* **2** ADJ An **athletic** person is fit, and able to perform energetic movements easily. *atlético* ❑ *Sandra is an athletic 36-year-old. Sandra es una persona atlética de 36 años.*

**ath|let|ics** /æθlɛtɪks/ N-UNCOUNT **Athletics** refers to any kind of physical sports, exercise, or games. *deportes, atletismo* ❑ *...college athletics. ...deportes universitarios.*

**at|las** /ætləs/ (**atlases**) N-COUNT An **atlas** is a book of maps. *atlas*

**ATM** /eɪ ti: ɛm/ (**ATMs**) N-COUNT An **ATM** is a machine built into the wall of a bank or other building, which allows people to take out money from their bank account by using a special card. **ATM** is an abbreviation for "automated teller machine." *cajero automático*

**Word Link** *sphere ≈ ball : atmosphere, blogosphere, hemisphere*

**at|mos|phere** /ætməsfɪər/ (**atmospheres**) **1** N-COUNT A planet's **atmosphere** is the layer of air or other gases around it. *atmósfera* ❑ *The shuttle Columbia will re-enter Earth's atmosphere tomorrow morning. El transbordador espacial Columbia ingresará a la atmósfera terrestre mañana temprano.* • **at|mos|pher|ic** /ætməsfɛrɪk/ ADJ *atmosférico* ❑ *...atmospheric gases. ...gases atmosféricos.* **2** N-COUNT The **atmosphere** of a place is the air that you breathe there. *atmósfera* ❑ *Gases from the power plant rise into the atmosphere. Los gases de la central eléctrica suben a la atmósfera.* **3** N-SING The **atmosphere** of a place is the general impression that you get of it. *atmósfera, ambiente* ❑ *The rooms are warm and the atmosphere is welcoming. Los cuartos tienen buena temperatura y el ambiente es agradable.* → see **air, biosphere, core, earth, greenhouse effect, moon, ozone, water**

**at|mos|pher|ic per|spec|tive** (**atmospheric perspectives**) N-VAR **Atmospheric perspective** means the same as **aerial perspective**. *perspectiva aérea*

**atmos|pher|ic pres|sure** (**atmospheric pressures**) N-VAR **Atmospheric pressure** is the amount of pressure that is produced by the weight of the Earth's atmosphere. *presión atmosférica*

**atom** /ætəm/ (**atoms**) N-COUNT An **atom** is the smallest amount of a substance that can take part in a chemical reaction. *átomo* → see **element**

**atom|ic** /ətɒmɪk/ ADJ **Atomic** means relating atoms or to power that is produced by splitting atoms. *atómico* ❑ *...atomic energy. ...energía atómica* ❑ *...the atomic number of an element. ...el número atómico de un elemento.*

**atom|ic mass** (**atomic masses**) N-VAR The **atomic mass** of a chemical element is the weight of one atom of that element, usually expressed in atomic mass units. *masa atómica* [TECHNICAL] → see **periodic table**

**atom|ic mass unit** (**atomic mass units**) N-COUNT An **atomic mass unit** is a unit that is used to measure the atomic mass of chemical elements. The abbreviation *amu* is also used. *unidad de masa atómica* [TECHNICAL]

**atom|ic num|ber** (**atomic numbers**) N-COUNT The **atomic number** of a chemical element is the number of protons in the nucleus of one atom of the element. *número atómico* [TECHNICAL]

**aton|al** /eɪtoʊnᵊl/ ADJ **Atonal** music is music that is not written or played in any key or system of scales. *atonal*

**ATP** /eɪ ti pi/ N-UNCOUNT **ATP** is a molecule that is found in all plant and animals cells and provides the cells with their main source of energy. **ATP** is an abbreviation for "adenosine triphosphate." *trifosfato de adenosina, ATP, adenosín trifosfato*

**atrium** /eɪtriəm/ (**atria**) N-COUNT The *left* **atrium** and the *right* **atrium** are the two upper chambers of the heart. *aurícula*

**atroc|ity** /ətrɒsɪti/ (**atrocities**) N-VAR An **atrocity** is a very cruel, shocking action. *atrocidad, monstruosidad* ❑ *The people who committed this atrocity should be punished. Quienes cometieron esa atrocidad deben ser castigados.*

**at|tach** /ətætʃ/ (**attaches, attaching, attached**) **1** V-T If you **attach** something **to** an object, you join it or fasten it to the object. *pegar, atar, adjuntar* ❑ *We attach labels to things before we store them. Pegamos etiquetas a las cosas antes de almacenarlas.* ❑ *Please use the attached form. Utilice la forma anexa.* **2** V-T In computing, if you **attach** a file **to** a message that you send to someone, you send it with the message but separate from it. *anexar, adjuntar* ❑ *It is possible to attach program files to e-mail. Se pueden anexar archivos de programa a los correos electrónicos.* **3** → see also **attached** **4 no strings attached** → see **string**

**at|tached** /ətætʃt/ ADJ If you are **attached to** someone or something, you like them very much. *apegado* ❑ *She is very attached to her family and friends. Es muy apegada a su familia y a sus amigos.*

**at|tach|ment** /ətætʃmənt/ (**attachments**) **1** N-VAR If you have an **attachment to** someone or something, you are fond of them. *cariño, apego, lazo, vínculo, relación* ❑ *Mother and child form a close attachment. El vínculo madre-hijo es muy estrecho.* **2** N-COUNT An **attachment** is a device that can be fixed onto a machine in order to enable it to do different jobs. *accesorio* ❑ *Some cleaners come with an attachment for brushing. Algunas aspiradoras vienen con un aditamento para tallar.* **3** N-COUNT In computing, an **attachment** is a file which is attached separately to a message that you send to someone. *anexo* ❑ *When you send an e-mail you can also send a file as an attachment. Cuando se manda un correo electrónico, también se puede enviar un archivo como anexo.*

A

**at|tack** /ətæ̱k/ (**attacks, attacking, attacked**) **1** V-T/V-I To **attack** a person or place means to try to hurt or damage them using physical violence. *atacar, agredir, asaltar* ❑ *I thought he was going to attack me. Pensé que me iba a agredir.* ❑ *He was in the yard when the dog attacked. Estaba en el patio cuando atacó el perro.* ● **Attack** is also a noun. *ataque, agresión, asalto* ❑ *...an attack on a police officer. ...un ataque contra un oficial de policía.* ● **at|tack|er** N-COUNT (**attackers**) *atacante* ❑ *She struggled with her attacker. Luchó con su agresor.* **2** V-T If you **attack** a person, belief, idea, or act, you criticize them strongly. *atacar, criticar* ❑ *He attacked bosses for giving themselves big pay raises. Criticó a los jefes por darse incrementos salariales altos.* ● **Attack** is also a noun. *ataque, crítica* ❑ *...his response to attacks on his work. ...su reacción ante las críticas a su trabajo.* **3** V-T If you **attack** a job or a problem, you start to deal with it in an energetic way. *atacar, abordar* ❑ *Parents shouldn't attack the problem on their own. Los padres no deben abordar el problema ellos solos.* **4** V-T/V-I In games such as soccer, when one team **attacks** the opponent's goal, they try to score a goal. *atacar* ❑ *Now the U.S. is attacking the other side's goal. Ahora los Estados Unidos están atacando la portería contraria.* ❑ *They attacked constantly in the second half. En la segunda mitad no dejaron de atacar.* **5** N-COUNT An **attack of** an illness is a short period in which you suffer badly from it. *ataque* ❑ *...an attack of asthma. ...un ataque de asma.* **6** → see also **counterattack, heart attack**
→ see **war**

**at|tain** /əteɪ̱n/ (**attains, attaining, attained**) V-T If you **attain** something, you gain it or achieve it, often after a lot of effort. *conseguir, alcanzar, lograr* [FORMAL] ❑ *Jim is about to attain his pilot's license. Jim está a punto de conseguir su licencia de piloto.* ● **at|tain|ment** N-UNCOUNT *logro, consecución, realización* ❑ *...the attainment of independence. ...la consecución de la independencia.*

**Word Link** **tempt ≈ trying : attempt, temptation, tempted**

**at|tempt** /ətɛ̱mpt/ (**attempts, attempting, attempted**) **1** V-T If you **attempt to** do something, you try to do it. *intentar, tratar, probar* ❑ *He attempted to enter law school. Trató de ingresar a la escuela de leyes.* ● **at|tempt|ed** ADJ *intentado* ❑ *...a case of attempted murder. ...un caso de intento de asesinato.* **2** N-COUNT If you make an **attempt to** do something, you try to do it, often without success. *intento, prueba, tentativa* ❑ *He was standing in the middle of the street in an attempt to stop the traffic. Se paró en medio de la calle en un intento por parar el tráfico.* **3** N-COUNT An **attempt on** someone's life is an attempt to kill them. *atentado, ataque* ❑ *...an attempt on the life of the president. ...un atentado en contra de la vida del presidente.*

**Thesaurus** *attempt* Ver también:

V. strive, tackle, take on, try **1**
N. effort, try, venture **2**

**Word Partnership** Usar *attempt* con:

V. attempt **to control/find/prevent/solve** **1**
**make an** attempt **2**
N. attempt **suicide** **1**
**assassination** attempt **3**
ADJ. **any** attempt, **desperate** attempt, **failed/successful** attempt **2**

**at|tend** /ətɛ̱nd/ (**attends, attending, attended**) **1** V-T/V-I If you **attend** a meeting or other event, you are present at it. *asistir, ir* ❑ *Thousands of people attended the wedding. Miles de personas asistieron a la boda.* ❑ *I was invited but was unable to attend. A mí me invitaron, pero no pude ir.* ● **at|tend|ance** N-UNCOUNT *asistencia, presencia* ❑ *...his poor attendance at classes. ...su mediocre asistencia a clase.* **2** V-T If you **attend** an institution such as a school, college, or church, you go there regularly. *asistir, ir* ❑ *They attended college together. Estaban juntos en la universidad.* ● **at|tend|ance** N-UNCOUNT *asistencia* ❑ *Attendance at the school is above average. La asistencia a la escuela es superior al promedio.* **3** V-I If you **attend to** something, you deal with it. If you **attend to** someone who is hurt or injured, you care for them. *atender, cuidar* ❑ *The staff will attend to your needs. El personal le atenderá.*

**attendance** /ətɛ̱ndəns/ (**attendances**) N-VAR The **attendance** at an event is the number of people who are present at it. *asistencia, concurrencia* ❑ *People had a good time, and attendance was high. La gente se divirtió, y hubo muchos espectadores.*

**at|tend|ant** /ətɛ̱ndənt/ (**attendants**) **1** N-COUNT An **attendant** is someone whose job is to serve or help people in a place such as a gas station or a parking lot. *asistente o asistenta, encargado o encargada* ❑ *Tony Williams was working as a parking lot attendant in Los Angeles. Tony Williams estaba como encargado de un estacionamiento de Los Ángeles.* **2** N-COUNT The **attendants** at a wedding are people such as the bridesmaids and the ushers, who accompany or help the bride and groom. *padrino o madrina* ❑ *The bride will choose the dresses her attendants will wear. La novia elegirá los vestidos de sus damas de honor.*

**at|tend|ee** /ətɛndi̱/ (**attendees**) N-COUNT The **attendees** at something such as a meeting or a conference are the people who are attending it. *participante, asistente* ❑ *Only half the attendees could fit into the large hall at any one time. Sólo la mitad de los asistentes podía estar al mismo tiempo en la gran sala.*

**at|ten|tion** /ətɛ̱nʃᵊn/ **1** N-UNCOUNT If you give someone or something your **attention,** you look at them, listen to them, or think about them carefully. *atención* ❑ *Can I have your attention? Su atención, por favor...* **2** N-UNCOUNT If someone or something is getting **attention,** they are being dealt with or cared for. *atención* ❑ *Each year more than two million people need medical attention. Cada año, más de dos millones de personas necesitan atención médica.* **3** PHRASE If you **pay attention to** someone, you watch them, listen to them, or take notice of them. If you **pay no attention to** someone, you behave as if you are not aware of them or as if they are not important. *prestar* *atención* ❑ *Everyone is paying attention. Todos están poniendo atención.*

**Word Partnership** Usar *attention* con:

| | |
|---|---|
| PREP. | attention **to detail** 1 |
| ADJ. | **careful/close/undivided** attention 1<br>**special** attention 1 2<br>**unwanted** attention 2 |
| V. | **attract** attention, **call/direct** ***someone's*** attention, **catch** ***someone's*** attention, **draw** attention, **focus** attention, **turn** attention **to** ***someone/something*** 1<br>**pay** attention 3 |
| N. | **center of** attention 2 |

**at|tic** /ætɪk/ (**attics**) N-COUNT An **attic** is a room at the top of a house just below the roof. *ático, desván*

→ see **house**

**at|ti|tude** /ætɪtud/ (**attitudes**) N-VAR Your **attitude to** something is the way that you think and feel about it. *actitud* ❑ *We needed to change our attitude. Necesitábamos cambiar de actitud.* ❑ *...negative attitudes to work. ...actitud negativa en el trabajo.*

**Word Partnership** Usar *attitude* con:

| | |
|---|---|
| PREP. | attitude **about/toward** |
| ADJ. | **bad** attitude, **negative/positive** attitude, **new** attitude, **progressive** attitude |
| V. | **change your** attitude |

**at|tor|ney** /ətɜrni/ (**attorneys**) N-COUNT In the United States, an **attorney** or **attorney-at-law** is a lawyer. *abogado o abogada, procurador o procuradora, agente legal* ❑ *...a prosecuting attorney. ...un fiscal.* ❑ *At the hearing, her attorney did not enter a plea. En la audiencia, su abogado no presentó ningún alegato.*

→ see **trial**

**at|tract** /ətrækt/ (**attracts, attracting, attracted**) 1 V-T If something **attracts** people or animals, it has features that cause them to come to it. *atraer* ❑ *The museum is attracting many visitors. El museo atrae a muchos visitantes.* 2 V-T If someone or something **attracts** you, they have particular qualities which cause you to like or admire them. *atraer* ❑ *May's boldness surprised and attracted him. El descaro de May lo sorprendía y atraía.* • **at|tract|ed** ADJ *atraído* ❑ *I wasn't very attracted to him. No me sentía muy atraída por él.* 3 V-T If something **attracts** support, publicity, or money, it receives it. *atraer, captar* ❑ *We're hoping to attract money into women's golf. Esperamos captar fondos para el golf femenil.*

**at|trac|tion** /ətrækʃᵊn/ (**attractions**) 1 N-UNCOUNT **Attraction** is a feeling of liking someone. *atracción* ❑ *His attraction to her was growing. La atracción que ejercía en él estaba creciendo.* 2 N-COUNT An **attraction** is a feature that makes something interesting or desirable. *atractivo* ❑ *...the attractions of living on the waterfront. ...el atractivo de vivir a orillas del lago.* 3 N-COUNT An **attraction** is something that people can go to for interest or enjoyment, for example, a famous building. *atracción* ❑ *Disney World is an important tourist attraction. Disney World es una atracción turística importante.* 4 N-UNCOUNT **Attraction** is the force that exists between two objects when they are pulled toward one another, for example by magnetism or gravity. *atracción*

**at|trac|tive** /ətræktɪv/ 1 ADJ An **attractive** person or thing is pleasant to look at. *atractivo, atrayente, interesante* ❑ *She's a very attractive woman. Es una mujer muy atractiva* ❑ *The apartment was small but attractive. El departamento era pequeño, pero tenía su encanto.* • **at|trac|tive|ness** N-UNCOUNT *atractivo* ❑ *...the attractiveness of the country. ...el atractivo del país.* 2 ADJ You can describe something as **attractive** when it seems worth having or doing. *atractivo, interesante* ❑ *Younger players are more attractive to major-league teams. Los jugadores jóvenes interesan más a los equipos de las ligas mayores.*

**Thesaurus** *attractive* Ver también:

ADJ. appealing, charming, good-looking, pleasant; (*ant.*) repulsive, ugly, unattractive 1

**Word Link** ***tribute*** ≈ ***giving*** : ***attribute, contribute, distribute***

**at|trib|ute** (**attributes, attributing, attributed**)

> The verb is pronounced /ətrɪbyut/. The noun is pronounced /ætrɪbyut/.

1 V-T If you **attribute** something **to** a person, thing, or event, you think that it was caused by that event or situation. *atribuir, asignar, imputar* ❑ *I attributed my success to luck. Le atribuí mi éxito a la suerte.* 2 V-T If a piece of writing, a work of art, or a remark **is attributed to** someone, people say that they wrote it, created it, or said it. *atribuir* ❑ *For a long time the painting was attributed to Rembrandt. Por mucho tiempo, la pintura se atribuyó a Rembrandt.* 3 N-COUNT An **attribute** is a quality or feature that someone or something has. *atributo, cualidad, característica* ❑ *He had most of the attributes of a really great reporter. Tenía casi todas las características de un gran reportero.*

**AU** /eɪ yu/ (**AU**) **AU** is an abbreviation for **astronomical unit.** *unidad astronómica, AU*

**auc|tion** /ɔkʃᵊn/ (**auctions, auctioning, auctioned**) 1 N-VAR An **auction** is a public sale where items are sold to the person who offers the highest price. *subasta, remate* ❑ *The painting sold for $400,000 at auction. La pintura se vendió en 400,000 dólares en una subasta.* 2 V-T If something **is auctioned,** it is sold in an auction. *subastar, rematar* ❑ *Eight drawings by French artist Jean Cocteau will be auctioned next week. La próxima semana se subastarán ocho dibujos de Jean Cocteau, artista francés.*

▸ **auction off** PHR-VERB If you **auction off** something, you sell it to the person who offers most for it, often at an auction. *subastar, rematar* ❑ *They're coming to auction off my farm. Van a venir a rematar mi granja.*

**auc|tion|eer** /ɔkʃənɪər/ (**auctioneers**) N-COUNT An **auctioneer** is a person in charge of an auction. *subastador o subastadora*

A

**Word Link** *audi ≈ hearing : audible, audience, audition*

**Word Link** *ible ≈ able to be : audible, flexible, possible*

**audible** /ɔdɪbᵊl/ ADJ A sound that is **audible** is loud enough to be heard. *audible, perceptible* ❑ *Her voice was barely audible. Su voz era apenas audible.*
• **audibly** /ɔdɪbli/ ADV *de modo audible* ❑ *Frank sighed audibly. Frank suspiró de forma audible.*

**audi|ence** /ɔdiəns/ (**audiences**) **1** N-COUNT The **audience** of a play, concert, movie, or television program is all the people who are watching or listening to it. *audiencia, público, auditorio* ❑ *...a TV audience of 35 million. ...una audiencia televisiva de 35 millones de personas.*
**2** N-COUNT The **audience** of a writer or artist is the people who read their books or look at their work. *auditorio, público* ❑ *His books reached a wide audience during his lifetime. Mientras vivió, sus libros llegaron a un amplio público.*
→ see **concert**

**Word Partnership** Usar *audience* con:

PREP. **before/in front of an** audience **1**
N. audience **participation**, **studio** audience, **television** audience **1**
ADJ. **captive** audience, **live** audience **1** **general** audience, **large** audience, **target** audience, **wide** audience **1** **2**
V. **reach an** audience **2**

**audio** /ɔdioʊ/ ADJ **Audio** equipment is used for recording and reproducing sound. *audio, sonido* ❑ *...audio and video files. ...archivos de sonido e imagen.*

**audit** /ɔdɪt/ (**audits, auditing, audited**) V-T When an accountant **audits** an organization's accounts, he or she examines the financial records officially in order to make sure that they are correct. *auditar, hacer una auditoría* ❑ *Each year they audit our financial records. Cada año auditan nuestros registros financieros.* • **Audit** is also a noun. *auditoría* ❑ *The bank learned of the problem when it carried out an internal audit. El banco se enteró del problema con la auditoría interna.* • **audi|tor** N-COUNT (**auditors**) *auditor o auditora* ❑ *...the group's internal auditors. ...los auditores internos del grupo.*

**audi|tion** /ɔdɪʃᵊn/ (**auditions, auditioning, auditioned**) **1** N-COUNT An **audition** is a short performance given by an actor, dancer, or musician so that a director or conductor can decide if they are good enough to be in a play, film, or orchestra. *audición, prueba* ❑ *...an audition for a Broadway musical. ...una audición para una obra musical de Broadway.* **2** V-T/V-I If you **audition** or if someone **auditions** you, you do an audition. *audicionar, hacer una audición* ❑ *They're auditioning new members for the cast of "Miss Saigon" today. Hoy hacen audiciones para nuevos miembros del elenco de "Miss Saigón".*
→ see **theater**

**audi|to|rium** /ɔdɪtɔriəm/ (**auditoriums** or **auditoria** /ɔdɪtɔriə/) **1** N-COUNT An **auditorium** is the part of a theater or concert hall where the audience sits. *auditorio* ❑ *...a 250-seat auditorium. ...un auditorio para 250 personas.* **2** N-COUNT An **auditorium** is a large room, hall, or building that is used for events such as meetings and concerts. *auditorio* ❑ *...a high school auditorium. ...un auditorio de secundaria.*

**aug|ment|ed in|ter|val** (**augmented intervals**) N-COUNT In music, an **augmented interval** is an interval that is increased by half a step or half a tone. *intervalo aumentado*

**August** /ɔgəst/ (**Augusts**) N-VAR **August** is the eighth month of the year in the Western calendar. *agosto* ❑ *The movie opened in August. La película se estrenó en agosto.*

**aunt** /ænt, ɑnt/ (**aunts**) N-COUNT; N-TITLE Your **aunt** is the sister of your mother or father, or the wife of your uncle. *tía* ❑ *She wrote to her aunt in Alabama. Le escribió a su tía de Alabama.*
→ see **family**

**Usage** **aunt** and **ant**

Be sure not to confuse *aunt* and *ant*, which many English speakers pronounce the same way. Your *aunt* is a sister of your parent; an *ant* is an insect: *Linh's aunt has an unusual fear—she's terrified of stepping on ants.*

**Aus|tra|lo|pithe|cine** also **australopithecine** /ɔstreɪloʊpɪθəsin, -saɪn, ɔstrə-/ (**Australopithecines**) N-COUNT **Austalopithecines** were a species of primates, resembling early human beings, that lived over 3 million years ago. *australopithecine*
→ see **evolution**

**authen|tic** /ɔθɛntɪk/ ADJ An **authentic** person, object, or emotion is genuine. *auténtico, genuino, verosímil, realista, legítimo, fidedigno* ❑ *...authentic Italian food. ...auténtica comida italiana.*
• **au|then|tic|ity** /ɔθɛntɪsɪti/ N-UNCOUNT *autenticidad, realismo, legitimidad, verosimilitud* ❑ *Some people doubt the statue's authenticity. Algunas personas dudan de la autenticidad de la estatua.*

**Word Link** *er, or ≈ one who does, that which does : author, painter, writer*

**author** /ɔθər/ (**authors**) **1** N-COUNT The **author** of a piece of writing is the person who wrote it. *autor o autora, creador o creadora* ❑ *...Jill Phillips, author of the book "Give Your Child Music." ...Jill Phillips, autora del libro "Dale música a tu hijo".* **2** N-COUNT An **author** is a person whose job is writing books. *autor o autora, escritor o escritora* ❑ *Haruki Murakami is Japan's best-selling author. Haruki Murakami es el autor más leído de Japón.*

**authori|ta|tive** /əθɔrɪteɪtɪv/ **1** ADJ Someone or something that is **authoritative** gives an impression of power and importance and is likely to be obeyed. *autoritario* ❑ *He has a deep, authoritative voice. Su voz es profunda, autoritaria.* **2** ADJ Someone or something that is **authoritative** has a lot of knowledge of a particular subject. *autorizado, fidedigno* ❑ *The first authoritative study of the disease. El primer estudio fidedigno sobre la enfermedad.*

**author|ity** /əθɔrɪti/ (**authorities**) **1** N-PLURAL **The authorities** are the people who have the power to make decisions and to make sure that laws are obeyed. *autoridad* ❑ *The authorities stopped more than 100 cars Friday. Las autoridades detuvieron más de 100 autos el viernes.* **2** N-COUNT An **authority**

is an official organization or government department that has the power to make decisions. *autoridad* ❑ *...the Philadelphia Parking Authority. ...el Departamento de Estacionamientos de Filadelfia.* **3** N-COUNT Someone who is an **authority on** a particular subject knows a lot about it. *autoridad, experto o experta* ❑ *He's an authority on Russian music. Es especialista en música rusa.* **4** N-UNCOUNT **Authority** is the right to command and control other people. *autoridad* ❑ *...a position of authority. ...un puesto de autoridad.* **5** N-UNCOUNT **Authority** is official permission to do something. *autorización, permiso, licencia* ❑ *They acted without authority. Lo hicieron sin autorización.*

**author|ize** /ɔθəraɪz/ (**authorizes, authorizing, authorized**) V-T If someone **authorizes** something, they give their official permission for it to happen. *autorizar, facultar, legalizar* ❑ *Only the president could authorize its use. Sólo el presidente podía autorizar que se utilizara.* ● **authori|za|tion** /ɔθərɪzeɪʃən/ N-VAR (**authorizations**) *autorización, permiso, licencia* ❑ *We didn't have authorization to go. No teníamos permiso para ir.*

**auto|bi|og|ra|phy** /ɔtəbaɪɒgrəfi/ (**autobiographies**) N-COUNT Your **autobiography** is an account of your life, which you write yourself. *autobiografía* ❑ *He published his autobiography last fall. El otoño pasado publicó su autobiografía.* ● **auto|bio|graphi|cal** /ɔtoʊbaɪəgræfɪkəl/ ADJ *autobiográfico* ❑ *...an autobiographical novel. ...una novela autobiográfica.*

| Word Link | *graph ≈ riting : autograph, biography, graph* |
|---|---|

**auto|graph** /ɔtəgræf/ (**autographs, autographing, autographed**) **1** N-COUNT An **autograph** is the signature of someone famous that is specially written for a fan to keep. *autógrafo* ❑ *He asked for her autograph. Le pidió su autógrafo.* **2** V-T If someone famous **autographs** something, they put their signature on it. *autografiar, firmar* ❑ *I autographed a copy of one of my books. Autografié un ejemplar de uno de mis libros.*

**auto|maker** /ɔtoʊmeɪkər/ (**automakers**) N-COUNT An **automaker** is a company that manufactures cars. *fabricante de automotores* ❑ *...General Motors Corp., the world's largest automaker. ...General Motors Corp., el fabricante de automóviles más grande del mundo.*

| Word Link | *auto ≈ self : automatic, automobile, autonomy* |
|---|---|

**auto|mat|ic** /ɔtəmætɪk/ (**automatics**) **1** ADJ An **automatic** machine or device can keep running without someone operating its controls. *automático* ❑ *Modern trains have automatic doors. Las puertas de los trenes modernos son automáticas.* **2** ADJ An **automatic** weapon is one that keeps firing shots until you stop pulling the trigger. *automático* ❑ *Three gunmen with automatic rifles opened fire. Tres gatilleros con armas automáticas abrieron fuego.* ● **Automatic** is also a noun. *automática* ❑ *He drew his automatic and began running in the direction of the sounds. Sacó su automática y empezó a correr en dirección de los ruidos.* **3** ADJ An **automatic** action is one that you do without thinking about it. *automático* ❑ *All of the automatic body functions, even breathing, are affected. Todas las funciones automáticas del organismo resultan afectadas, hasta la respiración.* ● **auto|mati|cal|ly** /ɔtəmætɪkli/ ADV *automáticamente* ❑ *You will automatically wake up after 30 minutes. Despertará de manera automática al cabo de 30 minutos.*

| Word Link | *mobil ≈ moving : automobile, mobile, mobilize* |
|---|---|

**auto|mo|bile** /ɔtəməbil/ (**automobiles**) N-COUNT An **automobile** is a car. *automóvil, carro, coche, auto* ❑ *...the automobile industry. ...la industria del automóvil.*
→ see car

| Word Link | *able ≈ able to be : acceptable, incurable, portable* |
|---|---|

**autono|my** /ɔtɒnəmi/ **1** N-UNCOUNT **Autonomy** is the control or government of a country, organization, or group by itself rather than by others. *autonomía* ❑ *Reagan spoke about his idea of greater autonomy for individual states. Reagan habló sobre su idea de conceder mayor autonomía a los estados.* ● **autono|mous** ADJ *autónomo* ❑ *...the autonomous region of Andalucia. ...la región autónoma de Andalucía.* **2** N-UNCOUNT **Autonomy** is the ability to make your own decisions about what to do rather than being influenced by someone else or told what to do. *autonomía* [FORMAL] ❑ *Each of the area managers has a great deal of autonomy in the running of his own area. Los gerentes de área tienen mucha autonomía para dirigir su propia área.* ● **autono|mous** ADJ *autónomo* ❑ *...autonomous business managers. ...administradores de negocios independientes.*

**auto|worker** /ɔtoʊwɜrkər/ (**autoworkers**) N-COUNT An **autoworker** is a person who works in the automobile manufacturing industry. *trabajador de la industria automotriz o trabajadora de la industria automotriz* ❑ *...an autoworker from Cleveland. ...un trabajador de la industria automotriz de Cleveland.*

**autumn** /ɔtəm/ (**autumns**) N-VAR **Autumn** is the season between summer and winter when the weather becomes cooler and the leaves fall off the trees. *otoño* [AM usually **fall**]

**aux|ilia|ry** /ɔgzɪlyəri, -zɪləri/ (**auxiliaries**) **1** ADJ **Auxiliary** equipment is extra equipment that is available for use when necessary. *auxiliar, accesorio, adicional* ❑ *...an auxiliary motor. ...un motor adicional.* **2** ADJ **Auxiliary** staff assist other staff. *auxiliar* ❑ *...auxiliary nurses. ...enfermeras auxiliares.* **3** N-COUNT An **auxiliary** is an organization that is connected with, but less important than, another organization. *adicional* ❑ *...the Stanford Hospital Auxiliary. ...el anexo del hospital de Stanford.* **4** N-COUNT An **auxiliary** is a person who is employed to assist other people in their work. Auxiliaries are often medical workers or members of the armed forces. *auxiliar* ❑ *Nursing auxiliaries provide basic care. Los auxiliares de enfermería prestan los cuidados básicos.* **5** N-COUNT In grammar, an **auxiliary** or **auxiliary verb** is a verb that is used with a main verb, for example, to form different tenses or to make the verb passive. In English, the basic auxiliary verbs are "be," "have," and "do." *verbo auxiliar, auxiliar*

**avail|able** /əveɪləbəl/ **1** ADJ If something you

A

want or need is **available,** you can find it or obtain it. *disponible* ❑ *Breakfast is available from 6 a.m. El desayuno se sirve a partir de las 6 am.* • **avail|abil|ity** /əveɪləbɪlɪti/ N-UNCOUNT *disponibilidad* ❑ *...the availability of health care. ...la disponibilidad de los servicios de salud.* **2** ADJ Someone who is **available** is not busy and is therefore free to talk to you or to do a particular task. *disponible* ❑ *Mr. Leach is not available for comment. Por el momento, el Sr. Leach no hará declaraciones.*

| **Thesaurus** | *available* Ver también: |
|---|---|
| ADJ. | accessible, handy, obtainable, usable **1** free **2** |

**ava|lanche** /ævəlæntʃ/ (**avalanches**) N-COUNT An **avalanche** is a large mass of snow that falls down the side of a mountain. *avalancha*
→ see **snow**

**avenge** /əvɛndʒ/ (**avenges, avenging, avenged**) V-T If you **avenge** a wrong or harmful act, you hurt or punish the person who is responsible for it. *vengar(se)* ❑ *He is determined to avenge his daughter's death. Está dispuesto a vengar la muerte de su hija.*

**av|enue** /ævɪnyu, -nu/ (**avenues**) **1** N-COUNT **Avenue** is sometimes used in the names of streets. The written abbreviation **Ave.** is also used. *avenida, Av., Ave.* ❑ *...the most expensive apartments on Park Avenue. ...los departamentos más costosos de Park Avenue.* **2** N-COUNT An **avenue** is a wide, straight road, especially one with trees on either side. *avenida, calle, boulevard*

**av|er|age** /ævərɪdʒ, ævrɪdʒ/ (**averages, averaging, averaged**) **1** N-COUNT An **average** is the result that you get when you add two or more numbers together and divide the total by the number of numbers you added together. *promedio* ❑ *The average age was 63. La edad promedio era de 63 años.* • **Average** is also an adjective. *promedio* ❑ *The average price of goods rose by just 2.2%. El precio promedio de los artículos se incrementó apenas 2.2 por ciento.* **2** N-SING An amount or quality that is **the average** is the normal amount or quality for a particular group of things or people. *promedio, lo normal* ❑ *Rainfall was nearly twice the average for this time of year. Las lluvias fueron casi del doble para esta época del año.* • **Average** is also an adjective. *promedio* ❑ *The average adult man burns 1,500 to 2,000 calories per day. El varón adulto promedio quema de 1,500 a 2,000 calorías diarias.* **3** V-T To **average** a particular amount means to do, get, or produce that amount as an average over a period of time. *promediar* ❑ *We averaged 42 miles per hour. Hicimos un promedio de 39 kilómetros por hora.* **4** PHRASE You say **on average** or **on the average** to indicate that a number is the average of several numbers. *en promedio* ❑ *Women are, on average, paid 25 per cent less than men. En promedio, a las mujeres les pagan 25 por ciento menos que a los hombres.*

**av|er|age speed** (**average speeds**) N-COUNT The **average speed** of a moving object is the overall rate at which it moves, which you calculate by dividing the distance that the object travels by the time it takes to travel that distance. *velocidad promedio*

**avert** /əvɜrt/ (**averts, averting, averted**) **1** V-T If you **avert** something unpleasant, you prevent it from happening. *desviar, evitar, prevenir* ❑ *They managed to avert war. Se las arreglaron para evitar la guerra.* **2** V-T If you **avert** your eyes or gaze **from** someone or something, you look away from them. *desviar, apartar* ❑ *I saw her but I averted my eyes. La ví, pero desvié la mirada.*

**aviary** /eɪviɛri/ (**aviaries**) N-COUNT An **aviary** is a large cage or covered area in which birds are kept. *aviario, pajarera*

**avia|tion** /eɪvieɪʃən/ N-UNCOUNT **Aviation** is the operation and production of aircraft. *aviación* ❑ *...the aviation industry. ...el sector de la aviación.*
→ see **oil**

**avo|ca|do** /ævəkɑdoʊ/ (**avocados**) N-VAR **Avocados** are pear-shaped fruit, with hard skins and large seeds, which are usually eaten raw. *aguacate*

**avoid** /əvɔɪd/ (**avoids, avoiding, avoided**) **1** V-T If you **avoid** something unpleasant that might happen, you take action in order to prevent it from happening. *evitar* ❑ *...a last-minute attempt to avoid a disaster. ...un intento de última hora por evitar un desastre.* **2** V-T If you **avoid** doing something, you choose not to do it, or you put yourself in a situation where you do not have to do it. *evitar* ❑ *I avoid working in places which are too public. Evito trabajar en lugares demasiado públicos.* **3** V-T If you **avoid** a person or thing, you keep away from them. *evitar* ❑ *She locked herself in the women's restroom to avoid him. Se encerró en el baño de mujeres para evitarlo.* **4** V-T If a person or vehicle **avoids** someone or something, they change the direction they are moving in, so that they do not hit them. *esquivar* ❑ *The driver only just avoided the woman. El chofer apenas logró esquivar a la mujer.*

**aw** /ɔ/ **1** EXCLAM People sometimes use **aw** to express disapproval, disappointment, or sympathy. *eh* [INFORMAL] ❑ *"Aw, leave her alone," Paul said. —¡Eh, déjala en paz! —le dijo Paul.* **2** EXCLAM People sometimes use **aw** to express encouragement or approval. *oh* [INFORMAL] ❑ *Aw, she's got her mother's nose! ¡Oh, sacó la nariz de su mamá!*

**await** /əweɪt/ (**awaits, awaiting, awaited**) **1** V-T If you **await** someone or something, you wait for them. *aguardar* [FORMAL] ❑ *We awaited the arrival of the chairman. Aguardamos la llegada del presidente.* **2** V-T Something that **awaits** you is going to happen or come to you in the future. *esperar* [FORMAL] ❑ *A surprise awaited them inside the store. Dentro de la tienda los esperaba una sorpresa.*

| **Word Link** | ***wak*** **≈ being awake : a*wak*e, a*wak*en, *wak*e** |
|---|---|

**awake** /əweɪk/ **1** ADJ Someone who is **awake** is not sleeping. *despierto* ❑ *I stayed awake worrying. Me quedé despierto, preocupado.* **2** PHRASE Someone who is **wide awake** is fully awake and unable to sleep. *completamente despierto* ❑ *I could not relax and still felt wide awake. No podía relajarme y seguía completamente despierto.*
→ see **sleep**

**Word Partnership** Usar *awake* con:

V. **keep** ***someone*** awake, **lie** awake, **stay** awake 1
ADV. **fully** awake, **half** awake 1
**wide** awake 2

**Word Link** *wak ≈ being awake : awake, awaken, wake*

**awak|en** /əweɪkən/ (**awakens, awakening, awakened**) 1 V-T To **awaken** a feeling in a person means to cause them to start having this feeling. despertar [LITERARY] ❑ *The aim of the cruise was to awaken an interest in foreign cultures.* *El propósito del crucero era despertar el interés en las culturas extranjeras.* ● **awak|en|ing** N-COUNT (**awakenings**) despertar ❑ *...the awakening of nationalism.* *...el despertar del nacionalismo.* 2 V-T/V-I When you **awaken**, or when something or someone **awakens** you, you wake up. despertar [LITERARY] ❑ *Grandma always awakens very early.* *La abuela siempre se despierta muy temprano.* ❑ *He was snoring when José awakened him.* *Estaba roncando cuando José lo despertó.*

**award** /əwɔrd/ (**awards, awarding, awarded**) 1 N-COUNT An **award** is a prize or certificate that a person is given for doing something well. premio ❑ *...the National Book Award for fiction.* *...el Premio Nacional al Libro para novela.* 2 N-COUNT In law, an **award** is a sum of money that a court decides should be given to someone. indemnización ❑ *He received an award of nearly $400,000.* *Recibió una indemnización de casi 400,000 dólares.* 3 V-T If someone **is awarded** something such as a prize or an examination mark, it is given to them. otorgar, dar ❑ *She was awarded the prize for both films.* *Le otorgaron el premio por las dos películas.* 4 V-T To **award** something **to** someone means to decide that it will be given to that person. dar ❑ *We have awarded the contract to a company in New York.* *Le dimos el contrato a una empresa de Nueva York.*

**Usage** award and reward

Be careful not to confuse *award* and *reward*. You get an *award* for doing something well, and you get a *reward* for doing a good deed or service: *Tuka got an award for writing the best short story, and Gina got a $50 reward for giving a lost wallet back to the owner—so they went out and had a fancy dinner at a fine restaurant.*

**Word Link** *war ≈ watchful : aware, beware, warning*

**aware** /əwɛər/ 1 ADJ If you are **aware of** something, you know about it. consciente ❑ *They are well aware of the danger.* *Están muy conscientes del peligro.* ● **aware|ness** N-UNCOUNT conciencia ❑ *...public awareness of the problem.* *...la conciencia pública del problema.* 2 ADJ If you are **aware of** something, you realize that it is present or is happening because you hear it, see it, smell it, or feel it. consciente ❑ *She was very aware of the noise of the city.* *Estaba muy consciente del ruido de la ciudad.*

**Word Partnership** Usar *aware* con:

ADV. **acutely/vaguely** aware, **fully** aware, **painfully** aware, **well** aware 1 2
V. **become** aware 1 2
PREP. aware **of** ***something/someone***, aware **that** 1 2

**away** /əweɪ/

**Away** is often used with verbs of movement, such as "go" and "drive," and also in phrasal verbs such as "do away with" and "fade away."

1 ADV If someone or something moves or is moved **away from** a place, they move or are moved so that they are no longer there. If you are **away from** a place, you are not in the place where people expect you to be. lejos, fuera ❑ *He walked away from his car.* *Se alejó de su carro.* ❑ *Jason was away from home.* *Jason estaba fuera de casa.* 2 ADV If you put something **away**, you put it where it should be. If you hide someone or something **away**, you put them in a place where nobody can see them or find them. guardar ❑ *I put my book away and went to bed.* *Guardé el libro y me fui a la cama.* ❑ *All her letters were carefully filed away.* *Todas sus cartas estaban cuidadosamente archivadas.* 3 ADV You use **away** to talk about future events. For example, if an event is a week **away**, it will happen after a week. faltar ❑ *Christmas is now only two weeks away.* *Ya sólo faltan dos semanas para la Navidad.* 4 ADV When a sports team plays **away**, it plays on its opponents' playing court or field. visitante ❑ *...a 4-3 victory for the team playing away.* *...una victoria 4 a 3 para el equipo visitante.* ● **Away** is also an adjective. fuera de casa, visitante ❑ *Pittsburgh is about to play an important away game.* *Pittsburgh está por enfrentar un importante juego fuera de casa.* 5 ADV You can use **away** to say that something slowly disappears, becomes less significant, or changes so that it is no longer the same. ❑ *The snow has already melted away.* *La nieve ya se derritió.* 6 ADV You can use **away** to emphasize a continuous or repeated action. ❑ *He often worked away late into the night.* *Solía trabajar hasta tarde en la noche.* 7 PHRASE If something is **away from** a person or place, it is at a distance from that person or place. lejos de, alejado ❑ *The two women were sitting as far away from each other as possible.* *Las dos mujeres estaban sentadas lo más lejos posible una de otra.*
8 **right away** → see **right**

**Word Partnership** Usar *away* con:

N. away **from home** 1
V. **back** away, **blow** away, **break** away, **chase** ***someone*** away, **drive** away, **get** away, **go** away, **hide** away, **move** away, **pull/take** ***something*** away, **walk** away 1
**stay** away 1 7
**put** away 2
ADJ. **far** away 1 7

**Word Link** *some ≈ causing : awesome, troublesome, worrisome*

**awe|some** /ɔsəm/ 1 ADJ An **awesome** person or thing is very impressive and often frightening. formidable ❑ *...the awesome power of the ocean waves.*

A

*...la formidable fuerza de las olas del mar.* **2** ADJ If you describe someone or something as **awesome,** you are emphasizing that they are very impressive or extraordinary. *impresionante* [INFORMAL] ❑ *He was awesome in the game. Hizo un juego impresionante.*

**aw|ful** /ɔfəl/ **1** ADJ If you say that someone or something is **awful,** you think they are very bad. *horrible, repugnante* ❑ *I thought he was awful. Me pareció horrible.* ❑ *...an awful smell of paint. ...un repugnante olor a pintura.* **2** ADJ You can use **awful** with noun groups that refer to an amount in order to emphasize how large that amount is. *enorme* ❑ *I've got an awful lot of work to do. Tengo una cantidad enorme de trabajo.* ● **aw|ful|ly** ADV *muy* ❑ *The cake looks awfully good. El pastel parece muy bueno.* **3** ADV You can use **awful** with adjectives that describe a quality in order to emphasize that particular quality. *tremendamente* [INFORMAL] ❑ *Gosh, you're awful pretty. ¡Caramba, eres tremendamente bonita!*

| **Thesaurus** | *awful* Ver también: |
|---|---|
| ADJ. | bad, dreadful, horrible, terrible; (*ant.*) good, nice, pleasing **1** |

**awk|ward** /ɔkwərd/ **1** ADJ An **awkward** situation is embarrassing and difficult to deal with. *incómodo* ❑ *...awkward questions. ...preguntas incómodas.* ● **awk|ward|ly** ADV *incómodo* ❑ *There was an awkwardly long silence. Se hizo un silencio muy largo e incómodo.* **2** ADJ Something that is **awkward to** use or carry is difficult to use or carry because of its design. A job that is **awkward** is difficult to do. *difícil* ❑ *It was small but awkward to carry. Era pequeño, pero difícil de cargar.* ● **awk|ward|ly** ADV *torpemente* ❑ *...an awkwardly shaped room. ...un cuarto mal diseñado.* **3** ADJ An **awkward** movement or position is uncomfortable or clumsy. *torpe* ❑ *Amy made an awkward movement with her hands. Amy hizo un movimiento torpe con las manos.* ● **awk|ward|ly** ADV *torpemente* ❑ *He fell awkwardly. Cayó torpemente.* **4** ADJ Someone who is **awkward** deliberately creates problems for other people. *difícil* ❑ *Please try not to be so awkward! ¡Por favor, trata de no ser tan difícil!*

| **Thesaurus** | *awkward* Ver también: |
|---|---|
| ADJ. | embarrassing, delicate, sticky, uncomfortable **1**<br>bulky, cumbersome, difficult **2**<br>blundering, bumbling, uncoordinated **3** |

**awoke** /əwoʊk/ **Awoke** is the past tense of **awake.** *pasado de **awake***

**awok|en** /əwoʊkən/ **Awoken** is the past participle of **awake.** *despertado*

**ax** /æks/ (**axes, axing, axed**) **1** N-COUNT An **ax** is a tool used for cutting wood. It consists of a heavy metal blade that is sharp at one edge and attached by its other edge to the end of a long handle. *hacha* **2** V-T If someone's job or something such as a public service or a television program **is axed,** it is ended suddenly and without discussion. *suprimir* ❑ *Thousands of jobs were axed. Miles de empleos fueron suprimidos.*

**ax|ial move|ment** /æksiəl muvmənt/ (**axial movements**) N-VAR **Axial movement** is movement such as bending or stretching, which does not involve moving from one place to another. *movimiento axial*

**axi|om** /æksiəm/ (**axioms**) N-COUNT An **axiom** is a statement or idea that people accept as being true. *axioma* [FORMAL]

**axis** /æksɪs/ (**axes**) **1** N-COUNT An **axis** is an imaginary line through the middle of something. *eje* ❑ *...the Earth's axis. ...el eje de la Tierra.* **2** N-COUNT An **axis** of a graph is one of the two lines on which the scales of measurement are marked. *eje*
→ see **graph, moon**

**axle** /æksᵊl/ (**axles**) N-COUNT An **axle** is a rod connecting a pair of wheels on a car or other vehicle. *eje*
→ see **wheel**

**axon** /æksɒn/ (**axons**) N-COUNT **Axons** are the long, thin parts of a nerve cell that carry electrical impulses to other parts of the nervous system. *axón* [TECHNICAL]

**azi|muth|al pro|jec|tion** /æzɪmʌθəl prədʒɛkʃən/ (**azimuthal projections**) N-VAR An **azimuthal projection** is an image of a map that is made by projecting the map on a globe onto a flat surface. *proyección acimutal* [TECHNICAL]

# Bb



**bab|ble** /bæbᵊl/ (**babbles, babbling, babbled**) **1** V-I If someone **babbles,** they talk in a confused or excited way. *balbucear, gruñir, parlotear* ❑ *Mom babbled on about how messy I was. Mamá siguió gruñendo sobre lo desordenado que soy.* ❑ *They all babbled together. Todos parloteaban al mismo tiempo.* **2** N-SING You can refer to people's voices as a **babble of** sound when they are excited and confused, preventing you from understanding what they are saying. *murmullo* ❑ *Kemp knocked loudly so that they could hear him above the babble of voices. Kemp tocó con fuerza para que pudieran oírlo por sobre el murmullo de voces.*

**babe** /beɪb/ (**babes**) N-VOC Some people use **babe** as an affectionate way of addressing someone they love. *nene o nena* [INFORMAL] ❑ *I'm sorry, babe. I didn't mean it. Discúlpame, nena; no era mi intención.*

**baby** /beɪbi/ (**babies**) **1** N-COUNT A **baby** is a very young child that cannot yet walk or talk. *bebé* ❑ *She used to take care of me when I was a baby. Ella me cuidaba cuando yo era bebé.* ❑ *My wife just had a baby. Mi esposa acaba de dar a luz.* **2** N-VOC; N-COUNT Some people use **baby** as an affectionate way of addressing someone. *nene o nena* [INFORMAL] ❑ *"Be careful, baby," he said. —Ten cuidado, nena —, le dijo.*
→ see **child**

**Word Partnership** Usar *baby* con:

| | |
|---|---|
| N. | baby **boy/girl/sister**, baby **clothes**, baby **food**, baby **names**, baby **talk** **1** |
| V. | **deliver a** baby, **have a** baby **1** |
| ADJ. | **new/newborn** baby, **unborn** baby **1** |

**ba|by car|riage** (**baby carriages**) N-COUNT A **baby carriage** is a small vehicle in which a baby can lie as it is pushed along. *cochecito, carriola*

**baby|sit** /beɪbisɪt/ (**babysits, babysitting, babysat**) V-T/V-I If you **babysit for** someone or **babysit** their children, you look after their children while they are out. *cuidar niños* ❑ *I promised to babysit for Mrs. Plunkett. Prometí que cuidaría a los hijos de la señora Plunkett.* ❑ *She was babysitting him and his little sister. Ella los estaba cuidando a él y a su hermanita.* • **baby|sitter** N-COUNT *niñera o muchacho que cuida niños* ❑ *It can be difficult to find a good babysitter. Puede ser difícil encontrar una buena niñera.*

**ba|by tooth** (**baby teeth**) N-COUNT Your **baby teeth** are the first teeth that grow in your mouth, which later fall out and are replaced by a second set. *diente de leche*

**bach|elor** /bætʃələr/ (**bachelors**) N-COUNT A **bachelor** is a man who has never married. *soltero*

**bach|elor|ette** /bætʃələrɛt/ (**bachelorettes**) N-COUNT A **bachelorette** is a woman who has never married. *soltera*

**bach|elor|ette par|ty** (**bachelorette parties**) N-COUNT A **bachelorette party** is a party for a woman who is getting married very soon, to which only women are invited. *despedida de soltera*

**bach|elor par|ty** (**bachelor parties**) N-COUNT A **bachelor party** is a party for a man who is getting married very soon, to which only men are invited. *despedida de soltero*
→ see **wedding**

**back**

1. ADVERB USES
2. OPPOSITE OF FRONT; NOUN AND ADJECTIVE USES
3. VERB USES

**1 back** /bæk/

In addition to the uses shown below, **back** is also used in phrasal verbs such as "date back" and "fall back on."

**1** ADV If you move **back,** you move in the opposite direction to the one in which you are facing or in which you were moving before. *apartar(se)* ❑ *She stepped back from the door. Se apartó de la puerta.* **2** ADV If you go **back** somewhere, you return to where you were before. *regresar, volver* ❑ *I went back to bed. Volví a acostarme.* ❑ *I'll be back as soon as I can. Regresaré tan pronto como pueda., Volveré tan pronto como pueda.* **3** ADV If someone or something is **back** in a particular state, they were in that state before and are now in it again. *volver* ❑ *The bus company expects service to get slowly back to normal. La empresa de autobuses espera que el servicio vuelva lentamente a la normalidad.* **4** ADV If you give or put something **back,** you return it to the person who had it or to the place where it was before you took it. If you get or take something **back,** you then have it again after not having it for a while. *devolver* ❑ *You'll get your money back. Te devolverán (devolveré) tu dinero.* ❑ *Put the meat back in the freezer. Vuelve a meter la carne en el refrigerador.* **5** ADV If you write or call **back,** you write to or telephone someone after they have written to or telephoned you. If you look **back** at someone, you look at them after they have started looking at you. *contestar, responder* ❑ *They wrote back to me and told me I didn't have to do it. Me contestaron (la carta) para decirme que no tenía que hacerlo.* ❑ *If the phone rings, you should say you'll call back after dinner. Si suena el teléfono, diles que tú les llamarás después de la cena.* **6** ADV If someone or something is kept or situated **back from** a place, they are at a distance away from it. *alejarse* ❑ *Keep back from the edge of the train platform. Aléjese de la*

B

*orilla del andén.* **7** ADV If you talk about something that happened **back** in the past or several years **back,** you are emphasizing that it happened quite a long time ago. *datar de* ❑ *The story starts back in 1950. La historia se inicia en 1950.* **8** PHRASE If someone moves **back and forth,** they repeatedly move in one direction and then in the opposite direction. *de un lado a otro, de atrás para adelante* ❑ *He paced back and forth. Caminaba de un lado a otro (de atrás para adelante).*

**❷ back** /bæk/ (**backs**) **1** N-COUNT Your **back** is the part of your body from your neck to your waist that is on the opposite side to your chest. *espalda* ❑ *Her son was lying on his back. Su hijo estaba acostado boca arriba.* ❑ *She turned her back to him. Le volvió la espalda.* **2** N-COUNT The **back of** something is the side or part of it that is toward the rear or farthest from the front. *atrás, parte posterior* ❑ *...a room at the back of the store. ...un cuarto atrás de la tienda., ...un cuarto en la parte posterior de la tienda.* ❑ *...the back of her neck. ...su nuca.* **3** ADJ **Back** is used to refer to the side or part of something that is toward the rear or farthest from the front. *trasero, de atrás* ❑ *She opened the back door. Abrió la puerta trasera., Abrió la puerta de atrás.* ❑ *Ann sat in the back seat of their car. Ann se sentó en la parte trasera del carro., Ann se sentó en el asiento de atrás (del carro).* **4** N-COUNT The **back** of a chair is the part that you lean against. *respaldo* ❑ *There was a pink sweater on the back of the chair. Había un suéter rosa en el respaldo de la silla.* **5** N-UNCOUNT You use **out back** to refer to the area behind a house or other building. You also use **in back** to refer to the rear part of something, especially a car or building. *afuera, atrás* ❑ *Dan was out back in the yard cleaning his shoes. Dan estaba afuera, en el patio, limpiando sus zapatos.* ❑ *...the trees in back of the building. ...los árboles de atrás del edificio.* **6** PHRASE If you say or do something **behind** someone's **back,** you do it without them knowing about it. *a espaldas de* ❑ *You eat at her house, and then criticize her behind her back. Comes en su casa y luego la criticas a sus espaldas.* **7** to **take a back seat** → see **seat**
→ see **body, horse**

**❸ back** /bæk/ (**backs, backing, backed**) **1** V-I If a building **backs onto** something, the back of it faces in the direction of that thing or touches the edge of that thing. *dar a, estar frente a* ❑ *He lives in an apartment that backs onto Friedman's Restaurant. Vive en un departamento que da al restaurante Friedman's., Vive en un departamento que está frente al restaurante Friedman's.* **2** V-T/V-I When you **back** a vehicle somewhere or when it **backs** somewhere, it moves backward. *dar marcha atrás, poner en reversa* ❑ *He backed his car out of the driveway. Dio marcha atrás para quitar su carro de la entrada., Puso su carro en reversa y lo quitó de la entrada.* **3** V-T If you **back** a person or a course of action, you support them. *respaldar, apoyar* ❑ *We told them what we wanted to do, and they agreed to back us. Les dijimos lo que queríamos hacer y estuvieron de acuerdo en respaldarnos (apoyarnos).*

▸ **back away** PHR-VERB If you **back away,** you move away, often because you are frightened of them. *retroceder, dar marcha atrás* ❑ *James stood up, but the girl backed away. James se levantó, pero la chica retrocedió.*

▸ **back down** PHR-VERB If you **back down,** you withdraw a claim or demand that you made earlier. *dar marcha atrás, echarse para atrás* ❑ *It's too late to back down now. Es demasiado tarde para dar marcha atrás.*

▸ **back off** PHR-VERB If you **back off,** you move away in order to avoid problems or a fight. *retroceder* ❑ *They backed off in fright. Retrocedieron atemorizados.*

▸ **back out** PHR-VERB If you **back out,** you decide not to do something that you previously agreed to do. *dar marcha atrás, echarse para atrás, abandonar* ❑ *The Hungarians backed out of the project. Los húngaros se echaron para atrás en el proyecto.*

▸ **back up** **1** PHR-VERB If someone or something **backs up** a statement, they supply evidence to suggest that it is true. *apoyar* ❑ *He didn't have any proof to back up his story. No tenía prueba alguna que apoyara su historia.* **2** PHR-VERB If you **back up** a computer file, you make a copy of it that you can use if the original file is damaged or lost. *respaldar, hacer una copia* [COMPUTING] ❑ *Make sure you back up your files every day. Asegúrate de respaldar tus archivos todos los días.* **3** PHR-VERB If you **back** someone **up,** you show your support for them. *apoyar, respaldar* ❑ *His employers backed him up. Sus patrones lo respaldaron.* **4** PHR-VERB If you **back** someone **up,** you help them by confirming that what they are saying is true. *respaldar, apoyar* ❑ *The girl denied being there, and the man backed her up. La muchacha negó haber estado ahí y el hombre lo confirmó.* **5** PHR-VERB When a car **backs up** or when you **back** it **up,** the car is driven backward. *retroceder, ir en reversa* **6** → see also **backup**

**back|board** /bækbɔrd/ (**backboards**) N-COUNT In basketball, the **backboard** is the flat board above each of the baskets. *tablero*
→ see **basketball**

**back|bone** /bækboʊn/ (**backbones**) **1** N-COUNT Your **backbone** is the column of small linked bones down the middle of your back. *columna vertebral (de todos los vertebrados), espina dorsal (de todos los vertebrados, menos del hombre)* **2** N-UNCOUNT If you say that someone has no **backbone,** you think that they do not have the courage to do things which need to be done. *fibra, valor, coraje* ❑ *He doesn't have the backbone to admit to his mistakes. No tiene el valor (coraje) para admitir sus errores.*

**back|court** /bækkɔrt/ (**backcourts**) N-COUNT In sports such tennis and badminton, the **backcourt** is the section of each side of the court that is furthest from the net. In basketball, the **backcourt** is the rear part of the court, where the defense plays. You can also use **backcourt** to refer to the members of a team who play mainly in this part of the court. *parte trasera de la cancha, defensa*

**back|er** /bækər/ (**backers**) N-COUNT A **backer** is someone who gives support or financial help to a person or project. *patrocinador o patrocinadora* ❑ *I was looking for a backer to help me with my business. Estaba buscando un patrocinador que me apoyara en mi negocio.*

**back|fire** /bækfaɪər/ (**backfires, backfiring, backfired**) **1** V-I If a plan or project **backfires,** it has the opposite result to the one that was intended. *fracasar, fallar* ❑ *This plan could backfire. Este plan podría fracasar.* **2** V-I When a motor vehicle or its engine **backfires,** it produces an explosion in the exhaust pipe. *producir explosiones*

❑ *Somewhere in the distance, a car backfired.* *En algún lugar, en la distancia, se oyó el escape de un carro.*

**Word Link** *ground ≈ bottom : background, groundwater, underground*

**back|ground** /bækgraʊnd/ (**backgrounds**) **1** N-COUNT Your **background** is the kind of family you come from and the kind of education you have had. *antecedente, ambiente* ❑ *The Warners were from a Jewish working-class background.* *Los Warner pertenecían a (venían de) la clase obrera judía.* **2** N-COUNT The **background** to an event or situation consists of the facts that explain what caused it. *antecedente* ❑ *...the background to the current problems.* *...los antecedentes de los problemas actuales.* **3** N-SING **The background** is sounds, such as music, that you can hear but that you are not listening to with your full attention. *fondo* ❑ *I heard the sound of music in the background.* *Oía el sonido de la música en el fondo.* **4** N-COUNT You can use **background** to refer to the things in a picture or scene that are less noticeable or important than the main things or people in it. *fondo* ❑ *...roses on a blue background.* *...rosas sobre un fondo azul.*

**Word Partnership** Usar *background* con:

| | |
|---|---|
| ADJ. | **cultural/ethnic/family** background, **educational** background **1** |
| N. | background **check** **1**<br>background **information/knowledge** **1** **2**<br>background **story** **2**<br>background **music/noise** **3** |
| PREP. | **in the** background **3** **4**<br>**against a** background **4** |
| V. | **blend into the** background **4** |

**back|hoe** /bækhoʊ/ (**backhoes**) N-COUNT A **backhoe** is a large vehicle which is used for moving large amounts of earth. *excavadora*

**back|ing** /bækɪŋ/ (**backings**) **1** N-UNCOUNT **Backing** is money, resources, or support given to a person or organization. *respaldo, apoyo* ❑ *He said the president had the full backing of his government.* *Dijo que el presidente tenía todo el respaldo de su gobierno.* **2** N-VAR A **backing** is a layer of something such as cloth that is put onto the back of something in order to strengthen or protect it. *refuerzo* ❑ *The placemats have a non-slip backing.* *Los mantelitos individuales tienen un refuerzo antideslizante.*

**back|lash** /bæklæʃ/ N-SING A **backlash against** a tendency or recent development in society or politics is a sudden, strong reaction against it. *reacción violenta* ❑ *...a backlash against healthy-eating messages.* *...una fuerte reacción contra los mensajes sobre la buena alimentación.*

**back|stage** /bæksteɪdʒ/ ADV In a theater, **backstage** refers to the areas behind the stage. *entre bastidores, entre bambalinas* ❑ *He went backstage and asked for her autograph.* *Fue a los camerinos a pedirle su autógrafo.*

**back talk** also **backtalk** N-UNCOUNT If you refer to something that someone says as **back talk**, you mean that it is rude or shows a lack of respect. *impertinencia*

**back|up** /bækʌp/ (**backups**) also **back-up** **1** N-VAR **Backup** consists of extra equipment, resources, or people that you can get help or support from if necessary. *respaldo, apoyo* ❑ *He drove to answer another officer's call for backup.* *Se dirigió en el coche a responder al llamado de apoyo de otro agente.* **2** N-VAR If you have something such as a second set of plans as **backup**, you have arranged for them to be available for use if the first one does not work. *respaldo* ❑ *Every part of the system has a backup.* *Cada parte del sistema tiene un respaldo.* **3** N-COUNT A **backup** is a long line of traffic stretching back along a road, which moves very slowly or not at all, for example, because of roadwork or an accident. *embotellamiento* ❑ *There was a seven-mile backup on the highway.* *Había un embotellamiento de once kilómetros en la autopista.*
→ see **concert**

**Word Link** *ward ≈ in the direction of : backward, forward, inward*

**back|ward** /bækwərd/ **1** ADJ A **backward** movement or look is in the direction that your back is facing. *hacia atrás* ❑ *...a backward glance.* *...una mirada (hacia) atrás.* **2** ADV If you move or look **backward**, you move or look in the direction that your back is facing. *hacia atrás* ❑ *He took two steps backward.* *Dio dos pasos hacia atrás.* **3** ADV If you do something **backward**, you do it in the opposite way to the usual way. *al revés, hacia atrás* ❑ *Start at the end of the alphabet and work backward.* *Empieza de la última letra del alfabeto para atrás., Recita el alfabeto al revés.* **4** PHRASE If someone or something moves **backward and forward**, they move repeatedly first in one direction and then in the opposite direction. *vaivén, de atrás para adelante* ❑ *I started moving backward and forward in time with the music.* *Empecé a balancearme al ritmo de la música.* **5** ADJ A **backward** country or society does not have modern industries and machines. *atrasado*

**back|yard** /bækyɑrd/ (**backyards**) also **back yard** N-COUNT A **backyard** is an area of land at the back of a house. *patio trasero*

**ba|con** /beɪkən/ N-UNCOUNT **Bacon** is salted or smoked meat which comes from the back or sides of a pig. *tocino, panceta* ❑ *...bacon and eggs.* *...huevos con tocino.*

**bac|te|ria** /bæktɪəriə/ N-PLURAL **Bacteria** are very small organisms which can cause disease. *bacteria* ❑ *Chlorine is added to the water to kill bacteria.* *Se añade cloro al agua para matar las bacterias.* ● **bac|te|rial** ADJ *bacteriano* ❑ *...a bacterial infection.* *...una infección bacteriana.*

**bad** /bæd/ (**worse, worst**) **1** ADJ Something that is **bad** is unpleasant, harmful, or undesirable. *mal, malo* ❑ *...bad weather.* *...mal tiempo.* ❑ *...a bad idea.* *...una mala idea.* ❑ *...bad news.* *...malas nuevas (noticias).* ❑ *Too much coffee is bad for you.* *Tomar demasiado café es malo para ti.* ❑ *The floods are the worst in nearly fifty years.* *Son las peores inundaciones en casi cincuenta años.* **2** ADJ Something that is **bad** is of an unacceptably low standard, quality, or amount. *malo* ❑ *...bad housing.* *...una mala vivienda.* ❑ *The school's main problem is that teachers' pay is so bad.* *El principal problema de la escuela es que el sueldo de los maestros es muy malo.* **3** ADJ Someone who is **bad at** doing something is not skillful or successful at it. *malo* ❑ *Howard was bad at basketball.* *Howard*

b

B

era malo para el básquetbol. ❑ He was a bad driver. Era un mal conductor., Era un chofer malo. **4** ADJ You can say that something is **not bad** to mean that it is quite good or acceptable, especially when you are rather surprised about this. mal, malo ❑ "How much is he paying you?" —"Oh, five thousand." —"Not bad." —¿Cuánto te está pagando? —Ah, cinco mil. —No está mal. ❑ That's not a bad idea. No es una mala idea. **5** ADJ If you are in a **bad** mood, you are angry and behave unpleasantly to people. mal ❑ She is in a bad mood because she had to get up early. Está de mal humor porque tuvo que levantarse temprano. **6** ADJ If you **feel bad about** something, you feel sorry or guilty about it. mal ❑ You don't have to feel bad about relaxing. No tienes que sentirte mal por descansar. ❑ I feel bad that he's doing most of the work. Me siento mal de que él esté haciendo la mayor parte del trabajo. **7** ADJ If you have a **bad** back, heart, leg, or eye, there is something wrong with it. mal, malo ❑ Joe has to be careful because of his bad back. Joe debe tener cuidado porque está mal de la espalda. **8** ADJ **Bad** language is language that contains vulgar or offensive words. malo ❑ I don't like to hear bad language in the street. No quiero oír palabrotas en la calle. **9** → see also **worse, worst** **10** **bad luck** → see **luck**

| **Thesaurus** | *bad* | Ver también: |
|---|---|---|
| ADJ. | damaging, dangerous, harmful; (*ant.*) good **1** | |
| | inferior, poor, unsatisfactory; (*ant.*) acceptable, good, satisfactory **2** **3** | |

**bad check** (**bad checks**) N-COUNT A **bad check** is a check that will not be paid because there is a mistake on it, or because there is not enough money in the account of the person who wrote it. cheque inservible (si hay error en él), cheque sin fondos

**badge** /bædʒ/ (**badges**) N-COUNT A **badge** is a piece of metal, cloth or plastic which you wear or carry to show that you work for a particular organization, or that you have achieved something. placa, chapa ❑ ...a police officer's badge. ...una placa de policía.

**bad|ly** /bædli/ (**worse, worst**) **1** ADV If something is done **badly** or goes **badly,** it is not very successful or effective. mal ❑ I was angry because I played so badly. Estaba enojado porque jugué (toqué) muy mal. ❑ The whole project was badly managed. Todo el proyecto se manejó muy mal. **2** ADV If someone or something is **badly** hurt or **badly** affected, they are severely hurt or affected. mal, gravemente ❑ The fire badly damaged a church. El fuego dañó gravemente una iglesia. ❑ One man was killed and another badly injured. Un hombre resultó muerto y otro malherido. **3** ADV If you want or need something **badly,** you want or need it very much. con desesperación ❑ Why do you want to go so badly? ¿Por qué tanta desesperación por ir? **4** → see also **worse, worst**

**bad|min|ton** /bædmɪntən/ N-UNCOUNT **Badminton** is a game played by two or four players on a rectangular court with a high net across the middle. The players try to score points by hitting a small object called a shuttlecock across the net using a racket. bádminton

**bad off** (**worse off, worst off**) **1** ADJ If you are **bad off,** you are in a bad situation. mal ❑ The people I write about are usually pretty bad off. La gente sobre la que escribo está muy mal (es muy pobre) por lo general. **2** ADJ If you are **bad off,** you do not have much money. pobre ❑ The owners are not so bad off; most are making money. Los propietarios no están tan pobres; la mayoría está ganando dinero.

**bad-tempered** ADJ Someone who is **bad-tempered** is not very cheerful and gets angry easily. malhumorado ❑ I usually feel tired and bad-tempered on Friday evening. Los viernes en la noche casi siempre me siento cansado y de mal humor (malhumorado).

**bag** /bæg/ (**bags**) **1** N-COUNT A **bag** is a container made of paper, plastic, or leather which is to carry things. bolsa ❑ ...a bag of candy. ...una bolsa de dulces. ❑ ...a shopping bag. ...una bolsa de compras. **2** N-PLURAL If you have **bags** under your eyes, you have folds of skin there, usually because you have not had enough sleep. bolsa, ojera ❑ The bags under his eyes have grown darker. Las ojeras se le han puesto más oscuras. **3** PHRASE If you say that something is **in the bag,** you mean that you are certain to get it or achieve it. en la bolsa [INFORMAL] ❑ "I'll win this time," he assured me. "It's in the bag." —Esta vez ganaré —me aseguró—, ya lo tengo en la bolsa. **4** PHRASE If you **are left holding the bag,** you are put in a situation where you are responsible for something, often in an unfair way because other people fail or refuse to take responsibility for it. cargar (con) el muerto [INFORMAL] ❑ I don't want to be left holding the bag if something goes wrong. No quiero cargar con el muerto si algo no sale bien. **5** → see also **sleeping bag**
→ see **container, tea**

**bag|gage** /bægɪdʒ/ **1** N-UNCOUNT Your **baggage** consists of the bags that you take with you when you travel. equipaje, maleta ❑ He collected his baggage and left the airport. Recogió su equipaje y salió del aeropuerto. **2** N-UNCOUNT You can use **baggage** to refer to someone's problems or prejudices. carga ❑ How much emotional baggage is he bringing with him into the relationship? ¿Cuánta carga emocional lleva consigo a la relación?

**bag|gage car** (**baggage cars**) N-COUNT A **baggage car** is a railroad car, often without windows, which is used to carry luggage, goods, or mail. furgón, vagón de equipaje

**bag|gage claim** N-SING At an airport, the **baggage claim** is the area where you collect your baggage at the end of your trip. recolección de equipaje ❑ Luke followed the signs to the baggage claim. Luke siguió las señales de la sala de recolección de equipaje.

**bag|ger** /bægər/ (**baggers**) N-COUNT A **bagger** is a person whose job is to put customers' purchases into bags at a supermarket or other store. empaquetador, empaquetadora, cerillo ❑ As well as being a bagger, he's worked at a fast-food restaurant. Además de ser cerillo, ha trabajado en un restaurante de comida rápida.

**bail** /beɪl/ (**bails, bailing, bailed**)

> The spelling **bale** is also used for meaning **3**, and for meaning **1** of the phrasal verb.

**1** N-UNCOUNT **Bail** is permission for an arrested person to be released after a sum of money has been paid as a guarantee that they will attend their trial. fianza ❑ He was held without bail after a court appearance in Detroit. Lo arrestaron sin derecho a fianza después de su presentación ante un tribunal de Detroit. **2** V-T/V-I If you **bail**, or **bail** water from a boat or from a place which is flooded, you use a container to remove water from it. achicar ❑ *We kept the boat afloat for a couple of hours by bailing frantically.* *Achicando frenéticamente, mantuvimos el bote a flote por un par de horas.* **3** PHRASE If someone who has been arrested **is freed on bail,** or **released on bail,** or **makes bail,** or if another person **makes bail** for them, the arrested person is released because a sum of money has been paid as a guarantee that they will attend their trial. pagar la fianza ❑ *Guerrero was finally arrested, but he made bail and fled to Colombia.* *Finalmente arrestaron a Guerrero, pero pagó la fianza y huyó a Colombia.* ❑ *He was freed on bail pending an appeal.* *Lo liberaron bajo fianza en espera de la apelación.*

▸ **bail out** **1** PHR-VERB If you **bail** someone **out,** you help them out of a difficult situation, often by giving them money. sacar de apuros ❑ *They will discuss how to bail out the country's banking system.* *Van a discutir cómo sacar de apuros a la banca del país.* **2** → see also **bailout** **3** PHR-VERB If you **bail** an arrested person **out,** you pay a sum of money as a guarantee that they will attend their trial. pagar la fianza ❑ *He has been arrested eight times. Each time, friends bailed him out.* *Lo han arrestado ocho veces y, cada vez, sus amigos han pagado la fianza.*

**bail|out** /beɪlaʊt/ (**bailouts**) N-COUNT A **bailout** of an organization or individual that has financial problems is the act of helping them by giving them money. rescate ❑ *...one of the biggest government bailouts of a private company in years.* *...uno de los mayores rescates gubernamentales de una empresa privada en muchos años.*

**bait** /beɪt/ (**baits, baiting, baited**) **1** N-VAR **Bait** is food which you put on a hook or in a trap in order to catch fish or animals. cebo, carnada ❑ *...a shop selling fishing bait.* *...una tienda que vende cebo para pescar.* **2** V-T If you **bait** a hook or trap, you put bait on it or in it. cebar ❑ *He baited his hook with worms.* *Cebó el anzuelo con gusanos.* **3** N-UNCOUNT; N-SING To use something as **bait** means to use it to trick or persuade someone to do something. cebo, carnada ❑ *Television programs are just bait to attract an audience for commercials.* *Los programas de televisión son sólo el cebo para hacer que el espectador vea los comerciales.* **4** V-T If you **bait** someone, you deliberately try to make them angry by teasing them. picar, provocar ❑ *He delighted in baiting his mother.* *Le gustaba mucho picar a su madre.* **5** **Bait and switch** is used to refer to a sales technique in which goods are advertised at low prices in order to attract customers, although only a small number of the low-priced goods are available. *Atraer a posibles clientes con la oferta de bienes a precios bajos, cuya existencia es reducida, e inducirlos a comprar otros de mayor precio.* ❑ *The restaurant really sells 11 dishes for the advertised price. There's no bait and switch here.* *El restaurante realmente vende los 11 platillos al precio anunciado. No hay trampa oculta.*

**bake** /beɪk/ (**bakes, baking, baked**) **1** V-T/V-I If you **bake,** you spend some time preparing and mixing together ingredients to make bread, cakes, pies, or other food which is cooked in the oven. hornear ❑ *How did you learn to bake cakes?* *¿Dónde aprendiste a hornear pasteles?* ❑ *I love to bake.* *Me encanta hornear.* ● **bak|ing** N-UNCOUNT hornear ❑ *On a Thursday she used to do all the baking.* *Acostumbraba hornearlo todo los jueves.* **2** V-T/V-I When a cake or bread **bakes** or when you **bake** it, it cooks in the oven without any extra liquid or fat. hornear ❑ *Bake the cake for 35 to 50 minutes.* *Hornee el pastel de 35 a 50 minutos.* ❑ *The batter rises as it bakes.* *La masa se levanta al hornearse.*
→ see **cook**

**bake-off** (**bake-offs**) N-COUNT A **bake-off** is a cooking competition. concurso de horneado ❑ *If you win the bake-off, you'll get a prize.* *Si ganas el concurso de horneado, obtienes un premio.*

**bak|er** /beɪkər/ (**bakers**) N-COUNT A **baker** is a person whose job is to bake and sell bread, pastries, and cakes. panadero o panadera, pastelero o pastelera

| Word Link | *ery ≈ place where something happens : bakery, cemetery, winery* |
|---|---|

**bak|ery** /beɪkəri, beɪkri/ (**bakeries**) N-COUNT A **bakery** is a building where bread, pastries, and cakes are baked, or the store where they are sold. panadería, pastelería ❑ *...the smell of bread from a bakery.* *...el olor a pan de una panadería.*

**bala|cla|va** /bæləklɑvə/ (**balaclavas**) N-COUNT A **balaclava** is a tight woolen hood that covers every part of your head except your face. pasamontañas
→ see **hat**

**bal|ance** /bæləns/ (**balances, balancing, balanced**) **1** V-T/V-I If you **balance** something somewhere, or if it **balances** there, it remains steady and does not fall. equilibrar, sostener en equilibrio ❑ *I balanced on the window ledge.* *Me sostuve en equilibrio en el antepecho de la ventana.* **2** N-UNCOUNT **Balance** is the ability to remain steady when you are standing up. equilibrio ❑ *The medicines you are taking could be affecting your balance.* *Las medicinas que estás tomando podrían afectar tu sentido del equilibrio.* **3** V-RECIP If you **balance** one thing **with** something different, each of the things has the same strength or importance. compensar ❑ *Balance spicy dishes with mild ones.* *Compensa los platillos condimentados con otros suaves.* ❑ *The government has to find some way to balance these two needs.* *El gobierno tiene que encontrar la manera de equilibrar ambas necesidades.* **4** N-SING A **balance** is a situation in which all the different parts are equal in strength or importance. equilibrio ❑ *...the ecological balance of the forest.* *...el equilibrio ecológico del bosque.* **5** V-T If you **balance** one thing **against** another, you consider its importance in relation to the other one. sopesar ❑ *...trying to balance professional success against motherhood.* *...tratando de sopesar los pros y contras del éxito profesional frente a los de la maternidad.* **6** V-T If someone **balances** their budget or if a government **balances** the economy of a country, they make sure that the amount of money that is spent is not greater than the amount that is received. equilibrar ❑ *He balanced his budgets by tightly controlling spending.* *Equilibró su presupuesto controlando estrechamente el gasto.* **7** V-T/V-I If you **balance** your books or make them **balance,** you prove by calculation that the amount of money you have received is equal to the amount

B

that you have spent. equilibrar ❑ ...teaching them to balance the books. ...enseñándoles a equilibrar los libros. 8 N-COUNT The **balance** in your bank account is the amount of money you have in it. saldo ❑ I'd like to check the balance in my account please. Quisiera verificar el saldo de mi cuenta, por favor. 9 N-SING **The balance** of an amount of money is what remains to be paid for something or what remains when part of the amount has been spent. saldo ❑ You sign the final agreement and pay the balance. Firmas el contrato definitivo y pagas el saldo. 10 N-UNCOUNT In a painting or drawing, **balance** is a sense of harmony in the arrangement of the different parts of the painting or drawing. equilibrio 11 N-UNCOUNT If two or more physical objects are in a state of **balance,** their weight is evenly distributed around a central point. equilibrio 12 N-COUNT A **balance** is a scientific instrument that is used for weighing things. balanza 13 PHRASE You can say **on balance** to indicate that you are stating an opinion after considering all the relevant facts or arguments. en resumidas cuentas, a fin de cuentas ❑ On balance he agreed with Christine. En resumidas cuentas, estuvo de acuerdo con Christine., A fin de cuentas, estuvo de acuerdo con Christine.
→ see **brain**

**Word Partnership** Usar *balance* con:

V. **keep/lose *your*** balance, **restore** balance 2
**check a** balance, **maintain a** balance 8
**pay a** balance 9
ADJ. **delicate** balance 4
balance **due, outstanding** balance 9
N. balance **a budget** 6
**account** balance, balance **transfer** 8

**bal|anced** /bælənst/ 1 ADJ A **balanced** account or report is fair and reasonable; used to show approval. equilibrado, ponderado ❑ ...a fair, balanced, comprehensive report. ...un informe exhaustivo, ponderado e imparcial. 2 ADJ Something that is **balanced** is pleasing or useful because its different parts or elements are in the correct proportions. equilibrado ❑ ...a balanced diet of nutritious food. ...una dieta equilibrada de alimentos nutritivos. 3 → see also **balance**

**bal|anced forces** N-PLURAL In physics, **balanced forces** are forces that are equal and opposite to each other, so that an object to which the forces are applied does not move. fuerzas equilibradas

**bal|co|ny** /bælkəni/ (**balconies**) 1 N-COUNT A **balcony** is a platform on the outside of a building, above ground level, with a wall or railing around it. balcón 2 N-SING The **balcony** in a theater is an area of seats above the main seating area. anfiteatro, galería

**bald** /bɔld/ (**balder, baldest**) 1 ADJ Someone who is **bald** has little or no hair on the top of their head. calvo ❑ He rubbed his hand across his bald head. Se frotó la calva con la mano. • **bald|ness** N-UNCOUNT calvicie ❑ He wears a cap to cover a spot of baldness. Usa una gorra para taparse la calvicie incipiente. 2 ADJ If a tire is **bald,** its surface has worn down and it is no longer safe to use. gastado, liso 3 ADJ A **bald** statement has no unnecessary words in it. puro ❑ The bald truth is that he's just not happy. La pura verdad es que no es feliz. • **bald|ly** ADV sin rodeos ❑ "I don't think these stories are true," said Phillips, baldly. —No creo que esas historias sean ciertas —dijo Phillips sin rodeos.

**ball** /bɔl/ (**balls**) 1 N-COUNT A **ball** is a round or oval object that is used in games such as tennis, baseball, football, basketball, and soccer. pelota ❑ ...a golf ball. ...una pelota de golf. 2 N-COUNT A **ball** is something that has a round shape. bola ❑ Thomas squeezed the letter up into a ball. Thomas hizo bola la carta. 3 N-COUNT **The ball of** your foot or **the ball of** your thumb is the rounded part where your toes join your foot or where your thumb joins your hand. base de los dedos del pie, base del pulgar 4 N-COUNT A **ball** is a large formal dance. baile ❑ My Mama and Daddy used to have a grand Christmas ball every year. Mamá y papá acostumbraban organizar un gran baile en Navidad todos los años. 5 PHRASE If you **are having a ball,** you are having a very enjoyable time. divertirse mucho, pasarla bien, pasar un buen rato [INFORMAL] ❑ The boys were sitting outside having a ball. Los muchachos estaban sentados afuera pasando un buen rato.
→ see **foot, golf, soccer**

**Word Partnership** Usar *ball* con:

V. **bounce/catch/hit/kick/throw a** ball 1
**roll into a** ball 2
N. **bowling/golf/soccer/tennis** ball, ball **field**, ball **game** 1
**snow** ball 2
PREP. ball **of *something*** 2

**bal|let** /bæleɪ/ (**ballets**) 1 N-UNCOUNT **Ballet** is a type of artistic dancing with carefully planned movements. ballet ❑ I trained as a ballet dancer. Me formé como bailarina de ballet. 2 N-COUNT A **ballet** is an artistic work that is performed by ballet dancers. ballet ❑ The performance will include three new ballets. La función incluirá tres ballets nuevos.
→ see **dance**

**ball game** (**ball games**) 1 N-COUNT **Ball games** are games that are played with a ball such as tennis, baseball, and football. juegos de pelota 2 N-COUNT A **ball game** is a baseball match. juego de béisbol ❑ I'd like to go to a ball game. Quisiera ir a un juego de béisbol. 3 N-SING You can use **ball game** to describe any situation or activity, especially one that involves competition. juego, jugada ❑ Two of his biggest competitors are out of the ball game. Dos de sus rivales más fuertes quedaron fuera de la jugada.

**bal|loon** /bəlun/ (**balloons, ballooning, ballooned**) 1 N-COUNT A **balloon** is a small, thin, rubber bag that you blow air into so that it becomes larger. globo ❑ She popped a balloon with her fork. Reventó el globo con su tenedor. 2 N-COUNT A **balloon** is a large, strong bag filled with gas or hot air, which can carry passengers in a container that hangs underneath it. globo aerostático ❑ They will attempt to circle the Earth by balloon. Tratarán de dar la vuelta a la tierra en globo. 3 V-I When something **balloons,** it increases rapidly in size or amount. hincharse, aumentar rápidamente ❑ The jail's female population has ballooned in recent years. La población femenina de la cárcel ha aumentado rápidamente en los últimos años.
→ see **fly**

**bal|lot** /bælət/ (**ballots**) N-COUNT A **ballot** is a secret vote in which people select a candidate in an election, or express their opinion about something. votación ❑ *The result of the ballot will not be known for two weeks.* No se conocerá el resultado de la votación antes de dos semanas.
→ see **election, vote**

**ball|player** /bɔlpleɪər/ (**ballplayers**) also **ball player** N-COUNT A **ballplayer** is a baseball player. jugador de béisbol o jugadora de béisbol, beisbolista

**ball|room danc|ing** N-UNCOUNT **Ballroom dancing** is a type of dancing in which a man and a woman dance together using fixed sequences of steps and movements. baile de salón
→ see **dance**

**ba|lo|ney** /bəloʊni/ N-UNCOUNT If you say that an idea or statement is **baloney,** you disapprove of it and think it is foolish or wrong. tonterías [INFORMAL] ❑ *That's a lot of baloney.* ¡Tonterías!

**bam|boo** /bæmbu/ (**bamboos**) N-VAR **Bamboo** is a tall tropical plant with hard, hollow stems. bambú ❑ *...huts with walls made of bamboo.* ...chozas con paredes de bambú.

**ban** /bæn/ (**bans, banning, banned**) **1** V-T To **ban** something means to state officially that it must not be done, shown, or used. prohibir, vedar ❑ *Scotland will ban hunting with dogs today.* Escocia prohibirá la cacería con perros hoy. **2** N-COUNT A **ban** is an official ruling that something must not be done, shown, or used. prohibición ❑ *The general lifted the ban on political parties.* El general levantó la prohibición de partidos políticos. **3** V-T If you **are banned from** doing something, you are officially prevented from doing it. prohibir ❑ *He was banned from driving for three years.* Le prohibieron manejar durante tres años.

**ba|na|na** /bənænə/ (**bananas**) N-VAR **Bananas** are long curved fruit with yellow skins. plátano, banana ❑ *...a bunch of bananas.* ...un racimo de plátanos.
→ see **fruit**

**band** /bænd/ (**bands, banding, banded**) **1** N-COUNT A **band** is a group of musicians who play popular music such as jazz, rock, or pop. banda, conjunto ❑ *He was a drummer in a rock band.* Era baterista de una banda de rock. **2** N-COUNT A **band** is a group of musicians who play brass and percussion instruments. banda ❑ *Bands played German marches.* Las bandas tocaron marchas alemanas. **3** N-COUNT A **band of** people is a group of people who have joined together because they share an interest or belief. banda, pandilla ❑ *...bands of rebels.* ...pandillas de rebeldes. **4** N-COUNT A **band** is a flat, narrow strip of cloth which you wear around your head or wrists, or which forms part of a piece of clothing. cinta, brazalete ❑ *Almost all hospitals use a wrist-band of some kind.* Casi todos los hospitales usan un brazalete de algún tipo. **5** N-COUNT A **band** is a strip or loop of metal or other strong material which strengthens something, or which holds several things together. abrazadera, fleje ❑ *His hand was like an iron band around her arm.* Sentía que su mano le apretaba el brazo como una garra. **6** N-COUNT A **band** is a range of numbers or values within a system of measurement. banda ❑ *A 10 megahertz-wide band of frequencies will be needed.* Se necesitará una banda de frecuencias de 10 megahercios de ancho.
→ see **concert, theater**
▸ **band together** PHR-VERB If people **band together,** they meet and act as a group in order to try and achieve something. unirse, hacer causa común ❑ *Women banded together to protect each other.* Las mujeres hicieron causa común para protegerse.

**band|age** /bændɪdʒ/ (**bandages, bandaging, bandaged**) **1** N-COUNT A **bandage** is a long strip of cloth that is wrapped around a wounded part of your body to protect or support it. venda, vendaje ❑ *We put a bandage on his knee.* Le pusimos una venda en la rodilla. **2** V-T If you **bandage** a wound or part of someone's body, you tie a bandage around it. vendar ❑ *Apply a dressing to the wound and bandage it.* Aplica un apósito en la herida y véndala.

**band|width** /bændwɪdθ, -wɪtθ/ (**bandwidths**) N-VAR A **bandwidth** is the range of frequencies used for a particular telecommunications signal, radio transmission, or computer network. ancho (amplitud, anchura) de banda ❑ *To cope with this amount of data, the system will need a bandwidth of around 100 megahertz.* Para procesar esta cantidad de datos, el sistema requerirá un ancho de banda de unos 100 megahercios.

**bang** /bæŋ/ (**bangs, banging, banged**) **1** N-COUNT A **bang** is a sudden loud noise such as the noise of an explosion. detonación, estallido ❑ *I heard four or five loud bangs.* Oí cuatro o cinco detonaciones fuertes., Oí cuatro o cinco estallidos fuertes. ❑ *She slammed the door with a bang.* Cerró la puerta de un portazo. **2** V-T/V-I If you **bang** a door, or if it **bangs,** it closes suddenly with a loud noise. cerrar de golpe, dar golpes, golpearse ❑ *...the sound of doors banging.* ...el sonido de puertas golpeándose. ❑ *All up and down the street the windows bang shut.* A todo lo largo de la calle, las ventanas se cierran de golpe. **3** V-T/V-I If you **bang on** something or if you **bang** it, you hit it hard, making a loud noise. golpear ❑ *We decided to bang on the desks and shout till they let us out.* Decidimos golpear sobre los escritorios hasta que nos dejaran salir. **4** V-T If you **bang** a part of your body, you accidentally knock it against something and hurt yourself. golpearse ❑ *She fainted and banged her head.* Se desmayó y se golpeó la cabeza. • **Bang** is also a noun. golpe ❑ *...a nasty bang on the head.* ...un fuerte golpe en la cabeza. **5** N-PLURAL **Bangs** are hair which is cut so that it hangs over your forehead. fleco ❑ *My bangs were cut short, but the rest of my hair was long.* Mi fleco estaba corto, pero el resto de mi pelo estaba largo.
→ see **hair**

**bang-up** also **bang up** ADJ Some people use **bang-up** to describe something they think is very good or enjoyable. súper [INFORMAL] ❑ *NET has done a bang-up job of designing its products for young people.* NET hizo un trabajo súper al diseñar sus productos para los jóvenes.

**bank**
❶ FINANCE AND STORAGE
❷ AREAS AND MASSES
❸ VERB USES

❶ **bank** /bæŋk/ (**banks**) **1** N-COUNT A **bank** is a place where people can keep their money. banco ❑ *Students should see which bank offers them the service*

B

*that best suits their financial needs. Los estudiantes deberían ver qué banco les ofrece el servicio que mejor satisfaga sus necesidades financieras.* **2** N-COUNT You use **bank** to refer to a store of something. For example, a blood **bank** is a store of blood. *banco* ❑ *...a national data bank of information on hospital employees. ...un banco de datos nacional con información sobre los empleados de los hospitales.*

**❷ bank** /bæŋk/ (**banks**) **1** N-COUNT The **banks of** a river, canal, or lake are the raised areas of ground along its edge. *ribera, orilla* ❑ *We walked along the east bank of the river. Caminamos a lo largo de la ribera oriente del río.* **2** N-COUNT A **bank** of ground is a raised area of it with a flat top and one or two sloping sides. *talud* ❑ *...resting on the grassy bank. ...descansando (apoyado) sobre el talud cubierto de hierba.* **3** N-COUNT A **bank of** something is a long high mass of it. *banco, masa* ❑ *...a bank of clouds. ...un banco de nubes., ...una masa de nubes.*

**❸ bank** /bæŋk/ (**banks, banking, banked**)
▸ **bank on** PHR-VERB If you **bank on** something happening, you rely on it happening. *contar con* ❑ *Everyone is banking on his recovery. Todos cuentan con su recuperación.*

**bank card** (**bank cards**) also **ATM card** N-COUNT A **bank card** is a plastic card which your bank gives you so you can get money from your bank account using a cash machine. *tarjeta de crédito, tarjeta bancaria*

**bank check** (**bank checks**) N-COUNT A **bank check** is a check that you can buy from a bank in order to pay someone who is not willing to accept a personal check. *cheque* ❑ *Payments should be made by bank check in U.S. dollars. Los pagos deberán hacerse con cheque en dólares estadounidenses.*

**bank|er** /bæŋkər/ (**bankers**) N-COUNT A **banker** is someone who works in banking at a senior level. *banquero o banquera* ❑ *...an investment banker. ...un ejecutivo de un banco de negocios.*

**bank|ing** /bæŋkɪŋ/ N-UNCOUNT **Banking** is the business activity of banks and similar institutions. *banca* ❑ *...online banking. ...banca en línea.*
→ see **industry**

**bank|rupt** /bæŋkrʌpt/ (**bankrupts, bankrupting, bankrupted**) **1** ADJ People or organizations that go **bankrupt** do not have enough money to pay their debts. *en quiebra, en bancarrota* [BUSINESS] ❑ *If the firm cannot sell its products, it will go bankrupt. Si la compañía no puede vender sus productos, irá a la quiebra.* **2** V-T To **bankrupt** a person or organization means to make them go bankrupt. *hacer quebrar, arruinar* [BUSINESS] ❑ *It became known as the most expensive film ever made and almost bankrupted the studio. Llegó a conocérsele como la película más cara de todos los tiempos y casi hizo quebrar a los estudios.* **3** ADJ If you say that something is **bankrupt,** you are emphasizing that it lacks any value or worth. *en quiebra, en bancarrota* ❑ *He thinks that European civilization is morally bankrupt. Él cree que la civilización europea está en bancarrota moral.*

**bank|rupt|cy** /bænkrʌptsi/ (**bankruptcies**) **1** N-UNCOUNT **Bankruptcy** is the state of being bankrupt. *quiebra, bancarrota* [BUSINESS] ❑ *He was brought in to rescue the company from bankruptcy. Lo trajeron para que rescatara a la compañía de la bancarrota.* **2** N-COUNT A **bankruptcy** is an instance of an organization or person going bankrupt. *quiebra, bancarrota* [BUSINESS] ❑ *The number of corporate bankruptcies climbed in August. El número de empresas quebradas aumentó en agosto.*

**Word Partnership** Usar *bankruptcy* con:

V. **force into** bankruptcy **1**
**avoid** bankruptcy **1 2**
**declare** bankruptcy, **file for** bankruptcy **2**
N. bankruptcy **law**, bankruptcy **protection 1 2**

**ban|ner** /bænər/ (**banners**) N-COUNT A **banner** is a long strip of cloth with something written on it. *pancarta* ❑ *The crowd danced and sang, and waved banners, flags, and caps. La multitud bailaba, cantaba y ondeaba pancartas, banderas y gorras.*

**ban|ner ad** (**banner ads**) N-COUNT A **banner ad** is a rectangular advertisement on a web page that contains a link to the advertiser's website. *báner* ❑ *See our banner ad at this site! ¡Vea nuestro báner publicitario en este sitio!*

**bar** /bɑr/ (**bars, barring, barred**) **1** N-COUNT A **bar** is a place where you can buy and drink alcoholic drinks. *bar* ❑ *...the city's most popular bar. ...el bar más popular de la ciudad.* **2** N-COUNT A **bar** is a counter on which alcoholic drinks are served. *bar* ❑ *Michael was standing alone by the bar when Brian joined him. Michael estaba solo junto al bar cuando Brian se le unió.* **3** N-COUNT A **bar** is a long, straight, stiff piece of metal. *barra* ❑ *...a building with bars across the ground floor windows. ...un edificio con barras atravesadas en las ventanas de la planta baja.* **4** N-COUNT A **bar of** something is a piece of it which is roughly rectangular. *tableta* ❑ *What is your favorite chocolate bar? ¿Cuál es tu tableta de chocolate preferida?* **5** V-T If you **bar** someone's way, you prevent them from going somewhere or entering a place, by blocking their path. *bloquear* ❑ *Harry moved to bar his way. Harry propuso que se le bloqueara el paso.* **6** V-T If someone **is barred from** a place or **from** doing something, they are officially forbidden to go there or to do it. *prohibir* ❑ *He has been barred from working in this country. Se le prohibió trabajar en el país.* **7** N-COUNT If something is a **bar to** doing a particular thing, it prevents someone from doing it. *obstáculo* ❑ *One of the bars to communication is the lack of a common language. Uno de los obstáculos para la comunicación es la falta de un lenguaje común.* **8** N-SING **The bar** is used to refer to the profession of any kind of lawyer in the United States, or of a barrister in England. *abogacía, cuerpo de abogados* ❑ *Very few graduates from the law school pass the bar exam on the first try. Muy pocos egresados de la escuela de derecho pasan el examen del cuerpo de abogados al primer intento.* **9** N-COUNT In music, a **bar** is one of the several short parts of the same length into which a piece of music is divided. *compás* ❑ *The opening bars of a waltz filled the room. El cuarto se llenó con los primeros compases de un vals.* **10** PHRASE If you say that someone is **behind bars,** you mean that they are in prison. *tras las rejas* ❑ *Fisher was behind bars last night, charged with*

*attempted murder.* *Fisher pasó la noche tras las rejas, acusado de intento de homicidio.*
→ see **soap**

**bar|becue** /bɑrbɪkyu/ (**barbecues, barbecuing, barbecued**) also **barbeque** or **Bar-B-Q**
1 N-COUNT A **barbecue** is a piece of equipment which you use for cooking on outdoors. *asador*
2 N-COUNT If someone has a **barbecue,** they cook food on a barbecue in the open air. *asado, parrillada* ❑ *On New Year's Eve we had a barbecue on the beach.* *La víspera de año nuevo hicimos una parrillada en la playa.* 3 V-T If you **barbecue** food, you cook it on a barbecue. *asar* ❑ *Tuna can be grilled, fried or barbecued.* *El atún se puede asar a la parrilla, a las brasas o freír.* ❑ *Here's a way of barbecuing fish that I learned from my uncle.* *Esta es una receta de pescado asado que aprendí de mi tío.*
→ see **cook**

**bar|bell** /bɑrbɛl/ (**barbells**) N-COUNT A **barbell** is a long bar with adjustable weights on either side that people lift to strengthen their arm and shoulder muscles. *barra de pesas* ❑ *She lifted the barbell in her left hand.* *Levantó la barra de pesas con la mano izquierda.*

**bar|ber** /bɑrbər/ (**barbers**) N-COUNT A **barber** is a person whose job is cutting men's hair. *peluquero o peluquera, barbero*

**bare** /bɛər/ (**barer, barest, bares, baring, bared**)
1 ADJ If a part of your body is **bare,** it is not covered by any clothing. *desnudo, descalzo* ❑ *Her feet were bare.* *Estaba descalza., Estaba con los pies descalzos.* 2 ADJ A **bare** surface is not covered or decorated with anything. *desnudo* ❑ *...bare wooden floors.* *...pisos de madera desnudos.* 3 ADJ If a room, cupboard, or shelf is **bare,** it is empty. *vacío* ❑ *His refrigerator was bare.* *Su refrigerador estaba vacío.*
4 ADJ If someone gives you the **bare** facts or the **barest** details of something, they tell you only the most basic and important things. *escueto* ❑ *Newspaper reporters were given only the bare facts by the officer in charge of the investigation.* *Los periodistas sólo recibieron los hechos escuetos de parte del agente a cargo de la investigación.* 5 ADJ If you talk about the **bare** minimum or the **bare** essentials, you mean the very least that is necessary. *lo estrictamente mínimo, necesario o esencial* ❑ *We learned that it was all right to do the bare minimum at school.* *Aprendimos que estaba bien hacer lo estrictamente mínimo en la escuela.* 6 V-T If you **bare** something, you uncover it and show it. *mostrar* [WRITTEN] ❑ *Walsh bared his teeth in a grin.* *Walsh sonrió burlonamente, mostrando los dientes.* 7 PHRASE If you do something **with** your **bare hands,** you do it without using any weapons or tools. *con las manos* ❑ *Rescuers used their bare hands to reach the trapped miners.* *Los rescatistas se valieron de sus propias manos para llegar hasta los mineros atrapados.*

**bare-bones** ADJ If you describe something as **bare-bones,** you mean that it is reduced to the smallest size, amount, or number that you need. *esencial* ❑ *...the city's bare-bones budget.* *...el presupuesto esencial para la ciudad.*

**bare|ly** /bɛərli/ 1 ADV You use **barely** to say that something is only just true or possible *apenas* ❑ *Anastasia could barely remember the ride to the hospital.* *Anastasia apenas podía recordar la ida al hospital.* ❑ *It was 90 degrees and the air conditioning barely cooled the room.* *Había 32 grados de temperatura y el aire acondicionado apenas enfriaba un poco el cuarto.* 2 ADV If you say that one thing had **barely** happened when something else happened, you mean that the first event was followed immediately by the second. *apenas* ❑ *She had barely sat down at the awards ceremony when she was called on stage.* *Apenas se había sentado en la ceremonia de entrega de premios, cuando la llamaron al escenario.*

**barf** (**barfs, barfing, barfed**) V-I If someone **barfs,** they vomit. *vomitar* [INFORMAL] ❑ *When I first tasted it I almost barfed.* *Cuando lo probé por primera vez, estuve a punto de vomitar.*

**bar|gain** /bɑrgɪn/ (**bargains, bargaining, bargained**) 1 N-COUNT Something that is a **bargain** is good value, usually because it has been sold at a lower price than normal. *ganga* ❑ *At this price the dress is a bargain.* *A este precio, el vestido es una ganga.* 2 N-COUNT A **bargain** is an agreement in which two people or groups agree what each of them will do, pay, or receive. *trato, negociación* ❑ *I'll make a bargain with you. I'll be the hostess if you'll include Matthew in your guest list.* *Hagamos un trato: yo seré la anfitriona si incluyes a Matthew en tu lista de invitados.* 3 V-I When people **bargain with** each other, they discuss what each of them will do, pay, or receive. *regatear* ❑ *They prefer to bargain with individual clients, for cash.* *Prefieren regatear al contado con cada cliente.* ● **bar|gain|ing** N-UNCOUNT *negociar* ❑ *The pay rise was the subject of intense bargaining last night.* *El aumento salarial fue motivo de intensas negociaciones anoche.* 4 PHRASE You use **into the bargain** or **in the bargain** when mentioning an additional quantity, feature, fact, or action, to emphasize the fact that it is also involved. *encima* ❑ *The taxis here are cheap, and you can have a great conversation with the driver thrown into the bargain.* *Los taxis aquí son baratos y, encima, puedes tener una gran conversación con el chofer.*
→ see **union**

▸ **bargain for** or **bargain on** PHR-VERB If you have not **bargained for** or **bargained on** something that happens, you did not expect it to happen and so feel surprised or worried by it. *no tener en cuenta* ❑ *The effects of this policy are more than the government bargained for.* *Los efectos de esta política son más que los esperados por el gobierno., Esta política tiene otros efectos que el gobierno no había tenido en cuenta.*

**Thesaurus** *bargain* Ver también:

| | |
|---|---|
| N. | deal, discount, markdown 1 |
| | agreement, deal, understanding 2 |
| V. | barter, haggle, negotiate 3 |

**Word Partnership** Usar *bargain* con:

| | |
|---|---|
| V. | **find/get a** bargain 1 |
| | **make/strike a** bargain 2 |
| N. | bargain **hunter**, bargain **price**, bargain **rates** 1 |
| | **part of the** bargain 2 |
| PREP. | bargain **with** ***someone*** 3 |

**barge** /bɑrdʒ/ (**barges, barging, barged**)
1 N-COUNT A **barge** is a long, narrow boat with a flat bottom, used for carrying heavy loads. *barcaza*

B

❑ *Carrying goods by train costs three times more than carrying them by barge.* *El transporte de mercancías en tren cuesta tres veces más que en barcaza.* **2** V-I If you **barge into** a place or **barge through** it, you rush or push into it in a rough and rude way. *entrar sin llamar* [INFORMAL] ❑ *Please knock before you barge into my room.* *Por favor, no entres en mi cuarto sin antes llamar.* **3** V-I If you **barge into** someone or **barge past** them, you bump against them roughly and rudely. *abrirse paso con los codos, abrirse paso a empujones* [INFORMAL] ❑ *He barged into them and kicked them.* *Se abrió paso a empujones entre ellos y los pateó.*
→ see **ship**

**bar graph** (**bar graphs**) N-COUNT A **bar graph** is a graph which uses parallel rectangular shapes to represent changes in the size, value or rate of something. *gráfica de barras*
→ see **chart, graph**

**bark** /bɑrk/ (**barks, barking, barked**) **1** V-I When a dog **barks,** it makes a short, loud noise. *ladrar* ❑ *Don't let the dogs bark.* *No dejes que ladren los perros.* • **Bark** is also a noun. *ladrido* ❑ *Your child may be afraid of a dog's bark, its smell or its size.* *Es posible que tu hijo tenga miedo del ladrido de los perros, de su olor o de su tamaño.* **2** N-UNCOUNT **Bark** is the tough material that covers the outside of a tree. *corteza*

**barn** /bɑrn/ (**barns**) N-COUNT A **barn** is a building on a farm in which animals, animal food, or crops can be kept. *establo, granero*
→ see Picture Dictionary: **barn**

**barn|yard** /bɑrnyɑrd/ (**barnyards**) N-COUNT On a farm, **the barnyard** is the area in front of or next to a barn. *corral, patio*
→ see **barn**

**ba|rom|eter** /bərɒmɪtər/ (**barometers**) N-COUNT A **barometer** is an instrument that measures air pressure and shows when the weather is changing. *barómetro*

**baro|met|ric** /bærəmɛtrɪk/ ADJ **Barometric** pressure is the atmospheric pressure that is shown by a barometer. *barométrico*
→ see **weather**

**bar|racks** /bærəks/ (**barracks**) N-COUNT A **barracks** is a building or group of buildings where soldiers or other members of the armed forces live and work. *cuartel* ❑ *...an army barracks in the north of the city.* *...un cuartel del ejército en el norte de la ciudad.*

**bar|rel** /bærəl/ (**barrels**) **1** N-COUNT A **barrel** is a large, round container for liquids or food. *barril, tonel* ❑ *...oak barrels.* *...toneles de roble.* **2** N-COUNT The **barrel** of a gun is the tube through which the bullet moves when the gun is fired. *cañón*

**barrel-chested** ADJ A **barrel-chested** man has a large, rounded chest. *fornido* ❑ *A barrel-chested young man entered the room.* *Un hombre joven y fornido entró al cuarto.*

**bar|ren** /bærən/ ADJ **Barren** land consists of soil that is so poor that plants cannot grow in it. *estéril, desierto* ❑ *...barren desert land.* *...tierra desértica y estéril., ...un desierto.*

**bar|rette** /bərɛt/ (**barrettes**) N-COUNT A **barrette** is a small metal or plastic device that a woman uses to hold her hair in position. *broche* ❑ *Sarah's hair was held back by a barrette.* *Un broche sostenía el pelo de Sara en la parte posterior de la cabeza.*

**bar|ri|cade** /bærɪkeɪd/ (**barricades, barricading, barricaded**) **1** N-COUNT A **barricade** is a line of vehicles or other objects placed across a road or open space to stop people from getting past, for example, during street fighting or as a protest. *barricada* ❑ *Large areas of the city were blocked by barricades.* *Grandes áreas de la ciudad estaban bloqueadas con barricadas.* **2** V-T If you **barricade** something such as a road or an entrance, you place a barricade or barrier across it, usually to

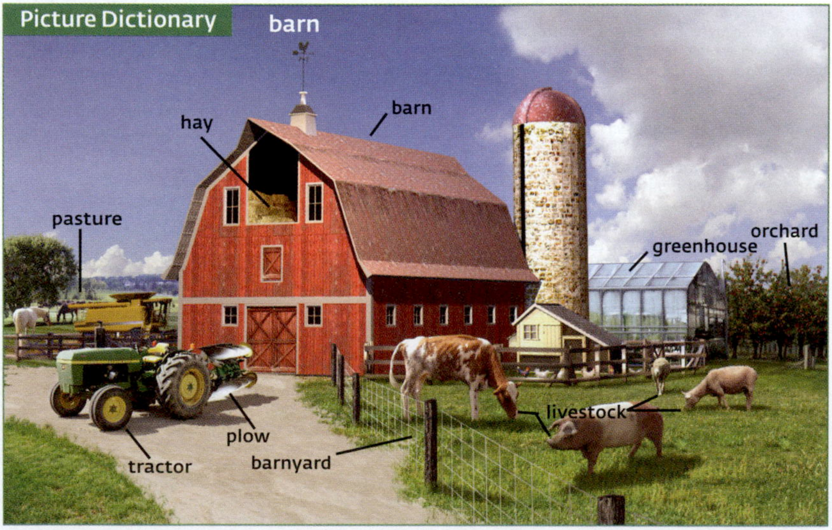

stop someone from getting in. cerrar con barricadas ❑ *Youths barricaded streets with burning tires.* *Los jóvenes cerraron las calles con barricadas de llantas encendidas.* 3 V-T If you **barricade** yourself inside a room or building, you place barriers across the door or entrance so that other people cannot get in. *atrincherarse* ❑ *The students have barricaded themselves into their dormitory building.* *Los estudiantes se han atrincherado en su dormitorio.*

**bar|ri|er** /bæriər/ (**barriers**) 1 N-COUNT A **barrier** is something such as a rule, law, or policy that makes it difficult or impossible for something to happen or be achieved. *barrera* ❑ *Taxes are the most obvious barrier to free trade.* *Los impuestos son la barrera más obvia al libre comercio.* 2 N-COUNT A **barrier** is something such as a fence or wall that prevents people or things from moving from one area to another. *valla* ❑ *A police barrier still blocked the road.* *Una valla de la policía seguía bloqueando la carretera (la avenida).*

barrier

**Word Partnership** Usar *barrier* con:

ADJ. **psychological** barrier, **racial** barrier 1
N. **language** barrier 1
**police** barrier 2
PREP. barrier **between** 1 2
V. **break down a** barrier, **cross a** barrier 1 2

**bar|rio** /bɑrioʊ/ (**barrios**) 1 N-COUNT A **barrio** is a mainly Spanish-speaking area in an American city. *barrio de hablantes del español en una ciudad estadounidense* ❑ *...the barrios of Santa Cruz.* *...los barrios de hispanohablantes de Santa Cruz.* 2 N-COUNT A **barrio** is an urban district in a Spanish-speaking country. *barrio* ❑ *...the barrios of Mexico City.* *...los barrios de la ciudad de México.*

**bar|ris|ter** /bærɪstər/ (**barristers**) N-COUNT In England and Wales, a **barrister** is a lawyer who represents clients in the higher courts of law. *abogado habilitado para llevar casos ante un tribunal superior*

**bar|tender** /bɑrtɛndər/ (**bartenders**) N-COUNT A **bartender** is a person who serves drinks behind a bar. *camarero o camarera, cantinero o cantinera, barman*

**bar|ter** /bɑrtər/ (**barters, bartering, bartered**) V-T/V-I If you **barter** goods, you exchange them for other goods, rather than selling them for money. *hacer trueque, cambiar* ❑ *They have been bartering wheat for cotton and timber.* *Han estado haciendo trueque de trigo por algodón y madera.* ❑ *The men were trading animal skins, bartering for jewellery.* *Los hombres hacían trueque de pieles de animales por joyería.* ● **Barter** is also a noun.
→ see **money**

**bas|alt** /bəsɔlt, beɪsɔlt/ N-UNCOUNT **Basalt** is a type of black rock that is produced by volcanoes. *basalto*

**base** /beɪs/ (**bases, basing, based**) 1 N-COUNT The **base** of something is its lowest edge or part. *base* ❑ *...a bright red candle with artificial roses around its base.* *...una vela rojo brillante con rosas artificiales alrededor de la base.* ❑ *...the base of the skull.* *...la base del cráneo.* 2 N-COUNT The **base** of an object is the lower surface or section of it. *base* ❑ *Put the base of the pan into a bowl of very cold water.* *Pon la base de la cacerola en una palangana con agua muy fría.* 3 N-COUNT A position or thing that is a **base** for something is one from which that thing can be developed or achieved. *base* ❑ *The company has developed a plan to establish a base for future growth.* *La empresa elaboró un plan para sentar (echar) las bases de su desarrollo futuro.* 4 V-T If you **base** one thing **on** another thing, the first thing develops from the second thing. *basar* ❑ *He based his conclusions on the evidence.* *Basó sus conclusiones en las pruebas.* ❑ *...products based on traditional herbal medicines.* *...productos basados en la herbolaria tradicional.* ❑ *The film is based on a novel by Alexander Trocchi.* *La película se basa en una novela de Alexander Trocchi.* 5 N-COUNT A military **base** is a place that part of the armed forces works from. *base* ❑ *...an army base close to the airport.* *...una base del ejército cercana al aeropuerto.* 6 N-COUNT Your **base** is the main place where you work, stay, or live. *domicilio principal* ❑ *For most of the summer her base was her home in Connecticut.* *Durante la mayor parte del verano, su domicilio principal fue su casa de Connecticut.* 7 N-COUNT A **base** in baseball or softball is one of the places at each corner of the diamond on the field. A player who is at **first base, second base,** or **third base,** is standing at the first, second, or third base in a counterclockwise direction from home plate. *base* ❑ *The first runner to reach second base was John Flaherty.* *El primer corredor en alcanzar la segunda base fue John Flaherty.* 8 N-COUNT In chemistry, a **base** is a substance which has the opposite effect to an acid. Bases react with acids to form salts and turn red litmus paper blue. *base* 9 PHRASE If you say that someone is **off base,** you mean that they are wrong. *estar equivocado, andar errado* [INFORMAL] ❑ *Am I way off base?* *¿Estoy muy equivocado?, ¿Ando muy errado?*
→ see **area, baseball**

**Word Partnership** Usar *base* con:

N. **knowledge** base, **tax** base 3
base **camp**, **home** base, base **of operation** 6
base **hit/run** 7
ADJ. **military/naval** base 5
**stolen** base 7

**base|ball** /beɪsbɔl/ N-UNCOUNT **Baseball** is a game played by two teams of nine players. Each player from one team hits a ball with a bat and then tries to run around three bases and get to home plate before the other team can get the ball back. *béisbol*
→ see Picture Dictionary: **baseball**
→ see **park**

**base|ball cap** (**baseball caps**) N-COUNT A **baseball cap** is a close-fitting cap with a curved part at the front that sticks out above your eyes. *gorra de béisbol* ❑ *He often wore a baseball cap.* *Casi siempre llevaba puesta una gorra de béisbol.*
→ see **clothing, hat**

B

## Picture Dictionary baseball

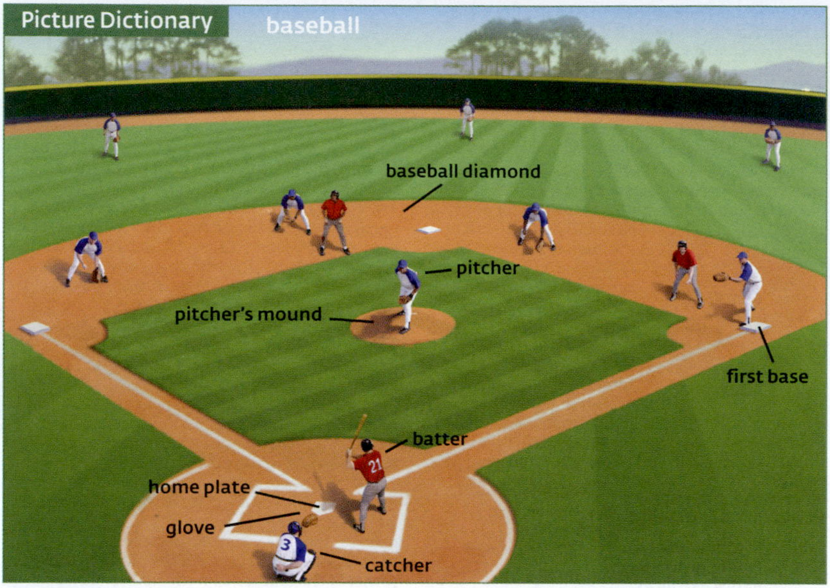


**base|ment** /beɪsmənt/ (**basements**) N-COUNT The **basement** of a building is a floor built partly or completely below ground level. *sótano* ❑ *They built a workshop in the basement. Instalaron un taller en el sótano.*
→ see **house**

**bases**

Pronounced /beɪsɪz/ for meaning **1**.
Pronounced /beɪsiz/ and hyphenated ba|ses for meaning **2**.

**1** **Bases** is the plural of **base**. *plural de **base***
**2** **Bases** is the plural of **basis**. *plural de **basis***

**base word** (**base words**) N-COUNT A **base word** is a word that you can add a prefix or suffix to in order to create other related words. *lexema* [TECHNICAL]

**bash** /bæʃ/ (**bashes, bashing, bashed**) **1** N-COUNT A **bash** is a party or celebration. *juerga, parranda* [INFORMAL] ❑ *...birthday bashes. ...parrandas de cumpleaños.* **2** V-T If you **bash** someone or something, you hit them hard in a rough way. *golpear, pegar, aporrear* [INFORMAL] ❑ *I bashed him on the head. Lo golpeé en la cabeza., Le pegué en la cabeza.* ❑ *Too many golfers try to bash the ball out of the sand. Muchos golfistas tratan de sacar la pelota a porrazos de la trampa de arena.*

**ba|sic** /beɪsɪk/ **1** ADJ You use **basic** to describe the most important or simplest aspects of something. *básico, fundamental* ❑ *...the basic skills of reading and writing. ...las habilidades básicas de lectura y escritura.* ❑ *Access to justice is a basic right. El acceso a la justicia es un derecho fundamental.* **2** ADJ **Basic** goods and services are very simple ones which every human being needs. *básico* ❑ *...shortages of even the most basic foods. ...escasez incluso de los alimentos más básicos.* ❑ *Hospitals lack even basic drugs for surgical operations. Los hospitales carecen incluso de las drogas básicas para las operaciones quirúrgicas.* **3** ADJ If one thing is **basic to** another, it is absolutely necessary to it. *básico, fundamental* ❑ *...an oily liquid, basic to the manufacture of many other chemical substances. ...un líquido aceitoso, básico (fundamental) para la fabricación de muchas otras sustancias químicas.* **4** ADJ You can use **basic** to describe something that has only the most necessary features, without any luxuries. *básico* ❑ *We provide basic cooking and camping equipment. Proveemos el equipo básico para cocinar y acampar.*

**Thesaurus** *basic* Ver también:

ADJ. essential, fundamental, key, main, necessary, principal, vital; (*ant.*) nonessential, secondary **1** – **4**

**Word Partnership** Usar *basic* con:

N. basic **right** **1**
basic **idea**, basic **principles/values**, basic **problem**, basic **questions**, basic **skills**, basic **understanding** **1**
basic **(health) care**, basic **needs** **2** **4**
ADJ. **most** basic, basic **types of *something*** **1** – **4**

**ba|si|cal|ly** /beɪsɪkli/ **1** ADV You use **basically** for emphasis when you are stating an opinion, or when you are making an important statement about something. *fundamentalmente* ❑ *Basically, the whole thing was extremely dull. En pocas (dos) palabras, la cosa fue (estuvo) muy aburrida.* **2** ADV You use **basically** to show that you are describing a situation in a simple, general way. *fundamentalmente* ❑ *Basically you have two choices. En* *pocas (dos) palabras, tienes dos opciones.*

**ba|sin** /beɪsᵊn/ (**basins**) **1** N-COUNT A **basin** is a large or deep bowl that you use for holding liquids. *cuenco, palangana, bol* ❑ *Water dripped into a basin at the back of the room. Las gotas de agua caían en una palangana en la parte trasera del cuarto.* **2** N-COUNT A **basin** is a sink. *lavabo* ❑ *...a white bathtub with a matching basin. ...una tina blanca con un lavabo que hacía juego.* **3** N-COUNT The **basin** of a large river is the area of land around it from which streams run down into it. *cuenca* ❑ *...the Amazon basin. ...la cuenca amazónica (del Amazonas).*
→ see **lake**

**ba|sis** /beɪsɪs/ (**bases** /beɪsiz/) **1** N-SING If something is done **on** a particular **basis**, it is done according to that method, system, or principle. *base* ❑ *We're going to be meeting there on a regular basis. Nos vamos a reunir ahí de manera regular.* ❑ *They want all groups to be treated on an equal basis. Quieren que se trate a todos los grupos de igual manera.* **2** N-SING If you say that you are acting **on the basis of** something, you are giving that as the reason for your action. *de acuerdo con* ❑ *McGregor must remain in bed, on the basis of the medical reports. De acuerdo con los informes médicos, McGregor debe permanecer en cama.* **3** N-COUNT The **basis** of something is the central or most important part of it from which it can be further developed. *base* ❑ *The UN plan is a possible basis for peace talks. El plan de las Naciones Unidas es una posible base para las pláticas de paz.*

**Word Partnership** Usar *basis* con:

| | |
|---|---|
| ADJ. | **equal** basis, **on a daily/regular/weekly** basis, **on a voluntary** basis **1** |
| PREP. | **on the** basis **of** *something* **2 3** basis **for** *something* **3** |
| V. | **provide a** basis, **serve as a** basis **3** |

**bas|ket** /bæskɪt/ (**baskets**) N-COUNT A **basket** is a stiff container that is used for carrying or storing objects. Baskets are made from thin strips of materials such as straw, plastic, or wire woven together. *canasta, canasto, cesta, cesto* ❑ *...picnic baskets filled with sandwiches. ...canastas de día de campo llenas de sándwiches.*

**basket|ball** /bæskɪtbɔl/ N-UNCOUNT **Basketball** is a game in which two teams of five players each try to score points by throwing a large ball through a circular net attached to a metal ring at each end of the court. *básquetbol*
→ see Picture Dictionary: **basketball**

**bas|ket sponge** (**basket sponges**) N-COUNT A

**Picture Dictionary** basketball

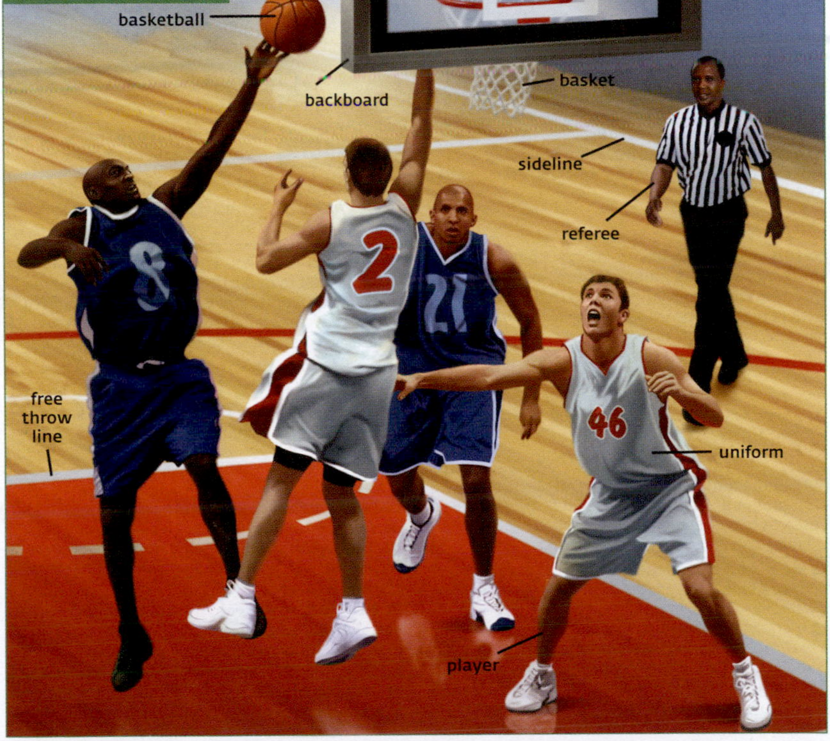

B

**Word Web** bat

**Bats** fly like birds, but they are **mammals**. Female bats give birth to their young and produce milk to feed them. Bats are **nocturnal**. They search for food at night and sleep during the day. They **roost** upside down in dark, quiet places such as caves and attics. People think that bats drink blood, but only **vampire bats** do this. Most bats eat fruit or insects. As bats fly they make high-pitched sounds that bounce off objects. This echolocation is a kind of **radar** that guides them as they fly.

**basket sponge** is a type of primitive sea creature with a hollow body that is open at the top. *esponja (euplectella aspergillus), cesta de Venus, regadera de Filipinas*

**bass** /beɪs/ (**basses**) **1** N-COUNT A **bass** is a man with a very deep singing voice. *bajo* ❑ *...the great Russian bass Chaliapin. ...el gran bajo ruso Chaliapin.* **2** ADJ A **bass** drum, guitar, or other musical instrument is one that produces a very deep sound. *bajo* ❑ *...bass guitarist Dee Murray. ...el bajista Dee Murray.*
→ see **percussion**

**bass clef** (**bass clefs**) N-COUNT A **bass clef** is a symbol that you use when writing music in order to show that the notes on the staff are below middle C. *clave de fa*

**bat** /bæt/ (**bats, batting, batted**) **1** N-COUNT A **bat** is a specially shaped piece of wood that is used for hitting the ball in baseball, softball, or cricket. *bate* ❑ *...a baseball bat. ...un bate de béisbol.* **2** V-I When you **bat**, you have a turn at hitting the ball with a bat in baseball, softball, or cricket. *batear* ❑ *Paxton hurt his elbow while he was batting. Paxton se lastimó el codo cuando estaba bateando.* **3** N-COUNT A **bat** is a small flying animal that looks like a mouse with wings made of skin. Bats are active at night. *murciélago*
→ see Word Web: **bat**
→ see **cave**

**batch** /bætʃ/ (**batches**) N-COUNT A **batch of** things or people is a group of things or people of the same kind, especially a group that is dealt with at the same time. *grupo, montón, hornada, tanda* ❑ *They announced the first batch of players for the team. Anunciaron el primer grupo de jugadores para el equipo.* ❑ *She brought a large batch of newspaper clippings. Trajo un gran montón de recortes de periódico.* ❑ *I baked a batch of cookies. Horneé una tanda (un montón) de galletas.*

**bath** /bæθ/ (**baths, bathing, bathed**)

When the form **baths** is the plural of the noun it is pronounced /bæðz/. When it is used in the present tense of the verb, it is pronounced /bɑθs/ or /bæθs/.

**1** N-COUNT A **bath** is the process of washing your body in a bathtub. *baño (de tina)* ❑ *The nurse gave him a warm bath. La enfermera le dio un baño de tina tibio.* **2** N-COUNT When you take a **bath**, you sit or lie in a bathtub filled with water in order to wash your body. *baño* ❑ *Take a shower instead of a bath. Date una ducha en lugar de bañarte en la tina (bañera).*

**bathe** /beɪð/ (**bathes, bathing, bathed**) **1** V-I When you **bathe**, you take a bath. *bañar(se)* ❑ *Most of us now bathe or shower once a day. La mayoría nos bañamos en la tina o en la regadera una vez al día.* **2** V-T If you **bathe** someone, especially a child, you wash them in a bathtub. *bañar* ❑ *Back home, Shirley feeds and bathes the baby. En casa, Shirley le da de comer al bebé y lo baña.* **3** V-T If you **bathe** a part of your body or a wound, you wash it gently or soak it in a liquid. *lavar* ❑ *Bathe the infected area in a salt solution. Lave la zona infectada con una solución salina.* **4** V-T If a place **is bathed in** light, it is covered with light, especially a gentle, pleasant light. *bañar* ❑ *The garden was bathed in warm sunshine. La cálida luz del sol bañaba el jardín.* ❑ *...a small room bathed in soft red light. ...un cuartito bañado por una suave luz roja.*

**bath|room** /bæθrum/ (**bathrooms**) **1** N-COUNT A **bathroom** is a room in a house that contains a bathtub or shower, a sink, and sometimes a toilet. *baño, cuarto de baño* **2** N-SING A **bathroom** is a room in a house or public building that contains a sink and toilet. *baño, cuarto de baño (casa), baño(s) (edificio público)* ❑ *She asked if she could use the bathroom. Preguntó si podía usar el baño.*
→ see Picture Dictionary: **bathroom**
→ see **house**

**Thesaurus** *bathroom* Ver también:

N. lavatory, boys'/girls'/ladies'/men's/ women's room; (*ant.*) powder room, restroom, toilet, washroom **2**

**bath salts** N-PLURAL You dissolve **bath salts** in bath water to make the water smell pleasant and as a water softener. *sales de baño* ❑ *She poured all of the bath salts into the swirling water of the tub. Vació todas las sales de baño en el agua arremolinada de la bañera.*

**bath|tub** /bæθtʌb/ (**bathtubs**) N-COUNT A **bathtub** is a long, usually rectangular container that you fill with water and sit in to wash your body. *bañera, tina* ❑ *...a huge pink marble bathtub. ...una enorme tina (bañera) rosa de mármol.*
→ see **bathroom**

**bats|man** /bætsmən/ (**batsmen**) N-COUNT The **batsman** in a game of cricket is the player who is batting. *bateador o bateadora* ❑ *He was the greatest batsman of his generation. Fue el mejor bateador de su generación.*

**bat|tal|ion** /bətælyən/ (**battalions**) N-COUNT A **battalion** is a large group of soldiers that consists of three or more companies. *batallón*

**bat|ter** /bætər/ (**batters, battering, battered**) **1** V-T To **batter** someone or something means to hit them many times. *apalear, aporrear, azotar* ❑ *The East Coast was battered by an unusually severe*

## Picture Dictionary bathroom

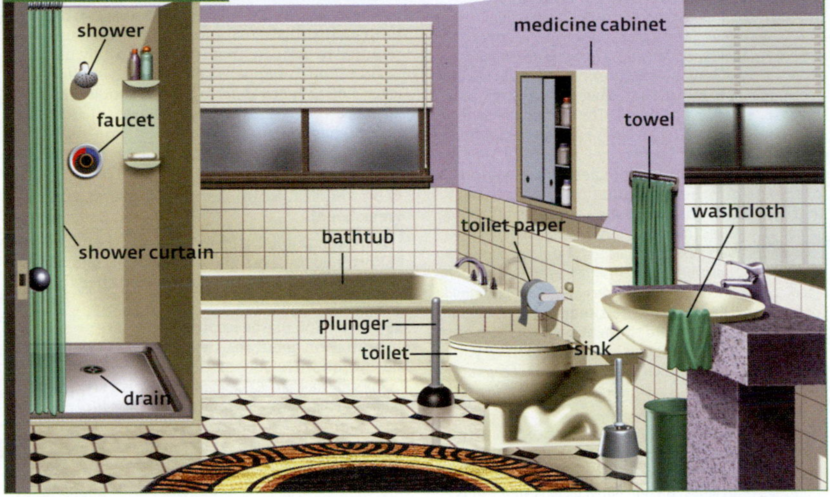


storm. La costa oriental fue azotada por una tormenta inusualmente fuerte. ❑ They were battering the door, trying to get in. Estaban aporreando la puerta, tratando de entrar. **2** N-VAR **Batter** is a mixture of flour, eggs, and milk that is used in cooking. masa ❑ ...pancake batter. ...masa para crepas. **3** N-COUNT In sports such as baseball and softball, a **batter** is a person who hits the ball. bateador o bateadora ❑ ...batters and pitchers. ...bateadores y lanzadores. **4** → see **baseball**

**bat|tery** /bætəri/ (**batteries**) **1** N-COUNT **Batteries** are small devices that provide the power for electrical items such as radios and children's toys. pila ❑ *The shavers come complete with batteries.* Las rasuradoras vienen con las pilas incluidas. ❑ *...a battery-operated watch.* ...un reloj de pilas. **2** N-COUNT A car **battery** is a rectangular box containing acid that is found in a car engine. It provides the electricity needed to start the car. batería ❑ *...a car with a dead battery.* ...un carro con la batería muerta. **3** N-UNCOUNT **Battery** is the crime of hitting or beating someone. lesión, agresión [LEGAL] ❑ *Lawrence was charged with battery.* Lawrence fue acusado de lesiones. **4** N-COUNT A **battery of** people or things is a very large number of them. multitud, ejército ❑ *...a battery of journalists and television cameras.* ...una multitud (un ejército) de periodistas y cámaras de televisión.
→ see **cellphone**

**bat|tle** /bætᵊl/ (**battles, battling, battled**) **1** N-VAR A **battle** is a violent fight between groups of people, especially one between military forces during a war. batalla, combate ❑ *...the Battle of the Boyne.* ...la Batalla del Boyne. ❑ *...a gun battle.* ...un tiroteo., ...un combate de artillería. **2** N-COUNT A **battle** is a conflict in which different people or groups compete in order to achieve success or control. lucha, batalla, combate ❑ *...a political battle over jobs and the economy.* ...una lucha política por el empleo y la economía. ❑ *...the eternal battle between good and evil in the world.* ...la eterna lucha entre el bien y el mal en el mundo. **3** V-RECIP To **battle with** an opposing group means to take part in a fight or contest against them. You can also say that one group or person **is battling** another. luchar, pelear ❑ *Thousands of people battled with police.* Miles de personas se enfrentaron a la policía. ❑ *The two players battled for a place in the final.* Los dos jugadores lucharon por un lugar en la final. **4** V-T/V-I To **battle** means to try hard to do something in spite of very difficult circumstances. You can also **battle** something, or **battle against** something or **with** something. luchar, combatir ❑ *Doctors battled throughout the night to save her life.* Los médicos lucharon toda la noche por salvarle la vida. ❑ *Firefighters are still battling the two blazes.* Los bomberos siguen combatiendo dos incendios.
→ see **army**

**Word Partnership** Usar *battle* con:

| | |
|---|---|
| ADJ. | **bloody** battle, **major** battle **1** **constant** battle, **legal** battle, **losing** battle, **uphill** battle **2** |
| V. | **prepare for** battle **1** **fight a** battle, **lose/win a** battle **1** **2** |
| N. | battle **of wills** **2** |

**battle|field** /bætᵊlfild/ (**battlefields**) **1** N-COUNT A **battlefield** is a place where a battle is fought. campo de batalla ❑ *...the struggle to save America's Civil War battlefields.* ...la lucha por salvar los campos de batalla de la guerra civil estadounidense. **2** N-COUNT You can refer to an issue or field of activity over which people disagree or compete as a **battlefield**. campo de batalla ❑ *...the battlefield of family life.* ...el campo de batalla de la vida familiar.

**battle|ship** /bætᵊlʃɪp/ (**battleships**) N-COUNT A **battleship** is a very large, heavily armed warship. acorazado

B

**bay** /beɪ/ (**bays, baying, bayed**) **1** N-COUNT A **bay** is a part of a coast where the land curves inward. *bahía* ❑ *...a short ferry ride across the bay.* *...un corto viaje en transbordador a través de la bahía.* ❑ *...the Bay of Bengal.* *...la bahía de Bengala.* **2** N-COUNT A **bay** is a partly enclosed area, inside or outside a building, that is used for a particular purpose. *corral, plataforma* ❑ *The animals are herded into a bay.* *Arriaron a los animales para hacerlos entrar al corral.* ❑ *...a cargo loading bay.* *...una plataforma de carga.* **3** V-I If a number of people **are baying for** something, they are demanding something angrily, usually that someone should be punished. *clamar* ❑ *...voices from the crowd baying for a penalty.* *...[se oyeron] voces entre la multitud que clamaban por un penalti.* ❑ *Opposition politicians have been baying for his blood.* *Los políticos de la oposición han estando clamando por su sangre.* **4** PHRASE If you **keep** something or someone **at bay,** or **hold** them **at bay,** you prevent them from reaching, attacking, or affecting you. *mantener a raya, acorralar* ❑ *Eating oranges keeps colds at bay.* *Comer naranjas mantiene a raya los resfríos.*
→ see **landform**

**BB gun** /bi bi gʌn/ (**BB guns**) N-COUNT A **BB gun** is a type of airgun that fires small round bullets that are called **BBs**. *escopeta de aire comprimido* ❑ *Sims was carrying a BB gun when he was shot.* *Sims llevaba una escopeta de aire comprimido cuando le dispararon (lo mataron).*

**BC** /bi si/ also **B.C.** You use **BC** in dates to indicate a number of years or centuries before the year in which Jesus Christ is believed to have been born. *antes de Jesucristo, a de J.C.* ❑ *The necklace dates back to the fourth century BC.* *El collar data del siglo IV antes de Jesucristo (a de J.C., a.C., de nuestra era)*

**BCE** /bi si i/ also **B.C.E.** Non-Christians often use **BCE** instead of **BC** in dates to indicate a number of years or centuries before the year in which Jesus Christ is believed to have been born. **BCE** is an abbreviation for "Before the Common Era." *antes de nuestra era* ❑ *...Lao-tzu, a sixth-century BCE Chinese teacher.* *...Lao-Tzu, maestro chino del siglo VI antes de nuestra era.* ❑ *The Babylonian Empire was conquered by the Persian Empire in 539 BCE.* *El Imperio Babilónico fue conquistado por el Imperio Persa en (el año) 539 antes de nuestra era.*

**be**

❶ AUXILIARY VERB USES
❷ OTHER VERB USES

❶ **be** /bi, STRONG bi/ (**am, are, is, being, was, were, been**)

In spoken English, forms of **be** are often shortened, for example "I am" can be shortened to "I'm" and "was not" can be shortened to "wasn't."

**1** AUX You use **be** with a present participle to form the continuous tenses of verbs. *estar* ❑ *This is happening in every school throughout the country.* *Esto está pasando en todas las escuelas del país.* ❑ *She didn't always think carefully about what she was doing.* *No siempre pensaba con cuidado en lo que estaba haciendo.* **2** **be going to** → see **going** **3** AUX You use **be** with a past participle to form the passive voice. *ser* ❑ *Her husband was killed in a car crash.* *Su marido murió en un choque de carros.* ❑ *Similar action is being taken by the U.S. government.* *El gobierno estadounidense está adoptando medidas similares.* **4** AUX You use **be** with an infinitive to indicate that something is planned to happen, that it will definitely happen, or that it must happen. *deber de + inf., ir a + inf., deber + inf.* ❑ *The talks are to begin tomorrow.* *Las pláticas deben empezar mañana.* ❑ *It was to be Johnson's first meeting with the board.* *Debía de (iba a, debía) ser la primera reunión de Johnson con la junta.* **5** **be about to** → see **about**

❷ **be** /bi, STRONG bi/ (**am, are, is, being, was, were, been**)

In spoken English, forms of **be** are often shortened, for example "I am" can be shortened to "I'm" and "was not" can be shortened to "wasn't."

**1** V-LINK You use **be** to introduce more information about the subject, such as its identity, nature, qualities, or position. *ser, estar, tener (años)* ❑ *She's my mother.* *Es mi madre.* ❑ *He is a very attractive man.* *Es un hombre muy atractivo.* ❑ *He is fifty and has been married twice.* *Tiene cincuenta años y ha estado casado dos veces.* ❑ *The sky was black.* *El cielo estaba negro.* ❑ *His house is next door.* *Su casa está al lado.* ❑ *He's still alive, isn't he?* *Todavía está vivo, ¿verdad?* **2** V-LINK You use **be,** with "it" as the subject, in clauses where you are describing something or giving your judgment of a situation. *hacer (impersonal), ser (impersonal)* ❑ *It was too chilly for swimming.* *Hacía mucho frío para nadar.* ❑ *Sometimes it is necessary to say no.* *A veces es necesario decir no.* ❑ *It is likely that investors will face losses.* *Es probable que los inversionistas enfrenten pérdidas.* ❑ *It's nice having friends to chat with.* *Es bueno tener amigos con quien platicar.* **3** V-LINK You use **be** with "there" in expressions like **there is** and **there are** to say that something exists or happens. *hay, había* ❑ *Clearly there is a problem here.* *Es evidente que hay un problema aquí.* ❑ *There are very few cars on this street.* *Hay muy pocos carros en esta calle.* **4** V-LINK You use **be** as a link between a subject and a clause and in certain other clause structures, as shown below. *ser* ❑ *Our greatest problem is convincing them.* *Nuestro mayor problema es convencerlos.* ❑ *All she knew was that she was feeling very lonely.* *Sólo sabía que se sentía muy sola (solitaria).* ❑ *Local residents say it was as if there were two explosions.* *Los vecinos dicen que fue como si hubiera habido dos explosiones.*

**beach** /bitʃ/ (**beaches**) N-COUNT A **beach** is an area of sand or stones beside the ocean. *playa* ❑ *...a beautiful sandy beach.* *...una hermosa playa arenosa.*
→ see Word Web: **beach**

**Word Partnership** Usar *beach* con:

| | |
|---|---|
| PREP. | **along the** beach, **at/on the** beach |
| N. | beach **chair**, beach **club/resort**, beach **vacation** |
| V. | **lie on the** beach, **walk on the** beach |
| ADJ. | **nude** beach, **private** beach, **rocky** beach, **sandy** beach |

**beach chair** (**beach chairs**) N-COUNT A **beach chair** is a simple chair with a folding frame, and a piece of canvas as the seat and back. *silla de playa, tumbona*

**Word Web** **beach**

**Beaches** have a natural cycle of build-up and **erosion. Ocean currents, wind,** and **waves** move **sand** along the **coast**. In certain spots, some of the sand gets left behind. The **surf** deposits it on the beach. Then the wind blows it into **dunes**. As currents change, they **erode** sand from the beach. High waves carry beach sand **seaward**. This process raises the seafloor. As the water gets shallower, the waves become smaller. Then they begin depositing sand on the beach. At the same time, small **pebbles** smash into each other. They break up and form new sand.

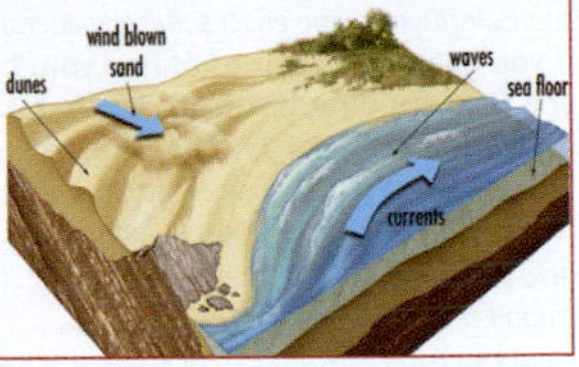


**bead** /bid/ (**beads**) **1** N-COUNT **Beads** are small pieces of colored glass, wood, or plastic with a hole through the middle which are used for jewelry or decoration. *cuenta* ❑ *...a string of beads. ...un collar de cuentas.* **2** N-COUNT A **bead of** liquid or moisture is a small drop of it. *gota* ❑ *...beads of blood. ...gotas de sangre.*
→ see **glass**

beak

**beak** /bik/ (**beaks**) N-COUNT A bird's **beak** is the hard curved or pointed part of its mouth. *pico* ❑ *...a black bird with a yellow beak. ...un pájaro negro con pico amarillo.*
→ see **bird**

**beak|er** /bikər/ (**beakers**) N-COUNT A **beaker** is a glass cup with straight sides used in a laboratory. *vaso (de precipitados)*
→ see **laboratory**

**beam** /bim/ (**beams, beaming, beamed**) **1** V-T/V-I If someone **is beaming,** they are smiling because they are happy. *sonreír radiante* [WRITTEN] ❑ *Frances beamed at her friend. Frances sonrió radiante a su amigo.* ❑ *"Welcome back," she beamed. —Bienvenido de vuelta —le dijo radiante.* **2** V-T/V-I If radio signals or television pictures **are beamed** somewhere, they are sent there by means of electronic equipment. *transmitir(se)* ❑ *The interview was beamed live across America. La entrevista se transmitió en vivo a todo Estados Unidos.* ❑ *The Sci-Fi Channel began beaming into 10 million American homes this week. El Canal Sci-Fi inició esta semana sus transmisiones a 10 millones de hogares estadounidenses.* **3** N-COUNT A **beam of** light is a line of light that shines from an object such as a lamp. *rayo (de luz)* **4** N-COUNT A **beam** is a long thick bar of wood, metal, or concrete, especially one used to support the roof of a building. *viga* ❑ *The ceilings are supported by oak beams. El techo descansa sobre vigas de roble.*
→ see **laser**

**bean** /bin/ (**beans**) **1** N-COUNT **Beans** are the pods of a climbing plant, or the seeds that the pods contain, eaten as a vegetable. *frijol, poroto* **2** N-COUNT Beans such as coffee **beans** or cocoa **beans** are the seeds of plants that are used to produce coffee, cocoa, and chocolate. *grano*

**bear**
❶ VERB USES
❷ NOUN USE

❶ **bear** /bɛər/ (**bears, bearing, bore, borne**) **1** V-T If someone or something **bears** something somewhere, they carry it there. *cargar, llevar* [LITERARY] ❑ *The wind bore coldness with it. El viento trajo el frío consigo.* **2** V-T If one thing **bears** the weight of something else, it supports the weight of that thing. *soportar, resistir, aguantar* ❑ *The ice was not thick enough to bear their weight. El hielo no era tan grueso como para aguantar su peso.* **3** V-T If you **bear** an unpleasant experience, you accept it because you are unable to do anything about it. *soportar* ❑ *They will have to bear the misery of living in constant fear. Tendrán que soportar el suplicio de vivir constantemente con miedo.* **4** V-T If you can't **bear** someone or something, you dislike them very much. *aguantar, soportar* ❑ *I can't bear people who talk during movies. No aguanto a la gente que habla en el cine.* **5** → see also **bore** **6** to **bear fruit** → see **fruit** **7** to **bear in mind** → see **mind**
▸ **bear out** PHR-VERB If someone or something **bears** a person **out** or **bears out** what that person is saying, they support what that person is saying. *confirmar* ❑ *Studies have borne out claims that perfume can change the way you feel. Los estudios dicen que es cierto que el perfume puede cambiar el estado de ánimo.*
▸ **bear with** PHR-VERB If you ask someone to **bear with** you, you are asking them to be patient. *aguantar, tener paciencia* ❑ *If you'll bear with me, Frank, just let me explain. Tenme paciencia, Frank, tan sólo déjame explicarte.*

**Thesaurus** *bear* Ver también:
v. carry, lug, move, transport ❶ **1**
endure, put up with, stand, tolerate ❶ **3**

bear

❷ **bear** /bɛər/ (**bears**) N-COUNT A **bear** is a large, strong wild animal with thick fur and sharp claws. *oso*
→ see **carnivore**

**beard** /bɪərd/ (**beards**) N-COUNT A man's **beard** is the hair that grows on his chin and cheeks. *barba* ❑ *He's decided to grow a beard. Decidió dejarse (crecer) la barba.*
→ see **hair**

B

**bear|ing** /bɛərɪŋ/ (**bearings**) **1** PHRASE If something **has a bearing on** a situation or event, it is relevant to it. *influencia* ❑ *The food you eat has an important bearing on your general health.* *Lo que comes influye mucho en tu salud en general.* **2** PHRASE If you **get** your **bearings** or **find** your **bearings,** you find out where you are or what you should do next. If you **lose** your **bearings,** you do not know where you are or what you should do next. *orientar(se)/desorientar(se)* ❑ *A bus tour of the city will help you get your bearings.* *Un recorrido en autobús por la ciudad te ayudará a orientarte.*

**beast** /bist/ (**beasts**) N-COUNT A **beast** is an animal, especially a large and dangerous one. *fiera* [LITERARY] ❑ *...wild beasts.* *...fieras salvajes*

**beat** /bit/ (**beats, beating, beaten**)

> The form **beat** is used in the present tense and is the past tense.

**1** V-T To **beat** someone or something means to hit them very hard. *golpear* ❑ *My wife tried to stop them and they beat her.* *Mi mujer trató de detenerlos y le dieron una golpiza.* ❑ *There was silence except for a fly beating against the glass.* *Todo estaba en silencio, salvo por el golpeteo de la mosca contra el vidrio.* ● **beat|ing** N-COUNT (**beatings**) *golpiza, golpeteo* ❑ *...the investigation into the beating of a car thief.* *...las investigaciones sobre la golpiza que recibió un ladrón de autos.* ❑ *All we heard was the beating of the rain.* *Sólo oíamos (oímos) el golpeteo de la lluvia.* **2** V-I When your heart or pulse **beats,** it continually makes regular rhythmic movements. *latir, palpitar* ❑ *I felt my heart beating faster.* *Sentí que mi corazón latía más rápido.* ● **Beat** is also a noun. *latido* ❑ *He could hear the beat of his heart.* *Podía oír los latidos de su corazón.* ● **beat|ing** N-SING *latir, palpitar* ❑ *I could hear the beating of my heart.* *Podía oír el latir (palpitar) de mi corazón.* **3** N-COUNT The **beat** of a piece of music is the main rhythm that it has. *ritmo* ❑ *...the pounding beat of rock music.* *...el ritmo martilleante del rock.* **4** V-T If you **beat** eggs, cream, or butter, you mix them thoroughly using a fork or beater. *batir* ❑ *Beat the eggs and sugar until they start to thicken.* *Bata los huevos y el azúcar hasta que empiecen a espesar.* **5** V-T If you **beat** someone in a competition or election, you defeat them. *vencer, derrotar, ganar* ❑ *In yesterday's game, Switzerland beat the United States two to one.* *Suiza derrotó a Estados Unidos dos a uno en el juego de ayer.* ● **beat|ing** N-SING *sacudida* ❑ *Our firm has taken a terrible beating in recent years.* *Nuestra compañía sufrió una terrible sacudida en los últimos años.* **6** to **beat** someone **at their own game** → see **game**
▸ **beat up** PHR-VERB If someone **beats** a person **up,** they hit or kick the person many times. *golpear* ❑ *Then they beat her up as well.* *Y luego también le dieron una golpiza.*

**Usage** beat

As a verb, *beat* is commonly used to talk about fighting an illness or addiction: *Lance Armstrong beat cancer. She just can't beat her addiction to cocaine.*

**Thesaurus** *beat* Ver también:

V. hit, pound, punch; (*ant.*) caress, pat, pet **1**
mix, stir, whip **4**

**Word Partnership** Usar *beat* con:

N. beat **a rug** **1**
**heart** beat **2**
beat **eggs** **4**
PREP. beat **against**, beat **on** **1**
**on/to a** beat **3**

**Word Link** *ful* ≈ *filled with* : *beautiful, careful, dreadful*

**beau|ti|ful** /byutɪfəl/ **1** ADJ A **beautiful** person is very attractive to look at. *hermoso, bello* ❑ *She was a very beautiful woman.* *Era una mujer muy hermosa (bella).* **2** ADJ Something that is **beautiful** is very attractive or pleasing. *bello, hermoso* ❑ *New England is beautiful.* *Nueva Inglaterra es bella.* ❑ *It was a beautiful morning.* *Era una mañana hermosa.* ● **beau|ti|ful|ly** /byutɪfli/ ADV *maravillosamente, de maravilla* ❑ *The children behaved beautifully.* *Los niños se portaron maravillosamente.* **3** ADJ You can describe something that someone does as **beautiful** when they do it very skillfully. *hermoso, lindo, magnífico* ❑ *...a beautiful throw to first base.* *...un magnífico lanzamiento a primera base.* ● **beau|ti|ful|ly** ADV *maravillosamente, de maravilla* ❑ *The Sixers played beautifully.* *Los Sixers jugaron de maravilla.*

**Thesaurus** *beautiful* Ver también:

ADJ. gorgeous, lovely, pretty, ravishing, stunning; (*ant.*) grotesque, hideous, homely, ugly **1**

**beau|ty** /byuti/ (**beauties**) **1** N-UNCOUNT **Beauty** is the state or quality of being beautiful. *belleza* ❑ *...an area of outstanding natural beauty.* *...un lugar de una belleza natural excepcional.* **2** N-COUNT A **beauty** is a beautiful woman. *belleza, bella, hermosura* ❑ *She is known as a great beauty.* *Se le conoce por su gran belleza.* **3** N-COUNT The **beauties** of something are its attractive qualities or features. *bello, belleza* [LITERARY] ❑ *He was beginning to enjoy the beauties of nature.* *Estaba empezando a disfrutar la belleza de la naturaleza.* **4** PHRASE If you say that a particular feature is **the beauty of** something, you mean that this feature is what makes the thing so good. *lo bueno* ❑ *The beauty of this type of paint is that it washes off easily.* *Lo bueno de este tipo de pintura es que se quita (sale) fácilmente con el lavado.*

**beau|ty mark** (**beauty marks**) N-COUNT A **beauty mark** is a small, dark spot on the skin that is supposed to add to a woman's beauty. *lunar*

**beau|ty pag|eant** (**beauty pageants**) N-COUNT A **beauty pageant** is a competition in which young women are judged to decide which one is the most beautiful. *concurso de belleza*

**beau|ty shop** (**beauty shops**) also **beauty parlor** N-COUNT A **beauty shop** is a place where women can go to have beauty treatments, for example, to have their hair, nails, or makeup done. *salón de belleza*

**be|came** /bɪkeɪm/ **Became** is the past tense of

become. *pasado de **become***

**be|cause** /bɪkɔz, -kɒz/ **1** CONJ You use **because** when stating the reason or explanation for something. *porque* ❑ *He is called Mitch, because his name is Mitchell. Le dicen Mitch, porque se llama Mitchell.* ❑ *Because it is an area of natural beauty, the number of boats on the river is limited. El número de botes en el río está limitado, porque es un área de belleza natural.* ❑ *I'm miserable because he didn't even ask me. Me siento triste, porque ni siquiera me preguntó (invitó).* **2** PHRASE If an event or situation occurs **because of** something, that thing is the reason or cause. *por, debido a, a causa de* ❑ *He's retiring because of ill health. Se va a jubilar debido a su mala salud.*

**be|come** /bɪkʌm/ (**becomes, becoming, became**)

> The form **become** is used in the present tense and is the past participle.

**1** V-LINK If someone or something **becomes** a particular thing, they start to change into that thing, or start to develop the characteristics mentioned. *convertirse en, empezar a* ❑ *I became interested in Islam while I was doing my nursing training. Empecé a interesarme en el Islam cuando estaba haciendo mi curso de enfermería.* **2** V-LINK If you wonder **what** has **become of** someone or something or **what** will **become of** them, you wonder what has happened to them or what will happen to them. *haber sido* ❑ *...the need for families to discover what has become of their relatives. ...la necesidad de las familias de descubrir qué ha sido de sus parientes.*

> **Usage** become
>
> Become is a linking verb and may be followed by a noun: *I'd like to become a teacher.* or by an adjective: *In the summer the weather becomes hot.*

**bed** /bɛd/ (**beds**) **1** N-COUNT A **bed** is a piece of furniture that you lie on when you sleep. *cama* ❑ *We finally went to bed at about 4 a.m. Finalmente me acosté como a las cuatro de la mañana.* ❑ *Nona was already in bed. Nona ya se había acostado.* **2** N-COUNT A **bed** in a garden or park is an area of ground that has been specially prepared so that plants can be grown in it. *arriate* ❑ *...beds of strawberries. ...arriates de fresas.* **3** N-COUNT The sea **bed** or a river **bed** is the ground at the bottom of the sea or of a river. *lecho* ❑ *...an operation to recover the wreckage from the sea bed. ...una operación para recuperar los restos del naufragio del lecho marino.* **4** → see also **bedding**

→ see Picture Dictionary: **bed**

→ see **lake, sleep**

> **Word Partnership** Usar *bed* con:
>
> ADJ. **asleep in** bed, **double/single/twin** bed, **ready for** bed **1**
>
> V. **be sick in** bed, **get into** bed, **go to** bed, **lie (down) in** bed, **put *someone* to** bed **1**
>
> PREP. **in/out of** bed, **under the** bed **1**
> bed **of *something*** **2**

**bed|ding** /bɛdɪŋ/ N-UNCOUNT **Bedding** is sheets, blankets, and covers that are used on beds. *ropa de cama* ❑ *...a crib with two full sets of bedding. ...una cuna con dos juegos completos de ropa de cama.*

**bed|room** /bɛdrum/ (**bedrooms**) **1** N-COUNT A **bedroom** is a room used for sleeping in. *cuarto, recámara* ❑ *...an extra bedroom. ...un cuarto (una recámara) extra.* **2** ADJ If you refer to a place as a **bedroom community** or **suburb**, you mean that most of the people who live there travel to work in a city or another, larger town a short distance away. *ciudad dormitorio* ❑ *This town is becoming a bedroom community of Columbus, 20 miles to the north. Este pueblo se está convirtiendo en una ciudad dormitorio de Columbus, 32 kilómetros al norte.*

→ see **house**

**Picture Dictionary** bed

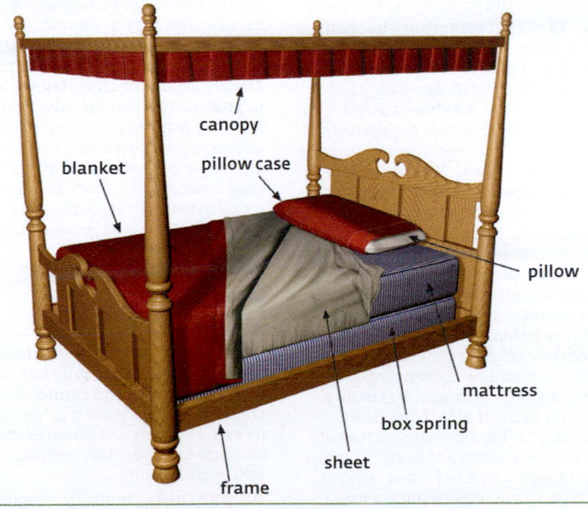

B

**bed|sore** /bɛdsɔr/ (**bedsores**) N-COUNT **Bedsores** are sore places on a person's skin, caused by having to lie in bed for a long time without changing position. *úlcera (por decúbito)*

**bee** /bi/ (**bees**) N-COUNT A **bee** is an insect with a yellow-and-black striped body that makes a buzzing noise as it flies. Bees make honey, and can sting. *abeja* ❑ *A bee buzzed in the flowers. Una abeja zumbaba entre las flores.*

**beef** /bif/ (**beefs, beefing, beefed**) N-UNCOUNT **Beef** is the meat of a cow, bull, or ox. *carne de res* ❑ *...roast beef. ...rosbif.* ❑ *...beef stew. ...puchero/estofado de res.*
→ see **meat**

▸ **beef up** PHR-VERB If you **beef up** something, you increase, strengthen, or improve it. *reforzar, fortalecer* ❑ *...to beef up security. ...reforzar la seguridad.* ❑ *Both sides are still beefing up their military strength. Ambos lados siguen fortaleciendo su poderío militar.*

**been** /bɪn/ **1** **Been** is the past participle of **be**. *sido, estado, ido* **2** V-I If you have **been** to a place, you have gone to it or visited it. *estar, ir* ❑ *He's already been to Tunisia, and has now moved on to Morocco. Ya estuvo en Túnez y ahora siguió a Marruecos., Ya fue a Túnez y ahora se fue a Marruecos.*

**beer** /bɪər/ (**beers**) N-VAR **Beer** is an alcoholic drink made from grain. A **beer** is a glass, can, or bottle of beer. *cerveza* ❑ *He sat in the kitchen drinking beer. Se sentó en la cocina a beber cerveza.* ❑ *Would you like a beer? ¿Quieres una cerveza?*

**beet** /bit/ (**beets**) **1** N-UNCOUNT **Beet** is a crop with a thick round root. *remolacha* ❑ *...fields of sweet corn and beet. ...campos de maíz tierno y remolacha.* **2** N-VAR **Beets** are dark red roots that are eaten as a vegetable. They are often preserved in vinegar. *betabel* ❑ *The roll comes with red beets, cottage cheese and blueberries. El bolillo lleva betabel, requesón y arándanos.*
→ see **sugar**

**bee|tle** /bitᵊl/ (**beetles**) N-COUNT A **beetle** is an insect with a hard covering on its body. *escarabajo*

**be|fore** /bɪfɔr/ **1** PREP If something happens **before** a particular date, time, or event, it happens earlier than that date, time, or event. *antes* ❑ *Annie was born a few weeks before Christmas. Annie nació unas semanas antes de Navidad.* ● **Before** is also a conjunction. *antes* ❑ *They decided to get married just before he got on the plane. Decidieron casarse justo antes de que él se subiera al avión.* **2** ADV You use **before** when you are talking about time. For example, if something happened the day **before**, it happened during the previous day. *antes* ❑ *Carlton's girlfriend had moved to Denver a month before. La novia de Carlton se había mudado a Denver un mes antes.* **3** ADV If someone has done something **before**, they have done it on a previous occasion. If someone has not done something **before**, they have never done it. *antes* ❑ *I've been here before. Ya he estado aquí antes.* ❑ *I have met Professor Lown before. Conocí al profesor Lown antes.* **4** PREP If someone is **before** something, they are in front of it. *ante, frente a, delante de* [FORMAL] ❑ *They drove through the tall gates, and stopped before a large white house. Cruzaron las altas puertas y detuvieron el coche frente a una casa blanca.* **5** PREP If you have something such as a trip, a task, or a stage of your life **before** you, you must do it or live through it in the future. *frente a* ❑ *Everyone in the room knew it was the hardest task before them. Todos en la habitación sabían que estaban frente a la tarea más difícil.* **6** **before long** → see **long**

| **Thesaurus** | *before* | Ver también: |
|---|---|---|
| ADV. | already, earlier, previously; (*ant.*) after **3** | |

**beg** /bɛg/ (**begs, begging, begged**) **1** V-T/V-I If you **beg** someone **to** do something, you ask them very anxiously or eagerly to do it. *rogar, suplicar* ❑ *I begged him to come back to New York with me. Le rogué que volviera a Nueva York conmigo.* ❑ *We are not going to beg for help anymore. Ya no vamos a rogar que nos ayuden.* **2** V-T/V-I If someone who is poor **is begging**, they are asking people to give them food or money. *mendigar* ❑ *I was surrounded by people begging for food. Estaba rodeado de gente que mendigaba comida.* ❑ *...homeless people begging on the streets. ...gente sin hogar que mendiga en la calle.* ❑ *She was living alone, begging food from neighbors. Vivía sola y mendigaba comida entre sus vecinos.* **3** **I beg your pardon** → see **pardon**

**be|gan** /bɪgæn/ **Began** is the past tense of **begin**. *pasado de **begin***

**beg|gar** /bɛgər/ (**beggars**) N-COUNT A **beggar** is someone who lives by asking people for money or food. *mendigo o mendiga, limosnero o limosnera* ❑ *There are no beggars on the streets in Vienna. En las calles de Viena no hay limosneros.*

**be|gin** /bɪgɪn/ (**begins, beginning, began, begun**) **1** V-T To **begin to** do something means to start doing it. *empezar, comenzar* ❑ *He stood up and began to move around the room. Se levantó y empezó a ir y venir por el cuarto.* ❑ *The damage began to look more serious. El daño empezó a parecer más grave.* ❑ *"Professor Theron," he began, "I'm very pleased to see you." —Profesor Theron —comenzó—, me da mucho gusto verlo.* **2** V-T/V-I When something **begins** or when you **begin** it, it takes place from a particular time onward. *comenzar, iniciar* ❑ *The problems began last November. Los problemas comenzaron en noviembre pasado.* ❑ *He has just begun his fourth year in hiding. Acaba de comenzar su cuarto año de estar escondido.* **3** PHRASE You use **to begin with** when you are talking about the first stage of a situation, event, or process, to introduce the first of several things that you want to say. *al principio, para empezar* ❑ *It was great to begin with but now it's difficult. Estuvo bien al principio, pero ahora es difícil.* ❑ *"What do scientists think about that?" —"Well, to begin with, they doubt it's going to work." —¿Qué piensan los científicos al respecto? —Pues, para empezar, dudan que vaya a servir.*

| **Thesaurus** | *begin* | Ver también: |
|---|---|---|
| V. | commence, kick off, start; (*ant.*) end, stop **1** **2** | |

**be|gin|ner** /bɪgɪnər/ (**beginners**) N-COUNT A **beginner** is someone who has just started learning to do something and cannot do it very well yet. *principiante o principianta* ❑ *The course is suitable for both beginners and advanced students. El curso es adecuado tanto para los estudiantes principiantes como para los avanzados.*

**be|gin|ning** /bɪgɪnɪŋ/ (**beginnings**) N-COUNT

The **beginning of** something is the first part of it. principio, inicio, comienzo ❑ *This was the beginning of her career.* *Ese fue el inicio de su carrera.* ❑ *The wedding will be at the beginning of March.* *La boda será a principios de marzo.* ❑ *I had the beginnings of a headache.* *Estaba empezando a dolerme la cabeza.*

**be|gun** /bɪgʌn/ **Begun** is the past participle of **begin**. *comenzado, principiado, iniciado*

**be|half** /bɪhæf/ PHRASE If you do something **on** someone's **behalf,** you do it for that person as their representative. *en nombre de* ❑ *She thanked us all on her son's behalf.* *Les dio las gracias a todos en nombre de su hijo.*

**be|have** /bɪheɪv/ (**behaves, behaving, behaved**) **1** V-I The way that you **behave** is the way that you do and say things, and the things that you do and say. *comportarse, portarse, actuar* ❑ *I couldn't believe these people were behaving in this way.* *No podía creer que esa gente actuara así.* **2** V-T/V-I If you **behave** or **behave yourself**, you act in the way that people think is correct and proper. *comportarse, portarse bien* ❑ *You have to behave.* *Tienes que comportarte bien.*

**be|hav|ior** /bɪheɪvyər/ (**behaviors**) **1** N-VAR A person's **behavior** is the way that they behave. *comportamiento, conducta* ❑ *Make sure that good behavior is rewarded.* *Asegúrese de recompensar el buen comportamiento.* ❑ *...human social behavior.* *...la conducta social humana.* **2** N-UNCOUNT In science, the **behavior** of something is the way that it behaves. *comportamiento, funcionamiento*

**Word Partnership** Usar *behavior* con:

| | |
|---|---|
| ADJ. | **aggressive/criminal** behavior, **bad/good** behavior, **learned** behavior |
| V. | **change** *someone's* behavior |
| N. | **human** behavior, behavior **pattern**, behavior **problems** |

**be|hav|ior|ism** /bɪheɪvyərɪzəm/ N-UNCOUNT **Behaviorism** is the belief held by some psychologists that the only valid method of studying the psychology of people or animals is to observe how they behave. *conductismo* • **be|hav|ior|ist** N-COUNT (**behaviorists**) *conductista* ❑ *Animal behaviorists have been studying these monkeys for years.* *Los especialistas en la conducta de los animales han estado estudiando a estos monos durante años.*

**be|hind** /bɪhaɪnd/ (**behinds**)

In addition to the uses shown below, **behind** is also used in a few phrasal verbs, such as "fall behind" and "lie behind."

**1** PREP If something is **behind** a thing or person, it is on the other side of them from you, or nearer their back rather than their front. *atrás* ❑ *I put one of the cushions behind his head.* *Le puse uno de los cojines atrás de la cabeza.* ❑ *They were parked behind the truck.* *Estaban estacionados atrás del camión.* • **Behind** is also an adverb. *atrás* ❑ *...wonderful views of the canal and the hills behind.* *...hermosas vistas del canal y de las colinas de atrás.* **2** PREP If you are walking or traveling **behind** someone or something, you are following them. *atrás* ❑ *Keith wandered along behind him.* *Keith caminaba sin rumbo fijo atrás de él.* • **Behind** is also an adverb. *atrás* ❑ *The other guards followed behind in a second vehicle.* *Los otros guardias iban atrás, en otro carro.* **3** N-COUNT Your **behind** is the part of your body that you sit on. *trasero* **4** PREP If something or someone is **behind** you, they support you and help you. *respaldar, apoyar* ❑ *The new government must get the country behind them.* *El nuevo gobierno debe buscar que el país lo respalde.* **5** PREP If something is **behind** schedule, it is not as far advanced as people had planned. If someone is **behind** schedule, they are not progressing as quickly at something as they had planned. *atrasado* ❑ *The work is 22 weeks behind schedule.* *El trabajo tiene 22 semanas de atraso.* **6** ADV If you stay **behind,** you remain in a place after other people have gone. *quedarse* ❑ *Some of us stayed behind to tidy up.* *Algunos nos quedamos para recoger.* **7** ADV If you leave something or someone **behind,** you do not take them with you when you go. *abandonar, dejar atrás* ❑ *The soldiers escaped into the mountains, leaving behind their weapons and supplies.* *Los soldados escaparon a las montañas, abandonando sus armas y provisiones.* **8** to **do** something **behind** someone's **back** → see **back** **9** **behind bars** → see **bar** **10** **behind the scenes** → see **scene**
→ see **location**

**Usage** **behind**

*Behind* and *in back of* have similar meanings, but *behind* is not generally used with *of*. *A police officer pulled up behind/in back of us and signaled us to stop.*

**beige** /beɪʒ/ COLOR Something that is **beige** is pale brown in color. *beige, ocre* ❑ *The walls are beige.* *Las paredes son de color beige.*

**be|ing** /biɪŋ/ (**beings**) **1** **Being** is the present participle of **be.** *siendo, estando* **2** N-COUNT You can refer to any real or imaginary creature as a **being.** *ser, ente* ❑ *Remember you are dealing with a living being—consider the horse's feelings too.* *Recuerda que estás tratando con un ser viviente; ten en cuenta también los sentimientos del caballo.* **3** → see also **human being** **4** N-UNCOUNT **Being** is existence. Something that is **in being** or comes **into being** exists. *existencia, vida* ❑ *Abraham Maslow described psychology as "the science of being."* *Abraham Maslow describía la psicología como "la ciencia de la existencia".* **5** → see also **well-being** **6** **for the time being** → see **time**

**be|jew|eled** /bɪdʒuᵊld/ also **bejewelled** ADJ A **bejeweled** person or object is wearing a lot of jewelry or is decorated with jewels. *enjoyado, tachonado de joyas* ❑ *...bejeweled women.* *...mujeres enjoyadas.*

**be|la|bor** /bɪleɪbər/ (**belabors, belaboring, belabored**) V-T If someone **belabors** a point, they keep on talking about it. *elaborar, extenderse* ❑ *I won't belabor the point, for this is a familiar story.* *No voy a extenderme en eso, pues es una historia familiar.*

**be|lief** /bɪlif/ (**beliefs**) N-VAR **Belief** is a feeling of certainty that something exists, is true, or is good. *creencia* ❑ *One billion people throughout the world are Muslims, united by belief in one god.* *Mil millones de personas en todo el mundo son musulmanes, unidos por la creencia en un dios.*

**be|lieve** /bɪliv/ (**believes, believing, believed**) **1** V-T If you **believe** that something is true, you think it is true. *creer* [FORMAL] ❑ *Many experts*

B

*believe that prices will continue to rise.* *Muchos expertos creen que los precios seguirán al alza.* ❑ *We believe them to be hidden here in this apartment.* *Creemos que se ocultan aquí, en este departamento.* **2** V-T If you **believe** someone, you accept that they are telling the truth. *creer a* ❑ *Of course I believe you!* *¡Claro que te creo!* ❑ *Never believe what you read in the newspapers.* *Nunca creas lo que lees en los periódicos.* **3** V-I If you **believe in** fairies, ghosts, or miracles, you are sure that they exist or happen. If you **believe in** a god, you are sure of the existence of that god. *creer en* ❑ *I don't believe in ghosts.* *No creo en los fantasmas.* **4** V-I If you **believe in** a way of life or an idea, you think it is good or right. *creer en* ❑ *He believed in honesty and trust.* *Creía en la honestidad y la confianza.*

**Thesaurus** *believe* Ver también:

V. consider, guess, speculate, think **1**
accept, buy, trust **2**

**bell** /bɛl/ (**bells**) **1** N-COUNT A **bell** is a device that makes a ringing sound and is used to attract people's attention. *timbre, campana* ❑ *I had just enough time to finish eating before the bell rang.* *Apenas tuve tiempo de terminar de comer antes de que sonara la campana.* **2** N-COUNT A **bell** is a hollow metal object with a loose piece hanging inside it that hits the sides and makes a sound. *campana* ❑ *My brother was born on a Sunday, when all the church bells were ringing.* *Mi hermano nació en domingo, cuando todas las campanas estaban repicando.*

**bell|hop** /bɛlhɒp/ (**bellhops**) N-COUNT A **bellhop** is a man or boy who works in a hotel, carrying bags or bringing things to the guests' rooms. *botones*
→ see **hotel**

**bell pep|per** (**bell peppers**) N-COUNT A **bell pepper** is a hollow green, red, or yellow vegetable with seeds. *pimiento dulce*

**bell|wether** /bɛlwɛðər/ (**bellwethers**) N-COUNT If you describe something as a **bellwether,** you mean that it is an indication of the way a situation is changing. *barómetro* [JOURNALISM] ❑ *IBM is considered the bellwether of the stock market.* *Se considera a IBM como el barómetro de la bolsa.*

**bel|ly** /bɛli/ (**bellies**) N-COUNT The **belly** of a person or animal is their stomach or abdomen. *vientre, barriga, panza* ❑ *She laid her hands on her swollen belly.* *Posó las manos sobre su vientre hinchado.*
→ see **horse**

**be|long** /bɪlɔŋ/ (**belongs, belonging, belonged**) **1** V-I If something **belongs to** you, you own it. *pertenecer* ❑ *The house had belonged to her family for three generations.* *La casa había pertenecido a su familia durante tres generaciones.* **2** V-I If someone or something **belongs to** a particular group, they are a member of that group. *pertenecer, ser socio* ❑ *I used to belong to a youth club.* *Antes era socio de un club juvenil.* **3** V-I If something or someone **belongs in** or **to** a particular category, type, or group, they are of that category, type, or group. *pertenecer* ❑ *The judges could not decide which category it belonged in.* *Los jueces no pudieron decidir a qué categoría pertenecía.*

**be|long|ings** /bɪlɔŋɪŋz/ N-PLURAL Your **belongings** are the things that you own. *pertenencias* ❑ *I collected my belongings and left.* *Recogí mis pertenencias y me fui.*

**be|lov|ed** /bɪlʌvɪd, -lʌvd/ ADJ A **beloved** person, thing, or place is one that you feel great affection for. *querido, amado* ❑ *He lost his beloved wife last year.* *Perdió a su amada esposa el año pasado.*

**be|low** /bɪloʊ/ **1** PREP If something is **below** something else, it is in a lower position. *abajo, debajo* ❑ *He appeared from the apartment directly below Leonard's.* *Se apareció del departamento que está exactamente debajo del de Leonard.* ❑ *The sun has already sunk below the horizon.* *El sol ya se hundió en el horizonte.* ● **Below** is also an adverb. *abajo* ❑ *We climbed down a rope-ladder to the boat below.* *Descendimos por una escala de cuerda al bote que estaba abajo.* ❑ *...a view to the street below.* *...con vista a la calle de abajo.* **2** PREP If something is **below** a particular amount, rate, or level, it is less than that amount, rate, or level. *por debajo de* ❑ *Night temperatures can drop below 15 degrees.* *Las medias de temperatura nocturnas pueden caer por debajo de los 15 grados.* ● **Below** is also an adverb. *bajo* ❑ *...temperatures at zero or below.* *...temperaturas de cero (grados) o bajo cero.* **3** **below par** → see **par**

**Word Partnership** Usar *below* con:

ADV. **directly** below, **far/significantly/substantially/well** below, **just/slightly** below **1**
N. below **the surface** **1**
below **cost**, below **freezing**, below **ground**, below **the poverty level/line**, below **zero** **2**
V. **dip/drop/fall** below **1** **2**
ADJ. below **average**, below **normal** **2**

**belt** /bɛlt/ (**belts, belting, belted**) **1** N-COUNT A **belt** is a strip of leather or cloth that you fasten around your waist. *cinturón* ❑ *He wore a belt with a large brass buckle.* *Llevaba un cinturón con una gran hebilla dorada.* **2** → see also **seat belt** **3** N-COUNT A **belt** in a machine is a circular strip of rubber that is used to drive moving parts or to move objects along. *correa, banda* ❑ *I started the car: the fan belt made a strange noise.* *Eché a andar el carro y la banda del ventilador hizo un ruido raro.* **4** N-COUNT A **belt** of land or sea is a long, narrow area of it that has some special feature. *región, franja, cinturón* ❑ *...the country's cocoa belt.* *...la región cacaotera del país.* **5** V-T If someone **belts** you, they hit you very hard. If someone belts something, they hit it very hard. *dar trancazos a* [INFORMAL] ❑ *She belted poor old George in the stomach.* *Le dio un trancazo en el estómago al pobre George.* ● **Belt** is also a noun. *trancazo* ❑ *She gave him a belt with her umbrella as he tried to run away.* *Le dio un trancazo con su paraguas cuando él trató de escapar.* **6** PHRASE If you have to **tighten** your **belt,** you have to manage without things because you have less money than you used to have. *apretarse el cinturón* ❑ *If you are spending more than your income, you'll need to tighten your belt.* *Si estás gastando más de lo que ganas, tendrás que apretarte el cinturón.* **7** PHRASE If you have something **under** your **belt,** you have already achieved it or done it. *en el haber de* ❑ *Clare is now a full-time author with six books under her belt.* *Clare ya es una escritora de tiempo completo con seis libros en su haber.*
→ see **button**

**bench** /bɛntʃ/ (**benches**) **1** N-COUNT A **bench**

is a long seat of wood or metal. *banca* ❑ *He sat down on a park bench.* *Se sentó en una banca del parque.* **2** N-COUNT A **bench** is a long, narrow table in a factory or laboratory. *mesa de trabajo* ❑ *...the laboratory bench.* *...la mesa de trabajo del laboratorio.* **3** N-SING In a court of law, **the bench** is the judge or magistrates. *estrado* ❑ *The Pollards and their lawyers approached the bench.* *Los Pollard y sus abogados se acercaron al estrado.*
→ see **location**

**bend** /bɛnd/ (**bends, bending, bent**) **1** V-I When you **bend**, you move the top part of your body downward and forward. *inclinarse, agacharse* ❑ *I bent over and kissed her cheek.* *Me incliné y le di un beso en la mejilla.* ❑ *She bent and picked up a plastic bucket.* *Se agachó y levantó una cubeta de plástico.* **2** V-T/V-I When you **bend** a part of your body such as your arm or leg, or when it **bends**, you change its position so that it is no longer straight. *doblar* ❑ *Bend your legs and leap as far as you can.* *Dobla las piernas y salta tan lejos como puedas.* ● **bent** ADJ *doblado* ❑ *Keep your knees slightly bent.* *Mantén las rodillas ligeramente dobladas.* **3** V-T If you **bend** something that is flat or straight, you use force to make it curved or to put an angle in it. *curvar* ❑ *Bend the bar into a horseshoe.* *Curva la barra hasta formar una herradura.* ● **bent** ADJ *torcido, doblado* ❑ *...a length of bent wire.* *...un tramo de alambre doblado.* **4** V-T/V-I When a road, beam of light, or other long thin thing **bends**, or when something **bends** it, it changes direction to form a curve or angle. *torcer, doblar, dar vuelta* ❑ *The road bent slightly to the right.* *El camino torcía ligeramente a la derecha.* **5** N-COUNT A **bend** in a road, pipe, or other long thin object is a curve or angle in it. *curva, codo* ❑ *The crash occurred on a sharp bend.* *El choque ocurrió en una curva muy cerrada.* **6** V-T If you **bend** rules or laws, you interpret them in a way that allows you to do something they would not normally allow you to do. *torcer* ❑ *A few officers were prepared to bend the rules.* *Unos cuantos agentes estaban dispuestos a torcer las reglas.* **7** → see also **bent**

| **Thesaurus** | *bend* | Ver también: |
|---|---|---|
| V. | arch, bow, hunch, lean; (*ant.*) straighten **1** contort, curl, twist **3** | |
| N. | angle, curve, deviation, turn **5** | |

**be|neath** /bɪniθ/ PREP Something that is **beneath** another thing is under the other thing. *bajo, abajo* ❑ *She could see the muscles of his shoulders beneath his T-shirt.* *Podía ver los músculos de sus hombros bajo la camiseta.* ❑ *Four levels of parking beneath the theater was not enough.* *Cuatro pisos de estacionamiento bajo el teatro eran suficientes.* ● **Beneath** is also an adverb. *bajo, abajo* ❑ *On a shelf beneath he spotted a photo album.* *En una repisa de abajo descubrió un álbum de fotos.*

**ben|efi|cial** /bɛnɪfɪʃᵊl/ ADJ Something that is **beneficial** helps people or improves their lives. *beneficioso* ❑ *...vitamins that are beneficial to our health.* *...vitaminas que son beneficiosas para nuestra salud.*

**ben|efit** /bɛnɪfɪt/ (**benefits, benefiting** or **benefitting, benefited** or **benefitted**) **1** N-VAR The **benefit of** something is the help that you get from it or the advantage that results from it. *beneficio* ❑ *It was his task to give them the benefit of his experience in academic matters.* *Su misión era ofrecerles el beneficio de su experiencia en cuestiones académicas.* ❑ *I'm a great believer in the benefits of this form of therapy.* *Tengo una gran fe en los beneficios de esta forma de terapia.* **2** N-UNCOUNT If something is **to your benefit** or is **of benefit to** you, it helps you or improves your life. *en beneficio de* ❑ *This could now work to Albania's benefit.* *Esto podría funcionar ahora en beneficio de Albania.* **3** V-T/V-I If you **benefit from** something or if it **benefits** you, it helps you or improves your life. *beneficiar(se)* ❑ *Both sides have benefited from the talks.* *Ambas partes se han beneficiado de las pláticas.* **4** N-UNCOUNT If you have the **benefit of** some information, knowledge, or equipment, you are able to use it so that you can achieve something. *beneficio* ❑ *Steve didn't have the benefit of a formal college education.* *Steve no contó con el beneficio de una educación universitaria formal.* **5** N-VAR **Benefits** are money or other advantages which come from your job, the government, or an insurance company. *prestación* ❑ *McCary will receive about $921,000 in retirement benefits.* *McCary recibirá aproximadamente 921,000 dólares en prestaciones cuando se jubile.* ❑ *...the rising cost of health care and medical benefits.* *...el costo en constante aumento de las prestaciones del seguro social.* **6** PHRASE If you give someone **the benefit of the doubt**, you treat them as if they are telling the truth or as if they have behaved properly, even though you are not sure that this is the case. *el beneficio de la duda* ❑ *At first I gave him the benefit of the doubt.* *Al principio, le concedí el beneficio de la duda.*

**bent** /bɛnt/ **1** **Bent** is the past tense and past participle of **bend**. *pasado y participio pasado de* **bend** **2** ADJ If someone is **bent on** doing something, especially something harmful, they are determined to do it. *empeñado en* ❑ *...the leader of a group bent on world domination.* *...el líder de un grupo empeñado en el dominio mundial.* **3** N-SING If you have a **bent for** something, you have a natural ability to do it or a natural interest in it. *aptitud* ❑ *His bent for natural history directed him toward his first job.* *Su aptitud para la historia natural lo llevó a du primer trabajo.*

**ben|thic en|vir|on|ment** /bɛnθɪk ɪnvaɪrənmənt, -vaɪərn-/ also **benthic zone** N-SING The **benthic environment** or **benthic zone** is the area on or near the bottom of seas, rivers, and lakes, and all the organisms that live there. Compare **pelagic**. *medio ambiente béntico* [TECHNICAL]

**ben|thos** /bɛnθɒs/ N-PLURAL **Benthos** are plants and animals that live in or near the bottoms of seas, rivers, and lakes. You can also use **benthos** to mean the areas at the bottoms of seas, rivers, and lakes. *bentos* [TECHNICAL]

**be|ret** /bəreɪ/ (**berets**) N-COUNT A **beret** is a circular, flat hat that is made of soft material and has no brim. *boina*
→ see **hat**

**Bernoulli's prin|ci|ple** /bərnuliz prɪnsɪpᵊl/ N-UNCOUNT **Bernoulli's principle** is a law in physics which states that the pressure of a moving fluid decreases as its speed increases. *principio de Bernoulli* [TECHNICAL]

b

B

**ber|ry** /bɛri/ (**berries**) N-COUNT **Berries** are small, round fruit that grow on a bush or a tree. baya

**be|side** /bɪsaɪd/ **1** PREP Something that is **beside** something else is at the side of it or next to it. junto a ❑ *On the table beside an empty plate was a pile of books.* En la mesa, junto a un plato vacío, había una pila de libros. **2** → see also **besides** **3** PHRASE If you are **beside yourself with** anger or excitement, you are extremely angry or excited. fuera de sí, no caber en sí ❑ *He shouted at her, beside himself with anxiety.* Le gritó fuera de sí por la ansiedad.

**be|sides** /bɪsaɪdz/ **1** PREP **Besides** something or **beside** something means in addition to it. además ❑ *She has many good qualities besides being very beautiful.* Tiene muchas buenas cualidades, además de ser muy bella. • **Besides** is also an adverb. también ❑ *You get to sample some baking, and take home some cookies besides.* Tienes la oportunidad de probar los pasteles y también llevarte unas galletitas a casa. **2** ADV **Besides** is used to emphasize an additional point that you are making. además ❑ *The house is out of our price range. Besides, I am fond of our little apartment.* La casa está fuera de nuestro presupuesto; además, estoy encariñado con nuestro departamentito. **3** → see also **except**

> **Usage** **besides**
>
> *Besides* and *beside* are often confused. *Besides* means "in addition (to)": *What are you doing today besides working? Beside* means "next to": *Come sit beside me.*

**be|siege** /bɪsiʤ/ (**besieges, besieging, besieged**) **1** V-T If you **are besieged by** people, many people want something from you and continually bother you. sitiar, asediar, cercar ❑ *She was besieged by journalists and the public.* Los periodistas y el público la asediaban. **2** V-T If soldiers **besiege** a place, they surround it and wait for the people in it to stop fighting or resisting. sitiar ❑ *The main part of the army moved to Sevastopol to besiege the town.* La mayor parte del ejército se desplazó a Sebastopol para sitiar la ciudad.

**best** /bɛst/ **1** **Best** is the superlative of **good**. mejor ❑ *The best thing to do is ask the driver as you get on the bus.* Lo mejor que puedes hacer es preguntar al chofer cuando te subas al autobús. **2** **Best** is the superlative of **well**. mejor ❑ *James Fox is best known as the author of "White Mischief."* Se conoce mejor a James Fox como el autor de "White Mischief". **3** N-SING **The best** is used to refer to things of the highest quality or standard. lo mejor ❑ *We offer only the best to our clients.* Sólo ofrecemos lo mejor a nuestros clientes. **4** N-SING Someone's **best** is the greatest effort or highest achievement or standard that they are capable of. mejor momento ❑ *Miss Blockey was at her best when she played the piano.* La señorita Blockey estaba en su mejor momento cuando tocaba el piano. **5** ADV If you like something **best** or like it **the best,** you prefer it. más ❑ *The thing I liked best about the show was the music.* Lo que más me gustó del espectáculo fue la música. ❑ *Mother liked it best when Daniel did the cooking.* A mamá le gustaba más cuando Daniel cocinaba. **6** **Best** is used to form the superlative of compound adjectives beginning with "good" and "well." For example, the superlative of "well-known" is "best-known." mejor **7** PHRASE You use **at best** to indicate that even if you describe something as favorably as possible or if it performs as well as it possibly can, it is still not very good. cuando mucho ❑ *At best his grade will be a B or B-minus.* Cuando mucho, su calificación será un 7 o un 8. **8** **to hope for the best** → see **hope** **9** **to the best of** your **knowledge** → see **knowledge** **10** **best of luck** → see **luck** **11** **the best of both worlds** → see **world**

**best man** N-SING The **best man** at a wedding is the man who assists the bridegroom. padrino de bodas
→ see **wedding**

**best-selling** also **bestselling** **1** ADJ A **best-selling** product such as a book is very popular and a large quantity of it has been sold. de mayor venta **2** ADJ A **best-selling** author is an author who has sold a very large number of copies of his or her book. de gran éxito

**bet** /bɛt/ (**bets, betting**)

> The form **bet** is used in the present tense and is the past tense and past participle.

**1** V-T/V-I If you **bet on** the result of a horse race, football game, or other event, you give someone a sum of money which they give you back with extra money if the result is what you predicted, or which they keep if it is not. apostar ❑ *Jockeys are forbidden to bet on the outcome of races.* Está prohibido que los jinetes apuesten al resultado de las carreras. ❑ *I bet $20 on a horse called Bright Boy.* Aposté 20 dólares al caballo Bright Boy. • **Bet** is also a noun. apuesta ❑ *Do you always have a bet on the Kentucky Derby?* ¿Siempre apuestas en el Derby de Kentucky? • **bet|ting** N-UNCOUNT apuestas ❑ *...his thousand-dollar fine for illegal betting.* ...su multa de 1,000 dólares por apuestas ilegales. **2** PHRASE You use expressions such as "**I bet,**" "**I'll bet,**" and "**you can bet**" to indicate that you are sure something is true. apostar a que [INFORMAL] ❑ *I bet you were good at games when you were at school.* Apuesto a que eras bueno para el juego cuando estabas en la escuela. ❑ *I'll bet they'll taste wonderful.* Apostaría a que saben sabroso.

**beta par|ti|cle** /beɪtəpɑrtɪkəl/ (**beta particles**) N-COUNT **Beta particles** are atomic particles that are released by the nuclei of certain radioactive substances. Compare *alpha particle* and *gamma ray*. partícula beta [TECHNICAL]

**be|tray** /bɪtreɪ/ (**betrays, betraying, betrayed**) **1** V-T If you **betray** someone who loves or trusts you, your actions hurt and disappoint them. traicionar ❑ *She betrayed him by starting a relationship with another writer.* Lo traicionó cuando inició una relación con otro escritor. **2** V-T If someone **betrays** their country or their friends, they give information to an enemy, putting their country's security or their friends' safety at risk. traicionar ❑ *They offered me money if I would betray my friends.* Me ofrecieron dinero si traicionaba a mis amigos. **3** V-T If you **betray** a feeling or quality, you show it without intending to. traslucir, revelar, delatar ❑ *She studied his face, but it betrayed nothing.* Escrutó su rostro, pero no traslucía nada.

b

**better**
1 COMPARING STATES AND QUALITIES
2 GIVING ADVICE

**1 bet|ter** /bɛtər/ 1 **Better** is the comparative of **good.** mejor, más, más que 2 **Better** is the comparative of **well.** mejor, más, más que 3 ADV If you like one thing **better than** another, you like it more. más que, más ❑ *I like your poem better than mine.* *Tu poema me gusta más que el mío.* ❑ *They liked it better when it rained.* *Les gustaba más cuando llovía.* 4 ADJ If you are **better** after an illness or injury, you have recovered from it. If you feel **better,** you no longer feel so ill. mejor ❑ *He is much better now; he's fine.* *Ya está mucho mejor; está bien.* 5 **Better** is used to form the comparative of compound adjectives beginning with "good" and "well." For example, the comparative of "well-off" is "better-off." mejor 6 PHRASE If something changes **for the better,** it improves. para bien ❑ *He dreams of changing the world for the better.* *Sueña con mejorar el mundo.* 7 PHRASE If a feeling such as jealousy, curiosity, or anger **gets the better of** you, it becomes too strong for you to hide or control. poder más que ❑ *She didn't allow her emotions to get the better of her.* *No permitió que sus emociones la dominaran.*

**Word Partnership** Usar *better* con:

| | |
|---|---|
| N. | better **idea**, **nothing** better 1 1 |
| V. | **make** *something* better 1 1 |
| | **look** better 1 1 4 |
| | **feel** better, **get** better 1 2 4 |
| ADV. | **any** better, **even** better, better **than** 1 1 2 |
| | **much** better 1 1 |

**2 bet|ter** /bɛtər/ PHRASE You use **had better** or **'d better** when you are advising, warning, or threatening someone, or expressing an opinion about what should happen. es mejor que, más vale que ❑ *It's half past two. I think we had better go home.* *Ya son las dos y media; es mejor que nos vayamos a la casa.* ❑ *You'd better run if you're going to get your ticket.* *Más vale que corras si quieres comprar tu boleto.* ● In spoken English, people sometimes use **better** without "had" or "be" before it. It has the same meaning. es mejor que, más vale que ❑ *Better not say too much aloud.* *Más vale no decir mucho en voz alta.*

**be|tween** /bɪtwin/

In addition to the uses shown below, **between** is used in a few phrasal verbs, such as "come between."

1 PREP If something is **between** two things or is **in between** them, it has one of the things on one side of it and the other thing on the other side. entre ❑ *She left the table to stand between the two men.* *Se levantó de la mesa para pararse entre los dos hombres.* 2 PREP If people or things travel **between** two places, they travel regularly from one place to the other and back again. entre ❑ *I spent a lot of time traveling between Waco and El Paso.* *Pasaba mucho tiempo viajando entre Waco y El Paso.* 3 PREP A relationship, discussion, or difference **between** two people, groups, or things is one that involves them both or relates to them both. entre ❑ *...the relationship between patients and doctors.* *...las relaciones entre pacientes y médicos.* ❑ *...long discussions between the two governments.* *...largas discusiones entre los dos gobiernos.* 4 PREP If something stands **between** you and what you want, it prevents you from having it. entre ❑ *His sense of duty often stood between him and his enjoyment of life.* *Su sentido del deber le impedía frecuentemente disfrutar de la vida.* 5 PREP If something is **between** two amounts or ages, it is greater or older than the first one and smaller or younger than the second one. entre ❑ *Increase the time you spend exercising by walking between 15 and 20 minutes every day.* *Aumenta el tiempo de ejercicio caminando entre 15 y 20 minutos al día.* 6 PREP If something happens **between** or **in between** two times or events, it happens after the first time or event and before the second one. entre ❑ *The canal was built between 1793 and 1797.* *El canal fue construido entre 1793 y 1797.* ● **Between** or **in between** is also an adverb. entre ❑ *My life had been a journey from one crisis to another with only a brief time in between.* *Mi vida había sido un ir de una crisis a otra con sólo breves respiros entre ellas.* 7 PREP If you must choose **between** two or more things, you must choose just one of them. entre ❑ *Students will be able to choose between English, French and Russian as their first foreign language.* *Los estudiantes podrán escoger entre inglés, francés y ruso como primera lengua extranjera.* 8 PREP If people or places have a particular amount of something **between** them, this is the total amount that they have. entre ❑ *The three companies employ 12,500 people between them.* *Entre las tres compañías emplean a 12,500 personas.* 9 PREP When something is divided or shared **between** people, they each have a share of it. entre ❑ *There is only one bathroom shared between eight bedrooms.* *Sólo hay un cuarto de baño para compartirlo entre ocho habitaciones.*

→ see **location**

**Usage** **between** and **among**

*Between* can be used to refer to two or more persons or things, but *among* can only be used to refer to three or more persons or things, or to a group. *Mr. Elliot's estate was divided between his two children. Mrs. Elliot's estate was divided between/among her three grandchildren.*

**Word Partnership** Usar *between* con:

| | |
|---|---|
| N. | **line** between, **link** between 1 |
| | between **countries/nations, difference** between, **relationship** between 3 |
| | **choice** between 7 |
| ADV. | ***somewhere* in** between 1 6 |
| V. | **caught** between 1 |
| | **choose/decide/distinguish** between 7 |

**bev|er|age** /bɛvərɪdʒ, bɛvrɪdʒ/ (**beverages**) N-COUNT **Beverages** are drinks. bebida [WRITTEN] ❑ *...artificially sweetened beverages.* *...bebidas endulzadas artificialmente.*, *...bebidas edulcoradas.*

→ see **sugar**

B

**Word Link** war ≈ watchful : aware, beware, warning

**be|ware** /bɪwɛər/

Beware is only used as an imperative or infinitive. It does not have any other forms.

V-I If you tell someone to **beware of** a person or thing, you are warning them that the person or thing may harm them or be dangerous. tener cuidado, poner atención ❑ *Beware of being too impatient with others. Ten cuidado de no ser demasiado impaciente con los demás.* ❑ *Drivers were warned to beware of icy conditions. Se advirtió a los conductores que estuvieran conscientes de la posibilidad de hielo en las carreteras.*

**be|yond** /bɪyɒnd/ **1** PREP If something is **beyond** a place or barrier, it is on the other side of it. más allá ❑ *On his right was a vegetable garden and beyond it a few apple trees. A su derecha había una hortaliza y, más allá, unos cuantos manzanos.* ● **Beyond** is also an adverb. a lo lejos ❑ *The house had a fabulous view out to the Strait of Georgia and the Rockies beyond. La casa tenía una magnífica vista del Estrecho de Georgia y las Rocallosas a lo lejos.* **2** PREP If something happens **beyond** a particular time or date, it continues after that time or date has passed. después de ❑ *Few jockeys continue riding beyond the age of 40. Pocos jockeys siguen montando después de los 40 (años de edad).* ● **Beyond** is also an adverb. después ❑ *...through the 1990s and beyond. ...a lo largo de los años 1990 y después.* **3** PREP If something extends **beyond** a particular thing, it affects or includes other things. más allá ❑ *His interests extended beyond the fine arts to politics and philosophy. Sus intereses van más allá de las bellas artes, hasta la política y la filosofía.* **4** PREP If something is, for example, **beyond** understanding or **beyond** belief, it is so extreme in some way that it cannot be understood or believed. superar ❑ *What Jock had done was beyond my comprehension. Lo que Jock había hecho superaba mi entendimiento.* **5** PREP If you say that something is **beyond** someone, you mean that they cannot deal with it. fuera de ❑ *The situation was beyond her control. La situación estaba fuera de su control.*

**B-grade** /bi greɪd/ ADJ A **B-grade** person or thing is one that you consider to be inferior or of poor quality. de segunda ❑ *...a B-grade action movie star. ...una estrella de películas de acción de segunda.*

**bias** /baɪəs/ (**biases**) N-VAR **Bias** is a tendency to prefer one person or thing to another, and to favor that person or thing. parcialidad ❑ *...his desire to avoid the appearance of bias in favor of one candidate or another. ...su deseo de evitar la apariencia de parcialidad en favor de un candidato u otro.*

**bi|ased** /baɪəst/ **1** ADJ If someone is **biased**, they prefer one group of people to another, and behave unfairly as a result. tendencioso, parcial, predispuesto ❑ *He seemed a bit biased against women in my opinion. En mi opinión, parecía un poco predispuesto contra las mujeres.* **2** ADJ If something is **biased toward** one thing, it is more concerned with it than with other things. parcial a ❑ *University funding was biased toward scientists. El financiamiento universitario era parcial a los científicos.*

**Bible** /baɪbəl/ (**Bibles**) N-PROPER **The Bible** is the sacred book of the Christian and Jewish religion. Biblia ● **biblical** /bɪblɪkəl/ ADJ bíblico ❑ *...the biblical story of creation. ...la historia bíblica de la creación.*

**bib|li|og|ra|phy** /bɪbliɒgrəfi/ (**bibliographies**) **1** N-COUNT A **bibliography** is a list of books on a particular subject. bibliografía ❑ *At the end of this chapter there is a bibliography of useful books. Al final del capítulo, hay una bibliografía de obras útiles.* **2** N-COUNT A **bibliography** is a list of the books and articles that are referred to in a particular book. bibliografía ❑ *The full bibliography is printed at the end of the second volume. Al final del segundo volumen, se encuentra la bibliografía completa.*

**Word Link** bi ≈ two : bicentennial, bicycle, bilingual

**Word Link** enn ≈ year : bicentennial, centennial, perennial

**bi|cen|ten|nial** /baɪsɛntɛniəl/ (**bicentennials**) **1** N-COUNT A **bicentennial** is a year in which you celebrate something important that happened exactly two hundred years ago. bicentenario ❑ *...the Bicentennial of the U.S. Constitution. ...el Bicentenario de la Constitución de Estados Unidos.* **2** ADJ **Bicentennial** celebrations are held to celebrate a bicentennial. bicentenario ❑ *...the bicentennial celebration of the American Revolution. ...la celebración del bicentenario de la Revolución de los Estados Unidos.*

**bi|coas|tal** /baɪkoʊstəl/ ADJ Someone or something that is **bicoastal** lives or occurs on both the east coast and the west coast of the U.S. *Aplicado a alguien o algo que vive u ocurre tanto en la costa este como en la oeste de Estados Unidos.*

**Word Link** cycl ≈ circle : bicycle, cycle, cyclist

**bi|cy|cle** /baɪsɪkəl/ (**bicycles**) N-COUNT A **bicycle** is a vehicle with two wheels which you ride by sitting on it and pushing two pedals with your feet. bicicleta
→ see Word Web: **bicycle**

**bid** /bɪd/ (**bids, bidding**)

The form **bid** is used in the present tense and is the past tense and past participle.

**1** N-COUNT A **bid for** something or a **bid to** do something is an attempt to obtain it or do it. intento ❑ *...the city's Olympic bid. ...el intento de la ciudad por obtener los Juegos Olímpicos.* **2** N-COUNT A **bid** is an offer to pay a particular amount of money for something that is being sold. oferta ❑ *They are hoping to make a bid for the company before Christmas. Esperan hacer una oferta por la compañía antes de Navidad.* **3** V-T/V-I If you **bid for** something or **bid to** do something, you try to obtain it or do it. pugnar ❑ *Several well-known firms are bidding for the work. Varias empresas bien conocidas están pugnando por el trabajo.* **4** V-T/V-I If you **bid for** something that is being sold, you offer to pay a particular amount of money for it. pujar, ofrecer ❑ *She wanted to bid for the painting. Quería pujar por el cuadro.* ❑ *The bank announced its intention to bid. El banco anunció su intención de hacer una oferta.* ❑ *The manager is prepared to bid $2 million for the soccer player. El entrenador está preparado a ofrecer dos millones de dólares por el futbolista.* ● **bid|der** N-COUNT (**bidders**) postor ❑ *The sale will be made to the highest bidder. La venta se hará al mejor postor.*

b

## Word Web bicycle

A Scotsman named Kirkpatrick MacMillan invented the first **bicycle** with **pedals** around 1840. Early bicycles had wooden or metal **wheels**. However, by the mid-1800s **tires** with tubes appeared. Modern **racing bikes** are very lightweight and aerodynamic. The wheels have fewer **spokes** and the tires are very thin and smooth. **Mountain bikes** allow riders to ride up and down steep hills on dirt trails. These bikes have fat, knobby tires for extra traction. The **tandem** is a bicycle for two people. It has about the same **wind resistance** as a one-person bike. But with twice the power, it goes faster.

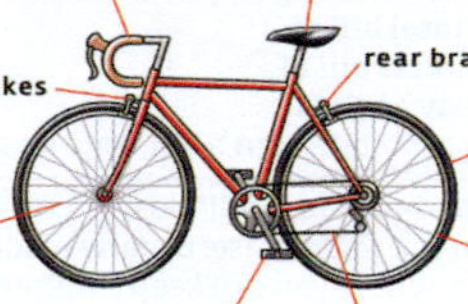


**Word Link** *er ≈ more : bigger, louder, taller*

**big** /bɪg/ (**bigger, biggest**) **1** ADJ A **big** person or thing is large in size or great in degree, extent, or importance. grande ❑ *Australia's a big country.* *Australia es un país grande.* ❑ *Her husband was a big man.* *Su esposo era un hombre grande.* ❑ *The crowd included a big group from Cleveland.* *Entre la multitud había un grupo numeroso de Cleveland.* ❑ *Her problem was just too big for her to solve on her own.* *Su problema era demasiado grande para resolverlo por sí sola.* ❑ *...one of the biggest companies in Italy.* *...una de las compañías más grandes de Italia.* **2** ADJ Children often refer to their older brother or sister as their **big** brother or sister. *(el/la) grande* ❑ *She always introduces me as her big sister.* *Ella siempre me presenta como su hermana la grande.*

**Thesaurus** *big* Ver también:
ADJ. enormous, huge, large, massive; (*ant.*) little, small, tiny **1**

**big bang theo|ry** N-SING In astronomy **the big bang theory** is a theory that suggests that the universe was created as a result of an extremely large explosion. *teoría del big bang, teoría de la gran explosión*

**big-box** ADJ A **big-box** store or retailer is a very large store where a great variety of goods is sold. *supertienda, megatienda* ❑ *...big-box stores spreading an hour west of Manhattan.* *...las megatiendas que se están multiplicando a una hora al oeste de Manhattan.*

**big bucks** N-PLURAL If someone earns or spends **big bucks,** they earn or spend a lot of money. *un dineral* [INFORMAL] ❑ *Plastic pipe is easy to install, and doing it yourself saves big bucks.* *La tubería de plástico es fácil de instalar y, si lo hace usted mismo, se ahorra un dineral.*

**big busi|ness** N-UNCOUNT Something that is **big business** is something which people spend a lot of money on, and which has become an important commercial activity. *un gran negocio* ❑ *Online dating is big business in the United States.* *Las agencias de contactos en línea son un gran negocio en Estados Unidos.*

**big-ticket** ADJ If you describe something as a **big-ticket** item, you mean that it costs a lot of money. *caro, costoso* ❑ *Supercomputers are big-ticket items.* *Las supercomputadoras son artículos muy caros.*

**big time** ADV You can use **big time** if you want to emphasize the importance or extent of something that has happened. *muchísimo, de veras* [INFORMAL] ❑ *You've upset her big-time.* *La molestaste de veras.*

**bike** /baɪk/ (**bikes**) N-COUNT A **bike** is a bicycle or a motorcycle. *bici, bicla, cicla, moto* [INFORMAL] ❑ *When you ride a bike, you exercise all of the leg muscles.* *Cuando montas en bici ejercitas todos los músculos de las piernas.*
→ see **bicycle**

**bike path** (**bike paths**) N-COUNT A **bike path** is a special path on which people can travel by bicycle separately from motor vehicles. *ciclopista*

**bik|er** /baɪkər/ (**bikers**) **1** N-COUNT **Bikers** are people who ride around on motorcycles, usually in groups. *motociclista* **2** N-COUNT People who ride bicycles are called **bikers.** *ciclista*

**bi|lat|er|al sym|met|ry** N-UNCOUNT An organism that has **bilateral symmetry** has a body that consists of two halves which are exactly the same, except that one half is the mirror image of the other. Compare **radial symmetry.** *simetría bilateral* [TECHNICAL]

**Word Link** *bi ≈ two : bicentennial, bicycle, bilingual*

**bi|lin|gual** /baɪlɪŋgwəl/ ADJ **Bilingual** means involving or using two languages. *bilingüe* ❑ *...bilingual education.* *...educación bilingüe.* ❑ *He is bilingual in Mandarin and English.* *Es bilingüe: habla mandarín e inglés.*

**bill** /bɪl/ (**bills, billing, billed**) **1** N-COUNT A **bill** is a written statement of money that you owe for goods or services. *cuenta, factura* ❑ *They couldn't afford to pay the bills.* *No tenían para pagar las cuentas.* ❑ *He paid his bill for the newspapers promptly.* *Pagó rápidamente la factura de los periódicos.* **2** V-T If you **bill** someone **for** goods or services you have provided them with, you give or send them a bill stating how much money they owe you for these goods or services. *facturar, pasar la cuenta* ❑ *Are you going to bill me for this?* *¿Va a facturarme esto?* **3** N-COUNT A **bill** is a piece of paper money. *billete (de banco)* ❑ *The case contained a large quantity of U.S. dollar bills.* *La maleta contenía una gran cantidad de billetes estadounidenses.* **4** N-COUNT In government, a **bill** is a formal statement of a proposed new law that is discussed and then voted on. *proyecto de ley* ❑ *This is the toughest crime bill that Congress has passed*

B

*in years.* *Este es el proyecto de ley contra el crimen más estricto que el Congreso ha aprobado en años.*

**Word Partnership** Usar *bill* con:

N. **electricity/gas/phone** bill, **hospital/hotel** bill 1
**dollar** bill 3
V. **pay a** bill 1
**pass a** bill, **sign a** bill, **vote on a** bill 4

**bill|fold** /bɪlfoʊld/ (**billfolds**) N-COUNT A **billfold** is a small flat folded case, usually made of leather or plastic, where you can keep banknotes and credit cards. *cartera, billetera*

**bil|lion** /bɪlyən/ (**billions**)

The plural form is **billion** after a number, or after a word or expression referring to a number, such as "several" or "a few."

1 NUM A **billion** is a thousand million. *mil millones* ❑ *The Ethiopian foreign debt has risen to 3 billion dollars.* *La deuda externa etíope aumentó a tres mil millones de dólares.* 2 QUANT You can use **billions** to mean an extremely large amount. *miles de millones* ❑ *The Universe is billions of years old.* *El universo tiene miles de millones de años de antigüedad.* • You can also use **billions** as a pronoun. *miles de millones* ❑ *It must be worth billions.* *Debe valer miles de millones.*

**bil|lion|aire** /bɪlyənɛər/ (**billionaires**) N-COUNT A **billionaire** is an extremely rich person who has money or property worth at least a thousand million dollars. *multimillonario o multimillonaria*

**bi|me|tal|lic strip** /baɪmətælɪk strɪp/ (**bimetallic strips**) N-COUNT A **bimetallic strip** is a long thin piece of material containing two different metals which expand at different rates when heated. Bimetallic strips are used in devices such as thermostats. *lámina bimetálica, plancha bimetálica* [TECHNICAL]

**bin** /bɪn/ (**bins**) N-COUNT A **bin** is a container that you keep or store things in. *cajón* ❑ *There is a storage bin under the passenger seat.* *Hay un cajón de almacenamiento bajo el asiento del pasajero.*

**bi|na|ry fis|sion** N-UNCOUNT **Binary fission** is the biological process by which a single cell divides to form two new cells. *fisión binaria* [TECHNICAL]

**bind** /baɪnd/ (**binds, binding, bound**) 1 V-T If something **binds** people **together**, it makes them feel as if they are all part of the same group. *unir, comprometer, obligar* ❑ *It is the threat of attack that binds them together.* *La amenaza de un ataque es lo que los une.* ❑ *The contract will bind the coach to the football team for two more seasons.* *El contrato comprometerá al entrenador con el equipo de fútbol por dos temporadas más.* 2 V-T If you **are bound** by something such as a rule, agreement, or restriction, you are forced or required to act in a certain way. *obligar* ❑ *You are bound by law to make sure that the information you receive remains secret.* *Estás obligado por ley a asegurarte de que la información que recibas permanezca en secreto.* ❑ *The authorities are legally bound to arrest any troublemakers.* *Las autoridades están obligadas por ley a arrestar a los alborotadores.* 3 V-T If you **bind** something or someone, you tie rope, string, tape, or other material around them so that they are held firmly. *atar, amarrar* ❑ *Bind the ends of the cord together with thread.* *Ate las puntas de la cuerda con hilo.* ❑ *...the red tape which was used to bind the files.* *...la cinta roja que se usaba para atar los expedientes.* 4 V-T When a book **is bound**, the pages are joined together and the cover is put on. *encuadernar, empastar* ❑ *Each volume is bound in bright-colored cloth.* *Cada volumen está encuadernado en tela de colores fuertes.* ❑ *Their business is from a few big publishers, all of whose books they bind.* *Hacen negocios con unas cuantas editoriales grandes, cuyos libros encuadernan.* 5 → see also **bound**

**bind|er** /baɪndər/ (**binders**) N-COUNT A **binder** is a hard cover with metal rings inside, which is used to hold loose pieces of paper. *carpeta*
→ see **office**

**bind|ing** /baɪndɪŋ/ (**bindings**) 1 ADJ A **binding** promise, agreement, or decision must be obeyed or carried out. *obligatorio* ❑ *It can take months to enter into a legally binding contract to buy a house.* *Puede tardar meses llegar a un contrato obligatorio para comprar una casa.* 2 N-VAR The **binding** of a book is its cover. *encuadernación, tapa, cubierta* ❑ *Its books are noted for the quality of their paper and bindings.* *Sus libros son famosos por la calidad del papel y la encuadernación.* 3 → see also **bind**

**bin|go** /bɪŋgoʊ/ N-UNCOUNT **Bingo** is a game in which each player has a card with numbers on it. Someone calls out numbers and if you are the first person to have all your numbers called out, you win the game. *lotería, bingo* ❑ *...a bingo hall.* *...un salón de lotería.*

binoculars

**bin|ocu|lars** /bɪnɒkyələrz/ N-PLURAL **Binoculars** consist of two small telescopes joined together side by side, which you look through in order to look at things that are a long distance away. *binoculares, gemelos*

**bi|no|mial** /baɪnoʊmiəl/ (**binomials**) 1 N-COUNT A **binomial** is an expression in algebra that consists of two terms, for example "3x + 2y." Compare **monomial, polynomial**. *binomio* [TECHNICAL] 2 ADJ **Binomial** means relating to binomials. *binomio*

**bi|no|mial dis|tri|bu|tion** (**binomial distributions**) N-COUNT A **binomial distribution** is a calculation that measures the probability of a particular outcome resulting from an event that has two possible outcomes. *distribución binómica* [TECHNICAL]

**bi|no|mial no|men|cla|ture** /baɪnoʊmiəl noʊmənkleɪtʃər/ N-UNCOUNT **Binomial nomenclature** is a system of scientifically classifying plants and animals by giving them a name consisting of two parts, first the genus and then the species. *nomenclatura binómica* [TECHNICAL]

**bi|no|mial theo|rem** (**binomial theorems**) N-COUNT The **binomial theorem** is a mathematical formula that is used to calculate the value of a binomial that has been multiplied by itself a particular number of times. *teorema binomio* [TECHNICAL]

**bio|chemi|cal** /baɪoʊkɛmɪkəl/ (**biochemicals**)

b

1 ADJ **Biochemical** changes, reactions, and mechanisms relate to the chemical processes that happen in living things. bioquímico ❑ *Starvation causes biochemical changes in the body.* *La privación extrema de alimento causa cambios bioquímicos en el cuerpo* 2 N-COUNT **Biochemicals** are chemicals that are made by living things, for example hormones and enzymes. sustancias bioquímicas

**Word Link** *chem ≈ chemical : biochemistry, chemical, chemistry*

**bio|chem|is|try** /baɪoʊkɛmɪstri/ N-UNCOUNT **Biochemistry** is the study of the chemical processes that occur in living things. bioquímica
● **bio|chem|ist** N-COUNT (**biochemists**) bioquímico o bioquímica

**bio|degrad|able** /baɪoʊdɪgreɪdəbəl/ ADJ Something that is **biodegradable** breaks down or decays naturally without any special scientific treatment, and can therefore be thrown away without causing pollution. biodegradable

**bio|di|ver|sity** /baɪoʊdaɪvɜrsɪti/ N-UNCOUNT **Biodiversity** is the existence of a wide variety of plant and animal species living in their natural environment. biodiversidad

**bi|og|raph|er** /baɪɒgrəfər/ (**biographers**) N-COUNT Someone's **biographer** is a person who writes an account of their life. biógrafo o biógrafa ❑ *...Picasso's biographer.* *...el biógrafo de Picasso.*

**Word Link** *bio ≈ life : biography, biology, biosphere*

**Word Link** *graph ≈ riting : autograph, biography, graph*

**bi|og|ra|phy** /baɪɒgrəfi/ (**biographies**) N-COUNT A **biography** of someone is an account of their life, written by someone else. biografía ❑ *...recent biographies of Stalin.* *...las biografías recientes de Stalin.*
● **bio|graphi|cal** /baɪəgræfɪkəl/ ADJ biográfico ❑ *The book contains few biographical details.* *El libro contiene pocos detalles biográficos.*
→ see **library**

**bio|logi|cal** /baɪəlɒdʒɪkəl/ 1 ADJ **Biological** is used to describe processes and states that occur in the bodies and cells of living things. biológico ❑ *...biological processes.* *...procesos biológicos.*
● **bio|logi|cal|ly** /baɪəlɒdʒɪkli/ ADV basado en la biología ❑ *Much of our behavior is biologically determined.* *Nuestra conducta es determinada en una gran medida por la biología.* 2 ADJ **Biological** is used to describe activities concerned with the study of living things. biológico, de la biología ❑ *...all aspects of biological research.* *...todos los aspectos de la investigación en el campo de la biología.* 3 ADJ **Biological** weapons and **biological** warfare involve the use of bacteria or other living organisms in order to attack human beings, animals, or plants. biológico ❑ *...chemical and biological weapons.* *...armas químicas y biológicas.*
→ see **sound, war, zoo**

**bio|logi|cal clock** (**biological clocks**) N-COUNT Your **biological clock** is your body's way of registering time. It does not rely on events such as day or night, but on factors such as your habits, your age, and chemical changes taking place in your body. reloj biológico

**Word Link** *logy, ology ≈ study of : biology, geology, mythology*

**bi|ol|ogy** /baɪɒlədʒi/ N-UNCOUNT **Biology** is the science which is concerned with the study of living things. biología ● **bi|olo|gist** /baɪɒlədʒɪst/ N-COUNT (**biologists**) biólogo o bióloga ❑ *...biologists studying the fruit fly.* *...los biólogos que estudian la mosca de la fruta.*

**bio|mass** /baɪoʊmæs/ 1 N-UNCOUNT The **biomass** of a particular area is the total number of organisms that live there. biomasa [TECHNICAL] 2 N-UNCOUNT **Biomass** is biological material such as dead plants that is used to provide fuel or energy. biomasa [TECHNICAL]

**bi|ome** /baɪoʊm/ (**biomes**) N-COUNT A **biome** is a group of plants and animals that live in a particular region because they are suited to its physical environment. bioma
→ see **habitat**

**bio|sphere** /baɪəsfɪər/ N-SING **The biosphere** is the part of the Earth's surface and atmosphere where there are living things. biosfera [TECHNICAL]
→ see Word Web: **biosphere**

**bio|tech|nol|ogy** /baɪoʊtɛknɒlədʒi/ N-UNCOUNT **Biotechnology** is the use of living parts such as cells or bacteria in industry and technology. biotecnología [TECHNICAL] ❑ *...the Scottish biotechnology company that developed Dolly the*

**Word Web** biosphere

Earth is the only place in the **universe** where we know that **life** exists. A **geologist**, Eduard Suess*, invented the word **biosphere** in 1875. For him this word described the **land**, **water**, and **atmosphere** where things live. Later scientists studied how living things and the biosphere affect each other. They created the word **ecosystem** to describe the whole system—living things and their biosphere. In the 1980s, scientists built a research center called Biosphere 2 in Arizona. They hoped to create an artificial biosphere for people to use on the moon. Today, the center studies the effects of **greenhouse gases** on the environment.

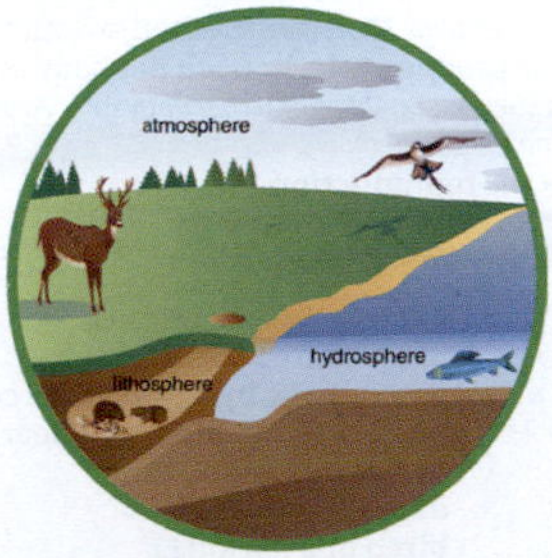


*Eduard Suess (1831–1914): an Austrian geologist.*

B

## Word Web bird

Many scientists today believe that birds evolved from avian dinosaurs. Recently many links have been found. Like birds, these dinosaurs laid their **eggs** in **nests**. Some had **wings**, **beaks**, and **claws** similar to modern birds. But perhaps the most dramatic link was found in 2001. Scientists in China discovered a well-preserved *Sinornithosaurus*, a bird-like dinosaur with **feathers**. This dinosaur is believed to be related to a prehistoric bird, the *Archaeopteryx*.

*cloned sheep. ...la compañía escocesa de biotecnología que creó la oveja clonada Dolly.*
→ see **technology**

**bi|ot|ic** /baɪɒtɪk/ ADJ **Biotic** means relating to plants, animals, and other living organisms. *biótico* [TECHNICAL]

**bio|weap|on** /baɪoʊwɛpən/ (**bioweapons**) N-COUNT **Bioweapons** are biological weapons. *arma biológica*

**bi|po|lar dis|or|der** (**bipolar disorders**) N-VAR **Bipolar disorder** is a mental illness in which a person's state of mind changes between extreme happiness and extreme depression. *desorden bipolar*

**bird** /bɜrd/ (**birds**) N-COUNT A **bird** is a creature with feathers and wings. *ave, pájaro*
→ see Word Web: **bird**
→ see **pet**

**bird feed|er** (**bird feeders**) also **birdfeeder** N-COUNT A **bird feeder** is an object that you fill with seeds or nuts and hang up outside in order to attract birds. *comedero para pájaros*

**bird flu** N-UNCOUNT **Bird flu** is a virus that can be transmitted from chickens, ducks, and other birds to people. *gripe aviar*

**bird|seed** /bɜrdsid/ N-UNCOUNT **Birdseed** is seeds that you give to birds as food. *alpiste* ❑ *She bought a supply of birdseed for the winter. Compró una buena provisión de alpiste para el invierno.*

**birth** /bɜrθ/ (**births**) **1** N-VAR When a baby is born, you refer to this event as his or her **birth**. *nacimiento* ❑ *His bad behavior started after the birth of his brother. Su mala conducta empezó después del nacimiento de su hermano.* ❑ *She weighed 5 lbs 7 oz at birth. Pesó 2.466 kilogramos al nacimiento.* **2** N-UNCOUNT You can refer to the beginning or origin of something as its **birth**. *nacimiento* ❑ *...the birth of democracy. ...el nacimiento de la democracia.* **3** PHRASE When a woman **gives birth**, she produces a baby from her body. *parir, dar a luz* ❑ *She's just given birth to a baby girl. Acaba de dar a luz una nena.*
→ see **reproduction**

### Word Partnership Usar *birth* con:

| | |
|---|---|
| PREP. | **at** birth, **before** birth **1** |
| ADJ. | **premature** birth **1** |
| N. | birth **of a baby/child**, birth **certificate**, birth **control**, birth **and death**, birth **defect**, birth **rate** **1** |
| | **date of** birth **1** **3** |
| | **birth of a** nation **2** |
| V. | **give** birth **3** |

**birth con|trol** N-UNCOUNT **Birth control** means planning whether to have children, and using contraception to prevent unwanted pregnancy. *control de la natalidad* ❑ *...today's methods of birth control. ...los métodos actuales de control de la natalidad.*

**birth|day** /bɜrθdeɪ, -di/ (**birthdays**) N-COUNT Your **birthday** is the anniversary of the date on which you were born. *cumpleaños* ❑ *On his birthday she sent him presents. El día de su cumpleaños le envió unos regalos.*

**birth|place** /bɜrθpleɪs/ (**birthplaces**) **1** N-COUNT Your **birthplace** is the place where you were born. *lugar de nacimiento, suelo natal* [WRITTEN] ❑ *...Bob Marley's birthplace in the village of Nine Mile. ...el lugar de nacimiento de Bob Marley en el poblado de Nine Mile.* **2** N-COUNT The **birthplace of** something is the place where it began. *cuna* ❑ *...Athens, the birthplace of the ancient Olympics. ...Atenas, la cuna de las antiguas olimpiadas.*

**birth rate** (**birth rates**) also **birth-rate** N-COUNT The **birth rate** is the number of babies born for every 1000 people during a particular period. *índice de natalidad, tasa de natalidad* ❑ *America's birth rate fell last year. La tasa de natalidad de Estados Unidos disminuyó el año pasado.*

**bish|op** /bɪʃəp/ (**bishops**) **1** N-COUNT; N-TITLE; N-VOC A **bishop** is a high-ranking member of the clergy. *obispo* **2** N-COUNT In chess a **bishop** is a piece that can be moved diagonally across the board on squares that are the same color. *alfil*
→ see **chess**

**bit** /bɪt/ (**bits**) **1** QUANT **A bit of** something is a small amount of it, or a small part or section of it. *un poquito, un pedacito, un cachito* ❑ *All it required was a bit of work. Todo lo que necesitaba era un poquito de trabajo.* ❑ *Only a bit of the barley remained. Sólo quedaba un poquito de la cebada.* ❑ *Now comes the really important bit. Ahora viene el pedacito que en verdad importa.* **2** PHRASE **A bit** means to a small extent or degree. It is sometimes used to make a statement less extreme. *un poco* ❑ *This girl was a bit strange. Esa chica era un poco rara.* ❑ *I think people feel a bit more confident. Creo que las personas se sienten un poco más confiadas.* **3** PHRASE You can use **a bit of** to make a statement less forceful. *poquito, agregar un diminutivo al final de la palabra tiene el mismo sentido eufemístico: -ito* ❑ *It's all a bit of a mess. Está un poquito desordenado.* ❑ *Students have always been portrayed as a bit of a joke. Los estudiantes siempre han sido representados un poquito en broma.* **4** PHRASE **Quite a bit** means quite a lot. *bastante* ❑ *They're worth quite a bit of money. Tienen bastante dinero.* ❑ *Things have changed quite a bit. Las cosas han* *cambiado bastante.* **5** PHRASE If you do something **a bit** or do something **for a bit,** you do it for a short time. *un poquito* ❑ *Let's wait a bit. Esperemos un poquito.* ❑ *I hope there will be time to talk a bit this evening. Espero que tengamos un poquito de tiempo para hablar esta tarde.* **6** N-COUNT In computing, a **bit** is the smallest unit of information that is held in a computer's memory. It is either 1 or 0. Several bits form a byte. *bit* **7** N-COUNT A **bit** is a piece of metal that is held in a horse's mouth and is used to control the horse when you are riding. *bocado* **8** **Bit** is the past tense of **bite**. *pasado de* ***bite*** **9** PHRASE If you say that something is **a bit much,** you are annoyed because you think someone has behaved in an unreasonable way. *un exceso* [INFORMAL] ❑ *Her bright red outfit was a bit much. Su brillante vestido rojo era un exceso.* **10** PHRASE You say that one thing is **every bit as** good, interesting, or important **as** another to emphasize that the first thing is just as good, interesting, or important as the second. *tan ... como* ❑ *My jacket is every bit as good as his. Mi chamarra es tan buena como la suya.*

**bitch** /bɪtʃ/ (**bitches**) N-COUNT A **bitch** is a female dog. *perra*

**bite** /baɪt/ (**bites, biting, bit, bitten**) **1** V-T/V-I If you **bite** something, you use your teeth to cut into it or through it. *morder* ❑ *Both sisters bit their nails as children. Ambas hermanas se mordían las uñas cuando eran niñas.* ❑ *He bit into his sandwich. Mordió su sándwich.* ❑ *She bit the end off the chocolate bar. Ella mordió una punta de su chocolate.*

bite

**2** N-COUNT A **bite** of something, especially food, is the action of biting it. *mordida* ❑ *He took another bite of apple. Le dio otra mordida a la manzana* **3** V-T/V-I If a snake or insect **bites** you, it makes a mark or hole in your skin. *picar, morder* ❑ *Mosquitoes spread the virus when they bite humans. Los mosquitos transmiten el virus cuando pican a los humanos.* ❑ *Do these flies bite? ¿Estas moscas muerden?* **4** N-COUNT A **bite** is an injury or a mark on your body where an animal, snake, or insect has bitten you. *mordida, piquete* ❑ *Any dog bite needs immediate medical attention. Una mordida de perro requiere de atención médica inmediata.* **5** V-I When an action or policy begins to **bite,** it begins to have a serious or harmful effect. *afectar* ❑ *The spending cuts will begin to bite from November onward. El recorte en el presupuesto empezará a afectar a partir de noviembre.* **6** PHRASE If you **bite** your **lip** or your **tongue,** you stop yourself from saying something that you want to say, because it would be the wrong thing to say in the circumstances. *morderse la lengua o los labios* ❑ *I must learn to bite my lip. Debo aprender a morderme la lengua.*

**bit|ten** /bɪtᵊn/ **Bitten** is the past participle of **bite.** *mordido*

**bit|ter** /bɪtər/ (**bitterest**) **1** ADJ In a **bitter** argument or conflict, people argue very angrily or fight very fiercely. *encarnizado* ❑ *...the scene of bitter fighting. ...la escena de la lucha encarnizada.* ❑ *...a bitter attack on the government. ...un ataque encarnizado contra el gobierno.* **2** ADJ If someone is **bitter,** they feel angry and resentful. *amargado* ❑ *She is very bitter about the way she was fired from her job. Ella está muy amargada por la forma en la que la despidieron de su trabajo.* • **bit|ter|ly** ADV *amargamente* ❑ *"And he sure didn't help us," Grant said bitterly. —Y no nos ayudó en lo absoluto —dijo amargamente Grant.* • **bit|ter|ness** N-UNCOUNT *amargura* ❑ *I still feel bitterness and anger toward the person who knocked me down. Todavía siento amargura y enojo contra la persona que me tiró al suelo.* **3** ADJ A **bitter** taste is sharp, not sweet, and often slightly unpleasant. *amargo* ❑ *The leaves taste bitter. Las hojas saben amargas.* **4** ADJ A **bitter** experience makes you feel very disappointed. You can also use **bitter** to emphasize feelings of disappointment. *amargo, penoso* ❑ *The decision was a bitter blow from which he never recovered. La decisión fue como un trago amargo del que nunca se recuperó.* ❑ *Bitter experience has taught him how to lose gracefully. La amarga experiencia le ha enseñado a perder con gracia.* • **bit|ter|ly** ADV *amargamente, penosamente* ❑ *I was bitterly disappointed to have lost yet another race. Estaba amargamente decepcionado de haber perdido una carrera más.* **5** ADJ **Bitter** weather, or a **bitter** wind, is extremely cold. *gélido, severo* ❑ *...a bitter east wind. ...un gélido viento del este.* • **bit|ter|ly** ADV *severamente, intensamente* ❑ *It's been bitterly cold here in Moscow. El clima ha sido gélido en Moscú.*
→ see **taste**

**bi|week|ly** /baɪwikli/ ADJ A **biweekly** event or publication happens or appears once every two weeks. *quincenal* ❑ *He used to see them at the biweekly meetings. Él solía verlos en las reuniones quincenales.*

**bi|zarre** /bɪzɑr/ ADJ Something that is **bizarre** is very odd and strange. *raro, extraño* ❑ *...the bizarre behavior of the team's manager. ...el extraño comportamiento del entrenador del equipo.* • **bi|zarre|ly** ADV *de modo extraño, extrañamente* ❑ *She dressed bizarrely. Ella se vestía de modo extraño.*

**black** /blæk/ (**blacker, blackest, blacks, blacking, blacked**) **1** COLOR Something that is **black** is of the darkest color that there is, the color of the sky at night when there is no light at all. *negro* ❑ *She was wearing a black coat with a white collar. Traía un abrigo negro con cuello blanco.* ❑ *He had thick black hair. Tenía el cabello negro y grueso.* • **black|ness** N-UNCOUNT *obscuridad* [LITERARY] ❑ *...the blackness of the night. ...la obscuridad de la noche.* **2** ADJ A **black** person belongs to a race of people with dark skins, especially a race originally from Africa. *negro* ❑ *He worked for the rights of black people. Trabajaba a favor de los derechos de los negros.* ❑ *Sharon is black, tall, and slender. Sherry es negra, alta y delgada.* **3** N-COUNT Black people are sometimes referred to as **blacks,** especially when comparing different groups of people. Other uses of the word could cause offense. *negros* ❑ *There are about thirty-one million blacks in the U.S. Hay como treinta y un millones de negros en los Estados Unidos.* **4** ADJ **Black** coffee or tea has no milk or cream added to it. *negro* ❑ *A cup of black tea or black coffee contains no calories. Una taza de café o té negro no tiene calorías.* **5** ADJ If you describe a situation as **black,** you are emphasizing that it is very bad indeed. *negro, obscuro* ❑ *It was one of the blackest days of his political career. Era uno de los días más negros de su carrera política.*
→ see **hair**

▸ **black out** PHR-VERB If you **black out,** you lose

consciousness for a short time. *desmayar* ❑ *I felt as if I was going to black out.* *Sentía que me iba a desmayar.*

**black and white** also **black-and-white** **1** COLOR In a **black and white** photograph or film, everything is shown in black, white, and gray. *blanco y negro* ❑ *...old black and white films.* *...películas viejas en blanco y negro.* ❑ *...a black-and-white photo of the two of us.* *...una foto en blanco y negro de los dos.* **2** PHRASE You say that something is **in black and white** when it has been written or printed, and not just said. *La frase significa ver algo impreso como prueba; "papelito habla", "lo hablado vuela, lo escrito permanece".* ❑ *He has seen the proof in black and white.* *Ha visto las pruebas impresas.*

**black|board** /blækbɔrd/ (**blackboards**) N-COUNT A **blackboard** is a dark-colored board that you can write on with chalk. *pizarrón* [AM also **chalkboard**]

**black eye** (**black eyes**) N-COUNT If someone has a **black eye,** they have a dark-colored bruise around their eye. *ojo morado* ❑ *He arrived at the hospital with a broken nose and a black eye.* *Llegó al hospital con la nariz rota y el ojo morado.*

**black-eyed pea** (**black-eyed peas**) N-COUNT **Black-eyed peas** are beige seeds with black marks that are eaten as a vegetable. They are from a plant called the cowpea. *frijol carita*

**black hole** (**black holes**) N-COUNT **Black holes** are areas in space where gravity is so strong that nothing, not even light, can escape from them. Black holes are thought to be formed by collapsed stars. *hoyo negro*

**black|jack** /blækdʒæk/ (**blackjacks**) **1** N-UNCOUNT **Blackjack** is a card game in which players try to obtain a combination of cards worth 21 points. *blackjack* ❑ *Vicky lost five hundred dollars playing blackjack.* *Vicky perdió quinientos dólares jugando al blackjack.* **2** N-COUNT A **blackjack** is a short, thick stick that is used as a weapon. *cachiporra* [INFORMAL] ❑ *Police searched the house for knives and blackjacks.* *La policía registró la casa en busca de cuchillos y cachiporras.*

**black|mail** /blækmeɪl/ (**blackmails, blackmailing, blackmailed**) **1** N-UNCOUNT **Blackmail** is the action of threatening to do something unpleasant to someone unless they do something you tell them to do, such as giving you money. *chantaje* ❑ *It looks like the pictures were being used for blackmail.* *Parece que las fotografías se estaban usando como chantaje.* **2** V-T If one person **blackmails** another person, they use blackmail against them. *chantajear* ❑ *He suddenly realized that she was blackmailing him.* *De pronto se dio cuenta que ella lo estaba chantajeando.* ❑ *The president insisted that he would not be blackmailed by violence.* *El presidente hizo énfasis en que no se iba a dejar chantajear por la violencia.* ● **black|mail|er** N-COUNT (**blackmailers**) *chantajista* ❑ *The nasty thing about a blackmailer is that his starting point is usually the truth.* *Lo peor de un chantajista es que normalmente empieza su chantaje a partir de una verdad.*

**black rhi|no** (**black rhinos**) also **black rhinoceros** N-COUNT A **black rhino** is a type of rhinoceros with gray skin and two horns on its nose, that lives in Africa. *rinoceronte negro*

**black|top** /blæktɒp/ N-UNCOUNT **Blacktop** is a hard black substance which is used as a surface for roads. *concreto asfáltico* ❑ *...waves of heat rising from the blacktop.* *...oleadas de calor que se desprendían del concreto asfáltico.*

blade

**blade** /bleɪd/ (**blades**) **1** N-COUNT The **blade** of a knife, ax, or saw is the edge, which is used for cutting. *cuchilla, hoja* ❑ *Many of them will have sharp blades.* *Muchas de ellas tendrán cuchillas afiladas.* **2** N-COUNT The **blades** of a propeller are the long, flat parts that turn around. *pala, paleta*
→ see **silverware**

**blame** /bleɪm/ (**blames, blaming, blamed**) **1** V-T If you **blame** a person or thing **for** something bad, or if you **blame** something bad **on** somebody, you believe or say that they are responsible for it or that they caused it. *culpar* ❑ *He can blame Greg for his failure.* *Puede culpar a Greg por su fracaso.* ❑ *The company blames its problems on the new computer system.* *La compañía culpa a los nuevos sistemas computacionales de sus problemas.* ● **Blame** is also a noun. *culpa* ❑ *Nothing could relieve my terrible sense of blame.* *Nada podía aliviar mi terrible sensación de culpa.* **2** N-UNCOUNT The **blame for** something bad that has happened is the responsibility for causing it or letting it happen. *culpa de* ❑ *I'm not going to take the blame for a mistake he made.* *No voy a asumir la culpa del error que cometió.* **3** V-T If you say that you do not **blame** someone **for** doing something, you mean that you consider it was a reasonable thing to do in the circumstances. *culpar* ❑ *I don't blame them for trying to make some money.* *No los culpo por tratar de hacer algo de dinero.* **4** PHRASE If someone is **to blame for** something bad that has happened, they are responsible for causing it. *el/la culpable* ❑ *You are not to blame for your illness.* *No eres el culpable de tu enfermedad.*

**Word Partnership** Usar *blame* con:

| | |
|---|---|
| N. | blame **the victim** **1** |
| V. | **tend to** blame **1** |
| | **lay** blame, **share the** blame **2** |
| | **can hardly** blame ***someone*** **3** |

**bland** /blænd/ (**blander, blandest**) **1** ADJ If you describe someone or something as **bland,** you mean that they are rather dull and unexciting. *insulso* ❑ *Serle has a blander personality than Howard.* *Serle es mucho más insulso que Howard.* ❑ *It sounds like a commercial: bland and forgettable.* *Suena como un comercial: insulso y fácilmente olvidable.* **2** ADJ Food that is **bland** has very little flavor. *insípido* ❑ *It tasted bland, like warmed cardboard.* *Era insípido, como cartón caliente.*
→ see **spice**

**blank** /blæŋk/ **1** ADJ Something that is **blank** has nothing on it. *en blanco, vacío* ❑ *We could put the pictures on that blank wall.* *Podríamos poner las pinturas en esa pared vacía.* ❑ *He tore a blank page from his notebook.* *Arrancó una hoja en blanco de su cuaderno.* **2** ADJ If you look **blank,** your face shows no feeling, understanding, or interest. *desconcertado* ❑ *Abbot looked blank. "I don't know him,*

sir." *Abbot se veía desconcertado. —No lo conozco, señor.*
• **blank|ly** ADV *con desconcierto* ❑ *She stared at him blankly. Ella lo miraba desconcertadamente.* **3** N-SING If your mind or memory is **a blank,** you cannot think of anything or remember anything. *mente en blanco* ❑ *I'm sorry, but my mind is a blank. Lo miraba con desconcierto., Lo siento, pero tengo la mente en blanco.* **4** PHRASE If your mind **goes blank,** you are suddenly unable to think of anything appropriate to say, for example in reply to a question. *ponerse en blanco*
→ see **answer**

**blank check** (**blank checks**) N-COUNT If someone is given a **blank check,** they are given the authority to spend as much money as they need or want. *cheque en blanco* ❑ *We will not write a blank check for companies that are in trouble. No extenderemos un cheque en blanco a las compañías en problemas.*

**blan|ket** /blæŋkɪt/ (**blankets, blanketing, blanketed**) **1** N-COUNT A **blanket** is a large square or rectangular piece of thick cloth, especially one that you put on a bed to keep you warm. *manta* **2** N-COUNT A **blanket of** something such as snow is a continuous layer of it which hides what is below or beyond it. *manto* ❑ *The mud disappeared under a blanket of snow. El lodo desapareció bajo un manto de nieve.* **3** V-T If something such as snow **blankets** an area, it covers it. *cubrir* ❑ *More than a foot of snow blanketed parts of Michigan. Más de treinta centímetros de nieve cubrieron parte de Michigan.* **4** ADJ You use **blanket** to describe something when you want to emphasize that it affects or refers to every person or thing in a group. *general* ❑ *...a blanket ban on courtroom cameras. ...una prohibición general de cámaras dentro de los juzgados.*
→ see **bed**

**blast** /blæst/ (**blasts, blasting, blasted**) **1** N-COUNT A **blast** is a big explosion, especially one caused by a bomb. *explosión* ❑ *250 people were killed in the blast. Doscientas cincuenta personas murieron en la explosión.* **2** V-T If something **is blasted** into a particular place or state, an explosion causes it to be in that place or state. If a hole **is blasted** in something, it is created by an explosion. *disparar, abrir un hueco* ❑ *There is a risk that harmful chemicals might be blasted into the atmosphere. Existe un riesgo de que químicos dañinos sean disparados a la atmósfera.* ❑ *The explosion blasted out the wall of her apartment. La explosión abrió un hueco en la pared de su departamento.* **3** V-T If workers **are blasting** rock, they are using explosives to make holes in it or destroy it, for example, so that a road or tunnel can be built. *volar, explotar* ❑ *Workers were blasting the rock beside the train track. Los trabajadores estaban volando la roca al lado de las vías del tren.* **4** V-T To **blast** someone means to shoot them with a gun. *disparar* ❑ *He blasted his rival to death. Le disparó a su rival hasta matarlo.* **5** N-SING If you say that something was a **blast,** you mean that you enjoyed it very much. *lo máximo* [INFORMAL] ❑ *He went skiing with his daughter. "It was a blast," he said later. Fue a esquiar con su hija. —Fue lo máximo —dijo después.*
▸ **blast off** PHR-VERB When a space rocket **blasts off,** it leaves the ground at the start of its journey. *despegar* ❑ *Columbia is expected to blast off at 1:20 a.m. Eastern Time tomorrow. Se espera que el Columbia despegue mañana a la 1:20 de la tarde, tiempo del este.*

**blaze** /bleɪz/ (**blazes, blazing, blazed**) **1** V-I When a building or a fire **blazes,** it burns strongly and brightly. *arder* ❑ *Three people died as the building blazed. Tres personas murieron mientras el edificio ardía.* ❑ *The log fire was blazing merrily. La fogata ardía vivamente* **2** N-COUNT A **blaze** is a large fire which is difficult to control and which destroys a lot of things. *incendio* ❑ *More than 4,000 firefighters are battling the blaze. Más de 4,000 bomberos combaten el incendio.* **3** V-I If something **blazes with** light or color, it is extremely bright. *resplandecer* [LITERARY] ❑ *The gardens blazed with color. Los jardines resplandecían, llenos de color.* • **Blaze** is also a noun. *esplendor* ❑ *I wanted the front garden to be a blaze of color. Quería que el jardín del frente resplandeciera de color.* **4** N-SING **A blaze of** publicity or attention is a great amount of it. *despliegue* ❑ *He was arrested in a blaze of publicity. Fue arrestado en medio de un despliegue publicitario.*

**bleach** /bliːtʃ/ (**bleaches, bleaching, bleached**) **1** V-T If you **bleach** something, you use a chemical to make it white or pale in color. *blanquear, decolorar* ❑ *These products don't bleach the hair. Estos productos no decoloran el cabello.* ❑ *...bleached pine tables. ...mesas de pino blanqueado.* **2** V-T/V-I If the sun **bleaches** something, or if something **bleaches,** its color gets paler until it is almost white. *decolorar* ❑ *The cloth was laid out on the grass to bleach in the sun. La tela fue tendida en el pasto para decolorarla al sol.* ❑ *His hair has been bleached by the sun. Su cabello ha sido decolorado por el sol.* **3** N-UNCOUNT **Bleach** is a chemical that is used to make cloth white, or to clean things thoroughly and kill germs. *cloro*

**bleach|ers** /bliːtʃərz/ N-PLURAL **The bleachers** are a part of an outdoor sports stadium, or the seats in that area, which are usually uncovered and are the least expensive place where people can sit. *gradería, tendido de sol*

**bleak** /bliːk/ (**bleaker, bleakest**) **1** ADJ If a situation is **bleak,** it is bad, and seems unlikely to improve. *sombrío, desolador* ❑ *The outlook remains bleak. La perspectiva es aún sombría.* • **bleak|ness** N-UNCOUNT *desolación* ❑ *We tried to get used to the bleakness of life after the war. Tratamos de acostumbrarnos a la desolación de la vida tras la guerra.* **2** ADJ If you describe a place as **bleak,** you mean that it looks cold, empty, and unattractive. *desolado* ❑ *The island's pretty bleak. La isla es bastante desolada.* **3** ADJ When the weather is **bleak,** it is cold, dull, and unpleasant. *sombrío, crudo* ❑ *The weather can be quite bleak on the coast. El clima puede ser bastante sombrío en la costa.* **4** ADJ If someone looks or sounds **bleak,** they look or sound depressed. *triste* ❑ *His face was bleak. Su semblante era triste.* • **bleak|ly** ADV *tristemente* ❑ *"There is nothing left," she says bleakly. —No queda nada —dijo tristemente.*

**bleed** /bliːd/ (**bleeds, bleeding, bled**) V-I When you **bleed,** you lose blood from your body as a result of injury or illness. *sangrar* ❑ *His lip was bleeding. Su labio sangraba.* ❑ *He was bleeding heavily from the cut on his arm. Sangraba profusamente por la herida en su brazo.* • **bleed|ing** N-UNCOUNT *sangrado* ❑ *We tried to stop the bleeding. Tratamos de detener el sangrado.*

B

**blend** /blɛnd/ (**blends, blending, blended**) **1** V-RECIP If you **blend** substances together or if they **blend,** you mix them together so that they become one substance. mezclar ❑ *Blend the butter with the sugar and beat until light and creamy.* *Mezcle el azúcar con la mantequilla y bata hasta que esté ligera y cremosa.* ❑ *Blend the ingredients until you have a smooth cream.* *Mezcle los ingredientes hasta que obtenga una crema suave.* **2** N-COUNT A **blend of** things is a mixture or combination of them that is useful or pleasant. mezcla ❑ *My album is a blend of jazz and rock'n'roll.* *Mi disco es una mezcla de jazz y rock.* ❑ *...a blend of natural cheeses and other fine ingredients.* *...una mezcla de quesos naturales con otros ingredientes finos.* **3** V-RECIP When colors, sounds, or styles **blend,** they come together or are combined in a pleasing way. armonizar ❑ *You could paint the walls and ceilings the same color so they blend together.* *Podrías pintar las paredes y el techo del mismo color para que armonicen.* **4** N-COUNT In linguistics, a **blend** is a combination of sounds that are represented by letters, for example the sound "spl" in "splash". combinación, mezcla [TECHNICAL]

**bless** /blɛs/ (**blesses, blessing, blessed**) **1** V-T When someone such as a priest **blesses** people or things, he or she asks for God's favor and protection for them. bendecir ❑ *We have come together to bless this couple and their love for each other.* *Nos hemos aquí reunido para bendecir a esta pareja y al amor que se profesan.* **2** CONVENTION **Bless** is used in expressions such as "God bless" or "bless you" to express affection, thanks, or good wishes. Dios te bendiga [INFORMAL, SPOKEN] ❑ *"Bless you, Eva," he whispered.* *—Dios te bendiga, Eva —susurró.* **3** CONVENTION You can say **"bless you"** to someone who has just sneezed. salud [SPOKEN] **4** → see also **blessing**

**bless|ing** /blɛsɪŋ/ (**blessings**) **1** N-COUNT A **blessing** is something good that you are grateful for. bendición ❑ *Rivers are a blessing for an agricultural country.* *Los ríos son una bendición para un país agrícola.* **2** N-COUNT If something is done with your **blessing,** it is done with your approval and support. bendición ❑ *Hailey quit school with the blessing of her parents.* *Hailey dejó la escuela con la bendición de sus padres.* **3** → see also **bless**

**blew** /bluː/ **Blew** is the past tense of **blow.** pasdo de **blow**

**blind** /blaɪnd/ (**blinds, blinding, blinded**) **1** ADJ Someone who is **blind** is unable to see because their eyes are damaged. ciego ❑ *I started helping him with the business when he went blind.* *Empecé a ayudarlo con el negocio cuando se quedó ciego.* • **The blind** are people who are blind. ciegos ❑ *He was a teacher of the blind.* *Era un maestro de ciegos.* • **blind|ness** N-UNCOUNT ceguera ❑ *Early treatment can usually prevent blindness.* *El tratamiento oportuno frecuentemente puede prevenir la ceguera.* **2** V-T If something **blinds** you, it makes you unable to see, either for a short time or permanently. cegar ❑ *The sun hit the windshield, momentarily blinding him.* *El sol dio de frente en el parabrisas, cegando al conductor momentáneamente.* **3** ADJ If you are **blind to** a fact or a situation, you ignore it or are unaware of it; used to show disapproval. ofuscar ante ❑ *David's good looks and manners made her blind to his faults.* *La hermosura y los buenos modales de David la ofuscaban ante sus faltas* • **blind|ness** N-UNCOUNT ceguera ❑ *...his blindness in the face of his son's guilt.* *...su ceguera ante la culpabilidad de su hijo.* **4** V-T If something **blinds** you **to** the real situation, it prevents you from realizing that it exists or from understanding it properly. ofuscar ante ❑ *He never allowed his love of Australia to blind him to its faults.* *Nunca permitió que su amor por Australia lo ofuscara ante sus faltas.* **5** ADJ You can describe someone's beliefs or actions as **blind** when you disapprove of them because they do not question or think about what they are doing. ciego ❑ *...her blind faith in the wisdom of the church.* *...su ciega fe en la sabiduría de la iglesia.* **6** N-COUNT A **blind** is a roll of cloth or paper which you can pull down over a window as a covering. persiana ❑ *Pulling the blinds up, she let some of the bright sunlight in.* *Abrió las persianas y dejó que entrara algo de la luz del sol.* **7** PHRASE If someone **is turning a blind eye to** something bad or illegal that is happening, they are pretending not to notice that it is happening so that they will not have to do anything about it. hacer la vista gorda ❑ *Officers say they are turning a blind eye to minor crimes.* *Los policías dicen que está haciendo la vista gorda ante los delitos menores.*
→ see **disability**

| **Word Partnership** | Usar *blind* con: |
|---|---|
| ADJ. | blind **and deaf** 1 |
| ADV. | **legally** blind, **partially** blind 1 |
| N. | blind **person** 1 |
| | blind **faith** 5 |

**blind|ers** /blaɪndərz/ N-PLURAL **Blinders** are two pieces of leather that are placed at the side of a horse's eyes so that it can only see straight ahead. anteojera

**blind|side** /blaɪndsaɪd/ (**blindsides, blindsiding, blindsided**) V-T If you say that you **were blindsided** by something, you mean that it surprised you in a negative way; used to show disapproval. sacar de onda ❑ *He complained about being blindsided by the decision.* *Se quejó de haber sido sacado de onda por la decisión.*

**bling** /blɪŋ/ also **bling-bling** N-UNCOUNT Some people refer to expensive or fancy jewelry or clothes as **bling** or **bling-bling.** bisutería o ropa vistosa [INFORMAL] ❑ *Famous jewelers want to get celebrities to wear their bling.* *Los joyeros de renombre desean que los famosos usen sus artículos de lujo.* ❑ *...the rap star's love of bling-bling.* *...el amor de la estrella del rap hacia las cosas lujosas y brillantes.*

**blink** /blɪŋk/ (**blinks, blinking, blinked**) **1** V-T/V-I When you **blink** or when you **blink** your eyes, you shut your eyes and very quickly open them again. parpadear ❑ *Kathryn blinked and forced a smile.* *Kathryn parpadeó y forzó una sonrisa.* ❑ *She was blinking her eyes rapidly.* *Ella estaba parpadeando rápidamente.* • **Blink** is also a noun. parpadeo ❑ *She gave a couple of blinks and her eyes cleared.* *Parpadeó un par de veces y su vista se aclaró.* **2** V-I When a light **blinks,** it flashes on and off. parpadear ❑ *Green and yellow lights blinked on the surface of the water.* *Luces verdes y amarillas parpadeaban en la superficie del agua.* ❑ *The plane was flying for about 15 minutes before a warning light blinked on.* *El avión había volado por unos 15 minutos cuando una luz de advertencia comenzó a parpadear.*

**bliz|zard** /blɪzərd/ (**blizzards**) N-COUNT A **blizzard** is a very bad snowstorm with strong winds. *tormenta de nieve*
→ see **snow, storm, weather**

**bloc** /blɒk/ (**blocs**) N-COUNT A **bloc** is a group of countries that have similar political aims and interests and that act together over some issues. *bloque* ❑ *...the former Soviet bloc. ...el antiguo bloque de países soviéticos.*

**block** /blɒk/ (**blocks, blocking, blocked**)
**1** N-COUNT A **block of** a substance is a large rectangular piece of it. *bloque* ❑ *...a block of ice. ...un bloque de hielo.*

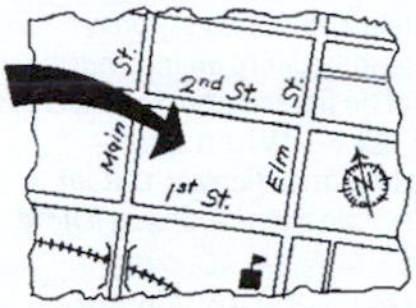

block

**2** N-COUNT A **block** in a town or city is an area of land with streets on all its sides, or the area or distance between such streets. *cuadra, manzana* ❑ *He walked around the block three times. Caminó tres veces alrededor de la cuadra.* ❑ *She walked four blocks down High Street. Caminó tres cuadras por High Street.* **3** V-T To **block** a road, channel, or pipe means to put an object across it or in it so that nothing can pass through it or along it. *bloquear* ❑ *Students blocked a highway through the center of the city. Los estudiantes han bloqueado una vía rápida que atraviesa la ciudad.* **4** V-T If something **blocks** your view, it prevents you from seeing something because it is between you and that thing. *tapar* ❑ *A row of trees blocked his view of the north slope of the mountain. Una fila de árboles le tapa la vista hacia la cara norte de la montaña.* **5** V-T If you **block** something that is being arranged, you prevent it from being done. *bloquear* ❑ *The country has tried to block imports of cheap foreign products. El país ha tratado de bloquear las importaciones de productos extranjeros de baja calidad.*
**6** → see also **stumbling block**
→ see **percussion**
▸ **block out** PHR-VERB If you **block out** a thought, you try not to think about it. *tratar de no pensar en* ❑ *She accused me of blocking out the past. Ella me acusó de tratar de no pensar en el pasado.*

**block|ade** /blɒkeɪd/ (**blockades, blockading, blockaded**) **1** N-COUNT A **blockade** of a place is an action that is taken to prevent goods or people from entering or leaving it. *bloqueo* ❑ *It's not yet clear who will enforce the blockade. Aún no está claro quién impondrá el bloqueo.* **2** V-T If a group of people **blockade** a place, they stop goods or people from reaching that place. If they **blockade** a road or a port, they stop people from using that road or port. *bloquear* ❑ *The town has been blockaded for 40 days. El pueblo ha estado bloqueado durante 40 días.*

**block and tackle** (**block and tackles** or **blocks and tackles**) N-COUNT A **block and tackle** is a device consisting of two or more pulleys connected by a rope or cable, which is used for lifting heavy objects. *aparejo de poleas*

**block|bust|er** /blɒkbʌstər/ (**blockbusters**) N-COUNT A **blockbuster** is a movie or book that is very popular and successful, usually because it is very exciting. *éxito* [INFORMAL] ❑ *...the latest Hollywood blockbuster. ...el último éxito de Hollywood.*

**blocked** /blɒkt/ also **blocked up** ADJ If something is **blocked** or **blocked up,** it is completely closed so that nothing can get through it. *tapado* ❑ *The main drain was blocked. El drenaje principal estaba tapado.* ❑ *His arteries were blocked up and he needed surgery. Tenía las arterias tapadas y necesitaba cirujía.*

**block|ing** **1** N-UNCOUNT In the theater, **blocking** is the process of planning the movements that the actors will make on the stage during the performance of a play. *marcar posiciones* [TECHNICAL] **2** → see also **block**

**block par|ty** (**block parties**) N-COUNT A **block party** is an outdoor party for all the residents of a block or neighborhood. *fiesta del barrio* ❑ *...the Fourth of July parade and block party. ...el desfile y la fiesta del barrio celebrando el 4 de julio.*

**blog** /blɒg/ (**blogs**) N-COUNT A **blog** is a website containing a diary or journal on a particular subject. *blog* [COMPUTING] ❑ *There are many ways to add entries and edit your blog. Existen muchas maneras de añadir entradas y editar tu blog.* • **blog|ger** N-COUNT (**bloggers**) *bloguero o bloguera* ❑ *Most bloggers comment on news reported elsewhere, while others do their own reporting. La mayoría de los blogueros comentan sobre noticias que se dieron en otro lugar, mientras que otros realizan sus propios reportes.* • **blog|ging** N-UNCOUNT *blogueo* ❑ *...the enormous popularity of blogging. ...la enorme popularidad del blogueo.*
→ see Word Web: **blog**

**Word Link** *sphere ≈ ball : atmosphere, blogosphere, hemisphere*

**blogo|sphere** /blɒgəsfɪər/ also **blogsphere** /blɒgsfɪər/ N-SING In computer technology, **the**

**Word Web** blog

The word **blog** is a combination of the words **web** and **log**. It is a **website** that has many dated **entries**. A blog can focus on one subject of interest. Most blogs are written by one person. But sometimes a political committee, corporation, or other group keeps a blog. Many blogs ask readers to leave comments on the site. This often results in a group of readers who write back and forth to each other. The total group of web logs is the blogosphere. A blogstorm occurs when there are many people using blogs about the same topic.

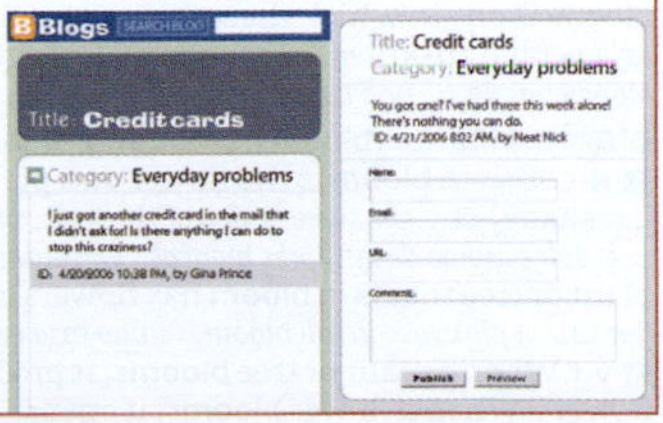

B

**blogosphere** or **the blogsphere** is all the blogs on the Internet, considered collectively. *blogósfera* ❑ *The blogosphere continues to expand. La blogósfera continúa expandiéndose.*
→ see **blog**

**blonde** /blɒnd/ (**blondes, blonder, blondest**) 1 COLOR Someone who has **blonde** hair has pale-colored hair. *rubio* ❑ *...a little girl with blonde hair. ...una niñita con el cabello rubio.* 2 ADJ Someone who is **blonde** has blonde hair. *rubio* ❑ *He was blonder than his brother. Era más rubio que su hermano.* 3 N-COUNT A **blonde** is a woman who has blonde hair. *rubia* ❑ *...a stunning blonde in her early thirties. ...una rubia despampanante de treinta y pico años.*
→ see **hair**

**blood** /blʌd/ 1 N-UNCOUNT **Blood** is the red liquid that flows inside your body, which you can see if you cut yourself. *sangre* ❑ *His shirt was covered in blood. Su camisa estaba cubierta de sangre.* 2 N-UNCOUNT You can use **blood** to refer to the race or social class of someone's parents or ancestors. *sangre* ❑ *There was Greek blood in his veins. Por sus venas corría sangre griega.* 3 PHRASE If something violent and cruel is done **in cold blood,** it is done deliberately and in an unemotional way. *a sangre fría* ❑ *The crime was committed in cold blood. El crimen se cometió a sangre fría.* 4 PHRASE You can use the expressions **new blood, fresh blood,** or **young blood** to refer to people who are brought into an organization to improve it by thinking of new ideas or new ways of doing things. *sangre nueva* ❑ *There's been a major effort to bring in new blood. Se ha hecho un esfuerzo por contratar sangre nueva.* 5 **own flesh and blood** → see **flesh**
→ see **cardiovascular system, donor**

**Word Partnership** Usar *blood* con:

| | |
|---|---|
| N. | (**red/white**) blood **cells**, blood **clot**, blood **disease**, blood **loss**, **pool of** blood, blood **sample**, blood **stream**, blood **supply**, blood **test**, blood **transfusion** 1 |
| ADJ. | **covered in** blood, blood **stained** 1 |
| V. | **donate/give** blood 1 |

**blood pres|sure** N-UNCOUNT Your **blood pressure** is the amount of force with which your blood flows around your body. *presión arterial, tensión arterial* ❑ *Your doctor will take your blood pressure. Tu doctor tomará tu presión arterial.* ❑ *What are the causes of high blood pressure? ¿Cuáles son las causas de la alta presión arterial?*
→ see **diagnosis**

**bloody** /blʌdi/ (**bloodier, bloodiest**) 1 ADJ Something that is **bloody** is covered in blood. *ensangrentado, sangriento* ❑ *...a bloody nose. ...una nariz sangrienta.* 2 A situation or event that is **bloody** is one in which there is a lot of violence and people are killed. *sangriento* ❑ *...a long and bloody battle. ...una batalla larga y sangrienta.*

**bloom** /blum/ (**blooms, blooming, bloomed**) 1 N-COUNT A **bloom** is the flower on a plant. *flor* [LITERARY] ❑ *...the sweet smell of the white blooms. ...el dulce aroma de las flores blancas.* 2 PHRASE A plant or tree that is **in bloom** has flowers on it. *en flor* ❑ *...a pink rose in full bloom. ...una rosa en flor.* 3 V-I When a plant or tree **blooms,** it produces flowers. When a flower **blooms,** it opens. *florecer* ❑ *This plant blooms between May and June. Esta planta florece entre mayo y junio.*

**bloop|er** /blupər/ (**bloopers**) N-COUNT A **blooper** is a silly mistake. *error* [INFORMAL] ❑ *...the funniest television bloopers. ...los más famosos errores de la televisión.*

**blos|som** /blɒsəm/ (**blossoms, blossoming, blossomed**) 1 N-VAR **Blossom** is the flowers that appear on a tree before the fruit. *flor* ❑ *...cherry blossoms. ...cerezos en flor.* 2 V-I If someone or something **blossoms,** they develop good, attractive, or successful qualities. *florecer* ❑ *Some people take longer than others to blossom. A algunas personas les toma más tiempo que a otras el florecer.* ❑ *Our local festival has blossomed into an international event. Nuestro festival local ha florecido hasta convertirse en un evento internacional.* 3 V-I When a tree **blossoms,** it produces blossom. *florecer* ❑ *Rain begins to fall and peach trees blossom. Empieza a llover y los duraznos florecen.*

**blouse** /blaʊs/ (**blouses**) N-COUNT A **blouse** is a kind of shirt worn by a girl or woman. *blusa*
→ see **clothing**

**blow**
❶ VERB USES
❷ NOUN USES

❶ **blow** /bloʊ/ (**blows, blowing, blew, blown**) 1 V-I When a wind or breeze **blows,** the air moves. *soplar* ❑ *A cold wind blew at the top of the hill. En lo alto de la colina soplaba un viento frío.* 2 V-T/V-I If the wind **blows** something somewhere or if it **blows** there, the wind moves it there. *volar con el viento* ❑ *The wind blew her hair back from her forehead. El cabello de su frente volaba con el viento.* ❑ *Sand blew in our eyes. Con el viento, la arena se nos metió en los ojos.* 3 V-I If you **blow,** you send out a stream of air from your mouth. *soplar(se)* ❑ *Danny blew on his fingers to warm them. Danny se sopló en los dedos para calentarlos.* 4 V-T/V-I When a whistle or horn **blows** or someone **blows** it, they make a sound by blowing into it. *sonar* ❑ *The whistle blew and the train moved forward. El silbato sonó y el tren avanzó.* 5 V-T When you **blow** your nose, you force air out of it through your nostrils in order to clear it. *sonarse* ❑ *He took out a handkerchief and blew his nose. Sacó un pañuelo y se sonó la nariz.* 6 V-T To **blow** something **out, off,** or **away** means to remove or destroy it violently with an explosion. *destrozar* ❑ *The can exploded, blowing out the kitchen windows. La lata explotó y destrozó las ventanas de la cocina.* 7 V-T If you **blow** a chance or attempt to do something, you make a mistake which wastes the chance or causes the attempt to fail. *echar a perder* [INFORMAL] ❑ *One careless word could blow the whole deal. Una palabra sin cuidado podría echar a perder todo el asunto.* ❑ *Oh you fool! You've blown it! ¡Ah, qué tonto! ¡Lo echaste a perder!* 8 V-T If you **blow** a large amount of money, you spend it quickly on luxuries. *gastar(se)* [INFORMAL] ❑ *My brother lent me some money and I went out and blew it all. Mi hermano me prestó algo de dinero y fui y me lo gasté todo.* 9 → see also **full-blown**
→ see **glass, wind**

▸ **blow off** PHR-VERB If you **blow** something **off,** you ignore it or choose not to deal with it. *hacer a*

un lado [INFORMAL] ❑ *I don't think we can just blow this off.* *No creo que podamos hacer esto a un lado.*
▸ **blow out** PHR-VERB If you **blow out** a flame or a candle, you blow at it so that it stops burning. *apagar* ❑ *I blew out the candle.* *Apagué la vela.*
▸ **blow over** PHR-VERB If something such as trouble or an argument **blows over,** it ends without any serious consequences. *caer en el olvido* ❑ *Wait, and it'll all blow over.* *Espera y todo caerá en el olvido.*
▸ **blow up** 1 PHR-VERB If someone **blows** something **up** or if it **blows up,** it is destroyed by an explosion. *explotar* ❑ *He was jailed for 45 years for trying to blow up a plane.* *Estuvo en la cárcel durante 45 años por tratar de explotar un avión.* 2 PHR-VERB If you **blow up** something such as a balloon or a tire, you fill it with air. *inflar* ❑ *Take some slow, deep breaths, as if you are blowing up a balloon.* *Respira lenta y hondamente, como si estuvieras inflando un globo.*

❷ **blow** /bloʊ/ (**blows**) 1 N-COUNT If someone receives a **blow,** they are hit with a fist or weapon. *golpe* ❑ *He went to the hospital after a blow to the face.* *Fue al hospital después de recibir un golpe en la cara.* 2 N-COUNT If something that happens is a **blow to** someone or something, it is very upsetting, disappointing, or damaging to them. *golpe* ❑ *The increase in tax was a blow to the industry.* *El aumento de impuestos fue un golpe para la industria.*

**Word Partnership** Usar *blow* con:

| | |
|---|---|
| ADV. | blow **away** ❶ 2 6 |
| N. | blow **bubbles**, blow **smoke** ❶ 3 |
| | blow **a whistle** ❶ 4 |
| | blow ***your* nose** ❶ 5 |
| V. | **deliver/strike a** blow ❷ 1 |
| | **cushion/soften a** blow, **suffer a** blow ❷ 1 2 |
| ADJ. | **crushing/devastating/heavy** blow ❷ 1 2 |
| PREP. | blow **to the head** ❷ 1 |
| | blow **to *someone*** ❷ 2 |

**blown** /bloʊn/ **Blown** is the past participle of **blow.** *participio pasado de* ***blow***

**blue** /blu/ (**bluer, bluest, blues**) 1 COLOR Something that is **blue** is the color of the sky on a sunny day. *azul* ❑ *...the cloudless blue sky...* *el cielo azul, sin nube alguna.* ❑ *...pale blue eyes.* *...ojos color azul claro.* 2 N-PLURAL **The blues** is a type of music which was developed by African American musicians in the southern United States. It is characterized by a slow tempo and a strong rhythm. *blues* ❑ *...to sing the blues...* *cantar el blues.* 3 ADJ If a U.S. state is described as **blue,** it means that the majority of its residents vote for the Democrats in elections, especially in the presidential elections. *En Estados Unidos, los estados azules son aquéllos donde la mayoría vota por el partido demócrata, especialmente en elecciones presidenciales.* ❑ *...the red and blue states.* *...los estados rojos y azules.*
→ see **color, rainbow**

**blue-collar** ADJ **Blue-collar** workers work in industry, doing physical work, rather than in offices. *obrero* ❑ *It wasn't just the blue-collar workers who lost their jobs, it was everyone.* *No sólo los obreros perdieron su empleo sino todos los trabajadores.*

**blunt** /blʌnt/ (**blunter, bluntest, blunts, blunting, blunted**) 1 ADJ If you are **blunt,** you say exactly what you think without trying to be polite. *franco* ❑ *She is blunt about her personal life.* *Es franca respecto a su vida personal.* • **blunt|ly** ADV *francamente* ❑ *"I don't believe you!" Jeanne said bluntly.* *—¡No te creo! —dijo Jeanne francamente.* • **blunt|ness** N-UNCOUNT *franqueza* ❑ *His bluntness got him into trouble.* *Su franqueza lo metió en problemas.* 2 ADJ A **blunt** object has a rounded or flat end rather than a sharp one. *desafilado* ❑ *Carefully draw round the shapes with a blunt pencil.* *Trace cuidadosamente las figuras con un lápiz romo.* 3 ADJ A **blunt** knife or blade is no longer sharp and does not cut well. *desafilado* ❑ *The edge is as blunt as a butter knife.* *El filo de la navaja está tan chato como si fuera cuchillo para mantequilla.* 4 V-T If something **blunts** an emotion, a feeling, or a need, it weakens it. *reducir* ❑ *Norway blunted England's hopes of qualifying for the Soccer World Cup by beating them 2-1.* *Noruega redujo las esperanzas de Inglaterra de calificar a la Copa del Mundo al ganarles 2-1.*

**blur** /blɜr/ (**blurs, blurring, blurred**) 1 N-COUNT A **blur** is a shape or area which you cannot see clearly because it has no distinct outline or because it is moving very fast. *algo borroso* ❑ *I saw a blur of movement on the other side of the glass door.* *Vi algo moverse tan rápido que no se apreciaba qué era, del otro lado de la puerta de vidrio.* 2 V-T/V-I When a thing **blurs** or when something **blurs** it, you cannot see it clearly because its edges are no longer distinct. *volver(se) algo borroso* ❑ *Removing your eyeglasses blurs the image.* *Quitarse los anteojos vuelve la imagen borrosa.* • **blurred** ADJ *borroso* ❑ *...blurred black and white photographs.* *...fotos borrosas en blanco y negro.* 3 V-T If something **blurs** an idea or a distinction between things, that idea or distinction no longer seems clear. *borrar* ❑ *She constantly blurs the line between work, personal life, and love.* *Constantemente borra la línea entre el trabajo, la vida personal y el amor.* • **blurred** ADJ *borroso* ❑ *The line between fact and fiction is becoming blurred.* *La línea entre los hechos y la ficción se está volviendo borrosa.*

**blush** /blʌʃ/ (**blushes, blushing, blushed**) V-I When you **blush,** your face becomes redder than usual because you are ashamed or embarrassed. *sonrojarse* ❑ *"Hello, Maria," he said, and she blushed again.* *—Hola, María —le dijo él, y ella se sonrojó de nuevo.* • **Blush** is also a noun. *sonrojo* ❑ *"The most important thing is to be honest," she says, without the trace of a blush.* *—Lo más importante es ser honesto —dice, sin traza alguna de sonrojo.*

**BMI** /bi ɛm aɪ/ **BMI** is an abbreviation for **body mass index.** *IMC (Índice de masa corporal)* [MEDICAL] ❑ *A BMI greater than 30 is considered obese.* *Se considera obesidad tener un IMC mayor a 30.*

**board** /bɔrd/ (**boards, boarding, boarded**) 1 N-COUNT A **board** is a flat, thin, rectangular piece of wood or plastic which is used for a particular purpose. *tabla* ❑ *After using cutting boards and knives, immediately wash them with hot soapy water.* *Después de utilizar cuchillo y una tabla de picar, lávelos con agua caliente con jabón.* 2 N-COUNT A **board** is a square piece of wood or stiff cardboard that you use for playing games such as chess. *tablero* ❑ *...a checkers board.* *...un tablero de damas.* 3 N-COUNT You can refer to a blackboard or a bulletin board as a **board.** *pizarrón, tablero* ❑ *He*

b

B

## Word Web boat

People once used **boats** only for transportation. But today millions of people enjoy boating as a form of recreation. Weekend **captains** enjoy quietly **sailing** their small boats along the shore. However, other boaters like to ride around in **motorboats**. Any **rowboat** can become a motorboat just by attaching an outboard **motor** to the back. Inboard motors are quieter, but they're more expensive. Fishermen usually like to use a rowboat with **oars**. That way they won't scare the fish away. For an even more peaceful ride, some people **paddle** around in **canoes**. But really adventurous folks like the thrill of white-water **rafting**.

*wrote a few more notes on the board.* *Escribió algunas notas más en el pizarrón.* **4** N-COUNT The **board** of a company or organization is the group of people who control it and direct it. *consejo* [BUSINESS] ❑ *The board has asked me to continue as chief executive.* *El consejo me ha pedido continuar como presidente.* **5** V-T When you **board** a train, ship, or aircraft, you get on it in order to travel somewhere. *abordar, embarcar(se)* [FORMAL] ❑ *I boarded the plane to Boston.* *Abordé el avión a Boston.* **6** N-UNCOUNT **Board** is the food which is provided when you stay somewhere, for example in a hotel. *alimentos* ❑ *Free room and board are provided for all hotel staff.* *Al personal del hotel se le proporciona habitación y alimentos.* **7** PHRASE If a policy or a situation applies **across the board,** it affects everything or everyone in a particular group. *en general, para todos* ❑ *The job cuts will take place across the board, from senior managers to mailmen.* *La reducción de personal aplicará en general, desde gerentes hasta carteros.* **8** PHRASE When you are **on board** a train, ship, or aircraft, you are on it or in it. *a bordo* ❑ *All 269 people on board the plane were killed.* *Los 269 pasajeros a bordo del avión murieron.* **9** PHRASE If you **take on board** an idea or a problem, you begin to accept it or understand it. *asumir* ❑ *We hope that they will take on board some of what you have said.* *Esperamos que asumirán algo de lo que has dicho.*
▸ **board up** PHR-VERB If you **board up** a door or window, you fix pieces of wood over it so that it is covered up. *tapiar* ❑ *Shopkeepers have boarded up their windows.* *Los tenderos han tapiado las ventanas.*

### Word Partnership Usar *board* con:

N. **cutting** board, **diving** board **1**
board **game** **2**
**bulletin** board, **message** board **3**
**chair/member of the** board, board **of directors**, board **meeting** **4**
board **a flight/plane/ship** **5**
**room and** board **6**

**board|ing pass** (**boarding passes**) N-COUNT A **boarding pass** is a card that a passenger must have when boarding a plane or a boat. *pase de abordar, tarjeta de embarque*

**board|walk** /bɔrdwɔk/ (**boardwalks**) N-COUNT A **boardwalk** is a path made of wooden boards, especially one along a beach. *malecón*

**boast** /boʊst/ (**boasts, boasting, boasted**) V-I If someone **boasts** about something that they have done or that they own, they talk about it very proudly, in a way that other people may find irritating or offensive. *presumir* ❑ *He boasted that the police would never catch him.* *Presumió que la policía nunca lo atraparía.* ❑ *Carol boasted about her costume.* *Carol presumía sobre su vestido.* ● **Boast** is also a noun. *presunción* ❑ *It is the charity's proud boast that it has never turned anyone away.* *Esta asociación caritativa alardea de que nunca ha rechazado a nadie.*

**boat** /boʊt/ (**boats**) **1** N-COUNT A **boat** is something in which people can travel across water. *bote* ❑ *One of the best ways to see the area is in a small boat.* *Una de las mejores maneras de conocer el área es en un pequeño bote.* **2** N-COUNT You can refer to a passenger ship as a **boat.** *barco* ❑ *When the boat reached Cape Town, we said goodbye.* *Cuando el barco llegó a Cape Town, nos dijimos adiós.*
→ see Word Web: **boat**
→ see **ship**

**bob** /bɒb/ (**bobs, bobbing, bobbed**) V-I If something **bobs,** it moves up and down, like something does when it is floating on water. *menearse* ❑ *Huge balloons bobbed about in the sky above.* *Enormes globos se meneaban arriba en el cielo.*

**bob|ble** /bɒbᵊl/ (**bobbles, bobbling, bobbled**) V-T If a player **bobbles** a ball, they drop it or fail to control it. *perder el control de* ❑ *The ball was bobbled momentarily, allowing Holloway to race home.* *Se perdió momentáneamente el control de la bola, permitiendo que Holloway corriera hasta home.*

**bob|by pin** /bɒbi pɪn/ (**bobby pins**) N-COUNT A **bobby pin** is a small piece of metal or plastic bent back on itself, which a woman uses to hold her hair in position. *pasador*

**bob|sled** /bɒbslɛd/ (**bobsleds**) N-COUNT A **bobsled** is a vehicle with long thin strips of metal fixed to the bottom, which is used for racing downhill on ice. *trineo*

**bo|da|cious** /boʊdeɪʃəs/ **1** ADJ If you say that someone or something is **bodacious,** you mean that they are very good or impressive. *increíble* [INFORMAL] ❑ *This is a bodacious opportunity for him.* *Es una oportunidad increíble para él.* **2** ADJ If you say that someone is **bodacious,** you mean that they are appealing or sexually attractive. *increíble* [INFORMAL] ❑ *...such bodacious models as Elle Macpherson and Rachel Williams.* *...modelos tan increíbles como Elle Macpherson y Rachel Williams.* ❑ *...a bodacious physique.* *...un físico increíble.*

**body** /bɒdi/ (**bodies**) **1** N-COUNT Your **body** is all your physical parts, including your head, arms, and legs. *cuerpo* ❑ *The largest organ in the body is the liver.* *El órgano más grande del cuerpo es el hígado.* **2** N-COUNT You can refer to the main part of your body, except for your arms, head, and legs, as your **body.** *tronco* ❑ *Lying flat on your back, twist your body onto one side.* *Acostado sobre su espalda, voltee su*

*tronco hacia un lado.* **3** N-COUNT You can refer to a person's dead body as a **body.** *cuerpo* ❑ *Two days later, her body was found in a wood.* *Dos días después, su cuerpo fue encontrado en el bosque.* **4** N-COUNT A **body** is an organized group of people who deal with something officially. *cuerpo* ❑ *She was elected student body president at the University of North Carolina.* *Fue elegida presidente del cuerpo estudiantil de la Universidad de Carolina del Norte.* **5** N-COUNT The **body** of a car or airplane is the main part of it, not including its engine, wheels, or wings. *fuselaje, carrocería* ❑ *The only shade was under the body of the plane.* *La única sombra se encontraba bajo el fuselaje del avión.*
→ see Picture Dictionary: **body**

**body|guard** /bɒdigɑrd/ (**bodyguards**) N-COUNT A **bodyguard** is a person or a group of people employed to protect someone. *guardaespaldas* ❑ *Three of his bodyguards were injured in the attack.* *Tres de sus guardaespaldas fueron heridos en el ataque.*

**body image** (**body images**) N-VAR A person's **body image** is their perception of their physical appearance. Someone with a good body image thinks they are attractive, while someone with a poor body image thinks they are unattractive. *imagen corporal*

**body mass in|dex** N-SING A person's **body mass index** is a measurement that represents the relationship between their weight and their height. *índice de masa corporal* [MEDICAL] ❑ *...those with a body mass index of 30 and over.* *...aquellos con un índice de masa corporal superior o igual a 30.*

**body odor** N-UNCOUNT **Body odor** is an unpleasant smell caused by sweat on a person's body. *olor corporal*

**body position** (**body positions**) N-VAR An actor's **body position** is their posture at a particular point in a play or other theatrical production, for example whether they are sitting or standing. *posición corporal* [TECHNICAL]

**bog** /bɒg/ (**bogs**) N-COUNT A **bog** is an area of land that is very wet and muddy. *ciénaga, pantano*
→ see **wetlands**

**boil** /bɔɪl/ (**boils, boiling, boiled**) **1** V-T/V-I When a hot liquid **boils** or when you **boil** it, bubbles appear in it and it starts to change into steam or vapor. *hervir* ❑ *I stood in the kitchen, waiting for the water to boil.* *Estaba parada en la cocina, esperando a que hirviera el agua.* ❑ *Boil the water in the saucepan and add the salt.* *Hierva el agua en la olla y añada la sal.* **2** V-T/V-I When you **boil** a pot or a kettle, or put it on to **boil,** you heat the water inside it until it boils. *poner a hervir* ❑ *He had nothing to do but boil the kettle and make the tea.* *No tenía nada que hacer más que poner la tetera a hervir y hacer el té.* **3** V-T/V-I When you **boil** food, or when it **boils,** it is cooked in boiling water. *cocer* ❑ *Boil the chickpeas, then add garlic and lemon juice.* *Cueza los garbanzos, luego añada ajo y jugo de limón.* ❑ *I peeled potatoes and put them in a pot to boil.* *Pelé las papas y las puse a cocer en una olla.* **4** N-COUNT A **boil** is a red, painful swelling on your skin. *forúnculo* **5** → see also **boiling** **6** PHRASE When you **bring** a liquid **to a boil,** you heat it until it boils. When it **comes to a boil,** it begins to boil. *romper el hervor* ❑ *Put the milk into a saucepan and bring it slowly to a boil.* *Coloque el agua en una olla y póngala a fuego lento a que rompa el hervor.*
→ see **cook, egg, thermometer**

▸ **boil down to** PHR-VERB If you say that a situation or problem **boils down to** a particular thing or can **be boiled down to** a particular thing, you mean that this is the most important or the most basic aspect of it. *se reduce a* ❑ *What they want boils down to just one thing: land.* *Lo que quieren se reduce a una sola cosa: tierra.*

▸ **boil over** PHR-VERB When a liquid that is being heated **boils over,** it rises and flows over the edge of the container. *derramarse* ❑ *Heat the liquid in a large, wide container so it doesn't boil over.* *Caliente el líquido en un recipiente grande y ancho para que no se derrame.*

**boil|ing** /bɔɪlɪŋ/ ADJ Something that is **boiling** or **boiling hot** is very hot. *hirviendo* ❑ *"It's boiling in here," complained Miriam.* *—Está hirviendo aquí —se quejó Miriam.*

**boil|ing point** N-UNCOUNT The **boiling point** of a liquid is the temperature at which it starts to change into steam or vapor. For example, the

**Picture Dictionary** **body**

boiling point of water is 212° Fahrenheit. *punto de ebullición*

**bold** /boʊld/ (**bolder, boldest**) **1** ADJ Someone who is **bold** is not afraid to do things that involve risk or danger. *audaz* ❑ *Amrita becomes a bold, daring rebel. Amrita se vuelve una rebelde audaz y atrevida.* ❑ *In 1960 this was a bold move. En 1960 esto era una decisión audaz.* ● **bold|ly** ADV *con audacia* ❑ *You must act boldly and confidently. Debes actuar con confianza y audacia.* ● **bold|ness** N-UNCOUNT *audacia* ❑ *...the boldness of his economic program. ...la audacia de su programa económico.* **2** ADJ A **bold** color or pattern is very bright and noticeable. *llamativo* ❑ *...bold flowers in shades of red, blue or white. ...llamativas flores en tonos rojos, azules o blancos.* **3** ADJ **Bold** lines or designs are drawn in a clear, strong way. *vigoroso* ❑ *Each picture is shown in color on one page and as a bold outline on the opposite page. Cada pintura se muestra a color en una página y como trazo vigoroso en la página opuesta.*

**bo|lo|gna** /bəloʊni/ (**bolognas**) N-VAR **Bologna** is a type of large smoked sausage, usually made of beef, veal, or pork. *tipo de salchicha ahumada* ❑ *...a bologna sandwich. ...un sandwich de salchicha ahumada.*

**bol|ster** /boʊlstər/ (**bolsters, bolstering, bolstered**) V-T If you **bolster** someone's confidence or courage, you increase it. *reafirmar* ❑ *The president is attempting to bolster confidence in the economy. El presidente intenta reafirmar la confianza en la economía.*

**bolt** /boʊlt/ (**bolts, bolting, bolted**) **1** N-COUNT A **bolt** is a long metal object that screws into a nut and is used to fasten things together. *tornillo* **2** V-T When you **bolt** one thing to another, you fasten them firmly together, using a bolt. *atornillar* ❑ *Perkins bolted the new parts to the old engine. Perkins atornilló las partes nuevas al viejo motor.* ❑ *Bolt the parts together. Atornille las piezas.* **3** N-COUNT A **bolt** on a door or window is a metal bar that you can slide across in order to fasten the door or window. *cerrojo* ❑ *I heard the sound of a bolt being slowly slid open. Escuché el sonido de un cerrojo que se abría lentamente.* **4** V-T When you **bolt** a door or window, you slide the bolt across to fasten it. *echar el cerrojo* ❑ *He locked and bolted the kitchen door after her. Cerró la puerta de la cocina con llave y pasó el cerrojo después que ella entró.* **5** V-I If a person or animal **bolts,** they suddenly start to run very fast, often because something has frightened them. *salir disparado* ❑ *The pig rose squealing, and bolted. El cerdo se levantó gruñendo y salió disparado.*

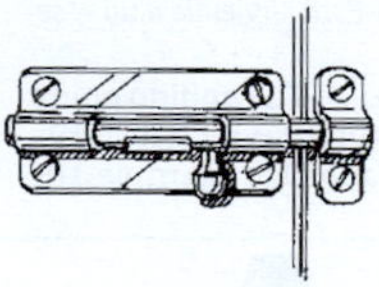

bolt

**bomb** /bɒm/ (**bombs, bombing, bombed**) **1** N-COUNT A **bomb** is a device that explodes and damages or destroys a large area. *bomba* ❑ *Bombs went off at two London train stations. Unas bombas explotaron en dos estaciones de trenes en Londres.* ❑ *It's not known who planted the bomb. No se sabe quién puso la bomba.* **2** V-T When people **bomb** a place, they attack it with bombs. *bombardear* ❑ *Air force jets bombed the airport. Los aviones de la fuerza aérea bombardearon el aeropuerto.* ● **bomb|ing** N-VAR (**bombings**) *bombardeo* ❑ *...the bombing of Pearl Harbor. ...el bombardeo de Pearl Harbor.*

| **Word Partnership** | Usar *bomb* con: |
|---|---|
| ADJ. | **atomic/nuclear** bomb, **live** bomb **1** |
| N. | bomb **blast**, **car** bomb, **pipe** bomb, bomb **shelter**, bomb **squad**, bomb **threat** **1** |
| V. | **drop/plant a** bomb, **set off a** bomb **1** |

**bomb|er** /bɒmər/ (**bombers**) **1** N-COUNT **Bombers** are people who cause bombs to explode in public places. *terrorista* ❑ *Detectives hunting the bombers will be eager to interview him. Los detectives que están en busca de los terroristas estarán ansiosos de entrevistarlo.* **2** N-COUNT A **bomber** is a military aircraft which drops bombs. *bombardero* ❑ *...a high-speed bomber with twin engines. ...un bombardero bimotor de alta velocidad.*

**bond** /bɒnd/ (**bonds, bonding, bonded**) **1** N-COUNT A **bond between** people is a strong feeling of friendship, love, or shared beliefs and experiences that unites them. *vínculo* ❑ *The experience created a very special bond between us. La experiencia creó un vínculo muy especial entre nosotros.* **2** V-RECIP When people **bond with** each other, they form a relationship based on love or shared beliefs and experiences. *establecer lazos de unión* ❑ *Belinda was having difficulty bonding with the baby. Belinda tenía dificultades para establecer lazos de unión con el bebé.* ❑ *They all bonded while writing the book together. Todos establecieron lazos de unión entre sí mientras escribían el libro.* **3** N-COUNT A **bond between** people or groups is a close connection that they have with each other. *lazo de unión* ❑ *...the strong bond between church and nation. ...el fuerte lazo de unión entre la Iglesia y la nación.* **4** V-RECIP When one thing **bonds with** another, it sticks to it or becomes joined to it in some way. *adherirse* ❑ *Strips of wood are bonded together and shaped by machine. Las tiras de madera se adhieren y se les da forma a máquina.* **5** N-COUNT When a government or company issues a **bond,** it borrows money from investors. The certificate that is issued to investors who lend money is also called a **bond.** *bono* [BUSINESS] ❑ *Most of it will be financed by government bonds. La mayor parte será financiada por bonos del gobierno.*
→ see **love**

**bone** /boʊn/ (**bones, boning, boned**) **1** N-VAR Your **bones** are the hard parts inside your body that together form your skeleton. *hueso* ❑ *Many passengers suffered broken bones. Muchos pasajeros sufrieron fracturas.* ❑ *The body is made up primarily of bone, muscle, and fat. El cuerpo está formado principalmente de huesos, músculos y grasa.* **2** V-T If you **bone** a piece of meat or fish, you remove the bones from it before cooking it. *deshuesar* ❑ *Make sure that you do not pierce the skin when boning the chicken thighs. Asegúrate de no perforar la piel cuando deshueses los muslos del pollo.*

**bon|net** /bɒnɪt/ (**bonnets**) N-COUNT A **bonnet** is a hat with ribbons that are tied under the chin. *gorro, sombrero*
→ see **hats**

**bo|nus** /boʊnəs/ (**bonuses**) **1** N-COUNT A **bonus** is an extra amount of money that is added to your pay, usually because you have worked very hard. *prima, bonificación* ❑ *Workers in big firms receive a part* *of their pay in the form of bonuses.* Los trabajadores de las grandes empresas reciben parte de su salario en forma de primas. ❑ *...a $60 bonus.* ...una prima de 60 dólares estadunidenses. **2** N-COUNT A **bonus** is something good that you get in addition to something else, and which you would not usually expect. ganancia ❑ *We might finish third. Any better would be a bonus.* Podríamos terminar en tercer lugar; el segundo o el primero serían ganancia.

**boo-boo** (**boo-boos**) **1** N-COUNT A **boo-boo** is a silly mistake or blunder. metida de pata [INFORMAL] ❑ *O.K. I made a boo-boo. I apologize.* Está bien, metí la pata. Discúlpame. **2** N-COUNT **Boo-boo** is a child's word for a cut or other minor injury. machucón [INFORMAL]

**book** /bʊk/ (**books, booking, booked**) **1** N-COUNT A **book** is a number of pieces of paper, usually with words printed on them, which are fastened together and fixed inside a cover of strong paper or cardboard. libro ❑ *His eighth book was an instant best-seller.* Su octavo libro fue un gran éxito de ventas inmediato. ❑ *...the author of a book on politics.* ...el autor de un libro sobre política. ❑ *...a new book by Rosella Brown.* ...un nuevo libro por Rosella Brown. **2** N-COUNT A **book of** something such as stamps, matches, or tickets is a small number of them fastened together between thin cardboard covers. libreta, talonario ❑ *Can I have a book of stamps please?* ¿Me puede dar una libreta de timbres (sellos), por favor? **3** V-T When you **book** something such as a hotel room or a ticket, you arrange to have it or use it at a particular time. reservar ❑ *The club has booked hotel rooms for the women and children.* El club reservó cuartos de hotel para las mujeres y los niños. ❑ *Laurie booked herself a flight home.* Laurie reservó un vuelo para su regreso a casa. **4** N-PLURAL A company's or organization's **books** are its records of money that has been spent and earned or of the names of people who belong to it. libro (de contabilidad) [BUSINESS] ❑ *He left the books to his managers and accountants.* Dejó los libros (de contabilidad) a sus gerentes y contadores. **5** PHRASE If transportation or a hotel, restaurant, or theater is **booked up, fully booked,** or **booked solid,** it has no tickets, rooms, or tables left for a particular time or date. agotado, completo ❑ *The ferries are often fully booked by February.* Las reservaciones para los transbordadores se agotan a menudo hacia febrero.
→ see **concert, library**

**Word Partnership** Usar *book* con:

| | |
|---|---|
| N. | **address** book, book **award**, **children's** book, book **club**, **comic** book, **copy of a** book, book **cover**, **library** book, **phone** book, book **review**, **subject of a** book, **title of a** book **1** |
| ADJ. | **latest/new/recent** book **1** |
| V. | **publish a** book, **read a** book, **write a** book **1** |

**book|case** /bʊkkeɪs/ (**bookcases**) N-COUNT A **bookcase** is a piece of furniture with shelves that you keep books on. librero, estante

**book group** (**book groups**) N-COUNT A **book group** is a group of people who meet regularly to discuss books that they have read. grupo de reseña literaria

**Word Link** *let* ≈ *little* : *booklet, caplet, pamphlet*

**book|let** /bʊklɪt/ (**booklets**) N-COUNT A **booklet** is a very thin book that has a paper cover and that gives you information about something. folleto ❑ *...a 48-page booklet of notes.* ...un cuaderno de notas de 48 páginas., ...un folleto ilustrativo de 48 páginas.

**Word Link** *mark* ≈ *boundary, sign* : *bookmark, earmark, landmark*

**book|mark** /bʊkmɑrk/ (**bookmarks, bookmarking, bookmarked**) **1** N-COUNT A **bookmark** is a narrow piece of card or leather that you put between the pages of a book so that you can find a particular page easily. marcador, señalador **2** N-COUNT In computing, a **bookmark** is the address of an Internet site that you put into a list on your computer so that you can return to it easily. marcador, favorito [COMPUTING] ❑ *It is simple to save what you find with an electronic bookmark; that way you can return to it later.* Es fácil guardar los sitios que encuentras con un marcador electrónico; de esa manera, puedes volver a ellos más tarde. ● **Bookmark** is also a verb. marcar [COMPUTING] ❑ *You should bookmark this website and use it in the future.* Deberías marcar este sitio y usarlo en el futuro.

**book|store** /bʊkstɔr/ (**bookstores**) N-COUNT A **bookstore** is a store where books are sold. librería

**boom** /bum/ (**booms, booming, boomed**) **1** N-COUNT If there is a **boom** in the economy, there is an increase in economic activity, for example, in the number of things that are being bought and sold. auge ❑ *An economic boom followed, especially in housing and construction.* El resultado fue (después hubo) un auge económico, especialmente en la vivienda y la construcción. ❑ *The 1980s were indeed boom years.* Los años 1980 fueron una época de auge. **2** V-T/V-I When something such as your voice, a cannon, or a big drum **booms,** it makes a loud, deep sound that lasts for several seconds. retumbar ❑ *"Ladies," boomed Helena, without a microphone, "We all know why we're here tonight."* —Señoras —dijo Helena con voz retumbante, sin micrófono—, todas sabemos por qué estamos aquí hoy. ❑ *Thunder boomed over Crooked Mountain.* Los truenos retumbaban sobre Crooked Mountain. ● **Boom out** means the same as **boom.** retumbar ❑ *Music boomed out from loudspeakers.* La música retumbaba por los altavoces., La música salía retumbando de los altavoces. ❑ *A megaphone boomed out, "This is the police."* La voz retumbó en el megáfono: "Es la policía". ● **Boom** is also a noun. trueno ❑ *...the boom of a cannon.* ...el trueno de un cañón.
→ see **sound**

**Thesaurus** *boom* Ver también:

| | |
|---|---|
| N. | explosion, roar **2** |

**boom box** (**boom boxes**) N-COUNT A **boom box** is a large portable machine for playing music, especially one that is played loudly in public by young people. grabadora portátil, reproductor portátil [INFORMAL]

**boost** /bust/ (**boosts, boosting, boosted**) **1** V-T If one thing **boosts** another, it causes it to increase, improve, or be more successful. estimular ❑ *Lower interest rates can boost the economy by reducing*

B

*borrowing costs for consumers and businesses.* *Las tasas de interés bajas pueden estimular la economía al reducir los costos del crédito para los consumidores y las empresas.* • **Boost** is also a noun. *estímulo* ❑ *It would get the economy going and give us the boost that we need.* *Echaría a andar la economía y nos daría el estímulo que necesitamos.* **2** V-T If something **boosts** your confidence or morale, it improves it. *elevar* ❑ *We need a big win to boost our confidence.* *Necesitamos un gran triunfo para elevar nuestra confianza.* • **Boost** is also a noun. *estímulo* ❑ *Scoring that goal gave me a real boost.* *Haber anotado ese tanto fue un gran estímulo para mí.*

**boot** /bu̲t/ (**boots, booting, booted**) **1** N-COUNT **Boots** are shoes that cover your whole foot and the lower part of your leg. *bota* ❑ *He reached down and pulled off his boots.* *Se agachó y se quitó las botas.* **2** N-COUNT **Boots** are strong, heavy shoes that cover your ankle and that have thick soles. *botín* ❑ *...the regular beat of the soldiers' boots.* *...el taconeo regular de los botines de los soldados.* **3** V-T To **boot** an illegally parked car means to fit a device to one of its wheels so that it cannot be driven away. *inmovilizar* ❑ *The city will no longer boot cars.* *El ayuntamiento dejará de inmovilizar vehículos.* **4** V-T/V-I If a computer **boots** or you **boot** it, it is made ready to use by putting in the instructions it needs in order to start working. *arrancar, encender* [COMPUTING] ❑ *The computer won't boot.* *La computadora no arranca.* ❑ *Put the CD into the drive and boot the machine.* *Ponga el disco compacto (el CD) en el lector y arranque la computadora.* • **Boot up** means the same as **boot.** *encender* ❑ *Go over to your PC and boot it up.* *Ve a tu computadora y enciéndela.* **5** PHRASE If you **get the boot** or **are given the boot,** you are told that you are not wanted anymore, either in your job or by someone you are having a relationship with. *poner de patitas en la calle* [INFORMAL] ❑ *She didn't enjoy her job, and after a year she got the boot.* *No disfrutaba haciendo su trabajo y después de un año la pusieron de patitas en la calle.*
→ see **clothing, shoe**

**boot camp** (**boot camps**) N-VAR In the United States, a **boot camp** is a camp where people who have just joined the army, navy, or marines are trained. *campamento de entrenamiento de reclutas de la infantería de marina, la marina de guerra y el ejército estadounidenses.*

**booth** /bu̲θ/ (**booths**) **1** N-COUNT A **booth** is a small area separated from a larger public area by screens or thin walls where, for example, people can make a telephone call or vote in private. *cabina* ❑ *...a public phone booth.* *...una cabina de teléfono público.* **2** N-COUNT A **booth** in a restaurant or café consists of a table with long fixed seats on two or sometimes three sides of it. *reservado* ❑ *They sat in a corner booth, away from other diners.* *Se sentaron en el reservado de un rincón, lejos de los otros comensales.* **3** N-COUNT A **booth** is a stall at an exhibition, for example with a display of goods for sale or with information leaflets. *puesto*

**booze** /bu̲z/ (**boozes, boozing, boozed**) **1** N-UNCOUNT **Booze** is alcoholic drink. *bebida, trago* [INFORMAL] **2** V-I If people **booze,** they drink alcohol. *beber, empinar el codo* [INFORMAL]

**bor|der** /bɔ̲rdər/ (**borders, bordering, bordered**) **1** N-COUNT The **border** between two countries or regions is the dividing line between them. Sometimes **the border** also refers to the land close to this line. *frontera* ❑ *They fled across the border.* *Huyeron al otro lado de la frontera.* ❑ *Soldiers closed the border between the two countries.* *Los soldados cerraron la frontera entre los dos países.* **2** V-T A country that **borders** another country, a sea, or a river is next to it. *limitar con, lindar con, bordear* ❑ *...the countries bordering the Mediterranean Sea.* *...los países que lindan con el Mediterráneo.*, *...los países que bordean el Mediterráneo.* **3** N-COUNT A **border** is a strip or band around the edge of something. *borde, cenefa* ❑ *...pillowcases trimmed with a lace border.* *...almohadas adornadas con una cenefa de encaje.*

border

| Thesaurus | *border* | Ver también: |
|---|---|---|
| N. | boundary, end, extremity, perimeter; (*ant.*) center, inside, middle **1** | |

**bore** /bɔ̲r/ (**bores, boring, bored**) **1** V-T If someone or something **bores** you, you find them dull and uninteresting. *aburrir* ❑ *Dickie bored him with stories of the navy.* *Dickie lo aburría con sus historias de la marina.* **2** N-COUNT You describe someone as a **bore** when you think that they talk in a very uninteresting way. *aburrido o aburrida* ❑ *He's a bore and a fool.* *Es (un) aburrido y (un) tonto.* **3** N-SING You can describe a situation as **a bore** when you find it annoying. *lata* ❑ *It's a bore to be sick.* *Estar enfermo es una lata.* **4** V-T If you **bore** a hole in something, you make a deep round hole in it using a special tool. *perforar, taladrar, hacer un agujero* ❑ *Bore a hole through the window frame and pass the cable through it.* *Haga un agujero en el marco de la ventana y pase el cable por ahí.* **5** **Bore** is the past tense of **bear.** *pasado de **bear*** **6** → see also **bored, boring**

**bored** /bɔ̲rd/ ADJ If you are **bored,** you feel tired and impatient because you have lost interest in something or because you have nothing to do. *aburrido* ❑ *I am getting very bored with this.* *Esto me está aburriendo mucho.*

| Word Link | *dom ≈ state of being : boredom, freedom, wisdom* |
|---|---|

**bore|dom** /bɔ̲rdəm/ N-UNCOUNT **Boredom** is the state of being bored. *aburrimiento* ❑ *Students never complain of boredom when great teachers are teaching.* *Los estudiantes nunca se quejan de aburrimiento cuando les enseñan los grandes maestros.*

**bor|ing** /bɔ̲rɪŋ/ ADJ Someone or something **boring** is so dull and uninteresting that they make people tired and impatient. *aburrido* ❑ *...boring work.* *...un trabajo aburrido.*

| Thesaurus | *boring* | Ver también: |
|---|---|---|
| ADJ. | dull, tedious; (*ant.*) exciting, fun, interesting, lively | |

**born** /bɔ̲rn/ **1** V-T PASSIVE When a baby **is born,** it comes out of its mother's body. In formal

English, if you say that someone **is born of** someone or **to** someone, you mean that person is their parent. *nacer* ❑ *She was born in Milan on April 29, 1923. Nació en Milán el 29 de abril de 1923.* ❑ *He was born of German parents and lived most of his life abroad. Nació de padres alemanes y vivió la mayor parte de su vida en el extranjero.* **2** ADJ You use **born** to describe someone who has a natural ability to do a particular activity or job. *nato, innato* ❑ *Jack was a born teacher. Jack era un maestro nato/innato.*

**bor|ough** /bɜroʊ/ (**boroughs**) N-COUNT A **borough** is a town, or a district within a large city, which has its own council, government, or local services. *municipio, distrito* ❑ *...the New York City borough of Brooklyn. ...el distrito de Brooklyn de la ciudad de Nueva York.*

**bor|row** /bɒroʊ/ (**borrows, borrowing, borrowed**) V-T If you **borrow** something that belongs to someone else, you take it or use it for a period of time, usually with their permission. *tomar prestado, pedir prestado* ❑ *Can I borrow a pen please? ¿Puede prestarme una pluma, por favor?, ¿Puedo tomar prestada una pluma?* ● **bor|row|ing** N-UNCOUNT *endeudamiento* ❑ *We have allowed spending and borrowing to rise. Permitimos que aumentaran el gasto y el endeudamiento.*
→ see **library**

> **Usage** **borrow** and **lend**
> *Borrow* means "to take something while intending to give it back later": *Jiao borrowed Terry's cell phone and then lost it! Lend* means "to give something to someone while expecting to get it back later": *Terry will never lend anything to Jiao again!*

**bor|row|er** /bɒroʊər/ (**borrowers**) N-COUNT A **borrower** is a person or organization that borrows money. *prestatario o prestataria* ❑ *Borrowers of more than $100,000 pay less interest. Los prestatarios de más de 100,000 dólares estadunidenses pagan menos intereses.*

**boss** /bɔs/ (**bosses, bossing, bossed**) **1** N-COUNT Your **boss** is the person in charge of the organization or department where you work. *jefe* ❑ *He hates his boss. Odia a su jefe.* **2** V-T If someone **bosses** you, they keep telling you what to do in a way that is irritating. *mandonear, ordenar* ❑ *We cannot boss them into doing more. No podemos ordenarles que hagan más.* ● **Boss around** means the same as **boss**. *mandonear* ❑ *He started bossing people around. Empezó a mandonear a todos.*

> **Thesaurus** *boss* Ver también:
> N. chief, director, employer, foreman, manager; (*ant.*) owner, superintendent, supervisor **1**

**bota|ny** /bɒtəni/ N-UNCOUNT **Botany** is the scientific study of plants. *botánica* ● **bo|tani|cal** /bətænɪkəl/ ADJ *botánico* ❑ *The area is of great botanical interest. La región (zona) reviste un gran interés botánico.* ● **bota|nist** N-COUNT (**botanists**) *botánico o botánica*

**both** /boʊθ/ **1** DET You use **both** when you are referring to two people or things and saying that something is true about each of them. *ambos, dos* ❑ *She threw both arms up to protect her face. Se protegió el rostro con ambos brazos., Se protegió la cara con los dos brazos.* ● **Both** is also a quantifier. *ambos, dos* ❑ *Both of these women have strong memories of the Vietnam War. Ambas mujeres tienen recuerdos muy intensos de la guerra de Vietnam.* ● **Both** is also a pronoun. *tanto... como, ambos* ❑ *Miss Brown and her friend are both from Brooklyn. Tanto la señorita Brown como su amiga son de Brooklyn.* ❑ *They both worked at the University of Havana. Ambas trabajaban en la Universidad de La Habana.* ● PREDET **Both** is also a predeterminer. *ambos* ❑ *Both the horses were out, ready for the ride. Ambos caballos estaban afuera, listos para el paseo.* **2** CONJ You use the structure **both... and** when you are giving two facts or alternatives and emphasizing that each of them is true or possible. *tanto...como* ❑ *Now women work both before and after having their children. Ahora las mujeres trabajan tanto antes como después de haber tenido a sus hijos.*

> **Usage** **both ... and**
> In sentences with *both... and* use a plural verb: *Both the president and the vice president are Texans.*

**both|er** /bɒðər/ (**bothers, bothering, bothered**) **1** V-T/V-I If you do not **bother to** do something or if you do not **bother with** it, you do not do it, consider it, or use it because you think it is unnecessary or because you are too lazy. *preocuparse, molestarse* ❑ *Lots of people don't bother to get married these days. Hoy en día, muchas personas no se preocupan por casarse.* ❑ *Nothing I do makes any difference anyway, so why bother? Nada de lo que haga cambia nada, así que, ¿para qué molestarme?* **2** N-UNCOUNT; N-SING **Bother** means trouble or difficulty. *molestia* ❑ *I usually buy sliced bread—it's less bother. Acostumbro comprar el pan rebanado; es menos molestia.* **3** V-T If something **bothers** you, it worries, annoys, or upsets you. *preocupar, molestar* ❑ *Is something bothering you? ¿Te preocupa algo?, ¿Te molesta algo?* ❑ *It bothered me that boys weren't interested in me. Me preocupaba que los muchachos no se interesaran en mí.* ● **both|ered** ADJ *preocupado* ❑ *I was bothered about the blister on my hand. Estaba preocupado por la ampolla que tenía en la mano.* **4** V-T If someone **bothers** you, they talk to you when you want to be left alone or they interrupt you when you are busy. *molestar* ❑ *...a man who keeps bothering me. ...un hombre que insiste en molestarme.* **5** PHRASE If you say that you **can't be bothered to** do something, you mean that you are not going to do it because you think it is unnecessary or because you are too lazy. *dar pereza, dar flojera, no tener ganas* ❑ *I can't be bothered to clean the house. No tengo ganas de limpiar la casa., Me da flojera limpiar la casa.*

**bot|tle** /bɒtəl/ (**bottles, bottling, bottled**) **1** N-COUNT A **bottle** is a glass or plastic container in which drinks and other liquids are kept. *botella* ❑ *There were two empty water bottles on the table. Había dos botellas de agua vacías sobre la mesa.* ❑ *She drank half a bottle of lemonade. Bebió media botella de limonada.* **2** V-T To **bottle** a drink or other liquid means to put it into bottles after it has been made. *embotellar* ❑ *...equipment to automatically bottle the soda. ...maquinaria automática para embotellar el refresco (la soda).*
→ see **container, glass**

B

**bot|tom** /bɒtəm/ (**bottoms**) 1 N-COUNT **The bottom of** something is the lowest or deepest part of it. *pie, fondo* ❑ *He sat at the bottom of the stairs. Se sentó al pie de las escaleras.* ❑ *Answers can be found at the bottom of page 8. Las respuestas se encuentran al pie de la página 8.* ❑ *...the bottom of their shoes. ...el fondo de sus zapatos.* 2 ADJ The **bottom** thing or layer in a series of things or layers is the lowest one. *inferior* ❑ *...the bottom drawer of the desk. ...el cajón inferior del escritorio.* 3 N-SING If someone is at **the bottom** in a survey, test, or league, their performance is worse than that of all the other people involved. *final, último* ❑ *He was always at the bottom of the class in school. Siempre era el último de su clase en la escuela.* 4 PHRASE If you want to **get to the bottom of** a problem, you want to solve it by finding out its real cause. *ir al fondo de* ❑ *I have to get to the bottom of this. Tengo que ir al fondo de esto.*

**Thesaurus** *bottom* Ver también:

N. base, floor, foundation, ground; (*ant.*) peak, top 1

**Word Partnership** Usar *bottom* con:

N. bottom **of a hill**, bottom **of the page/screen** 1
bottom **drawer**, bottom **of the pool**, bottom **of the sea**, **river** bottom 1 2
bottom **lip**, bottom **rung** 2
PREP. **along the** bottom, **on the** bottom 1 2
**at/near the** bottom 1–3
V. **reach the** bottom, **sink to the** bottom 1 3

**bought** /bɔt/ **Bought** is the past tense and past participle of **buy**. *pasado y participio pasado de buy*

**bouil|lon cube** (**bouillon cubes**) N-COUNT A **bouillon cube** is a solid cube made from dried meat or vegetable juices and other flavorings. *cubito para caldo*

**boul|der** /boʊldər/ (**boulders**) N-COUNT A **boulder** is a large rounded rock. *roca* ❑ *It is thought that the train hit a boulder. Se cree que el tren golpeó una roca.*

**bounce** /baʊns/ (**bounces, bouncing, bounced**) 1 V-T/V-I When an object such as a ball **bounces** or when you **bounce** it, it moves upward from a surface or away from it immediately after hitting it. *botar, rebotar* ❑ *My father came into the kitchen bouncing a tennis ball. Mi padre entró a la cocina botando una pelota de tenis.* ❑ *...a falling pebble, bouncing down the cliff. ...una piedra que caía, rebotando peñasco (risco) abajo.* ● **Bounce** is also a noun. *bote* ❑ *...two bounces of the ball.. . dos botes de la pelota.* 2 V-T/V-I If something **bounces** or if something **bounces** it, it swings or moves up and down. *balancear* ❑ *Her long black hair bounced as she walked. Su largo pelo negro se balanceaba al caminar.* ❑ *The car was bouncing up and down as if someone were jumping on it. El carro se balanceaba arriba y abajo como si alguien estuviera saltando sobre él.* 3 V-I If you **bounce** on a soft surface, you jump up and down on it repeatedly. *brincar* ❑ *She lets us do anything, even bounce on our beds. Nos deja hacer todo, hasta brincar en nuestra cama.* 4 V-T/V-I If a check **bounces** or if someone **bounces** it, the bank refuses to accept it and pay out the money, because the person who wrote it does not have enough money in their account. *rebotar* ❑ *Our only complaint would be if the check bounced. Nuestra única queja sería que el cheque rebotara.* 5 V-I If an e-mail or other electronic message **bounces,** it is returned to the person who sent it because the address was wrong or because of a problem with one of the computers involved in sending it. *devolver* [COMPUTING] ❑ *...a message saying that your mail has bounced or was unable to be delivered. ...un mensaje que decía que tu correo ha sido devuelto o que no fue posible entregarlo.*

**bound**
❶ BE BOUND
❷ OTHER USES

❶ **bound** /baʊnd/ 1 **Bound** is the past tense and past participle of **bind**. *pasado y participio pasado de bind* 2 PHRASE If something **is bound to** happen or be true, it is certain to happen or be true. *algo que tiene que suceder o está destinado a algo* ❑ *There are bound to be price increases next year. Es seguro que habrá aumentos de precios el próximo año.* ❑ *I'll show it to Benjamin. He's bound to know. Se lo mostraré a Benjamin. Seguro sabe.* 3 ADJ If a vehicle or person is **bound for** a particular place, they are traveling toward it. *con rumbo a, con destino a* ❑ *The ship was bound for Italy. El barco iba con destino a Italia.*

**Word Partnership** Usar *bound* con:

N. bound **by duty** ❶ 1
ADV. **legally** bound, **tightly** bound ❶ 1
V. bound **and gagged** ❶ 1
bound **to fail** ❶ 2
N. **feet/hands/wrists** bound, **leather** bound **spiral** bound, bound **with tape** ❶ 1
**a flight/plane/ship/train** bound **for** ❶ 3

❷ **bound** /baʊnd/ (**bounds, bounding, bounded**) 1 N-PLURAL **Bounds** are limits which normally restrict what can happen or what people can do. *límite* ❑ *You can use the time, within certain bounds, as you wish. Puedes emplear el tiempo como desees, dentro de ciertos límites.* ❑ *...beyond the bounds of polite conversation. ...excedía los límites de una conversación cortés.* 2 V-I If a person or animal **bounds** in a particular direction, they move quickly with large steps or jumps. *saltar* ❑ *He bounded up the steps. Subió la escalera a saltos.* 3 PHRASE If a place is **out of bounds,** people are not allowed to go there. *restringido* ❑ *For the last few days the area has been out of bounds to foreign journalists. Durante los últimos días, el lugar ha estado restringido a los periodistas extranjeros.*

**bounda|ry** /baʊndəri, -dri/ (**boundaries**) 1 N-COUNT The **boundary of** an area of land is an imaginary line that separates it from other areas. *límite, lindero, linde* ❑ *The river forms the western boundary of the wood. El río es el límite occidental del bosque.* 2 N-COUNT In linguistics, a **boundary** is a division between one word and another or between the different parts of a word. *frontera* [TECHNICAL]

**Word Partnership** Usar *boundary* con:

PREP. boundary **around places/things,** boundary **between places/things,** **beyond a** boundary, boundary **of** ***someplace/something*** 1
V. **cross a** boundary, **mark/set a** boundary 1
N. boundary **dispute,** boundary **line** 1

**bou|quet** /boʊkeɪ, bu-/ (**bouquets**) N-COUNT A **bouquet** is a bunch of flowers which is attractively arranged. ramo, ramillete ❑ *The woman carried a bouquet of dried roses.* *La mujer llevaba un ramo de rosas secas.*

**bout** /baʊt/ (**bouts**) 1 N-COUNT If you have a **bout of** an illness, you have it for a short period. ataque ❑ *He was recovering from a severe bout of flu.* *Se estaba recuperando de un fuerte ataque de gripa.* 2 N-COUNT A **bout of** something that is unpleasant is a short time during which it occurs a great deal. racha ❑ *...the latest bout of violence.* *...la última racha de violencia.*

**bow**
❶ BENDING OR SUBMITTING
❷ OBJECTS

❶ **bow** /baʊ/ (**bows, bowing, bowed**) 1 V-I When you **bow to** someone, you briefly bend your body toward them as a formal way of greeting them or showing respect. hacer una reverencia ❑ *They bowed low to the king and moved quickly out of his way.* *Hicieron una reverencia al rey y se apartaron rápidamente de su paso.* ● **Bow** is also a noun. reverencia ❑ *I gave a theatrical bow and waved.* *Hice una reverencia teatral y saludé con la mano.* 2 V-T If you **bow** your head, you bend it downward so that you are looking toward the ground. inclinar ❑ *The colonel bowed his head and whispered a prayer.* *El coronel inclinó la cabeza y murmuró una plegaria.* 3 V-I If you **bow to** pressure or to someone's wishes, you agree to do what they want you to do. ceder ❑ *Some stores are bowing to consumer pressure and offering organically grown vegetables.* *Algunas tiendas están cediendo a la presión de los consumidores y ofreciendo verduras cultivadas orgánicamente.*

▸ **bow out** PHR-VERB If you **bow out** of something, you stop taking part in it. retirar(se) [WRITTEN] ❑ *The executives were happy to let him bow out after 26 years in the job.* *Los ejecutivos estaban felices de permitirle retirarse después de 26 años en el trabajo.*

❷ **bow** /boʊ/ (**bows**) 1 N-COUNT A **bow** is a knot with two loops and two loose ends that is used in tying shoelaces and ribbons. moño, lazo ❑ *Add some ribbon tied in a bow.* *Añádale una cinta con un moño.* 2 N-COUNT A **bow** is a weapon for shooting arrows that consists of a long piece of curved wood with a string attached to both its ends. arco ❑ *Some of them were armed with bows and arrows.* *Algunos iban armados con arcos y flechas.* 3 N-COUNT The **bow** of a violin or other stringed instrument is a long thin piece of wood with fibers stretched along it that you move across the strings of the instrument in order to play it. arco

bow

**bowed**

Pronounced /boʊd/ for meaning 1, and /baʊd/ for meaning 2.

1 ADJ Something that is **bowed** is curved. arqueado ❑ *...an old lady with bowed legs.* *...una anciana con las piernas arqueadas.* 2 ADJ If a person's body is **bowed,** it is bent forward. encorvado ❑ *He walked along the street, head down and shoulders bowed.* *Caminó por la calle con la cabeza agachada y la espalda encorvada.*

**bow|el** /baʊəl/ (**bowels**) N-COUNT Your **bowels** are the tubes in your body through which digested food passes from your stomach to your anus. intestino ❑ *Eating fruit and vegetables can help to keep your bowels healthy.* *El consumo de frutas y verduras puede ayudarle a mantener saludable su intestino.*

**bowl** /boʊl/ (**bowls, bowling, bowled**) 1 N-COUNT A **bowl** is a round container with a wide uncovered top that is used for mixing and serving food. tazón ❑ *Put all the ingredients into a large bowl.* *Pon todos los ingredientes en un tazón grande.* ❑ *...a bowl of soup.* *...un tazón de sopa., ...una sopera.* 2 N-COUNT You can refer to the hollow rounded part of an object as its **bowl.** taza, inodoro ❑ *...toilet bowl cleaners.* *...limpiadores de inodoros.* 3 N-COUNT A **bowl** or **bowl game** is a competition in which the best college teams play, after the main season has ended. tazón ❑ *...the Fiesta college football bowl.* *...el tazón Fiesta del fútbol americano universitario.* 4 V-T/V-I In a sport such as bowling or lawn bowling, when a bowler **bowls,** or **bowls** a ball, he or she rolls it down a narrow track or field of grass. bolos, petanca (inglesa) ❑ *Neither finalist bowled a very strong game.* *Ninguno de los finalistas en los bolos (la petanca) logró un juego muy bueno.* 5 V-T/V-I In a sport such as cricket, when a bowler **bowls,** or **bowls** a ball, he or she throws it down the field toward a batsman. lanzar ❑ *Lee bowled a ball to Walsh at 161.8 kph.* *Lee le lanzó una pelota a Walsh a 161.8 kph.* 6 → see also **bowling**
→ see **dish, utensil**

**bowl|er** /boʊlər/ (**bowlers**) N-COUNT A **bowler** is someone who goes **bowling** or plays **lawn bowling.** jugador de bolos o petanca o jugadora de bolos o petanca

**bowl|ing** /boʊlɪŋ/ N-UNCOUNT **Bowling** is a game in which you roll a heavy ball down a narrow track toward a group of wooden objects and try to knock down as many of them as possible. bolos, boliche ❑ *I go bowling for relaxation.* *Voy a jugar al boliche para relajarme.*

**box** /bɒks/ (**boxes, boxing, boxed**) 1 N-COUNT A **box** is a square or rectangular container with hard or stiff sides. Boxes often have lids. caja ❑ *He reached into the cardboard box beside him.* *Metió la mano en la caja de cartón que estaba a su lado.* ❑ *They sat on wooden boxes.* *Se sentaron sobre cajas de madera.* ❑ *...boxes of chocolates.* *...cajas de chocolates.* 2 N-COUNT A **box** is a square or rectangle that is printed or drawn on a piece of paper, a road, or on some other surface. rectángulo, casilla ❑ *For more information, just check the box and send us the form.* *Para mayor información, marque la casilla y envíenos el formulario.* 3 N-COUNT A **box** is a small separate area in a theater or at a sports arena or stadium,

B

where a small number of people can sit to watch the performance or game. *palco* ❑ *Jim watched the game from a private box. Jim vio el juego desde un palco privado.* **4** V-I To **box** means to fight someone according to the rules of boxing. *boxear* ❑ *At school I boxed and played rugby. En la escuela boxeé y jugué al rugby.* ● **box|er** N-COUNT (**boxers**) *boxeador o boxeadora, pugilista* ❑ *...a professional boxer. ...un boxeador profesional.* **5** → see also **boxing**

▸ **box in** PHR-VERB If you **are boxed in,** you are unable to move from a particular place because you are surrounded by other people or cars. *cerrar el paso* ❑ *The police boxed in his white van outside his apartment. La policía le cerró el paso a su camioneta blanca afuera de su departamento.*

**box|ing** /bɒksɪŋ/ N-UNCOUNT **Boxing** is a sport in which two people wearing large padded gloves fight according to special rules. *box, boxeo*

**box lunch** (**box lunches**) N-COUNT A **box lunch** is food, for example sandwiches, which you take to work, to school, or on a trip and eat as your lunch. *lunch, almuerzo, refrigerio, box lunch*

**box of|fice** (**box offices**) also **box-office** **1** N-COUNT The **box office** in a theater or concert hall is the place where the tickets are sold. *taquilla, boletería* ❑ *...the long line of people outside the box office. ...la larga cola frente a la taquilla.* **2** N-SING When people talk about **the box office,** they are referring to the degree of success of a film or play in terms of the number of people who go to watch it or the amount of money it makes. *taquilla* ❑ *The film has earned $180 million at the box office. La película dejó 180 millones de dólares en taquilla.*

**box plot** (**box plots**) also **box-and-whisker plot** also **box-and-whisker chart** N-COUNT A **box plot** is a graph that shows the distribution of a set of data by using the middle fifty percent of the data. *gráfica de caja* [TECHNICAL]

**box spring** (**box springs**) N-COUNT A **box spring** is a frame containing rows of coiled springs that is used to provide support for a mattress. You can also use **box springs** to refer to the springs themselves. *box spring, box, cama*
→ see **bed**

**boy** /bɔɪ/ (**boys**) **1** N-COUNT A **boy** is a male child. *niño, chico, chamaco, muchacho, escuincle* ❑ *He was still just a boy. Seguía siendo un niño.* **2** N-COUNT You can refer to a young man as a **boy,** especially when talking about relationships between boys and girls. *niño, muchacho* ❑ *...the age when girls get interested in boys. ...la edad en que las niñas empiezan a interesarse por los niños.*

**boy band** (**boy bands**) N-COUNT A **boy band** is a band consisting of young men who sing pop music and dance. *boy band, banda*

**boy|cott** /bɔɪkɒt/ (**boycotts, boycotting, boycotted**) V-T If a country, group, or person **boycotts** a country, organization, or activity, they refuse to be involved with it in any way because they disapprove of it. *boicotear, hacer un boicot* ❑ *The main opposition parties are boycotting the elections. Los principales partidos de oposición están boicoteando las elecciones.* ● **Boycott** is also a noun. *boicot, boicoteo* ❑ *The boycott of British beef was finally lifted in June. El boicot a la carne de res británica finalmente terminó en junio.*

**boy|friend** /bɔɪfrɛnd/ (**boyfriends**) N-COUNT Someone's **boyfriend** is a man or boy with whom they are having a romantic or sexual relationship. *novio, galán* ❑ *...Brenda and her boyfriend Anthony. ...Brenda y su novio Anthony.*

**Boyle's law** /bɔɪlz lɔ/ N-UNCOUNT **Boyle's law** is a law in physics which describes the relationship between the pressure of a gas and its volume. *ley de Boyle* [TECHNICAL]

**bra** /brɑ/ (**bras**) N-COUNT A **bra** is a piece of underwear that women wear to support their breasts. *brasier, brassiere, sostén, sujetador, bra*

**brace** /breɪs/ (**braces, bracing, braced**) **1** V-T If you **brace yourself for** something unpleasant or difficult, you prepare yourself for it. *preparar(se)* ❑ *He braced himself for the icy dive into the black water. Se preparó para el helado chapuzón en la oscura agua.* **2** V-T If you **brace yourself against** something or **brace** part of your body **against** it, you press against something in order to steady your body or to avoid falling. *apoyarse, sujetarse* ❑ *Elaine braced herself against the table. Elaine se agarró de la mesa.* **3** N-COUNT A **brace** is a device attached to a part of a person's body to strengthen or support it. *aparato ortopédico* ❑ *They make wheelchairs and leg braces for children. Fabrican sillas de ruedas y aparatos ortopédicos infantiles.* **4** N-PLURAL **Braces** are a metal device that can be fastened to a person's teeth in order to help them grow straight. *frenos, brackets* ❑ *I used to have to wear braces. Yo tenía que usar brackets.*
→ see **teeth**

**brace|let** /breɪslɪt/ (**bracelets**) N-COUNT A **bracelet** is a piece of jewelry that you wear around your wrist. *pulsera, brazalete*
→ see **jewelry**

**braid** /breɪd/ (**braids, braiding, braided**) **1** N-UNCOUNT **Braid** is a narrow piece of decorated cloth or twisted threads, which is used to decorate clothes or curtains. *galón* ❑ *...a plum-colored uniform with lots of gold braid. ...un uniforme color ciruela con muchos galones dorados.* **2** V-T If you **braid** hair or a group of threads, you twist three or more lengths of the hair or threads over and under each other to make one thick length. *trenzar, hacer trenzas* ❑ *She has almost finished braiding Louisa's hair. Casi ha terminado de hacerle las trenzas a Louisa.* **3** N-COUNT A **braid** is a length of hair that has been divided into three or more lengths and then braided. *trenza* ❑ *...a woman with her hair in braids. ...una mujer peinada de trenzas.*

**brain** /breɪn/ (**brains**) **1** N-COUNT Your **brain** is the organ inside your head that controls your body's activities and enables you to think and to feel things such as heat and pain. *cerebro, encéfalo, sesos* **2** N-COUNT Your **brain** is your mind and the way that you think. *inteligencia, intelecto, cerebro* ❑ *Sports are good for your brain as well as your body. Los deportes desarrollan la mente y el cuerpo.* **3** N-COUNT If someone has **brains** or a good **brain,** they have the ability to learn and understand things quickly, to solve problems, and to make good decisions. *inteligencia* ❑ *The final competitors all had brains and imagination. Los últimos competidores tenían inteligencia e imaginación.* **4** PHRASE If someone is **the brains** behind an idea or an organization, he or she had that idea or makes the important decisions about

**Word Web** brain

The human **brain** weighs about three pounds. It contains seven distinct sections. The largest are the cerebrum, the cerebellum, and the medulla oblongata. The cerebrum wraps around the outside of the brain. It handles **learning**, **communication**, and voluntary **movement**. The cerebellum controls **balance**, **posture**, and movement. The medulla oblongata joins the **spinal cord** with other parts of the brain. This part of the brain controls automatic actions such as breathing, heartbeat, and swallowing. It also tells us when we are hungry and when we need to sleep.

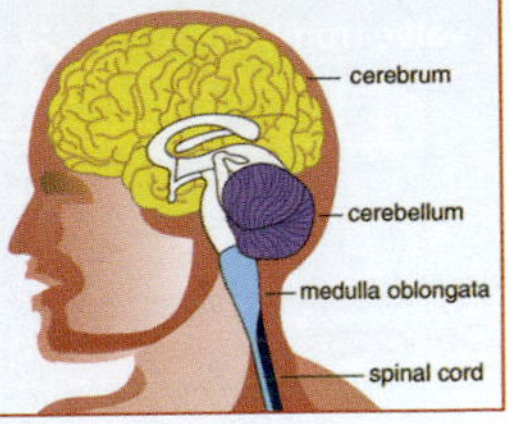


how that organization is managed. *cerebro, autor intelectual o autora intelectual* [INFORMAL] ❑ *Mr. White was the brains behind the plan. El Sr. White fue el autor intelectual del plan.*
→ see Word Web: **brain**
→ see **nervous system**

**brain|storm** /breɪnstɔrm/ N-COUNT If you have a **brainstorm,** you suddenly have a clever idea. *idea brillante, inspiración súbita* ❑ *"Look," she said, getting a brainstorm, "why don't you invite them here?" —Ya sé —dijo ella, cuando le llegó la inspiración— ¿por qué no los invitas aquí?*

**brake** /breɪk/ (**brakes, braking, braked**) **1** N-COUNT **Brakes** are devices in a vehicle that make it go slower or stop. *freno* **2** V-T/V-I When a vehicle or its driver **brakes,** the driver makes it slow down or stop by using the brakes. *frenar* ❑ *The car braked to avoid a collision. El auto frenó para evitar un choque.* ❑ *He braked the car slightly. Frenó ligeramente el vehículo.*

**Usage** **brake** and **break**

*Brake* and *break* sound the same, but they have very different meanings. You step on the *brake* to make your car slow down or stop: *Sometimes, Nayana steps on the accelerator when she means to step on the brake.* If you *break* something, you damage it: *I learned something today—if your laptop falls off your desk, it will probably break!*

**branch** /bræntʃ/ (**branches, branching, branched**) **1** N-COUNT The **branches** of a tree are the parts that grow out from its trunk. *rama* ❑ *...the upper branches of a row of pines. ...las ramas superiores de una hilera de pinos.* **2** N-COUNT A **branch of** a business or other organization is one of the offices, stores, or groups which belong to it and which are located in different places. *sucursal, agencia, delegación* ❑ *The local branch of Bank of America is handling the accounts. La sucursal local del Bank of America maneja las cuentas.* **3** N-COUNT A **branch of** a subject is a part or type of it. *rama* ❑ *Astronomy is a branch of science. La astronomía es una rama de la ciencia.*
▶ **branch off** PHR-VERB A road or path that **branches off** from another one starts from it and goes in a slightly different direction. If you **branch off** somewhere, you change the direction in which you are going. *bifurcarse* ❑ *After a few miles, a small road branched off to the right. Después de unos cuantos kilómetros, hacia la derecha salía un camino angosto.*
▶ **branch out** PHR-VERB If a person or an organization **branches out,** they do something that is different from their normal activities or work. *diversificar(se), ampliar las actividades* ❑ *I continued studying moths, and branched out to other insects. Seguí estudiando las palomillas e incluí otros insectos.*

**brand** /brænd/ (**brands, branding, branded**) **1** N-COUNT A **brand** of a product is the version of it that is made by one particular manufacturer. *marca* ❑ *...a brand of cereal. ...una marca de cereal.* ❑ *I bought one of the leading brands. Compré una de las marcas más conocidas.* **2** V-T If someone **is branded** as something bad, people think they are that thing. *etiquetar a, tachar de, tildar de, marcar, estigmatizar* ❑ *I was instantly branded as a rebel. De inmediato me pusieron la etiqueta de rebelde.* ❑ *Journalists who disagree have been branded unpatriotic. A los periodistas que discrepan los tachan de antipatriotas.* **3** V-T If you **brand** an animal, you put a permanent mark on its skin in order to show who it belongs to, usually by burning a mark onto its skin. *marcar (con hierro candente)* ❑ *The owner didn't bother to brand the cattle. El dueño no se preocupó por marcar el ganado.*

**brand-name prod|uct** (**brand-name products**) N-COUNT A **brand-name product** is one which is made by a well-known manufacturer and has the manufacturer's label on it. [BUSINESS] *producto de marca, marca registrada* ❑ *In buying footwear, 66% prefer brand-name products. Al comprar calzado, el 66% prefiere productos de marca.*

**brand-new** ADJ A **brand-new** object is completely new. *flamante, nuevo* ❑ *Yesterday he went off to buy himself a brand-new car. Ayer se fue a comprar un coche nuevecito.*

**brass** /bræs/ **1** N-UNCOUNT **Brass** is a yellow-colored metal made from copper and zinc. *latón* ❑ *The instrument is beautifully made in brass. Es un hermoso instrumento de latón.* **2** N-SING **The brass** is the section of an orchestra which consists of brass wind instruments such as trumpets and horns. *metales, bronces* ❑ *The drum solo gives the brass section a chance to recover. El solo de tambor da a los metales la oportunidad de recuperarse.* **3** N-SING In the army or in other organizations, **the brass** are the people in the highest positions. *alto mando, espadón* [INFORMAL] ❑ *Simmons admitted to being satisfied with most of the brass's answers. Simmons aceptó haber quedado satisfecho con casi todas las respuestas del alto mando.*
→ see Picture Dictionary: **brass**
→ see **orchestra**

B

## Picture Dictionary brass

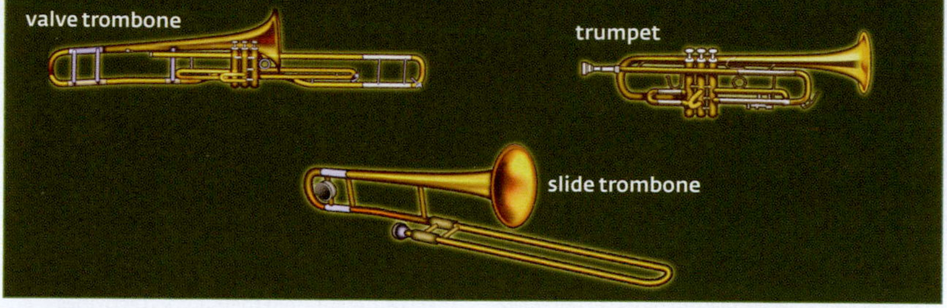


**brave** /breɪv/ (**braver, bravest, braves, braving, braved**) **1** ADJ Someone who is **brave** is willing to do things that are dangerous, and does not show fear in difficult or dangerous situations. valiente, bravo, valeroso ❑ *He was not brave enough to report the loss of the documents.* *No fue tan valiente como para informar de la pérdida de los documentos.* ● **brave|ly** ADV valerosamente, valientemente ❑ *The enemy fought bravely and well.* *El enemigo luchó con valor y bien.* **2** V-T If you **brave** unpleasant or dangerous conditions, you deliberately expose yourself to them, usually in order to achieve something. encarar, afrontar, hacer frente a, arrostrar, enfrentar(se) [WRITTEN] ❑ *Thousands have braved icy rain to show their support.* *Muchos han aguantado la helada lluvia para demostrar su apoyo.*
→ see **hero**

**brav|ery** /breɪvəri, breɪvri/ N-UNCOUNT **Bravery** is brave behavior or the quality of being brave. valentía, valor, coraje ❑ *He deserves the highest praise for his bravery.* *Merece los más grandes elogios por su valor.*

**breach** /britʃ/ (**breaches, breaching, breached**) **1** V-T If you **breach** an agreement, a law, or a promise, you break it. infringir, violar, quebrantar ❑ *The newspaper breached the rules on privacy.* *El periódico violó las reglas de privacidad.* **2** N-VAR A **breach of** an agreement, a law, or a promise is an act of breaking it. violación, infracción, contravención ❑ *Their actions are a breach of contract.* *Sus actos son una forma de incumplimiento del contrato* **3** N-COUNT A **breach in** a relationship is a serious disagreement which often results in the relationship ending. rompimiento [FORMAL] ❑ *...a serious breach in relations between the two countries.* *...una grave ruptura de relaciones entre los dos países.* **4** V-T If someone or something **breaches** a barrier, they make an opening in it, usually leaving it weakened or destroyed. romper [FORMAL] ❑ *Tree roots have breached the roof of the cave.* *Las raíces de los árboles penetraron el techo de la gruta.* **5** V-T If you **breach** security or someone's defenses, you manage to get through and attack an area that is heavily guarded and protected. violar, poner en peligro ❑ *The bomber breached security by hurling his dynamite from a roof.* *El terrorista violó la seguridad lanzando los explosivos desde un techo.* ● **Breach** is also a noun. infracción, violación ❑ *...serious breaches of security.* *...graves infracciones contra la seguridad.*

**bread** /brɛd/ (**breads**) N-VAR **Bread** is a food made from flour, water, and usually yeast. pan ❑ *...a loaf of bread.* *...una barra de pan., ...una hogaza de pan.* ❑ *...bread and butter.* *...pan con mantequilla.*
→ see Picture Dictionary: **bread**

## Picture Dictionary bread

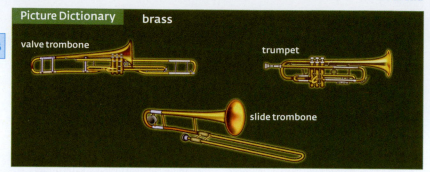

**break**
❶ DAMAGE OR DESTROY
❷ STOP OR CHANGE SOMETHING
❸ OTHER USES
❹ PHRASAL VERBS

❶ **break** /breɪk/ (**breaks, breaking, broke, broken**) 1 V-T/V-I When an object **breaks** or when you **break** it, it suddenly separates into two or more pieces, often because it has been hit or dropped. romper(se), quebrarse(se) ❑ *He fell through the window, breaking the glass.* *Se cayó por la ventana y rompió el vidrio.* ❑ *The plate broke.* *La placa se rompió.* ❑ *The plane broke into three pieces.* *El avión se rompió en tres pedazos.* 2 V-T/V-I If you **break** a part of your body such as your leg, your arm, or your nose, or if a bone **breaks,** you are injured because a bone cracks or splits. romper(se), fracturarse ❑ *She broke a leg in a skiing accident.* *Se rompió la pierna en un accidente de esquí.* ❑ *Old bones break easily.* *Los huesos viejos se fracturan con facilidad.* ● **Break** is also a noun. fractura, rompimiento ❑ *Gabriella had a bad break in her leg.* *Gabriella sufrió una grave fractura en la pierna.* 3 V-T/V-I When a tool or piece of machinery **breaks** or when you **break** it, it is damaged and no longer works. descomponer(se), averiar(se) ❑ *The cable on the elevator broke, and it crashed to the ground.* *El cable del elevador se descompuso y el aparato se estrelló en el piso.* 4 → see also **brake, tear**
→ see **crash, factory**

❷ **break** /breɪk/ (**breaks, breaking, broke, broken**) 1 V-T If someone **breaks** a habit, or a difficult or unpleasant situation that has existed for some time, they end it or change it. romper con ❑ *Here's a good way to break the habit of eating too quickly.* *Esta es una buena manera de acabar con el hábito de comer demasiado rápido.* ❑ *There have been suggestions of breaking the military's hold on power.* *Se ha sugerido acabar con el control del poder por los militares.* 2 V-I If someone **breaks for** a short period of time, they rest or change from what they are doing for a short period. interrumpir, parar, hacer una pausa ❑ *They broke for lunch.* *Interrumpieron para ir a comer.* 3 N-COUNT A **break** is a short period of time when you have a rest or a change from what you are doing, especially if you are working or if you are in a boring or unpleasant situation. pausa, break, descanso, intermedio, recreo ❑ *They may be able to help with childcare so that you can have a break.* *Ellos podrían ayudarte con el niño, para que te tomes un descanso.* ❑ *...a 15 minute break from work.* *...un descanso de 15 minutos.*

❸ **break** /breɪk/ (**breaks, breaking, broke, broken**) 1 V-T If you **break** a rule, promise, or agreement, you do something that you should not do according to that rule, promise, or agreement. romper, infringir, violar ❑ *We didn't know we were breaking the law.* *No sabíamos que estábamos violando la ley.* ❑ *...no more lies, no more broken promises.* *...no más mentiras, no más promesas incumplidas.* 2 V-I If you **break** free or loose, you free yourself from something or escape from it. escapar ❑ *She broke free by thrusting her elbow into his chest.* *Ella se liberó dándole un codazo en el pecho.* 3 V-T To **break** the force of something such as a blow or fall means to weaken its effect, for example, by getting in the way of it. interrumpir, disminuir ❑ *He suffered serious neck injuries after he broke someone's fall.* *Sufrió graves lesiones en el cuello por amortiguar la caída de alguien.* 4 V-T When you **break** a piece of bad news to someone, you tell it to them, usually in a kind way. decir, informar ❑ *Then Louise broke the news that she was leaving me.* *Entonces Louise me dio la noticia de que se iba.* 5 N-COUNT A **break** is a lucky opportunity that someone gets to achieve something. oportunidad, coyuntura feliz, chiripa [INFORMAL] ❑ *My first break came when I was 16.* *Tenía 16 años cuando se dio mi primer golpe de suerte.* 6 V-T If you **break** a record, you beat the previous record for a particular achievement. romper ❑ *Carl Lewis has broken the world record in the 100 meters.* *Carl Lewis batió el récord mundial de los 100 metros.* 7 V-I When day or dawn **breaks,** it starts to grow light after the night has ended. amanecer, salir el sol ❑ *They continued the search as dawn broke.* *Al alba siguieron con la búsqueda.* 8 V-I When a wave **breaks,** it passes its highest point and turns downward, for example, when it reaches the shore. romper (las olas) ❑ *Danny listened to the waves breaking against the shore.* *Danny oía las olas romper en la playa.* 9 V-T If you **break** a secret code, you work out how to understand it. descifrar ❑ *The machines worked on finding the numbers that would break the code.* *Las máquinas trabajaban en la búsqueda de los números con los que se descifraría el código.* 10 V-I When a boy's voice **breaks,** it becomes deeper and sounds more like a man's voice. cambiar ❑ *He sings with the strained discomfort of someone whose voice hasn't quite broken.* *Canta con la forzada incomodidad de aquel cuya voz no acaba de cambiar.* 11 → see also **broke, broken, outbreak** 12 to **break even** → see **even**

**Word Partnership** Usar *break* con:

| | |
|---|---|
| N. | break **a bone**, break **your arm/leg/neck** ❶ 2 |
| | break **a habit**, break **the silence** ❷ 1 |
| | **coffee/lunch** break ❷ 3 |
| | break **the law**, break **a promise**, break **a rule** ❸ 1 |
| | break **a record** ❸ 6 |
| V. | **need a** break, **take a** break ❷ 3 |

❹ **break** /breɪk/ (**breaks, breaking, broke, broken**)
▸ **break down** 1 PHR-VERB If a machine or a vehicle **breaks down,** it stops working. descomponer(se), averiar(se), estropear(se) ❑ *Their car broke down.* *Su coche se descompuso.* 2 PHR-VERB If a discussion, relationship, or system **breaks down,** it fails because of a problem or disagreement. fracasar ❑ *Talks with business leaders broke down last night.* *Anoche fracasaron las pláticas con los dirigentes empresariales.* 3 PHR-VERB When a substance **breaks down** or when something **breaks** it **down,** a biological or chemical process causes it to separate into the substances which make it up. descomponer(se) ❑ *White pasta breaks down into sugars almost as fast as table sugar does.* *La pasta de harina blanca se descompone en azúcares tan rápidamente como el azúcar normal.* 4 PHR-VERB If someone **breaks down,** they lose control of themselves and start crying. perder la compostura ❑ *Because he was being so kind and concerned, I broke down and cried.* *Mostró*

B

*tanta gentileza y preocupación, que perdí el control y lloré.* **5** PHR-VERB If you **break down** a door or barrier, you hit it so hard that it falls to the ground. *derribar, tumbar* ❑ *An angry mob broke down police barricades and rushed into the courtroom. Una enojada turba echó abajo las barricadas de la policía y se metió al tribunal.* **6** → see also **breakdown**

▸ **break in** **1** PHR-VERB If someone **breaks in,** they get into a building by force. *meterse, entrar por la fuerza* ❑ *Masked robbers broke in and stole $8,000. Se metieron unos ladrones enmascarados y se robaron 8,000 dólares.* **2** → see also **break-in** **3** PHR-VERB If you **break in** on someone's conversation or activity, you interrupt them. *interrumpir, meterse* ❑ *O'Leary broke in on his thoughts. O'Leary interrumpió sus pensamientos.* ❑ *"Oh yes, immediately!" Mollie broke in. —¡Claro que sí, ahora mismo! —interrumpió Mollie.*

▸ **break into** **1** PHR-VERB If someone **breaks into** a building, they get into it by force. *entrar por la fuerza, meterse* ❑ *There was no one nearby who might see him trying to break into the house. No había nadie cerca que lo hubiera visto tratando de meterse a la casa.* **2** PHR-VERB If someone **breaks into** something they suddenly start doing it. *empezar* ❑ *The moment she was out of sight she broke into a run. En cuanto ya no estuvo a la vista, ella se echó a correr.* **3** PHR-VERB If you **break into** a profession or area of business, especially one that is difficult to succeed in, you manage to have some success in it. *entrar, introducirse* ❑ *She finally broke into films after a successful stage career. Acabó por introducirse al cine, después de una exitosa carrera en los escenarios.*

▸ **break off** **1** PHR-VERB If part of something **breaks off** or if you **break** it **off,** it comes off or is removed by force. *partir(se), romper(se), desprender(se)* ❑ *The two wings of the aircraft broke off in the crash. Al estrellarse el avión, se desprendieron las dos alas.* ❑ *Grace broke off a large piece of the clay. Grace arrancó un pedazo grande de arcilla.* **2** PHR-VERB If you **break off** when you are doing or saying something, you suddenly stop doing it or saying it. *parar repentinamente* ❑ *Barry broke off in the middle of a sentence. Barry se quedó callado a mitad de una frase.* **3** PHR-VERB If someone **breaks off** a relationship, they end it. *romper, interrumpir* ❑ *The two West African states broke off relations two years ago. Los dos países del occidente de África rompieron relaciones hace dos años.*

▸ **break out** **1** PHR-VERB If something such as war, fighting, or disease **breaks out,** it begins suddenly. *empezar, desarrollar(se)* ❑ *He was 29 when war broke out. Tenía 29 años cuando estalló la guerra.* **2** PHR-VERB If you **break out in** a rash or a sweat, a rash or sweat appears on your skin. *aparecer* ❑ *My skin tends to break out in a rash when I get nervous. Mi piel tiene la tendencia a irritarse cuando me pongo nervioso.*

▸ **break through** **1** PHR-VERB If you **break through** a barrier, you succeed in forcing your way through it. *penetrar* ❑ *Protesters tried to break through a police barricade. Los manifestantes trataron de atravesar las barricadas de la policía.* **2** → see also **breakthrough**

▸ **break up** **1** PHR-VERB When something **breaks up** or when you **break** it **up,** it separates or is divided into several smaller parts. *dividir, separar* ❑ *There could be a civil war if the country breaks up. Si el país no se mantiene unido, podría haber una guerra civil.* ❑ *Break up the chocolate and melt it. Parta el chocolate y fúndalo.* **2** PHR-VERB If you **break up with** someone, your relationship with that person ends. *separarse* ❑ *My girlfriend has broken up with me. Mi novia rompió conmigo.* ❑ *He hated the idea of marriage so we broke up. Él detestaba la idea del matrimonio, así que nos separamos.* **3** PHR-VERB When a meeting or gathering **breaks up** or when someone **breaks** it **up,** it is brought to an end and the people involved in it leave. *disolver* ❑ *A neighbor asked for the music to be turned down and the party broke up. Un vecino pidió que se bajara el volumen de la música, así que se acabó la fiesta.* ❑ *Police used clubs to break up a demonstration. La policía se sirvió de macanas para disolver la manifestación.*

**break|down** /breɪkdaʊn/ (**breakdowns**) **1** N-COUNT The **breakdown of** something such as a relationship, plan, or discussion is its failure or ending. *rompimiento, interrupción* ❑ *...the breakdown of talks between the U.S. and European Union officials. ...el rompimiento de las pláticas entre los Estados Unidos y los funcionarios de la Unión Europea.* ❑ *...the breakdown of a marriage. ...el rompimiento de un matrimonio.* **2** N-COUNT If you have a **breakdown,** you become very depressed, so that you are unable to cope with your life. *breakdown, crisis nerviosa* ❑ *My mother died, and a couple of years later I had a breakdown. Mi madre murió y dos años después, tuve una crisis nerviosa.* **3** N-COUNT If a car or a piece of machinery has a **breakdown,** it stops working. *descompostura, falla, avería* ❑ *Her old car was unreliable, so the trip was ruined by breakdowns. Su viejo coche ya no era confiable, así que sus fallas nos arruinaron el viaje.*

breakdown

**4** N-COUNT A **breakdown of** something is a list of its separate parts. *desglose, análisis detallado* ❑ *The organizers were given a breakdown of the costs. A los organizadores les dieron el desglose de los costos.* → see **traffic**

**breaker zone** (**breaker zones**) N-COUNT The **breaker zone** is the area of water near a shoreline where waves begin to fall downward and hit the shore. *línea de rompimiento de las olas* [TECHNICAL]

**break|fast** /brɛkfəst/ (**breakfasts**) N-VAR **Breakfast** is the first meal of the day. It is usually eaten in the early part of the morning. *desayuno* ❑ *What's for breakfast? ¿Qué hay de desayuno?* → see **meal**

**break-in** (**break-ins**) N-COUNT If there is a **break-in,** someone gets into a building by force. *robo* ❑ *The break-in occurred just before midnight. El robo tuvo lugar poco antes de media noche.*

**break|ing point** N-UNCOUNT If something or someone has reached the **breaking point,** they have so many problems or difficulties that they can no longer cope with them, and may soon collapse or be unable to continue. *límite, colmo* ❑ *This race tests horse and rider to the breaking point. Esta carrera lleva al límite a caballo y jinete.*

**break|through** /breɪkθru/ (**breakthroughs**) N-COUNT A **breakthrough** is an important development or achievement. *gran avance* ❑ *The* *company is about to make a significant breakthrough in Europe.* La compañía está a punto de abrir significativamente el mercado en Europa.

**break|up** /breɪkʌp/ (**breakups**) N-COUNT The **breakup of** a marriage, relationship, or association is its end. ruptura, rompimiento ❑ *...the sudden breakup of the meeting.* ...la desintegración repentina de la reunión.

**breast** /brɛst/ (**breasts**) 1 N-COUNT A woman's **breasts** are the two soft, round parts on her chest that can produce milk to feed a baby. seno, pecho, mama 2 N-COUNT A person's **breast** is the upper part of his or her chest. pecho, tórax [LITERARY] ❑ *He struck his breast in a dramatic gesture.* Se estrujó el pecho en dramático gesto. 3 N-COUNT A bird's **breast** is the front part of its body. pechuga, pecho ❑ *...the robin's red breast.* ...el pecho rojo del petirrojo. 4 N-VAR You can refer to piece of meat that is cut from the front of a bird as **breast.** pechuga ❑ *...a chicken breast with vegetables.* ...pechuga de pollo con verduras.

**breath** /brɛθ/ (**breaths**) 1 N-VAR Your **breath** is the air that you let out through your mouth when you breathe. If someone has **bad breath,** their breath smells unpleasant. aliento, respiración, hálito ❑ *I could smell peppermint on his breath.* Podía sentir el olor de la menta en su aliento. 2 N-VAR When you take a **breath,** you breathe in once. respiración ❑ *He took a deep breath, and began to climb the stairs.* Hizo una respiración profunda antes de empezar a subir la escalera. ❑ *Gasping for breath, she leaned against the door.* Se recargó en la puerta, tratando de recuperar el aliento. 3 PHRASE If you describe something new or different as **a breath of fresh air,** you mean that it makes a situation or subject more interesting or exciting. soplo de aire fresco ❑ *I thought it was my job to bring a breath of fresh air to the company.* Yo pensaba que mi tarea era renovar la empresa. 4 PHRASE If you are **out of breath,** you are breathing very quickly and with difficulty because you have been doing something energetic. sin aliento ❑ *She was slightly out of breath from running.* Por correr, le faltó ligeramente el aliento. 5 PHRASE If you say something **under** your **breath,** you say it in a very quiet voice, often because you do not want other people to hear what you are saying. susurrar ❑ *Walsh muttered something under his breath.* Algo susurró Walsh.

**Word Partnership** Usar *breath* con:

| | |
|---|---|
| ADJ. | **bad** breath, **fresh** breath 1 **deep** breath 2 |
| V. | **gasp for** breath, **hold** *your* breath 1 **take a** breath 2 |

**breathe** /brið/ (**breathes, breathing, breathed**) V-T/V-I When people or animals **breathe,** they take air into their lungs and let it out again. When they **breathe** smoke or a particular kind of air, they take it into their lungs and let it out again as they breathe. respirar ❑ *He stood there breathing deeply and evenly.* Se detuvo ahí, respirando profunda y tranquilamente. ❑ *No American should have to drive out of town to breathe clean air.* Ningún estadounidense debería tener la necesidad de salir de la ciudad para respirar aire fresco. • **breath|ing** N-UNCOUNT respiración ❑ *Her breathing became slow and heavy.* Su respiración se tornó lenta y pesada. → see **sigh** → see **respiratory system**

▸ **breathe in** PHR-VERB When you **breathe in,** you take some air into your lungs. inspirar, respirar, tomar aire ❑ *She breathed in deeply.* Inspiró profundamente

▸ **breathe out** PHR-VERB When you **breathe out,** you send air out of your lungs through your nose or mouth. expirar, sacar el aire ❑ *Breathe out and bring your knees in toward your chest.* Suelta el aire y lleva las rodillas al pecho.

**breath|less** /brɛθlɪs/ ADJ If you are **breathless,** you have difficulty in breathing properly, for example, because you have been running or because you are afraid or excited. falto de aliento ❑ *I was a little breathless.* Jadeaba un poco. • **breath|less|ly** ADV entrecortadamente ❑ *"I'll go in," he said breathlessly.* —Voy a entrar —dijo jadeante. • **breath|less|ness** N-UNCOUNT dificultad para respirar ❑ *A slow heart rate causes breathlessness.* La desaceleración del ritmo cardíaco provoca dificultades para respirar.

**breed** /brid/ (**breeds, breeding, bred**) 1 N-COUNT A **breed** of animal is a particular type of it. For example, terriers are a breed of dog. raza, clase, especie ❑ *...rare breeds of cattle.* ...razas de ganado poco comunes. 2 V-T If you **breed** animals or plants, you keep them for the purpose of producing more animals or plants with particular qualities, in a controlled way. criar ❑ *He lived alone, breeding horses and dogs.* Vivía solo, criando caballos y perros. ❑ *He used to breed dogs for the police.* Acostumbraba criar perros para la policía. • **breed|er** N-COUNT (**breeders**) criador o criadora ❑ *Her father was a well-known racehorse breeder.* Su padre era un reputado criador de caballos de carrera. • **breed|ing** N-UNCOUNT cría ❑ *They are involved in the breeding of guide dogs for blind people.* Ellos crían perros guía para los ciegos. 3 V-I When animals **breed,** they have babies. procrear ❑ *Frogs will usually breed in any convenient pond.* Las ranas procrean en cualquier charco que les quede cerca. • **breed|ing** N-UNCOUNT cría, reproducción, crianza ❑ *During the breeding season the birds come ashore.* Las aves llegan a la playa durante la época de reproducción. 4 V-T If you say that something **breeds** bad feeling or bad behavior, you mean that it causes bad feeling or bad behavior to develop. producir, engendrar ❑ *If they are unemployed it may breed resentment.* El desempleo engendra resentimiento. → see **zoo**

**breeze** /briz/ (**breezes, breezing, breezed**) 1 N-COUNT A **breeze** is a gentle wind. brisa ❑ *...a cool summer breeze.* ...una brisa fresca de verano. 2 V-I If you **breeze into** a place or a position, you enter it in a very casual or relaxed manner. entrar tranquilamente ❑ *Lopez breezed into the finals of the tournament.* Lopez pasó cómodamente a las finales del torneo. → see **wind**

**brew** /bru/ (**brews, brewing, brewed**) 1 V-T If you **brew** tea or coffee, you make it by pouring hot water over tea leaves or ground coffee. preparar ❑ *He brewed a pot of coffee.* Preparó una jarra de café. 2 N-COUNT A **brew** is a particular kind of tea or coffee. It can also be a pot of tea or coffee. variedad, infusión ❑ *She swallowed a mouthful of the hot strong brew.* Tragó un sorbo de la infusión fuerte y caliente.

B

**3** V-T If someone **brews** beer, they make it. *fabricar* ❑ *I brew my own beer.* *Yo fabrico mi propia cerveza.* **4** V-I If an unpleasant or difficult situation **is brewing,** it is starting to develop. *avecinarse* ❑ *At home a crisis was brewing.* *En casa se estaba incubando una crisis.*
→ see **tea**

**brew|ery** /bruəri/ (**breweries**) N-COUNT A **brewery** is a place where beer is made. *fábrica de cerveza*

**bribe** /braɪb/ (**bribes, bribing, bribed**) **1** N-COUNT A **bribe** is a sum of money or something valuable that one person offers or gives to another in order to persuade him or her to do something. *soborno* ❑ *He was accused of receiving bribes.* *Fue acusado de recibir sobornos.* **2** V-T If one person **bribes** another, they give them a bribe. *sobornar* ❑ *He was accused of bribing a bank official.* *Fue acusado de sobornar a un funcionario del banco.*

**brick** /brɪk/ (**bricks**) N-VAR **Bricks** are rectangular blocks of baked clay used for building walls, which are usually red or brown. **Brick** is the material made up of these blocks. *ladrillo* ❑ *She built bookshelves out of bricks and boards.* *Construyó libreros a base de ladrillos y tablas.*

**bride** /braɪd/ (**brides**) N-COUNT A **bride** is a woman who is getting married or who has just gotten married. *novia* ❑ *...the bride and groom.* *...los novios.* • **brid|al** ADJ *nupcial* ❑ *She wore a floor length bridal gown.* *Llevaba puesto un vestido de novia largo hasta el piso.*
→ see **wedding**

**bride|groom** /braɪdgrum/ (**bridegrooms**) N-COUNT A **bridegroom** is a man who is getting married. *novio*

**brides|maid** /braɪdzmeɪd/ (**bridesmaids**) N-COUNT A **bridesmaid** is a woman or a girl who accompanies a bride on her wedding day. *dama de honor*
→ see **wedding**

**bridge** /brɪdʒ/ (**bridges, bridging, bridged**) **1** N-COUNT A **bridge** is a structure that is built over a railroad, river, or road so that people or vehicles can cross from one side to the other. *puente* ❑ *He walked back over the railroad bridge.* *Regresó caminando por el puente del ferrocarril.* **2** V-T To **bridge** the gap between two people or things means to reduce it or get rid of it. *salvar* ❑ *It is unlikely that the two sides will be able to bridge their differences.* *Es poco probable que los dos bandos sean capaces de salvar sus diferencias.* **3** V-T Something that **bridges** the gap between two very different things has some of the qualities of each of these things. *tender un puente* ❑ *...a singer who bridged the gap between pop music and opera.* *...una cantante que tendió un puente entre la música pop y la ópera.* **4** N-COUNT If something or someone acts as a **bridge** between two people, groups, or things, they connect them. *puente* ❑ *We hope this book will act as a bridge between doctor and patient.* *Esperamos que este libro sirva como puente entre el doctor y la paciente.* **5** N-UNCOUNT **Bridge** is a card game for four players in which the players begin by declaring how many tricks they expect to win. *bridge*
→ see Word Web: **bridge**

**bridge loan** (**bridge loans**) N-COUNT A **bridge loan** is money that a bank lends you for a short time, for example, so that you can buy a new house before you have sold the one you already own. *préstamo puente*

**brief** /brif/ (**briefer, briefest, briefs, briefing, briefed**) **1** ADJ Something that is **brief** lasts for only a short time. *breve* ❑ *She once made a brief appearance on television.* *Una vez hizo una breve aparición en televisión.* **2** ADJ A **brief** speech or piece of writing does not contain too many words or details. *breve* ❑ *In a brief statement, he concentrated on international affairs.* *En una breve declaración, se concentró en los asuntos internacionales.* **3** ADJ If you are **brief,** you say what you want to say in as few words as possible. *conciso* ❑ *Now please be brief—my time is valuable.* *Por favor, sean concisos, mi tiempo es valioso.* **4** ADJ You can describe a period of time as **brief** if you want to emphasize that it is very short. *fugaz* ❑ *For a few brief minutes we forgot our worries.* *Por unos fugaces minutos, olvidamos nuestras penas.* **5** N-PLURAL Men's or women's underpants can be referred to as **briefs.** *calzones* ❑ *...a pair of briefs.* *...unos calzones.* **6** V-T If someone **briefs** you, especially about a piece of work or a serious matter, they give you information that you need before you do it or consider it. *poner al día* ❑ *A Defense Department spokesman briefed reporters.* *El vocero del Departamento de Defensa informó a los reporteros.* **7** → see also **briefing**

**Word Partnership** Usar *brief* con:

N. brief **appearance**, brief **conversation**, brief **pause** **1**
brief **description**, brief **explanation**, brief **history**, brief **speech**, brief **statement** **2**

**Word Web** bridge

The world's longest and tallest **suspension bridge** is the Akashi Kaikyo Bridge. It is 12,828 feet long and almost 1,000 feet tall. It can withstand an 8.5 magnitude earthquake. Another famous **span**, the Brooklyn Bridge in New York City, dates from 1883. It was the first suspension bridge to use **steel** for its **cable** wire. More than 120,000 vehicles still use the bridge every day. The Evergreen Point Floating Bridge near Seattle, Washington, floats on pontoons. It's over a mile long. During windy weather the drawbridge in the middle must stay open to protect the bridge from damage.

**brief|case** /brifkeɪs/ (**briefcases**) N-COUNT A **briefcase** is a case used for carrying documents in. *portafolios*

**brief|ing** /brifɪŋ/ (**briefings**) **1** N-VAR A **briefing** is a meeting at which information or instructions are given to people. *reunión informativa* ❑ *They're holding a press briefing tomorrow. Mañana tendrán una conferencia de prensa.* **2** → see also **brief**

**brief|ly** /brifli/ **1** ADV Something that happens **briefly** happens for a very short period of time. *fugazmente* ❑ *He smiled briefly. Sonrió fugazmente.* **2** ADV If you say or write something **briefly,** you use very few words or give very few details. *en síntesis* ❑ *There are four basic choices; they are described briefly below. Hay cuatro opciones básicas; a continuación se describen resumidamente.* ❑ *Briefly, he believes that Europe should unite politically. En síntesis, él cree que Europa debería unirse políticamente.*

**bri|gade** /brɪgeɪd/ (**brigades**) N-COUNT A **brigade** is one of the groups which an army is divided into. *brigada* ❑ *...the soldiers of the 173rd Airborne Brigade. ...los soldados de la 173ava. brigada aerotransportada.*

**bright** /braɪt/ (**brights, brighter, brightest**) **1** ADJ A **bright** color is strong and noticeable, and not dark. *vivo* ❑ *...a bright red dress. ...un vestido rojo vivo.* • **bright|ly** ADV *vivamente* ❑ *...a display of brightly colored flowers. ...una exhibición de flores vivamente coloreadas.* **2** ADJ A **bright** light, object, or place is shining strongly or is full of light. *luminoso* ❑ *...a bright October day. ...un claro día de octubre.* • **bright|ly** ADV *claramente* ❑ *...a warm, brightly lit room. ...una habitación cálida, claramente iluminada.* • **bright|ness** N-UNCOUNT *brillo* ❑ *An astronomer can determine the brightness of each star. Un astrónomo puede determinar la intensidad luminosa de cada estrella.* **3** ADJ If you describe someone as **bright,** you mean that they are quick at learning things. *inteligente* ❑ *I was convinced that he was brighter than average. Yo estaba convencido de que él era más inteligente que la media.* **4** ADJ A **bright** idea is clever and original. *brillante* ❑ *There are lots of books filled with bright ideas. Hay un montón de libros llenos de ideas brillantes.* **5** ADJ If someone looks or sounds **bright,** they look or sound cheerful and lively. *animado* ❑ *Bamber spoke twice, sounding bright and eager. Bamber habló dos veces con ánimo y entusiasmo.* • **bright|ly** ADV *radiantemente* ❑ *He smiled brightly as Ben approached. Él sonreía radiantemente mientras Ben se acercaba.* **6** ADJ If the future is **bright,** it is likely to be pleasant or successful. *brillante* ❑ *Both had successful careers and the future looked bright. Ambos tenían carreras exitosas y el futuro se veía brillante.* **7** N-PLURAL The **brights** on a vehicle are its headlights when they are set to shine their brightest. *luces altas* ❑ *...a Bronco with its brights on, parked in the middle of the street. ...un Bronco con las luces altas encendidas, estacionado en medio de la calle.*

**bright|en** /braɪtᵊn/ (**brightens, brightening, brightened**) **1** V-I If someone **brightens** or their face **brightens,** they suddenly look happier. *iluminársele (una cara), animarse (una persona)* ❑ *Seeing him, she seemed to brighten a little. Al verlo, pareció animarse un poco.* • **Brighten up** means the same as **brighten**. *animarse* ❑ *He brightened up a bit when he saw the food. Se animó un poquito al ver la comida.* **2** V-T If someone or something **brightens** a place, they make it more colorful and attractive. *alegrar* ❑ *Pots planted with flowers brightened the area outside the door. Las macetas con flores alegraron el área de la entrada.* • **Brighten up** means the same as **brighten**. *alegrar* ❑ *She thought the pink lampshade would brighten up the room. Pensó que la pantalla rosa de la lámpara alegraría el cuarto.* **3** V-T/V-I If someone or something **brightens** a situation or the situation **brightens,** it becomes more pleasant, enjoyable, or favorable. *alegrar* ❑ *This piece of news should brighten your day. Esta noticia debería alegrarte el día.*

**bril|liant** /brɪlyənt/ **1** ADJ A **brilliant** person, idea, or performance is extremely clever or skillful. *brillante* ❑ *She had a brilliant mind. Tenía una mente brillante.* • **bril|liant|ly** ADV *brillantemente* ❑ *It is a very high quality show, brilliantly written and acted. Se trata de un espectáculo de muy buena calidad, brillantemente escrito y actuado.* • **bril|liance** N-UNCOUNT *talento* ❑ *He is a serious musician who showed his brilliance very early. Es un músico serio, que mostró su talento desde muy joven.* **2** ADJ A **brilliant** career or success is very successful. *brillante* • **bril|liant|ly** ADV *espléndidamente* ❑ *The strategy worked brilliantly. La estrategia funcionó espléndidamente.* **3** ADJ A **brilliant** light or color is extremely bright. *brillante* ❑ *The woman had brilliant green eyes. La mujer tenía ojos de un color verde brillante.* • **bril|liant|ly** ADV *brillantemente* ❑ *Many of the patterns show brilliantly colored flowers. Muchos de los patrones muestran flores coloreadas en tonos brillantes.* • **bril|liance** N-UNCOUNT *esplendor* ❑ *...a blue butterfly in all its brilliance. ...una mariposa azul en todo su esplendor.*

**bring** /brɪŋ/ (**brings, bringing, brought**) **1** V-T If you **bring** someone or something **with** you when you come to a place, they come with you or you have them with you. *traer* ❑ *Remember to bring an old shirt to protect your clothes. Recuerda traer una camiseta vieja para proteger tu ropa.* ❑ *Someone went upstairs and brought down a huge box. Alguien subió las escaleras y bajó una gran caja.* **2** V-T If you **bring** something somewhere, you move it there. *llevar* ❑ *Reaching into her pocket, she brought out a dollar bill. Buscó en su bolsa y sacó un billete de un dólar.* **3** V-T If you **bring** something that someone wants or needs, you get it for them or carry it to them. *llevar* ❑ *He poured a glass of milk for Dena and brought it to her. Sirvió un vaso de leche para Dena y se lo llevó.* **4** V-T To **bring** something or someone to a place or position means to cause them to come to the place or move into that position. *llevar, traer* ❑ *I told you what brought me here. Te dije qué fue lo que me trajo hasta aquí.* ❑ *The shock of her husband's arrival brought her to her feet. La sorpresa que le provocó la llegada de su marido la puso de pie.* **5** V-T To **bring** someone or something into a particular state or condition means to cause them to be in that state or condition. *provocar* ❑ *He brought the car to a stop in front of the store. Detuvo el carro frente a la tienda.* ❑ *They have brought down income taxes. Bajaron el impuesto a la renta.* **6** V-T If something **brings** a particular feeling, situation, or quality, it makes people experience it or have it. *dar* ❑ *He called on the United States to play a role in bringing peace to the region. Pidió a los Estados Unidos que interviniera para llevar la paz a la región.* ❑ *Her three children brought her much joy. Sus tres niños le dieron muchas alegrías.* **7** V-T

B

If you cannot **bring yourself to** do something, you cannot do it because you find it too upsetting, embarrassing, or disgusting. *tener fuerzas para* ❑ *It is all very sad and I just cannot bring myself to talk about it. Todo esto es muy triste y simplemente no tengo fuerzas para hablar de ello.*

▸ **bring about** PHR-VERB To **bring** something **about** means to cause it to happen. *provocar* ❑ *They can bring about political change. Ellos pueden provocar un cambio político.*

▸ **bring along** PHR-VERB If you **bring** someone or something **along**, you bring them with you when you come to a place. *traer, llevar* ❑ *They brought baby Michael along in a carrier. Trajeron/llevaron al pequeño Michael en una carriola.*

▸ **bring back** 1 PHR-VERB Something that **brings back** a memory makes you think about it. *recordar* ❑ *Your article brought back sad memories for me. Tu artículo me trajo a la memoria recuerdos tristes para mí.* 2 PHR-VERB When people **bring back** a practice or fashion that existed at an earlier time, they introduce it again. *revivir* ❑ *We've brought back long skirts so it's easier to walk. Hemos revivido las faldas largas de modo que sea más fácil caminar.*

▸ **bring down** PHR-VERB When people or events **bring down** a government or ruler, they cause the government or ruler to lose power. *derrocar* ❑ *They were threatening to bring down the government. Estaban amenazando con derrocar al gobierno.*

▸ **bring forward** PHR-VERB If you **bring forward** a meeting or event, you arrange for it to take place at an earlier date or time than had been planned. *adelantar* ❑ *He had to bring forward an 11 o'clock meeting. Tuvo que adelantar la reunión de las 11:00 hs.*

▸ **bring in** 1 PHR-VERB When a government or organization **brings in** a new law or system, they introduce it. *introducir* ❑ *The government brought in a law under which it could take any land it wanted. El gobierno promulgó una ley por la cual podía apropiarse de toda la tierra que quisiera.* 2 PHR-VERB Someone or something that **brings in** money makes it or earns it. *redituar* ❑ *I have three part-time jobs, which bring in about $24,000 a year. Tengo tres trabajos de medio tiempo, que me reditúan un total de cerca de 24,000 dólares al año.*

▸ **bring out** 1 PHR-VERB When a person or company **brings out** a new product, especially a new book or CD, they produce it and put it on sale. *sacar* ❑ *A journalist all his life, he's now brought out a book. Periodista de toda la vida, acaba de sacar un libro.* 2 PHR-VERB Something that **brings out** a particular kind of behavior or feeling in you causes you to show it, especially when it is something you do not normally show. *sacar a relucir* ❑ *He brings out the best in his pupils. Él saca a relucir lo mejor de sus alumnos.*

▸ **bring up** 1 PHR-VERB When someone **brings up** a child, they look after it until it is an adult. *criar* ❑ *She brought up four children on her own. Ella crió a cuatro niños sola.* ❑ *He was brought up in Nebraska. Él se crió en Alaska.* 2 PHR-VERB If you **bring up** a particular subject, you introduce it into a discussion or conversation. *plantear* ❑ *Her mother brought up the subject of going back to work. Su madre planteó el tema de regresar a trabajar.*

**Thesaurus** *bring* Ver también:

V. accompany, bear, carry, take; (*ant.*) drop, leave 1
move, take, transfer 2

**Word Partnership** Usar *bring* con:

N. bring **bad/good luck**, bring ***someone/something*** **home** 1
bring **to *someone's* attention**, bring **to a boil**, bring **to justice**, bring **to life**, bring **to mind**, bring **together** 5

**brink** /brɪŋk/ N-SING If you are **on the brink of** something important, terrible, or exciting, you are just about to do it or experience it. *a punto de* ❑ *Their economy is on the brink of collapse. Su economía está al borde del colapso.*

**brisk** /brɪsk/ (**brisker, briskest**) 1 ADJ A **brisk** activity or action is done quickly and in an energetic way. *rápido y enérgico* ❑ *He put out his hand for a brisk, firm handshake. Extendió la mano para darle un apretón firme y rápido.* ● **brisk|ly** ADV *rápida y enérgicamente* ❑ *Eve walked briskly down the hall to her son's room. Eve caminó con paso firme por el corredor hasta la habitación de su hijo.* 2 ADJ If the weather is **brisk**, it is cold and fresh. *frío* ❑ *...a brisk winter's day on the south coast. ...un día frío de invierno en la costa sur.* 3 ADJ Someone who is **brisk** behaves in a busy, confident way which shows that they want to get things done quickly. *expeditivo* ❑ *The chief was brisk and businesslike. El jefe era expeditivo y práctico.* ● **brisk|ly** ADV *enérgicamente* ❑ *"Anyhow," she added briskly, "it's none of my business." —De todos modos —agregó enérgicamente—, no es asunto mío*

**Brit|ish** /brɪtɪʃ/ 1 ADJ **British** means belonging or relating to the United Kingdom, or to its people or culture. *británico* 2 N-PLURAL **The British** are the people of Great Britain. *Los británicos son las personas de Gran Bretaña.*

**Brit|on** /brɪtᵊn/ (**Britons**) N-COUNT A **Briton** is a British citizen, or a person of British origin. *británico o británica* [FORMAL] ❑ *The role of the daughter is played by seventeen-year-old Briton Jane March. El papel de la hija es interpretado por la actriz británica de diecisiete años, Jane March.*

**bro** /broʊ/ (**bros**) 1 N-VOC Some men use **bro** as a friendly way of addressing other men when they are talking to them. *carnal* [INFORMAL] ❑ *What do you mean, bro? ¿Qué me quieres decir, carnal?* 2 N-COUNT **Bro** is the same as **brother**. *carnal* [INFORMAL] ❑ *Bryant said his bro did a great job. Bryant dijo que su carnal había hecho un gran trabajo.*

**broad** /brɔd/ (**broader, broadest**) 1 ADJ Something that is **broad** is wide. *ancho* ❑ *His shoulders were broad and his waist narrow. Su espalda era ancha y su cintura delgada.* ❑ *...the broad river. ...la parte ancha del río.* 2 ADJ A **broad** smile is one in which your mouth is stretched very wide. *amplio* ❑ *He greeted them with a wave and a broad smile. Los saludo con la mano y una amplia sonrisa.* ● **broad|ly** ADV *ampliamente* ❑ *Charles grinned broadly. Charles sonrió de oreja a oreja.* 3 ADJ You use **broad** to describe something that includes a large number of different things or people. *diverso* ❑ *A broad range of issues was discussed. Se discutió una amplia* *gama de temas.* • **broad|ly** ADV *diversamente* ❑ *It's a broadly-based group of people. Es un grupo conformado por personas muy diversas.* **4** ADJ You use **broad** to describe a word or meaning which covers or refers to a wide range of different things. *amplio* ❑ *A theater director is, in the broad sense of the word, an artist. Un director de teatro es, en el sentido amplio del término, un artista.* • **broad|ly** ADV *en un sentido amplio* ❑ *The authors define leadership broadly to include political figures and even parents. Los autores definen el liderazgo en un sentido amplio, incluyendo desde figuras políticas hasta los padres.* **5** ADJ You use **broad** to describe a feeling or opinion that is shared by many people, or by people of many different kinds. *generalizado* ❑ *The agreement won broad support in the U.S. Congress. El acuerdo contó con el apoyo generalizado del Congreso de Estados Unidos.* • **broad|ly** ADV *en general* ❑ *The law has been broadly welcomed. La ley fue en general bienvenida.* **6** → see also **broadly**

**Word Partnership** Usar *broad* con:

N. broad **expanse**, broad **shoulders** **1**
broad **smile** **2**
broad **range**, broad **spectrum** **3**
broad **definition**, broad **strokes**, broad **view** **4**

**broad|band** /brɔdbænd/ N-UNCOUNT **Broadband** is a method of sending many electronic messages at the same time by using a wide range of frequencies. *banda ancha* [COMPUTING] ❑ *The telecommunications company announced big price cuts for broadband customers. La compañía de telecomunicaciones anunció grandes descuentos para los clientes de banda ancha.*

**broad|cast** /brɔdkæst/ (**broadcasts, broadcasting**)

The form **broadcast** is used in the present tense and is the past tense and past participle of the verb.

**1** N-COUNT A **broadcast** is a program, performance, or speech on the radio or on television. *programa* ❑ *...a live television broadcast of Saturday's game. ...una transmisión en vivo por televisión del juego del sábado.* **2** V-T/V-I To **broadcast** a program means to send it out by radio waves, wires, or satellites so that it can be heard on the radio or seen on television. *transmitir* ❑ *The concert will be broadcast live on television and radio. El concierto será transmitido en vivo por radio y televisión.* ❑ *CNN also broadcasts in Europe. CNN también se transmite en Europa.* • **broad|cast|ing** N-UNCOUNT *transmisión, radiodifusión* ❑ *...religious broadcasting. ...las transmisiones religiosas.*

**broad|cast|er** /brɔdkæstər/ (**broadcasters**) N-COUNT A **broadcaster** is someone who gives talks or takes part in interviews and discussions on radio or television programs. *conductor o conductora (de televisión), locutor o locutora (de radio)* ❑ *...the naturalist and broadcaster, Sir David Attenborough. ...el naturalista y conductor de televisión, Sir David Attenborough.*

**broad|ly** /brɔdli/ **1** ADV You can use **broadly** to indicate that something is generally true. *en términos generales* ❑ *The president broadly got what he wanted out of his meeting. El presidente obtuvo en términos generales lo que quería de la reunión.* **2** → see also **broad**

**broad-minded** also **broadminded** ADJ If you describe someone as **broad-minded,** you approve of them because they are willing to accept types of behavior that other people consider immoral. *de mentalidad abierta* ❑ *...a fair and broad-minded man. ...un hombre agradable y de mentalidad abierta.*

**broc|co|li** /brɒkəli, brɒkli/ N-UNCOUNT **Broccoli** is a vegetable with green stalks and green or purple tops. *brócoli*
→ see **vegetable**

**bro|chure** /broʊʃʊər/ (**brochures**) N-COUNT A **brochure** is a thin magazine with pictures that gives you information about a product or service. *folleto* ❑ *...travel brochures. ...folletos de viaje.*

**broil** /brɔɪl/ (**broils, broiling, broiled**) V-T When you **broil** food, you cook it using very strong heat directly above it. *rostizar* ❑ *I'll broil the lobster. Voy a rostizar la langosta.*
→ see **cook**

**broil|er** /brɔɪlər/ (**broilers**) N-COUNT A **broiler** is a part of a stove which produces strong heat and cooks food placed underneath it. *parrilla superior del horno*

**broke** /broʊk/ **1** **Broke** is the past tense of **break.** *pasado de* ***break*** **2** ADJ If you are **broke,** you have no money. *quebrado* [INFORMAL] ❑ *I'm as broke as you are. Estoy tan quebrado como tú.* **3** PHRASE If a company or person **goes broke,** they lose money and are unable to continue in business or to pay their debts. *irse a la quiebra* [INFORMAL] ❑ *Balton went broke twice in his career. Balton quebró dos veces en su carrera.*

**Thesaurus** *broke* Ver también:

ADJ. bankrupt, destitute, impoverished, penniless, poor; (*ant.*) rich, wealthy, well-to-do **2**

**bro|ken** /broʊkən/ **1** **Broken** is the past participle of **break.** *participio pasado de* ***break*** **2** ADJ A **broken** line is not continuous but has gaps or spaces in it. *discontinuo* ❑ *...a broken blue line. ...una línea discontinua azul.* **3** ADJ You can use **broken** to describe a marriage that has ended in divorce, or a home in which the parents of the family are divorced, when you think this is a sad thing. *fracasado* ❑ *...the pain of a broken marriage. ...el dolor de un matrimonio fracasado.* **4** ADJ If someone talks in **broken** English, for example, or in **broken** French, they speak slowly and make a lot of mistakes because they do not know the language very well. *chapurreado* ❑ *Eric could only respond in broken English. Eric sólo pudo responder en un inglés chapurreado.*

**bro|ker** /broʊkər/ (**brokers, brokering, brokered**) **1** N-COUNT A **broker** is a person whose job is to buy and sell securities, foreign money, real estate, or goods for other people. *corredor* [BUSINESS] **2** V-T If a country or government **brokers** an agreement, a ceasefire, or a round of talks, they try to negotiate or arrange it. *concertar* ❑ *The United Nations brokered a peace agreement at the end of March. Las Naciones Unidas concertaron un acuerdo de paz a finales de marzo.*

B

**bron|chi** /brɒŋki, -kaɪ/ N-PLURAL The **bronchi** are the two large tubes in your body that connect your windpipe to your lungs. *bronquios* [TECHNICAL]

**Bronx cheer** /brɒŋks tʃɪər/ (**Bronx cheers**) N-COUNT A **Bronx cheer** is a sound that people make by vibrating their lips in order to express disapproval or contempt. *abucheo* [INFORMAL]

**bronze** /brɒnz/ **1** N-UNCOUNT **Bronze** is a yellowish-brown metal which is a mixture of copper and tin. *bronce* ❑ *...a bronze statue of Giorgi Dimitrov. ...una estatua de bronce de Giorgi Dimitrov.* **2** COLOR Something that is **bronze** is yellowish-brown in color. *bronce* ❑ *Her hair shone bronze and gold. Su cabello lucía tonos bronceados y dorados.*

**brooch** /broʊtʃ/ (**brooches**) N-COUNT A **brooch** is a piece of jewelry that has a pin at the back so it can be fastened on a dress, blouse, or coat. *broche, prendedor*
→ see **jewelry**

**broom** /brum/ (**brooms**) N-COUNT A **broom** is a kind of brush with a long handle. You use a broom for sweeping the floor. *escoba*

**broth|er** /brʌðər/ (**brothers**) **1** N-COUNT Your **brother** is a boy or a man who has the same parents as you. *hermano* ❑ *Oh, so you're Peter's younger brother. Así que tú eres el hermano menor de Peter.* **2** N-COUNT You can describe a man as your **brother** if he belongs to the same race, religion, country, or profession as you, or if he has similar ideas to you. *alguien que pertenece a tu misma raza, religión, país, profesión o que comparte tus ideas.* ❑ *He told reporters he'd come to be with his Latvian brothers. Le dijo a los reporteros que había venido a estar con sus hermanos letones.* **3** N-TITLE; N-COUNT; N-VOC **Brother** is a title given to a man who belongs to a religious community such as a monastery. *hermano* ❑ *...Brother Otto. ...hermano Otto.*
→ see **family**

**brother-in-law** (**brothers-in-law**) N-COUNT Someone's **brother-in-law** is the brother of their husband or wife, or the man who is married to their sister. *cuñado*
→ see **family**

**brought** /brɔt/ **Brought** is the past tense and past participle of **bring**. *pasado y participio pasado de* ***bring***

**brown** /braʊn/ (**browner, brownest, browns, browning, browned**) **1** COLOR Something that is **brown** is the color of earth or of wood. *café* ❑ *...her brown eyes. ...sus ojos cafés.* **2** ADJ **Brown** is used to describe grains that have not had their outer layers removed, and foods made from these grains. *integral* ❑ *...brown bread. ...pan integral.* ❑ *...brown rice. ...arroz integral.* **3** V-T/V-I When food **browns** or when you **brown** it, you cook it, usually for a short time on a high flame. *tostar* ❑ *Cook for ten minutes until the sugar browns. Cocine por diez minutos hasta que el azúcar se dore.*
→ see **hair**

**brown-bag** (**brown-bags, brown-bagging, brown-bagged**) **1** V-T If you **brown-bag** your lunch or you **brown-bag it**, you bring your lunch in a bag to work or school. *llevar un lunch al trabajo o a la escuela.* ❑ *Most of the time I brown-bagged my lunch. La mayoría de las veces me llevaba mi lunch.* **2** ADJ A **brown-bag** lunch is a meal that you bring in a bag to work or school. *lunch* ❑ *Members should bring a brown-bag lunch. Los miembros deben traerse su lunch.*

**brownie** /braʊni/ (**brownies**)

| The spelling **Brownie** is used for meaning **2**. |
|---|

**1** N-COUNT **Brownies** are small flat cookies or cakes. They are usually chocolate flavored and have nuts in them. *pastel de chocolate y nueces* ❑ *...chocolate brownies. ...pasteles de chocolate y nueces.* ❑ *...a tray of brownies. ...una charola de pasteles de chocolate y nueces.* **2** N-PROPER-COLL **The Brownies** is a junior version of the Girl Scouts for girls between the ages of six and eight. *niñas guías exploradoras, alitas* • A **Brownie** is a girl who is a member of the Brownies. *niña guía exploradora, alita*
→ see **dessert**

**brown sugar** N-UNCOUNT **Brown sugar** is sugar that has not been refined, or is only partly refined. It is golden brown in color. *azúcar morena*

**brows|er** /braʊzər/ (**browsers**) N-COUNT A **browser** is a piece of computer software that you use to search for information on the Internet, especially on the World Wide Web. *navegador* [COMPUTING] ❑ *You need an up-to-date Web browser. Necesitas un navegador de Web actualizado.*

**bruise** /bruz/ (**bruises, bruising, bruised**) **1** N-COUNT A **bruise** is an injury that appears as a purple mark on your body. *moretón* ❑ *How did you get that bruise on your cheek? ¿Cómo te hiciste ese moretón en la mejilla?* **2** V-T/V-I If you **bruise** a part of your body, a bruise appears on it, for example, because something hits you. If you **bruise** easily, bruises appear when something hits you only slightly. *lastimarse* ❑ *I bruised my knee. Me lastimé la rodilla.* • **bruised** ADJ *amoratado, con moretones* ❑ *I escaped with severely bruised legs. Salí con las piernas llenas de moretones.*

**brush** /brʌʃ/ (**brushes, brushing, brushed**) **1** N-COUNT A **brush** is an object that has a large number of bristles or hairs fixed to it. You use brushes for painting, for cleaning things, and for making your hair neat. *brocha, pincel, cepillo* ❑ *We gave him paint and brushes. Le dimos pintura y brochas/pinceles.* ❑ *...buckets of soapy water and scrubbing brushes. ...cubetas de agua jabonosa y cepillos para tallar.* **2** V-T If you **brush** something or **brush** something such as dirt off it, you clean it or make it neat using a brush. *cepillar* ❑ *Have you brushed your teeth? ¿Te cepillaste los dientes?* ❑ *She brushed the powder out of her hair. Se cepilló el cabello para quitarse el polvo.* • **Brush** is also a noun. *cepillada* ❑ *I gave my hair a quick brush. Me pasé el cepillo por el cabello.* **3** V-T If you **brush** something somewhere, you remove it with quick light movements of your hands. *sacudir, alisar* ❑ *He brushed his hair back with both hands. Se alisó el cabello con ambas manos.* ❑ *He brushed the snow off his suit. Se sacudió la nieve del traje.* **4** V-T/V-I If one thing **brushes against** another or if you **brush** one thing **against** another, the first thing touches the second thing lightly while passing it. *rozar* ❑ *Something brushed against her leg. Algo le rozó la pierna.* ❑ *I felt her dark hair brushing the back of my shoulder. Sentí que su oscuro cabello rozaba mi hombro.*
→ see **teeth**

▸ **brush aside** or **brush away** PHR-VERB If you

**brush aside** or **brush away** an idea, remark, or feeling, you refuse to consider it because you think it is not important or useful, even though it may be. *descartar* ❑ *Perhaps you shouldn't brush the idea aside. Quizá no debieras descartar esa idea.*
▸ **brush up on** PHR-VERB If you **brush up on** something, you practice it or improve your knowledge of it. *repasar* ❑ *I had hoped to brush up on my Spanish. Esperaba repasar mi español.*

**brus|sels sprout** /brʌsəlz spraʊt/ (**brussels sprouts**) also **Brussels sprout** N-COUNT **Brussels sprouts** are vegetables that look like tiny cabbages. *col de Bruselas*

**bru|tal** /brutᵊl/ **1** ADJ A **brutal** act or person is cruel and violent. *brutal* ❑ *...a brutal military dictator. ...un dictador militar brutal* ❑ *...brutal punishment. ...castigo brutal* • **bru|tal|ly** ADV *brutalmente* ❑ *Her parents were brutally murdered. Sus padres fueron brutalmente asesinados.* **2** ADJ If someone expresses something unpleasant with **brutal** honesty or frankness, they express it in a clear and accurate way, without attempting to disguise its unpleasantness. *crudo* ❑ *It was good to talk about our feelings with brutal honesty. Fue crudo, pero bueno, hablar de nuestros sentimientos como lo hicimos.* • **bru|tal|ly** ADV *crudamente* ❑ *The talks have been brutally frank. Han hablado crudamente al respecto.*

**BSE** /bi ɛs i/ N-UNCOUNT **BSE** is a disease that affects the nervous system of cattle and kills them. **BSE** is an abbreviation for "bovine spongiform encephalopathy." *EEB, encefalopatía espongiforme bovina, enfermedad de las vacas locas* ❑ *...meat from cattle infected with BSE, or mad cow disease. ...carne de res infectada con EEB, o enfermedad de las vacas locas.*

**BTW** **BTW** is the written abbreviation for "by the way," often used in e-mail. *PC* ❑ *BTW, the machine is simply amazing. PC, la máquina es realmente sorprendente.*

**bub|ble** /bʌbᵊl/ (**bubbles, bubbling, bubbled**) **1** N-COUNT **Bubbles** are small balls of air or gas in a liquid. *burbuja* ❑ *Air bubbles rise to the surface. Las burbujas de aire suben a la superficie.* **2** N-COUNT A **bubble** is a hollow ball of soapy liquid that is floating in the air or standing on a surface. *burbuja* ❑ *With soap and water, bubbles and boats, children love bathtime. A los niños les encanta la hora del baño con jabón y agua, burbujas y barquitos.* **3** V-I When a liquid **bubbles,** bubbles move in it, for example, because it is boiling or moving quickly. *burbujear, hacer burbujas* ❑ *Heat the soup until it is bubbling. Calienta la sopa hasta que haga burbujas.* ❑ *...the well where oil first bubbled up in Nigeria 43 years ago. ...el pozo en que por primera vez burbujeó el petróleo en Nigeria hace 43 años.*
→ see **soap**

**buck** /bʌk/ (**bucks, bucking, bucked**) **1** N-COUNT A **buck** is a U.S. or Australian dollar. *dólar* [INFORMAL] ❑ *That would probably cost you about fifty bucks. Eso te costaría unos cincuenta dólares* ❑ *Why can't you spend a few bucks on a coat? ¿Por qué no gastas unos dólares en un abrigo?* **2** N-COUNT A **buck** is the male of various animals, including the deer, antelope, rabbit, and kangaroo. *macho* **3** V-I If a horse **bucks,** it kicks both of its back legs wildly into the air, or jumps into the air wildly with all four feet off the ground. *corcovear* ❑ *The stallion bucked and kicked. El semental corcoveó y pateó.* **4** PHRASE If you **pass the buck,** you refuse to accept responsibility for something, and say that someone else is responsible. *pasar la bolita, no aceptar la responsabilidad de algo, hacer responsable a alguien* [INFORMAL] ❑ *They are trying to pass the buck and blame teachers. Están tratando de pasar la bolita a los maestros y hacerlos responsables.*

**buck|et** /bʌkɪt/ (**buckets**) N-COUNT A **bucket** is a round metal or plastic container with a handle attached to its sides. Buckets are often used for holding and carrying water. *cubeta, cubo* ❑ *...a blue bucket. ...una cubeta azul.* ❑ *...a bucket of water. ...una cubeta de agua.*

**buck|le** /bʌkᵊl/ (**buckles, buckling, buckled**) **1** N-COUNT A **buckle** is a piece of metal or plastic attached to one end of a belt or strap, which is used to fasten it. *hebilla* ❑ *He wore a belt with a large silver buckle. Usaba un cinturón con una gran hebilla de plata.* **2** V-T When you **buckle** a belt or strap, you fasten it. *abrochar, abrocharse* ❑ *A door slammed and a man came out buckling his belt. Se azotó una puerta y salió un hombre abrochándose el cinturón.* **3** V-T/V-I If an object **buckles** or if something **buckles** it, it becomes bent as a result of very great heat or force. *torcerse* ❑ *The door was beginning to buckle from the extreme heat. La puerta empezaba a torcerse por el intenso calor.* **4** V-I If your legs or knees **buckle,** they bend because they have become very weak or tired. *doblarse las piernas o las rodillas* ❑ *His knees buckled and he fell to the floor. Se le doblaron las rodillas y cayó al piso.*
→ see **button, crash**
▸ **buckle up** PHR-VERB When you **buckle up** in a car or airplane, you fasten your seat belt. *ponerse el cinturón, abrocharse el cinturón* [INFORMAL] ❑ *A sign ahead of me said, "Buckle Up. It's the Law in Illinois." Delante de mí había un letrero: "Abróchese el cinturón, es la Ley en Illinois".*

**bud** /bʌd/ (**buds**) **1** N-COUNT A **bud** is a small pointed lump that appears on a tree or plant and develops into a leaf or flower. *capullo* ❑ *Rosanna's favorite time is early summer, just before the buds open. La época favorita de Rosanna es el principio del verano, antes de que revienten los brotes.* **2** N-VOC Some men use **bud** as a way of addressing other men. *amigo* [INFORMAL] ❑ *You heard what the boss said, bud. Ya oíste lo que dijo el jefe, amigo.* **3** PHRASE If you **nip** something such as bad behavior **in the bud,** you stop it before it can develop very far. *cortar por lo sano* [INFORMAL] ❑ *It is important to recognize jealousy and to nip it in the bud. Es importante detectar los celos y cortarlos por lo sano.*
→ see **flower**

**Bud|dhism** N-UNCOUNT **Buddhism** is a religion which teaches that the way to end suffering is by overcoming your desires. *budismo*

**Bud|dhist** /budɪst, bud-/ (**Buddhists**) **1** N-COUNT A **Buddhist** is a person whose religion is Buddhism. *budista* **2** ADJ **Buddhist** means relating or referring to Buddhism. *budista* ❑ *...Buddhist monks. ...monjes budistas*

**bud|dy** /bʌdi/ (**buddies**) **1** N-COUNT A **buddy** is a close friend, usually a male friend of a man. *cuate* ❑ *We became great buddies. Nos hicimos grandes cuates.* **2** N-VOC Men sometimes address other

B

men as **buddy.** cuate [INFORMAL] ❑ *Hey, buddy, do me a favor.* *Oye, cuate, hazme un favor.* 3 PHRASE If one person is **buddy buddy with** another, they are very close friends. muy cuate [INFORMAL]

**budg|et** /bʌdʒɪt/ (**budgets, budgeting, budgeted**) 1 N-COUNT Your **budget** is the amount of money that you have available to spend. The **budget** for something is the amount of money that a person, organization, or country has available to spend on it. presupuesto [BUSINESS] ❑ *She will design a fantastic new kitchen for you—and all within your budget.* *Va a diseñar una fantástica cocina para ti, y dentro de tu presupuesto.* ❑ *Our low budget means we have to be careful with our money.* *Como tenemos un presupuesto bajo, tenemos que ser cuidadosos con nuestro dinero.* 2 V-T/V-I If you **budget** certain amounts of money for particular things, you decide that you can afford to spend those amounts on those things. presupuestar ❑ *The company has budgeted $10 million for advertising.* *La empresa presupuestó 10 millones de dólares para publicidad.* ❑ *The movie is only budgeted at $10 million.* *Se presupuestaron sólo 10 millones de dólares para la película.* ❑ *I'm learning how to budget.* *Estoy aprendiendo a presupuestar.* • **budg|et|ing** N-UNCOUNT hacer presupuestos, presupuesto ❑ *...our budgeting for the current year...* *nuestro presupuesto para el presente año.* 3 ADJ **Budget** is used in advertising to suggest that something is being sold cheaply. para presupuestos reducidos ❑ *Cheap flights are available from budget travel agents.* *Los agentes de viajes para presupuestos reducidos venden vuelos baratos.*

**Word Partnership** Usar *budget* con:

| | |
|---|---|
| V. | **balance a** budget 1 |
| N. | budget **crisis**, budget **crunch**, budget **cuts**, budget **deficit** 1 |
| ADJ. | **federal** budget, **tight** budget 1 |
| PREP. | **over** budget, **under** budget 1 |

**buf|fa|lo** /bʌfəloʊ/ (**buffalo**)

The plural can be either **buffaloes** or **buffalo.**

buffalo

N-COUNT A **buffalo** is a wild animal like a large cow with horns that curve upward. búfalo
→ see **grassland**

**buf|fet** (**buffets, buffeting, buffeted**)

Pronounced /bʊfeɪ/ for meaning 1 and /bʌfɪt/ for meaning 2.

1 N-COUNT A **buffet** is a meal of food that is displayed on a long table at a party or public occasion. Guests usually serve themselves. buffet ❑ *...a buffet lunch.* *...un almuerzo buffet.* 2 V-T If something **is buffeted** by strong winds or by stormy seas, it is repeatedly struck or blown around by them. sacudir, zarandear ❑ *Their plane was severely buffeted by storms.* *Las tormentas sacudieron fuertemente el avión en que venían.*

**bug** /bʌg/ (**bugs, bugging, bugged**) 1 N-COUNT A **bug** is an insect or similar small creature. bicho [INFORMAL] ❑ *We noticed tiny bugs that were all over the walls.* *Vimos que había bichitos por todas las paredes.* 2 N-COUNT A **bug** is an illness which is caused by small organisms such as bacteria. infección [INFORMAL] ❑ *I think I've got a stomach bug.* *Creo que tengo una infección estomacal.* 3 N-COUNT If there is a **bug** in a computer program, there is a mistake in it. falla, error [COMPUTING] ❑ *There is a bug in the software.* *El programa tiene un error/tiene una falla.* 4 V-T If someone **bugs** a place, they hide tiny microphones in it that transmit what people are saying. ocultar micrófonos ❑ *He heard that they were planning to bug his office.* *Supo que pensaban ocultar micrófonos en su oficina.* 5 V-T If someone or something **bugs** you, they worry or annoy you. fastidiar [INFORMAL] ❑ *I only did it to bug my parents.* *Nada más lo hice para fastidiar a mis padres.*

**Thesaurus** *bug* Ver también:

| | |
|---|---|
| N. | disease, germ, infection, microorganism, virus 2 |
| | breakdown, defect, error, glitch, hitch, malfunction 3 |

**build** /bɪld/ (**builds, building, built**) 1 V-T If you **build** something, you make it by joining things together. construir ❑ *They are going to build a hotel on the site.* *Van a construir un hotel en el terreno.* ❑ *The house was built in the early 19th century.* *La casa fue construida a principios del siglo XIX.* • **build|ing** N-UNCOUNT construcción ❑ *In Japan, the building of Kansai airport continues.* *Sigue la construcción del aeropuerto Kansai en Japón.* • **built** ADJ construido ❑ *Even newly built houses can need repairs.* *Incluso las casas recién construidas necesitan reparaciones.* ❑ *It's a product that has been built for safety.* *Es un producto que se construyó por seguridad.* 2 V-T If you **build** something **into** a wall or object, you make it in such a way that it is in the wall or object, or is part of it. empotrar ❑ *The TV was built into the wall.* *La TV estaba empotrada en el muro.* 3 V-T If people **build** an organization, a society, or a relationship, they gradually form it. crear, formar ❑ *He and a partner built a successful fashion company.* *Él y un socio crearon una exitosa empresa de modas.* ❑ *Their purpose is to build a fair society and a strong economy.* *Su objetivo es crear una sociedad justa y una economía fuerte.* • **build|ing** N-UNCOUNT construcción, creación ❑ *...the building of the great civilizations of the ancient world.* *...la construcción de las grandes civilizaciones del mundo antiguo.* 4 V-T If you **build** an organization, system, or product **on** something, you base it on it. basarse en ❑ *Science involves building theories from logical processes.* *La ciencia implica establecer teorías a partir de procesos lógicos.* 5 V-T If you **build** something **into** a policy, system, or product, you make it part of it. incorporar ❑ *We have to build computers into the school curriculum.* *Tenemos que incorporar las computadoras al currículum escolar.* 6 N-VAR Someone's **build** is the shape that their bones and muscles give to their body. complexión ❑ *He's described as six feet tall and of medium build.* *Lo describen como de 1.80 de estatura y complexión media.* 7 → see also **building, built**
→ see **muscle**

▸ **build up** 1 PHR-VERB If you **build up** something or if it **builds up,** it gradually becomes bigger, for example, because more is added to it. hacer crecer ❑ *I worked really hard building up the business.* *Realmente trabajé mucho para hacer crecer el negocio.* ❑ *The collection has been built up over the last seventeen* years. La colección ha crecido mucho en los últimos diecisiete años. 2 PHR-VERB If you **build** someone **up,** you help them to feel stronger or more confident, especially when they have had a bad experience or have been ill. fortalecer a, darle fuerzas a ❑ Build her up with kindness. Dale fuerzas con tus atenciones. 3 → see also **build-up, built-up**

**Thesaurus** *build* Ver también:

V. assemble, make, manufacture, produce, put together, set up; (*ant.*) demolish, destroy, knock down 1

**Word Partnership** Usar *build* con:

N. build **bridges**, build **roads**, build **schools** 1
V. **plan to** build 1
ADJ. **athletic** build, **slender** build, **strong** build 6

**build|er** /bɪldər/ (**builders**) N-COUNT A **builder** is a person whose job is to build or repair houses and other buildings. albañil ❑ The builders have finished the roof. Los albañiles terminaron el techo.

**build|ing** /bɪldɪŋ/ (**buildings**) N-COUNT A **building** is a structure that has a roof and walls. edificio ❑ They were on the upper floor of the building. Estaban en el piso más alto del edificio. → see **architecture**

**build-up** (**build-ups**) also **buildup** or **build up** 1 N-COUNT A **build-up** is a gradual increase in something. acumulación ❑ There will be a slight build-up of cloud later on this afternoon. La acumulación de nubes será ligeramente mayor por la tarde. 2 N-COUNT The **build-up** to an event is the way that journalists, advertisers, or other people talk about it a lot in the period of time immediately before it, and try to make it seem important and exciting. preparativos ❑ ...the excitement of the build-up to Christmas. ...la emoción de los preparativos de Navidad.

**built** /bɪlt/ 1 **Built** is the past tense and past participle of **build**. pasado y participio pasado de *build* 2 ADJ If you say that someone is **built** in a particular way, you are describing the kind of body they have. que tiene cierta complexión ❑ ...a strong, powerfully-built man of 60. ...un hombre de 60 años, fuerte y de complexión robusta.

**built-up** ADJ A **built-up** area is an area such as a town or city which has a lot of buildings in it. urbanizado ❑ A speed limit of 30 mph was introduced in built-up areas. En las áreas urbanizadas se impuso un límite de velocidad de 50 kph.

**bulb** /bʌlb/ (**bulbs**) 1 N-COUNT A **bulb** is the glass part of an electric light or lamp, which gives out light when electricity passes through it. foco ❑ The room was lit by a single bulb. En la habitación no había más que un foco. 2 N-COUNT A **bulb** is a root shaped like an onion that grows into a flower or plant. bulbo ❑ ...tulip bulbs. ...bulbos de tulipán. → see **flower**

**bulk** /bʌlk/ (**bulks, bulking, bulked**) 1 N-SING You can refer to the **bulk** of a person or thing when you want to emphasize that they are very large and heavy. tamaño, masa [WRITTEN] ❑ Despite its bulk, it's a beautiful bike. A pesar de su tamaño, es una hermosa bicicleta. ❑ Bannol lowered his bulk carefully into the chair. Bannol posó su masa en la silla con mucho cuidado. 2 QUANT The **bulk of** something is most of it. masa, mayor parte, el grueso de algo ❑ The bulk of the money will go to the children's hospital in Dublin. La mayor parte del dinero irá al hospital infantil de Dublín. ● **Bulk** is also a pronoun. mayor parte ❑ They come from all over the world, but the bulk is from India. Vienen de todo el mundo, pero la mayor parte es de la India. 3 PHRASE If you buy or sell something **in bulk,** you buy or sell it in large quantities. al mayoreo, al por mayor ❑ It is cheaper to buy supplies in bulk. Es más barato comprar las provisiones al mayoreo.

**bull** /bʊl/ (**bulls**) 1 N-COUNT A **bull** is a male animal of the cow family. toro 2 N-COUNT Some other male animals, including elephants and whales, are called **bulls.** macho ❑ ...a bull elephant with huge tusks. ...un elefante macho con enormes colmillos.

**bull|doze** /bʊldoʊz/ (**bulldozes, bulldozing, bulldozed**) V-T If people **bulldoze** something such as a building, they knock it down using a bulldozer. demoler ❑ They wanted to bulldoze her home to build a supermarket. Querían demoler su casa para construir un supermercado.

**bul|let** /bʊlɪt/ (**bullets**) N-COUNT A **bullet** is a small piece of metal which is fired out of a gun. bala ❑ Two of the police fired 16 bullets each. Dos de los policías dispararon 16 balas cada uno.

**bul|letin** /bʊlɪtɪn/ (**bulletins**) 1 N-COUNT A **bulletin** is a short news report on the radio or television. boletín ❑ ...the early morning news bulletin. ...el boletín noticioso de primeras horas de la mañana. 2 N-COUNT A **bulletin** is a regular newspaper or leaflet that is produced by an organization or group such as a school or church. boletín

**bul|letin board** (**bulletin boards**) 1 N-COUNT A **bulletin board** is a board which is usually attached to a wall in order to display notices giving information about something. tablero de anuncios 2 N-COUNT In computing, a **bulletin board** is a system that allows users to send and receive messages of general interest. tablero de anuncios ❑ The Internet is the largest computer bulletin board in the world, and it's growing. La Internet es el tablero de anuncios más grande del mundo, y sigue creciendo.

**bul|let point** (**bullet points**) N-COUNT A **bullet point** is one of a series of important items for discussion or action in a document, usually marked by a square or round symbol. inciso ❑ Use bold type for headings and bullet points for lists. Utilice negritas para los encabezados e incisos para las listas.

**bullet|proof** /bʊlɪtpruf/ also **bullet-proof** ADJ Something that is **bulletproof** is made of a strong material that bullets cannot pass through. a prueba de balas ❑ ...bulletproof glass. ...vidrio a prueba de balas. → see **glass**

**bull|horn** /bʊlhɔrn/ (**bullhorns**) N-COUNT A **bullhorn** is a device for making your voice sound louder in the open air. altavoz

**bull|pen** /bʊlpɛn/ (**bullpens**) N-COUNT In baseball, a **bullpen** is an area alongside the playing field, where pitchers can practice or warm up. bullpen ❑ Players from both bullpens ran onto the field.

B

*Los jugadores de ambos bullpens saltaron al campo.*

**bull ses|sion** (**bull sessions**) N-COUNT A **bull session** is an informal conversation among a small group of people. *charla* [INFORMAL] ❑ *The production actually started as an after-work bull session at a restaurant. En realidad, la producción se inició con una charla en un restaurante, después del trabajo.*

**bul|ly** /bʊli/ (**bullies, bullying, bullied**) 1 N-COUNT A **bully** is someone who uses their strength or power to hurt or frighten other people. *bravucón o bravucona, acosador o acosadora* ❑ *He was the office bully. Él era el bravucón de la oficina.* 2 V-T If someone **bullies** you, they use their strength or power to hurt or frighten you. *acosar* ❑ *I wasn't going to let him bully me. No lo iba a dejar que me acosara.* ● **bul|ly|ing** N-UNCOUNT *acoso* ❑ *...schoolchildren who were victims of bullying. ...niños en edad escolar que fueron víctimas de acoso.* 3 V-T If someone **bullies** you **into** something, they make you do it by using force or threats. *obligar a alguien a hacer algo* ❑ *Mary bullies me into a stroll every day. Mary me obliga a llevarla a pasear todos los días.* ❑ *She used to bully me into doing my schoolwork. Me obligaba a hacer la tarea.*

**bumble|bee** /bʌmbəlbi/ (**bumblebees**) also **bumble bee** N-COUNT A **bumblebee** is a large hairy bee. *abejorro*
→ see **insect**

**bump** /bʌmp/ (**bumps, bumping, bumped**) 1 V-T/V-I If you **bump** into something or someone, you accidentally hit them while you are moving. *chocar, golpear con* ❑ *They stopped walking and he almost bumped into them. Dejaron de caminar y él casi choca contra ellos.* ❑ *She bumped her head against a low branch. Se golpeó la cabeza con una rama baja.* ● **Bump** is also a noun. *golpe* ❑ *Small children often cry after a minor bump. Los niños pequeños suelen llorar por cualquier golpecito.* 2 N-COUNT A **bump** is a minor injury or swelling that you get if you bump into something or if something hits you. *chichón, chipote* ❑ *She fell against our coffee table and got a large bump on her forehead. Chocó contra la mesita de café y se hizo un gran chichón en la frente.* 3 V-I If a vehicle **bumps over** a surface, it travels in a rough, bouncing way because the surface is very uneven. *dar tumbos* ❑ *We left the road, and again bumped over the mountainside. Nos salimos del camino y dábamos tumbos de nuevo por la ladera de la montaña.*
▸ **bump into** PHR-VERB If you **bump into** someone you know, you meet them unexpectedly. *toparse con alguien* [INFORMAL] ❑ *I happened to bump into Mervyn Johns in the hallway. Resulta que me topé con Mervyn Johns en el corredor.*

**bump|er** /bʌmpər/ (**bumpers**) 1 N-COUNT **Bumpers** are bars at the front and back of a vehicle that protect it if it bumps into something. *defensa* ❑ *What stickers do you have on the bumper? ¿Qué etiquetas tienes en la defensa?* 2 ADJ A **bumper** crop or harvest is one that is larger than usual. *récord* ❑ *...a bumper crop of rice. ...una cosecha récord de arroz.*

**bumpy** /bʌmpi/ (**bumpier, bumpiest**) 1 ADJ A **bumpy** road or path has a lot of bumps on it. *lleno de baches* ❑ *...bumpy streets. ...calles llenas de baches.* 2 ADJ A **bumpy** ride is uncomfortable and rough, usually because you are traveling over an uneven surface. *incómodo* ❑ *...a hot and bumpy ride across the desert. ...un viaje caliente e incómodo por el desierto.*

**bun** /bʌn/ (**buns**) 1 N-COUNT **Buns** are small bread rolls. *bollo* ❑ *...a cinnamon bun. ...un bollo de canela.* 2 N-COUNT If a woman has her hair in a **bun**, she has fastened it tightly on top of her head or at the back of her head in the shape of a ball. *chongo*
→ see **bread**

**bunch** /bʌntʃ/ (**bunches, bunching, bunched**) 1 N-COUNT A **bunch of** people is a group of people who share one or more characteristics or who are doing something together. *montón de* [INFORMAL] ❑ *We were a pretty inexperienced bunch of people really. En realidad éramos un montón de gente más bien inexperta.* ❑ *Before she graduated, she and a bunch of friends started the Actors Company. Antes de graduarse, ella y un montón de amigos iniciaron la Actors Company.* 2 N-COUNT A **bunch of** flowers is a number of flowers with their stalks held or tied together. *ramo* ❑ *He left a huge bunch of flowers in her hotel room. Dejó un gran ramo de flores en su habitación del hotel.* 3 N-COUNT A **bunch of** bananas or grapes is a group of them growing on the same stem. *racimo* 4 QUANT A **bunch of** things is a number of things, especially a large number. *bonche de* [INFORMAL] ❑ *We recorded a bunch of songs together. Grabamos un bonche de canciones juntos.* ● **Bunch** is also a pronoun. *bonche*
▸ **bunch up** or **bunch together** PHR-VERB If people or things **bunch up** or if you **bunch** them **up**, they move close to each other so that they form a small tight group. **Bunch together** means the same as **bunch up**. *amontonar(se)* ❑ *They were bunching up, almost stepping on each other's heels. Se estaban amontonando, casi se pisaban los talones.* ❑ *People were bunched up at all the exits. La gente estaba amontonada en todas las salidas.*

**bun|dle** /bʌndəl/ (**bundles, bundling, bundled**) 1 N-COUNT A **bundle of** things is a number of them that are tied together or wrapped in a cloth or bag so that they can be carried or stored. *paquete* ❑ *...a bundle of papers. ...un paquete de papeles* ❑ *...bundles of clothing. ...paquetes de ropa.* 2 N-SING If you describe someone as, for example, a **bundle of** fun, you are emphasizing that they are full of fun. If you describe someone as a **bundle of** nerves, you are emphasizing that they are very nervous. *abundancia de* ❑ *I remember Mickey as a bundle of fun, great to be with. Recuerdo que Mickey era muy alegre, me encantaba estar con él.* ❑ *Life at high school wasn't a bundle of laughs. La vida en la secundaria no fue precisamente de risas.* 3 V-T If someone **is bundled** somewhere, someone pushes them there in a rough and hurried way. *echar a alguien hacia algún lado, aventar* ❑ *He was bundled into a car. Lo echaron/lo aventaron dentro de un auto.*

**bun|ga|low** /bʌŋgəloʊ/ (**bungalows**) N-COUNT A **bungalow** is a very small house that usually has only one level and no stairs. *casa de una planta*

**bun|ker** /bʌŋkər/ (**bunkers**) 1 N-COUNT A **bunker** is a place, usually underground, that has been built with strong walls to protect it against heavy gunfire and bombing. *búnker* ❑ *...an extensive network of underground bunkers. ...una extensa red de búnkers subterráneos.* 2 N-COUNT A **bunker** is a container for coal or other fuel. *depósito para combustibles* 3 N-COUNT On a golf course, a **bunker** is a large area filled with sand that is deliberately put there as an obstacle that golfers must try to avoid. *búnker, trampa de arena*

**bunt** /bʌnt/ (**bunts, bunting, bunted**) **1** V-T/V-I In baseball, if you **bunt** or if you **bunt** the ball, you deliberately hit the ball softly, in order to gain an advantage. *tocar, tocar la bola* ❑ *With runners on first and second, he tried to bunt. Con corredores en primera y segunda, trató de tocar.* ❑ *Richard Becker bunted a ball on the third-base side. Richard Becker tocó la bola hacia el lado de la tercera base.* **2** N-COUNT In baseball, a **bunt** is the act of bunting a ball or a hit made by bunting the ball. *toque de bola* ❑ *Then came a bunt from Russ Davis. Luego vino un toque de bola de Russ Davis.*

**buoy** /bui/ (**buoys, buoying, buoyed**) **1** N-COUNT A **buoy** is a floating object that is used to show ships and boats where they can go and to warn them of danger. *boya* **2** PHR-VERB If someone in a difficult situation **is buoyed up** by something, it makes them feel more cheerful and optimistic. *mantenerse a flote* ❑ *They are buoyed up by a sense of hope. Su esperanza los mantiene a flote.*

**buoy|ant force** (**buoyant forces**) N-COUNT The **buoyant force** of an object immersed in a fluid is the physical force that causes the object to float or to rise upward. *fuerza de flotación* [TECHNICAL]

**'burbs** /bɜrbz/ also **burbs** N-PLURAL The **'burbs** are the same as the **suburbs**. *suburbios* [INFORMAL] ❑ *...a quiet kid from the √burbs. ...un niño tranquilo de los suburbios*

**bur|den** /bɜrdᵊn/ (**burdens, burdening, burdened**) **1** N-COUNT If you describe a problem or a responsibility as a **burden**, you mean that it causes someone a lot of difficulty, worry, or hard work. *carga* ❑ *...the families who bear the burden of looking after aging relatives. ...las familias que llevan la carga de cuidar a sus parientes ancianos.* ❑ *Her death will be an impossible burden on Paul. Su muerte será una carga tremenda para Paul.* **2** N-COUNT A **burden** is a heavy load that is difficult to carry. *carga* [FORMAL] ❑ *...African women carrying burdens on their heads. ...mujeres africanas llevando la carga en la cabeza.* **3** V-T If someone **burdens** you **with** something that is likely to worry you, for example, a problem or a difficult decision, they tell you about it. *preocupar, agobiar* ❑ *We decided not to burden him with the news. Decidimos no agobiarlo con la noticia.*

**bu|reau** /byʊəroʊ/ (**bureaus**) **1** N-COUNT A **bureau** is an office, organization, or government department that collects and distributes information. *instituto, centro* ❑ *...the Federal Bureau of Investigation. ...la Oficina Federal de Investigación.* **2** N-COUNT A **bureau** is an office of a company or organization that has its main office in another city or country. *oficina* [BUSINESS] ❑ *...the Wall Street Journal's Washington bureau. Oficina en Washington del diario The Wall Street Journal.* **3** N-COUNT A **bureau** is a low piece of furniture with drawers in which you keep clothes or other things. *cómoda*

**bu|reau|cra|cy** /byʊrɒkrəsi/ (**bureaucracies**) **1** N-COUNT A **bureaucracy** is an administrative system operated by a large number of officials. *burocracia* ❑ *He blames the big bureaucracies for his troubles. Culpa a las grandes burocracias por sus problemas.* **2** N-UNCOUNT **Bureaucracy** refers to all the rules and procedures followed by government departments and similar organizations, especially when you think that these are complicated and cause long delays. *burocracia* ❑ *People usually complain about too much bureaucracy. La gente suele quejarse por las complicaciones de la burocracia.*

**bu|reau|crat** /byʊərəkræt/ (**bureaucrats**) N-COUNT **Bureaucrats** are officials who work in a large administrative system, especially ones who seem to follow rules and procedures too strictly. *burócrata* ❑ *The economy is still controlled by bureaucrats. La economía aún está bajo el control de los burócratas.*

**bu|reau|crat|ic** /byʊərəkrætɪk/ ADJ **Bureaucratic** means involving complicated rules and procedures which can cause long delays; used to show disapproval. *burocrático* ❑ *...bureaucratic delays. ...demoras burocráticas.*

**burg|er** /bɜrgər/ (**burgers**) N-COUNT A **burger** is a flat round mass of ground meat or minced vegetables that is fried and often eaten in a bread roll. *hamburguesa* ❑ *...a burger and fries. ...hamburguesa con papas a la francesa.*

**bur|glar** /bɜrglər/ (**burglars**) N-COUNT A **burglar** is a thief who enters a house or other building by force. *ladrón o ladrona de casas* ❑ *...the ability of the police to catch burglars. La capacidad policiaca para atrapar rateros.*

**bur|glar|ize** /bɜrgləraɪz/ (**burglarizes, burglarizing, burglarized**) V-T If a building **is burglarized**, a thief enters it by force and steals things. *robar* ❑ *Her home was burglarized. Su hogar fue robado.*

**bur|gla|ry** /bɜrgləri/ (**burglaries**) N-VAR If someone commits a **burglary**, they enter a building by force and steal things. **Burglary** is the act of doing this. *robo* ❑ *An 11-year-old boy committed a burglary. Un niño de 11 años de edad cometió un robo.*
→ see **crime**

**burka** /bɜrkə/ (**burkas**) → see **burqa**

**burn** /bɜrn/ (**burns, burning, burned** or **burnt**) **1** V-I If there is a fire or a flame somewhere, you say that there is a fire or flame **burning** there. *arder* ❑ *Fires were burning out of control in the center of the city. Los incendios estaban fuera de control en el centro de la ciudad.* ❑ *There was a fire burning in the fireplace. Ardía un fuego en la chimenea.* **2** V-I If something **is burning**, it is on fire. *estar en llamas* ❑ *When I arrived, one of the vehicles was still burning. Cuando llegué, uno de los vehículos aún estaba en llamas.* ❑ *The building burned for hours. El edificio ardió durante horas.* ● **burn|ing** N-UNCOUNT *quemazón, quemado* ❑ *When we arrived in our village, there was a terrible smell of burning. Cuando llegamos a nuestro pueblo, se percibía un terrible olor a quemado.* **3** V-T If you **burn** something, you destroy or damage it with fire. *quemar* ❑ *Protesters burned a building. Los manifestantes prendieron fuego a un edificio.* ❑ *They use the equipment to burn household waste. Usaron el equipo para quemar desperdicios.* ● **burn|ing** N-UNCOUNT *quema* ❑ *...the burning of a U.S. flag outside the American embassy. La quema de una bandera de Estados Unidos afuera de la embajada de ese país.* **4** V-T If you **burn** part of your body, **burn yourself**, or **are burned** or **burnt**, you are injured by fire or by something very hot. *quemar* ❑ *Take care not to burn your fingers. Ten cuidado de no quemarte los dedos.* ● **Burn** is also

**B**

a noun. _quemadura_ ❑ *She suffered burns to her back.* _Recibió quemaduras en la espalda._ 5 V-T If a substance **burns,** it produces flames or smoke when heated. _arder_ [TECHNICAL] 6 V-T To **burn** a CD means to write or copy data onto it. _quemar_ [COMPUTING] ❑ *I have the equipment to burn audio CDs.* _Tengo el equipo para quemar CDs de audio._ 7 → see also **burning**
→ see **fire**

▸ **burn down** PHR-VERB If a building **burns down** or if someone **burns** it **down,** it is completely destroyed by fire. _quedar reducido a cenizas_ ❑ *Six months after Bud died, the house burned down.* _Seis meses después de la muerte de Bud, la casa quedó reducida a cenizas._
→ see **fire**

**Thesaurus** *burn* Ver también:
V. ignite, incinerate, kindle, scorch, singe; (*ant.*) extinguish, put out 1 – 4

**Word Partnership** Usar *burn* con:
N. **fires** burn 1
burn **victim** 4
burn **a CD** 6
V. **watch** ***something*** burn 1 2
ADJ. **first/second/third degree** burn 4

**burn|er** /bɜrnər/ (**burners**) N-COUNT A **burner** is a device which produces heat or a flame, especially as part of a stove or heater. _quemador_ ❑ *He put the frying pan on the gas burner.* _Puso el sartén en el quemador de la estufa._
→ see **laboratory**

**burn|ing** /bɜrnɪŋ/ ADJ You use **burning** to describe something that is extremely hot. _ardiente_ ❑ *...the burning desert of central Asia.* _El ardiente desierto de Asia central._ ● **Burning** is also an adverb. _ardiendo_ ❑ *He touched the boy's forehead. It was burning hot.* _Tocó la frente del chico. Estaba ardiendo._

**burnt** /bɜrnt/ **Burnt** is a past tense and past participle of **burn**. _pasado y participio pasado de **burn**_

**burqa** /bɜrkə/ (**burqas**) also **burka** N-COUNT A **burqa** is a long garment that covers the head and body and is traditionally worn by some women in Islamic countries. _túnica_

**bur|ri|to** /bər͟itoʊ/ (**burritos**) N-COUNT A **burrito** is a tortilla containing a filling of ground beef, chicken, cheese, or beans. _taco_

**burst** /bɜrst/ (**bursts, bursting**)

The form **burst** is used in the present tense and is the past tense and past participle.

1 V-T/V-I If something **bursts** or if you **burst** it, it suddenly breaks open or splits open and the air or other substance inside it comes out. _explotar, reventar(se)_ ❑ *The driver lost control when a tire burst.* _El conductor perdió el control cuando se reventó una llanta._ ❑ *It is not a good idea to burst a blister.* _No es buena idea pinchar una ampolla._ 2 V-I To **burst into** or **out** of a place means to enter or leave it suddenly with a lot of energy or force. _irrumpir en, salir de_ ❑ *Gunmen burst into his home.* _Hombres armados irrumpieron en su casa._ 3 N-COUNT A **burst of** something is a sudden short period of it. _arranque, estallido_ ❑ *...a burst of energy.* _...un estallido de energía._
→ see **crash**

burst

▸ **burst into** 1 PHR-VERB If you **burst into** tears, laughter, or song, you suddenly begin to cry, laugh, or sing. _echarse a_ ❑ *She burst into tears and ran from the kitchen.* _Se echó a llorar y salió corriendo de la cocina._ 2 to **burst into flames** → see **flame**

▸ **burst out** PHR-VERB If someone **bursts out** laughing, crying, or making another noise, they suddenly start making that noise. _estallar_ ❑ *The class burst out laughing.* _La clase estalló en risas._
→ see **cry, laugh**

**Thesaurus** *burst* Ver también:
V. blow, explode, pop, rupture 1

**Word Partnership** Usar *burst* con:
N. burst **appendix, bubble** burst, **pipe** burst 1
burst **of air**, burst **of energy**, burst **of laughter** 3
ADJ. **ready to** burst 1
**sudden** burst 3

**bury** /bɛri/ (**buries, burying, buried**) 1 V-T To **bury** something means to put it into a hole in the ground and cover it up. _enterrar_ ❑ *They make the charcoal by burying wood in the ground and then slowly burning it.* _Para hacer el carbón entierran madera en el suelo y después la queman a fuego lento._ ❑ *Squirrels bury nuts and seeds.* _Las ardillas entierran nueces y semillas._ 2 V-T To **bury** a dead person means to put their body into a grave and cover it with earth. _enterrar_ ❑ *Soldiers helped to bury the dead.* _Los soldados ayudaron a enterrar a los muertos._ ❑ *People might think I was dead, and bury me alive.* _Podrían creerme muerto, y enterrarme vivo._ 3 V-T If something **buries** a place or person, it falls on top of them so that it completely covers them and often harms them in some way. _cubrir_ ❑ *Latest reports say that mud slides buried entire villages.* _Los informes más recientes indican que los deslaves de lodo cubrieron poblados enteros._ ❑ *The village was buried under seven feet of snow.* _El pueblo quedó cubierto debajo de más de dos metros de nieve._

**bus** /bʌs/ (**buses, busing, bused**)

The spellings **busses**, **bussing**, **bussed** are also used for the verb.

1 N-COUNT A **bus** is a large motor vehicle that carries passengers. _autobús_ ❑ *He missed his last bus home.* _Perdió el último autobús a su casa._ 2 V-T To **bus** tables means to clear away dirty dishes and reset the tables in a restaurant. _limpiar_ ❑ *I used to bus tables, and then I became a waitress.* _Antes limpiaba mesas, y luego me volví mesera._
→ see **transportation**

**bus boy** (**bus boys**) N-COUNT A **bus boy** is someone whose job is to set or clear tables in a restaurant. _garrotero_ o _garrotera, ayudante_ o _ayudanta de mesero_

**bush** /bʊʃ/ (**bushes**) 1 N-COUNT A **bush** is a large plant which is smaller than a tree and

has a lot of branches. arbusto ❑ *Trees and bushes grew down to the water's edge.* *Los árboles y arbustos crecían en las riberas de los arroyos.* **2** N-SING The wild, uncultivated parts of some hot countries are referred to as **the bush.** *monte, área silvestre* ❑ *They walked through the thick Mozambican bush for thirty-six hours.* *Caminaron por la densa área silvestre de Mozambique durante treinta y seis horas.*
→ see **plant**

**busi|ness** /bɪznɪs/ (**businesses**) **1** N-UNCOUNT **Business** is work relating to the production, buying, and selling of goods or services. *negocio* ❑ *...a career in business.* *...una carrera en los negocios.* ❑ *Jennifer has an impressive academic and business background.* *Los antecedentes académicos y administrativos de Jennifer son impresionantes.* ❑ *...Harvard Business School.* *...la Harvard Business School.* **2** N-UNCOUNT **Business** is used when talking about how many products or services a company is able to sell. If **business** is good, a lot of products or services are being sold and if **business** is bad, few of them are being sold. *ventas* ❑ *They worried that German companies would lose business.* *Les preocupaba que las empresas alemanas perdieran ventas.* **3** N-COUNT A **business** is an organization that produces and sells goods or that provides a service. *empresa, organización* ❑ *...a family business.* *...empresas familiar.* ❑ *...small businesses.* *...pequeñas empresas.* **4** N-UNCOUNT If you say that something is your **business,** you mean that it concerns you personally and that other people have no right to ask questions about it or disagree with it. *asunto* ❑ *If she doesn't want the police involved, that's her business.* *Si no quiere avisar a la policía, es asunto de ella.* **5** N-SING You can use **business** to refer in a general way to an event, situation, or activity. *situación* ❑ *I hope this unpleasant business will soon be over.* *Espero que esta desagradable situación termine pronto.* **6** → see also **big business, show business**
**7** PHRASE If you say that someone **has no business to** be in a place or **to** do something, you mean that they have no right to be there or to do it. *no tener nada que ver* ❑ *Really I had no business to be there at all.* *En verdad no tenía nada que ver con eso.*
→ see **city**

**Thesaurus** *business* Ver también:

N. company, corporation, firm, organization **3**

**Word Partnership** Usar *business* con:

N. **close of** business, business **opportunity,** business **school** **1**
business **administration,** business **decision,** business **expenses,** business **hours,** business **owner,** business **partner,** business **practices** **1**–**3**
ADJ. **family** business, **online** business, **small** business **1** **3**
**your own** business **1** **4**
V. **go out of** business **2**
**run a** business **3**

**business|man** /bɪznɪsmæn/ (**businessmen**) N-COUNT A **businessman** is a man who works in business. *hombre de negocios* ❑ *...a wealthy businessman who owns a printing business in Orlando.* *...un próspero hombre de negocios dueño de una imprenta en Orlando.*

**business|woman** /bɪznɪswʊmən/ (**businesswomen**) N-COUNT A **businesswoman** is a woman who works in business. *mujer de negocios* ❑ *...a successful businesswoman who runs her own cosmetics company.* *...una exitosa mujer de negocios que dirige su propia empresa de cosméticos.*

b

**bust** /bʌst/ (**busts, busting, busted**)

The form **bust** is used as the present tense of the verb, and can also be used as the past tense and past participle.

**1** V-T If you **bust** something, you break it or damage it so badly that it cannot be used. *romper* [INFORMAL] ❑ *They will have to bust the door to get him out.* *Tendrán que romper la puerta para sacarlo de allí.* **2** PHRASE If a company **goes bust,** it loses so much money that it is forced to close down. *quebrar* [INFORMAL] ❑ *...a Swiss company which went bust last May.* *...una empresa suiza que quebró en mayo pasado.* **3** N-COUNT A **bust** is a statue of the head and shoulders of a person. *busto* ❑ *...a bronze bust of Thomas Jefferson.* *...un busto de bronce de Thomas Jefferson.*

**bust**

**busy** /bɪzi/ (**busier, busiest, busies, busying, busied**) **1** ADJ When you are **busy,** you are working hard or concentrating on a task, so that you are not free to do anything else. *ocupado* ❑ *What is it? I'm busy.* *¿Qué pasa? Estoy ocupado.* ❑ *They are busy preparing for a day's activity on Saturday.* *Están ocupados con la preparación de la actividad del día para el sábado.* **2** V-T If you **busy yourself** with something, you occupy yourself by dealing with it. *entretenerse* ❑ *He busied himself with the camera.* *Se entretuvo con la cámara.* ❑ *She busied herself getting towels ready.* *Se entretuvo alistando las toallas.* **3** ADJ A **busy** place is full of people who are doing things or moving around. *ajetreado* ❑ *...a busy city street.* *...una calle urbana ajetreada.* **4** ADJ When a telephone line is **busy,** you cannot make your call because the line is already being used by someone else. *ocupado* ❑ *I tried to reach him, but the line was busy.* *Traté de comunicarme con él, pero la línea estaba ocupada.*

**busy sig|nal** (**busy signals**) N-COUNT If you try to make a telephone call and get a **busy signal,** it means that you cannot make the call because the line is already being used by someone else. *ocupado* ❑ *I tried the number again, but got a busy signal.* *Marqué otra vez el número, pero sonaba ocupado.*

**busy|work** /bɪziwɜrk/ N-UNCOUNT **Busywork** is work that is intended to keep someone occupied and is not completely necessary. *trabajo innecesario para mantenerse ocupado* ❑ *...meaningless busywork.* *...trabajo trivial.*

**but** /bət, STRONG bʌt/ **1** CONJ You use **but** to introduce something that contrasts with what you have just said, or to introduce something that adds to what you have just said. *pero* ❑ *"You said you'd stay till tomorrow." —"I know, but I think I would rather go back."* *—Dijiste que te quedarías hasta* mañana. —Ya sé, pero creo que prefiero regresar. ❑ Heat the cider until it is very hot but not boiling. Caliente la sidra hasta que esté muy caliente, pero no hirviendo. **2** CONJ You use **but** when you are about to add something further in a discussion or to change the subject. pero ❑ After three weeks, they reduced their sleep to eight hours. But another interesting thing happened. Después de tres semanas redujeron su sueño a ocho horas. Pero sucedió otra cosa interesante. **3** CONJ You use **but** after you have made an excuse or apologized for what you are just about to say. pero ❑ Please excuse me, but there is something I must say. Discúlpeme, pero debo decir algo. ❑ I'm sorry, but it's true. Lo siento, pero es cierto. **4** CONJ You use **but** to introduce a reply to someone when you want to indicate surprise, disbelief, refusal, or protest. pero ❑ "I don't think I should stay in this house." —"But why?" —Creo que debo irme de esta casa. —Pero, ¿por qué? **5** PREP **But** is used to mean "except." excepto, menos ❑ Europe will be represented in all but two of the seven races. Europa tendrá representantes en todas menos dos de las siete carreras. ❑ He didn't speak anything but Greek. No hablaba más que griego. **6** ADV **But** is used to mean "only." sólo [FORMAL] ❑ He is but one among many who are fighting for equality. Es sólo uno entre muchos que luchan por la igualdad. **7** PHRASE You use **but for** to introduce the only factor that causes a particular thing not to happen or not to be completely true. salvo por ❑ The street below was empty but for a white van. La calle estaba vacía, salvo por una camioneta blanca.

**Usage** **but** and **yet**

*But* is used to add something to what has been said: *Lisa tried to bake cookies, but she didn't have enough sugar. Yet* is used to indicate an element of surprise: *He doesn't eat much, yet he is gaining weight.*

**butch|er** /bʊtʃər/ (**butchers, butchering, butchered**) **1** N-COUNT A **butcher** is a storekeeper who cuts up and sells meat. carnicero o carnicera **2** V-T You can say that someone **has butchered** people when they have killed a lot of people in a very cruel way, and you want to express your horror and disgust. descuartizar ❑ Eight tourists were butchered in Bwindi national park. Ocho turistas fueron descuartizados en el parque nacional de Bwindi.

**butt** /bʌt/ (**butts, butting, butted**) **1** N-COUNT Someone's **butt** is the part of their body that they sit on. trasero [INFORMAL] **2** N-COUNT The **butt** or the **butt end of** a weapon or tool is the thick end of its handle. culata ❑ They beat him with their rifle butts. Lo golpearon con las culatas de sus rifles. **3** N-COUNT The **butt of** a cigarette or cigar is the small part of it that is left when someone has finished smoking it. colilla **4** N-SING If someone or something is **the butt of** jokes or criticism, people often make fun of them or criticize them. blanco ❑ He is still often the butt of cruel jokes. Aún suele ser el blanco de bromas pesadas.

▸ **butt in** PHR-VERB If you say that someone **is butting in,** you are criticizing the fact that they are joining in a conversation or activity without being asked to. entrometerse ❑ Sorry, I don't mean to butt in. Perdón, no quiero entrometerme.

▸ **butt out** PHR-VERB If someone tells you to **butt out,** they are telling you rudely to go away or not to interfere with what they are doing. largarse [INFORMAL] ❑ She wanted to tell him to butt out. Quería decirle que se largara.

**but|ter** /bʌtər/ (**butters, buttering, buttered**) **1** N-UNCOUNT **Butter** is a soft yellow substance made from cream. You spread it on bread or use it in cooking. mantequilla ❑ ...bread and butter. ...pan y mantequilla. **2** V-T If you **butter** something such as bread or toast, you spread butter on it. untar mantequilla ❑ She put two pieces of bread on the counter and buttered them. Puso dos rebanadas de pan en el mostrador y les untó mantequilla.

→ see **dish**

**butter|fly** /bʌtərflaɪ/ (**butterflies**) N-COUNT A **butterfly** is an insect with large colorful wings and a thin body. mariposa ❑ Butterflies are attracted to the wild flowers. Las flores silvestres atraen a las mariposas.

→ see **insect**

**but|tock** /bʌtək/ (**buttocks**) N-COUNT Your **buttocks** are the two rounded fleshy parts of your body that you sit on. nalga ❑ He had scars on his back and his buttocks. Tenía cicatrices en la espalda y en el trasero.

→ see **body**

**but|ton** /bʌtᵊn/ (**buttons, buttoning, buttoned**) **1** N-COUNT **Buttons** are small hard objects sewn onto shirts, coats, or other pieces of clothing. You fasten the clothing by pushing the buttons through holes called buttonholes. botón ❑ ...a coat with blue buttons. ...un abrigo con botones azules. **2** V-T If you **button** a shirt, coat, or other piece of clothing, you fasten it by pushing its buttons through the buttonholes. abotonar, abrochar ❑ Ferguson stood up and buttoned his coat. Ferguson se puso de pie y se abrochó el abrigo. ● **Button up** means the same as **button**. abotonar, abrochar ❑ I buttoned up my coat; it was chilly. Me abroché el abrigo; hacía frío. ❑ The young man put on the shirt and buttoned it up. El joven se puso la camisa y la abotonó. **3** N-COUNT A **button** is a small object on a machine or electrical device that you press in order to operate it. botón ❑ He pressed the "play" button. Oprimió el botón "play". **4** N-COUNT A **button** is a small piece of metal or plastic that you wear in order to show that you support a particular movement, organization, or person. You fasten a button to your clothes with a pin. broche ❑ People wore campaign buttons saying "Vote Clinton." La gente llevaba broches de campaña que decían "Vote por Clinton".

▸ **button up** → see **button 2**

→ see Picture Dictionary: **buttons and fasteners**

→ see **photography**

**Word Partnership** Usar *button* con:

| | |
|---|---|
| N. | **shirt** button **1** |
| V. | **sew on a** button **1** |
| | **press a** button, **push a** button **3** |
| PREP. | button **up** *something* **2** |

**button|hole** /bʌtᵊnhoʊl/ (**buttonholes**) N-COUNT A **buttonhole** is a hole that you push a button through in order to fasten a shirt, coat, or other piece of clothing. ojal

→ see **button**

b

## Picture Dictionary buttons and fasteners

button, buttonhole

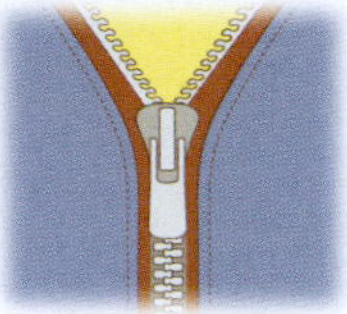
zipper

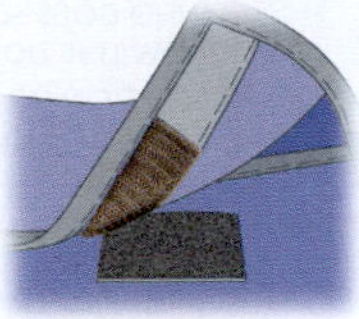
hook and loop tape

snap

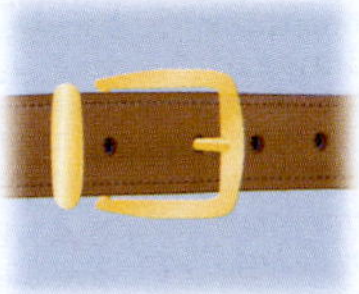
belt, buckle

shoelace

**Word Link** *ar, er ≈ one who acts as : buyer, registrar, seller*

**buy** /baɪ/ (**buys, buying, bought**) **1** V-T If you **buy** something, you obtain it by paying money for it. comprar ❑ *He could not afford to buy a house.* *No le alcanzaba para comprar una casa.* ❑ *Lizzie bought herself a bike.* *Lizzie se compró una bici.* ● **buy|er** N-COUNT (**buyers**) *comprador o compradora* ❑ *Car buyers are more interested in safety than speed.* *A quienes compran autos les interesa más la seguridad que la velocidad.* **2** V-T If you **buy** something like time, freedom, or victory, you obtain it but only by offering or giving up something in return. *ganar* ❑ *It was a risky operation, but might buy more time.* *Era una operación arriesgada, pero con ella podíamos ganar más tiempo.* **3** N-COUNT If something is a good **buy,** it is of good quality and not very expensive. *compra* ❑ *This was still a good buy even at the higher price.* *Fue una buena compra, aun con el precio más elevado.*

▸ **buy into** PHR-VERB If you **buy into** a company or an organization, you buy part of it, often in order to gain some control of it. *adquirir propiedad accionaria* [BUSINESS] ❑ *Other companies could buy into the firm.* *Otras empresas podrían comprar acciones de la compañía.*

▸ **buy out** PHR-VERB If you **buy** someone **out,** you buy their share of something such as a company or piece of property that you previously owned together. *comprar acciones de socios* [BUSINESS] ❑ *The bank bought out most of the 200 former partners.* *El banco compró la parte accionaria de la mayoría de los 200 socios anteriores.*

▸ **buy up** PHR-VERB If you **buy up** land, property, or a commodity, you buy large amounts of it, or all that is available. *comprar todo lo posible* ❑ *The mention of price increases sent people out to buy up as much as they could.* *Los anuncios de incrementos de precios hicieron que la gente comprara todo lo que podía.*

**Thesaurus** *buy* Ver también:

V. acquire, bargain, barter, get, obtain, pay, purchase **1**

**Word Partnership** Usar *buy* con:

V. **afford to** buy, buy **and/or sell** **1**

N. buy **in bulk**, buy **clothes**, buy **a condo/house**, buy **food**, buy **shares/stocks**, buy **tickets** **1**

ADV. buy **direct**, buy **online**, buy **retail**, buy **secondhand**, buy **wholesale** **1**

**buzz** /bʌz/ (**buzzes, buzzing, buzzed**) **1** V-I If something **buzzes** or **buzzes** somewhere, it makes a long continuous sound, like the noise a bee makes when it is flying. *zumbar, sonar* ❑ *Her doorbell buzzed.* *Sonó el timbre de su puerta.* ● **Buzz** is also a noun. *zumbido* ❑ *...the annoying buzz of an insect.* *...el molesto zumbido de un insecto.* **2** V-I If a place **is buzzing with** activity or conversation, there is a lot of activity or conversation there, especially because something important or exciting is about to happen. *bullicio de rumores* ❑ *The rehearsal studio is buzzing with lunchtime activity.* *El estudio de ensayos bulle de rumores a la hora del almuerzo.* **3** N-SING If a place or event has **a buzz** around it, it has a lively, interesting, and modern atmosphere. *bullir* ❑ *There is a real buzz around the place. Everyone is really excited.* *Hay un gran bullicio en ese lugar. Todos están de verdad emocionados.*

**buzz cut** (**buzz cuts**) N-COUNT A **buzz cut** is hairstyle in which the hair is cut very close to the head. *corte de pelo estilo militar* ❑ *He seemed even bigger than before, and he has a buzz cut now.* *Parecía incluso más alto que antes, y ahora tiene un corte de pelo estilo militar.*

**buzz|saw** /bʌzsɔ/ (**buzzsaws**) N-COUNT A **buzzsaw** is an electric saw consisting of a round metal disk with a row of V-shaped points along the edge. It is powered by an electric motor and is used for cutting wood and other materials. *sierra eléctrica*

B

**by**

❶ WHO DOES SOMETHING OR HOW IT IS DONE
❷ POSITION OR PLACE
❸ TIMES AND AMOUNTS

❶ **by** 1 PREP If something is done **by** a person or thing, that person or thing does it. *por* ❑ *The feast was served by his mother and sisters. El banquete fue servido por su madre y hermanas.* ❑ *She was woken by a loud noise in the street. Fue despertada por un fuerte ruido de la calle.* 2 PREP If you say that something such as a book, a piece of music, or a painting is **by** a particular person, you mean that this person wrote it or created it. *de, por* ❑ *...a painting by Van Gogh. ...una pintura de Van Gogh.* 3 PREP **By** is used to say how something is done. *en* ❑ *...traveling by car. ...viajar en auto.* ❑ *Make the sauce by boiling the cream and stock together. La salsa se elabora al hervir juntos la crema y el caldo.* 4 PREP If you hold someone or something **by** a particular part of them, you hold that part. *por* ❑ *He caught her by the shoulder and turned her around. La tomó del hombro e hizo que se diera la vuelta.* ❑ *She was led by the arm to a small room. La llevaron del brazo a un pequeño cuarto.* 5 PHRASE If you are **by yourself,** you are alone. *solo* ❑ *...a dark-haired man sitting by himself in a corner. ...un hombre de pelo oscuro, sentado solo en una esquina.* 6 PHRASE If you do something **by yourself,** you succeed in doing it without anyone helping you. *solo* ❑ *I didn't know if I could raise a child by myself. No sabía si podría criar a un niño yo solo.*

❷ **by** 1 PREP Someone or something that is **by** something else is beside it and close to it. *junto a* ❑ *Judith was sitting in a chair by the window. Judith estaba sentada en un sillón, junto a la ventana.* ❑ *Jack stood by the door, ready to leave. Jack se paró junto a la puerta, listo para irse.* ● **By** is also an adverb. *por ahí* ❑ *Large numbers of police stood by. Se mantuvieron al margen muchos policías.* 2 PREP If a person or vehicle goes **by** you, they move past you without stopping. *al lado de* ❑ *A few cars passed close by me. Unos cuantos autos pasaron cerca de mí.* ● **By** is also an adverb. *cerca* ❑ *Those who knew her waved or smiled as she went by. Quienes la conocían, saludaban o sonreían cuando pasaba.*

❸ **by** /baɪ/ 1 PREP If something happens **by** a particular time, it happens at or before that time. *antes de* ❑ *He arrived at my hotel by eight o'clock. Llegó a mi hotel antes de las ocho.* 2 PREP If something increases or decreases **by** a particular amount, that amount is gained or lost. *en* ❑ *Violent crime has increased by 10 percent since last year. Los crímenes violentos aumentaron en 10 por ciento desde el año pasado.* 3 PREP Things that are made or sold **by** the million or **by** the dozen are made or sold in those quantities. *por* ❑ *Packages arrived by the dozen from America. Los paquetes llegaron por docenas de Estados Unidos.* 4 PREP You use **by** in expressions such as "minute by minute" and "drop by drop" to talk about things that happen gradually, not all at once. *a* ❑ *His father began to lose his memory bit by bit. Su padre comenzó a perder la memoria poco a poco.*

In addition to the uses shown here, **by** is used in phrasal verbs such as "abide by," "put by," and "stand by."

The preposition is pronounced /baɪ/. The adverb is pronounced /b<u>aɪ</u>/.

**bye** /b<u>aɪ</u>/ also **bye-bye** CONVENTION **Bye** and **bye-bye** are informal ways of saying goodbye. *adiós* ❑ *Bye, Daddy. Adiós, papá.*

**by|law** /b<u>aɪ</u>lɔ/ (**bylaws**) N-COUNT A **bylaw** is a rule which controls the way an organization is run. *reglamento* ❑ *Under the company's bylaws, he can continue as chairman until the age of 70. Según los reglamentos de la empresa, puede ocupar su puesto de presidente hasta la edad de 70 años.*

**by|pass** /b<u>aɪ</u>pæs/ (**bypasses, bypassing, bypassed**) 1 V-T If you **bypass** someone or something that you would normally have to get involved with, you ignore them, often because you want to achieve something more quickly. *evitar* ❑ *The president gives radio interviews to bypass the newspapers. El presidente concede entrevistas a la radio para evitar los periódicos.* 2 N-COUNT A **bypass** is a surgical operation performed on or near the heart, in which the flow of blood is redirected so that it does not flow through a part of the heart that is diseased or blocked. *cirugía de puente coronario* ❑ *...heart bypass surgery. ...cirugía de puente coronario.* 3 N-COUNT A **bypass** is a main road that takes traffic around the edge of a town or city rather than through its center. *libramiento* ❑ *A new bypass around the city is being built. Se construye un nuevo libramiento alrededor de la ciudad.* 4 V-T If you **bypass** a place when you are traveling, you avoid going through it. *evitar* ❑ *His bus trip to the Midwest bypassed all the big cities. Su viaje en autobús al Medio Oeste evitó todas las ciudades grandes.*

**byte** /b<u>aɪ</u>t/ (**bytes**) N-COUNT In computing, a **byte** is a unit of storage approximately equivalent to one printed character. *byte* ❑ *...two million bytes of data. ...dos millones de bytes de datos.*

# Cc



**cab** /kæb/ (**cabs**) 1 N-COUNT A **cab** is a taxi. *taxi* ❑ *Can I call a cab? ¿Puedo pedir un taxi?* 2 N-COUNT The **cab** of a truck or train is the front part in which the driver sits. *cabina* ❑ *...the driver's cab. ...la cabina del conductor.*

**cab|bage** /kæbɪdʒ/ (**cabbages**) N-VAR A **cabbage** is a round vegetable with white, green, or purple leaves that is usually eaten cooked. *col*

**cab|in** /kæbɪn/ (**cabins**) 1 N-COUNT A **cabin** is a small wooden house, especially one in an area of forests or mountains. *cabaña* ❑ *...a log cabin. ...una cabaña de troncos.* 2 N-COUNT A **cabin** is a small room in a ship or boat. *camarote* ❑ *He showed her to a small cabin. La condujo a un pequeño camarote.* 3 N-COUNT A **cabin** is one of the areas inside a plane. *cabina* ❑ *He sat in the first-class cabin. Se sentó en la sección de primera clase.*

**cabi|net** /kæbɪnɪt/ (**cabinets**) 1 N-COUNT A **cabinet** is a cupboard used for storing things such as medicine or for displaying decorative things in. *gabinete, vitrina* ❑ *...the medicine cabinet. ...el botiquín.* 2 N-COUNT The **cabinet** is a group of the most senior advisers or ministers in a government. *gabinete* ❑ *...a cabinet meeting. ...una reunión de gabinete.*
→ see **office**

**ca|ble** /keɪbᵊl/ (**cables**) 1 N-VAR A **cable** is a kind of very strong, thick rope, made of wires twisted together. *cable* ❑ *...a cable made of steel wire. ...un cable de alambre de acero.* 2 N-VAR A **cable** is a thick wire, or a group of wires inside a rubber or plastic covering, which is used to carry electricity or electronic signals. *cable* ❑ *...underground power cables. ...cables eléctricos subterráneos.* 3 N-UNCOUNT **Cable** is used to refer to television systems in which the signals are sent along underground wires rather than by radio waves. *cable* ❑ *We don't have cable TV. No tenemos televisión por cable.*
→ see **bridge, computer, laser, television**

**ca|ble car** (**cable cars**) N-COUNT A **cable car** is a vehicle for taking people up mountains or steep hills. It is pulled by a moving cable. *teleférico, funicular*

**ca|boose** /kəbus/ (**cabooses**) N-COUNT On a freight train, a **caboose** is a small car, usually at the rear, in which the crew travels. *cabús, furgón de cola*

**cab stand** also **cabstand** (**cab stands**) N-COUNT A **cab stand** is a place where taxis wait for passengers, for example, at an airport or outside a station. *parada de taxi*

**cac|tus** /kæktəs/ (**cactuses** or **cacti** /kæktaɪ/) N-COUNT A **cactus** is a desert plant with a thick stem, often with spikes. *cactus*
→ see **desert**

cactus

**café** /kæfeɪ/ (**cafés**) also **cafe** N-COUNT A **café** is a place where you can buy drinks, simple meals, and snacks. *café*

**caf|eteria** /kæfɪtɪəriə/ (**cafeterias**) N-COUNT A **cafeteria** is a self-service restaurant, usually in a public building such as a hospital, college, or office. *cafetería*

**caf|feine** /kæfin/ N-UNCOUNT **Caffeine** is a chemical substance found in coffee, tea, and cocoa, which affects your brain and body and makes you more active. *cafeína*

**cage** /keɪdʒ/ (**cages**) N-COUNT A **cage** is a structure of wire or metal bars in which birds or animals are kept. *jaula* ❑ *I hate to see birds in cages. Odio ver a los pájaros enjaulados.*

**cake** /keɪk/ (**cakes**) 1 N-VAR A **cake** is a sweet food made by baking a mixture of flour, eggs, sugar, and fat. *pastel* ❑ *...a piece of chocolate cake. ...una rebanada de pastel de chocolate.* ❑ *...a birthday cake. ...un pastel de cumpleaños.* 2 N-COUNT Food that is formed into flat round shapes before it is cooked can be referred to as **cakes**. *tortitas* ❑ *...fish cakes. ...tortitas de pescado.* 3 PHRASE If someone has done something very stupid, rude, or selfish, you can say that they **take the cake** or that what they have done **takes the cake,** to emphasize your surprise at their behavior. *es el colmo (algo), no se mide (alguien)*
→ see **dessert**

**cake pan** (**cake pans**) N-COUNT A **cake pan** is a metal container that you bake a cake in. *molde para pastel*

**cake|walk** /keɪkwɔk/ N-SING If you describe something as a **cakewalk,** you mean that it is very easy to do or achieve. *pan comido* [INFORMAL] ❑ *Tomorrow's game against Italy should be a cakewalk. El partido de mañana contra Italia es pan comido.*

**cal|cium** /kælsiəm/ N-UNCOUNT **Calcium** is a soft white chemical element which is found in bones and teeth, and also in limestone, chalk, and marble. *calcio*

**cal|cu|late** /kælkyəleɪt/ (**calculates, calculating, calculated**) 1 V-T If you **calculate** a number or amount, you work it out using arithmetic. *calcular* ❑ *...a course in how to calculate business costs. ...un curso sobre cómo calcular costos en las empresas.* ❑ *We calculate that the average farm in Lancaster County is 65 acres. Calculamos que una granja promedio en el condado de Lancaster consta de 65 acres.* • **cal|cu|la|tion** /kælkyəleɪʃᵊn/ N-VAR (**calculations**) *cálculo* ❑ *Leonard made a quick calculation: he'd never get there in time. Leonard hizo un*

*rápido cálculo: nunca llegaría a tiempo.* **2** → see also **mathematics** **3** V-T If you **calculate** the effects of something, you consider what they will be. *evaluar* ❑ *We are calculating the consequences of his actions. Estamos evaluando las consecuencias de sus acciones.*
→ see **mathematics**

C

**cal|cu|lat|ed** /kælkyəleɪtɪd/ ADJ If something is **calculated,** it is deliberately planned to have a particular effect. *calculado* ❑ *Everything she said seemed calculated to make him feel guilty. Todo lo que ella decía parecía calculado para hacerlo sentir culpable.*

**cal|cu|la|tor** /kælkyəleɪtər/ (**calculators**) N-COUNT A **calculator** is a small electronic device that you use for making mathematical calculations. *calculadora* ❑ *...a pocket calculator. ...una calculadora de bolsillo.*
→ see **office**

**cal|de|ra** /kældɛərə/ (**calderas**) N-COUNT A **caldera** is a large crater at the top of a volcano that is formed when a volcano collapses. *caldera* [TECHNICAL]

**cal|en|dar** /kælɪndər/ (**calendars**) **1** N-COUNT A **calendar** is a chart or device which displays the date and the day of the week, and often the whole of a particular year. *calendario* ❑ *There was a calendar on the wall. Había un calendario en la pared.* **2** N-COUNT A **calendar** is a list of dates within a year that are important for a particular organization or activity. *agenda* ❑ *The meeting wasn't on the secretary's calendar. La reunión no figuraba en la agenda del secretario.*
→ see **year**

**call**

❶ NAMING
❷ DECLARING, ANNOUNCING, AND DEMANDING
❸ TELEPHONING AND VISITING
❹ PHRASAL VERBS

❶ **call** /kɔl/ (**calls, calling, called**) **1** V-T If you **call** someone or something **by** a particular name or title, you give them that name or title. *nombrar* ❑ *Everybody called each other by their first names. Todos se llamaban por su nombre de pila.* ❑ *I wanted to call the dog Mufty. Quería llamar al perro Mufty.* ❑ *There are two men called Buckley in the office. Hay dos hombres llamados Buckley en la oficina.* **2** V-T If you **call** a person or situation something, that is how you describe them. *llamar* ❑ *They called him a traitor. Lo llamaron traidor.* ❑ *She calls me lazy. Ella me dice perezoso.* **3** → see also **so-called** **4** to **call it quits** → see **quit**

❷ **call** /kɔl/ (**calls, calling, called**) **1** V-T If you **call** something, or if you **call** it **out**, you say it in a loud voice. *gritar* ❑ *He could hear the others calling his name. Podía oír a los otros gritando su nombre.* ● **Call out** means the same as **call**. *gritar* ❑ *The butcher called out a greeting. El carnicero soltó un grito de bienvenida.* **2** V-T If you **call** a meeting, you arrange for it to take place. *convocar* ❑ *We're going to call a meeting for next week. Estamos convocando a una reunión para la semana que entra.* **3** V-T To **call** a game or sporting event means to cancel it, for example because of rain or bad light. *suspender* ❑ *We called the next game. Suspendimos el partido siguiente.* **4** N-COUNT If there is a **call for** something, someone demands that it should happen. *requerimiento* ❑ *There have been calls for new security arrangements. Se han hecho requerimientos de nuevas medidas de seguridad.* **5** PHRASE If someone is **on call,** they are ready to go to work at any time if they are needed. *de turno* ❑ *...a doctor on call. ...un médico de turno.* **6** to **call** something **into question** → see **question**

| **Thesaurus** | *call* | Ver también: |
|---|---|---|
| V. | cry, holler, scream, shout ❷ **1** | |

❸ **call** /kɔl/ (**calls, calling, called**) **1** V-T If you **call** someone, you telephone them. *llamar* ❑ *Would you call me as soon as you find out? ¿Me llamas en cuanto lo averigües?* ❑ *I think we should call the doctor. Creo que deberíamos llamar al doctor.* ❑ *She told me to call this number. Me dijo que llamara a este número.* **2** V-I If you **call** somewhere, you make a short visit there. *hacer una visita corta* ❑ *A salesman called at the house. Un vendedor pasó por la casa.* ● **Call** is also a noun. *visita* ❑ *The police van was out on a call. La camioneta de la policía estaba haciendo una ronda.* **3** N-COUNT When you make a telephone **call,** you telephone someone. *llamada* ❑ *I made a phone call to the United States. Hice una llamada telefónica a Estados Unidos.* ❑ *I've had hundreds of calls from victims. He recibido cientos de llamadas de las víctimas.* **4** PHRASE If you **call collect** when you make a telephone call, the person who you are phoning pays the cost of the call and not you. *llamar por cobrar* **5** → see also **collect call**

❹ **call** /kɔl/ (**calls, calling, called**)

▸ **call back** PHR-VERB If you **call** someone **back,** you telephone them again or in return for a telephone call that they have made to you. *regresar la llamada* ❑ *We'll call you back. Te regresamos la llamada.*

▸ **call for** **1** PHR-VERB If something **calls for** a particular action or quality, it needs it. *requerir* ❑ *The situation calls for quick action. La situación requiere una respuesta rápida.* **2** PHR-VERB If you **call for** someone, you go to the building where they are, so that you can both go somewhere. *pasar por* ❑ *I'll call for you at seven o'clock. Paso por ti a las siete en punto.* **3** PHR-VERB If you **call for** something, you demand that it should happen. *exigir* ❑ *He called for further discussions on the issue. Exigió que se siguiera discutiendo el tema.*

▸ **call in** **1** PHR-VERB If you **call** someone **in,** you ask them to come and help you or do something for you. *llamar* ❑ *Call in a builder to do the work. Llama a un albañil para que haga el trabajo.* **2** PHR-VERB If you **call in** somewhere, you make a short visit there. *pasar por* ❑ *He calls in occasionally. Pasa por la casa de vez en cuando.*

▸ **call off** PHR-VERB If you **call off** an event that has been planned, you cancel it. *cancelar* ❑ *He called off the trip. Canceló el viaje.*

▸ **call on** or **call upon** **1** PHR-VERB If you **call on** someone **to** do something, you say publicly that you want them to do it. *hacer un llamado* ❑ *He called on the government to resign. Hizo un llamado al gobierno para que renuncie.* **2** PHR-VERB If you **call on** someone, you visit them for a short time. *pasar a ver* ❑ *Sofia was intending to call on Miss Kitts. Sofía tenía la intención de pasar a ver a la señorita Kitts.*

▸ **call out** **1** PHR-VERB If you **call** someone **out,**

## Word Web calories

**Calories** are a measure of **energy**. One calorie of heat raises the **temperature** of 1 gram of water by 1°C*. However, we usually think of calories in relation to food and exercise. A person eating a cup of vanilla ice cream **takes in** 270 calories. Walking a mile **burns** 66 calories. Different types of foods store different amounts of energy. **Proteins** and **carbohydrates** contain 4 calories per gram. However **fat** contains 9 calories per gram. Our bodies store extra calories in the form of fat. For every 3,500 extra calories we take in, we gain a pound of fat.

*0° Celsius = 32° Fahrenheit.*

C

you order them to come to help, especially in an emergency. *hacer venir* ❑ *Colombia has called out the army. Colombia ordenó la intervención del Ejército.* **2** → see also **call** ❷ **1**

▸ **call up** **1** PHR-VERB If you **call** someone **up,** you telephone them. *llamar* ❑ *When I'm in Pittsburgh, I call him up. Cuando estoy en Pittsburgh, lo llamo.* ❑ *He called up the museum. Llamó al museo.* **2** PHR-VERB If someone **is called up,** they are ordered to join the army, navy, or air force. *llamar a filas* ❑ *The United States Army has called up about 150,000 men and women. El Ejército de los Estados Unidos llamó a filas a 150,000 hombres y mujeres.*

▸ **call upon** → see **call on**

**call cen|ter** (**call centers**) N-COUNT A **call center** is an office where people work answering or making telephone calls for a company. *centro de atención telefónica*

**call|er** /kɔlər/ (**callers**) **1** N-COUNT A **caller** is a person who is making a telephone call. *una persona que hace una llamada telefónica* ❑ *A caller told police what happened. Una persona que llamó por teléfono le dijo a la policía lo que había sucedido.* **2** N-COUNT A **caller** is a person who comes to see you for a short visit. *visita* ❑ *She took her callers into the living room. Hizo pasar a las visitas a la sala.*

**call|er ID** N-UNCOUNT A telephone that has **caller ID** displays the telephone number and name of the person who is calling you. *identificador de llamadas* ❑ *The cellphone's caller ID display told her Frank Montoya was calling. El identificador de llamadas de su celular le indicó que Frank Montoya la estaba llamando.*

**calm** /kɑm/ (**calmer, calmest, calms, calming, calmed**) **1** ADJ A **calm** person does not show or feel any worry, anger, or excitement. *tranquilo* ❑ *...a calm, patient woman. ...una mujer paciente y tranquila.* ❑ *Try to keep calm. Trata de mantenerte calmada.* ● **Calm** is also a noun. *tranquilidad* ❑ *He felt a sudden sense of calm. Sintió una repentina sensación de tranquilidad.* ● **calm|ly** ADV *tranquilamente* ❑ *Alan said calmly, "I don't believe you." Alan dijo tranquilamente: —No te creo.* **2** ADJ If water is **calm,** it is not moving very much. *tranquilo, en calma* ❑ *...the calm waters of the canals. ...el agua tranquila de los canales.* **3** ADJ If the weather is **calm,** there is little or no wind. *sin viento* ❑ *It was a fine, calm day. Era un día despejado y sin viento.* **4** N-UNCOUNT **Calm** is a state of being quiet and peaceful. *calma* ❑ *...the calm of Grand Rapids, Michigan. ...la calma de Grand Rapids, en Michigan.* **5** V-T If you **calm** someone, you do something to make them less upset or excited. *calmar* ❑ *Isabella helped calm her fears. Isabella la ayudó a calmar sus temores.* ❑ *She tried to calm herself. Trató de calmarse.* ● **calm|ing** ADJ *calmante* ❑ *Yoga can have a very calming effect on the mind. El yoga puede tener un efecto muy calmante en la mente.*

▸ **calm down** PHR-VERB If you **calm down,** or if someone **calms** you **down,** you become less upset or excited. *calmar(se)* ❑ *Calm down for a minute and listen to me. Cálmate un minuto y escúchame.* ❑ *I'll try to calm him down. Voy a tratar de calmarlo.*

| **Thesaurus** | *calm* | Ver también: |
|---|---|---|
| ADJ. | laid-back, relaxed; (*ant.*) excited, upset **1** mild, peaceful, placid, serene, tranquil; (*ant.*) rough **1**–**3** | |

**calo|rie** /kæləri/ (**calories**) **1** N-COUNT **Calories** are units used to measure the energy value of food. *caloría* ❑ *Sweet drinks contain a lot of calories. Las bebidas dulces contienen muchas calorías.* **2** N-COUNT In physics, a **calorie** is the amount of heat that is needed to increase the temperature of one gram of water by one degree centigrade. **Calorie** is also sometimes used to mean a **kilocalorie.** *caloría* [TECHNICAL]
→ see Word Web: **calories**
→ see **diet**

**calo|rim|eter** /kælərɪmɪtər/ (**calorimeters**) N-COUNT A **calorimeter** is a scientific instrument that measures the amount of heat given off or absorbed in a chemical reaction. *calorímetro*

**came** /keɪm/ **Came** is the past tense of **come.** *pasado de* ***come***

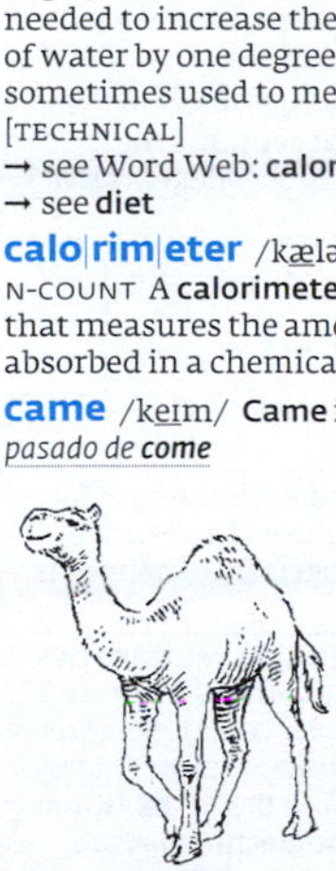
camel

**cam|el** /kæməl/ (**camels**) **1** N-COUNT A **camel** is a desert animal with one or two humps on its back. *camello* **2** **the straw that broke the camel's back** → see **straw**

**cam|era** /kæmrə/ (**cameras**) **1** N-COUNT A **camera** is a piece of equipment for taking photographs or making movies. *cámara* ❑ *...a video camera. ...una cámara de video.* **2** PHRASE If someone or something is **on camera,** they are being filmed. *en cámara* ❑ *I won't*

C

*be on camera, will I? No voy a estar en cámara, ¿o sí?*
→ see **photography**

**cam|era phone** (**camera phones**) N-COUNT A **camera phone** is a cellphone that can also take photographs. *celular (que también toma fotografías)*

**camp** /kæmp/ (**camps, camping, camped**) **1** N-COUNT A **camp** is a place where people live or stay in tents or trailers. *campamento* ❑ *...a refugee camp. ...un campamento de refugiados.* **2** V-I If you **camp** somewhere, you stay there in a tent or trailer. *acampar* ❑ *We camped near the beach. Acampamos cerca de la playa.* ❑ *They camped out in a meadow. Acamparon en una pradera.* ● **camp|ing** N-UNCOUNT *de campamento* ❑ *They went camping in the wild. Se fueron de campamento lejos de la civilización.*

**cam|paign** /kæmpeɪn/ (**campaigns, campaigning, campaigned**) **1** N-COUNT A **campaign** is a planned set of activities aimed at achieving a particular result. *campaña* ❑ *...a campaign to improve the training of staff. ...una campaña para mejorar la preparación del personal.* ❑ *...a bombing campaign. ...un operativo de bombardeo.* **2** V-I To **campaign** means to carry out a planned set of activities aimed at achieving a particular result. *hacer campaña* ❑ *We are campaigning for law reform. Estamos haciendo campaña por la reforma de la ley.*
● **cam|paign|er** N-COUNT (**campaigners**) *militante* ❑ *...anti-war campaigners. ...militantes antibélicos.*
→ see **army, election**

**camp|fire** /kæmpfaɪər/ (**campfires**) N-COUNT A **campfire** is a fire that you light out of doors when you are camping. *hoguera, fogata*
→ see **fire**

**camp|ground** /kæmpgraʊnd/ (**campgrounds**) N-COUNT A **campground** is the same as a **campsite**. *camping*

**camp|site** /kæmpsaɪt/ (**campsites**) N-COUNT A **campsite** is a place where people who are on vacation can stay in tents. *campamento*

**cam|pus** /kæmpəs/ (**campuses**) N-COUNT A **campus** is an area of land that contains the main buildings of a university or college. *ciudad universitaria*

**can**
❶ MODAL USES
❷ CONTAINER

❶ **can** /kən, STRONG kæn/

**Can** is a modal verb. It is used with the base form of a verb. The form **cannot** is used in negative statements. The usual spoken form of **cannot** is **can't**, pronounced /kænt/.

**1** MODAL If you **can** do something, you have the ability or opportunity to do it. *poder* ❑ *I can take care of myself. Puedo cuidarme solo.* ❑ *The United States will do whatever it can to help Greece. Estados Unidos hará todo lo que pueda para ayudar a Grecia.* **2** MODAL You use **can** to indicate that something is true sometimes or is true in some circumstances. *poder* ❑ *...long-term therapy that can last five years or more. ...una terapia de largo plazo que puede durar cinco años o más.* ❑ *Exercising alone can be boring. Hacer ejercicio solo puede llegar a ser aburrido.* **3** MODAL You use **cannot** and **can't** to state that you are certain that something is not the case or will not happen. *no poder* ❑ *Things can't be that bad. Las cosas no pueden estar tan mal.* ❑ *That person can't be Douglas! ¡Ése no puede ser Douglas!* **4** MODAL If you **can** do something, you are allowed to do it. *poder* ❑ *Can I have your jeans when you go? ¿Puedo usar tus pantalones de mezclilla cuando salgas?* ❑ *We can't answer any questions, I'm afraid. Me temo que no podemos contestar ninguna pregunta.* **5** MODAL You use **can** in order to make suggestions or requests, or to offer to do something. *poder* ❑ *You can always try the pasta. También puedes probar la pasta.* ❑ *Can I have a look at that? ¿Me dejas ver eso?* ❑ *Can I help you? ¿Me permites que te ayude?*

**Usage** **can** and **may**

Both *can* and *may* are used to talk about possibility and permission: *Highway traffic can/may be heavier in the summer than in the winter. Can/May I interrupt you for a moment?* To talk about ability, use *can* but not *may*: *Kazuo can run a mile in five minutes.*

❷ **can** /kæn/ (**cans, canning, canned**) **1** N-COUNT A **can** is a sealed metal container for food, drink, or paint. *lata* ❑ *Several young men were kicking a tin can along the middle of the road. Varios jóvenes estaban pateando una lata en medio de la calle.* **2** V-T When food or drink **is canned**, it is put into a metal container and sealed. *enlatar* ❑ *Fruit and vegetables were canned in large quantities. La fruta y los vegetales fueron enlatados en grandes cantidades.*
→ see **container**

**ca|nal** /kənæl/ (**canals**) N-COUNT A **canal** is a long, narrow, man-made stretch of water. *canal* ❑ *...the Grand Union Canal. ...el Grand Union Canal.*

**can|cel** /kænsᵊl/ (**cancels, canceling** or **cancelling, canceled** or **cancelled**) **1** V-T/V-I If you **cancel** something that has been arranged, you stop it from happening. If you **cancel** an order for goods or services, you tell the person or organization supplying them that you no longer wish to receive them. *cancelar* ❑ *The governor yesterday canceled his visit to Washington. El gobernador canceló ayer su visita a Washington.* ❑ *The customer called to cancel. El cliente llamó para cancelar.* ● **can|cel|la|tion** /kænsəleɪʃᵊn/ N-VAR (**cancellations**) *cancelación* ❑ *The cancellation of his visit has disappointed many people. La cancelación de su visita decepcionó a muchas personas.* **2** V-T If someone in authority **cancels** a document or a debt, they officially declare that it is no longer valid or no longer legally exists. *cancelar* ❑ *...a government order canceling his passport. ...una orden del gobierno de cancelar su pasaporte.* ● **can|cel|la|tion** N-UNCOUNT *cancelación* ❑ *...cancellation of Third World debt. ...cancelación de la deuda del Tercer Mundo.*
▸ **cancel out** PHR-VERB If one thing **cancels out** another thing, the two things have opposite effects which combine to produce no real effect. *anular* ❑ *The different influences might cancel each other out. Las diferentes influencias podrían anularse mutuamente.*

C

## Word Web cancer

The traditional **treatments** for **cancer** are **surgery**, **radiation therapy**, and **chemotherapy**. However, there is a new type of treatment called targeted therapy. This treatment uses new drugs that target specific types of cancer cells. Targeted therapy does not have many of the **toxic** effects on healthy **tissue** that traditional chemotherapy can have. One of these drugs helps stop blood vessels that feed a **tumor** from growing. Another drug kills cancer cells.

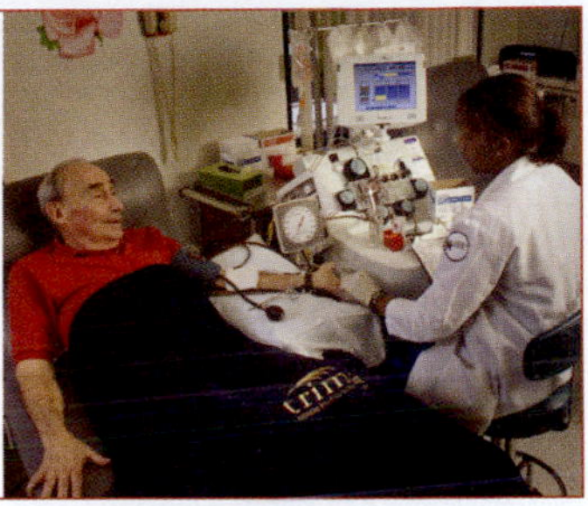

## Thesaurus *cancel* Ver también:

v. break, call off, scrap, undo 1

**can|cer** /kænsər/ (**cancers**) N-VAR **Cancer** is a serious disease in which abnormal body cells increase, producing growths. *cáncer* ❑ *Her mother died of breast cancer.* *Su madre murió de cáncer de pecho.* ❑ *Jane was 25 when she learned she had cancer.* *Jane tenía 25 años cuando supo que tenía cáncer.* • **can|cer|ous** ADJ *canceroso* ❑ *...the production of cancerous cells.* *...la producción de células cancerosas.*
→ see Word Web: **cancer**

**can|di|date** /kændɪdeɪt/ (**candidates**) 1 N-COUNT A **candidate** is someone who is being considered for a position, for example in an election or for a job. *candidato o candidata* ❑ *...the Democratic candidate.* *...el candidato demócrata* ❑ *He is a candidate for the office of governor.* *Es candidato al cargo de gobernador.* 2 N-COUNT A **candidate** is someone who is studying for a degree at a college. *candidato o candidata* ❑ *He is now a candidate for a master's degree in social work.* *Él es ahora candidato para el grado de maestría en trabajo social.*
→ see **election, vote**

**can|dle** /kændᵊl/ (**candles**) N-COUNT A **candle** is a stick of hard wax with a piece of string called a wick through the middle, that you set fire to in order to provide light. *vela* ❑ *The bedroom was lit by a single candle.* *El dormitorio estaba iluminado por una sola vela.*

**can|dy** /kændi/ (**candies**) N-VAR **Candy** is sweet foods such as chocolate or taffy. *dulce* ❑ *...a piece of candy.* *...un dulce.*

**can|dy apple** (**candy apples**) N-COUNT A **candy apple** is an apple coated with hard red sugar syrup and fixed on a stick. *manzana acaramelada*

**can|dy bar** (**candy bars**) N-COUNT A **candy bar** is a long, thin, sweet food, usually covered in chocolate. *un dulce en forma de barra generalmente cubierto con chocolate.*

**candy cane** (**candy canes**) N-COUNT A **candy cane** is a stick of red and white candy with a curve at one end. *bastón de dulce*

**cane** /keɪn/ (**canes**) 1 N-VAR **Cane** is the long, hollow, hard stems of plants such as bamboo. *caña, mimbre* ❑ *...cane furniture.* *...muebles de mimbre.* ❑ *...cane sugar.* *...caña de azúcar.* 2 N-COUNT A **cane** is a long narrow stick. *bastón* ❑ *He leaned heavily on his cane.* *Se apoyaba sobre su bastón.*
→ see **disability, sugar**

**can|non** /kænən/ (**cannons**) 1 N-COUNT A **cannon** is a large gun on wheels, which was used in battles in the past. *cañón* ❑ *The soldiers marched beside the gigantic cannons.* *Los soldados marchaban al lado de enormes cañones.* 2 N-COUNT A **cannon** is a heavy automatic gun, especially one fired from an aircraft. *cañón*

**can|not** /kænɒt, kənɒt/ **Cannot** is the negative form of **can**. *forma negativa de* ***can***

canoe

**ca|noe** /kənu/ (**canoes**) N-COUNT A **canoe** is a small, narrow boat that you move through the water using a paddle. *canoa*
→ see **boat**

**ca|no|la** /kənoʊlə/ N-UNCOUNT **Canola** or **canola oil** is a type of vegetable oil used in cooking. *canola*

**cano|py** /kænəpi/ (**canopies**) N-COUNT A **canopy** is a decorated cover which hangs above something such as a bed or a seat. *dosel, baldaquín*
→ see **bed**

**can't** /kænt/ **Can't** is the usual spoken form of "cannot." *forma hablada usual de* ***cannot***

**can|teen** /kæntin/ (**canteens**) N-COUNT A **canteen** is a place in a factory or military base where workers can have meals or snacks. *comedor* ❑ *Rennie ate his supper in the canteen.* *Rennie tomó su cena en el comedor.*

**can|vas** /kænvəs/ (**canvases**) 1 N-UNCOUNT **Canvas** is a strong, heavy cloth that is used for making tents, sails, and bags. *lona* ❑ *...a canvas bag.* *...un bolso de lona.* 2 N-VAR A **canvas** is a piece of canvas on which an oil painting is done, or the painting itself. *lienzo* ❑ *...canvases by Italian painters.* *...lienzos de pintores italianos.*
→ see **painting**

**can|yon** /kænyən/ (**canyons**) N-COUNT A **canyon** is a long, narrow valley with very steep sides. *cañón* ❑ *...the Grand Canyon.* *...el Gran Cañón del Colorado.*

**cap** /kæp/ (**caps, capping, capped**) 1 N-COUNT A **cap** is a soft, flat hat with a curved part at the front which is called a visor. *gorra* ❑ *...a dark-blue baseball cap.* *...una gorra de béisbol azul oscuro.* 2 N-COUNT The **cap** of a bottle is its lid. *tapa* ❑ *She unscrewed the cap of her water bottle and gave him a drink.* *Ella desenroscó la tapa de su botella de agua y* *le invitó un trago.* **3** V-T You can say that the last event in a series **caps** the others. *coronar* ❑ *The arrests capped a four-month investigation by the Internal Revenue Service. Los arrestos coronaron una investigación de cuatro meses del Internal Revenue Service.*

C

**ca|pable** /keɪpəbᵊl/ **1** ADJ If you are **capable of** doing something, you are able to do it. *capaz* ❑ *He was hardly capable of standing up. Apenas era capaz de ponerse de pie.* ● **ca|pa|bil|ity** /keɪpəbɪlɪti/ (**capabilities**) N-VAR *capacidad* ❑ *She has lost all her physical capabilities. Ha perdido todas sus capacidades físicas.* **2** ADJ Someone who is **capable** has the ability to do something well. *competente* ❑ *She's a very capable speaker. Ella es una oradora muy competente.* ● **ca|pably** /keɪpəbli/ ADV *competentemente* ❑ *It was all dealt with very capably. Todo se manejó de manera muy competente.*

**Thesaurus** *capable* Ver también:

ADJ. able, competent, skillful, talented; (*ant.*) incapable, incompetent **2**

**ca|pac|ity** /kəpæsɪti/ (**capacities**) **1** N-VAR Your **capacity for** something is your ability to do it. *capacidad* ❑ *...our capacity for giving care, love, and attention. ...nuestra capacidad de dar cuidados, amor y atención.* ❑ *Her mental capacity is remarkable. Su capacidad mental es notable.* **2** N-VAR The **capacity** of something is the maximum amount that it can hold or produce. *capacidad* ❑ *...containers with a maximum capacity of 200 gallons of water. ...recipientes con una capacidad máxima de 200 galones de agua.* ❑ *Each stadium had a seating capacity of about 50,000. Cada estadio tenía capacidad para 50,000 aficionados.* ❑ *Bread factories are working at full capacity. Las fábricas de pan están trabajando a su máxima capacidad.* **3** N-COUNT If you do something **in** a particular **capacity,** you do it as part of your job. *calidad* [WRITTEN] ❑ *She was there in her capacity as U.S. ambassador. Se encontraba allí en su calidad de embajadora de EE.UU.* **4** ADJ A **capacity** crowd or audience completely fills a theater, sports stadium, or other place. *lleno completo* ❑ *A capacity crowd of 76,000 people was at the stadium for the event. Había lleno completo de 76,000 personas en el estadio para el evento.*

**cape** /keɪp/ (**capes**) **1** N-COUNT A **cape** is a large piece of land that sticks out into the sea from the coast. *cabo* ❑ *...the storms of the cape. ...las tormentas en el cabo.* **2** N-COUNT A **cape** is a type of long coat with no sleeves that hangs from your shoulders. *capa* ❑ *...a woolen cape. ...una capa de lana.*

**ca|pil|lary** /kæpəlɛri/ (**capillaries**) N-COUNT **Capillaries** are tiny blood vessels in your body. *capilar*

**Word Link** *cap ≈ head : capital, capitalism, captain*

**capi|tal** /kæpɪtᵊl/ (**capitals**) **1** N-UNCOUNT **Capital** is a sum of money used to start a business or invested to make more money. *capital* [BUSINESS] ❑ *Companies are having difficulty in raising capital. Las compañías están teniendo problemas para conseguir capital.* **2** N-COUNT The **capital** of a country is the city where its government meets. *capital* ❑ *...Kathmandu, the capital of Nepal. ...Katmandú, la capital de Nepal.* **3** N-COUNT A **capital** or a **capital letter** is the large form of a letter used at the beginning of sentences and names. *mayúscula* ❑ *The name and address are written in capitals. El nombre y la dirección están escritos en mayúsculas.* **4** ADJ A **capital** offense is one that is punished by death. *sancionado con la pena capital*
→ see **city, country**

**capi|tal|ism** /kæpɪtᵊlɪzəm/ N-UNCOUNT **Capitalism** is an economic and political system in which property, business, and industry are owned by private individuals and not by the state. *capitalismo* ❑ *Nobody ever said capitalism was fair. Nadie dijo jamás que el capitalismo fuera justo.* ● **capi|tal|ist** (**capitalists**) N-COUNT *capitalista* ❑ *They argue that only private capitalists can remake Poland's economy. Argumentan que sólo los capitalistas privados pueden rehacer la economía polaca.* ❑ *...Western capitalists. ...capitalistas occidentales.*

**capi|tal pun|ish|ment** N-UNCOUNT **Capital punishment** is the legal killing of a person who has committed a serious crime. *pena capital* ❑ *Most democracies have outlawed capital punishment. La mayoría de las democracias han abolido la pena capital.*

**cap|i|tol** /kæpɪtᵊl/ (**capitols**) also **Capitol** **1** N-COUNT A **capitol** is a government building in which a state legislature meets. *capitolio* ❑ *...the construction of the state capitol in 1908. ...la construcción del capitolio del estado en 1908.* **2** N-PROPER **The Capitol** is the government building in Washington, D.C., in which the U.S. Congress meets. *El Capitolio* ❑ *Thousands of demonstrators gathered in front of the Capitol. Miles de manifestantes se reunieron frente al Capitolio.*

capitol

**Word Link** *let ≈ little : booklet, caplet, pamphlet*

**cap|let** /kæplɪt/ (**caplets**) N-COUNT A **caplet** is an oval tablet of medicine. *comprimido*

**cap|sule** /kæpsᵊl/ (**capsules**) **1** N-COUNT A **capsule** is a very small tube containing powdered or liquid medicine, which you swallow. *cápsula* **2** N-COUNT The **capsule** of a spacecraft is the part in which the astronauts travel. *cápsula* ❑ *...a Russian space capsule. ...una cápsula espacial rusa.*

**cap|tain** /kæptɪn/ (**captains, captaining, captained**) **1** N-COUNT; N-TITLE; N-VOC In the army, navy, and some other armed forces, a **captain** is an officer of middle rank. *capitán* ❑ *...Captain Mark Phillips. ...el capitán Mark Phillips.* ❑ *...a captain in the army. ...un capitán del ejército.* **2** N-COUNT The **captain of** a sports team is the player in charge of it. *capitán* ❑ *...Mickey Thomas, the captain of the tennis team. ...Mickey Thomas, el capitán del equipo de tenis.* **3** N-COUNT The **captain** of an airplane or ship is the person in charge of it. *capitán* ❑ *...the captain of the boat. ...el capitán del barco.* **4** N-COUNT; N-TITLE In the United States and some other countries, a **captain** is a high-ranking police officer or firefighter. *capitán* ❑ *...a former police captain. ...un antiguo capitán de policía.* **5** V-T If you **captain** a team or a ship, you are the captain of it. *capitanear* ❑ *He captained the winning*

*team in 1991.* *Capitaneó el equipo ganador en 1991.*
→ see **boat, ship**

**cap|tion** /kæpʃᵊn/ (**captions**) N-COUNT A **caption** of a picture consists of the words which are printed underneath. *subtítulo* ❑ *The photo had the caption "Home for the holidays."* *La fotografía tenía el subtítulo "En casa por las fiestas".*

**Word Link** *cap ≈ seize : captive, escape, capture*

**cap|tive** /kæptɪv/ (**captives**) **1** ADJ A **captive** animal or person is being kept in a place and is not allowed to escape. *cautivo* [LITERARY] ❑ *...captive rats, mice, and monkeys.* *...ratas, ratones y monos cautivos.* **2** • A **captive** is a prisoner. *cautivo o cautiva* ❑ *He survived for four months as a captive.* *Sobrevivió cuatro meses cautivo.* **3** PHRASE If you **take** someone **captive** or **hold** someone **captive,** you take or keep them as a prisoner. *tomar prisionero* ❑ *The kidnappers held Richard captive for a year.* *Los secuestradores mantuvieron preso a Richard durante un año.*

**cap|ture** /kæptʃər/ (**captures, capturing, captured**) **1** V-T If you **capture** someone or something, you catch them or take possession of them, especially in a war. *capturar* ❑ *The enemy shot down one airplane and captured the pilot.* *El enemigo derribó un avión y capturó al piloto.* • **Capture** is also a noun. *captura* ❑ *...the final battles which led to the army's capture of the town.* *...las batallas finales que llevaron a la captura del pueblo por parte del ejército.* **2** V-T If someone or something **captures** a quality, feeling, or atmosphere, they represent or express it successfully. *capturar* ❑ *...food that captures the spirit of the Mediterranean.* *...comida que captura el espíritu del Mediterráneo.*

**Word Partnership** Usar *capture* con:

V. **avoid** capture, **escape** capture, **fail to** capture **1**
N. capture **territory** **1**
capture **your attention**, capture **your imagination** **2**

**car** /kɑr/ (**cars**) **1** N-COUNT A **car** is a motor vehicle with room for a small number of passengers. *carro, coche* ❑ *He had left his tickets in his car.* *Había dejado sus boletos en el coche.* ❑ *They arrived by car.* *Llegaron en carro.* **2** N-COUNT A **car** is one of the separate, long sections of a train. *vagón* ❑ *The company manufactured railroad cars.* *La compañía fabricaba vagones de tren.* ❑ *He made his way into the dining car.* *Logró llegar hasta el vagón comedor.*
→ see Word Web: **car**
→ see **train**

**Word Link** *hydr ≈ water : carbohydrate, hydroelectric, hydroponics*

**car|bo|hy|drate** /kɑrboʊhaɪdreɪt/ (**carbohydrates**) N-VAR **Carbohydrates** are energy-giving substances found in foods such as sugar and bread. *carbohidrato* ❑ *...carbohydrates such as bread, pasta, or potatoes.* *...carbohidratos como el pan, la pasta o las papas.*
→ see **calorie, diet**

**car|bon** /kɑrbən/ N-UNCOUNT **Carbon** is a chemical element that diamonds and coal are made of. *carbono*
→ see **fossil**

**car|bon|at|ed** /kɑrbəneɪtɪd/ ADJ **Carbonated** drinks are drinks that contain small bubbles of carbon dioxide. *carbonatado, gaseoso* ❑ *...colas and other carbonated soft drinks.* *...colas y otras bebidas gaseosas.*

**car|bon di|ox|ide** /kɑrbən daɪɒksaɪd/ N-UNCOUNT **Carbon dioxide** is a gas that animals and people breathe out. *bióxido de carbono*
→ see **air, greenhouse effect, ozone, photosynthesis, respiratory system**

**car|bon mon|ox|ide** /kɑrbən mənɒksaɪd/ N-UNCOUNT **Carbon monoxide** is a poisonous gas produced especially by the engines of vehicles. *monóxido de carbono*
→ see **ozone**

**car|bu|re|tor** /kɑrbəreɪtər/ (**carburetors**) N-COUNT A **carburetor** is the part of an engine, usually in a car, in which air and gasoline are mixed together to form a vapor which can be burned. *carburador*

**card** /kɑrd/ (**cards, carding, carded**) **1** N-COUNT A **card** is a piece of stiff paper or thin cardboard on which something is written or printed. *tarjeta* ❑ *He wrote "I love you" on the card he sent with the*

**Word Web** car

The first mass-produced **automobile** in the U.S. was the Model T. In 1909, Ford sold over 10,000 of these **vehicles**. They all had the same basic **engine** and chassis. For years the only color choice was black. Three different bodies were available—roadster, sedan, and coupe. Today car makers offer many more choices. These include **convertibles**, sports cars, **station wagons**, **vans**, pick-up **trucks**, and SUVs. Laws now require **seat belts** and airbags to make **driving** safer. Some car makers now offer **hybrid** vehicles. They combine an electrical engine with an **internal combustion engine** to improve **fuel** economy.

flowers. Escribió "Te amo" en la tarjeta que envió con las flores. **2** N-COUNT A **card** is a small piece of cardboard or plastic that you use, for example, to prove your identity, to pay for things, or to give information about yourself. *credencial* ❑ *Members must show their membership card.* *Los miembros deben mostrar su credencial de afiliación.* ❑ *He paid the bill with a credit card.* *Pagó la cuenta con su tarjeta de crédito.* **3** N-COUNT A **card** is a piece of stiff paper with a picture and a message which you send to someone on a special occasion. *tarjeta* ❑ *She sends me a card on my birthday.* *Me manda una tarjeta de felicitación por mi cumpleaños.* **4** N-COUNT **Cards** are thin pieces of cardboard with numbers or pictures on them which are used to play various games. *carta* ❑ *...a deck of cards.* *...una baraja.* ❑ *They enjoy themselves playing cards.* *Se divierten jugando cartas.* **5** N-UNCOUNT **Card** is strong, stiff paper or thin cardboard. *cartón, cartulina* ❑ *She put the pieces of card in her pocket.* *Guardó los pedazos de cartón en su bolsillo.* **6** V-T If you **are carded,** someone asks you to show a document to prove that you are old enough to do something, for example, to buy alcohol. *pedir a alguien que muestre su identificación que pruebe que se es mayor de edad.* ❑ *For the first time in many years, I got carded.* *Por primera vez en muchos años, me pidieron mi identificación.* **7** → see also **bank card, credit card, debit card, greeting card, identity card, playing card**

**card|board** /kɑrdbɔrd/ N-UNCOUNT **Cardboard** is thick, stiff paper that is used to make boxes and other containers. *cartón* ❑ *...a cardboard box.* *...una caja de cartón.*

**car|di|ac** /kɑrdiæk/ ADJ **Cardiac** means relating to the heart. *cardiaco* [MEDICAL] ❑ *The man was suffering from cardiac weakness.* *El hombre sufría de debilidad cardiaca.*
→ see **muscle**

**car|di|ac mus|cle** (**cardiac muscles**) N-VAR **Cardiac muscle** is the muscle in the heart that pumps blood around the body by contracting. *músculo cardiaco*

**car|di|nal** /kɑrdənəl/ (**cardinals**) **1** N-COUNT; N-TITLE A **cardinal** is a high-ranking priest in the Catholic church. *cardenal* ❑ *In 1448, Nicholas became a cardinal.* *En 1448, Nicolás fue nombrado cardenal.* **2** ADJ A **cardinal** rule or quality is extremely important. *fundamental* [FORMAL] ❑ *As a salesman, your cardinal rule is to do everything you can to satisfy a customer.* *Como vendedor, tu regla fundamental es hacer todo lo posible para tener satisfecho al cliente.* **3** N-COUNT A **cardinal** is a common North American bird. The male has bright red feathers. *cardenal*

**car|di|nal di|rec|tion** (**cardinal directions**) N-COUNT The **cardinal directions** are the four main points of the compass, north, south, east, and west. *dirección cardinal*

**car|dio|vas|cu|lar sys|tem** (**cardiovascular systems**) N-COUNT The **cardiovascular system** carries blood to and from the body's cells. The organs in this system include the heart, the arteries, and the veins. *sistema cardiovascular*
→ see Word Web: **cardiovascular system**

**care** /kɛər/ (**cares, caring, cared**) **1** V-T/V-I If you **care** about something, you are concerned about it or interested in it. *preocuparse* ❑ *...a company that cares about the environment.* *...una empresa que se preocupa por el medio ambiente.* ❑ *...young men who did not care whether they lived or died.* *...hombres jóvenes a quienes no les importaba estar vivos o muertos.* **2** V-I If you **care for** someone, you feel a lot of affection for them. *querer* ❑ *He still cared for me.* *Todavía me quería.* **3** V-I If you **care for** someone or something, you look after them and keep them in a good state or condition. *cuidar* ❑ *They hired a nurse to care for her.* *Contrataron a una enfermera para que la cuidara.* • **Care** is also a noun. *cuidado* ❑ *Sensitive teeth need special care.* *Los dientes sensibles necesitan cuidados especiales.* **4** V-T/V-I You can ask someone if they would **care for** something or if they would **care to** do something as a polite way of asking if they would like to have or do something. *¿Le importaría...?, ¿Quiere...?* ❑ *Would you care for some orange juice?* *¿Quiere un poco de jugo de naranja?* **5** N-UNCOUNT If you do something **with care,** you do it with careful attention to avoid mistakes or damage. *con cuidado* ❑ *He took care to close the door.* *Cerró la puerta con cuidado.* **6** N-COUNT Your **cares** are your worries, anxieties, or fears. *preocupación* ❑ *Lean back in a hot bath and forget all the cares of the day.* *Recuéstese en un baño caliente y olvide todas las preocupaciones del día.* **7** → see also **caring, day care, intensive care** **8** PHRASE If you **take care of** someone or something, you look after them and prevent them from being harmed or damaged. *cuidar* ❑ *There was no one else to take care of their children.* *No había nadie más que cuidara a los niños.*

**Word Web** **cardiovascular system**

The **cardiovascular** or **circulatory system** carries **oxygen** and **nutrients** to **cells** in all parts of the body. It also removes waste from these cells. The **heart** pumps the **blood** through the **veins** and **arteries.** A human body contains more than 100,000 kilometers of veins and arteries. The blood follows two main routes. **Pulmonary circulation** carries blood through the **lungs** where it absorbs oxygen. The **systemic route** carries the oxygen-rich blood from the lungs to the rest of the body. Blood contains three types of cells. **Red blood cells** carry oxygen. **White blood cells** help fight disease. **Platelets** help the blood clot when there is an injury.

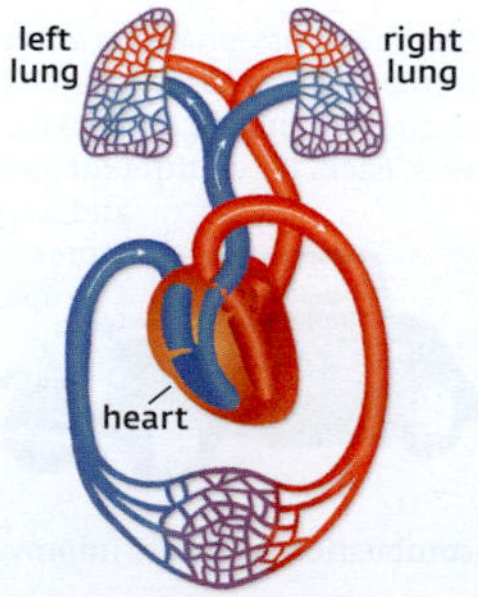

**Word Partnership** Usar *care* con:

ADJ. **good** care, **loving** care 3
V. **provide** care, **receive** care 3

**ca|reen** /kərin/ (**careens, careening, careened**) V-I If a person or vehicle **careens** somewhere, they move fast and in an uncontrolled way. *ir a toda velocidad* ❑ *He stood to one side as they careened past him.* *Se quitó del paso mientras lo pasaban a toda velocidad.*

**ca|reer** /kərɪər/ (**careers, careering, careered**) 1 N-COUNT A **career** is a job or profession. *carrera* ❑ *...a career as a fashion designer.* *...una carrera como diseñador grafico.* ❑ *...a political career.* *...una carrera política.* 2 N-COUNT Your **career** is the part of your life that you spend working. *carrera* ❑ *During his career, he wrote more than fifty plays.* *Escribió más de cincuenta obras durante su carrera.* 3 V-I If a person or vehicle **careers** somewhere, they move fast and in an uncontrolled way. *ir a toda velocidad* ❑ *His car careered into a river.* *Su carro iba a toda velocidad y cayó en un río.*

**Thesaurus** *career* Ver también:

N. field, job, profession, specialty, vocation, work 1

**Word Partnership** Usar *career* con:

N. career **advancement**, career **goals**, career **opportunities**, career **path** 1 2
ADJ. **political** career, **professional** career 1 2
V. **pursue a** career 1 2

**care|free** /kɛərfri/ ADJ A **carefree** person or period of time is without problems or responsibilities. *despreocupado* ❑ *Chantal remembered carefree summers at the beach.* *Chantal recordaba veranos despreocupados en la playa.*

**Word Link** *ful ≈ filled with : beautiful, careful, dreadful*

**care|ful** /kɛərfəl/ 1 ADJ If you are **careful**, you give serious attention to what you are doing, in order to avoid damage or mistakes. *cuidadoso* ❑ *Be very careful with this stuff, it can be dangerous.* *Sé muy cuidadoso con esto, puede ser peligroso.* ❑ *Careful on those stairs!* *¡Cuidado con las escaleras!* ● **care|ful|ly** ADV *con cuidado* ❑ *Have a nice time, and drive carefully.* *Pásenla bien, y manejen con cuidado.* 2 ADJ **Careful** work, thought, or examination is thorough and shows a concern for details. *cuidadoso* ❑ *The trip needs careful planning.* *El viaje requiere de planeación cuidadosa.* ● **care|ful|ly** ADV *cuidadosamente* ❑ *All her letters were carefully filed away.* *Todas sus cartas estaban cuidadosamente archivadas.*

**Word Partnership** Usar *careful* con:

ADV. **better be** careful 1
**extremely** careful, **very** careful 1 2
N. careful **attention**, careful **consideration**, careful **observation**, careful **planning** 2

**care|giv|er** /kɛərgɪvər/ (**caregivers**) also **care giver** N-COUNT A **caregiver** is someone who looks after another person, for example, a person who is disabled, ill, or very young. *persona que tiene a su cuidado a un incapacitado* ❑ *It is nearly always women who are the main caregivers.* *Casi siempre son mujeres las principales encargadas de los incapacitados.*

**care|less** /kɛərlɪs/ ADJ If you are **careless**, you do not pay enough attention to what you are doing, and so you make mistakes. *descuidado* ❑ *I'm sorry. How careless of me.* *Disculpe, qué descuidado de mi parte.* ❑ *Some parents are careless with their children's health.* *Algunos padres son descuidados respecto a la salud de sus hijos.* ● **care|less|ly** ADV *sin cuidado* ❑ *She was fined $200 for driving carelessly.* *Le pusieron una multa de 200 dólares por manejar sin cuidado.* ● **care|less|ness** N-UNCOUNT *descuido* ❑ *Errors are sometimes made from simple carelessness.* *Los errores a veces suceden por simple descuido.*

**Thesaurus** *careless* Ver también:

ADJ. absent-minded, forgetful, irresponsible, reckless, sloppy; (*ant.*) attentive, careful, cautious

**car|go** /kɑrgoʊ/ (**cargoes**) N-VAR The **cargo** of a ship or plane is the goods that it is carrying. *cargamento* ❑ *...a cargo of bananas.* *...un cargamento de plátanos.*
→ see **ship**

**car|go pants** N-PLURAL **Cargo pants** are large, loose pants with lots of pockets. *pantalones cargo* ❑ *...a pair of brown cargo pants.* *...un par de pantalones cargo cafés.*

**car|ing** /kɛərɪŋ/ ADJ A **caring** person is affectionate, helpful, and sympathetic. *bondadoso, afectuoso* ❑ *He is a lovely boy, very gentle and caring.* *Es un niño adorable, muy dulce y afectuoso.*

**car|ni|val** /kɑrnɪvəl/ (**carnivals**) 1 N-COUNT A **carnival** is a public festival with music, processions, and dancing. *carnaval* 2 N-COUNT A **carnival** is a traveling show held in a park or field, with machines to ride on, entertainments, and games. *feria*

**car|ni|vore** /kɑrnɪvɔr/ (**carnivores**) 1 N-COUNT A **carnivore** is an animal that eats meat. *carnívoro* [TECHNICAL] 2 N-COUNT If you describe someone as a **carnivore**, you are saying, especially in a humorous way, that they eat meat. *carnívoro o carnívora*
→ see Word Web: **carnivore**

**car|pen|ter** /kɑrpɪntər/ (**carpenters**) N-COUNT A **carpenter** is a person whose job is making and repairing wooden things. *carpintero o carpintera*

**car|pet** /kɑrpɪt/ (**carpets**) N-VAR A **carpet** is a thick covering of soft material which is laid over a floor or a staircase. *alfombra* ❑ *They laid new carpets.* *Colocaron alfombras nuevas.*

**carpet|bag|ger** /kɑrpɪtbægər/ (**carpetbaggers**) N-COUNT If you call someone a **carpetbagger**, you disapprove of them because they are trying to become a politician in an area which is not their home, because they think they are more likely to succeed there. *político oportunista que pretende representar una localidad que no es la suya* ❑ *He was called a carpetbagger because he lived outside the district.* *Se le llamó político oportunista porque vivía en otro distrito.*

**car|pool** /kɑrpul/ (**carpools, carpooling,**

C

**Word Web** carnivore

**Carnivores** are at the top of the **food chain**. These **predators** have to catch and kill their **prey**, so they must be fast and agile. They also have special teeth in the front of their mouths. These large, strong canine teeth allow them to **stab** their prey. Sharp **incisors** work almost like scissors. They tear animal **flesh**. Carnivores include large **wild** animals such as **lions** and **wolves**. Many people think **bears** are carnivores, but they are **omnivorous**. They eat plants and berries as well as **meat**. There are many more **herbivores** than carnivores in the world.

**carpooled**) also **car pool** or **car-pool** V-I If a group of people **carpool**, they take turns driving each other to work, or driving each other's children to school. *trasladarse en grupo al trabajo, en un sólo automóvil* ❏ *The government says fewer Americans are carpooling to work. El gobierno dice que cada vez menos estadounidenses se trasladan en grupos al trabajo.*

**car|rel** /kærəl/ (**carrels**) N-COUNT A **carrel** is a desk with low walls on three sides, at which a student can work in private, especially in a library. *cubículo*

**car|riage** /kærɪdʒ/ (**carriages**) N-COUNT A **carriage** is an old-fashioned vehicle pulled by horses. *carruaje* ❏ *...an open carriage pulled by six beautiful gray horses. ...un carruaje abierto, tirado por seis hermosos caballos grises.*

**car|ri|er** /kæriər/ (**carriers**) **1** N-COUNT A **carrier** is a vehicle that is used for carrying people, especially soldiers, or things. *portaaviones* ❏ *...a helicopter carrier. ...un portaaviones que transporta helicópteros.* **2** N-COUNT A **carrier** is a company that provides telecommunications services, such as telephone and Internet services. *compañía de telecomunicaciones* ❏ *The company is Japan's top wireless carrier. La empresa es la compañía de telecomunicaciones inalámbricas más grande de Japón.* **3** N-COUNT A **carrier** is a passenger airline. *línea aérea* ❏ *The airline is the third-largest carrier at Denver International Airport. La aerolínea es la tercera más grande en el Aeropuerto Internacional de Denver.*
→ see **ship**

**car|rot** /kærət/ (**carrots**) **1** N-VAR **Carrots** are long, thin, orange-colored vegetables that grow under the ground. *zanahoria* **2** N-COUNT Something that is offered to people in order to persuade them to do something can be referred to as a **carrot**. *incentivo* ❏ *They are given targets, with a carrot of extra pay if they achieve them. Se les dan metas, con incentivos extras si los logran.*
→ see **vegetable**

**car|ry** /kæri/ (**carries, carrying, carried**) **1** V-T If you **carry** something, you take it with you, holding it so that it does not touch the ground. *cargar* ❏ *He was carrying a briefcase. Cargaba un portafolios.* ❏ *She carried her son to the car. Cargó a su hijo hasta el coche.* **2** V-T If you **carry** something, you have it with you wherever you go. *llevar* ❏ *You have to carry a passport. Tienes que llevar tu pasaporte.* **3** V-T To **carry** someone or something means to take them somewhere. *llevar* ❏ *Insects carry the pollen from plant to plant. Los insectos llevan el polen de planta en planta.* ❏ *They were carrying a message of thanks to President Mubarak. Llevaban un mensaje de agradecimiento al Presidente Mubarak.* **4** V-T If someone **is carrying** a disease, they are infected with it and can pass it on to others. *portar* ❏ *...people carrying the virus. ...las personas que portan el virus.* **5** V-T If an action or situation **carries** a particular quality or consequence, it has it. *conllevar* ❏ *The medication carries no risk for your baby. El medicamento no conlleva riesgos para su bebé.* ❏ *It was a crime that carried the death penalty. Fue un crimen que conllevó a la pena de muerte.* **6** V-T If you **carry** an idea or a method to a particular extent, you use or develop it to that extent. *llevar* ❏ *It's not a new idea, but I carried it to extremes. No es una idea nueva, pero la llevé hasta el extremo.* **7** V-T If a newspaper or poster **carries** a picture or an article, it contains it. *llevar* ❏ *Several papers carry the photograph of Mr. Anderson. Varios periódicos llevan la fotografía del señor Anderson.* **8** V-T In a debate, if a proposal or motion **is carried**, a majority of people vote in favor of it. *aprobar* ❏ *The motion was carried by 322 votes to 296. La moción fue aprobada por 322 votos contra 296.* **9** V-I If a sound **carries**, it can be heard a long way away. *llegar* ❏ *He doubted if the sound would carry far. Dudaba que el sonido llegara tan lejos.* **10** PHRASE If you **get carried away**, you are so eager or excited about something that you do something hasty or foolish. *dejarse llevar* ❏ *I got completely carried away and almost cried. Me dejé llevar y casi lloré.*

▸ **carry on** **1** PHR-VERB If you **carry on** doing something, you continue to do it. *continuar* ❏ *The assistant carried on talking. El asistente continuó platicando.* ❏ *Her bravery has given him the will to carry on with his life. Su valor le ha dado la voluntad para continuar con su vida.* ❏ *His eldest son Joseph carried on his father's traditions. Joseph, su hijo mayor, continuó las tradiciones paternas.* **2** PHR-VERB If you **carry on** an activity, you do it or take part in it for a period of time. *mantener* ❏ *They carried on a conversation all morning. Mantuvieron la conversación toda la mañana.*

▸ **carry out** PHR-VERB If you **carry out** a threat, task, or instruction, you do it or act according to it. *llevar a cabo* ❏ *The Social Democrats could still carry out their threat to leave the government. Los social demócratas todavía podrían llevar a cabo su amenaza de dejar el gobierno.* ❏ *Police believe the attacks were carried out by nationalists. La policía cree que los nacionalistas llevaron a cabo los ataques.*

▸ **carry through** PHR-VERB If you **carry** something **through**, you do it, often in spite of difficulties. *sostener* ❏ *We don't have the confidence that the U.N. will carry through this program. No* tenemos la confianza de que las Naciones Unidas puedan sostener este programa.

| Thesaurus | carry | Ver también: |
|---|---|---|
| v. | bear, bring, cart, haul, lug, move, truck 1 | |

**car|ry|ing ca|pac|ity** (**carrying capacities**) N-COUNT The **carrying capacity** of a particular area is the maximum number of people or animals that can live there on a long-term basis. *capacidad de persistencia* [TECHNICAL]

**car|ry-on** ADJ Your **carry-on** bags are bags you have with you in an airplane, rather than ones that are carried in the hold. *bolsas de mano* ❑ *Passengers' carry-on bags are put through X-ray machines. Pasan las bolsas de mano de los pasajeros por máquinas de rayos X.*

**car|ry|over** /kæriouvər/ (**carryovers**) N-COUNT If something is a **carryover from** an earlier time, it began during an earlier time but still exists or happens now. *venir desde* ❑ *His team's success is a carryover from the high school season. El éxito de su equipo viene desde la temporada de la preparatoria.*

**car|sick** /kɑrsɪk/ ADJ If someone feels **carsick,** they feel sick as a result of traveling in a car. *mareado* ❑ *My son always gets carsick if we have to travel far. Mi hijo siempre se marea cuando hacemos viajes largos en coche.*

**cart** /kɑrt/ (**carts, carting, carted**) 1 N-COUNT A **cart** is an old-fashioned wooden vehicle, usually pulled by an animal. *carreta* ❑ *...a country where there are more horse-drawn carts than cars. ...un país donde hay más carretas tiradas por caballos, que autos.* 2 N-COUNT A **cart** is a small vehicle with a motor. *carrito* ❑ *Transportation is by electric cart. El transporte es por carrito eléctrico.* 3 N-COUNT A **cart** or a **shopping cart** is a large metal basket on wheels which is provided by stores such as supermarkets for customers to use while they are in the store. *carrito* 4 V-T If you **cart** things or people somewhere, you carry them or transport them there, often with difficulty. *transportar con dificultad* [INFORMAL] ❑ *He carted off the entire contents of the house. Se llevó todos los muebles de la casa (con dificultad).* ❑ *...a bag for carting around your child's books or toys. ...una maleta para cargar con los juguetes y libros de su hijo.*
→ see **golf, hotel**

**car|tel** /kɑrtɛl/ (**cartels**) N-COUNT A **cartel** is an association of similar companies or businesses that have grouped together in order to prevent competition and to control prices. *cártel* [BUSINESS] ❑ *...the OPEC oil cartel. ...el cártel OPEC de petróleo.*

**car|ti|lage** /kɑrtɪlɪdʒ/ (**cartilages**) N-VAR **Cartilage** is a strong, flexible substance which surrounds joints in your body. *cartílago* ❑ *The player tore cartilage in his chest. El jugador tuvo un desgarre en el cartílago del pecho.*
→ see **shark**

**car|ton** /kɑrtᵊn/ (**cartons**) 1 N-COUNT A **carton** is a plastic or cardboard container in which food or drink is sold. *cartón* ❑ *...a quart carton of milk. ...un envase de leche de un cuarto.* 2 N-COUNT A **carton** is a large, strong cardboard box. *caja* ❑ *There were 10,000 letters, 12 cartons full. Había 10,000 cartas, 12 cajas llenas.*
→ see **container**

**car|toon** /kɑrtun/ (**cartoons**) 1 N-COUNT A **cartoon** is a humorous drawing in a newspaper or magazine. *caricatura* ❑ *...cartoon characters. ...personajes de caricatura.* 2 N-COUNT A **cartoon** is a film in which all the characters and scenes are drawn rather than being real people or objects. *caricaturas* ❑ *...a TV set showing a cartoon comedy. ...una televisión con caricaturas.*
→ see **animation**

**car|tridge** /kɑrtrɪdʒ/ (**cartridges**) 1 N-COUNT In a gun, a **cartridge** is a tube containing a bullet and an explosive substance. *cartucho* 2 N-COUNT A **cartridge** is part of a machine that can be easily removed and replaced when it is worn out or empty. *cartucho* ❑ *Change the filter cartridge. Cambie el cartucho del filtro.*

**carve** /kɑrv/ (**carves, carving, carved**) 1 V-T/V-I If you **carve** an object, you cut it out of wood or stone. If you **carve** wood or stone, you make an object by cutting it out. *tallar* ❑ *One of the prisoners has carved a beautiful wooden chess set. Uno de los presos talló un hermoso juego de ajedrez de madera.* ❑ *I picked up a piece of wood and started carving. Tomé un pedazo de madera y comencé a tallar.* 2 → see also **carving** 3 V-T If you **carve** writing or a design **on** an object, you cut it into the surface. *grabar* ❑ *He carved his name on his desk. Grabó su nombre en su escritorio.* 4 V-T If you **carve** meat, you cut slices from it. *cortar* ❑ *Andrew began to carve the chicken. Andrew empezó a cortar el pollo.*

▸ **carve out** PHR-VERB If you **carve** or **carve out** a niche or a career, you succeed in getting the position or the career that you want by your own efforts. *forjar* ❑ *Vick carved out his niche as the fastest quarterback in football. Vick forjó su posición como el mariscal de campo más rápido del futbol americano.*

▸ **carve up** PHR-VERB If you say that someone **carves** something **up,** you disapprove of the way they have divided it into small parts. *dividir* ❑ *He has carved up the company that Smith created. Ha dividido la empresa que Smith creó.*

**case**
❶ INSTANCES AND OTHER ABSTRACT MEANINGS
❷ CONTAINERS
❸ GRAMMAR TERM USES

| Word Link | *cas ≈ box, hold : case, casette, suitcase* |
|---|---|

**❶ case** /keɪs/ (**cases**) 1 N-COUNT A **case** is a particular situation or instance, especially one that you are using as an example of something more general. *caso* ❑ *Prices of these goods have fallen, especially in the case of computers. Los precios de estos bienes han disminuido, en especial en el caso de las computadoras.* ❑ *In some cases, it can be very difficult. En algunos casos, puede ser muy difícil.* 2 N-COUNT A **case** is a person that a professional such as a doctor is dealing with. *caso* ❑ *Doctors were meeting to discuss her case. Los doctores estaban reunidos para analizar su caso.* 3 N-COUNT A crime, or the trial that takes place after a crime, can be called a **case.** *caso* ❑ *...a murder case. ...un caso de*

C

*asesinato.* ❑ *...court cases.* *...los casos de los tribunales.* **4** N-COUNT The **case for** or **against** a plan or idea consists of the facts and reasons used to support it or oppose it. *gumentos a favor, argumentos en contra* ❑ *He sat there while I made the case for his dismissal.* *Se sentó ahí mientras yo daba las razones para su despido.* **5** PHRASE You say **in any case** when you are adding another reason for something you have just said or done. *en cualquier caso, de todas formas* ❑ *The concert was sold out, and in any case, most people could not afford the price of a ticket.* *Los boletos para el concierto se agotaron, y en cualquier caso, la mayoría no podía pagar lo que costaban.* **6** PHRASE If you do something **in case** or **just in case** a particular thing happens, you do it because that thing might happen. *si acaso/por si acaso, por si las dudas* ❑ *In case anyone was following me, I jumped on a bus.* *Por si alguien me estuviera siguiendo, me subí a un autobús.* ❑ *Many stores along the route are closed in case of trouble.* *Muchas tiendas sobre la ruta están cerradas por si hay problemas.* ❑ *We've already talked about this but I'll ask you again just in case.* *Ya hablamos de eso pero te volveré a preguntar, por si acaso.* **7** PHRASE You say **in that case** or **in which case** to indicate that what you are going to say is true if the possible situation that has just been mentioned actually exists. *en ese caso, en cuyo caso* ❑ *Perhaps you've some doubts about the attack. In that case it may interest you to know that Miss Woods witnessed it.* *Quizá tengan algunas dudas sobre el ataque. En ese caso, les puede interesar saber que la señorita Woods lo presenció.* **8** PHRASE If you say that a task or situation is **a case of** a particular thing, you mean that it consists of that thing or can be described as that thing. *cuestión de* ❑ *Every team has a weakness; it's just a case of finding it.* *Cada equipo tiene una debilidad; sólo es cuestión de encontrarla.*
→ see **hospital**

**❷ case** /keɪs/ (**cases**) **1** N-COUNT A **case** is a container that is designed to hold or protect something. *estuche, caja* ❑ *...a black case for his glasses.* *...un estuche negro para sus lentes.* **2** → see also **bookcase, briefcase**

**❸ case** /keɪs/ (**cases**) N-COUNT In the grammar of many languages, the **case** of a group such as a noun group or adjective group is the form it has which shows its relationship to other groups in the sentence. *case*

**case-sensitive** ADJ If a word is **case-sensitive,** it must be written in a particular form, for example using all capital letters or all small letters, in order for a computer to recognize it. *que distingue mayúsculas y minúsculas* [COMPUTING]

**cash** /kæʃ/ (**cashes, cashing, cashed**) **1** N-UNCOUNT **Cash** is money, especially money in the form of bills and coins rather than checks. *dinero en efectivo* ❑ *...two thousand dollars in cash.* *...dos mil dólares en efectivo.* ❑ *...a financial-services group with plenty of cash.* *...un grupo de servicios financieros con bastante dinero.* **2** V-T If you **cash** a check, you exchange it at a bank for the amount of money that it is worth. *cobrar* ❑ *If you cash a check, they ask for an ID.* *Si cobras un cheque, te piden una identificación.*

▸ **cash in** PHR-VERB If someone **cashes in on** a situation, they use it to gain an advantage, often in an unfair or dishonest way. *aprovecharse de* ❑ *Private hospitals were trying to cash in on the growing elderly population.* *Los hospitales privados estaban tratando de aprovecharse del creciente número de ancianos.*

**cash bar** (**cash bars**) N-COUNT A **cash bar** is a bar at a party or similar event where guests can buy drinks. *barra* ❑ *At 6 p.m. there will be a reception and cash bar.* *A las 6 p.m. habrá una recepción y barra.*

**cash|ier** /kæʃɪər/ (**cashiers**) N-COUNT A **cashier** is a person who customers pay money to or get money from in places such as stores or banks. *cajero o cajera*

**cash|ier's check** (**cashier's checks**) N-COUNT A **cashier's check** is one which a cashier signs and which is drawn on a bank's own funds. *cheque de caja*

**cash on de|liv|ery** PHRASE If you pay for goods **cash on delivery,** you pay for them in cash when they are delivered. The abbreviation **C.O.D.** is also used. *entrega contra reembolso* ❑ *...an option of paying cash on delivery or by credit card.* *...la opción de pagar la entrega contra reembolso o con tarjeta de crédito.*

**ca|si|no** /kəsinoʊ/ (**casinos**) N-COUNT A **casino** is a place where people gamble. *casino*

**cas|ket** N-COUNT A **casket** is a **coffin.** *ataúd*

**cas|se|role** /kæsəroʊl/ (**casseroles**) **1** N-VAR A **casserole** is a meal made by cooking food slowly in a liquid. *guiso* ❑ *...a beef casserole.* *...un guiso de carne* **2** N-COUNT A **casserole** or a **casserole dish** is a large heavy container with a lid used for cooking casseroles. *cazuela* ❑ *Place all the chopped vegetables into a casserole dish.* *Colocar todas las verduras picadas en la cazuela.*

| Word Link | cas ≈ box, hold : case, casette, suitcase |
|---|---|

| Word Link | ette ≈ small : casette, cigarette, maquette |
|---|---|

**cas|sette** /kəsɛt/ (**cassettes**) N-COUNT A **cassette** is a small, flat, rectangular plastic case containing magnetic tape which is used for recording and playing back sound. *cassette*

**cast** /kæst/ (**casts, casting**)

> The form **cast** is used in the present tense and is the past tense and past participle.

**1** N-COUNT The **cast** of a play or movie is all the people who act in it. *elenco, reparto* ❑ *The show is very amusing and the cast is very good.* *El espectáculo es muy entretenido y el elenco es muy bueno.* **2** V-T To **cast** an actor means to choose them to act a particular role. *asignar, dar el papel de* ❑ *He was cast as a college professor.* *Le dieron el papel de profesor universitario.* **3** V-T If you **cast** your eyes or **cast** a look somewhere, you look there. *echar un vistazo* [WRITTEN] ❑ *He cast a glance at the two men.* *Echó un vistazo a los dos hombres.* ❑ *I cast my eyes down briefly.* *Bajé la mirada por poco tiempo.* **4** V-T If something **casts** a light or shadow somewhere, it causes it to appear there. *proyectar* [WRITTEN] ❑ *The moon cast a bright light over the yard.* *La luna proyectaba una luz brillante en el patio.* **5** V-T To **cast** doubt **on** something means to cause people to be unsure about it. *poner en duda algo* ❑ *Last night a top criminal psychologist cast doubt on the theory.* *Ayer en la noche*

un destacado criminólogo puso en duda la teoría. **6** V-T When you **cast** your vote in an election, you vote. *emitir* ❑ *The people will cast their votes in the country's first elections. El pueblo emitirá su voto en las primeras elecciones del país.* **7** V-T To **cast** an object means to make it by pouring a liquid such as hot metal into a specially-shaped container and leaving it there until it becomes hard. *fundir* ❑ *Our door knocker is cast in solid brass. La aldaba de nuestra puerta está fundida en latón.*
→ see **election, pan, theater, vote**

▸ **cast aside** PHR-VERB If you **cast aside** someone or something, you get rid of them. *hacer a un lado* ❑ *We need to cast aside outdated policies. Necesitamos hacer a un lado las políticas anticuadas.*

**caste** /kæst/ (**castes**) N-VAR A **caste** is one of the social classes into which people are divided in a Hindu society. *casta* ❑ *Most of the upper castes worship the goddess Kali. La mayoría de las castas superiores adoran a la diosa Kali.*

**cas|tle** /kæsᵊl/ (**castles**) N-COUNT A **castle** is a large building with thick, high walls that was built in the past to protect people during wars and battles. *castillo*

**cas|ual** /kæʒuəl/ **1** ADJ If you are **casual**, you are relaxed and not very concerned about what is happening. *despreocupado* ❑ *It's difficult for me to be casual about anything. Me es difícil ser despreocupado.* • **casu|al|ly** ADV *con toda tranquilidad* ❑ *"No need to hurry," Ben said casually. —No es necesario apurarse —dijo Ben con toda tranquilidad.* **2** ADJ A **casual** event or situation happens by chance or without planning. *casual, fortuito, ocasional* ❑ *...a casual remark. ...un comentario casual.* **3** ADJ **Casual** clothes are ones that you normally wear at home or on vacation, and not on formal occasions. *informal* ❑ *I also bought some casual clothes for the weekend. También compré ropa informal para el fin de semana.* • **casu|al|ly** ADV *informalmente, de manera informal* ❑ *They were casually dressed. Estaban vestidos de manera informal.*

**cas|ual Fri|day** (**casual Fridays**) also **Casual Friday** N-COUNT In some companies, a **casual Friday** is a Friday when employees are allowed to wear clothes that are more informal than usual. *viernes informal* ❑ *This denim shirt is as great with jeans as it is for work on casual Fridays. Esta camisa de mezclilla es fabulosa tanto para usar con jeans como para trabajar en viernes informal.*

**casu|al|ty** /kæʒuəlti/ (**casualties**) **1** N-COUNT A **casualty** is a person who is injured or killed in a war or in an accident. *víctima, baja, herido* ❑ *Police fired on the demonstrators causing many casualties. La policía disparó a los manifestantes causando muchas víctimas.* **2** N-COUNT A **casualty of** an event or situation is a person or a thing that has suffered badly as a result of it. *víctima* ❑ *One casualty of the battle for power may be the prime minister. Una víctima de la batalla por el poder puede ser el primer ministro.*

**cat** /kæt/ (**cats**) **1** N-COUNT A **cat** is a small furry animal that has a long tail and sharp claws. Cats are often kept as pets. *gato* **2** N-COUNT **Cats** are lions, tigers, and other animals in the same family. *felino* ❑ *The lion is perhaps the most famous member of the cat family. El león es quizás el miembro más famoso de los felinos.*
→ see **pet**

**cata|log** /kætᵊlɒg/ (**catalogs**) also **catalogue** **1** N-COUNT A **catalog** is a list of things such as the goods you can buy from a particular company, the objects in a museum, or the books in a library. *catálogo* ❑ *...the world's biggest seed catalog. ...el catálogo de semillas más grande del mundo.* **2** N-COUNT A **catalog of** similar things, especially bad things, is a number of them considered or discussed one after another. *serie, catálogo* ❑ *His story is a catalog of bad luck. Su historia es un catálogo de desgracias.*
→ see **library**

**cata|lyze** /kætᵊlaɪz/ (**catalyses, catalyzing, catalyzed**) **1** V-T If something **catalyzes** a change or event, it makes it happen. *catalizar* [FORMAL] ❑ *This new report should catalyze further public debate. Este nuevo reportaje debería catalizar el debate público.* **2** V-T In chemistry, if something **catalyzes** a reaction, it causes it to happen. *catalizar* [TECHNICAL] ❑ *The wires do not have a large enough surface to catalyze a big explosion. Los cables no tienen la superficie suficiente para catalizar una gran explosión.*

**ca|tas|tro|phe** /kətæstrəfi/ (**catastrophes**) N-COUNT A **catastrophe** is an unexpected event that causes great suffering or damage. *catástrofe* ❑ *From all points of view, war would be a catastrophe. Desde cualquier punto de vista, la guerra sería una catástrofe.*

**catch**
1 HOLD OR TOUCH
2 MANAGE TO SEE, HEAR, OR TALK TO
3 OTHER USES
4 PHRASAL VERBS

**1 catch** /kætʃ/ (**catches, catching, caught**) **1** V-T If you **catch** a person or animal, you capture them. *atrapar* ❑ *Police say they are confident of catching the gunman. La policía dice que confía en atrapar al pistolero.* ❑ *Where did you catch the fish? ¿Dónde atrapaste al pez?* **2** V-T If you **catch** an object that is moving through the air, you grab it with your hands. *atrapar, cachar* ❑ *I jumped up to catch a ball and fell over. Salté para cachar una pelota y me caí.* • **Catch** is also a noun. *atrapada* ❑ *He missed the catch and the game was lost. Perdió la atrapada y perdieron el juego.* **3** V-T If one thing **catches** another, it hits it. *pegar* ❑ *I caught him with my elbow but it was an accident. Le pegué con el codo pero fue un accidente.* **4** V-I If something **catches on** or **in** an object, it accidentally becomes attached to the object or stuck in it. *atorarse* ❑ *Her ankle caught on a root, and she fell over. Se le atoró el tobillo en una raíz, y se cayó.* **5** to **catch hold of** something → see **hold**

| **Thesaurus** | *catch* | Ver también: |
|---|---|---|
| v. | arrest, capture, grab, seize, snatch, trap; (*ant.*) free, let go, let off, release 1 **1** **2** | |

**2 catch** /kætʃ/ (**catches, catching, caught**) **1** V-T When you **catch** a bus, train, or plane, you get on it in order to travel somewhere. *tomar* ❑ *We were in plenty of time for Anthony to catch the ferry. Teníamos tiempo suficiente para que Anthony tomara el ferry.* **2** V-T If you **catch** someone doing something wrong, you see or find them doing it. *descubrir, cachar* ❑ *He caught a man breaking into a car.*

C

C

*Descubrió a un hombre robando un carro.* ❑ *They caught him with $30,000 cash in a briefcase.* *Lo descubrieron llevando en un portafolio $30,000 en efectivo.* **3** V-T If you **catch** something that someone has said, you manage to hear it. *escuchar* ❑ *I didn't catch your name.* *No escuché tu nombre.* **4** to **catch sight of** something → see **sight**

**❸ catch** /kætʃ/ (**catches, catching, caught**) **1** V-T If something **catches** your attention or your eye, you notice it or become interested in it. *llamar* ❑ *My shoes caught his attention.* *Mis zapatos llamaron su atención.* **2** V-T If you **catch** a cold or a disease, you become ill with it. *contagiarse de, contraer* ❑ *The more stress you are under, the more likely you are to catch a cold.* *Entre más estrés tengas, es más probable que contraigas un resfriado.* **3** V-T If something **catches** the light or if the light **catches** it, it reflects the light and looks bright or shiny. *reflejar* ❑ *They saw the ship's guns, catching the light of the moon.* *Vieron los cañones del barco, reflejando la luz de la luna.* **4** V-T PASSIVE If you **are caught** in a storm or other unpleasant situation, it happens when you cannot avoid its effects. *atrapar* ❑ *He was caught in a storm and almost drowned.* *Lo agarró la tormenta y casi se ahoga.* **5** N-COUNT A **catch** on a window, door, or container is a device that fastens it. *pasador, pestillo, cierre* ❑ *She opened the catch of her bag.* *Abrió el cierre de su bolsa.* **6** N-COUNT A **catch** is a hidden problem or difficulty in a plan or an offer. *problema del sistema* ❑ *The catch is that some of the students in need of help do not ask for it.* *El problema del sistema es que algunos de los estudiantes que necesitan ayuda, no la piden.*

**❹ catch** /kætʃ/ (**catches, catching, caught**)

▸ **catch on** **1** PHR-VERB If you **catch on to** something, you understand it, or realize that it is happening. *entender, captar* ❑ *I was slow to catch on to what she was trying to tell me.* *Me tardé en captar lo que trataba de decirme.* **2** PHR-VERB If something **catches on,** it becomes popular. *ponerse de moda* ❑ *The idea has been around for years without catching on.* *La idea ha circulado por años sin ponerse de moda.*

▸ **catch up** **1** PHR-VERB If you **catch up with** someone, you reach them by walking faster than they are walking. *alcanzar a* ❑ *I stopped and waited for her to catch up.* *Me detuve y esperé que ella me alcanzara.* **2** PHR-VERB To **catch up with** someone means to reach the same standard or level that they have reached. *alcanzar* ❑ *Most late developers will catch up with their friends.* *La mayoría de los alumnos de desarrollo tardío alcanzará el nivel de sus amigos.* ❑ *John began the season better than me but I fought to catch up.* *John comenzó la temporada mejor que yo pero luché por alcanzarlo.* **3** PHR-VERB If you **catch up on** an activity that you have not had much time to do, you spend time doing it. *ponerse al día* ❑ *I was catching up on a bit of reading.* *Estaba poniéndome al día con algunas lecturas.* **4** PHR-VERB If you **are caught up in** something, you are involved in it, usually unwillingly. *verse envuelto en* ❑ *The people weren't part of the conflict; they were just caught up in it.* *Las personas no eran parte del conflicto; sólo se vieron envueltas en él.*

▸ **catch up with** **1** PHR-VERB When people **catch up with** someone who has done something wrong, they succeed in finding them. *atrapar* ❑ *The police caught up with him yesterday.* *La policía lo atrapó ayer.* **2** PHR-VERB If something **catches up with** you, you are forced to deal with an unpleasant situation that you have been able to avoid until now. *poder más que uno* ❑ *His criminal past caught up with him.* *Su pasado criminal pudo más que él.*

**catch|er** /kætʃər/ (**catchers**) N-COUNT In baseball, the **catcher** is the player who stands behind the batter. The catcher has a special glove for catching the ball. *cátcher, receptor o receptora* → see **baseball**

**catch-up** PHRASE If someone **is playing catch-up,** they are trying to equal or better someone else's performance. *jugar para tratar de igualar a* ❑ *We were playing catch-up for most of the game.* *Jugamos para conseguir el empate casi todo el partido.*

**catch|word** also **catch phrase** /kætʃwɜrd/ (**catchwords**) N-COUNT A **catchword** is a word or phrase that becomes popular or well-known. *eslogan* ❑ *The catchword he and his supporters have been using is "consolidation."* *El eslogan que él y sus partidarios han estado usando es "consolidación".*

**cat|ego|ry** /kætɪgɔri/ (**categories**) N-COUNT If people or things are divided into **categories,** they are divided into groups according to their qualities and characteristics. *categoría* ❑ *This book clearly falls into the category of autobiography.* *Este libro evidentemente cae en la categoría de autobiografía.*

| **Thesaurus** | *category* | Ver también: |
|---|---|---|
| N. | class, grouping, kind, rank, sort, type | |

**ca|ter** /keɪtər/ (**caters, catering, catered**) V-I To **cater to** a group of people means to provide all the things that they need or want. *ofrecer servicios* ❑ *...businesses that cater to local trade.* *...negocios que ofrecen servicios al comercio local.*

**ca|ter|ing** /keɪtərɪŋ/ N-UNCOUNT **Catering** is the activity or business of providing food for large numbers of people. *catering* ❑ *His catering business made him a millionaire at 41.* *Su negocio de catering lo hizo millonario a los 41.*

**cat|er|pil|lar** /kætərpɪlər/ (**caterpillars**) N-COUNT A **caterpillar** is a small, worm-like animal that eventually develops into a butterfly or moth. *oruga*

**ca|thar|sis** /kəθɑrsɪs/ N-UNCOUNT **Catharsis** is getting rid of unhappy memories or strong emotions such as anger or sadness by expressing them in some way. *catarsis*

**ca|thedral** /kəθidrəl/ (**cathedrals**) N-COUNT A **cathedral** is a large and important church which has a bishop in charge of it. *catedral* ❑ *...St. Paul's Cathedral.* *...la catedral de San Pablo.*

**Catho|lic** /kæθlɪk/ (**Catholics**) **1** ADJ The **Catholic** Church is the branch of the Christian Church that accepts the Pope as its leader and is based in the Vatican in Rome. *católico* ❑ *...Catholic priests.* *...sacerdotes católicos.* • **Ca|tholi|cism** /kəθɒlɪsɪzəm/ N-UNCOUNT *catolicismo* ❑ *...her interest in Catholicism.* *...su interés en el catolicismo.* **2** N-COUNT A **Catholic** is a member of the Catholic Church. *católico o católica* ❑ *At least nine out of ten Mexicans are Catholics.* *Por lo menos nueve de cada diez mexicanos son católicos.*

**cat|nip** /kætnɪp/ N-UNCOUNT **Catnip** is an herb with scented leaves, which cats are fond of. *nébeda*

**cat|tle** /kæt^əl/ N-PLURAL **Cattle** are cows and bulls. ganado ❑ *...the finest herd of beef cattle for two hundred miles.* ...el mejor ganado vacuno en doscientas millas a la redonda.
→ see **dairy, herbivore**

**catty-corner** also **kitty-corner** ADV Something that is **catty-corner** or **kitty-corner** from another thing is placed or arranged diagonally from it. en diagonal ❑ *There was a police car catty-corner across the street.* Había una patrulla en diagonal al cruzar la calle. ❑ *Two tall steel and aluminum towers stood kitty-corner from each other.* Dos torres altas de acero y aluminio contra esquina una de la otra.

**caught** /kɔt/ **Caught** is the past tense and past participle of **catch**. pasado y participio pasado de *catch*

**cau|li|flow|er** /kɔliflaʊər/ (**cauliflowers**) N-VAR A **cauliflower** is a large, round, white vegetable surrounded by green leaves. coliflor
→ see **vegetable**

**caulk** /kɔk/ (**caulks, caulking, caulked**)
**1** V-T If you **caulk** something, you fill small cracks in its surface in order to prevent it from leaking. enmasillar, calafatear ❑ *He offered to caulk the windows.* Se ofreció a enmasillar las ventanas.
• **caulk|ing** /kɔkɪŋ/ N-UNCOUNT calafatear ❑ *...easy jobs like caulking.* ...trabajos sencillos como calafatear. **2** N-UNCOUNT **Caulk** is a soft substance that is used to caulk something. calafateado

**cause** /kɔz/ (**causes, causing, caused**)
**1** N-COUNT The **cause of** an event, usually a bad event, is the thing that makes it happen. causa ❑ *Pollution is the commonest cause of death for birds.* La contaminación es la causa más común de la muerte de pájaros. **2** N-COUNT A **cause** is an aim or principle which a group of people supports or is fighting for. causa ❑ *Refusing to have one leader has not helped the cause.* El rechazo a tener un líder único no ha ayudado a la causa. **3** V-T To **cause** something, usually something bad, means to make it happen. causar ❑ *Stress can cause health problems.* El estrés puede causar problemas de salud. ❑ *This was a genuine mistake, but it did cause me some worry.* Fue un error genuino, pero sí me causó preocupación. **4** N-UNCOUNT If you have **cause for** a particular feeling or action, you have good reasons for feeling it or doing it. motivo, razón ❑ *Only a few people can find any cause for celebration.* Sólo pocas personas pueden encontrar algún motivo para celebrar.

**Thesaurus** *cause* Ver también:
V. generate, make, produce, provoke; (*ant.*) deter, prevent, stop **3**

**Word Partnership** Usar *cause* con:
V. **determine the** cause **1**
**support a** cause **2**
N. cause **of death** **1**
cause **an accident**, cause **cancer**, cause **problems**, cause **a reaction** **3**
cause **for concern** **4**

**Word Link** *caut ≈ taking care : caution, cautious, precaution*

**cau|tion** /kɔʃ^ən/ (**cautions, cautioning, cautioned**) **1** N-UNCOUNT **Caution** is great care which you take in order to avoid possible danger. precaución, cautela ❑ *You should use caution when buying used tires.* Deberías tener precaución al comprar llantas usadas. **2** V-T/V-I If someone **cautions** you, they warn you about problems or danger. advertir ❑ *Tony cautioned against believing everything in the newspapers.* Tony advirtió no creer todo lo que sale en los periódicos. ❑ *His lawyers have cautioned him against saying anything.* Sus abogados le han advertido que no diga nada. • **Caution** is also a noun. advertencia ❑ *There was a note of caution in her voice.* Había un tono de advertencia en su voz. **3** to **err on the side of** caution → see **err**

**cau|tious** /kɔʃəs/ ADJ Someone who is **cautious** acts very carefully in order to avoid danger. cauteloso, prudente ❑ *Scientists are cautious about using the therapy on humans.* Los científicos son cautelosos al usar la terapia en humanos. • **cau|tious|ly** ADV cautelosamente ❑ *David moved cautiously forward and looked over the edge.* David avanzó cautelosamente y se asomó a la orilla.

**Thesaurus** *cautious* Ver también:
ADJ. alert, careful, guarded, watchful; (*ant.*) careless, rash, reckless

**cav|al|ry** /kæv^əlri/ **1** N-SING **The cavalry** is the part of an army that uses armored vehicles for fighting. caballería ❑ *...the 3rd Cavalry.* ...la tercera caballería. **2** N-SING In the past, **the cavalry** was the group of soldiers in an army who rode horses. caballería ❑ *...a young cavalry officer.* ...un joven oficial de caballería.

**cave** /keɪv/ (**caves, caving, caved**) N-COUNT A **cave** is a large hole in the side of a cliff or hill or under the ground. cueva
▶ **cave in** **1** PHR-VERB If a roof or a wall **caves in**, it collapses inward. derrumbarse ❑ *Part of the roof caved in.* Una parte del techo se derrumbó. **2** PHR-VERB If you **cave in**, you suddenly stop arguing or resisting. ceder ❑ *The judge caved in to political pressure.* El juez cedió a la presión política.
→ see Picture Dictionary: **cave**

**cav|ity** /kævɪti/ (**cavities**) **1** N-COUNT A **cavity** is a small space or hole in something solid. cavidad, hueco [FORMAL] ❑ *...a cavity in the roof.* ...un hueco en el techo. **2** N-COUNT In dentistry, a **cavity** is a hole in a tooth, caused by decay. cavidad [TECHNICAL]
→ see **smell, teeth**

**cc** /si si/ **1** **cc** is an abbreviation for "cubic centimeters," used when referring to the volume or capacity of something such as the size of a car engine. cc, cm3, centímetros cúbicos ❑ *...1,500 cc sports cars.* ...autos deportivos de 1,500 cc. **2** **cc** is used in e-mail headers or at the end of a business letter to indicate that a copy is being sent to another person. cc (con copia para) [BUSINESS] ❑ *...cc j.jones@harpercollins.co.uk.* ...cc j.jones@harpercollins.co.uk.

**CCTV** /si si ti vi/ N-UNCOUNT **CCTV** is an abbreviation for "closed-circuit television." televisión de circuito cerrado ❑ *...a CCTV camera.* ...una cámara de circuito cerrado.

**CD** /si di/ (**CDs**) N-COUNT A **CD** is a small shiny

C

## Picture Dictionary cave

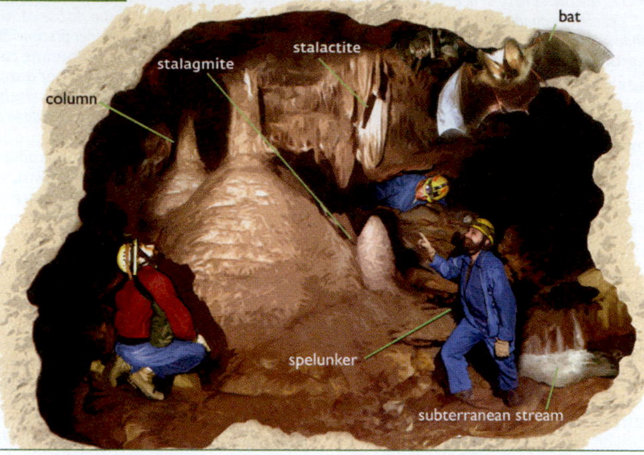


disc on which music or computer data is stored. *CD (disco compacto)*
→ see **laser**

**CD burn|er** (**CD burners**) N-COUNT A **CD burner** is a piece of computer equipment that you use for copying data from a computer onto a CD. *quemador de CDs* [COMPUTING]

**CD play|er** (**CD players**) N-COUNT A **CD player** is a machine on which you can play CDs. *reproductor de CDs*

**CD-ROM** /si di rɒm/ (**CD-ROMs**) N-COUNT A **CD-ROM** is a CD on which a very large amount of information can be stored and then read using a computer. *CD-ROM* [COMPUTING]
→ see **computer**

**CD writ|er** (**CD writers**) N-COUNT A **CD writer** is the same as a **CD burner**. *quemador de CDs* [COMPUTING]

**cease** /sis/ (**ceases, ceasing, ceased**) **1** V-I If something **ceases,** it stops happening or existing. *dejar de* [FORMAL] ❑ *At one o'clock the rain ceased. A la una dejó de llover.* **2** V-T If you **cease to** do something, you stop doing it. *dejar de* [FORMAL] ❑ *He never ceases to amaze me. Él nunca deja de sorprenderme.* ❑ *The newspaper ceased publication this week. El periódico dejó de publicarse esta semana.*

| **Thesaurus** | *cease* | Ver también: |
|---|---|---|
| v. | end, finish, halt, quit, shut down, stop; (*ant.*) begin, continue, start **1** | |

**cease|fire** /sisfaɪər/ (**ceasefires**) N-COUNT A **ceasefire** is an arrangement in which countries at war agree to stop fighting for a time. *cese al fuego* ❑ *They have agreed to a ceasefire after three years of conflict. Acordaron un cese al fuego después de tres años de conflicto.*

**ceil|ing** /silɪŋ/ (**ceilings**) **1** N-COUNT A **ceiling** is the top inside surface of a room. *techo* ❑ *The rooms were large, with high ceilings. Las habitaciones eran amplias, con techos altos.* **2** N-COUNT A **ceiling** is an official upper limit on prices or wages. *límite, tope* ❑ *...an informal agreement to put a ceiling on salaries. ...un acuerdo informal para poner un tope salarial.*

**cel|ebrate** /sɛlɪbreɪt/ (**celebrates, celebrating, celebrated**) **1** V-T/V-I If you **celebrate** something, you do something enjoyable because of a special occasion. *celebrar* ❑ *I was in a mood to celebrate. Tenía ganas de celebrar.* ❑ *Dick celebrated his 60th birthday Monday. Dick celebró el lunes su cumpleaños número 60.*
● **cel|ebra|tion** /sɛlɪbreɪʃ<sup>ə</sup>n/ (**celebrations**) N-VAR *celebración* ❑ *There was a celebration in our house that night. Esa noche hubo una celebración en nuestra casa.* ❑ *Few people can find any cause for celebration. Pocas personas pueden encontrar una causa para celebrar.* **2** V-T When priests **celebrate** Holy Communion or Mass, they officially perform the actions and ceremonies that are involved. *celebrar* ❑ *The Pope celebrated Mass today in Saint Peter's Square. Hoy el Papa celebró la Misa en la Plaza de San Pedro.*

**cel|ebrat|ed** /sɛlɪbreɪtɪd/ ADJ A **celebrated** person or thing is famous and much admired. *célebre, famoso* ❑ *...one of the most celebrated young painters in England. ...uno de los más célebres pintores jóvenes en Inglaterra.*

**ce|leb|rity** /sɪlɛbrɪti/ (**celebrities**) N-COUNT A **celebrity** is someone who is famous. *celebridad* ❑ *At the age of 30, Hersey suddenly became a celebrity. A los 30 años, Hersey de pronto se convirtió en una celebridad.*

**cel|ery** /sɛləri/ N-UNCOUNT **Celery** is a vegetable with long, pale-green stalks. *apio* ❑ *...a stick of celery. ...una rama de apio.*

**ce|les|tial** /sɪlɛstʃəl/ ADJ **Celestial** is used to describe things relating to heaven or to the sky. *celestial* [LITERARY] ❑ *...the Sun, Moon, and other celestial bodies. ...el Sol, la Luna y otros cuerpos celestiales.*
→ see **astronomer**

**cell** /sɛl/ (**cells**) **1** N-COUNT A **cell** is the smallest part of an animal or plant. Every animal or plant is made up of millions of cells. *célula* ❑ *...blood cells. ...células sanguíneas.* **2** N-COUNT A **cell** is a

small room in which a prisoner is locked. *celda* ❑ *How many prisoners were in each cell? ¿Cuántos prisioneros había en cada celda?* **3** N-COUNT A **cell** is a device that produces electricity as the result of a chemical reaction. *célula*
→ see **cardiovascular system, clone, electricity, skin**

**cell cy|cle** (**cell cycles**) N-COUNT A **cell cycle** is the series of changes that a biological cell goes through from the beginning of its life until its death. *ciclo celular*

**cell di|vi|sion** N-UNCOUNT **Cell division** is the biological process by which a cell inside an animal or a plant divides into two new cells during growth or reproduction. *división celular*

**cell mem|brane** (**cell membranes**) N-COUNT **Cell membranes** are the thin outer layers of the cells inside an animal. *membrana celular*

**cel|lo** /tʃɛloʊ/ (**cellos**) N-VAR A **cello** is a musical instrument that looks like a large violin. You hold it upright and play it sitting down. *violoncelo, violonchelo, chelo* • **cel|list** /tʃɛlɪst/ (**cellists**) N-COUNT *violoncelista, violonchelista* ❑ *...the world's greatest cellist. ...el mejor violoncelista del mundo.*
→ see **orchestra, string**

**cell|phone** /sɛlfoʊn/ (**cellphones**) N-COUNT A **cellphone** is a type of telephone which does not need wires to connect it to a telephone system. *teléfono celular, teléfono móvil, celular*
→ see Word Web: **cellphone**

**cell theo|ry** N-SING The **cell theory** is a set of basic principles relating to biological cells, such as the principle that all living creatures are composed of cells and that all cells come from other cells. *teoría celular*

**cel|lu|lar** /sɛlyələr/ ADJ **Cellular** means relating to the cells of animals or plants. *celular* ❑ *...cellular growth. ...crecimiento celular.*
→ see **cellphone**

**cel|lu|lar phone** (**cellular phones**) N-COUNT A **cellular phone** is the same as a **cellphone**. *teléfono celular, teléfono móvil, celular*
→ see **cellphone**

**cel|lu|lar res|pi|ra|tion** N-UNCOUNT **Cellular respiration** is the biological process by which cells convert substances such as sugar into energy. *respiración celular* [TECHNICAL]

**cell wall** (**cell walls**) N-COUNT **Cell walls** are the thin outer layers of the cells inside plants and bacteria. *pared celular, pared de la célula*

**Celsius** /sɛlsiəs/ ADJ **Celsius** is a scale for measuring temperature, in which water freezes at 0° and boils at 100°. *grados Celsius, grados centígrados* [TECHNICAL] ❑ *Highest temperatures 11° Celsius, that's 52° Fahrenheit. La temperatura más alta será de 11 grados Celsius, es decir, 52 grados Fahrenheit.*
→ see **measurement, thermometer**

**Usage** **Celsius and Fahrenheit**

The Celsius or centigrade scale is rarely used to express temperature in the U.S. The Fahrenheit scale is used instead.

**ce|ment** /sɪmɛnt/ (**cements, cementing, cemented**) **1** N-UNCOUNT **Cement** is a gray powder which is mixed with sand and water in order to make concrete. *cemento* **2** V-T Something that **cements** a relationship or agreement makes it stronger. *consolidar* ❑ *Nothing cements a friendship between countries so much as trade. Nada consolida tanto la amistad entre países como el comercio.* **3** V-T If things **are cemented** together, they are stuck or fastened together. *pegar* ❑ *...a street sign cemented into the wall. ...un letrero con el nombre de la calle pegado en la pared.*

**Word Link** *ery ≈ place where something happens : bakery, cemetery, winery*

**cem|etery** /sɛmətɛri/ (**cemeteries**) N-COUNT A **cemetery** is a place where dead people's bodies or their ashes are buried. *cementerio, panteón*

**Ce|no|zo|ic era** /sinəzoʊɪk, sɛn-/ N-SING **The Cenozoic era** is the most recent period in the history of the Earth, from 65 million years ago up to the present day. *era cenozoica* [TECHNICAL]

**cen|sus** /sɛnsəs/ (**censuses**) N-COUNT A **census** is an official survey of the population of a country. *censo* ❑ *...a detailed assessment of the latest census. ...una evaluación detallada del último censo.*

**Word Link** *cent ≈ hundred : cents, century, percentage*

**cent** /sɛnt/ (**cents**) N-COUNT A **cent** is a small unit of money worth one hundredth of some currencies, for example the dollar and the euro. *centavo* ❑ *...a cup of rice which cost thirty cents. ...un plato de arroz que costó treinta centavos.*

**Word Link** *enn ≈ year : bicentennial, centennial, perennial*

**cen|ten|nial** /sentɛniəl/ N-SING A **centennial**

**Word Web** **cellphone**

The word **"cell"** is not something inside the **cellular phone** itself. It describes the area around the **wireless transmitter** that your phone uses to make a call. The electrical system and **battery** in today's **mobile** phones are tiny. This makes their electronic **signals** weak. They can't travel very far. Therefore today's **cellular** phone systems need a lot of cells close together. When you make a call, your phone connects to the wireless transmitter with the strongest signal. Then it chooses a radio **channel** and connects you to the number you dialed. If you are riding in a car, **stations** in several different cells may handle your call.

is the one hundredth anniversary of an event. centenario [FORMAL] ❑ *The festival will conclude with the "grand finale" of the Oklahoma Centennial Year celebration.* *El festival terminará con el "gran final" de la celebración del año centenario de Oklahoma.*

**cen|ter** /sɛntər/ (**centers, centering, centered**) **1** N-COUNT The **center** of something is the middle of it. centro ❑ *...the center of the room.* *...el centro de la habitación.* **2** N-COUNT A **center** is a place where people have meetings, take part in a particular activity, or get help of some kind. centro ❑ *After school, Room 250 is a tutoring center.* *Después de clases, el salón 250 se utiliza como centro de tutorías.* **3** N-COUNT If an area or town is a **center** for an industry or activity, that industry or activity is very important there. centro ❑ *New York is a major international financial center.* *Nueva York es un centro finaciero internacional importante.* **4** N-COUNT If someone or something is the **center of** attention or interest, people are giving them a lot of attention. centro de atención ❑ *She was used to being the center of attention.* *Estaba acostumbrada a ser el centro de atención.* **5** V-T/V-I If something **centers** or **is centered on** a particular thing or person, that thing or person is the main subject of attention. centrar(se) en ❑ *...a plan which centered on academic achievement.* *...un plan que se centraba en los logros académicos.* ❑ *All his concerns were centered around himself rather than Rachel.* *Todas sus preocupaciones se centraban en torno a él mismo, más que en torno a Raquel.* • **-centered** ADJ centrado en, enfocado en ❑ *...child-centered teaching methods.* *...métodos pedagógicos centrados en los niños.* **6** V-T If something **is centered** in a place, it happens or is based there. centrarse, concentrarse ❑ *The fighting centered around the town of Vucovar.* *La batalla se concentró en torno al pueblo de Vucovar.* **7** → see also **shopping center**
→ see **soccer**

| **Word Partnership** | Usar *center* con: |
|---|---|
| N. | center **of a circle** 1<br>**convention** center, **research** center 2<br>center **of attention** 4 |

**cen|ter stage** N-UNCOUNT In a theater, **center stage** is the middle part of the stage. centro del escenario

**cen|ti|li|ter** /sɛntɪlitər/ (**centiliters**) N-COUNT A **centiliter** is a unit of volume in the metric system equal to ten milliliters or one-hundredth of a liter. centilitro

**cen|ti|me|ter** /sɛntɪmitər/ (**centimeters**) N-COUNT A **centimeter** is a unit of length in the metric system equal to ten millimeters or one-hundredth of a meter. centímetro ❑ *...a tiny plant, only a few centimeters high.* *...una plantita de sólo unos centímetros de alto.*
→ see **measurement**

**cen|ti|pede** /sɛntɪpid/ (**centipedes**) N-COUNT A **centipede** is a long, thin creature with a lot of legs. ciempiés

**cen|tral** /sɛntrəl/ **1** ADJ Something that is **central** is in the middle of a place or area. central ❑ *...Central America.* *...América Central, Centroamérica* • **cen|tral|ly** ADV céntrico ❑ *...a centrally-located office.* *...una oficina céntrica* **2** ADJ A **central** group or organization makes all the important decisions for a larger organization or a country. central ❑ *...the central government in Rome.* *...el gobierno central de Roma.* • **cen|tral|ly** ADV centralmente, desde el centro ❑ *...an international organization, centrally controlled by one country.* *...una organización internacional, controlada centralmente por un país.* **3** ADJ The **central** person or thing in a situation is the most important one. central, clave, principal ❑ *Black dance music has been central to pop since the early '60s.* *La música negra para bailar ha sido clave para el pop desde los primeros años sesenta.*

| **Word Partnership** | Usar *central* con: |
|---|---|
| N. | central **location** 1<br>central **government** 2 |

**cen|tral nerv|ous sys|tem** (**central nervous systems**) N-COUNT Your **central nervous system** is the part of your nervous system that consists of the brain and spinal cord. sistema nervioso central
→ see **nervous system**

**cen|trip|etal ac|cel|era|tion** /sɛntrɪpɪtᵊl æksɛləreɪʃᵊn/ N-UNCOUNT **Centripetal acceleration** is the acceleration that is required to keep an object traveling at a constant speed when it is moving in a circle. aceleración centrípeta [TECHNICAL]

**cen|tro|mere** /sɛntrəmɪər/ (**centromeres**) N-COUNT The **centromere** is the central part of a chromosome where the two ends of the chromosome are connected. centrómero [TECHNICAL]

| **Word Link** | *cent ≈ hundred : cents, century, percentage* |
|---|---|

**cen|tu|ry** /sɛntʃəri/ (**centuries**) **1** N-COUNT A **century** is a period of a hundred years that is used when stating a date. For example, the 19th century was the period from 1801 to 1900. siglo, centuria ❑ *...the late eighteenth century.* *...finales del siglo dieciocho* **2** N-COUNT A **century** is any period of a hundred years. siglo, centuria ❑ *The winter was the worst in a century.* *Este invierno fue el peor del siglo.*

**cephalo|tho|rax** /sɛfələθɔræks/ (**cephalothoraces** or **cephalothoraxes**) N-COUNT In animals such as spiders and crabs, the **cephalothorax** is the front part of the body consisting of the head and thorax. cefalotórax [TECHNICAL]

**ce|ram|ic** /sɪræmɪk/ (**ceramics**) **1** N-UNCOUNT **Ceramic** is clay that has been heated to a very high temperature so that it becomes hard. cerámica ❑ *...ceramic tiles.* *...baldosas/azulejos de cerámica.* **2** N-COUNT **Ceramics** are ceramic ornaments or objects. objetos de cerámica, cerámica ❑ *...a collection of Chinese ceramics.* *...una colección de cerámica china.* **3** N-UNCOUNT **Ceramics** is the art of making artistic objects out of clay. cerámica ❑ *...courses in ceramics and art.* *...cursos de cerámica y arte.*
→ see **pottery**

**ce|real** /sɪəriəl/ (**cereals**) **1** N-VAR **Cereal** is a food made from grain, usually mixed with milk and eaten for breakfast. cereal ❑ *I have a bowl of cereal every morning.* *Todas las mañanas me tomo un plato de cereal.* **2** N-COUNT **Cereals** are plants such as wheat, corn, or rice that produce grain. cereales ❑ ...*the cereal-growing districts of the Midwest.* ...*las zonas de cultivo de cereales del centro del país.*

**cer|ebel|lum** /sɛrəbɛləm/ (**cerebellums** or **cerebella**) N-COUNT The **cerebellum** is a part of the brain in humans and other mammals that controls the body's movements and balance. cerebelo [MEDICAL]

**cer|ebrum** /sərɪbrəm, sɛrə-/ (**cerebrums** or **cerebra**) N-COUNT The **cerebrum** is the large, front part of the brain, which is divided into two halves and controls activities such as thinking and memory. cerebro [MEDICAL]

**cer|emo|ny** /sɛrɪmoʊni/ (**ceremonies**) **1** N-COUNT A **ceremony** is a formal event such as a wedding. ceremonia ❑ *His grandmother's funeral was a private ceremony attended only by the family.* *El funeral de su abuela fue una ceremonia privada a la que asistió sólo la familia.* **2** N-UNCOUNT **Ceremony** consists of the special things that are said and done on very formal occasions. ceremonia, pompa ❑ *The historic meeting took place with great ceremony.* *La histórica reunión tuvo lugar con gran pompa.*
→ see **graduation, wedding**

| Word Link | *cert ≈ determined, true : certain, certificate, uncertain* |
|---|---|

**cer|tain** /sɜrtᵊn/ **1** ADJ If you are **certain** about something or if it is **certain,** you firmly believe it is true and have no doubt about it. seguro, cierto ❑ *She's absolutely certain she's going to make it.* *Está absolutamente segura de que lo va a lograr.* ❑ *We are not certain whether the airline will be able to stay profitable.* *No estamos seguros de que la línea aérea vaya a generar utilidades.* ❑ *One thing is certain, both have the greatest respect for each other.* *Una cosa es cierta, se tienen un gran respeto mutuo.* **2** ADJ You use **certain** to indicate that you are referring to one particular thing or person, although you are not saying exactly which it is. cierto, alguno ❑ *There will be certain people who'll say "I told you so!"* *Algunas personas te van a decir —¡Te lo advertí!* ❑ *You owe a certain person a sum of money.* *A cierta persona le debes dinero.* **3** PHRASE If you know something **for certain,** you have no doubt at all about it. con certeza, a ciencia cierta, con seguridad ❑ *She didn't know for certain if he'd go or not.* *No sabía con seguridad si él iba a ir.* **4** PHRASE If you **make certain that** something is the way you want or expect it to be, you take action to ensure that it is. asegurarse de ❑ *Parents should make certain that children spend enough time doing homework.* *Los padres deben asegurarse de que sus hijos le dediquen tiempo suficiente a la tarea.*

| Thesaurus | certain | Ver también: |
|---|---|---|
| ADJ. | definite, known, positive, sure, true; (*ant.*) unmistakable **1** | |

**cer|tain|ly** /sɜrtᵊnli/ **1** ADV You use **certainly** to emphasize what you are saying. seguro, desde luego, sin duda, no hay duda de ❑ *The public is certainly getting tired of hearing about it.* *No hay duda de que el público se está cansando de oir siempre lo mismo.* ❑ *The meeting will almost certainly start late.* *Es casi seguro que la reunión empezará tarde.* **2** ADV You use **certainly** when you are agreeing or disagreeing strongly with what someone has said. seguro, por supuesto ❑ *"In any case you remained friends." — "Certainly."* *—De todas formas siguen siendo amigos. —Por supuesto.* ❑ *"Perhaps it would be better if I left." — "Certainly not!"* *—Quizá sería mejor que me fuera. —¡Por supuesto que no!*

**cer|tain|ty** /sɜrtᵊnti/ (**certainties**) **1** N-UNCOUNT **Certainty** is the state of having no doubts at all. certeza, seguridad ❑ *I can tell you this with absolute certainty.* *Te lo digo con absoluta seguridad.* **2** N-COUNT **Certainties** are things that nobody has any doubts about. cosa segura, algo seguro ❑ *There are no certainties in modern life.* *En la vida moderna no hay nada seguro.*

**cer|tifi|cate** /sərtɪfɪkɪt/ (**certificates**) N-COUNT A **certificate** is an official document stating that particular facts are true, or that you have successfully completed a course of study or training. certificado, acta, constancia ❑ ...*birth certificates.* ...*actas de nacimiento.*
→ see **wedding**

**cer|ti|fied check** (**certified checks**) N-COUNT A **certified check** is a check that is guaranteed by a bank, because the bank has set aside sufficient money in the account. cheque certificado

**cer|ti|fied mail** N-UNCOUNT If you send a letter or package by **certified mail,** you send it using a mail service which gives you an official record of the fact that it has been mailed and delivered. correo certificado ❑ *We recommend that you send your certificates by certified mail.* *Recomendamos enviar las actas por correo certificado.*

**cer|ti|fied pub|lic ac|count|ant** (**certified public accountants**) N-COUNT A **certified public accountant** is someone who has received a certificate stating that he or she is qualified to work as an accountant within a particular state. The abbreviation **CPA** is also used. contador público titulado o contadora pública titulada, CPT

**CFC** /si ɛf si/ (**CFCs**) N-COUNT **CFCs** are chemicals that are used in aerosols, refrigerators, and cooling systems that can cause damage to the ozone layer. **CFC** is an abbreviation for "chlorofluorocarbon." CFC, clorofluorocarbono ❑ ...*the drop in CFC emissions.* ...*la reducción de las emisiones de CFC.*

**CGI** /si dʒi aɪ/ N-UNCOUNT **CGI** is a type of computer technology that is used to make special effects in movies and on television. **CGI** is an abbreviation for "computer-generated imagery." CGI, imágenes generadas por computadora

**chain** /tʃeɪn/ (**chains, chaining, chained**) **1** N-COUNT A **chain** consists of metal rings connected together in a line. cadena ❑ *Around his neck he wore a gold chain.* *Llevaba una cadena de oro en el cuello.* **2** N-COUNT A **chain of** things is a group of them existing or arranged in a line. cadena, serie ❑ ...*a chain of islands known as the Windward Islands.* ...*una cadena de islas conocidas como las islas Windward.* **3** N-COUNT A **chain of** stores, hotels, or other businesses is a number of them owned by the same company. cadena ❑ ...*a large supermarket chain.* ...*una gran cadena de supermercados.* **4** V-T If a person or thing **is chained to** something, they are fastened to it with a chain. estar encadenado a algo ❑ *The dogs were chained to a fence.* *Los perros estaban* *encadenados a una reja.* ❑ *We were sitting together in our cell, chained to the wall.* *Estábamos todos sentados en la celda, encadenados al muro.* **5** N-SING A **chain of** events is a series of them happening one after another. *cadena, serie* ❑ *...the chain of events that led to his departure.* *...la serie de acontecimientos que lo llevó a irse.*

C

**chair** /tʃɛər/ (**chairs, chairing, chaired**) **1** N-COUNT A **chair** is a piece of furniture for one person to sit on, with a back and four legs. *silla* ❑ *He rose from his chair and walked to the window.* *Se levantó de la silla y caminó hacia la ventana.* **2** N-COUNT At a university, a **chair** is the position or job of professor. *cátedra, presidencia* ❑ *He has been named chair of the sociology department.* *Lo nombraron presidente del departamento de sociología.* **3** N-COUNT The **chair of** a committee or meeting is the person in charge of it. *presidente o presidenta* ❑ *She is the chair of the Defense Advisory Committee on Women in the Military.* *Es la presidenta del Comité Asesor de la Defensa sobre las Mujeres en el Ejército.* **4** V-T If you **chair** a meeting or a committee, you are the person in charge of it. *presidir* ❑ *He was about to chair a meeting.* *Estaba a punto de presidir una reunión.*

**chair|man** /tʃɛərmən/ (**chairmen**) N-COUNT The **chairman** of a meeting or organization is the person in charge of it. *presidente* ❑ *He is chairman of the committee which produced the report.* *Es el presidente del comité que publicó el informe.*

**chair|person** /tʃɛərpɜrsᵊn/ (**chairpersons**) N-COUNT The **chairperson** of a meeting or organization is the person in charge of it. *presidente o presidenta* ❑ *She's the chairperson of the safety committee.* *Es la presidenta del comité de seguridad.*

**chair|woman** /tʃɛərwʊmən/ (**chairwomen**) N-COUNT The **chairwoman** of a meeting or organization is the woman in charge of it. *presidenta* ❑ *Primakov was meeting with the chairwoman of the Party.* *Primakov estaba en una reunión con la presidenta del Partido.*

**chalk** /tʃɔk/ (**chalks, chalking, chalked**) **1** N-UNCOUNT **Chalk** is a type of soft, white rock. *tiza, piedra caliza, gis* ❑ *...white cliffs made of chalk.* *...acantilados blancos de piedra caliza.* **2** N-VAR **Chalk** is small sticks of chalk used for writing or drawing. *tiza, gis* ❑ *...colored chalk.* *...gises de colores.*

▸ **chalk up** PHR-VERB If you **chalk up** a success, you achieve it. *anotarse, apuntarse* ❑ *The team chalked up another victory.* *El equipo se anotó otra victoria.*

**chalk|board** /tʃɔkbɔrd/ (**chalkboards**) N-COUNT A **chalkboard** is a dark-colored board that you can write on with chalk. *pizarrón, pizarra*

**chal|lenge** /tʃælɪndʒ/ (**challenges, challenging, challenged**) **1** N-VAR A **challenge** is something new and difficult which requires great effort and determination. *desafío, reto* ❑ *His first challenge was winning the respect of his players.* *Su primer reto fue ganarse el respeto de los jugadores.* **2** PHRASE If someone **rises to the challenge,** they act in response to a difficult situation which is new to them and are successful. *estar a la altura de algo, aceptar el reto* ❑ *Germany must rise to the challenge of its responsibilities.* *Alemania debe estar a la altura de sus responsabilidades.* **3** V-T If you **challenge** ideas or people, you question their truth, value, or authority. *cuestionar, poner en tela de juicio, poner en duda* ❑ *They challenged the laws and tried to change them.* *Pusieron en duda las leyes y trataron de cambiarlas.* ❑ *The move was challenged by two of the republics.* *La medida fue cuestionada por dos de las repúblicas.* • **Challenge** is also a noun. *reto, desafío, cuestionamiento* ❑ *...a challenge to his authority.* *...un reto para su autoridad.* **4** V-T If you **challenge** someone, you invite them to fight or compete with you in some way. *retar, desafiar* ❑ *Woods challenged O'Meara to a friendly game.* *Woods retó a O'Meara a un juego amistoso.* ❑ *He left a note at the crime scene, challenging detectives to catch him.* *Dejó una nota en la escena del crimen en la que retaba a los detectives a pescarlo.* • **Challenge** is also a noun. *reto* ❑ *Both the Swiss and the German team will provide a serious challenge for the gold medals.* *Tanto el equipo suizo como el alemán constituyen un verdadero reto para la medalla de oro.* **5** → see also **challenging**

**Word Partnership** Usar *challenge* con:

| | |
|---|---|
| ADJ. | **biggest** challenge, **new** challenge **1 3 4** |
| | **legal** challenge **3** |
| V. | **accept a** challenge, **present a** challenge **1 3 4** |
| | **dare to** challenge **3 4** |

**chal|leng|er** /tʃælɪndʒər/ (**challengers**) N-COUNT A **challenger** is someone who competes for a position or title. *contendiente, rival* ❑ *...a challenger for the Americas Cup.* *...un rival para la Copa de las Américas.*

**chal|leng|ing** /tʃælɪndʒɪŋ/ **1** ADJ A **challenging** task or job requires great effort and determination. *desafiante* ❑ *Mike found a challenging job as a computer programmer.* *Mike encontró un trabajo desafiante como programador de computadoras.* **2** ADJ **Challenging** behavior seems to be inviting people to argue or compete. *desafiante, retador* ❑ *Mona gave him a challenging look.* *Mona le lanzó una mirada desafiante.*

**cham|ber** /tʃeɪmbər/ (**chambers**) **1** N-COUNT A **chamber** is a large room that is designed and equipped for a particular purpose, for example for formal meetings. *sala, cámara* ❑ *...the council chamber.* *...la sala del consejo.* ❑ *...a burial chamber.* *...una cámara mortuoria.* **2** N-COUNT You can refer to a country's legislature or to one section of it as a **chamber.** *cámara* ❑ *...a two-chamber parliament.* *...un parlamento de dos cámaras.*

**cham|pagne** /ʃæmpeɪn/ (**champagnes**) N-VAR **Champagne** is an expensive French white wine with bubbles in it. *champaña*

**cham|pi|on** /tʃæmpiən/ (**champions, championing, championed**) **1** N-COUNT A **champion** is someone who has won the first prize in a competition. *campeón o campeona* ❑ *...a former Olympic champion.* *...un ex campeón olímpico. o ...una ex campeona olímpica.* ❑ *Kasparov became world champion.* *Kasparov llegó a ser campeón mundial.* **2** N-COUNT If you are a **champion of** a person, a cause, or a principle, you support or defend them. *paladín, defensor o defensora* ❑ *...a champion of freedom.* *...un defensor/una defensora de la libertad.* **3** V-T If you **champion** a person, a cause, or a principle, you support or defend them. *abogar* por, defender ❑ *He passionately championed the poor.* Abogaba fervientemente por los pobres.

**cham|pi|on|ship** /tʃæmpiənʃɪp/ (**championships**) **1** N-COUNT A **championship** is a competition to find the best player or team in a particular sport. campeonato ❑ *...the world chess championship.* ...el campeonato mundial de ajedrez. **2** N-SING **The championship** refers to the title or status of being a sports champion. campeonato ❑ *He went on to win the championship.* Siguió adelante, hasta que ganó el campeonato.

**chance** /tʃæns/ (**chances, chancing, chanced**) **1** N-VAR If there is a **chance of** something happening, it is possible that it will happen. posibilidad ❑ *Do you think they have a chance of beating Australia?* ¿Crees que tengan la posibilidad de ganarle a Australia? ❑ *There was very little chance that Ben would ever lead a normal life.* Había muy pocas posibilidades de que Ben llegara a tener una vida normal. **2** N-SING If you have a **chance to** do something, you have the opportunity to do it. oportunidad, chance ❑ *Everyone will get a chance to vote.* Todos tendrán la oportunidad de votar. ❑ *One hundred and fifty million never get the chance to go to school.* Ciento cincuenta millones de personas nunca tienen la oportunidad de ir a la escuela. **3** PHRASE Something that happens **by chance** was not planned by anyone. por casualidad ❑ *He met Mr. Maude by chance.* Se encontró con el Sr. Maude por casualidad. **4** PHRASE If you say that someone **stands a chance of** achieving something, you mean that they are likely to achieve it. If you say that someone doesn't **stand a chance of** achieving something, you mean that they cannot possibly achieve it. tener la oportunidad de ❑ *I stood a good chance of gaining high grades.* Tuve una gran oportunidad para sacar buenas calificaciones. **5** PHRASE When you **take a chance,** you try to do something although there is a large risk of danger or failure. correr el riesgo, arriesgarse ❑ *You take a chance on the weather if you vacation in Maine.* Si te vas de vacaciones a Maine, estás corriendo un riesgo con el clima. ❑ *Retailers are not taking any chances on unknown brands.* Los vendedores al menudeo no se arriesgan con marcas desconocidas.

**Word Partnership** Usar *chance* con:

| | |
|---|---|
| N. | chance **of success**, chance **of survival**, chance **of winning** **1** |
| ADJ. | **fair** chance, **good** chance, **slight** chance **1** **2** |
| V. | **give *someone/something*** a chance, **have a** chance, **miss a** chance **1** **2** **get a** chance **2** |

**chan|cel|lor** /tʃænsələr, -slər/ (**chancellors**) **1** N-TITLE; N-COUNT **Chancellor** is the title of the head of government in Germany and Austria. canciller ❑ *...Chancellor Angela Merkel of Germany.* ...la canciller Angela Merkel de Alemania. **2** N-COUNT The head of some American universities is called **the chancellor.** rector o rectora **3** N-COUNT In Britain, the **Chancellor** or **Chancellor of the Exchequer** is the minister in charge of finance and taxes. ministro o ministra de hacienda/economía, secretario o secretaria de hacienda/economía

**change** /tʃeɪndʒ/ (**changes, changing, changed**) **1** N-VAR If there is a **change in** something, it becomes different. cambio ❑ *...a change in U.S. policy.* ...un cambio en la política estadounidense ❑ *There are going to be some big changes.* Se harán grandes cambios. **2** N-SING If you say that something **is a change** or **makes a change,** you mean that it is enjoyable because it is different from what you are used to. ser un cambio, ser diferente ❑ *It is a complicated system, but it certainly makes a change.* Es un sistema complicado, pero no hay duda de que es diferente. **3** V-T/V-I When something **changes** or when you **change** it, it becomes different. cambiar, convertirse ❑ *We are trying to understand how the climate changes.* Estamos tratando de entender cómo cambia el clima. ❑ *The color of the sky changed from pink to blue.* El color del cielo cambió de rosado a azul. ❑ *She has now changed into a happy, self-confident woman.* Se ha convertido en una mujer feliz, con confianza en ella misma. ❑ *They should change the law.* Tienen que cambiar la ley. **4** V-T/V-I To **change** something means to replace it with something new or different. cambiar ❑ *All they did was change a light bulb.* Lo único que hicieron fue cambiar un foco. ❑ *He changed to a different medication.* Cambió a otro medicamento • **Change** is also a noun. cambio ❑ *A change of leadership alone will not be enough.* Un cambio de líder no va a ser suficiente. **5** V-T/V-I When you **change** your clothes, you take them off and put on different ones. cambiarse ❑ *Ben changed his shirt.* Ben se cambió de camisa. ❑ *They allowed her to shower and change.* Le permitieron bañarse y cambiarse. **6** V-T When you **change** a bed or **change** the sheets, you take off the dirty sheets and put on clean ones. cambiar ❑ *After changing the bed, I would usually fall asleep quickly.* Después de cambiar la cama, normalmente me dormía pronto. **7** V-T When you **change** a baby or **change** its diaper, you take off the dirty one and put on a clean one. cambiar ❑ *She criticizes me for the way I change him.* Me critica por la forma en que lo cambio. **8** V-T/V-I When you **change** buses, trains, or planes, you get off one and get on to another in order to continue your journey. cambiar de, transbordar ❑ *I changed planes in Chicago.* Cambié de avión en Chicago. **9** N-UNCOUNT Your **change** is the money that you receive when you pay for something with more money than it costs. cambio ❑ *"There's your change." — "Thanks very much."* —Su cambio. —Muchas gracias. **10** N-UNCOUNT **Change** is coins, rather than paper money. cambio, monedas, morralla ❑ *...a bag of loose change.* ...una bolsa de morralla. **11** PHRASE If you say that you are doing something or something is happening **for a change,** you mean that you do not usually do it or it does not usually happen, and you are happy to be doing it or that it is happening. para variar ❑ *Now let me ask you a question, for a change.* Ahora déjame hacerte una pregunta, para variar. **12** PHRASE When a substance undergoes a **change of state,** it changes from one form to another, for example from a solid to a liquid. cambio de estado **13** to change **for the better** → see **better** **14** to **change hands** → see **hand** **15** **a change of heart** → see **heart** **16** to **change** your **mind** → see **mind** **17** to **change tack** → see **tack** **18** to **change** your **tune** → see **tune** **19** to change **for the worse** → see **worse**

▸ **change over** PHR-VERB If you **change over from** one thing **to** another, you stop doing one thing and start doing the other. cambiar ❑ *We are gradually changing over to a completely metric system.*

*Estamos cambiando gradualmente a un sistema métrico.*

**Thesaurus** *change* Ver también:

N. adjustment, alteration 1
V. adapt, modify, transform, vary 3

C

**Word Partnership** Usar *change* con:

V. **adapt to** change, **resist** change 1
**make a** change 1 2
N. change **of pace**, **policy** change 1
change **of address**, change **clothes**, change **color**, change **direction**, change **the subject** 4 5
ADJ. **gradual** change, **social** change, **sudden** change 1
**loose** change, **spare** change 10

**chan|nel** /tʃænᵊl/ (**channels, channeling** or **channelling, channeled** or **channelled**) 1 N-COUNT A **channel** is a television station. *canal de televisión* ❑ *...the huge number of television channels in America. ...el enorme número de canales de televisión estadounidenses.* 2 N-COUNT If you do something through a particular **channel,** that is the system or organization that you use in order to do it. *canal* ❑ *Very few details of the talks are available through official channels. A través de los canales oficiales se consiguen muy pocos detalles de las pláticas.* 3 N-COUNT A **channel** is a narrow passage along which water flows. *canal* ❑ *...a drainage channel. ...un canal de drenaje.* 4 V-T If you **channel** money into something, you arrange for it to be used for that purpose. *canalizar* ❑ *...a system to channel funds to poor countries. ...un sistema para canalizar fondos a los países pobres.*
→ see **cellphone**

**channel-surfing** N-UNCOUNT **Channel-surfing** means switching quickly between different television channels looking for something interesting to watch. *navegar entre canales*

**chant** /tʃænt/ (**chants, chanting, chanted**) 1 N-COUNT A **chant** is a word or group of words that is repeated over and over again. *canto, cántico, consigna* ❑ *Then the crowd started the chant of "U-S-A!" Entonces la multitud empezó con el canto de "¡U-S-A!"* 2 N-COUNT A **chant** is a religious song or prayer that is sung on only a few notes. *canto* ❑ *...a Gregorian chant. ...canto gregoriano.* 3 V-T/V-I If you **chant** something, you repeat the same words over and over again. *cantar, recitar monótonamente, repetir una y otra vez* ❑ *The crowd chanted his name. La multitud recitaba su nombre.* ❑ *The crowd chanted "We are with you." La multitud repetía y repetía "Estamos contigo".* ● **chant|ing** N-UNCOUNT *consignas* ❑ *A lot of the chanting was in support of the prime minister. Muchas de las consignas eran para apoyar al primer ministro.*

**cha|os** /keɪɒs/ N-UNCOUNT **Chaos** is a state of complete disorder and confusion. *caos* ❑ *The race ended in chaos. La carrera acabó en un caos.*

**Word Partnership** Usar *chaos* con:

V. **bring** chaos, **cause** chaos
ADJ. **complete** chaos, **total** chaos
N. chaos **and confusion**

**chap|el** /tʃæpᵊl/ (**chapels**) 1 N-COUNT A **chapel** is a part of a church which has its own altar and which is used for private prayer. *capilla* 2 N-COUNT A **chapel** is a small church in or attached to a hospital, school, or prison. *capilla* ❑ *We married in the college chapel. Nos casamos en la capilla de la universidad.*

**chap|ter** /tʃæptər/ (**chapters**) 1 N-COUNT A **chapter** is one of the parts that a book is divided into. *capítulo* ❑ *See Chapter 4. Véase el capítulo 4.* 2 N-COUNT You can refer to part of your life or a period in history as a **chapter.** *capítulo* [WRITTEN] ❑ *This is a difficult chapter in Lebanon's history. Es un capítulo difícil de la historia del Líbano.*

**char|ac|ter** /kærɪktər/ (**characters**) 1 N-COUNT The **character** of a person or place consists of all the qualities they have that make them distinct. *carácter* ❑ *There is a negative side to his character that you haven't seen yet. Hay un aspecto negativo de su carácter que todavía no conoces.* 2 N-COUNT You can refer to a person as a **character,** especially when describing their qualities. *personaje, tipo* ❑ *It's his courage that makes him such a remarkable character. Su valor es lo que hace de él un personaje tan notable.* 3 N-COUNT The **characters** in a movie, book, or play are the people in it. *personaje* ❑ *The central character is played by Collard himself. El propio Collard hace el papel del personaje principal.* 4 N-COUNT A **character** is a letter, number, or other symbol that is written or printed. *carácter* ❑ *...a shopping list written in Chinese characters. ...una lista de compras escrita en caracteres chinos.* 5 N-VAR Your **character** is your reputation. *reputación* ❑ *...a series of personal attacks on my character. ...una serie de ataques personales contra mi reputación.*
→ see **printing**

**Word Partnership** Usar *character* con:

N. character **flaw**, character **trait** 1
character **development** 1 3
character **in a book/movie**, **cartoon** character 3
ADJ. **moral** character 1
**fictional** character, **main** character, **minor** character 3

**char|ac|ter|is|tic** /kærɪktərɪstɪk/ (**characteristics**) 1 N-COUNT A **characteristic** is a quality or feature that is typical of someone or something. *característica* ❑ *Genes determine the characteristics of every living thing. Los genes determinan las características de todos los seres vivientes.* 2 ADJ If something is **characteristic of** a person, thing, or place, it is typical of them. *característico* ❑ *Refusal to admit defeat was characteristic of Davis. El rechazo a admitir la derrota era característico de Davis.* ❑ *Churches are a characteristic feature of the English countryside. Las iglesias son un rasgo característico de la campiña inglesa.* ● **char|ac|ter|is|ti|cal|ly** /kærɪktərɪstɪkli/ ADV *de manera característica* ❑ *He was characteristically impatient. Era un impaciente.*

**char|ac|ter|is|tic prop|er|ty** (**characteristic properties**) N-COUNT A **characteristic property** of a substance is a quality of the substance that distinguishes it from other substances, for example the fact that it melts at a particular temperature. *propiedad característica*

**char|ac|teri|za|tion** /kærɪktərɪzeɪʃᵊn/ (**characterizations**) N-VAR **Characterization** is the way an author or an actor describes or shows what a character is like. caracterización

**char|ac|ter|ize** /kærɪktəraɪz/ (**characterizes, characterizing, characterized**) **1** V-T If something **is characterized by** a particular feature or quality, that feature or quality is an obvious part of it. caracterizar [FORMAL] ❑ *This election campaign has been characterized by violence. La campaña electoral se ha caracterizado por la violencia.* **2** V-T If you **characterize** someone or something **as** a particular thing, you describe them in that way. calificar [FORMAL] ❑ *Both companies characterized the relationship as "friendly." Ambas compañías calificaron la relación como "amistosa".* ● **char|ac|teri|za|tion** /kærɪktərɪzeɪʃᵊn/ (**characterizations**) N-VAR descripción ❑ *...his characterization of other designers as "thieves." ...su descripción de otros diseñadores como "ladrones".*

**char|broiled** /tʃɑrbrɔɪld/ also **char-grilled** ADJ **Charbroiled** meat or fish has been cooked so that it burns slightly and turns black. a las brasas, al carbón

**char|coal** /tʃɑrkoʊl/ N-UNCOUNT **Charcoal** is a black substance used as a fuel and for drawing, obtained by burning wood without much air. carbón (vegetal)
→ see **firework**

**charge** /tʃɑrdʒ/ (**charges, charging, charged**) **1** V-T/V-I If you **charge** someone an amount of money, you ask them to pay that amount for something. cobrar ❑ *The newspaper charges $5 a week for car ads. El periódico cobra 5 dólares semanales por los anuncios de autos.* ❑ *Some banks charge if you access your account to determine your balance. Algunos bancos cobran si consultas tu cuenta para averiguar tu saldo.* ❑ *The architect charged us a fee of seven hundred and fifty dollars. El arquitecto nos cobró setecientos cincuenta dólares de honorarios.* **2** V-T If you **charge** something **to** an organization or to your account, it will be paid for later by the organization or added to your account and paid for later. cargar ❑ *Go out and buy a pair of glasses, and charge it to us. Ve a comprar unos anteojos y los cargas a nuestra cuenta.* **3** V-T When the police **charge** someone, they formally accuse them of having done something illegal. inculpar ❑ *They have the evidence to charge him. Tienen las pruebas para inculparlo.* **4** V-I If you **charge** toward someone or something, you move quickly and aggressively toward them. cargar contra, abalanzarse ❑ *He charged through the door to my mother's office. Se abalanzó a la oficina de mi madre.* ❑ *He ordered us to charge. Nos ordenó atacar.* **5** V-T To **charge** a battery means to pass an electrical current through it in order to make it more powerful or to make it last longer. cargar ❑ *Alex forgot to charge the battery. Alex olvidó cargar la batería.* **6** N-COUNT An electrical **charge** is an amount of electricity that is held in or carried by something. carga [TECHNICAL] **7** N-COUNT A **charge** is an amount of money that you have to pay for a service. precio ❑ *We can arrange this for a small charge. Podemos arreglarlo por un buen precio.* **8** N-COUNT A **charge** is a formal accusation that someone has committed a crime. acusación ❑ *He may still face criminal charges. Todavía es posible que lo acusen de algún delito.* **9** N-UNCOUNT If you have **charge of** or are **in charge of** someone or something, you are responsible for them. hacerse cargo de, ser responsable de ❑ *A few years ago Bacryl took charge of the company. Hace unos años, Bacryl se hizo cargo de la compañía.* ❑ *Who's in charge here? ¿Quién está a cargo aquí?, ¿Quién es el responsable?* **10** PHRASE If something is **free of charge,** it does not cost anything. gratis, gratuitamente ❑ *The leaflet is available free of charge from post offices. El folleto está disponible gratuitamente en las oficinas de correos.*
→ see **lightning, magnet, trial**

**Word Partnership** Usar *charge* con:

| | |
|---|---|
| N. | charge **a fee** 1<br>charge **a battery** 5 |
| ADJ. | **criminal** charge, **guilty of a** charge 3 |
| V. | **deny a** charge 3<br>**lead a** charge 4 |

**charge card** (**charge cards**) N-COUNT A **charge card** is the same as a **credit card**. tarjeta de crédito

**chari|table** /tʃærɪtəbᵊl/ **1** ADJ A **charitable** organization or activity helps and supports people who are ill, disabled, or very poor. de beneficencia, benéfico ❑ *...charitable work. ...una obra de beneficencia.* **2** ADJ Someone who is **charitable** is kind and tolerant. caritativo, benevolente ❑ *They were not very charitable toward the referee. No fueron muy amables con el réferi.*

**char|ity** /tʃærɪti/ (**charities**) **1** N-VAR A **charity** is an organization which raises money in order to help people who are ill, disabled, or very poor. If you give money **to charity,** you give it to a charity. institución de beneficencia ❑ *...an AIDS charity. ...una institución de beneficencia de lucha contra el sida.* ❑ *Gooch is raising money for charity. Gooch está recaudando dinero para una obra de beneficencia.* **2** N-UNCOUNT People who live on **charity** live on money or goods which other people give them because they are poor. caridad ❑ *Her husband is unemployed and the family depends on charity. Su esposo está desempleado y la familia depende de la caridad.*

**Word Partnership** Usar *charity* con:

| | |
|---|---|
| V. | **collect for** charity, **donate to** charity, **give to** charity 1 |
| N. | **donation to** charity, charity **event**, **money for** charity, charity **organization**, charity **work** 1 |
| ADJ. | **local** charity, **private** charity 1 |

**Charles's law** /tʃɑrlzɪz lɔ/ also **Charles' law** N-UNCOUNT **Charles's law** is a principle in physics which states that the volume of a gas increases when the gas gets hotter. ley de Gay-Lussac [TECHNICAL]

**charm** /tʃɑrm/ (**charms, charming, charmed**) **1** N-VAR **Charm** is the quality of being pleasant and attractive. encanto ❑ *The original movie has lost none of its charm. La película original no ha perdido nada de su encanto.* **2** V-T If you **charm** someone, you please them by using your charm. encantar ❑ *He charmed all of us. Nos encantó a todos.* **3** N-COUNT A **charm** is an act, saying, or object that is believed to have magic powers. encanto, amuleto ❑ *...a good luck charm. ...un amuleto de buena suerte.*
→ see **jewelry**

C

## Picture Dictionary chart

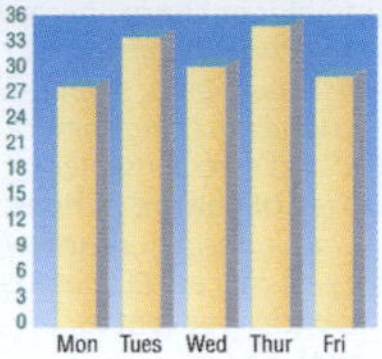


bar graph

35 students in class

| | | | | |
|---|---|---|---|---|
| Monday | 28 | 30 | 29 | 34 |
| Tuesday | 30 | 35 | 29 | 28 |
| Wednesday | 29 | 31 | 29 | 33 |
| Thursday | 28 | 34 | 33 | 29 |
| Friday | 30 | 33 | 35 | 31 |
| | 1 | 2 | 3 | 4 |

chart

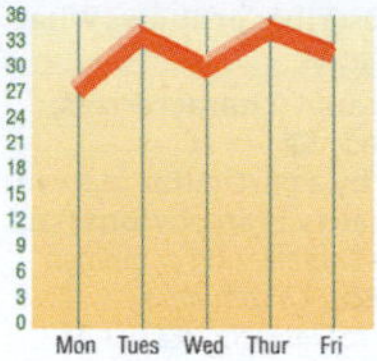


line graph

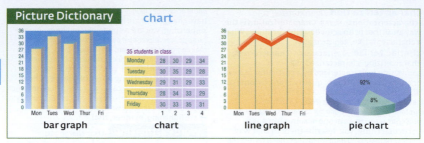

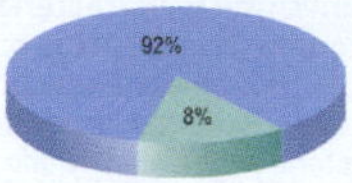


pie chart

**charm|ing** /tʃɑrmɪŋ/ ADJ If someone or something is **charming,** they are very pleasant and attractive. encantador ❑ *...a charming little fishing village. ...un pueblito pesquero encantador.* ❑ *...a charming young man. ...un joven encantador.* • **charm|ing|ly** ADV encantadoramente ❑ *Calder smiled charmingly. Calder sonrió encantadoramente.* ❑ *There's something charmingly old-fashioned about him. Hay algo encantadoramente anticuado en él.*

**chart** /tʃɑrt/ (**charts, charting, charted**) **1** N-COUNT A **chart** is a diagram or graph which displays information. gráfico, gráfica ❑ *Male unemployment was 14.2%, compared with 5.8% for women (see chart on next page). El desempleo masculino fue del 14.2%, en comparación con el 5.8% entre las mujeres (ver gráfica en la página siguiente).* **2** N-COUNT A **chart** is a map of the ocean or stars. carta, mapa ❑ *...charts of the Pacific Ocean. ...cartas del Océano Pacífico.* **3** V-T If you **chart** the development or progress of something, you observe and record it carefully. trazar, registrar ❑ *The book charts the history of four generations of the family. El libro traza la historia de cuatro generaciones de la familia.*
→ see Picture Dictionary: **chart**

**char|ter** /tʃɑrtər/ (**charters, chartering, chartered**) **1** N-COUNT A **charter** is a formal document describing the rights, aims, or principles of an organization. carta ❑ *...the United Nations Charter. ...la Carta de las Naciones Unidas.* **2** ADJ A **charter** plane or boat is one which is rented for use by a particular person or group. alquilado, fletado ❑ *The plane was a charter flight. El vuelo fue en un avión alquilado.* **3** V-T If someone **charters** a plane or boat, they rent it for their own use. alquilar, fletar ❑ *He chartered a jet to fly her home. Alquiló un avión para regresar a casa.*

**char|ter mem|ber** (**charter members**) N-COUNT A **charter member of** a club or organization is one of the people who first joined or started it. socio fundador o socia fundadora

**chase** /tʃeɪs/ (**chases, chasing, chased**) **1** V-T If you **chase** someone, you run after them or follow them in order to catch them or force them to leave a place. perseguir, echar, expulsar ❑ *She chased the thief for 100 yards. Persiguió al ladrón 100 metros.* ❑ *Many farmers will chase you off their land. Muchos campesinos te echan de sus tierras.* • **Chase** is also a noun. persecución ❑ *The chase ended at about 10:30 p.m. on Highway 522. La persecución terminó aproximadamente a las diez y media de la noche en la carretera 522.* **2** V-T/V-I If you **are chasing** something you want, such as work or money, you are trying hard to get it. andar en busca, andar detrás de, andar a la caza de ❑ *In some areas, 14 people are chasing every job. En algunos lugares, hasta catorce personas andan a la caza de cada empleo.* ❑ *There are too many schools chasing after too few students. Son muchas escuelas para tan pocos estudiantes.*
▸ **chase down** PHR-VERB If you **chase** someone **down,** you run after them or follow them quickly and catch them. perseguir y atrapar ❑ *Ness chased the thief down and held him until police arrived. Ness persiguió al ladrón hasta atraparlo y lo retuvo hasta que llegó la policía.*

**chat** /tʃæt/ (**chats, chatting, chatted**) V-RECIP When people **chat,** or **chat** to one another, they talk in an informal and friendly way. platicar, conversar, charlar ❑ *The women were chatting. Las mujeres estaban platicando.* ❑ *I was chatting to him the other day. Estaba platicando con él el otro día.* • **Chat** is also a noun. plática, conversación, charla ❑ *I had a chat with John. Tuve una charla con John.*

**chat room** (**chat rooms**) also **chatroom** N-COUNT A **chat room** is a site on the Internet where people can exchange messages about a particular subject. tertulia digital, charla digital [COMPUTING]

**chat|ter** /tʃætər/ (**chatters, chattering, chattered**) **1** V-I If you **chatter,** you talk quickly and continuously about unimportant things. parlotear, cotorrear, hablar por los codos ❑ *Everyone's chattering away in different languages. Todos estaban parloteando en diferentes idiomas.* ❑ *Erica chattered about Andrew's children. Erica hablaba hasta por los codos de los hijos de Andrew.* • **Chatter** is also a noun. parloteo, cotorreo, charla ❑ *...their noisy chatter. ...su ruidoso parloteo.* **2** V-I If your teeth **chatter,** they keep knocking together because you are cold. castañetear ❑ *She was so cold her teeth chattered. Tenía tanto frío que le castañeteaban los dientes.*

**cheap** /tʃip/ (**cheaper, cheapest**) **1** ADJ Goods or services that are **cheap** cost less money than usual or than you expected. barato ❑ *I'm going to live off campus if I can find somewhere cheap enough. Si encuentro algo lo suficientemente barato, dejaré de vivir en el dormitorio universitario.* ❑ *Costs are coming down because of cheaper fuel. Los costos están bajando gracias a que el combustible es más barato.* • **cheap|ly** ADV barato, a bajo costo, a bajo precio ❑ *It will produce electricity more cheaply than a nuclear plant. Producirá electricidad a menor costo que una planta nuclear.* **2** ADJ **Cheap** goods cost less money than similar products but their quality is poor. de pacotilla, corriente ❑ *Don't buy cheap imitations. No compres imitaciones corrientes.* **3** ADJ **Cheap** remarks are unkind and unnecessary. vil, de mal gusto ❑ ...a series of cheap insults. ...una serie de insultos de mal gusto. **4** ADJ If you describe someone as **cheap,** you are criticizing them for being unwilling to spend money. tacaño, agarrado, codo ❑ Oh, please, Dad, just this once don't be cheap. Por favor, papi, no seas tan codo esta vez.

| **Thesaurus** | *cheap* | Ver también: |
|---|---|---|
| ADJ. | budget, economical, low-cost, reasonable; (ant.) costly, expensive **1** second-rate **2** | |

**cheat** /tʃit/ (**cheats, cheating, cheated**) **1** V-I If someone **cheats,** they do not obey a set of rules which they should be obeying, for example in a game or exam. hacer trampa ❑ Students may be tempted to cheat in order to get into top schools. Los estudiantes pueden sentirse tentados a hacer trampa para ingresar a las mejores escuelas. ● **Cheat** is also a noun. tramposo, tramposa ❑ Cheats will be disqualified. Se descalificará a los tramposos. ● **cheat|ing** N-UNCOUNT hacer trampa ❑ He was accused of cheating by his opponent. Su oponente lo acusó de hacer trampa. **2** V-T If someone **cheats** you **out of** something, they get it from you by behaving dishonestly. estafar, timar ❑ It was a deliberate effort to cheat them out of their money. Fue un esfuerzo deliberado por estafarles su dinero.

▶ **cheat on** **1** PHR-VERB If someone **cheats on** their husband, wife, or partner, they have a sexual relationship with another person. engañar [INFORMAL] **2** PHR-VERB If someone **cheats on** something such as an agreement or their taxes, they do not do what they should do under a set of rules. burlar ❑ Their job is to check that none of the countries is cheating on the agreement. Su tarea consiste en verificar que ninguno de los países burle el acuerdo.

**cheat|er** /tʃitər/ (**cheaters**) N-COUNT A **cheater** is someone who cheats. tramposo o tramposa, embustero o embustera, estafador o estafadora

**check** /tʃɛk/ (**checks, checking, checked**) **1** V-T/V-I If you **check** something, you make sure that it is correct, satisfactory, or safe. comprobar, verificar ❑ Check the meanings of the words in a dictionary. Comprueba el significado de las palabras en un diccionario. ❑ I think there is an age limit, but I'd have to check. Creo que hay una edad límite, pero tendría que verificarlo. ❑ She checked whether she had a clean, ironed shirt. Se aseguró de tener una camisa limpia y planchada. ❑ Stephen checked on her several times during the night. Stephen fue a ver varias veces durante la noche que estuviera bien. ● **Check** is also a noun. revisión, verificación ❑ ...regular checks on his blood pressure. ...revisiones regulares de su presión sanguínea. **2** V-T If you **check** something that is written on a piece of paper, you put a mark, like a V with the right side extended, next to it. marcar ❑ Please check the box below. Por favor, marque la casilla de abajo. **3** V-T To **check** something, usually something bad, means to stop it from spreading or continuing. detener, parar, frenar ❑ How can we check the spread of this disease? ¿Cómo podemos detener la diseminación de esta enfermedad? **4** V-T When you **check** your luggage at an airport, you give it to an official so that it can be taken onto your plane. registrar ❑ We checked our baggage and walked around the gift shops. Registramos las maletas y fuimos a dar la vuelta por las tiendas de regalos. **5** N-COUNT The **check** in a restaurant is a piece of paper on which the price of your meal is written and which you are given before you pay. cuenta **6** N-COUNT A pattern of squares, usually of two colors, can be referred to as **checks** or a **check.** a cuadros, de cuadros ❑ Styles include stripes and checks. Los estilos incluyen rayas y cuadros. **7** N-COUNT A **check** is a printed form on which you write an amount of money and who it is to be paid to. Your bank then pays the money to that person from your account. cheque ❑ He handed me a check for $1,500. Me dio un cheque de 1,500 dólares. **8** → see also **blank check, traveler's check** **9** PHRASE If something or someone **is held in check** or **is kept in check,** they are controlled and prevented from becoming too great or powerful. tener a raya, contener ❑ Life on Earth will become impossible unless population growth is held in check. La vida en la Tierra será imposible a menos que se contenga el crecimiento demográfico. **10** → see also **rain check**

→ see **answer**

▶ **check in** **1** PHR-VERB When you **check in** or **check into** a hotel or clinic, you arrive and go through the necessary procedures before you stay there. registrar(se), internar(se) ❑ I'll tell the hotel we'll check in tomorrow. Avisaré al hotel que llegaremos mañana. ❑ He has checked into a clinic. Se internó en una clínica. **2** PHR-VERB When you **check in** at an airport, you arrive and show your ticket before going on a flight. registrar(se) ❑ He checked in at Amsterdam's Schiphol airport for a flight to Atlanta. Se registró para un vuelo a Atlanta en el aeropuerto Schiphol de Ámsterdam.

→ see **hotel**

▶ **check out** **1** PHR-VERB When you **check out of** a hotel, you pay the bill and leave. pagar la cuenta ❑ They packed and checked out of the hotel. Empacaron, pagaron la cuenta y abandonaron el hotel. ❑ They checked out yesterday morning. Pagaron la cuenta y se fueron ayer en la mañana. **2** PHR-VERB If you **check out** something or someone, you find out information about them. verificar, comprobar, investigar ❑ Maybe we ought to go down to the library and check it out. Tal vez deberíamos ir a la biblioteca y comprobarlo. ❑ We ought to check him out on the computer. Deberíamos investigarlo en la computadora. **3** → see also **checkout**

▶ **check up** **1** PHR-VERB If you **check up on** something or someone, you find out information about them. investigar ❑ Are you asking me to check up on my colleagues? ¿Está pidiéndome que investigue a mis colegas? **2** → see also **checkup**

| **Thesaurus** | *check* | Ver también: |
|---|---|---|
| V. | confirm, find out, make sure, verify; (ant.) ignore, overlook **1** | |

| **Word Partnership** | Usar *check* con: |
|---|---|
| PREP. | check **for/that** *something*, check **with** *someone* **1** |
| N. | **background** check, **credit** check, **security** check **1** check **your baggage/luggage** **4** |
| V. | **cash a** check, **deposit a** check, **pay with a** check, **write a** check **7** |

C

C

**checked** /tʃɛkt/ ADJ Something that is **checked** has a pattern of small squares, usually of two colors. *a cuadros, de cuadros* ❑ *...a checked shirt. ...una camisa de cuadros.*
→ see **pattern**

**checker|board** /tʃɛkərbɔrd/ (**checkerboards**) **1** N-COUNT A **checkerboard** is a square board with 64 squares of two different colors that is used for playing checkers or chess. *tablero de damas, tablero de ajedrez* **2** ADJ A **checkerboard** pattern is made up of equal-sized squares of two different colors, usually black and white. *de cuadros*

**check|ers** /tʃɛkərz/ N-UNCOUNT **Checkers** is a game for two people, played with 24 round pieces on a board. *damas*

**check|ing ac|count** (**checking accounts**) N-COUNT A **checking account** is a personal bank account that you can take money out of at any time. *cuenta de cheques, cuenta corriente*

**check mark** (**check marks**) N-COUNT A **check mark** is a written mark like a V with the right side extended. It is used to show that something is correct or has been selected or dealt with. *marca, palomita*

**check|out** /tʃɛkaʊt/ (**checkouts**) N-COUNT In a supermarket, a **checkout** is a counter where you pay for things you are buying. *caja*

**check|up** /tʃɛkʌp/ (**checkups**) N-COUNT A **checkup** is an examination by your doctor or dentist. *revisión médica, examen médico*

**cheek** /tʃik/ (**cheeks**) N-COUNT Your **cheeks** are the sides of your face below your eyes. *mejilla, cachete*
→ see **face, kiss**

**cheer** /tʃɪər/ (**cheers, cheering, cheered**) **1** V-T/V-I When people **cheer**, they shout loudly to show approval or encouragement. *vitorear, aclamar, ovacionar* ❑ *The crowd cheered as she went up the steps to the stage. La multitud gritaba entusiasmada mientras ella subía al escenario.* ❑ *Thousands of Americans cheered him on his return. Miles de estadounidenses lo vitorearon a su regreso.* • **Cheer** is also a noun. *ovación* ❑ *...a loud cheer. ...una fuerte ovación.* **2** V-T If you **are cheered by** something, it makes you happier. *levantar el ánimo* ❑ *The people around him looked cheered by his presence. La gente que lo rodeaba parecía animada por su presencia.* • **cheer|ing** ADJ *alentador* ❑ *...very cheering news. ...noticias muy alentadoras.*
▸ **cheer on** PHR-VERB When you **cheer** someone **on**, you shout loudly in order to encourage them, for example when they are taking part in a game. *animar, alentar* ❑ *A thousand supporters packed into the stadium to cheer them on. Mil partidarios se apretujaron en el estadio para animarlos.*
▸ **cheer up** PHR-VERB When you **cheer up** or when someone or something **cheers** you **up**, you stop feeling sad and become more cheerful. *animar, levantar el ánimo* ❑ *I think he misses her terribly. You might cheer him up. Creo que la extraña muchísimo. Tú podrías animarlo un poco.* ❑ *I wrote that song just to cheer myself up. Escribí esa canción sólo para levantarme el ánimo.*

**cheer|ful** /tʃɪərfəl/ **1** ADJ Someone who is **cheerful** is happy and shows this in their behavior. *alegre* ❑ *Paddy was always cheerful and jolly. Paddy siempre estaba alegre y de buen humor.* • **cheer|ful|ly** ADV *alegremente* ❑ *"We've come with good news," Pat said cheerfully. —Traemos buenas noticias —dijo Pat alegremente.* • **cheer|ful|ness** N-UNCOUNT *alegría* ❑ *...a youthful cheerfulness. ...una alegría juvenil.* **2** ADJ Something that is **cheerful** is pleasant and makes you feel happy. *alegre* ❑ *The nursery is bright and cheerful. La guardería tiene mucha luz y es alegre.*

**cheese** /tʃiz/ (**cheeses**) N-VAR **Cheese** is a solid food made from milk. It is usually white or yellow. *queso* ❑ *...bread and cheese. ...pan con queso.* ❑ *...delicious French cheeses. ...los deliciosos quesos franceses.*

**cheese|cake** /tʃizkeɪk/ (**cheesecakes**) N-VAR **Cheesecake** is a dessert that consists of a crust made from cookie or cracker crumbs covered with a soft sweet filling containing cream cheese. *pastel de queso, tarta de queso*
→ see **dessert**

**chef** /ʃɛf/ (**chefs**) N-COUNT A **chef** is a cook in a restaurant or hotel. *cocinero o cocinera, jefe de cocina o jefa de cocina, chef*

**chef's sal|ad** (**chef's salads**) N-VAR A **chef's salad** is a green salad with hard-boiled egg and strips of meat and cheese on top. *ensalada del chef*

| Word Link | **chem ≈ chemical : biochemistry, chemical, chemistry** |
|---|---|

**chemi|cal** /kɛmɪkᵊl/ (**chemicals**) **1** ADJ **Chemical** means involving or resulting from a reaction between two or more substances, or relating to the substances that something consists of. *químico* ❑ *...chemical reactions. ...reacciones químicas.* ❑ *Almost all of the natural chemical elements are found in the ocean. Casi todas las substancias químicas naturales se encuentran en el mar.* • **chemi|cal|ly** /kɛmɪkli/ ADV *químicamente* ❑ *...chemically-related drugs. ...drogas químicamente relacionadas.* **2** N-COUNT **Chemicals** are substances that are used in a chemical process or made by a chemical process. *substancia química, producto químico* ❑ *...the overuse of chemicals in agriculture. ...el uso excesivo de substancias químicas en la agricultura.*
→ see Word Web: **periodic table**
→ see **farm, firework, periodic table, war**

**chemi|cal bond** (**chemical bonds**) N-COUNT A **chemical bond** is the force that holds atoms together to make molecules. *enlace químico*

**chemi|cal bond|ing** N-UNCOUNT **Chemical bonding** is the joining together of atoms to make molecules. *enlace químico*

**chemi|cal change** (**chemical changes**) N-COUNT A **chemical change** is a change in a substance that results in a new or different substance, such as the conversion of wood to smoke and ash when it is burned. *cambio químico*

**chemi|cal en|er|gy** N-UNCOUNT **Chemical energy** is the energy that is released during a chemical reaction or a chemical change. *energía química*

**chemi|cal equa|tion** (**chemical equations**) N-COUNT A **chemical equation** is an equation that describes a chemical reaction. *ecuación química*

**chemi|cal for|mu|la** (**chemical formulas** or **chemical formulae**) N-COUNT A **chemical formula** is the scientific name for a substance, based on the number and type of atoms in one molecule of the substance. For example, H2O is the chemical formula for water. *fórmula química*

**chem|i|cal prop|er|ty** (**chemical properties**) N-COUNT The **chemical properties** of a substance are the physical qualities that determine how it will react with other substances. *propiedad química*

**chem|i|cal re|ac|tion** (**chemical reactions**) N-COUNT A **chemical reaction** is the change that happens when two or more substances are mixed and a new substance is formed. *reacción química*

**chem|i|cal weath|er|ing** N-UNCOUNT **Chemical weathering** is the change that takes place in the structure of rocks and minerals as a result of their exposure to water and the atmosphere. *descomposición química a la intemperie*

**Word Link** *ist ≈ one who practices : artist, chemist, pianist*

**chem|ist** /kɛmɪst/ (**chemists**) N-COUNT A **chemist** is a person who does research connected with chemistry or who studies chemistry. *químico o química*

**Word Link** *chem ≈ chemical : biochemistry, chemical, chemistry*

**chem|is|try** /kɛmɪstri/ N-UNCOUNT **Chemistry** is the scientific study of the structure of substances and of the way that they react with other substances. *química*

**cher|ry** /tʃɛri/ (**cherries**) **1** N-COUNT **Cherries** are small, round fruit with red skins. *cereza* **2** N-COUNT A **cherry** or a **cherry tree** is a tree that cherries grow on. *cerezo*

**chess** /tʃɛs/ N-UNCOUNT **Chess** is a game for two people, played on a chessboard. Each player has 16 pieces, including a king. The aim is to trap your opponent's king. *ajedrez* ❑ *He was playing chess with his uncle. Estaba jugando al ajedrez con su tío.*
→ see Word Web: **chess**

**chest** /tʃɛst/ (**chests**) **1** N-COUNT Your **chest** is the top part of the front of your body. *pecho, tórax* ❑ *He crossed his arms over his chest. Se cruzó los brazos sobre el pecho.* ❑ *He was shot in the chest. Le dispararon en el pecho.* **2** N-COUNT A **chest** is a large, heavy box used for storing things. *cofre* ❑ *...a treasure chest. ...un cofre de tesoro.*
→ see **body**

**chew** /tʃu/ (**chews, chewing, chewed**) V-T/V-I When you **chew** food, you break it up with your teeth so that it becomes easier to swallow. *masticar, mordisquear* ❑ *Eat slowly and chew your food well. Come lentamente y mastica bien la comida.* ❑ *He chewed on his toast. Mordisqueó su pan tostado.*

**Chi|ca|na** /tʃɪkɑnə/ (**Chicanas**) N-COUNT A **Chicana** is an American girl or woman whose family originally came from Mexico. *chicana* ❑ *...a Chicana from Michigan. ...una chicana de Michigan.*

**Chi|ca|no** /tʃɪkɑnoʊ/ (**Chicanos**) N-COUNT A **Chicano** is an American boy or man whose family originally came from Mexico. *chicano*

chick

**chick** /tʃɪk/ (**chicks**) **1** N-COUNT A **chick** is a baby bird. *pollo, polluelo* ❑ *...newly-hatched chicks. ...pollos recién salidos del cascarón.* **2** N-COUNT Some men refer to women as **chicks**. This use could cause offense. *muchacha bonita*

**chicka|dee** /tʃɪkədi/ (**chickadees**) N-COUNT A **chickadee** is a small North American bird with gray and black feathers. *paro carbonero*

**chick|en** /tʃɪkɪn/ (**chickens, chickening, chickened**) N-COUNT **Chickens** are birds which are kept on a farm for their eggs and for their meat. *pollo* ● **Chicken** is the flesh of this bird eaten as food. *pollo* ❑ *...roast chicken. ...pollo asado., ...pollo rostizado.*
→ see **meat**

▸ **chicken out** PHR-VERB If someone **chickens out of** something, they do not to do it because they are afraid. *acobardarse, rajarse* [INFORMAL] ❑ *He makes excuses to chicken out of family occasions such as weddings. Cuando hay alguna reunión familiar, como una boda, siempre pone algún pretexto para rajarse.*

**chick flick** (**chick flicks**) N-COUNT A **chick flick** is a romantic film that is not very serious and is intended to appeal to women. *película para mujeres* [INFORMAL]

**chief** /tʃif/ (**chiefs**) **1** N-COUNT The **chief** of an organization or group is its leader or the person who is in charge of it. *jefe o jefa* ❑ *The police chief has said very little about it. El jefe de la policía no ha dicho mucho al respecto.* **2** ADJ **Chief** is used in the job titles of the most senior worker or workers of a particular kind in an organization. *principal, en jefe* ❑ *...the chief test pilot. ...el piloto de pruebas principal.* **3** ADJ The **chief** cause, part, or member of something is the most important one. *principal*

C

**Word Web** chess

Scholars disagree on the origin of the game of **chess**. Some say it started in China around 570 AD. Others say it was invented later in India. In early versions of the **game**, the **king** was the most powerful **chess piece**. But when the game was brought to Europe in the Middle Ages, a new form appeared. It was called Queen's Chess. Modern chess is based on this game. The king is the most important piece, but the **queen** is the most powerful. Chess **players** use rooks, **bishops**, **knights**, and pawns to protect their king and to put their **opponent** in checkmate.

C

❑ *Lack of water is the chief problem in Ethiopia.* *La falta de agua es el principal problema de Etiopía.*

**Thesaurus** *chief* Ver también:

N. boss, director, head, leader **1**
ADJ. key, main, major; (*ant.*) minor, unimportant **3**

**chief jus|tice** (**chief justices**) N-COUNT; N-TITLE A **chief justice** is the most important judge in a court of law, especially a supreme court. *presidente de la corte o presidenta de la corte, presidente del tribunal o presidenta del tribunal*

**chief of staff** (**chiefs of staff**) N-COUNT The **chiefs of staff** are the highest-ranking officers of each service of the armed forces. *jefe del estado mayor o jefa del estado mayor*

**child** /tʃaɪld/ (**children**) **1** N-COUNT A **child** is a human being who is not yet an adult. *niño o niña* ❑ *When I was a child I lived in a village.* *Cuando era niño vivía en un pueblo.* ❑ *...a child of six..* *. un niño de seis años.* **2** N-COUNT Someone's **children** are their sons and daughters of any age. *hijos* ❑ *How are the children?* *¿Cómo están los niños?* ❑ *His children have left home.* *Sus hijos abandonaron el hogar.*
→ see Word Web: **child**
→ see **age**

**Word Partnership** Usar *child* con:

N. child **abuse**, child **care** **1**
V. **adopt a** child, **have a** child, **raise a** child **1**
ADJ. **difficult** child, **happy** child, **small/young** child, **unborn** child **1**

**Word Link** *hood ≈ state, condition : childhood, likelihood, manhood*

**child|hood** /tʃaɪldhʊd/ (**childhoods**) N-VAR A person's **childhood** is the period of their life when they are a child. *niñez, infancia* ❑ *She had a happy childhood.* *Tuvo una infancia feliz.* ❑ *...a story heard in childhood.* *...una historia que se oye en la niñez.*
→ see **child**

**child|ish** /tʃaɪldɪʃ/ **1** ADJ **Childish** means relating to or typical of a child. *infantil, pueril* ❑ *...childish enthusiasm.* *...entusiasmo infantil.* **2** ADJ If you describe someone, especially an adult, as **childish**, you disapprove of them because they behave in an immature way. *infantil, pueril* ❑ *...Penny's selfish and childish behavior.* *...la conducta infantil y egoísta de Penny.*

**chil|dren** /tʃɪldrən/ **Children** is the plural of **child**. *plural de* ***child***

**child sup|port** N-UNCOUNT If a parent pays **child support,** they legally have to pay money to help provide things such as food and clothing for a child with whom they no longer live. *pensión para el mantenimiento de los hijos* ❑ *He went to prison for failing to pay child support.* *Fue a la cárcel por no pagar la pensión para sus hijos.*

**chili** /tʃɪli/ (**chilies** or **chilis**) **1** N-VAR **Chilies** are small red or green peppers with a hot, spicy taste. *chile* **2** N-UNCOUNT **Chili** is a dish made from meat or beans, or sometimes both, with chilies and a thick sauce of tomatoes. *chile con carne, chile con frijoles*
→ see **spice**

**chil|i con car|ne** /tʃɪli kɒn kɑrni/ N-UNCOUNT **Chili con carne** is a dish made from meat, with chilies and a thick sauce of tomatoes. *chile con carne*

**chill** /tʃɪl/ (**chills, chilling, chilled**) **1** V-T/V-I To **chill** something means to make it cold. *enfriar, poner a enfriar* ❑ *Chill the fruit salad until serving time.* *Pon (ponga) a enfriar la ensalada de frutas hasta que sea hora de servirla.* ❑ *Put the pastry in the fridge to chill.* *Pon (ponga) a enfriar la masa en el regrigerador.* ❑ *Smith placed his chilled hands on the radiator.* *Smith puso sus frías manos sobre el radiador.* **2** N-COUNT If something sends a **chill** through you, it gives you a sudden feeling of fear or anxiety. *escalofrío* ❑ *He felt a chill of fear.* *Sintió un escalofrío (de temor).* **3** N-COUNT A **chill** is a mild illness which can give you a slight fever and headache. *enfriamiento* ❑ *He caught a chill.* *Le dio un enfriamiento.*
→ see **illness**

▸ **chill out** PHR-VERB To **chill out** means to relax after you have done something tiring or stressful. *relajarse* [INFORMAL] ❑ *After school, we used to chill out and watch TV.* *Después de la escuela, acostumbrábamos relajarnos y ver la tele.*

**chil|ly** /tʃɪli/ (**chillier, chilliest**) ADJ **Chilly** means uncomfortably cold. *frío* ❑ *It was a chilly afternoon.* *Era una tarde fría.* ❑ *I'm a bit chilly.* *Tengo un poco de frío.*

**chime** /tʃaɪm/ (**chimes, chiming, chimed**) **1** V-T/V-I When a bell or a clock **chimes,** it makes ringing sounds. *sonar* ❑ *He heard the front doorbell*

**Word Web** child

In the Middle Ages, only **infants** and **toddlers** enjoyed the freedoms of **childhood.** A **child** of seven or eight helped the family by working. In the countryside, **sons** started working on the family's farm. **Daughters** did important housework. In cities, children became laborers and worked along with adults. Today **parents** treat children with special care. **Babies** play with toys to help them learn. There are educational programs for preschoolers. The idea of **adolescence** as a separate stage of life appeared about 100 years ago. Today **teenagers** often have part-time jobs while they go to school.

C

chime. Oyó el timbre de la puerta del frente. ❑ The clock chimed three o'clock. Se oyeron las campanadas de las tres. **2** N-COUNT A **chime** is a ringing sound made by a bell, especially when it is part of a clock. campanada ❑ Did you hear a chime? ¿Oíste una campanada?
→ see **percussion**

▸ **chime in** PHR-VERB If you **chime in,** you say something just after someone else has spoken. hacerle eco a ❑ "Why?" Pete asked impatiently. — "Yes, why?" Bob chimed in. —¿Por qué? preguntó Pete con impaciencia. —Sí, ¿por qué? —le hizo eco Bob.

**chim|ney** /tʃɪmni/ (**chimneys**) N-COUNT A **chimney** is a pipe above a fireplace or furnace through which smoke can go up into the air. chimenea ❑ Smoke poured out of the chimneys. El humo salía de las chimeneas.

chimney

**chim|pan|zee** /tʃɪmpænzi/ (**chimpanzees**) N-COUNT A **chimpanzee** is a kind of small African ape. chimpancé
→ see **primate, zoo**

**chin** /tʃɪn/ (**chins**) N-COUNT Your **chin** is the part of your face that is below your mouth and above your neck. mentón, barbilla

**chi|na** /tʃaɪnə/ **1** N-UNCOUNT **China** is a hard white substance made from clay, used to make cups, plates, and ornaments. porcelana, loza ❑ ...a small bowl made of china. ...un pequeño tazón de porcelana. **2** N-UNCOUNT Cups, plates, and ornaments made of china are referred to as **china**. china ❑ Judy collects blue and white china. Judy colecciona porcelana azul y blanca.
→ see **pottery**

**chip** /tʃɪp/ (**chips, chipping, chipped**) **1** N-COUNT **Chips** or **potato chips** are very thin slices of fried potato that are eaten as a snack. papas fritas ❑ ...a package of potato chips. ...un paquete de papas fritas. **2** N-COUNT A silicon **chip** is a very small piece of silicon with electronic circuits on it. circuito integrado ❑ ...an electronic card containing a chip. ...una tarjeta electrónica con un circuito integrado. **3** N-COUNT A **chip** is a small piece of something or a small piece which has been broken off something. pedacito, trocito ❑ It contains real chocolate chips. Contiene trocitos de auténtico chocolate. **4** V-T If you **chip** something, a small piece is broken off it. despostillar, desportillar ❑ The apple chipped the woman's tooth. La manzana despostilló el diente de la mujer. • **chipped** ADJ descascarillado, saltado, desconchado ❑ The paint was badly chipped. La pintura estaba muy descascarillada.
→ see **computer**

▸ **chip in** PHR-VERB When a number of people **chip in,** each person gives some money so that they can pay for something together. cooperarse, contribuir [INFORMAL] ❑ They all chipped in for the gas. Todos se cooperaron para el gas.

**chlo|ro|phyll** /klɔrəfɪl/ N-UNCOUNT **Chlorophyll** is a green substance in plants which enables them to use the energy from sunlight in order to grow. clorofila
→ see **photosynthesis**

**chlo|ro|plast** /klɔrəplæst/ (**chloroplasts**) N-COUNT **Chloroplasts** are the parts of cells in plants and algae where photosynthesis takes place. cloroplasto [TECHNICAL]

**choco|late** /tʃɔkəlɪt, tʃɔklɪt/ (**chocolates**) **1** N-UNCOUNT **Chocolate** is a sweet food made from cocoa and eaten as a candy. chocolate ❑ ...a bar of chocolate. ...una tableta de chocolate. **2** N-VAR **Chocolate** or **hot chocolate** is a hot drink made from a powder containing chocolate. chocolate ❑ ...a small cafeteria where the visitors can buy tea, coffee and chocolate. ...una cafetería chica donde los visitantes pueden tomar té, café y chocolate. **3** N-COUNT **Chocolates** are small candies or nuts covered with a layer of chocolate. chocolate ❑ ...a box of chocolates. ...una caja de chocolates.
→ see **dessert**

**choice** /tʃɔɪs/ (**choices, choicer, choicest**) **1** N-COUNT If there is a **choice of** things, there are several of them and you can choose the one you want. selección, variedad ❑ It's available in a choice of colors. Lo hay en una variedad de colores. ❑ There's a choice between meat or a vegetarian dish. Se puede escoger entre un plato de carne o vegetariano. **2** N-COUNT Your **choice** is the thing or things that you choose. decisión, elección ❑ His choice of words made Rodney angry. Su vocabulario enojó a Rodney. ❑ ...tickets to see the football team of your choice. ...boletos para ver al equipo de fútbol que prefiera. **3** ADJ **Choice** means of very high quality. selecto [FORMAL] ❑ ...choice cuts of beef. ...cortes (de carne de res) de primera. **4** PHRASE If you **have no choice but** to do something or **have little choice but** to do it, you cannot avoid doing it. alternativa, opción ❑ They had little choice but to agree. Prácticamente no tenían más opción que estar de acuerdo. **5** PHRASE The item **of choice** is the one that someone likes best, or that most people prefer. preferido ❑ Coffee is their drink of choice. El café es su bebida preferida.

**Word Partnership** Usar *choice* con:

| | |
|---|---|
| ADJ. | **best/good** choice, **wide** choice **1** |
| N. | **freedom of** choice, choice **of *something*** **1** |
| V. | **given a** choice, **have a** choice, **make a** choice **1** **2** |

**choir** /kwaɪər/ (**choirs**) N-COUNT A **choir** is a group of people who sing together. coro ❑ He has been singing in his church choir since he was six. Ha estado cantando con el coro de su iglesia desde que tenía seis años.

**choke** /tʃoʊk/ (**chokes, choking, choked**) **1** V-T/V-I If you **choke** on something, it prevents you from breathing properly. ahogar(se), asfixiar(se), atragantar(se) ❑ A small child could choke on the toy. Un niño pequeño podría ahogarse con el juguete. ❑ The smoke was choking her. El humo la estaba asfixiando. ❑ The girl choked to death after breathing in smoke. La muchacha murió asfixiada después de haber inhalado humo. **2** V-T To **choke** someone means to squeeze their neck until they are dead. estrangular ❑ They choked him with his tie. Lo estrangularon con su corbata. **3** V-T If a place **is choked with** things or people, it is full of them and they prevent movement in it. atascar, embotellar, congestionar ❑ The village's roads are choked with traffic. Las calles del pueblo estaban congestionadas de tráfico.

C

**chol|era** /kɒlərə/ N-UNCOUNT **Cholera** is a serious disease that affects your digestive system. *cólera (m.)* ❑ *...a cholera epidemic. ...una epidemia de cólera.*

**cho|les|ter|ol** /kəlɛstərɔl/ N-UNCOUNT **Cholesterol** is a substance that exists in the fat, tissues, and blood of all animals. Too much cholesterol in the blood can cause heart disease. *colesterol* ❑ *...a dangerously high cholesterol level. ...un rango de colesterol muy alto.*

**choose** /tʃuz/ (**chooses, choosing, chose, chosen**) **1** V-T/V-I If you **choose** someone or something, you decide to have that person or thing. *elegir, escoger* ❑ *They will choose their own leaders in democratic elections. Elegirán a sus propios dirigentes en elecciones democráticas.* ❑ *There are several patterns to choose from. Hay varios patrones de dónde escoger.* **2** V-T/V-I If you **choose to** do something, you do it because you want to or because you feel that it is right. *decidir, optar* ❑ *They chose to ignore what was going on. Optaron por ignorar lo que estaba pasando.* ❑ *You have the right to remain silent if you choose. Tiene derecho a guardar silencio si así lo decide.*
→ see **answer**

| **Thesaurus** | *choose* | Ver también: |
|---|---|---|
| v. | decide on, opt, prefer, settle on; (*ant.*) pass over, refuse, reject **1** | |

**chop** /tʃɒp/ (**chops, chopping, chopped**) **1** V-T If you **chop** something, you cut it into pieces with a knife or an ax. *cortar* ❑ *Chop the butter into small pieces. Corte la mantequilla en trozos pequeños.* ❑ *We set to work chopping wood. Nos pusimos a trabajar cortando madera.* **2** N-COUNT A **chop** is a small piece of meat cut from the ribs of a sheep or pig. *costilla, chuleta* ❑ *...lamb chops.. . costillas de carnero.*
→ see **cut**

▸ **chop down** PHR-VERB If you **chop down** a tree, you cut through its trunk with an ax so that it falls to the ground. *cortar* ❑ *Sometimes they chop down a tree for firewood. A veces cortan un árbol para hacer leña.*

▸ **chop off** PHR-VERB To **chop off** something such as a part of your body means to cut it off. *cercenar, cortar* ❑ *She chopped off her hair. Se cortó el pelo.*

▸ **chop up** PHR-VERB If you **chop** something **up**, you chop it into small pieces. *picar* ❑ *Chop up three firm tomatoes. Pique (pica) tres jitomates firmes.*
→ see **cut**

**cho|rale** /kəræl, -rɑl/ (**chorales**) N-COUNT A **chorale** is a group of people who sing together. *coral, coro* ❑ *...the Seattle Symphony Chorale. ...el Coro de la Sinfónica de Seattle.*

**chord** /kɔrd/ (**chords**) N-COUNT A **chord** is a number of musical notes played or sung at the same time with a pleasing effect. *acorde* ❑ *I could play a few chords on the guitar. Podía tocar unos cuantos acordes en la guitarra.*

**chor|do|phone** /kɔrdəfoʊn/ (**chordophones**) N-COUNT A **chordophone** is any musical instrument which produces its sound by means of vibrating strings, for example a harp or a guitar. *instrumento de cuerda* [TECHNICAL]

**chore** /tʃɔr/ (**chores**) N-COUNT A **chore** is an unpleasant task. *lata* ❑ *She sees exercise as a chore. Ella cree que el ejercicio es una lata.*

**cho|rus** /kɔrəs/ (**choruses, chorusing, chorused**) **1** N-COUNT A **chorus** is a part of a song which is repeated after each verse. *estribillo* ❑ *Caroline sang two verses and the chorus of her song. Caroline cantó dos estrofas y el estribillo de su canción.* **2** N-COUNT A **chorus** is a large group of people who sing together. *coro* ❑ *The chorus was singing "The Ode to Joy." El coro estaba cantando la "Oda a la alegría".* **3** N-COUNT When there is a **chorus of** criticism, disapproval, or praise, that attitude is expressed by a lot of people at the same time. *coro* ❑ *There is a growing chorus of criticism against the government. Hay un coro de críticas cada vez más grande contra el gobierno.* **4** V-T When people **chorus** something, they say it or sing it together. *decir a una voz* [WRITTEN] ❑ *"Hi," they chorused. —Hola —dijeron a una voz.*

**chose** /tʃoʊz/ **Chose** is the past tense of **choose**. *pasado de* ***choose***

**cho|sen** /tʃoʊzᵊn/ **Chosen** is the past participle of **choose**. *participio pasado de* ***choose***

| **Word Link** | ***an, ian** ≈ one of, relating to : Christian, European, pedestrian* |
|---|---|

**Christian** /krɪstʃən/ (**Christians**) **1** N-COUNT A **Christian** is someone who follows the teachings of Jesus Christ. *cristiano o cristiana* **2** ADJ **Christian** means relating to Christianity or Christians. *cristiano* ❑ *...the Christian Church. ...la Iglesia Cristiana.* ❑ *Most of my friends are Christian. La mayoría de mis amigos son cristianos.*

**Chris|ti|an|ity** /krɪstʃiænɪti/ N-UNCOUNT **Christianity** is a religion based on the teachings of Jesus Christ. *cristianismo* ❑ *He converted to Christianity. Se convirtió al cristianismo.*

**Christ|mas** /krɪsməs/ (**Christmases**) N-VAR **Christmas** is the day or period around the day of the 25th of December, when Christians celebrate the birth of Jesus Christ. *Navidad* ❑ *...the day after Christmas. ...el día después de Navidad.* ❑ *...the Christmas holidays. ...las fiestas navideñas., ...las vacaciones de Navidad.*

**Christ|mas Eve** N-UNCOUNT **Christmas Eve** is the 24th of December, the day before Christmas Day. *Nochebuena*

**Christ|mas tree** (**Christmas trees**) N-COUNT A **Christmas tree** is a real or artificial fir tree, which people put in their houses at Christmas and decorate with lights and ornaments. *árbol de Navidad, árbol de Pascua*

**chro|ma|tid** /kroʊmətɪd/ (**chromatids**) N-COUNT A **chromatid** is one of the two identical halves of a chromosome. *cromátide* [TECHNICAL]

**chro|mo|sphere** /kroʊməsfɪər/ N-SING The **chromosphere** is the thin, middle layer of the sun's atmosphere. *cromosfera* [TECHNICAL]

**chron|ic** /krɒnɪk/ **1** ADJ A **chronic** illness lasts for a very long time. *crónico* ❑ *...chronic back pain. ...dolor de espalda crónico.* • **chroni|cal|ly** /krɒnɪkli/ ADV *crónicamente* ❑ *Most of them were chronically ill. La mayoría estaban enfermos crónicamente.* **2** ADJ A **chronic** situation is very severe and unpleasant. *crónico* ❑ *...chronic poverty. ...pobreza crónica.* • **chroni|cal|ly** ADV *permanentemente* ❑ *His wife is chronically ill. Su esposa padece de una enfermedad crónica.*

C

**chroni|cle** /krɒnɪkᵊl/ (**chronicles, chronicling, chronicled**) **1** V-T To **chronicle** a series of events means to describe them in the order in which they happened. *reseñar* ❑ *The series chronicles the adventures of two friends. En la serie se hace la reseña de las aventuras de dos amigos.* **2** N-COUNT A **chronicle** is an account or record of a series of events. *reseña, crónica* ❑ *...a chronicle of the civil rights movement. ...una crónica del movimiento pro derechos civiles.*
→ see **diary**

**chrysa|lis** /krɪsəlɪs/ (**chrysalises**) **1** N-COUNT A **chrysalis** is a butterfly or moth in the stage between being a larva and an adult. *crisálida* **2** N-COUNT A **chrysalis** is the hard, protective covering that a chrysalis has. *crisálida*

**chuck** /tʃʌk/ (**chucks, chucking, chucked**) V-T When you **chuck** something somewhere, you throw it there in a casual or careless way. *tirar, botar* [INFORMAL] ❑ *I chucked the clock in the trash. Tiré el reloj a la basura.*

**chunk** /tʃʌŋk/ (**chunks**) **1** N-COUNT **Chunks of** something are thick, solid pieces of it. *pedazo, trozo* ❑ *...floating chunks of ice. ...trozos de hielo flotantes.* ❑ *...a chunk of meat. ...un trozo de carne.* **2** N-COUNT A **chunk of** something is a large amount or large part of it. *pedazo* [INFORMAL] ❑ *...a chunk of farmland near the airport. ...un buen pedazo de tierra cerca del aeropuerto.*

**church** /tʃɜrtʃ/ (**churches**) **1** N-VAR A **church** is a building in which Christians worship. *iglesia* ❑ *...one of the country's most historic churches. ...una de las iglesias más históricas del país.* ❑ *...St Helen's Church. ...la iglesia de Santa Helena.* ❑ *The family has gone to church. La familia fue a la iglesia.* **2** N-COUNT A **Church** is one of the groups of people within the Christian religion that have their own beliefs, clergy, and forms of worship. *iglesia* ❑ *...the Catholic Church. ...la Iglesia Católica.*

**ci|der** /saɪdər/ (**ciders**) N-VAR **Cider** is a drink made from apples. In Britain, **cider** is an alcoholic drink made from apples. *sidra* ❑ *He ordered a cider. Pidió una sidra.*

**ci|gar** /sɪgɑr/ (**cigars**) N-COUNT **Cigars** are rolls of dried tobacco leaves which people smoke. *puro*

| Word Link | *ette ≈ small : casette, cigarette, maquette* |
|---|---|

**ciga|rette** /sɪgərɛt/ (**cigarettes**) N-COUNT **Cigarettes** are small tubes of paper containing tobacco which people smoke. *cigarrillo, cigarro*

**ci|lan|tro** /sɪlæntroʊ/ N-UNCOUNT **Cilantro** is the leaves of the coriander plant that are used as an herb. *cilantro* ❑ *Put a little cilantro on the side of each plate. Pon (ponga) un poco de cilantro en la orilla de cada plato.*

**cilia** /sɪliə/ N-PLURAL **Cilia** are short thin structures, resembling hairs, on the surfaces of some types of cells and organisms. *cilio* [TECHNICAL]

**cin|der** /sɪndər/ (**cinders**) N-COUNT **Cinders** are the pieces of blackened material that are left after wood or coal has burned. *ceniza, rescoldo*

**cin|der block** (**cinder blocks**) also **cinderblock** N-COUNT A **cinder block** is a large gray brick made from coal cinders and cement which is used for building. *ladrillo de cenizas, bloque de concreto de cenizas*

**cin|der cone** (**cinder cones**) also **cinder cone volcano** N-COUNT A **cinder cone** or a **cinder cone volcano** is a small volcano with steep sides, made from pieces of rock and ash. *cono volcánico*

**cin|ema** /sɪnɪmə/ (**cinemas**) N-UNCOUNT **Cinema** is the business and art of making movies. *cine* ❑ *...the history of cinema. ...la historia del cine.*
● **cin|emat|ic** /sɪnɪmætɪk/ ADJ *cinematográfico* ❑ *...the director's cinematic style. ...el estilo cinematográfico del director.*

**cin|na|mon** /sɪnəmən/ N-UNCOUNT **Cinnamon** is a sweet spice used for flavoring food. *canela*
→ see **spice**

**cir|ca** /sɜrkə/ PREP If you write **circa** in front of a date, you mean that the date is approximate. *alrededor de, cerca de* [FORMAL] ❑ *...circa 1850. ...alrededor de 1850.*

**cir|ca|dian rhythm** /sɜrkeɪdiən rɪðəm/ (**circadian rhythms**) N-COUNT **Circadian rhythms** are patterns in the function or behavior of living organisms that are repeated every 24 hours. *ritmo circadiano*

| Word Link | *circ ≈ around : circle, circuit, circulate* |
|---|---|

**cir|cle** /sɜrkᵊl/ (**circles, circling, circled**) **1** N-COUNT A **circle** is a round shape. Every part of its edge is the same distance from the center. *círculo* ❑ *The flag was red, with a large white circle in the center. La bandera era roja, con un gran círculo blanco en el centro.* ❑ *Cut out 4 circles of pastry. Corte cuatro círculos de masa.* **2** N-COUNT You can refer to a group of people as a **circle**. *círculo* ❑ *He has a small circle of friends. Tiene un círculo de amigos pequeño.* **3** V-T/V-I To **circle** someone or something means to move around them in a circle. *dar vueltas, volar en círculo* ❑ *The plane circled above the airport, waiting to land. El avión voló en círculos sobre el aeropuerto, esperando para aterrizar.* ❑ *There were two helicopters circling around. Había dos helicópteros volando en círculos.*
→ see **answer, shape, soccer**

**Word Partnership** Usar *circle* con:

| | |
|---|---|
| V. | **draw a** circle **1** |
| | **form a** circle, **make a** circle **1 2** |
| ADJ. | **big/large/small** circle **1 2** |
| PREP. | **inside/outside/within a** circle **1 2** |

**cir|cuit** /sɜrkɪt/ (**circuits**) **1** N-COUNT An electrical **circuit** is a complete route which an electric current can flow around. *circuito* ❑ *The electrical circuit was broken. El circuito eléctrico estaba cortado.* **2** → see also **closed-circuit** **3** N-COUNT A **circuit** is a series of places that are visited regularly by a person or group. *recorrido, circuito* ❑ *...the lecture circuit. ...el recorrido/circuito de las conferencias.*

**cir|cu|lar** /sɜrkyələr/ (**circulars**) **1** ADJ Something that is **circular** is shaped like a circle. *circular* ❑ *...a circular hole twelve feet wide. ...un agujero circular de 3.66 metros de diámetro.* **2** N-COUNT A **circular** is a letter or advertisement that is sent to a large number of people at the same time. *circular* ❑ *Information circulars were sent to 1,800 newspapers. Enviaron circulares de información a 1,800 periódicos.*

C

**Word Link** *circ ≈ around : circle, circuit, circulate*

**cir|cu|late** /sɜrkyəleɪt/ (**circulates, circulating, circulated**) **1** V-T/V-I When something **circulates** or **is circulated,** it is passed around or spread among a group of people. *circular, correr* ❑ *Rumors were beginning to circulate that the project might have to be abandoned. Empezaban a correr rumores de que podría tener que abandonarse el proyecto.* ❑ *She circulated a letter explaining why she was leaving. Hizo circular una carta en la que explicaba por qué se iba.* • **cir|cu|la|tion** /sɜrkyəleɪʃ<sup></sup>ᵊn/ N-UNCOUNT *circulación* ❑ *...the circulation of leaflets attacking him. ...la circulación de panfletos en los que se le atacaba.* **2** V-I When something **circulates,** it moves easily and freely within a closed place or system. *circular* ❑ *The virus circulates throughout the body. El virus circula por todo el cuerpo.* • **cir|cu|la|tion** N-UNCOUNT *circulación* ❑ *...the circulation of air. ...la circulación de aire.*

**cir|cu|la|tion** /sɜrkyəleɪʃᵊn/ (**circulations**) **1** N-COUNT The **circulation** of a newspaper or magazine is the number of copies that are sold each time it is produced. *circulación, tirada* ❑ *The Daily News once had the highest circulation in the country. El Daily News tuvo alguna vez la mayor tirada del país.* **2** N-UNCOUNT Your **circulation** is the movement of blood through your body. *circulación* ❑ *...cold spots in the fingers caused by poor circulation. ...áreas insensibles en los dedos (de la mano) causadas por la mala circulación.* **3** → see also **circulate** **4** PHRASE If something such as money is **in circulation,** it is being used by the public. *circulación* ❑ *In Spain, seven million credit cards are in circulation. En España circulan siete millones de tarjetas de crédito.*
→ see **cardiovascular system**

**cir|cu|la|tory** /sɜrkyələtɔri/ ADJ **Circulatory** means relating to the circulation of blood in the body. *circulatorio* [MEDICAL] ❑ *...the human circulatory system. ...el sistema circulatorio (humano).*
→ see **cardiovascular system**

**cir|cum|cise** /sɜrkəmsaɪz/ (**circumcises, circumcising, circumcised**) V-T If a boy or man **is circumcised,** the loose skin at the end of his penis is cut off. *circuncidar* ❑ *He was circumcised within eight days of birth. Le hicieron la circuncisión antes de cumplir ocho días de nacido.* • **cir|cum|ci|sion** /sɜrkəmsɪʒᵊn/ (**circumcisions**) N-VAR *circuncisión* ❑ *Jews and Moslems practice circumcision for religious reasons. Los judíos y los musulmanes practican la circuncisión por motivos religiosos.*

**cir|cum|fer|ence** /sərkʌmfrəns/ N-UNCOUNT The **circumference** of a circle, place, or round object is the distance around its edge. *circunferencia* ❑ *...the Earth's circumference. ...la circunferencia de la Tierra.*
→ see **area**

**cir|cum|stance** /sɜrkəmstæns/ (**circumstances**) **1** N-COUNT **Circumstances** are the conditions which affect what happens in a particular situation. *circunstancia* ❑ *Under certain circumstances, it may be necessary to fight a war. En ciertas circunstancias, puede ser necesario hacer la guerra.* ❑ *You're doing a wonderful job in the circumstances. Dadas las circunstancias, está (estás) haciendo un trabajo magnífico.* ❑ *I'm making inquiries about the circumstances of Mary Dean's murder. Estoy investigando las circunstancias del asesinato de Mary Dean.* **2** N-PLURAL Your **circumstances** are the conditions of your life, especially the amount of money that you have. *circunstancia* ❑ *...help and support for the single mother, whatever her circumstances. ...ayuda y apoyo para la madre soltera, sin importar su situación.*

**Word Partnership** Usar *circumstances* con:

ADJ. **certain** circumstances, **different/similar** circumstances, **difficult** circumstances, **exceptional** circumstances **1** **2**
PREP. **under the** circumstances **1** **2**

**cir|cus** /sɜrkəs/ (**circuses**) N-COUNT A **circus** is a group that consists of clowns, acrobats, and animals that travels around to different places and performs shows. *circo* ❑ *My real ambition was to work in a circus. Mi verdadera ambición era trabajar en un circo.*

**cir|rus** /sɪrəs/ (**cirri** /sɪraɪ/) N-VAR **Cirrus** is a type of thin white cloud that forms at high altitudes. *cirro* [TECHNICAL]
→ see **cloud**

**cite** /saɪt/ (**cites, citing, cited**) **1** V-T If you **cite** something, you quote it or mention it, especially as an example or proof of what you are saying. *citar, mencionar* [FORMAL] ❑ *She cited a favorite poem by George Herbert. Citó uno de sus poemas favoritos de George Herbert.* ❑ *Pilot error was cited as the main cause of the accident. Se mencionó que la causa del accidente había sido un error del piloto.* **2** V-T If someone **is cited,** they are officially ordered to appear before a court or criticized in court. *emplazar, citar* [LEGAL] ❑ *He was cited for driving without a license. La emplazaron a presentarse por conducir sin licencia.*

**citi|zen** /sɪtɪzᵊn/ (**citizens**) **1** N-COUNT Someone who is a **citizen** of a particular country is legally accepted as belonging to that country. *ciudadano o ciudadana* ❑ *...American citizens. ...ciudadanos estadunidenses.* **2** N-COUNT The **citizens of** a town or city are the people who live there. *habitante* ❑ *...the citizens of Buenos Aires. ...los habitantes de Buenos Aires.* **3** → see also **senior citizen**
→ see **election**

**citi|zen's ar|rest** (**citizen's arrests**) N-COUNT If someone **makes** a **citizen's arrest,** they catch someone who they believe has committed a crime and inform the police. *detención o aprehensión llevada a cabo por un ciudadano común* ❑ *Police do not advise the average person to make a citizen's arrest. La policía no aconseja a los ciudadanos comunes que detengan a los delincuentes.*

**citi|zens band** N-PROPER **Citizens band** is a range of radio frequencies which the general public is allowed to use to send messages to each other. The abbreviation **CB** is often used. *banda ciudadana* ❑ *...citizens band radios. ...radios de banda ciudadana.*

**Word Link** *ship ≈ condition or state : citizenship, friendship, membership*

**citi|zen|ship** /sɪtɪzᵊnʃɪp/ N-UNCOUNT If you have **citizenship** of a country, you are legally accepted as belonging to it. *ciudadanía* ❑ *He decided*

C

## Word Web city

For the past 6,000 years people have been moving from the **countryside** to **urban** centers. The world's oldest **capital** is Damascus, Syria. People have lived there for over 2,500 years. Cities are usually economic, commercial, cultural, political, social, and transportation centers. **Tourists** travel to cities for shopping and **sightseeing**. In some big cities, **skyscrapers** have **apartments**, **businesses**, **restaurants**, **theaters**, and **retail stores**. People never have to leave their building. Sometimes cities become **overpopulated** and **crime rates** soar. Then people move to the **suburbs**. In recent decades this trend has been reversed in some places and **inner cities** are being rebuilt.

*to apply for American citizenship. Decidió solicitar la ciudadanía estadunidense.*

**cit|rus** /sɪtrəs/ ADJ A **citrus** fruit is a juicy fruit with a sharp taste such as an orange, lemon, or grapefruit. *cítrico* ❑ *...citrus fruit. ...cítrico(s).*

**city** /sɪti/ (**cities**) N-COUNT A **city** is a large town. *ciudad* ❑ *...the city of Bologna. ...la ciudad de Bolonia*
→ see Word Web: **city**

**city cen|ter** (**city centers**) N-COUNT The **city center** is the busiest part of a city, where most of the stores and businesses are. *centro de la ciudad* ❑ *Our offices are in the city center. Nuestras oficinas están en el centro de la ciudad.*

**city plan|ning** N-UNCOUNT **City planning** is the planning and design of all the new buildings, roads, and parks in a place in order to make them attractive and convenient for the people who live there. *urbanismo* ❑ *...city planning officials. ...funcionarios de urbanismo.*

**Word Link** *wide ≈ extending throughout : citywide, nationwide, worldwide*

**city|wide** /sɪtiwaɪd/ ADJ **Citywide** activities or situations happen or exist in all parts of a city. *que abarca toda la ciudad* ❑ *This is a citywide problem. Este problema afecta a toda la ciudad.*

**Word Link** *civ ≈ citizen : civic, civil, civilian*

**civ|ic** /sɪvɪk/ **1** ADJ You use **civic** to describe people or things that have an official status in a city or town. *cívico, municipal, de la ciudad, del ayuntamiento* ❑ *Civic leaders say they want the city to look its best. Las autoridades dicen que quieren que la ciudad luzca lo mejor posible.* **2** ADJ You use **civic** to describe the duties or feelings that people have because they belong to a particular community. *cívico* ❑ *...a sense of civic pride. ...un sentimiento de orgullo cívico.*

**civic cen|ter** (**civic centers**) N-COUNT In a city or town, a **civic center** is a building or buildings that contain local government offices. Sporting events and concerts are also often held at **civic centers.** *edificios municipales* ❑ *The city council wants more parks and a civic center. El ayuntamiento quiere más parques y edificios municipales.*

**civ|ics** /sɪvɪks/ N-UNCOUNT **Civics** is the study of the rights and duties of the citizens of a society. *civismo* ❑ *...my high-school civics class. ...mi clase de civismo de secundaria.*

**civ|il** /sɪvᵊl/ **1** ADJ You use **civil** to describe things that relate to the people of a country, and their rights and activities, often in contrast with the armed forces. *civil* ❑ *He is a trained civil engineer. Es ingeniero civil recibido.* ❑ *...civil disturbances in the city. ...disturbios civiles en la ciudad.* ❑ *...civil and political rights. ...derechos civiles y políticos.* **2** ADJ Someone who is **civil** is polite in a formal way, but not particularly friendly. *cortés* [FORMAL] ❑ *The least we can do is be civil to people. Lo menos que podemos hacer es ser corteses con la gente.* ● **ci|vil|ity** /sɪvɪlɪti/ N-UNCOUNT *civismo, cortesía, urbanidad* ❑ *...an atmosphere of civility. ...un ambiente de urbanidad.*

**Word Partnership** Usar *civil* con:

N. civil **disobedience**, civil **liberties/rights**, civil **unrest** **1**

**civ|il de|fense** N-UNCOUNT **Civil defense** is the organization and training of ordinary people in a country so that they can help the armed forces in an emergency. *defensa civil* ❑ *...a civil defense exercise. ...un ejercicio de defensa civil.*

**ci|vil|ian** /sɪvɪlyən/ (**civilians**) **1** N-COUNT In a military situation, a **civilian** is anyone who is not a member of the armed forces. *civil* ❑ *He assured me the soldiers were not shooting at civilians. Me aseguró que los soldados no estaban disparando a los civiles.* **2** ADJ In a military situation, **civilian** is used to describe people or things that are not military. *civil* ❑ *...the country's civilian population. ...la población civil del país.*
→ see **war**

**civi|li|za|tion** /sɪvɪlɪzeɪʃᵊn/ (**civilizations**) **1** N-VAR A **civilization** is a human society with its own social organization and culture. *civilización* ❑ *...the ancient civilizations of Greece. ...las civilizaciones antiguas de Grecia.* **2** N-UNCOUNT **Civilization** is the state of having an advanced level of social organization and a comfortable way of life. *civilización* ❑ *...our advanced state of civilization. ...nuestro avanzado estado de civilización.*
→ see **history**

**civi|lized** /sɪvɪlaɪzd/ **1** ADJ A **civilized** society has an advanced level of social organization. *civilizado* ❑ *This is not what we expect of a civilized society. Esto no es lo que esperamos de una sociedad civilizada.* **2** ADJ If you describe a person or their behavior as **civilized,** you mean that they are polite and reasonable. *educado* ❑ *She was very civilized about it. Fue muy educada al respecto.*

C

**civ|il rights** N-PLURAL **Civil rights** are the rights that people have in a society to equal treatment and equal opportunities, whatever their race, sex, or religion. *derechos civiles* ❑ *...the civil rights movement. ...el movimiento pro derechos civiles.*

**civ|il serv|ant** (**civil servants**) N-COUNT A **civil servant** is a person who works for the **civil service**. *servidor público o servidora pública, funcionario público o funcionaria pública* ❑ *...two senior civil servants. ...dos servidores públicos de alta jerarquía.*

**civ|il ser|vice** N-SING **The civil service** of a country consists of its government departments and all the people who work in them. *servicio público, administración pública, servicio civil* ❑ *...a job in the civil service. ...un empleo en la administración pública.*

**civ|il war** (**civil wars**) N-COUNT A **civil war** is a war which is fought between different groups of people who live in the same country. *guerra civil* ❑ *...the American Civil War. ...la guerra civil estadounidense.*

**claim** /kleɪm/ (**claims, claiming, claimed**) **1** V-T If someone **claims that** something is true, they say that it is true but they have not proved it and it may be false. *afirmar* ❑ *He claimed that the people supported his action. Afirmaba que el pueblo apoyaba sus actos.* ❑ *...a man claiming to be a journalist. ...un hombre que afirma ser periodista.* **2** V-T If someone **claims** responsibility or credit for something, they say that they are responsible for it. *reivindicar, hacerse responsable* ❑ *A little-known group has claimed responsibility for the attack. Un grupo pequeño reivindicó el ataque.* **3** V-T If you **claim** something, you try to get it because you think you have a right to it. *reclamar* ❑ *Now they are returning to claim their land. Ahora están regresando a reclamar sus tierras.* • **Claim** is also a noun. *reclamo, reivindicación* ❑ *...claims for improved working conditions. ...los reclamos de mejores condiciones de trabajo.* ❑ *...rival claims to the territory. ...reivindicaciones opuestas por el territorio.* **4** V-T If something **claims** someone's life, they are killed by it or because of it. *cobrar* [FORMAL] ❑ *The civil war claimed the life of a U.N. official yesterday. La guerra civil cobró la vida de un oficial de las Naciones Unidas ayer.* **5** N-COUNT A **claim** is something which someone says which they have not proved and which may be false. *afirmación* ❑ *He repeated his claim that the people supported his actions. Reiteró su afirmación de que la gente apoyaba sus actos.* **6** N-COUNT If you have a **claim on** someone or their attention, you have the right to demand things from them or to demand their attention. *reclamación, exigencia* ❑ *She had no claims on him now. Ahora no tenía ninguna reclamación que hacerle.* **7** to **stake a claim** → see **stake**

**clam** /klæm/ (**clams**) N-COUNT **Clams** are a kind of shellfish. *almeja*
→ see **shellfish**

**clam|bake** /klæmbeɪk/ (**clambakes**) N-COUNT A **clambake** is a picnic at which clams and other food are served. *merienda campestre, especialmente en la playa, donde se sirven almejas y otros alimentos*

| Word Link | *claim, clam ≈ shouting : acclaim, clamor, exclaim* |
|---|---|

**clam|or** /klæmər/ (**clamors, clamoring, clamored**) V-I If people **are clamoring for** something, they are demanding it in a noisy or angry way. *clamar por* ❑ *Both parties are clamoring for the attention of the voter. Ambos partidos claman por la atención del votante.*

**clamp** /klæmp/ (**clamps, clamping, clamped**) **1** N-COUNT A **clamp** is a device that holds two things firmly together. *abrazadera* ❑ *Many can openers have a set of clamps to grip the lid. Muchos abrelatas tienen un juego de sujetadores para la tapa.* **2** V-T When you **clamp** one thing **to** another, you fasten the two things together with a clamp. *sujetar* ❑ *Clamp the microphone to the stand. Sujete el micrófono al pie.* **3** V-T To **clamp** something in a particular place means to put it or hold it there firmly and tightly. *afianzar, cerrar* ❑ *Simon clamped the phone to his ear. Simon afianzó el auricular en su oído.* ❑ *He clamped his lips together. Cerró los labios con fuerza.*
→ see **laboratory**

▸ **clamp down** PHR-VERB To **clamp down on** people or activities means to take strong official action to stop or control them. *ponerse severo, tomar medidas drásticas, apretar las clavijas* ❑ *The authorities are determined to clamp down on the media. Las autoridades están decididas a apretarles las clavijas a los medios de comunicación.*

**clan** /klæn/ (**clans**) N-COUNT A **clan** is a group which consists of families that are related to each other. *clan* ❑ *...enemy clans. ...clanes enemigos.*

**clang|or** /klæŋər, klæŋgər/ N-SING A **clangor** is a loud or harsh noise. *estrépito, estruendo* ❑ *Suddenly, the clangor and shouting ceased. Repentinamente, el estrépito y los gritos cesaron.*

**clap** /klæp/ (**claps, clapping, clapped**) **1** V-T/V-I When you **clap**, you hit your hands together to express appreciation or attract attention. *aplaudir* ❑ *The men danced and the women clapped. Los hombres bailaban y las mujeres marcaban el ritmo con palmadas.* ❑ *Midge clapped her hands. Midge aplaudió., Midge dio una palmada.* **2** V-T If you **clap** your hand or an object onto something, you put it there quickly and firmly. *dar una palmada* ❑ *I clapped a hand over her mouth. Rápidamente, le tapé la boca con la mano.* **3** N-COUNT A **clap of thunder** is a sudden and loud noise of thunder. *trueno*

| Word Link | *clar ≈ clear : clarify, clarity, declare* |
|---|---|

| Word Link | *ify ≈ making : claify, diversify, intensify* |
|---|---|

**clari|fy** /klærɪfaɪ/ (**clarifies, clarifying, clarified**) V-T To **clarify** something means to make it easier to understand, usually by explaining it in more detail. *aclarar, clarificar* [FORMAL] ❑ *Thank you for clarifying the position. Gracias por aclarar la posición.* • **clari|fi|ca|tion** /klærɪfɪkeɪʃən/ N-VAR (**clarifications**) *aclaración* ❑ *The union has asked for clarification of the situation. El sindicato pidió una aclaración sobre la situación.*

**clari|net** /klærɪnɛt/ (**clarinets**) N-VAR A **clarinet** is a wind instrument with a single reed in its mouthpiece. *clarinete*
→ see **orchestra**

**Word Link** *clar ≈ clear : clarify, clarity, declare*

**clar|ity** /klærɪti/ N-UNCOUNT **Clarity** is the quality of being clear and easy to understand. *claridad* ❑ *...the clarity of his writing.* *...la claridad de su escritura.*

**clash** /klæʃ/ (**clashes, clashing, clashed**) **1** V-RECIP When people **clash**, they fight, argue, or disagree with each other. *entrar en conflicto, discordar, chocar* ❑ *He often clashed with his staff when planning projects.* *Frecuentemente entraba en conflicto con su personal cuando planeaban algún proyecto.* ❑ *The two countries clashed over human rights.* *Los dos países entraron en conflicto respecto a los derechos humanos.* ● **Clash** is also a noun. *choque* ❑ *There have been a number of clashes between police and demonstrators.* *Ha habido algunos choques entre la policía y los manifestantes.* **2** V-RECIP Beliefs, ideas, or qualities that **clash with** each other are very different from each other and therefore are opposed. *entrar en conflicto* ❑ *We hope that the Internet will not clash with local customs and culture.* *Tenemos la esperanza de que la Internet no entre en conflicto con las costumbres y la cultura locales.* ● **Clash** is also a noun. *disparidad* ❑ *...a clash of views.* *...una disparidad de opiniones.* **3** V-RECIP If one color **clashes with** another, they look ugly together. *discordar, desentonar* ❑ *The red door clashed with the soft, natural color of the stone walls.* *La puerta roja desentonaba con el color suave de los muros de piedra al natural.*

**class** /klæs/ (**classes, classing, classed**) **1** N-COUNT A **class** is a group of students who are taught together. *clase, grupo* ❑ *He spent six months in a class with younger students.*, *Pasó seis meses en una clase con estudiantes más jóvenes.* **2** N-COUNT A **class** is a course of teaching in a particular subject. *clase* ❑ *She got her law degree by taking classes at night.* *Se licenció en derecho tomando clases nocturnas.* **3** N-COUNT A **class of** things is a group of them with similar characteristics. *clase* ❑ *Cauliflowers, cabbages and kale all belong to the same class of plants.* *Coliflor, col y col rizada todos pertenecen a la misma clase de plantas.* **4** N-UNCOUNT If you do something **in class,** you do it during a lesson in school. *en (la) clase* ❑ *We do lots of reading in class.* *Leemos mucho en clase.* **5** N-UNCOUNT If you say that someone or something has **class,** you mean that they are elegant and sophisticated. *clase* [INFORMAL] **6** N-SING The students in a school or college who finish their course in a particular year are often referred to as the **class of** that year. *clase, promoción* ❑ *...Evergreen High School's Class of 2002.* *...la Promoción 2002 de la Secundaria Evergreen.* **7** N-VAR **Class** refers to the division of people in a society into groups according to their social status. *clase* ❑ *...the relationship between social classes.* *...las relaciones entre las clases sociales.* **8** → see also **middle class, upper class, working class** **9** V-T If someone or something **is classed as** a particular thing, they are regarded as belonging to that group of things. *clasificar, considerar* ❑ *They cannot be classed as different species.* *No se puede clasificarlas como especies diferentes.* ❑ *I class myself as an ordinary working person.* *Me considero un trabajador común y corriente.* **10** → see also **second-class**

**Word Partnership** Usar *class* con:

| | |
|---|---|
| N. | class **for beginners**, class **size**, **students in a** class **1** |
| | **freshman/senior** class, **graduating** class **6** |
| | **leisure** class, class **struggle**, **working** class **7** |
| V. | **take a** class, **teach a** class **1 2** |
| ADJ. | **social** class **7** |

**class act** (**class acts**) N-COUNT If you describe someone or something as a **class act,** you mean that they are impressive and of high quality. *de primera* ❑ *This show will run a long time because it's a class act.* *Este espectáculo durará mucho tiempo porque es de primera.*

**clas|sic** /klæsɪk/ (**classics**) **1** ADJ A **classic** example of something has all the features which you expect such a thing to have. *clásico* ❑ *It's a classic example of racism in our country.* *Es un ejemplo clásico de racismo en nuestro país.* **2** ADJ A **classic** movie or piece of writing is of very high quality and has become a standard against which similar things are judged. *clásico* ❑ *...the classic movie "Huckleberry Finn."* *...la película clásica "Huckleberry Finn".* ● **Classic** is also a noun. *clásico* ❑ *...one of the classics of modern popular music.* *...uno de los clásicos de la música popular moderna.* **3** N-UNCOUNT **Classics** is the study of the ancient Greek and Roman civilizations, especially their languages, literature, and philosophy. *estudios clásicos* ❑ *...a classics degree.* *...un título en estudios clásicos.*

**clas|si|cal** /klæsɪkᵊl/ **1** ADJ You use **classical** to describe something that is traditional in form, style, or content. *clásico* ❑ *...classical ballet.* *...ballet clásico.* ❑ *...a classical composer like Beethoven.* *...un compositor clásico como Beethoven.* ● **clas|si|cal|ly** /klæsɪkli/ ADV *clásicamente* ❑ *...a classically-trained pianist.* *...un pianista formado en los clásicos.* **2** ADJ **Classical** is used to describe things which relate to the ancient Greek or Roman civilizations. *clásico* ❑ *...ancient Egypt and classical Greece.* *...el antiguo Egipto y la Grecia clásica.*
→ see **genre**

**clas|si|fied** /klæsɪfaɪd/ ADJ **Classified** information is officially secret. *confidencial, secreto* ❑ *He had access to classified information.* *Tenía acceso a información secreta.*

**clas|si|fy** /klæsɪfaɪ/ (**classifies, classifying, classified**) V-T To **classify** things means to divide them into groups or types so that things with similar characteristics are in the same group. *clasificar* ❑ *It is necessary to classify the headaches into certain types.* *Es necesario clasificar las jaquecas en ciertos tipos.* ● **clas|si|fi|ca|tion** /klæsɪfɪkeɪʃᵊn/ N-VAR (**classifications**) *clasificación* ❑ *...the classification of knowledge into fields of study.* *...la clasificación del conocimiento en campos de estudio.*

**class|mate** /klæsmeɪt/ (**classmates**) N-COUNT Your **classmates** are students who are in the same class as you at school or college. *compañero de clase o compañera de clase*

**class|room** /klæsrum/ (**classrooms**) N-COUNT A **classroom** is a room in a school where lessons take place. *salón de clases*

C

C

**class sched|ule** (**class schedules**) N-COUNT In a school or college, a **class schedule** is a list that shows the times when particular subjects are taught. *horario de clases*

**classy** /klæsi/ (**classier, classiest**) ADJ If you describe someone or something as **classy,** you mean they are stylish and sophisticated. *con estilo, con clase* [INFORMAL] ❑ *The German star gave a classy performance. La estrella alemana actuó con clase.*

**clause** /klɔz/ (**clauses**) **1** N-COUNT A **clause** is a section of a legal document. *cláusula* ❑ *There is a clause in his contract about company cars. En su contrato hay una cláusula sobre los vehículos de la empresa.* **2** N-COUNT In grammar, a **clause** is a group of words containing a verb. *oración, cláusula*

**claw** /klɔ/ (**claws, clawing, clawed**) **1** N-COUNT The **claws** of a bird or animal are the thin, hard, curved nails at the end of its feet. *garra* ❑ *The cat tried to cling to the edge by its claws. El gato trató de aferrarse al borde con las garras.* **2** V-I If an animal **claws at** something, it scratches or damages it with its claws. *arañar* ❑ *The wolf clawed at the tree and howled. El lobo arañó el árbol y aulló.* **3** V-I To **claw at** something means to try very hard to get hold of it. *aferrar(se)* ❑ *His fingers clawed at Blake's wrist. Buscó aferrarse con los dedos al brazo de Blake.*

claw

→ see **bird, shellfish**

**clay** /kleɪ/ N-UNCOUNT **Clay** is a kind of earth that is soft when it is wet and hard when it is dry. Clay is shaped and baked to make things such as pots and bricks. *arcilla, barro* ❑ *He shaped and squeezed the lump of clay. Le dio forma al terrón de arcilla y luego lo apretó.*

→ see **pottery**

**clean** /klin/ (**cleaner, cleanest, cleans, cleaning, cleaned**) **1** ADJ Something that is **clean** is free from dirt or unwanted marks. *limpio* ❑ *The subway is efficient and clean. El metro tiene un gran rendimiento y es limpio.* ❑ *Tiled kitchen floors are easy to keep clean. Es fácil mantener limpias las cocinas con pisos de baldosas.* **2** ADJ If something such as a book, joke, or lifestyle is **clean,** it is good because it is not immoral or offensive. *apropiado* ❑ *...clean, decent movies. ...películas decentes y apropiadas.* **3** ADJ If someone has a **clean** reputation or record, they have never done anything illegal or wrong. *limpio, sin tacha* ❑ *I've been driving for 40 years with a clean license. He manejado durante 40 años y nunca he tenido ni una sola infracción.* **4** V-T/V-I If you **clean** something, you make it free from dirt and unwanted marks. *limpiar* ❑ *Her father cleaned his glasses with a paper napkin. Su padre limpió sus lentes con una servilleta de papel.* ❑ *It took half an hour to clean the orange powder off the bathtub. Tomó media hora limpiar el polvo color naranja de la tina/bañera.* • **clean|ing** N-UNCOUNT *limpieza* ❑ *The windows were given a thorough cleaning. Las ventanas recibieron una limpieza concienzuda.*

→ see **soap**

▸ **clean out** PHR-VERB If you **clean out** something such as a closet or room, you take everything out of it and clean it thoroughly. *vaciar un lugar y limpiarlo, hacer una limpieza concienzuda* ❑ *Mr. Peters asked if I would help him clean out the basement. El señor Peters me preguntó si querría ayudarlo a hacer una limpieza concienzuda del sótano.*

▸ **clean up** PHR-VERB If you **clean up** something, you clean it thoroughly. *limpiar concienzudamente, limpiar a conciencia* ❑ *Hundreds of workers are cleaning up the beaches. Cientos de trabajadores están limpiando las playas a conciencia.*

| **Thesaurus** *clean* | Ver también: |
|---|---|
| ADJ. | neat, pure; (*ant.*) dirty, filthy **1** |
| V. | rinse, wash; (*ant.*) dirty, soil, stain **4** |

**clean|er** /klinər/ (**cleaners**) **1** N-COUNT A **cleaner** is someone who is employed to clean the rooms and furniture inside a building. *limpiador o limpiadora, afanador o afanadora* ❑ *...the hospital where Sid worked as a cleaner. ...el hospital donde Sid trabajó como afanador.* **2** N-COUNT A **cleaner** is a substance or device used for cleaning things. *quitamanchas, limpiador, purificador* ❑ *...oven cleaner. ...limpiador de hornos.* ❑ *...an air cleaner. ...un purificador de aire.* **3** → see also **vacuum cleaner** **4** N-COUNT A **cleaner** or a **cleaner's** is a store where things such as clothes are dry-cleaned. *tintorería* ❑ *Did you pick up my suit from the cleaner's? ¿Recogiste mi traje de la tintorería?*

**cleanse** /klɛnz/ (**cleanses, cleansing, cleansed**) **1** V-T To **cleanse** a place, person, or organization **of** something dirty, unpleasant, or evil means to make them free from it. *limpiar* ❑ *He tried to cleanse the house of bad memories. Trató de limpiar la casa de malos recuerdos.* **2** V-T If you **cleanse** your skin or a wound, you clean it. *limpiar* ❑ *Catherine demonstrated the proper way to cleanse the face. Catherine demostró la manera de limpiarse el rostro.*

**clear**

1. FREE FROM CONFUSION
2. FREE FROM PHYSICAL OBSTACLES
3. MORALLY OR LEGALLY RIGHT, POSSIBLE, OR PERMITTED
4. PHRASAL VERBS

**❶ clear** /klɪər/ (**clearer, clearest**) **1** ADJ Something that is **clear** is easy to understand, see, or hear. *claro* ❑ *The book is clear and readable. El libro es claro y ameno.* ❑ *The space telescope has taken the clearest pictures ever of Pluto. El telescopio espacial ha tomado las fotografías más claras de Plutón de toda la historia.* • **clear|ly** ADV *claramente* ❑ *Whales journey up the coast, clearly visible from the beach. Las ballenas viajan costa arriba, claramente visibles desde la playa.* **2** ADJ Something that is **clear** is obvious. *claro* ❑ *It was a clear case of homicide. Era un caso claro de homicidio.* ❑ *It became clear that I wouldn't be able to convince Mike. Se me hizo claro que no podría convencer a Mike.* • **clear|ly** ADV *obviamente* ❑ *Clearly, the police cannot break the law in order to enforce it. Obviamente, la policía no puede infringir la ley con el propósito de aplicarla.* **3** ADJ If you are **clear about** something, you understand it completely. *tener en claro* ❑ *It is important to be clear about what Chomsky is doing here. Es importante que tengamos en claro lo* que Chomsky quiere decir en este caso. **4** ADJ If your mind or your way of thinking is **clear,** you are able to think sensibly and logically. *claro, despejado* ❑ *She needed a clear head to carry out her instructions. Necesitaba tener la cabeza despejada para llevar a cabo sus instrucciones.* • **clear|ly** ADV *claramente, con claridad* ❑ *The only time I can think clearly is when I'm alone. El único momento en que puedo pensar con claridad es cuando estoy solo.*

❷ **clear** /klɪər/ (**clearer, clearest, clears, clearing, cleared**) **1** ADJ If a substance is **clear,** it has no color and you can see through it. *claro, transparente* ❑ *...a clear glass panel. ...un panel de vidrio transparente.* ❑ *...a clear gel. ...un gel transparente.* **2** ADJ If a surface, place, or view is **clear,** it is free of unwanted objects or obstacles. *despejado* ❑ *The runway is clear—go ahead and land. —La pista está despejada: puede aterrizar.* **3** ADJ If it is a **clear** day or if the sky is **clear,** there is no mist, rain, or cloud. *claro* ❑ *On a clear day you can see the coast. En un día claro, se puede ver la costa.* **4** ADJ **Clear** eyes or skin look healthy and attractive. *claro* ❑ *...clear blue eyes. ...ojos azul claro.* **5** ADJ If one thing is **clear of** another, it is not touching it or is a safe distance away from it. *salir, dejar atrás* ❑ *As soon as he was clear of the building he looked around. Tan pronto dejó atrás el edificio, miró a su alrededor.* **6** ADV If you drive **clear** to a place, especially a place that is far away, you go all the way there without delays. *sin obstáculos, sin inconvenientes* ❑ *They drove clear over to St Paul. Manejaron hasta St Paul sin dificultades.* **7** V-T When you **clear** an area or place, you remove unwanted things from it. *limpiar* ❑ *They needed to clear the land. Necesitaban limpiar la tierra.* ❑ *Workers could not clear the tunnels of smoke. Los trabajadores no pudieron limpiar de humo los túneles.* **8** V-I When fog or mist **clears,** it gradually disappears. *aclarar, levantar* ❑ *The early morning mist has cleared. Ya levantó la neblina matutina.* **9** to **clear the air** → see **air** **10** → see also **clearing** **11** to **clear your throat** → see **throat**

| **Thesaurus** | *clear* | Ver también: |
|---|---|---|
| ADJ. | obvious, plain, straightforward ❶ **1** | |
| | bright, cloudless, sunny ❷ **3** | |

| **Word Partnership** | Usar *clear* con: |
|---|---|
| N. | clear **goals/purpose,** clear **picture** ❶ **1** |
| | clear **idea,** clear **understanding** ❶ **1** **2** |
| | clear **the way** ❷ **7** |
| V. | **be** clear, **seem** clear ❶ **1** **2** |
| | **make it** clear ❶ **1** **2** |
| ADJ. | **crystal** clear ❶ **1**–**3** ❷ **1**–**3** |

❸ **clear** /klɪər/ (**clearer, clearest, clears, clearing, cleared**) **1** ADJ If you say that your conscience is **clear,** you mean you do not think you have done anything wrong. *limpio* ❑ *Mr. Garcia said his conscience was clear. El señor Garcia dijo que tenía la conciencia limpia.* **2** V-T If a course of action **is cleared,** people in authority give permission for it to happen. *autorizar* ❑ *The helicopter was cleared for take-off. Se autorizó al helicóptero que despegara.* **3** V-T If someone **is cleared,** they are proved to be not guilty of a crime or mistake. *absolver, exculpar* ❑ *She was cleared of the murder. La absolvieron del asesinato., La exculparon del asesinato.*

❹ **clear** /klɪər/ (**clearer, clearest, clears, clearing, cleared**)

▸ **clear away** PHR-VERB When you **clear** things **away** or **clear away,** you put away the things that you have been using. *recoger* ❑ *The waitress cleared away the plates. La mesera recogió los platos.*

▸ **clear out** **1** PHR-VERB If you tell someone to **clear out of** a place or to **clear out,** you are telling them rather rudely to leave. *irse, largarse* [INFORMAL] ❑ *She turned to the others in the room. "The rest of you clear out of here." Se volvió hacia los otros en la habitación y les dijo: —Todos los demás, ¡lárguense!* **2** PHR-VERB If you **clear out** a closet or place, you make it neat and throw away the things in it that you no longer want. *limpiar y ordenar* ❑ *I cleared out my desk before I left. Limpié y puse en orden mi escritorio antes de irme.*

▸ **clear up** **1** PHR-VERB When you **clear up** or **clear** a place **up,** you make things neat and put them away. *recoger* ❑ *After breakfast they played while I cleared up. Después del desayuno, ellos se pusieron a jugar mientras yo recogía.* **2** PHR-VERB To **clear up** a problem, misunderstanding, or mystery means to settle it or find a satisfactory explanation for it. *aclarar* ❑ *The purpose of the meeting is to clear up these disagreements. El propósito de la reunión es aclarar estos desacuerdos.* **3** PHR-VERB When the weather **clears up,** it stops raining or being cloudy. *aclarar* ❑ *It all depends on the weather clearing up. Todo depende de que el tiempo aclare.*

**clear|ance** /klɪərəns/ (**clearances**) **1** N-VAR **Clearance** is the removal of old buildings, trees, or other things that are not wanted from an area. *despeje, desmonte* ❑ *...the clearance of new lands for farming. ...el desmonte de nuevas tierras para la agricultura.* **2** N-VAR If you get **clearance to** do or have something, you get official approval or permission to do or have it. *autorización* ❑ *The plane was given clearance to land. Se dio la autorización al avión para que aterrizara.*

**clear-cut** also **clear cut** ADJ Something that is **clear-cut** is easy to understand and definite or distinct. *inequívoco* ❑ *There are no clear-cut answers. No hay respuestas inequívocas.*

**clear|ing** /klɪərɪŋ/ (**clearings**) N-COUNT A **clearing** is a small area in a forest where there are no trees or bushes. *claro* ❑ *The helicopter landed in a clearing in the dense jungle. El helicóptero aterrizó en un claro de la densa selva.*

**cleav|age** /klivɪdʒ/ (**cleavages**) N-COUNT **Cleavage** is the tendency of a mineral such as a gemstone to split along smooth, regular surfaces. *despegue* [TECHNICAL]

**clef** /klɛf/ (**clefs**) **1** N-COUNT A **clef** is a symbol at the beginning of a line of music that indicates the pitch of the written notes. *clave* **2** → see also **bass clef, treble clef**

**cler|gy** /klɜrdʒi/ N-PLURAL The **clergy** are the official religious leaders of a particular group of believers. *clero* ❑ *...Catholic clergy. ...el clero católico.*

**clerk** /klɜrk/ (**clerks, clerking, clerked**) **1** N-COUNT A **clerk** is a person who works in an office, bank, or law court and whose job is to keep the records or accounts, and sometimes to answer the telephone and deal with customers. *empleado o*

C

## Word Web climate

During the past 100 years, the air **temperature** of the earth has increased by about 1° **Fahrenheit** (F). Alaska has warmed by about 4° F. At the same time, **precipitation** over the northern hemisphere increased by 10%. This suggests that the increase in rain and snow has caused the sea level to rise 4-8 inches around the world. The years 1998, 2001, and 2002 were the three hottest ever recorded. This warm period followed what some scientists call the "Little Ice Age." Researchers found that from the 1400s to the 1800s the Earth cooled by about 6° F. Air and water temperatures were lower, **glaciers** grew quickly, and **ice** floes came further south than usual.

*St. Mark's Square in Venice flooded 111 times in 2002.*

*empleada, oficinista* ❑ *She works as a clerk with a travel agency. Trabaja como oficinista en una agencia de viajes.* **2** N-COUNT A **clerk** is someone who sells things to customers in a store. *dependiente o dependienta, vendedor o vendedora* ❑ *Thomas was working as a clerk in a store that sold leather goods. Thomas estaba trabajando de dependiente/vendedor en una tienda de artículos de piel.* **3** V-I To **clerk** means to work as a clerk. *trabajar (de empleado, oficinista, dependiente o vendedor)* ❑ *He clerked for a New York judge. Trabajaba de oficinista para un juez de Nueva York.*
→ see **hotel**

**clev|er** /klɛvər/ (**cleverer, cleverest**) **1** ADJ A **clever** idea, book, or invention is extremely effective and shows the skill of the people involved. *inteligente, ingenioso* ❑ *It is a clever novel. Es una novela ingeniosa.* • **clev|er|ly** ADV *inteligentemente, ingeniosamente* ❑ *...a cleverly-designed swimsuit. ...un traje de baño diseñado inteligentemente.* **2** ADJ Someone who is **clever** is intelligent and able to understand things easily or plan things well. *listo* ❑ *He's a very clever man. Es un hombre muy listo.* • **clev|er|ly** ADV *inteligentemente, ingeniosamente* ❑ *...asks cleverly thought-out questions. ...hace preguntas muy bien pensadas.* • **clev|er|ness** N-UNCOUNT *inteligencia, ingenio* ❑ *Her cleverness seems to get in the way of her emotions. Su inteligencia parece interferir con sus sentimientos.*

**Thesaurus** *clever* Ver también:
ADJ. bright, ingenious, smart; (*ant.*) dumb, stupid **1** **2**

**click** /klɪk/ (**clicks, clicking, clicked**) **1** V-T/V-I If something **clicks** or if you **click** it, it makes a short, sharp sound. *hacer click* ❑ *Hundreds of cameras clicked as she stepped out of the car. Cientos de cámaras hicieron click cuando ella se bajó del auto.* ❑ *He clicked off the radio. Hizo click para apagar el radio.* • **Click** is also a noun. *click* ❑ *I heard a click and then her recorded voice. Escuché un click y después la grabación de su voz.* **2** V-T/V-I If you **click** on an area of a computer screen, you point the cursor at that area and press one of the buttons on the mouse in order to make something happen. *dar click* [COMPUTING] ❑ *I clicked on a link. Di click en un link/vínculo.* • **Click** is also a noun. *click* ❑ *You can check your email with a click of your mouse. Puedes checar tu correo electrónico con un click del mouse.* **3** V-I When you suddenly understand something, you can say that it **clicks**. *captar, caer en la cuenta* [INFORMAL] ❑ *When I saw the television report it all clicked. Cuando vi la noticia en la televisión, caí en la cuenta.* **4** to **click into place** → see **place**

**cli|ent** /klaɪənt/ (**clients**) **1** N-COUNT A **client** is someone for whom a professional person or organization provides a service or does some work. *cliente* [BUSINESS] ❑ *...a lawyer and his client. ...un abogado y su cliente.* **2** → see also **customer**
→ see **sugar, trial**

**cliff** /klɪf/ (**cliffs**) N-COUNT A **cliff** is a high area of land with a very steep side, especially one next to the sea. *precipicio, acantilado* ❑ *The car rolled over the edge of a cliff. El auto rodó por el acantilado.*
→ see **landform, mountain**

**cli|mate** /klaɪmɪt/ (**climates**) **1** N-VAR The **climate** of a place is the general weather conditions that are typical of it. *clima* ❑ *...the hot and humid climate of Florida. ...el clima caliente y húmedo de Florida.* **2** N-COUNT You can use **climate** to refer to the general atmosphere or situation somewhere. *clima* ❑ *When the political climate changes, they will return to Cuba. Cuando el clima político cambie, regresarán a Cuba.*
→ see Word Web: **climate**

**cli|max** /klaɪmæks/ (**climaxes, climaxing, climaxed**) **1** N-COUNT The **climax of** something is the most exciting or important moment in it, usually near the end. *clímax* ❑ *Reaching the Olympics was the climax of her career. Llegar a las Olimpiadas fue el clímax de su carrera.* **2** V-T/V-I The event that **climaxes** a sequence of events is an exciting or important event that comes at the end. You can also say that a sequence of events **climaxes with** a particular event. *culminar* ❑ *The evening climaxed with an amazing firework display. La noche culminó con asombrosos fuegos artificiales.*

**climb** /klaɪm/ (**climbs, climbing, climbed**) **1** V-T/V-I If you **climb** something such as a tree, mountain, or ladder, or **climb up** it, you move toward the top of it. *escalar, subir, trepar* ❑ *Climbing* the hill took half an hour. Subir la colina tomó media hora. ❑ Climb up the steps onto the bridge. Sube los escalones hasta el puente. • **Climb** is also a noun. subida, ascenso ❑ ...an hour's climb through the woods. ...una hora de ascenso en medio del bosque. **2** V-I If you **climb** somewhere, you move there carefully, for example because you are moving into a small space or trying to avoid falling. subirse a ❑ The girls climbed into the car and drove off. Las chicas se subieron al auto y se fueron. ❑ He must have climbed out of his bed. Debió saltar de la cama. **3** V-I When something such as an airplane **climbs,** it moves upward. subir, ascender ❑ The plane lost an engine as it climbed. El avión perdió un motor mientras ascendía. **4** V-I When something **climbs,** it increases in value or amount. subir, ascender ❑ The nation's unemployment rate has been climbing steadily since last June. El índice de desempleo de la nación ha subido a un ritmo constante desde junio. ❑ Prices have climbed by 21% since the beginning of the year. Los precios han subido un 21% desde principios de año. **5** → see also **climbing**

**Word Partnership** Usar *climb* con:

N. climb **the stairs** **1**
**prices** climb **4**
PREP. climb **down/up**, climb **in/on** **1** **2**
V. **begin/continue to** climb **3** **4**

**climb|ing** /klaɪmɪŋ/ N-UNCOUNT **Climbing** is the activity of climbing rocks or mountains. alpinismo, montañismo ❑ I have done no skiing, no climbing, and no hiking. No he practicado el esquí, ni el alpinismo, ni el excursionismo.

**clinch** /klɪntʃ/ (**clinches, clinching, clinched**) V-T If you **clinch** something you are trying to achieve, you succeed in getting it. ganar ❑ The Lakers scored the next ten points to clinch the victory. Los Lakers anotaron los siguientes diez puntos para alcanzar la victoria.

**cling** /klɪŋ/ (**clings, clinging, clung**) **1** V-I If you **cling to** someone or something, you hold onto them tightly. aferrarse a ❑ The man was rescued as he clung to the riverbank. Rescataron al hombre mientras se aferraba a la orilla del río. ❑ She had to cling onto the door handle. Se tuvo que aferrar a la puerta. **2** V-I If you **cling to** a position or way of behaving, you try very hard to keep it or continue it. aferrarse a ❑ He appears determined to cling to power. Parece que está decidido a aferrarse al poder.

**clin|ic** /klɪnɪk/ (**clinics**) N-COUNT A **clinic** is a building where people receive medical advice or treatment. clínica

**clini|cal** /klɪnɪk^əl/ ADJ **Clinical** means involving or relating to the direct medical treatment or testing of patients. clínico [MEDICAL] ❑ ...her clinical training. ...su capacitación clínica. • **clini|cal|ly** /klɪnɪkli/ ADV clínicamente ❑ She was clinically depressed. Tenía depresión clínica. ADJ **Clinical** thought or behavior is very logical and does not involve any emotion, often when it would be more appropriate to show emotion. frío ❑ He didn't like the clinical way she talked about their love. No le gustaba la frialdad con la que hablaba de su amor.

**clip** /klɪp/ (**clips, clipping, clipped**) **1** N-COUNT A **clip** is a small metal or plastic device that is used for holding things together. clip, broche, pasador ❑ She took the clip out of her hair. Se quitó el broche del cabello. **2** N-COUNT A **clip** from a movie or a radio or television program is a short piece of it that is broadcast separately. clip ❑ ...a film clip of the Apollo moon landing. ...un videoclip del aterrizaje de la Apolo en la luna. **3** V-T/V-I When you **clip** things together or when things **clip** together, you fasten them together using a clip. sujetar (con un clip) ❑ Clip the rope onto the ring. Sujeta la cuerda al aro. **4** V-T If you **clip** something, you cut small pieces from it. cortar ❑ I saw an old man clipping his hedge. Ví a un hombre mayor cortando el seto.

**clock** /klɒk/ (**clocks**) **1** N-COUNT A **clock** is an instrument, for example in a room or on the outside of a building, that shows what time of day it is. reloj ❑ He could hear a clock ticking. Podía escuchar el tictac del reloj. **2** → see also **alarm clock, o'clock** **3** PHRASE If something is done **around the clock** or **round the clock,** it is done all day and all night without stopping. día y noche ❑ Rescue services have been working round the clock. Los servicios de rescate han estado trabajando día y noche.
→ see **time**

**Word Partnership** Usar *clock* con:

N. **hands of a** clock, clock **radio** **1**
V. **look at a** clock, **put/turn the** clock **back/forward**, **set a** clock, clock **strikes**, clock **ticks** **1**

**Word Link** *wise ≈ in the direction or manner of :* *clockwise, likewise, otherwise*

**clock|wise** /klɒkwaɪz/ ADV When something is moving **clockwise,** it is moving in a circle in the same direction as the hands on a clock. en el sentido de las agujas del reloj ❑ The children started moving clockwise around the room. Los niños comenzaron a moverse en la habitación en dirección de las agujas del reloj. • **Clockwise** is also an adjective. de las agujas del reloj ❑ Gently swing your right arm in a clockwise direction. Con cuidado dobla tu brazo derecho en dirección de las agujas del reloj.

clockwise

**clog** /klɒg/ (**clogs, clogging, clogged**) **1** V-T When something **clogs** a hole or place, it blocks it so that nothing can pass through. obstruir ❑ Traffic clogged the bridges. Los puentes se llenaron de tráfico. **2** N-COUNT **Clogs** are heavy leather or wooden shoes with thick, wooden soles. zuecos
→ see **shoe**

**clone** /kloʊn/ (**clones, cloning, cloned**) **1** N-COUNT A **clone** is an animal or plant that has been produced artificially from a cell of another animal or plant, and is exactly the same as it. clon ❑ ...the world's first human clone. ...el primer clon humano del mundo. **2** N-COUNT If someone or something is a **clone** of another person or thing, they are so similar to this person or thing that they seem to be exactly the same as them. clon ❑ Tom was in some ways a clone of his father. En ciertos aspectos, Tom era un clon de su padre. **3** V-T To **clone** an animal or plant means to produce it as a clone. clonar ❑ ...the scientist who helped to clone Dolly the

C

## Word Web clone

**Clones** have always existed. For example, a plant can be duplicated by using a leaf cutting to produce an **identical** new plant. Identical **twins** are also natural clones of each other. Recently however, scientists have started using **genetic engineering** to produce artificial clones of animals. The first step involves removing the genetic information called **DNA** from a **cell**. Next, the genetic information is placed into an egg cell. The egg then grows into a **copy** of the donor animal. The first animal experiments in the 1970s involved tadpoles. In 1997 a sheep named Dolly became the first successfully cloned mammal.

*sheep. ...el científico que ayudó a clonar a la oveja Dolly.* → see Word Web: **clone**

**close**
❶ SHUTTING OR COMPLETING
❷ NEARNESS; ADJECTIVE USES
❸ NEARNESS; VERB USES

❶ **close** /klouz/ (**closes, closing, closed**) **1** V-T/V-I When you **close** a door, window, or lid, or when it **closes,** it moves so that a hole, gap, or opening is covered. *cerrar* ❑ *If you are cold, close the window. Si tienes frío, cierra la ventana.* ❑ *Zac heard the door close. Zac escuchó que se cerró la puerta.* **2** V-T/V-I When a place **closes** or **is closed,** people cannot use it, or work or activity stops there. *cerrar* ❑ *Stores close only on Christmas Day and New Year's Day. Las tiendas sólo cierran en Navidad y en Año Nuevo.* ❑ *Government troops closed the airport. Las tropas del gobierno cerraron el aeropuerto.* • **clos|ing** N-SING *cierre, clausura* ❑ *...the closing of the steel mill in 1984. ...el cierre de la fábrica de acero en 1984.* **3** V-T To **close** a conversation, event, or matter means to bring it to an end. *cerrar, terminar, concluir* ❑ *Judge Isabel Oliva said last night: "I have closed the case." La juez Isabel Oliva dijo ayer en la noche: "He cerrado el caso."* ❑ *The governor now considers the matter closed. Ahora el gobernador considera el asunto concluido.* **4** to **close ranks** → see **rank**

▸ **close down** PHR-VERB If a business **closes down,** or if it is **closed down,** all work or activity stops there, usually for ever. *cerrar* ❑ *Minford closed down the business and went into politics. Minford cerró el negocio y se involucró en la política.*

**Thesaurus** *close* Ver también:
v. fasten, seal, shut, slam; (*ant.*) open ❶ **1**

❷ **close** /klous/ (**closer, closest**) **1** ADJ Something that is **close to** something else is near to it. *cercano, próximo* ❑ *Her lips were close to his head. Sus labios estaban cerca de su cabeza.* ❑ *The man moved closer. El hombre se acercó.* • **close|ly** ADV *estrechamente, cercano, de cerca* ❑ *They crowded more closely around the fire. Se aglomeraron cerca del fuego.* **2** ADJ People who are **close to** each other like each other very much and know each other very well. *cercano, allegado* ❑ *She was closest to her sister Gail. Era la más cercana a su hermana Gail.* ❑ *...a close friend from school. ...un amigo cercano de la escuela.* • **close|ness** N-UNCOUNT *cercanía, proximidad* ❑ *...her closeness to her mother. ...la estrecha relación con su madre.* **3** ADJ Your **close** relatives are the members of your family who are most directly related to you, for example your parents and your brothers or sisters. *cercano* ❑ *...the death of a close relative. ...la muerte de un pariente cercano.* **4** ADJ **Close** contact or cooperation involves seeing or communicating with someone often. *estrecho, directo* ❑ *Both nations are seeking closer links with the West. Ambas naciones están buscando lazos más estrechos con Occidente.* • **close|ly** ADV *estrechamente* ❑ *We work closely with local groups. Trabajamos estrechamente con grupos locales.* **5** ADJ If there is a **close** connection or resemblance between two things, they are strongly connected or are very similar. *estrecho* ❑ *There is a close connection between income and education. Hay una conexión cercana entre ingresos y educación.* • **close|ly** ADV *estrechamente* ❑ *The two problems are closely linked. Los dos problemas están estrechamente ligados.* **6** ADJ **Close** inspection or observation of something is careful and thorough. *detenido, detallado* ❑ *Let's have a closer look. Veámoslo con más detalle.* • **close|ly** ADV *detenidamente, atentamente* ❑ *You have to look closely to find the café. Tienes que mirar detenidamente para encontrar el café.* **7** ADJ A **close** competition or election is won or seems likely to be won by only a small amount. *reñido* ❑ *...a close contest for a Senate seat. ...una competencia reñida por una curul en el Senado.* • **close|ly** ADV *muy reñido* ❑ *This will be a closely-fought race. Ésta será una carrera muy reñida.* **8** ADJ If you are **close to** something, or if it is **close,** it is likely to happen or come soon. *cercano, próximo* ❑ *She sounded close to tears. Se escuchaba a punto del llanto.* ❑ *At the end of January, agreement seemed close. A fines de enero, el acuerdo parecía próximo.* **9** ADJ If the atmosphere somewhere is **close,** it is unpleasantly warm with not enough air. *bochornoso* **10** PHRASE Something that is **close by** or **close at hand** is near to you. *cerca* ❑ *Did a new hair salon open close by? ¿Abrieron una estética cerca?* **11** PHRASE **Close to** a particular amount or distance means slightly less than that amount or distance. *cerca de* ❑ *He spent close to 30 years in prison. Pasó cerca de 30 años en prisión.* **12** PHRASE If you look at something **close up,** you look at it when you are very near to it. *de cerca* ❑ *The airplane looked smaller close up. El avión se veía más pequeño de cerca.* **13** **at close quarters** → see **quarter**

**Word Partnership** Usar *close* con:

| | |
|---|---|
| N. | close **a door**, close ***your* eyes** ❶ 1<br>close **friend**, close **to *someone*** ❷ 2<br>close **family/relative** ❷ 2 3<br>close **attention/scrutiny** ❷ 6<br>close **election**, close **race** ❷ 7 |
| ADV. | close **enough, so/too/very** close ❷ 5 – 8 |

❸ **close** /kloʊz/ (**closes, closing, closed**) V-I If you **are closing on** someone or something that you are following, you are getting nearer and nearer to them. *acercarse a* ❑ *I was closing on the guy in second place. Me estaba acercando al chico que iba en segundo lugar.*

▸ **close in** PHR-VERB If a group of people **close in on** a person or place, they come nearer and nearer to them and gradually surround them. *cercar* ❑ *Soviet forces were closing in on Berlin. Las fuerzas soviéticas cercaron Berlín.*

**closed** /kloʊzd/ 1 ADJ A **closed** group of people does not welcome new people or ideas from outside. *cerrado* ❑ *It is a closed society. Es una sociedad cerrada.* 2 → see also **close** ❶

**closed-circuit** ADJ **Closed-circuit** television is a television system used to film people within a limited area such as a building. *circuito cerrado* ❑ *There's a closed-circuit television camera in the reception area. Hay una cámara de televisión de circuito cerrado en el área de recepción.*

**closed cir|cu|la|tory sys|tem** (**closed circulatory systems**) N-COUNT In animals that have a **closed circulatory system**, their blood flows through vessels such as veins and arteries and never flows through other parts of their body. *sistema circulatorio cerrado*

**closed sys|tem** (**closed systems**) N-COUNT In a **closed system**, matter cannot enter or leave the system and the system cannot be affected by anything outside it. *sistema cerrado*

**close-mouthed** ADJ Someone who is **close-mouthed** about something does not say much about it. *hermético* ❑ *Lionel was close-mouthed about his private life. Lionel fue hermético sobre su vida privada.*

**close|out** /kloʊzaʊt/ (**closeouts**) N-COUNT A **closeout** at a store is a sale at which goods are sold at reduced prices. *liquidación* ❑ *...a closeout sale at the department store. ...una venta de liquidación en la tienda departamental.*

**clos|et** /klɒzɪt/ (**closets**) 1 N-COUNT A **closet** is a very small room for storing things, especially clothing and linens. *clóset, armario* 2 ADJ **Closet** is used to describe a person who has beliefs, habits, or feelings which they keep secret. *de clóset* ❑ *He is a closet Fascist. Es un fascista de clóset.*
→ see **house**

**clos|ing ar|gu|ment** (**closing arguments**) N-COUNT In a court case, a lawyer's **closing argument** is their final speech, in which they give a summary of their case. *conclusiones finales* ❑ *Both sides presented closing arguments. Ambas partes presentaron sus conclusiones finales.*

**clos|ing date** (**closing dates**) N-COUNT The **closing date** for a competition or offer is the final date by which entries or applications must be received. *fecha límite, fecha tope* ❑ *The closing date for entries is Friday, January 11. La fecha límite para las inscripciones es el viernes 11 de enero.*

**clo|sure** /kloʊʒər/ (**closures**) 1 N-VAR The **closure** of a place such as a business or factory is the permanent ending of work or activity there. *cierre* ❑ *...the closure of the steel mill. ...el cierre de la fábrica de acero.* 2 N-COUNT The **closure** of a road or border is the blocking of it in order to prevent people from using it. *cierre* ❑ *Storms forced the closure of many roads. Las tormentas provocaron el cierre de muchos caminos.*

**cloth** /klɔθ/ (**cloths**) 1 N-UNCOUNT **Cloth** is fabric which is made by weaving or knitting a substance such as cotton or wool. *tela* ❑ *...a piece of cloth. ...un pedazo de tela.* 2 N-COUNT A **cloth** is a piece of cloth which you use for a particular purpose, such as cleaning. *trapo* ❑ *Clean the surface with a damp cloth. Limpia la superficie con un trapo húmedo.*

**clothed** /kloʊðd/ ADJ If you are **clothed in** a certain way, you are dressed in that way. *vestido* ❑ *He lay down on the bed fully clothed. Se acostó en la cama completamente vestido.* ❑ *She was clothed in a flowered dress. Traía un vestido floreado.*

**clothes** /kloʊz, kloʊðz/ N-PLURAL **Clothes** are the things that people wear, such as shirts, coats, pants, and dresses. *ropa* ❑ *Moira went upstairs to change her clothes. Moira subió a cambiarse de ropa.*

**cloth|ing** /kloʊðɪŋ/ N-UNCOUNT **Clothing** is the things that people wear. *ropa* ❑ *...a women's clothing store. ...una tienda de ropa para mujer.*
→ see Picture Dictionary: **clothing**

**cloud** /klaʊd/ (**clouds, clouding, clouded**) 1 N-VAR A **cloud** is a mass of water vapor that can be seen as a white or gray mass in the sky. *nube* ❑ *...the varied shapes of the clouds. ...las diferentes formas de las nubes.* ❑ *...a black mass of cloud. ...nubes negras.* 2 N-COUNT A **cloud of** smoke or dust is a mass of it floating in the air. *nube* ❑ *We saw a huge cloud of dust. Vimos una enorme nube de humo.* 3 V-T If you say that something **clouds** your view of a situation, you mean that it makes you unable to understand the situation or judge it properly. *nublar, ofuscar* ❑ *Perhaps anger clouded his vision. Quizá el enojo nubló su visión.* 4 V-T If something **clouds** an event or situation, it makes it less pleasant. *ofuscar, confundir* ❑ *Anger clouded his thinking. La ira ofuscó sus ideas.*
→ see Picture Dictionary: **clouds**
→ see **precipitation, sugar, water**

**cloudy** /klaʊdi/ (**cloudier, cloudiest**) 1 ADJ If it is **cloudy,** there are a lot of clouds in the sky. *nublado* ❑ *...a windy, cloudy day. ...un día nublado con viento.* 2 ADJ A **cloudy** liquid is less clear than it should be. *turbio* ❑ *The water was cloudy. El agua estaba turbia.*

**clove** /kloʊv/ (**cloves**) 1 N-VAR **Cloves** are small dried flower buds which are used as a spice. *clavo* ❑ *...chicken soup with cloves. ...sopa de pollo con clavos.* 2 N-COUNT A **clove of** garlic is one of the sections of a garlic bulb. *diente (de ajo)*

**clo|ver** /kloʊvər/ (**clovers**) N-VAR **Clover** is a small plant with pink or white ball-shaped flowers and usually three round leaves. *trébol* ❑ *...a four-leaf clover. ...un trébol de cuatro hojas.*

**clover|leaf** /kloʊvərlif/ (**cloverleafs,**

C

## Picture Dictionary clothing

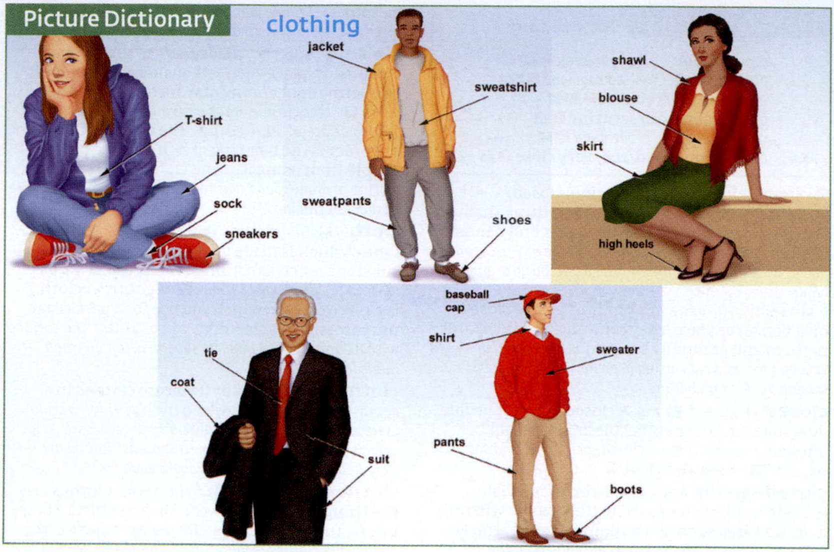


**cloverleaves**) N-COUNT A **cloverleaf** is an arrangement of curved roads, resembling a four-leaf clover, that joins two main roads. trébol ❑ *...the new route 29 cloverleaf.* *...el nuevo trébol de la ruta 29.*

**clown** /klaʊn/ (**clowns, clowning, clowned**) **1** N-COUNT A **clown** is a performer who wears funny clothes and bright makeup, and does silly things to make people laugh. *payaso o payasa* **2** V-I If you **clown around**, you do silly things in order to make people laugh. *hacer payasadas, payasear, hacerse el payaso* ❑ *He was clowning around with his umbrella.* *Se hizo el payaso con su sombrilla.*

**club** /klʌb/ (**clubs, clubbing, clubbed**) **1** N-COUNT A **club** is an organization of people who are all interested in a particular activity. *club* ❑ *...the Young Republicans Club.* *...el Club de Jóvenes Republicanos.* ❑ *...a chess club.* *...un club de ajedrez.* **2** N-COUNT A **club** is a place where the members of a club meet. *club* ❑ *I stopped in at the club.* *Pasé al club.* **3** N-COUNT A **club** is a team which competes in sports competitions. *club* ❑ *...the New York Yankees baseball club.* *...el club de béisbol de los Yankees de Nueva York.* **4** N-COUNT A **club** is the same as a **nightclub**. *discoteca* ❑ *It's a big dance hit in the clubs.* *Es un gran éxito para bailar en las discotecas.* **5** N-COUNT A **club** is a long, thin, metal stick with a piece of wood or metal at one end that you use to hit the ball in golf. *palo de golf* ❑ *...a six-iron club.* *...un fierro seis.* **6** N-COUNT A **club** is a thick, heavy stick that can be used as a weapon. *garrote* ❑ *...men armed with knives and clubs.* *...hombres armados con cuchillos y garrotes.* **7** V-T To **club** a person or animal means to hit them hard with a thick heavy stick or a similar weapon. *dar garrotazos* ❑ *Someone clubbed him over the head.* *Alguien le dio un garrotazo en la cabeza.* **8** N-UNCOUNT **Clubs** is one of the four suits in a pack of playing cards. Each card in the suit is marked with one or more black symbols: ♣. *basto, tréboles* ❑ *...the ace of clubs.* *...el as de tréboles.* ● A **club** is a playing card of this suit. *basto* ❑ *The next player put down a club.* *El siguiente jugador sacó un basto.*
→ see **golf**

**club|house** /klʌbhaʊs/ (**clubhouses**) N-COUNT A **clubhouse** is a place where the members of a sports club meet. *casa club*
→ see **golf**

**club soda** N-UNCOUNT **Club soda** is carbonated water used for mixing with alcoholic drinks and fruit juice. *agua mineral*

**clue** /klu/ (**clues**) **1** N-COUNT A **clue to** a problem, mystery, or puzzle is something that helps you to find the answer. *pista* ❑ *The police are looking for clues to his disappearance.* *La policía está buscando pistas de su desaparición.* ❑ *I'll give you a clue and then you have to think of the next word.* *Te daré una pista y luego tú tienes que pensar la siguiente palabra.* **2** PHRASE If you **don't have a clue** about something, you do not know anything about it or you have no idea what to do about it. *no tener idea* [INFORMAL] ❑ *I don't have a clue what I'll give Carl for his birthday.* *No tengo idea de qué le voy a dar a Carl por su cumpleaños.*

**clum|sy** /klʌmzi/ (**clumsier, clumsiest**) **1** ADJ A **clumsy** person moves or handles things in an awkward way. *torpe* ❑ *As a child she was very clumsy.* *Cuando niña, era muy torpe.* ● **clum|si|ly** /klʌmzɪli/ ADV *torpemente, con torpeza* ❑ *He fell clumsily onto the bed.* *Cayó con torpeza en la cama.* ● **clum|si|ness** N-UNCOUNT *torpeza* ❑ *His clumsiness embarrassed him.* *Su torpeza lo avergonzó.* **2** ADJ A **clumsy** action or statement is not skillful and is likely to fail or to upset people. *torpe, burdo* ❑ *...a clumsy attempt to bring down the government.* *...un burdo intento de derrocar al gobierno.* ● **clum|si|ly** ADV *torpemente, con*

Picture Dictionary clouds

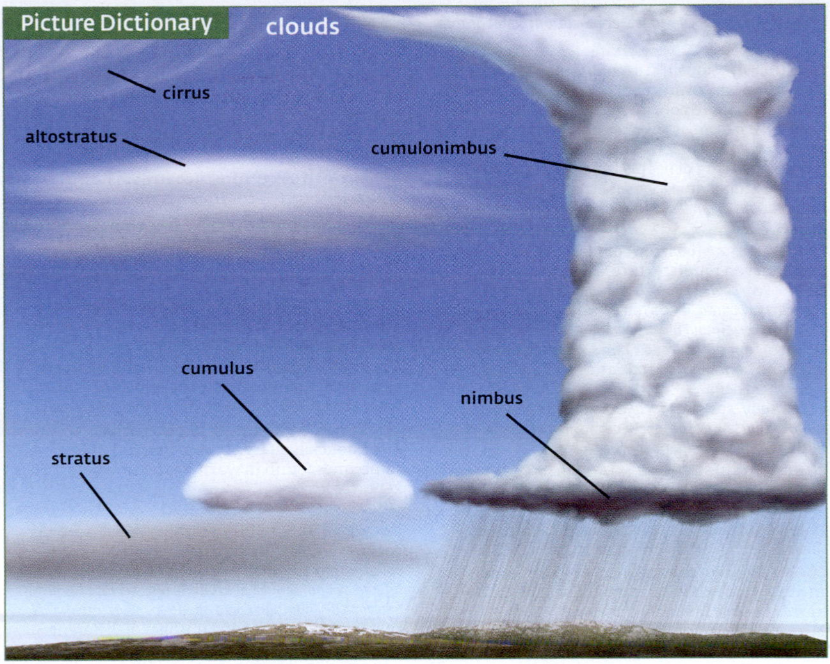


torpeza ❑ *The matter was handled clumsily.* *El problema se manejó con torpeza.* ● **clum|si|ness** N-UNCOUNT torpeza ❑ *My clumsiness upset him.* *Mi torpeza le molestó.*

**clung** /klʌŋ/ **Clung** is the past tense and past participle of **cling.** *pasado y participio pasado de **cling***

**clunk|er** /klʌŋkər/ (**clunkers**) N-COUNT If you describe a machine, especially a car, as a **clunker,** you mean that it is very old and almost falling apart. *carcacha, cacharro* [INFORMAL]

**clus|ter** /klʌstər/ (**clusters, clustering, clustered**) **1** N-COUNT A **cluster of** people or things is a small group of them close together. *grupo* ❑ *...clusters of men in formal clothes.* *...grupos de hombres con ropa formal.* **2** V-I If people **cluster together,** they gather together in a small group. *agruparse, concentrarse* ❑ *The passengers clustered together in small groups.* *Los pasajeros se concentraron en pequeños grupos.*

**clus|ter|ing** /klʌstərɪŋ/ N-UNCOUNT **Clustering** is a teaching method in which information is presented as a group of ideas in order to help students to remember it better. *estrategias de agrupamiento, clustering*

**clutch** /klʌtʃ/ (**clutches, clutching, clutched**) **1** V-T/V-I If you **clutch** something, you hold it very tightly. *agarrar con fuerza, apretar* ❑ *Michelle clutched my arm.* *Michelle me agarró con fuerza del brazo.* ❑ *I clutched at a chair for support.* *Me agarré con fuerza de una silla para apoyarme.* **2** N-PLURAL If you are in someone's **clutches,** they have power over you. *en las garras de* ❑ *Tony fell into the clutches of an evil gang.* *Tony cayó en las garras de una pandilla malvada.* **3** N-COUNT In a vehicle, the **clutch** is the pedal that you press before you change gear. *clutch* ❑ *Laura let out the clutch and pulled slowly away.* *Laura soltó el clutch y arrancó lentamente.*

**cm** **cm** is the written abbreviation for **centimeter** or **centimeters.** *cm, centímetro(s)*

**coach** /koʊtʃ/ (**coaches, coaching, coached**) **1** N-COUNT A **coach** is someone who is in charge of training a person or sports team. *entrenador o entrenadora* ❑ *...the women's soccer coach at Rowan University.* *...el entrenador de fútbol femenil de la Universidad Rowan.* **2** N-COUNT A **coach** is an enclosed vehicle with four wheels which is pulled by horses, and in which people used to travel. *carruaje, coche (tirado por caballos)* ❑ *...a coach pulled by six black horses.* *...un carruaje tirado por seis caballos negros.* **3** N-COUNT A **coach** is a large, comfortable bus that carries passengers on long trips. *autobús* **4** V-T If you **coach** someone, you help them to become better at a particular sport or subject. *entrenar, preparar, darle clases a* ❑ *She coached a golf team in San José.* *Entrenaba a un equipo de golf en San José.*

**coal** /koʊl/ (**coals**) **1** N-UNCOUNT **Coal** is a hard, black substance that is extracted from the ground and burned as fuel. *carbón* ❑ *Gas is cheaper than coal.* *El gas es más barato que el carbón.* **2** N-PLURAL **Coals** are burning pieces of coal. *carbón*
→ see **energy**

C

**Word Link** *co ≈ together : coalition, collaborate, collect*

**coa|li|tion** /koʊəlɪʃᵊn/ (**coalitions**) **1** N-COUNT A **coalition** is a government consisting of people from two or more political parties. *coalición* ❑ *The country has a coalition government. El país tiene un gobierno de coalición.* **2** N-COUNT A **coalition** is a group consisting of people from different political or social groups. *coalición* ❑ *.. a coalition of women's organizations. ...una coalición de organizaciones de mujeres.*

**coarse** /kɔrs/ (**coarser, coarsest**) **1** ADJ **Coarse** things have a rough texture. *burdo* ❑ *...a jacket made of very coarse cloth. ...una chamarra hecha de una tela muy burda.* • **coarse|ly** ADV *en trozos grandes* ❑ *...coarsely-ground black pepper. ...pimienta negra molida en trozos grandes.* **2** ADJ A **coarse** person talks and behaves in a rude and offensive way. *grosero, ordinario* ❑ *...coarse humor. ...humor ordinario.* • **coarse|ly** ADV *de manera ordinaria* ❑ *The women laughed coarsely at the joke. Las mujeres se rieron del chiste de manera ordinaria.*

**coarse ad|just|ment** N-UNCOUNT The part of a microscope that controls the **coarse adjustment** is the part that allows you to obtain the correct general focus for the object you are looking at. *ajuste grueso, ajuste aproximativo* [TECHNICAL]

**coast** /koʊst/ (**coasts**) N-COUNT The **coast** is an area of land that is next to the sea. *costa* ❑ *We stayed at a camp site on the coast. Nos quedamos en un campamento de la costa.* • **coast|al** /koʊstᵊl/ ADJ *costero* ❑ *...coastal areas. ...zonas costeras.*
→ see **beach**

**Coast Guard** N-PROPER The **Coast Guard** is a part of a country's military forces and is responsible for protecting the coast, carrying out rescues, and doing police work along the coast. *servicio costanero, guardacostas, resguardo marítimo* ❑ *The U.S. Coast Guard is searching for a missing airplane. La Guardia Costera de Estados Unidos está buscando un avión perdido.*

**coast|line** /koʊstlaɪn/ (**coastlines**) N-VAR A country's **coastline** is the edge of its coast. *costa* ❑ *...the Pacific coastline. ...la costa del (Océano) Pacífico.*

**coast-to-coast** ADJ A **coast-to-coast** journey or route is one that goes from one coast of a country or region to the opposite coast. *transcontinental, de una costa a (la) otra* ❑ *...a coast-to-coast tour across the United States. ...un viaje de costa a costa por los Estados Unidos.* • **Coast-to-coast** is also an adverb. *de una costa a otra* ❑ *I drove coast-to-coast in just over two hours. Manejé de una costa a la otra en sólo dos horas.*

**coat** /koʊt/ (**coats, coating, coated**) **1** N-COUNT A **coat** is a piece of clothing with long sleeves which you wear over your other clothes when you go outside. *abrigo* ❑ *He put on his coat and walked out. Se puso el abrigo y salió.* **2** N-COUNT An animal's **coat** is its fur or hair. *piel, pelo, pelaje, lana* **3** N-COUNT A **coat of** paint or varnish is a thin layer of it. *capa, mano* ❑ *The front door needs a new coat of paint. La puerta del frente necesita una nueva mano de pintura.* **4** V-T If you **coat** something **with** a substance, you cover it with a thin layer of the substance. *dar una mano, cubrir, enharinar* ❑ *Coat the fish with flour. Enharine el pescado.*
→ see **clothing, painting**

**coat check** (**coat checks**) also **coat-check** N-COUNT The **coat check** at a public building such as a theater or club is the place where customers can leave their coats. *guardarropa(s)* ❑ *Let's get our coats at the coat check. Vamos al guardarropa(s) por nuestros abrigos.*

**coat|room** /koʊtrum/ (**coatrooms**) also **coat room** N-COUNT A **coatroom** is the same as a **coat check**. *guardarropa(s)*

**co|caine** /koʊkeɪn/ N-UNCOUNT **Cocaine** is an addictive drug which some people take for pleasure. *cocaína*

**coch|lea** /kɒkliə, koʊ-/ (**cochleae**) N-COUNT The **cochlea** is the spiral-shaped part of the inner ear. *cóclea, caracol (del oído interno)*

**cock|pit** /kɒkpɪt/ (**cockpits**) N-COUNT In an airplane or racing car, the **cockpit** is the part where the pilot or driver sits. *cabina (de mando)*

**cock|roach** /kɒkroʊtʃ/ (**cockroaches**) N-COUNT A **cockroach** is a large brown insect that is sometimes found in warm places or where food is kept. *cucaracha*
→ see **insect**

**cock|tail** /kɒkteɪl/ (**cocktails**) **1** N-COUNT A **cocktail** is an alcoholic drink which contains several ingredients. *coctel, aperitivo* ❑ *Guests are offered a champagne cocktail. Se ofrece a los huéspedes una copa de champán como aperitivo.* **2** N-COUNT A **cocktail** is a mixture of a number of different things. *combinación* ❑ *...a cocktail of chemicals. ...una combinación de sustancias químicas.*

**co|coa** /koʊkoʊ/ **1** N-UNCOUNT **Cocoa** is a brown powder used in making chocolate. *cacao en polvo, cocoa* ❑ *The Ivory Coast became the world's leading cocoa producer. Costa de Marfil se convirtió en el principal productor mundial de cacao.* **2** N-UNCOUNT **Cocoa** is a hot drink made from cocoa powder and milk or water. *chocolate, cocoa* ❑ *...a cup of cocoa. ...una taza de chocolate.*

**coco|nut** /koʊkənʌt/ (**coconuts**) **1** N-COUNT A **coconut** is a very large nut with a hairy shell, white flesh, and milky juice inside it. *coco* **2** N-UNCOUNT **Coconut** is the white flesh of a coconut. *coco* ❑ *...two cups of grated coconut. ...dos tazas de coco rallado.*

**cod** /kɒd/ (**cod**) N-VAR A **cod** is a large sea fish with white flesh. *bacalao* • **Cod** is this fish eaten as food. *bacalao* ❑ *...fried cod. ...bacalao frito.*

**C.O.D.** /si oʊ di/ PHRASE **C.O.D.** is an abbreviation for **cash on delivery**. *contra reembolso, pago contra entrega, COD (cobro o devolución)* ❑ *Phone orders are accepted for C.O.D. payment. Se aceptan pedidos telefónicos de pago contra reembolso., Se aceptan pedidos telefónicos de COD.*

**code** /koʊd/ (**codes**) **1** N-COUNT A **code** is a set of rules about how people should behave or about how something must be done. *código* ❑ *...a strict moral code. ...un estricto código moral.* **2** N-COUNT A **code** is a system of replacing the words in a message with other words or symbols, so that nobody can understand it unless they know the system. *código, clave* ❑ *They used secret codes. Usaban claves secretas.* **3** N-COUNT A **code** is a group of numbers or letters which is used to identify something such as a mailing address. *código* ❏ *The area code for western Pennsylvania is 412. El código postal del oeste de Pensilvania es el 412.* **4** N-VAR A **code** is any system of signs or symbols that has a meaning. *código* ❏ *...digital code. ...código digital.* ❏ *She began writing software code at the age of nine. Empezó a escribir códigos digitales a la edad de nueve años.* **5** → see also **zip code**

**co|ed** /koʊɛd, -ɛd/ (**coeds**) **1** ADJ A **coed** school or facility is one that includes or involves both males and females. *mixto* ❏ *He was educated at a coed school. Estudió en una escuela mixta.* ❏ *You have a choice of coed or single-sex exercise classes. Puede escoger entre clases con ejercicios para sexos separados o mixtas.* **2** ADJ A **coed** sports facility or sport is one that both males and females use or take part in at the same time. *mixto* ❏ *We have coed and single-sex swimming pools. Tenemos albercas para sexos separados o mixtas.*

**co|ef|fi|cient** /koʊɪfɪʃənt/ (**coefficients**) N-COUNT A **coefficient** is a number that expresses a measurement of a particular quality of a substance or object under specified conditions. *coeficiente, factor, índice* [TECHNICAL]

**coe|lom** /siləm/ (**coeloms**) N-COUNT The **coelom** is a hollow space in the body of an animal which contains organs such as the heart and kidneys. *celoma* [TECHNICAL]

**co|evo|lu|tion** /koʊɛvəluʃᵊn/ N-UNCOUNT **Coevolution** is a process in which different species of animals or plants evolve in a particular way because of their close interaction with each other. *coevolución* [TECHNICAL]

**cof|fee** /kɔfi/ (**coffees**) **1** N-VAR **Coffee** is the roasted beans of the coffee plant. *café* ❏ *Brazil is the world's largest coffee producer. Brasil es el principal productor de café en el mundo.* **2** N-VAR **Coffee** is a drink made from boiling water and ground or powdered coffee beans. *café* ❏ *Would you like some coffee? ¿Quieres un café?* ● A **coffee** is a cup of coffee. *café* ❏ *We had a coffee. Nos tomamos un café.*

**cof|fee shop** (**coffee shops**) N-COUNT A **coffee shop** is an informal restaurant that sells food and drink, but not normally alcoholic drinks. *cafetería*

**cof|fin** /kɔfɪn/ (**coffins**) N-COUNT A **coffin** is a box in which a dead body is buried or cremated. *ataúd, féretro, caja, cajón*

**coin** /kɔɪn/ (**coins, coining, coined**) **1** N-COUNT A **coin** is a small piece of metal which is used as money. *moneda* ❏ *...a few loose coins. ...unas monedas.* **2** V-T If you **coin** a word or a phrase, you are the first person to use it. *acuñar* ❏ *Jaron Lanier coined the term "virtual reality." Jaron Lanier acuñó el término "realidad virtual".*
→ see **English, money**

**co|in|cide** /koʊɪnsaɪd/ (**coincides, coinciding, coincided**) **1** V-RECIP If one event **coincides with** another, they happen at the same time. *coincidir* ❏ *The exhibition coincides with the 50th anniversary of his death. La exposición coincide con el quincuagésimo aniversario de su muerte.* **2** V-RECIP If the ideas or interests of two or more people **coincide,** they are the same. *coincidir* ❏ *The kids' views on life don't always coincide. Los puntos de vista de los niños sobre la vida no siempre coinciden.*

**co|in|ci|dence** /koʊɪnsɪdəns/ (**coincidences**) N-VAR A **coincidence** is when two or more similar or related events occur at the same time by chance. *coincidencia* ❏ *Mr. Barry said the timing was a coincidence. El señor Barry dijo que la simultaneidad fue una coincidencia.*

**coke** /koʊk/ **1** N-UNCOUNT **Coke** is a solid, black substance that is produced from coal and is burned as a fuel. *coque* ❏ *...a coke-burning stove. ...una estufa de carbón de coque.* **2** N-UNCOUNT **Coke** is the same as **cocaine.** *coca* [INFORMAL]

**cola** /koʊlə/ (**colas**) N-VAR **Cola** is a sweet, brown, nonalcoholic carbonated drink. *refresco de cola* ❏ *...a can of cola. ...una cola en lata.*

**col|an|der** /kɒləndə, kʌl-/ (**colanders**) N-COUNT A **colander** is a container in the shape of a bowl with holes in it which you wash or drain food in. *coladera, colador, escurridor, escurridora*

**cold** /koʊld/ (**colder, coldest, colds**) **1** ADJ If something or someone is **cold,** they have a very low temperature. *frío* ❏ *...cold running water. ...agua corriente fría.* ❏ *The house is cold because I can't afford to turn the heat on. La casa está fría porque no puedo darme el lujo de encender la calefacción.* ❏ *I was freezing cold. Hacía un frío que calaba hasta los huesos.* ● **cold|ness** N-UNCOUNT *frialdad* ❏ *She complained about the coldness of his hands. Se quejó de sus manos frías.* **2** ADJ A **cold** person does not show much emotion or affection, and therefore seems unfriendly. *frío* ❏ *She was a cold, unfeeling woman. Era una mujer fría e insensible.* ● **cold|ly** ADV *fríamente* ❏ *"I'll see you in the morning," Hugh said coldly. —Te veré mañana —le dijo Hugh fríamente.* ● **cold|ness** N-UNCOUNT *frialdad* ❏ *His coldness angered her. Su frialdad la enojó.* **3** N-UNCOUNT Cold weather or low temperatures can be referred to as **the cold.** *(el) frío* ❏ *He must have come inside to get out of the cold. Debió haber entrado para quitarse del frío.* **4** **in cold blood** → see **blood** **5** N-COUNT If you have a **cold,** you have a mild, very common illness which makes you sneeze a lot and gives you a sore throat or a cough. *resfriado, catarro, resfrío* ❏ *I had a pretty bad cold. Tenía un resfriado muy fuerte.* **6** PHRASE If you **catch cold,** or **catch a cold,** you become ill with a cold. *resfriarse* ❏ *Let's dry our hair so we don't catch cold. Vamos a secarnos el pelo para no resfriarnos.*

| Thesaurus | *cold* | Ver también: |
|---|---|---|
| ADJ. | bitter, chilly, cool, freezing, frozen, raw; (*ant.*) hot, warm **1** | |
| | cool, distant; (*ant.*) friendly, warm **2** | |

| Word Partnership | Usar *cold* con: |
|---|---|
| N. | cold **air, dark and** cold, cold **night,** cold **rain,** cold **water,** cold **weather,** cold **wind** **1** |
| ADV. | **bitterly** cold **1** |
| | **freezing** cold **1** **3** |
| V. | **feel** cold, **get** cold **1** |
| | **catch/get a** cold **6** |

**cold-blooded** ADJ **Cold-blooded** animals have a body temperature that changes according to the surrounding temperature. Reptiles, for example, are cold-blooded. *de sangre fría*

**cold cuts** N-PLURAL **Cold cuts** are thin slices of cooked meat which are served cold. *fiambres, carnes frías*

**cold read|ing** (**cold readings**) N-COUNT A **cold reading** is a reading of the script of a play, read aloud for the first time by actors who are going to perform the play. *lectura sin preparación*

C

| Word Link | *co ≈ together : coalition, collaborate, collect* |
|---|---|

| Word Link | *labor ≈ working : collaborate, elaborate, laboratory* |
|---|---|

**col|labo|rate** /kəlæbəreɪt/ (**collaborates, collaborating, collaborated**) **1** V-RECIP When people **collaborate,** they work together on a particular project. *colaborar* ❑ *He collaborated with his son Michael on the English translation. Colaboró con su hijo Michael en la traducción al inglés.* ❑ *Students collaborate in group exercises. Los estudiantes colaboran en los ejercicios de grupo.* ● **col|labo|ra|tion** /kəlæbəreɪʃən/ (**collaborations**) N-VAR *colaboración* ❑ *...collaboration between parents and schools. ...la colaboración entre los padres y la escuela.* ❑ *...scientific collaborations. ...colaboraciones científicas.* ● **col|labo|ra|tor** /kəlæbəreɪtər/ N-COUNT (**collaborators**) *colaborador o colaboradora* ❑ *He and his collaborator completed the book in two years. Él y su colaboradora completaron el libro en dos años.* **2** V-I If someone **collaborates with** an enemy that is occupying their country during a war, they help them. *colaborar* ❑ *He was accused of collaborating with the secret police. Lo acusaron de colaborar con la policía secreta.* ● **col|labo|ra|tion** N-UNCOUNT *colaboración* ❑ *...collaboration with the enemy. ...colaboración con el enemigo.* ● **col|labo|ra|tor** N-COUNT *colaborador o colaboradora* ❑ *He was suspected of being a collaborator. Se sospechaba que hubiese sido un colaborador.*

**col|lapse** /kəlæps/ (**collapses, collapsing, collapsed**) **1** V-I If a building or other structure **collapses,** it falls down very suddenly. *derrumbarse, desplomarse* ❑ *A section of the Bay Bridge collapsed. Se desplomó una sección del puente de la bahía.* ● **Collapse** is also a noun. *derrumbe, desmoronamiento* ❑ *...an inquiry into the freeway's collapse. ...una investigación sobre el derrumbe de la autopista.* **2** V-I If a system or institution **collapses,** it fails completely and suddenly. *quebrar, fracasar, derrumbarse* ❑ *His business empire collapsed overnight. Su imperio comercial se derrumbó de la noche a la mañana.* ● **Collapse** is also a noun. *fracaso, ruina* ❑ *The medical system is facing collapse. El sistema médico enfrenta la ruina.* **3** V-I If you **collapse,** you suddenly fall down because you are very ill or tired. *desplomarse, sufrir un colapso* ❑ *He collapsed at his home. Sufrió un colapso en su casa.* ● **Collapse** is also a noun. *colapso, postración* ❑ *A few days after his collapse he was sitting up in bed. Unos cuantos días después de su postración, ya estaba sentado en la cama.*

collar

**col|lar** /kɒlər/ (**collars**) **1** N-COUNT The **collar** of a shirt or coat is the part which fits around the neck and is usually folded over. *cuello* ❑ *His tie was loose and his collar was open. Tenía la corbata floja y el cuello de la camisa abierto.* **2** → see also **blue-collar, white-collar** **3** N-COUNT A **collar** is a band of leather or plastic which is put around the neck of a dog or cat. *collar*

**col|league** /kɒlig/ (**colleagues**) N-COUNT Your **colleagues** are the people you work with, especially in a professional job. *colega, compañero de trabajo o compañera de trabajo* ❑ *...a business colleague. ...un colega de negocios.*

**col|lect** /kəlɛkt/ (**collects, collecting, collected**) **1** V-T If you **collect** a number of things, you bring them together from several places or from several people. *recolectar, recoger, reunir* ❑ *Two young girls were collecting firewood. Dos muchachas estaban recogiendo leña.* ● **col|lec|tion** N-UNCOUNT *recopilación* ❑ *Computer systems can speed up collection of information. Los sistemas informatizados pueden acelerar la recopilación de información.* **2** V-T If you **collect** things, such as stamps or books, as a hobby, you get a large number of them over a period of time because they interest you. *coleccionar* ❑ *I used to collect key rings. Acostumbraba coleccionar llaveros.* ● **col|lect|ing** N-UNCOUNT *colección* ❑ *...hobbies like stamp collecting. ...pasatiempos como la colección de timbres postales.* ● **col|lec|tor** (**collectors**) N-COUNT *coleccionista* ❑ *...a respected collector of Indian art. ...un respetado coleccionista de arte hindú.* **3** V-T/V-I If a substance **collects** somewhere, or if something **collects** it, it keeps arriving over a period of time and is held in that place or thing. *acumularse* ❑ *Gas does collect in the mines around here. El gas sí se acumula en las minas de los alrededores.* ❑ *...tanks which collect rainwater. ...tanques para recolectar el agua de lluvia.* **4** V-T/V-I If you **collect for** a charity or **for** a present for someone, you ask people to give you money for it. *recaudar* ❑ *Are you collecting for charity? ¿Está recaudando dinero para una obra de beneficencia?* ❑ *The organization has collected $2.5 million for the relief effort. La organización ha recaudado 2.5 millones de dólares para el esfuerzo de socorro.* ● **col|lec|tion** (**collections**) N-COUNT *recaudación* ❑ *We held a collection for a children's charity. Hicimos una recaudación de fondos para una institución de beneficencia infantil.*

| Thesaurus | *collect* | Ver también: |
|---|---|---|
| v. | accumulate, compile, gather; (*ant.*) scatter **1** | |

**col|lect call** (**collect calls**) **1** N-COUNT A **collect call** is a telephone call which is paid for by the person who receives the call, rather than the person who makes the call. *llamada por cobrar, llamada a cobro revertido* ❑ *I want to make a collect call. Quiero hacer una llamada por cobrar.* **2** → see also **call**

**col|lec|tion** /kəlɛkʃən/ (**collections**) **1** N-COUNT A **collection of** things is a group of similar or related things. *colección, recopilación* ❑ *...the world's largest collection of sculptures by Henry Moore. ...la colección más grande del mundo de esculturas de Henry Moore.* ❑ *...a collection of short stories called "Facing The Music." ...una recopilación de cuentos cortos titulada "Facing the Music".* ❑ *...a collection of modern glass office buildings. ...un grupo de modernos edificios de* *vidrio para oficinas.* **2** → see also **collect**

**col|lec|tion agen|cy** (**collection agencies**) N-COUNT A **collection agency** is an organization that obtains payments from people who owe money to others. *agencia de cobro* ❑ *...a debt collection agency. ...una agencia de cobro de deudas.*

**col|lec|tive** /kəlɛktɪv/ (**collectives**) **1** ADJ **Collective** means shared by every member of a group. *colectivo* ❑ *It was a collective decision. Fue una decisión colectiva.* ● **col|lec|tive|ly** ADV *colectivamente* ❑ *They collectively decided to move on. Decidieron colectivamente seguir adelante.* **2** N-COUNT A **collective** is a business or farm which is run, and often owned, by a group of people. *cooperativa* [BUSINESS] ❑ *He participates in all the decisions of the collective. Él participa en todas las decisiones de la cooperativa.*
→ see **union**

**col|lec|tor** /kəlɛktər/ (**collectors**) **1** N-COUNT A **collector** is someone whose job is to take something such as money, tickets, or garbage from people. *cobrador o cobradora, recaudador o recaudadora, recolector o recolectora* ❑ *He earned his living as a tax collector. Se ganaba la vida como recaudador (de impuestos).* **2** → see also **collect**

**col|lege** /kɒlɪdʒ/ (**colleges**) **1** N-VAR A **college** is an institution where students study after they have left secondary school. *universidad, colegio* ❑ *Joanna is taking business courses at a local college. Joanna está haciendo estudios de comercio en una universidad local.* ❑ *Stephanie left art college this summer. Stephanie terminó la carrera de bellas artes este verano.* **2** N-COUNT At some universities in the United States, **colleges** are divisions which offer degrees in particular subjects. *escuela* ❑ *...a professor at the University of Florida College of Law. ...profesor de la Escuela de Derecho de la Universidad de Florida.* **3** N-COUNT A **college** is one of the institutions which some British universities are divided into. *colegio* ❑ *He was educated at Balliol College, Oxford. Estudió en el Colegio Balliol de Oxford.*
→ see **graduation**

**col|legi|ate** /kəlidʒɪt, -dʒiɪt/ ADJ **Collegiate** means belonging or relating to a college or to college students. *universitario* ❑ *...the national collegiate football championship. ...el campeonato nacional de fútbol americano universitario.* ❑ *...collegiate life. ...vida universitaria.*

**col|lide** /kəlaɪd/ (**collides, colliding, collided**) V-RECIP If people or vehicles **collide**, they crash into one another. *chocar* ❑ *Two trains collided head-on. Dos trenes chocaron de frente.* ❑ *Racing up the stairs, he almost collided with Daisy. Cuando corría escaleras arriba, estuvo a punto de chocar con Daisy.*

| **Thesaurus** | *collide* | Ver también: |
|---|---|---|
| v. | bump, clash, crash, hit, smash; (*ant.*) avoid | |

**col|li|sion** /kəlɪʒ<sup></sup>ən/ (**collisions**) N-VAR A **collision** occurs when a moving object crashes into something. *colisión, choque* ❑ *Their van was involved in a collision with a car. Su camioneta chocó con un coche.*

**col|loid** /kɒlɔɪd/ (**colloids**) N-COUNT A **colloid** is a mixture containing tiny particles of a substance that do not dissolve or settle at the bottom of the mixture. *coloide* [TECHNICAL]

**co|lon** /koʊlən/ (**colons**) **1** N-COUNT A **colon** is the punctuation mark (:). *dos puntos* **2** N-COUNT Your **colon** is the part of your intestine above your rectum. *colon* ❑ *...deaths from colon cancer. ...muertes causadas por el cáncer de colon.*
→ see **punctuation**

**colo|nel** /kɜrnᵊl/ (**colonels**) N-COUNT; N-TITLE; N-VOC A **colonel** is a senior officer in an army, air force, or the marines. *coronel* ❑ *...an ex-army colonel. ...un antiguo coronel del ejército.*

**co|lo|nial** /kəloʊniəl/ **1** ADJ **Colonial** means relating to countries that are colonies, or to colonialism. *colonial* ❑ *...Jamaica's independence from British colonial rule. ...la independencia de Jamaica del gobierno colonial británico.* **2** ADJ A **colonial** building or piece of furniture was built or made in a style that was popular in America in the 17th and 18th centuries. *colonial* ❑ *...big white colonial houses. ...grandes casas coloniales blancas.*

**co|lo|ni|al|ism** /kəloʊniəlɪzəm/ N-UNCOUNT **Colonialism** is the practice by which a powerful country directly controls less powerful countries. *colonialismo* ❑ *...the fight against colonialism. ...la lucha contra el colonialismo.*

**colo|nist** /kɒlənɪst/ (**colonists**) N-COUNT **Colonists** are the people who start a colony or the people who are among the first to live in a particular colony. *colonizador o colonizadora, colono o colona* ❑ *...the early American colonists. ...los primeros colonizadores de América del Norte.*

**colo|nize** /kɒlənaɪz/ (**colonizes, colonizing, colonized**) V-T If people **colonize** a foreign country, they go to live there and take control of it. *colonizar* ❑ *...the first British attempt to colonize Ireland. ...el primer intento británico por colonizar Irlanda.*

**colo|ny** /kɒləni/ (**colonies**) **1** N-COUNT A **colony** is a country which is controlled by a more powerful country. *colonia* ❑ *...France's former North African colonies. ...las antiguas colonias norafricanas de Francia.* **2** N-COUNT A **colony** is a group of people or animals of a particular sort living together. *colonia* ❑ *...an artists' colony. ...una colonia de artistas.* ❑ *...colonies of sea birds. ...colonias de aves marinas.* **3** N-PLURAL **The colonies** means the 13 British colonies in North America which formed the original United States. *las colonias* ❑ *Philadelphia was the most important city in the colonies. Filadelfia era la ciudad más importante de las trece colonias.*

**col|or** /kʌlər/ (**colors, coloring, colored**) **1** N-COUNT The **color** of something is the appearance that it has as a result of the way in which it reflects light. Red, blue, and green are colors. *color* ❑ *"What color is the car?"— "Red." —¿De qué color es el coche? —Rojo.* ❑ *Judi's favorite color is pink. El color favorito de Judi es el rosa.* **2** N-COUNT Someone's **color** is the color of their skin. People often use **color** in this way to refer to a person's race. *color* ❑ *I don't care what color she is. No me importa de qué color sea.* **3** V-T If you **color** something, you use something such as dyes or paint to change its color. *pintar, colorear, teñir* ❑ *Many women begin coloring their hair in their mid-30s. Muchas mujeres empiezan a pintarse el pelo entre los 30 y los 40 años de edad.* **4** V-T If something **colors**

C

C

your opinion or judgment, it affects the way that you think about something. *empañar, influir* ❑ *He sometimes let emotion color his judgment. En ocasiones deja que sus emociones empañen su juicio.* **5** ADJ A **color** television, photograph, or picture is one that shows things in all their colors, and not just in black, white, and gray. *de color, a color* ❑ *...a color television set. ...una televisión a color.* **6** N-UNCOUNT **Color** is a quality that makes something especially interesting or exciting. *colorido* ❑ *Travel adds color to our lives. Los viajes dan colorido a la vida.* **7** → see also **colored**

→ see Picture Dictionary: **color**

→ see **painting**

▶ **color in** PHR-VERB If you **color in** a drawing, you give it different colors using crayons or paints. *pintar, colorear* ❑ *They colored in all the black and white pictures. Colorearon todas las ilustraciones que estaban en blanco y negro.*

**Word Partnership** Usar *color* con:

ADJ. **bright** color, **favorite** color **1**
N. color **blind**, **eye/hair** color **1**
**skin** color **2**
color **film/photograph**, color **television** **5**

**color-blind** **1** ADJ Someone who is **color-blind** cannot see the difference between colors, especially between red and green. *daltónico, daltoniano* ❑ *Far more men are color-blind than women. Hay muchos más hombres daltónicos que mujeres.* ● **color-blindness** N-UNCOUNT *daltonismo* ❑ *What exactly is color-blindness? ¿Qué es exactamente el daltonismo?* **2** ADJ A **color-blind** system or organization does not treat people differently according to their race or color. *imparcial, sin prejuicios* ❑ *Their goal is a color-blind society. Su objetivo es una sociedad sin prejuicios.*

**color-coded** ADJ Things that are **color-coded** use colors to represent different features or functions. *codificado con colores* ❑ *...color-coded buckets. ...cubetas codificadas con colores.*

**col|ored** /kʌlərd/ ADJ **Colored** means having a particular color. *de color* ❑ *...colored scarves. ...bufandas de color.*

**col|or|ful** /kʌlərfəl/ **1** ADJ Something that is **colorful** has bright colors or a lot of different colors. *colorido, vistoso* ❑ *The flowers were colorful. Las flores eran de colores muy vivos.* **2** ADJ **Colorful** means interesting and exciting. *interesante, original, pintoresco* ❑ *The story she told was certainly colorful. La historia que narró era original, sin duda alguna.* ❑ *...probably the most colorful character in baseball. ...probablemente el personaje más pintoresco del béisbol.*

**Thesaurus** *colorful* Ver también:

ADJ. bright, lively, vibrant, vivid; (*ant.*) bland, colorless, dull **1**
animated, dramatic, interesting **2**

**col|or|ing book** (**coloring books**) N-COUNT A **coloring book** is a book of simple drawings which children can color in. *libro para colorear, cuaderno para colorear*

**col|or re|la|tion|ship** (**color relationships**) also **color harmony** also **color scheme** **1** N-COUNT **Color relationships** are pleasing combinations of colors that are based on the position of colors on the color wheel. *relación de los colores* **2** → see also **color**

**col|or scheme** (**color schemes**) N-COUNT In a room or house, the **color scheme** is the way in which colors have been used to decorate it. *combinación (de colores)* ❑ *...a color scheme of green and pink. ...una combinación de verde y rosa.*

**Picture Dictionary** color

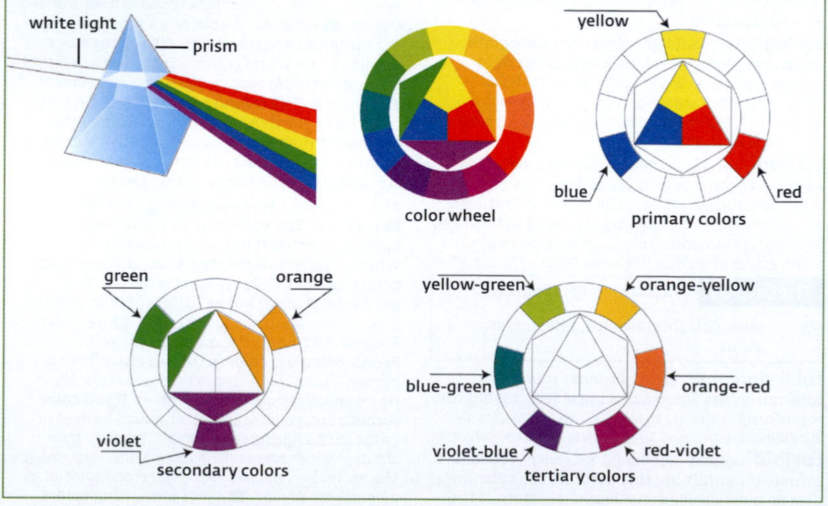

**col|or the|ory** (**color theories**) N-VAR **Color theory** is a set of rules for mixing colors in order to achieve a particular result in a painting. *teoría de los colores*

**col|umn** /kɒləm/ (**columns**) **1** N-COUNT A **column** is a tall, solid cylinder, especially one supporting part of a building. *columna* ❑ *The house had six white columns across the front. La casa tenía seis columnas en el frente.* **2** N-COUNT A **column** is something that has a tall, narrow shape. *columna* ❑ *...a column of smoke. ...una columna de humo.* **3** N-COUNT A **column** is a group of people or animals which moves in a long line. *columna* ❑ *...columns of military vehicles. ...columnas de vehículos militares.* **4** N-COUNT In a newspaper or magazine, or a printed chart, a **column** is a vertical section of writing, or a section that is always written by the same person. *columna* ❑ *He writes a column for the Wall Street Journal. Escribe una columna en el Wall Street Journal.*
→ see **cave**

**col|um|nist** /kɒləmnɪst, -əmɪst/ (**columnists**) N-COUNT A **columnist** is a journalist who writes a regular article in a newspaper or magazine. *columnista* ❑ *...a columnist for the Chicago Tribune. ...un columnista del Chicago Tribune.*

**comb** /koʊm/ (**combs, combing, combed**) **1** N-COUNT A **comb** is a flat piece of plastic or metal with narrow, pointed teeth along one side, which you use to make your hair neat. *peine* **2** V-T When you **comb** your hair, you make it neat using a comb. *peinar* ❑ *Salvatore combed his hair carefully. Salvatore se peinó con esmero.* **3** V-T If you **comb** a place for something, you search thoroughly for it. *peinar, rastrear* ❑ *Police combed the area for the boy. La policía rastreó la zona en busca del niño.*

**com|bat** (**combats, combating** or **combatting, combated** or **combatted**)

> The noun is pronounced /kɒmbæt/. The verb is pronounced /kəmbæt/.

**1** N-UNCOUNT **Combat** is fighting that takes place in a war. *combate* ❑ *Over 16 million men had died in combat. Más de 16 millones de hombres murieron en combate.* **2** V-T If people in authority **combat** something, they try to stop it from happening. *combatir* ❑ *...new laws to combat crime. ...nuevas leyes para combatir el crimen.*
→ see **sugar, war**

**Word Partnership** Usar *combat* con:

ADJ. **hand-to-hand** combat, **heavy** combat **1**
N. combat **forces/troops/units**, combat **gear** **1**
combat **crime**, combat **disease**, combat **terrorism** **2**

**com|bi|na|tion** /kɒmbɪneɪʃən/ (**combinations**) N-COUNT A **combination of** things is a mixture of them. *combinación* ❑ *...a fantastic combination of colors. ...una fantástica combinación de colores.*

**Word Link** *com ≈ with, together : combine, compact, companion*

**com|bine** /kəmbaɪn/ (**combines, combining, combined**) **1** V-RECIP If you **combine** two or more things or if they **combine**, they exist or join together. *combinar, mezclar* ❑ *Combine the flour with 3 tablespoons of water. Mezcla la harina con 3 cucharadas de agua.* ❑ *Disease and hunger combine to kill thousands. Las enfermedades y el hambre se combinan para matar a miles.* • **com|bined** /kəmbaɪnd/ ADJ *combinado, conjunto* ❑ *The companies had combined sales of $90 million. Las compañías tenían ventas conjuntas de $90 millones.* **2** V-T If someone or something **combines** two qualities or features, they have both of them. *combinar* ❑ *Their system seems to combine the two ideals. Su sistema parece combinar los dos ideales.* ❑ *His latest movie combines comedy with mystery. Su última película combina la comedia con el misterio.* **3** V-T If someone **combines** two activities, they do them both at the same time. *combinar* ❑ *It is possible to combine a career with being a mother. Es posible combinar una carrera con la maternidad.*

**Thesaurus** *combine* Ver también:

V. blend, fuse, incorporate, join, mix, unite; (*ant.*) detach, disconnect, divide, separate **1**–**3**

**com|bus|tion** /kəmbʌstʃən/ N-UNCOUNT **Combustion** is the act of burning something or the process of burning. *combustión* [TECHNICAL] ❑ *The energy is released by combustion. La combustión libera la energía.*
→ see **engine**

**come**
1. ARRIVE AT A PLACE
2. OTHER USES
3. PHRASAL VERBS

**❶ come** /kʌm/ (**comes, coming, came**)

> The form **come** is used in the present tense and is the past participle.

**1** V-I You use **come** to say that someone or something arrives somewhere, or moves toward you. *venir, llegar* ❑ *Two police officers came into the hall. Dos policías vinieron a la entrada.* ❑ *He came to a door. Llegó a una puerta.* ❑ *Eleanor came to see her. Eleanor vino a verla.* ❑ *Come here, Tom. Ven, Tom.* ❑ *We heard the train coming. Oímos que venía el tren.* ❑ *The windows broke and the sea came rushing in. Las ventanas se rompieron y el mar entró.* **2** V-I If something **comes to** a particular point, it reaches it. *llegar (a)* ❑ *The water came up to my chest. El agua me llegaba hasta el pecho.*

**❷ come** /kʌm/ (**comes, coming, came**)

> The form **come** is used in the present tense and is the past participle.

**1** V-I You can use **come** in expressions which state what happens to someone or something. *venir* ❑ *The lid won't come off. La tapa no va a salir.* ❑ *Their worst fears may be coming true. Sus peores miedos pueden volverse realidad.* **2** V-T If someone **comes to** do something, they gradually start to do it. *llegar a* ❑ *She said it so many times that she came to believe it. Lo dijo tantas veces que llegó a creerlo.* **3** V-I When a particular event or time **comes,** it arrives or happens. *llegar* ❑ *The announcement came after a meeting at the White House. El anuncio llegó después de una reunión en la Casa Blanca.* ❑ *There will come a time when they will have to negotiate. Llegará el momento en* *el que tendrán que negociar.* ● **com|ing** N-SING *llegada* ❑ *Most people welcome the coming of summer. Muchas personas se alegran por la llegada del verano.* 4 V-I If a thought, idea, or memory **comes to** you, you suddenly think of it or remember it. *llegar* ❑ *He was about to shut the door when an idea came to him. Estaba a punto de cerrar la puerta cuando le llegó una idea.* 5 V-I If something **comes to** a particular amount, it adds up to it. *llegar a* ❑ *Lunch came to $80. La comida llegó a los $80.* 6 V-I If someone or something **comes from** a particular place or thing, that place or thing is their origin, source, or starting point. *venir de* ❑ *Nearly half the students come from overseas. Cerca de la mitad de los estudiantes vienen del extranjero.* ❑ *Most of Germany's oil comes from the North Sea. La mayor parte del petróleo de Alemania viene del Mar del Norte.* 7 V-I Something that **comes from** something else or **comes of** it is the result of it. *venir de* ❑ *...a feeling of power that comes from driving fast. ...un sentimiento de poder que viene de conducir rápido.* ❑ *Some good might come of this. Algo bueno saldrá de esto.* 8 V-T If someone or something **comes** first, next, or last, they are first, next, or last in a series, list, or competition. *ir* ❑ *The two countries cannot agree what should come next. Los dos países no se ponen de acuerdo sobre qué debería seguir.* 9 V-I If a type of thing **comes in** a particular range of colors, forms, styles, or sizes, it can have any of those colors, forms, styles, or sizes. *venir* ❑ *Bikes come in all shapes and sizes. Hay bicicletas de muchos modelos y tamaños.*

❸ **come** /kʌm/ (**comes, coming, came**)

> The form **come** is used in the present tense and is the past participle.

▸ **come about** PHR-VERB When you say how or when something **came about,** you say how or when it happened. *suceder, ocurrir* ❑ *How did this situation come about? ¿Cómo sucedió esta situación?*

▸ **come across** 1 PHR-VERB If you **come across** something or someone, you find them or meet them by chance. *encontrar(se)* ❑ *I came across a photo of my grandparents. Encontré una foto de mis abuelos.* 2 PHR-VERB The way that someone **comes across** is the impression that they make on other people. *dar una impresión* ❑ *He comes across as an extremely pleasant young man. Da la impresión de ser un joven sumamente agradable.*

▸ **come along** 1 PHR-VERB You ask someone to **come along** to invite them in a friendly way to do something with you or go somewhere. *ir, llegar* ❑ *There's a party tonight and you're very welcome to come along. Hay una fiesta en la noche y sería muy grato que fueran.* 2 PHR-VERB When something or someone **comes along,** they occur or arrive by chance. *llegar* ❑ *It was lucky you came along. Fue una suerte que llegaras.* 3 PHR-VERB If something **is coming along,** it is developing or making progress. *ir* ❑ *The talks are coming along quite well. Las pláticas van muy bien.*

▸ **come around** 1 PHR-VERB If someone **comes around,** they come to your house to see you. *venir* ❑ *Beth came around this morning to apologize. Beth vino esta mañana a disculparse.* 2 PHR-VERB If you **come around to** an idea, you eventually change your mind and accept it. *aceptar* ❑ *It looks like they're coming around to our way of thinking. Parece que están aceptando nuestra forma de pensar.* 3 PHR-VERB When something **comes around,** it happens as a regular or predictable event. *llegar de nuevo* ❑ *I hope to be fit when the World Championship comes around. Espero estar en forma para el próximo campeonato mundial.* 4 PHR-VERB When someone who is unconscious **comes around,** they become conscious again. *volver en sí* ❑ *When I came around I was on the kitchen floor. Cuando volví en mí estaba en el piso de la cocina.*

▸ **come at** PHR-VERB If a person or animal **comes at** you, they move toward you in a threatening way and try to attack you. *venirse encima* ❑ *Mr. Cox came at him with a wild expression. El señor Cox se le fue encima con una expresión salvaje.*

▸ **come back** 1 PHR-VERB If someone comes back to a place, they return to it. *regresar, volver* ❑ *He wanted to come back to Washington. Quería regresar a Washington.* ❑ *She just wanted to go home and not come back. Sólo quería irse a casa y no volver.* 2 PHR-VERB If something that you had forgotten **comes back to** you, you remember it. *recordar* ❑ *I'll tell you his name when it comes back to me. Te diré su nombre en cuanto lo recuerde.* 3 PHR-VERB When something **comes back,** it becomes fashionable again. *volver a estar de moda* ❑ *I'm glad hats are coming back. Me alegra que los sombreros vuelvan a estar de moda.* 4 → see also **comeback**

▸ **come by** PHR-VERB To **come by** something means to obtain it or find it. *conseguir* ❑ *How did you come by that check? ¿Cómo conseguiste ese cheque?*

▸ **come down** 1 PHR-VERB If the cost, level, or amount of something **comes down,** it becomes less than it was before. *bajar* ❑ *Interest rates should come down. Las tasas de interés deberían bajar.* ❑ *If you buy three, the price comes down to $10. Si compras tres, el precio baja a $10.* 2 PHR-VERB If something **comes down,** it falls to the ground. *caer* ❑ *The cold rain came down for hours. La fría lluvia cayó durante horas.*

▸ **come down on** 1 PHR-VERB If you **come down on** one side of an argument, you declare that you support that side. *estar a favor de, ponerse de parte de* ❑ *He clearly came down on the side of the president. Claramente, estuvo a favor del presidente.* 2 PHR-VERB If you **come down on** someone, you criticize them severely or treat them strictly. *tratar con mano dura* ❑ *If Douglas comes down hard on him, Dale will rebel. Si Douglas lo trata con mano dura, Dale se rebelará.*

▸ **come down to** PHR-VERB If a problem, decision, or question **comes down to** a particular thing, that thing is the most important factor involved. *ser cuestión de, reducirse a* ❑ *The problem comes down to money. El problema es una cuestión de dinero.*

▸ **come down with** PHR-VERB If you **come down with** an illness, you get it. *contraer* ❑ *Thomas came down with a cold. Thomas contrajo un resfriado.*

▸ **come for** PHR-VERB If people such as soldiers or police **come for** you, they come to find you. *buscar* ❑ *Tanya was ready to fight if they came for her. Tanya estaba lista para pelear si venían a arrestarla.*

▸ **come forward** PHR-VERB If someone **comes forward,** they make themselves known and offer to help. *presentarse* ❑ *Police asked witnesses to come forward. La policía pidió a los testigos que se presentaran.*

▸ **come in** 1 PHR-VERB If information, a report, or a telephone call **comes in,** it is received. *recibir* ❑ *Reports are coming in of trouble at another jail. Se están recibiendo reportes de que hay problemas en otra* cárcel. **2** PHR-VERB If you have some money **coming in,** you receive it regularly as your income. ganar, entrar ❑ *She had no money coming in and no savings.* *No ganaba dinero y no tenía ahorros.* **3** PHR-VERB If someone or something **comes in,** they are involved in a situation or discussion. entrar ❑ *Rose asked again, "But where do we come in, Henry?"* *Rose preguntó de nuevo —¿Y nosotros en dónde entramos, Henry?* **4** PHR-VERB When a new idea, fashion, or product **comes in,** it becomes popular or available. ponerse de moda ❑ *Lots of new ideas were coming in.* *Muchas ideas nuevas se estaban poniendo de moda.*

▸**come in for** PHR-VERB If someone or something **comes in for** criticism or blame, they receive it. ser objeto de ❑ *The plans have already come in for criticism.* *Los planes ya son objeto de crítica.*

▸**come into** **1** PHR-VERB If someone **comes into** some money, some property, or a title, they inherit it. heredar ❑ *My father has just come into a fortune.* *Mi padre acaba de heredar una fortuna.* **2** PHR-VERB If someone or something **comes into** a situation, they have a role in it. tener un papel en ❑ *We don't really know where Harry comes into all this.* *En realidad no sabemos qué papel tiene Harry en esto.*

▸**come off** PHR-VERB If something **comes off,** it is successful or effective. tener éxito ❑ *It was a good try but it didn't really come off.* *Fue un buen intento pero en realidad no tuvo éxito.*

▸**come on** **1** CONVENTION You say **"Come on"** to someone to encourage them to do something or be quicker. vamos, ándale [SPOKEN] ❑ *Come on Doreen, let's dance.* *Vamos Doreen, vamos a bailar.* ❑ *Come on, or we'll be late.* *Vamos, o llegaremos tarde.* **2** PHR-VERB If you have an illness or a headache **coming on,** you can feel it starting. dar ❑ *Tiredness and fever are likely to be a sign of the flu coming on.* *El cansancio y la fiebre son señales probables de que te va a dar un resfriado.* **3** PHR-VERB If something or someone **is coming on,** they are developing well or making good progress. avanzar ❑ *Leah is coming on very well now.* *Leah está avanzando muy bien ahora.* **4** PHR-VERB When a machine **comes on,** it starts working. encenderse ❑ *The central heating came on.* *La calefacción central se encendió.*

▸**come out** **1** PHR-VERB When a new product **comes out,** it becomes available to the public. salir ❑ *The book comes out this week.* *El libro sale esta semana.* **2** PHR-VERB If a fact **comes out,** it becomes known to people. salir a la luz, revelarse ❑ *The truth is beginning to come out about what happened.* *La verdad sobre lo que sucedió está empezando a salir a la luz.* **3** PHR-VERB If you **come out for** or **against** something, you declare that you do or do not support it. declararse a favor/en contra ❑ *France came out against the plan on Friday.* *Francia se declaró en contra del plan el viernes.* **4** PHR-VERB When the sun, moon, or stars **come out,** they appear in the sky. salir ❑ *Oh, look! The sun's coming out!* *¡Ah, mira! ¡Está saliendo el sol!*

▸**come over** **1** PHR-VERB If a feeling **comes over** you, it affects you. invadir ❑ *A strange feeling came over me.* *Me invadió un sentimiento extraño.* **2** PHR-VERB The way that someone or something **comes over** is the impression they make on people. parecer ❑ *You come over as capable and amusing.* *Pareces capaz y divertido.*

▸**come round** → see **come around**

▸**come through** **1** PHR-VERB To **come through** a dangerous or difficult situation means to survive it and recover from it. sobrevivir ❑ *The city had faced the crisis and come through it.* *La ciudad enfrentó la crisis y sobrevivió a ella.* **2** PHR-VERB If something **comes through,** you receive it. llegar ❑ *The message that comes through is that taxes will have to be raised.* *El mensaje que llega es que los impuestos tendrán que subir.*

▸**come to** PHR-VERB When someone who is unconscious **comes to,** they become conscious. volver en sí ❑ *He came to and raised his head.* *Volvió en sí y levantó la cabeza.*

▸**come under** **1** PHR-VERB If you **come under** attack or pressure, for example, people attack you or put pressure on you. estar bajo ❑ *The police came under attack from angry crowds.* *La policía estuvo bajo el ataque de la multitud furiosa.* **2** PHR-VERB If something **comes under** a particular authority, it is managed or controlled by that authority. estar bajo ❑ *Their troops will come under U.S. command.* *Sus tropas estarán bajo el mando de Estados Unidos.*

▸**come up** **1** PHR-VERB If a person or animal **comes up to** you, they approach you. acercarse a ❑ *Her cat came up and rubbed itself against their legs.* *Su gato se les acercó y se les restregó en las piernas.* **2** PHR-VERB If something **comes up** in a conversation, it is mentioned. surgir ❑ *The subject came up at work.* *El tema surgió en el trabajo.* **3** PHR-VERB If something **is coming up,** it is about to happen or take place. acercarse ❑ *We do have elections coming up.* *Se acercan las elecciones.* **4** PHR-VERB If something **comes up,** it happens unexpectedly. surgir ❑ *I was delayed—something came up at home.* *Me retrasé—algo surgió en casa.* **5** PHR-VERB If a job **comes up** or if something **comes up for** sale, it becomes available. surgir ❑ *A job came up and I applied for it.* *Surgió un empleo y lo solicité.* **6** PHR-VERB When the sun or moon **comes up,** it rises. salir ❑ *It will be so great watching the sun come up.* *Será fabuloso ver salir el sol.*

▸**come up against** PHR-VERB If you **come up against** a problem or difficulty, you are faced with it and have to deal with it. tener que enfrentar ❑ *We came up against a few problems in dealing with the case.* *Tuvimos que enfrentar algunos problemas al resolver el caso.*

> **Come** is used in a large number of expressions which are explained under other words in this dictionary. For example, the expression "to come to terms with something" is explained at "term."

**come|back** (**comebacks**) **1** N-COUNT If a well-known person makes a **comeback,** they return to their profession or sport after a period away. retorno ❑ *At the age of 65 he's trying to make a comeback.* *A sus 65 años está tratando de reaparecer.* **2** N-COUNT If something makes a **comeback,** it becomes fashionable again. vuelta ❑ *Tight fitting T-shirts are making a comeback.* *Las camisetas ajustadas están de vuelta.*

**co|median** /kəmidiən/ (**comedians**) N-COUNT A **comedian** is an entertainer whose job is to make people laugh, by telling jokes or funny stories. cómico o cómica ❑ *...comedian Jay Leno.* *...el cómico Jay Leno.*

**com|edy** /kɒmədi/ (**comedies**) **1** N-UNCOUNT

C

C

**Comedy** consists of types of entertainment that are intended to make people laugh. *comedia* ❑ *...his career in comedy. ...su carrera en la comedia.* **2** N-COUNT A **comedy** is a play, movie, or television program that is intended to make people laugh. *comedia* ❑ *The movie is a romantic comedy. La película es una comedia romántica.*
→ see **genre**

**com|et** /kɒmɪt/ (**comets**) N-COUNT A **comet** is a bright object with a long tail that travels around the sun. *cometa* ❑ *Halley's Comet is going to come back in 2061. El cometa Halley va a regresar en el 2061.*
→ see **solar system**

**com|fort** /kʌmfərt/ (**comforts, comforting, comforted**) **1** N-UNCOUNT **Comfort** is the state of being physically or mentally relaxed. *comodidad, confort* ❑ *The audience can sit in comfort while watching the show. El público se puede sentar con comodidad mientras ve el espectáculo.* **2** N-UNCOUNT **Comfort** is a style of life in which you have enough money to have everything you need. *vivir desahogadamente* ❑ *We don't earn enough to live in comfort. No ganamos lo suficiente para vivir desahogadamente.* **3** N-UNCOUNT If something offers **comfort,** it makes you feel less worried or unhappy. *consuelo* ❑ *They will be able to take some comfort from the news. Podrán encontrar algún consuelo en la noticia.* **4** N-COUNT **Comforts** are things which make your life easier and more pleasant. *comodidades* ❑ *She enjoys the comforts married life has brought her. Disfruta de las comodidades que la vida marital le ha traído.* **5** V-T If you **comfort** someone, you make them feel less worried or unhappy. *consolar* ❑ *Ned put his arm around her, trying to comfort her. Ned la rodeó con su brazo, tratando de consolarla.*

**com|fort|able** /kʌmftəbəl, -fərtəbəl/ **1** ADJ If something such as furniture is **comfortable,** it makes you feel physically relaxed. *cómodo* ❑ *...a comfortable chair. ...una silla cómoda.* ❑ *A home should be comfortable and friendly. Un hogar debe ser cómodo y agradable.* ❑ *Lie down on your bed and make yourself comfortable. Acuéstate en la cama y ponte cómodo.* • **com|fort|ably** ADV *cómodamente, confortablemente* ❑ *...the comfortably-furnished living room. ...la sala cómodamente amueblada.* ❑ *Are you sitting comfortably? ¿Estás sentado cómodamente?* **2** ADJ If someone is **comfortable,** they have enough money to be able to live without financial problems. *de posición acomodada* ❑ *"Is he rich?" — "He's comfortable." —¿Es rico? —Es de posición acomodada.* • **com|fort|ably** ADV *holgadamente, con holgura* ❑ *Cayton lives very comfortably. Cayton vive muy holgadamente.* **3** ADJ If you feel **comfortable with** a particular situation or person, you feel confident and relaxed with them. *cómodo, a gusto (con)* ❑ *He liked me and I felt comfortable with him. Le caí bien y yo me sentí cómoda con él.*

| **Thesaurus** | *comfortable* | Ver también: |
|---|---|---|
| ADJ. | comfy, cozy, soft; (*ant.*) uncomfortable **1** well-off **2** | |

**com|fort|er** /kʌmfərtər/ (**comforters**) N-COUNT A **comforter** is a large cover filled with feathers or soft material which you put over yourself in bed. *edredón*

**com|ic** /kɒmɪk/ (**comics**) **1** ADJ Something that is **comic** makes you want to laugh. *cómico* ❑ *The novel is comic and tragic. La novela es cómica y trágica.* ❑ *Grodin is a fine comic actor. Grodin es un buen actor cómico.* **2** N-COUNT A **comic** is an entertainer who tells jokes in order to make people laugh. *cómico o cómica* ❑ *...the funniest comic in America. ...el cómico más divertido de América.*

**comi|cal** /kɒmɪkəl/ ADJ If something is **comical,** it makes you want to laugh because it is funny or silly. *cómico* ❑ *Her expression was comical. Su expresión era cómica.*

**com|ic book** (**comic books**) N-COUNT A **comic book** is a magazine that contains stories told in pictures. *cómic* ❑ *...comic book heroes such as Spider Man. ...héroes de los cómics como el Hombre Araña.*

**com|ing** /kʌmɪŋ/ **1** ADJ A **coming** event or time is an event or time that will happen soon. *próximo* ❑ *...the weather in the coming months. ...el clima de los próximos meses.* **2** → see also **come**

**com|ma** /kɒmə/ (**commas**) N-COUNT A **comma** is the punctuation mark (,). *coma*
→ see **punctuation**

**com|mand** /kəmænd/ (**commands, commanding, commanded**) **1** V-T If someone in authority **commands** you to do something, they tell you that you must do it. *ordenar, mandar* [mainly WRITTEN] ❑ *He commanded his troops to attack. Ordenó a sus tropas que atacaran.* ❑ *"Get in your car and follow me," she commanded. —Sube a tu carro y sígueme —me ordenó.* • **Command** is also a noun. *orden* ❑ *The driver failed to respond to a command to stop. El conductor no respondió a la orden de detenerse.* ❑ *I closed my eyes at his command. Cerré los ojos por orden suya.* **2** V-T If you **command** something such as respect or obedience, you obtain it because you are popular or important. *imponer, infundir, inspirar* ❑ *She commanded the respect of all her colleagues. Infundía respeto entre todos sus colegas.* **3** V-T An officer who **commands** part of an army, navy, or air force is responsible for controlling and organizing it. *estar al mando de* ❑ *...the French general who commands the U.N. troops in the region. ...el general francés que está al mando de las tropas de la ONU en la región.* • **Command** is also a noun. *mando* ❑ *The force will be under the command of an American general. Las fuerzas armadas estarán bajo el mando de un general estadounidense.* **4** N-UNCOUNT Your **command of** something is your knowledge of it and your ability to use it. *dominio* ❑ *His command of English was excellent. Su dominio del inglés era excelente.*

**com|mand|er** /kəmændər/ (**commanders**) **1** N-COUNT; N-TITLE; N-VOC A **commander** is an officer in charge of a military operation or organization. *comandante* ❑ *The commander and some of the men were released. El comandante y algunos de sus hombres fueron liberados.* **2** N-COUNT; N-TITLE; N-VOC A **commander** is an officer in the U.S. Navy or the Royal Navy. *capitán de fragata*

**com|mand mod|ule** (**command modules**) N-COUNT The **command module** is the part of a spacecraft in which the astronauts live and operate the controls. *módulo de maniobra y mando*

**com|media dell'ar|te** /kəmeɪdiədɛlɑrti, -teɪ/ N-UNCOUNT **Commedia dell'arte** was a form of improvised theater that began in Italy in the sixteenth century and used well-known characters and stories. comedia del arte

**Word Link** memor ≈ memory : commemorate, memorial, memory

**com|memo|rate** /kəmɛməreɪt/ (commemorates, commemorating, commemorated) V-T To **commemorate** an important event or person means to remember them by means of a special action, ceremony, or specially-created object. conmemorar ❑ *...paintings commemorating great moments in baseball history.* *...pinturas que conmemoran grandes momentos en la historia del béisbol.* • **com|memo|ra|tion** /kəmɛməreɪʃᵊn/ N-VAR (commemorations) conmemoración ❑ *...a commemoration of victory.* *...una conmemoración de la victoria.*

**com|men|sal|ism** /kəmɛnsəlɪzəm/ (commensalisms) N-VAR A **commensalism** between two species of plants or animals is a relationship which benefits one of the species and does not harm the other species. comensalismo [TECHNICAL]

**com|ment** /kɒmɛnt/ (comments, commenting, commented) **1** V-T/V-I If you **comment on** something, you give your opinion about it or make a statement about it. comentar ❑ *Mr. Cooke has not commented on these reports.* *El señor Cooke no ha comentado estos informes.* ❑ *You really can't comment until you know the facts.* *En realidad no puedes comentar hasta no conocer los hechos.* ❑ *One student commented that she preferred literature to social science.* *Una alumna comentó que prefería la literatura a las ciencias sociales.* **2** N-VAR A **comment** is a statement that you make or opinion that you give about something. comentario ❑ *He made his comments at a news conference.* *Hizo sus comentarios en una conferencia de prensa.* ❑ *There's been no comment so far from police.* *Hasta el momento no hay comentarios de la policía.*

**com|men|tary** /kɒmənteri/ (commentaries) **1** N-VAR A **commentary** is a description of an event that is broadcast on radio or television while the event is taking place. crónica ❑ *He turned on his car radio to listen to the commentary.* *Encendió el radio de su auto para escuchar la crónica.* **2** N-COUNT A **commentary** is an article or book which explains or discusses something. comentario ❑ *...a commentary on American society and culture.* *...un comentario sobre la sociedad y la cultura estadounidense.*

**com|men|ta|tor** /kɒmənteɪtər/ (commentators) **1** N-COUNT A **commentator** is a broadcaster who gives a commentary on an event. comentarista ❑ *...a sports commentator.* **2** N-COUNT A **commentator** is someone who often writes or broadcasts about a particular subject. comentarista ❑ *...a political commentator.* *...un comentarista de política.*

**Word Link** merc ≈ trading : commerce, merchandise, merchant

**com|merce** /kɒmɜrs/ N-UNCOUNT **Commerce** is the activities and procedures involved in buying and selling things. comercio ❑ *They made their fortunes from industry and commerce.* *Hicieron su fortuna en la industria y el comercio.*

**com|mer|cial** /kəmɜrʃᵊl/ (commercials) **1** ADJ **Commercial** means relating to the buying and selling of goods. comercial ❑ *...a major center of commercial activity.* *...un importante centro de actividad comercial.* **2** ADJ **Commercial** organizations and activities are concerned with making profits. comercial ❑ *The company has become more commercial over the past few years.* *La compañía se ha vuelto más comercial en los últimos años.* • **com|mer|cial|ly** ADV comercialmente ❑ *...a commercially successful movie.* *...una película que comercialmente ha sido un éxito.* **3** ADJ **Commercial** television and radio are paid for by advertising. comercial ❑ *...commercial radio stations.* *...estaciones de radio comercial.* **4** N-COUNT A **commercial** is an advertisement that is broadcast on television or radio. comercial ❑ *There are too many commercials.* *Hay demasiados comerciales.*

**com|mis|sion** /kəmɪʃᵊn/ (commissions, commissioning, commissioned) **1** V-T If you **commission** something or **commission** someone **to** do something, you formally arrange for someone to do a piece of work for you. encargarle (algo a alguien), comisionar ❑ *They have commissioned a study of the town's nightclubs.* *Encargaron un estudio de los clubs nocturnos de la ciudad.* ❑ *You can commission them to paint something especially for you.* *Puedes encargarles que pinten algo especialmente para ti.* • **Commission** is also a noun. encargo, comisión ❑ *He began making practical furniture by commission.* *Comenzó haciendo muebles prácticos por encargo.* **2** N-COUNT A **commission** is a piece of work that someone is asked to do and is paid for. encargo ❑ *Just a few days ago, I finished a commission.* *Hace unos días, terminé un encargo.* **3** N-VAR **Commission** is a sum of money paid to a salesperson for every sale that he or she makes. If a salesperson is paid **on commission**, the amount they receive depends on the amount they sell. comisión ❑ *The salespeople work on commission.* *Los vendedores trabajan por comisión.* **4** N-COUNT A **commission** is a group of people who have been appointed to find out about something or to control something. comisión ❑ *The government has set up a commission to look into those crimes.* *El gobierno ha creado una comisión para investigar esos crímenes.* **5** N-COUNT If a member of the armed forces receives a **commission**, he or she becomes an officer. nombramiento, cargo de oficial ❑ *He accepted a commission as a naval officer.* *Aceptó el nombramiento de oficial naval.*

**com|mis|sion|er** /kəmɪʃənər/ (commissioners) also **Commissioner** N-COUNT A **commissioner** is an important official in a government department or other organization. comisionado o comisionada ❑ *...Alaska's commissioner of education.* *...el comisionado de educación de Alaska.*

**com|mit** /kəmɪt/ (commits, committing, committed) **1** V-T If someone **commits** a crime or a sin, they do something illegal or bad. cometer ❑ *I have never committed any crime.* *Nunca he cometido un crimen.* **2** V-T If you **commit** money or resources **to** something, you decide to use them for a particular purpose. asignar ❑ *They called on Western nations to commit more money to the poorest nations.* *Hicieron un llamado a las naciones occidentales para que asignen más dinero a las naciones más pobres.* **3** V-T If you **commit yourself to** something, you accept it fully or say that you will definitely do it. comprometerse a ❑ *People should think carefully about committing*

C

themselves to working Sundays. *La gente debería pensar seriamente en comprometerse a trabajar los domingos.* **4** V-T If someone **is committed to** a mental hospital or prison, they are officially sent there. *internar* ❑ *Arthur was committed to the hospital.* *Arthur fue internado en el hospital.*

C

**com|mit|ment** /kəmɪtmənt/ (**commitments**) **1** N-UNCOUNT **Commitment** is a strong belief in an idea or system. *compromiso* ❑ *...his commitment to democracy.* *...su compromiso con la democracia.* **2** N-COUNT A **commitment** is a regular task that takes up some of your time. *responsabilidad* ❑ *I've got a lot of commitments.* *Tengo muchas responsabilidades.* **3** N-COUNT If you make a **commitment to** do something, you promise that you will do it. *compromiso* ❑ *We made a commitment to keep working together.* *Contrajimos el compromiso de seguir trabajando juntos.*

**Word Partnership** Usar *commitment* con:

| | |
|---|---|
| ADJ. | **deep/firm/strong** commitment **1** <br> **long-term** commitment, **prior** commitment **2** **3** |
| N. | ***someone's*** commitment **1** – **3** |
| PREP. | commitment **to** ***someone/something*** **1** **3** |
| V. | **make a** commitment **3** |

**com|mit|tee** /kəmɪti/ (**committees**) N-COUNT A **committee** is a group of people who meet to make decisions or plans for a larger group or organization that they represent. *comité* ❑ *...the school yearbook committee.* *...el comité para el anuario de la escuela.*

**com|mod|ity** /kəmɒdɪti/ (**commodities**) N-COUNT A **commodity** is something that is sold for money. *producto, artículo, mercancía* [BUSINESS] ❑ *...basic commodities like bread and meat.* *...productos básicos como pan y carne.*

**com|mon** /kɒmən/ (**commons**) **1** ADJ If something is **common,** it is found in large numbers or it happens often. *común* ❑ *His name was Hansen, a common name in Norway.* *Se llamaba Hansen, un nombre común en Noruega.* ❑ *Oil pollution is the most common cause of death for seabirds.* *La contaminación petrolífera es la causa de muerte más común de las aves marinas.* ● **com|mon|ly** ADV *comúnmente* ❑ *Parsley is one of the most commonly used herbs.* *El perejil es una de las hierbas que se utilizan más comúnmente.* **2** ADJ If something is **common to** two or more people or groups, it is done, possessed, or used by them all. *común* ❑ *The two groups share a common language.* *Los dos grupos comparten un lenguaje común.* **3** ADJ You can use **common** to describe knowledge, an opinion, or a feeling that is shared by people in general. *común* ❑ *It is common knowledge that swimming is one of the best forms of exercise.* *Todo el mundo sabe que nadar es una de las mejores formas de hacer ejercicio.* ● **com|mon|ly** ADV *comúnmente* ❑ *It was commonly believed that the Earth was just 6000 years old.* *Comúnmente se creía que la tierra tenía sólo 6000 años.* **4** N-COUNT A **common** is an area of grassy land, usually in or near a village or small town, where the public is allowed to go. *tierra comunal aledaña a una población* ❑ *We are warning women not to go out onto the common alone.* *Les estamos advirtiendo a las mujeres que no vayan solas afuera del pueblo.* **5** PHRASE If people or things have something **in common,** they have the same characteristics, features, or interests. *en común* ❑ *He had very little in common with his sister.* *Tenía muy poco en común con su hermana.*

**Thesaurus** *common* Ver también:

| | |
|---|---|
| ADJ. | frequent, typical, usual **1** <br> accepted, standard, universal **3** |

**Word Partnership** Usar *common* con:

| | |
|---|---|
| N. | common **belief,** common **language,** common **practice,** common **problem** **1** |
| ADV. | **fairly/increasingly/more/most** common **1** |
| V. | **have *something* in** common **5** |

**com|mon an|ces|tor** (**common ancestors**) N-COUNT The **common ancestor** of a group of human beings or animals is the individual who is an ancestor of all of them. *antepasado común*

**com|mon sense** also **commonsense** N-UNCOUNT Your **common sense** is your natural ability to make good judgments and to behave sensibly. *sentido común* ❑ *Use your common sense.* *Usa tu sentido común.*

**com|mon stock** N-UNCOUNT **Common stock** refers to the shares in a company that are owned by people who have a right to vote at the company's meetings and to receive part of the company's profits after the holders of preferred stock have been paid. *acciones ordinarias* [BUSINESS] ❑ *...2.7 million shares of common stock at 20 cents a share.* *...2.7 millones de acciones ordinarias a 20 centavos por acción.*

**com|mu|nal** /kəmyuːnᵊl/ **1** ADJ **Communal** means relating to particular groups in a country or society. *comunitario* ❑ *These groups developed strong communal ties.* *Estos grupos desarrollaron fuertes lazos comunitarios.* **2** ADJ You use **communal** to describe something that is shared by a group of people. *comunitario* ❑ *They ate in a communal dining room.* *Comieron en un comedor comunitario.*

**Word Link** *commun* ≈ *sharing* : *communicate, communism, community*

**com|mu|ni|cate** /kəmyuːnɪkeɪt/ (**communicates, communicating, communicated**) **1** V-RECIP If you **communicate with** someone, you share information, for example by speaking, writing, or sending radio signals. *comunicarse con* ❑ *They communicate with their friends by cellphone.* *Se comunican con sus amigos por celular.* ❑ *They use e-mail to communicate with each other.* *Utilizan el correo electrónico para comunicarse.* ● **com|mu|ni|ca|tion** /kəmyuːnɪkeɪʃᵊn/ N-UNCOUNT *comunicación* ❑ *There has been no direct communication with Moscow.* *No ha habido comunicación directa con Moscú.* ❑ *...communication between parents and teachers.* *...comunicación entre padres y maestros.* **2** V-RECIP If people are able to **communicate,** they are able to talk to each other openly, so that they understand each others feelings. *comunicarse* ❑ *We had to learn how to communicate with each other.* *Tuvimos que aprender a comunicarnos entre nosotros.* ● **com|mu|ni|ca|tion** N-UNCOUNT *comunicación* ❑ *There was a lack of communication between us.*

*Faltaba comunicación entre nosotros.* **3** V-T If you **communicate** an idea or a feeling **to** someone, you let them know about it. *comunicar* ❑ *They successfully communicate their knowledge to others. Comunican su conocimiento a otros con éxito.*

**com|mu|ni|ca|tion** /kəmyu̲nɪkeɪ̲ʃᵊn/ (**communications**) **1** N-PLURAL **Communications** are the systems and processes that are used to communicate or broadcast information. *comunicaciones* ❑ *...a communications satellite. ...un satélite de comunicaciones.* **2** N-COUNT A **communication** is a message. *comunicación* [FORMAL] ❑ *The ambassador has brought with him a communication from the president. El embajador ha traído consigo una comunicación del presidente.* **3** → see also **communicate**
→ see **brain, radio**

> **Word Link** *ism ≈ action or state : communism, optimism, tourism*

> **Word Link** *commun ≈ sharing : communicate, communism, community*

**com|mun|ism** /kɒ̲myənɪzəm/ also **Communism** N-UNCOUNT **Communism** is the political belief that all people are equal, that there should be no private ownership and that workers should control the means of producing things. *comunismo* ❑ *...the fight against communism. ...la lucha contra el comunismo.* ● **com|mun|ist** also **Communist** /kɒ̲myənɪst/ (**communists**) N-COUNT *comunista* ❑ *The communists seized power in 1947. Los comunistas tomaron el poder en 1947.* ADJ ❑ *...the Communist Party. ...el Partido Comunista.*

**com|mu|nity** /kəmyu̲nɪti/ (**communities**) **1** N-SING A **community** is a group of people who live in a particular area or are alike in some way. *comunidad* ❑ *He's well liked by people in the community. La gente de la comunidad lo quiere.* ❑ *...the black community. ...la comunidad negra.* **2** N-UNCOUNT **Community** is friendship between different people or groups, and a sense of having something in common. *comunidad* ❑ *...a neighborhood with no sense of community. ...un vecindario sin sentido de comunidad.* **3** N-COUNT A **community** is a group of plants and animals that live in the same region and interact with one another. *colonia*

> **Thesaurus** *community* Ver también:
> N. neighborhood, public, society **1**

**com|mu|nity col|lege** (**community colleges**) N-COUNT A **community college** is a local college where students from the surrounding area can take courses in practical or academic subjects. *escuela comunitaria*

**com|mu|nity ser|vice** **1** N-UNCOUNT **Community service** is unpaid work that criminals sometimes do as a punishment instead of being sent to prison. *servicio comunitario* ❑ *He was sentenced to 140 hours' community service. Fue sentenciado a 140 horas de servicio comunitario.* **2** N-UNCOUNT **Community service** is unpaid voluntary work that a person performs for the benefit of his or her local community. *trabajo comunitario* ❑ *I have been doing community service. He estado haciendo trabajo comunitario.*

**com|mute** /kəmyu̲t/ (**commutes, commuting, commuted**) V-I If you **commute**, you travel a long distance to work every day. *viajar todos los días (de la casa al trabajo)* ❑ *Mike commutes to Miami. Mike viaja todos los días a Miami.* ❑ *McLaren began commuting between Philadelphia and New York. McLaren empezó a viajar todos los días de Filadelfia a Nueva York.*
● **com|mut|er** (**commuters**) N-COUNT *persona que viaja a diario una distancia considerable de su casa al trabajo* ❑ *There are large numbers of commuters using our streets. Existe en nuestras calles un gran número de personas que viajan a diario para trabajar.*
→ see **traffic, transportation**

**comp** /kɒ̲mp/ (**comps, comping, comped**) **1** N-UNCOUNT **Comp** is short for **compensation**. *compensación, indemnización* [INFORMAL] ❑ *Workers' comp pays for work-related medical problems. Los pagos de indemnización a los trabajadores se hacen por problemas médicos relacionados con el trabajo.* **2** V-T If someone, or if a place such as a hotel or a restaurant **comps** you, they give you a room or a meal without charging you for it. *invitar* [INFORMAL] ❑ *I comped him his lunch. Le invité su comida.*

> **Word Link** *com ≈ with, together : combine, compact, companion*

**com|pact** /kəmpæ̲kt/ ADJ **Compact** things are small or take up very little space. *compacto* ❑ *...my compact office in Washington. ...mi oficina compacta en Washington.*

**com|pact bone** N-UNCOUNT **Compact bone** is very hard, dense bone that exists in the arms and legs and forms the outer layer of other bones. *hueso compacto* [MEDICAL]

**com|pact disc** (**compact discs**) also **compact disk** N-COUNT **Compact discs** are small shiny discs that contain music or computer information. The abbreviation **CD** is also used. *disco compacto*

**com|pact|ed** /kəmpæ̲ktɪd/ ADJ **Compacted** rock is rock that is formed when layers of material such as clay or sand press against each other over a long period of time. *compactado*

**com|pan|ion** /kəmpæ̲nyən/ (**companions**) N-COUNT A **companion** is someone who you spend time with or who you are traveling with. *compañero o compañera* ❑ *Her traveling companion was a middle-aged man. Su compañero de viaje era un hombre de mediana edad.*
→ see **pet**

**com|pa|ny** /kʌ̲mpəni/ (**companies**) **1** N-COUNT A **company** is a business organization that makes money by selling goods or services. *compañía* ❑ *...an insurance company. ...una compañía de seguros.* **2** N-COUNT A **company** is a group of opera singers, dancers, or actors who work together. *compañía* ❑ *...the Phoenix Dance Company. ...la Compañía de Danza de Phoenix.* **3** N-UNCOUNT **Company** is having another person or other people with you. *compañía* ❑ *"I won't stay long."—"No, please do stay. I need the company." —No me quedaré por mucho tiempo. —No, por favor quédate. Necesito la compañía.* **4** PHRASE If you **keep** someone **company**, you spend time with them and stop them from feeling lonely or bored. *acompañar*

❑ *Why don't you stay here and keep Emma company? ¿Por qué no te quedas aquí y le haces compañía a Emma?*
→ see **electricity**

| **Word Partnership** | Usar *company* con: |
|---|---|
| ADJ. | **foreign** company, **parent** company 1 |
| V. | **buy/own/sell/start a** company, company **employs**, company **makes** 1 **have** company, **keep** company, **part** company 4 |

**com|pa|rable** /kɒmpərəbᵊl/ 1 ADJ Something that is **comparable** to something else is roughly similar, for example in amount or importance. *comparable, equiparable* ❑ *Farmers' incomes should be comparable to those of townspeople. Los ingresos de los granjeros deberían ser comparables a los de aquéllos de la ciudad.* 2 ADJ If two or more things are **comparable,** they are similar and so they can reasonably be compared. *comparable, equiparable* ❑ *In comparable countries wages increased much more rapidly. En países comparables los salarios incrementaron mucho más rápido.*

**com|para|tive** /kəmpærətɪv/ (**comparatives**) 1 ADJ You use **comparative** to show that you are judging something against a previous or different situation. *relativo* ❑ *...a life of comparative ease. ...una vida de relativa facilidad.* • **com|para|tive|ly** ADV *relativamente* ❑ *...a comparatively small nation. ...una nación relativamente pequeña.* 2 ADJ A **comparative** study is a study that involves the comparison of two or more things of the same kind. *comparativo* ❑ *...a comparative study of the two writers. ...un estudio comparativo de ambos escritores.* 3 ADJ In grammar, the **comparative** form of an adjective or adverb shows that something has more of a quality than something else has. For example, "bigger" is the comparative form of "big." *comparativo* • **Comparative** is also a noun. *comparativo* ❑ *The comparative of "pretty" is "prettier." El comparativo de "pretty" es "prettier."*

| **Word Link** | ***par** ≈ equal : com**pare**, **par**t, **par**tner* |
|---|---|

**com|pare** /kəmpɛər/ (**compares, comparing, compared**) 1 V-T When you **compare** things, you consider them and discover the differences or similarities between them. *comparar* ❑ *Compare the two illustrations in Figure 60. Comparen las dos ilustraciones de la Figura 60.* ❑ *You can't compare my situation with hers. No puedes comparar mi situación con la suya.* 2 V-T If you **compare** one person or thing **to** another, you say that they are like the other person or thing. *comparar* ❑ *Some critics compared his work to that of James Joyce. Algunos críticos compararon su obra con la de James Joyce.* 3 → see also **compared**

| **Thesaurus** | *compare* Ver también: |
|---|---|
| V. | analyze, consider, contrast, examine 1 equate, match 2 |

**com|pared** /kəmpɛərd/ PHRASE If you say, for example, that one thing is large or small **compared with** another or **compared to** another, you mean that it is larger or smaller than the other thing. *comparado con* ❑ *Your bag is light compared to mine. Tu bolsa es ligera comparada con la mía.*

**com|pari|son** /kəmpærɪsən/ (**comparisons**) 1 N-VAR When you make a **comparison,** you consider two or more things and discover the differences between them. *comparación* ❑ *...a comparison of the two teams' performances this year. ...una comparación de la actuación de ambos equipos este año.* 2 N-COUNT When you make a **comparison,** you say that one thing is like another in some way. *comparación* ❑ *...the comparison of her life to a journey. ...la comparación de su vida con un viaje.*

**com|part|ment** /kəmpɑrtmənt/ (**compartments**) 1 N-COUNT A **compartment** is one of the separate parts of an object that is used for keeping things in. *compartimento* ❑ *The fire started in the baggage compartment. El fuego empezó en el compartimento del equipaje.* 2 N-COUNT A **compartment** is one of the separate spaces into which a railroad car is divided. *compartimento* ❑ *...a first-class compartment. ...un compartimento de primera clase.*

**com|pass** /kʌmpəs/ (**compasses**) N-COUNT A **compass** is an instrument that you use for finding directions. It has a dial and a magnetic needle that always points to the north. *brújula* ❑ *We had to use a compass to get here. Tuvimos que usar una brújula para llegar aquí.*
→ see **magnet, navigation**

compass

**com|pas|sion** /kəmpæʃᵊn/ N-UNCOUNT **Compassion** is a feeling of pity, sympathy, and understanding for someone who is suffering. *compasión* ❑ *Elderly people need compassion from their doctors. La gente mayor necesita la compasión de sus doctores.*

**com|pat|ible** /kəmpætɪbᵊl/ 1 ADJ If things, systems, or ideas are **compatible,** they work well together or can exist together successfully. *compatible* ❑ *He argues that religious beliefs are compatible with modern society. Sostiene que las creencias religiosas son compatibles con la sociedad moderna.* • **com|pat|ibil|ity** /kəmpætɪbɪlɪti/ N-UNCOUNT *compatibilidad* ❑ *...Islam and its compatibility with democracy. ...el Islam y su compatibilidad con la democracia.* 2 ADJ If you are **compatible** with someone, you have a good relationship with them because you have similar opinions and interests. *compatible* ❑ *Millie and I are very compatible. Millie y yo somos muy compatibles.* • **com|pat|ibil|ity** N-UNCOUNT *compatibilidad* ❑ *The basis of friendship is compatibility. La base de la amistad es la compatibilidad.*

| **Word Link** | ***pel** ≈ driving, forcing : com**pel**, ex**pel**, pro**pel**ler* |
|---|---|

**com|pel** /kəmpɛl/ (**compels, compelling, compelled**) V-T If a situation, a rule, or a person **compels** you **to** do something, they force you to do it. *obligar a, forzar a* ❑ *...a law to compel cyclists to wear a helmet. ...una ley que obliga a los ciclistas a usar casco.*

**com|pel|ling** /kəmpɛlɪŋ/ ADJ A **compelling**

argument or reason is one that convinces you that something is true or that something should be done. *convincente, persuasivo* ❑ *...a compelling reason to spend money. ...una razón convincente para gastar dinero.*

**com|pen|sate** /kɒmpənseɪt/ (**compensates, compensating, compensated**) **1** V-T To **compensate** someone **for** money or things that they have lost means to pay them money or give them something to replace those things. *indemnizar, compensar* ❑ *Some say that the government should compensate farmers for their losses. Algunos dicen que el gobierno debería indemnizar a los agricultores por sus pérdidas.* **2** V-I To **compensate for** something, especially something harmful or unwanted, means to do something which balances it or reduces its effects. *compensar, resarcir* ❑ *Her sense of humor and friendliness compensate for her lack of experience. Su sentido del humor y su simpatía compensan su falta de experiencia.*

**com|pen|sa|tion** /kɒmpənseɪʃən/ (**compensations**) **1** N-UNCOUNT **Compensation** is money that someone who has experienced loss or suffering claims from the person or organization responsible. *indemnización* ❑ *They want $20,000 in compensation. Quieren una indemnización de $20,000.* **2** N-VAR If something is a **compensation**, it reduces the effects of something bad that has happened. *compensación* ❑ *Age does have some compensations. La edad tiene algunas compensaciones.*

**com|pete** /kəmpit/ (**competes, competing, competed**) **1** V-RECIP When one firm or country **competes with** another **for** something, it tries to get that thing for themselves and stop the other from getting it. *competir (con alguien por algo)* ❑ *Hardware stores are competing for business. Las ferreterías están compitiendo por el negocio.* ❑ *Books compete with TV and movies for teenagers' attention. Los libros compiten con la televisión y el cine por la atención de los adolescentes.* **2** V-I If you **compete** in a contest or a game, you take part in it. *competir* ❑ *He will be competing in the 100 meter race. Competirá en la carrera de los 100 metros planos.*

**com|pe|tence** /kɒmpɪtəns/ N-UNCOUNT **Competence** is the ability to do something well or effectively. *competencia, capacidad* ❑ *No one doubts his competence. Nadie duda de su capacidad.*

**com|pe|tent** /kɒmpɪtənt/ ADJ Someone who is **competent** is efficient and effective. *competente* ❑ *He was a very competent salesman. Era un vendedor muy competente.* • **com|pe|tent|ly** ADV *competentemente* ❑ *The government performed competently. El gobierno actuó competentemente.*

**com|pe|ti|tion** /kɒmpɪtɪʃən/ (**competitions**) **1** N-UNCOUNT **Competition** is a situation in which two or more people or groups are trying to get something which not everyone can have. *competencia* ❑ *There's been a lot of competition for the prize. Ha habido mucha competencia por el premio.* **2** N-VAR A **competition** is an event in which many people take part in order to find out who is best at a particular activity. *competencia* ❑ *...a surfing competition. ...una competencia de surf.*

**com|peti|tive** /kəmpɛtɪtɪv/ **1** ADJ **Competitive** situations or activities are ones in which people or companies compete with each other. *competitivo* ❑ *Japan is a highly competitive market system. Japón es un sistema de mercado altamente competitivo.* • **com|peti|tive|ly** ADV *competitivamente* ❑ *He's now skiing competitively again. Ahora está esquiando competitivamente otra vez.* **2** ADJ A **competitive** person is eager to be more successful than other people. *competitivo* ❑ *He has always been very competitive. Siempre ha sido muy competitivo.* • **com|peti|tive|ly** ADV *competitivamente* ❑ *People do better when they work in teams than when they work competitively. La gente trabaja mejor en equipo que cuando lo hace competitivamente.* • **com|peti|tive|ness** N-UNCOUNT *competitividad* ❑ *I can't stand the competitiveness. No soporto la competitividad.* **3** ADJ Goods or services that are **competitive** are likely to be bought because they are less expensive than other goods of the same quality. *competitivo* ❑ *...homes for sale at competitive prices. ...casas en venta a precios competitivos.* • **com|peti|tive|ly** ADV *competitivamente* ❑ *...a competitively priced product. ...un producto a precio competitivo.* • **com|peti|tive|ness** N-UNCOUNT *competitividad* ❑ *...the competitiveness of the U.S. economy. ...la competitividad de la economía de EE.UU.*

**Word Partnership** Usar *competitive* con:

| | |
|---|---|
| N. | competitive **sport** 1<br>competitive **advantage** 1 3<br>competitive **person** 2 |
| ADV. | **fiercely** competitive, **highly** competitive, **more** competitive 1 2 |

**com|peti|tor** /kəmpɛtɪtər/ (**competitors**) **1** N-COUNT A company's **competitors** are companies that are trying to sell similar goods or services to the same people. *competidor* ❑ *The bank isn't performing as well as some of its competitors. El banco no está trabajando tan bien como algunos de sus competidores.* **2** N-COUNT A **competitor** is a person who takes part in a competition or contest. *concursante, participante* ❑ *One of the oldest competitors won the silver medal. Uno de los concursantes de más edad ganó la medalla de plata.*

**com|pile** /kəmpaɪl/ (**compiles, compiling, compiled**) V-T When you **compile** something such as a report, book, or program, you produce it by collecting and putting together many pieces of information. *compilar* ❑ *The book took 10 years to compile. Llevó 10 años compilar el libro.*

**com|plain** /kəmpleɪn/ (**complains, complaining, complained**) **1** V-T/V-I If you **complain about** something, you say that you are not satisfied with it. *quejarse (de)* ❑ *Voters complained that the government did not fulfill its promises. Los votantes se quejaron de que el gobierno no cumplió sus promesas.* ❑ *The couple complained about the high cost of visiting Europe. La pareja se quejó de lo caro que es visitar Europa.* ❑ *I shouldn't complain, I've got a good job. No debería de quejarme, tengo un buen trabajo.* ❑ *"I wish someone would do something about it," he complained. —Me gustaría que alguien hiciera algo al respecto —se quejó.* **2** V-I If you **complain of** pain or illness, you say that you are feeling pain or feeling ill. *quejarse de* ❑ *He complained of a headache. Se quejó de un dolor de cabeza.*

**com|plaint** /kəmpleɪnt/ (**complaints**) **1** N-VAR A **complaint** is a statement of dissatisfaction

C

or a reason for it. *queja* ❑ *...complaints about the standard of service. ...quejas por la calidad del servicio.* **2** N-COUNT A **complaint** is an illness. *afección* ❑ *...a common skin complaint. ...una afección común de la piel.*

C

**Word Link** *ple ≈ filling : complement, complete, deplete*

**com|ple|ment** (**complements, complementing, complemented**)

The verb is pronounced /kɒmplɪmɛnt/. The noun is pronounced /kɒmplɪmənt/.

**1** V-T If people or things **complement** each other, they have different qualities that go together well. *complementar* ❑ *There will be a written examination to complement the listening test. Habrá un examen escrito para complementar la prueba de comprensión auditiva.* **2** N-COUNT Something that is a **complement to** something else complements it. *complemento* ❑ *Our sauces are the perfect complement to your favorite dishes. Nuestras salsas son el complemento perfecto para su comida favorita.* **3** N-COUNT In grammar, the **complement** of a link verb is an adjective group or noun group which comes after the verb and describes or identifies the subject. For example, in the sentence "They felt very tired," "very tired" is the complement. In "They were students," "students" is the complement. *complemento, atributo* [TECHNICAL]

**com|plete** /kəmplit/ (**completes, completing, completed**) **1** ADJ You use **complete** to emphasize that something is as great in extent, degree, or amount as it possibly can be. *completo, total, absoluto* ❑ *The house is a complete mess. La casa es un completo desastre.* ❑ *His resignation came as a complete surprise. Su renuncia fue una absoluta sorpresa.* ● **com|plete|ly** ADV *completamente, totalmente* ❑ *Dozens of homes have been completely destroyed. Docenas de hogares han sido completamente destruidos.* **2** ADJ If something is **complete,** it contains all the parts that it should contain. *completo* ❑ *The list may not be complete. Puede ser que la lista no esté completa.* ❑ *...a complete set of novels by Henry James. ...la serie completa de las novelas de Henry James.* **3** ADJ If something is **complete,** it has been finished. *terminado, concluido* ❑ *The repairs to the house are complete. Las reparaciones de la casa están terminadas.* **4** V-T To **complete** a set or group means to provide the last item that is needed to make it a full set or group. *completar* ❑ *Children don't complete their set of 20 baby teeth until they are two to three years old. Los niños no completan sus 20 dientes de leche sino hasta que tienen dos o tres años.* **5** V-T If you **complete** something, you finish doing, making, or producing it. *acabar, terminar* ❑ *Peter Mayle has just completed his first novel. Peter Mayle ha terminado su primera novela.* ● **com|ple|tion** /kəmpliʃᵊn/ (**completions**) N-VAR *terminación, finalización* ❑ *The project is nearing completion. El proyecto está cerca de su terminación.* **6** V-T To **complete** a form means to write the necessary information on it. *llenar, rellenar* ❑ *Complete part 1 of the application. Llenen la parte 1 de la solicitud.* **7** PHRASE If one thing comes **complete with** another, it has that thing as an additional part. *incluir* ❑ *The diary comes complete with a gold pen. El diario incluye una pluma de oro.*

**Thesaurus** *complete* Ver también:
ADJ. total, utter **1**
entire, whole; (*ant.*) partial **2**

**com|plex** (**complexes**)

The adjective is pronounced /kəmplɛks/ or sometimes /kɒmplɛks/. The noun is pronounced /kɒmplɛks/.

**1** ADJ Something that is **complex** has many different parts, and is difficult to understand. *complejo* ❑ *...a complex system of voting. ...un complejo sistema de votación.* **2** N-COUNT A **complex** is a group of buildings used for a particular purpose. *complejo* ❑ *...a low-cost apartment complex. ...un complejo habitacional de bajo costo.*

**com|plex|ion** /kəmplɛkʃᵊn/ (**complexions**) N-COUNT Your **complexion** is the natural color or condition of the skin on your face. *tez* ❑ *She had a pale complexion. Tenía una tez pálida.*
→ see **makeup**

**com|plex|ity** /kəmplɛksɪti/ N-VAR **Complexity** is the state of having many different parts connected or related to each other in a complicated way. *complejidad* ❑ *...the complexity of the problem. ...la complejidad del problema.* ❑ *...the legal complexities of the issue. ...las complejidades legales del asunto.*

**com|plex num|ber** (**complex numbers**) N-COUNT **Complex numbers** are numbers of the form a+bi, where a and b are real numbers and i is the square root of -1. *números complejos* [TECHNICAL]

**Word Link** *ate ≈ causing to be : complicate, humiliate, motivate*

**com|pli|cate** /kɒmplɪkeɪt/ (**complicates, complicating, complicated**) V-T To **complicate** something means to make it more difficult to understand or deal with. *complicar* ❑ *This would only complicate the task. Esto sólo complicaría la tarea.*

**com|pli|cat|ed** /kɒmplɪkeɪtɪd/ ADJ Something that is **complicated** has many parts and is therefore difficult to understand. *complicado* ❑ *The situation is very complicated. La situación es muy complicada.*

**com|pli|ca|tion** /kɒmplɪkeɪʃᵊn/ (**complications**) N-COUNT A **complication** is a problem or difficulty. *complicación* ❑ *There were a number of complications. Hubo algunas complicaciones.*

**com|pli|ment** (**compliments, complimenting, complimented**)

The verb is pronounced /kɒmplɪmɛnt/. The noun is pronounced /kɒmplɪmənt/.

**1** N-COUNT A **compliment** is something nice that you say to someone about them. *cumplido* ❑ *You can do no harm by giving a compliment. No dañas a nadie haciendo un cumplido.* **2** V-T If you **compliment** someone, you give them a compliment. *elogiar* ❑ *They complimented me on the way I looked. Me felicitaron por cómo me veía.*

**Usage** **compliment**

*Compliment* and *complement* are easily confused. *Compliment* means to say something nice to or about someone. *Jack complimented Rita on her pronunciation.* *Complement* means to go well together or to make something good seem even better. *The wine complemented the meal.*

**com|pli|men|tary** /kɒmplɪmɛntəri, -mɛntri/ **1** ADJ If you are **complimentary** about something, you express admiration for it. elogioso ❑ *They have been very complimentary.* *Han sido muy elogiosos.* **2** ADJ A **complimentary** seat, ticket, or book is given to you free. de obsequio ❑ *He had complimentary tickets to see the movie.* *Tenía boletos de obsequio para ver la película.*

**com|ply** /kəmplaɪ/ (**complies, complying, complied**) V-I If you **comply with** a demand or rule, you do what is required. cumplir ❑ *Our changes comply with the new law.* *Nuestros cambios cumplen con la nueva ley.*

**com|po|nent** /kəmpoʊnənt/ (**components**) N-COUNT The **components** of something are its parts. componente ❑ *The plan has four main components.* *El plan tiene cuatro componentes principales.*

**Word Partnership** Usar *component* con:

ADJ. **key** component, **main** components, **separate** components
N. component **parts**

**com|pose** /kəmpoʊz/ (**composes, composing, composed**) **1** V-T The things that something **is composed of** are its parts or members. The separate things that **compose** something are the parts or members that form it. componer ❑ *The band is composed of police officers from all over the county.* *La banda está compuesta de policías de todo el condado.* ❑ *...the cells that compose muscles.* *...las células que componen los músculos.* **2** V-T/V-I When someone **composes** a piece of music, a speech, or a letter, they write it. componer ❑ *Vivaldi composed a large number of concertos.* *Vivaldi compuso un gran número de conciertos.* ❑ *I'd like more time to play the piano and compose.* *Quisiera tener más tiempo para tocar el piano y componer.*
→ see **music**

**com|pos|er** /kəmpoʊzər/ (**composers**) N-COUNT A **composer** is a person who writes music, especially classical music. compositor o compositora ❑ *...Mozart, Beethoven, and other great composers.* *...Mozart, Beethoven y otros grandes compositores.*
→ see **music**

**com|po|site** /kəmpɒzɪt/ (**composites**) ADJ A **composite** object or item is made up of several different things, parts, or substances. compuesto ❑ *...skis made from layers of different composite materials.* *...esquís hechos de capas de diferentes materiales compuestos.* ● **Composite** is also a noun. amalgama ❑ *The book is a composite of two real-life stories.* *El libro es una amalgama de dos historias reales.*

**com|pos|ite vol|ca|no** (**composite volcanoes**) N-COUNT A **composite volcano** is a volcano with steep sides composed of layers of lava and rock. estratovolcán, volcán cónico [TECHNICAL]

**com|po|si|tion** /kɒmpəzɪʃən/ (**compositions**) **1** N-UNCOUNT The **composition** of something is the things that it consists of and the way that they are arranged. composición, mezcla ❑ *...the composition of the audience.* *...la mezcla del público.* **2** N-COUNT A composer's **compositions** are the pieces of music that he or she has written. composición ❑ *Mozart's compositions are among the world's greatest.* *Las composiciones de Mozart están entre las mejores del mundo.* **3** N-COUNT A **composition** is a piece of written work that children do at school. composición ❑ *We had to write a composition on the subject "My Pet."* *Tuvimos que redactar una composición sobre "Mi mascota".* **4** N-UNCOUNT **Composition** is the technique or skill involved in composing something such as a piece of music or a poem. composición
→ see **orchestra**

**com|post** /kɒmpoʊst/ N-UNCOUNT **Compost** is a mixture of decayed plants that is used to improve soil. composta ❑ *...a small compost pile.* *...un montoncito de composta.*
→ see **dump**

**com|pound** /kɒmpaʊnd/ (**compounds, compounding, compounded**)

The noun is pronounced /kɒmpaʊnd/. The verb is pronounced /kəmpaʊnd/.

**1** N-COUNT A **compound** is an enclosed area of land that is used for a particular purpose. complejo ❑ *...a military compound.* *...un complejo militar.* **2** N-COUNT In chemistry, a **compound** is a substance that consists of two or more elements. compuesto ❑ *...a chemical compound consisting of two different elements.* *...un compuesto químico que consiste de dos elementos diferentes.* **3** V-T To **compound** a problem means to make it worse by adding to it. agravar ❑ *Additional loss of life will only compound the tragedy.* *La pérdida adicional de vidas sólo agravará la tragedia.* ❑ *The problem is compounded by the medical system here.* *El problema se agrava dado el sistema médico de aquí.* **4** ADJ In grammar, a **compound** noun, adjective, or verb is one that is made up of two or more words, for example "fire truck." compuesto **5** ADJ In grammar, a **compound** sentence is one that is made up of two or more main clauses. oración compuesta [TECHNICAL]
→ see **element, rock**

**com|pound eye** (**compound eyes**) N-COUNT A **compound eye** is a type of eye found in some creatures that is made up of many identical elements that work together. ojo compuesto

**com|pound light micro|scope** (**compound light microscopes**) N-COUNT A **compound light microscope** is a microscope that uses glass lenses and light to produce an image. microscopio compuesto

**com|pound ma|chine** (**compound machines**) N-COUNT A **compound machine** is a machine that consists of two or more smaller machines working together. Compare **simple machine.** máquina compuesta

**com|pound me|ter** (**compound meters**) N-VAR In a piece of music written in **compound meter,** the beat is divided into three parts. compás compuesto [TECHNICAL]

**com|pre|hen|sion** /kɒmprɪhɛnʃən/

**Picture Dictionary** computer

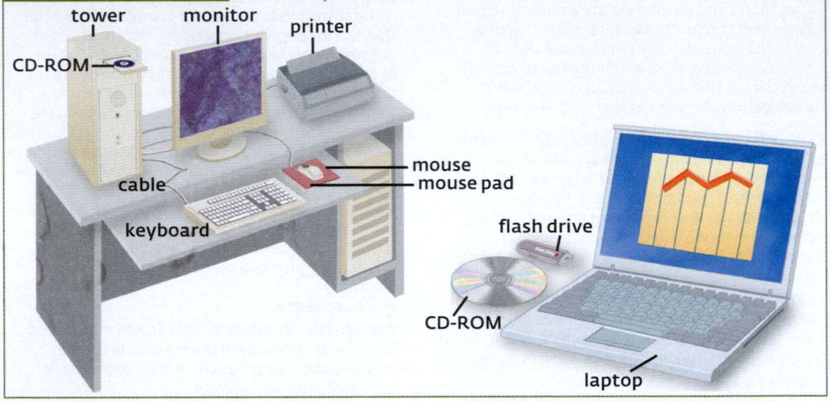


(**comprehensions**) N-UNCOUNT **Comprehension** is the ability to understand something or the process of understanding something. *comprensión* [FORMAL] ❑ *This was completely beyond her comprehension. Esto iba más allá de su comprensión.*

**com|pre|hen|sive** /kɒmprɪhɛnsɪv/ ADJ Something that is **comprehensive** includes everything that is needed or relevant. *exhaustivo* ❑ *...a comprehensive guide to the region. ...una guía exhaustiva de la región.* ● **com|pre|hen|sive|ly** /kɒmprɪhɛnsɪvli/ ADV *exhaustivamente* ❑ *The book is comprehensively illustrated. El libro está ilustrado exhaustivamente.*

**com|prise** /kəmpraɪz/ (**comprises, comprising, comprised**) V-T If something **comprises** or **is comprised of** a number of things or people, it has them as its parts or members. *constar* [FORMAL] ❑ *The exhibit comprises 50 paintings. La exhibición consta de 50 pinturas.* ❑ *American society is comprised of people from many different backgrounds. La sociedad estadounidense consta de gente de muchas nacionalidades diferentes.*

**com|pro|mise** /kɒmprəmaɪz/ (**compromises, compromising, compromised**) **1** N-VAR A **compromise** is a situation in which people accept something slightly different from what they really want. *arreglo* ❑ *Try to reach a compromise between what he wants and what you want. Trata de llegar a un arreglo entre lo que él quiere y lo que tú quieres.* **2** V-RECIP If you **compromise with** someone, you reach an agreement with them in which you both give up something that you originally wanted. *llegar a un arreglo* ❑ *The government has compromised with its critics. El gobierno ha llegado a un arreglo con sus críticos.* ❑ *"Nine," I said. "Nine thirty," he replied. We compromised on 9:15. —Nueve —dije yo. —Nueve y media —respondió. Llegamos a un arreglo: a las 9:15.* **3** V-T If someone **compromises** themselves or their beliefs, they do something which damages their reputation for honesty, loyalty, or high moral principles. *comprometer* ❑ *He would never compromise his principles. Nunca comprometería sus principios.*

**comp time** N-UNCOUNT **Comp time** is time off that an employer gives to an employee because the employee has worked overtime. **Comp time** is short for "compensation time." *Tiempo libre dado a los empleados en compensación por horas extras trabajadas.* ❑ *Comp time is often promised to firefighters and police officers. A los bomberos y policías, seguido se les promete tiempo libre en compensación por las horas trabajadas.*

**Word Link** *puls ≈ driving, pushing : compulsory, expulsion, impulse*

**com|pul|so|ry** /kəmpʌlsəri/ ADJ If something is **compulsory**, you must do it because a law or someone in authority says you must. *obligatorio* ❑ *In East Germany learning Russian was compulsory. En Alemania Oriental era obligatorio aprender ruso.*

**Word Link** *put ≈ thinking : computer, dispute, reputation*

**com|put|er** /kəmpyutər/ (**computers**) **1** N-COUNT A **computer** is an electronic machine that can store and deal with large amounts of information. *computadora, ordenador* ❑ *The data are then fed into a computer. Los datos son entonces capturados en la computadora.* ❑ *The company installed a $650,000 computer system. La empresa instaló un sistema de computadoras de 650,000 dólares.* **2** → see also **personal computer**
→ see Picture Dictionary: **computer**
→ see **office**

**com|put|er|ize** /kəmpyutəraɪz/ (**computerizes, computerizing, computerized**) V-T To **computerize** a system or type of work means to arrange for a lot of the work to be done by computer. *computarizar* ❑ *I'm trying to computerize everything. Estoy tratando de computarizar todo.* ● **com|put|er|ized** /kəmpyutəraɪzd/ ADJ ❑ *...a computerized system. ...un sistema computarizado.*

**com|pu|ting** /kəmpyutɪŋ/ N-UNCOUNT **Computing** is the activity of using a computer and writing programs for it. *computación* ❑ *Courses range from cooking to computing. Los cursos van desde cocina hasta computación.*

**con** /kɒn/ (**cons, conning, conned**) **1** V-T If someone **cons** you, they persuade you to do something or believe something by telling you things that are not true. *estafar, timar* [INFORMAL] ❑ *He claimed that the businessman conned him of $10,000. Afirmaba que el hombre de negocios le había timado 10,000 dólares.* ❑ *White conned his way into a job. White consiguió engatusarlos para tener el trabajo.* **2** N-COUNT A **con** is a trick in which someone deceives you by telling you something that is not true. *estafa* [INFORMAL] ❑ *It was all a con. Todo era una estafa.* **3** **pros and cons** → see **pro**

**con|cave** /kɒnkeɪv, kɒnkeɪv/ ADJ A surface that is **concave** curves inward in the middle. *cóncavo* ❑ *He has a concave stomach. Su estómago es cóncavo* → see **telescope**

**con|cave lens** (**concave lenses**) N-COUNT A **concave lens** is a lens that is thinner in the middle than at the edges. Compare **convex lens.** *lente cóncavo*

**con|ceal** /kənsil/ (**conceals, concealing, concealed**) V-T To **conceal** something means to hide it or keep it secret. *ocultar* ❑ *The hat concealed her hair. El sombrero ocultaba su cabello.* ❑ *Robert could not conceal his happiness. Robert no podía ocultar su felicidad.* • **con|ceal|ment** /kənsilmənt/ N-UNCOUNT *ocultamiento* ❑ *...the concealment of his true identity. ...el ocultamiento de su verdadera identidad.*

**con|cede** /kənsid/ (**concedes, conceding, conceded**) V-T If you **concede** something, you admit, often unwillingly, that it is true or correct. *reconocer* ❑ *Bess finally conceded that Nancy was right. Bess reconoció finalmente que Nancy tenía razón.* ❑ *"Well," he conceded, "there have been a few problems." —Bueno —reconoció—, ha habido algunos problemas.*

**con|ceive** /kənsiv/ (**conceives, conceiving, conceived**) **1** V-T/V-I If you cannot **conceive of** something, you cannot imagine it or believe it. *concebir* ❑ *I can't even conceive of that quantity of money. No puedo ni concebir tal cantidad de dinero.* ❑ *We could not conceive that he might soon be dead. No podíamos concebir que tal vez pronto estaría muerto.* **2** V-T If you **conceive** a plan or idea, you think of it and work out how it can be done. *concebir* ❑ *She conceived the idea of a series of novels. Concibió la idea de una serie de novelas.* **3** V-T/V-I When a woman **conceives,** she becomes pregnant. *concebir* ❑ *...women who want to conceive. ...mujeres que quieren concebir.* ❑ *...peoople trying to conceive a child. ...gente que trata de concebir un hijo.* • **con|cep|tion** /kənsɛpʃᵊn/ N-VAR (**conceptions**) *concepción* ❑ *Six weeks after conception your baby is the size of your little fingernail. Seis semanas después de la concepción, su bebé es del tamaño de la uña de tu dedo pequeño.*

**con|cen|trate** /kɒnsᵊntreɪt/ (**concentrates, concentrating, concentrated**) **1** V-I If you **concentrate on** something, you give it all your attention. *concentrarse en* ❑ *He should concentrate on his studies. Debería concentrarse en sus estudios.* ❑ *At work you need to be able to concentrate. Necesitas poder concentrarte en el trabajo.* **2** V-T If something **is concentrated in** one place, it is all there rather than being spread around. *concentrar* ❑ *Italy's industrial cities are concentrated in the north. Las ciudades industriales en Italia se concentran en el norte.*

**con|cen|trat|ed** /kɒnsᵊntreɪtɪd/ **1** ADJ A **concentrated** liquid has been increased in strength by having water removed from it. *concentrado* ❑ *...concentrated apple juice. ...jugo de manzana concentrado.* **2** ADJ A **concentrated** activity is done with great intensity in one place. *intenso* ❑ *...a concentrated effort to control his temper. ...un intenso esfuerzo por controlar su carácter.*

**con|cen|tra|tion** /kɒnsᵊntreɪʃᵊn/ (**concentrations**) **1** N-UNCOUNT **Concentration** on something involves giving all your attention to it. *concentración* ❑ *Neal kept talking, breaking my concentration. Neal no dejaba de hablar y yo no podía concentrarme.* **2** N-VAR A **concentration of** something is a large amount of it or large numbers of it in a small area. *concentración* ❑ *The area has one of the world's greatest concentrations of wildlife. El área tiene una de las concentraciónes más grandes de vida silvestre.* **3** N-VAR The **concentration of** a substance is the proportion of essential ingredients or substances in it. *concentración*

**con|cept** /kɒnsɛpt/ (**concepts**) N-COUNT A **concept** is an idea or abstract principle. *concepto* ❑ *...the concept of human rights. ...el concepto de los derechos humanos.* • **con|cep|tual** /kənsɛptʃuəl/ ADJ *conceptual* ❑ *...difficult conceptual problems. ...problemas conceptuales difíciles.*

**con|cep|tion** /kənsɛpʃᵊn/ (**conceptions**) **1** N-VAR A **conception of** something is an idea that you have of it in your mind. *noción* ❑ *...my conception of a garden. ...mi idea de un jardín.* **2** → see also **conceive**

**con|cern** /kənsɜrn/ (**concerns, concerning, concerned**) **1** N-UNCOUNT **Concern** is worry about a situation. *inquietud, preocupación* ❑ *There is no cause for concern. No hay por qué inquietarse.* **2** V-T If something **concerns** you, it worries you. *inquietar* ❑ *It concerns me that we're not being told about this. Me inquieta que no se nos comunique esto.* • **con|cerned** ADJ *inquieto* ❑ *I've been concerned about you lately. He estado inquieto por ti últimamente.* **3** V-T If you **concern yourself with** something, you give it attention because you think that it is important. *interesarse por* ❑ *I didn't concern myself with politics. No me interesaba por la política.* **4** V-T If a book or a piece of information **concerns** a particular subject, it is about that subject. *tratar de* ❑ *The book concerns Sandy's two children. El libro se trata de los dos niños de Sandy.* • **con|cerned** ADJ *tratar sobre* ❑ *Randolph's work is concerned with the effects of pollution. El trabajo de Randolph trata sobre los efectos de la contaminación.* **5** V-T If a situation, event, or activity **concerns** you, it affects or involves you. *concernir* ❑ *It doesn't concern you at all. No te concierne en absoluto.* • **con|cerned** ADJ *involucrado* ❑ *It's a very stressful situation for everyone concerned. Es una situación muy estresante para todos los involucrados.* **6** N-COUNT A **concern** is a fact or situation that worries you. *inquietud* ❑ *His concern was that people would know that he was responsible. Su inquietud era que la gente sabría que él era responsable.* **7** N-COUNT A **concern** is a company or business. *negocio* [FORMAL, BUSINESS] ❑ *The Minos Beach Hotel is a family concern. El Hotel Minos Beach es un negocio familiar.* **8** N-VAR **Concern for** someone is a feeling that you want them to be happy, safe, and well. *interés* ❑ *Without her care and concern, he had no chance at all. Sin los cuidados e interés de ella, él no tenía ninguna oportunidad.* **9** N-SING If a situation or problem

C

C

is your **concern,** it is your duty or responsibility. *asunto* ❑ *The technical details were the concern of the army. Los detalles técnicos eran asunto del ejército.*

**con|cern|ing** /kənsɜrnɪŋ/ PREP You use **concerning** to indicate what a question or piece of information is about. *con respecto a, acerca de* [FORMAL] ❑ *For more information concerning the club, contact Mr. Coldwell. Para más información acerca del club, contacte al señor Coldwell.*

**con|cert** /kɒnsərt/ (**concerts**) N-COUNT A **concert** is a performance of music. *concierto* ❑ *...a short concert of piano music. ...un pequeño concierto de piano.* ❑ *...live rock concerts. ...conciertos de rock en vivo.*
→ see Word Web: **concert**

**con|cer|to** /kəntʃɛərtoʊ/ (**concertos**) N-COUNT A **concerto** is a piece of music for one or more solo instruments and an orchestra. *concierto* ❑ *...Tchaikovsky's First Piano Concerto. ...el primer concierto para piano de Tchaikovsky.*
→ see **music**

**con|ces|sion** /kənsɛʃ^ən/ (**concessions**) **1** N-COUNT If you make a **concession to** someone, you agree to let them do or have something, especially in order to end an argument or conflict. *concesión* ❑ *We made too many concessions to the workers and we got too little in return. Hicimos demasiadas concesiones a los trabajadores y conseguimos poco a cambio.* **2** N-COUNT A **concession** is an arrangement where someone is given the right to sell a product or to run a business, especially in a building belonging to another business. *franquicia* [BUSINESS] ❑ *Concession sales at the airport are up 15%. Las ventas de franquicias en el aeropuerto subieron un 15%.*

**con|clude** /kənklud/ (**concludes, concluding, concluded**) **1** V-T If you **conclude that** something is true, you decide that it is true using the facts you know. *llegar a la conclusión* ❑ *Larry concluded that he had no choice but to accept. Larry llegó a la conclusión de que no tenía otra opción más que aceptar.* ❑ *So what can we conclude from this debate? ¿A qué conclusiones podemos llegar en este debate?* **2** V-T/V-I When something **concludes,** or when you **conclude** it, you end it. *concluir* [FORMAL] ❑ *The evening concluded with dinner and speeches. La velada concluyó con la cena y unos discursos.* **3** V-RECIP If people or groups **conclude** a treaty or business deal, they arrange it or agree to it. *concluir* [FORMAL] ❑ *We have concluded 81 trade agreements in the last two years. Hemos concluido 81 acuerdos comerciales en los últimos dos años.*

**con|clu|sion** /kənkluʒ^ən/ (**conclusions**) **1** N-COUNT When you come to a **conclusion,** you decide that something is true after you have thought about it carefully. *conclusión* ❑ *I've come to the conclusion that she's a great musician. He llegado a la conclusión de que es una gran música.* **2** N-SING The **conclusion** of something is its ending. *conclusión* ❑ *...the conclusion of the program. ...la conclusión del programa.* **3** PHRASE You say **"in conclusion"** to indicate that what you are about to say is the last thing that you want to say. *En conclusión* ❑ *In conclusion, walking is cheap, safe, and enjoyable. en conclusión, caminar es barato, seguro y agradable.*

**Word Partnership** Usar *conclusion* con:

| | |
|---|---|
| V. | **come to a** conclusion, **draw a** conclusion, **reach a** conclusion **1** |
| N. | conclusion **of *something*** **1** **2** |
| PREP. | **in** conclusion **3** |

**con|crete** /kɒŋkrit/ (**concretes, concreting, concreted**) **1** N-UNCOUNT **Concrete** is a substance used for building which is made from cement, sand, small stones, and water. *concreto* ❑ *The fence posts have to be set in concrete. Los postes de la barda deben ser de concreto.* ❑ *We sat on the concrete floor. Nos sentamos en el suelo de concreto.* **2** ADJ Something that is **concrete** is definite and specific. *concreto* ❑ *I had no concrete evidence. No tenía pruebas concretas.* ❑ *There were no concrete proposals. No había propuestas concretas.* **3** ADJ A **concrete** object is a real, physical object. A **concrete** image is an image of a real, physical object. *concreto*

**con|demn** /kəndɛm/ (**condemns, condemning, condemned**) **1** V-T If you **condemn** something, you say that it is very bad and unacceptable. *condenar* ❑ *Political leaders yesterday condemned the violence. Los líderes políticos condenaron ayer la violencia.* • **con|dem|na|tion** /kɒndɛmneɪʃ^ən/ (**condemnations**) N-VAR *condena* ❑ *There was widespread condemnation of the decision. Hubo una condena general a la decisión.* **2** V-T If someone **is condemned to** a punishment, they are given this punishment. *condenar* ❑ *He was condemned to life imprisonment. Fue condenado a cadena perpetua.* **3** V-T If authorities **condemn** a building, they officially decide that it is not safe and must be pulled down or repaired. *declarar en ruinas* ❑ *The town council has condemned all these houses. El ayuntamiento ha*

**Word Web** concert

A **rock concert** is much more than a group of **musicians** playing **music** on a **stage**. It is a full-scale **performance**. Each **band** must have a **manager** and an **agent** who **books** the **venue** and **promotes** the **show** in each new location. The band's assistants, called roadies, set up the stage, test the **microphones**, and tune the **instruments**. **Sound engineers** make sure the band sounds as good as possible. There's always **lighting** to **spotlight** the **lead singer** and **backup** singers. The bright, moving lights help to build excitement. The **fans** scream and yell when they hear their favorite **songs**. The **audience** never wants the show to end.

*declarado que todas estas casas están en ruinas.*

**con|den|sa|tion** /kɒndɛnseɪʃᵊn/ N-UNCOUNT **Condensation** consists of small drops of water which form when warm water vapor or steam touches a cold surface such as a window. *condensación*

**con|den|sa|tion point** (**condensation points**) N-VAR The **condensation point** of a gas or vapor is the temperature at which it becomes a liquid. *punto de condensación*

**con|dense** /kəndɛns/ (**condenses, condensing, condensed**) **1** V-T If you **condense** something, especially a piece of writing or a speech, you make it shorter. *condensar, resumir* ❑ *To save time, teachers condense lesson plans. Para ahorrar tiempo, los maestros resumen sus planes de clase.* **2** V-I When a gas or vapor **condenses,** or **is condensed,** it changes into a liquid. *condensarse* ❑ *Water vapor condenses to form clouds. El vapor de agua se condensa hasta formar nubes.*
→ see **matter, water**

**con|di|tion** /kəndɪʃᵊn/ (**conditions, conditioning, conditioned**) **1** N-SING The **condition** of someone or something is the state they are in. *condición* ❑ *He remains in a critical condition in a California hospital. Se mantiene en una condición crítica en un hospital de California.* ❑ *The two-bedroom house is in good condition. La casa de dos habitaciones está en buenas condiciones.* **2** N-PLURAL The **conditions** in which people live or do things are the factors which affect their comfort, safety, or success. *condiciones* ❑ *People are living in terrible conditions. La gente vive en terribles condiciones.* ❑ *...ideal weather conditions. ...condiciones climáticas ideales.* **3** N-COUNT A **condition** is something which must happen or be done in order for something else to be possible, especially when this is written into a contract or law. *condición* ❑ *A condition of our release was that we left the country immediately. Una de las condiciones para nuestra puesta en libertad fue que abandonáramos el país inmediatamente.* ❑ *...terms and conditions of employment. ...términos y condiciones de empleo.* **4** N-COUNT If someone has a particular **condition,** they have an illness or other medical problem. *afección* ❑ *Doctors suspect he may have a heart condition. Los doctores sospechan que tenga una afección cardiaca.* **5** V-T If someone **is conditioned** by their experiences or environment, they are influenced by them over a period of time so that they do certain things or think in a particular way. *condicionar* ❑ *We are all conditioned by early experiences. Todos estamos condicionados por nuestras experiencias tempranas.* ❑ *Some people are conditioned to eating particular foods, especially junk food. Algunas personas están condicionadas a comer ciertos tipos de comida, especialmente la chatarra.* • **con|di|tion|ing** N-UNCOUNT *condicionamiento* ❑ *...social conditioning. ...condicionamiento social.* **6** PHRASE When you agree to do something **on condition that** something else happens, you mean that you will only do it if this other thing also happens. *a condición de* ❑ *He agreed to speak to reporters on condition that he was not identified. Aceptó hablar con los reporteros a condición de que no se le identificara.*
→ see **factory**

**con|di|tion|al** /kəndɪʃənᵊl/ ADJ If a situation or agreement is **conditional on** something, it will only happen if this thing happens. *condicional* ❑ *Our second offer will be conditional on the success of the first. Nuestra segunda oferta será condicional, dependiendo del éxito de la primera.* ❑ *...a conditional offer. ...una oferta condicional.*

**con|dom** /kɒndəm/ (**condoms**) N-COUNT A **condom** is a rubber covering which a man wears on his penis as a contraceptive or as protection against disease during sex. *preservativo, condón*

**con|do|min|ium** /kɒndəmɪniəm/ (**condominiums**) **1** N-COUNT A **condominium** is an apartment building in which each apartment is owned by the person who lives there. *condominio* **2** N-COUNT A **condominium** is one of the privately-owned apartments in a condominium. *condominio*

C

**con|duct** (**conducts, conducting, conducted**)

> The verb is pronounced /kəndʌkt/. The noun is pronounced /kɒndʌkt/.

**1** V-T When you **conduct** an activity or task, you organize it and do it. *llevar a cabo* ❑ *I decided to conduct an experiment. Decidí llevar a cabo un experimento.* **2** V-T If you **conduct** yourself in a particular way, you behave in that way. *conducirse* ❑ *The way he conducts himself reflects on the family. La manera en que se conduce se refleja en la familia.* **3** V-T/V-I When someone **conducts** an orchestra or choir, they stand in front of it and direct its performance. *dirigir* ❑ *He will be conducting the orchestra and chorus. Dirigirá la orquesta y el coro.* ❑ *Solti continued to conduct here and abroad. Solti continuó dirigiendo aquí y en el extranjero.* **4** V-T If something **conducts** heat or electricity, it allows heat or electricity to pass through it or along it. *conducir* ❑ *Water conducts heat faster than air. El agua conduce el calor más rápidamente que el aire.* **5** N-SING The **conduct of** a task or activity is the way in which it is organized and carried out. *conducción* ❑ *...the conduct of free and fair elections. ...la conducción de elecciones libres y justas.* **6** N-UNCOUNT Someone's **conduct** is the way they behave in particular situations. *conducta* ❑ *...a prize for good conduct. ...un premio por buena conducta.*

**Thesaurus** *conduct* Ver también:

V. control, direct, manage **1**
N. attitude, behavior, manner **6**

**Word Partnership** Usar *conduct* con:

N. conduct **business**, conduct **an experiment** **1**
**code of** conduct **6**

**con|duc|tion** /kəndʌkʃᵊn/ N-UNCOUNT **Conduction** is the process by which heat or electricity passes through or along something. *conducción* [TECHNICAL]

**con|duc|tor** /kəndʌktər/ (**conductors**) **1** N-COUNT A **conductor** is a person who stands in front of an orchestra or choir and directs its performance. *director o directora* **2** N-COUNT On a train, a **conductor** is a person whose job is to travel on the train in order to help passengers and check tickets. *revisor o revisora* **3** N-COUNT On a streetcar or a bus, the **conductor** is the person whose job

is to sell tickets to the passengers. *cobrador o cobradora* **4** N-COUNT A **conductor** is a substance that heat or electricity can pass through or along. *conductor* ❑ *...a highly efficient conductor of electricity. ...un conductor de electricidad altamente eficiente.* **5** → see also **semiconductor**
→ see **metal**

C

**cone** /koʊn/ (**cones**) **1** N-COUNT A **cone** is a shape with a circular base ending in a point at the top. *cono* ❑ *...bright-orange traffic cones to stop people parking on the bridge. ...conos de tráfico en naranja brillante que no permitían estacionarse en el puente.* **2** N-COUNT A **cone** is the fruit of a tree such as a pine or fir. *piña, cono* ❑ *...a bowl of fir cones. ...un tazón de piñas de abetos.* **3** N-COUNT **Cones** are cells in the eye that detect bright light and help you to see colors. *cono* [MEDICAL]
→ see **solid, volcano, volume**

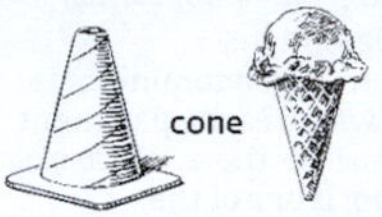


**con|fec|tion|ers' sug|ar** N-UNCOUNT **Confectioners' sugar** is very fine white sugar that is used for making frosting and candy. *azúcar glas(é)*

**con|fed|era|tion** /kənfɛdəreɪʃᵊn/ (**confederations**) N-COUNT A **confederation** is an organization or group consisting of smaller groups or states, especially one that exists for business or political purposes. *confederación* ❑ *...the Confederation of Indian Industry. La confederación de la industria india.*

**con|fer|ence** /kɒnfərəns, -frəns/ (**conferences**) **1** N-COUNT A **conference** is a meeting, often lasting a few days, which is organized on a particular subject. *congreso* ❑ *...a conference on education. ...un congreso sobre educación.* ❑ *...the Alternative Energy conference. ...el congreso "Energías Alternativas".* **2** → see also **press conference**

**con|fess** /kənfɛs/ (**confesses, confessing, confessed**) V-T/V-I If you **confess** to doing something wrong or something you are ashamed of, you admit that you did it. *confesar* ❑ *He confessed to seventeen murders. Confesó haber perpetrado diecisiete asesinatos.* ❑ *Ed confessed that he was worried. Ed confesó que estaba preocupado.* ❑ *He claimed that he was forced to confess. Afirmó que había sido obligado a confesar.*

**con|fes|sion** /kənfɛʃᵊn/ (**confessions**) **1** N-COUNT A **confession** is a signed statement by someone in which they admit that they have committed a particular crime. *confesión* ❑ *They forced him to sign a confession. Lo obligaron a firmar una confesión.* **2** N-VAR **Confession** is the act of admitting that you have done something that you are ashamed of or embarrassed about. *confesión* ❑ *I have a confession to make. Tengo algo que confesar.*

**con|fi|dence** /kɒnfɪdəns/ **1** N-UNCOUNT If you have **confidence in** someone, you feel that you can trust them. *confianza* ❑ *I have great confidence in you. Te tengo mucha confianza.* **2** N-UNCOUNT If you have **confidence,** you feel sure about your abilities, qualities, or ideas. *confianza* ❑ *The band is full of confidence. La banda se tiene mucha confianza.* **3** N-UNCOUNT If you tell someone something **in confidence,** you tell them a secret. *en confianza* ❑ *We told you all these things in confidence. Te dijimos todo esto en confianza.*

**con|fi|dent** /kɒnfɪdənt/ **1** ADJ If you are **confident** about something, you are certain that it will happen in the way you want it to. *seguro* ❑ *I am confident that everything will come out right. Confío en que todo salga bien.* ❑ *Mr. Ryan is confident of success. El Sr. Ryan confía en el éxito.* ● **con|fi|dent|ly** ADV *con confianza, con seguridad* ❑ *I can confidently promise that this year is going to be very different. Prometo con confianza que este año va a ser muy diferente.* **2** ADJ People who are **confident** feel sure about their own abilities, qualities, or ideas. *que tiene confianza en uno mismo* ❑ *In time he became more confident and relaxed. Con el tiempo llegó a tener más confianza en sí mismo y a estar más relajado.* ● **con|fi|dent|ly** ADV *con confianza, con seguridad* ❑ *She walked confidently across the hall. Atravesó el vestíbulo con toda confianza.*

**con|fi|den|tial** /kɒnfɪdɛnʃᵊl/ ADJ Information that is **confidential** is meant to be kept secret. *confidencial* ❑ *...confidential information about her private life. ...información confidencial sobre su vida privada.* ● **con|fi|den|tial|ly** ADV *con confidencialidad* ❑ *Any information they give will be treated confidentially. La información que nos proporcionen será confidencial.* ● **con|fi|den|ti|al|ity** /kɒnfɪdɛnʃiælɪti/ N-UNCOUNT *confidencialidad, reserva* ❑ *...the confidentiality of the doctor-patient relationship. ...la confidencialidad de la relación médico-paciente.*

| **Thesaurus** | *confidential* | Ver también: |
|---|---|---|
| ADJ. | private, restricted; (*ant.*) public | |

**con|fine** /kənfaɪn/ (**confines, confining, confined**) **1** V-T To **confine** something **to** a particular place or group means to prevent it from spreading beyond it or from leaving it. *confinar* ❑ *Health officials have confined the disease to the Tabatinga area. Los funcionarios de salud confinaron la enfermedad al área de Tabatinga.* ❑ *He was confined in a cell measuring 8 feet by 8 feet. Estaba confinado en una celda de 2.5 por 2.5 metros* ● **con|fine|ment** /kənfaɪnmənt/ N-UNCOUNT *confinamiento, estar confinado* ❑ *...my two-year confinement in a hospital. ...mis dos años de confinamiento en el hospital* **2** V-T If you **confine yourself** or your activities **to** something, you do only that thing. *limitar(se), restrigir(se)* ❑ *He did not confine himself to one language. No se limitaba a una sola lengua.*

**con|fined** /kənfaɪnd/ **1** ADJ If something is **confined to** a particular place, it exists only in that place. If it is **confined to** a particular group, only members of that group have it. *confinado, limitado* ❑ *The problem is not confined to Georgia. El problema no se limita a Georgia* **2** ADJ A **confined** space or area is small and enclosed by walls. *confinado, reducido* ❑ *I don't like confined spaces. No me gustan los espacios reducidos.*

| **Word Link** | *firm ≈ making strong : affirm, confirm, firm* |
|---|---|

**con|firm** /kənfɜrm/ (**confirms, confirming, confirmed**) **1** V-T If something **confirms** what you believe, it shows that it is definitely true. *confirmar* ❑ *Doctors have confirmed that he has not* *broken any bones.* *Los médicos confirmaron que no tenía huesos rotos.* ❑ *This news confirms our worst fears.* *Esta noticia confirma nuestros peores miedos.* • **con|fir|ma|tion** /kɒnfərmeɪʃən/ N-UNCOUNT *confirmación* ❑ *They took her words as confirmation of their suspicions.* *Tomaron sus palabras como confirmación de sus sospechas.* **2** V-T If you **confirm** something that has been stated or suggested, you say that it is true because you know about it. *confirmar* ❑ *Edith confirmed that every detail Peter gave was correct.* *Edith confirmó que todos los detalles que dio Peter estaban correctos.* • **con|fir|ma|tion** N-UNCOUNT *confirmación* ❑ *She glanced over at James for confirmation.* *Miró a James buscando una confirmación.* **3** V-T If you **confirm** an arrangement or appointment, you make it definite. *confirmar* ❑ *You make the reservation, and I'll confirm it in writing.* *Haz la reservación y yo la confirmo por escrito.* • **con|fir|ma|tion** N-UNCOUNT *confirmación* ❑ *Travel arrangements are subject to confirmation.* *Los arreglos del viaje están sujetos a confirmación.*

**con|flict** (**conflicts, conflicting, conflicted**)

> The noun is pronounced /kɒnflɪkt/. The verb is pronounced /kənflɪkt/.

**1** N-UNCOUNT **Conflict** is serious disagreement and argument. If two people or groups are **in conflict,** they have had a serious disagreement or argument and have not yet reached agreement. *conflicto* ❑ *I don't like being in conflict with people.* *No me gusta tener conflictos con la gente.* **2** N-VAR **Conflict** is fighting between countries or groups of people. *conflicto* [WRITTEN] ❑ *...a military conflict.* *...un conflicto militar.* **3** V-RECIP If ideas, beliefs, or accounts **conflict,** they are very different from each other and it seems impossible for them to exist together. *entrar en conflicto,* *discrepar* ❑ *He held firm opinions which usually conflicted with mine.* *Tenía opiniones muy firmes que solían discrepar de las mías.*
→ see **war**

**con|form** /kənfɔrm/ (**conforms, conforming, conformed**) **1** V-I If something **conforms to** something such as a law or standard, it is of the required type or quality. *ajustarse a,* *cumplir con* ❑ *The lamp conforms to new safety standards.* *La lámpara cumple con las nuevas normas de seguridad.* **2** V-I If you **conform,** you behave in the way that you are expected or supposed to behave. *someterse,* *acatar,* *avenirse a algo* ❑ *Many children who don't conform are bullied.* *Muchos niños que no se someten son acosados.*

**con|front** /kənfrʌnt/ (**confronts, confronting, confronted**) **1** V-T If you **are confronted with** a problem or task, you have to deal with it. *enfrentarse,* *hacer frente* ❑ *She was confronted with serious money problems.* *Tenía que hacer frente a graves problemas de dinero.* ❑ *We are learning how to confront death.* *Estamos aprendiendo a enfrentarnos a la muerte.* **2** V-T If you **confront** someone, you stand or sit in front of them, especially when you are going to fight or argue with them. *encarar,* *hacer frente,* *enfrentarse* ❑ *She confronted him face to face.* *Ella se le enfrentó cara a cara.* **3** V-T If you **confront** someone **with** evidence, you present it to them in order to accuse them of something. *confrontar con,* *enfrentarse con* ❑ *She decided to confront Kathryn with the truth.* *Decidió confrontar a Kathryn con la verdad.* ❑ *I could not bring myself to confront him about it.* *No me decidía a enfrentarme con él al respecto.*

**con|fron|ta|tion** /kɒnfrʌnteɪʃən/ (**confrontations**) N-VAR A **confrontation** is a dispute, fight, or battle. *confrontación* ❑ *...confrontation with the enemy.* *...confrontación con el enemigo.* • **con|fron|ta|tion|al** /kɒnfrʌnteɪʃənəl/ ADJ *polémico* ❑ *...his confrontational style.* *...su estilo polémico.*

C

**con|fuse** /kənfyuz/ (**confuses, confusing, confused**) **1** V-T If you **confuse** two things, you get them mixed up, so that you think one of them is the other one. *confundir* ❑ *I always confuse my left with my right.* *Siempre confundo la izquierda con la derecha.* • **con|fu|sion** /kənfyuʒən/ N-UNCOUNT *confusión* ❑ *Use different colors to avoid confusion.* *Usa diferentes colores para evitar confusiones.* **2** V-T To **confuse** someone means to make it difficult for them to know exactly what is happening or what to do. *confundir* ❑ *My words surprised and confused him.* *Mis palabras lo sorprendieron y confundieron.* **3** V-T To **confuse** a situation means to make it complicated or difficult to understand. *confundir,* *complicar,* *enredar* ❑ *In attempting to present two sides, you only confused the issue.* *Tratando de presentar las dos caras del asunto, acabaste por enredarlo todo.*

**con|fused** /kənfyuzd/ **1** ADJ If you are **confused,** you do not know exactly what is happening or what to do. *confundido* ❑ *People are confused about what they should eat to stay healthy.* *La gente está confundida sobre lo que debe comer para mantenerse sana.* **2** ADJ Something that is **confused** does not have any order or pattern and is difficult to understand. *confuso* ❑ *The situation remains confused.* *La situación sigue siendo confusa.*

**con|fus|ing** /kənfyuzɪŋ/ ADJ Something that is **confusing** makes it difficult for people to know exactly what is happening or what to do. *confuso* ❑ *The statement is really confusing.* *La declaración es realmente confusa.*

**con|fu|sion** /kənfyuʒən/ (**confusions**) **1** N-VAR If there is **confusion** about something, it is not clear what the true situation is. *confusión* ❑ *There's still confusion about the number of students.* *Sigue habiendo confusión sobre el número de estudiantes.* **2** N-UNCOUNT **Confusion** is a situation in which everything is in disorder, especially because there are lots of things happening at the same time. *confusión* ❑ *There was confusion when a man fired shots.* *Hubo confusión cuando un hombre hizo varios disparos.* **3** → see also **confuse**

> **Word Link** *grat ≈ pleasing : congratulate, gratify, gratitude*

**con|gratu|late** /kəngrætʃəleɪt/ (**congratulates, congratulating, congratulated**) V-T If you **congratulate** someone, you express pleasure about something nice has happened to them, or something good that they have done. *felicitar* ❑ *She congratulated him on the birth of his son.* *Lo felicitó por el nacimiento de su hijo.* • **con|gratu|la|tion** /kəngrætʃəleɪʃən/ N-UNCOUNT *felicitación* ❑ *...letters of congratulation.* *...cartas de felicitación.*

**con|gratu|la|tions** /kəngrætʃəleɪʃənz/ CONVENTION You say **"Congratulations"** to someone in order to congratulate them. *felicidades,*

C

*felicitaciones* ❑ *Congratulations, you have a healthy baby girl. Felicidades, tuvo una niña sana.* ❑ *Congratulations on your interesting article. Felicitaciones por su artículo tan interesante.*

**con|gre|ga|tion** /kɒŋgrɪgeɪʃᵊn/ (**congregations**) N-COUNT The people who attend a religious service are the **congregation.** *fieles, feligreses, miembros de la iglesia* ❑ *Members of the congregation began arriving. Empezaron a llegar los fieles.*

**con|gress** /kɒŋgrɪs/ (**congresses**) N-COUNT A **congress** is a large meeting that is held to discuss ideas and policies. *congreso* ❑ *A lot has changed after the party congress. Muchas cosas cambiaron después del congreso del partido.*

**Con|gress** N-PROPER **Congress** is the elected group of politicians that is responsible for making laws in the United States. *congreso* ❑ *We want to cooperate with both the administration and Congress. Queremos cooperar tanto con el gobierno como con el Congreso.* • **con|gres|sion|al** also **Congressional** /kəngrɛʃənᵊl/ ADJ *del congreso* ❑ *The president explained his plans to congressional leaders. El presidente explicó sus planes a los líderes del congreso*

**congress|man** /kɒŋgrɪsmən/ (**congressmen**) N-COUNT; N-TITLE A **congressman** is a male member of the U.S. Congress, especially of the House of Representatives. *congresista*

**congress|person** /kɒŋgrɪspɜrsᵊn/ (**congresspeople**) N-COUNT A **congressperson** is a member of the U.S. Congress, especially of the House of Representatives. *congresista*

**congress|woman** /kɒŋgrɪswʊmən/ (**congresswomen**) N-COUNT; N-TITLE A **congresswoman** is a female member of the U.S. Congress, especially of the House of Representatives. *congresista*

**con|gru|ent** /kɒŋgruənt, kəngru-/ ADJ In geometry, two shapes are **congruent** if they are the same size and shape but in different positions. *congruente* [TECHNICAL]

**con|ic pro|jec|tion** /kɒnɪk prədʒɛkʃən/ (**conic projections**) N-VAR A **conic projection** is an image of a map that is made by projecting the map on a globe onto a cone. Compare **azimuthal projection, Mercator projection.** *proyección cónica* [TECHNICAL]

**co|ni|fer** /kɒnɪfər/ (**conifers**) N-COUNT **Conifers** are a type of trees and shrubs such as pine trees and fir trees. They have fruit called cones, and very thin leaves called needles which they do not normally lose in winter. *conífera*
→ see **plant**

**con|junc|tion** /kəndʒʌŋkʃᵊn/ (**conjunctions**) **1** N-COUNT In grammar, a **conjunction** is a word or group of words that joins together words, groups, or clauses. For example, "and" and "or" are conjunctions. *conjunción* **2** PHRASE If one thing is done **in conjunction with** another, the two things are done or used together. *en conjunción con algo, en conjunción con alguien, coordinar* ❑ *Textbooks are designed to be used in conjunction with classroom teaching. El objetivo de los libros de texto es coordinarlos con las clases.*

**con|nect** /kənɛkt/ (**connects, connecting, connected**) **1** V-RECIP If something or someone **connects** one thing **to** another, or if one thing **connects to** another, or if two things **connect,** the two things are joined together. *conectar* ❑ *You can connect the speakers to your CD player. Puedes conectar las bocinas al reproductor de CD.* ❑ *I connected the wires. Conecté los cables.* **2** V-I If one train, plane, or boat **connects with** another, it arrives at a time which allows passengers to change to the other one in order to continue their trip. *conectar con, enlazar con* ❑ *The train connects with a ferry to Ireland. El tren conecta con el ferry a Irlanda.* **3** V-T If a piece of equipment or a place **is connected to** a source of power or water, it is joined to that source. *conectar* ❑ *The house is not yet connected to the water supply. La casa todavía no está conectada al suministro de agua.* • **Connect up** means the same as **connect.** *conectar* ❑ *The shower needs to be connected up to the hot and cold water supply. Se tiene que conectar la regadera al suministro de agua caliente y fría.* **4** V-T If you **connect** a person or thing **with** something, you realize that there is a link or relationship between them. *relacionar con* ❑ *I hoped he would not connect me with the article. Esperaba que no me relacionara con el artículo.*

**con|nect|ed** /kənɛktɪd/ **1** ADJ If one thing is **connected with** another, there is a link or relationship between them. *relacionado* ❑ *...problems connected with a high-fat diet. ...problemas relacionados con una dieta rica en grasas.* ❑ *Your breathing is directly connected to your heart rate. La respiración está directamente relacionada con el ritmo cardiaco.* **2** → see also **connect**

**con|nec|tion** /kənɛkʃᵊn/ (**connections**) **1** N-VAR A **connection** is a relationship between two things, people, or groups. *relación* ❑ *I felt a strong connection between us. Siento que nuestra relación es muy estrecha.* **2** N-COUNT A **connection** is a joint where two wires or pipes are joined together. *conexión* ❑ *...pipework connections. ...conexiones de la tubería.* **3** N-COUNT If a place has good road, rail, or air **connections,** many places can be directly reached from there by car, train, or plane. *conexiones* ❑ *New York has excellent air and rail connections. Nueva York tiene muy buenas conexiones aéreas y ferroviarias.* **4** N-COUNT If you get a **connection** at a station or airport, you continue your trip by catching another train, bus, or plane. *conexión* ❑ *My flight was late and I missed the connection. Mi vuelo se demoró y perdí la conexión.*

**con|nec|tive tis|sue** N-UNCOUNT **Connective tissue** is the substance in the bodies of animals and people which fills in the spaces between organs and connects muscles and bones. *tejido conjuntivo* [TECHNICAL]

**con|quer** /kɒŋkər/ (**conquers, conquering, conquered**) **1** V-T If one country or group of people **conquers** another, they take complete control of their land. *conquistar* ❑ *Germany conquered France in 1940. Alemania conquistó a Francia en 1940.* • **con|quer|or** /kɒŋkərər/ N-COUNT (**conquerors**) *conquistador o conquistadora* ❑ *They obeyed their conquerors because they wanted to go on living. Obedecieron a los conquistadores porque querían seguir viviendo.* **2** V-T If you **conquer** something such as a problem, you succeed in ending it or dealing with it. *vencer, superar, resolver* ❑ *Love was enough to conquer our differences. El amor bastó para superar nuestras diferencias.*
→ see **army, empire**

**Word Link** *sci ≈ knowing : conscience, conscious, science*

**con|science** /kɒnʃᵊns/ (**consciences**) **1** N-COUNT Your **conscience** is the part of your mind that tells you if what you are doing is wrong. If you have a **guilty conscience,** or if you have something **on** your **conscience,** you feel guilty about something because you know it was wrong. conciencia ❑ *My conscience is completely clear on this point. Tengo la conciencia limpia al respecto.* ❑ *He got a guilty conscience and brought it back. Le remordió la conciencia y lo devolvió.* **2** N-UNCOUNT **Conscience** is doing what you believe is right even though it might be unpopular or difficult. conciencia ❑ *He refused for reasons of conscience to eat meat. Se negó a comer carne por razones de conciencia.*

**con|scious** /kɒnʃəs/ **1** ADJ If you are **conscious of** something, you notice it or realize that it is happening. consciente de ❑ *She was very conscious of Max studying her. Estaba muy consciente de que Max la estaba analizando.* **2** ADJ If you are **conscious of** something, you think about it a lot, especially because you think it is important. consciente ❑ *I'm very conscious of my weight. Estoy muy consciente de mi peso.* **3** ADJ A **conscious** decision or effort is one that you are aware of making. deliberado, consciente ❑ *I don't think we ever made a conscious decision to have a big family. Creo que nunca decidimos deliberadamente tener una familia grande.* ● **con|scious|ly** ADV conscientemente ❑ *Sophie was not consciously seeking a replacement after her father died. Sophie no buscaba conscientemente un sustituo para su padre fallecido.* **4** ADJ Someone who is **conscious** is awake rather than asleep or unconscious. consciente ❑ *She was fully conscious throughout the operation. Estuvo totalmente consciente durante la operación.*

**Thesaurus** *conscious* Ver también:

ADJ. calculated, deliberate, intentional, rational **3**
awake, aware, responsive; (*ant.*) unaware, unconscious **4**

**Word Link** *ness ≈ state, condition : consciousness, sickness, weakness*

**con|scious|ness** /kɒnʃəsnɪs/ (**consciousnesses**) **1** N-COUNT Your **consciousness** is your mind, thoughts, beliefs, and attitudes. conciencia ❑ *...ideas about the nature of consciousness. ...ideas sobre la naturaleza de la conciencia.* **2** N-UNCOUNT If you **lose consciousness,** you become unconscious, and if you **regain consciousness,** you become conscious again. perder la conciencia, recobrar la conciencia ❑ *She banged her head and lost consciousness. Se golpeó la cabeza y quedó inconsciente.*

**con|secu|tive** /kənsɛkyətɪv/ ADJ **Consecutive** periods of time or events happen one after the other without interruption. consecutivo ❑ *The Cup was won for the third consecutive year by the Toronto Maple Leafs. Los Maple Leafs de Toronto ganaron la copa por tercer año consecutivo.*

**Word Link** *con ≈ together, with : consensus, construct, convene*

**con|sen|sus** /kənsɛnsəs/ N-SING A **consensus** is general agreement among a group of people. consenso ❑ *The consensus among scientists is that the world is likely to warm up. El consenso entre los científicos es que hay probabilidades de un calentamiento global.*

**con|sent** /kənsɛnt/ (**consents, consenting, consented**) **1** N-UNCOUNT If you give your **consent to** something, you give someone permission to do it. consentimiento [FORMAL] ❑ *Pollard finally gave his consent to the search. Finalmente Pollard dio su consentimiento para la búsqueda.* **2** V-T/V-I If you **consent to** something, you agree to do it or to allow it to be done. consentir, aceptar [FORMAL] ❑ *He finally consented to go. Por fin aceptó ir.* **3** → see also **age of consent**

**Word Link** *sequ ≈ following : consequence, sequel, sequence*

**con|se|quence** /kɒnsɪkwɛns, -kwəns/ (**consequences**) **1** N-COUNT The **consequences of** something are the results or effects of it. consecuencia ❑ *She understood the consequences of her actions. Entendió las consecuencias de sus actos.* **2** PHRASE If one thing happens and then another thing happens **in consequence** or **as a consequence,** the second thing happens as a result of the first. en consecuencia ❑ *His death was unexpected and, in consequence, no plans have been made for his replacement. Su muerte fue inesperada, y en consecuencia, no había planes para sustituirlo.*

**con|se|quent|ly** /kɒnsɪkwɛntli, -kwəntli/ ADV **Consequently** means as a result. consecuentemente, en consecuencia [FORMAL] ❑ *Grandfather broke his back while working in the mines. Consequently, he spent the rest of his life in a wheelchair. El abuelo se rompió la espalda cuando trabajaba en las minas y, en consecuencia, pasó el resto de su vida en una silla de ruedas.*

**con|ser|va|tion** /kɒnsərveɪʃᵊn/ **1** N-UNCOUNT **Conservation** is saving and protecting the environment. protección, conservación ❑ *...elephant conservation. ...protección de los elefantes.* **2** N-UNCOUNT The **conservation** of a supply of something is the careful use of it so that it lasts for a long time. ahorro

**con|ser|va|tion of en|er|gy** N-UNCOUNT The law of **conservation of energy** is a principle in physics which states that energy cannot be created or destroyed. conservación de la energía

**con|ser|va|tion of mass** also **conservation of matter** N-UNCOUNT The law of **conservation of mass** is a principle in physics which states that matter cannot be created or destroyed. conservación de la masa

**con|serva|tive** /kənsɜrvətɪv/ (**conservatives**)

The spelling **Conservative** is also used for meaning **4**.

**1** ADJ Someone who is **conservative** has views that are toward the political right. conservador ❑ *...the most conservative candidate. ...el candidato más conservador.* ● **Conservative** is also a noun. conservador o conservadora ❑ *The new judge is a conservative. El nuevo juez es Conservador.* ● **con|serva|tism** /kənsɜrvətɪzəm/ N-UNCOUNT conservadurismo ❑ *...the philosophy of modern conservatism. ...la filosofía del conservadurismo moderno.* **2** ADJ Someone who is **conservative**

C

is unwilling to accept changes and new ideas. *conservador* ❑ *People tend to be more conservative as they get older.* *Las personas tienden a ser más conservadoras conforme envejecen.* ● **con|serva|tism** N-UNCOUNT *tradicionalismo* ❑ *...the traditional conservatism of the countryside.* *...el tradicionalismo del campo.* **3** ADJ A **conservative** estimate is very cautious and probably less than the real amount. *conservador* ❑ *Conservative estimates put her wealth at $15 million.* *Un cálculo conservador es que su fortuna llega a los 15 millones de dólares.* ● **con|ser|va|tive|ly** ADV *conservadoramente* ❑ *The cost is conservatively estimated at $30 million.* *Se estima conservadoramente que el costo es de 30 millones de dólares.* **4** ADJ A **Conservative** politician or voter is a member of or votes for the Conservative Party in Britain and in various other countries. *conservador* ❑ *...Conservative MPs.* *...los MP del Partido Conservador* ● **Conservative** is also a noun. *conservador o conservadora* ❑ *The Conservatives won the election.* *Los Conservadores ganaron las elecciones.*

**Thesaurus** *conservative* Ver también:

ADJ. conventional, right-wing, traditional; (*ant.*) left-wing, liberal, radical **1**

**Word Link** ***serv ≈ keeping : conserve, observe, preserve***

**con|serve** /kənsɜrv/ (**conserves, conserving, conserved**) **1** V-T If you **conserve** a supply of something, you use it carefully so that it lasts for a long time. *ahorrar* ❑ *The factories have closed for the weekend to conserve energy.* *Las fábricas cerraron durante el fin de semana para ahorrar energía.* **2** V-T To **conserve** something means to protect it from harm, loss, or change. *conservar, preservar* ❑ *We want to conserve this natural beauty for ever.* *Queremos conservar para siempre esta belleza natural.*

**con|sid|er** /kənsɪdər/ (**considers, considering, considered**) **1** V-T If you **consider** a person or thing **to** be something, that is your opinion of them. *considerar* ❑ *We don't consider our customers to be just consumers.* *No consideramos a nuestros clientes sólo como clientes.* ❑ *I had always considered myself a strong, competent woman.* *Siempre me consideré una mujer fuerte y competente.* **2** V-T If you **consider** something, you think about it carefully. *considerar, tomar en consideración, analizar* ❑ *The administration continues to consider ways to resolve the situation.* *El gobierno sigue analizando la forma de resolver la situación.* ❑ *You do have to consider the feelings of those around you.* *Realmente tienes que tomar en consideración los sentimientos de quienes te rodean.* ● **con|sid|era|tion** N-UNCOUNT *consideración, análisis* ❑ *There should be careful consideration about the use of these chemicals.* *Se debe hacer un concienzudo análisis del uso de estas sustancias químicas.* **3** → see also **considering**

**Thesaurus** *consider* Ver también:

V. contemplate, examine, study, think about, think over; (*ant.*) dismiss, forget, ignore **2**

**con|sid|er|able** /kənsɪdərəbᵊl/ ADJ **Considerable** means great in amount or degree. *considerable, sustancial* [FORMAL] ❑ *...his considerable wealth.* *...su considerable riqueza.* ❑ *Their fees can be considerable.* *Sus honorarios son considerables.* ● **con|sid|er|ably** ADV *considerablemente* ❑ *Now the process is considerably faster now that we have our new computer system.* *Con nuestro nuevo sistema de cómputo, ahora el proceso es considerablemente más rápido.*

**Word Link** ***ate ≈ filled with : accurate, considerate, desperate***

**con|sid|er|ate** /kənsɪdərɪt/ ADJ Someone who is **considerate** pays attention to the needs, wishes, or feelings of other people. *considerado, atento* ❑ *He's the most considerate man I've ever known.* *Es el hombre más considerado que conozco.*

**con|sid|era|tion** /kənsɪdəreɪʃᵊn/ (**considerations**) **1** N-UNCOUNT If you show **consideration**, you pay attention to the needs, wishes, or feelings of other people. *consideración* ❑ *Show consideration for your neighbors.* *Demuestra tu consideración por los vecinos.* **2** N-COUNT A **consideration** is something that should be thought about when you are planning or deciding something. *preocupación, factor* ❑ *Price has become a more important consideration for shoppers.* *El precio ha llegado a ser el factor más importante para los compradores.* **3** → see also **consider** **4** PHRASE If you **take** something **into consideration**, you think about it because it is relevant to what you are doing. *tomar en consideración, tomar en cuenta, tener en cuenta* ❑ *Safe driving takes into consideration the lives of other people.* *Al manejar con precaución se toma en cuenta la vida de los demás.* **5** PHRASE If something is **under consideration**, it is being discussed. *en proceso de análisis, en estudio* ❑ *Several ideas are under consideration.* *Varias ideas están en estudio.*

**con|sid|er|ing** /kənsɪdərɪŋ/ PREP You use **considering** to indicate that you are thinking about a particular fact when making a judgment or giving an opinion. *considerando* ❑ *Considering the current situation, he may be hoping for too much.* *Considerando la situación actual, quizá espera demasiado.* ❑ *Graham did very well considering that he hasn't been playing regularly.* *La actuación de Graham fue muy buena, considerando que no había estado jugando regularmente.*

**con|sist** /kənsɪst/ (**consists, consisting, consisted**) V-I Something that **consists of** particular things or people is formed from them. *consistir en, constar de* ❑ *My diet consisted of cookies and milk.* *Mi dieta consistía en galletas y leche.*

**con|sist|ent** /kənsɪstənt/ **1** ADJ Someone who is **consistent** always behaves or responds in the same way. *constante, coherente, consistente* ❑ *He was a very consistent player.* *Era un jugador muy constante.* ● **con|sist|en|cy** N-UNCOUNT *regularidad, coherencia, consistencia* ❑ *She scores goals with great consistency.* *Hace goles con regularidad.* ● **con|sist|ent|ly** ADV *sistemáticamente, constantemente, consistentemente* ❑ *He has consistently denied it.* *Lo ha negado sistemáticamente.* **2** ADJ If one fact or idea is **consistent with** another, they do not contradict each other. *que concuerda* ❑ *This result is consistent with the theory.* *Este resultado concuerda con la teoría.*

**con|sole** (**consoles, consoling, consoled**)

The verb is pronounced /kənsoʊl/. The noun is pronounced /kɒnsoʊl/.

**1** V-T If you **console** someone who is unhappy, you try to make them feel more cheerful. *consolar* ❑ *"Never mind, Ned," he consoled me. —No te preocupes, Ned —dijo para consolarme.* ❑ *I can console myself with the fact that I'm not alone. Me consuela el hecho de no estar solo.* • **con|so|la|tion** /kɒnsəleɪʃᵊn/ N-VAR (**consolations**) *consuelo* ❑ *The only consolation for the team is that they will get another chance. El único consuelo para el equipo es que tendrán otra oportunidad.* **2** N-COUNT A **console** is a panel with a number of switches or knobs that is used to operate a machine. *consola* ❑ *...a console of flashing lights. ...una consola con luces parpadeantes.*

**con|soli|date** /kənsɒlɪdeɪt/ (**consolidates, consolidating, consolidated**) V-T If you **consolidate** something such as your power or success, you strengthen it so that it becomes more effective or secure. *consolidar* ❑ *The government consolidated its power by force. El gobierno consolidó su poder por la fuerza.*

**con|so|nant** /kɒnsənənt/ (**consonants**) N-COUNT A **consonant** is a sound such as "p" or "f" which you pronounce by stopping the air from flowing freely through your mouth. *consonante*

**con|so|nant dou|bling** N-UNCOUNT In grammar, **consonant doubling** is the repetition of the final consonant in certain words when a suffix is added, for example the repetition of the "r" in "occur" to make "occurred." *doble consonante* [TECHNICAL]

**con|sor|tium** /kənsɔrʃiəm, -ti-/ (**consortia** /kənsɔrʃiə, -ti-/ or **consortiums**) N-COUNT A **consortium** is a group of people or companies who have agreed to work together. *consorcio* [FORMAL] ❑ *The consortium includes some of the biggest firms in North America. El consorcio incluye a algunas de las empresas más grandes de los Estados Unidos.*

**con|spira|cy** /kənspɪrəsi/ (**conspiracies**) N-VAR **Conspiracy** is secret planning by a group of people to do something wrong or illegal. *conspiración* ❑ *Seven men admitted conspiracy to commit murder. Siete hombres aceptaron que había sido una conspiración para asesinarlo.*

**con|sta|ble** /kʌnstəbᵊl, kɒn-/ (**constables**) **1** N-COUNT; N-TITLE In the United States, a **constable** is an official who helps keep the peace in a town. They are lower in rank than a sheriff. *alguacil* ❑ *Courts cannot work without sheriffs and constables. Los tribunales no pueden funcionar sin sheriffs ni alguaciles.* **2** N-COUNT; N-TITLE; N-VOC In Britain and some other countries, a **constable** is a police officer of the lowest rank. *agente de policía*

**con|stant** /kɒnstənt/ **1** ADJ You use **constant** to describe something that happens all the time or is always there. *constante* ❑ *Women are under constant pressure to be thin. Las mujeres están sometidas a una presión constante por mantenerse delgadas.* • **con|stant|ly** ADV *constantemente* ❑ *The direction of the wind is constantly changing. La dirección del viento cambia constantemente.* **2** ADJ If an amount or level is **constant,** it stays the same over a particular period of time. *constante* ❑ *The temperature remains more or less constant. La temperatura se mantiene más o menos constante.*

**con|stel|la|tion** /kɒnstəleɪʃᵊn/ (**constellations**) N-COUNT A **constellation** is a group of stars which form a pattern. *constelación* ❑ *...the constellation of Orion. ...la constelación de Orión.*
→ see **star**

**con|stitu|en|cy** /kənstɪtʃuənsi/ (**constituencies**) **1** N-COUNT A **constituency** is a section of society that may give political support to a particular party or politician. *electores potenciales, grupo de votantes* ❑ *In Iowa, farmers are a powerful political constituency. En Iowa, los granjeros constituyen un grupo de votantes con gran poder.* **2** N-COUNT A **constituency** is an area for which someone is elected as the representative in a legislature or government. *distrito electoral* ❑ *Voters in 17 constituencies are voting today. Hoy se vota en 17 distritos electorales.*

**con|stitu|ent** /kənstɪtʃuənt/ (**constituents**) **1** N-COUNT A **constituent** is someone who lives in a particular constituency. *elector o electora* ❑ *He told his constituents that he would continue to represent them. Les dijo a sus electores que seguiría representándolos.* **2** N-COUNT A **constituent of** something is one of the things from which it is formed. *componente, elemento constitutivo* [FORMAL] ❑ *Caffeine is one of the main constituents of coffee. La cafeína es uno de los principales componentes del café.* • **Constituent** is also an adjective. *constituyente, constitutivo* ❑ *...a plan to split the company into its constituent parts. ...un plan para dividir la compañía en sus elementos constitutivos.*

**con|sti|tute** /kɒnstɪtut/ (**constitutes, constituting, constituted**) **1** V-LINK If something **constitutes** a particular thing, it can be regarded as being that thing. *constituir, representar* ❑ *Testing patients without their consent would constitute a legal offense. Hacer pruebas a los pacientes sin su consentimiento podría constituir un delito.* **2** V-LINK If a number of things or people **constitute** something, they are the parts or members that form it. *constituir* ❑ *Hindus constitute 83% of India's population. Los hindúes constituyen el 83% de la población de la India.*

**con|sti|tu|tion** /kɒnstɪtuʃᵊn/ (**constitutions**) **1** N-COUNT The **constitution** of a country or organization is the system of laws which formally states people's rights and duties. *constitución* ❑ *The king was forced to adopt a new constitution. Obligaron al rey a adoptar una nueva constitución.* • **con|sti|tu|tion|al** /kɒnstɪtuʃənᵊl/ ADJ *constitucional* ❑ *The issue is one of constitutional and civil rights. Es un asunto de derechos constitucionales y civiles.* **2** N-COUNT Your **constitution** is the state of your health. *constitución, complexión* ❑ *He must have an extremely strong constitution. Su constitución debe ser muy fuerte.*

**con|straint** /kənstreɪnt/ (**constraints**) **1** N-COUNT A **constraint** is something that limits or controls what you can do. *restricción, limitación* ❑ *...financial constraints. ...restricciones financieras.* **2** N-UNCOUNT **Constraint** is control over the way you behave which prevents you from doing what you want to do. *coacción, limitación* ❑ *Journalists must be free to report without constraint. Los periodistas deben tener la libertad de informar sin limitaciones.*

C

**con|struct** /kənstrʌkt/ (**constructs, constructing, constructed**) v-т If you **construct** something, you build, make, or create it. *construir* ❏ *His company recently constructed an office building in downtown Denver. Su empresa construyó recientemente un edificio de oficinas en el centro de Denver.* ❏ *He eventually constructed a huge business empire. A la larga construyó un enorme imperio empresarial.*

**con|struc|tion** /kənstrʌkʃən/ (**constructions**) **1** N-UNCOUNT **Construction** is the building or creating of something. *construcción, creación* ❏ *He has started construction on a swimming pool. Empezó la construcción de una alberca.* ❏ *…the construction of an equal society. …la creación de una sociedad igualitaria.* **2** N-COUNT A **construction** is an object that has been made or built. *construcción* ❏ *…an impressive steel and glass construction. …una impresionante construcción de acero y vidrio.*

**con|struc|tion pa|per** N-UNCOUNT **Construction paper** is a type of stiff, colored paper that children use for drawing and for making things. *cartón, cartulina* ❏ *…animals cut out of brown construction paper. …animales recortados de cartulina café.*

**con|struc|tive** /kənstrʌktɪv/ ADJ A **constructive** discussion, comment, or approach is useful and helpful. *constructivo* ❏ *She welcomes constructive criticism. Agradece la crítica constructiva.*

**con|sult** /kənsʌlt/ (**consults, consulting, consulted**) v-т/v-ı If you **consult** someone or something, you refer to them for advice or permission. *consultar a, consultar con* ❏ *Consult your doctor about how much exercise you should get. Consulta con tu médico cuánto ejercicio debes hacer.* ❏ *He needed to consult with an attorney. Necesitaba consultar a un abogado.* ● **con|sul|ta|tion** N-VAR (**consultations**) *consulta, asesoría* ❏ *…a consultation with a lawyer. …una consulta con un abogado.*

**con|sult|ant** /kənsʌltənt/ (**consultants**) N-COUNT A **consultant** is a person who gives expert advice on a particular subject. *consultor o consultora, asesor o asesora* ❏ *She is a consultant to the government. Es asesora del gobierno.*

**con|sul|ta|tion** /kɒnsəlteɪʃən/ (**consultations**) **1** N-VAR A **consultation** is a meeting to discuss something. *junta, reunión* ❏ *The unions want consultations with the employers. Los sindicatos quieren tener una junta con los patrones.* **2** → see also **consult**

**con|sume** /kənsum/ (**consumes, consuming, consumed**) **1** v-т If you **consume** something, you eat or drink it. *consumir, comerse, beberse* [FORMAL] ❏ *Martha consumed nearly a pound of cheese per day. Martha se comía casi medio kilo de queso al día.* **2** v-т To **consume** an amount of fuel, energy, or time means to use it up. *consumir* ❏ *The most efficient refrigerators consume 70 percent less electricity. Los refrigeradores más eficientes consumen un 70 por ciento menos de electricidad.* **3** → see also **consuming**

**con|sum|er** /kənsumər/ (**consumers**) **1** N-COUNT A **consumer** is a person who buys things or uses services. *consumidor o consumidora* ❏ *…consumer rights. …derechos de los consumidores.* **2** N-COUNT A **consumer** is a plant or animal that obtains energy by eating other plants or animals. *parásito, depredador* [TECHNICAL]

**con|sum|er con|fi|dence** N-UNCOUNT If there is **consumer confidence**, people generally are willing to spend money and buy things. *confianza del consumidor* ❏ *Consumer confidence rose in July. En julio se incrementó la confianza de los consumidores.*

**Con|sum|er Price In|dex** N-PROPER The **consumer price index** is an official measure of the rate of inflation within a country's economy. The abbreviation **CPI** is also used. *índice de precios al consumidor, IPC* ❏ *The Consumer Price Index fell by 1.1 per cent. El índice de precios al consumidor se redujo en 1.1 por ciento.*

**con|sum|ing** /kənsumɪŋ/ **1** ADJ A **consuming** passion or interest is more important to you than anything else. *absorbente* ❏ *He has developed a consuming passion for chess. Su pasión por el ajedrez es absorbente.* **2** → see also **consume**

**con|sump|tion** /kənsʌmpʃən/ **1** N-UNCOUNT The **consumption** of fuel or energy is the act of using it or the amount that is used. *consumo* ❏ *…a reduction in fuel consumption. …una reducción en el consumo de combustibles.* **2** N-UNCOUNT The **consumption** of food or drink is the act of eating or drinking something. *consumo* [FORMAL] ❏ *Most of the meat was unfit for human consumption. La mayor parte de la carne no era apta para el consumo humano.* **3** N-UNCOUNT **Consumption** is the act of buying and using things. *consumo* ❏ *…the production and consumption of goods and services. …la producción y el consumo de bienes y servicios.*

**con|tact** /kɒntækt/ (**contacts, contacting, contacted**) **1** N-UNCOUNT **Contact** involves meeting or communicating with someone. *contacto* ❏ *I had very little contact with teenagers. Tenía muy poco contacto con adolescentes.* ❏ *He was in direct contact with the kidnappers. Estaba en contacto directo con los secuestradores.* ❏ *How did you make contact with the author? ¿Cómo te pusiste en contacto con el autor?* **2** N-UNCOUNT If you come **into contact with** something, you have some experience of it in the course of your work or other activities. *en contacto con* ❏ *The college has brought me into contact with western ideas. La universidad me ha puesto en contacto con las ideas occidentales.* **3** N-UNCOUNT If people or things are in **contact**, they are touching each other. *contacto* ❏ *There was no physical contact. No hubo contacto físico.* **4** v-т If you **contact** someone, you telephone them or send them a message or letter. *contactar, ponerse en contacto con* ❏ *Contact our head office for further details. Para mayor información, póngase en contacto con la oficina principal.* **5** N-COUNT A **contact** is someone you know in an organization or profession who helps you or gives you information. *contacto* ❏ *Their contact at the United States embassy was Phil. Phil era su contacto en la embajada estadounidense.*

contact lens

**con|tact lens** (contact lenses) N-COUNT **Contact lenses** are small plastic lenses that you put on the surface of your eyes to help you see better. *lente de contacto*
→ see **eye**

**con|ta|gious** /kənteɪdʒəs/ **1** ADJ A **contagious** disease can be caught by touching people or things that are infected with it. *contagioso* ❑ *...a highly contagious disease of the lungs. ...una enfermedad de los pulmones muy contagiosa.* **2** ADJ A feeling or attitude that is **contagious** spreads quickly among a group of people. *contagioso* ❑ *Laughing is contagious. La risa es contagiosa.*

**con|tain** /kənteɪn/ (**contains, containing, contained**) **1** V-T If something such as a box or room **contains** things, those things are in it. *contener, haber* ❑ *The envelope contained a Christmas card. El sobre contenía una tarjeta de Navidad.* ❑ *The first two floors of the building contain stores and a restaurant. En los dos primeros pisos del edificio hay tiendas y un restaurante.* **2** V-T If something **contains** a substance, that substance is a part of it. *contener, tener* ❑ *Apples contain vitamins. Las manzanas tienen vitaminas.* **3** V-T To **contain** something means to control it and prevent it from spreading or increasing. *contener, detener* ❑ *Firefighters are still trying to contain the fire. Los bomberos siguen tratando de contener el fuego.* **4** → see also **self-contained**

**con|tain|er** /kənteɪnər/ (**containers**) **1** N-COUNT A **container** is something such as a box or bottle that is used to hold or store things. *recipiente* ❑ *The fish are stored in plastic containers. Los pescados están en recipientes de plástico.* **2** N-COUNT A **container** is a very large metal or wooden box used for transporting goods so that they can be loaded easily onto ships and trucks. *contenedor* ❑ *The train carried loaded containers. El tren llevaba contenedores cargados.*
→ see Picture Dictionary: **container**

**con|tain|er ship** (**container ships**) N-COUNT A **container ship** is a ship that is designed for carrying goods that are packed in large metal or wooden boxes. *buque/barco portacontenedores*
→ see **ship**

**con|tami|nate** /kəntæmɪneɪt/ (**contaminates, contaminating, contaminated**) V-T If something **is contaminated by** dirt, chemicals, or radiation, they make it dirty or harmful. *contaminar* ❑ *Have any fish been contaminated? ¿Se contaminaron los peces?* ● **con|tami|na|tion** /kəntæmɪneɪʃən/ N-UNCOUNT *contaminación* ❑ *...the contamination of the ocean. ...la contaminación del océano.*

**con|tem|plate** /kɒntəmpleɪt/ (**contemplates, contemplating, contemplated**) **1** V-T If you **contemplate** an action, you consider it as a possibility. *contemplar, considerar* ❑ *For a time he contemplated a career as a doctor. Durante un tiempo consideró hacer carrera como médico.* **2** V-T If you **contemplate** an idea or subject, you think about it carefully for a long time. *contemplar, pensar* ❑ *He cried as he contemplated his future. Lloró pensando en su futuro.* ● **con|tem|pla|tion** /kɒntəmpleɪʃən/ N-UNCOUNT *contemplación, reflexión, meditación* ❑ *It is a place of quiet contemplation. Es un tranquilo lugar de contemplación.* **3** V-T If you **contemplate** something or someone, you look at them for a long time. *contemplar* ❑ *He contemplated his hands. Contempló sus manos.*

**con|tem|po|rary** /kəntɛmpərɛri/ (**contemporaries**) **1** ADJ **Contemporary** means existing now or at the time you are talking about. *contemporáneo, actual* ❑ *...contemporary music. ...música contermporánea* **2** N-COUNT Someone's **contemporary** is a person who is or was alive at the same time as them. *contemporáneo* ❑ *...Shakespeare and his contemporaries. ...Shakespeare y sus contemporáneos.*

**con|tempt** /kəntɛmpt/ N-UNCOUNT If you have **contempt for** someone or something, you have no respect for them. *desprecio* ❑ *He has contempt for politicians of all parties. Muestra el desprecio que siente por los políticos de todos los partidos.*

**con|tend** /kəntɛnd/ (**contends, contending, contended**) **1** V-I If you have to **contend with** a problem or difficulty, you have to deal with it or overcome it. *lidiar con, enfrentar, enfrentarse a*

C

❑ *It is time, once again, to contend with racism.* *Otra vez llegó el momento de enfrentar el racismo* **2** V-T If you **contend that** something is true, you state or argue that it is true. *argüir, sostener, argumentar, afirmar* [FORMAL] ❑ *Evans contends that he has been falsely accused.* *Evans argumenta que la acusación es falsa.* **3** V-RECIP If you **contend with** someone **for** something, you compete with them to try to get it. *competir* ❑ *...the two main groups contending for power.* *...los dos grupos principales que compiten por el poder.* ❑ *Clubs such as the Kansas City Royals have had trouble contending with richer teams.* *Clubes como los Royals de Kansas City tienen problemas para competir con clubes más ricos.* • **con|tend|er** /kəntɛndər/ N-COUNT (**contenders**) *aspirante, contendiente* ❑ *...a strong contender for a place on the Olympic team.* *...un sólido aspirante a un puesto en el equipo olímpico.*

**content**
❶ NOUN USES
❷ ADJECTIVE USES

❶ **con|tent** /kɒntɛnt/ (**contents**) **1** N-PLURAL The **contents** of a container such as a bottle, box, or room are the things inside it. *contenido* ❑ *Empty the contents of the pan into a bowl.* *Vacía el contenido de la cacerola en un tazón.* **2** N-PLURAL The **contents** of a book are its different chapters and sections. *índice, tabla de contenidos* ❑ *There is no table of contents.* *No tiene tabla de contenidos.* **3** N-VAR The **content** of a book, television program, or website is its subject and the ideas expressed in it. *contenido* ❑ *She refused to discuss the content of the letter.* *Se negó a discutir el contenido de la carta.* **4** N-SING You can use **content** to refer to the amount or proportion of something that a substance contains. *contenido* ❑ *Margarine has the same fat content as butter.* *La margarina tiene el mismo contenido de grasa que la mantequilla.*

❷ **con|tent** /kəntɛnt/ **1** ADJ If you are **content with** something, you are willing to accept it, rather than wanting something more or something better. *contento, satisfecho, conforme* ❑ *I am content to admire the mountains from below.* *Estoy contento con admirar las montañas desde abajo.* ❑ *I'm perfectly content with the way the campaign has gone.* *Estoy perfectamente satisfecho de la forma en que se ha desarrollado la campaña.* **2** ADJ If you are **content**, you are happy or satisfied. *contento, feliz* ❑ *He says his daughter is quite content.* *Dice que su hija está contenta.*

**con|ten|tion** /kəntɛnʃᵊn/ (**contentions**) **1** N-COUNT Someone's **contention** is the opinion that they are expressing. *argumento, punto de vista, opinión* ❑ *It is my contention that everyone wants to be loved.* *Mi punto de vista es que todos desean ser amados.* **2** N-UNCOUNT If something is a cause **of contention,** it is a cause of disagreement or argument. *discusión, disputa* ❑ *What happened next is a matter of contention.* *Lo que pasó después, es motivo de discusión*

**con|test** (**contests, contesting, contested**)

The noun is pronounced /kɒntɛst/. The verb is pronounced /kəntɛst/.

**1** N-COUNT A **contest** is a competition or game. *competencia* ❑ *It was a thrilling contest.* *Fue una competencia emocionante.* **2** N-COUNT A **contest** is a struggle to win power or control. *contienda* ❑ *...next year's presidential contest.* *...la contienda del año próximo por la presidencia.* **3** V-T If you **contest** a statement or decision, you object to it formally. *refutar, impugnar* ❑ *He has to reply within 14 days in order to contest the case.* *Para impugnar el caso tiene que contestar en 14 días.*

**Thesaurus** *contest* Ver también:
N. competition, game, match **1**
fight, struggle **2**

**con|test|ant** /kəntɛstənt/ (**contestants**) N-COUNT A **contestant** in a competition or game show is a person who takes part in it. *competidor o competidora, concursante* ❑ *He applied to be a contestant on the television show.* *Se inscribió como concursante en un programa de televisión.*

**con|text** /kɒntɛkst/ (**contexts**) **1** N-VAR The **context of** an idea or event is the general situation in which it occurs. *contexto* ❑ *It helps to understand the historical context in which Chaucer wrote.* *Ayuda entender el contexto histórico en el cual escribió Chaucer.* **2** N-VAR The **context** of a word, sentence, or text consists of the words, sentences, or text before and after it which help to make its meaning clear. *contexto* ❑ *Thomas says that he has been quoted out of context.* *Thomas dice que lo citaron fuera de contexto.*

**con|text clue** (**context clues**) N-COUNT **Context clues** are words or phrases that surround a particular word and help the reader to understand the word's meaning or pronunciation. *clave contextual*

**con|ti|nent** /kɒntɪnənt/ (**continents**) N-COUNT A **continent** is a very large area of land, such as Africa or Asia, that consists of several countries. *continente* ❑ *She loved the African continent.* *Le encantaba el continente africano.* • **con|ti|nen|tal** ADJ *continental* ❑ *...continental Europe.* *...Europa continental.*
→ see Word Web: **continents**
→ see **earth**

**con|ti|nen|tal** /kɒntɪnɛntᵊl/ **1** ADJ The **continental** United States consists of all the states which are situated on the continent of North America, as opposed to Hawaii and territories such as the Virgin Islands. *continental* ❑ *Shipping is included on orders sent within the continental U.S.* *Envío incluido en las órdenes despachadas en los Estados Unidos continentales.* **2** → see also **continent**

**con|ti|nen|tal break|fast** (**continental breakfasts**) N-COUNT A **continental breakfast** is breakfast that consists of food such as bread, butter, jam, and a hot drink. There is no cooked food. *desayuno continental*
→ see **meal**

**con|ti|nen|tal drift** N-UNCOUNT **Continental drift** is the slow movement of the Earth's continents toward and away from each other. *deriva de los continentes*
→ see **continent**

**con|ti|nen|tal mar|gin** (**continental margins**) N-COUNT The **continental margin** is the part of the ocean floor between the edge of a continent and the deepest part of the ocean. *margen continental*

C

**Word Web** continents

In 1912, Alfred Wegener* made an important discovery. The shapes of the various **continents** seemed to fit together like the pieces of a puzzle. He decided they had once been a single **land mass** which he called **Pangaea**. He thought the continents had slowly moved apart. Wegener called this theory **continental drift**. He said the earth's **crust** is not a single, solid piece. It's full of cracks which allow huge pieces to move around on the earth's mantle. The movement of these tectonic **plates** increases the distance between Europe and North America by about 20 millimeters every year.

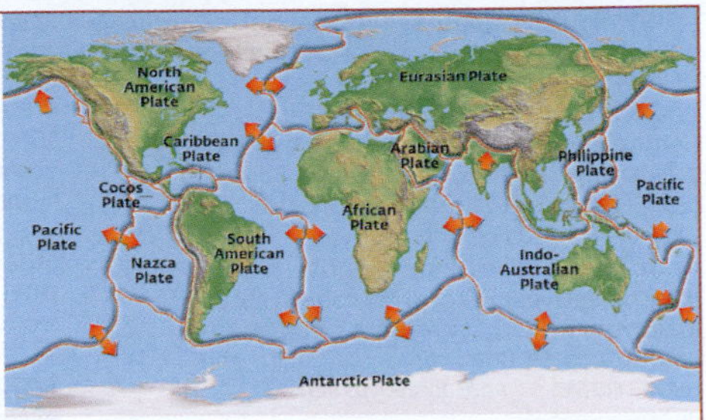


Major Plates of the Earth's Crust

*Alfred Wegener (1880-1930): a German scientist.*

**con|ti|nen|tal rise** (**continental rises**) N-COUNT The **continental rise** is the part of the ocean floor that lies at the base of a continental slope. *cuesta continental*

**con|ti|nen|tal shelf** N-UNCOUNT **The continental shelf** is the area which forms the edge of a continent, ending in a steep slope to the depths of the ocean. *plataforma continental*

**con|ti|nen|tal slope** (**continental slopes**) N-COUNT The **continental slope** is the steepest part of the continental margin. *declive continental*

**con|tin|gent** /kəntɪndʒᵊnt/ (**contingents**) N-COUNT A **contingent** is a group of people representing a country or organization at a meeting or other event. *contingente* [FORMAL] ❑ *The American contingent will stay overnight in London. El contingente estadounidense pasará la noche en Londres.*

**con|tin|ual** /kəntɪnyuəl/ ADJ **Continual** means happening without stopping or happening again and again. *continuo* ❑ *The school has been in continual use since 1883. La escuela ha estado en uso continuo desde 1883.* ❑ *...the government's continual demands for cash. ...las continuas solicitudes gubernamentales de efectivo.*
• **con|tinu|al|ly** ADV *continuamente, constantemente* ❑ *She cried almost continually. Lloraba casi constantemente.* ❑ *Malcolm was continually changing his mind. Malcolm cambiaba continuamente de idea.*

| **Thesaurus** | *continual* Ver también: |
|---|---|
| ADJ. | ongoing, constant, repeated, unending |

**con|tinue** /kəntɪnyu/ (**continues, continuing, continued**) **1** V-T/V-I If something **continues,** it does not stop. If you **continue to** do something, you do not stop doing it. *continuar, seguir* ❑ *The conflict continued for another four years. El conflicto continuó por cuatro años más.* ❑ *Outside the building people continue their protest. La gente sigue protestando frente al edificio.* ❑ *I hope they continue to fight for equal justice. Espero que sigan luchando por que la justicia sea equitativa.* ❑ *Diana and Roy are determined to continue working. Diana y Roy están decididos a seguir con su trabajo.* **2** V-T/V-I If something **continues** or if you **continue** it, it starts again after a break or interruption. *proseguir, continuar, seguir* ❑ *The trial continues today. El juicio continúa hoy.* ❑ *I went up to my room to continue with my packing. Me fui a mi cuarto a seguir empacando.* ❑ *She looked up for a minute and then continued drawing. Levantó la vista un minuto y después siguió dibujando.* **3** V-T/V-I If you **continue,** you begin speaking again after a pause or interruption. *proseguir, continuar* ❑ *"You have no right to threaten this man," Alison continued. —No tienes derecho a amenazar a este hombre —prosiguió Alison.* ❑ *Tony drank some coffee before he continued. Tony bebió un poco de café antes de continuar.* **4** V-I If you **continue** in a particular direction, you keep going in that direction. *seguir* ❑ *He continued rapidly up the path. Siguió rápidamente por el camino.*

| **Thesaurus** | *continue* Ver también: |
|---|---|
| V. | go on, persist; (*ant.*) stop **1**<br>carry on, resume **2** **3** |

**con|tinu|ous** /kəntɪnyuəs/ **1** ADJ A **continuous** process or event continues for a period of time without stopping. *continuo* ❑ *They heard continuous gunfire. Oyeron un tiroteo continuo.*
• **con|tinu|ous|ly** ADV *constantemente* ❑ *Detectives are working continuously on the case. Los detectives están constantemente trabajando en el caso.* **2** ADJ A **continuous** line or surface has no gaps or holes in it. *continuo* ❑ *...a continuous line of cars. ...una fila continua de autos.* **3** ADJ In English grammar, **continuous** verb groups are formed using the auxiliary "be" and the present participle of a verb, as in "I'm feeling a bit tired." Compare **simple**. *continuo*

**con|tour draw|ing** (**contour drawings**) N-VAR **Contour drawing** is a method of drawing in which you draw the outline of an object in a single, continuous line without looking at the drawing as a whole. A **contour drawing** is a drawing that is made using this method. *dibujo perfilado*

**con|tour feath|er** (**contour feathers**) N-COUNT **Contour feathers** are the outermost feathers on the body of an adult bird. *pluma de contorno*

**con|tour in|ter|val** (**contour intervals**) N-COUNT A **contour interval** on a map is the difference in height between one contour line and the contour line next to it. *distancia vertical*

C

**con|tour line** (**contour lines**) N-COUNT **Contour lines** on a map are the same as **contours**. *cota, curva de nivel*

**contra|cep|tion** /kɒntrəsɛpʃᵊn/ N-UNCOUNT **Contraception** refers to methods of preventing pregnancy. *anticoncepción, contracepción* ❑ *Use a reliable method of contraception. Utilice un método confiable de anticoncepción.*

**contra|cep|tive** /kɒntrəsɛptɪv/ (**contraceptives**) N-COUNT A **contraceptive** is a device or drug that prevents a woman from becoming pregnant. *anticonceptivo* ❑ *...oral contraceptives. ...anticonceptivos orales*

**Word Link** *tract ≈ dragging, drawing : contract, subtract, tractor*

**con|tract** (**contracts, contracting, contracted**)

The noun is pronounced /kɒntrækt/. The verb is pronounced /kəntrækt/.

1 N-COUNT A **contract** is a legal agreement, usually between two companies or between an employer and employee, which involves doing work for a stated sum of money. *contrato* ❑ *The company won a contract for work on Chicago's tallest building. La compañía ganó un contrato para trabajar en el edificio más alto de Chicago.* 2 V-T If you **contract with** someone **to** do something, you legally agree to do it for them or for them to do it for you. *contratar* [FORMAL] ❑ *You can contract with us to deliver your goods. Puede contratarnos para que entreguemos sus productos* 3 V-T/V-I When something **contracts**, or something **contracts** it, it becomes smaller or shorter. *contraerse* ❑ *When you are anxious, your muscles contract. Cuando estás ansioso, tus músculos se contraen.* • **con|trac|tion** /kəntrækʃᵊn/ N-VAR (**contractions**) *contracción* ❑ *...the contraction and expansion of blood vessels. ...la contracción y expansión de los vasos sanguíneos.* 4 V-T If you **contract** a serious illness, you become ill with it. *contraer, contagiarse* [FORMAL] ❑ *He contracted malaria in Africa. Contrajo la malaria en África.*
→ see **muscle**

**Word Partnership** Usar *contract* con:

V. **sign a** contract 1
N. **terms of a** contract 1
contract **with *someone*** 2
contract **a disease** 4

**con|trac|tor** /kɒntræktər, kəntræk-/ (**contractors**) N-COUNT A **contractor** is a person or company that does work for other people or organizations. *contratista* [BUSINESS] ❑ *...a building contractor. ...un contratista de la construcción.*

**Word Link** *contra ≈ against : contradict, contrary, contrast*

**Word Link** *dict ≈ speaking : contradict, dictate, predict*

**contra|dict** /kɒntrədɪkt/ (**contradicts, contradicting, contradicted**) 1 V-T If you **contradict** someone, you say or suggest that what they have just said is wrong. *contradecir* ❑ *She did not contradict him. Ella no lo contradijo.* 2 V-T If one statement or piece of evidence **contradicts** another, the first one makes the second one appear to be wrong. *contradecir* ❑ *Her version of the story contradicted her daughter's. Su versión de la historia contradecía a la de su hija.*

**contra|dic|tion** /kɒntrədɪkʃᵊn/ (**contradictions**) N-COUNT A **contradiction** is an aspect of a situation that appears to conflict with other aspects, so that they cannot all exist or be true. *contradicción* ❑ *...the contradiction between her private life and her public image. ...la contradicción entre su vida privada y su imagen pública.*

**Word Link** *ory ≈ relating to : advisory, contradictory, sensory*

**contra|dic|tory** /kɒntrədɪktəri/ ADJ If two or more facts, ideas, or statements are **contradictory**, they state or imply that opposite things are true. *contradictorio* ❑ *...a series of contradictory statements. ...una serie de declaraciones contradictorias.*

**con|tra|ry** /kɒntrɛri/ 1 ADJ **Contrary** ideas or opinions are completely different from each other. *contrario* ❑ *Contrary to popular belief, moderate exercise actually decreases your appetite. Contrario a lo que piensa la gente, de hecho el ejercicio moderado disminuye el apetito.* 2 PHRASE You use **on the contrary** when you disagree with something and are going to say that the opposite is true. *al contrario* ❑ *"People just don't do things like that."—"On the contrary, they do them all the time." —La gente no más no hace ese tipo de cosas. —Al contrario, lo hace todo el tiempo.* 3 PHRASE When a particular idea is being considered, evidence or statements **to the contrary** suggest that it is not true or that the opposite is true. *en contrario* ❑ *He continued to claim that he did nothing wrong, despite clear evidence to the contrary. Siguió afirmando que no había hecho nada malo, a pesar de las obvias pruebas en contrario.*

**con|trast** (**contrasts, contrasting, contrasted**)

The noun is pronounced /kɒntræst/. The verb is pronounced /kəntræst/.

1 N-VAR A **contrast** is a great difference between two or more things. *contraste* ❑ *...the contrast between town and country. ...el contraste entre el campo y la ciudad.* 2 PHRASE You say **by contrast** or **in contrast**, or **in contrast to** something, to show that you are mentioning a very different situation from the one you have just mentioned. *por el contrario, a diferencia de* ❑ *His brother, by contrast, has plenty of money to spend. Su hermano, sin embargo, tiene mucho dinero para gastar.* ❑ *In contrast, the lives of girls were often very restricted. Por el contrario, la vida de las niñas solía estar muy restringida.* 3 V-T If you **contrast** one thing **with** another, you show or consider the differences between them. *comparar* ❑ *She contrasted the situation then with the present crisis. Comparó la situación de entonces con la crisis actual.* ❑ *In this section we contrast four different ideas. En esta sección comparamos cuatro ideas.* 4 V-RECIP If one thing **contrasts with** another, it is very different from it. *contrastar, diferir* ❑ *The latest news contrasts with earlier reports. Las últimas noticias difieren de los primeros informes.* ❑ *Paint the wall in a contrasting color. Pinta la pared de un color que contraste.* 5 N-UNCOUNT **Contrast** is the degree of difference between

the darker and lighter parts of a photograph, television picture, or painting. *contraste*

**Word Link** *tribute ≈ giving : attribute, contribute, distribute*

**con|trib|ute** /kəntrɪbyut/ (**contributes, contributing, contributed**) **1** V-I If you **contribute to** something, you say or do something to help make it successful. *contribuir, aportar* ❑ *The three sons also contribute to the family business. También los tres hijos contribuyen al negocio familiar.* **2** V-T/V-I To **contribute** money or resources **to** something means to help pay for it or achieve it. *contribuir, colaborar* ❑ *The U.S. is contributing $4 billion in loans. Los Estados Unidos contribuyen con 4 mil millones de dólares en créditos.* ❑ *Local businesses have agreed to contribute. Las empresas locales han accedido a colaborar.* ● **con|tribu|tor** /kəntrɪbyətər/ N-COUNT (**contributors**) *donante, donador o donadora* ❑ *Candidates for Congress received 53 percent of their funds from individual contributors. Los candidatos al Congreso recibieron el 53 por ciento de los fondos de donantes particulares.* **3** V-I If something **contributes to** an event or situation, it is one of the causes of it. *contribuir a* ❑ *The wet road contributed to the accident. El pavimento mojado contribuyó al accidente.*

**Thesaurus** *contribute* Ver también:

V. aid, assist, chip in, commit, donate, give, grant, help, support; (*ant.*) neglect, take away **2**

**con|tribu|tor** /kəntrɪbyətər/ (**contributors**) N-COUNT You can use **contributor** to refer to one of the causes of an event or situation, especially if that event or situation is an unpleasant one. *que contribuye* ❑ *Old buses are major contributors to pollution in cities. Los autobuses viejos contribuyen mucho a la contaminación de las ciudades.*

**con|tri|bu|tion** /kɒntrɪbyuʃ°n/ (**contributions**) **1** N-COUNT If you make a **contribution to** something, you do something to help make it successful or to produce it. *contribución* ❑ *He received an award for his contribution to world peace. Le dieron un reconocimiento por contribuir a la paz mundial.* **2** N-COUNT A **contribution** is a sum of money that you give in order to help pay for something. *aportación, contribución, donación* ❑ *...contributions to charity. ...donaciones para obras de caridad.*

**Word Partnership** Usar *contribution* con:

ADJ. **important** contribution, **significant** contribution **1** **2**

V. **make a** contribution, **send a** contribution **1** **2**

**con|trol** /kəntroʊl/ (**controls, controlling, controlled**) **1** N-UNCOUNT **Control of** an organization, place, or system is the power to make all the important decisions about the way that it is run. *control* ❑ *Mr. Ronson is giving up control of the company. El Sr. Ronson está cediendo el control de la compañía.* ● PHRASE If you are **in control of** something, you have the power to make all the important decisions about the way it is run. *tener el control de, controlar* ❑ *Nobody knows who is in control of the club. Nadie sabe quién tiene el control en el club.* ● PHRASE If something is **under** your **control**, you have the power to make all the important decisions about the way that it is run. *bajo el control* ❑ *All the newspapers are under government control. El gobierno tiene el control de todos los periódicos.* **2** V-T If someone **controls** an organization, place, or system, they have the power to make all the important decisions about the way that it is run. *controlar, tener el control de* ❑ *He controls the largest software company in California. Controla la mayor compañía de software de California.* ● **con|trol|ler** (**controllers**) N-COUNT *controlador o controladora* ❑ *He became controller of Continental Airlines. Ahora es controlador de Continental Airlines.* **3** V-T If you **control** a person or machine, you are able to make them do what you want them to do. *controlar* ❑ *...a computerized system to control the gates. ...un sistema computarizado para controlar el portón.* ❑ *I can't control what the judge says. No puedo controlar lo que el juez dice.* ● **Control** is also a noun. *control* ❑ *He lost control of his car. Perdió el control de su auto.* **4** V-T To **control** prices, wages, or undesirable activities means to deal with them or restrict them to an acceptable level. *controlar* ❑ *The government tried to control rising health-care costs. El gobierno trató de controlar el alza en los costos de los servicios de salud.* ● **Control** is also a noun. *control* ❑ *...control of inflation. ...control de la inflación.* **5** PHRASE If something is **out of control**, it cannot be dealt with or restricted to an acceptable level. *fuera de control* ❑ *The fire is burning out of control. El fuego está fuera de control.* **6** PHRASE If something is **under control**, it is being dealt with or kept at an acceptable level. *bajo control, controlado* ❑ *The situation is under control. La situación está controlada.* **7** V-T If you **control yourself** or your feelings, you make yourself behave calmly even though you are feeling angry, excited, or upset. *controlarse* ❑ *Jo should learn to control herself. Jo debe aprender a controlarse.* ● **Control** is also a noun. *control* ❑ *Sometimes he would completely lose control. A veces perdía totalmente el control.* ● **con|trolled** ADJ *controlado* ❑ *Her manner was quiet and very controlled. Su actitud era de tranquilidad, y muy controlada.* **8** N-COUNT A **control** is a device such as a switch or lever which you use in order to operate a machine or piece of equipment. *control* ❑ *I practiced operating the controls. Practiqué la forma de operar los controles.* **9** N-VAR **Controls** are the methods an organization uses to restrict something. *control* ❑ *...price controls. ...controles de precios.* **10** N-COUNT In a scientific experiment such as a test of a new drug or treatment, a **control** is the use of a group of people or animals that do not receive the drug or treatment, so that the two groups can be compared to see if the drug or treatment works. *grupo de control, control* **11** V-I In a scientific experiment, to **control** *for* a particular variable means to carry out a second experiment in which the variable does not occur, so that the results of the two experiments can be compared and the effect of the variable seen. *controlar* **12** → see also **birth control, remote control**

**con|trolled ex|peri|ment** (**controlled experiments**) N-COUNT A **controlled experiment**

C

is a scientific experiment which examines the effect of a single variable by keeping all the other variables fixed. *experimento controlado*
→ see **experiment**

**con|tro|ver|sial** /kɒntrəvɜrʃᵊl/ ADJ Something or someone that is **controversial** is the subject of intense public argument, disagreement, or disapproval. *controvertido, polémico* ❑ *...a controversial new book. ...un nuevo libro polémico.*

C

**con|tro|ver|sy** /kɒntrəvɜrsi/ (**controversies**) N-VAR **Controversy** is a lot of discussion and argument about something, often involving strong anger or disapproval. *controversia* ❑ *The proposals have caused controversy. Las propuestas han sido motivo de controversias.*

**con|vec|tion** /kənvɛkʃᵊn/ N-UNCOUNT **Convection** is the process by which heat travels through air, water, and other gases and liquids. *convección* [TECHNICAL]

**con|vec|tion cur|rent** (**convection currents**) N-COUNT A **convection current** is a circular current within a substance such as air or water resulting from a difference in density between warm and cool parts of the substance. *corriente de convección* [TECHNICAL]

**con|vec|tive zone** /kənvɛktɪv zoʊn/ (**convective zones**) N-COUNT The **convective zone** is the area of the sun where energy is carried toward the surface by convection currents. *zona de convección* [TECHNICAL]

| Word Link | *con ≈ together, with : consensus, construct, convene* |
|---|---|

**con|vene** /kənvin/ (**convenes, convening, convened**) V-T/V-I If you **convene** a meeting, you arrange for it to take place. You can also say that people **convene** at a meeting. *convocar, reunirse* [FORMAL] ❑ *He convened a meeting of his closest advisers. Convocó a una reunión con sus asesores más cercanos.*

**con|veni|ence** /kənvinyəns/ (**conveniences**) **1** N-UNCOUNT If something is done for your **convenience,** it is done in a way that is useful or suitable for you. *conveniencia, comodidad* ❑ *We have enclosed a pre-paid envelope for your convenience. Para su comodidad, incluimos un sobre prepagado.* **2** N-COUNT A **convenience** is something that is very useful. *comodidad* ❑ *Mail order is a convenience for buyers who are too busy to shop. Las compras por correo son una comodidad para quien está demasiado ocupado como para ir a las tiendas.* **3** N-COUNT **Conveniences** are pieces of equipment designed to make your life easier. *comodidades* ❑ *...an apartment with all the modern conveniences. ...un departamento con todas las comodidades modernas.* **4** → see also **convenient**

**con|veni|ent** /kənvinyənt/ **1** ADJ Something that is **convenient** is easy, useful, or suitable for a particular purpose. *conveniente* ❑ *...a convenient way of paying. ...una forma de pago conveniente.* ● **con|veni|ence** N-UNCOUNT *conveniencia, comodidad* ❑ *They may use a credit card for convenience. Por comodidad podrían usar una tarjeta de crédito* ● **con|veni|ent|ly** ADV *convenientemente, de manera conveniente* ❑ *...conveniently-placed cupholders. ...soportes para las tazas colocados de manera conveniente.* **2** ADJ A place that is **convenient** is near to where you are, or near to another place where you want to go. *práctico, cómodo, muy a mano* ❑ *The town is convenient to Dulles Airport. El pueblo queda muy a mano del aeropuerto Dulles.* ● **con|veni|ent|ly** ADV *convenientemente* ❑ *It was very conveniently situated just across the road. Estaba muy convenientemente situado, al otro lado de la calle.* **3** ADJ A **convenient** time to do something is a time when you are free to do it or would like to do it. *oportuno, conveniente* ❑ *She will try to arrange a convenient time. Va a tratar de encontrar una hora conveniente.*

**con|ven|tion** /kənvɛnʃᵊn/ (**conventions**) **1** N-VAR A **convention** is an accepted way of behaving or of doing something. *convención, convencionalismo* ❑ *It's a social convention that men don't wear skirts. Es una convención social que los hombres no usen falda.* **2** N-COUNT A **convention** is an official agreement between countries or organizations. *convención* ❑ *...the U.N. convention on climate change. ...la convención de la ONU sobre el cambio climático.* **3** N-COUNT A **convention** is a large meeting of an organization or group. *convención, congreso* ❑ *...the annual convention of the Society of Professional Journalists. ...el congreso anual de la Asociación de Periodistas Profesionales.* **4** N-COUNT In art, literature, or the theater, a **convention** is a traditional method or style. *convención*

**con|ven|tion|al** /kənvɛnʃənᵊl/ **1** ADJ **Conventional** people behave in a way that is accepted as normal in their society. *convencional* ❑ *...a respectable married woman with conventional opinions. ...una respetable mujer casada con opiniones convencionales.* ● **con|ven|tion|al|ly** ADV *convencionalmente, de manera convencional* ❑ *Men still wore their hair short and dressed conventionally. Los hombres seguían llevando el cabello corto y vistiendo de manera convencional.* **2** ADJ A **conventional** method or product is one that is usually used. *tradicional, convencional* ❑ *...a conventional oven. ...un horno convencional* ● **con|ven|tion|al|ly** ADV *convencionalmente* ❑ *...conventionally-grown crops. ...cosechas cultivadas convencionalmente.* **3** ADJ **Conventional** weapons and wars do not include nuclear, chemical, or biological weapons. *convencional*

**con|ver|gent bound|a|ry** (**convergent boundaries**) N-COUNT A **convergent boundary** is an area in the Earth's crust where two tectonic plates are moving toward each other. *límite convergente* [TECHNICAL]

**con|ver|sa|tion** /kɒnvərseɪʃᵊn/ (**conversations**) N-COUNT If you have a **conversation with** someone, you talk with them, usually in an informal situation. *conversación* ❑ *I had an interesting conversation with him. Tuve una conversación interesante con él.* ● **con|ver|sa|tion|al** ADJ *familiar, coloquial* ❑ *...the author's easy, conversational style. ...el estilo coloquial y agradable del autor.*

| Word Link | *verg, vert ≈ turning : convert, divert, verge* |
|---|---|

**con|vert** (**converts, converting, converted**)

The verb is pronounced /kənvɜrt/. The noun is pronounced /kɒnvɜrt/.

**1** V-T/V-I To **convert** one thing **into** another means to change it into a different shape or form. *convertir* ❑ *The signal will be converted into digital code. La señal será convertida a código digital.* ❑ *He wants to convert County Hall into a hotel. Quiere convertir el County Hall en un hotel.* ● **con\ver\sion** /kənvɜrȝ°n/ (**conversions**) N-VAR *conversión* ❑ *...the conversion of unused rail lines into bike paths. ...la conversion de vías de ferrocarril que no se usan en ciclopistas.* **2** V-T/V-I If someone **converts** you, they persuade you to change your religious or political beliefs. *convertir(se)* ❑ *If you try to convert him, you could find he just walks away. Si tratas de convertirlo, verás que se va.* ❑ *He converted her to Catholicism. La convirtió al catolicismo.* ● **con\ver\sion** (**conversions**) N-VAR *conversión* ❑ *...his conversion to Christianity. ...su conversión al cristianismo.* **3** N-COUNT A **convert** is someone who has changed their religious or political beliefs. *converso o conversa* ❑ *She was a convert to Roman Catholicism. Se convirtió al catolicismo.*
→ see **measurement**

**con\vert\ible** /kənvɜrtɪb°l/ (**convertibles**) **1** N-COUNT A **convertible** is a car with a soft roof that can be folded down or removed. *convertible, descapotable* ❑ *Her car is a yellow convertible. Su auto es un convertible amarillo.* **2** ADJ In finance, **convertible** investments or money can be easily exchanged for other forms of investments or money. *convertible, canjeable* [BUSINESS] ❑ *...the introduction of a convertible currency. ...la introducción de una moneda convertible.*
→ see **car**

**con\vex lens** (**convex lenses**) N-COUNT A **convex lens** is a lens that is thicker in the middle than at the edges. Compare **concave**. *lente convexa*

**con\vey** /kənveɪ/ (**conveys, conveying, conveyed**) V-T To **convey** information or feelings means to cause them to be known or understood. *transmitir* ❑ *I tried to convey the wonder of this machine to my husband. Traté de transmitir a mi marido lo maravilloso que es esta máquina.*

**con\vict** (**convicts, convicting, convicted**)

The verb is pronounced /kənvɪkt/. The noun is pronounced /kɒnvɪkt/.

**1** V-T If someone **is convicted of** a crime, they are found guilty of it in a court of law. *condenar, declarar culpable* ❑ *He was convicted of murder. Lo declararon culpable de asesinato.* ❑ *There was insufficient evidence to convict him. Las evidencias no eran suficientes para condenarlo.* **2** N-COUNT A **convict** is someone who is in prison. *recluso o reclusa, presidiario o presidiaria, preso o presa, reo* ❑ *...escaped convicts. ...presos que escaparon.*

**con\vic\tion** /kənvɪkʃ°n/ (**convictions**) **1** N-COUNT A **conviction** is a strong belief or opinion. *convicción* ❑ *It is our firm conviction that a step forward has been taken. Tenemos la firme convicción de que se ha dado un paso adelante.* **2** N-COUNT If

someone has a **conviction,** they have been found guilty of a crime in a court of law. *condena* ❑ *He will appeal against his conviction. Apelará contra su condena.*

**con\vince** /kənvɪns/ (**convinces, convincing, convinced**) **1** V-T If someone or something **convinces** you **to** do something, they persuade you to do it. *convencer* ❑ *He convinced her to go ahead and marry Bud. La convenció de seguir adelante y casarse con Bud.* **2** V-T If someone or something **convinces** you **of** something, they make you believe that it is true or that it exists. *convencer* ❑ *I soon convinced him of my innocence. Pronto lo convencí de mi inocencia.* ● **con\vinced** /kənvɪnst/ ADJ *convencido* ❑ *He was convinced that I was part of the problem. Estaba convencido de que yo era parte del problema.*

**con\vinc\ing** /kənvɪnsɪŋ/ ADJ If someone or something is **convincing,** you believe them. *convincente* ❑ *There is no convincing evidence that power lines cause cancer. No hay pruebas convincentes de que los cables de energía eléctrica provoquen cáncer.* ● **con\vinc\ing\ly** ADV *convincentemente* ❑ *He argued convincingly. Argumentó convincentemente.*

**con\voy** /kɒnvɔɪ/ (**convoys**) N-COUNT A **convoy** is a group of vehicles or ships traveling together. *convoy* ❑ *...a U.N. convoy carrying food and medical supplies. ...un convoy de la ONU que lleva alimentos y suministros médicos.*

**cook** /kʊk/ (**cooks, cooking, cooked**) **1** V-T/V-I When you **cook** a meal, you prepare and heat food so it can be eaten. *cocinar, guisar, preparar comida* ❑ *I have to go and cook dinner. Tengo que ir a preparar la cena.* ❑ *...some basic instructions on how to cook a turkey. ...algunas instrucciones básicas para cocinar un pavo.* ❑ *Let the vegetables cook gently for about 10 minutes. Dejar que las verduras se cocinen ligeramente durante unos 10 minutos.* ❑ *Chefs at the restaurant once cooked for President Kennedy. Los chefs del restaurante cocinaron una vez para el presidente Kennedy.* ● **cook\ing** N-UNCOUNT *cocinar* ❑ *Her hobbies include dancing and cooking. Algunos de sus pasatiempos son bailar y cocinar.* **2** N-COUNT A **cook** is a person whose prepares and cooks food. *cocinero o cocinera* ❑ *They had a butler, a cook, and a maid. Tenían un mayordomo, un cocinero y una doncella.* ❑ *I'm a terrible cook. Soy malísima cocinera.*
→ see Picture Dictionary: **cook**
→ see **cooking**
▶ **cook up** PHR-VERB If someone **cooks up** a dishonest scheme, they plan it. *tramar* [INFORMAL] ❑ *They cooked up the plan between them. Tramaron el plan entre ellos.*

C

C

## Picture Dictionary cook

## Thesaurus *cook* Ver también:

V. heat up, make, prepare 1
N. chef 2

**cook|book** /kʊkbʊk/ (**cookbooks**) N-COUNT A **cookbook** is a book that contains recipes for preparing food. *libro de cocina, libro de recetas, recetario*

**cookie** /kʊki/ (**cookies**) 1 N-COUNT A **cookie** is a small sweet cake. *galleta, galletita* 2 N-COUNT A **cookie** is a piece of computer software which enables a website you have visited to recognize you if you visit it again. *cookie* [COMPUTING]
→ see **dessert**

**cookie cut|ter** (**cookie cutters**) also **cookie-cutter** 1 N-COUNT A **cookie cutter** is a tool that is used for cutting cookies into a particular shape. *molde para galletas* ❑ *...heart-shaped cookie cutters. ...moldes para galletas en forma de corazón.* 2 ADJ A **cookie-cutter** style is one in which the same approach is always used and there are not enough individual differences. *con molde* ❑ *Too many cookie-cutter houses were built. Construyeron demasiadas casas que parecen hechas con molde.*

**cookie sheet** (**cookie sheets**) N-COUNT A **cookie sheet** is a flat piece of metal on which you bake foods such as cookies in an oven. *charola metálica para hornear*

**cook|ing** /kʊkɪŋ/ 1 N-UNCOUNT **Cooking** is food which has been cooked. *comida, cocina* ❑ *...classic French cooking. ...cocina francesa clásica.* 2 N-UNCOUNT **Cooking** is the activity of preparing food. *cocinar, hacer la comida, preparar la comida* ❑ *He did the cooking, cleaning, and home repairs. Preparaba la comida y hacía la limpieza y algunas talachas.* 3 → see also **cook**
→ see Word Web: **cooking**

**cook|out** /kʊkaʊt/ (**cookouts**) N-COUNT A **cookout** is the same as a **barbecue**. *asado, parrillada*

**cool** /kul/ (**cooler, coolest, cools, cooling, cooled**) 1 ADJ Something that is **cool** has a low temperature but is not cold. *fresco* ❑ *I felt a current of cool air. Sentí una corriente de aire fresco.* ❑ *The water was cool. El agua estaba fresca.* 2 ADJ If you stay **cool** in a difficult situation, you remain calm. *tranquilo* ❑ *He was marvelously cool, smiling as if nothing had happened. Estaba maravillosamente tranquilo y sonreía como si nada hubiera pasado.* ● **cool|ly** ADV *tranquilamente, serenamente* ❑ *Everyone must think this situation through calmly and coolly. Todos deben analizar la situación tranquila y serenamente.* 3 ADJ If you say that a person or their behavior is **cool**, you mean that they are unfriendly or not enthusiastic. *hostil, frío* ❑ *The idea has received a cool response. La reacción ante la idea fue fría.* ● **cool|ly** ADV *fríamente, hostilmente* ❑ *"It's your choice, Nina," David said coolly. —Es tu decisión, Nina —dijo David fríamente.* 4 ADJ If you say that a person or thing is **cool**, you mean that they are fashionable and attractive. *cool, a la moda, en la onda, moderno, relajado* [INFORMAL] ❑ *He was trying to be really cool and trendy. Estaba tratando de mostrarse realmente relajado y moderno.* ❑ *That's a cool hat. Qué moderno sombrero.* 5 V-T/V-I When something **cools** or when you **cool** it, it becomes lower in temperature. *enfriar, enfriarse* ❑ *Drain the meat and allow it to cool. Escurre la carne y deja que se enfríe.* ❑ *Huge fans cool the room. Unos ventiladores enormes enfrían el salón.* ● To **cool down** means the same as to **cool**. *enfriar, enfriarse* ❑ *Avoid putting your*

## Word Web cooking

Scientists that study humans believe ancestors began to experiment with **cooking** about 1.5 million years ago. Cooking made some poisonous or **inedible** plants safe to **eat**. It made tough meat **tender** and easier for our bodies to **digest**. It also improved the flavor of the food they ate. **Heating up food** to a high **temperature** killed dangerous bacteria. **Cooked** food could be stored longer. This all helped increase the amount of food available to our ancestors.

car away until the engine has cooled down. No guardes tu auto hasta que no se enfríe el motor. 6 ADJ **Cool** colors are colors that suggest coolness, especially the colors blue, green, and violet.

▶ **cool down** 1 PHR-VERB → see cool 5
2 PHR-VERB If someone **cools down** or if you **cool** them **down,** they become less angry. *calmar, calmarse, tranquilizar, tranquilizarse* ❑ *He has had time to cool down. Tuvo tiempo para tranquilizarse.*

▶ **cool off** PHR-VERB If someone or something **cools off,** or if you **cool** them **off,** they become cooler after being hot. *refrescarse, enfriarse* ❑ *He's trying to cool off out there in the rain. Está afuera, tratando de refrescarse bajo la lluvia.* ❑ *She jumped in the pool to cool herself off. Saltó a la alberca para refrescarse.*

**Thesaurus** *cool* Ver también:
ADJ. chilly, cold, nippy; (*ant.*) warm 1
distant, unfriendly 3

**Word Partnership** Usar *cool* con:
N. cool **air,** cool **breeze** 1

**Word Link** *oper ≈ work : cooperate, opera, operation*

**co|oper|ate** /koʊɒpəreɪt/ (**cooperates, cooperating, cooperated**) 1 V-RECIP If you **cooperate with** someone, you work with them or help them. *cooperar* ❑ *The UN has been cooperating with the State Department. La ONU ha estado cooperando con el Departamento de Estado.*
● **co|opera|tion** /koʊɒpəreɪʃən/ N-UNCOUNT *cooperación* ❑ *...economic cooperation with East Asia. ...cooperación económica con Asia oriental.* 2 V-I If you **cooperate,** you do what someone has asked or told you to do. *cooperar* ❑ *He agreed to cooperate with the police investigation. Aceptó cooperar en la investigación policíaca.* ● **co|opera|tion** N-UNCOUNT *cooperación* ❑ *...the importance of the public's cooperation in the hunt for the bombers. ...la importancia de la cooperación del público en la búsqueda de los terroristas.*

**Word Partnership** Usar *cooperate* con:
V. **agree to** cooperate, **continue to** cooperate, **fail to** cooperate, **refuse to** cooperate 1 2
ADV. cooperate **fully** 1 2
N. **willingness to** cooperate 1 2

**Thesaurus** *cooperative* Ver también:
ADJ. combined, shared, united; (*ant.*) independent, private, separate 2
accommodating 3

**co|or|di|nate** (**coordinates, coordinating, coordinated**)

The verb is pronounced /koʊɔrdᵊneɪt/. The noun is pronounced /koʊɔrdənət/.

1 V-T If you **coordinate** an activity, you organize it. *coordinar* ❑ *...a committee to coordinate police work. ...un comité para coordinar las labores de la policía.* ● **co|or|di|nat|ed** ADJ *coordinado* ❑ *...a well-coordinated surprise attack. ...un ataque sorpresa bien coordinado.* ● **co|or|di|na|tion** /koʊɔrdᵊneɪʃən/ N-UNCOUNT *coordinación* ❑ *...the coordination of educational policy. ...la coordinación de las políticas educativas.* ● **co|or|di|na|tor** N-COUNT (**coordinators**) ❑ *...the party's campaign coordinator. ...el coordinador de la campaña del partido.* 2 V-T If you **coordinate** the parts of your body, you make them work together efficiently. *coordinar* ❑ *You need to coordinate legs, arms, and breathing. Necesitas coordinar piernas, brazos y respiración.* ● **co|or|di|na|tion** N-UNCOUNT *coordinación* ❑ *...clumsiness and lack of coordination. ...torpeza y falta de coordinación*
3 N-COUNT The **coordinates** of a point on a map or graph are the two sets of numbers or letters that you need in order to find that point. *coordenadas* [TECHNICAL] ❑ *Can you give me your coordinates? ¿Me puede dar sus coordenadas?*

**Thesaurus** *coordinate* Ver también:
V. direct, manage, organize 1

**co|or|di|nate sys|tem** (**coordinate systems**) N-COUNT A **coordinate system** is a system that uses coordinates to describe the position of objects on a map or graph. *sistema de coordenadas.*

**cootie** /kuti/ (**cooties**) N-COUNT **Cooties** are the same as **lice.** *piojo* [INFORMAL]

**cop** /kɒp/ (**cops, copping, copped**) N-COUNT A **cop** is a policeman or policewoman. *poli* [INFORMAL] ❑ *The cops know where to find him. Los polis sabían donde encontrarlo.*

▶ **cop to** PHR-VERB If you **cop to** something bad or wrong that you have done, you admit that you have done it. *confesar* [INFORMAL] ❑ *...a chance to cop to all the mistakes we made. ...una oportunidad de confesar todos los errores que cometimos.*

**cope** /koʊp/ (**copes, coping, coped**) V-I If you **cope with** a problem or task, you deal with it successfully. *afrontar, enfrentar, sobrellevar, arreglárselas* ❑ *My mother coped with bringing up three children on thirty dollars a week. Mi madre se las arregló para criar a tres hijos con treinta dólares a la semana.*

**Word Partnership** Usar *cope* con:
N. **ability to** cope, cope **with loss**
ADV. **how to** cope
V. **learn to** cope, **manage to** cope
ADJ. **unable to** cope

**copi|er** /kɒpiər/ (**copiers**) N-COUNT A **copier** is a machine which makes exact copies of writing or pictures on paper, usually by a photographic process. *copiadora*

**cop|per** /kɒpər/ N-UNCOUNT **Copper** is a soft reddish-brown metal. *cobre* ❑ *Chile is the world's largest producer of copper. Chile es el principal productor de cobre del mundo.*
→ see **metal, mineral, pan**

**cop|per wire** (**copper wires**) N-VAR **Copper wire** is a type of cable made of copper that is good at conducting heat and electricity. *alambre de cobre*

**copy** /kɒpi/ (**copies, copying, copied**)
1 N-COUNT If you make a **copy of** something, you produce something that looks like the original thing. *copia* ❑ *...a copy of Steve's letter. ...una copia de la carta de Steve.* 2 N-COUNT A **copy of** a book,

C

## Picture Dictionary core

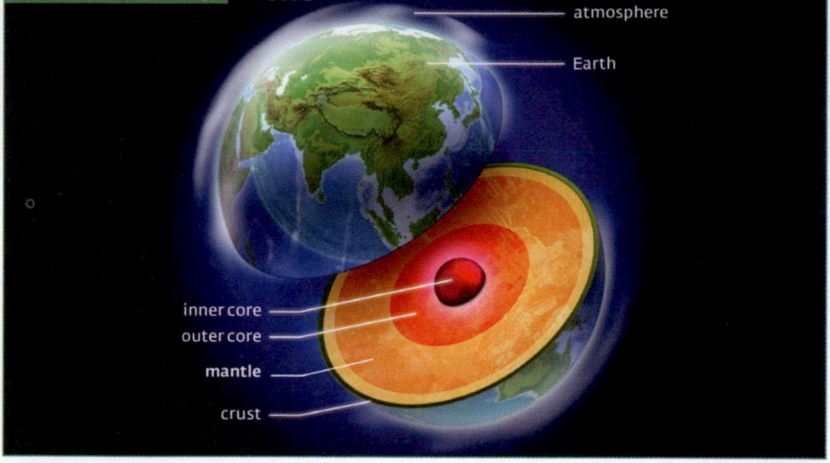


newspaper, or CD is one of many that are exactly the same. *ejemplar, copia* ❑ *...a copy of "USA Today." un ejemplar de "USA Today".* **3** V-T If you **copy** something, you produce or write something that is exactly like the original thing. *copiar* ❑ *...companies who unlawfully copy computer programs. ...empresas que copian programas de computadora ilegalmente.* ❑ *We're copying from textbooks. Estamos copiando de los libros de texto.* **4** V-T If you **copy** a person or their ideas, you try to do what they do or try to be like them. *copiar* ❑ *Children copy the behavior of people they admire. Los niños copian el comportamiento de las personas que admiran.*
→ see **clone, draw**

**Thesaurus** *copy* Ver también:
N. likeness, photocopy, replica, reprint; (*ant.*) master, original **1**
V. reproduce; (*ant.*) originate **3** imitate, mimic **4**

**copy ma|chine** (**copy machines**) N-COUNT A **copy machine** is the same as a **copier**. *copiadora*

**copy|right** /kɒpiraɪt/ (**copyrights**) N-VAR If someone has the **copyright** on a piece of writing or music, it is illegal to reproduce or perform it without their permission. *derechos, derechos de autor, copyright* ❑ *Who owns the copyright on this movie? ¿Quién tiene los derechos de autor de esta película?*

**cord** /kɔrd/ (**cords**) **1** N-VAR **Cord** is strong, thick string. *cuerda* ❑ *...a length of nylon cord. ...un pedazo de cuerda de nylon.* **2** N-VAR **Cord** is electrical wire covered in rubber or plastic. *cable* ❑ *...the iron's electrical cord. ...el cable eléctrico de la plancha.*

**core** /kɔr/ (**cores**) **1** N-COUNT The **core** of a fruit is the central part of it that contains seeds. *corazón* ❑ *...an apple core. ...un corazón de manzana.* **2** N-COUNT The **core** of something is the central or most important part of it. *centro, núcleo* ❑ *...the earth's core. ...el centro de la tierra.* ❑ *...the ability to get straight to the core of a problem. ...la habilidad para ir directamente al núcleo del problema.*
→ see Picture Dictionary: **core**

**Word Partnership** Usar *core* con:
N. **apple** core **1**
core **curriculum, Earth's** core, core **group** **2**

**Coriolis ef|fect** /kɔrioʊlɪs ɪfɛkt/ (**Coriolis effects**) N-COUNT **The Coriolis effect** is the tendency of moving objects to turn to the right in the northern hemisphere and to the left in the southern hemisphere, because of the Earth's rotation. *efecto Coriolis* [TECHNICAL]

**cork|screw** /kɔrkskru/ (**corkscrews**) N-COUNT A **corkscrew** is a device for pulling corks out of bottles. *sacacorcho, sacacorchos*

**corn** /kɔrn/ **1** N-UNCOUNT **Corn** is a tall plant which produces long vegetables covered with yellow seeds, or the seeds of this plant. *maíz* ❑ *...rows of corn in an Iowa field. ...hileras de maíz en un campo de Iowa.* **2** → see also **popcorn**
→ see **grain, vegetable**

**cor|nea** /kɔrniə/ (**corneas**) N-COUNT The **cornea** is the transparent skin covering the outside of your eye. *córnea*
→ see **eye**

**cor|ner** /kɔrnər/ (**corners, cornering, cornered**) **1** N-COUNT A **corner** is a point or an area where two sides or edges of something meet, or where a road meets another road. *rincón, esquina* ❑ *There was a table in the corner of the living room. En el rincón de la sala había una mesa.* ❑ *...street corners. ...las esquinas de las calles.* **2** V-T If you **corner** a person or animal, you force them into a place they cannot escape from. *acorralar* ❑ *The gang was cornered by armed police. Los policías armados acorralaron a la pandilla.* **3** V-T If a company or organization **corners** an area of trade, they gain control over it so that no one else can have any success in that area. acaparar, monopolizar [BUSINESS] ❑ *They have cornered the market in MP3 players.* *Acapararon el mercado de reproductores de MP3.* **4** PHRASE If you say that something is **around the corner,** you mean that it will happen very soon. *a la vuelta de la esquina, a punto de que algo suceda* ❑ *Economic recovery is just around the corner.* *La recuperación de la economía está a la vuelta de la esquina.*

**Word Partnership** Usar *corner* con:

ADJ. **far** corner, **sharp** corner **1**
V. **round/turn a** corner, **sit in a** corner **1**
N. **street** corner **1**
PREP. **in a** corner **1**
**around the** corner **4**

**corn|row** /kɔrnroʊ/ (**cornrows**) also **corn row** N-COUNT If someone wears their hair in **cornrows,** they braid their hair in parallel rows that lie flat upon their head. *trencitas* ❑ *...a tall woman in cornrows.* *...una mujer alta con el cabello en trencitas.* → see **hair**

**corn|starch** /kɔrnstɑrtʃ/ also **corn starch** N-UNCOUNT **Cornstarch** is a fine white powder made from corn that is used to make sauces thicker. *maicena*

**co|ro|na** /kəroʊnə/ N-SING The sun's **corona** is its outer atmosphere. *corona* [TECHNICAL]

**cor|po|ral pun|ish|ment** N-UNCOUNT **Corporal punishment** is the punishment of people by hitting them. *castigos corporales* ❑ *Corporal punishment in public schools is forbidden.* *Los castigos corporales están prohibidos en las escuelas públicas.*

**cor|po|rate** /kɔrpərɪt, -prɪt/ ADJ **Corporate** means relating to business corporations. *corporativo* [BUSINESS] ❑ *...top U.S. corporate executives.* *...los más altos ejecutivos corporativos de los EE.UU.*

**Word Partnership** Usar *corporate* con:

N. corporate **clients**, corporate **culture**, corporate **hospitality**, corporate **image**, corporate **lawyer**, corporate **sector**, corporate **structure**

**cor|po|ra|tion** /kɔrpəreɪʃᵊn/ (**corporations**) N-COUNT A **corporation** is a large business or company. *compañía* [BUSINESS] ❑ *...multinational corporations.* *...las compañías multinacionales.*

**corps** /kɔr/ (**corps**) **1** N-COUNT A **corps** is a part of the army which has special duties. *cuerpo* ❑ *...the Army Medical Corps.* *...el cuerpo médico del ejército.* **2** N-COUNT A **corps** is a small group of people who do a special job. *cuerpo* ❑ *...the U.S. diplomatic corps.* *...el cuerpo diplomático de los Estados Unidos.*

**corpse** /kɔrps/ (**corpses**) N-COUNT A **corpse** is a dead body. *cadáver*

**cor|ral** /kəræl/ (**corrals, corralling, corralled**) **1** N-COUNT A **corral** is a space surrounded by a fence where cattle or horses are kept. *corral* **2** V-T To **corral** a person or animal means to capture or trap them. *acorralar* ❑ *Within hours, police corralled the three men.* *En unas cuantas horas, la policía acorraló a los tres hombres.*

**Word Link** *rect* ≈ *right, straight* : *correct, rectangle, rectify*

**cor|rect** /kərɛkt/ (**corrects, correcting, corrected**) **1** ADJ If something is **correct,** it is right and true. *correcto* ❑ *The correct answers can be found on page 8.* *Las respuestas correctas se encuentran en la página 8.* • **cor|rect|ly** ADV *correctamente* ❑ *Did I pronounce your name correctly?* *¿Pronuncié su nombre correctamente?* • **cor|rect|ness** N-UNCOUNT *corrección, exactitud* ❑ *Ask him to check the correctness of what he has written.* *Pídale que revise la exactitud de lo que ha escrito.* **2** ADJ If you are **correct,** what you have said or thought is true. *tener razón* [FORMAL] ❑ *You are absolutely correct.* *Usted tiene toda la razón.* **3** ADJ The **correct** thing or method is the one that is most suitable in a particular situation. *correcto* ❑ *The use of the correct materials was essential.* *El uso de los materiales correctos era esencial.* • **cor|rect|ly** ADV *correctamente* ❑ *The exercises, correctly performed, will stretch and tone muscles.* *Los ejercicios, llevados a cabo correctamente, estirarán y tonificarán los músculos.* **4** ADJ **Correct** behavior is in accordance with social rules. *correcto* ❑ *He was very polite and very correct.* *Era muy correcto y cortés.* • **cor|rect|ly** ADV *con corrección* ❑ *She began speaking politely, even correctly.* *Comenzó hablando cortésmente, incluso con corrección* • **cor|rect|ness** N-UNCOUNT *corrección* ❑ *...his old-fashioned correctness.* *...su corrección pasada de moda.* **5** V-T If you **correct** a problem, mistake, or fault, you put it right. *corregir* ❑ *He may need surgery to correct the problem.* *Puede ser que necesite cirugía para corregir el problema.* • **cor|rec|tion** /kərɛkʃᵊn/ (**corrections**) N-VAR *corrección* ❑ *...the correction of factual errors.* *...la corrección de errores de hecho.* **6** V-T If you **correct** someone, you say something which is more accurate or appropriate than what they have just said. *corregir* ❑ *"Actually, that isn't what happened," George corrects me.* *—De hecho, eso no fue lo que sucedió —me corrigió George.* **7** V-T When someone **corrects** a piece of writing, they look at it and mark the mistakes in it. *corregir* ❑ *He was correcting his students' work.* *Estaba corrigiendo el trabajo de sus alumnos.*

**Thesaurus** *correct* Ver también:

ADJ. accurate, legitimate, precise, right, true; (*ant.*) false, inaccurate, incorrect, wrong **1**
V. fix, rectify, repair; (*ant.*) damage, hurt **5**

**Word Partnership** Usar *correct* con:

N. correct **answer**, correct **response** **1** **2**
correct **a mistake**, correct **a situation** **5**
correct ***someone*** **6**

**cor|rec|tion** /kərɛkʃᵊn/ (**corrections**) **1** N-COUNT **Corrections** are marks or comments made on a piece of written work which indicate where there are mistakes and what are the right answers. *corrección* ❑ *...corrections to the text.* *...correcciones al texto.* **2** N-UNCOUNT **Correction** is the punishment of criminals. *correctivo* ❑ *...jails and other parts of the correction system.* *...cárceles y otras partes del sistema correctivo.* • **cor|rec|tion|al** /kərɛkʃənᵊl/ ADJ *correccional* ❑ *He is currently in a city correctional center.* *Actualmente está en un centro correccional de la ciudad.* **3** → see also **correct**

C

C

**cor|rec|tion|al fa|cil|ity** (**correctional facilities**) N-COUNT A **correctional facility** is a prison or similar institution. *reformatorio* ❑ *...the Utah state correctional facility. ...el reformatorio estatal de Utah.*

**cor|rec|tions of|fic|er** (**corrections officers**) N-COUNT A **corrections officer** is someone who works as a guard at a prison. *guardia de la prisión*

**cor|re|la|tion|al de|sign** /kɔrəleɪʃənᵊl dɪzaɪn/ (**correlational designs**) N-VAR Research that has a **correlational design** involves studying the relationship between two or more things. *diseño correlacionado*

| Word Link | *cor ≈ with : accord, correspond, escort* |
|---|---|

**cor|re|spond** /kɔrɪspɒnd/ (**corresponds, corresponding, corresponded**) **1** V-RECIP If one thing **corresponds to** another, there is a close similarity or connection between them. *corresponder* ❑ *All buttons were clearly numbered to correspond to the chart on the wall Todos los botones estaban claramente numerados para que correspondieran al gráfico de la pared.* ❑ *The two maps of the Rockies correspond closely. Los dos mapas de las montañas Rocallosas corresponden estrechamente.* • **cor|re|spond|ing** ADJ *correspondiente* ❑ *...anger and its corresponding rise in blood pressure. ...el enojo y el correspondiente aumento en la presión sanguínea.* • **cor|re|spond|ing|ly** /kɔrɪspɒndɪŋli/ ADV *en proporción, en consecuencia* ❑ *As he gets older, he is growing correspondingly more dependent on his daughters. Al envejecer, se ha vuelto en consecuencia más dependiente de sus hijas.* **2** V-RECIP If you **correspond with** someone, you write letters to them. *mantener correspondencia con* ❑ *She still corresponds with her American friends. Todavía mantiene correspondencia con sus amigos estadounidenses.* ❑ *We corresponded regularly. Mantenemos una correspondencia regular.*

**cor|re|spond|ence** /kɔrɪspɒndəns/ (**correspondences**) **1** N-UNCOUNT; N-SING **Correspondence** is the act of writing letters to someone. *correspondencia* ❑ *...a long correspondence with a college friend. ...una larga correspondencia con un amigo de la universidad.* **2** N-UNCOUNT Someone's **correspondence** is the letters that they receive or send. *correspondencia* ❑ *He always replied to his correspondence. Siempre daba respuesta a su correspondencia.* **3** N-COUNT If there is a **correspondence between** two things, there is a similarity or connection between them. *correspondencia entre* ❑ *...a close correspondence between what government does and what the people want it to do. ...una clara correspondencia entre lo que hace el gobierno y lo que la gente quiera que haga.*

**cor|re|spond|ent** /kɔrɪspɒndənt/ (**correspondents**) N-COUNT A **correspondent** is a newspaper or television journalist. *corresponsal* ❑ *...White House correspondent for The New Republic magazine. ...el corresponsal de la revista The New Republic en la Casa Blanca.*

**cor|rupt** /kərʌpt/ (**corrupts, corrupting, corrupted**) **1** ADJ A **corrupt** person behaves in a way that is morally wrong, especially by doing illegal things for money. *corrupto* ❑ *...corrupt politicians. ...políticos corruptos.* **2** V-T/V-I If someone **is corrupted by** something, it causes them to become dishonest and unable to be trusted. *corromper(se)* ❑ *He was corrupted by the desire for money. Fue corrompido por su ambición de dinero.* ❑ *Power corrupts. El poder corrompe.*

**cor|rup|tion** /kərʌpʃᵊn/ N-UNCOUNT **Corruption** is dishonesty and illegal behavior by people in positions of power. *corrupción* ❑ *The president faces charges of corruption. El presidente enfrenta cargos por corrupción.*

**co|sine** /koʊsaɪn/ (**cosines**) N-COUNT A **cosine** is a mathematical calculation that is used especially in the study of triangles. The abbreviation **cos** is also used. *coseno* [TECHNICAL]

**cos|met|ic** /kɒzmɛtɪk/ (**cosmetics**) **1** N-COUNT **Cosmetics** are substances such as lipstick or face powder. *cosmético* ❑ *...the cosmetics counter of a department store. ...el mostrador de cosméticos de una tienda departamental.* **2** ADJ **Cosmetic** changes are not very effective because they improve the appearance of something without changing its basic character or solving a basic problem. *superficial* ❑ *...parts of the building where cosmetic improvements have been made. ...las partes del edificio donde se han hecho mejoras superficiales.*
→ see **makeup**

**cos|mic back|ground ra|dia|tion** N-UNCOUNT **Cosmic background radiation** is the heat that is present throughout the universe as a result of the original explosion which started the universe. *radiación del fondo cósmico*

**cos|mol|ogy** /kɒzmɒlədʒi/ N-UNCOUNT **Cosmology** is the study of the origin and nature of the universe. *cosmología*
→ see **myth**

**cost** /kɔst/ (**costs, costing, cost**) **1** N-COUNT The **cost of** something is the amount of money that is needed in order to buy, do, or make it. *costo* ❑ *The cost of a loaf of bread has increased. El costo de una hogaza de pan se ha incrementado.* ❑ *The price did not even cover the cost of production. El precio no cubría ni siquiera el costo de producción.* **2** V-T If something **costs** a particular amount of money, you can buy, do, or make it for that amount. *costar* ❑ *This course is limited to 12 people and costs $150. Este curso tiene cupo límite para 12 personas y cuesta 150 dólares.* ❑ *It's going to cost me over $100,000 to buy new trucks. Me va a costar más de 100,000 dólares comprar camiones nuevos.* **3** V-T If an event or mistake **costs** you something, you lose that thing as the result of it. *costar* ❑ *...an operation that cost him his sight. ...una operación que le costó la vista.* **4** N-SING The **cost of** something is the loss, damage, or injury that is involved in trying to achieve it. *a costa de* ❑ *He shut down the city's oil refinery at a cost of 5,000 jobs. Cerró la refinería de la ciudad a costa de 5,000 empleos.* **5** PHRASE If you say that something must be avoided **at all costs**, you are emphasizing that it must not be allowed to happen under any circumstances. *a toda costa* ❑ *A world trade war must be avoided at all costs. La guerra de comercio mundial debe ser evitada a toda costa.*

| Thesaurus | *cost* | Ver también: |
|---|---|---|
| N. | fee, price **1**<br>harm, loss, sacrifice **4** | |

C

**Word Partnership** Usar *cost* con:

ADJ. **additional** costs 1
N. cost **of living** 1
V. **cover the** cost, **cut** costs, **keep** costs **down** 1 4

**co|star** /koʊstɑr/ (**costars, costarring, costarred**) 1 N-COUNT An actor who is a **costar** in a movie has one of the main parts in it. coestrella ❑ *Curtis fell in love with his costar. Curtis se enamoró de su coestrella.* 2 V-RECIP If actors **costar** in a particular movie, they have the main parts in it. coprotagonizar ❑ *They costarred in the movie "State of Grace." Ellos coprotagonizaron la película "Estado de gracia".* ❑ *...a movie in which she costarred with her father. ...una película que coprotagonizó con su padre.*

**cost-effective** ADJ Something that is **cost-effective** saves or makes more money than it costs to make or run. redituable ❑ *The bank must be run in a cost-effective way. El banco debe operar de manera redituable.*

**cost|ly** /kɔstli/ (**costlier, costliest**) ADJ Something that is **costly** is very expensive. costoso ❑ *The project could be very costly. El proyecto podría ser muy costoso.*

**cos|tume** /kɒstum/ (**costumes**) 1 N-VAR A **costume** is a set of clothes worn as part of a performance. traje ❑ *His costume was stunning. Su traje estaba impresionante.* 2 N-UNCOUNT The clothes worn by people at a particular time in history, or in a particular country, are referred to as a particular type of **costume**. traje ❑ *...men and women in eighteenth-century costume. ...hombres y mujeres en trajes del siglo dieciocho.*
→ see **drama, theater**

**cos|tume par|ty** (**costume parties**) also **costume ball** N-COUNT A **costume party** or **costume ball** is a party at which the guests dress to look like famous people or people from history. fiesta de disfraces ❑ *I went to a costume party a few weeks ago. Fui a una fiesta de disfraces hace unas semanas.*

**cot|tage** /kɒtɪdʒ/ (**cottages**) N-COUNT A **cottage** is a small house, usually in the country. casita de campo ❑ *They have a cottage in Scotland. Tienen una casita de campo en Escocia.*

**cot|ton** /kɒtᵊn/ (**cottons**) 1 N-VAR **Cotton** is cloth made from the soft fibers of the cotton plant. algodón ❑ *...a cotton shirt. ...una camisa de algodón.* 2 N-UNCOUNT **Cotton** is a plant which produces soft fibers used in making cloth. algodón ❑ *...a large cotton plantation in Tennessee. ...una enorme plantación de algodón en Tennessee.* 3 N-UNCOUNT **Cotton** is a soft mass of cotton, used especially for putting liquids or creams onto your skin. algodón ❑ *...cotton balls. ...bolitas de algodón.*

**cot|ton can|dy** N-UNCOUNT **Cotton candy** is a pink or white mass of sugar threads that is eaten from a paper cone. algodón de azúcar

**cot|ton swab** (**cotton swabs**) N-COUNT A **cotton swab** is the same as a **swab**. cotonete

**cotton|tail** /kɒtənteɪl/ (**cottontails**) N-COUNT A **cottontail** is a type of rabbit commonly found in North America. conejo de cola de algodón, Sylvilagus, tapetí

**coty|ledon** /kɒtᵊlidᵊn/ (**cotyledons**) N-COUNT A **cotyledon** is the first leaf to grow after a seed germinates, before the proper leaves grow. cotiledón [TECHNICAL]

**couch** /kaʊtʃ/ (**couches**) N-COUNT A **couch** is a long, comfortable seat for two or three people. sofá

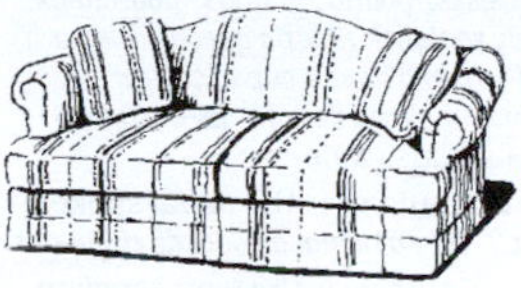
couch

**cou|gar** /kugər/ (**cougars**) N-COUNT A **cougar** is a wild member of the cat family that has brownish-gray fur and lives in mountain regions of North and South America. puma

**cough** /kɔf/ (**coughs, coughing, coughed**) 1 V-I When you **cough**, you force air out of your throat with a sudden, harsh noise. toser ❑ *Graham began to cough violently. Graham comenzó a toser violentamente.* • **Cough** is also a noun. tos ❑ *Coughs and sneezes spread infections. Los estornudos y la tos propagan las infecciones.* • **cough|ing** N-UNCOUNT tos ❑ *...a terrible fit of coughing. ...un terrible ataque de tos.* 2 V-T If you **cough** blood, it comes up out of your throat or mouth when you cough. toser ❑ *I started coughing blood. Comencé a toser sangre.* 3 N-COUNT A **cough** is an illness in which you cough. tos ❑ *I had a cough for over a month. Tuve tos por más de un mes.*
→ see **illness**

▸ **cough up** PHR-VERB If you **cough up** money, you pay or spend it, usually when you would prefer not to. soltar, aflojar [INFORMAL] ❑ *I'll have to cough up $30,000 a year for tuition. Tendré que soltar 30,000 dólares de colegiatura cada año.*

**could** /kəd, STRONG kʊd/

**Could** is a modal verb. It is used with the base form of a verb. **Could** is sometimes considered to be the past form of **can**, but in this dictionary the two words are dealt with separately.

1 MODAL If you **could** do something, you were able to do it. podía, podías, podíamos, podían ❑ *I could see that something was terribly wrong. Podía ver que algo andaba muy mal.* ❑ *When I left school at 16, I couldn't read or write. Cuando dejé la escuela a los 16, no podía leer ni escribir.* 2 MODAL You use **could** to indicate that something sometimes happened. podía, podías, podíamos, podían ❑ *He could be very pleasant when he wanted to. Podía ser muy agradable si se lo proponía.* 3 MODAL You use **could have** to indicate that something was a possibility in the past, although it did not actually happen. pude haber, pudiste haber, pudo haber, pudimos haber, pudieron haber ❑ *He could have made a lot of money as a lawyer. Pudo haber hecho mucho dinero como abogado.* 4 MODAL You use **could** to indicate that something is possibly true, or that it may possibly happen. podría, podrías, podríamos, podrían ❑ *Food which is high in fat could cause health problems. La comida alta en grasas podría causar problemas de salud.* 5 MODAL You use **could** after "if" when you are imagining what would happen if something was true. pudiera, pudieras, pudiéramos, pudieran ❑ *If I could afford it I'd have four television sets. Si pudiera costearlas, tendría cuatro televisiones.* 6 MODAL

C

You use **could** when you are making offers and suggestions. *podría, podrías, podríamos, podrían* ❑ *I could call the doctor. Podría llamar al doctor.* ❑ *Couldn't we call a special meeting? ¿Podríamos llamar a una junta extraordinaria?* **7** MODAL You use **could** in questions to make polite requests. *podría, podrías, podríamos, podrían* ❑ *Could I stay tonight? ¿Podría quedarme esta noche?* ❑ *He asked if he could have a cup of coffee. Preguntó si podía tomar una taza de café.* **8** **could do with** → see **do** **9** → see also **able**

**couldn't** /kʊdᵊnt/ **Couldn't** is the usual spoken form of "could not." *forma hablada usual de **could not***

**could've** /kʊdəv/ **Could've** is the usual spoken form of "could have" when "have" is an auxiliary verb. *forma hablada usual de **could have***

**coun|cil** /kaʊnsᵊl/ (**councils**) N-COUNT A **council** is a group of people who are elected to govern a local area such as a city. *ayuntamiento* ❑ *The city council has decided to build a new school. El ayuntamiento ha decidido construir una nueva escuela.*

**coun|ci|lor** /kaʊnsələr/ (**councilors**) N-COUNT; N-TITLE A **councilor** is a member of a local council. *consejero o consejera* ❑ *...Councilor Michael Poulter. ...el Consejero Michael Poulter.*

**coun|sel** /kaʊnsᵊl/ (**counsels, counseling** or **counselling, counseled** or **counselled**) **1** N-UNCOUNT **Counsel** is advice. *consejo* [FORMAL] ❑ *If you have a problem, it is a good idea to ask for help and counsel. Si tienes algún problema, es buena idea pedir ayuda y consejo.* **2** V-T If you **counsel** someone **to** do something, you advise them to do it. *aconsejar* [FORMAL] ❑ *My advisers counseled me to do nothing. Mis asesores me aconsejaron no hacer nada.* **3** V-T If you **counsel** people, you listen to them talk about their problems and help them to resolve them. *orientar* ❑ *She counsels people with eating disorders. Orienta a personas con desórdenes alimenticios.* • **coun|sel|ing** also **counselling** N-UNCOUNT *orientación* ❑ *She will need counseling to overcome the tragedy. Va a necesitar orientación para sobreponerse a la tragedia.* • **coun|se|lor** also **counsellor** N-COUNT (**counselors**) *orientador u orientadora* ❑ *Children who have suffered like this should see a counselor. Los niños que han sufrido así deberían consultar a un orientador.* **4** N-COUNT Someone's **counsel** is the lawyer who gives advice on a legal case and speaks for them in court. *abogado o abogada* ❑ *Singleton's counsel said that he would appeal. El abogado de Singleton dijo que apelaría.*

**coun|se|lor** /kaʊnsələr/ (**counselors**) also **counsellor** **1** N-COUNT A **counselor** is a young person who supervises children at a summer camp. *consejero o consejera* ❑ *Hicks worked with children as a camp counselor. Hicks trabajaba con niños cuando era consejero en campamentos.* **2** → see also **counsel**

**count** /kaʊnt/ (**counts, counting, counted**) **1** V-I When you **count,** you say all the numbers in order up to a particular number. *contar* ❑ *Nancy forced herself to count slowly to five. Nancy se forzó a contar lentamente hasta el cinco.* **2** V-T If you **count** all the things in a group, you add them up in order to find how many there are. *contar* ❑ *I counted the money. Conté el dinero.* ❑ *I counted 34 wild goats grazing. Conté 34 cabras salvajes pastando.* • **Count up** means the same as **count.** *contar* ❑ *They counted up all the hours the villagers work. Contaron todas las horas que trabajan los habitantes del pueblo.* **3** V-I If something or someone **counts for** something or **counts,** they are important or valuable. *contar* ❑ *It doesn't matter where charities get their money: what counts is what they do with it. No importa de dónde obtienen dinero las organizaciones de caridad: lo que cuenta es lo que hacen con ello.* **4** V-T/V-I If something **counts as** a particular thing, it is regarded as being that thing. *contar* ❑ *No one agrees on what counts as a desert. Nadie está de acuerdo en qué cuenta como desierto.* **5** N-COUNT A **count** is the action of counting, or the number that you get after counting. *cuenta* ❑ *The final count showed 56.7 percent in favor. La cuenta final mostró un 56.7 por ciento a favor.* **6** N-COUNT; N-TITLE; N-VOC A **count** is a European nobleman. *conde* ❑ *Her father was a Polish count. Su padre fue un conde polaco.* **7** PHRASE If you **keep count of** a number of things, you keep a record of how many have occurred. If you **lose count of** a number of things, you cannot remember how many have occurred. *llevar la cuenta, perder la cuenta* ❑ *Keep count of the number of hours you work. Lleve la cuenta de la cantidad de horas que trabaja.*
→ see **mathematics, zero**

▸ **count against** PHR-VERB If something **counts against** you, it may cause you to be rejected or punished. *perjudicar* ❑ *His youth might count against him. Su juventud puede perjudicarlo.*

▸ **count on** or **count upon** PHR-VERB If you **count on** someone or something, you rely on them to support you. *contar con* ❑ *They did not know how much support they could count on. No sabían con cuánto apoyo podían contar.*

▸ **count out** PHR-VERB If you **count out** a sum of money, you count the bills or coins as you put them in a pile one by one. *contar uno por uno* ❑ *Mr. Rohmbauer counted out the money. El señor Rohmbauer contó el dinero.*

▸ **count up** → see **count 2**

▸ **count upon** → see **count on**

**count|able noun** /kaʊntəbᵊl naʊn/ (**countable nouns**) N-COUNT A **countable noun** is the same as a **count noun.** *sustantivo contable, nombre contable*

**count|down** /kaʊntdaʊn/ N-SING A **countdown** is the counting aloud of numbers in reverse order before something happens. *cuenta regresiva* ❑ *The countdown has begun for the launch of the space shuttle. La cuenta regresiva para el lanzamiento del transbordador espacial ha comenzado.*

**coun|ter** /kaʊntər/ (**counters, countering, countered**) **1** N-COUNT In a store or café, a **counter** is a long flat surface at which customers are served. *mostrador* ❑ *...guys working behind the counter at our local DVD rental store. ...los muchachos que trabajan tras el mostrador en la tienda local de rentas de DVD.* **2** N-COUNT A **counter** is a device which keeps a count of something. *contador* ❑ *The new answering machine has a call counter. La nueva contestadora tiene un contador de llamadas.* **3** N-COUNT A **counter** is a very small object used in board games. *ficha* ❑ *...boards and counters for fifteen different games. ...tableros y fichas para quince juegos diferentes.* **4** V-T/V-I If you **counter** something that is being done, you take action to make it less effective. *contraatacar* ❑ *...more police officers* *to counter the increase in crime. ...más policías para contraatacar el incremento del crimen.* ❑ *He countered by filing a lawsuit. Contraatacó metiendo una demanda.* **5** N-SING If something is **counter to** something else, it is the opposite. *contrario a* ❑ *It was counter to what I believed in. Era contrario a lo que yo creía.*

**counter|bal|ance** /kaʊntərbæləns/ (**counterbalances**) N-COUNT A **counterbalance** is a weight that balances another weight. *contrapeso*

**counter|clockwise** /kaʊntərklɒkwaɪz/ ADV If something is moving **counterclockwise,** it is moving in a circle in the opposite direction to the hands of a clock. *en sentido contrario a las manecillas del reloj* ❑ *Winds blow counterclockwise around storm centers. Los vientos giran alrededor del centro de las tormentas en sentido contrario a las manecillas del reloj.*

counter clockwise

● **Counterclockwise** is also an adjective. ❑ *The dance moves in a counterclockwise direction. El baile se lleva a cabo en dirección contraria a las manecillas del reloj.*

**counter|feit** /kaʊntərfɪt/ (**counterfeits, counterfeiting, counterfeited**) **1** ADJ **Counterfeit** money, goods, or documents are not genuine, but have been made to look exactly like genuine ones in order to deceive people. *falso* ❑ *He admitted using counterfeit currency. Admitió que utiizaba dinero falso.* ● **Counterfeit** is also a noun. *falsificación* ❑ *Counterfeits of the company's jeans are flooding Europe. Hay falsificaciones de los jeans de la empresa por toda Europa.* **2** V-T To **counterfeit** something means to make a counterfeit version of it. *falsificar* ❑ *Davies was accused of counterfeiting the coins. Davies fue acusado de falsificar las monedas.*

**counter|of|fer** /kaʊntərɔfər/ (**counteroffers**) N-COUNT A **counteroffer** is an offer that someone makes in response to an offer by another person or group. *contraoferta* ❑ *Many would welcome a counteroffer from a foreign bidder. Muchos aceptarían una contraoferta de algun postor extranjero.*

**counter|part** /kaʊntərpɑrt/ (**counterparts**) N-COUNT Someone's or something's **counterpart** is another person or thing that has a similar function in a different place. *contraparte* ❑ *The Foreign Secretary telephoned his German and Italian counterparts. El Ministro de Relaciones Exteriores llamó a su contraparte alemana y a la italiana.*

**counter|top** /kaʊntərtɒp/ (**countertops**) N-COUNT A **countertop** is a flat surface in a kitchen on which you can prepare food. *cubierta de cocina*

**count|less** /kaʊntlɪs/ ADJ **Countless** means very many. *incontable* ❑ *She made countless people happy through her music. Hizo feliz a incontables personas con su música.*

**count noun** (**count nouns**) N-COUNT A **count noun** is a noun such as "bird," "chair," or "year" which has a singular and a plural form and is always used after a determiner in the singular. *sustantivo contable, nombre contable*

**coun|try** /kʌntri/ (**countries**) **1** N-COUNT A **country** is one of the political units which the world is divided into, covering a particular area of land. *país* ❑ *This is the greatest country in the world. Este es el mejor país del mundo.* ❑ *...the border between the two countries. ...la frontera entre los dos países.* **2** N-SING **The country** is land that is away from cities and towns. *campo* ❑ *...a healthy life in the country. ...una vida sana en el campo.* ❑ *She was cycling along a country road. Iba en bicicleta por un camino en el campo.* **3** N-UNCOUNT A particular kind of **country** is an area of land which has particular characteristics. *terreno* ❑ *...mountainous country. ...terreno montañoso.* **4** N-UNCOUNT **Country** music is a style of popular music from the southern United States. *country* ❑ *I just wanted to play country music. Sólo quería tocar música country.*
→ see Word Web: **country**

**coun|try and west|ern** also **country-and-western** N-UNCOUNT **Country and western** is the same as country music. *música country* ❑ *...a successful country and western singer. ...un exitoso cantante de música country.*
→ see **genre**

**country|side** /kʌntrisaɪd/ N-UNCOUNT **The countryside** is land that is away from cities and towns. *campiña* ❑ *I've always loved the English countryside. Siempre me ha encantado la campiña inglesa.*
→ see **city**

**coun|ty** /kaʊnti/ (**counties**) N-COUNT A **county** is a region of the U.S., Britain, or Ireland, which

C

**Word Web** country

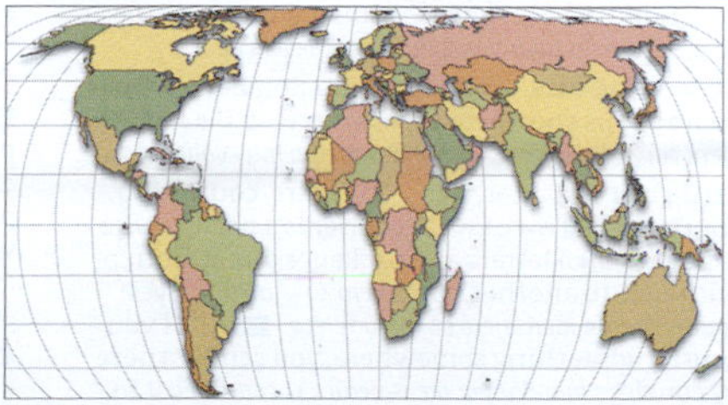

The largest **country** in the world geographically is Russia. It has an area of six million square miles and a **population** of more than 142 million people. Russia is a federal state with a republican form of **government**. The government is based in Russia's **capital** city, Moscow.

One of the smallest countries in the world is Nauru. This tiny island **nation** in the South Pacific Ocean is 8.1 square miles in size. Many of Nauru's more than 13,000 **residents** live in Yaren, which is the largest city, but not the capital. The Republic of Nauru is the only nation in the world without an official capital.

C

has its own local government. condado ❑ ...Palm Beach County. ...el condado de Palm Beach.

**coup** /ku/ (**coups**) 1 N-COUNT When there is a **coup**, a group of people seize power in a country. golpe de estado ❑ ...a military coup. ...un golpe de estado por parte de los militares. 2 N-COUNT A **coup** is an achievement which is thought to be especially good because it was very difficult. golpe maestro ❑ The sale is a big coup for them. La venta fue un golpe maestro para ellos.

**cou|ple** /kʌpᵊl/ (**couples, coupling, coupled**) 1 QUANT If you refer to **a couple of** people or things, you mean two or approximately two of them. par ❑ There are a couple of police officers outside. Hay un par de policías afuera. ❑ I think the trouble will clear up in a couple of days. Creo que el problema se resolverá en un par de días. • **Couple** is also a determiner in spoken American English. un par de ❑ ...a couple weeks before the election. ...un par de semanas antes de la elección. • **Couple** is also a pronoun. par ❑ I've got a couple that don't look too bad. Tengo un par que no se ven tan mal. 2 N-COUNT A **couple** is two people who are married or having a sexual or romantic relationship. pareja ❑ The couple have no children. La pareja no tiene hijos. 3 N-COUNT A **couple** is two people that you see together on a particular occasion or that have some association. pareja ❑ The four couples began the opening dance. Las cuatro parejas abrieron el baile. 4 V-T If one thing produces a particular effect when it **is coupled with** another, the two things combine to produce that effect. combinar ❑ High temperatures coupled with strong winds can mean fire danger. Las altas temperaturas, combinadas con fuertes vientos, pueden implicar peligro de fuego.

**cou|pon** /kupɒn, kyu-/ (**coupons**) 1 N-COUNT A **coupon** is a piece of printed paper which allows you to pay less money than usual for a product, or to get it free. cupón, vale ❑ ...a money-saving coupon. ...un cupón de descuento. 2 N-COUNT A **coupon** is a small form which you send off to ask for information, to order something, or to enter a competition. cupón ❑ Mail this coupon with your check. Mande este cupón junto con el cheque por correo.

| Word Link | **age ≈ state of, related to : courage, marriage, percentage** |
|---|---|

**cour|age** /kɜrɪdʒ/ N-UNCOUNT **Courage** is the quality shown by someone who does something difficult or dangerous, even though they may be afraid. valor ❑ The girl had the courage to tell the police. La niña tuvo el valor de contarle a la policía.

**cou|ra|geous** /kəreɪdʒəs/ ADJ Someone who is **courageous** shows courage. valiente ❑ The children were very courageous. Los niños fueron muy valientes.

**cou|ri|er** /kʊəriər, kɜr-/ (**couriers, couriering, couriered**) 1 N-COUNT A **courier** is a person who is paid to take letters and packages direct from one place to another. mensajero ❑ ...a motorcycle courier. ...un mensajero en motocicleta. 2 V-T If you **courier** something somewhere, you send it there by courier. mandar por mensajería ❑ I couriered it to Darren in New York. Se lo mandé a Darren a Nueva York por mensajería.

**course** /kɔrs/ (**courses**) 1 **Course** is often used in the expression "of course," or instead of "of course" in informal spoken English. See **of course**. claro 2 N-UNCOUNT; N-SING The **course** of a vehicle is the route along which it is traveling. rumbo ❑ Aircraft can avoid each other by altering course. Las aeronaves pueden evitarse mutuamente si alteran su rumbo. 3 N-COUNT A **course of** action is an action or a series of actions that you can take in a particular situation. camino ❑ My best course of action was to help Gill. Lo mejor que podía hacer era ayudar a Gill. 4 N-COUNT A **course** is a series of lessons or lectures on a particular subject. curso ❑ ...a course in business administration. ...un curso de administración de empresas. 5 N-COUNT A **course of** medical treatment is a series of treatments that a doctor gives someone. tratamiento ❑ ...a course of antibiotics. ...un tratamiento con antibióticos. 6 N-COUNT A **course** is one part of a meal. plato ❑ Lunch was excellent, especially the first course. La comida estuvo excelente, sobre todo el primer plato. 7 N-COUNT In sports, a **course** is an area of land where races are held or golf is played. campo, cancha ❑ Only 12 seconds separated the first three riders on the course. A los tres primeros puestos sólo los separaban 12 segundos en la pista. 8 **in due course** → see **due** 9 PHRASE If you are **on course for** something, you are likely to achieve it. en camino de ❑ The company is on course for profits of $20 million. La empresa está en camino de obtener 20 millones de dólares en ganancias.

**court**
❶ NOUN USES
❷ VERB USES

❶ **court** /kɔrt/ (**courts**) 1 N-COUNT A **court** is a place where legal matters are decided by a judge and jury or by a magistrate. You can also refer to a judge, jury, or magistrates as a **court**. court ❑ Would she be willing to testify in court? ¿Estaría dispuesta a testificar ante un tribunal? ❑ The court awarded the man one and a half million dollars. El tribunal le concedió un millón y medio de dólares. 2 N-COUNT A **court** is an area for playing a game such as tennis or squash. cancha ❑ The hotel has several tennis courts. El hotel tiene varias canchas de tenis. 3 N-COUNT The **court** of a king or queen is the place where he or she lives and carries out duties. corte ❑ ...the court of James I. ...la corte de Jaime I. 4 PHRASE Your **day in court** is your chance to give your side of an argument. audiencia ❑ All we wanted was our day in court. Todo lo que queríamos era que llegara nuestra audiencia.
→ see **park**

❷ **court** /kɔrt/ (**courts, courting, courted**) 1 V-T If you **court** something such as publicity or popularity, you try to attract it. buscar ❑ He spent a lifetime courting publicity. Se pasó la vida buscándose publicidad. 2 V-T If you **court** disaster, you act in a way that makes it likely to happen. atraer ❑ I knew I was courting disaster in asking her to stay. Sabía que estaba atrayéndome un desastre al pedirle que se quedara.

**cour|teous** /kɜrtiəs/ ADJ Someone who is **courteous** is polite and respectful. cortés ❑ He was a kind and courteous man. Era un hombre amable y cortés. • **cour|teous|ly** ADV cortésmente ❑ He nodded courteously to me. Me saludó cortésmente con la cabeza.

**cour|tesy** /kɜrtɪsi/ 1 N-UNCOUNT **Courtesy** is politeness, respect, and consideration for others.

*cortesía* [FORMAL] ❑ *...a gentleman who always behaves with courtesy. ...un caballero que siempre actúa con cortesía.* **2** N-COUNT A **courtesy** is something polite and respectful that you say or do. *cortesía* [FORMAL] ❑ *I wanted to give you the courtesy of returning your call. Quería tenerte la cortesía de regresar tu llamada.* **3** ADJ **Courtesy** is used to describe services that are provided free of charge by an organization to its customers, or to the general public. *cortesía* ❑ *A courtesy shuttle bus operates between the hotel and the town. Un autobús de cortesía va del hotel al pueblo y de regreso.*

**court|house** /kɔrthaʊs/ (**courthouses**) **1** N-COUNT A **courthouse** is a building in which a court of law meets. *juzgado* **2** N-COUNT A **courthouse** is a building used by the government of a county. *juzgado* ❑ *They were married at the Los Angeles County Courthouse. Se casaron en el Registro Civil del Condado de Los Angeles.*

**Court of Ap|peals** (**Courts of Appeals**) N-COUNT A **Court of Appeals** is a court which deals with appeals against legal judgments. *tribunal de apelaciones* ❑ *...the Oregon Court of Appeals. ...el tribunal de apelaciones de Oregon.*

**court|room** /kɔrtrum/ (**courtrooms**) N-COUNT A **courtroom** is a room in which a law court meets. *sala de justica, tribunal*

**court|yard** /kɔrtyɑrd/ (**courtyards**) N-COUNT A **courtyard** is an open area of ground which is surrounded by buildings or walls. *patio* ❑ *They walked into the courtyard. Caminaron al patio.*

**cous|in** /kʌzᵊn/ (**cousins**) N-COUNT Your **cousin** is the child of your uncle or aunt. *primo o prima* ❑ *My cousin Mark helped me to bring in the bags. Mi primo Mark me ayudó a meter las bolsas.*

**co|va|lent bond** /koʊveɪlənt bɒnd/ (**covalent bonds**) N-COUNT A **covalent bond** is the force that holds together two atoms that share a pair of electrons. *enlace covalente* [TECHNICAL]

**co|va|lent com|pound** /koʊveɪlənt kɒmpaʊnd/ (**covalent compounds**) N-COUNT A **covalent compound** is a chemical compound made of molecules in which the atoms are held together by covalent bonds. *compuesto covalente* [TECHNICAL]

**cover**
❶ VERB USES
❷ NOUN USES

❶ **cov|er** /kʌvər/ (**covers, covering, covered**) **1** V-T If you **cover** something, you place something else over it in order to protect it, hide it, or close it. *cubrir* ❑ *Cover the dish with a tight-fitting lid. Cubra el platillo con una tapa hermética.* ❑ *A black patch covered his left eye. Un parche negro le cubría el ojo izquierdo.* **2** V-T If one thing **covers** another, it forms a layer over its surface. *cubrir* ❑ *The clouds had spread and covered the entire sky. Las nubes se habían extendido y cubrían todo el cielo.* ❑ *The desk was covered with papers. El escritorio estaba cubierto de papeles.* **3** V-T If you **cover** a particular distance, you travel that distance. *recorrer* ❑ *It would not be easy to cover ten miles on that amount of gas. No sería fácil recorrer diez millas con esa cantidad de gasolina.* **4** V-T An insurance policy that **covers** a person or thing guarantees that money will be paid by the insurance company in relation to that person or thing. *cubrir* ❑ *Our insurance does not cover damage caused by floods. Nuestro seguro no cubre daños por inundaciones.* **5** V-T If you **cover** a particular topic, you discuss it in a lecture, course, or book. *cubrir* ❑ *Introduction to Chemistry aims to cover the main topics in chemistry. Introducción a la Química intenta cubrir los temas más importantes de esta materia.* **6** V-T If a sum of money **covers** something, it is enough to pay for it. *cubrir* ❑ *Send $2.50 to cover postage. Mande 2.50 dólares para cubrir el envío.*

▸ **cover up** **1** PHR-VERB If you **cover** something or someone **up**, you put something over them in order to protect or hide them. *tapar* ❑ *I covered him up with a blanket. Lo tapé con una manta.* **2** PHR-VERB If you **cover up** something that you do not want people to know about, you hide the truth about it. *ocultar* ❑ *They tried to cover up the crime. Trataron de ocultar el crimen.* ❑ *They knew they did something terribly wrong and lied to cover it up. Sabían que habían hecho algo terriblemente malo y mintieron para ocultarlo.*

| Thesaurus | *cover* | Ver también: |
|---|---|---|
| V. | conceal, drape, hide, screen; (*ant.*) uncover ❶ 1 2 guard, insure, protect ❶ 4 | |

❷ **cov|er** /kʌvər/ (**covers**) **1** N-COUNT A **cover** is something which is put over an object, usually in order to protect it. *cubierta* ❑ *...a sofa with washable covers. ....un sofá con cubierta lavable.* **2** N-COUNT The **cover** of a book or a magazine is the outside part of it. *tapa, portada* ❑ *...a small book with a green cover. ...un librito con tapa verde.* **3** N-UNCOUNT **Cover** is trees, rocks, or other things that give protection from the weather or from an attack. *refugio* ❑ *The rain started and they ran for cover. Empezó a llover y buscaron refugio.* **4** N-PLURAL Bed **covers** are sheets, blankets, and comforters. *cobijas* ❑ *She slid under the covers. Se metió entre las cobijas.* **5** → see also **covering**

| Word Partnership | Usar *cover* con: |
|---|---|
| N. | cover ***your face*** ❶ 1 2<br>covered **in *something*** ❶ 2 |
| V. | **run for** cover ❷ 3 |

**cov|er|age** /kʌvərɪdʒ/ **1** N-UNCOUNT The **coverage** of something in the news is the reporting of it. *cobertura* ❑ *A special TV network gives live coverage of most races. Una red televisiva especial brinda cobertura en vivo de la mayoría de las carreras.* **2** N-UNCOUNT **Coverage** is a guarantee from an insurance company that money will be paid by them in particular situations. *cobertura* ❑ *Make sure that your insurance coverage is adequate. Asegúrese de que la cobertura de su seguro sea la adecuada.*

**cover|alls** /kʌvərɔlz/ N-PLURAL **Coveralls** are a single piece of clothing that combines pants and a jacket, worn over your clothes to protect them. *overol* ❑ *...a man in white coveralls. ...un hombre de overol blanco.*

**cov|er|ing** /kʌvərɪŋ/ (**coverings**) N-COUNT A **covering** is a layer of something that protects or hides something else. *capa* ❑ *...a light covering of snow. ...una ligera capa de nieve.*

C

C

**cov|er let|ter** (**cover letters**) N-COUNT A **cover letter** is a letter that you send with something else in order to provide information about it. *carta adjunta*

**cow** /kaʊ/ (**cows, cowing, cowed**) 1 N-COUNT A **cow** is a large female animal that is kept on farms for its milk. *vaca* ❑ *He kept a few dairy cows. Tenía algunas vacas lecheras.* ❑ *Dad went out to milk the cows. Papá salió a ordeñar las vacas.* 2 N-COUNT Some female animals, including elephants and whales, are called **cows.** *hembra* ❑ *...a cow elephant. ...una elefanta.* 3 V-T If someone **is cowed,** they are made to behave in a particular way because they have been frightened. *intimidar* [FORMAL] ❑ *The government was not cowed by these threats. El gobierno no se intimidó ante estas amenazas.* • **cowed** ADJ *intimidado* ❑ *She was so cowed that she obeyed at once. La tenían tan intimidada que obedeció al momento.*
→ see **dairy, meat**

**cow|ard** /kaʊərd/ (**cowards**) N-COUNT A **coward** is someone who is easily frightened and avoids dangerous or difficult situations. *cobarde* ❑ *She accused her husband of being a coward. Lo acusó de ser un cobarde.*

**cow|boy** /kaʊbɔɪ/ (**cowboys**) 1 N-COUNT A **cowboy** is a male character in a western. *vaquero* ❑ *...cowboy movies. ...películas de vaqueros.* 2 N-COUNT A **cowboy** is a man employed to look after cattle in North America, especially in former times. *vaquero*
→ see **hat**

**cow|boy boots** N-PLURAL **Cowboy boots** are high leather boots, similar to those worn by cowboys. *botas vaqueras* ❑ *He showed up in jeans and cowboy boots. Llegó en pantalón de mezclilla y botas vaqueras.*

**cozy** /koʊzi/ (**cozier, coziest**) 1 ADJ A **cozy** house or room is comfortable and warm. *acogedor* ❑ *Guests can relax in the cozy lounge. Los huéspedes pueden relajarse en el acogedor salón.* 2 ADJ You use **cozy** to describe activities that are pleasant and friendly. *íntimo y agradable* ❑ *...a cozy chat between friends. ...una plática íntima y agradable entre amigos.*

**CPA** /si pi eɪ/ (**CPAs**) N-COUNT **CPA** is an abbreviation for **certified public accountant.** *C.P.* ❑ *He is a CPA in both New York and New Jersey. Es contador público certificado en Nueva York y Nueva Jersey.*

**CPI** /si pi aɪ/ N-SING **CPI** is an abbreviation for **consumer price index.** *IPC* ❑ *The CPI was up ¼ of a percent in October. El índice de precio al consumidor subió ¼ del porcentaje de octubre.*

**CPR** /si pi ɑr/ N-UNCOUNT **CPR** is a medical technique for reviving someone whose heart has stopped beating by pressing on their chest and breathing into their mouth. **CPR** is an abbreviation for "cardiopulmonary resuscitation." *RCP, reanimación cardiopulmonar* [MEDICAL] ❑ *McMullen performed CPR while someone called 911. McMullen llevaba a cabo la RCP mientras alguien llamaba al número de emergencias.*

**crab** /kræb/ (**crabs**) N-COUNT A **crab** is a sea creature with a flat round body covered by a shell, and five pairs of legs with large claws on the front pair. Crabs usually move sideways. *cangrejo* • **Crab** is the flesh of this creature eaten as food. *cangrejo* ❑ *I can't remember when I last had crab. No recuerdo cuándo fue la última vez que comí cangrejo.*
→ see **shellfish**

**crack**
❶ VERB USES
❷ NOUN AND ADJECTIVE USES

❶ **crack** /kræk/ (**cracks, cracking, cracked**) 1 V-T/V-I If something hard **cracks,** or if you **crack** it, it becomes slightly damaged, with lines appearing on its surface. *resquebrajar* ❑ *A gas pipe cracked and gas leaked into our homes. Una tubería de gas se resquebrajó y el gas se salió en nuestras casas.* ❑ *...a cracked mirror. ...un espejo resquebrajado.* 2 V-T When you **crack** something hard, you hit it and it breaks or is damaged. *partir* ❑ *Crack the eggs into a bowl. Parta los huevos en un tazón.* ❑ *He cracked his head on the pavement. Se partió la cabeza en la banqueta.* 3 V-T If you **crack** a problem or a code, you solve it, especially after a lot of thought. *descifrar* ❑ *He has finally cracked the system after years of research. Finalmente descifró el sistema después de años de investigación.* 4 V-I If someone **cracks,** they lose control of their emotions or actions because they are under a lot of pressure. *sufrir una crisis nerviosa* [INFORMAL] ❑ *She's calm and strong, and she is just not going to crack. Es tranquila y fuerte, no va a sufrir una crisis nerviosa.* 5 V-I If your voice **cracks** when you are speaking or singing, it changes in pitch because you are feeling a strong emotion. *quebrarse* ❑ *Her voice cracked and she began to cry. Se le quebró la voz y comenzó a llorar.* 6 V-T If you **crack** a joke, you tell it. *contar* ❑ *He cracked jokes, and talked about girls. Contaba chistes y hablaba de mujeres.*
→ see **crash**

▸ **crack down** PHR-VERB If people in authority **crack down on** a group of people, they become stricter in making them obey rules or laws. *tomar medidas enérgicas contra* ❑ *Police are cracking down on people who ride their bikes on the sidewalk. La policía está tomando medidas enérgicas contra aquéllos que andan en bicicleta sobre las banquetas.* → see also **crackdown**

▸ **crack up** PHR-VERB If someone **cracks up,** they are under such emotional strain that they become mentally ill. *sufrir un ataque de nervios* [INFORMAL] ❑ *She'll crack up if she doesn't have some fun. Le va a dar un ataque de nervios si no se divierte un poco.*

❷ **crack** /kræk/ (**cracks**) 1 N-COUNT A **crack** is a very narrow gap between two things. *rendija* ❑ *Kathryn saw him through a crack in the curtains. Kathryn lo vio a través de una rendija en las cortinas.* 2 N-COUNT A **crack** is a line that appears on the surface of something when it is slightly damaged. *rajadura* ❑ *The plate had a crack in it. El plato tenía una pequeña rajadura.* 3 N-COUNT A **crack** is a sharp sound, like the sound of a piece of wood breaking. *estallido* ❑ *Suddenly there was a loud crack and glass flew into the car. De pronto hubo un fuerte estallido y el vidrio voló dentro del coche.* 4 ADJ A **crack** soldier or sportsman is highly trained and very skillful. *de primera* ❑ *...a crack police officer. ...un oficial de policía de primera.* 5 N-COUNT A **crack** is a slightly rude or cruel joke. *comentario socarrón* ❑ *Tell Tracy you're sorry for that crack about her weight. Pídele perdón a Tracy por aquel comentario socarrón acerca de su peso.* 6 N-UNCOUNT **Crack** is a very pure form of the drug **cocaine.** *crack*

| **Word Partnership** | Usar *crack* con: |
|---|---|
| ADJ. | crack **open** ❶ 1 |
| N. | crack **a code,** crack **the system** ❶ 3 |
| | crack **jokes** ❶ 6 |
| ADJ. | **deep** crack ❷ 1 2 |
| V. | **have a** crack ❷ 1 2 |

**crack|down** /krækdaʊn/ (**crackdowns**) N-COUNT A **crackdown** is strong official action that is taken to punish people who break laws. *medidas enérgicas* ❑ *The unrest ended with a violent crackdown. El desorden acabó con la imposición de medidas enérgicas.*

**crack|er** /krækər/ (**crackers**) N-COUNT A **cracker** is a thin, crisp piece of baked bread which is often eaten with cheese. *galleta*

**crack-up** (**crack-ups**) 1 N-COUNT A **crack-up** is a mental breakdown. *sufrir un ataque de nervios* [INFORMAL] ❑ *You're clearly having some kind of a crack-up. Evidentemente estás sufriendo un ataque de nervios.* 2 N-COUNT A **crack-up** is a motor vehicle accident. *accidente automovilístico* [INFORMAL] ❑ *In one recent crack-up, two drivers survived with only minor injury. En un accidente automovilístico reciente, dos conductores sobrevivieron con sólo heridas menores.*

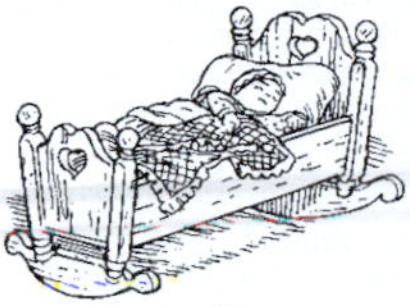

cradle

**cra|dle** /kreɪdᵊl/ (**cradles, cradling, cradled**) 1 N-COUNT A **cradle** is a baby's small bed with high sides, which can be rocked from side to side. *cuna* 2 V-T If you **cradle** someone or something **in** your arms, you hold them carefully and gently. *acunar* ❑ *I cradled her in my arms. La mecí en mis brazos.*

**craft** /kræft/ (**crafts, crafting, crafted**)

| **Craft** is both the singular and the plural form for meaning 1. |
|---|

1 N-COUNT You can refer to a boat, a spacecraft, or an aircraft as a **craft.** *nave, embarcación* ❑ *The fisherman guided his small craft close to the shore. El pescador guió su pequeña embarcación hasta la orilla.* 2 N-COUNT A **craft** is an activity such as weaving, carving, or pottery that involves making things skillfully with your hands. *artesanía* ❑ *...the crafts of the people of Oceania. ...las artesanías de la gente de Oceanía.* 3 V-T If something **is crafted,** it is made skillfully. *hacer con cuidado* ❑ *The windows were probably crafted in the late Middle Ages. Las ventanas fueron bien trabajadas probablemente durante el último periodo de la Edad Media.*
→ see **fly, ship**

**cram** /kræm/ (**crams, cramming, crammed**) V-T/V-I If you **cram** things or people **into** a container or place, or if they **cram into** it, there are so many of them in it at one time that it is completely full. *atiborrar* ❑ *Terry crammed the dirty clothes into his bag. Terry atiborró su ropa sucia en la bolsa.* ❑ *She crammed her mouth with cake. Se atiborró la boca de pastel.* ❑ *We crammed into my car and set off. Nos apretujamos en mi coche y nos fuimos.*

**cramp** /kræmp/ (**cramps**) N-VAR A **cramp** is a sudden strong pain caused by a muscle suddenly contracting. *calambre* ❑ *He had a cramp in his leg. Le dio un calambre en la pierna.*

**crane** /kreɪn/ (**cranes, craning, craned**) 1 N-COUNT A **crane** is a large machine that moves heavy things by lifting them in the air. *grúa* ❑ *...a huge crane. ...una enorme grúa.* 2 N-COUNT A **crane** is a kind of large bird with a long neck and long legs. *grulla* 3 V-T/V-I If you **crane** your neck or head, you stretch your neck in a particular direction in order to see or hear something better. *estirar* ❑ *She craned her neck to get a better view. Estiró el cuello para ver mejor.*

crane

**cranky** /kræŋki/ ADJ **Cranky** means bad-tempered. *cascarrabias* [INFORMAL] ❑ *Jack and I both started to get cranky. Jack y yo comenzábamos a ponernos de mal humor.*

**crap|shoot** /kræpʃut/ N-SING If you describe something as **a crapshoot,** you mean that what happens depends entirely on luck or chance. *volado* ❑ *Is buying a computer always a crapshoot? ¿Comprar una computadora siempre es un volado?*

**crash** /kræʃ/ (**crashes, crashing, crashed**) 1 N-COUNT A **crash** is an accident in which a moving vehicle hits something and is damaged or destroyed. *choque* ❑ *His elder son was killed in a car crash. A su hijo mayor lo mataron en un choque.* 2 N-COUNT A **crash** is a sudden, loud noise. *estrépito* ❑ *Two people recalled hearing a loud crash about 1:30 a.m. Dos personas recordaron haber escuchado gran estrépito a eso de la 1:30 a.m.* 3 V-T/V-I If a moving vehicle **crashes** or if the driver **crashes** it, it hits something and is damaged or destroyed. *chocar* ❑ *The plane crashed mysteriously. El avión chocó de manera misteriosa.* ❑ *Her car crashed into the rear of a van. Su auto chocó con la parte trasera de una camioneta.* 4 V-I To **crash** means to move or fall violently, making a loud noise. *derrumbarse* ❑ *The walls above us crashed down. Las paredes se derrumbaron sobre nosotros.* 5 V-I If a business or financial system **crashes,** it fails suddenly, often with serious effects. *quebrar* [BUSINESS] ❑ *When the market crashed, the deal was canceled. Cuando la bolsa se derrumbó, se canceló el trato.* ● **Crash** is also a noun. *crac, crack* ❑ *...a stock market crash. ...el crack del mercado financiero.* 6 V-I If a computer or a computer program **crashes,** it fails suddenly. *caerse* ❑ *My computer crashed for the second time in 10 days. Mi computadora se cayó por segunda ocasión en 10 días.*
→ see Word Web: **crash**

| **Thesaurus** | *crash* | Ver también: |
|---|---|---|
| N. | collision, wreck 1 | |
| | bang 2 | |
| V. | collide, hit, smash 3 | |
| | fail 5 6 | |

**cra|ter** /kreɪtər/ (**craters**) N-COUNT A **crater** is a very large hole in the ground, which has been caused by something hitting it or by an explosion.

## Word Web crash

Every year the National Highway Traffic Safety Administration* conducts crash tests on new cars. They evaluate exactly what happens during an accident. How fast do you have to be going to **buckle** a bumper during a collision? Does the gas tank **rupture**? Do the tires **burst**? What happens when the windshield **breaks**? Does it **crack**, or does it **shatter** into a thousand pieces? Does the force of the **impact crush** the front of the car completely? This is actually a good thing. It means that the engine and hood would protect the passengers during the crash.

*National Highway Traffic Safety Administration: a U.S. government agency that sets safety standards.*

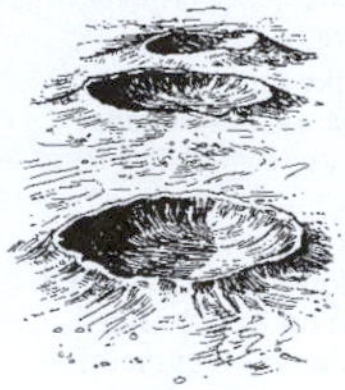

crater

cráter ❑ *The bomb left a ten-foot crater in the street.* *La bomba hizo un cráter de tres metros en la calle.*
→ see **astronomer, lake, meteor, moon, solar system**

**craw|fish** /krɔfɪʃ/ (**crawfish**) also **crayfish** N-COUNT A **crawfish** is a small shellfish with five pairs of legs which lives in rivers and streams. *cangrejo de río*
→ see **shellfish**

**crawl** /krɔl/ (**crawls, crawling, crawled**) **1** V-I When you **crawl**, you move forward on your hands and knees. *gatear* ❑ *Don't worry if your baby seems a little slow to crawl.* *No se preocupe si parece que su bebé tarda en gatear.* ❑ *I began to crawl on my hands and knees toward the door.* *Comencé a gatear hacia la puerta.* **2** V-I If something or someone **crawls** somewhere, they move there slowly. *arrastrarse* ❑ *He crawled from the car after the accident.* *Se arrastró fuera del coche después del accidente.* ● **Crawl** is also a noun. *paso de tortuga* ❑ *The traffic slowed to a crawl.* *El tráfico iba a paso de tortuga.* **3** V-I If you say that a place **is crawling with** people or things, you are emphasizing that it is full of them. *estar lleno de* [INFORMAL] ❑ *This place is crawling with police.* *Este lugar está lleno de policías.* **4** N-SING **The crawl** is a kind of swimming stroke which you do lying on your front, swinging one arm over your head, and then the other arm. *crol* ❑ *I did 50 lengths of the crawl.* *Di 50 vueltas de crol.*

crawl

**crawl space** (**crawl spaces**) N-COUNT A **crawl space** is a narrow space under the roof or floor of a building that provides access to the wiring or plumbing. *espacio estrecho bajo el techo o piso que permite el acceso a la plomería o a los cables.* ❑ *...a crawl space between the basement and the kitchen.* *...un espacio estrecho entre el sótano y la cocina.*

**cray|on** /kreɪɒn/ (**crayons**) N-COUNT A **crayon** is a stick of colored wax used for drawing. *crayón*

**cra|zy** /kreɪzi/ (**crazier, craziest, crazies**) **1** ADJ If you describe someone or something as **crazy**, you think they are very foolish or strange. *loco* [INFORMAL] ❑ *People thought they were crazy.* *La gente creía que estaban locos.* ● **cra|zi|ly** ADV *como loco* ❑ *...a flock of sheep running crazily in every direction.* *...un rebaño de ovejas que corrían como locas en todas direcciones.* **2** ADJ Someone who is **crazy** is insane. *loco* [INFORMAL] ❑ *If I sat home and worried about all this stuff, I'd go crazy.* *Si me sentara en casa a preocuparme de todo esto, me volvería loco.* ● **Crazy** is also a noun. *loco o loca* ❑ *...one of New York's crazies.* *...uno de los locos neoyorquinos.* **3** ADJ If you are **crazy about** something, you are very enthusiastic about it. If you are **crazy about** someone, you are deeply in love with them. *loco por* [INFORMAL] ❑ *He's still crazy about his work.* *Sigue loco por su trabajo.* ❑ *We're crazy about each other.* *Estamos locos el uno por el otro.*

**cream** /krim/ (**creams, creaming, creamed**) **1** N-UNCOUNT **Cream** is a thick liquid that is produced from milk. You can use it in cooking or put it on fruit or desserts. *crema* ❑ *...strawberries and cream.* *...fresas con crema.* **2** N-VAR A **cream** is a substance that you rub into your skin, for example, to keep it soft or to heal or protect it. *crema* ❑ *Gently apply the cream to the skin.* *Aplique la crema cuidadosamente sobre su piel.* **3** COLOR Something that is **cream** is yellowish-white in color. *crema* ❑ *...a cream silk shirt.* *...una camisa de seda color crema* **4** → see also **ice cream**

**cream|er** /krimər/ N-COUNT A **creamer** is a small pitcher used for pouring cream or milk. *cremera*
→ see **dish**

**cre|ate** /krieɪt/ (**creates, creating, created**) V-T To **create** something means to cause it to happen or exist. *crear, causar, provocar* ❑ *It is really great for a radio producer to create a show like this.* *Realmente es grandioso para un productor de radio crear un programa como éste.* ❑ *She could create a fight out of anything.* *Podía causar un problema de la nada.* ● **crea|tion** /krieɪʃᵊn/ N-UNCOUNT *creación* ❑ *...the creation of local jobs.* *...la creación de empleos locales.* ● **crea|tor** /krieɪtər/ (**creators**) N-COUNT *creador o creadora* ❑ *...Ian Fleming, the creator of James Bond.* *...Ian Fleming, creador de James Bond.*

**Thesaurus** *create* Ver también:

v. produce, make; (*ant.*) destroy

**Word Link** creat ≈ making : creation, creative, creature

**crea|tion** /krieɪʃən/ (creations) **1** N-UNCOUNT In many religions, **creation** is the making of the universe, earth, and creatures by God. *creación* ❑ *...the Creation of the universe as told in Genesis Chapter One. ...la creación del universo según el Génesis, capítulo uno.* **2** N-COUNT You can refer to something that someone has made as a **creation.** *creación* ❑ *The bathroom is entirely my own creation. El baño es enteramente creación mía.* **3** → see also **create**

**crea|tive** /krieɪtɪv/ **1** ADJ A **creative** person has the ability to invent and develop original ideas, especially in the arts. *creativo* ❑ *Like many creative people he was never satisfied. Como muchas personas creativas, nunca estaba satisfecho.* • **crea|tiv|ity** /krieɪtɪvɪti/ N-UNCOUNT *creatividad* ❑ *American art reached a peak of creativity in the '50s and '60s. El arte estadounidense alcanzó una cúspide de creatividad en los años 50 y 60.* **2** ADJ If you use something in a **creative** way, you use it in a new way that produces interesting and unusual results. *creativo* ❑ *...his creative use of words. ...la forma creativa en que utiliza las palabras.*

**crea|tive dra|ma** (creative dramas) N-VAR **Creative drama** is a form of improvised drama that is often used in teaching. *teatro, arte dramático*

**crea|tive writ|ing** N-UNCOUNT **Creative writing** is writing such as novels, stories, poems, and plays. *escritura creativa* ❑ *...a creative writing class. ...una clase de escritura creativa.*

**crea|ture** /kritʃər/ (creatures) N-COUNT You can refer to any living thing that is not a plant as a **creature.** *criatura* ❑ *Like all living creatures, birds need a good supply of water. Como todas las criaturas vivas, las aves necesitan abundante agua.*

**Word Link** cred ≈ to believe : credible, discredit, incredible

**cred|ible** /krɛdɪbəl/ **1** ADJ **Credible** means able to be trusted or believed. *creíble, verosímil* ❑ *Her claims seem credible to many. A muchos les parecen creíbles sus argumentos.* • **cred|ibil|ity** /krɛdɪbɪlɪti/ N-UNCOUNT *credibilidad* ❑ *The police have lost their credibility. La policía ha perdido credibilidad.* **2** ADJ A **credible** candidate, policy, or system is one that appears to have a chance of being successful. *plausible, viable* ❑ *Mr. Robertson is a credible candidate. El Sr. Robertson es un candidato viable.*

**cred|it** /krɛdɪt/ (credits, crediting, credited) **1** N-UNCOUNT If you are given **credit** for goods or services, or buy them **on credit,** you are allowed to pay for them several weeks or months after you have received them. *crédito* ❑ *The group can't get credit to buy farming machinery. El grupo no puede conseguir crédito para comprar maquinaria agrícola.* **2** N-UNCOUNT If you get **the credit for** something good, people praise you because you are thought to be responsible for it. *mérito, crédito* ❑ *We don't mind who gets the credit so long as we don't get the blame. No nos importa quién se lleve el crédito mientras no nos culpen.* ❑ *It would be wrong for us to take all the credit. No estaría bien que nos lleváramos todo el mérito.* **3** V-T If people **credit** someone **with** an achievement, people say or believe that they were responsible for it. *reconocer, atribuir el crédito* ❑ *The staff are crediting him with having saved Hythe's life. El personal le atribuye el crédito de haber salvado la vida de Hythe.* **4** N-COUNT A **credit** is one part of a course of study at a school or college that has been successfully completed. *crédito* ❑ *He doesn't have enough credits to graduate. Los créditos no le alcanzan para graduarse.* **5** N-PLURAL The list of people who helped to make a movie, a CD, or a television program is called **the credits.** *créditos* ❑ *It was fantastic seeing my name in the credits. Fue fantástico ver mi nombre entre los créditos.* **6** PHRASE If something is **to** your **credit,** you deserve praise for it. *decir mucho de alguien* ❑ *To her credit, she continued to look upon life as a positive experience. Que haya seguido viendo la vida como una experiencia positiva dice mucho de ella.*

**Word Partnership** Usar *credit* con:

| | |
|---|---|
| N. | credit **history, letter of** credit **1** |
| V. | **provide** credit **1** |
| | **deserve** credit, **take** credit **2** |
| ADJ. | **personal** credit **1** **2** |

**cred|it card** (credit cards) N-COUNT A **credit card** is a plastic card that you use to buy goods on credit. Compare **charge card.** *tarjeta de crédito*

**cred|it hour** (credit hours) N-COUNT A **credit hour** is a credit that a school or college awards to students who have completed a course of study. *crédito, materia* ❑ *Now he needs only two credit hours to graduate. Ya sólo le faltan dos materias para graduarse.*

**cred|it lim|it** (credit limits) N-COUNT Your **credit limit** is the amount of debt that you are allowed, for example, by a credit card company. *límite de crédito* ❑ *If you exceed your credit limit, we have the right to close your account. Estamos autorizados a cancelar su cuenta si rebasa su límite de crédito.*

**cred|it line** (credit lines) N-COUNT Your **credit line** is the same as your **credit limit.** *línea de crédito*

**credi|tor** /krɛdɪtər/ (creditors) N-COUNT Your **creditors** are the people who you owe money to. *acreedor, acreedora* ❑ *The company said it would pay all its creditors. Dijeron en la empresa que le pagarían a todos los acreedores.*

**cred|it trans|fer** (credit transfers) N-COUNT If a student has a **credit transfer** when they change to a new school or college, their credits are transferred from their old school or college to their new one. *transferencia de créditos*

**cred|it un|ion** (credit unions) N-COUNT A **credit union** is a financial institution that offers its members low-interest loans. *unión de crédito* ❑ *All our money is in a credit union. Todo nuestro dinero está en una unión de crédito.*

**creep** /krip/ (creeps, creeping, crept) **1** V-I To **creep** somewhere means to move there quietly and slowly. *moverse sigilosamente* ❑ *He crept up the stairs. Subió sigilosamente las escaleras.* ❑ *Mist crept in from the sea. La neblina llegó sigilosamente del mar.* **2** V-I If something **creeps** in or **creeps** back, it gradually starts happening or returning without people realizing or without them wanting it. *subrepticiamente, sin darse uno cuenta* ❑ *Problems can creep in. Los problemas empiezan sin que uno se dé cuenta.* ❑ *The inflation rate has been creeping up. La tasa de inflación ha estado subiendo poco a poco.* ❑ *Mistakes started to creep into her game. Empezaron*

C

C

## Picture Dictionary crime

graffiti mugging theft burglary shoplifting

*a aparecer errores en su juego.* **3** N-UNCOUNT In geology, **creep** is the very slow downhill movement of rocks and soil as a result of gravity. *deslizamiento lento, movimiento paulatino del terreno* [TECHNICAL]

**Word Partnership** Usar *creep* con:

PREP. creep **into**, creep **toward**, creep **up** **1**
creep **in** **2**

**creepy** /kripi/ (**creepier, creepiest**) ADJ If you say that something or someone is **creepy,** you mean they make you feel nervous or frightened. *escalofriante, repulsivo* [INFORMAL] ❑ *...places that were really creepy at night. ...lugares verdaderamente escalofriantes de noche.*

**crept** /krɛpt/ **Crept** is the past tense and past participle of **creep**. *pasado y participio pasado de **creep***

**Word Link** *cresc, creas ≈ growing : crescent, decrease, increase*

**cres|cent** /krɛsᵊnt/ (**crescents**) N-COUNT A **crescent** is a curved shape like the shape of the moon during its first and last quarters. It is the most important symbol of the Islamic faith. *media luna, creciente*
→ see **tool**

**crest** /krɛst/ (**crests**) **1** N-COUNT The **crest of** a hill or a wave is the top of it. *cima, cresta* **2** N-COUNT A **crest** is a design that is the symbol of a noble family, a town, or an organization. *emblema, divisa* ❑ *On the wall is the family crest. En el muro se ve el emblema familiar.*
→ see **sound**

**cre|vasse** /krɪvæs/ (**crevasses**) N-COUNT A **crevasse** is a large, deep crack in thick ice or rock. *grieta*

**crew** /kru/ (**crews**) **1** N-COUNT The **crew** of a ship, an aircraft, or a spacecraft is the people who work on and operate it. *tripulación* ❑ *...the crew of the space shuttle. ...la tripulación del transbordador espacial.* ❑ *These ships carry small crews, usually of around twenty men. La tripulación de esos barcos es reducida, normalmente unos veinte hombres.* **2** N-COUNT A **crew** is a group of people with special technical skills who work together on a task or project. *equipo* ❑ *...a two-man film crew. ...un equipo de filmación de dos personas.*
→ see **theater**

crib

**crib** /krɪb/ (**cribs**) N-COUNT A **crib** is a bed for a baby. *cuna*

**crick|et** /krɪkɪt/ (**crickets**) **1** N-UNCOUNT **Cricket** is an outdoor game played between two teams who try to score points, called runs, by hitting a ball with a wooden bat. *cricket, críquet* ❑ *During the summer term we played cricket. Jugábamos cricket durante el semestre de verano.* **2** N-COUNT A **cricket** is a small jumping insect that produces short, loud sounds by rubbing its wings together. *grillo*
→ see **insect**

**crime** /kraɪm/ (**crimes**) N-VAR A **crime** is an illegal action or activity for which a person can be punished by law. *crimen, delito* ❑ *...the scene of the crime. ...la escena del crimen.* ❑ *...the growing problem of organized crime. ...el creciente problema del crimen organizado.*
→ see Picture Dictionary: **crime**
→ see **city**

**Word Partnership** Usar *crime* con:

V. **commit a** crime, **fight against** crime
ADJ. **organized** crime, **terrible** crime, **violent** crime
N. **partner in** crime, crime **prevention**, crime **scene**, crime **wave**

**crimi|nal** /krɪmɪnᵊl/ (**criminals**) **1** N-COUNT A **criminal** is a person who has committed a crime. *criminal, delincuente* ❑ *They attacked the prison and set free nine criminals. Atacaron la cárcel y liberaron a nueve delincuentes.* **2** ADJ **Criminal** means connected with crime. *criminal, penal* ❑ *Her husband faces various criminal charges. Su esposo enfrenta varios cargos penales.*

**crip|ple** /krɪpᵊl/ (**cripples, crippling, crippled**) V-T If someone **is crippled** by an injury, it is so serious that they can never move their body properly again. *quedar lisiado, quedar inválido* ❑ *Mr. Easton was crippled in an accident. El Sr. Easton se quedó inválido a raíz de un accidente.* ❑ *Another bad fall could cripple him for life. Otra caída peligrosa y podría quedarse inválido de por vida.*

**cri|sis** /kraɪsɪs/ (**crises** /kraɪsiz/) **1** N-VAR A **crisis** is a situation in which something or someone is affected by one or more very serious problems. *crisis* ❑ *...the continent's economic crisis. ...la crisis económica del continente.* ❑ *...someone to turn to in moments of crisis. ...alguien a quien recurrir en momentos de crisis.* **2** N-COUNT The **crisis** is the most dramatic part of a play or movie, or the most important part of its plot. *crisis*

**crisp** /krɪsp/ (**crisper, crispest, crisps, crisping,**

crisped) 1 ADJ Food that is **crisp** is pleasantly hard and crunchy. *crujiente* ❑ *Bake the potatoes for 15 minutes, till they're nice and crisp.* *Fríe las papas 15 minutos, hasta que estén doradas y crujientes.* ❑ *...crisp bacon.* *...tocino crujiente.* 2 ADJ Weather that is pleasantly fresh, cold, and dry can be described as **crisp.** *despejado, frío* ❑ *...a crisp autumn day.* *...un despejado día de otoño.*

**cri|teri|on** /kraɪtɪəriən/ (**criteria** /kraɪtɪəriə/) N-COUNT A **criterion** is a factor on which you judge or decide something. *criterio* ❑ *The bank is reviewing its criteria for lending money.* *El banco está revisando sus criterios de otorgamiento de créditos.*

**Word Link** *crit ≈ to judge : critic, critical, criticize*

**crit|ic** /krɪtɪk/ (**critics**) 1 N-COUNT A **critic** is a person who writes about and expresses opinions about books, movies, music, or art. *crítico o crítica* ❑ *Mather was a film critic for many years.* *Mather fue crítico de cine durante muchos años.* 2 N-COUNT Someone who is a **critic** of a person or system disapproves of them and criticizes them publicly. *crítico o crítica* ❑ *He has been one of the most consistent critics of the government.* *Ha sido uno de los más constantes críticos del gobierno.*

**criti|cal** /krɪtɪkᵊl/ 1 ADJ A **critical** time or situation is extremely important. *crítico* ❑ *The incident happened at a critical point in the campaign.* *El incidente sucedió en un momento crítico de la campaña.* • **criti|cal|ly** /krɪtɪkli/ ADV *ser fundamental (algo)* ❑ *It is critically important for people to be prepared.* *Es fundamental que la gente se prepare.* 2 ADJ A **critical** situation is very serious and dangerous. *crítico* ❑ *The situation may become critical.* *La situación puede ponerse crítica.* • **criti|cal|ly** ADV *críticamente* ❑ *Food supplies are running critically low.* *La provisión de alimentos es críticamente baja.* 3 ADJ To be **critical of** someone or something means to criticize them. *crítico* ❑ *His report is highly critical of the trial judge.* *Su informe es muy crítico respecto del juez que llevó el caso.* • **criti|cal|ly** ADV *de manera crítica, en tono de desaprobación* ❑ *She spoke critically of Lara.* *Habló de Lara en tono de desaprobación.* 4 ADJ A **critical** approach to something involves examining and judging it carefully. *crítico* ❑ *...a critical examination of political ideas.* *...un análisis crítico de las ideas políticas.* • **criti|cal|ly** ADV *de manera crítica* ❑ *Wyman watched them critically.* *Wyman los miró de manera crítica.*

**Word Partnership** Usar *critical* con:

| | |
|---|---|
| N. | critical **issue**, critical **role** 1<br>critical **state** 1 2<br>critical **condition** 2 |
| V. | **become** critical 1 2 |
| PREP. | critical **of *someone***, critical **of *something*** 3 |

**criti|cism** /krɪtɪsɪzəm/ (**criticisms**) 1 N-VAR **Criticism** is the action of expressing disapproval of something or someone. A **criticism** is a statement that expresses disapproval. *crítica* ❑ *This policy has come under strong criticism.* *Esta política fue objeto de severas críticas.* 2 N-UNCOUNT **Criticism** is a serious examination and judgment of something such as a book or play. *crítica* ❑ *...film criticism.* *...crítica cinematográfica.*

**Thesaurus** *criticism* Ver también:

| | |
|---|---|
| N. | disapproval, judgment; (*ant.*) approval, flattery, praise 1<br>commentary, critique, evaluation, review 2 |

**Word Partnership** Usar *criticism* con:

| | |
|---|---|
| PREP. | criticism **against *something***, criticism **from *something***, criticism **of *something*** 1<br>**public** criticism 1 2 |
| ADJ. | **constructive** criticism, **open to** criticism 1 2 |
| N. | **literary** criticism 2 |

**criti|cize** /krɪtɪsaɪz/ (**criticizes, criticizing, criticized**) V-T If you **criticize** someone or something, you express your disapproval of them by saying what you think is wrong with them. *criticar* ❑ *His mother rarely criticized him.* *Su madre rara vez lo criticaba.*

**croco|dile** /krɒkədaɪl/ (**crocodiles**) N-COUNT A **crocodile** is a large reptile with a long body and strong jaws. Crocodiles live in rivers. *cocodrilo*

**crois|sant** /krwɑsɑn, krəsɑnt/ (**croissants**) N-VAR **Croissants** are bread rolls in the shape of a crescent that are eaten for breakfast. *cuerno, medialuna, croissant*
→ see **bread**

**Cro-Magnon** /kroʊ mægnən, mænyən/ (**Cro-Magnons**) N-COUNT **Cro-Magnons** were a species of early human being who lived between 50,000 and 100,000 years ago. *Cromañón, Cro-Magnon* • **Cro-Magnon** is also an adjective. *Cromañón, Cro-Magnon* ❑ *...Cro-Magnon man.* *...hombre de Cromañón*

**crook** /krʊk/ (**crooks**) 1 N-COUNT A **crook** is a dishonest person or a criminal. *pillo, sinvergüenza* [INFORMAL] ❑ *The man is a crook and a liar.* *El hombre es un pillo y un mentiroso.* 2 N-COUNT **The crook of** your arm or leg is the soft inside part where you bend your elbow or knee. *pliegue (del codo), corva (de la rodila)* ❑ *She hid her face in the crook of her arm.* *Escondió la cara en el pliegue del codo.*

**crook|ed** /krʊkɪd/ 1 ADJ If you describe something as **crooked,** especially something that is usually straight, you mean that it is bent or twisted. *torcido, chueco* ❑ *...the crooked line of his broken nose.* *...el perfil chueco de su nariz rota.* 2 ADJ If you describe a person or an activity as **crooked,** you mean that they are dishonest or criminal. *deshonesto, chueco* [INFORMAL] ❑ *...a crooked cop.* *...un policía deshonesto.*

**crop** /krɒp/ (**crops, cropping, cropped**) 1 N-COUNT **Crops** are plants such as wheat and potatoes that are grown in large quantities for food. *cosecha, cultivo* ❑ *Rice farmers here still plant and harvest their crops by hand.* *Aquí, los arroceros todavía siembran y recogen sus cosechas a mano.* 2 N-COUNT The plants or fruits that are collected at harvest time are referred to as a **crop.** *cosecha* ❑ *Each year it produces a fine crop of fruit.* *Cada año produce una buena cosecha de fruta.* ❑ *...this year's corn crop.* *...la cosecha de maíz de este año.* 3 N-SING You can refer to a group of people or things that have appeared together as a **crop of** people or things. *montón, lote*

C

[INFORMAL] ❑ *...a crop of books about Marilyn Monroe.* *...un lote de libros sobre Marilyn Monroe.* 4 V-T To **crop** your hair means to cut it short. *cortar al ras* ❑ *She cropped her hair and dyed it blonde.* *Se cortó el pelo al ras y se pintó de güera.*
→ see **farm, grain, plant, photography**

C

▸ **crop up** PHR-VERB If something **crops up,** it appears or happens unexpectedly. *surgir* ❑ *His name has cropped up at every meeting.* *Su nombre ha surgido en todas las reuniones.*

**crop dust|ing** also **crop-dusting** N-UNCOUNT **Crop dusting** is the spreading of pesticides on crops, usually from an aircraft. *fumigar* ❑ *...a crop-dusting plane.* *...un avión fumigador.*

**cross**
❶ MOVING ACROSS
❷ ANGRY

❶ **cross** /krɔs/ (**crosses, crossing, crossed**) 1 V-T/V-I If you **cross** a room, a road, or an area of land, you move to the other side of it. If you **cross to** a place, you move or travel over a room, road, or area in order to reach that place. *cruzar, cruzarse, atravesar, atravesarse* ❑ *She failed to look as she crossed the road.* *No se fijó al cruzar la calle.* ❑ *Egan crossed to the window and looked out.* *Egan cruzó hacia la ventana y miró afuera.* 2 V-T A road, railroad, or bridge that **crosses** an area of land or water passes over it. *cruzar* ❑ *The road crosses the river half a mile outside the town.* *El camino cruza el río a media milla, en las afueras del pueblo.* 3 V-T If an expression **crosses** your face, it appears briefly on your face. *cruzar* [WRITTEN] ❑ *A sad look crossed his face.* *Una mirada triste le cruzó por el rostro.* 4 V-T If you **cross** your arms, legs, or fingers, you put one of them on top of the other. *cruzar* ❑ *Jill crossed her legs.* *Jill cruzó las piernas.* 5 V-RECIP Lines or roads that **cross** meet and go across each other. *cruzarse* ❑ *...the place where Main and Center Streets cross.* *...donde se cruzan las calles de Main y Center.* 6 N-COUNT A **cross** is a shape that consists of a vertical line or piece with a shorter horizontal line or piece across it. It is the most important Christian symbol. *cruz* ❑ *Around her neck was a cross on a silver chain.* *Llevaba en el cuello una cruz con una cadena de plata.* 7 N-COUNT A **cross** is a written mark in the shape of an X. *cruz, tache* ❑ *Put a cross next to those activities you like.* *Marca con una cruz las actividades que te interesan.* 8 N-SING Something that is **a cross between** two things is neither one thing nor the other, but a mixture of both. *cruza, mezcla* ❑ *"Ha!" It was a cross between a laugh and a bark.* *"¡Ha!" Fue una mezcla de risa y ladrido.* 9 → see also **crossing** 10 to **cross** your **fingers** → see **finger** 11 to **cross** your **mind** → see **mind**
→ see **answer**

▸ **cross out** PHR-VERB If you **cross out** words, you draw a line through them. *tachar* ❑ *He crossed out her name and added his own.* *Tachó el nombre de ella y puso el propio.*

❷ **cross** /krɔs/ (**crosser, crossest**) ADJ Someone who is **cross** is angry or irritated. *enojado, enfadado* ❑ *I'm terribly cross with him.* *Estoy muy enojada con él.* • **cross|ly** ADV *con enojo, enojado* ❑ *"No, no, no," Morris said crossly.* *—No, no, no —dijo Morris con enojo.*

**cross-country** 1 N-UNCOUNT **Cross-country** is the sport of running, riding, or skiing across open countryside. *cross-country, campo traviesa* ❑ *She finished third in the world cross-country championships.* *Terminó en tercer lugar en los campeonatos mundiales de campo traviesa.* 2 ADJ A **cross-country** trip takes you from one side of a country to the other. *de extremo a extremo del país* ❑ *...cross-country rail services.* *...servicios ferroviarios de extremo a extremo del país.* • **Cross-country** is also an adverb. *de extremo a extremo, a través del país* ❑ *I drove cross-country in his van.* *Recorrí el país de extremo a extremo en su camioneta.*

**cross-examine** (**cross-examines, cross-examining, cross-examined**) V-T When a lawyer **cross-examines** someone during a trial or hearing, he or she questions them about the evidence that they have given. *contrainterrogar, repreguntar* ❑ *His lawyers will get a chance to cross-examine him.* *Sus abogados tendrán la oportunidad de contrainterrogarlo.* • **cross-examination** N-VAR (**cross-examinations**) *contrainterrogatorio* ❑ *...the cross-examination of a witness.* *...el contrainterrogatorio de un testigo.*
→ see **trial**

**cross|ing** /krɔsɪŋ/ (**crossings**) 1 N-COUNT A **crossing** is a boat journey to a place on the other side of an ocean, river, or lake. *crucero, travesía* ❑ *He made the crossing from Cape Town to Sydney.* *Hizo la travesía de Ciudad del Cabo a Sydney.* 2 N-COUNT A **crossing** is a place where you can cross something such as a road or a border. *cruce*

**cross|ing over** N-UNCOUNT In biology, **crossing over** is a process in which genetic material is exchanged between two chromosomes, resulting in new combinations of genes. *cruzamiento*

**cross|roads** /krɔsroʊdz/ (**crossroads**) 1 N-COUNT A **crossroads** is a place where two roads meet and cross each other. *cruce* ❑ *Turn right at the first crossroads.* *Da vuelta a la derecha en el primer cruce.* 2 N-SING A **crossroads** is an important or central place. *encrucijada* ❑ *...a small town at the crossroads of agriculture in central Florida.* *...un pueblito en la encrucijada agrícola del centro de la Florida.*

**cross|town** /krɔstaʊn/ also **cross-town** ADJ A **crosstown** bus or route is one that crosses the main roads or transportation lines of a city or town. *que cruza, que atraviesa* ❑ *...the crosstown bus that takes me to work.* *...me voy al trabajo en el autobús que atraviesa la ciudad.* ❑ *...a crosstown subway.* *...una línea de metro que cruza la ciudad.* • **Crosstown** is also an adverb. *atravesando* ❑ *I have trouble these days getting crosstown in Manhattan.* *Estos días he tenido problemas atravesando Manhattan.*

**cross|walk** /krɔswɔk/ (**crosswalks**) N-COUNT A **crosswalk** is a place where drivers must stop to let pedestrians cross a street. *cruce de peatones*

**cross|word** /krɔswɜrd/ (**crosswords**) N-COUNT A **crossword** or **crossword puzzle** is a word game in which you work out the answers and write them in the white squares of a pattern of black and white squares. *crucigrama* ❑ *He could do the Times crossword in 15 minutes.* *Hacía el crucigrama del Times en 15 minutos.*

crossword puzzle

**crouch** /kraʊtʃ/ (**crouches, crouching, crouched**) V-I If you **are crouching,** your legs are bent under you so that you are close to the ground and leaning forward slightly. acuclillarse, agazaparse, estar agachado ❑ *We were crouching in the bushes.* *Estábamos agachados entre los arbustos.* ❑ *I crouched on the ground.* *Me agaché en el suelo.* ● **Crouch** is also a noun. en cuclillas ❑ *They walked along in a crouch.* *Avanzaron en cuclillas.* ● **Crouch down** means the same as **crouch.** agacharse ❑ *He crouched down and reached under the bed.* *Se agachó y estiró la mano debajo de la cama.*

**crow** /kroʊ/ (**crows, crowing, crowed**) **1** N-COUNT A **crow** is a large black bird which makes a loud, harsh noise. cuervo **2** V-I When a rooster **crows,** it makes a loud sound, often early in the morning. cantar ❑ *The rooster crowed for many hours past dawn.* *El gallo cantó durante horas, después del amanecer*

**crowd** /kraʊd/ (**crowds, crowding, crowded**) **1** N-COUNT A **crowd** is a large group of people who have gathered together. gentío, multitud, muchedumbre ❑ *A huge crowd gathered in the square.* *Un gentío se reunió en la plaza.* **2** N-COUNT A particular **crowd** is a group of friends, or a set of people who share the same interests or job. gente, grupo [INFORMAL] ❑ *All the old crowd were there.* *Toda la gente de antes estaba ahí.* **3** V-I When people **crowd around** someone or something, they gather closely together around them. aglomerarse, amontonarse ❑ *The children crowded around him.* *Los niños se amontonaron alrededor de él.* **4** V-T/V-I If people **crowd into** a place or **are crowded into** a place, large numbers of them enter it so that it becomes very full. aglomerarse, amontonarse ❑ *Hundreds of thousands of people have crowded into the center.* *Cientos de miles de personas se han aglomerado en el centro.* ❑ *One group of journalists were crowded into a bus.* *Uno de los grupos de periodistas se amontonó en un autobús.*

**crowd|ed** /kraʊdɪd/ ADJ If a place is **crowded,** it is full of people. abarrotado, lleno ❑ *He looked slowly around the small crowded room.* *Revisó el saloncito, abarrotado de gente.* ❑ *...a crowded city of 2 million.* *...una ciudad abarrotada, de dos millones de habitantes.*

**crown** /kraʊn/ (**crowns, crowning, crowned**) **1** N-COUNT A **crown** is a circular ornament, usually made of gold and jewels, which a king or queen wears on their head at official ceremonies. corona **2** N-COUNT Your **crown** is the top part of your head, at the back. coronilla ❑ *He laid his hand gently on the crown of her head.* *Le puso suavemente la mano en la coronilla.* **3** N-COUNT A **crown** is an artificial top piece fixed over a broken or decayed tooth. corona ❑ *How long does it take to have crowns fitted?* *¿Cuánto se tarda en colocar las coronas?* **4** V-T When a king or queen **is crowned,** a crown is placed on their head as part of a ceremony in which they are officially made king or queen. coronar ❑ *Two days later, Juan Carlos was crowned king.* *Dos días después coronaron al rey Juan Carlos.*
→ see **teeth**

crown

**cru|cial** /kruʃᵊl/ ADJ Something that is **crucial** is extremely important. crucial, clave ❑ *He made all the crucial decisions himself.* *Las decisiones cruciales las tomó él.* ● **cru|cial|ly** ADV muy importante ❑ *Chewing properly is crucially important.* *Masticar adecuadamente es muy importante.*

**crud** /krʌd/ N-UNCOUNT You use **crud** to refer to any disgusting dirty or sticky substance. porquería [INFORMAL] ❑ *Remember the motel with all the crud in the pool?* *¿Te acuerdas del hotel en que la alberca estaba llena de porquerías?*

**crude** /krud/ (**cruder, crudest**) **1** ADJ Something that is **crude** is simple and rough rather than precise or sophisticated. ordinario, común, vulgar, rudimentario, burdo ❑ *...a crude way of assessing the risk of heart disease.* *...una forma rudimentaria de valorar el riesgo de enfermedad cardíaca.* ❑ *...crude wooden boxes.* *...burdas cajas de madera.* ● **crude|ly** ADV de forma rudimentaria, rudimentariamente ❑ *...a crudely-carved wooden form.* *...una forma de madera labrada de forma rudimentaria.* **2** ADJ If you describe someone as **crude,** you disapprove of them because they speak or behave in a rude or offensive way. vulgar ❑ *Must you be quite so crude?* *¿Tienes que ser tan vulgar?* ● **crude|ly** ADV vulgarmente, de manera vulgar ❑ *He hated it when she spoke so crudely.* *Le chocaba cuando ella hablaba tan vulgarmente.* **3** N-UNCOUNT **Crude** is the same as **crude oil.** crudo

**crude oil** N-UNCOUNT **Crude oil** is oil in its natural state before it has been processed or refined. petróleo crudo ❑ *...a thousand tons of crude oil.* *...mil toneladas de petróleo crudo.*
→ see **oil, petroleum**

**cru|el** /kruəl/ (**crueler** or **crueller, cruelest** or **cruellest**) ADJ Someone who is **cruel** deliberately causes pain or distress to people or animals. cruel ❑ *Children can be so cruel.* *Los niños pueden ser muy crueles.* ● **cru|el|ly** ADV cruelmente ❑ *Douglas was often treated cruelly by his jealous sisters.* *A Douglas sus hermanas celosas con frecuencia lo trataban cruelmente.* ● **cru|el|ty** /kruəlti/ N-VAR (**cruelties**) crueldad ❑ *...laws against cruelty to animals.* *...leyes en contra de la crueldad con los animales.*

**Thesaurus** *cruel* Ver también:
ADJ. harsh, mean, nasty, unkind; (*ant.*) gentle, kind **1**

**cruise** /kruz/ (**cruises, cruising, cruised**) **1** N-COUNT A **cruise** is a vacation during which you travel on a ship or boat and visit a number of places. crucero ❑ *He and his wife went on a world cruise.* *Él y su esposa se fueron a un crucero por el mundo.* **2** V-T/V-I If you **cruise** an ocean, river, or canal, you travel around it or along it on a cruise. hacer un crucero ❑ *She wants to cruise the canals of France.* *Quiere hacer un crucero por los canales de Francia.* ❑ *...a vacation cruising around the Caribbean.* *...vacacionar haciendo un crucero por el Caribe.* **3** V-I If a car, ship, or aircraft **cruises** somewhere, it moves there at a steady comfortable speed. desplazarse, circular ❑ *A black and white police car cruised past.* *Una patrulla circulaba por donde estábamos.*
→ see **ship**

**cruise con|trol** N-UNCOUNT In a car or

C

other vehicle, **cruise control** is a system that automatically keeps the vehicle's speed at the same level. *control de crucero* ❑ *My new car has cruise control. Mi auto nuevo tiene control de crucero.*

C

**crumb** /krʌm/ (**crumbs**) N-COUNT **Crumbs** are tiny pieces that fall from bread, cookies, or cake when you cut it or eat it. *miga, migaja, morona, borona* ❑ *I stood up, brushing crumbs from my pants. Me paré, sacudiéndome las migajas del pantalón.*

**crum|ble** /krʌmbᵊl/ (**crumbles, crumbling, crumbled**) **1** V-T/V-I If something **crumbles,** or if you **crumble** it, it breaks into a lot of small pieces. *desmoronar, desmoronarse* ❑ *The rock crumbled into pieces. La roca se desmoronó.* **2** V-I If an old building or piece of land **is crumbling,** parts of it keep breaking off. *desintegrarse, caerse* ❑ *Apartment buildings built in the 1960s are crumbling. Los edificios de departamentos que construyeron en los sesenta se están cayendo.* ● **Crumble away** means the same as **crumble**. *venirse abajo* ❑ *Much of the coastline is crumbling away. Gran parte de la costa se está viniendo abajo.* **3** V-I If something such as a system, relationship, or hope **crumbles,** it comes to an end. *derrumbarse* ❑ *Their economy crumbled as a result of the war. Su economía se derrumbó a causa de la guerra.*

**crunch** /krʌntʃ/ (**crunches, crunching, crunched**) **1** V-T/V-I If you **crunch** something hard, you crush it noisily between your teeth. *triturar, masticar haciendo ruido* ❑ *She crunched an ice cube loudly. Hizo mucho ruido masticando un hielito.* **2** V-T/V-I If something **crunches,** it makes a breaking or crushing noise, for example, when you step on it. *(hacer) crujir* ❑ *A piece of china crunched under my foot. Aplasté un pedazo de porcelana con el pie.* ● **Crunch** is also a noun. *crujido* ❑ *...the crunch of tires on the driveway. ...el crujido de las llantas en la terracería.*

**crush** /krʌʃ/ (**crushes, crushing, crushed**) **1** V-T To **crush** something means to press it very hard so that its shape is destroyed or so that it breaks into pieces. *aplastar, apachurrar, triturar* ❑ *Andrew crushed his empty can. Andrés aplastó la lata vacía.* ❑ *...crushed ice. ...hielo triturado., ...hielo frappé.* **2** V-T To **crush** a protest or movement, or a group of opponents, means to defeat it completely. *aplastar, acallar* ❑ *...a plan to crush the protests. ...un plan para acallar las protestas.* ● **crush|ing** N-UNCOUNT *represión* ❑ *...the violent crushing of anti-government demonstrations. ...la violenta represión de las manifestaciones anti gubernamentales.* **3** V-T If you **are crushed** against someone or something, you are pushed or pressed against them. *prensar, apretujar* ❑ *We were at the front, crushed against the stage. Estábamos adelante, apretujados contra el escenario.* **4** N-COUNT A **crush** is a crowd of people pressed close together. *aglomeración, tumulto* ❑ *His thirteen-year-old son somehow got separated in the crush. Nadie sabe cómo su hijo de trece años se separó de ellos en el tumulto.* **5** N-COUNT If you have a **crush on** someone, you are in love with them but do not have a relationship with them. *enamoramiento, estar enamorado* [INFORMAL] ❑ *She had a crush on you, you know. Ya sabes, estaba enamorada de ti.*
→ see **crash**

**crust** /krʌst/ (**crusts**) **1** N-COUNT The **crust** on a loaf of bread or pie is the hard, crisp outside part. *costra, corteza* ❑ *Cut the crusts off the bread. Quítale la corteza al pan.* **2** N-COUNT The earth's **crust** is its outer layer. *corteza terrestre* ❑ *Earthquakes leave scars in the earth's crust. Los terremotos dejan cicatrices en la corteza terrestre.*
→ see **continent, core, earthquake**

**cry** /kraɪ/ (**cries, crying, cried**) **1** V-I When you **cry,** tears come from your eyes, usually because you are unhappy or hurt. *llorar* ❑ *I hung up the phone and started to cry. Colgué la bocina y empecé a llorar.* ❑ *He cried with anger and frustration. Lloró de rabia y frustración.* ● **Cry** is also a noun. *llanto* ❑ *You have a good cry, dear. No contengas el llanto, linda.* ● **cry|ing** N-UNCOUNT *llanto* ❑ *She was unable to sleep because of her baby son's crying. El llanto de su bebé no la dejaba dormir.* **2** V-T If you **cry** something, you shout it or say it loudly. *gritar, exclamar* ❑ *"Nancy Drew," she cried, "you're under arrest!" —¡Nancy Drew, estás arrestada! —exclamó.* ● **Cry out** means the same as **cry**. *gritar* ❑ *"You're wrong, quite wrong!" Henry cried out. —¡Estas equivocado, muy equivocado! —gritó Enrique.* **3** N-COUNT A **cry** is a loud, high sound that you make when you feel a strong emotion such as fear, pain, or pleasure. *grito* ❑ *...a cry of horror. ...un grito de horror.* **4** N-COUNT A bird's or an animal's **cry** is the loud, high sound that it makes. *chillido* ❑ *...the cry of a seagull. ...el chillido de una gaviota.*
→ see Word Web: **cry**

▸ **cry out** PHR-VERB If you **cry out,** you call out loudly because you are frightened, unhappy, or in pain. *gritar* ❑ *He was crying out in pain when the ambulance arrived. Gritaba de dolor cuando llegó la ambulancia.* → see also **cry 2**

▸ **cry out for** PHR-VERB If you say that something **cries out for** a particular thing, you mean that it needs that thing very much. *clamar, exigir, pedir a*

**Word Web** cry

Have you ever seen someone **burst into tears** when something wonderful happened to them? We expect people to **cry** when they are **sad** or upset. But why do people sometimes **weep** when they are happy? Scientists have found there are three different types of **tears**. Basal tears keep the **eyes** moist. Reflex tears clear the eyes of dirt or smoke. The third type, emotional tears, occur when people experience strong feelings, either good or bad. These tears have high levels of chemicals called manganese and prolactin. Decreasing the amount of these chemicals in the body helps us feel better. When people experience strong feelings, **shedding tears** may help restore emotional balance.

**Word Web** crystal

The outsides of **crystals** have smooth flat planes. These surfaces form because of the repeating patterns of atoms, molecules, or ions inside the crystal. Evaporation, temperature changes, and pressure can all help to form crystals. Crystals grow when sea water evaporates and leaves behind **salt**. When water freezes, **ice** crystals form. When melted rock cools, it becomes **rock** with a crystalline structure. Pressure can also create one of the hardest, most beautiful crystals—the **diamond**.

*gritos* ❑ *His body was crying out for some exercise.* *Su cuerpo pedía a gritos algo de ejercicio.*

**Thesaurus** *cry* Ver también:

V. sob, weep 1
call, shout, yell 2
N. howl, moan, shriek 3

**Word Partnership** Usar *cry* con:

V. **begin to** cry, **start to** cry 1
N. cry **with anger** 1 2
cry **for help**, cry **of horror**, cry **with joy**, cry **of pain** 2

**crys|tal** /krɪstᵊl/ (**crystals**) 1 N-COUNT A **crystal** is a small piece of a substance that has formed naturally into a regular symmetrical shape. *cristal* ❑ *...salt crystals.* *...cristales de sal.* ❑ *...ice crystals.* *...cristales de hielo.* 2 N-VAR **Crystal** is a transparent rock used in jewelry and ornaments. *cristal* ❑ *...a string of crystal beads.* *...un collar de cuentas de cristal.* 3 N-UNCOUNT **Crystal** is high-quality glass, usually with patterns cut into its surface. *cristal, cristal cortado* ❑ *...finest drinking glasses made from crystal.* *...finísimos vasos de cristal cortado.*
→ see Word Web: **crystal**
→ see **precipitation, rock, sugar**

**crys|tal lat|tice** (**crystal lattices**) N-COUNT A **crystal lattice** is a symmetrical arrangement of atoms within a crystal. *red cristalina, retículo cristalino, estructura reticular del cristal* [TECHNICAL]

**CST** /si̱ ɛs ti̱/ **CST** is an abbreviation for "Central Standard Time." *CST, horario de la zona central* ❑ *Calls are taken between 7 a.m. and 8 p.m., CST.* *Se reciben llamadas de 7 a.m. a 8 p.m., CST.*

**cube** /kyu̱b/ (**cubes**) N-COUNT A **cube** is a solid object with six square surfaces which are all the same size. *cubo* ❑ *...cold water with ice cubes in it.* *...agua fría con hielo.* ❑ *...a box of sugar cubes.* *...un paquete de cubos de azúcar.*
→ see **solid, volume**

**cu|bic** /kyu̱bɪk/ ADJ **Cubic** is used to express units of volume. *cúbico* ❑ *...3 billion cubic meters of earth.* *...3 mil millones de metros cúbicos de tierra.*

**cu|bi|cle** /kyu̱bɪkᵊl/ (**cubicles**) N-COUNT A **cubicle** is a very small enclosed area, for example, one where you can take a shower or change your clothes. *cubículo* ❑ *...a separate shower cubicle.* *...cubículo independiente para bañarse.*
→ see **office**

**cu|cum|ber** /kyu̱kʌmbər/ (**cucumbers**) N-VAR A **cucumber** is a long dark-green vegetable that is eaten raw in salads. *pepino* ❑ *...a cheese and cucumber sandwich.* *...un sandwich de queso y pepino*
→ see **vegetable**

**cue** /kyu̱/ (**cues**) 1 N-COUNT A **cue** is something said or done by a performer that is a signal for another performer to begin speaking, playing, or doing something. *entrada, pie* ❑ *The actors sit at the side of the stage, waiting for their cues.* *Los actores se sientan a un lado del escenario, a esperar su pie.* 2 N-COUNT If you say that something that happens is a **cue for** an action, you mean that people start doing that action when it happens. *indicación, señal* ❑ *That was the cue for several months of fighting.* *Esa fue la señal para que empezaran varios meses de lucha.* 3 N-COUNT A **cue** is a long, thin wooden stick that is used to hit the ball in games such as billiards, pool, and snooker. *taco*

**cuff** /kʌ̱f/ (**cuffs**) 1 N-COUNT The **cuffs** of a shirt or dress are the end parts of the sleeves. *puño* ❑ *...a pale-blue shirt with white collar and cuffs.* *...una camisa azul claro con cuello y puños blancos.* 2 N-COUNT The **cuffs** on a pair of pants are the end parts of the legs which are folded up. *bastilla, dobladillo, valenciana* 3 PHRASE An **off-the-cuff** remark is made without being prepared or thought about in advance. *improvisado* ❑ *It was an off-the-cuff remark.* *Fue un comentario improvisado.*

**cui|sine** /kwɪzi̱n/ (**cuisines**) N-VAR The **cuisine** of a region is its characteristic style of cooking. *cocina* ❑ *The cuisine of Japan is low in fat.* *La cocina japonesa es baja en grasas.*

**cult** /kʌ̱lt/ (**cults**) 1 N-COUNT A **cult** is a fairly small religious group, especially one which is considered strange. *secta* 2 ADJ **Cult** is used to describe things that are very popular or fashionable among a particular group. *de culto* ❑ *The movie became a cult classic.* *La película llegó a ser un clásico de culto.*

**cul|ti|vate** /kʌ̱ltɪveɪt/ (**cultivates, cultivating, cultivated**) 1 V-T If you **cultivate** land, you prepare it and grow crops on it. *cultivar* ❑ *She cultivated a small garden of her own.* *Ella cultivaba un pequeño jardín de su propiedad.* ● **cul|ti|va|tion** /kʌ̱ltɪveɪʃᵊn/ N-UNCOUNT *cultivo* ❑ *...the cultivation of fruits and vegetables.* *...el cultivo de frutas y verduras.* 2 V-T If you **cultivate** an attitude, image, or skill, you develop it and make it stronger. *adoptar* ❑ *He has cultivated the image of an artist.* *Ha adoptado la imagen de artista.* ● **cul|ti|va|tion** N-UNCOUNT *cultivo* ❑ *...the cultivation of a positive approach to life.* *...el*

C

*cultivo de un enfoque positivo de la vida.*
→ see **farm, grain**

**cul|tur|al** /kʌltʃərəl/ ADJ **Cultural** means relating to the arts, or to the arts, ideas, and customs of a particular society. *cultural* ❑ *...sports and cultural events. ...eventos deportivos y culturales.* ❑ *...cultural and educational exchanges. ...intercambios culturales y educativos.* ● **cul|tur|al|ly** ADV *culturalmente, desde el punto de vista de la cultura* ❑ *Culturally, the two countries have much in common. Los dos países tienen mucho en común desde el punto de vista de la cultura.*

**cul|ture** /kʌltʃər/ (**cultures**) **1** N-UNCOUNT **Culture** consists of activities such as the arts and philosophy, which are considered to be important for the development of civilization and of people's minds. *cultura* ❑ *There is just not enough fun in culture today. Hoy día la cultura no es muy divertida.* ❑ *Movies are part of our popular culture. El cine es parte de nuestra cultura popular.* **2** N-COUNT A **culture** is a particular society or civilization, especially considered in relation to its beliefs, way of life, or art. *cultura* ❑ *...people from different cultures. ...gente de diferentes culturas.* **3** N-COUNT In science, a **culture** is a group of bacteria or cells grown in a laboratory as part of an experiment. *cultivo* [TECHNICAL] ❑ *...a culture of human cells. ...un cultivo de células humanas.*
→ see Word Web: **culture**
→ see **myth**

| **Word Partnership** | Usar *culture* con: |
|---|---|
| N. | culture **and religion**, **richness of** culture, culture **shock**, **society and** culture **1** |
| ADJ. | **ancient** culture, **popular** culture **1** **2** |

**cum laude** /cʊm laʊdeɪ/ ADV If a college student graduates **cum laude**, they receive the third-highest honor that is possible. *cum laude, con honores* ❑ *She graduated cum laude from Harvard. Se graduó con honores en Harvard.*

**cu|mu|lo|nim|bus** /kyumyəloʊnɪmbəs/ (**cumulonimbi** /kyumyəloʊnɪmbaɪ/) also **cumulo-nimbus** N-VAR **Cumulonimbus** is a type of cloud, similar to cumulus, that extends to a great height and is associated with thunderstorms. *cúmulonimbo* [TECHNICAL]
→ see **cloud**

**cu|mu|lus** /kyumyələs/ (**cumuli** /kyumyəlaɪ/) N-VAR **Cumulus** is a type of thick white cloud formed when hot air rises very quickly. *cúmulo*
→ see **cloud**

**cup** /kʌp/ (**cups, cupping, cupped**) **1** N-COUNT A **cup** is a small round container with a handle, that you drink from. *taza* ❑ *...cups and saucers. ...tazas y platos.* ❑ *...a cup of coffee. ...una taza de café.* **2** N-COUNT A **cup** is a unit of measurement used in cooking, equal to 16 tablespoons or 8 fluid ounces. *taza* ❑ *Gradually add 1 cup of milk. Agregar poco a poco una taza de leche.* ❑ *...half a cup of sugar. ...media taza de azúcar.* **3** N-COUNT Something that is small, round, and hollow can be referred to as a **cup**. *cáliz* ❑ *...flower cups. ...el cáliz de las flores* **4** N-COUNT A **cup** is a large metal cup with two handles that is given to the winner of a game or competition. *copa, trofeo* ❑ *The Stars won the Stanley Cup in 1999. Los Stars ganaron la Copa Stanley en 1999.* **5** V-T If you **cup** your **hands,** you make them into a curved shape like a cup. *ahuecar las manos, hacer una bocina con las manos* ❑ *He cupped his hands around his mouth and called out for Diane. Se puso las manos a los lados de la boca, a manera de bocina, y le gritó a Diana.* **6** V-T If you **cup** something in your hands, you make your hands into a curved dish-like shape and support it or hold it gently. *ahuecar las manos, tomar, coger algo con delicadeza* ❑ *He cupped her chin in his hand. Le tomó la barbilla con la mano.*
→ see **dish, office, tea, utensil**

**cup|board** /kʌbərd/ (**cupboards**) N-COUNT A **cupboard** is a piece of furniture with doors at the front and usually shelves inside. *alacena, aparador, armario, clóset* ❑ *The kitchen cupboard was full of cans of soup. La alacena estaba llena de latas de sopa.*

**curb** /kɜrb/ (**curbs, curbing, curbed**) **1** V-T If you **curb** something, you control it and keep it within limits. *frenar, refrenar, contener* ❑ *...advertisements aimed at curbing the spread of AIDS. ...publicidad enfocada a contener el avance del SIDA.* ● **Curb** is also a noun. *control* ❑ *He called for stricter curbs on immigration. Exigió controles más estrictos de la inmigración.* **2** N-COUNT **The curb** is the raised edge of a sidewalk which separates it from the road. *acera, banqueta, cuneta* ❑ *I pulled over to the*

curb

## Word Web culture

Each **society** has its own **culture** which influences how people live their lives. Culture includes **customs**, **language**, **art**, and other shared **traits**. When people move from one culture to another, there is often cultural **diffusion**. For example, European artists first saw Japanese art about 150 years ago. This caused a change in their painting style. The new style was called Impressionism. **Assimilation** happens when people enter a new culture. For instance, **immigrants** may start to follow American customs when they move to the U.S. People whose ideas differ from **mainstream** society may also form **subcultures** within the society.

curb. Me detuve al lado de la banqueta.

**curb|stone** /kɜrbstoʊn/ (**curbstones**) N-COUNT A **curbstone** is one of the stones that form a curb. *borde de la acera, borde de la banqueta* ❑ *There are people sitting on the curbstones. Hay personas sentadas en el borde de la banqueta.*

**cure** /kyʊər/ (**cures, curing, cured**) **1** V-T If doctors or medical treatments **cure** someone or **cure** an illness or injury, they make the person well again. *curar(se)* ❑ *An operation finally cured his leg injury. Por fin lograron curarle la pierna con la operación.* ❑ *Almost overnight I was cured. Me curé casi de la noche a la mañana.* **2** V-T If someone or something **cures** a problem, they bring it to an end. *remediar, poner remedio, solucionar* ❑ *We need to cure our economic problems. Necesitamos remediar nuestros problemas económicos.* **3** V-T When food, tobacco, or animal skin **is cured,** it is dried, smoked, or salted so that it will last for a long time. *curar* ❑ *Legs of pork were cured over the fire. Curaron al fuego las piernas de puerco.* **4** N-COUNT A **cure for** an illness is a medicine or other treatment that cures the illness. *cura* ❑ *There is still no cure for a cold. Aún no hay cura para el resfriado.*

**cur|few** /kɜrfyu/ (**curfews**) N-VAR A **curfew** is a law stating that people must stay inside their houses after a particular time at night. *toque de queda* ❑ *The village was placed under curfew. Impusieron el toque de queda en el pueblo.*

**cu|ri|os|ity** /kyʊəriɒsɪti/ (**curiosities**) **1** N-UNCOUNT **Curiosity** is a desire to know about something. *curiosidad* ❑ *Ryle accepted more out of curiosity than anything else. Ryle aceptó más por curiosidad que por otra cosa.* ❑ *...curiosity about the past. ...curiosidad por el pasado.* **2** N-COUNT A **curiosity** is something that is interesting and fairly rare. *curiosidad, objeto curioso* ❑ *...castles, curiosities, and museums. ...castillos, curiosidades y museos.*

**cu|ri|ous** /kyʊəriəs/ **1** ADJ If you are **curious about** something, you are interested in it and want to know more about it. *curioso* ❑ *Steve was curious about the place I came from. Steve sentía curiosidad por saber de dónde venía yo.* ● **cu|ri|ous|ly** ADV *curiosamente, con curiosidad* ❑ *The woman in the shop looked at them curiously. La mujer de la tienda los miró con curiosidad.* **2** ADJ If you describe something as **curious,** you mean that it is unusual or difficult to understand. *curioso, extraño* ❑ *...a curious mixture of old and new. ...una extraña mezcla de viejo y nuevo.* ● **cu|ri|ous|ly** ADV *curiosamente, extrañamente* ❑ *Harry was curiously silent. Harry estaba extrañamente silencioso.*

**curl** /kɜrl/ (**curls, curling, curled**) **1** N-COUNT If you have **curls,** your hair is in the form of curves and spirals. *rizo, chino, bucle* ❑ *...a little girl with blonde curls. ...una niñita de cabello rubio y con chinos.* **2** N-COUNT A **curl of** something is a piece or quantity of it that is curved or spiral in shape. *espiral* ❑ *...a thin curl of smoke. ...una fina espiral de humo.* **3** V-T/V-I If your hair **curls** or if you **curl** it, it is full of curls. *enchinar, enchinarse, rizar, rizarse* ❑ *She has hair that refuses to curl. Su cabello se niega a enchinarse.* ❑ *Maria curled her hair for the party. María se rizó el cabello para la fiesta.* **4** V-I If something **curls** somewhere, it moves there in a circles or spirals. *ondularse, serpentear* ❑ *Smoke was curling up the chimney. El humo serpenteaba por la chimenea.* **5** V-T/V-I If a person or animal **curls into** a ball, they move their arms and legs toward their stomach so that their body makes a rounded shape. *acurrucarse* ❑ *He wanted to curl into a tiny ball. Quería hacerse bolita y acurrucarse.* ● **Curl up** means the same as **curl.** *acurrucarse* ❑ *She curled up next to him. Se acurrucó cerca de él.* **6** V-I When a leaf, a piece of paper, or another flat object **curls,** its edges bend toward the center. *enroscarse* ❑ *The rose leaves have curled because of a disease. Las hojas del rosal se enroscaron por la plaga.* ● **Curl up** means the same as **curl.** *enroscarse* ❑ *The corners of the rug were curling up. Las esquinas del tapete estaban enroscadas.*

▸ **curl up** → see **curl 5, 6**

**curly** /kɜrli/ (**curlier, curliest**) **1** ADJ **Curly** hair is full of curls. *chino, rizado* ❑ *I've got naturally curly hair. Mi cabello es chino natural.* **2** ADJ **Curly** objects are curved or spiral in shape. *enroscado* ❑ *...cauliflowers with extra long curly leaves. ...coliflores con larguísimas hojas enroscadas.*

→ see **hair**

| **Word Link** | *curr, curs ≈ running, flowing : currency, current, cursor* |
|---|---|

**cur|ren|cy** /kɜrənsi/ (**currencies**) N-VAR The money used in a particular country is referred to as its **currency.** *moneda, divisas* ❑ *Tourism is the country's top earner of foreign currency. El mayor ingreso de divisas del país proviene del turismo.* ❑ *...a single European currency. ...una sola moneda europea.*

→ see **money**

**cur|rent** /kɜrənt/ (**currents**) **1** N-COUNT A **current** is a steady, continuous flowing movement of water or air. *corriente* ❑ *...the ocean currents of the Pacific. ...las corrientes oceánicas del Pacífico.* ❑ *I felt a current of cool air. Sentí una corriente de aire frío.* **2** N-COUNT An electric **current** is a flow of electricity through a wire or circuit. *corriente* ❑ *...a powerful electric current. ...una poderosa corriente eléctrica.* **3** ADJ **Current** means happening, being used, or being done at the present time. *vigente, actual* ❑ *The current situation is very different to that in 1990. La situación actual es muy diferente a la de 1990.* ● **cur|rent|ly** ADV *actualmente, hoy día* ❑ *He is currently unmarried. Actualmente no está casado.*

→ see **beach, erosion, ocean, tide**

**cur|rent af|fairs** also **current events** N-PLURAL → see **current events**

**cur|rent elec|tric|ity** N-UNCOUNT **Current electricity** is electricity that is flowing through a circuit. Compare **static electricity.** *electricidad dinámica*

**cur|rent ev|ents** also **current affairs** N-PLURAL **Current events** are political events and problems which are discussed in the media. *sucesos de actualidad* ❑ *I know nothing about current affairs. No sé nada de los sucesos de actualidad.*

**cur|ricu|lum** /kərɪkyələm/ (**curriculums** or **curricula** /kərɪkyələ/) **1** N-COUNT A **curriculum** is all the different courses of study that are taught in a school, college, or university. *plan de estudios* ❑ *Business skills should be part of the school curriculum. Las habilidades gerenciales deberían formar parte del plan de estudios de la carrera.* **2** N-COUNT A particular **curriculum** is one particular course of study.

*programa de una materia* ❑ *...the history curriculum.* *...el programa historia*

**cur|ry** /kɜri/ (**curries**) N-VAR **Curry** is a dish, originally from Asia, consisting of vegetables and sometimes meat cooked with hot spices. *curry* ❑ *...vegetable curry.* *...verduras con/al curry.*

C

**curse** /kɜrs/ (**curses, cursing, cursed**) 1 V-I If you **curse**, you use very impolite or offensive language, usually because you are angry about something. *maldecir, insultar* [WRITTEN] ❑ *I cursed and got to my feet.* *Maldije y me puse de pie.* ● **Curse** is also a noun. *maldición, insulto* 2 V-T If you **curse** someone or something, you say impolite or insulting things about them because you are angry. *insultar, maldecir* ❑ *He cursed her and rudely pushed her aside.* *La insultó y la empujó groseramente.* ❑ *We set off again, cursing the delay.* *Arrancamos de nuevo, maldiciendo.* 3 N-COUNT If you say that there is a **curse on** someone, you mean that there seems to be a supernatural power causing unpleasant things to happen to them. *maldición, estar maldito* ❑ *Maybe there is a curse on my family.* *Quizá una maldición pesa sobre mi familia.* 4 N-COUNT You can refer to something that causes a lot of trouble as a **curse.** *lacra* ❑ *...the curse of high unemployment.* *...la lacra del desempleo.*

> **Word Link** *curr, curs ≈ running, flowing : currency, current, cursor*

**cur|sor** /kɜrsər/ (**cursors**) N-COUNT On a computer screen, the **cursor** is a small shape that indicates where anything that is typed by the user will appear. *cursor* [COMPUTING] ❑ *He moved the cursor and clicked the mouse.* *Movió el cursor e hizo click con el ratón.*
→ see **computer**

**cur|tain** /kɜrtᵊn/ (**curtains**) 1 N-COUNT **Curtains** are pieces of material which hang from the top of a window. *cortinas* ❑ *...her bedroom curtains.* *...las cortinas de su habitación.* 2 N-SING In a theater, **the curtain** is the large piece of material that hangs in front of the stage until a performance begins. *telón* ❑ *The curtain rose.* *Se levantó el telón.*

**cur|tain rod** (**curtain rods**) N-COUNT A **curtain rod** is a long, narrow pole on which you hang curtains. *cortinero*

**cur|va|ture** /kɜrvətʃər, -tʃʊər/ N-UNCOUNT The **curvature of** something is its curved shape, especially when this shape is part of the circumference of a circle. *curvatura* [TECHNICAL]

**curve** /kɜrv/ (**curves, curving, curved**) 1 N-COUNT A **curve** is a smooth, gradually bending line, for example, part of the edge of a circle. *curva* ❑ *...the curve of his lips.* *...la curva de sus labios.* 2 N-COUNT You can refer to a change in something as a particular **curve,** especially when it is represented on a graph. *curva* ❑ *Youth crime is on a slow downward curve.* *La curva de la delincuencia juvenil va descendiendo lentamente.* 3 V-T/V-I If something **curves,** it has the shape of a curve or moves in a curve. *torcerse, curvearse, desviarse, hacer una curva* ❑ *Her spine curved.* *Tiene desviada la columna.* ❑ *The ball curved strangely in the air.* *El balón hizo una extraña curva en el aire.* ● **curved** ADJ *curvo* ❑ *...curved lines.* *...líneas curvas.*

**cur|vi|lin|ear** /kɜrvɪlɪniər/ ADJ A **curvilinear** shape has curving lines. Compare **rectilinear.** *curvilíneo*

**cush|ion** /kʊʃᵊn/ (**cushions, cushioning, cushioned**) 1 N-COUNT A **cushion** is a fabric case filled with soft material, which you put on a seat to make it more comfortable. *cojín* ❑ *...a velvet cushion.* *...un cojín de terciopelo.* 2 V-T To **cushion** an impact means to reduce its effect. *amortiguar* ❑ *We tried to cushion the blow.* *Tratamos de amortiguar el golpe.*

**cus|tard** /kʌstərd/ (**custards**) N-VAR **Custard** is a baked dessert made of milk, eggs, and sugar. *natilla* ❑ *...a custard with a caramel sauce.* *...una natilla con caramelo.*
→ see **dessert**

**cus|to|dy** /kʌstədi/ 1 N-UNCOUNT **Custody** is the legal right to keep and take care of a child, especially the right given to a child's mother or father when they get divorced. *custodia* ❑ *I'm going to court to get custody of the children.* *Voy a ir al tribunal por la custodia de mis hijos.* 2 PHRASE Someone who is **in custody** has been arrested and is being kept in prison. *detenido*

**cus|tom** /kʌstəm/ (**customs**) 1 N-VAR A **custom** is an activity, a way of behaving, or an event which is usual or traditional in a particular society or in particular circumstances. *costumbre* ❑ *...an ancient Japanese custom.* *...una antigua costumbre japonesa.* ❑ *It was the custom to give presents.* *La costumbre era dar regalos.* 2 → see also **customs**
→ see **culture**

**cus|tom|er** /kʌstəmər/ (**customers**) N-COUNT A **customer** is someone who buys goods or services, especially from a store. *cliente* ❑ *...a satisfied customer.* *...un cliente satisfecho.*

> **Usage** **customer, patients, and clients**
> Stores have *customers*: *Many small bookstores don't have enough customers to stay in business.* Professionals have *clients*: *The husband is a lawyer and the wife is an accountant, and they have many clients in common.* Doctors, dentists, nurses, and other medical practitioners have *patients*: *There were so many patients in my doctor's waiting room, I couldn't find a place to sit.*

> **Word Partnership** Usar *customer* con:
> N. customer **account**, customer **loyalty**, customer **satisfaction**
> V. **greet** customers, **satisfy a** customer

**cus|tom|er ser|vice** N-UNCOUNT **Customer service** refers to the way that companies behave toward their customers, for example, how well they treat them. *servicio al cliente* [BUSINESS] ❑ *...a business with a strong reputation for customer service.* *...una empresa que basa su reputación en el servico al cliente.*

**cus|toms** /kʌstəmz/ 1 N-PROPER **Customs** is the official organization responsible for collecting taxes on goods coming into a country and preventing illegal goods from being brought in. *aduana* ❑ *What right does Customs have to search my car?* *¿Con qué derecho revisan mi auto los de la aduana?*

**2** N-UNCOUNT **Customs** is the place where people arriving from a foreign country have to declare goods that they bring with them. aduana ❑ *He walked through customs.* *Pasó por la aduana.* **3** → see also **custom**

**cut**
❶ PHYSICAL ACTION
❷ SHORTEN OR REDUCE AMOUNT
❸ PHRASAL VERBS

❶ **cut** /kʌt/ (**cuts, cutting**)

The form **cut** is used in the present tense and is the past tense and past participle.

**1** V-T/V-I If you **cut** something, you use a knife or a similar tool to remove part of it, or to mark it or damage it. cortar, cortarse ❑ *Mrs. Haines cut the ribbon.* *La Sra. Haines cortó el listón.* ❑ *Cut the tomatoes in half.* *Corta los tomates a la mitad.* ❑ *The thieves cut a hole in the fence.* *Los ladrones cortaron un pedazo de la cerca.* ❑ *You had your hair cut, it looks great.* *Te cortaste el cabello, te ves muy bien.* ❑ *This little knife cuts really well.* *Este cuchillito corta muy bien.* ● **Cut** is also a noun. corte ❑ *Carefully make a cut in the shell with a small knife.* *Con un cuchillo pequeño haz con cuidado un corte en la concha.* **2** V-T If you **cut yourself**, you accidentally injure yourself on a sharp object so that you bleed. cortarse ❑ *Johnson cut himself shaving.* *Johnson se cortó mientras se afeitaba.* ❑ *I started to cry because I cut my finger.* *Empecé a llorar porque me corté el dedo.* ● **Cut** is also a noun. corte, cortada ❑ *He had a cut on his left eyebrow.* *Tenía una cortada en la ceja izquierda.*
→ see Picture Dictionary: **cut**

❷ **cut** /kʌt/ (**cuts, cutting**)

The form **cut** is used in the present tense and is the past tense and past participle.

**1** V-T If you **cut** something, you reduce it. cortar, achicar, reducir ❑ *The aim is to cut costs.* *El objetivo es reducir costos.* ❑ *The U.N. force is to be cut by 90%.* *Van a reducir en 90% los efectivos de Naciones Unidas.* ● **Cut** is also a noun. corte, reducción, recorte ❑ *...an immediate 2 percent cut in interest rates.* *...una reducción inmediata del 2 por ciento en las tasas de interés.* **2** V-T If you **cut** part of a piece of writing or a performance, you do not publish, broadcast, or perform that part of it. cortar, omitir, reducir, recortar ❑ *Branagh has cut the play a little.* *Branagh recortó un poco la obra.* ● **Cut** is also a noun. corte, recorte ❑ *It was necessary to make some cuts in the text.* *Fue necesario hacer algunos recortes al texto.* **3** V-I If you **cut across** or **through** a place, you go through it because it is the shortest route to another place. cortar por, tomar un atajo ❑ *Jesse cut across the parking lot.* *Jesse cortó por el estacionamiento.* **4** V-T To **cut** a supply of something means to stop providing it or stop it from being provided. interrumpir, cortar ❑ *Winds have knocked down power lines, cutting electricity to thousands of people.* *El viento tiró los cables y se interrumpió el suministro de electricidad para miles de personas.* ● **Cut** is also a noun. corte, recorte ❑ *...cuts in electricity and water supplies.* *...cortes en el suministro de electricidad y de agua.*

**Thesaurus** *cut* Ver también:

V. carve, slice, trim ❶ **1**
graze, nick, stab ❶ **2**
decrease, lower, reduce; (*ant.*) increase ❷ **1**
N. gash, incision, slit ❶ **1**
gash, nick, wound ❶ **2**

❸ **cut** /kʌt/ (**cuts, cutting**)

The form **cut** is used in the present tense and is the past tense and past participle.

▸ **cut across** PHR-VERB If an issue or problem **cuts across** the division between two or more groups of people, it affects or matters to people in all the groups. trascender, rebasar ❑ *The issue of health care cuts across all age groups.* *El problema de la atención de la salud trasciende los grupos de edad.*

▸ **cut back** PHR-VERB If you **cut back** something such as expenditure or **cut back on** it, you reduce it. recortar, reducir ❑ *Customers have cut back spending.* *Los clientes han recortado los gastos.* ❑ *The government has cut back on defense spending.* *El gobierno redujo el gasto en defensa.*

▸ **cut down** **1** PHR-VERB If you **cut down on** something or **cut down** something, you use or do less of it. reducir, disminuir, acortar ❑ *He cut down on coffee.* *Redujo su consumo de café.* ❑ *Car owners were asked to cut down travel.* *Se pidió a los propietarios de vehículos que disminuyeran el número de traslados.*

**Picture Dictionary** *cut*

C

**2** PHR-VERB If you **cut down** a tree, you cut through its trunk so that it falls to the ground. *cortar, talar* ❑ *They cut down several trees. Talaron varios árboles.*

▶ **cut off** **1** PHR-VERB If you **cut** something **off,** you remove it with a knife or a similar tool. *cortar* ❑ *Mrs. Johnson cut off a large piece of the meat. La Sra. Johnson cortó un buen pedazo de carne.* ❑ *He threatened to cut my hair off. Amenazó con cortarme el cabello.* **2** PHR-VERB To **cut** someone or something **off** means to separate them from things that they are normally connected with. *cortar* ❑ *They cut off the army from its supplies. Cortaron el envío de provisiones al ejército.* ● **cut off** ADJ *separse, aislarse* ❑ *Without a car we still felt very cut off. Sin el auto aún nos seguíamos sintiendo aislados.* **3** PHR-VERB To **cut off** a supply of something means to stop providing it or stop it from being provided. *cortar* ❑ *They have cut off the electricity. Cortaron la luz.* **4** PHR-VERB If you get **cut off** when you are on the telephone, the line is suddenly disconnected. *cortarse la línea, cortarse la comunicación, interrumpirse la comunicación* ❑ *You've got to speak quickly before you get cut off. Tienes que hablar rápido, antes de que se corte la comunicación.* **5** → see also **cutoff**

▶ **cut out** **1** PHR-VERB If you **cut** something **out,** you remove or separate it from what surrounds it using scissors or a knife. *recortar* ❑ *I cut the picture out and pinned it to my wall. Recorté la foto y la pegué en la pared.* **2** PHR-VERB If you **cut out** a part of a text, you do not print, publish, or broadcast that part, because to include it would make the text too long or unacceptable. *eliminar, suprimir* ❑ *They cut out all the best bits. Eliminaron lo mejor.* **3** PHR-VERB To **cut** something **out** something means to completely remove it or stop doing or having it. *suprimir* ❑ *It is wise to cut out coffee during pregnancy. Es conveniente suprimir el café durante el embarazo.* **4** PHR-VERB If an object **cuts out** the light, it prevents light from reaching a place. *tapar, no dejar pasar* ❑ *The curtains cut out the sunlight. Las cortinas no dejan pasar la luz del sol.* **5** PHR-VERB If an engine **cuts out,** it suddenly stops working. *pararse, apagarse* ❑ *The plane crashed when one of its engines cut out. El avión se estrelló cuando uno de sus motores se apagó.*

▶ **cut up** PHR-VERB If you **cut** something **up,** you cut it into several pieces. *cortar en pedazos, picar* ❑ *Halve the tomatoes, then cut them up. Parte los tomates a la mitad y luego pícalos.*

**cute** /kyut/ (**cuter, cutest**) **1** ADJ **Cute** means pretty or attractive. *mono, lindo* [INFORMAL] ❑ *Oh, look at that dog! He's so cute. ¡Mira qué lindo perro!* **2** ADJ If you describe someone as **cute,** you think they are pretty or attractive. *mono* [INFORMAL] ❑ *There was this girl, and I thought she was really cute. Y esa chica me pareció monísima.*

| Thesaurus | *cute* | Ver también: |
|---|---|---|
| ADJ. | adorable, charming, pretty; (*ant.*) homely, ugly **1** | |

**cu|ti|cle** /kyutɪkᵊl/ (**cuticles**) N-VAR **Cuticle** is a protective covering on the surface of leaves and other parts of a plant. *cutícula* [TECHNICAL]

**cut|off** /kʌtɔf/ (**cutoffs**) **1** N-COUNT A **cutoff** or a **cutoff** point is the level or limit at which you decide that something should stop happening. *límite, corte* ❑ *The cutoff has not yet been announced. Aún no se ha anunciado el límite.* **2** N-PLURAL **Cut-offs** are short pants made by cutting part of the legs off old pants. *shorts*

**cut|ting** /kʌtɪŋ/ (**cuttings**) **1** N-COUNT A **cutting** is a part of a plant that you have cut off so that you can grow a new plant from it. *gajo, esqueje* ❑ *Take cuttings from garden tomatoes in late summer. Sacar gajos de los jitomates de la huerta al final del verano.* **2** ADJ A **cutting** remark is unkind and hurts your feelings. *hiriente, cortante* ❑ *People make cutting remarks to help themselves feel superior. Hay personas que hacen comentarios hirientes para sentirse superiores.*

**cut|ting board** (**cutting boards**) N-COUNT A **cutting board** is a wooden or plastic board that you chop meat and vegetables on. *tabla de picar*

**cut|ting edge** N-SING If you are **at the cutting edge of** a field of activity, you are involved in its most important or most exciting developments. *estar a la vanguardia* ❑ *The company is at the cutting edge of modern design. La empresa está a la vanguardia del diseño moderno.*
→ see **technology**

**cuz** /kʌz/ also **'cuz** CONJ **Cuz** is an informal way of saying **because.** *porque* [SPOKEN] ❑ *I can't go 'cuz I'm a boy. No puedo ir porque soy pequeño.*

**cyano|bac|te|ria** /saɪənoʊbæktɪəriə/ N-PLURAL **Cyanobacteria** are bacteria that obtain their energy through photosynthesis. *cianobacteria* [TECHNICAL]

**cy|ber|space** /saɪbərspeɪs/ N-UNCOUNT In computer technology, **cyberspace** refers to data banks and networks, considered as a space. *cyberespacio, ciberespacio* [COMPUTING] ❑ *...a report circulating in cyberspace. ...un informe que circula por el ciberespacio.*

| Word Link | *cycl ≈ circle : bicycle, cycle, cyclist* |
|---|---|

**cy|cle** /saɪkᵊl/ (**cycles, cycling, cycled**) **1** N-COUNT A **cycle** is a series of events or processes that is repeated again and again, always in the same order. *ciclo* ❑ *...the life cycle of the plant. ...el ciclo de vida de la planta.* **2** N-COUNT A **cycle** is a single complete series of movements in an electrical, electronic, or mechanical process. *ciclo* ❑ *...10 cycles per second. ...10 ciclos por segundo.* **3** N-COUNT A **cycle** is the same as a **motorcycle.** *motocicleta, moto, bicla, cicla* **4** V-I If you **cycle,** you ride a bicycle. *andar en bici, andar en bicicleta* ❑ *He cycled to Ingwold. Se fue a Ingwold en bicicleta.* ● **cy|cling** N-UNCOUNT *ciclismo* ❑ *The quiet country roads are ideal for cycling. Los caminos rurales tranquilos son ideales para andar en bicicleta.*
→ see **hat**

**cy|clist** /saɪklɪst/ (**cyclists**) N-COUNT A **cyclist** is someone who rides a bicycle. *ciclista* ❑ *...better protection for cyclists. ...mejor protección para los ciclistas.*
→ see **park**

**cy|clone** /saɪkloʊn/ (**cyclones**) N-COUNT A **cyclone** is a violent tropical storm in which the air goes around and around. *ciclón* ❑ *The race was called off as a cyclone struck. La carrera se suspendió por la entrada del ciclón.*
→ see **hurricane**

**cyl|in|der** /sɪlɪndər/ (**cylinders**) N-COUNT A

**cylinder** is a shape or container with flat circular ends and long straight sides. cilindro, tanque ❑ *It was recorded on a wax cylinder.* *Lo registraron en un cilindro de cera.* ❑ *...oxygen cylinders.* *...tanques de oxígeno.*

→ see **engine, solid, volume**

**cyni|cal** /sɪnɪkᵊl/ ADJ If someone is **cynical,** they believe that people are usually selfish or dishonest. cínico, escéptico, amargado ❑ *...his cynical view of the world.* *...su visión amargada del mundo.* ❑ *It has made me more cynical about relationships.* *Me ha hecho un escéptico en cuanto a las relaciones.* ● **cyni|cal|ly** ADV cínicamente, con sorna ❑ *He laughed cynically.* *Se rió con sorna.* ● **cyni|cism** /sɪnɪsɪzəm/ N-UNCOUNT cinismo, escepticismo, sorna ❑ *...a time of growing cynicism about politicians.* *...una época de desconfianza cada vez mayor en los políticos.*

**cy|to|ki|nesis** /saɪtoʊkɪnɪsɪs/ N-UNCOUNT **Cytokinesis** is the stage in cell division at which the cytoplasm of the cell divides in two. citocinesis [TECHNICAL]

**cyto|plasm** /saɪtəplæzəm/ N-UNCOUNT **Cytoplasm** is the material that surrounds the nucleus of a plant or animal cell. citoplasma [TECHNICAL]

**cyto|sine** /saɪtəsin, -sɪn/ (**cytosines**) N-VAR **Cytosine** is one of the four basic components of the DNA molecule. It bonds with guanine. citosina [TECHNICAL]

# Dd

D

**D.A.** /di̲ eɪ/ (**D.A.s**) N-COUNT A **D.A.** is a **District Attorney**. *fiscal de distrito, procurador general o procuradora general*

**dad** /dæd/ (**dads**) N-COUNT Your **dad** is your father. *papá* [INFORMAL] ❑ *How are you, Dad? ¿Qué tal, papá?, Hola, papá.*

**dad|dy** /dædi/ (**daddies**) N-COUNT Children often call their father **daddy**. *papi, papito* [INFORMAL] ❑ *Look at me, Daddy! ¡Mira, papi!*

daffodil

**daf|fo|dil** /dæfədɪl/ (**daffodils**) N-COUNT A **daffodil** is a yellow spring flower with a central part shaped like a tube and a long stem. *narciso*

**dag|ger** /dægər/ (**daggers**) N-COUNT A **dagger** is a weapon like a knife with two sharp edges. *daga, puñal*

**dai|ly** /de̲ɪli/ **1** ADV If something happens **daily**, it happens every day. *diariamente, a diario, todos los días* ❑ *The airline flies daily to Hong Kong. La aerolínea vuela todos los días a Hong Kong.* ● **Daily** is also an adjective. *diario* ❑ *They had daily meetings. Tenían reuniones diarias.* **2** ADJ **Daily** quantities or rates relate to a period of one day. *diario* ❑ *...their daily dose of vitamins. ...su dosis diaria de vitaminas.* **3** PHRASE Your **daily life** is the things that you do every day as part of your normal life. *vida cotidiana* ❑ *Laughter was part of their daily life then. En ese entonces, la risa era parte de su vida cotidiana.*

**dairy** /dɛəri/ (**dairies**) **1** N-COUNT A **dairy** is a company that sells milk and food made from milk, such as butter, cream, and cheese. *lechería* ❑ *Local dairies bought milk from local farmers. Las lecherías locales compraban la leche a los ganaderos locales.* **2** ADJ **Dairy** is used to refer to foods such as butter and cheese that are made from milk. *lácteo* ❑ *He can't eat dairy products. No puede comer productos lácteos.* **3** ADJ **Dairy** is used to refer to cattle that produce milk rather than meat. *vacuno, lechero* ❑ *...a dairy farm. ...una granja lechera.*

→ see Word Web: **dairy**

**dam** /dæm/ (**dams**) N-COUNT A **dam** is a wall that is built across a river in order to stop the water from flowing and to make a lake. **Dams** are often used to produce electricity. *dique, presa, represa* ❑ *Before the dam was built, the Campbell River used to flood. El río Campbell solía desbordarse antes de que construyeran la presa.*

dam

→ see Word Web: **dam**

**dam|age** /dæmɪdʒ/ (**damages, damaging, damaged**) **1** V-T To **damage** something means to break it, harm it, or stop it from working properly. *dañar, perjudicar* ❑ *He damaged a car with a baseball bat. Dañó un automóvil con un bate de béisbol.* ❑ *Failure to pay will damage the company's reputation. El hecho de no pagar será perjudicial para el buen nombre de la empresa.* ● **dam|ag|ing** ADJ *dañino, perjudicial* ❑ *...the damaging effects of pollution on the environment. ...los efectos perjudiciales de la contaminación sobre el medio ambiente.* **2** N-UNCOUNT **Damage** is physical harm that is caused to an object. *daño* ❑ *The explosion caused a lot of damage to the house. La explosión causó muchos daños a la casa.* **3** N-PLURAL If a court of law awards **damages** to someone, it orders money to be paid to them by a person who has damaged their reputation or property, or who has injured them. *daños y perjuicios* ❑ *She won more than $75,000 in damages. Le concedieron más de 75,000 dólares en daños y perjuicios.*

→ see **disaster**

**Thesaurus** *damage* Ver también:

| | |
|---|---|
| V. | break, harm, hurt, ruin, wreck **1** |
| N. | harm, loss **2** |

**Word Web** dairy

Farmers no longer **milk** one **cow** at a time. Today most dairy **farms** use machines instead. The **milk** is taken from the cow by a vacuum-powered **milking machine**. Then it travels through a pipeline to be stored in a **refrigerated** storage tank. From there it goes to the factory for pasteurization and packaging. The largest such dairy farm in the world is the Al Safi Dairy Farm in Saudi Arabia. It has 24,000 head of **cattle** and produces about 33 million gallons of milk each year.

**Word Web** dam

The Egyptians built the world's first **dam** in about 2900 BC. The dam sent water into a **reservoir** near the capital city of Memphis*. Later they built another dam to prevent **flooding** south of Cairo*. Today, dams are used with **irrigation** systems to prevent **droughts**. Modern **hydroelectric** dams also provide more than 20% of the world's electricity. Brazil and Paraguay built the largest hydroelectric power station in the world—the Itaipu Dam. It took 18 years to build and cost 18 billion dollars! Hydroelectric power is non-polluting. However, the dams endanger some species of fish and sometimes destroy valuable forest lands.

*Memphis: an ancient city in Egypt.*
*Cairo: the capital of Egypt.*

**dame** /deɪm/ (**dames**) N-COUNT A **dame** is a woman. This use is old-fashioned and could cause offense. *tía, vieja* [INFORMAL] ❑ *Who does that dame think she is? ¿Quién se cree que es esa tía?*

**damn** /dæm/ (**damns, damning, damned**) V-T To **damn** someone or something means to criticize them severely. *criticar severamente* ❑ *His report damns the proposed law. Su informe critica severamente la propuesta de ley.*

**damp** /dæmp/ (**damper, dampest**) ADJ Something that is **damp** is slightly wet. *húmedo* ❑ *Her hair was still damp. Su pelo/cabello todavía estaba húmedo.* ❑ *...the damp, cold air. ...el aire frío y húmedo.* • **damp|ness** N-UNCOUNT *humedad* ❑ *It was cooler, and there was dampness in the air. Hacía más frío y el aire se sentía húmedo.*
→ see **weather**

**dance** /dæns/ (**dances, dancing, danced**) **1** V-I When you **dance**, you move your body and feet in a way which follows a rhythm, usually to music. *bailar* ❑ *He doesn't like to dance. No le gusta bailar.* • **danc|ing** N-UNCOUNT *baile* ❑ *Let's go dancing tonight. Vamos a bailar esta noche.* **2** N-COUNT A **dance** is a particular series of graceful movements of your body and feet, which you usually do in time to music. *baile, danza* ❑ *...a traditional Scottish dance. ...un baile escocés tradicional., ...una danza escocesa tradicional.* **3** N-COUNT A **dance** is a social event where people dance with each other. *baile* ❑ *At the school dance he talked to her all evening. En el baile de la escuela estuvo hablando con ella toda la noche.* **4** V-RECIP When you **dance with** someone, the two of you take part in a dance together, as partners. You can also say that two people **dance.** *bailar* ❑ *Nobody wanted to dance with him. Nadie quería bailar con él.* ❑ *Shall we dance? ¿Bailamos?* • **Dance** is also a noun. *baile* ❑ *Come and have a dance with me. Vamos a bailar.* **5** N-UNCOUNT **Dance** is the activity of performing dances, as a public entertainment or an art form. *baile, danza* ❑ *...international dance and music. ...música y bailes internacionales.*
→ see Picture Dictionary: **dance**

**Word Partnership** Usar *dance* con:

| | |
|---|---|
| V. | **let's** dance **1** **4**<br>**choreograph a** dance, **learn to** dance **2** **5** |
| N. | dance **class**, dance **moves**, dance **music**, dance **partner** **2** **5** |

**dance form** (**dance forms**) N-COUNT A **dance form** is a type of dancing, such as ballet or tap dancing. *estilo de baile*

**dance phrase** (**dance phrases**) N-COUNT A **dance phrase** is a short section of a dance consisting of a series of interconnected movements. *segmento (de baile/danza)*

**danc|er** /dænsər/ (**dancers**) N-COUNT A **dancer** is a person who earns money by dancing, or a person who is dancing. *bailarín o bailarina* ❑ *She was a dancer with the New York City Ballet. Era bailarina del Ballet de la Ciudad de Nueva York.*

**dance se|quence** (**dance sequences**) N-COUNT A **dance sequence** is a section of a dance that develops a particular theme or idea. *secuencia de pasos de baile*

**dance struc|ture** (**dance structures**) N-VAR **Dance structure** is the general way in which a dance is organized and the way that the parts of the dance relate to one another. *estructura del baile*

**dance study** (**dance studies**) N-VAR A **dance study** is a series of movements that a dance teacher or student performs in order to develop an idea for a dance. *estudio de baile, ejercicio de baile*

**dan|ger** /deɪndʒər/ (**dangers**) **1** N-UNCOUNT **Danger** is the possibility that someone may be harmed or killed. *peligro* ❑ *He faced great danger with wonderful bravery. Enfrentó un gran peligro con una valentía admirable.* **2** N-COUNT A **danger** is something or someone that can hurt or harm you. *riesgo* ❑ *...the dangers of speeding. ...los riesgos de conducir a gran velocidad.* **3** N-SING If there is a **danger that** something unpleasant will happen, it is possible that it will happen. *peligro, riesgo* ❑ *There is a real danger that this crisis will spread across the country. Existe un verdadero riesgo de que la crisis se extienda a todo el país.* ❑ *There was no danger that the*

**Picture Dictionary** **dance**

dancing

folk dancing

tap dancing

ballroom dancing

modern dance

ballet

*prisoner would escape. No se corría el riesgo de que el prisionero/preso escapara.*
→ see **hero**

**Word Link** ***ous* ≈ *having the qualities of*: *dangerous, fabulous, mysterious***

**dan|ger|ous** /deɪndʒərəs, deɪndʒrəs/ ADJ If something is **dangerous,** it is able or likely to hurt or harm you. *peligroso* ❑ *It's a dangerous road. Es una carretera peligrosa.* ❑ *...dangerous dogs. ...perros peligrosos.* ● **dan|ger|ous|ly** ADV *peligrosamente, arriesgadamente, gravemente* ❑ *He is dangerously ill. Está gravemente enfermo.*

**Thesaurus** *dangerous* Ver también:
ADJ. risky, threatening, unsafe

**Word Partnership** Usar *dangerous* con:
N. dangerous **area**, dangerous **criminal**, dangerous **driving**, dangerous **man**, dangerous **situation**
ADJ. **potentially** dangerous

**dare** /dɛər/ (**dares, daring, dared**) **1** V-T If you do not **dare to** do something, you do not have enough courage to do it, or you do not want to do it because you fear what might happen as a result. If you **dare to** do something, you do something which requires a lot of courage. *osar, atreverse* ❑ *Most people hate Harry but they don't dare to say so. La mayoría de la gente odia a Harry, pero no se atreven a decirlo.* ● **Dare** is also a modal. *atreverse, arriesgarse, animarse* ❑ *Dare she risk staying where she was? ¿Se atrevería/arriesgaría a quedarse donde está?* ❑ *She dare not leave the house. No se anima/atreve a salir de la casa.* **2** V-T If you **dare** someone **to** do something, you challenge them to prove that they are not frightened of doing it. *retar, desafiar* ❑ *His friends dared him to ask Randle for a job. Sus amigos lo retaron a que le pidiera trabajo a Randle.* **3** N-COUNT A **dare** is a challenge which one person gives to another to do something dangerous or frightening. *reto, desafío* ❑ *Jones stole the car on a dare. Jones robó el coche porque lo retaron a hacerlo.* **4** PHRASE You say "**how dare you**" when you are very shocked and angry about something that someone has done. *cómo te atreves/se atreve/se atreven* [SPOKEN] ❑ *How dare you pick up the phone and listen in on my conversations! ¡Cómo te atreves a descolgar el teléfono y escuchar mis conversaciones!*

**dar|ing** /dɛərɪŋ/ **1** ADJ A **daring** person is willing to do things that might be dangerous or shocking. *osado, audaz, temerario, atrevido* ❑ *His daring rescue saved the lives of the boys. Fue muy temerario, pero rescató a los niños y les salvó la vida.* ❑ *Bergit was more daring than I was. Bergit era más atrevida/osada que yo.* **2** N-UNCOUNT **Daring** is the courage to do things which might be dangerous or which might shock or anger other people. *audacia, osadía, arrojo* ❑ *We all admired his daring when we were boys. Todos admirábamos su osadía/arrojo/audacia cuando éramos niños.*

**dark** /dɑrk/ (**darker, darkest**) **1** ADJ When it is **dark,** there is not enough light to see properly. *oscuro* ❑ *It was too dark to see much. Estaba muy oscuro para poder ver algo.* ❑ *People usually shut the curtains when it gets dark. La gente suele cerrar las cortinas cuando oscurece.* ● **dark|ness** N-UNCOUNT *oscuridad* ❑ *The light went out, and we were in total darkness. Se apagó la luz y nos quedamos completamente a oscuras.* ● **dark|ly** ADV *oscuramente, secretamente, misteriosamente* ❑ *...a darkly lit hall. ...un pasillo muy oscuro/mal iluminado.* **2** ADJ If you describe something as **dark,** you mean that it is black in color, or a shade that is close to black. *oscuro* ❑ *He wore a dark suit. Llevaba un traje oscuro.* ❑ *...a dark blue dress. ...un vestido azul oscuro.* ● **dark|ly** ADV *oscuramente* ❑ *His skin was darkly tanned. Tenía la piel de un bronceado/moreno oscuro.* **3** ADJ If someone has **dark** hair, eyes, or skin, they have brown or black hair, eyes, or skin. *oscuro* ❑ *He had dark, curly hair. Tenía el pelo/cabello oscuro y rizado.* **4** ADJ **Dark** thoughts are sad, and show that you are expecting something unpleasant to happen. *sombrío* [LITERARY] ❑ *Troy's chatter stopped me from thinking dark thoughts. El parloteo de Troy me permitió hacer a un lado esos pensamientos sombríos.* ● **dark|ly** ADV *misteriosamente, sombríamente* ❑ *"I might need to talk to you," he said darkly. —Tal vez necesite hablar contigo —dijo misteriosamente/sombríamente.* **5** N-SING **The dark** is the lack of light in a place. *oscuridad* ❑ *Children are often afraid of the dark. Es frecuente que los niños tengan miedo a la oscuridad.* **6** PHRASE If you are **in the dark about** something, you do not know anything about it. *estar a oscuras* ❑ *He was still in the dark about what was happening. Todavía estaba a oscuras sobre lo que estaba pasando.*

| **Word Partnership** | Usar *dark* con: |
|---|---|
| V. | **get** dark **1**<br>**afraid of the** dark, **scared of the** dark **5** |
| N. | dark **clouds**, dark **suit** **2** |

**dark choco|late** N-UNCOUNT **Dark chocolate** is dark brown chocolate that has a stronger and less sweet taste than milk chocolate. *chocolate amargo, chocolate oscuro, chocolate sin leche* ❑ *I don't like dark chocolate. No me gusta el chocolate amargo.*

**dark|room** /dɑrkrum/ (**darkrooms**) N-COUNT A **darkroom** is a room which can be completely closed off from natural light and is lit only by red light. It is used for developing photographs. *cuarto oscuro*

**dar|ling** /dɑrlɪŋ/ (**darlings**) **1** N-VOC You call someone **darling** if you love them or like them very much. *amor, cariño, querido o querida* ❑ *Thank you, darling. Gracias, amor/cariño/querido/querida.* **2** ADJ Some people use **darling** to describe someone or something that they love or like very much. *precioso* [INFORMAL] ❑ *They have a darling baby boy. Tienen un bebé precioso., Tienen un bebé que es un amor., Tienen un bebé que es una preciosidad.* **3** N-COUNT If you describe someone as a **darling,** you are fond of them and think that they are nice. *amor* [INFORMAL] ❑ *He's such a darling. Es un amor.*

**dart** /dɑrt/ (**darts, darting, darted**) **1** V-I If a person or animal **darts** somewhere, they move there suddenly and quickly. *(salir, correr, lanzarse) como una flecha* [WRITTEN] ❑ *Ingrid darted across the street. Ingrid cruzó la calle como una flecha.* **2** V-T/V-I If you **dart** a look **at** someone or something, or if your eyes **dart to** them, you look at them very quickly. *lanzar rápidamente* [LITERARY] ❑ *She darted a sly glance at Bramwell. Lanzó una rápida mirada maliciosa/traviesa a Bramwell.* **3** N-COUNT A **dart** is a small, narrow object with a sharp point which can be thrown or shot. *dardo* ❑ *The idea was to burst a balloon by throwing a dart. La idea era reventar el globo arrojándole un dardo.* **4** N-UNCOUNT **Darts** is a game in which you throw darts at a round board which has numbers on it. *dardos* ❑ *I enjoy playing darts. Disfruto jugando (Me gusta jugar) a los dardos.*

**dash** /dæʃ/ (**dashes, dashing, dashed**) **1** V-I If you **dash** somewhere, you run or go there quickly and suddenly. *lanzarse* ❑ *Suddenly she dashed downstairs. Repentinamente, se lanzó escaleras abajo.* • **Dash** is also a noun. *carrera, vuelta* ❑ *...a quick dash to the store. ...una carrera/vuelta rápida a la tienda.* **2** V-T If an event or person **dashes** your hopes, it destroys them by making it impossible that the thing that is hoped for will ever happen. *hacer añicos* [LITERARY] ❑ *The fighting dashed hopes for a return to peace. Los combates hicieron añicos la esperanza del retorno a la paz.* **3** N-COUNT A **dash of** something is a small quantity or amount of it. *pizca* ❑ *Pour over olive oil and a dash of vinegar. Añada aceite de oliva y unas gotas de vinagre.* **4** N-COUNT A **dash** is a straight, horizontal line used in writing, for example, to separate two main clauses whose meanings are closely connected. *guión* ❑ *Sometimes the dash (—) is used in places where a colon could also be used. En ocasiones se usa el guión (—) cuando también se podría usar los dos puntos.* **5** N-COUNT A **dash** is a short fast race. *carrera*

▸ **dash off** **1** PHR-VERB If you **dash off to** a place, you go there very quickly. *irse corriendo, salir corriendo* ❑ *He dashed off to the restaurant. Se fue (Salió) corriendo al restaurante.* **2** PHR-VERB If you **dash off** a piece of writing, you write or compose it very quickly, without thinking about it very much. *escribir a la carrera* ❑ *In the waiting room, he dashed off a short poem. Escribió a la carrera un poema corto en la sala de espera.*

**dash|board** /dæʃbɔrd/ (**dashboards**) N-COUNT The **dashboard** in a car is the panel facing the driver's seat where most of the instruments and switches are. *tablero de instrumentos* ❑ *The clock on the dashboard said it was two o'clock. El reloj del tablero de instrumentos indicaba las dos en punto.*

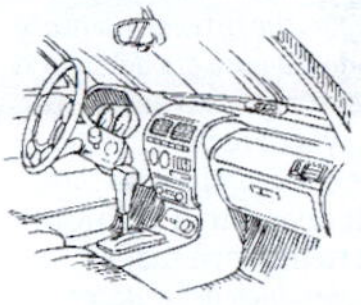

dashboard

**da|ta** /deɪtə, dætə/ **1** N-PLURAL You can refer to information as **data,** especially when it is in the form of facts or statistics that you can analyze. *datos* ❑ *The study was based on data from 2,100 women. El estudio se basó en los datos sobre 2,100 mujeres.* **2** N-UNCOUNT **Data** is information that can be stored and used by a computer program. *dato* [COMPUTING] ❑ *A CD-ROM can hold huge amounts of data. Un disco compacto puede almacenar una enorme cantidad de datos.*

→ see **forecast**

| **Thesaurus** | *data* | Ver también: |
|---|---|---|
| N. | facts, figures, information, results, statistics **1** | |

**data|base** /deɪtəbeɪs, dætə-/ (**databases**) also **data base** N-COUNT A **database** is a collection of data that is stored in a computer and that can easily be used and added to. *base de datos* ❑ *There is a database of names of people who are allowed to vote. Hay una base de datos con los nombres de las personas que pueden votar.*

**da|ta en|try** N-UNCOUNT **Data entry** is the activity of putting data into a computer, for example, by using a keyboard. *ingreso de datos, entrada de datos, captura de datos* ❑ *A simple data entry mistake was the cause of the computer error. Un simple error en la captura de datos fue la causa del error en la computadora.* ❑ *...data-entry clerks. ...capturistas de datos.*

**da|ta ta|ble** (**data tables**) N-COUNT A **data table** is a chart containing a set of data. *gráfica de datos*

**date** /deɪt/ (**dates, dating, dated**) **1** N-COUNT A **date** is a specific time that can be named, for example, a particular day or a particular year. *fecha* ❑ *What's the date today? ¿Qué fecha es hoy?*

D

**2** N-COUNT A **date** is an appointment to meet someone or go out with them, especially someone with whom you are having, or would like to have, a romantic relationship. *cita* ❑ *I have a date with Bob. Tengo una cita con Bob.* **3** V-RECIP If you **are dating** someone, you go out with them regularly because you are having a romantic relationship with them. You can also say that two people **are dating.** *salir con* ❑ *I dated a woman who was a teacher. Salí con una mujer que era maestra.* **4** N-COUNT If you have a date with someone with whom you are having, or may soon have, a romantic relationship, you can refer to that person as your **date.** *cita, pareja, compañero o compañera* ❑ *His date was one of the girls in the show. Su pareja era una de las muchachas del espectáculo.* **5** N-COUNT A **date** is a small, dark-brown, sticky fruit with a stone inside. Dates grow on palm trees in hot countries. *dátil* **6** V-T If you **date** something, you give or discover the date when it was made or when it began. *fechar, determinar la antigüedad de* ❑ *Experts have dated the jug to the fifteenth century. Los especialistas determinaron que la jarra era del siglo xv.* **7** V-T When you **date** something such as a letter or a check, you write that day's date on it. *fechar* ❑ *He dated and signed the letter. Fechó y firmó la carta.* **8** V-I If something **dates,** it goes out of fashion and becomes unacceptable to modern tastes. *pasar de moda* ❑ *...a classic style which never dates. ...un estilo clásico que nunca pasa de moda.* ● **dat|ed** ADJ *pasado de moda, anticuado* ❑ *Some of his ideas are dated. Tiene algunas ideas anticuadas.* **9** PHRASE **To date** means up until the present time. *hasta la fecha, hasta el momento* ❑ *"Dottie" is his best novel to date. Hasta la fecha, "Dottie" es su mejor novela.*

▸ **date back** PHR-VERB If something **dates back to** a particular time, it started or was made at that time. *remontarse* ❑ *The issue is not a new one. It dates back to the 1930s. La cuestión no es nueva; se remonta a los años 1930.*

**Word Partnership** Usar *date* con:

| | |
|---|---|
| N. | **birth** date, **cut-off** date, **due** date, **expiration** date **1** |
| V. | **set a** date **1** **2** |
| | date **and sign** **7** |

**date rape** N-UNCOUNT **Date rape** is when a man rapes a woman after having spent the evening socially with her. *violación (cometida durante una cita)*

**daugh|ter** /dɔtər/ (**daughters**) N-COUNT Someone's **daughter** is their female child. *hija* ❑ *...Flora and her daughter Catherine. ...Flora y su hija Catherine.* ❑ *...the daughter of a university professor. ...la hija de un profesor universitario.*
→ see **child**

**daugh|ter cell** (**daughter cells**) N-COUNT A **daughter cell** is one of the two cells that are formed when a single cell divides. *célula hija (plural: células hija)* [TECHNICAL]

**daughter-in-law** (**daughters-in-law**) N-COUNT Someone's **daughter-in-law** is the wife of their son. *nuera*

**dawn** /dɔn/ (**dawns, dawning, dawned**) **1** N-VAR **Dawn** is the time of day when light first appears in the sky, just before the sun rises. *amanecer, alba, crepúsculo* ❑ *Nancy woke at dawn. Nancy despertó al amanecer/alba.* **2** N-SING **The dawn of** a period of time or a situation is the beginning of it. *aurora* [LITERARY] ❑ *...the dawn of a new age in computing. ...la aurora de una nueva era en la computación.* **3** V-I If something **is dawning,** it is beginning to develop or come into existence. *nacer, alborear* [WRITTEN] ❑ *A new century was dawning. Un nuevo siglo estaba naciendo.* ● **dawn|ing** N-SING *albor* ❑ *...the dawning of the space age. ...los albores de la era espacial.*

▸ **dawn on** or **dawn upon** PHR-VERB If a fact or idea **dawns on** you, you realize it. *caer en la cuenta* ❑ *It took a while to dawn on me that I was trapped. Me llevó un tiempo caer en la cuenta de que estaba atrapado.*

**day** /deɪ/ (**days**) **1** N-COUNT A **day** is one of the seven twenty-four hour periods of time in a week. *día* ❑ *It snowed every day last week. La semana pasada nevó todos los días.* **2** N-COUNT You can refer to a particular period in history as a particular **day** or as particular **days.** *día, época* ❑ *...the most famous artist of his day. ...el artista más famoso de su época.* ❑ *...the early days of the war. ...los primeros días de la guerra.* **3** N-VAR **Day** is the time when it is light, or the time when you are up and doing things. *día* ❑ *Twenty-seven million working days are lost each year due to work accidents and sickness. Cada año se pierden 27 millones de días de trabajo debido a accidentes de trabajo y enfermedades.* ❑ *The streets are busy during the day. Las calles están concurridas/tienen mucho movimiento durante el día.* **4** PHRASE If you **call it a day,** you decide to stop what you are doing because you are tired of it or because it is not successful. *dejar las cosas para otro día o para el día siguiente* ❑ *They had no money left so decided to call it a day. No tenían dinero, así que decidieron dejarlo para otro día.* **5** PHRASE **One day** or **some day** or **one of these days** means at some time in the future. *un día/algún día/uno de estos días* ❑ *I dreamed of living in Dallas one day. Soñaba que un día viviría en Dallas.* ❑ *I hope some day you will find the woman who will make you happy. Espero que algún día encuentre(s) a la mujer que lo (te) haga feliz.*
→ see **year**

**day care** also **daycare** N-UNCOUNT **Day care** is care that is provided during the day for people who cannot take care of themselves, such as small children, old people, or people who are ill. Day care is provided by paid workers. *servicio de guardería infantil, centro de atención diurna para ancianos o minusválidos* ❑ *The day care for her 2-year-old son was canceled. Le cancelaron el servicio de guardería infantil para su hijo de dos años.* ❑ *...a daycare center for elderly people. ...un centro de atención diurna para ancianos.*

**day|dream** /deɪdrim/ (**daydreams, daydreaming, daydreamed**) **1** V-I If you **daydream,** you think about pleasant things for a period of time, usually about things that you would like to happen. *soñar despierto, fantasear, ilusionarse, hacerse ilusiones* ❑ *I've been daydreaming about a job in France. Me he estado haciendo ilusiones sobre un empleo en Francia.* ❑ *He daydreams of being a famous journalist. Se hace ilusiones de llegar a ser un periodista famoso.* **2** N-COUNT A **daydream** is a series of pleasant thoughts, usually about things that you would like to happen. *fantasía* ❑ *He escaped into daydreams of handsome men and beautiful* women. Se refugiaba en sus fantasías sobre hombres apuestos y mujeres bellas.

**Word Link** *light ≈ shining : daylight, headlight, moonlight*

**day|light** /deɪlaɪt/ **1** N-UNCOUNT **Daylight** is the natural light that there is during the day, before it gets dark. *luz de día, luz natural* ❑ *Lack of daylight often makes people feel depressed. La falta de luz natural frecuentemente hace que la gente se sienta deprimida.* **2** PHRASE If you say that a crime is committed **in broad daylight,** you are expressing your surprise that it is done during the day when people can see it, rather than at night. *a plena luz del día* ❑ *He was attacked in broad daylight. Lo atacaron a plena luz del día.*

**day|light sav|ing time** also **daylight savings time** or **daylight savings** N-UNCOUNT **Daylight saving time** is a period of time in the spring when the clocks are set one hour forward, so that people can have extra light in the evening. *horario (hora) de verano*

**day|time** /deɪtaɪm/ N-SING **The daytime** is the part of a day between the time when it gets light and the time when it gets dark. *día* ❑ *In the daytime he stayed in his room, sleeping, or listening to music. Durante el día permanecía/se quedaba en su habitación, durmiendo o escuchando música.*

**day-to-day** ADJ **Day-to-day** things or activities exist or happen every day as part of ordinary life. *cotidiano, diario, de cada día* ❑ *I pay our day-to-day expenses in cash. Nuestros gastos diarios los pago en efectivo.*

**dead** /dɛd/ **1** ADJ A person, animal, or plant that is **dead** is no longer living. *muerto* ❑ *"Do you live on your own?"—"Yes. My husband's dead." —¿Vive sola?—Sí, ya murió mi esposo.* ❑ *The group had shot dead another hostage. El grupo había matado a otro rehén.* • **The dead** are people who are dead. *los muertos* ❑ *Two soldiers were among the dead. Había dos soldados entre los muertos.* **2** ADJ A telephone or piece of electrical equipment that is **dead** is no longer functioning, for example, because it no longer has any electrical power. *desconectado, cortado* ❑ *I answered the phone and the line went dead. Respondí el teléfono y se cortó la línea.* **3** ADJ **Dead** is used to mean "complete" or "absolute," especially before the words "center," "silence," and "stop." *absoluto, total* ❑ *They hurried about in dead silence. Se dieron prisa en total silencio.* **4** ADV **Dead** means "precisely" or "exactly." *justo* ❑ *Mars was visible, dead in the center of the telescope. Marte era visible justo en el centro del telescopio.* **5** PHRASE To **stop dead** means to suddenly stop happening or moving. To **stop** someone or something **dead** means to cause them to suddenly stop happening or moving. *parar en seco* ❑ *We all stopped dead and looked at it. Todos nos paramos en seco y lo miramos.*

| **Thesaurus** | *dead* | Ver también: |
|---|---|---|
| ADJ. | deceased, lifeless; (*ant.*) alive, living **1** | |

**dead end** (**dead ends**) **1** N-COUNT If a street is a **dead end,** there is no way out at one end of it. *callejón sin salida* ❑ *There was another alleyway which came to a dead end. Había otra callejuela que llevaba a un callejón sin salida.* **2** ADJ A **dead-end** job or course of action is one that you think is bad because it does not lead to further developments or progress. *sin porvenir, sin futuro* ❑ *Waitressing was a dead-end job. Servir mesas era un trabajo sin porvenir/futuro., El trabajo de mesera no tenía porvenir/futuro.*

**dead|line** /dɛdlaɪn/ (**deadlines**) N-COUNT A **deadline** is a time or date before which a particular task must be finished or a particular thing must be done. *fecha límite, plazo* ❑ *We were not able to meet the deadline because of several delays. No pudimos cumplir con la fecha límite/el plazo debido a varias demoras.*

**dead|ly** /dɛdli/ (**deadlier, deadliest**) **1** ADJ If something is **deadly,** it is likely or able to cause death, or has already caused death. *mortal, mortífero* ❑ *...assault with a deadly weapon. ...un asalto con arma mortal.* ❑ *...a deadly disease currently affecting dolphins. ...una enfermedad mortífera que está afectando a los delfines.* **2** ADJ If you describe a person or their behavior as **deadly,** you mean that they will do or say anything to get what they want, without caring about other people. *letal* ❑ *She gave me a deadly look. Me lanzó una mirada letal.* **3** ADJ A **deadly** situation has unpleasant or dangerous consequences. *funesto, mortífero* ❑ *...a deadly combination of hunger and war. ...una combinación funesta/mortífera de hambre y guerra.*

**deaf** /dɛf/ (**deafer, deafest**) **1** ADJ Someone who is **deaf** is unable to hear anything or is unable to hear very well. *sordo* ❑ *She is now totally deaf. Ya se quedó completamente sorda.* • **The deaf** are people who are deaf. *los sordos o las sordas* ❑ *Many regular TV programs are captioned for the deaf. Muchos programas regulares de televisión tienen subtítulos para los sordos.* • **deaf|ness** N-UNCOUNT *sordera* ❑ *Because of her deafness she found conversations difficult. El conversar le parecía difícil debido a su sordera.*
→ see **disability**

**deal**
❶ QUANTIFIER USES
❷ VERB AND NOUN USES

❶ **deal** /dil/ QUANT If you say that you need or have **a great deal of** or **a good deal of** a particular thing, you are emphasizing that you need or have a lot of it. *mucho* ❑ *...a great deal of money. ...mucho dinero.* ❑ *She knew a good deal more than she admitted. Sabía mucho más de lo que quería admitir.*

❷ **deal** /dil/ (**deals, dealing, dealt**) **1** N-COUNT If you **make** a **deal,** do a **deal,** or **cut** a **deal,** you complete an agreement or an arrangement with someone, especially in business. *trato, arreglo, convenio, acuerdo* [BUSINESS] ❑ *They made a deal to split the money between them. Hicieron un trato para repartirse el dinero.* ❑ *Japan did a deal with the U.S. on rice imports. Japón cerró un acuerdo con EE.UU. sobre las importaciones de arroz.* **2** V-I If a person, company, or store **deals in** a particular type of goods, their business involves buying or selling those goods. *comerciar en, dedicarse a (la compraventa)* [BUSINESS] ❑ *They deal in antiques. Comercian en antigüedades., Se dedican a la compraventa de antigüedades.* • **deal|er** N-COUNT (**dealers**) *comerciante, corredor, corredora* ❑ *...an antique dealer. ...un comerciante/corredor en antigüedades.* **3** V-T If you **deal** playing cards, you give them out to the players in a game of

d

D

cards. repartir, dar ❑ *She dealt each player a card.* *Dio/Repartió una carta a cada jugador.* • **Deal out** means the same as **deal**. repartir, dar ❑ *Dalton dealt out five cards to each player.* *Dalton dio/repartió cinco cartas a cada jugador.* 4 → see also **dealings**

▸ **deal out** PHR-VERB 1 If someone **deals out** a punishment or harmful action, they punish or harm someone. dictar, aplicar, imponer [WRITTEN] ❑ *I'll leave you to deal out whatever punishment you feel is appropriate.* *Dejo en sus manos imponer el castigo/la pena que crea adecuada.* 2 → see also **deal** ❷ 3

▸ **deal with** 1 PHR-VERB When you **deal with** something or someone that needs attention, you give your attention to them, and often solve a problem or make a decision concerning them. ocuparse de, responder a ❑ *...the way that banks deal with complaints.* *...la manera en que los bancos se ocupan de/responden a las quejas.* 2 PHR-VERB If a book, speech, or movie **deals with** a particular thing, it has that thing as its subject or is concerned with it. tratar de ❑ *This is a sad story dealing with love and grief.* *Es una historia triste que trata del amor y el dolor.* 3 PHR-VERB If you **deal with** a particular person or organization, you have business relations with them. tratar con ❑ *When I worked in Florida I dealt with tourists all the time.* *Cuando trabajé en Florida, trataba con turistas todo el tiempo.*

**deal|ings** /dilɪŋz/ N-PLURAL Someone's **dealings with** a person or organization are the relations that they have with them or the business that they do with them. relación, trato ❑ *He has learned little in his dealings with the community.* *Ha aprendido poco a partir de sus relaciones/su trato con la comunidad.*

**dean** /din/ (**deans**) 1 N-COUNT A **dean** is an important official at a university or college. director, decano ❑ *She was dean of the University of Washington's Graduate School.* *Era el director de la Escuela de Posgrado de la Universidad de Washington.* 2 N-COUNT A **dean** is a priest who is the main administrator of a large church. deán ❑ *...Bob Gregg, dean of the Chapel, Stanford Memorial Church.* *...Bob Gregg, deán de la Capilla de la Iglesia Stanford Memorial.* 3 N-COUNT The **dean** of a group is the most important member of that group. decano ❑ *Aaron Copland was known as the dean of American composers.* *Aaron Copland era conocido como el decano de los compositores estadounidenses.*

**dear** /dɪər/ (**dearer, dearest, dears**) 1 ADJ You use **dear** to describe someone or something that you feel affection for. querido ❑ *Mrs. Cavendish is a dear friend of mine.* *La señora Cavendish es una amiga mía muy querida.* 2 ADJ If something is **dear to** you or **dear to** your **heart**, you care deeply about it. caro a ❑ *This is a subject very dear to the hearts of teachers.* *Este es un tema muy caro a los profesores.* 3 ADJ **Dear** is written at the beginning of a letter, followed by the name or title of the person you are writing to. querido, estimado ❑ *Dear Peter, How are you?* *Querido Peter, ¿cómo estás?* ❑ *...Dear Sir or Madam.* *...estimado Señor o Señora.* 4 N-VOC You can call someone **dear** as a sign of affection. querido o querida, cariño ❑ *Are you feeling better, dear?* *¿Te sientes mejor, querido?*

**death** /dɛθ/ (**deaths**) 1 N-VAR **Death** is the permanent end of the life of a person or animal. muerte ❑ *1.5 million people are in danger of death from hunger.* *Un millón y medio de personas están en peligro de muerte por hambre.* ❑ *...the thirtieth anniversary of her death.* *...el trigésimo aniversario de su muerte.* 2 PHRASE If you say that something is a matter **of life and death**, you are emphasizing that it is extremely important, often because someone may die or suffer great harm if people do not act immediately. de vida o muerte ❑ *Never mind, John, it's not a matter of life and death.* *Olvídalo, John, no es una cuestión de vida o muerte.* 3 PHRASE If someone **is put to death**, they are executed. ejecutar [FORMAL] ❑ *He was put to death for his crimes.* *Lo ejecutaron por sus crímenes.* 4 PHRASE You use **to death** after an adjective or a verb to emphasize the action, state, or feeling mentioned. For example, if you are **frightened to death** or **bored to death**, you are extremely frightened or bored. muerto de ❑ *I was scared to death just watching him climbing the cliff.* *Estaba muerto de miedo nada más de verlo trepar el acantilado.*

**Word Partnership** Usar *death* con:

| | |
|---|---|
| ADJ. | **accidental** death, **sudden** death, **violent** death 1 |
| N. | **brush with** death, **cause of** death, *someone's* death, death **threat** 1 |

**death row** /dɛθroʊ/ N-UNCOUNT If someone is **on death row**, they are in the part of a prison which contains the cells for criminals who have been sentenced to death. pabellón de los condenados a muerte ❑ *He was on death row for 11 years.* *Estuvo once años en el pabellón de los condenados a muerte.*

**death toll** (**death tolls**) also **death-toll** N-COUNT The **death toll** of an accident, disaster, or war is the number of people who die in it. número de víctimas, número de muertos ❑ *The death toll from the crash rose to 83.* *El número de víctimas/muertos por el choque/accidente ascendió a 83.*

**de|bate** /dɪbeɪt/ (**debates, debating, debated**) 1 N-VAR A **debate** is a discussion about a subject on which people have different views. discusión, deliberación ❑ *An intense debate is going on within the government.* *En el seno del gobierno está teniendo lugar una intensa discusión/deliberación.* ❑ *There has been a lot of debate among teachers about this subject.* *Ha habido muchos debates sobre el tema entre los maestros.* 2 N-COUNT A **debate** is a formal discussion, for example, in a parliament or institution, in which people express different opinions about a particular subject and then vote on it. debate ❑ *There was a debate in Congress on immigration reform.* *Hubo un debate en el Congreso sobre la reforma migratoria.* 3 V-RECIP If people **debate** a topic, they discuss it fairly formally, putting forward different views. You can also say that one person **debates** a topic **with** another person. discutir ❑ *The committee will debate the issue today.* *La comisión discutirá el asunto hoy.* ❑ *NASA officials are debating whether the space flight should end early.* *Los funcionarios de la NASA están discutiendo sobre si el viaje espacial debe terminar antes.* 4 V-T If you **debate** whether to do something or what to do, you think or talk about possible courses of action before deciding exactly what you are going to do. considerar, dar vueltas a ❑ *Emma was debating whether*

to go or not. *Emma estaba considerando si debía de ir o no/dándole vueltas a si debía de ir o no.*
→ see **election**

**Word Partnership** Usar *debate* con:

| | |
|---|---|
| V. | **open to** debate 1 |
| ADJ. | **major** debate, **ongoing** debate, **televised** debate 1 2 |
| | **political** debate, **presidential** debate 2 |
| N. | debate **the issue**, debate **over** ***something*** 3 4 |

**deb|it** /dɛbɪt/ (**debits, debiting, debited**) 1 V-T When your bank **debits** your account, money is taken from it and paid to someone else. *cargar, hacer un cargo* ❑ *We will confirm the amount before debiting your account. Le confirmaremos la suma antes de hacer el cargo a su cuenta.* 2 N-COUNT A **debit** is a record of the money taken from your bank account, for example, when you write a check. *débito, pasivo, debe* ❑ *The total of debits must balance the total of credits. El saldo deudor debe corresponder al saldo acreedor/a favor.*

**deb|it card** (**debit cards**) N-COUNT A **debit card** is a bank card that you can use to pay for things. When you use it the money is taken out of your bank account immediately. *tarjeta de débito*

**de|bris** /dəbri, deɪ-/ N-UNCOUNT **Debris** is pieces from something that has been destroyed or pieces of trash or unwanted material that are spread around. *escombros* ❑ *Several people were killed by flying debris. Los escombros que salieron volando mataron a varias personas.*

**debt** /dɛt/ (**debts**) 1 N-VAR A **debt** is a sum of money that you owe someone. *deuda* ❑ *He is still paying off his debts. Todavía está pagando sus deudas.* 2 → see also **bad debt** 3 N-UNCOUNT **Debt** is the state of owing money. *deuda* ❑ *...a report on the amount of debt people owe. ...un informe sobre el monto de las deudas de la gente.* • PHRASE If you are **in debt** or **get into debt**, you owe money. If you are **out of debt** or **get out of debt**, you succeed in paying all the money that you owe. *en deuda, endeudarse, salir de deudas* ❑ *Many students get into debt. Muchos estudiantes se endeudan.*

**Word Partnership** Usar *debt* con:

| | |
|---|---|
| V. | **incur** debt, **pay off a** debt, **reduce** debt, **repay a** debt 1 |
| ADV. | **deeply in** debt 2 |

**de|but** /deɪbyu/ (**debuts**) N-COUNT The **debut** of a performer or sports player is their first public performance, appearance, or recording. *debut* ❑ *She made her debut in a 1937 production of "Hamlet." Hizo su debut en una producción de "Hamlet" de 1937.*

**dec|ade** /dɛkeɪd/ (**decades**) N-COUNT A **decade** is a period of ten years, especially one that begins with a year ending in 0, for example, 1980 to 1989. *década, decenio* ❑ *...the last decade of the nineteenth century. ...la última década/el último decenio del siglo XIX.*

**de|cal** /dikæl/ (**decals**) N-COUNT **Decals** are pieces of paper with a design on one side. The design can be transferred onto a surface by heating it, soaking it in water, or pressing it hard. *calcomanía*

**de|cay** /dɪkeɪ/ (**decays, decaying, decayed**) 1 V-I When something such as a dead body, a dead plant, or a tooth **decays**, it is gradually destroyed by a natural process. *descomponerse, pudrirse* ❑ *The bodies slowly decayed. Los cuerpos se desompusieron lentamente.* • **Decay** is also a noun. *descomposición, caries* ❑ *Eating too much candy causes tooth decay. El comer muchos dulces causa caries dental.* • **de|cayed** ADJ *descompuesto, podrido, picado* ❑ *Even young children can have teeth so decayed they need to be pulled. Aun los niños muy pequeños pueden tener dientes tan cariados/picados que es necesario extraérselos.* 2 V-I If something such as a society, system, or institution **decays**, it gradually becomes weaker or its condition gets worse. *decaer, declinar* ❑ *The old standards have decayed. Los antiguos modelos/ejemplos/reglas han caído en decadencia.* • **Decay** is also a noun. *descomposición, decadencia, deterioro* ❑ *There are problems of urban decay. Hay problemas de deterioro urbano.*
→ see **teeth**

d

**de|ceased** /dɪsist/ (**deceased**) 1 N-SING OR N-PLURAL **The deceased** is used to refer to a particular person or to particular people who have recently died. *difunto o difunta, fallecido o fallecida* [LEGAL] ❑ *Police will inform the families of the deceased. La policía informará a las familias de los fallecidos/difuntos/muertos.* 2 ADJ A **deceased** person is one who has recently died. *difunto, fallecido* [FORMAL] ❑ *...his recently deceased mother. ...su madre, que recientemente falleció.*

**de|ceit** /dɪsit/ (**deceits**) N-VAR **Deceit** is behavior that is deliberately intended to make people believe something which is not true. *engaño* ❑ *Losing with honor is better than winning by lies and deceit. Perder con honor es mejor que ganar con mentiras y engaños.*

**de|ceive** /dɪsiv/ (**deceives, deceiving, deceived**) V-T If you **deceive** someone, you make them believe something that is not true, usually in order to get some advantage for yourself. *engañar, defraudar* ❑ *He has deceived us all. Nos engañó/defraudó a todos.*

**De|cem|ber** /dɪsɛmbər/ (**Decembers**) N-VAR **December** is the twelfth and last month of the year in the Western calendar. *diciembre* ❑ *...a bright morning in December. ...una soleada mañana de diciembre.*

**de|cent** /disᵊnt/ 1 ADJ **Decent** is used to describe something which is considered to be of an acceptable standard or quality. *decente* ❑ *He didn't get a decent explanation. No le dieron una explicación decente.* • **de|cent|ly** ADV *decentemente* ❑ *They treated their prisoners decently. Trataban decentemente a sus prisioneros.* 2 ADJ **Decent** is used to describe something which is morally correct or acceptable. *respetable, apropiado* ❑ *After a decent interval, she married again. Después de un tiempo apropiado/respetable, se casó nuevamente.* • **de|cent|ly** ADV *decentemente* ❑ *Can't you dress more decently? ¿No puedes vestirte más decentemente?*

**de|cen|tral|ize** /disɛntrəlaɪz/ (**decentralizes, decentralizing, decentralized**) V-T/V-I To **decentralize** government or a large organization means to move some departments away from the main administrative area, or to give more power to local departments. *descentralizar(se)* ❑ *The company began to decentralize thirty years ago.* *La empresa empezó a descentralizarse hace treinta años.* • **de|cen|trali|za|tion** /dɪsɛntrəlɪzeɪʃᵊn/ N-UNCOUNT *descentralización* ❑ *He is against the idea of increased decentralization.* *Está en contra de la idea de una mayor descentralización.*

**de|cep|tion** /dɪsɛpʃᵊn/ (**deceptions**) N-VAR **Deception** is the act of deceiving someone or the state of being deceived by someone. *engaño* ❑ *He admitted obtaining property by deception.* *Admitió haber obtenido la propiedad mediante engaños.*

**de|cide** /dɪsaɪd/ (**decides, deciding, decided**) **1** V-T/V-I If you **decide** to do something, you choose to do it, usually after you have thought carefully about the other possibilities. *decidir* ❑ *She decided to take a course in philosophy.* *Decidió seguir un curso de filosofía.* ❑ *Think about it very carefully before you decide.* *Piénselo muy bien antes de decidir.* **2** V-T If a person or group of people **decides** something, they choose what something should be like or how a particular problem should be solved. *decidir* ❑ *Schools need to decide the best way of testing students.* *Es necesario que las escuelas decidan la mejor manera de examinar a los estudiantes.* **3** V-T If an event or fact **decides** something, it makes it certain that a particular choice will be made or that there will be a particular result. *definir, determinar* ❑ *This goal decided the game.* *Este tanto/gol definió el partido.* ❑ *The election will decide if either party controls both houses of Congress.* *Las elecciones determinarán si alguno de los partidos controla las dos cámaras del Congreso.* **4** V-T If you **decide** that something is true, you form that opinion about it after considering the facts. *decidir* ❑ *He decided Franklin was suffering from a bad cold.* *Decidió que Franklin padecía de un fuerte resfrío.*
▸ **decide on** PHR-VERB If you **decide on** something or **decide upon** something, you choose it from two or more possibilities. *decidir(se)* ❑ *Have you decided on a name for the baby?* *¿Ya te decidiste por el nombre para el bebé?*

| **Thesaurus** | *decide* Ver también: |
|---|---|
| V. | choose, elect, pick, select **1** **2** |

| **Word Partnership** | Usar *decide* con: |
|---|---|
| V. | **help (to)** decide, **let** *someone* decide, **try to** decide **1** **2** |
| ADJ. | **unable to** decide **1** **2** **4** |

**de|cidu|ous** /dɪsɪdʒuəs/ ADJ A **deciduous** tree or bush is one that loses its leaves in the fall every year. *de hoja caduca, caducifolio*
→ see **plant, tree**

**deci|mal** /dɛsɪmᵊl/ (**decimals**) **1** ADJ A **decimal** system involves counting in units of ten. *decimal* ❑ *The mathematics of ancient Egypt used a decimal system.* *Las matemáticas del antiguo Egipto se basaban en el sistema decimal.* **2** N-COUNT A **decimal** is a fraction that is written in the form of a dot followed by one or more numbers which represent tenths, hundredths, and so on: for example, .5, .51, .517. *decimal* ❑ *...simple math concepts, such as decimals and fractions.* *...los conceptos matemáticos simples, como los decimales y las fracciones/los quebrados.*
→ see **fraction**

**deci|mal point** (**decimal points**) N-COUNT A **decimal point** is the dot in front of a decimal fraction. *punto decimal* ❑ *A waiter omitted the decimal point in the $13.09 bill.* *Un mesero omitió el punto decimal en la cuenta por 13.09 dólares.*

**de|ci|sion** /dɪsɪʒᵊn/ (**decisions**) **1** N-COUNT When you make a **decision**, you choose what should be done or which is the best of various possible actions. *decisión* ❑ *I don't want to make the wrong decision and regret it later.* *No quiero tomar una decisión equivocada/errónea y después arrepentirme.* **2** N-UNCOUNT **Decision** is the act of deciding something or the need to decide something. *decisión, resolución, determinación* ❑ *First plan carefully, then act with decision.* *Primero planéalo con todo cuidado y luego actúa con determinación/resolución/decisión.*

| **Word Partnership** | Usar *decision* con: |
|---|---|
| V. | **arrive at a** decision, **make a** decision, **postpone a** decision, **reach a** decision **1** |
| ADJ. | **difficult** decision, **final** decision, **important** decision, **right** decision, **wise** decision, **wrong** decision **1** |

**de|ci|sive** /dɪsaɪsɪv/ **1** ADJ If a fact, action, or event is **decisive**, it makes certain a particular result. *decisivo, contundente* ❑ *...his decisive victory in the presidential elections.* *...su decisiva/contundente victoria en las elecciones para presidente.* • **de|ci|sive|ly** ADV *decisivamente, terminantemente* ❑ *The plan was decisively rejected by Congress.* *El plan fue terminantemente rechazado por el Congreso.* **2** ADJ If someone is **decisive**, they have or show an ability to make quick decisions in a difficult or complicated situation. *resuelto* ❑ *He was a decisive leader.* *Era un dirigente resuelto.* • **de|ci|sive|ly** ADV *resueltamente, contundentemente* ❑ *"I'll call you at ten," she said decisively.* *—Te llamaré a las diez —dijo contundentemente.* • **de|ci|sive|ness** N-UNCOUNT *resolución, firmeza* ❑ *His supporters admire his decisiveness.* *Sus partidarios admiran su resolución.*

**deck** /dɛk/ (**decks**) **1** N-COUNT A **deck** on a vehicle such as a bus or ship is a lower or upper area of it. *cubierta* ❑ *...a luxury ship with five passenger decks.* *...un barco de lujo con cinco cubiertas para pasajeros.* **2** N-COUNT The **deck** of a ship is the top part of it that forms a floor in the open air which you can walk on. *cubierta* ❑ *She stood on the deck and waved as the boat moved off.* *Permaneció de pie en cubierta y dijo adiós con la mano cuando el barco se puso en marcha.* **3** N-COUNT A **deck** is a flat wooden area next to a house, where people can sit and relax or eat. *tarima* ❑ *A deck leads into the main room of the home.* *Un entarimado lleva a la habitación principal de la casa.*

deck

**4** N-COUNT A **deck** of cards is a complete set of playing cards. *mazo, baraja* ❑ *Matt picked up the cards and shuffled the deck.* *Matt recogió las cartas y barajó el mazo.*
→ see **ship**

**dec|la|ra|tion** /dɛklərei̲ʃ<sup></sup>n/ (**declarations**) **1** N-COUNT A **declaration** is an official announcement or statement. *declaración* ❑ *...a declaration of war. ...una declaración de guerra.* **2** N-COUNT A **declaration** is a firm, emphatic statement which shows that you have no doubts about what you are saying. *declaración* ❑ *...declarations of love. ...declaraciones de amor.*

**de|clara|tive** /dɪklɛ̲ərətɪv/ ADJ A **declarative** sentence is a sentence that expresses a statement, for example "My car is blue." *enunciativo, aseverativo*

| Word Link | *clar ≈ clear : clarify, clarity, declare* |
|---|---|

**de|clare** /dɪklɛ̲ər/ (**declares, declaring, declared**) **1** V-T If you **declare** that something is true, you say that it is true in a firm, deliberate way. You can also **declare** an attitude or intention. *declarar, manifestar, anunciar* [WRITTEN] ❑ *He declared he would not seek re-election as president. Anunció que no buscaría la reelección como presidente.* ❑ *He declared his intention to become the best golfer in the world. Anunció sus intenciones de llegar a ser el mejor golfista del mundo.* **2** V-T If you **declare** something, you state officially and formally that it exists or is the case. *declarar* ❑ *Neither leader was willing to declare an end to the war. Ninguno de los dirigentes estaba dispuesto a declarar el fin de la guerra.* ❑ *The judges declared Mr. Stevens innocent. Los jueces declararon inocente al señor Stevens.* **3** V-T If you **declare** goods that you have bought in another country or money that you have earned, you say how much you have bought or earned so that you can pay tax on it. *declarar, manifestar* ❑ *Declaring the wrong income will lead to a fine. El hecho de declarar ingresos incorrectos será motivo de una multa.*
→ see **war**

| Word Link | *clin ≈ leaning : decline, incline, recline* |
|---|---|

**de|cline** /dɪklai̲n/ (**declines, declining, declined**) **1** V-I If something **declines,** it becomes less in quantity, importance, or strength. *disminuir* ❑ *The number of staff has declined from 217,000 to 114,000. El número de empleados ha disminuido/disminuyó de 217,000 a 114,000.* ❑ *Exports rose 1.5% while imports declined 3.6%. Las exportaciones aumentaron el 1.5 por ciento, mientras que las importaciones disminuyeron el 3.6 por ciento.* **2** V-T/V-I If you **decline** something or **decline to** do something, you politely refuse to accept it or do it. *declinar, rehusar* [FORMAL] ❑ *He declined their invitation. Declinó su invitación.* ❑ *He offered the boys some coffee. They declined politely. Ofreció café a los muchachos, pero ellos lo rehusaron cortésmente.* **3** N-VAR If there is a **decline in** something, it becomes less in quantity, importance, or quality. *disminución* ❑ *Official records show a sharp decline in the number of foreign tourists. Los registros oficiales muestran una marcada disminución del número de turistas extranjeros.* **4** PHRASE If something is **in decline** or **on the decline,** it is gradually decreasing in importance, quality, or power. *en declive, en decadencia, en disminución* ❑ *Thankfully the disease is on the decline. Por fortuna, la enfermedad está cediendo.* **5** PHRASE If something **goes** or **falls into decline,** it begins to gradually decrease in importance, quality, or power. *entrar en decadencia* ❑ *Libraries should not be allowed to fall into decline. No se debería permitir que las bibliotecas entraran en decadencia.*

**de|cod|ing** /di̲koʊdɪŋ/ N-UNCOUNT **Decoding** is the process that is involved in understanding the meaning of a written word. *descodificar* [TECHNICAL]

**de|com|pos|er** /di̲kəmpo̲ʊzər/ (**decomposers**) N-COUNT **Decomposers** are organisms such as bacteria, fungi, and earthworms that feed on dead plants and animals and convert them into soil. *descomponedor* [TECHNICAL]

**de|com|po|si|tion re|ac|tion** (**decomposition reactions**) N-COUNT A **decomposition reaction** is a chemical reaction in which a compound is broken down into two or more simpler substances. *reacción de descomposición* [TECHNICAL]

**deco|rate** /dɛ̲kəreɪt/ (**decorates, decorating, decorated**) **1** V-T If you **decorate** something, you make it more attractive by adding things to it. *adornar, decorar* ❑ *He decorated his room with pictures of sports figures. Decoró su cuarto con fotografías de personajes deportivos.* **2** V-T/V-I If you **decorate** a room or the inside of a building, you put new paint or wallpaper on the walls and ceiling, and paint the woodwork. *empapelar, pintar* ❑ *They were decorating Jemma's bedroom. Estaban empapelando/pintando el cuarto de Jemma.* ❑ *They are planning to decorate when they get the time. Están pensando empapelar/pintar cuando tengan tiempo.*
● **deco|rat|ing** N-UNCOUNT *decorado* ❑ *I did a lot of the decorating myself. Yo mismo hice gran parte del decorado.* ● **deco|ra|tor** (**decorators**) N-COUNT *decorador o decoradora* ❑ *...Bloomberg's private palace, with its interior design by decorator Jamie Drake. ...la mansión privada de los Bloomberg, cuyo interior fue diseñado por el decorador Jamie Drake.*

**deco|ra|tion** /dɛkərei̲ʃ<sup></sup>n/ (**decorations**) **1** N-UNCOUNT The **decoration** of a room is its furniture, wallpaper, and ornaments. *decoración* ❑ *The decoration and furnishings were practical for a family home. La decoración y los muebles eran prácticos para una casa familiar.* **2** N-VAR **Decorations** are things that are added to something in order to make it look more attractive. *adorno* ❑ *The only wall decorations are candles and a single mirror. Los únicos adornos de las paredes son velas y un solo espejo.* ❑ *Colorful paper decorations were hanging from the ceiling. Del techo colgaban unos coloridos adornos de papel.* **3** → see also **decorate**

**deco|ra|tive** /dɛ̲kərətɪv, -əreɪtɪv/ ADJ Something that is **decorative** is intended to look pretty or attractive. *decorativo* ❑ *The drapes are for decorative purposes and do not open or close. Las cortinas eran decorativas y no se podía cerrarlas ni abrirlas.*

| Word Link | *cresc, creas ≈ growing : crescent, decrease, increase* |
|---|---|

**de|crease** (**decreases, decreasing, decreased**)

> The verb is pronounced /dɪkri̲s/. The noun is pronounced /di̲kris/ or /dɪkri̲s/.

**1** V-T/V-I When something **decreases** or when you **decrease** it, it becomes less in quantity, size, or intensity. *disminuir* ❑ *Population growth is decreasing by 1.4% each year. El crecimiento demográfico*

d

*está disminuyendo el 1.4 por ciento anual.* ❑ *The average price decreased from $134,000 to $126,000.* *EL precio promedio disminuyó de 134,000 dólares a 126,000.* ❑ *Since 1945 air forces have decreased in size.* *El tamaño de las fuerzas aéreas ha disminuido a partir de 1945.* **2** N-COUNT A **decrease in** the quantity, size, or intensity of something is a reduction in it. *disminución* ❑ *There has been a decrease in the number of people without a job.* *Ha habido una disminución del número de personas sin empleo.*

D

**Thesaurus** *decrease* Ver también:
v. decline, diminish, go down; (ant.) increase **1**

**de|cree** /dɪkri/ (**decrees, decreeing, decreed**) **1** N-COUNT A **decree** is an official order or decision, especially one made by the ruler of a country. *decreto* ❑ *The decree banned all meetings, strikes, parades and protests.* *El decreto prohibió/prohibía toda clase de reuniones, huelgas/paros, desfiles y manifestaciones.* **2** N-COUNT A **decree** is a judgment made by a law court. *sentencia* ❑ *...court decrees.* *...sentencias judiciales.* **3** V-T If someone in authority **decrees** that something must happen, they decide or state this officially. *decretar* ❑ *The government decreed that all children should have an education.* *El gobierno decretó que todos los niños debían recibir educación.*

**dedi|cate** /dɛdɪkeɪt/ (**dedicates, dedicating, dedicated**) **1** V-T If you say that someone **has dedicated** themselves **to** something, they have decided to give a lot of time and effort to it because they think that it is important. *dedicarse, consagrarse* ❑ *For the next few years, she dedicated herself to her work.* *Durante los años siguientes, se dedicó/consagró a su trabajo.* ● **dedi|cat|ed** ADJ *dedicado* ❑ *He's dedicated to his students.* *Está dedicado/consagrado a sus estudiantes.* ● **dedi|ca|tion** /dɛdɪkeɪʃᵊn/ N-UNCOUNT *dedicación* ❑ *We admire her dedication to achieving peace.* *Admiramos su dedicación al logro de la paz.* **2** V-T If someone **dedicates** something such as a book, play, or piece of music **to** you, they mention your name, for example, in the front of a book or when a piece of music is performed, as a way of showing affection or respect for you. *dedicar* ❑ *She dedicated her first book to her sons.* *Dedicó su primer libro a sus hijos.* ● **dedi|ca|tion** (**dedications**) N-COUNT *dedicatoria* ❑ *...the dedication at the beginning of the book.* *...la dedicatoria al comienzo del libro.*

**Word Link** *de ≈ from, down, away : deduct, descend, detach*

**de|duct** /dɪdʌkt/ (**deducts, deducting, deducted**) V-T When you **deduct** an amount from a total, you subtract it from the total. *deducir, restar* ❑ *The company deducted the money from his wages.* *La empresa dedujo el dinero de su salario.*

**de|duct|ible** /dɪdʌktɪbəl/ (**deductibles**) **1** ADJ If a payment or expense is **deductible,** it can be deducted from another sum such as your income, for example, when calculating how much income tax you have to pay. *deducible* ❑ *Travel is deductible as a business expense.* *Los viajes son deducibles como gastos empresariales.* ❑ *...deductible expenses.* *...gastos deducibles.* **2** N-COUNT A **deductible** is a sum of money which an insured person has to pay toward the cost of an insurance claim. The insurance company pays the rest. *deducible* ❑ *Each time they go to a hospital, they have to pay a deductible of $628.* *Cada vez que se internan en un hospital, tienen que pagar un deducible de 628 dólares.*

**de|duc|tion** /dɪdʌkʃᵊn/ (**deductions**) **1** N-COUNT A **deduction** is an amount that has been subtracted from a total. *deducción* ❑ *...an income tax deduction.* *...una deducción del ingreso sobre la renta.* **2** N-COUNT A **deduction** is a conclusion that you have reached about something because of other things that you know to be true. *deducción* ❑ *It was a pretty clever deduction.* *Fue una deducción muy inteligente/ingeniosa.*
→ see **science**

**deed** /did/ (**deeds**) **1** N-COUNT A **deed** is something that is done, especially something that is very good or very bad. *acto, hecho, acción, hazaña* [LITERARY] ❑ *The people who did this evil deed must be punished.* *Las personas que actuaron tan mal deben ser castigadas.* **2** N-COUNT A **deed** is a document containing the terms of an agreement, especially an agreement about the ownership of land or a building. *escritura* [LEGAL] ❑ *Do you have the deeds to the property?* *¿Tienes las escrituras de la propiedad?*

**dee|jay** /didʒeɪ/ (**deejays, deejaying, deejayed**) **1** N-COUNT A **deejay** is the same as a **disc jockey**. *disc-jockey* [INFORMAL] **2** V-I If someone **deejays,** they introduce and play music on the radio or at a nightclub. *trabajar de/como disc-jockey* ❑ *Ronson deejays every weekend.* *Ronson trabaja de/como disc-jockey todos los fines de semana.*

**deem** /dim/ (**deems, deeming, deemed**) V-T If something **is deemed to** have a particular quality or **to** do a particular thing, it is considered to have that quality or do that thing. *considerar, juzgar* [FORMAL] ❑ *A car was deemed essential to get around the many places to see and visit.* *Consideraron que era esencial tener un coche para ir a todos los lugares que querían ver.* ❑ *He will support the use of force if the government deems it necessary.* *Apoyará el uso de la fuerza si el gobierno lo juzga/considera necesario.*

**deep** /dip/ (**deeper, deepest**) **1** ADJ If something is **deep,** it extends a long way down from the ground or from the top surface of something. *profundo, hondo* ❑ *The water is very deep.* *El agua es muy profunda.* ❑ *Den dug a deep hole in the center of the garden.* *Den hizo un hoyo profundo en el centro del jardín.* ● **Deep** is also an adverb. *hondo* ❑ *She put her hand in deeper, to the bottom.* *Metió la mano más hondo, hasta el fondo.* ● **deep|ly** ADV *profundamente* ❑ *When planting a tree, the soil should be dug deeply.* *Cuando se planta un árbol, se debe cavar profundamente.* **2** ADJ A **deep** container, such as a closet, extends or measures a long distance from front to back. *profundo* ❑ *...a deep cupboard.* *...un armario/aparador profundo.* **3** ADJ You use **deep** to emphasize the seriousness, strength, importance, or degree of something. *profundo, sentido* ❑ *I had a deep admiration for Sartre.* *Tenía una profunda admiración por Sartre.* ❑ *He expressed his deep sympathy to the family.* *Expresó a la familia su más sentido pésame.* ● **deep|ly** ADV *profundamente* ❑ *He loved his brother deeply.* *Quería profundamente a su hermano.* **4** ADJ If you are in a **deep** sleep, you are sleeping peacefully and it is difficult to wake you. *profundo* ❑ *Una* fell into a deep sleep. Una se durmió profundamente. ● **deep|ly** ADV profundamente ❑ She slept deeply but woke early. Durmió profundamente, pero se despertó temprano. **5** ADJ A **deep** breath or sigh uses or fills the whole of your lungs. profundo ❑ Cal took a long, deep breath, struggling to control his emotions. Cal respiró larga y profundamente, luchando por dominar sus emociones. ● **deep|ly** ADV profundamente ❑ She sighed deeply. Dio un profundo suspiro. **6** ADJ A **deep** sound is low in pitch. grave ❑ His voice was deep. Su voz era grave. **7** ADJ If you describe something such as a problem or a piece of writing as **deep,** you mean that it is important, serious, or complicated. profundo ❑ They're adventure stories. They're not intended to be deep. Son historias de aventuras. No hay la intención de que sean profundas. **8** ADV If you experience or feel something **deep inside** you or **deep down,** you feel it very strongly even though you do not necessarily show it. hondo ❑ I have fear deep down, but I can't show it. Tengo miedo en lo más hondo de mí, pero no puedo mostrarlo. **9** ADJ You use **deep** to describe colors that are strong and fairly dark. intenso, subido ❑ ...cushions in deep colors. ...cojines en colores intensos. ❑ The sky was deep blue and starry. El cielo era de un azul intenso y estaba estrellado. **10** PHRASE If you say that something **goes deep** or **runs deep,** you mean that it is very serious or strong and is hard to change. venir de lo profundo de uno ❑ His anger clearly went deep. Era evidente que su enojo venía de lo más profundo.

**deep cur|rent** (**deep currents**) N-COUNT A **deep current** is a current of water that flows far below the surface of an ocean. corriente (oceánica) de aguas profundas

**deep|en** /dipən/ (**deepens, deepening, deepened**) **1** V-T/V-I If a situation or emotion **deepens** or if something **deepens** it, it becomes stronger and more intense. profundizar, estrechar ❑ These friendships will probably deepen in your teenage years. Es probable que esas amistades se estrechen en tu adolescencia. **2** V-T/V-I When a sound **deepens** or **is deepened,** it becomes lower in tone. hacer más grave ❑ "Go and speak to her," he said deepening his voice. —Ve a hablar con ella —le dijo en un tono de voz más grave. **3** V-T If people **deepen** something, they increase its depth by digging out its lower surface. ahondar ❑ There are plans to deepen the river from 40 to 45 feet, to allow for larger ships. Hay planes para ahondar el lecho del río de 12 a 13.5 metros y permitir el paso de barcos de más calado.

**deep ocean ba|sin** (**deep ocean basins**) N-COUNT The **deep ocean basin** is the part of the Earth's surface that lies beneath the ocean. cuenca abisal (oceánica)

**deep-water zone** (**deep-water zones**) N-COUNT The **deep-water zone** of a lake or pond is the area furthest from the surface, where no sunlight reaches. zona de aguas profundas

**deer** /dɪər/ (**deer**) N-COUNT A **deer** is a large wild animal that eats grass and leaves. A male deer usually has large, branching horns. venado, ciervo

**de|fault** /dɪfɔlt/ (**defaults, defaulting, defaulted**) **1** V-I If a person, company, or country **defaults on** something that they have legally agreed to do, such as paying some money or doing a piece of work before a particular time, they fail to do it. faltar, dejar de cumplir, incurrir en mora [LEGAL] ❑ More borrowers are defaulting on loan repayments. Más prestatarios están incurriendo en mora de pagos. ● **Default** is also a noun. falta, incumplimiento, mora ❑ ...a default on $1.3 billion in loans. ...una falta de pago de 1,300 millones de dólares en préstamos. **2** N-UNCOUNT In computing, the **default** is a particular set of instructions which the computer always uses unless the person using the computer gives other instructions. preestablecido [COMPUTING] ❑ The default setting on the printer is for color. La posición preestablecida de la impresora es para color. **3** PHRASE If something happens **by default,** it happens only because something else which might have prevented it or changed it has not happened. por omisión [FORMAL] ❑ He kept his title by default because no one else wanted to compete for it. Retuvo el título por omisión porque nadie más quiso disputárselo.

**de|feat** /dɪfit/ (**defeats, defeating, defeated**) **1** V-T If you **defeat** someone, you win a victory over them in a battle, game, or contest. derrotar, vencer ❑ They defeated the army in 1954. Derrotaron/Vencieron al ejército en 1954. **2** V-T If a task or a problem **defeats** you, it is so difficult that you cannot do it or solve it. frustrar ❑ The task of writing the book nearly defeated him. La tarea de escribir el libro casi lo dejó frustrado. **3** V-T To **defeat** an action or plan means to cause it to fail. derrotar ❑ The navy had an important role in defeating the rebellion. La marina tuvo un papel importante en la derrota de la rebelión. **4** N-VAR **Defeat** is the experience of being beaten in a battle, game, or contest, or of failing to achieve what you wanted to. derrota ❑ He didn't want to admit defeat. No quiso admitir la derrota. ❑ ...the team's 31-point defeat at Sacramento. ...la derrota del equipo por 31 puntos en Sacramento.

**de|fect** (**defects, defecting, defected**)

> The noun is pronounced /difɛkt/. The verb is pronounced /dɪfɛkt/.

**1** N-COUNT A **defect** is a fault or imperfection in a person or thing. defecto ❑ He was born with a hearing defect. Nació con un defecto de audición. ❑ The report shows the defects of the present system. El informe muestra los defectos del sistema actual. **2** V-I If you **defect,** you leave your country, political party, or other group, and join an opposing country, party, or group. desertar ❑ ...a Democrat who defected in 2004. ...un demócrata que desertó en 2004. ● **de|fec|tion** /dɪfɛkʃ$^{ə}$n/ (**defections**) N-VAR deserción ❑ ...the defection of ten Republicans. ...la deserción de diez republicanos. ● **de|fec|tor** /dɪfɛktər/ (**defectors**) N-COUNT desertor o desertora ❑ The government has attracted defectors from other parties. El gobierno ha atraído a algunos desertores de otros partidos.

**de|fec|tive** /dɪfɛktɪv/ ADJ If something is **defective,** there is something wrong with it and it does not work properly. defectuoso ❑ ...defective equipment. ...equipo defectuoso.

| Word Link | fend ≈ striking : defend, fender, offend |
|---|---|

**de|fend** /dɪfɛnd/ (**defends, defending, defended**) **1** V-T If you **defend** someone or something, you take action in order to protect

D

them. defender ❑ *He has always defended religious rights.* *Él siempre ha defendido los derechos religiosos.* **2** V-T If you **defend** someone or something when they have been criticized, you argue in support of them. defender ❑ *The president defended his decision to go to war.* *El presidente defendió su decisión de entrar en guerra.* **3** V-T When a lawyer **defends** a person who has been accused of something, the lawyer argues on their behalf in a court of law that the charges are not true. defender, abogar ❑ *...a lawyer who defended political prisoners.* *...un abogado que defendía a presos políticos.* ❑ *He has hired a lawyer to defend him in court.* *Contrató a un abogado que lo defienda en el juicio.* **4** V-T When a sports player plays in the tournament which they won the previous time it was held, you can say that they **are defending** their title. defender, refrendar, retener ❑ *Torrence hopes to defend her title successfully in the next Olympics.* *Torrence espera refrendar/retener su título en los próximos Juegos Olímpicos.*
→ see **hero**

| Word Link | *ant ≈ one who does, has : defendant, immigrant, occupant* |
|---|---|

**de|fend|ant** /dɪfɛndənt/ (**defendants**) N-COUNT A **defendant** is a person who has been accused of breaking the law and is being tried in court. acusado o acusada, demandado o demandada ❑ *The defendant pleaded guilty and was fined $500.* *El acusado/demandado se declaró culpable y fue multado con 500 dólares.*
→ see **trial**

**de|fend|er** /dɪfɛndər/ (**defenders**) **1** N-COUNT If you are a **defender of** a particular thing or person that has been criticized, you argue or act in support of that thing or person. defensor o defensora, abogado o abogada ❑ *He was known as a defender of human rights.* *Se le conocía como defensor/abogado de los derechos humanos.* **2** N-COUNT A **defender** in a game such as soccer or hockey is a player whose main task is to try and stop the other side from scoring. defensa ❑ *Lewis was the team's top defender.* *Lewis era el mejor defensa del equipo.*

**de|fense** /difɛns/ (**defenses**)

| Defense in meaning **7** is pronounced /diːfens/. |
|---|

**1** N-UNCOUNT **Defense** is action that is taken to protect someone or something against attack. defensa ❑ *The land was flat which made defense difficult.* *El terreno era llano y eso dificultó la defensa.* **2** N-UNCOUNT **Defense** is the organization of a country's armies and weapons, and their use to protect the country or its interests. defensa ❑ *Twenty-eight percent of the country's money is spent on defense.* *El 28 por ciento de los recursos del país se gasta en defensa.* ❑ *...the U.S. Defense Secretary.* *...el Secretario de Defensa de Estados Unidos.* **3** N-PLURAL The **defenses** of a country or region are all its armed forces and weapons. defensa ❑ *...his promise to rebuild the country's defenses.* *...su promesa de reconstruir las defensas del país.* **4** N-COUNT A **defense** is something that people or animals can use or do to protect themselves. defensa, protección ❑ *The immune system is the human body's main defense against disease.* *El sistema inmunitario es la principal defensa/protección del cuerpo humano contra las enfermedades.* **5** N-COUNT A **defense** is something that you say or write which supports ideas or actions that have been criticized or questioned. defensa ❑ *...his defense of the government's performance.* *...su defensa del desempeño del gobierno.* **6** N-SING **The defense** is the case that is presented by a lawyer in a trial for the person who has been accused of a crime. You can also refer to this person's lawyers as **the defense.** defensa ❑ *The defense was that the police had not kept full records of the interviews.* *La defensa se basó en que la policía no llevó registros completos de las entrevistas.* **7** N-SING In games such as soccer or hockey, the **defense** is the group of players in a team who try to stop the opposing players from scoring a goal or a point. defensa ❑ *Their defense was weak and allowed in 12 goals in six games.* *Su defensa era débil y permitió 12 goles en seis partidos.*

**de|fense mecha|nism** (**defense mechanisms**) N-COUNT A **defense mechanism** is a way of behaving or thinking which is not conscious or deliberate and is an automatic reaction to unpleasant experiences or feelings such as anxiety and fear. mecanismo de defensa

**de|fen|sive** /dɪfɛnsɪv/ **1** ADJ You use **defensive** to describe things that are intended to protect someone or something. defensivo ❑ *The Government organized defensive measures to protect the city.* *El gobierno organizó las medidas defensivas para proteger la ciudad.* **2** ADJ Someone who is **defensive** is behaving in a way that shows they feel unsure or threatened. a la defensiva ❑ *She heard the defensive note in his voice and knew that he was ashamed.* *Su voz denotaba que se había puesto a la defensiva y comprendió que se sentía avergonzado.* ● **de|fen|sive|ly** ADV a la defensiva ❑ *"I know," said Kate, defensively.* *—Lo sé—dijo Kate a la defensiva.* **3** PHRASE If someone is **on the defensive,** they are trying to protect themselves or their interests because they feel unsure or threatened. a la defensiva ❑ *Do not let one difficult student put you on the defensive.* *No permitas que un estudiante difícil te ponga a la defensiva.*

**de|fi|ance** /dɪfaɪəns/ N-UNCOUNT **Defiance** is behavior or an attitude which shows that you are not willing to obey someone. desafío, rebeldía ❑ *...his brave defiance of the government.* *...su valeroso desafío al gobierno.*, *...su valerosa rebeldía contra el gobierno.*

**de|fi|ant** /dɪfaɪənt/ ADJ If you say that someone is **defiant,** you mean they show aggression or independence by refusing to obey someone. desafiante, rebelde ❑ *The players are in a defiant mood as they prepare for tomorrow's game.* *Los jugadores se muestran desafiantes mientras se preparan para el partido de mañana.* ● **de|fi|ant|ly** ADV con actitud desafiante ❑ *They defiantly rejected the plan.* *Rechazaron el plan con una actitud desafiante.*

**de|fi|cien|cy** /dɪfɪʃᵊnsi/ (**deficiencies**) **1** N-VAR **Deficiency in** something, especially something that your body needs, is not having enough of it. deficiencia ❑ *He had blood tests for signs of vitamin deficiency.* *Le hicieron análisis de sangre en busca de indicios de deficiencia vitamínica.* **2** N-VAR A **deficiency** that someone or something has is a weakness or imperfection in them. deficiencia [FORMAL] ❑ *The company failed to correct deficiencies in the system.* *La empresa no logró corregir las deficiencias del sistema.*

**defi|cit** /dɛfəsɪt/ (**deficits**) N-COUNT A **deficit** is the amount by which something is less than is needed, especially the amount by which the total money received is less than the total money spent. *déficit* ❑ *...a deficit of five billion dollars. ...un déficit de cinco mil millones de dólares.* ● PHRASE If an account or organization is **in deficit**, more money has been spent than has been received. *en déficit, en descubierto*

**defi|cit spend|ing** N-UNCOUNT **Deficit spending** is an economic policy in which a government spends more money raised by borrowing than it receives in revenue. *uso de fondos obtenidos en préstamo* ❑ *...plans to end deficit spending. ...los planes para poner fin al uso de fondos obtenidos en préstamo.*

**de|fine** /dɪfaɪn/ (**defines, defining, defined**) V-T If you **define** something, you show, describe, or state clearly what it is and what its limits are, or what it is like. *definir* ❑ *The government defines a household as a group of people who live in the same house. El gobierno define una familia como un grupo de personas que viven bajo el mismo techo.*

**defi|nite** /dɛfɪnɪt/ 1 ADJ If something such as a decision or an arrangement is **definite,** it is firm and clear, and unlikely to be changed. *definitivo* ❑ *It's too soon to give a definite answer. Es muy pronto para dar una respuesta definitiva.* ❑ *She made no definite plans for her future. No hizo planes definitivos para su futuro.* 2 ADJ **Definite** evidence or information is true, rather than being an opinion or guess. *definitivo* ❑ *We didn't have any definite proof. No teníamos ninguna prueba definitiva.*

| **Thesaurus** | *definite* | Ver también: |
|---|---|---|
| ADJ. | clear-cut, distinct, precise, specific; (*ant.*) ambiguous, vague 1 | |

**defi|nite ar|ti|cle** (**definite articles**) N-COUNT The word "the" is sometimes called **the definite article.** *artículo definido, artículo determinado*

**defi|nite|ly** /dɛfɪnɪtli/ ADV You use **definitely** to emphasize that something is true, and will not change. *definitivamente, sin duda alguna* ❑ *This game is definitely more fun. Definitivamente, este juego es más divertido.* ❑ *The extra money will definitely help. El dinero extra ayudará, sin duda alguna.*

**defi|ni|tion** /dɛfɪnɪʃᵊn/ (**definitions**) 1 N-COUNT A **definition** is a statement giving the meaning of a word or expression, especially in a dictionary. *definición* ❑ *There is no agreement on a standard definition of intelligence. No hay acuerdo sobre una definición uniforme/general de la inteligencia.* ● PHRASE If you say that something has a particular quality **by definition**, you mean that it has this quality simply because of what it is. *por definición* 2 N-UNCOUNT **Definition** is the quality of being clear and distinct. *definición, claridad* ❑ *They criticized Prof. Johnson's program for its lack of definition. Criticaron el programa del profesor Johnson por su falta de claridad.*

**de|fini|tive** /dɪfɪnɪtɪv/ 1 ADJ Something that is **definitive** provides a firm conclusion that cannot be questioned. *definitivo* ❑ *The study provides definitive proof that the drug is safe. El estudio proporciona pruebas definitivas de que la droga es segura.* ● **de|fini|tive|ly** ADV *definitivamente* ❑ *He wasn't able to answer the question definitively. Fue incapaz de responder la pregunta de manera definitiva.* 2 ADJ A **definitive** book or performance is thought to be the best of its kind that has ever been done or that will ever be done. *decisivo, trascendental* ❑ *...a definitive book on Spanish history. ...un libro decisivo/trascendental en la historia española.*

**de|fla|tion** /dɪfleɪʃᵊn/ N-UNCOUNT In geology, **deflation** is the removal of soil and other material from the surface of the Earth by wind. *deflación* [TECHNICAL]

**de|fog|ger** /difɒgər/ (**defoggers**) N-COUNT A **defogger** is a device that removes condensation from the window of a vehicle by blowing warm air onto it. *desempañador* ❑ *...rear window defoggers. ...desempañadores traseros.*

**de|for|esta|tion** /difɔrɪsteɪʃᵊn/ N-UNCOUNT **Deforestation** is the cutting down of trees over a large area. *deforestación* ❑ *...the deforestation of the Amazon. ...la deforestación de la Amazonia.*
→ see **greenhouse effect**

**de|for|ma|tion** /difɔrmeɪʃᵊn/ (**deformations**) N-VAR **Deformation** is a change in the shape of a rock as a result of pressure, for example in an earthquake. *deformación* [TECHNICAL]

**defy** /dɪfaɪ/ (**defies, defying, defied**) 1 V-T If you **defy** someone or something that is trying to make you behave in a particular way, you refuse to obey them and behave in that way. *desobedecer, desacatar* ❑ *This was the first time I defied my mother. Era la primera vez que desobedecía a mi madre.* 2 V-T If you **defy** someone **to** do something, you challenge them to do it when you think that they will be unable to do it or too frightened to do it. *desafiar, retar* ❑ *I defy you to think of a better answer. Te reto a que pienses en una mejor respuesta.* 3 V-T If something **defies** description or understanding, it is so strange, extreme, or surprising that it is almost impossible to understand or explain. *desafiar* ❑ *This decision defies logic. La decisión desafía toda lógica.*

**de|gree** /dɪgri/ (**degrees**) 1 N-COUNT You use **degree** to indicate the extent to which something happens or is the case, or the amount which something is felt. *grado* ❑ *He treated her with a high degree of respect. La trató con un gran respeto.* ❑ *They tried it, with varying degrees of success. Lo intentaron con diferentes grados de éxito.* 2 N-COUNT A **degree** is a unit of measurement that is used to measure temperatures. It is often written as °, for example, 23°. *grado* ❑ *It's over 80 degrees outside. Hace más de 26 grados a la intemperie.* 3 N-COUNT A **degree** is a unit of measurement that is used to measure angles, and also longitude and latitude. It is often written as °, for example, 23°. *grado* ❑ *It was pointing outward at an angle of 45 degrees. Apuntaba hacia el exterior a un ángulo de 45 grados.* 4 N-COUNT A **degree** is a title or rank given by a university or college when you have completed a course of study there. It can also be given as an honorary title. *título* ❑ *...an engineering degree. ...un título de ingeniería.*
→ see **thermometer**

**Word Partnership** Usar *degree* con:

N. degree **of certainty**, degree **of difficulty** 1
**45/90** degree **angle** 3
**bachelor's/master's** degree, **college** degree, degree **program** 4
ADJ. **high** degree 1
**honorary** degree 4

D

**de|lay** /dɪleɪ/ (**delays, delaying, delayed**)
1 V-T/V-I If you **delay** doing something, you do not do it immediately or at the planned or expected time, but you leave it until later. retrasar, demorar, posponer ❑ *I delayed the decision until I had spoken to my mother.* *Pospuse la decisión hasta que hubiese hablado con mi madre.* ❑ *They delayed having children until they had more money.* *Decidieron no tener hijos hasta tener más dinero.* ❑ *There was no time to delay.* *No había tiempo qué perder.* 2 V-T To **delay** someone or something means to make them late or to slow them down. entretener, retrasar ❑ *Can you delay him in some way?* *¿Puedes entretenerlo de algún modo?* ❑ *Several problems delayed production.* *Varios problemas retrasaron la producción.* 3 N-VAR If there is a **delay,** something does not happen until later than planned or expected. retraso ❑ *He apologized for the delay.* *Se disculpó por el retraso.*

**Thesaurus** *delay* Ver también:

V. hold up, postpone, stall; (*ant.*) hurry, rush 1
N. interruption, lag; (*ant.*) rush 3

**del|egate** (**delegates, delegating, delegated**)

The noun is pronounced /dɛlɪgɪt/. The verb is pronounced /dɛlɪgeɪt/.

1 N-COUNT A **delegate** is a person who is chosen to vote or make decisions on behalf of a group of other people, especially at a conference or a meeting. delegado o delegada ❑ *The Canadian delegate didn't reply.* *El delegado canadiense no respondió/replicó/contestó.* 2 V-T/V-I If you **delegate** duties, responsibilities, or power **to** someone, you give them those duties, those responsibilities, or that power so that they can act on your behalf. delegar ❑ *He wants to delegate more tasks to his employees.* *Quiere delegar más responsabilidades en sus empleados.* ❑ *As a team leader, you must delegate effectively.* *Como cabeza del equipo, debe delegar realmente.* ● **del|ega|tion** N-UNCOUNT delegación ❑ *The delegation of responsibility is very important in a business.* *La delegación de responsabilidades es muy importante en los negocios.*

**del|ega|tion** /dɛlɪgeɪʃᵊn/ (**delegations**)
1 N-COUNT A **delegation** is a group of people who have been sent somewhere to have talks with other people on behalf of a larger group of people. delegación ❑ *...the Chinese delegation to the UN talks in New York.* *...la delegación china a las negociaciones de las Naciones Unidas en Nueva York.* 2 → see also **delegate**

**de|lete** /dɪlit/ (**deletes, deleting, deleted**) V-T If you **delete** something that has been written down or stored in a computer, you cross it out or remove it. suprimir, eliminar, borrar ❑ *He deleted files from the computer.* *Borró/Eliminó algunos archivos de la computadora.*

**Thesaurus** *delete* Ver también:

V. cut out, erase, remove

**deli** /dɛli/ (**delis**) N-COUNT A **deli** is a is a **delicatessen.** delicatessen [INFORMAL]

**de|lib|er|ate** (**deliberates, deliberating, deliberated**)

The adjective is pronounced /dɪlɪbərɪt/. The verb is pronounced /dɪlɪbəreɪt/.

1 ADJ If you do something that is **deliberate,** you planned or decided to do it beforehand, and so it happens on purpose rather than by chance. a propósito, adrede, intencional ❑ *It was a deliberate attempt to upset him.* *Trató de molestarlo a propósito/adrede.* ● **de|lib|er|ate|ly** ADV deliberadamente, intencionalmente ❑ *He started the fire deliberately.* *Inició el incendio intencionalmente.* 2 ADJ If a movement or action is **deliberate,** it is done slowly and carefully. cuidadoso ❑ *She folded her scarf with slow, deliberate movements.* *Dobló la bufanda con movimientos lentos y cuidadosos.* ● **de|lib|er|ate|ly** ADV pausadamente ❑ *He spoke slowly and deliberately, as if Rae were a very young child.* *Habló muy pausadamente, como si Rae fuese un niño chiquito.* 3 V-I If you **deliberate,** you think about something carefully, especially before making a very important decision. deliberar, considerar, meditar ❑ *She deliberated over the decision before she made up her mind.* *Meditó muy bien las cosas antes de tomar su decisión.*
→ see **trial**

**deli|cate** /dɛlɪkɪt/ 1 ADJ Something that is **delicate** is small and beautifully shaped. delicado, fino ❑ *He had delicate hands.* *Tenía manos muy finas.* ● **deli|ca|cy** N-UNCOUNT delicadeza ❑ *...the delicacy of a flower.* *...lo delicado de una flor.* ● **deli|cate|ly** ADV sutilmente ❑ *She was a delicately pretty girl.* *Era una muchacha sutilmente bonita.* 2 ADJ Something that is **delicate** has a color, taste, or smell which is pleasant and not strong or intense. delicado ❑ *The beans have a delicate flavor.* *Los granos tienen un gusto delicado.* ● **deli|cate|ly** ADV delicadamente ❑ *...a soup delicately flavored with nutmeg.* *...una sopa delicadamente sazonada con nuez moscada.* 3 ADJ If something is **delicate,** it is easy to harm, damage, or break, and needs to be handled or treated carefully. delicado ❑ *The china is very delicate.* *La porcelana es muy delicada.* 4 ADJ Someone who is **delicate** is not healthy and strong, and becomes ill easily. delicado, frágil ❑ *She was physically delicate.* *Su estado físico era delicado.* 5 ADJ You use **delicate** to describe a situation, problem, matter, or discussion that needs to be dealt with carefully and sensitively in order to avoid upsetting things or offending people. delicado ❑ *There's a delicate balance between the need for people to travel freely and the need for security.* *Hay un delicado equilibrio entre la necesidad de la gente de viajar libremente y la necesidad de seguridad.* ● **deli|ca|cy** N-UNCOUNT delicado ❑ *This was a subject of delicacy on which he wanted her advice.* *Era un asunto delicado sobre el que quería su consejo.* ● **deli|cate|ly** ADV con delicadeza ❑ *Shawn sent a delicately worded memo.* *Shawn (le) envió un memorándum redactado con delicadeza.*

**deli|ca|tes|sen** /dɛlɪkətɛsᵊn/ (**delicatessens**)

N-COUNT A **delicatessen** is a store that sells cold cuts, cheeses, salads, and often a selection of imported foods. *delicatessen*

**de|li|cious** /dɪlɪʃəs/ ADJ Food that is **delicious** has a very pleasant taste. *delicioso* ❑ *There was a wide choice of delicious meals. Había una amplia variedad de platillos (comidas) deliciosos.* • **de|li|cious|ly** ADV *deliciosamente* ❑ *This yogurt has a deliciously creamy flavor. Este yogur tiene un delicioso sabor cremoso.*

**de|light** /dɪlaɪt/ (**delights, delighting, delighted**) **1** N-UNCOUNT **Delight** is a feeling of very great pleasure. *deleite, placer* ❑ *He expressed delight at the news. Manifestó placer ante las noticias.* ❑ *Andrew laughed with delight. Andrew rió con deleite.* **2** PHRASE If someone **takes delight** or **takes a delight in** something, they get a lot of pleasure from it. *disfrutar* ❑ *Haig took obvious delight in his children. Era evidente que Haig disfrutaba con sus hijos.* **3** N-COUNT You can refer to someone or something that gives you great pleasure or enjoyment as a **delight.** *deleite, placer* ❑ *The aircraft was a delight to fly. Era un deleite/placer volar el avión.* **4** V-T If something **delights** you, it gives you a lot of pleasure. *deleitar* ❑ *She created a style of music which delighted audiences everywhere. Creó un estilo de música que deleitaba al auditorio en todas partes.*

**de|light|ed** /dɪlaɪtɪd/ ADJ If you are **delighted,** you are extremely pleased and excited about something. *encantado* ❑ *Frank was delighted to see her. Frank estaba encantado de verla.* • **de|light|ed|ly** ADV *con gran alegría* ❑ *"Look at that!" Jackson exclaimed delightedly. —¡Mira eso!—exclamó Jackson encantado.*

**de|light|ful** /dɪlaɪtfəl/ ADJ If you describe something or someone as **delightful,** you mean they are very pleasant. *agradable, delicioso, encantador* ❑ *...a delightful garden. ...un jardín encantador.* • **de|light|ful|ly** ADV *deliciosamente* ❑ *...a delightfully refreshing perfume. ...un perfume deliciosamente refrescante.*

**de|lin|quent** /dɪlɪŋkwənt/ (**delinquents**) ADJ Someone, usually a young person, who is **delinquent** repeatedly commits minor crimes. *delincuente* ❑ *...homes for delinquent children. ...hogares para niños delincuentes.* • **Delinquent** is also a noun. *delincuente* ❑ *...a nine-year-old delinquent. ...un delincuente de 9 años de edad.* • **de|lin|quen|cy** N-UNCOUNT *delincuencia* ❑ *...a study of delinquency. ...un estudio sobre la delincuencia.*

**de|liv|er** /dɪlɪvər/ (**delivers, delivering, delivered**) **1** V-T If you **deliver** something somewhere, you take it there. *entregar* ❑ *The Canadians plan to deliver more food to Somalia. Los canadienses tienen planeado entregar más alimentos a Somalia.* **2** V-T If you **deliver** a lecture or speech, you give it in public. *dar, pronunciar* [FORMAL] ❑ *The president will deliver a speech about schools. El presidente pronunciará un discurso sobre las escuelas.* **3** V-T When someone **delivers** a baby, they help the woman who is giving birth to the baby. *asistir en el parto, ayudar en el parto* ❑ *He didn't expect to deliver his own baby! ¡No esperaba ayudar en el parto de su propio bebé!* **4** V-T If someone **delivers** a blow to someone else, they hit them. *propinar, asestar* [WRITTEN] ❑ *He delivered the blow with a hammer. Le asestó el golpe con el martillo.*

**Word Partnership** Usar *deliver* con:

N. deliver **a letter**, deliver **mail**, deliver **a message**, deliver **news**, deliver **a package** **1**
deliver **a lecture**, deliver **a speech** **2**
deliver **a baby** **3**
deliver **a blow** **4**

d

**de|liv|ery** /dɪlɪvəri/ (**deliveries**) **1** N-VAR **Delivery** or a **delivery** is the bringing of letters, packages, or other goods to your house or to another place where you want them. *entrega* ❑ *Please allow 28 days for delivery. El plazo de entrega es de 28 días.* ❑ *The fighting is threatening the delivery of food and medicine. Los combates están poniendo en riesgo la entrega de alimentos y medicamentos.* **2** N-COUNT A **delivery** of something is the goods that are delivered. *entrega, remesa* ❑ *I got a delivery of fresh eggs this morning. Esta mañana recibí una entrega/remesa de huevos frescos.* **3** N-VAR **Delivery** is the process of giving birth to a baby. *parto, alumbramiento* ❑ *It was an easy delivery. Fue un parto fácil.* **4** N-UNCOUNT You talk about someone's **delivery** when you are referring to the way in which they give a speech or lecture. *expresión oral* ❑ *His speeches were well written but his delivery was hopeless. Sus discursos estaban bien escritos, pero su forma de expresarse era imposible.*

**de|liv|ery charge** (**delivery charges**) N-COUNT A **delivery charge** is the cost of transporting or delivering goods. *gastos de envío* [FORMAL] ❑ *Delivery charges are included in the price. Los gastos de envío están incluidos en el precio.*

**del|ta** /dɛltə/ (**deltas**) N-COUNT A **delta** is an area of low, flat land shaped like a triangle, where a river splits and spreads out into several branches before entering the sea. *delta* ❑ *...the Mississippi delta. ...el delta del Mississippi.*
→ see **landform, river**

**deluxe** /dɪlʌks/ ADJ **Deluxe** goods or services are better in quality and more expensive than ordinary ones. *de lujo* ❑ *...deluxe hotel suites. ...suites de lujo.*

**de|mand** /dɪmænd/ (**demands, demanding, demanded**) **1** V-T If you **demand** something such as information or action, you ask for it in a very forceful way. *exigir* ❑ *The victim's family is demanding an investigation into the shooting. La familia de la víctima está exigiendo que se investigue el tiroteo.* ❑ *He demanded that I give him an answer. Me exigió que le diera una respuesta.* **2** V-T If one thing **demands** another, the first needs the second in order to happen or be dealt with successfully. *exigir, requerir* ❑ *The job demands much patience and hard work. El empleo exige/requiere mucha paciencia y empeño.* **3** N-COUNT A **demand** is a firm request for something. *demanda, exigencia* ❑ *There were demands for better services. Hubo demandas/exigencias de mejores servicios.* **4** N-UNCOUNT If you refer to **demand,** or to the **demand for** something, you are referring to how many people want to have it, do it, or buy it. *demanda* ❑ *Demand for the product has increased. Ha aumentado la demanda del producto.* **5** N-PLURAL **The demands of** something or its **demands on** you are the things which it needs or the things which you have to do for it. *exigencia*

D

❑ ...*the demands and challenges of a new job.* ...*las exigencias y retos de un empleo nuevo.* **6** PHRASE If someone or something is **in demand** or **in great demand,** they are very popular and a lot of people want them. *de gran demanda, solicitado, popular* ❑ *He was much in demand as a lecturer in the U.S. Era un conferencista muy solicitado en Estados Unidos.* **7** PHRASE If something is available or happens **on demand,** you can have it or it happens whenever you want it or ask for it. *a solicitud, de libre acceso* ❑ ...*an entertainment system that offers 25 movies on demand.* ...*un sistema de entretenimiento que ofrece 25 películas a solicitud.*

| Thesaurus | *demand* | Ver también: |
|---|---|---|
| v. | command, insist on, order; (*ant.*) give, grant, offer **1**<br>necessitate, need, require; (*ant.*) give, supply **2** | |

**de|mand|ing** /dɪmændɪŋ/ **1** ADJ A **demanding** job or task requires a lot of your time, energy, or attention. *exigente* ❑ *He could no longer cope with his demanding job. Ya no podía hacer frente a las exigencias de su empleo.* **2** ADJ People who are **demanding** are not easily satisfied or pleased. *exigente* ❑ *Ricky was a very demanding child. Ricky era un niño muy exigente.*

**de|mise** /dɪmaɪz/ N-SING The **demise** of something or someone is their end or death. *fallecimiento, deceso* [FORMAL] ❑ ...*the demise of his father.* ...*el fallecimiento/deceso de su padre.*

**de|moc|ra|cy** /dɪmɒkrəsi/ (**democracies**) **1** N-UNCOUNT **Democracy** is a system of government in which people choose their rulers by voting for them in elections. *democracia* ❑ ...*the spread of democracy in Eastern Europe.* ...*la propagación de la democracia en Europa Oriental.* **2** N-COUNT A **democracy** is a country in which the people choose their government by voting for it. *democracia* ❑ *The new democracies face tough challenges. Las nuevas democracias enfrentan desafíos difíciles.*
→ see **vote**

**demo|crat** /dɛməkræt/ (**democrats**) **1** N-COUNT A **Democrat** is a member or supporter of a particular political party which has the word "democrat" or "democratic" in its title, for example, the Democratic Party in the United States. *demócrata* ❑ *Democrats voted against the plan. Los demócratas votaron contra el plan.* **2** N-COUNT A **democrat** is a person who believes in the ideals of democracy, personal freedom, and equality. *demócrata* ❑ *This is the time for democrats and not dictators. Es momento para demócratas, no para dictadores.*

**demo|crat|ic** /dɛməkrætɪk/ **1** ADJ A **democratic** country, government, or political system is governed by representatives who are elected by the people. *democrático* ❑ *Bolivia returned to democratic rule in 1982. Bolivia volvió al régimen democrático en 1982.* ● **demo|crati|cal|ly** /dɛməkrætɪkli/ ADV *democráticamente* ❑ *Yeltsin became Russia's first democratically elected president. Yeltsin fue el primer presidente de Rusia electo democráticamente.* **2** ADJ Something that is **democratic** is based on the idea that everyone should have equal rights and should be involved in making important decisions. *democrático* ❑ *Education is the basis of a democratic society. La educación es la base de una sociedad democrática.* ● **demo|crati|cal|ly** ADV *democráticamente* ❑ *This committee tries to make decisions democratically. Esta comisión trata de tomar las decisiones democráticamente.*

**de|mol|ish** /dɪmɒlɪʃ/ (**demolishes, demolishing, demolished**) **1** V-T To **demolish** something such as a building means to destroy it completely. *derribar* ❑ *The storm demolished buildings and flooded streets. La tormenta derribó algunos edificios e inundó algunas calles.* ● **demo|li|tion** /dɛməlɪʃᵊn/ (**demolitions**) N-VAR *demolición* ❑ ...*the total demolition of the old bridge.* ...*la demolición total del viejo puente.* **2** V-T If you **demolish** someone's ideas or arguments, you prove that they are completely wrong or unreasonable. *demoler, echar por tierra* ❑ *Our intention was to demolish the rumors about him. Nuestra intención era apagar/callar los rumores sobre él.*

**dem|on|strate** /dɛmənstreɪt/ (**demonstrates, demonstrating, demonstrated**) **1** V-T To **demonstrate** a fact means to make it clear to people. *demostrar* ❑ *Studies have demonstrated the link between what we eat and the diseases we may suffer from. Los estudios han demostrado la relación entre lo que comemos y las enfermedades que podemos padecer.* ❑ *The party wants to demonstrate to the voters that they have practical policies. El partido quiere demostrar a los votantes que cuenta con políticas prácticas.* ● **dem|on|stra|tion** /dɛmənstreɪʃᵊn/ (**demonstrations**) N-COUNT *demostración* ❑ *It was a demonstration of power by the people of Moscow. Fue una demostración de poder del pueblo moscovita.* **2** V-T If you **demonstrate** a particular skill, quality, or feeling, you show by your actions that you have it. *demostrar* ❑ *They have demonstrated their ability to work together. Ya demostraron su aptitud para trabajar juntos.* ● **dem|on|stra|tion** N-COUNT *manifestación* ❑ *There's been no public demonstration of opposition to the president. No ha habido ninguna manifestación pública de oposición al presidente.* **3** V-I When people **demonstrate,** they march or gather somewhere to show their opposition to something or their support for something. *manifestarse* ❑ *200,000 people demonstrated against the war. 200,000 personas se manifestaron en contra de la guerra.* ❑ *In the cities, crowds demonstrated for change. Las multitudes se manifestaron en las ciudades por un cambio.* ● **dem|on|stra|tion** N-COUNT *manifestación* ❑ ...*an anti-government demonstration.* ...*una manifestación en contra del gobierno.* ● **de|mon|stra|tor** (**demonstrators**) N-COUNT *manifestante* ❑ *Police were dealing with a crowd of demonstrators. La policía estaba negociando con una multitud de manifestantes.* **4** V-T If you **demonstrate** something, you show people how it works or how to do it. *demostrar* ❑ *Several companies will be demonstrating their new products. Varias compañías demostrarán sus nuevos productos.* ● **dem|on|stra|tion** N-COUNT *demostración* ❑ ...*a cooking demonstration.* ...*una demostración de cocina.*

| Thesaurus | *demonstrate* | Ver también: |
|---|---|---|
| v. | describe, illustrate, prove, show **1** **4**<br>march, picket, protest **3** | |

**den|drite** /dɛndraɪt/ (**dendrites**) N-COUNT **Dendrites** are thin fibers with which nerve cells receive messages from other nerve cells. *dendrita* [TECHNICAL]

**de|ni|al** /dɪnaɪəl/ (**denials**) **1** N-VAR A **denial** of something is a statement that it is not true, does not exist, or did not happen. *desmentido* ❑ *...official denials of the government's involvement. ...los desmentidos oficiales del involucramiento del gobierno.* **2** N-UNCOUNT The **denial of** something to someone is the act of refusing to let them have it. *denegación* [FORMAL] ❑ *...the denial of visas to international workers. ...la denegación de visas a trabajadores extranjeros.*

**den|im** /dɛnɪm/ N-UNCOUNT **Denim** is a thick cotton cloth, usually blue, which is used to make clothes. Jeans are made from denim. *mezclilla, tela vaquera* ❑ *...a denim jacket. ...una chamarra/un saco de mezclilla.*

**de|noue|ment** /deɪnumɑn/ (**denouements**) also **dénouement** N-COUNT In a book, play, or series of events, the **denouement** is the sequence of events at the end, when things come to a conclusion. *desenlace*

**de|noue|ment de|sign** (**denouement designs**) N-COUNT In a book or play, the **denouement design** is the way that the main theme of the book or play is resolved. *desenlace* [TECHNICAL]

**Word Link** *nounce ≈ repoting : announce, denounce, pronounce*

**de|nounce** /dɪnaʊns/ (**denounces, denouncing, denounced**) V-T If you **denounce** a person or an action, you criticize them severely and publicly because you feel strongly that they are wrong or evil. *denunciar* ❑ *German leaders denounced the attacks. Algunos dirigentes alemanes denunciaron los ataques.*

**dense** /dɛns/ (**denser, densest**) **1** ADJ Something that is **dense** contains a lot of things or people in a small area. *denso* ❑ *...a large, dense forest. ...un bosque grande y denso.* ● **dense|ly** ADV *densamente* ❑ *Java is a densely populated island. Java es una isla densamente poblada.* **2** ADJ **Dense** fog or smoke is difficult to see through because it is very heavy and dark. *denso* ❑ *Dense smoke rose several miles into the air. Un denso humo se elevó varios kilómetros en el aire.* **3** ADJ In science, a **dense** substance is very heavy in relation to its volume. *denso, compacto* [TECHNICAL] ❑ *...a small dense star. ...una estrella densa/compacta pequeña.*

**den|sity** /dɛnsɪti/ (**densities**) **1** N-VAR **Density** is the extent to which something is filled or covered with people or things. *densidad* ❑ *The area has a very high population density. El área tiene una densidad demográfica muy alta.* **2** N-VAR In science, the **density** of a substance or object is the relation of its mass or weight to its volume. *densidad* [TECHNICAL] ❑ *Jupiter's moon Io has a density of 3.5 grams per cubic centimeter. La luna Io de Júpiter es de una densidad de 3.5 gramos por centímetro cúbico.*

**dent** /dɛnt/ (**dents, denting, dented**) **1** V-T If you **dent** the surface of something, you make a hollow area in it by hitting or pressing it. *abollar* ❑ *The stone dented the car's fender. La piedra abolló la salpicadera del coche.* **2** V-T If something **dents** your confidence or your pride, it makes you realize that you are not as good or successful as you thought. *hacer mella, herir* ❑ *Her comments dented Sebastian's pride. Sus comentarios hirieron el orgullo de Sebastian/hirieron a Sebastian en su orgullo.* **3** N-COUNT A **dent** is a hollow in the surface of something which has been caused by hitting or pressing it. *abolladura* ❑ *There was a dent in the car door. La puerta del coche tenía una abolladura.*

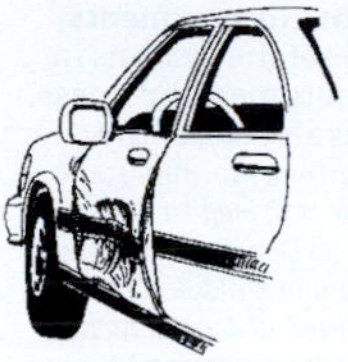
dent

**den|tal** /dɛntᵊl/ ADJ **Dental** is used to describe things that relate to teeth or to the care and treatment of teeth. *dental* ❑ *Regular dental care is important. El cuidado dental regular es importante.*

**den|tist** /dɛntɪst/ (**dentists**) N-COUNT A **dentist** is a medical practitioner who is qualified to examine and treat people's teeth. *dentista* ❑ *Visit your dentist twice a year for a checkup. Hágase revisar por su dentista dos veces al año.* ● **The dentist** or **the dentist's** is used to refer to the office or clinic where a dentist works. *dentista* ❑ *I'm going to the dentist's. Voy al dentista.*
→ see **teeth**

**den|tist's of|fice** (**dentist's offices**) N-COUNT A **dentist's office** is the room or house where a dentist works. *consultorio dental*

**den|tures** /dɛntʃərz/

The form **denture** is used as a modifier.

N-PLURAL **Dentures** are artificial teeth worn by people who no longer have all their own teeth. *dentadura (postiza), prótesis dental* ❑ *He had a new set of dentures. Tenía una nueva dentadura postiza.*
→ see **teeth**

**deny** /dɪnaɪ/ (**denies, denying, denied**) **1** V-T When you **deny** something, you state that it is not true. *negar* ❑ *She denied both accusations. Negó ambas acusaciones.* ❑ *He denied that he was involved in the crime. Negó que estuviera involucrado en el crimen.* **2** V-T If you **deny** someone something that they need or want, you refuse to let them have it. *denegar* ❑ *The military cannot deny prisoners access to lawyers. El ejército no puede denegar a los prisioneros la consulta con un abogado.*

**Word Partnership** Usar *deny* con:

V. **confirm or** deny **1**
N. deny **a charge, officials** deny **1**
deny **access**, deny **entry**, deny **a request** **2**

**de|odor|ant** /dioʊdərənt/ (**deodorants**) N-VAR **Deodorant** is a substance that you can use on your body to hide or prevent the smell of sweat. *desodorante*
→ see **petroleum**

**de|part** /dɪpɑrt/ (**departs, departing, departed**) V-T/V-I When something or someone **departs from** a place, they leave it and start a trip to another place. You can also say that someone **departs** a place *partir, salir, irse* ❑ *Flight 43 will depart from Denver at 11:45 a.m. El vuelo 43 partirá/saldrá de Denver* *a las 11:45 de la mañana.* ❑ *In the morning Mr. McDonald departed for Sydney. El señor McDonald salió para Sydney por la mañana.*

**de|part|ment** /dɪpɑrtmənt/ (**departments**) N-COUNT A **department** is one of the sections in an organization such as a government, business, or university. A department is also one of the sections in a large store. *departamento, ministerio, secretaría* ❑ *...the U.S. Department of Health and Human Services. ...la Secretaría (el Departamento) de Sanidad y Servicios Sociales de Estados Unidos.* ❑ *He moved to the sales department. Pasó al departamento de ventas.* ● **de|part|men|tal** /dipɑrtmɛntᵊl/ ADJ *departamental* ❑ *The Secretary of Education wants a bigger departmental budget. La Secretaría de Educación quiere un presupuesto más amplio.*

**de|part|ment store** (**department stores**) N-COUNT A **department store** is a large store which sells many different kinds of goods. *gran almacén, tienda de departamentos* ❑ *...famous department stores such as Macy's and Bloomingdales. ...tiendas de departamentos famosas, como Macy's y Bloomingdales.*

**de|par|ture** /dɪpɑrtʃər/ (**departures**) **1** N-VAR **Departure** or a **departure** is the act of going away from somewhere. *partida, salida* ❑ *...the president's departure for Helsinki. ...la partida del presidente para Helsinki.* ❑ *They wanted the departure of all foreign soldiers from the country. Querían la salida del país de todos los soldados extranjeros.* **2** N-COUNT If someone does something different or unusual, you can refer to their action as a **departure.** *desviación, alejamiento* ❑ *This was an unusual departure from tradition. Significaba apartarse de la tradición de manera inusual.*

**de|par|tures** /dɪpɑrtərz/ N-SING In an airport, **departures** is the place where passengers wait before they get onto their plane. *partida, salida*

**de|pend** /dɪpɛnd/ (**depends, depending, depended**) **1** V-I If you say that one thing **depends on** another, you mean that the first thing will be affected or determined by the second. *depender de* ❑ *The cooking time needed depends on the size of the potato. El tiempo de cocción necesario depende del tamaño de las papas.* **2** V-I If you **depend on** someone or something, you need them in order to be able to survive physically, financially, or emotionally. *depender de* ❑ *He depended on his writing for his income. Sus ingresos dependían de sus libros.* **3** V-I If you can **depend on** a person, organization, or law, you know that they will support you or help you when you need them. *depender de, contar con* ❑ *"You can depend on me," I assured him. —Puedes contar conmigo—le aseguré.* **4** V-I You use **depend** in expressions such as **it depends** to indicate that you cannot give a clear answer to a question because the answer will be affected or determined by other factors. *depender* ❑ *"How long can you stay?" — "I don't know. It depends." —¿Cuánto tiempo puedes quedarte?—No sé; depende.* **5** PHRASE You use **depending on** when you are saying that something varies according to the circumstances mentioned. *depender de* ❑ *The trip takes between two and three hours, depending on the traffic. El viaje toma entre dos y tres horas, dependiendo del tráfico.*

**de|pend|able** /dɪpɛndəbᵊl/ ADJ If you say that someone or something is **dependable,** you approve of them because you feel that you can be sure that they will always act consistently or sensibly, or do what you need them to do. *digno de confianza* ❑ *He was a dependable friend. Era un amigo con quien se podía contar.*

| Word Link | *ent ≈ one who does, has : dependent, resident, superintendent* |
|---|---|

**de|pend|ent** /dɪpɛndənt/ (**dependents**) also **dependant** **1** ADJ To be **dependent on** something or someone means to need them in order to succeed or be able to survive. *dependiente* ❑ *The local economy is dependent on oil. La economía local es dependiente del petróleo.* ● **de|pend|ence** N-UNCOUNT *dependencia* ❑ *...the city's dependence on tourism. ...la dependencia de la ciudad del turismo.* ● **de|pend|en|cy** N-UNCOUNT *dependencia* ❑ *...the dependency on chemicals for growing crops. ...la dependencia de los cultivos de las substancias químicas.* **2** N-COUNT Your **dependents** are the people you support financially, such as your children. *dependiente, persona a cargo* ❑ *...a single man with no dependents. ...un soltero sin personas a su cargo.*

**de|pict** /dɪpɪkt/ (**depicts, depicting, depicted**) V-T To **depict** someone or something means to show or represent them in a work of art such as a drawing or painting. *describir, representar* ❑ *...pictures depicting Lee's most famous battles. ...cuadros que representan las batallas más famosas de Lee.* ● **de|pic|tion** N-VAR (**depictions**) *descripción* ❑ *...their depiction in the book as thieves. ...su descripción en el libro como ladrones.*
→ see art

| Word Link | *ple ≈ filling : complement, complete, deplete* |
|---|---|

**de|plete** /dɪplit/ (**depletes, depleting, depleted**) V-T To **deplete** a stock or amount of something means to reduce it. *reducir, agotar* [FORMAL] ❑ *...substances that deplete the ozone layer. ...substancias que reducen la capa de ozono.* ● **de|plet|ed** ADJ *agotado, exhausto, reducido* ❑ *...Lee's tired and depleted army. ...el reducido y cansado ejército de Lee.* ● **de|ple|tion** /dɪpliʃᵊn/ N-UNCOUNT *reducción, disminución, agotamiento* ❑ *...the depletion of water supplies. ...la reducción del suministro de agua.*

**de|ploy** /dɪplɔɪ/ (**deploys, deploying, deployed**) V-T To **deploy** troops or military resources means to organize or position them so that they are ready to be used. *desplegar* ❑ *The president has no intention of deploying troops. El presidente no tiene intención de desplegar tropas.* ● **de|ploy|ment** N-VAR (**deployments**) *despliegue* ❑ *...the deployment of soldiers. ...el despliegue de soldados.*
→ see army

**de|port** /dɪpɔrt/ (**deports, deporting, deported**) V-T If a government **deports** someone, usually someone who is not a citizen of that country, it sends them out of the country because they have committed a crime or because it believes they do not have the right to be there. *deportar* ❑ *...a government decision to deport all illegal immigrants. ...una decisión gubernamental para deportar a todos los inmigrantes ilegales.* ● **de|por|ta|tion** /dipɔrteɪʃᵊn/ N-VAR (**deportations**) *deportación* ❑ *Thousands of* people face deportation. *Miles de personas enfrentan la deportación.*

**Word Link** *pos ≈ placing : deposit, preposition, repository*

**de|pos|it** /dɪpɒzɪt/ (**deposits, depositing, deposited**) **1** N-COUNT A **deposit** is a sum of money which is part of the full price of something, and which you pay when you agree to buy it or rent it. *depósito, entrega/pago inicial, enganche* ❑ *He put down a deposit of $500 for the car. Dio un enganche de 500 dólares por el carro.* **2** N-COUNT A **deposit** is an amount of a substance that has been left somewhere as a result of a chemical or geological process. *sedimento, yacimiento* ❑ *...underground deposits of gold. ...yacimientos de oro subterráneos.* **3** N-COUNT A **deposit** is a sum of money which you put into a bank account. *depósito* ❑ *I made a deposit every week. Hice un depósito cada semana.* **4** V-T If you **deposit** a sum of money, you put it into a bank account or savings account. *depositar* ❑ *The customer has to deposit a minimum of $100 monthly. El cliente debe depositar un mínimo mensual de 100 dólares.*

**depo|si|tion** /dɛpəzɪʃᵊn/ N-UNCOUNT **Deposition** is a geological process in which material that has been carried by the wind or water from one area is left on the surface of another area. *depósito, sedimento* [TECHNICAL]

**de|press** /dɪprɛs/ (**depresses, depressing, depressed**) **1** V-T If someone or something **depresses** you, they make you feel sad and disappointed. *deprimir* ❑ *The state of the country depresses me. La situación del país me deprime.* **2** V-T If something **depresses** prices, wages, or figures, it causes them to become less. *reducir* ❑ *The stronger U.S. dollar depressed sales. Un dólar estadounidense más fuerte redujo las ventas.*

**de|pressed** /dɪprɛst/ **1** ADJ If you are **depressed,** you are sad and feel that you cannot enjoy anything. *deprimido* ❑ *She was very depressed after her husband died. Estaba muy deprimida después de la muerte de su esposo.* **2** ADJ A **depressed** place or industry does not have enough business or employment to be successful. *deprimido, en crisis* ❑ *..plans to encourage more business in depressed areas. ...planes para impulsar más negocios en las áreas deprimidas.*

**de|press|ing** /dɪprɛsɪŋ/ ADJ Something that is **depressing** makes you feel sad and disappointed. *deprimente* ❑ *The view from the window was gray and depressing. La vista desde la ventana era gris y deprimente.* ● **de|press|ing|ly** ADV *que es deprimente* ❑ *The story sounded depressingly familiar to Janet. La historia le pareció familiar a Janet por lo deprimente.*

**de|pres|sion** /dɪprɛʃᵊn/ (**depressions**) **1** N-VAR **Depression** is a mental state in which you are sad and feel that you cannot enjoy anything. *depresión* ❑ *Mr. Thomas was suffering from depression. El señor Thomas sufría de una depresión.* **2** N-COUNT A **depression** is a time when there is very little economic activity, which causes a lot of unemployment and poverty. *depresión, crisis* ❑ *...the Great Depression of the 1930s. ...la gran depresión de los años 1930.* **3** N-COUNT A **depression** in a surface is an area which is lower than the parts surrounding it. *depresión* ❑ *...rain-filled depressions. ...depresiones inundadas por la lluvia.*

**de|prive** /dɪpraɪv/ (**deprives, depriving, deprived**) V-T If you **deprive** someone **of** something that they want or need, you take it away from them, or you prevent them from having it. *privar de* ❑ *They were deprived of fuel to heat their homes. Carecían del combustible para calentar sus hogares.* ● **dep|ri|va|tion** /dɛprɪveɪʃᵊn/ N-VAR (**deprivations**) *privación, falta* ❑ *Many people suffer from sleep deprivation caused by long work hours. Mucha gente sufre de falta de sueño causada por las jornadas de trabajo muy largas.* ● **de|prived** ADJ *desposeído, que padece carencias* ❑ *...the most severely deprived children in the country. ...los niños con carencias más severas/graves en el país.*

**depth** /dɛpθ/ (**depths**) **1** N-VAR The **depth** of something such as a river or hole is the distance downward from its top surface, or between its upper and lower surfaces. *profundidad* ❑ *The depth of the hole is 520 yards. La profundidad del hoyo es de 475.5 metros.* ❑ *The lake is fourteen feet in depth. El lago tiene una profundidad de 4.25 metros.* **2** N-VAR The **depth** of something such as a closet or drawer is the distance between its front surface and its back. *profundidad, fondo* **3** N-VAR If an emotion is very strongly or intensely felt, you can talk about its **depth**. *profundidad* ❑ *...the depth of feeling on the subject. ...la profundiad del sentimiento sobre el asunto.* **4** N-UNCOUNT The **depth** of a situation is its extent and seriousness. *profundidad* ❑ *The president underestimated the depth of the crisis. El presidente subestimó la profundidad de la crisis.* **5** N-UNCOUNT The **depth** of someone's knowledge is the great amount that they know. *profundidad* ❑ *We were impressed with the depth of her knowledge. Estábamos impresionados por la profundidad de sus conocimientos.* **6** N-PLURAL If you talk about **the depths of** an area, you mean the parts of it which are very far from the edge. *profundo* ❑ *...the depths of the countryside. ...lo profundo del campo/la campiña.* **7** N-PLURAL If you are **in the depths of** an unpleasant emotion, you feel that emotion very strongly. *en lo más hondo* ❑ *I was in the depths of despair before I met you. Estaba en la desesperación más profunda antes de conocerte.* **8** PHRASE If you deal with a subject **in depth,** you deal with it very thoroughly and consider all the aspects of it. *en profundidad* ❑ *We will discuss these three areas in depth. Discutiremos esos tres aspectos en profundidad.* **9** → see also **in-depth** **10** PHRASE If you say that someone is **out of** their **depth,** you mean that they are in a situation that is much too difficult for them to be able to cope with it. *no saber en qué terreno se pisa* ❑ *Mr. Gibson is intellectually out of his depth. Intelectualmente, el señor Gibson no sabe en qué terreno pisa.*

**depu|ty** /dɛpyəti/ (**deputies**) **1** N-COUNT A **deputy** is the second most important person in an organization such as a business or government department. Someone's deputy often acts on their behalf when they are not there. *segundo, asistente, vice-* ❑ *...Jack Lang, France's minister for culture, and his deputy, Catherine Tasca. ...Jack Lang, ministro de cultura de Francia, y su subsecretaria, Catherine Tasca.* **2** N-COUNT A **deputy** is a police officer. *ayudante (de la policía)* ❑ *Robyn asked the deputy if she could speak with Sheriff Adkins. Robyn preguntó al ayudante si podía hablar con el sheriff Adkins.*

d

D

**der|by** /dɜrbi/ (**derbies**) **1** N-COUNT A **derby** is a sports competition or race where there are no restrictions or limits on who can enter. *clásico, competencia, derby* ❑ *...the annual fishing derby at Lake Winnipesaukee. ...la competencia anual de pesca en el lago Winnipesaukee.* **2** N-COUNT A **derby** is a round, hard hat with a narrow brim which is worn by men. Derbies are no longer very common. *bombín, (sombrero) hongo*

**de|rive** /dɪraɪv/ (**derives, deriving, derived**) **1** V-T If you **derive** something such as pleasure or benefit **from** a person or from something, you get it from them. *obtener, derivar* [FORMAL] ❑ *Many people derive pleasure from helping others. Muchas personas obtienen placer de la ayuda a los demás.* **2** V-T/V-I If you say that something such as a word or feeling **derives** or **is derived from** something else, you mean that it comes from that thing. *derivar* ❑ *The name Anastasia is derived from a Greek word. El nombre Anastasia se deriva de una palabra griega.*

**der|ma|tolo|gist** /dɜrmətɒlədʒɪst/ (**dermatologists**) N-COUNT A **dermatologist** is a doctor who specializes in the study of skin and the treatment of skin diseases. *dermatólogo o dermatóloga* ● **der|ma|tol|ogy** N-UNCOUNT *dermatología* ❑ *...drugs used in dermatology. ...drogas que se emplean en la dermatología.*
→ see **skin**

**der|mis** /dɜrmɪs/ N-SING The **dermis** is the layer of skin beneath the epidermis. *dermis* [TECHNICAL]

**de|sali|na|tion** /disælɪneɪʃᵊn/ N-UNCOUNT **Desalination** is the process of removing salt from sea water so that it can be used for drinking, or for watering crops. *desalinización*

**des|cant** /dɛskænt/ (**descants**) N-COUNT A **descant** is a tune which is played or sung above the main tune in a piece of music. *contrapunto*

| Word Link | *de ≈ from, down, away : deduct, descend, detach* |
|---|---|

**de|scend** /dɪsɛnd/ (**descends, descending, descended**) **1** V-T/V-I If you **descend** or if you **descend** a staircase, you move downward from a higher to a lower level. *descender* [FORMAL] ❑ *We descended to the basement. Descendimos al sótano.* **2** V-I If a large group of people arrive to see you, especially if their visit is unexpected or causes you a lot of work, you can say that they **have descended on** you. *invadir* ❑ *Thousands of tourists descend on the area each year. Miles de turistas invaden la región cada año.* **3** V-I When you want to emphasize that the situation that someone is entering is very bad, you can say that they **are descending into** that situation. *caer, entrar* ❑ *The country descended into chaos. El país cayó en el caos.* **4** V-I If you say that someone **descends to** behavior which you consider unacceptable, you are expressing your disapproval of the fact that they do it. *rebajarse* ❑ *We're not going to descend to such methods. No vamos a rebajarnos a tales métodos.*

**de|scribe** /dɪskraɪb/ (**describes, describing, described**) **1** V-T If you **describe** a person, object, event, or situation, you say what they are like or what happened. *describir* ❑ *She described what she did in her spare time. Describió lo que hizo en su tiempo libre.* ❑ *The poem describes their life together. El poema describe su vida en común.* **2** V-T If you **describe** someone or something **as** a particular thing, you say that they are like that thing. *describir* ❑ *He described it as the worst job in the world. Lo describió como el peor trabajo del mundo.* ❑ *Even his closest friends describe him as forceful and determined. Incluso sus amigos íntimos lo describen como enérgico y resuelto.*

**de|scrip|tion** /dɪskrɪpʃᵊn/ (**descriptions**) N-VAR A **description** of someone or something is an account which explains what they are or what they look like. *descripción* ❑ *Police have issued a description of the man. La policía hizo pública una descripción del sujeto.* ❑ *He gave a detailed description of how the new system will work. Dio una descripción detallada de cómo va a funcionar el nuevo sistema.*

| Thesaurus | *description* | Ver también: |
|---|---|---|
| N. | account, characterization, summary | |

| Word Partnership | Usar *description* con: |
|---|---|
| ADJ. | **accurate** description, **brief** description, **detailed** description, **physical** description, **vague** description |
| V. | **fit a** description, **give a** description, **match a** description |

**de|scrip|tive** /dɪskrɪptɪv/ ADJ **Descriptive** language or writing indicates what someone or something is like. *descriptivo* ❑ *Being descriptive doesn't require a string of adjectives and adverbs. Often a strong verb gives a more precise picture in fewer words. Para ser descriptivo no se requiere una sarta de adjetivos y adverbios. Frecuentemente, un verbo bien seleccionado traza un cuadro más preciso con menos palabras.*

**de|scrip|tive de|sign** (**descriptive designs**) N-VAR Research that has a **descriptive design** involves studying the similarities and differences between two or more things. *diseño descriptivo*

**des|ert** (**deserts, deserting, deserted**)

The noun is pronounced /dɛzərt/. The verb is pronounced /dɪzɜrt/ and is hyphenated de|sert.

**1** N-VAR A **desert** is a large area of land, usually in a hot region, where there is almost no water, rain, trees, or plants. *desierto* ❑ *...the Sahara Desert. ...el desierto del Sáhara.* **2** V-T If people or animals **desert** a place, they leave it and it becomes empty. *abandonar* ❑ *Poor farmers are deserting their fields and coming to the cities to find jobs. Los agricultores pobres están abandonando sus campos y yendo a las ciudades en busca de trabajo.* ● **de|sert|ed** ADJ *desierto* ❑ *She led them into a deserted street. Los llevó a una calle desierta.* **3** V-T If someone **deserts** you, they go away and leave you, and no longer help or support you. *abandonar* ❑ *Mrs. Roding's husband deserted her years ago. El esposo de la señora Roding la abandonó hace años.* ● **de|ser|tion** /dɪzɜrʃᵊn/ N-VAR (**desertions**) *abandono* ❑ *...her father's desertion. ...el abandono de su padre.* **4** V-T/V-I If someone **deserts**, or **deserts** a job, especially a job in the armed forces, they leave that job without permission. *desertar* ❑ *He was an officer in the army until he deserted. Fue oficial del ejército hasta que desertó.* ❑ *He deserted from the army last month. Desertó del ejército el mes pasado.* ● **de|sert|er** /dɪzɜrtər/ N-COUNT (**deserters**) *desertor o desertora* ❑ *Two deserters were*

Picture Dictionary

shot. *Mataron a dos desertores.* • **de|ser|tion** N-VAR *deserción* ❑ *Two soldiers face charges of desertion. Dos soldados enfrentan cargos por deserción.*
→ see Picture Dictionary: **desert**
→ see **habitat**

**de|serve** /dɪzɜrv/ (**deserves, deserving, deserved**) V-T If you say that a person or thing **deserves** something, you mean that they should have it or receive it because of their actions or qualities. *merecer* ❑ *Government officials clearly deserve some of the blame. Es evidente que los funcionarios gubernamentales tienen parte de la culpa.* ❑ *These people deserve to get more money. Esta gente merece recibir más dinero.*

| Word Partnership | Usar *deserve* con: |
|---|---|
| N. | deserve **a chance**, deserve **credit**, deserve **recognition**, deserve **respect** |
| V. | **don't** deserve, deserve **to know** |
| PRON. | deserve **nothing** |

**de|sign** /dɪzaɪn/ (**designs, designing, designed**) **1** V-T When you **design** something new, you plan what it should be like. *diseñar* ❑ *They wanted to design a machine that was both attractive and practical. Querían diseñar una máquina que fuese atractiva y práctica a la vez.* **2** N-UNCOUNT **Design** is the process and art of planning and making detailed drawings of something. *diseño* ❑ *He had a talent for design. Tenía talento para el diseño.* **3** N-UNCOUNT The **design** of something is the way in which it has been planned and made. *diseño* ❑ *...a new design of clock. ...un nuevo diseño de reloj.* **4** N-COUNT A **design** is a drawing which someone produces to show how they would like something to be built or made. *diseño* ❑ *They drew up the design for the house. Dibujaron el diseño para la casa.* **5** N-COUNT A **design** is a pattern of lines, flowers, or shapes which is used to decorate something. *diseño* ❑ *Many pictures are based on simple designs. Muchos cuadros se basan en diseños simples.* **6** N-UNCOUNT In the theater, **design** is the planning and making of things such as the costumes, sets, and lighting for a play or other production. *diseño*
→ see **architecture, quilt**

**des|ig|nate** (**designates, designating, designated**)

> The verb is pronounced /dɛzɪgneɪt/. The adjective is pronounced /dɛzɪgnɪt/.

**1** V-T When you **designate** someone or something **as** a particular thing, you formally give them that description or name. *designar, declarar* ❑ *The president designated Sunday, February 3rd, as a national day of prayer for peace. El presidente declaró el domingo 3 de febrero como día nacional de oración por la paz.* ❑ *...plans to designate the hotel a historic building. ...planes para declarar el hotel como monumento histórico.* • **des|ig|na|tion** /dɛzɪgneɪʃᵊn/ N-VAR (**designations**) *clasificación* ❑ *The NC-17 designation for motion pictures stands for no children under 17 admitted. La clasificación NC-17 para las películas significa que no son aptas para menores de 17 años.* **2** V-T If something **is designated for** a particular purpose, it is set aside for that purpose. *designar* ❑ *Some of the rooms were designated as offices. Algunos de los cuartos fueron designados para oficinas.* **3** ADJ **Designate** is used to describe someone who has been formally chosen to do a particular job, but has not yet started doing it. *designado* ❑ *...Japan's prime minister-designate. ...el primer ministro designado de Japón.*

**de|sign|er** /dɪzaɪnər/ (**designers**) **1** N-COUNT A **designer** is a person whose job is to design things by making drawings of them. *diseñador o*

d

diseñadora ❑ *Carolyne is a fashion designer.* *Carolyne es diseñadora de modas.* **2** ADJ **Designer** clothes or **designer** labels are expensive, fashionable clothes made by a famous designer, rather than being made in large quantities in a factory. *de diseño (exclusivo)* ❑ *He wears designer clothes.* *Usa ropa de diseño (exclusivo).*

D

**de|sir|able** /dɪzaɪərəbᵊl/ ADJ Something that is **desirable** is worth having or doing because it is useful, necessary, or popular. *deseable, atractivo, conveniente* ❑ *The house is in a desirable neighborhood, close to schools.* *La casa está en un vecindario conveniente, cercano a las escuelas.* ● **de|sir|abil|ity** /dɪzaɪərəbɪlɪti/ N-UNCOUNT *conveniencia* ❑ *...the desirability of political change.* *...la conveniencia de un cambio político.* ● **de|sir|abil|ity** N-UNCOUNT *conveniencia* ❑ *...our attractiveness and desirability as a partner.* *...nuestro atractivo y conveniencia como socios.*

**de|sire** /dɪzaɪər/ (**desires, desiring, desired**) **1** N-COUNT A **desire** is a strong wish to do or have something. *deseo, anhelo* ❑ *I had a strong desire to help people.* *Tenía un fuerte anhelo de ayudar a la gente.* **2** V-T If you **desire** something, you want it. *desear, anhelar* [FORMAL] ❑ *She desired a child with her new husband.* *Deseaba tener un hijo con su nuevo esposo.* ● **de|sired** ADJ *deseado* ❑ *This will produce the desired effect.* *Esto producirá el efecto deseado.*

**Word Partnership** Usar *desire* con:

N. **heart's** desire **1**
ADJ. **sexual** desire, **strong** desire **1**
V. **express** desire, **have no** desire, **satisfy a** desire **1**
desire **to change** **1** **2**

**desk** /dɛsk/ (**desks**) **1** N-COUNT A **desk** is a table, often with drawers, which you sit at to write or work. *escritorio* **2** N-SING The place in a hotel, hospital, airport, or other building where you check in or obtain information is referred to as a particular **desk**. *mostrador* ❑ *They asked at the desk for Miss Minton.* *Preguntaron por la señorita Minton en el mostrador (de información).*
→ see **office**

**desk|top** /dɛsktɒp/ (**desktops**) also **desk-top** **1** ADJ **Desktop** computers are a convenient size for using on a desk or table, but are not designed to be portable. *de escritorio* ❑ *It was the smallest desktop computer ever produced.* *Era la computadora de escritorio más pequeña jamás fabricada.* ● **Desktop** is also a noun. *computadora de escritorio* ❑ *We have stopped making desktops.* *Ya dejamos de fabricar computadoras de escritorio.* **2** N-COUNT The **desktop** of a computer is the display of icons that you see on the screen when the computer is ready to use. *escritorio, pantalla* ❑ *You can rearrange the icons on the desktop.* *Puedes reordenar los iconos en la pantalla.*

**des|pair** /dɪspɛər/ (**despairs, despairing, despaired**) **1** N-UNCOUNT **Despair** is the feeling that everything is wrong and that nothing will improve. *desesperación* ❑ *I looked at my wife in despair.* *Miré a mi esposa con desesperación.* **2** V-I If you **despair,** you feel that everything is wrong and that nothing will improve. *desesperar* ❑ *"Oh, I despair sometimes," he said.* *—¡Oh! A veces desespero—dijo.* **3** V-I If you **despair of** something, you feel that there is no hope that it will happen or improve. If you **despair of** someone, you feel that there is no hope that they will improve. *perder la esperanza* ❑ *She despaired of making him understand her.* *Perdió la esperanza de hacerlo entender.*

**Word Link** *ate ≈ filled with : accurate, considerate, desperate*

**des|per|ate** /dɛspərɪt/ **1** ADJ If you are **desperate,** you are in such a bad situation that you are willing to try anything to change it. *desesperado* ❑ *Troops helped to get food to places where people are in desperate need.* *Las tropas ayudaron a llevar alimentos a los lugares donde la gente los necesitaba con mayor desesperación.* ● **des|per|ate|ly** ADV *desesperadamente* ❑ *Thousands of people are desperately trying to leave the country.* *Miles de personas están tratando desesperadamente de salir del país.* **2** ADJ If you are **desperate for** something or **desperate to** do something, you want or need it very much indeed. *desesperado* ❑ *June was desperate to have a baby.* *June estaba desesperada por tener un bebé.* ● **des|per|ate|ly** ADV *desesperadamente* ❑ *He was a boy who desperately needed affection.* *Era un niño que necesitaba afecto desesperadamente.* **3** ADJ A **desperate** situation is very difficult, serious, or dangerous. *desesperado* ❑ *...his desperate financial position.* *...su desesperada situación económica.*

**Word Partnership** Usar *desperate* con:

N. desperate **act**, desperate **attempt**, desperate **measures**, desperate **need**, desperate **struggle** **1**
desperate **situation** **3**
V. **sound** desperate **1**
**grow** desperate **1**–**3**

**de|spite** /dɪspaɪt/ PREP You use **despite** to introduce a fact which makes something surprising. *a pesar de* ❑ *The event was a success, despite the rain.* *El acto fue un éxito, a pesar de la lluvia.*

**des|sert** /dɪzɜrt/ (**desserts**) N-VAR **Dessert** is something sweet, such as fruit, pastry, or ice cream, that you eat at the end of a meal. *postre* ❑ *She had ice cream for dessert.* *Tomó helado como postre.*
→ see Picture Dictionary: **dessert**

**des|ti|na|tion** /dɛstɪneɪʃᵊn/ (**destinations**) N-COUNT Your **destination** is the place you are going to. *destino* ❑ *Ellis Island is one of America's most popular tourist destinations.* *La isla de Ellis es uno de los destinos turísticos más populares de Estados Unidos.*

**des|tined** /dɛstɪnd/ ADJ If something is **destined to** happen or if someone is **destined to** behave in a particular way, that thing seems certain to happen or be done. *destinado* ❑ *The plan is destined to fail.* *El plan está destinado al fracaso.*

**des|ti|ny** /dɛstɪni/ (**destinies**) **1** N-COUNT A person's **destiny** is everything that happens to them during their life, including what will happen in the future, especially when it is considered to be controlled by someone or something else. *destino* ❑ *Do we control our own destiny?* *¿Somos dueños de nuestro propio destino?* **2** N-UNCOUNT **Destiny** is the force which some people believe controls the things that happen to you in your life. *destino* ❑ *Is it destiny that brings people together, or is it accident?* *¿Es el destino lo que une a la gente o el azar?*

**Picture Dictionary** dessert

ice cream · cake · pie · cookies · cheesecake

custard · brownie · chocolate mousse · rice pudding · fruit salad

**de|stroy** /dɪstrɔɪ/ (**destroys, destroying, destroyed**) v-T To **destroy** something means to cause so much damage to it that it is completely ruined or does not exist any more. *destruir, arruinar* ❑ *The plan will destroy the economy. El plan arruinará la economía.* ● **de|struc|tion** /dɪstrʌkʃⁿn/ N-UNCOUNT *destrucción* ❑ *...an international agreement aimed at stopping the destruction of the ozone layer. ...un convenio internacional con el propósito de detener la destrucción de la capa de ozono.*

| **Thesaurus** | *destroy* | Ver también: |
|---|---|---|
| v. | annihilate, crush, demolish, eradicate, ruin, wipe out; (*ant.*) build, construct, create, repair | |

| **Word Link** | *struct ≈ building : con**struct**, de**struct**ive, in**struct*** |
|---|---|

**de|struc|tive** /dɪstrʌktɪv/ ADJ Something that is **destructive** causes or is capable of causing great damage, harm, or injury. *destructivo* ❑ *...the destructive power of nuclear weapons. ...el poder destructivo de las armas nucleares.*

| **Word Link** | *de ≈ from, down, away : **de**duct, **de**scend, **de**tach* |
|---|---|

**de|tach** /dɪtætʃ/ (**detaches, detaching, detached**) v-T/v-I If you **detach** one thing from another that it is attached to, you remove it. If one thing **detaches from** another, it becomes separated from it. *separar(se)* [FORMAL] ❑ *Detach the card and mail it to this address. Separe la tarjeta y envíela por correo a esta dirección.* ❑ *They tried to detach the kite from the tree. Trataron de desenredar el papalote del árbol.*

**de|tail** /dɪteɪl/ (**details, detailing, detailed**)

The pronunciation /dɪteɪl/ is also used for the noun.

**1** N-COUNT The **details of** something are its small, individual features or elements. *detalle* ❑ *The details of the plan are still being worked out. Todavía se está trabajando en los detalles del plan.* ❑ *They gave no details of the discussions. No dieron detalles sobre las negociaciones.* **2** N-PLURAL **Details** about someone or something are facts or pieces of information about them. *detalle* ❑ *See the bottom of this page for details of how to apply for this offer. Consulte en el pie de la página los detalles sobre cómo solicitar esta oferta.*

**3** v-T If you **detail** things, you list them or give information about them. *detallar* ❑ *The report detailed the mistakes which were made. En el informe estaban detallados los errores cometidos.* **4** PHRASE If you examine or discuss something **in detail**, you do it thoroughly and carefully. *en detalle* ❑ *Examine the contract in detail before signing it. Lee el contrato minuciosamente antes de firmarlo.*

| **Thesaurus** | *detail* | Ver también: |
|---|---|---|
| N. | component, element, feature, point **1** **2** fact, information **2** | |
| v. | depict, describe, specify; (*ant.*) approximate, generalize **3** | |

**de|tailed** /dɪteɪld/ ADJ A **detailed** report or plan contains a lot of details. *detallado* ❑ *The letter contains a detailed account of the decisions. La carta incluye una explicación detallada de las decisiones.*

| **Word Partnership** | Usar *detailed* con: |
|---|---|
| N. | detailed **account**, detailed **analysis**, detailed **description**, detailed **instructions**, detailed **plan**, detailed **record** |

**de|tain** /dɪteɪn/ (**detains, detaining, detained**) **1** v-T When people such as the police **detain** someone, they keep them in a place under their control. *detener* [FORMAL] ❑ *Police have detained two people in connection with the attack. La policía detuvo a dos personas relacionadas con el ataque.* **2** v-T To **detain** someone means to delay them, for example, by talking to them. *demorar* [FORMAL] ❑ *Could I ask just one more question—if I'm not detaining you? —No quisiera demorarlo, pero, ¿podría hacerle otra pregunta?*

**de|tain|ee** /dɪteɪni/ (**detainees**) N-COUNT A **detainee** is someone who is held prisoner by a government because of his or her political views or activities. *detenido, preso* ❑ *...the release of political detainees. ...la liberación de los presos políticos.*

| **Word Link** | *tect ≈ covering : de**tect**, pro**tect**, pro**tect**ive* |
|---|---|

**de|tect** /dɪtɛkt/ (**detects, detecting, detected**) v-T If you **detect** something, you find it or notice it. *detectar, notar, advertir* ❑ *...a piece of equipment used to detect heat. ...un dispositivo utilizado para detectar el calor.* ❑ *Arnold could detect a sadness in the* *old man's face. Arnold pudo advertir la tristeza en el rostro del anciano.* ● **de|tec|tion** N-UNCOUNT *detección, descubrimiento, diagnóstico* ❑ *...the early detection of cancer. ...el descubrimiento oportuno del cáncer.*

**de|tec|tive** /dɪtɛktɪv/ (**detectives**) N-COUNT
A **detective** is someone whose job is to discover what has happened in a crime or other situation and to find the people involved. Some detectives work in the police force and others work privately. *detective* ❑ *Detectives are appealing for witnesses to the attack. Los detectives están haciendo un llamado a que se presenten los testigos del ataque.*

**de|ten|tion** /dɪtɛnʃ°n/ (**detentions**)
■ N-UNCOUNT **Detention** is when someone is arrested or put into prison. *detención* ❑ *...the detention of people involved in crime. ...la detención de personas involucradas en el crimen.* ■ N-VAR **Detention** is a punishment for students who misbehave, who are made to stay at school after the other students have gone home. *castigo* ❑ *He kept most of the class after school for detention. Retuvo a la mayor parte del grupo después de clases como castigo.*

**de|ten|tion cen|ter** (**detention centers**)
N-COUNT A **detention center** is a sort of prison, for example, a place where people who have entered a country illegally are kept while a decision is made about what to do with them. *centro de detención*

**de|ter** /dɪtɜr/ (**deters, deterring, deterred**) V-T
To **deter** someone **from** doing something means to make them not want to do it or continue doing it. *disuadir* ❑ *High prices deter people from buying. Los precios altos disuaden a la gente de comprar.*

**de|ter|gent** /dɪtɜrdʒ°nt/ (**detergents**) N-VAR
**Detergent** is a chemical substance, usually in the form of a powder or liquid, which is used for washing things such as clothes or dishes. *detergente* ❑ *...a type of detergent. ...un tipo de detergente.*
→ see **soap, teeth**

**de|terio|rate** /dɪtɪəriəreɪt/ (**deteriorates, deteriorating, deteriorated**) V-I If something **deteriorates**, it becomes worse in some way. *deteriorar, degenerar en* ❑ *The situation might deteriorate into war. La situación podría degenerar en una guerra.* ● **de|terio|ra|tion** /dɪtɪəriəreɪʃ°n/ N-UNCOUNT *deterioro* ❑ *...concern about the deterioration in relations between the two countries. ...la preocupación por el deterioro de las relaciones entre los dos países.*

**de|ter|mi|na|tion** /dɪtɜrmɪneɪʃ°n/
■ N-UNCOUNT **Determination** is the quality that you show when you have decided to do something and you will not let anything stop you. *determinación* ❑ *Everyone behaved with courage and determination. Todos actuaron con valor y determinación.* ■ → see also **determine**

**de|ter|mine** /dɪtɜrmɪn/ (**determines, determining, determined**) ■ V-T If something **determines** what will happen, it controls it. *determinar* [FORMAL] ❑ *The size of the chicken pieces will determine the cooking time. El tamaño de las piezas de pollo determina el tiempo de cocción.*

● **de|ter|mi|na|tion** N-UNCOUNT *determinación* ❑ *This gene is responsible for eye color determination. Este gen es el responsable de la determinación del color de los ojos.* ■ V-T To **determine** a fact means to discover it as a result of investigation. *determinar* [FORMAL] ❑ *The investigation will determine what really happened. La indagación determinará lo que realmente pasó.* ❑ *Testing must be done to determine the long-term effects on humans. Se debe hacer pruebas para determinar los efectos en el largo plazo para los seres humanos.* ● **de|ter|mi|na|tion** N-UNCOUNT *determinación* ❑ *...a determination of guilt or innocence. ...la determinación de culpabilidad o inocencia.*

**de|ter|mined** /dɪtɜrmɪnd/ ADJ If you are **determined to** do something, you have made a firm decision to do it and will not let anything stop you. *determinado, decidido, resuelto* ❑ *His enemies are determined to ruin him. Sus enemigos están decididos a arruinarlo.*

**de|ter|min|er** /dɪtɜrmɪnər/ (**determiners**)
N-COUNT In grammar, a **determiner** is a word which is used at the beginning of a noun group to indicate, for example, which thing you are referring to or whether you are referring to one thing or several. Common English determiners are "a," "the," "some," "this," and "each." *determinante*

**de|tour** /dɪtʊər/ (**detours**) ■ N-COUNT If you make a **detour** on a trip, you go by a route which is not the shortest way, because you want to avoid something such as a traffic jam, or because there is something you want to do on the way. *rodeo* ❑ *He did not take the direct route to his home, but made a detour. No tomó el camino directo a su casa, sino que*

**detour**

*dio un rodeo.* ■ N-COUNT A **detour** is a special route for traffic to follow when the normal route is blocked, for example, because it is being repaired. *desviación* ❑ *A detour in the road is causing major problems for businesses. Una desviación en la carretera está causando grandes problemas a los negocios.*

**de|value** /divælyu/ (**devalues, devaluing, devalued**) ■ V-T To **devalue** something means to cause it to be thought less impressive or less deserving of respect. *subestimar, menospreciar* ❑ *They tried to devalue her work. Trataron de menospreciar su trabajo.* ■ V-T To **devalue** the currency of a country means to reduce its value in relation to other currencies. *devaluar* ❑ *India has devalued the rupee by about eleven percent. India devaluó la rupia en aproximadamente el once por ciento.* ● **de|valua|tion** /divælyueɪʃ°n/ N-VAR (**devaluations**) *devaluación* ❑ *It resulted in the devaluation of several currencies. El resultado fue la devaluación de varias monedas.*

**dev|as|tate** /dɛvəsteɪt/ (**devastates, devastating, devastated**) V-T If something **devastates** an area or a place, it damages it very badly or destroys it totally. *devastar, asolar* ❑ *The earthquake devastated parts of Indonesia. El terremoto devastó partes de Indonesia.* ● **dev|as|ta|tion** /dɛvəsteɪʃ°n/ N-UNCOUNT *devastación* ❑ *The war* brought massive devastation to the area. La guerra causó la devastación generalizada de la zona.

**dev|as|tat|ing** /dɛvəsteɪtɪŋ/ ADJ If you describe something as **devastating**, you are emphasizing that it is very harmful or upsetting. devastador, aniquilador ❑ We must find a cure for this devastating disease. Debemos encontrar una cura para esta enfermedad aniquiladora. ❑ When I heard about my dad's illness, it was devastating. Cuando me enteré de la enfermedad de mi papá, quedé destrozado.

**de|vel|op** /dɪvɛləp/ (**develops, developing, developed**) 1 V-I When something **develops**, it grows or changes over a period of time and usually becomes more advanced, complete, or severe. desarrollar, evolucionar, degenerar en ❑ It's difficult to know how the market will develop. Es difícil saber cómo evolucionará el mercado. ❑ This violence could develop into war. La violencia podría degenerar en una guerra. • **de|vel|oped** ADJ desarrollado ❑ Their bodies were well developed and super fit. Sus cuerpos estaban bien desarrollados y completamente en forma. • **de|vel|op|ment** N-UNCOUNT desarrollo, evolución ❑ ...the development of language. ...el desarrollo del lenguaje. 2 V-I If a problem or difficulty **develops**, it begins to occur. surgir, presentarse ❑ A problem developed with an experiment aboard the space shuttle. Surgió un problema con un experimento a bordo del transbordador espacial. 3 V-I If you say that a country **develops**, you mean that it changes from being a poor agricultural country to being a rich industrial country. progresar, desarrollarse ❑ All of these countries developed fast. Todos esos países progresaron rápidamente. • **de|vel|oped** ADJ desarrollado ❑ Family size is smaller in more developed countries. La familia es menos numerosa en los países más desarrollados. 4 → see also **developing** 5 V-T To **develop** land or property means to make it more profitable, by building houses or factories or by improving the existing buildings. establecer ❑ Local business people developed fashionable restaurants in the area. Los negociantes del lugar establecieron restaurantes modernos en el área. • **de|vel|oped** ADJ urbanizado ❑ Developed land grew from 5.3% to 6.9%. El área urbanizada pasó del 5.3 al 6.9 por ciento. • **de|vel|op|er** N-COUNT (**developers**) promotor inmobiliario o promotora inmobiliaria ❑ The land has a high value if it is sold to developers. La tierra aumenta de valor cuando se vende a las promotoras inmobiliarias. • **de|vel|op|ment** N-COUNT (**developments**) fraccionamiento, urbanización, complejo habitacional ❑ ...a 16-house development. ...un fraccionamiento de 16 casas. 6 V-T If someone **develops** a new product, they design it and produce it. desarrollar ❑ Several countries developed nuclear weapons secretly. Varios países desarrollaron armas nucleares en secreto. • **de|vel|op|er** N-COUNT diseñador o diseñadora ❑ ...a developer of computer software. ...un diseñador de programas de computación. • **de|vel|op|ment** N-VAR desarrollo ❑ The company is spending $850M on research and development. La empresa está gastando 850 millones de dólares en investigación y desarrollo. 7 V-T To **develop** photographs means to make negatives or prints from a photographic film. revelar ❑ She developed one roll of film. Reveló un rollo de película.
→ see **photography**

**de|vel|op|ing** /dɪvɛləpɪŋ/ ADJ If you talk about **developing** countries or the **developing** world, you mean the countries or the parts of the world that are poor and have few industries. en vías desarrollo ❑ In the developing world pollution is increasing. La contaminación está aumentando en los países en vías de desarrollo.

**de|vel|op|ment** /dɪvɛləpmənt/ (**developments**) 1 N-UNCOUNT **Development** is the growth of something such as a business or an industry. crecimiento [BUSINESS] ❑ A country's economic development is a key factor to progress. El crecimiento económico de un país es un factor clave para el progreso. 2 N-COUNT A **development** is an event or incident which has recently happened and is likely to have an effect on the present situation. suceso, acontecimiento, avance ❑ Police say this is an important development in the investigation. La policía afirma que se trata de un avance importante en la investigación.

**de|vice** /dɪvaɪs/ (**devices**) N-COUNT A **device** is an object that has been invented for a particular purpose, for example, for recording or measuring something. aparato, artefacto, dispositivo ❑ He used an electronic device to measure the rooms. Utilizó un aparato electrónico para medir los cuartos.
→ see **computer**

**dev|il** /dɛvᵊl/ (**devils**) 1 N-PROPER In Judaism, Christianity, and Islam, **the Devil** is the most powerful evil spirit. diablo 2 N-COUNT A **devil** is an evil spirit. diablo ❑ ...the idea of angels with wings and devils with horns. ...la idea de ángeles con alas y diablos con cuernos.

**de|vise** /dɪvaɪz/ (**devises, devising, devised**) V-T If you **devise** a plan, system, or machine, you have the idea for it and design it. idear, concebir ❑ We devised a plan to help him. Concebimos un plan para ayudarlo.

**de|vote** /dɪvoʊt/ (**devotes, devoting, devoted**) V-T If you **devote** yourself, your time, or your energy **to** something, you spend all or most of your time or energy on it. dedicar, consagrar, destinar ❑ He devoted the rest of his life to science. Consagró el resto de su vida a la ciencia. ❑ A lot of money was devoted to the project. Se dedicó mucho dinero al proyecto.

**de|vot|ed** /dɪvoʊtɪd/ ADJ Someone who is **devoted to** a person loves that person very much. devoto, dedicado ❑ ...a devoted husband. ...un esposo dedicado.

**de|vo|tion** /dɪvoʊʃᵊn/ N-UNCOUNT **Devotion to** someone or something is great love of them and commitment to them. devoción ❑ I've never seen such devotion between a brother and sister before. Nunca antes había visto tal devoción entre un hermano y una hermana. ❑ ...their devotion to religion. ...su devoción por la religión.

**dew point** (**dew points**) N-COUNT The **dew point** is the temperature at which water vapor in the air becomes liquid and dew begins to form. punto de rocío, punto de condensación, punto de saturación [TECHNICAL]

**dia|be|tes** /daɪəbitɪs, -tiz/ N-UNCOUNT **Diabetes** is a medical condition in which someone has too much sugar in their blood. diabetes
→ see **sugar**

**dia|bet|ic** /daɪəbɛtɪk/ (**diabetics**) 1 N-COUNT A **diabetic** is a person who suffers from diabetes.

d

*diabético o diabética* ❑ *...food that is suitable for diabetics. ...alimentos adecuados para los diabéticos.* • **Diabetic** is also an adjective. *diabético* ❑ *...diabetic patients. ...pacientes diabéticos.* **2** ADJ **Diabetic** means relating to diabetes. *diabético* ❑ *He found her in a diabetic coma. La encontró en un coma diabético.*

**Word Link** *dia ≈ across, through : diagnose, diagonal, dialogue*

**di|ag|nose** /daɪəgnoʊs/ (**diagnoses, diagnosing, diagnosed**) V-T If someone or something **is diagnosed as** having a particular illness or problem, their illness or problem is identified. If an illness or problem **is diagnosed,** it is identified. *diagnosticar* ❑ *The soldiers were diagnosed as having the flu. El diagnóstico fue que los soldados tenían gripe.* ❑ *His wife was diagnosed with diabetes. Le diagnosticaron diabetes a su esposa.*
→ see **diagnosis, illness**

**Word Link** *osis ≈ state or condition : diagnosis, mitosis, symbiosis*

**di|ag|no|sis** /daɪəgnoʊsɪs/ (**diagnoses**) N-VAR **Diagnosis** is the discovery and naming of what is wrong with someone who is ill or with something that is not working properly. *diagnóstico* ❑ *I had a second test to confirm the diagnosis. Me hicieron otro examen para confirmar el diagnóstico.*
→ see Word Web: **diagnosis**

**di|ago|nal** /daɪægən°l, -ægn°l/ ADJ A **diagonal** line or movement goes in a sloping direction, for example, from one corner of a square across to the opposite corner. *diagonal* ❑ *...a pattern of diagonal lines. ...un patrón de líneas diagonales.* • **di|ago|nal|ly** ADV *diagonalmente, en diagonal* ❑ *He ran diagonally across the field. Cruzó el campo en diagonal.*

square

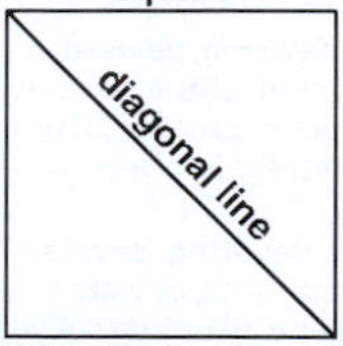


diagonal

**Word Link** *gram ≈ writing : diagram, grammar, program*

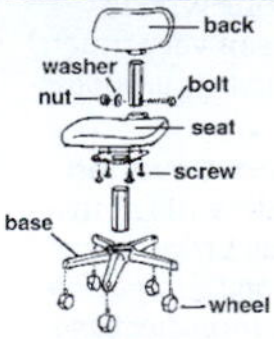


diagram

**dia|gram** /daɪəgræm/ (**diagrams, diagramming** or **diagraming, diagrammed** or **diagramed**) **1** N-COUNT A **diagram** is a simple drawing which consists mainly of lines and is used, for example, to explain how a machine works. *diagrama* ❑ *...a diagram of a computer. ...el diagrama de una computadora.* **2** V-T To **diagram** something means to draw a diagram of it or to explain it using a diagram. *hacer un diagrama* [FORMAL] ❑ *The process can be diagramed. Se puede hacer un diagrama del proceso.*

**Thesaurus** *diagram* Ver también:
N. blueprint, chart, design, illustration, plan **1**

**dial** /daɪəl/ (**dials, dialing, dialed**) **1** N-COUNT A **dial** is the part of a machine or instrument such as a clock or watch which shows you the time or a measurement that has been recorded. *esfera, cuadrante* ❑ *The dial on the clock showed five minutes to seven. La esfera del reloj mostraba las siete menos cinco.* **2** N-COUNT A **dial** is a control on a device or piece of equipment which you can move in order to adjust the setting, for example, to select or change the frequency on a radio or the temperature of a heater. *cuadrante, botón regulador, sintonizador* ❑ *He turned the dial on the radio. Dio vuelta al sintonizador del radio.* **3** V-T/V-I If you **dial** or if you **dial** a number, you press the buttons on a telephone, or turn the dial on an old-fashioned telephone, in order to phone someone. *marcar, discar* ❑ *He lifted the phone and dialed her number. Levantó el teléfono y marcó su número.*

dial

**dia|lect** /daɪəlɛkt/ (**dialects**) N-COUNT A **dialect** is a form of a language that is spoken in a particular area. *dialecto* ❑ *...speaking in the local dialect. ...hablando en el dialecto del lugar.*
→ see **English**

**dia|log box** (**dialog boxes**) N-COUNT A **dialog box** is a small area containing information or questions that appears on a computer screen when you are performing particular operations. *cuadro de diálogo* [COMPUTING] ❑ *Clicking this brings up another dialog box. Al hacer click aquí, se abre otra ventana de diálogo.*

**Word Link** *log ≈ reason, speech : apology, dialogue, logic*

**dia|logue** /daɪəlɔg/ (**dialogues**) also **dialog** **1** N-VAR **Dialogue** is communication or discussion between people or groups of people

**Word Web** diagnosis

Many doctors suggest that their **patients** get a routine **physical examination** once a year—even if they're feeling healthy. This enables the **physician** to see any **symptoms** early and **diagnose** possible **diseases** at an early stage. The doctor may begin by using a **tongue depressor** to look down the patient's throat for possible **infections**. Then he or she may use a **stethoscope** to listen to subtle sounds in the heart, lungs, and stomach. A **blood pressure** reading is always part of the physical exam.

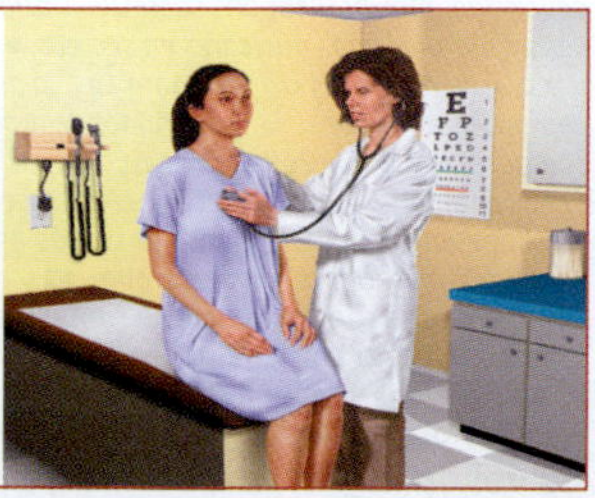

**Word Web** diary

Someone writes in a **diary** to tell about the things that happen in their daily life. Most diaries are private **documents** and are not shared with others. But sometimes an important diary is published as a book. One such example is *The Diary of a Young Girl*. This is Anne Frank's World War II **chronicle** of her family's experience as they hid from the Nazis. They were found and arrested, and later Anne died in a concentration camp. This **primary source** document tells Anne's story in her own words. It is full of rich details that are often missing from other historical **texts**. The book is now available in 60 different languages.

d

such as governments or political parties. *diálogo* ❑ *The dialogue continued for months.* *El diálogo continuó durante meses.* **2** N-VAR A **dialogue** is a conversation between two people in a book, film, or play. *diálogo* ❑ *He writes very funny dialogue.* *Escribe diálogos muy graciosos.*

**dial tone** (**dial tones**) N-COUNT The **dial tone** is the noise you hear when you pick up a telephone receiver, and which means that you can dial the number that you want. *tono de marcar*, *tono de discado*

**dial-up** ADJ A **dial-up** connection to the Internet is a connection that uses a modem and a conventional telephone line. *de acceso telefónico* ❑ *...more than 200 times the speed of a regular dial-up connection.* *...más de 200 veces la velocidad de una conexión de acceso telefónico normal.*

**di|am|eter** /daɪæmɪtər/ (**diameters**) N-COUNT The **diameter** of a round object is the length of a straight line that can be drawn across it, passing through the middle of it. *diámetro* ❑ *The tube is much smaller than the diameter of a human hair.* *El tubo es mucho más delgado que el diámetro de un cabello humano.*
→ see **area**

**dia|mond** /daɪmənd, daɪə-/ (**diamonds**) **1** N-VAR A **diamond** is a hard, bright, precious stone which is clear and colorless. Diamonds are used in jewelry and for cutting very hard substances. *diamante* ❑ *...a pair of diamond earrings.* *...un par de aretes de diamante(s).* **2** N-COUNT A **diamond** is a shape with four straight sides of equal length where the opposite angles are the same, but none of the angles is equal to 90°: ◇. *rombo* ❑ *He formed his hands into the shape of a diamond.* *Formó un rombo con las manos.* **3** N-UNCOUNT **Diamonds** is one of the four suits of cards in a pack of playing cards. Each card in the suit is marked with one or more red symbols in the shape of a diamond. *diamante* ❑ *He picked the seven of diamonds.* *Tomó el siete de diamantes.* ● A **diamond** is a playing card of this suit. *carta de diamantes* ❑ *Win the ace of clubs and play a diamond.* *Tome el as de tréboles y juegue una carta de diamantes.* **4** N-COUNT In baseball, the **diamond** is the square formed by the four bases, or the whole of the playing area. *diamante* ❑ *He was the best player to walk out onto the diamond.* *Fue el mejor jugador que haya ingresado al diamante.*
→ see **baseball, crystal, park**

**dia|per** /daɪpər, daɪə-/ (**diapers**) N-COUNT A **diaper** is a piece of soft towel or paper, which you fasten around a baby's bottom in order to contain its urine and feces. *pañal* ❑ *He never changed her diapers.* *Él nunca le cambió los pañales.*

**dia|phragm** /daɪəfræm/ (**diaphragms**) N-COUNT Your **diaphragm** is a muscle between your lungs and your stomach. It is used when you breathe. *diafragma* ❑ *...the skill of breathing from the diaphragm.* *...la habilidad de ayudarse a respirar con el diafragma.*
→ see **respiratory system**

**di|ar|rhea** /daɪəriə/ N-UNCOUNT If someone has **diarrhea**, a lot of liquid feces comes out of their body because they are ill. *diarrea* ❑ *Many team members suffered from diarrhea.* *Muchos miembros del equipo tuvieron diarrea.*

**dia|ry** /daɪəri/ (**diaries**) N-COUNT A **diary** is a book which has a separate space for each day of the year. You use a diary to write down things you plan to do, or to record what happens in your life day by day. *diario* ❑ *I read the entry from his diary for July 10, 1940.* *Leí la anotación que hizo en su diario el 10 de julio de 1940.*
→ see Word Web: **diary**
→ see **history**

**dia|ton|ic scale** /daɪətɒnɪk skeɪl/ (**diatonic scales**) N-COUNT A **diatonic scale** is the sequence of musical notes that make up a major or minor scale. *escala diatónica* [TECHNICAL]

**dice** /daɪs/ (**dices, dicing, diced**) **1** N-COUNT A **dice** is a small cube which has between one and six spots or numbers on its sides, and which is used in games to provide random numbers. In old-fashioned English, "dice" was used only as a plural form, and the singular was **die**, but now "dice" is used as both the singular and the plural form. *dado* ❑ *I throw both dice and get double 6.* *Tiré los dados y saqué un doble seis.* **2** V-T If you **dice** food, you cut it into small cubes. *cortar en cubitos*, *picar en cubitos* ❑ *Dice the onion and boil in the water.* *Pique finamente la cebolla y póngala a que hierva con el agua.*
→ see **cut**

**di|choto|mous key** /daɪkɒtəməs ki/ (**dichotomous keys**) N-COUNT A **dichotomous key** is a system for identifying species of plants or animals based on pairs of questions. *clave dicotómica* [TECHNICAL]

**Word Link** *dict ≈ speaking : contradict, dictate, predict*

**dic|tate** (**dictates, dictating, dictated**)

D

The verb is pronounced /dɪkteɪt, dɪkteɪt/. The noun is pronounced /dɪkteɪt/.

**1** V-T If you **dictate** something, you say or read it aloud for someone else to write down. *dictar* ❑ *She dictated a letter to her secretary.* *Dictó una carta a su secretaria.* **2** V-T If you **dictate to** someone, you tell them what they must do. *dictar, imponer* ❑ *Why should one country dictate the policy of another country?* *¿Por qué debe un país dictar la política de otro?* ❑ *What gives them the right to dictate to us what we should eat?* *¿Quién les da derecho de imponernos lo que debemos comer?* **3** V-T If one thing **dictates** another, the first thing causes or influences the second thing. *imponer, determinar* ❑ *The movie's budget dictated a tough schedule.* *El presupuesto para la película impuso un programa muy apretado.* ❑ *Several factors dictate how long an apple tree can live.* *Varios factores determinan el tiempo de vida de un manzano.*

**dic|ta|tion** /dɪkteɪʃ$^{ə}$n/ N-UNCOUNT **Dictation** is the speaking or reading aloud of words for someone else to write down. *dictado* ❑ *...taking dictation from the dean of the graduate school.* *...tomando dictado del director de la escuela de graduados.*

**dic|ta|tor** /dɪkteɪtər/ (**dictators**) N-COUNT A **dictator** is a ruler who has complete power in a country, especially power which was obtained by force and is used unfairly or cruelly. *dictador o dictadora* ❑ *...foreign dictators.* *...dictadores extranjeros.*

**dic|ta|tor|ship** /dɪkteɪtərʃɪp/ (**dictatorships**) **1** N-VAR **Dictatorship** is government by a dictator. *dictadura* ❑ *...a long period of military dictatorship in the country.* *...un largo período de dictadura militar en el país.* **2** N-COUNT A **dictatorship** is a country which is ruled by a dictator or by a very strict and harsh government. *dictadura* ❑ *Every country in the region was a military dictatorship.* *Todos los países de la región tuvieron dictaduras militares.*

**dic|tion** /dɪkʃ$^{ə}$n/ N-UNCOUNT Someone's **diction** is how clearly they speak or sing. *dicción*

**dic|tion|ary** /dɪkʃənɛri/ (**dictionaries**) N-COUNT A **dictionary** is a book in which the words and phrases of a language are listed alphabetically, together with their meanings or their translations in another language. *diccionario* ❑ *...a Spanish-English dictionary.* *...un diccionario español-inglés.*

**did** /dɪd/ **Did** is the past tense of **do**. *pasado de* ***do***

**didn't** /dɪd$^{ə}$nt/ **Didn't** is the usual spoken form of "did not." *forma hablada usual de* ***did not***

**die** /daɪ/ (**dies, dying, died**) **1** V-I When people, animals, and plants **die,** they stop living. *morir* ❑ *My dog died.* *Murió mi perro.* ❑ *Sadly, my mother died of cancer.* *Desgraciadamente, mi madre murió de cáncer.* **2** V-I You can say that you **are dying of** thirst, hunger, boredom, or curiosity to emphasize that you are very thirsty, hungry, bored, or curious. *morirse de* [INFORMAL] ❑ *Order me a drink, I'm dying of thirst.* *—Pídeme algo de tomar; me muero de sed.* **3** V-T/V-I You can say that you **are dying for** something or **are dying to** do something to emphasize that you very much want to have it or do it. *morirse por* [INFORMAL] ❑ *I'm dying for some fresh air.* *Me muero por un poco de aire fresco.* **4** → see also **dying** **5** V-I When something **dies,** or when it **dies away** or **dies down,** it gradually becomes weaker, until it no longer exists. *extinguirse, apagarse, amainar* ❑ *My love for you will never die.* *Mi amor por ti nunca se extinguirá.* ❑ *The thunder was dying away across the mountains.* *El ruido del trueno se extinguió poco a poco entre las montañas.* ❑ *The wind died down.* *El viento amainó.*

▶ **die out** PHR-VERB If something **dies out,** it becomes less and less common and eventually disappears completely. *caer en desuso* ❑ *Use of the Internet won't die out.* *La Internet no caerá en desuso.*

**Thesaurus** *die* Ver también:

| | |
|---|---|
| V. | pass away; (*ant.*) live **1** |

**Word Partnership** Usar *die* con:

| | |
|---|---|
| V. | **deserve to** die, **going to** die, **live or** die, **sentenced to** die, **want to** die, **would rather** die **1** |
| N. | **right to** die **1** |

**die|sel** /diz$^{ə}$l/ (**diesels**) **1** N-UNCOUNT **Diesel** or **diesel oil** is the heavy fuel used in a diesel engine. *diesel* **2** N-COUNT A **diesel** is a vehicle which has a diesel engine. *(vehículo) diesel* ❑ *Diesels are better now than they used to be.* *Los vehículos diesel son mejores ahora que antes.*

**diet** /daɪɪt/ (**diets, dieting, dieted**) **1** N-VAR Your **diet** is the type and variety of food that you regularly eat. *régimen (alimenticio), dieta* ❑ *It's never too late to improve your diet.* *Nunca es tarde para mejorar nuestro régimen alimenticio.* **2** N-VAR If you are on a **diet,** you eat special kinds of food or you eat less food than usual because you are trying to lose weight. *régimen (alimenticio), dieta* ❑ *Have you been on a diet? You've lost a lot of weight.* *—¿Estás a dieta? ¡Has adelgazado mucho!* • **di|et|er** /daɪətər/ N-COUNT (**dieters**) *persona que hace o se pone a dieta o sigue un régimen alimenticio* ❑ *More than 90 percent of dieters gain back every pound they lose.* *Más del 90 por ciento de los que se ponen a dieta recuperan cada kilo que pierden.* **3** V-I If you **are dieting,** you eat special kinds of food or you eat less food than usual because you are trying to lose weight. *hacer dieta, ponerse a dieta* ❑ *I've been dieting since the birth of my child.* *He estado haciendo dieta desde que di a luz.*

→ see Word Web: **diet**

→ see **vegetarian**

**Word Partnership** Usar *diet* con:

| | |
|---|---|
| ADJ. | **balanced** diet, **healthy** diet, **proper** diet, **vegetarian** diet **1** |
| | **strict** diet **2** |
| N. | diet **and exercise**, diet **supplements** **1** **2** |
| | diet **pills** **2** |
| PREP. | **on a** diet **2** |

**dif|fer** /dɪfər/ (**differs, differing, differed**) **1** V-RECIP If two or more things **differ,** they are unlike each other in some way. *diferir, ser diferente, ser distinto* ❑ *The story he told police differed from the one he told his mother.* *Lo que le dijo a la policía fue diferente de lo que le dijo a su madre.* **2** V-RECIP If people **differ** about something, they do not agree with each other about it. *discrepar, diferir* ❑ *The two leaders differed on the issue.* *Los dos dirigentes tenían*

**Word Web** diet

Recent U.S. government reports show that about 64% of American adults are **overweight** or **obese**. The number of people on **weight loss diets** is the highest ever. Many people are trying **fad** diets to lose weight. One diet tells people to eat mostly **protein**—meat, fish, and cheese—and very few **carbohydrates**. However, another diet tells people to eat at least 40% carbohydrates. A weight-loss diet works when you burn more **calories** than you eat. Most doctors agree that a balanced diet with plenty of exercise is the best way to lose weight.

*discrepancias sobre el asunto.* ❑ *That is where we differ. En eso discrepamos.*

**Usage** **differ**

Be sure to use the correct preposition after *differ*. *Differ from* means "are different from" or "are unlike": *Bicycles differ from tricycles in having two wheels instead of three.* *Differ with* means "disagree with": *Milagros differed with Armando about where to go this summer, to the beach or to the mountains.*

**dif|fer|ence** /dɪfərəns, dɪfrəns/ (**differences**) 1 N-COUNT The **difference** between two things is the way in which they are unlike each other. *diferencia* ❑ *That is the main difference between the two societies. Esa es la principal diferencia entre las dos sociedades.* ❑ *...the great difference in size. ...la gran diferencia de tamaño.* 2 N-COUNT If people have their **differences** about something, they disagree about it. *diferencia* ❑ *The two groups are learning how to resolve their differences. Los (dos) grupos están aprendiendo a resolver sus diferencias.* 3 N-SING A **difference** between two quantities is the amount by which one quantity is less than the other. *diferencia* ❑ *The difference is 8532. La diferencia es de 8,532.* 4 PHRASE If something **makes** a **difference** or **makes** a lot of **difference,** it affects you and helps you in what you are doing. If something **makes** no **difference,** it does not have any effect on what you are doing. *influir* ❑ *Where you live makes such a difference to the way you feel. El lugar donde se vive influye mucho en la manera de sentirse.*

**Word Partnership** Usar *difference* con:

ADJ. **big/major** difference 1
V. **know the** difference, **notice a** difference, **tell the** difference 1
**settle a** difference 2
**pay the** difference 3
**make a** difference 4
N. difference **in age**, difference **in price** 3

**dif|fer|ent** /dɪfərənt, dɪfrənt/ 1 ADJ If two people or things are **different,** they are not like each other. *diferente, distinto* ❑ *London was different from most European capital cities. Londres era diferente de la mayoría de las capitales europeas.* ❑ *Things would be different if he went to music school. Las cosas serían diferentes si asistiera a una escuela de música.*
• **dif|fer|ent|ly** ADV *diferentemente, de manera diferente* ❑ *Every person learns differently. Cada persona aprende de una manera diferente.* 2 ADJ You use **different** to indicate that you are talking about two or more separate and distinct things of the same kind. *diferente, distinto* ❑ *Different countries export different products. Países diferentes exportan productos diferentes.* 3 ADJ You can describe something as **different** when it is unusual and not like others of the same kind. *diferente, distinto* ❑ *The result is interesting and different. El resultado es interesante y diferente.*

**dif|fer|en|ti|ate** /dɪfərɛnʃieɪt/ (**differentiates, differentiating, differentiated**) 1 V-T/V-I If you **differentiate between** things or if you **differentiate** one thing **from** another, you recognize or show the difference between them. *diferenciar, distinguir* ❑ *A child may not differentiate between his imagination and the real world. Un niño puede no distinguir entre su imaginación y el mundo real.* 2 V-T A quality or feature that **differentiates** one thing **from** another makes the two things different. *distinguir* ❑ *...unusual policies that differentiate them from the other parties. ...políticas poco comunes que los distinguen de los otros partidos.*
• **dif|fer|en|tia|tion** /dɪfərɛnʃieɪʃᵊn/ N-UNCOUNT *diferenciación* ❑ *...a strict differentiation between men and women. ...una diferenciación estricta entre el hombre y la mujer.*

**dif|fi|cult** /dɪfɪkʌlt, -kəlt/ 1 ADJ Something that is **difficult** is not easy to do, understand, or deal with. *difícil* ❑ *The lack of childcare made it difficult for mothers to get jobs. La carencia de guarderías dificultaba el que las madres obtuvieran empleo.* ❑ *It was a very difficult decision to make. Era una decisión muy difícil.* 2 ADJ Someone who is **difficult** behaves in an unreasonable and unhelpful way. *difícil* ❑ *I knew you were going to be difficult about this. Sabía que ibas a ser difícil sobre esto.*

**Thesaurus** *difficult* Ver también:

ADJ. challenging, demanding, hard, tough; (*ant.*) easy, simple, uncomplicated 1
disagreeable, irritable; (*ant.*) accommodating, cooperative 2

**dif|fi|cul|ty** /dɪfɪkʌlti, -kəlti/ (**difficulties**) 1 N-COUNT A **difficulty** is a problem. *dificultad* ❑ *...the difficulty of getting information. ...la dificultad de obtener información.* 2 N-UNCOUNT If you have **difficulty** doing something, you are not able to do it easily. *dificultad* ❑ *Do you have difficulty walking? ¿Tienes dificultades para caminar?* 3 PHRASE If someone or something is **in difficulty,** they are having a lot of problems. *en dificultades* ❑ *The city's movie industry is in difficulty. La industria*

D

*cinematográfica de la ciudad está en dificultades.*

**dif|frac|tion** /dɪfrækʃən/ N-UNCOUNT In physics, **diffraction** is a change in the direction of a sound wave or a light wave caused by the presence of an obstacle in its path. *difracción* ❑ *...the diffraction of light that occurs in rainbows. ...la difracción de la luz que genera el arco iris.*

**dif|fuse** /dɪfyuz/ (**diffuses, diffusing, diffused**) V-T/V-I If something such as knowledge or information **is diffused,** or if it **diffuses** somewhere, it is made known over a wide area or to a lot of people. *difundir, esparcir* [WRITTEN] ❑ *The technology is diffused and used by other countries. La tecnología se difunde para que la utilicen otros países.* ❑ *...to diffuse new ideas obtained from elsewhere. ...difundir las nuevas ideas que se obtienen de todas partes.* ● **dif|fu|sion** /dɪfyuʒən/ N-UNCOUNT *difusión* ❑ *...the development and diffusion of ideas. ...la generación y difusión de ideas.*
→ see **culture**

**dig** /dɪg/ (**digs, digging, dug**) **1** V-T/V-I If people or animals **dig,** they make a hole in the ground or in a pile of something such as earth or stones. *excavar, cavar, escarbar* ❑ *I grabbed the shovel and started digging. Tomé la pala y empecé a escarbar.* ❑ *Dig a large hole. Escarba un hoyo grande.* **2** V-T/V-I If you **dig** one thing **into** another or if one thing **digs into** another, the first thing is pushed hard into the second, or presses hard into it. *clavar, meter* ❑ *She dug her spoon into the chocolate pudding. Clavó la cuchara en el pudín de chocolate.* **3** N-COUNT If you have a **dig at** someone, you say something which is intended to make fun of them or upset them. *comentario, indirecta* ❑ *She couldn't resist a dig at Dave after he lost the game. No pudo resistir el hacerle un comentario a Dave después de que éste perdió el juego.*

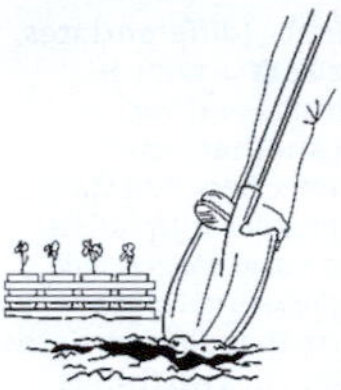
dig

▶ **dig out** PHR-VERB If you **dig** something **out,** you find it after it has been stored, hidden, or forgotten for a long time. *desempolvar* [INFORMAL] ❑ *Recently, I dug out the book and read it again. No hace mucho, desempolvé el libro y volví a leerlo.*

**di|gest** (**digests, digesting, digested**)

| |
|---|
| The verb is pronounced /dɪdʒɛst/. The noun is pronounced /daɪdʒɛst/. |

**1** V-T/V-I When food **digests** or when you **digest** it, it passes through your body to your stomach. Your stomach removes the substances that your body needs and gets rid of the rest. *digerir* ❑ *Do not swim for an hour after a meal to allow food to digest. No nade durante una hora después de comer para dar tiempo a la digestión.* ❑ *She couldn't digest food properly. No podía digerir bien la comida.* ● **di|ges|tion** /daɪdʒɛstʃən/ N-UNCOUNT *digestión* ❑ *Peppermint aids digestion. La menta ayuda a la digestión.* **2** V-T If you **digest** information, you think about it carefully so that you understand it. *asimilar, digerir* ❑ *You need time to digest the information. Se necesita tiempo para asimilar la información.*
→ see **cooking**

**di|ges|tive** /daɪdʒɛstɪv/ ADJ You can describe things that are related to the digestion of food as **digestive.** *digestivo, gástrico* ❑ *Digestive juices break down our food. Los jugos gástricos descomponen los alimentos.*

**dig|it** /dɪdʒɪt/ (**digits**) N-COUNT A **digit** is a written symbol for any of the ten numbers from 0 to 9. *dígito* ❑ *Her telephone number differs from mine by one digit. Su número de teléfono es diferente al mío por un dígito.*

**digi|tal** /dɪdʒɪtəl/ **1** ADJ **Digital** systems record or transmit information in the form of thousands of very small signals. *digital* ❑ *...the company had plans to introduce more digital products. ...la compañía tenía planes para introducir más productos digitales.* **2** ADJ **Digital** devices such as watches or clocks give information by displaying numbers rather than by having a pointer which moves around a dial. Compare **analog.** *digital* ❑ *...a digital watch. ...un reloj digital.*
→ see **technology, television, time**

**digi|tal cam|era** (**digital cameras**) N-COUNT A **digital camera** is a camera that produces digital images that can be stored on a computer. *cámara digital* ❑ *"Star Wars Attack of the Clones" was made using digital cameras. "El ataque de los clones", de la serie "La guerra de las galaxias", se filmó con cámaras digitales.*

**digi|tal ra|dio** (**digital radios**) **1** N-UNCOUNT **Digital radio** is radio in which the signals are transmitted in digital form and decoded by the radio receiver. *radio digital* ❑ *...people with access to digital radio. ...la gente con acceso a la radio digital.* **2** N-COUNT A **digital radio** is a radio that can receive digital signals. *radio digital* ❑ *...more than 100 digital radio channels. ...más de 100 canales de radio digital.*

**digi|tal tele|vi|sion** (**digital televisions**) **1** N-UNCOUNT **Digital television** is television in which the signals are transmitted in digital form and decoded by the television receiver. *televisión digital* ❑ *At present only 31 percent of the population has access to digital television. En el presente, sólo el 31 por ciento de la población tiene acceso a la televisión digital.* **2** N-COUNT A **digital television** is a television that can receive digital signals. *televisión digital, televisor digital* ❑ *...wide screen digital televisions. ...televisiones digitales de pantalla ancha.*

**dig|nity** /dɪgnɪti/ **1** N-UNCOUNT If someone behaves or moves with **dignity,** they are serious, calm, and controlled. *dignidad* ❑ *...her extraordinary dignity. ...su extraordinaria dignidad.* **2** N-UNCOUNT **Dignity** is the quality of being worthy of respect. *dignidad* ❑ *...the sense of human dignity. ...el sentido de dignidad humana.*

**di|graph** /daɪgræf/ (**digraphs**) N-COUNT A **digraph** is a combination of two letters that represents a single speech sound, such as "ea" in "bread." *dígrafo* [TECHNICAL]

**di|la|tion** /daɪleɪʃən/ (**dilations**) N-VAR In mathematics, a **dilation** is a procedure in which a figure such as a triangle is made bigger or smaller but its shape stays the same. *dilatación* [TECHNICAL]

| Word Link | *di ≈ two : **di**lemma, **di**verse, **di**vorce* |
|---|---|

**di|lem|ma** /dɪlɛmə/ (**dilemmas**) N-COUNT A **dilemma** is a difficult situation in which you have to choose between two or more alternatives. *dilema* ❑ *He was facing the dilemma of whether or not to return to his country. Enfrentaba el dilema de volver o no a su país.*

**di|lute** /daɪlut/ (**dilutes, diluting, diluted**) V-T If a liquid **is diluted,** it is added to water or another liquid, and becomes weaker. *diluir* ❑ *If you give your baby juice, dilute it with water. Si le da jugo a su bebé, dilúyalo en agua.* ❑ *The liquid is then diluted. Después se diluye el líquido.*

**dim** /dɪm/ (**dimmer, dimmest, dims, dimming, dimmed**) **1** ADJ **Dim** light is not bright. *tenue* ❑ *She waited in the dim light. Aguardó en la tenue luz.* • **dim|ly** ADV *tenuemente* ❑ *Two lamps burned dimly. Dos lámparas brillaban tenuemente.* **2** ADJ A **dim** figure, place or object is not very easy to see, because the light is not bright enough. *débil, borroso, vago* ❑ *Pete's flashlight showed the dim figures of Bob and Chang. La linterna de Pete mostró las siluetas borrosas de Bob y Chang.* • **dim|ly** ADV *vagamente* ❑ *The shoreline could be dimly seen. La costa podía verse vagamente.* **3** V-T/V-I If you **dim** a light or if it **dims,** it becomes less bright. *atenuar, bajar* ❑ *Dim the lighting. Baja la luz.* ❑ *Dim your lights behind that car. Pon las luces bajas cuando tengas un carro delante.*

**dime** /daɪm/ (**dimes**) N-COUNT A **dime** is a U.S. coin worth ten cents. *Moneda estadounidense de diez centavos, 'daim'.*

**di|men|sion** /dɪmɛnʃᵊn, daɪ-/ (**dimensions**) **1** N-COUNT A particular **dimension** of something is a particular aspect of it. *dimensión, aspecto* ❑ *There is a political dimension to the accusations. Las acusaciones tienen un aspecto político.* **2** N-PLURAL The **dimensions** of something are its measurements. *dimensión* ❑ *We do not yet know the exact dimensions of the new oilfield. Todavía no conocemos las dimensiones exactas del nuevo yacimiento petrolífero.*

**di|men|sion|al analy|sis** /dɪmɛnʃənᵊl ənælɪsɪs, daɪ-/ (**dimensional analyses**) N-VAR **Dimensional analysis** is a method used by scientists to understand the relationships between things that are measured in different sorts of units. *análisis dimensional* [TECHNICAL]

| Word Link | *min ≈ small, lessen : diminish, minus, minute* |
|---|---|

**di|min|ish** /dɪmɪnɪʃ/ (**diminishes, diminishing, diminished**) V-T/V-I When something **diminishes,** or when something **diminishes** it, it becomes reduced in size, importance, or intensity. *disminuir, reducirse, empañar* ❑ *The threat of war has diminished. La amenaza de guerra ha disminuido.* ❑ *This doesn't diminish what he has achieved. Esto no empaña lo que ha logrado.*

**di|min|ished in|ter|val** (**diminished intervals**) N-COUNT In music, a **diminished interval** is an interval that is reduced by half a step or half a tone. *intervalo disminuido* [TECHNICAL]

**dim sum** /dɪm sʊm, sʌm/ N-UNCOUNT **Dim sum** is a Chinese dish of dumplings filled with meat or other ingredients. *dim sum* ❑ *...dim sum restaurants. ...restaurantes de "dim sum".*

**dine** /daɪn/ (**dines, dining, dined**) V-I When you **dine,** you have dinner. *cenar* [FORMAL] ❑ *He dines alone most nights. Casi todas las noches cena solo.*

**ding|bat** /dɪŋbæt/ (**dingbats**) N-COUNT People sometimes refer to a person who they think is crazy or stupid as a **dingbat.** *menso, tonto* [INFORMAL] ❑ *I hope people realize I'm not a dingbat. Espero que la gente vea que no soy un menso.*

**din|ing room** (**dining rooms**) N-COUNT The **dining room** is the room in a house where people have their meals, or a room in a hotel where meals are served. *comedor*
→ see **house**

**din|ner** /dɪnər/ (**dinners**) **1** N-VAR **Dinner** is the main meal of the day, usually served in the early part of the evening. *cena* ❑ *She invited us for dinner. Nos invitó a cenar.* ❑ *Would you like to stay and have dinner? —¿Te gustaría quedarte a cenar?* **2** N-VAR Some people refer to the meal you eat in the middle of the day as **dinner.** *comida* **3** N-COUNT A **dinner** is a formal social event in the evening at which a meal is served. *cena* ❑ *...a series of official dinners. ...una serie de cenas oficiales.*
→ see **dish, meal**

**dino|flag|el|late** /daɪnoʊflædʒəlɪt, -leɪt/ (**dinoflagellates**) N-COUNT; ADJ **Dinoflagellates** are tiny organisms that live in sea water and fresh water and are found in plankton. *dinoflagelado* [TECHNICAL]

dinosaur

**di|no|saur** /daɪnəsɔr/ (**dinosaurs**) N-COUNT **Dinosaurs** were large reptiles which lived millions of years ago. *dinosaurio*

**dio|ra|ma** /daɪəræmə, -rɑmə/ (**dioramas**) N-COUNT A **diorama** is a miniature three-dimensional scene in which models of figures are arranged against a background. *diorama* ❑ *...a superb diorama of Quebec City. ...un magnífico diorama de la ciudad de Quebec.*

**dip** /dɪp/ (**dips, dipping, dipped**) **1** V-T If you **dip** something **in** a liquid, you put it in and then quickly take it out again. *meter, bañar, mojar* ❑ *Dip each apple in the syrup. Bañe cada manzana con el jarabe.* **2** N-COUNT A **dip** is a thick sauce that you dip pieces of food into before eating them. *salsa (espesa)* ❑ *...avocado dip. ...salsa de aguacate.* **3** V-I If something **dips,** it makes a downward movement. *descender, hundirse* ❑ *The boat dipped slightly as he got in. El bote se hundió ligeramente cuando él lo abordó.* **4** V-I If an area of land, a road, or a path **dips,** it goes down quite suddenly to a lower level. *descender, hundirse* ❑ *The road dipped and rose again. La carretera descendió y volvió a subir.* • **Dip** is also a noun. *declive* ❑ *Where the road makes a dip, turn right. Da vuelta a la derecha donde está el declive de la carretera.*

**di|plo|ma** /dɪploʊmə/ (**diplomas**) N-COUNT A **diploma** is a document which may be awarded to a student who has completed a course of study by a university or college, or by a high school in the United States. *diploma* ❑ *...a diploma in social work. ...un diploma de trabajo social.*
→ see **graduation**

**di|plo|ma|cy** /dɪploʊməsi/ **1** N-UNCOUNT **Diplomacy** is the activity or profession of managing relations between the governments

D

of different countries. *diplomacia* ❑ *...a success for American diplomacy.* *...un éxito para la diplomacia estadounidense.* 2 N-UNCOUNT **Diplomacy** is the skill of saying or doing things which will not offend people. *diplomacia* ❑ *...Jane's powers of persuasion and diplomacy.* *...la fuerza de persuasión y la diplomacia de Jane.*

**dip|lo|mat** /dɪpləmæt/ (**diplomats**) N-COUNT A **diplomat** is a senior official who discusses affairs with another country on behalf of his or her own country, usually working as a member of an embassy. *diplomático o diplomática* ❑ *...a Western diplomat with long experience in Asia.* *...un diplomático occidental con una amplia experiencia en Asia.*

**dip|lo|mat|ic** /dɪpləmætɪk/ 1 ADJ **Diplomatic** means relating to diplomacy and diplomats. *diplomático* ❑ *...diplomatic relations.* *...relaciones diplomáticas.* • **dip|lo|mati|cal|ly** /dɪpləmætɪkli/ ADV *diplomáticamente, con diplomacia* ❑ *The conflict was resolved diplomatically.* *El conflicto se resolvió diplomáticamente.* 2 ADJ Someone who is **diplomatic** is careful to say or do things without offending people. *diplomático* ❑ *She is very direct, but I'm more diplomatic.* *Ella es muy directa, pero yo soy más diplomático.* • **dip|lo|mati|cal|ly** ADV *diplomáticamente, con diplomacia* ❑ *"Of course," agreed Sloan diplomatically.* *—Claro—asintió Sloan diplomáticamente.*

**di|rect** /dɪrɛkt, daɪ-/ (**directs, directing, directed**) 1 ADJ **Direct** means moving toward a place or object, without changing direction and without stopping, for example, in a trip. *directo* ❑ *They took a direct flight to Athens.* *Tomaron un vuelo directo a Atenas.* • **Direct** is also an adverb. *directamente* ❑ *You can fly direct from Seattle to London.* *Puede volar directamente de Seattle a Londres.* • **di|rect|ly** ADV *directamente* ❑ *On arriving in New York, Dylan went directly to Greenwich Village.* *Al llegar a Nueva York, Dylan fue directamente a Greenwich Village.* 2 ADJ You use **direct** to describe an experience, activity, or system which only involves the people, actions, or things that are necessary to make it happen. *directo, de primera mano* ❑ *He has direct experience of the process.* *Tiene una experiencia de primera mano en el proceso.* • **Direct** is also an adverb. *directamente* ❑ *More farms are selling direct to consumers.* *Más agricultores están vendiendo directamente a los consumidores.* • **di|rect|ly** ADV *directamente* ❑ *We cannot measure pain directly.* *No podemos medir el dolor directamente.* 3 ADJ If you describe a person or their behavior as **direct,** you mean that they are honest and open, and say exactly what they mean. *franco, directo* ❑ *He avoided giving a direct answer.* *Evitó dar una respuesta directa.* • **di|rect|ly** ADV *directamente, de manera directa* ❑ *Explain simply and directly what you hope to achieve.* *Explique de manera simple y directa lo que espera lograr.* • **di|rect|ness** N-UNCOUNT *franqueza* ❑ *He spoke with rare directness.* *Habló con una franqueza inusual.* 4 V-T If something **is directed at** a particular person or thing, it is aimed at them or intended to affect them. *dirigir* ❑ *The question was directed toward her.* *La pregunta iba dirigida a ella.* ❑ *The abuse was directed at the manager.* *El abuso iba dirigido al gerente.* 5 V-T If you **direct** someone somewhere, you tell them how to get there. *indicar el camino* ❑ *Could you direct them to Dr. Lamont's office, please?* *—¿Podría indicarles el camino a la oficina del doctor Lamont, por favor?* 6 V-T When someone **directs** a project or a group of people, they are responsible for organizing the people and activities that are involved. *dirigir* ❑ *Christopher will direct day-to-day operations.* *Christopher dirigirá las operaciones cotidianas.* • **di|rec|tion** /dɪrɛkʃᵊn, daɪ-/ N-UNCOUNT *dirección* ❑ *Organizations need clear direction.* *Las organizaciones necesitan una dirección clara.* • **di|rec|tor** N-COUNT (**directors**) *director o directora* ❑ *...the director of the project.* *...el director del proyecto.* 7 V-T/V-I When someone **directs** a movie, play, or television program, they are responsible for the way in which it is performed and for telling the actors and assistants what to do. *dirigir* ❑ *He directed several TV shows.* *Dirigió varios programas de televisión.* ❑ *Branagh himself will star and direct.* *Branagh será el protagonista y dirigirá.* • **di|rec|tor** /dɪrɛktər, daɪ-/ N-COUNT (**directors**) *director o directora* ❑ *"Cut!" the director yelled. "That was perfect."* *—¡Corte!—gritó el director—. Estuvo perfecto.* 8 → see also **direction**

| **Thesaurus** | *direct* | Ver también: |
|---|---|---|
| ADJ. | nonstop, straight 1 | |
| | firsthand, personal 2 | |
| | candid, frank, plain 3 | |

**di|rect dis|course** N-UNCOUNT In grammar, **direct discourse** is speech which is reported by using the exact words that the speaker used. *estilo directo*

**di|rect|ing** /dɪrɛkt, daɪ-/ N-UNCOUNT **Directing** is the work that the director of a movie, play, or television program does. *dirección*

**di|rec|tion** /dɪrɛkʃᵊn, daɪ-/ (**directions**) 1 N-VAR A **direction** is the general line that someone or something is moving or pointing in. *dirección* ❑ *The nearest town was ten miles in the opposite direction.* *El pueblo más cercano estaba a 16 kilómetros en la dirección opuesta.* ❑ *He set off in the direction of Larry's shop.* *Partió en dirección de la tienda de Larry.* 2 N-PLURAL **Directions** are instructions that tell you what to do, how to do something, or how to get somewhere. *indicación* ❑ *She stopped the car to ask for directions.* *Detuvo el coche para pedir indicaciones.* 3 → see also **direct**

| **Word Partnership** | Usar *direction* con: |
|---|---|
| V. | **change** direction, **move in a** direction 1 |
| ADJ. | **general** direction, **opposite** direction, **right** direction, **wrong** direction 1 |
| N. | **sense of** direction 1 |

**di|rec|tive** /dɪrɛktɪv, daɪ-/ (**directives**) N-COUNT A **directive** is an official instruction that is given by someone in authority. *orden, mandato, disposición* ❑ *The new directive means that food labeling will be more specific.* *La nueva disposición significa que las etiquetas de los alimentos deberán ser más específicas.*

**di|rect ob|ject** (**direct objects**) N-COUNT In grammar, the **direct object** of a transitive verb is the noun group which refers to someone or something directly affected by or involved in the action performed by the subject. For example, in "I saw him yesterday," "him" is the direct object.

**Word Web** disability

Careful planning is making public places more **accessible** for people with **disabilities**. For hundreds of years **wheelchairs** have helped **paralyzed** people move around their homes. Today, **ramps** help these people cross the street, enter buildings, and get to work. Extra-wide doorways allow them to use public restrooms. **Blind** people are also more active and independent. **Seeing Eye dogs, canes**, and beeping crosswalks all help them get around town safely. Some movie theaters rent headsets for the **hearing-impaired**. Hearing dogs help **deaf** people stay connected. And sign language allows people who are deaf or **dumb** to communicate.

Compare **indirect object.** *objeto directo, complemento directo*

**di|rec|tor** /dɪrɛktər, daɪ-/ (**directors**) **1** N-COUNT The **directors** of a company are its most senior managers, who meet regularly to make important decisions about how it will be run. *directivo o directiva* [BUSINESS] ❑ *...the directors of the bank. ...los directivos del banco.* **2** N-COUNT The **director** of a choir is the person who is conducting it. *director o directora* **3** N-COUNT The **director** of a play, movie, or television program is the person who decides how it will appear on stage or screen, and who tells the actors and technical staff what to do. *director o directora*
→ see **theater**

**di|rec|tor gen|er|al** (**directors general**) N-COUNT The **director general** of a large organization is the person who is in charge of it. *director general o directora general* [BUSINESS]

**di|rec|tor's cut** (**director's cuts**) N-COUNT A **director's cut** is a version of a movie chosen by the movie's director, which expresses the director's artistic aims more fully than the original version. *versión del director* ❑ *I saw the director's cut of "Amadeus." Vi la versión del director de "Amadeus".*

**di|rec|tory** /dɪrɛktəri, daɪ-/ (**directories**) **1** N-COUNT A **directory** is a book which gives lists of facts, for example, people's names, addresses, and telephone numbers, or the names and addresses of business companies, usually arranged in alphabetical order. *directorio, guía* ❑ *...a telephone directory. ...un directorio telefónico.* **2** N-COUNT A **directory** is an area of a computer disk which contains one or more files or other directories. *directorio* [COMPUTING] ❑ *You can search the directory for files by date or name. Puede buscar los archivos en el directorio por fecha o nombre.*

**di|rec|tory as|sis|tance** N-UNCOUNT **Directory assistance** is a service which you can telephone to find out someone's telephone number. *servicio de información telefónica* ❑ *He dialed directory assistance. Llamó al servicio de información telefónica.*

**dirt** /dɜrt/ **1** N-UNCOUNT If there is **dirt** on something, there is dust, mud, or a stain on it. *suciedad, mugre* ❑ *I started to scrub off the dirt. Empecé a restregar la mugre.* **2** N-UNCOUNT You can refer to the earth on the ground as **dirt.** *tierra* ❑ *They all sat on the dirt under a tree. Todos se sentaron en la tierra bajo un árbol.*
→ see **erosion**

**dirty** /dɜrti/ (**dirtier, dirtiest, dirties, dirtying, dirtied**) **1** ADJ If something is **dirty,** it is marked or covered with stains, spots, or mud, and needs to be cleaned. *sucio* ❑ *She collected the dirty plates from the table. Recogió los platos sucios de la mesa.* **2** ADJ If you describe something such as a joke, a book, or someone's language as **dirty,** you mean that it refers to sex in a way that some people find offensive. *sucio, colorado, pícaro* ❑ *He laughed at their dirty jokes. Se rió de sus chistes colorados.* ● **Dirty** is also an adverb. *con un lenguaje vulgar* ❑ *"Don't talk dirty, Roger." —No seas vulgar, Roger.* **3** V-T To **dirty** something means to cause it to become dirty. *ensuciar* ❑ *The dog's hairs will dirty the seats. Los pelos del perro van a ensuciar los asientos.*

**dis|abil|ity** /dɪsəbɪlɪti/ (**disabilities**) N-COUNT A **disability** is a permanent injury, illness, or physical or mental condition that restricts the way that someone can live their life. *invalidez, incapacidad* ❑ *We're building a new changing room for people with disabilities. Estamos construyendo un nuevo vestidor para personas incapacitadas.*
→ see Word Web: **disability**

**dis|able** /dɪseɪbəl/ (**disables, disabling, disabled**) **1** V-T If an injury or illness **disables** someone, it affects them so badly that it restricts the way that they can live their life. *dejar lisiado* ❑ *The damage to her leg disabled her. El daño que sufrió en la pierna la dejó lisiada.* **2** V-T To **disable** a system or mechanism means to stop it from working. *inutilizar* ❑ *He disabled the car alarm. Desconectó (inutilizó) la alarma del carro.*

**dis|abled** /dɪseɪbəld/ ADJ Someone who is **disabled** has an illness, injury, or condition that tends to restrict the way that they can live their life, especially by making it difficult for them to move about. *lisiado, inválido, incapacitado, descapacitado, discapacitado, minusválido* ❑ *...the practical problems that disabled people face in the workplace. ...los problemas prácticos que enfrentan los discapacitados en el lugar de trabajo.* ● People who are disabled are sometimes referred to as **the disabled.** *discapacitado* ❑ *There are toilet facilities for the disabled. Hay instalaciones sanitarias para los discapacitados.*

**dis|ad|vant|age** /dɪsədvæntɪdʒ/ (**disadvantages**) **1** N-COUNT A **disadvantage** is a factor which makes someone or something less useful, acceptable, or successful than other people or things. *desventaja* ❑ *The big disadvantage of this computer is its size. La gran desventaja de esta computadora es su tamaño.* **2** PHRASE If you are **at a disadvantage,** you have a problem or difficulty that many other people do not have, which makes

d

it harder for you to be successful. *en desventaja* ❑ *The children from poor families were at a distinct disadvantage. Los hijos de las familias pobres estaban en clara desventaja.*

**Word Link** *dis ≈ negative, not : disagree, discomfort, disconnect*

D

**dis|agree** /dɪsəgri/ (**disagrees, disagreeing, disagreed**) **1** V-RECIP If you **disagree with** someone, you do not accept that what they say is true or correct. *discrepar, no estar de acuerdo con, estar en desacuerdo con* ❑ *You must continue to see them even if you disagree with them. Debes seguir viéndolos, aunque no estés de acuerdo con ellos.* ❑ *They can communicate even when they strongly disagree. Aun cuando no están en absoluto de acuerdo, pueden hablar (entre sí).* **2** V-I If you **disagree with** a particular action or proposal, you disapprove of it. *discrepar de, no estar de acuerdo con, estar en desacuerdo con* ❑ *I respect the president but I disagree with his decision. Respeto al presidente, pero no estoy de acuerdo con su decisión.*

**dis|agree|ment** /dɪsəgrimənt/ (**disagreements**) **1** N-UNCOUNT **Disagreement** means objecting to something. *desacuerdo* ❑ *Britain and France have expressed some disagreement with the plan. Gran Bretaña y Francia han expresado cierto desacuerdo con el plan.* **2** N-VAR When there is **disagreement** about something, people disagree or argue about what should be done. *desacuerdo, discrepancia* ❑ *The United States Congress and the president are still in disagreement over the plans. El Congreso y el presidente estadounidenses siguen estando en desacuerdo sobre los planes.*

**dis|ap|pear** /dɪsəpɪər/ (**disappears, disappearing, disappeared**) **1** V-I If someone or something **disappears,** they go away or are taken away somewhere where nobody can find them. *desaparecer* ❑ *She disappeared thirteen years ago. Desapareció hace trece años.* ● **dis|ap|pear|ance** N-VAR (**disappearances**) *desaparición* ❑ *Her disappearance is a mystery. Su desaparición es un misterio.* **2** V-I If something **disappears,** it stops existing or happening. *desaparecer, desvanecerse* ❑ *The immediate threat has disappeared. La amenaza inmediata ha desaparecido.* ● **dis|ap|pear|ance** N-UNCOUNT *desaparición* ❑ *...the disappearance of the dinosaurs. ...la desaparición de los dinosaurios.*

**dis|ap|point** /dɪsəpɔɪnt/ (**disappoints, disappointing, disappointed**) V-T If things or people **disappoint** you, they are not as good as you had hoped, or do not do what you hoped they would do. *decepcionar* ❑ *I don't want to disappoint him. No quiero decepcionarlo.* ● **dis|ap|point|ing** ADJ *decepcionante* ❑ *The restaurant looked lovely, but the food was disappointing. El restaurante era lindo, pero la comida era decepcionante.* ● **dis|ap|point|ing|ly** ADV *de manera decepcionante, decepcionantemente* ❑ *Progress is disappointingly slow. El avance es decepcionantemente lento.*

**dis|ap|point|ed** /dɪsəpɔɪntɪd/ ADJ If you are **disappointed,** you are sad because something has not happened or because something is not as good as you had hoped. *decepcionado* ❑ *Adamski was very disappointed with the mayor's decision. Adamski estaba muy decepcionado por la decisión del alcalde.* ❑ *I was disappointed that John was not there. Me decepcionó que John no estuviese (ahí).*

**dis|ap|point|ment** /dɪsəpɔɪntmənt/ (**disappointments**) **1** N-UNCOUNT **Disappointment** is the state of feeling disappointed. *decepción* ❑ *She couldn't hide the disappointment in her voice. No pudo ocultar su tono de decepción.* **2** N-COUNT Something or someone that is a **disappointment** is not as good as you had hoped. *decepción* ❑ *The result was a terrible disappointment. El resultado fue una decepción terrible.*

**dis|ap|prove** /dɪsəpruv/ (**disapproves, disapproving, disapproved**) V-I If you **disapprove of** something or someone, you feel or show that you do not like them or do not approve of them. *desaprobar* ❑ *Most people disapprove of such violent methods. La mayoría de la gente desaprueba esos métodos violentos.* ● **dis|ap|prov|ing** ADJ *desaprobatorio* ❑ *Janet gave him a disapproving look. Janet le lanzó una mirada de desaprobación.* ● **dis|ap|prov|ing|ly** ADV *con desaprobación* ❑ *Antonio looked at him disapprovingly. Antonio lo miró con desaprobación.*

**dis|as|ter** /dɪzæstər/ (**disasters**) **1** N-COUNT A **disaster** is a very bad accident such as an earthquake or a plane crash. *desastre, catástrofe* ❑ *It was the second air disaster that month. Era el segundo desastre aéreo de ese mes.* **2** N-COUNT If you refer to something as a **disaster,** you are emphasizing that you think it is extremely bad. *desastre, catástrofe* ❑ *The whole event was just a disaster! ¡Todo el acto fue un desastre!* **3** N-UNCOUNT **Disaster** is something which has very bad consequences for you. *desastre, catástrofe* ❑ *The government is facing financial disaster. El gobierno hace frente a una catástrofe económica.*
→ see Word Web: disaster

**dis|as|trous** /dɪzæstrəs/ ADJ A **disastrous**

**Word Web** disaster

We are learning more about nature's cycles. But natural **disasters** remain a big challenge. We can predict some disasters, such as **hurricanes** and **floods**. However, we still can't avoid the **damage** they do. Each year **monsoons** strike southern Asia. Monsoons are a combination of **typhoons**, **tropical storms**, and heavy **rains**. In addition to the damage caused by floods, **landslides** and **mudslides** add to the problem. In 2005 more than 90 million people suffered from disaster in China alone. Over 700 people died in that country and millions of acres of crops were destroyed. The **economic loss** totaled nearly 6 billion dollars.

event has extremely bad consequences and effects or is very unsuccessful. desastroso, catastrófico ❑ ...the recent, disastrous earthquake. ...el catastrófico terremoto reciente. ❑ ...their disastrous performance in the election. ...sus desastrosos resultados en las elecciones. • **dis|as|trous|ly** ADV desastrosamente, catastróficamente ❑ ...the company's disastrously low profits. ...las ganancias desastrosamente bajas de la empresa.

**dis|band** /dɪsbænd/ (**disbands, disbanding, disbanded**) V-T/V-I If someone **disbands** a group of people, or if the group **disbands,** it stops operating as a single unit. disolver, dispersar ❑ All the armed groups were disbanded. Todos los grupos armados fueron disueltos.

**dis|be|lief** /dɪsbɪlif/ N-UNCOUNT **Disbelief** is not believing that something is true or real. incredulidad, escepticismo ❑ She looked at him in disbelief. Lo miró con incredulidad.

**disc** /dɪsk/ → see **disk**

**dis|card** /dɪskɑrd/ (**discards, discarding, discarded**) V-T If you **discard** something, you get rid of it because you no longer want it or need it. desechar ❑ Read the instructions before discarding the box. Lea las indicaciones antes de desechar la caja.

**dis|charge** (**discharges, discharging, discharged**)

The verb is pronounced /dɪstʃɑrdʒ/. The noun is pronounced /dɪstʃɑrdʒ/.

**1** V-T When someone **is discharged from** a hospital, prison, or one of the armed services, they are officially allowed to leave, or told that they must leave. dar de alta (hospital), liberar (prisión), poner en libertad (prisión), dar de baja (ejército) ❑ He was discharged from hospital today. Lo dieron de alta hoy (en el hospital). • **Discharge** is also a noun. alta, liberación, baja ❑ ...his discharge from the army. ...su baja del ejército. **2** V-T If someone **discharges** their duties or responsibilities, they do everything that needs to be done in order to complete them. cumplir con [FORMAL] ❑ ...the quiet skill with which he discharged his duties. ...la discreta habilidad con que cumplió con sus obligaciones. **3** V-T If something **is discharged** from inside a place, it comes out. descargar, vaciar [FORMAL] ❑ The salty water was discharged at sea. Se vació el agua salada al mar. **4** N-VAR When there is a **discharge** of a substance, the substance comes out from inside somewhere. descarga, secreción [FORMAL] ❑ The disease causes a discharge from the eyes. La enfermedad provoca secreciones en los ojos. **5** N-COUNT The **discharge** of a river is the amount of water that it carries from one place to another in a particular period of time. caudal (volumétrico) [TECHNICAL]

**dis|ci|pli|nary** /dɪsɪplɪnɛri/ ADJ **Disciplinary** bodies or actions are concerned with making sure that people obey rules or regulations and that they are punished if they do not. disciplinario ❑ He is facing disciplinary action. Enfrenta medidas disciplinarias.

**dis|ci|pline** /dɪsɪplɪn/ (**disciplines, disciplining, disciplined**) **1** N-UNCOUNT **Discipline** is the practice of making people obey rules or standards of behavior, and punishing them when they do not. disciplina ❑ ...poor discipline in schools. ...la poca disciplina en las escuelas. **2** N-UNCOUNT **Discipline** is the quality of being able to behave and work in a controlled way which involves obeying particular rules or standards. disciplina ❑ He was impressed by their speed and discipline. Estaba impresionado por su rapidez y disciplina. **3** V-T If someone **is disciplined** for something that they have done wrong, they are punished for it. disciplinar, sancionar ❑ The workman was disciplined by his company but not dismissed. La empresa sancionó al trabajador, pero no lo despidió. **4** N-COUNT A **discipline** is a particular area of study, especially a subject of study in a college or university. disciplina [FORMAL] ❑ We're looking for people from a wide range of disciplines. Buscamos a profesionales de una amplia gama de disciplinas.

**disc jock|ey** (**disc jockeys**) also **disk jockey** N-COUNT A **disc jockey** is someone who plays and introduces music on the radio or at a disco. disc-jockey

**dis|close** /dɪsklo͟uz/ (**discloses, disclosing, disclosed**) V-T If you **disclose** new or secret information, you tell people about it. revelar ❑ They refused to disclose details of the deal. Se rehusaron a revelar los detalles del trato.

**dis|clo|sure** /dɪsklo͟uʒər/ (**disclosures**) N-VAR **Disclosure** is the act of giving people new or secret information. revelación ❑ ...disclosure of negative information about the company. ...la revelación de información negativa sobre la empresa.

**dis|co** /dɪskoʊ/ (**discos**) N-COUNT A **disco** is a place or event at which people dance to pop music. discoteca ❑ Fridays and Saturdays are regular disco nights. Regularmente, las noches de viernes y sábado son de discoteca.

**Word Link** dis ≈ negative, not : disagree, discomfort, disconnect

**dis|com|fort** /dɪskʌmfərt/ (**discomforts**) **1** N-UNCOUNT **Discomfort** is a painful feeling in part of your body when you have been hurt slightly or when you have been uncomfortable for a long time. incomodidad, malestar ❑ Steve had some discomfort, but no real pain. Steve tenía un poco de malestar, pero no le dolía realmente. **2** N-UNCOUNT **Discomfort** is a feeling of worry caused by shame or embarrassment. inquietud, desasosiego ❑ She hears the discomfort in his voice. Percibe la inquietud en su voz. **3** N-COUNT **Discomforts** are conditions which cause you to feel physically uncomfortable. incomodidad ❑ ...the discomforts of camping. ...las incomodidades de acampar.

**dis|con|nect** /dɪskənɛkt/ (**disconnects, disconnecting, disconnected**) V-T If you **disconnect** a piece of equipment, you separate it from its source of power or break a connection that it needs in order to work. desconectar ❑ Complete peace and quiet may mean disconnecting the telephone for a while. El poder disfrutar de paz y tranquilidad completas puede significar el tener que desconectar el teléfono por un rato.

**dis|count** (**discounts, discounting, discounted**)

Pronounced /dɪskaʊnt/ for meaning **1**, and /dɪskaʊnt/ for meaning **2**.

**1** N-COUNT A **discount** is a reduction in the usual price of something. descuento, rebaja ❑ You can buy them at a discount. Puede comprarlos con descuento.

❑ *All staff get a 20 percent discount.* *Todo el personal obtiene un descuento del 20 por ciento.* **2** V-T If you **discount** an idea, fact, or theory, you consider that it is not true, not important, or not relevant. *descartar, desechar* ❑ *He quickly discounted the idea.* *Rápidamente desechó la idea.*

**dis|count store** (**discount stores**) N-COUNT A **discount store** is a store that sells goods at lower prices than usual. *tienda de descuento* ❑ *A growing number of shoppers buy food at discount stores.* *Cada vez más personas compran sus alimentos en las tiendas de descuento.*

D

**dis|cour|age** /dɪskɜrɪdʒ/ (**discourages, discouraging, discouraged**) **1** V-T If someone or something **discourages** you, they cause you to lose your enthusiasm about your actions. *desalentar, desanimar* ❑ *It may be difficult to do at first. Don't let this discourage you.* *Al principio puede ser difícil, pero no dejes que eso te desanime.* ● **dis|cour|aged** ADJ *desalentado, desanimado* ❑ *He felt discouraged by his lack of progress.* *Se sintió desalentado porque no avanzaba.* ● **dis|cour|ag|ing** ADJ *desalentador* ❑ *Today's report is extremely discouraging for the economy.* *El informe de hoy es extremadamente desalentador para la economía.* **2** V-T To **discourage** an action or to **discourage** someone **from** doing it means to make them not want to do it. *desalentar, disuadir* ❑ *High prices discourage many people from traveling by train.* *Los precios altos disuaden a muchas personas de viajar en tren.* ● **dis|cour|age|ment** N-UNCOUNT *desaliento, desánimo* ❑ *Her family supported her when she experienced discouragement.* *Su familia la apoyó cuando se sintió desalentada.*

**dis|cov|er** /dɪskʌvər/ (**discovers, discovering, discovered**) **1** V-T If you **discover** something that you did not know about before, you become aware of it or learn of it. *descubrir* ❑ *She discovered that they'd escaped.* *Descubrió que habían escapado.* ❑ *They needed to discover who the thief was.* *Necesitaban descubrir quién fue el ladrón.* **2** V-T If a person or thing **is discovered,** someone finds them, either by accident or because they have been looking for them. *descubrir* ❑ *The car was discovered on a roadside outside the city.* *Descubrieron el coche al borde de una carretera en las afueras de la ciudad.* **3** V-T When someone **discovers** a new place, substance, scientific fact, or scientific technique, they are the first person to find it or become aware of it. *descubrir* ❑ *...the first European to discover America.* *...el primer europeo en descubrir América.*

**Thesaurus** *discover* Ver también:

v. detect, find out, learn, uncover; (*ant.*) ignore, miss, overlook **1**

**dis|cov|ery** /dɪskʌvəri/ (**discoveries**) **1** N-VAR If someone makes a **discovery,** they become aware of something that they did not know about before. *descubrimiento* ❑ *I made an incredible discovery.* *Hice un descubrimiento increíble.* **2** N-VAR If someone makes a **discovery,** they are the first person to find or become aware of a place, substance, or scientific fact that no one knew about before. *descubrimiento* ❑ *In that year, two important discoveries were made.* *Ese año hubo dos descubrimientos importantes.* **3** N-VAR When the **discovery** of people or objects happens, someone finds them. *descubrimiento* ❑ *...the discovery of a box of cellphones.* *...el descubrimiento de una caja de teléfonos celulares.*

**Word Link** *cred ≈ to believe : credible, discredit, incredible*

**dis|cred|it** /dɪskrɛdɪt/ (**discredits, discrediting, discredited**) V-T To **discredit** someone or something means to cause them to lose people's respect or trust. *desacreditar, desprestigiar, desautorizar* ❑ *...research which discredits the theory.* *...una investigación que desacredita la teoría.* ● **dis|cred|it|ed** ADJ *desacreditado* ❑ *The government is thoroughly discredited.* *El gobierno está totalmente desacreditado.*

**dis|creet** /dɪskrit/ ADJ If you are **discreet,** you are polite and careful in what you do or say, because you want to avoid embarrassing or offending someone. *discreto* ❑ *They were gossipy and not always discreet.* *Eran chismosos y no siempre discretos.* ● **dis|creet|ly** ADV *discretamente* ❑ *I took the phone, and she went discreetly into the living room.* *Levanté el teléfono y se dirigió discretamente a la sala.*

**dis|cre|tion** /dɪskrɛʃ͡ən/ **1** N-UNCOUNT **Discretion** is the quality of behaving in a quiet and controlled way without drawing attention to yourself or giving away personal or private information. *discreción* [FORMAL] ❑ *Angela was a model of discretion and didn't ask what had been in the letter.* *Ángela era un dechado de discreción y no preguntó qué decía la carta.* **2** N-UNCOUNT If someone in a position of authority uses their **discretion** or has **the discretion** to do something in a particular situation, they have the freedom and authority to decide what to do. *discreción* [FORMAL] ❑ *City departments have wide discretion on the contracts.* *Los departamentos municipales tienen facultades discrecionales sobre los contratos.* ❑ *We may change the rate at our discretion and will notify you of any change.* *Podemos cambiar la tasa a discreción nuestra, pero le notificaremos cualquier cambio.*

**dis|crimi|nate** /dɪskrɪmɪneɪt/ (**discriminates, discriminating, discriminated**) **1** V-I If you can **discriminate between** two things, you can recognize that they are different. *discriminar, distinguir* ❑ *He is unable to discriminate between a good idea and a terrible one.* *Es incapaz de distinguir entre una buena idea y una pésima.* **2** V-I To **discriminate against** a group of people or **in favor of** a group of people means to unfairly treat them worse or better than other groups. *discriminar* ❑ *They believe the law discriminates against women.* *Ellos creen que la ley discrimina a las mujeres.* ❑ *The company plan discriminated in favor of top executives.* *El plan de la empresa establecía distinciones que favorecían a los ejecutivos de alta jerarquía.*

**dis|crimi|na|tion** /dɪskrɪmɪneɪʃ͡ən/ **1** N-UNCOUNT **Discrimination** is the practice of treating one person or group of people less fairly or less well than other people or groups. *discriminación* ❑ *...sex discrimination laws.* *...leyes de discriminación sexual.* **2** N-UNCOUNT **Discrimination** is knowing what is good or of high quality. *discriminación, discernimiento* ❑ *They cooked without skill and ate without discrimination.* *Cocinaron sin habilidad y comieron indiscriminadamente.*

**dis|cuss** /dɪskʌs/ (**discusses, discussing, discussed**) V-T If people **discuss** something, they talk about it, often in order to reach a decision. *discutir* ❑ *I will discuss the situation with colleagues tomorrow.* *Mañana discutiré la situación con algunos colegas.*

**Word Partnership** Usar *discuss* con:

N. discuss **an issue**, discuss **a matter**, discuss **options**, discuss **plans**, discuss **problems**
V. **meet to** discuss, **refuse to** discuss

**dis|cus|sion** /dɪskʌʃᵊn/ (**discussions**) N-VAR If there is **discussion** about something, people talk about it, often in order to reach a decision. *discusión* ❑ *There was a lot of discussion about the report.* *Hubo una gran discusión sobre el informe.* ❑ *Managers are having informal discussions later today.* *Más tarde durante el día, los gerentes sostendrán discusiones informales.* PHRASE ● If something is **under discussion**, it is still being talked about and a final decision has not yet been reached. *estar discutiéndose*

**Thesaurus** *discussion* Ver también:

N. conference, conversation, debate, talk

**dis|ease** /dɪziz/ (**diseases**) N-VAR A **disease** is an illness which affects people, animals, or plants. *enfermedad* ❑ *...the rapid spread of disease.* *...la rápida propagación de la enfermedad.*
→ see **diagnosis, illness, medicine**

**Word Link** *grac ≈ pleasing : disgrace, grace, graceful*

**dis|grace** /dɪsgreɪs/ (**disgraces, disgracing, disgraced**) **1** N-UNCOUNT If you say that someone is **in disgrace**, you are emphasizing that other people disapprove of them and do not respect them because of something that they have done. *desgracia* ❑ *The vice president resigned in disgrace.* *El vicepresidente renunció por haber caído en desgracia.* **2** N-SING If you say that something is **a disgrace**, you are emphasizing that it is very bad or wrong, and that you find it completely unacceptable. *vergüenza* ❑ *His behavior was a complete disgrace.* *Su comportamiento fue completamente vergonzoso.* **3** V-T If you say that someone **disgraces** someone else, you are emphasizing that their behavior causes the other person to feel ashamed. *deshonrar* ❑ *I have disgraced my family.* *He deshonrado a mi familia.*

**dis|guise** /dɪsgaɪz/ (**disguises, disguising, disguised**) **1** N-VAR If you are **in disguise**, you are not wearing your usual clothes or you have altered your appearance in other ways, so that people will not recognize you. *disfrazado* ❑ *He traveled in disguise.* *Viajó disfrazado.* **2** V-T If you **disguise yourself**, you put on clothes which make you look like someone else or alter your appearance in other ways, so that people will not recognize you. *hacerse pasar por, disfrazar(se)* ❑ *She disguised herself as a man so she could fight on the battlefield.* *Se hizo pasar por un hombre para poder combatir.* ● **dis|guised** ADJ *disfrazado* ❑ *The robber entered the hospital disguised as a medical worker.* *El ladrón entró al hospital haciéndose pasar por un trabajador.* **3** V-T To **disguise** something means to hide it or make it appear different so that people will not know about it or will not recognize it. *ocultar, disimular* ❑ *He made no attempt to disguise his anger.* *No hizo ningún intento por disimular su enojo.* ● **dis|guised** ADJ *disimulado* ❑ *The book was actually a thinly disguised autobiography.* *El libro era realmente una autobiografía apenas disimulada.*

**dis|gust** /dɪsgʌst/ (**disgusts, disgusting, disgusted**) **1** N-UNCOUNT **Disgust** is a feeling of very strong dislike or disapproval. *indignación, repugnancia* ❑ *George watched in disgust.* *George observó con indignación.* **2** V-T To **disgust** someone means to make them feel a strong sense of dislike and disapproval. *indignar* ❑ *He disgusted many people with his behavior.* *Indignó a muchas personas con su conducta.*

**dis|gust|ed** /dɪsgʌstɪd/ ADJ If you are **disgusted**, you feel a strong sense of dislike and disapproval. *indignado* ❑ *I'm disgusted with the way that he was treated.* *Estoy indignado por la manera como fue tratado.* ● **dis|gust|ed|ly** ADV *con indignación* ❑ *"It's a little late for that," Ritter said disgustedly.* *—Ya es demasiado tarde para eso—dijo Ritter indignado.*

**dis|gust|ing** /dɪsgʌstɪŋ/ ADJ If you say that something is **disgusting**, you think it is extremely unpleasant or unacceptable. *repugnante, asqueroso, vergonzoso* ❑ *It tasted disgusting.* *Tenía un sabor asqueroso/repugnante.* ❑ *It's disgusting the way we were treated.* *Fue vergonzosa la manera como nos trataron.*

**dish** /dɪʃ/ (**dishes, dishing, dished**) **1** N-COUNT A **dish** is a shallow container used for cooking or serving food. *plato* ❑ *...plastic bowls and dishes.* *...tazones y platos de plástico.* **2** N-COUNT Food that is prepared in a particular style or combination can be referred to as a **dish**. *plato* ❑ *There are plenty of vegetarian dishes to choose from.* *Hay muchos platos vegetarianos de dónde escoger.* **3** N-COUNT You can use **dish** to refer to anything that is round and hollow in shape with a wide uncovered top. *antena parabólica* ❑ *...a dish used to receive satellite broadcasts.* *...una antena parabólica para recibir transmisiones por satélite.* **4** → see also **satellite dish**
→ see Picture Dictionary: **dish**
→ see **pottery**

▶ **dish out** **1** PHR-VERB If you **dish out** something, you distribute it among a number of people. *repartir* [INFORMAL] ❑ *...dishing out money.* *...repartiendo dinero.* **2** PHR-VERB If someone **dishes out** criticism or punishment, they give it to someone. *repartir* [INFORMAL] ❑ *It was his job to dish out the punishment.* *Su trabajo consistía en repartir los castigos.* **3** PHR-VERB If you **dish out** food, you serve it to people at the beginning of each course of a meal. *repartir* [INFORMAL] ❑ *Annie dished out the curry.* *Annie repartió el curry.*

▶ **dish up** PHR-VERB If you **dish up** food, you serve it. *servir, dar* [INFORMAL] ❑ *They dished up a lovely meal.* *Sirvieron una comida riquísima.*

**di|shev|eled** /dɪʃɛvᵊld/ also **dishevelled** ADJ If you describe someone's hair, clothes, or appearance as **disheveled**, you mean that it is very untidy. *desmelenado, desarreglado* ❑ *She arrived tired and disheveled.* *Llegó cansada y despeinada.*

**dis|hon|est** /dɪsɒnɪst/ ADJ If you say that a person or their behavior is **dishonest**, you mean that they are not truthful or honest and that you cannot trust them. *deshonesto, fraudulento* ❑ *I was dishonest with him.* *Fui deshonesto con él.* ● **dis|hon|est|ly** ADV *fraudulentamente,*

D

Picture Dictionary

deshonestamente ❑ *He dishonestly received $500,000.* *Recibió 500,000 dólares fraudulentamente.*

**dis|hon|or** /dɪsɒnər/ (**dishonors, dishonoring, dishonored**) **1** V-T If you **dishonor** someone, you behave in a way that damages their good reputation. *deshonrar* [FORMAL] ❑ *He had insulted and dishonored these people.* *Había insultado y deshonrado a esas personas.* **2** V-T If someone **dishonors** an agreement, they refuse to act according to its conditions. *incumplir, faltar a, quebrantar* ❑ *I do not think I dishonored my oath.* *No creo haber faltado a mi juramento.* **3** N-UNCOUNT **Dishonor** is a state in which people disapprove of you and lose their respect for you. *deshonor, deshonra* [FORMAL] ❑ *I have brought shame and dishonor on my family.* *He causado vergüenza y deshonra a mi familia.*

**dis|hon|or|able** /dɪsɒnərəbᵊl/ ADJ Someone who is **dishonorable** is not honest and does things which you consider to be morally unacceptable. *deshonroso, vergonzoso, indecoroso* ❑ *Actresses were considered slightly dishonorable in those days.* *En aquellos días se consideraba que el ser actriz era un poco indecoroso.* ● **dis|hon|or|ably** ADV *deshonrosamente, indecorosamente* ❑ *He didn't want to behave dishonorably.* *No quería comportarse deshonrosamente.*

**dish|rag** /dɪʃræg/ (**dishrags**) N-COUNT A **dishrag** is a cloth used for washing dishes, pans, and flatware. *estropajo, fregón, fregador*

**dish|washer** /dɪʃwɒʃər/ (**dishwashers**) **1** N-COUNT A **dishwasher** is an electrically operated machine that washes and dries dishes, pans and flatware. *lavaplatos, lavavajillas* **2** N-COUNT A **dishwasher** is a person who is employed to wash dishes, for example at a restaurant, or who usually washes the dishes at home. *lavaplatos* ❑ *I was a short-order cook and a dishwasher.* *Fui cocinero de comida rápida y lavaplatos.*

**dish|washing liq|uid** /dɪʃwɒʃɪŋlɪkwɪd/ (**dishwashing liquids**) N-VAR **Dishwashing liquid** is a thick soapy liquid which you add to hot water to clean dirty dishes. *líquido para lavaplatos/lavavajillas, detergente para lavaplatos/lavavajillas*

**dis|in|fect** /dɪsɪnfɛkt/ (**disinfects, disinfecting, disinfected**) V-T If you **disinfect** something, you clean it using a substance that kills germs. *desinfectar* ❑ *Chlorine is used for disinfecting water.* *El cloro se usa para desinfectar el agua.*

**dis|in|fect|ant** /dɪsɪnfɛktənt/ (**disinfectants**) N-VAR **Disinfectant** is a substance that kills germs. It is used, for example, for cleaning kitchens and bathrooms. *desinfectante* ❑ *They washed their hands with disinfectant.* *Se lavaron las manos con desinfectante.*

**dis|in|te|grate** /dɪsɪntɪgreɪt/ (**disintegrates, disintegrating, disintegrated**) **1** V-I If something **disintegrates,** it becomes seriously weakened, and is divided or destroyed. *desintegrarse* ❑ *The empire began to disintegrate.* *El imperio empezó a desintegrarse.* ● **dis|in|te|gra|tion** /dɪsɪntɪgreɪʃᵊn/ N-UNCOUNT *desintegración* ❑ *...the violent disintegration of Yugoslavia.* *...la violenta desintegración de Yugoslavia.* **2** V-I If an object or substance **disintegrates,** it breaks into many small pieces or parts and is destroyed. *desintegrarse* ❑ *At 420 mph the windshield disintegrated.* *El parabrisas se desintegró a las 420 millas por hora.*

**disk** /dɪsk/ (**disks**) also **disc** **1** N-COUNT A **disk** is a flat, circular shape or object. *disco* ❑ *The food processor has thin, medium, and thick slicing disks.* *El procesador de alimentos viene con discos rebanadores delgados, medianos y gruesos.* **2** N-COUNT A **disk** is one of the thin, circular pieces of cartilage which separate the bones in your back. *disco* ❑ *I had slipped a disk and was in pain.* *Tenía una hernia de disco y me dolía.* **3** N-COUNT In a computer, the **disk** is the part where information is stored. *disco* ❑ *The program takes up 2.5 megabytes of disk space.* *El programa ocupa 2.5 megabytes de la capacidad del disco.* **4** N-COUNT A disk is the same as a **compact disk.** *disco (compacto)* **5** → see also **floppy disk, hard disk**

**disk drive** (**disk drives**) N-COUNT The **disk drive** on a computer is the part that contains the disk or into which a disk can be inserted. The disk drive allows you to read information from the disk and store information on the disk. *unidad de disco*

**dis|like** /dɪslaɪk/ (**dislikes, disliking, disliked**) **1** V-T If you **dislike** someone or something, you think they are unpleasant and do not like them. *disgustar* ❑ *Many people dislike the taste.* *A mucha gente le disgusta el sabor.* **2** N-UNCOUNT **Dislike** is the feeling that you do not like someone or something. *aversión* ❑ *...his dislike of publicity.* *...su* *aversión a la publicidad.* **3** N-COUNT Your **dislikes** are the things that you do not like. *aversión* ❑ *Consider what your likes and dislikes are about your job. Piensa en los pros y los contras de tu trabajo.*

**dis|man|tle** /dɪsmæntᵊl/ (**dismantles, dismantling, dismantled**) V-T If you **dismantle** a machine or structure, you carefully separate it into its different parts. *desmantelar, desmontar, desarmar* ❑ *Expertly he dismantled the gun. Desarmó la pistola con una gran habilidad.*

**dis|may** /dɪsmeɪ/ (**dismays, dismaying, dismayed**) **1** N-UNCOUNT **Dismay** is a strong feeling of fear, worry, or sadness that is caused by something unpleasant and unexpected. *consternación, desánimo, desaliento* [FORMAL] ❑ *Local people reacted with dismay. Los lugareños se mostraron consternados.* **2** V-T If you **are dismayed** by something, it makes you feel afraid, worried, or sad. *consternado, desanimado, desalentado* [FORMAL] ❑ *The committee was dismayed by the news. Las noticias desalentaron a la comisión.* ● **dis|mayed** ADJ *consternado, desanimado, desalentado* ❑ *Glen was shocked and dismayed at her reaction. Glen se mostró horrorizado y consternado ante su reacción.*

**Word Link** *miss ≈ sending : dismiss, missile, missionary*

**dis|miss** /dɪsmɪs/ (**dismisses, dismissing, dismissed**) **1** V-T If you **dismiss** something, you decide or say that it is not important enough for you to think about or consider. *descartar, desechar, desestimar* ❑ *He dismissed the plan as nonsense. Descartó el plan porque consideró que eran tonterías.* **2** V-T When an employer **dismisses** an employee, the employer tells the employee that they are no longer needed to do the job that they have been doing. *despedir* ❑ *Locke was dismissed from the team after admitting to stealing an ATM card. Despidieron a Locke del equipo después de que admitió haber robado una tarjeta de crédito.* **3** V-T If you **are dismissed** by someone in authority, they tell you that you can go away from them. *despedir* ❑ *Two more witnesses were called, heard, and dismissed. Llamaron a dos testigos más, los escucharon y les dieron autorización para retirarse.*

**Word Partnership** Usar *dismiss* con:

ADJ. **easy to** dismiss **1**
N. dismiss **an idea,** dismiss **a possibility** **1**
dismiss **an employee** **2**

**dis|mis|sal** /dɪsmɪsᵊl/ (**dismissals**) **1** N-VAR When an employee is dismissed from their job, you call this their **dismissal.** *despido* ❑ *...Mr. Low's dismissal from his job. ...el despido del señor Low (de su empleo).* **2** N-UNCOUNT **Dismissal of** something means deciding or saying that it is not important. *desestimación, desprecio* ❑ *...dismissal of public opinion. ...el desprecio de la opinión pública.*

**dis|obedi|ence** /dɪsəbidiəns/ N-UNCOUNT **Disobedience** is deliberately not doing what someone tells you to do, or what a rule or law says that you should do. *desobediencia* ❑ *...an act of disobedience. ...un acto de desobediencia.*

**dis|obey** /dɪsəbeɪ/ (**disobeys, disobeying, disobeyed**) V-T/V-I When someone **disobeys** a person or an order, they deliberately do not do what they have been told to do. *desobedecer* ❑ *He often disobeyed his mother and father. Frecuentemente desobedecía a sus padres.* ❑ *He will not dare disobey. No se atreverá a desobedecer.*

**dis|or|der** /dɪsɔrdər/ (**disorders**) **1** N-VAR A **disorder** is a problem or illness which affects your mind or body. *afección* ❑ *...a rare blood disorder. ...una rara afección de la sangre.* **2** N-UNCOUNT **Disorder** is violence or rioting in public. *desorden, disturbio* ❑ *America's worst civil disorder erupted in the city of Los Angeles. Los peores disturbios civiles de Estados Unidos estallaron en Los Ángeles.* **3** N-UNCOUNT **Disorder** is a state of being untidy, badly prepared, or badly organized. *desorden* ❑ *The emergency room was in disorder. La sala de urgencias/emergencias era un desorden.*

**dis|or|der|ly con|duct** N-UNCOUNT In law, **disorderly conduct** is the offense of behaving in a dangerous or disruptive way in public. *alteración del orden público* ❑ *The group was charged with disorderly conduct. Acusaron al grupo de alteración del orden público.*

**dis|patch** /dɪspætʃ/ (**dispatches, dispatching, dispatched**) V-T If you **dispatch** someone or something to a place, you send them there. *despachar, enviar, mandar* [FORMAL] ❑ *He dispatched another letter to his cousin. Mandó otra carta a su primo.* ● **Dispatch** is also a noun. *despacho, envío, expedición* ❑ *We have 125 cases ready for dispatch. Tenemos 125 cajas listas para su envío.*

**dis|patch|er** /dɪspætʃər/ (**dispatchers**) N-COUNT A **dispatcher** is someone who works for an organization such as the police or the fire department and whose job is to send members of the organization to the places where they are needed. *despachador o despachadora* ❑ *The police dispatcher received the call at around 10:30 a.m. El despachador de la policía recibió la llamada a alrededor de las diez y media de la mañana.*

**dis|perse** /dɪspɜrs/ (**disperses, dispersing, dispersed**) **1** V-T/V-I When something **disperses** or when you **disperse** it, it spreads over a wide area. *dispersar, diseminar* ❑ *When the sandbags open, the sand is dispersed on the ocean floor. Cuando los sacos de arena se abren, la arena se dispersa en el fondo del mar.* **2** V-T/V-I When a group of people **disperses** or when someone **disperses** them, the group splits up and the people leave in different directions. *dispersar(se)* ❑ *Police used tear gas to disperse the demonstrators. La policía lanzó gas lacrimógeno para dispersar a los manifestantes.*

**dis|place** /dɪspleɪs/ (**displaces, displacing, displaced**) **1** V-T If one thing **displaces** another, it forces the other thing out and then occupies its position. *desplazar* ❑ *These factories have displaced tourism as the country's main source of income. Estas fábricas han desplazado al turismo como la principal fuente de ingresos del país.* **2** V-T If a person or group of people **is displaced,** they are forced to move away from the area where they live. *desplazar* ❑ *More than 600,000 people were displaced by the earthquake. Ha habido más de 600,000 desplazados debido al terremoto.* ● **dis|place|ment** N-UNCOUNT *desplazamiento* ❑ *...the gradual displacement of Native Americans. ...el desplazamiento gradual de los indios americanos.*

d

D

**dis|play** /dɪspleɪ/ (**displays, displaying, displayed**) **1** V-T If you **display** something, you put it in a place where people can see it. *exhibir, mostrar* ❑ *Old soldiers proudly displayed their medals. Los veteranos mostraron sus medallas con orgullo.* ● **Display** is also a noun. *exhibición, exposición* ❑ *...the artists whose work is on display. ...los artistas cuya obra está en exposición.* **2** V-T If you **display** a characteristic, quality, or emotion, you behave in a way which shows that you have it. *exteriorizar, manifestar, mostrar* ❑ *Gordon didn't often display his feelings. Gordon no exteriorizaba sus sentimientos a menudo.* ● **Display** is also a noun. *muestra, demostración* ❑ *He reserved displays of affection for his mother. Reservaba sus muestras de afecto para su madre.* **3** N-COUNT A **display** is an arrangement of things that have been put in a particular place, so that people can see them easily. *exposición* ❑ *...a display of your work. ...una exposición de tu trabajo.* **4** N-COUNT A **display** is a public performance or other event which is intended to entertain people. *exhibición, despliegue* ❑ *...a fireworks display. ...un despliegue de fuegos artificiales.*

**dis|pos|able** /dɪspoʊzəbᵊl/ ADJ A **disposable** product is designed to be thrown away after it has been used. *desechable* ❑ *...disposable diapers. ...pañales desechables.*

**dis|pos|al** /dɪspoʊzᵊl/ **1** PHRASE If you have something **at** your **disposal**, you are able to use it whenever you want, and for whatever purpose you want. If you are **at** someone's **disposal**, you are willing to help them in any way you can. *disposición* ❑ *Do you have this information at your disposal? ¿Está a tu disposición esa información?* **2** N-UNCOUNT **Disposal** is the act of getting rid of something that is no longer wanted or needed. *eliminación* ❑ *...the disposal of waste. ...la eliminación de los desechos.*

**dis|pose** /dɪspoʊz/ (**disposes, disposing, disposed**)
▸ **dispose of** PHR-VERB If you **dispose of** something that you no longer want or need, you get rid of it. *deshacerse de* ❑ *...the safest ways of disposing of nuclear waste. ...los métodos más seguros para deshacerse de los residuos radioactivos.*

**dis|prove** /dɪspruv/ (**disproves, disproving, disproved, disproven**) V-T To **disprove** an idea, belief, or theory means to show that it is not true. *desmentir, rebatir, refutar* ❑ *The research disproved his theory. Las investigaciones refutaron su teoría.*
→ see **science**

| Word Link | *put ≈ thinking : computer, dispute, reputation* |
|---|---|

**dis|pute** /dɪspyut/ (**disputes, disputing, disputed**) **1** N-VAR A **dispute** is an argument or disagreement between people or groups. *disputa, litigio, negociación* ❑ *They won a pay dispute with the government. Ganaron una negociación salarial con el gobierno.* **2** V-T If you **dispute** a fact, statement, or theory, you say that it is incorrect or untrue. *disputar, refutar, rebatir* ❑ *He disputed the idea that he had made a mistake. Refutó la idea de que hubiese cometido un error.* ❑ *Nobody disputed that Davey was clever. Nadie puso en disputa que Davey fuese listo.* **3** V-RECIP When people **dispute** something, they fight for control or ownership of it. *disputar* ❑ *Russia and Ukraine were disputing the ownership of the ships. Rusia y Ukrania se disputaban la propiedad de los barcos.* **4** PHRASE If something is **in dispute,** people are questioning it or arguing about it. *en disputa, en litigio* ❑ *The contract is in dispute. Están negociando el contrato.*

**dis|quali|fy** /dɪskwɒlɪfaɪ/ (**disqualifies, disqualifying, disqualified**) V-T When someone **is disqualified,** they are officially stopped from taking part in a particular event, activity, or competition. *descalificar* ❑ *Thomson was disqualified from the race. Thomson fue descalificado de la carrera.* ● **dis|quali|fi|ca|tion** /dɪskwɒlɪfɪkeɪʃᵊn/ N-VAR (**disqualifications**) *descalificación* ❑ *...her disqualification from next year's Olympic Games. ...su descalificación de los Juegos Olímpicos del año que viene.*

| Word Link | *rupt ≈ breaking : disrupt, erupt, interrupt* |
|---|---|

**dis|rupt** /dɪsrʌpt/ (**disrupts, disrupting, disrupted**) V-T If someone or something **disrupts** an event, system, or process, they cause difficulties that prevent it from continuing or operating in a normal way. *perturbar, afectar* ❑ *Anti-war protesters disrupted the debate. Las protestas contra la guerra afectaron el desarrollo del debate.* ● **dis|rup|tion** N-VAR (**disruptions**) *perturbación, trastorno* ❑ *The bad weather caused disruption at many airports. El mal tiempo provocó trastornos en muchos aeropuertos.*

**dis|sent** /dɪsɛnt/ (**dissents, dissenting, dissented**) **1** N-UNCOUNT **Dissent** is strong disagreement with a decision or opinion, especially one that is supported by most people or by people in authority. *disensión, desacuerdo* ❑ *...political dissent. ...desacuerdo político.* **2** V-I If you **dissent,** you express disagreement with a decision or opinion, especially one that is supported by most people or by people in authority. *discrepar, disentir, estar en desacuerdo* [FORMAL] ❑ *Just one of the 10 members dissented. Sólo uno de los 10 miembros mostró disconformidad.* ❑ *No one dissents from the decision. Nadie discrepa de la decisión.* ● **dis|sent|er** N-COUNT (**dissenters**) *disidente* ❑ *The party does not tolerate dissenters. El partido no tolera a los disidentes.* ● **dis|sent|ing** ADJ *disidente, discrepante* ❑ *He ignored dissenting views. Ignoró las opiniones discrepantes.*

**dis|ser|ta|tion** /dɪsərteɪʃᵊn/ (**dissertations**) N-COUNT A **dissertation** is a long formal piece of writing on a particular subject, especially for an advanced university degree. *disertación, tesis* ❑ *He is writing a dissertation on the civil war. Está escribiendo una disertación sobre la guerra civil.*

**dis|si|dent** /dɪsɪdənt/ (**dissidents**) N-COUNT **Dissidents** are people who disagree with and criticize their government, especially because it is undemocratic. *disidente* ❑ *...political dissidents. ...disidentes políticos.*

**dis|solve** /dɪzɒlv/ (**dissolves, dissolving, dissolved**) **1** V-T/V-I If a substance **dissolves** in liquid or if you **dissolve** it, it becomes mixed with the liquid and disappears. *disolver* ❑ *Heat the mixture gently until the sugar dissolves. Caliente la mezcla a fuego lento hasta que se disuelva el azúcar.* **2** V-T When something **is dissolved,** it is officially ended or broken up. *disolver* ❑ *The committee was* dissolved. La comisión fue disuelta. • **dis|so|lu|tion** /dɪsəluʃᵊn/ N-UNCOUNT; N-SING disolución ❑ *He stayed until the dissolution of the company.* *Él permaneció hasta la disolución de la compañía.*

**dis|tance** /dɪstəns/ (**distances, distancing, distanced**) **1** N-VAR The **distance between** two places is the amount of space between them. distancia ❑ *...the distance between the island and the shore.* *...la distancia entre la isla y la costa.* **2** N-UNCOUNT **Distance** is coolness or unfriendliness in the way that someone behaves toward you. distancia, distanciamiento [FORMAL] ❑ *There were periods of distance, of coldness.* *Hubo épocas de distanciamiento, de frialdad.* **3** V-T If you **distance yourself from** a person or thing, or if something **distances** you **from** them, you feel less friendly or positive toward them, or become less involved with them. distanciarse ❑ *The author distanced himself from some of the comments in his book.* *El autor se distanció de algunos de los comentarios de su libro.* • **dis|tanced** ADJ distanciado ❑ *She had become distanced from Derek.* *Se había distanciado de Derek.* **4** PHRASE If you are **at a distance** from something, or if you see it or remember it **from a distance,** you are a long way away from it in space or time. a distancia, desde lejos ❑ *At a distance, the lake looked beautiful.* *A distancia, el lago parecía hermoso.* ❑ *Now I can think about what happened from a distance of almost forty years.* *Ahora, a una distancia de casi cuarenta años, ya puedo reflexionar en lo que pasó.*

**Word Partnership** Usar *distance* con:

ADJ. **safe** distance, **short** distance **1**
PREP. distance **between, within walking** distance **1**
**at** a distance, **from a** distance **4**

**dis|tant** /dɪstənt/ **1** ADJ **Distant** means very far away. distante ❑ *The mountains were on the distant horizon.* *Las montañas estaban en el horizonte, a lo lejos.* • **dis|tant|ly** ADV en lontananza [LITERARY] ❑ *Distantly, she could just see the town of Chiffa.* *En lontananza, podía ver el poblado de Chiffa.* **2** ADJ You use **distant** to describe a time or event that is very far away in the future or in the past. distante, remoto ❑ *Things will improve in the not too distant future.* *Las cosas mejorarán en un futuro no muy distante.* **3** ADJ A **distant** relative is one who you are not closely related to. lejano ❑ *He's a distant relative of the mayor.* *Es pariente lejano del alcalde.* • **dis|tant|ly** ADV vagamente ❑ *The O'Shea girls are distantly related to our family.* *Las muchachas O'Shea son parientas lejanas de nuestra familia.* **4** ADJ If you describe someone as **distant,** you mean that you find them cold and unfriendly. distante ❑ *She seemed cold and distant.* *Parecía fría y distante.* **5** ADJ If you describe someone as **distant,** you mean that they are not concentrating on what they are doing because they are thinking about other things. ausente ❑ *There was a distant look in her eyes.* *Tenía una mirada ausente.* • **dis|tant|ly** ADV con ensimismamiento ❑ *"He's in the kitchen," she said distantly.* *—Está en la cocina—dijo como ausente.*

**Thesaurus** *distant* Ver también:

ADJ. faraway, remote; (*ant.*) close, near **1**
aloof, cool, unfriendly **4**

**dis|tinct** /dɪstɪŋkt/ **1** ADJ If something is **distinct from** something else of the same type, it is different or separate from it. distinto ❑ *Engineering and technology are distinct from one another.* *La ingeniería y la tecnología son distintas (una de otra).* • **dis|tinct|ly** ADV claramente ❑ *...a banking industry with two distinctly different sectors.* *...un sector bancario con dos ramas claramente diferentes.* **2** ADJ If something is **distinct,** you can hear, see, or taste it clearly. claro, distinto, inconfundible ❑ *Each vegetable has its own distinct flavor.* *Cada verdura tiene su propio sabor inconfundible.* • **dis|tinct|ly** ADV claramente ❑ *I distinctly heard the loudspeaker calling passengers for the Washington-Miami flight.* *Oí claramente que llamaban por el altavoz a los pasajeros del vuelo de Washington a Miami.* **3** ADJ If an idea, thought, or intention is **distinct,** it is clear and definite. claro, obvio ❑ *There was a distinct change in her attitude.* *Hubo un cambio obvio en su actitud.* • **dis|tinct|ly** ADV claramente, con toda claridad ❑ *I distinctly remember wishing I wasn't there.* *Recuerdo con toda claridad que deseé no haber estado ahí.*

**Usage** **distinct** and **distinctive**

*Distinct* and *distinctive* are easy to confuse. You use *distinct* to say that something is separate, different, clear, or noticeable; you use *distinctive* to say that something is special and easily recognized: *The distinct taste of lemon gave Elena's cake a distinctive and delicious flavor.*

**dis|tinc|tion** /dɪstɪŋkʃᵊn/ (**distinctions**) **1** N-COUNT A **distinction** is a difference **between** similar things. distinción ❑ *There are obvious distinctions between the two areas.* *Hay distinciones claras entre las dos áreas.* ❑ *...the distinction between craft and fine art.* *...la distinción entre los oficios (trabajos manuales) y las bellas artes.* • PHRASE If you **draw a distinction** or **make a distinction**, you say that two things are different. hacer una distinción, establecer una distinción ❑ *He draws a distinction between art and culture.* *Hace una distinción entre el arte y la cultura.* **2** N-UNCOUNT **Distinction** is the quality of being excellent. distinción [FORMAL] ❑ *Lewis is a writer of distinction.* *Lewis es un escritor distinguido.*

**dis|tinc|tive** /dɪstɪŋktɪv/ ADJ Something that is **distinctive** has a special quality or feature which makes it easily recognizable. característico ❑ *...the distinctive smell of gas.* *...el característico olor del gas.* • **dis|tinc|tive|ly** ADV característicamente, inconfundiblemente ❑ *...distinctively American music.* *...música inconfundiblemente estadounidense.* → see also **distinct**

**dis|tin|guish** /dɪstɪŋgwɪʃ/ (**distinguishes, distinguishing, distinguished**) **1** V-T/V-I If you can **distinguish** one thing **from** another or **distinguish between** two things, you can see or understand how they are different. distinguir ❑ *Could he distinguish right from wrong?* *¿Podía distinguir entre el bien y el mal?* ❑ *Research suggests that babies learn to see by distinguishing between areas of light and dark.* *Las investigaciones indican que*

d

D

los bebés aprenden a ver haciendo una distinción entre las áreas de luz y las de obscuridad. **2** V-T A feature or quality that **distinguishes** one thing **from** another causes the two things to be regarded as different. *distinguir* ❑ *There is something about music that distinguishes it from other art forms. La música tiene algo que la distingue de las demás formas de arte.* **3** V-T If you can **distinguish** something, you can see, hear, or taste it although it is very difficult to detect. *distinguir* [FORMAL] ❑ *He could distinguish voices. Podía distinguir unas voces.* **4** V-T If you **distinguish yourself**, you do something that makes you famous or important. *distinguirse* ❑ *He distinguished himself as a leading scientist. Se distinguió como científico destacado.*

**dis|tin|guished** /dɪstɪŋgwɪʃt/ ADJ If you describe a person or their work as **distinguished,** you mean that they have been very successful in their career and have a good reputation. *distinguido* ❑ *...a distinguished academic family. ...una familia de académicos distinguidos.*

**dis|tort** /dɪstɔrt/ (**distorts, distorting, distorted**) **1** V-T If you **distort** a statement, fact, or idea, you report or represent it in an untrue way. *distorsionar, deformar* ❑ *The media distorts reality. Los medios de comunicación distorsionan la realidad.* ● **dis|tort|ed** ADJ *distorsionado* ❑ *These figures give a distorted view of the situation. Estas cifras provocan un punto de vista distorsionado de la situación.* ● **dis|tor|tion** N-VAR (**distortions**) *distorsión* ❑ *...a gross distortion of reality. ...una burda distorsión de la realidad.* **2** V-T/V-I If something you can see or hear **is distorted** or **distorts,** its appearance or sound is changed so that it seems unclear. *distorsionar* ❑ *An artist may distort shapes in a painting. Un artista puede distorsionar las formas de una pintura.* ● **dis|tort|ed** ADJ *distorsionado* ❑ *The sound was becoming distorted. El sonido llegaba distorsionado.* ● **dis|tor|tion** N-VAR *distorsión* ❑ *Audio signals can travel along cables without distortion. Las señales de sonido pueden viajar por los cables sin distorsión.*

**dis|tress** /dɪstrɛs/ (**distresses, distressing, distressed**) **1** N-UNCOUNT **Distress** is a state of extreme sorrow, suffering, or pain. *angustia, aflicción* ❑ *Jealousy causes distress and painful emotions. Los celos causan angustia y emociones dolorosas.* **2** N-UNCOUNT **Distress** is the state of being in extreme danger and needing urgent help. *peligro* ❑ *The ship was in distress. El barco estaba en peligro.* **3** V-T If someone or something **distresses** you, they cause you to be upset or worried. *afligir, angustiar* ❑ *The idea distressed him greatly. La idea lo angustió profundamente.* ● **dis|tressed** ADJ *afligido, angustiado* ❑ *I feel very distressed about my problem. Me siento muy angustiado por mi problema.* ● **dis|tress|ing** ADJ *angustiante, penoso* ❑ *It is very distressing when your baby is sick. Es muy angustiante cuando un hijo está enfermo.* ● **dis|tress|ing|ly** ADV *penosamente, preocupantemente* ❑ *A distressingly large number of firms are ignoring the rules. Un número preocupantemente grande de empresas está ignorando las reglas.*

| Word Link | *tribute ≈ giving : attribute, contribute, distribute* |
|---|---|

**dis|trib|ute** /dɪstrɪbyut/ (**distributes, distributing, distributed**) **1** V-T If you **distribute** things, you hand them or deliver them to a number of people. *distribuir, repartir* ❑ *They distributed free tickets to young people. Repartieron boletos gratuitos a los jóvenes.* ● **dis|tri|bu|tion** /dɪstrɪbyuʃᵊn/ N-UNCOUNT *distribución* ❑ *...the distribution of information. ...la distribución de información.* **2** V-T When a company **distributes** goods, it supplies them to the stores or businesses that sell them. *distribuir* [BUSINESS] ❑ *We didn't understand how difficult it was to distribute a national paper. No entendíamos lo difícil que era distribuir un periódico nacional.* ● **dis|tri|bu|tion** /dɪstrɪbyuʃᵊn/ N-UNCOUNT *distribución* ❑ *...the distribution of goods and services. ...la distribución de bienes y servicios.* ● **dis|tribu|tor** N-COUNT (**distributors**) *distribuidor o distribuidora* ❑ *...Spain's largest distributor of food products. ...el mayor distribuidor de productos alimenticios de España.* **3** V-T To **distribute** a substance **over** something means to scatter it over it. *distribuir* [FORMAL] ❑ *Distribute the cheese evenly over the vegetables. Distribuya el queso uniformemente sobre las verduras.*

**dis|tri|bu|tion** /dɪstrɪbyuʃᵊn/ (**distributions**) N-VAR The **distribution** of something is how much of it there is in each place or at each time, or how much of it each person has. *distribución* ❑ *...a fairer distribution of wealth. ...una distribución más justa de la riqueza.*

**dis|trict** /dɪstrɪkt/ (**districts**) N-COUNT A **district** is a particular area of a town or country. *distrito* ❑ *I drove around the business district. Di unas vueltas por el distrito comercial.*

**dis|trict at|tor|ney** (**district attorneys**) N-COUNT A **district attorney** is a lawyer who works for a city, state, or federal government and puts on trial people who are accused of crimes. The abbreviation **D.A.** is also used. *fiscal de distrito, procurador general o procuradora general*

**dis|trict court** (**district courts**) N-COUNT In the United States, a **district court** is a state or federal court that has jurisdiction in a particular district. *tribunal de distrito* ❑ *A Miami district court has scheduled a hearing for Friday. Un tribunal de distrito de Miami fijó una audiencia para el viernes.*

**dis|turb** /dɪstɜrb/ (**disturbs, disturbing, disturbed**) **1** V-T If you **disturb** someone, you interrupt what they are doing and upset them. *perturbar, molestar* ❑ *I didn't want to disturb you. You looked so peaceful. No quería molestarte. Parecías tan tranquilo.* **2** V-T If something **disturbs** you, it makes you feel upset or worried. *perturbar* ❑ *My dreams are so vivid that they disturb me for days. Mis sueños son tan vívidos que me perturban durante días.* **3** V-T If something **is disturbed,** its position or shape is changed. *tocar, perturbar* ❑ *The books had not been disturbed for a long time and were covered in dust. Los libros no habían sido tocados durante mucho tiempo y estaban cubiertos de polvo.*

**Word Partnership** Usar *disturb* con:

| | |
|---|---|
| V. | **do not** disturb **1** |
| | **be sorry to** disturb **1 2** |
| | **be careful not to** disturb **1 3** |
| N. | disturb **the neighbors 2** |

**dis|turb|ance** /dɪstɜrbəns/ (**disturbances**) **1** N-COUNT A **disturbance** is an incident in which people behave violently in public. *disturbio* ❑ *During the disturbance, three men were hurt.* *Tres hombres resultaron heridos durante los disturbios.* **2** N-UNCOUNT **Disturbance** means upsetting or disorganizing something which was previously in a calm and well-ordered state. *perturbación* ❑ *There must be no disturbance in the treatment room.* *No debe haber perturbaciones en la sala de tratamiento.*

**dis|turbed** /dɪstɜrbd/ ADJ A **disturbed** person is very upset emotionally, and often needs special care or treatment. *perturbado, trastornado* ❑ *...emotionally disturbed children.* *...niños con trastornos emocionales.*

**dis|turb|ing** /dɪstɜrbɪŋ/ ADJ Something that is **disturbing** makes you feel worried or upset. *perturbador, inquietante, alarmante* ❑ *...disturbing news.* *...noticias alarmantes.* ● **dis|turb|ing|ly** ADV *perturbadoramente, inquietantemente, alarmantemente* ❑ *...the disturbingly high frequency of racial attacks.* *...la gran frecuencia alarmante de los ataques raciales.*

**ditch** /dɪtʃ/ (**ditches, ditching, ditched**) **1** N-COUNT A **ditch** is a long narrow channel cut into the ground at the side of a road or field. *zanja* ❑ *Both vehicles landed in a ditch.* *Los dos vehículos fueron a parar a una zanja.* **2** V-T If you **ditch** something, you get rid of it. *botar* [INFORMAL] ❑ *I decided to ditch the bed.* *Decidí botar la cama.*

**dive** /daɪv/ (**dives, diving, dived, dove, dived**) **1** V-I If you **dive into** some water, you jump in head first with your arms held straight above your head. *tirarse al agua, echarse un clavado* ❑ *He tried to escape by diving into a river.* *Trató de escapar lanzándose a un río.* ❑ *She was standing by a pool, about to dive in.* *Estaba junto a la piscina, a punto de echarse un clavado.* ● **Dive** is also a noun. *clavado* ❑ *Pam made a dive of 80 feet from the Chasm Bridge.* *Pam se lanzó al agua desde los 24 metros del puente Chasm.* ● **div|ing** N-UNCOUNT *clavado, salto de trampolín* ❑ *Weight is important in diving.* *El peso es importante para los clavadistas.* **2** V-I If you **dive,** you go under the surface of the sea or a lake, using special breathing equipment. *bucear* ❑ *Bezanik is diving to look at fish.* *Bezanik está buceando para ver los peces.* ● **Dive** is also a noun. *buceo* ❑ *He is already planning the next dive.* *Ya está planeando su próxima sesión de buceo.* ● **div|er** N-COUNT (**divers**) *buzo, buceador o buceadora* ❑ *Divers have discovered the wreck of a ship.* *Los buzos descubrieron un naufragio.* ● **div|ing** N-UNCOUNT *buceo* ❑ *...equipment for diving.* *...equipo para buceo.* **3** V-I When birds and animals **dive,** they go quickly downward, head first, through the air or through water. *zambullirse, sumergirse* ❑ *The pelican was diving for a fish.* *El pelícano se zambullía en busca de peces.* **4** V-I If you **dive** in a particular direction or into a particular place, you jump or move there quickly. *abalanzarse, precipitarse, arrojarse* ❑ *They dived into a taxi.* *Se metieron precipitadamente en un taxi.* ● **Dive** is also a noun. *movimiento rápido* ❑ *David made a dive for the door.* *David se abalanzó hacia la puerta.*

**di|ver|gent bounda|ry** (**divergent boundaries**) N-COUNT A **divergent boundary** is an area in the Earth's crust where two tectonic plates are moving away from each other. *límite divergente* [TECHNICAL]

| Word Link | *di ≈ two : dilemma, diverse, divorce* |
|---|---|

**di|verse** /dɪvɜrs, daɪ-/ ADJ If a group of things is **diverse,** it is made up of a wide variety of things. *diverso, variado* ❑ *...a diverse group of students.* *...un grupo variado de estudiantes.*

| Word Link | *ify ≈ making : claify, diversify, intensify* |
|---|---|

**di|ver|si|fy** /dɪvɜrsɪfaɪ, daɪ-/ (**diversifies, diversifying, diversified**) V-T/V-I When an organization or person **diversifies** into other things, or **diversifies** their product line, they increase the variety of things that they do or make. *diversificar(se)* ❑ *The company's troubles started when it diversified into new products.* *Los problemas de la empresa empezaron cuando diversificó su producción.* ❑ *Manufacturers need to diversify and improve quality.* *Los fabricantes necesitan diversificarse y mejorar la calidad.* ● **di|ver|si|fi|ca|tion** /dɪvɜrsɪfɪkeɪʃ<sup></sup>n, daɪ-/ N-VAR (**diversifications**) *diversificación* ❑ *...diversification of teaching methods.* *...la diversificación de los métodos de enseñanza.*

**di|ver|sity** /dɪvɜrsɪti, daɪ-/ (**diversities**) **1** N-VAR The **diversity** of something is the fact that it contains many very different elements. *diversidad* ❑ *...the cultural diversity of Latin America.* *...la diversidad cultural de América Latina.* **2** N-SING A **diversity of** things is a range of things which are very different from each other. *diversidad* ❑ *There was a diversity of attitudes about race.* *Había una diversidad de actitudes respecto a la raza.*
→ see **zoo**

| Word Link | *verg, vert ≈ turning : convert, divert, verge* |
|---|---|

**di|vert** /dɪvɜrt, daɪ-/ (**diverts, diverting, diverted**) **1** V-T/V-I To **divert** vehicles or travelers means to make them follow a different route or go to a different destination than they originally intended. You can also say that someone or something **diverts from** a particular route or **to** a particular place. *desviar, derivar* ❑ *We diverted a plane to rescue 100 passengers.* *Desviamos un avión para rescatar a 100 pasajeros.* ❑ *The hospital diverted patients to other hospitals because it did not have enough beds.* *El hospital derivó algunos pacientes a otros hospitales porque no tenía suficientes camas.* **2** V-T To **divert** money or resources means to cause them to be used for a different purpose. *desviar* ❑ *This will divert money from patient care.* *Esto significará un desvío del dinero destinado al cuidado de los pacientes.* ● **di|ver|sion** N-UNCOUNT *desvío* ❑ *...the diversion of funds from other parts of the economy.* *...el desvío de fondos de otras ramas de la economía.* **3** V-T If someone **diverts** your attention from something important or serious, they behave or talk in a way that stops you thinking about it. *distraer* ❑ *I don't want to divert attention from the project.* *No quiero distraer la atención del proyecto.*

**di|vide** /dɪvaɪd/ (**divides, dividing, divided**) **1** V-T/V-I When people or things **are divided** or **divide into** smaller groups or parts, they become separated into smaller parts. *dividir* ❑ *Divide the pastry in half and roll out each piece.* *Divida la masa en dos y enrolle cada mitad.* ❑ *The class was divided into two groups of six.* *EL grupo fue dividido en dos grupos de seis.* **2** V-T If you **divide** a larger number **by** a smaller number or **divide** a smaller number

D

into a larger number, you calculate how many times the smaller number can fit exactly into the larger number. *dividir* ❑ *Measure the floor area and divide it by six.* *Mida el área del piso y divídala entre/por seis.* **3** V-T If a border or line **divides** two areas or **divides** an area into two, it keeps the two areas separate from each other. *separar* ❑ *A long frontier divides Mexico from the United States.* *Una larga frontera separa a México de Estados Unidos.* **4** V-T/V-I If people **divide** over something or if something **divides** them, it causes strong disagreement between them. *dividir* ❑ *Major issues divided the country.* *Las cuestiones importantes dividieron al país.* • **di|vid|ed** ADJ *dividido* ❑ *The democrats are divided over whether to agree to the plan.* *Los demócratas están divididos entre quienes quieren aceptar el plan y quienes no.* **5** N-COUNT A **divide** is a significant distinction between two groups. *división* ❑ *...a deliberate attempt to create a Hindu-Muslim divide in India.* *...un intento deliberado por crear una división entre hindúes y musulmanes en la India.* **6** N-COUNT A **divide** is a line of high ground between areas that are drained by different rivers. *(línea) divisoria*

▸ **divide up** PHR-VERB If you **divide** something **up**, you separate it into smaller or more useful groups. *dividir* ❑ *The idea is to divide up the country into four areas.* *La idea es dividir el país en cuatro zonas.*

| **Thesaurus** | *divide* | Ver también: |
|---|---|---|
| V. | categorize, group, segregate, separate, split **1**<br>part, separate, split; (*ant.*) unite **4** | |

**di|vid|ed high|way** (**divided highways**) N-COUNT A **divided highway** is a road which has two lanes of traffic traveling in each direction with a strip of grass or concrete down the middle to separate the two lots of traffic. *carretera de dos carriles separados*

**divi|dend** /dɪvɪdɛnd/ (**dividends**) **1** N-COUNT A **dividend** is the part of a company's profits which is paid to people who own shares in the company. *dividendo* [BUSINESS] ❑ *The dividend has increased by 4 percent.* *Los dividendos aumentaron el cuatro por ciento.* **2** PHRASE If something **pays dividends,** it brings advantages at a later date. *pagar dividendos, rendir frutos* ❑ *Things you do now to improve your health will pay dividends later on.* *Las cosas que hagas ahora para mejorar tu salud rendirán sus frutos más adelante.*

**di|vine** /dɪvaɪn/ ADJ You use **divine** to describe something that is provided by or relates to a god or goddess. *divino* ❑ *...a divine punishment.* *...un castigo divino.* • **di|vine|ly** ADV *divinamente* ❑ *The work was divinely inspired.* *La obra fue de inspiración divina.* • **di|vin|ity** /dɪvɪnɪti/ N-UNCOUNT *divinidad* ❑ *...the divinity of Christ's word.* *...lo divino de la palabra de Cristo.*

**di|vi|sion** /dɪvɪʒᵊn/ (**divisions**) **1** N-UNCOUNT The **division of** something is the act of separating it **into** two or more distinct parts. *división* ❑ *...the unification of Germany, after its division into two states.* *...la unificación de Alemania después de su división en dos estados.* ❑ *The division of labor between workers and management will change.* *La división del trabajo entre obreros y administradores va a cambiar.* **2** N-UNCOUNT **Division** is the arithmetical process of dividing one number into another number. *división* ❑ *I taught my daughter how to do division.* *Le enseñé a mi hija la división.* **3** N-VAR A **division** is a significant distinction or argument between two groups. *división* ❑ *The division between the rich West and the poor East remains.* *Permanece la división entre el Occidente rico y el Este pobre.* **4** N-COUNT In a large organization, a **division** is a group of departments whose work is done in the same place or is connected with similar tasks. *división* ❑ *...the bank's Latin American division.* *...la división latinoamericana del banco.* • **di|vi|sion|al** ADJ *divisional* ❑ *She is divisional sales manager for the Philadelphia region.* *Es gerente de ventas divisional de la región de Filadelfia.*

→ see **mathematics**

| **Word Link** | *di ≈ two : dilemma, diverse, divorce* |
|---|---|

**di|vorce** /dɪvɔrs/ (**divorces, divorcing, divorced**) **1** N-VAR A **divorce** is the formal ending of a marriage by law. *divorcio* ❑ *Many marriages end in divorce.* *Muchos matrimonios terminan en divorcio.* **2** V-RECIP If a man and woman **divorce** or if one of them **divorces** the other, their marriage is legally ended. *divorciarse* ❑ *He and Lillian got divorced.* *Él y Lillian se divorciaron.* ❑ *He divorced me and married my friend.* *Nos divorciamos y se casó con mi amiga.* **3** V-T If one thing cannot **be divorced from** another, the two things cannot be considered as different and separate things. *divorciar* ❑ *Democracy cannot be divorced from social and economic progress.* *No se puede divorciar la democracia del progreso social y económico.*

**di|vor|cé** /dɪvɔrseɪ, -vɔrseɪ/ (**divorcés**) N-COUNT A **divorcé** is a man who is divorced. *divorciado*

**di|vorced** /dɪvɔrst/ **1** ADJ Someone who **is divorced** from their former husband or wife has separated from them and is no longer legally married to them. *divorciado* ❑ *He is divorced, with a young son.* *Es divorciado, con un hijo joven.* **2** ADJ If you say that one thing **is divorced from** another, you mean that the two things are very different and separate from each other. *divorciado* ❑ *...theories divorced from political reality.* *...teorías divorciadas de la realidad política.*

**di|vor|cée** /dɪvɔrseɪ, -si/ (**divorcées**) N-COUNT A **divorcée** is a woman who is divorced. *divorciada* ❑ *He married Clare Hollway, a divorcée.* *Se casó con Clare Hollway, una divorciada.*

**DIY** /di aɪ waɪ/ N-UNCOUNT **DIY** is the activity of making or repairing things yourself, especially in your home. **DIY** is an abbreviation for **do-it-yourself**. *práctica de hacer las cosas uno mismo* ❑ *He's useless at DIY. He won't even put up a shelf.* *Es un inútil para las cosas de la casa. ¡Ni siquiera sabe poner una repisa!*

**diz|zy** /dɪzi/ (**dizzier, dizziest**) ADJ If you feel **dizzy,** you feel that you are losing your balance and are about to fall. *mareado* ❑ *Her head hurt, and she felt slightly dizzy.* *Le dolía la cabeza y se sentía ligeramente mareada.* • **diz|zi|ness** N-UNCOUNT *mareo, vértigo* ❑ *His head injury caused dizziness.* *La herida en la cabeza le causaba mareos.*

**diz|zy|ing** /dɪziɪŋ/ ADJ You can use **dizzying** to emphasize that something impresses you, though it makes you a bit confused or unsteady. *vertiginoso* ❑ *...one of the dizzying changes that have taken place.* *...uno de los cambios vertiginosos que han tenido lugar.*

❑ *We're descending now at dizzying speed.* *Ahora estamos descendiendo a una velocidad vertiginosa.*

**DJ** /di̲ dʒeɪ/ (**DJs**) also **D.J.** or **dj** N-COUNT A **DJ** is the same as a **disc jockey**. *disc-jockey*

**DNA** /di̲ ɛn e̲ɪ/ N-UNCOUNT **DNA** is an acid in the chromosomes in the center of the cells of living things. DNA determines the particular structure and functions of every cell and is responsible for characteristics being passed on from parents to their children. **DNA** is an abbreviation for "deoxyribonucleic acid." *ADN, ácido desoxirribonucleico* ❑ *A DNA sample was taken.* *Tomaron una muestra de ADN.*

→ see **clone**

**DNA fi̲nger|print|ing** N-UNCOUNT **DNA fingerprinting** is the same as **genetic fingerprinting**. *análisis de muestras de ADN*

| do |
|---|
| ❶ AUXILIARY VERB USES |
| ❷ OTHER VERB USES |

❶ **do** /də, STRONG du/ (**does, doing, did, done**)

> **Do** is used as an auxiliary with the simple present tense. **Did** is used as an auxiliary with the simple past tense. In spoken English, negative forms of **do** are often shortened, for example, **do not** is shortened to **don't** and **did not** is shortened to **didn't**.

**1** AUX **Do** is used to form the negative of main verbs, by putting "not" after "do" and before the main verb without "to." *auxiliar negativo* ❑ *They don't work very hard.* *No ponen mucho empeño en el trabajo.* ❑ *I did not know Jamie had a knife.* *No sabía que Jamie tenía una navaja.* **2** AUX **Do** is used to form questions, by putting the subject after "do" and before the main verb without "to." *auxiliar para hacer preguntas; no se usa en español* ❑ *Do you like music?* *¿Te gusta la música?* ❑ *What did he say?* *¿Qué dijo?* **3** AUX **Do** is used in question tags. *auxiliar que se utiliza en las muletillas, ¿no?, ¿verdad?* ❑ *You know about Andy, don't you?* *Ya sabes lo de Andy, ¿no?* **4** AUX You use **do** when you are confirming or contradicting a statement containing "do," or giving a negative or positive answer to a question. *se usa en las respuestas a las preguntas que lo incluyen o en la respuesta afirmativa o negativa a una pregunta; no se usa en español.* ❑ *"Do you think he is telling the truth?"—"Yes, I do."* *—¿Crees que está diciendo la verdad?—Sí./Sí; sí lo creo.* **5** V-T/V-I **Do** can be used to refer back to another verb group when you are comparing or contrasting two things, or saying that they are the same. *se usa en el segundo miembro de la comparaciones para substituir al verbo, que en español se omite.* ❑ *I earn more money than he does.* *—Yo gano más dinero que él.* ❑ *I have dreams, as do all mothers, about what life will be like when my girls are grown.* *Sueño, como todas las madres, en lo que será la vida cuando mis hijas sean grandes.* **6** V-T You use **do** after "so" and "nor" to say that the same statement is true for two people or groups. *también* ❑ *You know that's true, and so do I.* *—Sabes que es cierto; y yo también (lo sé).*

❷ **do** /du̲/ (**does, doing, did, done**) **1** V-T When you **do** something, you take some action or perform an activity or task. **Do** is often used instead of a more specific verb, to talk about a common action involving a particular thing. *hacer; se traduce o no, dependiendo del objeto directo* ❑ *I was trying to do some work.* *Estaba tratando de trabajar un poco.* ❑ *After lunch Elizabeth and I did the dishes.* *Después de la comida (del almuerzo), Elizabeth y yo lavamos los trastes.* **2** V-T If you **do** something **about** a problem, you take action to try to solve it. *hacer* ❑ *They refuse to do anything about the real cause of crime: poverty.* *Se rehúsan a hacer algo respecto a la verdadera causa del crimen: la pobreza.* **3** V-T If an action or event **does** a particular thing, such as harm or good, it has that result or effect. *hacer, causar* ❑ *A few bombs can do a lot of damage.* *Unas cuantas bombas pueden hacer/causar mucho daño.* **4** V-T If you ask someone what they **do,** you want to know what their job or profession is. *hacer* ❑ *"What does your father do?"—"He's a doctor."* *—¿Qué hace tu papá?—Es médico.* **5** V-T If you **are doing** something, you are busy or active in some way, or have planned an activity for some time in the future. *hacer* ❑ *Are you doing anything tomorrow night?* *¿Vas a hacer algo mañana en la noche?* **6** V-I If someone or something **does** well or badly, they are successful or unsuccessful. *ir, salir* ❑ *Connie did well at school and graduated with honors.* *A Connie le fue bien en la escuela y se tituló con honores.* **7** V-T You can use **do** when referring to the speed or rate that something or someone achieves or is able to achieve. *ir a* ❑ *They were doing 70 miles an hour.* *Iban a 112.5 kilómetros por hora.* **8** V-T/V-I If you say that something **will do** or **will do** you, you mean that it is satisfactory. *bastar, ser suficiente* ❑ *Wear suitable clothes—anything warm will do.* *Use ropa adecuada; cualquier cosa caliente bastará.* ❑ *Twenty dollars will do me fine thanks.* *Veinte dólares me bastarán; gracias.* **9** PHRASE If you say that you **could do with** something, you mean that you need it or would benefit from it. *caer bien* ❑ *I could do with a cup of tea.* *Me caería bien una taza de té.* **10** PHRASE If you ask **what** someone or something **is doing** in a particular place, you are asking why they are there. *hacer* ❑ *"What are you doing here?" he said, clearly surprised.* *—¿Qué estás haciendo aquí?—le dijo, evidentemente sorprendido.* **11** PHRASE If you say that one thing **has** something **to do with** or **is** something **to do with** another thing, you mean that the two things are connected or that the first thing is about the second thing. *tener qué ver* ❑ *Mr. Butterfield denies having anything to do with it.* *El señor Butterfield niega que tenga algo qué ver con eso.*

▸ **do away with** PHR-VERB If you **do away with** something, you remove it completely or put an end to it. *eliminar* ❑ *This device does away with the need for batteries.* *Este dispositivo elimina la necesidad de baterías.*

▸ **do over** PHR-VERB If you **do** a task **over,** you perform it again from the beginning. *volver a hacer* ❑ *He made me do it over twice.* *Me hizo hacerlo dos veces. Me hizo volver a hacerlo.*

▸ **do up** PHR-VERB If you **do** something **up,** you fasten it. *abrochar, abotonar* ❑ *Mari did up the buttons.* *Mari abrochó los botones.*

▸ **do without** PHR-VERB If you **do without** something you need, want, or usually have, you are able to survive, continue, or succeed although you do not have it. *prescindir de, arreglárselas sin* ❑ *We can't do without the help of your organization.* *No podemos prescindir de la ayuda de su organización.*

d

D

**DOB** also **d.o.b.** **DOB** is a written abbreviation for **date of birth**, used especially on official forms. *fecha de nacimiento*

**dock** /dɒk/ (**docks, docking, docked**) **1** N-COUNT A **dock** is an enclosed area in a harbor where ships go to be loaded, unloaded, and repaired. *muelle, puerto* ❑ *She headed for the docks. Se dirigió a los muelles.* **2** N-COUNT A **dock** is a platform for loading vehicles or trains. *plataforma* ❑ *The truck left the loading dock. El camión salió de la plataforma de carga.* **3** N-COUNT A **dock** is a small structure at the edge of water where boats can tie up, especially one that is privately owned. *muelle, atracadero* ❑ *He had a house and a dock and a little boat. Tenía una casa y un atracadero con un bote pequeño.* **4** V-T/V-I When a ship **docks** or **is docked,** it is brought into a dock. *atracar, fondear* ❑ *The crash happened as the ferry tried to dock on Staten Island. El accidente ocurrió cuando el transbordador trataba de atracar en la isla Staten.* **5** V-T If you **dock** someone's pay or money, you take some of the money away. *descontar* ❑ *He threatens to dock her fee. Amenaza con descontarle sus honorarios.* **6** V-RECIP When one spacecraft **docks** or **is docked with** another, the two craft join together in space. *acoplarse* ❑ *The space shuttle Atlantis is scheduled to dock with Russia's Mir space station. Está programado que el transbordador espacial Atlantis se acople con la estación espacial rusa Mir.* **7** N-SING In a law court, **the dock** is where the person accused of a crime stands or sits. *banquillo de los acusados* ❑ *...the prisoner in the dock. ...el prisionero en el banquillo de los acusados.*

dock

**dock|et** /dɒkɪt/ (**dockets**) N-COUNT A **docket** is a list of cases waiting for trial in a law court. *lista de casos, registro de procedimientos* ❑ *The Court has 1,400 appeals on its docket. El tribunal tiene 1,400 apelaciones en su lista de casos.*

**doc|tor** /dɒktər/ (**doctors, doctoring, doctored**) **1** N-COUNT; N-TITLE; N-VOC A **doctor** is someone who has a degree in medicine and treats people who are sick or injured. *médico o médica* ❑ *Do not discontinue the treatment without consulting your doctor. No interrumpa el tratamiento sin antes consultar con su médico.* **2** N-COUNT; N-TITLE; N-VOC A **dentist** or **veterinarian** can also be called **doctor.** *dentista, veterinario o veterinaria* **3** N-COUNT; N-TITLE A **doctor** is someone who has been awarded the highest academic degree by a university. *doctor o doctora* ❑ *He is a doctor of philosophy. Es doctor en filosofía.* **4** V-T If someone **doctors** something, they change it in order to deceive people. *adulterar, falsificar, alterar* ❑ *...a doctored photo. ...una fotografía alterada.*

**doc|tor|ate** /dɒktərɪt/ (**doctorates**) N-COUNT A **doctorate** is the highest degree awarded by a university. *doctorado* ❑ *She has a doctorate in psychology from the University of Michigan. Tiene un doctorado en psicología por la Universidad de Michigan.*

**doc|tor of phi|los|o|phy** (**doctors of philosophy**) N-COUNT A **doctor of philosophy** is someone who has a **PhD.** *doctor en filosofía*

**doc|tor's of|fice** (**doctor's offices**) N-COUNT A **doctor's office** is the room or clinic where a doctor works. *consultorio (médico)* ❑ *...a visit to the doctor's office. ...una visita al consultorio del médico.*

**doc|trine** /dɒktrɪn/ (**doctrines**) **1** N-VAR A **doctrine** is a set of principles or beliefs. *doctrina* ❑ *...Christian doctrine. ...la doctrina cristiana.*
• **doc|tri|nal** /dɑktrɪnəl/ ADJ *doctrinal* [FORMAL] ❑ *...doctrinal differences. ...diferencias doctrinales.*
**2** N-COUNT A **doctrine** is a statement of official government policy, especially foreign policy. *doctrina* ❑ *...Bush's doctrine on terrorism. ...la doctrina de Bush sobre el terrorismo.*

**docu|ment** (**documents, documenting, documented**)

> The noun is pronounced /dɒkyəmənt/. The verb is pronounced /dɒkyəmɛnt/.

**1** N-COUNT A **document** is one or more official pieces of paper with writing on them. *documento* ❑ *...legal documents. ...documentos legales.* **2** N-COUNT A **document** is a piece of text or graphics that is stored as a file on a computer. *documento* [COMPUTING] ❑ *Remember to save your document. Recuerde salvar su documento.* **3** V-T If you **document** something, you make a detailed record of it in writing or on film or tape. *documentar* ❑ *He wrote a book documenting his prison experiences. Escribió un libro en el que documenta su experiencia en prisión.*
→ see **diary, history, printing**

**docu|men|tary** /dɒkyəmɛntəri, -tri/ (**documentaries**) **1** N-COUNT A **documentary** is a television or radio program, or a movie, which shows real events or provides information about a particular subject. *documental* ❑ *...a TV documentary on crime. ...un documental de televisión sobre el crimen.* **2** ADJ **Documentary** evidence consists of things that are written down. *documental* ❑ *The government has documentary evidence that the two countries are planning military action. El gobierno tiene pruebas documentales de que ambos países están planeando acciones militares.*

**docu|men|ta|tion** /dɒkyəmɛnteɪʃən/ N-UNCOUNT **Documentation** consists of documents which provide proof or evidence of something, or are a record of something. *documentación* ❑ *Passengers must carry proper documentation. Los pasajeros deben llevar consigo la documentación apropiada.*

**dodge** /dɒdʒ/ (**dodges, dodging, dodged**) **1** V-I If you **dodge,** you move suddenly, often to avoid being hit, caught, or seen. *esquivar, apartarse* ❑ *I dodged back into the alley and waited a minute. Volví rápidamente al callejón y esperé unos momentos.* **2** V-T If you **dodge** something, you avoid it by quickly moving aside or out of reach so that it cannot hit or reach you. *esquivar* ❑ *He desperately dodged a speeding car. Con desesperación, esquivó un coche que iba a gran velocidad.* **3** V-T If you **dodge** something, you deliberately avoid doing it, thinking about it or dealing with it, often by being deceitful. *eludir* ❑ *He dodged military service by pretending to be sick. Eludió el servicio militar aparentando que estaba enfermo.*

**dodo** /doʊdoʊ/ (**dodos** or **dodoes**) N-COUNT A **dodo** was a very large bird that was unable to fly. Dodos are now extinct. *dodo*

**does** /dəz, STRONG dʌz/ **Does** is the third person singular in the present tense of **do**. *tercera persona singular del presente de indicativo del verbo "do"*

**doesn't** /dʌzᵊnt/ **Doesn't** is the usual spoken form of "does not." *forma hablada usual de* ***does not***

**dog** /dɔg/ (**dogs, dogging, dogged**) 1 N-COUNT A **dog** is an animal that is often kept by people as a pet. *perro* ❑ *He was walking his dog. Andaba paseando a su perro.* 2 V-T If problems or injuries **dog** you, they are with you all the time. *perseguir* ❑ *His career has been dogged by bad luck. Lo ha perseguido la mala suerte en su carrera.*
→ see **pet**

**dog days** N-PLURAL The hottest part of the summer is sometimes referred to as the **dog days**. *canícula, días de mucho calor, época más calurosa del verano* ❑ *We're into the dog days of summer. Estamos en la época más calurosa del verano.*

**dog|gone** /dɔgɔn/ ADJ People sometimes use **doggone** to emphasize what they are saying, especially when they are annoyed. *maldito* [INFORMAL] ❑ *The doggone business just keeps getting worse. El maldito negocio nada más sigue empeorando.* • **Doggone** is also an adverb. *maldito, de los mil diablos, infernal* ❑ *It was so doggone hot. Hacía un calor de los mil diablos.*

**dog|house** /dɔghaʊs/ (**doghouses**) N-COUNT A **doghouse** is a small building made especially for a dog to sleep in. *perrera, casucha del perro*

**doh** /doʊ/ also **d'oh** EXCLAM People sometimes say **doh** to show that they have made a silly mistake. *¡oye!* [INFORMAL] ❑ *Doh! What are you doing? ¡Oye! ¿Qué estás haciendo?*

**doll** /dɒl/ (**dolls**) N-COUNT A **doll** is a child's toy which looks like a small person or baby. *muñeca, muñeco*

**dol|lar** /dɒlər/ (**dollars**) N-COUNT The **dollar** is the unit of money used in the U.S., Canada, Australia, and some other countries. It is represented by the symbol $. *dólar* ❑ *She earns seven dollars an hour. Gana siete dólares por hora.*

**doll|house** /dɒlhaʊs/ (**dollhouses**) N-COUNT A **dollhouse** is a toy in the form of a small house, which contains tiny dolls and furniture for children to play with. *casa de muñecas*

dolphin

**dol|phin** /dɒlfɪn/ (**dolphins**) N-COUNT A **dolphin** is a mammal with fins and a pointed mouth which lives in the sea. *delfín*
→ see **whale**

| Word Link | *dom, domin ≈ rule, master : domain, dominate, kingdom* |
|---|---|

| Word Link | *dom ≈ home : domain, dome, domestic* |
|---|---|

**do|main** /doʊmeɪn/ (**domains**) 1 N-COUNT A **domain** is a particular field of thought, activity, or interest. *dominio, terreno, campo* [FORMAL] ❑ *...a theory which is accepted in the domain of science. ...una teoría aceptada en el terreno de la ciencia.* 2 N-COUNT On the Internet, a **domain** is a set of addresses that shows, for example, the category or geographical area that an Internet address belongs to. *dominio* [COMPUTING] ❑ *...a domain name. ...un nombre de dominio.*

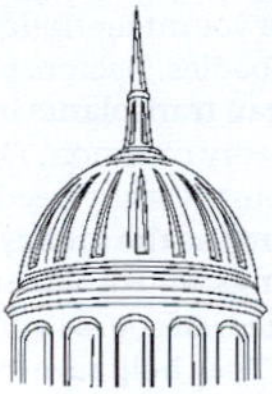
dome

**dome** /doʊm/ (**domes**) N-COUNT A **dome** is a round roof. *domo, cúpula* ❑ *...the dome of the building. ...el domo del edificio.*

**do|mes|tic** /dəmɛstɪk/ 1 ADJ **Domestic** political activities, events, and situations happen or exist within one particular country. *nacional* ❑ *...over 100 domestic flights a day. ...más de 100 vuelos nacionales al día.* 2 ADJ **Domestic** means relating to or concerned with the home and family. *doméstico, del hogar* ❑ *...a plan for sharing domestic chores. ...un plan para compartir los quehaceres domésticos.* ❑ *...domestic appliances such as washing machines. ...aparatos de uso doméstico, como las lavadoras.* 3 ADJ A **domestic** animal is one that is not wild and is kept either on a farm or as a pet. *doméstico* ❑ *...a domestic cat. ...un gato doméstico.*

**domi|nant** /dɒmɪnənt/ 1 ADJ Someone or something that is **dominant** is more powerful, successful, influential, or noticeable than other people or things. *dominante* ❑ *...his party's dominant position in politics. ...la posición dominante de su partido en la política.* • **domi|nance** N-UNCOUNT *dominio, dominación* ❑ *By 1942 Hitler had achieved dominance in all of Europe except Britain. Hacia 1942, Hitler había logrado el dominio en toda Europa, con excepción de la Gran Bretaña.* 2 ADJ A **dominant** gene is one that produces a particular characteristic, whether a person has only one of these genes from one parent, or two genes, one from each parent. Compare **recessive**. *dominante*

**domi|nate** /dɒmɪneɪt/ (**dominates, dominating, dominated**) 1 V-T/V-I To **dominate** a situation means to be the most powerful or important person or thing in it. *dominar, predominar* ❑ *The book dominated the bestseller lists. El libro predominaba en las listas de los éxitos de ventas.* ❑ *...countries where life is dominated by war. ...países donde la guerra predomina sobre la vida.* ❑ *At the conference, issues about the environment will dominate. Los temas sobre el medio ambiente predominarán en la conferencia.* • **domi|na|tion** /dɒmɪneɪʃᵊn/ N-UNCOUNT *dominación, dominio* ❑ *...the domination of the market by a small number of organizations. ...el dominio del mercado por un reducido número de grandes sociedades anónimas.* 2 V-T If one country or person **dominates** another, they have power over them. *dominar* ❑ *He denied that his country wants to dominate Europe. Negó que su país quiera dominar Europa.* ❑ *Women are no longer dominated by men. Los hombres ya no dominan a las mujeres.* • **domi|nat|ing** ADJ *dominante* ❑ *She was a dominating woman. Era una mujer dominante.* • **domi|na|tion** N-UNCOUNT *dominación* ❑ *...domination by a foreign country. ...la dominación de un país extranjero.*

| Word Link | *don ≈ giving : donate, donor, pardon* |
|---|---|

**do|nate** /doʊneɪt, doʊneɪt/ (**donates, donating, donated**) 1 V-T If you **donate** something **to** a charity or other organization, you give it to them.

D

**Word Web** donor

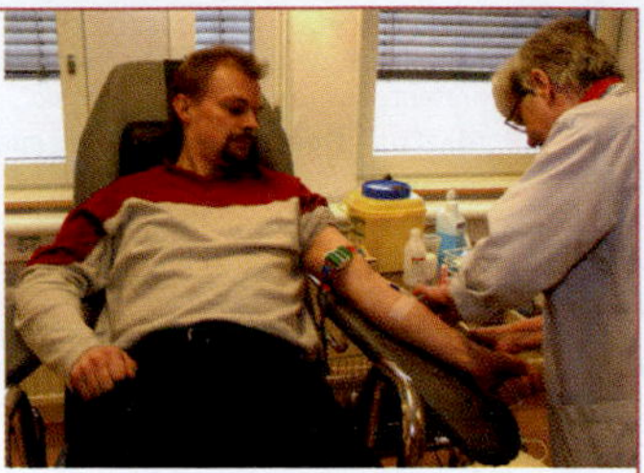

Many people **give donations**. They like to **help** others. They **donate money**, clothes, food, or volunteer their time. Some people even give parts of their bodies. Doctors performed the first successful human **organ transplants** in the 1950s. Today this type of operation is very common. The problem now is finding enough **donors** to meet the needs of potential **recipients**. Organs such as the **kidney** often come from a living donor. **Hearts, lungs**, and other vital organs come from donors who have died. Of course our health care system relies on **blood** donors. They help save lives every day.

*donar* ❑ *He often donates large amounts of money to charity.* *Frecuentemente dona grandes sumas de dinero a las instituciones de beneficencia.* • **do|na|tion** /doʊneɪʃᵊn/ N-VAR (**donations**) *donación* ❑ *...the donation of his collection to the art gallery.* *...la donación de su colección a la galería de arte.* ❑ *Employees make regular donations to charity.* *Los empleados hacen donaciones regulares a las instituciones de beneficencia.* **2** V-T If you **donate** your blood or a part of your body, you allow doctors to use it to help someone who is ill. *donar* ❑ *...people who donate their organs for use after death.* *...gente que dona sus órganos para que sean aprovechados después de su muerte.* • **do|na|tion** N-UNCOUNT *donación* ❑ *...ways of encouraging organ donation.* *...métodos para alentar la donación de órganos.*
→ see **donor**

**done** /dʌn/ **1** **Done** is the past participle of **do**. *participio pasado de **do*** **2** ADJ A task or activity that is **done** has been completed successfully. *terminado* ❑ *We thought the deal was done.* *Creíamos que ya se había cerrado el trato.* **3** ADJ When something that you are cooking is **done,** it has been cooked long enough and is ready. *listo, cocido* ❑ *As soon as the cake is done, remove it from the oven.* *Tan pronto como el pastel se haya horneado, sáquelo del horno.*

**don|key** /dɒŋki/ (**donkeys**) N-COUNT A **donkey** is an animal which is like a small horse with long ears. *burro, asno*

**Word Link** *don ≈ giving : donate, donor, pardon*

**do|nor** /doʊnər/ (**donors**) **1** N-COUNT A **donor** is someone who gives a part of their body or some of their blood to be used by doctors to help a person who is ill. *donador o donadora, donante* ❑ *...a blood donor.* *...donante de sangre.* **2** N-COUNT A **donor** is a person or organization who gives something, especially money, to a charity, organization, or country that needs it. *donador o donadora, donante* ❑ *The money was provided by a wealthy donor.* *El dinero fue donado por una persona acaudalada.*
→ see Word Web: **donor**

**don't** /doʊnt/ **Don't** is the usual spoken form of "do not." *forma hablada usual de **do not***

**do|nut** /doʊnʌt, -nət/ (**donuts**) → see **doughnut**

**doomed** /dumd/ **1** ADJ If something **is doomed to** happen, or if you **are doomed to** a particular state, something unpleasant is certain to happen, and you can do nothing to prevent it. *condenado, sentenciado, predestinado* ❑ *Their plans seemed doomed to failure.* *Sus planes parecían condenados al fracaso.* **2** ADJ Someone or something that is **doomed** is certain to fail or be destroyed. *condenado, sentenciado, predestinado* ❑ *The project was doomed from the start.* *El proyecto estaba condenado desde el principio.*

**door** /dɔr/ (**doors**) **1** N-COUNT A **door** is a piece of wood, glass, or metal, which is moved to open and close the entrance to a building, room, closet, or vehicle. *puerta* ❑ *I knocked at the front door but there was no answer.* *Toqué en la puerta del frente, pero no salió nadie.* **2** N-COUNT A **door** is the space in a wall when a door is open. *entrada* ❑ *She looked through the door of the kitchen.* *Miró a través de la entrada de la cocina.* **3** PHRASE When you **answer the door,** you go and open the door because a visitor has knocked on it or rung the bell. *abrir la puerta* ❑ *Carol answered the door as soon as I knocked.* *Carol abrió tan pronto llamé a su puerta.* **4** PHRASE If someone goes **from door to door** or goes **door to door,** they go along a street stopping at each house in turn, for example, selling something. *de puerta en puerta* ❑ *They are going from door to door collecting money.* *Están recolectando dinero de puerta en puerta.* **5** PHRASE When you are **out of doors,** you are not inside a building, but in the open air. *al aire libre* ❑ *The weather was fine enough for working out of doors.* *Hacía buen tiempo para trabajar al aire libre.*

**do-or-die** **1** ADJ A **do-or-die** battle or struggle is one that involves a determined or desperate effort to succeed. *de vida o muerte, a vencer o morir* ❑ *...a do-or-die effort to make the company into a successful business.* *...un esfuerzo decisivo para hacer de la empresa un negocio exitoso.* **2** PHRASE If something is **do-or-die for** someone or something, it will determine whether they succeed or fail. *de vida o muerte, a vencer o morir* ❑ *Nobody will know until Monday, when it is do-or-die for the deal.* *Nadie lo sabrá hasta el lunes, día decisivo para el trato.*

**door|step** /dɔrstɛp/ (**doorsteps**) **1** N-COUNT A **doorstep** is a step in front of a door on the outside of a building. *umbral* ❑ *I went and sat on the doorstep.* *Fui y me senté en el umbral.* **2** PHRASE If a place is **on your doorstep,** it is very near to where you live. *a la vuelta de la esquina* ❑ *It is easy to forget what is happening on our own doorstep.* *Es fácil olvidar lo que está pasando a la vuelta de la esquina.*

**door|way** /dɔrweɪ/ (**doorways**) N-COUNT A **doorway** is a space in a wall where a door opens and closes. *quicio* ❑ *David was standing in the doorway.* *David estaba parado en el quicio de la puerta.*

**dope** /doʊp/ (**dopes, doping, doped**)

**1** N-UNCOUNT **Dope** is an illegal drug, especially marijuana. *droga* [INFORMAL] **2** V-T If someone **dopes** a person or animal or **dopes** their food, they force them to take drugs or put drugs into their food. *poner droga, drogar* ❑ *He doped the drink. Puso una droga en la bebida.* ❑ *She was doped with painkilling drugs. Se drogó con analgésicos.*

**Word Link** *ory ≈ place where something happens : dormitory, factory, territory*

**dor|mi|tory** /dɔ̲rmɪtɔri/ (**dormitories**) **1** N-COUNT A **dormitory** is a building at a college or university where students live. *dormitorio, residencia* ❑ *She lived in a college dormitory. Vivía en una residencia universitaria.* **2** N-COUNT A **dormitory** is a large bedroom where several people sleep, for example, in a boarding school. *dormitorio* ❑ *...the boys' dormitory. ...el dormitorio de los muchachos.*

**dor|sal** /dɔ̲rsᵊl/ ADJ **Dorsal** means relating to the back of a fish or animal. *dorsal* [TECHNICAL] ❑ *...a dolphin's dorsal fin. ...la aleta dorsal del (de un) delfín.*
→ see **fish**

**dose** /doʊ̲s/ (**doses**) N-COUNT **A dose of** medicine or a drug is a measured amount of it which is intended to be taken at one time. *dosis* ❑ *One dose of penicillin can get rid of the infection. Una dosis de penicilina puede acabar con la infección.*

**dot** /dɒ̲t/ (**dots**) N-COUNT A **dot** is a very small round mark, for example, one that is used as the top part of the letter "i," as a period, or in the names of websites. *punto* ❑ *...a system of painting using small dots of color. ...un sistema de pintura mediante pequeños puntos de color.*

**dot-com** (**dot-coms**) also **dotcom** N-COUNT A **dot-com** is a company that does all or most of its business on the Internet. *empresa punto com* ❑ *In 1999, dot-coms spent more than $1 billion on TV advertising. En 1999, las empresas punto com gastaron más de mil millones de dólares en publicidad por televisión.*

**dot|ted** /dɒ̲tɪd/ **1** ADJ A **dotted** line is a line which is made of a row of dots. *punteado, de puntos* ❑ *Cut along the dotted line. Corte a lo largo de la línea punteada.* • PHRASE If you **sign on the dotted line**, you formally agree to something by signing an official document. *firmar sobre la línea punteada.* **2** ADJ If a place or object is **dotted with** things, it has many of those things scattered over its surface. *salpicado, esparcido* ❑ *The maps were dotted with the names of towns. Los mapas estaban salpicados de nombres de ciudades.* ❑ *Many plants are dotted around the house. Hay muchas plantas esparcidas alrededor de la casa.*

**dou|ble** /dʌ̲bᵊl/ (**doubles, doubling, doubled**) **1** ADJ You use **double** to indicate that something includes or is made of two things of the same kind. *doble* ❑ *...a pair of double doors. ...un par de puertas dobles.* ❑ *...a double murder. ...un doble asesinato.* **2** ADJ You use **double** to describe something which is twice the normal size or can hold twice the normal quantity of something. *doble* ❑ *...a double helping of ice cream. ...una ración doble de helado.* **3** ADJ A **double** room is a room intended for two people, usually a couple, to stay or live in. *doble* ❑ *The hotel charges $180 for a double room. El hotel cobra 180 dólares por un cuarto doble.* • **Double** is also a noun. *doble* ❑ *The Grand Hotel costs around $300 a night for a double. En el Gran Hotel, el cuarto doble cuesta alrededor de 300 dólares la noche.* **4** ADJ A **double** bed is a bed that is wide enough for two people to sleep in. *matrimonial, de matrimonio* ❑ *One bedroom had a double bed. Una de las habitaciones tenía una cama matrimonial.* **5** V-T/V-I When something **doubles** or when you **double** it, it becomes twice as great in number, amount, or size. *duplicar(se)* ❑ *The number of students has doubled from 50 to 100. El número de estudiantes se duplicó de 50 a 100.* **6** V-I If a person or thing **doubles as** someone or something else, they have a second job or purpose as well as their main one. *funcionar también como* ❑ *Lots of homes double as businesses. Muchos hogares también funcionan como negocios.* **7** N-UNCOUNT In tennis or badminton, when people play **doubles**, two teams consisting of two players on each team play against each other on the same court. *dobles* ❑ *In the doubles, they beat the Williams sisters. Derrotaron a las hermanas Williams en los dobles.* **8** in **double figures** → see **figure**
→ see **hotel, tennis**

▸ **double over** PHR-VERB If you **double over**, you bend your body quickly or violently, for example, because you are laughing a lot or because you are feeling a lot of pain. *doblarse (de dolor), desternillarse (de risa), morirse (de la risa)* ❑ *Everyone doubled over in laughter. Todo el mundo se moría de la risa.*

**double-barreled** **1** ADJ A **double-barreled** gun has two barrels. *de dos cañones* ❑ *...a double-barreled shotgun. ...una escopeta de dos cañones.* **2** ADJ **Double-barreled** is used to describe something such as a plan which has two main parts. *compuesto*

**dou|ble bass** /dʌ̲bᵊl beɪ̲s/ (**double basses**) also **double-bass** N-VAR A **double bass** is the largest instrument in the violin family. *contrabajo*
→ see **orchestra, string**

**double-click** (**double-clicks, double-clicking, double-clicked**) V-T If you **double-click on** an area of a computer screen, you point the cursor at that area and press one of the buttons on the mouse twice quickly in order to make something happen. *hacer doble clic* [COMPUTING] ❑ *Go to Control Panel and double-click on Sounds for a list of sounds. Vaya al Panel de Control y haga doble clic en Sonidos para ver la lista.*

**double-header** (**double-headers**) N-COUNT A **double-header** is a sporting contest between two teams that involves two separate games being played, often on the same day. *dos encuentros consecutivos*

**dou|ble he|lix** /dʌ̲bᵊl hi̲lɪks/ N-SING The **double helix** is a term used to describe the shape of the DNA molecule, which resembles a long ladder twisted into a coil. *doble hélice*

**dou|ble-re|place|ment re|ac|tion** (**double-replacement reactions**) N-COUNT A **double-replacement reaction** is a chemical reaction between two compounds in which some of the atoms in each compound switch places and form two new compounds. *reacción de doble substitución* [TECHNICAL]

**double-space** (**double-spaces, double-spacing, double-spaced**) also **double space** **1** V-T If you **double-space** something you are writing or

d

typing, you include a full line of space between each line of writing. escribir a doble espacio ❑ *Double-space the list.* *Escribe la lista a doble espacio.* • **double-spaced** ADJ *a doble espacio* ❑ *...forty pages of double-spaced text.* *...cuarenta páginas de texto a doble espacio.* • **dou|ble spac|ing** N-UNCOUNT *doble espacio* ❑ *Single spacing is used within paragraphs, double spacing between paragraphs.* *El espacio simple se usa para los párrafos y el doble espacio entre párrafos.* **2** N-COUNT A **double space** is a full line of space between each line of a piece of writing. *doble espacio* ❑ *Leave a double space between entries.* *Deja un doble espacio entre cada entrada.*

D

**doubt** /daʊt/ (**doubts, doubting, doubted**) **1** N-VAR If you have **doubt** or **doubts** about something, you feel uncertain about it. *duda* ❑ *Rendell raised doubts about the plan.* *Rendell suscitó/provocó dudas respecto al plan.* ❑ *There is little doubt that the Earth's climate is changing.* *Hay pocas dudas de que el clima de la Tierra esté cambiando.* **2** V-T If you **doubt** something, or if you **doubt** whether something is true, genuine or possible, you believe that it is probably not true, genuine or possible. *dudar* ❑ *Many people doubted whether it would happen.* *Mucha gente dudaba que ocurriera.* ❑ *He doubted if he would learn anything new from Marie.* *Dudaba que pudiera aprender algo nuevo de Marie.* ❑ *No one doubted his ability.* *Nadie dudaba de su habilidad.* **3** V-T If you **doubt** someone or **doubt** their word, you think that they may not be telling the truth. *dudar de* ❑ *No one doubted him.* *Nadie dudaba de él.* **4** PHRASE You say that something is **beyond doubt** or **beyond reasonable doubt** when you are certain that it is true and it cannot be contradicted or disproved. *fuera de duda* ❑ *The vote showed beyond doubt that people wanted independence.* *La votación mostró, fuera de duda, que el pueblo quería la independencia.* **5** PHRASE If you are **in doubt** about something, you feel unsure or uncertain about it. *en duda* ❑ *He is in no doubt about what to do.* *No tiene dudas sobre lo que debe hacer.* **6** PHRASE If you say that something is **in doubt** or **open to doubt,** you consider it to be uncertain or unreliable. *en duda* ❑ *The future of the business was still in doubt.* *El futuro del negocio todavía estaba en duda.* **7** PHRASE You use **no doubt** to emphasize that something seems certain or very likely to you. *sin duda* ❑ *She will no doubt be here soon.* *Sin duda llegará pronto.* **8** PHRASE If you say that something is true **without doubt** or **without a doubt,** you are emphasizing that it is definitely true. *sin duda alguna* ❑ *This was without doubt the best day of Amanda's life.* *Sin duda alguna, era el mejor día en la vida de Amanda.*

**doubt|ful** /daʊtfəl/ **1** ADJ If it is **doubtful that** something will happen, it seems unlikely to happen or you are uncertain whether it will happen. *dudoso* ❑ *After the accident, it seemed doubtful that he would be able to walk again.* *Después del accidente, parecía dudoso que pudiera caminar otra vez.* **2** ADJ If you are **doubtful about** something, you feel unsure or uncertain about it. *dudoso* ❑ *I was still very doubtful about the chances for success.* *Todavía tenía muchas dudas sobre las probabilidades de éxito.* • **doubt|ful|ly** ADV *dubitativamente* ❑ *Keeton shook his head doubtfully.* *Keeton sacudió la cabeza dubitativamente.*

**dough** /doʊ/ N-UNCOUNT **Dough** is a mixture of flour, water, and sometimes also fat and sugar. It can be cooked to make bread or pastry. *masa* ❑ *Roll out the dough into one large circle.* *Enrolle la masa y forme un círculo grande.*

**dough|nut** /doʊnʌt, -nət/ (**doughnuts**) also **donut** N-COUNT A **doughnut** is a piece of sweet dough that has been cooked in hot oil. *dona, rosquilla*

| down |
|---|
| ❶ PREPOSITION AND ADVERB USES |
| ❷ ADJECTIVE USES |
| ❸ NOUN USES |

**❶ down** /daʊn/

> **Down** is often used with verbs of movement, such as "fall" and "pull," and also in phrasal verbs such as "bring down" and "calm down."

**1** PREP **Down** means toward the ground or a lower level, or in a lower place. *abajo* ❑ *I marched down the hill.* *Caminé colina abajo.* ❑ *A man came down the stairs to meet them.* *Un hombre bajó por las escaleras para recibirlos.* ❑ *He was already halfway down the hill.* *Ya estaba a medio camino colina abajo.* ❑ *She was looking down at her papers.* *Estaba examinando los papeles.* • **Down** is also an adverb. *abajo* ❑ *She went down to the kitchen.* *Fue abajo, a la cocina.* **2** PREP If you go or look **down** something such as a road or river, you go or look along it. If you are **down** a road or river, you are somewhere along it. *abajo* ❑ *They set off up one street and down another.* *Salieron y fueron ora calle arriba, ora calle abajo.* **3** ADV If you put something **down,** you put it onto a surface. *dejar, depositar* ❑ *Danny put down his glass.* *Danny dejó su vaso.* **4** ADV If an amount or level of something goes **down,** it decreases. *bajar, descender* ❑ *Prices came down today.* *Los precios bajaron hoy.* ❑ *Inflation is down to three percent.* *La inflación descendió al tres por ciento.* **5** PHRASE If someone or something is **down for** a particular thing, it has been arranged that they will do that thing, or that thing will happen. *tener arreglado* ❑ *Mark was down for an interview.* *Mark tiene una cita.* **6** **up and down** → see **up**

**❷ down** /daʊn/ **1** ADJ If you are feeling **down,** you are feeling unhappy or depressed. *deprimido* [INFORMAL] ❑ *The man sounded really down.* *El tipo parecía realmente deprimido.* **2** ADJ If something is **down on** paper, it has been written on the paper. *por escrito, anotado* ❑ *That meeting wasn't down on the calendar.* *La reunión no estaba anotada en el calendario.* **3** ADJ If a piece of equipment, especially a computer system, is **down,** it is temporarily not working. Compare **up**. *descompuesto* ❑ *The computer's down again.* *La computadora está descompuesta otra vez.*

**❸ down** /daʊn/ N-UNCOUNT **Down** consists of the small, soft feathers on young birds. **Down** is used to make bed-covers and pillows. *plumón* ❑ *...goose down.* *...plumón de ganso.*

**down|draft** /daʊndræft/ (**downdrafts**) N-COUNT A **downdraft** is a downward current of air, usually accompanied by rain. *corriente descendente*

| Word Link | *down ≈ below, lower : downfall, download, downstairs* |
|---|---|

**down|fall** /daʊnfɔl/ (**downfalls**) **1** N-COUNT

The **downfall** of a successful or powerful person or institution is their loss of success or power. *ruina, perdición* ❑ *His lack of experience led to his downfall. Su falta de experiencia lo llevó a la ruina., La falta de experiencia lo llevó a su perdición.* **2** N-COUNT The thing that was a person's **downfall** caused them to fail or lose power. *perdición* ❑ *Jeremy's honesty was his downfall. La honradez de Jeremy fue su perdición.*

**down feath|er** (**down feathers**) N-COUNT **Down feathers** are the soft feathers on the bodies of young birds. *plumón* [TECHNICAL]

**down|grade** /daʊngreɪd/ (**downgrades, downgrading, downgraded**) V-T If someone or something **is downgraded,** their situation is changed to a lower level of importance or value. *reducir* ❑ *The boy's condition was downgraded from critical to serious. El estado del niño cambió de crítico a serio.* ❑ *There was no criticism of her work until after she was downgraded. Nadie había criticado su trabajo hasta que la bajaron de categoría.*

| Word Link | *down ≈ below, lower : downfall, download, downstairs* |
|---|---|

**down|load** /daʊnloʊd/ (**downloads, downloading, downloaded**) V-T To **download** data means to transfer it to or from a computer along a line such as a telephone line, a radio link, or a computer network. *descargar, trasvasar* ❑ *You can download the software from the Internet. Puede descargar el programa de Internet.*

**down|load|able** /daʊnloʊdəbᵊl/ ADJ If a computer file or program is **downloadable,** it can be downloaded to another computer. *descargable, trasvasable* [COMPUTING] ❑ *...downloadable computer games. ...juegos de computadora descargables.*

**down|scale** /daʊnskeɪl/ ADJ If you describe a product or service as **downscale,** you think that it is cheap and not very good in quality. *barato, de segunda* ❑ *...downscale stores. ...tiendas de artículos baratos.*

**down|stage** /daʊnsteɪdʒ/ ADV When an actor is **downstage** or moves **downstage,** he or she is or moves toward the front part of the stage. *proscenio* [TECHNICAL] • **Downstage** is also an adjective. *principal* ❑ *...downstage members of the cast. ...los principales miembros del reparto.*

**down|stairs** /daʊnstɛərz/ **1** ADV If you go **downstairs** in a building, you go down a staircase toward the ground floor. *escaleras abajo* ❑ *Denise went downstairs and made some tea. Denise fue abajo y preparó un poco de té.* **2** ADV If something or someone is **downstairs** in a building, they are on the ground floor or on a lower floor than you. *abajo* ❑ *The telephone was downstairs in the kitchen. El teléfono estaba abajo en la cocina.* **3** ADJ **Downstairs** means situated on the ground floor of a building or on a lower floor than you are. *abajo* ❑ *She painted the downstairs rooms. Pintó los cuartos de abajo.*

**Down's syn|drome** N-UNCOUNT **Down's syndrome** is a disorder that some people are born with. People who have Down's syndrome have a flat forehead and sloping eyes and lower than average intelligence. *síndrome de Down*

**down|time** /daʊntaɪm/ **1** N-UNCOUNT In computing, **downtime** is time when a computer is not working. *tiempo muerto, tiempo de inactividad* **2** N-UNCOUNT **Downtime** is time when people are not working. *tiempo muerto, tiempo de inactividad, período de descanso* ❑ *Downtime can cost businesses a lot of money. El tiempo de inactividad puede resultar muy costoso para las empresas.*

**down|town** /daʊntaʊn/ ADJ **Downtown** places are in or toward the center of a large town or city, where the stores and places of business are. *del centro* ❑ *...an office in downtown Chicago. ...una oficina en el centro de Chicago.* • **Downtown** is also an adverb. *en el centro* ❑ *He worked downtown for an insurance firm. Trabajaba en el centro para una compañía de seguros/una aseguradora.*

**down|ward** /daʊnwərd/

The form **downwards** is also used for the adverb.

**1** ADJ A **downward** movement or look is directed toward a lower place or a lower level. *descendente, hacia abajo* ❑ *...a downward movement of the hands. ...un movimiento descendente de las manos.* **2** ADJ If you refer to a **downward** trend, you mean that something is decreasing or that a situation is getting worse. *a la baja, al descenso* ❑ *There has actually been a downward trend in summer temperatures. En realidad, las temperaturas estivales han mostrado una tendencia a la baja.* **3** ADV If you move or look **downward,** you move or look toward the ground or a lower level. *hacia abajo* ❑ *Benedict pointed downward with his stick. Benedict señaló hacia abajo con su bastón.* **4** ADV If an amount or rate moves **downward,** it decreases. *hacia abajo* ❑ *Inflation is moving firmly downward. La inflación está descendiendo con constancia.*

**doze** /doʊz/ (**dozes, dozing, dozed**) V-I When you **doze,** you sleep lightly or for a short period. *dormitar* ❑ *She dozed for a while in the cabin. Dormitó un rato en el camarote.*
→ see **sleep**
▸ **doze off** PHR-VERB If you **doze off,** you fall into a light sleep. *adormecerse, quedarse dormido* ❑ *I closed my eyes and dozed off. Cerré los ojos y me quedé dormido.*

**doz|en** /dʌzᵊn/ (**dozens**)

The plural form is **dozen** after a number, or after a word or expression referring to a number, such as "several" or "a few."

**1** NUM **A dozen** means twelve. *docena* ❑ *The bus had room for two dozen people. El autobús tenía lugar para dos docenas de personas.* ❑ *In half a dozen words, he explained what was wrong. Explicó en unas cuantas palabras lo que estaba mal.* **2** QUANT If you refer to **dozens of** things or people, you are emphasizing that there are very many of them. *decenas* ❑ *The storm destroyed dozens of buildings. La tormenta destruyó decenas de edificios.*

**Dr.** (**Drs.**) **Dr.** is a written abbreviation for **Doctor**. *Dr.* ❑ *...Dr. John Hardy of St. Mary's Hospital. ...el Dr. John Hardy del Hospital St. Mary.*

**draft** /dræft/ (**drafts, drafting, drafted**) **1** N-COUNT A **draft** is an early version of a letter, book, or speech. *borrador* ❑ *I rewrote the rough draft. Volví a escribir el borrador.* ❑ *I e-mailed a first draft of the article to him. Le envié un primer borrador del artículo por correo electrónico.* **2** N-COUNT A **draft** is a current of air that comes into a place in an undesirable way. *corriente* ❑ *Block drafts around doors and windows. Ataje las corrientes en torno a las*

d

puertas y ventanas. **3** V-T When you **draft** a letter, book, or speech, you write the first version of it. redactar un borrador de ❑ *He drafted a letter to the manager.* *Redactó el borrador de una carta al gerente.* **4** V-T If you **are drafted,** you are ordered to serve in the armed forces, usually for a limited period of time. reclutar, llamar a filas ❑ *He was drafted into the U.S. Army.* *Lo llamó a filas el ejército estadounidense.* **5** V-T If people **are drafted** to do something, they are asked to do a particular job. asignar ❑ *Foxton was drafted to run the organization.* *Asignaron a Foxton para dirigir la organización.* **6** N-SING **The draft** is the practice of ordering people to serve in the armed forces, usually for a limited period of time. llamado a filas ❑ *...his effort to avoid the draft.* *...sus esfuerzos por evitar el llamado a filas.*

D

**Word Partnership** Usar *draft* con:

| | |
|---|---|
| ADJ. | **final** draft, **rough** draft **1** |
| V. | **revise a** draft, **write a** draft **1** |
| | **feel a** draft **2** |
| | **dodge the** draft **6** |
| N. | draft **a letter,** draft **a speech** **3** |

**draft dodg|er** (**draft dodgers**) N-COUNT A **draft dodger** is someone who avoids joining the armed forces when normally they would have to join. alguien que rehúye el servicio militar obligatorio

**drag** /dræg/ (**drags, dragging, dragged**) **1** V-T If you **drag** something, you pull it along the ground, often with difficulty. arrastrar ❑ *He dragged his chair toward the table.* *Arrastró su silla hacia la mesa.* **2** V-T If you **drag** a computer image, you use the mouse to move the position of the image on the screen, or to change its size or shape. arrastrar [COMPUTING] ❑ *Use your mouse to drag the pictures.* *Use el ratón para arrastrar las fotografías.* **3** V-T If someone **drags** you somewhere, they pull you there, or force you to go there by physically threatening you. arrastrar ❑ *They dragged the men out of the car.* *Sacaron a los hombres del coche a rastras.* **4** V-T If you **drag** someone somewhere they do not want to go, you make them go there. arrancar de/a ❑ *He's very friendly, when you can drag him away from his work!* *Es muy agradable, ¡cuando puedes arrancarlo de su trabajo!* ❑ *I find it really hard to drag myself out and exercise regularly.* *Me cuesta mucho trabajo forzarme a hacer ejercicio con regularidad.* **5** V-T If the police **drag** a river or lake, they pull nets or hooks across the bottom of it in order to look for something. dragar ❑ *Police are planning to drag the pond.* *La policía está considerando dragar el estanque.* **6** V-I If a period of time or an event **drags,** it is very boring and seems to last a long time. volverse pesado (conversación, trabajo), hacerse largo (película, espectáculo, tiempo), eternizarse/hacerse eterno (tiempo) ❑ *The minutes dragged past.* *Los minutos se hicieron eternos.* **7** N-UNCOUNT **Drag** is the resistance to movement that is experienced by something that is moving through air or through a fluid. resistencia al avance [TECHNICAL] **8** PHRASE If you **drag** your **feet** or **drag** your **heels,** you delay doing something or do it very slowly because you do not want to do it. arrastrar los pies, dar largas ❑ *The government was dragging its feet on the issue.* *El gobierno estaba dándole largas al problema.* **9** PHRASE If a man is **in drag,** he is wearing women's clothes; if a woman is **in drag,** she is wearing men's clothes. travestí/travesti

drag

▸ **drag out** **1** PHR-VERB If you **drag** something **out,** you make it last for longer than is necessary. alargar ❑ *They did everything they could to drag out the process.* *Hicieron todo lo posible por alargar el proceso.* **2** PHR-VERB If you **drag** something **out of** a person, you persuade them to tell you something that they do not want to tell you. sacar ❑ *She didn't want to tell me what happened, but I dragged it out of her.* *No quería decirme lo que pasó, pero se lo saqué.*

**drag and drop** (**drags and drops, dragging and dropping, dragged and dropped**) also **drag-and-drop** **1** V-T If you **drag and drop** computer files or images, you move them from one place to another by clicking on them with the mouse and moving them across the screen. arrastrar y soltar ❑ *Drag and drop the folder to the hard drive.* *Arrastre la carpeta y suéltela en el disco duro.* **2** N-UNCOUNT **Drag and drop** is a method of moving computer files or images from one place to another by clicking on them with the mouse and moving them across the screen. arrastrar y soltar ❑ *Copying software onto an iPod is as easy as drag and drop.* *Copiar los programas a una iPod es tan fácil como arrastrar y soltar.* • **Drag and drop** is also an adjective. que se arrastra y suelta ❑ *...a drag-and-drop text.* *...texto que se arrastra y suelta.*

**drag|on** /drægən/ (**dragons**) N-COUNT In stories and legends, a **dragon** is an animal like a big lizard. It has wings and claws, and breathes out fire. dragón

→ see **fantasy**

**dragon|fly** /drægənflaɪ/ (**dragonflies**) N-COUNT **Dragonflies** are brightly colored insects with long, thin bodies and two sets of wings. libélula, caballito del diablo

→ see **insect**

**drain** /dreɪn/ (**drains, draining, drained**) **1** V-T/V-I If you **drain** a liquid from a place or object, you remove the liquid by causing it to flow somewhere else. If a liquid **drains** somewhere, it flows there. drenar, desaguar ❑ *They built the tunnel to drain water out of the mines.* *Construyeron el túnel para drenar el agua de las minas.* ❑ *...springs and rivers that drain into lakes.* *...manantiales y ríos que desaguan en lagos.* **2** V-T/V-I If you **drain** a place or object, you dry it by causing water to flow out of it. If a place or object **drains,** water flows out of it until it is dry. drenar ❑ *...attempts to drain flooded land.* *...intentos por drenar las tierras inundadas.* **3** V-T/V-I If you **drain** food or if food **drains,** you remove the liquid that it has been in, especially after it has been cooked or soaked in water. escurrir ❑ *Drain the pasta well.* *Escurra bien la pasta.* **4** V-T If something **drains** you, it makes you feel physically and emotionally exhausted. agotar ❑ *All the worry drained me.* *Tanta preocupación me agotó.* • **drained** ADJ agotado ❑ *I suffer from headaches, which make me feel completely drained.* *Sufro de jaquecas y eso me hace sentirme completamente agotado.* • **drain|ing** ADJ agotador ❑ *This work is physically tiring and*

*emotionally draining.* *Este trabajo es agotador, física y emocionalmente.* **5** N-COUNT A **drain** is a pipe that carries water or sewage away from a place, or an opening in a surface that leads to the pipe. *drenaje* ❑ *Tony built his own house and laid his own drains.* *Tony construyó su propia casa e instaló el drenaje.* **6** N-SING If you say that something is **a drain on** an organization's finances or resources, you mean that it costs the organization a large amount of money, and you do not think that it is worth it. *sangría* ❑ *Her fuel bills were a constant drain on her cash.* *Las cuentas de combustible sangraban constantemente su efectivo.* **7** PHRASE If you say that something **is going down the drain,** you mean that it is being destroyed or wasted. *irse al caño, esfumarse* [INFORMAL] ❑ *These dreams were soon down the drain.* *Sus sueños se esfumaron pronto.*
→ see **bathroom**

**drain|age** /dreɪnɪdʒ/ N-UNCOUNT **Drainage** is the system or process by which water or other liquids are drained from a place. *drenaje* ❑ *Plant pots need good drainage.* *Las macetas requieren un buen drenaje.*
→ see **farm**

**drain|age ba|sin** (**drainage basins**) N-COUNT A **drainage basin** is the same as a **catchment area.** *cuenca (fluvial)* [TECHNICAL]

**dra|ma** /drɑmə, dræmə/ (**dramas**) **1** N-COUNT A **drama** is a serious play for the theater, television, or radio, or a serious movie. *obra dramática, drama* ❑ *He acted in radio dramas.* *Actuaba en obras radiofónicas.* ❑ *The movie is a drama about a woman searching for her children.* *La película es un drama sobre una mujer en búsqueda de sus hijos.* **2** N-UNCOUNT You use **drama** to refer to plays and the theater in general. *drama* ❑ *He knew nothing of Greek drama.* *No sabía nada del teatro dramático griego.* **3** N-VAR You can refer to a real situation which is exciting or distressing as **drama.** *drama* ❑ *He slept through all the drama.* *Se la pasó durmiendo durante todo el drama.*
→ see Picture Dictionary: **drama**
→ see **genre**

**dra|mat|ic** /drəmætɪk/ **1** ADJ A **dramatic** change or event happens suddenly and is very noticeable and surprising. *espectacular, drástico* ❑ *The reduction in sales had a dramatic effect on profits.* *La reducción de las ventas tuvo un efecto drástico en las ganancias.* ● **dra|mati|cal|ly** /drəmætɪkli/ ADV *dramáticamente, radicalmente* ❑ *The climate has changed dramatically.* *El clima ha cambiado radicalmente.* **2** ADJ A **dramatic** action, event, or situation is exciting and impressive. *dramático, espectacular* ❑ *His dramatic escape involved a helicopter and a submarine.* *En su espectacular escape intervinieron un helicóptero y un submarino.*

**dra|mat|ic play** N-UNCOUNT **Dramatic play** is children's play that involves imagined characters and situations. *juego dramático infantil*

**dra|mat|ic struc|ture** (**dramatic structures**) N-VAR The **dramatic structure** of a play or other story is the different parts into which it can be divided, such as the climax and the denouement. *trama*

**drama|turg** /dræmətɜrdʒ/ (**dramaturgs**) also **dramaturge** (**dramaturges**) N-COUNT A **dramaturg** is a person who works with writers and theaters to help them to develop and produce

**Picture Dictionary** drama

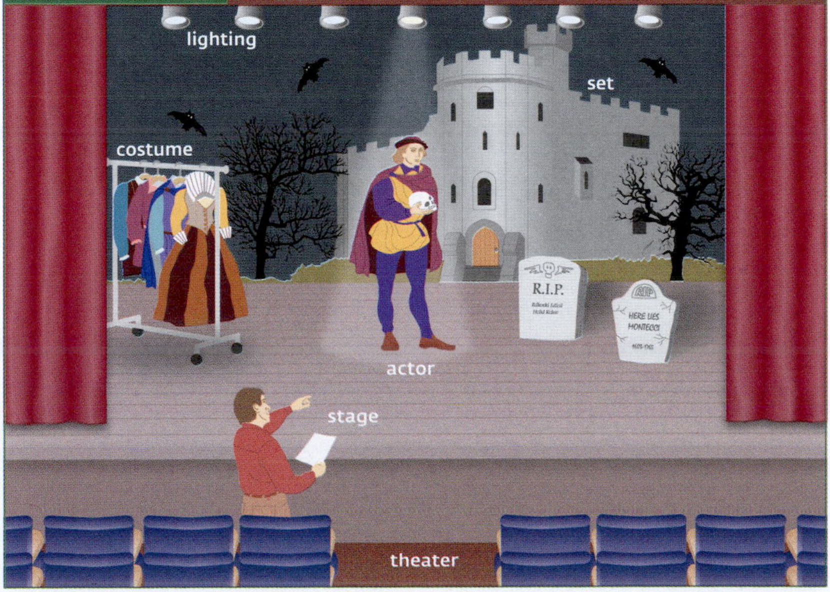

D

## Picture Dictionary draw

draw

trace

sketch

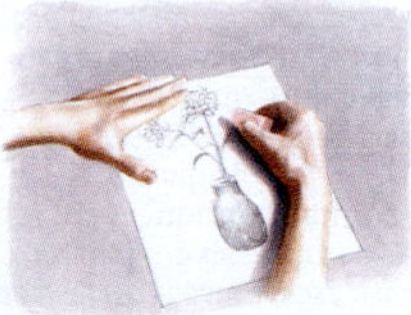
erase

paint

copy

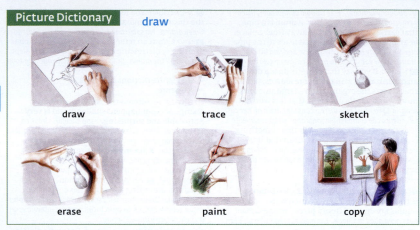

plays. *dramaturgo o dramaturga* [TECHNICAL]

**drank** /dræŋk/ **Drank** is the past tense of **drink.** *pasado de* **drink**

**dras|tic** /dræstɪk/ **1** ADJ If you have to take **drastic** action in order to solve a problem, you have to do something extreme to solve it. *drástico, radical* ❑ *Drastic measures are needed to improve the situation. Es necesario adoptar medidas radicales para mejorar la situación.* **2** ADJ A **drastic** change is a very great change. *radical* ❑ *...drastic alterations to Microsoft's products. ...modificaciones radicales a los productos de Microsoft.* ● **dras|ti|cal|ly** ADV *radicalmente* ❑ *As a result, services have been drastically reduced. Como resultado, los servicios han sido reducidos radicalmente.*

**draw**
1. MAKE A PICTURE
2. MOVE, PULL, OR TAKE
3. OTHER USES AND PHRASAL VERBS

**1 draw** /drɔ/ (**draws, drawing, drew, drawn**) **1** V-T/V-I When you **draw,** or when you **draw** something, you use a pencil or pen to produce a picture, pattern, or diagram. *dibujar* ❑ *She was drawing with a pencil. Estaba dibujando con un lápiz.* ● **draw|ing** N-UNCOUNT *dibujo, dibujar* ❑ *I like dancing, singing, and drawing. Me gusta bailar, cantar y dibujar., Me gustan el baile, el canto y el dibujo.* **2** to **draw the line** → see **line**
→ see Picture Dictionary: **draw**
→ see **animation**

**2 draw** /drɔ/ (**draws, drawing, drew, drawn**) **1** V-I If a person or vehicle **draws** somewhere, they move there. *irse, alejarse* [WRITTEN] ❑ *She drew away and did not smile. Se alejó y no sonrió.* ❑ *Claire saw the taxi drawing away. Claire vio que el taxi se alejaba.* **2** V-T If you **draw** something or someone in a particular direction, you move them in that direction. *arrimar, acercar* [WRITTEN] ❑ *He drew his chair nearer the fire. Arrimó su silla al fuego.* ❑ *He put his arm around Caroline's shoulders and drew her close to him. Puso el brazo en torno a los hombros de Caroline y la acercó.* **3** V-T When you **draw** a drape or blind, you pull it across a window, either to cover or to uncover it. *correr* ❑ *He went to the window and drew the drapes. Se dirigió a la ventana y corrió las cortinas.* **4** V-T If someone **draws** a gun, knife, or other weapon, they pull it out of its container so that it is ready to use. *desenfundar, sacar* ❑ *He drew his knife and turned to face them. Desenfundó el cuchillo y los enfrentó.* **5** V-T If you **draw** a deep breath, you breathe in deeply once. *aspirar, respirar* ❑ *He paused, and drew a deep breath. Hizo una pausa y aspiró profundamente.* **6** V-T To **draw** something such as water or energy **from** a particular source means to take it from that source. *extraer, sacar* ❑ *Villagers still have to draw their water from wells. Los aldeanos todavía tienen que sacar el agua de pozos artesanos.* **7** V-T If you **draw** money out of a bank account, you get it from the account so that you can use it. *retirar* ❑ *A few months ago he drew out nearly all his savings. Hace unos meses retiró casi todos sus ahorros.* **8** to **draw lots** → see **lot**

**3 draw** /drɔ/ (**draws, drawing, drew, drawn**) **1** V-T If you **draw** a comparison, conclusion, or distinction, you decide that it exists or is true. *establecer, llegar a, sacar* ❑ *Fonda's performance drew comparisons with his famous father, Henry. La actuación de Fonda hizo surgir las comparaciones con su célebre padre, Henry.* ❑ *He draws two conclusions from this. A partir de esto, saca dos conclusiones.* **2** V-T If you **draw** someone's attention to something, you make them aware of it or make them think about it. *atraer* ❑ *He was waving his arms to draw their attention. Estaba agitando los brazos para atraer su atención.* **3** V-T If someone or something **draws** a particular reaction, people react to it in that way. *provocar* ❑ *The suggestion drew laughter from everyone there. La sugerencia provocó la risa de todos los presentes.* **4** → see also **drawing** **5** PHRASE When an event or period of time **draws to a close** or **draws to an end,** it finishes. *llegar a su fin* ❑ *Another celebration drew to its close. Otra celebración llegó a su fin.*
▸ **draw in** PHR-VERB If you **draw** someone **in** or **draw** them **into** something you are involved with, you cause them to become involved with it.

*involucrar, hacer participar* ❑ *It won't be easy for you to draw him in. No te será fácil hacerlo participar.*

**Thesaurus** *draw* Ver también:

v. illustrate, sketch, trace ❶ 1
bring out, pull out, take out ❷ 4
inhale ❷ 5
extract, take ❷ 6
conclude, decide, make a decision, settle on ❸ 1

▸**draw on** PHR-VERB If you **draw on** or **draw upon** something such as your skill or experience, you make use of it in order to do something. *recurrir a, hacer uso de, inspirarse en* ❑ *He drew on his experience to write a book. Se inspiró en su experiencia para escribir un libro.*

▸**draw up** PHR-VERB If you **draw up** a document, list, or plan, you prepare it and write it out. *redactar* ❑ *They drew up a formal agreement. Redactaron un acuerdo formal.*

▸**draw upon** → see **draw on**

**draw|back** /drɔbæk/ (**drawbacks**) N-COUNT A **drawback** is an aspect of something or someone that you do not like. *inconveniente, desventaja* ❑ *The apartment's only drawback was that it was too small. El único inconveniente del departamento fue que era demasiado pequeño.*

**drawer** /drɔr/ (**drawers**) N-COUNT A **drawer** is part of a desk, chest, or other piece of furniture that is shaped like a box. You pull it toward you to open it. *cajón* ❑ *She opened her desk drawer and took out the book. Abrió el cajón de su escritorio y sacó el libro.*

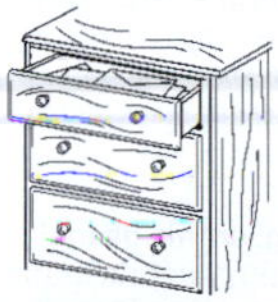
drawer

**draw|ing** /drɔɪŋ/ (**drawings**) 1 N-COUNT A **drawing** is a picture made with a pencil or pen. *dibujo* ❑ *She did a drawing of me. Hizo un dibujo de mí.* 2 → see also **draw 1**

**drawn** /drɔn/ 1 **Drawn** is the past participle of **draw**. *participio pasado de **draw*** 2 ADJ If someone or their face looks **drawn**, their face is thin and they look tired or ill. *demacrado* ❑ *She looked drawn and tired. Se veía demacrada y cansada.*

**drawn-out** ADJ You can describe something as **drawn-out** when it lasts or takes longer than you would like it to. *interminable* ❑ *...a long, drawn-out conversation. ...una conversación larga, interminable.*

**dread** /drɛd/ (**dreads, dreading, dreaded**) 1 V-T If you **dread** something which may happen, you feel very anxious and unhappy about it because you think it will be unpleasant or upsetting. *tener terror, temer, horrorizar* ❑ *I'm dreading Christmas this year. Me horroriza pensar en la Navidad de este año.* ❑ *I dreaded coming back. Tenía terror de volver.* 2 N-UNCOUNT **Dread** is a feeling of great anxiety and fear about something that may happen. *terror, horror* ❑ *She thought with dread of the cold winters. Pensó con horror en los gélidos inviernos.*

**Word Link** ***ful** ≈ filled with : beautiful, careful, dreadful*

**dread|ful** /drɛdfəl/ ADJ If you say that something is **dreadful**, you mean that it is very bad or unpleasant, or very poor in quality. *horrible, espantoso, terrible* ❑ *They told us the dreadful news. Nos dieron las horribles nuevas.* • **dread|fully** ADV *terriblemente* ❑ *You behaved dreadfully. Te comportaste terriblemente.*

**dream** /drim/ (**dreams, dreaming, dreamed** or **dreamt**) 1 N-COUNT A **dream** is a series of events that you experience only in your mind while you are asleep. *sueño* ❑ *He had a dream about Claire. Tuvo un sueño sobre Claire.* 2 N-COUNT You can refer to a situation or event as a **dream** if you often think about it because you would like it to happen. *sueño* ❑ *He finally achieved his dream of becoming a pilot. Finalmente logró su sueño de ser piloto.* 3 V-T/V-I When you **dream,** you experience events in your mind while you are asleep. *soñar (con/en)* ❑ *Ivor dreamed that he was on a bus. Ivor soñó que iba en un autobús.* ❑ *She dreamed about her baby. Soñó con su bebé.* 4 V-T/V-I If you often think about something that you would very much like to happen or have, you can say that you **dream of** it. *soñar* ❑ *She dreamed of becoming an actress. Soñaba con llegar a ser actriz.* ❑ *For most people, a life without work is something we can only dream about. Para la mayoría de la gente, una vida sin tener que trabajar es tan sólo un sueño.* ❑ *I dream that my son will attend college. Sueño que mi hijo irá a la universidad.* 5 V-I If you say that you **would not dream of** doing something, you are emphasizing that you would never do it because you think it is wrong or is not possible or suitable for you. *ni en sueños* ❑ *I wouldn't dream of laughing at you. Ni en sueños me reiría de ti.*

▸**dream up** PHR-VERB If you **dream up** a plan or idea, you work it out or create it in your mind. *idear* ❑ *I dreamed up a plan to solve the problem. Se me ocurrió un plan para resolver el problema.*

**Thesaurus** *dream* Ver también:

N. nightmare, reverie, vision 1
ambition, aspiration, design, hope, wish 2
V. hope, long for, wish 4

**Word Partnership** Usar *dream* con:

V. **have a** dream 1
**fulfill a** dream, **pursue a** dream, **realize a** dream 2
N. dream **interpretation** 1
dream **home**, dream **vacation** 2

**dress** /drɛs/ (**dresses, dressing, dressed**) 1 N-COUNT A **dress** is a piece of clothing worn by a woman or girl. It covers her body and part of her legs. *vestido* ❑ *She was wearing a black dress. Llevaba (puesto) un vestido negro.* 2 N-UNCOUNT You can refer to clothes worn by men or women as **dress**. *traje* ❑ *He wore formal evening dress. Iba vestido de etiqueta.* 3 V-T/V-I When you **dress** or **dress yourself**, you put on clothes. *vestir(se)* ❑ *Sarah waited while he dressed. Sara esperó mientras él se vestía.* 4 → see also **dressed, dressing**

▸**dress down** PHR-VERB If you **dress down**, you wear clothes that are less formal than usual. *vestir informalmente* ❑ *She dressed down in dark glasses and baggy clothes. Vestía informalmente, con ropas sueltas y lentes oscuros.*

▸ **dress up** PHR-VERB If you **dress up** or **dress** yourself **up**, you put on different clothes, in order to make yourself look more formal than usual or to disguise yourself. *vestirse elegante, ponerse elegante* ❑ *You do not need to dress up for dinner. No necesitas ponerte elegante para la cena.* ❑ *I love the fun of dressing up in nice clothing. Me encanta lo divertido que es ponerse elegante con ropa bonita.*
→ see **petroleum**

D

**Word Partnership** Usar *dress* con:

| | |
|---|---|
| V. | **put on a** dress, **wear a** dress 1 |
| ADJ. | **casual** dress, **formal** dress, **traditional** dress 2 |
| ADV. | dress **appropriately**, dress **casually**, dress **well** 3 |

**dressed** /drɛst/ 1 ADJ If you are **dressed,** you are wearing clothes rather than being naked or wearing your nightclothes. *vestido* ❑ *He was fully dressed, including shoes. Estaba completamente vestido y con los zapatos puestos.* 2 ADJ If you are **dressed** in a particular way, you are wearing clothes of a particular color or kind. *vestido (de)* ❑ *...a tall woman dressed in black. ...una mujer alta, vestida de negro.*

dresser

**dress|er** /drɛsər/ (**dressers**) N-COUNT A **dresser** is a chest of drawers, sometimes with a mirror on the top. *tocador*

**dress|ing** /drɛsɪŋ/ (**dressings**) 1 N-VAR A salad **dressing** is a mixture of oil, vinegar, and herbs or flavorings, which you pour over salad. *aderezo, aliño* ❑ *Mix the ingredients for the dressing. Mezcle los ingredientes para el aderezo.* 2 N-COUNT A **dressing** is a covering that is put on a wound to protect it while it heals. *apósito, vendaje* ❑ *He applied a fresh dressing to her hand. Le puso un apósito/vendaje nuevo en la mano.* 3 N-UNCOUNT **Dressing** is a mixture of food that is cooked and then put inside a bird such as a turkey before it is cooked and eaten. *relleno* ❑ *...cornbread dressing. ...relleno de pan de harina de maíz.*

**dress re|hears|al** (**dress rehearsals**) N-COUNT The **dress rehearsal** of a play, opera, or show is the final rehearsal before it is performed, in which the performers wear their costumes and the lights and scenery are all used as they will be in the performance. *ensayo general*

**dress-up** 1 N-UNCOUNT When children play **dress-up,** they put on special or different clothes and pretend to be different people. *disfraces* 2 ADJ **Dress-up** clothes are stylish clothes which you wear when you want to look elegant or formal. *elegante, formal* ❑ *The hotel is informal and you do not need dress-up clothes. El hotel es informal y no se necesita ropa formal.*

**drew** /dru/ **Drew** is the past tense of **draw**. *pasado de* ***draw***

**dried** /draɪd/ 1 ADJ **Dried** food or milk has had all the water removed from it so that it will last for a long time. *seco* ❑ *...dried herbs. ...hierbas secas.* 2 → see also **dry**

**dri|er** /draɪər/ → see **dry, dryer**

**drift** /drɪft/ (**drifts, drifting, drifted**) 1 V-I When something **drifts** somewhere, it is carried there by the movement of wind or water. *ir a la deriva, ir sin rumbo fijo* ❑ *We drifted up the river. Fuimos río arriba, sin saber a dónde nos dirigíamos.* 2 V-I To **drift** somewhere means to move there slowly or gradually. *dirigirse poco a poco* ❑ *People drifted toward the cities as there were fewer jobs on farms. La gente empezó a dirigirse poco a poco a las ciudades, pues cada vez había menos trabajo en el campo.* 3 N-COUNT A **drift** is a movement away from somewhere or something, or a movement toward somewhere or something different. *éxodo* ❑ *...the drift toward the cities. ...el éxodo a las ciudades.* 4 N-COUNT A **drift** is a mass of snow that has built up into a pile as a result of the movement of wind. *ventisquero* ❑ *A boy was trapped in a snow drift. Un niño quedó atrapado en un ventisquero.*
→ see **snow**

▸ **drift off** PHR-VERB If you **drift off** to sleep, you gradually fall asleep. *quedarse dormido* ❑ *He finally drifted off to sleep. Finalmente se quedó dormido.*

**drill** /drɪl/ (**drills, drilling, drilled**) 1 N-COUNT A **drill** is a tool or machine that you use for making holes. *taladro, taladradora* ❑ *...a dentist's drill. ...un taladro de dentista.* 2 V-T/V-I When you **drill into** something or **drill** a hole in something, you make a hole in it using a drill. *taladrar, perforar* ❑ *He drilled into the wall. Hizo un agujero en la pared con el taladro.* 3 N-VAR A **drill** is repeated training for a group of people, especially soldiers, so that they can do something quickly and efficiently. *ejercicio, simulacro* ❑ *...a drill that included 18 ships and 90 planes. ...un simulacro de guerra en el que participaron 18 barcos y 90 aviones.*
→ see **oil, tool**

**drink** /drɪŋk/ (**drinks, drinking, drank, drunk**) 1 V-T/V-I When you **drink** a liquid, you take it into your mouth and swallow it. *beber, tomar* ❑ *He drank his cup of tea. Bebió su taza de té.* ❑ *He drank thirstily. Bebió ansiosamente por la sed.* ● **drink|er** N-COUNT (**drinkers**) *bebedor o bebedora* ❑ *...coffee drinkers. ...bebedores de café.* 2 V-I To **drink** means to drink alcohol. *tomar, beber* ❑ *He drank too much. Tomó demasiado.* ● **drink|er** N-COUNT *bebedor empedernido o bebedora empedernida* ❑ *I'm not a heavy drinker. No soy un bebedor empedernido.* ● **drink|ing** N-UNCOUNT *bebida* ❑ *She left him because of his drinking. Lo dejó porque se daba a la bebida.* 3 N-COUNT A **drink** is an amount of a liquid which you drink. *trago, vaso* ❑ *I'll get you a drink of water. Te traeré un vaso de agua.* 4 N-COUNT A **drink** is an alcoholic drink. *trago, copa* ❑ *They only had one drink each. Sólo tomaron un trago/una copa cada uno.*

▸ **drink to** PHR-VERB When people **drink to** someone or something, they wish them success, good luck, or good health before having an alcoholic drink. *brindar* ❑ *We drank to our success. Brindamos por nuestro éxito.*

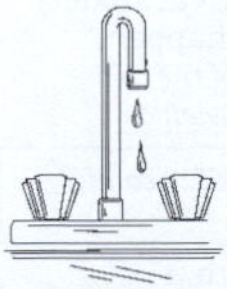
drip

**drip** /drɪp/ (**drips, dripping, dripped**) 1 V-T/V-I When liquid **drips** somewhere, or you **drip** it somewhere, it falls in individual small drops. *gotear* ❑ *The rain dripped down my face. Las gotas de lluvia me escurrían por la cara.* 2 V-I When something **drips,**

drops of liquid fall from it. gotear, chorrear, escurrir ❑ *A faucet in the kitchen was dripping.* Una llave del fregadero estaba goteando. ❑ *Lou was dripping with sweat.* Lou chorreaba de sudor., Lou estaba escurriendo de sudor. **3** N-COUNT A **drip** is a small individual drop of a liquid. gota, lágrima ❑ *...little drips of candle-wax.* ...gotitas de cera de una vela., ...lagrimitas de cera. **4** N-COUNT A **drip** is a piece of medical equipment by which a liquid is slowly passed through a tube into a patient's blood. gotero ❑ *He was put on a drip to treat his dehydration.* Le pusieron suero por goteo para reducir la deshidratación.

**drive** /draɪv/ (**drives, driving, drove, driven**) **1** V-T/V-I When you **drive** somewhere, you operate a car or other vehicle and control its movement and direction. manejar, conducir ❑ *I drove into town.* Fui en coche a la ciudad. ❑ *She never learned to drive.* Nunca aprendió a manejar. ❑ *We drove the car down to Richmond.* Fuimos en el coche a Richmond. ● **driv|ing** N-UNCOUNT manejo, conducción ❑ *...a driving instructor.* ...un profesor de manejo. ● **driv|er** N-COUNT (**drivers**) chofer, conductor o conductora ❑ *The driver got out of his truck.* El chofer se bajó del camión. **2** V-T If you **drive** someone somewhere, you take them there in a car or other vehicle. llevar (en automóvil) ❑ *She drove him to the train station.* Lo llevó en el coche a la estación del tren. **3** V-T If something **drives** a machine, it supplies the power that makes it work. mover, hacer funcionar ❑ *Electric motors drive the wheels.* Unos motores eléctricos mueven las ruedas. **4** V-T If you **drive** something such as a nail **into** something else, you push it in or hammer it in using a lot of effort. clavar, hincar ❑ *Drive the pegs into the ground.* Clave las estacas en el suelo. **5** V-T If you **drive** people or animals somewhere, you make them go to or from that place. arrear (animales), expulsar (gente) ❑ *The war drove thousands of people into Thailand.* La guerra obligó a miles de personas a buscar refugio en Tailandia. **6** V-T The desire or feeling that **drives** a person **to** do something, especially something extreme, is the desire or feeling that causes them to do it. obligar a, llevar a, impulsar a ❑ *His unhappiness drove him to ask for help.* Su infelicidad lo llevó a pedir ayuda. ❑ *Jealousy can drive people to murder.* Los celos pueden llevar a la gente a matar. **7** N-COUNT A **drive** is a trip in a car or other vehicle. paseo ❑ *Let's go for a drive on Sunday.* Vamos a dar un paseo el domingo. **8** N-COUNT A **drive** is a wide piece of hard ground, or sometimes a private road, that leads from the road to a person's house. camino de entrada ❑ *The boys followed Eleanor up the drive to the house.* Los muchachos siguieron a Eleanor por el camino de entrada a la casa. **9** N-COUNT You use **drive** to refer to the mechanical part of a computer which reads the data on disks and tapes, or writes data onto them. unidad de disco ❑ *The firm supplies tape drives and printers.* La empresa surte unidades de cinta e impresoras. **10** → see also **disk drive** **11** N-UNCOUNT **Drive** is energy and determination. empuje ❑ *John has a lot of drive and enthusiasm.* John tiene mucho empuje y entusiasmo. **12** N-SING A **drive** is a special effort made by a group of people for a particular purpose. búsqueda ❑ *...a drive toward personal happiness.* ...la búsqueda de la felicidad personal. **13** → see also **driving**

▸ **drive away** PHR-VERB To **drive** people **away** means to make them want to go away or stay away. alejar, distanciar ❑ *Patrick's rudeness drove Monica's friends away.* La mala educación de Patrick alejó a los amigos de Mónica.

**drive-by** ADJ A **drive-by** shooting or a **drive-by** murder involves shooting someone from a moving car. tiroteo desde un vehículo en movimiento ❑ *He was killed in a drive-by shooting.* Resultó muerto en un tiroteo desde un coche en movimiento.

**driv|er** /draɪvər/ (**drivers**) **1** → see also **drive 1** **2** N-COUNT A **driver** is a computer program that controls a device such as a printer. controlador [COMPUTING] ❑ *...printer driver software.* ...programa controlador de impresoras.

**driv|er's li|cense** (**driver's licenses**) N-COUNT A **driver's license** is a card showing that you are qualified to drive because you have passed a driving test. licencia de manejo, permiso para conducir

**drive-through** also **drive-thru** ADJ A **drive-through** store, bank, or restaurant is one where you can be served without leaving your car. servicio para automovilistas ❑ *...a drive-through restaurant.* ...un restaurante con servicio para automovilistas.

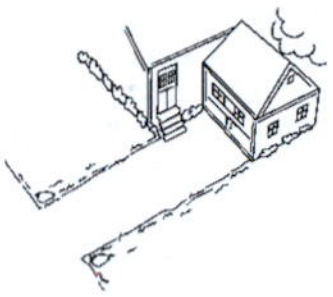
driveway

**drive|way** /draɪvweɪ/ (**driveways**) N-COUNT A **driveway** is a piece of hard ground that leads from the road to the front of a house, garage, or other building. camino de entrada ❑ *I ran down the driveway to the car.* Corrí hasta el coche por el camino de entrada de la casa.

**driv|ing** /draɪvɪŋ/ **1** ADJ The **driving** force or idea behind something that happens or is done is the main thing that has a strong effect on it and makes it happen or be done in a particular way. impulsor ❑ *Increased sales were the driving force behind the economic growth.* El aumento de las ventas fue la fuerza impulsora del crecimiento económico. **2** → see also **drive**
→ see **car**

**driz|zle** /drɪzᵊl/ (**drizzles, drizzling, drizzled**) **1** N-UNCOUNT; N-SING **Drizzle** is light rain falling in fine drops. llovizna ❑ *The drizzle stopped and the sun came out.* Dejó de lloviznar y salió el sol. **2** V-I If it **is drizzling**, it is raining very lightly. lloviznar ❑ *It was starting to drizzle.* Estaba empezando a lloviznar.
→ see **precipitation**

**drop** /drɒp/ (**drops, dropping, dropped**) **1** V-T/V-I If a level or amount **drops** or if someone or something **drops** it, it quickly becomes less. bajar, descender, reducir ❑ *Temperatures can drop to freezing at night.* Las temperaturas pueden descender a cero por la noche. ❑ *His blood pressure had dropped severely.* Su presión sanguínea había bajado marcadamente. ● **Drop** is also a noun. descenso, reducción ❑ *He took a drop in wages.* Tuvo que aceptar una reducción de su salario. **2** V-T/V-I If you **drop** something or it drops, it falls straight down. dejar caer, tirar, caer ❑ *I dropped my glasses and broke them.* Se me cayeron los lentes y se rompieron. ❑ *He felt tears dropping onto his fingers.* Sintió que unas lágrimas le caían en los dedos. **3** V-T/V-I If you **drop** something somewhere or if it **drops** there, you deliberately let it fall there. meter, soltar, caer ❑ *Drop the pasta into*

d

D

the water. *Meta la pasta en el agua.* ❏ *Bombs dropped on the city.* *Cayeron bombas sobre la ciudad.* ● **drop|ping** N-UNCOUNT *lanzamiento* ❏ *...the dropping of the first atomic bomb.* *...el lanzamiento de la primera bomba atómica.* **4** V-T/V-I If a person or a part of their body **drops** to a lower position, or if they **drop** a part of their body to a lower position, they move to that position, often in a tired and lifeless way. *dejar(se) caer, desplomarse* ❏ *Nancy dropped into a chair.* *Nancy se dejó caer en una silla.* ❏ *She let her head drop.* *Bajó la cabeza.* **5** V-T/V-I If your voice **drops** or if you **drop** your voice, you speak more quietly. *bajar* ❏ *Her voice dropped to a whisper.* *Su voz bajó hasta volverse un murmullo.* **6** V-T If you **drop** someone or something somewhere, you take them somewhere and leave them there, usually in a car or other vehicle. *dejar, llevar* ❏ *He dropped me outside the hotel.* *Me dejó fuera del hotel., Me llevó a la entrada del hotel.* ● **Drop off** means the same as **drop.** *llevar* ❏ *Just drop me off at the airport.* *Sólo déjame en el aeropuerto., Sólo llévame al aeropuerto.* **7** V-T If you **drop** an idea, course of action, or habit, you do not continue with it. *abandonar, renunciar a* ❏ *He decided to drop the idea.* *Decidió renunciar a la idea.* **8** N-COUNT A **drop of** a liquid is a very small amount of it shaped like a little ball. *gota* ❏ *...a drop of ink.* *...una gota de tinta.* **9** N-COUNT You use **drop** to talk about vertical distances. *descenso, caída* ❏ *The most impressive of the waterfalls had a drop of 741 feet.* *La más impresionante de las cascadas tenía una caída de 226 metros.*

▸ **drop by** PHR-VERB If you **drop by,** you visit someone informally. *pasar* ❏ *She will drop by later.* *Pasará más tarde.*

▸ **drop in** PHR-VERB If you **drop in on** someone, you visit them informally, usually without having arranged it. *pasar* ❏ *Why not drop in for a chat?* *¿Por qué no pasas para que platiquemos?*

▸ **drop off** **1** → see **drop 6** **2** PHR-VERB If you **drop off** to sleep, you go to sleep. *dormirse, quedarse dormido* [INFORMAL] ❏ *I lay down on the bed and dropped off to sleep.* *Me recosté en la cama y me quedé dormido.*

▸ **drop out** PHR-VERB If someone **drops out of** college or a race, for example, they leave it without finishing what they started. *abandonar, dejar* ❏ *He dropped out of high school at the age of 16.* *Abandonó la secundaria a los 16 años.*

**Word Partnership** Usar *drop* con:

| | |
|---|---|
| N. | drop **in sales** 1 |
| | drop **a ball** 2 |
| | drop **a bomb** 3 |
| | drop **of blood**, **tear** drop, drop **of water** 8 |
| ADJ. | **sudden** drop 1 |
| | **steep** drop 9 |

**drop-down menu** (**drop-down menus**) N-COUNT On a computer screen, a **drop-down menu** is a list of choices that appears when you give the computer a command. *desplegable* ❏ *In the drop-down menu right-click on any item.* *Haga clic con el botón derecho del ratón en cualquier artículo del menú desplegable.*

**drop kick** (**drop kicks**) N-COUNT In sports such as football and rugby, a **drop kick** is a kick in which the ball is dropped to the ground and kicked at the moment that it bounces. *patada a botepronto*

**drop|let** /drɒplɪt/ (**droplets**) N-COUNT A **droplet** is a very small drop of liquid. *gotita* ❏ *...droplets of sweat.* *...gotitas de sudor.*

→ see **precipitation**

**drop-off** (**drop-offs**) N-COUNT A **drop-off in** something such as sales or orders is a decrease in them. *disminución* ❏ *...a sharp drop-off in orders.* *...una marcada disminución de los pedidos.*

**drought** /draʊt/ (**droughts**) N-VAR A **drought** is a long period of time during which no rain falls. *sequía* ❏ *Drought and famines have killed more than two million people.* *Las sequías y las hambrunas han matado a más de dos millones de personas.*

→ see **dam**

**drove** /droʊv/ **Drove** is the past tense of **drive.** *pasado de **drive***

**drown** /draʊn/ (**drowns, drowning, drowned**) **1** V-T/V-I When someone **drowns** or **is drowned,** they die because they have gone under water and cannot breathe. *ahogar(se)* ❏ *A child can drown in only a few inches of water.* *Un niño se puede ahogar en tan sólo unos centímetros de agua.* ❏ *Last night a boy was drowned in the river.* *Un muchacho se ahogó anoche en el río.* **2** V-T If something **drowns** a sound, it is so loud that you cannot hear that sound properly. *ahogar* ❏ *Clapping drowned the speaker's words.* *Los aplausos ahogaron las palabras del orador.* ● **Drown out** means the same as **drown.** *ahogar* ❏ *Their cheers drowned out the protests of demonstrators.* *Sus vivas ahogaron las protestas de los manifestantes.*

**drug** /drʌg/ (**drugs, drugging, drugged**) **1** N-COUNT A **drug** is a chemical which is given to people in order to treat or prevent an illness or disease. *droga, medicamento* ❏ *The drug is useful to hundreds of thousands of people.* *La droga es útil para cientos de miles de personas.* **2** N-COUNT **Drugs** are illegal substances that some people take because they enjoy their effects. *droga, estupefaciente* ❏ *She hoped he wouldn't spend the money on drugs.* *Esperaba que no gastara el dinero en drogas.* ❏ *She was sure Leo was taking drugs.* *Estaba segura de que Leo estaba consumiendo drogas.* **3** V-T If you **drug** a person or animal, you give them a chemical substance in order to make them sleepy or unconscious. *drogar* ❏ *She was drugged and robbed.* *La drogaron para robarla.*

**drug ad|dict** (**drug addicts**) N-COUNT A **drug addict** is someone who is addicted to illegal drugs. *toxicómano o toxicómana, drogadicto o drogadicta*

**drug|store** /drʌgstɔr/ (**drugstores**) N-COUNT A **drugstore** is a store where medicines, cosmetics, and some other goods are sold. *farmacia, botica*

**drum** /drʌm/ (**drums, drumming, drummed**) **1** N-COUNT A **drum** is a musical instrument consisting of a skin stretched tightly over a round frame. *tambor* ● **drum|mer** N-COUNT (**drummers**) *tambor, baterista* ❏ *He was a drummer in a band.* *Era baterista de una banda.* **2** N-COUNT A **drum** is a large cylindrical container which is used to store fuel or other substances. *bidón, barril, tambor* ❏ *...an oil drum.* *...un barril de petróleo.* **3** V-T/V-I If something **drums on** a surface, or if you **drum** something **on** a surface, it hits it regularly, making a continuous beating sound. *tamborilear, golpetear* ❏ *He drummed his fingers on the top of his desk.* *Tamborileó con los*

*dedos sobre su escritorio.*
→ see **percussion**
▸ **drum into** PHR-VERB If you **drum** something **into** someone, you keep saying it to them until they understand it or remember it. *machacar, repetir* ❑ *The information was drummed into students' heads. Les machacaron la información a los estudiantes.*
▸ **drum up** PHR-VERB If you **drum up** support or business, you try to get it. *conseguir, obtener* ❑ *...drumming up new clients. ...consiguiendo nuevos clientes.*

**drum|beat** /drʌmbit/ (**drumbeats**) N-COUNT People sometimes describe a series of warnings or continuous pressure on someone to do something as a **drumbeat.** *machaqueo* [JOURNALISM] ❑ *...a continuous drumbeat of protest. ...un continuo machaqueo de protesta.*

**drum ma|jor** (**drum majors**) N-COUNT A **drum major** is a man who leads a marching band by walking in front of them. *tambor mayor*

**drum ma|jor|ette** (**drum majorettes**) N-COUNT A **drum majorette** is a girl or young woman who leads a marching band by walking in front of them. *bastonera*

**drunk** /drʌŋk/ (**drunks**) **1** ADJ Someone who is **drunk** has drunk so much alcohol that they cannot speak clearly or behave sensibly. *borracho, ebrio* ❑ *He got drunk and was carried home. Se emborrachó y lo llevaron a casa.* **2** N-COUNT A **drunk** is someone who is drunk or frequently gets drunk. *borracho o borracha* ❑ *A drunk lay in the alley. Había un borracho tirado en el callejón.* **3** **Drunk** is the past participle of **drink.** *participio pasado de **drink***

**drunk driv|er** (**drunk drivers**) N-COUNT A **drunk driver** is someone who drives after drinking more than the amount of alcohol that is legally allowed. *conductor ebrio o conductora ebria* ❑ *The car accident was caused by a drunk driver. El accidente de autos fue provocado por un conductor ebrio.* • **drunk driv|ing** N-UNCOUNT *conducir ebrio, conducir bajo la influencia del alcohol* ❑ *He was arrested for drunk driving. Fue arrestado por conducir bajo la influencia del alcohol.*

**dry** /draɪ/ (**drier** or **dryer, driest, dries, drying, dried**) **1** ADJ If something is **dry,** there is no water or moisture on it or in it. *seco* ❑ *Clean the metal with a soft dry cloth. Limpie el metal con un trapo suave seco.* ❑ *Pat it dry with a soft towel. Golpetéelo con una toalla suave hasta que se seque.* • **dry|ness** N-UNCOUNT *sequedad* ❑ *...the dryness of the air. ...la sequedad del aire.* **2** ADJ If your skin or hair is **dry,** it is less oily than, or not as soft as, normal. *seco* ❑ *She had dry, cracked lips. Tenía los labios secos y agrietados.* • **dry|ness** N-UNCOUNT *sequedad, resequedad* ❑ *...dryness of the skin. ...resequedad de la piel.* **3** ADJ If the weather, a place or a period of time is **dry,** there is no rain or there is much less rain than average. *seco, árido* ❑ *Exceptionally dry weather ruined crops. El clima excepcionalmente seco arruinó las cosechas.* ❑ *It was one of the driest places in Africa. Era uno de los lugares más áridos de África.* **4** ADJ **Dry** humor is subtle and clever. *mordaz* ❑ *He kept his dry humor in spite of all the stress. A pesar de tanta tensión, mantuvo su carácter mordaz.* • **dry|ly** ADV *mordazmente* ❑ *"I have been just a little busy," he said dryly. —He estado un poco ocupado—, dijo mordazmente.* **5** ADJ If you describe something such as a book, play, or activity as **dry,** you mean that it is dull and uninteresting. *árido* ❑ *...dry, academic phrases. ...áridas frases académicas.* **6** V-T/V-I When something **dries** or when you **dry** it, it becomes dry. *secar(se)* ❑ *Let your hair dry naturally whenever possible. Deje que su pelo se seque de manera natural siempre que sea posible.* ❑ *Mrs. Madrigal picked up a towel and began drying dishes. La señora Madrigal tomó un trapo de cocina y empezó a secar los trastes.*
→ see **weather**
▸ **dry out** PHR-VERB If something **dries out** or **is dried out,** it loses all the moisture that was in it and becomes hard. *secar(se)* ❑ *If the soil dries out, the tree could die. Si se seca el suelo, el árbol también podría secarse.*
▸ **dry up** **1** PHR-VERB If something **dries up** or if something **dries** it **up,** it loses all its moisture and becomes completely dry and shriveled or hard. *secarse* ❑ *The river dried up. El río se secó.* **2** PHR-VERB If a supply of something **dries up,** it stops. *agotarse* ❑ *With the economic crisis there, work has dried up. Con la crisis económica, el trabajó se agotó.*

**dry-clean** (**dry-cleans, dry-cleaning, dry-cleaned**) V-T When things such as clothes **are dry-cleaned,** they are cleaned with a liquid chemical rather than with water. *lavar en seco, limpiar en seco* ❑ *The suit must be dry-cleaned. El traje se debe lavar en seco.*

**dry|er** /draɪər/ (**dryers**) also **drier** **1** N-COUNT A **dryer** is a machine for drying things, for example, clothes or people's hair. *secadora* ❑ *...the hot air hand dryers in the restroom. ...las secadoras de manos del baño.* **2** → see also **dry**

**dry goods** N-PLURAL **Dry goods** are cloth, thread, flour, tea, and coffee, that contain no liquid. *artículos de confección, comestibles no perecederos*

**dry ice** N-UNCOUNT **Dry ice** is a form of solid carbon dioxide that is used to keep things cold and to create smoke in stage shows. *hielo seco*

**dry run** (**dry runs**) N-COUNT If you have a **dry run,** you practice something to make sure that you are ready to do it properly. *simulacro, ensayo* ❑ *The competition is a dry run for the World Cup finals. La competencia es un ensayo para las finales de la Copa Mundial.*

**DSL** /di es el/ **DSL** is a method of transmitting digital information at high speed over telephone lines. **DSL** is an abbreviation for "digital subscriber line." *DSL* [COMPUTING]

| Word Link | *du* ≈ *two* : ***du**al, **du**plex, **du**plicate* |
|---|---|

**dual** /duəl/ ADJ **Dual** means having two parts, functions, or aspects. *dual, doble* ❑ *...his dual role as head of the party and head of state. ...su doble papel como cabeza del partido y jefe de Estado.*

**dub** /dʌb/ (**dubs, dubbing, dubbed**) **1** V-T If someone or something **is dubbed** a particular thing, they are given that description or name. *apodar, llamar* ❑ *...a man dubbed as the "biggest nuisance in the U.S." ...un hombre llamado "el más pesado de Estados Unidos".* **2** V-T If a movie or soundtrack in a foreign language **is dubbed,** a new soundtrack is added with actors giving a translation. *doblar* ❑ *It was dubbed into Spanish for Mexican audiences. Estaba/Fue doblada al español para el público mexicano.*

d

D

**du|bi|ous** /dubiəs/ **1** ADJ If you describe something as **dubious,** you think it is not completely honest, safe, or reliable. *dudoso* ❑ *This claim seems to be rather dubious. Esta aseveración parece más bien dudosa.* • **du|bi|ous|ly** ADV *sospechosamente* ❑ *The government was dubiously re-elected. El gobierno fue reelecto sospechosamente.* **2** ADJ If you are **dubious about** something, you are not completely sure about it and have not yet made up your mind about it. *tener dudas o reservas* ❑ *Hayes was originally dubious about becoming involved with the project. En un principio, Hayes tenía dudas respecto a su participación en el proyecto.* • **du|bi|ous|ly** ADV *con recelo, con desconfianza* ❑ *He looked at Coyne dubiously. Miró a Coyne con desconfianza.*

**duck** /dʌk/ (**ducks, ducking, ducked**) **1** N-VAR A **duck** is a water bird with short legs, a short neck, and a large flat beak. *pato* ❑ *Chickens and ducks walk around outside. Afuera hay pollos y patos.* • **Duck** is the flesh of this bird when it is eaten as food. *pato* ❑ *...roasted duck. ...pato asado.* **2** V-T/V-I If you **duck,** you move your head or the top half of your body quickly downward to avoid something that might hit you or to avoid being seen. *agacharse, esquivar, eludir* ❑ *There was a loud noise and I ducked. Hubo un ruido fuerte y me agaché.* ❑ *Hans deftly ducked their blows. Hans esquivó hábilmente sus golpes.* **3** V-T If you **duck** your head, you move it quickly downward to hide the expression on your face. *bajar* ❑ *Davy ducked his head to hide his tears. Davy bajó el rostro para ocultar las lágrimas.* **4** V-T You say that someone **ducks** a duty or responsibility when you disapprove of the fact that they avoid it. *sacar la vuelta a* [INFORMAL] ❑ *The defense secretary ducked the question of whether the United States was winning the war. El secretario de defensa le sacó la vuelta a la pregunta sobre si Estados Unidos estaba ganando la guerra.*
▸ **duck out** PHR-VERB If you **duck out of** something that you are supposed to do, you avoid doing it. *escurrirse* [INFORMAL] ❑ *George ducked out of the meeting early. George se escurrió temprano de la reunión.*

**duct** /dʌkt/ (**ducts**) N-COUNT A **duct** is a pipe, tube, or channel which carries a liquid or gas. *conducto* ❑ *...a big air duct in the ceiling. ...un gran conducto de aire en el cielo raso.*

**duc|til|ity** /dʌktɪlɪti/ N-UNCOUNT The **ductility** of a metal is its ability to be stretched without breaking. *ductilidad* [TECHNICAL]

**duct tape** N-UNCOUNT **Duct tape** is a strong, sticky tape that you use to bind things together or to seal cracks in something. *cinta adhesiva* ❑ *...a broken lid held on with duct tape. ...una tapa rota sostenida con cinta adhesiva.*

**dude** /dud/ (**dudes**) N-COUNT A **dude** is a man. In very informal situations, **dude** is sometimes used as a greeting or form of address to a man. *cuate* [INFORMAL] ❑ *He's a real cool dude. Realmente es un buen cuate.*

**due** /du/ **1** PHRASE If an event or situation is **due to** something, it happens or exists as a direct result of that thing. *debido a* ❑ *She couldn't do the job, due to pain in her hands. No podía hacer el trabajo debido a un dolor de manos.* ❑ *Due to the large number of letters he receives, he cannot answer them all. Debido al gran número de cartas que recibe, no puede responderlas todas.* **2** PHRASE If you say that something will happen or take place **in due course,** you mean that you cannot make it happen any quicker and it will happen when the time is right for it. *a su debido tiempo* ❑ *In due course the baby was born. El niño nació a su debido tiempo.* **3** PHRASE You can say "**with due respect**" when you are about to disagree politely with someone. *con todo respeto* ❑ *With all due respect, I think you're asking the wrong question. Con todo respeto, creo que no es la pregunta adecuada.* **4** ADJ If something is **due** at a particular time, it is expected to happen, be done, or arrive at that time. *que debe ocurrir o hacerse en determinado momento* ❑ *The results are due at the end of the month. Los resultados estarán listos al final de mes.* ❑ *Mr. Carter is due in Washington on Monday. El señor Carter debe estar en Washington el lunes.* **5** ADJ **Due** attention or consideration is the proper, reasonable, or deserved amount of it under the circumstances. *debido* ❑ *We'll give due consideration to any serious offer. Le prestaremos la consideración debida a cualquier oferta seria.* **6** ADJ Something that is **due,** or that is **due to** someone, is owed to them, either as a debt or because they have a right to it. *vencido* ❑ *I was told that no more payments were due. Me dijeron que no debía más pagos., Me dijeron que no había más pagos vencidos.* **7** ADJ If someone is **due for** something, that thing is planned to happen or be given to them now, or very soon, often after they have been waiting for it for a long time. *que debe ocurrir o hacerse en determinado momento* ❑ *The prisoner is due for release next year. El preso deberá ser liberado el próximo año.*

**due pro|cess** N-UNCOUNT In law, **due process** refers to the carrying out of the law according to established rules and principles. *procedimiento debido* ❑ *The principles of fairness and due process were not followed. No se cumplió con los principios de imparcialidad y procedimiento debido.*

**dug** /dʌg/ **Dug** is the past tense and past participle of **dig**. *pasado y participio pasado de **dig***
→ see **tunnel**

**DUI** /di yu aɪ/ N-UNCOUNT **DUI** is the offense of driving after drinking more than the amount of alcohol that is legally allowed. **DUI** is an abbreviation for "driving under the influence." *conducir bajo la influencia del alcohol* ❑ *He was arrested for DUI. Lo arrestaron por conducir bajo la influencia del alcohol.* ❑ *...DUI offenders. ...infractores por conducir bajo la influencia del alcohol.*

**dull** /dʌl/ (**duller, dullest, dulls, dulling, dulled**) **1** ADJ If you describe someone or something as **dull,** you mean they are not interesting or exciting. *aburrido, soso* ❑ *I thought he was boring and dull. Yo creía que era aburrido y soso.* • **dull|ness** N-UNCOUNT *monotonía* ❑ *...the dullness of their routine life. ...la monotonía de su vida rutinaria.* **2** ADJ A **dull** color or light is not bright. *opaco, mate, pálido* ❑ *The stamp was a dark, dull blue color. La estampilla era de color azul oscuro mate.* • **dul|ly** ADV *pálidamente, débilmente* ❑ *The street lamps gleamed dully. Las lámparas de la calle brillaban débilmente.* **3** ADJ **Dull** sounds are not very clear or loud. *apagado, sordo* ❑ *The lid closed with a dull thud. La tapa se cerró con un ruido sordo.* • **dul|ly** ADV *débilmente* ❑ *He heard his heart thump dully but more quickly. Oía que su corazón latía débilmente, pero con mayor rapidez.* **4** ADJ **Dull** feelings are weak and not intense.

sordo ❑ *The pain was a dull ache.* *Era un dolor sordo.* ● **dul|ly** ADV sordo ❑ *His arm throbbed dully.* *Sentía un dolor punzante y sordo en el brazo.* **5** V-T/V-I If something **dulls** or if it **is dulled**, it becomes less intense, bright, or lively. opacar ❑ *Her eyes dulled.* *Su mirada se volvió opaca.*

**Thesaurus** *dull* Ver también:
ADJ. dingy, drab, faded, plain **2**

**dumb** /dʌm/ (**dumber, dumbest, dumbs, dumbing, dumbed**) **1** ADJ Someone who is **dumb** is completely unable to speak. mudo ❑ *...a young deaf and dumb man.* *...un hombre joven sordomudo.* **2** ADJ If someone is **dumb** on a particular occasion, they cannot speak because they are angry, shocked, or surprised. mudo [LITERARY] ❑ *The guards were struck dumb, in fear.* *El temor enmudeció a los guardias., Los guardias se quedaron mudos del temor.* **3** ADJ If you call a person **dumb**, you mean that they are stupid or foolish. tonto, bobo [INFORMAL] ❑ *He was a brilliant guy. He made me feel dumb.* *Era un tipo brillante que me hacía sentir como un tonto.* **4** ADJ If you say that something is **dumb**, you think that it is silly and annoying. tonto, bobo [INFORMAL] ❑ *He had this dumb idea.* *Tenía una idea muy tonta.*
→ see **disability**

▶ **dumb down** PHR-VERB If you **dumb down** something, you make it easier for people to understand, especially when this oversimplifies it. simplificar ❑ *The channel has dumbed down its news programs.* *El canal simplificó sus noticieros.* ● **dumb|ing down** N-UNCOUNT reducción del nivel intelectual ❑ *...the dumbing down of modern culture.* *...la reducción del alcance intelectual de la cultura moderna.*

**dump** /dʌmp/ (**dumps, dumping, dumped**) **1** V-T If you **dump** something somewhere, you put it or unload it there quickly and carelessly. tirar, botar [INFORMAL] ❑ *We dumped our bags at the hotel and went to the market.* *Botamos nuestras maletas en el hotel y nos fuimos al mercado.* **2** V-T If something **is dumped** somewhere, it is put or left there because it is no longer wanted or needed. tirar, botar [INFORMAL] ❑ *The getaway car was dumped near the freeway.* *Botaron cerca de la autopista el coche en el que huyeron.* ● **dump|ing** N-UNCOUNT vertido ❑ *German law forbids the dumping of hazardous waste.* *La ley alemana prohíbe el vertido de residuos peligrosos.* **3** N-COUNT A **dump** is a place where garbage and waste material are left. basurero, vertedero ❑ *He took his father's trash to the dump.* *Llevó la basura de su padre al basurero.* **4** N-COUNT If you say that a place is a **dump**, you think it is ugly and unpleasant to live in or visit. basurero, tiradero, muladar [INFORMAL] ❑ *"What a dump!" Christabel said, standing in the doorway of the house.* *—¡Qué muladar!—dijo Christabel, de pie en la entrada de la casa.*
→ see Word Web: **dump**

**dune** /dun/ (**dunes**) N-COUNT A **dune** is a hill of sand near the ocean or in a desert. duna ❑ *Large dunes make access to the beach difficult.* *Unas grandes dunas dificultan el acceso a la playa.*
→ see **beach**

**du|ple me|ter** /dupəl mitər/ (**duple meters**) N-VAR Music that is written in **duple meter** has a beat that is repeated in groups of two. compás binario [TECHNICAL]

**Word Link** *du ≈ two : dual, duplex, duplicate*

**du|plex** /dupleks/ (**duplexes**) N-COUNT A **duplex** is a house which has been divided into two separate units for two different families or groups of people. casa dúplex

**du|pli|cate** (**duplicates, duplicating, duplicated**)

The verb is pronounced /duplɪkeɪt/. The noun and adjective are pronounced /duplɪkɪt/.

**1** V-T If you **duplicate** something that has already been done, you repeat or copy it. duplicar, repetir ❑ *His task will be to duplicate his overseas success here at home.* *Su tarea será repetir en casa su éxito en el extranjero.* ● **Duplicate** is also a noun. duplicado, repetición ❑ *...a duplicate of the elections in Georgia and South Dakota last month.* *...una repetición de las elecciones de Georgia y Dakota del Sur del mes pasado.* ● **du|pli|ca|tion** /duplɪkeɪʃən/ N-UNCOUNT duplicación, repetición ❑ *...unnecessary duplication of resources.* *...una innecesaria duplicación de recursos.* **2** V-T To **duplicate** something which has been written, drawn, or recorded onto tape means to make exact copies of it. copiar, duplicar ❑ *The business duplicates video tapes for movie makers.* *La empresa hace copias de cintas de video para compañías cinematográficas.* ● **Duplicate** is also a noun. duplicado ❑ *I've lost my card. I've got to get a duplicate.* *Perdí mi tarjeta. Tengo que conseguir un duplicado.* **3** ADJ **Duplicate** is used to describe things that have been made as an exact copy of other things, usually in order to serve the same purpose. duplicado ❑ *He unlocked the door with a duplicate key.* *Abrió la puerta con un duplicado de la llave.*

**Word Web** dump

Most communities used to dispose of **solid waste** in **dumps**. However, more **environmentally friendly** methods are common today. There are alternatives to dumping **refuse** in a **landfill**. **Reduction** means creating less waste. For example, using washable napkins instead of paper napkins. **Reuse** involves finding a second use for something without processing it. For instance, giving old clothing to a charity. **Recycling** and **composting** involve finding a new use for something by processing it—using food scraps to fertilize a garden. **Incineration** involves burning solid waste and using the heat for another useful purpose.

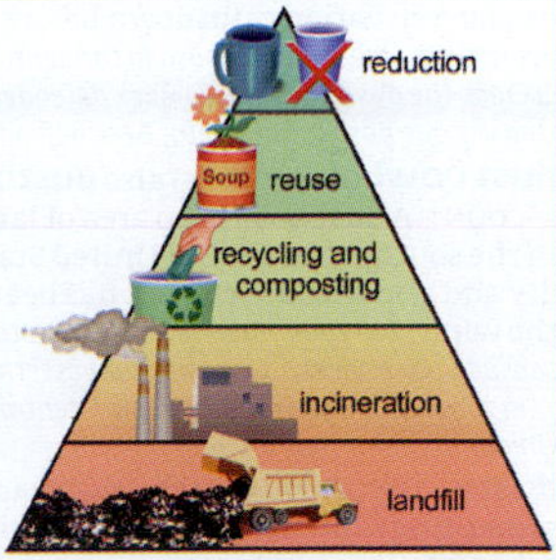


d

D

**du|rable** /dʊərəbᵊl/ ADJ Something that is **durable** is strong and lasts a long time without breaking or becoming weaker. durable ❑ *...a sofa covered with soft, durable leather. ...un sofá tapizado con piel suave y durable.* ● **du|rabil|ity** /dʊərəbɪlɪti/ N-UNCOUNT durabilidad ❑ *Airlines recommend hard-sided cases for durability. Las aerolíneas recomiendan las maletas con lados duros por su durabilidad.*

**du|ra|tion** /dʊəreɪʃᵊn/ N-UNCOUNT The **duration of** an event or state is the time during which it happens or exists. duración ❑ *The hotel was my home for the duration of my stay in New York. El hotel fue mi casa durante mi estancia en Nueva York.*

**dur|ing** /dʊərɪŋ/ **1** PREP If something happens **during** a period of time or an event, it happens continuously, or happens several times between the beginning and end of that period or event. durante ❑ *Storms are common during the winter. Las tormentas son comunes durante el invierno.* **2** PREP An event that happens **during** a period of time happens at some point or moment in that period. durante ❑ *During his visit, the president will visit the new hospital. El presidente visitará el nuevo hospital durante su estancia (en el lugar).*

**Usage** during

*During* and *for* are often confused. *During* answers the question "When?": *Bats hibernate during the winter. For* answers the question "How long?": *Carla talks on the phone to her boyfriend for an hour every night.*

**dusk** /dʌsk/ N-UNCOUNT **Dusk** is the time just before night when the daylight has almost gone but when it is not completely dark. anochecer ❑ *We arrived home at dusk. Llegamos a casa al anochecer.*

**dust** /dʌst/ (**dusts, dusting, dusted**) **1** N-UNCOUNT **Dust** is very small dry particles of earth, sand or dirt. polvo, polvareda ❑ *Tanks raise huge trails of dust when they move. Los tanques levantan grandes polvaredas cuando avanzan.* ❑ *I could see a thick layer of dust on the stairs. Pude ver una gruesa capa de polvo en la escalera.* **2** V-T/V-I When you **dust** something such as furniture, you remove dust from it, usually using a cloth. sacudir el polvo ❑ *I vacuumed and dusted and polished the living room. Pasé la aspiradora, sacudí el polvo y pulí toda la sala.* ❑ *I was dusting in his study. Yo estaba sacudiendo el polvo en su estudio.* **3** PHRASE If you say that something will happen when **the dust settles**, you mean that a situation will be clearer after it has calmed down. If you let **the dust settle** before doing something, you let a situation calm down before you try to do anything else. cuando pasa la tormenta [INFORMAL] ❑ *Once the dust had settled Beck defended his decision. Una vez que pasó la tormenta, Beck defendió su decisión.*

**dust bowl** (**dust bowls**) also **dustbowl** N-COUNT A **dust bowl** is an area of land, especially in the southern or central United States, that is dry and arid because the soil has been eroded by the wind. terreno semidesértico expuesto a la erosión causada por el viento ❑ *...the midwestern dust bowl. ...la zona semidesértica de la región central de Estados Unidos.*

**dusty** /dʌsti/ (**dustier, dustiest**) ADJ If something is **dusty**, it is covered with dust. polvoriento ❑ *...a dusty room. ...un cuarto polvoriento.*

**duty** /duti/ (**duties**) **1** N-VAR **Duty** is work that you have to do for your job. deber, trabajo, obligación ❑ *Staff must report for duty at 8 a.m. El personal debe presentarse a trabajar a las 8 de la mañana.* ❑ *I carried out my duties without complaining. Cumplí con mis obligaciones sin quejarme.* **2** N-SING If you say that something is your **duty**, you believe that you ought to do it because it is your responsibility. deber ❑ *I consider it my duty to write to you and thank you. Considero que es mi deber escribirle y darle las gracias.* **3** N-VAR **Duties** are taxes which you pay to the government on goods that you buy. impuesto, derecho de aduana ❑ *Import duties are around 30%. Los derechos de aduana son de aproximadamente el 30%.* **4** PHRASE If someone such as a police officer or a nurse is **off duty**, they are not working. If someone is **on duty**, they are working. libre de servicio, franco ❑ *I'm off duty. No estoy en servicio.*

**Thesaurus** duty Ver también:

N. assignment, responsibility, task **1** **2** obligation **2**

**Word Partnership** Usar duty con:

N. **guard** duty **1**
ADJ. **civic** duty, **military** duty, **patriotic** duty, **sense of** duty **2**
PREP. **off** duty, **on** duty **4**

**DVD** /di vi di/ (**DVDs**) N-COUNT A **DVD** is a disk on which a movie or music is recorded. DVD disks are similar to compact disks but hold a lot more information. **DVD** is an abbreviation for "digital video disk" or "digital versatile disk." disco de video ❑ *...a DVD player. ...un reproductor de discos de video.* → see **laser**

**DVD burn|er** (**DVD burners**) also **DVD writer** N-COUNT A **DVD burner** is a piece of computer equipment that you use for copying data from a computer onto a DVD. grabadora de discos de video [COMPUTING]

**dwarf** /dwɔrf/ (**dwarves, dwarfs, dwarfing, dwarfed**)

The spellings **dwarves** or **dwarfs** are used for the plural form of the noun.

**1** V-T If one person or thing **is dwarfed** by another, the second is so much bigger than the first that it makes them look very small. eclipsar, empequeñecer ❑ *The money he makes is dwarfed by his wife's salary. El salario de su esposa supera con mucho el dinero que él gana.* **2** N-COUNT In children's stories, a **dwarf** is an imaginary creature that is like a small man. Dwarfs often have magical powers. enano

**dwarf planet** (**dwarf planets**) N-COUNT A **dwarf planet** is a round object that orbits the sun and is larger than an asteroid but smaller than a planet. planeta enano

**dwelt** /dwɛlt/ **Dwelt** is the past tense and past participle of **dwell**. pasado y participio pasado de **dwell**

**DWI** /di dʌbəlyu aɪ/ N-UNCOUNT **DWI** is the offense of driving after drinking more than the amount of alcohol that is legally allowed. **DWI** is an abbreviation for "driving while intoxicated." conducir bajo la influencia del alcohol ❑ *He paid a fine* *for charges of DWI and reckless driving.* Pagó una multa por conducir bajo la influencia del alcohol y por manejo imprudente.

**dye** /daɪ/ (**dyes, dyeing, dyed**) **1** V-T If you **dye** something such as hair or cloth, you change its color by soaking it in a special liquid. teñir ❑ *The women spun and dyed the wool.* Las mujeres hilaron y tiñeron la lana. **2** N-VAR **Dye** is a substance made from plants or chemicals which is mixed into a liquid and used to change the color of something such as cloth or hair. tinte ❑ *...bottles of hair dye.* ...botellas de tinte para el pelo.

**dy|ing** /daɪɪŋ/ **1** **Dying** is the present participle of **die**. agonizante **2** ADJ A **dying** person or animal is very ill and likely to die soon. moribundo, agonizante ❑ *...a dying man.* ...un hombre moribundo. ● **The dying** are people who are dying. los moribundos ❑ *By the time our officers arrived, the dead and the dying were everywhere.* Para cuando nuestros agentes llegaron, había muertos y moribundos por todas partes. **3** ADJ A **dying** tradition or industry is becoming less important and is likely to disappear completely. en extinción ❑ *Shipbuilding is a dying business.* La construcción naval es un negocio en extinción.

**dy|nam|ic** /daɪnæmɪk/ (**dynamics**) **1** ADJ If you describe someone as **dynamic,** you approve of them because they are full of energy or full of new and exciting ideas. dinámico ❑ *He was a dynamic and energetic leader.* Era un dirigente muy activo y dinámico. ● **dy|nami|cal|ly** /daɪnæmɪkli/ ADV con dinamismo, enérgicamente, vívidamente ❑ *He's the most dynamically imaginative jazz musician of our time.* Es el jazzista con la imaginación más vívida de nuestra época. ● **dy|na|mism** /daɪnəmɪzəm/ N-UNCOUNT dinamismo ❑ *The situation needs dynamism and new thinking.* La situación exige dinamismo e ideas nuevas. **2** N-PLURAL The **dynamics** of a situation or group of people are the opposing forces within it that cause it to change. dinámica ❑ *...an understanding of family dynamics.* ...la comprensión de la dinámica familiar. **3** N-PLURAL **Dynamics** are forces which produce power or movement. dinámica [TECHNICAL] **4** N-UNCOUNT **Dynamics** is the scientific study of motion, energy, and forces. dinámica [TECHNICAL] **5** N-PLURAL The **dynamics** of a piece of music are how softly or loudly it is being played. dinámica [TECHNICAL]

**dy|nam|ic mark|ing** (**dynamic markings**) N-COUNT **Dynamic markings** are words and symbols in a musical score which show how softly or loudly the music should be played. marca dinámica [TECHNICAL]

**dyn|as|ty** /daɪnəsti/ (**dynasties**) N-COUNT A **dynasty** is a series of rulers of a country who all belong to the same family. dinastía ❑ *The Seljuk dynasty of Syria was founded in 1094.* La dinastía de los selyúcidas de Siria fue fundada en 1094.

**dys|lexia** /dɪslɛksiə/ N-UNCOUNT If someone has **dyslexia,** they have difficulty with reading because of a slight disorder of their brain. dislexia

# Ee

E

**each** /iːtʃ/ **1** DET If you refer to **each** thing or **each** person in a group, you are referring to every member of the group and considering them as individuals. *cada* ❑ *Each book is beautifully illustrated. Cada libro tiene bellísimas ilustraciones.* ❑ *The library buys $12,000 worth of books each year. La biblioteca compra 12,000 dólares de libros cada año.* ● **Each** is also a pronoun. *cada* ❑ *...two bedrooms, each with three beds. ...dos recámaras, cada una con tres camas.* ❑ *We each have different needs and interests. Cada uno de nosotros tiene diferentes necesidades e intereses.* ● **Each** is also an adverb. *cada* ❑ *Tickets are six dollars each. Cada boleto cuesta seis dólares.* ● **Each** is also a quantifier. *cada* ❑ *He handed each of them a page of photos. Le dio a cada uno una página de fotos.* ❑ *Each of these exercises takes one or two minutes to do. Cada ejercicio se lleva uno o dos minutos.* **2** QUANT If you refer to **each one of** the members of a group, you are emphasizing that something applies to every one of them. *cada uno* ❑ *He bought all her books and read each one of them. Le compró todos sus libros y leyó cada uno de ellos.* **3** PRON You use **each other** when you are saying that each member of a group does something to the others or has a particular connection with the others. *uno a otro, mutuamente* ❑ *We looked at each other in silence. Nos miramos mutuamente en silencio.*

> **Usage** each
>
> Sentences that begin with *each* take a singular verb. *Each of the drivers has a license.*

**eager** /iːgər/ ADJ If you are **eager to** do or have something, you want to do or have it very much. *impaciente, ansioso* ❑ *Robert was eager to talk. Robert estaba ansioso por hablar.* ❑ *I became eager for another baby. Estaba ansiosa por tener otro bebé* ● **eager|ly** ADV *ansiosamente* ❑ *"So what do you think will happen?" he asked eagerly. —Y, ¿qué crees que va a pasar? —preguntó ansiosamente.* ● **eager|ness** N-UNCOUNT *deseo, ansias* ❑ *...an eagerness to learn. ...ansias de aprender*

eagle

**eagle** /iːgᵊl/ (**eagles**) N-COUNT An **eagle** is a large bird that lives by eating small animals. *águila*

**ear** /ɪər/ (**ears**) **1** N-COUNT Your **ears** are the two parts of your body with which you hear sounds. *oreja, oído* ❑ *He whispered something in her ear. Le susurró algo al oído.* **2** N-SING If you have **an ear for** music or language, you are able to hear its sounds accurately and to interpret them or reproduce them well. *oído* ❑ *Moby certainly has a fine ear for a tune. No hay duda de que Moby tiene buen oído para las melodías.* **3** N-COUNT The **ears** of a cereal plant such as corn or barley are the top parts that contain the seeds. *espiga, mazorca* ❑ *...ears of wheat. ...espigas de trigo.*
→ see Word Web: **ear**
→ see **face**

**ear|drum** /ɪərdrʌm/ (**eardrums**) also **ear drum** N-COUNT Your **eardrums** are the thin pieces of tightly stretched skin inside each ear that vibrate when sound waves reach them. *tímpano* ❑ *The blast burst Ollie Williams' eardrum. La explosión le reventó un tímpano a Ollie Williams.*
→ see **ear**

**ear|li|er** /ɜrliər/ **1** **Earlier** is the comparative of **early**. *más temprano, antes* **2** ADV **Earlier** is used to refer to a point or period in time before the present or before the one you are talking about. *más temprano, antes, a principios de* ❑ *They finished*

## Word Web ear

The **ear** collects **sound waves** and sends them to the brain. First the **external ear** picks up sound waves. Then these sound **vibrations** travel along the **ear canal** and strike the **eardrum**. The eardrum pushes against a series of tiny bones. These bones carry the vibrations into the **inner ear**. There they are picked up by the hair cells in the **cochlea**. At that point, the vibrations turn into electronic impulses. The cochlea is connected to the hearing **nerve**. It sends the electronic impulses to the brain.

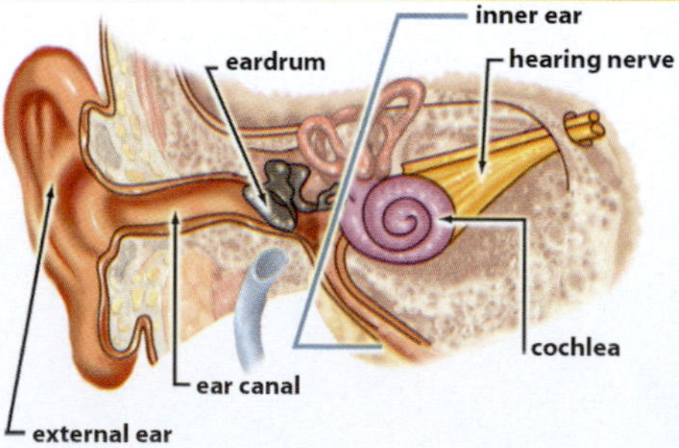

making the movie earlier this year. Terminaron de hacer la película hace algún tiempo este año. • **Earlier** is also an adjective. previo, anterior ❑ *Earlier reports suggested that the fire started accidentally.* En reportes anteriores se sugirió que el fuego se había iniciado accidentalmente.

**ear|li|est** /ɜrliɪst/ **1** **Earliest** is the superlative of **early**. lo más temprano **2** PHRASE **At the earliest** means not before the date or time mentioned. no antes de ❑ *The official results are not expected until Tuesday at the earliest.* No esperamos los resultados oficiales antes del martes.

**ear|lobe** /ɪərloʊb/ (**earlobes**) also **ear lobe** N-COUNT Your **earlobes** are the soft parts at the bottom of your ears. lóbulo de la oreja ❑ *...the holes in her earlobes.* ...las perforaciones del lóbulo de la oreja.
→ see **face**

**ear|ly** /ɜrli/ (**earlier, earliest**) **1** ADV **Early** means before the usual time that something happens or before the time that was arranged or expected. temprano ❑ *I knew I had to get up early.* Sabía que tenía que levantarme temprano. ❑ *She arrived early to get a place at the front.* Llegó temprano para encontrar lugar adelante. • **Early** is also an adjective. temprano ❑ *I want to get an early start in the morning.* Quiero empezar temprano por la mañana. **2** ADJ **Early** means near the beginning of an activity, process, or period of time. primero ❑ *...the early stages of pregnancy.* ...el principio del embarazo. ❑ *...the early 1980s.* ...los primeros años ochenta. ❑ *She was in her early teens.* Estaba empezando su adolescencia. • **Early** is also an adverb. al principio ❑ *We'll see you some time early next week.* Nos vemos al principio de la próxima semana. ❑ *...an accident that happened earlier in the week.* ...un accidente ocurrido al principio de la semana.

| Word Link | *mark ≈ boundary, sign : bookmark, earmark, landmark* |
|---|---|

**ear|mark** /ɪərmɑrk/ (**earmarks, earmarking, earmarked**) V-T If something **is earmarked for** a particular purpose, it is reserved for that purpose. destinar ❑ *Extra money is being earmarked for the new projects.* Dinero extra se está dedicando a los nuevos proyectos. ❑ *China has earmarked more than $20 billion for oil exploration.* China ha dedicado más de 20 mil millones de dólares a la exploración petrolera.

**earn** /ɜrn/ (**earns, earning, earned**) **1** V-T If you **earn** money, you receive money in return for work that you do. ganar, recibir ❑ *She earns $37,000 a year.* Gana 37,000 dólares al año. **2** V-T If something **earns** money, it produces money as profit or interest. producir, devengar ❑ *...a bank account that earns interest.* ...una cuenta bancaria que produce intereses. **3** V-T If you **earn** something such as praise, you get it because you deserve it. ganarse, hacerse de ❑ *Companies must earn a reputation for honesty.* Las empresas deben hacerse de una reputación por honestidad.

| Thesaurus | *earn* | Ver también: |
|---|---|---|
| v. | bring in, make, take in **1** | |

**ear|nest** /ɜrnɪst/ **1** PHRASE If something is done or happens **in earnest,** it happens to a much greater extent and more seriously than before. en serio ❑ *He'll start work in earnest next week.* Empezará a trabajar en serio la próxima semana. **2** ADJ **Earnest** people are very serious and sincere. serio ❑ *Catherine was an earnest woman.* Catherine era una mujer seria. • **ear|nest|ly** ADV con seriedad ❑ *She always listened earnestly.* Siempre escuchaba con seriedad.

**earn|ings** /ɜrnɪŋz/ N-PLURAL Your **earnings** are the sums of money that you earn by working. ingresos ❑ *Average weekly earnings rose by 1.5% in July.* En julio, los ingresos promedio por semana se incrementaron en 1.5%.

**ear|phone** /ɪərfoʊn/ (**earphones**) **1** N-COUNT **Earphones** are a small piece of equipment which you wear over or inside your ears so that you can listen to a radio or mp3 player without anyone else hearing. audífonos **2** N-COUNT An **earphone** is the part of a telephone receiver or other device that you hold up to your ear or put into your ear. audífono

**ear|ring** /ɪərɪŋ/ (**earrings**) N-COUNT **Earrings** are pieces of jewelry that you attach to your ears. arete, pendiente, zarcillo ❑ *...a pair of diamond earrings.* ...un par de aretes de brillantes.
→ see **jewelry**

**earth** /ɜrθ/ **1** N-PROPER **Earth** or **the Earth** is the planet on which we live. la Tierra ❑ *The space shuttle Atlantis returned safely to Earth today.* El transbordador espacial Atlantis volvió hoy a la Tierra sin novedad. **2** N-SING **The earth** is the land surface on which we live and move around. tierra ❑ *The earth shook and the walls fell around them.* La tierra se sacudió y los muros se derrumbaron en torno a ellos. **3** N-UNCOUNT **Earth** is the substance on the land surface of the earth in which plants grow. tierra, suelo ❑ *...a huge pile of earth.* ...un gran montón de tierra. **4** PHRASE **On earth** is used for emphasis in questions that begin with words such as "how," "why," "what," or "where." demonios, diablos ❑ *How on earth did that happen?* ¿Cómo diablos pasó? **5** PHRASE If you come **down to earth** or **back to earth,** you have to face the reality of everyday life after a period of great excitement. bajar de las nubes, poner los pies en la tierra ❑ *When he came down to earth after his win he admitted: "It was an amazing feeling."* Cuando puso los pies en la tierra, después de haber ganado, dijo: Fue una sensación maravillosa.
→ see Word Web: **earth**
→ see **core, eclipse, erosion, solar system**

**earth|quake** /ɜrθkweɪk/ (**earthquakes**) N-COUNT An **earthquake** is a shaking of the ground caused by movement of the Earth's crust. temblor, terremoto ❑ *...the San Francisco earthquake of 1906.* ...el terremoto de San Francisco de 1906.
→ see Word Web: **earthquake**

**earth sci|ence** (**earth sciences**) also **Earth science** N-VAR **Earth sciences** are sciences such as geology and geography that are concerned with the study of the earth. ciencias de la Tierra

**earth|worm** /ɜrθwɜrm/ (**earthworms**) N-COUNT An **earthworm** is a kind of worm that lives in the ground. lombriz (de tierra)

**ease** /iz/ (**eases, easing, eased**) **1** PHRASE If you do something **with ease,** you do it without difficulty or effort. fácilmente, con facilidad, sin problema ❑ *Anne passed her exams with ease.* Anne pasó sus exámenes sin problema. **2** N-UNCOUNT If you talk about the **ease of** a particular activity, you are

## Word Web earth

The **earth** is made of material left over after the **sun** formed. In the beginning, about 4 billion years ago, the earth was made of liquid **rock**. During its first million years, it cooled into solid rock. **Life**, in the form of bacteria, began in the **oceans** about 3.5 billion years ago. During the next billion years, the **continents** formed. At the same time, the level of **oxygen** in the **atmosphere** increased. **Life forms evolved**, and some of them began to use oxygen. **Evolution** allowed **plants** and **animals** to move from the oceans onto the **land**.

E

referring to the way that it has been made easier to do, or to the fact that it is already easy to do. *facilidad, facilitar* ❑ *For ease of reference, use the index to find the page. Para facilitar la consulta, busque la página en el índice.* **3** V-T/V-I If something unpleasant **eases** or if you **ease** it, it is reduced in degree, speed, or intensity. *disminuir, reducirse, aliviar* ❑ *Tensions had eased. Las tensiones se habían reducido.* ❑ *I gave him some aspirin to ease the pain. Le di aspirina para aliviar el dolor.* **4** V-T/V-I If you **ease** your **way** somewhere or **ease** somewhere, you move there slowly, carefully, and gently. If you **ease** something somewhere, you move it there slowly, carefully, and gently. *hacer algo con cuidado* ❑ *I eased my way toward the door. Me dirigí lentamente hacia la puerta.* ❑ *He eased his foot off the gas pedal. Quitó suavemente el pie del acelerador.* **5** PHRASE If you are **at ease,** you are feeling confident and relaxed, and are able to talk to people without feeling nervous or anxious. *cómodo, a gusto* ❑ *It is important that you feel at ease with your doctor. Es importante que te sientas a gusto con tu médico.* **6** PHRASE If you are **ill at ease,** you feel somewhat uncomfortable, anxious, or worried. *incómodo* ❑ *He seemed embarrassed and ill at ease. Parecía confundido e incómodo.*

▸ **ease up** **1** PHR-VERB If something **eases up,** it is reduced in degree, speed, or intensity. *disminuir, aminorar, calmar, calmarse* ❑ *The rain started to ease up. La lluvia empezó a calmarse.* **2** PHR-VERB If you **ease up,** you start to make less effort. *aflojar, bajar el ritmo* ❑ *He told supporters not to ease up even though he's in the lead. Dijo a sus partidarios que no bajaran el ritmo aun cuando él va a la cabeza.*

easel

**easel** /izəl/ (**easels**) N-COUNT An **easel** is a frame that supports a picture which an artist is painting or drawing. *caballete*
→ see **painting**

**easi|ly** /izɪli/ **1** ADV You use **easily** to emphasize that something is very likely to happen, or is very likely to be true. *por lo menos* ❑ *It could easily be another year before things improve. Por lo menos podría pasar otro año antes de que las cosas mejoren.* **2** ADV You use **easily** to say that something happens more quickly or more often than is usual or normal. *fácilmente, con facilidad* ❑ *He has always cried very easily. Siempre ha llorado con mucha facilidad.* **3** → see also **easy**

| **Thesaurus** *easily* | Ver también: |
|---|---|
| ADV. | quickly, readily **2** |

**east** /ist/ also **East** **1** N-UNCOUNT **The east** is the direction where the sun rises. *este, oriente* ❑ *The city lies to the east of the river. La ciudad se encuentra al oriente del río.* **2** N-SING **The east of** a place, country, or region is the part which is in the east. *este, oriente* ❑ *...a village in the east of the country. ...un pueblo al oriente del país.* ● **East** is also an adjective. *este, oriente* ❑ *...a line of hills along the east coast. ...una hilera de colinas a lo largo de la costa este.* **3** ADV **East** means toward the east, or positioned to the east of a place or thing. *al este, al oriente* ❑ *Go east on Route 9. Siga hacia el este por la carretera 9.* ❑ *...just east of the center of town. ...justo*

## Word Web earthquake

**Earthquakes** occur when two tectonic **plates** meet and start to move past each other. This meeting point is called the **focus**. It may be located anywhere from a few hundred meters to a few hundred kilometers below the surface of the earth. The resulting pressure causes a split in the earth's **crust** called a **fault**. Vibrations move out from the focus in all directions. These **seismic waves** cause little damage until they reach the surface. The **epicenter**, directly above the focus, receives the greatest damage. **Seismologists** use **seismographs** to measure the amount of ground movement during an earthquake.

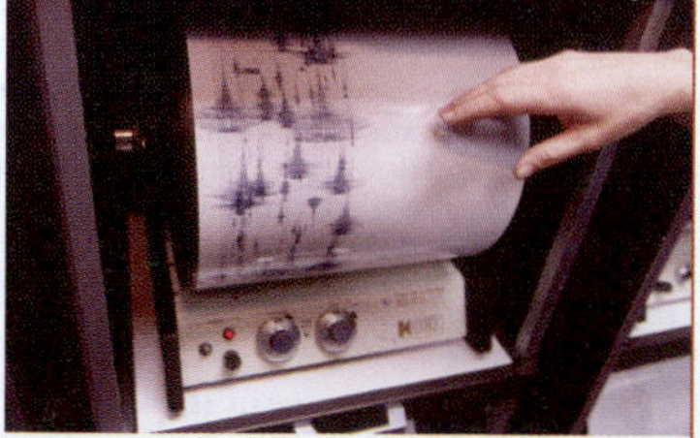

*A seismograph recording a major earthquake.*

al oriente del centro del pueblo. **4** ADJ An **east** wind is a wind that blows from the east. del este ❑ *...a cold east wind.* ...un frío viento del este. **5** N-SING **The East** is used to refer to the southern and eastern part of Asia, including India, China, and Japan. Este, Oriente ❑ *Every so often, a new fashion arrives from the East.* De vez en cuando llega de Oriente una nueva moda. **6** → see also **Middle East, Far East**

**East|er** /istər/ (**Easters**) N-VAR **Easter** is a Christian festival in March or April when Jesus Christ's return to life is celebrated. Pascua

**east|ern** /istərn/ **1** ADJ **Eastern** means in or from the east of a region, state, or country. oriental ❑ *...Eastern Europe.* ...Europa oriental. **2** ADJ **Eastern** means coming from or associated with the people or countries of the East, such as India, China, or Japan. oriental, de oriente ❑ *Exports to Eastern countries have gone down.* Se han reducido las exportaciones a los países de oriente.

**east|ward** /istwərd/

The form **eastwards** is also used.

ADV **Eastward** or **eastwards** means toward the east. en dirección este, hacia el este ❑ *A powerful snow storm is moving eastward.* Una intensa tormenta de nieve se dirige hacia el este. ● **Eastward** is also an adjective. hacia el este ❑ *...the eastward expansion of the city.* ...la expansión de la ciudad hacia el este.

**easy** /izi/ (**easier, easiest**) **1** ADJ If a job or action is **easy,** you can do it without difficulty. fácil ❑ *The shower is easy to install.* La regadera es fácil de instalar. ❑ *This is not an easy task.* No es una tarea fácil. ● **easi|ly** ADV fácilmente ❑ *Dress your baby in clothes you can remove easily.* Ponle a tu bebé ropa que puedas quitarle fácilmente. **2** ADJ If you say that someone has an **easy** life, you mean that they live comfortably without any problems or worries. fácil ❑ *She has not had an easy life.* Su vida no ha sido fácil. **3** PHRASE If someone tells you to **take it easy** or **take things easy,** they mean that you should relax and not do very much at all. tomarlo con calma, tomárselo con calma, tomar las cosas con calma [INFORMAL] ❑ *It is best to take things easy for a week or two.* Es mejor tomarse las cosas con calma durante una semana o dos. **4** → see also **easily**

**Thesaurus** *easy* Ver también:

ADJ. basic, elementary, simple, uncomplicated; (*ant.*) complicated, difficult, hard **1**

**easy|going** /izigoʊɪŋ/ ADJ If you describe someone as **easygoing,** you mean that they are not easily annoyed, worried, or upset, and you think this is a good quality. sin complicaciones ❑ *He was easygoing and good-natured.* No era complicado y tenía buen carácter.

**eat** /it/ (**eats, eating, ate, eaten**) **1** V-T/V-I When you **eat** something, you put it into your mouth, chew it, and swallow it. comer(se) ❑ *She was eating a sandwich.* Se estaba comiendo un sandwich. ❑ *I ate slowly and without speaking.* Comí con calma y sin hablar.
→ see **cooking, food**

▸ **eat away** PHR-VERB If one thing **eats away** another or **eats away at** another, it gradually destroys or uses it up. corroer, roer, desgastar, comerse ❑ *The sea eats away at rocks.* El mar desgasta las rocas.

▸ **eat into** PHR-VERB If something **eats into** your time or your resources, it uses them, when they should be used for other things. comerse, ocupar ❑ *Responsibilities at home and work eat into his time.* Las responsabilidades de la casa y del trabajo ocupan su tiempo.

**Thesaurus** *eat* Ver también:

V. chew, consume, munch, nibble, taste **1**

**Word Partnership** Usar *eat* con:

ADV. eat **alone**, eat **properly**, eat **together**, eat **too much**, eat **well** **1**
V. eat **and drink**, eat **and sleep**, **want** *something* **to** eat **1**

**eat|ing dis|or|der** (**eating disorders**) N-COUNT An **eating disorder** is a medical condition such as bulimia or anorexia in which a person does not eat in a normal or healthy way. trastorno alimenticio, trastorno de la alimentación, desorden alimenticio ❑ *Anyone can develop an eating disorder.* A cualquiera se le puede presentar un trastorno de la alimentación.

**eaves|drop** /ivzdrɒp/ (**eavesdrops, eavesdropping, eavesdropped**) V-I If you **eavesdrop on** someone, you listen secretly to what they are saying. escuchar a escondidas, espiar ❑ *The government illegally eavesdropped on his telephone conversations.* El gobierno escuchó ilegalmente las conversaciones telefónicas.

**ebb** /ɛb/ (**ebbs, ebbing, ebbed**) **1** V-I When the tide or the sea **ebbs,** its level gradually falls. bajar ❑ *When the tide ebbs, you can walk out for a mile.* Cuando la marea baja, se puede caminar un kilómetro y medio mar adentro. **2** N-COUNT **The ebb** or the **ebb** tide is one of the regular periods, usually two per day, when the sea gradually falls to a lower level as the tide moves away from the land. marea baja, reflujo **3** V-I If a feeling or the strength of something **ebbs,** it becomes weaker and gradually disappears. decaer, disminuir [FORMAL] ❑ *Were there times when enthusiasm ebbed?* ¿Hubo momentos en que decayó el entusiasmo? ● **Ebb away** means the same as **ebb.** decaer, disminuir ❑ *The government's popular support is ebbing away.* El apoyo popular al gobierno está disminuyendo. **4** PHRASE If someone or something is **at a low ebb** or **at** their **lowest ebb,** they are not very successful or profitable. de capa caída, decaído ❑ *...a time when everyone is tired and at a low ebb.* ...un momento en que todo el mundo se siente cansado y decaído.
→ see **ocean, tide**

**Ebola** /iboʊlə/ also **Ebola virus** N-UNCOUNT **Ebola** or the **Ebola virus** is a virus that causes a fever and internal bleeding, usually resulting in death. ébola, virus ébola

**Word Link** *ec ≈ away, from, out : eccentric, eclectic, ecstasy*

**ec|cen|tric** /ɪksɛntrɪk/ (**eccentrics**) ADJ If you say that someone is **eccentric,** you mean that they behave in a strange way, and have habits or opinions that are different from

e

## Word Web echo

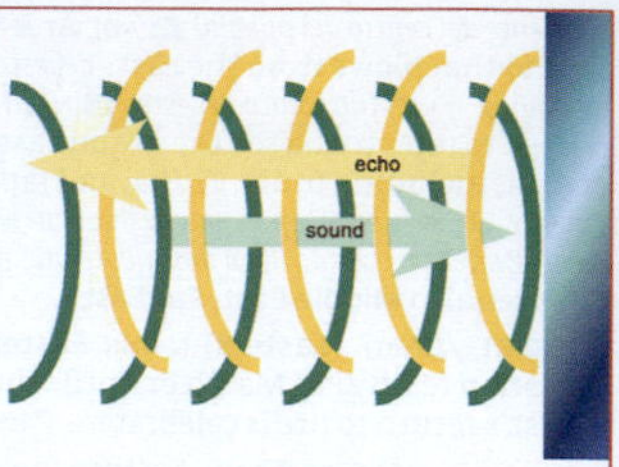


We can learn a lot from studyng **echoes.** Geologists use **sound reflection** to predict how earthquake waves will travel through the earth. They also use echolocation to find underground oil reservoirs. Oceanographers use **sonar** to expolore the ocean. Marine mammals, bats, and humans also use sonar for navigation. Architects study building materials and surfaces to understand how they absorb or **reflect** sound **waves.** They may use hard reflective surfaces to help create a noisy, exciting atmosphere in a restaurant. They may suggest soft drapes and carpeting to create a quiet, calm library.



those of most people. excéntrico, extraño ❑ *He is an eccentric character who likes wearing unusual clothes.* *Es un personaje excéntrico que gusta de vestir prendas extravagantes.* ● An **eccentric** is an eccentric person. excéntrico o excéntrica ❑ *Askew had a reputation as an eccentric.* *Askew tenía fama de excéntrico.* ● **ec|cen|tri|city** /ɛksɛntrɪsɪti/ N-VAR (**eccentricities**) excentricidad, extravagancia, rareza ❑ *She is unusual to the point of eccentricity.* *Es extraña, al punto de la extravagancia.* ❑ *We all have our eccentricities.* *Todos tenemos nuestras rarezas.*

**echo** /ɛkoʊ/ (**echoes, echoing, echoed**) **1** N-COUNT An **echo** is a sound caused by a noise being reflected off a surface such as a wall. eco ❑ *He heard nothing but the echoes of his own voice.* *No oía nada más que el eco de su propia voz.* **2** V-I If a sound **echoes,** or a place **echoes with** sounds, sounds are reflected off a surface there and can be heard again. resonar, retumbar ❑ *His feet echoed on the floor.* *Sus pasos resonaban en el piso.* ❑ *The hall echoed with the barking of a dozen dogs.* *El vestíbulo retumbaba con los ladridos de una docena de perros.* **3** V-T If you **echo** someone's words, you repeat what they have said or express the same opinion. repetir, hacerse eco ❑ *Their views often echo each other.* *Con frecuencia, sus opiniones se hacen eco.* **4** N-COUNT A detail or feature that reminds you of something else can be referred to as an **echo.** eco ❑ *The accident has echoes of past disasters.* *El accidente tiene ecos de pasados desastres.*
→ see Word Web: **echo**
→ see **sound**

**Word Link** *ec ≈ away, from, out : eccentric, eclectic, ecstasy*

**ec|lec|tic** /ɪklɛktɪk/ ADJ An **eclectic** collection of objects, ideas, or beliefs is wide-ranging and comes from many different sources. ecléctico [FORMAL] ❑ *...an eclectic collection of paintings, drawings, and prints.* *...una ecléctica colección de pinturas, dibujos y grabados.*

**eclipse** /ɪklɪps/ (**eclipses, eclipsing, eclipsed**) **1** N-COUNT An **eclipse of** the sun is an occasion when the moon is between the Earth and the sun, so that for a short time you cannot see part or all of the sun. An **eclipse of** the moon is an occasion when the Earth is between the sun and the moon, so that for a short time you cannot see part or all of the moon. eclipse ❑ *...the solar eclipse on May 21.* *...el eclipse de sol del 21 de mayo.* **2** V-T If one thing **is eclipsed by** a second thing that is bigger, newer, or more important than it, the first thing is no longer noticed because the second thing gets all the attention. eclipsar, desmerecer ❑ *The space program has been eclipsed by other needs.* *El programa espacial ha sido eclipsado por otras necesidades.*
→ see Word Web: **eclipse**

**eco-friendly** ADJ **Eco-friendly** products or services are less harmful to the environment than other similar products or services. inocuo para el ambiente, amigable con el ambiente, que no daña el ambiente ❑ *...eco-friendly laundry detergent.* *...detergente de lavandería que no daña el ambiente.*

**eco|logi|cal suc|ces|sion** N-UNCOUNT **Ecological succession** is the process in which one population of plants and animals gradually replaces another population in a particular area as a result of changing environmental conditions. sucesión ecológica [TECHNICAL]

**ecol|ogy** /ɪkɒlədʒi/ (**ecologies**) **1** N-UNCOUNT **Ecology** is the study of the relationships between plants, animals, people, and their environment, and the balances between these relationships.

## Word Web eclipse

There is more than one kind of eclipse. When the **earth** passes between the **sun** and the **moon,** we see a **lunar eclipse.** When the moon passes between the sun and the earth, we see a **solar eclipse.** A total eclipse of the sun happens when the moon covers the sun completely. In the past, people were frightened of eclipses. Some civilizations understood eclipses. Their leaders pretended to control the sun in order to gain the respect of their people. On July 22, 2009, a total eclipse of the sun will be visible in North America.

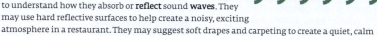

ecología ❑ ...a professor of ecology. ...un maestro de ecología. • **eco|lo|gist** N-COUNT (**ecologists**) ecologista ❑ *Ecologists are concerned that these chemicals might be polluting lakes.* *A los ecologistas les preocupa que estas sustancias químicas puedan contaminar los lagos.* **2** N-VAR When you talk about the **ecology** of a place, you are referring to the pattern and balance of relationships between plants, animals, people, and the environment in that place. *ecología* ❑ *...the ecology of the desert.* *...la ecología del desierto.* • **eco|logi|cal** /ɛkəlɒdʒɪkᵊl, i̱k-/ ADJ *ecológico* ❑ *...Siberia's delicate ecological balance.* *...el delicado equilibrio ecológico de Siberia.* • **eco|logi|cal|ly** /ɛkəlɒdʒɪkli, i̱k-/ ADV *ecológicamente, de manera ecológica* ❑ *This product can be recycled and is ecologically harmless.* *Este producto es reciblable y ecológicamente inocuo.*

→ see **amphibian**

**eco|nom|ic** /ɛkənɒmɪk, i̱k-/ **1** ADJ **Economic** means concerned with the organization of the money, industry, and trade of a country, region, or society. *económico* ❑ *...economic reforms.* *...reformas económicas.* ❑ *...economic growth.* *...crecimiento económico.* • **eco|nomi|cal|ly** /ɛkənɒmɪkli, i̱k-/ ADV *económicamente* ❑ *...an economically depressed area.* *un área deprimida económicamente.* **2** ADJ If something is **economic,** it produces a profit. *rentable* ❑ *The main purpose of most companies is economic and not charitable.* *El objetivo principal de la mayoría de las empresas es ser rentables, no de beneficencia.*

→ see **disaster**

**eco|nomi|cal** /ɛkənɒmɪkᵊl, i̱k-/ **1** ADJ Something that is **economical** does not require a lot of money to operate. *económico* ❑ *...smaller and more economical cars.* *...autos más pequeños y más económicos.* • **eco|nomi|cal|ly** ADV *económicamente, de manera económica* ❑ *Services could be operated more efficiently and economically.* *Los servicios podrían funcionar de manera más eficiente y económica.* **2** ADJ Someone who is **economical** spends money sensibly and does not want to waste it on things that are unnecessary. A way of life that is **economical** does not require a lot of money. *ahorrativo* ❑ *...ideas for economical housekeeping.* *...ideas para ser ahorrativo en la administración del gasto doméstico.*

| **Thesaurus** | *economical* | Ver también: |
|---|---|---|
| ADJ. | cost-effective, inexpensive **1** careful, frugal, practical, thrifty **2** | |

| **Word Link** | ***ics ≈ system, knowledge : economics, electronics, ethics*** |
|---|---|

**eco|nom|ics** /ɛkənɒmɪks, i̱k-/ N-UNCOUNT **Economics** is the study of the way in which money, industry, and commerce are organized in a society. *economía* ❑ *His sister is studying economics.* *Su hermana estudia economía.*

**econo|mist** /ɪkɒnəmɪst/ (**economists**) N-COUNT An **economist** is a person who studies, teaches, or writes about economics. *economista*

**econo|my** /ɪkɒnəmi/ (**economies**) **1** N-COUNT An **economy** is the system according to which the money, industry, and commerce of a country or region are organized. *economía* ❑ *The Indian economy is changing fast.* *La economía de la India está cambiando rápidamente.* **2** N-UNCOUNT **Economy** is the use of the minimum amount of money, time, or other resources needed to achieve something, so that nothing is wasted. *economía* ❑ *The biggest single step we can take to stop global warming is to raise the fuel economy of our vehicles.* *La medida más importante para detener el calentamiento global es hacer economías en el consumo de combustible de nuestros vehículos.*

**eco|sys|tem** /ɛkoʊsɪstəm, i̱k-/ (**ecosystems**) N-COUNT An **ecosystem** is all the plants and animals that live in a particular area together with the complex relationship that exists between them and their environment. *ecosistema* [TECHNICAL] ❑ *...the forest ecosystem.* *...el ecosistema de la selva.*

→ see **biosphere**

| **Word Link** | ***ec ≈ away, from, out : eccentric, eclectic, ecstasy*** |
|---|---|

**ec|sta|sy** /ɛkstəsi/ (**ecstasies**) N-VAR **Ecstasy** is a feeling of very great happiness. *éxtasis* ❑ *...a state of religious ecstasy.* *...un estado de éxtasis religioso.*

**ec|to|therm** /ɛktəθɜrm/ (**ectotherms**) N-COUNT An **ectotherm** is a cold-blooded animal, such as a reptile, whose body temperature depends on the temperature of the environment around it. Compare **endotherm.** *ectotérmico* [TECHNICAL]

**edge** /ɛdʒ/ (**edges, edging, edged**) **1** N-COUNT The **edge** of something is the place or line where it stops, or the part of it that is farthest from the middle. *orilla, borde, extremo* ❑ *We were on a hill, right on the edge of town.* *Estábamos en una colina, justo a las orillas del pueblo.* ❑ *She was standing at the water's edge.* *Estaba parada a la orilla del agua.* **2** N-COUNT The **edge** of something sharp such as a knife or an ax is its sharp or narrow side. *filo* ❑ *...the sharp edge of the sword.* *...el filo de la espada.* **3** V-I If someone or something **edges** somewhere, they move very slowly in that direction. *acercarse* ❑ *He edged closer to the telephone.* *Se acercó más al teléfono.* **4** N-SING If someone or something has an **edge,** they have an advantage. *ventaja* ❑ *Mature students have skills and experience that can give them the edge over younger graduates.* *Los estudiantes maduros tienen habilidades y experiencia que los ponen en ventaja respecto de los más jóvenes.* **5** → see also **cutting edge** **6** PHRASE If you or your nerves are **on edge,** you are tense, nervous, and unable to relax. *estar los nervios de punta, tener los nervios de punta* ❑ *My nerves were constantly on edge.* *Constantemente tenía los nervios de punta.*

edge

▸ **edge out** PHR-VERB If someone **edges out** someone else, they just manage to beat them or get in front of them in a game, race, or contest. *sacar ventaja* ❑ *France edged out the American team by less than a second.* *Francia le sacó menos de un segundo de ventaja al equipo estadounidense.*

| **Thesaurus** | *edge* | Ver también: |
|---|---|---|
| N. | border, boundary, rim; (*ant.*) center, middle **1** advantage **4** | |

e

E

**edge|wise** /ɛdʒwaɪz/ PHRASE If you say that you **cannot get a word in edgewise,** you are complaining that you do not have the opportunity to speak because someone else is talking so much. lograr decir una palabra [INFORMAL]

**ed|ible** /ɛdɪbᵊl/ ADJ If something is **edible,** it is safe to eat and not poisonous. comestible ❑ *...edible mushrooms. ...hongos comestibles.*

**edit** /ɛdɪt/ (**edits, editing, edited**) **1** V-T If you **edit** a text such as an article or a book, you correct and adapt it so that it is suitable for publishing. revisar, corregir ❑ *She helped him edit his book. Le ayudó a corregir su libro.* **2** V-T If you **edit** a book, you collect several pieces of writing by different authors and prepare them for publishing. editar ❑ *This collection of essays is edited by Ellen Knight. Ellen Knight editó esta recopilación de ensayos.* **3** V-T If you **edit** a movie or a television or radio program, you choose some of what has been filmed or recorded and arrange it in a particular order. editar ❑ *He taught me to edit film. Me enseñó a editar una película.* **4** V-T Someone who **edits** a newspaper, magazine, or journal is in charge of it. editar ❑ *I used to edit the college paper. Yo solía editar el periódico de la universidad.*

**edi|tion** /ɪdɪʃᵊn/ (**editions**) **1** N-COUNT An **edition** is a particular version of a book, magazine, or newspaper that is printed at one time. edición ❑ *The second edition was published only in Canada. La segunda edición sólo se publicó en Canadá.* ❑ *...a paperback edition. ...una edición en rústica.* **2** N-COUNT An **edition** is a single television or radio program that is one of a series about a particular subject. edición ❑ *...last week's edition of "60 Minutes." ...la edición de "60 minutos" de la semana pasada.*

**Word Partnership** Usar *edition* con:

| | |
|---|---|
| N. | **collector's** edition, **paperback** edition **1** |
| ADJ. | **limited** edition, **revised** edition **1** |
| | **new** edition, **special** edition **1** **2** |

**edi|tor** /ɛdɪtər/ (**editors**) **1** N-COUNT An **editor** is the person who is in charge of a newspaper or magazine, or a section of a newspaper or magazine, and who decides what will be published in each edition of it. editor o editora ❑ *Her father was the editor of the Saturday Review. Su padre era el editor del Saturday Review.* **2** N-COUNT An **editor** is a person who checks and corrects texts before they are published. corrector o correctora, revisor o revisora ❑ *He works as an editor of children's books. Es corrector de libros para niños.* **3** N-COUNT An **editor** is a person who prepares a movie, or a radio or television program, by selecting some of what has been filmed or recorded and putting it in a particular order. editor o editora ❑ *She worked at 20th Century Fox as a film editor. Trabajaba como editora de películas en 20th Century Fox.* **4** N-COUNT An **editor** is a person who collects pieces of writing by different authors and prepares them for publication in a book or a series of books. editor o editora ❑ *Michael Rosen is the editor of the book. El editor del libro es Michael Rosen.* **5** N-COUNT An **editor** is a computer program that enables you to change and correct stored data. editor [COMPUTING]

**edi|to|rial** /ɛdɪtɔriᵊl/ (**editorials**) **1** ADJ **Editorial** means involved in preparing a newspaper, magazine, or book for publication. editorial ❑ *I went to the editorial meetings when I had time. Iba a las reuniones editoriales cuando tenía tiempo.* **2** ADJ **Editorial** means involving the attitudes, opinions, and contents of something such as a newspaper, magazine, or television program. editorial ❑ *The editorial standpoint of the magazine is right-wing. El punto de vista editorial de la revista es de derecha.* **3** N-COUNT An **editorial** is an article in a newspaper, or an item on television or radio, that gives the opinion of the newspaper, network, or radio station. editorial ❑ *...an editorial in The New York Times. ...un editorial de The New York Times.*

**edu|cate** /ɛdʒʊkeɪt/ (**educates, educating, educated**) **1** V-T When someone **is educated,** he or she is taught at a school or college. educar(se) ❑ *He was educated at Yale and Stanford. Se educó en Yale y Stanford.* **2** V-T To **educate** people means to teach them better ways of doing something or a better way of living. concientizar, informar ❑ *...a program to help educate people about disabilities. ...un programa que ayuda a concientizar al público sobre las discapacidades.*

**Thesaurus** *educate* Ver también:

| | |
|---|---|
| V. | coach, instruct, teach, train **2** |

**edu|cat|ed** /ɛdʒʊkeɪtɪd/ ADJ Someone who is **educated** has a high standard of learning. culto, educado ❑ *...an educated and decent man. ...un hombre culto y respetable.*

**edu|ca|tion** /ɛdʒʊkeɪʃᵊn/ (**educations**) **1** N-VAR **Education** involves teaching and learning. educación ❑ *They're cutting funds for education. Están recortando los fondos para educación.* ❑ *...better health education. ...mejor educación para la salud.*
• **edu|ca|tion|al** /ɛdʒʊkeɪʃənᵊl/ ADJ educativo ❑ *...the Japanese educational system. ...el sistema educativo japonés.* **2** → see also **further education, higher education**

**Word Link** *ator ≈ one who does : educator, investigator, spectator*

**edu|ca|tor** /ɛdʒʊkeɪtər/ (**educators**) N-COUNT An **educator** is someone who is specialized in the theories and methods of education. educador o educadora, pedagogo o pedagoga

**eel** /il/ (**eels**) N-VAR An **eel** is a long, thin fish that looks like a snake. anguila • **Eel** is the flesh of this fish eaten as food. anguila ❑ *...smoked eel. ...anguila ahumada.*

**ef|fect** /ɪfɛkt/ (**effects, effecting, effected**) **1** N-VAR An **effect** is a change, reaction, or impression that is caused by something or is the result of something. efecto ❑ *Parents worry about the effect of junk food on their child's behavior. Los padres se preocupan por el efecto de la comida chatarra en el comportamiento de sus hijos.* ❑ *The overall effect is cool, light, and airy. El efecto es de tranquilidad, luz y espacio.* **2** V-T If you **effect** something that you are trying to achieve, you succeed in causing it to happen. llevar a cabo, efectuar, lograr [FORMAL] ❑ *Effecting real change does not come quickly. Lograr un verdadero cambio toma tiempo.* **3** → see also **greenhouse**

**effect, side effect, special effect** 4 PHRASE You add **in effect** to a statement or opinion that you feel is a reasonable description or summary of a particular situation. *de hecho* ❑ *The deal would create, in effect, the world's biggest airline. De hecho, con el trato se creará la línea aérea más grande del mundo.* 5 PHRASE When something **takes effect, comes into effect,** or is **put into effect,** it begins to apply or starts to have results. *entrar en vigor, hacer efecto* ❑ *The second injection should be given once the first drug takes effect. La segunda inyección debe ponerse una vez que el primer medicamento haga efecto.* ❑ *These measures were put into effect in 2005. Estas medidas entraron en vigor en 2005.* 6 PHRASE You use **effect** in expressions such as **to good effect** and **to no effect** in order to indicate how successful or impressive an action is. *resultado* ❑ *The museum is using advertising to good effect. El museo está utilizando la publicidad con buenos resultados.* 7 PHRASE You use **to this effect, to that effect,** or **to the effect that** to indicate that you have given or are giving a summary of something that was said or written, and not the actual words used. *en el sentido de* ❑ *A public warning was issued to this effect. Se hizo pública una advertencia en ese sentido.*

**Usage** **effect** and **affect**

*Effect* and *affect* are often confused. *Effect* means "to bring about": *Voters hope the election will effect change. Affect* means "to change": *The cloudy weather affected his mood.*

**Word Partnership** Usar *effect* con:

| | |
|---|---|
| ADJ. | **adverse** effect, **desired** effect, **immediate** effect, **lasting** effect, **negative/positive** effect 1 |
| V. | **have an** effect 1<br>**produce an** effect, **take** effect 5 |
| N. | effect **a change** 2 |

**ef|fec|tive** /ɪfɛktɪv/ 1 ADJ Something that is **effective** works well and produces the results that were intended. *efectivo* ❑ *We could be more effective in encouraging students to enter teacher training. Podríamos ser más efectivos entusiasmando a los estudiantes para que se formen como maestros.* ❑ *No drugs are effective against this disease. No hay medicamentos efectivos contra esta enfermedad.* ● **ef|fec|tive|ly** ADV *de manera efectiva* ❑ *Services need to be organized more effectively. Los servicios tienen que organizarse de manera más efectiva* ● **ef|fec|tive|ness** N-UNCOUNT *efectividad* ❑ *...the effectiveness of computers as an educational tool. ...la efectividad de las computadoras como herramienta de educación.* 2 ADJ **Effective** means having a particular role or result in practice, though not officially or in theory. *efectivo* ❑ *...an agreement giving Rubin effective control of the company. ...un convenio que concede a Rubin el control efectivo de la empresa.* 3 ADJ When something such as a law or an agreement becomes **effective,** it begins officially to apply or be valid. *en vigor* ❑ *The new rules will become effective in the next few days. Las nuevas reglas entrarán en vigor en unos días.*

**Usage** **effective** and **efficient**

*Effective* and *efficient* are often confused. If you are *effective*, you get the job done properly; if you are *efficient*, you get the job done quickly and easily: *Doing research at the library can be effective, but using the Internet is often more efficient.*

**Word Partnership** Usar *effective* con:

| | |
|---|---|
| N. | effective **means**, effective **method**, effective **treatment**, effective **use** 1 |
| ADV. | **highly** effective 1<br>effective **immediately** 3 |

**ef|fec|tive|ly** /ɪfɛktɪvli/ ADV You use **effectively** with a statement to show that it is not accurate in every detail, but that you feel it is a reasonable description of a particular situation. *en efecto* ❑ *The region was effectively independent. La región era en efecto independiente.*

**ef|fi|cient** /ɪfɪʃᵊnt/ ADJ If something or someone is **efficient,** they are able to do tasks successfully, without wasting time or energy. *eficiente* ❑ *Cycling is the most efficient form of transport. La bicicleta es la forma de transporte más eficiente.* ● **ef|fi|cien|cy** /ɪfɪʃᵊnsi/ N-UNCOUNT *eficiencia* ❑ *...ways to increase efficiency. ...formas de incrementar la eficiencia.* ● **ef|fi|cient|ly** ADV *de manera eficiente, eficientemente* ❑ *...a campaign to encourage people to use energy more efficiently. ...una campaña para impulsar a la gente a usar la energía de manera más eficiente.*
→ see also **effective**

**Word Partnership** Usar *efficient* con:

| | |
|---|---|
| N. | **energy** efficient, **fuel** efficient, efficient **method**, efficient **system**, efficient **use of** *something* |
| ADV. | **highly** efficient |

**ef|fort** /ɛfərt/ (**efforts**) 1 N-VAR If you make an **effort to** do something, you try very hard to do it. *esfuerzo* ❑ *He made no effort to hide his disappointment. No hizo ningún esfuerzo por ocultar su desilusión.* ❑ *Finding a cure takes a lot of time and effort. Se necesita mucho tiempo y esfuerzo para encontrar una cura.* 2 N-UNCOUNT; N-SING If you do something **with effort,** or if it is **an effort,** you mean it is difficult to do. *con esfuerzo, con trabajos* [WRITTEN] ❑ *She sat up slowly and with great effort. Se sentó lentamente y con gran esfuerzo.* ❑ *Carrying the equipment while hiking in the forest was an effort. Costaba trabajo llevar el equipo y caminar por la selva.*

**Thesaurus** *effort* Ver también:

| | |
|---|---|
| N. | attempt 1<br>exertion, labor, work 2 |

**ef|fort force** N-UNCOUNT In physics, **effort force** is force that is used to move an object. *fuerza de esfuerzo* [TECHNICAL]

**EFL** /i ɛf ɛl/ N-UNCOUNT **EFL** is the teaching of English to people whose first language is not English. **EFL** is an abbreviation for "English as a Foreign Language." *EFL, inglés como lengua extranjera* ❑ *...an EFL teacher. ...un maestro de inglés como lengua extranjera.*

**Picture Dictionary** **egg**

E

**e.g.** /i dʒi/ **e.g.** is an abbreviation that means "for example." It is used before a noun, or to introduce another sentence. por ejemplo ❑ *We need professionals of all types, e.g., teachers.* *Necesitamos profesionales de todo tipo, por ejemplo, maestros.*

**egg** /ɛg/ (**eggs, egging, egged**) **1** N-COUNT An **egg** is an oval object that is produced by a female bird and contains a baby bird. Other animals such as reptiles and fish also lay eggs. *huevo* ❑ *...a baby bird hatching from its egg.* *...un polluelo saliendo del cascarón.* **2** N-VAR In many countries, an **egg** means a hen's egg, eaten as food. *huevo* ❑ *Break the eggs into a shallow bowl.* *Rompe los huevos en un tazón poco profundo.* **3** N-COUNT An **egg** is a cell that is produced in the bodies of female animals and humans. If it is fertilized by a sperm, a baby develops from it. *óvulo* ❑ *It only takes one sperm to fertilize an egg.* *Basta con un espermatozoide para fertilizar un óvulo.*
→ see Picture Dictionary: **egg**
→ see **bird, reproduction**
▸**egg on** PHR-VERB If you **egg** a person **on,** you encourage them to do something, especially something dangerous or foolish. *incitar, azuzar* ❑ *She was laughing and egging him on.* *Se reía de él y lo azuzaba.*

**egg|plant** /ɛgplænt/ (**eggplants**) N-VAR An **eggplant** is a vegetable with a smooth, dark purple skin. *berenjena*
→ see **vegetable**

**ego** /igoʊ, ɛgoʊ/ (**egos**) N-VAR Someone's **ego** is their sense of their own worth. *ego, yo* ❑ *He had a big ego and never admitted that he was wrong.* *Tenía un ego enorme y nunca aceptaba que estaba equivocado.*

**eight** /eɪt/ (**eights**) NUM **Eight** is the number 8. *ocho* ❑ *The McEwans have eight children.* *Los McEwan tienen ocho hijos.*

| **Word Link** | ***teen** ≈ plus ten, from 13-19 : eighteen, seventeen, teenager* |
|---|---|

**eight|een** /eɪtin/ NUM **Eighteen** is the number 18. *dieciocho* ❑ *He worked for them for eighteen years.* *Trbajó para ellos durante dieciocho años.*

**eight|eenth** /eɪtinθ/ ORD The **eighteenth** item in a series is the one that you count as number eighteen. *decimoctavo, dieciochoavo* ❑ *The talks are now in their eighteenth day.* *Hoy es el decimoctavo día de pláticas.*

**eighth** /eɪtθ/ (**eighths**) **1** ORD The **eighth** item in a series is the one that you count as number eight. *octavo* ❑ *...the eighth prime minister of India.* *...el octavo primer ministro de la India.* **2** ORD An **eighth** is one of eight equal parts of something. *octavo, octava parte* ❑ *The area produces an eighth of Russia's grain, meat, and milk.* *En el área se produce la octava parte de los granos, la carne y la leche de Rusia.*

**eighth note** (**eighth notes**) N-COUNT An **eighth note** is a musical note that has a time value equal to half a quarter note. *octava*

**eighti|eth** /eɪtiəθ/ ORD The **eightieth** item in a series is the one that you count as number eighty. *octagésimo, ochentavo* ❑ *Mr. Stevens recently celebrated his eightieth birthday.* *El Sr. Stevens celebró recientemente su octagésimo aniversario.*

**eighty** /eɪti/ (**eighties**) **1** NUM **Eighty** is the number 80. *ochenta* ❑ *Eighty horses trotted up.* *Ochenta caballos iban al trote.* **2** N-PLURAL When you talk about the **eighties,** you are referring to numbers between 80 and 89. For example, if you are **in** your **eighties,** you are aged between 80 and 89. If the temperature is **in the eighties,** the temperature is between 80 and 89 degrees. *arriba de ochenta* ❑ *He was in his late eighties.* *Ya tenía más de ochenta, casi noventa años.* **3** N-PLURAL **The eighties** is the decade between 1980 and 1989. *los ochenta, los años ochenta* ❑ *He ran his own business in the eighties.* *En los años ochenta dirigía su propio negocio.*

**either** /iðər, aɪðər/ **1** CONJ You use **either** in front of the first of two or more alternatives, when you are stating the only possibilities or choices that there are. The other alternatives are introduced by "or." *o...o* ❑ *Either she goes or I go.* *O va ella, o voy yo.* ❑ *He should be either put on trial or set free.* *O lo juzgan, o lo dejan libre.* **2** CONJ You use **either** in a negative statement in front of the first of two alternatives to indicate that the negative statement refers to both the alternatives. *ni... ni* ❑ *There is no sign of either brain damage or memory loss.* *No hay signos ni de daño cerebral ni de pérdida de memoria.* ● **Either** is also a pronoun. *ni* ❑ *She said I'd never marry or have children. I don't want either.* *Dijo que nunca me casaría ni tendría hijos, yo ni quiero.* ● **Either** is also a quantifier. *ninguno* ❑ *There are no simple answers to either of those questions.* *No es fácil responder a ninguna de esas preguntas.* ● **Either** is also a determiner. *ninguno* ❑ *He couldn't remember either man's name.* *No pudo recordar el nombre de ninguno de los hombres.* **3** PRON You can use **either** to refer to one of two things, people, or situations, when you want to say that they are both possible and it does not matter which one is chosen or considered. *o* ❑ *You can contact him either by phone or by email.* *Te puedes poner en contacto con él por teléfono o por correo electrónico.* ● **Either** is also a quantifier. *alguno* ❑ *It's quick and convenient and requires little effort from either of you.* *Es rápido y cómodo, y requiere poco esfuerzo de alguno de los dos.* ● **Either** is also a determiner. *cualquier, cualquiera* ❑ *You can choose either date to send in your completed application form.* *Puedes escoger cualquiera de las dos fechas para llenar la solicitud y mandarla.* **4** ADV You use **either** by itself in negative statements to indicate that there is a similarity or connection with a person or thing that you have just mentioned. *tampoco* ❑ *He did not* say anything to her, and she did not speak to him either. *Él no le dijo nada, y ella tampoco le habló.* **5** DET You can use **either** to introduce a noun that refers to each of two things when you are talking about both of them. *cada, uno y otro* ❑ *The basketball nets hung down from the ceiling at either end of the gym. Las redes de básquetbol colgaban del techo en cada extremo del gimnasio.*

| Word Link | e ≈ away, out : eject, emigrate, emit |
|---|---|

**eject** /ɪdʒɛkt/ (**ejects, ejecting, ejected**) **1** V-T If you **eject** someone **from** a place, you force them to leave. *expulsar, echar* ❑ *Officials used guard dogs to eject the protesters. Los policías utilizaron perros guardianes para expulsar a los manifestantes.* ● **ejec|tion** /ɪdʒɛkʃᵊn/ N-VAR (**ejections**) *expulsión* ❑ *...the ejection of the New York Mets' manager from Saturday night's game. ...la expulsión del manager de los Mets de Nueva York del juego del sábado en la noche.* **2** V-T To **eject** something means to remove it or push it out forcefully. *expulsar, sacar* ❑ *Sometimes the disc can't be ejected from the computer. A veces no se puede expulsar el disco de la computadora.*

| Word Link | labor ≈ working : collaborate, elaborate, laboratory |
|---|---|

**elabo|rate** (**elaborates, elaborating, elaborated**)

> The adjective is pronounced /ɪlæbərɪt/. The verb is pronounced /ɪlæbəreɪt/.

**1** ADJ You use **elaborate** to describe something that is very complex because it has a lot of different parts. *complicado, complejo, elaborado* ❑ *...an elaborate research project. ...un complicado proyecto de investigación.* ● **elabo|rate|ly** ADV *minuciosamente, de manera minuciosa* ❑ *It was an elaborately planned operation. Fue una operación planeada minuciosamente.* **2** V-I If you **elaborate on** something that has been said, you say more about it, or give more details. *ampliar, entrar en detalles, explicar* ❑ *A spokesman declined to elaborate on yesterday's statement. Un vocero se negó a entrar en detalles sobre la declaración de ayer.*

**elapse** /ɪlæps/ (**elapses, elapsing, elapsed**) V-I When time **elapses,** it passes. *transcurrir, pasar* [FORMAL] ❑ *Forty-eight hours have elapsed since his arrest. Han pasado cuarenta y ocho horas desde que lo arrestaron.*

**elas|tic** /ɪlæstɪk/ **1** N-UNCOUNT **Elastic** is a rubber material that stretches when you pull it and returns to its original size and shape when you let it go. *liga, elástico* ❑ *It has a piece of elastic that goes around the back of the head. Lleva un elástico que se pasa por detrás de la cabeza.* **2** ADJ Something that is **elastic** is able to stretch easily. *elástico* ❑ *Beat the dough until it is slightly elastic. Bate la masa hasta que quede ligeramente elástica.*

**elas|tic re|bound** (**elastic rebounds**) N-VAR **Elastic rebound** is a geological process associated with earthquakes, in which rock is stretched and then contracts as a result of energy stored within it. *recuperación de la deformación elástica* [TECHNICAL]

**elat|ed** /ɪleɪtɪd/ ADJ If you are **elated,** you are extremely happy and excited because of something that has happened. *eufórico* ❑ *I was elated by the news. Las noticias me pusieron eufórico.* ● **ela|tion** /ɪleɪʃᵊn/ N-UNCOUNT *euforia, júbilo* ❑ *His supporters reacted to the news with elation. Las noticias causaron júbilo entre sus partidarios.*

**el|bow** /ɛlboʊ/ (**elbows, elbowing, elbowed**) **1** N-COUNT Your **elbow** is the joint where your arm bends in the middle. *codo* ❑ *He slipped and fell, badly bruising an elbow. Se lastimó mucho el codo por un resbalón que acabó en caída.* **2** V-T If you **elbow** people **aside** or **elbow** your **way** somewhere, you push people with your elbows in order to move somewhere. *dar codazos, empujar con los codos* ❑ *Jake came up to her, elbowing Susan aside. Jake se acercó a ella empujando a Susan con los codos.* **3** to **rub elbows with** → see **rub**
→ see **body**

**el|der** /ɛldər/ (**elders**) **1** ADJ **The elder of** two people is the one who was born first. *mayor* ❑ *...his elder brother. ...su hermano mayor.* **2** N-COUNT A person's **elder** is someone who is older than them, especially someone quite a lot older. *mayor* [FORMAL] ❑ *They have no respect for their elders. No muestran respeto por sus mayores.* **3** N-COUNT In some societies, an **elder** is one of the respected older people who have influence and authority. *anciano* ❑ *...a meeting of tribal elders. ...una reunión de los ancianos de la tribu.*

**el|der|ly** /ɛldərli/ ADJ You use **elderly** as a polite way of saying that someone is old. *anciano, de la tercera edad* ❑ *There was an elderly couple on the porch. Había una pareja de ancianos en el porche.* ● **The elderly** are people who are old. *personas de la tercera edad.* ❑ *...health care for the elderly. ...servicios de salud para los ancianos.*
→ see **age**

**eld|est** /ɛldɪst/ ADJ The **eldest** person in a group is the one who was born before all the others. *mayor* ❑ *The eldest child was a daughter. Su hijo mayor fue niña.* ❑ *David was the eldest of three boys. David fue el mayor de tres niños.*

**elect** /ɪlɛkt/ (**elects, electing, elected**) **1** V-T When people **elect** someone, they choose that person to represent them, by voting for them. *elegir, nombrar* ❑ *The people have voted to elect a new president. El pueblo ha votado para elegir al nuevo presidente.* ❑ *The University of Washington elected him dean in 1976. La Universidad de Washington lo nombró decano en 1976.* **2** V-T If you **elect to** do something, you choose to do it. *decidir* [FORMAL] ❑ *He elected to stay in India. Decidió quedarse en la India.*
→ see **election**

**elec|tion** /ɪlɛkʃᵊn/ (**elections**) **1** N-VAR An **election** is a process in which people vote to choose a person or group of people to hold an official position. *elección* ❑ *...the country's first free elections for more than fifty years. ...las primeras elecciones libres del país en más de cincuenta años.* ❑ *...his election campaign. ...su campaña para las elecciones.* **2** N-UNCOUNT The **election** of a particular person or group of people is their success in winning an election. *elección* ❑ *...the election of the Democrat candidate last year. ...la elección del candidato Demócrata el año pasado.* ❑ *...his election as president. ...su elección como presidente.*
→ see Word Web: **election**

e

E

## Word Web election

**Presidential candidates** spend millions of dollars on their **campaigns**. They give **speeches**. **They** appear on TV and **debate**. On election day, **voters cast** their **votes** at local **polling places**. **Citizens** living outside of the US mail in **absentee ballots**. But voters don't **elect** the **president** directly. States send representatives to the **electoral college**. There, representatives from all but two states must cast all their votes for one candidate—even if 49% of the people wanted the other candidate. Four times a candidate has **won** the popular vote and lost the election. This happened when George W. Bush won in 2000.

## Word Partnership Usar *election* con:

N. election **campaign**, election **day**, election **official**, election **results** 1

V. **hold an** election, **lose an** election, **vote in an** election, **win an** election 1

**elec|tive** /ɪlɛktɪv/ (**electives**) N-COUNT An **elective** is a subject which a student can choose to study as part of his or her course. *optativo* ❑ *I took most of my electives in English. Tomé casi todas mis optativas en inglés.*

**elector** /ɪlɛktə/ (**electors**) N-COUNT An **elector** is a person who has the right to vote in an election. *elector o electora*

**elec|tor|al** /ɪlɛktərəl/ ADJ **Electoral** is used to describe things that are connected with elections. *electoral* ❑ *...electoral reform. ...reforma electoral* ● **elec|tor|al|ly** ADV *en términos electorales, desde la perspectiva electoral* ❑ *The government's tax increases were electorally unpopular. En términos electorales, el alza de los impuestos no fue del gusto popular.*

**elec|tor|al col|lege** N-SING **The electoral college** is the system that is used in the United States in presidential elections. The electors in the electoral college act as representatives for each state, and they elect the president and vice president. *colegio electoral*

**elec|tor|ate** /ɪlɛktərɪt/ (**electorates**) N-COUNT The **electorate** of a country or area is all the people in it who have the right to vote in an election. *electorado* ❑ *He has the support of almost a quarter of the electorate. Cuenta con el apoyo de casi la cuarta parte del electorado.*

**elec|tric** /ɪlɛktrɪk/ 1 ADJ An **electric** device or machine works by means of electricity, rather than using some other source of power. *eléctrico* ❑ *...her electric guitar. ...su guitarra eléctrica.* 2 ADJ An **electric** current, voltage, or charge is one that is produced by electricity. *eléctrico* 3 ADJ **Electric** plugs, sockets, or power lines are designed to carry electricity. *eléctrico* 4 ADJ If you describe the atmosphere of a place or event as **electric**, you mean that people are in a state of great excitement. *electrizante, cargado de electricidad* ❑ *The mood in the hall was electric. El ambiente del salón estaba cargado de electricidad.*
→ see **keyboard, string**

**elec|tri|cal** /ɪlɛktrɪkᵊl/ 1 ADJ **Electrical** goods, equipment, or appliances work by means of electricity. *eléctrico* ❑ *...electrical equipment. ...equipo eléctrico* ● **elec|tri|cal|ly** /ɪlɛktrɪkli/ ADV *eléctricamente, con energía eléctrica* ❑ *...electrically powered vehicles. ...vehículos impulsados con energía eléctrica.* 2 ADJ **Electrical** industries, engineers, or workers are involved in the production and supply of electricity or electrical products. *eléctrico* ❑ *...company representatives from the electrical industry. ...representantes de empresas del sector eléctrico.*
→ see **electricity, energy**

**elec|tri|cal charge** N-SING The **law of electrical charges** is a principle in physics which states that two electrical charges will attract one another if they are opposite and repel one another if they are the same. *carga eléctrica* [TECHNICAL]

**elec|tri|cal en|er|gy** N-UNCOUNT **Electrical energy** is the form of energy that is produced by electricity. *energía eléctrica*

**elec|tric force** (**electric forces**) N-VAR An **electric force** is the force that exists between two objects with an electric charge. *fuerza eléctrica*

**elec|tric gen|era|tor** (**electric generators**) N-COUNT An **electric generator** is a machine which produces electricity. *generador de energía eléctrica, generador de electricidad*

**Word Link** *electr ≈ electric : electrician, electricity, electron*

**Word Link** *ician ≈ person who works at : electrician, musician, physician*

**elec|tri|cian** /ɪlɛktrɪʃᵊn, ilɛk-/ (**electricians**) N-COUNT An **electrician** is a person whose job is to install and repair electrical equipment. *electricista*

**elec|tric|ity** /ɪlɛktrɪsɪti, ilɛk-/ N-UNCOUNT **Electricity** is a form of energy that can be carried by wires and is used for heating and lighting, and to provide power for machines. *electricidad, energía eléctrica* ❑ *We moved into a house with electricity but no running water. Nos mudamos a una casa que tenía electricidad, pero no agua corriente.*
→ see Word Web: **electricity**
→ see **energy, light**

**elec|tric pow|er** N-UNCOUNT **Electric power** is the same as **electricity**. *energía eléctrica*

**elec|tric shock** (**electric shocks**) N-COUNT If you get an **electric shock**, you get a sudden painful feeling when you touch something connected to a supply of electricity. *descarga eléctrica, toque*

**Word Web** electricity

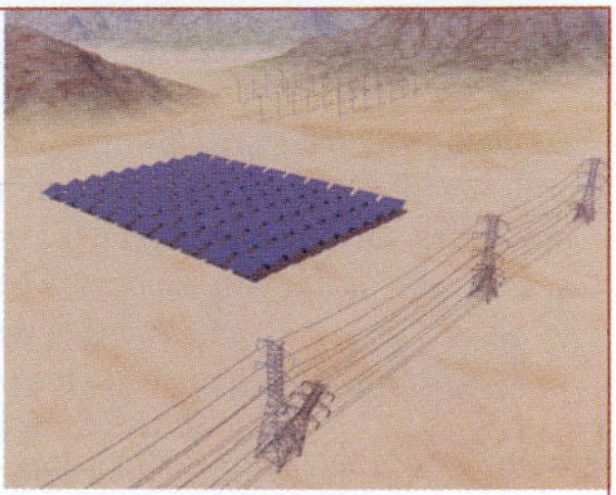

The need for **electrical** power in the U.S. may rise by 35 percent over the next 20 years. **Power companies** are working hard to meet this need. At the center of every **power station** are electrical **generators**. Traditionally, they ran on **hydroelectric** power or **fossil fuel**. However, today new sources of **energy** are available. On **wind farms**, wind **turbines** use the power of moving air to run generators. Seaside tidal power stations make use of the forces of rising and falling tides to turn turbines. And in sunny climates, **photovoltaic cells** produce electrical power from the sun's rays.

e

**elec|tro|cute** /ɪlɛktrəkyut/ (**electrocutes, electrocuting, electrocuted**) V-T If someone **is electrocuted,** they are killed or badly injured when they touch something connected to a source of electricity. *electrocutar(se)* ❑ *Three people were electrocuted by falling power lines. Tres personas se electrocutaron con unos cables de energía eléctrica que se cayeron.* • **elec|tro|cu|tion** /ɪlɛktrəkyuʃᵊn/ N-VAR (**electrocutions**) *electrocución* ❑ *The court sentenced him to death by electrocution. El tribunal lo condenó a morir en la silla eléctrica.*

**elec|tro|mag|net** /ɪlɛktroʊmægnɪt/ (**electromagnets**) N-COUNT An **electromagnet** is a magnet that consists of a piece of iron or steel surrounded by a coil. The metal becomes magnetic when an electric current is passed through the coil. *electroimán*

**elec|tro|mag|net|ic spec|trum** N-SING *The* **electromagnetic spectrum** is the complete range of electromagnetic radiation, from the longest radio waves to the shortest gamma rays. *espectro electromagnético*

**elec|tro|mag|net|ic wave** (**electromagnetic waves**) N-COUNT **Electromagnetic** waves are waves of energy inside an electromagnetic field. *onda electromagnética*

**Word Link** *electr ≈ electric : electrician, electricity, electron*

**elec|tron** /ɪlɛktrɒn/ (**electrons**) N-COUNT An **electron** is a tiny particle of matter that is smaller than an atom and has a negative electrical charge. *electrón* [TECHNICAL]

→ see **television**

**elec|tron cloud** (**electron clouds**) N-COUNT An **electron cloud** is an area inside an atom where electrons are likely to exist. *nube de electrones* [TECHNICAL]

**elec|tron|ic** /ɪlɛktrɒnɪk, i-/ **1** ADJ An **electronic** device has transistors or silicon chips that control and change the electric current passing through the device. *electrónico* ❑ *...expensive electronic equipment. ...equipo electrónico costoso.* **2** ADJ An **electronic** process or activity involves the use of electronic devices. *electrónico* ❑ *...electronic music. ...música electrónica* • **elec|troni|cal|ly** ADV *electrónicamente* ❑ *The gates are operated electronically. Las rejas funcionan electrónicamente.*

**elec|tron|ic me|dia** N-PLURAL **Electronic media** are means of communication such as radio, television, and the Internet, which use technology to produce information. Compare **print media.** *medios electrónicos*

**Word Link** *ics ≈ system, knowledge : economics, electronics, ethics*

**elec|tron|ics** /ɪlɛktrɒnɪks, i-/ N-UNCOUNT **Electronics** is the technology of using transistors and silicon chips, especially in devices such as radios, televisions, and computers. *electrónica* ❑ *...Ohio's three main electronics companies. ...las tres principales empresas de electrónica de Ohio.*

**elec|tron mi|cro|scope** (**electron microscopes**) N-COUNT An **electron microscope** is a type of very powerful microscope that uses electrons instead of light to produce a magnified image of something. *microscopio electrónico, microscopio de electrones*

**elec|tro|stat|ic dis|charge** /ɪlɛktrəstætɪk dɪstʃɑrdʒ/ (**electrocstatic discharges**) N-VAR An **electrostatic discharge** is the sudden release of static electricity that can occur when two objects with different electrical charges are brought close together. *descarga electrostática*

**el|egant** /ɛlɪgənt/ **1** ADJ If you describe a person or thing as **elegant,** you mean that they are pleasing and graceful in appearance or style. *elegante* ❑ *Patricia looked beautiful and elegant as always. Como siempre, Patricia lucía hermosa y elegante.* • **el|egance** N-UNCOUNT *elegancia* ❑ *...the elegance of the hotel. ...la elegancia del hotel.* • **el|egant|ly** ADV *elegantemente, con elegancia* ❑ *...a tall, elegantly dressed man. ...un hombre alto, elegantemente vestido.* **2** ADJ If you describe a piece of writing, an idea, or a plan as **elegant,** you mean that it is simple, clear, and clever. *elegante* ❑ *The document impressed me with its elegant simplicity. El documento me impresionó por su elegante sencillez.* • **el|egant|ly** ADV *elegantemente* ❑ *...an elegantly simple idea. ...una idea elegantemente sencilla.*

**Thesaurus** *elegant* Ver también:

ADJ. chic, exquisite, luxurious, stylish **1**

**el|ement** /ɛlɪmənt/ (**elements**) **1** N-COUNT The different **elements** of something are the different parts it contains. *elemento, parte* ❑ *The exchange of prisoners was a key element of the UN's peace plan. El intercambio de prisioneros fue un elemento clave del plan de paz de la ONU.* ❑ *Physical fitness has now become an important element in our lives. El acondicionamiento físico ya es parte importante de*

E

## Word Web element

**Elements**—like copper, sodium, and oxygen—are made from only one type of **atom**. Each element has its own unique **properties**. For example, oxygen is a gas at room temperature

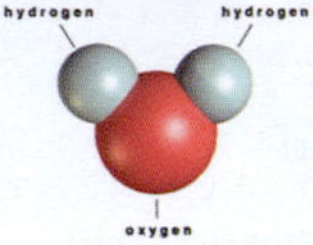


and copper is a solid. Often elements come together with other types of elements to make **compounds**. When the atoms in a compound bind together, they form a **molecule**. One of the best known molecules is $H_2O$. It is made up of two hydrogen atoms and one oxygen atom. This molecule is also known as water. The **periodic table** is a complete listing of all the elements.

**The Periodic Table of Elements**

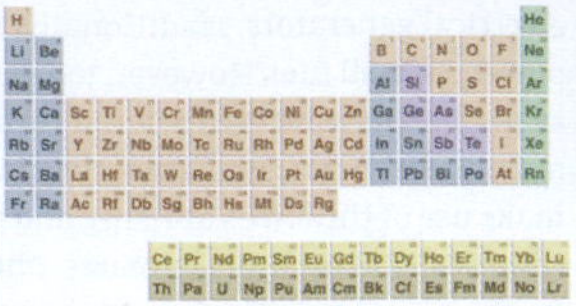


*nuestras vidas.* **2** N-COUNT When you talk about **elements** within a society or organization, you are referring to groups of people who have similar aims, beliefs, or habits. *elemento* ❑ *...criminal elements, such as thieves, murderers and hooligans. ...elementos delictivos, como ladrones, asesinos y vándalos.* **3** N-COUNT If something has an **element of** a particular quality or emotion, it has a certain amount of this quality or emotion. *parte, algo* ❑ *Many of the complaints contain an element of truth. Muchas de las quejas tienen algo de verdad.* **4** N-COUNT An **element** is a substance such as gold, oxygen, or carbon that consists of only one type of atom. *elemento* **5** N-COUNT The **element** in an electric or water heater is the metal part that changes the electric current into heat. *resistencia* **6** N-PLURAL You can refer to the weather, especially wind and rain, as **the elements.** *elementos* ❑ *Their open boat was exposed to the elements. Su embarcación abierta estuvo expuesta a los elementos.* **7** PHRASE If you say that someone is **in** their **element,** you mean that they are in a situation they enjoy. *en su elemento, como pez en el agua* ❑ *My mother was in her element, organizing everything. Mi madre estaba en su elemento, organizando todo.*
→ see Word Web: **element**
→ see **periodic table, rock**

**el|emen|ta|ry** /ɛlɪmɛntəri, -tri/ ADJ Something that is **elementary** is very simple and basic. *básico, elemental* ❑ *...elementary computer skills. ...conocimientos básicos de computación.*

**el|emen|ta|ry school** (**elementary schools**) N-VAR An **elementary school** is a school where children are taught for the first six or sometimes eight years of their education. *escuela primaria, escuela elemental*

**el|ements of art** N-PLURAL The **elements of art** are the basic components of a painting or drawing, such as line, color, and shape. *elementos artísticos* [TECHNICAL]

**el|ements of mu|sic** N-PLURAL The **elements of music** are the basic components of a piece of music, such as melody, harmony, and rhythm. *elementos musicales* [TECHNICAL]

**el|ephant** /ɛlɪfənt/ (**elephants**) N-COUNT An **elephant** is a very large animal with a long, flexible nose called a trunk. *elefante*
→ see **herbivore**

elephant

**el|evate** /ɛlɪveɪt/ (**elevates, elevating, elevated**) **1** V-T When someone or something **is elevated to** a more important rank or status, they achieve it. *elevar* [FORMAL] ❑ *He was elevated to the post of president. Lo elevaron al cargo de presidente.* • **el|eva|tion** /ɛlɪveɪʃən/ N-UNCOUNT *ascenso* ❑ *...the elevation of the assistant coach to the head coaching position. ...el ascenso del asistente del entrenador a entrenador principal.* **2** V-T To **elevate** something means to increase it in amount or intensity. *elevar, incrementar* [FORMAL] ❑ *Emotional stress can elevate blood pressure. La tensión emocional puede incrementar la presión sanguínea.* **3** V-T If you **elevate** something, you raise it higher. *elevar, subir, levantar* ❑ *I built a platform to elevate the bed. Construí una plataforma para subir la cama.*

**Word Link** *ation ≈ state of : elevation, humiliation, observation*

**el|eva|tion** /ɛlɪveɪʃən/ (**elevations**) N-COUNT The **elevation** of a place is its height above sea level. *altitud* ❑ *We're at an elevation of 13,000 feet above sea level. Estamos a una altitud de 13,000 pies sobre el nivel del mar.*

**el|eva|tor** /ɛlɪveɪtər/ (**elevators**) N-COUNT An **elevator** is a device that carries people or goods up and down inside tall buildings. *elevador, ascensor* ❑ *We took the elevator to the fourteenth floor. Tomamos el elevador al piso catorce.*

**elev|en** /ɪlɛvən/ (**elevens**) NUM **Eleven** is the number 11. *once* ❑ *Josh invited eleven friends to his party. Josh invitó a once amigos a la fiesta.*

**elev|enth** /ɪlɛvənθ/ ORD The **eleventh** item in a series is the one that you count as number eleven. *undécimo, onceavo* ❑ *We were working on the eleventh floor. Estamos trabajando en el onceavo piso.*

**elic|it** /ɪlɪsɪt/ (**elicits, eliciting, elicited**) **1** V-T If you **elicit** a response or a reaction, you do or say something that makes other people respond or react. *provocar, suscitar* ❑ *He was hopeful that his request would elicit a positive response. Tenía la* *esperanza de que su solicitud provocara una respuesta positiva.* **2** V-T If you **elicit** a piece of information, you get it by asking the right questions. *obtener* [FORMAL] ❑ *Several phone calls elicited no further information. Ni con varias llamadas telefónicas obtuve más información.*

**eli|gible** /ɛlɪdʒɪbᵊl/ ADJ Someone who is **eligible to** do something is qualified or able to do it, for example, because they are old enough. *elegible* ❑ *Almost half the population are eligible to vote. Casi la mitad de la población cumple con los requisitos para votar.* • **eli|gibil|ity** /ɛlɪdʒɪbɪlɪti/ N-UNCOUNT *elegibilidad* ❑ *...the rules covering eligibility for benefits. ...las reglas para tener derecho a recibir las prestaciones.*

**elimi|nate** /ɪlɪmɪneɪt/ (**eliminates, eliminating, eliminated**) **1** V-T To **eliminate** something means to remove it completely. *eliminar, acabar con* [FORMAL] ❑ *Recent measures have not eliminated discrimination in employment. Las recientes medidas no han acabado con la discriminación laboral.* • **elimi|na|tion** N-UNCOUNT *eliminación* ❑ *...the elimination of chemical weapons. ...la eliminación de las armas químicas.* **2** V-T PASSIVE When a person or team **is eliminated from** a competition, they are defeated and so stop participating in the competition. *eliminar* ❑ *I was eliminated from the 400 meters in the semi-finals. Me eliminaron de los 400 metros en las semifinales.*

**elite** /ɪlit, eɪ-/ (**elites**) N-COUNT You can refer to the most powerful, rich, or talented people within a particular group, place, or society as the **elite**. *élite* ❑ *...the political elite. ...la élite política* • **Elite** is also an adjective. *selecto, de élite* ❑ *...the elite troops of the president's bodyguard. ...el escuadrón de élite de la guardia presidencial.*

**Eliza|bethan thea|ter** /ɪlɪzəbiθᵊn θiətər/ N-UNCOUNT **Elizabethan theater** is the plays that were written or performed in England during the reign of Queen Elizabeth I. *teatro isabelino*

**el|lipse** /ɪlɪps/ (**ellipses**) N-COUNT An **ellipse** is an oval shape similar to a circle but longer and flatter. *elipse*
→ see **shape**

**el|lip|ti|cal gal|axy** (**elliptical galaxies**) N-COUNT An **elliptical galaxy** is a galaxy containing mainly older stars, which are distributed in an elliptical pattern. *galaxia elíptica* [TECHNICAL]

**El Niño** /ɛl ninyoʊ/ N-PROPER **El Niño** is a current of warm water that occurs every few years in the Pacific Ocean and can affect the weather throughout the world. *El niño*

**elo|quent** /ɛləkwənt/ ADJ A person who is **eloquent** is good at speaking and able to persuade people. *elocuente* ❑ *He was eloquent about his love of books. Fue elocuente sobre su amor por los libros.* ❑ *I heard him make a very eloquent speech. Le oí un discurso muy elocuente.* • **elo|quence** N-UNCOUNT *elocuencia* ❑ *...the eloquence of his writing. ...la elocuencia de sus escritos.* • **elo|quent|ly** ADV *elocuentemente, con elocuencia* ❑ *Juanita speaks eloquently about her art. Juanita habla con elocuencia de su arte.*

**else** /ɛls/ **1** ADJ You use **else** after words such as "anywhere," "someone," "what," "everyone," and "everything" to refer in a vague way to another person, place, or thing, or to all other people, places, or things. *más, los demás, otra cosa* ❑ *If I can't do it myself I'll ask someone else. Si no puedo hacerlo yo, le pediré a alguien más.* ❑ *She is much taller than everyone else. Es mucho más alta que todos los demás.* ❑ *I try to be truthful, and I expect everyone else to be truthful. Yo trato de ser sincero, y espero que todos los demás lo sean.* • **Else** is also an adverb. *otro lugar, otra parte* ❑ *I never wanted to live anywhere else. Nunca quise vivir en otra parte.* **2** PHRASE You use **or else** after stating a logical conclusion, to indicate that what you are about to say is evidence for that conclusion. *si no, de lo contrario, o* ❑ *No lessons were learned or else they would not have handled the problem so badly. No aprendieron la lección, de lo contrario no hubieran manejado tan mal el problema.* **3** PHRASE You use **or else** to introduce a possibility or alternative. *o...o, si no* ❑ *Hold on tight or else you will fall out. Agárrate fuerte, si no, te vas a caer.* ❑ *He is either a total genius or else totally crazy. O es todo un genio, o está totalmente loco.* **4** PHRASE You can say "**if nothing else**" to indicate that what you are mentioning is, in your opinion, the only good thing in a particular situation. *aparte de, además de, más que* ❑ *If nothing else, you'll really enjoy meeting them. Aparte de eso, realmente vas a disfrutar conocerlos.*

**else|where** /ɛlswɛər/ ADV **Elsewhere** means in other places or to another place. *en otro lugar, en otra parte, de otra parte* ❑ *Almost 80 percent of the state's residents were born elsewhere. Casi el 80 por ciento de los residentes del estado nacieron en otra parte.* ❑ *They were living well, in comparison with people elsewhere in the world. Vivían bien, a comparación de la gente de otras partes del mundo.*

**e-mail** (**e-mails, e-mailing, e-mailed**) also **E-mail** or **email** **1** N-VAR **E-mail** is a system of sending written messages electronically from one computer to another. **E-mail** is an abbreviation of **electronic mail**. *e-mail, correo electrónico, correo* ❑ *You can contact us by e-mail. Nos puedes contactar por e-mail.* ❑ *Do you want to send an e-mail? ¿Quieres mandar un correo?* **2** V-T If you **e-mail** someone, you send them an e-mail. *mandar un e-mail, mandar un correo electrónico* ❑ *Jamie e-mailed me to say he couldn't come. Jamie me mandó un e-mail para avisarme que no podría venir.*
→ see **Internet**

**em|bar|go** /ɪmbɑrgoʊ/ (**embargoes**) N-COUNT If one country or group of countries imposes an **embargo** against another, it forbids trade with that country. *embargo, prohibición* ❑ *The United Nations imposed an embargo. Las Naciones Unidas impusieron un embargo.*

**em|bark** /ɪmbɑrk/ (**embarks, embarking, embarked**) **1** V-I If you **embark on** something new, difficult, or exciting, you start doing it. *embarcarse en, emprender* ❑ *He's embarking on a new career as a writer. Está emprendiendo una nueva carrera de escritor.* **2** V-I When you **embark on** a ship, you go on board before the start of a journey. *embarcarse* ❑ *They embarked on a ship bound for Europe. Se embarcaron con rumbo a Europa.*

**em|bar|rass** /ɪmbærəs/ (**embarrasses, embarrassing, embarrassed**) **1** V-T If something or someone **embarrasses** you, they make you feel shy or ashamed. *avergonzar* ❑ *His clumsiness embarrassed him. Su torpeza le hizo sentir avergonzado.* • **em|bar|rass|ing** ADJ *embarazoso, penoso* ❑ *That*

e

was an embarrassing situation for me. Fue una situacion penosa para mí. • **em|bar|rass|ing|ly** ADV penosamente, embarazosamente ❑ It became embarrassingly clear that Lionel wasn't coming home for Christmas. Fue penosamente claro que Lionel no vendría a casa en Navidad. **2** V-T If something **embarrasses** a public figure such as a politician or an organization such as a political party, it causes problems for them. hacer pasar vergüenza, avergonzar ❑ They destroyed documents that would embarrass the governor. Destruyeron documentos que hubieran avergonzado al gobernador. • **em|bar|rass|ing** ADJ incómodo, vergonzoso ❑ He has put the administration in an embarrassing position. Puso a la administración en una posición incómoda.

E

**em|bar|rassed** /ɪmbærəst/ ADJ A person who is **embarrassed** feels shy, ashamed, or guilty about something. avergonzado, apenado ❑ He looked a bit embarrassed. Se veía un poco apenado.

**em|bar|rass|ment** /ɪmbærəsmənt/ (**embarrassments**) **1** N-VAR **Embarrassment** is the feeling you have when you are embarrassed. vergüenza, pena ❑ We apologize for any embarrassment this may have caused. Disculpe la vergüenza que le hayamos hecho pasar. **2** N-SING If you refer to a person as **an embarrassment,** you mean that you disapprove of them but cannot avoid your connection with them. vergüenza ❑ You have been an embarrassment to us from the day Doug married you. Has sido una vergüeza para nosotros desde el día en que Doug se casó contigo.

**em|bas|sy** /ɛmbəsi/ (**embassies**) N-COUNT An **embassy** is a group of government officials, headed by an ambassador, who represent their government in a foreign country. The building in which they work is also called an **embassy.** embajada ❑ The American embassy has already complained. La embajada americana ya interpuso su queja.

| Word Link | ***em ≈ making, putting : embellishment, emphasis, empower*** |
|---|---|

**em|bel|lish|ment** /ɪmbɛlɪʃmənt/ (**embellishments**) N-COUNT In music, **embellishments** are extra notes that area added to a melody or rhythm to make it more pleasing. floritura [TECHNICAL]

**em|brace** /ɪmbreɪs/ (**embraces, embracing, embraced**) **1** V-RECIP If you **embrace** someone, you put your arms around them in order to show affection for them. You can also say that two people **embrace.** abrazar(se) ❑ Penelope came forward and embraced her sister. Penélope se adelantó y abrazó a su hermana. ❑ People were crying for joy and embracing. La gente lloraba de alegría y se abrazaba. • **Embrace** is also a noun. abrazo ❑ ...a young couple locked in an embrace. ...una joven pareja fundida en un abrazo. **2** V-T If you **embrace** a change, political system, or idea, you accept it and start supporting it or believing in it. adoptar, aceptar, abrazar [FORMAL] ❑ He embraces the new information age. Acepta la nueva era de la información. • **Embrace** is also a noun. abrazo, adopción, aceptación ❑ ...James's embrace of the Catholic faith. ...la adopción de James de la fe católica. **3** V-T If something **embraces** a group of people, things, or ideas, it includes them in a larger group or category. incluir, abarcar, comprender [FORMAL] ❑ Paulin's poetry embraces a wide range of subjects. La poesía de Paulin abarca una amplia gama de temas.

**em|broi|dery** /ɪmbrɔɪdəri/ (**embroideries**) **1** N-VAR **Embroidery** consists of designs stitched into cloth. bordado ❑ The shorts had blue embroidery over the pockets. Los pantaloncillos tenían bordados azules en los bolsillos. **2** N-UNCOUNT **Embroidery** is the activity of stitching designs onto cloth. bordado ❑ She learned sewing, knitting, and embroidery. Aprendió costura, tejido y bordado.
→ see **quilt**

**em|bryo** /ɛmbrioʊ/ (**embryos**) N-COUNT An **embryo** is an unborn animal or human being in the very early stages of development. embrión
→ see **reproduction**

**em|cee** /ɛmsi/ (**emcees, emceeing, emceed**) **1** N-COUNT An **emcee** is the same as a **master of ceremonies.** presentador o presentadora, maestro de ceremonias o maestra de ceremonias **2** V-T To **emcee** an event means to act as master of ceremonies for it. presentar, hacer de maestro/maestra de ceremonias, ser el maestro/la maestra de ceremonias ❑ I'm going to be emceeing a costume contest. Voy a presentar un concurso de disfraces.

| Word Link | ***merg ≈ sinking : emerge, merge, submerge*** |
|---|---|

**emerge** /ɪmɜrdʒ/ (**emerges, emerging, emerged**) **1** V-I To **emerge** means to come out from a place where you could not be seen. salir, aparecer, surgir, revelarse ❑ Richard was waiting outside the door as she emerged. Richard estaba esperando afuera cuando ella apareció. ❑ She then emerged from the courthouse to thank her supporters. Entonces salió del tribunal a agradecer a quienes la apoyaban. **2** V-I If you **emerge from** a difficult or bad experience, you come to the end of it. salir de ❑ Emerging from the illness was like coming out of a fog. Salir de la enfermedad fue como salir de entre la niebla. **3** V-I When something such as an organization or an industry **emerges,** it comes into existence. surgir, emerger ❑ ...the new republic that emerged in October 1917. ...la nueva república surgida en octubre de 1917. • **emer|gence** N-UNCOUNT salida, aparición, surgimiento ❑ ...the emergence of new democracies in Latin America. ...el surgimiento de nuevas democracias en América Latina.

**emer|gen|cy** /ɪmɜrdʒᵊnsi/ (**emergencies**) **1** N-COUNT An **emergency** is an unexpected and serious situation, such as an accident, that must be dealt with quickly. emergencia ❑ He deals with emergencies promptly. Atiende prontamente las emergencias. **2** ADJ An **emergency** action is one that is done or arranged quickly and not in the normal way, because an emergency has occurred. de emergencia ❑ The board held an emergency meeting. El consejo tuvo una reunión de urgencia. **3** ADJ **Emergency** equipment or supplies are those intended for use in an emergency. de emergencia ❑ The plane is carrying emergency supplies for refugees. El avión lleva suministros de emergencia para los refugiados.
→ see **hospital**

**Word Partnership** Usar *emergency* con:

ADJ. **major** emergency, **medical** emergency, **minor** emergency 1
N. **state of** emergency 1
emergency **care**, emergency **surgery** 2
emergency **supplies**, emergency **vehicle** 3

**emer|gen|cy brake** (**emergency brakes**) N-COUNT In a vehicle, the **emergency brake** is a brake which the driver operates with his or her hand. *freno de mano, freno de emergencia*

**emer|gen|cy room** (**emergency rooms**) N-COUNT The **emergency room** is the room or department in a hospital where people who have severe injuries or sudden illnesses are taken for emergency treatment. The abbreviation **ER** is often used. *sala de urgencias, urgencias*

**Word Link** *e ≈ away, out : eject, emigrate, emit*

**Word Link** *migr ≈ moving, changing : emigrate, immigrant, migrant*

**emi|grate** /ɛmɪgreɪt/ (**emigrates, emigrating, emigrated**) V-I If you **emigrate**, you leave your own country to live in another country. *emigrar* ❑ *He emigrated to Belgium. Emigró a Bélgica.* • **emi|gra|tion** /ɛmɪgreɪʃᵊn/ N-UNCOUNT *emigración* ❑ *...the huge emigration of workers to the West. ...la intensa emigración de trabajadores hacia Occidente.*

**emi|nent** /ɛmɪnənt/ ADJ An **eminent** person is well-known and highly respected. *eminente, ilustre, prestigioso, prestigiado* ❑ *...an eminent scientist. ...una eminente científica.* • **emi|nence** /ɛmɪnəns/ N-UNCOUNT *eminencia, prestigio* ❑ *He was a man of great eminence. Era un hombre de gran prestigio.*

**emis|sion** /ɪmɪʃᵊn/ (**emissions**) N-VAR An **emission of** something such as gas or radiation is the release of it into the atmosphere. *emisión* [FORMAL] ❑ *...the emission of gases such as carbon dioxide. ...la emisión de gases como el bióxido de carbono.*
→ see **pollution**

**emit** /ɪmɪt/ (**emits, emitting, emitted**) V-T To **emit** a sound, smell, or substance means to produce it or send it out. *emitir* [FORMAL] ❑ *Whitney blinked and emitted a long, low whistle. Whitney parpadeó y emitió un prolongado y quedo silbido.*
→ see **light**

**emo|tion** /ɪmoʊʃᵊn/ (**emotions**) N-VAR **Emotion** is feeling such as joy or love. An **emotion** is one of these feelings. *emoción* ❑ *Mr. Anderson was a professional man who never showed his emotions at work. El Sr. Anderson era un profesional que en el trabajo nunca dejaba ver sus emociones.* ❑ *Wanda's voice was full of emotion and there were tears in her eyes. La voz de Wanda desbordaba emoción y había lágrimas en sus ojos.*
→ see Word Web: **emotion**

**emo|tion|al** /ɪmoʊʃənᵊl/ 1 ADJ **Emotional** means concerned with emotions and feelings. *emocional* ❑ *I needed emotional support. Yo necesitaba apoyo emocional.* • **emo|tion|al|ly** ADV *emocionalmente* ❑ *Are you becoming emotionally involved with her? ¿Te estás involucrando emocionalmente con ella?* 2 ADJ If someone is **emotional**, they show their feelings very openly, especially because they are upset. *emotivo* ❑ *He is a very emotional man. Es un hombre muy emotivo.*

**Word Link** *path ≈ feeling : empathy, pathetic, sympathy*

**em|pa|thy** /ɛmpəθi/ N-UNCOUNT **Empathy** is the ability to share another person's feelings and emotions as if they were your own. *empatía* ❑ *Very young children are capable of empathy. Los niños muy pequeños pueden sentir empatía.*

**em|per|or** /ɛmpərər/ (**emperors**) N-COUNT; N-TITLE An **emperor** is a man who rules an empire or is the head of state in an empire. *emperador* ❑ *...the emperor of Japan. ...el emperador de Japón.*
→ see **empire**

**Word Link** *em ≈ making, putting : embellishment, emphasis, empower*

**em|pha|sis** /ɛmfəsɪs/ (**emphases** /ɛmfəsiz/) 1 N-VAR **Emphasis** is special or extra importance that is given to an activity or to a part or aspect of something. *énfasis, importancia* ❑ *Too much emphasis is placed on research. Se da demasiada importancia a la investigación.* 2 N-VAR **Emphasis** is extra force that you put on a syllable, word, or phrase when you are speaking in order to make it seem more important. *énfasis, acento* ❑ *The emphasis is on the first syllable of the word. El acento va en la primera sílaba de la palabra.*

**em|pha|size** /ɛmfəsaɪz/ (**emphasizes, emphasizing, emphasized**) V-T To **emphasize** something means to indicate that it is particularly important or true, or to draw special attention to

**Word Web** emotion

Scientists believe that animals experience **emotions** such as **happiness** and **sadness** just like humans do. Research shows animals also feel **anger**, **fear**, **love**, and **hate**. Biochemical changes in mammals' brains cause these emotions. When an elephant gives birth, a **hormone** goes through her bloodstream. This causes feelings of **adoration** for her baby. The same thing happens to human mothers. When a dog chews on a bone, a chemical increases in its brain to produce feelings of **joy**. The same chemical produces elation in humans. Scientists aren't sure whether animals experience **shame**. However, they do know that animals experience **stress**.

e

it. *hacer énfasis, poner énfasis, subrayar, recalcar, hacer hincapié* ❑ *She emphasized that no major changes can be expected. Hizo hincapié en que no debíamos esperar cambios importantes.*

**em|phat|ic** /ɪmfætɪk/ **1** ADJ An **emphatic** response or statement is one made in a forceful way. *enfático, categórico, enérgico* ❑ *His response was immediate and emphatic. Su respuesta fue inmediata y categórica.* • **em|phati|cal|ly** /ɪmfætɪkli/ ADV *enfáticamente, rotundamente, categóricamente* ❑ *"No fast food," she said emphatically. —Nada de comida rápida—dijo rotundamente.* **2** ADJ An **emphatic** victory is one in which the winner has won by a large amount or distance. *rotundo, contundente* ❑ *Yesterday's emphatic victory was their fifth this season. La contundente victoria de ayer fue la quinta en esta temporada.*

E

**em|pire** /ɛmpaɪər/ (**empires**) **1** N-COUNT An **empire** is a number of individual nations that are all controlled by the government or ruler of one particular country. *imperio* ❑ *...the Roman Empire. ...el imperio Romano.* **2** N-COUNT You can refer to a group of companies controlled by one person as an **empire**. *imperio* ❑ *...a global media empire. ...un imperio mundial de medios.*
→ see Word Web: **empire**
→ see **history**

**em|piri|cal** /ɪmpɪrɪkᵊl/ ADJ **Empirical** evidence or knowledge is based on observation, experiment, and experience rather than theories. *empírico* ❑ *There is no empirical evidence to support his thesis. No existen pruebas empíricas que apoyen su tesis.* • **em|piri|cal|ly** ADV ❑ *They approached this part of their task empirically. Enfocaron esa parte del trabajo de una manera empírica.*
→ see **science**

**em|ploy** /ɪmplɔɪ/ (**employs, employing, employed**) **1** V-T If a person or company **employs** you, they pay you to work for them. *emplear, dar trabajo, dar empleo, contratar* ❑ *The company employs 18 workers. La empresa emplea a 18 trabajadores.* ❑ *More than 3,000 local workers are employed in the tourism industry. La industria turística da empleo a más de 3,000 trabajadores locales.* **2** V-T If you **employ** methods, materials, or expressions, you use them. *emplear, utilizar, usar* ❑ *All good teachers employ a variety of methods to teach reading. Todos los buenos maestros utilizan diferentes métodos para enseñar a leer.*

**em|ployee** /ɪmplɔɪi/ (**employees**) N-COUNT An **employee** is a person who is paid to work for an organization or for another person. *empleado o empleada* ❑ *He is an employee of Fuji Bank. Es empleado del Fuji Bank.*
→ see **factory, union**

**em|ploy|er** /ɪmplɔɪər/ (**employers**) N-COUNT Your **employer** is the person or organization that you work for. *patrón o patrona, empleador o empleadora, jefe o jefa* ❑ *He was sent to Rome by his employer. Su jefe lo mandó a Roma.*

**em|ploy|ment** /ɪmplɔɪmənt/ N-UNCOUNT **Employment** is the fact of having a paid job. *trabajo, empleo* ❑ *She was unable to find employment. No pudo encontrar trabajo.*

**Word Link** *em ≈ making, putting : embellishment, emphasis, empower*

**em|power** /ɪmpaʊər/ (**empowers, empowering, empowered**) V-T To **empower** someone means to give them the means or the power to achieve something for themselves. *empoderar, dar poder, conferir poder* ❑ *We must continue to empower young people. Debemos seguir el proceso de empoderar a los jóvenes.* • **em|pow|er|ment** N-UNCOUNT *empoderamiento* ❑ *...the empowerment of women. ...el empoderamiento de las mujeres.*

**em|press** /ɛmprɪs/ (**empresses**) N-COUNT; N-TITLE An **empress** is a woman who rules an empire or who is the wife of an emperor. *emperatriz* ❑ *...Catherine II, Empress of Russia. ...Catalina II, emperatriz de Rusia.*
→ see **empire**

**emp|ty** /ɛmpti/ (**emptier, emptiest, empties, emptying, emptied**) **1** ADJ An **empty** place, vehicle, or container is one that has no people or things in it. *vacío* ❑ *The room was bare and empty. El cuarto estaba desnudo y vacío.* ❑ *...empty cans of soda. ...latas de refresco vacías.* • **emp|ti|ness** N-UNCOUNT *vacío* ❑ *...the emptiness of the desert. ...el vacío del desierto.* **2** ADJ If you describe something as **empty**, you mean that it has no real value or meaning. *vacío, desocupado, hueco, falso* ❑ *She*

**Word Web** **empire**

An **empire** is formed when a strong nation-state **conquers** other states and creates a larger **political union**. An early example is the Roman Empire which began in 31 BC. The Roman **emperor** Augustus Caesar* ruled a large area from the Mediterranean Sea* to Western Europe. Later, the British Empire ruled from about 1600 to 1900 AD. Queen Victoria's* empire spread across oceans and continents. One of her many titles was **Empress** of India. Both of these empires spread their political influence as well as their language and culture over large areas.

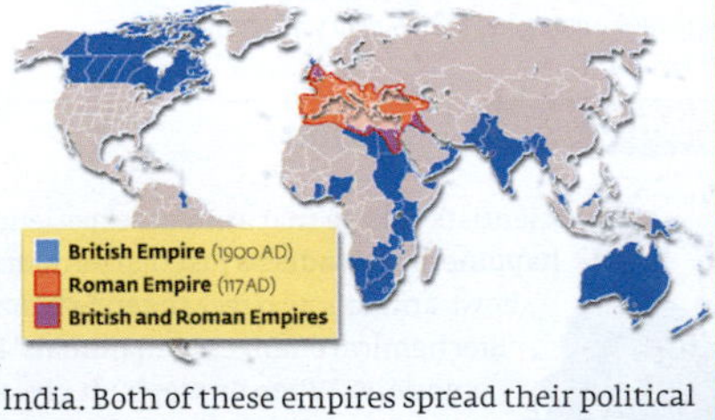


*Augustus Caesar: the first emperor of Rome.*
*Mediterranean Sea: between Europe and Africa.*
*Queen Victoria (1819-1901): queen of the United Kingdom.*

made empty threats to leave. Profirió falsas amenazas de irse. • **emp|ti|ness** N-UNCOUNT vacío ❑ ...feelings of emptiness and depression. ...sensaciones de vacío y depresión. **3** V-T If you **empty** a container, or **empty** something out of it, you remove its contents, especially by tipping it up. vaciar ❑ I emptied the wastepaper basket. Vacié el cesto de los papeles. ❑ Empty the noodles into a serving bowl. Vacía la pasta en un platón. **4** V-T/V-I If someone **empties** a room or place, or if it **empties**, everyone in it goes away. vaciar(se) ❑ The stadium emptied at the end of the game. El estadio se vació al terminar el juego.

**Thesaurus** *empty* Ver también:

ADJ. vacant; (ant.) full, occupied **1**
meaningless **2**
V. drain out, pour out **3**
evacuate, go out, leave **4**

**Word Partnership** Usar *empty* con:

N. empty **bottle**, empty **box**, empty **building**, empty **room**, empty **seat**, empty **space**, empty **stomach** **1**
empty **promise**, empty **threat** **2**
empty **the trash** **3**

**empty-handed** ADJ If you come away from somewhere **empty-handed,** you have failed to get what you wanted. con las manos vacías ❑ I have no intention of going home empty-handed. No tengo la intención de irme a casa con las manos vacías.

**Word Link** *en ≈ making, putting : enable, enact, endanger*

**en|able** /ɪneɪbᵊl/ (**enables, enabling, enabled**) V-T If someone or something **enables** you **to** do a particular thing, they make it possible for you to do it. permitir, hacer posible ❑ The new test should enable doctors to detect the disease early. La nueva prueba permitirá que los doctores detecten a tiempo la enfermedad.

**en|act** /ɪnækt/ (**enacts, enacting, enacted**) **1** V-T When a government or authority **enacts** a proposal, they make it into a law. promulgar, aprobar [TECHNICAL] ❑ President Johnson led the battle to enact civil-rights laws. El presidente Johnson encabezó la lucha para promulgar las leyes sobre los derechos civiles. • **en|act|ment** N-VAR (**enactments**) promulgación ❑ ...the enactment of a Bill of Rights. ...la promulgación de una declaración de derechos. **2** V-T If people **enact** a story or play, they perform it by acting. representar ❑ She often enacted the stories told to her by her father. A menudo representaba las historias que le contaba su padre.

**enam|el** /ɪnæmᵊl/ (**enamels**) N-UNCOUNT **Enamel** is a substance like glass that can be heated and put onto metal, glass, or pottery in order to decorate or protect it. esmalte ❑ ...a white enamel saucepan. ...una cacerola de esmalte blanco.

**en|close** /ɪnkloʊz/ (**encloses, enclosing, enclosed**) **1** V-T If a place or object **is enclosed** by something, the place or object is inside that thing or completely surrounded by it. envolver, envasar ❑ Samples must be enclosed in two watertight containers. Las muestras deben ir envasadas en dos recipientes herméticos. ❑ Enclose the meat in a plastic bag. Envuelve la carne con una bolsa de plástico. **2** V-T If you **enclose** something with a letter, you put it in the same envelope as the letter. adjuntar, anexar ❑ I have enclosed a check for $100. Anexé un cheque por 100 dólares.

**en|coun|ter** /ɪnkaʊntər/ (**encounters, encountering, encountered**) **1** V-T If you **encounter** problems or difficulties, you experience them. encontrar(se), enfrentar(se) ❑ Every day of our lives we encounter stress. Todos los días de nuestra vida nos enfrentamos al estrés. **2** V-T If you **encounter** someone, you meet them, usually unexpectedly. encontrarse con, toparse con [FORMAL] ❑ Did you encounter anyone in the building? ¿Te encontraste con alguien en el edificio? • **Encounter** is also a noun. encuentro ❑ ...a remarkable encounter with a group of soldiers. ...un encuentro sorprendente con un grupo de soldados.

**Thesaurus** *encounter* Ver también:

V. bump into, come across, run into; (ant.) avoid, miss **1** **2**

**en|cour|age** /ɪnkɜrɪdʒ/ (**encourages, encouraging, encouraged**) **1** V-T If you **encourage** someone, you give them confidence, for example by letting them know that what they are doing is good. animar, alentar, dar aliento, estimular ❑ When things aren't going well, he encourages me. Cuando las cosas no van bien, me anima. **2** V-T If someone **is encouraged by** something that happens, it gives them hope or confidence. alentar, dar aliento ❑ She has been encouraged by the support of her family. Ha sido alentada por el apoyo de su familia. • **en|cour|aged** ADJ animado ❑ He was encouraged that there seemed to be some progress. Estaba animado porque aparentemente se habían hecho progresos. **3** V-T If you **encourage** someone **to** do something, you try to persuade them to do it, for example, by trying to make it easier for them to do it. animar, entusiasmar, impulsar ❑ We want to encourage people to go fishing. Queremos entusiasmar a la gente para que vaya a pescar. ❑ Their task is to encourage private investment. Su labor es impulsar la inversión privada. **4** V-T If something **encourages** a particular activity or state, it causes it to happen or increase. fomentar ❑ ...a drug that encourages cell growth. ...un fármaco que fomenta el crecimiento de las células.

**en|cour|age|ment** /ɪnkɜrɪdʒmənt/ N-VAR **Encouragement** is the activity of encouraging someone, or something that is said or done in order to encourage them. ánimo, aliento ❑ Friends gave me a great deal of encouragement. Los amigos me dieron mucho ánimo.

**en|cour|ag|ing** /ɪnkɜrɪdʒɪŋ/ ADJ Something that is **encouraging** gives people hope or confidence. alentador, esperanzador ❑ The results have been encouraging. Los resultados han sido alentadores. • **en|cour|ag|ing|ly** ADV alentadoramente, de modo alentador ❑ ...encouragingly large audiences. ...un público alentadoramente numeroso.

**en|cy|clo|pedia** /ɪnsaɪkləpidiə/ (**encyclopedias**) also **encyclopaedia** N-COUNT An **encyclopedia** is a book, set of books, or CD-ROM in which facts about many different subjects or about one particular subject are arranged

e

for reference, usually in alphabetical order. *enciclopedia*

**end**
❶ NOUN USES
❷ VERB USES
❸ PHRASAL VERBS

E

❶ **end** /ɛnd/ (**ends**) 1 N-SING **The end of** something such as a period of time, an event, a book, or a movie is the last part of it or the final point in it. *fin, final* ❑ *The report is expected by the end of the year. Se espera el informe para fin de año.* ❑ *...families who settled in the region at the end of the 17th century. ...familias que se establecieron en la región a finales del siglo XVII.* 2 N-COUNT An **end to** something or the **end of** it is the fact that it finishes and does not continue any longer. You can also say that something **comes to an end** or **is at an end.** *fin, final* ❑ *The government today called for an end to the violence. El gobierno hizo hoy un llamado para acabar con la violencia* ❑ *The hot weather came to an end at the beginning of October. El clima cálido llegó a su fin a principios de octubre.* 3 N-COUNT The **end of** a long, narrow object is the tip or farthest part of it. *punta, extremo* ❑ *He tapped the ends of his fingers together. Juntó la punta de los dedos.* ❑ *...both ends of the tunnel. ...ambos extremos del túnel.* 4 N-COUNT An **end** is the purpose for which something is done or toward which you are working. *fin, objetivo* ❑ *The church should not be used for political ends. La iglesia no debe utilizarse con fines políticos.* 5 PHRASE If you find it difficult to **make ends meet,** you do not have enough money for the things you need. *tener apenas lo suficiente para vivir* ❑ *With Betty's salary they barely made ends meet. Con el salario de Betty apenas podían vivir.* 6 PHRASE When something happens for hours, days, weeks, or years **on end,** it happens continuously and without stopping for the amount of time that is mentioned. *sin interrupción, sin parar* ❑ *We can talk for hours on end. Podemos hablar sin parar durante horas.*

❷ **end** /ɛnd/ (**ends, ending, ended**) 1 V-T/V-I When a situation, process, or activity **ends,** or when something or someone **ends** it, it reaches its final point and stops. *terminar, acabar* ❑ *The meeting quickly ended. La reunión terminó rápidamente.* ❑ *She began to weep. That ended our discussion. Empezó a llorar y con eso acabó nuestra discusión.* • **end|ing** N-SING *final, fin* ❑ *...the ending of a marriage. ...el fin de un matrimonio.* 2 V-I A journey, road, or river that **ends** at a particular place stops there and goes no further. *terminar, acabar* ❑ *The highway ended at an intersection. La carretera terminaba en una intersección.*

| **Thesaurus** | *end* | Ver también: |
|---|---|---|
| N. | close, conclusion, finale, finish, stop; (*ant.*) beginning ❶ 1 2 | |
| V. | conclude, finish, wrap up ❷ 1 | |

❸ **end** /ɛnd/ (**ends, ending, ended**)
▸ **end up** PHR-VERB If you **end up** in a particular place or situation, you are in that place or situation after a series of events. *terminar en, acabar en* ❑ *The painting ended up at the Museum of Modern Art. La pintura acabó en el Museo de Arte Moderno.* ❑ *You might end up getting something you don't want. Podrías acabar con algo que no quieres.*

**Word Link** *en ≈ making, putting : enable, enact, endanger*

**en|dan|ger** /ɪndeɪndʒər/ (**endangers, endangering, endangered**) V-T To **endanger** something or someone means to put them in a situation where they might be harmed or destroyed completely. *poner en peligro, poner en riesgo* ❑ *The debate could endanger the peace talks. El debate podría poner en peligro las pláticas de paz.* ❑ *The beetles are on the list of endangered species. Los escarabajos están en la lista de especies en peligro.*

**en|deav|or** /ɪndɛvər/ (**endeavors, endeavoring, endeavored**) 1 V-T If you **endeavor to** do something, you try very hard to do it. *intentar, esforzarse* [FORMAL] ❑ *They are endeavoring to protect labor union rights. Se están esforzando por proteger los derechos sindicales de los trabajadores.* 2 N-VAR An **endeavor** is an attempt to do something, especially something new or original. *esfuerzo, intento, tentativa* [FORMAL] ❑ *...the company's creative endeavors. ...los esfuerzos creativos de la compañía.*

**end|ing** /ɛndɪŋ/ (**endings**) 1 N-COUNT You can refer to the last part of a book, story, play, or movie as the **ending,** especially when you are considering the way that the story ends. *final, desenlace, conclusión* ❑ *The film has a Hollywood happy ending. La película tiene un final feliz tipo Hollywood.* 2 → see also **end**

**en|dive** /ɛndaɪv/ (**endives**) N-VAR **Endive** is a type of a plant with crisp bitter leaves that can be cooked or eaten raw in salads. *endivia o endibia*

**Word Link** *less ≈ without : endless, hopeless, wireless*

**end|less** /ɛndlɪs/ ADJ If you say that something is **endless,** you mean that it is very large or lasts for a very long time, and it seems as if it will never stop. *interminable, eterno, infinito* ❑ *...the endless hours I spent on homework. ...las horas interminables que dediqué a la tarea.* • **end|less|ly** ADV *interminablemente* ❑ *They talk about it endlessly. Hablan interminablemente de ello.*

**endo|crine** /ɛndəkrɪn, -kraɪn/ ADJ The **endocrine** system is the system of glands that produce hormones for the bloodstream, such as the pituitary or thyroid glands. *endocrino* [MEDICAL]

**endo|cy|to|sis** /ɛndoʊsaɪtoʊsɪs/ N-UNCOUNT **Endocytosis** is a process in which a cell absorbs material from outside the cell by enclosing the material within a part of the cell membrane. Compare **exocytosis.** *endocitosis* [TECHNICAL]

**endo|plas|mic re|ticu|lum** /ɛndoʊplæzmɪk rɪtɪkyələm/ (**endoplasmic reticulums** or **endoplasmic reticula**) N-COUNT The **endoplasmic reticulum** is a network of tubes and membranes within cells that is involved in the making and movement of proteins. *retículo endoplásmico* [TECHNICAL]

**en|dorse** /ɪndɔrs/ (**endorses, endorsing, endorsed**) 1 V-T If you **endorse** someone or something, you say publicly that you support or approve of them. *aprobar, refrendar, respaldar* ❑ *I can* *endorse their opinion wholeheartedly.* *Puedo respaldar su opinión incondicionalmente.* • **en|dorse|ment** N-COUNT (**endorsements**) *aprobación, respaldo* ❑ *This is a powerful endorsement for his softer style of government.* *Es un poderoso respaldo a su estilo suave de gobierno.* **2** V-T If you **endorse** a product or company, you appear in advertisements for it. *promocionar* ❑ *The twins endorsed a line of household cleaning products.* *Los gemelos promocionaban una línea de productos de limpieza para el hogar.* • **en|dorse|ment** N-COUNT *promoción* ❑ *...his commercial endorsements for breakfast cereals.* *...su promoción comercial de cereales para el desayuno.*

**endo|skel|eton** /ɛndoʊskɛlɪtᵊn/ (**endoskeletons**) N-COUNT Animals with an **endoskeleton** have their skeleton inside their body, like humans. *endoesqueleto* [TECHNICAL]

**endo|therm** /ɛndəθɜrm/ (**endotherms**) N-COUNT An **endotherm** is a warm-blooded animal, such as a bird or mammal, that can keep its body temperature above or below that of the surrounding environment. Compare **ectotherm**. *endotermo* [TECHNICAL]

**endo|ther|mic** /ɛndoʊθɜrmɪk/ ADJ An **endothermic** chemical reaction or process is one that takes in heat from its surroundings, such as when ice melts. *endotérmico* [TECHNICAL]

**en|dow|ment** /ɪndaʊmənt/ (**endowments**) N-COUNT An **endowment** is a gift of money that is made to an institution or community in order to provide it with an annual income. *donación, legado, fideicomiso* ❑ *...the National Endowment for the Arts.* *...el Fideicomiso Nacional para las Artes.*

**en|dure** /ɪndʊər/ (**endures, enduring, endured**) **1** V-T If you **endure** a painful or difficult situation, you experience it, usually because you have no other choice. *soportar, aguantar, tolerar* ❑ *The company endured heavy financial losses.* *La compañía soportó enormes pérdidas financieras.* **2** V-I If something **endures**, it continues to exist without any loss in quality or importance. *perdurar* ❑ *Somehow the language endures and continues to survive.* *De alguna forma, la lengua perdura y continúa sobreviviendo.* • **en|dur|ing** ADJ *duradero* ❑ *...the start of an enduring friendship.* *...el inicio de una amistad duradera.*

**end user** (**end users**) N-COUNT The **end user** of a piece of equipment is the user that it has been designed for, rather than the person who installs or maintains it. *usuario final* [COMPUTING] ❑ *You have to describe things in a form that the end user can understand.* *Tiene que describir las cosas de manera que el usuario final las entienda.*

**en|emy** /ɛnəmi/ (**enemies**) **1** N-COUNT If someone is your **enemy**, they hate you or want to harm you. *enemigo* ❑ *...her many enemies.* *...sus muchos enemigos.* **2** N-SING **The enemy** is an army or other force that is opposed to you in a war, or a country with which your country is at war. *enemigo* ❑ *They pursued the enemy for two miles.* *Persiguieron al enemigo a lo largo de dos kilómetros.*

**en|er|get|ic** /ɛnərdʒɛtɪk/ ADJ An **energetic** person has a lot of energy. **Energetic** activities require a lot of energy. *lleno de energía* ❑ *Young children are incredibly energetic.* *Es increíble lo llenos de energía que están los niños pequeños.* • **en|er|geti|cal|ly** ADV *con energía, enérgicamente* ❑ *David chewed energetically on the steak.* *David masticó el bistec con energía.*

**e**

**en|er|gy** /ɛnərdʒi/ (**energies**) **1** N-UNCOUNT **Energy** is the ability and strength to do active physical things. *energía* ❑ *He was saving his energy for next week's race.* *Estaba ahorrando energía para la carrera de la semana siguiente.* **2** N-COUNT Your **energies** are the efforts and attention that you can direct toward a particular aim. *energía* ❑ *She started to devote her energies to teaching rather than performing.* *Empezó a dedicar su energía a la enseñanza, más que a la interpretación.* **3** N-UNCOUNT **Energy** is the power from sources such as electricity and coal that makes machines work or provides heat. *energía* ❑ *...nuclear energy.* *...energía nuclear.*
→ see Word Web: **energy**
→ see **calorie, electricity, food, petroleum, photosynthesis, solar**

**Word Partnership** Usar *energy* con:

| | |
|---|---|
| ADJ. | **full of** energy, **physical** energy, **sexual** energy **1** |
| | **atomic** energy, **nuclear** energy, **solar** energy **3** |
| V. | **focus** energy **1** **2** |
| | **conserve/save** energy **3** |

**en|er|gy con|ver|sion** N-UNCOUNT **Energy conversion** is the changing of energy from one form to another, for example from mechanical energy to electrical energy. *conversión de energía*

**en|er|gy ef|fi|cien|cy** N-UNCOUNT **Energy efficiency** is the careful use of resources such as electricity or fuel in order to reduce the amount of energy that is wasted. *eficiencia energética.*

**energy-efficient** also **energy efficient** ADJ A device or building that is **energy-efficient** uses

**Word Web** energy

**Wood** was the most important **energy** source for American settlers. Then, as industry developed, factories began to use **coal**. Coal was also used to **generate** most of the **electrical power** in the early 1900s. However, the popularity of automobile use soon made **petroleum** the most important **fuel**. **Natural gas** remains popular for home heating and industrial use. **Hydroelectric** power isn't a major source of energy in the U.S. It requires too much land and water to produce. Some companies built **nuclear** power plants to make **electricity** in the 1970s. Today **solar** panels convert sunlight and giant wind farms convert wind into electricity.

**Word Web** engine

In the **internal combustion engine** found in most cars, there are four, six, or eight **cylinders**. To start an engine, the **intake valve** opens and a small amount of **fuel** enters the **combustion** chamber of the cylinder. A **spark plug** ignites the fuel and air mixture, causing it to explode. This **combustion** moves the **cylinder head**, which causes the **crankshaft** to turn and the car to move. Next, the **exhaust valve** opens and the burned gases are drawn out. As the cylinder head returns to its original position, it compresses the new gas and air mixture and the process repeats itself.

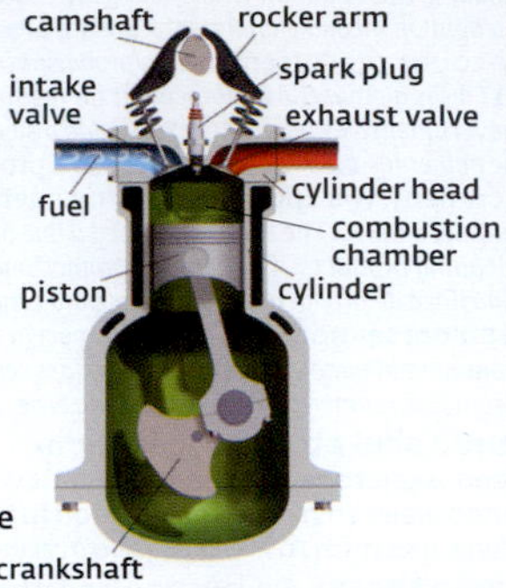


internal combustion engine

relatively little energy to provide the power it needs. *de gran rendimiento energético* ❑ *...energy-efficient light bulbs. ...focos de gran rendimiento energético.*

**en|er|gy pyra|mid** (**energy pyramids**) N-COUNT An **energy pyramid** is a diagram that shows the amount of energy that is available at each level of a food chain. *pirámide energética* [TECHNICAL]

**en|er|gy re|source** (**energy resources**) N-COUNT An **energy resource** is a source of energy such as oil, coal, and wind. *recurso energético*

**en|er|gy source** (**energy sources**) N-COUNT An **energy source** is any substance or system from which energy can be obtained, such as coal, gas, water, or sunlight. *fuente de energía, fuente energética*

**en|force** /ɪnfɔrs/ (**enforces, enforcing, enforced**) V-T If people in authority **enforce** a law or a rule, they make sure that it is obeyed, usually by punishing people who do not obey it. *hacer cumplir, hacer respetar, hacer obedecer* ❑ *Many states enforce drug laws. Muchos estados hacen cumplir la legislación contra las drogas.* • **en|force|ment** /ɪnfɔrsmənt/ N-UNCOUNT *cumplimiento* ❑ *The doctors want stricter enforcement of existing laws. Los médicos exigen el cumplimiento estricto de las leyes vigentes.*

**en|gage** /ɪngeɪdʒ/ (**engages, engaging, engaged**) **1** V-I If you **engage in** an activity, you do it or are actively involved with it. *dedicarse* [FORMAL] ❑ *They've never engaged in typical father-son activities like sports. Nunca se dedicaron a las típicas actividades padre-hijo, como los deportes.* **2** V-T If something **engages** you, it keeps you interested in it and thinking about it. *captar, atraer* ❑ *They never learned skills to engage the attention of the others. Nunca aprendieron habilidades para atraer la atención de los demás.* **3** V-T If you **engage** someone **in** conversation, you have a conversation with them. *entablar* ❑ *They tried to engage him in conversation. Trataron de entablar una conversación con él.* **4** V-T If you **engage** someone to do a particular job, you appoint them to do it. *contratar* [FORMAL] ❑ *We engaged the services of a famous engineer. Contratamos los servicios de un famoso ingeniero.* **5** → see also **engaged**

**en|gaged** /ɪngeɪdʒd/ **1** ADJ Someone who is **engaged in** a particular activity is doing that thing. *dedicado a* [FORMAL] ❑ *...the various projects he was engaged in. ...los diferentes proyectos a que estaba dedicado.* **2** ADJ When two people are **engaged,** they have agreed to marry each other. *comprometido* ❑ *We got engaged on my eighteenth birthday. Nos comprometimos el día que cumplí dieciocho años.*

**en|gage|ment** /ɪngeɪdʒmənt/ (**engagements**) **1** N-COUNT An **engagement** is an arrangement that you have made to do something at a particular time. *compromiso, cita* [FORMAL] ❑ *He had an engagement at a restaurant at eight. Tenía una cita a las ocho en un restaurante.* **2** N-COUNT An **engagement** is an agreement that two people have made with each other to get married. *compromiso* ❑ *I've broken off my engagement to Arthur. Rompí mi compromiso con Arthur.* **3** N-VAR A military **engagement** is a battle. *combate*
→ see **jewelry**

**en|gine** /ɛndʒɪn/ (**engines**) **1** N-COUNT The **engine** of a car or other vehicle is the part that produces the power which makes the vehicle move. *motor, máquina* ❑ *He got into the driving seat and started the engine. Ocupó el asiento del conductor y arrancó el motor.* **2** N-COUNT An **engine** is also the large vehicle that pulls a train. *locomotora, máquina* ❑ *In 1941, trains were pulled by steam engines. En 1941, los trenes eran jalados por máquinas de vapor.*
→ see Word Web: **engine**
→ see **car**

**en|gi|neer** /ɛndʒɪnɪər/ (**engineers, engineering, engineered**) **1** N-COUNT An **engineer** is a skilled person who uses scientific knowledge to design, construct, and maintain engines and machines or structures such as roads, railroads, and bridges. *ingeniero o ingeniera* **2** N-COUNT An **engineer** is a person who repairs mechanical or electrical devices. *ingeniero o ingeniera* ❑ *They sent a service engineer to fix the disk drive. Mandaron a un ingeniero de servicio a arreglar la unidad de disco.* **3** V-T When a vehicle, bridge, or building **is engineered,** it is planned and constructed using scientific methods. *construir* ❑ *The spaceship was engineered by Bert Rutan. La nave espacial fue construida por Bert Rutan.* **4** V-T If you **engineer** an event or situation, you arrange for it to happen, in a clever or indirect way. *planear, tramar* ❑ *Did she engineer the murder of her boss? ¿Ella tramó el asesinato de su jefe?*
→ see **concert**

**Word Web** **English**

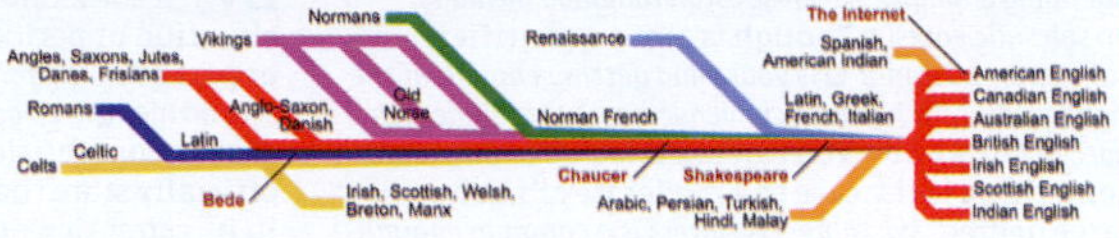


The **English language** has more **words** than any other language. Early English grew out of a Germanic language. Much of its **grammar** and basic **vocabulary** came from that language. But in 1066, England was conquered by the Normans. Norman French became the language of the rulers. Therefore many French and Latin words came into the English language. The playwright Shakespeare* **coined** over 1,600 new words in his plays. English has become an international language with many regional **dialects**.

*William Shakespeare (1564-1616): an English playwright and poet.*

**en|gi|neer|ing** /ɛndʒɪnɪərɪŋ/ **1** N-UNCOUNT **Engineering** is the work involved in designing and constructing engines and machinery or structures such as roads and bridges. **Engineering** is also the subject studied by people who want to do this work. *ingeniería* ❑ *...graduates with degrees in engineering. ...graduados de la escuela de ingeniería.* **2** → see also **genetic engineering**

**Eng|lish** /ɪŋglɪʃ/ **1** N-UNCOUNT **English** is the language spoken by people who live in Great Britain and Ireland, the United States, Canada, Australia, and many other countries. *inglés* **2** ADJ **English** means belonging or relating to England. *inglés* ❑ *...the English way of life. ...el estilo de vida inglés.* ● **The English** are English people. *los ingleses* ❑ *It is often said that the English are reserved. A menudo se dice que los ingleses son reservados.*
→ see Word Web: **English**

**Eng|lish muf|fin** (**English muffins**) N-COUNT **English muffins** are flat, round bread rolls that you split in half and usually eat hot with butter. *bollo inglés*

**en|hance** /ɪnhæns/ (**enhances, enhancing, enhanced**) V-T To **enhance** something means to improve its value, quality, or attractiveness. *realzar, mejorar* ❑ *They are eager to protect and enhance their reputation. Estan ansiosos por proteger y mejorar su reputación.* ● **en|hance|ment** N-VAR (**enhancements**) *mejora, realce, adorno* ❑ *Music is merely an enhancement to the power of her words. La música es un mero adorno para la fuerza de sus palabras.*

**Word Link** ***joy ≈ being glad : enjoy, enjoyable, enjoyment***

**en|joy** /ɪndʒɔɪ/ (**enjoys, enjoying, enjoyed**) **1** V-T If you **enjoy** something, you find pleasure and satisfaction in doing it or experiencing it. *disfrutar, gozar* ❑ *Ross has always enjoyed the company of women. Ross siempre ha disfrutado de la compañía de las mujeres.* ❑ *I enjoyed playing basketball. Yo disfrutaba jugando al básquetbol/baloncesto.* **2** V-T If you **enjoy yourself**, you do something that you like doing or you take pleasure in the situation that you are in. *disfrutar* ❑ *I am really enjoying myself at the moment. Ahora realmente estoy disfrutando.* **3** V-T If you **enjoy** something such as a privilege, you have it. *disfrutar de* [FORMAL] ❑ *The average German will enjoy 40 days' paid vacation this year. El alemán promedio disfrutará de 40 días de vacaciones pagadas este año.*

**en|joy|able** /ɪndʒɔɪəbᵊl/ ADJ Something that is **enjoyable** gives you pleasure. *agradable, placentero* ❑ *It was much more enjoyable than I expected. Fue mucho más agradable de lo que yo esperaba.*

**en|joy|ment** /ɪndʒɔɪmənt/ N-UNCOUNT **Enjoyment** is the feeling of pleasure and satisfaction that you have when you do or experience something that you like. *placer* ❑ *He took great enjoyment from traveling. Para él, los viajes eran un gran placer.*

**en|large** /ɪnlɑrdʒ/ (**enlarges, enlarging, enlarged**) **1** V-T/V-I When you **enlarge** something or when it **enlarges,** it becomes bigger. *agrandar(se)* ❑ *The college plans to enlarge its stadium. La universidad piensa agrandar el estadio.* ● **en|large|ment** N-UNCOUNT *ampliación* ❑ *There is not enough space for enlargement of the buildings. No hay suficiente espacio para la ampliación de los edificios.* **2** V-I If you **enlarge on** something that has been mentioned, you give more details about it. *abundar, extenderse, ampliar* [FORMAL] ❑ *He didn't enlarge on the form that the government would take. No abundó sobre la forma que asumiría el gobierno.*
→ see **photography**

**en|list** /ɪnlɪst/ (**enlists, enlisting, enlisted**) **1** V-T/V-I If someone **enlists** or **is enlisted,** they join the army, navy, marines, or air force. *alistarse, enrolarse* ❑ *He enlisted in the 82nd Airborne. Se alistó en el 82 batallón aéreo.* ❑ *He enlisted as a private in the Mexican War. Se enroló como soldado en la guerra contra México.* **2** V-T If you **enlist** the help of someone, you persuade them to help or support you in doing something. *conseguir* ❑ *I enlisted the help of several neighbors. Conseguí que varios de los vecinos me ayudaran.*

**enor|mous** /ɪnɔrməs/ ADJ Something that is **enormous** is extremely large in size, amount, or degree. *enorme, grande* ❑ *The main bedroom is enormous. La recámara principal es enorme.* ❑ *It was an enormous disappointment. Fue una gran desilusión.* ● **enor|mous|ly** ADV *enormemente, muchísimo* ❑ *I admired him enormously. Yo lo admiraba muchísimo.*

**enough** /ɪnʌf/ **1** DET **Enough** means as much as you need or as much as is necessary. *suficiente* ❑ *They had enough cash for a one-way ticket. Tenían suficiente efectivo para un boleto de ida.* ● **Enough** is also an adverb. *suficiente, suficientemente* ❑ *I was old enough to work and earn money. Tenía edad suficiente para trabajar y ganar dinero.* ❑ *Do you believe that sentences for criminals are tough enough? ¿Cree usted que las sentencias para los criminales son suficientemente duras?* ● **Enough** is also a pronoun. *suficiente* ❑ *Although efforts are being made, they are*

e

not doing enough. *Si bien se están tomando medidas, no son suficientes.* ● **Enough** is also a quantifier. *suficiente, bastante* ❑ *Is your child getting enough of the right foods? ¿Tu hijo está comiendo bastantes alimentos adecuados?* **2** ADV You can use **enough** to say that something is the case to a moderate or fairly large degree. *bastante* ❑ *Winters is a common enough surname. Winters es un apellido bastante común.* **3** ADV You use **enough** in expressions such as **strangely enough** and **interestingly enough** to indicate that you think a fact is strange or interesting. *curiosamente* ❑ *Strangely enough, the last thing he thought of was Tanya. Por extraño que parezca, en lo último en que pensó fue en Tanya.* **4** **fair enough** → see **fair** **5** **sure enough** → see **sure**

E

**Thesaurus** *enough* Ver también:

ADJ. adequate, complete, satisfactory, sufficient; (*ant.*) deficient, inadequate, insufficient **1**

**en|rich** /ɪnrɪtʃ/ (**enriches, enriching, enriched**) V-T To **enrich** something means to improve its quality, usually by adding something to it. *enriquecer* ❑ *It is important to enrich the soil before planting. Es importante enriquecer la tierra antes de sembrar.* ● **en|rich|ment** N-UNCOUNT *enriquecimiento* ❑ *...spiritual enrichment. ...enriquecimiento espiritual.*

**en|roll** /ɪnroʊl/ (**enrolls, enrolling, enrolled**) V-T/V-I If you **enroll** or **are enrolled** at an institution or in a class, you officially join it. *inscribir(se)* ❑ *Cherny was enrolled at the University in 1945. Cherny estuvo inscrito en la universidad en 1945.* ❑ *Her mother enrolled her in acting classes. Su madre la inscribió en clases de actuación.* ● **en|roll|ment** N-UNCOUNT *inscripción* ❑ *A fee is payable at enrollment. Se paga una cuota al momento de la inscripción.*

**en route** /ɒn rut/ → see **route**

**en|sem|ble** /ɑnsɑmbᵊl/ (**ensembles**) N-COUNT An **ensemble** is a group of musicians, actors, or dancers who regularly perform together. *conjunto, ensamble*

**en|sure** /ɪnʃʊər/ (**ensures, ensuring, ensured**) V-T To **ensure** something, or to **ensure that** something happens, means to make certain that it happens. *asegurar(se)* [FORMAL] ❑ *We must ensure that all patients have access to high quality care. Debemos asegurarnos de que todos los pacientes tengan acceso a atención de alta calidad.*

**Usage** **ensure** and **insure**

*Ensure* and *insure* both mean "to make certain." *Automobile inspections ensure that a car is safe to drive. Insure* can also mean "to protect against loss." *Drivers should insure their cars against theft.*

**en|ter** /ɛntər/ (**enters, entering, entered**) **1** V-T/V-I When you **enter** a place such as a room or building, you go into it or come into it. *entrar, entrar en, entrar a* [FORMAL] ❑ *He entered the room and stood near the door. Entró al salón y se paró cerca de la puerta.* ❑ *When Spinks entered they all turned to look at him. Cuando Spinks entró, todos voltearon a verlo.* **2** V-T If you **enter** an organization or institution, you start to work there or become a member of it. *ingresar, entrar* ❑ *He entered the firm as a junior assistant. Entró a la empresa como asistente junior.* **3** V-T If someone or something **enters** a particular situation or period of time, they start to be in it or part of it. *entrar a, llevar* ❑ *The war has entered its second month. La guerra lleva dos meses.* **4** V-T If you **enter** a competition, race, or examination, you officially state that you will compete or take part in it. *entrar, inscribirse* ❑ *I'm planning to enter some races. Estoy pensando en inscribirme en varias carreras.* ❑ *His wife entered him for the championship. Su esposa lo inscribió para el campeonato.* **5** V-T If you **enter** something in a book or computer, you write or type it in. *introducir, registrar* ❑ *When a baby is born, they enter that baby's name into the computer. Cuando nace un bebé, registran su nombre en la computadora.*

▸ **enter into** PHR-VERB If you **enter into** something such as an agreement, discussion, or relationship, you become involved in it. *participar, establecer, iniciar* [FORMAL] ❑ *I have not entered into any agreements with them. No he participado en ningún convenio con ellos.* ❑ *The strike was cancelled when the nurses entered into talks with the government. La huelga se conjuró cuando las enfermeras iniciaron pláticas con el gobierno.*

**en|ter|prise** /ɛntərpraɪz/ (**enterprises**) **1** N-COUNT An **enterprise** is a company or business. *empresa* [BUSINESS] ❑ *There are plenty of small industrial enterprises. Hay muchas empresas industriales pequeñas.* **2** N-COUNT An **enterprise** is something new, difficult, or important that you do or try to do. *empresa* ❑ *Horse breeding is indeed a risky enterprise. La cría de caballos es una empresa realmente riesgosa.* **3** N-UNCOUNT **Enterprise** is the ability and willingness to try out new ways of doing things, especially in order to make money. *empresa, proyecto, iniciativa* ❑ *...the spirit of enterprise. ...el espíritu de empresa.* ● **en|ter|pris|ing** ADJ *emprendedor* ❑ *...an enterprising young man. ...un joven emprendedor.*

**en|ter|tain** /ɛntərteɪn/ (**entertains, entertaining, entertained**) **1** V-T If you **entertain** people, you do something that amuses or interests them. *entretener, divertir, agasajar* ❑ *They were entertained by singers and dancers. Los entretuvieron con cantantes y bailarines.* ● **en|ter|tain|ing** ADJ *entretenido, ameno, divertido* ❑ *The sport needs to become more entertaining. El deporte tiene que ser más ameno.* **2** V-T/V-I If you **entertain** guests, you give them food and hospitality. *agasajar, tener invitados, invitar* ❑ *I don't like to entertain guests anymore. Ya no me gusta tener invitados.* ❑ *He loves to entertain. Le encanta invitar.* ● **en|ter|tain|ing** N-UNCOUNT *recibir invitados, invitar, divertirse* ❑ *...a cozy area for entertaining and relaxing. ...un área acogedora para divertirse y relajarse.* **3** V-T If you **entertain** an idea or suggestion, you consider it. *contemplar, considerar* [FORMAL] ❑ *They refused to entertain the idea. Se negaron a considerar la idea.*

**en|ter|tain|er** /ɛntərteɪnər/ (**entertainers**) N-COUNT An **entertainer** is a person whose job is to entertain audiences, for example, by telling jokes, singing, or dancing. *artista, animador o animadora* ❑ *Some people called him the greatest entertainer of the twentieth century. Algunos decían que era el más grande artista del siglo veinte.*

**en|ter|tain|ment** /ɛntərteɪnmənt/ (**entertainments**) N-VAR **Entertainment** consists of performances of plays and

movies, and activities such as reading and watching television, that give people pleasure. *entretenimiento, espectáculo* ❑ *...celebrities from the world of entertainment. ...celebridades del mundo del espectáculo.*
→ see **radio**

**en|thu|si|asm** /ɪnθuziæzəm/ (**enthusiasms**) **1** N-VAR **Enthusiasm** is great eagerness to be involved in a particular activity that you like and enjoy or that you think is important. *entusiasmo* ❑ *Their skill and enthusiasm has gotten them on the team. Su habilidad y entusiasmo los llevaron al equipo.* **2** N-COUNT An **enthusiasm** is an activity or subject that interests you very much and that you spend a lot of time on. *gusto* ❑ *Find out about his enthusiasms and future plans. Averigua sus gustos y sus planes futuros.*

| **Thesaurus** | *enthusiasm* | Ver también: |
|---|---|---|
| N. | eagerness, energy, excitement, passion, zest; (*ant.*) apathy, indifference **1** | |

**en|thu|si|ast** /ɪnθuziæst/ (**enthusiasts**) N-COUNT An **enthusiast** is a person who is very interested in a particular activity or subject and who spends a lot of time on it. *entusiasta, aficionado o aficionada* ❑ *He is a great sports enthusiast. Es un gran entusiasta de los deportes.*

**en|thu|si|as|tic** /ɪnθuziæstɪk/ ADJ If you are **enthusiastic about** something, you show how much you like or enjoy it by the way that you behave and talk. *entusiasta, entusiasmado* ❑ *Tom was very enthusiastic about the place. Tom estaba muy entusiasmado con el lugar.* • **en|thu|si|as|ti|cal|ly** /ɪnθuziæstɪkli/ ADV *con entusiasmo* ❑ *The announcement was greeted enthusiastically. El anuncio fue recibido con entusiasmo.*

**en|tire** /ɪntaɪər/ ADJ You use **entire** when you want to emphasize that you are referring to the whole of something, for example, the whole of a place, time, or population. *todo, entero* ❑ *He spent his entire life in China. Pasó toda su vida en China.* ❑ *There are only 60 swimming pools in the entire country. Sólo hay 60 albercas en todo el país.*

| **Thesaurus** | *entire* | Ver también: |
|---|---|---|
| ADJ. | absolute, complete, total, whole; (*ant.*) incomplete, limited, partial | |

**en|tire|ly** /ɪntaɪərli/ ADV **Entirely** means completely and not just partly. *totalmente, completamente* ❑ *...an entirely new approach. ...un enfoque enteramente nuevo.* ❑ *I agree entirely. Estoy totalmente de acuerdo.*

**en|ti|tle** /ɪntaɪtᵊl/ (**entitles, entitling, entitled**) **1** V-T If you **are entitled to** something, you have the right to have it or do it. *tener derecho, dar derecho* ❑ *A student card will entitle you to discounts at a variety of local clubs. Una credencial de estudiante le dará derecho a descuentos en varios clubes de la localidad.* ❑ *They are entitled to first class travel. Tienen derecho a viajar en primera clase.* • **en|ti|tle|ment** N-VAR (**entitlements**) *derecho a* [FORMAL] ❑ *They lose their entitlement to welfare when they start work. Perdieron su derecho a las prestaciones sociales cuando empezaron a trabajar.* **2** V-T You say that a book, movie, or painting **is entitled** a particular thing when you are mentioning its title. *titulado, intitulado* ❑ *...a performance entitled "United States." ...una representación titulada "United States".*

**en|tity** /ɛntɪti/ (**entities**) N-COUNT An **entity** is something that exists separately from other things and has a clear identity of its own. *entidad* [FORMAL] ❑ *The earth is a living entity. La tierra es una entidad viva.*

> **entrance**
> ❶ NOUN USES
> ❷ VERB USE

❶ **en|trance** /ɛntrəns/ (**entrances**) **1** N-COUNT The **entrance to** a place is the way into it, for example, a door or gate. *entrada* ❑ *Beside the entrance to the church, turn right. Date vuelta a la derecha junto a la entrada de la iglesia.* ❑ *He came out of a side entrance. Salió por una puerta lateral.* **2** N-COUNT Someone's **entrance** is their arrival in a room. *entrada, llegada* ❑ *She noticed her father's entrance. Se dio cuenta de la llegada de su padre.* **3** N-UNCOUNT If you gain **entrance to** a particular place, profession, or institution, you are allowed to go into it or accepted as a member of it. *ingreso* ❑ *Many students fail to gain entrance to the university of their choice. Muchos estudiantes no logran su ingreso a la universidad de su preferencia.*

| **Thesaurus** | *entrance* | Ver también: |
|---|---|---|
| N. | doorway, entry; (*ant.*) exit ❶ **1**<br>appearance, approach, debut ❶ **2** | |

❷ **en|trance** /ɪntræns/ (**entrances, entrancing, entranced**) V-T If something or someone **entrances** you, they cause you to feel delight and wonder. *fascinar* ❑ *He entranced me because he has a lovely voice. Me fascinó por su maravillosa voz.* • **en|tranced** ADJ *fascinado* ❑ *For the next three hours we sat entranced. Las siguientes tres horas las pasamos sentados, fascinados.*

**en|tre|pre|neur** /ɒntrəprənɜr, -nʊər/ (**entrepreneurs**) N-COUNT An **entrepreneur** is a person who sets up businesses and business deals. *empresario o empresaria* [BUSINESS] • **en|tre|pre|neur|ial** /ɒntrəprənɜriəl, -nʊər-/ ADJ *empresarial, emprendedor* ❑ *...her entrepreneurial husband. ...su emprendedor marido.*

**en|try** /ɛntri/ (**entries**) **1** N-UNCOUNT If you gain **entry to** a particular place, you are able to go in. *entrada, acceso* ❑ *No entry after 11 pm. Prohibida la entrada después de las 11 pm.* ❑ *Entry to the museum is free. El acceso al museo es gratis.* PHRASE • **No Entry** is used on signs to indicate that you are not allowed to go into a particular area or go through a particular door or gate. *Prohibida la entrada.* **2** N-UNCOUNT Someone's **entry into** a particular society or group is their joining of it. *entrada, ingreso* ❑ *...China's entry into the World Trade Organization. ...el ingreso de China a la Organización Mundial de Comercio.* **3** N-COUNT An **entry** in a diary or other book or in a computer file is a short piece of writing in it. *entrada, anotación* ❑ *...Violet's diary entry for April 20, 1917. ...la entrada del 20 de abril de 1917 en el diario de Violeta.* **4** N-COUNT An **entry for** a competition is something that you complete in order to take part, for example the answers to a

set of questions. participante ❑ *The closing date for entries is December 31.* *La fecha límite para la inscripción de participantes es el 31 de diciembre.* **5** N-COUNT The **entry to** a place is the way into it, for example a door or gate. entrada ❑ *The entry was blocked.* *La entrada estaba bloqueada.*
→ see **blog**

**en|vel|op** /ɪnvɛləp/ (**envelops, enveloping, enveloped**) V-T If one thing **envelops** another, it covers or surrounds it completely. envolver, rodear ❑ *The smell of the forest enveloped us.* *Nos envolvía el aroma del bosque.*

E

**en|velope** /ɛnvəloʊp, ɒn-/ (**envelopes**) N-COUNT An **envelope** is the rectangular paper cover in which you send a letter to someone through the mail. sobre
→ see **office**

**en|vi|ous** /ɛnviəs/ ADJ If you are **envious of** someone, you want something that they have. envidioso ❑ *I'm not envious of your success.* *No me da envidia tu éxito.* ● **en|vi|ous|ly** ADV envidiosamente, con envidia ❑ *People talked enviously about his good luck.* *La gente hablaba con envidia de su buena suerte.*

**en|vi|ron|ment** /ɪnvaɪrənmənt, -vaɪərn-/ (**environments**) **1** N-VAR Someone's **environment** is their surroundings, especially the conditions in which they grow up, live, or work. ambiente, entorno ❑ *Students in our schools are taught in a safe, secure environment.* *En nuestras escuelas, los estudiantes aprenden en un ambiente seguro y protegido.* **2** N-SING **The environment** is the natural world of land, sea, air, plants, and animals. medio ambiente, ambiente ❑ *...persuading people to respect the environment.* *...convenciendo a la gente de que respete el medio ambiente.* ● **en|vi|ron|men|tal** /ɪnvaɪrənmɛntᵊl, -vaɪərn-/ ADJ ambiental, ambientalista, ecologista ❑ *Environmental groups plan to hold public protests during the conference.* *Grupos ecologistas piensan protestar públicamente durante la conferencia.* ● **en|vi|ron|men|tal|ly** ADV ambientalmente, ecológicamente ❑ *...the high price of environmentally friendly goods.* *...el alto precio de los productos inocuos ecológicamente.*
→ see **amphibian, dump, habitat, pollution**

**Word Partnership** Usar *environment* con:

| | |
|---|---|
| ADJ. | **hostile** environment, **safe** environment, **supportive** environment, **unhealthy** environment **1** **natural** environment **2** |
| V. | **damage the** environment, **protect the** environment **2** |

**en|vi|ron|men|tal|ist** /ɪnvaɪrənmɛntəlɪst, -vaɪərn-/ (**environmentalists**) N-COUNT An **environmentalist** is a person who is concerned with protecting and preserving the natural environment. ecologista, ambientalista

**en|vis|age** /ɪnvɪzɪdʒ/ (**envisages, envisaging, envisaged**) V-T If you **envisage** something, you imagine that it is true, real, or likely to happen. pensar, considerar, imaginar ❑ *I don't envisage spending my whole life in this job.* *No pienso pasar toda mi vida en este trabajo.*

**en|vi|sion** /ɪnvɪʒᵊn/ (**envisions, envisioning, envisioned**) V-T If you **envision** something, you envisage it. imaginar(se) ❑ *We can envision a better future.* *Podemos imaginarnos un mejor futuro.*

**en|voy** /ɛnvɔɪ, ɒn-/ (**envoys**) **1** N-COUNT An **envoy** is someone who is sent as a representative from one government or political group to another. enviado ❑ *A U.S. envoy is expected in the region this month.* *Se espera que un enviado de los EE.UU. llegue a la región este mes.* **2** N-COUNT An **envoy** is a diplomat in an embassy who is immediately below the ambassador in rank. enviado plenipotenciario o enviada plenipotenciaria

**envy** /ɛnvi/ (**envies, envying, envied**) V-T If you **envy** someone, you wish that you had the same things or qualities that they have. envidiar ❑ *I don't envy young people.* *No envidio a los jóvenes.* ● **Envy** is also a noun. envidia ❑ *...his feelings of envy towards his mother.* *...la envidia que sentía por su madre.*

**en|zyme** /ɛnzaɪm/ (**enzymes**) N-COUNT An **enzyme** is a chemical substance found in living creatures that produces changes in other substances without being changed itself. enzima [TECHNICAL]

**epic** /ɛpɪk/ (**epics**) **1** N-COUNT An **epic** is a long book, poem, or movie whose story extends over a long period of time or tells of great events. epopeya ❑ *...Mel Gibson's historical epic "Braveheart."* *..."Corazón Valiente", la epopeya histórica de Mel Gibson.* ● **Epic** is also an adjective. épico ❑ *...epic narrative poems.* *...poemas narrativos épicos* **2** ADJ Something that is **epic** is very impressive or ambitious. épico, heroico, legendario ❑ *...Columbus's epic voyage of discovery.* *...el legendario viaje de descubrimientos de Colón.*
→ see **hero**

**epi|cen|ter** /ɛpɪsɛntər/ (**epicenters**) N-COUNT The **epicenter** of an earthquake is the place on the earth's surface directly above the point where it starts, and is the place where it is felt most strongly. epicentro
→ see **earthquake**

**epic thea|ter** N-UNCOUNT **Epic theater** is a style of theater that uses non-realistic devices such as songs and captions to illustrate social or political ideas. teatro épico

**epi|dem|ic** /ɛpɪdɛmɪk/ (**epidemics**) N-COUNT If there is an **epidemic of** a particular disease somewhere, it affects a very large number of people there and spreads quickly to other areas. epidemia ❑ *...a flu epidemic.* *...una epidemia de gripe.*
→ see **illness**

**epi|der|mis** /ɛpɪdɜrmɪs/ N-SING Your **epidermis** is the thin, protective, outer layer of your skin. epidermis [TECHNICAL]

**epi|di|dy|mis** /ɛpɪdɪdəmɪs/ (**epididymes**) N-COUNT The **epididymis** is a long, narrow tube behind the testicles of male animals, where sperm is stored. epidídimo [TECHNICAL]

**epi|sode** /ɛpɪsoʊd/ (**episodes**) **1** N-COUNT You can refer to an event or a short period of time as an **episode** if you want to suggest that it is important or unusual, or has some particular quality. episodio ❑ *This episode is deeply embarrassing for Washington.* *Este episodio es profundamente penoso para Washington.* **2** N-COUNT An **episode** is one of the separate parts of a story broadcast on television or radio, or published in a magazine. episodio, capítulo ❑ *The*

*final episode will be shown next Sunday.* El próximo domingo pasarán el último capítulo.
→ see **animation**

**epi|thelial tis|sue** /ɛpɪθi̲liəl tɪʃu/ (**epithelial tissues**) N-VAR **Epithelial tissue** is a layer of cells in animals that covers the skin and other surfaces of the body. tejido epitelial [TECHNICAL]

**equal** /i̲kwəl/ (**equals, equaling, equaled**) **1** ADJ If two things are **equal** or if one thing is **equal to** another, they are the same in size, number, or value. igual, mismo ❑ *Research and teaching are of equal importance.* La investigación y la enseñanza tienen la misma importancia. ❑ *...equal numbers of men and women.* ...mismo número de hombres y mujeres. • **equal|ly** ADV igualmente ❑ *All these techniques are equally effective.* Todas estas técnicas son igualmente efectivas ❑ *Eat three small meals a day, at equally spaced intervals.* Ingiera tres comidas pequeñas al día a intervalos regulares. **2** ADJ If different groups of people are **equal** or are given **equal** treatment, they have the same rights or are treated in the same way. igual, mismo ❑ *We demand equal rights at work.* Exigimos los mismos derechos laborales. ❑ *They have agreed to meet on equal terms.* Aceptaron reunirse en igualdad de condiciones. • **equal|ly** ADV igualmente, de la misma manera ❑ *The court system is supposed to treat everyone equally.* Se supone que el sistema judicial debe tratar de la misma manera a todos. **3** N-COUNT Someone who is your **equal** has the same ability, status, or rights as you have. igual ❑ *It was a marriage of equals.* Fue un matrimonio de iguales. **4** ADJ If someone is **equal to** a particular job or situation, they have the necessary ability, strength, or courage to deal successfully with it. capaz de, adecuado para, a la altura de ❑ *She is equal to any situation in which she finds herself.* Está a la altura de cualquier circunstancia en la que se encuentre. **5** V-LINK If something **equals** a particular number or amount, it is the same as that amount or the equivalent of that amount. ser igual a ❑ *9 minus 7 equals 2.* 9 menos 7 es igual a 2. **6** V-T To **equal** something or someone means to be as good or as great as them. ser igual a, igualar ❑ *The victory equaled the team's best in history.* El equipo igualó el mayor triunfo de toda su historia.

| Word Partnership | Usar *equal* con: |
|---|---|
| N. | equal **importance**, equal **number**, equal **parts**, equal **pay**, equal **share** **1** equal **rights**, equal **treatment** **2** |

**equali|ty** /ɪkwɒ̲lɪti/ N-UNCOUNT **Equality** is the same status, rights, and responsibilities for all the members of a society, group, or family. igualdad ❑ *...equality of the sexes.* ...igualdad de género.

**equal|ly** /i̲kwəli/ **1** ADV **Equally** is used to introduce another comment on the same topic, that balances or contrasts with the previous comment. igualmente, de igual modo, de todas maneras, aun así ❑ *I think it is a serious issue, but equally I don't think it is a matter of life and death.* Creo que es un asunto importante, pero de todas maneras no creo que sea de vida o muerte. **2** → see also **equal**

**equal op|por|tu|nity** N-UNCOUNT **Equal opportunity** refers to the policy of giving everyone the same opportunities for employment, pay, and promotion, without discriminating against particular groups. oportunidades iguales [BUSINESS] ❑ *...equal opportunity for women.* ...oportunidades iguales para las mujeres.

**equal op|por|tu|nity em|ploy|er** (**equal opportunity employers**) N-COUNT An **equal opportunity employer** is an employer who gives people the same opportunities for employment, pay, and promotion, without discrimination against anyone. empresa que ofrece las mismas oportunidades [BUSINESS]

**equate** /ɪkwe̲ɪt/ (**equates, equating, equated**) V-T/V-I If you **equate** one thing **with** another, or if you say that one thing **equates with** another, you believe that they are strongly connected. equivaler, equiparar, corresponder, identificar ❑ *I equate being thin with ill health.* Para mí, estar delgado equivale a tener mala salud. ❑ *The authors equate mind and brain.* Los autores identifican mente con cerebro.

**equa|tion** /ɪkwe̲ɪʒᵊn/ (**equations**) N-COUNT An **equation** is a mathematical statement saying that two amounts or values are the same, for example 6x4=24. ecuación

**equa|tor** /ɪkwe̲ɪtər/ N-SING **The equator** is an imaginary line around the middle of the earth at an equal distance from the North Pole and the South Pole. ecuador

**equi|lat|eral** /i̲kwɪlæ̲tərəl/ ADJ A shape or figure that is **equilateral** has sides that are all the same length. equilátero [TECHNICAL] ❑ *...an equilateral triangle.* ...un triángulo equilátero.
→ see **shape**

**equip** /ɪkwɪ̲p/ (**equips, equipping, equipped**) **1** V-T If you **equip** a person or thing **with** something, you give them the tools or equipment that are needed. equipar, preparar ❑ *Seattle police have equipped 16 cars with cameras since February.* Desde febrero, la policía de Seattle equipó 16 autos con cámaras. ❑ *Owners of restaurants have to equip them to admit disabled people.* Los propietarios de restaurantes tienen que prepararlos para recibir a discapacitados. **2** V-T If something **equips** you **for** a particular task or experience, it gives you the skills and attitudes you need for it, especially by educating you in a particular way. preparar ❑ *These skills will equip you for the future.* Estas habilidades te prepararán para el futuro.

**equip|ment** /ɪkwɪ̲pmənt/ N-UNCOUNT **Equipment** consists of the things that are used for a particular purpose, such as a hobby or job. equipo ❑ *...computers and electronic equipment.* ...computadoras y equipo electrónico.

| Thesaurus | *equipment* Ver también: |
|---|---|
| N. | accessories, facilities, gear, machinery, supplies; (*ant.*) tools, utensils |

**equiva|lent** /ɪkwɪ̲vələnt/ (**equivalents**) **1** N-SING If one amount or value is **the equivalent of** another, they are the same. equivalente ❑ *Mr. Li's pay is the equivalent of about $80 a month.* El pago del Sr. Li es el equivalente de unos 80 dólares al mes. • **Equivalent** is also an adjective. equivalente ❑ *If you don't have zucchini, you can use an equivalent amount of eggplant.* Si no tienes calabacitas, puedes utilizar una cantidad equivalente de berenjena. **2** N-COUNT The

e

equivalent of someone or something is a person or thing that has the same function in a different place, time, or system. *equivalente* ❑ *...the Red Cross, and its equivalent in Muslim countries, the Red Crescent. ...la Cruz Roja, y su equivalente en los países musulmanes, la Media Luna Roja.* ● **Equivalent** is also an adjective. *equivalente* ❑ *...a decrease of 10% compared with the equivalent period in 1991. ...una reducción del 10% respecto del periodo equivalente de 1991.*

**Thesaurus** *equivalent* Ver también:
ADJ. equal, similar; (*ant.*) different 1
N. counterpart, match, parallel, peer, substitute 2

E

**er** /ɜr/ **Er** is used in writing to represent the sound that people make when they hesitate, especially while they decide what to say next. *mmm, este* ❑ *I'm just, er, mentioning the opportunity as I see it. Yo, este, menciono la oportunidad como la veo.*

**ER** /i ɑr/ (**ERs**) N-COUNT The **ER** is the part of a hospital where people who have severe injuries or sudden illnesses are taken for emergency treatment. **ER** is an abbreviation for **emergency room.** *sala de urgencias, urgencias* ❑ *People come to the ER thinking they're having heart attacks. Hay gente que acude a urgencias creyendo que sufre un ataque cardiaco.*

**era** /ɪərə/ (**eras**) N-COUNT An **era** is a period of time that is considered as a single unit because it has a particular feature. *era, época, periodo* ❑ *...the nuclear era. ...la era nuclear.* ❑ *...the Reagan-Bush era. ...el periodo Reagan-Bush.*

**eradi|cate** /ɪrædɪkeɪt/ (**eradicates, eradicating, eradicated**) V-T To **eradicate** something means to get rid of it completely. *erradicar* [FORMAL] ❑ *We are trying to eradicate illnesses such as malaria. Estamos tratando de erradicar enfermedades como la malaria.* ● **eradi|ca|tion** /ɪrædɪkeɪʃᵊn/ N-UNCOUNT *erradicación* ❑ *...the eradication of corruption. ...la erradicación de la corrupción.*

**erase** /ɪreɪs/ (**erases, erasing, erased**) 1 V-T If you **erase** a thought or feeling, you destroy it completely so that you can no longer remember something or no longer feel a particular emotion. *borrar* ❑ *They are desperate to erase the memory of that last defeat. Están desesperados por borrar el recuerdo de la última derrota.* 2 V-T If you **erase** sound that has been recorded on a tape or information which has been stored in a computer, you completely remove or destroy it. *borrar* ❑ *The names were accidentally erased from computer files. Los nombres se borraron accidentalmente de los archivos de la computadora.* 3 V-T If you **erase** something such as writing or a mark, you remove it, usually by rubbing it. *borrar* ❑ *She erased his name from her address book. Borró el nombre de él de su libreta de direcciones.*
→ see **draw**

**eras|er** /ɪreɪsər/ (**erasers**) N-COUNT An **eraser** is an object, usually a piece of rubber or plastic, which is used for removing something that has been written using a pencil or a pen. *borrador, goma, goma de borrar* ❑ *...a large, pink eraser. ...una goma grande, de color rosa.*

**erect** /ɪrɛkt/ (**erects, erecting, erected**) 1 V-T If people **erect** something such as a building, bridge, or barrier, they build it or create it. *levantar, erigir, construir* [FORMAL] ❑ *The building was erected in 1900. El edificio fue construido en 1900.* ● **erec|tion** N-UNCOUNT *construcción, levantamiento* ❑ *...the erection of temporary fences. ...el levantamiento de barreras temporales.* 2 ADJ People or things that are **erect** are straight and upright. *erecto, derecho, erguido* ❑ *Stand erect, with your arms hanging naturally. Párate derecho, con los brazos en posición natural.*

**erode** /ɪroʊd/ (**erodes, eroding, eroded**) 1 V-T/V-I If rock or soil **erodes** or **is eroded** by the weather, sea, or wind, it cracks and breaks so that it is gradually destroyed. *erosionar(se)* ❑ *The storm washed away buildings and eroded beaches. La tormenta arrasó con los edificios y erosionó las playas.* ● **ero|sion** /ɪroʊʒᵊn/ N-UNCOUNT *erosión* ❑ *...erosion of the river valleys. ...erosión de los valles fluviales.* 2 V-T/V-I If something **erodes** or **is eroded,** it gradually weakens or loses value. *afectar, reducir* ❑ *Competition has eroded profits. La competencia ha reducido las utilidades.* ● **ero|sion** N-UNCOUNT *deterioro* ❑ *...the erosion of moral standards. ...el deterioro de las normas morales.*
→ see Word Web: **erosion**
→ see **beach, rock**

**erot|ic** /ɪrɒtɪk/ ADJ If you describe something as **erotic,** you mean that it involves sexual feelings or arouses sexual desire. *erótico* ❑ *It wasn't an erotic experience at all. No fue para nada una experiencia erótica.*

**err** /ɜr, ɛr/ (**errs, erring, erred**) 1 V-I If you **err,** you make a mistake. *errar, equivocarse, cometer un error* [FORMAL] ❑ *The firm erred in its estimates. La empresa se equivocó en sus estimados.* 2 PHRASE If you **err on the side of** caution, for example, you decide to act in a cautious way, rather than take risks. *pecar de, exagerar* ❑ *They may be wise to err on the side of caution. No está de más exagerar en cuanto a la precaución.*

**Word Web** erosion

There are two main causes of **soil erosion—water** and **wind. Rainfall,** especially heavy **thunderstorms,** breaks down **dirt.** Small particles of **earth, sand,** and **silt** are then carried away by the water. The run off may form **gullies** on hillsides. Heavy rain sometimes even causes a large, flat soil surface to wash away all at once. This is called sheet erosion. When the soil contains too much water, **mudslides** occur. Strong **currents** of **air** cause wind erosion. There are two major ways to prevent this damage. Permanent **vegetation** anchors the soil and windbreaks reduce the force of the wind.

**er|rand** /ɛrənd/ (**errands**) N-COUNT An **errand** is a short trip that you make in order to do a job, for example, when you go to a store to buy something. mandado, recado ❑ *She went off on some errand.* *Salió a unos mandados.*

**er|ro|neous** /ɪroʊniəs/ ADJ Beliefs, opinions, or methods that are **erroneous** are incorrect. erróneo, equivocado ❑ *They reached some erroneous conclusions.* *Llegaron a conclusiones equivocadas.* • **er|ro|neous|ly** ADV erróneamente, equivocadamente ❑ *It was erroneously reported that Armstrong refused to give evidence.* *Se informó erróneamente de que Armstrong se negó a presentar pruebas.*

**er|ror** /ɛrər/ (**errors**) N-VAR An **error** is a mistake. error, equivocación ❑ *There was a mathematical error in the calculations.* *Había un error matemático en los cálculos.* ❑ *The plane was shot down in error.* *Derribaron el avión por equivocación.*

**Word Partnership** Usar *error* con:

| | |
|---|---|
| ADJ. | **clerical** error, **common** error, **fatal** error, **human** error |
| V. | **commit an** error, **correct an** error, **make an** error |

**Word Link** *rupt ≈ breaking : disrupt, erupt, interrupt*

**erupt** /ɪrʌpt/ (**erupts, erupting, erupted**) **1** V-I When a volcano **erupts,** it throws out a lot of hot, melted rock called lava, as well as ash and steam. hacer erupción ❑ *The volcano erupted in 1980.* *El volcán hizo erupción en 1980.* • **erup|tion** /ɪrʌpʃən/ N-VAR (**eruptions**) erupción ❑ *...the volcanic eruption of Tambora in 1815.* *...la erupción volcánica de Tambora en 1815.* **2** V-I If something such as violence **erupts,** it suddenly begins or gets more intense. estallar ❑ *Heavy fighting erupted there today.* *Hoy estalló la violencia en ese lugar.* ❑ *The neighborhood erupted into riots.* *Estallaron los disturbios en el vecindario.* • **erup|tion** N-COUNT brote ❑ *...this sudden eruption of violence.* *...este repentino brote de violencia.*
→ see **rock, volcano**

**Word Link** *scal, scala ≈ ladder, stairs : escalate, escalator, scale*

**es|ca|late** /ɛskəleɪt/ (**escalates, escalating, escalated**) V-T/V-I If a bad situation **escalates** or if someone or something **escalates** it, it becomes worse. intensificar(se), aumentar, empeorar(se) ❑ *Nobody wants the situation to escalate; everybody wants the nation to return to peace and order.* *Nadie desea que la situación empeore; todos quieren que vuelvan al país el orden y la paz.* ❑ *The protests escalated into five days of rioting.* *Las protestas empeoraron y se convirtieron en cinco días de desmanes.* • **es|ca|la|tion** /ɛskəleɪʃən/ N-VAR (**escalations**) intensificación, escalada ❑ *...the threat of nuclear escalation.* *...la amenaza de una escalada nuclear.*

escalator

**es|ca|la|tor** /ɛskəleɪtər/ (**escalators**) N-COUNT An **escalator** is a moving staircase. escalera eléctrica ❑ *Take the escalator to the third floor.* *Utiliza la escalera eléctrica para ir al tercer piso.*

**Word Link** *cap ≈ seize : captivate, escape, capture*

**es|cape** /ɪskeɪp/ (**escapes, escaping, escaped**) **1** V-I If you **escape from** a place, you succeed in getting away from it. escapar(se), fugarse ❑ *A prisoner has escaped from a jail in northern Texas.* *Un prisionero escapó de una cárcel del norte de Texas.* ❑ *They escaped to the other side of the border.* *Escaparon al otro lado de la frontera.* • **Escape** is also a noun. escape, huida, fuga ❑ *The man made his escape.* *El hombre logró su fuga.* **2** V-T/V-I You can say that you **escape** when you survive something such as an accident. escapar, salvarse ❑ *The two officers were extremely lucky to escape serious injury.* *Los dos oficiales tuvieron mucha suerte de escapar sin lesiones graves.* ❑ *The man's girlfriend managed to escape unhurt.* *La novia del hombre se salvó de salir herida.* • **Escape** is also a noun. escape, fuga ❑ *I had a very narrow escape on the bridge.* *Fue milagroso mi escape en el puente.* **3** N-COUNT If something is an **escape,** it is a way of avoiding difficulties or responsibilities. escape ❑ *For me television is an escape.* *Para mí, la tele es un escape.* **4** V-T If something **escapes** you or **escapes** your attention, you do not know about it, do not remember it, or do not notice it. escaparse ❑ *His name escapes me for the moment.* *En este momento se me escapa su nombre.*

**Thesaurus** *escape* Ver también:

| | |
|---|---|
| V. | break out, flee, run away **1** |
| N. | breakout, flight, getaway **2** |

**Word Partnership** Usar *escape* con:

| | |
|---|---|
| N. | **chance to** escape, escape **from prison** **1** |
| V. | **try to** escape **1** |
| | **manage to** escape **1** **2** |
| | **make an** escape **2** |

**Word Link** *cor ≈ with : accord, correspond, escort*

**es|cort** (**escorts, escorting, escorted**)

The noun is pronounced /ɛskɔrt/. The verb is pronounced /ɪskɔrt/.

**1** V-T If you **escort** someone somewhere, you accompany them there, usually in order to make sure that they go. escoltar, acompañar, llevar ❑ *I escorted him to the door.* *Lo acompañé a la puerta.* **2** N-COUNT An **escort** is a person who travels with someone in order to protect or guard them. escolta, guardaespaldas, guarura ❑ *He arrived with a police escort.* *Llegó con una escolta de la policía.* PHRASE • If someone is taken somewhere **under escort,** they are accompanied by guards, either because they have been arrested or because they need to be protected. escoltado **3** N-COUNT An **escort** is a person who accompanies another person of the opposite sex to a social event. Sometimes people are paid to be escorts. acompañante ❑ *My sister needed an escort for a company dinner.* *Mi hermana necesitaba un acompañante para una cena de la empresa.*

**es|pe|cial|ly** /ɪspɛʃəli/ **1** ADV You use **especially** to emphasize that what you are saying applies more to one person, thing, time, or area than to

e

any others. especialmente, sobre todo ❑ *Millions of wild flowers grow in the valleys, especially in April and May.* *En los valles crecen millones de flores silvestres, especialmente en abril y mayo.* **2** ADV You use **especially** to emphasize a characteristic or quality. especialmente, particularmente ❑ *The brain and the heart are especially sensitive to lack of oxygen.* *El cerebro y el corazón son especialmente sensibles a la falta de oxígeno.*

**Thesaurus** *especially* Ver también:

ADV. exclusively, only, solely **1**
extraordinarily, particularly **2**

E

**es|say** /ɛseɪ/ (**essays**) N-COUNT An **essay** is a short piece of writing on a particular subject. ensayo, composición, trabajo ❑ *We asked Jason to write an essay about his hometown.* *Le pedimos a Jason que escribiera una composición sobre el pueblo en que nació.*

**es|sence** /ɛsᵊns/ (**essences**) N-UNCOUNT The **essence of** something is its basic and most important characteristic that gives it its individual identity. esencia ❑ *The essence of being a customer is having a choice.* *La esencia de ser cliente, es tener opciones.* ● PHRASE You use **in essence** to emphasize that you are talking about the most important or central aspect of an idea, situation, or event. en esencia, esencialmente [FORMAL] ❑ *Local taxes are in essence simple.* *En esencia, los impuestos locales son sencillos.* PHRASE ● If you say that something **is of the essence**, you mean that it is absolutely necessary in order for a particular action to be successful. esencial [FORMAL] ❑ *Speed was of the essence in a project of this type.* *La velocidad era esencial en un proyecto de esas características.*

**es|sen|tial** /ɪsɛnʃᵊl/ (**essentials**) **1** ADJ Something that is **essential** is absolutely necessary. esencial, indispensable ❑ *It was essential to separate crops from the areas used by animals.* *Era indispensable separar los cultivos de las áreas utilizadas por los animales.* ❑ *Play is an essential part of a child's development.* *El juego es parte esencial del desarrollo de los niños.* **2** N-COUNT The **essentials** are the things that are absolutely necessary in a situation. fundamentos, lo esencial, lo básico ❑ *The apartment contained the basic essentials.* *El departamento tenía lo básico.*

**Word Partnership** Usar *essential* con:

N. essential **element**, essential **function**, essential **information**, essential **ingredients**, essential **nutrients**, essential **personnel**, essential **services** **1**

**es|sen|tial|ly** /ɪsɛnʃəli/ **1** ADV You use **essentially** to emphasize a quality that someone or something has, and to say that it is their most important or basic quality. esencialmente, básicamente, en lo esencial [FORMAL] ❑ *He was essentially a simple man.* *Era un hombre sencillo, en lo esencial.* **2** ADV You use **essentially** to indicate that what you are saying is mainly true, although some parts of it are wrong or more complicated than has been stated. esencialmente, en esencia, en lo esencial [FORMAL] ❑ *His analysis proved essentially correct.* *Se demostró que, en lo esencial, su análisis estaba correcto.*

**Word Link** stab ≈ steady : establish, instability, stabilize

**es|tab|lish** /ɪstæblɪʃ/ (**establishes, establishing, established**) **1** V-T If someone **establishes** an organization or system, they create it. establecer, crear, formar ❑ *...the right to establish trade unions.* *...el derecho a formar sindicatos.* ● **es|tab|lish|ment** N-SING establecimiento ❑ *...the establishment of the regional government in 1980.* *...el establecimiento del gobierno regional en 1980.* **2** V-RECIP If you **establish** contact with someone, you start to have contact with them. You can also say that two people, groups, or countries **establish** contact. establecer [FORMAL] ❑ *We have already established contact with the museum.* *Ya establecimos contacto con el museo.* **3** V-T If you **establish that** something is true, you discover facts that show that it is definitely true. establecer, demostrar, definir [FORMAL] ❑ *Medical tests established that she had a heart defect.* *Se demostró mediante pruebas médicas que tenía un defecto cardíaco.* ❑ *We must establish how the money is being spent.* *Debemos definir cómo se gasta el dinero.* ● **es|tab|lished** ADJ comprobado, aceptado ❑ *This is an established medical fact.* *Es un hecho médico comprobado.*

**Word Partnership** Usar *establish* con:

N. establish **control**, establish **independence**, establish **rules** **1**
establish **contact**, establish **relations** **2**
establish ***someone's* identity** **3**

**es|tab|lished** /ɪstæblɪʃt/ ADJ If you use **established** to describe something such as an organization, you mean that it is well known because it has existed for a long time. establecido, de prestigio, de tradición ❑ *...old established companies.* *...empresas con años de prestigio.*

**es|tab|lish|ment** /ɪstæblɪʃmənt/ (**establishments**) **1** N-COUNT An **establishment** is a store, business, or organization occupying a particular building or place. establecimiento [FORMAL] ❑ *...food establishments such as cafeterias, coffee shops, delis, and restaurants.* *...establecimientos relacionados con alimentos, como cafeterías, salchichonerías y restaurantes.* **2** N-SING You refer to the people who have power and influence in the running of a country, society, or organization as **the establishment.** clase dirigente ❑ *Scientists are now part of the establishment.* *Los científicos ahora forman parte de la clase dirigente.* **3** → see also **establish**

**es|tate** /ɪsteɪt/ (**estates**) **1** N-COUNT An **estate** is a large area of land in the country which is owned by a person, family, or organization. propiedad, rancho ❑ *He spent the holidays at the 300-acre estate of his aunt and uncle.* *Pasó las vacaciones en la propiedad de 120 hectáreas de su tío y su tía.* **2** N-COUNT Someone's **estate** is all the money and property that they leave behind when they die. legado [LEGAL] ❑ *His estate was valued at $150,000.* *Valuaron su legado en 150,000 dólares.* **3** → see also **real estate**

**es|teem** /ɪstim/ **1** N-UNCOUNT **Esteem** is admiration and respect. estima, aprecio [FORMAL] ❑ *He is held in high esteem by colleagues.* *Sus colegas lo tienen en gran estima.* **2** → see also **self-esteem**

**es|ti|mate** (**estimates, estimating, estimated**)

The verb is pronounced /ɛstɪmeɪt/. The noun is pronounced /ɛstɪmɪt/.

**1** V-T If you **estimate** a quantity or value, you make an approximate judgment or calculation of it. *estimar, calcular* ❑ *It's difficult to estimate how much money is involved. Es difícil estimar de cuánto dinero estamos hablando.* ❑ *I estimate that the total cost for treatment will go from $9,000 to $12,500. Calculo que el costo total del tratamiento estará entre 9,000 y 12,500 dólares.* • **Estimate** is also a noun. *estimado, estimación, cálculo* ❑ *...the official estimate of the election result. ...el cálculo oficial de los resultados de la elección.* • **es|ti|mat|ed** ADJ *estimado* ❑ *There are an estimated 90,000 foreigners in the country. El número estimado de extranjeros en el país es de 90,000.* **2** N-COUNT An **estimate** is a judgment about a person or situation that you make based on the available evidence. *juicio, valoración, evaluación* ❑ *I was right in my estimate of his capabilities. Mi juicio sobre su capacidad era correcto.*

**Thesaurus** *estimate* Ver también:

V. appraise, gauge, guess, judge; (*ant.*) calculate **1**
N. evaluation, guess **1** **2**
appraisal, valuation **2**

**Word Partnership** Usar *estimate* con:

ADJ. **best** estimate, **conservative** estimate, **original** estimate, **rough** estimate **1**
V. **make an** estimate **1** **2**

**es|ti|va|tion** also **aestivation** /ɛstɪveɪʃᵊn/ N-UNCOUNT **Estivation** is a period during which some animals become inactive because the weather is very hot or dry. *estivación, letargo estival* [TECHNICAL]

**es|tranged** /ɪstreɪndʒd/ ADJ If you are **estranged from** your family or friends, you have quarreled with them and are not communicating with them. *distanciado, separado* [FORMAL] ❑ *...his estranged wife. ...su esposa, de quien está separado.* ❑ *Joanna was estranged from her father. Joanna estaba distanciada de su padre.* • **es|trange|ment** N-UNCOUNT *distanciamiento, alejamiento* ❑ *...years of estrangement between them. ...años de distanciamiento entre ellos.*

**etc.** /ɛt sɛtərə, -sɛtrə/ **etc.** is used at the end of a list to indicate that you have mentioned only some of the items involved and have not given a full list. **etc.** is a written abbreviation for "etcetera." *etc., etcétera* ❑ *She knew all about my schoolwork, my hospital work, etc. Sabía todo acerca de mis estudios, mi trabajo en el hospital, etc.*

**et|cet|era** /ɛtsɛtərə, -sɛtrə/ also **et cetera** → see **etc.**

**eter|nal** /ɪtɜrnᵊl/ ADJ Something that is **eternal** lasts forever. *eterno* ❑ *...the desire for eternal youth. ...el anhelo de la eterna juventud.* • **eter|nal|ly** ADV *eternamente, por siempre* ❑ *She is eternally grateful to her family for their support. Agradecerá eternamente a su familia el apoyo que le brindaron.*

**Word Link** *ics ≈ system, knowledge : economics, electronics, ethics*

**eth|ic** /ɛθɪk/ (**ethics**) **1** N-PLURAL **Ethics** are moral beliefs and rules about right and wrong. *ética* ❑ *Its members are bound by a strict code of ethics. Sus miembros se obligan a un estricto código de ética.* **2** N-SING An **ethic** of a particular kind is an idea or moral belief that influences the behavior, attitudes, and philosophy of a group of people. *ética* ❑ *...the ethic of public service. ...la ética del servicio público.*

**ethi|cal** /ɛθɪkᵊl/ **1** ADJ **Ethical** means relating to beliefs about right and wrong. *ético* ❑ *...the ethical issues surrounding terminally-ill people. ...los aspectos éticos relacionados con los enfermos terminales.* • **ethi|cal|ly** /ɛθɪkli/ ADV *éticamente, desde una perspectica ética, desde un punto de vista ético* ❑ *We can defend ethically everything we do. Todo lo que hacemos es defendible desde un punto de vista ético.* **2** ADJ If you describe something as **ethical,** you mean that it is morally right or morally acceptable. *ético* ❑ *...ethical business practices. ...prácticas comerciales éticas.* • **ethi|cal|ly** ADV *éticamente, con ética* ❑ *Companies should behave ethically. Las empresas deben comportarse éticamente.*

**eth|nic** /ɛθnɪk/ ADJ **Ethnic** means connected with or relating to different racial or cultural groups of people. *étnico* ❑ *...a survey of ethnic minorities. ...un estudio sobre las minorías étnicas.* • **eth|ni|cal|ly** /ɛθnɪkli/ ADV *étnicamente, desde un punto de vista étnico, desde una perspectiva étnica* ❑ *...a young, ethnically mixed audience. ...un público joven, étnicamente heterogéneo.*

**ety|mol|ogy** /ɛtɪmɒlədʒi/ (**etymologies**) **1** N-UNCOUNT **Etymology** is the study of the origins and historical development of words. *etimología* **2** N-COUNT The **etymology** of a particular word is its history. *etimología*

**EU** /i yu/ N-PROPER **The EU** is an organization of European countries that have the same policies on matters such as trade, agriculture, and finance. **EU** is an abbreviation for **European Union.** *UE*

**eu|bac|te|ria** /yubæktɪəriə/ N-PLURAL **Eubacteria** are bacteria that have a rigid cell wall. Compare **archaebacteria.** *eubacteria* [TECHNICAL]

**eu|glena** /yuglinə/ (**euglena**) N-COUNT **Euglena** is a type of single-celled organism that lives mainly in fresh water. *euglena* [TECHNICAL]

**eu|karyot|ic cell** /yukæriɒtɪk sɛl/ (**eukaryotic cells**) N-COUNT **Eukaryotic cells** are cells that have a nucleus, such as the cells in animals and plants. Compare **prokaryotic cell.** *célula eucariota* [TECHNICAL]

**eulo|gize** /yulədʒaɪz/ (**eulogizes, eulogizing, eulogized**) V-T If you **eulogize** someone who has died, you make a speech praising them. *hacer una apología, elogiar* ❑ *Leaders from around the world eulogized the president. Líderes de todo el mundo hicieron apologías del presidente.*

**eulogy** /yulədʒi/ (**eulogies**) N-COUNT A **eulogy** is a speech, usually at a funeral, in which a person who has just died is praised. *apología*

**euphemism** /yufəmɪzəm/ (**euphemisms**) N-COUNT A **euphemism** is a polite word or expression that is used to talk about something unpleasant or embarrassing, for example death or sex. *eufemismo* ❑ *He prefers the word "chubby" as a euphemism for fat. Prefiere usar la palabra "lleno" como un eufemismo para gordo.*

**euro** /yʊəroʊ/ (**euros**) N-COUNT The **euro** is a unit of currency that is used by most member countries of the European Union. *euro*

**Word Link** *an, ian ≈ one of, relating to : Christian, European, pedestrian*

E

**Euro|pean** /yʊərəpiən/ (**Europeans**) **1** ADJ **European** means belonging or relating to, or coming from Europe. *europeo* ❑ *...European countries. ...países europeos.* **2** N-COUNT A **European** is a person who comes from Europe. *europeo o europea*

**Euro|pean Un|ion** N-PROPER **The European Union** is an organization of European countries that have the same policies on matters such as trade, agriculture, and finance. *Unión Europea*

**Word Link** *vac ≈ empty : evacuate, vacant, vacuum*

**evacu|ate** /ɪvækyueɪt/ (**evacuates, evacuating, evacuated**) V-T If people are **evacuated from** a place, or if they **evacuate** a place, they move out of it because it has become dangerous. *evacuar* ❑ *The fire is threatening about sixty homes, and residents have evacuated the area. El fuego amenaza alrededor de sesenta casas y los habitantes han evacuado la zona.* ❑ *Officials ordered the residents to evacuate. Los oficiales les ordenaron a los habitantes que evacuaran.* ● **evacu|ation** /ɪvækyueɪʃən/ N-VAR (**evacuations**) *evacuación* ❑ *An evacuation of the city's four million inhabitants is planned. Se planea una evacuación de los cuatro millones de habitantes de la ciudad.*

**evalu|ate** /ɪvælyueɪt/ (**evaluates, evaluating, evaluated**) V-T If you **evaluate** something or someone, you consider them in order to make a judgment about them, for example about how good or bad they are. *evaluar* ❑ *The situation is difficult to evaluate. La situación es difícil de evaluar.* ● **evalu|ation** /ɪvælyueɪʃən/ N-VAR (**evaluations**) *evaluación* ❑ *...the opinions and evaluations of college supervisors. ...las opiniones y evaluaciones de supervisores en la universidad.*

**evapo|rate** /ɪvæpəreɪt/ (**evaporates, evaporating, evaporated**) V-I When a liquid **evaporates,** it changes into a gas, because its temperature has increased. *evaporar(se)* ❑ *Moisture is drawn to the surface of the fabric so that it evaporates. La humedad es atraída a la superficie de la tela, de donde se evapora.* ● **evapo|ra|tion** /ɪvæpəreɪʃən/ N-UNCOUNT *evaporación* ❑ *...the evaporation of sweat on the skin. ...la evaporación del sudor en la piel.*
→ see **matter, water**

**eve** /iv/ (**eves**) **1** N-COUNT **The eve of a** particular event or occasion is the day before it, or the period of time just before it. *víspera* ❑ *...on the eve of his 27th birthday. ...en la víspera de su vigésimo séptimo cumpleaños.* **2** → see also **Christmas Eve**

**even**
1. DISCOURSE USES
2. ADJECTIVE USES
3. PHRASAL VERB USES

**1 even** /ivən/ **1** ADV You use **even** to suggest that what comes just after or just before it in the sentence is rather surprising. *incluso, inclusive, aun* ❑ *He would call me and text me about 10 times a day, even when I asked him to stop. El me llamaba y me enviaba mensajes como 10 veces al día, incluso cuando le pedí que no lo hiciera más.* ❑ *Rob remains good-natured, even after the death of his wife. Rob se mantiene bondadoso, aun después de la muerte de su esposa.* **2** ADV You use **even** with comparative adjectives and adverbs to emphasize a quality that someone or something has. *todavía, aún* ❑ *On television he made an even stronger impact. En televisión su impacto era todavía más fuerte.* **3** PHRASE You use **even if** or **even though** to indicate that a particular fact does not make the rest of your statement untrue. *aun si, aun cuando* ❑ *Cynthia is not ashamed of what she does, even if she ends up doing something wrong. Cynthia no se avergüenza de lo que hace, aun si termina por hacer algo mal.* **4** PHRASE You use **even so** to introduce a surprising fact that relates to what you have just said. *de todos modos, de cualquier forma, de cualquier modo, aun así* ❑ *The bus was only half full. Even so, a man asked Nina if the seat next to her was taken. El autobús sólo estaba medio lleno. De cualquier modo, un hombre le preguntó a Nina si el asiento al lado de ella estaba disponible.*

**Usage** **even**
*Even* is used for emphasis or to say that something is surprising. *He didn't even try. How can you even think about that?*

**2 even** /ivən/ **1** ADJ An **even** measurement or rate stays at about the same level. *parejo, regular, uniforme* ❑ *How important is it to have an even temperature? ¿Qué tan importante es tener una temperatura uniforme?* ● **even|ly** ADV *regularmente* ❑ *He looked at Ellen, breathing evenly in her sleep. Él miró a Ellen, quien respiraba regularmente mientras dormía.* **2** ADJ An **even** surface is smooth and flat. *parejo, regular, uniforme* ❑ *The table has a glass top which provides an even surface. La mesa tiene una cubierta de vidrio, lo que la provee de una superficie uniforme.* **3** ADJ If there is an **even** distribution or division of something, each person, group, or area involved has an equal amount. *igual* ❑ *Divide the dough into 12 even pieces. Divida la masa en 12 partes iguales.* ● **even|ly** ADV *equitativamente* ❑ *The money was divided evenly. El dinero se repartió equitativamente.* **4** ADJ An **even** contest or competition is equally balanced between the two sides who are taking part. *parejo* ❑ *It was an even game. Era un juego parejo.* ● **even|ly** ADV *equitativamente* ❑ *...two evenly matched candidates. ...dos candidatos enfrentados equitativamente.* **5** ADJ An **even** number can be divided exactly by the number two. *par* **6** PHRASE When a company or a person running a business **breaks even,** they make neither a profit nor a loss. *recuperar los costos* [BUSINESS] ❑ *The airline hopes to break even next year. La aerolínea espera recuperar los costos el año próximo.* **7** to **be on an even keel** → see **keel**

**3 even** /iv^ən/ (**evens, evening, evened**)
▸ **even out** PHR-VERB If something **evens out,** or if you **even** it **out,** the differences between the different parts of it are reduced. *emparejar* ❑ *The power balance has evened out in the government. El balance del poder se ha emparejado en el gobierno.*

**eve|ning** /ivnɪŋ/ (**evenings**) N-VAR The **evening** is the part of each day between the end of the afternoon and the time when you go to bed. *tarde* ❑ *All he did that evening was sit around the house. Todo lo que hizo esa tarde fue estar en su casa sin hacer nada.* ❑ *Supper is from 5:00 to 6:00 in the evening. La cena se sirve de 5 a 6 de la tarde.*
→ see **time**

**event** /ɪvɛnt/ (**events**) **1** N-COUNT An **event** is something that happens. *suceso* ❑ *Yesterday's events took everyone by surprise. Los sucesos de ayer tomaron a todos por sorpresa.* **2** N-COUNT An **event** is a planned and organized occasion. *evento* ❑ *...major sports events. ...eventos deportivos importantes.* **3** PHRASE You use **in the event of, in the event that,** and **in that event** when you are talking about a possible future situation, especially when you are planning what to do if it occurs. *en caso de que* ❑ *The bank has agreed to give an immediate refund in the unlikely event of an error. El banco ha accedido a otorgar devoluciones inmediatas de dinero en el remoto caso de que se produjera un error.*
→ see **graduation, history**

| Thesaurus | *event* | Ver también: |
|---|---|---|
| N. | happening, occasion, occurrence **1** | |

**even|tual** /ɪvɛntʃuəl/ ADJ The **eventual** result of something is what happens at the end of it. *final* ❑ *There are many who believe that civil war will be the eventual outcome. Hay muchos quienes creen que el resultado final será la guerra civil.*

**even|tu|al|ly** /ɪvɛntʃuəli/ **1** ADV **Eventually** means in the end, especially after a lot of delays, problems, or arguments. *finalmente* ❑ *The flight eventually got away six hours late. El vuelo finalmente despegó seis horas tarde.* **2** ADV **Eventually** means at the end of a situation or process or as the final result of it. *con el tiempo, a la larga* ❑ *Eventually your child will leave home. Con el tiempo tu hijo se irá de casa.*

**ever** /ɛvər/

> **Ever** is an adverb that you use to add emphasis in negative sentences, commands, questions, and conditional structures.

**1** ADV **Ever** means at any time. It is used in questions and negative statements. *nunca, jamás, alguna vez* ❑ *I'm not sure I'll ever trust people again. No estoy seguro de que volveré a confiar en la gente alguna vez.* ❑ *Neither of us has ever skied. Ninguno de nosotros ha esquiado jamás.* ❑ *Have you ever seen anything like it? ¿Alguna vez viste algo así?* **2** ADV You use **ever** after comparatives and superlatives to emphasize the degree to which something is true. *Este uso es para dar énfasis y no se traduce o queda traducido con el verbo poder o con nunca o jamás.* ❑ *She is singing better than ever. Está cantando mejor que nunca.* ❑ *Japan is wealthier and more powerful than ever before. Japón es más rico y poderoso que nunca.* **3** PHRASE You say **as ever** in order to indicate that something is not unusual. *como siempre* ❑ *As ever, the meals are mainly fish-based. Como siempre, las comidas son principalmente de pescado.* **4** PHRASE If something has been the case **ever since** a particular time, it has been the case all the time from then until now. *desde que, desde entonces* ❑ *He's been there ever since you left! ¡Ha estado ahí desde que te fuiste!*
**5** → see also **forever** **6** **hardly ever** → see **hardly**

**ever|green** /ɛvərgrin/ (**evergreens**) N-COUNT An **evergreen** is a tree or bush that has green leaves all year long. *de hoja perenne* • **Evergreen** is also an adjective. *siempre verde* ❑ *Plant evergreen shrubs around the end of the month. Plante los arbustos de hoja perenne hacia el final del mes*
→ see **plant**

**every** /ɛvri/ **1** DET You use **every** to indicate that you are referring to all the members of a group or all the parts of something. *cada* ❑ *Every room has a window facing the ocean. Cada cuarto tiene una ventana con vista al mar.* ❑ *Record every purchase you make. Registra cada compra que hagas.* • **Every** is also an adjective. *todo* ❑ *....parents who fulfill his every need. ...padres que cubren todas sus necesidades.*
**2** DET You use **every** in order to say how often something happens or to indicate that something happens at regular intervals. *cada* ❑ *We had to attend meetings every day. Teníamos que asistir a juntas cada día.* ❑ *A burglary occurs every three minutes in the city. Un robo ocurre cada tres minutos en la ciudad.*
**3** DET You can use **every** before some nouns in order to emphasize what you are saying. *todo, mucho* ❑ *He has every intention of staying. Tiene toda la intención de quedarse.* ❑ *There is every chance that you will succeed. Hay mucha oportunidad de que lo logres.*
**4** PHRASE You use **every** in the expressions **every now and then, every now and again, every once in a while,** and **every so often** in order to indicate that something happens occasionally. *de vez en cuando, de vez en vez* ❑ *Stir the mixture every now and then to keep it from separating. Agite la mezcla de vez en cuando para evitar que se separe.* **5** PHRASE If something happens **every other day** or **every second day,** for example, it happens one day, then does not happen the next day, then happens the day after that, and so on. You can also say that something happens **every third week, every fourth year,** and so on. *cada tercer día, cada quince días, un día/semana sí y otro/otra no* ❑ *I went home every other week. Iba a casa cada quince días.* **6** **every bit as good as** → see **bit**

| Usage | every |
|---|---|
| Use *every* with *not, almost,* or *nearly*: *Not every employee received a bonus this year. Nearly every hand in the class went up. Almost every computer these days has a CD-ROM drive.* | |

**every|body** /ɛvribɒdi, -bʌdi/ **Everybody** means the same as **everyone.** *todos*

**every|day** /ɛvrideɪ/ ADJ You use **everyday** to describe something that happens or is used every day, or forms a regular and basic part of your life. *diario* ❑ *In the course of my everyday life, I had very little contact with teenagers. En el transcurso de mi vida diaria tuve poco contacto con adolescentes.*

**Usage** **everyday** and **every day**

*Everyday* and *every day* are often confused. *Everyday* means "ordinary, unsurprising"; *every day* means "something happens daily": *The everyday things are the things that happen every day.*

**every|one** /ɛvriwʌn/

The form **everybody** is also used.

PRON **Everyone** or **everybody** means all the people in a particular group or all people in general. *todos, todo el mundo* ❑ *Everyone on the street was shocked when they heard the news. Todos los que vivían en la calle se asombraron cuando oyeron la noticia.* ❑ *Not everyone thinks that the government is being fair. No todos piensan que el gobierno sea justo.* ❑ *Everyone feels like a failure at times. Todos se sienten un fracaso de vez en cuando.*

**Usage** **everyone** and **every one**

*Everyone* and *every one* are different. *Everyone* refers to all people or to all the people in some group being discussed, while *every one* refers to every single person or thing in some group being discussed: *Luisa offered everyone a copy of her new book; unfortunately, she had only twelve copies, and every one was gone before I could get one.*

**every|place** /ɛvripleɪs/ → see **everywhere**

**every|thing** /ɛvriθɪŋ/ **1** PRON You use **everything** to refer to all the objects, actions, activities, or facts in a situation. *todo* ❑ *Everything else in his life has changed. Todo lo demás en su vida ha cambiado.* ❑ *Najib and I do everything together. Najib y yo hacemos todo juntos.* **2** PRON You use **everything** to refer to a whole situation or to life in general. *todo* ❑ *She says everything is going smoothly. Dice que todo va sin contratiempos.* ❑ *Is everything all right? ¿Está todo bien?*

**every|where** /ɛvriwɛər/ also **everyplace** **1** ADV You use **everywhere** to refer to a whole area or to all the places in a particular area. *en/a/por todas partes, en/a/por todos lados* ❑ *Working people everywhere object to paying taxes. Los trabajadores de todas partes se quejan de tener que pagar impuestos.* ❑ *We went everywhere together. Íbamos a todos lados juntos.* **2** ADV You use **everywhere** to refer to all the places that someone goes to. *a todos lados, a todas partes* ❑ *Mary Jo is accustomed to traveling everywhere in style. Mary Jo está acostumbrada a viajar a todos lados lujosamente.* **3** ADV If you say that someone or something is **everywhere,** you mean that they are present in a place in very large numbers. *por/en todos lados, por/en todas partes* ❑ *There were ambulances and police cars everywhere. Había ambulancias y coches por todos lados.*

**evi|dence** /ɛvɪdəns/ **1** N-UNCOUNT **Evidence** is anything that makes you believe that something is true or has really happened. *prueba* ❑ *There is no evidence that he committed the offenses. No hay evidencia de que haya incurrido en esas faltas.* ❑ *The evidence against him is very strong. La evidencia en su contra es muy sólida.* **2** PHRASE If you **give evidence** in a court of law, you give a statement saying what you know about something. *dar testimonio* ❑ *Scientists will be called to give evidence. Científicos serán llamados a dar sus testimonios.* **3** PHRASE If someone or something **is in evidence,** they are present and can be clearly seen. *ser evidente, ser notorio* ❑ *Few soldiers were in evidence. Pocos soldados eran notorios.*

→ see **experiment, trial**

**Word Partnership** Usar *evidence* con:

ADJ. **circumstantial** evidence, **new** evidence, **physical** evidence, **scientific** evidence **1**
V. **find** evidence, **gather** evidence, **present** evidence, **produce** evidence, evidence **to support** *something* **1**

**evi|dent** /ɛvɪdənt/ ADJ If something is **evident,** you notice it easily and clearly. *evidente* ❑ *His footprints were clearly evident in the heavy dust. Sus pisadas eran evidentes en el polvo.* ❑ *It was evident that she had once been a beauty. Era evidente que ella había tenido gran belleza alguna vez.*

**evi|dent|ly** /ɛvɪdəntli, -dɛnt-/ ADV You use **evidently** to say that something is true, for example, because you have seen evidence of it yourself or because someone has told you it is true. *evidentemente* ❑ *The two Russians evidently knew each other. Los dos rusos evidentemente se conocían.*

**evil** /iːvəl/ (**evils**) **1** N-UNCOUNT **Evil** is used to refer to all the wicked and bad things that happen in the world. *el mal* ❑ *...a conflict between good and evil. Un conflicto entre el bien y el mal.* **2** N-COUNT An **evil** is a very unpleasant or harmful situation or activity. *lo nocivo* ❑ *...the evils of prejudice. ...lo nocivo de los prejuicios.* **3** ADJ If you describe something or someone as **evil,** you mean that you think they are morally very bad and cause harm to people. *malvado* ❑ *...the country's most evil terrorists. ...los terroristas más malvados del país.* ❑ *He condemned slavery as evil. Condenó la esclavitud como una práctica malvada.*

**evoke** /ɪvoʊk/ (**evokes, evoking, evoked**) V-T To **evoke** a particular memory, idea, emotion, or response means to cause it to occur. *evocar* [FORMAL] ❑ *The scene evoked memories of those old movies. La escena evocaba recuerdos de las viejas películas.*

**evo|lu|tion** /ɛvəluʃən, iv-/ (**evolutions**) **1** N-UNCOUNT **Evolution** is a process of gradual change that takes place over many generations, during which species of animals, plants, or insects slowly change some of their physical characteristics. *evolución* ❑ *...the evolution of plants and animals. La evolución de las plantas y animales.* **2** N-VAR **Evolution** is a process of gradual development in a particular situation or thing over a period of time. *desarrollo, evolución* [FORMAL] ❑ *...a crucial period in the evolution of modern physics. ...un periodo crucial en el desarrollo de la física moderna.*

→ see Word Web: **evolution**

→ see **earth**

**evolve** /ɪvɒlv/ (**evolves, evolving, evolved**) **1** V-I When animals or plants **evolve,** they gradually change and develop into different forms. *evolucionar* ❑ *Dinosaurs are believed to have evolved into birds. Se cree que los dinosaurios evolucionaron en pájaros.* ❑ *Corn evolved from a wild grass. El maíz evolucionó de pasto silvestre.* **2** V-T/V-I If something **evolves** or you **evolve** it, it gradually develops over a period of time into something

**Word Web** evolution

The **theory** of **human evolution** states that humans **evolved** from an ape-like ancestor. In 1856 the **fossils** of a **Neanderthal** were found. This was the first time that **scientists** realized that there were earlier forms of humans. **Anthropologists** have found other fossils that show how **hominids** changed over time. One of the earliest ancestors that has been found is called **Australopithecus**. This **species** lived about 4 million years ago in Africa. The most famous specimen of this species is named 'Lucy'. Scientists believe that she was among the first hominids to walk upright. The oldest fossils of **Homo sapiens** date back to approximately 130,000 years ago.

different and usually more advanced. *convertirse en, desarrollar, transformarse en, evolucionar* ❑ *...a tiny airline which eventually evolved into Pakistan International Airlines. ...una pequeña aerolínea que finalmente se convirtió en Aerolíneas Internacionales de Pakistán.* ❑ *Popular music evolved from folk songs. La música popular evolucionó a partir de canciones folclóricas.*
→ see **earth, evolution**

**ex|act** /ɪgzækt/ (**exacts, exacting, exacted**) **1** ADJ **Exact** means correct, accurate, and complete in every way. *exacto* ❑ *I don't remember the exact words. No recuerdo las palabras exactas.* ❑ *The exact number of protest calls has not been revealed. El número exacto de llamadas para protestar no ha sido revelado.* ● **ex|act|ly** ADV *exactamente* ❑ *Both drugs will be exactly the same. Ambas medicinas serán exactamente iguales.* **2** ADJ You use **exact** before a noun to emphasize that you are referring to that particular thing and no other. *exacto* ❑ *...the exact moment when he realized the truth. ...el momento exacto en el que se dio cuenta de la verdad.* ● **ex|act|ly** ADV *exactamente* ❑ *These are exactly the people who do not vote. Esas son exactamente las personas que no votan.* **3** V-T When someone **exacts** something, they demand and obtain it from another person. *arrancar* [FORMAL] ❑ *Already he has exacted a written apology from the chairman. Ya le arrancó una disculpa por escrito al director.* **4** → see also **exactly**

**Thesaurus** *exact* Ver también:

ADJ. accurate, clear, precise, true; (ant.) wrong **1**

**Word Partnership** Usar *exact* con:

N. exact **change**, exact **duplicate**, exact **number**, exact **opposite**, exact **replica**, exact **science**, exact **words** **1**
exact **cause**, exact **location**, exact **moment** **2**
exact **revenge** **3**

**ex|act|ly** /ɪgzæktli/ **1** ADV **Exactly** means precisely, and not just approximately. *exactamente* ❑ *The tower was exactly ten meters in height. La torre tenía exactamente diez metros de altura.* **2** ADV If you say **"Exactly,"** you are agreeing with someone or emphasizing the truth of what they say. If you say **"Not exactly,"** you are telling them politely that they are wrong in part of what they are saying. *exacto* ❑ *Eve nodded. "Exactly." Eva asintió.—Exacto.* **3** ADV You use **not exactly** to indicate that a meaning or situation is slightly different from what people think or expect. *no exactamente* ❑ *He's not exactly homeless, he just hangs out in this park. No es exactamente un vagabundo, simplemente le gusta estar en este parque.* **4** → see also **exact**

**ex|ag|ger|ate** /ɪgzædʒəreɪt/ (**exaggerates, exaggerating, exaggerated**) **1** V-T/V-I If you **exaggerate,** you indicate that something is bigger, worse, or more important than it really is. *exagerar* ❑ *He thinks I'm exaggerating. Piensa que exagero.* ❑ *She sometimes exaggerates the demands of her job. A veces exagera las exigencias de su trabajo.* ● **ex|ag|gera|tion** /ɪgzædʒəreɪʃᵊn/ N-VAR (**exaggerations**) *exageración* ❑ *He was accused of exaggeration. Fue acusado de exagerar.* **2** V-T If something **exaggerates** a situation, quality, or feature, it makes it appear greater, more obvious, or more important than it really is. *exagerar* ❑ *These figures exaggerate the size of the loss. Estas cifras exageran el tamaño de la pérdida.*

**ex|ag|ger|at|ed** /ɪgzædʒəreɪtɪd/ ADJ Something that is **exaggerated** is or seems larger, better, worse, or more important than it actually needs to be. *exagerado* ❑ *Western fears, he insists, are greatly exaggerated. Los miedos de Occidente, insiste, son muy exagerados.*

**exam** /ɪgzæm/ (**exams**) **1** N-COUNT An **exam** is a formal test that you take to show your knowledge of a subject. *examen* ❑ *I don't want to take any more exams. Ya no quiero hacer más exámenes.* **2** N-COUNT If you have a medical **exam,** a doctor looks at your body or does simple tests in order to check how healthy you are. *estudio, análisis* ❑ *These medical exams have shown I am in perfect physical condition. Estos estudios médicos han demostrado que estoy en perfecta condición física.*

**ex|ami|na|tion** /ɪgzæmɪneɪʃᵊn/ (**examinations**) N-COUNT An **examination** is the same as an **exam**. *examen* [FORMAL]
→ see **diagnosis**

**ex|am|ine** /ɪgzæmɪn/ (**examines, examining, examined**) **1** V-T If you **examine** something or someone, you look at them carefully. *examinar* ❑ *He examined her passport. Examinó su pasaporte.* ❑ *A doctor examined her and could find nothing wrong. Un doctor la examinó pero no encontró nada malo.* ● **ex|ami|na|tion** /ɪgzæmɪneɪʃᵊn/ N-VAR (**examinations**) inspección ❑ *The navy is to carry out an examination of the ship.* La marina va a llevar a cabo una inspección del barco. ❑ *The government said the proposals required careful examination.* El gobierno dijo que las propuestas requerían de una inspección minuciosa. **2** V-T If you **are examined,** you are given a formal test in order to show your knowledge of a subject. ser examinado ❑ *...the pressures of being judged and examined by our teachers.* ...la presión de ser juzgado y examinado por nuestros maestros.

E

**Thesaurus** *examine* Ver también:

V. analyze, go over, inspect, investigate, research; (*ant.*) scrutinize **1**

**ex|am|ple** /ɪgzæmpᵊl/ (**examples**) **1** N-COUNT An **example** is something that represents or is typical of a particular group of things. ejemplo ❑ *There are examples of this type of architecture among many different cultures around the world.* Hay ejemplos de este tipo de arquitectura entre muchas culturas diferentes del mundo. ❑ *This story was a perfect example of how men and women communicate differently.* Esta historia es un ejemplo perfecto de cómo los hombres y las mujeres se comunican de forma distinta. **2** N-COUNT If you refer to a person or their behavior as an **example to** other people, you mean that he or she behaves in a good way that other people should copy. ejemplo ❑ *He is an example to the younger boys.* Es un ejemplo para los muchachos más jóvenes. **3** PHRASE You use **for example** to introduce and emphasize something that shows that something is true. por ejemplo ❑ *Take, for example, the simple sentence: "The man climbed up the hill."* Tomemos, por ejemplo, la frase simple: "El hombre escaló el cerro." **4** PHRASE If you **follow** someone's **example,** you copy their behavior, especially because you admire them. seguir el ejemplo ❑ *Following the example set by her father, she has done her duty.* Siguiendo el ejemplo de su padre, ella ha cumplido con su deber. **5** PHRASE If you **set an example,** you encourage or inspire people by your behavior to behave or act in a similar way. poner el ejemplo, sentar un parámetro ❑ *An officer's job is to set an example.* El trabajo de un oficial es poner el ejemplo.

**Thesaurus** *example* Ver también:

N. model, representation, sample **1** ideal, role model, standard **2**

**Word Partnership** Usar *example* con:

ADJ. **classic** example, **good** example, **obvious** example, **perfect** example, **typical** example **1**
V. **give an** example **1** **follow an** example **4**

**Word Link** *ex ≈ away, from, out : exceed, exit, explode*

**ex|ceed** /ɪksid/ (**exceeds, exceeding, exceeded**) **1** V-T If something **exceeds** a particular amount, it is greater than that amount. exceder [FORMAL] ❑ *Its research budget exceeds $700 million a year.* Su presupuesto de investigación excede los 700 millones de dólares al año. **2** V-T If you **exceed** a limit, you go beyond it. exceder [FORMAL] ❑ *He accepts that he was exceeding the speed limit.* Acepta haber excedido el límite de velocidad.

**ex|cel** /ɪksɛl/ (**excels, excelling, excelled**) V-I If someone **excels in** something or **excels at** it, they are very good at doing it. sobresalir, destacar ❑ *Mary excelled at outdoor sports.* Mary sobresalía en los deportes al aire libre. ❑ *Academically he began to excel.* Comenzó a destacarse académicamente.

**Word Link** *ence ≈ state, condition : excellence, intelligence, patience*

**ex|cel|lence** /ɛksələns/ N-UNCOUNT **Excellence** is the quality of being extremely good in some way. excelencia ❑ *...the top award for excellence in journalism.* ...el premio más prestigioso a la excelencia periodística.

**ex|cel|lent** /ɛksələnt/ ADJ Something that is **excellent** is extremely good. excelente ❑ *The recording quality is excellent.* La calidad de la grabación es excelente. ● **ex|cel|lent|ly** ADV excelentemente ❑ *They're both playing excellently.* Ambos están tocando excelentemente.

**ex|cept** /ɪksɛpt/ PREP You use **except** or **except for** to introduce the only thing or person that a statement does not apply to, or a fact that prevents a statement from being completely true. excepto, excepto por ❑ *I wouldn't have accepted anything except a job in New York.* No habría aceptado nada excepto un trabajo en Nueva York. ❑ *He hasn't eaten a thing except for a bit of salad.* No ha comido nada, excepto un poco de ensalada. ● **Except** is also a conjunction. excepto, salvo ❑ *Freddie would tell me nothing about what he was writing, except that it was a play.* Freddie no me decía nada acerca de lo que estaba escribiendo, excepto que se trataba de una obra de teatro.

**Usage** **except** and **besides**

*Except* and *besides* are often confused. *Except* refers to someone or something that is not included: *I've taken all my required courses except psychology. I'm going to take it next term. Besides* means "in addition to." *What courses should I take next term besides psychology?*

**ex|cep|tion** /ɪksɛpʃᵊn/ (**exceptions**) **1** N-COUNT An **exception** is a particular thing, person, or situation that is not included in a general statement. excepción ❑ *Few guitarists can sing as well as they can play; Eddie, however, is an exception.* Pocos guitarristas pueden cantar tan bien como tocan; sin embargo, Eddie es una excepción. ❑ *The law makes no exceptions.* La ley no hace excepciones. **2** PHRASE If you **take exception to** something, you feel offended or annoyed by it, usually with the result that you complain about it. objetar, criticar ❑ *He took exception to being spied on.* Objetó el haber sido espiado.

**ex|cep|tion|al** /ɪksɛpʃənᵊl/ **1** ADJ You use **exceptional** to describe someone or something that has a particular quality, usually a good quality, to an unusually high degree. excepcional ❑ *...children with exceptional ability.* ...los niños con habilidades excepcionales. ● **ex|cep|tion|al|ly** ADV excepcionalmente ❑ *He's an exceptionally talented dancer.* Es un bailarín excepcionalmente talentoso. **2** ADJ **Exceptional** situations are very unusual or rare. extraordinario [FORMAL] ❑ *The time limit can*

be extended in exceptional circumstances. El tiempo límite se puede extender en situaciones extraordinarias.
• **ex|cep|tion|al|ly** ADV extraordinariamente ❑ *Exceptionally, in times of emergency, we may send a team of experts.* Extraordinariamente, en casos de emergencia, podríamos enviar a un equipo de expertos.

**ex|cerpt** /ɛ̲ksɜrpt/ (**excerpts**) N-COUNT An **excerpt** is a short piece of writing or music taken from a larger piece. resumen, extracto ❑ *...an excerpt from Tchaikovsky's "Nutcracker."* ...un extracto de "El cascanueces" de Tchaikovski.

**ex|cess** (**excesses**)

The noun is pronounced /ɪksɛ̲s/ or /ɛ̲ksɛs/. The adjective is pronounced /ɛ̲ksɛs/.

1 N-VAR An **excess of** something is a larger amount than is needed, allowed, or usual. exceso ❑ *...the problems created by an excess of wealth.* ...los problemas ocasionados por un exceso de riqueza. • **Excess** is also an adjective. excesivo, sobrante ❑ *After cooking the fish, pour off any excess fat.* Después de cocinar el pescado, elimine la grasa sobrante. 2 PHRASE **In excess of** means more than a particular amount. más que [FORMAL] ❑ *The value of the company is in excess of $2 billion.* El valor de la compañía excede los 2,000 millones de dólares. 3 PHRASE If you do something **to excess,** you do it too much; used showing disapproval. en exceso ❑ *At Christmas, people sometimes eat to excess.* En navidad, la gente a veces come en exceso.

**ex|ces|sive** /ɪksɛ̲sɪv/ ADJ If you describe the amount or level of something as **excessive,** you disapprove of it because it is more or higher than is necessary or reasonable. excesivo, desmedido ❑ *Their spending on research is excessive.* Su gasto en investigación es excesivo. • **ex|ces|sive|ly** ADV excesivamente ❑ *Managers are paying themselves excessively high salaries.* Los gerentes se pagan a sí mismos salarios excesivamente altos.

**ex|change** /ɪkstʃe̲ɪndʒ/ (**exchanges, exchanging, exchanged**) 1 V-RECIP If two or more people **exchange** things of a particular kind, they give them to each other at the same time. intercambiar ❑ *We exchanged addresses.* Intercambiamos direcciones. ❑ *The two men exchanged glances.* Ambos hombres intercambiaron miradas. • **Exchange** is also a noun. intercambio ❑ *He ruled out any exchange of prisoners.* Descartó cualquier intercambio de prisioneros. 2 V-T If you **exchange** something, you replace it with a different thing, especially something that is better or more satisfactory. canjear ❑ *...the chance to exchange goods.* ...la oportunidad de canjear bienes. 3 N-COUNT An **exchange** is a brief conversation. intercambio [FORMAL] ❑ *There have been some bitter exchanges between the two groups.* Ha habido unos cuantos intercambios duros entre los dos grupos. 4 → see also **foreign exchange, stock exchange** 5 PHRASE If you do or give something **in exchange for** something else, you do it or give it in order to get that thing. a cambio de ❑ *It is illegal for public officials to receive gifts or money in exchange for favors.* Es ilegal que los funcionarios públicos reciban regalos o dinero a cambio de favores.

**Word Partnership** Usar *exchange* con:

N. **currency** exchange, exchange **gifts**, exchange **greetings** 1
ADJ. **cultural** exchange 1
**brief** exchange 3

**ex|change rate** (**exchange rates**) N-COUNT The **exchange rate** of a country's unit of currency is the amount of another country's currency that you get in exchange for it. tipo de cambio ❑ *...a high exchange rate for the Canadian dollar.* ...un tipo de cambio alto por el dólar canadiense.

**ex|cite** /ɪksa̲ɪt/ (**excites, exciting, excited**) 1 V-T If something **excites** you, it makes you feel very happy or enthusiastic. emocionar ❑ *This is what excites me about the trip.* Esto es lo que me emociona sobre el viaje. 2 V-T If something **excites** a particular feeling or reaction, it causes it. despertar ❑ *Auto racing did not excite his interest.* Las carreras de autos no despertaban su interés.

**ex|cit|ed** /ɪksa̲ɪtɪd/ ADJ If you are **excited,** you are looking forward to something eagerly. entusiasmado, emocionado ❑ *I was excited about the possibility of playing football again.* Estaba entusiasmado por la posibilidad de jugar al fútbol otra vez. • **ex|cit|ed|ly** ADV agitadamente, emocionado ❑ *"You're coming?" he said excitedly. "That's fantastic!"* —¿Vas a venir?—dijo emocionado.—!Genial!

**ex|cite|ment** /ɪksa̲ɪtmənt/ (**excitements**) N-VAR You use **excitement** to refer to the state of being excited, or to something that excites you. entusiasmo, emoción ❑ *Everyone is in a state of great excitement.* Todo mundo está en un estado de gran emoción.

**ex|cit|ing** /ɪksa̲ɪtɪŋ/ ADJ If something is **exciting,** it makes you feel very happy or enthusiastic. emocionante ❑ *The race itself is very exciting.* La carrera misma es muy emocionante.

**Word Link** *claim, clam ≈ shouting : acclaim, clamor, exclaim*

**ex|claim** /ɪkskle̲ɪm/ (**exclaims, exclaiming, exclaimed**) V-T Writers sometimes use **exclaim** to show that someone is speaking suddenly, loudly, or emphatically, often because they are excited, shocked, or angry. exclamar ❑ *"There!" Jackson exclaimed delightedly.* —¡Allí!—Jackson exclamó lleno de alegría.

**ex|cla|ma|tion point** (**exclamation points**) also **exclamation mark** N-COUNT An **exclamation point** is the sign ! which is used in writing to show that a word, phrase, or sentence is an exclamation. signo de admiración
→ see **punctuation**

**ex|cla|ma|tory** /ɪksklæ̲mətɔri/ ADJ An **exclamatory** sentence is a sentence that is spoken suddenly, loudly, or emphatically, for example "We won!" exclamativo

**ex|clude** /ɪksklu̲d/ (**excludes, excluding, excluded**) 1 V-T If you **exclude** someone **from** a place or activity, you prevent them from entering it or taking part in it. excluir ❑ *The academy excluded women from its classes.* La academia excluía a las mujeres de sus clases. ❑ *Many of the youngsters feel excluded.* Muchos de los jóvenes se sienten excluidos.

e

E

● **ex|clu|sion** /ɪkskluʒ<sup></sup>ᵊn/ N-VAR (**exclusions**) exclusión ❑ *...women's exclusion from political power.* *...la exclusión de las mujeres del poder político.* **2** V-T If you **exclude** something that has some connection with what you are doing, you deliberately do not use it or consider it. excluir ❑ *The university excluded women from its classes until 1968.* *La universidad excluyó a las mujeres de sus aulas hasta 1968.* ● **ex|clu|sion** N-VAR exclusión ❑ *Their kids play video games to the exclusion of everything else.* *Sus niños juegan video juegos excluyendo todo lo demás.* **3** V-T To **exclude** a possibility means to decide or prove that it is wrong and not worth considering. descartar ❑ *They do not exclude the possibility of hiring a foreigner.* *No descartan la posibilidad de contratar a un extranjero.*

**ex|clud|ing** /ɪkskludɪŋ/ PREP You use **excluding** before mentioning a person or thing to show that you are not including them in your statement. con excepción de ❑ *Excluding water, half of the body's weight is protein.* *Con excepción del agua, la mitad del peso del cuerpo es proteína.*

**ex|clu|sive** /ɪksklusɪv/ (**exclusives**) **1** ADJ Something that is **exclusive** is available only to people who are rich or privileged. exclusivo ❑ *It used to be a private, exclusive club.* *Solía ser un club privado y exclusivo.* **2** ADJ **Exclusive** means used or owned by only one person or group. exclusivo ❑ *Our group will have exclusive use of a 60-foot boat.* *Nuestro grupo tendrá el uso exclusivo de de un bote de 60 pies.* **3** PHRASE If two things are **mutually exclusive,** they cannot exist together. mutuamente excluyente ❑ *Career ambition and successful fatherhood can be mutually exclusive.* *La ambición profesional y ser un buen padre pueden ser mutuamente excluyentes.*

**ex|clu|sive|ly** /ɪksklusɪvli/ ADV **Exclusively** is used to refer to situations or activities that involve only the thing or things mentioned, and nothing else. exclusivamente ❑ *...an exclusively male group.* *...un grupo exclusivamente de varones.*

**ex|cuse** (**excuses, excusing, excused**)

The noun is pronounced /ɪkskyus/. The verb is pronounced /ɪkskyuz/.

**1** N-COUNT An **excuse** is a reason that you give in order to explain why something has been done or has not been done, or in order to avoid doing something. pretexto ❑ *...trying to find excuses for their failure.* *...tratando de encontrar pretextos por su falla.* ❑ *Just stop making excuses and do it.* *Sólo deja de inventar pretextos y hazlo.* PHRASE ● If you say that there is **no excuse for** something, you are emphasizing that it should not happen, or expressing disapproval that it has happened. no hay excusa, no tiene excusa ❑ *There's no excuse for behavior like that.* *No hay excusas para ese tipo de comportamiento.* **2** V-T To **excuse** someone or **excuse** their behavior means to provide reasons for their actions, especially when other people disapprove of these actions. justificar(se) ❑ *He excused himself by saying that his English was not good enough.* *Se justificó diciendo que su inglés no era lo suficientemente bueno.* **3** V-T If you **excuse** someone **for** something wrong that they have done, you forgive them for it. disculpar, exculpar ❑ *I'm not excusing him for what he did.* *No lo estoy disculpando por lo que hizo.* **4** V-T If someone **is excused from** a duty or responsibility, they are told that they do not have to carry it out. exentar ❑ *She is usually excused from her duties during summer vacation.* *Normalmente está exenta de sus deberes durante las vacaciones de verano.* **5** V-T If you **excuse yourself**, you use a phrase such as "Excuse me" as a polite way of saying that you are about to leave. despedirse ❑ *He excused himself and went up to his room.* *Se despidió y se subió a su cuarto.* **6** CONVENTION You say "**Excuse me** " when you want to politely get someone's attention. disculpe, perdón ❑ *Excuse me, but are you Mr. Honig?* *Perdón, ¿es usted el Sr. Honig?* **7** CONVENTION You use **excuse me** to apologize to someone, for example when you interrupt them, bump into them, or do something slightly impolite such as burping or sneezing. perdón ❑ *Excuse me, but there's something I need to say.* *Perdón, pero hay algo que necesito decir.*

**Thesaurus** *excuse* Ver también:

N. apology, explanation, reason **1**
V. forgive, pardon, spare; (*ant.*) accuse, blame, punish **3**

**ex|ecute** /ɛksɪkyut/ (**executes, executing, executed**) **1** V-T To **execute** someone means to kill them as a punishment. ejecutar ❑ *Harris was executed this morning.* *Harris fue ejecutado esta mañana.* ❑ *One group claimed to have executed the hostage.* *Uno de los grupos dijo haber ejecutado al rehén.* ● **ex|ecu|tion** /ɛksɪkyuʃᵊn/ N-VAR (**executions**) ejecución ❑ *...execution by lethal injection.* *...ejecución por inyección letal.* ● **ex|ecu|tion|er** N-COUNT (**executioners**) verdugo ❑ *...the executioner's ax.* *...el hacha del verdugo.* **2** V-T If you **execute** a plan, you carry it out. llevar a cabo, ejecutar [FORMAL] ❑ *He decided to execute his plan to kill the king.* *Decidió llevar a cabo su plan para matar al rey.* ● **ex|ecu|tion** N-UNCOUNT ejecución ❑ *U.S. forces are fully prepared for the execution of any action.* *Las fuerzas de EE. UU. están completamente listas para la ejecución de cualquier acción.* **3** V-T If you **execute** a difficult action or movement, you successfully perform it. realizar ❑ *The landing was skillfully executed.* *El aterrizaje se realizó habilidosamente.*

**ex|ecu|tive** /ɪgzɛkyətɪv/ (**executives**) **1** N-COUNT An **executive** is someone who is employed by a business at a senior level. ejecutivo, ejecutiva ❑ *...an advertising executive.* *...un ejecutivo publicitario.* **2** N-SING The **executive** of an organization is a committee that has the authority to make important decisions. (la) directiva ❑ *Some members of the executive have called for his resignation.* *Algunos miembros de la directiva han pedido su renuncia.* **3** N-SING **The executive** is the part of the government of a country that is concerned with carrying out decisions or orders, as opposed to the part that makes laws or the part that deals with criminals. (poder) ejecutivo ❑ *Her brother, David, works for the Scottish Executive in Edinburgh.* *Su hermano, David, trabaja para el poder ejecutivo escocés en Edimburgo.*

**ex|ecu|tive or|der** (**executive orders**) N-COUNT An **executive order** is a regulation issued by a member of the executive branch of government. It has the same authority as a law. orden ejecutiva ❑ *The president issued an executive order.* *El presidente emitió una orden ejecutiva.*

**ex|empt** /ɪgzɛmpt/ (**exempts, exempting, exempted**) **1** ADJ If someone is **exempt from** a rule or duty, they do not have to obey it or perform it. *exento* ❑ *Men in college were exempt from military service. Los estudiantes hombres estaban exentos del servicio militar.* **2** V-T To **exempt** a person **from** a rule or duty means to state officially that they are not bound or affected by it. *exentar* ❑ *He was exempted from the full course because of his experience. Exentó el curso entero por su experiencia* • **ex|emp|tion** /ɪgzɛmpʃᵊn/ N-VAR (**exemptions**) *exención* ❑ *...the exemption of health insurance from taxation. ...la exención fiscal del seguro de enfermedad.*

**ex|er|cise** /ɛksərsaɪz/ (**exercises, exercising, exercised**) **1** V-T If you **exercise** something such as your authority, your rights, or a good quality, you use it or put it into effect. *ejercer* [FORMAL] ❑ *They are merely exercising their right to free speech. Simplemente están ejerciendo su derecho de libre expresión.* • **Exercise** is also a noun. *ejercicio* ❑ *...the exercise of political and economic power. ...el ejercicio de poder económico y político.* **2** V-I When you **exercise,** you move your body energetically in order to get in shape and to remain healthy. *hacer ejercicio* ❑ *She exercises two or three times a week. Hace ejercicio dos o tres veces por semana.* • **Exercise** is also a noun. *ejercicio* ❑ *Lack of exercise can lead to feelings of depression. La falta de ejercicio puede llevar a un sentimiento de depresión.* **3** N-COUNT **Exercises** are a series of movements or actions that you do in order to get in shape, remain healthy, or practice for a particular physical activity. *ejercicio* ❑ *I do special neck and shoulder exercises. Hago ejercicios especiales para cuello y hombros.* **4** N-COUNT **Exercises** are activities that you do in order to maintain or practice a skill. *ejercicios* ❑ *...military exercises. ...ejercicios militares.* ❑ *...creative writing exercises. ...ejercicios de redacción creativa.*
→ see **muscle**

**ex|ert** /ɪgzɜrt/ (**exerts, exerting, exerted**) **1** V-T If someone or something **exerts** influence or pressure, they use their influence or put pressure on someone else in order to produce a particular effect. *ejercer* [FORMAL] ❑ *Parents exert a huge influence over their children when it comes to diet and exercise. Los padres ejercen una gran influencia sobre sus hijos cuando se trata de dietas y ejercicio.* **2** V-T If you **exert yourself**, you make a physical or mental effort to do something. *hacer un gran esfuerzo* ❑ *Do not exert yourself unnecessarily. No te esfuerces innecesariamente.* • **ex|er|tion** N-UNCOUNT (**exertions**) *esfuerzo* ❑ *...the stress of physical exertion. ...la tensión del esfuerzo físico.*
→ see **motion**

**ex|hale** /ɛksheɪl/ (**exhales, exhaling, exhaled**) V-I When you **exhale,** you breathe out the air that is in your lungs. *exhalar* [FORMAL] ❑ *Hold your breath for a moment and exhale. Mantén la respiración por un momento y exhala.*
→ see **respiratory system**

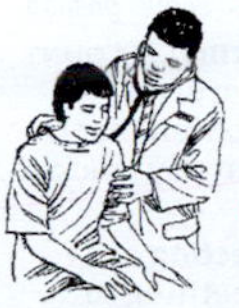
**exhale**

**ex|haust** /ɪgzɔst/ (**exhausts, exhausting, exhausted**) **1** V-T If something **exhausts** you, it makes you very tired. *agotar* ❑ *Don't exhaust him. No lo agotes.* • **ex|haust|ed** ADJ *exhausto* ❑ *She was too exhausted to talk. Estaba exhausta como para hablar.* • **ex|haust|ing** ADJ *agotador* ❑ *It was an exhausting schedule. Fue un programa agotador.* • **ex|haus|tion** /ɪgzɔstʃᵊn/ N-UNCOUNT *agotamiento* ❑ *He is suffering from exhaustion. Padece de agotamiento.* **2** V-T If you **exhaust** something such as money or food, you use or finish it all. *agotar* ❑ *We have exhausted all our material resources. Hemos agotado nuestros recursos materiales.* **3** V-T If you **have exhausted** a subject or topic, you have talked about it so much that there is nothing more to say about it. *agotar* ❑ *She and Chantal must have exhausted the subject of clothes. Chantal y ella deben de haber agotado el tema de la ropa.* **4** N-UNCOUNT **Exhaust** is the gas or steam that is produced when the engine of a vehicle is running. *gases* ❑ *...the exhaust from a car engine. ...los gases del motor de un carro.*
→ see **engine, pollution**

**ex|haust pipe** (**exhaust pipes**) N-COUNT The **exhaust pipe** is the pipe that carries the gas out of the engine of a vehicle. *escape, mofle*

**ex|hib|it** /ɪgzɪbɪt/ (**exhibits, exhibiting, exhibited**) **1** V-T To **exhibit** a particular quality, feeling, or type of behavior means to show it. *presentar, mostrar* [FORMAL] ❑ *He exhibited symptoms of anxiety. Presentó síntomas de ansiedad.* **2** V-T When an object of interest **is exhibited,** it is put in a public place such as a museum or art gallery so that people can come to look at it. *exhibir, exponer* ❑ *His work was exhibited in the best galleries. Su trabajo fue exhibido en las mejores galerías.* • **ex|hi|bi|tion** N-UNCOUNT *exposición* ❑ *Five of her paintings are currently on exhibition. Actualmente cinco de sus pinturas están en exposición.* **3** V-I When artists **exhibit,** they show their work in public. *exponer* ❑ *He has exhibited at galleries and museums in New York. Ha expuesto en galerías y museos en Nueva York.* **4** N-COUNT An **exhibit** is an object of interest that is displayed to the public in a museum or art gallery. *pieza en exposición* ❑ *Shona showed me around the exhibits. Shona me mostró las piezas en exposición.* **5** N-COUNT An **exhibit** is a public display of art or objects of interest in a museum or art gallery. *exposición* ❑ *...an exhibit at the Metropolitan Museum of Art. ...una exposición en el Museo Metropolitano de Arte.* **6** N-COUNT An **exhibit** is an object that a lawyer shows in court as evidence in a legal case. *prueba* ❑ *The jury has already asked to see more than 40 exhibits. El jurado ya ha solicitado ver mas de 40 pruebas.*

**ex|hi|bi|tion** /ɛksɪbɪʃᵊn/ (**exhibitions**) **1** N-COUNT An **exhibition** is a public event at which art or objects of interest are displayed, for example at a museum or art gallery. *exposición* ❑ *...an exhibition of modern art. ...una exposición de arte moderno.* **2** N-SING An **exhibition of** a particular skillful activity is a display or example of it. *espectáculo* ❑ *He treated the fans to an exhibition of power and speed. Les dio gusto a los fanáticos con un espectáculo de poder y velocidad.* **3** → see also **exhibit 2**

**ex|hi|bi|tion game** (**exhibition games**) N-COUNT In sports, an **exhibition game** is a game that is not part of a competition, and is played for entertainment or practice. *juego de exhibición*

**ex|ile** /ɛksaɪl, ɛgz-/ (**exiles, exiling, exiled**) **1** V-T If someone **is exiled,** they are living in a foreign country because they cannot live in their own country, usually for political reasons. *exiliar* ❑ *His* *wife, Hilary, was exiled from South Africa.* *Su esposa, Hilary, fue exiliada de Sudáfrica.* ❑ *They threatened to exile her in southern Spain.* *Amenazaron con exiliarla en el sur de España* • **Exile** is also a noun. *exilio* ❑ *He is now living in exile in Egypt.* *Ahora vive en el exilio en Egipto.* ❑ *He returned from exile earlier this year.* *Regresó del exilio a principios de año.* **2** N-COUNT An **exile** is someone who has been exiled. *exiliado o exiliada* ❑ *He is an exile who has given up the idea of going home.* *Es un exiliado que ha abandonado la idea de regresar a casa.*

E

**Word Partnership** Usar *exile* con:

V. **force into** exile, **go into** exile, **live in** exile, **return from** exile, **send into** exile **1**
ADJ. **self-imposed** exile **1**
**political** exile **1** **2**

**ex|ist** /ɪgzɪst/ (**exists, existing, existed**) V-I If something **exists,** it is present in the world as a real thing. *existir* ❑ *He thought that if he couldn't see something, it didn't exist.* *Pensó que si no podía ver algo, no existía.* ❑ *Research opportunities exist in a wide range of areas.* *Existen oportunidades de investigación en un amplio rango de áreas.*

**ex|ist|ence** /ɪgzɪstəns/ (**existences**) **1** N-UNCOUNT The **existence** of something is the fact that it is present in the world as a real thing. *existencia* ❑ *...the existence of other worlds.* *...la existencia de otros mundos.* **2** N-COUNT You can refer to someone's way of life as a particular **existence.** *existencia* ❑ *...a miserable existence.* *...una existencia miserable.*

**Word Partnership** Usar *existence* con:

V. **come into** existence, **deny the** existence **1**
ADJ. **continued** existence, **daily** existence, **everyday** existence **1** **2**

**ex|ist|ing** /ɪgzɪstɪŋ/ ADJ **Existing** is used to describe something that is now present, available, or in operation, especially when you are contrasting it with something that is planned for the future. *existente* ❑ *...the need to improve existing products.* *...la necesidad de mejorar los productos existentes.*

**Word Link** *ex ≈ away, from, out : exceed, exit, explode*

**exit** /ɛgzɪt, ɛksɪt/ (**exits, exiting, exited**) **1** N-COUNT The **exit** is the door through which you can leave a public building. *salida* ❑ *He picked up the box and walked toward the exit.* *Recogió la caja y caminó hacia la salida.* **2** N-COUNT An **exit** on a highway is a place where traffic can leave it. *salida* ❑ *She continued to the next exit.* *Continuó hasta la siguiente salida.* **3** N-COUNT If you refer to someone's **exit,** you are referring to the way that they left a room or building. *salida* [FORMAL] ❑ *I made a quick exit.* *Salí de manera rápida.* **4** V-T/V-I If you **exit** a room or building or **exit from** it, you leave it. *salir* [FORMAL] ❑ *She exited into the night.* *Salió hacia la noche.* ❑ *I exited the elevator and stepped into the lobby of the hotel.* *Salí del elevador y caminé al vestíbulo del hotel.* **5** V-T If you **exit** a computer program or system, you stop running it. *cerrar* [COMPUTING] ❑ *Do you want to exit this program?* *¿Quiere cerrar este programa?* • **Exit** is also a noun. *salida* ❑ *Press "exit" to return to your document.* *Pulse "salida" para regresar a su documento.*

**exit poll** (**exit polls**) N-COUNT An **exit poll** is a survey in which people who have just voted in an election are asked which candidate they voted for. *encuesta de salida*

**exit strat|egy** (**exit strategies**) N-COUNT In politics and business, an **exit strategy** is a way of ending your involvement in a situation. *estrategia de salida* ❑ *We have no exit strategy from this conflict.* *No tenemos una estrategia para salir del conflicto.*

**exo|cy|to|sis** /ɛksoʊsaɪtoʊsɪs/ N-UNCOUNT **Exocytosis** is a process in which a cell releases material from inside itself by sending the material to the surface of the cell. Compare **endocytosis.** *exocitosis* [TECHNICAL]

**exo|skel|eton** /ɛksoʊskɛlɪtᵊn/ (**exoskeletons**) N-COUNT Animals with an **exoskeleton** have their skeleton on the outside of their body, like insects. *exoesqueleto* [TECHNICAL]

**exo|sphere** /ɛksəsfɪər/ N-SING *The* **exosphere** is the highest layer of the Earth's atmosphere. *exosfera* [TECHNICAL]

**exo|ther|mic** /ɛksoʊθɜrmɪk/ ADJ An **exothermic** chemical reaction or process is one that releases heat. *exotérmico* [TECHNICAL]

**Word Link** *otic ≈ afecting, causing : antibiotic, exotic, patriotic*

**ex|ot|ic** /ɪgzɒtɪk/ ADJ Something that is **exotic** is unusual and interesting, usually because it comes from or is related to a distant country. *exótico* ❑ *...brilliantly colored, exotic flowers.* *...flores exóticas de colores brillantes.* • **ex|oti|cal|ly** ADV *exóticamente* ❑ *...exotically beautiful scenery.* *...paisaje exóticamente bello.*

**ex|pand** /ɪkspænd/ (**expands, expanding, expanded**) V-T/V-I If something **expands** or **is expanded,** it becomes larger. *expandir(se), aumentar* ❑ *The industry expanded toward the middle of the 19th century.* *La industria se expandió hacia mediados del siglo diecinueve.* ❑ *We have to expand the size of the image.* *Tenemos que aumentar el tamaño de la imagen.* • **ex|pan|sion** /ɪkspænʃᵊn/ N-VAR (**expansions**) *expansión* ❑ *...the rapid expansion of private health insurance.* *...la rápida expansión de seguros médicos privados.*

▸ **expand on** or **expand upon** PHR-VERB If you **expand on** or **expand upon** something, you give more information about it. *ahondar en* ❑ *The president used today's speech to expand on remarks he made last month.* *El presidente utilizó el discurso de hoy para ahondar en los comentarios que hizo el mes pasado.*

**ex|pand|ed form** (**expanded forms**) N-COUNT In mathematics, the **expanded form** of an expression is a version of the expression that is written in full, for example without any brackets. *forma desarrollada* [TECHNICAL]

**ex|pect** /ɪkspɛkt/ (**expects, expecting, expected**) **1** V-T If you **expect** something **to** happen, you believe that it will happen. *creer* ❑ *He expects to lose his job in the next few weeks.* *Cree que perderá su empleo en las próximas semanas.* ❑ *The talks* are expected to continue until tomorrow. Se cree que las pláticas continuarán hasta mañana. 2 V-T If you **are expecting** something or someone, you believe that they will be delivered or arrive soon. esperar ❑ *I wasn't expecting a visitor.* No esperaba a ningún visitante. 3 V-T If you **expect** something, or **expect** a person **to** do something, you believe that it is your right to have that thing, or the person's duty to do it for you. esperar ❑ *I don't expect your help.* No espero tu ayuda. ❑ *I do expect to have some time to myself.* Espero tener tiempo para mí mismo. 4 V-T/V-I If a woman **is expecting** a baby, she is pregnant. esperar (un bebé) ❑ *She was expecting another baby.* Estaba esperando otro bebé. ❑ *I hear Dawn's expecting.* Escuché que Dawn está esperando.

**ex|pec|ta|tion** /ɛkspɛkteɪʃᵊn/ (**expectations**) 1 N-VAR Your **expectations** are your beliefs that something will happen or that you will get something that you want. expectativa ❑ *Their expectation was that she was going to be found safe.* La expectativa era que la encontraran sana y salva. 2 N-COUNT A person's **expectations** are strong beliefs they have about the proper way someone should behave or something should happen. expectativas ❑ *He was determined to live up to the expectations of his parents.* Estaba decidido a estar a la altura de las expectativas de sus padres.

**ex|pedi|tion** /ɛkspɪdɪʃᵊn/ (**expeditions**) N-COUNT An **expedition** is an organized trip made for a particular purpose such as exploration. expedición ❑ *...an expedition to Antarctica.* ...una expedición a la Antártida.

| Word Link | pel ≈ driving, forcing : compel, expel, propeller |
|---|---|

**ex|pel** /ɪkspɛl/ (**expels, expelling, expelled**) 1 V-T If someone **is expelled from** a school or organization, they are officially told to leave because they have behaved badly. expulsar ❑ *High school students have been expelled for cheating.* Estudiantes de preparatoria han sido expulsados por hacer trampa. 2 V-T If people **are expelled from** a place, they are made to leave it, often by force. expulsar ❑ *An American was expelled from the country yesterday.* Un estadounidense fue expulsado ayer del país. 3 V-T To **expel** something means to force it out from a container or from your body. expulsar ❑ *He groaned, expelling the air from his lungs.* Se quejó, expulsando el aire de los pulmones.

**ex|pendi|ture** /ɪkspɛndɪtʃər/ (**expenditures**) N-VAR **Expenditure** is the spending of money on something, or the money that is spent on something. gasto [FORMAL] ❑ *The total expenditure of the administration was $11.4 billion.* El gasto total de la administración fue de $11,400 millones de dólares.

**ex|pense** /ɪkspɛns/ (**expenses**) 1 N-VAR **Expense** is the money that something costs you or that you need to spend in order to do something. gasto ❑ *He's bought a big TV at great expense.* Gastó muchísimo para comprarse una tele grande. 2 N-PLURAL **Expenses** are amounts of money that you spend while doing something in the course of your work, which will be paid back to you afterwards. gastos [BUSINESS] ❑ *Her hotel expenses were paid by the committee.* Los gastos de su hotel fueron pagados por el comité. 3 PHRASE If you do something **at** someone's **expense,** they provide the money for it. a expensas de (alguien) ❑ *Architects are trained for five years at public expense.* Los arquitectos son capacitados por cinco años a expensas del gasto público. 4 PHRASE If someone laughs or makes a joke **at** your **expense,** they do it to make you seem foolish. a costa de ❑ *I think he's having fun at our expense.* Creo que se está divirtiendo a costa de nosotros.

**ex|pen|sive** /ɪkspɛnsɪv/ ADJ If something is **expensive,** it costs a lot of money. caro ❑ *Broadband is still more expensive than dial-up services.* La banda ancha sigue siendo más cara que los servicios de dial-up. ● **ex|pen|sive|ly** ADV ostentosamente ❑ *She was expensively dressed.* Estaba vestida ostentosamente.

| Thesaurus | *expensive* Ver también: |
|---|---|
| ADJ. | costly, pricey, upscale; (*ant.*) cheap, economical, inexpensive |

**ex|peri|ence** /ɪkspɪəriəns/ (**experiences, experiencing, experienced**) 1 N-UNCOUNT **Experience** is knowledge or skill in a particular job or activity that you have gained because you have done that job or activity for a long time. experiencia ❑ *He has managerial experience.* Tiene experiencia gerencial. ● **ex|pe|ri|enced** ADJ experimentado ❑ *...a team packed with experienced professionals.* ...un equipo repleto de profesionales experimentados. 2 N-UNCOUNT **Experience** is used to refer to the past events, knowledge, and feelings that make up your life or character. experiencia ❑ *Experience has taught me caution.* La experiencia me ha enseñado a ser precavido. 3 N-COUNT An **experience** is something that you do or that happens to you, especially something important that affects you. experiencia ❑ *His only experience of gardening so far proved very satisfying.* Hasta ahora su única experiencia con la jardinería le ha sido satisfactoria. 4 V-T If you **experience** a particular situation or feeling, it happens to you or you are affected by it. experimentar ❑ *I have never experienced true love.* Nunca he experimentado amor verdadero.

| Thesaurus | *experience* Ver también: |
|---|---|
| N. | know-how, knowledge, wisdom; (*ant.*) inexperience 1 |

| Word Partnership | Usar *experience* con: |
|---|---|
| ADJ. | **professional** experience 1<br>**valuable** experience 1 – 3<br>**past** experience, **shared** experience 2 3<br>**learning** experience, **religious** experience, **traumatic** experience 3 |
| N. | **work** experience 1<br>**life** experience 2<br>experience **a loss**, experience **symptoms** 4 |

**ex|peri|ment** (**experiments, experimenting, experimented**)

| The noun is pronounced /ɪkspɛrɪmənt/. The verb is pronounced /ɪkspɛrɪmɛnt/. |
|---|

1 N-VAR An **experiment** is a scientific test done in order to discover what happens to something in particular conditions. experimento ❑ *...experiments to learn how the body reacts in space.* ...experimentos para aprender cómo reacciona el

E

**Word Web** experiment

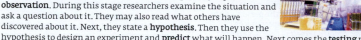

**Scientists** learn much of what they know through **controlled experiments.** The **scientific method** provides a dependable way to understand natural **phenomena.** The first step in any experiment is **observation.** During this stage researchers examine the situation and ask a question about it. They may also read what others have discovered about it. Next, they state a **hypothesis.** Then they use the hypothesis to design an experiment and **predict** what will happen. Next comes the **testing** phase. Often researchers do several experiments using different **variables.** If all of the **evidence** supports the hypothesis, it becomes a new **theory.**

*cuerpo en el espacio.* **2** V-I If you **experiment with** something or **experiment on** it, you do a scientific test on it in order to discover what happens to it in particular conditions. *experimentar* ❑ *The scientists have experimented on rats. Los científicos han experimentado con ratas.* ● **ex|peri|men|ta|tion** /ɪkspɛrɪmɛnteɪʃən/ N-UNCOUNT *experimentación* ❑ *...animal experimentation. ...experimentación animal.* **3** N-VAR An **experiment** is the trying out of a new idea or method in order to see what it is like and what effects it has. *experimento* ❑ *They started the magazine as an experiment. Comenzaron con la revista como un experimento.* **4** V-I To **experiment** means to try out a new idea or method to see what it is like and what effects it has. *experimentar* ❑ *I like cooking and have the time to experiment. Me gusta cocinar y tengo el tiempo para experimentar.* ● **ex|peri|men|ta|tion** N-UNCOUNT *experimentación* ❑ *Experimentation must be encouraged. La experimentación debe ser promovida.*

→ see Word Web: **experiment**
→ see **laboratory, science**

**Word Partnership** Usar *experiment* con:

V. **conduct an** experiment **1**
**perform an** experiment, **try an** experiment **1** **3**
ADJ. **scientific** experiment **1**
**simple** experiment **1** **3**

**ex|peri|men|tal** /ɪkspɛrɪmɛntəl/ **1** ADJ Something that is **experimental** is new or uses new ideas or methods. *experimental* ❑ *...an experimental air-conditioning system. ...un sistema de aire acondicionado experimental.* **2** ADJ **Experimental** means relating to scientific experiments. *experimental* ❑ *...experimental science. ...ciencia experimental.* ● **ex|peri|men|tal|ly** ADV *de manera experimental* ❑ *...a laboratory where animals can be studied experimentally. ...un laboratorio donde los animales pueden ser estudiados de manera experimental.*

**ex|peri|men|tal de|sign** (**experimental designs**) N-VAR Research that has an **experimental design** involves carrying out scientific experiments. *diseño experimental*

**ex|pert** /ɛkspɜrt/ (**experts**) **1** N-COUNT An **expert** is a person who is very skilled at doing something or who knows a lot about a particular subject. *experto o experta* ❑ *...a computer expert. ...un experto en computadoras.* ● **Expert** is also an adjective. *experto* ❑ *...an expert gardener. ...un jardinero experto.* ● **ex|pert|ly** ADV *con pericia* ❑ *He drove expertly down the twisting mountain road. Manejó con pericia cuesta abajo por el sinuoso camino de la montaña.* **2** ADJ **Expert** advice or help is given by someone who has studied a subject thoroughly or who is very skilled at a particular job. *experto* ❑ *We'll need an expert opinion. Vamos a necesitar una opinión experta.*

**Word Partnership** Usar *expert* con:

ADJ. **leading** expert **1**
N. expert **advice**, expert **opinion**, expert **witness** **2**

**ex|per|tise** /ɛkspɜrtiz/ N-UNCOUNT **Expertise** is special skill or knowledge. *experiencia, conocimientos, pericia* ❑ *She didn't have the expertise to deal with all the financial details. No tenía la experiencia para manejar todos los detalles financieros.*

**ex|pert wit|ness** (**expert witnesses**) N-COUNT In a court case, an **expert witness** is a professional person, such as a doctor, who testifies about issues that have been raised in the case. *testigo experto*

**ex|pi|ra|tion date** /ɛkspɪreɪʃən deɪt/ (**expiration dates**) N-COUNT The **expiration date** on a food container is the date by which the food should be sold or eaten. *fecha de caducidad* ❑ *We checked the expiration date on the carton and it was fine. Revisamos la fecha de caducidad en el empaque y estaba bien.*

**ex|pire** /ɪkspaɪər/ (**expires, expiring, expired**) V-I When something such as a contract, deadline, or visa **expires,** it comes to an end or is no longer valid. *caducar* ❑ *My passport has expired. Mi pasaporte caducó.*

**ex|plain** /ɪkspleɪn/ (**explains, explaining, explained**) **1** V-T/V-I If you **explain** something, you give details about it or describe it so that it can be understood. *explicar* ❑ *...the ability to explain the law in simple terms. ...la capacidad de explicar la ley en términos sencillos.* ❑ *Don't sign anything until your lawyer has explained the contract to you. No firmes nada hasta que tu abogado te haya explicado el contrato.* ❑ *Professor Griffiths explained how the drug works. El profesor Griffiths explicó cómo funciona la droga.* **2** V-T/V-I If you **explain,** or **explain** something that has happened, you give reasons for it. *explicar, dar explicaciones* ❑ *Let me explain, sir. Permítame dar una explicación, señor.* ❑ *Before she ran away, she left a note explaining her actions. Antes de escaparse, dejó una nota explicando sus acciones.* ❑ *Explain why you didn't telephone. Explica por qué no llamaste por teléfono.*

▸ **explain away** PHR-VERB If someone **explains away** a mistake or a bad situation they are responsible for, they try to indicate that it is unimportant or that it is not really their fault. *justificar* ❑ *They tried to explain away any problems as temporary.* *Trataron de justificar los problemas como temporales.*

**Thesaurus** *explain* Ver también:

V. describe, tell 1
account for, justify 2

**ex|pla|na|tion** /ɛkspləneɪʃᵊn/ **(explanations)** N-COUNT If you give an **explanation,** you give reasons why something happened, or describe something in detail. *explicación* ❑ *There was no apparent explanation for the crash.* *El choque no tenía ninguna explicación obvia.* ❑ *She gave a full explanation of the decision.* *Dio una explicación completa de la decisión.*

**Word Partnership** Usar *explanation* con:

ADJ. **brief** explanation, **detailed** explanation, **logical** explanation, **only** explanation, **possible** explanation
V. **give an** explanation, **offer an** explanation, **provide an** explanation

**ex|plana|tory** /ɪksplænətɔri/ ADJ Something that is **explanatory** explains something by giving details about it. *explicativo* [FORMAL] ❑ *...a series of explanatory notes.* *...una serie de notas explicativas.*

**ex|plic|it** /ɪksplɪsɪt/ 1 ADJ Something that is **explicit** is expressed or shown clearly and openly, without hiding anything. *explícito* ❑ *...the increase in explicit violence on television.* *...el aumento de la violencia explícita en la televisión.* • **ex|plic|it|ly** ADV *explícitamente* ❑ *...programs that deal explicitly with death.* *...los programas que lidian explícitamente con la muerte.* 2 ADJ If you are **explicit about** something, you speak about it very openly and clearly. *explícito, claro* ❑ *He was explicit about his intention to reform the party.* *Fue claro acerca de su intención de reformar el partido.* • **ex|plic|it|ly** ADV *explícitamente, claramente* ❑ *She has been talking very explicitly about AIDS.* *Ha estado hablando explícitamente acerca del SIDA.*

**Word Link** *ex ≈ away, from, out : exceed, exit, explode*

**ex|plode** /ɪksploʊd/ **(explodes, exploding, exploded)** 1 V-T/V-I If an object such as a bomb **explodes,** it bursts with great force. *explotar* ❑ *They were clearing up when the second bomb exploded.* *Estaban limpiando los escombros cuando la segunda bomba explotó.* ❑ *...gunfire which exploded the fuel tank.* *...las balas que hicieron explotar el tanque de gasolina.* 2 V-I If someone **explodes,** they express strong feelings suddenly and violently. *estallar* ❑ *Do you fear that you'll explode with anger?* *¿Temes que puedas llegar a estallar de ira?*
→ see **fireworks**

**Thesaurus** *explode* Ver también:

V. blow up, erupt, go off 1

**Word Partnership** Usar *explode* con:

N. **bombs** explode, **missiles** explode 1
ADJ. **about to** explode, **ready to** explode 1 2

**ex|ploit** **(exploits, exploiting, exploited)**

The verb is pronounced /ɪksplɔɪt/. The noun is pronounced /ɛksplɔɪt/.

1 V-T If someone **exploits** you, they treat you unfairly by using your work or ideas and giving you very little in return. *explotar* ❑ *They claim he exploited other musicians.* *Dicen que explotaba a otros músicos.* • **ex|ploi|ta|tion** /ɛksplɔɪteɪʃᵊn/ N-UNCOUNT *explotación* ❑ *We should prevent exploitation.* *Debemos prevenir actos de explotación.* 2 V-T To **exploit** a situation means to use it to gain an advantage for yourself. *aprovecharse de* ❑ *They exploit the troubles to their advantage.* *Ellos se aprovechan de los problemas.* • **ex|ploi|ta|tion** N-SING *aprovechamiento* ❑ *...the exploitation of the situation by local politicians.* *...el aprovechamiento de la situación por parte de los políticos locales.* 3 V-T To **exploit** resources or raw materials means to develop them and use them for industry or commercial activities. *explotar* ❑ *We're being very short-sighted in not exploiting our own coal.* *Estamos siendo muy miopes por no explotar nuestro propio carbón.* • **ex|ploi|ta|tion** N-UNCOUNT *utilización* ❑ *...the planned exploitation of oil and natural gas reserves.* *...la explotación planificada de las reservas de petróleo y gas natural.* 4 N-COUNT Someone's **exploits** are the brave or interesting things that they have done. *proeza, hazaña* ❑ *...his wartime exploits.* *...sus proezas durante la guerra.*

**ex|plore** /ɪksplɔr/ **(explores, exploring, explored)** 1 V-T/V-I If you **explore,** or **explore** a place, you travel around it to find out what it is like. *explorar* ❑ *I just wanted to explore on my own.* *Quería explorar por mí mismo.* ❑ *The best way to explore the area is in a boat.* *La mejor forma de explorar el área es en un bote.* • **ex|plo|ra|tion** /ɛkspləreɪʃᵊn/ N-VAR **(explorations)** *exploración* ❑ *...space exploration.* *...la exploración espacial.* • **ex|plor|er** N-COUNT **(explorers)** *explorador o exploradora* ❑ *...the travels of Columbus, Magellan, and many other explorers.* *...los viajes de Colón, Magallanes y muchos otros exploradores.* 2 V-T If you **explore** an idea, you carefully think about or discuss its different aspects. *sondear, examinar* ❑ *The movie explores the relationship between artist and model.* *La película examina la relación entre el artista y su modelo.* • **ex|plo|ra|tion** N-VAR *sondeo, examinación* ❑ *...the exploration of their theories.* *...la examinación de sus teorías.* 3 V-I If people **explore for** a substance such as oil or minerals, they study an area and do tests on the land to see whether they can find it. *ir en busca de* ❑ *They dug a mile-deep well to explore for oil.* *Cavaron un pozo de una milla de profundidad en busca de petróleo.* • **ex|plo|ra|tion** N-UNCOUNT *búsqueda* ❑ *...gas exploration.* *...la búsqueda de yacimientos de gas.*

**ex|plo|sion** /ɪksploʊʒᵊn/ **(explosions)** 1 N-COUNT An **explosion** is a sudden, violent burst of energy, such as one caused by a bomb. *explosión* ❑ *Six soldiers were injured in the explosion.* *Seis soldados resultaron heridos en la explosión.* 2 N-COUNT An **explosion** is a large rapid increase in the number or amount of something. *aumento*

e

*dramático* ❑ *...an explosion in the diet soft-drink market. ...un aumento dramático en el mercado de los refrescos dietéticos.*

**ex|plo|sive** /ɪksploʊsɪv/ (**explosives**) **1** N-VAR An **explosive** is a substance or device that can cause an explosion. *explosivo* ❑ *...150 pounds of explosive. ...150 libras de explosivos.* ● **Explosive** is also an adjective. *explosivo* ❑ *The explosive device was timed to go off at the rush hour. El aparato explosivo estaba calibrado para estallar en la hora pico.* **2** ADJ An **explosive** situation is likely to have serious or dangerous effects. *explosivo* ❑ *...a potentially explosive situation. ...una situación potencialmente explosiva.*
→ see **tunnel**

E

**ex|po|nen|tial func|tion** /ɛkspənɛnʃᵊl fʌŋkʃᵊn/ (**exponential functions**) N-COUNT An **exponential function** is a mathematical calculation that is used to study processes which increase at a constant rate, such as population growth or compound interest. *función exponencial* [TECHNICAL]

**Word Link** *port ≈ carrying : export, import, portable*

**ex|port** (**exports, exporting, exported**)

The verb is pronounced /ɪkspɔrt/. The noun is pronounced /ɛkspɔrt/.

**1** V-T/V-I To **export** products or raw materials means to sell them to another country. *exportar* ❑ *They also export beef. También exportan carne.* ❑ *The company now exports to Japan. La compañía ahora exporta a Japón.* ● **Export** is also a noun. *exportación* ❑ *A lot of our land is used to grow crops for export. Mucha de nuestra tierra es usada para cosecha de exportación.* ● **ex|port|er** /ɛkspɔrtər, ɪkspɔrtər/ N-COUNT (**exporters**) *exportador* ❑ *France is the world's second-biggest exporter of agricultural products. Francia es el segundo exportador más importante de productos del campo.* **2** N-COUNT **Exports** are goods sold to another country and sent there. *artículo de exportación* ❑ *Ghana's main export is cocoa. El artículo de exportación más importante de Ghana es el cacao.*

**ex|pose** /ɪkspoʊz/ (**exposes, exposing, exposed**) **1** V-T To **expose** something means to uncover it so that it can be seen. *exponer* ❑ *Water levels fell and exposed the wrecked boat. Descendieron los nieveles de agua y expusieron los restos del naufragio del bote.* **2** V-T To **expose** a person or situation means to reveal the truth about them. *desenmascarar* ❑ *Officials exposed him as a fake. Los policías lo desenmascararon como un impostor.* **3** V-T If someone **is exposed to** something dangerous or unpleasant, they are put in a situation in which it might affect them. *exponer, poner en peligro* ❑ *They have not been exposed to these diseases. No han sido expuestos a estas enfermedades.*

**ex|po|sure** /ɪkspoʊʒər/ (**exposures**) **1** N-UNCOUNT **Exposure to** something dangerous means being in a situation where it might affect you. *exposición* ❑ *Exposure to the sun can damage your skin. La exposición al sol puede dañar su piel.* **2** N-UNCOUNT **Exposure** is the harmful effect on your body caused by very cold weather. *hipotermia* ❑ *He was suffering from exposure and shock. Sufría de hipotermia y de shock.* **3** N-UNCOUNT The **exposure** of a well-known person is the revealing of the fact that they are bad or immoral in some way. *revelación* ❑ *...his exposure as a spy. ...se reveló que era un espía.* **4** N-UNCOUNT **Exposure** is publicity that a person, company, or product receives. *presencia, publicidad, tiempo aire* ❑ *All the candidates have been getting an enormous amount of exposure on television. Todos los candidatos han tenido una gran cantidad de presencia en la televisión.* **5** N-COUNT In photography, an **exposure** is a single photograph. *exposición* [TECHNICAL]

**ex|press** /ɪksprɛs/ (**expresses, expressing, expressed**) **1** V-T When you **express** an idea or feeling, or **express yourself**, you show what you think or feel. *expresar* ❑ *He expressed concern at American attitudes. Expresó su preocupación con respecto a las actitudes de los estadounidenses.* **2** V-T If an idea or feeling **expresses itself** in some way, it can be clearly seen in your actions or in its effects on a situation. *expresar* ❑ *Anxiety often expresses itself as anger. La ansiedad con frecuencia se expresa en forma de ira.* **3** ADJ An **express** command or order is one that is clearly and deliberately stated. *expreso, preciso* [FORMAL] ❑ *This power station was built on the express orders of the president. Esta estación eléctrica fue construida por órdenes precisas del presidente.* ● **ex|press|ly** ADV *expresamente, precisamente* ❑ *He has expressly forbidden her to go out on her own. Le ha prohibido expresamente salir sin ir acompañada.* **4** ADJ An **express** intention or purpose is deliberate and specific. *expreso* ❑ *The express purpose of the flights was to get Americans out of the danger zone. El propósito expreso de los vuelos era sacar a los estadounidenses de la zona de peligro.* ● **ex|press|ly** ADV *expresamente* ❑ *...projects expressly designed to support cattle farmers. ...proyectos expresamente diseñados para apoyar a los ganaderos.* **5** ADJ An **express** service is one in which things are sent or done faster than usual. *express, rápido* ❑ *A special express service is available. Tenemos disponible un servicio express especial.* ● **Express** is also an adverb. *express* ❑ *Send it express. Mándalo express.* **6** N-COUNT An **express** or an **express** train is a fast train that stops at very few stations. *expreso* ❑ *The express to Kuala Lumpur left Singapore station. El expreso a Kuala Lumpur abandonó la estación de Singapur.*

**Word Partnership** Usar *express* con:

N. express **appreciation**, express **your emotions**, express **gratitude**, express **sympathy**, **words to** express *something* **1**
express **purpose** **4**
express **mail**, express **service** **5**

**ex|pres|sion** /ɪksprɛʃᵊn/ (**expressions**) **1** N-VAR The **expression of** ideas or feelings is the showing of them through words, actions, or artistic activities. *expresión, manifestación* ❑ *Your baby's smiles are expressions of happiness. Las sonrisas de tu bebé son expresiones de su felicidad.* ❑ *...the rights of the individual to freedom of expression. ...el derecho de los individuos a la libertad de expresión.* **2** N-VAR Your **expression** is the way that your face looks at a particular moment. It shows what you are thinking or feeling. *expresión, aspecto* ❑ *Levin sat there, an expression of sadness on his face. Levin estaba ahí sentado, con una expresión de tristeza en el rostro.*

**3** N-COUNT An **expression** is a word or phrase. *frase* ❑ *When writing an essay it is important to avoid using slang expressions.* *Cuando se escribe, es importante evitar usar frases coloquiales.*

**ex|pres|sive con|tent** N-UNCOUNT **Expressive content** is writing, speech, or another form of communication which expresses someone's feelings about a particular subject. *contenido emocional*

**ex|pres|sive writ|ing** N-UNCOUNT **Expressive writing** is writing such as diaries and letters that describes the writer's feelings, ideas, or beliefs. *escritura emocional*

| Word Link | *puls ≈ driving, pushing : compulsory, expulsion, impulse* |
|---|---|

**ex|pul|sion** /ɪkspʌlʃᵊn/ (**expulsions**) **1** N-VAR **Expulsion** is when someone is forced to leave a school, university, or organization. *expulsión* ❑ *...her expulsion from high school.* *...su expulsión de la preparatoria.* **2** N-VAR **Expulsion** is when someone is forced to leave a place. *expulsión* [FORMAL] ❑ *...the expulsion of foreign workers.* *...la expulsión de los trabajadores extranjeros.*

**ex|quis|ite** /ɪkskwɪzɪt, ɛkskwɪzɪt/ ADJ **Exquisite** means extremely beautiful. *exquisito* ❑ *The Indians brought in exquisite things to sell.* *Los indígenas trajeron cosas exquisitas para vender.* ● **ex|quis|ite|ly** ADV *exquisitamente* ❑ *...exquisitely made dollhouses.* *...casas de muñecas exquisitamente hechas.*

**ex|tend** /ɪkstɛnd/ (**extends, extending, extended**) **1** V-I If you say that something, usually something large, **extends for** a particular distance or **extends from** one place **to** another, you are indicating its size or position. *extender* ❑ *The caves extend for 12 miles.* *Las cuevas se extienden por 12 millas.* ❑ *The main stem will extend to around 12 feet.* *El tallo principal alcanzará unos 12 pies.* **2** V-I If an object **extends from** a surface or place, it sticks out from it. *extenderse* ❑ *A table extended from the front of her desk.* *Una mesa se extendía desde el frente de su escritorio.* **3** V-I If something **extends to** a group of people, things, or activities, it includes or affects them. *extender* ❑ *The service extends to delivering gifts.* *El servicio se extiende a la entrega de los regalos.* **4** V-T If you **extend** something, you make it bigger, make it last longer, or make it include more. *extender, ampliar* ❑ *This year they have introduced three new products to extend their range.* *Este año han introducido tres nuevos productos para ampliar gama.* ❑ *They have extended the deadline by twenty-four hours.* *Han extendido la fecha límite por 24 horas.* **5** V-T If someone **extends** their hand, they stretch out their arm and hand to shake hands with someone. *extender* ❑ *The man extended his hand: "I'm Chuck."* *El hombre extendió su mano: —Me llamo Chuck.*

**ex|ten|sion** /ɪkstɛnʃᵊn/ (**extensions**) **1** N-COUNT An **extension** is a new room or building that is added to an existing building. *anexo, ampliación* ❑ *We are thinking of having an extension built.* *Estamos pensando en construir un anexo.* **2** N-COUNT An **extension** is an extra period of time for which something lasts or is valid, usually as a result of official permission. *extensión* ❑ *He was given a six-month extension to his visa.* *Le dieron una extensión de seis meses en la visa.* **3** N-COUNT Something that is an **extension of** something else is a development of it that includes or affects more people, things, or activities. *ampliación* ❑ *They did not agree with the extension of police powers.* *No estaban de acuerdo con la ampliación de los poderes policiacos.* **4** N-COUNT An **extension** is a telephone line that is connected to the switchboard of a company or institution, and that has its own number. The written abbreviation **ext.** is also used. *extensión* ❑ *She can get me on extension 308.* *Me puede encontrar en la extensión 308.*

**ex|ten|sive** /ɪkstɛnsɪv/ **1** ADJ Something that is **extensive** covers or includes a large physical area. *extensivo, extenso* ❑ *...an extensive tour of Latin America.* *...una gira extensiva por América Latina.* ● **ex|ten|sive|ly** ADV *extensivamente, extensamente* ❑ *Mark travels extensively.* *Mark viaja extensivamente.* **2** ADJ Something that is **extensive** covers a wide range of details, ideas, or items. *extensivo* ❑ *She recently completed an extensive study of elected officials.* *Recientemente ha completado un estudio extensivo de los funcionarios electos.* ● **ex|ten|sive|ly** ADV *extensivamente* ❑ *All these issues have been extensively researched.* *Todos estos problemas han sido extensivamente investigados.* **3** ADJ If something is **extensive,** it is very great. *extenso* ❑ *The security forces have extensive powers.* *Las fuerzas de seguridad tienen poderes extensos.* ● **ex|ten|sive|ly** ADV *extensamente* ❑ *Hydrogen is used extensively in industry.* *El hidrógeno es usado extensamente en la industria.*

**ex|ten|sor** /ɪkstɛnsər/ (**extensors**) N-COUNT **Extensors** are muscles that extend or straighten a part of your body. *extensor* [TECHNICAL]

**ex|tent** /ɪkstɛnt/ **1** N-SING If you are talking about how great, important, or serious a difficulty or situation is, you can refer to **the extent of** it. *alcance* ❑ *The government has little information on the extent of industrial pollution.* *El gobierno tiene poca información respecto al alcance de la contaminación industrial.* **2** N-SING **The extent of** something is its length, area, or size. *extensión* ❑ *Their commitment was to maintain the extent of forests.* *Su compromiso era mantener la extensión de los bosques.* **3** PHRASE You use expressions such as **to a large extent, to what extent,** or **to the extent that** in order to say how far something is true. *hasta cierto punto* ❑ *To some extent this was the truth.* *Hasta cierto punto, esa era la verdad.* ❑ *I was getting more nervous to the extent that I was almost physically sick.* *Me estaba poniendo cada vez más nervioso, hasta el punto en el que casi vomito.*

| Word Partnership | Usar *extent* con: |
|---|---|
| N. | extent **of the damage** **1** |
| V. | **determine the** extent, **know the** extent **1** |
| ADJ. | **lesser** extent **1** |
| | **full** extent **1** **2** |
| | **a certain** extent **3** |

**ex|te|ri|or** /ɪkstɪəriər/ (**exteriors**) **1** N-COUNT The **exterior** of something is its outside surface. *exterior* ❑ *...the exterior of the building.* *...el exterior del edificio.* **2** N-COUNT You can refer to someone's usual appearance or behavior as their **exterior.** *aspecto, apariencia* ❑ *Pat's tough exterior hides a shy and sensitive soul.* *El aspecto rudo de Pat oculta un alma tímida y sensible.* **3** ADJ You use **exterior** to refer to the outside parts of something or things that are outside something. exterior ❑ ...exterior walls. ...las paredes exteriores.

| Thesaurus | exterior | Ver también: |
|---|---|---|
| N. | coating, cover, shell, skin 1 | |
| ADJ. | external, outer, surface 3 | |

E

**ex|ter|nal** /ɪkstɜrnᵊl/ ADJ **External** means happening, coming from, or existing outside a place, person, or area. externo, exterior ❑ ...heat loss through external walls. ...la pérdida de calor a través de las paredes exteriores. ❑ ...the commissioner for external affairs. ...el comisionado para asuntos externos. ● **ex|ter|nal|ly** ADV externamente ❑ Vitamins can be applied externally to the skin. Las vitaminas se pueden aplicar externamente sobre la piel.
→ see **ear**

**ex|ter|nal com|bus|tion en|gine** (**external combustion engines**) N-COUNT An **external combustion engine** is an engine that burns fuel outside the engine. motor de combustión externa [TECHNICAL]

**ex|ter|nal fer|ti|li|za|tion** N-UNCOUNT **External fertilization** is a method of reproduction in some animals in which the egg and sperm join together outside the female's body, for example in water. Compare **internal fertilization**. fertilización externa [TECHNICAL]

**ex|ter|nal fuel tank** (**external fuel tanks**) N-COUNT An **external fuel tank** is a container for fuel that is fitted to the outside of a spacecraft. tanque de combustible externo

**ex|tinct** /ɪkstɪŋkt/ 1 ADJ A species of animal or plant that is **extinct** no longer has any living members. extinto ❑ Many animals could become extinct in less than 10 years. Muchos animales pueden estar extintos en diez años. 2 ADJ An **extinct** volcano does not erupt or is not expected to erupt anymore. extinto ❑ Its tallest volcano, long extinct, is Olympus Mons. Su volcán más alto, extinto desde hace mucho, es el monte Olimpo.

**ex|tra** /ɛkstrə/ (**extras**) 1 ADJ An **extra** amount, person, or thing is another one that is added to others of the same kind. adicional, suplementario ❑ Police warned drivers to allow extra time to get to work. La policía advirtió a los conductores que tomaran tiempo adicional para llegar a su trabajo. ❑ There's an extra blanket in the bottom drawer. Hay una cobija adicional en el cajón de abajo. ● **Extra** is also an adverb. extra ❑ You may be charged 10% extra for this service. Se le puede llegar a cobrar un 10% extra por este servicio. ● **Extra** is also a pronoun. extra, recargo ❑ She won't pay any extra. No pagará recargos. 2 N-COUNT **Extras** are additional amounts of money that are added to the price that you have to pay for something. cargo extra, sobreprecio ❑ There are no hidden extras. No hay cargos extra escondidos. 3 N-COUNT **Extras** are things that are not necessary in a situation, activity, or object, but that make it more comfortable, useful, or enjoyable. extra ❑ Optional extras include cooking classes. Los extras opcionales incluyen lecciones de cocina. 4 N-COUNT The **extras** in a movie are the people who play unimportant parts, for example, as members of a crowd. extra ❑ In 1944, Kendall entered films as an extra. En 1994, Kendall entró en el negocio de las películas como extra. 5 ADV You can use **extra** in front of adjectives and adverbs to emphasize the quality that they are describing. extremadamente [INFORMAL] ❑ You have to be extra careful. Debes ser extremadamente cuidadoso.

| Word Link | extra ≈ outside of : extract, extradite, extraordinary |
|---|---|

**ex|tract** (**extracts, extracting, extracted**)

The verb is pronounced /ɪkstrækt/. The noun is pronounced /ɛkstrækt/.

1 V-T To **extract** a substance means to obtain it from something else, for example, by using industrial or chemical processes. extraer ❑ ...the traditional method of extracting coal. ...el método tradicional para extraer el carbón. ● An **extract** is a substance that has been obtained in this way. exctracto ❑ ...plant extracts. ...extractos de plantas. ● **ex|trac|tion** N-UNCOUNT exctracción ❑ ...the extraction of oil. ...la extracción del petróleo. 2 V-T If you **extract** something **from** a place, you take it out or pull it out. extraer, sacar ❑ He extracted a small notebook from his pocket. Sacó un cuadernito de su bolsillo. 3 V-T When a dentist **extracts** a tooth, he or she removes it from a patient's mouth. sacar, extraer ❑ A dentist may decide to extract the tooth. Un dentista podría decidir extraer el diente. ● **ex|trac|tion** N-VAR (**extractions**) extracción ❑ The extraction was painless. La extracción fue indolora. 4 N-COUNT An **extract from** a book or piece of writing is a small part of it that is printed or published separately. fragmento, selección ❑ Read this extract from an information booklet. Lea este fragmento de un folleto informativo.
→ see **industry, mineral**

**extra|dite** /ɛkstrədaɪt/ (**extradites, extraditing, extradited**) V-T If someone **is extradited**, they are officially sent back to their own or another country or state to be tried for a crime. extraditar [FORMAL] ❑ A judge agreed to extradite him to Texas. Un juez accedió a extraditarlo a Texas. ● **extra|di|tion** /ɛkstrədɪʃᵊn/ N-VAR (**extraditions**) extradición ❑ A New York court turned down the British government's request for his extradition. Un juzgado de Nueva York rechazó la petición del gobierno inglés para que se le extraditara.

**extraor|di|nary** /ɪkstrɔrdᵊnɛri/ 1 ADJ If you describe something or someone as **extraordinary**, you mean that they have some extremely good or special quality. extraordinario ❑ We've made extraordinary progress. Hemos tenido un progreso extraordinario. ❑ The task requires extraordinary patience. La tarea requiere de paciencia extraordinaria. ● **extraor|di|nari|ly** /ɪkstrɔrdᵊnɛrɪli/ ADV extraordinariamente ❑ She's extraordinarily kind. Ella es extraordinarimente amable. 2 ADJ If you describe something as **extraordinary**, you mean that it is very unusual or surprising. extraordinario ❑ What an extraordinary thing to happen! ¡Qué cosa más extraordinaria ha sucedido! ● **extraor|di|nari|ly** ADV extraordinariamente ❑ Apart from the hair, he looked extraordinarily unchanged. Dejando a un lado el pelo, aparentaba estar extraordinariamente igual.

**ex|trava|gant** /ɪkstrævəgənt/ 1 ADJ Someone who is **extravagant** spends more money than they can afford or uses more of something than is reasonable. extravagante, carísimo ❑ We are not extravagant; restaurant meals are a luxury.

*No es que seamos extravagantes, es que las comidas en restaurante son un lujo.* • **ex|trava|gance** N-UNCOUNT *extravagancia* ❑ *Tales of his extravagance were common. Las historias de su extravagancia eran comunes.* • **ex|trava|gant|ly** ADV *de modo extravagante* ❑ *Jeff shopped extravagantly for presents. Jeff compraba los regalos de modo extravagante.* **2** ADJ Something that is **extravagant** costs more money than you can afford or uses more of something than is reasonable. *extravagante, carísimo* ❑ *Her aunt gave her an extravagant gift. Su tía le dio un regalo carísimo.* • **ex|trava|gant|ly** ADV *extravagantemente, excesivamente* ❑ *...an extravagantly expensive machine. ...un aparato extravagantemente caro.* **3** ADJ **Extravagant** behavior is extreme behavior that is often done for a particular effect. *extravagante* ❑ *He was extravagant in his admiration of her. Él era extravagante en su admiración hacia ella.* • **ex|trava|gant|ly** ADV *extravagantemente* ❑ *She praised him extravagantly. Lo elogiaba extravagantemente.*

**ex|treme** /ɪkstri̱m/ (**extremes**) **1** ADJ **Extreme** means very great in degree or intensity. *extremo* ❑ *The girls moved with extreme caution. Las chicas se movieron con precaución extrema.* ❑ *...people living in extreme poverty. ...la gente que vive en la pobreza extrema.* • **ex|treme|ly** ADV *extremadamente* ❑ *My cellphone is extremely useful. Mi teléfono celular es extremadamente útil.* **2** ADJ You use **extreme** to describe situations and behavior that are much more severe or unusual than you would expect, especially when you disapprove of them because of this. *extremo* ❑ *It is hard to imagine Jesse capable of anything so extreme. Es difícil imaginar a Jesse siendo capaz de algo tan extremo.* **3** N-COUNT You can use **extremes** to refer to situations or types of behavior that have opposite qualities to each other, especially when each situation or type of behavior has such a quality to the greatest degree possible. *extremo* ❑ *...a middle way between the extremes of success and failure. ...un punto medio entre los extremos del éxito y el fracaso.* **4** ADJ The **extreme** end or edge of something is its farthest end or edge. *fin, final, extremo* ❑ *...the room at the extreme end of the corridor. ...el cuarto al final del corredor.*

**Word Partnership** Usar *extreme* con:

| | |
|---|---|
| N. | extreme **caution**, extreme **difficulty** **1** extreme **case**, extreme **left**, extreme **right**, extreme **sports**, extreme **views** **2** |
| ADJ. | **the opposite** extreme **3** |

**ex|trem|ist** /ɪkstri̱mɪst/ (**extremists**) N-COUNT If you describe someone as an **extremist**, you disapprove of them because they try to bring about political change by using violent or extreme methods. *extremista, radical* ❑ *...foreign extremists. ...los extremistas extranjeros.* • **ex|trem|ism** N-UNCOUNT *extremismo, radicalismo* ❑ *...left and right-wing extremism. ...el radicalismo de la izquierda y de la derecha.*

**extro|vert** /ɛ̱kstrəvɜrt/ (**extroverts**) • An **extrovert** is someone who is extroverted. *extrovertido*

**extro|vert|ed** /ɛ̱kstrəvɜrtɪd/ ADJ Someone who is **extroverted** is very active, lively, and friendly. *extrovertido* ❑ *...young people who were easy-going and extroverted as children. ...los jóvenes que eran de fácil trato y extrovertidos cual niños.*

**ex|tru|sive** /ɪkstru̱sɪv/ ADJ **Extrusive** rock is rock that forms on the surface of the Earth after lava has been released and has cooled. Compare **intrusive.** *eruptivo, volcánico* [TECHNICAL]

**eye**
❶ PART OF THE BODY, ABILITY TO SEE
❷ PART OF AN OBJECT

❶ **eye** /a̱ɪ/ (**eyes, eyeing** or **eying, eyed**) **1** N-COUNT Your **eyes** are the parts of your body with which you see. *ojo* ❑ *I opened my eyes and looked. Abrí los ojos y miré.* ❑ *...a tall lady with dark brown eyes. ...una señora alta con ojos café obscuro.* **2** V-T If you **eye** someone or something in a particular way, you look at them carefully in that way. *echar un ojo/vistazo, contemplar, observar* ❑ *Sally eyed Claire with interest. Sally contempló a Calire con interés.* ❑ *Martin eyed the money. Martín le echó un ojo al dinero.* **3** N-COUNT You use **eye** when you are talking about a person's ability to judge things or about the way in which they are considering or dealing with things. *mirada, ojo para* ❑ *...a man with an eye for quality. ...un hombre con ojo para los productos de calidad.* ❑ *He learned to fish under the watchful eye of his grandmother. Aprendió a pescar bajo la mirada atenta de su abuela.* **4** → see also **black eye** **5** PHRASE If you say that something happens **before** your **eyes, in front of** your **eyes,** or **under** your **eyes,** you are emphasizing that it happens where you can see it clearly or while you are watching it. *ante (sus/los/mis propios) ojos* ❑ *A lot of them died in front of our eyes. Muchos de ellos murieron ante nuestros ojos.* **6** PHRASE If something **catches** your **eye,** you suddenly notice it. *llamar la atención* ❑ *A movement across the garden caught her eye. Un movimiento del otro lado del jardín le llamó la atención.* **7** PHRASE If you **catch** someone's **eye,** you do something to attract their attention, so that you can speak to them. *atraer la atención de* ❑ *He tried to catch Annie's eye. Intentó atraer la atención de Annie.* **8** PHRASE If you **keep** your **eyes open** or **keep an eye out for** someone or something, you watch for them carefully. *mantener ojos abiertos, vigilar, no perder de vista* [INFORMAL] ❑ *I asked the patrol to keep their eyes open. Le pedí a la vigilancia que mantuvieran sus ojos abiertos.* **9** PHRASE If you **have** your **eye on** something, you want to have it. *tener los ojos puestos en* [INFORMAL] ❑ *...a new outfit you've had your eye on. ...un nuevo traje en el que has tenido puestos los ojos.* **10** to **turn a blind eye** → see **blind** **11** **in** your **mind's eye** → see **mind**
→ see Word Web: **eye**
→ see **cry, face**

❷ **eye** /a̱ɪ/ (**eyes**) **1** N-COUNT An **eye** is a small metal loop that a hook fits into, as a fastening on a piece of clothing. *ojal* ❑ *...hooks and eyes. ...botones y ojales.* **2** N-COUNT The **eye** of a needle is the small hole at one end that the thread passes through. *ojo* ❑ *The difficult part was threading the cotton thread through the eye of the needle. La parte más difícil era pasar el hilo de algodón por el ojo de la aguja.*

**eye|ball** /a̱ɪbɔl/ (**eyeballs**) N-COUNT Your **eyeballs** are the parts of your eyes that are like

e

**Word Web** eye

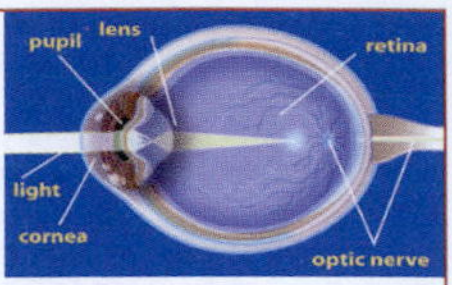


**Light** enters the **eye** through the **cornea.** The cornea bends the light and directs it through the **pupil.** The colored **iris** opens and closes the **lens.** This helps focus the **image** clearly on the **retina.** Nerve cells in the retina change the light into electrical signals. The **optic nerve** then carries these signals to the brain. In a **nearsighted** person the light rays focus in front of the lens. The image comes into focus in back of the lens in a **farsighted** person. An irregularity in the cornea can cause **astigmatism.** Glasses or **contact lenses** can correct all three problems.

E

white balls. *globo ocular*

**eye|brow** /aɪbraʊ/ (**eyebrows**) **1** N-COUNT Your **eyebrows** are the lines of hair that grow above your eyes. *ceja* **2** PHRASE If something causes you to **raise an eyebrow** or to **raise** your **eyebrows,** it causes you to feel surprised or disapproving. *levantar la ceja/las cejas, subir la ceja/las cejas* ❑ *He raised his eyebrows over some of the suggestions. Levantó las cejas cuando le dieron algunas sugerencias.*
→ see **face**

**eye can|dy** also **eye-candy** N-UNCOUNT **Eye candy** is used to refer to people or things that are attractive to look at but are not interesting in other ways. *simple decoración* [INFORMAL] ❑ *Back then, women on TV were mostly seen as eye candy. En aquel entonces, las mujeres que salían en televisión eran consideradas simple decoración.*

**eye|glasses** /aɪglæsɪz/ N-PLURAL **Eyeglasses** are the same as **glasses** or **spectacles.** *lentes, anteojos*

**eye|lash** /aɪlæʃ/ (**eyelashes**) N-COUNT Your **eyelashes** are the hairs that grow on the edges of your eyelids. *pestaña*
→ see **face**

**eye|lid** /aɪlɪd/ (**eyelids**) N-COUNT Your **eyelids** are the two pieces of skin that cover your eyes when they are closed. *párpado*
→ see **face**

**eye|liner** /aɪlaɪnər/ (**eyeliners**) N-MASS **Eyeliner** is a special kind of pencil which some women use on the edges of their eyelids next to their eyelashes in order to look more attractive. *delineador (de ojos)*

**eye|piece** /aɪpis/ (**eyepieces**) N-COUNT The **eyepiece** of a microscope or telescope is the piece of glass at one end, where you put your eye in order to look through the instrument. *ocular*

**eye-popping** ADJ Something that is **eye-popping** is very impressive or striking. *impactante* ❑ *...a plan to raise property taxes by an eye-popping $2 billion. ...un plan para aumentar el impuesto sobre la propiedad en una impactante cifra de 2,000 millones de dólares.*

**eye shad|ow** (**eye shadows**) also **eye-shadow** or **eyeshadow** N-MASS **Eye shadow** is a substance that you can brush on your eyelids in order to make them a different color. *sombra de ojos*
→ see **makeup**

**eye|sight** /aɪsaɪt/ N-UNCOUNT Your **eyesight** is your ability to see. *vista* ❑ *He suffered from poor eyesight. Tenía mala vista.*

**eye|witness** /aɪwɪtnɪs/ (**eyewitnesses**) N-COUNT An **eyewitness** is a person who was present at an event and can therefore describe it, for example in a law court. *testigo ocular, testigo presencial* ❑ *She was an eyewitness to the assassination of President Kennedy. Fue testigo presencial del asesinato de John F. Kennedy.*

# Ff

**fab|ric** /fæbrɪk/ (**fabrics**) **1** N-VAR **Fabric** is cloth produced by weaving together cotton, silk, or other threads. *tela* ❑ *...red cotton fabric.* *...tela roja de algodón.* **2** N-SING The **fabric** of a society or system is its basic structure, with all the customs and beliefs that make it work successfully. *estructura* ❑ *The fabric of society was damaged by the previous government.* *La estructura de la sociedad se vio dañada por el gobierno anterior.*
→ see **quilt**

| Word Link | *ous ≈ having the qualities of : dangerous, fabulous, mysterious* |
|---|---|

**fabu|lous** /fæbyələs/ ADJ If you describe something as **fabulous,** you like it a lot or think that it is very good. *fabuloso* [INFORMAL]

**face**
❶ NOUN USES
❷ VERB USES

❶ **face** /feɪs/ (**faces**) **1** N-COUNT Your **face** is the front part of your head from your chin to the top of your forehead. *cara*, *rostro* ❑ *She had a beautiful face.* *Tenía un rostro hermoso.* ❑ *He was hit in the face.* *Le pegaron en la cara.* **2** N-COUNT The **face** of a cliff, mountain, or building is a vertical surface or side of it. *ladera*, *lado*, *cara* ❑ *...the north face of the Eiger.* *...la ladera norte del Eiger.* **3** N-COUNT The **face** of a clock or watch is the surface with the numbers or hands on it, which shows the time. *carátula* **4** N-SING If you refer to one particular **face of** of something, you mean one particular aspect of it. *aspecto* ❑ *...the unacceptable face of politics.* *...el aspecto inaceptable de la política.* **5** N-UNCOUNT If you lose **face,** you do something which makes people respect or admire you less. If you do something in order to save **face,** you do it in order to avoid losing people's respect or admiration. *prestigio* ❑ *They don't want a war, but they don't want to lose face.* *No quieren una guerra, pero tampoco quieren desprestigiarse.* **6** → see also **face value** **7** PHRASE If you come **face to face** with someone, you meet them and can talk to them or look at them directly. *cara a cara*, *de frente* ❑ *We were walking into the town when we came face to face with Jacques Dubois.* *Caminábamos pueblo adentro cuando nos encontramos de frente con Jacques Dubois.* **8** PHRASE If an action or belief **flies in the face of** accepted ideas or rules, it seems to completely oppose or contradict them. *ignorar*, *hacer caso omiso de* ❑ *These ideas fly in the face of common sense.* *Estas ideas se oponen al sentido común.* **9** PHRASE If you take a particular action or attitude **in the face of** a problem or difficulty, you respond to that problem or difficulty in that way. *ante* ❑ *...Harrison's courage in the face of cancer.* *...el valor de Harrison ante al cáncer.* **10** PHRASE If you **make a face,** you show a feeling such as dislike for something by twisting your face into an ugly expression. *poner mala cara* ❑ *Opening the door, she made a face at the horrible smell.* *Al abrir la puerta, puso mala cara por el horrible olor.* **11** PHRASE If you manage to keep **a straight face,** you manage to look serious, although you want to laugh. *aguantarse la risa*
→ see Picture Dictionary: **face**
→ see **makeup**

❷ **face** /feɪs/ (**faces, facing, faced**) **1** V-T/V-I To **face** a particular direction means to look in that direction from a position directly opposite it. *estar de frente* ❑ *They stood facing each other.* *Estaban de pie uno frente a otro.* ❑ *Our house faces south.* *Nuestra casa da al sur.* **2** V-T If you **face** or **are faced** with something difficult or unpleasant, or if it **faces** you, you have to deal with it. *enfrentar* ❑ *Williams faces life in prison.* *Williams podría ser condenado a catena perpetua.* **3** V-T If you **cannot face** something, you do not feel able to do it because it seems so difficult or unpleasant. *no atreverse a* ❑ *I can't face telling my girlfriend.* *No me atrevo a decírselo a mi novia.*

**face card** (**face cards**) N-COUNT A **face card** is any of the twelve cards in a deck of cards which has a picture of a face. The face cards are kings, queens, and jacks. *figura*

**face mask** (**face masks**) **1** N-COUNT A **face mask** is something that you wear over your face to prevent yourself from breathing bad air or from spreading germs, or to protect your face. *mascarilla*, *máscara* **2** N-COUNT A **face mask** is a substance that you spread on your face, allow to dry and then remove, in order to clean your skin. *mascarilla*
→ see **football**

**face-off** (**face-offs**) N-COUNT A **face-off** is an argument or conflict that is intended to settle a dispute. *enfrentamiento* ❑ *...a face-off between Congress and the White House.* *...una enfrentamiento entre el Congreso y la Casa Blanca.*

**face value** **1** N-SING The **face value** of things such as coins, paper money, or tickets is the amount of money that they are worth, and that is written on them. *valor nominal* ❑ *Tickets were selling at twice their face value.* *Los boletos se estaban vendiendo al doble de su valor nominal.* **2** PHRASE If you take something **at face value,** you accept it and believe it without thinking about it very much, even though it might be untrue. *en sentido literal* ❑ *Public statements should not necessarily be taken at face value.* *No necesariamente se deben creer las declaraciones públicas.*

**fa|cial** /feɪʃ$^{\text{ə}}$l/ ADJ **Facial** means appearing on or

F

**Picture Dictionary** face

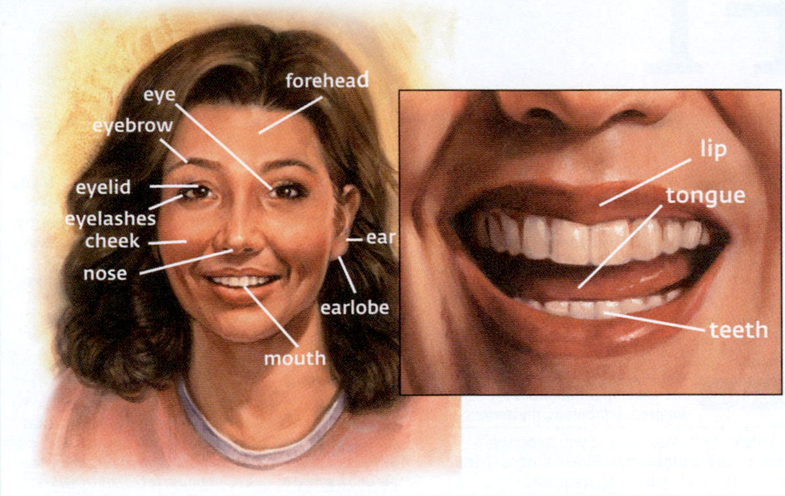


being part of your face. facial ❑ *His facial expression didn't change.* *Su expresión facial no cambió.*

**fa|cili|tate** /fəsɪlɪteɪt/ (**facilitates, facilitating, facilitated**) V-T To **facilitate** an action or process means to make it easier or more likely to happen. facilitar ❑ *The new airport will facilitate the development of tourism.* *El nuevo aeropuerto facilitará el desarrollo turístico.*

**fa|cil|ity** /fəsɪlɪti/ (**facilities**) **1** N-COUNT **Facilities** are buildings, pieces of equipment, or services that are provided for a particular purpose. instalación ❑ *...excellent kitchen and bathroom facilities.* *...excelentes instalaciones de baño y cocina.* **2** N-COUNT A **facility** is a useful service or feature provided by an organization or machine. medio, sistema ❑ *...a website's search facility.* *...el sistema de búsqueda de un sitio web.*

**fact** /fækt/ (**facts**) **1** N-COUNT **Facts** are pieces of information that are true. hecho ❑ *...the facts about the murder.* *...los hechos sobre el asesinato.* **2** PHRASE You use **the fact that** after some verbs or prepositions, especially in expressions such as **in view of the fact that, apart from the fact that,** and **despite the fact that,** to link the verb or preposition with a clause. el hecho de que ❑ *My family now accepts the fact that I don't eat sugar or bread.* *Mi familia ya acepta el hecho de que no como azúcar ni pan.* **3** PHRASE You use **in fact, in actual fact,** or **in point of fact** to indicate that you are giving more detailed information about what you have just said. de hecho ❑ *I don't watch television. In fact, I no longer even own a TV.* *No veo televisión. De hecho, ya ni siquiera tengo una.* **4** N-VAR When you refer to something as a **fact** or as **fact,** you mean that you think it is true or correct. hecho real ❑ *...a statement of historical fact.* *...una verdad histórica.*
→ see **history**

**Word Partnership** Usar *fact* con:

| | |
|---|---|
| V. | **accept a** fact, **check the** facts, **face a** fact **1** |
| N. | fact **and fiction** **1** |
| ADJ. | **hard** fact, **historical** fact, **important** fact, **obvious** fact, **random** fact, **simple** fact **1** |

**fac|tion** /fækʃən/ (**factions**) N-COUNT A **faction** is an organized group of people within a larger group, which opposes some of the ideas of the larger group and fights for its own ideas. facción ❑ *...the leaders of the country's warring factions.* *...los líderes de las facciones antagónicas del país.* ● **fac|tion|al** ADJ entre facciones ❑ *...factional disputes.* *...disputas entre facciones.*

**Word Link** ***fact, fic*** ≈ ***making : artificial, factor, manufacture***

**fac|tor** /fæktər/ (**factors, factoring, factored**) **1** N-COUNT A **factor** is one of the things that affects an event, decision, or situation. factor ❑ *Exercise is an important factor in maintaining physical and mental health.* *El ejercicio es un factor importante para mantener la salud física y mental.* **2** N-COUNT In mathematics, a **factor** is one of the numbers that you multiply when you multiply two or more numbers together. factor [TECHNICAL]
▸ **factor in** or **factor into** PHR-VERB If you **factor** a particular cost or element **into** a calculation you are making, or if you **factor** it **in,** you include it. tomar en cuenta ❑ *You'd better consider this and factor it into your decision making.* *Sería bueno que lo consideraras y lo tomaras en cuenta en tus decisiones.*

**Word Web** factory

Life in a 19th-century **factory** was very difficult. **Employees** often **worked** twelve hours a day, six days a week. **Wages** were low and **child labor** was common. Many **workers** were not allowed to take **breaks**. Some even had to eat while working. As early as 1832, doctors started warning about the dangers of **air pollution**. The 20th century brought some big changes. Workers began to join **unions**. During World War I, **government regulations** set standards for **minimum wages** and better **working conditions**. In addition, automation took over some of the most difficult and dangerous jobs.

f

**Word Link** *ory ≈ place where something happens : dormitory, factory, territory*

**fac|to|ry** /fæktəri, -tri/ (**factories**) N-COUNT A **factory** is a large building where machines are used to make large quantities of goods. *fábrica*
→ see Word Web: **factory**

**fac|ul|ty** /fækᵊlti/ (**faculties**) **1** N-COUNT Your **faculties** are your physical and mental abilities. *facultad* ❑ *X-rays showed fractures in my left arm, legs, and skull but I was in full control of my faculties. Los rayos X mostraban fracturas en mi brazo izquierdo, piernas y cráneo, pero yo estaba en pleno uso de mis facultades.* **2** N-VAR A **faculty** is all the teaching staff of a university or college, or of one department. *cuerpo docente, profesorado* ❑ *Good faculties are essential to a good college. Un buen cuerpo docente es esencial para una buena universidad.*

**fad** /fæd/ (**fads**) N-COUNT A **fad** is an activity or topic of interest that is very popular for a short time, but which people become bored with very quickly. *moda pasajera* ❑ *In 1981, some people thought the new mountain bikes were a fad. En 1981, algunas personas creyeron que las nuevas bicicletas de montaña serían una moda pasajera.*
→ see **diet**

**fade** /feɪd/ (**fades, fading, faded**) **1** V-T/V-I When a colored object **fades** or when the light **fades** it, it gradually becomes paler. *decolorar(se), apagar(se), perder color o intensidad* ❑ *Color fades under direct sunlight. El color se pierde bajo la luz directa del sol.* ❑ *No matter how soft the light is, it still fades carpets. No importa qué tan suave sea la luz, aún así hace que las alfombras se decoloren.* ● **fad|ed** ADJ *apagado, desteñido* ❑ *...a girl in a faded dress. ...una chica con un vestido desteñido.* **2** V-I If memories, feelings, or possibilities **fade,** they slowly become less intense or less strong. *desvanecerse* ❑ *My wish to live here has started to fade. Mi deseo de vivir aquí ha empezado a desvanecerse.*

**Word Partnership** Usar *fade* con:

| | |
|---|---|
| N. | **colors** fade, **images** fade **1** |
| | **memories** fade **2** |
| V. | **begin to** fade **1** **2** |
| ADV. | fade **quickly** **1** **2** |

**Fahr|en|heit** /færənhaɪt/ ADJ **Fahrenheit** is a scale for measuring temperature, in which water freezes at 32 degrees and boils at 212 degrees. It is represented by the symbol °F. *Fahrenheit* ❑ *The temperature was above 100 degrees Fahrenheit. La temperatura era superior a los 37.8 grados centígrados.*
→ see **climate, measurement, thermometer**

**Usage** **Fahrenheit** and **Celsius**

The Fahrenheit scale is commonly used to express temperature in the U.S. rather than the Celsius (or centigrade) scale.

**fail** /feɪl/ (**fails, failing, failed**) **1** V-T/V-I If you **fail** to do something that you were trying to do, you do not succeed in doing it. *no hacer, no lograr, fracasar* ❑ *The party failed to win the election. El partido no logró ganar la elección.* ❑ *He failed in his attempt to take control of the company. Fracasó en su intento por hacerse con el control de la compañía.* **2** V-T If someone or something **fails** to do a particular thing that they should have done, they do not do it. *no cumplir con algo* [FORMAL] ❑ *He failed to file his tax return. No cumplió con la presentación de su declaración de impuestos.* **3** V-T If someone **fails** you, they do not do what you had expected or trusted them to do. *fallar* ❑ *All the doctors have failed me—they don't know what's wrong. Todos los doctores me han fallado; no saben qué tengo.* **4** V-T If someone **fails** a test or examination, they do not reach the standard that is required. *reprobar* ❑ *I lived in fear of failing my final exams. Tenía miedo de reprobar los exámenes finales.* **5** PHRASE You use **without fail** to emphasize that something always happens or must definitely happen. *sin falta* ❑ *He attended every meeting without fail. Asistió a todas las reuniones sin falta.* ❑ *You must without fail give the money to Alex. Debes darle el dinero a Alex sin falta.*

**fail|ure** /feɪlyər/ (**failures**) **1** N-UNCOUNT **Failure** is a lack of success in doing or achieving something. *fracaso* ❑ *This policy is doomed to failure. Esta política está destinada al fracaso.* ❑ *Three attempts on the 200-meter record ended in failure. Tres intentos por batir el récord de los 200 metros terminaron en fracaso.* **2** N-UNCOUNT Your **failure to** do a particular thing is the fact that you do not do it. *no hacer algo* ❑ *They were upset by his failure to tell the truth. Estaban molestos porque no dijo la verdad.* **3** N-COUNT If something is **a failure,** it is not a success. *fracaso* ❑ *The marriage was a failure. El matrimonio era un fracaso.* **4** N-VAR If there is a **failure** of something, it goes wrong and stops working or developing properly. *falla* ❑ *Several accidents were caused by engine failures. Varios accidentes fueron causados por fallas en los motores.*

**Word Partnership** Usar *failure* con:

ADJ. **afraid of** failure, **doomed to** failure 1
**complete** failure 1–3
**dismal** failure 3
N. **feelings of** failure, **risk of** failure, **success or** failure 1
**engine** failure, **heart** failure, **kidney** failure, **liver** failure 3
V. failure **to communicate** 1 2

F

**faint** /feɪnt/ (**fainter, faintest, faints, fainting, fainted**) 1 ADJ A **faint** sound, color, mark, or quality is not strong or intense. *débil, tenue, ligero* ❑ *...the soft, faint sounds of water dripping. ...el suave y débil sonido del agua goteando.* ❑ *There was still the faint hope that she might return. Aún existía una ligera esperanza de que volviera.* • **faint|ly** ADV *apenas, ligeramente, débilmente* ❑ *The room smelled faintly of paint. La habitación olía ligeramente a pintura.* 2 ADJ Someone who is **faint** feels weak and unsteady as if they are about to lose consciousness. *débil, mareado* ❑ *He was unsteady on his feet and felt faint. Sus pies apenas podían sostenerlo y se sentía mareado.* 3 V-I If you **faint,** you lose consciousness for a short time. *desmayarse* ❑ *She suddenly fell forward and fainted. Repentinamente se desmayó y cayó al suelo.*

**fair** /fɛər/ (**fairer, fairest, fairs**) 1 ADJ Something or someone that is **fair** is reasonable and right. *justo* ❑ *It didn't seem fair to leave out her father. No parecía justo excluir a su padre.* ❑ *Do you feel they're paying their fair share? ¿Crees que están pagando lo justo?* ❑ *I wanted them to get a fair deal. Quería que tuvieran un trato justo.* • **fair|ly** ADV *limpiamente, equitativamente* ❑ *We solved the problem quickly and fairly. Resolvimos el problema rápida y equitativamente.* • **fair|ness** N-UNCOUNT *justicia, imparcialidad* ❑ *...concerns about the fairness of the election campaign. ...inquietud sobre la imparcialidad de la campaña electoral.* 2 ADJ A **fair** amount, degree, size, or distance is quite a large amount, degree, size, or distance. *considerable* ❑ *My neighbors travel a fair amount. Mis vecinos viajan bastante.* 3 ADJ Someone who is **fair,** or who has **fair** hair, has light-colored hair. *rubio* 4 ADJ **Fair** skin is very pale and usually burns easily under strong sunlight. *blanco* 5 ADJ When the weather is **fair,** it is quite sunny and not raining. *despejado* [FORMAL] 6 N-COUNT A county, state, or country **fair** is an event where there are, for example, displays of goods and animals, and amusements, games, and competitions. *feria, exposición* 7 N-COUNT A **fair** is an event at which people display and sell goods. *feria, bazar* ❑ *...an antiques fair. ...un bazar de antigüedades.* 8 PHRASE You use **fair enough** when you want to say that a statement, decision, or action seems reasonable to a certain extent, but that perhaps there is more to be said or done. *bueno, está bien* [mainly SPOKEN] ❑ *"I need a holiday."— "That's fair enough. Can I come too?" —Necesito unas vacaciones.—Me parece bien; pero ¿puedo ir yo también?*

**Usage** **fair** and **fare**

Avoid confusing *fair* and *fare*, which sound exactly the same. The adjective *fair* means reasonable, or attractive, or light in color; the noun *fare* refers to the price of a bus, train, ferry, or airplane ticket, while the verb *fare* refers to how well someone is doing in a particular situation: *Was it fair that all the fair-haired people on the boat fared well, while all the dark-haired people got seasick? After all, everyone had paid the same fare.*

**Word Partnership** Usar *fair* con:

ADJ. fair **and balanced** 1
N. fair **chance**, fair **deal**, fair **fight**, fair **game**, fair **play**, fair **price**, fair **share**, fair **trade**, fair **treatment**, fair **trial** 1
fair **amount** 2
fair **hair** 3
fair **skin** 4
**craft** fair, **science** fair 7

**fair|ly** /fɛərli/ 1 ADV **Fairly** means to quite a large degree. *bastante, más o menos* ❑ *We did fairly well. Lo hicimos bastante bien.* ❑ *Were you always fairly bright at school? ¿Siempre fuiste muy inteligente en la escuela?* 2 → see also **fair**

**fairy** /fɛəri/ (**fairies**) N-COUNT A **fairy** is an imaginary creature with magical powers. Fairies are often represented as small people with wings. *hada*
→ see **fantasy**

**fairy tale** (**fairy tales**) also **fairytale** N-COUNT A **fairy tale** is a story for children involving magical events and imaginary creatures. *cuento de hadas*

**faith** /feɪθ/ (**faiths**) 1 N-UNCOUNT If you have **faith in** someone or something, you feel confident about their ability or goodness. *fe, confianza* ❑ *People have lost faith in the government. La gente ha perdido la confianza en el gobierno.* 2 N-UNCOUNT **Faith** is strong religious belief in a particular God. *fe, creencia* ❑ *They respect his faith. Respetan su fe.* 3 N-COUNT A **faith** is a particular religion, for example, Christianity, Buddhism, or Islam. *fe* ❑ *The college welcomes students of all faiths. La universidad acepta a estudiantes de todas las creencias.* 4 PHRASE If you do something **in good faith,** you seriously believe that what you are doing is right, even though it may not be. *de buena fe*

**faith|ful** /feɪθfəl/ 1 ADJ Someone who is **faithful to** a person, organization, or idea, remains firm in their support for them. *fiel* ❑ *Help your brothers and sisters and be faithful to your friends. Ayuda a tus hermanos y se fiel a tus amigos.* • **The faithful** are people who are faithful to someone or something. *los incondicionales* ❑ *...the gathering of the Democratic Party faithful. ...la reunión de los incondicionales del Partido Demócrata.* • **faith|ful|ly** ADV *fielmente* ❑ *He has faithfully supported every twist and turn of government policy. Ha apoyado fielmente todos los cambios de la política gubernamental.* 2 ADJ Someone who is **faithful to** their husband, wife, or lover does not have a sexual relationship with anyone else. *fiel* 3 ADJ A **faithful** account, translation, or copy of something represents or reproduces the original accurately. *fiel* ❑ *His movie is not faithful to the book.* *Su película no es fiel al libro.* ● **faith|ful|ly** ADV *fielmente* ❑ *The story is told faithfully.* *La historia está contada fielmente.*

**faith|ful|ly** /feɪθfəli/ **1** CONVENTION When you start a formal or business letter with "Dear Sir" or "Dear Madam," you can write **Yours faithfully** before your signature at the end. *Atentamente* **2** → see also **faithful**

**fa|ji|ta** /fəhitə/ (**fajitas**) N-COUNT A **fajita** is a Mexican dish consisting of a tortilla wrapped around strips of meat and vegetables. *fajita* ❑ *...chicken fajitas.* *...fajitas de pollo.*

**fake** /feɪk/ (**fakes, faking, faked**) **1** ADJ **Fake** things have been made to look valuable or genuine, although they are not. *falso* ❑ *The bank manager issued fake certificates.* *El gerente del banco emitió certificados falsos.* ● A **fake** is something that is fake. *falsificación, imitación* ❑ *Every one of the works of art is a fake.* *Cada una de las obras de arte es una falsificación.* **2** V-T If someone **fakes** something, they try to make it look genuine although it is not. *falsificar, falsea, simular* ❑ *It's easy to fake a suntan with make-up.* *Es fácil simular un bronceado con maquillaje.* ❑ *...faked evidence.* *...pruebas falsas.*

| **Thesaurus** | *fake* | Ver también: |
|---|---|---|
| ADJ. | artificial, counterfeit, imitation **1** | |
| V. | falsify, pretend **2** | |

**fall** /fɔl/ (**falls, falling, fell, fallen**) **1** V-I If someone or something **falls,** they move quickly downward, by accident or because of a natural force. *caer(se)* ❑ *He has fallen from his horse.* *Se cayó del caballo.* ❑ *Bombs fell on the town.* *Las bombas cayeron en la ciudad.* **2** V-I If a person or structure that is standing somewhere **falls,** they move from their upright position, so that they are then lying on the ground. *caer(se)* ❑ *The woman tried to stop herself from falling.* *La mujer intentó no caerse.* ❑ *He lost his balance and fell backwards.* *Perdió el equilibrio y cayó de espaldas.* ● **Fall** is also a noun. *caída* ❑ *She broke her right leg in a bad fall.* *Cayó mal y se rompió la pierna derecha.* ● **Fall down** means the same as **fall.** *caer* ❑ *I hit him so hard he fell down.* *Le pegué tan fuerte que se cayó.* **3** V-I When rain or snow **falls,** it comes down from the sky. *caer* **4** V-I If something **falls,** it decreases in amount, value, or strength. *bajar, disminuir, descender* ❑ *His income will fall by almost 70 percent.* *Su ingreso disminuirá casi el 70 por ciento.* ❑ *The number of Americans without jobs has fallen to 9.8 million.* *El número de estadounidenses sin empleo ha disminuido a 9.8 millones.* ● **Fall** is also a noun. *caída, descenso* ❑ *...a sharp fall in the value of the dollar.* *...una brusca caída del valor del dólar.* **5** V-I If a powerful or successful person **falls,** they suddenly lose their power or position. *caer* ❑ *Leaders fall, revolutions come and go, but places never really change.* *Los líderes caen, las revoluciones van y vienen, pero los lugares nunca cambian del todo.* ● **Fall** is also a noun. *caída* ❑ *...the fall of the military dictator.* *...la caída del dictador militar.* **6** V-I If you say that something or someone **falls into** a particular group or category, you mean that they belong in that group or category. *clasificar* ❑ *The problems fall into two categories.* *Los problemas se clasifican en dos categorías.* **7** V-I When light or shadow **falls** on something, it covers it. *caer, cubrir* ❑ *A shadow suddenly fell across the doorway.* *Repentinamente, una sombra cubrió la puerta.* **8** V-I When night or darkness **falls,** night begins and it becomes dark. *caer* ❑ *As darkness fell outside, they sat down to eat.* *Mientras afuera caía la noche, se sentaron a comer.* **9** V-LINK You can use **fall** to show that someone or something passes into another state. For example, if someone **falls ill,** they become ill. *caer* ❑ *...she suddenyl fell ill and was rushed to hospital.* *...de repente cayó enferma y la llevaron urgentemente al hospital.* ❑ *Shakespeare's tragic heroine, Desdemona, fell victim to the jealousy of her husband.* *Desdémona, la heroína trágica de Shakespeare, cayó víctima de los celos de su esposo.* **10** N-PLURAL You can refer to a **waterfall** as **the falls.** *cascada, caída de agua, catarata(s)* **11** N-VAR **Fall** is the season between summer and winter when the weather becomes cooler. *otoño* ❑ *...the fall of 1991.* *...el otoño de 1991.* **12** → see also **fallen** **13** to **fall foul of** → see **foul** **14** to **fall into place** → see **place**

▸ **fall apart** **1** PHR-VERB If something **falls apart,** it breaks into pieces because it is old or badly made. *deshacerse, desmoronarse* ❑ *Bit by bit the building fell apart.* *Poco a poco el edificio se desmoronó.* **2** PHR-VERB If an organization or system **falls apart,** it becomes disorganized and inefficient. *venirse abajo* ❑ *Europe's monetary system is falling apart.* *El sistema monetario europeo está viniéndose abajo.*

▸ **fall back on** PHR-VERB If you **fall back on** something, you do it or use it after other things have failed. *recurrir a, echar mano de* ❑ *When things get tricky, you fall back on your experience.* *Cuando las cosas se ponen difíciles, se echa mano de la experiencia.*

▸ **fall behind** PHR-VERB If you **fall behind,** you do not make progress or move forward as fast as other people. *rezagarse, quedarse a la zaga* ❑ *He is falling behind all the top players.* *Se está quedando a la zaga de los mejores jugadores.*

▸ **fall for** **1** PHR-VERB If you **fall for** someone, you are strongly attracted to them and start loving them. *enamorarse de* ❑ *I just fell for him right away.* *Me enamoré de él de inmediato.* **2** PHR-VERB If you **fall for** a lie or trick, you believe it or are deceived by it. *tragarse* ❑ *He pretended he was famous, but none of us fell for it.* *Quería hacer creer que era famoso, pero ninguno de nosotros se lo tragó.*

▸ **fall off** PHR-VERB If something **falls off,** it separates from the thing to which it was attached. *caerse, soltarse* ❑ *When the exhaust pipe falls off your car, you have to replace it.* *Cuando el tubo de escape de tu auto se desprende, tienes que reemplazarlo.*

▸ **fall out** **1** PHR-VERB If a person's hair or a tooth **falls out,** it comes out. *caerse* **2** PHR-VERB If you **fall out** with someone, you have an argument and stop being friendly with them. You can also say that two people **fall out.** *pelearse* ❑ *She fell out with her husband.* *Se peleó con su esposo.* **3** → see also **fallout**

▸ **fall through** PHR-VERB If an arrangement, plan, or deal **falls through,** it fails to happen. *no concretarse* ❑ *They wanted to turn the estate into a private golf course, but the deal fell through.* *Querían convertir la propiedad en un campo de golf privado, pero el trato no se concretó.*

▸ **fall to** PHR-VERB If a responsibility, duty, or opportunity **falls to** someone, it becomes their responsibility, duty, or opportunity. *tocarle,* corresponderle ❑ *It fell to me to make a speech.* *Me tocó hacer un discurso.*

**Thesaurus** *fall* Ver también:

V. fall down, plunge, topple 1 2
come down 3
drop, plunge; (*ant.*) increase, rise 4

**fall|en** /fɔlən/ **Fallen** is the past participle of **fall**. *participio pasado de **fall***

**fal|lo|pian tube** /fəloʊpiən tub/ (**fallopian tubes**) N-COUNT A woman's **fallopian tubes** are the two tubes in her body along which eggs pass from her ovaries to her womb. *trompa de Falopio*

F

**fall|out** /fɔlaʊt/ N-UNCOUNT **Fallout** is the radiation that affects a place after a nuclear explosion. *lluvia radiactiva* ❑ *...radioactive fallout.* *...lluvia radiactiva.*

**false** /fɔls/ 1 ADJ If something is **false**, it is incorrect, untrue, or mistaken. *falso, postizo* ❑ *The president received false information from those around him.* *El presidente recibió información falsa de quienes lo rodean.* ❑ *You do not know whether what you're told is true or false.* *No sabes si lo que te dicen es verdadero o falso.* ● **false|ly** ADV *falsamente, con falsedad* ❑ *She falsely accused him of the crime.* *Lo acusó falsamente del crimen.* 2 ADJ You use **false** to describe objects which are artificial but which are intended to look like the real thing or to be used instead of the real thing. *falso* ❑ *...a set of false teeth.* *...una dentadura postiza.* 3 ADJ If you describe a person or their behavior as **false**, you are criticizing them for being insincere or for hiding their real feelings. *falso, fingido* ❑ *"Thank you," she said with false enthusiasm.* *—Gracias—dijo con un entusiasmo fingido.* ● **false|ly** ADV *fingidamente, falsamente, con falsedad* ❑ *They smiled at one another, somewhat falsely.* *Se sonrieron uno al otro, un poco fingidamente.*

**false alarm** (**false alarms**) N-COUNT When you think something dangerous is about to happen, but then discover that you were mistaken, you can say that it was a **false alarm**. *falsa alarma* ❑ *The bomb threat turned out to be a false alarm.* *La amenaza de bomba resultó ser una falsa alarma.*

**false cau|sal|ity** N-UNCOUNT In logic, **false causality** is an error that occurs when one event is wrongly considered to be the cause of another event. *causalidad falsa* [TECHNICAL]

**fame** /feɪm/ N-UNCOUNT If you achieve **fame**, you become very well-known. *fama* ❑ *The film earned him international fame.* *La cinta le valió la fama internacional.*

**Word Partnership** Usar *fame* con:

V. **bring** fame, **gain** fame, **rise to** fame
N. **claim to** fame, fame **and fortune**, **hall of** fame
ADJ. **international** fame

**fa|mili|ar** /fəmɪlyər/ 1 ADJ If someone or something is **familiar** to you, you recognize them or know them well. *familiar* ❑ *...a culture that was quite familiar to him.* *...una cultura que le era muy familiar.* ❑ *They are already familiar faces on our TV screens.* *Ya son rostros familiares en nuestras pantallas de televisión.* ● **fa|mili|ar|ity** /fəmɪliærɪti/ N-UNCOUNT *familiaridad* ❑ *...the comforting familiarity of her face.* *...la reconfortante familiaridad de su rostro.* 2 ADJ If you are **familiar with** something, you know or understand it well. *familiarizado con* ❑ *Are you familiar with the region?* *¿Conoces la región?* ● **fa|mili|ar|ity** N-UNCOUNT *familiaridad* ❑ *...familiarity with advanced technology.* *...familiaridad con la tecnología de punta.* 3 ADJ If someone you do not know well behaves in a **familiar** way toward you, they treat you very informally in a way that you might find offensive. *con demasiada confianza* ❑ *The women suggested that his behavior was "too familiar."* *La mujer insinuó que la trató "con demasiada confianza."* ● **fa|mili|ar|ity** N-UNCOUNT *confianza* ❑ *She spoke to the waiter with easy familiarity.* *Le habló al mesero con confianza.* ● **fa|mili|ar|ly** ADV *confianzudamente, con demasiada confianza* ❑ *"Gerald, isn't it?" I began familiarly.* *—¿Gerald, verdad?" le dije confiazudamente.*

**fami|ly** /fæmɪli, fæmli/ (**families**) 1 N-COUNT A **family** is a group of people who are related to each other, especially parents and their children. *familia* ❑ *...a family of five.* *...una familia de cinco* ❑ *Does he have any family?* *¿Tiene familia?* 2 N-COUNT When people talk about their **family**, they sometimes mean their ancestors. *familia* ❑ *My father's family came from Ireland.* *La familia de mi padre vino de Irlanda.* 3 N-COUNT A **family** of animals or plants is a group of related species. *familia*
→ see Picture Dictionary: **family**

**fami|ly room** (**family rooms**) N-COUNT A **family room** in a house is a room where a family watches television or plays games. *cuarto de la tele, cuarto de televisión* ❑ *The present owners added a new kitchen, a front porch and a family room.* *Los propietarios actuales agregaron una cocina, un pórtico al frente y un cuarto de televisión.*
→ see **house**

**fami|ly values** N-PLURAL People sometimes refer to traditional moral values and standards as **family values**. *valores familiares, valores tradicionales* ❑ *Reverend Jackson called for a return to family values.* *El reverendo Jackson hizo un llamado a recuperar los valores tradicionales.*

**fam|ine** /fæmɪn/ (**famines**) N-VAR **Famine** is a situation in which large numbers of people have little or no food, and many of them die. *hambruna* ❑ *...refugees trapped by war and famine.* *...refugiados atrapados por la guerra y la hambruna.*

**fa|mous** /feɪməs/ ADJ Someone or something that is **famous** is very well known. *famoso, muy conocido* ❑ *...one of Kentucky's most famous landmarks.* *...uno de los edificios más conocidos de Kentucky.*

**Thesaurus** *famous* Ver también:

ADJ. acclaimed, celebrated, prominent, renowned; (*ant.*) anonymous, obscure, unknown

**fan** /fæn/ (**fans, fanning, fanned**) 1 N-COUNT If you are a **fan** of someone or something, you like them very much and are very interested in them. *aficionado o aficionada, admirador o admiradora, fanático o fanática* ❑ *If you're a Billy Crystal fan, you'll love this movie.* *Si eres admirador de Billy Crystal, te va a encantar esta película.* ❑ *I am a great fan of rave music.*

*Soy muy aficionado a la música rave.* **2** N-COUNT A **fan** is a piece of electrical equipment that keeps a room or machine cool. *ventilador* **3** N-COUNT A **fan** is a flat object that you wave to keep yourself cool. *abanico* **4** V-T If you **fan** yourself when you are hot, you wave a fan or other flat object in order to make yourself feel cooler. *abanicar(se)* ❑ *She waited in the truck, fanning herself with a piece of cardboard. Esperó en el camión, abanicándose con un pedazo de cartón.*

fan

→ see **concert**

▸**fan out** PHR-VERB If a group of people or things **fan out,** they move forward away from a particular point in different directions. *desplegar(se)* ❑ *The troops have fanned out to the west. Las tropas se desplegaron hacia el oeste.*

**fa|nat|ic** /fənætɪk/ (**fanatics**) **1** N-COUNT If you describe someone as a **fanatic,** you disapprove of them because you think their behavior or opinions are very extreme. *fanático o fanática* ❑ *I am not a religious fanatic but I am a Christian. No soy fanático de la religión, pero soy cristiano.* ● **fa|nati|cal** ADJ *fanático* ❑ *They're fanatical about what they eat. Son fanáticos de lo que comen.* **2** N-COUNT If you say that someone is a **fanatic,** you mean that they are very enthusiastic about a particular activity, sport, or way of life. *fanático o fanática, aficionado o aficionada* ❑ *...football fanatics. ...fanáticos del fútbol.* **3** ADJ **Fanatic** means the same as **fanatical.** *fanático*

**fan base** (**fan bases**) also **fanbase** N-COUNT The **fan base** of a pop star or a pop group is their fans, considered as a whole. *admiradores o admiradoras* ❑ *His fan base is mostly middle-aged ladies. Sus admiradoras son básicamente mujeres de edad madura.*

**fancy**
❶ ELABORATE OR EXPENSIVE
❷ WANTING, LIKING, OR THINKING

❶ **fan|cy** /fænsi/ (**fancier, fanciest**) **1** ADJ If you describe something as **fancy,** you mean that it is special, unusual, or elaborate, for example because it has a lot of decoration. *estrambótico, extravagante, caprichoso* ❑ *...fancy jewelry. ...joyería extravagante.* **2** ADJ If you describe something as **fancy,** you mean that it is very expensive or of very high quality, and you often dislike it because of this. *lujoso, elegante, muy chic* [INFORMAL] ❑ *My parents sent me to a fancy private school. Mis padres me mandaron a una escuela privada muy chic.*

❷ **fan|cy** /fænsi/ **1** EXCLAM You say "**fancy**" or "**fancy that**" when you want to express surprise or disapproval. *¡mira nada más!, ¡qué barbaridad!, ¡imagínate!* **2** PHRASE If something **takes** your **fancy,** you like it a lot when you see it or think of it. *encantar, fascinar, gustar, llamar la atención* ❑ *She makes her own clothes, copying any fashion which takes her fancy. Ella se hace su propia ropa y copia cualquier modelo que le llame la atención.*

**fan mail** N-UNCOUNT **Fan mail** is mail that is sent to a famous person by their fans. *cartas a una personalidad*

**fan|ny pack** (**fanny packs**) N-COUNT A **fanny**

fanny pack

**pack** is a small bag attached to a belt which you wear around your waist. You use it to carry things such as money and keys. _cangurera_

**fan|ta|size** /fæntəsaɪz/ (**fantasizes, fantasizing, fantasized**) V-I If you **fantasize** about something, you give yourself pleasure by imagining it, although it is unlikely to happen. _fantasear, soñar con algo_ ❑ *I fantasized about writing music.* _Soñaba con escribir música._



**fan|tas|tic** /fæntæstɪk/ **1** ADJ If you say that something is **fantastic,** you are emphasizing that you think it is very good. _fantástico_ [INFORMAL] ❑ *I have a fantastic social life.* _Mi vida social es fantástica._ **2** ADJ A **fantastic** amount or quantity is an extremely large one. _fantástico_ ❑ *...fantastic sums of money.* _...cantidades fantásticas de dinero_ • **fan|tas|ti|cal|ly** /fæntæstɪkli/ ADV _fantásticamente, increíblemente_ ❑ *...a fantastically expensive restaurant.* _...un restaurante increíblemente caro._

**fan|ta|sy** /fæntəsi/ (**fantasies**) **1** N-COUNT A **fantasy** is a pleasant situation or event that you think about and that you want to happen, especially one that is unlikely to happen. _fantasía_ ❑ *...fantasies of romance and true love.* _...fantasías románticas y de amor verdadero._ **2** N-VAR You can refer to a story or situation that someone creates from their imagination and that is not based on reality as **fantasy.** _fantasía_ ❑ *The film is a science-fiction fantasy.* _Esa película es una fantasía de ciencia ficción._

→ see Word Web: **fantasy**

**FAQ** /fæk/ (**FAQs**) N-COUNT **FAQ** is used especially on websites to refer to questions about a particular topic. **FAQ** is an abbreviation for "frequently asked questions." _preguntas frecuentes_

**far**
- ❶ DISTANT IN SPACE OR TIME
- ❷ THE EXTENT TO WHICH SOMETHING HAPPENS
- ❸ EMPHATIC USES

**❶ far** /fɑr/ **1** ADV If one place, thing, or person is **far** away from another, there is a great distance between them. _lejos_ ❑ *He was too far from the car to go back now.* _Ya estaba demasiado lejos del auto como para regresarse._ ❑ *My sisters moved even farther away from home.* _Mis hermanas se mudaron aún más lejos de casa._ **2** ADV You use **far** in questions and statements about distances. _a qué distancia, hasta, qué tan lejos_ ❑ *How far is it to San Francisco?* _¿Qué tan lejos está San Francisco?_ ❑ *She followed the tracks as far as the road.* _Siguió las vías hasta el camino._ **3** ADV A time or event that is **far** away in the future or the past is a long time from the present or from a particular point in time. _lejano, a más de_ ❑ *...conflicts whose roots lie far back in time.* _...conflictos cuyas raíces están en un pasado muy lejano._ ❑ *I can't plan any farther than the next six months.* _No puedo planear nada a más de seis meses._ **4** ADJ You can use **far** to refer to the part of an area or object that is the greatest distance from the center in a particular direction. _extremo_ ❑ *Port Angeles is in the far north of Washington State.* _Port Angeles está en el extremo norte del estado de Washington._

**❷ far** /fɑr/ **1** ADV You can use **far** to talk about the extent to which something happens. _hasta dónde, hasta qué punto_ ❑ *How far did the film tell the truth about his life?* _¿Hasta qué punto la película dice la verdad sobre su vida?_ **2** ADV You can talk about how **far** someone or something gets to describe the progress that they make. _mucho, hasta dónde_ ❑ *Discussions never progressed very far.* _Las discusiones nunca avanzaron mucho._ ❑ *Think of how far we have come in a short time.* _Piensa en lo mucho que avanzamos en poco tiempo._ **3** ADV You can talk about how **far** a person or action goes to describe the degree to which someone's behavior or actions are extreme. _pasarse de la raya, ir demasiado lejos_ ❑ *This time he's gone too far.* _Esta vez se pasó de la raya._ **4** PHRASE If you talk about what has happened **so far,** you talk about what has happened up until the present point in a situation or story. _hasta ahora, hasta el momento, hasta este momento_ ❑ *So far, they have failed.* _Hasta ahora, han fallado._

**❸ far** /fɑr/ **1** ADV You can use **far** to mean "very much" when you are comparing two things and emphasizing the difference between them. _mucho_ ❑ *Women who eat a healthy diet are far less likely to suffer anxiety.* _Las mujeres cuya dieta es saludable son mucho menos propensas a padecer ansiedad._ ❑ *The police say the response has been far better than expected.* _La policía dijo que la respuesta ha sido mucho mejor de lo esperado._ **2** PHRASE You use the expression **by far** when you are comparing something or someone with others of the same kind, in order to emphasize how great the difference is between them. _por mucho, con_

**Word Web** **fantasy**

All **fictional** writing involves the use of **imaginary** situations and characters. However, **fantasy** goes even further. This **genre** uses more **imagination** than **reality**. Authors create new creatures, **myths**, and **legends**. A **novelist** may use **realistic** people and settings. But a fantasy writer is free to create a whole different world where earthly laws no longer apply. Contemporary movies have found a rich source of stories in the genre. Today you can see many different films about **fairies**, **wizards**, and **dragons**.

mucho ❑ *By far the most important issue for them is unemployment.* *Con mucho, el problema más importante para ellos es el desempleo.* **3** PHRASE If you say that something is **far from** a particular thing or **far from** being true, you are emphasizing that it is not that particular thing or not true at all. *lejos de, al contrario, ni mucho menos* ❑ *Much of what they said was far from the truth.* *Gran parte de lo que dijeron estaba lejos de ser verdad.* ❑ *Far from being relaxed, we both felt very uncomfortable.* *Lejos de sentirnos relajados, los dos nos sentíamos muy incómodos.*

> **Far** has two comparatives, **farther** and **further**, and two superlatives, **farthest** and **furthest**. **Farther** and **farthest** are used mainly in sense **1**, and are dealt with here. **Further** and **furthest** are dealt with in separate entries.

**far|away** /fɑrəweɪ/ ADJ A **faraway** place is a long distance from you or from a particular place. *lejano, remoto* ❑ *...photographs of a faraway country.* *...fotografías de un país lejano.*

**fare** /fɛər/ (**fares, faring, fared**) **1** N-COUNT A **fare** is the money that you pay for a trip that you make, for example, in a bus, train, or taxi. *boleto, pasaje, billete* ❑ *He could not afford the fare.* *No le alcanzaba para el boleto.* **2** V-I If you say that someone or something **fares** well or badly, you are referring to the degree of success they have in a particular situation or activity. *irle bien a alguien, irle mal a alguien* ❑ *Of course, some vice presidents fare better than others.* *Obviamente, a algunos vicepresidentes les va mejor que a otros.*
→ see also **fair**

**Far East** N-PROPER **The Far East** consists of all the countries of Eastern Asia, including China, Japan, North and South Korea, and Indonesia. *Lejano Oriente, Extremo Oriente*

**far-fetched** ADJ If you describe a story or idea as **far-fetched**, you are criticizing it because you think it is unlikely to be true or practical. *exagerado*

**farm** /fɑrm/ (**farms, farming, farmed**) **1** N-COUNT A **farm** is an area of land, together with the buildings on it, that is used for growing crops or raising animals. *rancho, granja, hacienda, finca* ❑ *Both boys like to work on the farm.* *A los dos muchachos les gusta trabajar en el rancho.* **2** V-T/V-I If you **farm** an area of land, you grow crops or keep animals on it. *cultivar, trabajar la tierra, criar animales, sembrar* ❑ *They farmed some of the best land in the country.* *Sembraban en algunas de las mejores tierras del país.* ❑ *Bease has been farming for 30 years.* *Bease ha trabajado la tierra durante 30 años.*
→ see Word Web: **farm**
→ see **dairy**

**farm|er** /fɑrmər/ (**farmers**) N-COUNT A **farmer** is a person who owns or manages a farm. *ranchero o ranchera, granjero o granjera, agricultor o agricultora*
→ see **farm**

**farm|ing** /fɑrmɪŋ/ N-UNCOUNT **Farming** is the activity of growing crops or keeping animals on a farm. *agricultura, cultivo, labranza, crianza de animales*

**far off** (**further off, furthest off**) **1** ADJ **Far-off** time is a long way in the future or past. *remoto, lejano, distante* ❑ *In those far-off days no one imagined that a woman could be prime minister.* *En esa lejana época nadie se imaginaba que una mujer pudiera ser primera ministra.* **2** ADJ A **far-off** place is a long distance away. *lejano, distante, alejado* ❑ *...far-off galaxies.* *...galaxias distantes.* ❑ *The woman was too far off to hear.* *La mujer estaba muy lejos para poder oír.* • **Far off** is also an adverb. *a lo lejos* ❑ *The band was playing far off.* *A lo lejos se oía la banda.*

**Farsi** /fɑrsi/ N-UNCOUNT **Farsi** is a language that is spoken in Iran. *lengua persa, dari*

**far-sighted** ADJ **Far-sighted** people cannot see things clearly that are close to them, and therefore need to wear glasses. *présbite, miope*
→ see **eye**

**far|ther** /fɑrðər/ **Farther** is a comparative of **far**. *más lejos*

**far|thest** /fɑrðɪst/ **Farthest** is a superlative of **far**. *lo más lejos, lejísimos*

**fas|ci|nate** /fæsɪneɪt/ (**fascinates, fascinating, fascinated**) V-T If something **fascinates** you, you find it extremely interesting. *fascinar(se)* ❑ *Politics fascinated Franklin's father.* *La política le fascinaba al padre de Franklin.*

**fas|ci|nat|ing** /fæsɪneɪtɪŋ/ ADJ If you describe something as **fascinating**, you find it extremely interesting. *fascinante* ❑ *Madagascar is a fascinating place.* *Madagascar es un lugar fascinante.*

**fas|cist** /fæʃɪst/ (**fascists**) ADJ Someone with **fascist** views has right-wing political beliefs that include strong control by the state and a powerful role for the armed forces. *fascista* ❑ *...extreme fascist organizations.* *...organizaciones fascistas.* • A **fascist** is someone who has fascist views. *fascista*
• **fas|cism** N-UNCOUNT *fascismo* ❑ *...the rise of fascism in the 1930s.* *...el ascenso del fascismo en la década de 1930.*

**fash|ion** /fæʃᵊn/ (**fashions**) **1** N-UNCOUNT **Fashion** is the area of activity that involves styles of clothing and appearance. *moda* ❑ *...20 full-*

**Word Web** farm

Farmers no longer simply plant a **crop** and **harvest** it. Today's **farmer** uses engineering and technology to make a living. Careful **irrigation** and **drainage** control the amount of water **plants** receive. **Insecticides** protect plants from insects. **Fertilizers** make things grow. High-tech **agricultural** methods may increase the world's **food** supply. Using **hydroponic** methods, farmers use **chemical** solutions to **cultivate** plants. This has several advantages. **Soil** can contain **pests** and diseases not present in water alone. Growing plants hydroponically also requires less water and less labor than conventional growing methods.

color pages of fashion for men. *...20 páginas a color de moda masculina.* **2** N-COUNT A **fashion** is a style of clothing or a way of behaving that is popular at a particular time. *moda* ❑ *Long dresses were in fashion back then. En esa época estuvieron de moda los vestidos largos.* **3** N-SING If you do something **in** a particular **fashion** or **after** a particular **fashion**, you do it in that way. *manera, forma* ❑ *According to investigators, all of the fires were set in a similar fashion. Según los investigadores, todos los incendios fueron iniciados de la misma forma.* **4** → see also **old-fashioned** **5** PHRASE If something is **in fashion**, it is popular and approved of at a particular time. If it is **out of fashion**, it is not popular or approved of. *de moda, en boga* ❑ *That sort of house is back in fashion. Ese tipo de casa está otra vez de moda.*

F

**fash|ion|able** /fæʃənəbᵊl/ ADJ Something or someone that is **fashionable** is popular or approved of at a particular time. *a la moda, de moda* ❑ *It became fashionable to eat certain kinds of fish. Se puso de moda comer cierto tipo de pescado.* • **fash|ion|ably** ADV *a la moda* ❑ *She is fashionably dressed. Está vestida a la moda.*

**fast** /fæst/ (**faster, fastest, fasts, fasting, fasted**) **1** ADJ **Fast** means happening, moving, or doing something at great speed. You also use **fast** in questions or statements about speed. *rápido, veloz* ❑ *...fast cars. ...autos veloces.* ❑ *How fast will the process will be? ¿Qué tan rápido será el proceso?* • **Fast** is also an adverb. *rápidamente, velozmente, rápido, veloz* ❑ *They work terrifically fast. Trabajan terriblemente rápido.* ❑ *It would be nice to go faster and break the world record. Sería muy agradable ir más rápido y romper el récord del mundo.* **2** ADJ If a watch or clock is **fast**, it is showing a time that is later than the real time. *adelantado* ❑ *That clock's an hour fast. Ese reloj está adelantado una hora.* **3** ADV You use **fast** to say that something happens without any delay. *rápidamente, inmediatamente, de inmediato* ❑ *You need professional help—fast! Necesitas ayuda especializada,—¡pero de inmediato!* • **Fast** is also an adjective. *rápido* ❑ *...surprisingly fast action by Congress. ...medidas sorprendentemente rápidas del Congreso.* **4** ADV If you hold something **fast**, you hold it tightly and firmly. If something is stuck **fast**, it is stuck very firmly and cannot move. *con firmeza, firmemente* ❑ *She climbed the staircase cautiously, holding fast to the rail. Subió con cuidado la escalera, sujetándose con firmeza del barandal.* **5** ADV If you hold **fast** to a principle or idea, or if you stand **fast**, you do not change your mind about it, even though people are trying to persuade you to. *firme* ❑ *We try to hold fast to the values of honesty and concern for others. Tratamos de mostrarnos firmes en cuanto a valores como la honestidad y la preocupación por los demás.* **6** V-I If you **fast**, you eat no food for a period of time, usually for either religious or medical reasons, or as a protest. *ayunar* • **Fast** is also a noun. *ayuno* ❑ *The fast is over at sunset. El ayuno termina al ponerse el sol.* **7** PHRASE Someone who is **fast asleep** is completely asleep. *profundamente dormido* ❑ *When he went upstairs five minutes later, she was fast asleep. Cuando subió cinco minutos después, ya estaba profundamente dormida.*

| **Thesaurus** | *fast* | Ver también: |
|---|---|---|
| ADJ. | hasty, quick, rapid, speedy, swift; (*ant.*) leisurely, slow **1** | |
| ADV. | quickly, rapidly, soon, swiftly; (*ant.*) leisurely, slowly **3** | |
| | firmly, tightly; (*ant.*) loosely, unsteadily **4** | |

**fas|ten** /fæsᵊn/ (**fastens, fastening, fastened**) **1** V-T/V-I When you **fasten** something, you close it by means of buttons or a strap, or some other device. If something **fastens** with buttons or straps, you can close it in this way. *asegurar(se), abrochar(se), cerrar(se), sujetar(se)* ❑ *She got quickly into her car and fastened the seat-belt. Se subió rápidamente al auto y se abrochó el cinturón de seguridad.* ❑ *Her long hair was fastened at her neck by an elastic band. Tenía el largo cabello recogido en la nuca, sujeto con una liga.* **2** V-T If you **fasten** one thing **to** another, you attach the first thing to the second. *pegar, fijar, sujetar* ❑ *...instructions on how to fasten the strap to the box. ...instrucciones sobre cómo sujetar la correa a la caja.*

**fast food** N-UNCOUNT **Fast food** is hot food, such as hamburgers and French fries, which is served quickly after you order it. *comida rápida*
→ see **meal**

**fast lane** (**fast lanes**) **1** N-COUNT On a highway, **the fast lane** is the part of the road where the vehicles that are traveling fastest go. *carril de alta velocidad* **2** N-SING If someone is living **in the fast lane,** they have a very busy, exciting life, although they sometimes seem to take a lot of risks. *vivir a tope* ❑ *...a tale of life in the fast lane. ...la historia de una vida vivida a tope.*

**fat** /fæt/ (**fats, fatter, fattest**) **1** ADJ A **fat** person has a lot of flesh on his or her body and weighs too much. *gordo, obeso* ❑ *I ate what I liked and began to get fat. Comía lo que quería y empecé a engordar.* • **fat|ness** N-UNCOUNT *gordura, obesidad* ❑ *...an increase in fatness in adults. ...un incremento de la obesidad entre los adultos.* **2** N-VAR **Fat** is a substance contained in foods such as meat, cheese, and butter which stores energy in your body. *grasa* ❑ *Cut the amount of fat in your diet by avoiding red meats. Reduce la cantidad de grasa de tu dieta evitando la carne roja.* **3** N-VAR **Fat** is a solid or liquid substance obtained from animals or vegetables, which is used in cooking. *grasa* ❑ *Use as little oil or fat as possible. Usa lo menos posible de aceite o grasa.* **4** ADJ A **fat** object, especially a book, is very thick or wide. *grueso, gordo* **5** N-UNCOUNT **Fat** is the extra flesh that animals and humans have under their skin, which is used to store energy and to help keep them warm. *grasa* ❑ *If you don't exercise, everything you eat turns to fat. Si no haces ejercicio, todo lo que comes se convierte en grasa.*
→ see **calorie**

| **Thesaurus** | *fat* | Ver también: |
|---|---|---|
| ADJ. | big, chunky, heavy, obese, overweight, stout, thick; (*ant.*) lean, skinny, slim, thin **1** | |

**fa|tal** /feɪtᵊl/ **1** ADJ A **fatal** action has very undesirable effects. *fatal, mortal, desastroso* ❑ *He made the fatal mistake of lending her some money.*

*Cometió el fatal error de prestarle dinero.* • **fa|tal|ly** ADV *fatalmente* ❑ *This could fatally damage his chances of becoming president. Esto podría tener consecuencias funestas para sus probabilidades de llegar a presidente.* **2** ADJ A **fatal** accident or illness causes someone's death. *fatal, mortal* ❑ *...the fatal stabbing of a police officer. ...el apuñalamiento mortal de un oficial de policía.* • **fa|tal|ly** ADV *fatalmente, mortalmente, de muerte* ❑ *The soldier was fatally wounded in the chest. El soldado fue herido de muerte en el pecho.*

**fa|tal|ity** /fətælɪti/ (**fatalities**) N-COUNT A **fatality** is a death caused by an accident or by violence. *muerto, víctima mortal, fatalidad* [FORMAL] ❑ *...rising highway fatalities. ...el incremento de los accidentes fatales en las carreteras.*

**fate** /feɪt/ (**fates**) **1** N-UNCOUNT **Fate** is a power that some people believe controls and decides everything that happens. *suerte, destino* ❑ *I believe in fate and that things happen for a reason. Yo creo en el destino y en que por algo pasan las cosas.* **2** N-COUNT A person's or thing's **fate** is what happens to them. *suerte, destino* ❑ *His fate is now in the hands of the governor. Su suerte está ahora en manos del gobernador.*

**fa|ther** /fɑðər/ (**fathers, fathering, fathered**) **1** N-COUNT Your **father** is your male parent. *padre, papá, progenitor* ❑ *His father was a painter. Su papá era pintor.* **2** V-T When a man **fathers** a child, he makes a woman pregnant and their child is born. *engendrar, ser el padre* ❑ *She claims Mark fathered her child. Ella afirma que Mark es el padre de su hijo.* **3** N-COUNT The man who invented or started something is sometimes referred to as the **father of** that thing. *padre* ❑ *...Max Dupain, the father of modern photography. ...Max Dupain, el padre de la fotografía moderna.*
→ see **family**

**father-in-law** (**fathers-in-law**) N-COUNT Your **father-in-law** is the father of your husband or wife. *suegro*
→ see **family**

**fa|tigue** /fətig/ (**fatigues**) **1** N-UNCOUNT **Fatigue** is a feeling of extreme physical or mental tiredness. *fatiga, cansancio* ❑ *She continued to have severe stomach cramps and fatigue. Seguía con fuertes dolores de estómago y fatiga.* **2** N-PLURAL **Fatigues** are clothes that soldiers wear when they are fighting or when they are doing routine jobs. *uniforme de faena*

**fat|so** /fætsoʊ/ (**fatsos** or **fatsoes**) N-COUNT; N-VOC If someone calls another person a **fatso,** they are saying in an unkind way that the person is fat. *gordo, gorda, gordinflón, gordinflona* [INFORMAL]

**fat|ty** /fæti/ (**fattier, fattiest**) **1** ADJ **Fatty** food contains a lot of fat. *grasoso* ❑ *Don't eat fatty food or chocolates. No comas alimentos grasosos ni chocolates.* **2** ADJ **Fatty** acids or **fatty** tissues contain a lot of fat. *graso*

**fau|cet** /fɔsɪt/ (**faucets**) N-COUNT A **faucet** is a device that controls the flow of a liquid or gas from a pipe or container. Sinks and baths have faucets attached to them. *llave, grifo, canilla* ❑ *She turned off the faucet and dried her hands. Cerró la llave del agua y se secó las manos.*
→ see **bathroom**

**fault** /fɔlt/ (**faults, faulting, faulted**) **1** N-SING If a bad or undesirable situation is your **fault,** you caused it or are responsible for it. *culpa, responsabilidad* ❑ *The accident was my fault. El accidente fue culpa mía, El accidente fue mi culpa.* **2** N-COUNT A **fault** in someone or something is a weakness in them or something that is not perfect. *defecto, falla* ❑ *His manners made her forget his faults. Su buena educación la hizo pasar por alto sus defectos.* **3** N-COUNT A **fault** is a large crack in the surface of the Earth. *falla* ❑ *...the San Andreas Fault. ...la falla de San Andrés.* **4** V-T If you **cannot fault** someone, you cannot find any reason for criticizing them or the things that they are doing. *criticar, encontrar defectos a alguien, censurar* ❑ *You can't fault their determination. No puedes criticar su determinación.* **5** PHRASE If someone or something is **at fault,** they are responsible for something that has gone wrong. *ser culpable, tener la culpa* ❑ *He could not accept that he was at fault. No podía aceptar que era culpable.* **6** PHRASE If you **find fault with** something or someone, you complain about them. *criticar, censurar, desaprobar* ❑ *He says you're always finding fault with him. Él dice que siempre lo estás criticando.*
→ see **earthquake**

| **Thesaurus** | *fault* | Ver también: |
|---|---|---|
| N. | blunder, error, mistake, wrongdoing **1**<br>defect, flaw, imperfection, weakness **2** | |

**fault block** (**fault blocks**) N-COUNT A **fault block** is a large area of rock that is separated from other rock by faults in the Earth's surface. *roca de dislocación* [TECHNICAL]

**fault-block moun|tain** (**fault-block mountains**) N-COUNT A **fault-block mountain** is a mountain that is formed when the land between two fault lines rises up or the land outside the fault lines drops down. *bloque fallado, bloque de falla* [TECHNICAL]

**fava bean** /fɑvəbin/ (**fava beans**) N-COUNT **Fava beans** are flat round beans that are light green in color and are eaten as a vegetable. *haba*

**fa|vor** /feɪvər/ (**favors, favoring, favored**) **1** N-UNCOUNT If you regard something or someone with **favor,** you like or support them. *aprecio, estimación, gusto* ❑ *She wished that she could look with favor on her new boss. Deseaba poder sentir estimación por su nueva jefa.* **2** N-COUNT If you **do** someone **a favor,** you do something to help them even though you do not have to. *favor* ❑ *I've come to ask you to do me a favor. Vine a pedirte que me hicieras un favor.* **3** V-T If you **favor** something, you prefer it to the other choices available. *preferir, estar a favor de* ❑ *The majority of Americans favor raising taxes on the rich. La mayoría de los americanos están a favor de que se incrementen los impuestos a los ricos.* **4** V-T If you **favor** someone, you treat them better or in a kinder way than you treat other people. *favorecer, privilegiar* ❑ *The company favors U.S. citizens. La empresa favorece a los ciudadanos estadounidenses.* **5** PHRASE If you are **in favor of** something, you support it and think that it is a good thing. *a favor de* ❑ *I wouldn't be in favor of income tax cuts. Yo no estaría a favor de que se redujera el impuesto sobre la renta.* **6** PHRASE If someone makes a judgment **in your favor,** they say that you are right about

F

something. *en favor de, a favor de* ❑ *The Supreme Court ruled in Fitzgerald's favor. La Suprema Corte falló a favor de Fitzgerald.* **7** PHRASE If something is **in** your **favor,** it helps you or gives you an advantage. *en favor de, a favor de* ❑ *This is a career where age works in your favor. Ésta es una carrera en la que la edad está a tu favor.* **8** PHRASE If one thing is rejected **in favor of** another, the second thing is done or chosen instead of the first. *en pro* ❑ *The writing program is being rejected in favor of computer classes. El programa de redacción fue rechazado en pro de las clases de computación.* **9** PHRASE If someone or something is **in favor,** people like or support them. If they are **out of favor,** people no longer like or support them. *en el favor de* ❑ *Governments only remain in favor with the public for so long. Los gobiernos sólo gozan del favor del público por un tiempo.*

**fa|vor|able** /feɪvərəbəl/ **1** ADJ If your opinion or your reaction is **favorable** to something, you agree with it and approve of it. *favorable* ❑ *The president's speech received favorable reviews. El discurso del presidente recibió críticas favorables.* **2** ADJ **Favorable** conditions make something more likely to succeed or seem more attractive. *favorable* ❑ *Under favorable conditions, these tiny cells divide every 22 minutes. En condiciones favorables, estas diminutas células se dividen cada 22 minutos.* **3** ADJ If you make a **favorable** comparison between two things, you say that the first is better than or as good as the second. *favorable*

**fa|vor|ite** /feɪvərɪt, feɪvrɪt/ (**favorites**) **1** ADJ Your **favorite** thing or person is the one you like most. *favorito, favorita* ❑ *...his favorite music. ...su música favorita* • **Favorite** is also a noun. *favorito* ❑ *That hotel is my favorite. Ese hotel es mi favorito.* **2** N-COUNT The **favorite** in a race or contest is the competitor that is expected to win. *favorito* ❑ *The U.S. team is one of the favorites in next month's games. El equipo de Estados Unidos es uno de los favoritos de los juegos del mes próximo.*

**fa|vor|it|ism** /feɪvərɪtɪzəm, feɪvrɪt-/ N-UNCOUNT If you accuse someone of **favoritism,** you disapprove of them because they unfairly help or favor one person or group much more than another. *favoritismo* ❑ *Maria loved both the children. There was never a hint of favoritism. María quería a los dos niños, nunca mostró ni asomo de favoritismo por ninguno.*

**fax** /fæks/ (**faxes, faxing, faxed**) **1** N-COUNT A **fax** or a **fax machine** is a piece of equipment used to send and receive documents electronically using a telephone line. *fax* **2** N-COUNT You can refer to a copy of a document that is sent or received by a fax machine as a **fax.** *fax* ❑ *I sent him a long fax. Le mandé un fax largo.* **3** V-T If you **fax** a document to someone, you send it from one fax machine to another. *mandar por fax, enviar por fax* ❑ *I faxed a copy of the agreement to each of the investors. Mandé por fax una copia del acuerdo a cada uno de los inversionistas.* ❑ *Did you fax him a reply? ¿Le enviaste el fax con la respuesta?*

**FDA** /ɛf di eɪ/ N-PROPER **FDA** is an abbreviation for **Food and Drug Administration.** *FDA* ❑ *The FDA has approved a new treatment for a rare blood disorder. La FDA aprobó un nuevo tratamiento para un raro trastorno de la sangre.*

**fear** /fɪər/ (**fears, fearing, feared**) **1** N-VAR **Fear** is the unpleasant feeling you have when you think that you are in danger. *miedo, temor* ❑ *I sat shivering with fear because a bullet was fired through a window. Me senté temblando de miedo porque dispararon un tiro a través de la ventana.* **2** N-VAR A **fear** is a thought that something unpleasant might happen or might have happened. *miedo, temor* ❑ *These youngsters have a fear of failure. Estos jóvenes tienen temor a fracasar.* ❑ *His worst fears were confirmed. Se confirmaron sus peores temores.* **3** N-VAR If you have **fears for** someone or something, you are very worried because you think that they might be in danger. *temor* ❑ *He also spoke of his fears for the future of his country. También habló de sus temores por el futuro de su país.* **4** V-T If you **fear** something unpleasant or undesirable, you are worried that it might happen or might have happened. *temer* ❑ *She feared she was losing her memory. Temía estar perdiendo la memoria.* **5** V-I If you **fear for** someone or something, you are very worried because you think that they might be in danger. *temer, sentir temor* ❑ *Carla fears for her son. Carla teme por su hijo.* **6** PHRASE If you do not do something **for fear of** another thing happening, you do not do it because you do not wish that other thing to happen. *por miedo de* ❑ *He did not move his feet for fear of making a noise. No movió un pie por temor a hacer ruido.*
→ see **emotion**

**Thesaurus** *fear* Ver también:

N. alarm, dread, panic, terror **1**
concern, worry **2**

**Word Partnership** Usar *fear* con:

ADJ. **constant** fear **1**
**irrational** fear **1** **2**
**worst** fear **2**
V. **face** *your* fear, **hide** *your* fear, **live in** fear, **overcome** *your* fear **1** **2**
N. fear **of failure,** fear **of rejection,** fear **of the unknown** **2**
fear **change, nothing to** fear, fear **the worst** **4**

**fear|ful** /fɪərfəl/ **1** ADJ If you are **fearful of** something, you are afraid of it. *temeroso, miedoso* [FORMAL] ❑ *Bankers were fearful of a world banking crisis. Los banqueros temían que se produjera una crisis bancaria mundial.* **2** ADJ You use **fearful** to emphasize how serious or bad a situation is. *espantoso, horrible* [FORMAL] ❑ *The world's in such a fearful mess. La confusión que reina en el mundo es espantosa.*

**feast** /fist/ (**feasts, feasting, feasted**) **1** N-COUNT A **feast** is a large and special meal. *banquete, festín* ❑ *...wedding feasts. ...banquetes nupciales.* **2** V-I If you **feast on** a particular food, you eat a large amount of it with great enjoyment. *festejar, agasajarse, darse un festín* ❑ *They feasted on Indian food. Se dieron un festín de comida hindú.* **3** V-I If you **feast,** you take part in a feast. *festejar* ❑ *They feasted in the castle's main hall. Festejaron en el salón principal del castillo.*

**feat** /fit/ (**feats**) N-COUNT If you refer to something as a **feat,** you admire it because it is an impressive and difficult achievement. *hazaña, proeza* ❑ *A racing car is an extraordinary feat of engineering. Un carro de carreras es una hazaña extraordinaria de ingeniería.*

feather

**feath|er** /fɛðər/ (**feathers**) **1** N-COUNT A bird's **feathers** are the light soft things covering its body. *pluma* ❑ *...black ostrich feathers. ...plumas negras de avestruz.*
→ see **bird**

**fea|ture** /fitʃər/ (**features, featuring, featured**) **1** N-COUNT A **feature of** something is an interesting or important part or characteristic of it. *característica, rasgo distintivo* ❑ *The flower gardens are a special feature of this property. Los jardines de flores son una característica especial de esta propiedad.* **2** N-COUNT A **feature** is a special article in a newspaper or magazine, or a special program on radio or television. *artículo, programa especial* ❑ *There was a feature on Marvin Gaye in the New York Times. Había un artículo sobre Marvin Gaye en el New York Times.* **3** N-COUNT A **feature** or a **feature** film or movie is a full-length film about a fictional situation. *película* **4** N-PLURAL Your **features** are your eyes, nose, mouth, and other parts of your face. *facciones, rasgos* ❑ *...his mother's fine, delicate features. ...las finas y delicadas facciones de su madre.* **5** V-T When something such as a movie or exhibition **features** a particular person or thing, they are an important part of it. *incluir, destacar* ❑ *The program will feature highlights from recent games. En el programa se incluirán aspectos interesantes de los juegos recientes.* **6** V-I If someone or something **features in** something such as a show, exhibition, or magazine, they are an important part of it. *participar, actuar, aparecer* ❑ *Jon featured in one of the show's most thrilling episodes. Jon apareció en uno de los episodios más emocionantes de la serie.*

| Word Partnership | Usar *feature* con: |
|---|---|
| ADJ. | **key** feature **1**<br>**special** feature **1 2**<br>**best** feature, **striking** feature **1 4**<br>**animated** feature, **double** feature, **full-length** feature **3**<br>**facial** feature **4** |

**Feb|ru|ary** /fɛbyuɛri, fɛbru-/ (**Februaries**) N-VAR **February** is the second month of the year in the Western calendar. *febrero* ❑ *His exhibition opens on February 5. Su exposición se inaugura el 5 de febrero.*

**fed** /fɛd/ (**feds**) **1** **Fed** is the past tense and past participle of **feed**. *pasado y participio pasado de feed* **2** → see also **fed up** **3** N-SING **The Fed** is the **Federal Reserve**. *Reserva Federal* [INFORMAL] ❑ *The Fed has lowered interest rates three times since late October. La Reserva Federal ha reducido tres veces las tasas de interés desde finales de octubre.* **4** N-COUNT The **feds** are federal agents, for example of the American security agency, the FBI. *agentes federales, agentes del FBI* [INFORMAL]

**fed|er|al** /fɛdərəl/ **1** ADJ In a **federal** country or system, a group of states is controlled by a central government. *federal* **2** ADJ **Federal** means belonging or relating to the national government of a federal country rather than to one of the states within it. *federal, nacional* ❑ *...federal judges. ...jueces federales.* ● **fed|er|al|ly** ADV *a escala federal* ❑ *...federally-regulated companies. ...empresas reguladas a escala federal.*

**Fed|er|al Re|serve** N-SING In the United States, the **Federal Reserve** is the central banking system, responsible for national financial matters such as interest rates. *Reserva Federal*

**fed|era|tion** /fɛdəreɪʃən/ (**federations**) **1** N-COUNT A **federation** is a federal country. *federación* ❑ *...the Russian Federation. ...la Federación Rusa.* **2** N-COUNT A **federation** is a group of organizations which have joined together for a common purpose. *federación* ❑ *...the American Federation of Government Employees. ...la Federación Estadounidense de Empleados Públicos.*

**fe|do|ra** /fɪdɔrə/ (**fedoras**) N-COUNT A **fedora** is a type of hat which has a brim and is made from a soft material such as velvet. *sombrero de fieltro de ala ancha*
→ see **hat**

**fed up** ADJ If you are **fed up**, you are unhappy, bored, or tired of something. *harto, hasta el copete, hasta el gorro* [INFORMAL] ❑ *He became fed up with city life. Se hartó de vivir en la ciudad.*

**fee** /fi/ (**fees**) **1** N-COUNT A **fee** is a sum of money that you pay to be allowed to do something. *derechos, cuota* ❑ *He paid his license fee, and walked out with a new driver's license. Pagó los derechos y salió con su nueva licencia para conducir.* **2** N-COUNT A **fee** is the amount of money that a person or organization is paid for a particular job or service that they provide. *honorarios* ❑ *...lawyer's fees. ...honorarios del abogado.*

**feed** /fid/ (**feeds, feeding, fed**) **1** V-T If you **feed** a person or animal, you give them food. *alimentar, dar de comer* ❑ *We brought along pieces of old bread and fed the birds. Llevamos pan duro y les dimos de comer a los pájaros.* ● **feed|ing** N-UNCOUNT *alimento, alimentación* ❑ *...the feeding of dairy cows. ...la alimentación de las vacas lecheras.* **2** V-T To **feed** a family or a community means to supply food for them. *alimentar* ❑ *Feeding a hungry family can be expensive. Alimentar a una familia hambrienta puede ser costoso.* **3** V-I When an animal **feeds,** it eats or drinks something. *alimentarse* ❑ *Some insects feed on wood. Algunos insectos se alimentan de madera.* **4** V-T/V-I When a baby **feeds,** or when you **feed** it, it drinks breast milk or milk from a bottle. *alimentar(se), comer, amamantar, dar de mamar, dar de comer, dar el biberón, dar la mamila* ❑ *When a baby is thirsty, it feeds more often. Cuando un bebé tiene sed, come más seguido.* **5** V-T To **feed** something to a place, means to supply it to that place in a steady flow. *proveer, llevar* ❑ *The blood vessels feed blood to the brain. Los vasos sanguíneos llevan la sangre al cerebro.*

| Word Partnership | Usar *feed* con: |
|---|---|
| N. | feed **the baby**, feed **the cat**, feed **the children**, feed ***your* family**, feed **the hungry** **1** |
| V. | feed **and clothe** **2** |

**feed|back** /fidbæk/ N-UNCOUNT If you get

**feedback on** your work or progress, someone tells you how well or badly you are doing. retroalimentación ❑ *Continue to ask for feedback on your work.* *No dejes de pedir retroalimentación sobre tu trabajo.*

**feed|back con|trol** N-UNCOUNT **Feedback control** is a system that regulates a process by using the output of the system in order to make changes to the input of the system. *control de retroalimentación* [TECHNICAL]

**feel** /fi̲l/ (**feels, feeling, felt**) **1** V-LINK If you **feel** a particular emotion or physical sensation, you experience it. *sentir(se)* ❑ *I am feeling very depressed.* *Me siento muy deprimida.* ❑ *I felt a sharp pain in my shoulder.* *Sentí un dolor punzante en el hombro.* **2** V-LINK If you talk about how an experience or event **feels,** you talk about the emotions and sensations connected with it. *sentir(se), hacer sentir, dejar una sensación* ❑ *It feels good to finish a piece of work.* *Terminar un trabajo hace que uno se sienta bien.* ❑ *The speed at which everything moved felt strange.* *La velocidad a la que todo se movía dejaba una sensación extraña.* **3** V-LINK If you talk about how an object **feels,** you talk about the physical quality that you notice when you touch or hold it. *sentirse* ❑ *The metal felt smooth and cold.* *El metal se sentía suave y frío.* ● **Feel** is also a noun. *sensación, tacto* ❑ *...the feel of her skin.* *...el tacto de su piel.* **4** V-T/V-I If you **feel** an object, you touch it deliberately with your hand, so that you learn what it is like. *tocar, sentir, palpar* ❑ *The doctor felt his head.* *El doctor le palpó la cabeza.* ❑ *Feel how soft the skin is.* *Siente la suavidad de la piel.* **5** V-T If you can **feel** something, you are aware of it because you touch it or it touches you. *sentir* ❑ *Joe felt a bump on the back of his brother's head.* *Joe sintió una protuberancio en la parte trasera de la cabeza de su hermano.* ❑ *She felt something being pressed into her hands.* *Sintió que trataba de ponerle algo entre las manos.* **6** V-T If you **feel yourself** doing something or being in a particular state, you are aware that something is happening to you which you are unable to control. *sentir(se)* ❑ *I felt myself blush.* *Sentí que me sonrojaba.* **7** V-T If you **feel** the presence of someone or something, you become aware of them, even though you cannot see or hear them. *sentir* ❑ *He felt her eyes on him.* *Sintió que estaba mirándolo.* ❑ *I could feel that a man was watching me.* *Podía sentir que un hombre me observaba.* **8** V-T If you **feel** that something is true, you have a strong idea in your mind that it is true. *sentir, pensar, creer* ❑ *I feel that not enough is being done.* *Creo que no se está haciendo lo suficiente.* ❑ *She felt certain that it wasn't the same guy.* *Tenía la seguridad de que no era el mismo hombre.* **9** V-T If you **feel** that you should do something, you think that you should do it. *sentir, pensar, creer* ❑ *I feel that I should resign.* *Creo que debo renunciar.* **10** V-I If you talk about how you **feel about** something, you talk about your opinion, attitude, or reaction to it. *pensar sobre, sentir(se), opinar* ❑ *We'd like to know what you feel about the new rules.* *Nos gustaría saber tu opinión sobre las nuevas reglas.* ❑ *She feels guilty about spending less time lately with her two kids.* *Se siente culpable de que últimamente pasa menos tiempo con sus dos hijos.* **11** V-I If you **feel like** doing something or having something, you want to do it or have it because you are in the right mood for it and think you would enjoy it. *antojarse, querer algo, tener ganas, apetecer* ❑ *Neither of them felt like going back to sleep.* *Ninguno de los dos tenía ganas de volver a dormirse.* **12** → see also **feeling, felt** **13** **feel free** → see **free**

▸ **feel for** **1** PHR-VERB If you **feel for** something, you try to find it by moving your hand around until you touch it. *palpar, buscar(se)* ❑ *I felt for my wallet in my pocket.* *Me busqué la cartera en el bolsillo.* **2** PHR-VERB If you **feel for** someone, you have sympathy for them. *compadecer(se), sentir lástima por, dar lástima* ❑ *She cried on the phone and I really felt for her.* *Lloró en el teléfono y realmente me dio lástima.*

**feel|ing** /fi̲lɪŋ/ (**feelings**) **1** N-COUNT A **feeling** is an emotion. *sensación* ❑ *It gave me a feeling of satisfaction.* *Me dio una sensación de satisfacción.* **2** N-COUNT If you have **a feeling that** something is the case or that something is going to happen, you think that it is probably the case or that it is probably going to happen. *sensación, sentimiento* ❑ *I have a feeling that everything will be all right.* *Tengo la sensación de que todo va a salir bien.* **3** N-PLURAL Your **feelings** about something are the things that you think and feel about it, or your attitude toward it. *sentimiento, sensación, impresión, opinión* ❑ *They have strong feelings about politics.* *Sus opiniones políticas son muy firmes.* **4** N-PLURAL When you refer to your **feelings,** you are talking about the things that might embarrass, offend, or upset you. For example, if someone hurts your **feelings,** he or she upsets you by something that he or she says or does. *sentimiento* ❑ *I'm sorry if I hurt your feelings.* *Discúlpame si herí tus sentimientos.* **5** N-UNCOUNT **Feeling** for someone is love, affection, sympathy, or concern for them. *sentir afecto* ❑ *Thomas never lost his feeling for Harriet.* *Thomas nunca dejó de sentir afecto por Harriet.* **6** N-UNCOUNT **Feeling** in part of your body is the ability to experience the sense of touch in this part of the body. *sensación* ❑ *After the accident he had no feeling in his legs.* *Después del accidente no tenía sensación en las piernas.* **7** N-SING If you have a **feeling of** being in a particular situation, you feel that you are in that situation. *sensación* ❑ *I had the terrible feeling of being left behind to bring up the baby on my own.* *Tuve la horrible sensación de que me abandonaban y de tenía que criar sola a mi bebé.* **8** → see also **feel** **9** PHRASE **Bad feeling** or **ill feeling** is bitterness or anger which exists between people. *resentimiento* ❑ *There's been some bad feeling between the two families.* *Ha habido cierto resentimiento entre las dos familias.*

**feet** /fi̲t/ **Feet** is the plural of **foot.** *plural de* ***foot***

**feld|spar** /fɛ̲ldspɑr, fɛ̲l-/ (**feldspars**) N-VAR **Feldspar** is a mineral that forms rocks and makes up most of the Earth's crust. *feldespato*

**fell** /fɛ̲l/ (**fells, felling, felled**) **1** **Fell** is the past tense of **fall.** *pasado de* ***fall*** **2** V-T If trees **are felled,** they are cut down. *derribar, talar*

**fel|low** /fɛ̲loʊ/ (**fellows**) **1** ADJ You use **fellow** to describe people who are in the same situation as you, or people you feel you have something in common with. *colega, compañero, correligionario* ❑ *...a talent for making her fellow guests laugh.* *...tenía facilidad para hacer reír a los otros invitados.* **2** N-COUNT A **fellow of** an academic or professional association is someone who is a specially elected member of it. *miembro* ❑ *...a fellow of the New York Academy of Medicine.* *...miembro*

*de la Academia de Medicina de Nueva York.*
→ see **hospital**

**felo|ny** /fɛləni/ (**felonies**) N-COUNT A **felony** is a very serious crime such as armed robbery. *delito grave* [LEGAL] ❑ *He was guilty of six felonies. Era culpable de seis delitos graves.*

**fel|sic** /fɛlsɪk/ ADJ **Felsic** rocks are igneous rocks that contain a lot of lighter elements such as silicon, aluminum, sodium, and potassium. Compare **mafic**. *félsico* [TECHNICAL]

**felt** /fɛlt/ **1** **Felt** is the past tense and past participle of **feel**. *pasado y participio pasado de* ***feel*** **2** N-UNCOUNT **Felt** is a thick cloth made from wool or other fibers packed tightly together. *fieltro* ❑ *...an old felt hat. ...un viejo sombrero de fieltro.*

| Word Link | *fem, femin ≈ woman : female, feminine, feminist* |
|---|---|

**fe|male** /fimeɪl/ (**females**) **1** ADJ Someone who is **female** is a woman or a girl. *mujer, de sexo femenino* ❑ *...a female singer. ...una cantante.* **2** ADJ **Female** matters and things relate to or affect women rather than men. *de mujeres, femenino, del sexo femenino* ❑ *...female diseases. ...enfermedades del sexo femenino., ...enfermedades de las mujeres.* **3** N-COUNT Women and girls are sometimes referred to as **females** when they are being considered as a type. *mujeres* ❑ *Hay fever affects males more than females. La fiebre del heno afecta más a los varones que a las mujeres.* **4** N-COUNT You can refer to any creature that can lay eggs or produce babies from its body as a **female**. *hembra* ❑ *Each female will lay just one egg. Cada hembra pone un sólo huevo.* ● **Female** is also an adjective. *femenino* ❑ *...the female gorillas. ...los gorilas hembra.*
→ see **reproduction**

**Usage** **female and woman**

In everyday situations, you should avoid using *female* to refer to women, because that can sound offensive. When used as a noun, *female* is mainly used in scientific or medical contexts. *The leader of the herd of elephants is usually the oldest female.*

**femi|nine** /fɛmɪnɪn/ ADJ **Feminine** qualities and things relate to or are considered typical of women, in contrast to men. *femenino* ❑ *...traditional feminine roles. ...papeles femeninos tradicionales.* ● **femi|nin|ity** /fɛmɪnɪnɪti/ N-UNCOUNT *feminidad* ❑ *...ideals of femininity. ...ideales de feminidad.*

**femi|nist** /fɛmɪnɪst/ (**feminists**) **1** N-COUNT A **feminist** is a person who believes in and supports feminism. *feminista* ❑ *...one of the earliest feminists to speak up in this country. ...una de las primeras feministas de este país que dijeron lo que pensaban.* **2** ADJ **Feminist** groups, ideas, and activities are involved in feminism. *feminista* ❑ *...the feminist movement. ...el movimiento feminista.*

**fence** /fɛns/ (**fences, fencing, fenced**) **1** N-COUNT A **fence** is a barrier made of wood or wire supported by posts. *cerca, valla* **2** V-T If you **fence** an area of land, you surround it with a fence. *cercar* ❑ *The owner has fenced the property. El propietario cercó su propiedad.* **3** PHRASE If you **sit on the fence**, you avoid supporting a particular side in a discussion or argument. *no definirse, mirar los toros desde la barrera, no tomar partido* ❑ *I'm sitting on the fence until I know what happened. No tomaré partido hasta saber qué pasó.*

**fenc|ing** /fɛnsɪŋ/ **1** N-UNCOUNT **Fencing** is a sport in which two competitors fight each other using very thin swords. *esgrima* **2** N-UNCOUNT Materials such as wood or wire that are used to make fences are called **fencing**. *material para cercas*

**fend** /fɛnd/ (**fends, fending, fended**) V-I If you have to **fend for** yourself, you have to look after yourself without relying on anyone else. *valerse por sí mismo, arreglárselas solo* ❑ *The woman and her young baby were left to fend for themselves. La mujer y su bebé tuvieron que arreglárselas solos.*

▸ **fend off** **1** PHR-VERB If you **fend off** someone or something, you defend yourself against them using words. *eludir, evadir* ❑ *Henry fended off questions about his future. Henry evadió las preguntas sobre su futuro.* **2** PHR-VERB If you **fend off** someone who is attacking you, you use your arms or something such as a stick to defend yourself from their blows. *esquivar* ❑ *He raised his hand to fend off the blow. Levantó la mano para esquivar el golpe.*

| Word Link | *fend ≈ striking : defend, fender, offend* |
|---|---|

**fend|er** /fɛndər/ (**fenders**) N-COUNT The **fender** of a car is a bar at the front or back that protects the car if it bumps into something. *defensa*

**fer|ment** (**ferments, fermenting, fermented**)

The noun is pronounced /fɜrmɛnt/. The verb is pronounced /fərmɛnt/.

**1** N-UNCOUNT **Ferment** is excitement and trouble caused by change or uncertainty. *agitación, conmoción* ❑ *The whole country was in a state of political ferment. Todo el país se encontraba en un estado de agitación política.* **2** V-T/V-I If a food, drink, or other natural substance **ferments**, or if it is **fermented**, a chemical change takes place in it so that alcohol is produced. *fermentar* ❑ *The dried grapes are allowed to ferment until there is no sugar left. Se deja fermentar las uvas secas hasta que ya no les quede azúcar.* ● **fer|men|ta|tion** /fɜrmɛnteɪʃᵊn/ N-UNCOUNT *fermentación* ❑ *Fermentation produces alcohol. La fermentación produce alcohol.*
→ see **fungus**

**Fer|ris wheel** (**Ferris wheels**) also **ferris wheel** N-COUNT A **Ferris wheel** is a very large wheel with carriages for people to ride in, especially at a theme park or fair. *rueda de la fortuna*

**fer|ry** /fɛri/ (**ferries, ferrying, ferried**) **1** N-COUNT A **ferry** is a boat that transports passengers and sometimes also vehicles, usually across rivers or short stretches of sea. *ferry, transbordador* ❑ *They crossed the River Gambia by ferry. Cruzaron el río Gambia en transbordador.* **2** V-T If a vehicle **ferries** people or goods, it transports them, usually by means of regular trips between the same two places. *transportar, llevar* ❑ *A plane arrived to ferry guests to and from Bird Island Lodge. Llegó un avión para transportar de ida y vuelta a los huéspedes del hotel Bird Island.*
→ see **ship**

**fer|tile** /fɜrtᵊl/ **1** ADJ Land or soil that is **fertile** is able to support the growth of a large number of

strong healthy plants. *fértil* • **fer|til|ity** /fɜrtɪlɪti/ N-UNCOUNT *fertilidad* ❑ *...the fertility of the soil. ...la fertilidad del suelo* **2** ADJ A situation or environment that is **fertile** in relation to a particular activity or feeling encourages the activity or feeling. *fértil, fecundo* ❑ *She says Seattle is fertile ground for small businesses. Dice que Seattle es tierra fértil para las pequeñas empresas.* **3** ADJ A person or animal that is **fertile** is able to reproduce and have babies or young. *fértil* • **fer|til|ity** N-UNCOUNT *fertilidad* ❑ *In the cities, fertility levels are lower. En las ciudades, los niveles de fertilidad son más bajos.*
→ see **grassland**

F

**fer|ti|lize** /fɜrtəlaɪz/ (**fertilizes, fertilizing, fertilized**) **1** V-T When an egg from the ovary of a woman or female animal **is fertilized,** a sperm from the male joins with the egg, causing a baby or young animal to begin forming. A female plant **is fertilized** when its reproductive parts come into contact with pollen from the male plant. *fertilizar* ❑ *...the normal sperm levels needed to fertilize the egg. ...el número normal de espermatozoides necesarios para fertilizar el óvulo.* • **fer|ti|li|za|tion** /fɜrtəlɪzeɪʃən/ N-UNCOUNT *fertilización* ❑ *From fertilization until birth is about 266 days. De la fertilización al nacimiento transcurren más o menos 266 días.* **2** V-T To **fertilize** land means to improve its quality in order to make plants grow well on it, by spreading solid animal waste or a chemical mixture on it. *fertilizar* ❑ *The fields are fertilized, usually with animal manure. Los campos se fertilizan normalmente con estiércol.*
→ see **reproduction**

**fer|ti|liz|er** /fɜrtəlaɪzər/ (**fertilizers**) N-UNCOUNT **Fertilizer** is a substance such as solid animal waste or a chemical mixture that you spread on the ground in order to make plants grow more successfully. *fertilizante*
→ see **farm, pollution**

**fes|ti|val** /fɛstɪvəl/ (**festivals**) **1** N-COUNT A **festival** is an organized series of events such as musical concerts or drama productions. *festival* ❑ *...festivals of music, theater, and dance. ...festivales de música, teatro y danza.* **2** N-COUNT A **festival** is a day or time of the year when people do not go to work or school and celebrate some special event, often a religious event. *fiesta, celebración* ❑ *Shavuot is a two-day festival for Jews. El Shavuot es una celebración judía que dura dos días.*

| Thesaurus | *festive* | Ver también: |
|---|---|---|
| ADJ. | happy, joyous, merry; (*ant.*) gloomy, somber **1** | |

**fe|tal po|si|tion** (**fetal positions**) N-COUNT If someone is in the **fetal position,** their body is curled up like a fetus in the womb. *posición fetal* ❑ *She lay in a fetal position, turned away from him. Se acostó en posición fetal, dándole la espalda.*

**fetch** /fɛtʃ/ (**fetches, fetching, fetched**) **1** V-T If you **fetch** something or someone, you go and get them from the place where they are. *buscar, recoger, ir por, traer* ❑ *Sylvia fetched a towel from the bathroom. Silvia fue al baño por una toalla.* ❑ *Fetch me a glass of water. Tráeme un vaso de agua.* **2** V-T If something **fetches** a particular sum of money, it is sold for that amount. *vender* ❑ *The painting fetched three million dollars. La pintura se vendió en tres millones de dólares.* **3** → see also **far-fetched**

**fe|tus** /fitəs/ (**fetuses**) N-COUNT A **fetus** is an animal or human being in its later stages of development before it is born. *feto*
→ see **reproduction**

**fe|ver** /fivər/ (**fevers**) N-VAR If you have a **fever** when you are ill, your body temperature is higher than usual. *fiebre, temperatura, calentura* ❑ *Jim had a high fever. Jim tenía mucha calentura.*
→ see **illness**

**fe|ver blis|ter** (**fever blisters**) N-COUNT **Fever blisters** are small sore spots that sometimes appear on someone's lips and nose when they have a cold. *boquera, fuego*

**few** /fyu/ (**fewer, fewest**) **1** DET You use **a few** to indicate that you are talking about a small number of people or things. *algunos, unos cuantos* ❑ *...a dinner party for a few close friends. ...una cena para unos cuantos amigos cercanos.* ❑ *Here are a few more ideas to consider. Estas son algunas otras ideas que podemos considerar.* • **Few** is also a pronoun. *poco, alguno, algún* ❑ *Most were Americans but a few were British. La mayoría eran estadounidenses, pero algunos eran británicos.* • **Few** is also a quantifier. *alguno, algún* ❑ *There are many ways eggs can be prepared; here are a few of them. Hay muchas maneras de preparar los huevos; estas son algunas de ellas.* **2** DET You use **few** to indicate that you are talking about a small number of people or things. *poco* ❑ *She had few friends. Tenía pocos amigos.* • **Few** is also a pronoun. *poco* ❑ *Few can survive more than a week without water. Pocos pueden sobrevivir más de una semana sin agua.* • **Few** is also a quantifier. *alguno* ❑ *Few of the houses still had lights on. Algunas de las casas todavía tenían prendidas las luces.* • **Few** is also an adjective. *poco* ❑ *She spent her few waking hours in front of the TV. Pasaba sus pocas horas de vigilia frente a la tele.* **3** PHRASE You use **as few as** before a number to suggest that it is surprisingly small. *apenas* ❑ *Some people put on weight eating as few as 800 calories a day. Algunas personas suben de peso con apenas 800 calorías diarias.* **4** PHRASE Things that are **few and far between** are very rare or do not happen very often. *muy de cuando en cuando, muy de vez en cuando, muy rara vez* ❑ *Kelly's trips to the hairdresser were few and far between. Kelly iba al salón de belleza muy de vez en cuando.* **5** PHRASE You use **no fewer than** to emphasize that a number is surprisingly large. *no menos de* ❑ *No fewer than thirteen foreign ministers attended the session. No menos de trece ministros de relaciones exteriores asistieron a la sesión.*
→ see also **less**

**Usage** — **few and a few**

Be careful to use *few* and *a few* correctly. *Few* means "not many," and is used to emphasize that the number is very small: *He had few complaints about his workload.* *A few* means "more than one or two," and is used when we wish to imply a small but significant number: *He had a few complaints about his workload.*

**fi|an|cé** /fiɑnseɪ, fiɑnseɪ/ (**fiancés**) N-COUNT A woman's **fiancé** is the man to whom she is engaged to be married. *prometido, novio*

**fi|an|cée** /fiɑnseɪ, fiɑnseɪ/ (**fiancées**) N-COUNT

A man's **fiancée** is the woman to whom he is engaged to be married. prometida, novia

**fi|ber** /faɪbər/ (**fibers**) **1** N-COUNT A **fiber** is a thin thread of a natural or artificial substance, especially one that is used to make cloth or rope. *fibra* ❑ *If you look at the paper under a microscope you will see the fibers. Si observas el papel al miscroscopio, verás las fibras.* **2** N-COUNT A **fiber** is a thin piece of flesh like a thread which connects nerve cells in your body or which muscles are made of. *fibra* **3** N-UNCOUNT **Fiber** consists of the parts of plants or seeds that your body cannot digest. *fibra* ❑ *Most vegetables contain fiber. Casi todos los vegetales contienen fibra.*
→ see **paper**

**fiber|glass** /faɪbərglæs/ N-UNCOUNT **Fiberglass** is a material made from short, thin threads of glass which can be used to stop heat from escaping. *fibra de vidrio*

**fi|ber op|tics**

The form **fiber optic** is used as a modifier.

**1** N-UNCOUNT **Fiber optics** is the use of long thin threads of glass to carry information in the form of light. *por fibra óptica* **2** ADJ **Fiber optic** means relating to or involved in fiber optics. *de fibra óptica* ❑ *...fiber optic cables. ...cables de fibra óptica.*
→ see **laser**

**fi|brous root** (**fibrous roots**) N-COUNT Plants with **fibrous roots** have a series of thin roots which branch out from the stem of the plant. *raíces fibrosas* [TECHNICAL]

**fic|tion** /fɪkʃᵊn/ **1** N-UNCOUNT **Fiction** refers to books and stories about imaginary people and events. *ficción, narrativa* • **fictional** ADJ *ficticio* ❑ *...fictional characters. ...personajes ficticios.* **2** N-UNCOUNT A statement or account that is **fiction** is not true. *ficción* ❑ *The truth or fiction of this story has never really been determined. Nunca se ha determinado realmente si esta historia era verdad o ficción.*
→ see **fantasy, genre, library**

**fid|dle** /fɪdᵊl/ (**fiddles, fiddling, fiddled**) **1** V-I If you **fiddle with** an object, you keep moving it or touching it with your fingers. *jugar, juguetear* ❑ *Harriet fiddled with a pen. Harriet jugueteaba con una pluma.* **2** N-VAR Some people call violins **fiddles**. *Algunos personas llaman fiddle al violín.*

**field** /fild/ (**fields, fielding, fielded**) **1** N-COUNT A **field** is an enclosed area of land where crops are grown, or where animals are kept. *campo, sembradío, potrero* ❑ *...a field of wheat. ...un sembradío de trigo.* **2** N-COUNT A sports **field** is an area of grass where sports are played. *campo, cancha, terreno de juego* ❑ *...a baseball field. ...un campo de béisbol.* **3** N-COUNT A **field** is an area of land or seabed under which large amounts of a particular mineral have been found. *yacimiento* ❑ *...a natural gas field in Alaska. ...un yacimiento de gas natural en Alaska.* **4** N-COUNT A particular **field** is a particular subject of study or type of activity. *campo, especialidad* ❑ *Each of the authors is an expert in his field. Cada uno de los autores es experto en su campo.* **5** N-COUNT Your **field** of vision is the area that you can see without turning your head. *campo visual* **6** ADJ **Field** work involves research that is done in a real, natural environment rather than in a theoretical way or in controlled conditions. *de campo* ❑ *She did her field work in Somalia in the late 1980s. Hizo su trabajo de campo en Somalia, a finales de los años ochenta.* **7** V-I In a game of baseball or cricket, the team that **is fielding** is trying to catch the ball, while the other team is trying to hit it. *fildear* • **field|er** N-COUNT (**fielders**) *fildeador o fildeadora, jardinero o jardinera* ❑ *He hit 10 home runs and he's also a good fielder. Bateó 10 jonrones y también es un buen jardinero.*

**Word Partnership** Usar *field* con:

| | |
|---|---|
| ADJ. | **open** field **1** |
| N. | **ball** field, field **hockey**, **track and** field **2** |
| | **oil** field **3** |
| | **expert in a** field, field **trip** **4** |
| | field **of vision** **5** |
| V. | **work in a** field **4** |

**field goal** (**field goals**) N-COUNT In football, a **field goal** is a score of three points that is gained by kicking the ball through the opponent's goalposts above the crossbar. *gol de campo*

**field hand** (**field hands**) N-COUNT A **field hand** is someone who is employed to work on a farm. *bracero o bracera, jornalero o jornalera, peón de campo*

**field hock|ey** N-UNCOUNT **Field hockey** is an outdoor game played between two teams of 11 players who use long curved sticks to hit a small ball and try to score goals. *hockey, hockey sobre pasto*

**field trip** (**field trips**) N-COUNT A **field trip** is a trip made by students and a teacher to see or study something, for example a museum, a factory, or a historical site. *viaje de estudio*

**fierce** /fɪərs/ (**fiercer, fiercest**) **1** ADJ A **fierce** animal or person is very aggressive or angry. *feroz, fiero, violento* • **fierce|ly** ADV *violentamente, con violencia, con una gran dureza, implacablemente* ❑ *"Go away!" she said fiercely. —Vete!—, le dijo con una gran dureza.* **2** ADJ **Fierce** feelings or actions are very intense or enthusiastic, or involve great activity. *feroz* ❑ *Consumers have a wide range of choices and price competition is fierce. Los consumidores tienen una amplia gama de opciones y la competencia de precios es feroz.* • **fierce|ly** ADV *ferozmente, tremendamente, muy* ❑ *He is ambitious and fiercely competitive. Es ambicioso y extremadamente competitivo.*

**fif|teen** /fɪftin/ (**fifteens**) NUM **Fifteen** is the number 15. *quince*

**fif|teenth** /fɪftinθ/ ORD The **fifteenth** item in a series is the one that you count as number fifteen. *décimoquinto, quince, quinceavo* ❑ *...the fifteenth century. ...el siglo quince.*

**fifth** /fɪfθ/ (**fifths**) **1** ORD The **fifth** item in a series is the one that you count as number five. *quinto* ❑ *...his fifth trip to Australia. ...su quinto viaje a Australia.* **2** N-COUNT A **fifth** is one of five equal parts of something. *quinto* ❑ *India spends over a fifth of its budget on defense. India gasta más de la quinta parte de su presupuesto en defensa.*

**Fifth Amend|ment** N-SING In American law, if someone **takes the Fifth Amendment,** they refuse to answer a question because they think it might show that they are guilty of a crime. *la Quinta Enmienda*

**fif|ti|eth** /fɪftiəθ/ ORD The **fiftieth** item in a

f

series is the one that you count as number fifty. *quincuagésimo, cincuentavo* ❑ *...his fiftieth birthday. ...su quincuagésimo cumpleaños.*

**fif|ty** /fɪfti/ (**fifties**) **1** NUM **Fifty** is the number 50. *cincuenta* **2** N-PLURAL When you talk about the **fifties,** you are referring to numbers between 50 and 59. For example, if you are **in** your **fifties,** you are aged between 50 and 59. If the temperature is **in the fifties,** the temperature is between 50 and 59 degrees. *cincuenta* **3** N-PLURAL **The fifties** is the decade between 1950 and 1959. *los años cincuenta, la década de 1950* ❑ *They first met in the early Fifties. Se conocieron a principios de los años cincuenta.*

F

**fig** /fɪg/ (**figs**) N-COUNT A **fig** is a soft sweet fruit full of tiny seeds. Figs grow on trees in hot countries. *higo*
→ see **fruit**

**fight** /faɪt/ (**fights, fighting, fought**) **1** V-T/V-I If you **fight** something unpleasant, you try in a determined way to prevent it or stop it from happening. *luchar, combatir, pelear* ❑ *Prison inmates are being trained to fight forest fires. Están entrenando a los presos para combatir incendios forestales.* ❑ *I've spent a lifetime fighting against racism and prejudice. Llevo toda la vida luchando contra el racismo y los prejuicios.* ● **Fight** is also a noun. *combate, lucha, pelea* ❑ *...the fight against crime. ...la lucha contra el crimen.* **2** V-I If you **fight** for something, you try in a determined way to get it or achieve it. *luchar por* ❑ *Lee had to fight hard for his place on the team. Lee tuvo que luchar mucho por su lugar en el equipo.* ❑ *I told him how we had fought to hold on to the company. Le conté lo mucho que habíamos luchado para conservar la compañía.* ● **Fight** is also a noun. *lucha* ❑ *...the fight for justice. ...la lucha por la justicia.* **3** V-T/V-I If a person or army **fights** or **fights in** a battle or a war, they take part in it. *combatir, luchar, pelear, emprender una guerra* ❑ *He fought in the war and was taken prisoner. Luchó en la guerra y lo hicieron prisionero.* ❑ *I would sooner go to prison than fight for this country. Antes iría a prisión que luchar por este país.* ❑ *The United States is fighting a new war against terrorism. Los Estados Unidos han emprendido una nueva guerra contra el terrorismo* ● **fight|ing** N-UNCOUNT *lucha, pelea, combate* ❑ *More than nine hundred people have died in the fighting. Más de novecientas personas han muerto en los combates.* **4** V-T If you **fight** your way to a place, you move toward it with great difficulty, because there are a lot of people or things in your way. *abrirse camino, abrirse paso* ❑ *The firefighters fought their way through the flames into the house. Los bomberos se abrieron paso entre las llamas para entrar a la casa.* **5** V-T If you **fight** an election, you are a candidate in the election and try to win it. *participar en una elección* **6** V-T If you **fight** an emotion or desire, you try very hard not to feel it, show it, or act on it. *tratar de contener* ❑ *I desperately fought the urge to giggle. Traté desesperadamente de contener las ganas de reírme.* **7** V-RECIP If one person **fights** with another, the two people hit or kick each other because they want to hurt each other. *pelearse* ❑ *As a child she fought with her younger sister. De niña se peleaba con su hermana menor.* ❑ *He looked like he wanted to fight with me. Parecía tener ganas de pelearse conmigo.* ● **Fight** is also a noun. *pelea* ❑ *He had a fight with Smith. Tuvo una pelea con Smith.* **8** V-RECIP If one person **fights** with another, they have an angry disagreement or quarrel. *pelearse con, discutir* [INFORMAL] ❑ *She was always fighting with him. Siempre estaba peleándose con él.* ● **Fight** is also a noun. *discusión, pelea* ❑ *He ran away because he had a big fight with his dad. Se fue porque tuvo una horrible discusión con su papá.*
→ see **army**

▸ **fight back** **1** PHR-VERB If you **fight back** against someone or something that is attacking or harming you, you defend yourself by taking action against them. *defenderse, oponerse* ❑ *The passengers and crew chose to fight back against the hijackers. Los pasajeros y la tripulación decidieron defenderse de los secuestradores.* **2** PHR-VERB If you **fight back** an emotion, you try very hard not to feel it, show it, or act on it. *luchar, reprimir* ❑ *She fought back the tears. Ella reprimió las lágrimas.*

▸ **fight off** **1** PHR-VERB If you **fight off** something such as an illness or an unpleasant feeling, you succeed in getting rid of it and in not letting it overcome you. *combatir, resistir(se)* ❑ *...the body's ability to fight off infection. ...la capacidad del organismo para combatir las infecciones.* **2** PHR-VERB If you **fight off** someone who has attacked you, you fight with them, and succeed in making them go away or stop attacking you. *lograr, rechazar* ❑ *She fought off three armed robbers. Logró rechazar el asalto de tres ladrones armados.*

**Thesaurus** *fight* Ver también:

N. fist fight **7**
argument, disagreement, squabble, tiff **8**
V. scuffle **7**
argue, bicker, quarrel, squabble **8**

**Word Partnership** Usar *fight* con:

N. fight **crime**, fight **fire** **1**
fight **a battle/war**, fight **an enemy** **3** **8**
V. **join a** fight **1** **2** **8**
**lose a** fight, **win a** fight **1** **2** **7** **8**
**stay and** fight **1** **3** **8**
**break up a** fight, **have a** fight, **pick a** fight, **start a** fight **7** **8**

**fight|er** /faɪtər/ (**fighters**) **1** N-COUNT A **fighter** or a **fighter plane** is a fast military aircraft that is used for destroying other aircraft. *caza, avión de combate* **2** N-COUNT A **fighter** is a person who physically fights another person, especially a professional boxer. *luchador o luchadora, boxeador o boxeadora, peleador o peleadora, púgil* ❑ *...a real street fighter. ...un verdadero peleador callejero.* **3** → see also **firefighter**

**fight|ing chance** N-SING If you say that someone has a **fighting chance** of success, you are emphasizing that they have some chance of success after a hard struggle. *tener posibilidades de algo, tener la oportunidad de algo* ❑ *The airline has a fighting chance of surviving. La aerolínea tiene posibilidades de sobrevivir.*

**fig|ura|tive** /fɪgyərətɪv/ **1** ADJ If you use a word or expression in a **figurative** sense, you use it with a more abstract or imaginative meaning than its ordinary literal one. *figurado, metafórico* ❑ *"Like I said before, I'm in a different place." His statement was both literal and figurative. Su declaración fue tan* *literal como metafórica:—Como dije antes, estoy en otro lugar—.* • **fig|ura|tive|ly** ADV *metafóricamente, en sentido figurado* ❑ *Figuratively, the world is standing still, waiting to see what will happen. Hablando metafóricamente, el mundo se ha detenido, en espera de lo que pueda ocurrir.* **2** ADJ **Figurative** art is a style of art in which people and things are shown in a realistic way. *figurativo*

**fig|ure** /fɪgyər/ (**figures, figuring, figured**) **1** N-COUNT A **figure** is a particular amount expressed as a number, especially a statistic. *cifra, número* ❑ *We need a true figure of how many people in this country do not have a job. Necesitamos la cifra exacta de cuántas personas están desempleadas en este país.* **2** N-COUNT A **figure** is any of the ten written symbols from 0 to 9 that are used to represent a number. *número, cifra, guarismo* ❑ *...the glowing red figures on the radio alarm clock. ...los números rojos parpadeantes del radio reloj despertador.* **3** N-COUNT A **figure** is the shape of a person you cannot see clearly. *silueta, figura* ❑ *Ernie saw the dim figure of Rose in the chair. Ernie vio la tenue silueta de Rose en la silla.* **4** N-COUNT In art, a **figure** is a person in a drawing or a painting, or a statue of a person. *figura* ❑ *...a life-size bronze figure of a woman. ...la figura de bronce de una mujer, de tamaño natural.* **5** N-COUNT Your **figure** is the shape of your body. *figura* ❑ *Take pride in your health and your figure. Siéntase orgullosa de su salud y su figura.* **6** N-COUNT Someone who is referred to as a **figure** of a particular kind is a person who is well-known and important in some way. *personaje, personalidad, figura* ❑ *...key figures in the three main political parties. ...figuras clave de los tres principales partidos políticos.* **7** N-COUNT If you say that someone is, for example, a mother **figure** or a hero **figure**, you mean that other people regard them as the type of person stated or suggested. *figura* **8** N-PLURAL An amount or number that is in single **figures** is between zero and nine. An amount or number that is in double **figures** is between ten and ninety-nine. *dígito, cifra* **9** V-T If you **figure** that something is true, you think or guess that it is true. *figurarse, imaginarse* [INFORMAL] ❑ *She figured that she had learned a lot from the experience. Se figuraba que la experiencia le había enseñado mucho.* **10** V-I If a person or thing **figures in** something, they appear in or are included in it. *figurar, aparecar* ❑ *Human rights violations figured heavily in the report. Las violaciones de los derechos humanos aparecían reiteradamente en el informe.*

▸ **figure out** PHR-VERB If you **figure out** a solution to a problem or the reason for something, you succeed in solving it or understanding it. *entender* [INFORMAL] ❑ *It took them about one month to figure out how to use the equipment. Les tomó cerca de un mes entender cómo usar el equipo.*

▸ **figure up** PHR-VERB If you **figure up** a cost or amount, you add numbers together to get the total. *sumar, calcular* ❑ *He figured up the balance in their checking account. Calculó el saldo de su cuenta de cheques.*

**fig|ure eight** (**figure eights**) N-COUNT A **figure eight** is something that has the same shape as a number 8, for example a movement done by a skater. *ocho*

**file** /faɪl/ (**files, filing, filed**) **1** N-COUNT A **file** is a box or folder in which letters or documents are kept. *expediente, archivo* ❑ *...a file of insurance papers. ...un expediente de documentos de seguros.* **2** N-COUNT A **file** is a collection of information about a particular person or thing. *expediente, archivo* ❑ *We have files on people's tax details. Tenemos expedientes con la información fiscal detallada de las personas.* **3** N-COUNT In computing, a **file** is a set of related data that has its own name. *archivo* ❑ *Save the revised version of the file under a new filename. Guarde la versión revisada del archivo con otro nombre.* **4** N-COUNT A **file** is a tool which is used for rubbing hard objects to make them smooth or to shape them. *lima* **5** V-T If you **file** a document, you put it in the correct file. *archivar, clasificar* ❑ *They are all filed alphabetically under author. Están todos archivados alfabéticamente por autor.* **6** V-T If you **file** a formal or legal accusation, complaint, or request, you make it officially. *presentar una demanda, entablar una demanda* ❑ *I filed for divorce. Presenté una demanda de divorcio.* **7** V-T If you **file** an object, you smooth it, shape it, or cut it with a file. *limar(se)* ❑ *She was shaping and filing her nails. Se estaba limando las uñas.* **8** PHRASE A group of people who are walking or standing **in single file** are in a line, one behind the other. *en fila, en fila india*
→ see **office, tool**

**file|name** /faɪlneɪm/ (**filenames**) N-COUNT In computing, a **filename** is a name that you give to a particular document. *nombre del archivo*

**file-sharing** also **file sharing** N-UNCOUNT **File-sharing** is a method of distributing computer files, for example, files containing music, among a large number of users. *compartir archivos* [COMPUTING]

**fi|let** /fɪleɪ, fɪleɪ/ (**filets**) N-COUNT A **filet** of meat or fish is the same as a **fillet**. *filete*

**fili|bus|ter** /fɪlɪbʌstər/ (**filibusters**) N-COUNT A **filibuster** is a long slow speech made to use up time so that a vote cannot be taken and a law cannot be passed. *maniobra dilatoria, obstruccionismo*

**fil|ings** N-PLURAL Court **filings** are cases filed in a court of law. *expediente judicial* ❑ *In court filings, they argued that the payment was inadequate. En los expedientes judiciales argumentaron que el pago no era el adecuado.*

**fill** /fɪl/ (**fills, filling, filled**) **1** V-T/V-I If you **fill** a container or area, or if it **fills**, an amount of something enters it that is enough to make it full. *llenar* ❑ *She went to the bathroom and filled a glass with water. Fue al baño y llenó de agua un vaso* ❑ *The boy's eyes filled with tears. Los ojos del niño se llenaron de lágrimas* • **Fill up** means the same as **fill**. *llenar* ❑ *Warehouses fill up with sacks of rice and flour. Bodegas llenas de costales de arroz y harina* **2** V-T If something **fills** a space, it is so big, or there are such large quantities of it, that there is very little room left. *llenar, atiborrar* ❑ *Rows of cabinets filled the enormous work area. La enorme área de trabajo estaba atiborrada de archiveros.* • **Fill up** means the same as **fill**. *llenar, atiborrar* ❑ *Complicated machines fill up today's laboratories. Los laboratorios de hoy están llenos de aparatos complicados.* • **filled** ADJ *lleno, repleto* ❑ *...museum buildings filled with historical objects. ...edificios de museos repletos de objetos históricos.* **3** V-T If you **fill** a crack or hole, you put a substance

f

into it in order to make the surface smooth again. rellenar ❑ *You should fill cracks between plaster walls and window frames.* *Tienes que rellenar las grietas entre las paredes de yeso y los marcos de las ventanas.* ● **Fill in** means the same as **fill**. rellenar ❑ *Start by filling in any cracks.* *Empieza por rellenar todas las grietas.* **4** V-T If something **fills** you **with** an emotion, you experience this emotion strongly. llenar(se) de ❑ *My father's work filled me with awe.* *El trabajo de mi padre me llenaba de admiración.* **5** V-T If you **fill** a period of time with a particular activity, you spend the time in this way. ocupar ❑ *We fill our days with swimming and sailing.* *Nos pasamos los días nadando y navegando en bote de vela.* ● **Fill up** means the same as **fill**. ocupar ❑ *She went to her yoga class, glad to have something to fill up the evening.* *Se fue a la clase de yoga, contenta de tener algo con qué ocupar la tarde.* **6** V-T If something **fills** a need or a gap, it makes this need or gap no longer exist. llenar ❑ *Her sense of fun filled a gap in his life.* *Su sentido de la diversión llenaba un hueco en su vida.* **7** V-T If something **fills** a role or position, that is their role or function. desempeñar(se) ❑ *Dena filled the role of diplomat's wife with skill.* *Dena desempeñaba hábilmente su papel de esposa de un diplomático.*
→ see **answer**

▸**fill in** **1** PHR-VERB If you **fill in** a form, you write information in the spaces on it. llenar ❑ *Fill in the coupon and send it to the address shown.* *Llene el cupón y mándelo a la dirección indicada.* **2** PHR-VERB If you **fill** someone **in**, you give them more details about something that you know about. poner al corriente, informar [INFORMAL] ❑ *He filled her in on Wilbur Kantor's visit.* *La puso al corriente sobre la visita de Wilbur Kantor.* **3** PHR-VERB If you **fill in** for someone, you do the work that they normally do because they are unable to do it. cubrir, sustituir, reemplazar **4** → see also **fill 3**

▸**fill out** PHR-VERB If you **fill out** a form, you write information in the spaces on it. llenar ❑ *Fill out the application carefully.* *Llene cuidadosamente la solicitud.*

▸**fill up** **1** PHR-VERB A type of food that **fills** you **up** makes you feel that you have eaten a lot, even though you have only eaten a small amount. llenar **2** → see also **fill 1, 2, 5**

| Thesaurus | *fill* | Ver también: |
|---|---|---|
| V. | inflate, load, pour into, put into; (*ant.*) empty, pour out **1** | |
| | crowd, take up **2** | |
| | block, close, plug, seal **3** | |

**fill|ing** /fɪlɪŋ/ (**fillings**) **1** N-COUNT A **filling** is a small amount of metal or plastic that a dentist puts in a hole in a tooth. tapadura, incrustación, empaste **2** N-VAR The **filling** in a cake, pie, or sandwich is what is inside it. relleno **3** ADJ Food that is **filling** makes you feel full when you have eaten it. llenador
→ see **teeth**

**film** /fɪlm/ (**films, filming, filmed**) **1** N-COUNT A **film** consists of moving pictures that have been recorded so that they can be shown in a theater or on television. película, film, filme ❑ *Everything about the film was good.* *Todo en la película era bueno.* **2** N-COUNT A **film of** powder, liquid, or oil is a very thin layer of it. capa ❑ *The sea is coated with a film of oil.* *El mar está cubierto por una capa de aceite.* **3** V-T If you **film** something, you use a camera to take moving pictures of it. filmar, rodar ❑ *He filmed her life story.* *Filmó la historia de su vida.* ● **film|ing** N-UNCOUNT filmación ❑ *Filming is due to start next month.* *La filmación debe empezar el mes próximo.* **4** N-VAR A **film** is the narrow roll of plastic that is used in a camera to take photographs. película ❑ *...rolls of film.* *...rollos de película.*
→ see **genre, photography**

| Word Partnership | Usar *film* con: |
|---|---|
| N. | film **clip**, film **critic**, film **director**, film **festival**, film **producer**, film **studio** **1** **roll of** film **4** |
| V. | **direct a** film, **edit** film, **watch a** film **1** **develop** film **4** |

**fil|ter** /fɪltər/ (**filters, filtering, filtered**) **1** V-T To **filter** a substance means to pass it through a device which is designed to remove certain particles contained in it. filtrar ❑ *The best prevention for cholera is to boil or filter water.* *La mejor manera de prevenir el cólera es hervir o filtrar el agua.* **2** V-I If light or sound **filters into** a place, it comes in faintly. filtrarse ❑ *Light filtered into my kitchen through the tree.* *La luz se filtraba en mi cocina a través del árbol.* **3** V-I When news or information **filters** through to people, it gradually reaches them. filtrarse, esparcirse ❑ *It took months before the findings began to filter through to the politicians.* *Pasaron meses antes de que los resultados empezaran a filtrarse a los políticos.* ❑ *News of the attack filtered through the college.* *Las noticias sobre el ataque se esparcieron por la universidad.* **4** N-COUNT A **filter** is a device through which a substance is passed when it is being filtered. filtro ❑ *...a coffee filter.* *...un filtro para café.* **5** N-COUNT A **filter** is a device through which sound or light is passed and which blocks or reduces particular sound or light frequencies. filtro ❑ *A blue filter gives the correct color balance.* *Un filtro azul proporciona el equilibrio correcto de color.*

**filthy** /fɪlθi/ (**filthier, filthiest**) ADJ Something that is **filthy** is very dirty. sucio, mugroso, asqueroso, cochino ❑ *He always wore a filthy old jacket.* *Siempre llevaba una chamarra vieja y asquerosa.*

**fin** /fɪn/ (**fins**) **1** N-COUNT A fish's **fins** are the flat parts which stick out of its body and help it to swim. aleta **2** N-COUNT A **fin** on something such as an airplane, rocket, or bomb is a flat part which sticks out and helps control its movement. aleta, alerón
→ see **fish**

| Word Link | *fin ≈ end : final, finish, infinite* |
|---|---|

**fi|nal** /faɪnᵊl/ (**finals**) **1** ADJ In a series of events, things, or people, the **final** one is the last one. último, final ❑ *Astronauts will make a final attempt today to rescue a communications satellite.* *Los astronautas harán hoy un último intento por rescatar un satélite de comunicaciones.* **2** ADJ If a decision is **final**, it cannot be changed or questioned. definitiva, inapelable ❑ *The judges' decision is final.* *La decisión de los jueces es inapelable.* **3** N-COUNT The **final** is the last game or contest in a series and decides who is the winner. final ❑ *...the Gold*

*Cup final. ...la final de la Copa de Oro.* **4** → see also **quarterfinal, semifinal**

**Thesaurus** *final* Ver también:

ADJ. last, ultimate **1**
absolute, decisive, definite, settled **2**

**Word Link** *ize ≈ making : finalize, modernize, publicize*

**fi|nal|ize** /faɪnᵊlaɪz/ (**finalizes, finalizing, finalized**) V-T If you **finalize** something such as a plan or an agreement, you complete the arrangements for it. *terminar, finalizar, concluir, acabar* ❑ *James Baker arrived in Israel to finalize the details of the conference. James Baker llegó a Israel a finalizar los detalles de la conferencia.*

**fi|nal|ly** /faɪnᵊli/ **1** ADV You use **finally** to suggest that something happens after a long period of time, usually later than you wanted or expected it to happen. *finalmente, por fin* ❑ *The food finally arrived at the end of last week. Por fin llegó la comida a finales de la semana pasada.* **2** ADV You use **finally** to indicate that something is last in a series of actions or events. *por último, al final* ❑ *The action slips from comedy to melodrama and finally to tragedy. La acción va de la comedia al melodrama y por último a la tragedia.*

**fi|nance** /faɪnæns, fɪnæns/ (**finances, financing, financed**) **1** V-T When someone **finances** a project or a purchase, they provide the money to pay for it. *financiar(se), costear(se)* ❑ *The fund has been used to finance the building of prisons. El fondo se ha utilizado para financiar la construcción de cárceles.* ● **Finance** is also a noun. *financiamiento, financiación, finanzas* ❑ *They are looking for finance for a major new project. Están buscando financiamiento para un proyecto importante y novedoso.* **2** **Finance** is the commercial or government activity of managing money. *finanzas* ❑ *It is their job to inform consumers about the world of finance. Su tarea es informar a los consumidores sobre el mundo de las finanzas.* **3** N-PLURAL You can refer to the amount of money that you have and how well it is organized as your **finances.** *finanzas* ❑ *Take control of your finances now and save thousands. Tome el control de sus finanzas ahora y ahorre miles.*

**fi|nance charge** (**finance charges**) N-COUNT **Finance charges** are fees or interest that you pay when you borrow money or buy something on credit. *cargo financiero* ❑ *...credit cards with reduced finance charges. ...tarjetas de crédito con cargos financieros reducidos.*

**fi|nan|cial** /faɪnænʃᵊl, fɪn-/ ADJ **Financial** means relating to or involving money. *financiero* ❑ *The company is in financial difficulties. La empresa tiene problemas financieros.* ● **fi|nan|cial|ly** ADV *en lo financiero* ❑ *She would like to be more financially independent. Le gustaría ser más independiente en lo financiero*

**fi|nan|cial ad|vis|er** (**financial advisers**) N-COUNT A **financial adviser** is someone whose job it is to advise people about financial products and services. *asesor financiero o asesora financiera* [BUSINESS]

**fi|nan|cial ser|vices**

The form **financial service** is used as a modifier.

N-PLURAL A company or organization that provides **financial services** is able to help you do things such as make investments or get a mortgage. *servicio financiero* [BUSINESS]

**find** /faɪnd/ (**finds, finding, found**) **1** V-T If you **find** someone or something, you see them or learn where they are. *encontrar* ❑ *The police found a pistol. La policía encontró una pistola.* **2** V-T If you **find** something that you need or want, you succeed in getting it. *encontrar* ❑ *Many people here cannot find work. Aquí mucha gente no puede encontrar trabajo.* ❑ *We have to find him a job. Tenemos que encontrarle un trabajo.* **3** V-T If you **find yourself** doing something, you are doing it without deciding or intending to do it. *encontrarse, descubrir* ❑ *It's not the first time that you've found yourself in this situation. No es la primera vez que te encuentras en esta situación.* ❑ *I found myself having a good time. Descubrí que me la estaba pasando bien.* **4** V-T If you **find** that something is true, you become aware of it or realize that it is true. *percatarse, darse cuenta* ❑ *They awoke to find that he was no longer there. Al despertar se percataron de que él ya no estaba ahí.* ❑ *I find that I am very happy in my life at the moment. Me doy cuenta de que en este momento estoy contento con mi vida.* **5** V-T When a court or jury decides that a person on trial is guilty or innocent, you say that the person **has been found** guilty or not guilty. *declarar, hallar* **6** V-T You can use **find** to express your reaction to someone or something. *parecer, resultar* ❑ *I find his behavior extremely rude. Su comportamiento me resulta muy grosero.* ❑ *I find it shocking that nothing has been done to protect passengers from fire. Me parece escandaloso que no se haya hecho nada para proteger a los pasajeros del fuego.* **7** V-T PASSIVE If something **is found** in a particular place or thing, it exists in that place. *encontrarse* ❑ *Many species of flowering plants are found in the park. En el parque se encuentran muchas especies de plantas en flor.* **8** N-COUNT If you describe someone or something that has been discovered as a **find,** you mean that they are valuable, interesting, good, or useful. *hallazgo* ❑ *...a lucky find at a local yard sale. ...un afortunado hallazgo en una venta de garaje en ese lugar.* **9** → see also **finding, found** **10** PHRASE If you **find** your **way** somewhere, you successfully get there by choosing the right way to go. *encontrar el camino, orientarse* ❑ *He was an expert at finding his way, even in strange surroundings. Se orientaba perfectamente, incluso en lugares desconocidos.* **11** to **find fault with** → see **fault**

▸ **find out** **1** PHR-VERB If you **find** something **out,** you learn something that you did not already know, especially by making a deliberate effort to do so. *descubrir, averiguar, saber, enterarse* ❑ *I'll watch the next episode to find out what happens. Voy a ver el próximo capítulo para descubrir qué pasa.* ❑ *I was relieved to find out that my illness was not serious. Me sentí aliviada al enterarme de que mi enfermedad no era grave.* **2** PHR-VERB If you **find** someone **out,** you discover that they have been doing something dishonest. *descubrir* ❑ *I've spent months filled with shame that they might find me out. Ha pasado meses llena de verguenza de que puedan descubrirme.*

f

F

**find|ing** /faɪndɪŋ/ (**findings**) N-COUNT Someone's **findings** are the information they get as the result of an investigation or some research. resultado, hallazgo ❑ *...one of the main findings of the survey.* *...uno de los principales resultados de la encuesta.*
→ see **laboratory, science**

**fine**
❶ ADJECTIVE USES
❷ PUNISHMENT

❶ **fine** /faɪn/ (**finer, finest**) **1** ADJ You use **fine** to describe something that you think is very good. magnífico, excelente, fino ❑ *There is a fine view of the countryside.* *Hay una excelente vista del campo.* • **fine|ly** ADV magníficamente, excelentemente ❑ *They are finely engineered boats.* *Estos botes han sido excelentemente diseñados.* **2** ADJ If you say that you are **fine,** you mean that you are in good health or reasonably happy. bien ❑ *Lina is fine and sends you her love.* *Lina está bien y te manda saludos.* **3** ADJ If you say that something is **fine,** you mean that it is satisfactory or acceptable. bien ❑ *Everything was going to be just fine.* *Todo iba a salir bien.* • **Fine** is also an adverb. bien ❑ *All the instruments are working fine.* *Todos los instrumentos están funcionando bien.* **4** ADJ Something that is **fine** is very delicate, narrow, or small. fino, delgado ❑ *...the fine hairs on her arms.* *...el fino vello de sus brazos.* • **fine|ly** ADV finamente ❑ *Chop the onions finely.* *Pique finamente las cebollas.* **5** ADJ A **fine** detail or distinction is very small or exact. fino, preciso, sutil, pequeño ❑ *Johnson likes the broad outline but is critical of the fine detail.* *A Johnson le gusta el proyecto en general, pero se muestra crítico de los pequeños detalles.* • **fine|ly** ADV delicadamente ❑ *The smallest mistake could ruin the whole finely-balanced process.* *El más pequeño error podría arruinar todo el proceso, tan delicadamente equilibrado.* **6** ADJ When the weather is **fine,** the sun is shining and it is not raining. bueno

❷ **fine** /faɪn/ (**fines, fining, fined**) **1** N-COUNT A **fine** is a punishment in which a person is ordered to pay a sum of money because they have done something illegal or broken a rule. multa **2** V-T If someone **is fined,** they are punished by being ordered to pay a sum of money because they have done something illegal or broken a rule. multar, imponer una multa, poner una multa ❑ *She was fined $300 and banned from driving for one month.* *La multaron con 300 dólares y le prohibieron manejar durante un mes.*

**fine ad|just|ment** N-UNCOUNT The part of a microscope that controls the **fine adjustment** is the part that allows you to obtain the best possible focus for the object you are looking at. ajuste fino [TECHNICAL]

**fine-tune** (**fine-tunes, fine-tuning, fine-tuned**) V-T If you **fine-tune** something, you make very small and precise changes to it in order to make it work better. afinar, ajustar, poner a punto ❑ *The staff help to fine-tune business plans.* *El personal ayudó a afinar los planes de negocios.*

**fin|ger** /fɪŋgər/ (**fingers, fingering, fingered**) **1** N-COUNT Your **fingers** are the long thin parts at the end of each hand. dedo ❑ *She ran her fingers through her hair.* *Se pasó los dedos por el cabello.* **2** V-T If you **finger** something, you touch or feel it with your fingers. palpar, tentar, tocar ❑ *He fingered the coins in his pocket.* *Palpó las monedas que traía en el bolsillo.* **3** PHRASE If you **cross** your **fingers,** you put one finger on top of another and hope for good luck. If you say that someone **is keeping their fingers crossed,** you mean they are hoping for good luck. cruzar los dedos, poner changuitos **4** PHRASE If you **point the finger at** someone, you blame them or accuse them of doing something wrong. señalar con el dedo, acusar ❑ *He said he wasn't pointing an accusing finger at anyone in the government.* *Dijo que no estaba señalando con el dedo a nadie del gobierno.* **5** PHRASE If you **put** your **finger on** something, for example, a reason or problem, you see and identify exactly what it is. dar con algo, acertar ❑ *We couldn't put our finger on what went wrong.* *No pudimos dar con lo que estaba mal.*
→ see **hand**

**finger|nail** /fɪŋgərneɪl/ (**fingernails**) N-COUNT Your **fingernails** are the thin hard areas at the end of each of your fingers. uña
→ see **hand**

**finger|print** /fɪŋgərprɪnt/ (**fingerprints**) N-COUNT **Fingerprints** are marks made by a person's fingers which show the lines on the skin. huella digital ❑ *His fingerprints were found on the murder weapon.* *Encontraron sus huellas digitales en el arma homicida.* PHRASE • If the police **take** someone's **fingerprints,** they make that person press their fingers onto a pad covered with ink, and then onto paper, so that they know what that person's fingerprints look like. tomar las huellas digitales

**Word Link** *fin ≈ end : final, finish, infinite*

**fin|ish** /fɪnɪʃ/ (**finishes, finishing, finished**) **1** V-T When you **finish** doing something, you do the last part of it, so that there is no more for you to do. terminar, acabar, concluir ❑ *As soon as he finished eating, he excused himself.* *En cuanto terminó de comer, se disculpó y se retiró.* ❑ *Mr. Gould was given loud cheers when he finished his speech.* *El Sr. Gould recibió fuertes aclamaciones cuando terminó su discurso.* • **Finish up** means the same as **finish.** terminar, acabar, concluir ❑ *We waited a few minutes outside his office while he finished up his meeting.* *Esperamos unos minutos fuera de su oficina mientras terminaba su reunión.* **2** V-I When something such as a course, show, or sale **finishes,** especially at a planned time, it ends. terminar, acabar ❑ *The teaching day finishes at around 4 p.m.* *Las clases terminan más o menos a las 4 de la tarde.* **3** N-SING **The finish** of something is the end of it or the last part of it. fin, final ❑ *I'll see the job through to the finish.* *Yo me ocuparé del trabajo hasta el final.* **4** N-COUNT If the surface of something that has been made has a particular kind of **finish,** it has the appearance or texture mentioned. terminado, acabado ❑ *The anchors are made from stainless steel and are polished to a shiny finish.* *Las anclas son de acero inoxidable y las pulen para darles un terminado brillante.* **5** → see also **finished** **6** PHRASE If you add **the finishing touches** to something, you add or do the last things that are necessary to complete it. toque final, último toque, toque ❑ *She was adding the finishing touches to her novel.* *Estaba*

*dando los últimos toques a su novela.*
▸ **finish off** 1 PHR-VERB If you **finish off** something that you have been eating or drinking, you eat or drink the last part of it with the result that there is none left. *terminar(se), acabar(se)* ❑ *Kelly finished off his coffee. Kelly se terminó el café.* 2 → see also **finish 2** 3 PHR-VERB If you **finish up** something that you have been eating or drinking, you eat or drink the last part of it. *terminar(se), acabar(se)* ❑ *Finish up your soup now, please. Ya termínate la sopa, por favor.* 4 → see also **finish 1, 2**

**Thesaurus** *finish* Ver también:

V. conclude, end, wrap up; (*ant.*) begin, start 1 2

**Word Partnership** Usar *finish* con:

N. finish **a conversation**, finish **school**, finish **work** 1
finish **a job**, **time to** finish 1 2

**fin|ished** /fɪnɪʃt/ 1 ADJ Someone who is **finished with** something is no longer doing it or dealing with it or is no longer interested in it. *haber acabado con, estar harto de* ❑ *He says he is finished with police work. Dice que ya está harto de ser policía.* 2 ADJ Someone or something that is **finished** is no longer important, powerful, or effective. *acabado* ❑ *Her power over me is finished. Se acabó su poder sobre mí.*

**fin|ish line** (**finish lines**) N-COUNT In a race, the **finish line** is the place on the track or course where the race officially ends. *meta, línea de llegada*

**fire**
❶ BURNING, HEAT
❷ SHOOTING OR ATTACKING
❸ DISMISSAL

❶ **fire** /faɪər/ (**fires**) 1 N-UNCOUNT **Fire** is the hot, bright flames produced by things that are burning. *fuego, lumbre* ❑ *They saw a huge ball of fire reaching hundreds of feet into the sky. Vieron una enorme bola de fuego que alcanzaba una altura de cientos de metros.* 2 N-VAR **Fire** or a **fire** is an occurrence of uncontrolled burning which destroys buildings, forests, or other things. *incendio* ❑ *87 people died in a fire at the Social Club. En el incendio del Social Club murieron 87 personas.* ❑ *...a forest fire. ...un incendio forestal.* 3 N-COUNT A **fire** is a burning pile of wood, coal, or other fuel that you make. *fogata, fuego, hoguera* ❑ *There was a fire in the fireplace. Había fuego en la chimenea.* 4 PHRASE If an object or substance **catches fire,** it starts burning. *incendiarse* ❑ *The blast caused several buildings to catch fire. La explosión provocó que varios edificios se incendiaran.* 5 PHRASE If something is **on fire,** it is burning and being damaged by a fire. *quemarse, incendiarse* 6 PHRASE If you **set fire to** something or if you **set** it **on fire,** you start it burning in order to damage or destroy it. *prender fuego, encender, incendiar*
→ see Word Web: **fire**

❷ **fire** /faɪər/ (**fires, firing, fired**) 1 V-T/V-I If someone **fires** a gun or a bullet, or if they **fire,** a bullet is sent from a gun that they are using. *disparar, hacer fuego* ❑ *Soldiers fired rubber bullets into the crowd. Los soldados dispararon balas de goma contra la multitud.* • **fir|ing** N-UNCOUNT *balacera, disparo* ❑ *The firing got heavier and we moved inside the building. Se intensificó la balacera y nos refugiamos en el edificio.* 2 V-T If you **fire** questions at someone, you ask them a lot of questions very quickly, one after another. *preguntar, hacer preguntas* 3 N-UNCOUNT You can use **fire** to refer to the shots fired from a gun or guns. *fuego, disparo* ❑ *...fire from automatic weapons. ...fuego de armas automáticas*

❸ **fire** /faɪər/ (**fires, firing, fired**) V-T If an employer **fires** you, they dismiss you from your job. *despedir, correr* ❑ *This guy's lying. Do we fire him? Este tipo está mintiendo, ¿lo corremos?*

**fire alarm** (**fire alarms**) N-COUNT A **fire alarm** is a device that makes a noise, for example, with a bell, to warn people when there is a fire. *alarma contra incendio*

**fire|arm** /faɪərɑrm/ (**firearms**) N-COUNT **Firearms** are guns. *armas de fuego* [FORMAL] ❑ *Security guards were carrying firearms. Los guardias de seguridad portaban armas de fuego.*
→ see **war**

**fire blan|ket** (**fire blankets**) N-COUNT A **fire blanket** is a thick cloth made from fire-resistant material that is designed to put out small fires. *manta contra incendios*

**fire de|part|ment** (**fire departments**) N-COUNT **The fire department** is an organization which has the job of putting out fires. *departamento de bomberos*

**fire en|gine** (**fire engines**) N-COUNT A **fire engine** is a large vehicle which carries firefighters and equipment for putting out fires. *camión de bomberos, carro de bomberos*

**fire ex|tin|guish|er** (**fire extinguishers**) also **fire-extinguisher** N-COUNT A **fire extinguisher**

**Word Web** fire

A single **match**, a **campfire**, or even a bolt of lightning can **spark** a **wild fire**. Wild fires can spread across grasslands and **burn down** forests. Huge firestorms can **burn** out of control for days. They cause death and destruction. However, some ecosystems depend on fire. Once the fire passes, the **smoke** clears, the **smoldering** embers cool, and the **ash** settles, then the cycle of life begins again. Humans have learned to use fire. The **heat** cooks our food. People build fires in **fireplaces** and **wood** stoves. The **flames** warm our hands. And before electricity, the **glow** of **candle light** lit our homes.

is a metal cylinder which contains water or chemicals at high pressure which can put out fires. extintor de incendios, extinguidor de incendios

**fire|fight|er** /faɪərfaɪtər/ (**firefighters**) N-COUNT A **firefighter** is a person whose job is to put out fires. bombero o bombera

**fire|place** /faɪərpleɪs/ (**fireplaces**) N-COUNT In a room, the **fireplace** is the place where a fire can be lit and the area on the wall and floor surrounding this place. chimenea, hogar
→ see **fire**

**fire|storm** (**firestorms**) N-COUNT If you say that there is a **firestorm of** protest or criticism, you are emphasizing that there is a great deal of fierce protest or criticism. tormenta
→ see **fire**

**fire truck** (**fire trucks**) N-COUNT A **fire truck** is a large vehicle which carries firefighters and equipment for putting out fires. carro de bomberos, camión de bomberos

**fire|work** /faɪərwɜrk/ (**fireworks**) N-COUNT **Fireworks** are small objects that are lit to entertain people on special occasions. They burn brightly in an attractive way, and often make a loud noise. fuegos artificiales, fuegos pirotécnicos, fuegos de artificio
→ see Word Web: **fireworks**

**Word Link** *firm ≈ making strong : affirm, confirm, firm*

**firm** /fɜrm/ (**firms, firmer, firmest**) **1** N-COUNT A **firm** is an organization which sells or produces something or which provides a service which people pay for. empresa, compañía, despacho ❑ *...a Chicago law firm.* *...un despacho de abogados de Chicago.* **2** ADJ If something is **firm**, it does not change much in shape when it is pressed but is not completely hard. firme ❑ *Fruit should be firm and in excellent condition.* *La fruta tiene que estar firme y en excelentes condiciones.* **3** ADJ A **firm** physical action is strong and controlled. firme, fuerte, enérgico ❑ *The quick handshake was firm and cool.* *El rápido apretón de manos fue enérgico y frío.* ● **firm|ly** ADV firmemente, con firmeza ❑ *She held me firmly by the elbow.* *Me sujetó firmemente por el codo.* **4** ADJ A **firm** person behaves in a way that shows that they are not going to change their mind. firme, enérgico ❑ *She had to be firm with him. "I don't want to see you again."* *Tenía que ser firme con él. Le dijo:—No quiero volver a verte.* ● **firm|ly** ADV firmemente, con firmeza ❑ *"A good night's sleep is what you want," he said firmly.* *—Lo que necesitas es una buena noche de sueño,—le dijo con firmeza.* **5** ADJ A **firm** decision or opinion is definite and unlikely to change. firme, definitiva ❑ *He made a firm decision to leave.* *Tomó la firme decisión de irse.* ● **firm|ly** ADV firmemente, con firmeza ❑ *Political values and opinions are firmly held.* *Las opiniones y los valores políticos se arraigan firmemente.* **6** ADJ **Firm** evidence or information is based on facts and so is likely to be true. sólido **7** PHRASE If someone **stands firm,** they refuse to change their mind about something. mantenerse firme ❑ *The council is standing firm against the protest.* *El ayuntamiento se mantiene firme en contra de la protesta.*

**Thesaurus** *firm* Ver también:

| | |
|---|---|
| N. | business, company, enterprise, organization **1** |
| ADJ. | dense, hard, sturdy **2** |

**first** /fɜrst/ **1** ORD The **first** thing, person, event, or period of time is the one that happens or comes before all the others of the same kind. primero, primer ❑ *...the first month of the year.* *...el primer mes del año.* ❑ *...the first few flakes of snow.* *...los primeros copos de nieve.* ● **First** is also a pronoun. primero, primer ❑ *I've seen the movie twice and the second time I liked it even better than the first.* *He visto dos veces la película y la segunda me gustó mucho más que la primera.* **2** ORD You use **first** to refer to the best or most important thing or person of a particular kind. primero, principal ❑ *The first duty of any government must be to protect the interests of the taxpayers.* *El principal deber de todo gobierno debe ser la protección de los intereses de los contribuyentes.* **3** ADV If you do something **first,** you do it before anyone else does, or before you do anything else. primero, para empezar ❑ *I do not remember who spoke first.* *No recuerdo quién habló primero.* ❑ *First, tell me what you think of my products.* *Para empezar, dime qué piensas de mis productos.* **4** ADV You use **first** when you are talking about what happens in the early part of an event or experience, in contrast to what happens later. al principio ❑ *When we first came here there were a lot of kids.* *Al principio, cuando llegamos, había muchos niños.* ● **First** is also an ordinal. primero ❑ *She told him that her first reaction was disgust.* *Le dijo que su primera reacción fue de disgusto.* **5** N-SING An event that is described as **a first** has never happened before and is important or exciting. acontecimiento sin precedentes ❑ *It is a first for New York: an outdoor exhibition of Botero's sculpture on Park Avenue.* *La exposición al aire libre de las esculturas de Botero en Park Avenue es un acontecimiento sin precedentes en Nueva York.* **6** PRON **The first** you hear of something or **the first** you know about it is the time when you

**Word Web** fireworks

**Fireworks** were created in China more than a thousand years ago. Historians believe that the discovery was made by alchemists. They heated **sulfur, potassium nitrate, charcoal,** and arsenic together and the mixture **exploded.** It made a very hot, bright fire. Later they mixed these **chemicals** in a hollow bamboo tube and threw it in the fire. Thus the firecracker was born. Marco Polo brought firecrackers to Europe from the Orient in 1292. Soon the Italians began experimenting with ways of producing elaborate, colorful fireworks displays. This launched the era of modern pyrotechnics.

first become aware of it. *lo primero* ❑ *We heard it on TV last night—that was the first we heard of it. Nos enteramos por primera vez en la tele anoche.* **7** PHRASE You use **first of all** to introduce the first of a number of things that you want to say. *en primer lugar, antes que nada* ❑ *First of all, he's far too old to work as a spy, and secondly, he's completely honest. En primer lugar, es demasiado viejo para ser espía y, en segundo, totalmente honesto.* **8** PHRASE You use **at first** when you are talking about what happens in the early stages of an event or experience, or just after something else has happened, in contrast to what happens later. *al principio* ❑ *At first, he seemed surprised by my questions. Al principio pareció sorprendido de mis preguntas.*

**first aid** N-UNCOUNT **First aid** is simple medical treatment given as soon as possible to a sick or injured person. *primeros auxilios* ❑ *...emergencies which need prompt first aid treatment. ...emergencias que exigen la administración inmediata de los primeros auxilios.*

**first aid kit** (**first aid kits**) N-COUNT A **first aid kit** is a bag or case containing basic medical supplies that are designed to be used on someone who is injured or who suddenly becomes ill. *equipo de primeros auxilios, botiquín*

**First Amend|ment** N-SING The **First Amendment** is the part of the U.S. Constitution that guarantees people the right of free speech, and freedom of religion, assembly, and petition. *Primera Enmienda a la Constitución de los Estados Unidos*

**First Fami|ly** N-SING The **First Family** is the U.S. president and their spouse and children. *la familia del presidente*

**first floor** (**first floors**) N-COUNT **The first floor** of a building is the one at ground level. *planta baja*

**First Lady** (**First Ladies**) N-COUNT **The First Lady** in a country or state is the wife of the president or state governor, or a woman who performs the official duties normally performed by the wife. *Primera Dama*

**first name** (**first names**) N-COUNT Your **first name** is the first of the names that were given to you when you were born. *nombre, nombre de pila* ❑ *Her first name was Mary. Se llamaba Mary.*

**fis|cal** /fɪskᵊl/ ADJ **Fiscal** is used to describe something that relates to government money or public money, especially taxes. *fiscal* ❑ *...fiscal policy. ...política fiscal.*

**fish** /fɪʃ/ (**fish** or **fishes, fishes, fishing, fished**) **1** N-COUNT A **fish** is a creature that lives in water and has a tail and fins. *pez* **2** N-UNCOUNT **Fish** is the flesh of a fish eaten as food. *pescado* **3** V-I If you **fish,** you try to catch fish, either for food or as a form of sport or recreation. *pescar* ❑ *Brian learned to fish in the Colorado River. Brian aprendió a pescar en el río Colorado.* **4** → see also **fishing**
→ see Picture Dictionary: **fish**
→ see **pet, shark**

**fish and chips** N-PLURAL **Fish and chips** are fish fillets coated with batter and deep-fried, eaten with French fries. *pescado capeado con papas fritas*

**fish|bowl** /fɪʃboʊl/ (**fishbowls**) also **fish bowl** **1** N-COUNT A **fishbowl** is a glass bowl in which you can keep fish as pets. *pecera* **2** N-COUNT You can use **fishbowl** to describe a place or situation that is open to observation. *estar en un aparador, a la vista de todo el mundo* ❑ *The yacht's crew must get used to working in a fishbowl. La tripulación del yate tiene que acostumbrarse a trabajar como si estuviera en un aparador.*

**fisher|man** /fɪʃərmən/ (**fishermen**) N-COUNT A **fisherman** is a person who catches fish as a job or for sport. *pescador o pescadora*

**fish|ing** /fɪʃɪŋ/ N-UNCOUNT **Fishing** is the sport, hobby, or business of catching fish. *pesca*

**fish stick** (**fish sticks**) N-COUNT **Fish sticks** are small long pieces of fish covered in breadcrumbs, usually sold in frozen form. *dedo de pescado, palito de pescado*

**fish|tail** /fɪʃteɪl/ (**fishtails, fishtailing, fishtailed**) V-I If a vehicle **fishtails,** the rear of the vehicle swings around in an uncontrolled way while the vehicle is moving. *colear(se)*

**fist** /fɪst/ (**fists**) N-COUNT Your hand is referred to as your **fist** when you have bent your fingers in toward the palm in order to hit someone, to make an angry gesture, or to hold something. *puño* ❑ *He shouted and shook his fist at me. Me gritó y me amenazó con el puño.*

**fist|fight** /fɪstfaɪt/ (**fistfights**) also **fist fight** N-COUNT A **fistfight** is a fight in which people punch each other. *pelea a puñetazos, pleito a puñetazos* ❑ *Their argument almost ended in a fistfight. Su discusión casi acabó en un pleito a puñetazos.*

f

**Picture Dictionary** fish

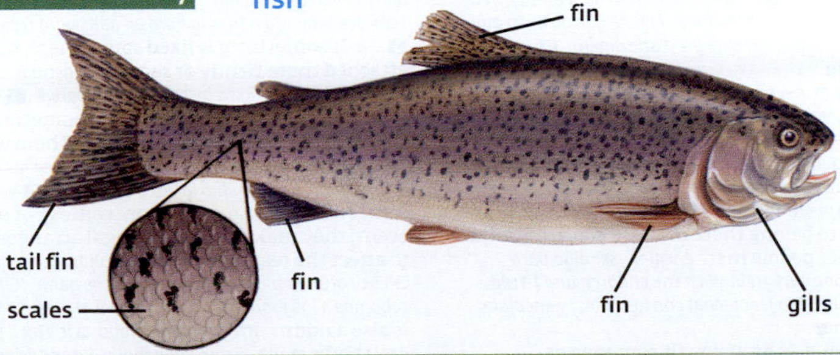

F

**fit**
1 BEING RIGHT OR GOING IN THE RIGHT PLACE
2 HEALTHY
3 UNCONTROLLABLE MOVEMENTS OR EMOTIONS

**1 fit** /fɪt/ (**fits, fitting, fitted** or **fit**) → Please look at category 9 to see if the expression you are looking for is shown under another headword. **1** V-T/V-I If something **fits**, it is the right size and shape to go onto a person's body or onto a particular object. *ajustar, quedar bien* ❑ *The kimono fit the child perfectly. El kimono le quedó perfectamente al niño.* ❑ *She has to go to the men's department to find trousers that fit at the waist. Tiene que ir al departamento de hombres para encontrar pantalones que le queden bien de la cintura.* **2** V-I If something **fits** somewhere, it can be put there or is designed to be put there. *caber* ❑ *The pocket computer is small enough to fit into your pocket. La computadora de bolsillo es tan pequeña que, como su nombre la indica, cabe en el bolsillo.* **3** V-T If you **fit** something into a particular space or place, you put it there. *poner, colocar* ❑ *She fitted the book back on the shelf. Puso de nuevo el libro en el estante.* **4** V-T If you **fit** something somewhere, you attach it there, or put it there carefully and securely. *instalar, poner, colocar* ❑ *Fit locks on outside doors and install a visible burglar alarm. Instale cerraduras en las puertas exteriores y una alarma contra robo en un lugar visible.* ❑ *Peter built the overhead ladders and fitted them to the wall. Peter construyó las escaleras elevadas y las fijó al muro.* **5** N-SING If something is a good **fit**, it fits well. *ajustar, quedar bien* ❑ *He was happy that the doors were a reasonably good fit. Le dio gusto que las puertas ajustaran razonablemente bien.* **6** ADJ If something is **fit** for a particular purpose, it is suitable for that purpose. *adecuado* ❑ *Only two of the bicycles were fit for the road. Sólo dos de las bicicletas eran adecuadas para el camino.* **7** ADJ If someone is **fit** to do something, they have the appropriate qualities or skills that will allow them to do it. *capacitado, digno* ❑ *You're not fit to be a mother! ¡No eres digna de ser madre!* ● **fit|ness** N-UNCOUNT *capacidad, aptitud* ❑ *There is a debate about his fitness for the job. Se está discutiendo su aptitud para el trabajo.* **8** PHRASE If you say that someone **sees fit to** do something, you mean that they are entitled to do it, but that you disapprove of their decision to do it. *parecer conveniente o parecer adecuado, parecer apropiado* [FORMAL] ❑ *He's not a friend, you say, yet you saw fit to lend him money. Dijiste que no es tu amigo, pero te pareció conveniente prestarle dinero.* **9** → see also **fitting**

▸**fit in** **1** PHR-VERB If you manage to **fit** a person or task **in**, you manage to find time to deal with them. *acomodar, cuadrar* ❑ *We work long hours and we rush around trying to fit everything in. Trabajamos muchas horas y nos apuramos para tratar de acomodar todo.* **2** PHR-VERB If you **fit in** as part of a group, you seem to belong there because you are similar to the other people in it. *encajar, ser algo para alguien* ❑ *She was great with the children and fitted in beautifully. Era fenomenal con los niños, y encajaba perfectamente.*

▸**fit out** PHR-VERB If you **fit** someone or something **out**, or you **fit** them **up**, you provide them with equipment and other things that they need. *proveer de algo, equipar* ❑ *We helped to fit him out for a trip to the Baltic. Lo ayudamos a equiparse para un viaje al Báltico.* ❑ *Within an hour, Saab had fitted me up with another car. En menos de una hora Saab me había provisto con otro auto.*

**2 fit** /fɪt/ (**fitter, fittest**) ADJ Someone who is **fit** is healthy and physically strong. *en forma* ❑ *An averagely fit person can master easy ski runs within a few days. Una persona razonablemente en forma puede dominar las pistas fáciles de ski en unos días.* ● **fit|ness** N-UNCOUNT *buena forma física, buen estado físico, buena condición física* ❑ *Squash was once thought to offer all-round fitness. En algún momento se pensó que el squash ponía en buena forma física general.*

**3 fit** /fɪt/ (**fits**) **1** N-COUNT If you have a **fit of** coughing or laughter, you suddenly start coughing or laughing in an uncontrollable way. *ataque* ❑ *Part of the way through my speech I had a fit of coughing. Me dio un ataque de tos en medio de mi discurso.* **2** N-COUNT If someone has a **fit** they suddenly lose consciousness and their body makes uncontrollable movements. *ataque* ❑ *Place a pillow under the head of the person suffering a fit. Coloque una almohada bajo la cabeza de la persona que esté sufriendo un ataque.*

**fit|ting** /fɪtɪŋ/ (**fittings**) **1** ADJ Something that is **fitting** is right or suitable. *adecuado, digno* ❑ *A solitary man, it was perhaps fitting that he died alone. Era un hombre solitario, quizá fue digno que muriera solo.* ● **fit|ting|ly** ADV *adecuadamente, dignamente* ❑ *He ended his baseball career, fittingly, by hitting a home run. Terminó su carrera como beisbolista dignamente, anotando un jonrón.* **2** N-COUNT A **fitting** is one of the smaller parts on the outside of a piece of equipment or furniture, for example, a handle or a faucet. *accesorio* ❑ *...brass light fittings. ...accesorios de bronce para iluminación.* **3** N-PLURAL **Fittings** are things such as ovens or heaters, that are fitted inside a building, but can be removed if necessary. *accesorios, aditamentos*

**five** /faɪv/ (**fives**) NUM **Five** is the number 5. *cinco* ❑ *I spent five years there. Pasé cinco años allá.*

**fix** /fɪks/ (**fixes, fixing, fixed**) **1** V-T If you **fix** something which is damaged or which does not work properly, you repair it. *arreglar, reparar* ❑ *This morning, a man came to fix my washing machine. Esta mañana vino un hombre a reparar la lavadora.* **2** V-T If you **fix** something, for example, a date, price, or policy, you decide and say exactly what it will be. *fijar, concretar, decidir* ❑ *He's going to fix a time when I can see him. Va a fijar la hora en que podrá recibirme.* **3** V-T If something **is fixed** somewhere, it is attached there firmly or securely. *instalar* ❑ *It is fixed on the wall. Está instalado en la pared.* **4** V-T/V-I If you **fix** your eyes **on** someone or something or if your eyes **fix on** them, you look at them with complete attention. *fijar* ❑ *Gregory fixed his eyes on the floor. Gregory fijó la vista en el piso.* **5** V-T If someone **fixes** a race, election, contest, or other event, they make unfair or illegal arrangements to affect the result. *arreglar, amañar, comprar* ❑ *They offered players bribes to fix the game. Ofrecieron sobornos a los jugadores para arreglar el juego.* ● **Fix** is also a noun. *arreglo, chanchullo* ❑ *It's all a fix, a deal they've made. Es un chanchullo, ya se pusieron de* *acuerdo.* **6** → see also **fixed**

▸ **fix up** PHR-VERB If you **fix** someone **up with** something they need, you provide it for them. *conseguir* ❑ *We'll fix him up with a tie. Le conseguiremos una corbata.*

| **Thesaurus** | *fix* | Ver también: |
|---|---|---|
| v. | adjust, correct, repair, restore **1**<br>agree on, decide, establish, work out **2** | |

**fixed** /fɪkst/ **1** ADJ You use **fixed** to describe something which stays the same and does not or cannot vary. *fijo* ❑ *The company issues a fixed number of shares. La compañía emite un número fijo de acciones.* ❑ *...fixed-price menus. ...menús de precio fijo.* **2** → see also **fix**

**fixed pul|ley** (**fixed pulleys**) N-COUNT A **fixed pulley** is a pulley that is attached to something that does not move. *polea fija*

| **Word Link** | *fix ≈ fastening : fixture, prefix, suffix* |
|---|---|

**fix|ture** /fɪkstʃər/ (**fixtures**) N-COUNT **Fixtures** are fittings or furniture which belong to a building and are legally part of it, for example, a bathtub or a toilet. *aditamentos* ❑ *...fixtures and fittings are included in the purchase price. ...los aditamentos y los accesorios están incluidos en el precio.*

**flag** /flæg/ (**flags, flagging, flagged**) **1** N-COUNT A **flag** is a piece of colored cloth which can be attached to a pole and is used as a sign for something or as a signal. *bandera, banderín* ❑ *...the American flag. ...la bandera estadounidense.* **2** V-I If you **flag** or if your spirits **flag,** you begin to lose enthusiasm or energy. *flaquear, disminuir, decaer*

**fla|gella** /flədʒɛlə/ N-PLURAL **Flagella** are the long, thin extensions of cells in some microorganisms that help them move. *flagelo* [TECHNICAL]

**flame** /fleɪm/ (**flames**) **1** N-VAR A **flame** is a hot bright stream of burning gas that comes from something that is burning. *flama, llama* ❑ *The heat from the flames was so intense that roads melted. El calor de las llamas era tan intenso que los caminos se fundían.* **2** PHRASE If something **bursts into flames** or **bursts into flame,** it suddenly starts burning strongly. *estallar en llamas* **3** PHRASE Something that is **in flames** is on fire. *en llamas*
→ see **laboratory, fire**

**fla|min|go** //fləmɪŋgoʊ// (**flamingos** or **flamingoes**) N-COUNT A **flamingo** is a bird with pink feathers, long thin legs, a long neck, and a curved beak. Flamingos live near water in warm areas. *flamenco*

**flank** /flæŋk/ (**flanks, flanking, flanked**) **1** N-COUNT An animal's **flank** is its side, between the ribs and the hip. *costado* **2** N-COUNT A **flank** of an army or navy force is one side of it when it is organized for battle. *flanco* **3** V-T If something **is flanked by** things, it has them on both sides of it, or sometimes on one side of it. *flanquear* ❑ *The altar was flanked by two Christmas trees. El altar estaba flanqueado por dos árboles de navidad.*
→ see **horse**

**flap** /flæp/ (**flaps, flapping, flapped**) **1** V-T/V-I If something such as a piece of cloth or paper **flaps** or if you **flap** it, it moves quickly up and down or from side to side. *ondear, agitar(se)* ❑ *Gray sheets flapped on the clothes line. Unas sábanas grises se agitaban en los tendederos.* **2** V-T/V-I If a bird or insect **flaps** its wings or if its wings **flap,** the wings move quickly up and down. *batir las alas, aletear* **3** N-COUNT A **flap** of cloth or skin is a flat piece of it that can move freely up and down or from side to side because it is attached by only one edge. *colgajo, faldón* ❑ *He drew back the tent flap. Levantó el faldón de la tienda.*

**flare** /flɛər/ (**flares, flaring, flared**) **1** N-COUNT A **flare** is a small device that produces a bright flame. Flares are used as distress signals, for example, on ships. *bengala* **2** V-I If a fire **flares,** the flames suddenly become larger. *llamear, flamear* ● **Flare up** means the same as **flare.** *llamear, flamear, encenderse* ❑ *Don't spill too much fat on the barbecue as it could flare up. No rocíes demasiada grasa en la parrillada porque podría encenderse.* **3** V-I If something such as trouble, violence, or conflict **flares,** it starts or becomes more violent. *enardecer(se), estallar, recrudecer(se)* ❑ *Trouble flared in several American cities. Los problemas se recrudecieron en varias ciudades americanas.* ● **Flare up** means the same as **flare.** *enardecer(se), estallar, recrudecer(se)* ❑ *Dozens of people were injured as fighting flared up. Decenas de personas resultaron lesionadas al enardecerse los combates.*

**flash** /flæʃ/ (**flashes, flashing, flashed**) **1** N-COUNT A **flash** is a sudden burst of light or of something shiny or bright. *chispazo, destello, fogonazo, flash, flashazo* ❑ *...a sudden flash of lightning. ...un repentino destello luminoso.* **2** V-T/V-I If a light **flashes** or if you **flash** a light, it shines with a sudden bright light, especially as quick, regular flashes of light. *brillar, destellar, hacer señales con una luz* ❑ *Lightning flashed among the dark clouds. Los relámpagos brillaron entre las nubes oscuras.* ❑ *Frightened drivers flashed their headlights at him as he drove down the wrong side of the road. Los asustados conductores le hacían señales con los faros porque circulaba en sentido contrario.* **3** V-I If something **flashes** past or by, it moves past you so fast that you cannot see it properly. *pasar como rayo, pasar volando* ❑ *It was a busy road, and cars flashed by every few minutes. Era un camino muy concurrido y los autos pasaban volando cada pocos minutos.* **4** N-COUNT A **flash** is the same as a **flashlight**. *linterna* [INFORMAL] ❑ *Stopping to rest, Pete shut off the flash. Cuando se detuvo a descansar, Pete apagó la linterna.* **5** PHRASE If you say that something happens **in a flash,** you mean that it happens suddenly and lasts only a very short time. *de repente* ❑ *The answer came to him in a flash. De repente se le ocurrió la respuesta.*

**flash drive** (**flash drives**) N-COUNT A **flash drive** is a small, lightweight smart card that can be plugged into a computer where it functions as a portable hard drive. *unidad de disco portátil, usb*
→ see **computer**

**flash flood** (**flash floods**) N-COUNT A **flash flood** is a sudden rush of water over dry land, usually caused by a great deal of rain. *inundación repentina, torrente*

**flash|light** /flæʃlaɪt/ (**flashlights**) N-COUNT A **flashlight** is a small electric light which gets

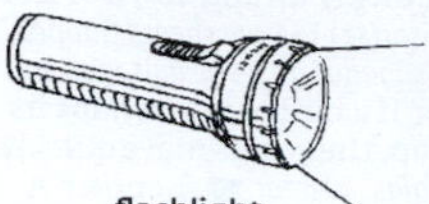
flashlight

its power from batteries and which you can carry in your hand. *linterna*

**flask** /flæsk/ (**flasks**) N-COUNT A **flask** is a bottle which you use for carrying alcoholic or hot drinks around with you. *frasco, termo* ❑ *...a flask of coffee. ...un termo de café.*

**flat**
❶ SURFACES, SHAPES, AND POSITIONS
❷ OTHER USES

❶ **flat** /flæt/ (**flatter, flattest**) **1** ADJ Something that is **flat** is level, smooth, or even, rather than sloping, curved, or uneven. *plano, llano* ❑ *Tiles can be fixed to any surface as long as it's flat. Las losetas se pueden pegar en cualquier superficie, siempre que sea plana.* ❑ *...a flat roof. ...un techo plano.* **2** ADJ A **flat** object is not very tall or deep in relation to its length and width. *plano* ❑ *...a square flat box. ...una caja cuadrada y plana.* **3** ADJ A **flat** tire or ball does not have enough air in it. *desinflado, ponchado*

| **Thesaurus** | *flat* | Ver también: |
| --- | --- | --- |
| ADJ. | even, horizontal, level, smooth ❶ 1 | |

❷ **flat** /flæt/ (**flatter, flattest**) **1** ADJ If you say that something happened, for example, in ten seconds **flat** or ten minutes **flat,** you are emphasizing that it happened surprisingly quickly and only took ten seconds or ten minutes. *en sólo, en apenas* ❑ *The engine will take you from 0 to 60 mph in six seconds flat. El motor lo llevará de 0 a 96 kph en apenas seis segundos.* **2** ADJ A **flat** rate, price, or percentage is one that is fixed and which applies in every situation. *fijo* ❑ *Fees are charged at a flat rate. Las cuotas se cobran a tasa fija.* **3** ADJ **Flat** is used after a letter representing a musical note, to show that the note should be played or sung half a tone lower than the note which otherwise matches that letter. **Flat** is often represented by the symbol ♭ after the letter. *bemol* ❑ *...Schubert's B flat Piano Trio. ...el Trío para Piano en Si Bemol de Schubert.* **4** ADV If someone sings **flat** or if a musical instrument is **flat,** their singing or the instrument is slightly lower in pitch than it should be. *desafinado* • **Flat** is also an adjective. *desafinado* ❑ *He was fired from the choir because his singing was flat. Lo despidieron del coro por cantar desafinado.* **5** ADJ A **flat** denial or refusal is definite and firm. *categórico, rotundo, terminante* ❑ *The Foreign Ministry has issued a flat denial of any involvement. El Ministerio del Exterior emitió una rotunda negativa de participación.* • **flat|ly** ADV *de plano, rotundamente* ❑ *He flatly refused to discuss it. Se negó rotundamente a discutirlo.* **6** PHRASE If an event or attempt **falls flat** or **falls flat on** its **face,** it is unsuccessful. *fracasar, no ser bien recibido* ❑ *Liz meant it as a joke but it fell flat. Liz pretendía hacer un chiste, pero fracasó rotundamente.* **7** PHRASE If you do something **flat out,** you do it as fast or as hard as you can. *lo más rápidamente, a toda velocidad, a todo vapor* ❑ *Everyone is working flat out to try to find those responsible. Todos están trabando lo más rápidamente posible para tratar de dar con los responsables.* ❑ *...almost 20 minutes of flat-out rowing. ...casi 20 minutos remando a todo vapor.*

**flat|lands** /flætlændz/ N-PLURAL **Flatlands** are areas where the land is very flat. *llano, llanura* ❑ *...the featureless flatlands of the Midwest. ...las monótonas llanuras del Medio Oeste.*

**flat|ten** /flætᵊn/ (**flattens, flattening, flattened**) **1** V-T/V-I If you **flatten** something or if it **flattens,** it becomes flat or flatter. *aplanar, aplastar, agachar* ❑ *Flatten the dough with your hands to a thickness of about 1 inch. Aplane la masa con las manos a que tenga unos dos centímetros de grueso.* ❑ *The dog's ears flattened slightly as Chris spoke his name. El perro agachó ligeramente las orejas cuando Chris lo llamó.* • **Flatten out** means the same as **flatten.** *aplanar(se), aplastar* ❑ *The hills flattened out just south of the mountain. Los cerros se desplomaron justo al sur de la montaña.* **2** V-T If you **flatten yourself against** something, you press yourself flat against it, for example, to avoid getting in the way or being seen. *aplastar(se) contra, pegar(se) contra* ❑ *He flattened himself against a brick wall as I passed. Se aplastó contra la pared de ladrillo cuando yo pasaba.*

**flat|ter** /flætər/ (**flatters, flattering, flattered**) **1** V-T If someone **flatters** you, they praise you in an exaggerated way that is not sincere. *halagar, adular* ❑ *I knew she was just flattering me. Yo sabía que nada más me estaba adulando.* **2** V-T If you **flatter yourself that** something good is true, you believe that it is true, although others may disagree. *considerarse* ❑ *I flatter myself that I've done it all very well. Considero que lo he hecho todo muy bien.* **3** → see also **flat**

**flat|ware** /flætwɛər/ N-UNCOUNT You can refer to knives, forks, and spoons that you eat food with as **flatware.** *cubiertos*

**fla|vor** /fleɪvər/ (**flavors, flavoring, flavored**) **1** N-VAR The **flavor** of a food or drink is its taste. *sabor* ❑ *I always add some paprika for extra flavor. Siempre le agrego un poco de pimentón para realzar el sabor.* **2** V-T If you **flavor** food or drink, you add something to it to give it a particular taste. *sazonar, dar sabor* ❑ *Flavor your favourite dishes with herbs and spices. Sazone sus platos favoritos con hierbas y especias.*

**fla|vored** /fleɪvərd/ ADJ If a food is **flavored,** various ingredients have been added to it so that it has a distinctive flavor. *sazonado* ❑ *Many of these recipes are highly flavored. Muchas de estas recetas están muy sazonadas.*

**fla|vor|ful** /fleɪvərfəl/ ADJ **Flavorful** food has a strong, pleasant taste and is good to eat. *sabroso, rico*

**fla|vor|ing** /fleɪvərɪŋ/ (**flavorings**) N-VAR **Flavorings** are substances that are added to food or drink to give it a particular taste. *sazonador, saborizante, condimento*

**fla|vor|less** /fleɪvərlɪs/ ADJ **Flavorless** food is uninteresting because it does not taste strongly of anything. *insípido, soso, sin sabor*

**fled** /flɛd/ **Fled** is the past tense and past participle of **flee.** *pasado y participio pasado de* ***flee***

**flee** /fli/ (**flees, fleeing, fled**) V-T/V-I If you **flee** from something or someone, or **flee** a person or thing, you escape from them. *escapar, huir, darse a la fuga, echar(se) a correr* [WRITTEN] ❑ *He slammed the door behind him and fled. Azotó la puerta tras sí y huyó.* ❑ *...refugees fleeing torture. ...refugiados que huyen de la tortura.*

**fleet** /flit/ (**fleets**) **1** N-COUNT A **fleet** is a group of ships organized to do something together. *flota* ❑ *...local fishing fleets. ...flotas pesqueras locales.* **2** N-COUNT A **fleet** of vehicles is a group of them, especially when they all belong to a particular organization or business. *flotilla* ❑ *With its own fleet of trucks, the company delivers most orders overnight. La compañía entrega casi todas las órdenes de un día para otro con su propia flotilla de camiones.*

**flesh** /flɛʃ/ (**fleshes, fleshing, fleshed**) **1** N-UNCOUNT **Flesh** is the soft part of a person's or animal's body between the bones and the skin. *carne* ❑ *...the pale pink flesh of trout. ...la carne rosa pálido de la trucha.* **2** N-UNCOUNT You can use **flesh** to refer to human skin and the human body. *cuerpo* ❑ *...the warmth of her flesh. ...la calidez de su cuerpo.* **3** N-UNCOUNT The **flesh** of a fruit or vegetable is the soft inside part. *pulpa* **4** PHRASE If you say that someone is your **own flesh and blood,** you are emphasizing that they are a member of your family. *pariente, familiar, consanguíneo* **5** PHRASE If you meet or see someone **in the flesh,** you actually meet or see them in person. *en persona* ❑ *The first thing people usually say when they see me in the flesh is "You're smaller than you look on TV." Lo primero que suelen decirme cuando me ven en persona es "Eres más bajo de lo que parece en la televisión".* → see **carnivore**

→ see **carnivore**

▸**flesh out** PHR-VERB If you **flesh out** something such as a story or plan, you add details and more information to it. *desarrollar, dar cuerpo* ❑ *We need to flesh out the details of the agreement. Necesitamos desarrollar los detalles del acuerdo.*

**flesh-colored** ADJ Something that is **flesh-colored** is yellowish pink in color. *color carne*

**flew** /flu/ **Flew** is the past tense of **fly**. *pasado de fly*

| Word Link | *flex ≈ bending : flexible, flextime, reflex* |
|---|---|

| Word Link | *ible ≈ able to be : audible, flexible, possible* |
|---|---|

**flex|ible** /flɛksɪbᵊl/ **1** ADJ A **flexible** object or material can be bent easily without breaking. *flexible* ❑ *...brushes with long, flexible bristles. ...pinceles de cerdas largas y flexibles.* • **flexi|bil|ity** /flɛksɪbɪlɪti/ N-UNCOUNT *flexibilidad, elasticidad* ❑ *...exercises to enhance the body's flexibility and strength. ...ejercicios para incrementar la flexibilidad y la fuerza del cuerpo.* **2** ADJ If you say that something or someone is **flexible,** you approve of them because they are able to change easily and adapt to different conditions and circumstances. *flexible* ❑ *...flexible working hours. ...horario laboral flexible.* • **flexi|bil|ity** N-UNCOUNT *flexibilidad* ❑ *...the flexibility of the seating arrangements. ...la flexibilidad para organizar los asientos.*

**flex|or** /flɛksər/ (**flexors**) N-COUNT A **flexor** is a muscle that bends a part of your body. *flexor* [TECHNICAL]

**flex|time** /flɛkstaɪm/ also **flexitime** N-UNCOUNT **Flextime** is a system that allows employees to vary the time that they start or finish work, provided that an agreed total number of hours are spent at work. *horario flexible* [BUSINESS]

**flick** /flɪk/ (**flicks, flicking, flicked**) **1** V-T/V-I If something **flicks** in a particular direction, or if someone **flicks** it, it moves with a short, sudden movement. *quitar, chasquear, sacudir* ❑ *His tongue flicked across his lips. Chasqueó la lengua entre los labios.* ❑ *He shook his head to flick hair out of his eyes. Sacudió la cabeza para quitarse el cabello de los ojos.* • **Flick** is also a noun. *chasquido, sacudida, trazo rápido* ❑ *...a flick of a paintbrush. ...una pincelada.* **2** V-T If you **flick** a switch, or **flick** an electrical appliance on or off, you press the switch quickly. *accionar un interruptor repetidamente* ❑ *Sam was flicking a flashlight on and off. Sam estaba prendiendo y apagando una linterna.* **3** V-I If you **flick through** a book or magazine, you turn its pages quickly. *hojear*

**flight** /flaɪt/ (**flights**) **1** N-COUNT A **flight** is a trip made by flying, usually in an airplane. *vuelo* ❑ *The flight will take four hours. El vuelo durará cuatro horas.* **2** N-COUNT You can refer to an airplane carrying passengers on a particular trip as a particular **flight.** *vuelo* ❑ *BA flight 286 was two hours late. El vuelo 286 de British Airlines se retrasó dos horas.* **3** N-COUNT A **flight of** steps or stairs is a set of steps or stairs that lead from one level to another. *tramo* **4** N-UNCOUNT **Flight** is the action of flying, or the ability to fly. *volar* ❑ *...the first commercial space flight. ...el primer vuelo comercial al espacio.* **5** N-UNCOUNT **Flight** is the act of running away from a dangerous or unpleasant situation or place. *huida, fuga, a salto de mata* ❑ *The family was often in flight, hiding out in friends' houses. La familia andaba a salto de mata con frecuencia, ocultándose en casas de amigos.*

→ see **fly**

**flight deck** (**flight decks**) **1** N-COUNT On an aircraft carrier, **the flight deck** is the flat open surface on the deck where aircraft take off and land. *cubierta de vuelo* **2** N-COUNT On a large airplane, **the flight deck** is the area at the front where the pilot works and where all the controls are. *cabina de mando*

→ see **ship**

**fling** /flɪŋ/ (**flings, flinging, flung**) **1** V-T If you **fling** something somewhere, you throw it there using a lot of force. *lanzar, arrojar, aventar* ❑ *The woman flung the cup at him. La mujer le arrojó la taza.* **2** N-COUNT If two people have **a fling,** they have a brief romantic relationship. *aventura* [INFORMAL] ❑ *She had a brief fling with him 30 years ago. Hace 30 años tuvo una breve aventura con él.*

**flip** /flɪp/ (**flips, flipping, flipped**) **1** V-I If you **flip** through the pages of a book, you turn the pages quickly. *hojear* ❑ *He was flipping through a magazine in the living room. Estaba hojeando una revista en la sala.* **2** V-T/V-I If something **flips** over, or if you **flip** it over or into a different position, it moves or is moved into a different position. *volcar(se), voltear(se)* ❑ *The car flipped over and burst into flames. El auto se volcó y estalló en llamas.*

**flip-flop** (**flip-flops, flip-flopping, flip-flopped**)

f

F

**1** N-PLURAL **Flip-flops** are open shoes which are held on your feet by a strap that goes between your toes. *chanclas* **2** V-I If you say that someone, especially a politician, **flip-flops** on a decision, you are critical of them because they change their decision, so that they do or think the opposite. *dar virajes* [INFORMAL] ❑ *He was criticized for flip-flopping on several key issues.* *Lo criticaron por dar virajes en varios aspectos clave.*

**flirt** /flɜrt/ (**flirts, flirting, flirted**) **1** V-RECIP If you **flirt with** someone, you behave as if you are attracted to them, in a playful or not very serious way. *coquetear, flirtear* ❑ *He's flirting with all the ladies.* *Está coqueteando con todas las mujeres.* ● **flir|ta|tion** /flɜrteɪʃᵊn/ N-VAR (**flirtations**) *coqueteo* ❑ *She was aware of his attempts at flirtation.* *Ella estaba consciente de sus coqueteos.* **2** N-COUNT Someone who is a **flirt** likes to flirt a lot. *coqueto o coqueta* ❑ *I'm not a flirt. I like being with one person.* *No soy un coqueteo, me gusta estar con una sola persona.* **3** V-I If you **flirt with** the idea of something, you consider it but do not do anything about it. *coquetear* ❑ *Sadat also flirted with socialism.* *Sadat también coqueteó con el socialismo.* ● **flir|ta|tion** N-VAR *coqueteo* ❑ *...a flirtation with danger that excited me.* *...un coqueteo con el peligro que me emocionaba.*

**float** /floʊt/ (**floats, floating, floated**) **1** V-T/V-I If something or someone **is floating** in a liquid, they are in the liquid, on or just below the surface, and are being supported by it. You can also **float** something on a liquid. *flotar* ❑ *They noticed fifty-dollar bills floating in the water.* *Vieron billetes de cincuenta dólares flotando en el agua.* ❑ *It's below freezing and small icebergs are floating by.* *Estamos bajo cero y se ven pequeños icebergs flotando.* **2** V-I Something that **floats** in or through the air hangs in it or moves slowly and gently through it. *flotar* ❑ *The white cloud of smoke floated away.* *La nubecilla de humo blanco se alejó flotando.* **3** V-T If a company director **floats** their company, they start to sell shares in it to the public. *emitir acciones, cotizar en bolsa, colocar en bolsa* [BUSINESS] ❑ *He floated his firm on the stock market.* *Colicó las acciones de su empresa en el mercado de valores* **4** N-COUNT A **float** is a light object that is used to help someone or something float. *flotador* ❑ *First, the children learn to swim using floats.* *Al principio, los niños aprenden a nadar con flotadores.*

**flock** /flɒk/ (**flocks, flocking, flocked**) **1** N-COUNT A **flock of** birds, sheep, or goats is a group of them. *bandada, rebaño* **2** N-COUNT You can refer to a group of people or things as a **flock of** them to emphasize that there are a lot of them. *multitud, tropel* ❑ *A flock of small children came running.* *Un tropel de niñitos llegó corriendo.* **3** V-I If people **flock to** a particular place or event, a lot of them go there. *acudir en tropel, ir en tropel* ❑ *The public has flocked to the show.* *El público acudió en tropel al espectáculo.* ❑ *The criticisms will not stop people from flocking to see the film.* *Las críticas no impedirán que la gente vaya en tropel a ver la película.*

**flood** /flʌd/ (**floods, flooding, flooded**) **1** N-VAR If there is a **flood,** a large amount of water covers an area which is usually dry, for example, when a river flows over its banks or a pipe bursts. *inundación* ❑ *More than 70 people died in the floods.* *Más de 70 personas murieron en las inundaciones.* **2** V-T/V-I If something such as a river or a burst pipe **floods** an area that is usually dry or if the area **floods,** it becomes covered with water. *inundar(se), anegar(se), saturar(se)* ❑ *The kitchen flooded.* *La cocina se inundó.* ● **flood|ing** N-UNCOUNT *inundación* ❑ *The flooding is the worst in sixty-five years.* *La inundación es la peor en sesenta y cinco años.* **3** V-I If you say that people or things **flood** into a place, you are emphasizing that they arrive there in large numbers. *saturar* ❑ *Thousands of immigrants flooded into the area.* *Miles de inmigrantes saturaron el área.* **4** N-COUNT If you say that a **flood of** people or things arrive somewhere, you are emphasizing that a very large number of them arrive there. *raudal* ❑ *...the flood of refugees out of Haiti and into Florida.* *...los raudales de refugiados que llegaban de Haití a Florida.*
→ see **dam, disaster, storm**

**flood plain** (**flood plains**) also **floodplain** N-COUNT A **flood plain** is a flat area on the edge of a river, where the ground consists of soil, sand, and rock left by the river when it floods. *terreno aluvial, terreno de aluvión*

**floor** /flɔr/ (**floors, flooring, floored**) **1** N-COUNT **The floor** of a room is the part of it that you walk on. *piso, suelo* ❑ *Jack's sitting on the floor watching TV.* *Jack está sentado en el suelo, viendo la tele.* **2** N-COUNT A **floor** of a building is all the rooms that are on a particular level. *piso* ❑ *The café was on the top floor.* *El café estaba en el último piso.* **3** N-COUNT **The** ocean **floor** is the ground at the bottom of an ocean. **The** valley **floor** is the ground at the bottom of a valley. *fondo* **4** V-T If you **are floored by** something, you are unable to respond to it because you are so surprised by it. *dejar helado* ❑ *He was floored by the announcement.* *El anuncio lo dejó helado.* **5** → see also **dance floor, first floor, shop floor**

**Word Partnership** Usar *floor* con:

| | |
|---|---|
| V. | **fall on the** floor, **sit on the** floor, **sweep the** floor **1** |
| N. | floor **to ceiling**, floor **space** **1** |
| | floor **plan** **2** |
| | **forest** floor, **ocean** floor **3** |

**floor lamp** (**floor lamps**) N-COUNT A **floor lamp** is a tall electric light which stands on the floor in a living room. *lámpara de pie*

**flop** /flɒp/ (**flops, flopping, flopped**) **1** V-I If you **flop** into a chair, for example, you sit down suddenly and heavily because you are so tired. *dejarse caer, desplomarse* ❑ *Ben flopped down upon the bed and rested his tired feet.* *Ben se desplomó en la cama para reposar sus cansados pies.* **2** V-I If something **flops** onto something else, it falls there heavily or untidily. *caer de golpe* ❑ *The briefcase flopped onto the desk.* *El portafolios cayó de golpe en el escritorio.* **3** V-I If something **flops,** it is completely unsuccessful. *fracasar estrepitosamente* [INFORMAL] ❑ *The movie flopped badly at the box office.* *La película fracasó estrepitosamente en taquilla.* **4** N-COUNT If something is a **flop,** it is completely unsuccessful. *fracaso, fiasco* [INFORMAL] ❑ *It is the public who decides whether a film is a hit or a flop.* *Es el público quien decide si una película es un éxito o un fracaso.*

Picture Dictionary **flowers**

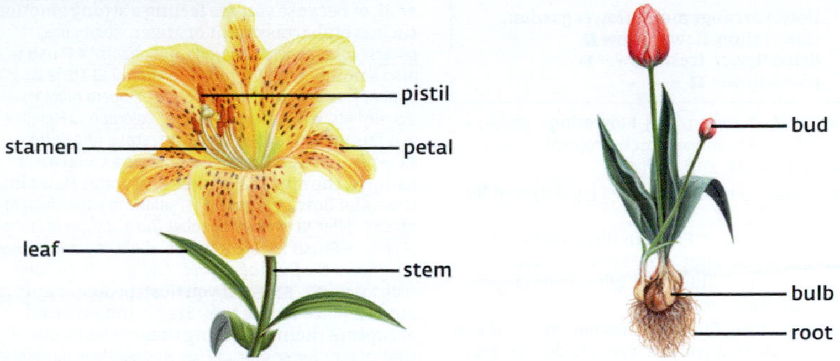


**flop|py** /flɒpi/ (**floppier, floppiest**) ADJ **Floppy** things are loose rather than stiff, and hang downward. *flexible, blando, aguado* ❑ *...the girl with the floppy hat. ...la chica del sombrero aguado.*

**flop|py disk** (**floppy disks**) N-COUNT A **floppy disk** is a small magnetic disk that is used for storing computer data and programs. *disquet, disquete, disco flexible, flopy*

**flo|rist** /flɔrɪst/ (**florists**) **1** N-COUNT A **florist** is a storekeeper who arranges and sells flowers and sells houseplants. *florista* **2** N-COUNT A **florist** or a **florist's** is a store where flowers and houseplants are sold. *florería*

**floun|der** /flaʊndər/ (**flounders, floundering, floundered**) **1** V-I If something **is floundering,** it has many problems and may soon fail completely. *tambalearse, fallar* ❑ *What a pity that his career was left to flounder. Qué lastima que su carrera haya fallado.* **2** V-I If you say that someone **is floundering,** you are criticizing them for not making decisions or for not knowing what to say or do. *dar tumbos, perder pie* ❑ *Right now, you've got a president who's floundering. Ahora mismo, tienen un presidente que anda dando tumbos.*

**flour** /flaʊər/ N-UNCOUNT **Flour** is a white or brown powder that is made by grinding grain. It is used to make bread, cakes, and pastry. *harina*
→ see **grain**

**flour|ish** /flɜrɪʃ/ (**flourishes, flourishing, flourished**) **1** V-I If something **flourishes,** it is successful, active, or common, and is developing quickly and strongly. *florecer, prosperar* ❑ *Translations of Western literature have flourished in China since the 19th century. Las traducciones de la literatura occidental han florecido en China desde el siglo diecinueve.* • **flour|ish|ing** ADJ *próspero, floreciente* ❑ *Boston quickly became a flourishing port. Boston pronto llegó a ser un puerto próspero.* **2** V-I If a plant or animal **flourishes,** it grows well or is healthy. *darse, crecer bien, prosperar* ❑ *The plant flourishes well in warm climates. La planta se da bien en climas cálidos.* • **flour|ish|ing** ADJ *floreciente* ❑ *...a flourishing fox population. ...una floreciente población de zorros.* **3** N-COUNT If you do something with a **flourish,** you do it with a bold sweeping movement, intended to make people notice it. *gesto ceremonioso* ❑ *He took his cap from under his arm with a flourish. Se sacó la gorra de debajo del brazo con un gesto ceremonioso.*

**flow** /floʊ/ (**flows, flowing, flowed**) **1** V-I If a liquid, gas, or electrical current **flows** somewhere, it moves there steadily and continuously. *fluir, manar, correr* ❑ *A stream flowed gently down into the valley. Un arroyo corría suavemente hacia el valle.* • **Flow** is also a noun. *flujo* ❑ *In the veins, the blood flow is slower. En las venas, el flujo de la sangre es lento.* **2** V-I If a number of people or things **flow** from one place to another, they move there steadily in large groups. *fluir, salir* ❑ *Large numbers of refugees continue to flow from the troubled region. Grandes cantidades de refugiados siguen fluyendo de las regiones turbulentas.* • **Flow** is also a noun. *flujo* ❑ *...the flow of cars and buses along the street. ...el flujo de autos y camiones por la calle.* **3** V-I If information or money **flows** somewhere, it moves freely between people or organizations. *fluir libremente* ❑ *A lot of this information flowed through other police departments. Gran parte de esta información fluía libremente entre otros departamentos de policía.* • **Flow** is also a noun. *flujo* ❑ *...the opportunity to control the flow of information. ...la oportunidad de controlar el flujo de información.*
→ see **ocean, traffic**

**flow chart** (**flow charts**) N-COUNT A **flow chart** or a **flow diagram** is a diagram which represents the sequence of actions in a particular process or activity. *diagrama de flujo*

**flow|er** /flaʊər/ (**flowers, flowering, flowered**) **1** N-COUNT A **flower** is the part of a plant which is often brightly colored and grows at the end of a stem. *flor* ❑ *...a bunch of flowers. ...un ramo de flores.* **2** V-I When a plant or tree **flowers,** its flowers appear and open. *florecer* ❑ *These plants will flower this year for the first time. Estas plantas florecerán por primera vez este año.* **3** V-I When something **flowers,** for example, a political movement or a relationship, it gets stronger and more successful. *florecer* • **flow|er|ing** N-UNCOUNT *florecimiento* ❑ *...the flowering of new thinking. ...el florecimiento de una nueva forma de pensamiento.*
→ see Picture Dictionary: **flowers**
→ see **plant**

f

F

**Word Partnership** Usar *flower* con:

| | |
|---|---|
| N. | flower **arrangement**, flower **garden**, flower **shop**, flower **show** 1 |
| ADJ. | **dried** flower, **fresh** flower 1 |
| V. | **pick a** flower 1 |

**flow|er|ing** /flaʊərɪŋ/ ADJ **Flowering** shrubs, trees, or plants are those which produce noticeable flowers. *en flor, florido*

**flown** /floʊn/ **Flown** is the past participle of **fly**. *participio pasado de **fly***

**flu** /flu/ N-UNCOUNT **Flu** is an illness which is similar to a bad cold but more serious. It is an abbreviation for "influenza." *gripa, gripe* ❑ *I got the flu. Tengo gripa.*

**flub** /flʌb/ (**flubs, flubbing, flubbed**) 1 V-T If you **flub** something that you are trying to do, you are unsuccessful or you do it badly. *fallar, echar a perder, meter la pata* [INFORMAL] ❑ *If you try a sales technique and flub it, will you try it again? Si pruebas una técnica de ventas y metes la pata, ¿la vuelves a probar?* 2 N-COUNT A **flub** is a mistake or an unsuccessful attempt to do something. *metida de pata, error* [INFORMAL] ❑ *...her biggest flub of the day. ...su gran metida de pata del día.*

**flu|ent** /fluənt/ 1 ADJ Someone who is **fluent in** a particular language can speak the language easily and correctly. You can also say that someone speaks **fluent** French, Chinese, or some other language. *hablar con fluidez una lengua, tener dominio de una lengua, dominar una lengua* ● **flu|en|cy** /fluənsi/ N-UNCOUNT *fluidez* ❑ *To work as a translator, you need fluency in at least one foreign language. Para ser traductor, necesita dominar con fluidez cuando menos una lengua extranjera.* ● **flu|ent|ly** ADV *fluidamente, con fluidez* ❑ *He spoke three languages fluently. Hablaba con fluidez tres idiomas.* 2 ADJ If your speech, reading, or writing is **fluent,** you speak, read, or write easily, smoothly, and clearly with no mistakes. *fluido, elocuente* ❑ *...a fluent debater. ...un polemista elocuente.* ● **flu|ent|ly** ADV *con fluidez, fluidamente* ❑ *Alex didn't read fluently till he was nearly seven. Alex solo logró leer con fluidez ya tenía casi los siete años.*

**flu|id** /fluɪd/ (**fluids**) 1 N-VAR A **fluid** is a liquid. *fluido, líquido* [FORMAL] ❑ *Make sure that you drink plenty of fluids. Asegúrese de consumir líquidos en abundancia.* 2 ADJ **Fluid** movements, lines, or designs are smooth and graceful. *fluido* ❑ *His painting became more fluid. Su pintura se hizo más fluida.*

**flung** /flʌŋ/ **Flung** is the past tense and past participle of **fling**. *pasado y participio pasado de **fling***

**flunk** /flʌŋk/ (**flunks, flunking, flunked**) V-T If you **flunk** an exam or a course, you fail to reach the required standard. *reprobar, tronar* [INFORMAL]

**fluo|res|cent** /flʊrɛsᵊnt/ 1 ADJ A **fluorescent** surface, substance, or color has a very bright appearance when light is directed onto it. *fluorescente* ❑ *...a piece of fluorescent tape. ...un trozo de cinta fluorescente.* 2 ADJ A **fluorescent** light shines with a very hard, bright light and is usually in the form of a long strip. *fluorescente, tubo fluorescente, lámpara fluorescente*
→ see **light bulb**

**flush** /flʌʃ/ (**flushes, flushing, flushed**) 1 V-I If you **flush,** your face gets red because you are hot or ill, or because you are feeling a strong emotion such as embarrassment or anger. *sonrojarse, ponerse rojo, ponerse colorado, ruborizarse* ● **Flush** is also a noun. *sonrojo, rubor, bochorno* ❑ *There was a slight flush on his cheeks. Había un ligero rubor en sus mejillas.* ● **flushed** ADJ *rojo, colorado* ❑ *Her face was flushed with anger. Su rostro estaba rojo de ira.* 2 V-T/V-I When someone **flushes** a toilet after using it, they press a handle and water flows into the toilet bowl, cleaning it. *jalarle al baño, jalar la cadena, jalar* ❑ *I heard the toilet flush. Oí que le jalaron al baño.* ● **Flush** is also a noun. *ruido del baño al jalarle* ❑ *He heard the flush of a toilet. Oyó el ruido del baño cuando jalaron.* 3 V-T If you **flush** people or animals **out** of a place where they are hiding, you find or capture them by forcing them to come out of that place. *hacer salir* ❑ *They flushed them out of their hiding places. Los hicieron salir de sus escondrijos.*

**flute** /flut/ (**flutes**) N-VAR A **flute** is a musical instrument of the woodwind family. You play it by blowing over a hole near one end while holding it sideways to your mouth. *flauta*
→ see **orchestra**

**flut|ist** /flutɪst/ (**flutists**) N-COUNT A **flutist** is someone who plays the flute. *flautista*

**fly** /flaɪ/ (**flies, flying, flew, flown**) 1 N-COUNT A **fly** is a small insect with two wings. *mosca* 2 N-COUNT The front opening on a pair of pants is referred to as the **fly.** *bragueta* 3 V-I When something such as a bird, insect, or aircraft **flies,** it moves through the air. *volar* ❑ *The planes flew through the clouds. Los aviones volaron entre las nubes.* ● **fly|ing** ADJ *volador* ❑ *...flying insects. ...insectos voladores.* 4 V-I If you **fly** somewhere, you travel there in an aircraft. *volar, viajar en avión* ❑ *He flew to Los Angeles. Voló a Los Angeles.* 5 V-T/V-I When someone **flies** an aircraft, they control its movement in the air. *volar* ❑ *He flew a small plane to Cuba. Voló una avioneta a Cuba.* ❑ *I learned to fly in Vietnam. Aprendí a volar en Vietnam.* ● **fly|er** N-COUNT (**flyers**) *aviador o aviadora* ❑ *The American flyers ran for their planes and got in. Los aviadores estadounidenses corrieron a sus aviones y los abordaron.* 6 V-T To **fly** someone or something somewhere means to take or send them there in an aircraft. *mandar en avión* ❑ *It may be possible to fly the women out on Thursday. Podríamos mandar a las mujeres en avión el jueves.* 7 V-I If something such as your hair **is flying** about, it is moving about freely and loosely in the air. *ondear* ❑ *His long, uncovered hair flew back in the wind. Su largo cabello suelto ondeaba al viento.* 8 V-T/V-I If you **fly** a flag or if it **is flying,** you display it at the top of a pole. *ondear, flotar en el aire* ❑ *He flies the American flag on his front lawn. La bandera americana ondea en su jardín delantero.* 9 V-I If you say that someone or something **flies** in a particular direction, you are emphasizing that they move there with a lot of speed or force. *volar* ❑ *She flew to their bedsides when they were ill. Volaba a su cabecera cuando estaban enfermos.* 10 → see also **flying** 11 to **fly in the face of** → see **face**
→ see Word Web: **fly**
→ see **insect**

▸ **fly into** PHR-VERB If you **fly into** a bad temper or a panic, you suddenly become very angry or

## Word Web fly

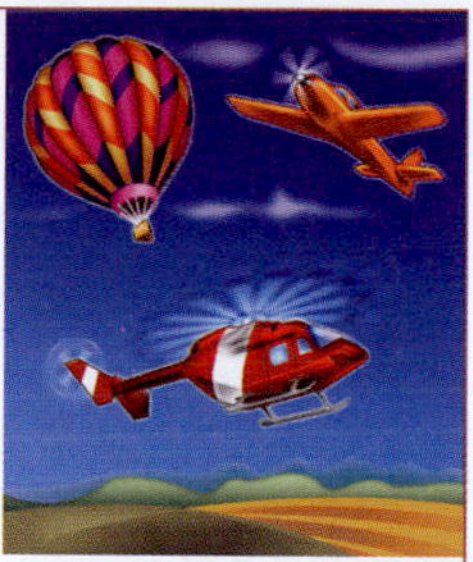

About 500 years ago, Leonardo da Vinci* designed some simple flying machines. His sketches look a lot like modern **parachutes** and **helicopters**. About 300 years later, the Montgolfier Brothers amazed the king of France with **hot-air balloon** flights. Soon inventors in many countries began experimenting with blimps, **hang gliders**, and human-powered **aircraft**. Most inventors tried to imitate the **flight** of birds. Then in 1903, the Wright brothers invented the first true **airplane**. Their gasoline-powered **craft** carried one **passenger**. The trip lasted 59 seconds. And amazingly, 70 years later **jumbo jets** carrying 400 passengers became an everyday occurrence.

*Leonardo da Vinci (1452-1519): an Italian artist.*

anxious and show this in your behavior. montar en cólera, ponerse hecho una furia ❑ *Losing a game would cause him to fly into a rage.* *Perder un juego lo hacía ponerse hecho una furia.*

**fly ball** (**fly balls**) also **flyball** N-COUNT In baseball, a **fly ball** is a ball that is hit very high. *globo*

**fly|er** /flaɪər/ (**flyers**) also **flier** N-COUNT A **flyer** is a small printed notice which is used to advertise a particular company, service, or event. *folleto, volante* ❑ *Flyers advertising the tour were handed out.* *Se repartieron folletos en que se anunciaba el recorrido.*

**fly|ing** /flaɪɪŋ/ PHRASE If someone or something **gets off to a flying start**, or **makes a flying start**, they start very well. *empezar con el pie derecho, arrancar bien* ❑ *The bank has gotten off to a flying start and profits are well ahead of last year.* *El banco empezó con el pie derecho y las utilidades son muy superiores a las del año pasado.*

**fo|cus** /foʊkəs/ (**focuses, focusing** or **focussing, focused** or **focussed**)

> The plural of the noun can be either **focuses** or **foci** /foʊsaɪ/.

**1** V-T/V-I If you **focus on** a particular topic or if your attention **is focused on** it, you concentrate on it and deal with it, rather than dealing with other topics. *concentrar(se), enfocar(se)* ❑ *The research focused on these effects.* *La investigación se enfocó en dichos efectos.* **2** V-T/V-I If you **focus** your eyes or if your eyes **focus**, your eyes adjust so that you can clearly see the thing that you want to look at. If you **focus** a camera, telescope, or other instrument, you adjust it so that you can see clearly through it. *enfocar(se)* ❑ *Kelly couldn't focus his eyes well enough to tell if the figure was male or female.* *Kelly no pudo enfocar bien la vista como para decir si la figura era masculina o femenina.* ❑ *His eyes began to focus on what looked like a small ball.* *Su mirada empezó a enfocarse en lo que parecía una pelotita.* **3** V-T If you **focus** rays of light on a particular point, you pass them through a lens or reflect them from a mirror so that they meet at that point. *enfocar* ❑ *They move the mirrors to focus the sun's rays onto a piece of glass.* *Mueven los espejos para enfocar los rayos del sol en un pedazo de vidrio.* **4** N-COUNT **The focus** of something is the main topic or main thing that it is concerned with. *centro, foco* ❑ *The new system is the focus of controversy.* *El nuevo sistema está en el centro de la controversia.* **5** N-COUNT Your **focus** on something is the special attention that you pay it. *atención, interés* ❑ *...his sudden focus on foreign policy.* *...su repentino interés por la política exterior.* **6** N-COUNT The **focus** of an earthquake is the point within the Earth where the earthquake starts. *epicentro* **7** PHRASE If an image or a camera, telescope, or other instrument is **in focus**, the edges of what you see are clear and sharp. *enfocado, en foco* **8** PHRASE If an image or a camera, telescope, or other instrument is **out of focus**, the edges of what you see are unclear. *fuera de foco, desenfocado*
→ see **photography, telescope**

**fo|cus group** (**focus groups**) N-COUNT A **focus group** is a specially selected group of people who are intended to represent the general public. Focus groups have discussions in which their opinions are recorded as a form of market research. *grupo de sondeo*

**fog** /fɒg/ (**fogs**) N-VAR When there is **fog**, there are tiny drops of water in the air which form a thick cloud and make it difficult to see things. *niebla, neblina* ❑ *The crash happened in thick fog.* *El choque se produjo en medio de una espesa niebla.*

fog

**fog|gy** /fɒgi/ (**foggier, foggiest**) ADJ When it is **foggy**, there is fog. *brumoso, nebuloso*

**foil** /fɔɪl/ (**foils, foiling, foiled**) **1** N-UNCOUNT **Foil** consists of sheets of metal as thin as paper. It is used to wrap food in. *papel aluminio* **2** V-T If someone **foils** your plan or attempt to do something, he or she succeeds in stopping you from doing what you want. *frustrar* ❑ *A brave police chief foiled an armed robbery.* *Un valiente jefe de policía frustró un asalto a mano armada.*

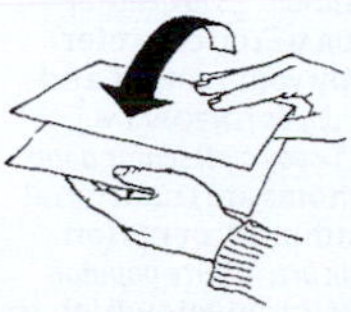

fold

**fold** /foʊld/ (**folds, folding, folded**) **1** V-T If you **fold** a piece of paper or cloth, you bend it so that one part covers another part. *doblar* ❑ *He folded the paper carefully.* *Dobló cuidadosamente el papel.* ❑ *Fold the towel in* half. Dobla la toalla a la mitad. **2** V-T/V-I If a piece of furniture or equipment **folds** or if you can **fold** it, you can make it smaller by bending or closing parts of it. plegar(se), doblar(se) ❑ *The back of the bench folds forward to make a table.* El respaldo de la banca se dobla hacia delante para formar una mesa. ❑ *This portable seat folds flat for easy storage.* Este asiento portátil se pliega para poder guardarlo fácilmente. • **Fold up** means the same as **fold**. doblarse, plegarse ❑ *When not in use, the table folds up out of the way.* La mesa puede plegarse para que no estorbe cuando no esté en uso. **3** V-T If you **fold** your arms or hands, you bring them together and cross or link them, for example, over your chest. cruzar **4** N-COUNT A **fold** in a piece of paper or cloth is a bend that you make in it when you put one part of it over another part and press the edge. pliegue, doblez ❑ *Make another fold and turn the ends together.* Haz otro doblez y únelo por las puntas. **5** N-COUNT The **folds** in a piece of cloth are the curved shapes which are formed when it is not hanging or lying flat. pliegue **6** N-COUNT A **fold** is a bend in a layer of rock that occurs when the rock is compressed. pliegue • **fold|ing** N-UNCOUNT pliegue ❑ *...where the fracturing has resulted from folding of the rock.* ...donde la fractura es producto de los pliegues de la roca.

▸ **fold up** **1** PHR-VERB If you **fold** something **up**, you make it into a smaller, neater shape by folding it, usually several times. doblar, plegar ❑ *I folded up the map and put it away.* Doblé el mapa y lo puse en su lugar. **2** → see also **fold 2**

**Word Partnership** Usar *fold* con:

ADV. fold **carefully**, fold **gently**, fold **neatly** **1**
N. fold **clothes**, fold **paper** **1**
fold ***your* arms/hands** **3**

**fold|ed moun|tain** (**folded mountains**) N-COUNT A **folded mountain** is a mountain that forms when rock is bent or folded because of stresses in the Earth's crust. montaña de plegamiento [TECHNICAL]

**fold|er** /foʊldər/ (**folders**) **1** N-COUNT A **folder** is a thin piece of cardboard in which you can keep loose papers. fólder, carpeta **2** N-COUNT A **folder** is a group of files that are stored together on a computer. fólder, carpeta
→ see **office**

**fo|li|at|ed** /foʊlieɪtɪd/ ADJ **Foliated** rock is rock that consists of lots of thin layers. roca lamelar [TECHNICAL]

**folk** /foʊk/ (**folks**)

Folk can also be used as the plural form for meaning **1**.

**1** N-PLURAL You can refer to people as **folk** or **folks**. gente ❑ *...country folk.* ...gente del pueblo ❑ *These are the folks from the local TV station.* Es la gente de la estación de TV local. **2** N-PLURAL You can refer to your close family, especially your mother and father, as your **folks**. padres, papás [INFORMAL] ❑ *I'll introduce you to my folks.* Te voy a presentar a mis papás **3** ADJ **Folk** art and customs are traditional or typical of a particular community or nation. popular ❑ *...South American folk art.* ...arte popular sudamericano. **4** ADJ **Folk** music is music which is traditional or typical of a particular community or nation. música popular, música folklórica
→ see **dance**

**folk|lore** /foʊklɔr/ N-UNCOUNT **Folklore** consists of the traditional stories, customs, and habits of a particular community or nation. folklor, tradición ❑ *In Chinese folklore the bat is a symbol of good fortune.* En el folklor chino, el murciélago es símbolo de buena suerte.

**Word Link** *cle ≈ small : article, follicle, particle*

**fol|li|cle** /fɒlɪkəl/ (**follicles**) N-COUNT A **follicle** is one of the small hollows in the skin which hairs grow from. folículo

**follow**
❶ GO OR COME AFTER
❷ ACT ACCORDING TO SOMETHING, OBSERVE SOMETHING
❸ UNDERSTAND
❹ PHRASAL VERBS

❶ **fol|low** /fɒloʊ/ (**follows, following, followed**) **1** V-T/V-I If you **follow** someone who is going somewhere, you move along behind them. seguir ❑ *We followed him up the steps.* Lo seguimos escaleras arriba. ❑ *Please follow me, madam.* Sígame por favor, señora. ❑ *They took him into a small room and I followed.* Lo llevaron a una habitación pequeña y yo los seguí. **2** V-T If you **follow** someone who is going somewhere, you move along behind them without their knowledge, in order to catch them or find out where they are going. seguir, perseguir ❑ *She realized that the car was following her.* Se dio cuenta de que el auto iba seguiéndola. **3** V-T If you **follow** someone to a place, you join them there at a later time. alcanzar ❑ *He followed Janice to New York.* Él alcanzó a Janice en Nueva York. **4** V-T/V-I An event, activity, or period of time that **follows** a particular thing happens or comes after that thing, at a later time. seguir ❑ *Great celebrations followed the announcement.* Al anuncio siguieron grandes celebraciones. ❑ *Other problems may follow.* Otros problemas podrían seguir. **5** V-T If you **follow** one thing **with** another, you do or say the second thing after you have done or said the first thing. seguir con ❑ *Warm up first then follow this with a series of simple stretching exercises.* Haz primero unos ejercicios calentamiento y después sigues con una serie de ejercicios de estiramiento sencillos. • **Follow up** means the same as **follow**. seguir, perseguir, seguir con ❑ *The Phillies followed up a five-game winning streak with three straight losses.* Después de una racha de cinco victorias, los Phillies siguieron con tres derrotas consecutivas. **6** V-T/V-I If it **follows** that a particular thing is true, that thing is a logical result of something else being true. deducir(se) ❑ *With ten new families moving to the neighborhood, it follows that there will be more children in school.* De la llegada de diez nuevas familias al vecindario se deduce que habrá más niños en la escuela. ❑ *If the explanation is right, two things follow.* Si la explicación es correcta, se deducen dos cosas. **7** V-T If you **follow** a path, route, or set of signs, you go somewhere using the path, route, or signs to direct you. seguir ❑ *All we had to do was follow the map.* Lo único que teníamos que hacer, era seguir el mapa. **8** PHRASE You use **as follows** in writing or speech to introduce something such as a list, description, or an explanation. *siguiente, como sigue* ❑ *The winners are as follows: E. Walker; R. Foster; R. Gates. Los ganadores son los siguientes: E. Walker; R. Foster; R. Gates.* 9 PHRASE You use **followed by** to say what comes after something else in a list or ordered set of things. *seguido de* ❑ *Potatoes are still the most popular food, followed by white bread. Las papas siguen siendo el alimento más popular, seguidas del pan blanco.* 10 → see also **following** 11 **to follow in** someone's **footsteps** → see **footstep**

**❷ fol|low** /fɒloʊ/ (**follows, following, followed**) 1 V-T If you **follow** advice, an instruction, or a recipe, you act or do something in the way that it indicates. *seguir* ❑ *Follow the instructions carefully. Sigue cuidadosamente las instrucciones.* 2 V-T If you **follow** something, you take an interest in it and keep informed about what happens. *seguir, tener interés en algo, interesarse por algo* ❑ *Millions of people follow football. Millones de personas siguen el fútbol.*

**❸ fol|low** /fɒloʊ/ (**follows, following, followed**) 1 V-T/V-I If you are able to **follow** something such as an explanation or the story of a movie, you understand it. *entender* ❑ *Can you follow the plot so far? ¿Entiendes el argumento hasta ahora?* ❑ *I'm sorry, I don't follow. Perdón, no entiendo.* 2 → see also **following**

**Word Partnership** Usar *follow* con:

ADV. **closely** follow ❶ 1 2
**blindly** follow ❷ 1 2
N. follow **a road**, follow **signs**, follow **a trail** ❶ 7
follow **orders**, follow **rules** ❷ 1
follow **advice**, follow **directions**, follow **instructions**, follow **a story** ❸ 1

**❹ fol|low** /fɒloʊ/ (**follows, following, followed**)
▸ **follow through** PHR-VERB If you **follow through** an action, plan, or idea or **follow through** with it, you continue doing or thinking about it until you have done everything possible. *continuar, seguir adelante con algo* ❑ *The leadership has been unwilling to follow through with these ideas. Los líderes no han estado dispuestos a seguir adelante con esas ideas.* ❑ *I was trained to be an actress but I didn't follow it through. Me preparé para ser actriz, pero no seguí adelante.*

**fol|low|er** /fɒloʊər/ (**followers**) N-COUNT A **follower** of a particular person, group, or belief is someone who supports or admires this person, group, or belief. *seguidor o seguidora, discípulo o discípula* ❑ *...followers of Judaism. ...seguidores del judaísmo.*

**fol|low|ing** /fɒloʊɪŋ/ (**followings**) 1 PREP **Following** a particular event means after that event. *lo siguiente, después de* ❑ *He took four months off work following the birth of his first child. Tomó cuatro meses de licencia después del nacimiento de su primer hijo.* 2 ADJ The **following** day, week, or year is the day, week, or year after the one you have just mentioned. *siguiente* ❑ *We went to dinner the following Monday evening. Fuimos a cenar la noche del lunes siguiente.* 3 ADJ You use **following** to refer to something that you are about to mention. *siguiente* ❑ *Write down the following information: name of product, date purchased, and price. Escriba la siguiente información: nombre del producto, fecha de compra y precio.* • **The following** refers to the thing or things that you are about to mention. *el siguiente, lo siguiente, la siguiente, lo que sigue* ❑ *The following is a summary of what was said. Lo que sigue es un resumen de lo que se dijo.* 4 N-COUNT A person or organization that has a **following** has a group of people who support or admire their beliefs or actions. *seguidor o seguidora, admirador o admiradora* ❑ *Australian rugby league enjoys a huge following in New Zealand. La liga australiana de rugby tiene muchos seguidores en Nueva Zelanda.*

**follow-up** (**follow-ups**) N-VAR A **follow-up** is something that is done to continue or add to something done previously. *seguimiento, continuación* ❑ *They are recording a follow-up to their 2005 album. Están grabando la continuación de su álbum de 2005.*

**fond** /fɒnd/ (**fonder, fondest**) 1 ADJ If you are **fond of** someone, you feel affection for them. *encariñado con, aficionado de* ❑ *I am very fond of Michael. Estoy muy encariñada con Michael.* • **fond|ness** N-UNCOUNT *cariño, afición* ❑ *...a great fondness for children. ...un gran cariño por los niños.* 2 ADJ You use **fond** to describe people or their behavior when they show affection. *cariñoso, complaciente* ❑ *...a fond father. ...un padre complaciente.* • **fond|ly** ADV *cariñosamente, con cariño* ❑ *Their eyes met fondly across the table. Se miraron cariñosamente a través de la mesa.* 3 ADJ If you are **fond of** something, you like it or you like doing it very much. *ser aficionado a algo, gustarle mucho algo a uno* ❑ *He was fond of singing. Le gustaba mucho cantar.* • **fond|ness** N-UNCOUNT *afición, gusto* ❑ *...a fondness for chocolate cake. ...un gusto por el pastel de chocolate.* 4 ADJ If you have **fond** memories of someone or something, you remember them with pleasure. *buen, bueno* • **fond|ly** ADV *cariñosamente, con cariño* ❑ *My dad took us there and I remembered it fondly. Mi papá nos llevó ahí, y me acordé con cariño.*

**food** /fud/ (**foods**) 1 N-VAR **Food** is what people and animals eat. *comida, alimento* ❑ *Enjoy your food. Disfruta tu comida.* ❑ *...frozen foods. ...alimentos congelados.* 2 → see also **fast food** 3 PHRASE If you give someone **food for thought**, you make them think carefully about something. *hacer reflexionar* ❑ *Her speech offers much food for thought. Su discurso hace reflexionar mucho.*
→ see Word Web: **food**
→ see **cooking, farm, habitat, meal, rice, sugar, vegetarian**

**Food and Drug Ad|min|is|tra|tion** N-PROPER In the United States, the **Food and Drug Administration** is a government department that is responsible for making sure that foods and drugs are safe. *Dirección de Alimentos y Medicinas*

**food bank** (**food banks**) N-COUNT A **food bank** is a place that collects food that has been donated and gives it to people who are poor or homeless. *banco de alimentos*

**food chain** (**food chains**) N-COUNT **The food chain** is a series of living things which are linked to each other because each thing feeds on the one next to it in the series. *cadena alimenticia, cadena alimentaria, cadena trófica*
→ see **carnivore, food**

**food court** (**food courts**) N-COUNT A **food court**

f

## Word Web food

The **food chain** begins with sunlight. Green **plants** absorb and store **energy** from the sun through **photosynthesis**. This energy is passed on to an **herbivore** (such as a mouse) that **eats** these plants. The mouse is then eaten by a **carnivore** (such as a snake). The snake may be eaten by a **top predator** (such as a hawk). When the hawk dies, its body is broken down by bacteria. Soon its **nutrients** become food for plants and the cycle begins again.

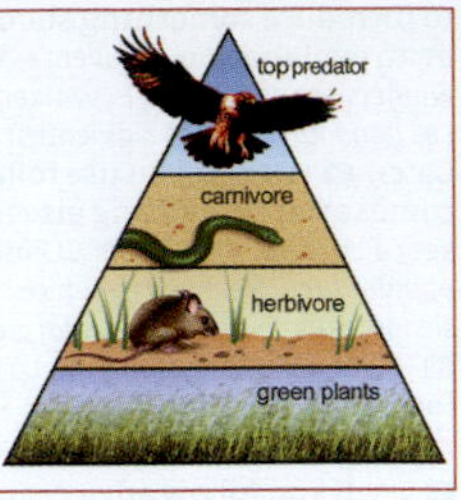


**Food chain**

F

is a place, for example, in a shopping mall, that has several small restaurants and a common eating area. *zona de restaurantes de comida rápida, zona de alimentos*

**food web** (**food webs**) N-COUNT A **food web** is a network of interconnected food chains. *red de cadenas alimenticias, trama alimentaria*

**fool** /fu̲l/ (**fools, fooling, fooled**) **1** N-COUNT If you call someone a **fool**, you are indicating that you think they are not at all sensible and show a lack of good judgment. *idiota, tonto o tonta* ❑ *"You fool!" she shouted. —¡Eres un idiota!—le gritó ella.* **2** V-T If someone **fools** you, they deceive or trick you. *engañar, hacer creer* ❑ *Art dealers fool a lot of people. Los comerciantes de arte engañan a mucha gente.* ❑ *Don't be fooled by his appearance. No te dejes engañar por su aspecto.* **3** PHRASE If you **make a fool of** someone, you make them seem silly by telling people about something stupid that they have done, or by tricking them. *poner(se) en ridículo* ❑ *Your brother is making a fool of you. Tu hermano te está poniendo en ridículo.*

▸ **fool around** PHR-VERB If you **fool around**, you behave in a silly or dangerous way. *bromear, tontear, hacerse guaje, hacerse el tonto* ❑ *They fool around and get into trouble at school. Tuvieron problemas en la escuela por hacerse guajes.*

**fool|ish** /fu̲lɪʃ/ ADJ If your behavior or action is **foolish**, it is not sensible and shows a lack of good judgment. *insensato, estúpido, tonto* ❑ *It would be foolish to raise their hopes. Sería tonto que se hicieran ilusiones.* ● **fool|ish|ly** ADV *tontamente, a lo tonto* ❑ *He admitted that he had acted foolishly. Aceptó haberlo hecho a lo tonto.* ● **fool|ish|ness** N-UNCOUNT *insensatez, tontería, estupidez* ❑ *They don't accept any foolishness. Ellos no aceptan tonterías.*

**foot**

❶ PART OF BODY
❷ UNIT OF MEASUREMENT
❸ LOWER END OF SOMETHING

❶ **foot** /fʊ̲t/ (**feet**) **1** N-COUNT Your **feet** are the parts of your body that are at the ends of your legs, and that you stand on. *pie* ❑ *She stamped her foot again. Dio otra patada en el suelo.* ❑ *...a foot injury. ...una lesión del pie.* **2** → see also **footing** **3** PHRASE If you go somewhere **on foot**, you walk, rather than using any form of transport. *a pie, caminando* ❑ *We rowed ashore, then explored the island on foot. Remamos hasta la orilla y después exploramos la isla a pie.* **4** PHRASE If you are **on** your **feet**, you are standing up. *de pie, parado* ❑ *Everyone was on their feet applauding. Todos aplaudieron de pie.* **5** PHRASE If you say that someone or something is **on** their **feet** again after an illness or difficult period, you mean that they have recovered and are back to normal. *recuperarse, levantarse* ❑ *You need someone to help you get back on your feet. Necesitas que alguien te ayude a levantarte.* **6** PHRASE If someone **puts** their **foot down**, they use their authority in order to stop something from happening. *no ceder, mantenerse firme* ❑ *He wanted to go skiing in March but his wife put her foot down. Él quería ir a esquiar en marzo, pero su esposa no cedió.* **7** PHRASE If you **put** your **feet up**, you relax or have a rest, especially by sitting or lying with your feet supported off the ground. *descansar con los pies en alto* ❑ *After supper he put his feet up and read. Después de la cena se fue a descansar con los pies en alto y a leer.* **8** PHRASE If you get or rise **to** your **feet**, you stand up. *levantarse, pararse, ponerse de pie* ❑ *Malone got to his feet and followed us out. Malone se paró y nos siguió afuera.* **9** to **drag** your **feet** → see **drag**

→ see Picture Dictionary: **foot**

→ see **body, measurement**

❷ **foot** /fʊ̲t/ (**feet**) N-COUNT A **foot** is a unit of length equal to 12 inches or 30.48 centimeters. The plural form **foot** is also sometimes used. *pie* ❑ *...six thousand feet above sea level. ...1,830 metros sobre el nivel del mar.* ❑ *...a cell 10 foot long, 6 foot wide and 10 foot high. ...una celda de 3 metros de largo, 2 de ancho y 3 de alto.*

❸ **foot** /fʊ̲t/ N-SING **The foot of** something is the part that is farthest from its top. *pie* ❑ *...the foot of the stairs. ...el pie de la escalera.*

**foot|age** /fʊ̲tɪdʒ/ N-UNCOUNT **Footage** of a particular event is a film of it or the part of a film which shows this event. *metraje, secuencia* ❑ *...footage from this summer's festivals. ...secuencias de los festivales de este verano.*

**foot|ball** /fʊ̲tbɔl/ (**footballs**) **1** N-UNCOUNT **Football** is a game played by two teams of eleven players using an oval ball. Players carry the ball in their hands or throw it to each other as they try to score goals that are called touchdowns. *futbol americano o fútbol americano* ❑ *...a field where boys played football. ...una cancha donde los niños jugaban al futbol americano.* **2** N-COUNT A **football** is a ball that is used for playing football. *balón de futbol, pelota de futbol* ❑ *...a heavy leather football. ...un pesado balón de cuero.*

→ see Picture Dictionary: **football**

## Picture Dictionary foot

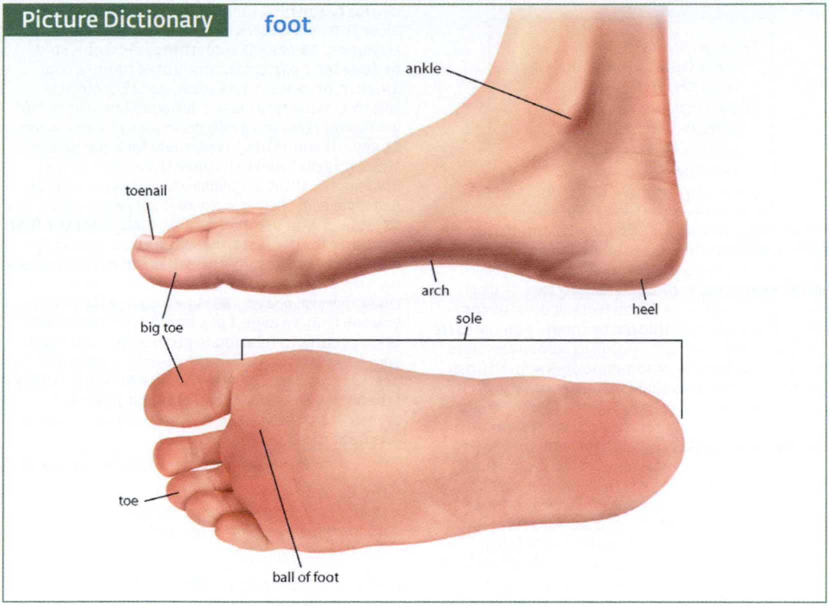


**foot|ball field** (**football fields**) N-COUNT A **football field** is an area of grass where football is played. *cancha de futbol o cancha de fútbol, campo de futbol o campo de fútbol*

**foot|ing** /fʊtɪŋ/ **1** N-UNCOUNT You use **footing** to describe the basis on which something is done or exists. *base, fundamento* ❑ *The research is aimed at placing training on a more scientific footing. La investigación tiende a dar bases más científicas a la capacitación.* **2** N-UNCOUNT You use **footing** to refer to your position and how securely your feet are placed on the ground. *equilibrio* ❑ *He lost his footing and slid into the water. Perdió el equilibrio y cayó al agua.*

**foot|locker** /fʊtlɔkər/ (**footlockers**) also **foot locker** N-COUNT A **footlocker** is a large box for keeping personal possessions in, especially one that is placed at the end of a bed. *baúl*

**foot|note** /fʊtnoʊt/ (**footnotes**) N-COUNT A **footnote** is a note at the bottom of a page in a book which provides more detailed information about something that is mentioned on that page. *nota de pie de página, nota a pie de página, nota al pie*

**foot|print** /fʊtprɪnt/ (**footprints**) N-COUNT A **footprint** is the mark of a person's or animal's foot left on a surface. *huella, pisada*
→ see **fossil**

**foot|step** /fʊtstɛp/ (**footsteps**) **1** N-COUNT A **footstep** is the sound that is made by someone walking each time their foot touches the ground. *paso* ❑ *I heard footsteps outside. Oí pasos en el exterior.* **2** PHRASE If you **follow in** someone's **footsteps**, you do the same things as he or she did earlier. *seguir los pasos* ❑ *My father is proud that I followed in his footsteps and became a doctor. Mi padre está orgulloso de que haya seguido sus pasos y sea médico.*

**foot|wall** /fʊtwɔl/ (**footwalls**) N-COUNT A **footwall** is the rock beneath a geological fault. Compare **hanging wall**. *pared baja de una falla inclinada* [TECHNICAL]

## Picture Dictionary football

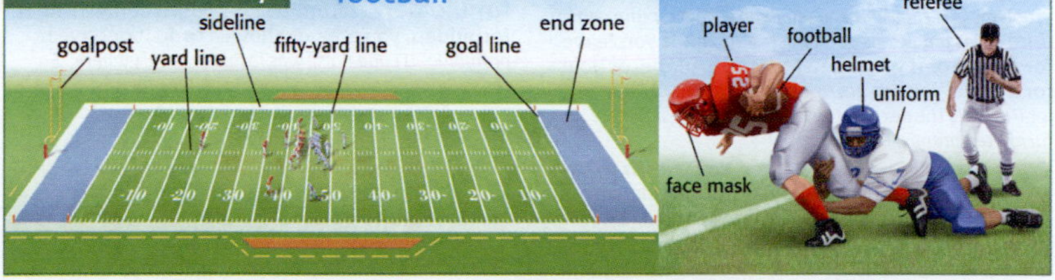

**for**

❶ SAYING WHO OR WHAT SOMETHING RELATES TO, OR WHO BENEFITS
❷ MENTIONING A PURPOSE, REASON, OR DESTINATION
❸ BEFORE NUMBERS, AMOUNTS, AND TIMES
❹ WANTING OR SUPPORTING

F

❶ **for** /fər, STRONG fɔr/ **1** PREP If something is **for** someone, they are intended to have it or benefit from it. *para* ❑ *Isn't that enough for you? ¿No es suficiente para ti?* ❑ *...a table for two. ...una mesa para dos.* **2** PREP If you work or do a job **for** someone, you are employed by them. *para, en* ❑ *He worked for a security firm. Trabajaba para una empresa de seguridad.* **3** PREP If someone does something **for** you, they do it so that you do not have to do it. *para* ❑ *I held the door open for the next person. Mantuve la puerta abierta para quien venía después.* **4** PREP If you feel a particular emotion **for** someone or something, they are the object of that emotion. *por* ❑ *I'm sorry for Steve, but I think you've made the right decision. Lo siento por Steve, pero creo que tomaste la decisión correcta.* **5** PREP You use **for** after words such as "time," "space," "money," or "energy" when you say how much there is or whether there is enough of it in order to be able to do or use a particular thing. *para* ❑ *...a huge house with plenty of room for books. ...una casa enorme, con mucho espacio para libros.* **6** PREP After some adjective, noun, and verb phrases, you use **for** when you are saying how something affects someone. *para* ❑ *I have made arrangements for my affairs to be dealt with by my children. Hice arreglos para que mis hijos se ocupen de mis asuntos.* **7** PREP A word or term **for** something, is another way of referring to it. *para* ❑ *The technical term for sunburn is erythema. El término técnico para quemadura de sol es eritema.* **8** PREP To be named **for** someone means to be given the same name as them. *por, en honor de* ❑ *The Brady Bill is named for former White House Press Secretary James Brady. La ley Brady se llama así por el ex secretario de prensa de la Casa Blanca, James Brady.* **9** **as for** → see **as** **10** **but for** → see **but** **11** **for all** → see **all**

❷ **for** /fər, STRONG fɔr/ **1** PREP You use **for** when you are describing the purpose of something. *para* ❑ *...laboratory equipment for genetic research. ...equipo de laboratorio para investigación genética.* ❑ *...a knife for cutting sausage. ...un cuchillo para salchichas.* **2** PREP You use **for** when you are describing the reason for something or the cause of something. *para, de* ❑ *...his reasons for going. ...sus razones para irse.* ❑ *The hospital could find no physical cause for Sumner's problems. En el hospital no pudieron encontrar una causa física de los problemas de Sumner.* **3** PREP If you leave **for** a place or if you take a bus, train, plane, or boat **for** a place, you are going there. *a, para* ❑ *They left for Rio early the next morning. A la mañana siguiente se fueron temprano a Río.*

❸ **for** /fər, STRONG fɔr/ **1** PREP You use **for** to say how long something lasts or continues. *durante, por* ❑ *The toaster was on for more than an hour. El tostador estuvo prendido por más de una hora* ❑ *They talked for a bit. Hablaron durante un rato.* **2** PREP You use **for** to say how far something extends. ❑ *We drove on for a few miles. Seguimos manejando varios kilómetros.* **3** PREP If something is bought, sold, or done **for** a particular amount of money, that amount of money is its price. *en* ❑ *The Martins sold their house for about 1.4 million dollars. Los Martin vendieron su casa en 1.4 millones de dólares, más o menos.* **4** PREP If something is planned **for** a particular time, it is planned to happen then. *para* ❑ *The Baltimore Boat Show is planned for January 21–29. El Baltimore Boat Show está planeado para enero, del 21 al 29.* **5** PHRASE You use expressions such as **for the first time** and **for the last time** when you are talking about how often something has happened before. *por* ❑ *He was married for the second time. Estaba casado por segunda vez.* **6** PREP You use **for** when you say that an aspect of something or someone is surprising in relation to other aspects of them. *para* ❑ *He was tall for an eight-year-old. Estaba alto para sus ocho años.* **7** PREP You use **for** with "every" when you state the second part of a ratio. *por* ❑ *There is one manager for every six employees. Hay un gerente por cada seis empleados.*

**Usage** **for**

Use *for* to describe a length of time. *Noriko has studied English for seven years. She lived in Japan for the first fifteen years of her life and has lived in the U.S. for two years.*

❹ **for** /fər, STRONG fɔr/ **1** PREP If you say that you are **for** a particular activity, you mean that this is what you want or intend to do. *en favor de, por* ❑ *Who's for a toasted sandwich? ¿Quién vota por un sándwich tostado?* **2** PREP If you are **for** something, you agree with it or support it. *a favor de, en favor de* ❑ *He wasn't sure whether he was for or against what Quayle had said. No estaba seguro de si estaba a favor o en contra de lo que Quayle había dicho.*

In addition to the uses shown here, **for** is used after some verbs, nouns, and adjectives in order to introduce extra information, and in phrasal verbs such as "account for" and "make up for." It is also used with some verbs that have two objects in order to introduce the second object.

**for|bid** /fərbɪd, fɔr-/ (**forbids, forbidding, forbade, forbidden**) **1** V-T If you **forbid** someone **to** do something, or if you **forbid** an activity, you order that it must not be done. *prohibir* ❑ *They'll forbid you to marry. Te van a prohibir que te cases.* ❑ *...regulations that forbid the use of torture. ...normas que prohíben la tortura.* **2** V-T If something **forbids** a particular course of action or state of affairs, it makes it impossible. *prohibir, impedir* ❑ *His own pride forbids him to ask for Arthur's help. Su propio orgullo le impide pedirle ayuda a Arthur.*

**for|bid|den** /fərbɪdᵊn, fɔr-/ ADJ If something is **forbidden**, you are not allowed to do it or have it. *prohibido* ❑ *Loud noise was forbidden everywhere. En todos lados estaban prohibidos los ruidos fuertes.*

**force**

❶ VERB USES
❷ NOUN USES: POWER OR STRENGTH
❸ THE ARMY, POLICE, ETC.

❶ **force** /fɔrs/ (**forces, forcing, forced**) **1** V-T If

someone **forces** you **to** do something, they make you do it even though you do not want to. *forzar, obligar* ❑ *He forced them to drive away from the area. Lo obligaron a alejarse del lugar.* ❑ *They were grabbed by three men who forced them into a car. Los agarraron tres hombres que los obligaron a subir a un carro.* **2** V-T If you **force** something into a particular position, you use a lot of strength to make it move there. *forzar, meter a fuerza* ❑ *She forced her key into the lock. Metió a fuerza la llave en la cerradura.* **3** V-T If someone **forces** a lock, a door, or a window, they break the lock or fastening in order to get into a building without using a key. *forzar* ❑ *Police forced the door of the apartment and arrested Mr. Roberts. La policía forzó la puerta del departamento y arrestó al Sr. Roberts.*
→ see **motion**

**❷ force** /fɔrs/ (**forces**) **1** N-UNCOUNT If someone uses **force** to do something, strong and violent physical action is taken in order to achieve it. *fuerza* ❑ *The government decided against using force to break up the demonstrations. El gobierno decidió no usar la fuerza para disolver las manifestaciones.* **2** N-UNCOUNT **Force** is the power or strength which something has. *fuerza* ❑ *...the force of the explosion. ...la fuerza de la explosión.* **3** N-COUNT If you refer to someone or something as a **force** in a particular type of activity, you mean that they have a strong influence on it. *fuerza, poder, figura, personalidad* ❑ *The army was the most powerful political force in the country. El ejército era la fuerza política más poderosa del país.* ❑ *Christopher Wheeldon is a creative force in dance. Christopher Wheeldon es una personalidad creativa en la danza.* **4** N-VAR In physics, a **force** is the pulling or pushing effect that something has on something else. *fuerza* ❑ *...the Earth's gravitational force. ...la fuerza de gravitación de la Tierra.* **5** PHRASE A law, rule, or system that is **in force** exists or is being used. *vigente* ❑ *The new tax is already in force. El nuevo impuesto ya está vigente.* **6** PHRASE If you **join forces with** someone, you work together in order to achieve a common aim or purpose. *unir fuerzas* ❑ *He joined forces with his brother to start the company. Unió fuerzas con su hermano para iniciar la empresa.*

**Thesaurus** *force* Ver también:

V. coerce, make ❶ **1**
push, thrust ❶ **2**
break in, break open ❶ **3**
N. energy, pressure, strength ❷ **2**

**❸ force** /fɔrs/ (**forces**) **1** N-COUNT **Forces** are groups of soldiers or military vehicles that are organized for a particular purpose. *fuerza* ❑ *...the presence of American forces in the region. ...la presencia de fuerzas estadounidenses en la región.* **2** → see also **air force, armed forces, labor force, workforce**

**Word Partnership** Usar *force* con:

V. force **to resign** ❶ **1**
N. force **a smile** ❶ **2**
**use of** force ❷ **1** **2**
force **of gravity** ❷ **4**
ADJ. **excessive** force, **necessary** force ❷ **1**
**driving** force, **powerful** force ❷ **3**
**enemy** forces, **military** forces ❸ **1**

**force field** (**force fields**) N-COUNT A **force field** is an area of energy, such as magnetic energy, that surrounds an object or place. *campo de fuerza* ❑ *A giant force field protects the planet from solar winds. Un campo de fuerza gigantesco protege el planeta de los vientos solares.*

**fore|arm** /fɔrɑrm/ (**forearms**) N-COUNT Your **forearm** is the part of your arm between your elbow and your wrist. *antebrazo*

**Word Link** *fore ≈ before : forecast, foreman, foresee*

**fore|cast** /fɔrkæst/ (**forecasts, forecasting, forecasted**)

The forms **forecast** and **forecasted** can both be used for the past tense and past participle.

**1** N-COUNT A **forecast** is a statement of what is expected to happen in the future, especially in relation to a particular event or situation. *pronóstico, previsión* ❑ *...a forecast of a 2.25 percent growth in the economy. ...un pronóstico de crecimiento económico del 2.25 por ciento.* **2** V-T If you **forecast** future events, you say what you think is going to happen in the future. *pronosticar, prever, predecir* ❑ *They forecast a defeat for the president. Pronostican la derrota del presidente.* • **fore|cast|er** N-COUNT (**forecasters**) *analista* ❑ *...the nation's top economic forecasters. ...los principales analistas económicos del país.*
→ see Word Web: **forecast**

**fore|head** /fɔrhɛd, fɔrɪd/ (**foreheads**) N-COUNT Your **forehead** is the area at the front of your head between your eyebrows and your hair. *frente*
→ see **face**

f

**Word Web** forecast

**Meteorologists** depend on good information. They make **observations**. They gather **data** about **barometric pressure**, **temperature**, and **humidity**. They track **storms** with **radar** and **satellites**. They track cold **fronts** and warm fronts. They put all of this information into their computers and **model** possible weather patterns. Today scientists are trying to make better **weather forecasts**. They are installing thousands of small, inexpensive **radar** units on rooftops and cellphone towers. They will gather information near the Earth's surface and high in the sky. This will give meteorologists more information to help them **predict** tomorrow's weather.

**for|eign** /fɔrɪn/ **1** ADJ Something or someone that is **foreign** comes from or relates to a country that is not your own. extranjero ❑ *...her first foreign vacation without her parents.* *...sus primeras vacaciones en el extranjero sin sus padres.* ❑ *...a foreign language.* *...una lengua extranjera.* **2** ADJ In politics and journalism, **foreign** is used to describe people, jobs, and activities relating to countries that are not the country of the person or government concerned. exterior ❑ *...the German foreign minister.* *...el ministro alemán de relaciones exteriores.* ❑ *...American foreign policy.* *...la política exterior estadounidense.* **3** ADJ A **foreign** object is something that has got into something else, usually by accident, and should not be there. *extraño* [FORMAL] ❑ *...a foreign body in the eye.* *...un cuerpo extraño en el ojo.*

F

**Thesaurus** *foreign* Ver también:

ADJ. alien, exotic, strange; (*ant.*) domestic, native **1** **3**

**for|eign|er** /fɔrɪnər/ (**foreigners**) N-COUNT A **foreigner** is someone who belongs to a country that is not your own. *extranjero o extranjera*

**for|eign ex|change** (**foreign exchanges**) **1** N-PLURAL **Foreign exchanges** are the institutions or systems involved with changing one currency into another. *mercado de divisas* ❑ *On the foreign exchanges, the U.S. dollar is up point forty-five.* *El tipo de cambio del dólar estadounidense subió 0.45 en el mercado de divisas.* **2** N-UNCOUNT **Foreign exchange** is used to refer to foreign currency that is obtained through the foreign exchange system. *divisas* ❑ *...an important source of foreign exchange.* *...una fuente importante de divisas.*

**for|eign ser|vice** N-SING **The foreign service** is the government department that employs diplomats to work in foreign countries. *servicio exterior, servicio diplomático*

**Word Link** *fore ≈ before : forecast, foreman, foresee*

**Word Link** *man ≈ human being : foreman, humanity, woman*

**fore|man** /fɔrmən/ (**foremen**) N-COUNT A **foreman** is a person who is in charge of a group of workers. *capataz*

**fore|see** /fɔrsi/ (**foresees, foreseeing, foresaw, foreseen**) V-T If you **foresee** something, you expect and believe that it will happen. *prever* ❑ *He did not foresee any problems.* *No previó ningún problema.*

**for|est** /fɔrɪst/ (**forests**) N-VAR A **forest** is a large area where trees grow close together. *bosque, selva*
→ see Word Web: **forest**
→ see **habitat**

**for|est land** (**forest lands**) also **forestland** N-VAR **Forest land** is land that is mainly covered by forest. *superficie forestal, terreno forestal*

**for|est|ry** /fɔrɪstri/ N-UNCOUNT **Forestry** is the science or skill of growing and taking care of trees in forests. *silvicultura*
→ see **industry**

**for|ever** /fɔrɛvər, fər-/ **1** ADV If you say that something will happen or continue **forever**, you mean that it will always happen or continue. *siempre, por siempre* ❑ *I think that we will live together forever.* *Creo que viviremos juntos por siempre.* **2** ADV If something has gone or changed **forever**, it has gone or changed and will never come back or return to the way it was. *para siempre, permanentemente, eternamente* ❑ *His pain was gone forever.* *Se le quitó el dolor para siempre.*

**Thesaurus** *forever* Ver también:

ADV. always, endlessly, eternally **1** permanently **2**

**for|gave** /fərgeɪv/ **Forgave** is the past tense of **forgive**. *pasado de* ***forgive***

**forge** /fɔrdʒ/ (**forges, forging, forged**) **1** V-RECIP If one person or institution **forges** an agreement or relationship with another, they succeed in creating it. *forjar, fraguar* ❑ *The prime minister is determined to forge a good relationship with the country's new leader.* *El primer ministro está decidido a forjar una buena relación con el nuevo líder del país.* ❑ *They agreed to forge closer economic ties.* *Convinieron en forjar vínculos económicos más estrechos.* **2** V-T If someone **forges** paper money, a document, or a painting, they make false copies of it in order to deceive people. *falsificar* ❑ *He admitted forging passports.* *Aceptó que falsificaba pasaportes.* ❑ *They used forged documents to leave the country.* *Utilizaron documentos falsificados para salir del país.* • **forg|er** N-COUNT (**forgers**) *falsificador o falsificadora* ❑ *...an art forger.* *...un falsificador de obras de arte.*

▸ **forge ahead** PHR-VERB If you **forge ahead** with something, you continue with it and make a lot of progress with it. *seguir adelante, seguir* ❑ *He forged ahead with his plans for reform.* *Siguió adelante con sus planes de reforma.*

**Word Web** forest

Four hundred years ago, settlers in North America found endless **forests**. This large supply of **wood** helped them. They used **timber** to build homes and make furniture. They burned wood for cooking and heat. They cut down the **woods** to create farmland. By the late 1800s, most of the old growth forests on the East Coast had disappeared. The **lumber** industry has also destroyed millions of trees. Reforestation has replaced some of them. However, **logging** companies usually plant single species forests. Some people say these are not really forests at all—just **tree** farms.

**Word Partnership** Usar *forge* con:

N. forge **a bond**, forge **a friendship**, forge **links**, forge **a relationship**, forge **ties** 1
forge **documents**, forge **an identity**, forge **a signature** 2

**for|gery** /fɔrdʒəri/ (**forgeries**) 1 N-UNCOUNT **Forgery** is the crime of forging money, documents, or paintings. falsificación 2 N-COUNT You can refer to a forged document, bill, or painting as a **forgery**. falsificación ❑ *The letter was a forgery.* *La carta era una falsificación.*

**for|get** /fərgɛt/ (**forgets, forgetting, forgot, forgotten**) 1 V-T If you **forget** something or **forget** how to do something, you cannot think of it or think how to do it, although you knew in the past. olvidar(se) ❑ *She forgot where she left the car.* *Se le olvidó dónde había dejado el auto.* 2 V-T/V-I If you **forget** something or **forget** to do it, you do not remember it or remember to do it. olvidar(se) ❑ *She never forgets her dad's birthday.* *Nunca se le olvida el cumpleaños de su papá.* ❑ *She forgot to lock her door.* *Se olvidó de cerrar con llave la puerta.* ❑ *When I close my eyes, I forget about everything.* *Cuando cierro los ojos, me olvido de todo.* ❑ *I meant to ask you about it but I forgot.* *Tenía la intención de preguntarte, pero se me olvidó.* 3 V-T If you **forget** something that you had intended to bring with you, you do not remember to bring it. olvidar ❑ *Once when we were going to Paris, I forgot my passport.* *Una vez, cuando íbamos a París, olvidé mi pasaporte.* 4 V-T/V-I If you **forget** something or someone, you deliberately put them out of your mind and do not think about them any more. olvidar(se) ❑ *I hope you will forget the bad experience you had today.* *Espero que olvides la desagradable experiencia que tuviste hoy.* ❑ *I found it very easy to forget about Sumner.* *Me resultó muy fácil olvidarme de Sumner.*

**Thesaurus** *forget* Ver también:

V. disregard, ignore, neglect, overlook 2

**Word Partnership** Usar *forget* con:

ADV. **never** forget, **quickly** forget, **soon** forget 1
**almost** forget 1 – 3
ADJ. **easy/hard to** forget 1 – 4

**for|get|ful** /fərgɛtfəl/ ADJ Someone who is **forgetful** often forgets things. olvidadizo ❑ *My mother has become very forgetful and confused.* *Mi madre se ha vuelto muy olvidadiza y se confunde mucho.*

**for|give** /fərgɪv/ (**forgives, forgiving, forgave, forgiven**) V-T If you **forgive** someone who has done something bad or wrong, you stop being angry with them and no longer want to punish them. perdonar(se) ❑ *Hopefully Jane will understand and forgive you.* *Espero que Jane entienda y te perdone.* ❑ *Irene forgave Terry for stealing her money.* *Irene perdonó a Terry que le robara dinero.* • **for|giv|ing** ADJ indulgente, comprensivo ❑ *I don't think people are in a very forgiving mood.* *No creo que la gente esté muy comprensiva.* • **for|give|ness** N-UNCOUNT perdón ❑ *...a spirit of forgiveness.* *...un espíritu de perdón.*

**for|got** /fərgɒt/ **Forgot** is the past tense of **forget**. pasado de **forget**

**for|got|ten** /fərgɒtᵊn/ **Forgotten** is the past participle of **forget**. participio pasado de **forget**

**fork** /fɔrk/ (**forks, forking, forked**) 1 N-COUNT A **fork** is a tool used for eating food which has a row of three or four long metal points at the end. tenedor ❑ *...knives and forks.* *...cuchillos y tenedores.* 2 N-COUNT A **fork** in a road, path, or river is a point at which it divides into two parts and forms a "Y" shape. y griega, bifurcación ❑ *We arrived at a fork in the road.* *Llegamos a una bifurcación en el camino.* 3 V-I If a road, path, or river **forks**, it forms a fork. bifurcarse, dividirse
→ see **lightning, silverware**

▸ **fork out** PHR-VERB If you **fork out for** something, you spend a lot of money on it. gastar(se), desembolsar [INFORMAL] ❑ *Visitors to the castle had to fork out for a guidebook.* *Los visitantes tuvieron que aflojar para una guía del castillo.* ❑ *I forked out $530 on a ticket for a month's train travel in Europe.* *Tuve que desembolsar 530 dólares para un boleto de tren para viajar un mes por Europa.*

**form** /fɔrm/ (**forms, forming, formed**) 1 N-COUNT A **form of** something is a type or kind of it. forma, tipo ❑ *...a rare form of the disease.* *...una forma rara de la enfermedad.* ❑ *I am against violence in any form.* *Me opongo a todo tipo de violencia.* 2 N-COUNT The **form** of something is its shape. forma ❑ *...the form of the body.* *...la forma del cuerpo.* 3 N-COUNT You can refer to something that you can see as a **form** if you cannot see it clearly, or if its outline is the clearest aspect of it. forma ❑ *His form lay still under the blankets.* *Su forma yacía inmóvil bajo las mantas.* 4 N-COUNT A **form** is a paper with questions on it and spaces marked where you should write the answers. forma, formulario ❑ *You will be asked to fill in a form with details of your birth and occupation.* *Te van a pedir que pongas tu fecha de nacimiento y tu ocupación en un formulario.* 5 V-T/V-I When a particular shape **forms** or **is formed**, people or things move or are arranged so that this shape is made. formar(se) ❑ *A line formed to use the bathroom.* *Se formó una cola para usar el baño.* ❑ *The 12 students formed a circle with their arms around each other.* *Los 12 estudiantes se abrazaron entre sí y formaron un círculo.* 6 V-T If something is arranged or changed so that it becomes similar to a thing with a particular structure or function, you can say that it **forms** that thing. formar ❑ *The case opens to form a supporting easel.* *El estuche se abre para formar un caballete de apoyo.* 7 V-T If something consists of particular things, people, or features, you can say that they **form** that thing. formar, constituir ❑ *These articles formed the basis of Randolph's book.* *Estos artículos constituyen la base del libro de Randolph.* 8 V-T If you **form** an organization, group, or company, you start it. formar, crear, constituir ❑ *They tried to form a study group on human rights.* *Trataron de formar un grupo de estudio sobre derechos humanos.* 9 V-T/V-I When something natural **forms** or **is formed**, it begins to exist and develop. formar(se) ❑ *The stars formed 10 to 15 billion years ago.* *Las estrellas se formaron hace 10 a 15 mil millones de años atrás.* 10 N-UNCOUNT In sports, **form** refers to the ability or success of a person or animal over a period of time. forma ❑ *His form this season has been brilliant.* *Ha estado en*

f

*excelente forma esta temporada.*

**Thesaurus** *form* Ver también:

N. class, description, kind 1
body, figure, frame, shape 2
application, document, sheet 4
V. construct, create, develop, establish 5 – 9

**for|mal** /fɔrməl/ 1 ADJ **Formal** speech or behavior is very correct and serious rather than relaxed and friendly, and is used especially in official situations. *formal* ❑ *...a very formal letter of apology. ...una carta de disculpa muy formal.* ● **for|mal|ly** ADV *formalmente* ❑ *He took her home, saying goodnight formally on the doorstep. La llevó a su casa y se despidió muy formalmente en la puerta.* ● **for|mal|ity** N-UNCOUNT *formalidad* ❑ *Lillith's formality and seriousness amused him. La formalidad y seriedad de Lillith le divertían.* 2 ADJ A **formal** action, statement, or request is an official one. *formal* ❑ *No formal announcement has been made. No se ha hecho un anuncio formal.* ● **for|mal|ly** ADV *formalmente* ❑ *Officials haven't formally agreed to Anderson's plan. Los funcionarios no han aceptado formalmente el plan de Anderson.* 3 ADJ **Formal** education or training is given officially, usually in a school, college, or university. *formal* ❑ *Wendy didn't have any formal dance training. Wendy no tenía una educación formal como bailarina.* ● **for|mal|ly** ADV *formalmente* ❑ *...formally-trained artists from established schools. ...artistas que han hecho estudios formales en instituciones de prestigio.*
→ see also **formerly**

**for|mal thea|ter** N-UNCOUNT **Formal theater** is entertainment consisting of plays performed before an audience in a theater. *teatro convencional*

**for|mat** /fɔrmæt/ (**formats, formatting, formatted**) 1 N-COUNT The **format** of something is the way or order in which it is arranged and presented. *formato, estilo* ❑ *I met with him to explain the format of the program. Me reuní con él para explicarle el formato del programa.* 2 V-T To **format** a computer disk means to run a program so that the disk can be written on. *formatear* [COMPUTING]

**for|ma|tion** /fɔrmeɪʃən/ (**formations**) 1 N-UNCOUNT **The formation of** something is the starting or creation of it. *formación, creación* ❑ *...the formation of a new government. ...la formación de un nuevo gobierno.* 2 N-COUNT If people or things are **in formation,** they are arranged in a particular pattern as they move. *en formación* ❑ *He was flying in formation with seven other jets. Volaba en formación con otros siete jets.* 3 N-COUNT A rock or cloud **formation** is rock or cloud of a particular shape or structure. *formación*

**for|mer** /fɔrmər/ 1 ADJ **Former** is used to describe someone who used to have a particular job, position, or role, but no longer has it. *ex, antiguo, anterior* ❑ *The unemployed executives include former sales managers, directors and accountants. Entre los ejecutivos desempleados se encuenteran antiguos gerentes de ventas, directores y contadores.* ❑ *...former president Richard Nixon. ...el ex presidente Richard Nixon.* 2 PRON When two people, things, or groups have just been mentioned, you can refer to the first of them as **the former.** The second of them is called **the latter.** *el primero, lo primero* ❑ *If you want a career and children, then plan the latter as carefully as the former. Si quieres una carrera e hijos, entonces planea esto último tan cuidadosamente como lo primero.*

**Thesaurus** *former* Ver también:

ADJ. past 1
prior 2

**for|mer|ly** /fɔrmərli/ ADV If something happened or was true **formerly,** it happened or was true in the past. *antes, anteriormente* ❑ *He was formerly in the navy. Antes estuvo en la marina.*

**Usage** **formerly** and **formally**

*Formerly* and *formally* sound very similar but have very different meanings. *Formerly* is used to talk about something that used to be true but isn't true now; *formally* means "in a formal manner": *Jacques was formerly the president of our club, but he formally resigned last week by sending a letter to the club secretary.*

**form-fitting** ADJ **Form-fitting** clothes fit very closely to the body of the person who is wearing them. *pegado, ceñido, ajustado* ❑ *...a black, form-fitting designer dress. ...un exclusivo vestido negro ceñido.*

**for|mi|dable** /fɔrmɪdəbəl, fərmɪd-/ ADJ If you describe something or someone as **formidable,** you mean that you feel slightly frightened by them because they are very great or impressive. *extraordinario, monumental* ❑ *We have a formidable task ahead of us. Tenemos una tarea monumental ante nosotros.*

**form let|ter** (**form letters**) N-COUNT A **form letter** is a single copy of a letter that has been reproduced in large numbers and sent to many people. *circular*

**for|mu|la** /fɔrmyələ/ (**formulae** /fɔrmyəli/ or **formulas**) 1 N-COUNT A **formula** is a plan that is invented in order to deal with a particular problem. *fórmula, receta* ❑ *...a formula for peace. ...una fórmula para la paz.* 2 N-COUNT A **formula** is a group of letters, numbers, or other symbols which represents a scientific or mathematical rule. *fórmula* ❑ *This mathematical formula describes the distances of the planets from the Sun. Esta fórmula matemática sirve para calcular las distancias entre los planetas y el sol.* 3 N-COUNT In science, the **formula** for a substance tells you what amounts of other substances are needed in order to make that substance. *fórmula* ❑ *They have the same chemical formula. Tienen la misma fórmula química.*

**for|mu|late** /fɔrmyəleɪt/ (**formulates, formulating, formulated**) 1 V-T If you **formulate** something such as a plan or proposal, you invent it, thinking about the details carefully. *formular, idear, concebir* ❑ *Little by little, he formulated his plan for escape. Poco a poco concibió su plan para escapar.* ● **for|mu|la|tion** N-UNCOUNT *formulación* ❑ *...the formulation of U.S. environmental policies. ...la formulación de las políticas ambientales estadounidenses.* 2 V-T If you **formulate** a thought, opinion, or idea, you express it or describe it in words. *formular, expresar* ❑ *I was impressed by the way he formulated his ideas. Me impresionó la forma en que expresó sus ideas.*

• **for|mu|la|tion** N-UNCOUNT *formulación, manera de plantear* ❑ *The formulation of the question is important. La manera de plantear la pregunta es importante.*

**for-profit** ADJ A **for-profit** organization is one that is run with the aim of making a profit. *lucrativo, comercial, con fines de lucro* [BUSINESS] ❑ *Gerber has been running her own for-profit school in southern Florida for 17 years. Gerber ha estado operando durante 17 años su propia escuela con fines de lucro en el sur de Florida.*

**fort** /fɔrt/ (**forts**) N-COUNT A **fort** is a strong building that is used as a military base. *fuerte*

**forth** /fɔrθ/

In addition to the uses shown below, **forth** is also used in the phrasal verbs "put forth" and "set forth."

1 ADV When someone goes **forth** from a place, they leave it. *salir a, marchar a, ir a* [LITERARY] ❑ *Go forth into the desert. Marchad al desierto.* 2 ADV If one thing brings **forth** another, the first thing produces the second. *producir, provocar, suscitar, llevar a* [LITERARY] ❑ *My reflections brought forth no conclusion. Mis reflexiones no me llevaron a ninguna conclusión.* 3 **back and forth** → see **back**

**forth|com|ing** /fɔrθkʌmɪŋ/ 1 ADJ A **forthcoming** event is planned to happen soon. *próximo, futuro* ❑ *...the forthcoming elections. ...las próximas elecciones.* 2 ADJ If something that you want, need, or expect is **forthcoming,** it is given to you or it happens. *próximo, que está por llegar* [FORMAL] ❑ *They promised that the money would be forthcoming. Me prometieron que el dinero llegaría próximamente.* ❑ *No major shift in policy will be forthcoming. No se esperan cambios políticos importantes.* 3 ADJ If you say that someone is **forthcoming,** you mean that they willingly give information when you ask them. *comunicativo* ❑ *William was not very forthcoming about where he lived. William no fue muy comunicativo respecto de dónde vivía.*

**for|ti|eth** /fɔrtiəθ/ ORD The **fortieth** item in a series is the one that you count as number forty. *cuadragésimo, cuarentavo* ❑ *It was the fortieth anniversary of the death of the composer. Fue el cuadragésimo aniversario de la muerte del compositor.*

**for|tu|nate** /fɔrtʃənɪt/ ADJ If someone or something is **fortunate,** they are lucky. *afortunado, suertudo* ❑ *He was extremely fortunate to survive. Fue muy afortunado de sobrevivir.* ❑ *She is in the fortunate position of having plenty of choice. Está en la afortunada situación de tener múltiples opciones.*

**for|tu|nate|ly** /fɔrtʃənɪtli/ ADV **Fortunately** is used to introduce or indicate a statement about an event or situation that is good. *afortunadamente, por fortuna, por suerte* ❑ *Fortunately, the weather last winter was reasonably mild. Por fortuna, el invierno pasado fue razonablemente benigno.*

**for|tune** /fɔrtʃən/ (**fortunes**) 1 N-COUNT You can refer to a large sum of money as **a fortune** or **a small fortune** to emphasize how large it is. *fortuna* ❑ *He made a small fortune in the property boom. Hizo una pequeña fortuna con el auge de los bienes raíces.* 2 N-COUNT Someone who has a **fortune** has a very large amount of money. *fortuna* ❑ *He made his fortune in car sales. Hizo su fortuna vendiendo automóviles.* 3 N-UNCOUNT **Fortune** or good **fortune** is good luck. Ill **fortune** is bad luck. *suerte* ❑ *Investors are starting to wonder how long their good fortune can last. Los inversionistas están empezando a preguntarse cuánto puede durar su buena suerte.* 4 N-PLURAL If you talk about someone's **fortunes** or the **fortunes** of something, you are talking about the extent to which they are doing well or being successful. *trayectoria, vicisitudes* ❑ *The company had to do something to reverse its sliding fortunes. La empresa tenía que hacer algo para revertir su trayectoria descendente.*

**for|ty** /fɔrti/ (**forties**) 1 NUM **Forty** is the number 40. *cuarenta* 2 N-PLURAL **The forties** is the decade between 1940 and 1949. *cuarenta, años cuarenta, década de 1940* ❑ *They met in London in the Forties. Se conocieron en Londres en los años cuarenta.*

**fo|rum** /fɔrəm/ (**forums**) N-COUNT A **forum** is a place, situation, or group in which people exchange ideas and discuss issues. *foro* ❑ *The discussion groups are an open forum for listening. Los grupos de discusión son foros abiertos donde escuchar.*

**Word Link** *ward ≈ in the direction of: backward, forward, inward*

**for|ward** /fɔrwərd/ (**forwards, forwarding, forwarded**) 1 ADV If you move or look **forward,** you move or look in a direction that is in front of you. *hacia adelante* ❑ *He came forward with his hand out. "Mr. and Mrs. Selby?" he said. Se adelantó con la mano extendida.—¿Los señores Selby?—preguntó.* ❑ *She fell forward on to her face. Se fue de bruces.* 2 ADV **Forward** means in a position near the front of something such as a building or a vehicle. *adelante* ❑ *The best seats in the theater are as far forward as possible. Las mejores localidades del teatro son las de hasta adelante.* • **Forward** is also an adjective. *adelantado* ❑ *The troops moved to forward positions. Las tropas se movilizaron a posiciones adelantadas.* 3 ADV You use **forward** to indicate that something progresses or improves. *hacia adelante* 4 ADV If something or someone is put **forward,** or comes **forward,** they are suggested or offered as suitable for a particular purpose. *presentar(se), proponer(se)* ❑ *Several similar theories have been put forward. Se han propuesto varias teorías parecidas.* ❑ *No witnesses came forward. No se presentó ningún testigo.* 5 V-T If a letter or message **is forwarded to** someone, it is sent to the place where they are, after having been sent to a different place earlier. *enviar, reenviar, transmitir, mandar, remitir* ❑ *When he's out on the road, office calls are forwarded to his cellphone. Cuando está de viaje, las llamadas a la oficina son retransmitidas a su celular.* 6 **backward and forward** → see **backward**

**for|ward slash** (**forward slashes**) N-COUNT A **forward slash** is the sloping line / that separates letters, words, or numbers. *barra oblicua, barra diagonal, diagonal*

**fos|sil** /fɒsᵊl/ (**fossils**) N-COUNT A **fossil** is the hard remains of a prehistoric animal or plant that are found inside a rock. *fósil*
→ see Word Web: **fossil**
→ see **evolution**

**fos|sil fuel** (**fossil fuels**) also **fossil-fuel** N-VAR **Fossil fuel** is fuel such as coal or oil that is formed from the decayed remains of plants or animals. *combustible fósil* ❑ *Burning fossil fuels uses oxygen and*

f

## Word Web fossil

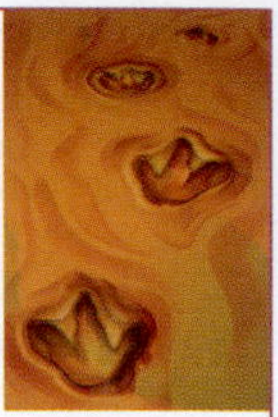

There are two types of animal **fossils**—body fossils and **trace** fossils. Body fossils help us understand how the animal looked when it was alive. Trace fossils, such as **tracks** and **footprints**, show us how the animal moved. Since we don't find tracks of dinosaurs' tails, we know they lifted them up as they walked. Footprints tell us about the weight of the dinosaur and how fast it moved. Scientists use two methods to calculate the date of a fossil. They sometimes count the number of **rock** layers covering it. They also use **carbon** dating.

F

*produces carbon dioxide.* *La quema de los combustibles fósiles consume oxígeno y genera produce dióxido de carbono.*
→ see **electricity, greenhouse effect, solar**

**fos|sil rec|ord** (**fossil records**) N-COUNT The **fossil record** is the history of life on Earth that is recorded in fossils found in rocks. *registro fósil*

**fos|ter** /fɔstər/ (**fosters, fostering, fostered**) **1** ADJ **Foster** parents are people who officially take a child into their family for a period of time, without becoming the child's legal parents. The child is referred to as their **foster** child. *de acogida, sustituto* **2** V-T If you **foster** a child, you take it into your family for a period of time, without becoming its legal parent. *acoger* **3** V-T If you **foster** a feeling, activity, or idea, you help it to develop. *fomentar, promover* ❑ *These organizations fostered a strong sense of pride within the black community.* *Estas organizaciones fomentaron un intenso orgullo entre la comunidad negra.*

**fought** /fɔt/ **Fought** is the past tense and past participle of **fight**. *pasado y participio pasado de* ***fight***

**foul** /faʊl/ (**fouler, foulest, fouls**) **1** ADJ If you describe something as **foul**, you mean it is dirty and smells or tastes unpleasant. *nauseabundo, fétido, repugnante* ❑ *...foul, polluted water.* *...agua fétida y contaminada.* **2** ADJ **Foul** language is offensive and contains swear words or rude words. *lenguaje obsceno* **3** ADJ If someone has a **foul** temper or is in a **foul** mood, they become angry or violent very suddenly and easily. *mal, malo* **4** N-COUNT A **foul** is an act in a game or sport that is not allowed according to the rules. *falta, faul* **5** PHRASE If you **run foul of** someone or **fall foul of** them, you do something which gets you into trouble with them. *tener problemas* ❑ *He had fallen foul of the FBI.* *Había tenido problemas con el FBI.*

**foul line** (**foul lines**) N-COUNT In basketball, **the foul line** is the line from which a player tries to throw the ball through the basket after they have been fouled. *línea de faul*

**found** /faʊnd/ (**founds, founding, founded**) **1** **Found** is the past tense and past participle of **find**. *pasado y participio pasado de* ***find*** **2** V-T When an institution, company, or organization **is founded** by someone, he or she gets it started, often by providing the necessary money. *fundar, crear, establecer* ❑ *The New York Free-Loan Society was founded in 1892.* *La New York Free-Loan Society fue fundada en 1892.* ❑ *His father founded the American Socialist Party.* *Su padre creó el partido socialista estadounidense.* • **foun|da|tion** /faʊndeɪʃən/ N-SING *fundación, creación* ❑ *...the foundation of the National Association of Evangelicals in 1942.* *...la fundación de la National Association of Evangelicals en 1942.* • **found|er** N-COUNT (**founders**) *fundador o fundadora, creador o creadora* ❑ *...one of the founders of the United Nations.* *...uno de los fundadores de las Naciones Unidas.* • **found|ing** N-SING *fundación, creación* ❑ *The firm has had great success since its founding 65 years ago.* *La empresa ha tenido un gran éxito desde su fundación, hace 65 años.*

**Word Link** *found ≈ base : foundation, founder, profound*

**foun|da|tion** /faʊndeɪʃən/ (**foundations**) **1** N-COUNT **The foundation of** something such as a belief or way of life is the things on which it is based. *base, fundamento* ❑ *Best friends are the foundation of my life.* *La base de mi vida son mis mejores amigos.* ❑ *The issue strikes at the very foundation of our community.* *El problema afecta a los fundamentos mismos de nuestra comunidad.* **2** N-COUNT A **foundation** is an organization which provides money for a special purpose. *fundación* ❑ *...the National Foundation for Educational Research.* *...la Fundación Nacional para la Investigación Educativa.* **3** N-PLURAL The **foundations** of a building or other structure are the layer of bricks or concrete below the ground that it is built on. *cimientos* **4** N-UNCOUNT If a story, idea, or argument has **no foundation,** there are no facts to prove that it is true. *fundamento* ❑ *The rumors were without foundation.* *Los rumores no tenían fundamento.* **5** → see also **found**

**found|er** /faʊndər/ (**founders, foundering, foundered**) V-I If something such as a plan or project **founders,** it fails. *fallar, fracasar, zozobrar* ❑ *The talks foundered, without agreement.* *Las pláticas fracasaron, no hubo acuerdo.*

**found|ing mem|ber** (**founding members**) N-COUNT A **founding member** of a club, group, or organization is one of the first members, often one who was involved in setting it up. *miembro fundador*

**foun|tain** /faʊntɪn/ (**fountains**) **1** N-COUNT A **fountain** is an ornamental feature in a pool or lake which consists of a jet of water that is forced up into the air by a pump. *fuente, manantial* **2** N-COUNT A **fountain of** a liquid is an amount of it which is sent up into the air and falls back. *chorro, surtidor* [LITERARY] ❑ *A fountain of liquid rock rose from the volcano.* *Del volcán brotó un manantial de roca líquida.*

**four** /fɔr/ (**fours**) **1** NUM **Four** is the number 4. *cuatro* **2** PHRASE If you are **on all fours,** your knees, feet, and hands are on the ground. *en cuatro patas, a gatas* ❑ *She crawled on all fours over to the window. Se arrastró a gatas hasta la ventana.*

**four|teen** /fɔrtin/ (**fourteens**) NUM **Fourteen** is the number 14. *catorce*

**four|teenth** /fɔrtinθ/ ORD The **fourteenth** item in a series is the one that you count as number fourteen. *decimocuarto, catorceavo* ❑ *The festival is now in its fourteenth year. Es el decimocuarto año del festival.*

**fourth** /fɔrθ/ (**fourths**) **1** ORD The **fourth** item in a series is the one that you count as number four. *cuarto* ❑ *Last year's winner is in fourth place. El ganador del año pasado está en cuarto lugar.* **2** N-COUNT A **fourth** is one of four equal parts of something. *cuarto, cuarta parte* ❑ *Three-fourths of the public say they favor a national vote on the issue. Tres cuartas partes del público están en favour de una votación nacional sobre el tema.*

**four-wheel drive** (**four-wheel drives**) N-COUNT A **four-wheel drive** is a vehicle in which all four wheels receive power from the engine to help with steering. *transmisión en las cuatro ruedas, tracción integral, propulsión total*

**fowl** /faʊl/ (**fowls**)

> The form **fowl** is usually used for the plural, but **fowls** can also be used.

N-COUNT A **fowl** is a bird, especially one that can be eaten as food, such as a duck or a chicken. *ave de corral*

**fox** /fɒks/ (**foxes**) N-COUNT A **fox** is a wild animal which looks like a dog and has reddish-brown fur, a pointed face and ears, and a thick tail. *zorro o zorra*

fox

**foxy** /fɒksi/ (**foxier, foxiest**) ADJ If a man calls a woman **foxy,** he means that she is physically attractive. *sexy* [INFORMAL] ❑ *...a foxy blonde. ...una rubia sexy.*

**Word Link** *fract, frag ≈ breaking : fraction, fracture, fragile*

**frac|tion** /frækʃən/ (**fractions**) **1** N-COUNT A **fraction of** something is a tiny amount or proportion of it. *fracción* ❑ *She hesitated for a fraction of a second before answering. Dudó una fracción de segundo antes de contestar.* **2** N-COUNT A **fraction** is a number that can be expressed as a proportion of two whole numbers. For example, ½ and ¾ are both fractions. *fracción*
→ see Picture Dictionary: **fractions**

**frac|ture** /fræktʃər/ (**fractures, fracturing, fractured**) **1** N-COUNT A **fracture** is a crack or break in something, especially a bone. *fractura* ❑ *...a hip fracture. ...una fractura de cadera* **2** V-T/V-I If something such as a bone **is fractured** or **fractures,** it gets a crack or break in it. *fracturar(se)* ❑ *You've fractured a rib, maybe more than one. Se te fracturó una costilla, quizá más de una.* ❑ *The mast of his boat fractured in two places and fell into the sea. El mástil de su bote se fracturó en dos lugares y cayó al mar.*

**frag|ile** /frædʒəl/ **1** ADJ If you describe a situation as **fragile,** you mean that it is weak or uncertain, and is unlikely to be able to resist strong pressure or attack. *frágil* ❑ *The fragile economies of several southern African nations could be damaged. Las frágiles economías de varios países del sur de África podrían resultar afectadas.* ● **fra|gil|ity** /frədʒɪlɪti/ N-UNCOUNT *fragilidad* ❑ *...the fragility of the peace process. ...la fragilidad del proceso de paz.* **2** ADJ Something that is **fragile** is easily broken or damaged. *frágil* ❑ *...fine, fragile crystal. ...cristal delgado y frágil* ● **fra|gil|ity** N-UNCOUNT *fragilidad* ❑ *...the fragility of their bones. ...la fragilidad de sus huesos.*

**Thesaurus** *fragile* Ver también:
ADJ. unstable, weak **1**
breakable, delicate; (*ant.*) sturdy **2**

**frag|ment** (**fragments, fragmenting, fragmented**)

> The noun is pronounced /frægmənt/. The verb is pronounced /frægmɛnt/.



## Picture Dictionary — fractions

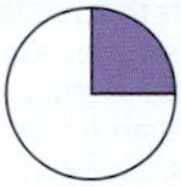

| fraction | decimal | percentage |
|---|---|---|
| 1/4 | 0.25 | 25% |

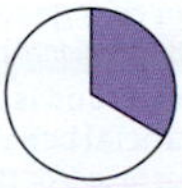

| fraction | decimal | percentage |
|---|---|---|
| 1/3 | 0.33 | 33% |

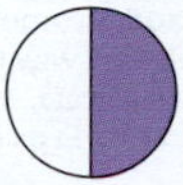

| fraction | decimal | percentage |
|---|---|---|
| 1/2 | 0.50 | 50% |

**adding fractions**

| problem: | solution: |
|---|---|
| 1 1/4 | 1 1/4 |
| +2 1/2 | +2 2/4 |
| ? | 3 3/4 |

**subtracting fractions**

| problem: | solution: |
|---|---|
| 5 2/3 | 5 4/6 |
| - 1 1/6 | - 1 1/6 |
| ? | 4 3/6 = 4 1/2 |

**1** N-COUNT A **fragment of** something is a small piece or part of it. *fragmento, trozo* ❑ *...tiny fragments of glass. ...diminutos fragmentos de vidrio.* ❑ *She read every fragment of news. Leyó hasta el último trozo de información.* **2** V-T/V-I If something **fragments** or **is fragmented,** it breaks or separates into small pieces or parts. *fragmentar(se), abrirse (las nubes)* ❑ *The clouds fragmented and out came the sun. Las nubes se abrieron y salió el sol.* ● **frag|men|ta|tion** /frægmɛnteɪʃᵊn/ N-UNCOUNT *fragmentación* ❑ *...the fragmentation of the Soviet Union. ...la fragmentación de la Unión Soviética.*

**frag|men|ta|tion** /frægmɛnteɪʃᵊn/ **1** N-UNCOUNT **Fragmentation** is a type of reproduction in some worms and other organisms, in which the organism breaks into several parts and each part grows into a new individual. *escisión, fragmentación* [TECHNICAL] **2** → see also **fragment**

**fra|grance** /freɪgrəns/ (**fragrances**) N-VAR A **fragrance** is a pleasant or sweet smell. *fragancia, aroma* ❑ *...a plant with a strong fragrance. ...una planta de intensa fragancia.*

**fra|grant** /freɪgrənt/ ADJ Something that is **fragrant** has a pleasant, sweet smell. *fragante* ❑ *...fragrant oils and perfumes. ...fragantes aceites y perfumes.*

**frame** /freɪm/ (**frames, framing, framed**) **1** N-COUNT The **frame** of a picture or mirror is the wood, metal, or plastic that is fitted around it. *marco* ❑ *...a photograph of her mother in a silver frame. ...una fotografía de su madre en marco de plata.* **2** N-COUNT The **frame** of an object such as a building, chair, or window is the arrangement of wooden, metal, or plastic bars between which other material is fitted, and which gives the object its strength and shape. *marco, armazón* ❑ *He supplied builders with door and window frames. Era proveedor de marcos de puertas y ventanas para la construcción.* ❑ *With difficulty he released the mattress from the metal frame. Le costó trabajo sacar el colchón del marco de metal.* **3** N-COUNT A **frame** of movie film is one of the many separate photographs that it consists of. *cuadro* ❑ *...films shot at 4000 frames per second. ...películas filmadas a 4000 cuadros por segundo.* **4** V-T When a picture or photograph **is framed,** it is put in a frame. *enmarcar* ❑ *The picture is now ready to be mounted and framed. La foto ya está lista para montarse y enmarcarse.* **5** V-T If someone **frames** an innocent person, they make other people think that that person is guilty of a crime, by lying or inventing evidence. *incriminar* [INFORMAL] ❑ *I'm trying to find out who tried to frame me. Estoy tratando de averiguar quien intentó incriminarme.* **6** N-COUNT You can refer to someone's body as their **frame,** especially when you are describing the general shape of it. *cuerpo* ❑ *Their belts are pulled tight against their bony frames. Sus cinturones quedan ajustados contra sus cuerpos huesudos.*
→ see **animation, bed, painting**

**frame|work** /freɪmwɜrk/ (**frameworks**) **1** N-COUNT A **framework** is a particular set of rules, ideas, or beliefs which you use in order to decide what to do. *marco de referencia, parámetro* ❑ *...the framework of federal regulations. ...el marco de referencia de la reglamentación federal.* **2** N-COUNT A **framework** is a structure that forms a support or frame for something. *marco, estructura, armazón* ❑ *...wooden shelves on a steel framework. ...entrepaños de madera en una armazón de acero.*

**fran|chise** /fræntʃaɪz/ (**franchises**) **1** N-COUNT A **franchise** is an authority that is given by an organization to someone, allowing them to sell its goods or services or to take part in an activity which the organization controls. *franquicia, concesión* [BUSINESS] ❑ *...a franchise to develop Hong Kong's first cable TV system. ...una concesión para desarrollar el primer sistema de televisión por cable en Hong Kong.* **2** N-UNCOUNT **Franchise** is the right to vote in an election. *sufragio, derecho de voto* ❑ *...the introduction of universal franchise. ...la introducción del sufragio universal.*

**frank** /fræŋk/ (**franker, frankest**) ADJ If someone is **frank,** they state or express things in an open and honest way. *franco, sincero* ❑ *My husband has not been frank with me. Mi esposo no ha sido sincero conmigo.* ● **frank|ly** ADV *francamente, con franqueza* ❑ *You can talk frankly to me. Conmigo puedes hablar con franqueza.* ● **frank|ness** N-UNCOUNT *franqueza* ❑ *The reaction to his frankness was hostile. La reacción ante su franqueza fue de hostilidad.*

**frank|ly** /fræŋkli/ **1** ADV You use **frankly** when you are expressing an opinion or feeling to emphasize that you mean what you are saying, especially when the person you are speaking to may not like it. *francamente* ❑ *Frankly, this whole thing is getting boring. Francamente todo esto se está poniendo aburrido.* **2** → see also **frank**

**fran|tic** /fræntɪk/ ADJ If you are **frantic,** you are behaving in a wild and uncontrolled way because you are frightened or worried. *desesperado, frenético, furioso, desequilibrado* ❑ *A bird was trapped in the room and was by now quite frantic. Había un pájaro atrapado en el cuarto y para entonces ya estaba bastante desesperado.* ● **fran|ti|cal|ly** /fræntɪkli/ ADV *desesperadamente, con desesperación* ❑ *She clutched frantically at Emily's arm. Se aferró desesperadamente al brazo de Emily.*

**fra|ter|nity** /frətɜrnɪti/ (**fraternities**) **1** N-COUNT You can refer to people who have the same profession or the same interests as a particular **fraternity.** *fraternidad, hermandad, asociación, organización* ❑ *...the spread of stolen guns among the criminal fraternity. ...la proliferación de armas robadas entre las organizaciones criminales.* **2** N-UNCOUNT **Fraternity** refers to friendship and support between people who feel they are closely linked to each other. *apoyo fraterno* [FORMAL] ❑ *Bob needs the fraternity of others who share his ideas. Bob necesita el apoyo fraterno de otros que compartan sus ideas.* **3** N-COUNT In the United States, a **fraternity** is a society of male university or college students. *asociación estudiantil masculina, club estudiantil masculino*

**fraud** /frɔd/ (**frauds**) **1** N-VAR **Fraud** is the crime of gaining money or financial benefits by a trick or by lying. *fraude* ❑ *He was jailed for two years for fraud and deception. Lo encarcelaron dos años por fraude y estafa.* **2** N-COUNT A **fraud** is something or someone that deceives people in a way that is illegal or dishonest. *impostor o impostora, simulador o simuladora* ❑ *He's a fraud and a cheat. Es un impostor y un simulador.*

**fraudu|lent** /frɔdʒələnt/ ADJ A **fraudulent**

activity is deceitful or dishonest. fraudulento ❑ ...fraudulent claims about being a nurse. ...afirmaciones fraudulentas de que era enfermera. • **fraudu|lent|ly** ADV fraudulentamente, de manera fraudulenta ❑ She was fraudulently using a credit card. Usaba una tarjeta de crédito de manera fraudulenta.

**fraz|zle** /fræzəl/ PHRASE If you **wear** yourself **to a frazzle,** or if you **are worn to a frazzle,** you feel mentally and physically exhausted because you have been working too hard or because you have been constantly worrying about something. hecho polvo, agotado, muerto de cansancio ❑ *She's worn to a frazzle preparing for the competition.* Acabó muerta de cansancio preparándose para la competencia.

**fraz|zled** /fræzəld/ ADJ If you are **frazzled,** or if your nerves are **frazzled,** you feel mentally and physically exhausted. hecho polvo, rendido, agotado ❑ *...a place to calm the most frazzled tourist.* ...un lugar que ofrece tranquilidad al más agotado de los turistas.

**freak** /fri̱k/ (**freaks**) **1** ADJ A **freak** event or action is one that is a very unusual or extreme example of its type. raro, inesperado, inusitado, insólito ❑ *Weir broke his leg in a freak accident playing golf.* Weir se rompió la pierna en un raro accidente, jugando al golf. **2** N-COUNT People are sometimes referred to as **freaks** when their behavior or attitude is very different from that of the majority of people and other people do not like them because of this. fenómeno, monstruo, bicho raro, fenómeno de circo, freak ❑ *It's the story of a troupe of circus freaks.* Es la historia de una compañía de fenómenos de circo.

**free** /fri/ (**freer, freest, frees, freeing, freed**) **1** ADJ If something is **free,** you can have it or use it without paying for it. gratis, libre, abierto, sin costo ❑ *The classes are free, with lunch provided.* Las clases son gratis, con almuerzo incluido. **2** **free of charge** → see **charge** **3** ADJ Someone or something that is **free** is not restricted, controlled, or limited, for example, by rules, customs, or other people. libre, en libertad de ❑ *The government will be free to pursue its economic policies.* El gobierno estará en libertad de continuar sus políticas económicas. ❑ *The elections were free and fair.* Las elecciones fueron libres y justas. • **free|ly** ADV libremente, con libertad ❑ *They cast their votes freely on election day.* El día de las elecciones emitieron libremente su voto. **4** ADJ Someone who is **free** is no longer a prisoner or a slave. libre ❑ *He walked from the court house a free man.* Salió del tribunal en calidad de hombre libre. **5** ADJ If someone or something is **free of** or **free from** an unpleasant thing, they do not have it or they are not affected by it. libre de, exento de, sin ❑ *...a future free of fear.* ...un futuro sin miedo. ❑ *She still has her slim figure and is free of wrinkles.* Su figura aún es esbelta, y no tiene arrugas. **6** ADJ If you have a **free** period of time or are **free** at a particular time, you are not working or occupied then. libre, desocupado ❑ *She spent her free time shopping.* Dedicó su tiempo libre a ir de compras. ❑ *I used to write during my free periods at school.* Solía escribir en el tiempo que tenía libre en la escuela. **7** ADJ If something such as a table or seat is **free,** it is not being used or occupied by anyone, or is not reserved for anyone to use. desocupado, libre **8** ADJ If you get something **free** or if it gets **free,** it is no longer trapped by anything or attached to anything. suelto, libre ❑ *He pulled his arm free.* Jaló hasta que su brazó quedo libre. **9** V-T If you **free** someone of something that is unpleasant or restricting, you remove it from them. liberar(se) ❑ *It will free us of debt.* Esto nos liberará de deudas. **10** V-T To **free** a prisoner or a slave means to release them. poner en libertad, liberar, soltar **11** V-T To **free** someone or something means to make them available for a task or function that they were previously not available for. liberar, dejar en libertad, dejar libre ❑ *Choosing the play early frees the director to make other decisions.* Escoger la obra con anterioridad deja en libertad al director para tomar otras decisiones. ❑ *His contract will run out soon, freeing him to pursue his own projects.* Su contrato terminará dentro de poco, lo cual lo dejará en libertad para dedicarse a sus propios proyectos. **12** V-T If you **free** someone or something, you remove them from the place in which they have been trapped or become fixed. liberar ❑ *Rescue workers freed him by cutting away part of the car.* Los rescatistas lo liberaron cortando parte del carro. **13** PHRASE You say "**feel free**" when you want to give someone permission to do something, in a very willing way. con confianza [INFORMAL] ❑ *If you have any questions at all, please feel free to ask me.* Si tiene alguna pregunta, hágamela con confianza. **14** to **give** someone **a free hand** → see **hand** **15** to **give** someone **free rein** → see **rein**

| Thesaurus | *free* | Ver también: |
|---|---|---|
| ADJ. | complimentary **1** | |
| | independent, unrestricted **3** | |
| | available, vacant **7** | |
| V. | emancipate, let go, liberate **8** **9** | |

**free agent** (**free agents**) N-COUNT If a sports player is a **free agent,** he or she is free to sign a contract with any team. agente libre

**free as|so|cia|tion** N-UNCOUNT **Free association** is a psychological technique in which words or images are used to suggest other words or images in a non-logical way. asociación libre

| Word Link | *dom* ≈ *state of being : boredom, freedom, wisdom* |
|---|---|

**free|dom** /fri̱dəm/ (**freedoms**) **1** N-VAR **Freedom** is the state of being allowed to do what you want to do. libertad ❑ *...individual freedoms and human rights.* ...las libertades y los derechos humanos de los individuos. **2** N-UNCOUNT When prisoners or slaves are set free or escape, they gain their **freedom.** libertad ❑ *...the agreement under which all hostages would gain their freedom.* ...el acuerdo mediante el cual todos los rehenes podrían recuperar su libertad. **3** N-UNCOUNT **Freedom from** something you do not want means not being affected by it. inmunidad ❑ *...the freedom from pain that medicine could provide.* ...la inmunidad contra el dolor que la medicina podría proporcionar.

| Word Partnership | Usar *freedom* con: |
|---|---|
| ADJ. | **artistic** freedom, **political** freedom, **religious** freedom **1** |
| N. | freedom **of choice**, **feeling/sense of** freedom, freedom **of the press**, freedom **of speech** **1** |
| | **struggle for** freedom **1** **2** |

f

**free|dom of speech** N-UNCOUNT **Freedom of speech** is the same as **free speech.** *libertad de expresión.* ❑ *...a country where freedom of speech may not be allowed. ...un país en el que quizá no exista libertad de expresión.*

**free fall** (**free falls**) also **free-fall** N-UNCOUNT An object that is **in free fall** is falling through the air because of gravity, and no other forces are affecting it. *caída libre*

**freely** /fri̲li/ **1** ADV **Freely** means many times or in large quantities. *profusamente, a manos llenas* ❑ *We have referred freely to his ideas. Nos hemos referido profusamente a sus ideas.* ❑ *George was spending very freely. George estaba gastando a manos llenas.* **2** ADV If you can talk **freely,** you can talk without needing to be careful about what you say. *libremente* **3** ADV If someone gives or does something **freely,** they give or do it willingly, without being ordered or forced to do it. *voluntariamente, libremente, de buen grado* ❑ *Danny shared his knowledge freely with anyone interested. Danny compartía de buen grado sus conocimientos con quien se interesara en ellos.* **4** ADV If something or someone moves **freely,** they move easily and smoothly, without any obstacles or resistance. *sin restricciones, libremente* ❑ *Traffic is flowing freely. El tráfico está fluyendo libremente.* **5** → see also **free**

F

**free ride** (**free rides**) N-COUNT If you say that someone is getting **a free ride** in a particular situation, you mean that they are getting some benefit from it without putting any effort into achieving it themselves, and you disapprove of this. *aprovechar(se)* ❑ *I didn't want anyone to think I was getting a free ride from the boss. No quería que nadie pensara que me estaba aprovechando de mi jefe.*

**free speech** N-UNCOUNT **Free speech** is the right to express your opinions in public. *libertad de expresión*

**free trade** N-UNCOUNT **Free trade** is trade between different countries that is carried on without particular government regulations such as subsidies or taxes. *libre comercio* ❑ *...the idea of a free trade pact between the U.S. and Mexico. ...la idea de un tratado de libre comercio entre los Estados Unidos y México.*

| Word Link | *free ≈ without : freeway, hands-free, toll-free* |
|---|---|

**free|way** /fri̲weɪ/ (**freeways**) N-COUNT A **freeway** is a major road that has been specially built for fast travel over long distances. *autopista*

**freeze** /fri̲z/ (**freezes, freezing, froze, frozen**) **1** V-T/V-I If a liquid or a substance containing a liquid **freezes,** or if something **freezes** it, it becomes solid because of low temperatures. *congelar* ❑ *If the temperature drops below 32° F, water freezes. Si la temperatura desciende a menos de 0 grados centigrados, el agua se congela.* ❑ *The ground froze solid. La tierra se congeló.* ● **freez|ing** N-UNCOUNT *congelación* ❑ *...damage due to freezing and thawing. ...daños debidas a la congelación y el deshielo.* **2** V-T If you **freeze** something such as food, you preserve it by storing it at a temperature below freezing point. *congelar(se)* **3** V-I If you **freeze,** you feel extremely cold. *congelarse, helarse* ❑ *The windows didn't fit properly so in winter we froze. Las ventanas no cerraban bien, así que en invierno nos helábamos.* **4** V-I If someone who is moving **freezes,** they suddenly stop and become completely still and quiet. *congelarse, quedarse inmóvil, paralizarse* [WRITTEN] ❑ *She froze when the beam of the flashlight struck her. Se quedó inmóvil cuando la luz de la linterna la iluminó.* **5** V-T If the government or a company **freeze** things such as prices or wages, they state officially that they will not allow them to increase for a fixed period of time. *inmovilizar, congelar* [BUSINESS] ❑ *They want the government to freeze prices. Quieren que el gobierno congele los precios* ● **Freeze** is also a noun. *congelación, congelamiento* ❑ *A wage freeze was imposed on all staff. Se impuso la congelación de salaries a todo el personal.* **6** V-T If someone in authority **freezes** something such as a bank account, fund, or property, they obtain a legal order which states that it cannot be used or sold for a particular period of time. *congelar* [BUSINESS] **7** → see also **freezing, frozen**

**freez|er** /fri̲zər/ (**freezers**) N-COUNT A **freezer** is a large container like a refrigerator in which the temperature is kept below freezing point so that you can store food inside it for long periods. *congelador o congeladora*

**freez|ing** /fri̲zɪŋ/ **1** ADJ If you say that something is **freezing** or **freezing cold,** you are emphasizing that it is very cold. *congelado, helado* ❑ *The movie theater was freezing. El cine estaba helado.* **2** ADJ If you say that you are **freezing** or **freezing cold,** you are emphasizing that you feel very cold. *helado* ❑ *"You must be freezing," she said. —Debes estar helándote—, le dijo.* **3** → see also **freeze**
→ see **precipitation, thermometer, water**

**freez|ing point** (**freezing points**) also **freezing-point** **1** N-UNCOUNT **Freezing point** is 32° Fahrenheit or 0° Celsius, the temperature at which water freezes. Freezing point is often used when talking about the weather. *punto de congelación* **2** N-COUNT The **freezing point** of a particular substance is the temperature at which it freezes. *punto de congelación*

**freight** /fre̲ɪt/ **1** N-UNCOUNT **Freight** is the movement of goods by trucks, trains, ships, or airplanes. *carga, flete* ❑ *Most shipments went by air freight. La mayoría de los embarques se hicieron por carga aérea.* **2** N-UNCOUNT **Freight** is goods that are transported by trucks, trains, ships, or airplanes. *carga* ❑ *...26 tons of freight. ...26 toneladas de carga.*
→ see **train**

**freight car** (**freight cars**) N-COUNT On a train, a **freight car** is a large container in which goods are transported. *vagón de carga, carro de carga*

**French fries** N-PLURAL **French fries** are long, thin pieces of potato fried in oil or fat. *papas fritas, papas a la francesa*

**French toast** N-UNCOUNT **French toast** is toast made by dipping a slice of bread into beaten egg and milk and then frying it. *torreja, pan francés*

**fre|quen|cy** /fri̲kwənsi/ (**frequencies**) **1** N-UNCOUNT The **frequency** of an event is the number of times it happens. *frecuencia* ❑ *The frequency of Kara's phone calls increased. Aumentó la frecuencia de las llamadas telefónicas de Kara.* **2** N-VAR The **frequency** of a sound wave or a radio wave is the number of times it vibrates within a period

of time. *frecuencia* ❑ *You can't hear waves of such a high frequency. No se puede escuchar las ondas de una frecuencia tan alta.*
→ see **sound, wave**

**fre|quent** /frɪkwənt/ ADJ If something is **frequent,** it happens often. *frecuente* ❑ *Bordeaux is on the main Paris-Madrid line so there are frequent trains. Burdeos está en la línea principal de París a Madrid, así que los trenes son frecuentes.* • **fre|quent|ly** ADV *frecuentemente, con frecuencia* ❑ *He was frequently unhappy. Con frecuencia se sentía infeliz.*

**Thesaurus** *frequent* Ver también:
ADJ. common, everyday, habitual; (*ant.*) occasional, rare

**fresh** /frɛʃ/ (**fresher, freshest**) **1** ADJ A **fresh** thing or amount replaces or is added to a previous thing or amount. *nuevo, adicional, otro* ❑ *He asked the police to make fresh inquiries. Pidió a la policía que hiciera nuevas investigaciones.* **2** ADJ Something that is **fresh** has been done, made, or experienced recently. *fresco, nuevo, reciente* ❑ *There were fresh car tracks in the snow. En la nieve había huellas recientes de un automóvil.* • **fresh|ly** ADV *recién, recientemente* ❑ *...freshly-baked bread. ...pan recién horneado.* **3** ADJ **Fresh** food has been picked or produced recently, and has not been preserved. *fresco* ❑ *...locally-caught fresh fish. ...pescado fresco del lugar.* **4** ADJ If you describe something as **fresh,** you like it because it is new and exciting. *nuevo, fresco* ❑ *These designers are full of fresh ideas. Estos diseñadores tienen muchas ideas nuevas.* **5** ADJ If something smells, tastes, or feels **fresh,** it is clean or cool. *fresco* ❑ *The air was fresh and for a moment she felt revived. El aire estaba fresco y por un momento sintió que revivía.* **6** ADJ **Fresh** paint is not yet dry. *fresca* ❑ *There was fresh paint on the walls. La pintura de las paredes estaba fresca.*

**fresh|man** /frɛʃmən/ (**freshmen**) N-COUNT In the United States, a **freshman** is a student who is in their first year at a high school or college. *novato o novata, estudiante de primer año de universidad*

**fresh|water** /frɛʃwɔtər/ ADJ A **freshwater** lake contains water that is not salty, usually in contrast to the sea. *agua dulce*
→ see **glacier, wetland**

**fric|tion** /frɪkʃ<sup>ə</sup>n/ (**frictions**) **1** N-UNCOUNT **Friction** between people is disagreement and argument between them. *fricción* ❑ *Sara sensed that there had been friction between her children. Sara intuyó que había habido fricciones entre sus hijos.* **2** N-UNCOUNT **Friction** is the force that makes it difficult for things to move freely when they are touching each other. *fricción*

**Fri|day** /fraɪdeɪ, -di/ (**Fridays**) N-VAR **Friday** is the day after Thursday and before Saturday. *viernes* ❑ *He is intending to go home on Friday. Pretende irse a casa el viernes.* ❑ *...Friday November 6. ...viernes 6 de noviembre.*

**fridge** /frɪdʒ/ (**fridges**) N-COUNT A **fridge** is the same as a **refrigerator.** *refrigerador, refri, heladera* [INFORMAL]

**friend** /frɛnd/ (**friends**) **1** N-COUNT A **friend** is someone who you know well and like, but who is not related to you. *amigo o amigo, cuate o cuata* ❑ *...my best friend. ...mi mejor amigo.* ❑ *She never was a close friend of mine. Ella nunca fue mi amiga íntima.* **2** N-PLURAL If you are **friends with** someone, you are their friend and they are yours. *en buenos términos, ser amigos* ❑ *I still wanted to be friends with Alison. Yo aún quería estar en buenos términos con Alison.* ❑ *We remained good friends. Seguimos siendo buenos amigos.* **3** N-PLURAL The **friends of** a country, cause, or organization are the people and organizations who help and support them. *amigos, partidarios, aliados, favorecedores* ❑ *...the friends of Israel. ...los aliados de Israel.* **4** PHRASE If you **make friends with** someone, you begin a friendship with them. *hacer amistad, hacer amigos, trabar amistad* ❑ *He has made friends with the kids on the street. Ha hecho amistad con los niños que viven en la misma calle.* ❑ *Dennis made friends easily. Dennis hacía amigos con facilidad*

**Word Partnership** Usar *friend* con:
ADJ. **best** friend, **close** friend, **dear** friend, **faithful** friend, **former** friend, **good** friend, **loyal** friend, **mutual** friend, **old** friend, **personal** friend, **trusted** friend **1**
N. **childhood** friend, friend **of the family,** friend **or relative** **1**
friend **or foe** **1** **2**
V. **tell a** friend **1**
**make a** friend **1** **4**

**friend|ly** /frɛndli/ (**friendlier, friendliest, friendlies**) **1** ADJ If someone is **friendly,** they behave in a pleasant, kind way, and like to be with other people. *amistoso, amable, simpático, cordial* ❑ *Godfrey was friendly to me. Godfrey fue cordial conmigo.* ❑ *The man had a pleasant, friendly face. El hombre tenía un rostro agradable y amistoso.* • **friend|li|ness** N-UNCOUNT *afabilidad, cordialidad, amabilidad* ❑ *She loves the friendliness of the people there. Le encanta la afabilidad de la gente de allá.* **2** ADJ If you are **friendly with** someone, you like each other and enjoy spending time together. *amistoso* ❑ *I'm friendly with his mother. Soy amistoso con su madre.*

**Word Partnership** Usar *friendly* con:
N. friendly **atmosphere,** friendly **face,** friendly **neighbors,** friendly **service,** friendly **voice** **1**
friendly **relationship** **2**
V. **become** friendly **2**

**friend|ly fire** N-UNCOUNT If you come under **friendly fire** during a battle, you are accidentally shot at by people on your own side, rather than by your enemy. *fuego amigo* ❑ *A high percentage of casualties were caused by friendly fire. Un alto porcentaje de las víctimas fue producto del fuego amigo.*

**Word Link** *ship* ≈ *condition or state* : *citizenship, friendship, membership*

**friend|ship** /frɛndʃɪp/ (**friendships**) N-VAR A **friendship** is a relationship between two or more friends. *amistad*

**fries** /fraɪz/ N-PLURAL **Fries** are the same as **French fries.** *papas fritas, papas a la francesa*

**fright** /fraɪt/ (**frights**) **1** N-UNCOUNT **Fright**

is a sudden feeling of fear. *miedo, susto* ❑ *The steam pipes rattled suddenly, and Franklin jumped with fright.* *De repente tronaron las tuberías del vapor y Franklin brincó del susto.* **2** N-COUNT **A fright** is an experience which makes you suddenly afraid. *susto, miedo* ❑ *The snake raised its head, which gave everyone a fright.* *La serpiente levantó la cabeza y a todos les dio miedo.*

**fright|en** /fraɪtᵊn/ (**frightens, frightening, frightened**) V-T If something or someone **frightens** you, they cause you to suddenly feel afraid, anxious, or nervous. *asustar, espantar, atemorizar* ❑ *He knew that Soli was trying to frighten him.* *Sabía que Soli estaba tratando de asustarlo.*

▸ **frighten away** or **frighten off** **1** PHR-VERB If you **frighten away** a person or animal or **frighten** them **off**, you make them afraid so that they run away or stay some distance away from you. *asustar* ❑ *The boats were frightening away the fish.* *Los botes estaban asustando a los peces.* **2** PHR-VERB To **frighten** someone **away** or **frighten** them **off** means to make them nervous so that they decide not to become involved with a particular person or activity. *asustar, alejar* ❑ *High prices have frightened buyers off.* *Los altos precios han alejado a los compradores.*

▸ **frighten off** → see **frighten away**

**fright|ened** /fraɪtᵊnd/ ADJ If you are **frightened**, you are anxious or afraid. *estar asustado, tener miedo* ❑ *She was frightened of making a mistake.* *Tenía miedo de cometer un error.*

**fright|en|ing** /fraɪtᵊnɪŋ/ ADJ If something is **frightening**, it makes you feel afraid, anxious, or nervous. *espantoso, aterrador, alarmante* ❑ *It was a very frightening experience.* *Fue una experiencia aterradora.* ● **fright|en|ing|ly** ADV *de manera alarmante* ❑ *The country is frighteningly close to war.* *El país se acerca a la guerra de manera alarmante.*

**fringe** /frɪndʒ/ (**fringes**) **1** N-COUNT A **fringe** is a decoration attached to clothes, or other objects such as curtains, consisting of a row of hanging threads. *fleco, cenefa* ❑ *The jacket had leather fringes.* *La chamarra tenía flecos de piel.* **2** N-COUNT To be **on the fringe** or **the fringes of** a place means to be on the outside edge of it. *en las afueras, en la periferia* ❑ *...a small town on the fringes of the city.* *...un pueblo pequeño en las afueras de la ciudad.* **3** N-COUNT **The fringe** or **the fringes of** an activity or organization are its less important, least typical, or most extreme parts. *margen* ❑ *This political party is the fringe of the political scene.* *Este partido político está al margen de la escena política.*

**frog** /frɒg/ (**frogs**) N-COUNT A **frog** is a small creature with smooth skin, big eyes, and long back legs which it uses for jumping. *rana*
→ see **amphibian**

**from**
❶ MENTIONING THE SOURCE, ORIGIN, OR STARTING POINT
❷ MENTIONING A RANGE OF TIMES, AMOUNTS, OR THINGS
❸ MENTIONING SOMETHING YOU WANT TO PREVENT OR AVOID

❶ **from** /frəm, STRONG frʌm/ **1** PREP If something comes **from** a particular person or thing, or if you get something **from** them, they give it to you or they are the source of it. *de* ❑ *He appealed for information from anyone who saw the attackers.* *Solicitó información de quien hubiera visto a los atacantes.* ❑ *...an anniversary present from his wife.* *...un regalo de aniversario de su esposa.* **2** PREP Someone who comes **from** a particular place lives in that place or originally lived there. Something that comes **from** a particular place was made in that place. *de* ❑ *...an art dealer from Zurich.* *...un comerciante de arte de Zurich.* **3** PREP If someone or something moves or is moved **from** a place, they leave it or are removed, so that they are no longer there. *de* ❑ *The guests watched as she fled from the room.* *Los invitados la observaban mientras salía del cuarto.* **4** PREP If you take one thing or person **from** another, you move that thing or person so that they are no longer with the other or attached to the other. *de* ❑ *In many bone transplants, bone can be taken from other parts of the patient's body.* *En muchos trasplantes óseos, se puede tomar hueso de otras partes del cuerpo del paciente.* **5** PREP If you take something **from** an amount, you reduce the amount by that much. *de* ❑ *The $103 was deducted from Mrs. Adams' salary.* *Los 103 dólares fueron deducidos del salario de la Sra. Adams.* **6** PREP If you return **from** a place or an activity, you return after being in that place or doing that activity. *de* ❑ *My son has just returned from Amsterdam.* *Mi hijo acaba de regresar de Amsterdam.* **7** PREP If you see or hear something **from** a particular place, you are in that place when you see it or hear it. *a través de* ❑ *Visitors see the painting from behind a plate glass window.* *Los visitantes ven la pintura a través de un placa cristal.* **8** PREP If something hangs or sticks out **from** an object, it is attached to it or held by it. *de* ❑ *Hanging from her right wrist is a gold bracelet.* *De su muñeca derecha cuelga una pulsera de oro.* ❑ *Large fans hang from the ceilings.* *Del techo cuelgan grandes ventiladores.* **9** PREP You can use **from** when giving distances. For example, if a place is fifty miles **from** another place, the distance between the two places is fifty miles. *de* ❑ *The park is only a few hundred yards from Zurich's main shopping center.* *El parque está sólo a unos metros del principal centro comercial de Zurich.* ❑ *How far is it from here?* *¿Qué tan lejos de aquí está?* **10** PREP If a road or railroad line goes **from** one place to another, you can travel along it between the two places. *de* ❑ *...the road from St. Petersburg to Tallinn.* *...el camino de San Petersburgo a Tallinn.* **11** PREP **From** is used, especially in the expression **made from,** to say what substance has been used to make something. *de* ❑ *...bread made from white flour.* *...pan de harina blanca.* **12** PREP If something changes **from** one thing **to** another, it stops being the first thing and becomes the second thing. *de* ❑ *The expression on his face changed from sympathy to surprise.* *La expresión de su cara cambió de simpatía a sorpresa.* ❑ *Unemployment has fallen from 7.5 to 7.2%.* *El desempleo se ha reducido del 7.5 al 7.2%.* **13** PREP You use **from** after some verbs and nouns when mentioning the cause of something. *de* ❑ *The problem simply resulted from a difference of opinion.* *El problema se derivó sencillamente de una diferencia de opiniones.* **14** PREP You use **from** when you are giving the reason for an opinion. *por* ❑ *She knew from experience that Dave was telling her the truth.* *Ella* *supo por experiencia que Dave estaba diciéndole la verdad.*

**❷ from** /frəm, STRONG frʌm/ **1** PREP You can use **from** when you are talking about the beginning of a period of time. *desde, a partir de* ❑ *She studied painting from 1926. Estudió pintura desde 1926.* ❑ *Breakfast is available from 6 a.m. El desayuno se sirve a partir de las 6 a.m.* **2** PREP You say **from** one thing **to** another when you are stating the range of things that are possible. *de* ❑ *There are 94 countries represented, from Algeria to Zimbabwe. Hay 94 países representados, de Argelia a Zimbabwe.*

**❸ from** /frəm, STRONG frʌm/ PREP **From** is used after verbs with meanings such as "protect," "free," "keep," and "prevent" to introduce the action that does not happen, or that someone does not want to happen. *de* ❑ *Such laws could protect the consumer from harm. Dichas leyes podrían proteger de daños al consumidor.*

In addition to the uses shown here, **from** is used in phrasal verbs such as "date from" and "grow away from."

**front** /frʌnt/ (**fronts**) **1** N-COUNT **The front of** something is the part of it that faces you, or that faces forward. *frente* ❑ *Stand at the front of the line. Párate frente a la línea.* **2** N-COUNT In a war, the **front** is a line where two opposing armies are fighting each other. *frente, frente de batalla* ❑ *Sonja's husband is fighting at the front. El esposo de Sonja está luchando en el frente de batalla.* **3** → see also **front line** **4** N-COUNT If you say that something is happening on a particular **front,** you mean that it is happening with regard to a particular situation or field of activity. *campo* ❑ *...research across a wide academic front. ...investigación en un amplio campo académico.* **5** N-COUNT If someone puts on a particular kind of **front,** they pretend to have a particular quality. *cara* ❑ *Michael kept up a brave front to the world. Michael seguía poniendo buena cara al mundo.* **6** N-COUNT An organization or activity that is **a front for** one that is illegal or secret is used to hide it. *pantalla* ❑ *...The charity was set up as a front for their criminal activities. ...la caridad era la pantalla de sus actividades criminales.* **7** N-COUNT In relation to the weather, a **front** is a line where a mass of cold air meets a mass of warm air. *frente* **8** PHRASE If a person or thing is **in front,** they are ahead of others in a moving group. *adelante* ❑ *Don't drive too close to the car in front. No manejes demasiado cerca del carro de adelante.* **9** PHRASE Someone who is **in front** in a competition or contest at a particular point is winning at that point. *al frente* ❑ *Richard Dunwoody is in front in the race. Richard Dunwoody va al frente de la carrera.* **10** PHRASE If someone or something is **in front of** a particular thing, they are facing it, ahead of it, or close to the front part of it. *frente a, en frente de* ❑ *She sat down in front of her mirror. Se sentó frente a su espejo.* ❑ *Something ran out in front of my car. Algo pasó corriendo frente a mi carro.* **11** PHRASE If you do or say something **in front of** someone else, you do or say it when they are present. *en frente de* ❑ *They never argued in front of their children. Nunca discutieron en frente de sus hijos.*
→ see **forecast, location**

**front and cen|ter** ADJ If a topic or question is **front and center,** a lot of attention is being paid to it or a lot of people are talking about it. *centro de la atención* ❑ *The media has kept the story front and center. Los medios han mantenido la historia en el centro de atención.*

**front desk** N-SING The **front desk** in a hotel is the desk or office that books rooms for people and answers their questions. *recepción* ❑ *Call the hotel's front desk and cancel your morning wake-up call. Llama a la recepción del hotel y cancela la llamada para que te despierten por la mañana.*
→ see **hotel**

**fron|tier** /frʌntɪər, frɒn-/ (**frontiers**) **1** N-COUNT **The frontiers** of something are the limits to which it extends. *frontera, límite* ❑ *...expanding the frontiers of science. ...ampliar las fronteras de la ciencia.* **2** N-COUNT A **frontier** is a border between two countries. *frontera* ❑ *They showed their passports at the Russian frontier. Mostraron sus pasaportes en la frontera rusa.*

**front line** (**front lines**) also **front-line** N-COUNT **The front line** is the place where two opposing armies are fighting each other. *primera línea* ❑ *...taking supplies to soldiers on the front line. ...llevar suministros a los soldados de la primera línea.*

**front of|fice** (**front offices**) N-COUNT The **front office** of a company or other organization is the room or rooms where staff deal with the public. The executives of a company or other organization are sometimes referred to collectively as the **front office.** *oficina de atención al público* ❑ *Information is available at the front office of the Cultural Center. La información está disponible en la oficina de atención al público del Centro Cultural.*

**front-page** ADJ A **front-page** article or picture appears on the front page of a newspaper because it is very important or interesting. *primera plana*

**frost** /frɔst/ (**frosts, frosting, frosted**) **1** N-VAR When there is **frost** or a **frost,** the temperature outside falls below freezing point and the ground becomes covered in ice crystals. *escarcha, helada* ❑ *There is frost on the ground and snow is forecast. Hay escarcha en la tierra y se pronostica nieve.* **2** V-T If you **frost** a cake, you cover and decorate it with frosting. *embetunar, cubrir con azúcar glaseada*
→ see **snow**

**frost|ing** /frɔstɪŋ/ N-UNCOUNT **Frosting** is a sweet substance made from powdered sugar that is used to decorate cakes. *betún*

**frosty** /frɔsti/ (**frostier, frostiest**) **1** ADJ If the weather is **frosty,** the temperature is below freezing. *helado, con escarcha* ❑ *...winter's cold and frosty nights. ...las frías noches de escarcha de invierno.* **2** ADJ You describe the ground or an object as **frosty** when it is covered with frost. *cubierto de escarcha* ❑ *...the frosty road. ...el camino cubierto de escarcha.*

**frown** /fraʊn/ (**frowns, frowning, frowned**) V-I When someone **frowns,** their eyebrows become drawn together, because they are annoyed, worried, or puzzled, or because they are concentrating. *fruncir el ceño, fruncir el entrecejo* ❑ *Nancy shook her head, frowning. Nancy sacudió la cabeza, frunciendo el ceño.* ❑ *He frowned at her anxiously. La miró frunciendo con ansiedad el entrecejo.* ● **Frown** is also a noun. *ceño fruncido, cara de enojo/concentración* ❑ *There was a deep frown on the boy's face. En la cara del*

f

F

niño se reflejaba su profundo desagrado.

▸ **frown upon** or **frown on** PHR-VERB If something **is frowned upon** or **is frowned on,** people disapprove of it. estar mal visto, desaprobar ❑ *This practice is frowned upon as being wasteful.* *Esta costumbre está mal vista porque se considera un desperdicio.*

**froze** /froʊz/ **Froze** is the past tense of **freeze.** pasado de **freeze**

**fro|zen** /froʊz$^{ə}$n/ **1** **Frozen** is the past participle of **freeze.** participio pasado de **freeze** **2** ADJ If the ground is **frozen** it has become very hard because the weather is very cold. congelado ❑ *It was bitterly cold and the ground was frozen hard.* *Hacía un frío tremendo y la tierra estaba totalmente congelada.* **3** ADJ **Frozen** food has been preserved by being kept at a very low temperature. congelado ❑ *Frozen fish is a healthy convenience food.* *El pescado congelado es un alimento saludable y práctico.* **4** ADJ If you say that you are **frozen,** or a part of your body is **frozen,** you are emphasizing that you feel very cold. congelado, helado ❑ *He put one hand up to his frozen face.* *Se llevó la mano a la helada cara.* ❑ *I'm frozen out here.* *Aquí me estoy congelando.*
→ see **glacier**

**fruit** /frut/ (**fruit, fruits**)

> The plural form is usually **fruit**, but can also be **fruits.**

**1** N-VAR **Fruit** is something which grows on a tree or bush and which contains seeds or a pit covered by a substance that you can eat. fruta ❑ *Fresh fruit and vegetables provide fiber and vitamins.* *La fruta y las verduras frescas proporcionan fibra y vitaminas.* ❑ *...bananas and other tropical fruits.* *...plátanos y otras frutas tropicales.* **2** N-COUNT **The fruits** or **the fruit of** your work or activity are the good things that result from it. fruto ❑ *We will have a meeting to share the fruits of your investigations.* *Vamos a tener una reunión para compartir el fruto de sus investigaciones.* **3** PHRASE If an action **bears fruit,** it produces good results. dar fruto, fructificar ❑ *Eleanor's work will, I hope, bear fruit.* *Espero que el trabajo de Eleanor fructifique.*
→ see Picture Dictionary: **fruit**
→ see **dessert, grain**

**frus|trate** /frʌstreɪt/ (**frustrates, frustrating, frustrated**) **1** V-T If something **frustrates** you, it upsets or angers you because you are unable to do anything about the problems it creates. frustrar(se) ❑ *These questions frustrated me.* *Estas cuestiones me frustraron.* ● **frus|trat|ed** ADJ frustrado ❑ *Roberta felt frustrated and angry.* *Roberta se sintió frustrada y enojada.* ● **frus|trat|ing** ADJ frustrante ❑ *This situation is very frustrating for us.* *Esta situación es muy frustrante para nosotros* ● **frus|tra|tion** /frʌstreɪʃ$^{ə}$n/ N-VAR (**frustrations**) frustración ❑ *...frustration among hospital doctors.* *...frustración entre los médicos de hospital.* **2** V-T If someone or something **frustrates** a plan or attempt to do something, they prevent it from succeeding. frustrar ❑ *The government has frustrated his efforts to employ foreign workers.* *El gobierno ha frustrado sus esfuerzos para emplear a trabajadores extranjeros.*
→ see **anger**

**fry** /fraɪ/ (**fries, frying, fried**) **1** V-T When you **fry** food, you cook it in a pan that contains hot fat or oil. freír ❑ *Fry the breadcrumbs until golden brown.* *Fría el pan molido hasta que tome un color café dorado.* **2** N-PLURAL **Fries** are the same as **French fries.** papas fritas, papas a la francesa
→ see **cook, egg**

**fry|ing pan** (**frying pans**) N-COUNT A **frying pan** is a flat metal pan with a long handle, in which you fry food. sartén
→ see **pan**

**fuel** /fyuəl/ (**fuels**) N-VAR **Fuel** is a substance such as coal, oil, or gasoline that is burned to provide heat or power. combustible, carburante ❑ *They ran out of fuel.* *Se les acabó el combustible.*
→ see **car, energy, engine, oil, petroleum**

**Word Partnership** Usar *fuel* con:

N. **cost of** fuel, fuel **oil**, fuel **pump**, fuel **shortage**, fuel **supply**, fuel **tank**
ADJ. **unleaded** fuel

**fuel cell** (**fuel cells**) N-COUNT A **fuel cell** is a device, similar to a battery, that converts chemicals into electricity. célula electroquímica, célula de combustible o celda de combustible

**Picture Dictionary** fruit

**fueled** /fyuəld/ also **fuelled** ADJ A machine or vehicle that **is fueled by** a particular substance works by burning that substance. *alimentado* ❑ *She's cooking on a stove fueled by natural gas. Está cocinando en una estufa alimentada con gas natural.*

**fu|gi|tive** /fyudʒɪtɪv/ (**fugitives**) N-COUNT A **fugitive** is someone who is running away or hiding, usually in order to avoid being caught by the police. *fugitivo o fugitiva* ❑ *The rebel leader was a fugitive from justice. El líder rebelde era fugitivo de la justicia.*

**fugue** /fyug/ (**fugues**) N-COUNT A **fugue** is a piece of music that begins with a simple tune which is then repeated by other voices or instrumental parts with small variations. *fuga* [TECHNICAL]

**ful|crum** /fʊlkrəm/ N-SING In physics, *the* **fulcrum** is the central point on which a lever balances when it is lifting or moving something. *fulcro, punto de apoyo*

**ful|fill** /fʊlfɪl/ (**fulfills, fulfilling, fulfilled**) **1** V-T If you **fulfill** a promise, dream, or hope, you do what you said or hoped you would do. *cumplir, hacer realidad* ❑ *She fulfilled her dream of starting law school. Hizo realidad su sueño de entrar a la escuela de leyes.* **2** V-T To **fulfill** a task, role, or requirement means to do or be what is required, necessary, or expected. *llevar a cabo, desempeñar, realizar* ❑ *Without their help you will not be able to fulfill the tasks you have before you. Sin su ayuda, no podrás llevar a cabo las tareas que tienes delante.* **3** V-T If something **fulfills** you, you feel happy and satisfied with what you are doing or with what you have achieved. *satisfacer, llenar* ❑ *Rachel knew that a life of luxury could not fulfill her. Rachel sabía que una vida de lujos no la llenaría.* • **ful|filled** ADJ *satisfecho, de satisfacciones, pleno* ❑ *...a fulfilled life. ...una vida plena.* • **ful|fil|ling** ADJ *pleno, satisfactorio* ❑ *...a fulfilling career. ...una carrera satisfactoria.* • **ful|fill|ment** N-UNCOUNT *satisfacción* ❑ *...professional fulfillment. ...satisfacción profesional.*

**full**

❶ CONTAINING AS MANY PEOPLE/ THINGS AS POSSIBLE
❷ COMPLETE, INCLUDING THE MAXIMUM POSSIBLE
❸ OTHER USES

❶ **full** /fʊl/ (**fuller, fullest**) **1** ADJ If something is **full,** it contains as much of a substance or as many objects as it can. *lleno* ❑ *Once the container is full, close it. Una vez lleno el recipiente, tápalo.* **2** ADJ If a place or thing **is full of** things or people, it contains a large number of them. *lleno* ❑ *The case was full of clothes. La caja estaba llena de ropa.* ❑ *The streets are still full of garbage from two nights of rioting. Las calles todavía están llenas de basura, después de dos noches de disturbios.* **3** ADJ If you feel **full,** you have eaten or drunk so much that you do not want anything else. *lleno, satisfecho* ❑ *It's healthy to eat when you're hungry and to stop when you're full. Lo saludable es comer cuando se tiene hambre y dejar de comer cuando se está satisfecho.* • **full|ness** N-UNCOUNT *plenitud, llenura, saciedad* ❑ *High-fiber diets give the feeling of fullness. Las dietas ricas en fibra dan la sensación de saciedad.*

| Thesaurus | *full* | Ver también: |
|---|---|---|
| ADJ. | brimming; (*ant.*) ;, empty ❶ **1** | |
| | loaded ❶ **1** **2** | |
| | bursting ❶ **2** | |

❷ **full** /fʊl/ (**fuller, fullest**) **1** ADJ If someone or something **is full of** a particular feeling or quality, they have a lot of it. *lleno* ❑ *I feel full of confidence. Me siento llena de confianza.* ❑ *Mom's face was full of pain. La cara de mamá reflejaba su gran dolor.* **2** ADJ You use **full** before a noun to indicate that you are referring to all the details, things, or people that it can possibly include. *completo, total, todo* ❑ *Full details will be sent to you once your application has been accepted. Una vez que se acepte su solicitud, se le enviarán todos los detalles.* ❑ *May I have your full name? ¿Me da su nombre completo?* **3** ADJ **Full** is used to describe a sound, light, or physical force which is being produced with the greatest possible power or intensity. *todo, pleno* ❑ *...the sound of Mahler, playing at full volume. ...la música de Mahler, a todo volumen.* ❑ *The operation will be carried out in full daylight. La operación se llevará a cabo a plena luz del día.* **4** ADJ If you say that someone has or leads a **full** life, you approve of the fact that they are always busy and do a lot of different things. *pleno* **5** PHRASE You say that something has been done or described **in full** when everything that was necessary has been done or described. *completamente, íntegramente, en detalle* ❑ *The medical experts have yet to report in full. Los expertos médicos aún tienen que informar en detalle.* **6** PHRASE Something that is done or experienced **to the full** is done to as great an extent as is possible. *al máximo* ❑ *A good mind should be used to the full. Una gran inteligencia debe aprovecharse al máximo.* **7** **full blast** → see **blast** **8** **in full swing** → see **swing**

❸ **full** /fʊl/ (**fuller, fullest**) **1** ADJ A **full** flavor is strong and rich. *intenso, concentrado* ❑ *Italian plum tomatoes have a full flavor. Los pequeños jitomates pera italianos tienen un sabor intenso.* **2** ADJ When there is a **full** moon, the moon appears as a bright, complete circle. *lleno*

**full-blown** ADJ **Full-blown** means having all the characteristics of a particular type of thing or person. *verdadero, auténtico, en toda la extensión de la palabra, todo* ❑ *Before becoming a full-blown director, he worked as a film editor. Antes de ser todo un director, era editor de películas.*

**full-flavored** ADJ **Full-flavored** food or drink has a pleasant fairly strong taste. *de sabor intenso*

**full-length** **1** ADJ A **full-length** book, record, or movie is the normal length, rather than being shorter than normal. *de largo normal, completo* **2** ADJ A **full-length** coat or skirt is long enough to reach the lower part of a person's leg. *largo* **3** ADJ A **full-length** mirror or painting shows the whole of a person. *de cuerpo entero* **4** ADV Someone who is lying **full-length** is lying down flat and stretched out. *cuan largo es* ❑ *She stretched herself out full-length. Se estiró cuan larga era.*

**full-scale** **1** ADJ **Full-scale** means as complete, intense, or great in extent as possible. *declarado, de gran envergadura* ❑ *...a full-scale nuclear war. ...una*

f

guerra nuclear declarada. **2** ADJ A **full-scale** drawing or model is the same size as the thing that it represents. de tamaño natural ❑ *The artist drew a full-scale sketch.* *El artista hizo un bosquejo de tamaño natural.*

**full-time** also **full time** ADJ **Full-time** work or study involves working or studying for the whole of each normal working week. de tiempo completo ❑ *...a full-time job.* *...un empleo de tiempo completo.* • **Full-time** is also an adverb. tiempo completo ❑ *Deirdre works full-time.* *Deirdre trabaja tiempo completo.*

F

**ful|ly** /fʊli/ **1** ADV **Fully** means to the greatest degree or extent possible. completamente, totalmente ❑ *She was fully aware of my thoughts.* *Estaba totalmente consciente de mis pensamientos.* **2** ADV If you describe, answer, or deal with something **fully,** you leave out nothing that should be mentioned or dealt with. del todo, por completo, en detalle, de lleno ❑ *He promised to answer fully and truthfully.* *Prometió contestar en detalle y verazmente.*

**Word Partnership** Usar *fully* con:

ADJ. fully **adjustable**, fully **aware**, fully **clothed**, fully **functional**, fully **operational**, fully **prepared** **1**
V. fully **agree**, fully **expect**, fully **extend**, fully **understand** **1**
fully **explain** **2**

**fun** /fʌn/ **1** N-UNCOUNT You refer to an activity or situation as **fun** if you think it is pleasant and enjoyable. diversión ❑ *It's been a learning adventure and it's also been great fun.* *Ha sido una aventura didáctica y también una gran diversión.* ❑ *It could be fun to watch them.* *Podría ser divertido verlos.* **2** N-UNCOUNT If you say that someone is **fun,** you mean that you enjoy being with them because they say and do interesting or amusing things. divertido ❑ *Liz was fun to be with.* *Era divertido estar con Liz.* **3** PHRASE If you do something **in fun,** you do it as a joke or for amusement, without intending to cause any harm. de chiste ❑ *Don't say such things, even in fun.* *No digas esas cosas, ni de chiste.* **4** PHRASE If you **make fun of** someone or something or **poke fun at** them, you laugh at them, tease them, or make jokes about them in a way that causes them to seem ridiculous. burlarse, reírse de ❑ *Don't make fun of me.* *No te burles de mí.*

**Thesaurus** *fun* Ver también:

N. amusement, enjoyment, play; (*ant.*) misery **1**
ADJ. amusing, enjoyable, entertaining, happy, pleasant; (*ant.*) boring **2**

**func|tion** /fʌŋkʃᵊn/ (**functions, functioning, functioned**) **1** N-COUNT The **function** of something or someone is the useful thing that they do or are intended to do. función ❑ *The main function of fat is as a store of energy.* *La principal función de la grasa es almacenar energía.* **2** N-COUNT A **function** is a large formal dinner or party. recepción, ceremonia, función ❑ *...a private function hosted by one of his students.* *...uno de sus estudiantes fue el anfitrión de la función privada.* **3** V-I If a machine or system **is functioning,** it is working or operating. funcionar ❑ *The prison is now functioning normally.* *La prisión ya está funcionando normalmente.* **4** V-I If someone or something **functions as** a particular thing, they do the work or fulfill the purpose of that thing. funcionar, hacer las veces de ❑ *On weekdays, one third of the living room functions as workspace.* *Durante la semana, una tercera parte de la sala funciona como lugar de trabajo.* **5** N-COUNT If you say that one thing is a **function** of another, you mean that its amount or nature depends on the other thing. función [FORMAL]

**func|tion|al** /fʌŋkʃənᵊl/ **1** ADJ **Functional** things are useful rather than decorative. funcional, práctico ❑ *...modern, functional furniture.* *...muebles modernos y funcionales.* **2** ADJ **Functional** equipment works or operates in the way that it is supposed to. en buen estado ❑ *We have fully functional smoke alarms on all staircases.* *Las alarmas de humo de todas las escaleras están en buen estado.*

**fund** /fʌnd/ (**funds, funding, funded**) **1** N-PLURAL **Funds** are amounts of money that are available to be spent, especially money that is given to an organization or person for a particular purpose. fondos, dinero ❑ *The concert will raise funds for research into cancer.* *El concierto es para recaudar fondos para la investigación sobre el cáncer.* **2** → see also **fund-raising** **3** N-COUNT A **fund** is an amount of money that is collected or saved for a particular purpose. fondo ❑ *...a scholarship fund for undergraduate engineering students.* *...un fondo para becar a estudiantes de la licenciatura en ingeniería.* **4** V-T When a person or organization **funds** something, they provide money for it. financiar ❑ *The Foundation has funded a variety of programs.* *La Fundación ha financiado diversos programas.*

**fun|da|men|tal** /fʌndəmɛntᵊl/ ADJ You use **fundamental** to describe things, activities, and principles that are very important or essential. fundamental ❑ *...the fundamental principles of democracy.* *...los principios fundamentales de la democracia.* ❑ *...a fundamental human right.* *...un derecho humano fundamental.* • **fun|da|men|tal|ly** ADV fundamentalmente, esencialmente ❑ *He is fundamentally a good man.* *Fundamentalmente es un buen hombre.*

**fun|da|men|tal|ism** /fʌndəmɛntᵊlɪzəm/ N-UNCOUNT **Fundamentalism** is the belief in the original form of a religion or theory, without accepting any later ideas. fundamentalismo ❑ *...religious fundamentalism.* *...fundamentalismo religioso.* • **fun|da|men|tal|ist** N-COUNT (**fundamentalists**) fundamentalista ❑ *...Christian fundamentalists.* *...fundamentalistas cristianos.*

**fun|da|men|tals** /fʌndəmɛntᵊlz/ N-PLURAL **The fundamentals** of something are its simplest, most important elements, ideas, or principles. fundamento, principio, base ❑ *Come and learn the fundamentals of effective speaking.* *Venga a aprender los fundamentos de la buena expresión.*

**fund|ing** /fʌndɪŋ/ N-UNCOUNT **Funding** is money which a government or organization provides for a particular purpose. financiación, financiamiento, fondos, recursos ❑ *They hope for government funding for the program.* *Esperan obtener fondos del gobierno para el programa.*

**fund man|ag|er** (**fund managers**) N-COUNT

A **fund manager** is someone whose job involves investing the money contained in a fund, for example, a mutual fund, on behalf of another person or organization. *administrador financiero o administradora financiera*

**fund|rais|er** /fʌndreɪzər/ (**fundraisers**) also **fund-raiser** 1 N-COUNT A **fundraiser** is an event which is intended to raise money for a particular purpose. *evento para recaudar fondos* ❑ *Organize a fundraiser for your church. Organiza un evento para recaudar fondos para tu iglesia.* 2 N-COUNT A **fundraiser** is someone who works to raise money for a particular purpose, for example, for a charity. *recaudador de fondos o recaudadora de fondos* ❑ *...a fundraiser for the Democrats. ...un recaudador de fondos para los Demócratas.*

**fund-raising** also **fundraising** N-UNCOUNT **Fund-raising** is the activity of collecting money to support a charity or political campaign or organization. *recaudación de fondos*

**fu|ner|al** /fyunərəl/ (**funerals**) N-COUNT A **funeral** is the ceremony that is held when the body of someone who has died is buried or cremated. *funeral* ❑ *The funeral will be held in Joplin, Missouri. El funeral tendrá lugar en Joplin, Missouri.*

**fu|ner|al home** (**funeral homes**) N-COUNT A **funeral home** is a place where the body of a dead person is taken to be prepared for burial or cremation. *funeraria*

**fu|ner|al par|lor** (**funeral parlors**) N-COUNT A **funeral parlor** is the same as a **funeral home**. *funeraria*

**fun|gus** /fʌŋgəs/ (**fungi** /fʌndʒaɪ, -ŋgaɪ/ or **funguses**) N-VAR A **fungus** is a plant that has no flowers, leaves, or green coloring, such as a mushroom or a toadstool. *hongo* ● **fun|gal** ADJ *micótico, de los hongos* ❑ *...fungal growth. ...brote de hongos.*
→ see Word Web: **fungus**

**funky** /fʌŋki/ (**funkier, funkiest**) ADJ If you describe something or someone as **funky,** you like them because they are unconventional or unusual. *en la onda, original* [INFORMAL] ❑ *It had a certain funky charm, but it wasn't a place to raise a kid. Tenía cierto encanto original, pero no era lugar para criar a un niño.*

**fun|ny** /fʌni/ (**funnier, funniest**) 1 ADJ Someone or something that is **funny** is amusing and likely to make you smile or laugh. *divertido, chistoso, cómico, gracioso* ❑ *I'll tell you a funny story. Te voy a contar una historia chistosa.* 2 ADJ If you describe something as **funny,** you think it is strange, surprising, or puzzling. *raro, extraño, curioso, ocurrente* ❑ *Children get some very funny ideas sometimes! ¡A veces los niños tienen ideas ocurrentes!* ❑ *There's something funny about him. Hay algo extraño en él.* 3 ADJ If you feel **funny,** you feel slightly ill. *raro, medio mal* [INFORMAL] ❑ *My head began to ache and my stomach felt funny. Me empezó a doler la cabeza y me sentí medio mal del estómago.*

**Thesaurus** *funny* Ver también:
ADJ. amusing, comical, entertaining; (*ant.*) serious 1
bizarre, odd, peculiar 2

**fur** /fɜr/ (**furs**) 1 N-UNCOUNT **Fur** is the thick and usually soft hair that grows on the bodies of many mammals. *piel, pelo, pelaje* ❑ *This creature's fur is short, dense, and silky. El pelo de este animal es corto, denso y sedoso.* 2 N-COUNT A **fur** is a coat made from fur. *pieles* ❑ *...women in furs. ...mujeres ataviadas con pieles.*

**fu|ri|ous** /fyʊəriəs/ 1 ADJ Someone who is **furious** is extremely angry. *furioso, furibundo* ❑ *He is furious at the way his wife has been treated. Está furioso por la forma en que han tratado a su esposa.* ● **fu|ri|ous|ly** ADV *furiosamente* ❑ *He stormed out of the apartment, slamming the door furiously behind him. Se salió del departamento y azotó furiosamente la puerta tras él.* 2 ADJ **Furious** is used to describe something that is done with great energy, effort, speed, or violence. *febril, feroz, frenético* ❑ *...a furious gunbattle. ...una balacera feroz.* ● **fu|ri|ous|ly** ADV *febrilmente, intensamente* ❑ *Doctors worked furiously to save their friend's life. Los médicos trabajaron intensamente para salvar la vida de su amigo.*
→ see **anger**

**fur|nace** /fɜrnɪs/ (**furnaces**) N-COUNT A **furnace** is a container or enclosed space in which a very hot fire is made, for example, to melt metal, burn trash, or produce heat for a building or house. *horno, caldera, alto horno*

**fur|nish** /fɜrnɪʃ/ (**furnishes, furnishing, furnished**) 1 V-T If you **furnish** a room or building, you put furniture and furnishings into it. *amueblar, amoblar* ❑ *Many owners try to furnish their hotels with antiques. Muchos propietarios tratan de amueblar sus hoteles con antigüedades.* ● **fur|nished** ADJ *amueblado* ❑ *...his sparsely furnished house. ...su casa apenas amueblada.* 2 V-T If you **furnish** someone **with** something, you provide or supply

**Word Web** **fungus**

**Fungi** can be both harmful and helpful. For example, **mold** and **mildew** destroy crops, ruin clothing, cause diseases, and can even lead to death. But many fungi are useful. For instance, a single-cell fungus called **yeast** makes bread rise. Another form of yeast makes wine **ferment**. It turns the sugar in grape juice into alcohol. And **mushrooms** are a part of the diet of people all over the world. Cheese makers use a specific fungus to produce the creamy white skin on brie. A different **microorganism** gives blue cheese its characteristic color. Truffles, the most expensive fungi, cost more than $100 an ounce.

it. proveer, surtir, proporcionar [FORMAL] ❑ *They'll be able to furnish you with the rest of the details.* Ellos podrán proporcionarle los demás detalles.

**fur|ni|ture** /fɜrnɪtʃər/ N-UNCOUNT **Furniture** consists of large objects such as tables, chairs, or beds that are used in a room for sitting or lying on or for putting things on. muebles ❑ *Each piece of furniture suited the style of the house.* Cada mueble era adecuado al estilo de la casa.

**fur|ther** /fɜrðər/ (**furthers, furthering, furthered**)

> **Further** is a comparative form of **far**. It is also a verb.

1 ADV **Further** means to a greater extent or degree. más, aún más, todavía más ❑ *Inflation is below 5% and set to fall further.* La inflación está por debajo del 5% y bajará aún más. ❑ *The rebellion further damaged the country's image.* La rebelión perjudicó todavía más la imagen del país. 2 ADV If you go or get **further with** something, or take something **further,** you make some progress. más allá, más adelante ❑ *We've got a great chance of going further in this competition.* Tenemos una gran oportunidad de avanzar más en la competencia. 3 ADV **Further** means a greater distance than before or than something else. más lejos, más allá ❑ *People are living further away from their jobs.* La gente vive cada vez más lejos de su trabajo. ❑ *...a main road fifty yards further on.* ...un camino principal cincuenta metros más allá. 4 ADV **Further** is used in expressions such as "**further back**" and "**further ahead**" to refer to a point in time that is earlier or later than the time you are talking about. remontarse, retroceder, adelantarse, anticiparse ❑ *Looking still further ahead, by the end of the next century world population is expected to be about ten billion.* Anticipándonos aún más, se espera que hacia finales del próximo siglo, la población del mundo sea de unos diez mil millones. 5 ADJ A **further** thing, number of things, or amount of something is an additional thing, number of things, or amount. otro, adicional ❑ *...further evidence of slowing economic growth.* ...pruebas adicionales de la desaceleración del crecimiento económico. 6 V-T If you **further** something, you help it to progress, to be successful, or to be achieved. adelantar, favorecer, fomentar ❑ *Education isn't only about furthering your career.* La educación no es sólo para avanzar en tu carrera.

**fur|ther edu|ca|tion** N-UNCOUNT **Further education** is the education of people who have left school but who are not at a university or a college of education. educación continua, educación para adultos, programas de extensión universitaria

**further|more** /fɜrðərmɔr/ ADV **Furthermore** is used to introduce a piece of information or opinion that adds to or supports the previous one. además, por otra parte [FORMAL] ❑ *It's nearly dark, and furthermore it's going to rain.* Ya casi ha anochecido; además, va a llover.

**fur|thest** /fɜrðɪst/

> **Furthest** is a superlative form of **far**.

1 ADV **Furthest** means to a greater extent or degree than ever before or than anything or anyone else. aún más, todavía más ❑ *Prices have fallen furthest in the south.* Los precios han caído aún más en el sur. 2 ADV **Furthest** means at a greater distance from a particular point than anyone or anything else, or for a greater distance than anyone or anything else. más lejano, extremo ❑ *...those areas furthest from the coast.* ...esas áreas más lejanas de la costa. ● **Furthest** is also an adjective. ...más lejano ❑ *...the furthest point from Earth that any spacecraft has ever been.* ...el punto más lejano de la Tierra en que haya alcanzado una nave espacial.

**fury** /fyʊəri/ N-UNCOUNT **Fury** is violent or very strong anger. furia, ira, furor ❑ *She screamed, her face distorted with fury.* Gritó con el rostro congestionado por la ira.

**fuse** /fyuz/ (**fuses, fusing, fused**)

> The spelling **fuze** is also used for meaning 2.

1 N-COUNT A **fuse** is a safety device in an electric plug or circuit. It contains a piece of wire which melts when there is a fault so that the flow of electricity stops. fusible, tapón ❑ *The fuse blew as he pressed the button to start the motor.* El fusible se quemó cuando apretó el botón de arranque del motor. 2 N-COUNT A **fuse** is a device on a bomb or firework which delays the explosion so that people can move a safe distance away. fusible ❑ *Some witnesses said he lit the fuse, others that he made the bomb.* Algunos testigos dicen que él hizo estallar la bomba, otros, encendió la mecha, otros, que él la hizo. 3 V-RECIP When things **fuse** or **are fused,** they join together physically or chemically, usually to become one thing. fundir(se), fusionar(se), amalgamar(se) ❑ *The skull bones fuse between the ages of fifteen and twenty-five.* Los huesos del cráneo se fusionan entre los quince y los veinticinco años de edad. ❑ *Manufactured glass is made by fusing various types of sand.* El vidrio manufacturado se produce fusionando varios tipos de arena.

**fu|sion** /fyuʒᵊn/ (**fusions**) 1 N-VAR The **fusion** of two or more things involves joining them together to form one thing. fusión ❑ *...a delicate fusion of Eastern and Western art.* ...una delicada fusión de arte oriental y occidental. 2 N-UNCOUNT In physics, **fusion** is the process in which atomic particles combine and produce a large amount of nuclear energy. fusión ❑ *...research into nuclear fusion.* ...la investigación sobre la fusión nuclear.
→ see **sun**

**fuss** /fʌs/ (**fusses, fussing, fussed**) 1 N-SING **Fuss** is anxious or excited behavior which serves no useful purpose. alboroto, escándalo, agitación ❑ *I don't know what all the fuss is about.* No entiendo por qué tanto alboroto. 2 V-I If you **fuss,** you worry or behave in a nervous, anxious way about unimportant matters or rush around doing unnecessary things. preocupar(se), inquietar(se), ir de aquí para allá, complicar(se)la existencia ❑ *Carol fussed about getting me a drink.* Carol se complicó la existencia preparándome algo de tomar. ❑ *My wife was fussing over the clothing we were going to take.* Mi esposa iba de aquí para allá por la ropa que íbamos a llevar. 3 V-I If you **fuss over** someone, you pay them a lot of attention and do things to make them happy or comfortable. mimar, consentir, hacer fiestas ❑ *Aunt Laura fussed over him all afternoon.* La tía Laura le estuvo haciendo fiestas toda la tarde.

**fu|ture** /fyu̲tʃər/ (**futures**) **1** N-SING **The future** is the period of time that will come after the present. futuro, porvenir ❑ *No decision on the proposal is likely in the immediate future.* *No es probable que se decida sobre la propuesta en el futuro inmediato.* ❑ *He was making plans for the future.* *Estaba haciendo planes para el futuro.* **2** ADJ **Future** things will happen or exist after the present time. futuro ❑ *...the future king and queen.* *...los futuros rey y reina.* **3** N-COUNT Someone's **future,** or **the future of** something, is what will happen to them or what they will do after the present time. futuro, porvenir ❑ *His future depends on the outcome of the elections.* *Su futuro depende del resultado de las elecciones.* **4** PHRASE You use **in the future** when you are saying what will happen from now on, and you are emphasizing that this will be different from what has previously happened. en el futuro, en un futuro ❑ *I asked her to be more careful in the future.* *Le pedí que en el futuro fuera más cuidadosa.*

**Word Partnership** Usar *future* con:

ADJ. **bright** future, **distant** future, **immediate** future, **near** future, **uncertain** future **1**
V. **discuss the** future, **have a** future, **plan for the** future, **predict/see the** future **1**
N. future **date**, future **events**, future **generations**, future **plans**, **for** future **reference** **2**

**fuzzy** /fʌ̲zi/ (**fuzzier, fuzziest**) **1** ADJ **Fuzzy** hair sticks up in a soft, curly mass. chino, rizado, crespo **2** ADJ A **fuzzy** picture, image, or sound is unclear and hard to see or hear. borroso, confuso ❑ *A couple of fuzzy pictures have been published.* *Se publicó un par de imágenes borrosas.*

**FYI** **FYI** is a written abbreviation for "for your information," often used in notes and documents when giving someone additional information about something. para su información ❑ *The town's postmaster is called Jamie Ablerd [FYI she's a female].* *El administrador de correos del pueblo se llama Jamie Ablerd [para su información, es mujer].*

# Gg



**gadg|et** /gædʒɪt/ (**gadgets**) N-COUNT A **gadget** is a small machine or device which does something useful. *instrumento, artefacto, artilugio, aparato, chisme* ❑ *...kitchen gadgets such as can openers and bottle openers. ...instrumentos de cocina, como abrelatas y destapadores.*
→ see **technology**

**gag or|der** (**gag orders**) N-COUNT If a judge puts a **gag order** on information relating to a legal case, people involved in the case are banned from discussing it in public or writing about it. *orden mordaza*

**gag rule** (**gag rules**) N-COUNT A **gag rule** is an official restriction that forbids people from discussing something in a particular place. *ley mordaza*

**gain** /geɪn/ (**gains, gaining, gained**) **1** V-T If you **gain** something, you acquire it gradually. *ganar, adquirir* ❑ *Students can gain valuable experience by working during their vacations. Los estudiantes pueden adquirir una experiencia valiosa trabajando durante las vacaciones.* **2** V-T/V-I If you **gain from** something such as an event or situation, you get some advantage from it. *ganar, salir ganando* ❑ *The company expects to gain billions from the deal. La empresa espera ganar miles de millones con el contrato.* ❑ *Everybody is going to gain from working together. Todos van a salir ganando al trabajar juntos.* **3** V-T To **gain** something such as weight or speed means to have an increase in that particular thing. *subir, cobrar, aumentar* ❑ *Some women gain weight after they have a baby. Algunas mujeres suben de peso despúes de tener un bebé.* ❑ *The car was gaining speed as it approached. El carro cobraba velocidad conforme se acercaba.* • **Gain** is also a noun. *ganancia, incremento* ❑ *Sales showed a gain of nearly 8% last month. El mes pasado, las ventas tuvieron un incremento de casi el 8 por ciento.* **4** V-T If you **gain** something, you obtain it, usually after a lot of effort. *conseguir, lograr* ❑ *To gain a promotion, you might have to work overtime. Para conseguir el ascenso, quizá tengas que trabajar horas extra.* **5** PHRASE If something such as an idea or an ideal **gains ground,** it gradually becomes more widely known or more popular. *ganar terreno* ❑ *His views are gaining ground. Sus opiniones están ganando terreno.*

**gal|axy** /gæləksi/ (**galaxies**) also **Galaxy** N-COUNT A **galaxy** is an extremely large group of stars and planets that extends over many billions of light years. *galaxia* ❑ *Astronomers have discovered a distant galaxy. Los astrónomos descubrieron una galaxia lejana.*
→ see Word Web: **galaxy**
→ see **star**

**gale** /geɪl/ (**gales**) N-COUNT A **gale** is a very strong wind. *vendaval* ❑ *There could be gales over the next few days. Podría haber vendavales durante los próximos días.*
→ see **wind**

**gal|lery** /gæləri/ (**galleries**) **1** N-COUNT A **gallery** is a place where people go to look at works of art. *galería* ❑ *...an art gallery. ...una galería de arte.* **2** N-COUNT **The gallery** in a theater or concert hall is an area high above the ground that usually contains the cheapest seats. *galería* ❑ *They got cheap tickets in the gallery. Consiguieron boletos baratos para la galería.*

**gal|lon** /gælən/ (**gallons**) N-COUNT A **gallon** is a unit of measurement for liquids that is equal to eight pints or 3.785 liters. *galón* ❑ *...80 million gallons of water. ...302,833 m3 de agua.*
→ see **measurement**

**gam|ble** /gæmb$^{ə}$l/ (**gambles, gambling, gambled**) **1** N-COUNT A **gamble** is a risky action or decision that you take in the hope of gaining money, success, or an advantage over other people. *apuesta, riesgo* ❑ *She took a gamble and started up her own business. Corrió el riesgo e inició su propio negocio.* **2** V-T/V-I If you **gamble on** something, you take

**Word Web** **galaxy**

The word **galaxy** with a small g refers to an extremely large group of **stars** and **planets.** It measures billions of **light years** wide. There are about 100 billion galaxies in the **universe. Astronomers** classify galaxies into four different types. Irregular galaxies have no particular shape. Elliptical galaxies look like flattened spheres. Spiral galaxies have long curving arms. A barred spiral galaxy has straight lines of stars extending from its nucleus. Galaxy with a capital G refers to our own **solar system.** The name of this galaxy is the **Milky Way.** It is about 100,000 light years wide.

a risky action or decision in the hope of gaining money, success, or an advantage over other people. *jugársela* ❑ *Companies sometimes have to gamble on new products. A veces las empresas tienen que jugársela con los nuevos productos.* ❑ *He gambled his career on this movie. Se jugó la carrera con esta película.* **3** V-T/V-I If you **gamble,** you bet money in a game or on the result of a race or competition. *apostar* ❑ *Most people visit Las Vegas to gamble their money. La mayoría de la gente visita Las Vegas para apostar su dinero.* ❑ *John gambled heavily on horse racing. John apostó mucho en las carreras de caballos.*

**gam|bling** /gæmblɪŋ/ N-UNCOUNT **Gambling** is the act or activity of betting money, for example in card games or on horse racing. *juego* ❑ *The gambling laws are quite tough. Las leyes sobre los juegos de azar son muy estrictas.*

**game** /geɪm/ (**games**) **1** N-COUNT A **game** is an activity or sport usually involving skill, knowledge, or chance, in which you follow fixed rules and try to win against an opponent or to solve a puzzle. *juego, deporte, juego de azar* ❑ *Football is a popular game. El futbol es un deporte popular.* ❑ *...a game of cards. ...un juego de cartas.* **2** N-COUNT A **game** is one particular occasion on which a game is played. *juego* ❑ *It was the first game of the season. Fue el primer juego de la temporada.* **3** N-COUNT In sports such as tennis, a **game** is a part of a match. *juego* ❑ *She won the first game of the tennis match. Ella ganó el primer juego del partido de tenis.* **4** N-PLURAL **Games** are an organized event in which competitions in several sports take place. *juegos* ❑ *...the 1996 Olympic Games in Atlanta. ...las Olimpiadas de 1996 en Atlanta.* **5** N-COUNT You can describe a way of behaving as a **game** when a person uses it to gain an advantage. *juego* ❑ *The Americans are playing a very delicate political game. Los estadounidenses participan en un juego político muy delicado.* **6** N-UNCOUNT **Game** is wild animals or birds that are hunted for sport or food. *caza, animal de caza* ❑ *The men shot game for food. Los hombres cazaron para la comida.* **7** ADJ If you are **game for** something, you are willing to do something new, unusual, or risky. *estar dispuesto* ❑ *He's always game for a challenge. Siempre está dispuesto para el reto.* **8** PHRASE If you beat someone **at** their **own game,** you use the same methods that they have used, but more successfully, so that you gain an advantage over them. *ganarle a alguien con sus propias armas* ❑ *He must beat the other lawyers at their own game. Debe vencer a los otros abogados con sus propias armas.* **9** PHRASE If someone or something **gives the game away,** they reveal a secret or reveal their feelings, and this puts them at a disadvantage. *abrir las cartas, descubrir el pastel, delatarse* ❑ *Their faces gave the game away. Su cara los delató.*

→ see **chess, mammal**

**ga|meto|phyte** /gəmitəfaɪt/ (**gametophytes**) N-COUNT A **gametophyte** is a stage in the life of a plant when it produces eggs and sperm, or a plant during this stage of its life. *gametofito* [TECHNICAL]

**gam|ing** /geɪmɪŋ/ N-UNCOUNT **Gaming** means the same as **gambling**. *juego* ❑ *Gaming is illegal in some places. El juego es ilegal en algunos lugares.*

**gam|ma rays** N-PLURAL **Gamma rays** are a type of electromagnetic radiation that has a shorter wavelength and higher energy than X-rays. *rayos gamma*

→ see **telescope**

**gang** /gæŋ/ (**gangs, ganging, ganged**) **1** N-COUNT A **gang** is a group of people, especially young people, who go around together and often deliberately cause trouble. *pandilla, banda, grupo, grupito* ❑ *...a fight with a rival gang. ...una pelea con una banda rival.* **2** N-COUNT A **gang** is a group of criminals who work together to commit crimes. *banda* ❑ *Police are hunting for a gang that have stolen several cars. La policía busca una banda que ha robado varios automóviles.* **3** N-COUNT A **gang** is a group of workers who do physical work together. *cuadrilla, brigada* ❑ *...a gang of laborers. ...una cuadrilla de peones.*

▸ **gang up** PHR-VERB If people **gang up on** someone, they unite against them. *confabularse contra, tomarla contra* [INFORMAL] ❑ *Harrison complained that his colleagues ganged up on him. Harrison se quejó de que sus colegas la habían tomado contra él.* ❑ *All the other parties ganged up to keep them out of power. Los demás partidos se confabularon para mantenerlo alejado del poder.*

| **Thesaurus** | *gang* | Ver también: |
|---|---|---|
| N. | crowd, group, pack **1** | |
| | mob, ring **2** | |

**gan|gli|on** /gæŋgliən/ (**ganglia**) N-COUNT **Ganglia** are groups of nerve cells, usually outside the central nervous system. *ganglio* [TECHNICAL]

**gang|ster** /gæŋstər/ (**gangsters**) N-COUNT A **gangster** is a member of an organized group of violent criminals. *gángster, pandillero o pandillera, pistolero o pistolera* ❑ *...a gangster movie. ...una película de gángsters.*

**gap** /gæp/ (**gaps**) **1** N-COUNT A **gap** is a space between two things or a hole in the middle of something solid. *espacio, abertura, brecha, separación* ❑ *There was a narrow gap between the curtains. Había una pequeña separación entre las cortinas.* **2** N-COUNT A **gap** is a period of time when you are not busy or when you stop doing something that you normally do. *intervalo* ❑ *There was a gap of five years between the birth of her two children. Había un intervalo de cinco años entre sus dos hijos.* **3** N-COUNT If there is something missing from a situation that prevents it from being complete or satisfactory, you can say that there is a **gap.** *brecha, espacio, hueco* ❑ *We need more young teachers to fill the gap left by retirements. Necesitamos más maestros jóvenes para llenar los huecos que han dejado las jubilaciones.* **4** N-COUNT A **gap between** two groups of people, things, or sets of ideas is a big difference between them. *brecha* ❑ *...the gap between rich and poor. ...la brecha entre ricos y pobres.*

**gap hy|poth|esis** N-SING The **gap hypothesis** is a theory in geology which states that strong earthquakes are more likely to occur close to fault lines that have had few earthquakes in the past. *hipótesis de la falla* [TECHNICAL]

**gar|age** /gərɑʒ/ (**garages**) **1** N-COUNT A **garage** is a building in which you keep a car. *garage, garaje* ❑ *They have turned the garage into a study. Convirtieron el garage en estudio.* **2** N-COUNT A **garage** is a place where you can get your car repaired. *taller* ❑ *Nancy* *took her car to a local garage. Nancy llevó su auto a un taller local.*

**gar|age sale** (**garage sales**) N-COUNT If you have a **garage sale,** you sell things such as clothes, toys, and household items that you do not want, usually in your garage. *venta de garage*

**gar|bage** /gɑrbɪdʒ/ **1** N-UNCOUNT **Garbage** is waste material, especially waste from a kitchen. *basura* ❑ *...a garbage bag. ...una bolsa de basura.* **2** N-UNCOUNT If someone says that an idea or opinion is **garbage,** they are emphasizing that they believe it is untrue or unimportant. *basura, porquería* [INFORMAL] ❑ *I think this theory is garbage. Pienso que esa teoría es basura.*

→ see **pollution**

G

**Thesaurus** *garbage* Ver también:

N. junk, litter, rubbish, trash **1**
foolishness, nonsense **2**

garbage can

**gar|bage can** (**garbage cans**) N-COUNT A **garbage can** is a container that you put rubbish into. *bote de basura, basurero*

**gar|bage col|lec|tor** (**garbage collectors**) N-COUNT A **garbage collector** is a person whose job is to take people's garbage away. *basurero*

**gar|bage dis|pos|al** (**garbage disposals**) N-COUNT A **garbage disposal** or a **garbage disposal unit** is a small machine in the kitchen sink that breaks down waste matter so that it does not block the sink. *triturador o trituradora*

**gar|bage dump** (**garbage dumps**) N-COUNT A **garbage dump** is a place where garbage is left. *basurero, relleno sanitario, tiradero*

**gar|bage man** (**garbage men**) N-COUNT A **garbage man** is the same as a **garbage collector**. *basurero*

**gar|bage truck** (**garbage trucks**) N-COUNT A **garbage truck** is a large truck which collects the garbage from outside people's houses. *carro de la basura, camión de la basura*

**gar|den** /gɑrdᵊn/ (**gardens, gardening, gardened**) **1** N-COUNT A **garden** is the part of a yard which is used for growing flowers and vegetables. *jardín* ❑ *She had a beautiful garden. Tenía un lindo jardín.* **2** V-I If you **garden,** you do work in your garden such as weeding or planting. *trabajar en el jardín, jardinear, hacer el jardín* ❑ *Jim gardened on weekends. Jim hacía el jardín los fines de semana.* ● **gar|den|er** N-COUNT *jardinero o jardinera* (**gardeners**) ❑ *She employed a gardener. Ella contrataba un jardinero.* ● **gar|den|ing** N-UNCOUNT *jardinería* ❑ *My favorite hobby is gardening. Mi pasatiempo favorito es la jardinería.* **3** N-PLURAL **Gardens** are places with plants, trees, and grass, that people can visit. *jardines* ❑ *The gardens are open from 10:30 a.m. until 5:00 p.m. Los jardines están abiertos de 10:30 am a 5:00 pm.*

→ see Picture Dictionary: **garden**

→ see **park**

**garden-variety** ADJ You can use **garden-variety** to describe something you think is ordinary and not special in any way. *lugar común, común y corriente, casero* ❑ *The experiment is garden-variety science. El experimento es de ciencia común y corriente.*

**gar|lic** /gɑrlɪk/ N-UNCOUNT **Garlic** is the small, white, round bulb of a plant. It has a strong flavor and is used in cooking. *ajo* ❑ *...a clove of garlic. ...un diente de ajo.*

→ see **spice**

**gar|ment** /gɑrmənt/ (**garments**) N-COUNT A **garment** is a piece of clothing. *prenda de vestir, ropa* ❑ *Exports of garments to the U.S. fell 3%. La exportación de prendas de vestir a EU cayó 3 por ciento.*

**gas** /gæs/ (**gases, gasses, gassing, gassed**)

The form **gases** is the plural of the noun. The form **gasses** is the third person singular of the verb.

**1** N-VAR A **gas** is any substance that is neither

**Picture Dictionary** garden

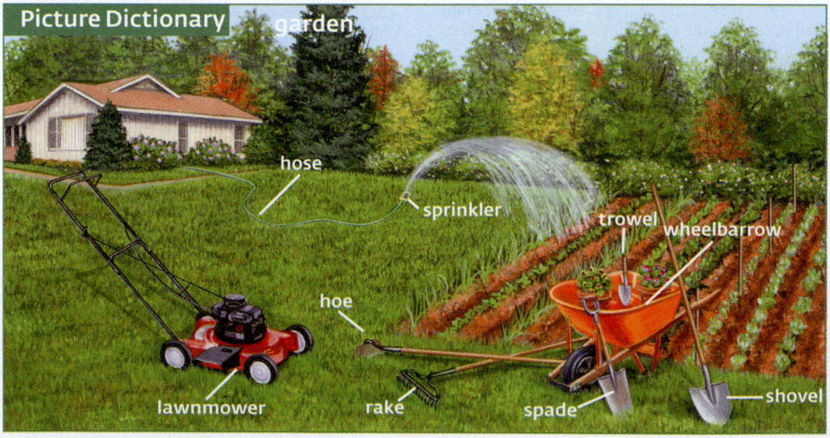

liquid nor solid, for example oxygen or hydrogen. *gas* ❑ *Hydrogen is a gas, not a metal.* *El hidrógeno es un gas, no un metal.* **2** N-VAR **Gas** is a poisonous gas that can be used as a weapon. *gas* ❑ *...a gas attack.* *...un ataque con gases.* **3** N-UNCOUNT **Gas** is the fuel which is used to drive motor vehicles. *gasolina* ❑ *...a tank of gas.* *...un tanque de gasolina.* **4** V-T To **gas** a person or animal means to kill them by making them breathe poisonous gas. *gasear, asfixiar con gas, matar en la cámara de gases* ❑ *They attempted to gas the rats.* *Trataron de asfixiar con gas a las ratas.* **5** PHRASE If you **step on the gas** when you are driving a vehicle, you go faster. *pisar el acelerador, acelerar* [INFORMAL] **6** → see also **greenhouse gas**
→ see **air, greenhouse effect, matter, petroleum, solar system**

**gas ex|change** N-UNCOUNT **Gas exchange** is the same as **respiration**. *intercambio de gases, respiración* [TECHNICAL]

**gas gi|ant** (**gas giants**) N-COUNT A **gas giant** is a large planet that is composed mainly of gas, such as Neptune or Jupiter. *gigante gaseoso* [TECHNICAL]

**gas guz|zler** (**gas guzzlers**) also **gas-guzzler** N-COUNT If you say that a car is a **gas guzzler** you mean that it uses a lot of fuel and is not cheap to run. *tragón de gasolina* [INFORMAL] ❑ *He drives one of those big gas guzzlers.* *Tiene uno de esos enormes coches tragones de gasolina.*

**gaso|hol** /gæsəhɔl/ N-UNCOUNT **Gasohol** is a mixture of gasoline and alcohol that can be used instead of gasoline in cars. *gasohol*

**gaso|line** /gæsəlin/ N-UNCOUNT **Gasoline** is the fuel which is used to drive motor vehicles. *gasolina*
→ see **oil, petroleum**

**gasp** /gæsp/ (**gasps, gasping, gasped**)
**1** N-COUNT A **gasp** is a short, quick breath of air that you take in through your mouth, especially when you are surprised, shocked, or in pain. *resuello, suspiro, exclamación* ❑ *A gasp went around the court as the jury announced the verdict.* *Cuando el juez anunció el veredicto, se oyó una exclamación en el tribunal.* **2** V-I When you **gasp**, you take a short, quick breath through your mouth, especially when you are surprised, shocked, or in pain. *suspirar, jadear, respirar con dificultad* ❑ *She gasped for air.* *Ella respiró con dificultad.* **3** PHRASE You describe something as **the last gasp** to emphasize that it is the final part of something or happens at the last possible moment. *último suspiro, últimos momentos* ❑ *...the last gasp of the Roman Empire.* *...los últimos momentos del Imperio Romano.*

**gas pe|dal** (**gas pedals**) N-COUNT **The gas pedal** is another name for the **accelerator**. *acelerador*

**gas sta|tion** (**gas stations**) N-COUNT A **gas station** is a place where you can buy fuel for your car. *gasolinera, estación de gasolina*

**gas tank** (**gas tanks**) N-COUNT The **gas tank** in a motor vehicle is the container for gas. *tanque de gasolina* ❑ *The gas tank holds 15 gallons.* *Al tanque de gasolina le caben 57 litros.*

**gate** /geɪt/ (**gates**) **1** N-COUNT A **gate** is a structure like a door which is used at the entrance to a field, a garden, or the grounds of a building. *reja, portón, puerta* ❑ *He opened the gate and walked up to the house.* *Abrió la reja y caminó hacia la casa.* **2** N-COUNT In an airport, a **gate** is a place where passengers leave the airport and get on their airplane. *puerta de embarque, puerta* ❑ *Please go to gate 15.* *Favor de dirigirse a la puerta 15.*

**gat|ed com|mu|nity** (**gated communities**) N-COUNT A **gated community** is an area of houses and sometimes stores that is surrounded by a wall or fence and has an entrance that is guarded. *fraccionamiento cerrado*

**gath|er** /gæðər/ (**gathers, gathering, gathered**)
**1** V-T/V-I If people **gather** somewhere, or if someone **gathers** them, they come together in a group. *reunir(se), juntar(se)* ❑ *We gathered around the fireplace and talked.* *Nos reunimos a platicar en torno a la chimenea.* **2** V-T If you **gather** things, you collect them together so that you can use them. *juntar, reunir, recoger, acumular* ❑ *They gathered enough firewood to last the night.* *Juntaron suficiente leña para toda la noche.* ❑ *He used a hidden tape recorder to gather information.* *Utilizó una grabadora oculta para reunir información.* ● **Gather up** means the same as **gather**. *juntar, reunir, recoger, acumular* ❑ *Steve gathered up his papers and went out.* *Steve juntó sus papeles y se fue.* **3** V-T If something **gathers** speed, momentum, or force, it gradually becomes faster or more powerful. *cobrar* ❑ *Demands for reform gathered momentum.* *Las demandas de reformas cobraron ímpetu.* **4** V-T You use **gather** in expressions such as "**I gather**" and "**as far as I can gather**" to introduce information that you have found out, especially when you have found it out in an indirect way. *tener entendido, deducir* ❑ *I gather he didn't enjoy the show.* *Tengo entendido que no le gustó el espectáculo.* ❑ *"He speaks English," she said to Graham. "I gathered that."* *—Tengo entendido que habla inglés—le dijo a Graham.—Ya lo había deducido.* **5** **to gather dust** → see **dust**
▸ **gather up** → see **gather 2**

**gath|er|ing** /gæðərɪŋ/ (**gatherings**) N-COUNT A **gathering** is a group of people meeting together for a particular purpose. *reunión, asamblea* ❑ *...a large family gathering.* *...una gran reunión familiar.*

**gator** /geɪtər/ (**gators**) also **'gator** N-COUNT A **gator** is the same as an **alligator**. *caimán, lagarto, cocodrilo* [INFORMAL]

**gauge** /geɪdʒ/ (**gauges, gauging, gauged**)
**1** V-T If you **gauge** something, you measure it or judge it. *calcular, medir, ponderar, evaluar, valorar, estimar, juzgar* ❑ *She found it hard to gauge his mood.* *Le costó trabajo juzgar su estado de ánimo.* **2** N-COUNT A **gauge** is a device that measures the amount or quantity of something and shows the amount measured. *medidor* ❑ *...temperature gauges.* *...medidores de temperatura.* **3** N-SING A **gauge of** a situation is a fact or event that can be used to judge it. *indicio* ❑ *Letters to the newspapers are a gauge of how people feel.* *Las cartas a los periódicos son un indicio de lo que la gente siente.*

**gave** /geɪv/ **Gave** is the past tense of **give**. *pasado de give*

**gay** /geɪ/ (**gays**) ADJ A **gay** person is homosexual. *gay, homosexual* ❑ *The quality of life for gay men has improved.* *La calidad de vida de los varones homosexuales ha mejorado.* ● **Gay** people are sometimes referred to as **gays**, especially when comparing different groups of people. Other uses of the word could cause offense. *homosexuales* ❑ *It's a friendly city for gays to move to.* *Es una ciudad donde los homosexuales se sienten bienvenidos.*

**gaze** /geɪz/ (**gazes, gazing, gazed**) **1** V-I If you **gaze at** someone or something, you look steadily at them for a long time, for example because you find them attractive or interesting, or because you are thinking about something else. *mirar fijamente, fijar la mirada, quedarse mirando* ❑ *She was gazing at herself in the mirror.* *Estaba mirándose al espejo.* ❑ *He gazed into the fire.* *Se quedó mirando el fuego.* **2** N-COUNT You can talk about someone's **gaze** as a way of describing how they are looking at something, especially when they are looking steadily at it. *mirada fija, mirada penetrante* [WRITTEN] ❑ *She felt uncomfortable under the woman's steady gaze.* *Se sintió incómoda por la penetrante mirada de la mujer.*

G

**gear** /gɪər/ (**gears, gearing, geared**) **1** N-COUNT The **gears** on a machine or vehicle are a device for changing the rate at which energy is changed into motion. *transmisión de velocidad, caja de transmisión, velocidades* ❑ *On a hill, use low gears.* *En una colina, utiliza las velocidades bajas.* ❑ *The car was in fourth gear.* *El carro iba en cuarta.* **2** N-UNCOUNT The **gear** involved in a particular activity is the equipment or special clothing that you use. *equipo, herramienta, ropa, uniforme, avíos* ❑ *...100 police officers in riot gear.* *...100 policías con equipo para disturbios.* ❑ *...fishing gear.* *...avíos de pesca.* **3** V-T PASSIVE If someone or something **is geared to** or **toward** a particular purpose, they are organized or designed in order to achieve that purpose. *orientar, preparar* ❑ *Colleges are not always geared to the needs of part-time students.* *Las universidades no siempre están preparadas para cubrir las necesidades de los estudiantes de tiempo parcial.* ❑ *My training was geared toward winning the gold medal.* *Mi entrenamiento estaba orientado a ganar la medalla de oro.*

▸ **gear up** PHR-VERB If someone **is gearing up for** a particular activity, they are preparing to do it. If they **are geared up to** do a particular activity, they are prepared to do it. *prepararse, orientarse* ❑ *The country is gearing up for an election.* *El país se está preparando para la elección.*

**gear|shift** /gɪərʃɪft/ (**gearshifts**) N-COUNT The **gearshift** is the lever that you use to change gear in a car or other vehicle. *palanca de velocidades*

**GED** /dʒi i di/ (**GEDs**) N-COUNT A **GED** is an American educational qualification which is equivalent to a high school diploma. **GED** is an abbreviation for "General Equivalency Diploma." *GED, General Equivalency Diploma, Diploma de Equivalencias Generales*

**geese** /gis/ **Geese** is the plural of **goose**. *plural de* ***goose***

**gel** /dʒɛl/ (**gels, gelling, gelled**)

> The spelling **jell** is sometimes used for meanings **1** and **2**.

**1** V-RECIP If people **gel with** each other, or if two groups of people **gel**, they work well together because their skills and personalities fit together well. *ser compatible, compaginar* ❑ *He has gelled very well with the rest of the team.* *Era muy compatible con el resto del grupo.* ❑ *The two writers gelled, and scriptwriting for television followed.* *Los dos escritores compaginaron, y luego vino la redacción de guiones para televisión.* **2** V-I If a vague shape, thought, or creation **gels**, it becomes clearer or more definite. *cuajar* ❑ *Her idea has not yet gelled into a satisfying whole.* *Su idea no ha cuajado satisfactoriamente.* **3** N-VAR **Gel** is a thick, jelly-like substance, especially one used to keep your hair in a particular style. *gel*

**gela|tin** /dʒɛlətᵊn/ (**gelatins**) also **gelatine** N-VAR **Gelatin** is a clear tasteless powder that is used to make liquids become firm, for example when you are making desserts. *gelatina*

**gen|der** /dʒɛndər/ (**genders**) **1** N-VAR A person's **gender** is the fact that they are male or female. *género, sexo* ❑ *Women are sometimes denied opportunities because of their gender.* *En ocasiones, a las mujeres se les niegan oportunidades por su sexo.* **2** N-COUNT You can refer to all male people or all female people as a particular **gender.** *género* ❑ *She made some general comments about the male gender.* *Hizo algunos comentarios generales sobre el género masculino.* **3** N-VAR In grammar, the **gender** of a noun, pronoun, or adjective is whether it is masculine, feminine, or neuter. A word's gender can affect its form and behavior. In English, only personal pronouns such as "she," reflexive pronouns such as "itself," and possessive determiners such as "his" have gender. *género* ❑ *In French the word for "moon" is of feminine gender.* *En francés, el género de la palabra "luna" es femenino.*

**gene** /dʒin/ (**genes**) N-COUNT A **gene** is the part of a cell in a living thing which controls its physical characteristics, growth, and development. *gen* ❑ *...the gene for left-handedness.* *...el gen de la zurdera.*

**gen|er|al** /dʒɛnərəl/ (**generals**) **1** N-COUNT; N-TITLE; N-VOC A **general** is a high-ranking officer in the armed forces, usually in the army. *general* ❑ *The troops received a visit from the general.* *Las tropas recibieron la visita del general.* **2** ADJ If you talk about the **general** situation somewhere or talk about something in **general** terms, you are describing the situation as a whole rather than considering its details or exceptions. *general, en general* ❑ *There has been a general fall in unemployment.* *Ha habido una disminución general del desempleo.* ❑ *In general terms life has gotten better.* *En términos generales, la vida ha mejorado.* **3** ADJ You use **general** to describe something that involves or affects most people, or most people in a particular group. *general, generalizado* ❑ *There is not enough general awareness of this problem.* *La conciencia sobre este problema no está suficientemente generalizada.* **4** ADJ If you describe something as **general,** you mean that it is not limited to any one thing or area. *general, generalizado* ❑ *...a general ache across her upper body.* *...un dolor generalizado en la parte superior del cuerpo.* **5** ADJ **General** is used to describe a person's job, usually as part of their title, to indicate that they have complete responsibility for the administration of an organization or business. *general* [BUSINESS] ❑ *He became general manager of the company.* *Llegó a ser gerente general de la compañía.* **6** → see also **generally** **7** PHRASE You use **in general** to indicate that you are talking about something as a whole, rather than about part of it. *en general* ❑ *We need to improve our educational* *system in general. Necesitamos mejorar nuestro sistema educativo en general.* **8** PHRASE You say **in general** to indicate that you are referring to most people or things in a particular group. *en general, generalidad* ❑ *People in general will support us. La generalidad de la gente nos va a apoyar.*

**gen|er|al elec|tion** (**general elections**) N-COUNT In the United States, a **general election** is a local, state, or national election where the candidates have been selected by a primary election. Compare **primary**. *elecciones generales*

**gen|er|al hos|pi|tal** (**general hospitals**) N-COUNT A **general hospital** is a hospital that does not specialize in the treatment of particular illnesses or patients. *hospital general*

**gen|er|al|ize** /dʒɛnrəlaɪz/ (**generalizes, generalizing, generalized**) V-I If you **generalize**, you say something that seems to be true in most situations or for most people, but that may not be completely true in all cases. *generalizar* ❑ *You shouldn't generalize and say that all men are the same. No debes generalizar y decir que todos los hombres son iguales.* ● **gen|er|ali|za|tion** /dʒɛnrəlaɪzeɪʃən/ N-VAR (**generalizations**) *generalización* ❑ *He made sweeping generalizations about politicians. Hizo burdas generalizaciones sobre los políticos.*

**gen|er|al|ly** /dʒɛnrəli/ **1** ADV You use **generally** to give a summary of a situation, activity, or idea without referring to the particular details of it. *generalmente, en general* ❑ *Teachers generally are enthusiastic about their subjects. Los maestros en general se entusiasman por su especialidad.* **2** ADV You use **generally** to say that something happens or is used on most occasions but not on every occasion. *generalmente* ❑ *It is generally true that darker fruits contain more iron. En general es cierto que las frutas oscuras tienen más hierro.*

| Thesaurus | *generally* Ver también: |
|---|---|
| ADV. | commonly, mainly, usually **1** **2** |

**gen|er|al store** (**general stores**) N-COUNT A **general store** is a store, especially in a small town, where many different sorts of goods are sold. *tienda de abarrotes, miscelánea*

**gen|er|ate** /dʒɛnəreɪt/ (**generates, generating, generated**) **1** V-T To **generate** something means to cause it to begin and develop. *generar, producir, provocar* ❑ *The reforms will generate new jobs. Las reformas generarán nuevos empleos.* **2** V-T To **generate** a form of energy or power means to produce it. *generar, producir* ❑ *We burn coal to generate power. Quemamos carbón para generar energía.*
→ see **energy**

**gen|era|tion** /dʒɛnəreɪʃən/ (**generations**) **1** N-COUNT A **generation** is all the people in a group or country who are of a similar age, especially when they are considered as having the same experiences or attitudes. *generación* ❑ *...the current generation of teens. ...la generación actual de adolescentes.* **2** N-COUNT A **generation** is the period of time, usually considered to be about thirty years, that it takes for children to grow up and become adults and have children of their own. *generación* ❑ *Within a generation, flying has become a very common method of travel. En una generación se ha hecho muy común viajar por aire.* **3** N-COUNT You can use **generation** to refer to a stage of development in the design and manufacture of machines or equipment. *generación* ❑ *...a new generation of computers. ...una nueva generación de computadoras.*

**gen|era|tion time** (**generation times**) N-VAR The **generation time** of an organism is the average time between the birth of one generation of the organism and the birth of the next generation. *periodo generacional* [TECHNICAL]

**gen|era|tor** /dʒɛnəreɪtər/ (**generators**) N-COUNT A **generator** is a machine which produces electricity. *generador* ❑ *The house has its own power generators. La casa tiene sus propios generadores de energía.*
→ see **electricity**

**ge|ner|ic** /dʒɪnɛrɪk/ (**generics**) **1** ADJ You use **generic** to describe something that refers or relates to a whole class of similar things. *genérico, general* ❑ *As a boy, I said "pop" as a generic term for all soft drinks. De niño utilizaba "pop" como término genérico para todas las bebidas refrescantes.* **2** ADJ A **generic** drug or other product is one that does not have a trademark and that is known by a general name, rather than the manufacturer's name. *génerico, no de marca* ❑ *Doctors sometimes prescribe cheaper generic drugs instead of more expensive brand names. En ocasiones los médicos recetan medicamentos genéricos en lugar de marcas comerciales caras.* ● **Generic** is also a noun. *genérico* ❑ *The program saved $11 million by substituting generics for brand-name drugs. El programa ahorró 11 millones de dólares sustituyendo los medicamentos de marca con genéricos.*

**gen|er|ous** /dʒɛnərəs/ **1** ADJ A **generous** person gives more of something, especially money, than is usual or expected. *generoso* ❑ *He is generous with his money. Es generoso con su dinero* ● **gen|er|os|ity** /dʒɛnərɒsɪti/ N-UNCOUNT *generosidad* ❑ *There are many stories about his generosity. Hay muchas historias sobre su generosidad.* ● **gen|er|ous|ly** ADV *generosamente, con generosidad* ❑ *We would like to thank everyone who generously gave their time. Quisiéramos agradecer a quienes tan generosamente cedieron su tiempo.* **2** ADJ A **generous** person is friendly, helpful, and willing to see the good qualities in someone or something. *generoso* ❑ *He was always generous in sharing his knowledge. Siempre fue generoso para compartir sus conocimientos.* ● **gen|er|ous|ly** ADV *generosamente* ❑ *He generously offered some advice. Generosamente ofreció asesoría.* **3** ADJ A **generous** amount of something is much larger than is usual or necessary. *amplio* ❑ *The house has a generous amount of storage space. La casa tiene amplios espacios para almacenamiento.* ● **gen|er|ous|ly** ADV *generosamente, abundamente* ❑ *Season the steaks generously with salt and pepper. Sazona abundantemente los bistecs con sal y pimienta.*

| Thesaurus | *generous* Ver también: |
|---|---|
| ADJ. | charitable, kind; (*ant.*) mean, selfish, stingy **1** **2**<br>abundant, overflowing; (*ant.*) meager **3** |

**ge|net|ic** /dʒɪnɛtɪk/ ADJ You use **genetic** to describe something that is concerned with genetics or with genes. *genético* ❑ *...a rare genetic disease. ...una rara enfermedad genética.*

• **ge|neti|cal|ly** /dʒɪnɛtɪkli/ ADV *genéticamente* ❑ *Some people are genetically more likely to suffer from diabetes. Algunas personas son genéticamente más propensas a la diabetes.*

**ge|neti|cal|ly-modi|fied** ADJ **Genetically-modified** plants and animals have had one or more genes changed. The abbreviation **GM** is often used. *modificado genéticamente* ❑ *...genetically-modified foods. ...alimentos genéticamente modificados.*

**ge|net|ic en|gi|neer|ing** N-UNCOUNT **Genetic engineering** is the science or activity of changing the genetic structure of an animal, plant, or other organism in order to make it stronger or more suitable for a particular purpose. *ingeniería genética*
→ see **clone**

G

**ge|net|ics** /dʒɪnɛtɪks/ N-UNCOUNT **Genetics** is the study of how characteristics are passed on from one generation to another by means of genes. *genética* ❑ *Genetics is changing our understanding of cancer. La genética está cambiando nuestra forma de ver el cáncer.*

**ge|ni|us** /dʒinyəs/ (**geniuses**) **1** N-UNCOUNT **Genius** is very great ability or skill in a particular subject or activity. *genio, genialidad, don* ❑ *...her genius as a designer. ...sus dones de diseñadora.* **2** N-COUNT A **genius** is a highly talented, creative, or intelligent person. *genio* ❑ *Chaplin was a genius. Chaplin fue un genio.*

| Word Link | ***cide ≈ killing : genocide, pesticide, suicide*** |
|---|---|

**geno|cide** /dʒɛnəsaɪd/ N-UNCOUNT **Genocide** is the deliberate murder of a whole community or race. *genocidio*

**geno|type** /dʒinətaɪp, dʒɛn-/ (**genotypes**) N-VAR A **genotype** is the particular set of genes possessed by an individual organism. Compare **phenotype**. *genotipo* [TECHNICAL]

**gen|re** /ʒɒnrə/ (**genres**) N-COUNT A **genre** is a particular type of literature, painting, music, film, or other art form which people consider as a class because it has special characteristics. *género* [FORMAL] ❑ *...novels in the romance genre. ...novelas del género romántico.*
→ see Word Web: **genre**
→ see **fantasy**

**gen|tle** /dʒɛntᵊl/ (**gentler, gentlest**) **1** ADJ Someone who is **gentle** is kind, mild, and calm. *suave, moderado, discreto, tierno, cortés* ❑ *My husband was a quiet and gentle man. Mi esposo era un hombre tranquilo y discreto.* • **gen|tly** ADV *suavemente, dulcemente* ❑ *She smiled gently at him. Ella le sonrió dulcemente.* • **gen|tle|ness** N-UNCOUNT *suavidad, dulzura, delicadeza* ❑ *She treated her mother with great gentleness. Trataba a su madre con gran delicadeza.* **2** ADJ **Gentle** actions or movements are performed in a calm and controlled manner, with little force. *cortés, caballeroso* ❑ *...a gentle game of tennis. ...un caballeroso juego de tenis.* • **gen|tly** ADV *cortésmente, caballerosamente* ❑ *Patrick took her gently by the arm. Patrick la tomó caballerosamente del brazo.* **3** ADJ A **gentle** slope or curve is not steep or severe. *suave* ❑ *...an easy walk up a gentle slope. ...una caminata tranquila, por pendientes suaves.* • **gen|tly** ADV *suavemente* ❑ *Tuscany is known for its gently rolling hills. La Toscana es renombrada por sus colinas, que se pierden suavemente en el horizonte.* **4** ADJ A **gentle** heat is a fairly low heat. *suave, bajo* ❑ *Cook the sauce over a gentle heat. Cocina la salsa a fuego bajo.* • **gen|tly** ADV *suavemente, poco a poco* ❑ *Cook the onion gently for about 15 minutes. Cocina la cebolla poco a poco durante unos 15 minutos.*

**gentle|man** /dʒɛntᵊlmən/ (**gentlemen**) **1** N-COUNT A **gentleman** is a man who is polite and educated, and can be trusted. *caballero, señor* ❑ *He was always such a gentleman. Fue siempre un perfecto caballero.* **2** N-COUNT A **gentleman** is a man who comes from a family of high social standing. *caballero* ❑ *Her parents wanted her to marry a gentleman. Sus padres querían que se casara con un caballero.* **3** N-COUNT; N-VOC You can address men as **gentlemen,** or refer politely to them as **gentlemen.** *caballero* ❑ *This way, please, ladies and gentlemen. Por aquí, por favor, damas y caballeros.*

**genu|ine** /dʒɛnyuɪn/ **1** ADJ **Genuine** is used to describe people and things that are exactly what they appear to be, and are not false or an imitation. *genuino, verdadero, auténtico, legítimo* ❑ *He's a genuine American hero. Es un auténtico héroe americano.* ❑ *...genuine leather. ...piel legítima.* **2** ADJ **Genuine** refers to things such as emotions that are real and not pretended. *sincero* ❑ *This is a genuine offer to help. Se trata de un sincero ofrecimiento de ayuda.* • **genu|ine|ly** ADV *realmente, verdaderamente, de verdad* ❑ *He was genuinely surprised. Estaba realmente sorprendido* **3** ADJ Someone who is **genuine** is honest, truthful, and sincere. *sincero, honesto* ❑ *She is very caring and very genuine. Es muy cariñosa y muy sincera.*

**Word Web** **genre**

Each of the arts includes several different types called **genre**. The four basic types of **literature** are **fiction**, nonfiction, **poetry**, and **drama**. In painting, some of the special areas are **realism**, **expressionism**, and **Cubism**. In music, they include **classical**, **jazz**, and **popular** forms. Each genre contains several parts. For example, popular music takes in country and western, **rap music**, and **rock**. Modern movie-making has produced a wide variety of genres. These include **horror films**, **comedies**, **action movies**, film noir, and **westerns**. Some artists don't like working within just one genre.

**Thesaurus** *genuine* Ver también:

ADJ. actual, original, real, true; (*ant.*) bogus, fake 1 2
honest, open, sincere, true, valid; (*ant.*) dishonest 3

**geo|graphi|cal** /dʒiəgræfɪkᵊl/ also **geographic** /dʒiəgræfɪk/ ADJ **Geographical** or **geographic** means concerned with or relating to geography. *geográfico* ❑ *...a vast geographical area. ...una vasta área geográfica.* • **geo|graphi|cal|ly** /dʒiəgræfɪkli/ ADV *geográficamente* ❑ *It is geographically a very diverse continent. Es un continente geográficamente muy variado.*

**Word Link** *geo ≈ earth : geography, geology, geothermal energy*

**ge|og|ra|phy** /dʒiɒgrəfi/ 1 N-UNCOUNT **Geography** is the study of the countries of the world and of such things as the land, seas, climate, towns, and population. *geografía* 2 N-UNCOUNT The **geography** of a place is the way that features such as rivers, mountains, towns, or streets are arranged within it. *geografía* ❑ *...policemen who knew the local geography. ...policías que conocían la geografía local.*

**geo|logi|cal time scale** (**geological time scales**) also **geological timescale** N-COUNT The **geological time scale** is an arrangement of the main geological and biological events in the history of the Earth. *escala del tiempo geológico*

**Word Link** *logy, ology ≈ study of : biology, geology, mythology*

**ge|ol|ogy** /dʒiɒlədʒi/ 1 N-UNCOUNT **Geology** is the study of the Earth's structure, surface, and origins. *geología* ❑ *He was professor of geology at the University of Georgia. Fue profesor de geología en la Universidad de Georgia.* • **geo|logi|cal** /dʒiəlɒdʒɪkᵊl/ ADJ *geológico* ❑ *...a geological survey. ...un levantamiento geológico.* • **ge|olo|gist** N-COUNT (**geologists**) *geólogo o geóloga* ❑ *Geologists have studied the way that heat flows from the Earth. Los geólogos han estudiado la forma en que el calor mana de la tierra.* 2 N-UNCOUNT The **geology** of an area is the structure of its land, together with the types of rocks and minerals that exist within it. *geología* ❑ *...the geology of Asia. ...la geología de Asia.* → see **biosphere**
→ see **biosphere**

**geo|met|ric se|quence** (**geometric sequences**) also **geometric progression** N-COUNT A **geometric sequence** is a series of numbers in which there is the same ratio between each number and the next one, for example the series 1, 2, 4, 8, 16. *secuencia geométrica* [TECHNICAL]

**ge|om|etry** /dʒiɒmɪtri/ 1 N-UNCOUNT **Geometry** is the branch of mathematics concerned with the properties and relationships of lines, angles, curves, and shapes. *geometría* ❑ *...the way in which mathematics and geometry describe nature. ...la forma en que las matemáticas y la geometría describen la naturaleza.* 2 N-UNCOUNT The **geometry** of an object is its shape or the relationship of its parts to each other. *geometría* ❑ *...the geometry of the curved roof. ...la geometría de un techo curvo.*
→ see **mathematics**

**geo|sta|tion|ary** /dʒioʊsteɪʃənɛri/ also **geosynchronous** /dʒioʊsɪŋkrənəs/ ADJ A satellite that is in **geostationary** orbit is positioned directly above the equator and moves at the same speed as the Earth's rotation, so that it appears to be stationary. *geoestacionario*

**geo|ther|mal en|er|gy** /dzioʊθɜrmᵊl ɛnərdʒi/ ADJ **Geothermal** energy is heat that comes from hot water and steam beneath the Earth's surface. *geotérmico* [TECHNICAL] ❑ *The house is heated and cooled with geothermal energy. La casa se calienta y enfría con energía geotérmica.*

**germ** /dʒɜrm/ (**germs**) 1 N-COUNT A **germ** is a very small organism that causes disease. *germen, microbio* ❑ *This chemical is used to kill germs. Esta sustancia química se utiliza para matar gérmenes.* 2 N-SING The **germ of** something such as an idea is the beginning of it. *germen, origen* ❑ *The incident gave him the germ of a book. El incidente fue el origen de su libro.*
→ see **medicine, spice, thermometer**

**Ger|man shep|herd** /dʒɜrmən ʃɛpərd/ (**German shepherds**) N-COUNT A **German shepherd** is a large, usually fierce dog that is used to guard buildings or by the police to help them find criminals. *pastor alemán*

**ger|mi|nate** /dʒɜrmɪneɪt/ (**germinates, germinating, germinated**) 1 V-T/V-I If a seed **germinates** or if it **is germinated,** it starts to grow. *germinar* ❑ *Some seeds germinate in just a few days. Algunas semillas germinan en unos cuantos días.* • **ger|mi|na|tion** /dʒɜrmɪneɪʃᵊn/ N-UNCOUNT *germinación* ❑ *If the soil is too cold it can stop germination. Si el suelo está demasiado frío, la germinación puede interrumpirse.* 2 V-I If an idea, plan, or feeling **germinates,** it comes into existence and begins to develop. *germinar, tomar forma* ❑ *A book was germinating in his mind. Un libro estaba tomando forma en su mente.*
→ see **tree**

**ges|ta|tion pe|ri|od** (**gestation periods**) N-COUNT The **gestation period** of a particular species of animal is the length of time that animals belonging to that species are pregnant for. *periodo de gestación, gestación* [TECHNICAL]

**ges|ture** /dʒɛstʃər/ (**gestures, gesturing, gestured**) 1 N-COUNT A **gesture** is a movement that you make with a part of your body, especially your hands, to express emotion or information. *ademán, seña, gesto* ❑ *Sarah made a gesture with her fist. Sarah hizo un ademán con el puño.* 2 N-COUNT A **gesture** is something that you say or do in order to express your attitude or intentions, often something that you know will not have much effect. *gesto* ❑ *He asked the government to make a gesture of good will. Pidió al gobierno que hiciera un gesto de buena voluntad.* 3 V-I If you **gesture,** you use movements of your hands or head in order to tell someone something or draw their attention to something. *hacer gestos, hacer señas, señalar* ❑ *I gestured toward the house. Hice señas hacia la casa.*

**ges|ture draw|ing** (**gesture drawings**) N-COUNT A **gesture drawing** is a quick, simple drawing that aims to represent the movements or gestures of a body. dibujo gestual [TECHNICAL]

**get**
1 CHANGING, CAUSING, MOVING, OR REACHING
2 OBTAINING, RECEIVING, OR CATCHING
3 PHRASAL VERBS

**1 get** /gɛt/ (**gets, getting, got, gotten** or **got**)

In most of its uses **get** is a fairly informal word.

1 V-LINK You use **get** with adjectives to mean "become." For example, if someone **gets cold,** they become cold, and if they **get angry,** they become angry. *llegar a ser, llegar a estar* ❑ *The boys were getting bored. Los niños se estaban aburriendo.* ❑ *Things will get better. Las cosas mejorarán.* 2 V-LINK **Get** is used with expressions referring to states or situations. For example, to **get into trouble** means to start being in trouble. *preparar, prepararse, empezar a* ❑ *She was getting ready to go out for the evening. Se estaba preparando para salir en la noche.* ❑ *If you do that you might get into trouble. Si haces eso, podrías meterte en problemas.* 3 V-T To **get** someone or something into a particular state or situation means to cause them to be in it. *lograr* ❑ *I can't get the windows clean. No logro limpiar las ventanas.* ❑ *Brian will get them out of trouble. Brian logrará sacarlos de problemas.* 4 V-T If you **get** someone **to** do something, you cause them to do it by asking, persuading, or telling them to do it. *convencer, persuadir* ❑ *...a campaign to get politicians to take AIDS more seriously. ...una campaña para persuadir a los políticos de tomar más en serio el SIDA.* 5 V-T If you **get** something done, you cause it to be done. *hacer que alguien haga algo* ❑ *Why don't you get your car fixed? ¿Por qué no te arreglan tu coche?* 6 V-I To **get** somewhere means to move there. *salir, levantarse, pasar* ❑ *I got off the bed and opened the door. Me levanté de la cama y fui a abrir la puerta.* ❑ *How can I get past her without her seeing me? ¿Cómo pasar junto a ella sin que me vea?* 7 V-T To **get** something or someone into a place or position means to cause them to move there. *sacar, poner(se)* ❑ *Mack got his wallet out. Mack sacó su cartera.* ❑ *Go and get your coat on. Ve a ponerte el abrigo.* 8 AUX **Get** is often used in place of "be" as an auxiliary verb to form passives. *se* ❑ *A window got broken. Se rompió la ventana.* 9 V-T If you **get to** do something, you manage to do it or have the opportunity to do it. *poder, hacer, lograr* ❑ *How did he get to be the boss of a major company? ¿Cómo le hizo para llegar a jefe de una compañía importante?* ❑ *Do you get to see him often? ¿Logras verlo con frecuencia?* 10 V-T You can use **get** in expressions like **get moving, get going,** and **get working** when you want to tell people to begin moving, going, or working quickly. *hacer que alguien haga algo* ❑ *The train leaves in 30 minutes, so let's get moving. El tren sale en 30 minutos, vámonos yendo.* 11 V-I If something that has continued for some time **gets to** you, it starts causing you to suffer. *afectar* ❑ *The pressure was getting to him and he lost his temper. La presión estaba empezando a afectarlo y perdió los estribos.*

**Usage** get
In conversation *get* is often used instead of *become. We're getting worried about her.*

**2 get** /gɛt/ (**gets, getting, got, gotten** or **got**)
1 V-T If you **get** something that you want or need, you obtain it. *conseguir* ❑ *I got a job at the store. Conseguí un empleo en la tienda.* 2 V-T If you **get** something, you receive it or are given it. *recibir, dar* ❑ *I'm getting a bike for my birthday. Me van a dar una bici en mi cumpleaños.* ❑ *He gets a lot of letters from fans. Recibe muchas cartas de sus admiradores.* 3 V-T If you **get** someone or something, you go and bring them to a particular place. *traer* ❑ *I went downstairs to get the newspaper. Bajé a traer el periódico.* ❑ *Go and get me a drink of water. Ve a traerme un vaso de agua.* 4 V-T If you **get** a particular price **for** something that you sell, you obtain that amount of money by selling it. *conseguir, vender* ❑ *He can't get a good price for his crops. No puede vender a buen precio sus cosechas.* 5 V-T If you **get** an idea, impression, or feeling, you begin to have that idea, impression, or feeling as you learn or understand more about something. *sentir, tener la sensación* ❑ *I get the feeling that you're an honest man. Tengo la sensación de que eres un hombre honesto.* 6 V-T If you **get** a joke or **get** the point of something that is said, you understand it. *entender* ❑ *Did you get that joke? ¿Entendiste ese chiste?* 7 V-T If you **get** an illness or disease, you become ill with it. *contraer, darle a uno una enfermedad* ❑ *When I was five I got the measles. A los cinco años me dieron paperas.* 8 V-T When you **get** a train, bus, plane, or boat, you leave a place on a particular train, bus, plane, or boat. *tomar* ❑ *It's quicker to get the bus. Es más rápido tomar el camión.* 9 → see also **got**

| **Thesaurus** | *get* | Ver también: |
|---|---|---|
| V-LINK. | become 1 1 | |
| V. | bring, collect, pick up 2 3 | |
| | know, sense 2 5 | |

**3 get** /gɛt/ (**gets, getting, got, gotten** or **got**)
▸ **get across** PHR-VERB When an idea **gets across** or when you **get** it **across,** you succeed in making other people understand it. *hacer(se) entender* ❑ *People felt their opinions were not getting across to the government. La gente sentía que no lograba hacerse entender por el gobierno.*
▸ **get along** PHR-VERB If you **get along with** someone, you have a friendly relationship with them. You can also say that two people **get along.** *llevarse bien* ❑ *It's impossible to get along with him. Es imposible llevarse bien con él.*
▸ **get around** 1 PHR-VERB To **get around** a problem or difficulty means to overcome it. *sortear, evitar* ❑ *We need to find a way to get around the problem of kids missing school. Tenemos que encontrar la manera de evitar el problema de que los niños pierdan clases.* 2 PHR-VERB If you **get around** a rule or law, you find a way of doing something that the rule or law is intended to prevent, without actually breaking it. *sacarle la vuelta a, eludir* ❑ *Companies find ways to get around the ban. Las empresas encuentran la manera de eludir la prohibición.* 3 PHR-VERB If news **gets around,** it becomes well known as a result of being told to lots of people.

corer, circular ❑ Word got around that he was going to leave. Corrió el rumor de que se iba. **4** PHR-VERB If you **get around,** you visit a lot of different places as part of your way of life. viajar ❑ He was a journalist, and he got around. Era periodista, y viajaba. **5** PHR-VERB The way that someone **gets around** is the way that they walk or go from one place to another. desplazarse, caminar ❑ It is difficult for Gail to get around since she broke her leg. A Gail le cuesta trabajo caminar desde que se rompió la pierna.

▶ **get around to** PHR-VERB When you **get around to** doing something that you have delayed doing or have been too busy to do, you finally do it. encontrar el momento para ❑ I said I would write you, but I never got around to it. Te dije que te escribiría, pero nunca encontré el momento.

▶ **get at** **1** PHR-VERB To **get at** something means to succeed in reaching it. llegar ❑ She walked on the grass to get at the flowers in front of the house. Caminó por el pasto para llegar a las flores del frente de la casa. **2** PHR-VERB If you **get at** the truth about something, you succeed in discovering it. llegar, descubrir ❑ We want to get at the truth. Who killed him? And why? Queremos descubrir la verdad. ¿Quién lo mató? ¿Y por qué? **3** PHR-VERB If you ask someone what they **are getting at,** you are asking them to explain what they mean, usually because you think that they are being unpleasant or are suggesting something that is untrue. querer decir, querer llegar ❑ I don't understand what you're getting at. No entiendo a dónde quieres llegar.

▶ **get away** **1** PHR-VERB If you **get away,** you succeed in leaving a place or a person's company. irse, alejarse, salir ❑ She wanted to get away from the city for a while. Ella quería alejarse de la ciudad por un tiempo. **2** PHR-VERB If you **get away,** you go away for a period of time in order to have a vacation. irse, salir de vacaciones ❑ He is too busy to get away. Él está demasiado ocupado como para irse de vacaciones. **3** PHR-VERB When someone or something **gets away,** or when you **get** them **away,** they escape. escaper(se) ❑ The thieves got away through an upstairs window. Los ladrones se escaparon por una ventana del piso de arriba.

▶ **get away with** PHR-VERB If you **get away with** doing something wrong or risky, you do not suffer any punishment or other bad consequences because of it. salirse con la suya, escaparse ❑ Criminals know how to steal and get away with it. Los delincuentes saben cómo robar y salirse con la suya.

▶ **get back** PHR-VERB If you **get** something **back** after you have lost it or after it has been taken from you, you then have it again. recuperar ❑ You have the right to cancel the contract and get your money back. Usted tiene derecho a cancelar el contrato y recuperar su dinero.

▶ **get back to** **1** PHR-VERB If you **get back to** an activity, you start doing it again after you have stopped doing it. regresar, volver ❑ Let's get back to work. Regresemos al trabajo. **2** PHR-VERB If you **get back to** someone, you contact them again after a short period of time, often by telephone. volver a ponerse en contacto, llamar ❑ We'll get back to you as soon as possible. Lo llamaremos lo antes posible.

▶ **get by** PHR-VERB If you can **get by** with what you have, you can manage to live or do things in a satisfactory way. arreglárselas ❑ I'm a survivor. I'll get by. Soy un sobreviviente, me las arreglaré.

▶ **get down** **1** PHR-VERB If something **gets** you **down,** it makes you unhappy. deprimir ❑ Sometimes my work gets me down. En ocasiones mi trabajo me deprime. **2** PHR-VERB If you **get down,** you lower your body until you are sitting, kneeling, or lying on the ground. agacharse, ponerse en el piso ❑ Everybody got down and started looking for the earring. Todos se agacharon y empezaron a buscar el arete.

▶ **get down to** PHR-VERB If you **get down to** something, you begin doing it. empezar, ponerse a ❑ It's time for us to stop talking and get down to business. Ya es hora de dejar de hablar y de ponerse a trabajar.

▶ **get in** **1** PHR-VERB If a political party or a politician **gets in,** they are elected. ser electo, resultar electo, ganar ❑ If the Democrats get in everything will change. Si los demócratas ganan, todo va a cambiar. **2** PHR-VERB If you **get** something **in,** you manage to do it at a time when you are very busy doing other things. lograr, arreglárselas ❑ I managed to get a trip to the gym in. Me las arreglé para ir un rato al gimnasio. **3** PHR-VERB When a train, bus, or plane **gets in,** it arrives. llegar ❑ Our flight got in late. Nuestro vuelo llegó tarde.

▶ **get into** **1** PHR-VERB If you **get into** a particular kind of work or activity, you manage to become involved in it. entrar en, participar, meterse ❑ He wanted to get into politics. Él quería meterse en política. **2** PHR-VERB If you **get into** a school, college, or university, you are accepted there as a student. ser aceptado, ser admitido ❑ I was working hard to get into Yale. Yo estaba trabajando duro para que me aceptaran en Yale.

▶ **get off** **1** PHR-VERB If someone who has broken a law or rule **gets off,** they are not punished, or are given only a very small punishment. librar(se) ❑ He got off with a small fine. La libró con una pequeña multa. **2** PHR-VERB If you tell someone to **get off** a piece of land or a property, you are telling them to leave, because they have no right to be there and you do not want them there. salir(se) ❑ I told the dog to get off the grass. Le dije al perro que se saliera del pasto.

▶ **get on** PHR-VERB If you **get on with** something, you continue doing it or start doing it. seguir adelante ❑ Jane got on with her work. Jane siguió adelante con su trabajo.

▶ **get on to** PHR-VERB If you **get on to** a topic when you are speaking, you start talking about it. llegar a, pasar a ❑ We got on to the subject of relationships. Llegamos al tema de las relaciones.

▶ **get out** **1** PHR-VERB If you **get out,** you leave a place because you want to escape from it, or because you are made to leave it. irse ❑ They wanted to get out of the country. Querían irse del país. **2** PHR-VERB If you **get out,** you go to places and meet people, usually in order to have a more enjoyable life. salir ❑ Get out and enjoy yourself, make new friends. Sal y diviértete, haz nuevos amigos. **3** PHR-VERB If news or information **gets out,** it becomes known. saberse, hacerse público ❑ News got out about their relationship. Se supo de su relación.

▶ **get out of** PHR-VERB If you **get out of** doing something that you do not want to do, you succeed in avoiding doing it. librarse de, salvarse de ❑ Some people will do anything to get out of paying taxes. Algunos personas harían cualquier cosa para librarse de pagar impuestos.

G

▸ **get over** 1 PHR-VERB If you **get over** an unpleasant or unhappy experience or an illness, you recover from it. *recuperarse, superar* ❑ *It took me a long time to get over her death. Me llevó mucho tiempo recuperarme de su muerte.* 2 PHR-VERB If you **get over** a problem or difficulty, you overcome it. *resolver, superar* ❑ *I don't know how they'll get over that problem. No sé cómo resolverán ese problema.*

▸ **get through** 1 PHR-VERB If you **get through** a task or an amount of work, you complete it. *terminar* ❑ *I managed to get through the first two chapters. Me las arreglé para terminar los dos primeros capítulos.* 2 PHR-VERB If you **get through** a difficult or unpleasant period of time, you manage to live through it. *sobrevivir, superar, pasar* ❑ *It is hard to see how people will get through the winter. Es difícil imaginarse cómo la gente sobrevivirá al invierno.* 3 PHR-VERB If you **get through to** someone, you succeed in making them understand something that you are trying to tell them. *lograr comunicarse, conseguir comunicarse* ❑ *An old friend might be able to get through to her and help her. Un viejo amigo podría lograr comunicarse con ella y ayudarle.* 4 PHR-VERB If you **get through to** someone, you succeed in contacting them on the telephone. *lograr comunicarse* ❑ *I can't get through to this number. No logro comunicarme a este número.*

▸ **get together** 1 PHR-VERB When people **get together,** they meet in order to discuss something or to spend time together. *reunirse, juntarse* ❑ *This is a time for families to get together and enjoy themselves. Es una época en que las familias se reúnen y disfrutan juntas.* 2 PHR-VERB If you **get** something **together,** you organize it. *reunir, formar, organizar* ❑ *Paul and I got a band together. Paul y yo formamos una banda.* 3 PHR-VERB If you **get** an amount of money **together,** you succeed in getting all the money that you need in order to pay for something. *reunir, juntar* ❑ *We've finally got enough money together to buy a home. Por fin juntamos suficiente dinero para comprar una casa.*

▸ **get up** 1 PHR-VERB When someone who is sitting or lying down **gets up,** they rise to a standing position. *levantarse, pararse* ❑ *I got up and walked over to where he was. Me levanté y fui a donde él estaba.* 2 PHR-VERB When you **get up,** you get out of bed. *levantarse, pararse* ❑ *They have to get up early in the morning. Ellos tienen que levantarse temprano en la mañana.*

**get-go** PHRASE If something happens or is true **from the get-go,** it happens or is true from the beginning of a process or activity. *desde el principio* [INFORMAL] ❑ *From the get-go, we knew he could do the job. Desde el principio supimos que él podía hacer el trabajo.*

**ghet|to** /gɛtoʊ/ (**ghettos** or **ghettoes**) N-COUNT A **ghetto** is a part of a city in which many poor people or many people of a particular race, religion, or nationality live separately from everyone else. *gueto* ❑ *...the ghettos of New York. ...los guetos de Nueva York.*

**ghost** /goʊst/ (**ghosts**) N-COUNT A **ghost** is the spirit of a dead person that someone believes they can see or feel. *fantasma* ❑ *...the ghost of Marie Antoinette. el fantasma de María Antonieta.*

**GI** /dʒi aɪ/ (**GIs**) N-COUNT A **GI** is a soldier in the United States armed forces, especially the army. *soldado estadounidense, GI* ❑ *...the GIs who came to Europe to fight the Nazis. ...los soldados estadounidenses que llegaron a Europa a combatir a los nazis.*

**gi|ant** /dʒaɪənt/ (**giants**) 1 ADJ Something that is described as **giant** is much larger or more important than most others of its kind. *gigante, gigantesco* ❑ *America's giant car makers are located in Detroit. Los gigantes estadounidenses de la fabricación de autos están en Detroit.* ❑ *...a giant oak table. ...una mesa gigante de roble* 2 N-COUNT **Giant** is often used to refer to any large, successful business organization or country. *gigante* ❑ *Japan is an electronics giant. Japón es un gigante de la electrónica.* 3 N-COUNT A **giant** is an imaginary person who is very big and strong, especially one mentioned in old stories. *gigante*

| **Thesaurus** | *giant* | Ver también: |
|---|---|---|
| ADJ. | colossal, enormous, gigantic, huge, immense, mammoth; (*ant.*) miniature 1 | |

**gi|ant pan|da** (**giant pandas**) N-COUNT A **giant panda** is the same as a **panda.** *panda, panda gigante*

**gift** /gɪft/ (**gifts**) 1 N-COUNT A **gift** is something that you give someone as a present. *regalo, presente, obsequio* ❑ *...a birthday gift. ...un regalo de cumpleaños.* 2 N-COUNT If someone has a **gift for** doing something, they have a natural ability for doing it. *don, talento* ❑ *He found he had a gift for teaching. Descubrió que tenía talento para la enseñanza.*

**gift cer|tifi|cate** (**gift certificates**) N-COUNT A **gift certificate** is a card or piece of paper that you buy at a store and give to someone, which entitles the person to exchange it for goods worth the same amount. *certificado de regalo* ❑ *...a $25 gift certificate. ...un certificado de regalo por 25 dólares.*

**gift|ed** /gɪftɪd/ 1 ADJ Someone who is **gifted** has a natural ability to do something well. *de talento, talentoso* ❑ *...one of the most gifted players in the world. ...uno de los jugadores más talentosos del mundo.* 2 ADJ A **gifted** child is much more intelligent or talented than average. *talentoso*

**gig** /gɪg/ (**gigs**) N-COUNT A **gig** is a live performance by someone such as a musician or a comedian. *tocada, performance* [INFORMAL] ❑ *We went to a gig at Madison Square Garden. Fuimos a una tocada en el Madison Square Garden.*

**gi|ga|byte** /gɪgəbaɪt/ (**gigabytes**) N-COUNT In computing, a **gigabyte** is one thousand and twenty-four megabytes. *gigabyte*

**gi|gan|tic** /dʒaɪgæntɪk/ ADJ If you describe something as **gigantic,** you are emphasizing that it is extremely large in size, amount, or degree. *gigantesco* ❑ *There are gigantic rocks along the roadside. Hay unas rocas gigantescas a ambos lados de la carretera.*

**gig|gle** /gɪgᵊl/ (**giggles, giggling, giggled**) V-T/V-I If someone **giggles,** they laugh in a childlike way, because they are amused, nervous, or embarrassed. *reírse nerviosamente* ❑ *The girls began to giggle. Las niñas comenzaron a reírse nerviosamente.* ❑ *"I beg your pardon?" she giggled. —¿Perdón?—dijo entre risas.* ● **Giggle** is also a noun. *risa nerviosa* ❑ *He gave a little giggle. Soltó una risita nerviosa.*
→ see **laugh**

**gill** /gɪl/ (**gills**) N-COUNT **Gills** are the organs on the sides of fish and other water creatures

through which they breathe. branquia
→ see **amphibian, fish**

**gilt** /gɪlt/ ADJ A **gilt** object is covered with a thin layer of gold or gold paint. dorado, enchapado en oro ❑ *...thick paper with gilt edges.* *...papel grueso con bordes dorados.*

**gin|ger** /dʒɪndʒər/ **1** N-UNCOUNT **Ginger** is the root of a plant that is used to flavor food. It has a sweet, spicy flavor and is often sold in powdered form. jengibre **2** COLOR **Ginger** is used to describe things that are orangey-brown in color. anaranjado, pelirrojo ❑ *She had ginger hair and pale skin.* *Era pelirroja y de piel blanca.*

**gi|raffe** /dʒɪræf/ (**giraffes**) N-COUNT A **giraffe** is a large African animal with a very long neck, long legs, and dark patches on its body. jirafa

giraffe

**girl** /gɜrl/ (**girls**) **1** N-COUNT A **girl** is a female child. niña, muchacha ❑ *...an eleven-year-old girl.* *...una niña de once años.* ❑ *They have two girls and a boy.* *Tienen dos niñas y un niño.* **2** N-COUNT Young women are often referred to as **girls**. This use could cause offense. niña ❑ *He married a girl twenty years younger than him.* *Se casó con una muchacha veinte años menor que él.*

**Usage** girl

Don't refer to an adult female as a *girl*. This may cause offense. Use *woman*. *I'm studying with Diana. She's a woman from my English class*

**girl|friend** /gɜrlfrɛnd/ (**girlfriends**) **1** N-COUNT Someone's **girlfriend** is a girl or woman with whom they are having a romantic or sexual relationship. novia ❑ *Does he have a girlfriend?* *¿Tiene novia?* **2** N-COUNT A **girlfriend** is a female friend. amiga ❑ *I had lunch with my girlfriends.* *Almorcé con mis amigas.*

**give**

❶ USED WITH NOUNS DESCRIBING ACTIONS
❷ TRANSFERRING
❸ OTHER USES, PHRASES, AND PHRASAL VERBS

❶ **give** /gɪv/ (**gives, giving, gave, given**) **1** V-T You can use **give** with nouns that refer to physical actions. The whole expression refers to the performing of the action. For example, **She gave a smile** means almost the same as "She smiled." dar ❑ *She gave a big yawn.* *Dio un gran bostezo.* ❑ *He gave her a friendly smile.* *Le sonrió amigablemente.* **2** V-T You use **give** to say that a person does something for another person. For example, if you **give** someone a lift, you take them somewhere in your car. dar ❑ *I gave her a lift back to her house.* *Le di un aventón a su casa.* ❑ *She began to give piano lessons to some of the local children.* *Comenzó a darles clases de piano a algunos niños de la zona.* **3** V-T You use **give** with nouns that refer to information, opinions, or greetings to indicate that something is communicated. For example, if you **give** someone some news, you tell it to them. dar ❑ *He gave no details.* *No dio detalles.* ❑ *Would you please give me your name?* *¿Podría darme su nombre, por favor?* **4** V-T You use **give** to say how long you think something will last or how much you think something will be. dar ❑ *The doctors gave her less than a year to live.* *Los doctores le dieron menos de un año de vida.* **5** V-T If someone or something **gives** you a particular idea, impression, or feeling, they cause you to have it. dar ❑ *They gave me the impression that they were very happy.* *Me dieron la impresión de ser muy felices.* ❑ *He gave me a shock.* *Me dio un susto.* **6** V-T If you **give** a performance or speech, you perform or speak in public. dar ❑ *She gives a wonderful performance in her new movie.* *Ella actúa maravillosamente en su nueva película.* **7** V-T If you **give** something thought or attention, you think about it, concentrate on it, or deal with it. pensar en, prestar atención ❑ *I've given the matter some thought.* *He estado pensando en el asunto.* **8** V-T If you **give** a party or other social event, you organize it. hacer ❑ *I gave a dinner party for a few friends.* *Hice una cena para nos pocos amigos.*
→ see **donor**

❷ **give** /gɪv/ (**gives, giving, gave, given**) **1** V-T/V-I If you **give** someone something that you own or have bought, you provide them with it, so that they have it or can use it. dar, donar ❑ *They gave us T-shirts and stickers.* *Nos dieron playeras y calcomanías.* ❑ *He gave money to the World Health Organization.* *Le donó dinero a la Organización Mundial de la Salud* ❑ *Most Americans give to charity.* *La mayoría de los estadounidenses hace donaciones para obras de caridad.* **2** V-T If you **give** someone something that you are holding or that is near you, you pass it to them, so that they are then holding it. dar ❑ *Give me that pencil.* *Dame ese lápiz.* **3** V-T To **give** someone or something a particular power or right means to allow them to have it. otorgar ❑ *The new law would give the president more power.* *La nueva ley le otorgaría más poder al presidente.*

❸ **give** /gɪv/ (**gives, giving, gave, given**)
→ Please look at category **7** to see if the expression you are looking for is shown under another headword. **1** V-I If something **gives,** it collapses or breaks under pressure. dar de sí, ceder, doblarse ❑ *My knees gave under me.* *Se me doblaron las rodillas.* **2** V-T PASSIVE You say that you **are given to** understand or believe that something is the case when you do not want to say how you found out about it, or who told you. dar a entender, hacer creer [FORMAL] ❑ *We were given to understand that he was sick.* *Se nos dio a entender que estaba enfermo.* **3** → see also **given** **4** PHRASE You use **give me** to say that you would rather have one thing than another, especially when you have just mentioned the thing that you do not want. preferir ❑ *I hate rain. Give me cold, dry weather any day.* *Odio la lluvia. Siempre voy a preferir un día seco y frío.* **5** PHRASE If you say that something requires **give-and-take,** you mean that people must compromise or cooperate for it to be successful. concesiones mutuas, toma y daca ❑ *In a happy relationship there has to be give-and-take.* *En una buena relación tiene que haber concesiones mutuas.* **6** PHRASE **Give or take** is used to indicate that an amount is approximate. For example, if you say that something is fifty years old, **give or take** a few years, you mean that it is approximately fifty years old. más o menos ❑ *They grow to a height of 12*

g

## Word Web glacier

Two-thirds of all **fresh water** is **frozen**. The largest **glaciers** in the world are the **polar ice caps** of Antarctica and Greenland. They cover more than six million square miles. Their average depth is almost one mile. If all the glaciers **melted**, the average **sea level** would rise by more than 250 feet. Glaciologists have noted that the Antarctic is about 1° C* warmer than it was 50 years ago. Some of them are worried. Continued warming might cause floating **ice** shelves there to begin to fall apart. This, in turn, could cause disastrous coastal flooding around the world.

*1° Celsius = 33.8° Fahrenheit.*

*inches—give or take a couple of inches.* *Crecen a una altura de 30 centímetros, centímetros más centímetros menos.* **7** to **give the game away** → see **game** **8** to **give notice** → see **notice** **9** to **give rise to** → see **rise**

▸ **give away** **1** PHR-VERB If you **give away** something that you own, you give it to someone, rather than selling it, often because you no longer want it. *pasar, regalar* ❑ *She likes to give away plants from her garden.* *Le gusta regalar plantas de su jardín.* **2** PHR-VERB If you **give away** information that should be kept secret, you reveal it to other people. *revelar, traslucir* ❑ *Her face gave nothing away.* *Su cara no dejaba traslucir nada.*

▸ **give back** PHR-VERB If you **give** something **back**, you return it to the person who gave it to you. *devolver, regresar* ❑ *I gave the book back to him.* *Le regresé el libro.* ❑ *Give me back my camera.* *Devuélmeme mi cámara.*

▸ **give in** **1** PHR-VERB If you **give in**, you admit that you are defeated or that you cannot do something. *rendirse* ❑ *It was tough, but we were determined not to give in.* *Era difícil, pero estábamos decididos a no rendirnos.* **2** PHR-VERB If you **give in**, you agree to do something that you do not want to do. *acceder* ❑ *My parents finally gave in and let me have driving lessons.* *Mis padres finalmente accedieron y me dejaron tomar clases de manejo.*

▸ **give off** or **give out** PHR-VERB If something **gives off** or **gives out** a gas, heat, or a smell, it produces it and sends it out into the air. *despedir* ❑ *Natural gas gives off less carbon dioxide than coal.* *El gas natural despide menos dióxido de carbono que el carbón.*

▸ **give out** **1** PHR-VERB If you **give out** a number of things, you distribute them among a group of people. *repartir* ❑ *There were people at the entrance giving out tickets.* *Había personas en la puerta repartiendo entradas.* **2** → see **give off**

▸ **give over to** or **give up to** PHR-VERB If something **is given over** or **given up to** a particular use, it is used entirely for that purpose. *dedicar, reservar* ❑ *Much of the garden was given over to vegetables.* *Buena parte del jardín había sido dedicada a los vegetales.*

▸ **give up** **1** PHR-VERB If you **give up** something, you stop doing it or having it. *abandonar* ❑ *The Coast Guard have given up all hope of finding the divers alive.* *La Guardia Costera ha abandonado toda esperanza de encontrar a los buzos con vida.* **2** PHR-VERB If you **give up**, you decide that you cannot do something and stop trying to do it. *rendirse, dares por vencido, renunciar* ❑ *I give up. I'll never understand this.* *Me rindo. Nunca voy a entender esto.* **3** PHR-VERB If you **give up** your job, you resign from it. *renunciar* ❑ *She gave up her job to join her husband's campaign.* *Renunció a su trabajo para unirse a la campaña de su esposo.*

▸ **give up to** → see **give over to**

**giv|en** /gɪvᵊn/ **1** **Given** is the past participle of **give**. *participio pasado de **give*** **2** ADJ If you talk about, for example, any **given** position or a **given** time, you mean any particular position or any particular time. *dado, determinado* ❑ *There are usually about 250 students in the building at any given time.* *Normalmente, hay alrededor de 250 estudiantes en el edificio en cualquier momento determinado.* **3** PREP **Given** is used when indicating a possible situation in which someone has the opportunity or ability to do something. For example, **given the chance** means "if I had the chance." *de tener* ❑ *Given the opportunity, I'd like to travel more.* *De tener la oportunidad, me gustaría viajar más.* **4** PHRASE If you say **given** something, or **given that** something is true, you mean taking that thing into account. *dado* ❑ *Given the difficulties, I think we did very well.* *Dadas las dificultades, creo que lo hicimos muy bien.* ❑ *I have to be careful with money, given that I don't earn very much.* *Debo ser cuidadoso con el dinero, dado que no gano mucho.*

**gla|cial** /gleɪʃᵊl/ ADJ **Glacial** means relating to or produced by glaciers or ice. *glacial* [TECHNICAL] ❑ *...a glacial landscape.* *...un paisaje glacial.* → **lake**

**gla|cial drift** N-UNCOUNT **Glacial drift** is rocks that have been carried and left by a glacier. *morena* [TECHNICAL]

**glaci|er** /gleɪʃər/ (**glaciers**) N-COUNT A **glacier** is an extremely large mass of ice which moves very slowly, often down a mountain valley. *glaciar* → see Word Web: **glacier**

**glad** /glæd/ **1** ADJ If you are **glad** about something, you are happy and pleased about it. *contento* ❑ *They seemed glad to see me.* *Parecían contentos de verme.* ❑ *I'd be glad if the boys slept a little longer.* *Me gustaría que los niños durmieran un poco más.* ● **glad|ly** ADV *gustosamente* ❑ *Malcolm gladly accepted the invitation.* *Malcolm gustosamente aceptó la invitación.* **2** ADJ If you say that you will be **glad to** do something, usually for someone else, you mean that you are willing and eager to do it. *con gusto*

❑ *I'll be glad to show you everything.* *Con mucho gusto te muestro todo.* • **glad|ly** ADV *gustosamente* ❑ *She'll gladly babysit for you if she's free.* *Si está libre, con todo gusto cuidará de tus hijos.*

**glam|or** /glæmər/ N-UNCOUNT → see **glamour**

**glam|or|ous** /glæmərəs/ ADJ If you describe someone or something as **glamorous**, you mean that they are more attractive, exciting, or interesting than ordinary people or things. *glamoroso* ❑ *...beautiful and glamorous women.* *...mujeres hermosas y glamorosas.*

**glam|our** /glæmər/ also **glamor** N-UNCOUNT **Glamour** is the quality of being more attractive, exciting, or interesting than ordinary people or things. *glamour* ❑ *...the glamour of show biz.* *...el glamour de la farándula.*

**glance** /glæns/ (**glances, glancing, glanced**) **1** V-I If you **glance at** something or someone, you look at them very quickly and then look away again immediately. *echar un vistazo* ❑ *He glanced at his watch.* *Le echó un vistazo a su reloj.* **2** V-I If you **glance through** or **at** a newspaper, report, or book, you spend a short time looking at it without reading it very carefully. *ojear, hojear* ❑ *I picked up the book and glanced through it.* *Tomé el libro y lo estuve hojeando.* **3** N-COUNT A **glance** is a quick look at someone or something. *mirada* ❑ *Trevor and I exchanged a glance.* *Trevor y yo intercambiamos miradas.* **4** PHRASE If you say that something is true or seems to be true **at first glance,** you mean that it seems to be true when you first see it or think about it, but that your first impression may be wrong. *a primera vista* ❑ *At first glance, the new car does not look very different from the old one.* *A primera vista, el carro nuevo no se ve muy diferente del viejo.*

**gland** /glænd/ (**glands**) N-COUNT A **gland** is an organ in the body which produces chemical substances for the body to use or get rid of. *glándula* ❑ *...sweat glands.* *...glándulas sudoríparas*

**glare** /glɛər/ (**glares, glaring, glared**) **1** V-I If you **glare at** someone, you look at them with an angry expression on your face. *mirar furiosamente* ❑ *The old woman glared at him.* *La anciana le echó una mirada furiosa.* ❑ *Jacob glared angrily.* *Jacob lo miró enojado.* **2** N-COUNT A **glare** is an angry, hard, and unfriendly look. *mirada furiosa* ❑ *She gave him a furious glare.* *Le echó una mirada furiosa.* **3** V-I If the sun or a light **glares,** it shines with a very bright light which is difficult to look at. *deslumbrar* ❑ *Blinding white light glared in his eyes.* *Una cegadora luz blanca lo deslumbró.* **4** N-UNCOUNT **Glare** is very bright light that is difficult to look at. *resplandor* ❑ *...the glare of a car's headlights.* *...el resplandor de las luces delanteras del carro.* **5** N-SING If someone is in **the glare of** publicity or public attention, they are constantly being watched and talked about by a lot of people. *bajo los reflectores* ❑ *The president's wife disliked the glare of publicity.* *A la esposa del presidente le disgustaba estar bajo los reflectores.*

**glar|ing** /glɛərɪŋ/ **1** ADJ If you describe something bad as **glaring,** you are emphasizing that it is very obvious and easily seen or noticed. *flagrante* ❑ *This was a glaring mistake.* *Era un error flagrante.* • **glar|ing|ly** ADV *flagrantemente, absolutamente* ❑ *It was glaringly obvious.* *Era absolutamente obvio.* **2** → see also **glare**

**glass** /glɑs, glæs/ (**glasses**) **1** N-UNCOUNT **Glass** is a hard, transparent substance that is used to make things such as windows and bottles. *vidrio* ❑ *...a bowl made of glass.* *...un tazón de vidrio.* **2** N-COUNT A **glass** is a container made from glass, which you can drink from and which does not have a handle. *vaso* ❑ *He picked up his glass and drank.* *Tomó su vaso y le dio un trago.* ❑ *...a glass of milk.* *...un vaso de leche.* **3** N-UNCOUNT **Glass** is used to mean objects made of glass. *objetos de vidrio* ❑ *They sell beautiful silver and glass.* *Venden hermosos objetos de plata y vidrio.* **4** N-PLURAL **Glasses** are two lenses in a frame that some people wear in front of their eyes in order to help them see better. *lentes, anteojos* ❑ *He took off his glasses.* *Se quitó los lentes.*
→ see Word Web: **glass**
→ see **light**

**glass slide** (**glass slides**) → see **slide**

**glazed** /gleɪzd/ **1** ADJ If someone's eyes are **glazed,** their expression is dull or dreamy, because they are tired or having difficulty concentrating. *vidrioso* ❑ *He sat with glazed eyes in front of the TV.* *Se sentó frente al televisor con la mirada vidriosa.* **2** ADJ **Glazed** pottery is covered with a thin layer of a hard, shiny substance. *vidriado* ❑ *...a large glazed pot.* *...una gran vasija vidriada.* **3** ADJ A **glazed** window or door has glass in it. *con vidrio* ❑ *Her new office had a glazed door with her name on it.* *Su nueva oficina tenía una puerta con una vidriera y su nombre en ella.*
→ see **pottery**

**gleam** /glim/ (**gleams, gleaming, gleamed**) **1** V-I If an object or a surface **gleams,** it reflects light because it is shiny and clean. *resplandecer*

**Word Web** glass

The basic ingredients for **glass** are **silica** (found in **sand**) and **ash** (left over from burning wood). The earliest glass objects are glass **beads** made in Egypt around 3500 BC. By 14 AD, the Syrians had learned how to **blow** glass to form hollow containers. These included primitive **bottles** and **vases**. By 100 AD, the Romans were making clear glass **windowpanes**. Modern factories now produce **safety glass** which doesn't **shatter** when it breaks. It includes a layer of cellulose between two **sheets** of glass. **Bulletproof** glass consists of several layers of glass with a tough, **transparent** plastic between the layers.

❑ *His black hair gleamed in the sun.* *Su cabello negro resplandecía bajo el sol.* **2** N-COUNT A **gleam of** something is a faint sign of it. *atisbo* ❑ *There was a gleam of hope for peace.* *Había un atisbo de esperanza de paz.*

**glid|er** /glaɪdər/ (plural) N-COUNT A **glider** is an aircraft without an engine, which flies by floating on air currents. *planeador*

**glimpse** /glɪmps/ (**glimpses, glimpsing, glimpsed**) **1** N-COUNT If you get a **glimpse of** someone or something, you see them very briefly and not very well. *vistazo* ❑ *Fans waited outside the hotel to catch a glimpse of the star.* *Los admiradores de la estrella la esperaban fuera del hotel para siquiera echarle un vistazo.* **2** V-T If you **glimpse** someone or something, you see them very briefly and not very well. *vislumbrar, divisar* ❑ *She glimpsed a boat out on the ocean.* *Divisó una embarcación en el océano.* **3** N-COUNT A **glimpse of** something is a brief experience of it or an idea about it that helps you understand or appreciate it better. *probadita* ❑ *The movie offers a glimpse into the lives of these women.* *La película ofrece una breve mirada de las vida de esas mujeres.*

G

**glit|ter** /glɪtər/ (**glitters, glittering, glittered**) **1** V-I If something **glitters,** light comes from or is reflected off different parts of it. *destellar* ❑ *The bay glittered in the sunshine.* *La bahía destellaba bajo la luz del sol.* **2** N-UNCOUNT You can use **glitter** to refer to superficial attractiveness or to the excitement connected with something. *brillo* ❑ *She loved the glitter of show business.* *Le encantaba el brillo del mundo del espectáculo*

**glob|al** /gloʊbᵊl/ **1** ADJ **Global** means concerning or including the whole world. *global* ❑ *...a global ban on nuclear testing.* *...una prohibición global de pruebas nucleares.* • **glob|al|ly** ADV *globalmente* ❑ *The company employs 5,800 people globally, including 2,000 in Colorado.* *La compañía emplea globalmente a 5,800 personas, 2,000 de ellas en Colorado.* **2** ADJ A **global** view or vision of a situation is one in which all the different aspects of it are considered. *global* ❑ *We need to take a global view of economic and social problems.* *Necesitamos adoptar una visión global de los problemas sociales y económicos.*

**glob|al po|si|tion|ing sys|tem** (**global positioning systems**) N-COUNT A **global positioning system** is a system that uses signals from satellites to find out the position of an object. The abbreviation **GPS** is also used. *sistema de posicionamiento global*

**glob|al vil|lage** N-SING People sometimes refer to the world as a **global village** when they want to emphasize that all the different parts of the world form one community linked together by electronic communications, especially the Internet. *aldea global* ❑ *We are all part of the global village.* *Todos formamos parte de la aldea global.*

**glob|al warm|ing** N-UNCOUNT **Global warming** is the gradual rise in the Earth's temperature caused by high levels of carbon dioxide and other gases in the atmosphere. *calentamiento global* ❑ *...the threat of global warming.* *...la amenaza del calentamiento global.*
→ see **air, greenhouse effect, ozone**

**globe** /gloʊb/ (**globes**) **1** N-SING You can refer to the world as **the globe** when you are emphasizing how big it is or that something happens in many different parts of it. *Tierra, globo, mundo* ❑ *...people from every part of the globe.* *...gente de todas partes del globo.* ❑ *70% of our globe's surface is water.* *El 70% de la superficie de nuestro mundo está cubierta de agua.* **2** N-COUNT A **globe** is a ball-shaped object with a map of the world on it. It is usually fixed on a stand. *globo terráqueo* ❑ *A large globe stood on his desk.* *Un gran globo terráqueo estaba sobre su escritorio.*

**globu|lar clus|ter** (**globular clusters**) N-COUNT A **globular cluster** is a dense group of older stars that is roughly the shape of a sphere. *cúmulo globular* [TECHNICAL]

**gloom** /glum/ **1** N-SING **The gloom** is a state of near darkness. *penumbra* ❑ *...the gloom of a foggy November morning.* *...la penumbra de una mañana neblinosa de noviembre.* **2** N-UNCOUNT **Gloom** is a feeling of sadness and lack of hope. *desaliento* ❑ *There is increasing gloom over the economy.* *Existe un desaliento creciente respecto de la economía.*

**gloomy** /glumi/ (**gloomier, gloomiest**) **1** ADJ If a place is **gloomy,** it is almost dark so that you cannot see very well. *sombrío, tétrico* ❑ *Inside it's gloomy after all that sunshine.* *Adentro estaba sombrío luego de toda esa luz del sol.* **2** ADJ If people are **gloomy,** they are unhappy and have no hope. *desalentado* ❑ *He is gloomy about the future of television.* *Se siente desalentado respecto del futuro de la televisión.* • **gloomi|ly** ADV *con tristeza, con melancolía* ❑ *He told me gloomily that he had to leave.* *Me dijo con tristeza que tenía que irse.* **3** ADJ If a situation is **gloomy,** it does not give you much hope of success or happiness. *desalentador* ❑ *The economic prospects for next year are gloomy.* *Las perspectivas económicas para el año próximo son desalentadoras.*
→ see **weather**

**glo|ri|ous** /glɔriəs/ **1** ADJ Something that is **glorious** is very beautiful and impressive. *espléndido, magnífico, soberbio* ❑ *...a glorious rainbow.* *...un arcoíris soberbio.* • **glo|ri|ous|ly** ADV *magníficamente, espléndidamente, soberbiamente* ❑ *The trees are gloriously colored in the fall.* *Los árboles se tiñen de colores espléndidos en el otoño.* **2** ADJ If you describe something as **glorious,** you are emphasizing that it is wonderful and it makes you feel very happy. *glorioso* ❑ *...glorious memories of his days as a champion.* *...recuerdos de sus gloriosos días de campeón.* • **glo|ri|ous|ly** ADV *magníficamente, espléndidamente, soberbiamente* ❑ *...a gloriously sunny morning.* *...una mañana espléndidamente soleada.* **3** ADJ A **glorious** career, victory, or occasion involves great fame or success. *glorioso, espléndido, magnífico* ❑ *He had a glorious career as a broadcaster and writer.* *Tenía una magnífica carrera como locutor y escritor.* • **glo|ri|ous|ly** ADV *magníficamente, espléndidamente, soberbiamente* ❑ *The mission was gloriously successful.* *La misión fue muy exitosa.*

**glo|ry** /glɔri/ (**glories**) **1** N-UNCOUNT **Glory** is the fame and admiration that you gain by doing something impressive. *gloria* ❑ *He had his moment of glory when he won a 20-km race.* *Tuvo su momento de gloria cuando ganó una carrera de 20 km.* **2** N-PLURAL A person's **glories** are the occasions when they have done something people greatly admire which makes them famous. glorias ❑ *Instead of remembering past glories we need to create something new.* *En vez de recordar las glorias pasadas necesitamos crear algo nuevo.*

**Word Partnership** Usar *glory* con:

V. **bask in the** glory 1
N. **blaze of** glory, glory **days, hope and** glory, **moment of** glory 1

**glove** /glʌv/ (**gloves**) N-COUNT **Gloves** are pieces of clothing which cover your hands and wrists and have individual sections for each finger. You wear gloves to keep your hands warm or dry or to protect them. *guante* ❑ *He put his gloves in his pocket.* *Se metió los guantes en la bolsa.*
→ see **baseball**

**glow** /gloʊ/ (**glows, glowing, glowed**)
1 N-COUNT A **glow** is a dull, steady light, for example the light produced by a fire when there are no flames. *resplandor* ❑ *She saw the red glow of a fire.* *Vio el rojo resplandor de un fuego.* 2 N-SING A **glow** is a pink color on a person's face, usually because they are healthy or have been exercising. *rubor* ❑ *The moisturizer gave my face a healthy glow.* *La crema hidratante le dio a mi rostro un rubor saludable.* 3 N-SING If you feel a **glow of** satisfaction or achievement, you have a strong feeling of pleasure because of something that you have done or that has happened. *oleada* ❑ *Exercise will give you a glow of satisfaction.* *El ejercicio te dará una sensación de gran satisfacción.* 4 V-I If something **glows,** it produces a dull, steady light. *brillar con luz tenue* ❑ *The lantern glowed softly in the darkness.* *La linterna brillaba tenuemente en la oscuridad.* 5 V-I If someone's skin **glows,** it looks pink because they are healthy or excited, or have been doing physical exercise. *enrojecer* ❑ *Her skin glowed with health.* *Su piel estaba rozagante.* 6 V-I If someone **glows with** an emotion such as pride or pleasure, the expression on their face shows how they feel. *resplandecer* ❑ *Her mother glowed with pride.* *Su madre resplandecía de orgullo.*
→ see **fire, light**

**Thesaurus** *glow* Ver también:

N. beam, glimmer, light 1
blush, flush, radiance 2
V. gleam, radiate, shine 4 6

**glu|cose** /glukoʊs/ N-UNCOUNT **Glucose** is a type of sugar. *glucosa*
→ see **photosynthesis**

**glue** /glu/ (**glues, glueing** or **gluing, glued**)
1 N-VAR **Glue** is a sticky substance used for joining things together. *pegamento* ❑ *...a tube of glue.* *...un tubo de pegamento.* 2 V-T If you **glue** one object to another, you stick them together using glue. *pegar* ❑ *Glue the fabric around the picture.* *Pega la tela alrededor de la foto.* ❑ *The material is cut and glued in place.* *El material se corta y pega en su lugar.*
3 V-T PASSIVE If you say that someone **is glued to** something, you mean that they are giving it all their attention. *pegar(se), clavar(se)* ❑ *They were all glued to the game on TV.* *Estaban todos pegados a la television viendo el partido.*

**GM** /dʒi ɛm/ ADJ **GM** crops have had one or more genes changed, for example in order to make them resist pests better. **GM** is an abbreviation for **genetically modified**. *transgénico* ❑ *We may be eating food containing GM ingredients without realizing it.* *Podríamos estar comiendo alimentos que contienen ingredientes transgénicos sin saberlo.*

**GM-free** ADJ **GM-free** products or crops are products or crops that do not contain any genetically-modified material. *no transgénicos* ❑ *...GM-free soy.* *...soya no transgénica.*

**GMO** /dʒi ɛm oʊ/ (**GMOs**) N-COUNT A **GMO** is an animal, plant, or other organism whose genetic structure has been changed by genetic engineering. **GMO** is an abbreviation for "genetically-modified organism." *organismo transgénico* ❑ *...the presence of GMOs in many processed foods.* *...la presencia de organismos transgénicos en muchas alimentos preparados.*

**GMT** /dʒi ɛm ti/ **GMT** is the standard time in Great Britain which is used to calculate the time in the rest of the world. **GMT** is an abbreviation for **Greenwich Mean Time.** *hora (media) de Greenwich* ❑ *New Mexico is seven hours behind GMT.* *La hora de Nuevo México tiene una diferencia de siete horas menos con el meridiano de Greenwich.*

**go**
1 MOVING OR LEAVING
2 LINK VERB USE
3 OTHER VERB USES, NOUN USES, AND PHRASES
4 PHRASAL VERBS

1 **go** /goʊ/ (**goes, going, went, gone**)

In most cases the past participle of **go** is **gone,** but occasionally you use "been:" see **been.**

1 V-T/V-I When you **go** somewhere, you move or travel there. *ir, avanzar* ❑ *We went to Rome.* *Fuimos a Roma.* ❑ *I went home for the weekend.* *Fui a casa por el fin de semana.* ❑ *It took an hour to go three miles.* *Tomó una hora avanzar cinco kilómetros.* 2 V-I When you **go,** you leave the place where you are. *irse* ❑ *It's time for me to go.* *Es hora de irme.* 3 V-T/V-I You use **go** to say that someone leaves the place where they are and does an activity, often a leisure activity. *ir(se)* ❑ *We went swimming early this morning.* *Fuimos a nadar temprano en la mañana.* ❑ *They've gone shopping.* *Se fueron de compras.* ❑ *He went for a walk.* *Fue a caminar.* 4 V-I When you **go** do something, you move to a place in order to do it and you do it. You can also **go and** do something, but you always say that someone **went and** did something. *ir* ❑ *I have to go see the doctor.* *Tengo que ir a ver al médico.* ❑ *I finished my drink, then went and got another.* *Terminé mi trago y luego fui por otro.* 5 V-I If you **go to** school, work, or church, you attend it regularly as part of your normal life. *ir* ❑ *Does your daughter go to school yet?* *¿Ya va tu hija a la escuela?* 6 V-I When you say where a road or path **goes,** you are saying where it begins or ends, or what places it is in. *ir* ❑ *There's a road that goes from Blairstown to Millbrook Village.* *Hay un camino que va de Blairstown a Millbrook Village.* 7 V-I If you say where money **goes,** you are saying what it is spent on. *irse* ❑ *Most of my money goes toward bills.* *La mayor parte de mi dinero se va en pagar cuentas.*
8 V-I If you say that something **goes to** someone,

you mean that it is given to them. *corresponder* ❑ *A lot of credit should go to his father. Buena parte del crédito debería corresponder a su padre.* **9** V-I If something **goes,** someone gets rid of it. *deshacerse, perderse* ❑ *Hundreds of jobs could go. Podrían perderse cientos de empleos.* **10** V-I If something **goes into** something else, it is put in it as one of the parts or elements that form it. *entrar, llevar* ❑ *...the ingredients that go into the dish. ...los ingredientes que lleva el platillo.* **11** V-I If something **goes** in a particular place, it belongs there or should be put there, because that is where you normally keep it. *ir* ❑ *The shoes go on the shoe shelf. Los zapatos van en la zapatera.* **12** V-I If one of a person's senses, such as their sight or hearing, **is going,** it is getting weak and they may soon lose it completely. *estar perdiendo* [INFORMAL] ❑ *His eyes are going. Está perdiendo la vista.* **13** V-I If something such as a light bulb or a part of an engine **goes,** it is no longer working and needs to be replaced. *descomponerse, fundirse* ❑ *A light bulb has gone in the bathroom. Se fundió un foco del baño.*

G

**Usage** go

Go is often used to mean *visit. Sarah has gone to London twice this year, and Tony went three times last year. It's their favorite city.*

**❷ go** /goʊ/ (**goes, going, went, gone**) V-LINK You can use **go** to say that a person or thing changes to another state or condition. For example, if someone **goes crazy,** they become crazy, and if something **goes bad,** it deteriorates. *volverse* ❑ *I'm going bald. Me estoy quedando calvo.* ❑ *The meat has gone bad. La carne se echó a perder.*

**❸ go** /goʊ/ (**goes, going, went, gone**) **1** V-I You use **go** to talk about the way something happens. For example, if an event or situation **goes well,** it is successful. *ir, salir* ❑ *Everything is going wrong. Todo está saliendo mal.* **2** V-I If a machine or device **is going,** it is working. *andar* ❑ *Can you get my car going again? ¿Puedes echar a andar mi carro otra vez?* **3** V-RECIP If something **goes with** something else, or if two things **go together,** they look or taste good together. *quedar bien* ❑ *Those pants would go with my new shirt. Esos pantalones quedarían bien con mi nueva playera.* ❑ *Some colors go together and some don't. Algunos colores van bien entre sí y otros no.* **4** N-COUNT A **go** is an attempt at doing something. *intento, prueba* ❑ *I wanted to have a go at football. Quise probar en el futbol.* ❑ *She won on her first go. Ganó en el primer intento.* **5** N-COUNT If it is your **go** in a game, it is your turn to do something, for example to play a card or move a piece. *turno* ❑ *Now whose go is it? ¿A quién le toca ahora?* **6** → see also **going, gone** **7** PHRASE If you say that someone **is making a go of** something such as a business or relationship, you mean that they are having some success with it. *salir adelante, sacar adelante* ❑ *I knew we could make a go of it and be happy. Sabía que podríamos salir adelante y ser felices.* **8** PHRASE If you say that someone is always **on the go,** you mean that they are always busy and active. *no parar, no descansar* [INFORMAL] ❑ *In my job I am on the go all the time. En mi trabajo me paso todo el tiempo sin parar.* **9** PHRASE If you say that there is a certain amount of time **to go,** you mean that there is that amount of time left before something happens or ends. *faltar* ❑ *There is a week to go until the party. Falta una semana para la fiesta.* **10** PHRASE If you are in a café or restaurant and ask for an item of food **to go,** you mean that you want to take it with you and not eat it there. *para llevar* ❑ *...large fries to go. ...una porción grande de papas para llevar.*

**❹ go** /goʊ/ (**goes, going, went, gone**)

▸ **go about** **1** PHR-VERB The way you **go about** a task or problem is the way you approach it and deal with it. *abordar, emprender, empezar* ❑ *I want to work in journalism, but I don't know how to go about it. Quiero trabajar en periodismo, pero no sé por dónde empezar.* **2** PHR-VERB When you **are going about** your normal activities, you are doing them. *estar ocupado en* ❑ *People were going about their business when they heard an explosion. Las personas estaban ocupadas en sus asuntos cuando oyeron la explosión.*

▸ **go after** PHR-VERB If you **go after** something, you try to get it, catch it, or hit it. *ir por* ❑ *This year he's going after the championship. Este año va a ir por el campeonato.*

▸ **go against** PHR-VERB If a person or their behavior **goes against** your wishes, beliefs, or expectations, their behavior is the opposite of what you want, believe in, or expect. *ir en contra de* ❑ *These changes go against my principles. Estos cambios van en contra de mis principios.*

▸ **go ahead** **1** PHR-VERB If someone **goes ahead with** something, they begin to do it or make it, especially after planning, promising, or asking permission to do it. *seguir adelante* ❑ *The board will vote on whether to go ahead with the plan. El consejo votará si seguimos adelante o no con el plan.* **2** PHR-VERB If a process or an organized event **goes ahead,** it takes place or is carried out. *llevarse a cabo* ❑ *The event will go ahead as planned next summer. El evento se llevará a cabo el próximo verano, de acuerdo a lo planeado.*

▸ **go along with** PHR-VERB If you **go along with** a rule, decision, or policy, you accept it and obey it. *secundar, estar de acuerdo* ❑ *I'll go along with whatever the others decide. Secundaré lo que los otros decidan.*

▸ **go around** **1** PHR-VERB If you **go around to** someone's house, you go to visit them at their house. *ir* ❑ *He went around to her house to see if she was there. Fue a su casa a ver si la encontraba.* **2** PHR-VERB If there is enough of something **to go around,** there is enough of it to be shared among a group of people, or to do all the things for which it is needed. *alcanzar* ❑ *In the future we may not have enough water to go around. En el futuro es posible que el agua no alcance para todo el mundo.*

▸ **go away** **1** PHR-VERB If you **go away,** you leave a place or a person's company. *irse* ❑ *I need to go away and think about this. Necesito un rato para considerar esto.* **2** PHR-VERB If you **go away,** you leave a place and spend a period of time somewhere else, especially as a vacation. *salir* ❑ *Why don't you and I go away this weekend? ¿Por qué no salimos tú y yo este fin de semana?*

▸ **go back on** PHR-VERB If you **go back on** a promise or agreement, you do not do what you promised or agreed to do. *no cumplir con* ❑ *The president has gone back on his promise. El presidente no cumplió con su promesa.*

▸ **go back to** PHR-VERB If you **go back to** a task or activity, you start doing it again after you have

stopped doing it for a period of time. regresar a ❑ *I want to go back to work as soon as possible.* *Quiero regresar a trabajar tan pronto como sea posible.*
▸ **go before** PHR-VERB To **go before** a judge, tribunal, or court of law means to be present there as part of an official or legal process. presentar ante ❑ *The case went before the judge on December 23.* *El caso se presentó ante el juez el 23 de diciembre.*
▸ **go by** PHR-VERB If you say that time **goes by,** you mean that it passes. pasar ❑ *I gradually forgot about him as the years went by.* *Me fui olvidando gradualmente de él a medida que pasaban los años.*
▸ **go down** **1** PHR-VERB If a price, level, or amount **goes down,** it becomes lower or less than it was. bajar ❑ *Inflation went down last month.* *La inflación bajó el mes pasado.* ❑ *Crime has gone down 70 percent.* *El crimen ha bajado en un 70 por ciento.* **2** PHR-VERB If you **go down on** your knees or **on** all fours, you lower your body until it is supported by your knees, or by your hands and knees. ponerse ❑ *I went down on my knees and prayed.* *Me puse de rodillas y recé.* **3** PHR-VERB When the sun **goes down,** it goes below the horizon. ponerse ❑ *It gets cold after the sun goes down.* *Hace frío después de que se pone el sol.* **4** PHR-VERB If a ship **goes down,** it sinks. If a plane **goes down,** it crashes out of the sky. hundirse, caerse ❑ *Their aircraft went down.* *Su avión se cayó.*
▸ **go for** **1** PHR-VERB If you **go for** a particular thing or way of doing something, you choose it. decidirse por, optar por ❑ *He decided to go for a smaller computer.* *Se decidió por una computadora más chica.* **2** PHR-VERB If you **go for** someone, you attack them. irse sobre ❑ *The dog suddenly went for him.* *El perro se le fue encima de repente.*
▸ **go in** PHR-VERB If the sun **goes in,** a cloud comes in front of it and it can no longer be seen. meterse ❑ *The sun went in, and it felt cold.* *Se metió el sol y se sintió frío.*
▸ **go in for** PHR-VERB If you **go in for** a particular activity, you do it as a hobby. practicar ❑ *They go in for tennis and bowling.* *Ellos practican tenis y boliche.*
▸ **go into** **1** PHR-VERB If you **go into** something, you describe or examine it fully or in detail. entrar en, meterse ❑ *I don't want to go into details about what was said.* *No quiero entrar en detalles sobre lo que se dijo.* **2** PHR-VERB If you **go into** something, you decide to do it as your job or career. entrar en ❑ *Sam has gone into the tourism business.* *Sam entró en el negocio del turismo.*
▸ **go off** **1** PHR-VERB If an explosive device or a gun **goes off,** it explodes or fires. explotar ❑ *A bomb went off, destroying the vehicle.* *Una bomba explotó y destruyó el vehículo.* **2** PHR-VERB If an alarm bell **goes off,** it makes a sudden loud noise. activarse ❑ *The fire alarm went off and everybody ran out.* *Se activó la alarma contra incendios y todos salieron corriendo.* **3** PHR-VERB If an electrical device **goes off,** it stops operating. apagarse ❑ *All the lights went off.* *Todas las luces se apagaron.*
▸ **go on** **1** PHR-VERB If you **go on** doing something, or **go on with** an activity, you continue to do it. seguir ❑ *Go on with your work.* *Sigue con tu trabajo.* **2** PHR-VERB If something **is going on,** it is happening. suceder, transcurrir ❑ *While this conversation was going on, I was listening.* *Mientras transcurría esta conversación, yo estaba escuchando.* **3** PHR-VERB If a process or institution **goes on,** it continues to happen or exist. continuar ❑ *Why is it necessary for the war to go on?* *¿Por qué es necesario que continúe la guerra?* **4** PHR-VERB If an electrical device **goes on,** it begins operating. encender ❑ *A light went on at seven every evening.* *Todos los días se encendía una luz a las siete de la tarde.*
▸ **go out** **1** PHR-VERB If you **go out,** you leave your home in order to do something enjoyable, for example to go to a party, a bar, or the movies. salir ❑ *I'm going out tonight.* *Voy a salir esta noche.* **2** PHR-VERB If you **go out with** someone, the two of you have a romantic or sexual relationship. salir ❑ *I once went out with a French man.* *Una vez salí con un francés.* **3** PHR-VERB If a light **goes out,** it stops shining. apagarse ❑ *The bedroom light went out after a moment.* *La luz del cuarto se apagó luego de un momento.* **4** PHR-VERB If something that is burning **goes out,** it stops burning. apagarse ❑ *The fire seemed to be going out.* *El fuego parecía estar apagándose.* **5** PHR-VERB When the tide **goes out,** the water in the sea gradually moves back to a lower level. bajar ❑ *The tide was going out.* *La marea estaba bajando.*
▸ **go over** PHR-VERB If you **go over** a document, incident, or problem, you examine, discuss, or think about it very carefully. revisar ❑ *We went over everything, searching for errors.* *Revisamos todo, buscando errores.*
▸ **go round** → see **go around**
▸ **go through** **1** PHR-VERB If you **go through** a difficult experience or a period of time, you experience it. atravesar, pasar por ❑ *He was going through a very difficult time.* *Estaba pasando por un momento muy difícil.* **2** PHR-VERB If you **go through** a lot of things such as papers or clothes, you look at them, usually in order to sort them into groups or to search for a particular item. revisar ❑ *Someone has gone through my possessions.* *Alguien estuvo revisando mis cosas.* **3** PHR-VERB If a law, agreement, or official decision **goes through,** it is approved by a legislature or committee. pasar ❑ *The bill probably won't go through.* *El proyecto de ley probablemente no va a pasar.*
▸ **go through with** PHR-VERB If you **go through with** an action you have decided on, you do it, even though it may be very unpleasant or difficult for you. llevar a cabo, cumplir ❑ *Richard pleaded with Bella not to go through with the divorce.* *Richard le suplicó a Bella que no llevara a cabo el trámite del divorcio.*
▸ **go under** PHR-VERB If a business or project **goes under,** it becomes unable to continue in operation or in existence. hundirse, quebrar [BUSINESS] ❑ *Many small businesses have gone under.* *Muchas empresas pequeñas quebraron.*
▸ **go up** **1** PHR-VERB If a price, amount, or level **goes up,** it becomes higher or greater than it was. subir ❑ *Interest rates went up.* *Las tasas de interés subieron.* ❑ *The cost has gone up to $1.95 a minute.* *El costo ha subido a 1.95 dólares el minuto.* **2** PHR-VERB If something **goes up,** it explodes or starts to burn, usually suddenly and with great intensity. estallar, incendiarse ❑ *The hotel went up in flames.* *El hotel se incendió.*
▸ **go with** **1** PHR-VERB If one thing **goes with** another thing, the two things officially belong together, so that if you get one, you also get the other. ir acompañado de ❑ *A $250,000 salary goes with the job.* *El empleo va acompañado de un salario de*

250,000 dólares. **2** PHR-VERB If one thing **goes with** another thing, it is usually found or experienced together with the other thing. *acompañar* ❑ *...the pain that goes with defeat. ...el dolor que acompaña a la derrota.*

▸ **go without** PHR-VERB If you **go without** something that you need or usually have or do, you do not get it or do it. *arreglárselas sin* ❑ *They had to go without food for days. Tuvieron que arreglárselas sin comida durante varios días.*

**go-ahead** **1** N-SING If you give someone or something **the go-ahead,** you give them permission to start doing something. *visto bueno, luz verde* ❑ *He got the go-ahead to start the project. Obtuvo el visto bueno para comenzar el proyecto.* **2** ADJ A **go-ahead** person or organization tries hard to succeed, often by using new methods. *emprendedor, decidido, con empuje*

G

**goal** /goʊl/ (**goals**) **1** N-COUNT In games such as soccer or hockey, the **goal** is the space into which the players try to get the ball in order to score a point for their team. *portería* ❑ *The ball went straight into the goal. El balón entró directamente en la portería.* **2** N-COUNT In games such as soccer or hockey, a **goal** is when a player gets the ball into the goal, or the point that is scored by doing this. *gol* ❑ *They scored five goals in the first half of the match. Anotaron cinco goles en la primera mitad del partido.* **3** N-COUNT Your **goal** is something that you hope to achieve, especially when much time and effort will be needed. *meta* ❑ *You need to decide your own goals. Tienes que escoger tus propias metas.*
→ see **football, soccer**

| **Word Partnership** | Usar *goal* con: |
|---|---|
| V. | **shoot at a** goal **1** |
| | **score a** goal **2** |
| | **accomplish a** goal, **share a** goal **3** |
| ADJ. | **winning** goal **2** |
| | **attainable** goal, **main** goal **3** |

**goalie** /goʊli/ (**goalies**) N-COUNT A **goalie** is the same as a **goalkeeper.** *portero o portera* [INFORMAL]

**goal|keeper** /goʊlkipər/ (**goalkeepers**) N-COUNT A **goalkeeper** is the player on a sports team whose job is to guard the goal. *portero o portera*

**goal|post** /goʊlpoʊst/ (**goalposts**) also **goal post** N-COUNT A **goalpost** is one of the two upright wooden posts that are connected by a crossbar and form the goal in games such as soccer and hockey. *poste de la portería*
→ see **football**

**goat** /goʊt/ (**goats**) N-COUNT A **goat** is an animal that is about the size of a sheep. Goats have horns, and hairs on their chin which resemble a beard. *chivo, cabra*

**gob** /gɒb/ (**gobs**) **1** N-COUNT A **gob of** something is a lump of it. *pedazo* ❑ *...a gob of ice. ...un pedazo de hielo.* **2** N-PLURAL **Gobs of** something means a lot of it. *montón* [INFORMAL] ❑ *We're getting input from gobs of sources. Estamos recibiendo aportaciones de un montón de fuentes.*

**go-cart** (**go-carts**) also **go-kart** N-COUNT A **go-cart** is a very small motor vehicle with four wheels, used for racing. *go kart*

**god** /gɒd/ (**gods**) **1** N-PROPER The name **God** is given to the spirit or being who is worshipped as the creator and ruler of the world, especially by Jews, Christians, and Muslims. *Dios* ❑ *He believes in God. Él cree en Dios.* **2** CONVENTION People sometimes use **God** in exclamations to emphasize something that they are saying, or to express surprise, fear, or excitement. This use could cause offense. *Dios* ❑ *Oh my God, it's snowing. ¡Dios mío, está nevando!* ❑ *Good God, it's Mr. Harper! ¡Dios mío, si es el Sr. Harper!* **3** N-COUNT In many religions, a **god** is one of the spirits or beings that are believed to have power over a particular part of the world or nature. *dios* ❑ *...Zeus, king of the gods. ...Zeus, rey de los dioses.* **4** **thank God** → see **thank**

**god|dess** /gɒdɪs/ (**goddesses**) N-COUNT In many religions, a **goddess** is a female spirit or being that is believed to have power over a particular part of the world or nature. *diosa* ❑ *...Diana, the goddess of hunting. ...Diana, la diosa de la caza.*

**GOES** /dʒi oʊ i ɛs/ N-SING The **GOES** program is a series of satellites that send back information to Earth about environmental and weather conditions. **GOES** is an abbreviation for "Geostationary Operational Environmental Satellite." *satélites meteorológicos geoestacionarios*

goggles

**gog|gles** /gɒgəlz/ N-PLURAL **Goggles** are large glasses that fit closely to your face around your eyes to protect them from such things as water or wind. *goggles, gafas*

**going** /goʊɪŋ/ **1** PHRASE If you say that something **is going to** happen, you mean that it will happen in the future, usually quite soon. *ir a* ❑ *I think it's going to be successful. Creo que va a ser un éxito.* ❑ *You're going to enjoy this. Esto te va a gustar.* **2** PHRASE You say that you **are going to** do something to express your intention or determination to do it. *ir a* ❑ *I'm going to go to bed. Me voy a la cama.* ❑ *He announced that he's going to resign. Anunció que va a renunciar.* **3** N-UNCOUNT You use **the going** to talk about how easy or difficult it is to do something. You can also say that something is, for example, **hard going** or **tough going.** *las cosas* ❑ *She will support him when the going gets tough. Ella lo va a apoyar cuando las cosas se pongan mal.* **4** ADJ The **going** rate for something is the usual amount of money that you expect to pay or receive for it. *actual* ❑ *...the going price for oil. ...el precio actual del petróleo.* **5** → see also **go** **6** PHRASE If someone or something **has** a lot **going for** them, they have a lot of advantages. *tener a su favor* ❑ *This school has a lot going for it. La escuela tiene mucho a su favor.* **7** PHRASE When you **get going,** you start doing something or start a journey, especially after a delay. *moverse* ❑ *The plane leaves in two hours so I've got to get going. El avión sale en dos horas, así que tengo que moverme.* **8** PHRASE If you **keep going,** you continue doing things or doing a particular thing. *seguir adelante* ❑ *She kept going even when she was sick. Siguió adelante, a pesar de que estaba enferma.*
→ see also **will**

**Usage** **going to**

*Going to* and the present continuous are both used to talk about the future. *Going to* is used to describe things that you intend to do: *I'm going tocall my sister tonight*. The present continuous is used to talk about things that are already planned or decided: *We are meeting for lunch on Saturday at noon*.

**goings-on** N-PLURAL If you describe events or activities as **goings-on**, you mean that they are strange, interesting, amusing, or dishonest. *tejemanejes* ❑ *A reporter found out about the goings-on in the company. Un periodista descubrió los tejemanejes que había en la empresa.*

**gold** /goʊld/ (**golds**) **1** N-UNCOUNT **Gold** is a valuable, yellow-colored metal that is used for making jewelry and ornaments, and as an international currency. *oro* ❑ *...a ring made of gold. ...un anillo de oro.* ❑ *The price of gold was going up. El precio del oro estaba subiendo.* **2** N-UNCOUNT **Gold** is jewelry and other things that are made of gold. *objeto de oro* ❑ *We handed over all our gold and money. Entregamos todos nuestros objetos de oro y nuestro dinero.* **3** COLOR Something that is **gold** is a bright-yellow color, and is often shiny. *dorado* ❑ *He wore a black and gold shirt. Llevaba puesta una playera dorada y negra.*
→ see **metal, mineral, money**

**gold|en** /goʊldᵊn/ **1** ADJ Something that is **golden** is bright yellow in color. *dorado* ❑ *She combed her golden hair. Se peinaba su cabello dorado.* **2** ADJ **Golden** things are made of gold. *de oro* ❑ *...a golden chain. ...una cadena de oro.* **3** ADJ If you describe something as **golden**, you mean it is wonderful because it is likely to be successful and rewarding, or because it is the best of its kind. *excelente* ❑ *This is a golden opportunity for peace. Es una oportunidad excelente para la paz.*

**gold|fish** /goʊldfɪʃ/ (**goldfish**) N-COUNT **Goldfish** are small gold or orange fish which are often kept as pets. *pez dorado*
→ see **aquarium**

**gold med|al** (**gold medals**) N-COUNT A **gold medal** is a medal made of gold which is awarded as first prize in a contest or competition. *medalla de oro* ❑ *Her dream is to win a gold medal at the Winter Olympics. Su sueño es ganar la medalla de oro en los Juegos Olímpicos de Invierno.*

**golf** /gɒlf/ N-UNCOUNT **Golf** is a game in which you use long sticks called clubs to hit a small, hard ball into holes that are spread out over a large area of grassy land. *golf* ❑ *Do you play golf? ¿Juegas al golf?* ● **golf|er** N-COUNT (**golfers**) *golfista* ❑ *...one of the world's best golfers. ...uno de los mejores golfistas del mundo.* ● **golf|ing** N-UNCOUNT *golf, jugar al golf* ❑ *You can play tennis or go golfing. Puedes jugar al tenis o al golf.* ❑ *...golfing buddies. ...amigos del golf.*
→ see Picture Dictionary: **golf**

**golf club** (**golf clubs**) **1** N-COUNT A **golf club** is a long, thin, metal stick with a piece of wood or metal at one end that you use to hit the ball in golf. *palo de golf* **2** N-COUNT A **golf club** is a social organization which provides a golf course and a building to meet in for its members. *club de golf*

**Golgi com|plex** /gɔldʒi kɒmplɛks, goʊl-/ (**Golgi complexes**) also **Golgi body** also **Golgi apparatus** N-COUNT *The* **Golgi complex** is a structure inside the cells of animals and plants, which controls the production and secretion of substances such as proteins. *aparato de Golgi* [TECHNICAL]

**gone** /gɔn/ **1** **Gone** is the past participle of **go**. *ido* **2** ADJ When someone is **gone,** they have left the place where you are and are no longer there. When something is **gone,** it is no longer present or no longer exists. *retirado, ausente* ❑ *Things were hard for her while he was gone. Las cosas se pusieron difíciles para ella mientras él estuvo ausente.* ❑ *He's already been gone four hours! ¡Tiene cuatro horas de haberse ido!*

**gong** /gɔŋ/ (**gongs**) N-COUNT A **gong** is a large, flat, circular piece of metal that you hit with a hammer to make a sound like a loud bell. Gongs are sometimes used as musical instruments, or to give a signal that it is time to do something. *gong*
→ see **percussion**

**gon|na** /gɔnə/ **Gonna** is used in written English to represent the words "going to" when they are pronounced informally. *ir a* ❑ *What am I gonna do? ¿Qué voy a hacer?*

**Picture Dictionary** **golf**

**good**
1. DESCRIBING QUALITY, EXPRESSING APPROVAL
2. BENEFIT
3. MORALLY RIGHT
4. OTHER USES

**❶ good** /gʊd/ (**better, best**) **1** ADJ **Good** means pleasant or enjoyable. bueno ❑ *We had a really good time.* *Nos la pasamos muy bien.* ❑ *They wanted a better life.* *Ellos querían una vida mejor.* **2** ADJ **Good** means of a high quality, standard, or level. bueno ❑ *Good food is important to health.* *La buena comida es importante para la salud.* ❑ *His parents wanted him to have the best possible education.* *Sus padres querían que tuviera la mejor educación.* **3** ADJ If you are **good at** something, you are skillful and successful at doing it. bueno en ❑ *He was very good at his work.* *Era muy bueno en su trabajo.* ❑ *I'm not very good at singing.* *No soy muy bueno para el canto.* **4** ADJ A **good** idea, reason, method, or decision is a sensible or valid one. bueno ❑ *It's a good idea to keep your desk tidy.* *Sería bueno que mantuvieras ordenado tu escritorio.* ❑ *There is good reason to suspect that he's guilty.* *Hay buenas razones para sospechar que es culpable.* **5** ADJ Someone who is in a **good** mood is cheerful and pleasant to be with. bueno ❑ *She woke up in a good mood.* *Despertó de buen humor.* ❑ *He is full of charm and good humor.* *Tiene mucho encanto y buen humor.* **6** ADJ You use **good** to emphasize the great extent or degree of something. bueno ❑ *We waited a good fifteen minutes.* *Esperamos unos buenos quince minutos.* **7** → see also **best, better**

| **Thesaurus** | *good* Ver también: |
|---|---|
| ADJ. | agreeable, enjoyable, nice, pleasant; (*ant.*) unpleasant ❶ **1**<br>able, capable, skilled; (*ant.*) unqualified, unskilled ❶ **3** |

**❷ good** /gʊd/ **1** N-SING If something is done for **the good** of a person or organization, it is done in order to benefit them. bien ❑ *He should resign for the good of the country.* *Debería renunciar por el bien del país.* **2** N-UNCOUNT If you say that doing something is **no good** or does **not** do **any good,** you mean that doing it is not of any use or will not bring any success. no sirve de nada ❑ *It's no good worrying about it now.* *No sirve de nada preocuparse por eso ahora.* ❑ *We gave them water and kept them warm, but it didn't do any good.* *Les dimos agua y los mantuvimos calientes, pero no sirvió de nada.* **3** → see also **goods**

**❸ good** /gʊd/ (**better, best**) **1** N-UNCOUNT **Good** is what is considered to be right according to moral standards or religious beliefs. bien ❑ *...the battle between good and evil.* *...la lucha entre el bien y el mal.* **2** ADJ Someone, especially a child, who is **good** is well-behaved. bueno ❑ *The children were very good.* *Los niños eran muy buenos.* ❑ *I'm going to be a good boy now.* *Ahora voy a portarme bien.* **3** ADJ Someone who is **good** is kind and thoughtful. bueno, considerado ❑ *You are good to me.* *Eres bueno conmigo.* ❑ *Her good intentions did not work out the way she wanted.* *Sus buenas intenciones no dieron el resultado que ella esperaba.* **4** → see also **best, better**

**❹ good** /gʊd/ **1** PHRASE "**As good as**" can be used to mean "almost." a punto ❑ *His career is as good as finished.* *Su carrera está a punto de terminar.* **2** PHRASE If something changes or disappears **for good,** it never changes back or comes back as it was before. para siempre ❑ *These forests may be gone for good.* *Estos bosques pueden haberse perdido para siempre.* **3** PHRASE If someone **makes good** a threat or promise or **makes good on** it, they do what they have threatened or promised to do. cumplir ❑ *I am sure they will make good on their promises.* *Estoy segura de que van a cumplir su promesa.*

**good after|noon** CONVENTION You say "**Good afternoon**" when you are greeting someone in the afternoon. buenas tardes [FORMAL]

**good|bye** /gʊdbaɪ/ (**goodbyes**) also **good-bye** **1** CONVENTION You say "**Goodbye**" to someone when you or they are leaving, or at the end of a telephone conversation. adiós **2** N-COUNT When you say your **goodbyes,** you say something such as "Goodbye" when you leave. despedida ❑ *They said their goodbyes at the airport.* *Se despidieron en el aeropuerto.* ❑ *Perry and I exchanged goodbyes.* *Perry y yo nos despedimos.*

**good guy** (**good guys**) N-COUNT You can refer to the good characters in a movie or story as the **good guys.** You can also refer to the **good guys** in a situation in real life. bueno [INFORMAL] ❑ *We're the good guys in this situation.* *Somos los buenos en esta situación.*

**good-humored** ADJ A **good-humored** person or atmosphere is pleasant and cheerful. de buen humor, alegre, jovial, amistoso ❑ *Charles remained very good-humored.* *Charles siguió de muy buen humor.* ❑ *It was a good-humored meeting.* *Fue una junta amistosa.*

**good-looking** (**better-looking, best-looking**) ADJ Someone who is **good-looking** has an attractive face. guapo ❑ *Katy noticed him because he was good-looking.* *Katy notó su presencia porque era guapo.*

**good-natured** ADJ A **good-natured** person or animal is naturally friendly and does not get angry easily. de buen carácter ❑ *He seems like a good-natured person.* *Parece una persona de buen carácter.*

**good|ness** /gʊdnɪs/ **1** EXCLAM People sometimes say "**goodness**" or "**my goodness**" to express surprise. Válgame Dios, Dios mío ❑ *Goodness, I wonder how that happened?* *¡Válgame Dios! ¿Cómo pudo pasar eso?* **2** **thank goodness** → see **thank** **3** N-UNCOUNT **Goodness** is the quality of being kind, helpful, and honest. bondad ❑ *He has faith in human goodness.* *Tiene fe en la bondad humana.*

**goods** /gʊdz/ N-PLURAL **Goods** are things that are made to be sold. productos, bienes ❑ *Companies sell goods or services.* *Las empresas venden bienes o servicios*

| **Word Partnership** | Usar *goods* con: |
|---|---|
| V. | **buy** goods, **sell** goods, **transport** goods |
| N. | **consumer** goods, **delivery of** goods, **exchange of** goods, **variety of** goods |
| ADJ. | **sporting** goods, **stolen** goods |

**good|will** /gʊdwɪl/ N-UNCOUNT **Goodwill** is a friendly or helpful attitude toward other people, countries, or organizations. buena voluntad ❑ *I invited them to dinner to show my goodwill.* *Los invité a* cenar para demostrarles mi buena voluntad.

**goody bag** (**goody bags**) 1 N-COUNT A **goody bag** is a bag of little gifts, often given away by manufacturers in order to encourage people to try their products. muestra gratis [INFORMAL] 2 N-COUNT A **goody bag** is a bag of little gifts or candy that children are sometimes given at a children's party. bolsita de dulces

**goof** /guf/ (**goofs, goofing, goofed**)
▸ **goof off** PHR-VERB If someone **goofs off,** they spend their time doing nothing, often when they should be working. flojear [INFORMAL] ❑ *I goofed off all day.* *Estuve flojeando todo el día.*

**goose** /gus/ (**geese**) 1 N-COUNT A **goose** is a large bird that has a long neck and webbed feet. ganso ❑ *Geese are often raised for their meat.* *Los gansos generalmente se crían para aprovechar su carne.* 2 N-UNCOUNT **Goose** is the meat from a goose that has been cooked. ganso ❑ *...roast goose.* *...ganso asado.*

**gore** /gɔr/ (**gores, goring, gored**) 1 V-T If someone **is gored** by an animal, they are badly wounded by its horns or tusks. cornear ❑ *The farmer was gored by a bull.* *El granjero fue corneado por un toro.* 2 N-UNCOUNT **Gore** is blood from a wound that has become thick. sangre coagulada ❑ *There was blood and gore on the sidewalk.* *Había sangre fresca y coagulada en la acera.*

**gorge** /gɔrdʒ/ (**gorges, gorging, gorged**) 1 N-COUNT A **gorge** is a deep, narrow valley with very steep sides, usually where a river passes through mountains or an area of hard rock. desfiladero ❑ *...the deep gorge between the hills.* *...el profundo desfiladero entre las colinas.* 2 V-T/V-I If you **gorge on** something or **gorge yourself on** it, you eat lots of it in a very greedy way. hartarse de ❑ *We gorged on chocolate.* *Nos hartamos de chocolate.*
→ see **river**

**gor|geous** /gɔrdʒəs/ ADJ Someone or something that is **gorgeous** is very pleasant or attractive. guapísimo, magnífico [INFORMAL] ❑ *It's a gorgeous day.* *Es un día magnífico.* ❑ *You look gorgeous.* *Te ves guapísima.*

**go|ril|la** /gərɪlə/ (**gorillas**) N-COUNT A **gorilla** is a very large ape. gorila
→ see **primate**

**gos|pel** /gɒspəl/ (**gospels**) 1 N-COUNT In the New Testament of the Bible, the **Gospels** are the four books which describe the life and teachings of Jesus Christ. evangelio ❑ *...St. Matthew's Gospel.* *...el Evangelio según San Mateo.* 2 N-UNCOUNT **Gospel** or **gospel music** is a style of religious music that uses strong rhythms and vocal harmony. gospel ❑ *I used to sing gospel.* *Yo acostumbraba cantar música gospel.* 3 N-UNCOUNT If you take something **as gospel,** or as **the gospel truth,** you believe that it is completely true. pura verdad ❑ *This is the gospel truth, I promise.* *Es la pura verdad, te lo juro.*

**gos|sip** /gɒsɪp/ (**gossips, gossiping, gossiped**) 1 N-UNCOUNT; N-SING **Gossip** is informal conversation, often about other people's private business. chisme ❑ *There has been gossip about the reasons for his absence.* *Han corrido chismes sobre los motivos de su ausencia.* 2 V-RECIP If you **gossip with** someone, you talk informally, especially about other people or local events. You can also say that people **gossip.** chismear ❑ *They sat at the kitchen table gossiping.* *Se sentaron a chismear en la mesa de la cocina.* ❑ *Eva gossiped with Sarah.* *Eva estuvo chismeando con Sarah.* 3 N-COUNT If you describe someone as a **gossip,** you disapprove of them because they enjoy talking about the private business of other people. chismoso o chismosa ❑ *He was a terrible gossip.* *Era un chismoso terrible.*

**got** /gɒt/ 1 **Got** is the past tense and sometimes the past participle of **get**. pasado y una de los participios pasados de **get** 2 PHRASE You use **have got** to say that someone has a particular thing, or to mention a quality or characteristic that someone or something has. In informal American English, people sometimes just use "got." tener [SPOKEN] ❑ *I've got a coat just like this.* *Tengo un abrigo igualito a este.* ❑ *He asked, "You got any identification?"* *—¿Tiene una identificación?—me preguntó* 3 PHRASE You use **have got to** when you are saying that something is necessary or must happen in the way stated. In informal American English, the "have" is sometimes omitted. tener que [SPOKEN] ❑ *I'm not happy with the situation, but I've got to accept it.* *No me gusta la situación, pero tengo que aceptarla.* ❑ *Sometimes you got to admit you're wrong.* *A veces tienes que admitir que estás equivocado.* 4 PHRASE People sometimes use **have got to** in order to emphasize that they are certain that something is true, because of the facts or circumstances involved. In informal American English, the "have" is sometimes omitted. deber [SPOKEN] ❑ *"You've got to be joking!" he replied.* *—¡Estas bromeando!—contestó*

**got|ta** /gɒtə/ **Gotta** is used in written English to represent the words "got to" when they are pronounced informally, with the meaning "have to" or "must." tener que ❑ *We gotta eat.* *Tenemos que comer.*

**got|ten** /gɒtən/ **Gotten** is the past participle of **get** in American English. participio pasado de **get** en el inglés de E.U.

**gov|ern** /gʌvərn/ (**governs, governing, governed**) 1 V-T To **govern** a place such as a country, or its people, means to officially control and organize its economic, social, and legal systems. gobernar ❑ *The people choose who they want to govern their country.* *El pueblo decide quién quiere que gobierne su país.* 2 V-T If a situation or activity **is governed by** a particular factor, rule, or force, it is controlled by that factor, rule, or force. regir ❑ *The insurance industry is governed by strict rules.* *El sector de los seguros está regida por leyes estrictas.*

| **Thesaurus** | *govern* | Ver también: |
|---|---|---|
| v. | administer, command, control, direct, guide, head up; (*ant.*) lead, manage, reign 1 | |

**gov|ern|ment** /gʌvərnmənt/ (**governments**) 1 N-COUNT The **government** of a country is the group of people who are responsible for governing it. gobierno ❑ *The government has decided to make changes.* *El gobierno ha decidido hacer cambios.* ❑ *...democratic governments in countries like Britain and the U.S.* *...gobiernos democráticos en países como Gran Bretaña y Estados Unidos.* 2 N-UNCOUNT **Government** consists of the activities, methods,

g

and principles involved in governing a country or other political unit. gobierno ❑ ...our system of government. ...nuestro sistema de gobierno.

• **gov|ern|men|tal** /gʌvərnmɛntᵊl/ ADJ gubernamental **Governmental** means relating to a particular government, or to the practice of governing a country. gubernamental ❑ ...a governmental agency. ...una oficina gubernamental.

→ see **country**

**gov|er|nor** /gʌvərnər/ (**governors**) **1** N-COUNT; N-TITLE In some systems of government, a **governor** is a person who is in charge of the political administration of a state, colony, or region. gobernador o gobernadora ❑ He was governor of Iowa. Fue gobernador de Iowa. **2** N-COUNT A **governor** is a member of a committee which controls an organization such as a university or a hospital. consejero o consejera ❑ ...the board of governors at City University, Bellevue. ...la junta de gobierno de la Universidad de Bellevue.

G

gown

**gown** /gaʊn/ (**gowns**) **1** N-COUNT A **gown** is a long dress which women wear on formal occasions. vestido de gala ❑ She was wearing a ball gown. Traía puesto un vestido de gala. **2** N-COUNT A **gown** is a loose black garment worn on formal occasions by people such as lawyers and academics. toga ❑ ...a headmaster in a long black gown. ...un director en una larga toga negra.

**GP** /dʒi pi/ (**GPs**) also **G.P.** N-COUNT A **GP** is a doctor who does not specialize in any particular area of medicine, but who has a medical practice in which he or she treats all types of illness. **GP** is an abbreviation for "general practitioner." médico familiar o médica familiar, médico de cabecera o médica de cabecera ❑ Her husband called their local GP. Su marido llamó a su médico familiar.

**GPA** /dʒi pi eɪ/ (**GPAs**) N-COUNT **GPA** is an abbreviation for **grade point average.** promedio ❑ You need a good GPA to get into graduate school. Necesitas un buen promedio para entrar a un posgrado.

**GPS** /dʒi pi ɛs/ (**GPSs**) N-COUNT **GPS** is an abbreviation for **global positioning system.** GPS ❑ GPS operates best near the equator. El GPS funciona mejor cerca del ecuador. ❑ ...a GPS receiver. ...un receptor GPS.

→ see **navigation**

**grab** /græb/ (**grabs, grabbing, grabbed**) **1** V-T If you **grab** something, you take it or pick it up suddenly and roughly. agarrar ❑ I grabbed her hand. Le agarré la mano. **2** V-I If you **grab at** something, you try to grab it. alcanzar ❑ He was trying to grab at the handle. Estaba tratando de alcanzar la manija. • **Grab** is also a noun. intento de agarrar ❑ I made a grab for the letter. Traté de agarrar la carta. **3** to **grab hold of** → see **hold** **4** PHRASE If something is **up for grabs,** it is available to anyone who is interested. libre, disponible [INFORMAL] ❑ His old job is up for grabs. Su antiguo puesto está libre.

**Thesaurus** *grab* Ver también:

v. capture, catch, seize, snap up; (ant.) release **1**

**grab bag** (**grab bags**) **1** N-COUNT A **grab bag** is a game in which you take a prize out of a container full of hidden prizes. bolsa de sorpresas, caja de sorpresas **2** N-COUNT A **grab bag of** things, ideas, or people is a varied group of them. montón de cosas varias ❑ The movie is just a grab bag of jokes. La película es sólo un montón de chistes.

**Word Link** *grac ≈ pleasing : disgrace, grace, graceful*

**grace** /greɪs/ (**graces, gracing, graced**) **1** N-UNCOUNT If someone moves with **grace,** they move in a smooth, controlled, and attractive way. gracia ❑ He moved with the grace of a dancer. Se movía con la gracia de un bailarín. **2** V-T If you say that something **graces** a place or a person, you mean that it makes them more attractive. adornar [FORMAL] ❑ Beautiful antique furniture graces their home. Hermosos muebles antiguos adornan su casa. **3** N-VAR When someone says **grace** before or after a meal, they say a prayer in which they thank God for the food and ask Him to bless it. dar las gracias ❑ Will you say grace? ¿Das tú las gracias?

**grace|ful** /greɪsfəl/ **1** ADJ Someone or something that is **graceful** moves in a smooth and controlled way that is attractive to watch. elegante ❑ His movements were smooth and graceful. Sus movimientos eran suaves y elegantes. • **grace|ful|ly** ADV graciosamente ❑ She stepped gracefully onto the stage. Subió graciosamente al escenario. **2** ADJ Something that is **graceful** is attractive because it has a pleasing shape or style. elegante ❑ His handwriting was flowing and graceful. El trazo de su escritura era suelto y elegante.

**grad** /græd/ (**grads**) N-COUNT A **grad** is a **graduate.** licenciado o licenciada, graduado o graduada [INFORMAL]

**grade** /greɪd/ (**grades, grading, graded**) **1** V-T If something **is graded,** its quality is judged, and it is often given a number or a name that indicates how good or bad it is. calificar ❑ Restaurants are graded according to the quality of the food and service. Los restaurantes se califican de acuerdo a la calidad de la comida y el servicio. ❑ Teachers grade the students' work from A to E. Los maestros califican el trabajo de sus estudiantes de la A a la E. **2** N-COUNT The **grade** of a product is its quality. calidad ❑ ...a good grade of wood. ...una madera de buena calidad. **3** N-COUNT Your **grade** in an examination or piece of written work is the mark you get, usually in the form of a letter or number, that indicates your level of achievement. calificación ❑ The best grade you can get is an A. La calificación más alta que puedes obtener es una A. **4** N-COUNT Your **grade** in a company or organization is your level of importance or your rank. grado, categoría ❑ She thinks she should move to a higher grade. Cree que debería ascender a una categoría más alta. **5** N-COUNT In the United States, a **grade** is a group of classes in which all the children are of a similar age. When you are six years old you go into the first grade and you leave school after the twelfth grade. grado ❑ Mr. White teaches first grade. El señor White enseña en primer grado. **6** N-COUNT A **grade** is a slope. pendiente ❑ She drove up a steep grade. Condujo el carro por una cuesta empinada. **7** N-COUNT Someone's **grade** is their military rank. grado ❑ I was a naval officer, lieutenant junior grade. Era oficial naval, con grado de subteniente. 8 PHRASE If someone **makes the grade,** they succeed, especially by reaching a particular standard. dar la talla, tener éxito ❏ *She wanted to be a dancer but failed to make the grade.* Quería ser bailarina, pero no dio la talla.

**grade point av|er|age** (**grade point averages**) also **grade-point average** N-COUNT A student's **grade point average** is a measure of their academic achievement, based on an average of all the grades they receive. promedio ❏ *She had the highest grade point average in the class.* Obtuvo el promedio más alto de la clase.

**grad|ual** /grædʒuəl/ ADJ A **gradual** change or process occurs in small stages over a long period of time, rather than suddenly. gradual ❏ *Losing weight is a gradual process.* Perder peso es un proceso gradual. ● **gradu|al|ly** /grædʒuəli/ ADV gradualmente ❏ *We are gradually learning to use the new computer system.* Gradualmente estamos aprendiendo a usar el nuevo sistema informático.

**gradu|ate** (**graduates, graduating, graduated**)

The noun is pronounced /grædʒuɪt/. The verb is pronounced /grædʒueɪt/.

1 N-COUNT A **graduate** is a student who has successfully completed a course at a high school, college, or university. licenciado o licenciada, egresado o egresada, graduado o graduada ❏ *His parents are both college graduates.* Sus padres son egresados universitarios. 2 V-I When a student **graduates,** they complete their studies successfully and leave their school or university. graduarse ❏ *Her son just graduated from high school.* Su hijo acaba de graduarse de la preparatoria. 3 V-I If you **graduate from** one thing **to** another, you go from a less important job or position to a more important one. ascender ❏ *He graduated to a job as assistant manager.* Ascendió al puesto de subgerente.
→ see **graduation**

**gradu|at|ed** /grædʒueɪtɪd/ ADJ **Graduated** jars are marked with lines and numbers which show particular measurements. graduado

**gradu|ate stu|dent** (**graduate students**) N-COUNT In the United States, a **graduate student** is a student with a first degree from a university who is studying or doing research at a more advanced level. estudiante de posgrado

**gradua|tion** /grædʒueɪʃᵊn/ (**graduations**) 1 N-UNCOUNT **Graduation** is the successful completion of a course of study at a university, college, or school, for which you receive a degree or diploma. graduación ❏ *What are your plans after graduation?* ¿Cuáles son tus planes para después de graduarte? 2 N-COUNT A **graduation** is a special ceremony at a university, college, or school, at which certificates are given to students who have completed their studies. graduación ❏ *Her parents came to her graduation.* Sus padres vinieron a su graduación.
→ see Word Web: **graduation**

**graf|fi|ti** /grəfiti/ N-UNCOUNT **Graffiti** is words or pictures that are written or drawn in public places, for example on walls or posters. grafiti ❏ *There was graffiti all over the walls.* Todas las paredes estaban llenas de grafiti.
→ see **crime**

**gra|ham crack|er** /greɪəm krækər/ (**graham crackers**) N-COUNT A **graham cracker** is a thin, crisp cookie made from wholewheat flour. galleta delgada rectangular de harina de trigo integral

**grain** /greɪn/ (**grains**) 1 N-COUNT A **grain of** wheat, rice, or other cereal crop is a seed from it. grano ❏ *...a grain of wheat.* ...grano de trigo. 2 N-VAR **Grain** is a cereal crop, especially wheat or corn, that has been harvested and is used for food or in trade. grano ❏ *...a bag of grain.* ...una bolsa de granos. 3 N-COUNT A **grain of** something such as sand or salt is a tiny, hard piece of it. grano ❏ *...a grain of sand.* ...un grano de arena. 4 N-SING A **grain of** a quality is a very small amount of it. pizca ❏ *There's a grain of truth in what he says.* Hay una pizca de verdad en lo que dice. 5 N-SING **The grain** of a piece of wood is the direction of its fibers. You can also refer to the pattern of lines on the surface of the wood as **the grain.** veta ❏ *Paint the wood in the direction of the grain.* Pinta la madera siguiendo la dirección de la veta. 6 PHRASE If an idea or action **goes against the grain,** it is very difficult for you to accept it or do it, because it conflicts with your ideas, beliefs, or principles. ir a contracorriente, ir contra ❏ *Paying more taxes goes against the grain for him.* Pagar más impuestos va en contra de sus principios.
→ see Word Web: **grain**
→ see **rice**

**gram** /græm/ (**grams**) N-COUNT A **gram** is a unit of weight. One thousand grams are equal to one kilogram. gramo ❏ *A soccer ball weighs about 400 grams.* Un balón de futbol pesa aproximadamente 400 gramos.

**Word Link** *gram ≈ writing : diagram, grammar, program*

**gram|mar** /græmər/ 1 N-UNCOUNT **Grammar** is the ways that words can be put together in order to make sentences. gramática ❏ *You need to know*

g

**Word Web** graduation

**High school** and **college graduations** are important **events** for students. This **ceremony** tells the world that the **student** is educated. In college, **graduates** receive different types of **diplomas** depending on their subject and level of study. After four years of study, students earn a Bachelor of Arts or Bachelor of Science degree. A Master of Arts or Master of Science usually takes one or two more years. The **PhD**, or doctor of philosophy degree, may require several more years. In addition, a PhD student must write a **thesis** and defend it in front of a group of **professors**.

**Word Web** grain

People first began **cultivating grain** about 10,000 years ago in Asia. Working in groups made growing and **harvesting** the **crop** easier. This probably led Stone Age people to live in communities. Today grain is still the principal food source for humans and domestic animals. Half of all the farmland in the world is used to produce grain. The most popular are **wheat, rice, corn**, and **oats**. An individual kernel of grain is actually a dry, one-seeded **fruit**. It combines the walls of the seed and the flesh of the fruit. Grain is often **ground** into **flour** or meal.

*the basic rules of grammar.* *Necesitas conocer las reglas básicas de la gramática.* **2** N-UNCOUNT Someone's **grammar** is the way in which they obey or do not obey the rules of grammar when they write or speak. *redacción, expresión* ❑ *His vocabulary was large and his grammar was excellent.* *Su vocabulario era amplio y su manera de expresarse excelente.*
→ see **English**

**gram|mati|cal** /grəmætɪk$^{ə}$l/ **1** ADJ **Grammatical** is used to indicate that something relates to grammar. *gramatical* ❑ *...a book of grammatical rules.* *...un libro de reglas gramaticales.* **2** ADJ If language is **grammatical,** it is considered correct because it obeys the rules of grammar. *correcto* ❑ *The test will show whether students can write grammatical English.* *El examen mostrará si los estudiantes son capaces de escribir en un correcto inglés.*

**gramme** /græm/ (**grammes**) → see **gram**

**grand** /grænd/ (**grander, grandest, grand**)

The form **grand** is used as the plural for meaning **5**.

**1** ADJ If you describe a building or a piece of scenery as **grand,** you mean that its size or appearance is very impressive. *majestuoso* ❑ *The courthouse is a grand building in the center of town.* *El Palacio de Justicia es un edificio majestuoso en el centro de la ciudad.* **2** ADJ **Grand** plans or actions are intended to achieve important results. *grande* ❑ *He had a grand design to change the entire future of the United States.* *Tenía grandes planes para cambiar completamente el futuro de los Estados Unidos.* **3** ADJ People who are **grand** think they are important or socially superior. *que se cree superior, creído* ❑ *He is grander than the Prince of Wales.* *Se cree más que el Príncipe de Gales.* **4** ADJ A **grand** total is one that is the final amount or the final result of a calculation. *gran* ❑ *We collected a grand total of $220,329.* *Recabamos un gran total de 220,329 dólares.* **5** N-COUNT A **grand** is a thousand dollars or a thousand pounds. *mil dólares o mil libras.* [INFORMAL] ❑ *She makes at least 80 grand a year.* *Ella gana al menos 80 mil dólares al año.*

**grand|child** /græntʃaɪld/ (**grandchildren**) N-COUNT Someone's **grandchild** is the child of their son or daughter. *nieto o nieta* ❑ *Mary loves her grandchildren.* *Mary adora a sus nietos.*

**grand|dad** /grændæd/ (**granddads**) N-COUNT; N-VOC Your **granddad** is your grandfather. *abuelito* [INFORMAL] ❑ *My granddad is 85.* *Mi abuelito tiene 85 años.*

**grand|daughter** /grændɔtər/ (**granddaughters**) N-COUNT Someone's **granddaughter** is the daughter of their son or daughter. *nieta* ❑ *This is my granddaughter Amelia.* *Esta es mi nieta Amelia.*

**grand|father** /grænfɑðər/ (**grandfathers**) N-COUNT Your **grandfather** is the father of your father or mother. *abuelo* ❑ *His grandfather was a professor.* *Su abuelo era catedrático.*
→ see **family**

**grand jury** (**grand juries**) N-COUNT A **grand jury** is a jury, usually in the United States, which considers a criminal case in order to decide if someone should be tried in a court of law. *jurado de acusación* ❑ *They gave evidence before a grand jury in Washington.* *Presentaron declaración ante el jurado de acusación de Washington.*

**grand|ma** /grænmɑ/ (**grandmas**) N-COUNT Your **grandma** is your grandmother. *abuelita* [INFORMAL] ❑ *Grandma was from Scotland.* *Mi abuelita era de Escocia.*

**grand|mother** /grænmʌðər/ (**grandmothers**) N-COUNT Your **grandmother** is the mother of your father or mother. *abuela* ❑ *My grandmothers were both teachers.* *Mis dos abuelas eran maestras.*
→ see **family**

**grand|pa** /grænpɑ/ (**grandpas**) N-COUNT Your **grandpa** is your grandfather. *abuelito* [INFORMAL] ❑ *Grandpa was sitting in the yard.* *Mi abuelito estaba sentado en el patio.*

**grand|parent** /grænpɛərənt, -pær-/ (**grandparents**) N-COUNT Your **grandparents** are the parents of your father or mother. *abuelo o abuela* ❑ *Tammy was raised by her grandparents.* *Tammy fue criada por sus abuelos.*

**grand slam** (**grand slams**) **1** ADJ In sports, a **grand slam** tournament is a major one. *gran slam* ❑ *She won 39 grand slam titles.* *Ella ganó 39 títulos de gran slam.* • **Grand slam** is also a noun. *gran slam* ❑ *It's my first grand slam.* *Este es mi primer gran slam.* **2** N-COUNT If someone wins a **grand slam,** they win all the major tournaments in a season in a particular sport, for example in golf or tennis. *gran slam* ❑ *They won the grand slam in 1990.* *Ellos ganaron el gran slam en 1990.* **3** N-COUNT In baseball, a **grand slam** is a home run that is hit when there are players standing at all of the bases. *jonrón con las bases llenas*

**grand|son** /grænsʌn/ (**grandsons**) N-COUNT Someone's **grandson** is the son of their son or daughter. *nieto* ❑ *My grandson's birthday was on Tuesday.* *El cumpleaños de mi nieto fue el martes.*

**gran|ny** /græni/ (**grannies**) also **grannie** N-COUNT Some people refer to their grandmother

**Word Web** graph

There are three main elements in a **line** or **bar graph**:

- a **vertical axis** (the y-axis)
- a **horizontal axis** (the x-axis)
- at least one line or set of bars.

To understand a **graph**, do the following:

1. Read the **title** of the graph.
2. Read the **labels** and the **range** of numbers along the side (the **scale** or vertical axis).
3. Read the information along the bottom (horizontal axis) of the graph.
4. Determine what **units** the graph uses. This information can be found on the axis or in the **key**.
5. Look for patterns, groups, and differences.

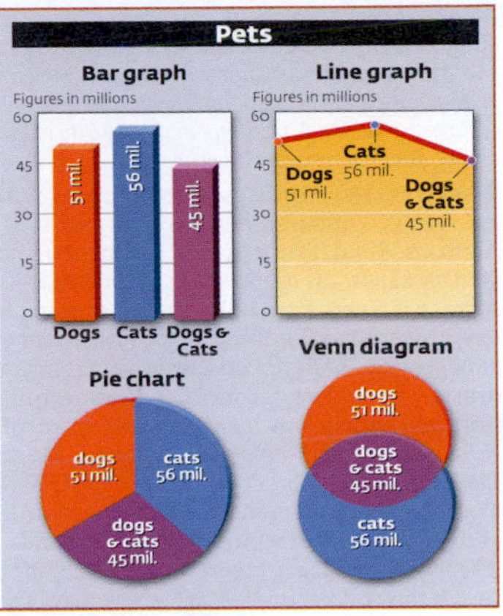


g

as **granny.** *abuelita* [INFORMAL] ❑ *I hugged my granny. Le di un abrazo a mi abuelita.*

**gra|no|la** /grənoʊlə/ N-UNCOUNT **Granola** is a breakfast cereal that contains cereals, dried fruit and nuts. *granola* ❑ *I usually have granola for breakfast. Por lo general desayuno granola.*

**grant** /græ̲nt/ (**grants, granting, granted**) **1** N-COUNT A **grant** is an amount of money that a government or other institution gives to an individual or to an organization for a particular purpose such as education or home improvements. *subsidio, beca* ❑ *They got a grant to research the disease. Obtuvieron un subsidio para investigar la enfermedad.* **2** V-T If someone in authority **grants** you something, you are allowed to have it. *otorgar* [FORMAL] ❑ *France granted him political asylum. Francia le otorgó asilo político.* ❑ *We should grant more independence to our children. Deberíamos darles más independencia a nuestros niños.* **3** V-T If you **grant that** something is true, you accept that it is true, even though your opinion about it does not change. *reconocer* ❑ *We grant that we made a mistake, but it was not intentional. Reconocemos que cometimos un error, pero no fue intencional.* **4** PHRASE If you say that someone **takes** you **for granted,** you are complaining that they benefit from your help, efforts, or presence without showing that they are grateful. *no valorar* ❑ *She feels that her family take her for granted. Siente que su familia no la valora.* **5** PHRASE If you **take** something **for granted,** you believe that it is true or accept it as normal without thinking about it. *dar por sentado o dar por descontado* ❑ *We take things like electricity and running water for granted. Damos por descontadas cosas como la electricidad o el agua corriente.* **6** PHRASE If you **take it for granted that** something is true, you believe that it is true or you accept it as normal without thinking about it. *dar por sentado o dar por descontado* ❑ *He seemed to take it for granted that everyone agreed with him. Parecía dar por descontado que todos estaban de acuerdo con él.*

**grape** /gre̲ɪp/ (**grapes**) **1** N-COUNT **Grapes** are small green or purple fruit which grow in bunches. *uva* ❑ *...a bunch of grapes. ...un racimo de uvas.* **2** PHRASE If you describe someone's attitude as **sour grapes,** you mean that they say something is worthless or undesirable because they want it themselves but cannot have it. *inalcanzable, carente de valor* ❑ *These accusations are just sour grapes. Esas acusaciones carecen de valor.*
→ see **fruit**

**grape|fruit** /gre̲ɪpfrut/ (**grapefruit**)

The plural can also be **grapefruits.**

N-VAR A **grapefruit** is a large, round, yellow fruit that has a sharp, slightly bitter taste. *toronja*

**grape|vine** /gre̲ɪpvaɪn/ N-SING If you hear or learn something **on** or **through the grapevine,** you hear it or learn it in casual conversation with other people. *por vía secreta, contado por un pajarito* ❑ *I heard through the grapevine that he was planning to visit. Me contó un pajarito que estaba pensando venir a vernos.*

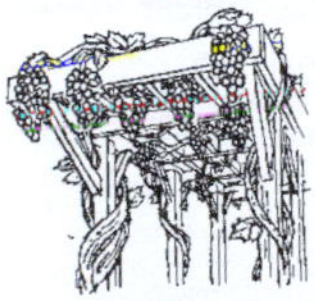
grapevines

**Word Link** *graph ≈ riting : autograph, biography, graph*

**graph** /græf/ (**graphs**) N-COUNT A **graph** is a mathematical diagram which shows the relationship between two or more sets of numbers or measurements. *gráfica* ❑ *The graph shows that prices have risen about 20 percent over the past five years. La gráfica muestra que los precios han subido cerca de un 20 por ciento durante los últimos cinco años.*
→ see Word Web: **graph**

**graph|ic** /græ̲fɪk/ (**graphics**) **1** ADJ If you say that a description or account of something unpleasant is **graphic,** you are emphasizing that it is clear and detailed. *gráfico* ❑ *...graphic descriptions of violence. ...descripciones de violencia muy gráficas.* ● **graphi|cal|ly** /græ̲fɪkli/ ADV *gráficamente, vívidamente* ❑ *War was very graphically depicted in the movie. La guerra estaba representada muy vívidamente en la película.* **2** N-UNCOUNT **Graphics** is the activity of drawing or making pictures, especially in publishing, industry, or computing. *gráficas* ❑ *...a computer manufacturer that specializes in graphics.*

...*un productor de computadoras que se especializa en gráficas.* **3** N-COUNT **Graphics** are drawings and pictures that are composed using simple lines. *diseño gráfico* ❑ *The organization chose a new graphic to replace the old logo. La compañía escogió un nuevo diseño gráfico para reemplazar el viejo logotipo.*

**grasp** /græsp/ (**grasps, grasping, grasped**) **1** V-T If you **grasp** something, you take it in your hand and hold it very firmly. *agarrar* ❑ *He grasped both my hands. Me agarró las dos manos.* **2** N-SING A **grasp** is a very firm hold or grip. *apretón* ❑ *He took her hand in a firm grasp. Tomó su mano con un firme apretón.* **3** N-SING If something is **in** your **grasp,** you possess or control it. If something slips **from** your **grasp,** you lose it or lose control of it. *en las manos (tener), de las manos (perder)* ❑ *Victory slipped from her grasp. La victoria se le fue de las manos.* **4** V-T If you **grasp** something that is complicated or difficult to understand, you understand it. *comprender* ❑ *I don't think you have grasped how serious this problem is. No creo que hayan comprendido la gravedad de este problema.* **5** N-SING A **grasp of** something is an understanding of it. *comprensión* ❑ *They have a good grasp of foreign languages. Tienen una buena comprensión de las lenguas extranjeras.* **6** PHRASE If something is **within** someone's **grasp,** it is very likely that they will achieve it. *al alcance* ❑ *Peace is now within our grasp. La paz está ahora a nuestro alcance.*

G

**grass** /græs/ (**grasses**) N-VAR **Grass** is a very common plant consisting of large numbers of thin, spiky, green leaves that cover the surface of the ground. *pasto* ❑ *We sat on the grass and ate our picnic. Nos sentamos en el pasto y nos pusimos a comer.*
→ see **habitat, grassland, herbivore, plant**

**grass|land** /græslænd/ (**grasslands**) N-VAR **Grassland** is land covered with wild grass. *pastizal, pradera* ❑ *...areas of open grassland. ...áreas de grandes pastizales.*
→ see Word Web: **grassland**
→ see **habitat**

**grass|roots** /græsruts/ N-PLURAL The **grassroots** of an organization or movement are the ordinary people who form the main part of it, rather than its leaders. *bases* ❑ *The grassroots of the party should help to choose its leader. Las bases del partido deberían ayudar a escoger a su líder.*

**grate** /greɪt/ (**grates, grating, grated**) **1** N-COUNT A **grate** is a framework of metal bars in a fireplace, which holds the wood or coal. *chimenea* ❑ *A fire burned in the grate. El fuego ardía en la chimenea.* **2** V-T If you **grate** food such as cheese or carrots, you rub it over a metal tool called a grater so that the food is cut into very small pieces. *rallar* ❑ *Grate the cheese into a bowl. Ralla el queso en un tazón.* **3** V-I When something **grates,** it rubs against something else, making a harsh, unpleasant sound. *chirriar* ❑ *His chair grated as he stood up. Su silla chirrió cuando se levantó.* **4** V-I If something such as someone's behavior **grates on** you or **grates,** it makes you feel annoyed. *irritar* ❑ *His voice grates on me. Su voz me irrita.*
→ see **cut**

**grate|ful** /greɪtfəl/ ADJ If you are **grateful for** something that someone has given you or done for you, you have warm, friendly feelings towards them and wish to thank them. *agradecido* ❑ *She was grateful to him for being so helpful. Le estaba agradecida por toda su ayuda.* ● **grate|ful|ly** ADV *con agradecimiento* ❑ *"That's kind of you," Claire said gratefully. —Es muy amable de tu parte—dijo Claire con agradecimiento.*

**grat|er** /greɪtər/ (**graters**) N-COUNT A **grater** is a kitchen tool which has a rough surface that you use for cutting food into very small pieces. *rallador*
→ see **utensil**

**Word Link** — ***grat ≈ pleasing : congratulate, gratify, gratitude***

**grati|fy** /grætɪfaɪ/ (**gratifies, gratifying, gratified**) **1** V-T If you **are gratified** by something, it gives you pleasure or satisfaction. *satisfacer* [FORMAL] ❑ *The teacher was gratified by her students' success. La maestra estaba satisfecha con el éxito de sus alumnos.* ● **grati|fy|ing** ADJ *satisfactorio* ❑ *It's very gratifying when people appreciate what you do. Es muy satisfactorio cuando la gente aprecia lo que haces.* ● **grati|fi|ca|tion** /grætɪfɪkeɪʃən/ N-UNCOUNT *satisfacción* ❑ *To his gratification, they all knew who he was. Para su satisfacción, todos sabían quién era.* **2** V-T If you **gratify** your own or another person's desire, you do what is necessary to please yourself or them. *satisfacer* [FORMAL] ❑ *Gratify my curiosity and tell me why you're here. Satisface mi curiosidad y dime por qué estás aquí.* ● **grati|fi|ca|tion** N-UNCOUNT *satisfacción* ❑ *Children want instant gratification. Los niños quieren satisfacción inmediata.*

**grati|tude** /grætɪtud/ N-UNCOUNT **Gratitude** is the state of feeling grateful. *gratitud* ❑ *I want to express my gratitude to everyone who has helped. Quiero*

**Word Web** grassland

**Grasslands** are flat, open areas of land covered with **grass**. They get from 10 to 30 inches of rain per year. The **soil** there is deep and **fertile**. The **prairies** in the American Midwest used to be mostly grasslands. At that time, herds of bison, or buffalo, lived there along with antelopes. Because of the rich soil, almost all this prairie land has been converted to **agricultural** use. Very few buffalo or antelopes are still there. There are grasslands on every continent except Antarctica. In South America they are called pampas. In Europe they call them steppes and in Africa, **savannas**.

*expresar mi gratitud a todos los que han ayudado.*

**grave** /greɪv/ (**graves, graver, gravest**)
**1** N-COUNT A **grave** is a place where a dead person is buried. *tumba* ❑ *They visit her grave twice a year. Visitan su tumba dos veces al año.* **2** ADJ A **grave** event or situation is very serious, important, and worrying. *grave* ❑ *The situation in his country is very grave. La situación en su país es muy grave.* ● **grave|ly** ADV *gravemente* ❑ *They have gravely damaged the government's reputation. Han dañado gravemente la reputación del gobierno.* **3** ADJ A **grave** person is quiet and serious in their appearance or behavior. *serio* ❑ *He looked grave and worried. Se veía serio y preocupado.* ● **grave|ly** ADV *gravamente, con un tono grave* ❑ *She said gravely that they were in danger. Dijo con un tono grave que estaban en peligro.*

**grav|eled** /grævᵊld/ ADJ A **graveled** path, road, or area has a surface made of gravel. *de grava*

**grave|yard shift** (**graveyard shifts**) N-COUNT If someone works **the graveyard shift,** they work during the night. *turno de noche, turno nocturno*

**gravi|ta|tion|al** /grævɪteɪʃənᵊl/ ADJ **Gravitational** means relating to or resulting from the force of gravity. *gravitacional* [TECHNICAL] ❑ *...the Earth's gravitational pull. ...la fuerza gravitacional de la tierra.*
→ see **tide**

**gravi|ta|tion|al po|ten|tial en|er|gy** N-UNCOUNT **Gravitational potential energy** is the stored energy that an object has because of its height above the Earth. *energía potencial gravitacional* [TECHNICAL]

**gra|vit|ro|pism** /grævɪtrəpɪzəm/ N-UNCOUNT **Gravitropism** is the tendency of a plant to grow either downward or upward in response to the force of gravity. *gravitropismo* [TECHNICAL]

**grav|ity** /grævɪti/ **1** N-UNCOUNT **Gravity** is the force that causes things to drop to the ground. *gravedad* ❑ *...the force of gravity. ...la fuerza de gravedad.* **2** N-UNCOUNT The **gravity of** a situation or event is its extreme importance or seriousness. *gravedad* ❑ *We didn't understand the gravity of the situation. No entendíamos la gravedad de la situación.*
→ see **moon**

**gra|vy** /greɪvi/ N-UNCOUNT **Gravy** is a sauce made from the juices that come from meat when it cooks. *salsa hecha con el jugo de la carne asada*
→ see **dish**

**gray** /greɪ/ (**grayer, grayest**) COLOR **Gray** is the color of ashes or of clouds on a rainy day. *gris* ❑ *...a gray suit. ...un traje gris.*
→ see **hair**

| Word Partnership | Usar *gray* con: |
|---|---|
| N. | gray **eyes**, gray **hair**, **shades of** gray, gray **sky**, gray **suit** |

**gray area** (**gray areas**) N-COUNT If you refer to something as a **gray area,** you mean that it is unclear. *terreno o materia poco definidos* ❑ *At the moment, the law on discrimination is a gray area. Por el momento, la ley sobre la discriminación es un terreno poco definido.*

**gray mat|ter** N-UNCOUNT You can refer to your intelligence or your brains as **gray matter.** *materia gris* [INFORMAL] ❑ *These puzzles will exercise your gray matter. Estos rompecabezas ejercitarán tu materia gris.*

**graze** /greɪz/ (**grazes, grazing, grazed**) **1** V-T/V-I When animals **graze** or **are grazed,** they eat the grass or other plants that are growing in a particular place. You can also say that a field **is grazed** by animals. *pastar* ❑ *Cows were grazing peacefully in the field. Las vacas pastaban plácidamente en el campo.* ❑ *Horses grazed the meadow. Los caballos pastaban en la pradera.* **2** V-T If you **graze** a part of your body, you injure your skin by scraping against something. *rasparse, arañarse* ❑ *I fell and grazed my knees. Me caí y me raspé las rodillas.* **3** N-COUNT A **graze** is a small wound caused by scraping against something. *rasguño* ❑ *Cuts and grazes can be quite painful. Los rasguños y las cortadas pueden ser muy dolorosos.* **4** V-T If something **grazes** another thing, it touches that thing lightly as it passes by. *rozar* ❑ *The ball grazed the hitter's face. La pelota rozó la cara del bateador.*
→ see **herbivore**

**grease** /gris/ (**greases, greasing, greased**)
**1** N-UNCOUNT **Grease** is a thick, oily substance which is put on the moving parts of cars and other machines in order to make them work smoothly. *grasa* ❑ *His hands were covered in grease. Sus manos estaban llenas de grasa.* **2** V-T If you **grease** a part of a car, machine, or device, you put grease on it in order to make it work smoothly. *engrasar* ❑ *I greased the wheels. Engrasé las llantas.* **3** N-UNCOUNT **Grease** is an oily substance that is produced by your skin. *grasa* ❑ *He needs to wash the grease out of his hair. Necesita lavarse para quitar la grasa de los cabellos.* **4** N-UNCOUNT **Grease** is animal fat that is produced by cooking meat. *grasa* ❑ *I could smell bacon grease. Podía oler la grasa del tocino.* **5** V-T If you **grease** a dish, you put a small amount of fat or oil around the inside of it in order to prevent food from sticking to it during cooking. *engrasar* ❑ *Grease two baking sheets. Engrase dos charolas de horno.*

| Word Link | *est ≈ most : greatest, kindest, loudest* |
|---|---|

**great** /greɪt/ (**greater, greatest**) **1** ADJ You use **great** to describe something that is very large. *grande* ❑ *Inside the castle was a great hall. Dentro del castillo había un gran vestíbulo.* **2** ADJ **Great** means large in amount or degree. *grande* ❑ *She lived to a great age. Vivió hasta muy grande.* ● **great|ly** ADV *muy, mucho* [FORMAL] ❑ *He will be greatly missed. Se le echará mucho de menos.* **3** ADJ You use **great** to describe someone or something that is important, famous, or exciting. *grande* ❑ *...great scientific discoveries. ...grandes descubrimientos científicos.* ❑ *He has the ability to be a great player. Tiene la habilidad de ser un gran jugador.* ● **great|ness** N-UNCOUNT *grandeza* ❑ *She dreamed of achieving greatness. Soñaba con alcanzar la grandeza.* **4** EXCLAM If something is **great,** it is very good. *¡maravilloso!, ¡qué bien!* ❑ *I thought it was a great idea. Creí que era una gran idea.* ❑ *Oh great! You made a cake. ¡Qué bien! Hiciste un pastel.*

g

**Thesaurus** *great* Ver también:

ADJ. enormous, immense, vast; (*ant.*) small 1 2
distinguished, famous, important; (*ant.*) remarkable 3

**Great Red Spot** N-SING *The* **Great Red Spot** is a large area in the atmosphere of the planet Jupiter where a powerful storm has been taking place for hundreds of years. *La Gran Mancha Roja*

**greed** /grid/ N-UNCOUNT **Greed** is the desire to have more of something, such as food or money, than is necessary or fair. *codicia* ❑ *People say that the world economy is based on greed. La gente dice que la economía mundial está basada en la codicia.*

G

**greedy** /gridi/ (**greedier, greediest**) ADJ If you describe someone as **greedy,** you mean that they want to have more of something such as food or money than is necessary or fair. *codicioso* ❑ *He criticized greedy bosses for giving themselves big raises. Criticaba a los jefes codiciosos por darse grandes aumentos.* ● **greedi|ly** ADV *avaramente, glotonamente* ❑ *Laurie ate the pastries greedily. Laurie se comió los pastelillos con glotonería.*

**Greek thea|ter** N-UNCOUNT **Greek theater** is the style of theater associated with ancient Greece. *teatro griego*

**green** /grin/ (**greener, greenest, greens**) 1 COLOR **Green** is the color of grass or leaves. *verde* ❑ *She wore a green dress. Traía un vestido verde.* 2 ADJ A place that is **green** is covered with grass, plants, and trees. *verde* ❑ *The city has lots of parks and green spaces. La ciudad tiene muchos parques y áreas verdes.* ● **green|ness** N-UNCOUNT *verdor* ❑ *...the greenness of the river valley. ...el verdor del valle del río.* 3 ADJ **Green** issues and political movements relate to or are concerned with the protection of the environment. *verde* ❑ *...the Green movement. ...el movimiento verde.* 4 N-COUNT A **green** is a smooth, flat area of grass around a hole on a golf course. *hoyo* ❑ *...the 18th green. ...el hoyo 18.*
→ see **color, golf, rainbow**

**green|house** /grinhaʊs/ (**greenhouses**) N-COUNT A **greenhouse** is a glass building in which you grow plants that need to be protected from bad weather. *invernadero*
→ see **barn**

**green|house ef|fect** N-SING **The greenhouse effect** is the problem caused by increased quantities of gases such as carbon dioxide in the air. *efecto invernadero* ❑ *...gases that contribute to the greenhouse effect. ...los gases que contribuyen al efecto invernadero.*
→ see Word Web: **greenhouse effect**
→ see **ozone**

**green|house gas** (**greenhouse gases**) N-VAR **Greenhouse gases** are the gases responsible for causing the greenhouse effect. The main greenhouse gas is carbon dioxide. *gas invernadero* ❑ *...an international treaty to limit greenhouse gases. ...un tratado nternacional para limitar los gases invernadero.*
→ see **biosphere**

**green on|ion** (**green onions**) N-COUNT **Green onions** are small onions with long green leaves. *cebollita, cebolla cambray, cebollino*

**green plant** (**green plants**) N-COUNT **Green plants** are plants that get their energy by means of photosynthesis. *planta verde*

**green tea** (**green teas**) N-VAR **Green tea** is tea made from tea leaves that have been steamed and dried quickly. *té verde* ❑ *...a cup of green tea. ...una taza de té verde.*

**greet** /grit/ (**greets, greeting, greeted**) 1 V-T When you **greet** someone, you say "Hello" or shake hands with them. *saludar* ❑ *She greeted him when he came in from school. Lo saludó cuando llegó de la escuela.* 2 V-T If something **is greeted** in a particular way, people react to it in that way. *acoger, recibir* ❑ *His comments were greeted with anger. Sus comentarios provocaron enojo.*

**greet|ing** /gritɪŋ/ (**greetings**) N-VAR A **greeting** is something friendly that you say or do when you meet someone. *saludo* ❑ *...a friendly greeting. ...un saludo cariñoso.* ❑ *They exchanged greetings. Intercambiaron saludos.*

**greet|ing card** (**greeting cards**) N-COUNT A **greeting card** is a folded card with a picture on the front and greetings inside that you give or send to someone, for example on their birthday. *tarjeta de felicitación*

**grew** /gru/ **Grew** is the past tense of **grow**. *pasado de* ***grow***

**grid|lock** /grɪdlɒk/ 1 N-UNCOUNT **Gridlock** is the situation that exists when all the roads in a particular place are so full of vehicles that none of them can move. *paralización del tráfico* ❑ *There was an accident on the freeway, creating gridlock. Hubo un accidente en la autopista, lo cual resultó en la paralización del tráfico.* 2 N-UNCOUNT You can use **gridlock** to refer to a situation in an argument

**Word Web** greenhouse effect

Over the past 100 years, the global average **temperature** has risen dramatically. Researchers believe that this **global warming** comes from added **carbon dioxide** and other **gases** in the **atmosphere**. With **water vapor**, they form a layer that holds in heat. It acts like the glass in a greenhouse. Scientists call this the **greenhouse effect**. Some natural causes of this warming may include increased **solar radiation** and tiny changes in the earth's orbit. However, human activities, such as **deforestation**, and the use of **fossil fuels**, seem to be an important cause.

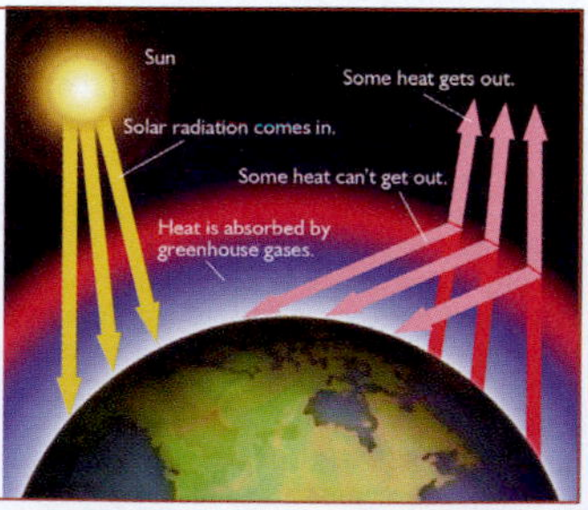

or dispute when neither side is prepared to give in, so no agreement can be reached. *punto muerto* ❑ *...political gridlock. ...un punto muerto en la política.*
→ see **traffic**

**grief** /grif/ (**griefs**) 1 N-VAR **Grief** is a feeling of extreme sadness. *pena, dolor* ❑ *She experienced terrible grief after he died. Experimentó una profunda pena después de que él murió.* 2 PHRASE If something **comes to grief,** it fails. If someone **comes to grief,** they fail in something they are doing, and may be hurt. *irse al traste* ❑ *Their friendship came to grief over lack of money. Su amistad se fue al traste por la falta de dinero.*

**grieve** /griv/ (**grieves, grieving, grieved**) V-I If you **grieve over** something, especially someone's death, you feel very sad about it. *estar de luto por alguien, llorar a alguien* ❑ *He's grieving over his dead wife. Está de luto por la muerte de su esposa.* ❑ *I didn't have any time to grieve. No tuve tiempo para llorarlo.*

**grill** /grɪl/ (**grills, grilling, grilled**) 1 N-COUNT A **grill** is a flat frame of metal bars on which food can be cooked over a fire. *parrilla* ❑ *We cooked the fish on a grill over the fire. Cocinamos el pescado a la parrilla.* 2 V-T When you **grill** food, or when it **grills,** you cook it on metal bars above a fire or barbecue. *asar a la parrilla* ❑ *Grill the steaks for about 5 minutes each side. Ase los filetes a la parrilla durante aproximadamente 5 minutos de cada lado.* 3 V-T If you **grill** someone **about** something, you ask them a lot of questions for a long period of time. *acribillar a preguntas* [INFORMAL] ❑ *The teacher grilled us about what had happened. El maestro nos acribilló a preguntas sobre lo que había pasado.* ● **grill|ing** N-COUNT (**grillings**) *interrogatorio, acribillar a preguntas* ❑ *He got a grilling from the committee. El comité lo acribilló a preguntas.*

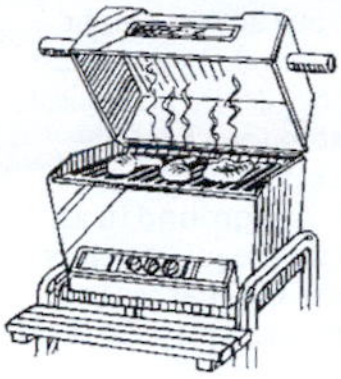
grill

**grim** /grɪm/ (**grimmer, grimmest**) 1 ADJ A situation or piece of information that is **grim** is unpleasant, depressing, and difficult to accept. *desalentador, sombrío* ❑ *There was grim news about the economy yesterday. Las noticias sobre la economía el día de ayer fueron desalentadoras.* ❑ *With rising crime and violence, the situation is grim. Dado el incremento del crimen y la violencia, la situación es sombría.* 2 ADJ A place that is **grim** is unattractive and depressing. *lúgubre* ❑ *...a grim, industrial city. ...una lúgubre ciudad industrial.*

**grin** /grɪn/ (**grins, grinning, grinned**) 1 V-I When you **grin,** you smile broadly. *sonreír* ❑ *He grinned, delighted at the memory. Sonrió, encantado con el recuerdo.* ❑ *Phillip grinned at her. Phillip le sonrió.* 2 N-COUNT A **grin** is a broad smile. *sonrisa* ❑ *She had a big grin on her face. Traía una gran sonrisa.*

**grind** /graɪnd/ (**grinds, grinding, ground**) 1 V-T If you **grind** a substance such as corn, you crush it until it becomes a fine powder. *moler* ❑ *Grind some pepper into the sauce. Muela un poco de pimienta y añádala a la salsa.* 2 V-T If you **grind** something **into** a surface, you press and rub it hard into the surface using small circular or sideways movements. *incrustar, meter* ❑ *He ground the toe of his boot into the gravel path. Metió la puntera de la bota entre la grava del sendero con un suave movimiento circular.* 3 N-SING If you refer to routine tasks or activities as a **grind,** you mean they are boring and take up a lot of time and effort. *talacha* [INFORMAL] ❑ *Life is a terrible grind for most people. La vida es una talacha terrible para la mayoría de la gente.* 4 PHRASE If a country's economy or something such as a process **grinds to a halt,** it gradually becomes slower or less active until it stops. *estancarse* ❑ *The peace process has ground to a halt. El proceso de paz se ha estancado.* 5 PHRASE If a vehicle **grinds to a halt,** it stops slowly and noisily. *detenerse con gran chirrido de frenos.* ❑ *The truck ground to a halt after a hundred yards. El camión se detuvo cien metros más adelante con un gran chirrido de frenos.*

▸**grind down** PHR-VERB If you say that someone **grinds** you **down,** you mean that they treat you very harshly and cruelly, reducing your confidence or your will to resist them. *avasallar* ❑ *Don't let people grind you down. No dejes que la gente te avasalle.*



**grip** /grɪp/ (**grips, gripping, gripped**) 1 V-T If you **grip** something, you take hold of it with your hand and continue to hold it firmly. *agarrar* ❑ *She gripped the rope. Agarró la cuerda.* 2 N-COUNT A **grip** is a firm, strong hold on something. *acto de sujetar algo con fuerza* ❑ *He pulled the bag from her grip. Jaló la bolsa que ella sujetaba con fuerza.* 3 N-SING Someone's **grip on** something is the power and control they have over it. *control* ❑ *The president maintains a strong grip on his country. El presidente continúa teninedo un gran control sobre su país.* 4 V-T If you **are gripped by** something, it affects you strongly and your attention is concentrated on it. *atrapado* ❑ *The audience was gripped by the dramatic story. La dramática historia atrapó al público.* ● **grip|ping** ADJ *que lo atrapa a uno* ❑ *The film was a gripping thriller. La película era una película de suspenso que te atrapaba.* 5 PHRASE If you **come to grips with** a problem, you consider it seriously, and start taking action to deal with it. *enfrentarse a* ❑ *Our first job is to come to grips with the economy. Nuestro primer trabajo es controlar la economía.* 6 PHRASE If you **get a grip** on yourself, you make an effort to control or improve your behavior or work. *dominarse* ❑ *I was very frightened and I had to get a grip on myself. Estaba muy asustado y tuve que dominarme.*

**groan** /groʊn/ (**groans, groaning, groaned**) 1 V-I If you **groan,** you make a long, low sound because you are in pain, or because you are upset or unhappy about something. *gemir* ❑ *He began to groan with pain. Empezó a gemir de dolor.* ❑ *The man on the floor was groaning. El hombre que estaba en el suelo gemía.* ● **Groan** is also a noun. *gemido* ❑ *She let out a groan. Dejó escapar un gemido.* 2 V-T If you **groan** something, you say it in a low, unhappy voice. *gemir* ❑ *"My head hurts," Eric groaned. —Me duele la cabeza—gimió Eric.*

**gro|cer** /groʊsər/ (**grocers**) N-COUNT A **grocer** is a storekeeper who sells foods such as flour, sugar, and canned foods. *tendero o tendera*

**gro|cery** /groʊsəri, groʊsri/ (**groceries**) 1 N-COUNT A **grocery** or a **grocery store** is a small store that sells foods such as flour, sugar, and canned goods. *tienda de abarrotes* ❑ *They run a small grocery store. Tienen una pequeña tienda de abarrotes.* 2 → see also **supermarket** 3 N-PLURAL **Groceries**

are foods you buy at a grocery or at a supermarket. *abarrotes, comestibles* ❑ *...a small bag of groceries. ...una pequeña bolsa de comestibles.*

**groin** /grɔɪn/ **(groins)** N-COUNT Your **groin** is the front part of your body between your legs. *ingle, entrepierna* ❑ *He felt a pain in his groin. Sintió dolor en la ingle.*

**groom** /grum/ **(grooms, grooming, groomed)** 1 N-COUNT A **groom** is the same as a **bridegroom**. *novio* ❑ *...the bride and groom. ...los novios.* 2 N-COUNT A **groom** is someone whose job is to look after the horses in a stable and to keep them clean. *mozo de cuadra* 3 V-T If you **groom** an animal, you clean its fur, usually by brushing it. *cepillar* ❑ *She groomed the horses regularly. Cepillaba regularmente a los caballos.* 4 V-T If you **are groomed for** a special job, someone prepares you for it by teaching you the skills you will need. *preparar* ❑ *George was being groomed for the manager's job. A George lo estaban preparando para el puesto de gerente.*

G

**groove** /gruv/ **(grooves)** N-COUNT A **groove** is a deep line cut into a surface. *ranura* ❑ *Grooves had been worn in the table. El uso había formado estrías en la mesa.*

**gross** /groʊs/ **(grosser, grossest)** 1 ADJ You use **gross** to describe something unacceptable or unpleasant to a very great amount, degree, or intensity. *extremo* ❑ *...gross abuse of human rights. ...el abuso extremo contra los derechos humanos.* • **gross|ly** ADV *escandalosamente* ❑ *He was sentenced to nine years in prison after a grossly unfair trial. Lo sentenciaron a nueve años de prisión después de un juicio escandalosamente injusto.* 2 ADJ If you describe someone or something as **gross,** you think they are very unpleasant. *asqueroso* [INFORMAL] ❑ *Some scenes in the movie were really gross. Algunas escenas de la película eran realmente asquerosas.* 3 ADJ **Gross** means the total amount of something, especially money, before any has been taken away, for example in tax. *bruto* ❑ *The account gives 10.4% gross interest or 7.8% net interest. La cuenta da un interés bruto de 10.4% o un interés neto de 7.8%.* • **Gross** is also an adverb. *en bruto* ❑ *Interest is paid gross. Los intereses se pagan en bruto.*

**Word Partnership** Usar *gross* con:

N. **act of** gross **injustice**, gross **mismanagement**, gross **negligence** 1
gross **income**, gross **margin** 3
V. **feel** gross 2

**ground**
❶ NOUN USES
❷ VERB AND ADJECTIVE USES
❸ PHRASES

❶ **ground** /graʊnd/ **(grounds)** 1 N-SING **The ground** is the surface of the earth or the floor of a room. *suelo* ❑ *They were sitting on the ground. Estaban sentados en el suelo.* ❑ *He fainted and fell to the ground. Se desmayó y cayó al suelo.* 2 N-SING If you say that something takes place **on the ground,** you mean it takes place on the surface of the earth and not in the air. *en (la) tierra* ❑ *Repairs are done while the plane is on the ground. Las reparaciones se llevan a cabo mientras el avión está en tierra.* 3 N-COUNT You can use **ground** to refer to an area of land, sea, or air which is used for a particular activity. *terreno, lugar, área* ❑ *There are great fishing grounds around the islands. Alrededor de las islas hay lugares muy buenos para la pesca.* 4 N-PLURAL The **grounds** of a large or important building are the garden or area of land which surrounds it. *jardines* ❑ *...the palace grounds. ...los jardines de palacio.* 5 N-VAR You can use **ground** to refer to a place or situation in which particular methods or ideas can develop and be successful. *terreno* ❑ *This company is a developing ground for new ideas. Esta compañía es terreno de desarrollo de nuevas ideas.* 6 N-UNCOUNT **Ground** is used in expressions such as **gain ground, lose ground,** and **give ground** in order to indicate that someone gets or loses an advantage. *terreno* ❑ *The team has won its last three games and is gaining ground. El equipo ha ganado sus últimos tres juegos y está ganando terreno.* 7 N-VAR If something is **grounds for** a feeling or action, it is a reason for it. If you do something **on the grounds** of a particular thing, that thing is the reason for your action. *razón* ❑ *There are some grounds for optimism. Hay algunas razones para ser optimistas.* ❑ *They denied his request on the grounds that it would cost too much money. Rechazaron su solicitud aduciendo que que costaría demasiado dinero.* 8 N-COUNT The **ground** in an electric plug or piece of electrical equipment is the wire through which electricity passes into the ground and which makes the equipment safe. *tierra*

❷ **ground** /graʊnd/ **(grounds, grounding, grounded)** 1 V-T If an argument, belief, or opinion **is grounded** in something, that thing is used to justify it. *fundamentar* ❑ *Her argument was grounded in fact. Su argumento estaba fundamentado en los hechos.* 2 V-T If an aircraft or its passengers **are grounded,** they are made to stay on the ground and are not allowed to take off. *detener en tierra* ❑ *Planes were grounded because of the bad weather. Los aviones fueron detenidos en tierra a causa del mal tiempo.* 3 ADJ **Ground** meat has been cut into very small pieces in a machine. *molido* ❑ *The sausages are made of ground pork. Las salchichas están hechas de carne de puerco molida.* 4 **Ground** is the past tense and past participle of **grind.** *pasado y participio pasado de* ***grind*** → see **grain**

❸ **ground** /graʊnd/ 1 PHRASE If something such as a project gets **off the ground,** it begins or starts functioning. *despegar* ❑ *We help small companies to get off the ground. Les ayudamos a despegar a las pequeñas empresas.* 2 PHRASE If you **stand** your **ground** or **hold** your **ground,** you do not run away from a situation, but face it bravely. *no ceder terreno, mantenerse firme* ❑ *He was angry, but she stood her ground. Él estaba enojado, pero ella se mantuvo firme.* 3 PHRASE In a painting, the **middle ground** is the area between the foreground and the background. *medio plano*

**grounds|keeper** /graʊndzkipər/ **(groundskeepers)** N-COUNT A **groundskeeper** is a person whose job is to look after a park or sports ground. *encargado o encargada*

**Word Link** ***ground ≈ bottom : background, groundwater, underground***

**ground|water** /gr<u>aʊ</u>ndwɔtər/ N-UNCOUNT **Groundwater** is water that is found under the ground. Groundwater has usually passed down through the soil and become trapped by rocks. *aguas freáticas, agua subterránea, agua del subsuelo*

**ground zero** also **Ground Zero** N-UNCOUNT People sometimes use **ground zero** to refer to the site of a disaster such as a nuclear explosion. It is used especially to refer to the site of the destruction of the World Trade Center in New York City on September 11, 2001. *zona cero*

**group** /grup/ (**groups, grouping, grouped**) 1 N-COUNT A **group of** people or things is a number of people or things that are together in one place at one time. *grupo* ❑ *A small group of people stood on the street corner. Había un pequeño grupo de personas en la esquina.* 2 N-COUNT A **group** is a set of people who have the same interests or aims, and who organize themselves to work or act together. *grupo* ❑ *...members of an environmental group. ...miembros de un grupo ambientalista.* 3 N-COUNT A **group** is a set of people, organizations, or things which are considered together because they have something in common. *grupo* ❑ *She is among the best players in her age group. Está entre los mejores jugadores de su generación.* 4 N-COUNT A **group** is a number of musicians who perform together, especially ones who play popular music. *grupo* ❑ *He played guitar in a rock group. Tocaba la guitarra en un grupo de rock.* 5 V-T/V-I If a number of things or people **are grouped together** or **group together,** they are together in one place or within one organization or system. *agrupar* ❑ *Plants are grouped into botanical "families." Las plantas se agrupan en familias botánicas.* ❑ *We group the students together according to ability. Agrupamos a los alumnos de acuerdo con sus habilidades.* 6 N-COUNT In chemistry, a **group** of elements is a number of them that are in the same column in the periodic table of elements. *grupo*
→ see **periodic table**

**Thesaurus** *group* Ver también:

N. collection, crowd, gang, organization, society 1
V. arrange, categorize, class, order, rank, sort 5

**grove** /gr<u>oʊ</u>v/ (**groves**) N-COUNT A **grove** is a group of trees that are close together. *arboleda* ❑ *...an olive grove. ...un olivar.*
→ see **tree**

**grow** /gr<u>oʊ</u>/ (**grows, growing, grew, grown**) 1 V-I When people, animals, and plants **grow,** they increase in size and change physically over a period of time. *crecer* ❑ *All children grow at different rates. Todos los niños crecen a diferente ritmo.* 2 V-I If a plant or tree **grows** in a particular place, it is alive there. *crecer* ❑ *There were roses growing by the side of the door. Habían unos rosales creciendo al lado de la puerta.* 3 V-T If you **grow** a particular type of plant, you put seeds or young plants in the ground and take care of them as they develop. *cultivar* ❑ *I always grow a few red onions. Siempre cultivo unas cuantas cebollas moradas.* • **grow|er** N-COUNT (**growers**) *cultivador o cultivadora* ❑ *...apple growers. ...cultivadores de manzanas.* 4 V-T/V-I When your hair or nails **grow,** they gradually become longer. If you **grow** your hair or nails, you stop cutting them so that they become longer. *crecer, dejarse crecer* ❑ *My hair grows really fast. Mi cabello crece muy rápido.* ❑ *He's growing a beard. Se está dejando crecer la barba.* 5 V-LINK You use **grow** to say that someone or something gradually changes until they have a new quality, feeling, or attitude. *volverse* ❑ *I grew a little afraid of him. Me volví un poco temerosa de él.* ❑ *He's growing old. Se está volviendo viejo.* 6 V-I If something **grows,** it becomes bigger, greater or more intense. *aumentar* ❑ *The number of unemployed people grew to 4 million. El número de gente desempleada ha aumentado a 4 millones.* ❑ *The public's anger is growing. El enojo del público está aumentando.* ❑ *The economy continues to grow. La economía continúa aumentando.* 7 → see also **grown**

▸ **grow apart** PHR-VERB If people who have a close relationship **grow apart,** they gradually start to have different interests and opinions from each other, and their relationship starts to fail. *distanciarse* ❑ *He and his wife grew apart. Él y su esposa se distanciaron.*

▸ **grow into** PHR-VERB When a child **grows into** an item of clothing, they become taller or bigger so that it fits them properly. *ajustar, ir bien, quedar* ❑ *The coat is too big, but she'll soon grow into it. El abrigo es demasiado grande; pero va a crecer y le quedará.*

▸ **grow on** PHR-VERB If someone or something **grows on** you, you start to like them more and more. *empezar a gustar* ❑ *Slowly the place began to grow on me. Poco a poco el lugar empezó a gustarme.*

▸ **grow out of** 1 PHR-VERB If you **grow out of** a type of behavior or an interest, you stop behaving in that way or having that interest, as you develop or change. *pasar una etapa, dejar algo atrás* ❑ *Most children who bite their nails grow out of it. A la mayoría de los niños que se muerden las uñas se les pasa al crecer.* 2 PHR-VERB When a child **grows out of** an item of clothing, they become so tall or big that it no longer fits them properly. *dejar de quedar* ❑ *You've grown out of your shoes again. Otra vez ya no te quedan los zapatos.*

▸ **grow up** 1 PHR-VERB When someone **grows up,** they gradually change from being a child into being an adult. *criarse, madurar* ❑ *She grew up in Tokyo. Se crió en Tokio.* 2 → see also **grown-up** 3 PHR-VERB If something **grows up,** it starts to exist and then becomes larger or more important. *surgir* ❑ *New housing grew up alongside the port. Surgieron nuevas viviendas a lo largo del puerto.*

**Word Partnership** Usar *grow* con:

V. **continue to** grow 1 – 3
**try to** grow 3
N. grow **food** 3
ADJ. grow **older** 5

**grown** /gr<u>oʊ</u>n/ ADJ A **grown** man or woman is one who is fully developed and mature, both physically and mentally. *adulto* ❑ *Why do grown men love games so much? ¿Por qué les gustan tanto los juegos a los hombres adultos?*

g

**grown-up** (**grown-ups**)

The spelling **grownup** is also used. The syllable **up** is not stressed when it is a noun.

**1** N-COUNT A **grown-up** is an adult; used by or to children. *adulto* ❑ *Jan was almost a grown-up. Jan era casi un adulto.* **2** ADJ Someone who is **grown-up** is physically and mentally mature and no longer depends on their parents or another adult. *mayor* ❑ *She has two grown-up children who both live nearby. Tiene dos hijos ya mayores que viven cerca.*

**growth** /groʊθ/ (**growths**) **1** N-UNCOUNT The **growth of** something such as an industry, organization, or idea is its development in size, wealth, or importance. *crecimiento* ❑ *...the growth of nationalism. ...el crecimiento del nacionalismo.* ❑ *...Japan's enormous economic growth. ...el enorme crecimiento económico de Japón.* **2** N-UNCOUNT **Growth** in a person, animal, or plant is the process of increasing in physical size and development. *crecimiento* ❑ *...hormones which control growth. ...las hormonas que controlan el crecimiento.* **3** N-COUNT A **growth** is a lump caused by a disease that grows inside or on a person, animal, or plant. *tumor* ❑ *He had a growth on his back. Tenía un tumor en la espalda.*

**grudge** /grʌdʒ/ (**grudges**) N-COUNT If you have or bear a **grudge against** someone, you have unfriendly feelings toward them because of something they did in the past. *rencor* ❑ *He seems to have a grudge against me. Parece que me tiene rencor.*

**grudg|ing** /grʌdʒɪŋ/ ADJ A **grudging** feeling or action is felt or done very unwillingly. *con renuencia, a regañadientes* ❑ *He earned his opponents' grudging respect. Se ganó el respeto de sus oponentes, a pesar de su renuencia a otorgárselo.* ● **grudg|ing|ly** ADV *a regañadientes* ❑ *The company grudgingly agreed to allow him to continue working. La empresa aceptó a regañadientes dejarlo seguir trabajando.*

**grunge** /grʌndʒ/ **1** N-UNCOUNT **Grunge** is the name of a fashion and of a type of music. **Grunge** fashion involves wearing clothes which look old and untidy. **Grunge** music is played on guitars and is very loud. *grunge* **2** N-UNCOUNT **Grunge** is dirt. *mugre* [INFORMAL] ● **grungy** ADJ *mugroso* ❑ *...grungy motel rooms. ...cuartos mugrosos de motel.*

**grunt work** N-UNCOUNT **The grunt work** is the hard work or the less interesting part of the work that needs to be done. *trabajo pesado, talacha* [INFORMAL] ❑ *She didn't have enough patience for the grunt work. No tenía la paciencia necesaria para la talacha.*

**gua|nine** /gwɑnin, -nin/ (**guanines**) N-VAR **Guanine** is one of the four basic components of the DNA molecule. It bonds with cytosine. *guanina* [TECHNICAL]

**guar|an|tee** /gærənti/ (**guarantees, guaranteeing, guaranteed**) **1** V-T If one thing **guarantees** another, the first is certain to cause the second thing to happen. *garantizar* ❑ *Hard work does not guarantee success. El trabajar duro no garantiza el éxito.* **2** N-COUNT Something that is a **guarantee of** something else makes it certain that it will happen or that it is true. *garantía de* ❑ *A famous company name is not a guarantee of quality. Una marca famosa no es garantía de calidad.* **3** V-T If you **guarantee** something, you promise that it will definitely happen, or that you will do or provide it for someone. *garantizar* ❑ *We guarantee the safety of our products. Garantizamos la seguridad de nuestros productos.* ❑ *I guarantee that you will enjoy this movie. Te garantizo que vas a disfrutar esta película.* ● **Guarantee** is also a noun. *garantía* ❑ *He gave me a guarantee he would finish the job. Me dio garantías de que terminaría el trabajo.* **4** N-COUNT A **guarantee** is a written promise by a company to replace or repair a product free of charge if it has any faults within a particular time. *garantía* ❑ *Keep the guarantee in case something goes wrong. Guarda la garantía por si acaso algo sale mal.* **5** V-T If a company **guarantees** its product or work, they provide a guarantee for it. *garantizar* ❑ *Some builders guarantee their work. Algunos constructores garantizan su trabajo.* ❑ *All our computers are guaranteed for 12 months. Todas nuestras computadoras están garantizadas por doce meses.*

**guard** /gɑrd/ (**guards, guarding, guarded**) **1** V-T If you **guard** a place, person, or object, you stand near them in order to watch and protect them. *vigilar* ❑ *Armed police guarded the court. Unos policías armados vigilaban el tribunal.* **2** V-T If you **guard** someone, you watch them and keep them in a particular place to stop them from escaping. *custodiar* ❑ *Marines with rifles guarded them. Los custodiaban unos marines armados de rifles.* **3** N-COUNT A **guard** is someone such as a soldier, police officer, or prison officer who is guarding a particular place or person. *vigilante, custodio* ❑ *The prisoners attacked their guards. Los prisioneros atacaron a sus custodios.* **4** N-SING A **guard** is a specially-organized group of people, such as soldiers or police officers, who protect or watch someone or something. *guardia* ❑ *We have a security guard around the whole area. Tenemos una guardia de seguridad alrededor de toda el área.*

guard

**5** V-T If you **guard** some information or advantage that you have, you try to protect it or keep it for yourself. *proteger* ❑ *He closely guarded his information. Protegía cuidadosamente su información.* **6** N-COUNT A **guard** is a protective device which covers a part of your body or a dangerous part of a piece of equipment. *barbiquejo, barboquejo* ❑ *...the chin guard of my helmet. ...el barbiquejo de mi casco.* **7** → see also **bodyguard** **8** PHRASE If someone **catches** you **off guard,** they surprise you by doing something you do not expect. If something **catches** you **off guard,** it surprises you by happening when you are not expecting it. *coger a alguien desprevenido* ❑ *He likes to catch the audience off guard. Le gusta coger desprevenido al público.* **9** PHRASE If you are **on** your **guard** or **on guard,** you are being very careful because you think a situation might become difficult or dangerous. *en guardia* ❑ *He was on his guard because the police were asking questions. Estaba en guardia porque la policía estaba haciendo preguntas.*

▸ **guard against** PHR-VERB If you **guard against** something, you are careful to prevent it from happening, or to avoid being affected by it. *prevenir* ❑ *Wear gloves to guard against infection. Utiice guantes*

*para prevenir infecciones.*
→ see **soccer**

**Word Partnership** Usar *guard* con:

N. guard **a door/house/prisoner** 1 2
**prison** guard, **security** guard 3 4
V. **catch *someone* off** guard 8
***be* on** guard 9

**guard cell** (**guard cells**) N-COUNT **Guard cells** are pairs of cells on the leaves of plants, which control things such as how much air a plant takes in and how much water it releases. *célula oclusiva, célula de guarda*

**guard|ian** /gɑrdiən/ (**guardians**) 1 N-COUNT A **guardian** is someone who has been legally appointed to take charge of the affairs of another person, for example a child or someone who is mentally ill. *tutor o tutora* ❑ *Diana's grandmother was her legal guardian. La abuela de Diana era su tutora legal.* 2 N-COUNT The **guardian of** something is someone who defends and protects it. *defensor o defensora, custodio* ❑ *He sees himself as the guardian of democracy. Se considera el custodio de la democracia.*

**guer|ril|la** /gərɪlə/ (**guerrillas**) also **guerilla** N-COUNT A **guerrilla** is someone who fights as part of an unofficial army. *guerrillero o guerrillera* ❑ *...a guerrilla war. ...una guerra de guerillas.*

**guess** /gɛs/ (**guesses, guessing, guessed**) 1 V-T/V-I If you **guess** something, you give an answer or provide an opinion which may not be true because you do not have definite knowledge about the matter concerned. *adivinar, pensar* ❑ *Yvonne guessed that he was around 40 years old. Yvonne pensaba que tenía cerca de 40 años.* ❑ *You can only guess at what they are thinking. Sólo podemos tratar de adivinar lo que están pensando.* ❑ *Guess what I did. Adivina qué hice.* 2 V-T If you **guess that** something is the case, you correctly form the opinion that it is the case, although you do not have definite knowledge about it. *adivinar* ❑ *I guessed that he was American. Adiviné que era estadounidense.* ❑ *He should have guessed what would happen. Debió haber adivinado lo que sucedería.* 3 N-COUNT A **guess** is an attempt to give an answer or provide an opinion which may not be true because you do not have definite knowledge about the matter concerned. *cálculos, intento de calcular algo* ❑ *My guess is that this solution will not work. Yo calculo que esta solución no va a funcionar.* ❑ *He made a guess at her age. Hizo un cálculo de su edad.* 4 PHRASE You say "**I guess**" to show that you are slightly uncertain or reluctant about what you are saying. *supongo* [INFORMAL] ❑ *I guess he's right. Supongo que tiene razón.* ❑ *"I think we should stop." — "Yeah. I guess so." —Creo que deberíamos parar.—Sí; creo que sí.*

**Thesaurus** *guess* Ver también:

V. estimate, predict, suspect 1
N. assumption, prediction, theory 3

**Word Partnership** Usar *guess* con:

N. guess **a secret** 2
ADJ. **educated** guess, **good** guess, **wild** guess 3
V. **make a** guess 3

**guest** /gɛst/ (**guests**) 1 N-COUNT A **guest** is someone who is visiting you or is at an event because you have invited them. *invitado o invitada* ❑ *She was a guest at the wedding. Estuvo de invitada en la boda.* 2 N-COUNT A **guest** is someone who visits a place or organization or appears on a radio or television show because they have been invited to do so. *invitado o invitada* ❑ *...a frequent talk show guest. ...un invitado frecuente a los programas de entrevistas.* ❑ *Dr. Gerald Jeffers is the guest speaker. El orador invitado es el Dr. Gerald Jeffers.* 3 N-COUNT A **guest** is someone who is staying in a hotel. *huésped* ❑ *A few guests were having breakfast. Algunos huéspedes estaban desayunando.*
→ see **hotel**

**Word Partnership** Usar *guest* con:

ADJ. **unwelcome** guest 1 2
V. **be *someone's*** guest, **entertain a** guest 1 2
**accommodate a** guest 1 – 3
N. guest **appearance**, guest **list**, guest **speaker** 1 2
**hotel** guest 3

**guest house** (**guest houses**) N-COUNT A **guest house** is a small house on the grounds of a large house, where visitors can stay. *casa de huéspedes*

**guest of hon|or** (**guests of honor**) N-COUNT The **guest of honor** at a dinner or other social occasion is the most important guest. *invitado de honor o invitada de honor*

**GUI** /gui/ (**GUIs**) N-COUNT In computing, a **GUI** is a type of screen interface that is found on most computers, consisting of menus and icons that can be controlled by a mouse. **GUI** is an abbreviation for "graphical user interface." *Interfaz Gráfica de Usuario (GUI por sus siglas en inglés)*

**guid|ance** /gaɪdᵊns/ N-UNCOUNT **Guidance** is help and advice. *orientación, consejos* ❑ *My tennis game improved under his guidance. Mi manera de jugar al tenis mejoró con sus consejos.*

**guid|ance coun|se|lor** (**guidance counselors**) N-COUNT A **guidance counselor** is a person who works in a school giving students advice about careers and personal problems. *orientador vocacional u orientadora vocacional*

**guide** /gaɪd/ (**guides, guiding, guided**) 1 N-COUNT A **guide** is a book that gives you information or instructions to help you do or understand something. *guía* ❑ *...a step-by-step guide to building your own home. ...una guía para construir tu propia casa paso a paso.* 2 N-COUNT A **guide** is a book that gives tourists information about a town, area, or country. *guía* ❑ *The guide to Paris lists hotel rooms for as little as $35 a night. La guía de París incluye hoteles con cuartos de apenas 35 dólares la noche.* 3 N-COUNT A **guide** is someone who shows tourists around places such as museums or cities. *guía* ❑ *A guide will take you on a tour of the city. Un guía los llevará a un recorrido por la ciudad.* 4 V-T If you **guide** someone around a city, museum, or building, you show it to them and explain points of interest. *guiar* ❑ *She guided him around Berlin. Lo guió por Berlín.* 5 N-COUNT A **guide** is someone who shows people the way to a place in a difficult or dangerous region. *guía* ❑ *With guides, the journey* can be done in fourteen days. Con guías, se puede realizar el viaje en catorce días. 6 N-COUNT A **guide** is something that can be used to help you plan your actions or to form an opinion about something. guía, idea ❑ As a rough guide, you need about half a loaf of bread per person. Para darte una idea, necesitas alrededor de media barra de pan por persona. 7 V-T If you **guide** someone somewhere, you go there with them in order to show them the way. guiar ❑ He took her by the arm and guided her out. La tomó del brazo y la guió afuera. 8 V-T If you **guide** a vehicle somewhere, you control it carefully to make sure that it goes in the right direction. conducir ❑ Captain Shelton guided his plane along the runway. El Capitán Shelton condujo su avión por la pista. 9 V-T If something or someone **guides** you, they influence your actions or decisions. guiar ❑ Let your thoughts and feelings guide you. Déjate guiar por tus pensamientos y emociones.

G

**Thesaurus** *guide* Ver también:

N. directory, handbook, information 1 2
V. accompany, direct, instruct, lead, navigate; (*ant.*) follow 4 7

**guide|line** /gaɪdlaɪn/ (**guidelines**) N-COUNT If an organization issues **guidelines on** something, it issues official advice about how to do it. pauta ❑ The government has issued new guidelines on religious education. El gobierno ha emitido nuevas pautas para la educación religiosa.

**guild** /gɪld/ (**guilds**) N-COUNT A **guild** is an organization of people who do the same job. gremio ❑ ...the Writers' Guild of America. ...el Gremio de Escritores de América.

**guilt** /gɪlt/ 1 N-UNCOUNT **Guilt** is an unhappy feeling that you have because you have done something wrong or think that you have done something wrong. culpa ❑ She felt a lot of guilt about her children's unhappiness. Sentía mucha culpa por la infelicidad de sus hijos. 2 N-UNCOUNT **Guilt** is the fact that you have done something wrong or illegal. culpabilidad ❑ The jury was convinced of his guilt. El jurado estaba convencido de su culpabilidad.

**Word Partnership** Usar *guilt* con:

N. **burden of** guilt, **feelings of** guilt, **sense of** guilt, guilt **trip** 1
V. **admit** guilt 2

**guilty** /gɪlti/ (**guiltier, guiltiest**) 1 ADJ If you feel **guilty**, you feel unhappy because you think that you have done something wrong or have failed to do something which you should have done. culpable ❑ I feel so guilty, leaving all this work to you. Me siento tan culpable, dejándote a ti todo este trabajo. ● **guilti|ly** ADV con aire de culpabilidad ❑ He looked up guiltily when I walked in. Alzó la vista con aire de culpabilidad cuando yo entré. 2 ADJ You use **guilty** to describe an action or fact that you feel guilty about. vergonzoso ❑ He discovered her guilty secret. Descubrió su vergonzoso secreto. 3 **guilty conscience** → see **conscience** 4 ADJ If someone is **guilty of** doing something wrong or of committing a crime or offense, they have done that thing or committed that crime. culpable de ❑ They were found guilty of murder. Los declararon culpables de asesinato. ❑ He was guilty of making some serious mistakes. Su culpa fue haber cometido algunos errores muy graves.
→ see **trial**

**Word Partnership** Usar *guilty* con:

V. **feel** guilty, **look** guilty 1
**find someone** guilty, **plead (not)** guilty, **prove someone** guilty 4
N. guilty **conscience**, guilty **secret** 2
guilty **party**, guilty **plea**, guilty **verdict** 4
PREP. guilty **of something** 4

**gui|tar** /gɪtɑr/ (**guitars**) N-VAR A **guitar** is a musical instrument with six strings that are plucked or strummed. guitarra ● **gui|tar|ist** /gɪtɑrɪst/ N-COUNT (**guitarists**) guitarrista ❑ ...the world's best jazz guitarists. ...los mejores guitarristas de jazz del mundo.
→ see **string**

**gulch** /gʌltʃ/ (**gulches**) N-COUNT A **gulch** is a long narrow valley with steep sides which has been made by a stream flowing through it. barranco ❑ ...California Gulch. ...el Barranco de California

**gulf** /gʌlf/ (**gulfs**) 1 N-COUNT A **gulf** is an important or significant difference between two people, things, or groups. abismo ❑ There is a growing gulf between rich and poor. Hay un abismo que se acrecienta entre los ricos y los pobres. 2 N-COUNT A **gulf** is a large area of sea which extends a long way into the surrounding land. golfo ❑ ...the Gulf of Mexico. ...el Golfo de México.

**gul|ly** /gʌli/ (**gullies**) also **gulley** N-COUNT A **gully** is a long, narrow valley with steep sides. barranco, hondonada ❑ They fell down a steep gully. Cayeron por un barranco muy escarpado.
→ see **erosion**

**gum** /gʌm/ (**gums**) 1 N-UNCOUNT **Gum** is a flavored substance, which you chew for a long time but do not swallow. chicle ❑ I do not chew gum in public. Yo no masco chicle en público. 2 N-COUNT Your **gums** are the areas of firm, pink flesh inside your mouth, which your teeth grow out of. encía ❑ Gently brush your teeth and gums. Cepille cuidadosamente sus dientes y encías.
→ see **teeth**

**gum|ball** /gʌmbɔl/ (**gumballs**) N-COUNT **Gumballs** are round, brightly-colored balls of chewing gum. bolita de chicle

**gun** /gʌn/ (**guns, gunning, gunned**) 1 N-COUNT A **gun** is a weapon from which bullets or other things are fired. arma ❑ He pointed the gun at officers as they chased him. Apuntó el arma a los policías mientras lo perseguían. 2 → see also **shotgun** 3 PHRASE If you **stick to** your **guns,** you continue to have your own opinion about something even though other people are trying to tell you that you are wrong. mantenerse firme [INFORMAL] ❑ He stuck to his guns and refused to meet her. Se mantuvo firme y rehusó encontrarse con ella.

▸ **gun down** PHR-VERB If someone **is gunned down,** they are shot and severely injured or killed. tumbar a tiros, matar a tiros ❑ He had been gunned down and killed. Lo mataron a tiros.

**gun|fire** /gʌnfaɪr/ N-UNCOUNT **Gunfire** is the

repeated shooting of guns. *disparos* ❑ *The sound of gunfire grew closer.* *El ruido de disparos se acercaba.*

**gun|man** /gʌnmən/ (**gunmen**) N-COUNT A **gunman** is a man who uses a gun to commit a crime. *pistolero* ❑ *A gunman fired at police.* *Un pistolero disparó a la policía.*

**gun|point** /gʌnpɔɪnt/ PHRASE If you are held **at gunpoint,** someone threatens to shoot and kill you if you do not obey them. *a punta de pistola* ❑ *They were held at gunpoint by a thief.* *Un ladrón los mantuvo a punta de pistola.*

**gur|ney** /gɜrni/ (**gurneys**) N-COUNT A **gurney** is a bed on wheels that is used in hospitals for moving sick or injured people. *camilla*

**gut** /gʌt/ (**guts, gutting, gutted**) **1** N-PLURAL A person's or animal's **guts** are all the organs inside them. *vísceras, tripas* ❑ *She cleaned out all the fish guts.* *Limpió completamente el pescado.* **2** V-T When someone **guts** a dead animal or fish, they prepare it for cooking by removing all the organs from inside it. *destripar, limpiar* ❑ *We gut the fish and then freeze them.* *Limpiamos el pescado y luego lo congelamos.* **3** N-SING **The gut** is the tube inside the body of a person or animal through which food passes while it is being digested. *intestino* ❑ *The food then passes into the gut.* *La comida pasa entonces al intestino.* **4** N-UNCOUNT **Guts** is the will and courage to do something that is difficult or unpleasant, or which might have unpleasant results. *agallas* [INFORMAL] ❑ *She has the guts to say what she thinks.* *Tiene las agallas de decir lo que piensa.* **5** ADJ A **gut** feeling is based on instinct or emotion rather than reason. *reacción instintiva, reacción visceral* ❑ *My gut reaction was not to believe him.* *Mi reacción instintiva fue no creerle.* **6** V-T To **gut** a building means to destroy the inside of it so that only its outside walls remain. *destruir el interior de un edificio* ❑ *Fire gutted a building where 60 people lived.* *El fuego destruyó el interior de un edificio donde vivían 60 personas.*

**guy** /gaɪ/ (**guys**) **1** N-COUNT A **guy** is a man. *tipo* [INFORMAL] ❑ *I was working with a guy from Milwaukee.* *Estaba trabajando con un tipo de Milwaukee.* **2** N-VOC; N-PLURAL You can address a group of people, whether they are male or female, as **guys** or **you guys.** *chavos* [INFORMAL] ❑ *Hi, guys. How are you doing?* *Hola, chavos. ¿Cómo les va?*

**gym** /dʒɪm/ (**gyms**) **1** N-COUNT A **gym** is a club, building, or large room, usually containing special equipment, where people go to do physical exercise and get fit. *gimnasio* ❑ *Twice a week, I go to the gym.* *Voy dos veces a la semana al gimnasio.* **2** N-UNCOUNT **Gym** is the activity of doing physical exercises in a gym, especially at school. *gimnasia* ❑ *...gym classes.* *...clases de gimnasia.*

**gym|na|sium** /dʒɪmneɪziəm/ (**gymnasiums** or **gymnasia** /dʒɪmneɪziə/) N-COUNT A **gymnasium** is the same as a **gym**. *gimnasio* [FORMAL]

**gym|no|sperm** /dʒɪmnəspɜrm/ (**gymnosperms**) N-PLURAL A **gymnosperm** is a plant that produces seeds but does not produce flowers. *gimnosperma* [TECHNICAL]

**gyro** /dʒaɪroʊ/ (**gyros**) N-COUNT A **gyro** is the same as a **gyroscope.** *giroscopio* [INFORMAL] ❑ *We have six gyros on board.* *Tenemos seis giroscopios a bordo.*

| Word Link | *scope ≈ looking : gyroscope, microscope, telescope* |
| --- | --- |

**gyro|scope** /dʒaɪrəskoʊp/ (**gyroscopes**) N-COUNT A **gyroscope** is a device that contains a disc turning on an axis that can turn freely in any direction, so that the disc maintains the same position whatever the position or movement of the surrounding structure. *giroscopio* ❑ *Crewmen inspected the gyroscope.* *Los miembros de la tripulación revisaron el giroscopio.*

# Hh



**H** On a weather map, **H** is an abbreviation for "high pressure." *alta presión*

**Usage** **a** and **an** with the letter **h**

Before a word beginning with *h*: *a* is used if the *h* is pronounced and the first syllable is stressed at all: *Paul has a hidden agenda. That is a harmonica. I'm staying at a hotel. A* or *an* is used if the *h* is pronounced by the speaker: *This is a/an historic moment. He is making a/an habitual mistake.* (If *an* is used, the *h* isn't pronounced.) *An* is used if the *h* is never pronounced: *It is an honor to meet you.*

**hab|it** /hæbɪt/ (**habits**) **1** N-VAR A **habit** is something that you do often or regularly. *hábito* ❑ *He has a habit of licking his lips. Tiene el hábito de chuparse los labios.* ❑ *He had a habit of taking a 30-minute bath each morning. Tenía el hábito de darse un baño de 30 minutos cada mañana.* **2** N-COUNT A drug **habit** is an addiction to a drug such as heroin or cocaine. *drogadicción.* **3** PHRASE If you **are in the habit of** doing something or **make a habit of** doing it, you do it regularly or often. If you **get into the habit of** doing something, you begin to do it regularly or often. *(hacerse el) hábito* ❑ *They were in the habit of watching TV every night. Tenían la costumbre de ver televisión en la noche.* ❑ *Make a habit of hanging your clothes up each night. Hazte el hábito de colgar tu ropa todas las noches.*

**habi|tat** /hæbɪtæt/ (**habitats**) N-VAR The **habitat** of an animal or plant is the natural environment in which it normally lives or grows. *hábitat* ❑ *In its natural habitat, the plant will grow up to 25 feet. En su hábitat natural, la planta crecerá hasta 25 pies.*
→ see Word Web: **habitat**

**hack** /hæk/ (**hacks, hacking, hacked**) **1** V-T/V-I If you **hack** something or **hack away at** it, you cut it with strong, rough strokes using a sharp tool such as an ax or a knife. *cortar* ❑ *He hacked the wood with an ax. Cortó la madera con un hacha.* ❑ *He started to hack away at the tree bark. Empezó a cortar la corteza del árbol.* **2** V-I If someone **hacks into** a computer system, they break into the system, especially in order to get secret information. *hackear* ❑ *Criminals hacked into websites owned by the bank. Los sitios web del banco fueron hackeados por delincuentes.* ● **hack|er** N-COUNT (**hackers**) *hacker* ❑ *...a hacker who steals credit card numbers. ...un hacker que roba números de tarjetas de crédito.* ● **hack|ing** N-UNCOUNT *hackear* ❑ *...the common crime of computer hacking. ...el crimen común de hackear computadoras.* **3** N-COUNT If you refer to a professional writer, such as a journalist, as a **hack**, you disapprove of them because they write for money and do not worry very much about the quality of their writing. *escritor mercenario o escritora mercenaria* ❑ *...newspaper hacks, always eager to find something to write about. ...los mercenarios del periodismo, siempre ansiosos por encontrar algo sobre qué escribir.*
→ see **Internet**

**had**

The auxiliary verb is pronounced /həd, STRONG hæd/. For the main verb, the pronunciation is /hæd/.

**Had** is the past tense and past participle of **have**. *pasado y participio pasado de* ***have***

**Word Web** **habitat**

The **environment** where a plant or animal lives is its **habitat**. The habitat provides **food**, **water**, and **shelter**. Each habitat has different **temperatures**, **rainfall**, and amounts of **sunlight**. A **desert** is a sunny, dry habitat where few plants and animals can live. The **tropical rainforest** gets heavy rain every day and has many types of **vegetation** and animal life. **Grasslands** or **prairies** get little rain but are home to many **grass**-eating animals. The boreal **forest** is the largest **biome** in the world. Its winters are cold and snowy, and summers are warm, rainy, and humid.

desert

boreal forest

rainforest

grassland

## Picture Dictionary hair

**hadn't** /hædᵊnt/ **Hadn't** is the usual spoken form of "had not." *forma hablada usual de **had not***

**hail** /heɪl/ (**hails, hailing, hailed**) **1** V-T If a person, event, or achievement **is hailed as** important or successful, they are praised publicly. *ser aclamado* ❑ *He was hailed as a hero after rescuing a boy from the fire. Fue aclamado como héroe tras rescatar a un niño del fuego.* **2** N-UNCOUNT **Hail** consists of small balls of ice that fall like rain from the sky. *granizo* ❑ *...a storm with hail. ...una tormenta con granizo.* **3** V-T If you **hail** a taxi, you wave at it in order to stop it because you want the driver to take you somewhere. *hacerle señas a* ❑ *We tried to hail a taxi after the movie. Intentamos parar un taxi después de la película.*
→ see **precipitation, storm**

**hair** /hɛər/ (**hairs**) **1** N-VAR Your **hair** is the fine threads that grow on your head. *cabello, pelo* ❑ *I wash my hair every night. Me lavo el cabello todas las noches.* ❑ *My Mom gets some gray hairs but she pulls them out. A mi mamá le salen algunas canas, pero se las arranca.* **2** N-VAR **Hair** is the short, fine threads that grow on different parts of your body. *vello, pelo* ❑ *Most men have hair on their chest. La mayoría de los hombres tiene pelo en el pecho.* **3** N-VAR **Hair** is the threads that cover the body of an animal such as a dog, or make up a horse's mane and tail. *pelo* ❑ *She had dog hair on her clothes. Tenía pelos de perro en la ropa.*
→ see Picture Dictionary: **hair**

**Word Partnership** Usar *hair* con:

| | |
|---|---|
| ADJ. | **black/blonde/brown/gray** hair, **curly/straight/wavy** hair **1** |
| V. | **bleach your** hair, **brush/comb your** hair, **color your** hair, **cut your** hair, **do your** hair, **dry your** hair, **fix your** hair, **lose your** hair, **pull *someone's*** hair, **wash your** hair **1** |
| N. | **lock of** hair **1** |

**hair|cut** /hɛərkʌt/ (**haircuts**) **1** N-COUNT If you get a **haircut,** someone cuts your hair for you. *corte de pelo* ❑ *You need a haircut. Necesitas un corte de pelo.* **2** N-COUNT A **haircut** is the style in which your hair has been cut. *corte (de pelo)* ❑ *Who's that guy with the funny haircut? ¿Quién es ese chavo del corte chistoso?*

**hairy** /hɛəri/ (**hairier, hairiest**) **1** ADJ Someone or something that is **hairy** is covered with hairs. *peludo* ❑ *He was wearing shorts which showed his hairy legs. Andaba de shorts y se le veían las piernas peludas.* **2** ADJ If you describe a situation as **hairy,** you mean that it is exciting, worrying, and somewhat frightening. *escalofriante* [INFORMAL] ❑ *His driving was slightly hairy. Manejaba de forma escalofriante.*

**half** /hæf/ (**halves** /hævz/) **1** ORD **Half of** a number, an amount, or an object is one of two equal parts that together make up the whole number, amount, or object. *(la) mitad* ❑ *More than half of all U.S. houses are heated with gas. En los EE.UU., más de la mitad de las casas son calentadas con gas.* ● **Half** is also a predeterminer. *media, mitad*

❑ *We sat and talked for half an hour.* *Nos sentamos y hablamos durante media hora.* ❑ *They only received half the money that they were expecting.* *Recibieron solamente la mitad del dinero que esperaban.* • **Half** is also an adjective. *medio* ❑ *I'll stay with you for the first half hour.* *Me quedaré contigo la primera media hora.* 2 ADV You use **half** to say that something is only partly true or only partly happens. *medio* ❑ *His eyes were half closed.* *Tenía los ojos medio cerrados.* ❑ *The glass was half empty.* *El vaso estaba medio vacío.* 3 N-COUNT In games such as football, soccer, rugby, and basketball, games are divided into two equal periods of time which are called **halves.** *mitades, tiempos* ❑ *Jakobsen scored a goal early in the second half.* *Jakobsen anotó un gol muy pronto en el segundo tiempo.* 4 ADV You use **half** to say that someone has parents of different nationalities. For example, if you are **half** German, one of your parents is German. *mitad* ❑ *She was half Italian and half American.* *Era mitad italiana y mitad americana.*

H

**half-hour** (**half-hours**) N-COUNT A **half-hour** is a period of thirty minutes. *media hora* ❑ *...a talk followed by a half-hour of discussion.* *...una plática seguida de media hora de discusión.*

**half-life** (**half-lives**) also **half life** N-COUNT The **half-life** of a radioactive substance is the amount of time that it takes to lose half its radioactivity. *vida media.*

**half note** (**half notes**) N-COUNT A **half note** is a musical note that has a time value equal to two quarter notes. *blanca, mitad*

**half|time** /hæftaɪm/ N-UNCOUNT **Halftime** is the short period of time between the two parts of a sports event such as a football, hockey, or basketball game, when the players take a short rest. *medio tiempo.* ❑ *We bought something to eat during halftime.* *Compramos algo para comer durante el medio tiempo.*

**half|way** /hæfweɪ/ 1 ADV **Halfway** means in the middle of a place or between two points, at an equal distance from each of them. *a la mitad* ❑ *He was halfway up the ladder.* *Estaba a la mitad de la escalera.* 2 ADV **Halfway** means in the middle of a period of time or of an event. *a la mitad de* ❑ *We were more than halfway through our tour.* *Estábamos a más de la mitad de nuestro viaje.* • **Halfway** is also an adjective. *a medio* ❑ *Cleveland was winning at the halfway point in the game.* *Cleveland iba ganando a medio juego.*
→ see **soccer**

**hall** /hɔl/ (**halls**) 1 N-COUNT The **hall** in a house or an apartment is the area just inside the front door, into which some of the other rooms open. *vestíbulo* ❑ *The lights were on in the hall.* *Las luces estaban encendidas en el vestíbulo.* 2 N-COUNT A **hall** in a building is a long passage with doors into rooms on both sides of it. *pasillo, corredor* ❑ *There are 10 rooms along each hall.* *Hay 10 cuartos a lo largo de cada pasillo.* 3 N-COUNT A **hall** is a large room or building which is used for public events such as concerts, exhibitions, and meetings. *salón, sala* ❑ *We went into the lecture hall.* *Fuimos a la sala de conferencias.*
→ see **house**

**Word Partnership** Usar *hall* con:

| | |
|---|---|
| PREP. | **across the** hall, **down the** hall, **in the** hall 1 2 |
| N. | **concert** hall, **lecture** hall, **meeting** hall, **pool** hall 3 |

**Hal|ley's com|et** /hæliz kɒmɪt, heɪ-/ N-PROPER **Halley's comet** is a comet that is visible from the Earth every 76 years. *cometa Halley*

**Hal|low|een** /hæloʊwin/ also **Hallowe'en** N-UNCOUNT **Halloween** is the night of October 31st and is traditionally said to be the time when ghosts and witches can be seen. *noche de brujas, Halloween*

**hall|way** /hɔlweɪ/ (**hallways**) 1 N-COUNT A **hallway** in a building is a long passage with doors into rooms on both sides of it. *pasillo* ❑ *They walked along the quiet hallway.* *Recorrieron el silencioso pasillo.* 2 → see also **hall** 3 N-COUNT A **hallway** in a house or an apartment is the area just inside the front door, into which some of the other rooms open. *recibidor* ❑ *...the coats hanging in the hallway.* *...los abrigos colgados en el recibidor.*

**halo|gen** /hælədʒən/ (**halogens**) N-VAR A **halogen** is one of a group of chemical elements that includes chlorine, fluorine, and iodine. Halogens are often used in lighting and heating devices. *halógeno* ❑ *...a halogen lamp.* *...una lámpara de halógeno.*

**halo|phile** /hæləfaɪl/ (**halophiles**) N-COUNT **Halophiles** are bacteria that need salt in order to grow. *halófila* [TECHNICAL]

**halt** /hɔlt/ (**halts, halting, halted**) 1 V-T/V-I When a person or a vehicle **halts** or when something **halts** them, they stop moving in the direction they were going and stand still. *detener* ❑ *Judges halted the race at 5:30 p.m. yesterday.* *Ayer los jueces detuvieron la carrera a las 5:30 p.m.* 2 V-T/V-I When something such as growth, development, or activity **halts** or when you **halt** it, it stops completely. *parar* ❑ *Last week's storm halted business.* *La tormenta de la semana pasada paró los negocios.* 3 PHRASE If someone or something comes **to a halt,** they stop moving. *detener(se), parar(se)* ❑ *The elevator came to a halt at the first floor.* *El elevador se detuvo en el primer piso.* 4 PHRASE If something such as growth, development, or activity **comes** or **grinds to a halt** or **is brought to a halt,** it stops completely. *interrumpir* ❑ *Her career came to a halt in December 2005.* *Su carrera se interrumpió en diciembre de 2005.*

**halve** /hæv/ (**halves, halving, halved**) 1 V-T/V-I When you **halve** something or when it **halves,** it is reduced to half its previous size or amount. *reducir a la mitad.* ❑ *People who exercise may halve their risk of getting heart disease.* *La gente que hace ejercicio puede reducir a la mitad el riesgo de sufrir una enfermedad del corazón.* 2 V-T If you **halve** something, you divide it into two equal parts. *partir en dos, dividir en dos* ❑ *Halve the peppers and remove the seeds.* *Parte los pimientos a la mitad y quítales las semillas.* 3 **Halves** is the plural of **half**. *plural de **half***

**ham** /hæm/ (**hams**) N-VAR **Ham** is meat from the top of the back leg of a pig, specially treated so that it can be kept for a long period of time. *jamón*

❑ *...ham sandwiches.* *...sándwiches de jamón.*

**ham|burg|er** /hæmbɜrgər/ (**hamburgers**) N-COUNT A **hamburger** is ground meat which has been shaped into a flat circle. Hamburgers are fried or grilled and often eaten on a bun. *hamburguesa*

→ see **bread**

**ham|mer** /hæmər/ (**hammers, hammering, hammered**) 1 N-COUNT A **hammer** is a tool that consists of a heavy piece of metal at the end of a handle. It is used, for example, to hit nails into something, or to break things into pieces. *martillo* ❑ *He used a hammer to knock the nail in.* *Utilizó un martillo para clavar el clavo.* 2 V-T If you **hammer** an object such as a nail, you hit it with a hammer. *clavar* ❑ *She hammered a nail into the window frame.* *Clavó un clavo en el marco de la ventana.* 3 V-I If you **hammer on** a surface, you hit it several times in order to make a noise, or to emphasize something you are saying when you are angry. *golpear* ❑ *We had to hammer on the door before they opened it.* *Tuvimos que golpear la puerta antes de que la abrieran.* 4 V-T If you say that someone **hammers** another person, you mean that they attack, criticize, or punish the other person severely. *castigar* ❑ *Sports officials hammered him with a 15-day ban.* *Los dirigentes del deporte lo castigaron con una suspensión de 15 días.*

→ see **tool**

▸ **hammer out** PHR-VERB If people **hammer out** an agreement or treaty, they succeed in producing it after a long or difficult discussion. *negociar* ❑ *I think we can hammer out a solution.* *Creo que podemos negociar una solución.*

**ham|per** /hæmpər/ (**hampers, hampering, hampered**) 1 V-T If someone or something **hampers** you, they make it difficult for you to do what you are trying to do. *dificultar* ❑ *The bad weather hampered rescue operations.* *El mal tiempo dificultó las labores de rescate.* 2 N-COUNT A **hamper** is a large basket with a lid, used especially for carrying food. *canasta* ❑ *...a picnic hamper.* *...una canasta para picnic.* 3 N-COUNT A **hamper** is a storage container for soiled laundry. *cesto* ❑ *He threw his wet towel into the laundry hamper.* *Echó su toalla húmeda al cesto de la ropa sucia.*

**hand**

❶ NOUN USES AND PHRASES
❷ VERB USES

❶ **hand** /hænd/ (**hands**) 1 N-COUNT Your **hands** are the parts of your body at the end of your arms. *manos* ❑ *I put my hand into my pocket and pulled out the letter.* *Metí la mano en el bolsillo y saqué la carta.* 2 N-SING If you ask someone for **a hand** with something, you are asking them to help you in what you are doing. *(echar la) mano* ❑ *Come and give me a hand in the kitchen.* *Ven y échame la mano en la cocina.* 3 N-COUNT In a game of cards, your **hand** is the set of cards that you are holding in your hand at a particular time or the cards that are dealt to you at the beginning of the game. *juego* ❑ *He carefully looked at his hand.* *Observó atentamente su juego.* 4 N-COUNT The **hands** of a clock or watch are the thin pieces of metal, plastic, or other material that indicate what time it is. *manecillas* ❑ *The hands of the clock on the wall moved with a slight click.* *Las manecillas del reloj de pared hicieron clic al moverse.* 5 PHRASE If something is **at hand, near at hand,** or **close at hand,** it is very near in place or time. *a la mano* ❑ *She sat down, with the phone close at hand.* *Se sentó con el teléfono a la mano.* 6 PHRASE If you do something **by hand,** you do it using your hands rather than a machine. *a mano* ❑ *...a dress made entirely by hand.* *...un vestido todo hecho a mano.* 7 PHRASE When something **changes hands,** its ownership changes, usually because it is sold to someone else. *pasar de mano en mano* ❑ *The firm has changed hands many times.* *La empresa ha cambiado de dueño muchas veces.* 8 PHRASE If someone gives you **a free hand,** they give you the freedom to use your own judgment and to do exactly as you wish. *entera libertad* ❑ *He gave Stephanie a free hand in the decoration of the house.* *Le dio entera libertad a Stephanie en la decoración de la casa.* 9 PHRASE If two things **go hand in hand,** they are closely connected and cannot be considered separately from each other. *ir (tomado) de la mano* ❑ *Research and teaching go hand in hand.* *La investigación y la enseñanza van de la mano.* 10 PHRASE If you **have a hand in** something such as an event or activity, you are involved in it. *tener que ver con* ❑ *He thanked everyone who had a hand in the event.* *Agradeció a todos los que participaron en el evento.* 11 PHRASE If a situation is **in hand,** it is under control. *bajo control* ❑ *The Olympic organizers say that plans are well in hand.* *Los organizadores olímpicos dicen que los planes están bajo control.* 12 PHRASE If someone **lives hand to mouth** or **lives from hand to mouth,** they have hardly enough food or money to live on. *vivir al día* ❑ *I have a wife and two children and we live from hand to mouth on what I earn.* *Tengo una esposa y dos niños y vivimos al día con lo que gano.* 13 PHRASE If someone or something is **on hand,** they are near and able to be used if they are needed. *a la mano* ❑ *There are experts on hand to give you all the help you need.* *Hay expertos a la mano para darte toda la ayuda que necesites.* 14 PHRASE You use **on the one hand** to introduce the first of two contrasting points, facts, or ways of looking at something. It is always followed by "on the other hand" or "on the other." *por una parte* ❑ *On the one hand, the body cannot survive without fat. On the other hand, if the body has too much fat, our health starts to suffer.* *Por una parte, el cuerpo humano no puede sobrevivir sin grasa, pero por la otra, el exceso de grasa perjudica la salud.* 15 PHRASE You use **on the other hand** to introduce the second of two contrasting points, facts, or ways of looking at something. You do not need to use **on the one hand** before it. *sin embargo* ❑ *The movie lost money; reviews, on the other hand, were mostly favorable.* *La película perdió dinero; las reseñas, sin embargo, fueron en su mayoría favorables.* 16 PHRASE If a person or a situation gets **out of hand,** you are no longer able to control them. *salir(se) de control, fuera de control* ❑ *Officials tried to stop the demonstration from getting out of hand.* *Los oficiales intentaron que la manifestación no se saliera de control.* 17 PHRASE If you **try** your **hand at** an activity, you attempt to do it, usually for the first time. *probar suerte* ❑ *He tried his hand at fishing, but he wasn't very good at it.* *Probó suerte en la pesca, pero no era muy bueno.* 18 PHRASE If you **wash** your **hands of** someone or something, you refuse to be involved with them any more or to take responsibility for them. *lavarse las manos* ❑ He

**Picture Dictionary** hand

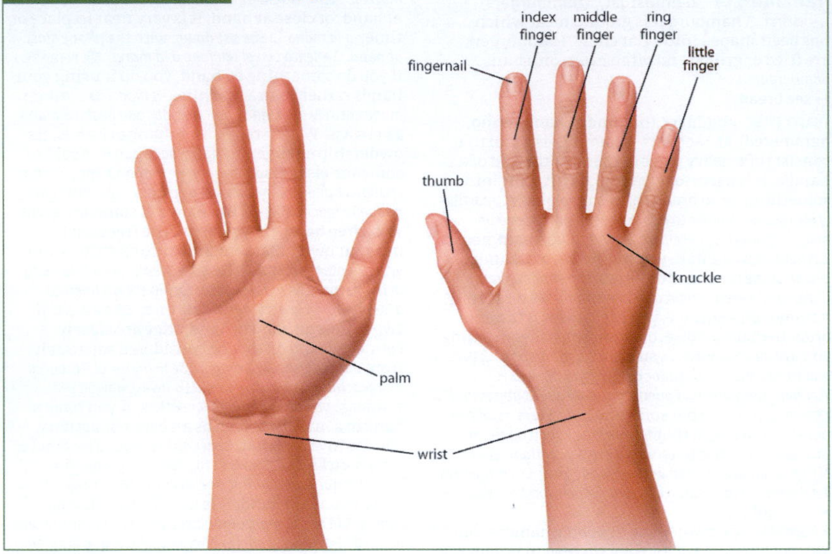


*has washed his hands of the job.* *Se lavó las manos sobre el trabajo.* **19** **with** one's **bare hands** → see **bare** **20** to **shake** someone's **hand** → see **shake** **21** to **shake hands** → see **shake**

→ see Picture Dictionary: **hand**

→ see **body, time**

**❷ hand** /hænd/ (**hands, handing, handed**) V-T If you **hand** something **to** someone, you pass it to them. *dar (con la mano)* ❑ *He handed me a piece of paper.* *Me dio un papel.*

▸ **hand down** PHR-VERB If you **hand down** something such as knowledge, a possession, or a skill, you give or leave it to people who belong to a younger generation. *transmitir* ❑ *The idea of handing down knowledge to your children is important.* *La idea de transmitirles conocimientos a tus hijos es importante.*

▸ **hand in** PHR-VERB If you **hand in** something such as homework or something that you have found, you give it to a teacher, police officer, or other person in authority. *entregar* ❑ *I need to hand in my homework today.* *Hoy necesito entregar mi tarea.*

▸ **hand on** → see **hand down**

▸ **hand out** **1** PHR-VERB If you **hand** things **out** to people, you give one or more to each person in a group. *repartir, entregar* ❑ *My job was to hand out the prizes.* *Mi trabajo era entregar los premios.* **2** → see also **handout**

▸ **hand over** PHR-VERB If you **hand over to** someone or **hand** something **over to** them, you give them the responsibility for dealing with a particular situation or problem. *dar, transferir* ❑ *The chairman handed over control to someone younger.* *El presidente le dio el control a alguien más joven.*

**hand|bag** /hændbæg/ (**handbags**) N-COUNT A **handbag** is a small bag which a woman uses to carry things such as her money and keys in when she goes out. *bolsa (de mano)*

**hand|ful** /hændfʊl/ (**handfuls**) **1** N-SING A **handful of** people or things is a small number of them. *(unos) cuantos* ❑ *Only a handful of people knew his secret.* *Sólo unas cuantas personas sabían su secreto.* **2** N-COUNT A **handful of** something is the amount of it that you can hold in your hand. *puñado* ❑ *...a handful of sand.* *...un puñado de arena.* **3** N-SING If you say that someone, especially a child, is a **handful,** you mean that they are difficult to control. *travieso o traviesa* [INFORMAL] ❑ *Sarah is a handful sometimes.* *Sarah es una traviesa a veces.*

**handi|cap** /hændikæp/ (**handicaps, handicapping, handicapped**) **1** N-COUNT A **handicap** is a physical or mental disability. *impedimento* ❑ *He lost his leg when he was ten, but learned to live with his handicap.* *Perdió la pierna cuando tenía diez años, pero aprendió a vivir con su impedimento.* **2** N-COUNT A **handicap** is an event or situation that makes it harder for you to do something. *desventaja* ❑ *Being a foreigner was not a handicap.* *El ser extranjero no fue una desventaja.* **3** V-T If an event or a situation **handicaps** someone or something, it makes it harder for them to do something. *(poner en) desventaja* ❑ *Their nationality handicaps them in the job market.* *Su nacionalidad los pone en desventaja en el mercado laboral.*

**handi|capped** /hændikæpt/ ADJ Someone who is **handicapped** has a physical or mental disability. Some people find this term offensive and prefer to use **disabled.** *impedido* ❑ *She teaches handicapped kids to fish.* *Enseña a niños impedidos a pescar.*

**hand|ker|chief** /hæŋkərtʃɪf/ (**handkerchiefs**) N-COUNT A **handkerchief** is a small square piece of fabric which you use for blowing your nose. *pañuelo*

**han|dle** /hændᵊl/ (**handles, handling, handled**) **1** N-COUNT A **handle** is a small round object or a lever that is attached to a door and is used for opening and closing it. *manija* ❑ *I turned the handle and the door opened. Bajé la manija y la puerta se abrió.* **2** N-COUNT A **handle** is the part of an object such as a tool, bag, or cup that you hold in order to be able to pick up and use the object. *mango, asa* ❑ *...a knife handle. ...el mango de un cuchillo.* **3** V-T If you **handle** a problem or situation, you deal with it. *manejar, poder (manejar una situación)* ❑ *I don't know if I can handle the job. No sé si pueda con el trabajo.* ❑ *I think I handled the meeting very badly. Creo que manejé muy mal la reunión.* ● **han|dling** N-UNCOUNT *manejo, tratamiento* ❑ *He questioned them about their handling of the case. Los cuestionó sobre el manejo del caso.* **4** V-T If you **handle** a particular area of work, you have responsibility for it. *ocuparse (de algo), encargarse (de algo)* ❑ *She handles travel plans for the company's managers. Se encarga de los planes de viaje para los gerentes de la compañía.* **5** V-T When you **handle** something, you hold it or move it with your hands. *manipular* ❑ *Wash your hands before handling food. Lávate las manos antes de manipular los alimentos.*

handle

→ see **silverware**

**Word Partnership** Usar *handle* con:

N. handle **a job/problem/situation**, handle **pressure/responsibility** **3** **4**
**ability to** handle *something* **3** – **5**
ADJ. **difficult/easy/hard to** handle **3** – **5**

**hand|made** /hændmeɪd/ also **hand-made** ADJ **Handmade** objects have been made by someone using their hands or using tools rather than by machines. *hecho a mano* ❑ *...handmade jewelry. ...joyería hecha a mano.*

**hand-me-down** (**hand-me-downs**) **1** N-COUNT **Hand-me-downs** are things, usually clothes, which someone else has already used and which are given to you to use. *ropa heredada* ❑ *Edward wore Andrew's hand-me-downs. Edward usaba la ropa que dejaba Andrew.* **2** ADJ **Hand-me-down** is used to describe things, usually clothes, which someone else has already used and which are given to you to use. *ropa heredada* ❑ *Most of the boys wore hand-me-down shirts from their fathers. La mayoría de los niños usaba camisas heredadas de sus papás.*

**hand|out** /hændaʊt/ (**handouts**) **1** N-COUNT A **handout** is a gift of money, clothing, or food, which is given free to poor people. *dádiva* ❑ *Each family got a cash handout of six thousand rupees after the fire. Cada familia recibió una dádiva de seis mil rupias después del incendio.* **2** N-COUNT A **handout** is a document which contains news or information about something. *folleto informativo, notas* ❑ *Turn to the first page of the handout. Ve a la primera página de las notas.*

**Word Link** *free ≈ without : freeway, hands-free, toll-free*

**hands-free** ADJ A **hands-free** telephone or other device can be used without being held in your hand. *manos libres* ❑ *...laws to ban handheld and hands-free cellphones in moving cars. ...leyes para prohibir celulares en mano y manos libres en autos en movimiento.*

**hand|shake** /hændʃeɪk/ (**handshakes**) N-COUNT If you give someone a **handshake,** you take their right hand with your own right hand and hold it firmly or move it up and down, as a sign of greeting or to show that you have agreed about something. *apretón de manos* ❑ *He has a strong handshake. Aprieta fuerte al saludar.*

**hands-off** ADJ A **hands-off** policy or approach to something consists of not being personally or directly involved in it. *de no intromisión* ❑ *...the government's hands-off attitude toward large businesses. ...la actitud de no intromisión del gobierno hacia las compañías grandes.*

**hand|some** /hænsəm/ **1** ADJ A **handsome** man has an attractive face with regular features. *guapo* ❑ *...a tall, handsome farmer. ...un granjero alto y guapo.* **2** ADJ A **handsome** sum of money is a large or generous amount. *bueno, generoso* [FORMAL] ❑ *They will make a handsome profit when they sell the house. Obtendrán una buena ganancia cuando vendan la casa.*

**hand|writing** /hændraɪtɪŋ/ N-UNCOUNT Your **handwriting** is your style of writing with a pen or pencil. *letra* ❑ *The address was in Anna's handwriting. La dirección estaba escrita con la letra de Anna.*

**hand|written** /hændrɪtᵊn/ ADJ A piece of writing that is **handwritten** is one that someone has written using a pen or pencil rather than by typing it. *escrito a mano, manuscrito* ❑ *...a handwritten note. ...una nota escrita a mano.*

**handy** /hændi/ (**handier, handiest**) **1** ADJ Something that is **handy** is useful. *práctico* ❑ *The book gives handy hints on growing plants. El libro da consejos prácticos sobre el cultivo de plantas.* **2** ADJ A thing or place that is **handy** is nearby and therefore easy to get or reach. *a la mano* ❑ *Make sure you have a pencil and paper handy. Asegúrate de tener lápiz y papel a la mano.*

**hang** /hæŋ/ (**hangs, hanging, hung** or **hanged**)

The form **hanged** is used as the past tense and past participle for meaning **3**.

**1** V-T/V-I If something **hangs** in a high place or position, or if you **hang** it there, it is attached there so it does not touch the ground. *colgar* ❑ *Posters hang at every entrance. En cada entrada cuelga un poster.* ● **Hang up** means the same as **hang.** *colgar* ❑ *His jacket was hanging up in the hallway. Su chamarra estaba colgada en el pasillo.* **2** V-I If something **hangs** in a particular way or position, that is how it is worn or arranged. *caerle a alguien* ❑ *...a coat that hung down to her ankles. ...un abrigo que le llegaba a los tobillos.* ❑ *Her long hair hung loose about her shoulders. El largo pelo le llegaba a la altura de los hombros.* **3** V-T/V-I If someone **is hanged** or if they **hang,** they are killed by having a rope tied around their neck and the support taken away from under their feet. *ahorcar(se)* ❑ *The five men were hanged on Tuesday. A los cinco hombres los ahorcaron el martes.* ❑ *He hanged himself in prison. Él mismo se ahorcó en la prisión.* **4** V-I If a possibility **hangs over** you,

h

it worries you and makes your life unpleasant or difficult because you think it might happen. amenazar ❑ *The threat of unemployment hangs over many workers.* *La posibilidad de desempleo amenaza a muchos trabajadores.* 5 → see also **hung** 6 PHRASE If you **get the hang of** something such as a skill or activity, you begin to understand or realize how to do it. agarrarle la onda (a algo) [INFORMAL] ❑ *Driving is difficult at first until you get the hang of it.* *Manejar es difícil, hasta que le agarras la onda.*

▸ **hang back** PHR-VERB If you **hang back,** you move or stay slightly behind a person or group, usually because you are shy or nervous about something. hacer(se) para atrás ❑ *He hung back while the others moved forward.* *Se hizo para atrás mientras los otros se movieron hacia adelante.*

▸ **hang on** 1 PHR-VERB If you ask someone to **hang on,** you ask them to wait or stop what they are doing or saying for a moment. esperar [INFORMAL] ❑ *Can you hang on for a minute?* *¿Puedes esperar un minuto?* 2 PHR-VERB If you **hang on,** you manage to survive, achieve success, or avoid failure in spite of great difficulties or opposition. aguantar ❑ *He hung on to finish second in the race.* *Aguantó y logró terminar segundo en la carrera.* 3 PHR-VERB If you **hang on to** or **hang onto** something that gives you an advantage, you succeed in keeping it for yourself. mantener ❑ *The tennis player was unable to hang on to his lead and lost the game.* *El tenista fue incapaz de mantener su ventaja y perdió el juego.* 4 PHR-VERB If you **hang on to** or **hang onto** something, you hold it very tightly. aferrarse a ❑ *He hung on to the rail as he went downstairs.* *Se aferró al barandal mientras bajaba.* ❑ *The child hung onto his legs.* *El niño se aferró a sus piernas.* 5 PHR-VERB If one thing **hangs on** another, it depends on it in order to be successful. depender de ❑ *The success of the agreement hangs on this meeting.* *El éxito del acuerdo depende de esta junta.*

▸ **hang out** 1 PHR-VERB If you **hang out** clothes that you have washed, you hang them on a clothes line to dry. tender ❑ *I hung my laundry out.* *Tendí mi ropa.* 2 PHR-VERB If you **hang out** in a particular place or area, you go and stay there for no particular reason, or spend a lot of time there. pasar el rato [INFORMAL] ❑ *I often hang out at the mall.* *Con frecuencia paso el rato en el centro comercial.*

▸ **hang up** 1 → see **hang** 1 2 PHR-VERB If you **hang up** or you **hang up** the phone, you end a phone call. If you **hang up on** someone you are speaking to on the phone, you end the phone call suddenly and unexpectedly. colgar ❑ *Mom hung up the phone.* *Mamá colgó el teléfono.* ❑ *Don't hang up on me!* *¡No me cuelgues!*

**hang|er** /hæŋər/ (**hangers**) N-COUNT A **hanger** is the same as a **coat hanger**. colgador, gancho

**hang|ing val|ley** (**hanging valleys**) N-COUNT A **hanging valley** is a type of valley associated with glaciers. It is smaller and higher than the main glacial valley, to which it is connected. valle pendiente [TECHNICAL]

**hang|ing wall** (**hanging walls**) N-COUNT A **hanging wall** is the rock above a geological fault. Compare **footwall**. pared colgante [TECHNICAL]

**hap|pen** /hæpən/ (**happens, happening, happened**) 1 V-I Something that **happens** occurs or is done without being planned. suceder ❑ *We don't know what will happen.* *No sabemos lo que sucederá.* 2 V-I When something **happens to** you, it takes place and affects you. ocurrir ❑ *What's the worst thing that has ever happened to you?* *¿Qué es lo peor que te ha pasado?* 3 V-T If you **happen to** do something, you do it by chance. suceder ❑ *We happened to be there at the same time.* *Sucedió que estuvimos ahí al mismo tiempo.* 4 PHRASE You use **as it happens** in order to introduce a statement, especially one that is rather surprising. sucede que ❑ *As it happened, I was the first to arrive.* *Da la casualidad de que fui el primero en llegar.*

**hap|pi|ly** /hæpɪli/ 1 ADV You can add **happily** to a statement to indicate that you are glad that something happened. afortunadamente ❑ *Happily, most kittens are adopted within days of arriving at the shelter.* *Afortunadamente, la mayoría de los gatitos son adoptados a unos cuántos días de llegar al albergue.* 2 → see also **happy**

**hap|py** /hæpi/ (**happier, happiest**) 1 ADJ Someone who is **happy** has feelings of pleasure. feliz ❑ *Marina was a happy child.* *Marina era una niña feliz.* ● **hap|pi|ly** ADV felizmente ❑ *Albert leaned back happily and drank his coffee.* *Albert se recargó plácidamente y le dio un trago al café.* ● **hap|pi|ness** N-UNCOUNT felicidad ❑ *I think she was looking for happiness.* *Creo que ella buscaba la felicidad.* 2 ADJ A **happy** time, place, or relationship is full of happy feelings and pleasant experiences, or has an atmosphere in which people feel happy. feliz ❑ *She had a happy childhood.* *Ella tuvo una niñez feliz.* ❑ *It was always a happy place.* *Siempre fue un sitio feliz.* 3 ADJ If you are **happy about** or **with** a situation or arrangement, you are satisfied with it. contento, feliz ❑ *I'm not happy with what I've written.* *No me encanta lo que escribí.* 4 ADJ If you say you are **happy to** do something, you mean that you are very willing to do it. contento de ❑ *I'm happy to answer any questions.* *Con gusto responderé cualquier pregunta.* ● **hap|pi|ly** ADV ❑ *I will happily apologize if I've upset anyone.* *Con gusto pediré disculpas si he molestado a alguien.* 5 ADJ **Happy** is used in greetings and other conventional expressions to say that you hope someone will enjoy a special occasion. feliz ❑ *Happy Birthday!* *¡Feliz cumpleaños!*
→ see **emotion**

**Thesaurus** *happy* Ver también:

ADJ. cheerful, content, delighted, glad, pleased, upbeat; (*ant.*) sad, unhappy 1

**Word Partnership** Usar *happy* con:

ADV. **extremely/perfectly/very** happy 1
V. **feel** happy, **make** *someone* happy, **seem** happy 1
N. happy **ending**, happy **family**, happy **marriage** 2

**har|bor** /hɑrbər/ (**harbors, harboring, harbored**) 1 N-COUNT A **harbor** is an area of water which is partly enclosed by land or strong walls, so that boats can be left there safely. puerto ❑ *The fishing boats left the harbor and motored out to sea.* *Los barcos pesqueros dejaron el puerto y enfilaron hacia alta mar.* 2 V-T If you **harbor** an emotion, thought, or secret, you have it in your mind over a long period of time. guardar ❑ *She harbored a lot of anger about her childhood.* Abrigaba un intenso enojo por su niñez. 3 V-T If a person or country **harbors** someone who is wanted by the police, they let them stay in their house or country and offer them protection. albergar ❑ *...states that harbored terrorists.* ...estados que albergaban a terroristas.

**har|bor|master** /hɑrbərmæstər/ (**harbormasters**) also **harbor master** N-COUNT A **harbormaster** is the official in charge of a harbor. capitán o capitana de puerto

**hard** /hɑrd/ (**harder, hardest**) 1 ADJ Something that is **hard** is very firm and stiff to touch and is not easily bent, cut, or broken. duro ❑ *...the hard wooden floor.* ...el duro piso de madera. • **hard|ness** N-UNCOUNT dureza ❑ *...the hardness of the iron railing.* ...la dureza del barandal de hierro. 2 ADJ Something that is **hard** is very difficult to do or deal with. difícil ❑ *That's a very hard question.* Qué pregunta tan difícil. ❑ *She had a hard life.* Ella tuvo una vida muy difícil. 3 ADV If you work **hard** doing something, you are very active or work intensely, with a lot of effort. duro ❑ *If I work hard, I'll finish the work by tomorrow.* Si trabajo duro, terminaré este trabajo para mañana. • **Hard** is also an adjective. duro ❑ *I admired him as a hard worker.* Lo admiraba por ser muy trabajador. ❑ *...a hard day's work.* ...un duro día de trabajo. 4 ADV If you strike or take hold of something **hard,** you strike or take hold of it with a lot of force. con dureza ❑ *I kicked a trash can very hard and broke my toe.* Le di una dura patada al bote de basura y me rompí un dedo del pie. • **Hard** is also an adjective. fuerte ❑ *She gave me a hard push and I fell over.* Ella me dio un fuerte empujón y me caí. 5 ADJ If a person or their expression is **hard,** they show no kindness or sympathy. duro ❑ *His father was a hard man.* Su padre era un hombre duro. 6 ADJ **Hard** evidence or facts are definitely true and do not need to be questioned. concreto, definitivo ❑ *You should base your decision on hard facts.* Debes basar tu decisión en hechos concretos. 7 PHRASE If you say that something is **hard going,** you mean it is difficult and requires a lot of effort. muy difícil ❑ *The job was hard going at the start.* El trabajo fue muy difícil al principio.
→ see **hat**

| **Thesaurus** | *hard* | Ver también: |
|---|---|---|
| ADJ. | firm, solid, tough; (*ant.*) gentle, soft 1 complicated, difficult, tough; (*ant.*) easy 2 | |

**hard|ball** /hɑrdbɔl/ PHRASE If someone **plays hardball,** they will do anything that is necessary to achieve or get what they want, even if this involves being harsh or unfair. ser despiadado ❑ *She is playing hardball in a difficult business.* Se muestra despiadada en un asunto difícil.

**hard ci|der** (**hard ciders**) N-UNCOUNT **Hard cider** is an alcoholic drink that is made from apples. sidra

**hard core** also **hard-core** N-SING You can refer to the members of a group who are the most committed to its activities or who are the most involved in them as a **hard core of** members or as the **hard-core** members. de hueso colorado ❑ *The violence was started by a hard core of troublemakers.* La violencia la inició un pequeño grupo de alborotadores de hueso colorado. ❑ *Hard-core Harry Potter fans criticized the film for changing important parts of the book.* Los fanáticos a ultranza de Harry Potter criticaron la película porque cambia partes importantes del libro.

**hard|cover** /hɑrdkʌvər/ (**hardcovers**) N-COUNT A **hardcover** is a book which has a stiff hard cover. Compare **softcover.** libro de pasta dura ❑ *The book was published in hardcover last October.* El libro fue publicado en pasta dura en octubre.

**hard disk** (**hard disks**) N-COUNT A computer's **hard disk** is a stiff magnetic disk on which data and programs can be stored. disco duro

**hard drive** (**hard drives**) N-COUNT The **hard drive** on a computer is the part that contains the computer's hard disk. disco duro ❑ *You can play music from the PC's hard drive.* Puedes tocar música del disco duro de la computadora.

**hard-earned** ADJ A **hard-earned** victory or **hard-earned** cash is a victory or money that someone deserves because they have worked hard for it. ganado con dificultad ❑ *Don't waste any more of your hard-earned money on that dress!* ¡No gastes más dinero que no te regalaron en ese vestido!

**hard|en** /hɑrdᵊn/ (**hardens, hardening, hardened**) 1 V-T/V-I When something **hardens** or when you **harden** it, it becomes stiff or firm. endurecer(se) ❑ *Mold the mixture before it hardens.* Dale forma a la mezcla antes de que endurezca. 2 V-T/V-I When an attitude or opinion **hardens** or **is hardened,** it becomes harsher, stronger, or fixed. endurecer(se) ❑ *Their actions will harden the government's attitude.* Sus acciones endurecerán la actitud del gobierno. • **hard|en|ing** N-SING endurecimiento ❑ *...a hardening of public opinion.* ...un endurecimiento de la opinión pública. 3 V-T/V-I When events **harden** people or when people **harden,** they become less easily affected emotionally and less sympathetic and gentle than they were before. endurecer(se) ❑ *Nina's heart hardened against her father.* El corazón de Nina se endureció en contra de su padre.

**hard la|bor** N-UNCOUNT **Hard labor** is hard physical work which people have to do as punishment for a crime. trabajos forzados ❑ *The sentence of the court was twelve years' hard labor.* La sentencia de la corte fue de doce años de trabajos forzados.

**hard-line** also **hardline** ADJ If you describe someone's policy or attitude as **hard-line,** you mean that it is strict or extreme, and they refuse to change it. de línea dura ❑ *...the country's hard-line government.* ...el gobierno de línea dura del país.

**hard|ly** /hɑrdli/ 1 ADV You use **hardly** to say that something is only just true. apenas ❑ *I hardly know you.* Apenas te conozco. ❑ *I've hardly slept for three days.* Apenas si he dormido los últimos tres días. 2 ADV You use **hardly** in expressions such as **hardly ever, hardly any,** and **hardly anyone** to mean almost never, almost none, or almost no one. apenas, casi ❑ *We hardly ever eat fish.* Nosotros casi nunca comemos pescado. ❑ *...young workers with hardly any experience.* ...trabajadores jóvenes con casi ninguna experiencia. 3 ADV You use **hardly** to mean "not" when you want to suggest that you are expecting your listener or reader to agree with your comment. apenas ❑ *It's hardly surprising his ideas didn't work.* No es de extrañar que sus ideas no hayan funcionado.

h

**Usage** **hardly** and **hard**

*Hardly* is not the adverb form of *hard*. *Hard* is used for both the adjective: *The test was very hard*. and the adverb: *The staff worked hard*. However, to say: "*The staff hardly worked*." means that they did not work hard. The adverbs *hardly* and *hard* means just about the opposite of each other.

**hard|ship** /hɑrdʃɪp/ (**hardships**) N-VAR **Hardship** is a situation in which your life is difficult or unpleasant. *apuro, privación* ❑ *Higher bus fares are a hardship on elderly people. Subir el costo del transporte en autobús es una penuria para la gente mayor.*

**Word Link** *ware ≈ merchandise : hardware, software, warehouse*

H

**hard|ware** /hɑrdwɛər/ **1** N-UNCOUNT In computer systems, **hardware** refers to the machines themselves as opposed to the programs which tell the machines what to do. Compare **software.** *hardware* ❑ *The hardware costs about $200. El hardware cuesta aproximadamente 200 US dólares.* **2** N-UNCOUNT **Hardware** refers to tools and equipment that are used in the home and garden, for example nuts and bolts, screwdrivers, and hinges. *ferretería* ❑ *...a hardware store. ...una ferretería.*

**har|dy** /hɑrdi/ (**hardier, hardiest**) ADJ People, animals and plants that are **hardy** are strong and able to survive difficult conditions. *resistente* ❑ *The plant is hardy and easy to grow. La planta es resistente y fácil de cultivar.*

**harm** /hɑrm/ (**harms, harming, harmed**) **1** V-T To **harm** someone or something means to injure or damage them. *lastimar* ❑ *They didn't mean to harm anyone. No tenían intención de lastimar a nadie.* ❑ *...a warning that the product may harm the environment. ...una advertencia de que el producto podría dañar al ambiente.* **2** N-UNCOUNT **Harm** is injury or damage to a person or thing. *daño* ❑ *All dogs are capable of doing harm to people. Todos los perros son capaces de hacerle daño a la gente.* **3** PHRASE If you say **it does no harm to** do something or **there is no harm in** doing something, you mean that it might be worth doing, and you will not be blamed for doing it. *no hacer daño* ❑ *I don't think he'll help, but there's no harm in asking. No creo que él ayude, pero no hace daño pedírselo.*

**Thesaurus** *harm* Ver también:

| | |
|---|---|
| V. | abuse, damage, hurt, injure, ruin, wreck; (*ant.*) benefit **1** |
| N. | abuse, damage, hurt, injury, ruin, violence **2** |

**Word Partnership** Usar *harm* con:

| | |
|---|---|
| N. | harm **the environment** **1** |
| ADJ. | **bodily** harm **2** |
| V. | **cause** harm, **not mean any** harm **2** |

**harm|ful** /hɑrmfəl/ ADJ Something that is **harmful** has a bad effect on someone or something. *dañino* ❑ *...the harmful effects of the sun. ...los efectos dañinos del sol.*

**harm|less** /hɑrmlɪs/ **1** ADJ Something that is **harmless** does not have any bad effects. *inofensivo* ❑ *These bugs don't bite and are harmless. Estos insectos no pican y son inofensivos.* **2** ADJ If you describe someone or something as **harmless,** you mean that they are unlikely to annoy other people or cause trouble. *inofensivo* ❑ *He seemed harmless. Parecía inofensivo.*

**har|mon|ic pro|gres|sion** (**harmonic progressions**) N-COUNT A **harmonic progression** is a series of chords or harmonies within a piece of music. *progresión armónica* [TECHNICAL]

**har|mo|ny** /hɑrməni/ (**harmonies**) **1** N-UNCOUNT If people are living **in harmony with** each other, they are living together peacefully rather than fighting or arguing. *en armonía* ❑ *People should live in harmony with each other and with nature. La gente debería vivir en armonía con los demás y con la naturaleza.* **2** N-VAR **Harmony** is the pleasant combination of different notes of music played at the same time. *armonía* ❑ *...singing in harmony. ...cantando en armonía.* **3** N-UNCOUNT The **harmony** of something is the way in which its parts are combined into a pleasant arrangement. *armonía* ❑ *...the beauty and harmony of the design. ...la belleza y armonía del diseño.*

**harp** /hɑrp/ (**harps, harping, harped**) N-VAR A **harp** is a large musical instrument consisting of a row of strings stretched from the top to the bottom of a frame. You play the harp by plucking the strings with your fingers. *arpa* → see **string**

▸ **harp on** PHR-VERB If someone **harps on** a subject, or **harps on about** it, they keep on talking about it in a way that other people find annoying. *insistir en, machacar acerca de* ❑ *Jones harps on this subject more than on any other. Jones insiste en ese tema más que en cualquier otro.*

**har|row|ing** /hæroʊɪŋ/ ADJ A **harrowing** experience is extremely upsetting or disturbing. *espeluznante* ❑ *Soldiers who fought together during World War II talked openly about their harrowing experiences. Los soldados que pelearon juntos durante la Segunda Guerra Mundial hablaban abiertamente acerca de sus espeluznantes experiencias.*

**harsh** /hɑrʃ/ (**harsher, harshest**) **1** ADJ **Harsh** climates or conditions are very difficult for people, animals, and plants to live in. *áspero* ❑ *...the harsh desert climate. ...el áspero clima del desierto.* ● **harsh|ness** N-UNCOUNT *aspereza, dureza* ❑ *...the harshness of their living conditions. ...la dureza de sus condiciones de vida.* **2** ADJ **Harsh** actions or speech are unkind and show no understanding or sympathy. *duro* ❑ *He said many harsh things about his opponents. Dijo muchas cosas duras acerca de sus adversarios.* ● **harsh|ly** ADV *duramente* ❑ *He was harshly treated in prison. Fue tratado muy duramente en la cárcel.* ● **harsh|ness** N-UNCOUNT *dureza* ❑ *...the harshness of her words. ...la dureza de sus palabras.* **3** ADJ Something that is **harsh** is so hard, bright, or rough that it seems unpleasant or harmful. *áspero* ❑ *The harsh light made the room look very unattractive. El cuarto no lucía por lo artificial de la luz.*

**har|vest** /hɑrvɪst/ (**harvests, harvesting, harvested**) **1** N-SING **The harvest** is the gathering of a crop. *cosecha* ❑ *The bean harvest starts in January.*

*La cosecha del frijol comienza en enero.* **2** N-COUNT A **harvest** is the crop that is gathered in. *cosecha* ❑ *...the potato harvest. ...la cosecha de la papa.* **3** V-T When you **harvest** a crop, you gather it in. *cosechar* ❑ *Farmers here still plant and harvest their crops by hand. Los campesinos aquí todavía plantan y cosechan sus cultivos a mano.*
→ see **farm, grain**

**has**

> The auxiliary verb is pronounced /həz, STRONG hæz/. The main verb is usually pronounced /hæz/.

**Has** is the third person singular of the present tense of **have**. *tercera persona singular del presente de* ***have***

**hasn't** /hæzᵊnt/ **Hasn't** is the usual spoken form of "has not." *forma hablada usual de la forma negativa de la tercera persona singular de* ***have***

**has|ty** /heɪsti/ (**hastier, hastiest**) **1** ADJ A **hasty** movement, action, or statement is sudden, and often done in reaction to something that has just happened. *apresurado* ❑ *Donald knocked over a chair in his hasty departure. Donald tiró una silla por su apresurada salida.* ● **hasti|ly** /heɪstɪli/ ADV *apresuradamente* ❑ *A meeting was hastily arranged to discuss the problem. Apresuradamente, se arregló una reunión para discutir el problema.* **2** ADJ If you describe a person or their behavior as **hasty,** you are critical of them because they act too quickly, without thinking carefully. *apresurado* ❑ *Don't make a hasty decision. No tomes una decisión apresurada.* ● **hasti|ly** ADV *apresuradamente* ❑ *I decided that I wouldn't do anything hastily. Decidí que no haría nada apresuradamente.*

**hat** /hæt/ (**hats**) N-COUNT A **hat** is a head covering. *sombrero* ❑ *...a woman in a red hat. ...una mujer con un sombrero rojo.*
→ see Picture Dictionary: **hats**

**hatch** /hætʃ/ (**hatches, hatching, hatched**) **1** V-T/V-I When a baby bird, insect, or other animal **hatches,** or when it **is hatched,** it comes out of its egg by breaking the shell. You can also say that an egg **hatches.** *salir del cascarón (las crías), romperse (el cascarón)* ❑ *The young birds died soon after they were hatched. Los pajaritos murieron poco después de salir del cascarón.* ❑ *The eggs hatch after a week. Los huevos se rompen a la semana.* **2** V-T If you **hatch** a plot or a scheme, you think of it and work it out. *tramar* ❑ *He hatched a plot to embarrass the president. Tramó un complot para avergonzar al presidente.* **3** N-COUNT A **hatch** is an opening in the deck of a ship, through which people or cargo can go. *escotilla* ❑ *He moved through the hatch to the passageway. Pasó a través de la escotilla hacia el pasillo.*

**hate** /heɪt/ (**hates, hating, hated**) **1** V-T If you **hate** someone or something, you have an extremely strong feeling of dislike for them. *odiar* ❑ *Most people hate him. La mayoría de la gente lo odia.* ❑ *He hates to lose. Odia perder.* ● **Hate** is also a noun. *odio* ❑ *I was 17 and full of hate. Tenía 17 años y estaba llena de odio.* **2** V-T You can use **hate** in expressions such as **"I hate to say it"** or **"I hate to tell you"** when you want to express regret about what you are about to say, because you think it is unpleasant or should not be the case. *odiar* ❑ *I hate to say it but I think he's too old for the job. Odio decírtelo pero creo que es demasiado viejo para ese trabajo.*
→ see **emotion**

**ha|tred** /heɪtrɪd/ N-UNCOUNT **Hatred** is an extremely strong feeling of dislike for someone



## Picture Dictionary

### hats

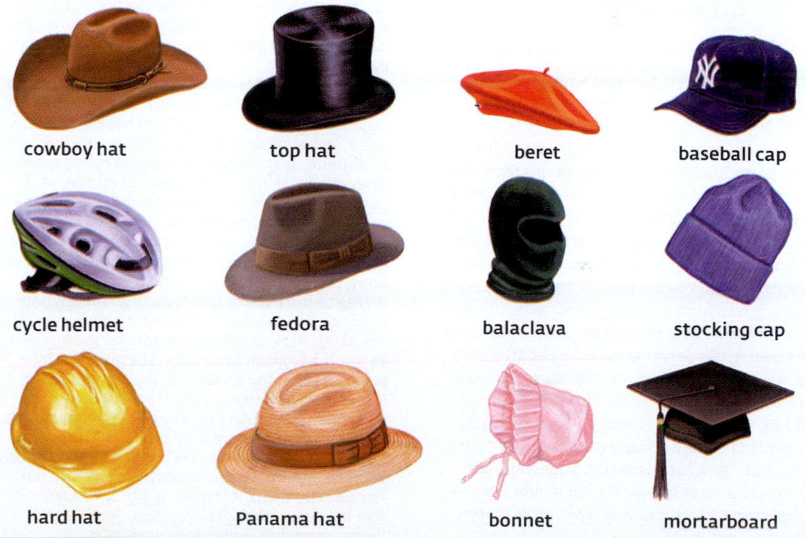

or something. *odio* ❑ *...her hatred of her daughter's killer.* *...su odio por el asesino de su hija.*

**haul** /hɔl/ (**hauls, hauling, hauled**) 1 V-T If you **haul** something which is heavy or difficult to move, you move it using a lot of effort. *arrastrar* ❑ *They used a crane to haul the car out of the water.* *Usaron una grúa para sacar el carro del agua.* 2 PHRASE If you say that a task or a journey is a **long haul,** you mean that it takes a long time and a lot of effort. *viaje largo y cansado* ❑ *It's been a long haul since leaving Miami at 7 a.m.* *Fue una tirada larga, salimos de Miami a las 7 a.m.*

**haunt** /hɔnt/ (**haunts, haunting, haunted**) 1 V-T If something unpleasant **haunts** you, you keep thinking or worrying about it over a long period of time. *perseguir* ❑ *The memory of the accident haunted him for a long time.* *El recuerdo del accidente lo persiguió durante mucho tiempo.* 2 N-COUNT A place that is the **haunt** of a particular person is one which they often visit because they enjoy going there. *lugar favorito* ❑ *The islands are a favorite summer haunt for tourists.* *Las islas son el lugar favorito de los turistas en verano.* 3 V-T A ghost or spirit that **haunts** a place or a person regularly appears in the place, or is seen by the person and frightens them. *rondar* ❑ *His ghost is believed to haunt the room.* *Se cree que su fantasma ronda la habitación.*

H

**have**

❶ AUXILIARY VERB USES
❷ USED WITH NOUNS DESCRIBING ACTIONS
❸ OTHER VERB USES AND PHRASES
❹ MODAL PHRASES

❶ **have** /həv, STRONG hæv/ (**has, having, had**)

In spoken English, forms of **have** are often shortened, for example **I have** is shortened to **I've** and **has not** is shortened to **hasn't**.

1 AUX You use the forms **have** and **has** with a past participle to form the present perfect tense of verbs. *he, has, hemos, ha, han* ❑ *Alex hasn't left yet.* *Alex no se ha ido todavía.* ❑ *What have you found?* *¿Qué has encontrado?* ❑ *Frankie hasn't been feeling well for a long time.* *Frankie no se ha sentido bien desde hace mucho tiempo.* 2 AUX You use the form **had** with a past participle to form the past perfect tense of verbs. *había, habías, habíamos, habían* ❑ *You could tell she had been crying.* *Se notaba que había estado llorando.* 3 AUX **Have** is used in question tags. *¿No es así?* ❑ *You haven't seen her, have you?* *No la has visto, ¿o sí?* 4 AUX You use **have** when you are confirming or contradicting a statement containing "have," "has," or "had," or answering a question. *así es* ❑ *"You've never seen the Marilyn Monroe film?"—"No I haven't."* *—¿Nunca viste la película de Marilyn Monroe?—No, nunca.*

**Usage** **have**

In speech, when *have* follows verbs such as *could, should, would, might,* and *must*, contracting *have* makes it sound like *of*: *could've* sounds like "could of"; *might've* sounds like "might of"; and so on. Be sure to say (and write) *have* when you don't use contractions: *could have; might have;* and so on.

❷ **have** /hæv/ (**has, having, had**)

**Have** is used in combination with a wide range of nouns, where the meaning of the combination is mostly given by the noun.

1 V-T You can use **have** followed by a noun to talk about an action or event, when it would be possible to use the same word as a verb. For example, you can say "**I had a look at the photos**" instead of "I looked at the photos." *tener, tomar* ❑ *I went out and had a walk around.* *Salí y di un paseo por ahí.* 2 V-T In normal spoken or written English, people use **have** with a wide range of nouns to talk about actions and events, often instead of a more specific verb. For example people are more likely to say "**we had ice cream**" or "**he's had a shock**" than "we ate ice cream," or "he's suffered a shock." *tener, tomar* ❑ *Come and have a meal with us tonight.* *Ven a cenar con nosotros hoy en la noche.* ❑ *We are having a meeting to decide what to do.* *Vamos a reunirnos para decidir qué hacer.*

❸ **have** /hæv/ (**has, having, had**) 1 V-T You use **have** to say that someone or something owns a particular thing, or when you are mentioning one of their qualities or characteristics. *tener* ❑ *Billy has a new bicycle.* *Billy tiene una nueva bicicleta.* ❑ *She had a good job.* *Tenía un buen trabajo.* ❑ *You have beautiful eyes.* *Qué lindos ojos tienes.* ❑ *Do you have any brothers and sisters?* *¿Tienes hermanos?* 2 V-T If you **have** something **to** do, you are responsible for doing it or must do it. *tener qué hacer* ❑ *He had plenty of work to do.* *Tenía mucho trabajo.* 3 V-T If you **have** something such as a part of your body in a particular position or state, it is in that position or state. *tener* ❑ *Mary had her eyes closed.* *Mary tenía los ojos cerrados.* ❑ *They had the windows open.* *Tenían las ventanas abiertas.* 4 V-T If you **have** something done, someone does it for you or you arrange for it to be done. *mandar hacer* ❑ *I had your room cleaned.* *Hice que limpiaran tu cuarto.* ❑ *He had his hair cut.* *Le cortaron el pelo.* 5 V-T If someone **has** something unpleasant happen to them, it happens to them. *suceder* ❑ *We had our money stolen.* *Nos robaron el dinero.* 6 V-T If someone **has** you **by** a part of your body, they are holding you there and they are trying to hurt you or force you to go somewhere. *tener(se)* ❑ *She had the child by the arm and was pulling him along.* *Tenía al niño por el brazo y lo estaba jalando.* 7 V-T If a woman **has** a baby, she gives birth to it. If she **is having** a baby, she is pregnant. *dar a luz, estar embarazada* ❑ *My wife has just had a baby.* *Mi esposa acaba de dar a luz a un niño.* 8 PHRASE You can use **has it** in expressions such as "**rumor has it that**" or "**as legend has it**" when you are quoting something that you have heard, but you do not necessarily think it is true. *se dice* ❑ *Rumor has it that tickets were being sold for $300.* *Se dice que los boletos se estaban vendiendo en 300 dólares.*

❹ **have** /hæv, hæf/ (**has, having, had**) PHRASE You use **have to** when you are saying that something is necessary or required, or must happen. If you do not **have to** do something, it is not necessary or required. tener que ❑ *He had to go to work.* *Tenía que ir a trabajar.* ❑ *You have to be careful what you say on TV.* *Tienes que ser cuidadoso con lo que dices en TV.*

**ha|ven** /heɪvᵊn/ (**havens**) 1 N-COUNT A **haven** is a place where people or animals feel safe, secure, and happy. refugio ❑ *...Lake Baringo, a haven for birds.* *...Lago Baringo, un refugio para las aves.* 2 → see also **safe haven**

**haven't** /hævᵊnt/ **Haven't** is the usual spoken form of "have not." forma hablada usual de la forma negativa de **have**

**hawk** /hɔk/ (**hawks**) N-COUNT A **hawk** is a large bird that catches and eats small birds and animals. halcón

hawk

**hay** /heɪ/ N-UNCOUNT **Hay** is grass which has been cut and dried so that it can be used to feed animals. heno

**haz|ard** /hæzərd/ (**hazards, hazarding, hazarded**) 1 N-COUNT A **hazard** is something which could be dangerous to you, your health or safety, or your plans or reputation. peligro, riesgo ❑ *A report says that chewing gum may be a health hazard.* *Se dice en un informe que mascar chicle puede representar un riesgo para la salud.* 2 V-T If you **hazard a guess**, you make a suggestion about something which is only a guess and which you know might be wrong. aventurar ❑ *We can only hazard a guess at the reasons for this.* *Sólo podemos aventurar una opinión acerca de las razones de ello.*

**haz|ing** /heɪzɪŋ/ (**hazings**) N-VAR **Hazing** is a ritual practiced in some universities and other institutions, in which a new member of a club or organization is forced to do something embarrassing or dangerous. novatada ❑ *She was a victim of hazing but escaped serious injury.* *Fue víctima de una novatada, pero no sufrió lesiones graves.* ❑ *...a vicious hazing ritual.* *...una horrenda costumbre de hacer novatadas.*

**hazy** /heɪzi/ (**hazier, haziest**) 1 ADJ **Hazy** weather makes things difficult to see, because of light mist, hot air, or dust. brumoso ❑ *Tomorrow's weather will be hazy sunshine.* *Mañana va a estar brumoso, pero soleado.* 2 ADJ If you are **hazy about** ideas or details, or if they are **hazy**, you are uncertain or confused about them. vago, incierto ❑ *I have only a hazy memory of what he was like.* *No tengo más que un recuerdo vago de cómo era él.*

**HDTV** /eɪtʃdi ti vi/ N-UNCOUNT **HDTV** is a television system that provides a clearer image than conventional television systems. **HDTV** is an abbreviation for "high-definition television." HDTV ❑ *The quality of digital TV is better, especially HDTV.* *La calidad de la TV digital es mejor, especialmente la HDTV.*
→ see **television**

**he** /hi, i, STRONG hi/

> **He** is a third person singular pronoun. **He** is used as the subject of a verb.

PRON You use **he** to refer to a man, boy, or male animal. él ❑ *He couldn't remember my name.* *Él no podía recordar mi nombre.*

> **head**
> ❶ NOUN USES
> ❷ VERB USES
> ❸ PHRASES

❶ **head** /hɛd/ (**heads**) 1 N-COUNT Your **head** is the top part of your body, which has your eyes, mouth, and brain in it. cabeza ❑ *She turned her head away from him.* *Volteó la cabeza para no verlo.* 2 N-COUNT You can use **head** to refer to your mind and your mental abilities. cabeza, mente ❑ *He could do difficult math in his head.* *Podía hacer cálculos difíciles en la mente.* 3 N-COUNT The **head** of a company or organization is the person in charge of it and in charge of the people in it. jefe o jefa, cabeza ❑ *Heads of government from more than 100 countries will meet in Geneva tomorrow.* *Los jefes de gobierno de más de 100 países se reunirán en Ginebra mañana.* 4 N-COUNT The **head** of something is the top, start, or most important end of it. cabecera, principio, cabeza ❑ *She sat at the head of the table.* *Se sentó a la cabecera de la mesa.* ❑ *He went to the head of the line.* *Se fue al principio de la fila.* 5 ADV If you flip a coin and it comes down **heads**, you can see the side of the coin which has a picture of a head on it. cara, sol ❑ *Let's flip a coin for it. If it's heads, then we'll talk.* *Echemos un volado, si cae sol, entonces hablamos.*
→ see **body**

❷ **head** /hɛd/ (**heads, heading, headed**) 1 V-T If someone or something **heads** a line or procession, they are at the front of it. encabezar, ir al frente, dirigir ❑ *I headed the line walking down the sidewalk.* *Yo iba al frente de quienes caminaban por la banqueta.* 2 V-T If something **heads** a list or group, it is at the top of it. encabezar, estar a la cabeza ❑ *She heads the list of the most popular actors in the U.S.* *Encabeza la lista de actores más populares de los Estados Unidos.* 3 V-T If you **head** a department, company, or organization, you are the person in charge of it. dirigir, encabezar, estar a la cabeza ❑ *Michael Williams heads the department's Office of Civil Rights.* *Michael Williams encabeza la Oficina de Derechos Civiles del departamento.* 4 V-T If you **are heading** or **are headed** for a particular place, you are going toward that place. dirigirse, ir(se) ❑ *He headed for the bus stop.* *Se fue a la parada del camión.* ❑ *Many people are heading back to Washington tomorrow.* *Mucha gente regresa a Washington mañana.* 5 V-T/V-I If something or someone **is heading for** or **is headed for** a particular result, it means that the result is very likely. ir hacia ❑ *The talks seem to be heading for failure.* *Parece que las pláticas van camino al fracaso.* 6 V-T If you **head** a ball in soccer, you hit it with your head in order to make it go in a particular direction. cabecear ❑ *He headed the ball into the goal.* *Cabeceó y metió el gol.*

❸ **head** /hɛd/ (**heads**) 1 EXCLAM If someone shouts "**Heads up!**" to you, they are warning you to move out of the way, usually because someth is falling on you from above, or because something is coming towards you very quickly. *¡Cuidado!* ❑ *Heads up! Watch out for the baseball! ¡Aguas con la pelota!* **2** PHRASE The cost or amount **a head** or **per head** is the cost or amount for one person. *cada uno, por cabeza, por persona* ❑ *This simple meal costs less than $3 a head. Esta comida sencilla cuesta menos de 3 dólares por cabeza.* **3** PHRASE If a problem or disagreement **comes to a head** or **is brought to a head,** it becomes so bad that something must be done about it. *hacer crisis* ❑ *Things came to a head on Saturday when they had a fight. Las cosas llegaron al colmo el sábado, cuando se pelearon.* **4** PHRASE If you **get** a fact or idea **into** your **head,** you suddenly realize or think that it is true and you usually do not change your opinion about it. *meterse algo en la cabeza* ❑ *Once they get an idea into their heads, they never give up. Una vez que se les mete algo en la cabeza, no se dan por vencidos nunca.* **5** PHRASE If something such as praise or success **goes to** someone's **head,** they start to believe that they are better than they really are. *subírsele a la cabeza, subírsele* ❑ *Ford is not the type of man to let success go to his head. Ford no es el tipo de hombre al que el éxito se le sube a la cabeza.* **6** PHRASE If you **keep** your **head,** you remain calm in a difficult situation. If you **lose** your **head,** you panic or do not remain calm in a difficult situation. *mantener la calma, perder la calma, perder la cabeza* ❑ *She was able to keep her head and not panic. Pudo mantener la calma y no entró en pánico* **7** PHRASE If something such as an idea, joke, or comment goes **over** someone's **head,** it is too difficult for them to understand. *no entender* ❑ *A lot of the ideas at the meeting went over my head. Muchas de las ideas expresadas en la reunión rebasaron mi capacidad de entendimiento.*

**head|ache** /hɛdeɪk/ (**headaches**) **1** N-COUNT If you have a **headache,** you have a pain in your head. *dolor de cabeza, cefalea* ❑ *I have a terrible headache. Me duele muchísimo la cabeza.* **2** N-COUNT If you say that something is a **headache,** you mean that it causes you difficulty or worry. *problema, preocupación, quebradero de cabeza, dolor de cabeza* ❑ *The biggest headache for mothers who want to return to work is childcare. El principal dolor de cabeza de las madres que quieren volver a trabajar es la atención de los hijos.*

| Word Link | *light ≈ shining : daylight, headlight, moonlight* |
|---|---|

**head|light** /hɛdlaɪt/ (**headlights**) N-COUNT A vehicle's **headlights** are the large powerful lights at the front. *faro* ❑ *He turned on the car's headlights in the tunnel. Para atravesar el túnel prendió los faros.*

**head|line** /hɛdlaɪn/ (**headlines**) **1** N-COUNT A **headline** is the title of a newspaper story, printed in large letters at the top of it. *encabezado, encabezamiento* ❑ *The headline said: "New government plans." El encabezado decía: "Nuevos planes de gobierno".* **2** N-PLURAL **The headlines** are the main points of the news which are read on radio or television. *resumen de noticias* ❑ *Claudia Polley read the news headlines. Claudia Polley leyó el resumen informativo.* **3** PHRASE Someone or something that **hits the headlines** or **grabs the headlines** gets a lot of publicity from the media. *ser noticia, aparecer en las noticias* ❑ *Johnson first hit the world headlines last year. El año pasado, Johnson ocupó por primera vez los titulares en todo el mundo.*

**head|master** /hɛdmæstər/ (**headmasters**) N-COUNT A **headmaster** is the principal of a private school. *director (de escuela), rector (de escuela)*

**head of state** (**heads of state**) N-COUNT A **head of state** is the leader of a country, for example a president, king, or queen. *jefe de estado o jefa de estado* ❑ *...the Algerian head of state. ...el jefe de estado argelino.*

**head-on** **1** ADV If two vehicles hit each other **head-on,** they hit each other with their fronts pointing toward each other. *de frente* ❑ *The car crashed head-on into a truck. El coche se dio de frente contra un camión.* ● **Head-on** is also an adjective. *de frente* ❑ *There was a serious head-on crash. Hubo un choque durísimo, de frente.* **2** ADJ A **head-on** conflict or approach is direct, without any attempt to compromise or avoid the issue. *frontal* ❑ *...a head-on clash between the president and the government. ...un enfrentamiento frontal entre el presidente y el gobierno.* ● **Head-on** is also an adverb. *frontalmente* ❑ *I dealt with the issue head-on. Me enfrenté sin ambages con el problema.*

**head|phones** /hɛdfoʊnz/ N-PLURAL **Headphones** are small speakers which you wear over your ears in order to listen to music or other sounds without other people hearing it. *audífonos, auriculares* ❑ *I listened to the program on headphones. Oí el programa con los audífonos.*

headphones

**head|quarters** /hɛdkwɔrtərz/ N-SING The **headquarters** of an organization are its main offices. *oficina central, cuartel general, jefatura de policía* ❑ *...Chicago's police headquarters. ...la jefatura de policía de Chicago.*

**heads-up** N-SING If you give someone a **heads-up** about something that is going to happen, you tell them about it before it happens. *aviso* ❑ *They changed the rules without giving anyone a heads-up. Cambiaron las reglas sin advertirle a nadie.*

**head|waters** /hɛdwɔtərz/ also **head-waters** or **head waters** N-PLURAL The **headwaters** of a river are smaller streams which flow into the river near its source. *naciente, cabecera* ❑ *...the headwaters of the Amazon River. ...el naciente del río Amazonas.*

**heal** /hil/ (**heals, healing, healed**) **1** V-I When a broken bone or other injury **heals,** it becomes healthy and normal again. *curar, sanar, cicatrizar, soldar* ❑ *It took six months for her injuries to heal. Sus lesiones tardaron seis meses en sanar.* **2** V-T/V-I If you **heal** something such as a disagreement, or if it **heals,** the situation is put right so that people are friendly or happy again. *remediar(se), componer(se), corregir* ❑ *When you remember the other person is your friend, you can begin to heal the disagreement. Cuando recuerdas que la otra persona es tu amiga, puedes empezar a reconcialiarte.*

**health** /hɛlθ/ **1** N-UNCOUNT A person's **health** is the condition of their body. *salud* ❑ *Too much fatty food is bad for your health. Es malo para la salud consumir demasiados alimentos grasosos.*

**2** N-UNCOUNT **Health** is a state in which a person is fit and well. salud ❑ *In the hospital they nursed me back to health.* *En el hospital me cuidaron hasta que recuperé la salud.* **3** N-UNCOUNT The **health** of something such as an organization or a system is its success and the fact that it is working well. bienestar, prosperidad ❑ *...the health of the banking industry.* *...la prosperidad del sector bancario.*

**health care** also **healthcare** N-UNCOUNT **Health care** is the various services for the prevention or treatment of illness and injuries. atención de la salud, política sanitaria ❑ *Nobody wants to pay more for health care.* *Nadie quiere pagar más por la atención de la salud.* ❑ *...the nation's health care system.* *...las políticas sanitarias del país.*

**health cen|ter** (**health centers**) N-COUNT A **health center** is a building in which a group of doctors have offices where their patients can visit them. centro de salud, centro médico

**health main|te|nance or|gani|za|tion** (**health maintenance organizations**) N-COUNT A **health maintenance organization** is an organization to which you pay a fee and that allows you to use only doctors and hospitals which belong to the organization. The abbreviation **HMO** is often used. servicios médicos exclusivos para un grupo específico ❑ *...a health maintenance organization for retired workers in northern California.* *...servicios médicos para trabajadores retirados del norte de California.*

**healthy** /hɛlθi/ (**healthier, healthiest**) **1** ADJ Someone who is **healthy** is well and is not suffering from any illness. saludable, sano ❑ *Most of us need to exercise more to be healthy.* *La mayoría necesita hacer más ejercicio para estar bien de salud.* ● **healthi|ly** /hɛlθɪli/ ADV saludablemente ❑ *I want to live healthily for as long as possible.* *Quiero conservar la salud el mayor tiempo posible.* **2** ADJ Something that is **healthy** is good for your health. saludable, sano ❑ *...a healthy diet.* *...una dieta sana.* **3** ADJ A **healthy** organization or system is successful. robusto, floreciente ❑ *...an economically healthy country.* *...un país próspero económicamente.* **4** ADJ A **healthy** amount of something is a large amount that shows success. abundante ❑ *...healthy profits.* *...utilidades sustanciales.*

**Word Partnership** Usar *healthy* con:

N. healthy **baby** **1**
healthy **diet/food**, healthy **lifestyle** **2**

**heap** /hip/ (**heaps, heaping, heaped**) **1** N-COUNT A **heap of** things is an untidy pile of them. montón, pila ❑ *...a heap of clothes.* *...un montón de ropa.* **2** V-T If you **heap** things in a pile, you arrange them in a large pile. amontonar, apilar, acumular ❑ *His mother heaped more carrots onto Michael's plate.* *Su madre amontonó más zanahorias en el plato de Michael.* ● **Heap up** means the same as **heap**. amontonar, apilar, acumular ❑ *He was heaping up wood for the fire.* *Estaba juntando leña para el fuego.* **3** V-T If you **heap** praise or criticism **on** someone or something, you give them a lot of praise or criticism. colmar de, prodigar(se) ❑ *They heaped praise on the president for his efforts.* *Se prodigaron en elogios por los esfuerzos del presidente.* **4** QUANT **Heaps of** something or a **heap of** something is a large quantity of it. montones, muchos [INFORMAL] ❑ *You have heaps of time.* *Tienes muchísimo tiempo.*

**heap|ing** /hipɪŋ/ ADJ A **heaping** spoonful has the contents of the spoon piled up above the edge. colmado ❑ *Add one heaping tablespoon of salt.* *Agregue una cucharada copeteada de sal.*

**hear** /hɪər/ (**hears, hearing, heard** /hɜrd/) **1** V-T/V-I When you **hear** a sound, you become aware of it through your ears. oír, escuchar ❑ *She heard no further sounds.* *Ya no oyó nada.* ❑ *I heard him say, "Thanks."* *Lo oí decir "gracias".* ❑ *He doesn't hear very well.* *No oye muy bien.* **2** V-T When a judge or a court of law **hears** a case, or evidence in a case, they listen to it officially in order to make a decision about it. ver, oír [FORMAL] ❑ *The court will hear the case next week.* *El tribunal oirá del caso la próxima semana.* **3** V-I If you **hear from** someone, you receive a letter or telephone call from them. saber de, oír de ❑ *It's always great to hear from you.* *Siempre es agradable saber de ti.* **4** V-T/V-I If you **hear** some news or information about something, you find out about it by someone telling you, or from the radio or television. oír ❑ *My mother heard of the school from Karen.* *Mi madre se enteró de la escuela por Karen.* ❑ *He heard that the house was sold.* *Supo que la casa se había vendido.* **5** V-I If you **have heard of** something or someone, you know about them, but not in great detail. llegar a saber ❑ *I've heard of him.* *He oído hablar de él.* **6** PHRASE If you say that you **won't hear of** someone doing something, you mean that you refuse to let them do it. no querer saber nada de algo ❑ *I wanted to be an actor but Dad wouldn't hear of it.* *Yo quería ser actor, pero papá no quería ni oír hablar de ello.*

**Thesaurus** *hear* Ver también:

V. detect, listen, pick up **4**

**hear|ing** /hɪərɪŋ/ (**hearings**) **1** N-UNCOUNT **Hearing** is the sense which makes it possible for you to be aware of sounds. oído, audición ❑ *His hearing was excellent.* *Su oído era excelente.* **2** N-COUNT A **hearing** is an official meeting which is held in order to collect facts about an incident or problem. audiencia, vista, sesión, juicio ❑ *The hearing will last about two weeks.* *El proceso durará unas dos semanas.* **3** PHRASE If someone gives you **a fair hearing** or **a hearing,** they listen to you when you give your opinion about something. escuchar con imparcialidad ❑ *Weber gave a fair hearing to anyone who had a different opinion.* *Weber permitía que quien tuviera una opinión diferente se expresara.*
→ see **disability**

**Word Partnership** Usar *hearing* con:

N. hearing **impairment/loss** **1**
**court** hearing **2**
V. **hold a** hearing, **testify at/before a** hearing **2**

**heart**
❶ NOUN USES
❷ PHRASES

❶ **heart** /hɑrt/ (**hearts**) **1** N-COUNT Your **heart** is the organ in your chest that pumps the blood

h

around your body. People also use **heart** to refer to the area of their chest that is closest to their heart. *corazón, miocardio* ❑ *...the beating of his heart. ...los latidos de su corazón.* **2** N-COUNT You can refer to your **heart** when you are talking about your deep feelings and beliefs. *corazón, espíritu* [LITERARY] ❑ *Alik's words filled her heart with joy. Las palabras de Alik llenaron su alma de gozo.* **3** N-VAR You use **heart** when you are talking about someone's character and attitude toward other people, especially when they are kind and generous. *generosidad* ❑ *She's got a good heart. Tiene buen corazón.* **4** N-SING **The heart of** something is the most central and important part of it. *centro, núcleo* ❑ *The heart of the problem is money. El meollo del problema es el dinero.* **5** N-SING **The heart of** a place is its center. *corazón, centro* ❑ *...a busy hotel in the heart of the city. ...un hotel muy concurrido en el centro de la ciudad.* **6** N-COUNT A **heart** is a shape that is used as a symbol of love:♥. *corazón* ❑ *...heart-shaped chocolates. ...chocolates en forma de corazón* **7** N-UNCOUNT **Hearts** is one of the four suits in a deck of playing cards. Each card in the suit is marked with one or more symbols in the shape of a heart. *corazón* ● A **heart** is a playing card of this suit. *corazón* ❑ *West had to decide whether to play a heart. West tuvo que decidir si tiraba un corazón.*

→ see **cardiovascular system, donor**

**❷ heart** /hɑ̲rt/ (**hearts**) **1** PHRASE If you say that someone is a particular kind of person **at heart,** you mean that that is what they are really like, even though they may seem very different. *en el fondo* ❑ *He was a gentle boy at heart. En el fondo era un chico amable.* **2** PHRASE If someone or something **breaks** your **heart,** they make you very unhappy. *romper el corazón, arrancar el alma* [LITERARY] ❑ *I fell in love on vacation but the girl broke my heart. Me enamoré en las vacaciones, pero la niña me rompió el corazón.* **3** PHRASE If you know something such as a poem **by heart,** you have learned it so well that you can remember it without having to read it. *de memoria* ❑ *Mike knew this song by heart. Mike se sabía al dedillo la canción.* **4** PHRASE If someone has a **change of heart,** their attitude toward something changes. *cambiar de opinión* ❑ *She was surprised by David's change of heart. Se sorprendió con el cambio de actitud de David.* **5** PHRASE If something such as a subject or project is **close to** your **heart** or **near to** your **heart,** it is very important to you and you are very interested in it and concerned about it. *muy importante* ❑ *This is a subject very close to my heart. Ese tema me interesa muchísimo.* **6** PHRASE If you say something **from the heart** or **from the bottom of** your **heart,** you sincerely mean what you say. *con toda sinceridad* ❑ *He spoke from the heart. Lo dijo desde el fondo del corazón.* **7** PHRASE If you **take heart from** something, you are encouraged and made to feel optimistic by it. *tomar aliento* ❑ *The company should take heart from its success. La compañía debe animarse con su éxito.* **8** PHRASE If you **take** something **to heart,** you are deeply affected and upset by it. *tomar a pecho* ❑ *If someone says something unpleasant, I take it to heart. Si alguien dice algo desagradable, me llega.* **9** PHRASE If you feel or believe something **with all** your **heart,** you feel or believe it very strongly. *profundamente* ❑ *I loved him with all my heart. Yo lo quería con todo el corazón.*

**heart at|tack** (**heart attacks**) N-COUNT If someone has a **heart attack,** their heart begins to beat very irregularly or stops completely. *ataque al corazón, ataque cardíaco* ❑ *He died of a heart attack. Murió de un infarto.*

**heart-stopping** also **heartstopping** **1** ADJ A **heart-stopping** moment is one that makes you anxious or frightened because it seems that something bad is likely to happen. *impresionante, que quita el aliento* ❑ *There was a heart-stopping moment when she fell backward. Fue impresionante cuando cayó de espaldas.* **2** ADJ A **heart-stopping** event or sight is very impressive or exciting. *impresionante, emocionante* ❑ *The restaurant has a heart-stopping sea view. La vista del mar desde el restaurante te deja sin habla.*

**heart|worm** /hɑ̲rtwɜrm/ (**heartworms**) N-VAR **Heartworms** are parasitic worms that are spread through mosquito bites and affect cats, dogs, foxes and some other animals. You can also use **heartworm** to mean the disease caused by heartworms. *gusano del corazón*

**hearty** /hɑ̲rti/ (**heartier, heartiest**) **1** ADJ **Hearty** people or actions are loud, cheerful, and energetic. *sincero, cordial, enérgico* ❑ *Wade was a hearty, athletic sort of guy. Wade era un tipo cordial, de tipo atlético.* ● **hearti|ly** ADV *con entusiasmo, mucho* ❑ *He laughed heartily. Se rió de corazón.* **2** ADJ **Hearty** feelings or opinions are strongly felt or strongly held. *sincero, espontáneo* ❑ *Arnold was in hearty agreement with her. Arnold no tuvo empacho en estar de acuerdo con ella.* ● **hearti|ly** ADV *completamente* ❑ *I'm heartily sick of him. ¡Me tiene hasta el copete!* **3** ADJ A **hearty** meal is large and very satisfying. *abundante* ❑ *The men ate a hearty breakfast. Los hombres ingirieron un sustancioso desayuno.* ● **hearti|ly** ADV *abundantemente* ❑ *He ate heartily but drank only water. Comió en abundancia, pero bebió sólo agua.*

**heat** /hi̲t/ (**heats, heating, heated**) **1** V-T When you **heat** something, you raise its temperature. *calentar* ❑ *Heat the tomatoes and oil in a pan. Calienta los jitomates y el aceite en una sartén.* **2** N-UNCOUNT **Heat** is warmth or the quality of being hot. *calor* ❑ *...the strong heat of the sun. ...el intenso calor del sol.* **3** N-UNCOUNT The **heat** of something that is warm or being heated is its temperature. *calor* ❑ *...the heat of the oven. ...el calor del horno.* **4** N-SING You use **heat** to refer to a source of heat, for example a burner on a stove or the heating system of a house. *calor* ❑ *Remove the pan from the heat. Quita la sartén de la lumbre.* **5** N-SING **The heat of** a particular activity is the point when there is the greatest activity or excitement. *calor* ❑ *People say all kinds of things in the heat of an argument. Al calor de la discusión, se dice todo tipo de cosas.*

→ see **fire, pan, petroleum, weather**

▸ **heat up** **1** PHR-VERB When you **heat** something **up,** especially food which has already been cooked and allowed to go cold, you make it hot. *calentar, recalentar* ❑ *Freda heated up a pie for me. Freda recalentó un pay para mí.* **2** PHR-VERB When something **heats up,** it gradually becomes hotter. *calentarse* ❑ *In the summer her house heats up like an oven. En verano su casa es un horno.*

→ see **cooking**

**heat|ed** /hi̲tɪd/ **1** ADJ A **heated** discussion or quarrel is one where the people involved are angry and excited. acalorado ❑ It was a heated argument. Fue una discusión acalorada. 2 ADJ If someone gets **heated about** something, they get angry and excited about it. acalorado, caldeado ❑ People get heated about issues such as these. Son temas candentes. ● **heat|ed|ly** ADV acaloradamente ❑ The crowd continued to argue heatedly. La multitud seguía discutiendo con vehemencia.

**heat en|gine** (**heat engines**) N-COUNT A **heat engine** is a machine that uses energy from heat to do work. máquina térmica, termomotor, motor térmico [TECHNICAL]

**heat|er** /hitər/ (**heaters**) N-COUNT A **heater** is a piece of equipment or a machine which is used to raise the temperature of something. calentador, calefactor, calentón ❑ There's an electric heater in the bedroom. En la recámara hay un calentador eléctrico.

**heav|en** /hɛvən/ (**heavens**) 1 N-PROPER In some religions, **heaven** is said to be the place where God lives, where good people go when they die. cielo, paraíso ❑ I believe that when I die I will go to heaven. Creo que cuando muera me iré al cielo. 2 EXCLAM You say "**Good heavens!**" or "**Heavens!**" to express surprise or to emphasize that you agree or disagree with someone. ¡Por Dios!, ¡Dios mío! [SPOKEN] ❑ Good Heavens! That explains a lot! ¡Dios mío, eso explica todo! 3 PHRASE You can say "**Heaven knows**" to emphasize that you do not know something, or that you find something very surprising. no saber nadie [SPOKEN] ❑ Heaven knows what he'll do next! ¡Sepa Dios qué hará después! 4 PHRASE You can say "**Heaven knows**" to emphasize something that you feel or believe very strongly. no saber nadie [SPOKEN] ❑ Heaven knows they have enough money. Dios sabe que tienen suficiente dinero. 5 **thank heavens** → see **thank**

**heavy** /hɛvi/ (**heavier, heaviest**) 1 ADJ Something that is **heavy** weighs a lot. pesado ❑ The bag is very heavy. La bolsa es muy pesada. ● **heavi|ness** N-UNCOUNT peso ❑ ...the heaviness of lead. ...el peso del plomo. 2 ADJ You use **heavy** to ask or talk about how much someone or something weighs. pesado ❑ How heavy are you? ¿Cuánto pesas? 3 ADJ **Heavy** means great in amount, degree, or intensity. intenso, fuerte ❑ There was heavy fighting in the area. Las peleas eran intensas en el área. ● **heavi|ly** ADV intensamente, abundantemente ❑ It rained heavily all day. Llovió mucho todo el día. ● **heavi|ness** N-UNCOUNT peso, pesadez ❑ ...the heaviness of his blood loss. ...la intensidad de su pérdida de sangre. 4 ADJ If a person's breathing is **heavy**, it is very loud and deep. profundo ❑ Her breathing was slow and heavy. Su respiración era lenta y profunda. ● **heavi|ly** ADV pesadamente ❑ She was breathing heavily as if asleep. Respiraba profundo, como si estuviera dormida. 5 ADJ A **heavy** movement or action is done with a lot of force or pressure. fuerte, pesado ❑ ...a heavy blow on the back of the head. ...un fuerte golpe en la parte posterior de la cabeza. ● **heavi|ly** ADV pesadamente ❑ I sat down heavily on the ground. Caí como un plomo en el piso. 6 ADJ If you describe a period of time or a schedule as **heavy**, you mean it involves a lot of work. cargado ❑ It's been a heavy day and I'm tired. Ha sido un día pesado y estoy cansada. 7 ADJ **Heavy** work requires a lot of strength or energy. pesado ❑ John does all the heavy work. John hace todo el trabajo pesado. 8 ADJ Air or weather that is **heavy** is unpleasantly still, hot, and damp. pesado ❑ The outside air was heavy and damp. Afuera el aire era pesado y húmedo. 9 ADJ A situation that is **heavy** is serious and difficult to cope with. duro, difícil [INFORMAL] ❑ It was a heavy conversation when I told her I didn't love her any more. Fue muy difícil cuando le dije que ya no la amaba.

| **Thesaurus** | *heavy* | Ver también: |
|---|---|---|
| ADJ. | hefty, overweight; (*ant.*) light 1 | |
| | forceful, powerful 5 | |
| | complex, difficult, tough 9 | |

**heavy cream** N-UNCOUNT **Heavy cream** is very thick cream. doble crema

**heavy-duty** ADJ A **heavy-duty** piece of equipment is very strong and can be used a lot. muy resistente ❑ ...a heavy-duty plastic bag. ...una bolsa de plástico para uso industrial.

**heavy|weight** /hɛviweɪt/ (**heavyweights**) 1 N-COUNT A **heavyweight** is a boxer weighing more than 175 pounds and therefore in the heaviest class. peso pesado 2 N-COUNT If you refer to a person or organization as a **heavyweight**, you mean that they have a lot of influence, experience, and importance in a particular field. peso pesado, pez gordo ❑ He was a political heavyweight. Era un pez gordo de la política.

**he'd** /hid, id, STRONG hid/ 1 **He'd** is the usual spoken form of "he had," especially when "had" is an auxiliary verb. forma hablada de he had ❑ He'd seen her before. Él la había visto antes. 2 **He'd** is a spoken form of "he would." forma hablada de **he would** ❑ He'd like to come with us. Le gustaría ir con nosotros.

**hedge** /hɛdʒ/ (**hedges, hedging, hedged**) 1 N-COUNT A **hedge** is a row of bushes or small trees, usually along the edge of a lawn, garden, field, or road. seto 2 V-I If you **hedge against** something unpleasant or unwanted that might affect you, especially losing money, you do something which will protect you from it. cubrirse, protegerse ❑ You can hedge against illness with insurance. Puedes protegerte de las enfermedades con un seguro. 3 PHRASE If you **hedge** your **bets**, you reduce your chances of losing by supporting more than one person or thing. cubrirse, protegerse ❑ The organization may support one candidate, or hedge its bets by supporting several candidates. La organización puede apoyar a un candidato, o protegerse apoyando a varios.

**hedge|hog cac|tus** (**hedgehog cacti**) N-VAR **Hedgehog cactus** is a name given to several types of cactus with short prickly spines, especially a type that has edible fruit. cactus erizo

**heel** /hil/ (**heels**) 1 N-COUNT Your **heel** is the back part of your foot, just below your ankle. talón ❑ He hurt his heel. Se lastimó el talón. 2 N-COUNT The **heel** of a shoe is the raised part on the bottom at the back. tacón, taco ❑ ...shoes with high heels. ...zapatos de tacón alto. 3 to **drag** your **heels** → see **drag**
→ see **foot**

**height** /haɪt/ (**heights**) 1 N-VAR The **height** of a person or thing is their size or length from the bottom to the top. altura, estatura ❑ Her weight

h

*is normal for her height. Su peso es normal para su estatura.* ❑ *I am five feet six inches in height. Mido 1.70 m.* **2** N-UNCOUNT **Height** is the quality of being tall. *altura* ❑ *He is almost her height. Está casi de su altura.* **3** N-VAR A particular **height** is the distance that something is above the ground. *altitud, altura* ❑ *...the speed and height at which the plane was moving. ...la velocidad y la altitud a las cuales se movía el avión.* **4** N-COUNT A **height** is a high position or place above the ground. *altura* ❑ *I'm not afraid of heights. No le tengo miedo a las alturas.* **5** N-SING When an activity, situation, or organization is **at** its **height,** it is at its most successful, powerful, or intense. *en la cima, en la cumbre* ❑ *...the time when his career was at its height. ...cuando su carrera estaba en la cúspide.* **6** N-SING If you say that something is **the height of** a particular quality, you are emphasizing that it has that quality to the greatest degree possible. *lo más alto* ❑ *The dress was the height of fashion. El vestido era el último grito de la moda.*
→ see **area**

H

**Word Partnership** Usar *height* con:

ADJ. **average** height, **medium** height, **the right** height **1**
N. height **and weight,** height **and width** **1**
**the** height **of *someone's* career** **5**
**the** height **of fashion/popularity/style** **6**
V. **reach a** height **1** **5**

**height|en** /haɪtᵊn/ (**heightens, heightening, heightened**) V-T/V-I If something **heightens** a feeling or if the feeling **heightens,** the feeling increases in degree or intensity. *aumentar, acrecentar, incrementar(se)* ❑ *It heightened awareness of the differences between them. Los hizo más conscientes de las diferencias entre ellos.* ❑ *Chris's interest in her heightened. Aumentó el interés de Chris por ella.*

**heir** /ɛər/ (**heirs**) N-COUNT An **heir** is someone who has the right to inherit a person's money, property, or title when that person dies. *heredero o heredera* ❑ *He is the heir to a fortune. Es el heredero de una fortuna.*

**held** /hɛld/ **Held** is the past tense and past participle of **hold**. *pasado y participio pasado de **hold***

**heli|cop|ter** /hɛlikɒptər/ (**helicopters**) N-COUNT A **helicopter** is an aircraft with long blades on top that go around very fast. It is able to stay still in the air and to move straight upward or downward. *helicóptero*
→ see **fly**

helicopter

**he|lix** /hilɪks/ (**helixes**) N-COUNT A **helix** is a spiral shape or form. *hélice* [TECHNICAL]
→ see **solid**

**hell** /hɛl/ (**hells**) **1** N-PROPER; N-COUNT In some religions, **hell** is the place where the Devil lives, and where bad people are sent when they die. *infierno* ❑ *I don't believe in heaven or hell. No creo en el cielo ni en el infierno.* **2** N-VAR If you say that a particular situation or place is **hell,** you are emphasizing that it is extremely unpleasant. *infierno, lo peor* ❑ *...the hell of prison. ...el infierno de la prisión.*

**he'll** /hɪl, il, STRONG hil/ **He'll** is the usual spoken form of "he will." *forma hablada de **he will*** ❑ *He'll be very successful, I'm sure. Estoy segura de que tendrá mucho éxito.*

**hel|lo** /hɛloʊ/ (**hellos**) also **hullo** **1** CONVENTION You say **"Hello"** to someone when you meet them. *saludo* ❑ *Hello, Trish. How are you? Qué tal, Trish, ¿cómo estás?* ● **Hello** is also a noun. *saludo* ❑ *The salesperson greeted me with a warm hello. El saludo del vendedor fue cálido.* **2** CONVENTION You say **"Hello"** to someone at the beginning of a telephone conversation, either when you answer the phone or before you give your name or say why you are phoning. *bueno, diga* ❑ *Cohen picked up the phone. "Hello?" Cohen levantó la bocina. —Bueno...*

**hel|met** /hɛlmɪt/ (**helmets**) N-COUNT A **helmet** is a hat made of a strong material which you wear to protect your head. *casco, yelmo, careta (de esgrima)*
→ see **army, football, hat**

helmet

**help** /hɛlp/ (**helps, helping, helped**) **1** V-T/V-I If you **help** someone, you make it easier for them to do something, for example by doing part of the work for them or by giving them advice or money. *ayudar, socorrer, asistir, colaborar* ❑ *He helped to raise money. Ayudó a reunir fondos.* ❑ *You can help by giving them some money. Puedes ayudar dándoles algo de dinero.* ● **Help** is also a noun. *ayuda, asistencia* ❑ *Thanks very much for your help. Muchas gracias por su colaboración.* **2** V-T/V-I If you say that something **helps,** you mean that it makes something easier to do or get, or that it improves a situation. *ayudar, favorecer* ❑ *The right clothes can help to make you look slim. La ropa adecuada te hará ver delgada.* ❑ *The new president will help the country at home and abroad. El nuevo presidente ayudará al país aquí y en el extranjero.* ❑ *I'm happy to help. Con gusto ayudo.* ● **Help** is also a noun. *ayuda* ❑ *Thank you. You've been a great help. Gracias, fuiste de gran ayuda.* **3** N-UNCOUNT **Help** is action taken to rescue a person who is in danger. You shout **"help!"** when you are in danger in order to attract someone's attention so that they can come and rescue you. *auxilio, socorro* ❑ *He shouted for help. Gritó pidiendo auxilio.* **4** V-T If you **help yourself to** something, you serve yourself or you take it for yourself. If someone tells you to **help yourself,** they are telling you politely to serve yourself anything you want or to take anything you want. *servir(se)* ❑ *There's bread on the table. Help yourself. Hay pan en la mesa, sírvase.* **5** PHRASE If you **can't help** the way you feel or behave, you cannot control it or stop it from happening. You can also say that you **can't help yourself.** *evitar* ❑ *I can't help feeling sorry for the poor man. No puedo evitar sentir pena por el pobre hombre.* **6** PHRASE If someone or something **is of help,** they make a situation easier or better. *ayudar, ser útil* ❑ *Can I be of help to you? ¿Puedo ayudarles?*

▸ **help out** PHR-VERB If you **help** someone **out,**

you help them by doing some work for them or by lending them some money. *ayudar, echar una mano* ❑ *I help out with the secretarial work. Ayudo con el trabajo secretarial.* ❑ *I didn't have enough money so my mother helped me out. No tenía suficiente dinero, así que mi madre me ayudó.*
→ see **donor**

**Usage** **help**

After *help*, you can use the infinitive with or without *to*: *Budi helped Lastri study for the exam; then he asked her to help him towrite an e-mail to the professor.*

**Thesaurus** *help* Ver también:

V. aid, assist, support; (*ant.*) hinder 1
N. aid, assistance, guidance, support 1

**Word Partnership** Usar *help* con:

ADJ. **financial** help, **professional** help 1
V. **ask for** help, **get** help, **need** help, **want to** help 1
**try to** help 1 3
**cry/scream/shout for** help 3
**can't** help **feeling/thinking** *something* 5

**help desk** (**help desks**) N-COUNT A **help desk** is a special service that you can telephone or e-mail in order to get information about a particular product or subject. *help desk, centro de ayuda (remota)* ❑ *Our help desk can solve any kind of problem. En nuestro centro de soporte pueden resolver todo tipo de problemas.*

**help|er** /hɛlpər/ (**helpers**) N-COUNT A **helper** is a person who helps another person or group with a job they are doing. *ayudante, asistente o asistenta* ❑ *Phyllis and her helpers gave us some food. Phyllis y sus ayudantes nos sirvieron algo de comer.*

**help|ful** /hɛlpfəl/ 1 ADJ If someone is **helpful**, they help you by doing part of your job for you or by giving you advice or information. *útil, servicial, conveniente* ❑ *The staff in the hotel are helpful. El personal del hotel es servicial.* ● **help|ful|ly** ADV *con amabilidad* ❑ *They helpfully told us how to find the house. Amablemente nos dijeron cómo encontrar la casa.* 2 ADJ Something that is **helpful** makes a situation more pleasant or more easy to tolerate. *beneficioso* ❑ *It is helpful to have someone with you when you go to the doctor. Es conveniente que alguien te acompañe cuando vas al médico.*

**help|less** /hɛlpləs/ ADJ If you are **helpless**, you do not have the strength or power to do anything useful or to control or protect yourself. *impotente, sin recursos, desvalido* ❑ *Parents often feel helpless when their kids are sick. Los padres suelen sentirse impotentes cuando sus hijos se enferman.* ● **help|less|ly** ADV *con impotencia* ❑ *They watched helplessly as the house burned to the ground. Vieron con impotencia cómo se quemaba la casa hasta los cimientos.* ● **help|less|ness** N-UNCOUNT *indefensión, desamparo* ❑ *I remember my feelings of helplessness. Recuerdo mi sensación de impotencia.*

**hema|tol|ogy** /himətɒlədʒi/ N-UNCOUNT **Hematology** is the branch of medicine that is concerned with diseases of the blood. *hematología* ❑ *...the American Society of Hematology. ...la Sociedad Estadounidense de Hematología.*

**Word Link** *sphere ≈ ball : atmosphere, blogosphere, hemisphere*

**hemi|sphere** /hɛmɪsfɪər/ (**hemispheres**) N-COUNT A **hemisphere** is one half of the earth. *hemisferio* ❑ *...the northern hemisphere. ...el hemisferio norte.*
→ see **solid**

**hen** /hɛn/ (**hens**) N-COUNT A **hen** is a female chicken. *gallina*

**hence** /hɛns/ ADV You use **hence** to indicate that the statement you are about to make is a consequence of what you have just said. *por lo tanto* [FORMAL] ❑ *This problem is likely to happen again. Hence we need a new plan. Es probable que el problema vuelva a presentarse, así que necesitamos un nuevo plan.*

**her** /hər, ər, STRONG hɜr/

**Her** is a third person singular pronoun. **Her** is used as the object of a verb or a preposition. **Her** is also a possessive determiner.

1 PRON You use **her** to refer to a woman, girl, or female animal. *la/le/se/ella* ❑ *I told her that dinner was ready. Le avisé que la cena estaba lista.* ● **Her** is also a possessive determiner. *su/sus* ❑ *Liz traveled around the world with her husband, James. Liz recorrió el mundo con su esposo, James.* 2 PRON **Her** is sometimes used to refer to a country or nation. *su/sus* [FORMAL OR WRITTEN] ● **Her** is also a possessive determiner. *su/sus* ❑ *America and her partners are helping to rebuild roads and buildings. Los Estados Unidos y sus socios están ayudando a reconstruir caminos y edificios.* 3 PRON People sometimes use **her** to refer to a car, machine, or ship. *la/le/se* ❑ *Fill her up, please. Lleno, por favor.* ● **Her** is also a possessive determiner. *su/sus* ❑ *This photograph of the ship was taken by one of her passengers. Esta fotografía del barco fue tomada por uno de los pasajeros.*

**her|ald** /hɛrəld/ (**heralds, heralding, heralded**) 1 V-T Something that **heralds** a future event or situation is a sign that it is going to happen or appear. *anunciar, presagiar, proclamar* [FORMAL] ❑ *This discovery could herald a cure for cancer. Este descubrimiento podría presagiar una cura para el cáncer.* 2 N-COUNT Something that is a **herald of** a future event or situation is a sign that it is going to happen or appear. *portavoz, precursor o precursora, heraldo* [FORMAL] ❑ *These cool mornings are a herald of fall. Estas frías mañanas anuncian el otoño.*

**herb** /ɜrb/ (**herbs**) N-COUNT An **herb** is a plant whose leaves are used in cooking to add flavor to food, or as a medicine. *hierba, yerba* ❑ *...herbs such as basil and coriander. ...yerbas como albahaca y cilantro.* ● **herb|al** ADJ *de hierbas* ❑ *...herbal remedies for colds. ...remedios de hierbas para el resfriado.*

**her|bi|vore** /hɜrbɪvɔr, ɜr-/ (**herbivores**) N-COUNT A **herbivore** is an animal that only eats plants. *herbívoro*
→ see Word Web: **herbivore**
→ see **carnivore**

**herbivorous** /hɜrbɪvərəs, ɜr-/ ADJ **Herbivorous** animals only eat plants. *herbívoro*

**herd** /hɜrd/ (**herds, herding, herded**) 1 N-COUNT A **herd** is a large group of animals of one kind that

Word Web **herbivore**

**Herbivores** come in all shapes and sizes. The tiny **aphid** lives on the juices found in **plants**. The **elephant** eats 100 to 1,000 pounds of **vegetation** a day. Some herbivores prefer a single plant. For example, the **koala** eats only eucalyptus **leaves**. **Cattle graze** on **grass** all day long. In the evening they regurgitate food from their stomachs and chew it again. **Rodents** have two pairs of long teeth in the front of their mouths. These teeth never stop growing. They use them to gnaw on hard **seeds**.

live together. *hato, rebaño, manada* ❑ *...herds of elephants. ...manadas de elefantes.* **2** V-T If you **herd** people or animals somewhere, you make them move there in a group. *agrupar, arriar* ❑ *He began to herd the prisoners out. Empezó a sacar a los prisioneros.* ❑ *Stefano used a dog to herd the sheep. Stefano usaba un perro para arriar a las ovejas.*

H

**here** /hɪər/ **1** ADV You use **here** when you are referring to the place where you are. *aquí* ❑ *I can't stand here talking all day. No puedo estar aquí parado todo el día, hablando.* **2** ADV You use **here** when you are pointing toward a place that is near you, in order to draw someone else's attention to it. *aquí* ❑ *Come and sit here. Ven y siéntate aquí.* **3** ADV You use **here** in order to draw attention to something or someone who has just arrived in the place where you are, or to draw attention to the place you have just arrived at. *anunciar* ❑ *"Here's the taxi," she said. —Llegó el taxi—les dijo.* **4** ADV You use **here** to refer to a particular point or stage of a situation or subject that you have come to or that you are dealing with. *en este punto* ❑ *It's here that our problems started. Aquí es donde empezaron nuestros problemas.* **5** ADV You use **here** when you are offering or giving something to someone. *anunciar algo* ❑ *Here's your coffee. Aquí está tu café.*

**he|red|ity** /hɪrɛdɪti/ N-UNCOUNT **Heredity** is the process by which features and characteristics are passed on from parents to their children before the children are born. *herencia*

**her|it|age** /hɛrɪtɪdʒ/ (**heritages**) N-VAR A country's **heritage** is all the qualities, traditions, or features of life there that have continued over many years and have been passed on from one generation to another. *patrimonio, legado* ❑ *Old buildings are part of our heritage. Los edificios antiguos forman parte de nuestro patrimonio.*

**hero** /hɪəroʊ/ (**heroes**) **1** N-COUNT The **hero** of a book, play, movie, or story is the main male character, who usually has good qualities. *héroe o heroína, protagonista* ❑ *The actor Daniel Radcliffe plays the hero in the Harry Potter movies. El actor Daniel Radcliffe representa al héroe en Harry Potter.* **2** N-COUNT A **hero** is someone who has done something brave, new, or good, and who is admired by a lot of people. *héroe o heroína* ❑ *He called Mr. Mandela a hero who had inspired millions. Del Sr. Mandela dijo que era un héroe que había inspirado a millones de personas.*
→ see Word Web: **hero**
→ see **myth**

**he|ro|ic** /hɪroʊɪk/ (**heroics**) **1** ADJ If you describe a person or their actions as **heroic,** you admire them because they show extreme bravery. *heroico* ❑ *People praised his heroic deeds. El pueblo aclamó sus hazañas heroicas.* • **he|roi|cal|ly** /hɪroʊɪkli/ ADV *heroicamente* ❑ *He acted heroically when the boat started to sink. Se comportó heroicamente cuando el bote empezó a hundirse.* **2** ADJ If you describe an action or event as **heroic,** you admire it because it involves great effort or determination to succeed. *heroico, colosal* ❑ *The company made heroic efforts to reduce costs. La empresa hizo esfuerzos heroicos para reducir costos.* • **he|roi|cal|ly** ADV *heroicamente* ❑ *Single parents manage heroically in*

Word Web **hero**

Odysseus is a **hero** from Greek **mythology**. He is a warrior. He is brave in battle. He faces many **dangers**. However he knows he must return home after the Trojan War*. During his **epic** journey home, Odysseus faces many trials. He must survive wild storms at sea and fight a monster. He must also resist the temptations of Sirens and outsmart the goddess Circe*. At home Penelope, Odysseus' wife, **defends** their home and **protects** their son. She remains **loyal** and **brave** through many trials. She is the **heroine** of the story.

*Trojan War: a legendary war between Greece and Troy.*
*Circe: a Greek goddess.*

*Odysseus saves his men from the Cyclops.*

*doing the job of two people.* *Los padres solteros se las arreglan maravillosamente para hacer el trabajo de dos personas.*

**hero|in** /hɛroʊɪn/ N-UNCOUNT **Heroin** is a powerful illegal drug which some people take for pleasure, but which they can become addicted to. *heroína*

**hero|ine** /hɛroʊɪn/ (**heroines**) **1** N-COUNT The **heroine** of a book, play, movie, or story is the main female character, who usually has good qualities. *heroína, protagonista* ❑ *The heroine is a young doctor.* *La protagonista es una joven doctora.* **2** N-COUNT A **heroine** is a woman who has done something brave, new, or good, and is admired by a lot of people. *heroína* ❑ *China's first gold medal winner became a national heroine.* *La primera china que ganó una medalla de oro se convirtió en heroína nacional.*

→ see **hero**

**hers** /hɜrz/

Hers is a third person possessive pronoun.

PRON You use **hers** to indicate that something belongs or relates to a woman, girl, or female animal. *de ella* ❑ *His hand as it shook hers was warm and firm.* *Al tomar la mano de ella, la sintió cálida y firme.*

**her|self** /hərsɛlf/

**Herself** is a third person singular reflexive pronoun. **Herself** is used when the object of a verb or preposition refers to the same person as the subject of the verb.

**1** PRON You use **herself** to refer to a woman, girl, or female animal. *se, ella misma* ❑ *She made herself a sandwich.* *Se hizo un sándwich.* ❑ *Jennifer didn't feel good about herself.* *Jennifer no se sintió bien con ella misma.* **2** PRON You use **herself** to emphasize the person or thing that you are referring to. *ella (se expresa el pronombre en lugar de omitirse)* ❑ *She herself was not hungry.* *Ella no tenía hambre.*

**Hertz|sprung-Rus|sell dia|gram** /hɛərtsprʊŋrʌsᵊl daɪəgræm/ (**Hertzsprung-Russell diagrams**) N-COUNT The **Hertzsprung-Russell diagram** is a chart used in astronomy to show the relationships between different types of stars. The abbreviations H-R *diagram* and HRD are also used. *diagrama de Hertzsprung-Russell, diagrama HR*

**he's** /hiz, iz, STRONG hiz/ **He's** is the usual spoken form of "he is" or "he has," especially when "has" is an auxiliary verb. *forma hablada de* ***he is*** *o* ***he has*** ❑ *He's coming home tomorrow.* *Llega a la casa mañana.*

**hesi|tate** /hɛzɪteɪt/ (**hesitates, hesitating, hesitated**) **1** V-I If you **hesitate,** you do not speak or act for a short time, usually because you are uncertain, embarrassed, or worried about what you are going to say or do. *dudar, vacilar* ❑ *Catherine hesitated before answering.* *Catherine titubeó antes de responder.* ● **hesi|ta|tion** /hɛzɪteɪʃᵊn/ N-VAR (**hesitations**) *duda, titubeo* ❑ *After some hesitation, she replied, "I'll have to think about that."* *Tendré que pensarlo, respondió después de cierta vacilación.* **2** V-T If you **hesitate to** do something, you are unwilling to do it, usually because you are not certain it would be right. *dudar en* ❑ *Don't hesitate to ask if you have any questions.* *No dudes en preguntar si lo necesitas.* ● **hesi|ta|tion** N-VAR *duda, titubeo, vacilación* **Hesitation** is an unwillingness to do something, or a delay in doing it, because you are uncertain, worried, or embarrassed about it. *duda* ❑ *He said there would be no more hesitation in making changes.* *Dijo que no más vacilación ante cambios necesarios.*

| **Thesaurus** | *hesitate* Ver también: |
| --- | --- |
| V. | falter, pause, wait **1** **2** |

**hetero|geneous** /hɛtərədʒiniəs, -dʒinyəs/ ADJ A **heterogeneous** group consists of many different types of things or people. *heterogéneo, mixto* [FORMAL]

**hetero|geneous mix|ture** (**heterogeneous mixtures**) N-COUNT In chemistry, a **heterogeneous mixture** is a mixture of two or more substances that remain separate, for example oil and water. *mezcla heterogénea*

**hetero|sex|ual** /hɛtəroʊsɛkʃuəl/ (**heterosexuals**) ADJ Someone who is **heterosexual** is sexually attracted to people of the opposite sex. *heterosexual* ❑ *...heterosexual couples.* *...parejas heterosexuales.* ● **Heterosexual** is also a noun. *heterosexual* ❑ *...unmarried heterosexuals.* *...heterosexuales solteros.* ● **hetero|sexu|al|ity** /hɛtəroʊsɛkʃuælɪti/ N-UNCOUNT *heterosexualidad* ❑ *He is proud of his heterosexuality.* *Está orgulloso de su heterosexualidad.*

**hexa|gon** /hɛksəgɒn/ (**hexagons**) N-COUNT A **hexagon** is a shape that has six straight sides. *hexágono*

→ see **shape**

**hey** /heɪ/ **1** CONVENTION In informal situations, you say or shout **"hey"** to attract someone's attention, or to show surprise, interest, or annoyance. *¡eh!, ¡oye!, ¡oiga!* ❑ *"Hey! Look out!" shouted Patty.* *—¡Oye, fíjate! —gritó Patty.* **2** CONVENTION In informal situations, you can say **"hey"** to greet someone. *hola* ❑ *He smiled and said "Hey, Kate."* *Sonrió y dijo —hola, Kate.*

**hi** /haɪ/ CONVENTION In informal situations, you say **"hi"** to greet someone. *hola* ❑ *"Hi, Liz," she said.* *—Hola, Liz —dijo ella.*

**hi|ber|nate** /haɪbərneɪt/ (**hibernates, hibernating, hibernated**) V-I Animals that **hibernate** spend the winter in a state like a deep sleep. *hibernar, invernar*

**hi|ber|na|tion** /haɪbərneɪʃᵊn/ N-UNCOUNT **Hibernation** is the act or state of hibernating. *hibernación*

**hicko|ry** /hɪkəri/ (**hickories**) N-VAR A **hickory** is a tree which has large leaves, greenish flowers, and nuts with smooth shells. *nogal americano* ❑ *They cut down many trees, including oaks and hickories.* *Derriban muchos árboles, hasta robles y nogales.* ● **Hickory** is the wood of this tree. *nogal americano* ❑ *The first skis were long, thin strips of hickory.* *Los primeros esquís fueron unas tiras de nogal americano delgadas y largas.*

**hid** /hɪd/ **Hid** is the past tense of **hide.** *pasado de* ***hide***

**hid|den** /hɪdᵊn/ **1** **Hidden** is the past participle of **hide.** *participio pasado de hide* **2** ADJ **Hidden** facts, feelings, activities, or problems are not easy to notice or discover. *oculto, secreto, escondido* ❑ *There are hidden dangers on the beach.* *En la playa hay*

h

peligros ocultos. **3** ADJ A **hidden** place is difficult to find. *oculto, escondido* ❑ *As you go down the hill, you suddenly see the hidden waterfall. Conforme bajas la colina, aparece de repente una cascada que no se veía.*

**hide** /haɪd/ (**hides, hiding, hid, hidden**) **1** V-T If you **hide** something or someone, you put them in a place where they cannot easily be seen or found. *esconder* ❑ *He hid the bicycle behind the wall. Escondió la bicicleta detrás del muro.* **2** V-T/V-I If you **hide** or if you **hide yourself**, you go somewhere where you cannot easily be seen or found. *esconderse* ❑ *The little boy ran and hid. El niñito corrió a esconderse.* **3** V-T To **hide** something means to cover it so that people cannot see it. *esconder, ocultar* ❑ *She hid her face in her hands. Se tapó la cara con las manos.* **4** V-T If you **hide** what you feel or know, you keep it a secret, so that no one knows about it. *ocultar* ❑ *Lee tried to hide his excitement. Lee trató de ocultar su emoción.* **5** N-VAR A **hide** is the skin of a large animal which can be used for making leather. *piel, pellejo* ❑ *...cow hides. ...pieles de vaca.* **6** → see also **hidden, hiding**

H

**Thesaurus** *hide* Ver también:

v. camouflage, cover, lock up **1** **3**

**Word Partnership** Usar *hide* con:

ADV. **nowhere to** hide **1** **2**
V. **attempt/try to** hide **1** – **4**
**run and** hide **2**
N. hide *your* **face** **3**
hide **a fact/secret,** hide *your* **disappointment/fear/feelings/tears** **4**

**hid|eous** /hɪdiəs/ ADJ If you say that someone or something is **hideous,** you mean that they are very ugly or unpleasant. *espantoso, horrible, monstruoso, horroroso, horrendo* ❑ *She saw a hideous face at the window and screamed. Vio una cara horrible en la ventana y gritó.* ❑ *He was the victim of a hideous attack. Fue víctima de un espantoso ataque.* ● **hid|eous|ly** ADV *espantosamente, horriblemente* ❑ *He was hideously ugly. Era espantosamente feo.*

**hid|ing** /haɪdɪŋ/ N-UNCOUNT If someone is **in hiding,** they have secretly gone somewhere where they cannot be seen or found. *escondido* ❑ *Cohen is in hiding with his wife. Cohen está en un escondite con su mujer.*

**hi|er|ar|chy** /haɪərɑrki/ (**hierarchies**) **1** N-VAR A **hierarchy** is a system of organizing people into different ranks or levels of importance, for example in society or in a company. *jerarquía* ❑ *Workers and managers did not mix in the company hierarchy. En la jerarquía de la empresa obreros y administrativos no se mezclan.* ● **hi|er|ar|chi|cal** /haɪərɑrkɪkᵊl/ ADJ *jerárquico* ❑ *...a hierarchical society. ...una sociedad organizada jerárquicamente.* **2** N-COUNT The **hierarchy** of an organization is the group of people who manage and control it. *jerarquía* ❑ *The church hierarchy feels that the church needs to modernize. La jerarquía eclesiástica piensa que la iglesia tiene que modernizarse.*

**high** /haɪ/ (**higher, highest, highs**) **1** ADJ Something that is **high** extends a long way from the bottom to the top when it is upright. You do not use **high** to describe people, animals, or plants. *alto, elevado* ❑ *...a house with a high wall around it. ...una casa rodeada por un alto muro.* ❑ *Mount Marcy is the highest mountain in the Adirondacks. Mount Marcy es la montaña más alta de los Adirondacks.* ● **High** is also an adverb. *arriba, en alto, por encima* ❑ *...wagons packed high with goods. ...vagones llenos hasta el tope.* **2** ADJ You use **high** to talk or ask about how much something upright measures from the bottom to the top. *alto* ❑ *How high is the door? ¿Cuánto mide la puerta?* ❑ *The grass in the yard was a foot high. En el patio, el pasto ya llegaba a los 30 cm.* **3** ADJ If something is **high,** it is a long way above the ground, above sea level, or above a person or thing. *alto, arriba* ❑ *I looked down from the high window. Miré desde la ventana de arriba.* ❑ *The sun was high in the sky. El sol estaba alto en el cielo.* ● **High** is also an adverb. *alto* ❑ *She can jump higher than other people. Puede brincar más alto que los demás.* PHRASE ● If something is **high up,** it is a long way above the ground, above sea level, or above a person or thing. *en lo alto, muy arriba* ❑ *His farm was high up in the hills. Su granja estaba en lo alto de las colinas.* **4** ADJ **High** means great in amount, degree, or intensity. *fuerte, intenso, violento* ❑ *High winds knocked down trees. Los fuertes vientos derribaron árboles.* ❑ *The number of people injured was high. Un número considerable de personas resultaron heridas.* ● **High** is also an adverb. *alto, elevado* ❑ *Unemployment rose even higher last year. El desempleo se incrementó aún más el año pasado.* PHRASE ● You can use phrases such as **"in the high 80s"** to indicate that a number or level is, for example, more than 85 but not as much as 90. *entre* **5** ADJ If a food or other substance is **high in** a particular ingredient, it contains a large amount of that ingredient. *rico en, abundante* ❑ *Foods such as ice cream and pizza are high in fat. Alimentos como el helado y la pizza tienen mucha grasa.* **6** N-COUNT If something reaches a **high of** a particular amount or degree, that is the greatest it has ever been. *lo más alto* ❑ *Sales have reached an all-time high. Las ventas alcanzaron el nivel más alto de todos los tiempos.* **7** ADJ If you say that something is a **high** priority or is **high on** your list, you mean that you consider it to be one of the most important things you have to do or deal with. *prioritario, lo más importante* ❑ *The government made education a high priority. La educación es prioritaria para el gobierno.* **8** ADJ Someone who is **high in** a particular profession or society, or has a **high** position, has a very important position and has great authority and influence. *alto, importante* ❑ *He was very high in the administration. Ocupaba un puesto muy alto en la administración.* PHRASE ● Someone who is **high up in** a profession or society has a very important position. *muy alto, muy elevado, muy importante* ❑ *He is quite high up in the navy. Tiene un rango bastante alto en la marina.* **9** ADJ If the quality or standard of something is **high,** it is extremely good. *gran, alto, muy bueno* ❑ *This is high quality stuff. Es un producto de gran calidad.* **10** ADJ A **high** sound or voice is close to the top of a particular range of notes. *agudo* ❑ *She spoke in a high voice. Habló con voz aguda.* **11** ADJ If your spirits are **high,** you feel happy and excited. *animado, contento* ❑ *Her spirits were high with the hope of seeing Nick. Estaba muy entusiasmada porque iba a ver a Nick.*

**Thesaurus** *high* Ver también:

ADJ. tall 1 2
elevated, lofty, tall; (*ant.*) low 3

**high beams** N-PLURAL A car's or truck's **high beams** are its headlights when they are set to shine their brightest. *luces altas* ❑ *Claire switched on her high beams for a better look at the road. Claire prendió las luces altas para ver mejor el camino.*

**high-class** ADJ If you describe something as **high-class,** you mean that it is of very good quality or of superior social status. *de gran clase* ❑ *...a high-class jeweler. ...un joyero de gran clase.*

**high|er edu|ca|tion** N-UNCOUNT **Higher education** is education at universities and colleges. *educación superior* ❑ *...students in higher education. ...los alumnos de educación superior.*

**high fi|del|ity** also **high-fidelity** N-UNCOUNT **High fidelity** is the use of electronic equipment to reproduce a sound or image with very little distortion or loss of quality. *alta fidelidad* ❑ *...a digital, high-fidelity audio system. ...un sistema de audio digital de alta fidelidad*

**high-frequency word** (**high-frequency words**) N-COUNT **High-frequency words** are words that occur much more often than most other words in written or spoken language. *palabra de uso frecuente*

**high-impact** ADJ **High-impact** exercise puts a lot of stress on your body. *de alto impacto*

**high|lands** /haɪləndz/ N-PLURAL **Highlands** are mountainous areas of land. *tierras altas, altiplanicie*

**high|light** /haɪlaɪt/ (**highlights, highlighting, highlighted**) 1 V-T If someone or something **highlights** a point or problem, they emphasize it or make you think about it. *destacar, sacar a relucir* ❑ *Collins wrote a song which highlighted the problems of homeless people. Collins escribió una canción que sacaba a relucir los problemas de la gente sin hogar.* 2 N-COUNT The **highlights of** an event, activity, or period of time are the most interesting or exciting parts of it. *evento más importante* ❑ *The match was one of the highlights of the tournament. El partido fue la atracción principal del torneo.*

**high|light|er** /haɪlaɪtər/ (**highlighters**) 1 N-COUNT A **highlighter** is a pen with brightly colored ink that is used to mark parts of a document. *marcador, rotulador* 2 N-MASS **Highlighter** is a pale-colored cosmetic that someone puts above their eyes or on their cheeks to emphasize the shape of their face. *sombra clara de ojos*
→ see **office**

**high|ly** /haɪli/ 1 ADV **Highly** is used before some adjectives to mean "very." *sumamente* ❑ *Mr. Singh was a highly successful salesman. El señor Singh era un vendedor sumamente exitoso.* ❑ *It seems highly unlikely that she will win. Parece sumamente improbable que ella gane.* 2 ADV You use **highly** to indicate that someone has an important position in an organization or set of people. *alto* ❑ *...a highly placed government advisor. ...un alto consejero gubernamental* 3 ADV If you think **highly** of something or someone, you think they are extremely good. *tener un gran concepto de* ❑ *Michael thought highly of the school. Michael tenía muy buen concepto de su escuela.*

**Word Partnership** Usar *highly* con:

ADJ. highly **addictive**, highly **competitive**, highly **contagious**, highly **controversial**, highly **critical**, highly **educated**, highly **intelligent**, highly **qualified**, highly **skilled**, highly **successful**, highly **technical**, highly **trained**, highly **unlikely**, highly **visible** 1
V. highly **recommended**, highly **respected** 1

**high-maintenance** also **high maintenance** ADJ If you describe something or someone as **high-maintenance,** you mean that they require a lot of time, money, or effort. *de mucho mantenimiento* ❑ *Small gardens can be high maintenance. Los jardines pequeños pueden requerir mucho mantenimiento.* ❑ *She was a high-maintenance girl who needed lots of attention. Era una muchacha que requería mucha atención.*

**high power lens** (**high power lenses**) N-COUNT A **high power lens** is a very powerful lens on an instrument such as a microscope. *de gran aumento*

**high road** N-SING If you say that someone is taking **the high road** in a situation, you mean that they are taking the most positive and careful course of action. *camino del éxito, el mejor camino* ❑ *He tried to start an argument with her, but she took the high road and ignored him. Trató de comenzar una discusión con ella, pero ella tomó el mejor camino y lo ignoró.*

**high school** (**high schools**) N-VAR; N-COUNT A **high school** is a school for children usually aged between fourteen and eighteen. *bachillerato, preparatoria, liceo* ❑ *My daughter has just started high school. Mi hija acaba de empezar el bachillerato.*
→ see **graduation**

**high-stakes** ADJ A **high-stakes** game or contest is one in which the people involved can gain or lose a lot. *Hay mucho en juego* ❑ *...the high-stakes television debate. ...el debate televisivo en el que hay mucho en juego*

**high-strung** ADJ If someone is **high-strung,** they are very nervous and easily upset. *muy nervioso* ❑ *The pressure of his job was making the high-strung man sick. De tan nervioso que era, la presión del trabajo lo estaba enfermando.*

**high-tech** /haɪ tɛk/ also **high tech** or **hi tech** ADJ **High-tech** activities or equipment involve or use high technology. *de alta tecnología* ❑ *...high-tech industries such as computers and telecommunications. ...industrias de alta tecnología, como la computación y las telecomunicaciones.*

**high tech|nol|ogy** N-UNCOUNT **High technology** is the development and use of advanced electronics and computers. *alta tecnología* ❑ *...the high technology section of the newspaper. ...la sección de alta tecnología del periódico.*

**high tide** N-UNCOUNT At the coast, **high tide** is the time when the sea is at its highest level because the tide is in. *marea alta*
→ see **tide**

**high|way** /haɪweɪ/ (**highways**) N-COUNT A

highway is a main road, especially one that connects towns or cities. *carretera* ❑ *I crossed the highway. Crucé la carretera.*
→ see **traffic**

**high|way pa|trol** (**highway patrols**) N-COUNT In the United States, the **highway patrol** is the part of the police force within a particular state that is responsible for making sure that the roads are safe and for dealing with drivers who break the law. *policía de caminos* ❑ *The Florida Highway Patrol shut a 20-mile stretch of the interstate. La policía de caminos de Florida cerró un tramo de 20 millas de la carretera interestatal.* ❑ *...highway patrol officers. ...los oficiales de la policía de caminos*

**hike** /haɪk/ (**hikes, hiking, hiked**) **1** N-COUNT A **hike** is a long walk in the country, especially one that you go on for pleasure. *caminata, excursión* ❑ *We went for a 30-minute hike through a forest. Fuimos a una caminata de 30 minutos por el bosque.* **2** V-I If you **hike,** you go for a long walk in the country. *ir de caminata, ir de excursión* ❑ *You can hike through the Fish River Canyon. Puedes ir de excursión por el Fish River Canyon.* ● **hik|er** N-COUNT (**hikers**) *caminante, excursionista* ❑ *The hikers spent the night in the mountains. Los excursionistas pasaron la noche en las montañas.* ● **hik|ing** N-UNCOUNT *ir de caminata, ir de excursión* ❑ *I love hiking and horseback riding in the mountains. Me encanta ir de caminata y cabalgar en las montañas.* **3** V-T To **hike** prices, rates, taxes, or quantities means to increase them suddenly or by a large amount. *subir, incrementar* [INFORMAL] ❑ *The company hiked its prices by 5 percent. La compañía subió sus precios en un cinco por ciento.* ● **Hike up** means the same as **hike.** *subir, incrementar* ❑ *The government hiked up the tax on air travel. El gobierno subió los impuestos en tarifas aéreas.*
→ see **shoe**

H

**hi|lari|ous** /hɪlɛəriəs/ ADJ If something is **hilarious,** it is extremely funny. *comiquísimo, muy cómico* ❑ *He told me a hilarious story. Me contó una historia comiquísima.* ● **hi|lari|ous|ly** ADV *de manera muy cómica* ❑ *She found it hilariously funny. Se le hizo extremadamente gracioso.*

**hill** /hɪl/ (**hills**) N-COUNT A **hill** is an area of land that is higher than the land that surrounds it. *colina* ❑ *I walked up the hill. Subí la colina.*

**hilly** /hɪli/ (**hillier, hilliest**) ADJ A **hilly** area has many hills. *accidentado* ❑ *The area is hilly and densely wooded. El terreno es accidentado y muy boscoso.*

**him** /hɪm/

> **Him** is a third person singular pronoun. **Him** is used as the object of a verb or a preposition.

**1** PRON You use **him** to refer to a man, boy, or male animal. *él* ❑ *Elaine met him at the railroad station. Elaine lo conoció en la estación del tren.* ❑ *Is Sam there? Let me talk to him. ¿Está Sam? Déjame hablar con él.* **2** PRON In written English, **him** is sometimes used to refer to a person without saying whether that person is a man or a woman. Some people dislike this use and prefer to use "him or her" or "them." *lo, le* ❑ *If I see a person who is new, I ask him why he is here. Si veo a alguien nuevo, le pregunto porqué está aquí.*

**him|self** /hɪmsɛlf/

> **Himself** is a third person singular reflexive pronoun. **Himself** is used when the object of a verb or preposition refers to the same person as the subject of the verb.

**1** PRON You use **himself** to refer to a man, boy, or male animal. *se, sí mismo* ❑ *He poured himself a cup of coffee. Se sirvió una taza de café.* ❑ *He was talking to himself. Hablaba consigo mismo.* **2** PRON You use **himself** to emphasize the person or thing that you are referring to. *él mismo, en persona* ❑ *The president himself is on a visit to Beijing. El presidente en persona está de visita en Beijing.*

**Hin|du** /hɪndu/ (**Hindus**) **1** N-COUNT A **Hindu** is a person who believes in Hinduism. *hindú* **2** ADJ **Hindu** is used to describe things that belong or relate to Hinduism. *hindú* ❑ *...a Hindu temple. ...un templo hindú*

**hint** /hɪnt/ (**hints, hinting, hinted**) **1** N-COUNT A **hint** is a suggestion about something that is made in an indirect way. *indirecta, insinuación* ❑ *I gave him a hint about coming to visit me. Le hice la insinuación de que viniera a visitarme.* **2** V-I If you **hint at** something, you suggest it in an indirect way. *insinuar* ❑ *She hinted at a trip to her favorite store. Le insinuó una visita a su tienda favorita.* **3** N-COUNT A **hint** is a helpful piece of advice. *consejo, tip* ❑ *Here are some helpful hints to make your trip easier. Aquí hay algunos tips que pueden facilitarles el viaje.* **4** N-SING A **hint of** something is a very small amount of it. *dejo* ❑ *...pancakes with a hint of vanilla. ...panqueques con un dejo de vainilla.*

> **Word Partnership** Usar *hint* con:
>
> V. **take a** hint **1**
> **drop a** hint, **give a** hint **1 3**
> ADJ. **slight** hint **1**
> **helpful** hint **3**

**hip** /hɪp/ (**hips**) **1** N-COUNT Your **hips** are the two areas or bones at the sides of your body between the tops of your legs and your waist. *cadera* ❑ *Tracey put her hands on her hips and laughed. Tracey puso los brazos en jarras y se rió.* ❑ *Surgeons replaced both hips. Los cirujanos remplazaron ambas caderas.* **2** ADJ If you say that someone is **hip,** you mean that they are very modern and follow all the latest fashions, for example in clothes and ideas. *in, en la onda* [INFORMAL] ❑ *...a hip young man. ...un joven muy in., ...un joven muy en onda.*

**hire** /haɪər/ (**hires, hiring, hired**) V-T If you **hire** someone, you employ them or pay them to do a particular job for you. *contratar* ❑ *He just hired a new secretary. Acaba de contratar a una nueva secretaria.*
▸ **hire out** PHR-VERB If you **hire out** a person's services, you allow them to be used in return for payment. *ofrecer un servicio* ❑ *His agency hires out bodyguards. Su agencia ofrece el servicio de guardaespaldas.*

**his**

> The determiner is pronounced /hɪz/. The pronoun is pronounced /hɪz/.

> **His** is a third person singular possessive determiner. **His** is also a possessive pronoun.

DET You use **his** to indicate that something

belongs or relates to a man, boy, or male animal. *su* ❑ *He spent part of his career in Hollywood.* *Pasó parte de su carrera en Hollywood.* ● **His** is also a possessive pronoun. *suyo* ❑ *Staff say the decision was his.* *El personal dice que la decisión fue de él.*

**His|pan|ic** /hɪspæ̱nɪk/ (**Hispanics**) ADJ A **Hispanic** person is a citizen of the United States of America who originally came from Latin America, or whose family originally came from Latin America. *latino, hispano* ❑ *...a group of Hispanic doctors.* *...un grupo de doctores latinos.* ● A **Hispanic** is someone who is Hispanic. *latino* ❑ *About 80 percent of Hispanics here are U.S. citizens.* *Alrededor del 80 por ciento de los latinos son ciudadanos estadounidenses.*

**his|to|gram** /hɪ̱stəgræm/ (**histograms**) N-COUNT A **histogram** is a graph that uses vertical bars with no spaces between them to represent the distribution of a set of data. *histograma, gráfica de barras* [TECHNICAL]

**his|to|rian** /hɪstɔ̱riən/ (**historians**) N-COUNT A **historian** is a person who specializes in the study of history, and who writes books and articles about it. *historiador o historiadora*
→ see **history**

**his|tor|ic** /hɪstɔ̱rɪk/ ADJ Something that is **historic** is important in history, or likely to be considered important at some time in the future. *histórico* ❑ *...the historic changes in Eastern Europe.* *...los cambios históricos de Europa Oriental.*

**his|tori|cal** /hɪstɔ̱rɪkəl/ **1** ADJ **Historical** people, situations, or things existed in the past and are considered to be a part of history. *histórico* ❑ *...an important historical figure.* *...un importante personaje histórico.* ● **his|tori|cal|ly** ADV *históricamente* ❑ *Historically, royal marriages have been unhappy.* *Históricamente, los matrimonios de la realeza han sido desdichados.* **2** ADJ **Historical** books, works of art, or studies are concerned with people, situations, or things that existed in the past. *histórico* ❑ *...a historical novel about nineteenth-century France.* *...una novela histórica sobre Francia en el siglo diecinueve.* ❑ *...historical records.* *...registros históricos.*

**Word Partnership** Usar *historical* con:

N. historical **events**, historical **figure**, historical **impact**, historical **significance** **1**
historical **detail/fact**, historical **records**, historical **research** **2**

**his|to|ry** /hɪ̱stəri, -tri/ (**histories**) **1** N-UNCOUNT You can refer to the events of the past as **history.** You can also refer to the past events which concern a particular topic or place as its **history.** *historia* ❑ *He studied history at Indiana University.* *Estudió historia en la Universidad de Indiana.* ❑ *...great moments in football history.* *...grandes momentos de la historia del fútbol.* **2** N-COUNT A **history** is an account of events that have happened in the past. *historia* ❑ *...the history of the modern world.* *...la historia del mundo moderno.* **3** N-COUNT If a person or a place has **a history of** something, it has been very common or has happened frequently in their past. *historial, antecedentes* ❑ *He had a history of health problems.* *Tenía un historial de problemas de salud.* **4** N-COUNT Someone's **history** is the set of facts that are known about their past. *historial* ❑ *He couldn't get a new job because of his medical history.* *No podía conseguir otro trabajo por sus antecedentes clínicos.* **5** PHRASE Someone who **makes history** does something that is thought to be important and significant in the development of the world or of a particular society. *hacer historia* ❑ *Willy Brandt made history by visiting East Germany in 1970.* *Willy Brandt hizo historia al visitar Alemania Oriental en 1970.* **6** PHRASE If someone or something **goes down in history,** people in the future remember them because of a particular thing they have done or because of particular events that have happened. *pasar a la historia* ❑ *John Paul will go down in history as the most important world leader of the 20th century.* *El Papa Juan Pablo II pasará a la historia como el líder más importante del siglo XX.*
→ see Word Web: **history**

**Word Web** history

**3800 BC** The wheel is invented.

**2600 BC** The Pyramid of Giza is built.

**31 BC** Roman Empire founded.

**700 AD** The Great Wall of China is started.

**1200 AD** Incan empire is founded.

**1492** Columbus sails for America.

**1969** Humans land on the Moon.

Open any history textbook and you will find **timelines.** They show important dates for **ancient civilizations**—when **empires** appeared and disappeared, and when **wars** were fought. But how much of what we read in **history** books is **fact**? **Accounts** of the **past** are often based on how **archeologists** interpret the **artifacts** they find. **Scholars** often rely on the **records** of the people who were in power. These **historians** included certain facts and left out others. Historians today look beyond official records. They research **documents** such as **diaries.** They describe **events** from different **points of view.**

**Word Partnership** Usar *history* con:

V. **go down in** history, **make** history, **teach** history 1
N. **the course of** history, **world** history 1
**family** history 1 4
**life** history 4

**hit** /hɪt/ (**hits, hitting**)

The form **hit** is used in the present tense and is the past and present participle.

1 V-T If you **hit** someone or something, you deliberately touch them with a lot of force, with your hand or an object held in your hand. *golpear* ❑ *She hit the ball hard. Golpeó la pelota muy fuerte.* 2 V-T When one thing **hits** another, it touches it with a lot of force. *golpear* ❑ *The car hit a traffic sign. El carro golpeó una señal de tránsito.* ● **Hit** is also a noun. *golpe* ❑ *The building took a direct hit from the bomb. El edificio recibió el golpe directo de la bomba.* 3 V-T If something **hits** a person, place, or thing, it affects them very badly. *afectar* ❑ *The earthquake hit northern Peru. El terremoto afectó el norte de Perú.* 4 V-T When a feeling or an idea **hits** you, it suddenly affects you or comes into your mind. *darse cuenta* ❑ *It hit me that I had a choice. Me di cuenta de que tenía una opción.* 5 N-COUNT If a CD, movie, or play is a **hit,** it is very popular and successful. *éxito* ❑ *The song was a big hit. La canción fue un gran éxito.* 6 N-COUNT A **hit** is a single visit to a website. *visita* [COMPUTING] ❑ *The company has had 78,000 hits on its Internet pages. La compañía ha recibido 78,000 visitas a su página de Internet.* 7 N-COUNT If someone who is searching for information on the Internet gets a **hit,** they find a website where there is that information. *atinar* 8 PHRASE If two people **hit it off,** they like each other and become friendly as soon as they meet. *congeniar* [INFORMAL] ❑ *Dad and Walter hit it off straight away. Papá y Walter congeniaron inmediatamente.* 9 to **hit the headlines** → see **headline** 10 to **hit the roof** → see **roof**

▸ **hit on** or **hit upon** PHR-VERB If you **hit on** an idea or a solution to a problem, or **hit upon** it, you think of it. *dar con* ❑ *We finally hit on a solution to the problem. Finalmente dimos con una solución para el problema.*

▸ **hit up** PHR-VERB If you **hit** somebody **up** for something, especially for money, you ask them for it. *pedir* [INFORMAL] ❑ *They hit up Harry for the last $250. Le pidieron a Harry los últimos 250 dólares.*

**Thesaurus** *hit* Ver también:

V. bang, beat, knock, pound, slap, smack, strike 1
N. smash, success, triumph; (*ant.*) failure 5

**Word Partnership** Usar *hit* con:

N. hit **a ball**, hit **a button**, hit **the brakes** 1
**earthquakes/famine/storms** hit ***someplace*** 3
**a** hit **movie/show/song** 5

**hit-and-miss** also **hit and miss** ADJ If something is **hit-and-miss** or **hit-or-miss,** it is sometimes successful and sometimes not. *un volado, una lotería* ❑ *Their new album is a hit-and-miss collection of songs. El conjunto de canciones de su nuevo disco es un volado.*

**hit-and-run** ADJ A **hit-and-run** accident is an accident in which the driver of a vehicle hits someone and then drives away without stopping. *accidente en el que el conductor se da a la fuga* ❑ *He was the victim of a hit-and-run accident. Fue víctima de un accidente en que el conductor se dio a la fuga.*

**hi tech** → see **high-tech**

**HIV** /eɪtʃaɪ vi/ 1 N-UNCOUNT **HIV** is a virus which reduces people's resistance to illness and can cause AIDS. **HIV** is an abbreviation for "human immunodeficiency virus." *VIH* 2 PHRASE If someone is **HIV positive,** they are infected with the HIV virus, and may develop AIDS. If someone is **HIV negative,** they are not infected with the virus. *VIH positivo/negativo*

**HMO** /eɪtʃɛm oʊ/ (**HMOs**) N-COUNT An **HMO** is an organization to which you pay a fee and that allows you to use only doctors and hospitals which belong to the organization. **HMO** is an abbreviation for **health maintenance organization**. *servicios médicos exclusivos para un grupo específico*

**hoarse** /hɔrs/ (**hoarser, hoarsest**) ADJ If your voice is **hoarse** or if you are **hoarse,** your voice sounds rough and unclear, for example because your throat is sore. *ronco* ❑ *"What do you think?" she said in a hoarse whisper. -¿Qué opinas? -preguntó en un susurro ronco.* ● **hoarse|ly** ADV *de manera ronca* ❑ *"Thank you," Maria said hoarsely. —Gracias —dijo ella con voz ronca.*

**hob|by** /hɒbi/ (**hobbies**) N-COUNT A **hobby** is an activity that you enjoy doing in your spare time. *pasatiempo, hobby* ❑ *My hobbies are music and tennis. Mis pasatiempos son la música y el tenis.*

**Thesaurus** *hobby* Ver también:

N. activity, craft, interest, pastime

**hobo** /hoʊboʊ/ (**hobos** or **hoboes**) 1 N-COUNT A **hobo** is a person who has no home, especially one who travels from place to place and gets money by begging. *vagabundo o vagabunda* 2 N-COUNT A **hobo** is a worker, especially a farm worker, who goes from place to place in order to find work. *trabajador o trabajadora itinerante*

**hock|ey** /hɒki/ N-UNCOUNT **Hockey** is a game played on ice between two teams who use long curved sticks to hit a small rubber disk, called a puck, and try to score goals. *hockey* ❑ *...a new hockey rink. ...una nueva pista de hockey*

**hoe** /hoʊ/ (**hoes**) N-COUNT A **hoe** is a gardening tool with a long handle and a small square blade, which you use to remove small weeds and break up the surface of the soil. *azadón*
→ see **garden**

**hog** /hɔg/ (**hogs, hogging, hogged**) 1 N-COUNT A **hog** is a pig. *puerco* ❑ *We fed the corn to the hogs. Les dimos el maíz a los puercos.* 2 V-T If you **hog** something, you take all of it in a greedy or impolite way. *acaparar* [INFORMAL] ❑ *Have you finished hogging the bathroom? ¿Qué te crees que el baño es sólo para ti?*

**hold**
1 PHYSICALLY TOUCHING, SUPPORTING, OR CONTAINING
2 HAVING OR DOING
3 CONTROLLING OR REMAINING
4 PHRASES
5 PHRASAL VERBS

**1 hold** /hoʊld/ (**holds, holding, held**) **1** V-T When you **hold** something, you carry or support it, using your hands or your arms. *sujetar, tomar* ❑ *I held the baby in my arms. Tomé al bebé entre mis brazos.* • **Hold** is also a noun. ❑ *He let go his hold on the door. Dejó de sujetar la puerta.* **2** N-UNCOUNT **Hold** is used in expressions such as **grab hold of, catch hold of,** and **get hold of,** to indicate that you close your hand tightly around something. *agarrar, asir* ❑ *I woke up when someone grabbed hold of my sleeping bag. Me desperté cuando alguien agarró mi bolsa de dormir.* ❑ *A doctor and a nurse caught hold of his arms. Un doctor y una enfermera lo asieron de los brazos.* **3** V-T When you **hold** a part of your body in a particular position, you put it into that position and keep it there. *mantener* ❑ *Hold your hands in front of your face. Mantenga las manos frente a la cara.* **4** V-T If one thing **holds** another in a particular position, it keeps it in that position. *mantener* ❑ *The doorstop held the door open. La cuña mantenía la puerta abierta.* **5** V-T If one thing is used to **hold** another, it is used to store it. *guardar* ❑ *Two drawers hold her favorite T-shirts. Tiene sus camisetas favoritas en dos cajones.* **6** N-COUNT In a ship or airplane, a **hold** is a place where cargo or luggage is stored. *bodega* ❑ *A fire started in the hold. El fuego comenzó en la bodega.* **7** V-T If something **holds** a particular amount of something, it can contain that amount. *contener* ❑ *One CD-ROM disk can hold over 100,000 pages of text. Un disco CD-ROM puede contener hasta 100,000 páginas de texto.*

| **Thesaurus** | *hold* | Ver también: |
|---|---|---|
| v. | carry, support 1 1 | |

**2 hold** /hoʊld/ (**holds, holding, held**)

**Hold** is often used to indicate that someone or something has the particular thing, characteristic, or attitude that is mentioned. Therefore it takes most of its meaning from the word that follows it.

**1** V-T If you **hold** an opinion or belief, that is your opinion or belief. *tener una opinión* ❑ *He held opinions which were usually different from mine. Normalmente sus opiniones eran diferentes a las mías.* **2** V-T **Hold** is used with words such as "fear" or "mystery" to say that something has a particular quality or characteristic. *causar* ❑ *Death doesn't hold any fear for me. La muerte no me causa ningún miedo.* **3** V-T **Hold** is used with nouns such as "office," "power," and "responsibility" to indicate that someone has a particular position of power or authority. *tener una posición de poder o autoridad* ❑ *She has never held an elected office. Nunca ha tenido un cargo de elección.* **4** V-T **Hold** is used with nouns such as "permit," "degree," or "ticket" to indicate that someone has a particular document that allows them to do something. *tener* ❑ *He did not hold a driver's license. No tenía licencia de conducir.* • **holder** N-COUNT (**holders**) *poseedor* ❑ *...season-ticket holders. ...los poseedores de boletos de la temporada.* **5** V-T **Hold** is used with nouns such as "party," "meeting," "talks," "election," and "trial" to indicate that people are organizing a particular activity. *celebrar, llevar a cabo* ❑ *The country will hold elections within a year. El país celebrará elecciones dentro de un año.* **6** V-RECIP **Hold** is used with nouns such as "conversation," "interview," and "talks" to indicate that two or more people meet and discuss something. *tener* ❑ *The prime minister is holding talks to finalize the agreement. El primer ministro está celebrando pláticas para finalizar los acuerdos.* **7** V-T **Hold** is used with nouns such as "attention" or "interest" to indicate that what you do or say keeps someone interested or listening to you. *mantener* ❑ *If you want to hold someone's attention, look straight into their eyes. Si quiere mantener la atención de una persona, mírela directamente a los ojos.*

**3 hold** /hoʊld/ (**holds, holding, held**) **1** V-T If someone **holds** you in a place, they keep you there as a prisoner and do not allow you to leave. *mantener* ❑ *Two angry motorists held a man prisoner in his own car. Dos automovilistas enojados mantuvieron a un hombre preso en su propio vehículo.* **2** N-SING If you have a **hold over** someone, you have power or control over them. *control* ❑ *Because he once loved her, she still has a hold on him. Como alguna vez la amó, ella aún tiene control sobre él.* **3** V-T/V-I If you ask someone to **hold,** or to **hold the line,** when you are answering a telephone call, you are asking them to wait for a short time, for example so that you can find the person they want to speak to. *esperar* ❑ *Could you hold on? I'll just get a pen. ¿Puede esperar? Voy por una pluma.* **4** V-I If something **holds,** it remains the same. *mantener* ❑ *Will the weather hold? ¿Irá a seguir así el tiempo?*

**4 hold** /hoʊld/ (**holds, holding, held**) **1** PHRASE If you **get hold of** an object or information, you obtain it, usually after some difficulty. *conseguir* ❑ *It is hard to get hold of medicines in poor countries. Es difícil conseguir medicinas en países pobres.* **2** PHRASE If you **get hold of** someone, you succeed in contacting them. *encontrar* ❑ *I tried to call him but I couldn't get hold of him. Traté de llamarle pero nunca lo encontré.* **3** CONVENTION If you say "**Hold it,**" you are telling someone to stop what they are doing and to wait. *¡espere!, ¡alto!* ❑ *Hold it! Don't move! ¡Alto! ¡No se mueva!* **4** PHRASE If you can do something well enough to **hold** your **own,** you do not appear foolish when you are compared with someone who is generally thought to be very good at it. *saber defenderse* ❑ *She can hold her own against almost any player. Se sabe defender casi de cualquier jugador.* **5** PHRASE If you put something **on hold,** you decide not to do it, deal with it, or change it now, but to leave it until later. *posponer algo* ❑ *He put his retirement on hold to help to find a solution. Pospuso su retiro para ayudar a encontrar una solución.* **6** PHRASE If something **takes hold,** it gains complete control or influence over a person or thing. *apoderarse* ❑ *Excitement took hold of her. La emoción se apoderó de ella.* **7** to **hold** something **at bay** → see **bay** **8** to **hold** something **in check** → see **check** **9** to **hold fast** → see **fast** **10** to **hold** your ground → see **ground** **11** to **hold sway** → see **sway**

**6 hold** /hoʊld/ (**holds, holding, held**)

▸ **hold against** PHR-VERB If you **hold** something **against** someone, you dislike them because of something they did in the past. *guardar rencor a* ❑ *Bernstein lost the case, but didn't hold it against Grundy. Bernstein perdió el caso, pero no le guardó rencor a Grundy.*

▸ **hold back** **1** PHR-VERB If you **hold back** or if something **holds** you **back**, you hesitate before you do something because you are not sure whether it is the right thing to do. *contenerse* ❑ *I was holding back a little. Me estaba conteniendo un poco.* **2** PHR-VERB To **hold** someone or something **back** means to prevent someone from doing something, or to prevent something from happening. *inhibir(se)* ❑ *He wanted to help but something held him back. Quería ayudar, pero algo se lo impidió.* **3** PHR-VERB If you **hold** something **back**, you do not include it in the information you are giving about something. *ocultar* ❑ *You're holding something back. Estás ocultando algo.*

H

▸ **hold down** PHR-VERB If you **hold down** a job or a place on a team, you manage to keep it. *mantener* ❑ *He couldn't hold down a job. No podía mantener un empleo.*

▸ **hold off** PHR-VERB If you **hold off** doing something, you delay doing it or delay making a decision about it. *posponer* ❑ *I held off buying it in case the price dropped. Pospuse la compra por si bajaba el precio.*

▸ **hold on** or **hold onto** **1** PHR-VERB If you **hold on,** or **hold onto** something, you keep your hand on it or around it. *aferrarse* ❑ *He held on to a coffee cup. No soltó la taza de café.* ❑ *He was holding onto a rock on the cliff. Se aferró a una roca del acantilado.* **2** PHR-VERB If you **hold on,** you manage to achieve success or avoid failure in spite of great difficulties or opposition. *Mantener la ventaja* ❑ *The Rams held on to defeat the Nevada Wolf Pack, 32–28. Los Rams mantuvieron la ventaja para derrotar al Nevada Wolf Pack 32 a 28.*

▸ **hold out** **1** PHR-VERB If you **hold out** your hand or something you have in your hand, you move your hand away from your body, for example to shake hands with someone. *tender la mano* ❑ *"I'm Nancy," she said, holding out her hand. —Soy Nancy —dijo dándole la mano.* **2** PHR-VERB If you **hold out for** something, you refuse to accept something inferior or you refuse to surrender. *aguantar* ❑ *He held out for a better deal. Se aguantó para lograr un mejor acuerdo.* ❑ *The soldiers held out for two weeks until they were rescued. Los soldados aguantaron dos semanas hasta ser rescatados.*

▸ **hold up** **1** PHR-VERB To **hold up** a person or process means to make them late or delay them. *retrasar* ❑ *Why were you holding everyone up? ¿Por qué retrasó a todos?* **2** PHR-VERB If someone **holds up** a place such as a bank or a store, they point a weapon at someone there to make them give them money or valuable goods. *asaltar* ❑ *He held up a gas station with a toy gun. Asaltó una gasolinera con un arma de juguete.*

**hold|er** /hoʊldər/ (**holders**) N-COUNT A **holder** is a container in which you put an object. *contenedor* ❑ *...a toothbrush holder. ...un soporte para cepillos de dientes*

**hold|ing** /hoʊldɪŋ/ (**holdings**) N-COUNT If you have a **holding** in a company, you own shares in it. *inversión* [BUSINESS] ❑ *Their holdings grew by 40 percent. Sus inversiones crecieron en un 40 por ciento.*

**hold|ing pat|tern** (**holding patterns**) **1** N-COUNT If an aircraft is put **in a holding pattern,** it is instructed to continue flying while waiting for permission to land. *vuelo en círculos, mantener un avión en vuelo esperando permiso para aterrizar* ❑ *Planes were kept in a holding pattern until they were allowed to land. Los aviones estuvieron volando en círculos hasta que les permitieron aterrizar.* **2** N-COUNT If something or someone is **in a holding pattern,** they remain in the same state or continue to do the same thing while waiting for something to happen. *estancado* ❑ *The computer market is in a kind of holding pattern. Podría decirse que el mercado de computadoras está estancado.*

**hold|over** /hoʊldoʊvər/ (**holdovers**) N-COUNT A **holdover from** an earlier time is a person or thing which existed or occurred at that time and which still exists or occurs today. *miembro veterano, resto, vestigio* ❑ *There are only four holdovers from last season's football team. Sólo quedan cuatro jugadores del equipo de fútbol de la temporada pasada.*

**hole** /hoʊl/ (**holes**) **1** N-COUNT A **hole** is an opening or hollow space in something. *hoyo* ❑ *He dug a hole 45 feet wide and 15 feet deep. Hizo un hoyo de 45 pies de ancho y 15 de profundidad.* ❑ *...kids with holes in the knees of their jeans. ...niños con las rodillas de los pantalones agujeradas.* **2** PHRASE If a person or organization is **in the hole,** they owe money to someone else. *en números rojos* [INFORMAL] ❑ *The business is $14,000 in the hole. El negocio tiene deudas por 14,000 dólares.*

→ see **golf**

**Word Partnership** Usar *hole* con:

| | |
|---|---|
| ADJ. | **big/huge/small** hole, **deep** hole, **gaping** hole **1** |
| V. | **bore/drill a** hole **in** ***something***, **cut/punch a** hole **in** ***something***, **dig a** hole, **fill/plug a** hole **1** |

**holi|day** /hɒlɪdeɪ/ (**holidays** N-COUNT A **holiday** is a day when people do not go to work or school because of a religious or national celebration. *día feriado* ❑ *New Year's Day is a public holiday. Año Nuevo es día feriado.*

**hol|low** /hɒloʊ/ (**hollows**) **1** ADJ Something that is **hollow** has a space inside it. *hueco* ❑ *...a hollow tree. ...un árbol hueco* **2** ADJ A surface that is **hollow** curves inward. *hundido* ❑ *He was young, with hollow cheeks. Era joven, con las mejillas hundidas.* **3** N-COUNT A **hollow** is an area that is lower than the surrounding surface. *hondonada* ❑ *Below him the town lay in the hollow of the hill. Detrás de él, el pueblo yacía en la hondonada de la colina.* **4** ADJ If you describe a statement, situation, or person as **hollow,** you mean they have no real value, worth, or effectiveness. *vano, falso* ❑ *Any threat to tell the police is a hollow one. Cualquier amenaza de decirle a la policía es vana.* • **hol|low|ness** N-UNCOUNT *falsedad* ❑ *I saw the hollowness of his promises. Vi la falsedad de sus promesas.* **5** ADJ A **hollow** sound is dull and echoing. *hueco* ❑ *...the hollow sound of a baseball bat* *on the road.* *...el sonido hueco de un bate de béisbol en el camino.*

**holy** /hoʊli/ (**holier, holiest**) ADJ Something that is **holy** is considered to be special because it is connected with God or a particular religion. *sagrado* ❑ *This is a holy place.* *Éste es un lugar sagrado.*

**Holy Land** N-SING People sometimes refer to the part of the Middle East where most of the Bible is set as **the Holy Land.** *Tierra Santa* ❑ *We went on a trip to the Holy Land.* *Hicimos un viaje a Tierra Santa.*

**holy war** (**holy wars**) N-COUNT A **holy war** is a war that people fight in order to defend or support their religion. *guerra santa* ❑ *More than 1,000 young men have joined the holy war.* *Más de mil jóvenes se han unido a la guerra santa.*

**home** /hoʊm/ (**homes**) **1** N-COUNT Someone's **home** is the house or apartment where they live. *casa* ❑ *Last night they stayed home and watched TV.* *Anoche se quedaron en casa y vieron televisión.* ❑ *Hi, Mom, I'm home!* *¡Mamá, ya llegué!* **2** N-UNCOUNT You can use **home** to refer in a general way to the house, town, or country where someone lives now or where they were born. *hogar* ❑ *Ms. Highsmith has made Switzerland her home.* *La señorita Highsmith ha hecho de Suiza su hogar.* ❑ *His father worked away from home most of the time.* *Su padre trabajaba lejos del hogar la mayor parte del tiempo.* **3** ADV **Home** means to or at the place where you live. *casa* ❑ *She wasn't feeling well and she wanted to go home.* *No se sentía bien y quería irse a casa.* ❑ *I'll call you as soon as I get home.* *Te llamo en cuanto llegue a casa.* **4** N-COUNT A **home** is a building where people who cannot care for themselves live and are cared for. *hogar, asilo* ❑ *It's a home for elderly people.* *Es un asilo para ancianos.* **5** N-SING If you refer to the **home of** something, you mean the place where it began or where it is most typically found. *tierra* ❑ *Greece is the home of the Olympics.* *Grecia es la tierra de las Olimpiadas.* **6** ADV If you drive, or hammer something **home,** you explain it to people as forcefully as possible. *hacer entender* ❑ *I want to drive home the point that exercise is as important as eating healthily.* *Quiero hacerles entender que el ejercicio es tan importante como comer saludable.* **7** N-UNCOUNT When a sports team plays **at home,** they play a game on their own field, rather than on the opposing team's field. *en casa* ❑ *I scored in both games; we lost at home and won away.* *Anoté en ambos juegos, pero perdimos en casa y ganamos como visitantes.* ● **Home** is also an adjective. *en casa, local* ❑ *They see all home games together.* *Ven todos los juegos locales juntos.* **8** PHRASE If you feel **at home,** you feel comfortable in the place or situation that you are in. *en casa* ❑ *We soon felt at home.* *Pronto nos sentimos como en casa.*

**Thesaurus** *home* Ver también:

N. dwelling, house, residence **1**
birthplace **2**

**Word Partnership** Usar *home* con:

ADJ. **new** home **1** **2**
**close to** home **1** – **3**

V. **bring/take** ***someone/something*** home, **build a** home, **buy a** home, **call/phone** home, **come** home, **drive** home, **feel at** home, **fly** home, **get** home, **go** home, **head for** home, **leave** home, **return** home, **ride** home, **sit** ***at*** home, **stay** ***at*** home, **walk** home, **work at** home **1** – **3**

**home|body** /hoʊmbɒdi/ (**homebodies**) N-COUNT If you describe someone as a **homebody,** you mean that they enjoy being at home and spend most of their time there. *hogareño u hogareña* ❑ *We're both homebodies. We don't like going to parties.* *Ambos somos hogareños. No nos gusta ir a fiestas.*

**home field** (**home fields**) N-COUNT A sports team's **home field** is their own playing field, as opposed to that of other teams. *campo local*

**home front** N-SING If something is happening on **the home front,** it is happening within the country where you live. *frente interno* ❑ *I wanted to find out what was happening on the home front.* *Quería saber qué estaba pasando en el frente interno.*

**home|land** /hoʊmlænd/ (**homelands**) N-COUNT Your **homeland** is your native country. *patria* [mainly WRITTEN] ❑ *Many people are planning to return to their homeland.* *Muchas personas planean regresar a su patria.*

**home|less** /hoʊmlɪs/ ADJ **Homeless** people have nowhere to live. *sin hogar* ❑ *...the growing number of homeless families.* *...el creciente número de familias sin hogar.* ● **The homeless** are people who are homeless. *los que no tienen hogar* ❑ *...raising money for the homeless.* *...reunir dinero para los que no tienen hogar.* ● **home|less|ness** N-UNCOUNT *falta de vivienda* ❑ *The only way to solve homelessness is to build more homes.* *La única manera de resolver la falta de vivienda es construir más casas.*

**home|made** /hoʊmmeɪd/ ADJ Something that is **homemade** has been made in someone's home, rather than in a store or factory. *casero* ❑ *...homemade bread.* *...pan casero.*

**home|maker** /hoʊmmeɪkər/ (**homemakers**) **1** N-COUNT A **homemaker** is a woman who spends a lot of time taking care of her home and family. A **homemaker** usually does not have another job. *ama de casa* **2** → see also **housewife**

**homeo|sta|sis** /hoʊmiəsteɪsɪs/ N-UNCOUNT An organism or a system that is capable of **homeostasis** is able to regulate processes such as its temperature so that it can function normally when external conditions change. *homeostasis* [TECHNICAL] ● **homeo|stat|ic** /hoʊmiəstætɪk/ ADJ *homeostático* ❑ *...a homeostatic mechanism.* *...un mecanismo homeostático.*

**home plate** N-UNCOUNT In baseball, **home plate** is the piece of rubber or other material that the batter stands beside. It is the last of the four bases that a runner must touch in order to score a run. *base del bateador, home* ❑ *He broke his ankle in a fall at home plate.* *Se rompió el tobillo por una caída en home.*
→ see **baseball**

h

**home|room** /hoʊmrum, -rʊm/ (**homerooms**) N-VAR In a school, **homeroom** is the class or room where students in the same grade meet to get general information and where their homeroom teacher checks attendance. aula del curso ❑ *Twice a week in homeroom, teachers help students work through a math problem.* *Los maestros ayudan a los estudiantes a resolver problemas de matemáticas dos veces a la semana, en su salón de clase.*

**home run** (**home runs**) N-COUNT In baseball, a **home run** is a hit that allows the batter to run around all four bases and score a run. *jonrón* ❑ *Ruth hit sixty home runs that year.* *Ruth anotó sesenta jonrones ese año.*

**home school|ing** also **home-schooling** N-UNCOUNT **Home schooling** is the practice of educating your child at home rather than in a school. *educación en casa* ❑ *All fifty American states allow home schooling.* *En todo Estados Unidos se permite la educación en casa.*

H

**home|sick** /hoʊmsɪk/ ADJ If you are **homesick,** you feel unhappy because you are away from home and are missing your family and friends. *sentir nostalgia por*, *añorar* ❑ *He was homesick for his family.* *Añoraba a su familia.* ● **home|sick|ness** N-UNCOUNT *añoranza* ❑ *...feelings of homesickness.* *...sentimientos de añoranza.*

**home|work** /hoʊmwɜrk/ **1** N-UNCOUNT **Homework** is schoolwork that teachers give to students to do at home in the evening or on the weekend. *tarea* ❑ *Have you done your homework, Gemma?* *¿Hiciste la tarea, Gemma?* **2** N-UNCOUNT If you **do** your **homework,** you find out what you need to know in preparation for something. *prepararse*, *investigar* ❑ *Before you buy a new computer, do your homework on the best prices.* *Antes de comprar una nueva computadora, investiga cuáles son los mejores precios.*

**homey** /hoʊmi/ ADJ If you describe a room or house as **homey,** you like it because you feel comfortable and relaxed there. *acogedor* [INFORMAL] ❑ *...a large, homey dining room.* *...un comedor grande y acogedor.*

**homi|nid** /hɒmɪnɪm/ (**hominids**) N-COUNT **Hominids** are members of a group of animals that includes human beings and early ancestors of human beings. *homínido* [TECHNICAL]
→ see **evolution**

**homo|geneous mixture** (**homogeneous mixtures**) N-COUNT In chemistry, a **homogeneous mixture** is a mixture of two or more substances that have mixed completely, for example salt and water. *mezcla homogénea*

**homo|graph** /hɒməgræf/ (**homographs**) N-COUNT **Homographs** are words that are spelled the same but have different meanings and are sometimes pronounced differently. For example, "bow" (in the sense of a weapon) and "bow" (meaning the front of a ship) are homographs. *homógrafo* [TECHNICAL]

**ho|molo|gous** /həmɒləgəs/ ADJ **Homologous** chromosomes are pairs of chromosomes that contain the same genetic information but come from different parents. *homólogo* [TECHNICAL]

**homo|pho|bia** /hɒməfoʊbiə/ N-UNCOUNT **Homophobia** is a strong and unreasonable dislike of gay people, especially gay men. *homofobia* ● **ho|mo|pho|bic** /hɒməfoʊbɪk/ ADJ *homofóbico* ❑ *I'm not homophobic in any way.* *No soy homofóbico en ningún sentido.*

**homo|phone** /hɒməfoʊn/ (**homophones**) N-COUNT In linguistics, **homophones** are words with different meanings which are pronounced in the same way but are spelled differently. For example, "write" and "right" are homophones. *homófono*

**homo sa|pi|ens** /hoʊmoʊ sæpiɛnz/ N-UNCOUNT **Homo sapiens** is used to refer to modern human beings as a species, in contrast to other species of ape or animal, or earlier forms of human. *Homo sapiens* [TECHNICAL] ❑ *What distinguishes homo sapiens from every other living creature is the mind.* *La mente es lo que distingue al Homo sapiens de los demás seres vivos.*
→ see **evolution**

**homo|sex|ual** /hoʊmoʊsɛkʃuəl/ (**homosexuals**) ADJ Someone who is **homosexual** is sexually attracted to people of the same sex. *homosexual* ❑ *I knew from an early age that I was homosexual.* *Supe desde temprana edad que era homosexual.* ● **Homosexual** is also a noun. *homosexual* ❑ *The organization wants equality for homosexuals in South African society.* *La organización busca igualdad para los homosexuales en la sociedad sudafricana.* ● **homo|sex|ual|ity** /hoʊmoʊsɛkʃuælɪti/ N-UNCOUNT *homosexualidad* ❑ *...a place where they could openly discuss homosexuality.* *...un lugar donde se pueda hablar abiertamente sobre la homosexualidad.*

**hon|est** /ɒnɪst/ **1** ADJ If you describe someone as **honest,** you mean that they always tell the truth, and do not try to deceive people or break the law. *honesto* ❑ *She's honest and reliable.* *Ella es honesta y confiable.* ● **hon|est|ly** ADV *honestamente* ❑ *Lawrence acted fairly and honestly.* *Lawrence actuó limpia y honestamente.* **2** ADJ If you are **honest** in a particular situation, you tell the complete truth or give your sincere opinion, even if this is not very pleasant. *honesto* ❑ *I was honest about what I was doing.* *Fui honesto sobre lo que estaba haciendo.* ● **hon|est|ly** ADV *honestamente* ❑ *She answered the question honestly* *Respondió honestamente la pregunta.* **3** ADV You say **"honest"** before or after a statement to emphasize that you are telling the truth and that you want people to believe you. *te lo juro* [INFORMAL] ❑ *I'm not sure, honest.* *No estoy seguro, te lo juro.* ● **hon|est|ly** ADV *honestamente* ❑ *Honestly, I don't know anything about it.* *Honestamente, no sé nada al respecto.*

**Thesaurus** *honest* Ver también:
ADJ. fair, genuine, sincere, true, truthful, upright **1**
candid, frank, straight, truthful **2**

**hon|est|ly** /ɒnɪstli/ **1** ADV You use **honestly** to indicate that you are annoyed or impatient. *¡por favor!* [SPOKEN] ❑ *Honestly, Brian! I wish you weren't so rude to him.* *¡Por favor, Brian! Me gustaría que no fueras tan grosero con él.* **2** → see also **honest**

**hon|es|ty** /ɒnɪsti/ N-UNCOUNT **Honesty** is the quality of being honest. *honestidad* ❑ *I can answer you with complete honesty.* *Te puedo responder con toda honestidad.*

**hon|ey** /hʌni/ (**honeys**) **1** N-VAR **Honey** is a sweet, sticky, yellowish substance that is made by bees. *miel* **2** N-VOC You call someone **honey** as a sign of affection. *cariño* ❑ *Honey, I don't think that's a good idea. Cariño, no creo que sea una buena idea.*

**honey|moon** /hʌnimun/ (**honeymoons, honeymooning, honeymooned**) **1** N-COUNT A **honeymoon** is a vacation taken by a man and a woman who have just gotten married. *luna de miel* ❑ *We went to Florida on our honeymoon. Fuimos a Florida en nuestra luna de miel.* **2** V-I When a recently married couple **honeymoon** somewhere, they go there on their honeymoon. *ir de luna de miel* ❑ *They honeymooned in Venice. Se fueron de luna de miel a Venecia.*
→ see **wedding**

**hon|or** /ɒnər/ (**honors, honoring, honored**) **1** N-UNCOUNT **Honor** means doing what you believe to be right and being confident that you have done what is right. *honor* ❑ *He behaved with honor. Se comportó con honor.* **2** N-COUNT An **honor** is a special award that is given to someone, usually because they have done something good or because they are greatly respected. *honor* ❑ *He won many honors—among them an Oscar. Recibió muchos honores – entre ellos un Oscar.* **3** V-T If someone **is honored,** they are given public praise or an award for something they have done. *honrar* ❑ *Maradona was honored with an award presented by Argentina's soccer association. Maradona fue honrado con un premio otorgado por la asociación de fútbol de Argentina.* **4** N-SING If you describe doing or experiencing something as an **honor,** you mean you think it is something special and desirable. *honor* ❑ *...the honor of hosting the Olympic Games. ...el honor de ser la sede de los Juegos Olímpicos.* **5** V-T PASSIVE If you say that you **would be honored to** do something, you are saying very politely and formally that you would be pleased to do it. If you say that you **are honored by** something, you are saying that you are grateful for it and pleased about it. *sería un honor* ❑ *Ms. Payne said she was honored to accept the job. La señora Payne dijo que sería un honor aceptar el empleo.* **6** V-T If you **honor** an arrangement or promise, you do what you said you would do. *cumplir (con)* ❑ *I wanted to see if he was ready to honor the agreement. Quería ver si estaba listo para cumplir con el acuerdo.* **7** N-VOC Judges and mayors are sometimes called **your honor** or referred to as **his honor** or **her honor.** *su Señoría* ❑ *I say this, your honor, because I think it is important. Digo esto, su Señoría, porque creo que es importante.* **8** PHRASE If something is arranged **in honor of** a particular event, it is arranged in order to celebrate that event. *en honor de* ❑ *They're holding a dinner in honor of the president's visit. Ofrecen una cena para honrar la visita del presidente.*

**Thesaurus** *honor* Ver también:

| | |
|---|---|
| N. | award, distinction, recognition **2** |
| V. | commend, praise, recognize **3** |

**Word Partnership** Usar *honor* con:

| | |
|---|---|
| N. | **code of** honor, **sense of** honor **1**<br>honor **a ceasefire** **6** |
| ADJ. | **great/highest** honor **2** **4** |

**hon|or|able men|tion** (**honorable mentions**) N-VAR If something that you do in a competition is given an **honorable mention,** it receives special praise from the judges although it does not actually win a prize. *mención honorífica* ❑ *His designs received an honorable mention. Sus diseños recibieron una mención honorífica.*

**hon|or roll** (**honor rolls**) N-COUNT An **honor roll** is a list of the names of people who are admired or respected for something they have done, such as doing very well in a sport or in school. *cuadro de honor* ❑ *If you study hard, you can be on the honor roll. Si estudias mucho, puedes estar en el cuadro de honor.*

**hon|or sys|tem** N-SING If a service such as an arrangement for buying something is based on an **honor system,** people are trusted to use the service honestly and without cheating or lying. *atendiendo sólo a la palabra* ❑ *Readers can borrow or buy on the honor system. Los lectores pueden pedir prestados los libros o comprarlos, sin más requisitos.*

**hood** /hʊd/ (**hoods**) **1** N-COUNT A **hood** is a part of a coat or other garment which you can pull up to cover your head. *capucha* ❑ *She pushed back the hood of her coat. Se hizo para atrás la capucha del abrigo.* **2** N-COUNT The **hood** of a car is the metal cover over the engine at the front. *cofre* ❑ *He raised the hood of the truck. Levantó el cofre del camión.* **3** N-COUNT A **hood** is a covering on a vehicle or a piece of equipment, which is usually curved and can be removed. *cubierta*

**hoof** /hʊf, huf/ (**hoofs** or **hooves**) N-COUNT The **hooves** of an animal such as a horse are the hard lower parts of its feet. *casco, pezuña* ❑ *He heard the sound of horses' hooves. Escuchó el sonido de los cascos de los caballos.*
→ see **horse**

**hook** /hʊk/ (**hooks, hooking, hooked**) **1** N-COUNT A **hook** is a bent piece of metal or plastic that is used for catching or holding things, or for hanging things up. *gancho* ❑ *His jacket hung from a hook. Su chamarra colgaba de un gancho.* **2** V-T/V-I If you **hook** one thing **to** another, you attach it there using a hook. If something **hooks** somewhere, it can be hooked there. *enganchar* ❑ *Paul hooked his tractor to the car and pulled it to safety. Paul enganchó su tractor al auto y lo jaló a un lugar seguro.* **3** N-COUNT A **hook** is a short sharp blow with your fist that you make with your elbow bent. *gancho* ❑ *Lewis tried to stay away from Ruddock's big left hook. Lewis trató de librarse del gran gancho de izquierda de Ruddock.* **4** PHRASE If someone gets **off the hook** or is let **off the hook,** they manage to get out of the awkward or unpleasant situation that they are in. *librarse* [INFORMAL] ❑ *You're not getting off the hook that easily! ¡No te vas a librar tan fácilmente!* **5** PHRASE If you take a phone **off the hook,** you take the receiver off the part that it normally rests on, so that the phone will not ring. *descolgar* ❑ *I took my phone off the hook to try to get some sleep. Descolgué el teléfono para intentar dormir un rato.* **6** PHRASE If your phone **is ringing off the hook,** so many people are trying to telephone you that it is ringing constantly. *sonar constantemente* ❑ *After the earthquake, the phones at donation centers were ringing off the hook. Después del terremoto, los teléfonos en los centros de donación sonaban constantemente.*

▸ **hook up** **1** PHR-VERB If someone **hooks up with**

h

another person, they begin a sexual or romantic relationship with that person. You can also say that two people **hook up.** *engancharse, relacionarse, ligar(se)* [INFORMAL] ❑ *I hooked up with an intelligent, beautiful girl. Me ligué a una chica hermosa e inteligente.* ❑ *We haven't hooked up yet. Todavía no somos pareja.* **2** PHR-VERB If you **hook up with** someone, you meet them and spend time with them. You can also say that two people **hook up.** *relacionarse, hacer buenas migas, unirse* [INFORMAL] ❑ *He hooked up with other cyclists and joined a club. Se enganchó con otros ciclistas y se unió al club.* ❑ *This afternoon Jude and Chris hooked up. Esta tarde Jude y Chris se hicieron novios.* **3** PHR-VERB When someone **hooks up** a computer or other electronic machine, they connect it to other similar machines or to a central power supply. *conectar(se)* ❑ *...technicians who hook up computer systems and networks. ...técnicos que conectan sistemas y redes de cómputo.* ❑ *He hooked the machine up and we got it to work. Conectó la máquina y pudimos trabajar.*

H

**hoop|la** /hu̲plɑ/ N-UNCOUNT **Hoopla** is great fuss or excitement. *con bombo y platillo* [INFORMAL] ❑ *He didn't want a lot of hoopla. No quería bombo y platillo.*

**hooves** /hu̲vz/ **Hooves** is a plural of **hoof.** *plural de **hoof***

**hop** /hɒ̲p/ (**hops, hopping, hopped**) **1** V-I If you **hop,** you move along by jumping on one foot. *saltar con un pie, saltar en un pie, brincar de cojito* ❑ *I hopped down three steps. Bajé tres escalones brincando en un pie.* • **Hop** is also a noun. *salto con un pie* ❑ *"This is a great tune," he said, with a few little hops. —Me encanta esta canción —dijo saltando en un pie.* **2** V-I When birds and some small animals **hop,** they move along by jumping on both feet or all four feet together. *dar saltitos* ❑ *A small brown bird hopped in front of them. Un pajarito café dio saltitos frente a ellos.* • **Hop** is also a noun. *saltito* ❑ *The rabbit took four hops. El conejo dio cuatro saltitos.* **3** V-I If you **hop** somewhere, you move there quickly or suddenly. *ir rápidamente* [INFORMAL] ❑ *We hopped on the train. Nos subimos rápidamente al tren.* **4** N-COUNT A **hop** is a short, quick trip, usually by plane. *vuelo corto* [INFORMAL] ❑ *They went for a short hop in the plane. Tomaron un vuelo corto.*

**hope** /ho̲ʊp/ (**hopes, hoping, hoped**) **1** V-T/V-I If you **hope** that something is true, or if you **hope** for something, you want it to be true or to happen, and you usually believe that it is possible or likely. *esperar* ❑ *I hope that's OK. Espero que esté bien.* ❑ *He waited and looked as if he was hoping for an answer. No se fue, con la esperanza de que le dieran una respuesta.* **2** N-UNCOUNT **Hope** is a feeling of desire and expectation that things will go well in the future. *esperanza* ❑ *Many people have hope for genuine changes in the system. Muchas personas tienen la esperanza de que haya cambios genuinos en el sistema.* ❑ *Kevin hasn't given up hope of losing weight. Kevin no ha perdido la esperanza de perder peso.* **3** N-COUNT If someone wants something to happen, and considers it likely or possible, you can refer to their **hopes of** that thing, or to their **hope that** it will happen. *esperanza* ❑ *They have hopes of reaching the final. Tienen la esperanza de llegar a la final.* ❑ *My hope is that, in the future, I will move to Australia. Tengo la esperanza de irme algún día a Australia.* **4** PHRASE If you are in a difficult situation and do something and **hope for the best,** you hope that everything will happen in the way you want, although you know that it may not. *esperar que (alguien) tenga suerte* ❑ *Some companies are cutting costs and hoping for the best. Algunas compañías están reduciendo costos y esperando tener suerte.* **5** PHRASE If you do one thing **in the hope of** another thing happening, you do it because you think it might cause or help the other thing to happen, which is what you want. *con la esperanza de* ❑ *He was studying in the hope of going to college. Estaba estudiando con la esperanza de ir a la universidad.*

| **Thesaurus** | *hope* | Ver también: |
|---|---|---|
| V. | aspire, desire, dream, wish **1** | |
| N. | ambition, aspiration, desire, dream, wish **3** | |

| **Word Partnership** | Usar *hope* con: |
|---|---|
| ADJ. | **faint** hope, **false** hope, **little** hope **2** **3** |
| V. | **give *someone*** hope, **give up *all*** hope, **hold out** hope, **lose *all*** hope **2** **3** |
| N. | **glimmer of** hope **3** |

**hope|ful** /ho̲ʊpfəl/ **1** ADJ If you are **hopeful,** you are fairly confident that something that you want to happen will happen. *esperanzado, optimista* ❑ *I am hopeful that with help she will recover. Tengo la esperanza de que con ayuda se recuperará.* **2** ADJ If something such as a sign or event is **hopeful,** it makes you feel that what you want to happen will happen. *esperanzador* ❑ *He welcomed the news as a hopeful sign. Recibió la noticia como una señal esperanzadora.*

**hope|ful|ly** /ho̲ʊpfəli/ ADV You say **hopefully** when mentioning something that you hope will happen. Some careful speakers of English think that this use of **hopefully** is not correct, but it is very frequently used. *con suerte* ❑ *Hopefully, you won't have any more problems. Con suerte, no tendrás ningún problema.*

| **Word Link** | ***less*** **≈ without : end*less*, hope*less*, wire*less*** |
|---|---|

**hope|less** /ho̲ʊplɪs/ **1** ADJ If you feel **hopeless,** you feel very unhappy because there seems to be no possibility of a better situation or success. *desesperado, sin esperanzas* ❑ *He had not heard her cry before in this uncontrolled, hopeless way. Nunca la había oído llorar así, desesperadamente y sin control.* • **hope|less|ly** ADV *sin esperanzas* ❑ *I looked around hopelessly. Miré alrededor sin esperanzas.* • **hope|less|ness** N-UNCOUNT *desesperanza* ❑ *She had a feeling of hopelessness about the future. Tenía un sentimiento de desesperanza en cuanto al futuro.* **2** ADJ Someone or something that is **hopeless** is certain to fail or be unsuccessful. *no tener remedio* ❑ *I don't believe your situation is as hopeless as you think it is. No creo que tu situación sea tan desesperada como piensas.* **3** ADJ You use **hopeless** to emphasize how bad or inadequate something or someone is. *un desastre* ❑ *He's hopeless without her. Es un desastre sin ella.* • **hope|less|ly** ADV *sin esperanzas* ❑ *Harry was hopelessly lost. Harry estaba totalmente perdido.*

**ho|ri|zon** /həra̲ɪzᵊn/ (**horizons**) **1** N-SING The

horizon is the line in the far distance where the sky seems to meet the land or the sea. *horizonte* ❑ *A small boat appeared on the horizon. Un pequeño bote apareció en el horizonte.* **2** N-COUNT Your **horizons** are the limits of what you want to do or of what you are interested or involved in. *horizonte* ❑ *Children's horizons open up when they start school. Los niños abren sus horizontes cuando entran a la escuela.* **3** PHRASE If something is **on the horizon,** it is almost certainly going to happen or be done quite soon. *en puerta* ❑ *There is more bad news on the horizon. Hay más malas noticias en puerta.*

**hori|zon|tal** /hɒrɪzɒntᵊl/ ADJ Something that is **horizontal** is flat and level with the ground, rather than at an angle to it. *horizontal* ❑ *...vertical and horizontal lines. ...líneas verticales y horizontales.* • **Horizontal** is also a noun. *horizontal* ❑ *Do not raise your left arm above the horizontal. No rebases la horizontal con el brazo izquierdo.* • **hori|zon|tal|ly** ADV *horizontalmente* ❑ *The wind blew the snow almost horizontally. El viento soplaba y echaba la nieve casi horizontalmente.*
→ see **graph**

**hor|mone** /hɔrmoʊn/ (**hormones**) N-COUNT A **hormone** is a chemical, usually occurring naturally in your body, that makes an organ of your body do something. *hormona* ❑ *...female hormones. ...hormonas femeninas.* • **hor|mo|nal** /hɔrmoʊnᵊl/ ADJ *hormonal* ❑ *...a hormonal weight problem. ...un problema de peso por cuestiones hormonales.*
→ see **emotion**

**horn** /hɔrn/ (**horns**) **1** N-COUNT On a vehicle such as a car, the **horn** is the device that makes a loud noise, and is used as a signal or warning. *claxon* ❑ *He sounded the car horn. Tocó el claxon.* **2** N-COUNT The **horns** of an animal such as a cow or deer are the hard pointed things that grow from its head. *cuerno* ❑ *A mature cow has horns. Una vaca madura tiene cuernos.* **3** N-COUNT A **horn** is a musical instrument, which is part of the brass section in an orchestra or band. It is a long circular metal tube, wide at one end, which you play by blowing. *cuerno* ❑ *He started playing the horn when he was eight. Empezó a tocar el cuerno cuando tenía ocho años.* **4** N-COUNT A **horn** is a musical instrument consisting of a metal tube that is wide at one end and narrow at the other. *cuerno* ❑ *...a hunting horn. ...un cuerno de caza.* **5** N-COUNT In geology, a **horn** is a sharp peak that forms when the sides of a mountain are eroded. *pico piramidal* [TECHNICAL]

**hor|ri|ble** /hɔrɪbᵊl, hɒr-/ ADJ If you describe something or someone as **horrible,** you mean that they are very unpleasant. *horrible* [INFORMAL] ❑ *Her voice sounds horrible. Su voz suena horrible.* ❑ *The situation was a horrible mess. La situación era un desastre horrible.* • **hor|ri|bly** /hɔrɪbli, hɒr-/ ADV *horriblemente* ❑ *When trouble comes they behave selfishly and horribly. Cuando hay problemas actúan egoísta y horriblemente.* ❑ *Our plans have gone horribly wrong. Nuestros planes resultaron horriblemente mal.*

**hor|ri|fy** /hɔrɪfaɪ, hɒr-/ (**horrifies, horrifying, horrified**) V-T If someone **is horrified,** they feel shocked or disgusted. *horrorizar* ❑ *His family was horrified by the news. Su familia se horrorizó por la noticia.* • **hor|ri|fy|ing** ADJ *horroroso* ❑ *It was a horrifying sight. Era una vista horrorosa.*

**hor|ror** /hɔrər, hɒr-/ (**horrors**) **1** N-UNCOUNT **Horror** is a feeling of great shock, fear, and worry caused by something extremely unpleasant. *horror* ❑ *I felt sick with horror. El horror me dio náuseas.* **2** N-SING If you have a **horror of** something, you are afraid of it or dislike it very much. *horror a* ❑ *...his horror of death. ...le tiene horror a la muerte.* **3** N-COUNT You can refer to extremely unpleasant or frightening experiences as **horrors.** *horror* ❑ *...the horrors of war. ...los horrores de la guerra.* **4** ADJ A **horror** film or story is intended to be very frightening. *de horror*
→ see **genre**

**horse** /hɔrs/ (**horses**) N-COUNT A **horse** is a large animal which people can ride. *caballo* ❑ *...a man on a gray horse. ...un hombre en un caballo gris.*
→ see Picture Dictionary: **horse**

**Picture Dictionary** **horse**

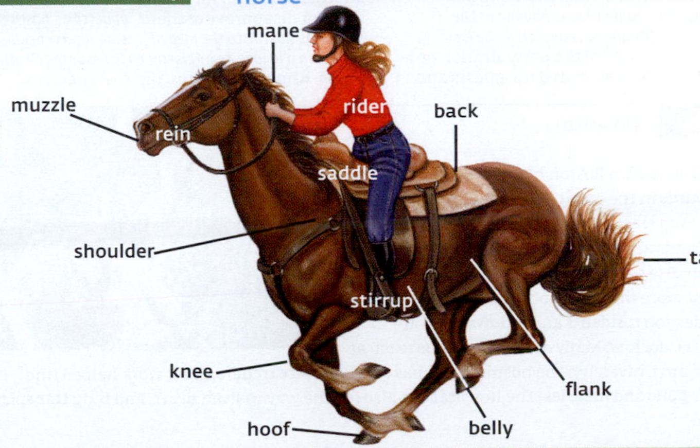


h

**horse|back rid|ing** N-UNCOUNT **Horseback riding** is the activity of riding a horse. *equitación, montar*

**hose** /hoʊz/ (**hoses, hosing, hosed**) **1** N-COUNT A **hose** is a long, flexible pipe made of rubber or plastic. Water is directed through a hose in order to do things such as put out fires, clean cars, or water gardens. *manguera* ❑ *You've left the garden hose on. Dejaste abierta la manguera del jardín.* **2** V-T If you **hose** something, you wash or water it using a hose. *regar* ❑ *We hose our gardens without thinking about how much water we use. Regamos nuestros jardines sin pensar en cuánta agua utilizamos.*
→ see **garden**

**hos|pice** /hɒspɪs/ (**hospices**) N-COUNT A **hospice** is a special hospital for people who are dying. *residencia para enfermos desahuciados* ❑ *...a hospice for cancer patients. ...una residencia para enfermos de cáncer desahuciados.*

H

**Word Link** *hosp, host ≈ guest : hospital, hospitality, hostage*

**hos|pi|tal** /hɒspɪtᵊl/ (**hospitals**) N-VAR A **hospital** is a place where people who are ill are cared for by nurses and doctors. *hospital* ❑ *...a children's hospital. ...un hospital infantil.*
→ see Word Web: **hospital**

**Word Partnership** Usar *hospital* con:

V. **admit** ***someone*** **to a** hospital, **bring/rush/take** ***someone*** **to a** hospital, **end up in a** hospital, **go to a** hospital, **visit** ***someone*** **in a** hospital

**hos|pi|tal|ity** /hɒspɪtælɪti/ N-UNCOUNT **Hospitality** is friendly, welcoming behavior toward guests or people you have just met. *hospitalidad* ❑ *Every visitor to Georgia notices the kindness and hospitality of the people. Todo visitante de Georgia nota la amabilidad y la hospitalidad de la gente.*

**host** /hoʊst/ (**hosts, hosting, hosted**) **1** N-COUNT The **host** at a party is the person who has invited the guests and provides the food, drink, or entertainment. *anfitrión o anfitriona* ❑ *Apart from my host, I didn't know anyone at the party. Además del anfitrión, no conocía a nadie en la fiesta.* **2** V-T If someone **hosts** a party, dinner, or other function, they have invited the guests and provide the food, drink, or entertainment. *ofrecer* ❑ *She hosted a party for 300 guests. Ofreció una fiesta para 300 invitados.* **3** N-COUNT A country, city, or organization that is the **host** of an event provides the facilities for that event to take place. *sede* ❑ *Atlanta was the host of the 1996 Olympic games. Atlanta fue la sede de los Juegos Olímpicos de 1996.* **4** V-T If a country, city, or organization **hosts** an event, they provide the facilities for the event to take place. *ser la sede de* ❑ *New Bedford hosts several festivals in the summer. New Bedford es la sede de varios festivales en verano.* **5** N-COUNT The **host** of a radio or television show is the person who introduces it and talks to the people who appear in it. *presentador o presentadora* ❑ *I am the host of a live radio program. Soy el presentador de un programa de radio en vivo.* **6** V-T The person who **hosts** a radio or television show introduces it and talks to the people who appear in it. *presentar* ❑ *She hosts a show on St. Petersburg Radio. Presenta un programa en la radio de St Petersburg.* **7** QUANT A **host of** things is a lot of them. *gran cantidad* ❑ *A host of problems delayed the opening of the new bridge. Una gran cantidad de problemas retrasó la inauguración del nuevo puente.* **8** N-COUNT The **host** of a parasite is the plant or animal which it lives on or inside and from which it gets its food. *huésped* [TECHNICAL]

**hos|tage** /hɒstɪdʒ/ (**hostages**) **1** N-COUNT A **hostage** is someone who has been captured by a person or organization and who may be killed or injured if people do not do what that person or organization demands. *rehén* ❑ *The two hostages were freed yesterday. Los dos rehenes fueron liberados ayer.* **2** PHRASE If someone **is taken hostage** or **is held hostage,** they are captured and kept as a hostage. *tomar a alguien como rehén* ❑ *He was taken hostage on his first trip to the country. Fue tomado como rehén en su primer viaje al país.*

**host|ess** /hoʊstɪs/ (**hostesses**) N-COUNT The **hostess** at a party is the woman who has invited the guests and provides the food, drink, or entertainment. *anfitriona* ❑ *The hostess introduced them. La anfitriona los presentó.*

**hos|tile** /hɒstᵊl/ **1** ADJ If you are **hostile to** another person or an idea, you disagree with them or disapprove of them. *opuesto a, hostil* ❑ *He was hostile to the idea of foreign intervention. Se oponía a la idea de intervenir en los asuntos de otra nación.* ● **hos|til|ity** /hɒstɪlɪti/ N-UNCOUNT

**Word Web** hospital

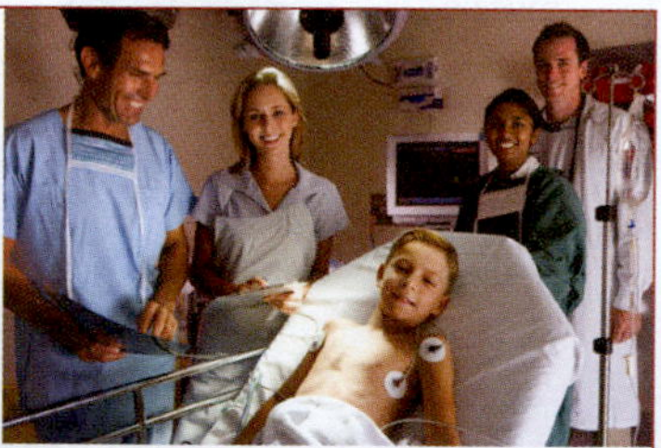

Children's **Hospital** in Boston has one of the best **pediatric wards** in the country. Its Advanced Fetal Care Center can even treat babies before they are born. The hospital records about 18,000 inpatient **admissions** every year. It also has over 150 outpatient programs and takes care of more than 300,000 **emergency cases**. The staff includes 700 **residents** and **fellows**, who are studying to be doctors. Many of its **physicians** teach at nearby Harvard University. The hospital also has excellent **researchers**. Their work helped find **vaccines** for **polio** and **measles**. The hospital has also led the way in liver, heart, and lung **transplants** in children.

*hostilidad* ❑ *There's a lot of hostility in the city. Hay gran hostilidad en la ciudad.* **2** ADJ Someone who is **hostile** is unfriendly and aggressive. *hostil* ❑ *He was angry, hostile and had a bad attitude toward his boss. Estaba enojado, hostil y tenía una mala actitud hacia su jefe.* ● **hos|til|ity** N-UNCOUNT *hostilidad* ❑ *He felt the hostility toward him from other players. Sintió la hostilidad de otros jugadores.* **3** ADJ **Hostile** situations and conditions make it difficult for you to achieve something. *hostil* ❑ *...some of the most hostile weather conditions in the world. ...algunas de las condiciones de clima más hostiles en el mundo.*

**Word Partnership** Usar *hostile* con:

N. hostile **attitude/feelings/intentions** **1**
hostile **act/action**, hostile **environment**, hostile **takeover** **3**
ADV. **increasingly** hostile **1** – **3**

**hos|til|ities** /hɒstɪlɪtiz/ N-PLURAL You can refer to fighting between two countries or groups who are at war as **hostilities.** *hostilidades* [FORMAL] ❑ *Hostilities broke out in many areas of the country. Las hostilidades estallaron en muchas áreas del país.*

**hot** /hɒt/ (**hotter, hottest**) **1** ADJ Something that is **hot** has a high temperature. *caliente* ❑ *When the oil is hot, add the sliced onion. Cuando se caliente el aceite, ponga la cebolla rebanada.* ❑ *He needed a hot bath and a good sleep. Necesitaba un baño caliente y una buena siesta.* **2** ADJ **Hot** is used to describe the weather or the air in a room or building when the temperature is high. *caluroso* ❑ *It was too hot even for a gentle walk. Hacía demasiado calor incluso para pasear sin prisas.* **3** ADJ If you are **hot,** you feel as if your body is at an unpleasantly high temperature. *tener calor* ❑ *I was too hot and tired to eat much. Tenía demasiado calor y sueño para comer mucho.* **4** ADJ You can say that food is **hot** when it has a strong, burning taste caused by spices. *picoso* ❑ *...hot curries. ...curries picosos.* **5** ADJ You can use **hot** to describe an issue or event that is very important, exciting, or popular at the present time. *popular, de actualidad* [INFORMAL] ❑ *...the hottest movie of the summer. ...la película más taquillera del verano.* ❑ *The magazine contains hot news about TV celebrities. La revista contiene noticias de actualidad sobre las celebridades de la TV.*
→ see **weather**

**Thesaurus** *hot* Ver también:

ADJ. sweltering; (*ant.*) chilly, cold **1**
spicy; (*ant.*) bland, mild **4**
cool, popular; (*ant.*) unpopular **5**

**hot but|ton** (**hot buttons**) N-COUNT A **hot button** is a subject or problem that people have very strong feelings about. *punto caliente* ❑ *Health care is a political hot button. La salud pública es un punto caliente en política.*

**hot dog** (**hot dogs**) N-COUNT A **hot dog** is a long bun with a hot sausage inside it. *hot dog*
→ see **bread**

**ho|tel** /hoʊtɛl/ (**hotels**) N-COUNT A **hotel** is a building where people stay, paying for their rooms and meals. *hotel*
→ see Word Web: **hotel**

**Word Partnership** Usar *hotel* con:

V. **check into a** hotel, **check out of a** hotel, **stay at a** hotel
N. hotel **guest**, hotel **reservation**, hotel **room**
ADJ. **luxury** hotel, **new** hotel

**hot spot** (**hot spots**) also **hotspot** N-COUNT In geology, **hot spots** are areas beneath the Earth's surface where lava rises and often forms volcanoes. *punto caliente* [TECHNICAL]

**hound** /haʊnd/ (**hounds, hounding, hounded**) **1** N-COUNT A **hound** is a type of dog that is often used for hunting or racing. *sabueso* ❑ *Rainey's main interest is hunting with hounds. El principal interés de Rainey es cazar con sabuesos.* **2** V-T If someone **hounds** you, they constantly disturb or speak to you in an annoying or upsetting way. *acosar* ❑ *People were always hounding him for advice. La gente siempre lo acosaba buscando su consejo.*

**hour** /aʊər/ (**hours**) **1** N-COUNT An **hour** is a period of sixty minutes. *hora* ❑ *They waited for about two hours. Esperaron cerca de dos horas.* ❑ *I only slept about half an hour last night. Sólo dormí cerca de media hora anoche.* **2** N-PLURAL You can refer to the period of time during which something happens or operates each day as the **hours** during which it happens or operates. *horas* ❑ *...the hours of darkness. ...las horas de oscuridad.* ❑ *Call us on this number during office hours. Llámenos a este número en horas de oficina.* **3** → see also **rush hour** **4** PHRASE If something happens **on the hour,** it happens every hour at, for

**Word Web** hotel

When making **reservations** at a **hotel**, most people request a **single** or a **double** room. Sometimes the **clerk** invites the person to **upgrade** to a **suite**. When arriving at the hotel, the first person to greet the **guest** is the **bellhop**. He will put the person's suitcases on a **luggage cart** and later deliver them to their room. The guest then goes to the **front desk** and **checks in**. The clerk often describes **amenities** such as a **fitness club** or **spa**. Most hotels provide **room service** for late night snacks. There is often a concierge to help arrange dinners and other entertainment outside of the hotel.

h

example, nine o'clock, ten o'clock, and so on. *a la hora en punto* ❑ *There are newscasts every hour on the hour.* *Hay noticieros cada hora, a la hora en punto.*
→ see **time**

**house** (**houses, housing, housed**)

The noun is pronounced /haʊs/. The verb is pronounced /haʊz/. The form **houses** is pronounced /haʊzɪz/.

1 N-COUNT A **house** is a building in which people live. *casa* ❑ *She has moved to a small house.* *Se mudó a una casa pequeña.* 2 N-SING You can refer to all the people who live together in a house as **the house.** *los de la casa* ❑ *He set his alarm clock for midnight, and it woke the whole house.* *Puso su despertador a la medianoche y despertó a todos los de la casa.* 3 N-COUNT **House** is used in the names of types of places where people go to eat and drink. *casa* ❑ *...a steak house.* *...restaurante de carnes.*
4 N-COUNT **House** is used in the names of types of companies, especially ones which publish books, lend money, or design clothes. *casa* ❑ *The clothes came from the world's top fashion houses.* *La ropa venía de las mejores casas de moda del mundo.*
5 N-COUNT You can refer to one of the two bodies of the U.S. Congress as a **House.** The House of Representatives is sometimes referred to as **the House.** *Cámara* ❑ *Some members of the House and Senate worked all day yesterday.* *Algunos miembros de la Cámara y el Senado trabajaron todo el día de ayer.* 6 V-T To **house** someone means to provide a house or apartment for them to live in. *alojar* ❑ *...homes that house up to nine people.* *...hogares que alojan hasta nueve personas.* 7 V-T A building or container that **houses** something is the place where it is located or from where it operates. *albergar* ❑ *The building houses a museum.* *El edificio alberga un museo.* 8 → see also **White House**
→ see Picture Dictionary: **house**

**Thesaurus** *house* Ver también:
N. dwelling, home, place, residence 1

**Word Partnership** Usar *house* con:
V. **break into a** house, **build a** house, **buy a** house, **find a** house, **live in a** house, **own a** house, **rent a** house, **sell a** house 1
ADJ. **empty** house, **expensive** house, **little** house, **new/old** house 1
N. house **prices, a room in a** house 1

**house|hold** /haʊshoʊld/ (**households**)
1 N-COUNT A **household** is all the people in a family or group who live together in a house. *casa, familia, personal* ❑ *...growing up in a large household.* *...crecer en una familia grande.* 2 N-SING The **household** is your home and everything that is connected with taking care of it. *hogar* ❑ *...household duties.* *...deberes del hogar.* 3 ADJ Someone or something that is a **household** name or word is very well known. *conocido* ❑ *Today, fashion designers are household names.* *Hoy, los diseñadores de modas son nombres conocidos.*

**house-sit** (**house-sits, house-sitting, house-sat**) V-I If someone **house-sits** for you, they stay at your house and look after it while you are away. *cuidar la casa* ❑ *Bill was house-sitting for me.* *Bill me estaba cuidando la casa.*

**house|wife** /haʊswaɪf/ (**housewives**)
1 N-COUNT A **housewife** is a woman who does not have a paid job, but instead takes care of her home and children. *ama de casa* ❑ *She was a housewife and mother of four children.* *Era ama de casa y madre de cuatro hijos.* 2 → see also **homemaker**

**house|work** /haʊswɜrk/ N-UNCOUNT **Housework** is the work such as cleaning, washing, and ironing that you do in your home. *tareas domésticas* ❑ *Men are doing more housework nowadays.* *En la actualidad los hombres están haciendo más tareas domésticas.*

**hous|ing** /haʊzɪŋ/ N-UNCOUNT **Housing** is the buildings that people live in. *viviendas* ❑ *...a housing shortage.* *...la escasez de viviendas.*

**hous|ing proj|ect** (**housing projects**) N-COUNT A **housing project** is a group of homes for poorer families which is funded and controlled by the

**Picture Dictionary** *house*

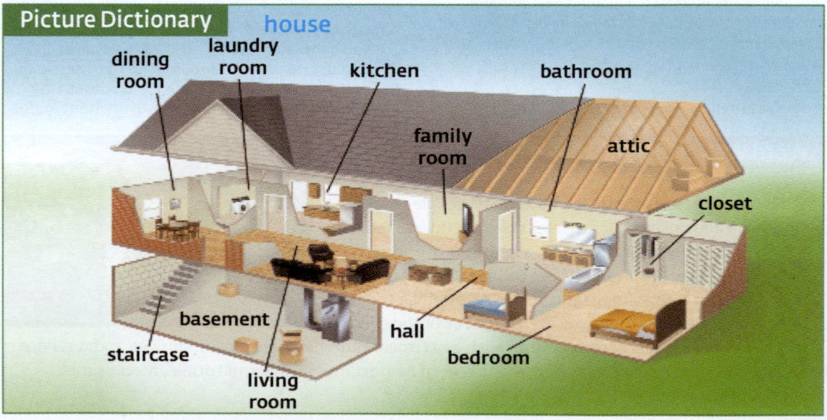

local government. *complejo de viviendas*

**hov|er** /hʌvər/ (**hovers, hovering, hovered**) **1** V-I To **hover** means to stay in the same position in the air without moving forward or backward. *mantenerse inmóvil en el aire* ❑ *Butterflies hovered above the flowers. Las mariposas se quedaban inmóviles en el aire, sobre las flores.* **2** V-I If you **hover,** you stay in one place and move slightly in a nervous way, for example because you cannot decide what to do. *vacilar* ❑ *Judith was hovering in the doorway. Judith dudaba en el portal.*

**how** /haʊ/

The conjunction is pronounced /haʊ/.

**1** ADV You use **how** to ask about the way in which something happens or is done. *cómo* ❑ *How do I put money into my account? ¿Cómo deposito dinero en mi cuenta?* ❑ *How do you manage to keep the place so neat? ¿Cómo logras mantener el lugar tan arreglado?* ● **How** is also a conjunction. *cómo* ❑ *I don't want to know how he died. No quiero saber cómo murió.* **2** ADV You use **how** to ask questions about the quantity or degree of something. *cuánto* ❑ *How much money do you have? ¿Cuánto dinero tienes?* ❑ *How many people work there? ¿Cuántas personas trabajan ahí?* ❑ *How long will you stay? ¿Cuánto tiempo te quedarás?* ❑ *How old is your son now? ¿Cuántos años tiene ahora tu hijo?* **3** ADV You use **how** when you are asking someone whether something was successful or enjoyable. *qué tal* ❑ *How was your trip to Orlando? ¿Qué tal estuvo tu viaje a Orlando?* ❑ *How did your meeting go? ¿Qué tal estuvo tu junta?* **4** ADV You use **how** to ask about someone's health or to find out their news. *cómo (estás)* ❑ *Hi! How are you doing? ¡Hola! ¿Cómo estás?* ❑ *How's Rosie? ¿Cómo está Rosie?* **5** ADV You use **how** to emphasize the degree to which something is true. *qué tan, qué tanto* ❑ *I didn't know how heavy the bag was. No sabía qué tan pesada estaba la bolsa.* **6** ADV You use **how** in expressions such as "**How about...**" or "**How would you like...**" when you are making an offer or a suggestion. *qué tal* ❑ *How about a cup of coffee? ¿Qué tal una taza de café?* **7** CONVENTION If you ask someone "**How about you?**" you are asking them what they think or want. *¿y tú?* ❑ *Well, I enjoyed that. How about you two? Bueno, yo lo disfruté, ¿y ustedes dos?*

**how|dy** /haʊdi/ CONVENTION "**Howdy**" is an informal way of saying "Hello." *hola* [DIALECT]

**how|ever** /haʊɛvər/ **1** ADV You use **however** when you are adding a comment which is surprising or which contrasts with what has just been said. *sin embargo* ❑ *This is not an easy decision. It is, however, a decision that we have to make. No es una decisión fácil, pero tenemos que tomarla.* **2** ADV You use **however** before an adjective or adverb to say that the degree or extent of something cannot change a situation. *sin importar* ❑ *You should try to achieve more, however well you have done before. Deberías intentar lograr más, no importa qué tan bien lo hayas hecho antes.* ❑ *However hard she tried, nothing seemed to work. No importa cuánto se esforzara, nada parecía funcionar.* **3** CONJ You use **however** when you want to say that it makes no difference how something is done. *como sea* ❑ *Wear your hair however you want. Lleva el cabello como quieras.* **4** ADV You can use **however** to ask in an emphatic way how something has happened which you are very surprised about. Some speakers of English think that this form is incorrect and prefer to use "how ever." *cómo* ❑ *However did you find this place in such bad weather? ¿Cómo encontraste este lugar con tan mal tiempo?*

**Usage** however

Be sure to punctuate sentences with *however* correctly. When *however* expresses contrast, it is followed by a comma (and preceded by a period or a semicolon): *Dae's parents sent her a new computer; however, she can't figure out how to set it up.* In other uses, *however* isn't followed by a comma: *I'm surprised—Dae can usually figure anything out, however difficult it seems to be.*

**howl** /haʊl/ (**howls, howling, howled**) **1** V-I If an animal such as a wolf or a dog **howls,** it makes a long, loud, crying sound. *aullar* ❑ *A dog suddenly howled. De pronto un perro aulló.* ● **Howl** is also a noun. *aullido* ❑ *The dog let out a long howl. El perro soltó un largo aullido.* **2** V-I If a person **howls,** they make a long, loud cry expressing pain, anger, or unhappiness. *dar alaridos* ❑ *He howled like a wounded animal. Dio alaridos como un animal herido.* ● **Howl** is also a noun. *alarido* ❑ *He gave a howl of pain. Dio un alarido de dolor.* **3** V-I When the wind **howls,** it blows hard and makes a loud noise. *aullar* ❑ *The wind howled all night. El viento aulló toda la noche.* **4** V-I If you **howl with** laughter, you laugh very loudly. *estallar de risa, carcajearse* ❑ *Joe and Tom howled with delight. Joe y Tom se atacaron de risa.* ● **Howl** is also a noun. *ataque de risa* ❑ *His stories caused howls of laughter. Sus historias provocaron carcajadas.*
→ see **laugh**

**how-to** ADJ A **how-to** book provides instructions on how to do or make a particular thing, especially something that you do or make as a hobby. *con información práctica* ❑ *...a simple how-to book that explains each step in taking a photo. ...un libro sencillo con información práctica que explica paso a paso cómo tomar una foto.*

**HQ** /eɪtʃkyu/ (**HQs**) N-VAR **HQ** is an abbreviation for **headquarters**. *oficina central* ❑ *The HQ is a large office in downtown Seattle. La oficina central es una oficina grande en el centro de Seattle.*

**hr** (**hrs**) **hr** is a written abbreviation for **hour**. *abreviatura de hour* ❑ *Cook the meat for another 1 hr 15 mins. Dejar la carne en la lumbre otra hora y cuarto.*

**H-R dia|gram** (**H-R diagrams**) also **HRD** N-COUNT An **H-R diagram** or **HRD** is the same as a **Hertzsprung-Russell diagram**. *diagrama H-R*

**HTML** /eɪtʃti ɛm ɛl/ N-UNCOUNT **HTML** is a system of codes for producing documents for the Internet. **HTML** is an abbreviation for "hypertext markup language." *html* [COMPUTING] ❑ *...HTML documents. ...documentos html.*

**hug** /hʌg/ (**hugs, hugging, hugged**) **1** V-T When you **hug** someone, you put your arms around them and hold them tightly, for example because you like them or are pleased to see them. *abrazar* ❑ *She hugged him and invited him to dinner the next day. Lo abrazó y lo invitó a cenar al día siguiente.* ● **Hug** is also a noun. *abrazo* ❑ *She leapt out of the car, and gave him a hug. Salió del auto de un salto y le dio un abrazo.* **2** V-T If you **hug** something, you hold it close to your body with your arms tightly around it. abrazar, llevar en los brazos ❑ *He walked toward them, hugging a large box.* *Caminó hacia ellos, cargando una gran caja.* **3** V-T Something that **hugs** the ground or a stretch of land or water stays very close to it. ir pegado a [WRITTEN] ❑ *The road hugs the coast for hundreds of miles.* *El camino va pegado a la costa por cientos de millas.*

**huge** /hyudʒ/ (**huger, hugest**) ADJ Something or someone that is **huge** is extremely large in size, amount or degree. enorme ❑ *...a little woman with huge black glasses.* *...una mujer pequeña con unos lentes negros enormes.* ❑ *I have a huge number of ties because I never throw them away.* *Tengo un número enorme de corbatas porque nunca me deshago de ellas.* ● **huge|ly** ADV enormemente, tremendamente ❑ *This hotel is hugely popular.* *Este hotel es tremendamente popular.*

H

**hull** /hʌl/ (**hulls**) N-COUNT The **hull** of a boat or tank is the main body of it. casco ❑ *The ship is new, with a steel hull.* *El barco es nuevo, tiene casco de acero.*

**hum** /hʌm/ (**hums, humming, hummed**) **1** V-I If something **hums**, it makes a low continuous noise. zumbar ❑ *The birds sang and the bees hummed.* *Los pájaros cantaban y las abejas zumbaban.* ● **Hum** is also a noun. zumbido ❑ *...the hum of traffic.* *...el zumbido del tráfico.* **2** V-T/V-I When you **hum**, or **hum** a tune, you sing a tune with your lips closed. tararear ❑ *She was humming a tune.* *Estaba tarareando una canción.*

**hu|man** /hyumən/ (**humans**) **1** ADJ **Human** means relating to or concerning people. humano ❑ *...the human body.* *...el cuerpo humano.* **2** N-COUNT You can refer to people as **humans**, especially when you are comparing them with animals or machines. humano ❑ *Like humans, cats and dogs can eat meat and plants.* *Como los humanos, los gatos y los perros pueden comer carne y plantas.*
→ see **evolution, primate**

**Word Partnership** Usar *human* con:

N. human **behavior**, human **body**, human **brain**, human **dignity**, human **life** **1**

**hu|man be|ing** (**human beings**) N-COUNT A **human being** is a man, woman, or child. ser humano ❑ *Can't we discuss this like sensible human beings?* *¿No podemos hablar de esto como seres humanos sensatos?*

**Hu|man Ge|nome Proj|ect** /hyumən dʒinoʊm prɒdʒɛkt/ N-SING **The Human Genome Project** is an international research program that is designed to provide a complete set of information about human DNA. Proyecto del Genoma Humano

**Word Link** *arian ≈ believing in, having : humanitarian, sectarian, vegetarian*

**hu|mani|tar|ian** /hyumænɪtɛəriən/ ADJ If a person or society has **humanitarian** ideas or behavior, they try to avoid making people suffer or they help people who are suffering. humanitario ❑ *The soldiers were there for humanitarian reasons, to give out food and medicines.* *Los soldados estaban ahí por razones humanitarias, para repartir comida y medicinas.*

**Word Link** *man ≈ human being : foreman, humanity, woman*

**hu|man|ity** /hyumænɪti/ (**humanities**) **1** N-UNCOUNT All the people in the world can be referred to as **humanity.** humanidad ❑ *...an act of humanity* *...un acto de humanidad* **2** N-UNCOUNT A person's **humanity** is their state of being a human being. humanidad [FORMAL] ❑ *He was in prison and it made him feel he had lost his humanity.* *Estando en prisión sentía que había perdido su calidad de humano.* **3** N-UNCOUNT **Humanity** is the quality of being kind, thoughtful, and sympathetic. humanidad ❑ *Her speech showed great humanity.* *Su discurso mostró una gran humanidad.* **4** N-PLURAL **The humanities** are the subjects such as history, philosophy, and literature which are concerned with human ideas and behavior. humanidades ❑ *The number of students studying the humanities has fallen by more than 50%.* *El número de estudiantes de humanidades ha disminuido más del 50 por ciento.*

**hu|man na|ture** N-UNCOUNT **Human nature** is the natural qualities and ways of behavior that most people have. naturaleza humana ❑ *It is human nature to worry.* *Preocuparse es parte de la naturaleza humana.*

**hu|man rights** N-PLURAL **Human rights** are basic rights which many societies believe that all people should have. derechos humanos ❑ *Both sides promised to respect human rights.* *Ambas partes prometieron respetar los derechos humanos.*

**hum|ble** /hʌmbəl/ (**humbler, humblest, humbles, humbling, humbled**) **1** ADJ A **humble** person is not proud and does not believe that they are better than other people. humilde, modesto ❑ *He gave a great performance, but he was very humble.* *Qué gran actuación, pero él se mostró muy modesto.* ● **hum|bly** ADV con humildad, humildemente ❑ *"I'm a lucky man, and I don't deserve it," he said humbly.* *—Soy un hombre con suerte, y no lo merezco —dijo con humildad.* **2** ADJ People with low social status are sometimes described as **humble.** humilde ❑ *He started his career as a humble fisherman.* *Empezó su carrera como un humilde pescador.* **3** ADJ A **humble** person, place, or thing is ordinary and not special in any way. humilde ❑ *This is our humble home.* *Este es nuestro humilde hogar.* **4** V-T If something or someone **humbles** you, they make you realize that you are not as important or good as you thought you were. dar una lección de humildad ❑ *Ted's words humbled me.* *Las palabras de Ted me dieron una lección de humildad.* ● **hum|bling** ADJ lección de humildad ❑ *It's humbling to know that so many people care.* *Es una lección de humildad saber que a tanta gente le importa.*

**hu|mid** /hyumɪd/ ADJ You use **humid** to describe an atmosphere or climate that is very damp, and usually very hot. húmedo ❑ *We can expect hot and humid conditions.* *Es de esperar que el clima esté caliente y húmedo.*
→ see **weather**

**hu|mid|ity** /hyumɪdɪti/ N-UNCOUNT **Humidity** is the amount of water in the air. humedad ❑ *The humidity is relatively low.* *La humedad es relativamente baja.*
→ see **forecast**

**Word Link** *ate ≈ causing to be : complicate, humiliate, motivate*

**hu|mili|ate** /hyumɪlieɪt/ (**humiliates, humiliating, humiliated**) V-T To **humiliate** someone means to say or do something which makes them feel ashamed or stupid. *humillar* ❑ *He enjoyed humiliating me. Disfrutaba humillándome.* • **hu|mili|at|ed** ADJ *humillado* ❑ *I have never felt so humiliated in my life. Nunca me había sentido tan humillado en mi vida.* • **hu|mili|at|ing** /hyumɪlieɪtɪŋ/ ADJ *humillante* ❑ *...a humiliating defeat. ...una derrota humillante.*

**Word Link** *ation ≈ state of : elevation, humiliation, observation*

**hu|milia|tion** /hyumɪlieɪʃᵊn/ (**humiliations**) **1** N-UNCOUNT **Humiliation** is the embarrassment and shame you feel when someone makes you appear stupid, or when you make a mistake in public. *humillación* ❑ *He faced the humiliation of forgetting his wife's birthday. Enfrentó la humillación de olvidar el cumpleaños de su esposa.* **2** N-COUNT A **humiliation** is an occasion or a situation in which you feel embarrassed and ashamed. *humillación* ❑ *The result is a humiliation for the president. El resultado es una humillación para el presidente.*

**hu|mil|ity** /hyumɪlɪti/ N-UNCOUNT Someone who has **humility** is not proud and does not believe they are better than other people. *humildad* ❑ *Bernal knows that there are other actors who are more talented than him, and this humility is unusual in Hollywood. Bernal sabe que hay otros actores con más talento que él, y esa humildad no es común en Hollywood.*

**hu|mor** /hyumər/ (**humors, humoring, humored**) **1** N-UNCOUNT You can refer to the amusing things that people say as their **humor**. *humor* ❑ *He told his story with humor. Contó su historia con humor.* **2** → see also **sense of humor** **3** N-UNCOUNT **Humor** is a quality in something that makes you laugh, for example in a situation, in someone's words or actions, or in a book or movie. *humor* ❑ *She felt sorry for the man but she couldn't ignore the humor of the situation. Sintió pena por el hombre, pero no pudo ignorar lo cómico de la situación.* **4** N-VAR If you are **in** a good **humor**, you feel cheerful and happy, and are pleasant to people. If you are **in** a bad **humor**, you feel bad tempered and unhappy, and are unpleasant to people. *de buen /mal humor* ❑ *She wondered why he was in such bad humor. Se preguntaba por qué él estaba de tan mal humor.* **5** V-T If you **humor** someone who is behaving strangely, you try to please them or pretend to agree with them, so that they will not become upset. *seguir la corriente* ❑ *I agreed, partly to humour him. Estuve de acuerdo, en parte para seguirle la corriente.*
→ see **laugh**

**Word Partnership** Usar *humor* con:

| | |
|---|---|
| N. | **brand of** humor, **sense of** humor **1** |
| ADJ. | **good** humor **4** |

**hu|mor|less** /hyumərlɪs/ ADJ Someone who is **humorless** is very serious about everything and does not find things amusing. *sin sentido del humor* ❑ *This man was as humorless as a dictionary. Este hombre tenía tan poco sentido del humor como un diccionario.*

**hu|mor|ous** /hyumərəs/ ADJ If someone or something is **humorous**, they are amusing, especially in a clever or witty way. *divertido, gracioso* ❑ *He was quite humorous, and I liked that. Era muy divertido, y eso me gustaba.* • **hu|mor|ous|ly** ADV *con humor* ❑ *He looked at me humorously. Me miró con humor.*

**hump** /hʌmp/ (**humps**) **1** N-COUNT A **hump** is a small hill or raised area. *montículo* ❑ *The path goes over a large hump by a tree. El sendero continúa sobre un gran montículo cerca de un árbol.* **2** N-COUNT A camel's **hump** is the large lump on its back. *joroba* ❑ *Camels store water in their hump. Los camellos almacenan agua en su joroba.*

**hump|back whale** /hʌmpbæk weɪl/ (**humpback whales**) N-COUNT A **humpback whale** is a large whale with long front fins. *ballena jorobada*

**hu|mus** /hyuməs/ N-UNCOUNT **Humus** is the part of soil which consists of dead plants that have begun to decay. *humus*

**hun|dred** /hʌndrɪd/ (**hundreds**)

> The plural form is **hundred** after a number, or after a word or expression referring to a number, such as "several" or "a few."

**1** NUM **A hundred** or **one hundred** is the number 100. *cien* ❑ *More than a hundred people were there. Había más de cien personas.* **2** QUANT You can use **hundreds** to mean an extremely large number of things or people. *cientos, centenares, montones* ❑ *He received hundreds of letters. Le mandaron montones de cartas.* • You can also use **hundreds** as a pronoun. *cientos* ❑ *Hundreds were killed in the fighting. En la batalla murieron centenares.* **3** PHRASE You can use **a hundred percent** or **one hundred percent** to emphasize that you agree completely with something or that it is completely right or wrong. *cien por ciento, totalmente, absolutamente* [INFORMAL] ❑ *I'm a hundred percent sure that's what I saw. Estoy completamente segura de que eso vi.*

**hun|dredth** /hʌndrɪdθ, -drɪtθ/ (**hundredths**) **1** ORD The **hundredth** item in a series is the one that you count as number one hundred. *centésimo* ❑ *The bank's hundredth anniversary is in December. En diciembre es el centésimo aniversario del banco.* **2** ORD A **hundredth of** something is one of a hundred equal parts of it. *centésimo, centésima parte* ❑ *Mitchell beat Lewis by three-hundredths of a second. Mitchell le ganó a Lewis por tres centésimas de segundo.*

**hung** /hʌŋ/ **1** **Hung** is the past tense and past participle of most of the senses of **hang**. *pasado y participio pasado de casi todos los sentidos de* ***hang*** **2** ADJ A **hung** jury is the situation that occurs when a jury is unable to reach a decision. *jurado en desacuerdo* ❑ *His trial ended in a hung jury. El juicio terminó con el jurado en desacuerdo.*

**hun|ger** /hʌŋgər/ (**hungers, hungering, hungered**) **1** N-UNCOUNT **Hunger** is the feeling of weakness or discomfort that you get when you need something to eat. *hambre* ❑ *Hunger is the body's signal that you need to eat. El hambre es la señal del organismo de que se necesita comer.* **2** N-UNCOUNT **Hunger** is a severe lack of food which causes suffering or death. hambre ❑ *Three hundred people in this town are dying of hunger every day.* *En este pueblo, todos los días mueren de hambre trescientas personas.* **3** N-SING If you have a **hunger for** something, you want or need it very much. *ansias, deseo* [WRITTEN] ❑ *Geffen has a hunger for success.* *Geffen anhela el éxito.* **4** V-I If you **hunger for** something or **hunger after** it, you want it very much. *desear, anhelar, ansiar* [FORMAL] ❑ *Jules hungered for adventure.* *Jules tenía ansias de aventura.*

**hun|gry** /hʌŋgri/ (**hungrier, hungriest**) **1** ADJ When you are **hungry,** you want some food. *estar hambriento, tener hambre* ❑ *My friend was hungry, so we drove to a shopping mall to get some food.* *Mi amigo tenía hambre, así que fuimos a un centro comercial a comprar algo de comer.* • **hun|gri|ly** /hʌŋgrɪli/ ADV *ávidamente* ❑ *James ate hungrily.* *James comió con avidez.* **2** PHRASE If people **go hungry,** they do not have enough food to eat. *pasar hambre* ❑ *Nobody went hungry, even for a day.* *Nadie pasó hambre, ni siquiera un día.* **3** ADJ If you are **hungry** for something, you want it very much. *ansioso, deseoso* [LITERARY] ❑ *He's hungry for power.* *Tiene sed de poder.* • **hun|gri|ly** ADV *ávidamente* ❑ *They were hungrily waiting for news.* *Esperaban ávidamente noticias.*

| **Thesaurus** | *hungry* | Ver también: |
|---|---|---|
| ADJ. | starving; (*ant.*) full **1** eager **3** | |

**hunker** /hʌŋkər/ (**hunkers, hunkering, hunkered**)

▸ **hunker down** **1** PHR-VERB If you **hunker down,** you bend your knees so that you are in a low position, balancing on your feet. *agacharse, ponerse en cuclillas* ❑ *Betty hunkered down on the floor.* *Betty se agachó al suelo.* ❑ *He hunkered down beside her.* *Él se puso en cuclillas a su lado.* **2** PHR-VERB If you say that someone **hunkers down,** you mean that they are trying to avoid doing things that will make them noticed or put them in danger. *agacharse* ❑ *They hunkered down until the situation became calmer.* *Se agacharon hasta que la situación se calmó.*

**hunt** /hʌnt/ (**hunts, hunting, hunted**) **1** V-I If you **hunt for** something or someone, you try to find them by searching carefully or thoroughly. *buscar* ❑ *He hunted for an apartment.* *Buscaba afanosamente un departamento.* • **Hunt** is also a noun. *búsqueda* ❑ *Several people helped in the hunt for the children.* *Varias personas colaboraron en la búsqueda de los niños.* • **hunt|ing** N-UNCOUNT *búsqueda* ❑ *Job hunting is not easy.* *No es fácil andar a la caza de un trabajo.* **2** V-T If you **hunt** a criminal or an enemy, you search for them in order to catch or harm them. *buscar* ❑ *Detectives have been hunting him for seven months.* *Los detectives lo han estado buscando durante siete meses.* • **Hunt** is also a noun. *búsqueda* ❑ *More than 70 police officers are involved in the hunt for her killer.* *Más de 70 policías están participando en la búsqueda del asesino de la mujer.* **3** V-T/V-I When people or animals **hunt,** or **hunt** something, they chase and kill wild animals for food or as a sport. *cazar* ❑ *I learned to hunt and fish when I was a child.* *De niño aprendí a cazar y pescar.* • **Hunt** is also a noun. *caza, cacería* ❑ *He went on a nineteen-day moose hunt.* *Fue a una cacería de alces que duró diecinueve días.* • **hunt|ing** N-UNCOUNT *caza, cacería* ❑ *He went deer hunting with his cousins.* *Fue a la caza de venados con sus primos.*

▸ **hunt down** PHR-VERB If you **hunt down** a criminal or an enemy, you find them after searching for them. *acorralar, capturar, dar caza* ❑ *They hunted down and killed one of the gang members.* *Acorralaron y mataron a uno de los miembros de la banda.*

**hunt|er** /hʌntər/ (**hunters**) **1** N-COUNT A **hunter** is a person who hunts wild animals for food or as a sport. *cazador, cazadora* ❑ *...deer hunters.* *...cazadores de venados.* **2** N-COUNT People who are searching for things of a particular kind are often referred to as **hunters.** *cazador, cazadora, buscador, buscadora* ❑ *...job-hunters.* *...los caza empleos.*

**hur|dle** /hɜrdᵊl/ (**hurdles**) **1** N-COUNT A **hurdle** is a problem, difficulty, or part of a process that may prevent you from achieving something. *obstáculo* ❑ *Writing a résumé is the first hurdle in a job search.* *El primer obstáculo de la búsqueda de un empleo es hacer el currículum.* **2** N-COUNT **Hurdles** is a race in which people have to jump over a number of obstacles that are also called hurdles. *vallas, carrera de obstáculos* ❑ *...the 400 meter hurdles.* *...los 400 metros con vallas.*

**hurl** /hɜrl/ (**hurls, hurling, hurled**) **1** V-T If you **hurl** something, you throw it violently and with a lot of force. *lanzar, arrojar* ❑ *Groups of boys hurled stones at police.* *Grupos de muchachos aventaban piedras a la policía.* ❑ *Simon caught the book and hurled it back.* *Simon cachó el libro y lo lanzó de regreso.* **2** V-T If you **hurl** abuse or insults **at** someone, you shout insults at them aggressively. *lanzar* ❑ *The driver of the other car hurled abuse at him.* *El conductor del otro auto lo insultó.*

**hur|ri|cane** /hɜrɪkeɪn, hʌr-/ (**hurricanes**) N-COUNT A **hurricane** is an extremely violent storm that begins over ocean water. *huracán*
→ see Word Web: **hurricane**
→ see **disaster**

**hur|ry** /hɜri, hʌr-/ (**hurries, hurrying, hurried**) **1** V-I If you **hurry** somewhere, you go there as quickly as you can. *apurarse, darse prisa* ❑ *Claire hurried along the road.* *Claire caminó de prisa por la calle.* **2** V-T If you **hurry to** do something, you start doing it as soon as you can, or try to do it quickly. *apurarse, apresurarse* ❑ *Latecomers hurried to find a seat.* *Los que llegaron tarde se apresuraron a encontrar un lugar.* **3** N-SING If you are **in a hurry to** do something, you need or want to do something quickly. If you do something **in a hurry,** you do it quickly. *prisa, premura* ❑ *Mike was in a hurry to get back to work.* *A Mike le urgía regresar al trabajo.* **4** V-T To **hurry** something or someone means to try to make something happen more quickly. *apresurar, apurar, apremiar* ❑ *Sorry to hurry you, John.* *Perdón por apurarte, John.* **5** V-T If you **hurry** someone to a place or into a situation, you try to make them go to that place or get into that situation quickly. *apresurar, apurar, apremiar* ❑ *I won't hurry you into a decision.* *No te voy a presionar para que tomes la decisión.*

▸ **hurry along** → see **hurry up 2**

▸ **hurry up** **1** PHR-VERB If you tell someone to

**Word Web** hurricane

A **hurricane** is a violent **storm** or tropical **cyclone** that develops in the Atlantic Ocean or Caribbean Sea. When a hurricane develops in the Pacific Ocean it is known as a typhoon. A hurricane begins as a **tropical depression**. It becomes a **tropical storm** when its winds reach 39 miles per hour (mph). When wind speeds reach 74 mph, a distinct **eye** forms in the center. Then the storm is officially a hurricane. It has heavy **rains** and very high **winds**. When a hurricane makes landfall or moves over cool water, it loses some of its power.

**hurry up,** you are telling them do something more quickly than they were doing. apurarse, apresurarse ❑ *Hurry up and get ready.* *Apúrate a estar listo.* **2** PHR-VERB If you **hurry** something **up** or **hurry** it **along,** you make it happen faster or sooner than it would otherwise have done. ir de prisa, apurarse, apresurarse ❑ *We could hurry the wedding plans along if you want to.* *Podemos apresurar los planes de la boda, si quieres.*

**Thesaurus** *hurry* Ver también:

V. run, rush; (*ant.*) relax, slow down **1**

**hurt** /hɜrt/ (**hurts, hurting, hurt**) **1** V-T If you **hurt yourself** or **hurt** a part of your body, you feel pain because you have injured yourself. lastimar(se), herir(se), hacer(se) daño ❑ *Yasin hurt himself while trying to escape.* *Yasin se lastimó tratando de escapar.* **2** V-I If a part of your body **hurts,** you feel pain there. doler, tener dolor ❑ *His arm hurt.* *Le dolía el brazo.* **3** ADJ If you are **hurt,** you have been injured. herido, lastimado ❑ *His friends asked him if he was hurt.* *Sus amigos le preguntaron si se había lastimado.* **4** V-T/V-I If you **hurt** someone, you cause them to feel pain. herir, lastimar, hacer daño ❑ *I didn't mean to hurt her.* *No era mi intención lastimarla.* ❑ *That hurts!* *¡Me duele!* **5** V-T/V-I If someone or something **hurts,** or **hurts** you, they say or do something that makes you unhappy. herir, hacer sufrir, lastimar ❑ *He is afraid of hurting Bessy's feelings.* *Tiene miedo de herir los sentimientos de Bessy.* ❑ *What hurts most is that I had to find out for myself.* *Lo que más me dolió es haber tenido que enterarme por mi cuenta.* **6** ADJ If you are **hurt,** you are upset because of something that someone has said or done. herido, ofendido ❑ *She was deeply hurt by what Smith said.* *Estaba muy dolida por lo que dijo Smith.* **7** V-T To **hurt** someone or something means to have a bad effect on them. dañar, estropear ❑ *The hot weather is hurting many businesses.* *El calor está perjudicando a muchos negocios.*

**Thesaurus** *hurt* Ver también:

V. harm, injure, wound **1** **4**
ache, smart, sting **2**
ADJ. injured, wounded **3**
saddened, upset **6**

**Word Partnership** Usar *hurt* con:

ADV. **badly/seriously** hurt **1** **3**
V. **get** hurt **3**
**feel** hurt **6**
N. hurt *someone's* **chances**, hurt **the economy**, hurt *someone's* **feelings**, hurt **sales** **7**

**hus|band** /hʌzbənd/ (**husbands**) N-COUNT A woman's **husband** is the man she is married to. esposo, marido ❑ *Eva married her husband in 1957.* *Eva se casó con su esposo en 1957.*
→ see **family, love**

**hut** /hʌt/ (**huts**) N-COUNT A **hut** is a small simple building, especially one made of wood, mud, grass, or stones. cabaña, choza, casucha

**hy|brid** /haɪbrɪd/ (**hybrids**) **1** N-COUNT A **hybrid** is an animal or plant that has been bred from two different species of animal or plant. híbrido [TECHNICAL] ❑ *These brightly colored hybrids are so lovely in the garden.* *Estos híbridos de brillantes colores lucen mucho en el jardín.* • **Hybrid** is also an adjective. híbrido ❑ *...the hybrid corn seed.* *...la semilla de maíz híbrido.* **2** N-COUNT A **hybrid** or a **hybrid car** is a car that can be powered by either gasoline or electricity. híbrido ❑ *Hybrid cars can go almost 600 miles between refueling.* *Los autos híbridos pueden recorrer casi 1,000 kilómetros sin rellenar el tanque.* **3** N-COUNT You can use **hybrid** to refer to anything that is a mixture of other things, especially two other things. híbrido ❑ *...a hybrid of solid and liquid fuel.* *...un híbrido de combustible sólido y líquido.* • **Hybrid** is also an adjective. híbrido ❑ *...a hybrid system.* *...un sistema híbrido.*
→ see **car**

**hydro|car|bon** /haɪdroʊkɑrbᵊn/ (**hydrocarbons**) N-COUNT A **hydrocarbon** is a chemical compound that is a mixture of hydrogen and carbon. hidrocarburo

**Word Link** *hydr ≈ water : carbohydrate, hydroelectric, hydroponics*

**hydro|elec|tric** /haɪdroʊɪlɛktrɪk/ also **hydro-electric** ADJ **Hydroelectric** means relating to or involving electricity made from the energy of running water. hidroeléctrico
→ see **dam, electricity, energy**

**hydro|elec|tric|ity** /haɪdroʊɪlɛktrɪsɪti/ N-UNCOUNT **Hydroelectricity** is electricity made from the energy of running water. hidroelectricidad

h

**hydro|gen** /haɪdrədʒ^ə^n/ N-UNCOUNT **Hydrogen** is a colorless gas that is the lightest and most common element in the universe. *hidrógeno*
→ see **sun**

**hydro|log|ic cy|cle** /haɪdrəlɒdʒɪk saɪk^ə^l/ N-SING *The* **hydrologic cycle** is the process by which the earth's water is circulated from the surface to the atmosphere through evaporation and back to the surface through rainfall. *ciclo hidrológico, ciclo del agua* [TECHNICAL]
→ see **water**

| Word Link | *hydr ≈ water : carbohydrate, hydroelectric, hydroponics* |
|---|---|

**hydro|pon|ics** /haɪdrəpɒnɪks/ N-UNCOUNT **Hydroponics** is a method of growing plants without the use of soil, by using water through which nutrients are pumped. *hidroponia, hidroponía* ❑ *Is hydroponics a cheaper way of producing food? ¿Es la hidroponia una forma más barata de producir alimentos?* ● **hydro|pon|ic** ADJ *hidropónico* ❑ *...hydroponic strawberries. ...fresas hidropónicas.* ● **hydro|poni|cal|ly** ADV *de manera hidropónica* ❑ *...hydroponically grown plants. ...plantas cultivadas de forma hidropónica.*
→ see **farm**

**hydro|power** /haɪdrəpaʊər/ N-UNCOUNT **Hydropower** is the use of energy from running water, especially in hydroelectricity. *energía hidroeléctrica, fuerza hidroeléctrica*

**hype** /haɪp/ (**hypes, hyping, hyped**) **1** N-UNCOUNT **Hype** is the use of a lot of publicity and advertising to make people interested in something such as a product. *promoción intensa* ❑ *There's been a lot of hype about her new book. Han hecho gran escándalo por su nuevo libro.* **2** V-T To **hype** a product means to advertise or praise it a lot. *promocionar intensamente* ❑ *We hyped the film to raise money. Hicimos una gran campaña publicitaria sobre la película para reunir dinero.* ● **Hype up** means the same as **hype**. *promocionar intensamente* ❑ *...hyping up famous people. ...grandes campañas publicitarias sobre personas famosas.*

**hyper|link** /haɪpərlɪŋk/ (**hyperlinks**) N-COUNT In an HTML document, a **hyperlink** is a link to another part of the document or to another document. Hyperlinks are shown as words with a line under them. *hipervínculo* [COMPUTING] ❑ *...Web pages full of hyperlinks. ...páginas web llenas de hipervínculos.*

**hyper|son|ic** /haɪpərsɒnɪk/ ADJ A **hypersonic** rocket or missile travels at five times the speed of sound or faster. *hipersónico* ❑ *...hypersonic aircraft. ...aeronave hipersónica.*

**hy|phen** /haɪf^ə^n/ (**hyphens**) N-COUNT A **hyphen** is the punctuation sign used to join words together to make a compound, as in "left-handed." *guión*
→ see **punctuation**

**hypo|thala|mus** /haɪpoʊθæləməs/ (**hypothalami**) N-COUNT The **hypothalamus** is the part of the brain that controls functions such as hunger and thirst. *hipotálamo* [MEDICAL]

**hy|poth|esis** /haɪpɒθɪsɪs/ (**hypotheses**) N-VAR A **hypothesis** is an idea which is suggested as a possible explanation for a particular situation or condition, but which has not yet been proved to be correct. *hipótesis* [FORMAL] ❑ *Work will now begin to test the hypothesis in rats. Ahora dará comienzo el trabajo de probar la hipótesis en ratas.*
→ see **hypothesis, science**

**hys|teri|cal** /hɪstɛrɪk^ə^l/ **1** ADJ Someone who is **hysterical** is in a state of uncontrolled excitement, anger, or panic. *histérico* ❑ *Calm down. Don't get hysterical. Cálmate, no te pongas histérica.* ● **hys|teri|cal|ly** /hɪstɛrɪkli/ ADV *de forma histérica* ❑ *The woman screamed hysterically. La mujer gritaba histéricamente.* **2** ADJ **Hysterical** laughter is loud and uncontrolled. *histérico, incontrolable* [INFORMAL] ❑ *He burst into hysterical laughter. Le dio un ataque de risa histérica.* ● **hys|teri|cal|ly** ADV *histéricamente, de forma incontrolable* ❑ *Everyone was laughing hysterically. A todos les dio un ataque de risa.* **3** ADJ If you describe something or someone as **hysterical**, you think that they are very funny. *muy gracioso* [INFORMAL] ❑ *His stories were hysterical. Sus relatos eran para morirse de risa.* ● **hys|teri|cal|ly** ADV *muy divertido* ❑ *His new play is hysterically funny. Su nueva obra es divertidísima.*

**hys|ter|ics** /hɪstɛrɪks/ **1** N-PLURAL If someone is **in hysterics** or is having **hysterics**, they are in a state of uncontrolled excitement, anger, or panic. *histeria, histerismo* [INFORMAL] ❑ *I'm sick of you having hysterics. Estoy harto de tu histerismo.* **2** N-PLURAL You can say that someone is **in hysterics** or is having **hysterics** when they are laughing loudly in an uncontrolled way. *ataque de risa* [INFORMAL] ❑ *We were all in hysterics when we saw his silly hat. Todos nos atacamos de risa al ver su ridículo sombrero.*

H

# Ii

**I** /aɪ/ PRON A speaker or writer uses **I** to refer to himself or herself. **I** is used as the subject of a verb. *yo* ❑ *Jim and I are getting married. Jim y yo vamos a casarnos.*

**ice** /aɪs/ (**ices**) **1** N-UNCOUNT **Ice** is frozen water. *hielo* ❑ *The ground was covered with ice. La tierra estaba cubierta de hielo.* **2** → see also **iced** **3** PHRASE If you **break the ice** at a party or meeting, or in a new situation, you say or do something to make people feel relaxed and comfortable. *romper el hielo* ❑ *Her friendly manner helped break the ice. Su amistosa forma de ser ayudó a romper el hielo.*
→ see **climate, crystal, glacier, precipitation, snow**

**Ice Age** N-PROPER **The Ice Age** was a period of time lasting many thousands of years, during which a lot of the earth's surface was covered with ice. *glaciación, edad de hielo, periodo glaciar*
→ see **glacier**

**ice|berg** /aɪsbɜrg/ (**icebergs**) N-COUNT An **iceberg** is a large tall mass of ice floating in the sea. *iceberg, témpano de hielo*

**ice cream** (**ice creams**) **1** N-VAR **Ice cream** is a very cold sweet food made from frozen cream or a substance like cream and has a flavor such as vanilla, chocolate, or strawberry. *helado, nieve* ❑ *I'll get you some ice cream. Te traigo un poco de helado.* **2** N-COUNT An **ice cream** is a portion of ice cream. *helado* ❑ *Do you want an ice cream? ¿Quieres un helado?*
→ see **dessert**

**iced** /aɪst/ ADJ An **iced** drink has been made very cold, often by putting ice in it. *helado* ❑ *...iced tea. ...té helado.*

**ice wa|ter** N-UNCOUNT **Ice water** is very cold water served as a drink. *agua fría, agua helada, agua con hielo*

**ice wedg|ing** /aɪs wɛdʒɪŋ/ N-UNCOUNT **Ice wedging** is a geological process in which rocks are broken because water freezes in gaps or cracks in the rocks. *gelifracción, crioclastia* [TECHNICAL]

**ici|cle** /aɪsɪkᵊl/ (**icicles**) N-COUNT An **icicle** is a long pointed piece of ice hanging down from a surface. *carámbano*
→ see **snow**

**icky** /ɪki/ **1** ADJ If you describe something as **icky**, you dislike it because it is very emotional or sentimental. *empalogoso* [INFORMAL] ❑ *...an icky photo of the loving couple. ...una empalagosa foto de la pareja de enamorados.* **2** ADJ If you describe a substance as **icky**, you mean that it is disgustingly sticky. *pegajoso* [INFORMAL] ❑ *She felt something icky on her fingers. Sintió algo pegajoso en los dedos.*

**ID** /aɪ di/ (**IDs**) N-VAR If you have **ID** or an **ID**, you are carrying a document such as an identity card or driver's license that tells who you are. *identificación, ID* ❑ *I had no ID so I couldn't prove that it was my car. No traía identificación, así que no pude demostrar que era mi coche.*

**I'd** /aɪd/ **1** **I'd** is the usual spoken form of "I had," especially when "had" is an auxiliary verb. *forma hablada usual de* ***I had*** ❑ *I was sure I'd seen her before. Yo estaba segura de que la había visto antes.* **2** **I'd** is the usual spoken form of "I would." *forma hablada usual de* ***I would*** ❑ *There are some questions I'd like to ask. Hay algunas preguntas que me gustaría hacerle.*

**ID card** (**ID cards**) N-COUNT An **ID card** is the same as an **identity card, identification card**. *identificación, credencial, carné de identidad, carnet de identidad, documento de identificación* ❑ *You have to carry an ID card. Tienes que llevar una identificación.*

**idea** /aɪdiə/ (**ideas**) **1** N-COUNT An **idea** is a plan, suggestion, or possible course of action. *idea* ❑ *I really like the idea of helping people. Realmente me gusta la idea de ayudar a la gente.* **2** N-COUNT An **idea** is an opinion or belief about what something is like or should be like. *opinión, idea, concepto, noción* ❑ *Everyone has different ideas about how to raise children. Todos tienen diferentes ideas sobre cómo criar a los niños.* **3** N-SING If you have an **idea** of something, you have some knowledge or information about it. *idea* ❑ *We had no idea what was happening. No teníamos idea de lo que estaba pasando.* **4** N-SING **The idea** of an action or activity is its aim or purpose. *idea, objetivo* ❑ *The idea is to have fun. La idea es divertirnos.*

**Word Partnership** Usar *idea* con:

ADJ. **bad** idea, **bright** idea, **brilliant** idea, **great** idea **1**
**crazy** idea, **different** idea, **dumb** idea, **interesting** idea, **new** idea, **original** idea **1** **2**
**the main** idea, **the whole** idea **1** **4**
V. **get an** idea, **have an** idea **1** **3**

**Word Link** *ide, ideo ≈ idea : ideal, idealistic, ideology*

**ideal** /aɪdiəl/ (**ideals**) **1** N-COUNT An **ideal** is a principle, idea, or standard that seems very good and worth trying to achieve. *ideal* ❑ *He stayed true to his ideals. Se mantuvo fiel a sus ideales.* **2** N-SING Your **ideal of** something is the person or thing that seems to you to be the best possible example of it. *ideal* ❑ *...the American ideal of equality. ...el ideal americano de igualdad.* **3** ADJ The **ideal** person or thing for a particular task or purpose is the best possible person or thing for it. *ideal* ❑ *You are the ideal person to do the job. Eres la persona ideal para el trabajo.* • **ideal|ly** ADV *idealmente, perfectamente, inmejorablemente* ❑ *They were a happy couple, ideally* matched. Eran una pareja feliz, hechos el uno para el otro. 4 ADJ An **ideal** society or world is the best possible one that you can imagine. *ideal* ❑ *We do not live in an ideal world. No vivimos en un mundo ideal.*

**Word Link** *ide, ideo ≈ idea : ideal, idealistic, ideology*

**ideal|is|tic** /aɪdiəlɪstɪk, aɪdiə-/ ADJ If you describe someone as **idealistic,** you mean that they have ideals, and base their behavior on these ideals, even though this may be impractical. *idealista* ❑ *Idealistic young people died for the cause. Jóvenes idealistas murieron por la causa.*

**ideal|ly** /aɪdiəli/ ADV If you say that **ideally** a particular thing should happen or be done, you mean that this is what you would like to happen or be done, but you know that it may not be possible or practical. *lo ideal, de preferencia, lo recomendable* ❑ *Ideally, you should drink every 10 – 15 minutes during exercise. Lo ideal es que durante el ejercicio bebas cada 10 a 15 minutos.*

I

**ideal ma|chine** (**ideal machines**) N-COUNT An **ideal machine** is a machine that is a hundred percent efficient but cannot exist in reality because of forces such as friction. *máquina ideal* [TECHNICAL]

**Word Link** *ident ≈ same : identical, identification, unidentified*

**iden|ti|cal** /aɪdɛntɪkᵊl/ ADJ Things that are **identical** are exactly the same. *idéntico, igual, mismo* ❑ *The houses were almost identical. Las casas eran casi idénticas.* ● **iden|ti|cal|ly** /aɪdɛntɪkli/ ADV *idénticamente* ❑ *...nine identically dressed dancers. ...nueve bailarinas vestidas idénticamente.*
→ see **clone**

**iden|ti|fi|ca|tion** /aɪdɛntɪfɪkeɪʃᵊn/ N-UNCOUNT If someone asks you for some **identification,** they want to see something such as a driver's license that proves who you are. *identificación* ❑ *The police asked him to show some identification. La policía le pidió que mostrara alguna identificación.*
→ see **jewelry**

**iden|ti|fi|ca|tion card** (**identification cards**) N-COUNT An **identification card** is the same as an **identity card.** The abbreviation **ID card** is also used. *identificación, credencial, carné de identidad, carnet de identidad*

**iden|ti|fy** /aɪdɛntɪfaɪ/ (**identifies, identifying, identified**) 1 V-T If you can **identify** someone or something, you are able to recognize them or distinguish them from others. *identificar, reconocer* ❑ *Now we have identified the problem, we must decide how to fix it. Ya que identificamos el problema, debemos decidir cómo solucionarlo.* ● **iden|ti|fi|ca|tion** /aɪdɛntɪfɪkeɪʃᵊn/ N-VAR (**identifications**) *identificación* ❑ *Early identification of the disease is important. Es importante la identificación oportuna de la enfermedad.* 2 V-T If you **identify** someone or something, you name them and say who or what they are. *identificar* ❑ *Police have already identified 10 murder suspects. La policía ya identificó a 10 sospechosos de asesinato.* ● **iden|ti|fi|ca|tion** N-VAR (**identifications**) *identificación, reconocimiento* ❑ *He made a formal identification of the body. Hizo la identificación formal del cuerpo.* 3 V-T If you **identify** something, you discover or notice its existence. *identificar, reconocer* ❑ *Scientists have identified drugs which are able to fight cancer. Los científicos han identificado fármacos para combatir el cáncer.* 4 V-T If a particular thing **identifies** someone or something, it makes them easy to recognize, by making them different in some way. *identificar* ❑ *She wore a nurse's hat to identify her. Llevaba una toca de enfermera para que la identificaran.* 5 V-T If you **identify** one person or thing **with** another, you think that they are closely associated or involved in some way. *identificarse* ❑ *He identified himself with modern Russian composers. Se identificaba con los compositores rusos modernos.* ● **iden|ti|fi|ca|tion** N-VAR *identificación* ❑ *...the identification of Spain with Catholicism. ...la identificación de España con el catolicismo.*

**iden|tity** /aɪdɛntɪti/ (**identities**) 1 N-COUNT Your **identity** is who you are. *identidad* ❑ *He uses the name Abu to hide his identity. Usa el nombre de Abu para ocultar su identidad.* 2 N-VAR The **identity** of a person or place is the characteristics that distinguish them from others. *identidad* ❑ *I wanted a sense of my own identity. Yo quería sentir mi propia identidad.*

**Word Partnership** Usar *identity* con:

| | |
|---|---|
| N. | identity **theft** 1<br>identity **crisis, sense of** identity 2 |
| ADJ. | **ethnic** identity, **national** identity, **personal** identity 2 |

**iden|tity card** (**identity cards**) N-COUNT An **identity card** is a card with a person's name, photograph, date of birth, and other information on it. In some countries, people are required to carry identity cards in order to prove who they are. The abbreviation **ID card** is also used. *carné de identidad, credencial de identificación, cédula de identidad, identificación, identificación personal*

**iden|tity cri|sis** (**identity crises**) N-COUNT If someone or something is having an **identity crisis,** it is not clear what kind of person or thing they are, or what kind of person or thing they would like to be. *crisis de identidad* ❑ *Halfway through his career he suffered an identity crisis. A mitad de la carrera sufrió una crisis de identidad.*

**iden|tity theft** N-UNCOUNT **Identity theft** is the crime of getting personal information about another person without their knowledge, for example, in order to gain access to their bank account. *robo de identidad* ❑ *...how to protect yourself from identity theft. ...cómo protegerse del robo de identidad.*

**ideol|ogy** /aɪdiɒlədʒi, ɪdi-/ (**ideologies**) N-VAR An **ideology** is a set of beliefs, especially the political beliefs on which people, parties, or countries base their actions. *ideología* ❑ *...capitalist ideology. ...ideología capitalista.* ● **ideo|logi|cal** /aɪdiəlɒdʒɪkᵊl, ɪdi-/ ADJ *ideológico* ❑ *Others left the party for ideological reasons. Otros salieron del partido por razones ideológicas.* ● **ideo|logi|cal|ly** /aɪdiəlɒdʒɪkli, ɪdi-/ ADV *ideológicamente* ❑ *He was ideologically opposed to the plan. Se oponía ideológicamente al plan.*

**idi|om** /ɪdiəm/ (**idioms**) N-COUNT An **idiom** is a group of words that have a different meaning when used together from the one they would have if you took the meaning of each word separately. For example, "to live from hand to mouth" is an idiom meaning to have very little food or money to live on. *modismo, expresión idiomática, locución idiomática* [TECHNICAL]

**idio|phone** /ɪdiəfoʊn/ (**idiophones**) N-COUNT An **idiophone** is any musical instrument that produces its sound by being hit or shaken. *idiófono*

**id|iot** /ɪdiət/ (**idiots**) N-COUNT If you call someone an **idiot**, you are showing that you think they are very stupid or have done something very stupid. *idiota, imbécil, necio* ❑ *You were an idiot to stay there. Qué idiota por quedarte.*

**idle** /aɪdᵊl/ **1** ADJ If people who were working are **idle**, they have no jobs or work. *inactivo, desocupado, sin trabajo* ❑ *4,000 workers have been idle for 12 weeks. 4,000 trabajadores han estado inactivos durante 12 semanas.* **2** ADJ If machines or factories are **idle**, they are not working or being used. *en paro, parado* ❑ *The machine is lying idle. La máquina está parada.* **3** ADJ If you say that someone is **idle**, you disapprove of them because they are not doing anything and you think they should be. *ocioso, perezoso, flojo, haragán* ❑ *...idle men who spent the day reading newspapers. ...hombres flojos que pasaban el día leyendo periódicos.* ● **idly** ADV *despreocupadamente, pasando el rato* ❑ *We were idly sitting around. Estábamos pasando el rato.* **4** ADJ **Idle** is used to describe something that you do for no particular reason. *ocioso, sin importancia, fútil* ❑ *We filled the time with idle talk. Ocupábamos el tiempo con pláticas sin importancia.* ● **idly** ADV *ociosamente, despreocupadamente* ❑ *We talked idly about baseball. Hablábamos despreocupadamente de béisbol.*

**if** /ɪf/

| |
|---|
| Often pronounced /ɪf/ at the beginning of the sentence. |

**1** CONJ You use **if** in conditional sentences to introduce the circumstances in which an event or situation might happen, might be happening, or might have happened. *si* ❑ *She gets very upset if I disagree with her. Se molesta mucho si no estoy de acuerdo con ella.* ❑ *You can go if you want. Puedes ir si quieres.* **2** CONJ You use **if** in indirect questions where the answer is either "yes" or "no." *si* ❑ *He asked if I wanted some water. Me preguntó si quería agua.* **3** CONJ You use **if** to suggest that something might be slightly different from what you are stating in the main part of the sentence, for example, that there might be slightly more or less of a particular quality. *si no es que, si es que, por no decir* ❑ *That standard is quite difficult, if not impossible, to achieve. Ese nivel es bastante difícil de cumplir, por no decir imposible.* ❑ *What one quality, if any, do you dislike about your partner? ¿Qué cualidad en particular te disgusta de tu pareja, si es que hay alguna?* **4** PHRASE You use **if only** with past tenses to introduce what you think is a fairly good reason for doing something, although you realize it may not be a very good one. *aunque* ❑ *She writes me once a month, if only to remind me that I haven't answered her last letter. Ella me escribe una vez al mes, aunque sea sólo para recordarme que no he contestado su última carta.* **5** PHRASE You use **if only** to express a wish or desire, especially one that cannot be fulfilled. *si* ❑ *If only you had told me that earlier. Me lo hubieras dicho antes., Cómo no me lo dijiste antes.* **6** PHRASE You use **as if** to describe something or someone by comparing them with another thing or person. *como si* ❑ *He made a movement with his hand, as if he were writing something. Hizo un movimiento con la mano, como si estuviera escribiendo algo.*
→ see also **whether**

**ig|ne|ous** /ɪgniəs/ ADJ In geology, **igneous** rocks are rocks that were once so hot that they were liquid. *ígneo* [TECHNICAL]
→ see **rock**

**ig|no|rant** /ɪgnərənt/ **1** ADJ If you describe someone as **ignorant**, you mean that they do not know things they should know. If someone is **ignorant of** a fact, they do not know it. *ignorante* ❑ *People don't want to appear ignorant. A la gente no le gusta parecer ignorante.* ● **ig|no|rance** /ɪgnərəns/ N-UNCOUNT *ignorancia, desconocimiento* ❑ *I feel embarrassed by my ignorance of world history. Me avergüenza mi desconocimiento de la historia del mundo.* **2** ADJ People are sometimes described as **ignorant** when they do something that is not polite or kind. *maleducado* ❑ *Some ignorant people called me names. Algunas personas maleducadas me insultaron.*
→ see also **stupid**

**ig|nore** /ɪgnɔr/ (**ignores, ignoring, ignored**) V-T If you **ignore** someone or something, you pay no attention to them. *ignorar, no hacer caso* ❑ *Her husband ignored her. Su esposo la ignoró.*

**ill** /ɪl/ (**ills**) **1** ADJ Someone who is **ill** is suffering from a disease or a health problem. *enfermo, malo, indispuesto* ❑ *He was seriously ill with pneumonia. Estaba gravemente enfermo de neumonía.* ● People who are ill in some way can be referred to as, for example, **the** mentally **ill**. *enfermo* ❑ *She visits the seriously ill. Visita a los enfermos graves.* **2** N-COUNT Difficulties and problems are sometimes referred to as **ills**. *mal, desgracia, infortunio* [FORMAL] ❑ *He's responsible for many of the country's ills. Es el responsable de muchas de las desgracias del país.* **3** ADJ You can use **ill** in front of some nouns to indicate that you are referring to something harmful or unpleasant. *negativo, adverso, malo* [FORMAL] ❑ *She brought ill luck into her family. Ella llevó la mala suerte a su familia.* **4** N-UNCOUNT **Ill** is evil or harm. *mal, desgracia* [LITERARY] ❑ *I don't wish them any ill. No les deseo ningún mal.* **5** to **speak ill of** someone → see **speak**

| Word Partnership | Usar *ill* con: |
|---|---|
| V. | **become** ill, **feel** ill, **look** ill **1** |
| ADV. | **critically** ill, **mentally** ill, **physically** ill, **seriously** ill, **terminally** ill, **very** ill **1** |

**I'll** /aɪl/ **I'll** is the usual spoken form of "I will" or "I shall." *forma hablada usual de **I will** o **I shall*** ❑ *I'll go there tomorrow. Mañana iré para allá.*

| Word Link | *il ≈ not : illegal, illegitimate, illiterate* |
|---|---|

**il|legal** /ɪligᵊl/ ADJ If something is **illegal**, the law says that it is not allowed. *ilegal, contra las reglas, contra la ley* ❑ *It is illegal for the governor to take gifts of more than $10 in value. Es ilegal que el gobernador acepte obsequios cuyo valor sea superior a 10 dólares.* ❑ *...illegal activities. ...actividades ilegales.* ● **il|legal|ly**

i

I

**Word Web** illness

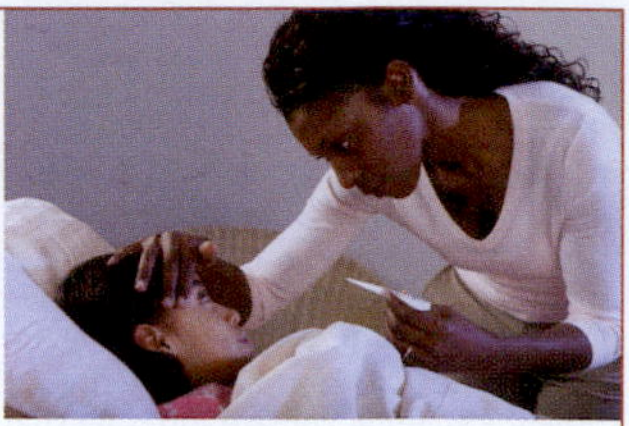

Most **infectious diseases** pass from person to person. However, some people have caught **viruses** from animals. During the 2002 SARS **epidemic**, doctors discovered that the disease came from birds. SARS caused more than 800 deaths in 32 countries. The disease had to be stopped quickly. Hospitals **quarantined** SARS patients so they would not make other people sick. Medical workers used **symptoms** such as **fever, chills**, and a **cough** to help **diagnose** the disease. **Treatment** was not easy. By the time the symptoms appeared, the disease had already caused a lot of damage. **Patients** received oxygen and **physical therapy** to help clear the lungs.

ADV *ilegalmente* ❑ *He was fined for parking illegally. Lo multaron por estacionarse en lugar prohibido.*

**Word Link** ***il*** *≈* ***not*** *:* ***illegal, illegitimate, illiterate***

**il|legiti|mate** /ɪlɪdʒɪtɪmɪt/ **1** ADJ A person who is **illegitimate** was born to parents who were not married to each other. *ilegítimo* ❑ *He learned that he had an illegitimate child. Se enteró de que tenía un hijo ilegítimo.* **2** ADJ **Illegitimate** is used to describe activities and institutions that are not allowed by law or are not acceptable according to standards of what is right. *ilegítimo* ❑ *He called the new government illegitimate. Se refirió al nuevo gobierno como ilegítimo.*

**Word Link** ***liter*** *≈* ***letter*** *:* ***illiterate, literally, literature***

**il|lit|er|ate** /ɪlɪtərɪt/ ADJ Someone who is **illiterate** does not know how to read or write. *analfabeto* ❑ *Many people are illiterate. Muchas personas son analfabetas.*

**ill|ness** /ɪlnɪs/ (**illnesses**) **1** N-UNCOUNT **Illness** is the fact or experience of being ill. *enfermedad* ❑ *He was away from school because of illness. No iba a la escuela por razones de salud.* **2** N-COUNT An **illness** is a particular disease such as measles or pneumonia. *enfermedad, mal, padecimiento* ❑ *She is recovering from a serious illness. Se está recuperando de una enfermedad grave.*

→ see Word Web: **illness**

**Thesaurus** *illness* Ver también:

N. ailment, disease, sickness; (*ant.*) health **1** **2**

**Word Partnership** Usar *illness* con:

N. **signs/symptoms of** ***an*** illness **1** **2**
ADJ. **mental** illness, **serious** illness, **terminal** illness **1** **2**
**long/short** illness, **mysterious** illness, **sudden** illness **2**
V. **suffer from** ***an*** illness, **treat** ***an*** illness **1** **2**
**diagnose an** illness, **have an** illness **2**

**il|lu|sion** /ɪluʒᵊn/ (**illusions**) **1** N-COUNT An **illusion** is something that appears to exist or be a particular thing but does not actually exist or is in reality something else. *ilusión, impresión* ❑ *Large windows can give the illusion of more space. Las ventanas grandes dan la impresión de más espacio.* **2** N-VAR An **illusion** is a false idea or belief. *ilusión, impresión* ❑ *He's under the illusion that money automatically makes people happy. Tiene la impresión de que el dinero hace automáticamente felices a las personas.*

**Word Partnership** Usar *illusion* con:

V. **create an** illusion, **give an** illusion **about/of/that** ***something*** **1** **2**
PREP. **be under an** illusion **2**

**il|lus|trate** /ɪləstreɪt/ (**illustrates, illustrating, illustrated**) **1** V-T If something **illustrates** a situation or point, it makes it clearer or shows that it exists or is right. *ilustrar, ejemplificar, mostrar, demostrar, aclarar* ❑ *Let me give an example to illustrate my point. Déjeme darle un ejemplo que demuestra mi punto.* ❑ *The accident illustrates how difficult it is to design a safe system. El accidente muestra lo difícil que es diseñar un sistema seguro.* ● **il|lus|tra|tion** /ɪləstreɪʃᵊn/ N-VAR (**illustrations**) *ejemplo* ❑ *This is a good illustration of how an essay should be written. Éste es un buen ejemplo de cómo se debe escribir un ensayo.* **2** V-T If you **illustrate** a book, you put pictures, photographs or diagrams into it. *ilustrar* ❑ *She illustrates children's books. Ilustra libros para niños.* ● **il|lus|tra|tion** N-VAR (**illustrations**) *ilustración* ❑ *...a book with beautiful illustrations. ...un libro con bellas ilustraciones.*

→ see **animation**

**IM** /aɪ ɛm/ (**IMs**) **1** N-VAR **IM** is an abbreviation for **instant messaging**. *abreviatura de instant message, mensaje instantáneo* ❑ *The device lets you chat via IM. El dispositivo te permite chatear por IM.* **2** N-VAR **IM** is an abbreviation for **instant message**. *mensaje instantáneo, IM*

**I'm** /aɪm/ **I'm** is the usual spoken form of "I am." *forma usual hablada de* ***I am*** ❑ *I'm sorry. Discúlpame*

**im|age** /ɪmɪdʒ/ (**images**) **1** N-COUNT If you have an **image** of something or someone, you have a picture or idea of them in your mind. *imagen, idea* ❑ *If you talk about California, people have an image of sunny blue skies. Cuando se habla de California, la gente se hace una idea de cielos azules y soleados.* **2** N-COUNT The **image** of a person, group, or organization is the way that they appear to other people. *imagen* ❑ *The government does not have a good public image. El gobierno no tiene una buena imagen pública.* **3** N-COUNT An **image** is a picture of someone or something. *imagen, representación* [FORMAL] ❑ *...photographic images of* children. ...imágenes fotográficas de niños. **4** N-COUNT An **image** is a poetic description of something. imagen [FORMAL] ❑ *He uses a lot of images from nature in his poetry.* *Usa muchas imágenes de la naturaleza en su poesía.*

→ see **eye, photography, telescope, television**

**Word Partnership** Usar *image* con:

N. **body** image, **self-**image **1** **2**
image **on a screen** **3**
ADJ. **corporate** image, **negative/positive** image, **public** image **2**
V. **project an** image **2** **3**
**display an** image **3**

**im|agi|nary** /ɪmædʒɪneri/ ADJ An **imaginary** person, place, or thing exists only in your mind or in a story, and not in real life. imaginario ❑ *Lots of children have imaginary friends.* *Muchos niños tienen amigos imaginarios.*

→ see **fantasy**

**im|agi|na|tion** /ɪmædʒɪneɪʃən/ (**imaginations**) N-VAR Your **imagination** is the ability that you have to form pictures or ideas in your mind of new, exciting, or imaginary things. imaginación, fantasía ❑ *Children have lively imaginations.* *Las fantasías de los niños son muy vívidas.*

→ see **fantasy**

**Word Partnership** Usar *imagination* con:

ADJ. **active** imagination, **lively** imagination, **vivid** imagination
PREP. **beyond** *(someone's)* imagination
N. **lack of** imagination

**im|agi|na|tive** /ɪmædʒɪnətɪv/ ADJ If you describe someone or their ideas as **imaginative**, you are praising them because they are easily able to think of or create new or exciting things. imaginativo ❑ *...an imaginative writer.* *...un escritor imaginativo.* ● **im|agi|na|tive|ly** ADV imaginativamente, con imaginación, de manera imaginativa ❑ *The hotel is decorated imaginatively.* *La decoración del hotel es imaginativa.*

**im|ag|ine** /ɪmædʒɪn/ (**imagines, imagining, imagined**) **1** V-T If you **imagine** something, you think about it and your mind forms a picture or idea of it. imaginar(se) ❑ *He could not imagine a more peaceful scene.* *No pudo imaginarse una escena más tranquila.* **2** V-T If you **imagine** that something is true, you think that it is true. imaginar, suponer ❑ *I imagine that you're hungry.* *Supongo que tienen hambre.* **3** V-T If you **imagine** something, you think that you have seen, heard, or experienced that thing, although actually you have not. imaginar, imaginarse, figurarse ❑ *I realize that I imagined the whole thing.* *Me di cuenta de que todo eran figuraciones mías.*

**Thesaurus** *imagine* Ver también:

V. picture, see, visualize **1**
believe, guess, think **2**

**Word Partnership** Usar *imagine* con:

V. **can/can't/could/couldn't** imagine *something*, **try to** imagine **1** **2**
ADJ. **difficult/easy/hard/impossible to** imagine **1** **2**

**Word Link** *im ≈ not : imbalance, immature, impossible*

**im|bal|ance** /ɪmbæləns/ (**imbalances**) N-VAR If there is an **imbalance** in a situation, the things involved are not the same size, or are not the right size in relation to each other. desequilibrio, desproporción ❑ *There is an imbalance between people and water resources in the east of the country.* *Hay un desequilibrio entre el número de habitantes y la cantidad de agua disponible en la parte este del país.*

**imi|tate** /ɪmɪteɪt/ (**imitates, imitating, imitated**) **1** V-T If you **imitate** someone, you copy what they do or produce. imitar, copiar, remedar ❑ *Birds are starting to imitate the ringtones of cellphones.* *Los pájaros están empezando a imitar el sonido de los teléfonos celulares.* ● **imi|ta|tor** /ɪmɪteɪtər/ N-COUNT (**imitators**) imitador ❑ *He has had many imitators but no equals.* *Tiene muchos imitadores, pero ninguno lo iguala.* **2** V-T If you **imitate** a person or animal, you copy the way they speak or behave, usually because you are trying to be funny. imitar, copiar, remedar ❑ *I didn't like the way he imitated my voice.* *No me gustaba cómo imitaba mi voz.*

**im|ma|ture** /ɪmətʃʊər, -tʊər/ **1** ADJ Something or someone that is **immature** is not yet completely grown or fully developed. inmaduro ❑ *She is emotionally immature.* *Es emocionalmente inmadura.* **2** ADJ If you describe someone as **immature**, you are being critical of them because they do not behave in a sensible or responsible way. inmaduro ❑ *You're being silly and immature.* *Te estás comportando como un tonto y un inmaduro.*

**Thesaurus** *immature* Ver también:

ADJ. underdeveloped, unripe **1**
childish, foolish, juvenile **2**

**im|medi|ate** /ɪmidiɪt/ **1** ADJ An **immediate** result, action, or reaction happens or is done without any delay. inmediato ❑ *The changes in the law had an immediate effect.* *Los cambios en las leyes tienen efecto inmediato.* ● **im|medi|ate|ly** ADV inmediatamente, de inmediato ❑ *He immediately fell to the floor.* *De inmediato cayó al piso.* **2** ADJ **Immediate** needs and concerns must be dealt with quickly. inmediato, urgente ❑ *The immediate problem is that people have no clean water.* *El problema urgente es que la gente carece de agua limpia.* **3** ADJ The **immediate** person or thing comes just before or just after another person or thing in a sequence. inmediato ❑ *Her immediate boss refused to help, so she went to his boss.* *Su jefe inmediato se negó a ayudar, así que ella recurrió al jefe de él.* ● **im|medi|ate|ly** ADV inmediatamente ❑ *...the weeks immediately before the war.* *...las semanas inmediatamente anteriores a la guerra.* **4** ADJ You use **immediate** to describe an area or position that is next to or very near a particular place or person. inmediato ❑ *People had* to leave the immediate area. *La gente tuvo que desalojar el área inmediata.* **5** ADJ Your **immediate** family are your parents, children, brothers, and sisters. *inmediato, cercano* ❑ *Only their immediate family came to the wedding. Sólo sus familiares cercanos vinieron a la boda.*

**Word Partnership** Usar *immediate* con:

N. immediate **action**, immediate **plans**, immediate **reaction**, immediate **response**, immediate **results** **1**
immediate **future** **3**
immediate **surroundings** **4**
immediate **family** **5**

**im|medi|ate|ly** /ɪmidiɪtli/ **1** ADV If something is **immediately** obvious, it can be seen or understood without any delay. *inmediatamente, de inmediato* ❑ *The cause of the accident was not immediately clear. La causa del accidente no se hizo obvia de inmediato.* **2** ADV **Immediately** is used to emphasize that something comes next, or is next to something else. *inmediatamente* ❑ *The speeches began immediately after dinner. Los discursos empezaron inmediatamente después de la cena.*

I

**im|mense** /ɪmɛns/ ADJ If you describe something as **immense,** you mean that it is extremely large or great. *inmenso, enorme, grandísimo* ❑ *...an immense cloud of smoke. ...una inmensa nube de humo.*

**im|merse** /ɪmɜrs/ (**immerses, immersing, immersed**) **1** V-T If you **immerse** yourself in something that you are doing, you become completely involved in it. *sumergirse, enfrascarse* ❑ *She immersed herself in her studies. Ella se enfrascó en sus estudios.* • **im|mersed** ADJ *inmerso, enfrascado, sumergido* ❑ *He was immersed in his work. Estaba inmerso en su trabajo.* **2** V-T If you **immerse** something in a liquid, you put it into the liquid so that it is completely covered. *sumergir* ❑ *His whole body was immersed in the water. Todo su cuerpo estaba sumergido en el agua.*

**Word Link** ***ant*** ***≈ one who does, has : defendant, immigrant, occupant***

**Word Link** ***migr*** ***≈ moving, changing : emigrate, immigrant, migrant***

**im|mi|grant** /ɪmɪgrənt/ (**immigrants**) N-COUNT An **immigrant** is a person who has come to live in a country from some other country. Compare **emigrant.** *inmigrante* ❑ *...immigrant workers. ...trabajadores inmigrantes.*
→ see **culture**

**im|mi|gra|tion** /ɪmɪgreɪʃən/ **1** N-UNCOUNT **Immigration** is the fact or process of people coming into a country in order to live and work there. *inmigración* ❑ *...laws controlling immigration. ...leyes para controlar la inmigración.* **2** N-UNCOUNT **Immigration** or **immigration control** is the place at a port, airport, or international border where officials check the passports of people who wish to come into the country. *migración, inmigración* ❑ *You have to go through immigration and customs when you enter the country. Al llegar al país, tienen que pasar por migración y por la aduana.*

**im|mi|nent** /ɪmɪnənt/ ADJ If something is **imminent,** it is almost certain to happen very soon. *inminente* ❑ *We are not in any imminent danger. No estamos ante un peligro inminente.*

**im|mor|al** /ɪmɔrəl/ ADJ If you describe someone or their behavior as **immoral,** you believe that their behavior is morally wrong. *inmoral* ❑ *Some people think that earning a lot of money is immoral. Algunas personas piensan que ganar mucho dinero es inmoral.*

**im|mune** /ɪmyun/ **1** ADJ If you are **immune to** a particular disease, you cannot be affected by it. *inmune* ❑ *Some people are naturally immune to measles. Algunas personas son inmunes al sarampión por naturaleza.* • **im|mun|ity** /ɪmyunɪti/ N-UNCOUNT *inmunidad* ❑ *Immunity to the common cold increases with age. La inmunidad ante el resfriado común se incrementa con la edad.* **2** ADJ If you are **immune to** something that happens or is done, you are not affected by it. *inmune* ❑ *She is immune to criticism. Es inmune a las críticas.* **3** ADJ Someone or something that is **immune from** a particular process or situation is able to avoid it. *inmune* ❑ *Nobody's life is immune from pain. Mientras esté vivo, nadie es inmune al dolor.* • **im|mun|ity** N-UNCOUNT *inmunidad* ❑ *His official status gave him immunity from inspection at the airport. Su estatus oficial le concedía inmunidad ante la inspección en el aereopuerto.*

**im|mune sys|tem** (**immune systems**) N-COUNT Your **immune system** consists of all the organs and processes in your body that protect you from illness and infection. *sistema inmunitario, sistema inmune* ❑ *The disease affects the immune system. La enfermedad afecta al sistema imunitario.*

**im|mun|ize** /ɪmyənaɪz/ (**immunizes, immunizing, immunized**) V-T If people or animals **are immunized,** they are made immune to a particular disease, often by being given an injection. *vacunar, inmunizar* ❑ *Every student is immunized against hepatitis B. Se vacuna contra la hepatitis B a todos los estudiantes.* • **im|mun|iza|tion** /ɪmyənɪzeɪʃən/ N-VAR (**immunizations**) *inmunización, vacunación* ❑ *...immunization against childhood diseases. ...vacunación contra las enfermedades de la infancia.*

**im|mu|no|de|fi|cien|cy** /ɪmyənoʊdɪfɪʃənsi/ N-UNCOUNT **Immunodeficiency** is a weakness in a person's immune system or the failure of a person's immune system. *inmunodeficiencia* [MEDICAL] ❑ *...a type of immunodeficiency disease. ...es algún tipo de inmunodeficiencia.*

**im|pact** (**impacts, impacting, impacted**)

The noun is pronounced /ɪmpækt/. The verb is pronounced /ɪmpækt/ or /ɪmpækt/.

**1** N-COUNT If something has an **impact on** a situation, process, or person, it has a strong effect on them. *impacto, repercusión, efecto* ❑ *The experience had a strong impact on him. La experiencia produjo un gran efecto en él.* **2** N-VAR An **impact** is the action of one object hitting another, or the force with which one object hits another. *impacto, choque, colisión* ❑ *The impact of the crash threw the truck off the roadway. El impacto sacó al camión de la carretera.* **3** V-T To **impact** a situation, process, or person means to affect them. *impactar, afectar* ❑ *The new law has impacted small businesses. La nueva ley afectó a los negocios pequeños.*
→ see **crash**

**Word Partnership** Usar *impact* con:

ADJ. **historical** impact, **important** impact 1
V. **have an** impact, **make an** impact 1
**die on** impact 2
PREP. **on** impact 2

**im|pa|tient** /ɪmpeɪʃᵊnt/ 1 ADJ If you are **impatient,** you are annoyed because you have to wait too long for something. impaciente, intolerante ❑ *People are impatient for the war to be over.* *El pueblo está impaciente por que la guerra termine.* • **im|pa|tient|ly** ADV impacientemente, con impaciencia ❑ *She waited impatiently for the mail to arrive.* *Esperaba con impaciencia que llegara el correo.* • **im|pa|tience** /ɪmpeɪʃᵊns/ N-UNCOUNT impaciencia ❑ *I remember his impatience with long speeches.* *Recuerdo la impaciencia que le provocan los discursos largos.* 2 ADJ If you are **impatient,** you are easily irritated by things. impaciente, intolerante ❑ *Try not to be impatient with your kids.* *Trata de no ser intolerante con tus hijos.* • **im|pa|tient|ly** ADV impacientemente, con impaciencia ❑ *"Come on, David," Harry said impatiently.* *—Vámonos, David —dijo Harry con impaciencia.* • **im|pa|tience** N-UNCOUNT impaciencia ❑ *She tried to hide her growing impatience with him.* *Trató de disimular que cada vez era mayor su impaciencia con él.* 3 ADJ If you are **impatient to** do something or **impatient for** something to happen, you are eager to do it or for it to happen and do not want to wait. impaciente, ansioso ❑ *He was impatient to get home.* *Estaba ansioso por llegar a su casa.* • **im|pa|tience** N-UNCOUNT impaciencia, ansiedad ❑ *He didn't hide his impatience to leave.* *No ocultó su ansiedad por irse.*

**im|pede** /ɪmpid/ (**impedes, impeding, impeded**) V-T If you **impede** someone or something, you make their movement, development, or progress difficult. dificultar, obstaculizar, impedir [FORMAL] ❑ *Bad weather conditions are impeding the progress of rescue workers.* *El mal estado del tiempo está obstaculizando el avance de los rescatistas.*

**im|pend|ing** /ɪmpɛndɪŋ/ ADJ An **impending** event is one that is going to happen very soon. inminente [FORMAL] ❑ *I had a feeling of impending disaster.* *Tengo la sensación de que el desastre es inminente.*

**im|pen|etrable** /ɪmpɛnɪtrəbᵊl/ 1 ADJ An **impenetrable** barrier or forest is impossible or very difficult to get through. impenetrable ❑ *The mountains form an almost impenetrable barrier between the two countries.* *Las montañas forman una barrera casi impenetrable entre los dos países.* 2 ADJ If you describe something such as a book or a theory as **impenetrable,** you are emphasizing that it is impossible or very difficult to understand. incomprensible, impenetrable, inescrutable ❑ *His writing is impenetrable.* *Su escritura es incomprensible.*

**im|perial** /ɪmpɪəriəl/ 1 ADJ **Imperial** is used to refer to things or people that are or were connected with an empire. imperial ❑ *...the Imperial Palace in Tokyo.* *...el Palacio Imperial de Tokio.* 2 ADJ The **imperial** system of measurement uses inches, feet, yards, and miles to measure length, ounces and pounds to measure weight, and pints, quarts, and gallons to measure volume. sistema inglés de pesos y medidas

**im|peri|al|ism** /ɪmpɪəriəlɪzəm/ N-UNCOUNT **Imperialism** is a system in which a rich and powerful country controls other countries. imperialismo ❑ *...nations which have been victims of imperialism.* *...naciones que han sido víctima del imperialismo.* • **im|peri|al|ist** N-COUNT (**imperialists**) imperialista ❑ *He called his enemies "imperialists."* *Él calificaba de "imperialistas" a sus enemigos.*

**im|per|son|al** /ɪmpɜrsənᵊl/ 1 ADJ If you describe a place, organization, or activity as **impersonal,** you dislike it because it is not very friendly and makes you feel unimportant. impersonal ❑ *...expensive impersonal hotels.* *...costosos hoteles impersonales.* 2 ADJ If you describe someone's behavior as **impersonal,** you mean that they do not show any emotion about the person they are dealing with. impersonal ❑ *Doctors must often make decisions in an impersonal way.* *A veces los médicos deben tomar decisiones de manera impersonal.*

**im|per|son|ate** /ɪmpɜrsəneɪt/ (**impersonates, impersonating, impersonated**) V-T If someone **impersonates** a person, they pretend to be that person, either to deceive people or to make people laugh. hacerse pasar por, fingir ser, imitar ❑ *As a child I was always impersonating family and friends.* *Cuando era niño siempre imitaba a familiares y amigos.* • **im|per|sona|tion** /ɪmpɜrsəneɪʃᵊn/ N-VAR (**impersonations**) suplantación, imitación, representación ❑ *...his impersonations of his teachers.* *...las imitaciones de sus maestros.*

**im|ple|ment** (**implements, implementing, implemented**)

The verb is pronounced /ɪmplɪmɛnt/ or /ɪmplɪmənt/. The noun is pronounced /ɪmplɪmənt/.

1 V-T If you **implement** a plan, system, or law, you carry it out. implementar, instrumentar, poner en práctica, ejecutar ❑ *The government implemented a new system for inspecting schools.* *El gobierno puso en práctica un nuevo sistema de inspección para las escuelas.* • **im|ple|men|ta|tion** /ɪmplɪmənteɪʃᵊn, -mɛn-/ N-UNCOUNT implementación, puesta en práctica, ejecución ❑ *...the implementation of the peace agreement.* *...la implementación del acuerdo de paz.* 2 N-COUNT An **implement** is a tool or other piece of equipment. implemento, utensilio, herramienta, instrumento [FORMAL] ❑ *...kitchen implements.* *...utensilios de cocina.*

**im|pli|ca|tion** /ɪmplɪkeɪʃᵊn/ (**implications**) N-COUNT **The implications of** something are the things that are likely to happen as a result. implicación, consecuencia, repercusión ❑ *What are the implications of his decision?* *¿Cuáles son las implicaciones de su decisión?*

**Word Partnership** Usar *implication* con:

ADJ. **clear** implication, **important** implication, **obvious** implication 1

**im|plic|it** /ɪmplɪsɪt/ 1 ADJ Something that is **implicit** is expressed in an indirect way. implícito, tácito, sobrentendido ❑ *Some people laughed at the implicit joke.* *Algunas personas se rieron del chiste implícito.* • **im|plic|it|ly** ADV implícitamente, tácitamente ❑ *He implicitly agreed.* *Aceptó* *implícitamente.* **2** ADJ If you have an **implicit** belief or faith in something, you have complete faith in it and no doubts at all. *incondicional, total, absoluto* ❑ *He had implicit faith in the democratic system. Su fe en el sistema democrático era absoluta.* • **im|plic|it|ly** ADV *incondicionalmente, totalmente, absolutamente* ❑ *I trust him implicitly. Confío en él incondicionalmente.*

**im|ply** /ɪmplaɪ/ (**implies, implying, implied**) **1** V-T If you **imply that** something is true, you say something that indicates in an indirect way that it is true. *sugerir, insinuar, dar a entender* ❑ *Are you implying that this is my fault? ¿Estás queriendo decir que es mi culpa?* **2** V-T If an event or situation **implies** that something is true, it makes you think that it is true. *sugerir, dar a entender* ❑ *The news article implies that he is guilty. La noticia sugiere que él es culpable.*

**Usage** imply and infer

*Imply* and *infer* are often confused. When you *imply* something, you say or suggest it indirectly, but when you *infer* something, you figure it out: *Xian-li smiled to imply that she thought Dun was nice, but Dun inferred that she thought he was silly.*

**Thesaurus** *imply* Ver también:

V. hint, insinuate, point to, suggest **1** **2**

**Word Link** *port ≈ carrying : export, import, portable*

**im|port** (**imports, importing, imported**)

The verb is pronounced /ɪmpɔrt/ or /ɪmpɔrt/. The noun is pronounced /ɪmpɔrt/.

**1** V-T To **import** products or raw materials means to buy them from another country for use in your own country. *importar* ❑ *The U.S. imports over half of its oil. Los Estados Unidos importan más de la mitad de su petróleo.* • **Import** is also a noun. *importación* ❑ *Pizza is an import from Italy. La pizza es una importación de Italia.* • **im|por|ta|tion** /ɪmpɔrteɪʃən/ N-UNCOUNT *importación, entrada, internación* ❑ *...rules about the importation of birds. ...reglas sobre la importación de aves.* • **im|port|er** N-COUNT (**importers**) *importador o importadora* ❑ *Japan is the biggest importer of U.S. beef. Japón es el mayor importador de carne de res estadounidense.* **2** N-COUNT **Imports** are products or raw materials bought from another country for use in your own country. *productos importados* ❑ *...cheap imports from other countries. ...productos baratos importados de otros países.*

**im|por|tant** /ɪmpɔrtᵊnt/ **1** ADJ Something that is **important** is very significant, is highly valued, or is necessary. *importante, significativo, valioso* ❑ *The most important thing in my life is my career. Lo más importante en mi vida es mi carrera.* ❑ *It's important to answer her questions honestly. Es importante contestar sus preguntas con honestidad.* • **im|por|tance** N-UNCOUNT *importancia* ❑ *The teacher stressed the importance of doing our homework. El profesor subrayó la importancia de hacer la tarea.* • **im|por|tant|ly** ADV *lo más importante, importantemente* ❑ *I was hungry, and, more importantly, my children were hungry. Yo tenía hambre, pero lo más importante es que mis hijos tenían hambre.* **2** ADJ Someone who is **important** has influence or power within a society or a particular group. *importante* ❑ *She's an important person in the world of television. Ella es un personaje importante en el mundo de la televisión.* • **im|por|tance** N-UNCOUNT *importancia, peso, valor* ❑ *I didn't realize his importance in the company. No me di cuenta de su valor en la compañía.*

**Thesaurus** *important* Ver también:

ADJ. critical, essential, principal, significant; (ant.) unimportant **1** distinguished **2**

**Word Partnership** Usar *importance* con:

ADJ. **critical** importance, **enormous** importance, **growing/increasing** importance, **utmost** importance **1**
V. **place less/more** importance **on** *something*, **recognize the** importance, **understand the** importance **1**
N. **self**-importance, **sense of** importance **2**

**im|pose** /ɪmpoʊz/ (**imposes, imposing, imposed**) **1** V-T If you **impose** something **on** people, you force them to accept it. *imponer* ❑ *We impose fines on drivers who break the speed limit. Imponemos multas a los conductores que rebasan el límite de velocidad.* • **im|po|si|tion** /ɪmpəzɪʃən/ N-UNCOUNT *imposición* ❑ *...the imposition of a new property tax. ...la imposición de un nuevo impuesto a la propiedad.* **2** V-T If you **impose** your opinions or beliefs **on** other people, you try to make people accept them as a rule or as a model to copy. *imponer* ❑ *He tries to impose his own taste on all of us. Trata de imponernos sus propios gustos.* **3** V-I If someone **imposes on** you, they unreasonably expect you to do something for them which you do not want to do. *imponerse, hacerse aceptar* ❑ *I won't stay overnight because I don't want to impose on you. No voy a dormir aquí porque no quiero abusar.* • **im|po|si|tion** N-COUNT *imposición* ❑ *He brought all his friends with him, which was a real imposition. Vino con todos sus amigos, lo cual fue una verdadera imposición.*

**im|pos|ing** /ɪmpoʊzɪŋ/ ADJ If you describe someone or something as **imposing**, you mean that they have an impressive appearance or manner. *imponente, impresionante* ❑ *He was an imposing man. Era un hombre imponente.*

**Word Link** *im ≈ not : imbalance, immature, impossible*

**im|pos|sible** /ɪmpɒsɪbᵊl/ **1** ADJ Something that is **impossible** cannot be done or cannot happen. *imposible* ❑ *It was impossible for anyone to get in because no one knew the password. Para todos era imposible entrar porque nadie conocía la contraseña.* ❑ *Heavy snow in New York made it impossible to play the game. La intensa nevada hizo imposible que se jugara en Nueva York.* • **The impossible** is something that is impossible. *lo imposible* ❑ *They expected us to do the impossible. Esperaban que nosotros hiciéramos lo imposible.* • **im|pos|sibly** ADV *extremadamente, increíblemente, imposiblemente* ❑ *Mathematical physics is an almost impossibly difficult subject. La física matemática es una materia increíblemente difícil.* • **im|pos|sibil|ity** /ɪmpɒsɪbɪlɪti/ N-VAR (**impossibilities**) imposibilidad, cosa imposible ❑ ...the impossibility of knowing the whole truth. ...la imposibilidad de saber toda la verdad. 2 ADJ An **impossible** situation or an **impossible** position is one that is very difficult to deal with. imposible ❑ He was in an impossible position. Estaba en una posición imposible. 3 ADJ If you describe someone as **impossible**, you are annoyed that their bad behavior or strong views make them difficult to deal with. intolerable, imposible, insoportable ❑ You are an impossible man! ¡Eres insoportable!

**Word Partnership** Usar *impossible* con:

V. impossible **to describe**, impossible **to find**, impossible **to ignore**, impossible **to prove**, impossible **to say/tell**, **seem** impossible 1
ADV. **absolutely** impossible, **almost** impossible, **nearly** impossible 1 2
N. **an** impossible **task** 1 2

**Word Link** *potent ≈ ability, power : impotent, potent, potential*

**im|po|tent** /ɪmpətənt/ 1 ADJ If someone feels **impotent**, they feel that they have no power to influence people or events. impotente, inerme, desvalido ❑ Bullying makes children feel depressed and impotent. El acoso hace que los niños se sientan deprimidos y desvalidos. ● **im|po|tence** /ɪmpətəns/ N-UNCOUNT impotencia ❑ ...a sense of national impotence. ...una sensación de impotencia nacional. 2 ADJ If a man is **impotent**, he is unable to get an erection. impotente ● **im|po|tence** N-UNCOUNT impotencia ❑ Impotence affects 10 million men in the U.S. La impotencia afecta a 10 millones de hombres en los Estados Unidos.

**im|prac|ti|cal** /ɪmpræktɪkᵊl/ ADJ If you describe an object, idea, or course of action as **impractical**, you mean that it is not sensible or realistic. poco práctico, impráctico, no ser práctico ❑ It is impractical to get there by train. Es poco práctico ir allá en tren.

**im|press** /ɪmprɛs/ (**impresses, impressing, impressed**) 1 V-T If something **impresses** you, you feel great admiration for it. impresionar, impactar ❑ Their speed impressed everyone. Impresionaron a todos con su velocidad. ● **im|pressed** ADJ impresionado ❑ I was very impressed by his lecture. Me impresionó mucho su conferencia. 2 V-T If you **impress** something **on** someone, you make them understand its importance or degree. recalcar, subrayar, inculcar ❑ I impressed the importance of hard work on the children. Les inculqué a los niños la importancia de trabajar duro.

**im|pres|sion** /ɪmprɛʃᵊn/ (**impressions**) 1 N-COUNT Your **impression** of a person or thing is what you think they are like. Your **impression** of a situation is what you think is going on. impresión, efecto ❑ What were your first impressions of college? ¿Cuáles fueron tus primeras impresiones de la universidad? ❑ My impression is that the kids are totally out of control. Mi impresión es que los niños están totalmente fuera de control. 2 N-SING If someone gives you a particular **impression**, they cause you to believe that something is true, often when it is not. impresión ❑ I don't want to give the impression that I'm running away. No quiero dar la impresión de que me estoy escapando 3 N-COUNT An **impression** is an amusing imitation of someone's behavior or way of talking, usually someone well-known. imitación ❑ ...a great impression of the teacher. ...una fabulosa imitación del maestro. 4 N-COUNT An **impression** of an object is a mark or outline that it has left after being pressed hard onto a surface. huella, marca, señal, impresión ❑ ...impressions of dinosaur bones in the rock. ...huellas de huesos de dinosaurio en la roca. 5 PHRASE If someone or something **makes an impression**, they have a strong effect on people or a situation. causar buena impresión, causar mala impresión ❑ It's her first day at work and she has already made an impression. Es su primer día de trabajo y ya causó una buena impresión. 6 PHRASE If you are **under the impression that** something is true, you believe that it is true. tener la impresión ❑ I was under the impression that you were angry. Yo tenía la impresión de que estabas enojado.

**im|pres|sive** /ɪmprɛsɪv/ ADJ Something that is **impressive** impresses you, for example, because it is great in size or degree, or is done with a lot of skill. impresionante, emocionante, notable, admirable, digno de admiración, imponente ❑ ...an impressive amount of cash: $390.8 million. ...una cantidad impresionante de dinero: 390.8 millones de dólares. ● **im|pres|sive|ly** ADV admirablemente, impresionantemente, imponentemente ❑ ...an impressively bright woman. ...una mujer impresionantemente brillante.

**im|pris|on** /ɪmprɪzᵊn/ (**imprisons, imprisoning, imprisoned**) V-T If someone **is imprisoned**, they are locked up or kept somewhere. encarcelar, encerrar, meter en la cárcel, meter a la cárcel ❑ He was imprisoned for 18 months. Estuvo en la cárcel 18 meses. ● **im|pris|on|ment** /ɪmprɪzᵊnmənt/ N-UNCOUNT encarcelamiento, prisión ❑ She was sentenced to seven years' imprisonment. Fue sentenciado a siete años de prisión.

**im|prop|er** /ɪmprɒpər/ 1 ADJ **Improper** activities are illegal or dishonest. indebido, incorrecto, erróneo [FORMAL] ❑ The two men were arrested for improper use of a computer. Los dos hombres fueron arrestados por hacer uso indebido de una computadora. ● **im|prop|er|ly** ADV indebidamente, incorrectamente, erróneamente ❑ I did not act improperly. Yo no actué incorrectamente. 2 ADJ **Improper** conditions or methods of treatment are not suitable or good enough for a particular purpose. impropio, inadecuado [FORMAL] ❑ The improper use of medicine could be dangerous. El uso inadecuado de una medicina puede ser peligroso. ● **im|prop|er|ly** ADV impropiamente, inadecuadamente ❑ Many doctors were improperly trained. Muchos doctores fueron capacitados de manera inadecuada. 3 ADJ If you describe someone's behavior as **improper**, you mean it is offensive or shocking. impropio, indecoroso, deshonesto ❑ He considered it improper for a young lady to go out alone. Consideró impropio que una joven saliera sola. ● **im|prop|er|ly** ADV impropiamente, inadecuadamente ❑ He showed up at his job interview improperly dressed. Se presentó a la entrevista de trabajo inadecuadamente vestido.

**im|prove** /ɪmpruv/ (**improves, improving, improved**) 1 V-T/V-I If something **improves** or if you **improve** it, it gets better. mejorar(se), hacer mejoras, perfeccionar(se) ❑ Your general health *will improve if you drink more water.* *Su salud general mejorará si bebe más agua.* ❑ *Their French has improved enormously.* *Su francés ha mejorado enormemente.*

● **im|prove|ment** /ɪmpruvmənt/ N-VAR (**improvements**) *mejora, mejoría, perfeccionamiento* ❑ *...the dramatic improvements in technology in recent years.* *...el asombroso perfeccionamiento de la tecnología en los últimos años.* **2** V-I If you **improve on** a previous achievement of your own or of someone else, you achieve a better standard or result. *mejorar, superar* ❑ *We need to improve on our successes.* *Tenemos que superar nuestros logros.* ● **im|prove|ment** N-COUNT (**improvements**) *mejora, mejoría* ❑ *The new governor is an improvement on the previous one.* *El nuevo gobernador es superior al anterior.*

**Word Partnership** Usar *improve* con:

V. **continue to** improve, **expected to** improve, **need to** improve, **try to** improve **1** **2**
ADV. **significantly** improve, improve **slightly** **1** **2**

**Word Partnership** Usar *improvement* con:

ADJ. **big** improvement, **dramatic** improvement, **gradual** improvement, **marked** improvement, **significant** improvement, **slight** improvement **1** **2**
N. **home** improvement, **self-**improvement, **signs of** improvement **1** **2**

**im|pro|vise** /ɪmprəvaɪz/ (**improvises, improvising, improvised**) **1** V-T/V-I If you **improvise**, you make or do something using whatever you have or without having planned it in advance. *improvisar* ❑ *If children don't have toys to play with, they improvise.* *Si los niños no tienen juguetes para entretenerse, improvisan.* ❑ *I used socks to improvise a pair of gloves.* *Improvisé un par de guantes con unos calcetines.* **2** V-T/V-I When performers **improvise**, they invent music or words as they play, sing, or speak. *improvisar* ❑ *The jazz band improvised on well-known tunes.* *La banda de jazz improvisó a partir de tonadas muy conocidas.* ❑ *Richard improvised a prayer.* *Richard improvisó una plegaria.* ● **im|provi|sa|tion** /ɪmprɒvɪzeɪʃən/ N-UNCOUNT *improvisación*

**Word Link** *puls ≈ driving, pushing : compulsory, expulsion, impulse*

**im|pulse** /ɪmpʌls/ (**impulses**) **1** N-VAR An **impulse** is a sudden desire to do something. *impulso, arranque* ❑ *She couldn't resist the impulse to look at him.* *Ella no pudo resistir el impulso de voltear a verlo.* **2** N-COUNT An **impulse** is a short electrical signal that is sent along a wire or nerve or through the air, usually as one of a series. *impulso* ❑ *The machine reads the electrical impulses and turns them into messages.* *La máquina interpreta los impulsos eléctricos y los convierte en mensajes.* **3** PHRASE If you do something **on impulse**, you suddenly decide to do it, without planning it. *dejarse llevar por un impulso, en un arranque* ❑ *Sean usually acts on impulse.* *Sean normalmente se deja llevar por sus impulsos.*

**Word Partnership** Usar *impulse* con:

ADJ. **first** impulse, **strong** impulse, **sudden** impulse **1**
V. **control an** impulse, **resist an** impulse **1** **act on** impulse **3**

**im|pul|sive** /ɪmpʌlsɪv/ ADJ If you describe someone as **impulsive**, you mean that they do things suddenly without thinking about them carefully first. *impulsivo* ❑ *He is too impulsive to be a parent.* *Es demasiado impulsivo como para ser padre.* ● **im|pul|sive|ly** ADV *impulsivamente* ❑ *He said impulsively: "Let's get married."* *—Vamos a casarnos —le dijo impulsivamente.*

**in**

1. POSITION OR MOVEMENT
2. INCLUSION OR INVOLVEMENT
3. TIME AND NUMBERS
4. STATES AND QUALITIES
5. OTHER USES AND PHRASES

**1 in**

The preposition is pronounced /ɪn/. The adverb is pronounced /ɪn/.

In addition to the uses shown below, **in** is used after some verbs, nouns, and adjectives in order to introduce extra information. **In** is also used with verbs of movement such as "walk" and "push," and in phrasal verbs such as "give in" and "dig in."

**1** PREP Someone or something that is **in** something else is enclosed by it or surrounded by it. If you put something **in** a container, you move it so that it is enclosed by the container. *en* ❑ *He was in his car.* *Estaba en su auto.* **2** PREP If something happens **in** a place, it happens there. *en* ❑ *We spent a few days in a hotel.* *Pasamos unos días en un hotel.* **3** ADV If you **are in**, you are present at your home or place of work. *estar en algún lugar, haber llegado* ❑ *My mother was in at the time.* *Mi madre estaba en ese momento.* **4** ADV When someone comes **in**, they enter a room or building. *dentro, adentro* ❑ *She looked up as he came in.* *Ella lo miró cuando iba entrando.* **5** ADV If a train, boat, or plane has come **in** or is **in**, it has arrived at a station, port, or airport. *haber llegado, llegar* ❑ *A plane was coming in from Los Angeles.* *Un avión llegaba de Los Angeles.* **6** ADV When the ocean or tide comes **in**, the ocean moves toward the shore rather than away from it. *subir (la marea)* ❑ *The tide rushed in, covering the sand.* *La marea subió y cubrió la arena.* **7** PREP Something that is **in** a window, especially a store window, is just behind the window so that you can see it from outside. *en* ❑ *There was a camera for sale in the window.* *En el aparador había una cámara en oferta.* **8** PREP When you see something **in** a mirror, the mirror shows an image of it. *en* ❑ *I looked at my reflection in the mirror.* *Miré mi imagen en el espejo.* **9** PREP If you are dressed **in** a piece of clothing, you are wearing it. *de* ❑ *He was in a suit and tie.* *Iba de traje y corbata.*
→ see **location**

**2 in** /ɪn/ **1** PREP If something is **in** a book, movie, play, or picture, you can read it or see it there. en ❑ *I'll read you what it says in the book.* *Te voy a leer lo que dice en el libro.* **2** PREP If you are **in** something such as a play or a race, you are one of the people involved with it. en ❑ *Alfredo offered her a part in his play.* *Alfredo le ofreció un papel en su obra.* **3** PREP Something that is **in** a group or collection is a member of it or part of it. de ❑ *The New England team is the worst in the country.* *El equipo de Nueva Inglaterra es el peor del país.* **4** PREP You use **in** to specify a general subject or field of activity. en ❑ *He works in the music industry.* *Trabaja en la industria de la música.*

**❸ in** /ɪn/ **1** PREP If something happens **in** a particular year, month, or other period of time, it happens during that time. en ❑ *He was born in April 1996.* *Nació en abril de 1996.* ❑ *Sales improved in the last month.* *En el último mes mejoraron las ventas.* **2** PREP If you do something **in** a particular period of time, that is how long it takes you to do it. en ❑ *He walked two hundred miles in eight days.* *Caminó 200 kilómetros en ocho días.* **3** PREP If something will happen **in** a particular length of time, it will happen after that length of time. en ❑ *Breakfast will be ready in a few minutes.* *El desayuno estará listo en unos minutos.* **4** PREP You use **in** to indicate roughly how old someone is. For example, if someone is **in** their fifties, they are between 50 and 59 years old. de ❑ *...young people in their twenties.* *...jóvenes de veintitantos años.* **5** PREP You use **in** to indicate roughly how many people or things do something. por ❑ *People came in their thousands to hear him speak.* *Vinieron miles y miles a oirlo hablar.* **6** PREP You use **in** to express a relationship between numbers. de ❑ *One in three children can't find the U.S. on a map.* *Uno de cada tres niños no sabe localizar los Estados Unidos en un mapa.*

**❹ in** /ɪn/ **1** PREP If something or someone is **in** a particular state or situation, that is their present state or situation. en ❑ *The economy was in trouble.* *La economía estaba en problemas.* ❑ *Dave was in a hurry to get back to work.* *Dave tenía prisa de regresar al trabajo.* **2** PREP You use **in** to indicate the feeling or desire that someone has when they do something, or which causes them to do it. con ❑ *Simpson looked at them in surprise.* *Simpson los miró sorprendido.* **3** PREP You use **in** to indicate how someone is expressing something. por ❑ *Can you give me the information in writing?* *¿Puede darme la información por escrito?* **4** PREP You use **in** in expressions such as **in a row** or **in a ball** to describe the arrangement or shape of something. en ❑ *She put her shoes in a row on the floor.* *Acomodó sus zapatos en fila, en el suelo.* **5** PREP You use **in** to specify which feature or aspect of something you are talking about. de ❑ *The movie is nearly two hours in length.* *La película dura casi dos horas.*

**❺ in**

Pronounced /ɪn/ for meanings **1** and **3** to **5**, and /ɪn/ for meaning **2**.

**1** ADJ If you say that something is **in**, or is the **in** thing, you mean it is fashionable or popular. a la moda, in [INFORMAL] ❑ *A few years ago jogging was the in thing.* *Hace unos años lo in era salir a correr.* **2** PHRASE If you say that someone **is in for** a shock or a surprise, you mean that they are going to experience it. esperar algo ❑ *You might be in for a shock at how hard you have to work.* *Te va a dar un ataque cuando veas cuánto trabajo hay.* **3** PHRASE If someone **has it in for** you, they dislike you and try to cause problems for you. venganza, enojo [INFORMAL] ❑ *The other kids had it in for me.* *Los otros niños estaban enojados conmigo.* **4** PHRASE If you are **in on** something, you are involved in it or know about it. participación ❑ *She suspected him of being in on the plan.* *Ella sospechaba que él era parte del plan.* **5** PHRASE You use **in that** to introduce an explanation of a statement you have just made. en el sentido de, porque, ya que ❑ *I'm lucky in that I've got four sisters.* *Tengo suerte de tener cuatro hermanas.*

| Word Link | *in ≈ not : inability, inaccurate, inadequate* |
|---|---|

**in|abil|ity** /ɪnəbɪlɪti/ N-UNCOUNT Someone's **inability to** do something is the fact that they are unable to do it. incapacidad, ineptitud ❑ *Her inability to concentrate could cause an accident.* *Su incapacidad para concentrarse podría causar un accidente.*

**in|ac|cu|rate** /ɪnækyərɪt/ ADJ If a statement or measurement is **inaccurate,** it is not accurate or correct. inexacto, incorrecto, erróneo ❑ *The book is inaccurate and untrue.* *El libro es inexacto y falso.* • **in|ac|cu|ra|cy** /ɪnækyərəsi/ N-VAR (**inaccuracies**) inexactitud, imprecisión ❑ *He was upset by the inaccuracy of the answers.* *Estaba molesto por la inexactitud de las respuestas.*

**in|ac|tive** /ɪnæktɪv/ ADJ Someone or something that is **inactive** is not doing anything or is not working. inactivo ❑ *He has always been politically inactive.* *En política siempre ha estado inactivo.* • **in|ac|tiv|ity** /ɪnæktɪvɪti/ N-UNCOUNT inactividad, inacción ❑ *Long periods of inactivity are bad for you.* *Los largos periodos de inactividad no te hacen ningún bien.*

**in|ad|equate** /ɪnædɪkwɪt/ **1** ADJ If something is **inadequate,** there is not enough of it or it is not good enough. insuficiente, inadecuado ❑ *Supplies of food are inadequate.* *El abasto de alimentos es insuficiente.* • **in|ad|equa|cy** /ɪnædɪkwəsi/ N-VAR (**inadequacies**) insuficiencia, deficiencia ❑ *...the inadequacy of the water supply.* *...deficiencias en el suministro de agua.* • **in|ad|equate|ly** ADV inadecuadamente, no adecuado ❑ *The schools were inadequately funded.* *El financiamiento para las escuelas no era adecuado.* **2** ADJ If someone feels **inadequate,** they feel that they do not have the qualities and abilities necessary to do something or to cope with life in general. inadecuado, incompetente, no preparado ❑ *Many people are inadequately prepared for old age.* *Muchas personas no están preparadas para la ancianidad.* • **in|ad|equa|cy** N-UNCOUNT ineptitud, incompetencia, deficiencia ❑ *I had a feeling of inadequacy.* *Tenía la sensación de incompetencia.*

**in|ap|pro|pri|ate** /ɪnəproʊpriɪt/ ADJ Something that is **inappropriate** is not suitable for a particular situation or purpose. inadecuado, inoportuno, poco apropiado ❑ *The movie is inappropriate for young children.* *La película es poco apropiada para chiquitos.*

**in|box** /ɪnbɒks/ (**inboxes**) also **in-box** **1** N-COUNT An **inbox** is a shallow container used in offices to put letters and documents in before they are dealt with. bandeja de entrada **2** N-COUNT On a computer, your **inbox** is the part of your

i

mailbox which stores e-mails that have arrived for you. *bandeja de entrada* ❑ *I went home and checked my inbox. Llegué a casa y revisé mi bandeja de entrada.*

**Inc.** **Inc.** is an abbreviation for **Incorporated** when it is used after a company's name. *Inc.* [BUSINESS] ❑ *...BP America Inc. ...BP America Inc.*

**in|ca|pable** /ɪnkeɪpəbᵊl/ ADJ Someone who is **incapable of** doing something is unable to do it. *inútil, incapaz, incompetente* ❑ *She seemed incapable of deciding what to do. Parecía incapaz de tomar una decisión.*

**in|cen|tive** /ɪnsɛntɪv/ (**incentives**) N-VAR An **incentive** is something that encourages you to do something. *incentivo, estímulo* ❑ *We want to give our employees an incentive to work hard. Queremos dar un incentivo a nuestros empleados para que se esfuercen.*

**in|cest** /ɪnsɛst/ N-UNCOUNT **Incest** is the crime of two members of the same family having sexual intercourse. *incesto*

**inch** /ɪntʃ/ (**inches, inching, inched**) **1** N-COUNT An **inch** is a unit of length, approximately equal to 2.54 centimeters. There are twelve inches in a foot. *pulgada* ❑ *Dig a hole 18 inches deep. Haga una perforación de 18 pulgadas de profundidad.* **2** V-T/V-I To **inch** somewhere or to **inch** something somewhere means to move there very slowly and carefully, or to make something do this. *lentamente, paso a paso* ❑ *A climber was inching up the wall of rock. Un escalador subía lentamente por la pared de roca.* ❑ *He inched the van forward. Avanzó poco a poco la camioneta.*
→ see **measurement**

I

**in|ci|dent** /ɪnsɪdənt/ (**incidents**) N-COUNT An **incident** is something that happens, often something that is unpleasant. *incidente, lo que pasó* [FORMAL] ❑ *He was furious about the whole incident. Estaba furioso por todo lo que pasó.*

**Thesaurus** *incident* Ver también:

N. episode, event, fact, happening, occasion, occurrence

**in|ci|den|tal** /ɪnsɪdɛntᵊl/ ADJ If one thing is **incidental** to another, it is less important than the other thing or is not a major part of it. *secundario, incidental* ❑ *...scenes in the movie that are incidental to the plot. ...escenas de la película que son secundarias a la trama.*

**in|ci|den|tal|ly** /ɪnsɪdɛntli/ ADV You use **incidentally** to introduce a point that is not directly relevant to what you are saying, often a question or extra information that you have just thought of. *a propósito, por cierto* ❑ *She introduced me to her boyfriend (who, incidentally, doesn't speak a word of English). Me presentó a su novio (quien, por cierto, no habla una palabra de inglés).*

**in|cin|er|ate** /ɪnsɪnəreɪt/ (**incinerates, incinerating, incinerated**) V-T When authorities **incinerate** garbage or waste material, they burn it completely in a special container. *incinerar, quemar* ❑ *They were incinerating leaves. Estaban quemando hojas.* ● **in|cin|era|tion** /ɪnsɪnəreɪʃᵊn/ N-UNCOUNT *incineración, cremación, quema* ❑ *...the incineration of the weapons. ...la quema de las armas.*
→ see **dump**

**in|ci|sor** /ɪnsaɪzər/ (**incisors**) N-COUNT Your **incisors** are the teeth at the front of your mouth that you use for biting into food. *incisivo*
→ see **carnivore**

**Word Link** *clin ≈ leaning : decline, incline, recline*

**in|cline** (**inclines, inclining, inclined**)

The noun is pronounced /ɪnklaɪn/. The verb is pronounced /ɪnklaɪn/.

**1** N-COUNT An **incline** is land that slopes at an angle. *pendiente, cuesta, declive* [FORMAL] ❑ *He stopped at the edge of a steep incline. Se detuvo a la orilla de una cuesta empinada.* **2** V-T If you **incline to** think or act in a particular way, or if something **inclines** you **to** it, you are likely to think or act in that way. *inclinar(se), predisponer* [FORMAL] ❑ *...factors that incline us toward particular beliefs. ...factores que nos predisponen a ciertas creencias.*

**in|clined** /ɪnklaɪnd/ **1** ADJ If you say that you are **inclined to** have a particular opinion, you mean that you hold this opinion but you are not expressing it strongly. *proclive, dispuesto* ❑ *I am inclined to agree with Alan. Me inclino a pensar como Alan.* **2** ADJ Someone who is mathematically **inclined** or artistically **inclined**, for example, has a natural talent for mathematics or art. *con la inclinación, con aptitud* ❑ *...students who are musically inclined. ...estudiantes con aptitudes para la música.*
**3** → see also **incline**

**in|clined plane** (**inclined planes**) N-COUNT An **inclined plane** is a flat surface that is sloping at a particular angle. *plano inclinado*

**in|clude** /ɪnklud/ (**includes, including, included**) V-T If one thing **includes** another thing, it has it as one of its parts. *incluir, abarcar, contener* ❑ *The trip will include a day at the beach. El viaje incluirá un día en la playa.*

**Usage** include

Saying that a group *includes* one or more people or things implies that the group has additional people or things in it also. For instance, the sentence: *Cities in Japan include Tokyo and Kyoto* implies that Japan has additional cities.

**in|clud|ing** /ɪnkludɪŋ/ PREP You use **including** to introduce examples of people or things that are part of the group of people or things that you are talking about. *incluido, incluso* ❑ *Thousands were killed, including many women and children. Miles murieron, incluso muchas mujeres y niños.*

**in|come** /ɪnkʌm/ (**incomes**) N-VAR A person's or organization's **income** is the money that they earn or receive. *ingreso* [BUSINESS] ❑ *...families on low incomes. ...familias de bajos ingresos.*

**Word Partnership** Usar *income* con:

ADJ. **average** income, **fixed** income, **large/small** income, **a second** income, **steady** income, **taxable** income
V. **earn** ***an*** income, **supplement** ***your*** income
N. **loss of** income, **source of** income

**in|come tax** (**income taxes**) N-VAR **Income tax** is a part of your income that you have to pay regularly to the government. *impuesto sobre la renta* [BUSINESS] ❑ *You pay income tax every month. Usted* *paga mensualmente el impuesto sobre la renta.*

**in|com|ing** /ɪnkʌmɪŋ/ **1** ADJ An **incoming** message or phone call is one that you receive. *entrante, que llega* ❑ *We keep a record of incoming calls. Llevamos un registro de las llamadas que entran.* **2** ADJ An **incoming** plane or passenger is one that is arriving at a place. *que llega* ❑ *The airport was closed to incoming flights. El aeropuerto estaba cerrado a los vuelos de llegada.*

**in|com|pe|tent** /ɪnkɒmpɪtənt/ ADJ If you describe someone as **incompetent,** you are criticizing them because they are unable to do their job or a task properly. *incompetente, inepto* ❑ *He threatened to fire incompetent employees. Amenazó con despedir a los empleados ineptos.* ● **in|com|pe|tence** N-UNCOUNT *incompetencia, ineptitud* ❑ *The incompetence of government officials is shocking. La incompetencia de los funcionarios del gobierno es asombrosa.*

**in|com|plete** /ɪnkəmplit/ ADJ Something that is **incomplete** is not yet finished, or does not have all the parts or details that it needs. *incompleto, inconcluso* ❑ *The data we have is incomplete. Los datos que tenemos están incompletos.*

**in|con|ven|ient** /ɪnkənvinyənt/ ADJ Something that is **inconvenient** causes problems or difficulties for someone. *poco conveniente, inoportuno, inconveniente* ❑ *I know it's inconvenient, but I have to see you now. Sé que es inoportuno, pero tengo que verte ahora.*

**in|cor|po|rate** /ɪnkɔrpəreɪt/ (**incorporates, incorporating, incorporated**) V-T If one thing **incorporates** another thing, it includes the other thing. *incluir, incorporar algo* [FORMAL] ❑ *The new cars will incorporate a number of major changes. Los nuevos autos incluirán varios cambios importantes.*

**In|cor|po|rated** /ɪnkɔrpəreɪtɪd/ ADJ **Incorporated** is used after a corporation's name to show that it is a legally established company in the United States. *constituido legalmente, Incorporated* [BUSINESS] ❑ *...MCA Incorporated. ...MCA Incorporated.*

**in|cor|rect** /ɪnkərɛkt/ ADJ Something that is **incorrect** is wrong or untrue. *incorrecto, equivocado, erróneo* ❑ *The answer he gave was incorrect. La respuesta de él fue incorrecta.* ● **in|cor|rect|ly** ADV *incorrectamente, erróneamente, equivocadamente* ❑ *The article suggested, incorrectly, that he was planning to retire. El artículo sugería, erróneamente, que estaba pensando en retirarse.*

**Word Link** *cresc, creas ≈ growing : crescent, decrease, increase*

**in|crease** (**increases, increasing, increased**)

The verb is pronounced /ɪnkris/. The noun is pronounced /ɪnkris/.

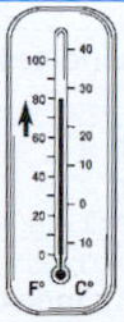
increase

**1** V-T/V-I If something **increases** or you **increase** it, it becomes greater in number, level, or amount. *aumentar, incrementar, crecer* ❑ *The population continues to increase. La población sigue incrementándose.* ❑ *Japanese exports increased by 2% last year. Las exportaciones japonesas aumentaron 2% el año pasado.* **2** N-COUNT If there is an **increase in** the number, level, or amount of something, it becomes greater. *incremento, aumento* ❑ *...a sharp increase in cost. ...un notable incremento en los costos.* **3** PHRASE If something is **on the increase,** it is happening more often or becoming greater in number or intensity. *ir en aumento* ❑ *Crime is on the increase. Los delitos van en aumento.*

**Thesaurus** *increase* Ver también:
V. expand, extend, raise; (*ant.*) decrease, reduce **1**
N. gain, hike, raise, rise; (*ant.*) decrease, reduction **2**

**Word Partnership** Usar *increase* con:
ADV. increase **dramatically**, increase **rapidly** **1**
N. **population** increase, **price** increase, **salary** increase **1**
increase **in crime**, increase **in demand**, increase **in size**, increase **in spending**, increase **in temperature**, increase **in value** **2**
ADJ. **big** increase, **marked** increase, **sharp** increase **1** **2**

**in|creas|ing|ly** /ɪnkrisɪŋli/ ADV You can use **increasingly** to indicate that a situation or quality is becoming greater in intensity or more common. *cada vez más, en aumento* ❑ *He was finding it increasingly difficult to make decisions. Cada vez le era más difícil tomar decisiones.*

**Word Link** *cred ≈ to believe : credible, discredit, incredible*

**in|cred|ible** /ɪnkrɛdɪbᵊl/ **1** ADJ If you describe something or someone as **incredible,** you like them very much or are impressed by them, because they are extremely or unusually good. *increíble* ❑ *The food was incredible. La comida estuvo increíble.* ● **in|cred|ibly** /ɪnkrɛdɪbli/ ADV *increíblemente* ❑ *Their father was incredibly good-looking. Su padre era increíblemente guapo.* **2** ADJ If you say that something is **incredible,** you mean that it is very unusual or surprising, and you cannot believe it is really true, although it may be. *increíble* ❑ *It seemed incredible that people still wanted to play football during a war. Es increíble que la gente siguiera queriendo jugar futbol durante una guerra.* ● **in|cred|ibly** ADV *increíblemente* ❑ *Incredibly, some people don't like the name. Increíblemente, a algunas personas no les gusta el nombre.* **3** ADJ You use **incredible** to emphasize the degree, amount, or intensity of something. *increíble* ❑ *I work an incredible number of hours. Trabajo un número increíble de horas.* ● **in|cred|ibly** ADV *increíblemente* ❑ *It was incredibly hard work. Era un trabajo increíblemente pesado.*

**Word Partnership** Usar *incredible* con:
N. incredible **discovery**, incredible **prices** **1**
incredible **experience** **1** – **3**
ADV. **absolutely** incredible **1** – **3**

**in|cum|bent** /ɪnkʌmbənt/ (**incumbents**) N-COUNT An **incumbent** is someone who holds an official post at a particular time. *funcionario o funcionaria, titular* [FORMAL] ❑ *Incumbents usually have a high chance of being re-elected. Los titulares suelen tener grandes oportunidades de ser reelegidos.* • **Incumbent** is also an adjective. *titular* ❑ *...the only candidate who defeated an incumbent senator. ...el único candidato que venció a un senador en funciones.*

**in|cur** /ɪnkɜr/ (**incurs, incurring, incurred**) V-T If you **incur** something unpleasant, it happens to you because of something you have done. *incurrir en, acarrear* [WRITTEN] ❑ *The government incurred huge debts. El gobierno incurrió en deudas enormes.*

> **Word Link** *able ≈ able to be : acceptable, incurable, portable*

**in|cur|able** /ɪnkyʊərəbᵊl/ **1** ADJ An **incurable** disease cannot be cured. *incurable* ❑ *He is suffering from an incurable skin disease. Sufre una enfermedad incurable de la piel* • **in|cur|ably** /ɪnkyʊərəbli/ ADV *incurablemente* ❑ *...youngsters who are incurably ill. ...jóvenes que padecen una enfermedad incurable.* **2** ADJ You can use **incurable** to indicate that someone has a particular quality or attitude and will not change. *incurable, incorregible* ❑ *Bill is an incurable romantic. Bill es un romántico incurable.* • **in|cur|ably** ADV *incurablemente, incorregiblemente* ❑ *I know you think I'm incurably nosy, but I'm worried about you. Sé que piensas que soy incorregiblemente metiche, pero estoy preocupada por ti.*

I

**in|debt|ed** /ɪndɛtɪd/ ADJ If you say that you are **indebted to** someone, you mean that you are very grateful to them for something. *en deuda* ❑ *I am indebted to him for his help. Estoy en deuda con él por su ayuda.*

**in|de|cent** /ɪndisᵊnt/ ADJ If you describe something as **indecent**, you mean that it is shocking and offensive, usually because it relates to sex or nakedness. *obsceno, indecente, indecoroso* ❑ *...indecent material on the Internet. ...material obsceno en Internet.* • **in|de|cen|cy** /ɪndisᵊnsi/ N-UNCOUNT *indecencia, lo obsceno, obscenidad* ❑ *...the indecency of their language. ...lo obsceno de su lenguaje.* • **in|de|cent|ly** ADV *indecorosamente, indecentemente* ❑ *...an indecently short skirt. ...una falda indecentemente corta.*

**in|deed** /ɪndid/ **1** ADV You use **indeed** to confirm or agree with something that has just been said. *efectivamente, claro está, de hecho* ❑ *He admitted that he had indeed paid him. Él aceptó que efectivamente le había pagado.* ❑ *"Did you know him?" — "I did indeed." —¿Lo conocías? —Claro que lo conocía.* **2** ADV You use **indeed** to introduce a further comment or statement that strengthens the point you have already made. *de hecho* ❑ *We have nothing against change; indeed, we encourage it. No tenemos nada contra el cambio, de hecho, lo fomentamos.* **3** ADV You use **indeed** at the end of a clause to give extra force to the word "very," or to emphasize a particular word. *¡no me digas!, de veras, en serio* ❑ *The results were very strange indeed. Los resultados fueron de veras muy extraños.*

**in|defi|nite** /ɪndɛfɪnɪt/ **1** ADJ If a situation or period is **indefinite**, people have not decided when it will end. *indefinido, indeterminado* ❑ *He was sent to jail for an indefinite period. Lo metieron a la cárcel por tiempo indefinido.* • **in|defi|nite|ly** ADV *indefinidamente* ❑ *The visit has been postponed indefinitely. La visita se pospuso indefinidamente.* **2** ADJ Something that is **indefinite** is not exact or clear. *incierto, vago, impreciso, indefinido* ❑ *...indefinite fears about the future. ...vagos temores acerca del futuro.*

**in|defi|nite ar|ti|cle** (**indefinite articles**) N-COUNT The words "a" and "an" are sometimes called **the indefinite article.** *artículo indefinido*

**in|defi|nite pro|noun** (**indefinite pronouns**) N-COUNT An **indefinite pronoun** is a pronoun such as "someone," "anything," or "nobody" that you use to refer in a general way to a person or thing. *pronombre indefinido*

**in|de|pend|ent** /ɪndɪpɛndənt/ **1** ADJ If one thing or person is **independent of** another, they are separate and not connected, so the first one is not affected or influenced by the second. *independiente* ❑ *The two organizations are completely independent of one another. Las dos organizaciones son completamente independientes una de otra.* ❑ *We need an independent review. Necesitamos una revisión independiente.* • **in|de|pen|dent|ly** ADV *de manera independiente, por separado, independientemente* ❑ *...people working independently in different parts of the world. ...personas que trabajan de manera independiente en diferentes partes del mundo.* **2** ADJ If someone is **independent,** they do not need help or money from anyone else. *independiente* ❑ *Children become more independent as they grow. Los niños se van haciendo más independientes conforme crecen.* • **in|de|pend|ence** N-UNCOUNT *independencia* ❑ *Her financial independence was very important to her. Para ella, su independencia financiera era muy importante.* • **in|de|pen|dent|ly** ADV *de manera independiente, por separado, independientemente* ❑ *We want to help disabled students to live independently. Queremos ayudar a los estudiantes discapacitados a vivir de manera independiente.* **3** ADJ **Independent** countries and states are not ruled by other countries but have their own government. *independiente* ❑ *Papua New Guinea became independent from Australia in 1975. Papua Nueva Guinea se independizó de Australia en 1975.* • **in|de|pend|ence** N-UNCOUNT *independencia* ❑ *Argentina declared its independence from Spain in 1816. Argentina declaró su independencia de España en 1816.*

> **Word Partnership** Usar *independence* con:
>
> V. **fight for** independence, **gain** independence **1**–**3**
> N. **a struggle for** independence **1** **3**
> ADJ. **economic/financial** independence **2**

**in-depth** ADJ An **in-depth** analysis or study of something is a very detailed and complete study of it. *a fondo, exhaustivo* ❑ *...an in-depth look at film-making. ...una mirada profunda a cómo se hacen las películas.*

**in|dex** /ɪndɛks/ (**indices, indexes, indexing, indexed**)

> The usual plural is **indexes**, but the form **indices** can be used for meaning **1**.

**1** N-COUNT An **index** is a system by which changes in the value of something can be recorded, measured, or interpreted. *índice* ❑ *...a change in the consumer price index. ...un cambio en el índice de precios al consumidor.* **2** N-COUNT An **index** is an alphabetical list that is printed at the back of a book and tells you on which pages important topics are referred to. *índice, índice analítico* ❑ *There's a subject index at the back of the book. Al final del libro hay un índice analítico.* **3** V-T If you **index** a book or a collection of information, you make an alphabetical list of the items in it. *hacer un índice, poner en un índice* ❑ *Songs are indexed alphabetically by title. Las canciones están en un índice alfabético por título.* **4** V-T If a quantity or value **is indexed to** another, a system is arranged so that it increases or decreases whenever the other one increases or decreases. *indexar* ❑ *My bonus is indexed to the company's profits. Mi bono está indexado a las utilidades de la empresa.*

**in|dex con|tour** (**index contours**) also **index contour line** N-COUNT An **index contour** is a thick contour line on a map which shows the height of the area marked by the line. *curva de nivel* [TECHNICAL]

**in|di|cate** /ɪndɪkeɪt/ (**indicates, indicating, indicated**) **1** V-T If one thing **indicates** another, the first thing shows that the second is true or exists. *indicar, señalar, denotar* ❑ *The survey indicates that most people agree. La encuesta indica que la mayoría de la gente está de acuerdo.* **2** V-T If you **indicate** an opinion, an intention, or a fact, you mention it in an indirect way. *dar indicios, dar a entender* ❑ *Mr. Rivers indicated that he might leave the company. El Sr. Rivers dio a entender que podría irse de la empresa.* **3** V-T If you **indicate** something to someone, you show them where it is. *indicar, señalar* [FORMAL] ❑ *He indicated a chair. "Sit down." Él señaló una silla. —Siéntese.*

| **Thesaurus** | *indicate* | Ver también: |
|---|---|---|
| v. | demonstrate, hint, mean, reveal, show **1** **2** | |

**in|di|ca|tion** /ɪndɪkeɪʃᵊn/ (**indications**) N-VAR An **indication** is a sign that suggests, for example, what people are thinking or feeling. *indicio, idea, pauta* ❑ *We have no indication of where he is. No tenemos idea de dónde está.*

**in|di|ca|tor** /ɪndɪkeɪtər/ (**indicators**) N-COUNT An **indicator** is a measurement or value that gives you an idea of what something is like. *indicador* ❑ *The phone has a low battery indicator. El teléfono tiene un indicador de batería baja.*

**in|di|ces** /ɪndɪsiz/ **Indices** is a plural form of **index**. *plural de* ***index***

**in|dif|fer|ent** /ɪndɪfərənt/ **1** ADJ If you accuse someone of being **indifferent to** something, you mean that they have a complete lack of interest in it. *indiferente, insensible* ❑ *People have become indifferent to the suffering of others. La gente se ha vuelto insensible al sufrimiento de los demás.* ● **in|dif|fer|ence** N-UNCOUNT *indiferencia* ❑ *...his cruel indifference to his son. ...su cruel indiferencia hacia su hijo.* ● **in|dif|fer|ent|ly** ADV *indiferentemente, con indiferencia* ❑ *"It doesn't really matter," said Tom indifferently. —Realmente no importa —dijo Tom con indiferencia.* **2** ADJ If you describe something or someone as **indifferent,** you mean that their standard or quality is not very good, and often quite bad. *mediocre, regular, del montón* ❑ *She starred in several very indifferent movies. Protagonizó varias películas muy mediocres.*

**in|dig|enous** /ɪndɪdʒɪnəs/ ADJ **Indigenous** people or things belong to the country in which they are found, rather than coming there or being brought there from another country. *indígena, autóctono* [FORMAL] ❑ *...the country's indigenous population. ...la población autóctona del país.*

**in|di|ges|tion** /ɪndɪdʒɛstʃᵊn, -daɪ-/ N-UNCOUNT If you have **indigestion,** you have pains in your stomach and chest that are caused by difficulties in digesting food. *indigestión*

**in|dig|nant** /ɪndɪgnənt/ ADJ If you are **indignant,** you are shocked and angry, because you think that something is unjust or unfair. *indignado* ❑ *He is indignant at suggestions that they were spies. Está indignado de que hayan sugerido que eran espías.* ● **in|dig|nant|ly** ADV *de manera indignante, con indignación, indignantemente* ❑ *"That is not true," Erica said indignantly. "Eso no es cierto", dijo Erica con indignación.*

**in|di|rect** /ɪndaɪrɛkt, -dɪr-/ **1** ADJ An **indirect** result or effect is not caused immediately and obviously by a thing or person, but happens because of something else that they have done. *indirecto* ❑ *Millions could die of hunger as an indirect result of the war. Millones podrían morir de hambre como resultado indirecto de la guerra* ● **in|di|rect|ly** ADV *indirectamente, de manera indirecta* ❑ *The government is indirectly responsible for the violence. El gobierno es indirectamente responsable de la violencia.* **2** ADJ An **indirect** route or journey does not use the shortest or easiest way between two places. *indirecto* ❑ *He took an indirect route back home. De regreso a la casa tomó un camino indirecto.* **3** ADJ **Indirect** remarks and information suggest something or refer to it, without actually mentioning it or stating it clearly. *indirecto* ❑ *...an indirect criticism of the president. ...una crítica indirecta al presidente.* ● **in|di|rect|ly** ADV *indirectamente* ❑ *He referred indirectly to their divorce. Se refirió indirectamente a su divorcio.*

**in|di|rect dis|course** N-UNCOUNT **Indirect discourse** tells you what someone said but does not use the person's actual words: for example, "They said you didn't like it," "I asked him what his plans were," and "People complained about the smoke." *estilo indirecto*

**in|di|rect ob|ject** (**indirect objects**) N-COUNT An **indirect object** is an object that is used with a transitive verb to indicate who benefits from an action or gets something as a result. For example, in "She gave him her address", "him" is the indirect object. Compare **direct object**. *objeto indirecto*

**in|di|rect speech** N-UNCOUNT **Indirect speech** is the same as **indirect discourse.** *estilo indirecto*

**in|dis|pen|sable** /ɪndɪspɛnsəbᵊl/ ADJ If you say that someone or something is **indispensable,** you mean that they are absolutely essential and other people or things cannot function without them. *indispensable, imprescindible, esencial* ❑ *She was indispensable to the company. Era imprescindible en la compañía.*

**in|di|vid|ual** /ɪndɪvɪdʒuᵊl/ (**individuals**) **1** ADJ **Individual** means relating to one person or thing, rather than to a large group. *individual, cada, personal* ❑ *You should decide as* a group rather than making individual decisions. Ustedes deben decidir como grupo, en vez de tomar decisiones individuales. • **in|di|vid|ual|ly** ADV individualmente ❑ ...individually made pies. ...pays hechos individualmente. **2** N-COUNT An **individual** is a person. individuo, persona, tipo ❑ We want to reward individuals who do good within our community. Queremos premiar a las personas que hacen el bien en nuestra comunidad.

**Thesaurus** *individual* Ver también:

N. human being, person **2**
PRON. somebody, someone **2**

**in|door** /ɪndɔr/ ADJ **Indoor** activities or things are ones that happen or are used inside a building and not outside. dentro, adentro, en el interior, bajo techo ❑ The matches were moved to an indoor tennis club 40 miles away. Los partidos de tenis se pasaron a unas canchas bajo techo a 40 kilómetros de distancia.

**in|doors** /ɪndɔrz/ ADV If something happens **indoors,** it happens inside a building. en el interior, bajo techo, adentro, dentro ❑ I think we should go indoors. Creo que debemos meternos.

**in|duce** /ɪndus/ (**induces, inducing, induced**) **1** V-T To **induce** a state or condition means to cause it. inducir, provocar, producir ❑ Doctors said surgery could induce a heart attack. Los médicos dicen que la cirugía podría provocar un ataque cardíaco. **2** V-T If you **induce** someone **to** do something, you persuade or influence them to do it. convencer, inducir, persuadir ❑ More than 4,000 teachers were induced to retire early. Más de 4,000 maestros fueron convencidos de retirarse anticipadamente.

**in|duct** /ɪndʌkt/ (**inducts, inducting, inducted**) V-T If someone **is inducted into** the army, they are officially made to join the army. reclutar ❑ He was inducted into the army. Fue reclutado por el ejército.

**in|dulge** /ɪndʌldʒ/ (**indulges, indulging, indulged**) **1** V-T/V-I If you **indulge in** something or if you **indulge yourself**, you allow yourself to have or do something that you know you will enjoy. consentir, consentirse, darse un gusto, ser complaciente, disfrutar ❑ She occasionally indulges in a candy bar. Ocasionalmente se da el gusto de comerse un caramelo. ❑ In New York you can indulge your passion for art. En Nueva York puedes entregarte a tu pasión por el arte. **2** V-T If you **indulge** someone, you let them have or do what they want, even if this is not good for them. consentir, mimar ❑ He did not agree with indulging children. No estaba de acuerdo en consentir a los niños.

**in|dul|gent** /ɪndʌldʒᵊnt/ ADJ If you are **indulgent,** you treat a person with special kindness, often in a way that is not good for them. indulgente, consentidor, complaciente, condescendiente ❑ His indulgent mother gave him anything he wanted. Su madre, complaciente, le daba todo lo que quería.
• **in|dul|gence** N-VAR (**indulgences**) indulgencia ❑ A teacher should not show too much indulgence. Un maestro no debe demostrar demasiada indulgencia.
• **in|dul|gent|ly** ADV con indulgencia, indulgentemente ❑ Najib smiled at him indulgently. Najib le sonrió con indulgencia.

**in|dus|trial** /ɪndʌstriəl/ **1** ADJ You use **industrial** to describe things that relate to or are used in industry. industrial ❑ ...industrial machinery and equipment. ...maquinaria y equipo industrial. **2** ADJ An **industrial** city or country is one in which industry is important or highly developed. industrial, industrializado ❑ ...Western industrial countries. ...los países industrializados de Occidente.

**Word Partnership** Usar *industrial* con:

N. industrial **machinery**, industrial **production**, industrial **products** **1** industrial **area**, industrial **city**, industrial **country** **2**

**in|dus|tri|al|ist** /ɪndʌstriəlɪst/ (**industrialists**) N-COUNT An **industrialist** is a person who owns or controls large industrial companies or factories. industrial, industrialista ❑ ...well-known Japanese industrialists. ...renombrados industriales japoneses.

**in|dus|tri|al|ize** /ɪndʌstriəlaɪz/ (**industrializes, industrializing, industrialized**) V-T/V-I When a country **industrializes** or **is industrialized,** it develops a lot of industries. industrializar, industrializarse ❑ By the late nineteenth century, both Russia and Japan had begun to industrialize. Hacia finales del siglo diecinueve, tanto Rusia como Japón habían empezado a industrializarse. • **in|dus|tri|ali|za|tion** /ɪndʌstriəlɪzeɪʃᵊn/ N-UNCOUNT industrialización ❑ Industrialization began early in Spain. La industrialización en España empezó muy pronto.

**in|dus|trial park** (**industrial parks**) N-COUNT An **industrial park** is an area which has been specially planned for a lot of factories. parque industrial, zona industrial

**in|dus|try** /ɪndəstri/ (**industries**) **1** N-UNCOUNT **Industry** is the work and processes involved in making things in factories. industria ❑ Industry needs to carry out more research. La industria necesita hacer más investigación. **2** N-COUNT A particular **industry** consists of all the people and activities involved in making a particular product or providing a particular service. industria, sector ❑ ...the tourism industry. ...el sector turístico.
→ see Word Web: **industry**
→ see **cooking**

**in|ed|ible** /ɪnɛdɪbᵊl/ ADJ If something is **inedible,** you cannot eat it, for example, because it tastes bad or is poisonous. incomestible, incomible ❑ The food was so bad it was inedible. La comida, de tan mala, estaba incomible.
→ see **cooking**

**in|ef|fec|tual** /ɪnɪfɛktʃuəl/ ADJ If someone or something is **ineffectual,** they fail to do what they are expected to do or are trying to do. inútil, incapaz ❑ ...a weak and ineffectual president. ...un presidente débil e incapaz. • **in|ef|fec|tu|al|ly** ADV ineficazmente ❑ Her voice trailed off ineffectually. Su voz se apagaba sin ningún efecto.

**in|ef|fi|cient** /ɪnɪfɪʃᵊnt/ ADJ **Inefficient** people, organizations, systems, or machines do not use time, energy, or other resources in the best way. ineficiente, incompetente ❑ Their communication systems are inefficient. Sus sistemas de comunicación son ineficientes. • **in|ef|fi|cien|cy** N-VAR (**inefficiencies**) ineficiencia ❑ The inefficiency of the marketing department has lost millions of dollars for the company. La ineficiencia del departamento de ventas ha hecho perder

**Word Web** **industry**

There are three general categories of **industry**. Primary industry means **extracting raw materials** from the environment. Examples include **agriculture, forestry,** and **mining**. In secondary industry people **refine** raw materials to make new **products**. It also includes **assembling** parts made by other **manufacturers**. There are two types of secondary industry—**light industry** (such as **textile weaving**) and **heavy industry** (such as **shipbuilding**). The third industry, tertiary industry, is **services**, which do not produce a product. Some examples are **banking**, **tourism**, and education. Recently, computers have created millions of jobs in the **information technology** field. Some researchers describe this as a fourth type of industry.

*millones de dólares a la empresa.* • **in|ef|fi|cient|ly** ADV *de manera ineficiente, ineficientemente* ❑ *Too many of us use energy inefficiently. Demasiados de nosotros utilizamos la energía de manera ineficiente.*

**in|er|tia** /ɪnɜrʃə/ **1** N-UNCOUNT If you have a feeling of **inertia,** you feel very lazy and unwilling to move or be active. *apatía* ❑ *He was annoyed by her inertia, her lack of energy. Le molestaba la apatía de ella, su falta de energía.* **2** N-UNCOUNT **Inertia** is the tendency of a physical object to remain still or to continue moving, unless a force is applied to it. *inercia* [TECHNICAL]

**in|evi|table** /ɪnɛvɪtəbᵊl/ ADJ If something is **inevitable,** it is certain to happen and cannot be prevented or avoided. *inevitable, ineludible* ❑ *Suffering is an inevitable part of life. El sufrimiento es ineludible en la vida.* • **The inevitable** is something that is inevitable. *lo inevitable* ❑ *Be realistic and prepare yourself for the inevitable. Afronta la realidad y prepárate para lo inevitable.* • **in|evi|tabil|ity** /ɪnɛvɪtəbɪlɪti/ N-VAR (**inevitabilities**) *inevitabilidad, lo inevitable* ❑ *...the inevitability of death. ...lo inevitable de la muerte.* • **in|evi|tably** /ɪnɛvɪtəbli/ ADV *inevitablemente* ❑ *Technological changes will inevitably lead to unemployment. Los cambios tecnológicos resultarán inevitablemente en desempleo.*

**in|ex|pen|sive** /ɪnɪkspɛnsɪv/ ADJ Something that is **inexpensive** does not cost very much. *barato, económico, poco costoso* ❑ *There are a number of good, inexpensive restaurants. Hay muchos restaurantes buenos y baratos.*

**in|ex|pe|ri|enced** /ɪnɪkspɪəriənst/ ADJ If you are **inexperienced,** you have little knowledge or experience of a particular situation or activity. *inexperto, sin experiencia, novato* ❑ *...inexperienced young doctors. ...médicos jóvenes sin experiencia.*

**in|fa|mous** /ɪnfəməs/ ADJ **Infamous** people or things are well-known because of something bad. *de triste memoria, de mala reputación, infame* [FORMAL] ❑ *He was infamous for his part in a racist attack. Tenía mala reputación por haber participado en un ataque racista.*

**in|fan|cy** /ɪnfənsi/ **1** N-UNCOUNT **Infancy** is the period of your life when you are a baby or very young child. *infancia, niñez* ❑ *...the way our brains develop during infancy. ...la forma en que se desarrolla nuestro cerebro en la infancia.* **2** N-UNCOUNT If something is **in its infancy,** it is new and has not developed very much. *en pañales* ❑ *Computing science was still in its infancy. La ciencia de la computación todavía estaba en pañales.*

**in|fant** /ɪnfənt/ (**infants**) N-COUNT An **infant** is a baby or very young child. *bebé, criatura* [FORMAL] ❑ *He held the infant in his arms. Cargó en sus brazos a la criatura.* ❑ *...their infant son. ...su hijo bebé.*
→ see **age, child**

**in|fan|try** /ɪnfəntri/ N-UNCOUNT **Infantry** are soldiers who fight on foot. *infantería* ❑ *...an infantry division. ...una división de infantería.*

**in|fect** /ɪnfɛkt/ (**infects, infecting, infected**) **1** V-T To **infect** people, animals, or plants means to cause them to have a disease or illness. *infectar, contagiar, contaminar* ❑ *A single mosquito can infect a large number of people. Un sólo mosquito puede infectar a gran número de personas.* ❑ *You can't catch the disease just by touching an infected person. La enfermedd no se contagia sólo con tocar a una persona infectada.* • **in|fec|tion** /ɪnfɛkʃᵊn/ N-UNCOUNT *infección* ❑ *Any form of cut can lead to infection. Cualquier cortada puede dar lugar a una infección.* **2** V-T If a virus **infects** a computer, it damages or destroys files or programs. *infectar* [COMPUTING] ❑ *This virus infected thousands of computers across the world. Ese virus infectó miles de computadoras en todo el mundo.*

**Word Partnership** Usar *infect* con:

PRON. infect **others** **1**
N. **bacteria** infect, infect **cells**, infect **people** **1**
**viruses** infect, infect **with a virus** **1** **2**

**in|fec|tion** /ɪnfɛkʃᵊn/ (**infections**) **1** N-COUNT An **infection** is a disease caused by germs or bacteria. *infección, enfermedad* ❑ *Ear infections are common in young children. Las infecciones del oído son frecuentes en los niños pequeños.* **2** → see also **infect**
→ see **diagnosis**

**Word Partnership** Usar *infection* con:

N. **cases of** infection, **rates of** infection, **risk of** infection, **symptoms of** infection **1**
V. **cause an** infection, **have an** infection, **prevent** infection, **spread an** infection **1**

**in|fec|tious** /ɪnfɛkʃəs/ **1** ADJ A disease that is **infectious** can be caught by being near a person who has it. Compare **contagious.** *infeccioso* ❑ *...infectious diseases such as measles. ...enfermedades infecciosas, como el sarampión.* **2** ADJ If a feeling is **infectious,** it spreads to other people. *contagioso* ❑ *She has an infectious enthusiasm for everything she does. Su entusiasmo por todo lo que hace es contagioso.*
→ see **illness**

**in|fer** /ɪnfɜr/ (**infers, inferring, inferred**) V-T If you **infer** that something is true, you decide that it is true on the basis of information that you already have. *inferir, deducir* ❑ *I inferred from what she said that you were sick. Deduje que estabas enfermo por lo que ella dijo.*
→ see also **imply**

**in|fe|ri|or** /ɪnfɪəriər/ (**inferiors**) **1** ADJ Something that is **inferior** is not as good as something else. *inferior, mediocre* ❑ *The fruit was of inferior quality. La fruta era de menor calidad.* **2** ADJ If one person is regarded as **inferior to** another, they are regarded as less important because they have less status or ability. *inferior* ❑ *Successful people made him feel inferior. La gente de éxito lo hacía sentirse inferior.* ● **Inferior** is also a noun. *inferior, subordinado* ❑ *The general was always polite, even to his inferiors. El general siempre era cortés, incluso con sus subordinados.* ● **in|fe|ri|or|ity** /ɪnfɪriɔrɪti/ N-UNCOUNT *inferioridad* ❑ *I felt a sense of social inferiority. Me dio la sensación de inferioridad social.*

I

**in|fer|tile** /ɪnfɜrtᵊl/ **1** ADJ A person or animal that is **infertile** is unable to produce babies. *infértil, estéril, infecundo* ❑ *One woman in eight is infertile. Una de cada ocho mujeres es estéril.* ● **in|fer|til|ity** /ɪnfɜrtɪlɪti/ N-UNCOUNT *infertilidad* ❑ *Male infertility is becoming more common. La infertilidad masculina es cada vez más común.* **2** ADJ **Infertile** soil is of poor quality because it lacks substances that plants need. *infértil* ❑ *The land was poor and infertile. La tierra era pobre e infértil.*

**in|fi|del|ity** /ɪnfɪdɛlɪti/ (**infidelities**) N-VAR **Infidelity** occurs when a person who is married or in a steady relationship has sex with another person. *infidelidad* ❑ *George ignored his partner's infidelities. George ignoró las infidelidades de su pareja.*

**in|field** /ɪnfild/ (**infields**) **1** N-COUNT In baseball, the **infield** is the part of the playing field that is inside the area marked by the four bases. *diamante* ❑ *...the right side of the infield. ...a la derecha del diamante.* **2** ADV In sports such as soccer and rugby, if players move **infield,** they move toward the center of the playing field. *centro* ❑ *Farrell threw himself infield and caught the ball. Farrell se lanzó al centro y cachó la pelota.*

**in|fil|trate** /ɪnfɪltreɪt/ (**infiltrates, infiltrating, infiltrated**) V-T If people **infiltrate** a place or organization, they enter it secretly in order to spy on it or influence it. *infiltrar, infiltrarse en* ❑ *Spies infiltrated the organization. La organización fue infiltrada por espías.* ● **in|fil|tra|tion** /ɪnfɪltreɪʃᵊn/ N-VAR (**infiltrations**) *infiltración* ❑ *...the recent infiltration by a terrorist group. ...la reciente infiltración por un grupo terrorista.*

| Word Link | *fin ≈ end : final, finish, infinite* |
|---|---|

**in|fi|nite** /ɪnfɪnɪt/ **1** ADJ If you describe something as **infinite,** you are emphasizing that it is extremely great in amount or degree. *infinito, ilimitado, inmenso* ❑ *...an infinite variety of plants. ...una infinita variedad de plantas.* ❑ *With infinite care, John laid down the baby. John acostó al bebé con inmenso cuidado.* ● **in|fi|nite|ly** ADV *infinitamente, muchísimo* ❑ *His design was infinitely better than anything I could have done. Su diseño era infinitamente mejor que cualquier cosa que yo hubiera hecho.* **2** ADJ Something that is **infinite** has no limit, end, or edge. *infinito, ilimitado* ❑ *...an infinite number of stars. ...un número infinito de estrellas* ● **in|fi|nite|ly** ADV *infinitamente* ❑ *A centimeter can be infinitely divided into smaller units. Un centímetro puede dividirse infinitamente en unidades más pequeñas.*

**in|fini|tive** /ɪnfɪnɪtɪv/ (**infinitives**) N-COUNT The **infinitive** of a verb is the basic form, for example, "do," "be," "take," and "eat." The infinitive is often used with "to" in front of it. *infinitivo*

**in|fin|ity** /ɪnfɪnɪti/ **1** N-UNCOUNT **Infinity** is a number that is larger than any other number and can never be given an exact value. *infinito* **2** N-UNCOUNT **Infinity** is a point that is further away than any other point and can never be reached. *infinito* ❑ *...job applicants whose experience ranged from zero to infinity. ...solicitantes de empleo cuya experiencia va de cero a infinito.*

**in|flam|ma|tion** /ɪnfləmeɪʃᵊn/ (**inflammations**) N-VAR An **inflammation** is a painful redness or swelling of a part of your body that results from an infection, injury, or illness. *inflamación* ❑ *The drug can cause inflammation of the heart. El fármaco puede provocar una inflamación del corazón.*

**in|flat|able** /ɪnfleɪtəbᵊl/ ADJ An **inflatable** object is one that you fill with air when you want to use it. *inflable, que se infla* ❑ *The children were playing on the inflatable castle. Los niños estaban jugando en el castillo inflable.*

**in|flate** /ɪnfleɪt/ (**inflates, inflating, inflated**) V-T/V-I If you **inflate** something such as a balloon or tire, or if it **inflates,** it becomes bigger as it is filled with air or a gas. *inflar(se), hinchar(se)* ❑ *The children's parents inflated the balloons. Los padres de los niños inflaron los globos.*

inflate

**in|fla|tion** /ɪnfleɪʃᵊn/ N-UNCOUNT **Inflation** is a general increase in the prices of goods and services in a country. *inflación* [BUSINESS] ❑ *...rising unemployment and high inflation. ...creciente desempleo e inflación alta.*

| Word Partnership | Usar *inflation* con: |
|---|---|
| V. | **control** inflation, **reduce** inflation |
| N. | inflation **fears, increase in** inflation, inflation **rate** |
| ADJ. | **high/low** inflation |

**in|flec|tion** /ɪnflɛkʃᵊn/ (**inflections**) N-VAR An **inflection** in your voice is a change in its tone or pitch as you are speaking. *inflexión, entonación,* *modulación* [WRITTEN] ❑ *A question has an upward inflection.* *En las preguntas la inflexión de la voz es hacia arriba.*

**in|flict** /ɪnflɪkt/ (**inflicts, inflicting, inflicted**) V-T To **inflict** harm or damage **on** someone or something means to make them suffer it. *infligir, imponer, causar* ❑ *...sports which inflict pain on animals.* *...deportes que causan dolor a los animales.*

**in|flu|ence** /ɪnfluəns/ (**influences, influencing, influenced**) **1** N-UNCOUNT **Influence** is the power to make other people agree with your opinions or do what you want. *influencia, ascendiente, autoridad* ❑ *He used his influence to get his son into medical school.* *Se sirvió de su influencia para que su hijo entrara a la escuela de medicina.* **2** V-T If you **influence** someone, you use your power to make them agree with you or do what you want. *influir, inducir, persuadir, influenciar* ❑ *He tried to influence a witness.* *Trató de influir en un testigo.* **3** N-COUNT To have an **influence on** people or situations means to affect what they do or what happens. *influencia, influir* ❑ *Van Gogh had a big influence on the development of modern painting.* *Van Gogh influyó mucho en el desarrollo de la pintura moderna.* **4** V-T If someone or something **influences** a person or situation, they have an effect on that person's behavior or that situation. *influir, influenciar* ❑ *We became the best of friends and he influenced me deeply.* *Nos hicimos grandes amigos y él influyó mucho en mí.* **5** N-COUNT Someone or something that is a good or bad **influence on** people has a good or bad effect on them. *influencia* ❑ *I thought Sonny would be a good influence on you.* *Pensé que Sonny sería una buena influencia para ti.*

**in|flu|en|tial** /ɪnfluɛnʃᵊl/ ADJ Someone or something that is **influential** has a lot of influence over people or events. *influyente* ❑ *It helps to have influential friends.* *Ayuda tener amigos influyentes.* ❑ *He was influential in changing the law.* *Influyó en los cambios de la ley.*

**info** /ɪnfoʊ/ N-UNCOUNT **Info** is information. *información* [INFORMAL] ❑ *For more info call 414-3935.* *Para más información, llame al 414-3935.*

**in|form** /ɪnfɔrm/ (**informs, informing, informed**) V-T If you **inform** someone **of** something, you tell them about it. *informar, comunicar, enterar* ❑ *We will inform you of any changes.* *Le informaremos de cualquier cambio.* ❑ *My daughter informed me that she was pregnant.* *Mi hija me dijo que estaba embarazada.*

**in|for|mal** /ɪnfɔrmᵊl/ ADJ **Informal** speech, behavior, or situations are relaxed and friendly rather than serious, very correct, or official. *informal, sin ceremonias* ❑ *Her style of teaching is very informal.* *Su estilo de enseñanza es muy informal.* ❑ *The house has an informal atmosphere.* *El ambiente de la casa no es nada ceremonioso.* ● **in|for|mal|ly** ADV *informalmente, con familiaridad* ❑ *She was chatting informally to the children.* *Estaba platicando informalmente con los niños.*

**Thesaurus** *informal* Ver también:

N. casual, natural, relaxed, unofficial; (ant.) formal

**in|for|mal thea|ter** N-UNCOUNT **Informal theater** is drama that is performed in somewhere such as a classroom or workshop and is not usually intended to be seen by the general public. *teatro informal*

**in|for|ma|tion** /ɪnfərmeɪʃᵊn/ **1** N-UNCOUNT **Information** about someone or something consists of facts about them. *información, datos* ❑ *Pat did not give her any information about Sarah.* *Pat no le dio ninguna información sobre Sarah.* ❑ *We can provide information on training.* *Podemos dar información sobre capacitación.* **2** N-UNCOUNT **Information** is a service that you can telephone to find out someone's telephone number. *información* ❑ *He called information, and they gave him the number.* *Llamó a información y le dieron el número.*

**Word Partnership** Usar *information* con:

ADJ. **additional** information, **background** information, **classified** information, **important** information, **new** information, **personal** information **1**

V. **find** information, **get** information, **have** information, **need** information, **provide** information, **retrieve** information, **store** information, **want** information **1**

**in|for|ma|tion tech|nol|ogy** N-UNCOUNT **Information technology** is the theory and practice of using computers to store and analyze information. The abbreviation **IT** is often used. *tecnología de la información, TI, IT* ❑ *...the information technology industry.* *...el sector de la tecnología de la información.*
→ see **industry**

**in|forma|tive** /ɪnfɔrmətɪv/ ADJ Something that is **informative** gives you useful information. *informativo, instructivo* ❑ *The meeting was friendly and informative.* *La reunión fue amistosa e informativa.*

**in|formed** /ɪnfɔrmd/ **1** ADJ Someone who is **informed** knows about a subject or what is happening in the world. *informado, sabedor, al corriente* ❑ *Informed people know the company is in trouble.* *Las personas informadas saben que la empresa está en problemas.* **2** ADJ An **informed** guess or decision is one that is likely to be good, because it is based on definite knowledge or information. *informado, fundamentado* ❑ *We can now make informed choices about medical treatment.* *Ahora podemos tomar decisiones fundamentadas sobre tratamientos médicos.*
**3** → see also **inform**

**in|frac|tion** /ɪnfrækʃᵊn/ (**infractions**) N-COUNT An **infraction** of a rule or law is an instance of breaking it. *infracción, transgresión, violación* ❑ *...an infraction of school rules.* *...una infracción a las reglas de la escuela.*

**infra|red** /ɪnfrərɛd/ **1** ADJ **Infrared** radiation is similar to light but has a longer wavelength, so you cannot see it without special equipment. *infrarrojo* **2** ADJ **Infrared** equipment detects infrared radiation. *infrarrojo* ❑ *...infrared scanners.* *...escáneres infrarrojos.*
→ see **sun**

**infra|struc|ture** /ɪnfrəstrʌktʃər/ (**infrastructures**) N-VAR The **infrastructure** of a country, society, or organization consists of the basic facilities such as transportation, communications, power supplies, and buildings, which enable it to function. infraestructura ❑ *...improvements in the country's infrastructure. ...mejoras a la infraestructura del país.*

**in|furi|ate** /ɪnfyʊərieɪt/ (**infuriates, infuriating, infuriated**) V-T If something or someone **infuriates** you, they make you extremely angry. *enfurecer, poner furioso* ❑ *His behavior infuriated her. Su comportamiento la enfureció.* ● **in|furi|at|ing** ADJ *exasperante, irritante* ❑ *It's infuriating to watch them play so badly. Es exasperante verlos jugar tan mal.*

**in|grained** /ɪngreɪnd/ ADJ **Ingrained** habits and beliefs are difficult to change or remove. *arraigado* ❑ *People's beliefs about right and wrong are often deeply ingrained. La idea de lo que es correcto y lo que es incorrecto suele estar profundamente arraigada.*

**in|gre|di|ent** /ɪngridiənt/ (**ingredients**) **1** N-COUNT **Ingredients** are the things that are used to make something, especially all the different foods you use when you are cooking a particular meal. *ingrediente* ❑ *Mix together all the ingredients. Mezclar todos los ingredientes.* **2** N-COUNT An **ingredient** of a situation is one of the essential parts of it. *ingrediente, elemento* ❑ *The movie has all the ingredients of a Hollywood success. La película tiene todos los elementos de un éxito de Hollywood.*

**Word Partnership** Usar *ingredient* con:

ADJ. **active** ingredient, **a common** ingredient, **secret** ingredient **1**
**important** ingredient, **key** ingredient, **main** ingredient **1** **2**

**in|hab|it** /ɪnhæbɪt/ (**inhabits, inhabiting, inhabited**) V-T If a place or region **is inhabited** by a group of people or a species of animal, those people or animals live there. *habitar, vivir en* ❑ *The house next to mine is inhabited by a 90-year-old. En la casa de junto vive una persona de 90 años.* ❑ *...the people who inhabit these islands. ...la gente que habita en estas islas.*

**in|hab|it|ant** /ɪnhæbɪtənt/ (**inhabitants**) N-COUNT The **inhabitants** of a place are the people who live there. *habitante* ❑ *...the inhabitants of the town. ...los habitantes del pueblo.*

**in|hale** /ɪnheɪl/ (**inhales, inhaling, inhaled**) V-T/V-I When you **inhale**, you breathe in. When you **inhale** something such as smoke, you take it into your lungs when you breathe in. *inhalar, aspirar* ❑ *He took a long slow breath, inhaling deeply. Respiró largo y lento, inhalando profundamente.* ● N-VAR **Inhalation** is the process or act of breathing in, taking air and sometimes other substances into your lungs. *inhalación* [FORMAL] ❑ *Take several deep inhalations.*

inhale

**in|her|ent** /ɪnhɛrənt, -hɪər-/ ADJ The **inherent** qualities of something are the necessary and natural parts of it. *inmanente, inherente, intrínseco* ❑ *Stress is an inherent part of life. El estrés es inherente a la vida.* ● **in|her|ent|ly** ADV *intrínsecamente* ❑ *Airplanes are not inherently dangerous. Los aviones no son intrínsecamente peligrosos.*

**in|her|it** /ɪnhɛrɪt/ (**inherits, inheriting, inherited**) **1** V-T If you **inherit** money or property, you receive it from someone who has died. *heredar, recibir una herencia* ❑ *He has no child to inherit his house. No tiene hijos que hereden su casa.* **2** V-T If you **inherit** something such as a task, problem, or attitude, you get it from the people who used to have it. *heredar* ❑ *The government has inherited a difficult situation. El gobierno heredó una situación difícil.* **3** V-T If you **inherit** a characteristic or quality, you are born with it, because your parents or ancestors also had it. *heredar* ❑ *We inherit a lot of our behavior from our parents. De nuestros padres heredamos gran parte de nuestro comportamiento.* ❑ *Her children have inherited her love of sports. Los hijos de ella heredaron su gusto por los deportes.*

**in|hib|it** /ɪnhɪbɪt/ (**inhibits, inhibiting, inhibited**) V-T If something **inhibits** an event or process, it prevents it or slows it down. *inhibir, impedir, detener* ❑ *This law inhibits freedom of speech. Esta ley inhibe la libertad de expresión.*

**in|hi|bi|tion** /ɪnɪbɪʃən/ (**inhibitions**) N-VAR **Inhibitions** are feelings of fear or embarrassment that make it difficult for you to behave naturally. *inhibición* ❑ *When you dance you can lose all your inhibitions. Cuando bailas, puedes perder todas tus inhibiciones.*

**in|hibi|tor** /ɪnhɪbɪtər/ (**inhibitors**) N-COUNT An **inhibitor** is a substance that slows down or stops a chemical reaction. *inhibidor, retardador* [TECHNICAL]

**in|hu|man** /ɪnhyumən/ **1** ADJ If you describe treatment or an action as **inhuman**, you mean that it is extremely cruel. *inhumano, cruel* ❑ *The prisoners are held in inhuman conditions. Tienen a los prisioneros en condiciones inhumanas.* **2** ADJ If you describe someone or something as **inhuman**, you mean that they are strange or bad because they do not seem human in some way. *inhumano* ❑ *...inhuman screams. ...gritos inhumanos.*

**ini|tial** /ɪnɪʃəl/ (**initials, initialing, initialed**) **1** ADJ You use **initial** to describe something that happens at the beginning of a process. *inicial, primero* ❑ *The initial reaction has been excellent. La reacción inicial ha sido excelente.* **2** N-COUNT **Initials** are the capital letters that begin each word of a name. *inicial* ❑ *...a silver car with her initials JB on the side. ...un auto color plata con sus iniciales, JB, en el costado.* **3** V-T If someone **initials** an official document, they write their initials on it, to show that they have seen it or that they accept or agree with it. *poner sus iniciales, firmar con sus iniciales, inicialar* ❑ *Would you mind initialing this check? ¿Le importaría poner sus iniciales en este cheque?*

**ini|tial con|so|nant** (**initial consonants**) also **initial blend** N-COUNT In linguistics, **initial consonants** are two or more letters that begin a word and are pronounced in their normal way when they are joined, for example the letters "b" and "l" in "blue". *consonante inicial* [TECHNICAL]

**ini|tial|ly** /ɪnɪʃəli/ ADV **Initially** means soon after the beginning of a process or situation, rather than in the middle or at the end of it. *inicialmente, en un principio, al principio* ❑ *The storms are not as bad as we initially thought. Las tormentas no* *son tan fuertes como pensamos en un principio.*

**ini|ti|ate** /ɪnɪʃieɪt/ (**initiates, initiating, initiated**) **1** V-T If you **initiate** something, you start it or cause it to happen. *iniciar, empezar, principiar* ❑ *He wanted to initiate a discussion on education. Quería empezar una discusión sobre la educación.* ● **ini|tia|tion** /ɪnɪʃieɪʃᵊn/ N-UNCOUNT *inicio, principio, comienzo* ❑ *...the initiation of a program of changes. ...el principio de un programa de cambios.* **2** V-T If someone **is initiated into** something such as a religion, secret society, or social group, they become a member of it during a special ceremony. *iniciar a alguien en algo* ❑ *In many societies, young people are formally initiated into their adult roles. En muchas sociedades, los jóvenes son iniciados formalmente en su función de adultos.* ● **ini|tia|tion** N-VAR (**initiations**) *iniciación, comienzo, principio* ❑ *This was my initiation into the peace movement. Esa fue mi iniciación en el movimiento pacifista.*

**ini|tia|tive** /ɪnɪʃiətɪv, -ʃətɪv/ (**initiatives**) **1** N-COUNT An **initiative** is an important act or statement that is intended to solve a problem. *iniciativa* ❑ *...new initiatives to help young people. ...nuevas iniciativas para ayudar a los jóvenes.* **2** N-SING If you have **the initiative,** you are in a stronger position than your opponents because you are able to do something first. *iniciativa* ❑ *We'll make sure we don't lose the initiative. Nos aseguraremos de no perder la iniciativa.* **3** N-UNCOUNT If you have **initiative,** you have the ability to decide what to do next and to do it, without needing other people to tell you what to do. *iniciativa* ❑ *Don't keep asking me for help—use your initiative. Deja de pedirme ayuda; usa tu iniciativa.* **4** N-COUNT An **initiative** is a political procedure in which a group of citizens propose a new law or a change to the law, which all voters can then vote on. *iniciativa* ❑ *The public will vote on the initiative in November. El público votará sobre la iniciativa en noviembre.* **5** PHRASE If you **take the initiative** in a situation, you are the first person to act, and are therefore able to control the situation. *tomar la iniciativa* ❑ *We must take the initiative and end the war. Debemos tomar la iniciativa y poner fin a la guerra.*

**in|ject** /ɪndʒɛkt/ (**injects, injecting, injected**) **1** V-T To **inject** a substance such as a medicine into someone means to put it into their body using a device with a needle called a syringe. *inyectar, inyectarse* ❑ *She was injected with painkillers. Le inyectaron analgésicos.* ❑ *The doctor injected morphine into him. El doctor le inyectó morfina.* **2** V-T If you **inject** a new, exciting, or interesting quality **into** a situation, you add it. *inyectar* ❑ *She tried to inject a little fun into their relationship. Ella trató de inyectar alegría a su relación.* **3** V-T If you **inject** money or resources **into** a business or organization, you provide more money or resources for it. *inyectar* [BUSINESS] ❑ *We need to inject money into the economy. Necesitamos inyectar dinero a la economía.*

**in|jec|tion** /ɪndʒɛkʃᵊn/ (**injections**) **1** N-COUNT If you have an **injection,** a doctor or nurse puts a medicine into your body using a device with a needle called a syringe. *inyección* ❑ *They gave me an injection to help me sleep. Me pusieron una inyección para dormir.* **2** N-COUNT An **injection of** money or resources into an organization is the act of providing it with more money or resources, to help it become more efficient or profitable. *inyección* [BUSINESS] ❑ *An injection of cash is needed to fund these projects. Para financiar estos proyectos se necesita una inyección de fondos.*

**in|jure** /ɪndʒər/ (**injures, injuring, injured**) V-T If you **injure** a person or animal, you damage some part of their body. *herir, lastimar, lesionar* ❑ *The bomb seriously injured at least five people. La bomba hirió gravemente cuando menos a cinco personas.*
→ see **war**

**Word Partnership** Usar *injure* con:

| | |
|---|---|
| V. | **kill or** injure |
| ADV. | **seriously** injure |
| PRON. | injure ***someone***, injure ***yourself*** |

**in|jured** /ɪndʒərd/ **1** ADJ An **injured** person or animal has physical damage to part of their body, usually as a result of an accident or fighting. *herido, lesionado* ❑ *Nurses helped the injured man. Las enfermeras ayudaron al herido.* ● **The injured** are people who are injured. *los heridos* ❑ *Army helicopters moved the injured. Los heridos fueron trasladados en helicópteros del ejército.* **2** ADJ If you have **injured** feelings, you feel upset because you believe someone has been unfair or unkind to you. *herir, ofender, agraviar* ❑ *...a look of injured pride. ...una mirada de orgullo herido.*

**Word Partnership** Usar *injured* con:

| | |
|---|---|
| N. | injured **in an accident/attack**, injured **people** 1 |
| ADV. | **badly** injured, **critically** injured, **seriously** injured 1 |
| ADJ. | **dead/killed and** injured 1 |
| V. | **get** injured, **rescue the** injured 1 |

**in|ju|ry** /ɪndʒəri/ (**injuries**) **1** N-VAR An **injury** is damage done to a person's or an animal's body. *herida, lesión* ❑ *He died from his injuries at Hope Hospital. Murió en el Hospital Hope a causa de sus heridas.* **2** to **add insult to injury** → see **insult**

**Word Partnership** Usar *injury* con:

| | |
|---|---|
| ADJ. | **bodily** injury, **internal** injury, **minor** injury, **personal** injury, **serious** injury, **severe** injury 1 |
| V. | **escape** injury, **suffer an** injury 1 |

**in|jus|tice** /ɪndʒʌstɪs/ (**injustices**) N-VAR **Injustice** is a lack of fairness in a situation. *injusticia, arbitrariedad* ❑ *They'll continue to fight injustice. Ellos seguirán luchando contra la injusticia.*

**ink** /ɪŋk/ (**inks**) N-VAR **Ink** is the colored liquid used for writing or printing. *tinta* ❑ *She wrote in black ink. Escribió con tinta negra.*

**in|land**

The adverb is pronounced /ɪnlænd, -lənd/. The adjective is pronounced /ɪnlənd/.

**1** ADV If something is situated **inland,** it is away from the coast, toward or near the middle of a country. *tierra adentro, interior de un país* ❑ *Most of the population live inland. Gran parte de la población vive en el interior del país.* ❑ *It's about 15 minutes' drive inland from Pensacola. De Pensacola, está a unos 15 minutos de*

i

*camino hacia el interior del país.* **2** ADJ **Inland** areas, lakes, and places are not on the coast, but in or near the middle of a country. *tierra adentro, interior de un país* ❑ *...a quiet inland town. ...un tranquilo pueblo del interior del país.*

**in-laws** N-PLURAL Your **in-laws** are the parents and close relatives of your husband or wife. *parientes políticos, familia política* ❑ *He spent Thanksgiving with his in-laws. Pasó el Día de Acción de Gracias con su familia política.*

**in|let** /ɪnlɛt, -lɪt/ (**inlets**) N-COUNT An **inlet** is a narrow strip of water that goes from an ocean or lake into the land. *ensenada* ❑ *...a fishing village by a rocky inlet. ...un pueblo de pescadores en una ensenada pedregosa.*

**in-line skate** (**in-line skates**) N-COUNT **In-line skates** are a type of roller skates with a single line of wheels along the bottom. *patines en línea* ❑ *She glided past on in-line skates. Pasó patinando con sus patines en línea.*

inline skates

**in|mate** /ɪnmeɪt/ (**inmates**) N-COUNT The **inmates** of a prison or mental hospital are the prisoners or patients who live there. *interno, preso, recluso, enfermo* ❑ *...education for prison inmates. ...educación para los internos de las cárceles.*

**inn** /ɪn/ (**inns**) N-COUNT An **inn** is a hotel, or restaurant, often one in the country. *hotel, posada, hostería, taberna, inn* ❑ *...the Waterside Inn. ...el hotel Waterside.*

**in|ner** /ɪnər/ **1** ADJ The **inner** parts of something are the parts contained or enclosed inside the other parts, closest to the center. *interno, interior* ❑ *The room opened onto an inner courtyard. El cuarto daba a un patio interior.* **2** ADJ Your **inner** feelings are feelings that you have but do not show to other people. *íntimo* ❑ *Loving relationships give a child an inner sense of security. Una relación cálida da al niño una íntima sensación de seguridad.*
→ see **ear**

**in|ner city** (**inner cities**) N-COUNT You use **inner city** to refer to the areas in or near the center of a large city where people live and where there are often social and economic problems. *zonas urbanas deprimidas* ❑ *...problems of crime in the inner city. ...problemas de delincuencia en las zonas urbanas deprimidas.*
→ see **city**

**in|ner core** (**inner cores**) N-COUNT The **inner core** of the Earth is the central part of the Earth's interior. It is solid and made of nickel and iron. *centro de la tierra*
→ see **core**

**in|no|cence** /ɪnəsəns/ **1** N-UNCOUNT **Innocence** is the quality of having no experience or knowledge of the more complex or unpleasant aspects of life. *inocencia* ❑ *...the sweet innocence of youth. ...la dulce inocencia de la juventud.* **2** N-UNCOUNT If someone proves their **innocence,** they prove that they are not guilty of a crime. *inocencia* ❑ *She has information which could prove his innocence. Ella tiene información que serviría para demostrar su inocencia.*

**in|no|cent** /ɪnəsənt/ (**innocents**) **1** ADJ If someone is **innocent,** they did not commit a crime that they have been accused of. *inocente* ❑ *He was sure that the man was innocent. Estaba seguro de que el hombre era inocente.* **2** ADJ If someone is **innocent,** they have no experience or knowledge of the more complex or unpleasant aspects of life. *inocente* ❑ *They seemed so young and innocent. Parecían tan jóvenes e inocentes.* ● An **innocent** is someone who is innocent. *inocente* ❑ *Greg was a complete innocent regarding women. Greg era totalmente inocente respecto de las mujeres.* ● **in|no|cent|ly** ADV *inocentemente, con inocencia* ❑ *She smiled innocently. Ella sonrió con inocencia.* **3** ADJ **Innocent** people are those who are not involved in a crime or conflict, but are injured or killed as a result of it. *inocente* ❑ *The bombing had many innocent victims. El bombardeo dejó muchas víctimas inocentes.* **4** ADJ An **innocent** question, remark, or comment is not intended to offend or upset people, even if it does so. *inocente* ❑ *It was an innocent question, I didn't mean to upset her. Fue una pregunta inocente, no era mi intención molestarla.*

**Word Partnership** Usar *innocent* con:

V. **plead** innocent, **presumed** innocent, **proven** innocent **1**
N. innocent **man/woman** **1**
innocent **children** **2**
innocent **bystander**, innocent **civilians**, innocent **people**, innocent **victim** **3**
ADV. **perfectly** innocent **4**

**Word Link** *nov ≈ new : innovation, novel, renovate*

**in|no|va|tion** /ɪnəveɪʃᵊn/ (**innovations**) **1** N-COUNT An **innovation** is a new thing or a new method of doing something. *innovación, novedad* ❑ *Vegetarian burgers were an innovation which quickly spread across the world. Las hamburguesas vegetarianas fueron una innovación que pronto se difundió por el mundo.* **2** N-UNCOUNT **Innovation** is the introduction of new ideas, methods, or things. *innovación* ❑ *Technological innovation is very important to business. La innovación tecnológica es muy importante en los negocios.*

**in|no|va|tive** /ɪnəveɪtɪv/ **1** ADJ Something that is **innovative** is new and original. *innovador* ❑ *...innovative products. ...productos innovadores.* **2** ADJ An **innovative** person introduces changes and new ideas. *innovador* ❑ *He was one of the most creative and innovative engineers of his generation. Fue uno de los ingenieros más creativos e innovadores de su generación.*
→ see **technology**

**in|put** /ɪnpʊt/ (**inputs, inputting, input**) **1** N-VAR **Input** consists of information or resources that someone receives. *aportación* ❑ *We value the students' input in planning the class. Valoramos las aportaciones de los estudiantes para la planeación de las clases.* **2** N-UNCOUNT **Input** is information that is put into a computer. *input, entrada, información introducida* [COMPUTING] ❑ *The computer processes input to produce reports. La computadora procesa las entradas para producir reportes.* **3** V-T If you **input** information into a computer, you put it in, for example, by typing it on a keyboard. *introducir, capturar* [COMPUTING] ❑ *We need more keyboarders to input the data. Necesitamos más capturistas que introduzcan los datos.*

**in|put force** (**input forces**) N-VAR In physics, the **input force** is the effort that is applied to a machine such as a lever or pulley in order to do work. Compare **output force.** *potencia de entrada* [TECHNICAL]

**in|quire** /ɪnkwaɪər/ (**inquires, inquiring, inquired**) **1** V-T/V-I If you **inquire** about something, you ask for information about it. *preguntar, informarse, averiguar, inquirir* [FORMAL] ❑ *"What are you doing here?" she inquired. —¿Qué estás haciendo aquí?—preguntó ella.* ❑ *He called them to inquire about job possibilities. Él les llamó para informarse sobre posibilidades de trabajo.* **2** V-I If you **inquire into** something, you investigate it carefully. *investigar, inquirir, averiguar* ❑ *Inspectors will inquire into the company's affairs. Los investigadores averiguarán sobre los asuntos de la empresa.*

**Thesaurus** *inquire* Ver también:
v. ask, question, quiz **1**

**in|quiry** /ɪnkwaɪəri, ɪŋkwɪri/ (**inquiries**) **1** N-COUNT An **inquiry** is a question you ask in order to get some information. *pregunta, averiguación, investigación, indagación* ❑ *He made some inquiries and discovered she had gone to Connecticut. Hizo algunas averiguaciones y se enteró de que ella se había ido a Connecticut.* **2** N-COUNT An **inquiry** is an official investigation. *investigación, averiguación* ❑ *...an official murder inquiry. ...una investigación oficial sobre el asesinato.*

**in|quis|i|tive** /ɪnkwɪzɪtɪv/ ADJ An **inquisitive** person likes finding out about things, especially secret things. *inquisitivo, preguntón, curioso* ❑ *Barrow has an inquisitive nature. Barrow es un preguntón.*

**in|roads** /ɪnroʊdz/ PHRASE If one thing **makes inroads into** another, the first thing starts affecting or destroying the second. *afectar, adentrarse* ❑ *Television has made inroads into movie audiences. La televisión ha reducido el público del cine.*

**Word Link** *san ≈ health : insane, sane, sanitary*

**in|sane** /ɪnseɪn/ **1** ADJ Someone who is **insane** is severely mentally ill. *loco, demente, chiflado* ❑ *Some people cannot cope and just go insane. Algunas personas no pueden afrontarlo y se vuelven locas.* • **in|san|ity** /ɪnsænɪti/ N-UNCOUNT *locura, demencia* ❑ *...a psychiatrist who specialized in diagnosing insanity. ...un psiquiatra especializado en el diagnóstico de la demencia.* **2** ADJ If you describe a decision or action as **insane,** you think it is very foolish or excessive. *insensato, descabellado* ❑ *I thought the idea was completely insane. Me pareció que la idea era totalmente descabellada.* • **in|sane|ly** ADV *locamente, como loco* ❑ *Try to arrive early during the insanely busy months of July and August. Trata de llegar pronto en julio y agosto, que son meses de locura.* • **in|san|ity** N-UNCOUNT *insensatez, locura* ❑ *...the insanity of war. ...la insensatez de la guerra.*

**Word Link** *sat, satis ≈ enough : insatiable, satisfy, unsatisfactory*

**in|sa|tiable** /ɪnseɪʃəbəl, -ʃiə-/ ADJ If someone has an **insatiable** desire for something, they want as much of it as they can possibly get. *insaciable* ❑ *The public has an insatiable appetite for stories about famous people. La avidez del público por enterarse de la vida de los famosos es insaciable.*

**in|scrip|tion** /ɪnskrɪpʃən/ (**inscriptions**) N-COUNT An **inscription** is writing carved into something, or written on a book or photograph. *inscripción, letrero, dedicatoria* ❑ *The inscription in the book reads "for Frankie." La dedicatoria del libro dice "para Frankie".*

**in|sect** /ɪnsɛkt/ (**insects**) N-COUNT An **insect** is a very small animal that has six legs. Most insects have wings. *insecto*
→ see Picture Dictionary: **insects**

**in|sec|ti|cide** /ɪnsɛktɪsaɪd/ (**insecticides**) N-VAR **Insecticide** is a chemical substance that is used to kill insects. *insecticida* ❑ *Spray the plants with insecticide. Rocía las plantas con insecticida.*
→ see **farm**

**in|secure** /ɪnsɪkyʊər/ **1** ADJ If you are **insecure,** you lack confidence because you think that you are not good enough or are not loved. *inseguro* ❑ *Most people are a little insecure about their looks. La mayoría de la gente se siente un poco insegura sobre su apariencia.* • **in|secu|rity** /ɪnsɪkyʊərɪti/ N-VAR (**insecurities**) *inseguridad* ❑ *She is full of emotional insecurity. Está llena de inseguridad emocional.* **2** ADJ Something that is **insecure** is not safe or protected. *inseguro* ❑ *...low-paid, insecure jobs. ...trabajos mal pagados e inseguros.* • **in|secu|rity** N-UNCOUNT *inseguridad* ❑ *Crime creates feelings of insecurity in the population. La delincuencia crea una sensación de inseguridad en la población.*

**in|sen|si|tive** /ɪnsɛnsɪtɪv/ ADJ If you describe someone as **insensitive,** you are criticizing them for being unaware of or unsympathetic to other people's feelings. *insensible, duro* ❑ *My husband is very insensitive to my problem. Mi esposo es insensible respecto de mi problema.* • **in|sen|si|tiv|ity** /ɪnsɛnsɪtɪvɪti/ N-UNCOUNT *insensibilidad, falta de sensibilidad* ❑ *I was sorry about my insensitivity toward her. Me dolió mi falta de sensibilidad hacia ella.*

**in|sepa|rable** /ɪnsɛpərəbəl/ **1** ADJ If one thing **is inseparable from** another, the two things cannot be considered separately. *inseparable* ❑ *Olive oil is inseparable from any well-made salad. El aceite de oliva y una buena ensalada son inseparables.* **2** ADJ If two people are **inseparable,** they are very good friends and spend a lot of time together. *inseparable* ❑ *She and her best friend were inseparable. Ella y su mejor amiga eran inseparables.*

**in|sert** (**inserts, inserting, inserted**)

The verb is pronounced /ɪnsɜrt/. The noun is pronounced /ɪnsɜrt/.

**1** V-T If you **insert** an object **into** something, you put the object inside it. *insertar, introducir, meter* ❑ *He took a key from his pocket and inserted it into the lock. Sacó una llave del bolsillo y la introdujo en la cerradura.* • **in|ser|tion** /ɪnsɜrʃən/ N-VAR (**insertions**) *inserción, introducción* ❑ *...an experiment involving the insertion of chemicals into a human being.*

i

## Picture Dictionary insects

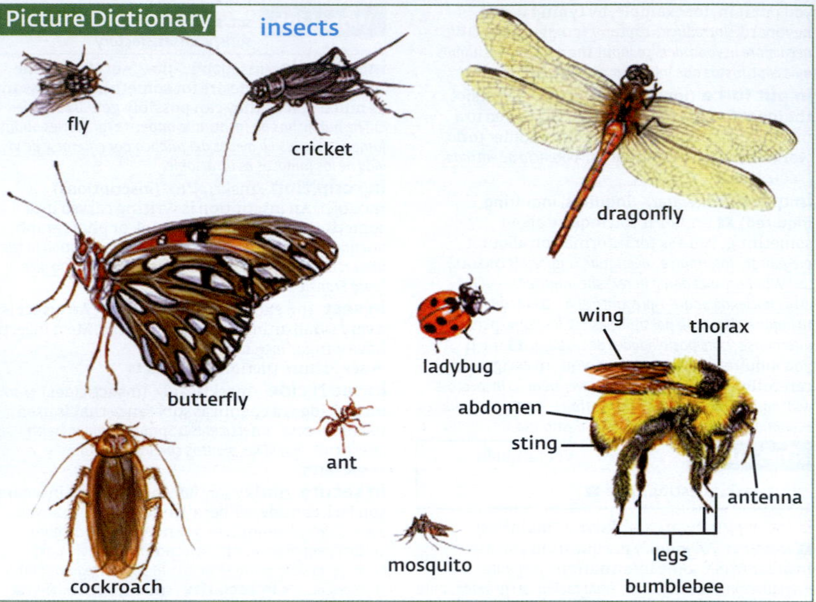


I

*...un experimento que implica dar sustancias químicas a un ser humano.* 2 V-T If you **insert** a comment into a piece of writing or a speech, you add it. *insertar, agregar, añadir* ❑ *He inserted a paragraph about the recent accident.* *Agregó un párrafo sobre el último accidente.* • **in|ser|tion** N-VAR *inserción* ❑ *Here are two more names for insertion in the list.* *Aquí están otros dos nombres para agregar a la lista.*

**in|side** /ɪnsaɪd/ (**insides**)

The preposition is usually pronounced /ɪnsaɪd/.

1 PREP Something or someone that is **inside** or **inside of** a place, container, or object is in it or is surrounded by it. *dentro, adentro, en* ❑ *Inside the envelope was a photograph.* *Dentro del sobre había una foto.* ❑ *Have you ever looked inside of a piano?* *¿Alguna vez has mirado adentro de un piano?* • **Inside** is also an adverb. *en el interior, dentro, adentro* ❑ *The couple chatted on the doorstep before going inside.* *La pareja conversó en la puerta antes de meterse.* • **Inside** is also an adjective. *interior, interno* ❑ *...an inside wall.* *...una pared interior.* 2 N-COUNT The **inside** of something is the part or area that its sides surround or contain. *interior* ❑ *The doors were locked from the inside.* *Cerraron las puertas desde el interior.* ❑ *The paper has a photo feature on its inside pages.* *El periódico tiene un artículo sobre fotografía en sus páginas interiores.* 3 ADJ **Inside** information is obtained from someone who is involved in a situation and therefore knows a lot about it. *de dentro, de adentro, confidencial* ❑ *I have no inside knowledge.* *No tengo información confidencial.* 4 N-PLURAL Your **insides** are your internal organs, especially your stomach. *entrañas, órganos internos, vísceras* [INFORMAL] ❑ *The pill made my insides hurt.* *La píldora hizo que me doliera la panza.* 5 PHRASE If something such as a piece of clothing is **inside out,** the part that is normally inside now faces outward. *al revés* ❑ *The wind blew her umbrella inside out.* *El viento volteó su paraguas al revés.*

**Thesaurus** *inside* Ver también:

| | | |
|---|---|---|
| PREP. | in; (*ant.*) outside | 1 |
| ADV. | indoors | 2 |
| N. | interior, middle | 2 |

**in|sid|er** /ɪnsaɪdər/ (**insiders**) N-COUNT An **insider** is someone who is involved in a situation and who knows more about it than other people. *persona informada, miembro de un grupo* ❑ *An insider told the newspaper that the couple were getting married.* *Alguien informado dijo al periódico que la pareja iba a casarse.*

**in|sight** /ɪnsaɪt/ (**insights**) N-VAR If you gain **insight into** a complex situation or problem, you gain an accurate and deep understanding of it. *conocimiento de* ❑ *...new insights into what is happening to the Earth.* *...nuevos conocimientos sobre lo que le está pasando a la Tierra.*

**in|sig|nifi|cant** /ɪnsɪgnɪfɪkənt/ ADJ Something that is **insignificant** is unimportant, especially because it is very small. *insignificante, pequeño, sin importancia* ❑ *In 1949 Bonn was a small, insignificant city.* *En 1949, Bonn era una ciudad pequeña y sin importancia.* • **in|sig|nifi|cance** N-UNCOUNT *insignificancia* ❑ *With this book, he went from insignificance to worldwide fame.* *Con este libro, pasó de la insignificancia a la fama mundial.*

**in|sist** /ɪnsɪst/ (**insists, insisting, insisted**) 1 V-T/V-I If you **insist that** something should be done, you say so very firmly. *insistir, obstinarse,*

*persistir* ❑ *He insisted that I should stay for dinner.* *Insistió en que me tenía que quedar a cenar.* ❑ *She insisted on being present.* *Insistió en estar presente*
• **in|sist|ence** N-UNCOUNT *insistencia, obstinación* ❑ *...her insistence on personal privacy.* *...su insistencia en la privacidad personal.* **2** V-T/V-I If you **insist** that something is true, you say so very firmly and refuse to change your mind. *insistir* ❑ *He insisted that he never accepted any gifts.* *Insistió en que nunca aceptó regalos.* ❑ *He insisted on his innocence.* *Insistió en su inocencia.*

**in|sist|ent** /ɪnsɪstənt/ **1** ADJ Someone who is **insistent** keeps insisting that a particular thing should be done or is true. *insistente, obstinado* ❑ *She is insistent that she has done nothing wrong.* *Ella sigue insistiendo en que no ha hecho nada malo.* • **in|sist|ent|ly** ADV *insistentemente, con insistencia* ❑ *"What is it?" she asked insistently.* *—¿Qué pasa?—preguntó con insistencia.* **2** ADJ An **insistent** noise or rhythm keeps going on for a long time and holds your attention. *insistente* ❑ *...the insistent rhythms of American rock music.* *...los insistentes ritmos del rock americano.*

**in|som|nia** /ɪnsɒmniə/ N-UNCOUNT Someone who suffers from **insomnia** finds it difficult to sleep. *insomnio*
→ see **sleep**

**in|spect** /ɪnspɛkt/ (**inspects, inspecting, inspected**) V-T If you **inspect** something, you examine it or check it carefully. *inspeccionar, revisar, examinar* ❑ *He inspected the car carefully before he bought it.* *Revisó cuidadosamente el coche antes de comprarlo.* • **in|spec|tion** /ɪnspɛkʃᵊn/ N-VAR (**inspections**) *inspección, revisión* ❑ *Officials will make an inspection of the site.* *Los oficiales harán una inspección del sitio.*

**in|spec|tor** /ɪnspɛktər/ (**inspectors**) **1** N-COUNT An **inspector** is a person whose job is to find out whether people are obeying official regulations. *inspector o inspectora, revisor o revisora* ❑ *Health and safety inspectors are still examining the incident.* *Los inspectores de salud y seguridad siguen analizando el incidente.* **2** N-COUNT; N-TITLE; N-VOC An **inspector** is an officer in the police who is next in rank to a superintendent or police chief. *inspector o inspectora* ❑ *...San Francisco police inspector Tony Camileri.* *...Tony Camileri, inspector de la policía de San Francisco.*

**in|spi|ra|tion** /ɪnspɪreɪʃᵊn/ **1** N-UNCOUNT **Inspiration** is a feeling of enthusiasm you get from someone or something, that gives you new ideas. *inspiración* ❑ *My inspiration comes from poets like Walt Whitman.* *Mi inspiración viene de poetas como Walt Whitman.* **2** N-SING If something or someone is **the inspiration for** a particular book, work of art, or action, they are the source of the ideas in it or act as a model for it. *inspiración* ❑ *The garden was the inspiration for a series of flower paintings.* *El jardín fue la fuente de inspiración de una serie de cuadros de flores.*

| Word Link | *spir ≈ breath : aspiration, inspire, respiratory* |
|---|---|

**in|spire** /ɪnspaɪər/ (**inspires, inspiring, inspired**) **1** V-T If someone or something **inspires** you, they give you new ideas and a strong feeling of enthusiasm. *inspirar, influir* ❑ *Guitarist Jimi Hendrix inspired a generation.* *El guitarrista Jimi Hendrix inspiró a una generación.* • **in|spir|ing** ADJ *inspirador* ❑ *She was one of the most inspiring people I ever met.* *Ella fue una de las personas más inspiradoras que conocí.* **2** V-T If a book, work of art, or action **is inspired by** something, that thing is the source of the idea for it. *inspirarse* ❑ *The book was inspired by a real person.* *El libro se inspiró en una persona real.* **3** V-T Someone or something that **inspires** a particular emotion or reaction in people makes them feel that emotion or reaction. *inspirar* ❑ *The way he manages people certainly inspires confidence.* *La forma en que trata a la gente sin duda inspira confianza.*

| Word Link | *stab ≈ steady : establish, instability, stabilize* |
|---|---|

**in|stabil|ity** /ɪnstəbɪlɪti/ (**instabilities**) N-VAR **Instability** is a lack of stability in a place, situation, or person. *inestabilidad* ❑ *...political instability.* *...inestabilidad política.*

**in|stall** /ɪnstɔl/ (**installs, installing, installed**) **1** V-T If you **install** a piece of equipment, you put it somewhere so that it is ready to be used. *instalar, colocar, montar* ❑ *They installed a new phone line in the apartment.* *Instalaron una nueva línea telefónica en el departamento.* • **in|stal|la|tion** N-UNCOUNT *instalación, colocación* ❑ *The installation of smoke alarms could save hundreds of lives.* *La instalación de alarmas de humo podría salvar cientos de vidas.* **2** V-T If someone **is installed** in a new job or important position, they are officially given the job or position. *instalar, tomar posesión* ❑ *A temporary government was installed.* *Se instaló un gobierno provisional.* ❑ *He was installed as defense secretary yesterday.* *Ayer tomó posesión como secretario de defensa.*

| Word Partnership | Usar *install* con: |
|---|---|
| ADJ. | **easy to** install **1** |
| N. | install **equipment**, install **machines**, install **software** **1** |

**in|stal|la|tion art** N-UNCOUNT **Installation art** is art that uses a variety of materials such as everyday objects, video, and sound to create an artistic work. *instalación*

**in|stall|ment** /ɪnstɔlmənt/ (**installments**) **1** N-COUNT If you pay for something in **installments,** you pay small sums of money at regular intervals over a period of time. *a plazos* ❑ *You can choose to pay your tax in installments.* *Se puede optar por pagar los impuestos a plazos.* **2** N-COUNT An **installment** of a story or plan is one of its parts that are published or carried out separately one after the other. *capítulo, entrega, fascículo* ❑ *The next installment of this four-part series is about Africa.* *El siguiente capítulo de esta serie de cuatro partes es sobre África.*

**in|stall|ment plan** (**installment plans**) N-COUNT An **installment plan** is a way of buying goods gradually. You make regular payments to the seller until you have paid the full price and the goods belong to you. *plan de pagos, facilidades de pago, con financiamiento*

**in|stance** /ɪnstəns/ (**instances**) **1** PHRASE You use **for instance** to introduce a particular event, situation, or person that is an example of what you are talking about. *por ejemplo, como* ❑ *...the important issues that face us all, for instance,* global warming. ...los problemas importantes que todos enfrentamos, por ejemplo, el calentamiento global. **2** N-COUNT An **instance** is a particular example or occurrence of something. *caso, ejemplo* ❑ *This was an instance of bad timing. Ese fue un caso de mala organización.* **3** PHRASE You say **in the first instance** to mention something that is the first step in a series of actions. *en primer lugar, en primer término* [INFORMAL] ❑ *In the first instance you should visit your doctor. Para empezar, usted debe consultar a su médico.*

**in|stant** /ɪnstənt/ (**instants**) **1** N-COUNT An **instant** is an extremely short period of time or a point in time. *instante, momento* ❑ *For an instant, I wanted to cry. Por un momento quise llorar.* ❑ *At that instant all the lights went out. En ese instante se apagaron todas las luces.* **2** PHRASE To do something **the instant** something else happens means to do it immediately. *en el instante, en el momento* ❑ *I knew who he was the instant I saw him. Supe quién era desde el momento en que lo vi.* **3** ADJ You use **instant** to describe something that happens immediately. *instantáneo, inmediato* ❑ *Her book was an instant hit. Su libro fue un éxito instantáneo.* • **in|stant|ly** ADV *instantáneamente, al instante, al momento* ❑ *The man was killed instantly. El hombre murió al instante.* **4** ADJ **Instant** food is food that you can prepare very quickly, for example, by just adding water. *instantáneo* ❑ *He stirred instant coffee into a mug of hot water. Puso café instantáneo en una taza de agua caliente.*

**Thesaurus** *instant* Ver también:

N. minute, second **1**

**Word Partnership** Usar *instant* con:

PREP. **for an** instant, **in an** instant **1**
ADJ. **the next** instant **1** **2**
N. instant **access**, instant **messaging**, instant **success** **3**

**in|stant mes|sage** (**instant messages, instant messaging, instant messaged**) **1** N-VAR An **instant message** is a written message that is sent from one computer to another. The message appears immediately on the screen of the computer you send it to, provided the computer is using the service. The abbreviation **IM** is also used. *mensaje instantáneo, IM* ❑ *Instructors answer student questions by e-mail, instant message, phone or fax. Los instructores responden las preguntas de los estudiantes por correo electrónico, mensaje instantáneo, teléfono o fax.* **2** V-T If you **instant message** someone, you send them an **instant message**. *mandar un mensaje instantáneo* ❑ *You can instant message your friends whenever you like. Puedes mandar mensajes instantáneos a tus amigos siempre que quieras.*

**in|stant mes|sag|ing** N-UNCOUNT **Instant messaging** is the sending of written messages from one computer to another. The message appears immediately on the screen of the computer you send it to, provided the computer is using the service. The abbreviation **IM** is also used. *mandar mensajes instantáneos, mensajería instantánea.* ❑ *...instant-messaging services. ...servicios de mensajería instantánea.*

**in|stant re|play** (**instant replays**) N-COUNT An **instant replay** is a repeated showing, usually in slow motion, of an event that has just been on television. *repetición instantánea.*

**in|stead** /ɪnstɛd/ **1** PHRASE If you do one thing **instead of** another, you do the first thing and not the second thing, as the result of a choice or a change of behavior. *en lugar de, en vez de* ❑ *Why don't you try to help, instead of complaining? ¿Por qué no tratas de ayudar, en lugar de quejarte?* **2** ADV If you do not do something, but do something else **instead**, you do the second thing and not the first thing. *en lugar de, en vez de, más bien* ❑ *I'm going to forget about dieting and eat normally instead. Me voy a olvidar de las dietas, más bien voy a comer normalmente.*

**in|stinct** /ɪnstɪŋkt/ (**instincts**) **1** N-VAR **Instinct** is the natural tendency that a person or animal has to behave or react in a particular way. *instinto* ❑ *She had a strong maternal instinct. Su instinto maternal era muy fuerte.* **2** N-VAR **Instinct** is a feeling, rather than an opinion or idea based on facts, that something is true. *intuición, presentimiento* ❑ *I have an instinct that he may be right. Tengo el presentimiento de que él podría tener razón.*

**Word Partnership** Usar *instinct* con:

ADJ. **basic** instinct, **maternal** instinct, **natural** instinct **1**
N. **survival** instinct **1**

**in|stinc|tive** /ɪnstɪŋktɪv/ ADJ An **instinctive** feeling, idea, or action is one that you have or do without thinking or reasoning. *instintivo* ❑ *It's an instinctive reaction—if a child falls you pick him or her up. Es una reacción instintiva—si un niño se cae, lo levantas.* • **in|stinc|tive|ly** ADV *instintivamente, por intuicion* ❑ *Jane instinctively knew something was wrong. Jane supo por intuición que algo no estaba bien.*

**in|sti|tute** /ɪnstɪtut/ (**institutes, instituting, instituted**) **1** N-COUNT An **institute** is an organization or building where a particular type of work is done, especially research or teaching. *instituto* ❑ *...the National Cancer Institute. ...el Instituto Nacional del Cáncer.* **2** V-T If you **institute** a system, rule, or course of action, you start it. *instituir, establecer* [FORMAL] ❑ *We will institute a number of changes to improve public safety. Instituiremos varios cambios para incrementar la seguridad pública.*

**in|sti|tu|tion** /ɪnstɪtuʃᵊn/ (**institutions**) **1** N-COUNT An **institution** is a large important organization such as a university, church, or bank. *institución* ❑ *...financial institutions. ...instituciones financieras.* **2** N-COUNT An **institution** is a building where certain people are cared for, such as people who are mentally ill. *institución, asilo, manicomio, orfanatorio* ❑ *Larry has been in an institution since he was four. Larry ha estado en un orfanatorio desde los cuatro años.* **3** N-COUNT An **institution** is a custom or system that is considered an important or typical feature of a particular society or group, usually because it has existed for a long time. *institución* ❑ *I believe in the institution of marriage. Yo creo en el matrimonio como institución.*

**in-store** ADJ **In-store** facilities are facilities that are available within a department store, supermarket or other large store. *dentro de una* *tienda* ❑ *...in-store banking. ...banco en la tienda.* ❑ *...an in-store bakery. ...una panadería dentro de la tienda.* • **In-store** is also an adverb. *adentro de la tienda* ❑ *Ask in-store for details. Pida información adentro de la tienda.*

**Word Link** *struct ≈ building : construct, destructive, instruct*

**in|struct** /ɪnstrʌkt/ (**instructs, instructing, instructed**) **1** V-T If you **instruct** someone to do something, you formally tell them to do it. *instruir, ordenar, dar instrucciones, enseñar, mandar* [FORMAL] ❑ *A doctor will often instruct patients to exercise. Con frecuencia el médico manda a sus pacientes que hagan ejercicio.* ❑ *"Go and speak to her," Ken instructed. —Ve y habla con ella —le ordenó Ken.* **2** V-T Someone who **instructs** people **in** a subject or skill teaches it to them. *enseñar, instruir* ❑ *He instructed us in nursing techniques. Nos enseñó técnicas de enfermería.*

**in|struc|tion** /ɪnstrʌkʃᵊn/ (**instructions**) **1** N-COUNT An **instruction** is something that someone tells you to do. *instrucción, orden* ❑ *We had instructions not to leave the building. Teníamos órdenes de no salir del edificio.* **2** N-UNCOUNT If someone gives you **instruction** in a subject or skill, they teach it to you. *instrucción, educación, enseñanza* [FORMAL] ❑ *Each new member is given instruction in safety. A todos los nuevos miembros se les dan las instrucciones de seguridad.* **3** N-PLURAL **Instructions** are detailed information on how to do something. *instrucciones* ❑ *The instructions that come with the software are easy to understand. Las instrucciones que vienen con el programa son fáciles de entender.*

**Thesaurus** *instruction* Ver también:

N. direction, order **1**
education, learning **2**

**Word Partnership** Usar *instruction* con:

ADJ. **explicit** instruction **1** **2**
N. **classroom** instruction, instruction **manual** **2**
V. **give** instruction, **provide** instruction, **receive** instruction **2**

**in|struc|tive** /ɪnstrʌktɪv/ ADJ Something that is **instructive** gives useful information. *instructivo, educativo, didáctico* ❑ *...an entertaining and instructive program. ...un programa divertido y educativo.*

**in|struc|tor** /ɪnstrʌktər/ (**instructors**) N-COUNT An **instructor** is someone who teaches a skill such as driving or skiing. An **instructor** can also be used to refer to a schoolteacher or to a college teacher of low rank. *instructor o instructora, profesor auxiliar o profesora auxiliar* ❑ *...a swimming instructor. ...un instructor de natación.*

**Thesaurus** *instructor* Ver también:

N. educator, leader, professor, teacher

**in|stru|ment** /ɪnstrəmənt/ (**instruments**) **1** N-COUNT An **instrument** is a tool or device that is used to do a particular task. *instrumento, herramienta, utensilio* ❑ *...instruments for cleaning and polishing teeth. ...instrumentos para limpiar y pulir los dientes.* **2** N-COUNT A musical **instrument** is an object such as a piano, guitar, or flute, which you play in order to produce music. *instrumento* ❑ *Learning a musical instrument helps a child to understand music. Aprender a tocar un instrumento musical ayuda al niño a apreciar la música.*
→ see **concert, orchestra**

**in|stru|men|tal** /ɪnstrəmɛntᵊl/ (**instrumentals**) **1** ADJ Someone or something that is **instrumental in** a process or event helps to make it happen. *decisivo en* ❑ *He was instrumental in the company's success. Su participación fue clave para el éxito de la empresa.* **2** ADJ **Instrumental** music is performed by instruments and not by voices. *instrumental* ❑ *...a CD of vocal and instrumental music. un CD de música vocal e instrumental.* • **Instrumentals** are pieces of instrumental music. *música instrumental* ❑ *There's a short instrumental after each of the songs. Después de cada canción viene una pieza instrumental corta.*

**in|suf|fi|cient** /ɪnsəfɪʃᵊnt/ ADJ Something that is **insufficient** is not large enough in amount or degree for a particular purpose. *insuficiente, escaso* [FORMAL] ❑ *There was insufficient evidence to charge him with murder. Las evidencias eran insuficientes como para acusarlo de asesinato.* • **in|suf|fi|cient|ly** ADV *insuficientemente, de modo insuficiente* ❑ *Food that is insufficiently cooked can cause food poisoning. Los alimentos que se cuecen de manera insuficiente pueden provocar intoxicaciones.*

**Word Link** *insula ≈ island : insulate, insulation, peninsula*

**in|su|late** /ɪnsəleɪt/ (**insulates, insulating, insulated**) **1** V-T To **insulate** something such as a building means to protect it from cold, heat, or noise by placing a layer of other material around it or inside it. *aislar* ❑ *People should insulate their homes to save energy. Para ahorrar energía se deben aislar las casas.* **2** V-T If a piece of equipment **is insulated,** it is covered with rubber or plastic to prevent electricity from passing through it and giving the person using it an electric shock. *aislar* ❑ *In order to make it safe, the equipment is electrically insulated. Por seguridad, el equipo se aísla eléctricamente.* **3** V-T If a person or group **is insulated from** the rest of society or from outside influences, they are protected from them. *aislar de* ❑ *Small towns are no longer insulated from the problems of big cities. Las poblaciones pequeñas ya no están aisladas de los problemas de las grandes ciudades.*

**Word Link** *insula ≈ island : insulate, insulation, peninsula*

**in|su|la|tion** /ɪnsəleɪʃᵊn/ **1** N-UNCOUNT **Insulation** is a thick layer of a substance that keeps something warm, especially a building. *aislante, aislamiento* ❑ *Better insulation could cut your heating bills. Un mejor aislante podría reducir sus cuentas de calefacción.* **2** → see also **insulate**

insulation

**in|su|la|tor** /ɪnsəleɪtər/ (**insulators**) N-COUNT An **insulator** is a material that insulates something. *aislante*

**in|su|lin** /ɪnsəlɪn/ N-UNCOUNT **Insulin** is a substance that most people produce naturally in their body and that controls the level of sugar in their blood. insulina ❑ *...cells that produce insulin.* *...células que producen insulina.*

**in|sult** (**insults, insulting, insulted**)

| The verb is pronounced /ɪnsʌlt/. The noun is pronounced /ɪnsʌlt/. |
|---|

**1** V-T If someone **insults** you, they say or do something that is rude or offensive. insultar, ofender ❑ *I didn't intend to insult you.* *No fue mi intención ofenderte.* • **in|sult|ed** ADJ insultado, ofendido ❑ *I was really insulted by the way he spoke to me.* *Realmente me sentí ofendido por la forma en que me habló.* • **in|sult|ing** ADJ insultante, ofensivo ❑ *...insulting language.* *...lenguaje insultante.* **2** N-COUNT An **insult** is a rude remark, or something a person says or does which insults you. insulto, ofensa, injuria ❑ *They shouted insults at each other.* *Se gritaron insultos mutuamente.* **3** PHRASE You say **to add insult to injury** when mentioning an action or fact that makes an unfair or unacceptable situation even worse. por si fuera poco, para acabarla de amolar, para colmo, para colmo de males ❑ *To add insult to injury, when the package finally arrived the contents were damaged.* *Para colmo, cuando finalmente llegó el paquete, el contenido estaba dañado.*

I

**Word Link** *ance ≈ quality, state : insurance, performance, resistance*

**in|sur|ance** /ɪnʃʊərəns/ **1** N-UNCOUNT **Insurance** is an arrangement in which you pay money to a company, and they pay you if something bad happens to you, for example, if your property is stolen. seguro ❑ *His employer provided health insurance.* *Su patrón proporcionaba un seguro de gastos médicos.* **2** N-SING If you do something as **insurance against** something bad happening, you do it to protect yourself in case the bad thing happens. prevención ❑ *Farmers grow a mixture of crops as insurance against crop failure.* *Los campesinos siembran granos de diferentes tipos por si alguna de las cosechas se echa a perder.*

**Word Partnership** Usar *insurance* con:

| | |
|---|---|
| V. | **buy/purchase** insurance, **carry** insurance, **sell** insurance **1** |
| N. | insurance **claim**, insurance **company**, insurance **coverage**, insurance **payments**, insurance **policy** **1** |

**in|sure** /ɪnʃʊər/ (**insures, insuring, insured**) V-T/V-I If you **insure** yourself or your property, you pay money to an insurance company so that, if you become ill or if your property is damaged or stolen, the company will pay you a sum of money. asegurar, asegurarse, comprar un seguro ❑ *It costs a lot of money to insure your car.* *Cuesta mucho dinero asegurar tu coche.* ❑ *Many people insure against death or long-term sickness.* *Muchas personas compran seguros contra enfermedades mortales o largas.*
→ see also **ensure**

**Word Partnership** Usar *insure* con:

| | |
|---|---|
| N. | insure ***your* car/health/house/property**, insure ***your* safety** |
| ADJ. | **difficult to** insure, **necessary to** insure |

**in|sur|er** /ɪnʃʊərər/ (**insurers**) N-COUNT An **insurer** is a company that sells insurance. aseguradora, compañía de seguros [BUSINESS]

**in|sur|rec|tion** /ɪnsərɛkʃᵊn/ (**insurrections**) N-VAR An **insurrection** is violent action by a group of people against the rulers of their country. insurrección, rebelión, levantamiento [FORMAL] ❑ *...an armed insurrection.* *...un levantamiento armado.*

**in|tact** /ɪntækt/ ADJ Something that is **intact** is complete and has not been damaged or changed. intacto, entero, íntegro ❑ *The roof was still intact.* *El techo seguía intacto.*

**in|take** /ɪnteɪk/ N-SING Your **intake** of a particular kind of food or drink is the amount that you eat or drink. ingestión, consumo ❑ *Your intake of salt should be no more than a few grams per day.* *Su consumo de sal no debe ser de más de unos gramos al día.*
→ see **engine**

**in|te|ger** /ɪntɪdʒər/ (**integers**) N-COUNT In mathematics, an **integer** is an exact whole number such as 1, 7, or 24 as opposed to a number with fractions or decimals. entero, número entero [TECHNICAL]

**in|te|grate** /ɪntɪgreɪt/ (**integrates, integrating, integrated**) **1** V-T/V-I If someone **integrates** into a social group, or **is integrated** into it, they behave in such a way that they become part of the group or are accepted into it. When different races **integrate,** they begin to live and work together, instead of separately. integrar(se) ❑ *He didn't integrate successfully into the Italian way of life.* *No logró integrarse al estilo de vida de los italianos.* ❑ *Integrating the kids with the community is essential.* *Es esencial que los niños se integren a la comunidad.* • **in|te|grat|ed** ADJ integrado ❑ *...a fully integrated, supportive society.* *...una sociedad bien integrada y que ofrezca apoyo.* • **in|te|gra|tion** /ɪntɪgreɪʃᵊn/ N-UNCOUNT integración, incorporación ❑ *...the integration of robots into the daily lives of humans.* *...la incorporación de los robots a la vida cotidiana del hombre.* **2** V-RECIP If you **integrate** things, you combine them so that they become closely linked or so that they form one thing. integrar, combinar, mezclar ❑ *The two airlines will integrate their services.* *Las dos líneas aéreas combinarán sus servicios.* • **in|te|grat|ed** ADJ integrado ❑ *...integrated computer systems.* *...sistemas de cómputo integrados.*

**Thesaurus** *integrate* Ver también:

| | |
|---|---|
| V. | assimilate, combine, consolidate, incorporate, synthesize, unite; (*ant.*) separate **2** |

**in|teg|rity** /ɪntɛgrɪti/ N-UNCOUNT If you have **integrity,** you are honest and firm in your moral principles. integridad, ser íntegro ❑ *I regard him as a man of integrity.* *Yo lo consideraba como un hombre íntegro.*

**in|tegu|men|tary sys|tem** /ɪntɛgyəmɛntəri sɪstəm/ (**integumentary systems**) N-COUNT The **integumentary system** of animals and people is a group of body parts which includes the skin, hair, and nails. sistema integumentario, sistema tegumentario [TECHNICAL]

**in|tel|lect** /ɪntɪlɛkt/ (**intellects**) **1** N-VAR **Intellect** is the ability to understand or deal with ideas and information. inteligencia, intelecto ❑ *Puzzles and games can help develop the intellect. Los acertijos y los juegos favorecen el desarrollo del intelecto.* 2 N-VAR **Intellect** is the quality of being intelligent. inteligencia ❑ *She is famous for her intellect. Es famosa por su inteligencia.*

**in|tel|lec|tual** /ɪntɪlɛktʃuəl/ (**intellectuals**) 1 ADJ **Intellectual** means involving a person's ability to think and to understand ideas and information. intelectual ❑ *...the intellectual development of children. ...el desarrollo intelectual del niño.* • **in|tel|lec|tual|ly** ADV intelectualmente, mediante la inteligencia ❑ *...intellectually satisfying work. ...trabajo intelectualmente satisfactorio.* 2 N-COUNT An **intellectual** is someone who spends a lot of time studying and thinking about complicated ideas. intelectual ❑ *...teachers, artists and other intellectuals. ...maestros, artistas y otros intelectuales.* • **Intellectual** is also an adjective. intelectual, inteligente ❑ *They were very intellectual and witty. Eran muy inteligentes e ingeniosos.*

**in|tel|lec|tual prop|er|ty** N-UNCOUNT **Intellectual property** is something such as an invention or a copyright which is officially owned by someone. propiedad intelectual [LEGAL] ❑ *...music and movies that are defined as intellectual property. ...música y películas definidas como propiedad intelectual.*

| Word Link | *ence ≈ state, condition : excellence, intelligence, patience* |
|---|---|

**in|tel|li|gence** /ɪntɛlɪdʒᵊns/ 1 N-UNCOUNT **Intelligence** is the ability to understand and learn things. inteligencia ❑ *She's a woman of great intelligence. Es una mujer de gran inteligencia.* 2 N-UNCOUNT **Intelligence** is the ability to think, reason, and understand instead of doing things by instinct. inteligencia ❑ *Your intelligence can help you solve your problems. Tu inteligencia te ayudará a resolver tus problemas.* 3 N-UNCOUNT **Intelligence** is information that is gathered by the government or the army about their country's enemies and their activities. inteligencia, información ❑ *...the need for better military intelligence. ...la necesidad de mejor inteligencia militar.*

| Word Partnership | Usar *intelligence* con: |
|---|---|
| ADJ. | **human** intelligence 2<br>**secret** intelligence 3 |
| N. | intelligence **agent**, intelligence **expert**, **military** intelligence 3 |

**in|tel|li|gent** /ɪntɛlɪdʒᵊnt/ 1 ADJ A person or animal that is **intelligent** has the ability to think, understand, and learn things quickly and well. inteligente ❑ *Susan's a very intelligent woman. Susan es una mujer muy inteligente.* • **in|tel|li|gent|ly** ADV inteligentemente, de manera inteligente, con inteligencia ❑ *They don't think intelligently about politics. No piensan de manera inteligente sobre política.* 2 ADJ Something that is **intelligent** can think and understand instead of doing things automatically or by instinct. inteligente ❑ *Intelligent computers will soon be an important tool for every doctor. Pronto las computadoras inteligentes serán una herramienta importante para los médicos.*

| Thesaurus | *intelligent* Ver también: |
|---|---|
| ADJ. | bright, clever, sharp, smart; (*ant.*) dumb, stupid 1 |

**in|tend** /ɪntɛnd/ (**intends, intending, intended**) 1 V-T If you **intend** to do something, you have decided or planned to do it. proponerse, pensar en, querer hacer ❑ *Maybe he intends to resign. Quizá él está pensando en renunciar* ❑ *What do you intend to do when you leave college? ¿Qué quieres hacer cuando salgas de la universidad?* 2 V-T If something **is intended** for a particular purpose, it has been planned to fulfill that purpose. If something **is intended** for a particular person, it has been planned to be used by that person or to affect them in some way. destinar a, dedicar a, ser para ❑ *This money is intended for schools. Este dinero está destinado a las escuelas.* ❑ *The big windows were intended to make the room brighter. Las ventanas grandes eran para dar más luz al cuarto.*

**in|tense** /ɪntɛns/ 1 ADJ **Intense** is used to describe something that is very great or extreme in strength or degree. intenso, profundo, apasionado ❑ *He was sweating from the intense heat. Estaba sudando por el intenso calor.* ❑ *...intense hatred. ...odio profundo.* • **in|tense|ly** ADV intensamente, profundamente ❑ *The fast-food business is intensely competitive. El negocio de la comida rápida es tremendamente competitivo.* • **in|ten|sity** /ɪntɛnsɪti/ N-UNCOUNT intensidad ❑ *The intensity of the attack was a shock. La intensidad del ataque provocó un shock.* 2 ADJ An **intense** person is very serious. intenso, vehemente, apasionado ❑ *He's a very intense player who loves to win. Es un jugador muy apasionado, que gusta de ganar.*

| Word Link | *ify ≈ making : claify, diversify, intensify* |
|---|---|

**in|ten|si|fy** /ɪntɛnsɪfaɪ/ (**intensifies, intensifying, intensified**) V-T/V-I If you **intensify** something or if it **intensifies,** it becomes greater in strength, amount, or degree. intensificar, agudizar, recrudecer ❑ *We must intensify our efforts to find a solution. Debemos intensificar nuestros esfuerzos para encontrar una solución.*

**in|ten|sity** /ɪntɛnsɪti/ (**intensities**) 1 N-COUNT The **intensity** of a color is how bright or dull it is. intensidad, fuerza 2 → see also **intense**

**in|ten|sive** /ɪntɛnsɪv/ 1 ADJ **Intensive** activity involves concentrating a lot of effort or people on one particular task. intenso, intensivo ❑ *...several days of intensive negotiations. ...varios días de negociaciones intensivas.* • **in|ten|sive|ly** ADV intensamente, intensivamente ❑ *He is working intensively on his book. Está trabajando intensamente en su libro.* 2 ADJ **Intensive** farming involves producing as many crops or animals as possible from your land, usually with the aid of chemicals. intensivo ❑ *...intensive methods of growing larger tomatoes. ...métodos intensivos para producir jitomates más grandes.*

**in|ten|sive care** N-UNCOUNT If someone is **in intensive care,** they are being given extremely thorough care in a hospital because they are very ill or very badly injured. cuidados intensivos, terapia intensiva ❑ *She spent the night in intensive care. Pasó la* *noche en cuidados intensivos.*

**in|tent** /ɪntɛnt/ (**intents**) **1** ADJ If you are **intent on** doing something, you are eager and determined to do it. *estar decidido, estar resuelto* ❑ *We are intent on winning this competition. Estamos decididos a ganar esta competencia.* **2** ADJ If someone does something in an **intent** way, they pay great attention to what they are doing. *decidido, resuelto* [WRITTEN] ❑ *There was an intent expression of concentration on her face. Su cara reflejaba decisión y concentración.* • **in|tent|ly** ADV *atentamente, resueltamente* ❑ *He listened intently. Escuchó atentamente.* **3** N-UNCOUNT; N-SING A person's **intent** is their intention to do something. *intención, propósito, intento* [FORMAL] ❑ *It was our intent to keep the wedding as private as possible. Nuestra intención es que la boda sea lo más privada posible.* ❑ *...an intent to frighten us. ...un intento por asustarnos.* **4** PHRASE You say **for all intents and purposes** to suggest that a situation is not exactly as you describe it but the effect is the same as if it were. *prácticamente, en el fondo, para efectos prácticos* ❑ *He sees me as his second son, which I am, for all intents and purposes. Me considera como un segundo hijo, que para efectos prácticos, soy.*

**in|ten|tion** /ɪntɛnʃᵊn/ (**intentions**) **1** N-VAR An **intention** is an idea or plan of what you are going to do. *intención, propósito* ❑ *The company has every intention of keeping the share price high. La empresa tiene el firme propósito de mantener alto el precio de sus acciones.* ❑ *It is my intention to retire later this year. Mi intención es jubilarme a finales del año.* **2** PHRASE If you say that you **have no intention of** doing something, you are emphasizing that you are not going to do it. If you say that you **have every intention of** doing something, you are emphasizing that you intend to do it. *tener la intención de* ❑ *I have no intention of going without you. No tengo intenciones de irme sin ti.*

| Word Link | *inter ≈ between : interact, interfere, internal* |
|---|---|

**inter|act** /ɪntərækt/ (**interacts, interacting, interacted**) **1** V-RECIP When people **interact with** each other or **interact,** they communicate as they work or spend time together. *interactuar, relacionarse* ❑ *The other children interacted and played together. Los otros niños interactuaron y jugaron juntos.* • **inter|ac|tion** /ɪntərækʃᵊn/ N-VAR (**interactions**) *interacción, relación* ❑ *...social interactions with other people. ...relaciones sociales con otras personas.* **2** V-RECIP When one thing **interacts with** another or two things **interact,** the two things affect each other's behavior or condition. *interactuar, relacionarse* ❑ *You have to understand how cells interact. Tienes que entender cómo interactúan las células.* • **inter|ac|tion** N-VAR *interacción* ❑ *...the interaction between physical and emotional illness. ...la interacción entre las enfermedades físicas y las emocionales.*

**inter|ac|tive** /ɪntəræktɪv/ ADJ An **interactive** computer program or electronic device is one that allows direct communication between the user and the machine. *interactivo* ❑ *This will make computer games more interactive than ever. Con esto, los juegos de computadora van a ser más interactivos que nunca.* • **inter|ac|tiv|ity** /ɪntəræktɪvɪti/ N-UNCOUNT *interactividad* ❑ *...digital television, with more channels and interactivity. ...televisión digital con más canales e interactividad.*

**inter|cept** /ɪntərsɛpt/ (**intercepts, intercepting, intercepted**) V-T If you **intercept** someone or something that is traveling from one place to another, you stop them before they get to their destination. *interceptar* ❑ *We can easily intercept emails on non-secure Web sites. Fácilmente podemos interceptar correos electrónicos en sitios web inseguros.* • **inter|cep|tion** /ɪntərsɛpʃᵊn/ N-VAR (**interceptions**) *intercepción* ❑ *...the interception of a ship off the coast of Oregon. ...la intercepción de un barco frente a la costa de Oregon.*

**inter|col|legi|ate** /ɪntərkəlidʒɪt, -dʒiɪt/ ADJ **Intercollegiate** means involving or related to more than one college or university. *intercolegial* ❑ *...an intercollegiate basketball team championship. ...un torneo intercolegial de equipos de basketball.*

**inter|course** /ɪntərkɔrs/ N-UNCOUNT **Intercourse** is the act of having sex. *coito, acto sexual, relaciones sexuales* [FORMAL]

**in|ter|est** /ɪntrɪst, -tərɪst/ (**interests, interesting, interested**) **1** N-UNCOUNT; N-SING If you have an **interest in** something, you want to learn or hear more about it. *interés* ❑ *There has been a lot of interest in the elections in the last two weeks. En las últimas dos semanas, ha habido gran interés por las elecciones.* ❑ *She liked him at first, but soon lost interest. Primero le gustó, pero pronto perdió interés en él.* **2** N-COUNT Your **interests** are the things that you enjoy doing. *interés, gusto* ❑ *Encourage your child in her interests and hobbies. Fomenta en tu hija sus pasatiempos e intereses.* **3** V-T If something **interests** you, you want to learn or hear more about it or continue doing it. *interesar, interesarse por, estar interesado en* ❑ *Your financial problems do not interest me. No estoy interesado en tus problemas financieros.* **4** N-COUNT If something is in the **interests** of a particular person or group, it will benefit them in some way. *en beneficio de, en provecho de* ❑ *He has a duty to act in the best interests of the company. Tiene la obligación de actuar en beneficio de la compañía.* **5** N-COUNT A person or organization that has an **interest** in an area, a company, a property, or in a particular type of business owns stock in it. *intereses, negocios* [BUSINESS] ❑ *My father had many business interests in Vietnam. Mi padre tenía muchos intereses comerciales en Vietnam.* **6** N-COUNT If a person, country, or organization has an **interest in** a possible event or situation, they want that event or situation to happen because they are likely to benefit from it. *interés, convenir algo* ❑ *The West has an interest in promoting democracy. A Occidente le conviene fomentar la democracia.* **7** N-UNCOUNT **Interest** is extra money that you receive if you have invested a sum of money. **Interest** is also the extra money that you pay if you have borrowed money. *interés* ❑ *Does your checking account pay interest? ¿Tu cuenta de cheques paga intereses?* **8** → see also **interested, interesting, self-interest** **9** PHRASE If you do something **in the interests of** a particular result or situation, you do it in order to achieve that result or maintain that situation. *en pro de, en beneficio de* ❑ *The president agreed to meet with the country's leader in the interests of peace. El presidente aceptó reunirse con el líder del país en pro de la paz.*

**Word Partnership** Usar *interest* con:

ADJ. **great** interest, **little** interest, **strong** interest **1**
N. **level of** interest, **places of** interest, **self-**interest **1**
**conflict of** interest **5** **6** **9**
interest **charges**, interest **expenses**, interest **payments** **7**
V. **attract** interest, **express** interest, **lose** interest **1**
**earn** interest, **pay** interest **7**

**in|ter|est|ed** /ɪntərəstɪd, -trɪstɪd/ **1** ADJ If you are **interested in** something, you think it is important and want to learn more about it or spend time doing it. *interesado* ❑ *I thought you might be interested in this article. Pensé que podrías estar interesado en este artículo.* **2** ADJ An **interested** party or group of people is affected by or involved in a particular event or situation. *parte interesada* ❑ *All the interested parties eventually agreed to the idea. Finalmente, todos los interesados aceptaron la idea.*

**Word Partnership** Usar *interested* con:

V. **become** interested, interested **in buying**, **get** interested, interested **in getting**, interested **in helping**, interested **in learning**, interested **in making**, **seem** interested **1**
ADV. **really** interested, **very** interested **1**

**in|ter|est|ing** /ɪntərɛstɪŋ, -trɪstɪŋ/ ADJ If you find something **interesting**, it attracts you or holds your attention. *interesante, de interés* ❑ *It was interesting to be in a new town. Fue interesante estar en una población diferente.* • **in|ter|est|ing|ly** /ɪntərɛstɪŋli, -trɪstɪŋli/ ADV *de modo interesante, curiosamente* ❑ *Interestingly, a few weeks later, he married again. Curiosamente, unas semanas después volvió a casarse.*

**Word Partnership** Usar *interesting* con:

ADV. **especially** interesting, **really** interesting, **very** interesting
N. interesting **idea**, interesting **people**, interesting **point**, interesting **question**, interesting **story**, interesting **things**

**inter|face** /ɪntərfeɪs/ (**interfaces**) **1** N-COUNT The **interface** between two subjects or systems is the area in which they affect each other or have links with each other. *interfaz, interfase* ❑ *...a funny story about the interface between bureaucracy and the working world. ...una historia divertida sobre la interfase entre la burocracia y el mundo laboral.* **2** N-COUNT The user **interface** of a piece of computer software is its presentation on the screen and how easy it is to operate. *interfase* [COMPUTING] ❑ *...the development of better user interfaces. ...el desarrollo de mejores interfases de usuario.*

**Word Link** *inter ≈ between : interact, interfere, internal*

**inter|fere** /ɪntərfɪər/ (**interferes, interfering, interfered**) **1** V-I If someone **interferes in** a situation, they get involved in it although it does not concern them and their involvement is not wanted. *interferir, entrometerse, inmiscuirse* ❑ *I wish everyone would stop interfering and just leave me alone. Cómo quisiera que dejaran de inmiscuirse y me dejaran en paz.* **2** V-I Something that **interferes with** a situation, activity, or process has a damaging effect on it. *interferir, afectar* ❑ *Many things can interfere with a good night's sleep. Muchas cosas pueden impedir que se duerma bien en la noche.*

**inter|fer|ence** /ɪntərfɪərəns/ **1** N-UNCOUNT **Interference** is unwanted or unnecessary involvement in something. *interferencia, intromisión* ❑ *She didn't appreciate her mother's interference in her life. Ella no aceptaba la interferencia de su madre en su vida.* **2** N-UNCOUNT When there is **interference**, a radio signal is affected by other radio waves or electrical activity so that it cannot be received properly. *interferencia* ❑ *There was too much interference and we couldn't hear the broadcast. Había demasiada interferencia y no pudimos oir la transmisión.*

**in|ter|im** /ɪntərɪm/ **1** ADJ **Interim** is used to describe something that is intended to be used until something permanent is done or established. *interino, provisional* ❑ *...an interim government. ...un gobierno interino.* **2** PHRASE **In the interim** means until a particular thing happens or until a particular thing happened. *en el ínterin, entretanto* [FORMAL] ❑ *She will return in the fall, and in the interim we have hired a temporary teacher. Ella regresa en otoño, y en el ínterin contratamos un maestro temporal.*

**in|te|ri|or** /ɪntɪəriər/ (**interiors**) **1** N-COUNT The **interior** of something is the inside part of it. *interior, parte interna* ❑ *The interior of the house was dark and old-fashioned. El interior de la casa estaba oscuro y pasado de moda.* **2** N-SING The **interior** of a country or continent is the central area of it. *interior* ❑ *The country's interior is very mountainous. El interior del país es muy montañoso.*

**Thesaurus** *interior* Ver también:

N. inside; (*ant.*) exterior, outside **1**

**inter|lude** /ɪntərlud/ (**interludes**) N-COUNT An **interlude** is a short period of time when an activity or situation stops and something else happens. *intervalo, paréntesis, intermedio*

**Word Link** *med ≈ middle : intermediate, media, medium*

**inter|medi|ate** /ɪntərmidiɪt/ **1** ADJ An **intermediate** stage, level, or position is one that occurs between two other stages, levels, or positions. *intermedio* ❑ *Do you make any intermediate stops between your home and work? ¿Haces alguna parada intermedia entre tu casa y tu trabajo?* **2** ADJ **Intermediate** learners of something have some knowledge or skill but are not yet advanced. *intermedio* ❑ *We teach beginner, intermediate, and advanced level students. Nuestros estudiantes son principiantes, intermedios y avanzados.*

**inter|mit|tent** /ɪntərmɪtᵊnt/ ADJ Something that is **intermittent** happens occasionally rather than continuously. *intermitente, recurrente* ❑ *After three hours of intermittent rain, the game was abandoned. Después de tres horas de lluvia intermitente,*

**Word Web** Internet

The **Internet** allows information to be shared by users around the world. The **World-Wide Web** allows users to access **servers** anywhere. **User names** and **passwords** give access and protect information. **E-mail** travels through **networks**. **Websites** are created by companies and individuals to share information. **Web pages** can include images, words, sound, and video. Some organizations built private **intranets**. These groups have to guard the **gateway** between their system and the larger Internet. **Hackers** can break into computer networks. They sometimes steal information or damage the system. **Webmasters** usually build firewalls for protection.

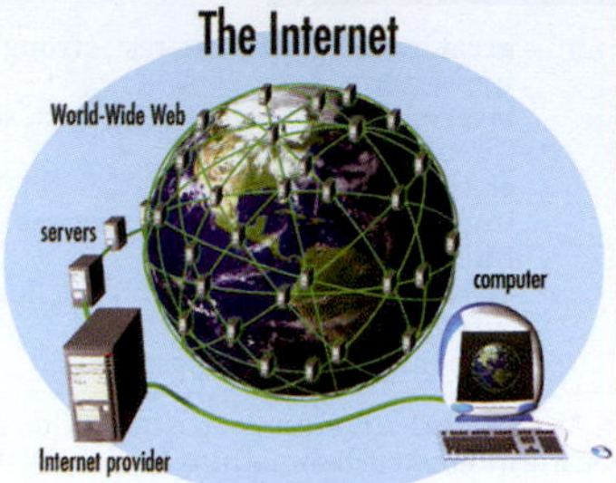


*se canceló el juego.* • **inter|mit|tent|ly** ADV *de manera intermitente, intermitentemente* ❑ *The talks went on intermittently for years. Las pláticas siguieron intermitentemente durante años.*

I

**in|tern** (**interns, interning, interned**)

The verb is pronounced /ɪntɜrn/. The noun is pronounced /ɪntɜrn/.

**1** V-T If someone **is interned,** they are put in prison or in a prison camp for political reasons. *internar, recluir* ❑ *He was interned as a prisoner of war. Estuvo recluido como prisionero de guerra.* **2** N-COUNT An **intern** is an advanced student or a recent graduate, especially in medicine, who is being given practical training under supervision. *interno* ❑ *...a medical intern. ...un interno con especialidad en medicina.*

**Word Link** *inter* ≈ *between* : *interact, interfere, internal*

**in|ter|nal** /ɪntɜrnᵊl/ **1** ADJ **Internal** is used to describe things that exist or happen inside a country or organization. *interno* ❑ *The country improved its internal security. El país mejoró la seguridad interna.* ❑ *...Russia's Ministry of Internal Affairs. ...el Ministerio de Asuntos Internos de Rusia.* • **in|ter|nal|ly** ADV *internamente* ❑ *We need to fight terrorism both internally and abroad. Necesitamos combatir el terrorismo, tanto internamente como en el exterior.* **2** ADJ **Internal** is used to describe things that exist or happen inside a particular person, object, or place. *interno* ❑ *He suffered internal bleeding. Tuvo una hemorragia interna.* • **in|ter|nal|ly** ADV *internamente* ❑ *The herb has calming effects when taken internally. Ingerida, la hierba tiene efectos calmantes.*

**in|ter|nal com|bus|tion en|gine** (**internal combustion engines**) N-COUNT An **internal combustion engine** is an engine that creates its energy by burning fuel inside itself. Most cars have internal combustion engines. *motor de combustión interna*
→ see **car, engine**

**in|ter|nal fer|ti|li|za|tion** N-UNCOUNT **Internal fertilization** is a method of reproduction in which the egg and sperm join together inside the female's body. Compare **external fertilization.** *fertilización interna* [TECHNICAL]

**In|ter|nal Rev|enue Ser|vice** N-PROPER **The Internal Revenue Service** is the U.S. government authority that collects taxes. The abbreviation **IRS** is often used. *IRS, agencia de impuestos interiores estadounidense*

**inter|na|tion|al** /ɪntərnæʃənᵊl/ ADJ **International** means between or involving different countries. *internacional* ❑ *...an international organization that brings fun and games to children in refugee camps. ...una organización internacional que lleva diversión y juegos a los niños de los campos de refugiados.* • **inter|na|tion|al|ly** ADV *internacionalmente* ❑ *...rules that have been internationally agreed upon. ...reglas acordadas internacionalmente.*

**In|ter|net** /ɪntərnɛt/ also **internet** N-PROPER **The Internet** is the network that allows computer users to connect with computers all over the world, and that carries e-mail. *Internet*
→ see Word Web: **Internet**

**In|ter|net café** (**Internet cafés**) N-COUNT An **Internet café** is a café with computers where people can pay to use the Internet. *café internet, cibercafé, cybercafé*

**in|tern|ist** /ɪntɜrnɪst/ (**internists**) N-COUNT An **internist** is a doctor who specializes in the nonsurgical treatment of disorders occurring inside people's bodies. *internista* ❑ *I've been to see an internist. Fui a consultar con un internista.*

**in|tern|ship** /ɪntɜrnʃɪp/ (**internships**) N-COUNT An **internship** is the position held by an intern, or the period of time when someone is an intern. *internado*

**in|ter|pret** /ɪntɜrprɪt/ (**interprets, interpreting, interpreted**) **1** V-T If you **interpret** something in a particular way, you decide that this is its meaning or significance. *interpretar* ❑ *I interpreted her look as a sign she didn't approve. Interpreté su mirada como un signo de desaprobación.* ❑ *The judge has to interpret the law. El juez tiene que interpretar la ley.* **2** V-T/V-I If you **interpret** what someone is saying, you translate it immediately into another language. *interpretar* ❑ *She spoke little English, so her husband came with her to interpret. Ella hablaba poco inglés, así que su esposo fue con ella para interpretar.* • **in|ter|pret|er** /ɪntɜrprɪtər/ N-COUNT (**interpreters**) *intérprete* ❑ *Speaking through an interpreter, he said that he was very pleased with the result. En voz de un intérprete, dijo que estaba muy complacido con el resultado.*

**in|ter|pre|ta|tion** /ɪntɜrprɪteɪʃᵊn/

(**interpretations**) 1 N-VAR An **interpretation** of something is an opinion about what it means. *interpretación* ❑ *Professor Wolfgang gives the data a very different interpretation. El profesor Wolfgang da una interpretación muy diferente de los datos.* 2 N-COUNT A performer's **interpretation** of something such as a piece of music or a role in a play is the particular way in which they choose to perform it. *interpretación* ❑ *...the pianist's interpretation of Chopin. ...como interpreta a Chopin el pianista.*
→ see **art**

**Word Link** *rupt ≈ breaking : disrupt, erupt, interrupt*

**in|ter|rupt** /ɪntərʌpt/ (**interrupts, interrupting, interrupted**) 1 V-T/V-I If you **interrupt** someone who is speaking, you say or do something that causes them to stop. *interrumpir* ❑ *I'm sorry to interrupt, but there's a phone call for you. Disculpe la interrupción, le hablan por teléfono.* ❑ *Don't interrupt the teacher when she's speaking. No interrumpan a la maestra cuando está hablando.* ● **in|ter|rup|tion** /ɪntərʌpʃᵊn/ N-VAR (**interruptions**) *interrupción* ❑ *The sudden interruption stopped Justin in the middle of a sentence. Interrumpieron repentinamente a Justin a mitad de una frase.* 2 V-T If someone or something **interrupts** a process or activity, they stop it for a period of time. *interrumpir* ❑ *She kept coming into the room, interrupting my work. Siguió entrando al cuarto e interrumpiendo mi trabajo.* ● **in|ter|rup|tion** N-VAR *interrupción* ❑ *...telephone interruptions. ...interrupciones por llamadas telefónicas.*

**inter|state** /ɪntərsteɪt/ (**interstates**) 1 ADJ **Interstate** means between states, especially the states of the United States. *interestatal* ❑ *...interstate commerce. ...comercio interestatal.* 2 N-COUNT An **interstate** or **interstate highway** is a major road linking states. *carretera interestatal, interestatal* ❑ *We were traveling on Interstate 75. Íbamos por la Interestatal 75.*

**in|ter|val** /ɪntərvᵊl/ (**intervals**) 1 N-COUNT An **interval** between two events or dates is the period of time between them. *intervalo, interrupción* ❑ *After an interval of six months, doctors repeat the test. Después de un intervalo de seis meses, los médicos repiten la prueba.* 2 N-COUNT An **interval** in music is the distance in pitch between two tones. *intervalo* 3 PHRASE If something happens **at intervals,** it happens several times with gaps or pauses in between. *a intervalos* ❑ *She woke him for his medication at intervals throughout the night. Lo estuvo despertando toda la noche para que tomara su medicina.* 4 PHRASE If things are placed **at** particular **intervals,** there are spaces of a particular size between them. *a intervalos* ❑ *White barriers marked the road at intervals of about a mile. El camino estaba marcado con barreras blancas a intervalos de un kilómetro.*

**inter|vene** /ɪntərvin/ (**intervenes, intervening, intervened**) V-I If you **intervene in** a situation, you become involved in it and try to change it. *intervenir* ❑ *The situation calmed down when police intervened. La situación se calmó cuando intervino la policía.* ● **inter|ven|tion** /ɪntərvɛnʃᵊn/ N-VAR (**interventions**) *intervención* ❑ *...the intervention of the U.S. in the affairs of other countries. ...la intervención de los Estados Unidos en los asuntos de otros países.*

**inter|view** /ɪntərvyu/ (**interviews, interviewing, interviewed**) 1 N-VAR An **interview** is a formal meeting at which someone is asked questions in order to find out if they are suitable for a job. *entrevista laboral* ❑ *The interview went well. La entrevista estuvo bien.* 2 V-T If you **are interviewed** for a particular job, someone asks you questions about yourself to find out if you are suitable for it. *entrevistar, ser entrevistado, entrevistarse con alguien* ❑ *She was interviewed for a management job. La entrevistaron para un puesto administrativo.* 3 N-COUNT An **interview** is a conversation in which a journalist asks a famous person a series of questions. *entrevista* ❑ *Allan gave an interview to the Chicago Tribune last month. Allan le concedió una entrevista al Chicago Tribune el mes pasado.* 4 V-T When a journalist **interviews** someone such as a famous person, they ask them a series of questions. *entrevistar* ❑ *She has interviewed many famous actors. Ha entrevistado a muchos actores famosos.* ● **inter|view|er** N-COUNT (**interviewers**) *entrevistador o entrevistadora* ❑ *Being a good interviewer requires preparation and skill. Para ser un buen entrevistador se necesita preparación y habilidad.*

**Word Partnership** Usar *interview* con:

N. **job** interview 1
**(tele)phone** interview 1 3
**radio/magazine/newspaper/television** interview 3
V. **conduct an** interview, **give an** interview, **request an** interview 1 3

**in|tes|tine** /ɪntɛstɪn/ (**intestines**) N-COUNT Your **intestines** are the tubes in your body through which food passes when it has left your stomach. *intestino* ❑ *He has a problem with his intestines. Tiene un problema con los intestinos.* ● **in|tes|ti|nal** /ɪntɛstɪnᵊl/ ADJ *intestinal* [FORMAL] ❑ *...the intestinal wall. ...la pared intestinal.*

**in|ti|mate** (**intimates, intimating, intimated**)

The adjective is pronounced /ɪntɪmɪt/. The verb is pronounced /ɪntɪmeɪt/.

1 ADJ If you have an **intimate** friendship with someone, you know them very well and like them a lot. *íntimo* ❑ *I told my intimate friends I wanted to have a baby. Le dije a mis amigos más íntimos que quería tener un bebé.* ● **in|ti|mate|ly** ADV *íntimamente* ❑ *He knew them quite well, but not intimately. Los conocía bastante bien, pero no íntimamente.* 2 ADJ If two people are in an **intimate** relationship, they are involved with each other in a loving or sexual way. *íntimo* ❑ *...a private and intimate moment between two people. ...un momento privado e íntimo entre dos personas.* 3 ADJ If you use **intimate** to describe an occasion or the atmosphere of a place, you like it because it is quiet and pleasant, and seems suitable for close conversations between friends. *íntimo* ❑ *...an intimate dinner for two. ...una cena íntima para dos.* 4 ADJ An **intimate** knowledge of something is a deep and detailed knowledge of it. *profundo* ❑ *She surprised me with her intimate knowledge of football. Me sorprendió con su profundo conocimiento del fútbol.* ● **in|ti|mate|ly** ADV *a profundidad* ❑ *...musicians whose work she knew intimately. ...músicos cuyo trabajo ella conocía a*

*profundidad.* **5** V-T If you **intimate** something, you say it in an indirect way. *insinuar* [FORMAL] ❑ *He intimated that things were going to change dramatically. Insinuó que las cosas iban a cambiar dramáticamente.*

**in|timi|date** /ɪntɪmɪdeɪt/ (**intimidates, intimidating, intimidated**) V-T If you **intimidate** someone, you frighten them, often deliberately in order to make them do what you want them to do. *intimidar* ❑ *My new boss tried to intimidate me. Mi nuevo jefe trató de intimidarme.* • **in|timi|dat|ed** /ɪntɪmɪdeɪtɪd/ ADJ *intimidado* ❑ *Children often feel intimidated starting in a new school. Los niños se sienten a menudo intimidados cuando entran a una nueva escuela.* • **in|timi|dat|ing** /ɪntɪmɪdeɪtɪŋ/ ADJ *intimidatorio* ❑ *He was a huge, intimidating man. Era un hombre enorme e intimidante.* • **in|timi|da|tion** /ɪntɪmɪdeɪʃᵊn/ N-UNCOUNT *intimidación* ❑ *Witnesses may not give evidence because they are afraid of intimidation. Los testigos pueden no proporcionar la evidencia porque tienen miedo a la intimidación*

**into** /ɪntu/

Pronounced /ɪntu/ or /ɪntu/, particularly before pronouns.

In addition to the uses shown below, **into** is used after some verbs and nouns in order to introduce extra information. **Into** is also used with verbs of movement, such as "walk" and "push," and in phrasal verbs such as "enter into" and "talk into."

**1** PREP If you put one thing **into** another, you put the first thing inside the second. *en* ❑ *Put the apples into a dish. Ponga las manzanas en un plato* **2** PREP If you go **into** a place or vehicle, you move from being outside it to being inside it. *dentro* ❑ *She got into the car and started the engine. Se metió dentro del carro y arrancó el motor.* **3** PREP If you bump **into** something or crash **into** something, you hit it accidentally. *contra* ❑ *A train crashed into the barrier at the end of the track. Un tren chocó contra la barrera al final de las vías.* **4** PREP When you get **into** a piece of clothing, you put it on. *ponerse algo de ropa* ❑ *I'll change into some warmer clothes. Me voy a poner ropa más calientita.* **5** PREP If someone or something gets **into** a particular state, they start being in that state. *en* ❑ *He got into a panic. Entró en pánico.* **6** PREP If you talk someone **into** doing something, you persuade them to do it. *convencer* ❑ *They talked him into selling the farm. Lo convencieron de vender la granja.* **7** PREP If something changes **into** something else, it then has a new form, shape, or nature. *transformar* ❑ *Malmsten turned her hobby into a business. Malmstem transformó su pasatiempo en un negocio.* **8** PREP If something is cut or split **into** a number of pieces or sections, it is divided so that it becomes several smaller pieces or sections. *en* ❑ *Sixteen teams are taking part, divided into four groups. Participan dieciséis equipos, divididos en cuatro grupos.* **9** PREP An investigation **into** a subject or event is concerned with that subject or event. *sobre* ❑ *...research into AIDS. ...investigación sobre SIDA.*

**Word Link** *intra ≈ inside, within : intramural, intranet, intravenous*

**intra|mu|ral** /ɪntrəmyʊərəl/ ADJ **Intramural** activities happen within one college or university, rather than between different colleges or universities. *intramuros* ❑ *...a program of intramural sports. ...un programa deportivo intramuros.*

**in|tra|net** /ɪntrənɛt/ (**intranets**) N-COUNT An **intranet** is a network of computers, similar to the Internet, within a particular company or organization. *intranet, red interna*
→ see **Internet**

**in|tran|si|tive** /ɪntrænsɪtɪv/ ADJ An **intransitive** verb does not have an object. *intransitivo*

**intra|venous** /ɪntrəvinəs/ ADJ **Intravenous** foods or drugs are put into people's bodies through their veins, rather than their mouths. *intravenoso* [MEDICAL] ❑ *...intravenous fluids. ...fluidos intravenosos* • **intra|venous|ly** ADV *por vía intravenosa* ❑ *Premature babies have to be fed intravenously. A los bebés prematuros se les debe alimentar por vía intravenosa.*

**in|tri|cate** /ɪntrɪkɪt/ ADJ You use **intricate** to describe something that has many small parts or details. *intrincado, complejo, delicado* ❑ *...carpets with very intricate patterns. ...alfombras de estampados muy complicados.* • **in|tri|ca|cy** /ɪntrɪkəsi/ N-UNCOUNT *complejidad, lo intrincado* ❑ *The price depends on the intricacy of the work. El precio depende de la complejidad del trabajo.* • **in|tri|cate|ly** ADV *delicadamente* ❑ *...intricately carved sculptures. ...esculturas delicadamente talladas.*

**in|trigue** (**intrigues, intriguing, intrigued**)

The noun is pronounced /ɪntrig/. The verb is pronounced /ɪntrig/.

**1** N-VAR **Intrigue** is the making of secret plans to harm or deceive people. *intriga* ❑ *...political intrigue. ...intriga política.* **2** V-T If something, especially something strange, **intrigues** you, it interests you and you want to know more about it. *intrigar* ❑ *Her remark intrigued him. Su comentario lo intrigó.* • **in|trigued** ADJ *intrigado* ❑ *I would be intrigued to hear his views. A mí me intrigaría escuchar sus puntos de vista.*

**in|tri|guing** /ɪntrigɪŋ/ **1** ADJ If you describe something as **intriguing**, you mean that it is interesting or strange. *fascinante* ❑ *This is an intriguing story. Es una historia fascinante.* • **in|tri|guing|ly** ADV *de manera intrigante* ❑ *The results are intriguingly different each time. Los resultados varían de manera intrigante cada vez.* **2** → see also **intrigue**

**intro|duce** /ɪntrədus/ (**introduces, introducing, introduced**) **1** V-T To **introduce** something means to cause it to enter a place or exist in a system for the first time. *introducir* ❑ *They are introducing new rules for student visas. Están introduciendo nuevas reglas para las visas de estudiante.* • **intro|duc|tion** /ɪntrədʌkʃᵊn/ N-UNCOUNT *introducción* ❑ *...the introduction of a computerized payment system. ...la introducción de un sistema computarizado de pagos.* **2** V-T If you **introduce** one person **to** another, or you **introduce** two people, you tell them each other's names, so that they can get to know each other. If you **introduce yourself** to someone, you tell them your name. *presentar* ❑ *Tim, may I introduce you to my wife? Tim, ¿te presento a mi esposa?* ❑ *We haven't been introduced. My name is Ned Taylor. No nos han* *presentado. Mi nombre es Ned Taylor.* • **intro|duc|tion** N-VAR (**introductions**) *presentaciones* ❑ *Elaine, the hostess, performed the introductions. Elaine, la anfitriona, hizo las presentaciones.* **3** V-T If you **introduce** someone **to** something, you cause them to learn about it or experience it for the first time. *introducir* ❑ *He introduced us to the delights of Spanish food. Nos introdujo a los deleites de la cocina española.* • **intro|duc|tion** N-SING *introducción* ❑ *The vacation was a gentle introduction to camping. Las vacaciones fueron una sutil introducción al campismo.* **4** V-T The person who **introduces** a television or radio program speaks at the beginning of it, and often between the different items in it, in order to explain what the program or the items are about. *presentar* ❑ *The show is introduced by Abby Clarke. El espectáculo es presentado por Abby Clarke.*

**Word Partnership** Usar *introduce* con:

N. introduce **a bill**, introduce **changes**, introduce **legislation**, introduce **reform** **1**
V. **allow me to** introduce, **let me** introduce, **want to** introduce **2**

**intro|duc|tion** /ɪntrədʌkʃᵊn/ (**introductions**) **1** N-COUNT The **introduction to** a book or talk is the part that comes at the beginning and tells you what the rest of the book or talk is about. *introducción* ❑ *Ellen Malos wrote the introduction to the book. Ellen Malos escribió la introducción del libro.* **2** N-COUNT If you refer to a book as an **introduction to** a particular subject, you mean that it explains the basic facts about that subject. *introducción* ❑ *The book is a simple introduction to physics. El libro no es más que una introducción a la física.* **3** → see also **introduce**

**in|tui|tion** /ɪntuɪʃᵊn/ (**intuitions**) N-VAR Your **intuition** or your **intuitions** are unexplained feelings that something is true even when you have no evidence or proof of it. *intuición* ❑ *Her intuition told her that something was wrong. Su intuición le decía que algo andaba mal.*

**in|vade** /ɪnveɪd/ (**invades, invading, invaded**) **1** V-T/V-I To **invade** a country means to enter it by force with an army. *invadir* ❑ *In autumn 1944 the Allies invaded the Italian mainland. En el otoño de 1944 los aliados invadieron la masa territorial italiana.* ❑ *...invading armies. ...ejércitos invasores.* • **in|vad|er** N-COUNT (**invaders**) *invasor o invasora* **Invaders** are soldiers who are invading a country. *invasores* ❑ *The city was destroyed by foreign invaders. La ciudad fue destruida por invasores extranjeros.* **2** V-T If you say that people or animals **invade** a place, you mean that they enter it in large numbers, often in a way that is unpleasant or difficult to deal with. *invadir* ❑ *Every so often ants invaded the kitchen. De vez en cuando las hormigas invadían la cocina.*

**in|va|lid** (**invalids**)

The noun is pronounced /ɪnvəlɪd/. The adjective is pronounced /ɪnvælɪd/ and is hyphenated in|val|id.

**1** N-COUNT An **invalid** is someone who needs to be cared for because they have an illness or disability. *inválido o inválida* ❑ *I hate being called an invalid. Odio que me llamen inválido.* **2** ADJ If an action, procedure, or document is **invalid**, it cannot be accepted, because it breaks the law or some official rule. *inválido* ❑ *The trial was stopped and the results were declared invalid. El juicio fue detenido y los resultados fueron declarados inválidos.* **3** ADJ An **invalid** argument or conclusion is wrong because it is based on a mistake. *inválido* ❑ *The facts show that this argument is invalid. Los hechos muestran que su argumento es inválido.*

**in|valu|able** /ɪnvælyuəbᵊl/ ADJ If you describe something as **invaluable**, you mean that it is extremely useful. *invaluable* ❑ *I gained invaluable experience during that year. Gané experiencia invaluable durante ese año.*

**in|vari|ably** /ɪnvɛəriəbli/ ADV If something **invariably** happens or is **invariably** true, it always happens or is always true. *invariablemente* ❑ *He is invariably late. Llega tarde invariablemente.*

**in|va|sion** /ɪnveɪʒᵊn/ (**invasions**) **1** N-VAR If there is an **invasion** of a country, a foreign army enters it by force. *invasión* ❑ *...the German invasion of Poland in 1939. ...la invasión alemana a Polonia en 1939.* **2** N-VAR If you refer to the arrival of a large number of people or things as an **invasion**, you are emphasizing that they are unpleasant or difficult to deal with. *invasión* ❑ *...the annual summer invasion of flies. ...la invasión veraniega anual de moscas.* **3** N-VAR If you describe an action as an **invasion**, you disapprove of it because it affects someone or something in a way that is not wanted. *invasión, intromisión* ❑ *Reading someone's diary is an invasion of privacy. Leer un diario ajeno es una invasión a la privacidad.*

**in|vent** /ɪnvɛnt/ (**invents, inventing, invented**) **1** V-T If you **invent** something such as a machine or process, you are the first person to think of it or make it. *inventar* ❑ *He invented the first electric clock. Inventó el primer reloj eléctrico.* • **in|ven|tor** N-COUNT (**inventors**) *inventor o inventora* ❑ *...Alexander Graham Bell, the inventor of the telephone. ...Alexander Graham Bell, inventor del teléfono.* **2** V-T If you **invent** a story or excuse, you try to make other people believe that it is true when in fact it is not. *inventar* ❑ *I tried to invent a good excuse. Intenté inventar un buen pretexto.*

**in|ven|tion** /ɪnvɛnʃᵊn/ (**inventions**) **1** N-COUNT An **invention** is a machine, device, or system that has been invented by someone. *invento* ❑ *Paper was a Chinese invention. El papel fue un invento de los chinos.* **2** N-UNCOUNT **Invention** is the act of inventing something that has never been made or used before. *invención* ❑ *...the invention of the telephone. ...la invención del teléfono.* **3** N-VAR If you refer to someone's account of something as an **invention**, you think that it is untrue and that they have made it up. *invento* ❑ *His story was an invention from start to finish. Su historia era un invento de pies a cabeza.*

**in|ven|tory** /ɪnvᵊntɔri/ (**inventories**) **1** N-VAR An **inventory** is a supply or stock of something. *inventario* ❑ *...an inventory of ten items at $15 each. ...un inventario de diez artículos a 15 dólares cada uno.* **2** N-COUNT An **inventory** is a written list of all the objects in a particular place such as all the merchandise in a store. *inventario* ❑ *He made an inventory of everything that was in the apartment. Hizo un inventario de todo lo que había en el departamento.*

**in|vert** /ɪnvɜrt/ (**inverts, inverting, inverted**) V-T If you **invert** something, you turn it upside down or back to front. *invertir, voltear* [FORMAL] ❑ *Invert the cake onto a serving plate. Voltee el pastel en un plato para servir.*

**in|ver|te|brate** /ɪnvɜrtɪbrɪt/ (**invertebrates**) N-COUNT An **invertebrate** is a creature that does not have a spine such as an insect, a worm, or an octopus. *invertebrado* [TECHNICAL] ● **Invertebrate** is also an adjective. *invertebrado* ❑ *...invertebrate creatures. ...criaturas invertebradas*

**in|vest** /ɪnvɛst/ (**invests, investing, invested**) **1** V-T/V-I If you **invest in** something, or if you **invest** a sum of money, you use your money in a way that you hope will increase its value, for example, by buying securities or property. *invertir* ❑ *Many people don't like to invest in stocks. A mucha gente no le gusta invertir en acciones.* ❑ *He invested millions of dollars in the business. Invirtió millones de dólares en el negocio.* ● **in|ves|tor** N-COUNT (**investors**) *inversionista* ❑ *The main investor in the project is the French bank Crédit National. El inversionista principal en el proyecto es el banco francés Credit National.* **2** V-T/V-I If you **invest in** something useful, you buy it, because it will help you to do something more efficiently or more cheaply. *invertir* ❑ *We decided to invest in new computers. Decidimos invertir en computadoras nuevas.* **3** V-T If you **invest** time or energy **in** something, you spend a lot of time or energy on it because you think it will be useful or successful. *invertir* ❑ *I would rather invest time in my children than in my work. Prefiero invertir tiempo en mis hijos que en mi trabajo.* **4** V-T To **invest** someone **with** rights or responsibilities means to give them those rights or responsibilities legally or officially. *investir* [FORMAL] ❑ *The president invested him with special powers. El presidente lo invistió con poderes especiales.*

**in|ves|ti|gate** /ɪnvɛstɪgeɪt/ (**investigates, investigating, investigated**) V-T/V-I If someone, especially an official, **investigates** an event, situation, or claim, they try to find out what happened or what is the truth. *investigar* ❑ *Officials are still investigating the cause of the explosion. Los oficiales están aún investigando la causa de la explosión.* ❑ *Police are investigating how the accident happened. La policía está investigando cómo sucedió el accidente.* ● **in|ves|ti|ga|tion** /ɪnvɛstɪgeɪʃᵊn/ N-VAR (**investigations**) *investigación* ❑ *He ordered an investigation into the affair. Ordenó que se hiciera una investigación del asunto.*

| Word Link | *ator ≈ one who does : educ**ator**, investig**ator**, spect**ator*** |
|---|---|

**in|ves|ti|ga|tor** /ɪnvɛstɪgeɪtər/ (**investigators**) N-COUNT An **investigator** is someone who carries out investigations, especially as part of their job. *investigador o investigadora, detective* ❑ *...a private investigator. ...un investigador privado*

**in|vest|ment** /ɪnvɛstmənt/ (**investments**) **1** N-UNCOUNT **Investment** is the activity of investing money. *inversión* ❑ *...rules on investment. ...reglas de inversión* **2** N-VAR An **investment** is an amount of money that you invest, or the thing that you invest it in. *inversión* ❑ *...an investment of twenty-eight million dollars. ...una inversión de veintiocho millones de dólares.* **3** N-COUNT If you describe something you buy as an **investment,** you mean that it will be useful, especially because it will help you to do a task more cheaply or efficiently. *inversión* ❑ *Buying good quality leather boots is a wise investment. Comprar botas de piel de buena calidad es una sabia inversión.*

**in|vis|ible** /ɪnvɪzɪbᵊl/ **1** ADJ If something is **invisible,** you cannot see it, for example, because it is transparent, hidden, or very small. *invisible* ❑ *The mark is invisible from a distance. La marca es invisible a cierta distancia.* **2** ADJ If you say that a person, problem, or situation is **invisible,** you are complaining that they are being ignored. *invisible* ❑ *He felt completely invisible in the room. Sintió que era invisible en el cuarto.* ● **in|vis|ibil|ity** /ɪnvɪzɪbɪlɪti/ N-UNCOUNT *invisibilidad* ❑ *She talked about the invisibility of women in society. Habló acerca de la invisibilidad de las mujeres en la sociedad.*
→ see **sun**

**in|vi|ta|tion** /ɪnvɪteɪʃᵊn/ (**invitations**) **1** N-COUNT An **invitation** is a written or spoken request to come to an event such as a party, a meal, or a meeting. *invitación* ❑ *I accepted her invitation to lunch. Acepté su invitación a almorzar.* **2** N-COUNT An **invitation** is the card or paper on which an invitation is written or printed. *invitación* ❑ *Hundreds of invitations are being sent out this week. Se están mandando cientos de invitaciones esta semana.* **3** N-SING If you believe that someone's action is likely to have a particular result, especially a bad one, you can refer to the action as an **invitation to** that result. *invitación* ❑ *Don't leave your purse in your car—it's an invitation to theft. No dejes tu monedero en el coche, es una invitación a que te roben.*

| Word Partnership | Usar *invitation* con: |
|---|---|
| V. | **accept an** invitation, **decline an** invitation, **extend an** invitation **1** **get/receive an** invitation **1** **2** |

**in|vi|ta|tion|al** /ɪnvɪteɪʃᵊnᵊl/ (**invitationals**) ADJ An **invitational** tournament or event is a sports competition in which only players who have been asked to take part can compete. *por invitación* ❑ *The golf tournament in Spain is an invitational tournament. En España, el torneo de golf es por invitación.* ● **Invitational** is also a noun. *evento al que sólo se puede asistir con invitación* ❑ *...a 59-team invitational. Un torneo entre 59 equipos que han sido invitados.*

**in|vite** (**invites, inviting, invited**)

> The verb is pronounced /ɪnvaɪt/. The noun is pronounced /ɪnvaɪt/.

**1** V-T If you **invite** someone to something such as a party or a meal, you ask them to come to it. *invitar* ❑ *She invited him to her 26th birthday party. Lo invitó a su fiesta de cumpleaños número 26.* ❑ *Barron invited her to go with him to the theater. Barron la invitó a ir con él al teatro.* **2** V-T If you **are invited to** do something, you are formally asked or given permission to do it. *invitar* ❑ *Managers were invited to buy stocks in the company. Se invitó a los gerentes a comprar acciones de la empresa.* ❑ *He invited me to go into partnership with him. Me invitó a asociarme con él.* **3** V-T If something you say or do **invites** trouble or criticism, it makes trouble or criticism more likely. *atraer* ❑ *Their refusal to compromise will* *invite more criticism.* *Su negativa a ceder atraerá más críticas.* **4** N-COUNT An **invite** is an invitation to something such as a party or a meal. *invitación* [INFORMAL] ❑ *She tried to get an invite to the party.* *Trató de obtener una invitación a la fiesta.*

**Word Partnership** Usar *invite* con:

N. invite *someone* **to dinner**, invite **friends**, invite **people** **1**
invite **criticism**, invite **questions** **3**

**in|vo|ca|tion** /ɪnvoʊkeɪʃᵊn/ (**invocations**) N-COUNT An **invocation** is a prayer at a public meeting, usually at the beginning. *invocación* ❑ *Dr. Jerome Taylor will give the invocation.* *El Dr. Jerome Taylor hará la invocación.*

**in|voice** /ɪnvɔɪs/ (**invoices, invoicing, invoiced**) **1** N-COUNT An **invoice** is a document that lists goods that have been supplied or services that have been done, and says how much money you owe for them. *factura* ❑ *We will send you an invoice for the course fees.* *Le mandaremos una factura por las colegiaturas del curso.* **2** V-T If you **invoice** someone, you send them a bill for goods or services you have provided them with. *pasarle factura a* ❑ *The agency invoiced the client.* *La agencia le facturó al cliente.*

**in|vol|un|tary** /ɪnvɒlənteri/ ADJ If you make an **involuntary** movement or sound, you make it suddenly and without intending to because you are unable to control yourself. *involuntario* ❑ *Pain in my ankle caused me to give an involuntary scream.* *El dolor del tobillo me hizo dar un grito involuntario.* • **in|vol|un|tari|ly** /ɪnvɒlənteərɪli/ ADV *involuntariamente* ❑ *I smiled involuntarily.* *Sonreí involuntariamente.*
→ see **muscle**

**in|volve** /ɪnvɒlv/ (**involves, involving, involved**) **1** V-T If a situation or activity **involves** something, that thing is a necessary part or consequence of it. *involucrar* ❑ *Running a household involves lots of organizational skills.* *Llevar una casa involucra muchas habilidades de organización.* **2** V-T If a situation or activity **involves** someone, they are taking part in it. *involucrar* ❑ *The case involved people at the highest levels of government.* *El caso involucraba a gente de los niveles más altos del gobierno.* **3** V-T If you **involve** someone **in** something, you get them to take part in it. *involucrar* ❑ *We involve the children in everything we do as a family.* *Involucramos a los niños en todo lo que hacemos como familia.*

**in|volved** /ɪnvɒlvd/ **1** ADJ If you are **involved in** a situation or activity, you are taking part in it or have a strong connection with it. *involucrado* ❑ *She has been involved in business since she was a young woman.* *Ha estado involucrada en el negocio desde que era joven.* **2** ADJ If you are **involved in** something, you give a lot of time, effort, or attention to it. *comprometido* ❑ *The family was deeply involved in their local church.* *La familia le dedicaba mucho tiempo a su iglesia.* **3** ADJ The things **involved in** something such as a job or system are the necessary parts or consequences of it. *implicado* ❑ *There is a lot of hard work involved in the job.* *Este empleo implica mucho trabajo duro.* **4** ADJ If a situation or activity is **involved,** it is very complicated. *complejo* ❑ *The surgery can be quite involved.* *La cirugía puede ser bastante compleja.*

**in|volve|ment** /ɪnvɒlvmənt/ N-UNCOUNT Your **involvement in** or **with** something is the fact that you are taking part in it. *participación* ❑ *His parents didn't like his involvement with the group.* *A sus padres no les gustaba su participación en el grupo.*

**Word Link** *ward ≈ in the direction of : backward, forward, inward*

**in|ward** /ɪnwərd/ **1** ADJ Your **inward** thoughts or feelings are the ones that you do not express or show to other people. *interno* ❑ *I felt inward relief.* *Sentí un alivio interno.* • **in|ward|ly** ADV *por dentro* ❑ *Sara was inwardly furious.* *Sara estaba furiosa por dentro.* **2** ADJ An **inward** movement is one toward the inside or center of something. *interno* ❑ *...a sharp, inward breath.* *...una respiración intensa y profunda.* **3** ADV If something moves or faces **inward,** it moves or faces toward the inside or center of something. *hacia adentro* ❑ *He pushed the front door, which swung inward.* *Empujó la puerta principal, que se abrió hacia adentro.*

**ion** /aɪən, aɪɒn/ (**ions**) N-COUNT **Ions** are electrically charged atoms. *ión* [TECHNICAL]

**ion|ic bond** /aɪɒnɪk bɒnd/ (**ionic bonds**) N-COUNT An **ionic bond** is a force that holds together two atoms with opposite electric charges. *enlace iónico* [TECHNICAL]

**ion|ic com|pound** (**ionic compounds**) N-COUNT An **ionic compound** is a chemical compound, consisting of a metal and a nonmetal, in which the atoms are held together by ionic bonds. *compuesto iónico* [TECHNICAL]

**IP ad|dress** /aɪ pi ædrɛs/ (**IP addresses**) N-COUNT An **IP address** is a series of numbers that identify which particular computer or network is connected to the Internet. **IP** is an abbreviation for "Internet Protocol." *dirección IP* [COMPUTING] ❑ *Every computer on the Internet has an unique IP address.* *Toda computadora conectada a internet tiene una dirección IP única.*

**IQ** /aɪ kyu/ (**IQs**) N-VAR Your **IQ** is your level of intelligence, as indicated by a special test that you take. **IQ** is an abbreviation for "intelligence quotient." *IQ, coeficiente intelectual* ❑ *His IQ is above average.* *Su IQ es superior al promedio.*

**iris** /aɪrɪs/ (**irises**) N-COUNT The **iris** is the round colored part of a person's eye. *iris*
→ see **eye, muscle**

**iron** /aɪərn/ (**irons, ironing, ironed**) **1** N-UNCOUNT **Iron** is an element that usually takes the form of a hard, dark gray metal. *hierro* ❑ *...a gate made of iron.* *...una reja de hierro.* **2** N-COUNT An **iron** is an electrical device with a flat metal base. You heat it until the base is hot, then rub it over clothes to remove creases. *plancha* **3** V-T If you **iron** clothes, you remove the creases from them using an iron. *planchar* ❑ *She used to iron his shirts.* *Ella solía planchar sus camisas.* • **iron|ing** N-UNCOUNT *planchado* ❑ *I did all the ironing this morning.* *Planché toda la ropa hoy en la mañana.* **4** ADJ You can

iron

i

use **iron** to describe the character or behavior of someone who is very firm in their decisions and actions, or who can control their feelings well. acero ❑ *...a man of iron determination.* *...un hombre con una voluntad de acero.*
→ see **pan**
▸ **iron out** PHR-VERB If you **iron out** difficulties, you resolve them and bring them to an end. resolver, superar ❑ *We had to iron out a lot of problems.* *Tuvimos que superar muchos problemas.*

**Word Partnership** Usar *iron* con:

| | |
|---|---|
| ADJ. | **cast** iron, **wrought** iron 1<br>**a hot** iron 2 |
| N. | iron **bar**, iron **gate** 1<br>iron **a shirt** 3<br>**an** iron **fist/hand** 4 |

**iron|ic** /aɪrɒnɪk/ also **ironical** /aɪrɒnɪkəl/ 1 ADJ When you make an **ironic** remark, you say the opposite of what you really mean, as a joke. irónico ❑ *The comment was meant to be ironic.* *Se trataba de hacer un comentario irónico.* • **ironi|cal|ly** /aɪrɒnɪkli/ ADV irónicamente ❑ *His enormous dog is ironically called "Tiny."* *Irónicamente, su enorme perro se llamaba "Pequeño".* 2 ADJ An **ironic** situation is odd or amusing because it involves a contrast. irónico ❑ *It is ironic that so many women are anti-feminist.* *Es irónico que tantas mujeres sean antifeministas.* • **ironi|cal|ly** ADV irónicamente ❑ *Ironically, many people who drown know how to swim.* *Irónicamente, muchas personas que se ahogan sí saben nadar.*

**iro|ny** /aɪrəni, aɪər-/ (**ironies**) 1 N-UNCOUNT **Irony** is a subtle form of humor that involves saying things that are the opposite of what you really mean. ironía ❑ *His tone was full of irony.* *Su tono estaba lleno de ironía.* 2 N-VAR If you talk about the **irony** of a situation, you mean that it is odd or amusing because it involves a contrast. ironía ❑ *The irony is that although we all know we should save money for the future, few of us do.* *La ironía es que, a pesar de que todos sabemos que debemos ahorrar para el futuro, pocos lo hacemos.*

**Word Link** *ir ≈ not : irrational, irregular, irresponsible*

**Word Link** *ratio ≈ reasoning : irrational, ratio, rational*

**ir|ra|tion|al** /ɪræʃənəl/ ADJ **Irrational** feelings and behavior are not based on logical reasons or clear thinking. irracional, irrazonable, absurdo ❑ *...an irrational fear of science.* *...un temor absurdo a la ciencia.* • **ir|ra|tion|al|ly** ADV irracionalmente ❑ *My husband is irrationally jealous of my ex-boyfriends.* *Mi esposo está irracionalmente celoso de mis ex novios.* • **ir|ra|tion|al|ity** /ɪræʃənælɪti/ N-UNCOUNT irracionalidad, lo irracional ❑ *...the irrationality of his behavior.* *...lo irracional de su comportamiento.*

**ir|ra|tion|al num|ber** (**irrational numbers**) N-COUNT An **irrational number** is a number that cannot be written as a simple fraction, for example the square root of 2. número irracional [TECHNICAL]

**ir|regu|lar** /ɪrɛgyələr/ 1 ADJ If events or actions occur at **irregular** intervals, the periods of time between them are of different lengths. irregular, discontinuo ❑ *Cars passed at irregular intervals.* *Pasaban coches a intervalos irregulares.* ❑ *Two years of irregular rainfall have brought problems for farmers.* *Dos años de lluvias irregulares han provocado problemas a los agricultores.* • **ir|regu|lar|ly** ADV irregularmente, de manera irregular ❑ *He was eating irregularly and losing weight.* *Estaba comiendo de manera irregular y perdiendo peso.* • **ir|regu|lar|ity** /ɪrɛgyəlærɪti/ N-VAR (**irregularities**) irregularidad ❑ *...a dangerous irregularity in her heartbeat.* *...una peligrosa irregularidad de su ritmo cardíaco.* 2 ADJ Something that is **irregular** is not smooth or straight, or does not form a regular pattern. irregular ❑ *The irregular surface makes it difficult for plants to grow.* *Lo irregular de la superficie dificulta el crecimiento de las plantas.* • **ir|regu|lar|ly** ADV irregularmente, con irregularidad ❑ *The lake was irregularly shaped.* *El lago era de forma irregular.* 3 ADJ **Irregular** behavior is dishonest or not in accordance with the normal rules. irregular, inadmisible ❑ *...irregular business practices.* *...prácticas comerciales irregulares.* • **ir|regu|lar|ity** N-VAR irregularidad ❑ *We are investigating financial irregularities in the company.* *Estamos investigando las irregularidades financieras de la empresa.* 4 ADJ An **irregular** verb, noun, or adjective has different forms from most other verbs, nouns, or adjectives in the language. For example, "break" is an irregular verb because its past form is "broke," not "breaked." irregular • **ir|regu|lar|ity** N-VAR (**irregularities**) irregularidad, anomalía ❑ *...irregularities such as irregular plurals (sheep, oxen, phenomena).* *...anomalías del tipo de los plurales irregulares (sheep, oxen, phenomena).* [TECHNICAL]

**ir|regu|lar gal|axy** (**irregular galaxies**) N-COUNT An **irregular galaxy** is a galaxy with an irregular shape that does not belong to the other main types of galaxy such as spiral or elliptical galaxies. galaxia irregular [TECHNICAL]

**ir|rel|evant** /ɪrɛlɪvənt/ ADJ If you describe something as **irrelevant,** you mean that it is not important to or connected with what you are discussing or dealing with. irrelevante, intrascendente, no pertinente ❑ *...irrelevant details.* *...detalles irrelevantes.* ❑ *Your age is irrelevant—what matters is whether you can do your job.* *Tu edad no importa, lo que importa es que puedas hacer el trabajo.* • **ir|rel|evance** N-UNCOUNT irrelevancia ❑ *...the irrelevance of the debate.* *...la irrelevancia del debate.*

**ir|re|sist|ible** /ɪrɪzɪstɪbəl/ 1 ADJ If a desire or force is **irresistible,** it is so powerful that it makes you act in a certain way, and there is nothing you can do to prevent this. irresistible ❑ *He had an irresistible urge to yawn.* *Sentía un ansia irresistible de bostezar.* • **ir|re|sist|ibly** /ɪrɪzɪstɪbli/ ADV irresistiblemente ❑ *I found myself irresistibly drawn to Steve.* *Me sentía irresistiblemente atraída por Steve.* 2 ADJ If you describe something or someone as **irresistible,** you mean that they are so good or attractive that you cannot stop yourself from liking them or wanting them. irresistible [INFORMAL] ❑ *The music is irresistible.* *La música es irresistible.* • **ir|re|sist|ibly** ADV irresistiblemente ❑ *She had a charm that men found irresistibly attractive.* *Su encanto era tal, que para los hombres era irresistiblemente atractiva.*

**Word Link** ir ≈ not : irrational, irregular, irresponsible

**ir|re|spon|sible** /ɪrɪspɒnsɪbəl/ ADJ If you describe someone as **irresponsible**, you are criticizing them because they do things without properly considering their possible consequences. *irresponsable* ❑ *It is irresponsible to leave such a young child alone. Es irresponsable dejar solo a un niño pequeño.* ● **ir|re|spon|sibly** /ɪrɪspɒnsɪbli/ ADV *irresponsablemente, de manera irresponsable* ❑ *They behaved irresponsibly. Se comportaron irresponsablemente.* ● **ir|re|spon|sibil|ity** /ɪrɪspɒnsɪbɪlɪti/ N-UNCOUNT *irresponsabilidad, lo irresponsable* ❑ *I am surprised at the irresponsibility of their behavior. Me sorprendió lo irresponsable de su comportamiento.*

**ir|re|vers|ible** /ɪrɪvɜrsɪbəl/ ADJ If a change is **irreversible**, things cannot be changed back to the way they were before. *irreversible, irrevocable* ❑ *He suffered irreversible brain damage. Sufrió un daño cerebral irreversible.*

**ir|ri|gate** /ɪrɪgeɪt/ (**irrigates, irrigating, irrigated**) V-T To **irrigate** land means to supply it with water in order to help crops grow. *irrigar, regar* ❑ *Water from Lake Powell is used to irrigate the area. El agua del lago Powell se utiliza para regar la zona.* ● **ir|ri|ga|tion** /ɪrɪgeɪʃən/ N-UNCOUNT *irrigación, riego* ❑ *The irrigation of the surrounding agricultural land is poor. El riego de la tierra cultivable de los alrededores es deficiente.*
→ see **dam, farm**

**ir|ri|tate** /ɪrɪteɪt/ (**irritates, irritating, irritated**) **1** V-T If something **irritates** you, it keeps annoying you. *irritar, molestar, enojar* ❑ *Their attitude irritates me. La actitud de ellos me irrita.* ● **ir|ri|tat|ed** ADJ *irritado, enojado* ❑ *Her teacher got irritated with her. Su maestra se enojó con ella.* ● **ir|ri|tat|ing** ADJ *irritante, molesto* ❑ *They have an irritating habit of interrupting. Tienen la molesta costumbre de interrumpir.* ● **ir|ri|tat|ing|ly** ADV *insufriblemente* ❑ *He is irritatingly indecisive. Él es insufriblemente indeciso.* **2** V-T If something **irritates** a part of your body, it causes it to itch or become sore. *irritar* ❑ *Chilies can irritate the skin. Los chiles pueden irritar la piel.*

**ir|ri|ta|tion** /ɪrɪteɪʃən/ (**irritations**) **1** N-UNCOUNT **Irritation** is a feeling of annoyance. *irritación, molestia, enfado* ❑ *He tried not show his irritation. Él trató de no demostrar su enfado.* **2** N-COUNT An **irritation** is something that keeps annoying you. *molestia, enojo* ❑ *Don't let a minor irritation at work make you unhappy. No dejes que un enojo sin importancia te quite el gusto por el trabajo.* **3** N-VAR **Irritation** in a part of your body is a feeling of slight pain and discomfort there. *irritación* ❑ *These oils may cause irritation to sensitive skins. Estos aceites pueden provocar irritación en pieles sensibles.*

**Is|lam** /ɪslɑm/ N-UNCOUNT **Islam** is the religion of the Muslims, which was started by Mohammed. *islam, islamismo* ❑ *He converted to Islam at the age of 16. Se convirtió al islam/islamismo a los 16 años.* ● **Is|lam|ic** /ɪslæmɪk, -lɑ-/ ADJ *islámico, musulmán* ❑ *...Islamic law. ...la ley islámica.*

**is|land** /aɪlənd/ (**islands**) N-COUNT An **island** is a piece of land that is completely surrounded by water. *isla* ❑ *...the Canary Islands. ...las Islas Canarias.*
→ see **landform**

**isle** /aɪl/ (**isles**) N-COUNT An **isle** is an island; often used as part of an island's name, or in literary English. *isla* ❑ *...the Isle of Pines. ...la Isla de Pinos.*

**isn't** /ɪzənt/ **Isn't** is the usual spoken form of "is not." *forma hablada usual de* **is not**

**iso|bar** /aɪsəbɑr/ (**isobars**) N-COUNT An **isobar** is a line on a weather map that connects points of equal atmospheric pressure. *isobara*

**iso|late** /aɪsəleɪt/ (**isolates, isolating, isolated**) V-T To **isolate** someone or something means to make them become separate from other people or things of the same kind, either physically or socially. *aislar, separar, apartar* ❑ *His difficult behavior isolated him from other children. Lo difícil de su comportamiento lo apartaba de los otros niños.* ● **iso|lat|ed** ADJ *aislado, apartado* ❑ *She was completely isolated, living alone in a big house. Estaba completamente aislada; vivía sola en una enorme casa.* ● **iso|la|tion** /aɪsəleɪʃən/ N-UNCOUNT *aislamiento, incomunicación* ❑ *Boredom and isolation were starting to upset her. El aburrimiento y la incomunicación empezaban a molestarle.*

**iso|lat|ed** /aɪsəleɪtɪd/ **1** ADJ An **isolated** place is a long way away from large towns and is difficult to reach. *aislado, apartado* ❑ *Their village is in an isolated area. Su pueblo se encuentra en un área apartada.* **2** ADJ An **isolated** example is an example of something that is not very common. *aislado, único* ❑ *There was one isolated case of cheating. Fue el único caso en que hicieron trampa.*

**iso|la|tion** /aɪsəleɪʃən/ (**isolations**) **1** N-VAR In dance, an **isolation** is a movement or exercise that involves only one part of your body, for example shrugging your shoulders or rolling your head. *aislamiento* [TECHNICAL] **2** → see also **isolate** **3** PHRASE If someone does something **in isolation**, they do it without other people present or without their help. *por sí solo, solo* ❑ *She is good at working in isolation. Ella es buena para trabajar sola.*

**iso|tope** /aɪsətoʊp/ (**isotopes**) N-COUNT **Isotopes** are atoms that have the same number of protons and electrons but different numbers of neutrons and therefore have different physical properties. *isótopo* [TECHNICAL]

**ISP** /aɪ ɛs pi/ (**ISPs**) N-COUNT An **ISP** is a company that provides Internet and e-mail services. **ISP** is an abbreviation for "Internet service provider." *proveedor de servicios de internet*

**is|sue** /ɪʃu/ (**issues, issuing, issued**) **1** N-COUNT An **issue** is an important subject that people are arguing about or discussing. *problema, cuestión, asunto, tema* ❑ *She raised the issue of money with her boss. Tocó el tema del dinero con su jefe.* **2** N-SING If something is **the issue**, it is the thing you consider to be the most important part of a situation or discussion. *lo más importante* ❑ *Job satisfaction is the issue for me, not money. Para mí, lo más importante no es el dinero, sino estar satisfecho con el trabajo.* **3** N-COUNT An **issue** of something such as a magazine or newspaper is the version of it that is published, for example, in a particular month or on a particular day. *número* ❑ *...the latest issue of the "Scientific American." ...el último número de*

"Scientific American". **4** V-T If you **issue** a statement or a warning, you make it known formally or publicly. emitir, expedir, publicar ❑ *The government issued a warning of possible terrorist attacks.* El gobierno emitió un boletín de advertencia sobre posibles ataques terroristas. **5** V-T If you **are issued with** something, it is officially given to you. entregar algo a alguien ❑ *He was issued with a new passport.* Le entregaron su nuevo pasaporte. ● **Issue** is also a noun. reparto, expedición, entrega ❑ *...a pair of army issue boots.* ...un par de botas del ejército. **6** PHRASE The question or point **at issue** is the question or point that is being argued about or discussed. de lo que se trata ❑ *The point at issue is who controls the company.* El punto en cuestión es quién controla la empresa.
→ see **philosophy**

**it** /ɪt/

**It** is a third person singular pronoun. **It** is used as the subject or object of a verb, or as the object of a preposition.

I

**1** PRON You use **it** to refer to an object, animal, or other thing that has already been mentioned, or to a situation that you have just described. pronombre neutro, tercera persona singular, sujeto u objeto ❑ *It's a wonderful city. I'll show it to you.* Es una ciudad maravillosa, te la voy a enseñar. ❑ *She has a health problem but is embarrassed to ask the doctor about it.* Tiene un problema de salud, pero le da pena preguntarle al doctor al respecto. ❑ *He quit sports, not because of injury but because he wanted it that way.* Abandonó los deportes, no por lesiones, sino porque así lo quiso. **2** PRON You use **it** before certain nouns, adjectives, and verbs to introduce your feelings or point of view about a situation. pronombre sujeto neutro ❑ *It was nice to see Steve again.* Fue agradable volver a ver a Steve. ❑ *It's a pity you can't come, Sarah.* Qué lástima que no puedas venir, Sarah. **3** PRON You use **it** in passive clauses that report a situation or event. pronombre sujeto neutro ❑ *It is said that stress can cause cancer.* Se dice que el estrés puede provocar cáncer. **4** PRON You use **it** as the subject of "be" to say what the time, day, or date is. pronombre sujeto de construcciones impersonales ❑ *It's three o'clock in the morning.* Son las tres de la mañana. ❑ *It was a Monday, so she was at home.* Era lunes, así que estaba en su casa. **5** PRON You use **it** as the subject of a linking verb to describe the weather, the light, or the temperature. pronombre sujeto de construcciones impersonales ❑ *It was very wet and windy.* Estaba muy húmedo y airoso. **6** PRON You use **it** when you are telling someone who you are, or asking them who they are, especially at the beginning of a phone call. You also use **it** in statements and questions about the identity of other people. pronombre personal sujeto ❑ *"Who is it?" he called.— "It's your neighbor."* —¿Quién es? —dijo él. —Soy tu vecino. **7** PRON When you are emphasizing or drawing attention to something, you can put that thing immediately after **it** and a form of the verb "be." pronombre personal neutro ❑ *It's my father they're talking about.* Es de mi padre de quien están hablando.

**ital|ic** /ɪtælɪk/ (**italics**) **1** N-PLURAL **Italics** are letters that slope to the right. Italics are often used to emphasize a particular word or sentence. The examples in this dictionary are printed in italics. itálica, cursiva, bastardilla ❑ *The title is printed in italics.* El título está impreso en itálicas. **2** ADJ **Italic** letters slope to the right. itálico ❑ *She wrote to them in her beautiful italic handwriting.* Les escribió con su espléndida letra manuscrita.

**itch** /ɪtʃ/ (**itches, itching, itched**) **1** V-I When a part of your body **itches,** you have an unpleasant feeling on your skin that makes you want to scratch. picar, tener comezón, arder ❑ *Her perfume made my eyes itch.* Su perfume hizo que me ardieran los ojos. ● **Itch** is also a noun. picor, picazón, comezón, prurito ❑ *Scratch my back—I've got an itch.* Ráscame la espalda, tengo comezón. ● **itch|ing** N-UNCOUNT irritación, comezón, prurito ❑ *The disease can cause severe itching.* La enfermedad puede provocar un prurito intenso. ● **itchy** ADJ irritado, ardoroso ❑ *...itchy, sore eyes.* ...ojos irritados y ardorosos. **2** V-T If you **are itching** to do something, you are very eager or impatient to do it. ansioso, impaciente [INFORMAL] ❑ *I was itching to start.* Estaba ansioso por empezar. ● **Itch** is also a noun. comezón, picazón, ansia, impaciencia ❑ *...TV viewers with an itch to switch from channel to channel.* ...espectadores de televisión con ansias de andar de canal en canal.

**it'd** /ɪtəd/ **1** **It'd** is a spoken form of "it would." forma hablada usual de **it would** ❑ *It'd be better to keep quiet.* Lo mejor sería que me quedara callado. **2** **It'd** is a spoken form of "it had," especially when "had" is an auxiliary verb. forma hablada usual de **it had** ❑ *Marcie was watching a movie. It'd just started.* Marcie estaba viendo una película que acababa de empezar.

**item** /aɪtəm/ (**items**) **1** N-COUNT An **item** is one of a collection or list of objects. artículo, objeto, pieza ❑ *The most valuable item on show was a Picasso drawing.* El objeto más valioso de la exposición era un dibujo de Picasso. **2** N-COUNT An **item** is one of a list of things for someone to do, deal with, or talk about. tema, punto ❑ *The other item on the agenda is sales.* El otro punto de la agenda son las ventas. **3** N-COUNT An **item** is a report or article in a newspaper or magazine, or on television or radio. artículo ❑ *There was an item in the paper about him.* Había un artículo sobre él en el periódico.

**Thesaurus** *item* Ver también:

N. issue, subject, task **2**
article, story **3**

**it'll** /ɪtᵊl/ **It'll** is a spoken form of "it will." forma hablada usual de **it will** ❑ *It'll be nice to see them next weekend.* Sería agradable verlos el próximo fin de semana.

**its** /ɪts/

**Its** is a third person singular possessive determiner.

DET You use **its** to indicate that something belongs or relates to a thing, place, or animal that has just been mentioned or whose identity is known. su ❑ *He held the knife by its handle.* Tomó el cuchillo por el mango.

**it's** /ɪts/ **It's** is the usual spoken form of "it is" or "it has," when "has" is an auxiliary verb. forma hablada usual de **it is**, forma hablada usual de **it has**

**Usage** **its and it's**

*Its* is the possessive form of *it*, and *it's* is the contraction of *it is* or *it has*. They are often confused because they are pronounced the same and because the possessive *its* doesn't have an apostrophe: *It's been a month since Maricel's store lost its license, but it's still doing business.*

**it|self** /ɪtsɛlf/ **1** PRON **Itself** is used as the object of a verb or preposition when it refers to something that is the same thing as the subject of the verb. *a sí mismo, por sí solo* ❑ *The body refreshes itself while we sleep. El cuerpo se refresca por sí solo mientras dormimos.* **2** PRON You use **itself** to emphasize the thing you are referring to. *mismo, en sí* ❑ *Life itself is a learning process. La vida en sí es un proceso de aprendizaje.* **3** PRON If you say that someone is, for example, politeness **itself** or kindness **itself,** you are emphasizing that they are extremely polite or extremely kind. *mismo, personificación* ❑ *I wasn't really happy there, though the people were kindness itself. En realidad no estaba muy contento ahí, pero la gente no podía haber sido más amable.*

**IV** /aɪ vi/ (**IVs**) **1** N-COUNT An **IV** or an **IV drip** is a piece of medical equipment by which a liquid is slowly passed through a tube into a patient's blood. *vía intravenosa, sistema intravenoso, IV* ❑ *She was attached to an IV. Estaba conectada a un sistema intravenoso.* **2** ADJ **IV** is an abbreviation for **intravenous.** *abreviatura de* ***intravenous*** ❑ *...a plastic bottle of IV fluids. ...un envase de plástico para líquidos intravenosos.*

**I've** /aɪv/ **I've** is the usual spoken form of "I have," especially when "have" is an auxiliary verb. *forma hablada usual de* ***I have*** ❑ *I've been invited to a party. Me han invitado a una fiesta.*

**IVF** /aɪ vi ɛf/ N-UNCOUNT **IVF** is a method of helping a woman to have a baby in which an egg is removed from one of her ovaries, fertilized outside her body, and then replaced in her womb. **IVF** is an abbreviation for "in vitro fertilization." *abreviatura de* ***in vitro fertilization*** ❑ *After years of trying for a baby she had IVF. Después de años de tratar de concebir, se sometió a una fertilización in vitro.*

**ivo|ry** /aɪvəri/ N-UNCOUNT **Ivory** is a hard cream-colored substance that forms the tusks of elephants. *marfil* ❑ *...the international ban on the sale of ivory. ...la proscripción internacional a las ventas de marfil.*

**Ivy League** **1** N-PROPER **The Ivy League** is a group of eight colleges in the northeastern United States, which have high academic and social status. *Ivy League* ❑ *...an Ivy League college. ...universidad que forma parte de la Ivy League* **2** ADJ You use **Ivy League** to describe fashions and attitudes typical of students at Ivy League colleges. *tipo Ivy League* ❑ *...Ivy League shirts. ...camisas muy Ivy League.*

# Jj



**jack** /dʒæk/ (**jacks**) **1** N-COUNT A **jack** is a piece of equipment for lifting a heavy object, such as a car, off the ground. gato **2** N-COUNT A **jack** is a playing card whose value is between a ten and a queen. jota ❑ *...the jack of spades.* *...la jota de espadas.*

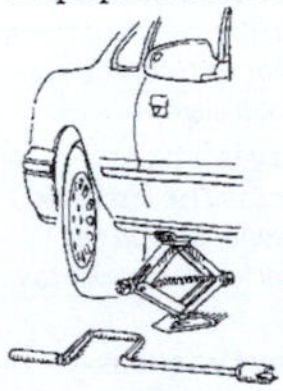

jack

**jack|et** /dʒækɪt/ (**jackets**) **1** N-COUNT A **jacket** is a short coat with long sleeves. chamarra ❑ *...a black leather jacket.* *...una chamarra de piel negra.* **2** N-COUNT The **jacket** of a book is the paper cover that protects the book. cubierta ❑ *There's a picture of a beautiful girl on the jacket of this book.* *Hay una imagen de una chica guapa en la cubierta de este libro.* ❑ *The back cover of the book's jacket.* *La contraportada de la cubierta del libro.*
→ see **clothing**

**jack|ham|mer** /dʒækhæmər/ (**jackhammers**) N-COUNT A **jackhammer** is a large powerful hammer that is used for breaking up rocks and other hard material. martillo neumático.

**jack-o'-lantern** /dʒæk əlæntərn/ (**jack-o'-lanterns**) also **jack o'lantern** N-COUNT A **jack-o'-lantern** is a lantern made from a hollow pumpkin that has been carved to look like a face. calabaza de Halloween

**jade** /dʒeɪd/ N-UNCOUNT **Jade** is a hard green type of stone used for making jewelry and ornaments. jade

**jag|ged** /dʒægɪd/ ADJ Something that is **jagged** has a rough, uneven shape or edge with lots of sharp points. dentado, escarpado ❑ *...jagged black cliffs.* *...acantilados negros escarpados.*

**jail** /dʒeɪl/ (**jails, jailing, jailed**) **1** N-VAR A **jail** is a place where criminals are kept in order to punish them. cárcel ❑ *Three prisoners escaped from a jail.* *Tres prisioneros escaparon de una cárcel.* **2** V-T If someone **is jailed,** they are put into jail. mandar a la cárcel ❑ *He was jailed for twenty years.* *Lo condenaron a veinte años de cárcel.*

**jail|house** /dʒeɪlhaʊs/ (**jailhouses**) N-COUNT A **jailhouse** is a small prison. cárcel (local)

**jam** /dʒæm/ (**jams, jamming, jammed**) **1** V-T If you **jam** something somewhere, you push it there roughly. meter a presión ❑ *Pete jammed his hands into his pockets.* *Pete metió las manos con fuerza en los bolsillos.* **2** V-T/V-I If something **jams,** or if you **jam** it, it becomes fixed in position and is unable to move freely or work properly. atorar(se), trabar(se) ❑ *When he tried to open the door, it jammed.* *Cuando intentó abrir la puerta, se trabó.* ❑ *He jammed the key in the lock.* *Se le atoró la llave en la cerradura.* **3** V-T/V-I If a lot of people **jam** a place, or **jam into** a place, they are pressed tightly together so that they can hardly move. abarrotar ❑ *Hundreds of people jammed the streets.* *Cientos de personas abarrotaron las calles.* ● **jammed** ADJ repleto ❑ *The stadium was jammed.* *El estadio estaba repleto.* **4** N-COUNT If there is a traffic **jam** on a road, there are so many vehicles there that they cannot move. embotellamiento ❑ *Trucks sat in a jam for ten hours.* *Los camiones estuvieron en un embotellamiento durante diez horas.* **5** V-T To **jam** a radio or electronic signal means to interfere with it and prevent it from being received or heard clearly. bloquear ❑ *The plane is used to jam radar equipment.* *El avión se utiliza para bloquear equipo de radar.* ● **jam|ming** N-UNCOUNT interferencia ❑ *...electronic signal jamming equipment.* *...equipo electrónico de interferencia de señal.*

| **Word Partnership** | Usar *jam* con: |
| --- | --- |
| N. | **traffic** jam **4** |

**Jane Doe** /dʒeɪn doʊ/ (**Jane Does**) N-COUNT **Jane Doe** is used to refer to a woman whose real name is not known or cannot be revealed, for example, for legal reasons. Juana N ❑ *...the patient, known as "Jane Doe."* *...la paciente, conocida como "Juana N".*

**jani|tor** /dʒænɪtər/ (**janitors**) N-COUNT A **janitor** is a person whose job is to take care of a building. conserje ❑ *...a school janitor.* *...el conserje de la escuela*

**Janu|ary** /dʒænyuɛri/ (**Januaries**) N-VAR **January** is the first month of the year in the Western calendar. enero ❑ *We always have snow in January.* *Siempre tenemos nieve en enero.*

**jar** /dʒɑr/ (**jars, jarring, jarred**) **1** N-COUNT A **jar** is a glass container with a lid that is used for storing food. frasco, bote ❑ *...candy in glass jars.* *...dulces en frascos de vidrio.* **2** V-T/V-I If something **jars,** or **jars** you, you find it unpleasant or shocking. crispar (los nervios) ❑ *The question jarred her a little.* *La pregunta la crispó un poco.* ● **jar|ring** ADJ discordante ❑ *...the jarring sound of the machine.* *...el discordante sonido de la máquina.* **3** V-T/V-I If an object **jars,** or if something **jars** it, the object moves with a fairly hard shaking movement. sacudir(se), (hacer) temblar ❑ *The ship jarred a little.* *El barco se sacudió un poco.* ❑ *The sudden movement jarred the box.* *el movimiento repentino hizo temblar la caja.*
→ see **container**

jar

**java** /dʒɑvə/ N-UNCOUNT **Java** is coffee. café

[INFORMAL] ❑ *...a cup of hot java.* *...una taza de café caliente.*

**jaw** /dʒɔ/ (**jaws**) **1** N-COUNT Your **jaw** is the lower part of your face *quijada* ❑ *Andrew broke his jaw in two places.* *Andrew tenía dos fracturas en la quijada.* **2** N-COUNT A person's or animal's **jaws** are the two bones in their head that their teeth are attached to. *mandíbulas, fauces* ❑ *...an animal with powerful jaws.* *...un animal con fauces poderosas.*

**jazz** /dʒæz/ N-UNCOUNT **Jazz** is a style of music that was invented by African American musicians in the early part of the twentieth century. Jazz music has very strong rhythms and often involves improvisation. *jazz* ❑ *The club plays live jazz on Sundays.* *El club toca jazz en vivo los domingos.*
→ see **genre**

**jazz dance** N-UNCOUNT **Jazz dance** is a form of dance that developed in America in the twentieth century, based on jazz-influenced music and complex rhythmic movements. *danza jazz*

**jeal|ous** /dʒɛləs/ **1** ADJ If someone is **jealous,** they feel angry or bitter because they think that another person is trying to take a lover or friend, or a possession, away from them. *celoso* ❑ *She got jealous and there was a fight.* *Se puso celosa y hubo una pelea.* ● **jeal|ous|ly** ADV *celosamente* ❑ *Her recipe for chocolate cake was a jealously guarded secret.* *Su receta de pastel de chocolate era un secreto celosamente guardado.* **2** ADJ If you are **jealous of** another person's possessions or qualities, you feel angry or bitter because you do not have them. *envidioso* ❑ *She was jealous of his wealth.* *Ella envidiaba su riqueza.* ● **jeal|ous|ly** ADV *con envidia* ❑ *Gloria looked jealously at the red sports car.* *Gloria miró con envidia el carro deportivo rojo.*

**jeal|ousy** /dʒɛləsi/ **1** N-UNCOUNT **Jealousy** is the feeling of anger or bitterness that someone has when they think that another person is trying to take a lover or friend, or a possession, away from them. *celos* ❑ *He could not control his jealousy when he saw her new husband.* *No pudo controlar sus celos cuando vio a su nuevo esposo.* **2** N-UNCOUNT **Jealousy** is the feeling of anger or bitterness that someone has when they wish that they could have the qualities or possessions that another person has. *envidia* ❑ *...jealousy of her beauty.* *...envidia de su belleza.*

**jeans** /dʒinz/ N-PLURAL **Jeans** are casual pants that are usually made of strong cotton cloth called denim. *jeans* ❑ *...a young man in jeans and a T-shirt.* *...un joven en jeans y una playera.*
→ see **clothing**

**jel|ly** /dʒɛli/ (**jellies**) N-VAR **Jelly** is a sweet food made by cooking fruit with a large amount of sugar, that is usually spread on bread. *mermelada* ❑ *...peanut butter and jelly sandwiches.* *...sandwiches de crema de cacahuate y mermelada.*

**jelly|fish** /dʒɛlifɪs/ (**jellyfish**) N-COUNT A **jellyfish** is a sea creature that has a clear soft body and can sting you. *aguamala, medusa, aguaviva*

**jel|ly roll** (**jelly rolls**) N-VAR **Jelly roll** is a long cake made from a thin, flat cake which is covered with jam or cream on one side, then rolled up. *brazo de gitano*

**jerk** /dʒɜrk/ (**jerks, jerking, jerked**) **1** V-T/V-I If you **jerk** something or someone in a particular direction, or they **jerk** in a particular direction, they move a short distance very suddenly and quickly. *mover (bruscamente), mover (repentinamente)* ❑ *Mr. Griffin jerked forward in his chair.* *El señor Griffin se movió bruscamente hacia adelante en su silla.* ❑ *"This is Brady," said Sam, jerking his head in my direction.* *—Este es Brady —dijo Sam, moviendo repentinamente su cabeza hacia mí.* ● **Jerk** is also a noun. *sacudida* ❑ *He gave a jerk of his head to the other two men.* *Sacudió su cabeza señalando a los otros dos hombres.* **2** N-COUNT If you call someone a **jerk,** you are insulting them because you think they are stupid or you do not like them. *imbécil* [INFORMAL]

**jer|sey** /dʒɜrzi/ (**jerseys**) N-VAR **Jersey** is a knitted, slightly stretchy fabric used especially to make women's clothing. *tejido de punto* ❑ *...a black jersey top.* *...un top negro de tejido de punto.*

**Jesus** /dʒizəs/ N-PROPER **Jesus** or **Jesus Christ** is the name of the man who Christians believe was the son of God, and whose teachings are the basis of Christianity. *Jesús, Jesucristo*

**jet** /dʒɛt/ (**jets, jetting, jetted**) **1** N-COUNT A **jet** is an aircraft that is powered by jet engines. *jet, avión a reacción* ❑ *...her private jet.* *...su jet privado.* ❑ *He arrived from Key West by jet.* *Llegó de Key West en un jet.* **2** V-I If you **jet** somewhere, you travel there in a fast plane. *viajar en jet* ❑ *The president will jet off to Germany today.* *El presidente viajará hoy en jet a Alemania.* **3** N-COUNT A **jet** of liquid or gas is a strong, fast, thin stream of it. *chorro* ❑ *A jet of water poured through the windows.* *Un chorro de agua entró por las ventanas.*
→ see **fly**

**jet en|gine** (**jet engines**) N-COUNT A **jet engine** is an engine in which hot air and gases are forced out at the back. *motor de reacción*

**jet|liner** /dʒɛtlaɪnər/ (**jetliners**) N-COUNT A **jetliner** is a large aircraft, especially one which carries passengers. *avión de pasajeros*

**jet stream** (**jet streams**) N-COUNT The **jet stream** is a very strong wind that blows high in the Earth's atmosphere and has an important influence on the weather. *corriente en chorro*

**jet|ty** /dʒɛti/ (**jetties**) N-COUNT A **jetty** is a wide stone wall or wooden platform where boats stop to let people get on or off, or to load or unload goods. *embarcadero, malecón, muelle*

**Jew** /dʒu/ (**Jews**) N-COUNT A **Jew** is a person who believes in and practices the religion of Judaism. *judío o judía*

**jew|el** /dʒuəl/ (**jewels**) N-COUNT A **jewel** is a precious stone used to decorate valuable things, such as rings or necklaces. *joya* ❑ *...precious jewels.* *...joyas preciosas.*

**jew|el|er** /dʒuələr/ (**jewelers**) **1** N-COUNT A **jeweler** is a person who makes, sells, and repairs jewelry and watches. *joyero o joyera* **2** N-COUNT A **jeweler** is a store where jewelry and watches are made, sold, and repaired. *joyería* ❑ *...a jeweler on Fifth Avenue.* *una joyería en la Quinta Avenida.*

**jew|el|ry** /dʒuəlri/ N-UNCOUNT **Jewelry** is ornaments that people wear, such as rings and bracelets. *joyería* ❑ *...a selection of expensive watches and jewelry.* *...una selección de relojes y joyería caros.*
→ see Picture Dictionary: **jewelry**

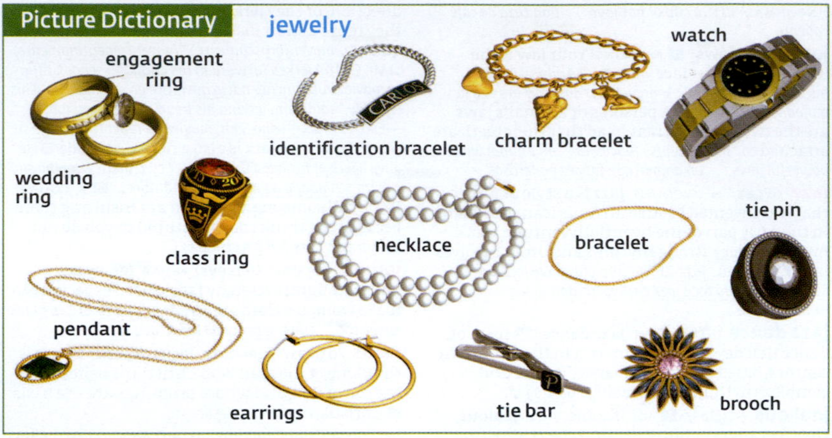


**Jew|ish** /dʒuɪʃ/ ADJ **Jewish** means belonging or relating to the religion of Judaism, or to Jews as an ethnic group. judío ❑ *...the Jewish festival of Passover.* *...el festival judío de Pascua.*

**jin|gle** /dʒɪŋgəl/ (**jingles, jingling, jingled**) **1** V-T/V-I When something **jingles** or when you **jingle** it, it makes a gentle ringing noise, like small bells. tintinear ❑ *Brian put his hands in his pockets and jingled some coins. Brian metió las manos en sus bolsillos e hizo tintinear algunas monedas.* **2** N-COUNT A **jingle** is a short, simple tune, often with words, that is used to advertise a product or program on radio or television. jingle, canción publicitaria ❑ *...advertising jingles. ...jingles publicitarios.*

**jive** /dʒaɪv/ **1** N-UNCOUNT **Jive** is rock and roll or swing music that you dance to. jive **2** N-UNCOUNT **Jive** or **jive talk** is a kind of informal language used by some African Americans. jerga jive

**job** /dʒɒb/ (**jobs**) **1** N-COUNT A **job** is the work that someone does to earn money. empleo, trabajo ❑ *I want to get a job. Quiero conseguir un empleo.* ❑ *Terry was looking for a new job. Terry estaba buscando un nuevo trabajo.* **2** N-COUNT A **job** is a particular task. tarea ❑ *I'm glad I don't have the job of replacing him. Me alegra no tener la tarea de reemplazarlo.* **3** N-COUNT The **job** of a particular person or thing is their duty or function. trabajo ❑ *Drinking a lot of water helps the kidneys do their job. Beber mucha agua ayuda a que los riñones hagan su trabajo.* **4** N-SING If you say that someone is doing a good **job,** you mean that they are doing something well. trabajo ❑ *He did a far better job of managing the project than I did. Hizo un mucho mejor trabajo administrando el proyecto que yo.*

| **Thesaurus** *job* | Ver también: |
| --- | --- |
| N. | employment, occupation, profession, vocation; (*ant.*) work **1** |

**job|less** /dʒɒblɪs/ ADJ Someone who is **jobless** does not have a job, but would like one. desempleado ❑ *...millions of jobless Americans. ...millones de americanos desempleados.*

**job sat|is|fac|tion** N-UNCOUNT **Job satisfaction** is the pleasure that you get from doing your job. satisfacción con el empleo ❑ *I'll never be rich, but I get job satisfaction. Nunca seré rico, pero estoy satisfecho con lo que hago.*

**job share** (**job shares, job sharing, job shared**) V-I If two people **job share,** they share the same job by working part-time, for example, one person working in the mornings and the other in the afternoons. alternar (el trabajo) ❑ *They both want to job share. Ambos quieren alternar.*

**jock|ey** /dʒɒki/ (**jockeys**) N-COUNT A **jockey** is someone who rides a horse in a race. jinete

**jog** /dʒɒg/ (**jogs, jogging, jogged**) **1** V-I If you **jog,** you run slowly, often as a form of exercise. correr (lentamente) ❑ *I got up early the next morning to jog. Me levanté temprano a la mañana siguiente para correr.* • **Jog** is also a noun. vuelta corriendo ❑ *He went for another early morning jog. Fue a correr temprano en la mañana.* • **jog|ger** N-COUNT (**joggers**) corredor o corredora ❑ *The park was full of joggers. El parque estaba lleno de corredores.* • **jog|ging** N-UNCOUNT correr ❑ *The jogging helped him to lose weight. Correr le ayudó a perder peso.* **2** V-T If you **jog** something, you push or bump it slightly so that it moves. mover ❑ *Avoid jogging the camera. Evita mover la cámara.*

**John Doe** /dʒɑn doʊ/ (**John Does**) N-COUNT **John Doe** is used to refer to a man whose real name is not known or cannot be revealed, for example, for legal reasons. Juan N ❑ *...a letter from someone who signed himself "John Doe." ...una carta que alguien firmó como "Juan N".*

**join** /dʒɔɪn/ (**joins, joining, joined**) **1** V-T If one person or vehicle **joins** another, they move or go to the same place. acompañar ❑ *She joined him in a trip to France. Lo acompañó en un viaje a Francia.* **2** V-T If you **join** an organization, you become a member of it. afiliarse a, alistarse en ❑ *He joined the Army five years ago. Se alistó en el ejército hace cinco años.* **3** V-T/V-I If you **join** an activity, or **join in** an activity, you take part in it or become involved with it. integrarse, participar en ❑ *The United States joined the war in April 1917. Los Estados Unidos entró a la guerra en Abril de 1917.* ❑ *Thousands of people will join in the celebrations. Miles de personas participarán en las* *celebraciones.* **4** V-T If you **join** a line, you stand at the end of it so that you are part of it. *formarse* ❑ *He joined the line of people waiting to board the plane. Se formó en la línea de la gente que esperaba abordar el avión.* **5** V-T To **join** two things means to attach or fasten them together. *unir* ❑ *"And" is often used to join two sentences. "Y" se usa a menudo para unir dos oraciones.* **6** **join forces** → see **force**

▸**join in** PHR-VERB If you **join in** an activity, you take part in it or become involved in it. *participar en, unirse a* ❑ *I hope everyone will join in the fun. Espero que todos se unan a la diversión.*

▸**join up** PHR-VERB If someone **joins up,** they become a member of the army, the navy, or the air force. *alistarse* ❑ *When the war started, he joined up. Cuando la guerra inició, se alistó.*

**joint** /dʒɔɪnt/ (**joints**) **1** ADJ **Joint** means shared by or belonging to two or more people. *conjunto* ❑ *...a joint bank account. ...una cuenta bancaria conjunta.* ● **joint|ly** ADV *conjuntamente* ❑ *They jointly write and direct every film themselves. Ellos mismos escriben y dirigen conjuntamente cada película.* **2** N-COUNT A **joint** is a part of your body such as your elbow or knee where two bones meet and are able to move together. *articulación* ❑ *Her joints ache if she exercises. Sus articulaciones le duelen si hace ejercicio.* **3** N-COUNT A **joint** is the place where two things are fastened or joined together. *junta* ❑ *...the joint between two layers of wood. ...la junta entre dos capas de madera.*

**joint ven|ture** (**joint ventures**) N-COUNT A **joint venture** is a business or project in which two or more companies or individuals have invested, with the intention of working together. *alianza estratégica, empresa conjunta* [BUSINESS] ❑ *...a joint venture between Dow Jones and Westinghouse Broadcasting. ...una alianza estratégica entre Dow Jones y Westinghouse Broadcasting.*

**joke** /dʒoʊk/ (**jokes, joking, joked**) **1** N-COUNT A **joke** is something that is said or done to make you laugh, such as a funny story. *chiste* ❑ *He made a joke about it. Hizo un chiste al respecto.* **2** V-I If you **joke,** you tell funny stories or say amusing things. *bromear* ❑ *She often joked about her appearance. Con frecuencia bromeaba sobre su apariencia.* ❑ *I was only joking! ¡Sólo estaba bromeando!* **3** N-SING If you say that something or someone is **a joke,** you think they are ridiculous and do not deserve respect. *burla* [INFORMAL] ❑ *The whole idea is a joke. Toda la idea es una burla.* **4** PHRASE If you describe a situation as **no joke,** you are emphasizing that it is very difficult or unpleasant. *no es un chiste* [INFORMAL] ❑ *Eight hours on a bus is no joke. Estar ocho horas en autobús no es un chiste.* **5** CONVENTION You say **you're joking** or **you must be joking** to someone when they have just told you something that is so surprising or unreasonable that you find it difficult to believe. *¡Estás bromeando!, ¡Debes estar bromeando!* [SPOKEN] ❑ *You're joking. Are you serious? ¡Estás bromeando! ¿O hablas en serio?* ❑ *You've got to be joking if you choose him instead of me. Debes estar bromeando si lo escoges a él en vez de a mí.*

**jok|er** /dʒoʊkər/ (**jokers**) N-COUNT The **joker** in a deck of playing cards is the card that does not belong to any of the four suits. *comodín*

**jol|ly** /dʒɒli/ (**jollier, jolliest**) ADJ Someone who is **jolly** is happy and cheerful. *alegre, jovial* ❑ *She was a jolly, kindhearted woman. Era un mujer alegre, de buen corazón.*

**joule** /dʒul/ (**joules**) N-COUNT In physics, a **joule** is a unit of energy or work. *julio* [TECHNICAL]

**jour|nal** /dʒɜrnᵊl/ (**journals**) **1** N-COUNT A **journal** is a magazine or newspaper, especially one that deals with a specialized subject. *revista, periódico* ❑ *The results were published in scientific journals. Los resultados se publicaron en revistas científicas.* **2** N-COUNT A **journal** is a notebook or diary. *diario* ❑ *Sara wrote her private thoughts in her journal. Sara escribió sus pensamientos íntimos en su diario.*

**jour|nal|ist** /dʒɜrnəlɪst/ (**journalists**) N-COUNT A **journalist** is a person whose job is to collect news and write about it for newspapers, magazines, television, or radio. *periodista* ● **jour|nal|ism** N-UNCOUNT *periodismo* ❑ *He began a career in journalism. Comenzó una carrera en el periodismo.*

**jour|ney** /dʒɜrni/ (**journeys, journeying, journeyed**) **1** N-COUNT When you make a **journey,** you travel from one place to another. *viaje* [FORMAL] ❑ *...the 3,000-mile journey from New York to San Francisco. ...el viaje de 3,000 millas de Nueva York a San Francisco.* **2** V-I If you **journey** somewhere, you travel there. *viajar* [FORMAL] ❑ *Naomi journeyed to the United States for the first time. Naomi viajó a los Estados Unidos por primera vez.*

**Thesaurus** *journey* Ver también:

N. adventure, trip, visit, voyage **1**
V. cruise, fly, go, travel **2**

**Word Partnership** Usar *journey* con:

V. **begin a** journey, **complete a** journey, **make a** journey **1**
N. journey **of discovery, end of a** journey, **first/last leg of a** journey **1**

**joy** /dʒɔɪ/ (**joys**) **1** N-UNCOUNT **Joy** is a feeling of great happiness. *júbilo* ❑ *She shouted with joy. Gritó con júbilo.* **2** N-COUNT A **joy** is something or someone that makes you feel happy or gives you great pleasure. *alegría* ❑ *Spending evenings outside is one of the joys of summer. Pasar las tardes fuera es una de las alegrías del verano.*
→ see **emotion**

**Word Partnership** Usar *joy* con:

V. **bring** *someone* joy, **cry/weep for** joy, **feel** joy **1**
ADJ. **filled with** joy, **great** joy, **pure** joy, **sheer** joy **1**
N. **tears of** joy **1**

**judge** /dʒʌdʒ/ (**judges, judging, judged**) **1** N-COUNT; N-TITLE A **judge** is the person in a court of law who decides how the law should be applied, for example how criminals should be punished. *juez* ❑ *A state judge sent him to jail for 100 days. Un juez estatal lo envió a prisión por 100 días.* **2** N-COUNT A **judge** is a person who decides who will be the winner of a competition. *juez* ❑ *A panel of judges is now choosing the winner. Un panel de jueces está escogiendo ahora al ganador.* **3** V-T If you **judge** a competition, you decide who or what

is the winner. arbitrar ❑ *He was asked to judge the competition.* *Le pidieron arbitrar la competencia.* **4** V-T If you **judge** something or someone, you form an opinion about them based on the evidence or information that you have. juzgar ❑ *People should judge his music for themselves.* *La gente debería juzgar su música por sí misma.* ❑ *I want to judge myself on how I play.* *Yo quiero ser el juez de mí mismo en cuanto a mi juego.* ❑ *Other people can judge how much I have improved.* *Otras personas pueden juzgar cuánto he mejorado.* **5** N-COUNT If someone is a good **judge of** something, they understand it and can make sensible decisions about it. juez de ❑ *I'm a pretty good judge of character.* *Soy bastante buen juez de carácter.*
→ see **trial**

**judg|ment** /dʒʌdʒmənt/ (**judgments**) **1** N-VAR A **judgment** is an opinion that you have or express after thinking carefully about something. opinión ❑ *In your judgment, what has changed?* *En tu opinión, ¿qué ha cambiado?* **2** N-UNCOUNT **Judgment** is the ability to make sensible guesses about a situation or sensible decisions about what to do. buen juicio, criterio ❑ *I respect his judgment and I'll follow any advice he gives me.* *Respeto su buen juicio y seguiré cualquier consejo que él me dé.* **3** N-VAR A **judgment** is a decision made by a judge or by a court of law. fallo ❑ *We are waiting for a judgment from the Supreme Court.* *Estamos esperando el fallo de la Suprema Corte.*

J

**ju|di|cial** /dʒudɪʃᵊl/ ADJ **Judicial** means relating to the legal system and to judgments made in a court of law. judicial ❑ *...our judicial system.* *...nuestro sistema judicial.*

**ju|di|ci|ary** /dʒudɪʃiɛri/ N-SING **The judiciary** is the branch of authority in a country that is concerned with law and the legal system. judicatura [FORMAL] ❑ *...the head of the judiciary committee.* *...el dirigente del comité de la judicatura.*

**jug|gle** /dʒʌgᵊl/ (**juggles, juggling, juggled**) **1** V-T If you **juggle** lots of different things, you try to give enough time or attention to all of them. balancear, abarcar ❑ *He was finding it hard to juggle both careers.* *Le estaba costando trabajo balancear las dos carreras.* **2** V-T/V-I If you **juggle**, you entertain people by throwing things into the air, catching each one, and throwing it up again so that there are several of them in the air at the same time. hacer malabares ❑ *She was juggling five eggs.* *Estaba haciendo malabares con cinco huevos.* ● **jug|gler** N-COUNT (**jugglers**) malabarista ❑ *...a professional juggler.* *...un malabarista profesional.* ● **jug|gl|ing** N-UNCOUNT malabarismo ❑ *...a children's show with juggling and comedy.* *...un espectáculo para niños con malabarismo y chistes.*

**juice** /dʒus/ (**juices**) **1** N-VAR **Juice** is the liquid that can be obtained from a fruit or vegetable. jugo ❑ *...fresh orange juice.* *...jugo de naranja fresco.* **2** N-PLURAL The **juices** of a piece of meat are the liquid that comes out of it when you cook it. jugos ❑ *Pour off the juices and put the meat in a frying pan.* *Saque el jugo y ponga la carne en el sartén.*

**Word Partnership** Usar *juice* con:

| | |
|---|---|
| N. | **bottle of** juice, **fruit** juice, **glass of** juice **1** |
| ADJ. | **fresh-squeezed** juice **1** |

**juicy** /dʒusi/ (**juicier, juiciest**) **1** ADJ If food is **juicy,** it has a lot of juice in it and is very enjoyable to eat. jugoso ❑ *...a thick, juicy steak.* *un bistec grueso y jugoso.* **2** ADJ **Juicy** gossip or stories contain exciting or scandalous details. sabroso [INFORMAL] ❑ *...drinking coffee and sharing juicy gossip.* *...tomando café e intercambiando chismes sabrosos.*

**July** /dʒʊlaɪ/ (**Julys**) N-VAR **July** is the seventh month of the year in the Western calendar. julio ❑ *In July 1969, Neil Armstrong walked on the moon.* *En julio de 1969, Neil Armstrong caminó sobre la luna.*

**jum|bo** /dʒʌmboʊ/ (**jumbos**) **1** ADJ **Jumbo** means very large. enorme ❑ *...a jumbo box of tissues.* *...una caja enorme de pañuelos desechables.* **2** N-COUNT A **jumbo** or a **jumbo jet** is a very large jet aircraft. jumbo jet
→ see **fly**

**jump** /dʒʌmp/ (**jumps, jumping, jumped**) **1** V-T/V-I If you **jump,** you bend your knees, push against the ground with your feet, and move quickly upward into the air. saltar ❑ *I jumped over the fence.* *Salté sobre la barda.* ❑ *He jumped out of a first-floor window.* *Saltó desde una ventana del primer piso.* ❑ *I jumped seventeen feet in the long jump.* *Salté cinco metros en el salto de longitud.* ● **Jump** is also a noun. salto ❑ *...the longest jump by a man.* *...el salto más largo de un hombre.* **2** V-T If you **jump** something such as a fence, you move quickly up and through the air over or across it. saltar ❑ *He jumped the first fence beautifully.* *Saltó la primera valla de maravilla.* **3** V-I If you **jump** somewhere, you move there quickly and suddenly. saltar, brincar ❑ *Adam jumped from his seat when he heard the girl's cry.* *Adam brincó de su asiento cuando escuchó el grito de la niña.* **4** V-I If something **makes** you **jump,** it makes you make a sudden movement because you are frightened or surprised. sobresaltar ❑ *The phone rang and made her jump.* *El teléfono sonó y la sobresaltó.* **5** V-T/V-I If an amount or level **jumps,** it suddenly increases by a large amount in a short time. dispararse, subir repentinamente ❑ *Sales jumped from $94 million to $101 million.* *Las ventas se dispararon de 94 millones a 101 millones de dólares.* ❑ *The number of crimes jumped by ten percent.* *El número de crímenes subió repentinamente un 10 por ciento.* ❑ *The company's shares jumped $2.50 in value.* *El valor de las acciones de la compañía subió 2.50 dólares.* ● **Jump** is also a noun. alza abrupta ❑ *...a big jump in sales.* *...una gran alza en las ventas.* **6** V-I If you **jump at** an offer or opportunity, you accept it quickly and eagerly. aceptar inmediatamente ❑ *She'd jump at the chance to be on TV.* *Aceptaría inmediatamente la oportunidad de estar en televisión.*

**Thesaurus** *jump* Ver también:

| | |
|---|---|
| V. | bound, hop, leap, lunge **1**<br>hurdle **2**<br>startle **4**<br>increase, rise, shoot up **5** |

**Word Partnership** Usar *jump* con:

| | |
|---|---|
| ADJ. | **big** jump **1** **5** |
| N. | jump **to *your* feet** **3**<br>jump **in prices,** jump **in sales** **5** |

**jump|er** /dʒʌmpər/ (**jumpers**) N-COUNT A

jumper is a sleeveless dress that is worn over a blouse or sweater. *jumper* ❑ *She wore a blue jumper. Traía puesto un jumper azul.*

**jump|er ca|bles** N-PLURAL **Jumper cables** are thick wires that can be used to start a car when its battery does not have enough power. *cables de arranque*

**jump rope** (**jump ropes**) N-COUNT A **jump rope** is a piece of rope, usually with handles at each end, that you use for exercising by jumping over it as you turn it round and round. *cuerda de saltar*

**June** /dʒun/ (**Junes**) N-VAR **June** is the sixth month of the year in the Western calendar. *junio* ❑ *He spent two weeks with us in June 2006. Pasó dos semanas con nosotros en junio de 2006.*

**jun|gle** /dʒʌŋgᵊl/ (**jungles**) **1** N-VAR A **jungle** is a forest in a tropical country where large numbers of tall trees and plants grow very close together. *selva* ❑ *...the mountains and jungles of Papua New Guinea. ...las montañas y selvas de Papúa-Nueva Guinea.* **2** N-SING If you describe a situation as **a jungle,** you dislike it because it is complicated and difficult to get what you want from it. *maraña* ❑ *...a jungle of complex rules. ...una maraña de reglas complejas.*

**jun|ior** /dʒunyər/ (**juniors**) **1** ADJ A **junior** official or employee holds a low-ranking position in an organization or profession. *subalterno* ❑ *His father was a junior officer in the army. Su padre era un oficial subalterno del ejército.* ● **Junior** is also a noun. *auxiliar* ❑ *...a job as an office junior. ...un trabajo como auxiliar de oficina.* **2** N-SING If you are someone's **junior,** you are younger than they are. *menor* ❑ *She lives with actor Denis Lawson who is 10 years her junior. Vive con el actor Denis Lawson quien es 10 años menor que ella.* **3** N-COUNT In the United States, a student in the third year of high school or college is called a **junior.** *estudiante de tercer año* ❑ *Amy is a junior at the University of Evansville. Amy es estudiante de tercer año en la Universidad de Evansville.*

**jun|ior col|lege** (**junior colleges**) N-COUNT In the United States, a **junior college** is a college that provides a two-year course that is usually equivalent to the first two years of a 4-year undergraduate course of study. *escuela técnica, escuela semisuperior* ❑ *He went to a junior college and majored in computer programming. Asistió a una escuela técnica y obtuvo un grado en programación de computadoras.*

**jun|ior high school** (**junior high schools**) also **junior high** N-VAR; N-COUNT A **junior high school** or a **junior high** is a school for students from 7th through 9th or 10th grade. *escuela secundaria* ❑ *I teach junior high school and I love it. Doy clases en una escuela secundaria y me encanta.* ❑ *...Benjamin Franklin Junior High. ...escuela secundaria Benjamin Franklin.*

**junk** /dʒʌŋk/ **1** N-UNCOUNT **Junk** is old and useless things that you do not want or need. *chatarra* [INFORMAL] ❑ *What are you going to do with all that junk, Larry? ¿Qué vas a hacer con toda esa chatarra, Larry?* **2** N-UNCOUNT **Junk** is old and used goods that people buy and collect. *remates* ❑ *Rose buys her furniture in junk shops. Rose compra sus muebles en tiendas de remates.*

**Ju|pi|ter** /dʒupɪtər/ N-PROPER **Jupiter** is the fifth planet from the sun and the largest in our solar system. *Júpiter*
→ see **solar system**

**ju|ror** /dʒʊərər/ (**jurors**) N-COUNT A **juror** is a member of a jury. *miembro del jurado* ❑ *The jurors reached a verdict. Los miembros del jurado llegaron a un veredicto.*

**jury** /dʒʊəri/ (**juries**) **1** N-COUNT In a court of law, the **jury** is the group of people who have been chosen from the general public to listen to the facts about a crime and to decide whether the person accused is guilty or not. *jurado* ❑ *I sat on a jury two years ago. Formé parte de un jurado hace dos años.* **2** N-COUNT A **jury** is a group of people who choose the winner of a competition. *jurado* ❑ *The jury chose to award the prize to this novel. El jurado decidió otorgar el premio a esta novela.*
→ see **trial**

**Word Partnership** Usar *jury* con:

| | |
|---|---|
| N. | jury **duty, trial by** jury **1** |
| V. | jury **convicts** **1** |
| | jury **announces** **1** **2** |
| ADJ. | **hung** jury **1** |
| | **unbiased** jury **1** **2** |

**just**

❶ ADVERB USES
❷ ADJECTIVE USE

❶ **just** /dʒʌst/ **1** ADV If you say that something **just happened** or **has just happened,** you mean that it happened a very short time ago. *acabar de* ❑ *I just had the most awful dream. Acabo de tener un sueño horrible.* **2** ADV If you say that you are **just** doing something, you mean that you will finish doing it soon. If you say that you are **just about to** do something, or **just going to** do it, you mean that you will do it very soon. *en este momento* ❑ *I'm just making the sauce for the cauliflower. En este momento estoy haciendo la salsa para la coliflor.* ❑ *I'm just going to go mail a letter. En este momento voy a enviar la carta.* **3** ADV You use **just** to indicate that something is no more important, interesting, or difficult, for example, than you say it is. *solamente* ❑ *It's just a thought. Solamente es una idea.* **4** ADV You use **just** to indicate that what you are saying is true, but only by a very small degree or amount. *apenas* ❑ *I arrived just in time for my flight. Llegué apenas a tiempo para mi vuelo.* **5** ADV You use **just** to put emphasis on the word that follows, in order to express feelings such as annoyance, admiration, or certainty. *simplemente* ❑ *She just won't relax. Ella simplemente no se relaja.* **6** ADV You can use **just** with instructions or polite requests to make your request seem less difficult than someone might think. *sólo* ❑ *I'm just going to ask you a bit more about your father's business. Te voy a preguntar sólo un poco más sobre el negocio de tu padre.* **7** ADV You use **just** to mean exactly or precisely. *exactamente, justamente* ❑ *They are just like the rest of us. Son exactamente iguales al resto de nosotros.* ❑ *My arm hurts too, just here. También me duele el brazo, justamente aquí.* **8** PHRASE You use **just about** to indicate that what you are talking about is so close to being true that it can be accepted as being true. *prácticamente* ❑ *He is just* *about the best golfer in the world.* *Él es prácticamente el mejor golfista del mundo.* **9** **not just** → see **not** **10** **just now** → see **now**

**❷ just** /dʒʌst/ ADJ If you describe a situation, action, or idea as **just,** you mean that it is right or acceptable according to moral principles. *justo* [FORMAL] ❑ *They believe that they are fighting a just war.* *Ellos creen que están librando una guerra justa.* ● **just\|ly** ADV *con justicia* ❑ *They were not treated justly in the past.* *No se les trató con justicia en el pasado.*

**jus\|tice** /dʒʌstɪs/ (**justices**) **1** N-UNCOUNT **Justice** is fairness in the way that people are treated. *justicia* ❑ *We want freedom, justice and equality.* *Queremos libertad, justicia e igualdad.* **2** N-UNCOUNT The **justice of** a cause, claim, or argument is its quality of being reasonable, fair, or right. *legitimidad* ❑ *We must convince people of the justice of our cause.* *Debemos convencer a la gente de la legitimidad de nuestra lucha.* **3** N-UNCOUNT **Justice** is the system that a country uses in order to deal with people who break the law. *sistema judicial* ❑ *Many young people feel that the justice system does not treat them fairly.* *Muchos jóvenes sienten que el sistema judicial los trata injustamente.* **4** N-COUNT A **justice** is a judge. *juez* ❑ *He is a justice on the Supreme Court.* *Es juez de la Suprema Corte.* **5** N-TITLE **Justice** is used before the names of judges. *juez* ❑ *...Justice Hutchison.* *...el Juez Hutchison.* **6** PHRASE If a criminal is **brought to justice,** he or she is punished for a crime by being arrested and tried in a court of law. *capturar y enjuiciar* ❑ *The people responsible for the crime should be brought to justice.* *Los responsables del crimen deberían ser capturados y enjuiciados.* **7** PHRASE If you **do justice to** someone or something, you deal with them properly and completely. *hacer justicia* ❑ *This article doesn't do the topic justice.* *Este artículo no le hace justicia al tema.*

**Word Partnership** Usar *justice* con:

| | |
|---|---|
| V. | **seek** justice **1** |
| ADJ. | **racial** justice, **social** justice **1** |
| | **criminal** justice, **equal** justice **3** |
| N. | **obstruction of** justice, justice **system** **3** |

**jus\|ti\|fi\|ca\|tion** /dʒʌstɪfɪkeɪʃᵊn/ (**justifications**) N-VAR A **justification for** something is an acceptable reason or explanation for it. *justificación* ❑ *There is no justification for this huge price rise.* *No hay justificación para este alto incremento de precio.*

**jus\|ti\|fied** /dʒʌstɪfaɪd/ ADJ A decision, action, or idea that is **justified** is reasonable and acceptable. *justificado* ❑ *In my opinion, the decision was justified.* *En mi opinión, la decisión estaba justificada.* ❑ *We felt justified in blaming him.* *Nos sentimos justificados para culparlo.*

**jus\|ti\|fy** /dʒʌstɪfaɪ/ (**justifies, justifying, justified**) V-T To **justify** a decision, action, or idea means to show or prove that it is reasonable or necessary. *justificar* ❑ *Is there anything that can justify a war?* *¿Hay algo que justifique una guerra?*

**ju\|venile** /dʒuvənᵊl, -naɪl/ (**juveniles**) N-COUNT A **juvenile** is a child or young person who is not yet old enough to be treated as an adult. *joven* [FORMAL] ❑ *...the number of juveniles in the general population.* *...el número de jóvenes en la población general.*

# Kk

**K-12** /keɪ twɛlv/ ADJ **K-12** education is education for children from kindergarten through twelfth grade. *El sistema escolar, que consta de doce años, desde la educación elemental hasta la pre-universitaria* ❑ *...all of the state's 11,000 K-12 schools. ...todas las escuelas estatales de educación básica a media superior*

**Ka|bu|ki** /kəbuki/ N-UNCOUNT **Kabuki** is a form of traditional Japanese theater that uses dance and music as well as acting. *kabuki*

**kan|ga|roo** /kæŋgəru/ (**kangaroos**) N-COUNT A **kangaroo** is a large Australian animal. Female kangaroos carry their babies in a pocket on their stomach. *canguro*

kangaroo

**kan|ga|roo rat** (**kangaroo rats**) N-COUNT A **kangaroo rat** is a small rodent that lives in North and Central America. It has long back legs, which it uses in order to hop. *rata canguro*

**kar|at** /kærət/ N-COUNT A **karat** is a unit for measuring the purity of gold. The purest gold is 24-karat gold. *quilate* ❑ *...a twenty-four-karat gold necklace. ...un collar de oro de veinticuatro quilates.*

**ka|ra|te** /kərɑti/ N-UNCOUNT **Karate** is a martial art in which people fight using their hands, elbows, feet, and legs. *karate*

**karst to|pog|r|aphy** /kɑrst təpɒgrəfi/ N-UNCOUNT **Karst topography** is land where rainwater has dissolved the rock, and features such as caves and underground streams have formed. *topografía kárstica* [TECHNICAL]

**Kb** also **kb** **Kb** or **kb** is a written abbreviation for **kilobit** or **kilobits**. *Kb, kilobit* [COMPUTING]

**KB** also **K** **KB** or **K** is a written abbreviation for **kilobyte** or **kilobytes**. *KB, kilobyte* [COMPUTING]

**Kbps** also **kbps** **Kbps** or **kbps** is a written abbreviation for "kilobits per second." *kilobits por segundo* [COMPUTING] ❑ *...a 28.8 Kbps modem. ...un modem de 28.8 kilobits por segundo*

**keel** /kil/ (**keels, keeling, keeled**) PHRASE If something is **on an even keel**, it is working or progressing smoothly and steadily, without any sudden changes. *estabilidad* ❑ *There is enough money to keep the family on an even keel. Hay suficiente dinero para mantener a la familia con estabilidad.*

▸ **keel over** PHR-VERB If someone **keels over**, they fall down because they are tired or sick. *desplomarse* [INFORMAL] ❑ *He keeled over and fell flat on his back. Se desplomó y cayó sobre su espalda.*

**keen** /kin/ (**keener, keenest**) **1** ADJ If you have a **keen** eye or ear, you are able to notice things that are difficult to detect. *con mucha visión, con un olfato agudo* ❑ *...an artist with a keen eye for detail. ...un artista con una aguda visión para los detalles.* ● **keen|ly** ADV *con entusiasmo* ❑ *Charles listened keenly. Carlos escuchaba con entusiasmo.* **2** ADJ If someone has a **keen** mind, they are very clever and aware of what is happening around them. *gran, aguda* ❑ *...a man of keen intelligence. ...un hombre de gran inteligencia* ● **keen|ly** ADV *profundamente* ❑ *I am keenly aware of the things that we share as Americans. Estoy profundamente consciente de lo que compartimos como americanos.*

**keep**

1. REMAIN, STAY, OR CONTINUE TO HAVE/DO
2. STOP OR PREVENT
3. COST OF LIVING
4. PHRASAL VERBS

**❶ keep** /kip/ (**keeps, keeping, kept**) **1** V-LINK If someone **keeps** or **is kept** in a particular state, they remain in it. *mantener (v-t)* ❑ *The noise kept him awake. El ruido lo mantuvo despierto* ❑ *People had to burn wood to keep warm. Tenían que quemar madera para mantener el calor.* **2** V-T/V-I If you **keep** or you **are kept** in a particular position or place, you remain in it. *mantener* ❑ *Keep away from the doors while the train is moving. Manténgase lejos de las puertas mientras el tren esté en movimiento.* ❑ *He kept his head down, hiding his face. Mantenía la cabeza gacha, ocultando su cara.* **3** V-T If you **keep** doing something, you do it repeatedly or continue to do it. *hacer algo repetidamente, continuar haciendo algo* ❑ *I keep forgetting it's December. Se me sigue olvidando que es diciembre.* ❑ *She forced herself to keep going. Se forzó a continuar.* ● **Keep on** means the same as **keep**. *hacer algo repetidamente, continuar haciendo algo* ❑ *Did he give up or keep on trying? ¿Se rindió o siguió intentando?* **4** V-T If you **keep** something, you continue to have it. If you **keep** it somewhere, you store it there. *guardar* ❑ *We must decide what to keep and what to give away. Debemos decidir qué guardar y qué regalar.* ❑ *She kept her money under the bed. Guardaba su dinero abajo de la cama.* **5** V-T **Keep** is used with some nouns to indicate that someone does something for a period of time or continues to do it. For example, if you **keep a grip on** something, you continue to hold or control it. *seguir, mantener* ❑ *One of them would keep watch on the road. Uno de ellos vigilaría el camino.* **6** V-T When you **keep** something such as a promise or an appointment, you do what you said you would do. *cumplir* ❑ *I'm hoping you'll keep your promise to come. Espero que cumplirás tu promesa de venir.* **7** V-T

k

If you **keep** a record of a series of events, you write down details of it so that they can be referred to later. *llevar* ❑ *Eleanor began to keep a diary. Eleanor comenzó a llevar un diario.* **8** PHRASE If one thing is **in keeping with** another, it is suitable because of that thing. *de acuerdo con* ❑ *This job is in keeping with his experience. Este trabajo va de acuerdo con su experiencia.* **9** PHRASE If you **keep** something **to yourself**, you do not tell anyone else about it. *callarse algo* ❑ *I have to tell someone. I can't keep it to myself. Tengo que decirle a alguien. No puedo callármelo.* **10** PHRASE If you **keep to yourself**, you stay on your own most of the time and do not mix socially with other people. *ser muy reservado* ❑ *He was a quiet man who always kept to himself. Era un hombre tranquilo que no se mezclaba con la gente.* **11** to **keep** someone **company** → see **company** **12** to **keep a straight face** → see **face** **13** to **keep** your **head** → see **head** **14** to **keep pace** → see **pace** **15** to **keep quiet** → see **quiet** **16** to **keep track** → see **track**

**❷ keep** /kip/ (**keeps, keeping, kept**) **1** V-T If someone or something **keeps** you **from** doing something, they prevent you from doing it. *impedir* ❑ *Embarrassment has kept me from doing all sorts of things. La pena me ha impedido hacer todo tipo de cosas.* **2** V-T If someone or something **keeps** you, they delay you and make you late. *detener* ❑ *Sorry to keep you, Jack. Discúlpame por detenerte, Jack.* **3** V-T If you **keep** something **from** someone, you do not tell them about it. *ocultar* ❑ *She knew that Gabriel was keeping something from her. Sabía que Gabriel le ocultaba algo.*

**❸ keep** /kip/ N-SING Someone's **keep** is the cost of food and other things that they need in their daily life. *sustento* ❑ *Ray will earn his keep on local farms while he is a student. Ray se ganará el sustento en granjas locales mientras estudia.*

**❹ keep** /kip/ (**keeps, keeping, kept**)

▶ **keep down** PHR-VERB If you **keep** the amount of something **down**, you do not let it increase. *Mantener bajo, limitar* ❑ *The aim is to keep prices down. El objetivo es mantener los precios bajos*

▶ **keep on** **1** → see **keep❶** **3** **2** PHR-VERB If you **keep** someone **on**, you continue to employ them, for example after other employees have lost their jobs. *mantener a alguien como empleado* ❑ *Firing him would be more damaging than keeping him on. Despedirlo sería más perjudicial que mantenerlo empleado.*

▶ **keep to** **1** PHR-VERB If you **keep to** a rule, plan, or agreement, you do exactly what you are expected or supposed to do. *respetar* ❑ *You've got to keep to the speed limit. Debes respetar el límite de velocidad.* **2** PHR-VERB If you **keep** something **to** a particular number or quantity, you limit it to that number or quantity. *limitar* ❑ *Keep costs to a minimum. Limita los costos al mínimo.*

▶ **keep up** **1** PHR-VERB If you **keep up with** someone or something, you move at the same speed or progress at the same rate. *mantener* ❑ *He walked faster to keep up with his father. Caminaba más rápidamente para mantener el paso de su padre.* ❑ *Cellphones are changing so fast it's hard to keep up. Los teléfonos celulares cambian tan rápidamente que es difícil mantenerse actualizado.* **2** PHR-VERB If you **keep** something **up**, you continue to do it or provide it. *mantener* ❑ *I could not keep the diet up for longer than a month. No pude mantener la dieta más de un mes.*

**keep|er** /kipər/ (**keepers**) N-COUNT A **keeper** is a person who takes care of something; a **keeper** at a zoo is a person who takes care of the animals. *guardia*

**ken|nel** /kɛnəl/ (**kennels**) N-COUNT A **kennel** is a place where dogs are bred and trained, or cared for when their owners are away. *criadero, pensión, guardería (de perros)* ❑ *Mrs Wray said the dogs would stay at the kennels until tomorrow. La Sra. Wray dijo que los perros se quedarían en la pensión hasta mañana.*

**kept** /kɛpt/ **Kept** is the past tense and past participle of **keep**. *pasado y participio pasado de* ***keep***

**kero|sene** /kɛrəsin/ N-UNCOUNT **Kerosene** is a strong-smelling liquid which is used as a fuel in heaters and lamps. *queroseno, petróleo* ❑ *...a kerosene lamp. ...una lámpara de queroseno.*

**ket|tle** /kɛtəl/ (**kettles**) **1** N-COUNT A **kettle** is a covered container that you use for boiling water. *cafetera (para hervir agua), pava* ❑ *I'll put the kettle on and make us some tea. Pondré la cafetera para hacer un poco de té.* **2** N-COUNT A **kettle** is a metal pot for boiling or cooking things in. *olla* ❑ *Put the meat into a small kettle. Ponga la carne en una olla pequeña*

**key** /ki/ (**keys**) **1** N-COUNT A **key** is a specially shaped piece of metal that fits in a lock and is turned in order to open something, or start an engine. *llave* ❑ *They put the key in the door and entered. Insertaron la llave de la puerta y entraron.* **2** N-COUNT The **keys** on a computer keyboard or typewriter are the buttons that you press in order to operate it. *tecla* ❑ *Finally, press the "Delete" key. Para finalizar, presione la tecla "borrar".* **3** N-COUNT The **keys** of a piano or organ are the white and black bars that you press in order to play it. *tecla* **4** N-VAR In music, a **key** is a scale of musical notes that starts on one specific note. *tono* ❑ *...the key of A minor. ...en el tono de La menor.* **5** ADJ The **key** person or thing in a group is the most important one. *clave* ❑ *He is expected to be the key witness at the trial. Se espera que él sea el testigo clave en el juicio.* **6** N-COUNT The **key to** something good is the things that help you achieve it. *clave* ❑ *The key to getting good grades is to work hard. La clave para obtener buenas notas es trabajar duro.*

**Thesaurus** *key* Ver también:

ADJ. critical, important, major, vital **5**

**Word Partnership** Usar *key* con:

V. **turn a** key **1**
ADJ. key **component**, key **decision**, key **factor**, key **figure**, key **ingredient**, key **issue**, key **official**, key **player**, key **point**, key **question**, key **role**, key **word** **5**
key **to success** **6**

**key|board** /kibɔrd/ (**keyboards**) **1** N-COUNT The **keyboard** of a typewriter or computer is the set of keys that you press in order to operate it. *teclado* **2** N-COUNT The **keyboard** of a piano or organ is the set of black and white keys that you press in order to play it. *teclado*
→ see Picture Dictionary: **keyboard**
→ see **computer**

K

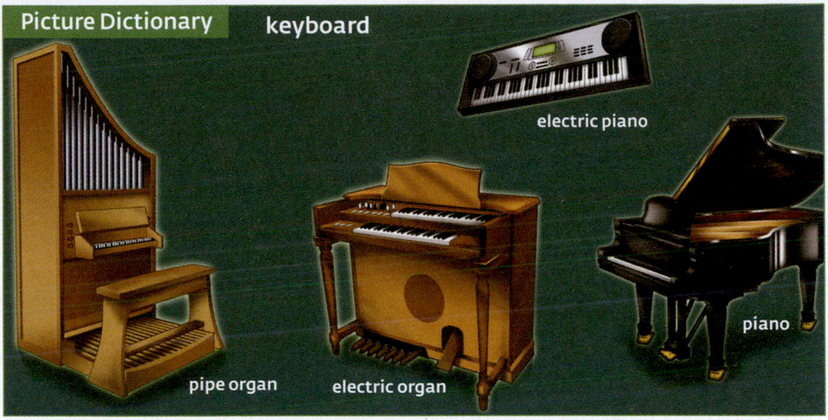


**key card** (**key cards**) N-COUNT A **key card** is a small plastic card which you can use instead of a key to open a door or barrier, for example in some hotels and parking lots. tarjeta que funciona como llave electrónica ❏ *The electronic key card to Julie's room didn't work.* *La tarjeta que abre la puerta de Julie no funcionó.*

**key|stone** /kistoʊn/ (**keystones**) **1** N-COUNT A **keystone of** a policy, system, or process is an important part of it, which is the basis for later developments. piedra angular ❏ *The government's determination to beat inflation has so far been the keystone of its economic policy.* *Hasta ahora, la piedra angular de la política económica del gobierno ha sido su determinación de abatir la inflación.* **2** N-COUNT A **keystone** is a stone at the top of an arch, which keeps the other stones in place by its weight and position. sillar de clave [TECHNICAL]
→ see **architecture**

**key|word** /kiwɜrd/ (**keywords**) also **key word** **1** N-COUNT A **keyword** is a word or phrase that is associated with a particular document in Internet searches. palabra clave ❏ *Users can search by title, by author, by subject, and by keyword.* *Los usuarios podrán realizar la búsqueda por título, autor, tema, o palabra clave.* **2** N-COUNT The **keyword** in a situation is a word or phrase that is very important in that situation. palabra clave ❏ *Compromise is the keyword.* *La palabra clave es acuerdo.*

**kg** **kg** is a written abbreviation for **kilogram** or **kilograms.** kg, kilogramo

**kha|ki** /kæki/ COLOR Something that is **khaki** is greenish-brown or yellowish-brown in color. caqui ❏ *He was dressed in khaki trousers.* *Llevaba unos pantalones color caqui.*

kick

**kick** /kɪk/ (**kicks, kicking, kicked**) **1** V-T/V-I If you **kick** someone or something, you hit them with your foot. patear ❏ *He kicked the door hard.* *Pateó fuertemente la puerta.* ❏ *He kicked the ball away.* *Pateó la pelota muy lejos.* ❏ *He threw the ball on the ground and started to kick.* *Arrojó la pelota al suelo y comenzó a dar de patadas.* ● **Kick** is also a noun. patada ❏ *He suffered a kick to the knee.* *Le dieron una patada en la rodilla.* **2** V-T/V-I If you **kick** or if you **kick** your legs, you move your legs with very quick, small, and forceful movements, once or repeatedly. patalear ❏ *They were dragged away struggling and kicking.* *Los arrastraron mientras forcejeaban y pataleaban.* ❏ *The baby smiled and kicked her legs.* *La bebé sonrió y pataleó.* **3** V-T If you **kick** a bad habit, you stop having it. dejar un mal hábito [INFORMAL] ❏ *Nail-biting is a difficult habit to kick.* *Dejar de morderse las uñas es un hábito difícil de dejar.* **4** N-SING If something gives you **a kick,** it gives you pleasure or excitement. gusto [INFORMAL] ❏ *I got a kick out of seeing my name in print.* *Me dio gusto ver mi nombre impreso.*

▸ **kick in** **1** PHR-VERB If something **kicks in,** it begins to take effect. surtir efecto ❏ *I hoped the aspirin would kick in soon.* *Esperaba que la aspirina surtiera efecto.* **2** PHR-VERB If someone **kicks in** a particular amount of money, they provide that amount of money to help pay for something. aportar ❏ *Kansas City churches kicked in $35,000 to support the event.* *Las iglesias de Kansas City aportaron $35,000 para apoyar el evento.*

▸ **kick off** PHR-VERB If an event, game, series, or discussion **kicks off,** or **is kicked off,** it begins. comenzar ❏ *The show kicks off on October 24th.* *El espectáulo comenzará el 24 de octubre.* ❏ *The mayor kicked off the party.* *El alcalde dio comienzo a la fiesta.*

▸ **kick out** PHR-VERB To **kick** someone **out of** a place or an organization means to force them to leave it. correr, echar [INFORMAL] ❏ *They kicked five foreign journalists out of the country.* *Corrieron a cinco reporteros extranjeros del país.*

| **Thesaurus** | *kick* | Ver también: |
|---|---|---|
| V. | abandon, give up, quit, stop; (*ant.*) start, take up **3** | |
| N. | enjoyment, excitement, fun, thrill **4** | |

**Word Partnership** Usar *kick* con:

N. kick **a ball**, kick **a door**, **penalty** kick 1
kick **a habit**, kick **smoking** 3

**kick|er** /kɪkər/ (**kickers**) N-COUNT In sports such as football and rugby, the **kicker** is a player whose role includes kicking the ball. pateador o pateadora ❑ *...Broncos' kicker Jason Elam.* *...el pateador de los Broncos, Jason Elam.*

**kick|off** /kɪkɔf/ (**kickoffs**) 1 N-VAR In football or soccer, the **kickoff** is the time at which a particular game starts. *patada inicial* ❑ *Officials expect about 65,000 fans for the 7:30 kickoff.* *Se espera que haya alrededor de 65,000 fanáticos para la patada inicial a las 7:30.* 2 N-COUNT In football, a **kickoff** is the kick that begins play, for example at the beginning of a half or after a touchdown or goal has been scored. *patada*

**kick|stand** /kɪkstænd/ (**kickstands**) N-COUNT A **kickstand** is a metal bar attached to a bicycle or motorcycle that holds it upright when it is not being used. *Pie de bicicleta o motocicleta que sirve para mantenerla derecha.* ❑ *He put down the kickstand and took off his helmet.* *Bajó el pie de la bicicleta y se quitó el casco.*

K

**kick-start** (**kick-starts, kick-starting, kick-started**) also **kickstart** V-T To **kick-start** a process that has stopped working or progressing is to take a course of action that will quickly start it going again. *arrancar* ❑ *He's raising money to kick-start a youth basketball league.* *Está recolectando dinero para comenzar una liga de basquetbol juvenil.*

**kid** /kɪd/ (**kids, kidding, kidded**) 1 N-COUNT You can refer to a child as a **kid.** *niño o niña* [INFORMAL] ❑ *They have three kids.* *Tienen tres niños.* 2 V-I If you **are kidding,** you are saying something that is not really true, as a joke. *bromear* [INFORMAL] ❑ *I thought he was kidding but he was serious.* *Creí que estaba bromeando, pero hablaba en serio.* ❑ *I'm just kidding.* *Sólo estoy bromeando* 3 V-T If people **kid themselves,** they allow themselves to believe something that is not true because they wish that it was true. *Hacerse tontos* ❑ *We're kidding ourselves, Bill. We're not winning, we're not even doing well.* *Nos estamos haciendo tontos, Bill. No vamos a ganar, ni siquiera nos está yendo bien.* 4 N-COUNT A **kid** is a young goat. *cabrito*

**Word Partnership** Usar *kid* con:

ADJ. **fat** kid, **friendly** kid, **good** kid, **little** kid, **new** kid, **nice** kid, **poor** kid, **skinny** kid, **smart** kid, **tough** kid, **young** kid 1
N. **school** kid, kid **stuff** 1
V. **raise a** kid 1 4

**kiddo** /kɪdoʊ/ (**kiddos**) N-VOC You can call someone **kiddo,** especially someone who is younger than you, as a sign of affection. *amigo* [INFORMAL] ❑ *I'll miss you, kiddo.* *Te voy a extrañar, amigo.*

**kid|nap** /kɪdnæp/ (**kidnaps, kidnapping** or **kidnaping, kidnapped** or **kidnaped**) 1 V-T To **kidnap** someone is to take them away illegally and by force, and usually to hold them prisoner in order to demand something from their family, employer, or government. *secuestrar* ❑ *The police uncovered a plot to kidnap him.* *La policía descubrió un plan para secuestrarlo.* ● **kid|nap|per** N-COUNT (**kidnappers**) *secuestrador o secuestradora* ❑ *His kidnappers have threatened to kill him.* *Sus secuestradores amenazaron con matarlo.* ● **kid|nap|ping** N-VAR (**kidnappings**) *secuestro* ❑ *Two men have been arrested and charged with kidnapping.* *Dos hombres fueron arrestados y hallados culpables de secuestro.* 2 N-VAR **Kidnap** or a **kidnap** is the crime of taking someone away by force. *secuestro* ❑ *He was charged with the kidnap of a 25-year-old woman.* *Lo hallaron culpable del secuestro de una mujer de 25 años.*

**kid|ney** /kɪdni/ (**kidneys**) N-COUNT Your **kidneys** are the two organs in your body that take waste matter from your blood and send it out of your body as urine. *riñón* ❑ *...a kidney transplant.* *...un trasplante de riñón.*
→ see **donor**

**kid|ney bean** (**kidney beans**) N-COUNT **Kidney beans** are small, reddish-brown beans that are eaten as a vegetable. They are the seeds of a bean plant. *frijol*

**kill** /kɪl/ (**kills, killing, killed**) 1 V-T/V-I If a person, animal, or other living thing **is killed,** something or someone causes them to die. *matar* ❑ *More than 1,000 people have been killed by the armed forces.* *Las fuerzas armadas han matado a más de 1,000 personas.* ❑ *Drugs can kill.* *Las drogas pueden matar.* ● **kill|ing** N-UNCOUNT *homicidio* ❑ *...the killing of seven civilians.* *...el homicidio de siete civiles.* 2 V-T If something or someone **kills** an activity, process, or feeling, they prevent it from continuing. *acabar con* ❑ *His objective was to kill the project altogether.* *Su objetivo era acabar con el proyecto de una vez.* ● **Kill off** means the same as **kill.** *matar* ❑ *Global warming might kill off polar bears.* *El calentamiento global podría matar a los osos polares.* 3 V-T If you **are killing** time, you are doing something because you have some time available, not because you really want to do it. *matar* ❑ *To kill the hours while she waited, Anna worked in the yard.* *Para matar las horas mientras esperaba, Anna trabajaba en el patio.* 5 to **be killed outright** → see **outright**
▸ **kill off** 1 → see **kill 2** 2 PHR-VERB If you **kill** things **off,** you destroy or kill all of them. *matar, exterminar* ❑ *Author J K Rowling is going to kill off a character in her next book.* *La escritora JK Rowling matará a un personaje en su próximo libro.* ❑ *...poison to kill off the rats.* *...un veneno para exterminar a las ratas.*
→ see **war**

**Thesaurus** *kill* Ver también:

V. execute, murder, put down, slay, wipe out 1

**kill|er** /kɪlər/ (**killers**) 1 N-COUNT A **killer** is a person who has killed someone. *homicida, asesino o asesina* ❑ *The police are searching for the killers.* *La policía busca a los homicidas.* 2 N-COUNT You can refer to anything that causes death as a **killer.** *causa de muerte* ❑ *Heart disease is the biggest killer of men in some countries.* *Las enfermedades cardiacas son la principal causa de muerte en algunos países.*

**kilo** /kiloʊ/ (**kilos**) N-COUNT A **kilo** is the same as a **kilogram.** *kilo* ❑ *He'd lost ten kilos in weight.* *Había perdido diez kilos de peso.*

**kilo|bit** /kɪləbɪt/ (**kilobits**) N-COUNT In computing, a **kilobit** is 1,024 bits of data. kilobit ❑ *...a 256-kilobit chip.* *...un chip de 256 kilobits.* [COMPUTING]

**Word Link** *kilo ≈ thousand : kilobyte, kilogram, kilometer*

**kilo|byte** /kɪləbaɪt/ (**kilobytes**) N-COUNT In computing, a **kilobyte** is 1,024 bytes of data. *kilobyte* [COMPUTING]

**kilo|calo|rie** /kɪləkæləri/ (**kilocalories**) N-COUNT A **kilocalorie** is a unit of energy that is equal to one thousand calories. *kilocaloría* [TECHNICAL]

**kilo|gram** /kɪləgræm/ (**kilograms**) N-COUNT A **kilogram** is a metric unit of mass. One kilogram is a thousand grams, and is equal to 2.2 pounds. *kilogramo* ❑ *...a box weighing around 4.5 kilograms.* *...una caja que pesa cerca de 4.5 kilogramos*

**Word Link** *meter ≈ measuring : kilometer, meter, perimeter*

**kilo|meter** /kɪləmitər, kɪlɒmɪtər/ (**kilometers**) N-COUNT A **kilometer** is a metric unit of distance or length. One kilometer is a thousand meters, and is equal to 0.62 miles. *kilómetro* ❑ *...only one kilometer from the border.* *...a solo un kilómetro de la frontera.*
→ see **measurement**

**kin** /kɪn/ PHRASE Your **next of kin** is your closest relative, especially in official or legal documents. *pariente* [FORMAL] ❑ *We have notified the next of kin.* *Ya notificamos a los parientes más cercanos.*

**kind**
❶ NOUN USES AND PHRASES
❷ ADJECTIVE USE

❶ **kind** /kaɪnd/ (**kinds**) **1** N-COUNT If you talk about a particular **kind of** thing, you are talking about one of the types or sorts of that thing. *estilo, tipo* ❑ *The party needs a different kind of leadership.* *El partido necesita un estilo de liderazgo diferente.* ❑ *Has Jamie ever been in any kind of trouble?* *¿Ha tenido Jamie alguna vez algún tipo de problema?* **2** PHRASE You use **kind of** when you want to say that something or someone can be roughly described in a particular way. *algo* [SPOKEN] ❑ *It was kind of sad, really.* *Fue algo triste, en verdad.* **3** PHRASE Payment **in kind** is payment in the form of goods or services and not money. *pago en especie* ❑ *...gifts in kind.* *...donaciones en especie*

**Thesaurus** *kind* Ver también:
N. sort, type ❶ **1**
ADJ. affectionate, considerate, gentle ❷ **1**

**Word Link** *est ≈ most : greatest, kindest, loudest*

❷ **kind** /kaɪnd/ (**kinder, kindest**) ADJ Someone who is **kind** behaves in a gentle, caring, and helpful way toward other people. *amable* ❑ *I must thank you for being so kind to me.* *Debo agradecerte que seas tan amable conmigo.* ● **kind|ly** ADV *amablemente* ❑ *"You seem tired this morning, Jenny," she said kindly.* *—Te ves cansada esta mañana, Jenny—comentó amablemente.* ● **kind|ness** N-UNCOUNT *amabilidad* ❑ *We have been treated with such kindness by everybody.* *Todos nos han tratado con tanta amabilidad.*

**kin|der|gar|ten** /kɪndərgɑrtᵊn/ (**kindergartens**) N-VAR A **kindergarten** is a school for children aged 4 to 6 years old, that prepares them to go into the first grade. *jardín de niños* ❑ *She's in kindergarten now.* *Está ahora en el jardín de niños.*

**kind|ly** /kaɪndli/ **1** ADJ A **kindly** person is kind, caring, and sympathetic. *amable* ❑ *He was an extremely kindly man.* *Era un hombre extremadamente amable.* **2** ADV If someone asks you to **kindly** do something, they are asking you in a way which shows that they have authority over you, or that they are angry with you. *¿Sería tan amable de...?* [FORMAL] ❑ *Will you kindly obey the instructions?* *¿Sería tan amable de seguir las instrucciones?* **3** → see also **kind**

**kin|es|thet|ic** /kɪnɪsθɛtɪk/ also **kinaesthetic** ADJ **Kinesthetic** means relating to sensations caused by movement of the body. *cinestético* [TECHNICAL]

**ki|net|ic en|er|gy** N-UNCOUNT In physics, **kinetic energy** is the energy that is produced when something moves. *energía cinética* [TECHNICAL]

**king** /kɪŋ/ (**kings**) **1** N-TITLE; N-COUNT A **king** is a man who is a member of the royal family of his country, and who is the head of state of that country. *rey* ❑ *...the king and queen of Spain.* *...el rey y la reina de España.* **2** N-COUNT A **king** is a playing card with a picture of a king on it. *rey* ❑ *...the king of diamonds.* *...el rey de diamantes.* **3** N-COUNT In chess, the **king** is the piece which each player must try to capture. *rey*
→ see **chess**

**Word Link** *dom, domin ≈ rule, master : domain, dominate, kingdom*

**king|dom** /kɪŋdəm/ (**kingdoms**) **1** N-COUNT A **kingdom** is a country or region that is ruled by a king or queen. *reino* ❑ *The kingdom's power grew.* *El poder del reino creció.* **2** N-SING All the animals, birds, and insects in the world can be referred to together as the animal **kingdom.** All the plants can be referred to as the plant **kingdom.** *reino* ❑ *The animal kingdom is full of wonderful creatures.* *El reino animal está lleno de maravillosas criaturas.*

**ki|osk** /kiɒsk/ (**kiosks**) N-COUNT A kiosk is a small structure with an open window at which people can buy things like newspapers, pay an attendant at a parking lot, or get information about something. *kiosko* ❑ *I was getting a newspaper at the kiosk.* *Estaba yo comprando un periódico en el kiosco.*

**kiss** /kɪs/ (**kisses, kissing, kissed**) V-RECIP If you **kiss** someone, you touch them with your lips to show affection or to greet them. *besar* ❑ *She leaned up and kissed him on the cheek.* *Ella se inclinó y lo besó en la mejilla.* ❑ *Her parents kissed her goodbye as she set off from their home.* *Sus padres la besaron al despedirla cuando salió de su casa.* ❑ *They kissed for almost half a minute.* *Se besaron por casi medio minuto.* ● **Kiss** is also a noun. *beso* ❑ *I put my arms around her and gave her a kiss.* *La abracé y le di un beso.*
→ see Word Web: **kiss**

k

## Word Web kiss

Some anthropologists believe mothers invented the **kiss**. They chewed a bit of food and then used their lips to place it in their child's mouth. Others believe that kissing started with primates. There are many types of kisses. Kisses express affection or accompany a greeting or a goodbye. Friends and family members exchange **social kisses** on the **lips** or sometimes on the **cheek**. When people are about to kiss they pucker their lips. In European countries, friends kiss each other lightly on both cheeks. And in the Middle East, a kiss between two leaders shows support for each other.

**kit** /kɪt/ (**kits, kitting, kitted**) **1** N-COUNT A **kit** is a group of items that are kept together because they are used for a similar purpose. *equipo, juego* ❑ *...a first aid kit. ...un equipo o juego de primeros auxilios.* **2** N-COUNT A **kit** is a set of parts that can be put together in order to make something. *equipo, juego, maqueta* ❑ *...model airplane kits. ...maquetas de aeromodelismo.*

**kitch|en** /kɪtʃ$^{ə}$n/ (**kitchens**) N-COUNT A **kitchen** is a room that is used for cooking and for household jobs such as washing dishes. *cocina.*
→ see **house**

**kite** /kaɪt/ (**kites**) N-COUNT A **kite** is an object consisting of a light frame covered with paper or cloth, which you fly in the air at the end of a long string. *papalote, cometa* ❑ *Bill asked if I'd ever flown a kite before. Bill me preguntó si alguna vez había yo volado un papalote.*

**kitsch** /kɪtʃ/ N-UNCOUNT You can refer to a work of art or an object as **kitsch** if it is showy and in bad taste. *ostentoso y de mal gusto* ❑ *...an embarrassing piece of kitsch. ...un objeto de cursilería que da pena verlo.* ● **Kitsch** is also an adjective. *cursi* ❑ *She was wearing kitsch green eyeshadow. Ella traía sombra de ojos de un verde muy cursi.*

**kit|ten** /kɪt$^{ə}$n/ (**kittens**) N-COUNT A **kitten** is a very young cat. *gatito*

**kit|ty** /kɪti/ (**kitties**) **1** N-COUNT A **kitty** is an amount of money gathered from several people, which is used to buy things that they will share or use together. *caja de ahorros* ❑ *You haven't put any money in the kitty. No le has puesto nada de dinero a la caja.* **2** N-COUNT A **kitty** is a cat, especially a young one. *gatito* [INFORMAL]

**kitty-corner** ADJ → see **catty-corner**

**kiwi** /kiwi/ (**kiwis**) A **kiwi** is the same as a **kiwi fruit.** *kiwi*
→ see **fruit**

**kiwi fruit** (**kiwi fruits**)

> **Kiwi fruit** can also be used as the plural form.

N-VAR A **kiwi fruit** is a fruit with a brown hairy skin and green flesh. *kiwi*

**klutz** /klʌts/ (**klutzes**) N-COUNT You can refer to someone who is very clumsy as a **klutz.** *desmañado, torpe* [INFORMAL]

**km** (**kms**) **km** is a written abbreviation for **kilometer.** *abreviación que significa kilómetro*

**knack** /næk/ (**knacks**) N-COUNT If you have the **knack** of doing something difficult or skillful, you are able to do it easily. *habilidad de hacer algo difícil* ❑ *He's got the knack of getting people to listen. Tiene la habilidad de hacer que la gente lo escuche.*

**knead** /nid/ (**kneads, kneading, kneaded**) V-T When you **knead** dough, you press and squeeze it with your hands to make it smooth. *amasar* ❑ *Knead the dough for a few minutes. Amasa la masa durante algunos minutos.*

**knee** /ni/ (**knees**) **1** N-COUNT Your **knee** is the place where your leg bends. *rodilla* ❑ *He will receive physical therapy on his left knee. Va a recibir terapia física en la rodilla izquierda.* **2** N-COUNT If something or someone is **on** your **knee** or **on** your **knees,** they are resting or sitting on the upper part of your legs when you are sitting down. *piernas, rodillas* ❑ *He sat with the package on his knees. Se sentó con el paquete en las piernas.* **3** N-PLURAL If you are **on** your **knees,** your legs are bent and your knees are on the ground. *arrodillado* ❑ *She fell to the ground on her knees and prayed. Cayó de rodillas al suelo y rezó.* **4** PHRASE If a country or organization **is brought to its knees,** it is almost completely destroyed by someone or something. *aniquilar, destruir* ❑ *The country was being brought to its knees by the loss of 2.4 million manufacturing jobs. El país estaba siendo aniquilado por la pérdida de 2.4 millones de empleos en la manufactura.*
→ see **body, horse**

### Word Partnership Usar *knee* con:

| | |
|---|---|
| N. | knee **injury** **1** |
| ADJ. | **left/right** knee, **weak**-kneed **1** |
| V. | **bend your** knees, knees **buckle** **1** |
| | **fall on your** knees **3** |

**kneel** /nil/ (**kneels, kneeling, kneeled** or **knelt**) V-I When you **kneel,** you bend your legs so that your knees are touching the ground. *arrodillarse, hincarse* ❑ *She knelt by the bed and prayed. Se arrodilló a un lado de la cama y rezó.* ❑ *Other people were kneeling, but she just sat. Otras personas estaban arrodilladas, pero ella permaneció sentada.* ● **Kneel down** means the same as **kneel.** *hincarse* ❑ *She kneeled down beside him. Se hincó junto a él.*

**knew** /nu/ **Knew** is the past tense of **know.** *pasado de* ***know***

**knife** /naɪf/ (**knives, knifes, knifing, knifed**)

> **Knives** is the plural form of the noun and **knifes** is the third person singular of the present tense of the verb.

**1** N-COUNT A **knife** is a tool consisting of a sharp flat piece of metal attached to a handle, used to cut things or as a weapon. *cuchillo* ❑ *...a knife and fork. ...un cuchillo y un tenedor.* **2** V-T To **knife** someone means to attack and injure them with a knife. *acuchillar.* ❑ *Julius Caesar was knifed to death. Julio César fue acuchillado a muerte.*
→ see **tool**

**knight** /naɪt/ (**knights, knighting, knighted**) **1** N-COUNT In medieval times, a **knight** was a man of noble birth, who served his king or lord in battle. *caballero* ❑ *...King Arthur's faithful knight, Gawain. ...Gawain, el fiel caballero del Rey Arturo.* **2** V-T If someone **is knighted,** they are given a knighthood. *armar caballero* ❑ *He was knighted in June 1988. Fue armado caballero en junio de 1988.* **3** N-COUNT In chess, a **knight** is a piece which is shaped like a horse's head. *caballo*
→ see **chess**

**knit** /nɪt/ (**knits, knitting, knitted**) V-T/V-I If you **knit** something, especially an article of clothing, you make it from wool or a similar thread by using two long needles or a machine. *tejer* ❑ *I had endless hours to knit and sew. Tuve largas horas para tejer y coser.* ❑ *I have already started knitting baby clothes. Ya comencé a tejer ropa de bebé.* ● **knit|ting** N-UNCOUNT *tejer* ❑ *...a relaxing hobby, such as knitting. ...un hobby que te relaje, como tejer.*

**knit|ting** /nɪtɪŋ/ N-UNCOUNT **Knitting** is something, such as an article of clothing, that is being knitted. *el tejido* ❑ *She had been sitting with her knitting. Había estado sentada con su tejido.*

**knives** /naɪvz/ **Knives** is the plural of **knife**. *plural de* **knife**

**knob** /nɒb/ (**knobs**) N-COUNT A **knob** is a round handle or switch. *perilla, interruptor* ❑ *He turned the knob and pushed against the door. Hizo girar la perilla y empujó la puerta.* ❑ *...the volume knob. ...la perilla del volumen.*

**knock** /nɒk/ (**knocks, knocking, knocked**) **1** V-I If you **knock on** something such as a door or window, you hit it, usually several times, to attract someone's attention. *tocar, golpear* ❑ *She went directly to Simon's apartment and knocked on the door. Fue directamente al apartamento de Simón y tocó en la puerta.* ● **Knock** is also a noun. *golpe* ❑ *They heard a knock at the front door. Oyeron un golpe de alguien en la puerta de adelante.* ● **knock|ing** N-SING *golpes* ❑ *...a loud knocking at the door. ...golpes fuertes en la puerta.* **2** V-T If you **knock** something, you touch or hit it roughly, especially so that it falls or moves. *Pegar, tocar o golpear.* ❑ *She accidentally knocked the glass off the shelf. Ella accidentalmente golpeó el vaso que se cayó de la repisa.* ❑ *The raccoons knock over the garbage cans in search of food. Los mapaches tiran los botes de basura al buscar alimento.* ● **Knock** is also a noun. *golpe* ❑ *...tough materials to protect against knocks. ...materiales resistentes que protejan contra los golpes.* **3** V-T To **knock** someone into a particular position, state, or condition means to hit them very hard so that they fall over or become unconscious. *Golpear, aventar.* ❑ *The third wave was so strong it knocked me backward. La tercera ola fue tan fuerte que me aventó de espaldas.* ❑ *He nearly knocked me over. Casi me avienta al suelo.* **4** V-T If you **knock** something or someone, you criticize them. *hablar mal, criticar.* [INFORMAL] ❑ *I'm not knocking them: if they want to do it, it's up to them. No los critico: si quieren hacerlo, depende de ellos.*

knock

▸ **knock down 1** PHR-VERB To **knock down** a building or part of a building means to demolish or destroy it. *derribar, demoler, destruir* ❑ *Why doesn't he just knock the wall down? ¿Porqué no simplemente derriba la pared y ya?* **2** PHR-VERB To **knock down** a price or amount means to decrease it. *rebajar, disminuir* ❑ *The market might knock down its price. El mercado podría hacer que baje el precio.*

▸ **knock off** PHR-VERB To **knock off** an amount from a price, time, or level means to reduce it by that amount. *rebajar, reducir.* ❑ *We have knocked 10% off admission prices. Hemos rebajado 10% del precio de entrada.*

▸ **knock out 1** PHR-VERB To **knock** someone **out** means to cause them to become unconscious. *poner a alguien fuera de combate, noquear* ❑ *He was knocked out in a fight. Lo noquearon en una pelea.* **2** PHR-VERB If a person or team **is knocked out** of a competition, they are defeated in a game, so that they take no more part in the competition. *poner fuera de combate, derrotar* ❑ *He got knocked out in the first inning. Fue puesto fuera de combate en la primera entrada.* **3** → see also **knockout**

**Word Partnership** Usar *knock* con:

| | |
|---|---|
| V. | **answer a** knock, **hear a** knock **1** |
| N. | knock **at/on a door 1** |
| ADJ. | **loud** knock **1** |
| | knock ***someone*** **out cold**, knock ***someone*** **unconscious 3** |

**knock|out** /nɒkaʊt/ (**knockouts**) also **knock-out 1** N-COUNT In boxing, a **knockout** is a situation in which a boxer wins the fight by making his opponent fall to the ground and be unable to stand up before the referee has counted to ten. *nocaut* ❑ *Lewis ended the fight with a knockout in the eighth round. Lewis terminó la pelea con un nocaut en el octavo asalto.* **2** ADJ A **knockout** blow is an action or event that completely defeats an opponent. *golpe de nocaut* ❑ *He delivered a knockout blow to all of his enemies. Les dio un golpe fatal a todos sus enemigos.*

**knot** /nɒt/ (**knots, knotting, knotted**) **1** V-T If you **knot** a piece of string, rope, cloth, or other material, you pass one end or part of it through a loop and pull it tight. *anudar* ❑ *He knotted the laces securely together. Anudó las agujetas firmemente.* ❑ *He knotted the scarf around his neck. Se anudó la bufanda alderedor*

knot

k

*del cuello.* • **Knot** is also a noun. *nudo* ❑ *One lace had broken and been tied in a knot.* *Una agujeta se había roto y había sido atada en forma de nudo.* **2** V-T/V-I If your stomach **knots** or if something **knots** it, it feels tight because you are afraid or excited. *hacerse nudos* ❑ *My stomach knotted with fear.* *Mi estómago se hizo nudos por el temor.* • **Knot** is also a noun. *nudo* ❑ *There was a knot of tension in his stomach.* *Tenía un nudo de tensión en el estómago.* **3** N-COUNT A **knot** is a unit used for measuring the speed of ships, aircraft, and wind. *nudo* ❑ *They travel at speeds of up to 30 knots.* *Viajan a velocidades de hasta 30 nudos.*

**know**
❶ VERB USES
❷ PHRASES

❶ **know** /noʊ/ (**knows, knowing, knew, known**) **1** V-T/V-I If you **know** a fact, a piece of information, or an answer, you have it correctly in your mind. *saber* ❑ *I don't know the name of the place.* *No sé el nombre del lugar.* ❑ *"People like doing things for nothing."— "I know they do."* *—A la gente le gusta hacer las cosas por nada.—Yo sé que así es.* ❑ *I don't know what happened to her husband.* *No sé lo que le sucedió a su marido.* ❑ *"How did he meet your mother?" — "I don't know."* *—¿Cómo conoció a tu mamá?—No lo sé.* **2** V-T If you **know** a person or place, you are familiar with them. *conocer* ❑ *I'd known him for nine years.* *Yo ya lo conocía desde hacía nueve años.* ❑ *No matter how well you know this city, it is easy to get lost.* *No importa qué tan bien conozcas esta ciudad, es fácil perderse.* **3** V-I If you **know of** something, you have heard about it but you do not necessarily have a lot of information about it. *saber de* ❑ *We know of the accident but have no further details.* *Sabemos del accidente pero no tenemos más detalles.* **4** V-T/V-I If you **know about** something or **know** it, you understand it, or have the necessary skills and understanding to do it. *saber de* ❑ *Hire someone with experience, someone who knows about real estate.* *Contrata a alguien con experiencia, alguien que sepa acerca de bienes raíces.* ❑ *She didn't know anything about music.* *Ella no sabía nada acerca de música.* ❑ *It helps to know French.* *Ayuda saber francés.* ❑ *The health authorities now know how to deal with the disease.* *Las autoridades de salud ya saben cómo tratar la enfermedad.* **5** V-T If someone or something **is known as** a particular name, they are called by that name. *conocerse* ❑ *Rubella is more commonly known as German measles.* *La rubeola es mejor conocida como sarampión alemán.* ❑ *Everyone knew him as Dizzy.* *Todo el mundo lo conocía como Dizzy.* **6** → see also **known**

K

| **Thesaurus** | *know* | Ver también: |
| --- | --- | --- |
| v. | comprehend, recognize, understand ❶ **1** | |

❷ **know** /noʊ/ (**knows, knowing, knew, known**) **1** PHRASE If you **get to know** someone, you find out what they are like by spending time with them. *conocerse* ❑ *The new neighbors were getting to know each other.* *Los nuevos vecinos estaban comenzando a conocerse.* **2** CONVENTION You say **"I know"** to show that you agree with what has just been said. *—lo sé* ❑ *"This country is so awful."— "I know, I know."* *—Este país es tan terrible.—Lo sé, lo sé.* **3** PHRASE Someone who is **in the know** has information about something that only a few people have. *al tanto* ❑ *It was good to be in the know about important people.* *Era bueno estar al tanto acerca de la gente importante.* **4** CONVENTION You say **"You never know"** or **"One never knows"** to indicate that it is not definite or certain what will happen in the future, and to suggest that there is some hope that things will turn out well. *nunca sabes* ❑ *You never know, I might get lucky.* *Nunca sabes, podría yo tener suerte.* **5** CONVENTION You use **you know** to emphasize or to draw attention to what you are saying. *¿sabes?* [SPOKEN] ❑ *The conditions in there are awful, you know.* *Las condiciones allá son terribles, ¿sabes?* **6** to **let** someone **know** → see **let**

**know-how** N-UNCOUNT **Know-how** is knowledge of the methods or techniques of doing something. *conocimiento* [INFORMAL] ❑ *He doesn't have the know-how to run a farm.* *Él no tiene la pericia para administrar una granja.*

**know|ing|ly** /noʊɪŋli/ ADV If you **knowingly** do something wrong, you do it even though you know it is wrong. *a sabiendas* ❑ *The company is knowingly breaking the law.* *La compañía está haciendo algo ilegal a sabiendas.*

**know-it-all** (**know-it-alls**) N-COUNT If you say that someone is a **know-it-all,** you are critical of them because they think that they know a lot more than other people. *sabelotodo* [INFORMAL]

**knowl|edge** /nɒlɪdʒ/ **1** N-UNCOUNT **Knowledge** is information and understanding about a subject which a person has, or which all people have. *conocimiento* ❑ *He has a wide knowledge of sports.* *Tiene un gran conocimiento acerca de deportes.* **2** PHRASE If you say that something is true **to** your **knowledge** or **to the best of** your **knowledge,** you mean that you believe it to be true but it is possible that you do not know all the facts. *hasta donde se sabe* ❑ *The president, to my knowledge, hasn't commented on it.* *El presidente, hasta donde yo sé, no ha hecho ningún comentario al respecto.*

| **Word Partnership** | Usar *knowledge* con: |
| --- | --- |
| v. | **acquire** knowledge, **gain** knowledge, **have** knowledge, **lack** knowledge, **require** knowledge, **test** ***your*** knowledge, **use** ***your*** knowledge **1** |
| ADJ. | **background** knowledge, **common** knowledge, **general** knowledge, **prior** knowledge, **scientific** knowledge, **useful** knowledge, **vast** knowledge **1** |
| N. | knowledge **base** **1** |

**knowl|edge|able** /nɒlɪdʒəbᵊl/ also **knowledgable** ADJ Someone who is **knowledgeable** knows a lot about many different things or a lot about a particular subject. *conocedor o conocedora* ❑ *Do you think you are more knowledgeable about life than your parents were at your age?* *¿Consideras que conoces más de la vida que lo que sabían tus padres a tu edad?*

**known** /noʊn/ **1** **Known** is the past participle of **know**. *participio pasado de* ***know*** **2** ADJ You use **known** to describe someone or something that is clearly recognized by or familiar to all people or to a particular group of people. *conocido* ❑ *He was a known face at the cafés along Broadway.* *Era una cara* *conocida en los cafés a lo largo de Broadway.* **3** PHRASE If you **let it be known that** something is true, or you **let** something **be known,** you make sure that people know it or can find out about it. *hacer saber* ❑ *The president has let it be known that he is against it. El presidente ha hecho saber que está en contra de ello.*

**knuck|le** /nʌkᵊl/ (**knuckles**) **1** N-COUNT Your **knuckles** are the rounded pieces of bone where your fingers join your hands, and where your fingers bend. *nudillo de la mano* ❑ *Brenda's knuckles were white as she gripped the arms of the chair. Los nudillos de Brenda estaban blancos mientras asía los brazos de la silla.* **2** a **rap on the knuckles** → see **rap** → see **hand**

**kook** /kuk/ (**kooks**) N-COUNT You can refer to someone who you think is slightly strange or eccentric as a **kook.** *loquito o loquita* [INFORMAL]

**Ko|ran** /kɔran, -ræn/ N-PROPER **The Koran** is the sacred book on which the religion of Islam is based. *Corán*

**Kuiper belt** /kaɪpər bɛlt/ N-SING **The Kuiper belt** is a region of the solar system beyond Neptune where there are many small, icy comets. *cinturón de Kuiper* [TECHNICAL]

**Kurd** /kɜrd/ (**Kurds**) N-COUNT A **Kurd** is a member of a race of people who live mainly in parts of Turkey, Iran, and Iraq. *kurdo o kurda* ❑ *...a group of Iraqi Kurds. ...un grupo de kurdos iraquíes.*

**Kur|dish** /kɜrdɪʃ/ **1** ADJ **Kurdish** means belonging or relating to the Kurds, or to their language or culture. *kurdo* ❑ *...Kurdish villages. ...pueblos kurdos.* **2** N-UNCOUNT **Kurdish** is the language spoken by Kurds. *kurdo* ❑ *...schoolchildren speaking Kurdish. ...niños de escuela hablando kurdo.*

**kvetch** /kvɛtʃ/ (**kvetches, kvetching, kvetched**) V-I If someone **kvetches** about something, they complain about it constantly or in a bad-tempered way. *quejarse constantemente o de un modo malhumorado.* [INFORMAL] ❑ *The woman kept kvetching about how he should change into something nicer. La mujer constantemente se quejaba de que él debería vestirse más elegantemente.* ❑ *I just really love to kvetch. A mí me fascina quejarme con mucha pasión.*

**kW** also **KW** **kW** or **KW** is a written abbreviation for **kilowatt.** *KW, kilovatio*

# Ll

**L** On a weather map, **L** is an abbreviation for "low pressure." *baja presión*

**lab** /læb/ (**labs**) N-COUNT A **lab** is the same as a **laboratory**. *laboratorio, lab, labo*

**laba|no|ta|tion** /lɑbənoʊteɪʃᵊn, leɪb-/ N-UNCOUNT **Labanotation** is a system for recording dance movements that uses symbols to represent points on the dancer's body. *labanotación* [TECHNICAL]

**lab apron** (**lab aprons**) N-COUNT A **lab apron** is a piece of clothing that you wear when you are working in a laboratory, in order to prevent your clothes from getting dirty. *bata de laboratorio*

**la|bel** /leɪbᵊl/ (**labels, labeling** or **labelling, labeled** or **labelled**) **1** N-COUNT A **label** is a piece of paper or plastic that is attached to an object in order to give information about it. *etiqueta, rótulo* ❑ *He looked at the label on the bottle. Se fijó en la etiqueta de la botella.* **2** V-T If something **is labeled**, a label is attached to it giving information about it. *etiquetar, rotular, poner una etiqueta* ❑ *All foods must be clearly labeled. Todos los alimentos deben estar claramante etiquetados.* ❑ *The radio was labeled "Made in China." La etiqueta del radio decía "Made in China".* **3** V-T If you say that someone or something **is labeled as** a particular thing, you mean that people generally describe them that way and you think that this is unfair. *etiquetar, catalogar, calificar* ❑ *He was labeled as a difficult child. Le pusieron la etiqueta de niño difícil.*
→ see **graph**

| **Thesaurus** | *label* | Ver también: |
|---|---|---|
| N. | sticker, tag, ticket **1** | |
| V. | brand, characterize, classify **3** | |

**la|bor** /leɪbər/ (**labors, laboring, labored**) **1** N-VAR **Labor** is very hard work, usually physical work. *gran esfuerzo, trabajo duro, faena* ❑ *...the labor of moving heavy rocks. ...la faena de mover rocas pesadas.* **2** V-I Someone who **labors** works hard using their hands. *trabajar con las manos, trabajar incansablemente* ❑ *The miners labored 1400 yards below ground. Los mineros trabajaban 1300 metros bajo tierra.* **3** V-T/V-I If you **labor to** do something, you do it with difficulty. *esforzarse, luchar por algo* ❑ *The police labored for months to try to solve the case. La policía trabajó durante meses tratando de resolver el caso.* ❑ *He could feel his heart laboring in his chest. Podía sentir el esfuerzo del corazón en su pecho.* **4** N-UNCOUNT **Labor** is used to refer to the workers of a country or industry. *trabajadores, mano de obra, fuerza laboral* ❑ *Employers want cheap labor. Los patrones quieren mano de obra barata.* **5** N-UNCOUNT **Labor** is the last stage of pregnancy, in which the mother gradually pushes the baby out. *parto* ❑ *Her labor was long and difficult. Su parto fue largo y difícil.*
→ see **factory**

| **Word Link** | *labor ≈ working : collaborate, elaborate, laboratory* |
|---|---|

**la|bora|tory** /læbrətɔri/ (**laboratories**) N-COUNT A **laboratory** is a building or a room where scientific experiments and research are carried out. *laboratorio* ❑ *...a research laboratory at Columbia University. ...un laboratorio de investigación en Columbia University.*
→ see Picture Dictionary: **laboratory equipment**
→ see Word Web: **laboratory**

| **Word Partnership** | Usar *laboratory* con: |
|---|---|
| N. | laboratory **conditions**, laboratory **equipment**, laboratory **experiment**, **research** laboratory, laboratory **technician**, laboratory **test** |

**la|bor camp** (**labor camps**) N-COUNT A **labor camp** is a kind of prison, where the prisoners are forced to do hard, physical work, usually outdoors. *campo de trabajos forzados*

**la|bored** /leɪbərd/ **1** ADJ If your breathing is

**Picture Dictionary** laboratory equipment

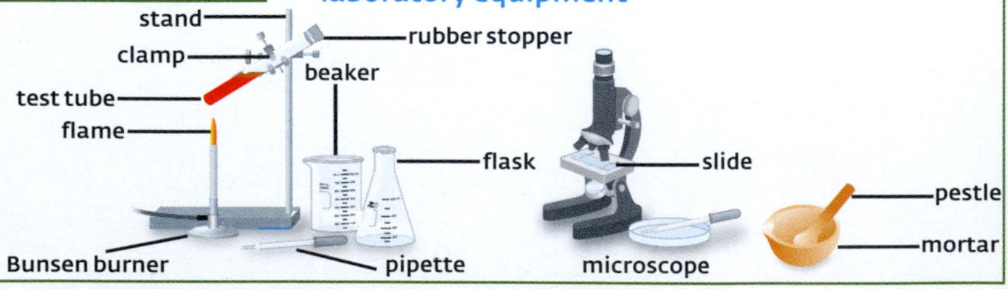


L

**Word Web** **laboratory**

The discovery of the life-saving drug penicillin was a lucky accident. While cleaning his **laboratory**, a **researcher** named Alexander Fleming* noticed that the bacteria in one **Petri dish** had been killed by some kind of **mold**. He took a **sample** and found that it was a form of penicillin. Fleming and others did further **research** and **published** their **findings** in 1928, but few people took notice. However, ten years later a team at Oxford University in England read Fleming's **study** and began animal and human **experiments**. Within ten years, drug companies were manufacturing 650 billion units of penicillin a month!

*Alexander Fleming (1881-1955): a Scottish biologist and pharmacologist.*

**labored,** it is slow and seems to take a lot of effort. *trabajoso, difícil, fatigoso* ❑ *She could hear Max's harsh, labored breathing. Podía oír la respiración de Max, difícil y laboriosa.* **2** ADJ If something such as someone's writing or speech is **labored,** they have put too much effort into it so it seems awkward and unnatural. *forzado, torpe*

**la|bor|er** /leɪbərər/ (**laborers**) N-COUNT A **laborer** is a person who does a job which involves a lot of hard physical work. *obrero u obrera, trabajador o trabajadora, trabajador agrícola o trabajadora agrícola, peón* ❑ *...a farm laborer. ...un trabajador agrícola.*
→ see **union**

**la|bor force** (**labor forces**) N-COUNT **The labor force** consists of all the people who are able to work in a country or area, or all the people who work for a particular company. *fuerza laboral, mano de obra, trabajadores* [BUSINESS] ❑ *At least 20% of the labor force is unemployed. Cuando menos el 20% de los trabajadores están desempleados.*

**labor-intensive** ADJ **Labor-intensive** industries or methods of making things involve a lot of workers. Compare **capital-intensive.** *intensivo en mano de obra* [BUSINESS] ❑ *Making clothing is very labor-intensive. La fabricación de ropa es muy intensiva en mano de obra.*

**la|bor mar|ket** (**labor markets**) N-COUNT When you talk about **the labor market,** you are referring to all the people who are able to work and want jobs in a country or area, in relation to the number of jobs there are available. *mercado laboral* [BUSINESS] ❑ *Women's wages are still less than men's in today's labor market. En el mercado laboral de hoy, los salarios de las mujeres siguen siendo inferiores a los de los hombres.*

**la|bor re|la|tions** N-PLURAL **Labor relations** refers to the relationship between employers and employees in industry, and the political decisions and laws that affect it. *relación laboral* ❑ *We have to balance good labor relations against the need to cut costs. Tenemos que equilibrar una buena relación laboral con la necesidad de reducir los costos.*

**labor-saving** ADJ A **labor-saving** device or idea makes it possible for you to do something with less effort than usual. *que ahorra esfuerzo, economizador de trabajo* ❑ *...labor-saving devices such as washing machines. ...máquinas que ahorran trabajo, como las lavadoras.*

**la|bor un|ion** (**labor unions**) N-COUNT A **labor union** is an organization that represents the rights and interests of workers to their employers. *sindicato, gremio*

**lace** /leɪs/ (**laces, lacing, laced**) **1** N-UNCOUNT **Lace** is a very delicate cloth which is made by twisting together very fine threads leaving holes in between. *encaje* ❑ *...a wedding gown made of lace. ...un vestido de encaje para novia.* **2** N-COUNT **Laces** are thin pieces of material that are used to fasten some types of clothing, especially shoes. *agujeta, cordón* ❑ *Barry put on his shoes and tied the laces. Barry se puso los zapatos y se amarró las agujetas.* **3** V-T If you **lace** something such as a pair of shoes, you tighten the shoes by pulling the laces through the holes, and tying them together. *amarrar(se)* ❑ *I laced my ice-skates tightly. Me amarré bien apretadas las agujetas de los patines de hielo.* ● **Lace up** means the same as **lace.** *amarrar(se)* ❑ *He sat on the steps, and laced up his boots. Se sentó en el escalón a amarrarse las botas.* **4** V-T To **lace** food or drink with something harmful means to put a small amount of the substance into the food or drink. *rociar* ❑ *She laced his food with poison. Le echó veneno a la comida de él.*

lace

**lack** /læk/ (**lacks, lacking, lacked**)
**1** N-UNCOUNT; N-SING If there is a **lack of** something, there is not enough of it or it does not exist at all. *falta de, carencia de* ❑ *Despite his lack of experience, he got the job. A pesar de su inexperiencia, le dieron el trabajo.* ❑ *The police dropped the charges for lack of evidence. La policía retiró los cargos por falta de pruebas.* **2** V-T/V-I If you say that someone or something **lacks** a particular quality or that a particular quality **is lacking** in them, you mean that they do not have any or enough of it. *faltar, carecer* ❑ *The meal lacked flavor. A la comida le faltaba sabor.* ❑ *It lacked the power of Italian cars. Carecía de la potencia de los automóviles italianos.* ● **lack|ing** /lækɪŋ/ ADJ *falta, carencia, deficiencia* ❑ *She felt nervous and lacking in confidence. Ella se sentía nerviosa y falta de confianza.* **3** PHRASE If you say there is **no lack of** something, you are emphasizing that there is a great deal of it. *no faltar* ❑ *There was no lack of things for them to talk about. No les faltaban temas de qué hablar.*

**Word Partnership** Usar *lack* con:

N. lack *of* **confidence**, lack *of* **control**, lack *of* **enthusiasm**, lack *of* **evidence**, lack *of* **exercise**, lack *of* **experience**, lack *of* **food**, lack *of* **information**, lack *of* **knowledge**, lack *of* **money**, lack *of* **progress**, lack *of* **resources**, lack *of* **skills**, lack *of* **sleep**, lack *of* **support**, lack *of* **trust**, lack *of* **understanding** 1

**lad|der** /lædər/ (**ladders**) N-COUNT A **ladder** is a piece of equipment used for climbing up something or down from something. It consists of two long pieces of wood, metal, or rope with steps fixed between them. *escalera, escalera de mano* ❑ *He climbed the ladder so he could see over the wall. Se subió a la escalera para poder ver por arriba del muro.*
→ see **utensil**

**la|dle** /leɪdᵊl/ (**ladles, ladling, ladled**) 1 N-COUNT A **ladle** is a large, round, deep spoon with a long handle, used for serving soup, stew, or sauce. *cucharón* 2 V-T If you **ladle** food such as soup or stew, you serve it, especially with a ladle. *servir (con cucharón)* ❑ *Barry held the bowls while Liz ladled soup into them. Barry sostenía los platos, mientras Liz servía la sopa.* ❑ *Mrs. King went to the big black stove and ladled out steaming soup. La señora King se dirigió a la enorme estufa negra y (se) sirvió un poco de sopa humeante.*

L

**lady** /leɪdi/ (**ladies**) 1 N-COUNT You can use **lady** when you are referring to a woman, especially when you are showing politeness or respect. *dama, señora* ❑ *She's a very sweet old lady. Es una señora muy amable* ❑ *Here's the lady's purse. Aquí está la bolsa de la dama.* 2 N-VOC **"Lady"** is sometimes used by men as a form of address when they are talking to a woman that they do not know, especially in stores and on the street. *señora* [INFORMAL] ❑ *What seems to be the trouble, lady? ¿Hay algún problema, señora?*

**lady|bug** /leɪdibʌg/ (**ladybugs**) A **ladybug** is a small round beetle that is red with black spots. *mariquita, catarina*
→ see **insect**

**lag** /læg/ (**lags, lagging, lagged**) 1 V-I If you **lag behind** someone or something, you make slower progress than them. *quedarse atrás, rezagarse, atrasarse* ❑ *She's still lagging behind the other students in her class. Se sigue quedando atrás de los otros estudiantes de su clase* 2 N-COUNT A time **lag** or a **lag** of a particular length of time is a period of time between one event and another related event. *intervalo, demora, lapso, retraso* ❑ *There's a time lag between becoming infected and getting sick. Hay un intervalo entre infectarse y enfermarse.*

**laid** /leɪd/ **Laid** is the past tense and past participle of **lay**. *pasado y participio pasado de* ***lay***

**lain** /leɪn/ **Lain** is the past participle of **lie**. *participio pasado de lie*

**lake** /leɪk/ (**lakes**) N-COUNT A **lake** is a large area of fresh water, surrounded by land. *lago* ❑ *They went fishing in the lake. Fueron a pescar al lago.*
→ see Word Web: **lake**
→ see **landform, river**

**lake|front** /leɪkfrʌnt/ also **lake front** or **lake-front** N-SING The **lakefront** is the area of land around the edge of a lake. *orilla del lago, ribera del lago* ❑ *...a cabin down on the lakefront. ...una cabaña a orillas del lago.*

**lamb** /læm/ (**lambs**) N-COUNT A **lamb** is a young sheep. *cordero, borrego* • **Lamb** is the flesh of a lamb eaten as food. *cordero* ❑ *For supper she served lamb and vegetables. En la cena sirvió cordero con verduras.*

**lame** /leɪm/ (**lamer, lamest**) 1 ADJ If someone is **lame,** they are unable to walk properly because of damage to one or both of their legs. *cojo, rengo, renco, inválido* ❑ *She was lame in one leg. Ella cojeaba de una pierna.* • **The lame** are people who are lame. *cojo, inválido* ❑ *...the wounded and the lame of the last war. ...los heridos y los inválidos de la última guerra.* 2 ADJ If you describe an excuse, argument, or remark as **lame,** you mean that it is poor or weak. *pobre, malo, débil* ❑ *He gave me some lame excuse about being too busy to call me. Me dio una excusa poco convincente de que estaba demasiado ocupado como para llamarme.* • **lame|ly** ADV *débilmente, sin convicción* ❑ *"I've forgotten my phone number," I said lamely. —Se me olvidó mi número de teléfono —dije sin convicción.*

**lamp** /læmp/ (**lamps**) N-COUNT A **lamp** is a light that works by using electricity or by burning oil or gas. *lámpara* ❑ *She switched on the bedside lamp. Encendió la lámpara de buró.*

**land** /lænd/ (**lands, landing, landed**)
1 N-UNCOUNT **Land** is an area of ground, especially one that is used for a particular purpose such as farming or building. *tierra, terreno, campo* ❑ *There is not enough good agricultural land. No hay suficientes tierras cultivables de buena calidad.* ❑ *...160 acres of land. ...64 hectáreas de terreno.* ❑ *It isn't clear whether the plane crashed on land or in the ocean. No está claro si el avión se estrelló en tierra o en el mar.* 2 N-COUNT You can use **land** to refer to a country in a poetic or emotional way. *tierra, país* [LITERARY] ❑ *...America, land of opportunity. ...Estados Unidos,*

**Word Web** lake

Several forces create **lakes**. The movement of a glacier can carve out a deep **basin** in the soil. The Great Lakes between the U.S. and Canada are **glacial** lakes. Very deep lakes appear when large pieces of the earth's crust suddenly shift. Lake Baikal in Russia is over a mile deep. When a volcano erupts, it creates a **crater**. Crater Lake in Oregon is the perfectly round remains of a volcanic cone. It contains **water** from melted snow and rain. Erosion also creates lakes. When the wind blows away sand, the hole left behind forms a natural lake **bed**.

*tierra de oportunidades.* **3** V-I When someone or something **lands,** they come down to the ground after moving through the air or falling. *aterrizar, caer, ir a parar* ❑ *He was sent flying into the air and landed 20 feet away. Lo lanzaron hacia arriba y cayó a 6 metros de distancia.* **4** V-T/V-I When someone **lands** a plane, ship, or spacecraft, or when it **lands,** it arrives somewhere after a journey. *aterrizar, atracar* ❑ *The plane landed after a flight of three hours. El avión aterrizó después de un vuelo de tres horas.* ❑ *He landed his boat on the western shore. Atracó su bote en la orilla oeste.* ● **land|ing** N-VAR (**landings**) *aterrizaje* ❑ *The pilot made a controlled landing into the sea. El piloto hizo un aterrizaje controlado en el mar.* **5** V-T/V-I If you **land in** an unpleasant situation or place or if something **lands** you **in** it, something causes you to be in it. *ir a parar, ir a dar, meter en problemas, meter en líos* [INFORMAL] ❑ *His big ideas have landed him in trouble again. Sus grandiosas ideas lo han metido en problemas otra vez.*
→ see **biosphere, continent, earth**

**Thesaurus** *land* Ver también:

N. area, country, real estate **1**
V. arrive, touch down; (*ant.*) take off **3** **4**

**Word Partnership** Usar *land* con:

N. **acres of** land, **area of** land, **desert** land, land **development**, land **management**, land **ownership**, **parcel of** land, **piece of** land, **plot of** land, **strip of** land, **tract of** land, land **use** **1**
ADJ. **agricultural** land, **fertile** land, **flat** land, **grazing** land, **private** land, **public** land, **undeveloped** land, **vacant** land, **vast** land **1**
V. **buy** land, **own** land, **sell** land **1**

**land|fill** /lændfɪl/ (**landfills**) **1** N-UNCOUNT **Landfill** is a method of getting rid of very large amounts of garbage by burying it in a large deep hole. *vertedero, relleno sanitario* ❑ *...the high cost of landfill. ...el alto costo de los rellenos sanitarios.* **2** N-COUNT A **landfill** is a large deep hole in which very large amounts of garbage are buried. *vertedero* ❑ *The trash in modern landfills does not decompose easily. La basura no se descompone tan fácilmente en los vertederos modernos.*
→ see **dump**

**land|form** /lændfɔrm/ (**landforms**) also **land form** N-COUNT A **landform** is any natural feature of the Earth's surface, such as a hill, a lake, or a beach. *accidente geográfico* ❑ *This small country has a huge variety of landforms. Este pequeño país tiene una enorme variedad de accidentes geográficos.*
→ see Picture Dictionary: **landforms**

**land|ing** /lændɪŋ/ (**landings**) N-COUNT In a house or other building, the **landing** is the area at the top of the staircase which has rooms leading off it. *rellano, descanso, descansillo, pasillo*

**land|lord** /lændlɔrd/ (**landlords**) N-COUNT Someone's **landlord** is the man who allows them to live or work in a building which he owns, in return for rent. *casero, dueño, arrendador, propietario* ❑ *His landlord doubled the rent. Su casero duplicó la renta.*

**Word Link** *mark ≈ boundary, sign : bookmark, earmark, landmark*

**land|mark** /lændmɑrk/ (**landmarks**) **1** N-COUNT A **landmark** is a building or feature which is easily noticed and can be used to judge your position or the position of other buildings or features. *hito, edificio representativo, característica* ❑ *The Empire State Building is a New York landmark. El Empire State es un edificio representativo de Nueva York.* **2** N-COUNT You can refer to an important stage in the development of something as a **landmark.** *hito, acontecimiento importante* ❑ *The baby was a*

**Picture Dictionary** **landforms**

l

*landmark in our lives.* *El bebé fue un hito en nuestras vidas.*

**land mass** (**land masses**) also **landmass** N-COUNT A **land mass** is a very large area of land such as a continent. *masa continental* ❑ *...the Antarctic landmass.* *...la masa continental antártica.* ❑ *...the country's large land mass of 768 million hectares.* *...la gran masa continental del país, de 768 millones de hectáreas.*
→ see **continent**

**land|scape** /lændskeɪp/ (**landscapes, landscaping, landscaped**) **1** N-VAR The **landscape** is everything you can see when you look across an area of land, including hills, rivers, buildings, trees, and plants. *paisaje, vista, panorama* ❑ *...Arizona's desert landscape.* *...el paisaje desértico de Arizona.* **2** N-COUNT A **landscape** is a painting which shows a scene in the countryside. *paisaje* **3** V-T If an area of land **is landscaped,** it is changed to make it more attractive. *ajardinar, construir un jardín, arreglar un jardín, enjardinar* ❑ *The back garden was landscaped.* *Arreglaron el jardín de atrás.* ❑ *They landscaped their property with trees, shrubs, and lawns.* *Ajardinaron su propiedad con árboles, arbustos y prados.* ● **land|scap|ing** N-UNCOUNT *paisajismo, jardín* ❑ *The house and the landscaping are lovely.* *La casa y el jardín están hermosos.*
→ see **art, painting**

L

**land|slide** /lændslaɪd/ (**landslides**) **1** N-COUNT A **landslide** is a victory in an election in which a person or political party gets far more votes or seats than their opponents. *victoria arrolladora* ❑ *He won the election by a landslide.* *Ganó las elecciones con una victoria arrolladora.* **2** N-COUNT A **landslide** is a large amount of earth and rocks falling down a cliff or the side of a mountain. *derrumbamiento, derrumbe, deslizamiento de tierra* ❑ *The storm caused landslides and flooding.* *La tormenta provocó deslizamientos de tierra e inundaciones.*
→ see **disaster**

**lane** /leɪn/ (**lanes**) **1** N-COUNT A **lane** is a narrow road, especially in the country. *camino, sendero* ❑ *...a quiet country lane.* *...un tranquilo sendero campirano.* ❑ *They had a house on Spring Park Lane in East Hampton.* *Tenían una casa en el camino a Spring Park, en East Hampton.* **2** N-COUNT A **lane** is a part of a main road which is marked by the edge of the road and a painted line, or by two painted lines. *carril* ❑ *The truck was traveling at 20 mph in the slow lane.* *El camión circulaba a 30 kph por el carril de baja velocidad.* **3** N-COUNT At a swimming pool, athletics track, or bowling alley, a **lane** is a long narrow section which is separated from other sections, for example by lines or ropes. *carril* ❑ *Who is the runner in the inside lane?* *¿Quién corre en el carril interior?* **4** N-COUNT A **lane** is a route that is frequently used by aircraft or ships. *ruta de navegación* ❑ *...one of the busiest shipping lanes in the world.* *...una de las rutas de navegación más transitadas del mundo.*
→ see **traffic**

**lan|guage** /læŋgwɪdʒ/ (**languages**) **1** N-COUNT A **language** is a system of communication which consists of a set of sounds and written symbols which are used by the people of a particular country or region for talking or writing. *lengua, idioma, lenguaje* ❑ *...the English language.* *...la lengua inglesa.* ❑ *Students must learn to speak a second language.* *Los estudiantes deben aprender a hablar una segunda lengua.* **2** N-UNCOUNT **Language** is the use of a system of communication which consists of a set of sounds or written symbols. *lenguaje, lengua* ❑ *Students studied how children develop language.* *Los alumnos estudiaron el desarrollo del lenguaje en los niños.* **3** N-UNCOUNT You can refer to the words used in connection with a particular subject as **the language of** that subject. *vocabulario, lengua* ❑ *...the language of business.* *...el vocabulario de los negocios.* **4** N-UNCOUNT The **language** of a piece of writing or speech is the style in which it is written or spoken. *palabra, lenguaje, expresión* ❑ *Why can't they explain things in plain language?* *¿Por qué no pueden explicar las cosas con palabras sencillas?* ❑ *The tone of his language was polite.* *Se expresó con un lenguaje cortés.*
→ see **culture, English**

**Thesaurus** *language* Ver también:

N. communication, dialect **1** **2** **4**
jargon, slang, terminology **4**

**Word Partnership** Usar *language* con:

V. **know a** language, **learn a** language, **speak a** language, **study a** language, **teach a** language, **understand a** language, **use a** language **1**

ADJ. **a different** language, **foreign** language, **native** language, **official** language, **second** language, **universal** language **1**
**bad** language, **foul** language, **plain** language, **simple** language, **technical** language, **vulgar** language **4**

N. language **acquisition**, language **barrier**, language **of children**, language **classes**, language **comprehension**, language **development**, **proficiency in a** language, language **skills** **1** **2**

lantern

**lan|tern** /læntərn/ (**lanterns**) N-COUNT A **lantern** is a lamp in a metal frame with glass sides. *linterna, farol*

**lap** /læp/ (**laps, lapping, lapped**) **1** N-COUNT Your **lap** is the flat area formed by your thighs when you are sitting down. *regazo* ❑ *She waited quietly with her hands in her lap.* *Esperó tranquilamente, con las manos en el regazo.* **2** N-COUNT In a race, a competitor completes a **lap** when they have gone around a course once. *vuelta* ❑ *...the last lap of the race.* *...la última vuelta de la carrera.* **3** V-T In a race, if you **lap** another competitor, you go past them while they are still on the previous lap. *sacar ventaja* ❑ *Schumacher lapped every other driver in the race.* *Schumacher les sacó a los demás corredores.* **4** V-T/V-I When water **laps** against something such as the shore or the side of a boat, it touches it gently and makes a soft sound. *chapalear, bañar* [WRITTEN] ❑ *Water lapped against the shore.* *El agua bañaba la playa.* ❑ *...white beaches lapped by warm blue seas.* *...playas blancas acariciadas por cálidos mares azules.* ● **lap|ping** N-UNCOUNT *chapaleo* ❑ *The only sound was the lapping of the waves.* *El único sonido era el chapaleo de las olas.* **5** V-T

**Word Web** laser

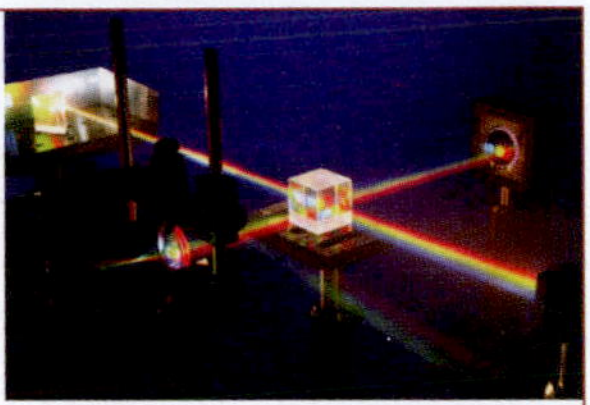

Lasers are an amazing form of technology. Laser **beams** read **CDs** and **DVDs**. They can create three-dimensional holograms. Laser **light shows** add excitement at concerts. **Fiber optic cables** carry intense flashes of laser light. This allows a single cable to transmit thousands of e-mail and phone messages at the same time. Laser **scanners** read prices from bar codes. Lasers are also used as scalpels in **surgery**, and to remove hair, birthmarks, and tattoos. Dentists use lasers to remove cavities. Laser eye surgery has become very popular. In manufacturing, lasers make precise cuts in everything from fabric to steel.

When an animal **laps** a drink, it uses short quick movements of its tongue to take liquid up into its mouth. *lamer, dar lengüetazos* ❑ *The cat lapped milk from a dish. El gato bebía a lengüetazos la leche del plato.* • **Lap up** means the same as **lap**. *lamer, dar lengüetazos* ❑ *She poured some water into a bowl and the dog lapped it up eagerly. Ella sirvió un poco de agua en un tazón y el perro dio ávidos lengüetazos.*

▸ **lap up** PHR-VERB If someone **laps up** something such as information or attention, they accept it eagerly. *deleitarse* ❑ *Children lap up adult attention. Los niños se encantan con la atención de los adultos.*

**lap|top** /læptɒp/ (**laptops**) N-COUNT A **laptop** or a **laptop computer** is a small portable computer. *lap, laptop, computadora portátil* ❑ *She was working at her laptop. Ella estaba trabajando en su laptop.*
→ see **computer**

**large** /lɑrdʒ/ (**larger, largest**) **1** ADJ A **large** thing or person is greater in size than usual or average. *grande, amplio, vasto* ❑ *This fish lives mainly in large rivers and lakes. Este pez vive principalmente en ríos y lagos grandes.* ❑ *In the largest room a few people were sitting on the carpet. Algunas pesonas estaban sentadas en la alfombra del salón más grande.* **2** ADJ A **large** amount or number of people or things is more than the average amount or number. *grande, importante, abundante* ❑ *The gang got away with a large amount of cash. La pandilla huyó con una buena cantidad de efectivo.* ❑ *There are a large number of places where you can take full-time courses. Hay numerosos lugares en los que puedes tomar cursos de tiempo completo.* **3** ADJ **Large** is used to indicate that a problem or issue is very important or serious. *grande, importante, grave* ❑ *One large problem remains. Queda un problema grave.* **4** PHRASE You use **at large** to indicate that you are talking in a general way about most of the people mentioned. *en general* ❑ *He wanted to get the public at large interested in modern art. Quería que el público en general se interesara por el arte moderno.*

**Thesaurus** *large* Ver también:
ADJ. big, sizable, spacious, substantial; (*ant.*) small **1**

**large|ly** /lɑrdʒli/ **1** ADV You use **largely** to say that a statement is not completely true but is mostly true. *en buena parte, en gran medida, mayormente* ❑ *The project is largely funded by donations. En buena parte, el proyecto es financiado por donaciones.* ❑ *The government is largely to blame for this. El gobierno es mayormente culpable de esto.* **2** ADV **Largely** is used to introduce the main reason for a particular event or situation. *sobre todo, principalmente, en gran medida* ❑ *She failed her exams, largely because she did no work. No le fue bien en los exámenes, sobre todo porque no trabajó.*

**large-scale** also **large scale** **1** ADJ A **large-scale** action or event happens over a very wide area or involves a lot of people or things. *en grande, en gran escala* ❑ *...a large-scale military operation. ...una operación militar en grande.* **2** ADJ A **large-scale** map or diagram represents a small area of land or a building or machine in a way that allows small details to be shown. *a gran escala*

**lar|va** /lɑrvə/ (**larvae** /lɑrvi/) N-COUNT A **larva** is an insect at the stage of its life after it has developed from an egg and before it changes into its adult form. *larva* ❑ *The eggs quickly hatch into larvae. Los huevecillos se transforman rápidamente en larvas.*
→ see **amphibian**

**lar|ynx** /lærɪŋks/ (**larynxes**) N-COUNT Your **larynx** is the top part of the passage that leads from your throat to your lungs and contains your vocal cords. *laringe* [MEDICAL]

**la|ser** /leɪzər/ (**lasers**) N-COUNT A **laser** is a narrow beam of concentrated light produced by a special machine. *láser, rayo láser* ❑ *...new laser technology. ...nueva tecnología láser.*
→ see Word Web: **laser**

**lash** /læʃ/ (**lashes, lashing, lashed**) **1** N-COUNT Your **lashes** are the hairs that grow on the edge of your eyelids. *pestaña* ❑ *His eyes had very long lashes. Sus pestañas eran larguísimas.* **2** V-T If you **lash** two or more things together, you tie one of them firmly to the other. *amarrar, atar* ❑ *He held the boxes tightly while Rita used rope to lash them together. Sostenía firmemente las cajas mientras Rita las amarraba con una cuerda.* ❑ *We built the shelter by lashing poles together. Construimos el refugio amarrando postes.* **3** V-T/V-I If wind, rain, or water **lashes** someone or something, it hits them violently. *azotar* [WRITTEN] ❑ *Storms lashed the east coast of North America. Las tormentas azotaron la costa este de Norteamérica.* ❑ *Rain lashed against the windows. La lluvia azotaba contra las ventanas.* **4** N-COUNT A **lash** is a blow with a whip, especially a blow on someone's back as a punishment. *latigazo, azote* ❑ *The villagers sentenced one man to five lashes for stealing. Los habitantes del pueblo sentenciaron a un hombre a recibir cinco latigazos por haber robado.*

▸ **lash out** **1** PHR-VERB If you **lash out**, you attempt to hit someone quickly and violently with a weapon or with your hands or feet. *atacar, arremeter contra* ❑ *They held his arms to stop him from*

I

*lashing out.* *Lo retuvieron por los brazos para impedir que siguiera atacando.* **2** PHR-VERB If you **lash out at** someone or something, you speak to them or about them very angrily or critically. *atacar verbalmente* ❑ *His laughter made her angry and she lashed out at him.* *Ella lo increpó porque su risa la había enfurecido.*

**Lasik** /leɪsɪk/ also **LASIK** N-UNCOUNT **Lasik** is a form of eye surgery that uses lasers to improve or correct people's eyesight. **Lasik** is an abbreviation for "laser-assisted in situ keratomileusis." *Lasik* ❑ *...Lasik surgery.* *...cirugía Lasik.*

**last** /læst/ (**lasts, lasting, lasted**) **1** DET You use **last** in expressions such as **last Friday, last night,** and **last year** to refer, for example, to the most recent Friday, night, or year. *pasado, último* ❑ *I got married last July.* *Me casé en julio pasado.* ❑ *He didn't come home last night.* *Anoche no llegó a casa.* **2** ADJ The **last** event, person, thing, or period of time is the most recent one. *último* ❑ *Much has changed since my last visit.* *Ha habido muchos cambios desde mi última visita.* ❑ *I split up with my last boyfriend three years ago.* *Hace tres años que terminé con mi último novio.* ● **Last** is also a pronoun. *último, anterior* ❑ *Each song was better than the last.* *Cada canción era mejor que la anterior.* **3** ADV If something **last** happened on a particular occasion, that is the most recent occasion on which it happened. *último* ❑ *When were you there last?* *¿Cuándo fue la última vez que fuiste?* ❑ *He is a lot taller than when I last saw him.* *Está mucho más alto que la última vez que lo vi.* **4** ORD The **last** thing, person, event, or period of time is the one that happens or comes after all the others of the same kind. *último* ❑ *...the last three pages of the chapter.* *...las tres últimas páginas del capítulo.* ● **Last** is also a pronoun. *último* ❑ *It wasn't the first time he had cried and it wouldn't be the last.* *No fue la primera vez que lloró, y tampoco sería la última.* **5** ADV If you do something **last,** you do it after everyone else does, or after you do everything else. *último* ❑ *I arrived home last.* *Fui la última en llegar a la casa.* ❑ *I was always picked last for the football team at school.* *En la escuela siempre era el último al que escogían para el equipo de futbol.* **6** PRON If you are **the last to** do or know something, everyone else does or knows it before you. *último* ❑ *She was the last to go to bed.* *Fue la última en acostarse.* **7** ADJ **Last** is used to refer to the only thing, person, or part of something that remains. *último* ❑ *Can I have the last piece of pizza?* *¿Puedo comerme la última rebanada de pizza?* ● **Last** is also a noun. *lo último, lo que queda* ❑ *He finished off the last of the coffee.* *Se acabó lo que quedaba de café.* **8** ADJ You can use **last** to indicate that something is extremely undesirable or unlikely. *lo último* ❑ *The last thing I wanted to do was teach.* *Lo último que quería hacer era dar clases.* ● **Last** is also a pronoun. *último* ❑ *I'm the last to say that science explains everything.* *Sería el último en decir que la ciencia lo explica todo.* **9** V-T/V-I If an event, situation, or problem **lasts** for a particular length of time, it continues to exist or happen for that length of time. *durar* ❑ *The marriage lasted for less than two years.* *El matrimonio duró menos de dos años.* ❑ *The games lasted only half the normal time.* *Los juegos duraron sólo la mitad de lo normal.* **10** V-T/V-I If something **lasts** for a particular length of time, it continues to be able to be used for that time, for example, because there is some of it left or because it is in good enough condition. *durar* ❑ *You only need a small amount of glue, so one tube lasts for a long time.* *Se utiliza muy poquito pegamento, así que un tubo dura mucho.* ❑ *This battery lasts twice as long as the smaller size.* *Esta batería dura el doble que la más pequeña.* **11** → see also **lasting** **12** PHRASE If you say that something has happened **at last** or **at long last,** you mean it has happened after you have been hoping for it for a long time. *por fin, al fin, finalmente* ❑ *I'm so glad that we've found you at last!* *¡Estoy muy contento de que por fin te hayamos encontrado!* ❑ *Here, at long last, was the moment he was waiting for.* *Por fin llegó el momento que había estado esperando.* **13** PHRASE You use expressions such as **the night before last, the election before last** and **the leader before last** to refer to the period of time, event, or person that came immediately before the most recent one in a series. *anterior* ❑ *I went out with Helen the night before last.* *Antenoche salí con Helen.* **14** PHRASE You can use expressions such as **the last I heard** and **the last she heard** to introduce a piece of information that is the most recent that you have on a particular subject. *lo último* ❑ *The last I heard, Joe and Irene were still happily married.* *Lo último que supe es que Joe e Irene seguían felizmente casados.* **15** **the last straw** → see **straw** **16** **last thing** → see **thing**

**Usage** **last** and **latter**

Both *last* and *latter* refer to the final person or thing mentioned. Use *last* when more than two persons or things have been mentioned: *Whales, dolphins, and sharks all have fins and live in the ocean, but only the last is a fish.* Use *latter* when exactly two persons or things have been mentioned: *Jorge and Ana applied for the same scholarship, which was awarded to the latter.*

**last|ing** /læstɪŋ/ **1** ADJ You can use **lasting** to describe a situation, result, or agreement that continues to exist or have an effect for a very long time. *duradero, perdurable, durable* ❑ *Everyone wants a lasting peace.* *Todos quieren que la paz perdure.* **2** → see also **last**

**last-minute** → see **minute**

**late** /leɪt/ (**later, latest**) **1** ADV **Late** means near the end of a day, week, year, or other period of time. *tarde, tardío* ❑ *It was late in the afternoon.* *Ya era casi el final de la tarde.* ❑ *He married late in life.* *Se casó ya mayor.* ● **Late** is also an adjective. *a finales, al final* ❑ *We went on vacation in late spring.* *Salimos de vacaciones a finales de la primavera.* ❑ *He was in his late 20s.* *Tenía cerca de treinta años.* **2** ADJ If it is **late,** it is near the end of the day or it is past the time that you feel something should have been done. *tarde* ❑ *It was very late and the streets were empty.* *Ya era muy tarde y las calles estaban vacías.* ● **late|ness** N-UNCOUNT *lo tarde* ❑ *A crowd gathered despite the lateness of the hour.* *Se juntó una multidad a pesar de lo tarde.* **3** ADV **Late** means after the time that was arranged or expected. *tarde* ❑ *Steve arrived late.* *Steve llegó tarde.* ❑ *The talks began fifteen minutes late.* *Las pláticas empezaron quince minutos tarde.* ● **Late** is also an adjective. *atraso, demora, retraso* ❑ *His campaign got off to a late start.* *Su campaña tuvo un arranque tardío.* ❑ *The train was 40 minutes late.* *El tren tenía 40 minutos de retraso.* ● **late|ness** N-UNCOUNT *tardanza, atraso, demora* ❑ *He apologized for his*

lateness. *Se disculpó por su tardanza.* 4 ADV **Late** means after the usual time that a particular event or activity happens. *tarde* ❑ *We went to bed very late. Nos acostamos muy tarde.* • **Late** is also an adjective. *tarde* ❑ *They had a late lunch. Comieron tarde.* 5 ADJ You use **late** when you are talking about someone who is dead, especially someone who has died recently. *difunto, fallecido* ❑ *...my late husband. ...mi difunto marido.* 6 → see also **later, latest** 7 PHRASE If an action or event is **too late,** it is useless or ineffective because it occurs after the best time for it. *demasiado tarde* ❑ *It was too late to change her mind. Era demasiado tarde como para que cambiara de idea.*
8 **a late night** → see **night**

**late|ly** /leɪtli/ ADV You use **lately** to describe events in the recent past, or situations that started a short time ago. *últimamente, recientemente, a últimas fechas* ❑ *Dad's health hasn't been good lately. Papá no ha estado bien de salud últimamente.* ❑ *Have you talked to her lately? ¿Has hablado con ella recientemente?*
→ see also **recently**

**lat|er** /leɪtər/ 1 **Later** is the comparative of **late.** *comparativo de late* 2 ADV You use **later** to refer to a time or situation that is after the one that you have been talking about or after the present one. *más tarde, después* ❑ *He left his job ten years later. Dejó su trabajo diez años después.* 3 PHRASE You use **later on** to refer to a time or situation that is after the one that you have been talking about or after the present one. *más tarde, después* ❑ *Later on I'll be speaking to Patty Davis. Más tarde voy a hablar con Patty Davis.* 4 ADJ You use **later** to refer to an event, period of time, or other thing which comes after the one that you have been talking about or after the present one. *posterior, más adelante* ❑ *The competition was re-scheduled for a later date. Reprogramaron la competencia para una fecha posterior.* 5 ADJ You use **later** to refer to the last part of someone's life or career or the last part of a period of history. *último, más tarde* ❑ *He found happiness in later life. Encontró la felicidad en la última etapa de su vida.* ❑ *...the later part of the 20th century. ...la última parte del siglo veinte.* 6 → see also **late**

**lat|er|al line sys|tem** (**lateral line systems**) N-COUNT A **lateral line system** is a row of sense organs along each side of a fish's body that helps it to detect movement in the water. *línea lateral* [TECHNICAL]

**lat|est** /leɪtɪst/ 1 **Latest** is the superlative of **late.** *superlativo de late* 2 ADJ You use **latest** to describe something that is the most recent thing of its kind. *último, más reciente* ❑ *...her latest book. ...su obra más reciente.* 3 ADJ You can use **latest** to describe something that is very new and modern and is better than older things of a similar kind. *último* ❑ *Criminals are using the latest laser photocopiers to produce fake dollars. Los delincuentes están usando las últimas copiadoras láser para producir dólares falsos.* ❑ *I got to drive the latest model of the car. Me tocó manejar el último modelo del auto.* 4 → see also **late** 5 PHRASE You use **at the latest** in order to indicate that something must happen at or before a particular time and not after that time. *a más tardar, cuando mucho* ❑ *She'll be back by ten o'clock at the latest. Cuando muy tarde, regresa a las diez.*

**La|ti|na** /lætinə/ (**Latinas**) N-COUNT A **Latina** is a female citizen of the United States who originally came from Latin America, or whose family originally came from Latin America. *latina* ❑ *He married a Latina. Se casó con una latina.*

**Lat|in Ameri|can** /lætɪn əmɛrɪkən/ ADJ **Latin American** means belonging or relating to the countries of South America, Central America, and Mexico. **Latin American** also means belonging or relating to the people or culture of these countries. *latinoamericano* ❑ *...Latin American writers. ...escritores latinoamericanos.*

**La|ti|no** /lætinoʊ/ (**Latinos**) also **latino** N-COUNT A **Latino** is a citizen of the United States who originally came from Latin America, or whose family originally came from Latin America. *latino* ❑ *...Emilio Estevez and other famous Latinos. ...Emilio Estevez y otros latinos famosos.*

**lati|tude** /lætɪtud/ (**latitudes**) 1 N-VAR The **latitude** of a place is its distance from the equator. Compare **longitude.** *latitud* ❑ *In the middle to high latitudes rainfall has risen over the last 20–30 years. En los últimos 20 a 30 años, las lluvias se han incrementado en las latitudes medias y altas.* • **Latitude** is also an adjective. *latitud* ❑ *...places above 36° latitude north. ...lugares a más de 36 grados de latitud norte.* 2 N-UNCOUNT **Latitude** is freedom to choose the way in which you do something. *libertad, laxitud* [FORMAL] ❑ *He was given every latitude in forming a new government. Le dieron toda la libertad para formar un nuevo gobierno.*
→ see **navigation**

**lat|ter** /lætər/ 1 PRON When two people, things, or groups have just been mentioned, you can refer to the second of them as **the latter.** You can refer to the first of them as **the former.** *último, segundo* ❑ *He found his cousin and uncle. The latter was sick. Encontró a su primo y su tío; el segundo estaba enfermo.* • **Latter** is also an adjective. *último* ❑ *Some people like public speaking and some don't. Mike belongs in the latter group. A algunas personas les gusta hablar en público y a otras no. Mike forma parte del segundo grupo.* 2 ADJ You use **latter** to describe the later part of a period of time or event. *último* ❑ *...in the latter years of his career. ...en los últimos años de su carrera.* 3 → see also **last**

**laugh** /læf/ (**laughs, laughing, laughed**) 1 V-T/V-I When you **laugh,** you make a sound with your throat while smiling and show that you are happy or amused. People also sometimes laugh when they feel nervous or are being unfriendly. *reír(se)* ❑ *When I saw what he was wearing, I started to laugh. Cuando vi lo que llevaba puesto, me empecé a reír.* ❑ *I couldn't laugh at his jokes the way I used to. No podía reírme de sus chistes como antes.* ❑ *"We need some help," he laughed. —Necesitamos ayuda —dijo riendo.* • **Laugh** is also a noun. *risa* ❑ *Lysenko gave a deep laugh at his own joke. Lysenko soltó una sonora carcajada por su propio chiste.* 2 V-I If people **laugh at** someone or something, they mock them or make jokes about them. *reírse de alguien* ❑ *When I competed in the high jump as a kid, people laughed at me because I was so small. Cuando de niño yo competía en salto alto, la gente se reía de mí de tan pequeño que era.*

▸ **laugh off** PHR-VERB If you **laugh off** a difficult or serious situation, you try to suggest that it is amusing and unimportant. *tomar a broma, reírse de algo* ❑ *He laughed off reports that he is to be replaced as the team manager. Los reportes de que le iban a quitar el*

**Word Web** laugh

There is an old saying, "**Laughter** is the best medicine." New scientific research supports the idea that **humor** really is good for your health. For example, laughing 100 times provides the same exercise benefits as a 15-minute bike ride. When a person **bursts out laughing**, levels of stress hormones in the bloodstream immediately drop. And laughter is more than just a sound. **Howling with laughter** gives face, stomach, leg, and back muscles a good workout. From polite **giggles** to noisy guffaws, laughter allows the release of anger, sadness, and fear. And that has to be good for you.

*puesto de gerente del grupo le hacían gracia.*
→ see Word Web: **laugh**

**Thesaurus** *laugh* Ver también:

v. chuckle, crack up, giggle, howl; (*ant.*) cry 1

**Word Partnership** Usar *laugh* con:

v. **begin/start to** laugh, **hear** *someone* laugh, **make** *someone* laugh, **try to** laugh 1
ADJ. **big** laugh, **good** laugh, **hearty** laugh, **little** laugh 1

L

**laugh|ter** /læftər/ N-UNCOUNT **Laughter** is the sound of people laughing. *risotada, carcajada* ❑ *Their laughter filled the room. El salón se lleno de carcajadas.*
→ see **laugh**

**Word Partnership** Usar *laughter* con:

v. **burst into** laughter, **hear** laughter, **roar with** laughter
N. **burst of** laughter, **sound of** laughter
ADJ. **hysterical** laughter, **loud** laughter, **nervous** laughter

**launch** /lɔntʃ/ (**launches, launching, launched**) 1 V-T To **launch** a rocket, missile, or satellite means to send it into the air or into space. *lanzar* ❑ *NASA plans to launch a new satellite. La NASA piensa lanzar un nuevo satélite.* • **Launch** is also a noun. *lanzamiento* ❑ *...the launch of the space shuttle Columbia. ...el lanzamiento del transbordador espacial Columbia.* 2 V-T To **launch** a ship or a boat means to put it into water, often for the first time after it has been built. *botar* ❑ *The "Titanic" was launched in 1911. El "Titanic" fue botado en 1911.* • **Launch** is also a noun. *botadura* ❑ *The launch of a ship was a big occasion. La botadura de un barco era un gran acontecimiento.* 3 V-T To **launch** a large and important activity means to start it. *lanzar, iniciar, emprender* ❑ *The police have launched an investigation into the incident. La policía ha iniciado una investigación sobre el incidente.* • **Launch** is also a noun. *lanzamiento, principio* ❑ *...the launch of a campaign for healthy eating. ...el lanzamiento de una campaña sobre alimentación saludable.* 4 V-T If a company **launches** a new product, it makes it available to the public. *lanzar* ❑ *The company launched a low-cost computer. La compañía lanzó un computadora de bajo costo.* • **Launch** is also a noun. *lanzamiento* ❑ *...the launch of a new Sunday magazine. el lanzamiento de una nueva revista dominical.*
→ see **satellite**
▸ **launch into** PHR-VERB If you **launch into** something such as a speech, task, or fight, you enthusiastically start it. *embarcarse, lanzarse, emprender* ❑ *Horrigan launched into a speech about the importance of new projects. Horrigan se embarcó en un discurso sobre la importancia de nuevos proyectos.*

**launch|er** /lɔntʃər/ (**launchers**) N-COUNT A missile **launcher** or a grenade **launcher** is a device that is used for firing missiles or grenades. *lanzador*

**launch pad** (**launch pads**) N-COUNT A **launch pad** or **launching pad** is a platform from which rockets, missiles, or satellites are launched. *plataforma de lanzamiento*

**launch ve|hi|cle** (**launch vehicles**) N-COUNT A **launch vehicle** is a rocket that is used to launch a satellite or spacecraft. *lanzacohetes*

**laun|dro|mat** /lɔndrəmæt/ (**laundromats**) N-COUNT A **laundromat** is a place where people can pay to use machines to wash and dry their clothes. *lavandería automática pública*

**laun|dry** /lɔndri/ (**laundries**) 1 N-UNCOUNT **Laundry** is used to refer to clothes, sheets, and towels that are about to be washed, are being washed, or have just been washed. *ropa lavada, ropa para lavar* ❑ *I'll do your laundry. Yo lavo tu ropa.* ❑ *...the room where I hang the laundry. ...el cuarto donde cuelgo la ropa lavada.* 2 N-COUNT A **laundry** is a business that washes and irons clothes, sheets, and towels for people. *lavandería* ❑ *He gets his washing done at the laundry. Lleva su ropa a la lavandería.* 3 N-COUNT A **laundry** or a **laundry room** is a room in a house, hotel, or institution where clothes, sheets, and towels are washed. *lavandería* ❑ *...the prison laundry. ...la lavandería de la prisión.*
→ see **house, soap**

**lava** /lɑvə, lævə/ N-UNCOUNT **Lava** is the very hot liquid rock that comes out of a volcano. *lava* ❑ *...the lava and ash that came out of Mexico's Mount Colima. ...la lava y las cenizas que arrojó el volcán de Colima de México.*
→ see **rock, volcano**

**lav|ish** /lævɪʃ/ (**lavishes, lavishing, lavished**) 1 ADJ If you describe something as **lavish**, you mean that it is very elaborate and impressive and a lot of money has been spent on it. *suntuoso, espléndido* ❑ *...a lavish party. ...una fiesta espléndida.* • **lav|ish|ly** ADV *espléndidamente, magníficamente* ❑ *The apartment was lavishly decorated. El* departamento estaba magníficamente decorado. **2** ADJ If you say that spending, praise, or the use of something is **lavish,** you mean that someone spends a lot or that something is praised or used a lot. derrochador, generoso, extravagante ❑ *Some people disapprove of his lavish spending.* *Algunos desaprueban sus extravagantes gastos.* **3** V-T If you **lavish** money, affection, or praise **on** someone or something, you spend a lot of money on them or give them a lot of affection or praise. derrochar, no escatimar, desvivirse ❑ *Walmsley lavished gifts on family and friends.* *Walmsley derrochaba en regalos para la familia y los amigos.*

**law** /lɔ/ (**laws**) **1** N-SING **The law** is a system of rules that a society or government develops in order to deal with crime, business agreements, and social relationships. You can also use **the law** to refer to the people who work in this system. ley ❑ *Threatening phone calls are against the law.* *Las llamadas telefónicas amenazantes van contra la ley.* ❑ *We will punish those who break the law.* *Castigaremos a quien infrinja la ley.* ❑ *The book looks at how the law treats young people who commit crimes.* *El libro es sobre cómo tratan las leyes a los jóvenes que delinquen.* **2** N-COUNT A **law** is one of the rules in a system of law which deals with a particular type of agreement, relationship, or crime. ley ❑ *...a new law to protect young people.* *...una nueva ley para proteger a los jóvenes.* **3** N-PLURAL **The laws of** an organization or activity are its rules, which are used to organize and control it. leyes ❑ *...the laws of the Catholic Church.* *...las leyes de la iglesia católica.* **4** N-COUNT A **law** is a rule or set of rules for good behavior which is considered right and important by the majority of people for moral, religious, or emotional reasons. ley ❑ *...laws of morality.* *...las leyes morales.* **5** N-COUNT A **law** is a natural process in which a particular event or thing always leads to a particular result, or a scientific rule that someone has invented to explain such a process. ley ❑ *A falling apple led Isaac Newton to discover the law of gravity.* *Una manzana que cayó llevó a Isaac Newton a descubrir la ley de la gravedad.* **6** N-UNCOUNT **Law** or **the law** is all the professions which deal with advising people about the law, representing people in court, or giving decisions and punishments. leyes, abogacía, derecho ❑ *He is interested in a career in law.* *Está interesado en una carrera relacionada con las leyes.* **7** N-UNCOUNT **Law** is the study of systems of law and how laws work. leyes, derecho ❑ *He studied law.* *Él estudió derecho.*

**law and or|der** N-UNCOUNT When there is **law and order** in a country, the laws are generally accepted and obeyed, so that society there functions normally. orden público ❑ *...the breakdown of law and order.* *...el colapso del orden público.*

**law enforcement** N-UNCOUNT Agencies or officials whose job is **law enforcement** are responsible for catching people who break the law. aplicación de la ley, ejecución de la ley ❑ *...increased funding for prisons and local law enforcement.* *...más fondos para las cárceles y para la aplicación de la ley en la localidad.* ❑ *...law enforcement agencies such as the police.* *...instituciones dedicadas a hacer cumplir la ley, como la policía.*

**law|maker** /lɔmeɪkər/ (**lawmakers**) N-COUNT A **lawmaker** is someone such as a politician who is responsible for proposing and passing new laws. legislador o legisladora

**lawn** /lɔn/ (**lawns**) N-VAR A **lawn** is an area of grass that is kept cut short and is usually part of someone's yard, or part of a park. prado, césped, pasto ❑ *They were sitting on the lawn.* *Estaban sentados en el pasto.*

**lawn bowl|ing** N-UNCOUNT **Lawn bowling** is a game in which players try to roll large wooden balls as near as possible to a small wooden ball. Lawn bowling is usually played outdoors on grass. lawn bowling ❑ *...a revival of lawn bowling in the U.S.* *...el renacimiento del lawn bowling en los Estados Unidos.*

**lawn chair** (**lawn chairs**) N-COUNT A **lawn chair** is a simple chair with a folding frame. Lawn chairs are usually used outdoors. silla para jardín

**lawn|mow|er** /lɔnmoʊər/ (**lawnmowers**) N-COUNT A **lawnmower** is a machine for cutting grass on lawns. podadora de pasto, cortadora de pasto
→ see **garden**

**law|suit** /lɔsut/ (**lawsuits**) N-COUNT A **lawsuit** is a case in a court of law which concerns a dispute between two people or organizations. pleito, juicio, litigio, proceso [FORMAL] ❑ *Some of the dead soldiers' families filed a million-dollar lawsuit against the army.* *Algunas familias de los soldados muertos demandaron al ejército por un millón de dólares.*

**law|yer** /lɔɪər, lɔyər/ (**lawyers**) N-COUNT A **lawyer** is a person who is qualified to advise people about the law and represent them in court. abogado o abogada, licenciado o licenciada ❑ *His lawyers say that he is innocent.* *Sus abogados dicen que él es inocente.*
→ see **trial**

**lay**
❶ VERB AND NOUN USES
❷ ADJECTIVE USES

❶ **lay** /leɪ/ (**lays, laying, laid**)

> In standard English, the form **lay** is also the past tense of the verb **lie** in some meanings. In informal English, people sometimes use the word **lay** instead of **lie** in those meanings.

**1** V-T If you **lay** something somewhere, you put it there in a careful, gentle, or neat way. poner, colocar, depositar ❑ *Lay a sheet of newspaper on the floor.* *Ponga una hoja de periódico en el piso.* ❑ *Mothers usually lay babies on their backs to sleep.* *Las mamás normalmente ponen a los bebés de espaldas, para que se duerman.* **2** V-T If you **lay** something such as carpets, cables, or foundations, you put them into their permanent position. colocar, instalar ❑ *Workmen are currently laying new drains.* *En este momento, los trabajadores están instalando las nuevas tuberías.* **3** V-T/V-I When a female bird **lays** or **lays** an egg, it produces an egg by pushing it out of its body. poner huevos, desovar **4** V-T **Lay** is used with some nouns to talk about making official preparations for something. For example, if you **lay the basis** for something or **lay plans** for it, you prepare it carefully. sentar las bases, hacer planes, preparar ❑ *We have already laid plans for our next trip.* *Ya hicimos planes para nuestro próximo viaje.* **5** V-T **Lay** is used with some nouns in expressions about accusing or blaming someone. For example, if you

**lay the blame** for a mistake on someone, you say it is their fault. *culpar* ❑ *She refused to lay the blame on any one person. Ella se negó a echar la culpa a otra persona.*
→ see also **lie**

▸ **lay aside** PHR-VERB If you **lay aside** a feeling or belief, you reject it or give it up in order to progress with something. *dejar de lado, apartar* ❑ *We laid aside our differences, and got on with the job. Dejamos de lado nuestras diferencias y nos pusimos a trabajar.*

▸ **lay down** PHR-VERB If rules or people in authority **lay down** what people should do or must do, they officially state what they should or must do. *imponer, determinar* ❑ *Not all companies lay down written guidelines. No todas las empresas ponen por escrito sus reglamentos.*

▸ **lay off** **1** PHR-VERB If workers **are laid off,** they are told by their employers to leave their job, usually because there is no more work for them to do. *despedir a un empleado, suspender a un empleado* [BUSINESS] ❑ *100,000 employees will be laid off to cut costs. 100,000 empleados serán despedidos para reducir costos.*

▸ **lay out** **1** PHR-VERB If you **lay out** a group of things, you spread them out and arrange them neatly, for example, so that they can all be seen clearly. *preparar, disponer, exhibir* ❑ *We spread the blanket and laid out the food. Extendimos la manta y pusimos la comida.* **2** PHR-VERB To **lay out** ideas, principles, or plans means to explain or present them clearly, for example, in a document or a meeting. *plantear, exponer* ❑ *Maxwell listened as Johnson laid out his plan. Maxwell escuchaba mientras Johnson exponía su plan.*

L

❷ **lay** /leɪ/ **1** ADJ You use **lay** to describe people who are involved with a Christian church but are not members of the clergy or are not monks or nuns. *lego, laico, seglar* ❑ *Edwards is a Methodist lay preacher. Edwards es un predicador metodista laico.* **2** ADJ You use **lay** to describe people who are not experts or professionals in a particular subject or activity. *lego, no especialista* ❑ *He was able to understand the science and explain it to a lay person. Él tenía la capacidad de entender la ciencia y explicarla a los legos.*

**lay|er** /leɪər/ (**layers, layering, layered**) **1** N-COUNT A **layer** of a material or substance is a quantity or piece of it that covers a surface or that is between two other things. *capa* ❑ *A fresh layer of snow covered the street. Una capa de nieve fresca cubría la calle.* **2** N-COUNT If something such as a system or an idea has many **layers,** it has many different levels or parts. *capa, estrato, interpretación* ❑ *...the layers of meaning in the artist's paintings. ...los varios significados de las pinturas del artista.* **3** V-T If you **layer** something, you arrange it in layers. *acomodar en capas* ❑ *Layer the onion slices on top of the potatoes. Ponga una capa de rebanadas de cebolla sobre las papas.*
→ see **ozone**

**Word Partnership** Usar *layer* con:

ADJ. **bottom/top** layer, **lower/upper** layer, **outer** layer, **protective** layer, **single** layer, **thick/thin** layer **1**
N. layer **cake**, layer **of dust**, layer **of fat**, **ozone** layer, layer **of skin**, **surface** layer **1**

**lay|over** /leɪoʊvər/ (**layovers**) N-COUNT A **layover** is a short stay in a place in between parts of a journey, especially a plane journey. *parada, escala* ❑ *She booked a plane for Denver with a layover in Dallas. Ella reservó un vuelo a Denver con escala en Dallas.*

**lazy** /leɪzi/ (**lazier, laziest**) **1** ADJ If someone is **lazy,** they do not want to work or make any effort to do anything. *flojo, perezoso, holgazán* ❑ *I'm not lazy: I hate lounging about, doing nothing. No soy flojo, me choca desperdiciar el tiempo sin hacer nada.*
• **la|zi|ness** N-UNCOUNT *flojera, pereza, holgazanería* ❑ *Through laziness, he didn't bother to learn our names. Por flojera ni siquiera se molestó en aprenderse nuestros nombres.* **2** ADJ You can use **lazy** to describe an activity or event in which you are very relaxed and which you do or take part in without making much effort. *relajado, descansado* ❑ *Her novel is perfect for a lazy summer's afternoon reading. Su novela es perfecta para leerla en una tarde de verano en que echas flojera.* • **la|zi|ly** /leɪzɪli/ ADV *perezosamente* ❑ *Liz stretched lazily. Liz se estiró perezosamente.*

**lb.**

The plural is **lbs.** or **lb.**.

**lb.** is a written abbreviation for **pound,** when it refers to weight. *abreviatura de libra* ❑ *The baby weighed 8 lbs. 5 oz. El bebé pesó 8 lbs. 5 oz.*

**lead**
❶ BEING AHEAD OR TAKING SOMEONE SOMEWHERE
❷ SUBSTANCES

❶ **lead** /lid/ (**leads, leading, led**) **1** V-T If you **lead** a group of people, you walk or ride in front of them. *encabezar, guiar, dirigir* ❑ *A brass band led the parade. Una banda de metales iba al frente del desfile.* ❑ *He led his soldiers into battle. Condujo a sus soldados a la batalla.* **2** V-T If you **lead** someone to a particular place or thing, you take them there. *dirigir, llevar* ❑ *He took Dick's hand and led him into the house. Tomó a Dick de la mano y lo llevó a la casa.* **3** V-I If a road, gate, or door **leads** somewhere, you can get there by following the road or going through the gate or door. *llevar, conducir* ❑ *The door led to the yard. La puerta llevaba al patio.* ❑ *A hallway leads to the living room. Un pasillo conduce a la sala.* **4** V-T/V-I If you **are leading** at a particular point in a race or competition, you are winning at that point. *ir a la cabeza, llevar la delantera* ❑ *He's leading the presidential race. Encabeza la carrera presidencial.* ❑ *So far Fischer leads by five wins to two. Hasta ahora, Fischer va ganando por cinco victorias a dos.* ❑ *Drury led 49 – 41 at halftime. Drury ganaba 49 – 41 al medio tiempo.* **5** N-SING If you have **the lead** or are **in the lead** in a race or competition, you are winning. *ir a la cabeza, llevar la delantera* ❑ *Harvard took the lead early in the game. Desde el principio del juego, Harvard se puso a la cabeza.* **6** V-T If you **lead** a group of people, an organization, or an activity, you are in control or in charge of the people or the activity. *dirigir* ❑ *He led the country between 1949 and 1984. Dirigió al país entre 1949 y 1984.* **7** V-T You can use **lead** when you are saying what kind of life someone has. For example, if you **lead** a busy life, your life is busy. *llevar* ❑ *She led a normal, happy life. Llevaba*

*una vida normal y feliz.* **8** V-I If something **leads to** a situation or event, usually an unpleasant one, it begins a process which causes that situation or event to happen. *provocar, llevar a, conducir a* ❑ *Every time we talk about money it leads to an argument. Cada vez que hablamos de dinero, discutimos.* **9** V-T If something **leads** you **to** do something, it influences or affects you in such a way that you do it. *llevar a, conducir a* ❑ *What led you to write this book? ¿Qué te llevó a escribir este libro?* **10** V-T You can say that one point or topic in a discussion or piece of writing **leads** you **to** another in order to introduce a new point or topic that is linked with the previous one. *llevar a* ❑ *That leads me to the real point. Esto me lleva a donde quería llegar.* **11** N-COUNT A **lead** is a piece of information or an idea which may help people to discover the facts in a situation where many facts are not yet known, for example, in the investigation of a crime or in a scientific experiment. *pista* ❑ *The police are following up possible leads after receiving 400 calls from the public. La policía está siguiendo las posibles pistas después de recibir 400 llamadas del público.* **12** N-COUNT A **lead** in a piece of equipment is a piece of wire covered in plastic which supplies electricity to the equipment or carries it from one part of the equipment to another. *cable* ❑ *This lead plugs into the camcorder. Este cable se conecta a la cámara de video.* **13** N-COUNT **The lead** in a play, film, or show is the most important part in it. The person who plays this part can also be called the **lead.** *papel principal, primer actor o primera actriz, protagonista* ❑ *Neve Campbell is the lead, playing one of the dancers. Neve Campbell es la protagonista, y representa a una de las bailarinas.* **14** → see also **leading**
→ see **concert**

▸ **lead up to** **1** PHR-VERB The events that **lead up to** a particular event happen one after the other until that event occurs. *preceder, llevar a, culminar en* ❑ *...the events that led up to his death. ...los acontecimientos que concluyeron con su muerte.* **2** PHR-VERB If someone **leads up to** a particular subject, they gradually guide a conversation to a point where they can introduce it. *preparar el terreno, llevar gradualmente a un tema* ❑ *I wondered what he was leading up to. Me preguntaba hacia dónde iba él.*

| **Thesaurus** | *lead* | Ver también: |
|---|---|---|
| v. | escort, guide, precede; (*ant.*) follow ❶ **1** **2** | |
| | govern, head, manage ❶ **6** | |

❷ **lead** /lɛd/ (**leads**) **1** N-UNCOUNT **Lead** is a soft, gray, heavy metal. *plomo* ❑ *...old-fashioned lead pipes. ...tuberías de plomo obsoletas.* **2** N-COUNT The **lead** in a pencil is the center part of it which makes a mark on paper. *punta, mina* ❑ *He started writing with pencil, but the lead immediately broke. Empezó a escribir con lápiz, pero de inmediato se le rompió la punta.*
→ see **mineral**

**lead|er** /li̲dər/ (**leaders**) **1** N-COUNT The **leader** of a group of people or an organization is the person who is in charge of it. *líder, dirigente, jefe, cabecilla, guía* ❑ *Illinois Republicans met Monday to elect a new leader. Los Republicanos de Illinois se reunieron el lunes para elegir a su nuevo líder.* **2** N-COUNT The **leader** at a particular point in a race or competition is the person who is winning at that point. *líder, puntero o puntera* ❑ *The leader came in two minutes before the other runners. El puntero llegó dos minutos antes que los otros corredores.*

**lead|er|ship** /li̲dərʃɪp/ (**leaderships**) **1** N-COUNT You refer to people who are in control of a group or organization as the **leadership.** *liderazgo, conducción, autoridad, mando* ❑ *He held talks with the Croatian and Slovenian leaderships. Tuvo pláticas con los mandos croatas y eslovenos.* **2** N-UNCOUNT Someone's **leadership** is their position or state of being in control of a group of people. *liderazgo, dirección* ❑ *The company doubled in size under her leadership. Mientras ella estuvo al mando, la compañía creció al doble de su tamaño.*

**lead|ing** /li̲dɪŋ/ **1** ADJ The **leading** person or thing in a particular area is the one which is most important or successful. *principal, destacado, importante* ❑ *...a leading member of the city's Sikh community. ...un destacado miembro de la comunidad sikh de la ciudad.* **2** ADJ The **leading** role in a play or movie is the main role. A **leading** lady or man is an actor who plays this role. *protagonista, primer actor o primera actriz* ❑ *He played the leading role in an Arthur Miller play. Fue el primer actor de una obra de Arthur Miller.*

leaf

**leaf** /li̲f/ (**leaves, leafs, leafing, leafed**) N-COUNT The **leaves** of a tree or plant are the parts that are flat, thin, and usually green. *hoja* ❑ *The leaves of the tree moved gently in the wind. Las hojas del árbol se movían suavemente con el viento.*
→ see **flower, herbivore, tea**

▸ **leaf through** PHR-VERB If you **leaf through** something such as a book or magazine, you turn the pages without reading or looking at them very carefully. *hojear* ❑ *She enjoyed leafing through old photo albums. Le encantaba hojear viejos álbumes de fotografías.*

**leaf|let** /li̲flɪt/ (**leaflets**) N-COUNT A **leaflet** is a little book or a piece of paper containing information about a particular subject. *folleto* ❑ *Officials handed out leaflets to workers. Los funcionarios repartieron folletos entre los trabajadores.*

**league** /li̲g/ (**leagues**) **1** N-COUNT A **league** is a group of people, clubs, or countries that have joined together for a particular purpose, or because they share a common interest. *liga, asociación, federación* ❑ *...the League of Nations. ...la Liga de las Naciones.* **2** N-COUNT A **league** is a group of teams that play the same sport or activity against each other. *liga* ❑ *...the American League series between the Boston Red Sox and World Champion Oakland Athletics. ...la serie de la Liga Americana entre los Medias Rojas de Boston y los campeones mundiales, los Atléticos de Oakland.* **3** N-COUNT You use **league** to make comparisons between different people or things, especially in terms of their quality. *nivel, categoría* ❑ *Her success has taken her out of my league. Por sus éxitos ya no estamos a la misma altura.* **4** PHRASE If you say that someone is **in league with** another person to do something bad, you mean that they are working together to do that

l

thing. confabulado con ❑ *They stole billions of dollars in league with the mafia.* *Se aliaron con la mafia y robaron miles de millones de dólares.*

**leak** /li̲k/ (**leaks, leaking, leaked**) **1** V-I If a container **leaks,** there is a hole or crack in it which lets a substance such as liquid or gas escape. You can also say that liquid or gas **leaks** from a container. *filtrarse, gotear* ❑ *The roof leaked.* *El techo goteaba.* ❑ *The swimming pool's sides cracked and the water leaked out.* *Los costados de la alberca se resquebrajaron y el agua se filtraba.* • **Leak** is also a noun. *filtración, fuga* ❑ *A gas leak may have caused the explosion.* *Una fuga de gas puede haber provocado la explosión.* **2** N-COUNT A **leak** is a crack, hole, or other gap that a substance such as a liquid or gas can pass through. *fuga* ❑ *...a leak in the radiator.* *...una fuga en el radiador.* **3** V-T/V-I If a secret document or piece of information **leaks** or **is leaked,** someone lets the public know about it. *filtrarse, filtrar* ❑ *The police were leaking information to a newspaper.* *La policía estaba filtrando información a un periódico.* ❑ *We don't know how the story leaked.* *No sabemos cómo se filtró la historia.* • **Leak** is also a noun. *filtración* ❑ *A leak to a newspaper made the story public.* *Una filtración a un periódico hizo pública la historia.*

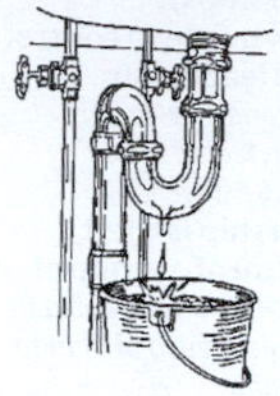

leak

**Thesaurus** *leak* Ver también:

V. drip, ooze, seep, trickle **1**
come out, divulge, pass on **3**
N. crack, hole, opening **2**

**Word Partnership** Usar *leak* con:

V. **cause a** leak, **spring a** leak **1**
N. **fuel** leak, **gas** leak, **oil** leak, leak **in the roof, water** leak **1** **2**
leak **information,** leak **news,** leak **a story** **3**

**lean** /li̲n/ (**leans, leaning, leaned, leaner, leanest**) **1** V-I When you **lean** in a particular direction, you bend your body in that direction. *inclinarse, doblarse, ladearse, encorvarse* ❑ *The driver leaned across and opened the passenger door.* *El chofer se inclinó y abrió la puerta del pasajero.* **2** V-T/V-I If you **lean on** or **against** someone or something, you rest against them so that they partly support your weight. If you **lean** an object **on** or **against** something, you place the object so that it is partly supported by that thing. *apoyar(se)* ❑ *She was feeling tired and leaned against him.* *Se sentía cansada y se apoyó en él.* ❑ *Lean the plants against a wall.* *Apoya las plantas en una pared.* **3** ADJ If you describe someone as **lean,** you mean that they are thin but look strong and healthy. *delgado, atlético, musculoso* ❑ *Like most athletes, she was lean and muscular.* *Como la mayoría de los atletas, estaba delgada y musculosa.* **4** ADJ If meat is **lean,** it does not have very much fat. *magro* **5** ADJ If you describe periods of time as **lean,** you mean that people have less of something, such as money, than they used to have, or are less successful than they used to be. *de escasez, de vacas flacas* ❑ *My parents lived through the lean years of the 1930s.* *Mis padres vivieron los años treinta, que fueron de escasez.*

lean

▸ **lean on** or **lean upon** PHR-VERB If you **lean on** someone or **lean upon** them, you depend on them for support and encouragement. *depender de, apoyarse en* ❑ *She leaned on him to help her to solve her problems.* *Se apoyaba en él para resolver sus problemas.*

**Thesaurus** *lean* Ver también:

V. bend, incline, prop, tilt **1**
recline, rest **2**
ADJ. angular, slender, slim, wiry **3**

**Word Partnership** Usar *lean* con:

ADV. lean **heavily** **2**
ADJ. **long and** lean, **tall and** lean **3**
N. lean **body** **3**
lean **beef,** lean **meat** **4**

**leap** /li̲p/ (**leaps, leaping, leaped** or **leapt**) **1** V-I If you **leap,** you jump high in the air or jump a long distance. *saltar, brincar* ❑ *He leaped in the air and waved his hands.* *Saltó en el aire y agitó las manos.* • **Leap** is also a noun. *salto, brinco* ❑ *Phillips won the long jump with a leap of 27 feet, 5 inches.* *Phillips ganó en el salto largo con 8.4 m.* **2** V-I To **leap** somewhere means to move there suddenly and quickly. *moverse rápidamente* ❑ *The two men leaped into the car and sped off.* *Los dos hombres se metieron de un salto al carro y aceleraron.* ❑ *The dog leapt forward again.* *El perro volvió a saltar hacia adelante.* **3** N-COUNT A **leap** is a large and important change, increase, or advance. *salto* ❑ *There was a giant leap in productivity at the factory.* *En la fábrica se dio un gran salto en la productividad.* ❑ *...a further leap in prices.* *...otro salto en los precios.* **4** V-I If you **leap to** a particular place or position, you make a large and important change, increase, or advance. *saltar a* ❑ *The song leapt to the top of the charts.* *La canción saltó a los primeros lugares de clasificación.*

**leap year** (**leap years**) N-COUNT A **leap year** is a year which has 366 days. The extra day is February 29th. There is a leap year every four years. *año bisiesto*
→ see **year**

**learn** /lɜ̲rn/ (**learns, learning, learned** or **learnt**) **1** V-T/V-I If you **learn** something, you obtain knowledge or a skill through studying or training. *aprender, estudiar, instruirse* ❑ *Where did you learn English?* *¿Dónde aprendiste inglés?* ❑ *He is learning to play the piano.* *Está aprendiendo a tocar el piano.* ❑ *These guys learn quickly.* *Estos cuates aprenden rápido.* • **learn|er** N-COUNT (**learners**) *estudiante, principiante* ❑ *Clint was a quick learner and soon settled into the job.* *Clint aprendió rápidamente y pronto se asentó en el trabajo.* • **learn|ing** N-UNCOUNT *aprendizaje* ❑ *...the learning of English.* *...el aprenizaje del inglés.* **2** V-T/V-I If you **learn,** or **learn of,** something, you find out about it. *enterarse, saber, conocer* ❑ *We first learned of her plans in a newspaper* report. Supimos de sus planes en un reportaje periodístico. ❑ *She wasn't surprised to learn that he was involved.* A ella no le sorprendió enterarse de que él estaba implicado. **3** V-T If people **learn to** behave or react in a particular way, they gradually start to behave in that way as a result of a change in their attitude. aprender ❑ *She's learning to talk about her problems.* Está aprendiendo a hablar de sus problemas. **4** V-T/V-I If you **learn from** an unpleasant experience, you change the way you behave so that it does not happen again or so that, if it happens again, you can deal with it better. aprender ❑ *It's important to learn from your mistakes.* Es importante aprender de los propios errores. ❑ *I hope we all learn some lessons from this.* Espero que todos nos aprendamos esta lección. **5** V-T If you **learn** something such as a poem or a role in a play, you study or repeat the words so that you can remember them. aprenderse, memorizar ❑ *He learned this song as a child.* De niño se aprendió esa canción. **6** → see also **learned**

→ see **brain**

**Usage** **learn** and **teach**

*Learn* means "to get information or knowledge about something": *Kim can read English well but hasn't learned to speak it.* *Teach* means "to give someone information or knowledge about something": *Michael enjoys teaching his friends how to drive.*

**Thesaurus** *learn* Ver también:

V. master, pick up, study **1**
discover, find out, understand **2**

**learn|ed** /lɜrnɪd/ ADJ A **learned** person has gained a lot of knowledge by studying. culto, sabio, erudito, ilustrado

**learned be|hav|ior** (**learned behaviors**) N-VAR **Learned behavior** is a way of behaving that someone has learned through experience or observation rather than because it is a natural instinct. comportamiento aprendido

**learn|er's per|mit** (**learner's permits**) N-COUNT A **learner's permit** is a license that allows you to drive a vehicle before you have passed your driving test. permiso para conducir ❑ *She's still too young to get a learner's permit.* Ella todavía es muy joven como para sacar su permiso.

**lease** /lis/ (**leases, leasing, leased**) **1** N-COUNT A **lease** is a legal agreement by which the owner of a building, a piece of land, or something such as a car allows someone else to use it for a period of time in return for money. arrendamiento, alquiler ❑ *He took up a 10-year lease on the house.* Le dieron la casa en arrendamiento por diez años. **2** V-T If you **lease** property or something such as a car from someone or if they **lease** it **to** you, they allow you to use it in return for regular payments of money. arrendar, rentar, alquilar ❑ *He leased an apartment in Toronto.* Rentó un departamento en Toronto. ❑ *She's going to lease the building to students.* Va a rentar el edificio a estudiantes.

**least** /list/

**Least** is often considered to be the superlative form of **little**.

**1** PHRASE You use **at least** to say that a number or amount is the minimum that is possible or likely and that more may be possible. The forms **at the least** and **at the very least** are also used. cuando menos, al menos, por lo menos ❑ *Drink at least half a pint of milk each day.* Bébase cuando menos un cuarto de litro de leche al día. ❑ *You could at least say thank you.* Por lo menos podrías dar las gracias. **2** PHRASE You use **at least** to indicate an advantage that exists in a bad situation. cuando menos, al menos, por lo menos ❑ *At least we know he is still alive.* Al menos sabemos que todavía está vivo. **3** ADJ You use **the least** to mean a smaller amount than anyone or anything else, or the smallest amount possible. lo menos, lo mínimo ❑ *He wants to save money and to spend the least amount of money on a car.* Quiere ahorrar dinero y gastar lo mínimo en un coche. ● **Least** is also a pronoun. lo menos ❑ *On education, Japan performs best but spends the least per student.* En educación, Japón es el mejor, pero es el que menos gasta por estudiante. ● **Least** is also an adverb. menos ❑ *The extra money may benefit those who need it the least.* El dinero extra podría beneficiar a quienes menos lo necesitan. ❑ *He is one of the least friendly people I have ever met.* Es una de las personas menos amables que conozco. **4** ADJ You use **least** when you are emphasizing that a particular situation or event is much less important or serious than other possible or actual ones. menos, menor ❑ *Getting up at three o'clock every morning was the least of her worries.* Levantarse a las tres todas las mañanas era su problema menos importante. **5** PHRASE You can use **in the least** and **the least bit** to emphasize a negative. en lo más mínimo, de ninguna manera ❑ *I'm not like that at all. Not in the least.* Yo no soy así, de ninguna manera. ❑ *Alice wasn't the least bit frightened.* Alice no estaba asustada en lo más mínino. **6** PHRASE You can use **not least** to emphasize an important example or reason. hasta, incluido ❑ *Everyone is more worried about traveling these days, not least Americans.* A todos les preocupa más viajar en estos días, incluidos los americanos. **7** PHRASE You can use **to say the least** to suggest that a situation is actually much more extreme or serious than you say it is. por no decir más, para decir lo menos ❑ *The experience was interesting, to say the least.* La experiencia fue interesante, por no decir más.

**Thesaurus** *least* Ver también:

ADJ. fewest, lowest, minimum, smallest **3**

**leath|er** /lɛðər/ (**leathers**) N-VAR **Leather** is treated animal skin which is used for making shoes, clothes, bags, and furniture. piel ❑ *...a leather jacket.* ...una chamarra de piel.

**leave**

❶ VERB USES
❷ NOUN USE
❸ PHRASAL VERBS

❶ **leave** /liv/ (**leaves, leaving, left**) **1** V-T/V-I If you **leave** a place or person, you go away from that place or person. dejar, irse, salir ❑ *He couldn't leave the country.* No podía dejar el país. ❑ *My flight leaves in less than an hour.* Mi vuelo sale en menos de una hora. **2** V-T/V-I If you **leave** an institution, group, or job, you permanently stop attending that institution, being a member of that group, or doing that job.

dejar, irse ❑ *He left school before graduating.* *Dejó la escuela antes de graduarse.* ❑ *I am leaving to spend more time with my family.* *Me voy para dedicar más tiempo a mi familia.* **3** V-T If you **leave** your husband, wife, or some other person with whom you have had a close relationship, you stop living with them or you end the relationship. *dejar, abandonar* ❑ *He'll never leave you. You needn't worry.* *Él nunca te va a dejar, no tienes que preocuparte por eso.* **4** V-T If you **leave** something or someone in a particular place, you let them remain there when you go away. If you **leave** something or someone with a person, you let them remain with that person so they are safe while you are away. *dejar* ❑ *I left my bags in the car.* *Dejé mis maletas en el coche.* ❑ *Leave your key with a neighbor.* *Deja tu llave con un vecino.* **5** V-T If you **leave** someone **to** do something, you go away from them so that they do it on their own. If you **leave** someone **to** himself or herself, you go away from them and allow them to be alone. *dejar, irse* ❑ *I'll leave you to get to know each other.* *Los dejo para que se conozcan.* ❑ *I can see you're busy—I'll leave you to it.* *Veo que estás ocupado, no te interrumpo.* **6** V-T To **leave** an amount of something means to keep it available after the rest has been used or taken away. *dejar* ❑ *He always left a little food for the next day.* *Él siempre dejaba un poco de comida para el día siguiente.* **7** V-T If an event **leaves** people or things in a particular state, they are in that state when the event has finished. *producir un efecto* ❑ *An auto accident left him unable to walk.* *No puede caminar a raíz de un accidente automovilístico.* **8** V-T If something **leaves** a mark, effect, or sign, it causes that mark, effect, or sign to remain as a result. *dejar* ❑ *The wound healed well and only left a small scar.* *La herida sanó bien y sólo quedó una pequeña cicatriz.* **9** V-T If you **leave** something **until** a particular time, you delay doing it or dealing with it until then. *dejar* ❑ *Don't leave it all until the last minute.* *No dejes todo al último minuto.* **10** PHRASE If you **leave** something **too late,** you delay doing it so that when you eventually do it, it is useless or ineffective. *ser demasiado tarde* **11** V-T If you **leave** property or money **to** someone, you arrange for it to be given to them after you have died. *dejar a, heredar* ❑ *He left everything to his wife when he died.* *Cuando murió, le dejó todo a su esposa.* **12** V-T If you **leave** something somewhere, you forget to bring it with you. *dejar, olvidar* ❑ *I left my purse back there in the gas station.* *Olvidé mi bolsa en la gasolinera.* **13** → see also **left**

| **Thesaurus** | *leave* | Ver también: |
|---|---|---|
| v. | abandon, depart, go away; (*ant.*) arrive, come, stay ❶ **1** | |
| | give up, quit, resign; (*ant.*) remain, stay ❶ **2** | |
| | abandon, desert, ditch, take off ❶ **3** | |

❷ **leave** /liv/ N-UNCOUNT **Leave** is a period of time when you are not working at your job, because you are on vacation, or for some other reason. If you are **on leave,** you are not working at your job. *permiso, licencia* ❑ *Why don't you take a few days' leave?* *¿Por qué no pides unos días de permiso?* ❑ *...maternity leave.* *...licencia de maternidad.*

❸ **leave** /liv/ (**leaves, leaving, left**)

▸ **leave behind** **1** PHR-VERB If you **leave** someone or something **behind,** you go away permanently from them. *abandonar, dejar atrás, irse sin* ❑ *He left his friends and family behind in Canada.* *Dejó a sus amigos y su familia en Canadá.* **2** PHR-VERB If you **leave behind** an object or a situation, it remains after you have left a place. *olvidar* ❑ *He left his glasses behind in his office.* *Olvidó sus anteojos en la oficina.* **3** PHR-VERB If a person, country, or organization **is left behind,** they remain at a lower level than others because they are not as quick at understanding things or developing. *rezagarse, quedarse atrás* ❑ *We're going to be left behind by the rest of the world.* *Nos vamos a rezagar del resto del mundo.* ❑ *I'm slow at reading, so I got left behind at school.* *Leo muy despacio, así que me retrasé en la escuela.*

▸ **leave off** PHR-VERB If someone or something **is left off** a list, they are not included on that list. *dejar fuera, no incluir* ❑ *She was left off the guest list.* *No la incluyeron en la lista de invitados.*

▸ **leave out** PHR-VERB If you **leave** someone or something **out** of an activity, collection, discussion, or group, you do not include them in it. *dejar fuera, exluir* ❑ *They shouldn't have left her out of the team.* *No debieron excluirla del equipo.* ❑ *If you like mild flavors, leave out the chili.* *Si te gustan los sabores suaves, olvídate del chile.*

**leav|ened** /lɛvᵊnd/ ADJ **Leavened** bread or dough is made with yeast. *hecho con levadura*

**leaves** /livz/ **Leaves** is the plural form of **leaf**, and the third person singular form of **leave**. *plural de leaf*

**lec|ture** /lɛktʃər/ (**lectures, lecturing, lectured**) **1** N-COUNT A **lecture** is a talk someone gives in order to teach people about a particular subject, usually at a university or college. *conferencia, disertación* ❑ *...a lecture by Professor Eric Robinson.* *...una conferencia del profesor Eric Robinson.* **2** V-I If you **lecture on** a particular subject, you give a lecture or a series of lectures about it. *enseñar sobre, dictar cátedra sobre* ❑ *She invited him to Atlanta to lecture on the history of art.* *Lo invitó a Atlanta a dar conferencias sobre historia del arte.* **3** V-T If someone **lectures** you about something, they criticize you or tell you how they think you should behave. *sermonear, dar sermones* ❑ *They lectured us about our eating habits.* *Nos sermonearon sobre nuestros hábitos alimenticios.* ❑ *Chuck lectured me about getting a haircut.* *Chuck me echó un sermón, dice que necesito un corte de pelo.* ● **Lecture** is also a noun. *conferencia, sermón, cátedra, plática* ❑ *We had a lecture on safety.* *Tuvimos una plática sobre seguridad.*

**lec|tur|er** /lɛktʃərər/ (**lecturers**) N-COUNT A **lecturer** is a teacher at a university or college. *conferencista, catedrático, conferenciante, profesor universitario* ❑ *...a lecturer in law.* *...un profesor universitario de leyes.*

**left**

❶ REMAINING
❷ DIRECTION AND POLITICAL GROUPINGS

❶ **left** /lɛft/ **1** **Left** is the past tense and past participle of **leave**. *pasado y participio pasado de **leave*** **2** ADJ If there is a certain amount of something **left,** or if you have a certain amount of it **left,** it remains when the rest has gone or been used.

dejar, quedar ❑ *Is there any milk left? ¿Quedó algo de leche?* ❑ *They still have six games left to play. Todavía les quedan seis partidos por jugar.* **3** PHRASE If there is a certain amount of something **left over,** or if you have it **left over,** it remains when the rest has gone or been used. *lo que sobra, lo que queda* ❑ *She spends so much money on clothes, there's never any left over to buy books. Gasta tanto dinero en ropa, que nunca sobra nada para comprar libros.*

**❷ left** /lɛft/

The spelling **Left** is also used for meanings **3** and **4**.

**1** N-SING The **left** is one of two opposite directions, sides, or positions. If you are facing north and you turn to the left, you will be facing west. In the word "to," the "t" is to the left of the "o." *izquierda* ❑ *Take a left at the end of the road. Dé vuelta a la izquierda al final del camino.* ❑ *...the brick wall to the left of the building. ...el muro de ladrillo que está del lado izquierdo del edificio.* ● **Left** is also an adverb. *hacia la izquierda* ❑ *Turn left at the corner. En la esquina da vuelta a la izquierda.* **2** ADJ Your **left** arm, leg, or ear, for example, is the one which is on the left side of your body. Your **left** shoe or glove is the one which is intended to be worn on your left foot or hand. *izquierdo* ❑ *Fred fell and twisted his left leg. Fred se cayó y se torció la pierna izquierda.* **3** N-SING In the U.S., **the left** refers to people who want to use legislation and the tax system to improve social conditions. In most other countries, **the left** refers to people who support the ideas of socialism. *izquierda* ❑ *...the political parties of the left. ...los partidos políticos de izquierda.* **4** N-SING If you say that a person or political party has moved **to the left,** you mean that their political beliefs have become more left-wing. *hacia la izquierda*

**left-hand** ADJ If something is on the **left-hand** side of something, it is positioned on the left of it. *izquierda* ❑ *The Japanese drive on the left-hand side of the road. Los japoneses circulan por el lado izquierdo del camino.*

**left-of-center** ADJ **Left-of-center** people or political parties support the ideals of the political left. *centro izquierda*

**left-wing** also **left wing** **1** ADJ **Left-wing** people support the ideas of the political left. *de izquierda, izquierdista* ❑ *They will not be voting for him because he is too left-wing. No votarán por él porque su postura es demasiado de izquierda.* **2** N-SING **The left wing** of a group of people, especially a political party, consists of the members of it whose beliefs are closer to those of the political left than are those of its other members. *izquierda* ❑ *She belongs on the left wing of the Democratic Party. Ella forma parte de la izquierda del Partido Demócrata.*

**lefty** /lɛfti/ (**lefties**) N-COUNT A **lefty** is someone, especially a sports player, who is left-handed. *zurdo* [INFORMAL]

**leg** /lɛg/ (**legs**) **1** N-COUNT A person's or animal's **legs** are the long parts of their body that they use to stand on. *pata, pierna* ❑ *He broke his right leg in a motorcycle accident. Se rompió la pierna derecha en un accidente de motocicleta.* **2** N-COUNT The **legs** of a pair of pants are the parts that cover your legs. *pierna, pernera* ❑ *Anthony dried his hands on the legs of his jeans. Anthony se secó las manos en los jeans.* **3** N-COUNT A **leg** of lamb, pork, chicken, or other meat is a piece of meat that consists of the animal's or bird's leg, especially the thigh. *pierna* ❑ *...a chicken leg. ...una pierna de pollo.* **4** N-COUNT The **legs** of a table, chair, or other piece of furniture are the parts that rest on the floor and support the furniture's weight. *pata* ❑ *She sat on his knee. Then the chair legs broke. Ella se sentó en las rodillas de él, y después se rompieron las patas de la silla.* **5** N-COUNT A **leg** of a long journey is one part of it, usually between two points where you stop. *etapa, trecho, tramo* ❑ *The first leg of the journey was by boat to Lake Naivasha in Kenya. La primera etapa del recorrido fue en barco, al Lago Naivasha, en Kenia.*
→ see **body, insect, shellfish**

**lega|cy** /lɛgəsi/ (**legacies**) **1** N-COUNT A **legacy** is money or property which someone leaves to you when they die. *legado, herencia* ❑ *His father left him a generous legacy. Su padre le dejó una generosa herencia.* **2** N-COUNT A **legacy of** an event or period of history is something which is a direct result of it and which continues to exist after it is over. *legado* ❑ *...the legacy of slavery. ...el legado de la esclavitud.*

**le|gal** /ligᵊl/ **1** ADJ **Legal** is used to describe things that relate to the law. *legal, jurídico* ❑ *He promised to take legal action. Prometió tomar medidas legales.* ❑ *...the legal system. ...el sistema jurídico.* ● **le|gal|ly** ADV *legalmente, jurídicamente, por vías legales* ❑ *It could be difficult, legally speaking. Podría ser difícil, jurídicamente hablando.* **2** ADJ An action or situation that is **legal** is allowed or required by law. *legal* ❑ *What I did was perfectly legal. Lo que hice fue perfectamente legal.* ● **le|gal|ity** /ligælɪti/ N-UNCOUNT *legalidad, legitimidad* ❑ *Some people question the legality of the contracts. Algunas personas cuestionan la legalidad de los contratos.*

**Word Partnership** Usar *legal* con:

| | |
|---|---|
| N. | legal **action**, legal **advice**, legal **battle**, legal **bills**, legal **costs/expenses**, legal **defense**, legal **department**, legal **documents**, legal **expert**, legal **fees**, legal **guardian**, legal **issue**, legal **liability**, legal **matters**, legal **obligation**, legal **opinion**, legal **problems/troubles**, legal **procedures/proceedings**, legal **profession**, legal **responsibility**, legal **rights**, legal **services**, legal **status**, legal **system** **1** |
| ADV. | **perfectly** legal **2** |

**leg|end** /lɛdʒᵊnd/ (**legends**) **1** N-VAR A **legend** is a very old and popular story that may be true. *leyenda, mito* ❑ *...the legends of ancient Greece. ...los mitos de la antigua Grecia.* **2** N-COUNT If you refer to someone as a **legend,** you mean that they are very famous and admired by a lot of people. *leyenda, mito* ❑ *...singing legend Frank Sinatra. ...Frank Sinatra, mito de la canción.*
→ see **fantasy**

**leg|end|ary** /lɛdʒᵊndɛri/ **1** ADJ If you describe someone or something as **legendary,** you mean that they are very famous and that many stories are told about them. *legendario* ❑ *...the legendary jazz singer Adelaide Hall. ...Adelaide Hall, legendaria cantante de jazz.* **2** ADJ A **legendary** person, place, or event is mentioned or described in an old

l

legend. *legendario* ❑ *...the legendary King Arthur. ...el legendario Rey Arturo.*

**leg|gings** /lɛgɪŋz/ N-PLURAL **Leggings** are close-fitting pants, usually made out of a stretchy fabric, that are worn by women and girls. *leggings, leotardos, mallas, mallones*

**leg|is|la|tion** /lɛdʒɪsleɪʃᵊn/ N-UNCOUNT **Legislation** consists of a law or laws passed by a government. *legislación* [FORMAL] ❑ *...legislation to protect women's rights. ...legislación que proteja los derechos de las mujeres.*

**Word Partnership** Usar *legislation* con:

V. **draft** legislation, **enact** legislation, **introduce** legislation, **oppose** legislation, **pass** legislation, **support** legislation, **veto** legislation
ADJ. **federal** legislation, **new** legislation, **proposed** legislation

**leg|is|la|tive** /lɛdʒɪsleɪtɪv/ ADJ **Legislative** means involving or relating to the process of making and passing laws. *legislativo* [FORMAL] ❑ *Today's hearing was just the first step in the legislative process. La audiencia de hoy sólo fue el primer paso del proceso legislativo.*

**leg|is|la|ture** /lɛdʒɪsleɪtʃər/ (**legislatures**) N-COUNT The **legislature** of a particular state or country is the group of people in it who have the power to make and pass laws. *legislatura, poder legislativo, cuerpo legislativo* [FORMAL]

L

**le|giti|mate** /lɪdʒɪtɪmɪt/ **1** ADJ Something that is **legitimate** is acceptable according to the law. *legítimo, legal, válido, auténtico* ❑ *...a legitimate driver's license with my picture on it. ...una licencia de manejo válida, con mi fotografía.* ● **le|giti|ma|cy** /lɪdʒɪtɪməsi/ N-UNCOUNT *legitimidad, validez, lo legítimo* ❑ *...the political legitimacy of his government. ...la legitimidad política de su gobierno* ● **le|giti|mate|ly** ADV *legítimamente* ❑ *The government was legitimately elected by the people. El gobierno fue elegido legítimamente por el pueblo.* **2** ADJ If you say that something such as a feeling or claim is **legitimate,** you think that it is reasonable and justified. *legítimo, válido, justificado* ❑ *That's a perfectly legitimate fear. Su miedo está perfectamente justificado.* ● **le|giti|ma|cy** N-UNCOUNT *justificación, validez* ❑ *He refused to accept the legitimacy of Helen's anger. Se negó a aceptar la justificación del temor de Helen.* ● **le|giti|mate|ly** ADV *justificadamente* ❑ *They argued quite legitimately with some of my choices. Argumentaron de manera justificada con algunas de mis opciones.*

**leg|work** /lɛgwɜrk/ N-UNCOUNT You use **legwork** to refer to work that involves physical activity such as interviewing people or gathering information, especially when this work forms the basis of other, more intellectual work. *trabajo preliminar, trabajo de campo, talacha* ❑ *He helped with the routine legwork in the investigation. Ayudó con el trabajo rutinario previo a la investigación.*

**lei|sure** /liʒər, lɛʒ-/ **1** N-UNCOUNT **Leisure** is the time when you are not working and you can relax and do things that you enjoy. *ratos de ocio, tiempo libre* ❑ *They spend their leisure time painting or drawing. Dedicaban su tiempo libre a pintar o dibujar.* **2** PHRASE If someone does something **at leisure** or **at** their **leisure,** they enjoy themselves by doing it when they want to, without hurrying. *cuando uno quiere, cuando se tiene tiempo, al gusto de cada quien* ❑ *You can walk at leisure through the gardens. Puedes caminar a tu gusto por los jardines.*

**lem|on** /lɛmən/ (**lemons**) N-VAR A **lemon** is a bright yellow fruit with very sour juice. Lemons grow on trees in warm countries. *limón* ❑ *...a slice of lemon. ...una rebanada de limón.*
→ see **fruit**

**lem|on|ade** /lɛməneɪd/ (**lemonades**) N-VAR **Lemonade** is a drink that is made from lemons, sugar, and water. *limonada* ❑ *He was pouring ice and lemonade into tall glasses. Estaba sirviendo hielo y limonada en vasos altos.* ❑ *They ordered two lemonades. Ellos ordenaron dos limonadas.*

**lend** /lɛnd/ (**lends, lending, lent**) **1** V-T/V-I When people or organizations such as banks **lend** you money, they give it to you and you agree to pay it back at a future date, often with an extra amount as interest. *prestar, proporcionar* ❑ *Banks are not the only institutions that lend money. Los bancos no son las únicas instituciones que prestan dinero.* ❑ *The government will lend you money at very good rates, between zero percent and 3 percent. El gobierno le prestará dinero a tasas atractivas, entre cero y tres por ciento.* ❑ *Banks have never been more ready to lend. Los bancos nunca habían estado más dispuestos a prestar.* ● **lend|er** N-COUNT (**lenders**) *prestamista, entidad crediticia* ❑ *...the six leading mortgage lenders. ...las seis principales entidades hipotecarias.* ● **lend|ing** N-UNCOUNT *préstamo* ❑ *...a financial institution that specializes in lending money. ...una institución financiera que se especializa en préstamos de efectivo.* **2** V-T If you **lend** something that you own, you allow someone to have it or use it for a period of time. *prestar* ❑ *Will you lend me your pen? ¿Me prestas tu pluma?* **3** V-T If you **lend** your support **to** someone or something, you help them with what they are doing or with a problem that they have. *ayudar, apoyar* ❑ *He was asked to lend support to a charity. Le pidieron que apoyara una obra de caridad.* **4** V-T If something **lends itself to** a particular activity or result, it is easy for it to be used for that activity or to achieve that result. *prestarse a* ❑ *The piano lends itself to all styles of music. El piano se presta para todo tipo de música.* **5** → see also **lent, borrow**

**length** /lɛŋθ/ (**lengths**) **1** N-VAR The **length** of something is the amount that it measures from one end to the other. *longitud, largo* ❑ *It is about a meter in length. Mide más o menos un metro de largo.* ❑ *...the length of the fish. ...el largo del pescado.*

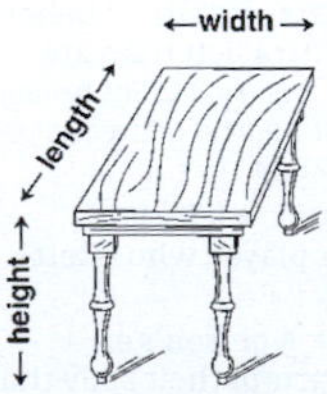

length

**2** N-VAR The **length** of something such as a piece of writing is the amount of writing that is contained in it. *largo* ❑ *...a book of at least 100 pages in length. ...un libro de cuando menos 100 páginas de largo.* **3** N-VAR The **length** of an event, activity, or situation is the period of time from beginning to end for which something lasts or during which something happens. duración ❑ *The length of each class may vary.* *La duración de las clases puede variar.* **4** N-COUNT A **length of** rope, cloth, wood, or other material is a piece of it that is intended to be used for a particular purpose or that exists in a particular situation. tramo, pedazo ❑ *...a three-foot length of rope.* *...un tramo de cuerda de un metro.* **5** N-UNCOUNT The **length of** something is its quality of being long. tiempo, lapso ❑ *We were surprised at the length of time it took him to make up his mind.* *Nos sorprendió el tiempo que le llevó tomar la decisión.* **6** PHRASE If someone does something **at length,** they do it for a long time or in great detail. extensamente, detalladamente, con detenimiento ❑ *They spoke at length.* *Hablaron largo y tendido.* **7** PHRASE If someone **goes to great lengths** to achieve something, they try very hard and perhaps do extreme things in order to achieve it. hacer todo lo posible ❑ *She went to great lengths to hide from reporters.* *Hizo hasta lo imposible por esconderse de los reporteros.* **8** → see also **full-length**

**Word Partnership** Usar *length* con:

ADJ. **average** length, **entire** length **1** – **4**
N. length **and width** **1** **4**
length **of** ***your*** **stay**, length **of time**, length **of treatment** **3** **5**

**lengthy** /lɛŋθi/ (**lengthier, lengthiest**) **1** ADJ You use **lengthy** to describe an event or process which lasts for a long time. largo, prolongado ❑ *There was a lengthy meeting to decide the company's future.* *Fue una reunión prolongada para decidir el futuro de la compañía.* **2** ADJ A **lengthy** report, article, book, or document contains a lot of speech, writing, or other material. largo ❑ *The U.N. issued a lengthy report on the subject.* *La ONU publicó un extenso informe sobre el tema.*

**Word Partnership** Usar *lengthy* con:

N. lengthy **period** **1**
lengthy **description**, lengthy **discourse**, lengthy **discussion**, lengthy **report** **2**

**lens** /lɛnz/ (**lenses**) **1** N-COUNT A **lens** is a thin, curved piece of glass or plastic used in things such as cameras, telescopes, and pairs of glasses. You look through a lens in order to make things look larger, smaller, or clearer. lente ❑ *...a powerful lens for my camera.* *...un lente de gran potencia para mi cámara.* **2** N-COUNT In your eye, the **lens** is the part behind the pupil that focuses light and helps you to see clearly. cristalino **3** → see also **contact lens** → see **eye**

**lent** /lɛnt/ **Lent** is the past tense and past participle of **lend**. pasado y participio pasado de ***lend***

**len|til** /lɛntɪl, -tᵊl/ (**lentils**) N-COUNT **Lentils** are the seeds of a lentil plant. They are usually dried and are used to make soups and stews. lenteja

**lep|re|chaun** /lɛprəkɒn/ (**leprechauns**) N-COUNT In Irish folklore, a **leprechaun** is an imaginary creature that looks like a little old man. duende, gnomo

**les|bian** /lɛzbiən/ (**lesbians**) ADJ **Lesbian** is used to describe homosexual women. lesbiana ❑ *...in the lesbian community.* *...en la comunidad lesbiana.* • A **lesbian** is a woman who is lesbian. lesbiana ❑ *...a group for lesbians, gays and bisexuals.* *...un grupo para lesbianas, gays y bisexuales.*

**less** /lɛs/

**Less** is often considered to be the comparative form of **little**.

**1** DET You use **less** to indicate that there is a smaller amount of something than before or than average. menos ❑ *People should eat less fat.* *La gente debería comer menos grasa.* ❑ *This dishwasher uses less water than older machines.* *Esta lavadora de platos necesita menos agua que las anteriores.* • **Less** is also a pronoun. menos ❑ *He thinks people should spend less and save more.* *Piensa que las personas deberían gastar menos y ahorrar más.* • **Less** is also a quantifier. menos ❑ *I see less of my cousins now that they've moved out of town.* *Veo menos a mis primos ahora que se mudaron a otra ciudad.* **2** PHRASE You use **less than** before a number or amount to say that the actual number or amount is smaller than this. menos de ❑ *The population of the country is less than 12 million.* *La población del país es de menos de 12 millones.* **3** PREP When you are referring to amounts, you use **less** in front of a number or quantity to indicate that it is to be subtracted from another number or quantity already mentioned. menos ❑ *You will pay between ten and twenty five percent, less tax.* *Usted pagará entre diez y veinticinco por ciento, menos impuestos.* **4** PHRASE You use **less than** to say that something does not have a particular quality. For example, if you describe something as **less than** perfect, you mean that it is not perfect at all. menos que ❑ *Her greeting was less than welcoming.* *Su saludo fue menos que acogedor.*

**Usage** **less** and **fewer**

*Less* is used to describe general amounts (or noncount nouns). *Less snow fell in December than in January.* *Fewer* is used to describe amounts of countable items. *Maria is working fewer hours this semester.*

**less|er** /lɛsər/ ADJ You use **lesser** in order to indicate that something is smaller in extent, degree, or amount than another thing that has been mentioned. menor, inferior ❑ *He watches sports to a lesser degree than he did five years ago.* *Ahora ve menos deportes que hace cinco años.* • **Lesser** is also an adverb. menos ❑ *...lesser-known works by famous artists.* *...obras menos conocidas de artistas famosos.*

**les|son** /lɛsᵊn/ (**lessons**) **1** N-COUNT A **lesson** is a fixed period of time when people are taught about a particular subject or taught how to do something. clase ❑ *Johanna took piano lessons.* *Johanna tomó clases de piano.* **2** N-COUNT You use **lesson** to refer to an experience which acts as a warning to you or an example from which you should learn. lección ❑ *I learned an important lesson: never think you know everything.* *Aprendí una lección importante: nunca pensar que lo sabes todo.* **3** PHRASE If you say that you are going to **teach** someone **a lesson,** you mean that you are going to punish them for something that they have done so that they do not do it again. darle una lección a

**Thesaurus** *lesson* Ver también:

N. class, course, instruction, session 1

**Word Partnership** Usar *lesson* con:

ADJ. **private** lesson 1
**hard** lesson, **important** lesson, **painful** lesson, **valuable** lesson 2
V. **get a** lesson, **give a** lesson 1 2
**learn a** lesson, **teach *someone* a** lesson 2

**let** /lɛt/ (**lets, letting, let**)

The form **let** is used in the present tense and is the past tense and past participle.

1 V-T If you **let** something happen, you allow it to happen without doing anything to stop or prevent it. *dejar, permitir, permitirse* ❑ *Thorpe let him talk. Thorpe lo dejó hablar.* ❑ *I couldn't let myself cry. No pude permitirme llorar.* 2 V-T If you **let** someone do something, you give them your permission to do it. *permitir, dar permiso, dejar* ❑ *I love candy but Mom doesn't let me have it very often. Me encantan los dulces, pero mamá no me deja comerlos muy seguido.* 3 V-T If you **let** someone into, out of, or through a place, you allow them to enter, leave, or go through it, for example, by opening a door or making room for them. *dejar, permitir* ❑ *I had to let them into the building because they had lost their keys. Tuve que permitirles la entrada al edificio porque habían perdido sus llaves.* 4 V-T You use **let me** when you are introducing something you want to say. *dejar, permitir* ❑ *Let me tell you what I saw. Permítame decirle lo que vi.* ❑ *Let me explain why. Déjeme explicarle porqué.* 5 V-T You use **let me** when you are offering politely to do something. *permitir* ❑ *Let me take your coat. Permítame llevarme su abrigo* 6 V-T You say **let's** or, in formal English, **let us,** when you are making a suggestion. *sugerir* ❑ *I'm bored. Let's go home. Ya me aburrí, vámonos a la casa.* 7 PHRASE **Let alone** is used after a statement, usually a negative one, to indicate that the statement is even more true of the person, thing, or situation that you are going to mention next. *menos aún, mucho menos* ❑ *It is amazing that the child could reach the pedals, let alone drive the car. Es sorprendente que el niño hubiera podido alcanzar los pedales, mucho menos manejar el coche.* 8 PHRASE If you **let go of** someone or something, you stop holding them. *soltar, liberar* ❑ *She let go of Mona's hand. Soltó la mano de Mona.* 9 PHRASE If you **let** someone **know** something, you tell them about it or make sure that they know about it. *hacer saber, informar, comunicar* ❑ *I want to let them know that I'm safe. Quiero que sepan que estoy bien.*

▸ **let down** PHR-VERB If you **let** someone **down,** you disappoint them, by not doing something that you have said you will do or that they expected you to do. *desilusionar, fallar, decepcionar* ❑ *I didn't want to let him down by not going out with him. No quería desilusionarlo no saliendo con él.*

▸ **let in** PHR-VERB If an object **lets in** something such as air, light, or water, it allows air, light, or water to get into it. *dejar entrar, dejar pasar* ❑ *These materials let in air but not light. Estos materiales dejan entrar el aire, pero no la luz.*

▸ **let off** 1 PHR-VERB If a situation, or someone in authority, **lets** you **off** a task or duty, they make it possible for you, or give you permission, not to do it. *perdonar, permitir* ❑ *The teachers let us off afternoon classes to watch the game. Los maestros nos perdonaron las clases de la tarde para que viéramos el juego.* 2 PHR-VERB If you **let** someone **off,** you give them a lighter punishment than they expect or no punishment at all. *no castigar, perdonar* ❑ *He thought that if he said he was sorry, the judge would let him off. Pensó que si se disculpaba, el juez no lo castigaría.* 3 PHR-VERB If you **let off** an explosive or a gun, you explode or fire it. *hacer estallar, disparar* ❑ *They let off fireworks to celebrate New Year's. Lanzaron fuegos artificiales para celebrar el Año Nuevo.*

▸ **let out** PHR-VERB If something or someone **lets** water, air, or breath **out,** they allow it to flow out or escape. *dejar salir* ❑ *Nancy let out the breath she'd been holding. Nancy soltó la respiración que había estado conteniendo.*

▸ **let up** PHR-VERB If an unpleasant, continuous process **lets up,** it stops or becomes less intense. *amainar, disminuir, parar* ❑ *The traffic in this city never lets up. En esta ciudad siempre hay tráfico.*

**Thesaurus** *let* Ver también:

V. allow, approve, permit; (*ant.*) prevent, stop 1 2

**le|thal** /liθᵊl/ ADJ A substance that is **lethal** can kill people or animals. *letal, mortal, mortífero* ❑ *...a lethal dose of sleeping pills. ...una dosis mortal de somníferos.*

**let's** /lɛts/ **Let's** is the usual spoken form of "let us." *forma hablada usual de **let us***

**Usage** **let's**

Be sure to include the apostrophe when you write *let's* (the contraction of *let us*), in order to avoid confusing it with *lets*: *Nisim sometimes lets his workers go home early, and when he does, he always laughs and says, "Let's stop now. We've done enough damage for one day!"*

**let|ter** /lɛtər/ (**letters**) 1 N-COUNT If you write a **letter** to someone, you write a message on paper and send it to them. *carta* ❑ *I received a letter from a friend. Recibí una carta de una amiga.* ❑ *...a letter offering me the job. ...una carta en la que me ofrecen el trabajo.* 2 N-COUNT **Letters** are written symbols which represent one of the sounds in a language. *letra* ❑ *...the letters of the alphabet. ...las letras del alfabeto.* 3 V-I If a student **letters** in sports or athletics by being part of the high school, university, or college team, they are entitled to wear on their jacket the initial letter of the name of their high school, university, or college. *ser seleccionado* ❑ *Burkoth lettered in soccer. Burkoth era seleccionado de futbol.* 4 N-COUNT If a student earns a **letter** in sports or athletics by being part of the high school, university, or college team, they are entitled to wear on their jacket the initial letter of the name of their high school, university, or college. *ser seleccionado* ❑ *Valerie earned letters in volleyball and basketball. A Valerie la seleccionaron en voleibol y basketball.*

**let|ter car|ri|er** (**letter carriers**) N-COUNT A **letter carrier** is a person whose job is to collect and deliver letters and parcels that are sent by mail. *cartero o cartera*

**levee** /lɛvi/ (**levees**) N-COUNT A **levee** is a raised bank alongside a river. dique ❑ *Water poured over a levee and flooded about 75 percent of Montegut.* *El agua se desbordó del dique e inundó cerca del 75 por ciento de Montegut.*

**lev|el** /lɛvᵊl/ (**levels, leveling** or **levelling, leveled** or **levelled**) **1** N-COUNT A **level** is a point on a scale, for example, a scale of amount, quality, or difficulty. nivel ❑ *We have the lowest level of inflation for some years.* *Tenemos el nivel de inflación más bajo en varios años.* **2** N-SING The **level** of something is its height or the height of its surface. nivel ❑ *The water level of the Mississippi River is 6.5 feet below normal.* *El nivel del agua del río Mississippi está unos dos metros por abajo del normal.* ❑ *Liz sank down in the tub until the water came up to her chin and the bubbles were at eye level.* *Liz se sumergió en la tina hasta que el agua le llegó a la barbilla y las burbujas al nivel de los ojos.* **3** → see also **sea level** **4** N-COUNT A **level** of a building is one of its different stories, which is situated above or below other stories. nivel, piso ❑ *Thurlow's rooms were on the second level.* *Las habitaciones de Thurlow estaban en el segundo nivel.* **5** N-COUNT A **level** is a device for testing to see if a surface is level. It consists of a plastic, wood, or metal frame containing a glass tube of liquid with an air bubble in it. nivel **6** ADJ If one thing is **level with** another thing, it is at the same height as it. al mismo nivel, a la misma altura ❑ *He leaned over the counter so his face was level with the boy's.* *Se inclinó por encima del mostrador, de modo que su cara quedó al mismo nivel que la del niño.* **7** ADJ When something is **level,** it is completely flat. plano, horizontal, igual ❑ *The floor was level, but the ceiling sloped.* *El piso estaba plano, pero el techo tenía declive.* **8** ADV If you draw **level** with someone or something, you get closer to them until you are by their side. alcanzar ❑ *Courtney walked past me but I drew level with a few quick steps.* *Courtney me rebasó, pero yo la alcancé acelerando un poco el paso.* ● **Level** is also an adjective. a nivel, igual, parejo ❑ *He waited until they were level with the door.* *Esperó hasta que llegaron a la puerta.* **9** V-T If someone or something such as a violent storm **levels** a building or area of land, they destroy it completely or make it completely flat. arrasar ❑ *The storm leveled areas of forest and destroyed homes.* *La tormenta arrasó bosques y destruyó casas.* **10** V-T If an accusation or criticism **is leveled at** someone, they are accused of doing wrong or they are criticized for something they have done. criticar, acusar ❑ *Many criticisms have been leveled at the president.* *El presidente ha recibido muchas críticas.* **11** N-COUNT In the theater, an actor's **level** is their height above the stage at a particular time, for example when they are sitting or lying down. altura, nivel

▸ **level off** or **level out** PHR-VERB If a changing number or amount **levels off** or **levels out,** it stops increasing or decreasing at such a fast speed. nivelarse, estabilizarse ❑ *The rate of unemployment is beginning to level off.* *La tasa de desempleo está empezando a estabilizarse.*

**Word Partnership** Usar *level* con:

ADJ. **basic** level, **increased** level, **intermediate** level, **top** level, **upper** level **1** **high/low** level **1** **2**
N. level **of activity**, level **of awareness**, **cholesterol** level, **college** level, **comfort** level, level **of difficulty**, **energy** level, **noise** level, **reading** level, **skill** level, **stress** level, level **of violence** **1** **eye** level, **ground** level, **street** level **2**

**lev|el|er** /lɛvələr/ (**levelers**) also **leveller** N-COUNT If you describe something as a **leveler,** you mean that it makes all people seem the same, in spite of their differences in, for example, age or social status. nivelador, igualador ❑ *War is a great leveler—everyone helps each other, whoever they are.* *Como en tiempo de guerra todos están en la misma situación, todos se ayudan, no importa de quién se trate.*

**lev|er|age** /lɛvərɪdʒ/ N-UNCOUNT **Leverage** is the ability to influence situations or people so that you can control what happens. influencia, poder ❑ *His senior position gives him leverage to get things done.* *Su mayor rango le permite lograr que las cosas se hagan.*

**levy** /lɛvi/ (**levies, levying, levied**) **1** N-COUNT A **levy** is a sum of money that you have to pay, for example, as a tax to the government. gravamen, impuesto ❑ *...an annual levy on all drivers.* *...un impuesto anual a todos los conductores.* **2** V-T If a government or organization **levies** a tax or other sum of money, it demands it from people or organizations. recaudar, imponer ❑ *States levy their own taxes.* *Los estados recaudan sus propios impuestos.*

**lia|bil|ity** /laɪəbɪlɪti/ (**liabilities**) **1** N-COUNT If you say that someone or something is **a liability,** you mean that they cause a lot of problems or embarrassment. desventaja, riesgo, pasivo ❑ *We want to be an asset to the city, not a liability.* *Queremos ser un activo para la ciudad, no una desventaja.* **2** N-COUNT A company's or organization's **liabilities** are the sums of money which it owes. pasivo, deuda [BUSINESS OR LEGAL] ❑ *The company had assets of $138 million and liabilities of $120.5 million.* *Los activos de la empresa representan 138 millones de dólares, y los pasivos, 120.5 millones.* **3** → see also **liable**

**lia|ble** /laɪəbᵊl/ **1** PHRASE When something **is liable to** happen, it is very likely to happen. ser susceptible de, tener la tendencia a ❑ *...equipment that is liable to break.* *...equipo susceptible de descomponerse.* **2** ADJ If people or things are **liable to** something unpleasant, they are likely to experience it or do it. propenso a, susceptible de ❑ *...a woman liable to depression.* *...una mujer propensa a la depresión.* **3** ADJ If you are **liable for** something such as a debt, you are legally responsible for it. ser sujeto de ❑ *Companies who pollute the river are liable for damages to wildlife.* *Las empresas que contaminan el río son responsables de los daños a la vida silvestre.* ● **lia|bil|ity** N-UNCOUNT responsabilidad ❑ *The delivery company does not accept liability for breakages.* *La empresa transportadora no acepta responsabilidad por descomposturas.*

**li|bel** /laɪbᵊl/ (**libels, libeling** or **libelling, libeled** or **libelled**) **1** N-VAR **Libel** is a written statement which wrongly accuses someone of something, and which is therefore against the law. Compare **slander.** *libelo, escrito difamatorio* [LEGAL] ❑ *Warren sued him for libel over the remarks in the newspaper. Warren lo demandó por difamación respecto de lo publicado en el periódico.* **2** V-T To **libel** someone means to write or print something in a book, newspaper, or magazine which wrongly damages that person's reputation and is therefore against the law. *difamar, calumniar* [LEGAL] ❑ *The newspaper which libeled him offered him a large amount of money. El periódico que lo difamó le ofreció una cantidad importante de dinero.*

**li|bel|ous** /laɪbələs/ also **libellous** ADJ If a statement in a book, newspaper, or magazine is **libelous,** it wrongly accuses someone of something, and is therefore against the law. *difamatorio, injurioso* ❑ *The stories are inaccurate or even libelous. Los relatos son inexactos, incluso difamatorios.*

**Word Link** *liber ≈ free : liberal, liberate, liberty*

**lib|er|al** /lɪbərəl, lɪbrəl/ (**liberals**) **1** ADJ Someone who has **liberal** views believes people should have a lot of freedom in deciding how to behave and think. *liberal, tolerante* ❑ *She has liberal views on divorce. Sus opiniones sobre el divorcio son liberales.* ● **Liberal** is also a noun. *liberal* ❑ *...a nation of liberals. ...una nación de liberales.* **2** ADJ A **liberal** system allows people or organizations a lot of political or economic freedom. *liberal* ❑ *...a liberal democracy. ...una democracia liberal* ● **Liberal** is also a noun. *liberal* ❑ *...the free-market liberals. ...los liberales del libre mercado.* **3** ADJ A **Liberal** politician or voter is a member of a Liberal Party or votes for a Liberal Party. *Liberal* ❑ *My father was always a Liberal voter. Mi padre siempre votó por los Liberales.* ● **Liberal** is also a noun. *liberal* ❑ *The Liberals did well in the election. A los Liberales les fue bien en las elecciones.* **4** ADJ **Liberal** means giving, using, or taking a lot of something, or existing in large quantities. *generoso, abundante* ❑ *He is liberal with his jokes. Cuenta muchos chistes.* ● **lib|er|al|ly** ADV *liberalmente, generosamente* ❑ *Season the steaks liberally with salt and pepper. Sazona los bisteces con abundante sal y pimienta.*

**lib|er|al arts** N-PLURAL At a university or college, **liberal arts** courses are on subjects such as history or literature rather than science, law, medicine, or business. *humanidades*

**lib|er|al|ize** /lɪbərəlaɪz, lɪbrəl-/ (**liberalizes, liberalizing, liberalized**) V-T/V-I When a country or government **liberalizes,** or **liberalizes** its laws or its attitudes, it allows people more freedom in their actions. *liberalizar* ❑ *Some states are only beginning to liberalize. Algunos estados apenas empiezan a liberalizarse.* ● **lib|er|ali|za|tion** /lɪbərəlɪzeɪʃᵊn, lɪbrəl-/ N-UNCOUNT *liberalización* ❑ *...the liberalization of divorce laws. ...la liberalización de las leyes sobre el divorcio.*

**lib|er|ate** /lɪbəreɪt/ (**liberates, liberating, liberated**) **1** V-T To **liberate** a place or the people in it means to free them from the political or military control of another country, area, or group of people. *liberar, libertar* ❑ *They planned to liberate the city. Piensan liberar la ciudad.* ● **lib|era|tion** /lɪbəreɪʃᵊn/ N-UNCOUNT *liberación* ❑ *...a mass liberation movement. ...un movimiento de liberación masiva.* **2** V-T To **liberate** someone **from** something means to help them escape from it or overcome it, and lead a better way of life. *liberar* ❑ *The leadership is committed to liberating its people from poverty. Los líderes están comprometidos con liberar a su pueblo de la pobreza.* ● **lib|er|at|ing** ADJ *liberador* ❑ *Talking to a therapist can be a very liberating experience. Hablar con un terapista puede resultar una experiencia liberadora.* ● **lib|era|tion** N-UNCOUNT *liberación* ❑ *...the women's liberation movement. ...el movimiento de liberación de las mujeres.*

**Thesaurus** *liberate* Ver también:

V. free, let out, release; (*ant.*) confine **1**

**lib|er|at|ed** /lɪbəreɪtɪd/ ADJ If you describe someone as **liberated,** you approve of them because they do not accept their society's traditional values or restrictions on behavior. *liberado* ❑ *...a liberated businesswoman. ...una mujer de negocios liberada.*

**lib|er|ty** /lɪbərti/ (**liberties**) **1** N-VAR **Liberty** is the freedom to live your life in the way that you want and go where you want to. *libertad* ❑ *We are united because the attack on America was an attack on the liberty of us all. Nos hemos unido porque el ataque contra los Estados Unidos fue un ataque contra la libertad de todos nosotros.* **2** PHRASE If someone is **at liberty to** do something, they have been given permission to do it. *ser libre de, tener permiso para, estar autorizado para, tener la libertad de* ❑ *I'm not at liberty to tell you where he lives. No estoy autorizado para decirte dónde vive.*

**Thesaurus** *liberty* Ver también:

N. freedom, independence, privilege **1**

**Word Partnership** Usar *liberty* con:

ADJ. **human** liberty, **individual** liberty, **personal** liberty, **religious** liberty **1**

**li|brar|ian** /laɪbrɛəriən/ (**librarians**) N-COUNT A **librarian** is a person who is in charge of a library or who has been specially trained to work in a library. *bibliotecario, bibliotecaria*
→ see **library**

**li|brary** /laɪbrɛri/ (**libraries**) N-COUNT A public **library** is a building where things such as books, newspapers, videos, and music are kept for people to read, use, or borrow. *biblioteca* ❑ *...the local library. ...la biblioteca local.*
→ see Word Web: **library**

**lice** /laɪs/ N-PLURAL **Lice** are small insects that live on the bodies of people or animals. **Lice** is the plural of **louse.** *plural de* ***louse***

**li|cense** /laɪsᵊns/ (**licenses, licensing, licensed**) **1** N-COUNT A **license** is an official document which gives you permission to do, use, or own something. *licencia, permiso, autorización* ❑ *You need a license to teach foreign students. Necesitas un permiso para enseñar a estudiantes extranjeros.* **2** V-T To **license** a person or activity means to give official permission for the person to do something or for the activity to take place. *autorizar, otorgar un*

**Word Web** library

**Public libraries** are changing. Many new **services** are now available. Websites often allow you to search the library's **catalog** of books and **periodicals** from your own computer. Many libraries have computers with Internet access for the public. Some offer literacy classes, tutoring, and homework assistance. Of course, you can still **borrow** and **return books, magazines,** DVDs, CDs, and other **media** free of charge. You can still go to the **fiction** section to find a good **novel**. You can also search the nonfiction bookshelves for an interesting **biography**. And if you need help, the **librarian** is still there to answer your questions.

permiso, otorgar una licencia ❑ *...to license songs for films or video games.* ...autorizar el uso de canciones en películas o juegos de video.

**Word Partnership** Usar *license* con:

N. **driver's** license, license **fees**, **hunting** license, **liquor** license, **marriage** license, **pilot's** license, **software** license 1
V. **get/obtain a** license, **renew a** license, **revoke a** license 1
ADJ. **suspended** license, **valid** license 1

**li|censed** /laɪsᵊnst/ 1 ADJ If you are **licensed to** do something, you have official permission from the government or from the authorities to do it. autorizado ❑ *There were about 250 people on board, 100 more than the ferry was licensed to carry.* Había unas 250 personas a bordo, 100 más de las autorizadas para viajar en el ferry. 2 ADJ If something that you own or use is **licensed,** you have official permission to own it or use it. registrado, autorizado ❑ *...a licensed rifle.* ...un rifle registrado.

**li|cense num|ber** (**license numbers**) N-COUNT The **license number** of a car or other road vehicle is the series of letters and numbers that are shown at the front and back of it. número de placa

**li|cense plate** (**license plates**) N-COUNT A **license plate** is a sign on the back, and in some places also on the front, of a vehicle that shows its license number. placa, chapa ❑ *...a car with Austrian license plates.* ...un coche con placas de Austria.

**lick** /lɪk/ (**licks, licking, licked**) V-T When people or animals **lick** something, they move their tongue across its surface. lamer ❑ *She licked the stamp and pressed it onto the envelope.* Lamió la estampilla y la pegó en el sobre. ● **Lick** is also a noun. lamedura, lamida ❑ *The cat took a lick of milk.* El gato dio una lamida a la leche.

**lickety-split** /lɪkətisplɪt/ ADV If you do something **lickety-split,** you do it very quickly. a toda mecha, de volada, rapidísimo [INFORMAL] ❑ *The waiter returned lickety-split with our meal.* El mesero volvió rapidísimo con nuestra comida.

**lid** /lɪd/ (**lids**) N-COUNT A **lid** is the top of a box or other container which can be removed or raised when you want to open the container. tapa, tapadera ❑ *She lifted the lid of the box.* Levantó la tapa de la caja.

**lie**
❶ POSITION OR SITUATION
❷ THINGS THAT ARE NOT TRUE

❶ **lie** /laɪ/ (**lies, lying, lay, lain**) 1 V-I If you **are lying** somewhere, you are in a horizontal position and are not standing or sitting. echarse, acostarse, estar situado, extenderse ❑ *There was a man lying on the ground.* Había un hombre echado en el piso. 2 V-I If an object **lies** in a particular place, it is in a flat position in that place. estar ❑ *The newspaper was lying on a chair.* El periódico estaba en una silla. 3 V-I If you say that a place **lies** in a particular position or direction, you mean that it is situated there. estar situado, situarse, encontrarse ❑ *The islands lie at the southern end of Florida.* Las islas están situadas en el extremo sur de Florida. 4 V-LINK You can use **lie** to say that something is or remains in a particular state or condition. For example, if something **lies forgotten,** it has been and remains forgotten. estar ❑ *The picture lay hidden in the library for over 40 years.* El cuadro estuvo escondido en la biblioteca más de 40 años. 5 V-I You can talk about where something such as a problem, solution, or fault **lies** to say what you think it consists of, involves, or is caused by. radicar, estribar, estar ❑ *Some of the blame lies with the president.* Parte de la culpa la tiene el presidente. 6 V-I You use **lie** in expressions such as **lie ahead, lie in store,** and **lie in wait** when you are talking about what someone is going to experience in the future, especially when it is something unpleasant or difficult. tener por delante ❑ *She'll need all her strength to cope with what lies ahead.* Necesitará toda su fuerza para afrontar lo que le espera.

▸ **lie around** PHR-VERB If things are left **lying around,** they are not put away but left casually somewhere where they can be seen. dejar botado, dejar tirado ❑ *People should not leave their possessions lying around.* La gente no debe dejar botadas sus pertenencias.

▸ **lie behind** PHR-VERB If you refer to what **lies behind** a situation or event, you are referring to the reason the situation exists or the event happened. haber detrás de ❑ *Worries about money lay behind their problems.* Sus problemas se derivaban de su preocupación por el dinero.

▸ **lie down** PHR-VERB When you **lie down,** you move into a horizontal position, usually in order to rest or sleep. acostarse, tumbarse, echarse ❑ *Why don't you go upstairs and lie down?* ¿Por qué no subes y te acuestas?

**Usage** **lie** and **lay**

*Lie* and *lay* are often confused. *Lie* is generally used without an object: *Please lie down. Lay* usually requires an object: *Lay your head on the pillow.*

❷ **lie** /laɪ/ (**lies, lying, lied**) 1 N-COUNT A **lie** is something that someone says or writes which they know is untrue. mentira ❑ *"Who else do you work for?" — "No one." — "That's a lie." —¿Para quién más trabajas? —Para nadie. —Mentira.* 2 V-I If someone **is lying,** they are saying something which they know is not true. mentir, decir mentiras ❑ *I know he's lying. Yo sé que está diciendo mentiras.* ● **ly|ing** N-UNCOUNT mentiras ❑ *Lying is something that I hate. Odio las mentiras.*

**Thesaurus** *lie* Ver también:

V. recline, rest; (*ant.*) stand ❶ 1 2
deceive, distort, fake, falsify, mislead ❷ 2
N. dishonesty ❷ 1

**lieu|ten|ant** /lutɛnənt/ (**lieutenants**) N-COUNT; N-TITLE; N-VOC A **lieutenant** is a junior officer in the army, navy, marines, or air force, or in the U.S. police force. teniente ❑ *Lieutenant Campbell ordered the man to stop. El teniente Campbell le ordenó al hombre que se detuviera.*

L

**lieu|ten|ant gov|er|nor** (**lieutenant governors**) 1 N-COUNT A **lieutenant governor** is an elected official who acts as the deputy of a state governor in the United States. vicegobernador o vicegobernadora 2 N-COUNT A **lieutenant governor** is an official elected by the Canadian government to act as a representative of the British king or queen in a province of Canada. lugarteniente del gobernador, lugarteniente de la gobernadora

**life** /laɪf/ (**lives** /laɪvz/) 1 N-UNCOUNT **Life** is the quality which people, animals, and plants have when they are not dead. vida, existencia ❑ *...a baby's first minutes of life. ...los primeros minutos de vida de un bebé.* 2 N-UNCOUNT You can use **life** to refer to things or groups of things which are alive. vida ❑ *Is there life on Mars? ¿Hay vida en Marte?* 3 N-COUNT Someone's **life** is their state of being alive, or the period of time during which they are alive. vida ❑ *Your life is in danger. Tu vida está en peligro.* ❑ *A nurse tried to save his life. Una enfermera trató de salvarle la vida.* ❑ *He spent the last fourteen years of his life in France. Los últimos catorce años de su vida los pasó en Francia.* 4 N-COUNT You can use **life** to refer to particular activities which people regularly do during their lives. vida ❑ *My personal life has suffered because of my career. Mi vida personal se resintió por mi carrera.* 5 N-UNCOUNT You can use **life** to refer to the things that people do and experience that are characteristic of a particular place, group, or activity. vida, forma de vida ❑ *How do you like college life? ¿Te gusta la vida universitaria?* ❑ *He loves the challenges of political life. Le encantan los retos de la vida política.* 6 N-UNCOUNT If you say that someone or something is full of **life,** you like them because they give an impression of excitement, energy, or cheerfulness. vida, vitalidad ❑ *The town was full of life and character. La ciudad tenía gran vitalidad y personalidad.* 7 N-UNCOUNT If someone is sentenced to **life,** they are sentenced to stay in prison for the rest of their life or for a very long time. de por vida, prisión perpetua [INFORMAL] ❑ *He could get life in prison, if he is found guilty. Lo podrían encerrar de por vida si lo consideran culpable.* 8 N-COUNT The **life** of something such as a machine, organization, or project is the period of time that it lasts for. vida, duración ❑ *The repairs did not increase the value or the life of the equipment. Las reparaciones no incrementaron el valor ni la duración de la máquina.* 9 PHRASE If you say that someone **is fighting for** their **life,** you mean that they are in a very serious condition and may die as a result of an accident or illness. luchar por la vida ❑ *The robbery left a man fighting for his life. El robo dejó a un hombre luchando por su vida.*
→ see **biosphere, earth**

**life pre|serv|er** (**life preservers**) N-COUNT A **life preserver** is something such as a ring or a jacket, which helps you to float when you have fallen into deep water. salvavidas

**life sci|ence** (**life sciences**) N-COUNT The **life sciences** are sciences such as zoology, botany, and anthropology which are concerned with human beings, animals, and plants. ciencias de la vida, ciencias biológicas

**life|style** /laɪfstaɪl/ (**lifestyles**) also **life-style** or **life style** 1 N-VAR The **lifestyle** of a particular person or group of people is the living conditions, behavior, and habits that are typical of them or are chosen by them. estilo de vida, tren de vida ❑ *They had a lifestyle that many people would envy. Tenían un estilo de vida que muchos envidiarían.* 2 ADJ **Lifestyle** magazines, television programs, and products are aimed at people who are interested in glamorous and successful lifestyles. estilo de vida ❑ *The footwear ads will appear this fall in fashion and lifestyle magazines. Los anuncios de calzado se publicarán este otoño en revistas de modas y de estilo de vida.*

**life support** N-UNCOUNT **Life support** is a system that is used to keep a person alive when they are very ill and cannot breathe without help. respirador artificial, máquina corazón-pulmón, equipo para mantener la vida ❑ *She was on life support for several weeks. Pasó varias semanas en un respirador artificial.*

**life|time** /laɪftaɪm/ (**lifetimes**) N-COUNT A **lifetime** is the length of time that someone is alive. vida, curso de la vida ❑ *He traveled a lot during his lifetime. Viajó mucho durante su vida.*

**lift** /lɪft/ (**lifts, lifting, lifted**) 1 V-T If you **lift** something, you move it to another position, especially upward. levantar, recoger, alzar, cargar ❑ *He lifted the bag onto his shoulder. Levantó la bolsa y se la colgó al hombro.* ● **Lift up** means the same as **lift.** levantar, recoger, alzar, cargar ❑ *She lifted the baby up and gave him to me. Cargó al bebé y me lo dio.* 2 V-T If people in authority **lift** a law or rule that prevents people from doing something, they end it. revocar, suprimir ❑ *France finally lifted its ban on importing British beef. Por fin en Francia revocaron la prohibición de importar carne de res del Reino Unido.* 3 N-COUNT If you give someone a **lift** somewhere, you take them there in your car as a favor to them. dar un aventón, dar un "ride", llevar ❑ *He had a car and often gave me a lift home. Tenía coche y muy seguido me daba un aventón a la casa.* 4 N-UNCOUNT **Lift** is the force that makes an aircraft leave the ground and stay in the air. *fuerza ascensional*

| Thesaurus | *lift* | Ver también: |
|---|---|---|
| V. | boost, hoist, pick up; (*ant.*) drop, lower, put down 1 | |

**light**
1 BRIGHTNESS OR ILLUMINATION
2 NOT GREAT IN WEIGHT, AMOUNT, OR INTENSITY
3 UNIMPORTANT OR NOT SERIOUS

1 **light** /laɪt/ (**lights, lighting, lit** or **lighted, lighter, lightest**) 1 N-UNCOUNT **Light** is the brightness that lets you see things. Light comes from sources such as the sun, moon, lamps, and fire. *luz, claridad, iluminación* ❑ *Cracks of light came through the dirty window. Por la ventana sucia se filtraban destellos de luz.* ❑ *...ultraviolet light. ...luz ultravioleta* 2 N-COUNT A **light** is something such as an electric lamp which produces light. *luz* ❑ *The janitor comes around to turn the lights out. El conserje se da su vuelta para apagar las luces.* 3 V-T If a place or object **is lit** by something, it has light shining on it. *iluminar* ❑ *The moon lit the road brightly. La luna arrojaba una luz brillante sobre el camino.* ❑ *The room was lit by only one light. Una sola luz iluminaba el cuarto.* 4 ADJ If it is **light,** the sun is providing light at the beginning or end of the day. *ser de día, haber luz, haber sol, estar claro el día* ❑ *It was still light when we arrived at Lalong Creek. Aún había luz cuando llegamos a Lalong Creek.* 5 ADJ If a room or building is **light,** it has a lot of natural light in it. *tener luz, estar iluminado* ❑ *It is a light room with tall windows. Es un cuarto con mucha luz y grandes ventanas.* • **light|ness** N-UNCOUNT *luminosidad, claridad* ❑ *...the lightness of the bedroom. ...la luminosidad de la recámara.* 6 V-T/V-I If you **light** something such as a candle or a fire, or if it **lights,** it starts burning. *prender, encender* ❑ *Stephen leaned forward to light the candle. Stephen se inclinó hacia adelante para prender la vela.* ❑ *The fire wouldn't light. El fuego no prendía.* 7 N-COUNT If something is presented in a particular **light,** it is presented so that you think about it in a particular way or so that it appears to be of a particular nature. *luz, aspecto* ❑ *He worked hard to show New York in a better light. Se esforzó mucho para mostrar a Nueva York bajo una luz favorable.* 8 → see also **lighting** 9 PHRASE If something **comes to light** or **is brought to light,** it becomes obvious or is made known to a lot of people. *salir a la luz, sacar a la luz, revelar* ❑ *Nothing about this money has come to light. Nada ha salido a la luz respecto de este dinero.* 10 PHRASE If something is possible **in the light of** particular information, it is only possible because you have this information. *a la luz de, en vista de* ❑ *People often change their opinions in the light of new information. Las personas suelen cambiar de opinión a la luz de nuevos datos.* 11 PHRASE To **shed light on, throw light on,** or **cast light on** something means to make it easier to understand, because more information is known about it. *echar luz, arrojar luz, aclarar* ❑ *No one could shed light on her secret past. Nadie podía aclarar su secreto pasado.*
→ see **color, eye, laser, ozone, telescope, wave**

▸ **light up** 1 PHR-VERB If you **light** something **up** or if it **lights up,** it becomes bright. *iluminarse, encenderse la luz, prenderse* ❑ *The coffee maker lights up when you switch it on. Cuando prendes la cafetera, se enciende la luz.* 2 PHR-VERB If your face or your eyes **light up,** you suddenly look very surprised or happy. *iluminarse* ❑ *Sue's face lit up with surprise. La cara de Sue se iluminó por la sorpresa.*

| Thesaurus | *light* | Ver también: |
|---|---|---|
| N. | brightness, glow, radiance, shine 1 1 | |
| ADJ. | bright, sunny 1 4 5 | |

2 **light** /laɪt/ (**lighter, lightest**) 1 ADJ Something that is **light** does not weigh very much. *ligero, liviano* ❑ *I'm about 30 pounds lighter than I was. Peso unos 15 kilos menos que antes.* ❑ *...weight training with light weights. ...entrenamiento con pesas ligeras.* • **light|ness** N-UNCOUNT *ligereza, lo liviano, lo ligero* ❑ *It is made of steel for lightness and strength. Es de acero, para ligereza y resistencia.* 2 ADJ Something that is **light** is not very great in amount, degree, or intensity. *ligero, escaso, poco* ❑ *It's a Sunday, with the usual light traffic in the city. Es domingo, y como siempre, hay poco tráfico en la ciudad.* ❑ *Trading on the stock exchange was very light. Los movimientos de la bolsa de valores no fueron muchos.* • **light|ly** ADV *ligeramente, poco, apenas* ❑ *Cook the onions until they are lightly browned. Fríe las cebollas a que se oscurezcan ligeramente.* 3 ADJ Something that is **light** is pale in color. *claro, pálido* ❑ *He is light haired with gray eyes. Tiene el cabello claro y los ojos grises.* ❑ *...a light green van. ...una camioneta verde pálido.* 4 ADJ **Light** work does not involve much physical effort. *ligero*

3 **light** /laɪt/ (**lighter, lightest**) 1 ADJ If you describe things such as books, music, and movies as **light,** you mean that they entertain you without making you think very deeply. *ligero, frívolo, superficial* ❑ *He doesn't like reading light novels. No le gusta leer novelas frívolas.* ❑ *...light classical music. ...música clásica ligera.* 2 ADJ If you say something in a **light** way, you sound as if you think that something is not important or serious. *a la ligera* ❑ *Talk to him in a friendly, light way about the relationship. Habla con él de la relación amistosamente, restándole importancia.* • **light|ly** ADV *ligeramente, a la ligera* ❑ *"Sure," he said lightly. —Claro —dijo a la ligera.*

**light bulb** (**light bulbs**) N-COUNT A **light bulb** is the round glass part of an electric light or lamp which light shines from. *foco, bombilla*
→ see Word Web: **light bulb**
→ see **light**

**light cream** N-UNCOUNT **Light cream** is thin cream that does not have a lot of fat in it. *crema ligera*

**light en|er|gy** N-UNCOUNT **Light energy** is energy in the form of electromagnetic waves. *energía de luz*

**light|ing** /laɪtɪŋ/ N-UNCOUNT The **lighting** in a place is the way that it is lit, or the quality of the light in it. *iluminación* ❑ *...bright fluorescent lighting. ...iluminación fluorescente brillante.* ❑ *The whole room has soft lighting. La iluminación es suave en todo el salón.*
→ see **concert, drama, photography, theater**

**light min|ute** (**light minutes**) N-COUNT A **light minute** is the distance that light travels in one minute. *minuto luz* [TECHNICAL]

## Word Web light bulb

The incandescent **light bulb** has changed little since the 1870s. It consists of a **glass** globe containing an inert gas, such as argon, some wires, and a filament. **Electricity** flows through the wires and the tungsten filament. The filament heats up and **glows**. Light bulbs aren't very efficient. They give off more heat than **light**. **Fluorescent** lights are much more efficient. They contain liquid mercury and argon gas. A layer of phosphorus covers the inside of the tube. When electricity begins to flow, the mercury becomes a gas and **emits** ultraviolet light. This causes the phosphorus coating to **shine**.

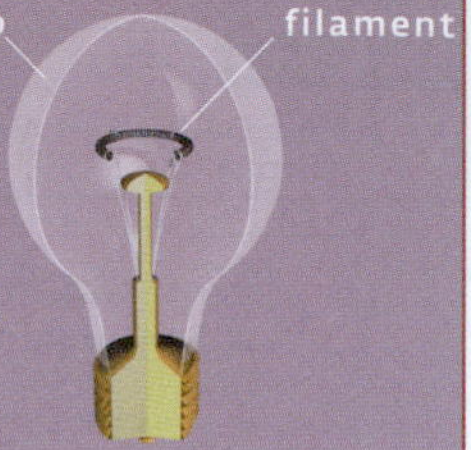


**light|ning** /laɪtnɪŋ/ **1** N-UNCOUNT **Lightning** is the very bright flashes of light in the sky that happen during thunderstorms. rayo, relámpago ❑ *One man died when he was struck by lightning.* *Un hombre cayó fulminado por un rayo.* ❑ *Another flash of lightning lit up the cave.* *Otro relámpago iluminó la gruta.* **2** ADJ **Lightning** describes things that happen very quickly or last for only a short time. como rayo, como de rayo, a gran velocidad ❑ *He drove off at lightning speed.* *Se fue manejando como rayo.*
→ see Word Web: **lightning**
→ see **storm**

**light|ning rod** (**lightning rods**) **1** N-COUNT A **lightning rod** is a long thin piece of metal on top of a building that attracts lightning and allows it to reach the ground safely. pararrayos **2** PHRASE If you say that someone **is a lightning rod for** something, you mean that they attract that thing to themselves. que atrae algo ❑ *He is a lightning rod for trouble.* *Él atrae los problemas.*

**light source** (**light sources**) N-COUNT A **light source** is any object or device that gives off light, such as the sun or an electric light bulb. fuente luminosa

**light|weight** /laɪtweɪt/ (**lightweights**) also **light-weight** **1** ADJ Something that is **lightweight** weighs less than most other things of the same type. ligero, de poco peso ❑ *...lightweight denim.* *...mezclilla ligera* **2** N-UNCOUNT **Lightweight** is a category in some sports, such as boxing, judo, or rowing, based on the weight of the athlete. peso ligero ❑ *...the junior lightweight champion.* *...el campeón junior de peso ligero.* **3** N-COUNT If you describe someone as a **lightweight**, you are critical of them because you think that they are not very important or skillful in a particular area of activity. superficial, poco serio ❑ *Critics say that she is an intellectual lightweight.* *Los críticos dicen que es una intelectual poco seria.* ● **Lightweight** is also an adjective. superficial, poco serio ❑ *Some of the discussion in the book is lightweight and unconvincing.* *Parte de lo expresado en el libro es superficial y poco convincente.*

**light year** (**light years**) **1** N-COUNT A **light year** is the distance that light travels in a year. año luz ❑ *...a star system millions of light years away.* *...un sistema estelar a millones de años luz de distancia.* **2** N-COUNT You can say that two things are **light years** apart to emphasize a very great difference or a very long distance or period of time between them. años luz, millones de años, miles de años [INFORMAL] ❑ *Our computer system is light years ahead of anyone else's.* *Nuestro sistema de computación está muchísimo más adelantado que los demás.*
→ see **galaxy**

**like**
1. PREPOSITION AND CONJUNCTION USES
2. VERB USES
3. NOUN USES AND PHRASES

**1 like** /laɪk, laɪk/ **1** PREP If you say that one person or thing is **like** another, you mean that they share some of the same qualities or features. como, a la manera de, similar ❑ *He looks like Father Christmas.* *Parece Santa Claus.* ❑ *When I was in New York City, I kept thinking, "This is just like the movies."* *Estando en la ciudad de Nueva York, no podía dejar de pensar "es como en las películas".* ❑ *It's nothing like what happened last year.* *No es en nada como lo que sucedió el año pasado.* **2** PREP If you talk about what something or someone is **like**, you are talking about their qualities or features. como, qué tal

## Word Web lightning

**Lightning** forms in storm clouds. Strong winds cause tiny **particles** within the clouds to rub together violently. This creates **positive charges** on some particles and **negative charges** on others. The negatively charged particles sink to the bottom of the cloud. There they are attracted by the positively charged surface of the earth. Gradually a large negative charge accumulates in a cloud. When it is large enough, a **bolt** of lightning strikes the earth. When a bolt branches out in several directions, the result is called **forked lightning**. Sheet lightning occurs when the bolt **discharges** within a cloud, instead of on the earth.

L

❑ *What was Bulgaria like? ¿Qué tal Bulgaria?* ❑ *What did she look like? ¿Qué tal se veía?* 3 PREP You can use **like** to introduce an example of the set of things or people that you have just mentioned. *como, por ejemplo* ❑ *...large cities like New York. ...ciudades grandes, como Nueva York.* 4 PREP If you say that someone is behaving **like** something or someone else, you mean that they are behaving in a way that is typical of that kind of thing or person. **Like** is used in this way in many fixed expressions, for example, **to cry like a baby** and **to watch someone like a hawk.** *como* ❑ *I was shaking all over, trembling like a leaf. No dejaba de moverme, temblaba como una hoja* 5 CONJ **Like** is sometimes used as a conjunction in order to say that something appears to be true when it is not. Some people consider this use to be incorrect. *que, como* ❑ *His arms are so thin that they look like they might break. Sus brazos son tan delgados, que dan la impresión de que van a romperse.* 6 CONJ **Like** is sometimes used as a conjunction in order to indicate that something happens or is done in the same way as something else. Some people consider this use to be incorrect. *como, igual* ❑ *People are walking around the park, just like they do every Sunday. La gente camina alrededor del parque, como todos los domingos.* ❑ *He spoke exactly like I did. Hablaba exactamente como yo.* 7 PREP You can use **like** in expressions such as **nothing like** to make an emphatic negative statement. *énfasis negativo* ❑ *Three hundred million dollars will be nothing like enough. Trescientos millones de dólares para nada bastarían.*

**❷ like** /laɪk/ (**likes, liking, liked**) 1 V-T If you **like** something or someone, you think they are interesting, enjoyable, or attractive. *gustar algo* ❑ *He likes baseball. A él le gusta el béisbol.* ❑ *I don't like being in crowds. No me gustan los tumultos.* ❑ *Do you like to go swimming? ¿Te gusta ir a nadar?* 2 V-T If you say that you **would like** something or **would like** to do something, you are indicating a wish or desire that you have. *quisiera* ❑ *I'd like a bath. Me gustaría darme un baño.* ❑ *Would you like to have some coffee? ¿Quieres un café?*

| **Thesaurus** | *like* | Ver también: |
|---|---|---|
| ADJ. | alike, comparable, similar ❶ 1 | |
| V. | admire, appreciate, enjoy; (ant.) dislike ❷ 1 | |

**❸ like** /laɪk/ (**likes**) 1 N-PLURAL Someone's **likes** are the things that they enjoy or find pleasant. *preferencia* ❑ *I knew all Jemma's likes and dislikes. Yo sabía todo lo que le gustaba y no le gustaba a Jemma.* 2 3 PHRASE You say **if you like** when you are making or agreeing to an offer or suggestion in a casual way. *si quieres* ❑ *You can stay here if you like. Puedes quedarte si quieres.* 4 PHRASE You say **like this, like that,** or **like so** when you are showing someone how something is done. *así, de cierto modo* ❑ *It opens and closes, like this. Se abre y se cierra, así.* 5 PHRASE You use the expression **something like** with an amount, number, or description to indicate that it is approximately accurate. *más o menos, aproximado* ❑ *They can get something like $3,000 a year. Pueden recibir unos 3,000 dólares al año.*

| **Word Link** | *hood ≈ state, condition : childhood, likelihood, manhood* |
|---|---|

**like|li|hood** /laɪklihʊd/ N-UNCOUNT The **likelihood of** something happening is how likely it is to happen. *probabilidad, posibilidd* ❑ *The likelihood of getting the disease is small. Hay pocas probabilidades de contraer la enfermedad.*

**like|ly** /laɪkli/ (**likelier, likeliest**) 1 ADJ You use **likely** to indicate that something is probably true or will probably happen in a particular situation. *probable, posible* ❑ *Experts say a "yes" vote is still the likely outcome. Los expertos dicen que todavía es posible que el voto sea positivo.* ● **Likely** is also an adverb. *probablemente, lo probable* ❑ *Profit will most likely rise by about $25 million. Lo más probable es que las utilidades se incrementen en unos 25 millones de dólares.* 2 ADJ If someone or something is **likely to** do a particular thing, they will very probably do it. *probable, posible* ❑ *The problem seems likely to continue. Es probable que el problema continúe.*

| **Word Link** | *like ≈ similar : alike, likewise, unlike* |
|---|---|

| **Word Link** | *wise ≈ in the direction or manner of : clockwise, likewise, otherwise* |
|---|---|

**like|wise** /laɪkwaɪz/ 1 ADV You use **likewise** when you are comparing two methods, states, or situations and saying that they are similar. *asimismo, así mismo, de la misma manera* ❑ *What is fair for you likewise should be fair to me. Lo que es justo para ti, también debe ser justo para mí.* 2 ADV If you do something and someone else does **likewise,** they do the same or a similar thing. *lo mismo, otro tanto* ❑ *He gave money to charity and encouraged others to do likewise. Donó dinero para una obra de caridad y animó a otros a hacer lo mismo.*

**lily** /lɪli/ (**lilies**) N-VAR A **lily** is a plant with large sweet-smelling flowers. *lirio, azucena*

**limb** /lɪm/ (**limbs**) 1 N-COUNT Your **limbs** are your arms and legs. *miembro, extremidad* ❑ *She stretched out her aching limbs. Estiró sus adoloridas extremidades.* 2 PHRASE If someone goes **out on a limb,** they do something they strongly believe in even though it is risky or extreme. *aventurarse* ❑ *I'm going to go out on a limb here and say this is good news. Me voy a arriesgar en cuanto a esto y diré que son buenas noticias.*
→ see **mammal**

**lime** /laɪm/ (**limes**) 1 N-VAR A **lime** is a round, green fruit that tastes like a lemon. *limón (verde)* ❑ *...slices of lime. ...rebanadas de limón.* 2 N-UNCOUNT **Lime** is a substance containing calcium. It is found in soil and water. *cal* ❑ *If your soil is very acidic, add lime. Si el suelo es muy ácido, ponle cal.*

**lim|it** /lɪmɪt/ (**limits, limiting, limited**) 1 N-COUNT A **limit** is the greatest amount, extent, or degree of something that is possible. *límite* ❑ *Her love for him was tested to its limits. Su amor por él fue puesto a prueba a más no poder.* ❑ *There is no limit to how much fresh fruit you can eat in a day. No hay límite en cuanto a la cantidad de fruta fresca que puedes comer al día.* 2 N-COUNT A **limit** of a particular kind is the largest or smallest amount of something such as time or money that is allowed because of a rule, law, or decision. *límite* ❑ *The three-month time limit will be over in June. El límite de tres meses se cumple en junio.* 3 V-T If you **limit** something, you prevent it

L

from becoming greater than a particular amount or degree. *limitar, restringir* ❑ *Residents must limit water use to 15,000 gallons per month. Los residentes deben limitar el consumo de agua a 15,000 galones al mes.* ● **limi|ta|tion** /lɪmɪteɪʃᵊn/ N-UNCOUNT *limitación, restricción* ❑ *...the limitation of nuclear weapons. ...la restricción de armas nucleares.* **4** V-T If you **limit yourself** to something, or if someone or something **limits** you, the number of things that you have or do is reduced. *limitarse* ❑ *Limit yourself to three meals and a snack each day. Limítate a tres comidas y una colación al día.* ● **lim|it|ing** ADJ *limitante, restrictivo* ❑ *I found the conditions very limiting. Me parece que las condiciones son muy limitantes.* **5** V-T If something **is limited to** a particular place or group of people, it exists only in that place, or is had or done only by that group. *limitarse a* ❑ *The protests were not limited to New York. Las protestas no fueron exclusivas de Nueva York.* **6** → see also **limited** **7** PHRASE If an area or a place is **off limits,** you are not allowed to go there. *de acceso prohibido* ❑ *Parts of the church are off limits to visitors. Ciertas partes de la iglesia están cerradas al público.*

**limi|ta|tion** /lɪmɪteɪʃᵊn/ (**limitations**) **1** N-VAR A **limitation on** something is a rule or decision which prevents that thing from growing or extending beyond certain limits. *limitación, restricción* ❑ *...a limitation on the amount of tax you pay in a year. ...una limitación al monto de impuestos que se pagan anualmente.* **2** N-PLURAL The **limitations** of someone or something are the things that they cannot do, or the things that they do badly. *limitaciones* ❑ *Parents often blame schools for the limitations of their children. Los padres suelen culpar a las escuelas de las limitaciones de sus hijos.* **3** N-VAR A **limitation** is a fact or situation that allows only some actions and makes others impossible. *limitación* ❑ *She has ongoing pain and limitation of movement in her arm. Le duele constantemente el brazo y casi no puede moverlo.* **4** → see also **limit**

L

**lim|it|ed** /lɪmɪtɪd/ ADJ Something that is **limited** is not very great in amount, range, or degree. *limitado, restringido* ❑ *They had only a limited amount of time to talk. Les limitaban el tiempo para hablar.*

**lim|it|ing fac|tor** (**limiting factors**) N-COUNT A **limiting factor** is a feature of the environment, such as space, sunlight or water, which is only available in small amounts and therefore limits the size of a population of animals or plants. *factor limitante*

**limp** /lɪmp/ (**limps, limping, limped, limper, limpest**) **1** V-I If a person or animal **limps,** they walk with difficulty or in an uneven way because one of their legs or feet is hurt. *cojear, caminar con dificultad* ❑ *James limps because of a hip injury. James cojea por una lesión de la cadera.* ● **Limp** is also a noun. *cojera* ❑ *Anne walks with a limp. Anne camina con dificultad.* **2** ADJ If something is **limp,** it is soft or weak when it should be firm or strong. *flácido, flojo, aguado* ❑ *...people with limp handshakes. ...personas que no aprietan la mano al saludar.* ● **limp|ly** ADV *sin fuerza, lánguido* ❑ *Flags hung limply in the still air. Las banderas colgaban inmóviles porque no había viento.*

**line**

❶ NOUN USES
❷ PHRASES
❸ VERB USES
❹ PHRASAL VERB

❶ **line** /laɪn/ (**lines**) **1** N-COUNT A **line** is a long, thin mark which is drawn or painted on a surface. *línea, raya* ❑ *Draw a line at the bottom of the page. Trace una línea en la parte inferior de la página.* ❑ *...a dotted line. ...una línea punteada.* **2** N-COUNT The **lines** on your skin, especially on your face, are long thin marks that appear there as you grow older. *arruga* ❑ *He has a large round face with deep lines. Su cara es grande y redonda, surcada por profundas arrugas.* **3** N-COUNT A **line** of people or vehicles is a number of them that are waiting one behind another or side by side. *cola, fila* ❑ *I saw a line of people waiting to get into the building. Vi a gente haciendo cola para entrar al edificio.* **4** N-COUNT An actor's **lines** are the words they speak in a play or movie. *papel, parte* ❑ *He is having trouble memorizing his lines. Le está costando trabajo memorizar su parte.* **5** N-VAR You can refer to a long piece of wire, string, or cable as a **line** when it is used for a particular purpose. *cuerda, cable* ❑ *She put her washing on the line. Colgó en el tendedero la ropa que lavó.* ❑ *...a piece of fishing-line. ...un pedazo de cuerda de pescar.* **6** N-COUNT A **line** is a route along which people or things move or are sent. *línea* ❑ *The telephone lines went dead. Las líneas telefónicas quedaron muertas.* ❑ *They've got to stay on the train all the way to the end of the line. Tienen que quedarse en el tren hasta la última estación.* **7** N-COUNT A state or county **line** is a boundary between two states or counties. *línea divisoria, límite* ❑ *...the California state line. ...el límite del estado de California.* **8** N-COUNT The particular **line** that a person has toward a problem is the attitude that they have toward it. *postura, línea* ❑ *The official company line is that we will continue as planned. La posición oficial de la empresa es que seguiremos de acuerdo con lo planeado.* **9** N-COUNT Your **line of** business or work is the kind of work that you do. *línea de negocio* [BUSINESS] ❑ *So what was your father's line of business? Así que, ¿a qué se dedicaba tu papá?* **10** → see also **bottom line, front line**
→ see **basketball, football, graph, mathematics, soccer, train**

| Thesaurus | *line* | Ver también: |
|---|---|---|
| N. | cable, rope, wire ❶ **5** | |

❷ **line** /laɪn/ (**lines**) **1** PHRASE If you **draw the line at** a particular activity, you refuse to do it, because you disapprove of it or because it is more extreme than what you normally do. *no ir más allá, poner un límite, pintar su raya* ❑ *They decided to draw the line at raising taxes. Decidieron poner un límite al incremento de impuestos.* **2** PHRASE If one thing is **in line with** another, or is brought **into line with** it, the first thing is, or becomes, similar to the second, especially in a way that has been planned or expected. *de acuerdo con, de conformidad con* ❑ *Prices go up in line with people's incomes. Los precios se incrementan en función de los ingresos de la gente.* ❑ *This brings the law into line with most medical opinion.*

*Esto pone a la ley en la misma línea que la opinión de los médicos.* **3** PHRASE If you do something **on line,** you do it using a computer or a computer network. *en línea* ❑ *They can order their books on line. Pueden solicitar sus libros en línea.* **4** → see also **online** **5** PHRASE When people **stand in line** or **wait in line,** they stand one behind the other in a line, waiting their turn for something. *hacer cola, formarse* ❑ *For the homeless, standing in line for meals is part of the daily routine. Hacer cola para comer es parte de la rutina diaria de las personas sin hogar.* **6** to **sign on the dotted line** → see **dotted**

**❸ line** /laɪn/ (**lines, lining, lined**) **1** V-T If people or things **line** a road, room, or other place, they are present in large numbers along its edges or sides. *llenar, ocupar* ❑ *Thousands of local people lined the streets. Miles de lugareños hacían valla en las calles.* **2** V-T If you **line** a wall, container, or other object, you put a layer of something such as leaves or paper on the inside surface of it in order to make it stronger, warmer, or cleaner. *forrar, recubrir* ❑ *Line the basket with a napkin before adding the cookies. Ponle una servilleta en el canastito antes de poner las galletas.* **3** → see also **lining**

**❹ line** /laɪn/ (**lines, lining, lined**)

▸ **line up** **1** PHR-VERB If people **line up** or if you **line** them **up,** they move so that they are standing in a line. *ponerse en fila, hacer cola, formarse* ❑ *The leaders lined up behind him in rows. Los líderes hicieron filas detrás de él.* ❑ *The gym teachers lined us up against the walls. Los maestros de gimnasia nos alinearon contra la pared.* **2** PHR-VERB If you **line** things **up,** you move them into a straight row. *poner en fila* ❑ *I would line up my toys and play. Haría una fila con mis juguetes para ponerme a jugar.* **3** PHR-VERB If you **line up** an event or activity, you arrange for it to happen. If you **line** someone **up** for an event or activity, you arrange for them to be available for that event or activity. *organizar, planear* ❑ *She lined up all her friends to be on the committee. Organizó a todas sus amigas para que estuvieran en el comité.* **4** → see also **lineup**

**lin|ear equa|tion** (**linear equations**) N-COUNT A **linear equation** is a mathematical equation that contains linear expressions. *ecuación lineal* [TECHNICAL]

**lin|ear ex|pres|sion** (**linear expressions**) N-COUNT A **linear expression** is a mathematical expression that contains a variable and does not contain any exponents such as squared or cubed numbers. *expresión lineal* [TECHNICAL]

**lin|ear per|spec|tive** (**linear perspectives**) N-VAR **Linear perspective** is a technique that is used in painting and drawing to create the appearance of three dimensions on a flat surface. *perspectiva lineal* [TECHNICAL]

**line di|rec|tion** (**line directions**) N-VAR **Line direction** is the direction in which a line is drawn or painted, for example vertically or horizontally. *dirección lineal*

**line drive** (**line drives**) N-COUNT In baseball, a **line drive** is a ball that is hit hard and travels straight and close to the ground. *recta* ❑ *...a line drive into the left-field corner. ...una recta hacia el rincón del jardín izquierdo.*

**line graph** (**line graphs**) N-COUNT A **line graph** is a graph in which the data are represented by points connected by one or more lines. *gráfica lineal* → see **chart**

**line|man** /laɪnmən/ (**linemen**) N-COUNT In football, a **lineman** is one of the players on the line of scrimmage at the start of each play. *delantero* ❑ *He is a defensive lineman for the Atlanta Falcons. Juega como defensa delantera de los Halcones de Atlanta.*

**lin|en** /lɪnɪn/ (**linens**) N-VAR **Linen** is a kind of cloth that is made from a plant called flax. *lino* ❑ *...a white linen suit. ...un traje blanco de lino.*

**line of credit** (**lines of credit**) N-COUNT A **line of credit** is the same as a **credit line.** *línea de crédito*

**line of scrim|mage** N-SING In football, **the line of scrimmage** is an imaginary line on either side of which the offense and defense line up. *línea de scrimmage* ❑ *The Bears stacked the line of scrimmage with extra defenders to stop the run. Los Osos reforzaron la línea de scrimmage con defensores extra para detener la carrera.*

**line qual|ity** (**line qualities**) N-VAR **Line quality** is all the characteristics of a drawn or painted line, such as its direction, darkness, and thickness. *características de la línea*

**lin|er** /laɪnər/ (**liners**) N-COUNT A **liner** is a large ship in which people travel long distances, especially on vacation. *barco de pasajeros* ❑ *...luxury ocean liners. ...lujosos transatlánticos de pasajeros.* → see **ship**

**lin|er note** (**liner notes**) N-COUNT The **liner notes** on CD jackets are short pieces of writing that tell you something about the CD or the musicians playing on the CD. *comentarios de la funda del CD*

**line|up** /laɪnʌp/ (**lineups**) N-COUNT A **lineup** is a group of people or a series of things that have been gathered together to be part of a particular event. *integrantes* ❑ *...a new show with a great lineup of musicians. ...un nuevo espectáculo con muchos músicos.*

**lin|ger** /lɪŋgər/ (**lingers, lingering, lingered**) **1** V-I When something such as an idea, feeling, or illness **lingers,** it continues to exist for a long time. *quedarse, persistir* ❑ *The scent of her perfume lingered on in the room. El aroma de su perfume persistía en el salón.* ❑ *He was ashamed. That feeling lingered for some time. Estaba avergonzado; esa sensación duró bastante tiempo.* **2** V-I If you **linger** somewhere, you stay there for a longer time than is necessary. *quedarse, tardar en irse* ❑ *Customers are welcome to linger over coffee until around midnight. Los clientes pueden prolongar la sobremesa y el café hasta la medianoche.*

**lin|gui|ne** /lɪŋgwini/ also **linguini** N-UNCOUNT **Linguine** is a kind of pasta in the shape of thin, flat strands. *linguine*

**lin|guis|tics** /lɪŋgwɪstɪks/ (**linguistic**) **1** N-PLURAL **Linguistics** is the study of the way in which language works. *lingüística* ❑ *...courses in linguistics. ...clases de lingüística.* **2** ADJ **Linguistic** abilities or ideas relate to language or linguistics. *lingüístico* ❑ *...linguistic skills. ...habilidades lingüísticas.*

**lin|ing** /laɪnɪŋ/ (**linings**) **1** N-VAR The **lining** of something such as a piece of clothing or a curtain is a layer of cloth attached to the inside of it in order to make it thicker or warmer, or in order to make it hang better. forro, revestimiento ❑ *...a black jacket with a red lining.* *...un saco negro con forro rojo.* **2** N-COUNT The **lining** of your stomach or other organ is a layer of tissue on the inside of it. pared interior **3** → see also **line**

**link** /lɪŋk/ (**links, linking, linked**) **1** N-COUNT If there is a **link between** two things or situations, there is a relationship between them, for example, because one thing causes or affects the other. vínculo, relación, eslabón, conexión ❑ *...the link between fast food and being overweight.* *...la relación entre la comida rápida y el sobrepeso.* ● **Link** is also a verb. vincular, conectar, relacionar ❑ *Studies have linked television violence with aggressive behavior in children.* *Los investigadores han relacionado la violencia de la televisión con el comportamiento agresivo de los niños.* **2** N-COUNT A **link between** two things or places is a physical connection between them. vínculo, unión, conexión ❑ *...the railroad link between Boston and New York.* *...el enlace ferroviario entre Boston y Nueva York.* ● **Link** is also a verb. vincular, unir, conectar ❑ *The Rama Road links the capital, Managua, with the Caribbean coast.* *La carretera Rama une la capital, Managua, con la costa del Caribe.* **3** N-COUNT A **link** between people, organizations, or places is a connection between them. relación, vínculo ❑ *Kiev hopes to develop close links with Bonn.* *Kiev espera desarrollar vínculos estrechos con Bonn.* ❑ *She was my only link with the past.* *Ella era lo único que me conectaba con el pasado.* ❑ *The Red Cross was created to provide a link between soldiers in battle and their families at home.* *La Cruz Roja se creó como vínculo entre los soldados combatientes y sus familias, en su país de origen.* **4** V-T If you **link** one person or thing to another, you claim that there is a relationship or connection between them. relacionar ❑ *The DNA evidence linked him to the crime.* *La prueba del ADN lo relacionó con el crimen.* **5** N-COUNT In computing, a **link** is a connection between different documents, or between different parts of the same document, using hypertext. link, enlace, vínculo ❑ *The website has links to other tourism sites.* *El sitio web tiene vínculos con otros sitios de turismo.* ● **Link** is also a verb. vincular, enlazar ❑ *Hypertext is used to link Internet documents.* *El hipertexto se utiliza para vincular documentos de Internet.* **6** N-COUNT A **link** is one of the rings in a chain. eslabón ❑ *...a chain of heavy gold links.* *...una cadena de oro de eslabones pesados.* **7** V-T If you **link** one thing with another, you join them by putting one thing through the other. enlazar ❑ *She linked her arm through his.* *Ella lo tomó del brazo.*

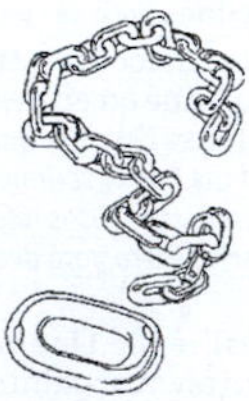

link

▸ **link up** **1** PHR-VERB If you **link up with** someone, you join them for a particular purpose. reunirse, encontrarse ❑ *I linked up with them on the walk.* *Me encontré con ellos en el camino.* **2** PHR-VERB If one thing **is linked up to** another, the two things are connected to each other. conectar, enlazar ❑ *The machine was linked up to a computer.* *La máquina estaba conectada a una computadora.*

**Word Partnership** Usar *link* con:

| | |
|---|---|
| ADJ. | **direct** link, **possible** link, **vital** link **1**–**3** **5** |
| | **strong/weak** link **1**–**3** **6** |
| V. | **establish a** link, **find a** link **1**–**3** |
| | **attempt to** link **1** **2** **4** **5** **7** |

**lint** /lɪnt/ N-UNCOUNT **Lint** is small unwanted threads or fibers that collect on clothes. pelusa, hilacho

**lion** /laɪən/ (**lions**) N-COUNT A **lion** is a large wild member of the cat family that is found in Africa. Lions have yellowish fur, and male lions have long hair on their head and neck. león
→ see **carnivore**

**lip** /lɪp/ (**lips**) N-COUNT Your **lips** are the two outer parts of the edge of your mouth. labio ❑ *He kissed her gently on the lips.* *La besó suavemente en los labios.*
→ see **face, kiss**

**lip|id** /lɪpɪd, laɪp-/ (**lipids**) N-COUNT **Lipids** are fatty substances that do not dissolve in water and are found in living cells. lípidos [TECHNICAL]

**lip|stick** /lɪpstɪk/ (**lipsticks**) N-VAR **Lipstick** is a colored substance in the form of a stick which women put on their lips. bilé, pintura de labios, lápiz de labios, labial, pintalabios, barra de labios ❑ *She was wearing red lipstick.* *Se pintó de rojo los labios.*
→ see **makeup**

**liq|uid** /lɪkwɪd/ (**liquids**) N-VAR A **liquid** is a substance which is not solid but which flows and can be poured, for example, water. líquido ❑ *Drink plenty of liquid.* *Beba muchos líquidos.*
→ see **matter**

**liq|uor** /lɪkər/ (**liquors**) N-VAR Strong alcoholic drinks such as whiskey, vodka, and gin can be referred to as **liquor**. bebida alcohólica, alcohol, bebida, bebida espirituosa ❑ *The room was filled with cases of liquor.* *El cuarto estaba lleno de cajas de bebidas alcohólicas.*

**liq|uor store** (**liquor stores**) N-COUNT A **liquor store** is a store which sells beer, wine, and other alcoholic drinks. licorería, tienda de vinos y licores

**list** /lɪst/ (**lists, listing, listed**) **1** N-COUNT A **list** of things such as names or addresses is a set of them which all belong to a particular category, written down one below the other. lista, relación ❑ *...a shopping list.* *...una lista de compras* ❑ *There were six names on the list.* *En la lista había seis nombres.* **2** V-T To **list** several things such as reasons or names means to write or say them one after another, usually in a particular order. hacer una lista, enumerar ❑ *The students were asked to list the sports they liked best.* *Se pidió a los estudiantes que hicieran una lista de deportes preferidos.*

L

**Word Partnership** Usar *list* con:

V. **add *someone/something* to a** list, list **includes**, **make a** list 1
N. list **of candidates**, list **of demands**, **guest** list, list **of ingredients**, list **of items**, list **of names**, **price** list, list **of questions**, **reading** list, list **of things**, **wine** list, **wish** list, list **of words** 1
ADJ. **complete** list, **disabled** list, **injured** list, **long** list, **short** list 1

**lis|ten** /lɪsᵊn/ (**listens, listening, listened**) 1 V-I If you **listen to** someone who is talking or **to** a sound, you give your attention to them or it. *oír, escuchar* ❑ *He spent his time listening to the radio.* *Se pasaba el tiempo oyendo el radio.* • **lis|ten|er** N-COUNT (**listeners**) *oyente, escucha, radioescucha* ❑ *A few listeners fell asleep while the president was speaking.* *Algunos oyentes se durmieron mientras el presidente hablaba.* 2 V-I If you **listen for** a sound, you keep alert and are ready to hear it if it occurs. *estar atento, prestar atención* ❑ *We listened for footsteps.* *Estábamos atentos, por si oíamos pasos.* 3 V-I If you **listen to** someone, you do what they advise you to do, or you believe them. *hacer caso, oír razones* ❑ *Anne, please listen to me this time.* *Anne, por favor, esta vez hazme caso.* 4 CONVENTION You say **listen** when you want someone to pay attention to you because you are going to say something. *hacer caso, oír razones* ❑ *Listen, there's something I should warn you about.* *Escúchame, tengo que hacerte una advertencia.* 5 CONVENTION You say **listen up** when you want someone to listen to what you are going to say. *escuchar* [SPOKEN] ❑ *Okay, listen up, guys. We've got to talk a little about how you look.* *Muy bien, escúchenme muchachos. Tenemos que hablar un poco sobre su aspecto.*

▸ **listen in** PHR-VERB If you **listen in** to a private conversation, you secretly listen to it. *escuchar a escondidas, espiar una conversación* ❑ *He was sure that someone was listening in on his phone calls.* *Estaba seguro de que alguien escuchaba sus llamadas telefónicas.*

**Thesaurus** *listen* Ver también:

V. catch, pick up, tune in; (*ant.*) ignore 1
heed, mind 3

**Word Partnership** Usar *listen* con:

V. listen **to *someone's* voice** 1
**sit up and** listen, **willing to** listen 1
ADV. listen **carefully**, listen **closely** 1

**lis|ten|er** /lɪsənər, lɪsnər/ (**listeners**) 1 N-COUNT A **listener** is a person who listens to the radio or to a particular radio program. *radioescucha, oyente* ❑ *I'm a regular listener to her show.* *Oigo regularmente su programa.* 2 → see also **listen**
→ see **radio, transportation**

**list|serv** /lɪstsɜrv/ (**listservs**) N-COUNT A **listserv** is a computerized list of names and e-mail addresses that a company or organization keeps, so that they can send people e-mails containing information or advertisements. *listserv, lista de correo*

**li|ter** /lɪtər/ (**liters**) N-COUNT A **liter** is a metric unit of volume that is a thousand cubic centimeters. It is equal to 2.11 pints. *litro* ❑ *...a 13-thousand liter water tank.* *...un tanque de 13,000 litros de agua.* ❑ *It costs eight cents a liter.* *Cuesta ocho centavos el litro.*
→ see **measurement**

**Word Link** *liter ≈ letter : illiterate, literally, literature*

**lit|er|al|ly** /lɪtərəli/ ADV You can use **literally** to emphasize an exaggeration. Some careful speakers of English think that this use is incorrect. *literalmente* ❑ *The view is literally breathtaking.* *La vista es literalmente asombrosa.*

**lit|er|ary** /lɪtərɛri/ 1 ADJ **Literary** means connected with literature. *literario* ❑ *...literary criticism.* *...crítica literaria.* ❑ *She's the literary editor of the "Sunday Review."* *Es la editora literaria de "Sunday Review".* 2 ADJ **Literary** words and expressions are often unusual in some way and are used to create a special effect in a piece of writing such as a poem, speech, or novel. *literario*

**lit|er|ary analy|sis** N-UNCOUNT **Literary analysis** is the academic study of the techniques used in the creation of literature. *análisis literario*

**lit|er|ary criti|cism** N-UNCOUNT **Literary criticism** is the analysis and judgment of works of literature. *crítica literaria*

**lit|era|ture** /lɪtərətʃər, -tʃʊər/ 1 N-UNCOUNT Novels, plays, and poetry are referred to as **literature**, especially when they are considered to be good or important. *literatura* ❑ *...classic works of literature.* *...obras clásicas de la literatura* 2 N-UNCOUNT **Literature** is written information produced by people who want to sell you something or give you advice. *impresos, información* ❑ *I am sending you literature from two other companies.* *Le mando información de otras dos empresas.*
→ see **genre**

**litho|sphere** /lɪθəsfɪər/ N-SING **The lithosphere** is the outer layer of the Earth's surface, consisting of the crust and the outer mantle. *litosfera, litósfera* [TECHNICAL]

litter

**lit|ter** /lɪtər/ (**litters, littering, littered**) 1 N-UNCOUNT **Litter** is garbage or trash that is left lying around. *basura, tiradero* ❑ *If you see litter in the corridor, pick it up.* *Si ves basura en el corredor, recógela.* 2 V-T If a number of things **litter** a place, they are scattered around it or over it. *ensuciar, tirar basura* ❑ *Broken glass litters the sidewalk.* *La banqueta está llena de vidrios rotos* • **lit|tered** ADJ *desordenado, sucio* ❑ *The room was littered with toys.* *Había juguetes regados por el cuarto.* 3 ADJ If something is **littered with** things, it contains many examples of it. *lleno de* ❑ *History is littered with war plans that went wrong.* *La historia está plagada de planes de guerra que no funcionaron.*

**Thesaurus** *litter* Ver también:

N. clutter, debris, garbage, trash 1
V. clutter, scatter 2

L

**litter|bug** /lɪtərbʌg/ (**litterbugs**) N-COUNT If you refer to someone as a **litterbug**, you disapprove of the fact that they drop litter in public places. *alguien que tira basura en la calle* ❑ *...a city full of litterbugs.* *...una ciudad que se caracteriza por tiraderos de basura en lugares públicos.*

**little**
❶ DETERMINER, QUANTIFIER, AND ADVERB USES
❷ ADJECTIVE USES

**❶ lit|tle** /lɪtᵊl/ **1** DET You use **little** to indicate that there is only a very small amount of something. *poco, escaso* ❑ *I had little money and little free time.* *Tenía poco dinero y poco tiempo libre.* ❑ *I get very little sleep these days.* *Estos días he dormido poco.* ● **Little** is also a quantifier. *poco* ❑ *Little of the existing housing is of good enough quality.* *En pocos casos las viviendas son de regular calidad.* ● **Little** is also a pronoun. *poco* ❑ *He ate little, and drank less.* *Comió poco, y bebió menos.* ❑ *In general, employers do little to help the single working mother.* *En general, los patrones hacen poco por ayudar a las madres solteras que trabajan.* **2** ADV **Little** means not very often or to only a small extent. *poco* ❑ *They spoke very little.* *Hablaron muy poco.* **3** DET **A little** of something is a small amount of it. *algo, un poco* ❑ *Mrs. Patel needs a little help getting her groceries home.* *La Sra. Patel necesita algo de ayuda para llevar su compra a casa.* ❑ *A little sugar in your diet does no harm.* *Un poco de azúcar en la dieta no hace daño.* ● **Little** is also a pronoun. *poco* ❑ *They get paid for it. Not much. Just a little.* *Les pagan por eso, no mucho, sólo un poquito.* ● **Little** is also a quantifier. *poco* ❑ *Pour a little of the sauce over the chicken.* *Ponle un poco de salsa al pollo.* **4** ADV If you do something **a little,** you do it for a short time. *por corto tiempo* ❑ *He walked a little by himself.* *Caminó solo por un rato.* **5** ADV **A little** or **a little bit** means to a small extent or degree. *un poco* ❑ *He complained a little of a pain between his shoulders.* *Se quejó un poco de un dolor entre los hombros.* ❑ *He was a little bit afraid of the dog.* *Le tenía un poco de miedo al perro.*

**❷ lit|tle** /lɪtᵊl/ (**littler, littlest**)

The comparative **littler** and the superlative **littlest** are sometimes used in spoken English for meanings **1** and **2**, but otherwise the comparative and superlative forms of the adjective **little** are not used.

**1** ADJ **Little** things are small in size. **Little** is slightly more informal than **small**. *pequeño, chico* ❑ *We sat around a little table, eating.* *Nos sentamos a comer en torno a una mesa pequeña.* **2** ADJ **A little** distance, period of time, or event is short in length. *un poco* ❑ *Go down the road a little way, turn left, and cross the bridge.* *Sigue por el camino un poquito, da vuelta a la izquierda y cruza el puente.* ❑ *Why don't we wait a little while and see what happens?* *¿Por qué no esperamos un poco y vemos qué pasa?* **3** ADJ You use **little** to indicate that something is not serious or important. *sin importancia, insignificante* ❑ *...annoying little habits.* *...hábitos molestos.*

**Thesaurus** *little* Ver también:

DET. bit, dab, hint, touch, trace ❶ **1** **3**
ADJ. miniature, petite, slight, small, young; (*ant.*) big ❷ **1**
casual, insignificant, minor, small, unimportant; (*ant.*) important ❷ **3**

**lit|to|ral zone** /lɪtərəl zoʊn/ (**littoral zones**) N-COUNT The **littoral zone** is the area along the edge of a pond, lake or sea. *litoral* [TECHNICAL]

**live**
❶ VERB USES
❷ ADJECTIVE USES

**❶ live** /lɪv/ (**lives, living, lived**) **1** V-I If someone **lives** in a particular place or with a particular person, their home is in that place or with that person. *vivir, habitar* ❑ *She lived there for 10 years.* *Vivió ahí durante 10 años.* ❑ *Where do you live?* *¿Dónde vives?* **2** V-T/V-I If you say that someone **lives** in particular circumstances or that they **live** a particular kind of life, you mean that they are in those circumstances or that they have that kind of life. *vivir* ❑ *We live very well.* *Vivimos muy bien* ❑ *She lived a life of luxury in Paris.* *Llevó una vida de lujo en París.* ❑ *...people living a hundred years ago.* *...los que vivieron hace cien años.* **3** V-I If you say that someone **lives for** a particular thing, you mean that it is the most important thing in their life. *vivir para* ❑ *He lived for his work.* *Vivió para trabajar.* **4** V-T/V-I To **live** means to be alive. If someone **lives to** a particular age, they stay alive until they are that age. *estar vivo, vivir* ❑ *He's very ill and will not live long.* *Está muy enfermo y no va a vivir mucho.* ❑ *He lived to be 103.* *Vivió a los 103 años.* **5** V-I If people **live by** doing a particular activity, they get the money, food, or clothing they need by doing that activity. *vivir de* ❑ *...the last people to live by hunting.* *...los últimos que vivieron de la cacería.* **6** → see also **living** **7** PHRASE If you **live it up,** you have a very enjoyable and exciting time. *darse la gran vida* [INFORMAL] ❑ *There is no reason why you shouldn't live it up sometimes.* *No veo por qué no te puedas dar la gran vida de vez en cuando.* **8** to **live hand to mouth** → see **hand**

▸ **live down** PHR-VERB If you are unable to **live down** a mistake, failure, or bad reputation, you are unable to make people forget about it. *hacer olvidar* ❑ *You can't live down a mistake like this.* *No puedes hacer que se olviden de un error así.*

▸ **live off** PHR-VERB If you **live off** another person, you rely on them to provide you with money. *vivir de* ❑ *He lived off his father.* *Vivía a costa de su padre.*

▸ **live on** or **live off** **1** PHR-VERB If you **live on** or **live off** a particular amount of money, you have that amount of money to buy things. *vivir con* ❑ *They are trying to live on $100 a week.* *Están tratando de vivir con 100 dólares a la semana.* **2** PHR-VERB If an animal **lives on** or **lives off** a particular food, this is the kind of food that it eats. *vivir de* ❑ *The fish live on smaller fish.* *Estos peces se alimentan de peces más pequeños.*

▸ **live up to** PHR-VERB If someone or something **lives up to** what they were expected to be, they are as good as they were expected to be. *estar a la altura de, cumplir con* ❑ *Sales have not lived up to expectations* this year. Este año las ventas no han sido lo esperado.

❷ **live** /laɪv/ **1** ADJ **Live** animals or plants are alive, rather than being dead or artificial. vivo ❑ *...a protest against the company's tests on live animals.* ...una protesta en contra de que la compañía experimente en animales vivos. **2** ADJ A **live** television or radio program is one in which an event or performance is broadcast at the time that it happens. en vivo, en directo ❑ *They watch all the live games.* Ven todos los juegos en vivo. ● **Live** is also an adverb. en vivo ❑ *The game was broadcast live in 50 countries.* El juego fue transmitido en directo en 50 países. **3** ADJ A **live** performance is given in front of an audience, rather than being recorded. vivo, en vivo ❑ *...live music.* ...música viva. ❑ *A live audience will ask the questions.* El público presente hará las preguntas. ● **Live** is also an adverb. en vivo ❑ *Kat Johnson has been playing live with her new band.* Kat Johnson ha estado tocando en vivo con su nueva banda. **4** ADJ A **live** wire or piece of electrical equipment is directly connected to a source of electricity. con corriente, cargado ❑ *The plug broke, showing live wires.* El enchufe se rompió y se veían los cables vivos.

**Thesaurus** *live* Ver también:

| | |
|---|---|
| V. | dwell, inhabit, occupy, reside ❶ **1**<br>manage, subsist, survive ❶ **2** **5**<br>exist ❶ **4** |
| ADJ. | active, alive, living, vigorous ❷ **1** |

**live|ly** /laɪvli/ (**livelier, liveliest**) **1** ADJ You can describe someone as **lively** when they behave in an enthusiastic and cheerful way. vivaz, animado, bullicioso ❑ *She has a lively personality.* Tiene una personalidad muy entusiasta. ● **live|li|ness** N-UNCOUNT vivacidad, animación ❑ *The first thing you notice about him is his liveliness.* Lo primero que notas en él es su vivacidad. **2** ADJ A **lively** event or a **lively** discussion, for example, has lots of interesting and exciting things happening or being said in it. animado, vigoroso ❑ *...a lively debate.* ...un debate acalorado. **3** ADJ Someone who has a **lively** mind is intelligent and interested in a lot of different things. vivaz ❑ *She was an intelligent girl with a lively mind.* Era una chica inteligente, de mente despierta.

**Word Partnership** Usar *lively* con:

| | |
|---|---|
| ADV. | **very** lively **1** – **3** |
| N. | lively **atmosphere**, lively **conversation**, lively **debate**, lively **discussion**, lively **music**, lively **performance** **2**<br>lively **imagination**, lively **interest**, lively **sense of humor** **3** |

**liv|er** /lɪvər/ (**livers**) **1** N-COUNT Your **liver** is a large organ in your body which processes your blood and helps to clean unwanted substances out of it. hígado **2** N-VAR **Liver** is the liver of some animals, especially lambs, pigs, and cows, which is cooked and eaten. hígado ❑ *...grilled calves' liver.* ...hígado de ternera a la parrilla.

**liv|er|wort** /lɪvərwɜrt, -wɔrt/ (**liverworts**) N-COUNT A **liverwort** is a plant with no leaves or stem that grows in wet places and resembles seaweed or moss. hepática, empeine

**lives**

Pronounced /laɪvz/ for meaning **1**, and /lɪvz/ for meaning **2**.

**1** **Lives** is the plural of **life**. plural de *life* **2** **Lives** is the third person singular form of **live**. tercera persona singular de *live*

**live|stock** /laɪvstɒk/ N-UNCOUNT Animals such as cattle and sheep which are kept on a farm are referred to as **livestock**. ganado, ganadería, res ❑ *The heavy rains killed a lot of livestock.* Muchas reses murieron a causa de las intensas lluvias.
→ see **barn**

**liv|ing** /lɪvɪŋ/ (**livings**) **1** N-COUNT The work that you do for a **living** is the work that you do in order to earn the money that you need. sustento, medios de vida ❑ *Dad never talked about what he did for a living.* Papá nunca hablaba de lo que hacía para ganarse la vida. **2** N-UNCOUNT You use **living** when you are talking about the quality of people's daily lives. forma de vida ❑ *She believes in healthy living.* Ella cree en un estilo de vida saludable.

**liv|ing room** (**living rooms**) also **living-room** N-COUNT The **living room** in a house is the room where people sit and relax. sala ❑ *We were sitting on the couch in the living room watching TV.* Estábamos sentados en el sillón de la sala, viendo la tele.
→ see **house**

**liz|ard** /lɪzərd/ (**lizards**) N-COUNT A **lizard** is a reptile with short legs and a long tail. lagartija, lagarto
→ see **desert**

**load** /loʊd/ (**loads, loading, loaded**) **1** V-T If you **load** a vehicle or a container, you put a large quantity of things into it. cargar, llenar ❑ *The men finished loading the truck.* Los hombres acabaron de cargar el camión. ❑ *Mr. Dambar loaded his plate with food.* El Sr. Dambar llenó su plato de comida. **2** N-COUNT A **load** is something, usually a large quantity or heavy object, which is being carried. carga, peso ❑ *This car is easy to drive and takes a big load.* Este carro es fácil de manejar y aguanta mucho peso. **3** QUANT If you refer to **a load of** people or things or **loads of** them, you are emphasizing that there are a lot of them. mucho, gran número [INFORMAL] ❑ *I've got loads of money.* Tengo montones de dinero. ❑ *...a load of kids.* ...un montón de niños. **4** V-T When someone **loads** a weapon such as a gun, they put a bullet or missile in it so that it is ready to use. cargar ❑ *I knew how to load and handle a gun.* Yo sabía como cargar y usar un arma. ❑ *He carried a loaded gun.* Llevaba un arma cargada. **5** V-T To **load** a camera or other piece of equipment means to put film, tape, or data into it so that it is ready to use. cargar ❑ *A photographer from the newspaper was loading his camera with film.* Un fotógrafo del periódico estaba poniéndole rollo a su cámara. **6** N-COUNT A **load** is any electrical device that is connected to a source of electricity such as a generator or circuit. carga [TECHNICAL] **7** N-VAR A river's **load** is the sediment and other material that it carries with it. carga [TECHNICAL] **8** → see also **loaded**
→ see **photography**

**Thesaurus** *load* Ver también:

V. arrange, fill, pack, pile up, stack 1
N. bundle, cargo, freight, haul, shipment 2

**Word Partnership** Usar *load* con:

N. load **a truck** 1
ADJ. **big** load, **full** load, **heavy** load 2
V. **carry a** load, **handle a** load, **lighten a** load, **take on a** load 2

**load|ed** /loʊdɪd/ 1 ADJ A **loaded** question or word has more meaning or purpose than it appears to have, because the person who uses it hopes it will cause people to respond in a particular way. *tendencioso* ❑ *That's a loaded question. Ésa es una pregunta tendenciosa.* 2 ADJ If a place or object is **loaded with** things, it has very many of them in it or it is full of them. *cargado de, lleno de* ❑ *...a tray loaded with cups. ...una charola con tazas.* ❑ *The store was loaded with jewelry. La tienda estaba repleta de joyas.* 3 ADJ If you say that something is **loaded in favor of** someone, you mean it works unfairly to their advantage. If you say it is **loaded against** them, you mean it works unfairly to their disadvantage. *inclinado, cargado* ❑ *The education system is loaded in favor of the rich. El sistema educativo se inclina a favor de los ricos.*

L

**loaf** /loʊf/ (**loaves**) N-COUNT A **loaf** of bread is bread which has been shaped and baked in one piece and can be cut into slices. *hogaza, barra, baguette*
→ see **bread**

**loam** /loʊm/ N-UNCOUNT **Loam** is soil that is good for growing crops and plants in because it contains a lot of decayed vegetable matter and does not contain too much sand or clay. *tierra negra*

**loan** /loʊn/ (**loans, loaning, loaned**) 1 N-COUNT A **loan** is a sum of money that you borrow. *préstamo, crédito, empréstito* ❑ *She didn't have enough money to buy the car, so she got a loan. No le alcanzaba el dinero para comprar el coche y pidió un préstamo.* 2 → see also **bridge loan** 3 N-SING If someone gives you a **loan of** something, you borrow it from them. *préstamo* ❑ *I need a loan of a bike for a few weeks. Necesito que me presten una bici durante unas semanas.* 4 V-T If you **loan** something to someone, you lend it to them. *prestar* ❑ *He offered to loan us his car. Nos ofreció prestarnos su coche.* 5 PHRASE If something is **on loan,** it has been borrowed. *prestado* ❑ *...paintings on loan from the Metropolitan Museum. ...pinturas prestadas por el Metropolitan Museum.*

**Word Partnership** Usar *loan* con:

N. loan **agreement**, loan **application**, **bank** loan, **home** loan, **interest on a** loan, **mortgage** loan, loan **payment/repayment**, **savings and** loan, **student** loan 1
V. **apply for a** loan, **get/receive a** loan, **make a** loan, **pay off a** loan, **repay a** loan 1

**loaves** /loʊvz/ **Loaves** is the plural of **loaf**. *plural de loaf*

**lob|by** /lɒbi/ (**lobbies, lobbying, lobbied**) 1 V-T/V-I If you **lobby** someone such as a member of a government or council, you try to persuade them that a particular law should be changed or that a particular thing should be done. *cabildear, buscar aprobación, presionar* ❑ *Mr. Bass lobbied city officials for money to build a community center. El Sr. Bass trató de conseguir dinero con funcionarios de la ciudad para construir un centro comunitario.* ❑ *The group lobbies for women's rights. El grupo cabildea en favor de los derechos de las mujeres.* 2 N-COUNT A **lobby** is a group of people who represent a particular organization or campaign, and try to persuade a government or council to help or support them. *cabilderos, grupo de pesión* ❑ *The American Association of Retired Persons is one of the most powerful lobbies in the United States. La Asociación Americana de Personas Jubiladas es uno de los grupos de presión más poderosos de los Estados Unidos.* 3 N-COUNT In a hotel or other large building, the **lobby** is the area near the entrance that usually has corridors and staircases leading off it. *vestíbulo, hall, entrada* ❑ *I met her in the lobby of the museum. Me encontré con ella en el vestíbulo del museo.*

**lobe** /loʊb/ (**lobes**) N-COUNT The **lobe** of your ear is the soft, fleshy part at the bottom. *lóbulo*

**lob|ster** /lɒbstər/ (**lobsters**) N-VAR A **lobster** is a sea creature that has a hard shell, two large claws, and eight legs. *langosta* ❑ *She sold me two live lobsters. Me vendió dos langostas vivas.* ● **Lobster** is the flesh of a lobster eaten as food. *langosta* ❑ *...lobster on a bed of fresh vegetables. ...langosta sobre verduras frescas.*
→ see **shellfish**

lobster

**lo|cal** /loʊkᵊl/ (**locals**) ADJ **Local** means existing in or belonging to the area where you live, or to the area that you are talking about. *local* ❑ *...the local paper. ...el periódico local* ❑ *Some local residents joined the students' protest. Algunos residentes locales se unieron a la protesta de los estudiantes.* ● The **locals** are local people. *vecinos del lugar, habitantes* ❑ *Camping is a great way to meet the locals. El campismo es una buena manera de conocer a los lugareños.* ● **lo|cal|ly** ADV *localmente, en la localidad* ❑ *She bought her clothes locally. Ella compraba su ropa en la ciudad.*

**Word Partnership** Usar *local* con:

N. local **area**, local **artist**, local **business**, local **community**, local **customs**, local **government**, local **group**, local **hospital**, local **library**, local **news**, local **office**, local **officials**, local **newspaper**, local **people**, local ***phone*** **call**, local **police**, local **politicians**, local **politics**, local **residents**, local **restaurant**, local **store**

**lo|cal col|or** N-UNCOUNT **Local color** is used to refer to customs, traditions, dress, and other things which give a place or period of history its own particular character. *color local* ❑ *There's plenty of local color in the book. Hay mucho color local en el libro.*

Picture Dictionary
location
The squirrel is above/over the bench.
The squirrel is in the tree.
The squirrel is on the bench.
The squirrel is between the bench and the tree.
The squirrel is behind the bench.
The squirrel is under/underneath the bench.
The squirrel is in front of the bench.

**lo|cal gov|ern|ment** N-UNCOUNT **Local government** is the system of electing representatives to be responsible for the administration of public services and facilities in a particular area. gobierno local

**lo|cate** /loʊkeɪt/ (**locates, locating, located**) **1** V-T If you **locate** something or someone, you find out where they are. localizar, ubicar [FORMAL] ❑ *They couldn't locate the missing ship.* *No pudieron encontrar el barco desaparecido.* **2** V-T If you **locate** something in a particular place, you put it there or build it there. ubicar, situar [FORMAL] ❑ *Business people voted Atlanta the best city in which to locate a business.* *Gente de negocios votaron por Atlanta como la mejor ciudad para abrir un negocio.* ● **lo|cat|ed** ADJ situado, ubicado ❑ *A shop and beauty salon are located in the hotel.* *En el hotel hay una tienda y un salón de belleza.* **3** V-I If you **locate** in a particular place, you move there or open a business there. ubicarse, situarse [BUSINESS] ❑ *...businesses that locate in poor neighborhoods.* *...negocios que se establecen en barrios pobres.*

**lo|ca|tion** /loʊkeɪʃən/ (**locations**) **1** N-COUNT A **location** is the place where something happens or is situated. posición, ubicación ❑ *Rand pointed out the location of the different school buildings.* *Rand señaló la ubicación de los diferentes planteles escolares.* **2** N-VAR A **location** is a place away from a studio where a movie or part of a movie is made. en locación, en exteriores ❑ *...a movie with many locations.* *...una película con muchas tomas fuera del estudio.*
→ see Picture Dictionary: **location**

**Word Partnership** Usar *location* con:

ADJ. **central** location, **convenient** location, **exact** location, **geographic** location, **present** location, **secret** location, **specific** location **1**
V. **pinpoint a** location **1**

**lock** /lɒk/ (**locks, locking, locked**) **1** V-T When you **lock** something, you fasten it with a key. cerrar con llave, echar llave ❑ *Are you sure you locked the front door?* *¿Estás seguro de haber echado llave a la puerta de afuera?* **2** N-COUNT The **lock** on something such as a door or a drawer is the device which is used to keep it shut. Locks are opened with a key. chapa, cerradura, cerrojo ❑ *He heard Gill's key turning in the lock.* *Oyó cuando la llave de Gill giró en la cerradura.* **3** V-T If you **lock** something or someone in a place, room, or container, you put them there and fasten the lock. guardar bajo llave ❑ *She locked the case in the closet.* *Guardó el estuche en el clóset y echó llave.* **4** V-T/V-I If you **lock** something in a particular position, or if it **locks** there, it is held or fitted firmly in that position. inmovilizar, bloquear ❑ *He locked his fingers behind his head.* *Cruzó los dedos tras la nuca.* **5** N-COUNT On a canal or river, a **lock** is a place where walls have been built with gates at each end so that boats can move to a higher or lower section of the canal or river, by gradually changing the water level inside the gates. esclusa ❑ *The lock slowly filled with water.* *La esclusa se llenó lentamente de agua.* **6** N-COUNT A **lock of** hair is a small bunch of hairs on your head that grow together in the same direction. mechón

▸ **lock away** **1** PHR-VERB If you **lock** something **away** in a place or container, you put or hide it there and fasten the lock. guardar bajo llave ❑ *She carefully cleaned her jewelry and locked it away in a case.* *Limpió minuciosamente sus joyas y las guardó bajo llave en un estuche.* **2** PHR-VERB To **lock** someone **away** means to put them in prison. encerrar ❑ *You can't lock someone away because they are mentally ill.* *No puedes encerrar a alguien porque sea un enfermo mental.*

▸ **lock up** **1** PHR-VERB To **lock** someone **up** means to put them in prison. encarcelar, encerrar ❑ *He is a criminal: they should lock him up.* *Es un criminal, deberían encerrarlo.* **2** PHR-VERB When you **lock up** a building or car, or **lock up,** you make sure that all the doors and windows are locked so that nobody can get in. *cerrar con llave, asegurar* ❑ *Don't forget to lock up. No se te olvide cerrar con llave.*

> **Word Partnership** Usar *lock* con:
>
> N. lock **a car**, lock **a door**, lock **a room** **1** **combination** lock, **door** lock, lock **and key, key in a** lock **2**
>
> V. **change a** lock, **open a** lock, **pick a** lock **2**

**lock|smith** /lɒksmɪθ/ (**locksmiths**) N-COUNT A **locksmith** is a person whose job is to make or repair locks. *cerrajero o cerrajera*

**lock-up** (**lock-ups**) also **lockup** N-COUNT A **lock-up** is the same as a **jail**. *prisión* [INFORMAL] ❑ *...the 450 prisoners at the lock-up in Lucasville. ...los 450 presos de la cárcel de Lucasville.*

**lo|co|mo|tive** /loʊkəmoʊtɪv/ (**locomotives**) N-COUNT A **locomotive** is a large vehicle that pulls a train. *locomotora* [FORMAL]
→ see **train**

**lo|co|mo|tor** /loʊkəmoʊtər/ ADJ **Locomotor** movements are actions such as walking or running, which involve moving from one place to another. *locomotor, locomotriz*

**lodge** /lɒdʒ/ (**lodges, lodging, lodged**) **1** N-COUNT A **lodge** is a house or hotel in the country or in the mountains where people stay on vacation. *casa de campo, hotel campestre* ❑ *...a hunting lodge. ...un pabellón de caza.* **2** V-T If you **lodge** a complaint, protest, accusation, or claim, you officially make it. *denunciar, interponer, poner* ❑ *He has four weeks in which to lodge an appeal. Tiene cuatro semanas para interponer una denuncia.* **3** V-T/V-I If you **lodge** somewhere, such as in someone else's house or if you **are lodged** there, you live there, usually paying rent. *alojar(se), hospedar(se)* ❑ *She lodged with a farming family when she was a young teacher. Cuando era una joven maestra se alojó con una familia de campesinos.* ● **lodg|er** N-COUNT (**lodgers**) *inquilino o inquilina, huésped* ❑ *Jennie took in a lodger to help pay the mortgage. Jennie tuvo un inquilino para ayudarse a pagar la hipoteca.* **4** V-T/V-I If an object **lodges** or **is lodged** somewhere, it becomes stuck there. *alojar(se), atorarse* ❑ *The bullet lodged in the policeman's leg. La bala se alojó en la pierna del policía.*

**lo|ess** /loʊɪs, lɛs, lɜrs/ N-UNCOUNT **Loess** is a mixture of sand, soil, and other material that has been deposited by the wind. *loes, loess* [TECHNICAL]

**log** /lɔg/ (**logs, logging, logged**) **1** N-COUNT A **log** is a thick piece of wood cut from a branch or the trunk of a tree. *tronco, leña* ❑ *He put the logs near the fireplace. Puso los troncos cerca de la chimenea.*

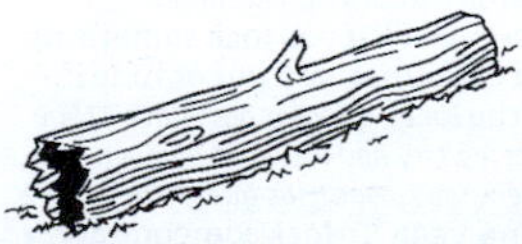

log

**2** N-COUNT A **log** is an official written account of what happens each day, for example, on board a ship. *bitácora, diario de navegación* ❑ *He wrote about his experience in his ship's log. Anotó sus experiencias en la bitácora de su barco.* **3** V-T If you **log** an event or fact, you record it officially in writing or on a computer. *registrar, anotar, tomar nota* ❑ *They log everything that comes in and out of here. Registran todo lo que entra y sale de aquí.*
→ see **blog, forest**

▸ **log in** or **log on** PHR-VERB When someone **logs in, logs on,** or **logs into** a computer system, they start using the system, usually by typing their name and a password. *entrar al sistema* ❑ *Customers pay to log on and speak to other users. Los clientes pagan por entrar al sistema y hablar con otros usuarios.*

▸ **log out** or **log off** PHR-VERB When someone who is using a computer system **logs out** or **logs off,** they finish using the system by typing a particular command. *salir del sistema, cerrar el sistema* ❑ *Remember to log off when you have finished. No se te olvide cerrar el sistema cuando termines.*

**loga|rithm** /lɔgərɪðəm/ (**logarithms**) N-COUNT In mathematics, the **logarithm** of a number is a number that it can be represented by in order to make a difficult multiplication or division sum simpler. *logaritmo*

**log|ger** /lɔgər/ (**loggers**) N-COUNT A **logger** is a man whose job is to cut down trees. *leñador, maderero, explotador forestal*

**log|ger|head tur|tle** /lɔgərhɛd tɜrt$^{ə}$l/ (**loggerhead turtles**) N-COUNT A **loggerhead turtle** is a large, carnivorous sea turtle. *tortuga mordedora, tortuga boba*

> **Word Link** *log ≈ reason, speech : apology, dialogue, logic*

**log|ic** /lɒdʒɪk/ N-UNCOUNT **Logic** is a method of reasoning that involves a series of statements, each of which must be true if the statement before it is true. *lógica* ❑ *Students study philosophy and logic. Los alumnos estudian filosofía y lógica.*
→ see **philosophy**

**logi|cal** /lɒdʒɪk$^{ə}$l/ **1** ADJ In a **logical** argument or method of reasoning, each step must be true if the step before it is true. *lógico* ❑ *Each logical step is checked by other mathematicians. Cada paso lógico es verificado por otros matemáticos.* ● **logi|cal|ly** /lɒdʒɪkli/ ADV *lógicamente, con lógica* ❑ *I have learned to think about things logically. He aprendido a pensar las cosas lógicamente.* **2** ADJ The **logical** conclusion or result of a series of facts or events is the only one which can come from it, according to the rules of logic. *lógica* ❑ *Brown and Harris lost their jobs and the logical conclusion is that I'll be next. Brown y Harris fueron despedidos, y la conclusión lógica es que sigo yo.* ● **logi|cal|ly** ADV *lógicamente, con lógica* ❑ *We worked it all out logically. Todo lo resolvimos con lógica.* **3** ADJ Something that is **logical** seems reasonable or sensible in the circumstances. *lógico, razonable* ❑ *Connie seemed the logical person to go with her. Lo razonable parecía que Connie fuera con ella.* ❑ *There was a logical explanation. Había una explicación lógica.*

**lo|gis|tics** /loʊdʒɪstɪks/ N-UNCOUNT If you refer to the **logistics** of doing something complicated that involves a lot of people or equipment, you are referring to the skillful organization of it so that it can be done successfully and efficiently. *logística* ❑ *...the logistics of getting such a big show on the road. ...los problemas logísticos de llevar de gira un espectáculo tan grande.*

**logo** /loʊgoʊ/ (**logos**) N-COUNT The **logo** of a

company or organization is the special design or way of writing its name that it puts on all its products, stationery, or advertisements. *logo, logotipo* ❑ *...the famous MGM logo of the roaring lion. ...el famoso logo del león que ruge de la MGM.*

**LOL** **LOL** is a written abbreviation for "laughing out loud" or "lots of love," often used in e-mail and text messages. *LOL*

**lone** /loʊn/ ADJ A **lone** person or thing is alone. *solitario* ❑ *A lone walker disappeared over the top of the hill. Un paseante solitario desapareció hacia lo alto de la colina.*

**lone|ly** /loʊnli/ (**lonelier, loneliest**) **1** ADJ Someone who is **lonely** is unhappy because they are alone or do not have anyone they can talk to. *solo, solitario, triste* ❑ *He has been lonely since his wife died. Ha estado solo desde que murió su esposa.* ● **lone|li|ness** N-UNCOUNT *soledad, melancolía* ❑ *I have a fear of loneliness. Le tengo miedo a la soledad.* **2** ADJ A **lonely** place is one where very few people come. *solitario, aislado* ❑ *It felt like the loneliest place in the world. Parecía el lugar más solitario del mundo.*

**lone|some** /loʊnsəm/ **1** ADJ Someone who is **lonesome** is unhappy because they do not have any friends or do not have anyone to talk to. *solitario, triste* ❑ *I get lonesome without anybody to talk to. Me pone triste no tener con quién hablar.* **2** ADJ A **lonesome** place is one which very few people come to and which is a long way from places where people live. *solitario, alejado* ❑ *...lonesome little towns like Acorn and Hatfield. ...pequeños pueblos lejanos, como Acorn y Hatfield.*

**long**

❶ TIME
❷ DISTANCE AND SIZE
❸ PHRASES
❹ VERB USE

❶ **long** /lɔŋ/ (**longer** /lɔŋgər/ (**longest** /lɔŋgɪst/) **1** ADV **Long** means a great amount of time or for a great amount of time. *mucho* ❑ *The repairs did not take too long. Las reparaciones no tardaron mucho.* ❑ *Have you known her parents long? ¿Hace mucho que conoce a sus padres?* ❑ *It all happened so long ago. Todo pasó hace mucho tiempo.* **2** PHRASE The expression **for long** is used to mean "for a great amount of time." *mucho tiempo* ❑ *"Did you live there?"— "Not for long." —¿Viviste ahí?—No mucho tiempo.* **3** ADJ A **long** event or period of time lasts for a great amount of time or takes a great amount of time. *largo* ❑ *We had a long meeting. La reunión se prolongó.* ❑ *She is planning a long vacation in Europe. Está planeando unas largas vacaciones por Europa.* **4** ADV You use **long** to ask or talk about amounts of time. *cuánto* ❑ *How long have you lived around here? ¿Hace cuánto que vives por aquí?* ● **Long** is also an adjective. *largo* ❑ *So how long is the movie? ¿Así que cuánto dura la película?* **5** ADJ A **long** speech, book, movie, or list contains a lot of information or a lot of items and takes a lot of time to listen to, read, watch, or deal with. *largo, prolongado* ❑ *He made a long speech. Su discurso fue largo.*

❷ **long** /lɔŋ/ (**longer** /lɔŋgər/ (**longest** /lɔŋgɪst/) **1** ADJ Something that is **long** measures a great distance from one end to the other. *largo* ❑ *...a long table. ...una mesa larga.* ❑ *Lucy had long dark hair. Lucy tenía el cabello largo y oscuro.* **2** ADJ A **long** distance is a great distance. A **long** journey or route covers a great distance. *largo, grande* ❑ *These people were a long way from home. Esas personas estaban muy lejos de su casa.* ❑ *The long journey made him tired. Se agotó con el largo viaje.* **3** ADJ You use **long** to talk or ask about the distance something measures from one end to the other. *largo* ❑ *The cut on his arm was an inch long. La cortada que tenía en el brazo era de tres centímetros.* ❑ *How long is the tunnel? ¿Qué tan largo es el túnel?* ❑ *...a three-foot-long hole in the ship's side. ...un agujero de un metro en el costado del barco.*

❸ **long** /lɔŋ/ (**longer** /lɔŋgər/) **1** PHRASE If you say that something is true **as long as** or **so long as** something else is true, you mean that it is only true if the second thing is true. *siempre que, con tal que* ❑ *They can do what they want as long as they are not breaking the law. Pueden hacer lo que quieran, siempre que no violen la ley.* **2** PHRASE If you say that something will happen or happened **before long,** you mean that it happened or will happen soon. *dentro de poco* ❑ *Prices will fall before long. Los precios no tardarán en bajar.* **3** PHRASE Something that is **no longer** the case used to be the case but is not the case now. You can also say that something is not the case **any longer.** *no más* ❑ *Food shortages are no longer a problem. La escasez de alimentos ha dejado de ser un problema.* ❑ *She couldn't afford to pay the rent any longer. Ya no podía pagar la renta.* **4** PHRASE If you say that someone **won't be long,** you mean that you think they will arrive or be back soon. If you say that it **won't be long** before something happens, you mean that you think it will happen soon. *no mucho* ❑ *"What's happened to her?"— "I'm sure she won't be long." —¿Qué pasa con ella?—Seguro ya no tarda.* **5** **at long last** → see **last** **6** **in the long run** → see **run** **7** **a long shot** → see **shot** **8** **in the long term** → see **term**

❹ **long** /lɔŋ/ (**longs, longing, longed**) V-T/V-I If you **long for** something, you want it very much. *echar de menos, extrañar, añorar* ❑ *Steve longed for his old life. Steve echaba de menos su antigua vida.* ❑ *I'm longing to meet her. Añoro verla.* ● **long|ing** N-VAR (**longings**) *nostalgia, añoranza* ❑ *She never lost the longing for her own home and country. Nunca dejó de sentir nostalgia por su casa y su país.*

**long-distance** **1** ADJ **Long-distance** is used to describe travel between places that are far apart. *larga distancia* ❑ *Trains are best for long-distance travel. La mejor manera de viajar largas distancias es en tren.* **2** ADJ **Long-distance** is used to describe communication that takes place between people who are far apart. *de larga distancia* ❑ *...a long-distance phone call. ...una llamada telefónica de larga distancia.*

**lon|gi|tu|di|nal wave** /lɒndʒɪtudᵊnᵊl weɪv/ (**longitudinal waves**) N-COUNT **Longitudinal waves** are waves such as sound waves in which the material that the waves are passing through moves in the same direction as the waves. Compare **transverse wave.** *onda longitudinal* [TECHNICAL]

**long-lost** ADJ You use **long-lost** to describe someone or something that you have not seen for a long time. *perdido de vista* ❑ *...a reunion with her* *long-lost sister.* *...una reunión con su hermana, de quien no había sabido nada en mucho tiempo.*

**long-range** ADJ A **long-range** plan or prediction relates to a period extending a long time into the future. *de largo plazo* ❑ *...the need for long-range planning.* *...la necesidad de planes de largo plazo.*

**long|shore cur|rent** /lɔŋʃɔr kɜrənt/ (**longshore currents**) N-COUNT A **longshore current** is an ocean current that flows close to, and parallel to, the shore. *corriente litoral, corriente costera longitudinal, corriente longitudinal de la costa* [TECHNICAL]

**long|shore|man** /lɔŋʃɔrmən/ (**longshoremen**) N-COUNT A **longshoreman** is a person who works in the docks, loading and unloading ships. *estibador, cargador*

**long-standing** ADJ A **long-standing** situation has existed for a long time. *de años atrás, duradero* ❑ *They resolved their long-standing dispute over money.* *Resolvieron su añeja discusión sobre el dinero.*

**long-time** ADJ You use **long-time** to describe something that has existed or been a particular thing for a long time. *de siempre, de tiempo atrás* ❑ *...long-time sweethearts.* *...novios de toda la vida.*

**look**
❶ USING YOUR EYES OR YOUR MIND
❷ APPEARANCE

❶ **look** /lʊk/ (**looks, looking, looked**) **1** V-I If you **look** in a particular direction, you direct your eyes there in order to see what is there. *ver, mirar, fijarse, observar* ❑ *I looked down the hallway.* *Miré por el corredor.* ❑ *If you look, you'll see a lake.* *Si te fijas, verás un lago* ● **Look** is also a noun. *mirada, ojeada* ❑ *Lucille took a last look in the mirror.* *Lucille se vio al espejo por última vez.* **2** V-I If you **look for** something or someone, you try to find them. *buscar* ❑ *I'm looking for a child.* *Estoy buscando a un niño.* ❑ *I looked everywhere for ideas.* *Busqué ideas por todas partes.* ● **Look** is also a noun. *vistazo, mirada, ojeada* ❑ *Go and have another look.* *Ve a echar otro vistazo.* **3** V-I If you **look at** a subject, problem, or situation, you examine, it, consider it, or judge it. *analizar, examinar, ver* ❑ *Next term we'll be looking at the Second World War.* *El próximo periodo analizaremos la segunda guerra mundial.* ❑ *Anne Holker looks at ways of making changes to your home.* *Anne Holker piensa en cómo hacerle cambios a tu casa.* ❑ *Brian learned to look at her with new respect.* *Brian aprendió a verla con respeto.* ● **Look** is also a noun. *mirada, ojeada, vistazo* ❑ *...a quick look at the morning newspapers.* *...un rápido vistazo a los diarios matutinos.* **4** CONVENTION You say **look** when you want someone to pay attention to you because you are going to say something important. *mira* ❑ *Look, I'm sorry. I didn't mean it.* *Mira, discúlpame, no era mi intención.* **5** V-T/V-I You can use **look** to draw attention to a particular situation, person, or thing, for example because you find it very surprising, significant, or annoying. *fijarse en* ❑ *Look at the time! We've got to go.* *¡Fíjate en la hora! Tenemos que irnos.* ❑ *Look at how many people watch television and how few read books.* *Fíjate en cuántas personas ven televisón y cuántas leen libros.* ❑ *Look what you've done!* *¡Mira lo que hiciste!* **6** V-I If something such as a building or window **looks** somewhere, it has a view of a particular place. *dar hacia, ver hacia un lugar* ❑ *The apartment looks over a park.* *El departamento da a un parque.* **7** EXCLAM If you say or shout "**look out!**" to someone, you are warning them that they are in danger. *¡cuidado!* ❑ *"Look out!" somebody shouted, as the truck started to roll toward the sea.* *—¡Cuidado! —gritó alguien, cuando el camión empezó a deslizarse hacia el mar.*

▸ **look after** **1** PHR-VERB If you **look after** someone or something, you do what is necessary to keep them healthy, safe, or in good condition. *cuidar de, atender* ❑ *I love looking after the children.* *Me encanta atender a los niños.* **2** PHR-VERB If you **look after** something, you are responsible for it and deal with it. *ocuparse de, atender* ❑ *The farm manager looks after the day-to-day business.* *El administrador de la granja está encargado de los asuntos cotidianos.*

▸ **look around** PHR-VERB If you **look around** or **look round** a building or place, you walk round it and look at the different parts of it. *ver, examinar* ❑ *She left Annie looking around the store.* *Dejó a Annie curioseando en la tienda.*

▸ **look back** PHR-VERB If you **look back**, you think about things that happened in the past. *mirar atrás, recordar, reflexionar* ❑ *Looking back, I am surprised how easy it was.* *Recordando, me sorprendo de lo fácil que era.*

▸ **look down on** PHR-VERB To **look down on** someone means to consider that person to be inferior or unimportant, usually when this is not true. *menospreciar* ❑ *They looked down on me because I wasn't successful.* *Me veían por encima del hombro porque no había tenido éxito.*

▸ **look forward to** PHR-VERB If you **look forward to** something that is going to happen, you want it to happen because you think you will enjoy it. *desear, esperar con ansias* ❑ *He was looking forward to working with the new manager.* *Ya quería trabajar con el nuevo gerente.*

▸ **look into** PHR-VERB If you **look into** something, you find out about it. *considerar* ❑ *He once looked into buying his own island.* *Alguna vez pensó en comprarse su propia isla.*

▸ **look on** PHR-VERB If you **look on** while something happens, you watch it happening without taking part yourself. *contemplar, mirar* ❑ *Local people looked on in silence as he walked past.* *Silenciosa, la gente del lugar lo vio pasar.*

▸ **look on** or **look upon** PHR-VERB If you **look on** or **look upon** someone or something in a particular way, you think of them in that way. *considerar como, estimar* ❑ *I looked upon him as a friend.* *Yo lo consideraba un amigo.* ❑ *A lot of people look on it like that.* *Muchas personas lo piensan de esa manera.*

▸ **look out** → see **look❶ 7**

▸ **look out for** PHR-VERB If you **look out for** something, you pay attention so that you notice it if or when it occurs. *buscar, estar atento a* ❑ *Look out for special deals.* *Busca las ofertas especiales.*

▸ **look round** → see **look around**

▸ **look through** PHR-VERB If you **look through** a book, a magazine, or a group of things, you get an idea of what is in it by examining a lot of the items in it. *revisar, echar un vistazo* ❑ *Peter started looking through the mail at once.* *De inmediato, Peter empezó a checar el correo.*

▸ **look to** PHR-VERB If you **look to** someone or something for a particular thing, you expect or hope that they will provide it. esperar, confiar ❑ *The nation looks to them for help.* *La nación espera que ellos ayuden.*

▸ **look up** 1 PHR-VERB If you **look up** a fact or a piece of information, you find it out by looking in something such as a reference book or a list. buscar ❑ *I looked your address up in the phone book.* *Busqué tu dirección en el directorio telefónico.* 2 PHR-VERB If you **look** someone **up,** you visit them after not having seen them for a long time. visitar, ir a ver ❑ *I'll look him up when I'm in New York.* *Lo visito cuando voy a Nueva York.*

▸ **look up to** PHR-VERB If you **look up to** someone, especially someone older than you, you respect and admire them. admirar, respetar ❑ *A lot of the younger girls look up to you.* *Muchas de las chicas más pequeñas te admiran.*

**Usage** **look, see,** and **watch**

If you *look* at something, you purposely direct your eyes at it: *Daniel kept turning around to look at the big-screen TV—he had never seen one before.* If you *see* something, it is visible to you: *Maria couldn't see the TV because Hector was standing in front of her and watching it.* If you *watch* something, you pay attention to it and keep it in sight: *Everyone was watching TV instead of looking at the photo album.*

❷ **look** /lʊ̲k/ (**looks, looking, looked**) 1 V-LINK You use **look** when describing the appearance of a person or thing or the impression that they give. aspecto, apariencia ❑ *Sheila was looking sad.* *Sheila se veía triste* ❑ *In time, owners begin to look like their dogs.* *Con el tiempo, los dueños se parecen a sus perros.* ❑ *He looked as if he was going to smile.* *Parecía como si fuera a sonreír.* 2 N-SING If someone or something has a particular **look,** they have a particular appearance or expression. aspecto, apariencia ❑ *She had the look of someone with a secret.* *Parecía que ocultaba un secreto.* ❑ *The kitchen has a country look.* *La cocina parece de casa de campo.* 3 N-PLURAL When you refer to someone's **looks,** you are referring to how beautiful or ugly they are. aspecto físico ❑ *I never chose friends just because of their looks.* *Nunca escojo amigos sólo por que sean atractivos.* 4 V-LINK You use **look** when indicating what you think will happen in the future or how a situation seems to you. parecer ❑ *He had lots of time to think about the future, and it didn't look good.* *Tuvo mucho tiempo para pensar en el futuro, y no le pareció halagüeño.* ❑ *It looks like we're going to win.* *Parece que vamos a ganar.* ❑ *The 90 degree heat looks like it will return for the weekend.* *Parece que para el fin de semana otra vez llegaremos a los 30 grados.* 5 PHRASE You use expressions such as **by the look of him** and **by the looks of it** when you want to indicate that you are giving an opinion based on the appearance of someone or something. según parece ❑ *He was not a well man by the look of him.* *Por lo que se veía, no estaba bien de salud.* 6 PHRASE If you **don't like the look of** something or someone, you feel that they may be dangerous or cause problems. desconfiar ❑ *I don't like the look of those clouds.* *No me gustan esas nubes.*

**loom** /lu̲m/ (**looms, looming, loomed**) 1 V-I If something **looms over** you, it appears as a large or unclear shape, often in a frightening way. aparecer algo amenazador, asomarse algo vagamente ❑ *She loomed over me, pale and gray.* *Se me acercó, pálida y gris.* 2 V-I If a worrying or threatening situation or event **is looming,** it seems likely to happen soon. amenazar, avecinarse ❑ *Another economic crisis is looming.* *Se avecina otra crisis económica.* ❑ *The threat of war looms ahead.* *La amenaza de la guerra surge amenazadora.* 3 N-COUNT A **loom** is a machine that is used for weaving thread into cloth. telar

loom

**loop** /lu̲p/ (**loops, looping, looped**) 1 N-COUNT A **loop** is a curved or circular shape in something long, for example, in a piece of string. vuelta, lazo, lazada ❑ *...a loop of garden hose.* *...una vuelta de la manguera del jardín.* 2 V-T If you **loop** something such as a piece of rope around an object, you tie a length of it in a loop around the object, for example, in order to fasten it to the object. enrollar, enlazar ❑ *He looped the rope over the wood.* *Sujetó la madera enrollando la cuerda.* 3 V-I If something **loops** somewhere, it goes there in a circular direction that makes the shape of a loop. dar la vuelta ❑ *The enemy was looping around the south side.* *El enemigo daba la vuelta por el lado sur.* 4 PHRASE If someone is **in the loop,** they are part of a group of people who make decisions about important things, or they know about these decisions. If they are **out of the loop,** they do not make or know about important decisions. (no) estar enterado, (no) formar parte de algo [INFORMAL] ❑ *I think that the vice president was in the loop.* *Yo creo que el vicepresidente estaba en el ajo.*

**loose** /lu̲s/ (**looser, loosest**) 1 ADJ Something that is **loose** is not firmly held or fixed in place. suelto, flojo ❑ *If a tooth feels very loose, your dentist may recommend that it be taken out.* *Si un diente está flojo, quizá el dentista te recomiende sacarlo.* ❑ *Two wooden beams came loose from the ceiling.* *Se soltaron dos vigas de madera del techo.* • **loose|ly** ADV sin apretar ❑ *Tim held his hands loosely in front of his belly.* *Tim se sujeto el vientre con las manos, sin apretarlo.* 2 ADJ If people or animals break **loose** or are set **loose,** they are no longer held, tied, or kept somewhere and can move around freely. soltarse ❑ *They tried to stop her but she broke loose.* *Ellos trataron de detenerla, pero se soltó.* 3 ADJ Clothes that are **loose** are somewhat large and do not fit closely. suelto, holgado ❑ *...a loose shirt.* *...una camisa suelta.* • **loose|ly** ADV sin apretar, flojamente ❑ *A scarf hung loosely round his neck.* *Del cuello le colgaba flojamente una bufanda.* 4 ADJ A **loose** grouping, arrangement, or organization is flexible rather than strictly controlled or organized. flexible, sin rigidez ❑ *Murray and Alison came to some sort of loose arrangement.* *Murray y Alison llegaron a una especie de arreglo flexible.* • **loose|ly** ADV sin cohesión, poco rígido ❑ *...a loosely-organized group of criminals.* *...un grupo de delincuentes más o menos organizados.* 5 PHRASE If a person or an animal is **on the loose,** they are free because they have escaped from a person or place. en libertad ❑ A

*dangerous criminal is on the loose after escaping from jail.* *Un peligroso criminal anda suelto porque se escapó de la cárcel.*
→ see also **lose**

| Thesaurus | *loose* | Ver también: |
|---|---|---|
| ADJ. | slack, wobbly 1<br>free 2<br>baggy 3 | |

**loos|en** /lusᵊn/ (**loosens, loosening, loosened**) **1** V-T If someone **loosens** restrictions or laws, for example, they make them less strict or severe. *relajar, aflojar* ❑ *It looks like the government will loosen controls on the newspapers.* *Parece que el gobierno reducirá el control sobre los periódicos.* • **loos|en|ing** N-SING *distensión, relajación* ❑ *...the loosening of trade restrictions.* *...restricciones comerciales menos estrictas.* **2** V-T/V-I If your clothing or something that is tied or fastened **loosens**, or you **loosen** it, you undo it slightly so that it is less tight or less firmly held in place. *aflojarse* ❑ *He reached up to loosen the scarf around his neck.* *Levantó los brazos para aflojarse la bufanda que le apretaba el cuello.*
▸ **loosen up** **1** PHR-VERB If a person or situation **loosens up,** they become more relaxed and less tense. *relajarse* ❑ *Relax, smile; loosen up.* *Tranquilízate, sonríe; relájate.* **2** PHR-VERB If you **loosen up** your body, or if it **loosens up,** you do simple exercises to get your muscles ready for a difficult physical activity, such as running or playing sports. *relajar, estirar* ❑ *Squeeze your foot with both hands to loosen up tight muscles.* *Apriétate el pie con ambas manos para relajar los músculos tensos.*

**L**

**loot** /lut/ (**loots, looting, looted**) V-T/V-I If people **loot** stores or houses, or if they **loot** things from them, they steal things from them, for example, during a war or riot. *saquear, pillar, robar* ❑ *People started breaking windows and looting shops.* *La gente empezó a romper vidrieras y a saquear las tiendas.* ❑ *The men looted food supplies.* *Los hombres robaron productos alimenticios.* ❑ *People came into the city to look for food and to loot.* *La gente llegó a la ciudad en busca de comida y de un botín.* • **loot|ing** N-UNCOUNT *saqueo* ❑ *There has been rioting and looting.* *Ha habido disturbios y saqueos.* • **loot|er** N-COUNT (**looters**) *saqueador o saqueadora* ❑ *Looters took thousands of dollars' worth of food.* *Los saqueadores se llevaron miles de dólares en alimentos.*

**lord** /lɔrd/ (**lords**) **1** N-COUNT; N-TITLE A **lord** is a man who has a high rank in the nobility, for example, an earl, a viscount, or a marquis. *lord, señor, noble* ❑ *She married a lord.* *Se casó con un noble.* **2** N-PROPER In the Christian church, people refer to God and to Jesus Christ as the **Lord.** *Señor* ❑ *She prayed now. "Lord, help me to find courage."* *Entonces oró. "Señor, ayudame a encontrar el valor".*

**lose** /luz/ (**loses, losing, lost**) **1** V-T/V-I If you **lose** a contest, a fight, or an argument, someone defeats you. *perder, ser derrotado* ❑ *The Golden Bears lost three games this season.* *Los Osos Dorados perdieron tres juegos en esta temporada.* ❑ *The government lost the argument.* *El gobierno salió derrotado en la discusión.* ❑ *No one likes to lose.* *A nadie le gusta perder.* **2** V-T If you **lose** something, you do not know where it is, for example, because you have forgotten where you put it. *perder* ❑ *I lost my keys.* *Perdí mis llaves.* **3** V-T You say that you **lose** something when you no longer have it because it has been taken away from you. *perder* ❑ *I lost my job when the company moved to another state.* *Me quedé sin trabajo cuando la empresa se trasladó a otro estado.* ❑ *He lost his license for six months.* *Le retiraron la licencia durante seis meses.* **4** V-T If someone **loses** a quality, characteristic, attitude, or belief, they no longer have it. *perder* ❑ *He lost all sense of reason.* *Estaba totalmente fuera de sus cabales.* **5** V-T If someone or something **loses** heat, their temperature becomes lower. *perder* ❑ *Babies lose heat much faster than adults.* *Los bebés se enfrían mucho más rápido que los adultos.* **6** V-T If you **lose** blood or fluid from your body, it leaves your body so that you have less of it. *perder* ❑ *The victim lost a lot of blood.* *La víctima perdió mucha sangre.* **7** V-T If you **lose** weight, you become less heavy, and usually look thinner. *bajar de peso, adelgazar* ❑ *I lost a lot of weight.* *Adelgacé mucho.* **8** V-T If someone **loses** their life, they die. *perder (la vida)* ❑ *192 people lost their lives in the disaster.* *192 personas murieron en el desastre.* **9** V-T If you **lose** a close relative or friend, they die. *perder* ❑ *My Grandma lost her brother in the war.* *El hermano de mi abuela murió en la guerra.* **10** V-T If you **lose** time, something slows you down so that you do not make as much progress as you hoped. *perder* ❑ *Police lost time in the early part of the investigation.* *La policía perdió tiempo al principio de la investigación.* **11** V-T If you **lose** an opportunity, you do not take advantage of it. *perder* ❑ *If you don't do it soon, you're going to lose your opportunity.* *Si no lo haces pronto, vas a perder tu oportunidad.* ❑ *They did not lose the opportunity to say what they thought.* *No desaprovecharon la oportunidad de decir lo que pensaban.* **12** V-T If a business **loses** money, it earns less money than it spends, and is therefore in debt. *perder* [BUSINESS] ❑ *His stores might lose millions of dollars.* *Sus tiendas podrían perder millones de dólares.* **13** → see also **lost** **14** PHRASE If you **lose** your **way,** you become lost when you are trying to go somewhere. *perderse* ❑ *The men lost their way in a storm.* *Los hombres se perdieron en una tormenta.* **15** to **lose face** → see **face** **16** to **lose** your **head** → see **head** **17** to **lose sight of** → see **sight** **18** to **lose** your **temper** → see **temper** **19** to **lose track of** → see **track** **20** → see also **miss**
▸ **lose out** PHR-VERB If you **lose out,** you suffer a loss or disadvantage because you have not succeeded in what you were doing. *salir perdiendo* ❑ *We both lost out.* *Ambos salimos perdiendo.* ❑ *Laura lost out to Tom.* *Laura salió perdiendo con Tom.*

**Usage** **lose** and **loose**

Be careful not to write *loose* when you mean *lose*. *Lose* means that you no longer have something, and *loose* describes something that is not held firmly or attached. *Loose* rhymes with *goose*, while *lose* rhymes with *shoes*: *You might lose your dog if you let him run loose.*

**los|er** /luzər/ (**losers**) **1** N-COUNT The **losers** of a game, contest, or struggle are the people who are defeated or beaten. *perdedor o perdedora* ❑ *...the losers of this year's Super Bowl.* *...los perdedores del Super Bowl de este año.* **2** PHRASE If someone is a **good loser,** they accept that they have lost a game or contest without complaining. If someone is a **bad loser,** they hate losing and complain about it.

*(no) saber perder* ❑ *I try to be a good loser.* *Trato de ser un buen perdedor.*

**loss** /lɔs/ (**losses**) **1** N-VAR **Loss** is the fact of no longer having something or having less of it than before. *pérdida* ❑ *...loss of sight.* *...pérdida de la vista.* ❑ *...hair loss.* *...pérdida del cabello.* **2** N-UNCOUNT The **loss** of a relative or friend is their death. *pérdida* ❑ *They talked about the loss of Thomas.* *Hablaron sobre la muerte de Thomas.* **3** N-UNCOUNT **Loss** is the feeling of sadness you experience when someone or something you like is taken away from you. *pérdida* ❑ *...feelings of loss and grief.* *...sensación de pérdida y dolor.* **4** N-COUNT A **loss** is the disadvantage you suffer when a valuable and useful person or thing leaves or is taken away. *pérdida* ❑ *His death was a great loss to his family.* *Su muerte fue una gran pérdida para la familia.* ❑ *...a terrible loss of human life.* *...una terrible pérdida de vidas humanas.* **5** N-VAR If a business makes a **loss,** it earns less than it spends. *perder* ❑ *...the company's continuing losses.* *...las constantes pérdidas de la compañía.* **6** PHRASE If you say that you are **at a loss,** you mean that you do not know what to do in a particular situation. *sentirse perdido* ❑ *I was at a loss for what to do next.* *No sabía qué hacer después.*
→ see **diet, disaster**

**Word Partnership** Usar *loss* con:

N. loss **of appetite, blood** loss, loss **of control, hair** loss, **hearing** loss, loss **of income,** loss **of a job, memory** loss, **weight** loss **1**
ADJ. **great/huge/substantial** loss **1**–**4**
**tragic** loss **2** **3**
**net** loss **5**

**lost** /lɔst/ **1** **Lost** is the past tense and past participle of **lose.** *pasado y participio pasado de* ***lose*** **2** ADJ If you are **lost** or if you get **lost,** you do not know where you are or are unable to find your way. *perdido, extraviado* ❑ *I realized I was lost.* *Me di cuenta de que estaba perdida.* **3** ADJ If something is **lost,** or gets **lost,** you cannot find it. *perdido* ❑ *...a lost book.* *...un libro perdido.* ❑ *His pen was lost under the sheets of paper.* *Su pluma estaba escondida entre las hojas de papel.* **4** ADJ If you feel **lost,** you feel very uncomfortable because you are in an unfamiliar situation. *perdido, confundido, desorientado* ❑ *He remembered feeling very lost at the funeral.* *Recuerda que en el funeral estaba totalmente confundido.*

**Thesaurus** *lost* Ver también:

ADJ. adrift **2**
missing **3**

**lost and found** **1** N-SING **Lost and found** is the place where lost property is kept. *objetos perdidos* **2** ADJ **Lost-and-found** things are things which someone has lost and which someone else has found. *objeto perdido*

**lot** /lɒt/ (**lots**) **1** QUANT **A lot of** something or **lots of** it is a large amount of it. *cantidad sustancial* ❑ *A lot of our land is used to grow crops.* *Gran parte de nuestra tierra se utiliza para sembrar.* ❑ *He drank lots of milk.* *Bebe mucha leche.* ● **Lot** is also a pronoun. *mucho* ❑ *I like to be in a town where there's lots going on.* *Me gusta estar en una ciudad en la que pasan muchas cosas.* ❑ *I learned a lot from him.* *Aprendí mucho de él.* **2** ADV **A lot** means to a great extent or degree. *mucho* ❑ *Matthew goes out quite a lot.* *Matthew sale bastante.* ❑ *I like you, a lot.* *Me gustas, y mucho.* **3** N-COUNT You can use **lot** to refer to a set or group of things or people. *lote, montón* ❑ *He bought two lots of 1,000 shares in the company.* *Compró dos lotes de 1,000 acciones de la compañía.* **4** N-SING You can refer to a specific group of people as a particular **lot.** *grupo* [INFORMAL] ❑ *Our grandchildren will think that we were a boring lot.* *Nuestros nietos pensarán que éramos una bola de aburridos.* **5** N-COUNT A **lot** is a small area of land that belongs to a person or company. *lote, terreno, solar* ❑ *Oil was discovered under their lot.* *En su terreno encontraron petróleo.* **6** → see also **parking lot** **7** N-COUNT A **lot** in an auction is one of the objects or groups of objects that are being sold. *lote* ❑ *They want to sell the furniture as one lot.* *Quieren vender los muebles en lote.* **8** PHRASE If people **draw lots** to decide who will do something, they each take a piece of paper from a container. One or more pieces of paper is marked, and the people who take marked pieces are chosen. *echar suertes, echar un volado, rifarse* ❑ *They drew lots to decide who would finish second and third.* *Echaron un volado para decidir quién quedaría en segundo y quién en tercero.*

**Usage** lot

Both *a lot* and *lots* mean "very many," "a large number," or "a large amount," and both can be followed by a singular or plural verb, depending on what's being talked about: *Lots/A lot of people are here. A lot is also an adverb: I like him a lot.*

**lot|tery** /lɒtəri/ (**lotteries**) **1** N-COUNT A **lottery** is a type of gambling game in which people buy numbered tickets. Several numbers are then chosen, and the people who have those numbers on their tickets win a prize. *lotería* ❑ *...the national lottery.* *...la lotería nacional.* **2** N-SING If you describe something as **a lottery,** you mean that what happens depends entirely on luck or chance. *lotería, volado* ❑ *The stockmarket is a lottery.* *La bolsa de valores es una lotería.*

**Word Link** *er ≈ more : bigger, louder, taller*

**Word Link** *est ≈ most : greatest, kindest, loudest*

**loud** /laʊd/ (**louder, loudest**) **1** ADJ If a noise is **loud,** the level of sound is very high and it can be easily heard. Someone or something that is **loud** produces a lot of noise. *fuerte, intenso* ❑ *There was a loud bang.* *Se oyó un fuerte impacto.* ❑ *His voice was harsh and loud.* *Su voz era áspera y fuerte.* ● **Loud** is also an adverb. *fuerte, alto* ❑ *He turned the volume on the television up very loud.* *Puso muy alto el volumen de la televisión.* ● **loud|ly** ADV *fuertemente* ❑ *His footsteps sounded loudly in the hall.* *Sus pasos sonaron ruidosamente en el vestíbulo.* **2** ADJ If you describe something, especially a piece of clothing, as **loud,** you dislike it because it has very bright colors or very large, bold patterns which look unpleasant. *escandaloso, chillón, llamativo* ❑ *He wore gold chains and loud clothes.* *Él usaba cadenas de oro y ropa escandalosa.* **3** PHRASE If you say or read something **out loud,** you say it or read it so that it

**Word Web** love

Until the Middle Ages, **romance** was not an important part of **marriage.** Parents decided who their children would marry. The social class and political connections of a future **spouse** were very important. No one expected a couple to **fall in love.** However, during the Middle Ages, poets and musicians began to write about love in a new way. These **romantic** poems and songs describe a new type of courtship. In them, the man **woos** a woman for her **affection.** This is the basis for the modern idea of a romantic **bond** between **husband** and **wife.**

can be heard, rather than just thinking it. *en voz alta* ❑ *Parts of the book made me laugh out loud.* *Partes del libro me hicieron reír a carcajadas.*

**Word Partnership** Usar *loud* con:

N. loud **bang,** loud **crash,** loud **explosion,** loud **music,** loud **noise,** loud **voice** 1
ADJ. loud **and clear** 1
V. **laugh out** loud, **read out** loud, **say** ***something*** **out** loud, **think out** loud 3

**lounge** /laʊndʒ/ (**lounges, lounging, lounged**) 1 N-COUNT In a hotel, club, or other public place, a **lounge** is a room where people can sit and relax. *salón, sala de estar* ❑ *Afternoon tea is served in the hotel lounge.* *El té de la tarde se sirve en la sala de estar del hotel.* 2 N-COUNT In an airport, a **lounge** is a very large room where people can sit and wait for aircraft to arrive or leave. *sala de espera* ❑ *...the departure lounge.* *...la sala de espera de salida.* 3 V-I If you **lounge** somewhere, you sit or lie there in a relaxed or lazy way. *no hacer nada, relajarse* ❑ *They ate and drank and lounged in the shade.* *Comieron, bebieron y descansaron a la sombra.*

**louse** /laʊs/ (**lice**) N-COUNT **Lice** are small insects that live on the bodies of people or animals. *piojo*

**love** /lʌv/ (**loves, loving, loved**) 1 V-T If you **love** someone, you feel romantically or sexually attracted to them, and they are very important to you. *querer, amar, gustar, tener cariño por* ❑ *Oh, Amy, I love you.* *Oh, Amy, te amo.* 2 N-UNCOUNT **Love** is a very strong feeling of affection toward someone who you are romantically or sexually attracted to. *amor* ❑ *In the four years since we married, our love has grown stronger.* *Nuestro amor se ha fortalecido en los cuatro años que llevamos casados.* ❑ *...a old-fashioned love story.* *...una historia de amor a la antigua.* 3 V-T You say that you **love** someone when their happiness is very important to you, so that you behave in a kind and caring way toward them. *querer* ❑ *You'll never love anyone the way you love your baby.* *Nunca querrás a nadie como quieres a tu bebé.* 4 N-UNCOUNT **Love** is the feeling that a person's happiness is very important to you, and the way you show this feeling in your behavior toward them. *amor* ❑ *...my love for my children.* *...el amor por mis hijos.* 5 V-T If you **love** something, you like it very much. *gustar mucho algo* ❑ *I love food, I love cooking and I love eating.* *Me encanta la comida, me encanta cocinar y me encanta comer.* ❑ *They love to be in the outdoors.* *Disfrutan estar al aire libre.* 6 V-T You can say that you **love** something when you consider that it is important and want to protect or support it. *amar* ❑ *I love my country.* *Amo a mi patria.* 7 N-UNCOUNT **Love** is a strong liking for something, or a belief that it is important. *amor* ❑ *This is no way to encourage a love of literature.* *Esta no es manera de fomentar el amor por la literatura.* 8 V-T If you **would love to** have or do something, you very much want to have it or do it. *desear algo* ❑ *I would love to be thinner.* *Me gustaría estar más delgada.* ❑ *I would love a hot bath.* *Cómo deseo un baño caliente.* 9 NUM In tennis, **love** is a score of zero. *cero* ❑ *He beat Thomas Muster three sets to love.* *Le ganó a Thomas Muster tres sets a cero.* 10 CONVENTION You can use expressions such as **love, love from,** and **all my love,** followed by your name, as an informal way of ending a letter to a friend or relative. *con todo cariño, besos, TQM* ❑ *...with love from Grandma.* *...besos de la abuela.* 11 → see also **loving** 12 PHRASE If you **fall in love with** someone, you start to be in love with them. *enamorarse* ❑ *I fell in love with him because he was so kind.* *Me enamoré de él por su gentileza.*
→ see Word Web: **love**
→ see **emotion**

**Thesaurus** *love* Ver también:

V. adore, cherish, treasure; (*ant.*) dislike, hate 1 3 5
N. adoration, devotion, tenderness; (*ant.*) hate 2 4 7

**love|ly** /lʌvli/ (**lovelier, loveliest**) ADJ If you describe someone or something as **lovely,** you mean that they are very beautiful and therefore pleasing to look at or listen to. *bonito, lindo, encantador, adorable* ❑ *You look lovely, Marcia.* *Te ves muy bien, Marcia.* ❑ *He had a lovely voice.* *Tenía una hermosa voz.*

**lov|er** /lʌvər/ (**lovers**) 1 N-COUNT Someone's **lover** is someone who they are having a sexual relationship with but are not married to. *amante, querido, novio* ❑ *Every Thursday she met her lover Leon.* *Todos los jueves se reunía con Leon, su amante.* 2 N-COUNT If you are a **lover** of something such as animals or the arts, you enjoy them very much and take great pleasure in them. *aficionado o aficionada* ❑ *She is a great lover of horses.* *Es muy aficionada a los caballos.*

**lov|ing** /lʌvɪŋ/ 1 ADJ Someone who is **loving** feels or shows love to other people. *afectuoso, cariñoso, amoroso* ❑ *...a loving husband.* *...un esposo cariñoso.* ● **lov|ing|ly** ADV *cariñosamente, afectuosamente* ❑ *Brian gazed lovingly at Mary.* *Brian*

L

*miró cariñosamente a Mary.* **2** ADJ **Loving** actions are done with great enjoyment and care. *amoroso, afectuoso* ❑ *The house has been decorated with loving care. Decoraron la casa con amoroso cuidado.* ● **lov|ing|ly** ADV *amorosamente* ❑ *...lovingly-prepared food. ...comida preparada con gran cuidado.*

**low** /loʊ/ (**lower, lowest, lows**) **1** ADJ Something that is **low** measures only a short distance from the bottom to the top, or from the ground to the top. *bajo, de poca altura* ❑ *...the low garden wall. ...el muro bajo del jardín.* ❑ *...the low hills of the country. ...las colinas de poca altura del país.* **2** ADJ If something is **low,** it is close to the ground, to sea level, or to the bottom of something. *bajo* ❑ *He bumped his head on the low beams. Se golpeó la cabeza en las vigas bajas.* ❑ *It was late afternoon and the sun was low in the sky. Ya era tarde y el sol estaba bajo en el horizonte.* **3** ADJ You can use **low** to indicate that something is small in amount or that it is at the bottom of a particular scale. You can use phrases such as **in the low 80s** to indicate that a number or level is less than 85 but not as little as 80. *bajo* ❑ *...low incomes. ...ingresos bajos.* ❑ *They are still living on very low incomes. Siguen viviendo con muy pocos ingresos.* **4** ADJ **Low** is used to describe people who are not considered to be very important because they are near the bottom of a particular scale or system. *bajo* ❑ *...a soldier of low rank. ...un soldado de rango inferior.* **5** N-COUNT If something reaches a **low** of a particular amount or degree, that is the smallest it has ever been. *mínimo, más bajo* ❑ *Prices dropped to a low of about $1.12. Los precios cayeron al mínimo de 1.12 dólares, más o menos.* **6** ADJ If the quality or standard of something is **low,** it is very poor. *bajo* ❑ *...low-quality work. ...trabajo de baja calidad.* ❑ *The hospital was criticized for its low standard of care. Criticaron al hospital porque el estándar de atención es bajo.* **7** ADJ If you have a **low** opinion of someone or something, you disapprove of them or dislike them. *malo* ❑ *...his low opinion of rap music. ...su mala opinión de la música de rap.* **8** ADJ A **low** sound or noise is deep and quiet. *bajo* ❑ *Her voice was so low he couldn't hear it. La voz de ella era tan baja, que él no podía oírla.* **9** ADJ A light that is **low** is not bright or strong. *bajo, opaco* ❑ *Their eyesight is poor in low light. No ven bien con poca luz.* **10** ADJ If a radio, oven, or light is on **low,** it has been adjusted so that only a small amount of sound, heat, or light is produced. *bajo* ❑ *She turned her radio on low. Puso su radio a volumen bajo.* ❑ *We keep the light on low beside her bed. La luz de su buró la dejamos baja.* **11** ADJ If you are **low,** you are depressed. *deprimido, desanimado, desganado* [INFORMAL] ❑ *She tried to make him smile when he was feeling low. Ella trataba de hacerlo sonreír cuando estaba deprimido.* **12** → see also **lower** **13** **low profile** → see **profile**

**low-end** ADJ **Low-end** products, especially electronic products, are the least expensive of their kind. *low-end, chafa, de baja calidad, económica* ❑ *...a low-end laser printer. ...una impresora láser económica.*

**low|er** /loʊər/ (**lowers, lowering, lowered**) **1** ADJ You can use **lower** to refer to the bottom one of a pair of things. *inferior, de abajo* ❑ *She bit her lower lip. Se mordió el labio de abajo.* ❑ *...the lower of the two holes. ...de las dos perforaciones, la de abajo.* **2** V-T If you **lower** something, you move it slowly downward. *bajar* ❑ *They lowered the coffin into the grave. Bajaron el ataúd a la tumba.* ❑ *Chris lowered himself into the chair. Chris se dejó caer en la silla.* **3** V-T If you **lower** something, you make it less in amount, degree, value, or quality. *bajar, reducir* ❑ *The Central Bank lowered interest rates. El Banco Central bajó las tasas de interés.* ● **low|er|ing** N-UNCOUNT *reducción* ❑ *...the lowering of the retirement age. ...la reducción de la edad de jubilación.* **4** → see also **low**

**low|er class** (**lower classes**) also **lower-class** N-COUNT Some people use **the lower class** or **the lower classes** to refer to the division of society that they consider to have the lowest social status. *de clase baja* ❑ *Education offers the lower classes better job opportunities. La educación ofrece mejores oportunidades de empleo a las clases bajas.* ● **Lower class** is also an adjective. *clase baja* ❑ *...lower-class families. ...familias de clase baja.*

**low|er man|tle** N-SING *The* **lower mantle** is the part of the Earth's interior that lies between the upper mantle and the outer core. *corteza inferior*

**low-impact** ADJ **Low-impact** exercise does not put a lot of stress on your body. *bajo impacto*

**low-maintenance** also **low maintenance** ADJ If you describe something or someone as **low-maintenance,** you mean that they require very little time, money, or effort. *fácil de mantener* ❑ *...a small, low-maintenance yard. ...un pequeño jardín fácil de conservar.*

**low-rise** (**low-rises**) ADJ **Low-rise** buildings are modern buildings which have only a few stories. *de poca altura, bajo* ❑ *...low-rise apartment buildings. ...edificios de departamentos de poca altura.* ● **Low-rise** is also a noun. *edificio de poca altura* ❑ *...a mix of low-rises and town houses. ...una mezcla de edificios de pocos pisos y casas.*

**low tide** (**low tides**) N-VAR At the coast, **low tide** is the time when the sea is at its lowest level because the tide is out. *marea baja* → see **tide**

**loy|al** /lɔɪəl/ ADJ Someone who is **loyal** remains firm in their friendship or support for a person or thing. *leal, fiel* ❑ *They stayed loyal to the Republican party. Siguieron siendo leales al partido republicano.* ● **loy|al|ly** ADV *lealmente, fielmente* ❑ *They loyally supported their leader. Siguieron apoyando fielmente a su líder.* → see **hero**

**loy|al|ty** /lɔɪəlti/ (**loyalties**) **1** N-UNCOUNT **Loyalty** is the quality of staying firm in your friendship or support for someone or something. *lealtad, fidelidad* ❑ *I believe in family loyalty. Creo en la lealtad de la familia.* **2** N-COUNT **Loyalties** are feelings of friendship, support, or duty toward someone or something. *fidelidad* ❑ *She had developed strong loyalties to the Manet family. Había desarrollado una gran lealtad hacia la familia Manet.*

**LP** /ɛl pi/ (**LPs**) N-COUNT An **LP** is a vinyl disk which usually has about 25 minutes of music or speech on each side. **LP** is an abbreviation for "long-playing record." *LP, disco de larga duración*

**LPN** /ɛl pi ɛn/ (**LPNs**) N-COUNT An **LPN** is a nurse who is trained to provide patients with basic care under the supervision of a doctor or a registered nurse. **LPN** is an abbreviation for "licensed

l

practical nurse." ayudante de enfermería, ayudante de enfermera ❑ *She'll become an LPN after graduating next March.* Será ayudante de enfermera después de graduarse en marzo.

**LSAT** /ɛlsæt/ (**LSATs**) N-PROPER The **LSAT** is an examination which is often taken by students who wish to enter a law school. **LSAT** is an abbreviation for "Law School Admission Test." examen de admisión a la escuela de derecho ❑ *These students are preparing to take their LSAT.* Estos estudiantes se están preparando para el examen de admisión a la escuela de derecho.

**lub|ri|cant** /lubrɪkənt/ (**lubricants**) N-COUNT A **lubricant** is a substance which you put on the surfaces or parts of something, especially something mechanical, to make the parts move smoothly. lubricante

**luck** /lʌk/ (**lucks, lucking, lucked**) **1** N-UNCOUNT **Luck** or **good luck** is success or good things that happen to you, that do not come from your own abilities or efforts. suerte, buena suerte ❑ *I knew I needed a bit of luck to win.* Sabía que necesitaba un poco de suerte para ganar. ❑ *We are having no luck with the weather.* No hemos tenido suerte con el clima. **2** N-UNCOUNT **Bad luck** is lack of success or bad things that happen to you, that have not been caused by yourself or other people. mala suerte ❑ *I had a lot of bad luck during the first half of this season.* Tuve muy mala suerte en la primera mitad de la temporada. **3** CONVENTION You can say "**Bad luck**" or "**Hard luck**" to someone when you want to express sympathy to them. mala suerte [INFORMAL] ❑ *Bad luck, man, just bad luck.* Mala suerte, amigo, mala suerte nada más. **4** CONVENTION If you say "**Good luck**" or "**Best of luck**" to someone, you are telling them that you hope they will be successful in something they are trying to do. buena suerte [INFORMAL] ❑ *He kissed her on the cheek. "Best of luck!"* La besó en la mejilla. —¡Mucha suerte! **5** PHRASE You can say someone **is in luck** when they are in a situation where they can have what they want or need. estar de suerte, tener suerte ❑ *You're in luck. The doctor's still here.* Tienes suerte, el doctor no se ha ido.

▶ **luck out** PHR-VERB If you **luck out**, you get some advantage or are successful because you have good luck. estar de suerte ❑ *Was he born to be successful, or did he just luck out?* ¿Nació para tener éxito o sólo tiene buena suerte?

**Word Partnership** Usar *luck* con:

ADJ. **dumb** luck, **good** luck, **just** luck, **pure** luck, **sheer** luck **1**
V. **bring *someone*** luck, **need a little** luck, **need some** luck, **push *your*** luck, **try *your*** luck, **wish *someone*** luck **1**
**have any/bad/better/good/no** luck **1** **2**

**lucky** /lʌki/ (**luckier, luckiest**) **1** ADJ You say that someone is **lucky** when they have something that is very desirable or when they are in a very desirable situation. afortunado, suertudo ❑ *I am luckier than most people round here. I have a job.* Soy más afortunado que muchos de por aquí, tengo trabajo. ❑ *He is very lucky to be alive.* Tiene suerte de estar vivo. **2** ADJ Someone who is **lucky** seems to always have good luck. suertudo, afortunado, con suerte ❑ *Some people are born lucky, aren't they?* Muchos nacen con suerte, ¿o no? **3** ADJ If you describe an action or experience as **lucky,** you mean that it was good or successful, and that it happened by chance and not as a result of planning or preparation. por suerte, por casualidad ❑ *I got the answer right, but it was just a lucky guess.* Tuve bien la respuesta, pero fue por pura casualidad. **4** ADJ A **lucky** object is something that people believe helps them to be successful. que trae suerte ❑ *He says this pair of green socks is lucky.* Él dice que estos calcetines verdes le dan suerte. **5** PHRASE If you say that someone **will be lucky to** do or get something, you mean that they are very unlikely to do or get it. correr con suerte ❑ *You'll be lucky if you get any breakfast.* Me extrañaría si te dieran de desayunar. ❑ *Those remaining in work will be lucky to get a pay increase.* Los que todavía tengan trabajo tendrán mucha suerte si les suben el sueldo.

**Word Partnership** Usar *lucky* con:

V. **be** lucky, **feel** lucky, **get** lucky, lucky **to get *something***, lucky **to have *something*** **1**
ADV. lucky **enough**, **pretty** lucky, **really** lucky, **so** lucky, **very** lucky **1**
N. lucky **break**, lucky **guess** **3**

**lu|cra|tive** /lukrətɪv/ ADJ A **lucrative** activity, job, or business deal is very profitable. lucrativo, provechoso ❑ *...his lucrative career as a filmmaker.* ...su lucrativa carrera de cineasta.

luggage

**lug|gage** /lʌgɪdʒ/ N-UNCOUNT **Luggage** is the suitcases and bags that you take with you when you travel. equipaje, maletas ❑ *Leave your luggage in the hotel.* Deja tu equipaje en el hotel.
→ see **hotel**

**lug|gage rack** N-COUNT A **luggage rack** is a shelf for putting luggage on, in a vehicle such as a train or bus. portaequipaje, portaequipajes

**lum|ber** /lʌmbər/ (**lumbers, lumbering, lumbered**) **1** N-UNCOUNT **Lumber** consists of trees and large pieces of wood that have been roughly cut up. madera **2** V-I If someone or something **lumbers** from one place to another, they move there very slowly and clumsily. avanzar pesadamente ❑ *He lumbered back to his chair.* Se dirigió pesadamente a su silla.
→ see **forest**

**lumber|man** /lʌmbərmən/ (**lumbermen**) N-COUNT A **lumberman** is a man who sells timber. leñador

**lumber|yard** /lʌmbəryɑrd/ (**lumberyards**) also **lumber yard** N-COUNT A **lumberyard** is a place where wood is stored and sold. maderería, depósito de madera

**lump** /lʌmp/ (**lumps, lumping, lumped**) **1** N-COUNT A **lump of** something is a solid piece of it. trozo ❑ *...a lump of wood.* ...un trozo de madera. **2** N-COUNT A **lump** on or in your body is a small, hard swelling that has been caused by an injury or an illness. bulto, protuberancia, chichón, chipote ❑ *I've got a lump on my shoulder.* Tengo una bolita en el hombro.

▸ **lump together** PHR-VERB If a number of different people or things **are lumped together,** they are considered as a group rather than separately. *agrupar, englobar* ❑ *Policemen, bankers and butchers are all lumped together in one group. Policías, banqueros y carniceros, todos en el mismo grupo.*

**lu|nar** /lunər/ ADJ **Lunar** means relating to the moon. *lunar* ❑ *...the lunar landscape. ...el paisaje lunar.*

**lu|nar eclipse** (**lunar eclipses**) N-COUNT A **lunar eclipse** is an occasion when the Earth is between the sun and the moon, so that for a short time you cannot see part or all of the moon. Compare **solar eclipse.** *eclipse de luna, eclipse lunar*
→ see **eclipse**

**lun|ar mod|ule** (**lunar modules**) N-COUNT A **lunar module** is a part of a spacecraft that is designed to separate from the rest of the spacecraft and land on the moon. *módulo lunar*

**lunch** /lʌntʃ/ (**lunches, lunching, lunched**) **1** N-VAR **Lunch** is the meal that you have in the middle of the day. *comida, almuerzo* ❑ *Shall we meet somewhere for lunch? ¿Nos vemos para comer en algún lado?* ❑ *He did not enjoy business lunches. No le gustan las comidas de negocios.* **2** V-I When you **lunch,** you have lunch, especially at a restaurant. *comer* [FORMAL] ❑ *Only very rich people can afford to lunch at the Mirabelle. Sólo los muy ricos pueden darse el lujo de comer en el Mirabelle.*
→ see **meal**

**Word Partnership** Usar *lunch* con:

| | |
|---|---|
| V. | **break for** lunch, **bring** ***your*** lunch, **buy** ***someone*** lunch, **eat** lunch, **go** ***somewhere*** **for** lunch, **go to** lunch, **have** lunch, **pack a** lunch, **serve** lunch **1** |
| ADJ. | **free** lunch, **good** lunch, **hot** lunch, **late** lunch **1** |

**lunch meat** (**lunch meats**) N-VAR **Lunch meat** is meat that you eat in a sandwich or salad, and that is usually cold and either sliced or formed into rolls. *carnes frías, embutido, fiambre*

**lunch|room** /lʌntʃrum/ (**lunchrooms**) also **lunch room** N-COUNT A **lunchroom** is the room in a school or at work where you buy and eat your lunch. *comedor, refectorio*

**lunch|time** /lʌntʃtaɪm/ (**lunchtimes**) also **lunch time** N-VAR **Lunchtime** is the period of the day when people have their lunch. *hora de la comida, hora de comer* ❑ *Could we meet at lunchtime? ¿Nos vemos a la hora de comer?*

**lung** /lʌŋ/ (**lungs**) N-COUNT Your **lungs** are the two organs inside your chest which fill with air when you breathe in. *pulmón* ❑ *...lung disease. ...enfermedad de los pulmones.*
→ see **amphibian, cardiovascular system, donor, respiratory system**

**lure** /lʊər/ (**lures, luring, lured**) **1** V-T To **lure** someone means to trick them into a particular place or to trick them into doing something that they should not do. *atraer, seducir, tentar* ❑ *They lured him into a trap. Lo hicieron caer en la trampa.* **2** N-COUNT A **lure** is an attractive quality that something has, or something that you find attractive. *tentación, atractivo, señuelo* ❑ *The lure of country life is as strong as ever. La tentación de vivir en el campo es tan fuerte como siempre.*

**lus|ter** /lʌstər/ N-UNCOUNT **Luster** is gentle shining light that is reflected from a surface, for example from polished metal. *lustre, brillo, fulgor*

**Lu|ther|an** /luθərən/ (**Lutherans**) **1** ADJ **Lutheran** means belonging or relating to a Protestant church, founded on the teachings of Martin Luther, which emphasizes the importance of faith and the authority of the Bible. *luterano* ❑ *...the Lutheran church. ...la iglesia luterana.* ❑ *...a Lutheran hymn. ...un himno luterano.* **2** N-COUNT A **Lutheran** is a member of the Lutheran church. *luterano o luterana* ❑ *...a school run by Lutherans. ...una escuela dirigida por luteranos.*

**luxu|ry** /lʌkʃəri, lʌgʒə-/ (**luxuries**) **1** N-UNCOUNT **Luxury** is very great comfort, especially among beautiful and expensive surroundings. *lujo, pompa, suntuosidad* ❑ *He leads a life of luxury. Vive rodeado de lujos.* **2** N-COUNT A **luxury** is something expensive which is not necessary but which gives you pleasure. *lujo* ❑ *A week by the sea is a luxury they can no longer afford. Ya no pueden darse el lujo de una semana en la playa.* **3** ADJ A **luxury** item is something expensive which is not necessary but which gives you pleasure. *lujoso, suntuoso* ❑ *...luxury leather goods. ...lujosos artículos de piel.* **4** N-SING A **luxury** is a pleasure which you do not often have the opportunity to enjoy. *lujo* ❑ *Hot baths are my favorite luxury. Mi mayor lujo es un baño caliente.*

**Thesaurus** *luxury* Ver también:

| | |
|---|---|
| N. | comfort, splendor **1** <br> extra, extravagance, nonessential, treat **2** **3** |

**lymph** /lɪmf/ N-UNCOUNT **Lymph** is a liquid that flows through your body and contains cells that help your body to fight infection. *linfa* [TECHNICAL]

**lym|phat|ic sys|tem** /lɪmfætɪk sɪstəm/ (**lymphatic systems**) N-COUNT The **lymphatic system** is the network of tissues and organs in your body that produces white blood cells and carries lymph. *sistema linfático* [TECHNICAL]

**lym|phat|ic ves|sel** (**lymphatic vessels**) N-COUNT **Lymphatic vessels** are thin tubes that carry lymph through your body. *vaso capilar* [TECHNICAL]

**lymph ca|pil|lary** (**lymph capillaries**) N-COUNT **Lymph capillaries** are tiny tubes that join together to form lymphatic vessels. *capilar linfático* [TECHNICAL]

**lymph node** /lɪmf noʊd/ (**lymph nodes**) N-COUNT **Lymph nodes** are small bean-shaped masses of tissue that help to protect the body against infection by killing bacteria. *nódulo linfático* [TECHNICAL]

**lym|pho|cyte** /lɪmfəsaɪt/ (**lymphocytes**) N-COUNT **Lymphocytes** are white blood cells that are involved in fighting infection and disease. *linfocito* [TECHNICAL]

**lynch** /lɪntʃ/ (**lynches, lynching, lynched**) V-T If an angry crowd of people **lynch** someone, they kill that person by hanging them, without letting them have a trial, because they believe that that person has committed a crime. linchar ❑ *They broke into his house and threatened to lynch him.* *Se metieron a su casa y amenazaron con lincharlo.*

**lyr|ic** /lɪrɪk/ (**lyrics**) **1** ADJ **Lyric** poetry is written in a simple and direct style, and usually expresses personal emotions such as love. lírico **2** N-COUNT The **lyrics** of a song are its words. letra ❑ *...a Broadway opera with lyrics by Langston Hughes.* *...una ópera de Broadway con letra de Langston Hughes.*

**lyso|some** /laɪsəsoʊm/ (**lysosomes**) N-COUNT A **lysosome** is a part of a cell that contains enzymes which can break down many different substances. lisosoma [TECHNICAL]

L

# Mm

**ma'am** /mæm/ N-VOC People sometimes say **ma'am** as a polite way of addressing a woman whose name they do not know, especially in the American South. señora ❑ *Would you repeat that please, ma'am? —¿Podría repetírmelo, por favor, señora?*

**ma|ca|ro|ni and cheese** /mækəroʊni ən tʃiz/ N-UNCOUNT **Macaroni and cheese** is a dish made from macaroni pasta and a cheese sauce. *macarrones con queso*

**ma|chine** /məʃin/ (**machines**) **1** N-COUNT A **machine** is a piece of equipment that uses electricity or an engine in order to do a particular kind of work. *máquina* ❑ *I put the coin in the machine. Puse la moneda en la máquina.* **2** N-COUNT You can use **machine** to refer to a large and well-controlled system or organization. *maquinaria* ❑ *...the New York political machine. ...la maquinaria política de Nueva York.*

**Thesaurus** *machine* Ver también:

N. appliance, computer, gadget, mechanism **1**
organization, structure, system **2**

**Word Partnership** Usar *machine* con:

N. **copy** machine, machine **oil**, machine **parts**, machine **shop** **1**
V. **design a** machine, **invent a** machine, **use a** machine **1**
ADJ. **heavy** machine, **new** machine, machine **washable** **1**

**ma|chine gun** (**machine guns**) N-COUNT A **machine gun** is a gun which fires a lot of bullets one after the other very quickly. *ametralladora* ❑ *Attackers fired machine guns at the car. Los asaltantes dispararon contra el automóvil con ametralladoras.*

**ma|chin|ery** /məʃinəri/ **1** N-UNCOUNT You can use **machinery** to refer to machines in general, or machines that are used in a factory or on a farm. *maquinaria* ❑ *...machinery for making cars. ...maquinaria para fabricar automóviles.* **2** N-SING **The machinery** of a government or organization is the system that it uses to deal with things. *maquinaria* ❑ *...the machinery of the legal system. ...la maquinaria del sistema legal.*

**macho** /mɑtʃoʊ/ ADJ You use **macho** to describe men who are very conscious and proud of their masculinity. *macho* [INFORMAL] ❑ *He tried to be macho by opening the bottle with his teeth. Trató de hacerse el muy macho abriendo la botella con los dientes.*

**macro|eco|nom|ics** /mækroʊɛkənɒmɪks, -ik-/ also **macro-economics** N-UNCOUNT **Macroeconomics** is the branch of economics that is concerned with the major, general features of a country's economy, such as the level of inflation, employment, or interest rates. *macroeconomía* ❑ *He teaches macroeconomics. Enseña macroeconomía.* ● **macro|eco|nom|ic** ADJ *macroeconómico* ❑ *The goal of macroeconomic policy is a growing economy. El objetivo de la política macroeconómica es una economía floreciente.*

**mad** /mæd/ (**madder, maddest**) **1** ADJ If you say that someone is **mad**, you mean that they are very angry. *furioso* [INFORMAL] ❑ *You're just mad at me because I'm late. Estás furioso conmigo sólo porque llegué tarde.* **2** ADJ You use **mad** to describe people or things that you think are very foolish. *loco* ❑ *You'd be mad to work with him again. Estarías loco si trabajaras con él otra vez.* ● **mad|ness** N-UNCOUNT *locura* ❑ *It is madness to spend $1,000 on a dress. Es una locura gastar 1,000 dólares en un vestido.* **3** ADJ Someone who is **mad** has a mental illness which makes them behave in a strange way. *loco* ❑ *She was afraid of going mad. Tenía miedo de volverse loca.* ● **mad|ness** N-UNCOUNT *locura* ❑ *What or who caused his madness? ¿Qué o quién provocó su locura?* **4** ADJ If you are **mad about** something or someone, you like them very much. *estar loco por, volver loco* [INFORMAL] ❑ *I'm mad about sports. Los deportes me vuelven loco.* ❑ *He's mad about you. Está loco por ti.* **5** ADJ **Mad** behavior is wild and uncontrolled. *desenfrenado, alocado* ❑ *There was a mad rush to get out of the building. Todos corrieron alocadamente para salir del edificio.* ● **mad|ly** ADV *desenfrenadamente, con locura* ❑ *People on the streets were waving madly. Las gentes en la calle agitaban los brazos como locos.* **6** PHRASE If you say that someone or something **drives** you **mad**, you mean that you find them extremely annoying. *volver loco* [INFORMAL] ❑ *The noise was driving me mad. El ruido estaba volviéndome loco.* **7** PHRASE If you do something **like mad**, you do it very energetically or enthusiastically. *como loco* [INFORMAL] ❑ *He was training for the competition like mad. Estaba entrenando como loco para la competencia.*

**Thesaurus** *mad* Ver también:

ADJ. angry, furious **1**
crazy, foolish, senseless **2**
deranged, insane **3**
crazy **5**

**mad|am** /mædəm/ also **Madam** N-VOC **Madam** is a very formal and polite way of addressing a woman whose name you do not know. *señora* ❑ *Good morning, madam. Buenos días, señora.*

**made** /meɪd/ **1** **Made** is the past tense and past participle of **make**. *Pasado y participio pasado de* ***make***

**2** ADJ If something is **made of** or **made out of** a particular substance, that substance was used to build it. *hecho* ❑ *The top of the table is made of glass.* *La cubierta de la mesa está hecha de vidrio.*

**made to or|der** also **made-to-order** ADJ If something is **made to order,** it is made according to your special requirements. *a la medida, de/por encargo, sobre pedido* ❑ *The dining room table was made to order.* *La mesa del comedor fue hecha a la medida.* ❑ *...a maker of made-to-order jewelry.* *...fabricante de joyería sobre pedido/a la medida.*

**Ma|fia** /mɑfiə/ (**Mafias**) also **mafia** **1** N-PROPER **The Mafia** is a criminal organization that makes money illegally, especially by threatening people and dealing in drugs. *mafia* ❑ *Italian television does not ignore the Mafia.* *La televisión italiana no ignora a la mafia.* **2** N-COUNT You can use **mafia** to refer to an organized group of people who you disapprove of because they use unfair or illegal means in order to get what they want. *mafia* ❑ *I will not let the fashion mafia tell me what to wear.* *No permitiré que la mafia de la moda me diga qué debo ponerme.*

**maf|ic** /mæfɪk/ ADJ **Mafic** rocks are igneous rocks that contain a lot of heavier elements such as magnesium and iron. Compare **felsic.** *fémico (máfico)* [TECHNICAL]

**mag** /mæg/ (**mags**) N-COUNT A **mag** is the same as a magazine. *revista* [INFORMAL] ❑ *...a music mag for girls.* *...una revista de música para mujeres.*

M

**maga|zine** /mægəzin, -zin/ (**magazines**) **1** N-COUNT A **magazine** is a monthly or weekly publication which contains articles, stories, photographs, and advertisements. *revista* ❑ *Her face is often on the cover of magazines.* *Su rostro aparece a menudo en portadas de revistas.* **2** N-COUNT In an automatic gun, the **magazine** is the part that contains the bullets. *recámara, cargador* ❑ *He took the empty magazine out of his gun.* *Sacó el cargador vacío de su pistola.*
→ see **library**

**mag|got** /mægət/ (**maggots**) N-COUNT **Maggots** are creatures that look like very small worms and turn into flies. *cresa, larva, gusano*

**mag|ic** /mædʒɪk/ **1** N-UNCOUNT **Magic** is the power to use supernatural forces to make impossible things happen, such as making people disappear or controlling events in nature. *magia* ❑ *They believe in magic.* *Creen en la magia.* **2** ADJ You use **magic** to describe something that does things, or appears to do things, by magic. *mágico* ❑ *...the magic ingredient in the face cream that helps to keep skin looking smooth.* *...el ingrediente mágico de la crema facial que ayuda a mantener la apariencia de frescura de la piel.* **3** N-UNCOUNT **Magic** is the art and skill of performing tricks to entertain people, for example by making things appear and disappear. *magia* ❑ *He loves performing magic tricks.* *Le encanta hacer trucos de magia.* **4** N-UNCOUNT **The magic of** something is a special mysterious quality which makes it seem wonderful and exciting. *magia* ❑ *Children love the magic of the movies.* *A los niños les encanta la magia del cine.* ● **Magic** is also an adjective. *mágico* ❑ *We had some magic moments together.* *Juntos pasamos algunos momentos mágicos.*

| **Thesaurus** | *magic* | Ver también: |
|---|---|---|
| N. | enchantment, illusion, sorcery, witchcraft **1**<br>appeal, beauty, charm **4** | |

**magi|cal** /mædʒɪkᵊl/ **1** ADJ Something that is **magical** seems to use magic or to be able to produce magic. *mágico* ❑ *...the story of a little boy who has magical powers.* *...la historia de un niño que tiene poderes mágicos.* ● **magi|cal|ly** /mædʒɪkli/ ADV *como por arte de magia, como por encanto* ❑ *You can't magically turn back the clock to a happier time.* *No puedes hacer retroceder el tiempo a una época más feliz como por arte de magia.* **2** ADJ You can say that a place or object is **magical** when it has a special mysterious quality that makes it seem wonderful and exciting. *maravilloso, mágico* ❑ *Bermuda is a magical place to get married.* *Las Bermudas es un lugar maravilloso para casarse., Las Bermudas es un lugar mágico, como para casarse allí.*

**ma|gi|cian** /mədʒɪʃᵊn/ (**magicians**) N-COUNT A **magician** is a person who entertains people by doing magic tricks. *mago o maga*

**mag|is|trate** /mædʒɪstreɪt/ (**magistrates**) N-COUNT A **magistrate** is an official who acts as a judge in law courts which deal with minor crimes or disputes. *juez o jueza* ❑ *The magistrate did not believe our story.* *El juez no creyó nuestra historia.*

**mag|ma** /mægmə/ N-UNCOUNT **Magma** is molten rock that is formed in very hot conditions inside the Earth. *magma (m.)* [TECHNICAL] ❑ *The volcano threw magma and ash into the air.* *El volcán arrojó lava y cenizas al aire.*
→ see **volcano**

**mag|net** /mægnɪt/ (**magnets**) N-COUNT A **magnet** is a piece of iron or other material which attracts iron toward it. *imán* ❑ *The children used a magnet to find objects made of iron.* *Los niños utilizaron un imán para encontrar objetos de hierro.*
→ see Word Web: **magnet**

**mag|net|ic** /mægnɛtɪk/ **1** ADJ If something metal is **magnetic,** it acts like a magnet. *magnético* ❑ *...iron-rich magnetic minerals.* *...minerales magnéticos ricos en hierro.* **2** ADJ You use **magnetic** to describe tapes and other objects which have a coating of a magnetic substance and contain coded information that can be read by computers or other machines. *magnético* ❑ *...an ID card with a magnetic strip.* *...una credencial con banda magnética.* **3** ADJ If you describe something or someone as **magnetic,** you mean that they are very attractive to people because they have unusual, powerful, and exciting qualities. *con magnetismo* ❑ *The park has a beauty that is magnetic.* *El parque es de una belleza llena de magnetismo.*

**mag|net|ic dec|li|na|tion** /mægnɛtɪk dɛklɪneɪʃᵊn/ (**magnetic declinations**) N-VAR **Magnetic declination** is the angle between the magnetic North Pole of the Earth and the geographic North Pole. *declinación magnética* [TECHNICAL]

**mag|net|ic field** (**magnetic fields**) N-COUNT A **magnetic field** is an area around a magnet, or something functioning as a magnet, in which

**Word Web** magnet

**Magnets** have a north **pole** and a south pole. One side has a **negative charge** and the other side has a **positive** charge. The negative side of a magnet **attracts** the positive side of another magnet. Two sides that have the same charge will **repel** each other. The earth itself is a huge magnet, with a North Pole and a South Pole. A **compass** uses a magnetized needle to indicate directions. The "north" end of the needle always points toward the earth's North Pole.

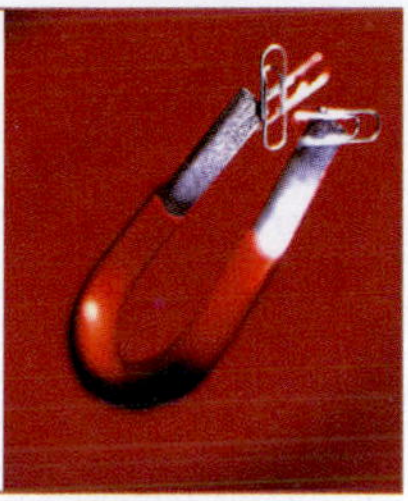

the magnet's power to attract things is felt. *campo magnético*

**mag|net|ic pole** (**magnetic poles**) N-COUNT The **magnetic poles** of a magnet are the two areas at opposite ends of the magnet where the magnetic field is strongest. The **magnetic poles** of the Earth are the two areas near the North and South Poles where the Earth's magnetic field is strongest. *polo magnético*

**mag|net|ic re|ver|sal** (**magnetic reversals**) N-VAR **Magnetic reversal** is the process which causes the Earth's magnetic North Pole and its magnetic South Pole to reverse their positions. *inversión magnética* [TECHNICAL]

**mag|net|ize** /mæɡnɪtaɪz/ (**magnetizes, magnetizing, magnetized**) V-T If you **magnetize** something, you make it magnetic. *imantar, magnetizar* ❑ *Make a Mobius strip out of a ribbon of mild steel and magnetize it. Haga una cinta de Möbius con una tira de acero dulce y magnetícela.* ❑ *...a small metal chessboard with magnetized playing pieces. ...un pequeño tablero metálico de ajedrez con piezas imantadas.*
→ see **magnet**

**mag|nifi|cent** /mæɡnɪfɪsənt/ ADJ Something or someone that is **magnificent** is extremely good, beautiful, or impressive. *magnífico, espléndido* ❑ *...a magnificent country house. ...una casa de campo magnífica.* ● **mag|nifi|cence** N-UNCOUNT *magnificencia, esplendor* ❑ *...the magnificence of the Swiss mountains. ...la magnificencia de las montañas suizas.* ● **mag|nifi|cent|ly** ADV *magníficamente, espléndidamente* ❑ *The team played magnificently. El equipo jugó espléndidamente.*

**mag|ni|fy** /mæɡnɪfaɪ/ (**magnifies, magnifying, magnified**) **1** V-T To **magnify** an object means to make it appear larger than it really is, by means of a special lens or mirror. *agrandar, aumentar, amplificar* ❑ *This telescope magnifies images 11 times. Este telescopio agranda las imágenes once veces.* ❑ *A lens magnified the picture so it was like looking at a large TV screen. Una lente agrandaba la imagen, por lo que era como estar viendo en una gran pantalla de televisión.* ● **mag|ni|fi|ca|tion** /mæɡnɪfɪkeɪʃən/ N-UNCOUNT *aumento, amplificación* ❑ *Some creatures are too small to see without magnification. Algunas criaturas son demasiado pequeñas para poder verlas sin aumento.* **2** V-T To **magnify** something means to increase its effect, size, loudness, or intensity. *amplificar* ❑ *The space in the church seemed to magnify every sound. El espacio de la iglesia parecía amplificar todos los sonidos.*

**maid** /meɪd/ (**maids**) N-COUNT A **maid** is a woman who cleans rooms in a hotel or private house. *recamarera, sirvienta, mucama* ❑ *A maid brought me breakfast. Una recamarera me llevó el desayuno.*

**maid|en** /meɪdən/ (**maidens**) **1** N-COUNT A **maiden** is a young girl or woman. *doncella* [LITERARY] ❑ *...beautiful maidens. ...hermosas doncellas.* **2** ADJ The **maiden** voyage or flight of a ship or aircraft is the first official journey that it makes. *inaugural* ❑ *In 1912, the Titanic sank on her maiden voyage. El Titánic se hundió en su viaje inaugural en 1912.*

**maid of hon|or** (**maids of honor**) N-COUNT A **maid of honor** is the chief bridesmaid at a wedding. *dama de honor*
→ see **wedding**

**mail** /meɪl/ (**mails, mailing, mailed**) **1** N-SING **The mail** is the public service or system by which letters and packages are collected and delivered. *correo* ❑ *Your check is in the mail. Su cheque ya está en el correo.* **2** N-UNCOUNT You can refer to letters and packages that are delivered to you as **mail**. *correo, correspondencia* ❑ *There was no mail this morning. No hubo correo esta mañana.* **3** V-T If you **mail** something to someone, you send it to them by mail. *enviar por correo, mandar por correo* ❑ *He mailed the documents to French journalists. Envió los documentos por correo a algunos periodistas franceses.* ❑ *He mailed me the contract. Me envió/mandó el contrato por correo.* **4** V-T To **mail** a message to someone means to send it to them by means of e-mail or a computer network. *enviar/mandar por correo electrónico* ● **Mail** is also a noun. *mensaje* ❑ *If you have any problems then send me a mail. Si tiene problemas, entonces envíeme un mensaje.* **5** → see also **e-mail**

▸ **mail out** PHR-VERB If someone **mails out** things such as letters, leaflets, or bills, they send them to a large number of people at the same time. *enviar por correo* ❑ *We have mailed out our wedding invitations. Ya enviamos nuestras invitaciones a la boda.*

**Word Partnership** Usar *mail* con:

| | |
|---|---|
| PREP. | **by** mail, **in the** mail, **through the** mail **1** |
| N. | mail **carrier**, **fan** mail **2** |
| V. | **deliver** mail, **get** mail, **open** mail, **read** mail, **receive** mail, **send** mail **2** |

**mail|box** /meɪlbɒks/ (**mailboxes**) **1** N-COUNT A **mailbox** is a box outside your house where your letters are delivered. *buzón* ❑ *The next day there was a letter in her mailbox. Al día siguiente, había una carta en su buzón.* **2** N-COUNT A **mailbox** is a metal box in a public place, where you put letters and small packages to be collected. *buzón* ❑ *He dropped the*

m

*letters into the mailbox.* *Echó las cartas en el buzón.* **3** N-COUNT On a computer, your **mailbox** is the file where your e-mail is stored. *buzón* ❑ *There were 30 new messages in his mailbox.* *Había 30 mensajes nuevos en su buzón.*

**mail|er** /meɪlər/ (**mailers**) **1** N-COUNT A **mailer** is a box, large envelope, or other container for mailing things. *sobre, paquete* ❑ *Put the CD in this mailer and send it back to us.* *Ponga el disco compacto en este sobre y envíenoslo de regreso.* **2** N-COUNT A **mailer** is a letter advertising something or appealing for money for a particular charity. Mailers are sent out to a large number of people at once. *folleto publicitario enviado por correo* ❑ *Thousands of mailers go straight into the trash.* *Miles de folletos publicitarios enviados por correo van directamente a la basura.* **3** N-COUNT A **mailer** is a company that sends out mail. *remitente* ❑ *The group represents mailers who send only a small volume of mail.* *El grupo representa a las empresas que sólo envían poca correspondencia.*

**mail|man** /meɪlmæn/ (**mailmen**) N-COUNT A **mailman** is a man whose job is to collect and deliver letters and packages that are sent by mail. *cartero*

**mail or|der** N-UNCOUNT **Mail order** is a system of buying and selling goods. You choose them from a catalog, and the company sends them to you by mail. *compraventa por correo* ❑ *The toys are available by mail order.* *Puede comprar los juguetes mediante venta por correo.*

M

**main** /meɪn/ (**mains**) **1** ADJ The **main** thing is the most important one of several similar things in a particular situation. *principal* ❑ *The main reason I came today was to say sorry.* *La principal razón por la que vine fue para disculparme.* **2** PHRASE If you say that something is true **in the main,** you mean that it is generally true, although there may be exceptions. *por lo general, en general* ❑ *Nurses are, in the main, women.* *Por lo/En general, los que atienden a los enfermos son mujeres., Por lo/En general, hay más enfermeras que enfermeros.* **3** N-COUNT The **mains** are the pipes which supply gas or water to buildings, or which take sewage away from them. *tubería principal, red de suministro, cañería principal* ❑ *...the water supply from the mains.* *...el agua de la red de suministro.*

| **Thesaurus** | *main* | Ver también: |
|---|---|---|
| ADJ. | chief, major, primary, principal **1** | |

**main clause** (**main clauses**) N-COUNT A **main clause** is a clause that can stand alone as a complete sentence. Compare **subordinate clause.** *oración principal*

**main drag** N-SING **The main drag** in a town is its main street. *calle principal* [INFORMAL] ❑ *Michigan Avenue is the town's main drag.* *La Avenida Michigan es la calle principal de la ciudad.*

**main|frame** /meɪnfreɪm/ (**mainframes**) N-COUNT A **mainframe** or **mainframe computer** is a large, powerful computer which can be used by many people at the same time. *computadora central* ❑ *The names of all patients are on the hospital mainframe.* *Los nombres de todos los pacientes están en la computadora central del hospital.*

**main idea** (**main ideas**) N-COUNT The **main idea** of a piece of writing is the most important subject or point of view that it discusses or expresses. *idea central*

**main|land** /meɪnlænd/ N-SING You can refer to the largest part of a country or continent as **the mainland** when contrasting it with the islands around it. *tierra firme, continente, territorio continental* ❑ *She caught a boat to the mainland.* *Tomó un barco para ir a tierra firme.*

**main|ly** /meɪnli/ ADV You use **mainly** to say that a statement is true in most cases or to a large extent. *principalmente* ❑ *The African people there were mainly from Senegal.* *Los africanos que estaban ahí eran principalmente del Senegal.*

**main-sequence star** (**main-sequence stars**) N-COUNT A **main-sequence star** is the most common type of star, which gets its energy by converting hydrogen into helium. *estrella de secuencia principal* [TECHNICAL]

**main|stream** /meɪnstrim/ N-SING People, activities, or ideas that are part of the **mainstream** are regarded as typical, normal, and conventional. *corriente principal* ❑ *Some people like to live outside the mainstream.* *A algunas personas les gusta apartarse de la corriente principal.*
→ see **culture**

**Main Street** **1** N-PROPER In small towns in the United States, the street where most of the stores are is often called **Main Street.** *Calle Mayor, Calle Principal* **2** N-UNCOUNT **Main Street** is used by journalists to refer to the ordinary people of America who live in small towns rather than big cities or are not very rich. *provincia, ciudad pequeña* ❑ *This financial crisis had a big impact on Main Street.* *Esta crisis financiera tuvo su mayor impacto en (los habitantes de) provincia.*

**main|tain** /meɪnteɪn/ (**maintains, maintaining, maintained**) **1** V-T If you **maintain** something, you continue to have it, and do not let it stop or grow weaker. *mantener* ❑ *France maintained close contacts with Jordan during the Gulf War.* *Francia mantuvo un estrecho contacto con Jordania durante la guerra del golfo.* **2** V-T If you **maintain that** something is true, you state your opinion strongly. *mantener, sostener, afirmar* ❑ *He maintained that he had not stolen the money.* *Él sostuvo que no había robado el dinero.* ❑ *"Not all women want to have children," Jo maintains.* *Jo afirma que no todas las mujeres quieren tener hijos.* **3** V-T If you **maintain** something **at** a particular rate or level, you keep it at that rate or level. *mantener* ❑ *She maintained her weight at 150 pounds.* *Mantuvo su peso en 68 kilos.* **4** V-T If you **maintain** a road, building, vehicle, or machine, you keep it in good condition by regularly checking it and repairing it when necessary. *mantener* ❑ *The house costs a lot to maintain.* *El mantenimiento de la casa cuesta mucho.* **5** V-T If you **maintain** someone, you provide them with money and other things that they need. *mantener* ❑ *...the costs of maintaining a child in college.* *...el costo de mantener a un niño que está en la escuela.*

| **Thesaurus** | *maintain* | Ver también: |
|---|---|---|
| V. | carry on, continue; (*ant.*) neglect **1** | |
| | keep up, look after, protect, repair **4** | |

**main|te|nance** /meɪntɪnəns/ **1** N-UNCOUNT The **maintenance** of a building, vehicle, road, or machine is the process of keeping it in good condition by regularly checking it and repairing it when necessary. *mantenimiento* ❑ *...maintenance work on government buildings. ...las obras de mantenimiento de los edificios gubernamentales.* ❑ *They replaced the window during routine maintenance. Reemplazaron la ventana durante el mantenimiento regular/de rutina.* **2** N-UNCOUNT If you ensure the **maintenance of** a state or process, you make sure that it continues. *mantenimiento* ❑ *...the maintenance of peace in Asia. ...el mantenimiento de la paz en Asia.* **3** N-UNCOUNT **Maintenance** is money that someone gives regularly to another person to pay for the things that the person needs. *pensión alimenticia* ❑ *He pays a lot in maintenance for his children. Paga mucho de pensión alimenticia para sus hijos.*

**mai|tre d'** /meɪtrədi, meɪtər-/ (**maitre d's, maitres d'**) N-COUNT At a restaurant, the **maitre d'** is the head waiter. *jefe de comedor, capitán de meseros* ❑ *We found a table and the maitre d' told us that we would be served quickly. Encontramos (una) mesa y el capitán de meseros nos dijo que nos servirían rápidamente.*

**ma|jes|tic** /mədʒɛstɪk/ ADJ If you describe something or someone as **majestic,** you think they are very beautiful, dignified, and impressive. *majestuoso* ❑ *...a majestic country home. ...una casa de campo majestuosa.* ● **ma|jes|ti|cal|ly** /mədʒɛstɪkli/ ADV *majestuosamente* ❑ *The ship sailed majestically in from the Atlantic Ocean. El barco arribó majestuosamente después de recorrer el Océano Atlántico.*

**maj|es|ty** /mædʒɪsti/ (**majesties**) **1** N-VOC; PRON You use majesty in expressions such as **Your Majesty** or **Her Majesty** when you are addressing or referring to a king or queen. *majestad* ❑ *His Majesty would like to see you now. Su Majestad lo verá ahora.* **2** N-UNCOUNT **Majesty** is the quality of being beautiful, dignified, and impressive. *majestuosidad* ❑ *...the majesty of the mountains. ...la majestuosidad de las montañas.*

| Word Link | *major ≈ larger : major, majority, majorleague* |
|---|---|

**ma|jor** /meɪdʒər/ (**majors, majoring, majored**) **1** ADJ You use **major** when you want to describe something that is more important, serious, or significant than other things in a group or situation. *muy importante* ❑ *His family was a major factor in his decision to leave his job. Su familia fue un factor muy importante en su decisión de dejar su empleo.* ❑ *Homelessness is a major problem in some cities. La falta de vivienda es un gran problema en algunas ciudades.* **2** N-COUNT; N-TITLE; N-VOC A **major** is an officer who is one rank above captain in the United States Army, Air Force, or Marines. *mayor, comandante* ❑ *I was a major in the war, you know. Tuve el grado de mayor en la guerra, ¿sabes?* **3** N-COUNT At a university or college, a student's **major** is the main subject that they are studying. *materia principal* ❑ *"What's your major?"—"Chemistry." —¿Qué estás estudiando?—Química.* **4** N-COUNT At a university or college, if a student is, for example, a geology **major,** geology is the main subject they are studying. *materia principal* ❑ *She was a history major at the University of Oklahoma. Estudió historia en la Universidad de Oklahoma.* **5** V-I If a student at a university or college **majors in** a particular subject, that subject is the main one they study. *especializarse* ❑ *He majored in finance at Claremont Men's College in California. Se especializó en finanzas en el Colegio Claremont para Hombres de California.* **6** N-PLURAL **The majors** are groups of professional sports teams that compete against each other, especially in baseball. *liga mayor* ❑ *I just wanted a chance to play in the majors. Sólo quería una oportunidad para jugar en las grandes ligas.*

| Thesaurus | *major* | Ver también: |
|---|---|---|
| ADJ. | chief, critical, crucial, key, main, principal; (*ant.*) little, minor, unimportant **1** | |

**ma|jor|ity** /mədʒɔrɪti/ (**majorities**) **1** N-SING The **majority** of people or things in a group is more than half of them. *mayoría* ❑ *The majority of my patients are women. La mayoría de mis pacientes son mujeres.* PHRASE ● If a group is **in a majority** or **in the majority**, they form more than half of a larger group. *mayoría* ❑ *Supporters of the proposal are still in the majority. Los que apoyan la propuesta siguen siendo la mayoría.* **2** N-COUNT A **majority** is the difference between the number of votes or seats in a legislature or parliament that the winner gets in an election, and the number of votes or seats that the next person or party gets. *mayoría* ❑ *After the November elections, the Democrats had a majority of 32 seats. Después de las elecciones de noviembre, los demócratas obtuvieron la mayoría con 32 escaños de diferencia.*

| Word Partnership | Usar *majority* con: |
|---|---|
| N. | majority **of people**, majority **of the population** **1**<br>majority **leader** **2** |
| ADJ. | **overwhelming** majority, **vast** majority **1** **2** |

**ma|jor key** N-COUNT In music, the **major key** is based on the major scale, in which the third note is two tones higher than the first. *si/do mayor*

**ma|jor league** (**major leagues**) **1** N-PLURAL **The major leagues** are groups of professional sports teams that compete against each other, especially in baseball. *gran liga* ❑ *At 47, he was the oldest player in the major leagues last season. Con sus 47 años, fue el jugador más viejo de las grandes ligas en la última temporada.* **2** ADJ **Major league** means connected with the major leagues in baseball. *gran liga* ❑ *I live in a town with no major league baseball. Vivo en una ciudad que no tiene equipo en las grandes ligas de béisbol.* **3** ADJ **Major-league** people or institutions are important or successful. *de primera línea* ❑ *His first film has major-league stars. En su primera película actúan estrellas de primera línea.*

**make**
❶ CARRYING OUT AN ACTION
❷ CAUSING OR CHANGING
❸ CREATING OR PRODUCING
❹ LINK VERB USES
❺ ACHIEVING OR REACHING
❻ PHRASAL VERBS

❶ **make** /meɪk/ (**makes, making, made**)

**Make** is used in a large number of expressions which are explained under other words in this dictionary. For example, the expression "to make sense" is explained at "sense."

**1** V-T You can use **make** with a wide range of nouns to indicate that someone performs an action or says something. *hacer* ❑ *I'd just like to make a comment. Sólo quisiera hacer un comentario.* ❑ *I made a few phone calls. Hice unas cuantas llamadas por teléfono.* **2** PHRASE If you **make do with** something, you use or have it instead of something else that you do not have, although it is not as good. *conformarse* ❑ *Why make do with a copy if you can afford the real thing? ¿Por qué conformarse con una copia cuando se puede tener el original?*

❷ **make** /meɪk/ (**makes, making, made**) **1** V-T If something **makes** you do something, it causes you to do it. *hacer* ❑ *Dirt from the highway made him cough. El polvo de la carretera lo hizo toser.* ❑ *Her long dress made her look like a movie star. Su vestido largo la hacía parecer una estrella de cine.* **2** V-T If you **make** someone do something, you force them to do it. *obligar* ❑ *You can't make me do anything. No puedes obligarme a hacer nada.* **3** V-T You use **make** to talk about causing someone or something to be a particular thing or to have a particular quality. For example, to **make** someone a star means to cause them to become a star, and to **make** someone angry means to cause them to become angry. *hacer* ❑ *Home-schooling made me a better person. El estudio/La educación que recibí en casa me hizo una mejor persona.* ❑ *She made life very difficult for me. Me hizo la vida muy difícil.* **4** V-T If you **make yourself** understood, heard, or known, you succeed in getting people to understand you, hear you, or know that you are there. *hacerse* ❑ *He was able to make himself understood in Spanish. Lograba hacerse entender en español.* **5** V-T If you **make** something **into** something else, you change it in some way so that it becomes that other thing. *convertir* ❑ *We made it into a beautiful home. La convertimos en una casa hermosa.* **6** to **make friends** → see **friend**

❸ **make** /meɪk/ (**makes, making, made**) **1** V-T To **make** something means to produce, construct, or create it. *hacer* ❑ *She made her own bread. Hacía su propio pan.* ❑ *Having curtains made can be expensive. Mandar hacer las cortinas puede ser muy caro.* **2** V-T If you **make** a note or list, you write something down in that form. *hacer, escribir* ❑ *Mr. Perry made a note in his book. El señor Perry escribió una nota en su libro.* **3** V-T If you **make** rules or laws, you decide what these should be. *hacer, establecer* ❑ *The police don't make the laws. La policía no hace las reglas.* **4** V-T If you **make** money, you get it by working for it, by selling something, or by winning it. *hacer, ganar* ❑ *I think every business's goal is to make money. Creo que el objetivo de todo negocio es ganar dinero.* **5** N-COUNT The **make** of something such as a car or radio is the name of the company that made it. *marca* ❑ *What make of car do you drive? ¿De qué marca es su coche?*

**Thesaurus** *make* Ver también:
v. build, compose, create, fabricate, produce; (*ant.*) destroy ❸ **1**

❹ **make** /meɪk/ (**makes, making, made**) **1** V-LINK You can use **make** to say that someone or something has the right qualities for a particular task or role. *ser* ❑ *She'll make a good actress, if she gets the right training. Será una buena actriz, si recibe la capacitación adecuada.* ❑ *You've a very good idea there. It will make a good book. Tu idea es muy buena; serviría para escribir un buen libro.* **2** V-LINK You can use **make** to say what two numbers add up to. *ser* ❑ *Four twos make eight. Cuatro por dos son ocho.*

❺ **make** /meɪk/ (**makes, making, made**) **1** V-T If someone **makes** a particular team or **makes** a particular high position, they do so well that they are put on that team or get that position. *formar parte, lograr, alcanzar* ❑ *The athletes are just happy to make the team. Los atletas están felices de formar parte del equipo.* **2** PHRASE If you **make it** somewhere, you succeed in getting there, especially in time to do something. *lograr llegar* ❑ *So you did make it to America, after all. Así que lograste llegar a Estados Unidos, después de todo.* **3** PHRASE If you **make it,** you are successful in achieving something difficult, or in surviving through a very difficult period. *lograr* ❑ *I believe I have the talent to make it. Creo tener el talento para lograrlo.*

❻ **make** /meɪk/ (**makes, making, made**)
▸ **make for** PHR-VERB If you **make for** a place, you move toward it. *dirigirse a* ❑ *He made for the door. Se dirigió hacia la puerta.*
▸ **make of** PHR-VERB If you ask a person what they **make of** something, you want to know what their impression, opinion, or understanding of it is. *pensar de* ❑ *Nancy wasn't sure what to make of Mick's apology. Nancy no sabía qué pensar de la disculpa de Mick.*
▸ **make off** PHR-VERB If you **make off,** you leave somewhere as quickly as possible, often in order to escape. *escapar, salir corriendo* ❑ *They made off in a stolen car. Escaparon en un coche robado.*
▸ **make out 1** PHR-VERB If you **make** something **out,** you can see, hear or understand it. *distinguir, comprender, entender* ❑ *I could just make out a tall figure of a man. Sólo pude distinguir la silueta de un hombre alto.* ❑ *She thought she heard a name. She couldn't make it out, though. Creyó oír un nombre, aunque no logró distinguir qué nombre era.* ❑ *I couldn't make out what he was saying. No pude entender lo que estaba diciendo.* **2** PHR-VERB If you **make out that** something is true or **make** something **out to** be true, you try to cause people to believe that it is the case. *dar a entender* ❑ *They were trying to make out that I stole the money. Estaban tratando de dar a entender que yo robé el dinero.* ❑ *They made him out to be an awful guy. Dieron a entender que era un tipo horrible.* **3** PHR-VERB When you **make out** a check, receipt, or order form, you write all the necessary information on it. *hacer* ❑ *I'll make the check out to you and put it in the mail this*

**Word Web** makeup

The women of ancient Egypt were among the first to **wear makeup**. They **applied foundation** to lighten their skin and used kohl as **eye shadow** to darken their eyelids. Greek women used charcoal as an eyeliner and rouge on their cheeks. In 14th century Europe, the most popular **cosmetic** was a **powder** made from wheat flour. Women whitened their faces to show their high social class. A light **complexion** meant the woman didn't have to work outdoors. **Cosmetics** containing poisons, such as lead and arsenic, sometimes caused illness and death. Makeup use grew in the early 1900s. For the first time many women could afford mass-produced **lipstick**, **mascara**, and **face powder**.

*afternoon. Haré el cheque a tu nombre y lo pondré en el correo esta tarde.*

▸ **make up** 1 PHR-VERB The people or things that **make up** something are the members or parts that form that thing. *representar, constituir* ❑ *Women officers make up 13 percent of the police force. Las mujeres policía representan el 13 por ciento de la fuerza policiaca.* 2 PHR-VERB If you **make up** something such as a story or excuse, you invent it. *inventar* ❑ *It's very unkind of you to make up stories about him. Es muy poco amable de tu parte inventar historias sobre él.* 3 PHR-VERB If two people **make up** after a quarrel or disagreement, they become friends again. *reconciliarse* ❑ *She came back and they made up. Ella regresó y se reconciliaron.*

**mak|er** /meɪkər/ (**makers**) N-COUNT The **maker** of something is the person or company that makes it. *fabricante* ❑ *...Japan's two largest car makers. ...los dos principales fabricantes de autos de Japón.*

**make|up** /meɪkʌp/ 1 N-UNCOUNT **Makeup** consists of things such as lipstick, eye shadow, and powder which some women put on their faces to make themselves look more attractive. *maquillaje* ❑ *Normally she wore little makeup. Normalmente, se maquillaba poco.* 2 N-UNCOUNT The **makeup** of something consists of its different parts and the way these parts are arranged. *composición, estructura* ❑ *The makeup of the unions has changed a lot. La composición de los sindicatos ha cambiado mucho.* 3 N-UNCOUNT **Makeup** consists of things such as lipstick, eye shadow, and powder, and sometimes hairstyles, which an actor wears on stage. *maquillaje*
→ see Word Web: **makeup**
→ see **theater**

**mak|ing** /meɪkɪŋ/ (**makings**) 1 N-UNCOUNT The **making** of something is the act or process of producing or creating it. *hechura, elaboración* ❑ *...Salamon's book about the making of the movie. ...el libro de Salamon sobre la filmación de la película.* 2 PHRASE If you describe a person or thing as something **in the making,** you mean that they are going to become known or recognized as that thing. *en ciernes* ❑ *Her drama teacher thinks Julie is a star in the making. El maestro de teatro de Julie cree que ella es una estrella en ciernes.* 3 PHRASE If something **is the making of** a person or thing, it is the reason that they become successful or become very much better than they used to be. *ser decisivo para* ❑ *This new school might be the making of him. La nueva escuela puede ser decisiva para él.* 4 PHRASE If you say that a person or thing **has the makings of** something, you mean it seems possible or likely that they will become that thing, as they have the necessary qualities. *tener el potencial para* ❑ *Godfrey had the makings of a successful journalist. Godfrey tenía el potencial para llegar a ser un gran periodista.* 5 PHRASE If you say that something such as a problem you have is **of** your **own making,** you mean you have caused or created it yourself. *hechura de uno, obra* ❑ *Some of his problems are of his own making. Algunos de sus problemas son obra suya.*

**male** /meɪl/ (**males**) 1 N-COUNT A **male** is a person or animal that belongs to the sex that cannot lay eggs or have babies. *macho, varón, hombre* ❑ *...males and females of all ages. ...hombres y mujeres de todas las edades.* ● **Male** is also an adjective. *varón, macho* ❑ *...male dancers. ...bailarines varones.* ❑ *...male cats. ...felinos machos.* 2 ADJ **Male** means relating to, belonging to, or affecting men rather than women. *masculino* ❑ *...male unemployment. ...desempleo masculino.*
→ see **reproduction**

**ma|lig|nant** /məlɪgnənt/ ADJ A **malignant** tumor or disease is out of control and likely to cause death. *maligno* [MEDICAL] ❑ *The lump in her breast was not malignant. El bulto que tenía en el pecho no era maligno.*

**mall** /mɔl/ (**malls**) N-COUNT A **mall** is a very large, enclosed shopping area. *centro comercial*

**mal|le|able** /mæliəbᵊl/ 1 ADJ Someone who is **malleable** is easily influenced or controlled by other people. *maleable* [WRITTEN] ❑ *She was young enough to be malleable. Era una mujer todavía joven y maleable.* 2 ADJ A substance that is **malleable** is soft and can easily be made into different shapes. *maleable* ❑ *Silver is the most malleable of all metals. La plata es el más maleable de los metales.* ● **mal|le|abil|ity** /mæliəbɪlɪti/ N-UNCOUNT *maleabilidad* ❑ *Red-hot metals rapidly lose their malleability as they cool. Los metales al rojo vivo pierden la maleabilidad rápidamente al enfriarse.*

**mal|prac|tice** /mælpræktɪs/ (**malpractices**) N-VAR If you accuse someone of **malpractice,** you are accusing them of breaking the law or the rules of their profession. *negligencia profesional* [FORMAL] ❑ *They accused the doctor of malpractice. Acusaron al médico de negligencia profesional.*

**mama** /mɑmə, məmɑ/ (**mamas**) also **mamma** N-COUNT; N-VOC **Mama** means the same as **mother**. *mamá* [INFORMAL]

**mam|bo** /mɑmboʊ/ (**mambos**) N-COUNT The **mambo** is a lively dance that comes from Cuba.

m

**Word Web** **mammal**

Elephants, dogs, mice, and humans all belong to the class of animals called **mammals**. Mammals have live babies rather than laying eggs. The females also feed their **young** with milk from their bodies. Mammals are **warm-blooded** and usually have hair on their bodies. Some, such as the brown bear and the raccoon, are omnivorous—they eat meat and plants. Deer and zebras are herbivorous, living mostly on grass and leaves. Lions and tigers are carnivorous—they eat meat. They must have a supply of large **game** to survive. Mammals have a variety of different types of **limbs**. Monkeys have long arms for climbing. Seals have **flippers** for swimming.

*mambo* ❑ *The mambo was very popular in the 1940s and 1950s. El mambo fue muy popular en los decenios de 1940 y 1950.* ❑ *...mambo music. ...mambo.*

**mam|mal** /mæməl/ (**mammals**) N-COUNT **Mammals** are animals such as humans, dogs, lions, and whales. In general, female mammals give birth to babies rather than laying eggs, and feed their young with milk. *mamífero o mamífera*
→ see Word Web: **mammal**
→ see **bat, pet, whale**

**mam|ma|ry** /mæməri/ ADJ **Mammary** means relating to the breasts. *mamario* [TECHNICAL]

**mam|ma|ry glands** N-COUNT **Mammary glands** are milk-producing glands in mammals. *glándula mamaria* [TECHNICAL]

M

**mam|mog|ra|phy** /məmɑgrəfi/ N-UNCOUNT **Mammography** is the use of X-rays to examine women's breasts in order to detect cancer. *mamografía* ❑ *Mammography is not always available in poor countries. La mamografía no es una técnica que siempre esté disponible en los países pobres.*

**man** /mæn/ (**men, mans, manning, manned**) **1** N-COUNT A **man** is an adult male human being. *hombre* ❑ *A young man walked into the room. Un hombre joven entró en la habitación.* ❑ *Both men and women will enjoy this movie. Tanto los hombres como las mujeres disfrutarán esta película.* **2** N-VAR **Man** and **men** are sometimes used to refer to all human beings, including both males and females. Some people dislike this use. *hombre* ❑ *...when man first arrived in the Americas. ...cuando el hombre llegó al Continente Americano por primera vez.* **3** CONVENTION Some people address a man as **my man**. *hombre (en ocasiones no se traduce)* [INFORMAL] ❑ *"Get the guy in the purple shirt."— "All right, my man." —Llama al hombre de la camisa morada. —Está bien.* **4** V-T If you **man** something such as a place or machine, you operate it or are in charge of it. *manejar, manipular, ocuparse de* ❑ *Two officers manned the aircraft. Dos agentes tripularon el avión.* ❑ *...the person manning the phone. ...la persona que se ocupa del teléfono.* **5** → see also **manned, no-man's land**
→ see **age**

**man|age** /mænɪdʒ/ (**manages, managing, managed**) **1** V-T If you **manage** an organization, business, or system, or the people who work in it, you are responsible for controlling them. *administrar* ❑ *Within two years he was managing the store. En menos de dos años, ya era el administrador de la tienda.* **2** V-T If you **manage** time, money, or other resources, you deal with them carefully and do not waste them. *administrar* ❑ *In a busy world, managing your time is very important. En este mundo tan atareado, la administración del tiempo es muy importante.* **3** V-T If you **manage to** do something, especially something difficult, you succeed in doing it. *arreglárselas* ❑ *Somehow, he managed to persuade Kay to buy a computer for him. De alguna manera, se las arregló para persuadir a Kate de que le comprara una computadora.* ❑ *I managed to pull myself out of the water. Me las arreglé para salir del agua.* **4** V-I If you **manage**, you succeed in coping with a difficult situation. *arreglárselas* ❑ *She managed without medication for three years. Se las arregló sin medicinas durante tres años.*

**man|aged care** N-UNCOUNT **Managed care** is a method of controlling the cost of medical care by fixing a doctor's fees and limiting a patient's choice of doctors and hospitals. *asistencia médica dirigida*

**Word Link** *ment ≈ state, condition : agreement, management, movement*

**man|age|ment** /mænɪdʒmənt/ (**managements**) **1** N-UNCOUNT **Management** is the control and organizing of a business or other organization. *administración* ❑ *The zoo needed better management rather than more money. Antes bien que más dinero, el zoológico necesitaba una mejor administración.* **2** N-VAR You can refer to the people who control and organize a business or other organization as the **management**. *gerencia, administración* [BUSINESS] ❑ *The management is trying hard to keep employees happy. La gerencia está haciendo grandes esfuerzos por mantener contento al personal.* ❑ *We need to get more women into top management. Necesitamos que haya más mujeres entre los altos ejecutivos.*

**Word Partnership** Usar *management* con:

N. **business** management, **crisis** management, management **skills**, management **style**, **waste** management **1**
management **team**, management **training** **2**
ADJ. **new** management, **senior** management **2**

**man|ag|er** /mænɪdʒər/ (**managers**) N-COUNT A **manager** is a person who is responsible for

running part of or the whole of a business organization. *gerente, administrador o administradora, director o directora* ❑ *The chef, staff, and managers are all Chinese. Tanto el cocinero como el personal y los administradores/gerentes son chinos.*
→ see **concert**

**mana|tee** /mænəti/ (**manatees**) N-COUNT A **manatee** is a mammal which lives in the sea and looks like a small whale with a broad, flat tail. *manatí*

**man|date** /mændeɪt/ (**mandates, mandating, mandated**) **1** N-COUNT A government's **mandate** is the authority it has to carry out a particular policy or task as a result of winning an election or vote. *mandato* ❑ *The election result gave the new leader a mandate for change. El resultado de las elecciones significó un mandato de cambio para el nuevo dirigente.* **2** N-COUNT If someone is given a **mandate** to carry out a particular policy or task, they are given the official authority to do it. *orden, instrucción, directriz* ❑ *The company has a mandate to help their clients. Las instrucciones de la empresa son ayudar a sus clientes.* **3** V-T When someone **is mandated to** carry out a particular policy or task, they are given the official authority to do it. *orden, instrucción* [FORMAL] ❑ *The organization was mandated to look after the country's blood supplies. La organización tiene instrucciones de encargarse del suministro de sangre del país., Se encargó a la organización el suministro de sangre del país.* **4** V-T To **mandate** something means to make it mandatory. *estipular, resolver* ❑ *The law mandates a 40-hour work week. La ley estipula que la semana laboral es de 40 horas.* ❑ *Congress mandated that all 4th graders take the reading test. El Congreso resolvió que todos los alumnos de 40. grado hagan el examen de lectura.*

**man|di|ble** /mændɪbᵊl/ (**mandibles**) N-COUNT A **mandible** is the bone in the lower jaw of a person or animal. *mandíbula inferior* [TECHNICAL]

**mane** /meɪn/ (**manes**) N-COUNT The **mane** on a horse or lion is the long, thick hair that grows from its neck. *crin, melena* ❑ *You can wash the horse's mane at the same time as his body. Puede lavar la crin del caballo al mismo tiempo que el cuerpo.*
→ see **horse**

**ma|neu|ver** /mənuvər/ (**maneuvers, maneuvering, maneuvered**) **1** V-T If you **maneuver** something into or out of an awkward position, you skillfully move it there. *maniobrar, abrirse paso* ❑ *He maneuvered the car through the narrow gate. Maniobró para pasar con el coche por la angosta puerta.* ❑ *I maneuvered my way among the tables to the back of the restaurant. Me abrí paso por entre las mesas hasta el fondo del restaurante.* • **Maneuver** is also a noun. *maniobra* ❑ *The airplanes performed some difficult maneuvers. Los pilotos de los aviones ejecutaron unas maniobras difíciles.* **2** N-COUNT A **maneuver** is something clever which you do to change a situation to your advantage. *maniobra, estratagema* ❑ *...dishonest maneuvers to make him sell his house. ...maniobras fraudulentas para obligarlo a vender su casa.* **3** N-PLURAL Military **maneuvers** are training exercises which involve the movement of soldiers and equipment over a large area. *maniobra* ❑ *The army begins maneuvers tomorrow. El ejército iniciará las maniobras mañana.*

| Word Link | *hood ≈ state, condition : childhood, likelihood, manhood* |
|---|---|

**man|hood** /mænhʊd/ N-UNCOUNT **Manhood** is the state of being a man rather than a boy. *madurez* ❑ *Fathers must help their sons grow from boyhood to manhood. Los padres deben ayudar a sus hijos a pasar de la pubertad a la madurez.*

**mani|fest** /mænɪfɛst/ (**manifests, manifesting, manifested**) **1** ADJ If you say that something is **manifest**, you mean that it is clearly true and that nobody would disagree with it if they saw it or considered it. *manifiesto, patente, evidente* [FORMAL] ❑ *...the manifest power of prayer. ...la fuerza manifiesta de la oración.* • **mani|fest|ly** ADV *manifiestamente, evidentemente* ❑ *It is manifestly clear that she hates me. Es evidente que me odia.* **2** V-T If you **manifest** a particular quality, feeling, or illness, or if it **manifests itself**, it becomes visible or obvious. *mostrar, hacerse evidente* [FORMAL] ❑ *He manifested health problems when he was a child. Ya tenía problemas de salud evidentes cuando era niño.* ❑ *The virus needs two weeks to manifest itself. Tienen que pasar dos semanas para que el virus se haga evidente.* • **Manifest** is also an adjective. *evidente* ❑ *Fear is manifest everywhere. El miedo es evidente en todas partes.*

**mani|fes|to** /mænɪfɛstoʊ/ (**manifestos** or **manifestoes**) N-COUNT A **manifesto** is a statement published by a person or group of people, especially a political party or a government, in which they say what their aims and policies are. *manifiesto* ❑ *The Republicans are preparing their election manifesto. Los republicanos están preparando su manifiesto sobre las elecciones.*

| Word Link | *man ≈ hand : manipulate, manual, manuscript* |
|---|---|

**ma|nipu|late** /mənɪpyəleɪt/ (**manipulates, manipulating, manipulated**) **1** V-T If you say that someone **manipulates** people or events, you disapprove of them because they use or control them for their own benefit. *manipular* ❑ *She was unable to control and manipulate events. Era incapaz de controlar y manipular los acontecimientos.* ❑ *She's always manipulating me to give her money. Siempre está manipulándome para que le dé dinero.* • **ma|nipu|la|tion** /mənɪpyəleɪʃᵊn/ N-VAR *manipulación* ❑ *Crying can be a form of emotional manipulation. El llanto puede ser una forma de manipulación afectiva.* **2** V-T If you **manipulate** something that requires skill, such as a complicated piece of equipment or a difficult idea, you operate it or process it. *manipular* ❑ *The technology uses a pen to manipulate a computer. Con esta tecnología se emplea una pluma para manipular la computadora.* • **ma|nipu|la|tion** N-VAR *manipulación* ❑ *...mathematical manipulations. ...manipulaciones matemáticas.*

**man|kind** /mænkaɪnd/ N-UNCOUNT You can refer to all human beings as **mankind** when considering them as a group. Some people dislike this use. *humanidad, género humano* ❑ *...a better future for all mankind. ...un futuro mejor para toda la humanidad.*

**man-made** also **manmade** ADJ **Man-made** things are created or caused by people, rather than occurring naturally. *artificial, sintético, hecho por el*

m

hombre ❑ *Some of the world's problems are man-made. Algunos de los problemas del mundo han sido provocados por el hombre.* ❑ *...man-made lakes. ...lagos artificiales.*

**manned** /mænd/ ADJ A **manned** vehicle such as a spacecraft has people in it who are operating its controls. *tripulado* ❑ *In thirty years from now, the United States should have a manned spacecraft on Mars. Dentro de treinta años, Estados Unidos habrá enviado una nave tripulada a Marte.*

**man|ner** /mænər/ (**manners**) **1** N-SING The **manner** in which you do something is the way that you do it. *manera, modo* ❑ *She smiled again in a friendly manner. Volvió a sonreír amistosamente.* **2** N-SING Someone's **manner** is the way in which they behave and talk when they are with other people. *actitud* ❑ *He has a very confident manner. Tiene una actitud muy confiada.* ● **-mannered** ADJ *de ciertas maneras, de ciertos modales* ❑ *...a quiet-mannered woman. ...una mujer de modales tranquilos.* **3** N-PLURAL If someone has **good manners,** they are polite and observe social customs. If someone has **bad manners,** they are impolite and do not observe these customs. *buenos modales* ❑ *He dressed well and had perfect manners. Vestía bien y tenía muy buenos modales.*

**Word Partnership** Usar *manner* con:

ADJ. **effective** manner, **efficient** manner **1**
**abrasive** manner, **abrupt** manner, **appropriate** manner, **businesslike** manner, **different** manner, **friendly** manner, **usual** manner **1** **2**

M

**man|sion** /mænʃᵊn/ (**mansions**) N-COUNT A **mansion** is a very large, impressive house. *mansión* ❑ *...an eighteenth-century mansion in New Hampshire. ...una mansión del siglo XVIII en Nueva Hampshire.*

**man|tle** /mæntᵊl/ (**mantles**) N-SING In geology, **the mantle** is the part of the earth that lies between the crust and the core. It is divided into the upper mantle and the lower mantle. *manto* [TECHNICAL]
→ see **core**

**Word Link** *man ≈ hand : manipulate, manual, manuscript*

**manu|al** /mænyuəl/ (**manuals**) **1** ADJ **Manual** work is work in which you use your hands or your physical strength. *manual* ❑ *...manual workers. ...obreros (manuales).* **2** ADJ **Manual** means operated by hand, rather than by electricity or a motor. *manual* ❑ *We used a manual pump to get the water out of the hole. Utilizamos una bomba manual para sacar el agua del agujero.* ● **manu|al|ly** ADV *manualmente, a mano* ❑ *We cut the weeds down manually. Cortamos la maleza a mano.* **3** N-COUNT A **manual** is a book which tells you how to do something or how a piece of machinery works. *manual* ❑ *...the instruction manual. ...el manual de operación.*

**Word Link** *fact, fic ≈ making : artificial, factor, manufacture*

**manu|fac|ture** /mænyəfæktʃər/ (**manufactures, manufacturing, manufactured**) **1** V-T To **manufacture** something means to make it in a factory. *fabricar, manufacturar* [BUSINESS] ❑ *The company manufactures plastics. La compañía fabrica plásticos.* ● **Manufacture** is also a noun. *manufactura, fabricación, elaboración* ❑ *...the manufacture of steel. ...la elaboración de acero.* ● **manu|fac|tur|ing** N-UNCOUNT *manufactura* ❑ *Manufacturing in China has increased dramatically. Las manufacturas han aumentado espectacularmente en China.* **2** V-T If you say that someone **manufactures** information, you are criticizing them because they invent information that is not true. *fabricar, inventar* ❑ *The criminals had manufactured their story completely. La historia que contaron los criminales era completamente inventada.*

**manu|fac|tured home** (**manufactured homes**) N-COUNT A **manufactured home** is a house built with parts which have been made in a factory and then quickly put together at the place where the house is located. *casa prefabricada*

**manu|fac|tur|er** /mænyəfæktʃərər/ (**manufacturers**) N-COUNT A **manufacturer** is a business or company which makes goods in large quantities. *fabricante* [BUSINESS] ❑ *...the world's largest doll manufacturer. ...el mayor fabricante de muñecas del mundo.*
→ see **industry**

**Word Link** *script ≈ writing : manuscript, prescription, transcript*

**manu|script** /mænyəskrɪpt/ (**manuscripts**) N-COUNT A **manuscript** is a handwritten or typed document, especially a writer's first version of a book before it is published. *manuscrito, original* ❑ *He has seen a manuscript of the book. Vio el manuscrito del libro.*

**many** /mɛni/ **1** DET You use **many** to indicate a large number of people or things. *mucho* ❑ *I don't think many people would argue with that. Creo que no mucha gente estaría en desacuerdo.* ❑ *Not many films are made in Finland. En Finlandia no se hacen muchas películas.* ● **Many** is also a pronoun. *mucho* ❑ *He made a list of his friends. There weren't many. Hizo una lista de sus amigos, pero no eran muchos.* ● **Many** is also a quantifier. *mucho* ❑ *Why do many of us feel the need to get married? ¿Por qué muchos sentimos la necesidad de casarnos?* ● **Many** is also an adjective. *mucho* ❑ *His many hobbies include swimming and reading. Entre sus muchos pasatiempos están la natación y la lectura.* **2** ADV You use **many** in expressions such as "not many," "not very many," and "too many" when replying to questions about numbers of things or people. *mucho* ❑ *"How many of their songs were hits?" — "Not very many." —¿Cuántas de sus canciones fueron éxitos? —No muchas.* **3** DET You use **many** after "how" to talk and ask questions about numbers or quantities. *cuánto* ❑ *How many years have you been here? ¿Cuántos años ha estado aquí?* ● **Many** is also a pronoun. *cuánto o cuánta, cuántos o cuántas* ❑ *There were some mistakes, but I'm not sure how many. Había algunos errores, pero no estoy seguro (de) cuántos.* **4** PHRASE You use **as many as** before a number to suggest that it is surprisingly large. *no menos de* ❑ *As many as 4 million people watched today's parade. No menos de cuatro millones de personas vieron el desfile de hoy.*

**map** /mæp/ (**maps, mapping, mapped**) **1** N-COUNT A **map** is a drawing of a particular area such as a city, a country, or a continent, showing its main features as they would appear if you looked at them from above. *mapa* ❑ *He unfolded the map and put it on the floor. Desdobló el mapa y lo extendió en el piso.* **2** N-COUNT A **map** is a model or representation of the Earth's surface. *mapa, planisferio, mapa mundi*

▸ **map out** PHR-VERB If you **map out** something that you are intending to do, you work out in detail how you will do it. *trazar, planear, planificar* ❑ *I went home and mapped out my plan. Me fui a casa y tracé mi plan.* ❑ *Before writing a play he sits down and maps it out. Antes de escribir una obra, se pone a elaborar la trama.*

**Word Partnership** Usar *map* con:

ADJ. **detailed** map **1** **2**
V. **draw a** map, **look at a** map, **open a** map, **read a** map **1** **2**

**map key** (**map keys**) N-COUNT A **map key** is a list which explains the meaning of the symbols and abbreviations used on a map. *explicación (de símbolos, distancias, etcétera)*

**ma|ple** /meɪpᵊl/ (**maples**) N-VAR A **maple** or a **maple tree** is a tree with five-pointed leaves which turn bright red or gold in the fall. *arce* ● **Maple** is the wood of this tree. *arce (madera de)* ❑ *...a solid maple table. ...una sólida mesa de arce.*

**Word Link** *ette ≈ small : casette, cigarette, maquette*

**ma|quette** /mækɛt/ (**maquettes**) N-COUNT A **maquette** is a small model of a sculpture. Sculptors often use maquettes as a preparation for a larger sculpture. *maqueta* [TECHNICAL]

**mar** /mɑr/ (**mars, marring, marred**) V-T **To mar** something means to spoil or damage it. *estropear* ❑ *A number of problems marred the event. Varios problemas estropearon el acto.*

**mara|thon** /mærəθɒn/ (**marathons**) **1** N-COUNT A **marathon** is a race in which people run a distance of 26 miles, which is about 42 km. *maratón* ❑ *He is running in his first marathon. Está corriendo su primer/primera maratón.* **2** ADJ A **marathon** event or task takes a long time and is very tiring. *maratónico* ❑ *People make marathon journeys to buy glass here. La gente viaja desde muy lejos para comprar cristalería aquí.*

**mar|ble** /mɑrbᵊl/ (**marbles**) **1** N-UNCOUNT **Marble** is a type of very hard rock which feels cold when you touch it. Statues and parts of buildings are sometimes made of marble. *mármol* **2** N-UNCOUNT **Marbles** is a children's game played with small balls made of colored glass. You roll a ball along the ground and try to hit an opponent's ball with it. *canicas, bolitas* ❑ *Two boys were playing marbles. Dos niños estaban jugando a las canicas.* **3** N-COUNT A **marble** is one of the small balls used in the game of marbles. *canica* ❑ *...a glass marble. ...una canica de vidrio.*

**march** /mɑrtʃ/ (**marches, marching, marched**) **1** V-T/V-I When soldiers **march** somewhere, or when a commanding officer **marches** them somewhere, they walk there with very regular steps, as a group. *marchar, hacer marchar* ❑ *Some soldiers were marching down the street. Unos soldados marchaban por la calle.* ❑ *Captain Ramirez marched them off to the main camp. El capitán Ramírez los hizo marchar hasta el campo principal.* ● **March** is also a noun. *marcha* ❑ *After a short march, the soldiers entered the village. Después de una corta marcha, los soldados llegaron al pueblo.* **2** V-I When a large group of people **march** for a cause, they walk somewhere together in order to express their ideas or to protest about something. *marchar* ❑ *The demonstrators marched through the capital city. Los manifestantes marcharon a través de la capital.* ● **March** is also a noun. *marcha, manifestación* ❑ *Organizers expect 300,000 protesters to join the march. Los organizadores esperan que se unan a la marcha unos 300,000 manifestantes.* ● **march|er** N-COUNT (**marchers**) *manifestante* ❑ *The police arrested several marchers. La policía arrestó a varios manifestantes.* **3** V-I If someone **marches** somewhere, they walk there quickly and in a determined way, for example because they are angry. *ir, entrar* ❑ *He marched into the kitchen without knocking. Entró a/en la cocina sin anunciarse.* **4** V-T If you **march** someone somewhere, you force them to walk there with you, for example by holding their arm tightly. *llevar* ❑ *The teacher marched me into the principal's office. El maestro me llevó a la oficina del director.* **5** N-SING **The march of** something is its steady development or progress. *avance* ❑ *The march of technology brings more and more new products. El avance de la tecnología genera más y más productos nuevos.*

**March** /mɑrtʃ/ (**Marches**) N-VAR **March** is the third month of the year in the Western calendar. *marzo* ❑ *I flew to Milwaukee in March. Fui en avión a Milwaukee en marzo.* ❑ *She was born on March 6, 1920. Nació el 6 de marzo de 1920.*

**mare** /mɛər/ (**mares**) N-COUNT A **mare** is an adult female horse. *yegua*

**mar|gin** /mɑrdʒɪn/ (**margins**) **1** N-COUNT A **margin** is the difference between two amounts, especially the difference in the number of votes or points between the winner and the loser in an election or other contest. *margen* ❑ *They won with a 50-point margin. Ganaron con un margen de 50 puntos.* **2** N-COUNT The **margin** of a written or printed page is the empty space at the side of the page. *margen* ❑ *She added her comments in the margin. Añadió sus comentarios al margen.* **3** N-VAR If there is a **margin** for something in a situation, there is some freedom to choose what to do or decide how to do it. *margen* ❑ *There is no margin for error in dangerous sports. En los deportes peligrosos no hay margen para el error.*

**Word Partnership** Usar *margin* con:

ADJ. **comfortable** margin, **large** margin, **slim** margin **1**
**narrow** margin, **wide** margin **1** **2**
N. margin **for error** **3**

**mar|gin|al** /mɑrdʒɪnᵊl/ ADJ If you describe something as **marginal**, you mean that it is small or not very important. *secundario, mínimo* ❑ *This is a marginal improvement. Es una mejora mínima.* ● **mar|gin|al|ly** /mɑrdʒɪnᵊli/ ADV *ligeramente* ❑ *Sales last year were marginally higher. Las ventas del* *año pasado fueron ligeramente superiores.*

**mari|achi** /mæriɑtʃi/ N-UNCOUNT In Mexico, a **mariachi** band is a small group of musicians who can be hired to play at parties or to serenade people. *mariachi* ❑ *My father was a singer in a mariachi band. Mi padre cantaba en un conjunto de mariachis.* ❑ *...joyous mariachi music. ...alegre música de mariachi.*

**ma|ri|jua|na** /mærɪwɑnə/ N-UNCOUNT **Marijuana** is an illegal drug which can be smoked. *mariguana, mota, yerba, marihuana, marijuana, de la verde*

**mari|nate** /mærɪneɪt/ (**marinates, marinating, marinated**) V-T/V-I If you **marinate** meat or fish, or if it **marinates,** you soak it in oil, vinegar, spices, and herbs before cooking it, so that it develops a special flavor. *marinar(se)* ❑ *Marinate the chicken for 4 hours. Ponga a marinar el pollo 4 horas.*

| Word Link | *mar ≈ sea : marine, maritime, submarine* |
|---|---|

**ma|rine** /mərin/ (**marines**) **1** N-COUNT; N-PROPER A **marine** is a soldier, for example in the U.S. Marine Corps or the Royal Marines, who is specially trained for military duties at sea as well as on land. *infante de marina, marines* ❑ *A small number of Marines were wounded. Unos cuantos marines resultaron heridos.* **2** ADJ **Marine** is used to describe things relating to the sea. *marino, marítimo* ❑ *...the colorful marine life in the Indian Ocean. ...la vistosa vida marina del Océano Índico.*
→ see **ship**

M

**mari|tal** /mærɪtᵊl/ ADJ **Marital** means relating to marriage. *marital, conyugal, nupcial* ❑ *Their marital home was in Pittsburgh. Su hogar conyugal estaba en Pittsburgh.*

**mari|time** /mærɪtaɪm/ ADJ **Maritime** means relating to the sea and to ships. *marítimo, náutico* ❑ *...a maritime museum. ...un museo marítimo.*

**mark** /mɑrk/ (**marks, marking, marked**) **1** N-COUNT A **mark** is a small area of something such as dirt that has accidentally gotten onto a surface or piece of clothing. *mancha* ❑ *There was a red paint mark on the wall. Había una mancha de pintura roja en la pared.* **2** V-T/V-I If something **marks** a surface, or if the surface **marks,** the surface is damaged by marks or a mark. *marcar(se), dejar una marca* ❑ *His shoes marked the carpet. Sus zapatos dejaron una marca en el tapete.* **3** N-COUNT A **mark** is a written or printed symbol, for example a letter of the alphabet. *marca, señal, signo* ❑ *He made marks with a pencil. Hizo las marcas con un lápiz.* **4** V-T If you **mark** something with a particular word or symbol, you write that word or symbol on it. *señalar, marcar, poner una marca, poner una señal* ❑ *She marked the letter "sent." Marcó la carta como "enviada".* ❑ *Each farmer marks his sheep with a different symbol. Cada ganadero marca sus ovejas con un símbolo diferente.* **5** N-COUNT A **mark** is a point that is given for a correct answer or for doing something well in an exam or competition. A mark can also be a written symbol such as a letter that indicates how good a student's work is. *calificación, punto, nota* ❑ *He scored 9 marks out of 10. Obtuvo 9 puntos de 10.* **6** V-T When a teacher **marks** a student's work, the teacher decides how good it is and writes a number or letter on it to indicate this opinion. *calificar* ❑ *He was marking essays in his small study. Estaba calificando las composiciones en su pequeño estudio.* • **mark|ing** N-UNCOUNT *calificar, calificación* ❑ *Marking students' work can take a long time. La calificación de los trabajos de los estudiantes puede llevar mucho tiempo.* **7** N-COUNT A particular **mark** is a particular number, point, or stage which has been reached or might be reached, especially a significant one. *marca, punto de referencia, hito, indicador, meta* ❑ *Unemployment is almost at the one million mark. El desempleo casi ha llegado a la marca del millón.* **8** N-SING If you say that a type of behavior or an event is **a mark of** a particular quality, feeling, or situation, you mean it shows that that quality, feeling, or situation exists. *señal, muestra* ❑ *She put her arm around him: a mark of how caring she was. Lo abrazó como muestra de lo cariñosa que era.* **9** V-T If something **marks** a place or position, it shows where a particular thing is or was. *marcar* ❑ *A big hole in the road marks the place where the bomb landed. Un gran agujero en el camino marca dónde cayó la bomba.* • **mark|er** N-COUNT (**markers**) *marcador, señalador* ❑ *He put a marker in his book. Puso un señalador en su libro.* **10** V-T An event that **marks** a particular stage or point is a sign that something different is about to happen. *marcar* ❑ *The announcement marks the end of an extraordinary period in European history. El anuncio marca el fin de un extraordinario periodo de la historia europea.* **11** → see also **marked** **12** → see also **punctuation mark, question mark** **13** PHRASE If someone or something **leaves** their **mark** or **leaves a mark,** they have a lasting effect on another person or thing. *dejar marca en alguien, dejar marcado a alguien, marcar a alguien* ❑ *Her parents' unhappy marriage left its mark on her. El infeliz matrimonio de sus padres la marcó.* **14** PHRASE If you **make** your **mark** or **make a mark,** you become noticed or famous by doing something impressive or unusual. *dejar marca* ❑ *She made her mark in the movie business in the 1960s. Ella dejó su marca en el negocio del cine de los años sesenta.* **15** PHRASE If something such as a claim or estimate is **wide of the mark,** it is incorrect or inaccurate. *errado, equivocado, no dar en el blanco* ❑ *His answer was wide of the mark. Su respuesta estuvo equivocada.*

▸ **mark down** **1** PHR-VERB To **mark** an item **down** or **mark** its price **down** means to reduce its price. *rebajar, bajar, reducir* ❑ *The toy store marked down many computer games. En la juguetería rebajaron muchos juegos de computadora.* **2** PHR-VERB If you **mark** something **down,** you write it down. *anotar, escribir, apuntar* ❑ *I forget things unless I mark them down. Si no apunto las cosas, se me olvidan.*

▸ **mark up** PHR-VERB If you **mark** something **up,** you increase its price. *incrementar, subir* ❑ *We sell goods to stores at one price, then the stores mark them up. Nosotros vendemos los productos a las tiendas a un precio y después, las tiendas lo suben.*

**marked** /mɑrkt/ ADJ A **marked** change or difference is very obvious and easily noticed. *marcado, claro, evidente, notable* ❑ *There has been a marked increase in traffic on the roads. Ha habido un notable aumento del tráfico en las carreteras.*
• **mark|ed|ly** /mɑrkɪdli/ ADV *claramente, marcadamente, muy* ❑ *The movie is markedly different from the play. La película es muy diferente de la obra.*

**mar|ket** /mɑrkɪt/ (**markets, marketing, marketed**) **1** N-COUNT A **market** is a place where goods are bought and sold, usually outdoors. *mercado, plaza, tianguis* ❑ *They usually buy fruit and vegetables at the market. Normalmente compran la fruta y la verdura en el mercado.* **2** N-COUNT The **market** for a particular type of thing is the number of people who want to buy it, or the area of the world in which it is sold. *mercado* [BUSINESS] ❑ *The foreign market is very important. El mercado exterior es muy importante.* **3** N-SING The **market** refers to the total amount of a product that is sold each year, especially when you are talking about the competition between the companies who sell that product. *mercado* [BUSINESS] ❑ *The two big companies control 72% of the market. Las dos compañías grandes controlan el 72% del mercado.* **4** V-T To **market** a product means to organize its sale, by deciding on its price, where it should be sold, and how it should be advertised. *vender, comercializar, vender, poner a la venta, distribuir* [BUSINESS] ❑ *They market our music in a very different way than pop music. Comercializan nuestra música de una manera muy diferente a la música pop.* • **mar|ket|ing** N-UNCOUNT *mercadotecnia, marketing* ❑ *...the marketing department. ...el departamento de mercadotecnia.* **5** → see also **black market** **6** PHRASE If something is **on the market,** it is available for people to buy. If it comes **onto the market,** it becomes available for people to buy. *en el mercado, a la venta* [BUSINESS] ❑ *There are many empty offices on the market. Hay muchas oficinas vacías en el mercado de bienes raíces.*

**mar|quee** /mɑrki/ (**marquees**) **1** N-COUNT A **marquee** is a large tent which is used at a fair, garden party, or other outdoor event, usually for eating and drinking in. *carpa* **2** N-COUNT A **marquee** is a cover over the entrance of a building, for example a hotel or a theater, that has a sign with the name of the film or play on it. *marquesina, toldo* ❑ *...the marquees of Broadway. ...las marquesinas de Broadway.*

| Word Link | *age ≈ state of, related to : courage, marriage, percentage* |
|---|---|

**mar|riage** /mærɪdʒ/ (**marriages**) **1** N-COUNT A **marriage** is the relationship between a husband and wife, or the state of being married. *matrimonio, vida de casado* ❑ *In a good marriage, both husband and wife are happy. En un buen matrimonio, tanto el esposo como la esposa son felices.* ❑ *When I was 35 my marriage ended. Cuando mi matrimonio terminó, yo tenía 35 años.* **2** N-VAR A **marriage** is the act of marrying someone, or the ceremony at which this is done. *matrimonio, enlace, boda, nupcias, casamiento* ❑ *Her marriage to Darryl was a mistake. Su matrimonio con Darryl fue un error.*
→ see **love, wedding**

**mar|riage li|cense** (**marriage licenses**) N-COUNT A **marriage license** is an official document that you need in order to get married. *licencia de matrimonio, licencia matrimonial, licencia para casarse* ❑ *They got the marriage license the day before the ceremony. Les dieron la licencia de matrimonio al día anterior a la ceremonia.*

**mar|ried** /mærid/ **1** ADJ If you are **married,** you have a husband or wife. *casado* ❑ *We have been married for 14 years. Hemos estado casados 14 años.* ❑ *She is married to an Englishman. Está casada con un inglés.* **2** ADJ **Married** means relating to marriage or to people who are married. *casado* ❑ *For the first ten years of our married life we lived in a farmhouse. Los primeros diez años de casados vivimos en un rancho.*

**mar|ry** /mæri/ (**marries, marrying, married**) **1** V-RECIP When two people **get married** or **marry,** they legally become husband and wife in a special ceremony. *casarse, contraer matrimonio, contraer nupcias* ❑ *I thought he would change after we got married. Pensé que él cambiaría después de que nos casáramos.* ❑ *They married a month after they met. Se casaron un mes después de conocerse.* ❑ *He wants to marry her. Quiere casarse con ella.* **2** V-T When a priest or official **marries** two people, he or she conducts the ceremony in which the two people legally become husband and wife. *casar, unir en matrimonio* ❑ *The minister has agreed to marry us next week. El pastor aceptó casarnos la próxima semana.*

**Mars** /mɑrz/ N-PROPER **Mars** is the fourth planet from the sun, between the Earth and Jupiter. *Marte*
→ see **solar system**

**marsh** /mɑrʃ/ (**marshes**) N-VAR A **marsh** is a wet, muddy area of land. *pantano, ciénaga, marisma*
→ see **wetland**

**mar|shal** /mɑrʃᵊl/ (**marshals, marshaling** or **marshalling, marshaled** or **marshalled**) **1** V-T If you **marshal** people or things, you gather them together and arrange them for a particular purpose. *formar, reunir, organizar* ❑ *Napoleon marshalled his troops. Napoleón organizó sus tropas.* **2** N-COUNT A **marshal** is an official who helps to supervise a public event, especially a sports event. *supervisor o supervisora, vigilante* ❑ *Several marshals control the race. Varios supervisores controlan la carrera.* **3** N-COUNT In the United States and some other countries, a **marshal** is a police officer, often one who is responsible for a particular area. *jefe de policía* ❑ *A federal marshal arrested him. Fue arrestado por un jefe de la policía federal.* **4** N-COUNT A **marshal** is an officer in a fire department. *jefe de bomberos* ❑ *A fire marshal told her there was a gas leak. Un jefe de los bomberos le dijo que había una fuga de gas.*

**mar|su|pial** /mɑrsupiəl/ (**marsupials**) N-COUNT A **marsupial** is an animal such as a kangaroo or an opossum. Female marsupials carry their babies in a pouch on their stomach. *marsupial*

**mar|tial** /mɑrʃᵊl/ **1** ADJ **Martial** is used to describe things relating to soldiers or war. *marcial* [FORMAL] ❑ *...a martial court. ...una corte marcial.* **2** → see also **court martial**

**mar|tial art** (**martial arts**) N-COUNT A **martial art** is one of the methods of fighting, often without weapons, that come from the Far East, for example kung fu or karate. *arte marcial*

**mar|vel|ous** /mɑrvələs/ ADJ If you describe someone or something as **marvelous,** you are emphasizing that they are very good. *maravilloso, prodigioso, espléndido* ❑ *It's a marvelous piece of music. Es una espléndida composición musical.* • **mar|vel|ous|ly** ADV *maravillosamente, de maravilla, a las mil maravillas* ❑ *We want people to think he's doing marvelously. Queremos que la gente piense que lo está haciendo de maravilla.*

m

**Marx|ism** /mɑrksɪzəm/ N-UNCOUNT **Marxism** is a political philosophy based on the writings of Karl Marx which stresses the importance of the struggle between different social classes. *marxismo*

**Marx|ist** /mɑrksɪst/ (**Marxists**) **1** ADJ **Marxist** means based on Marxism or relating to Marxism. *marxista* ❑ *...a Marxist state. ...un estado marxista.* **2** N-COUNT A **Marxist** is a person who believes in Marxism or who is a member of a Marxist party. *marxista* ❑ *...a 78-year-old former Marxist. ...un ex marxista de 78 años de edad.*

**mas|cara** /mæskærə/ N-UNCOUNT **Mascara** is a substance used to make eyelashes darker. *máscara, rímel*
→ see **makeup**

**mas|cu|line** /mæskyəlɪn/ ADJ **Masculine** qualities and things relate to or are considered typical of men, in contrast to women. *masculino, varonil* ❑ *...masculine characteristics like a deep voice and hair on the face. ...características masculinas, como la voz grave y la barba.* ● **mas|cu|lin|ity** /mæskyəlɪnɪti/ N-UNCOUNT *masculinidad* ❑ *Some men think doing dangerous things is a sign of masculinity. Algunos hombres piensan que hacer cosas peligrosas es signo de masculinidad.*

**mask** /mæsk/ (**masks, masking, masked**) **1** N-COUNT A **mask** is something which you wear over your face for protection or to disguise yourself. *máscara, careta, antifaz, mascarilla* ❑ *The gunman's mask slipped so we could see his face. Se le deslizó la máscara al pistolero, así que pudimos verle la cara.* ❑ *You must wear goggles and a mask that will protect you against the smoke. Tienes que usar gafas de seguridad y mascarilla para protegerte del humo.* **2** N-COUNT If you describe someone's behavior as a **mask,** you mean that they do not show their real feelings or character. *fachada, máscara, disfraz* ❑ *Her happy face is just a mask. Su cara de felicidad no es más que un disfraz.* **3** V-T If you **mask** your feelings, you deliberately do not show them in your behavior, so that people cannot know what you really feel. *ocultar, disimular, disfrazar* ❑ *She tried to mask her anger by laughing. Trató de disimular su enojo riéndose.* **4** V-T If one thing **masks** another, it prevents people from noticing or recognizing the other thing. *ocultar, cubrir, disimular* ❑ *The smoke masked their faces. El humo ocultaba sus rostros.* **5** → see also **gas mask**

mask

**masked** /mæskt/ ADJ If someone is **masked,** they are wearing a mask. *enmascarado, disfrazado, encubierto* ❑ *I looked directly into his masked face. Miré directamente su rostro enmascarado.*

**ma|son jar** (**mason jars**) also **Mason jar** N-COUNT A **mason jar** is a glass jar with a lid that you screw on, which is used for preserving food. *frasco para conservas*

**mass** /mæs/ (**masses, massing, massed**) **1** N-SING A **mass of** things is a large number of them grouped together. *montón, masa, cúmulo, abundancia* ❑ *On his desk is a mass of books and papers. En su escritorio hay un montón de libros y papeles.* **2** N-SING A **mass of** something is a large amount of it. *masa, gran cantidad, mucho* ❑ *She had a mass of black hair. Tenía una abundante cabellera negra.* **3** QUANT **Masses of** something means a large amount of it. *montones, mucho* [INFORMAL] ❑ *She has masses of work to do. Tiene montones de trabajo por hacer.* **4** ADJ **Mass** is used to describe something which involves or affects a very large number of people. *masivo, generalizado* ❑ *Mass unemployment is a big problem. El desempleo generalizado es un gran problema.* **5** N-PLURAL **The masses** are the ordinary people in society. *masas* ❑ *His music is aimed at the masses. Su música está destinada a las masas.* **6** V-T/V-I When people or things **mass,** or when you **mass** them, they gather together into a large crowd or group. *concentrar, concentrarse, juntar, juntarse* ❑ *Police began to mass outside the football stadium. La policía empezó a concentrarse fuera del estadio de futbol.* ● **massed** ADJ *concentrado* ❑ *The massed crowd began to shout. La multitud concentrada empezó a gritar.* **7** N-VAR In physics, the **mass** of an object is the amount of physical matter that it has. *masa* [TECHNICAL] ❑ *...the mass of a single atom. ...la masa de un sólo átomo.* **8** N-VAR **Mass** is a Christian church ceremony, especially in a Roman Catholic or Orthodox church, during which people eat bread and drink wine in order to remember the last meal of Jesus Christ. *misa* ❑ *She went to Mass each day. Ella fue a misa todos los días.*
→ see **continent**

**mas|sa|cre** /mæsəkər/ (**massacres, massacring, massacred**) **1** N-VAR A **massacre** is the killing of a large number of people at the same time in a violent and cruel way. *masacre, matanza, carnicería* ❑ *Her mother died in the massacre. Su madre murió en la masacre.* **2** V-T If people **are massacred,** a large number of them are attacked and killed in a violent and cruel way. *masacrar, matar en masa, asesinar con crueldad* ❑ *300 people were massacred by the soldiers. Los soldados asesinaron cruelmente a 300 personas.*

**mas|sage** /məsɑʒ/ (**massages, massaging, massaged**) **1** N-VAR **Massage** is the action of rubbing someone's body, as a way of making them relax or reducing their pain. *masaje* ❑ *Alex asked me if I wanted a massage. Alex me preguntó si quería un masaje.* **2** V-T If you **massage** someone or a part of their body, you rub their body, in order to make them relax or reduce their pain. *masajear(se), dar(se) masaje* ❑ *She continued massaging her right foot. Ella siguió dándose masaje en el pie derecho.*

**m|ass ex|tinc|tion** (**mass extinctions**) N-VAR A **mass extinction** is a period of time when many different species of animals and plants become extinct. *extinción masiva, extinción en masa*

**mas|sive** /mæsɪv/ ADJ Something that is **massive** is very large in size, quantity, or extent. *sólido, masivo, enorme, cuantioso, muy grande, grandísimo* ❑ *They borrowed massive amounts of money. Pidieron prestadas enormes cantidades de dinero.* ❑ *...a massive new store. ...una nueva tienda grandísima.* ● **mas|sive|ly** ADV *enormemente* ❑ *...a massively popular game. ...un juego enormemente popular.*

**mass me|dia**

Mass media can take the singular or plural form of the verb.

N-SING The **mass media** are television, radio, newspapers, and magazines. *medios de comunicación (de masas)* ❑ *Reports in the mass media affect people's opinions. Los informes de los medios de comunicación influyen en la opinión de la gente.*

**mass move|ment** (**mass movements**) N-VAR In geology, **mass movement** is the downhill movement of rocks and soil as a result of gravity. Compare **creep**. *deslizamiento masivo* [TECHNICAL]

**mass num|ber** (**mass numbers**) N-VAR The **mass number** of a chemical element is the total number of protons and neutrons in the atomic nucleus of that element. *número de masa, número másico* [TECHNICAL]

**mass-produce** (**mass-produces, mass-producing, mass-produced**) V-T To **mass-produce** something means to make it in large quantities, usually by machine. *producir en masa, producir en serie, fabricar en masa, fabricar en serie* [BUSINESS] ❑ *...machines to mass-produce shoes. ...máquinas para fabricar calzado en serie.* ● **mass-produced** ADJ *producido en serie, producido en masa, fabricado en serie, fabricado en masa* ❑ *...the first mass-produced bike. ...la primera bicicleta producida en serie.*

**mass trans|it** N-UNCOUNT **Mass transit** is the transportation of people by means of buses, trains, or other vehicles running on fixed routes within a city or town. *transporte público* ❑ *The president wants to spend $105 billion to improve the nation's mass transit systems. El presidente quiere invertir 105,000 millones de dólares en el mejoramiento de los sistemas de transporte público del país.*
→ see **transportation**

**mast** /mæst/ (**masts**) 1 N-COUNT The **masts** of a boat are the tall, upright poles that support its sails. *mástil* 2 N-COUNT A radio **mast** is a tall upright structure that is used to transmit radio or television signals. *antena*

**mas|ter** /mæstər/ (**masters, mastering, mastered**) 1 N-COUNT A servant's **master** is the man that he or she works for. *amo, patrón, jefe* ❑ *My master ordered me to deliver a message. Mi patrón me ordenó entregar un mensaje.* 2 N-COUNT If you say that someone is a **master** of a particular activity, you mean that they are extremely skilled at it. *maestro, experto* ❑ *She was a master of the English language. Era una experta en la lengua inglesa.* ● **Master** is also an adjective. *experto, maestro* ❑ *...a master craftsman. ...un artesano experto.* 3 N-VAR If you are **master** of a situation, you have complete control over it. *amo, señor, dueño* ❑ *Sometimes he didn't feel master of his own thoughts. En ocasiones no se sentía dueño de sus propios pensamientos.* 4 V-T If you **master** something, you learn how to do it properly or you succeed in understanding it completely. *dominar* ❑ *David soon mastered the skills of soccer. David dominó pronto las técnicas del futbol.*

**Thesaurus** *master* Ver también:

| | |
|---|---|
| N. | owner; (*ant.*) servant, slave 1 |
| | artist, expert, professional 2 |
| V. | learn, study, understand 4 |

**master|piece** /mæstərpis/ (**masterpieces**) N-COUNT A **masterpiece** is an extremely good painting, novel, movie, or other work of art. *obra maestra* ❑ *His book is a masterpiece. Su libro es una obra maestra.*

**mat** /mæt/ (**mats**) 1 N-COUNT A **mat** is a small piece of something such as cloth, wood, or plastic which you put on a table to protect it from plates or cups. *mantel individual, mantelito* ❑ *The food is served on big tables with mats. La comida se sirve en grandes mesas con manteles individuales.* 2 N-COUNT A **mat** is a small piece of carpet or other thick material which is put on the floor. *tapete, felpudo* ❑ *There was a letter on the mat. Había una carta en el tapete.* 3 → see also **matte**

**match** /mætʃ/ (**matches, matching, matched**) 1 N-COUNT A **match** is an organized game of tennis, soccer, cricket, or some other sport. *juego, partido* ❑ *He was watching a soccer match. Estaba viendo un partido de futbol.* 2 N-COUNT A **match** is a small wooden or paper stick with a substance on one end that produces a flame when you rub it along a rough surface. *cerillo, fósforo, cerilla*

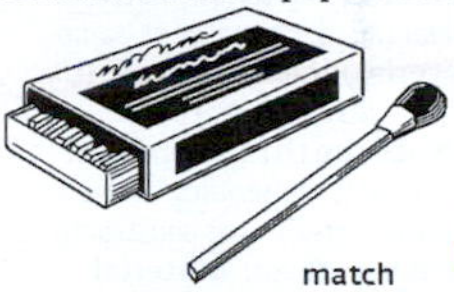
match

3 V-RECIP If something of a particular color or design **matches** another thing, they have the same color or design, or have a pleasing appearance when they are used together. *combinar, hacer juego, casar* ❑ *Your shoes match your dress. Tus zapatos combinan con el vestido.* ❑ *All the chairs matched. Todas las sillas hacían juego.* ● **match|ing** ADJ *que combina, que hace juego, a juego* ❑ *...a hat and a matching scarf. ...un sombrero y una bufanda a juego.* 4 V-RECIP If something such as an amount or a quality **matches with** another amount or quality, they are both the same or equal. *ser comparable, ser similar, concordar* ❑ *Their skills in basketball matched. Su habilidad para el basketball era comparable.* ❑ *Our opinion does not match with their opinion. Nuestra opinión no concuerda con la de ellos.* 5 V-T If you **match** something, you are as good as it or equal to it, for example in speed, size, or quality. *equiparar, estar a la altura, comparar, ser igual* ❑ *They're a good team, but I think we matched them in that game. Es un buen equipo, pero creo que en ese juego estuvimos a la altura.* 6 → see also **matched**
→ see **answer, fire**

**Word Partnership** Usar *match* con:

| | |
|---|---|
| N. | **boxing** match, **chess** match, **tennis** match, **wrestling** match 1 |
| V. | **strike** a match 2 |

**match|book** /mætʃbʊk/ (**matchbooks**) N-COUNT A **matchbook** is a folded piece of cardboard with paper matches inside. *carterita de cerillos, cerillos de carterita*

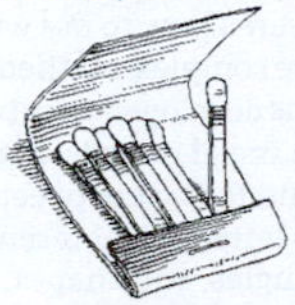
matchbook

**matched** /mætʃt/ 1 ADJ If two people are well **matched,** they have qualities that will enable them to have a good relationship. *que hace pareja*

m

❑ *My parents were not very well matched.* *Mis padres no hacían buena pareja.* **2** ADJ In sports and other competitions, if the opponents or teams are well **matched,** they are both of the same standard in strength or ability. *comparable, ser digno rival* ❑ *The two teams were pretty well-matched.* *Los dos equipos eran dignos rivales.*

**mate** /meɪt/ (**mates, mating, mated**) **1** N-COUNT An animal's **mate** is its sexual partner. *pareja* ❑ *The male shows its colorful feathers to attract a mate.* *El macho muestra sus coloridas plumas para atraer una pareja.* **2** V-RECIP When animals **mate,** a male and a female have sex in order to produce young. *aparearse* ❑ *Some females eat the males after they mate.* *Algunas hembras se comen al macho después de aparearse.* ❑ *They want the males to mate with wild females.* *Quieren que los machos se apareen con hembras silvestres.* **3** → see also **classmate, roommate, running mate**

**ma|terial** /mətɪəriəl/ (**materials**) **1** N-VAR A **material** is a solid substance. *material, materia* ❑ *...a material such as a metal.* *...un material, como un metal.* **2** N-VAR **Material** is cloth. *tela* ❑ *...the thick material of her skirt.* *...la tela gruesa de su falda.* **3** N-PLURAL **Materials** are the things that you need for a particular activity. *materiales* ❑ *The builders needed some more materials.* *Los constructores necesitaban algunos materiales.* **4** ADJ **Material** things are related to possessions or money, rather than to more abstract things such as ideas or values. *material* ❑ *Every room was full of material things.* *Todas las habitaciones estaban llenas de cosas materiales.* • **ma|teri|al|ly** ADV *materialmente* ❑ *He tried to help the child materially and spiritually.* *Trató de ayudar al niño material y espiritualmente.*
→ see **industry**



**Word Partnership** Usar *material* con:

ADJ. **genetic** material, **hazardous** material **1**
**new** material, **original** material **2** **3**
**raw** materials **3**

**ma|ter|nal** /mətɜrnᵊl/ ADJ **Maternal** is used to describe feelings or actions which are typical of those of a kind mother toward her child. *maternal, materno* ❑ *...maternal love.* *...amor materno.*

**ma|ter|nity** /mətɜrnɪti/ ADJ **Maternity** is used to describe things relating to the help and medical care given to a woman when she is pregnant and when she gives birth. *maternidad* ❑ *Sam was born in the maternity hospital.* *Sam nació en la maternidad.*

**math** /mæθ/ N-UNCOUNT **Math** is the same as **mathematics.** *matemáticas* ❑ *He studied math in college.* *Estudio matemáticas en la universidad.*
→ see **mathematics**

**math|emati|cal** /mæθəmætɪkᵊl/ ADJ Something that is **mathematical** involves numbers and calculations. *matemático* ❑ *...mathematical calculations.* *...cálculos matemáticos.* • **math|emati|cal|ly** /mæθəmætɪkli/ ADV *matemáticamente* ❑ *...a mathematically complicated problem.* *...un problema matemáticamente complicado.*
→ see **mathematics**

**math|ema|ti|cian** /mæθəmətɪʃᵊn/ (**mathematicians**) N-COUNT A **mathematician** is a person who is trained in the study of mathematics. *matemático o matemática*
→ see **mathematics**

**math|emat|ics** /mæθəmætɪks/ N-UNCOUNT **Mathematics** is the study of numbers, quantities, or shapes. *matemáticas* ❑ *...a professor of mathematics at Boston College.* *...un profesor de matemáticas del Boston College.*
→ see Word Web: **mathematics**

**mati|nee** /mætᵊneɪ/ (**matinees**) N-COUNT A **matinee** is a performance of a play or a showing of a movie which takes place in the afternoon. *matiné*

**ma|tron of hon|or** /meɪtrən əv hɒnər/ (**matrons of honor**) N-COUNT A **matron of honor** is a married woman who serves as the chief bridesmaid at a wedding. *dama de honor, madrina de boda* ❑ *My sister was the matron of honor at our wedding.* *Mi hermana fue la dama de honor en nuestra boda.*
→ see **wedding**

**matte** /mæt/ also **matt** or **mat** ADJ A **matte** color, paint, or surface is dull rather than shiny. *mate* ❑ *...a white matte paint.* *...una pintura blanca mate.*

**mat|ter** /mætər/ (**matters, mattering, mattered**) **1** N-COUNT A **matter** is a task, situation, or event which you have to deal with or think about. *asunto, cuestión* ❑ *She wanted to discuss some private matter.* *Ella quería discutir algunos asuntos privados.* ❑ *Business matters took him to Louisville.* *Tuvo que ir a Louisville por cuestiones de negocios.* **2** N-PLURAL You use **matters** to refer to the situation you are talking about. *cosas* ❑ *We are*

**Word Web** **mathematics**

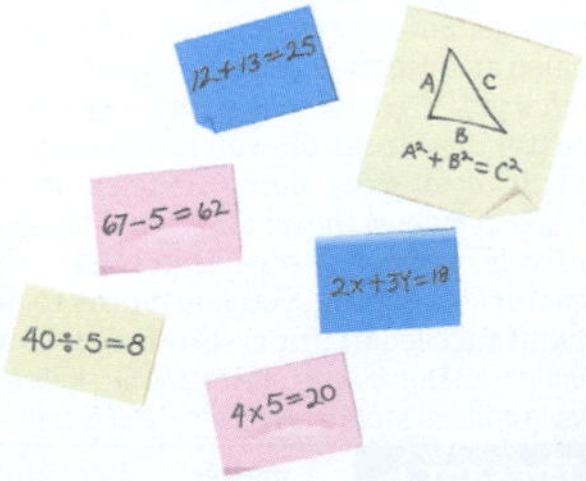


During prehistoric times people **counted** things they could see—for example, four sheep. Later they began to use **numbers** with abstract **quantities** like time—for example, two days. This led to the development of basic **arithmetic**—**addition, subtraction, multiplication,** and **division**. When people discovered how to use written numerals, they could do more complex **mathematical calculations**. **Mathematicians** developed new types of **math** to **measure** land and keep financial records. **Algebra** and **geometry** developed in the Middle East between 2,000 and 3,000 years ago. Algebra uses letters to represent possible quantities. Geometry deals with the relationships among **lines**, **angles**, and **shapes**.

**Word Web** matter

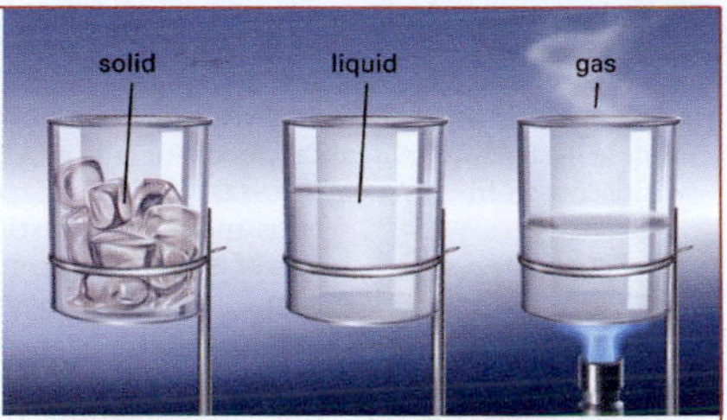


**Matter** exists in three states—**solid, liquid,** and **gas.** Changes in the state of matter happen frequently. For example, when a solid becomes hot enough, it **melts** and becomes a liquid. When a liquid is hot enough, it **evaporates** into a gas. The process also works the other way around. A gas which becomes very cool will **condense** into a liquid. And a liquid that is cooled enough will freeze and become a solid. Other changes in **state** are possible. Sublimation describes what happens when a solid, dry ice, turns directly into a gas, carbon dioxide. And did you know that glass is actually a liquid, not a solid?

*hoping that this change will improve matters.* *Esperamos que con este cambio mejorarán las cosas.* ❑ *If it would make matters easier, I will come to New York.* *Iré a Nueva York si eso facilita las cosas.* **3** N-UNCOUNT Printed **matter** consists of books, newspapers, and other texts that are printed. Reading **matter** consists of things that are suitable for reading, such as books and newspapers. *material impreso, impresos* ❑ *The government plans to put a tax on printed matter.* *El gobierno piensa poner un impuesto a los materiales impresos.* **4** N-UNCOUNT **Matter** is the physical part of the universe consisting of solids, liquids, and gases. *materia* ❑ *The universe is made up of matter and energy.* *El universo está compuesto de materia y energía.* **5** N-SING You use **matter** in expressions such as **"What's the matter?"** or **"Is anything the matter?"** when you think that someone has a problem and you want to know what it is. *problema, situación, circunstancia* ❑ *Carole, what's the matter? You don't seem happy.* *Carole, ¿qué pasa? No pareces contenta.* **6** N-SING You use **matter** in expressions such as **"a matter of weeks"** when you are emphasizing how small an amount is or how short a period of time is. *cosa* ❑ *Within a matter of days she was back at work.* *En cosa de días había vuelto al trabajo.* **7** V-T/V-I If you say that something does not **matter,** you mean that it is not important to you because it does not have an effect on you or on a particular situation. *importar, dar igual* ❑ *A lot of the food goes on the floor but that doesn't matter.* *Gran parte de la comida va a dar al piso, pero da igual.* ❑ *It does not matter how long your essay is.* *No importa qué tan largo sea tu ensayo.* **8** → see also **subject matter** **9** PHRASE If you say that something is **another matter** or **a different matter,** you mean that it is very different from the situation that you have just discussed. *otro asunto, otra cosa, diferente* ❑ *Taking care of yourself is one thing, but taking care of someone else is a different matter.* *Cuidar de uno es una cosa, pero cuidar de alguien más es otro asunto.* **10** PHRASE If you are going to do something **as a matter of** urgency or priority, you are going to do it as soon as possible, because it is important. *asunto* ❑ *You need to go to your doctor as a matter of urgency.* *Necesitas ir al doctor con urgencia.* **11** CONVENTION You say **"it doesn't matter"** to tell someone who is apologizing to you that you are not angry or upset, and that they should not worry. *no importar, no tener importancia, dar igual* ❑ *"Did I wake you?" — "Yes, but it doesn't matter."* *—¿Te desperté? —Sí, pero no importa.* **12** PHRASE You use **no matter** in expressions such as **"no matter how"** and **"no matter what"** to say that something is true or happens in all circumstances. *sin importar, no importar* ❑ *Anyone can learn to swim, no matter what their age.* *Cualquiera puede aprender a nadar, sin importar su edad.* **13** a matter of **life and death** → see **death**
→ see Word Web: **matter**

**mat|tress** /mætrɪs/ (**mattresses**) N-COUNT A **mattress** is the large, flat object which is put on a bed to make it comfortable to sleep on. *colchón*
→ see **bed**

**ma|ture** /mətyʊər, -tʊər, -tʃʊər/ (**matures, maturing, matured, maturer, maturest**) **1** V-I When a child or young animal **matures,** it becomes an adult. *madurar, crecer, desarrollarse* ❑ *You will learn what to expect as your child matures physically.* *Ya sabrás qué esperar conforme tu hijo se desarrolle físicamente.* **2** ADJ A **mature** person or animal is fully grown. *maduro, adulto, desarrollado* • **maturity** /mətyʊərɪti, -tʊər-, -tʃʊər-/ N-UNCOUNT *madurez* ❑ *We stop growing at maturity.* *En la madurez, dejamos de crecer.* **3** V-I When something **matures,** it reaches a state of complete development. *madurar, desarrollarse, crecer* ❑ *When the trees matured they cut them down.* *Cuando los árboles maduraron, los cortaron.* **4** ADJ If you describe someone as **mature,** you think that their behavior is responsible and sensible. *maduro* ❑ *Fiona was mature for her age.* *Fiona era madura para su edad.* • **ma|tur|ity** N-UNCOUNT *madurez* ❑ *Her speech showed great maturity.* *Su forma de expresarse demostraba una gran madurez.*

**ma|ven** /meɪvən/ (**mavens**) N-COUNT A **maven** is a person who is an expert on a particular subject. *experto* ❑ *...style maven Andre Leon Talley.* *...Andre Leon Talley, el experto en diseño.*

**maxi|mum** /mæksɪməm/ **1** ADJ You use **maximum** to describe an amount which is the largest that is possible, allowed, or required. *máximo* ❑ *The maximum height for a garden fence is 6 feet.* *La altura máxima para una cerca de jardín es de 1.80 metros.* • **Maximum** is also a noun. *máximo* ❑ *...a maximum of two years in prison.* *...un máximo de dos años en prisión.* **2** ADJ You use **maximum** to indicate how great an amount is. *máximo* ❑ *I need the maximum amount of information you can give me.* *Necesito el máximo de información que puedas darme.* **3** ADV If you say that something is a particular amount **maximum,** you mean that this is the greatest amount it should be or could possibly be, although a smaller amount is acceptable or very

m

## Word Web meal

Customs for eating meals are very different around the world. In the Middle East, popular **breakfast** foods include pita bread, olives and white cheese. In China, favorite **fast food** breakfast items are steamed buns and fried breadsticks. The **continental breakfast** in Europe consists of bread, butter, jam, and a hot drink. In many places **lunch** is a light **meal**, like a **sandwich**. But in Germany, lunch is the main meal of the day. In most places, **dinner** is the name of the meal eaten in the evening. However, some people say they eat dinner at noon and supper at night.

possible. máximo, cuando mucho ❑ *We need 6 grams of salt a day maximum.* Cuando mucho necesitamos 6 gramos de sal al día.

**Thesaurus** *maximum* Ver también:

ADJ. biggest, greatest, highest, most; (ant.) lowest, minimum 1 2

**Word Partnership** Usar *maximum* con:

N. maximum **benefit**, maximum **charge**, maximum **efficiency**, maximum **fine**, maximum **flexibility**, maximum **height**, maximum **penalty**, maximum **rate**, maximum **sentence**, maximum **speed** 1

M

**may** /meɪ/

**May** is a modal verb. It is used with the base form of a verb.

1 MODAL You use **may** to indicate that there is a possibility that something will happen or is true. poder(se), quizá/quizás ❑ *We may have some rain today.* Hoy podría llover. ❑ *I may be back next year.* Quizá regrese el año próximo. 2 MODAL You use **may** in statements where you are accepting the truth of a situation, but contrasting it with something that is more important. poder ❑ *I may be almost 50, but I can remember most things.* Podré tener casi 50, pero puedo recordar la mayoría de las cosas. 3 MODAL You use **may** to indicate that someone is allowed to do something. ser posible ❑ *If you will be away on election day, you may vote by mail.* Si vas a estar fuera el día de las elecciones, podrás votar por correo. ❑ *May we come in?* ¿Podemos entrar? 4 **may as well** → see **well**
→ see also **can**

**May** /meɪ/ (**Mays**) N-VAR **May** is the fifth month of the year in the Western calendar. mayo ❑ *We went on vacation in early May.* Nos fuimos de vacaciones a principios de mayo.

**may|be** /meɪbi/ 1 ADV You use **maybe** to express uncertainty, for example when you do not know that something is definitely true. quizá, posiblemente, tal vez ❑ *Maybe she is in love.* Tal vez esté enamorada ❑ *I do think about having children, maybe when I'm 40.* Sí pienso tener hijos, tal vez cuando cumpla 40. ❑ *"Is she coming back?" — "Maybe."* —¿Va a regresar? —Quizá. 2 ADV You use **maybe** when you are making suggestions or giving advice. acaso, quizá, tal vez ❑ *Maybe we can go to the movies or something.* Tal vez podamos ir al cine, o algo así. ❑ *Maybe you should go there and look at it.* Tal vez deberías ir a verlo. 3 ADV You use **maybe** when you are making a rough guess at a number, quantity, or value, rather than stating it exactly. tal vez, quizá, posiblemente ❑ *The men were maybe a hundred feet away and coming closer.* Los hombres estaban tal vez a unos treinta metros y venían acercándose.

**Usage** maybe

*Maybe* is often confused with *may be*. *Maybe* is an adverb: *Maybe we'll be a little late*. *May be* is a verb form that means the same thing as *might be*: *We may be a little late.*

**may|on|naise** /meɪəneɪz/ N-UNCOUNT **Mayonnaise** is a thick, pale sauce made from egg yolks and oil. mayonesa

**mayor** /meɪər, mɛər/ (**mayors**) N-COUNT The **mayor** of a city or town is the person who has been elected for a fixed period of time to run its government. alcalde o alcaldesa, presidente o presidenta municipal ❑ *...the mayor of New York.* ...el alcalde de Nueva York.

**me** /mi, STRONG mi/ PRON A speaker or writer uses **me** to refer to himself or herself. **Me** is a first person singular pronoun. **Me** is used as the object of a verb or a preposition. a mí, me, mí ❑ *I had to make decisions that would affect me for the rest of my life.* Tuve que tomar decisiones que me afectarían para el resto de mi vida. ❑ *He asked me to go to California with him.* Me pidió que fuera a California con él.

**meal** /mil/ (**meals**) 1 N-COUNT A **meal** is an occasion when people sit down and eat. comida ❑ *She sat next to him throughout the meal.* Estuvo sentada junto a él durante toda la comida. 2 N-COUNT A **meal** is the food you eat during a meal. comida ❑ *Steil finished his meal in silence.* Steil terminó de comer en silencio.
→ see Word Web: **meal**

**Thesaurus** *meal* Ver también:

N. breakfast, dinner, lunch, supper 1

**Word Partnership** Usar *meal* con:

V. **enjoy a** meal, **miss a** meal, **skip a** meal 1 **cook a** meal, **eat a** meal, **have a** meal, **order a** meal, **prepare a** meal, **serve a** meal 2
ADJ. **big** meal, **delicious** meal, **good** meal, **hot** meal, **large** meal, **simple** meal, **well-balanced** meal 2

**mean**
❶ VERB USES
❷ ADJECTIVE USES
❸ NOUN USE

❶ **mean** /mi̲n/ (**means, meaning, meant**) 1 V-T If you want to know what a word, code, signal, or gesture **means,** you want to know what it refers to or what its message is. *significar, querer decir* ❑ *"Unable" means "not able." "Incapaz" quiere decir "no ser capaz".* ❑ *What does "disapproving" mean? ¿Qué significa "desaprobación"?* 2 V-T If something **means** something **to** you, it is important to you in some way. *significar* ❑ *Her feelings meant nothing to him. Sus sentimientos no significaban nada para él.* 3 V-T If one thing **means** another, it shows that the second thing is true or makes it certain that it will happen. *significar, traducirse en* ❑ *The new factory means more jobs for people who live here. La nueva fábrica se traducirá en más empleos para la gente que vive aquí.* 4 V-T If you **mean** what you are saying, you are serious about it and are not joking. *significar, decir en serio* ❑ *He said he loves her. And I think he meant it. Él dice que la ama, y yo creo que lo dice en serio.* 5 V-T If someone **meant to** do something, they did it deliberately. *tener la intención* ❑ *I didn't mean to hurt you. Mi intención no era lastimarte.* 6 PHRASE You can use **"I mean"** to introduce a statement, when you are explaining, justifying, or correcting something that you have just said. *es decir, querer decir, después de todo* [SPOKEN] ❑ *I'm sure he wouldn't mind. I mean, I was the one who asked him. Estoy seguro de que no le importaría. Después de todo, yo fui quien le preguntó.* ❑ *It was English or Spanish—I mean French or Spanish. Era inglés o español; qué digo, francés o español.* 7 → see also **meaning, means, meant**

❷ **mean** /mi̲n/ (**meaner, meanest**) 1 ADJ If someone is being **mean,** they are being unkind to another person, for example by not allowing them to do something. *malo* ❑ *Their older brother was being mean to them. Su hermano mayor estaba siendo malo con ellos.* ● **mean|ness** N-UNCOUNT *maldad* ❑ *You took his toys out of meanness. Te llevaste sus juguetes por maldad.* 2 ADJ If you describe a person or animal as **mean,** you are saying that they are very bad-tempered and cruel. *malo, cruel* ❑ *...the meanest fighter in the world. ...el peleador más cruel del mundo.*

**Thesaurus** *mean* Ver también:

V. aim, intend, plan ❶ 5
ADJ. nasty, unfriendly, unkind; (*ant.*) kind ❷ 1

❸ **mean** /mi̲n/ 1 N-SING **The mean** is a number that is the average of a set of numbers. *promedio, media* ❑ *Take a hundred numbers and calculate the mean. Escoge cien números y calcula el promedio.* 2 → see also **means**

**mean|ing** /mi̲nɪŋ/ (**meanings**) 1 N-VAR The **meaning** of a word, expression, or gesture is the thing or idea that it refers to or represents and which can be explained using other words. *significado, sentido, acepción* ❑ *What is the meaning of the word "disgusting"? ¿Cuál es el significado de la palabra "asqueroso"?* 2 N-UNCOUNT If an activity or action has **meaning,** it has a purpose and is worthwhile. *significado, intención, propósito* ❑ *Art has real meaning when it helps people to understand themselves. El arte adquiere un verdadero significado cuando ayuda a la gente a entenderse.*

**Word Partnership** Usar *meaning* con:

N. meaning **of a term,** meaning **of a word** 1
ADJ. **literal** meaning 1
**deeper** meaning, **new** meaning, **real** meaning, **true** meaning 1 2
V. **explain the** meaning **of** ***something,*** **understand the** meaning **of** ***something*** 1 2

**mean|ing|ful** /mi̲nɪŋfəl/ 1 ADJ If you describe something as **meaningful,** you mean that it is serious, important, or useful in some way. *significativo, importante, con sentido* ❑ *He does meaningful work, working with children with AIDS. Su labor es significativa: trabaja con niños con SIDA.* ● **mean|ing|ful|ly** ADV *significativamente, seriamente* ❑ *We need to talk meaningfully about these problems. Tenemos que hablar seriamente de estos problemas.* 2 ADJ A **meaningful** look or gesture is one that is intended to express something, usually to a particular person. *significativo* ❑ *She gave Jane a meaningful look. Le lanzó a Jane una mirada significativa.* ● **mean|ing|ful|ly** ADV *significativamente* ❑ *He glanced meaningfully at the other policeman. Miró significativamente a los otros policías.*

**mean|ing|less** /mi̲nɪŋlɪs/ ADJ Something that is **meaningless** has no meaning or purpose. *sin sentido* ❑ *The sentence "kicked the ball the man" is meaningless. La oración "pelota pateó la hombre el" no tiene sentido.* ❑ *...a meaningless life. ...una vida sin sentido.*

**means** /mi̲nz/ 1 N-COUNT A **means** of doing something is a method, instrument, or process which can be used to do it. **Means** is both the singular and the plural form for this use. *medio, instrumento, manera* ❑ *She used tears as a means to get his attention. Se valió de las lágrimas como un medio para atraer su atención.* ❑ *The army used terror as a means of controlling the people. El ejército utilizó el terror como instrumento de control de la gente.* 2 N-PLURAL You can refer to the money that someone has as their **means.** *recursos, medios, ingresos* [FORMAL] ❑ *...a person of means. ...una persona de recursos.* 3 PHRASE If you do something **by means of** a particular method, instrument, or process, you do it using that method, instrument, or process. *por medio de, mediante* ❑ *This course is taught by means of lectures and seminars. Este curso se imparte mediante conferencias y seminarios.* 4 CONVENTION You can say **"by all means"** to tell someone that you are very willing to allow them to do something. *¡cómo no!, por supuesto* ❑ *"Can I come to your house?"— "Yes, by all means." —¿Puedo ir a tu casa?—Sí, por supuesto.*

**meant** /mɛ̲nt/ 1 **Meant** is the past tense and past participle of **mean.** *pasado y participio pasado de **mean*** 2 ADJ You use **meant to** to say that something or someone was intended to be or do a particular thing, especially when they have failed to be or do it. *suponer, tener la intención* ❑ *I can't say any more, it's meant to be a big secret. Ya no puedo decir más, supuestamente es un gran secreto.* ❑ *Everything is meant to be informal. La intención*

**Picture Dictionary** measurements

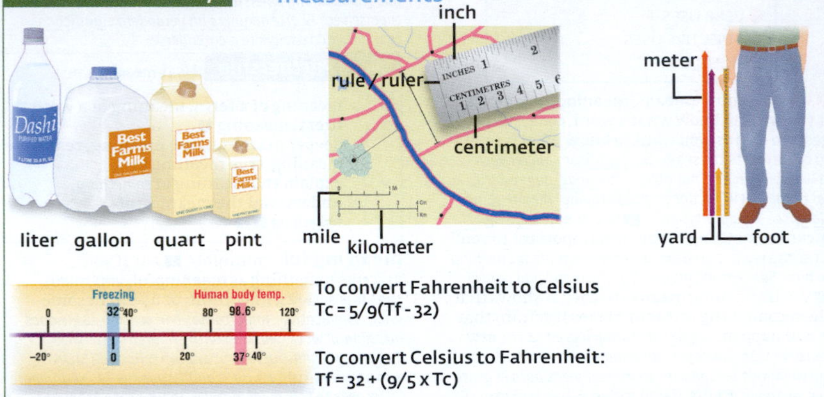


To convert Fahrenheit to Celsius
Tc = 5/9(Tf - 32)

To convert Celsius to Fahrenheit:
Tf = 32 + (9/5 x Tc)

*es que todo sea informal.* **3** ADJ If something **is meant for** particular people or for a particular situation, it is intended for those people or for that situation. *estar destinado a, ser para* ❑ *These stories aren't just meant for children. Estas historias no son solamente para niños.* **4** PHRASE If you say that something **is meant to** have a particular quality or characteristic, you mean that it has a reputation for being like that. *se supone que* ❑ *They're meant to be one of the best teams in the league. Se supone que son uno de los mejores equipos de la liga.*

**mean|time** /mi̲ntaɪm/ PHRASE **In the meantime** or **meantime** means in the period of time between two events. *entretanto, mientras, mientras tanto, por lo pronto* ❑ *Elizabeth wants to go to college but in the meantime she has to work. Elizabeth quiere ir a la universidad, pero mientras tiene que trabajar.*

**mean|while** /mi̲nwaɪl/ ADV **Meanwhile** means in the period of time between two events or while a particular thing is happening. *mientras tanto, entretanto* ❑ *I'll be ready to meet them. Meanwhile, I'm going to talk to Karen. Estaré listo para reunirme con ellos, mientras tanto, voy a hablar con Karen.*

**mea|sles** /mi̲zᵊlz/ N-UNCOUNT **Measles** is an infectious illness that gives you a high temperature and red spots. *sarampión*
→ see **hospital**

**meas|ure** /mɛ̲ʒər/ (**measures, measuring, measured**) **1** V-T If you **measure** the quality, quantity, or value of something, you find out or judge how great it is. *medir* ❑ *Measure the length of the table. Mida el largo de la mesa.* ❑ *I measured his height against the chart in the doctor's office. Medí su estatura con la tabla del consultorio del doctor.* **2** V-T If something **measures** a particular length, width, or amount, that is its size or intensity, expressed in numbers. *medir* ❑ *The football field measures 400 feet. El campo de futbol mide 122 metros de largo.* **3** N-SING A **measure of** a particular quality, feeling, or activity is a fairly large amount of it. *en una gran medida* [FORMAL] ❑ *Everyone achieved a measure of success. Todos lograron el éxito en una gran medida.* **4** N-SING If something is **a measure of** a situation, it shows that the situation is very serious or has developed to a very great extent. *indicador* ❑ *That is a measure of how bad things have become at the bank. Eso es un indicador de lo mal que están las cosas en el banco.* **5** N-COUNT When someone takes **measures** to do something, they carry out particular actions in order to achieve a particular result. *tomar medidas* [FORMAL] ❑ *The police are taking measures to deal with the problem. La policía está tomando medidas para resolver el problema.* **6** N-COUNT In music, a **measure** is one of the several short parts of the same length into which a piece of music is divided. *compás* ❑ *The music changes style for a few measures. El estilo de la música cambia a lo largo de algunos compases.* **7** → see also **tape measure**
→ see **mathematics, thermometer, utensil**

▸ **measure up** PHR-VERB If you do not **measure up to** a standard or to someone's expectations, you are not good enough to achieve the standard or fulfill the person's expectations. *estar a la altura, ponerse a la altura* ❑ *I was trying to measure up to her high standards. Estaba tratando de ponerme a la altura de sus expectativas*

**Word Partnership** Usar *measure* con:

N. measure **intelligence**, measure **performance**, measure **progress**, **tests** measure **1**

**meas|ure|ment** /mɛ̲ʒərmənt/ (**measurements**) **1** N-COUNT A **measurement** is a result that you obtain by measuring something. *medida* ❑ *We took lots of measurements. Tomamos muchas medidas.* **2** N-VAR **Measurement** of something is the process of measuring it. *medida* ❑ *Tests include measurement of height and weight. Las pruebas incluyen medir y pesar a la persona.* **3** N-PLURAL Your **measurements** are the size of your waist, chest, hips, and other parts of your body, which you need to know when you are buying clothes. *medida* ❑ *I know all her measurements and find it easy to buy clothes she likes. Me sé todas sus medidas y no me cuesta trabajo comprarle la ropa que le gusta.*
→ see Picture Dictionary: **measurements**

M

## Word Web meat

The English language has different words for animals and the **meat** that comes from those animals. This is because of influences from other

languages. In the year 1066 AD the Anglo-Saxons of England lost a major battle to the French-speaking Normans. As a result, the Normans became the ruling class and the Anglo-Saxons worked on farms. The Anglo-Saxons tended the animals. They tended **sheep, cows, chickens,**

and **pigs** in the fields. The wealthier Normans, who purchased and ate the meat from these animals, used different words. They bought "mouton," which became the word **mutton**, "bouef," which became **beef**, "poulet," which became **poultry**, and "porc," which became **pork**.

**meat** /mit/ (**meats**) N-VAR **Meat** is flesh taken from a dead animal that people cook and eat. *carne* ❑ *I don't eat meat or fish. Yo no como carne ni pescado.* ❑ *...imported meat products. ...productos de carne importados.*
→ see Word Web: **meat**
→ see **carnivore, vegetarian**

**meat|pack|ing** /mitpækɪŋ/ also **meat-packing** or **meat packing** N-UNCOUNT **Meatpacking** is the processing and packaging of meat for sale. *empacado de carne* ❑ *...the local meatpacking plant. ...la empacadora local de carne.*

**me|chan|ic** /mɪkænɪk/ (**mechanics**) **1** N-COUNT A **mechanic** is someone whose job is to repair and maintain machines and engines, especially car engines. *mecánico o mecánica* ❑ *If you smell burning in your car, take it to your mechanic. Si tu auto huele a quemado, llévalo al mecánico.* **2** N-PLURAL **The mechanics of** a process, system, or activity are the way in which it works or the way in which it is done. *mecánica, mecanismo* ❑ *What are the mechanics of this new process? ¿Cuál es la mecánica de este nuevo proceso?*

**me|chani|cal** /mɪkænɪkᵊl/ **1** ADJ A **mechanical** device has parts that move when it is working, often using power from an engine or from electricity. *mecánico, maquinal* ❑ *...mechanical parts for trains. ...partes mecánicas para trenes.* ❑ *...a working mechanical clock. ...un reloj mecánico que funciona.* ● **me|chani|cal|ly** /mɪkænɪkli/ ADV *mecánicamente, de manera mecánica* ❑ *The machine is mechanically operated. El aparato funciona de manera mecánica.* **2** ADJ A **mechanical** action is done automatically, without thinking about it. *mecánico, automático* ❑ *He reacted in a mechanical way. Reaccionó de manera mecánica.* ● **me|chani|cal|ly** ADV *mecánicamente* ❑ *He nodded his head mechanically. Asintió mecánicamente con la cabeza.*

**me|chani|cal ad|van|tage** (**mechanical advantages**) N-VAR The **mechanical advantage** of a machine such as a lever or pulley is a measure of the difference between the force applied to the machine and the force exerted by the machine. *rendimiento mecánico* [TECHNICAL]

**me|chani|cal en|er|gy** N-UNCOUNT **Mechanical energy** is the energy that an object such as a machine has because of its movement or position. *energía mecánica*

**me|chani|cal weath|er|ing** N-UNCOUNT **Mechanical weathering** is a geological process in which rock is broken down into smaller pieces, for example because of frost. *desgaste mecánico* [TECHNICAL]

**mecha|nism** /mɛkənɪzəm/ (**mechanisms**) **1** N-COUNT In a machine or piece of equipment, a **mechanism** is a part which performs a particular function. *mecanismo* ❑ *...the locking mechanism on the car door. ...el mecanismo de cierre de la puerta del automóvil.* **2** N-COUNT A **mechanism** is a special way of getting something done within a particular system. *mecanismo* ❑ *There's no mechanism for making changes. No existe un mecanismo para hacer cambios.*

**mecha|nize** /mɛkənaɪz/ (**mechanizes, mechanizing, mechanized**) V-T If someone **mechanizes** a process, they cause it to be done by a machine or machines. *mecanizar, automatizar* ❑ *Technologies are developing to mechanize the job. Se están desarrollando tecnologías para mecanizar el trabajo.* ● **mecha|ni|za|tion** /mɛkənɪzeɪʃᵊn/ N-UNCOUNT *mecanización* ❑ *Mechanization happened years ago. Hace años que se hizo la mecanización.*

**med|al** /mɛdᵊl/ (**medals**) N-COUNT A **medal** is a small metal disk which is given as an award for bravery or as a prize in a sports event. *medalla, condecoración* ❑ *...the country's highest medal for bravery. ...la más alta condecoración que el país otorga al valor.*

medal

**med|al|ist** /mɛdᵊlɪst/ (**medalists**) N-COUNT A **medalist** is a person who has won a medal in sports. *medallista* ❑ *...the Olympic gold medalists. ...los medallistas de oro de los Juegos Olímpicos.*

**Med|al of Hon|or** (**Medals of Honor**) N-COUNT The **Medal of Honor** is a medal that is given to members of the U.S. armed forces who have shown special courage or bravery in battle. *Medalla*

m

*de Honor* ❑ *He won the Medal of Honor for his actions in 1943.* *En 1943 recibió la Medalla de Honor por sus actos.*

**Word Link** **med ≈ middle : intermediate, media, medium**

**me|dia** /midiə/ **1** N-SING You can refer to television, radio, newspapers, and magazines as **the media.** *medios de comunicación*

**Media** can take the singular or plural form of the verb.

❑ *A lot of people in the media have written bad things about him.* *Mucha gente de los medios de comunicación ha escrito cosas desfavorables sobre él.* ❑ *They told their story to the news media.* *Contaron su historia a los noticiarios.* **2** → see also **mass media, multimedia** **3** **Media** is a plural of **medium.** *plural de* ***medium***
→ see **library**

**me|dia cir|cus** (**media circuses**) N-COUNT If an event is described as a **media circus,** a large group of people from the media are there to report on it and take photographs. *circo mediático* ❑ *The couple married in the Caribbean to avoid a media circus.* *La pareja se casó en el Caribe para evitar un circo mediático.*

**me|dian** /midiən/ (**medians**) ADJ The **median** value of a set of values is the middle one when they are arranged in order. For example, if a group of five students take a test and their scores are 5, 7, 7, 8, and 10, the median score is 7. *valor medio, mediana* [TECHNICAL]

**me|dian strip** /midiən strɪp/ (**median strips**) N-COUNT The **median strip** is the strip of ground, often covered with grass, that separates the two sides of a major road. *camellón, mediana*

**me|dia source** (**media sources**) N-COUNT You can refer to television, radio, newspapers, the Internet, and other forms of mass communication as **media sources.** *fuente de los medios, fuente mediática*

**me|di|ate** /midieɪt/ (**mediates, mediating, mediated**) V-T/V-I If someone **mediates between** two groups of people, or **mediates** an agreement **between** them, they try to settle an argument between them. *mediar, hacer de mediador, actuar como mediador, arbitrar* ❑ *My mom mediated between Zelda and her mom.* *Mi mamá medió entre Zelda y su mamá.* ❑ *United Nations officials have mediated a series of peace meetings between the two sides.* *Los funcionarios de la ONU han fungido como mediadores en una serie de reuniones de paz entre los dos bandos.*
• **me|dia|tion** /midieɪʃᵊn/ N-UNCOUNT *mediación* ❑ *...to solve disputes informally through mediation.* *...dirimir controversias informalmente con la mediación.*
• **me|dia|tor** N-COUNT (**mediators**) *mediador o mediadora* ❑ *A religious leader acted as mediator between the rebels and the government.* *Un dirigente religioso actuó como mediador entre los rebeldes y el gobierno.*
→ see **war**

**med|ic** /mɛdɪk/ (**medics**) **1** N-COUNT A **medic** is a doctor who works with the armed forces, as part of a medical corps. *médico o médica* ❑ *...an army medic.* *...un médico militar.* **2** N-COUNT A **medic** is a doctor or medical student. *médico o médica, estudiante de medicina* [INFORMAL]

**Medi|caid** /mɛdɪkeɪd/ N-PROPER In the United States, **Medicaid** is a government program that helps to pay medical costs for poor people. *Medicaid, programa estadounidense de asistencia médica para los pobres* ❑ *For her medical care, the family used Medicaid.* *La familia recibía asistencia médica a través de Medicaid.* ❑ *Some doctors won't accept Medicaid patients.* *Algunos doctores no aceptan pacientes inscritos a Medicaid.*

**medi|cal** /mɛdɪkᵊl/ (**medicals**) ADJ **Medical** means relating to illness and injuries and to their treatment or prevention. *médico* ❑ *Several police officers received medical treatment for cuts and bruises.* *Varios policías recibieron tratamiento médico para las cortadas y contusiones.* • **medi|cal|ly** /mɛdɪkli/ ADV *médicamente, desde el punto de vista médico, médico* ❑ *Most teachers are not medically trained.* *La mayoría de los maestros carece de formación médica.*

**Word Partnership** Usar *medical* con:

N. medical **advice**, medical **attention**, medical **bills**, medical **care**, medical **center**, medical **doctor**, medical **emergency**, medical **practice**, medical **problems**, medical **research**, medical **science**, medical **supplies**, medical **tests**, medical **treatment** **1**

**medi|cal ex|am|in|er** (**medical examiners**) N-COUNT A **medical examiner** is a medical expert who is responsible for investigating the deaths of people who have died in a sudden, violent, or unusual way. *médico o médica forense, el forense o la forense*

**Medi|care** /mɛdɪkɛər/ N-PROPER In the United States, **Medicare** is a government program that provides health insurance to cover medical costs for people aged 65 and older. *Medicare, programa estadounidense de asistencia médica para ancianos*

**medi|ca|tion** /mɛdɪkeɪʃᵊn/ (**medications**) N-VAR **Medication** is medicine that is used to treat and cure illness. *medicación, medicamento, medicina, remedio* ❑ *Are you taking any medication?* *¿Estás tomando algún medicamento?*

**medi|cine** /mɛdɪsɪn/ (**medicines**) **1** N-UNCOUNT **Medicine** is the treatment of illness and injuries by doctors and nurses. *medicina* ❑ *He decided on a career in medicine.* *Decidió seguir la carrera de medicina.* **2** N-VAR **Medicine** is a substance that you drink or swallow in order to treat or cure an illness. *medicina, medicamento, remedio, medicación* ❑ *The medicine saved his life.* *La medicina le salvó la vida.*
→ see Word Web: **medicine**

**Word Partnership** Usar *medicine* con:

V. **practice** medicine, **study** medicine **1**
**give *someone*** medicine, **take** medicine, **use** medicine **2**

**me|di|eval** /midiivᵊl, mɪdivᵊl/ ADJ Something that is **medieval** relates to or was made in the period of European history between the end of the Roman Empire in A.D. 476 and about A.D. 1500. *medieval, de la Edad Media* ❑ *...a medieval castle.* *...un castillo medieval*

**me|dio|cre** /midioʊkər/ ADJ If you describe something as **mediocre,** you mean that it is of

M

## Word Web **medicine**

**Medicine** began in the Western Hemisphere in ancient Greece. The Greek philosopher Hippocrates separated medicine from religion and **disease** from supernatural explanations. He created the Hippocratic **oath** which describes a **physician's** duties. During the Middle Ages, Andreas Vesalius helped to advance medicine through his **research** on **anatomy**. Another major step forward was Friedrich Henle's development of **germ** theory. An understanding of germs led to Joseph Lister's demonstrations of the effective use of **antiseptics**, and Alexander Fleming's discovery of the **antibiotic** penicillin.

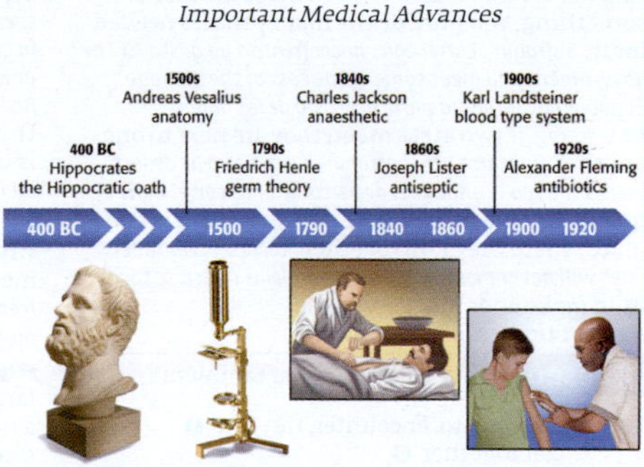


average quality but you think it should be better. *mediocre, ordinario* ❑ *His school test results were mediocre. Los resultados de sus exámenes escolares fueron mediocres.* • **me|di|oc|rity** /miːdiɒkrɪti/ N-UNCOUNT *mediocridad* ❑ *...the mediocrity of her work. ...la mediocridad de su trabajo.*

**medi|tate** /mɛdɪteɪt/ (**meditates, meditating, meditated**) **1** V-I If you **meditate on** something, you think about it very carefully and deeply for a long time. *meditar, reflexionar, cavilar* ❑ *She meditated on how to be a good mother. Reflexionó sobre cómo ser una buena madre.* **2** V-I If you **meditate,** you remain in a silent and calm state for a period of time, often as part of a religious training. *meditar* ❑ *When you meditate, you think about nothing. Cuando meditas, no piensas en nada.* • **medi|ta|tion** /mɛdɪteɪʃᵊn/ N-UNCOUNT *meditación* ❑ *I enjoy yoga and meditation. Disfruto el yoga y la meditación.*

**Word Link** **med ≈ middle : intermediate, media, medium**

**me|dium** /miːdiəm/ (**mediums** or **media**) **1** ADJ If something is of **medium** size, it is neither large nor small, but approximately halfway between the two. *mediano* ❑ *Mix the cream and eggs in a medium bowl. Mezcla la crema y los huevos en un tazón mediano.* **2** ADJ You use **medium** to describe something that is average in degree or amount, or approximately halfway along a scale between two extremes. *medio, intermedio* ❑ *Bread and cakes contain only medium levels of salt. El pan y los pasteles sólo contienen un grado intermedio de sal.* • **Medium** is also an adverb. *medio* ❑ *Andrea has medium brown hair. El cabello de Andrea es medio castaño.* **3** N-COUNT A **medium** is a way or means of expressing your ideas or of communicating with people. *medio, instrumento* ❑ *English is a medium of communication in many countries. El inglés es un medio de comunicación en muchos países.* **4** N-COUNT A **medium** is a substance or material which is used for a particular purpose or in order to produce a particular effect. *medio* **5** → see also **media**

**me|dul|la** /mədʌlə/ (**medullas** or **medullae** /mədʌli/) N-COUNT The **medulla** is a part of the brain in humans and other animals that connects the brain to the spinal cord. It controls functions such as breathing and swallowing. The form **medulla oblongata** is also used. *médula, médula oblonga, bulbo raquídeo* [TECHNICAL]

**me|du|sa** /mədusə/ (**medusas** or **medusae**) N-COUNT A **medusa** is a type of jellyfish. *medusa, aguamala, malagua* [TECHNICAL]

**meet** /miːt/ (**meets, meeting, met**) **1** V-RECIP If you **meet** someone, you happen to be in the same place as them and start talking to them. *conocer(se), encontrar(se)* ❑ *I have just met an amazing man. Acabo de conocer a un hombre sorprendente.* ❑ *He's the kindest person I've ever met. Él es la persona más amable que he conocido.* • **Meet up** means the same as **meet.** *conocer(se), encontrar(se)* ❑ *Last night he met up with a friend from school. Anoche se encontró con un amigo de la escuela.* **2** V-RECIP If two or more people **meet,** they go to the same place, which they have earlier arranged to do, so that they can talk or do something together. *verse, juntarse, reunirse* ❑ *We could meet for a game of tennis after work. Podríamos juntarnos para jugar al tenis después del trabajo.* • **Meet up** means the same as **meet.** *verse, juntarse, reunirse* ❑ *We meet up for lunch once a week. Nos vemos para comer juntas una vez por semana.* **3** V-T If you **meet** someone at their train, plane, or bus, you go to the station, airport, or bus stop in order to be there when they arrive. *recibir a alguien, recoger a alguien* ❑ *Mama met me at the station. Mamá me recogió en la estación.* **4** V-I If you **meet with** someone, you have a meeting with them. *reunirse* ❑ *A group of lawyers met with the president yesterday. Un grupo de abogados se reunió ayer con el presidente.* **5** V-T/V-I If something such as a suggestion, proposal, or new book **meets with** or **is met with** a particular reaction, it gets that reaction from people. *aceptar, recibir* ❑ *We hope today's offer will meet with your approval. Esperamos que la oferta de hoy reciba su aprobación.* **6** V-T If something **meets** a need, requirement, or condition, it is good enough to do what is required. *satisfacer, cumplir* ❑ *This hospital does not meet some patients' needs. Este hospital no satisface las necesidades de algunos pacientes.* **7** V-T If you **meet** something such as a problem or challenge, you deal with it satisfactorily or do what is required. *resolver, hacer frente, enfrentar* ❑ *Some people can't meet the problems of daily life.*

Algunas personas no pueden hacer frente a los problemas de la vida cotidiana. 8 V-T If you **meet** the cost of something, you provide the money that is needed for it. sufragar, correr con, hacer frente a un gasto ❑ *The government will meet some of the cost of the damage.* *El gobierno sufragará parte del costo de los daños.*
9 V-RECIP If two areas **meet,** they are next to one another. juntarse, encontrarse ❑ *...where the desert meets the sea.* *...donde el desierto se junta con el mar.*
10 V-RECIP The place where two lines **meet** is the place where they join together. tocarse ❑ *Parallel lines will never meet.* *Las líneas paralelas nunca se tocan.*
11 to **make ends meet** → see **end**
▸ **meet up** → see **meet 1, 2**

| Thesaurus | *meet* | Ver también: |
|---|---|---|
| v. | bump into, encounter, run into 1 | |
| | get together 2 | |
| | comply with, follow, fulfill 6 | |
| | accomplish, achieve, complete, make 7 | |

**meet|ing** /mitɪŋ/ (**meetings**) 1 N-COUNT A **meeting** is an event in which a group of people come together to discuss things or make decisions. reunión, junta ❑ *Can we have a meeting to discuss that?* *¿Podemos tener una reunión para discutirlo?* ● You can also refer to the people at a meeting as **the meeting.** junta ❑ *The meeting decided that more work was necessary.* *La junta decidió que era necesario trabajar más.* 2 N-COUNT A **meeting** is an occasion when you meet someone. encuentro ❑ *In January, 37 years after our first meeting, I was back in the studio with Dennis.* *En enero, 37 años después de nuestro primer encuentro, estaba de vuelta en el estudio con Dennis.*

M

| Word Partnership | Usar *meeting* con: |
|---|---|
| N. | meeting **agenda**, **board** meeting, **business** meeting 1 |
| V. | **attend a** meeting, **call a** meeting, **go to a** meeting, **have a** meeting, **hold a** meeting 1 |
| | **plan a** meeting, **schedule a** meeting 1 2 |

**mega|byte** /mɛgəbaɪt/ (**megabytes**) N-COUNT In computing, a **megabyte** is one million bytes of data. megabyte ❑ *...256 megabytes of memory.* *...256 megabytes de memoria.*

**meio|sis** /maɪoʊsɪs/ N-UNCOUNT **Meiosis** is a type of cell division that results in egg and sperm cells with only half the usual number of chromosomes. meiosis [TECHNICAL]

**mela|nin** /mɛlənɪn/ N-UNCOUNT **Melanin** is a dark substance in the skin, eyes, and hair of people and animals, which gives them color and can protect them against strong sunlight. melanina

**meld** /mɛld/ (**melds, melding, melded**) 1 V-T/V-I If several things **meld,** or if something **melds** them, they combine or blend in a pleasant or useful way. unir, mezclar, fusionar [FORMAL] ❑ *She listened to the way the words melded with the music.* *Escuchaba la manera como la letra se fusionaba con la música.* ❑ *Leave the sauce for 30 minutes for the flavors to meld.* *Deje reposar la salsa durante 30 minutos para que se mezclen los sabores.* 2 V-T/V-I If several things **meld into** another thing, or if they **are melded into** another thing, they combine and become the other thing. fusionar(se) [FORMAL] ❑ *Fact and fiction seemed to meld into a familiar legend.* *Los hechos y la ficción parecían fusionarse en una leyenda familiar.* ❑ *Two unions were melded into one group.* *Dos sindicatos se fusionaron en un solo grupo.* 3 N-COUNT A **meld of** things is a mixture or combination of them that is useful or pleasant. mezcla [FORMAL] ❑ *...a perfect meld of art and news.* *...una mezcla perfecta de arte y noticias.*

**melo|dy** /mɛlədi/ (**melodies**) N-COUNT A **melody** is a tune. melodía ❑ *I whistle melodies from my favorite TV shows.* *Silbo las melodías de mis programas de televisión preferidos.*

**mel|on** /mɛlən/ (**melons**) N-VAR A **melon** is a large fruit which is sweet and juicy inside and has a hard green or yellow skin. melón ❑ *...some juicy slices of melon.* *...unas jugosas rebanadas de melón.*

**melt** /mɛlt/ (**melts, melting, melted**) 1 V-T/V-I When a solid substance **melts** or when you **melt** it, it changes to a liquid, usually because it has been heated. derretir(se), fundir(se) ❑ *The snow melted.* *La nieve se derritió.* ❑ *Melt the chocolate in a bowl.* *Funda el chocolate en un tazón.* ● **melting** N-UNCOUNT fusión ❑ *This experiment investigates if mass also changes during melting.* *Con este experimento se investiga si la masa también cambia durante la fusión.* 2 V-I If something **melts,** it suddenly disappears. desvanecerse, disiparse [LITERARY] ❑ *His feelings of worry melted, but returned later.* *Su sentimiento de preocupación se disipó, pero después volvió.* ● **Melt away** means the same as **melt.** disiparse ❑ *Scot felt his doubts melt away.* *Scot sintió que sus dudas se habían disipado.* 3 V-I If a person or thing **melts into** something such as darkness or a crowd of people, they become difficult to see. desaparecer [LITERARY] ❑ *He turned and melted into the darkness.* *Se volvió y desapareció en la oscuridad.* 4 N-COUNT A **melt** is a piece of bread which has meat or fish on it, and melted cheese on top. derretido ❑ *...a tuna melt.* *...un sándwich de atún con queso derretido.*
→ see **glacier, matter**

**melt|ing point** (**melting points**) N-COUNT The **melting point** of a substance is the temperature at which it melts when you heat it. punto de fusión

**mem|ber** /mɛmbər/ (**members**) N-COUNT A **member** of a group or organization is one of the people, animals, or things belonging to that group. miembro, asociado o asociada, socio o socia ❑ *Britain is a full member of NATO.* *Gran Bretaña es socio de pleno derecho de la OTAN.* ❑ *A member of the public saw the accident.* *Un transeúnte presenció el accidente.* ❑ *The support of our members is very important to the organization.* *El apoyo de nuestros socios es muy importante para la organización.*

**Mem|ber of Par|lia|ment** (**Members of Parliament**) N-COUNT A **Member of Parliament** is a person who has been elected by the people in a particular area to represent them in a country's parliament. The abbreviation **MP** is often used. parlamentario o parlamentaria, miembro del parlamento

| Word Link | *ship ≈ condition or state : citizenship, friendship, membership* |
|---|---|

**mem|ber|ship** /mɛmbərʃɪp/ (**memberships**) 1 N-UNCOUNT **Membership** in an organization is the state of being a member of it. *afiliación, calidad de socio, calidad de asociado* ❑ *...his membership in the Communist Party. ...su afiliación al Partido Comunista.* **2** N-VAR The **membership** of an organization is the people who belong to it, or the number of people who belong to it. *nómina de socios* ❑ *By 1890 the organization had a membership of 409,000. Hacia 1890, la organización tenía una nómina de 409,000 socios.*

**mem|bra|no|phone** /mɛmbreɪnəfoʊn/ (**membranophones**) N-COUNT A **membranophone** is any musical instrument that produces its sound by the vibration of a stretched skin, for example a drum. *membranófono* [TECHNICAL]

**memo** /mɛmoʊ/ (**memos**) N-COUNT A **memo** is a short official note that is sent by one person to another within the same company or organization. *memorándum, circular* ❑ *He sent a memo to all staff. Envió una circular/un memorándum a todo el personal.*

**mem|oirs** /mɛmwɑrz/ N-PLURAL A person's **memoirs** are a written account of the people who they have known and events that they remember. *memorias* ❑ *He published his memoirs after he retired from work. Publicó sus memorias después de jubilarse.*

**memo|rable** /mɛmərəbᵊl/ ADJ Something that is **memorable** is worth remembering or likely to be remembered, because it is special or very enjoyable. *memorable* ❑ *Our wedding was a very memorable day. El día de nuestra boda fue memorable.*

**Word Link** *memor ≈ memory : commemorate, memorial, memory*

**me|mo|rial** /mɪmɔriəl/ (**memorials**) **1** N-COUNT A **memorial** is a structure built in order to remind people of a famous person or event. *monumento* ❑ *He wanted to build a memorial to Columbus. Quería construir un monumento a Colón.* **2** ADJ A **memorial** event, object, or prize is in honor of someone who has died, so that they will be remembered. *conmemorativo* ❑ *A memorial service was held for her at St. Paul's Church. Se llevó a cabo un oficio religioso en su memoria en la iglesia de St. Paul.*

memorial

**memo|rize** /mɛməraɪz/ (**memorizes, memorizing, memorized**) V-T If you **memorize** something, you learn it so that you can remember it exactly. *memorizar* ❑ *He tried to memorize the way to Rose's street. Trató de memorizar el camino a la calle donde vivía Rose.*

**memo|ry** /mɛməri/ (**memories**) **1** N-VAR Your **memory** is your ability to remember things. *memoria* ❑ *All the details of the meeting are fresh in my memory. Tengo frescos en la memoria todos los detalles del encuentro/de la reunión.* ❑ *He had a good memory for faces. Tenía buena memoria para los rostros.* **2** N-COUNT A **memory** is something that you remember from the past. *recuerdo* ❑ *She doesn't like to watch the film because of the bad memories it brings back. No le gusta ver la película por los malos recuerdos que le trae.* **3** N-COUNT A computer's **memory** is the part of the computer where information is stored, especially for a short time before it is transferred to disks or magnetic tapes. *memoria* [COMPUTING] ❑ *The data are stored in the computer's memory. La información está almacenada en la memoria de la computadora.* **4** N-SING If you talk about the **memory** of someone who has died, especially someone who was loved or respected, you are referring to the thoughts, actions, and ceremonies by which they are remembered. *memoria, recuerdo* ❑ *I planted a tree in memory of my grandmother. Planté un árbol en recuerdo de mi abuelita.* **5** PHRASE If you do something **from memory**, for example speak the words of a poem or play a piece of music, you do it without looking at it, because you know it very well. *de memoria* ❑ *Many members of the church sang from memory. Muchos feligreses cantan de memoria.*

**Word Partnership** Usar *memory* con:

ADJ. **conscious** memory, **failing** memory, **fresh in** *your* memory, **long-/short-term** memory, **poor** memory, **in recent** memory **1**
**bad** memory, **good** memory **1** **2**
**happy** memory, **painful** memory, **sad** memory, **vivid** memory **2**

N. **computer** memory, **random access** memory, memory **storage** **3**

**memo|ry card** (**memory cards**) N-COUNT A **memory card** is a type of card containing computer memory that is used in digital cameras and other devices. *tarjeta de memoria* [COMPUTING]

**men** /mɛn/ **Men** is the plural of **man**. *plural de man*

**mend** /mɛnd/ (**mends, mending, mended**) **1** V-T If you **mend** a tear or a hole in a piece of clothing, you repair it by sewing it. *zurcir, remendar* ❑ *He earns money by mending clothes. Gana dinero remendando ropa.* **2** V-T/V-I If a person or a part of their body **mends** or **is mended,** they get better after they have been ill or have had an injury. *curar(se)* ❑ *I'm feeling a lot better. The cut aches, but it's mending. Me siento mucho mejor. La herida me duele, pero ya se está curando.* **3** PHRASE If you are **on the mend** after an illness or injury, you are recovering from it. *mejorar, reponerse* [INFORMAL] ❑ *The baby has been ill, but is on the mend now. El bebé ha estado enfermo, pero ya está mejorando.*

**me|nis|cus** /mɪnɪskəs/ (**menisci**) N-COUNT A **meniscus** is the curved surface of a liquid in a narrow tube. *menisco* [TECHNICAL]

**Men|no|nite** /mɛnənaɪt/ (**Mennonites**) **1** N-COUNT **Mennonites** are members of a Protestant sect who do not baptize their children and who are opposed to military service. *menonita* **2** ADJ **Mennonite** means relating to the religious beliefs or practices of Mennonites. *menonita* ❑ *...Pennsylvania's Mennonite communities. ...las comunidades menonitas de Pensilvania.*

**meno|pause** /mɛnəpɔz/ N-SING **Menopause** is the time during which a woman gradually stops menstruating, usually when she is about fifty. *menopausia* • **meno|pau|sal** ADJ *menopáusico* ❑ *...a menopausal woman. ...una mujer menopáusica.*

**me|no|rah** /mənɔrə, -noʊrə/ (**menorahs**) N-COUNT A **menorah** is a candelabra consisting of

m

seven or sometimes eight branches. It is a symbol of Judaism. *menorá* ❑ *We lit the menorah. Encendimos la menorá.*

**men's room** (**men's rooms**) N-COUNT **The men's room** is a bathroom for men in a public building. *baño de hombres*

**men|stru|ate** /mɛnstrueɪt/ (**menstruates, menstruating, menstruated**) V-I When a woman **menstruates,** a flow of blood comes from her uterus. *menstruar* [FORMAL] ❑ *Women athletes may menstruate less frequently. Las atletas pueden menstruar con menos frecuencia.* ● **men|strua|tion** /mɛnstrueɪʃᵊn/ N-UNCOUNT *menstruación* ❑ *Menstruation stops when a woman is between forty-five and fifty. La menstruación desaparece cuando la mujer tiene entre 45 y 50 años de edad.*

**men|tal** /mɛntᵊl/ **1** ADJ **Mental** means relating to the process of thinking. *mental* ❑ *...the mental development of the children. ...el desarrollo mental de los niños.* ● **men|tal|ly** ADV *mentalmente* ❑ *I think you are mentally tired. Creo que estás cansado mentalmente.* **2** ADJ A **mental** act is one that involves only thinking and not physical action. *mental* ❑ *Allen did a quick mental calculation. Allen hizo un rápido cálculo mental.* ● **men|tal|ly** ADV *mentalmente* ❑ *This technique will help people mentally organize information. Esta técnica ayudará a la gente a organizar mentalmente la información.*

**men|tion** /mɛnʃᵊn/ (**mentions, mentioning, mentioned**) V-T If you **mention** something, you say something about it, usually briefly. *mencionar, decir* ❑ *She did not mention her mother's name. No mencionó el nombre de su madre.* ❑ *I may not have mentioned it to her. Quizá no se lo mencioné.* ❑ *I mentioned that I didn't really like pop music. Dije que realmente no me gustaba la música pop.*

M

**Word Partnership** Usar *mention* con:

V. **fail to** mention, **forget to** mention, **neglect to** mention

**men|tor** /mɛntɔr/ (**mentors**) N-COUNT A person's **mentor** is someone who gives them help and advice over a period of time. *mentor o mentora* ❑ *Leon Sullivan was my mentor and my friend. Leon Sullivan fue mi mentor y amigo.*

**menu** /mɛnyu/ (**menus**) **1** N-COUNT In a restaurant or café, the **menu** is a list of the meals and drinks that are available. *carta, menú* ❑ *A waiter offered him the menu. Un mesero le presentó la carta/el menú.* **2** N-COUNT On a computer screen, a **menu** is a list of choices of things that you can do using the computer. *menú* ❑ *Press F7 to show the print menu. Pulse/Oprima la tecla F7 para ver el menú de impresión.*

**MEP** /ɛm i pi/ (**MEPs**) N-COUNT An **MEP** is a person who has been elected to the European Parliament. **MEP** is an abbreviation for "Member of the European Parliament." *eurodiputado*

**Mercator pro|jec|tion** /mərkeɪtər prəjɛkʃᵊn/ (**Mercator projections**) N-VAR A **Mercator projection** is an image of a map that is made by projecting the map on a globe onto a cylindrical surface. Compare **azimuthal projection, conic projection.** *proyección de/conforme a Mercator* [TECHNICAL]

**Word Link** *merc ≈ trading : commerce, merchandise, merchant*

**mer|chan|dise** /mɜrtʃəndaɪz, -daɪs/ N-UNCOUNT **Merchandise** is products that are bought, sold, or traded. *mercancía, mercadería* [FORMAL] ❑ *The company provides merchandise for elderly people. La empresa suministra mercancías para ancianos.*

**mer|chan|dis|er** /mɜrtʃəndaɪzər/ (**merchandisers**) N-COUNT A **merchandiser** is a person or company that sells goods to the public. *comerciante, minorista* [BUSINESS] ❑ *...a fashion merchandiser. ...un comerciante/minorista en moda.*

**mer|chant** /mɜrtʃənt/ (**merchants**) **1** N-COUNT A **merchant** is a person who buys or sells goods in large quantities. *comerciante* ❑ *His father was a successful wool merchant. Su padre fue un próspero comerciante en lana.* **2** N-COUNT A **merchant** is a person who owns or runs a store or shop. *comerciante* ❑ *The family buys most of the things it needs from local merchants. La familia compra la mayoría de las cosas que necesita a los comerciantes del lugar.* **3** ADJ **Merchant** seamen or ships are involved in carrying goods for trade. *mercante* ❑ *...the merchant navy. ...la marina mercante.*

**mer|ci|ful|ly** /mɜrsɪfəli/ ADV You can use **mercifully** to show that you are glad that something good has happened, or that something bad has not happened or has stopped. *por fortuna, felizmente* ❑ *Mercifully, a friend saw what was happening and came to help. Por fortuna, un amigo vio lo que estaba pasando y fue a ayudar.*

**mer|cu|ry** /mɜrkyəri/ N-UNCOUNT **Mercury** is a silver-colored liquid metal that is used especially in thermometers and barometers. *mercurio*
→ see **thermometer**

**Mer|cu|ry** /mɜrkyəri/ N-PROPER **Mercury** is the planet that is closest to the sun. *Mercurio*
→ see **solar system**

**mer|cy** /mɜrsi/ (**mercies**) **1** N-UNCOUNT If someone in authority shows **mercy,** they choose not to harm or punish someone they have power over. *piedad* ❑ *His attacker showed no mercy. Sus asaltantes no tuvieron piedad.* **2** PHRASE If one person or thing is **at the mercy of** another, the first person or thing is in a situation where they cannot prevent themselves from being harmed or affected by the second. *a merced de* ❑ *We slept outside, at the mercy of the mosquitoes. Dormimos al aire libre, a merced de los mosquitos.*

**mere** /mɪər/ (**merest**)

**Mere** does not have a comparative form. The superlative form **merest** is used to emphasize how small something is, rather than in comparisons.

ADJ You use **mere** to emphasize how unimportant, insufficient, or small something is. *mero, simple, apenas* ❑ *Sixty percent of teachers are women, but a mere five percent of women are principals. El sesenta por ciento de los maestros son mujeres, pero apenas el cinco por ciento de las mujeres son directoras.* ❑ *Some people are terrified at the mere sight of a spider. A algunas personas les aterroriza la simple vista de una araña.*
● **mere|ly** ADV *simplemente, meramente, apenas*

❑ *The brain accounts for merely three percent of body weight.* *El cerebro representa apenas el tres por ciento del peso corporal.*

**mere|ly** /mɪərli/ **1** ADV You use **merely** to emphasize that something is only what you say and not better, more important, or more exciting. *simplemente, apenas* ❑ *Michael is now merely a good friend.* *Michael ya es simplemente un buen amigo.* **2** PHRASE You use **not merely** before the less important of two contrasting statements, as a way of emphasizing the more important statement. *no simplemente, no solamente* ❑ *The team needs players who want to play for Canada, not merely any country that will have them.* *El equipo necesita jugadores que quieran jugar por Canadá, no solamente por cualquier país que los acepte.*

**Word Link** *merg ≈ sinking : emerge, merge, submerge*

**merge** /mɜrdʒ/ (**merges, merging, merged**) V-RECIP If one thing **merges with** another, or **is merged with** another, they combine or come together to make one whole thing. *fusionar(se), confluir, unir(se)* ❑ *Bank of America merged with another bank.* *El Bank of America se fusionó con otro banco* ❑ *The rivers merge just north of here.* *Los ríos confluyen justo al norte de aquí.* ❑ *The two countries merged into one.* *Los dos países se unieron en uno.*

**mer|ger** /mɜrdʒər/ (**mergers**) N-COUNT A **merger** is the joining together of two separate companies or organizations so that they become one. *fusión* [BUSINESS] ❑ *...a merger between two of America's biggest companies.* *...una fusión de las dos empresas más grandes de Estados Unidos.*

**mer|it** /mɛrɪt/ (**merits, meriting, merited**) **1** N-UNCOUNT If something has **merit,** it has good or worthwhile qualities. *mérito* ❑ *The argument had considerable merit.* *El argumento tenía mucho mérito.* **2** N-PLURAL The **merits** of something are its advantages or other good points. *ventaja* ❑ *We need to persuade them of the merits of peace.* *Necesitamos persuadirlos de las ventajas de la paz.* **3** V-T If someone or something **merits** a particular action or treatment, they deserve it. *merecer, ameritar* [FORMAL] ❑ *He made a mistake, but that does not merit going to jail.* *Cometió un error, pero no por ello merece la cárcel.*

**mer|ry** /mɛri/ (**merrier, merriest**) ADJ **Merry** means happy and cheerful. *alegre, feliz* ❑ *...a merry little tune.* *...una tonadilla alegre.* ❑ *Merry Christmas, everyone.* *—¡Feliz Navidad a todos!* • **mer|ri|ly** ADV *alegremente* ❑ *Chris laughed merrily.* *Chris rió alegremente.*

**me|sa** /meɪsə/ (**mesas**) N-COUNT A **mesa** is a large hill with a flat top and steep sides, especially in the southwestern United States. *meseta, mesa*

**meso|sphere** /mɛzəsfɪər/ **1** N-SING **The mesosphere** is the layer of the Earth's atmosphere that is directly above the stratosphere. *mesosfera* [TECHNICAL] **2** N-SING **The mesosphere** is the part of the Earth's interior that lies between the upper mantle and the outer core. *mesosfera* [TECHNICAL]

**Meso|zo|ic era** /mɛzəzoʊɪk ɪərə/ N-SING **The Mesozoic era** is a period in the history of the Earth that began around 250 million years ago and ended around 65 million years ago. *mesozoico* [TECHNICAL]

**mess** /mɛs/ (**messes, messing, messed**) **1** N-SING If something is **a mess** or **in a mess,** it is not neat. *desorden, revoltijo* ❑ *The house is a mess.* *La casa es un desorden.* **2** N-VAR If you say that a situation is **a mess,** you mean that it is full of trouble or problems. You can also say that something is **in a mess.** *desastre, caos* ❑ *I've made such a mess of my life.* *He hecho un verdadero desastre de mi vida.* ❑ *...the reasons why the economy is in such a mess.* *...las razones de que la economía se encuentre en ese caos.*

▸ **mess around** **1** PHR-VERB If you **mess around,** you spend time doing things without any particular purpose or without achieving anything. *entretenerse* ❑ *We were just messing around playing with paint.* *Sólo estábamos entreteniéndonos, jugando con pintura.* **2** PHR-VERB If you say that someone **is messing around with** something, you mean that they are interfering with it in a harmful way. *meterse con* ❑ *You don't want to go messing around with bears.* *—Que no se te ocurra meterte con los osos.*

▸ **mess up** **1** PHR-VERB If you **mess** something **up** or if you **mess up,** you cause something to fail or be spoiled. *echar a perder, arruinar* [INFORMAL] ❑ *When politicians mess things up, it is the people who suffer.* *Cuando los políticos echan a perder las cosas, el que sufre es el pueblo.* ❑ *He has messed up one career.* *Ya echó a perder una carrera.* **2** PHR-VERB If you **mess up** a place or a thing, you make it dirty or not neat. *desarreglar, desordenar* [INFORMAL] ❑ *I hope they haven't messed up your video tapes.* *Espero que no hayan desordenado tus cintas de video.*

**Word Partnership** Usar *mess* con:

| | |
|---|---|
| v. | **clean up a** mess, **leave a** mess, **make a** mess **1** **2**<br>**get into a** mess **2** |

**mes|sage** /mɛsɪdʒ/ (**messages, messaging, messaged**) **1** N-COUNT A **message** is a piece of information or a request that you send to someone or leave for them when you cannot speak to them directly. *mensaje, recado* ❑ *I got a message you were trying to find me.* *Recibí el recado de que estaba buscándome.* **2** N-COUNT The **message** that someone is trying to communicate is the idea or point that they are trying to communicate. *mensaje* ❑ *The report's message was clear.* *El mensaje del informe era claro.* ❑ *We've been getting the message from you that we're useless.* *Nos has estado dando a entender que somos unos inútiles.* **3** V-T/V-I If you **message** someone, you send them a message electronically using a computer or another device such as a cellphone. *enviar mensajes electrónicos* ❑ *People who message a lot feel unpopular if they don't get many back.* *Las personas que envían muchos mensajes electrónicos creen que le caen mal a la gente si a su vez no reciben muchos.*

m

## Word Web **metal**

copper

aluminum

gold

In their natural state, most **metals** are not pure. They are usually combined with other materials in mixtures known as **ores**. Almost all metals are **shiny**. Many metals share these special properties. They are ductile, meaning that they can be made into **wire**. They are malleable and can be formed into thin, flat sheets. And they are also good **conductors** of heat and electricity. Except for **copper** and **gold**, metals are generally gray or silver in color.

## Word Partnership Usar *message* con:

V. **give** ***someone*** **a** message, **leave a** message, **read a** message, **take a** message 1
**deliver a** message, **get a** message, **hear a** message, **send a** message 1 2
**get a** message **across**, **spread a** message 2

ADJ. **clear** message, **important** message, **urgent** message 1 2
**powerful** message, **simple** message, **strong** message, **wrong** message 2

**mes|sage board** (**message boards**) N-COUNT A **message board** is a **bulletin board**, especially on the Internet. *tablero de anuncios*

**mes|sen|ger** /mɛsɪndʒər/ (**messengers**) N-COUNT A **messenger** takes a message or package to someone, or takes them regularly as their job. *mensajero* ❑ *There will be a messenger at the airport to collect the photographs. Habrá un mensajero en el aeropuerto para recoger las fotografías.*

M

**Messiah** /mɪsaɪə/ N-PROPER For Jews, **the Messiah** is a king or leader who will be sent to them by God. For Christians, **the Messiah** is Jesus Christ. *Mesías*

**messy** /mɛsi/ (**messier, messiest**) 1 ADJ A **messy** person or activity makes things dirty or not neat. *desordenado, sucio* ❑ *She was a messy cook. Era una cocinera desordenada.* 2 ADJ Something that is **messy** is dirty or not neat. *sucio y descuidado* ❑ *His writing is very messy. Su escritura es muy sucia y descuidada.* 3 ADJ If you describe a situation as **messy,** you are emphasizing that it is confused or complicated, and therefore unsatisfactory. *desagradable* ❑ *John's divorce was very messy. El divorcio de John fue muy desagradable.*

**met** /mɛt/ **Met** is the past tense and past participle of **meet**. *pasado y participio pasado de* ***meet***

## Word Link ***meta*** *≈ beyond, change* : ***meta****bolism,* ***meta****morphic,* ***meta****phor*

**me|tabo|lism** /mɪtæbəlɪzəm/ (**metabolisms**) N-VAR Your **metabolism** is the way that chemical processes in your body cause food to be used in an efficient way, for example to make new cells and to give you energy. *metabolismo* ❑ *If you don't eat breakfast, your metabolism slows down. Si no desayunas, tu metabolismo se hace lento.*

**met|al** /mɛtəl/ (**metals**) N-VAR **Metal** is a hard substance such as iron, steel, gold, or lead. *metal* ❑ *...a table with metal legs. ...una mesa con patas de metal.*
→ see Word Web: **metal**
→ see **mineral**

**me|tal|lic bond** (**metallic bonds**) N-COUNT A **metallic bond** is the kind of chemical bond that occurs in metals. *enlace metálico* [TECHNICAL]

**met|al|loid** /mɛtəlɔɪd/ (**metalloids**) N-COUNT **Metalloids** are chemical elements that have some of the properties of metals and some of the properties of nonmetals. *metaloide* [TECHNICAL]
● **metalloid** is also an adjective *metaloide* ❑ *...metalloid elements. ...metaloides.*

**meta|mor|phic** /mɛtəmɔrfɪk/ ADJ **Metamorphic** rock is rock that is formed from other rock as a result of heat or pressure beneath the surface of the Earth. Compare **igneous**, **sedimentary**. *metamórfico*
→ see **rock**

**meta|mor|pho|sis** /mɛtəmɔrfəsɪs/ (**metamorphoses**) N-VAR When a **metamorphosis** occurs, a person or thing develops and changes into something completely different. *metamorfosis, conversión* [FORMAL] ❑ *...his metamorphosis from a Republican to a Democrat. ...su conversión de republicano a demócrata.* ❑ *It undergoes its metamorphosis from a caterpillar to a butterfly. Pasa por su metamorfosis de oruga a mariposa.*
→ see **amphibian**

**meta|phase** /mɛtəfeɪz/ (**metaphases**) N-VAR **Metaphase** is a stage in the process of cell division in which the chromosomes line up before they separate. *metafase* [TECHNICAL]

**meta|phor** /mɛtəfɔr/ (**metaphors**) N-VAR A **metaphor** is an imaginative way of describing something by referring to something else which is the same in a particular way. *metáfora* ❑ *She uses a lot of religious metaphors in her writing. Emplea muchas metáforas religiosas en su narrativa.*

**me|tas|ta|size** /mətæstəsaɪz/ (**metastasizes, metastasizing, metastasized**) V-I If cancer cells **metastasize**, they spread to another part of the body. *extenderse/diseminarse por metástasis* [MEDICAL] ❑ *A small tumor on his left lung has started to metastasize. Tiene un pequeño tumor en el pulmón izquierdo que ha empezado a diseminarse.*

**me|teor|oid** /mitiərɔɪd/ (**meteoroids**) N-COUNT A **meteoroid** is a piece of rock or dust that travels around the sun. *meteoroide* [TECHNICAL]

**me|teor|ol|ogy** /mitiərɒlədʒi/ N-UNCOUNT **Meteorology** is the study of the processes in the

Earth's atmosphere that cause particular weather conditions, especially in order to predict the weather. *meteorología*
→ see **forecast**

**Word Link** *meter ≈ measuring : kilometer, meter, perimeter*

**me|ter** /mitər/ (**meters**) **1** N-COUNT A **meter** is a device that measures and records something such as the amount of gas or electricity that you have used. *medidor* ❑ *He was there to read the electricity meter. Se presentó para leer el medidor de electricidad.* **2** N-COUNT A **meter** is a metric unit of length equal to 100 centimeters. *metro* ❑ *She's running the 1,500 meters race. Está corriendo los 1,500 metros.* **3** N-VAR In music, **meter** is the rhythmic arrangement of beats according to particular patterns. *compás* [TECHNICAL] **4** PHRASE **Meters per second** is a unit of speed in physics. An object that is moving at a particular number of **meters per second** travels that number of meters in one second. The abbreviation *m/s* is also used. *metros por segundo*
→ see **measurement**

**metha|done** /mɛθədoʊn/ N-UNCOUNT **Methadone** is a drug that is sometimes prescribed to heroin addicts as a substitute for heroin. *metadona*

**metha|no|gen** /məθænədʒən/ (**methanogens**) N-COUNT **Methanogens** are bacteria that produce methane. *bacterias productoras de metano* [TECHNICAL]

**metha|nol** /mɛθənɔl/ N-UNCOUNT **Methanol** is a colorless, poisonous liquid, used as a solvent and fuel. *metanol* ❑ *Methanol is a cleaner fuel than oil. El metanol es un combustible menos contaminante/más limpio que el petróleo.*

**meth|od** /mɛθəd/ (**methods**) N-COUNT A **method** is a particular way of doing something. *método* ❑ *...new teaching methods. ...nuevos métodos de enseñanza.*

**Thesaurus** *method* Ver también:

N. manner, procedure, process, system, technique

**Word Partnership** Usar *method* con:

ADJ. **alternative/traditional** method, **best** method, **effective** method, **new** method, **preferred** method, **scientific** method
V. **develop a** method, **use a** method
N. method **of payment**, **teaching** method

**me|thodi|cal** /məθɒdɪkᵊl/ ADJ If you describe someone as **methodical**, you mean that they do things carefully, thoroughly, and in order. *metódico* ❑ *Da Vinci was methodical in his research. Da Vinci era metódico en sus investigaciones.* • **me|thodi|cal|ly** /məθɒdɪkli/ ADV *metódicamente* ❑ *She methodically put her things into her suitcase. Acomodó metódicamente sus cosas en la maleta.*

**met|ric** /mɛtrɪk/ ADJ **Metric** means relating to the metric system. *métrico* ❑ *...80,000 metric tons of food. ...80,000 toneladas de alimento.*

**met|ric sys|tem** N-SING **The metric system** is the system of measurement that uses meters, grams, and liters. *sistema métrico decimal*

**met|ric ton** (**metric tons**) N-COUNT A **metric ton** is 1,000 kilograms. *tonelada (métrica)* ❑ *The Wall Street Journal uses 220,000 metric tons of paper each year. El Wall Street Journal usa 220,000 toneladas de papel al año.*

**met|ro** /mɛtroʊ/ (**metros**) also **Metro** N-COUNT **The metro** is the subway system in some cities, for example in Washington or Paris. *metro, metropolitano, tren subterráneo* ❑ *A new metro runs under the square. Bajo la plaza corre una nueva línea del tren subterráneo.*

**Word Link** *poli ≈ city : metropolitan, politics, police*

**met|ro|poli|tan** /mɛtrəpɒlɪtᵊn/ ADJ **Metropolitan** means belonging to or typical of a large, busy city. *metropolitano* ❑ *...the metropolitan district of Miami. ...el distrito metropolitano de Miami.* ❑ *...major metropolitan hospitals. ...grandes hospitales metropolitanos.*

**mez|za|nine** /mɛzənin/ (**mezzanines**) **1** N-COUNT A **mezzanine** is a small floor which is built between two main floors of a building. *mezzanine* ❑ *...the mezzanine floor. ...el mezzanine.* **2** N-COUNT The **mezzanine** is the lowest balcony in a theater, or the front rows in the lowest balcony. *platea, primer balcón*

**mg** **mg** is a written abbreviation for **milligram** or **milligrams**. *miligramo (mg)* ❑ *...300 mg of calcium. ...300 mg de calcio.*

**MIA** /ɛm aɪ eɪ/ (**MIAs**) ADJ **MIA** is used to describe members of the armed forces who do not return from a military operation but who are not known to have been killed or captured. **MIA** is an abbreviation for "missing in action." *desaparecido en acción* ❑ *Hundreds of soldiers were MIA. Cientos de soldados desaparecieron en acción.* • An **MIA** is a member of the armed forces who is missing in action. *desaparecido en acción* ❑ *...the families of MIAs. ...las familias de los desaparecidos en acción.*

**mice** /maɪs/ **Mice** is the plural of **mouse**. *plural de* ***mouse***

**Word Link** *micro ≈ small : microchip, microeconomics, microscope*

**micro|chip** /maɪkroʊtʃɪp/ (**microchips**) N-COUNT A **microchip** is a very small piece of silicon inside a computer that has electronic circuits on it. *microcircuito*

**micro|cli|mate** /maɪkroʊklaɪmɪt/ (**microclimates**) also **micro-climate** N-COUNT A **microclimate** is the climate that exists in a particular small area, which may be different from the climate of the surrounding area. *microclima*

**micro|eco|nom|ics** /maɪkroʊɛkənɒmɪks, -ik-/ also **micro-economics** N-UNCOUNT **Microeconomics** is the branch of economics that is concerned with individual areas of economic activity, such as those within a particular company or relating to a particular market. *microeconomía* ❑ *...a theory based on microeconomics. ...una teoría basada en la microeconomía.* • **micro|eco|nom|ic** /maɪkroʊɛkənɒmɪk, -ik-/

m

ADJ *microeconómico* ❑ *...microeconomic theory. ...teoría microeconómica.*

**micro|fiber** /maɪkroʊfaɪbər/ (**microfibers**) N-VAR **Microfibers** are extremely light artificial fibers that are used to make cloth. *microfibra* ❑ *...microfiber fabric. ...tela de microfibras.*

**micro|organism** /maɪkroʊɔrgənɪzəm/ (**microorganisms**) N-COUNT A **microorganism** is a very small living thing which you can only see if you use a microscope. *microorganismo*
→ see **fungus**

| Word Link | *phon ≈ sound : microphone, symphony, telephone* |
|---|---|

**micro|phone** /maɪkrəfoʊn/ (**microphones**) N-COUNT A **microphone** is a device that is used to make sounds louder or to record them on a tape recorder. *micrófono*
→ see **concert**

| Word Link | *micro ≈ small : microchip, microeconomics, microscope* |
|---|---|

| Word Link | *scope ≈ looking : gyroscope, microscope, telescope* |
|---|---|

**micro|scope** /maɪkrəskoʊp/ (**microscopes**) N-COUNT A **microscope** is a scientific instrument which makes very small objects look bigger so that more detail can be seen. *microscopio*
→ see **laboratory**

M

**micro|scop|ic** /maɪkrəskɒpɪk/ ADJ **Microscopic** objects are extremely small, and usually can be seen only through a microscope. *microscópico* ❑ *...microscopic cells. ...células microscópicas.*

**micro|wave** /maɪkroʊweɪv/ (**microwaves, microwaving, microwaved**) **1** N-COUNT A **microwave** or a **microwave oven** is an oven which cooks food very quickly by electromagnetic radiation rather than by heat. *horno de microondas* **2** V-T To **microwave** food or drink means to cook or heat it in a microwave oven. *calentar/cocinar en horno de microondas* ❑ *Microwave the vegetables first. Caliente primero las verduras en el horno de microondas.*
→ see **cook, wave**

**mid-Atlantic** ADJ A **mid-Atlantic** accent is a mixture of British and American accents. *mezcla de acento británico y estadounidense* ❑ *He had a mid-Atlantic accent. Tenía un acento que era una mezcla del británico y el estadounidense.*

**mid|dle** /mɪdᵊl/ (**middles**) **1** N-COUNT **The middle of** something is the part of it that is farthest from its edges, ends, or outside surface. *centro, medio, en medio/enmedio* ❑ *Howard stood in the middle of the room. Howard estaba de pie en medio/enmedio de la habitación.* ❑ *They had a tennis court in the middle of the garden. Tenían una cancha de tenis enmedio del jardín.* **2** **the middle of nowhere** → see **nowhere** **3** ADJ The **middle** object in a row of objects is the one that has an equal number of objects on each side. *medio, de enmedio* ❑ *...the middle button of his uniform jacket. ...el botón de enmedio del saco de su uniforme.* **4** N-SING **The middle of** an event or period of time is the part that comes after the first part and before the last part. *en medio de* ❑ *I woke up in the middle of the night and could hear a noise outside. Desperté en medio de la noche y oí un ruido afuera.* ● **Middle** is also an adjective. *medio, de enmedio* ❑ *He was now in his middle years, and looked even better than before. Ya estaba en la madurez y se veía aun mejor que antes.* **5** PHRASE If you are **in the middle of** doing something, you are busy doing it. *en medio de* ❑ *I'm in the middle of cooking for nine people. Estoy atareado cocinando para nueve personas.*
→ see **hand**

**mid|dle age** N-UNCOUNT **Middle age** is the period in your life when you are between the ages of about 40 and 60. *madurez, mediana edad* ❑ *Men often gain weight in middle age. Los hombres suelen subir de peso en la madurez., Los hombres de mediana edad suelen subir de peso.*

**middle-aged** ADJ A **middle-aged** person is between the ages of about 40 and 60. *de mediana edad, maduro* ❑ *...middle-aged, married businessmen. ...hombres de negocios casados de mediana edad.*
→ see **age**

**mid|dle class** (**middle classes**) N-COUNT **The middle class** or **middle classes** are the people in a society who are not lower class or upper class, for example business people, managers, doctors, lawyers, and teachers. *clase media* ❑ *The middle class is leaving the cities. La clase media está abandonando las ciudades.* ● **Middle class** is also an adjective. *de clase media* ❑ *...middle-class families. ...familias de clase media.*

**Mid|dle East** N-PROPER **The Middle East** is the area around the eastern Mediterranean that includes Iran and all the countries in Asia to the west and southwest of Iran. *Medio Oriente, Oriente Medio* ❑ *...the two great rivers of the Middle East. ...los dos grandes ríos del Medio Oriente.*

**middle|man** /mɪdᵊlmæn/ (**middlemen**) **1** N-COUNT A **middleman** is a person or company which buys things from the people who produce them and sells them to the people who want to buy them. *intermediario* [BUSINESS] ❑ *Brian bought his sofas from a middleman who wouldn't tell him where they came from. Brian compró sus sofás a un intermediario que no quiso decirle de dónde provenían.* **2** N-COUNT A **middleman** is a person who helps in negotiations between people who are unwilling to meet each other directly. *intermediario* ❑ *The two sides would only meet indirectly, through middlemen. Las partes no aceptaban reunirse directamente; sólo trataban a través de intermediarios.*

**mid|field** /mɪdfild/ N-UNCOUNT In football and soccer, the **midfield** is the central area of the playing field between the two goals, or the players whose usual position is in this area. *centro del campo, centro/centrocampista, medio/mediocampista* ❑ *In the last two years, I played a lot of games in midfield. En los últimos dos años, jugué muchos partidos como medio.* ❑ *...the best midfield player in the world. ...el mejor mediocampista del mundo.*

**mid|field|er** /mɪdfildər/ (**midfielders**) N-COUNT In soccer, a **midfielder** is a player whose usual position is in the midfield. *centro, medio* ❑ *The young French midfielder scored a goal. El joven centro/medio francés anotó un gol.*

| Word Link | *mid ≈ middle : midnight, midst, midterm* |
|---|---|

**mid|night** /mɪdnaɪt/ N-UNCOUNT **Midnight** is twelve o'clock in the middle of the night. *medianoche* ❑ *It was well after midnight. Ya era bastante más de (la) medianoche.*
→ see **time**

**mid-ocean ridge** (**mid-ocean ridges**) also **mid-oceanic ridge** N-COUNT A **mid-ocean ridge** is a range of mountains beneath the ocean. *cordillera oceánica central*

**mid|ship|man** /mɪdʃɪpmən/ (**midshipmen**) N-COUNT; N-TITLE A **midshipman** is a cadet who is training to become a junior officer in the navy. *guardia marina/guardiamarina* ❑ *He became a midshipman at age sixteen. Se enroló como guardiamarina a los dieciséis años.* ❑ *...midshipman Edward Brooke of the U.S. Navy. ...el guardiamarina Edward Brooke de la Armada (Marina de Guerra) estadounidense.*

| Word Link | *mid ≈ middle : midnight, midst, midterm* |
|---|---|

**midst** /mɪdst/ **1** PHRASE If you are **in the midst of** doing something, you are doing it at the moment. *en medio de* ❑ *We are in the midst of one of the worst wars for many, many years. Estamos en medio de una de las peores guerras en muchos, muchos años.* **2** PHRASE If something happens **in the midst of** an event, it happens during it. *en medio de* ❑ *Eleanor arrived in the midst of a storm. Eleanor llegó en medio de una tormenta.* **3** PHRASE If someone or something is **in the midst of** a group of people or things, they are among them or surrounded by them. *en medio de, entre* ❑ *I was surprised to see him in the midst of a large crowd. Me sorprendió verlo en medio de una gran multitud.*

**mid|term** /mɪdtɜrm/ (**midterms**) **1** ADJ A **midterm** election is an election that takes place approximately halfway through a president's or a government's term of office. *mitad de un período* ❑ *...midterm congressional elections in November. ...las elecciones de la mitad del período en noviembre.* **2** N-COUNT A **midterm** or a **midterm exam** is a test which a student takes in the middle of a school or college term. *mitad de un período* ❑ *She walked into a midterm exam for a subject she knew very little about. Entró a un examen de mitad de período de una materia que conocía muy poco.*

**mid|town** /mɪdtaʊn/ ADJ **Midtown** places are in the center of a city. *del centro* ❑ *...a midtown Manhattan hotel. ...un hotel del centro de Manhattan.* • **Midtown** is also a noun. *centro* ❑ *He drove around midtown. Se paseó en el coche por el centro.*

**mid|wife** /mɪdwaɪf/ (**midwives**) N-COUNT A **midwife** is a nurse who is trained to deliver babies and to advise pregnant women. *comadrona, partera* ❑ *The midwife placed the baby in his mother's arms. La partera puso al recién nacido en los brazos de su madre.*

**might**
❶ MODAL USES
❷ NOUN USES

**❶ might** /maɪt/

**Might** is a modal verb. It is used with the base form of a verb.

**1** MODAL You use **might** to indicate that something will possibly happen or be true in the future. *subjuntivo y potencial de **may*** ❑ *The baby might be born early. El niño podría nacer antes/ser prematuro.* ❑ *I might regret it later. Podría arrepentirme después.* **2** MODAL You use **might** to indicate that there is a possibility that something is true. *subjuntivo y potencial de **may*** ❑ *They still hope that he might be alive. Todavía tienen esperanzas de que pudiera/pueda estar vivo.* ❑ *You might be right. Podrías tener razón.* **3** MODAL You use **might** to make a suggestion or to give advice in a very polite way. *subjuntivo y potencial de **may*** ❑ *Next time you see them you might thank them for their help. La próxima vez que los veas podrías agradecerles su ayuda.* **4** MODAL You use **might** as a polite way of interrupting someone, asking a question, making a request, or introducing what you are going to say next. *subjuntivo y potencial de **may*** [FORMAL, SPOKEN] ❑ *Might I make a suggestion? ¿Podría hacer una sugerencia?* ❑ *Might I ask what you're doing here? ¿Podría preguntarle qué está haciendo aquí?*

**❷ might** /maɪt/ N-UNCOUNT **Might** is power or strength. *poder, poderío* [FORMAL] ❑ *They were powerless against the might of the army. Eran impotentes contra el poderío del ejército.*

**mightn't** /maɪtᵊnt/ **Mightn't** is a spoken form of "might not." *forma hablada de **might not***

**might've** /maɪtəv/ **Might've** is the usual spoken form of "might have," especially when "have" is an auxiliary verb. *forma hablada usual de **might have***

**mighty** /maɪti/ (**mightier, mightiest**) **1** ADJ **Mighty** is used to describe something that is very large or powerful. *poderoso, fortísimo* [LITERARY] ❑ *There was a flash and a mighty bang. Hubo un destello y un estrépito fortísimo.* **2** ADV **Mighty** is used in front of adjectives and adverbs to emphasize the quality that they are describing. *muy, sumamente* [INFORMAL] ❑ *I'm mighty proud of my son. Estoy orgullosísimo/sumamente orgulloso de mi hijo*

**mi|graine** /maɪgreɪn/ (**migraines**) N-VAR A **migraine** is an extremely painful headache that makes you feel very ill. *jaqueca, migraña* ❑ *Her mother suffered from migraines. Su madre sufría de jaquecas/migrañas.*

| Word Link | *migr ≈ moving, changing : emigrate, immigrant, migrant* |
|---|---|

**mi|grant** /maɪgrənt/ (**migrants**) N-COUNT A **migrant** is a person who moves from one place to another, especially in order to find work. *trabajador extranjero o trabajadora extranjera* ❑ *Most of his workers were migrants from the South. La mayoría de sus trabajadores venían de países del Sur.*

**mi|grate** /maɪgreɪt/ (**migrates, migrating, migrated**) **1** V-I If people **migrate,** they move from one place to another, especially in order to find work. *emigrar* ❑ *People migrate to cities like Jakarta searching for work. La gente emigra a ciudades como Yakarta en busca de trabajo.* • **mi|gra|tion** /maɪgreɪʃᵊn/ N-VAR (**migrations**) *emigración* ❑ *...the migration of Jews to Israel. ...la emigración de judíos a Israel.* **2** V-I When birds, fish, or animals **migrate,** they move at a particular season from one part of the world or from one part of a country

m

to another, usually in order to breed or to find food. *migrar/emigrar* ❑ *Most birds have to fly long distances to migrate.* *La mayoría de las aves recorren grandes distancias cuando emigran.* • **mi|gra|tion** N-VAR *migración* ❑ *...the migration of animals in the Serengeti.* *...la migración de animales en el Serengeti.*

**mild** /maɪld/ (**milder, mildest**) **1** ADJ **Mild** is used to describe something that is not very strong or severe. *ligero, suave* ❑ *Teddy turned to Mona with a look of mild confusion.* *Teddy se volvió hacia Mona con una mirada de ligera confusión.* ❑ *This cheese has a soft, mild flavor.* *Este queso tiene un sabor suave.* • **mild|ly** ADV *ligeramente* ❑ *She had the disease very mildly because she felt fine.* *La enfermedad la atacó muy ligeramente, porque se sentía bien.* **2** ADJ **Mild** weather is pleasant because it is neither extremely hot nor extremely cold. *benigno* ❑ *The area has very mild winters.* *Los inviernos son muy benignos en la región.*

**mile** /maɪl/ (**miles**) **1** N-COUNT A **mile** is a unit of distance equal to 1760 yards or approximately 1.6 kilometers. *milla terrestre inglesa = 1.609 kilómetros* ❑ *They drove 600 miles across the desert.* *Condujeron 600 millas (965.6 kilómetros) a través del desierto.* ❑ *She lives just half a mile away.* *Vive a sólo milla y media (dos kilómetros y medio).* **2** N-PLURAL **Miles** is used, especially in the expression **miles away,** to refer to a long distance. *lejísimos* ❑ *The gym is miles away from her home.* *El gimnasio está lejísimos de su casa.*
→ see **measurement**

**Word Partnership** Usar *mile* con:

ADJ. mile **high**, mile **long**, **nautical** mile, **square** mile, mile **wide** **1**

M

**mile|age** /maɪlɪdʒ/ (**mileages**) **1** N-VAR **Mileage** refers to the distance that you have traveled, measured in miles. *kilometraje* ❑ *Most of their mileage is in and around town.* *La mayor parte de sus recorridos los hacen en la ciudad o en los alrededores.* **2** N-UNCOUNT The **mileage** in a particular course of action is its usefulness in getting you what you want. *provecho* ❑ *It's important to get as much mileage out of the meeting as possible.* *Es importante que la reunión sea lo más provechosa posible.*

**Word Link** *milit ≈ soldier : militant, military, militia*

**mili|tant** /mɪlɪtənt/ (**militants**) ADJ You use **militant** to describe people who believe in something very strongly and are active in trying to bring about political or social change, often in extreme ways that other people find unacceptable. *militante, combativo* ❑ *Militant workers voted to go on strike.* *Los obreros combativos votaron por declarar la huelga.* • **Militant** is also a noun. *militante* ❑ *...terrorist acts committed by militants.* *...actos terroristas cometidos por militantes.* • **mili|tan|cy** N-UNCOUNT *militancia* ❑ *...the rise of militancy in the labor unions.* *...el aumento de la militancia de los sindicatos.*

**mili|tary** /mɪlɪteri/ (**militaries**) **1** ADJ **Military** means relating to the armed forces of a country. *militar* ❑ *Military action may become necessary.* *Podría ser necesaria la acción militar.* ❑ *...a meeting of military leaders.* *...una reunión de dirigentes militares.* • **mili|tari|ly** /mɪltɛərɪli/ ADV *militarmente* ❑ *...militarily useful weapons.* *...armas útiles militarmente.* **2** N-SING **The military** are the armed forces of a country, especially officers of high rank. **Military** can take the singular or plural form of the verb. *militar, ejército* ❑ *The military have said little about the attacks.* *Los militares no se han manifestado mucho respecto a los ataques.*
→ see **army**

**mi|li|tia** /mɪlɪʃə/ (**militias**) N-COUNT A **militia** is an organization that operates like an army but whose members are not professional soldiers. *milicia* ❑ *Young men formed their own militias.* *Los jóvenes formaron sus propias milicias.*
→ see **army**

**milk** /mɪlk/ (**milks, milking, milked**) **1** N-UNCOUNT **Milk** is the white liquid produced by cows, goats, and some other animals, which people drink and use to make butter, cheese, and yogurt. *leche* ❑ *He went out to buy a quart of milk.* *Salió a comprar un litro de leche.* **2** V-T If someone **milks** a cow or goat, they get milk from it, using either their hands or a machine. *ordeñar* ❑ *Farm workers milked cows by hand.* *Los granjeros ordeñaban las vacas a mano.* • **milk|ing** N-UNCOUNT *ordeña* ❑ *...helping to bring the cows in for milking.* *...ayuda a llevar las vacas a la ordeña.* **3** N-UNCOUNT **Milk** is the white liquid produced by women to feed their babies. *leche* ❑ *Milk from the mother's breast is a perfect food for the human baby.* *La leche materna es el alimento perfecto para el niño.* **4** V-T If you say that someone **milks** something, you are critical of them for getting as much benefit or profit as they can from it, without caring about the effects this has on other people. *ordeñar, aprovecharse de* ❑ *A few people tried to milk the insurance companies.* *Unas cuantas personas trataron de aprovecharse de las aseguradoras.*
→ see **dairy**

**Milky Way** N-PROPER **The Milky Way** is the pale strip of light consisting of many stars that you can see stretched across the sky at night. *Vía Láctea*
→ see **galaxy**

**mill** /mɪl/ (**mills, milling, milled**) **1** N-COUNT A **mill** is a building in which grain is crushed to make flour. *molino* ❑ *The old mill is now a restaurant.* *El antiguo molino es un restaurante ahora.* **2** N-COUNT A **mill** is a small device used for grinding something such as coffee or pepper. *molino* ❑ *...a pepper mill.* *...un molino de pimienta.* **3** N-COUNT A **mill** is a factory used for making and processing materials such as steel, wool, or cotton. *acería/fundición (acero), aserradero (madera), fábrica (algodón)* ❑ *...a steel mill.* *...una acería.*
▸ **mill around** PHR-VERB When a crowd of people **mill around,** they move around in a disorganized way. *dar vueltas, arremolinarse* ❑ *Quite a few people were milling around.* *Unas cuantas personas estaban dando vueltas.*

**Word Link** *mill ≈ thousand : milligram, million, millionaire*

**mil|li|gram** /mɪlɪgræm/ (**milligrams**) N-COUNT A **milligram** is a metric unit of weight that is equal to a thousandth of a gram. *miligramo* ❑ *...0.5 milligrams of sodium.* *...0.5 miligramos de sodio.*

**mil|li|meter** /mɪlɪmitər/ (**millimeters**) N-COUNT A **millimeter** is a metric unit of length that is equal to a tenth of a centimeter or a thousandth of a meter. *millímetro* ❑ *The creature is tiny, just 10 millimeters long. El animalito es diminuto, de apenas 10 milímetros de largo.*

**Word Link** *mill ≈ thousand : milligram, million, millionaire*

**mil|lion** /mɪlyən/ (**millions**)

The plural form is **million** after a number, or after a word or expression referring to a number, such as "several" or "a few."

**1** NUM A **million** or one **million** is the number 1,000,000. *millón* ❑ *Five million people visit the county each year. Cinco millones de personas visitan el condado cada año.* **2** QUANT If you talk about **millions of** people or things, you mean that there is a very large number of them. *millón* ❑ *The program was watched on television in millions of homes. El programa fue visto por la televisión en millones de hogares.*

**mil|lion|aire** /mɪlyənɛər/ (**millionaires**) N-COUNT A **millionaire** is a person who has money or property worth at least a million dollars. *millonario o millonaria* ❑ *By the time he died, he was a millionaire. Cuando murió, era millonario.*

**mil|lionth** /mɪlyənθ/ (**millionths**) ORD The **millionth** item in a series is the one you count as number one million. *millonésimo* ❑ *It seemed like the millionth time she asked the question. Parecía que hacía la pregunta por millonésima vez.*

**mince** /mɪns/ (**minces, mincing, minced**) V-T If you **mince** food such as meat or vegetables, you cut or chop it up into very small pieces. *picar* ❑ *Mince the onions and mix in well. Pique las cebollas y mézclelas bien (con los demás ingredientes).*
→ see **cut**

**mind**
❶ NOUN USES
❷ VERB USES

❶ **mind** /maɪnd/ (**minds**) **1** N-COUNT You refer to someone's **mind** when talking about their thoughts. *mente, cabeza, cerebro* ❑ *I'm trying to clear my mind of bad thoughts. Estoy tratando de alejar los malos pensamientos de mi mente.* ❑ *There was no doubt in his mind that the man was serious. No tenía duda alguna de que el hombre hablaba en serio.* **2** N-COUNT Your **mind** is your ability to think and reason. *mente* ❑ *You have a good mind. Tienes buena cabeza.* ❑ *Studying improved my mind and got me thinking about things. El estudio mejoró mi inteligencia y me hizo pensar más.* **3** N-COUNT If you have a particular type of **mind,** you have a particular way of thinking which is part of your character, or a result of your education or professional training. *mente* ❑ *Andrew, you have a very suspicious mind. Andrew, eres muy suspicaz.* ❑ *You need a logical mind to solve this problem. Es necesario tener lógica para resolver este problema.* **4** → see also **state of mind** **5** PHRASE If you tell someone to **bear** something **in mind** or to **keep** something **in mind,** you are reminding or warning them about something important which they should remember. *tener en mente, tener presente, tener en cuenta* ❑ *Bear in mind that there aren't many gas stations out of town. Ten en cuenta que no hay muchas gasolinerías fuera de la ciudad.* **6** PHRASE If you **change** your **mind,** or if someone or something **changes** your **mind,** you change a decision you have made or an opinion that you had. *cambiar de opinión* ❑ *I was going to vote for him, but I changed my mind. Iba a votar por él, pero cambié de opinión.* **7** PHRASE If you say that an idea or possibility never **crossed** your **mind,** you mean that you did not think of it. *ocurrirse, pasar(se) por la cabeza* ❑ *It didn't cross his mind that there might be a problem. No se le ocurrió que podría haber un problema.* **8** PHRASE If you see something **in** your **mind's eye,** you imagine it and have a clear picture of it in your mind. *como estarlo viendo* ❑ *In his mind's eye, he can imagine the effect he's having. Puede imaginar el efecto que hace como si lo estuviera viendo.* **9** PHRASE If you **make up** your **mind** or **make** your **mind up,** you decide which of a number of possible things you will have or do. *decidirse* ❑ *He made up his mind to call Kathy. Se decidió a llamar a Kathy.* **10** PHRASE If something is **on** your **mind,** you are worried or concerned about it and think about it a lot. *tener en la cabeza, pensar en* ❑ *The game was on my mind all week. Estuve pensando en el juego toda la semana.* **11** PHRASE If your **mind is on** something or you **have** your **mind on** something, you are thinking about that thing. *tener la mente puesta en, concentrarse* ❑ *At school my mind was never on my work. En la escuela, nunca me concentraba en el estudio.* **12** PHRASE If you have **an open mind,** you avoid forming an opinion or making a decision until you know all the facts. *tener una actitud abierta* ❑ *Try to keep an open mind until you have all the facts. Trata de mantener una actitud abierta hasta contar con todos los hechos.* **13** PHRASE If you say that someone is **out of their mind,** you mean that they are crazy or very foolish. *estar loco* [INFORMAL] ❑ *What are you doing? Are you out of your mind? —¿Qué estás haciendo? ¿Estás loco?* **14** PHRASE If something **takes** your **mind off** a problem or unpleasant situation, it helps you to forget about it for a while. *distraer* ❑ *I thought a game of tennis might take his mind off his problems. Pensé que un juego de tenis podría distraerlo de sus problemas.* **15** PHRASE You say or write **to my mind** to indicate that the statement you are making is your own opinion. *en opinión de* ❑ *To my mind, this play is too violent. En mi opinión, esta obra es demasiado violenta.*

❷ **mind** /maɪnd/ (**minds, minding, minded**) **1** V-T/V-I If you do not **mind** something, you are not annoyed or bothered by it. *importar* ❑ *I don't mind the noise during the day. No me importa el ruido durante el día.* ❑ *I hope you don't mind me calling you so late. Espero que no le importe que llame tan tarde.* ❑ *I opened a window and nobody seemed to mind. Abrí una ventana y a nadie pareció importarle.* **2** V-T If someone does not **mind** what happens or what something is like, they do not have a strong preference for any particular thing. *importar* ❑ *I don't mind what we play, really. No me importa a qué juguemos, de veras.* **3** V-T If you **mind** something such as a store or luggage, you take care of it, usually while the person who owns it or is usually responsible for it is somewhere else. *cuidar, atender* ❑ *Jim Coulters will mind the store while I'm away. Jim Coulters cuidará la tienda mientras yo no estoy.* **4** PHRASE You use **never mind** to tell someone that they do not have to do something or worry about something, because it is not important or because you will do it yourself. *importar, olvidar* ❑ *"Was his name David?"*

— "No I don't think it was, but never mind, go on." —¿Se llamaba David? —No, creo que no; pero olvídalo; ¿qué sigue? ❑ Dorothy, come on. Never mind your coat. We'll drive. Anda, Dorothy; olvida el abrigo. Vamos a ir en coche. **5** PHRASE You use **never mind** after a statement, often a negative one, to indicate that the statement is even more true of the person, thing, or situation that you are going to mention next. ni hablar de, ya no decir para ❑ He's too shy even to look at her, never mind talk to her! —Es demasiado tímido para atreverse a mirarla, ¡ya no digamos para hablarle! **6** PHRASE If you say that you **wouldn't mind** something, you mean that you would like it. no venir mal ❑ I wouldn't mind a cup of coffee. No me vendría mal una taza de café.

**mind|less** /maɪndlɪs/ **1** ADJ If you describe a violent action as **mindless,** you mean that it is done without thought and will achieve nothing. insensato, sin sentido, ciego ❑ ...mindless violence. ...violencia ciega. **2** ADJ If you describe an activity as **mindless,** you mean that it is so dull or boring that people do it or take part in it without thinking. mecánico ❑ It was mindless work, but it gave me something to do. Era un trabajo mecánico, pero me mantenía ocupado. ● **mind|less|ly** ADV mecánicamente ❑ I spent many hours mindlessly hitting a tennis ball against the wall. Me pasé muchas horas lanzando mecánicamente la pelota de tenis contra la pared.

**mine**
❶ PRONOUN USE
❷ NOUN AND VERB USES

M

❶ **mine** /maɪn/ PRON **Mine** is the first person singular possessive pronoun. A speaker or writer uses **mine** to refer to something that belongs or relates to himself or herself. mí/mío ❑ Her right hand was close to mine. Su mano derecha estaba cerca de la mía. ❑ That wasn't his bag, it was mine. No era su bolsa, era la mía.
→ see **industry, tunnel**

❷ **mine** /maɪn/ (**mines, mining, mined**) **1** N-COUNT A **mine** is a place where deep holes and tunnels are dug under the ground in order to obtain minerals such as coal, diamonds, or gold. mina ❑ ...coal mines. ...minas de carbón. **2** V-T When a mineral **is mined,** it is obtained from the ground by digging deep holes and tunnels. extraer, explotar ❑ Diamonds are mined in South Africa. Las minas de diamantes están en Sudáfrica. ● **min|er** N-COUNT (**miners**) minero o minera ❑ My father was a miner. Mi padre fue minero. ● **min|ing** N-UNCOUNT minería ❑ ...industries such as coal mining and steel making. ...industrias como la minería del carbón y la fundición de acero. **3** N-COUNT A **mine** is a bomb which is hidden in the ground or in water and which explodes when people or things touch it. mina

**min|er|al** /mɪnərəl/ (**minerals**) N-COUNT A **mineral** is a substance such as tin, salt, or sulfur that is formed naturally in rocks and in the earth. mineral
→ see Word Web: **mineral**
→ see **photosynthesis, rock**

**min|er|al wa|ter** (**mineral waters**) N-VAR **Mineral water** is water that comes out of the ground naturally and is considered healthy to drink. agua mineral

**Word Link** *mini ≈ very small : miniature, minibus, minivan*

**minia|ture** /mɪniətʃər, -tʃʊər/ (**miniatures**) **1** ADJ **Miniature** is used to describe something that is very small, especially a smaller version of something which is normally much bigger. miniatura ❑ ...miniature roses. ...rosas miniatura. **2** PHRASE If you describe one thing as another thing **in miniature,** you mean that it is much smaller in size or scale than the other thing, but is otherwise exactly the same. en miniatura ❑ Ecuador is like the whole of South America in miniature. El Ecuador es como toda Sudamérica en miniatura. **3** N-COUNT A **miniature** is a very small, detailed painting, often of a person. miniatura

**mini|bus** /mɪnibʌs/ (**minibuses**) also **mini-bus** N-COUNT A **minibus** is a large van which has seats in the back for passengers, and windows along its sides. minibús ❑ A minibus drove them to the airport. Fueron al aeropuerto en un minibús.

**Word Link** *minim ≈ smallest : minimal, minimize, minimum*

**mini|mal** /mɪnɪməl/ ADJ Something that is **minimal** is very small in quantity, value, or degree. mínimo ❑ The difference between the two computers is minimal. La diferencia entre las dos computadoras es mínima. ● **mini|mal|ly** ADV mínimamente, en grado mínimo ❑ They paid him, but only minimally. Le pagaron, pero sólo lo mínimo.

**mini|mal|ism** /mɪnɪməlɪzəm/ N-UNCOUNT **Minimalism** is a style in which a small number of

**Word Web** mineral

The **extraction** of **minerals** from ore is an ancient process. Neolithic man discovered **copper** around 8000 BC. Using fire and charcoal, they **reduced** the ore to its pure **metal** form. About 4,000 years later, Egyptians learned to pour molten copper into molds. **Silver** ore often contains large amounts of copper and **lead**. Silver **refineries** often use the **smelting** process to remove these other metals from the silver. Most **gold** does not exist as an ore. Instead, veins of gold run through the earth. Refiners use chemicals such as cyanide to get pure gold.

very simple things are used to create a particular effect. *minimalismo* ❑ *...the minimalism of her home. ...el estilo minimalista de su casa.*

**Word Link** *minim ≈ smallest : minimal, minimize, minimum*

**mini|mize** /mɪnɪmaɪz/ (**minimizes, minimizing, minimized**) **1** V-T If you **minimize** a risk, problem, or unpleasant situation, you reduce it to the lowest possible level, or prevent it from increasing beyond that level. *reducir al mínimo* ❑ *People want to minimize the risk of getting cancer. La gente quiere reducir al mínimo el riesgo de desarrollar cáncer.* **2** V-T If you **minimize** something, you make it seem smaller or less significant than it really is. *desestimar* ❑ *Do not minimize the danger. No desestimes el peligro.*

**mini|mum** /mɪnɪməm/ **1** ADJ You use **minimum** to describe an amount which is the smallest that is possible, allowed, or required. *mínimo* ❑ *He was only five feet nine, the minimum height for a policeman. Medía sólo 1.75 metros, la estatura mínima para ser policía.* ● **Minimum** is also a noun. *mínimo o mínima* ❑ *This will take a minimum of one hour. Esto tardará un mínimo de una hora.* **2** ADJ You use **minimum** to state how small an amount is. *mínimo* ❑ *This book tells you how to get through college with minimum work and maximum fun. Este libro te dice cómo cursar la universidad con el mínimo de trabajo y el máximo de diversión.* ● **Minimum** is also a noun. *mínimo o mínima* ❑ *It is better to travel with a minimum of baggage. Es mejor viajar con el mínimo de equipaje.*
→ see **factory**

**Word Partnership** Usar *minimum* con:

N. minimum **age**, minimum **balance**, minimum **payment**, minimum **purchase**, minimum **requirement**, minimum **salary** **1**
ADJ. **absolute** minimum, **bare** minimum **1** **2**

**mini|mum se|cu|rity pris|on** (**minimum security prisons**) N-COUNT A **minimum security prison** is a prison where there are fewer restrictions on prisoners than in a normal prison. *prisión de baja seguridad, cárcel abierta, cárcel de puertas abiertas*

**min|is|ter** /mɪnɪstər/ (**ministers**) **1** N-COUNT A **minister** is a member of the clergy, especially in Protestant churches. *ministro o ministra, pastor o pastora* ❑ *His father was a Baptist minister. Su padre era pastor bautista.* **2** N-COUNT A **minister** is a person who officially represents their government in a foreign country and has a lower rank than an ambassador. *cónsul, secretario o secretaria* ❑ *...the Danish minister in Washington. ...el cónsul danés en Washington.* **3** N-COUNT In some countries outside the United States, a **minister** is a person who is in charge of a particular government department. *ministro o ministra, secretario o secretaria* ❑ *He was named minister of culture. Lo nombraron secretario de cultura.*

**min|is|terial** /mɪnɪstɪəriəl/ ADJ You use **ministerial** to refer to people, events, or jobs that are connected with government ministers. *ministerial, administrativo, de gabinete* ❑ *...a series of ministerial meetings in Brussels. ...una serie de reuniones ministeriales en Bruselas.*

**min|is|try** /mɪnɪstri/ (**ministries**) **1** N-COUNT The **ministry** of a religious person is the work that they do that is inspired by their religious beliefs. *ministerio* ❑ *His ministry is among poor people. Su ministerio está dedicado a los pobres.* **2** N-SING Members of the clergy belonging to some branches of the Christian church are referred to as **the ministry**. *clero, clerecía* ❑ *What made him enter the ministry? ¿Qué lo hizo unirse al clero?* **3** N-COUNT In many countries, a **ministry** is a government department which deals with a particular thing or area of activity, for example trade, defense, or transportation. *ministerio, secretaría* ❑ *...the Ministry of Justice. ...el Ministerio de Justicia.*

**Word Link** *mini ≈ very small : miniature, minibus, minivan*

**mini|van** /mɪnivæn/ (**minivans**) N-COUNT A **minivan** is a large, tall car whose seats can be moved or removed, for example, so that it can carry large loads. *minivan* ❑ *A minivan drove by with five faces looking out of the window. Pasó una minivan y cinco caras se asomaban por la ventanilla.*

**mi|nor** /maɪnər/ (**minors**) **1** ADJ You use **minor** when you want to describe something that is less important, serious, or significant than other things in a group or situation. *menor, poco importante, menos importante* ❑ *She had a number of minor roles in films. Ella tuvo varios papeles menores en películas.* **2** N-COUNT A **minor** is a person who is still legally a child. In most states in the United States, people are minors until they reach the age of eighteen. *menor, menor de edad* ❑ *Minors are not allowed to vote. Los menores de edad no tienen derecho al voto.*

**Thesaurus** *minor* Ver también:

ADJ. insignificant, lesser, small, unimportant; (*ant.*) important, major, significant **1**

**Word Partnership** Usar *minor* con:

N. minor **adjustment**, minor **damage**, minor **detail**, minor **illness**, minor **injury**, minor **operation**, minor **problem**, minor **surgery** **1**
ADV. **relatively** minor **1**

**mi|nor|ity** /mɪnɔrɪti, maɪ-/ (**minorities**) **1** N-SING If you talk about a **minority** of people or things in a larger group, you are referring to a number of them that forms less than half of the larger group, usually much less than half. *minoría* ❑ *A minority of mothers go out to work. Las madres que trabajan fuera de casa son una minoría.* PHRASE ● If people are **in a minority** or **in the minority**, they belong to a group of people or things that form less than half of a larger group. *ser una minoría, formar parte de una minoría* ❑ *Male nurses are in a minority. Los enfermeros son una minoría.* **2** N-COUNT A **minority** is a group of people of the same race, culture, or religion who live in a place where most of the people around them are of a different race, culture, or religion. *minoría* ❑ *...the region's ethnic minorities. ...las minorías étnicas de la región.*

m

**Word Partnership** Usar *minority* con:

N. minority **leader**, minority **party** 1
minority **applicants**, minority **community**, minority **group**, minority **population**, minority **students**, minority **voters**, minority **women** 2

**mi|nor key** N-COUNT In music, the **minor key** is based on the minor scale, in which the third note is three semitones higher than the first. *tono menor*

**mi|nor league** (**minor leagues**) 1 N-COUNT In baseball, a **minor league** is a professional league that is not one of the major leagues. *liga menor* ❑ *In 1952, there were 43 minor leagues. En 1952 había 43 ligas menores.* 2 ADJ **Minor-league** people are not very important or not very successful. *de segunda, menor* ❑ *...minor-league actors. ...actores de segunda.*

**min|strel show** /mɪnstrəl ʃoʊ/ (**minstrel shows**) N-COUNT In the past, a **minstrel show** was a form of entertainment consisting of songs, dances, and comedy performed by actors wearing black face make-up. *espectáculo cómico en que actores blancos representaban a personajes negros, minstrel show*

**mint** /mɪnt/ (**mints, minting, minted**) 1 N-UNCOUNT **Mint** is an herb with fresh-tasting leaves. *menta* ❑ *The lamb was served with mint. Sirvieron el cordero con menta.* 2 N-COUNT A **mint** is a candy with a peppermint flavor. Some people suck mints in order to make their breath smell fresher. *menta, pastilla de menta* ❑ *She put a mint into her mouth. Se llevó una menta a la boca.* 3 N-COUNT **The mint** is the place where the official coins of a country are made. *casa de moneda, casa de la moneda* ❑ *In 1965 the mint stopped putting silver in dimes. En 1965, la casa de moneda dejó de poner plata en las monedas de diez centavos.* 4 V-T To **mint** coins or medals means to make them in a mint. *acuñar* ❑ *...the right to mint coins. ...el derecho a acuñar monedas.* • **mint|ing** N-UNCOUNT *acuñación* ❑ *...the minting of new gold coins. ...la acuñación de nuevas monedas de oro.*
→ see **money**

**Word Link** *min ≈ small, lessen : diminish, minus, minute*

**mi|nus** /maɪnəs/ (**minuses**) 1 CONJ You use **minus** to show that one number or quantity is being subtracted from another. *menos* ❑ *One minus one is zero. Uno menos uno igual a cero.* 2 ADJ **Minus** before a number or quantity means that the number or quantity is less than zero. *menos* ❑ *...temperatures of minus 65 degrees. ...temperaturas de menos 65 grados.* 3 PREP To be **minus** something means not to have that thing. *sin* [INFORMAL] ❑ *The company closed, leaving Chris minus a job. La compañía cerró y Chris se quedó sin trabajo.* 4 N-COUNT A **minus** is a disadvantage. *desventaja, deficiencia, contra* [INFORMAL] ❑ *The idea had a lot more pluses than minuses. La idea tiene muchos más pros que contras.*

**Thesaurus** *minus* Ver también:

PREP. without 3
N. deficiency, disadvantage, drawback 4

**minute**
❶ NOUN AND VERB USES
❷ ADJECTIVE USE

❶ **mi|nute** /mɪnɪt/ (**minutes**) 1 N-COUNT A **minute** is one of the sixty parts that an hour is divided into. People often say **"a minute"** or **"minutes"** when they mean a short length of time. *minuto, rato, instante, momento* ❑ *The pizza will take twenty minutes to cook. La pizza tarda veinte minutos en cocinarse.* ❑ *Bye Mom, see you in a minute. Adiós ma, te veo al rato.* 2 N-PLURAL The **minutes** of a meeting are the written records of the things that are discussed or decided at it. *minuta, acta* ❑ *He read the minutes of the last meeting. Leyó la minuta de la última reunión.* 3 PHRASE If you say that something will or may happen **at any minute** or **any minute now,** you are emphasizing that it is likely to happen very soon. *en cualquier momento, ya* ❑ *It looked as though it might rain at any minute. Parecía como si en cualquier momento fuera a llover.* 4 PHRASE A **last-minute** action is one that is done at the latest time possible. *de último momento, a ultima hora* ❑ *He made a last-minute decision to stay at home. A última hora decidió quedarse en casa.* 5 PHRASE If you say that something happens **the minute** something else happens, you are emphasizing that it happens immediately after the other thing. *en el momento, tan pronto como* ❑ *The minute he lay down on his bed, he fell asleep. Se quedó dormido tan pronto como se acostó en la cama.* 6 CONVENTION People often use expressions such as **wait a minute** or **just a minute** when they want to stop you from doing or saying something. *un momento* ❑ *Wait a minute, something is wrong here. Un momento, hay algo mal aquí.*
→ see **time**

❷ **mi|nute** /maɪnut/ (**minutest**) ADJ If something is **minute,** it is very small. *muy pequeño, diminuto, muy poco, poquito* ❑ *Only a minute amount of glue is needed. Se necesita poquito pegamento.*
• **mi|nute|ly** /maɪnutli/ ADV *mínimamente, apenas, minuciosamente, detalladamente* ❑ *Then the pain changed minutely. Luego, el dolor se redujo mínimamente.*

**mira|cle** /mɪrəkᵊl/ (**miracles**) 1 N-COUNT If you say that something is a **miracle,** you mean that it is very surprising and fortunate. *milagro* ❑ *It's a miracle that he survived the accident. Es un milagro que haya sobrevivido al accidente.* 2 ADJ A **miracle** drug or product does something that was thought almost impossible. *milagroso* ❑ *...the miracle drugs that keep him alive. ...los medicamentos milagrosos que lo mantienen con vida.* 3 N-COUNT A **miracle** is a wonderful and surprising event that is believed to be caused by God. *milagro* ❑ *...Jesus's ability to perform miracles. ...la capacidad de Jesús para hacer milagros.*

**Word Partnership** Usar *minute* con:

DET. a minute **or two**, **another** minute, **each** minute, **every** minute, **half a** minute ❶ 1
V. **take a** minute ❶ 1
**wait a** minute ❶ 6
N. minute **detail**, minute **quantity of** *something* ❷

**mir|ror** /mɪrər/ (**mirrors, mirroring, mirrored**) **1** N-COUNT A **mirror** is a flat piece of glass in which you can see your reflection. *espejo* ❑ *He looked at himself in the mirror. Se miró al espejo.* **2** V-T If something **mirrors** something else, it has similar features to it, and therefore seems like a copy or representation of it. *reflejar* ❑ *The book mirrors the author's own experiences. El libro refleja las experiencias personales del autor.* **3** V-T If you see something reflected in water, you can say that the water **mirrors** it. *reflejar(se)* [LITERARY] ❑ *The river mirrors the sky. El cielo se refleja en el río.*
→ see **telescope**

**Word Partnership** Usar *mirror* con:

V. **glance in a** mirror, **look in a** mirror, **reflect in a** mirror, **see in a** mirror **1**
PREP. **in front of a** mirror **1**
N. **reflection in a** mirror **1**

**mis|be|hav|ior** /mɪsbɪheɪvyər/ N-UNCOUNT **Misbehavior** is behavior that is not acceptable to other people. *mala conducta, mal comportamiento* [FORMAL] ❑ *What was causing their son's misbehavior? ¿Cuál era la causa del mal comportamiento de su hijo?*

**mis|car|riage** /mɪskærɪdʒ, -kær-/ (**miscarriages**) N-VAR If a pregnant woman has a **miscarriage,** she gives birth to her baby before it is properly formed, and it dies. *aborto espontáneo, aborto no provocado*

**mis|cel|la|neous** /mɪsəleɪniəs/ ADJ A **miscellaneous** group consists of many different kinds of things or people that are difficult to put into a particular category. *mixto, heterogéneo, variado, de todo tipo* ❑ *...a box of miscellaneous junk. ...una caja de cachivaches de todo tipo.*

**mis|chief** /mɪstʃɪf/ **1** N-UNCOUNT **Mischief** is playing harmless tricks on people or doing things you are not supposed to do. It can also refer to the desire to do this. *travesura, diablura* ❑ *He's a typical little boy—full of mischief. Es el típico niñito, siempre pensando en travesuras.* **2** N-UNCOUNT **Mischief** is behavior that is intended to cause trouble for people. It can also refer to the trouble that is caused. *maldad, daño, engorro* ❑ *Brandi loves to cause mischief. A Brandi le encanta hacer maldades.*

**mis|con|duct** /mɪskɒndʌkt/ N-UNCOUNT **Misconduct** is bad or unacceptable behavior, especially by a professional person. *mala conducta, falta de ética profesional, inmoralidad* ❑ *A doctor was found guilty of serious misconduct yesterday. Ayer declararon culpable de falta de ética profesional a un médico.*

**mis|er|able** /mɪzərəbᵊl/ **1** ADJ If you are **miserable,** you are very unhappy. *infeliz, desgraciado, desdichado* ❑ *I had a job which made me really miserable. Yo tenía un trabajo que verdaderamente me hacía infeliz.* ● **mis|er|ably** /mɪzərəbli/ ADV *miserablemente, con abatimiento* ❑ *He looked miserably down at his plate. Abatido, fijo la mirada en su plato.* **2** ADJ A **miserable** place or **miserable** weather makes you feel unhappy or depressed. *pésimo, atroz, lamentable* ❑ *There was nothing in this miserable place to enjoy. No había nada que disfrutar en ese lamentable lugar.* ❑ *It was a gray, wet, miserable day. Fue un día pésimo, gris y húmedo.*

**Thesaurus** *miserable* Ver también:

ADJ. unhappy **1**
unfortunate, wretched **2**

**mis|ery** /mɪzəri/ (**miseries**) **1** N-VAR **Misery** is great unhappiness. *miseria, infelicidad, desdicha, desgracia, sufrimiento* ❑ *All that money brought nothing but sadness and misery. Todo ese dinero no trajo más que tristeza y sufrimiento.* **2** N-UNCOUNT **Misery** is the way of life and unpleasant living conditions of people who are very poor. *miseria* ❑ *...the misery of some African people. ...la miseria de algunos pueblos africanos.*

**Word Link** *mis ≈ bad : misfit, misleading, misunderstood*

**mis|fit** /mɪsfɪt/ (**misfits**) N-COUNT A **misfit** is a person who is not easily accepted by other people, often because their behavior is very different from that of everyone else. *inadaptado o inadaptada, raro o rara* ❑ *I feel like a misfit because I don't want children. Me siento como un indaptado porque no quiero hijos.*

**mis|lead** /mɪslid/ (**misleads, misleading, misled**) V-T If you say that someone or something **has misled** you, you mean that they have made you believe something that is not true. *engañar, inducir a error* ❑ *...government lawyers who have misled the court. ...abogados del gobierno que engañaron al tribunal.*

**mis|lead|ing** /mɪslidɪŋ/ ADJ If you describe something as **misleading,** you mean that it gives you a wrong idea or impression. *engañoso* ❑ *It would be misleading to say that we were friends. Sería engañoso decir que éramos amigos.* ● **mis|lead|ing|ly** ADV *engañosamente, de manera equívoca* ❑ *The facts have been presented misleadingly. Los hechos fueron presentados de manera equívoca.*

**mis|led** /mɪslɛd/ **Misled** is the past tense and past participle of **mislead**. *pasado y participio pasado de* **mislead**

**mis|per|cep|tion** /mɪspərsɛpʃᵊn/ (**misperceptions**) N-COUNT A **misperception** is an idea or impression that is not correct. *idea falsa, error* ❑ *There's a misperception that all women want to have children. Existe la falsa idea de que todas las mujeres quieren tener hijos.*

**mis|placed** /mɪspleɪst/ ADJ If you describe a feeling or action as **misplaced,** you are critical of it because you think it is inappropriate, or directed toward the wrong thing or person. *no venir al caso, equivocado* ❑ *We believed that she would be honest with us; that trust was misplaced. Pensábamos que sería honesta con nosotros; pero nos equivocamos al confiar en ella.*

**mis|read** /mɪsrid/ (**misreads, misreading**)

The form **misread** is used in the present tense, and is the past tense and past participle, when it is pronounced /mɪsrɛd/.

**1** V-T If you **misread** a situation or someone's behavior, you do not understand it properly. *entender mal, interpretar mal, malinterpretar* ❑ *I misread the signals, and thought she wanted me to kiss her. Malinterpreté sus señales y pensé que ella quería que la besara.* ● **mis|read|ing** N-COUNT (**misreadings**) *mala interpretación* ❑ *...a misreading of public opinion in France.* *...una mala interpretación de la opinión pública en Francia.* **2** V-T If you **misread** something that has been written or printed, you look at it and think that it says something that it does not say. *leer mal, malinterpretar* ❑ *He misread his route and took a wrong turn.* *Interpretó mal la guía y dio vuelta donde no debía.*

**miss**
❶ USED AS A TITLE OR A FORM OF ADDRESS
❷ VERB AND NOUN USES

❶ **Miss** /mɪs/ (**Misses**) N-TITLE You use **Miss** in front of the name of a girl or unmarried woman when you are speaking to her or referring to her. *señorita* [FORMAL] ❑ *It was nice talking to you, Miss Ellis.* *Me dio gusto hablar con usted, señorita Ellis.*

❷ **miss** /mɪs/ (**misses, missing, missed**) **1** V-T/V-I If you **miss** something you are trying to hit, you fail to hit it. *errar, fallar* ❑ *She threw her glass across the room, and it missed my head by an inch.* *Lanzó su vaso a través del salón y no me dio en la cabeza por escasos centímetros.* ❑ *His first shot missed the goal completely.* *Su primer disparo erró por completo la portería.* ● **Miss** is also a noun. *fallo, falla* ❑ *After more misses, they finally put two arrows into the lion's chest.* *Después de fallar varias veces, por fin le atinaron al león en el pecho con dos flechas.* **2** V-T If you **miss** something, you fail to notice it. *pasar por alto, omitir, escapársele a uno algo, írsele a uno algo* ❑ *He watched, never missing a detail.* *Observaba y nunca se le iba un detalle.* **3** V-T If you **miss** the meaning or importance of something, you fail to understand or appreciate it. *escapársele a uno algo, pasar por alto* ❑ *He totally missed the point of the question.* *Se le escapó totalmente el meollo del asunto.* **4** V-T If you **miss** someone who is no longer with you or who has died, you feel sad and wish that they were still with you. *extrañar, echar de menos* ❑ *Your mama and I are going to miss you at Thanksgiving.* *Tu mamá y yo te vamos a extrañar el día de acción de gracias.* **5** V-T If you **miss** something, you feel sad because you no longer have it or are no longer doing or experiencing it. *echar de menos, extrañar, hacer falta algo* ❑ *If I moved into an apartment I'd miss my garden.* *Si me mudara a un departamento, echaría de menos mi jardín.* **6** V-T If you **miss** something such as a plane or train, you arrive too late to catch it. *perder, írsele a uno algo* ❑ *He missed the last bus home and had to stay with a friend.* *Se le fue el último autobús de regreso y tuvo que quedarse con un amigo.* **7** V-T If you **miss** something such as a meeting or an activity, you do not go to it or take part in it. *perderse uno algo, faltar* ❑ *Martha and I had to miss our class last week.* *Martha y yo tuvimos que faltar a la clase de la semana pasada.* **8** → see also **missing**

▸ **miss out** PHR-VERB If you **miss out on** something that would be enjoyable or useful to you, you are not involved in it or do not take part in it. *dejar pasar, desaprovechar* ❑ *We're missing out on a great opportunity.* *Estamos dejando pasar una gran oportunidad.*

M

**Usage** miss and lose

*Miss* and *lose* have similar meanings. *Miss* is used to express something you didn't do: *I missed class yesterday.* *Lose* is used when you can't find something you once had. *Cancel your ATM card if you lose your wallet.*

**Word Link** *miss ≈ sending : dismiss, missile, missionary*

**mis|sile** /mɪsᵊl/ (**missiles**) **1** N-COUNT A **missile** is a tube-shaped weapon that travels long distances through the air and explodes when it reaches its target. *misil, proyectil* ❑ *They fired missiles all night.* *Lanzaron misiles toda la noche.* **2** N-COUNT Anything that is thrown as a weapon can be called a **missile.** *proyectil* ❑ *The football fans threw missiles onto the field.* *Los fanáticos del futbol lanzaron proyectiles al campo.*

**miss|ing** /mɪsɪŋ/ **1** ADJ If something is **missing** or has **gone missing,** it is not in its usual place, and you cannot find it. *perdido, traspapelado* ❑ *I discovered that my cellphone was missing.* *Descubrí que mi celular no estaba donde lo dejé.* **2** ADJ If a part of something is **missing,** it has been removed or has come off, and has not been replaced. *que falta* ❑ *Three buttons were missing from his shirt.* *A su camisa le faltaban tres botones.* **3** ADJ Someone who is **missing** cannot be found, and it is not known whether they are alive or dead. *desaparecido* ❑ *Five people died in the explosion and one person is still missing.* *Cinco personas murieron en la explosión y otra sigue desaparecida.* PHRASE ● If a member of the armed forces is **missing in action**, they have not returned from a battle, their body has not been found, and they are not thought to have been captured. *desaparecido en acción* **4** → see also **MIA**

**Word Partnership** Usar *missing* con:

ADV. **still** missing **1** **3**
N. missing **piece** **1** **2**
missing **information**, missing **ingredient** **2**
missing **children**, missing **girl**, missing **people**, missing **soldiers** **3**

**mis|sion** /mɪʃᵊn/ (**missions**) **1** N-COUNT A **mission** is an important task that people are given to do, especially one that involves traveling to another country. *misión* ❑ *His government sent him on a mission to North America.* *Su gobierno le encomendó una misión en los Estados Unidos.* **2** N-COUNT A **mission** is a group of people who have been sent to a foreign country to carry out an official task. *delegación* ❑ *...the head of the trade mission to Zimbabwe.* *...el jefe de la delegación comercial en Zimbabue.* **3** N-COUNT A **mission** is a special journey made by a military airplane or spacecraft. *misión* ❑ *The plane crashed during a training mission in the mountains.* *El avión se estrelló durante una misión de entrenamiento en las montañas.* **4** N-SING If you have a **mission,** you have a strong commitment and sense of duty to do or achieve something. *misión* ❑ *His mission in life was to tell people about Jesus.* *Su misión en la vida era dar testimonio de Jesús a la gente.*

**Word Partnership** Usar *mission* con:

ADJ. **dangerous** mission, **secret** mission, **successful** mission 1
N. **peacekeeping** mission 1 2
**combat** mission, **rescue** mission, **training** mission 1 3
V. **accomplish a** mission, **carry out a** mission 1 3 4

**Word Link** *miss ≈ sending : dismiss, missile, missionary*

**mis|sion|ary** /mɪʃənɛri/ (**missionaries**) N-COUNT A **missionary** is a Christian who has been sent to a foreign country to teach people about Christianity. misionero o misionera ❑ *My mother would like me to be a missionary in Africa.* *Mi madre quisiera que fuera misionero en África.*

**mis|state** /mɪssteɪt/ (**misstates, misstating, misstated**) V-T If you **misstate** something, you state it incorrectly or give false information about it. exponer mal, exponer falsamente ❑ *The report misstated important facts.* *En el informe se exponían mal hechos importantes.*

**mis|state|ment** /mɪssteɪtmənt/ (**misstatements**) N-COUNT A **misstatement** is an incorrect statement, or the giving of false information. declaración tergiversada, relato inexacto, inexactitud, hecho erróneo ❑ *He finally corrected his misstatement.* *Finalmente corrigió las inexactitudes de su declaración.* ❑ *This book is filled with misstatements of fact.* *Este libro está lleno de hechos erróneos.*

**mis|step** /mɪsstɛp/ (**missteps**) N-COUNT A **misstep** is a mistake. desliz, paso en falso ❑ *A single misstep could make him lose his job.* *Un sólo paso en falso podría hacer que perdiera su empleo.*

**mist** /mɪst/ (**mists, misting, misted**) 1 N-VAR **Mist** consists of a large number of tiny drops of water in the air, which make it difficult to see very far. neblina, bruma ❑ *Thick mist made flying impossible.* *La espesa neblina hacía imposible volar.* 2 V-T/V-I If a piece of glass **mists** or **is misted**, it becomes covered with tiny drops of moisture, so that you cannot see through it easily. empañar(se) ❑ *The windows misted, and I couldn't see out.* *Las ventanas se empañaron y yo no podía ver hacia afuera.* • **Mist over** means the same as **mist**. empañar(se), cubrir(se) de neblina ❑ *The front windshield was misting over.* *El parabrisas se estaba empañando.*

**mis|take** /mɪsteɪk/ (**mistakes, mistaking, mistook, mistaken**) 1 N-COUNT If you make a **mistake,** you do something which you did not intend to do, or which produces a result that you do not want. error, equivocación ❑ *They made the big mistake of thinking they would win easily.* *Cometieron el grave error de pensar que ganarían fácilmente.* ❑ *There must be some mistake.* *Debe haber una equivocación.* 2 N-COUNT A **mistake** is something or part of something that is incorrect or not right. error, equivocación ❑ *Her mother erased a mistake in her letter.* *Su madre borró un error de la carta.* 3 V-T If you **mistake** one person or thing **for** another, you wrongly think that they are the other person or thing. confundir ❑ *People are always mistaking her for her sister.* *La gente siempre la confunde con su hermana.* 4 PHRASE You can say **there is no mistaking** something when you are emphasizing that you cannot fail to recognize or understand it. ser inconfundible algo, no caber duda ❑ *There's no mistaking he comes from Mexico.* *No cabe duda de que viene de México.*

**Word Partnership** Usar *mistake* con:

ADJ. **fatal** mistake, **honest** mistake, **tragic** mistake 1
**big** mistake, **common** mistake, **costly** mistake, **huge** mistake, **serious** mistake, **terrible** mistake 1 2
V. **admit a** mistake, **correct a** mistake, **fix a** mistake, **make a** mistake, **realize a** mistake 1 2

**mis|tak|en** /mɪsteɪkən/ 1 ADJ If you are **mistaken about** something, you are wrong about it. equivocado ❑ *I was mistaken about you.* *Estaba equivocada respecto de ti.* 2 ADJ A **mistaken** belief or opinion is incorrect. equivocado, falso ❑ *I had a mistaken view of what was happening.* *Yo tenía una opinión equivocada de lo que estaba pasando.* • **mis|tak|en|ly** ADV equivocadamente, falsamente ❑ *They mistakenly believed there was no one in the house.* *Equivocadamente pensaban que no había nadie en la casa.*

**mis|ter** /mɪstər/ N-VOC Men are sometimes addressed as **mister,** especially by children and especially when the person talking to them does not know their name. señor [INFORMAL] ❑ *Look, Mister, don't try to tell us what to do.* *Por favor, señor, no trate de decirnos qué hacer.*

**mis|took** /mɪstʊk/ **Mistook** is the past tense and past participle of **mistake**. pasado y participio pasado de *mistake*

**mis|tri|al** /mɪstraɪəl/ (**mistrials**) N-COUNT A **mistrial** is a legal trial which ends without a verdict, for example because the jury cannot agree on one. juicio nulo ❑ *The judge refused to declare a mistrial.* *El juez se negó a declarar nulo el juicio.*

**mis|trust** /mɪstrʌst/ (**mistrusts, mistrusting, mistrusted**) 1 N-UNCOUNT **Mistrust** is the feeling that you have toward someone who you do not trust. desconfianza, recelo ❑ *There was a lot of mistrust between the two men.* *Había un gran recelo entre los dos hombres.* 2 V-T If you **mistrust** someone or something, you do not trust them. desconfiar de, recelar de ❑ *He mistrusts all journalists.* *Desconfía de todos los periodistas.*

**mis|under|stand** /mɪsʌndərstænd/ (**misunderstands, misunderstanding, misunderstood**) 1 V-T/V-I If you **misunderstand** someone or something, you do not understand them properly. interpretar mal, no entender, no comprender, entender mal, comprender mal ❑ *I misunderstood you.* *No te entendí.* ❑ *They have misunderstood what rock and roll is.* *No han entendido lo que es el rock and roll.* 2 → see also **misunderstood**

**Word Link** *mis ≈ bad : misfit, misleading, misunderstood*

**mis|under|stood** /mɪsʌndərstʊd/ 1 **Misunderstood** is the past tense and past participle of **misunderstand**. pasado y participio pasado de *misunderstand* 2 ADJ If you describe someone or something as **misunderstood,** you mean that people do not understand them and have a wrong impression or idea of them. incomprendido ❑ *Eric is very badly misunderstood.* *Eric es un gran incomprendido.*

**mito|chon|drion** /maɪtəkɒndriən/ (**mitochondria**) N-COUNT **Mitochondria** are the parts of a cell that convert nutrients into energy. mitocondria [TECHNICAL]

| Word Link | *osis ≈ state or condition : diagnosis, mitosis, symbiosis* |
|---|---|

**mi|to|sis** /maɪtoʊsɪs/ N-UNCOUNT **Mitosis** is the process by which a cell divides into two identical halves. mitosis [TECHNICAL]

**mix** /mɪks/ (**mixes, mixing, mixed**) **1** V-RECIP If two substances **mix** or if you **mix** one substance **with** another, they combine to become a single substance. mezclar(se), juntar(se), combinar(se) ❑ *Oil and water don't mix.* *El aceite y el agua no se mezclan.* ❑ *A quick stir will mix them thoroughly.* *Agitando rápidamente se mezclan por completo.* ❑ *Mix the sugar with the butter.* *Mezcle el azúcar y la mantequilla.* **2** V-T If you **mix** something, you prepare it by mixing other things together. mezclar, combinar ❑ *He spent several hours mixing cement.* *Pasó varias horas mezclando el cemento.* **3** N-VAR A **mix** is a powder containing all the substances that you need in order to make something. When you want to use it, you add liquid. preparado, mezcla, mixtura ❑ *...a package of cake mix.* *...un paquete de preparado para pastel.* **4** N-COUNT A **mix of** different things or people is two or more of them together. mezcla, combinación ❑ *The story is a mix of fact and fiction.* *La historia es una combinación de realidad y ficción.* **5** V-RECIP If you **mix with** other people, you meet them and talk to them. mezclarse, juntarse ❑ *He loved to mix with the rich and famous.* *Le encantaba juntarse con los ricos y famosos.* ❑ *The meeting gave younger and older students the chance to mix.* *La reunión fue una oportunidad para que los estudiantes jóvenes se juntaran con los mayores.*

▸ **mix up** **1** PHR-VERB If you **mix up** two things or people, you confuse them, so that you think that one of them is the other one. confundir, revolver ❑ *People often mix me up with other actors.* *La gente suele confundirme con otros actores.* ❑ *Children often mix up their words.* *En ocasiones, los niños confunden las palabras.* **2** → see also **mixed up**

| Word Partnership | Usar *mix* con: |
|---|---|
| N. | mix **ingredients**, mix **with water** **1** **2** |
| ADV. | mix **thoroughly**, mix **together** **1** **2** |

**mixed** /mɪkst/ **1** ADJ If you have **mixed** feelings about something or someone, you feel uncertain about them because you can see both good and bad points about them. encontrado, ambivalente ❑ *I came home from the meeting with mixed feelings.* *Regresé a casa de la reunión con sentimientos encontrados.* **2** ADJ You use **mixed** to describe something which includes or consists of different things or people of the same general kind. de todo tipo, diverso ❑ *...a very mixed group of people.* *...un grupo de personas de todo tipo.* ❑ *...a teaspoon of mixed herbs.* *...una cucharadita de hierbas mixtas.* **3** ADJ **Mixed** is used to describe something that involves people from two or more different races. mixto, mezclado ❑ *I went to a racially mixed school.* *Asistí a una escuela en la que aceptaban alumnos de todas las razas.* **4** ADJ **Mixed** education or accommodations are intended for both males and females. mixto ❑ *Girls who go to a mixed school know how to speak to boys.* *Las niñas que van a escuelas mixtas saben cómo relacionarse con los niños.*

**mixed me|dia** N-UNCOUNT **Mixed media** is the use of more than one medium or material in a work of art, for example the use of both painting and collage. técnica mixta [TECHNICAL]

**mixed me|ter** (**mixed meters**) N-VAR Music that is written in **mixed meter** combines two or more meters, for example duple and triple meters. compás mixto [TECHNICAL]

**mixed up** **1** ADJ If you are **mixed up,** you are confused. confundido, confuso, desorientado ❑ *He's a rather mixed-up kid.* *Es un chico con problemas.* **2** ADJ To be **mixed up in** something bad, or **with** someone you disapprove of, means to be involved in it or with them. enredado, liado, mezclado ❑ *Why did I ever get mixed up with you?* *¿Por qué llegué a enredarme contigo?*

**mix|ture** /mɪkstʃər/ (**mixtures**) **1** N-SING A **mixture of** things consists of several different things together. mezcla, mixtura, mescolanza ❑ *They looked at him with a mixture of horror and surprise.* *Lo miraron con una mezcla de horror y sorpresa.* **2** N-COUNT A **mixture** is a substance that consists of other substances which have been stirred or shaken together. mezcla, mescolanza ❑ *...a mixture of water and sugar and salt.* *...una mescolanza de agua con azúcar y sal.*

| Thesaurus | *mixture* | Ver también: |
|---|---|---|
| N. | blend, collection, variety **1** | |
| | blend, compound **2** | |

**ml** **ml** is a written abbreviation for **milliliter** or **milliliters.** ml, mL, mililitro ❑ *Boil the sugar and 100 ml of water.* *Hierva el azúcar en 100 ml de agua.*

**mm** **mm** is a written abbreviation for **millimeter** or **millimeters.** mm, milímetro ❑ *...a 135 mm lens.* *...una lente de 135 mm.*

**moan** /moʊn/ (**moans, moaning, moaned**) **1** V-I If you **moan,** you make a low sound, usually because you are unhappy or in pain. quejarse, protestar, gemir ❑ *Tony moaned in his sleep.* *Tony se quejaba dormido.* • **Moan** is also a noun. quejido, queja, gemido, lamento ❑ *A moan came from the crowd.* *Se oyó el lamento de la multitud.* **2** V-I To **moan** means to complain or speak in a way which shows that you are very unhappy. quejarse ❑ *She moans if she doesn't get more than six hours' sleep at night.* *Se queja si por la noche no duerme más de seis horas.* ❑ *...moaning about the weather.* *...quejándose del clima.*

**mob** /mɒb/ (**mobs, mobbing, mobbed**) **1** N-COUNT A **mob** is a large, disorganized, and often violent crowd of people. turba ❑ *...a mob of angry men.* *...una turba de hombres enojados.* **2** V-T If you say that someone **is being mobbed by** a crowd of people, you mean that the people are trying to talk to them or get near them in an enthusiastic or threatening way. asediar ❑ *Her car was mobbed by reporters.* *Su carro fue asediado por los reporteros*

M

**Word Link** *mobil ≈ moving : automobile, mobile, mobilize*

**mo|bile** /moʊbᵊl/ **1** ADJ You use **mobile** to describe something large that can be moved easily from place to place. móvil, ambulante ❑ *...a mobile theater.* *...un teatro ambulante.* **2** ADJ If you are **mobile,** you can move or travel easily from place to place. móvil ❑ *I'm still very mobile.* *Todavía tengo mucha movilidad.* ● **mo|bil|ity** /moʊbɪlɪti/ N-UNCOUNT movilidad ❑ *The car gave him much more mobility.* *El carro le dio mucho más movilidad.* **3** ADJ In a **mobile** society, people move easily from one job, home, or social class to another. móvil ❑ *We are a very mobile society and like to take everything with us.* *Somos una sociedad muy móvil y nos gusta llevar todo con nosotros.* ● **mo|bil|ity** N-UNCOUNT movilidad ❑ *Before the nineteenth century, there was little mobility among the classes.* *Antes del siglo diecinueve, había poca movilidad entre las clases.*
→ see **cellphone**

**Word Partnership** Usar *mobile* con:

N. mobile **device,** mobile **service** **1**

**mo|bi|lize** /moʊbɪlaɪz/ (**mobilizes, mobilizing, mobilized**) **1** V-T If you **mobilize** support or **mobilize** people to do something, you succeed in encouraging people to take action. movilizar ❑ *The government could not mobilize public support.* *El gobierno no pudo movilizar el apoyo público.* ● **mo|bi|li|za|tion** /moʊbɪlɪzeɪʃᵊn/ N-UNCOUNT movilización ❑ *...the mobilization of opinion in support of the revolution.* *...la movilización de la opinión en apoyo de la revolución.* **2** V-T/V-I If a country **mobilizes,** or **mobilizes** its armed forces, or if its armed forces **mobilize,** orders are given to prepare for a conflict. movilizar(se) ❑ *Sudan threatened to mobilize.* *Sudán amenazó con movilizarse.* ● **mo|bi|li|za|tion** N-UNCOUNT movilización ❑ *...mobilization to defend the republic.* *...movilización para defender la república.*

**mo|cha** /moʊkə/ (**mochas**) **1** N-VAR **Mocha** is a drink that is a mixture of coffee and chocolate. A **mocha** is a cup of mocha. café moca/moka ❑ *...a cup of mocha.* *...una taza de café moca/moka.* **2** N-UNCOUNT **Mocha** is a type of strong coffee. café moca/moka

**mock** /mɒk/ (**mocks, mocking, mocked**) **1** V-T If you **mock** someone, you laugh at them, tease them, or try to make them look foolish. burlarse de ❑ *I thought you were mocking me.* *Pensé que te estabas burlando de mí.* ● **mock|ing** /mɒkɪŋ/ ADJ burlón ❑ *She gave a mocking smile.* *Esbozó una sonrisa burlona* **2** ADJ You use **mock** to describe something which is not real or genuine, but which is intended to be very similar to the real thing. simulado, fingido ❑ *"It's tragic!" said Jeffrey in mock horror.* *—¡Es trágico! —dijo Jeffrey con horror fingido.*

**Word Link** *mod ≈ measure, manner : mode, model, modern*

**mode** /moʊd/ (**modes**) **1** N-COUNT A **mode** of life or behavior is a particular way of living or behaving. estilo de vida, modo de vida [FORMAL] ❑ *He decided to completely change his mode of life.* *Decidió cambiar por completo su estilo de vida.* **2** N-COUNT A **mode** is a particular style in art, literature, or dress. estilo, modo ❑ *...a formal mode of dress.* *...un estilo de vestir formal.* **3** N-COUNT In statistics, the **mode** of a set of numbers is the number that occurs most often. modo [TECHNICAL] **4** N-COUNT In music, a **mode** is a scale with a particular arrangement of intervals. modo [TECHNICAL]

**mod|el** /mɒdᵊl/ (**models, modeling, modelling, modeled, modelled**) **1** N-COUNT A **model** of an object is a physical representation that shows what it looks like or how it works. The model is often smaller than the object it represents. modelo, maqueta ❑ *...a model of a house.* *...una maqueta de una casa.* ❑ *I made a model out of paper and glue.* *Hice un modelo con papel y pegamento.* ● **Model** is also an adjective. a escala, en miniatura ❑ *...model trains.* *...trenes a escala/en miniatura.* **2** N-COUNT A **model** is a system that is being used and that people might want to copy in order to achieve similar results. modelo [FORMAL] ❑ *...the old-fashioned model of teaching.* *...el antiguo modelo de enseñanza.* **3** N-COUNT If you say that someone or something is **a model of** a particular quality, you approve of them because they have that quality to a large degree. modelo ❑ *He is a model of good manners.* *Es un modelo de la buena educación.* **4** ADJ You use **model** to express approval of someone when you think that they perform their role or duties extremely well. modelo ❑ *She was a model student.* *Era una estudiante modelo.* **5** V-T If one thing **is modeled on** another, the first thing is made so that it is like the second thing in some way. inspirar ❑ *The system was modeled on the one used in Europe.* *El sistema se inspiró en el que se aplica en Europa.* **6** N-COUNT A particular **model** of a machine is a particular version of it. modelo ❑ *You don't need an expensive computer, just a basic model.* *No necesitas una computadora cara, sólo un modelo básico.* **7** N-COUNT An artist's **model** is a person who is drawn, painted or sculpted by them. modelo ❑ *The model for his painting was his sister.* *La modelo de su pintura fue su hermana.* **8** N-COUNT A fashion **model** is a person whose job is to display clothes by wearing them. modelo ❑ *...Paris's top fashion model.* *...supermodelo de la moda en París.* **9** V-T/V-I If someone **models** clothes, they display them by wearing them. modelar ❑ *She began modeling at age 15.* *Comenzó a modelar a los 15 años.* ● **mod|el|ing** N-UNCOUNT modelaje ❑ *Modeling is not an easy job.* *El modelaje no es un trabajo fácil.* **10** → see also **role model**
→ see **forecast**

**Word Partnership** Usar *model* con:

V. **build a** model, **make a** model **1**
**base** *something* **on a** model, **follow a** model, **serve as a** model **1** – **3**
N. **business** model **2**
ADJ. **basic** model, **current** model, **latest** model, **new** model, **standard** model **6**

**mod|er|ate** (**moderates, moderating, moderated**)

The adjective and noun are pronounced /mɒdərɪt/. The verb is pronounced /mɒdəreɪt/.

**1** ADJ **Moderate** political opinions or policies are not extreme. moderado ❑ *He has very moderate views.* *Tiene opiniones muy moderadas.* **2** ADJ You use **moderate** to describe people or groups who have moderate political opinions or policies. moderado ❑ *...a moderate Democrat.* *...un demócrata moderado.* • A **moderate** is someone with moderate political opinions. moderado o moderada ❑ *He needs the moderates on his side.* *Necesita a los moderados de su lado.* **3** ADJ You use **moderate** to describe something that is neither large nor small in amount or degree. mediano, moderado ❑ *A moderate amount of stress can be good for you.* *Un poco de estrés te puede ser benéfico.* • **mod|er|ate|ly** ADV moderadamente, medianamente ❑ *...a moderately large animal.* *...un animal medianamente grande.* **4** V-T/V-I If you **moderate** something or if it **moderates,** it becomes less extreme or violent and easier to deal with or accept. moderar ❑ *Will he ever moderate his views?* *¿Alguna vez moderará sus opiniones?* • **mod|era|tion** /mɒdəreɪʃən/ N-UNCOUNT moderación ❑ *...a moderation in food prices.* *...una moderación en los precios de los alimentos.*

**Word Partnership** Usar *moderate* con:

N. moderate **approach**, moderate **position**, moderate **view** **1**
moderate **amount**, moderate **exercise**, moderate **growth**, moderate **heat**, moderate **improvement**, moderate **prices**, moderate **speed** **3**

**Word Link** *mod ≈ measure, manner : mode, model, modern*

M

**mod|ern** /mɒdərn/ **1** ADJ **Modern** means relating to the present time, for example the present decade or present century. moderno ❑ *...the problems in modern society.* *...los problemas de la sociedad moderna.* **2** ADJ Something that is **modern** is new and involves the latest ideas or equipment. moderno ❑ *It was a very modern school for its time.* *Era una escuela muy moderna para su época.*

**Thesaurus** *modern* Ver también:

ADJ. contemporary, current, present **1**
state-of-the-art, up-to-date **2**

**Word Partnership** Usar *modern* con:

N. modern **civilization**, modern **culture**, modern **era**, modern **life**, modern **science**, modern **society**, modern **times**, modern **warfare** **1**
modern **conveniences**, modern **equipment**, modern **methods**, modern **techniques**, modern **technology** **2**

**mod|ern dance** N-UNCOUNT **Modern dance** is a form of dance that developed in the twentieth century and uses movement to express emotion and abstract ideas. danza contempóranea, danza moderna
→ see **dance**

**Word Link** *ize ≈ making : finalize, modernize, publicize*

**mod|ern|ize** /mɒdərnaɪz/ (**modernizes, modernizing, modernized**) V-T To **modernize** something such as a system or a factory means to change it by replacing old equipment or methods with new ones. modernizar ❑ *...to modernize our schools.* *...modernizar nuestras escuelas.* • **mod|erni|za|tion** /mɒdərnɪzeɪʃən/ N-UNCOUNT modernización ❑ *...a five-year modernization program.* *...un programa de modernización de 5 años.*

**mod|est** /mɒdɪst/ **1** ADJ A **modest** house or other building is not large or expensive. modesto ❑ *They spent the night at a modest hotel.* *Pasaron la noche en un modesto hotel.* **2** ADJ You use **modest** to describe something such as an amount, rate, or improvement which is fairly small. moderado ❑ *Unemployment rose to the still modest rate of 0.7%.* *La tasa de desempleo fue de un todavía moderado 0.7%.* • **mod|est|ly** ADV moderadamente ❑ *The results improved modestly.* *Los resultados mejoraron moderadamente.* **3** ADJ If you say that someone is **modest,** you approve of them because they do not talk much about their abilities or achievements. modesto ❑ *He's modest, as well as being a great player.* *Es tan modesto como buen jugador/intérprete.* • **mod|est|ly** ADV modestamente ❑ *"You really must be very good at what you do." — "I suppose I am," Kate said modestly.* *—Debes ser realmente muy buena en lo que haces. —Supongo que sí —dijo Kate con modestia.*

**mod|es|ty** /mɒdɪsti/ N-UNCOUNT Someone who shows **modesty** does not talk much about their abilities or achievements. modestia ❑ *He speaks about his achievements with modesty.* *Habla de sus logros con modestia.*

**modi|fi|er** /mɒdɪfaɪər/ (**modifiers**) N-COUNT A **modifier** is a word or group of words that modifies another word or group. In some descriptions of grammar, only words that are used before a noun are called **modifiers.** modificador

**modi|fy** /mɒdɪfaɪ/ (**modifies, modifying, modified**) V-T If you **modify** something, you change it slightly, usually in order to improve it. modificar ❑ *We all modify our behavior in different situations.* *Todos modificamos nuestro comportamiento en distintas situaciones.* • **modi|fi|ca|tion** /mɒdɪfɪkeɪʃən/ N-VAR (**modifications**) modificación ❑ *A few small modifications were needed.* *Unas cuantas pequeñas modificaciones fueron necesarias.*

**Moho** /moʊhoʊ/ also **Mohorovicic Discontinuity** N-SING **The Moho** is the boundary between the Earth's crust and its mantle. Discontinuidad de Mohorovicic [TECHNICAL]

**moist** /mɔɪst/ (**moister, moistest**) ADJ Something that is **moist** is slightly wet. húmedo ❑ *The soil is moist after the September rain.* *La tierra está húmeda tras las lluvias de Septiembre.*

**mois|ture** /mɔɪstʃər/ N-UNCOUNT **Moisture** is tiny drops of water in the air, on a surface, or in the ground. humedad ❑ *When the soil is dry, more moisture is lost from the plant.* *Cuando la tierra está seca, la planta pierde más humedad.*

**mold** /moʊld/ (**molds, molding, molded**) **1** N-COUNT A **mold** is a hollow container that you pour liquid into. When the liquid becomes solid, it takes the same shape as the mold. molde ❑ *...a plastic jelly mold.* *...un molde de plástico para gelatina.* **2** V-T If you **mold** a soft substance such as plastic or clay, you make it into a particular shape or into an object. moldear, modelar ❑ *He began to mold the clay into a different shape.* *Comenzó a modelar una figura diferente con la arcilla/la plastilina.* **3** V-T To

**mold** someone or something means to change or influence them over a period of time so that they develop in a particular way. *moldear* ❑ *My mother molded my ideas a lot. Mi madre moldeó mucho mis ideas.* **4** N-UNCOUNT **Mold** is a soft gray, green, or blue substance that sometimes forms in spots on old food or on damp walls or clothes. *moho* ❑ *She discovered black and green mold growing in her closet. Descubrió que se estaba formando un moho negro y verde en su ropero.*
→ see **fungus, laboratory**

**mol|ecule** /mɒlɪkyul/ (**molecules**) N-COUNT A **molecule** is the smallest amount of a chemical substance which can exist by itself. *molécula* ❑ *...water molecules. ...moléculas de agua.*
→ see **element**

**mo|lest** /məlɛst/ (**molests, molesting, molested**) V-T A person who **molests** someone touches them in a sexual way against their will. *abusar sexualmente (de alguien)*

**mol|ten** /moʊltᵊn/ ADJ **Molten** rock, metal, or glass has been heated to a very high temperature and has become a hot, thick liquid. *fundido* ❑ *The molten metal is extremely hot. El metal fundido es extremadamente caliente.*
→ see **volcano**

**molt|ing** /moʊltɪŋ/ N-UNCOUNT **Molting** is a process in which an animal or bird gradually loses its coat or feathers so that a new coat or feathers can grow. *muda (piel, pelo, plumaje)*

**mom** /mɒm/ (**moms**) N-COUNT; N-VOC Your **mom** is your mother. *ma, mamá* [INFORMAL] ❑ *We waited for Mom and Dad to get home. Esperamos a que llegaran a casa mamá y papá.*

**mo|ment** /moʊmənt/ (**moments**) **1** N-COUNT You can refer to a very short period of time, for example a few seconds, as a **moment** or **moments**. *instante, momento* ❑ *In a moment he was gone. En un instante se había ido.* ❑ *In moments, I was asleep again. En unos momentos, estaba dormido otra vez.* **2** N-COUNT A particular **moment** is the point in time at which something happens. *momento* ❑ *At that moment a car stopped at the house. En ese momento, un carro se detuvo en la casa.* **3** PHRASE You use expressions such as **at the moment, at this moment,** and **at the present moment** to indicate that a particular situation exists at the time when you are speaking. *en este momento, por el momento* ❑ *At the moment, no one is talking to me. Por el momento, nadie me habla.* ❑ *He's in South America at this moment in time. Está en sudamérica en este momento.* **4** PHRASE You use **for the moment** to indicate that something is true now, even if it will not be true in the future. *hasta este momento, por el momento* ❑ *For the moment, everything is fine. Hasta este momento, todo esta bien.* **5** PHRASE If you say that something happens **the moment** something else happens, you are emphasizing that it happens immediately after the other thing. *en cuanto, en el momento* ❑ *The moment I closed my eyes, I fell asleep. En cuanto cerré los ojos, me quedé dormido.* **6** **spur of the moment** → see **spur**

**Word Partnership** Usar *moment* con:

| | |
|---|---|
| ADV. | a moment **ago, just a** moment **1** |
| N. | moment **of silence,** moment **of thought** **1** |
| V. | **stop for a** moment, **take a** moment, **think for a** moment, **wait a** moment **1** |
| ADJ. | **an awkward** moment, **a critical** moment, **the right** moment **2** |

**mo|men|tum** /moʊmɛntəm/ **1** N-UNCOUNT If a process or movement gains **momentum,** it keeps developing or happening more quickly and keeps becoming less likely to stop. *impulso* ❑ *This campaign is really gaining momentum. Esta campaña realmente está cobrando impulso.* **2** N-UNCOUNT In physics, **momentum** is the mass of a moving object multiplied by its speed in a particular direction. *momento, momentum* [TECHNICAL]
→ see **motion**

**Word Partnership** Usar *momentum* con:

| | |
|---|---|
| V. | **build** momentum, **gain** momentum, **gather** momentum, **have** momentum, **lose** momentum, **maintain** momentum **1** **2** |

**mom|ma** /mɒmə/ (**mommas**) N-COUNT; N-VOC **Momma** means the same as **mommy**. *mamá* [INFORMAL]

**mom|my** /mɒmi/ (**mommies**) N-COUNT; N-VOC Some people, especially young children, call their mother **mommy**. *mami* [INFORMAL] ❑ *Mommy and I went in an airplane. Mi mami y yo fuimos en avión.*

**mon|arch** /mɒnərk, -ɑrk/ (**monarchs**) N-COUNT The **monarch** of a country is the king, queen, emperor, or empress. *monarca*

**mon|ar|chy** /mɒnərki/ (**monarchies**) N-VAR A **monarchy** is a system in which a country has a monarch. *monarquía* ❑ *...a discussion about the future of the monarchy. ...una discusión sobre el futuro de la monarquía.*

**mon|as|tery** /mɒnəstɛri/ (**monasteries**) N-COUNT A **monastery** is a building in which monks live. *monasterio*

**Mon|day** /mʌndeɪ, -di/ (**Mondays**) N-VAR **Monday** is the day after Sunday and before Tuesday. *lunes* ❑ *I went back to work on Monday. Regresé al trabajo el Lunes.* ❑ *The first meeting was last Monday. La primera junta fue el lunes pasado.*

**mon|etary** /mɑnɪtɛri/ ADJ **Monetary** means relating to money, especially the total amount of money in a country. *monetario* [BUSINESS] ❑ *The U.S. monetary system is a decimal system, with 100 cents in one dollar. El sistema monetario de EE.UU. es decimal: un dólar es igual a 100 centavos/céntimos.*

**mon|ey** /mʌni/ **1** N-UNCOUNT **Money** is the coins or banknotes that you use to buy things, or the sum that you have in an account. *dinero* ❑ *Cars cost a lot of money. Los autos cuestan mucho dinero.* ❑ *A lot of football players earn money from advertising. Muchos jugadores de fútbol ganan dinero de la publicidad* ❑ *Companies have to make money. Las compañías tienen que hacer dinero.* **2** PHRASE If you **get** your **money's worth,** you get something which is worth the money that it costs or the effort you have put in.

m

**Word Web** money

Early traders used a system of **barter** which didn't involve **money**. For example, a farmer might trade a cow for a wooden cart. In China, India, and Africa, cowrie shells* became a form of **currency**. The first **coins** were crude lumps of metal. Uniform circular coins appeared in China around 1500 BC. In 1150 AD, the Chinese started using paper bills. In 560 BC, the Lydians (living in what is now Turkey) **minted** three types of coins—a **gold** coin, a **silver** coin, and a mixed metal coin. Their use quickly spread through Asia Minor and Greece.

*cowrie shell: a small, shiny, oval shell.*

*sacarle jugo al dinero, verse recompensado* ❑ *The team's fans get their money's worth. Los fanáticos del equipo se ven recompensados por lo que pagan.*
→ see Word Web: **money**
→ see **donor**

**Thesaurus** *money* Ver también:
N. capital, cash, currency, funds, wealth 1

**mon|ey or|der** (**money orders**) N-COUNT A **money order** is a piece of paper representing a sum of money which you can buy at a post office and send to someone as a way of sending them money by mail. *giro postal*

M

**moni|tor** /mɒnɪtər/ (**monitors, monitoring, monitored**) 1 V-T If you **monitor** something, you regularly check its development or progress. *observar, seguir de cerca* ❑ *Officials monitored the voting. Los funcionarios siguieron de cerca la votación.* 2 N-COUNT A **monitor** is a machine that is used to check or record things. *monitor* ❑ *The monitor shows his heartbeat. El monitor muestra su ritmo cardíaco.* 3 N-COUNT A **monitor** is a screen which is used to display certain kinds of information. *monitor* ❑ *He was watching a game of tennis on a television monitor. Estaba viendo un juego de tenis en un monitor de televisión.*
→ see **computer**

**Word Partnership** Usar *monitor* con:
ADV. **carefully** monitor, **closely** monitor 1
N. monitor **activity**, monitor **elections**, monitor **performance**, monitor **progress**, monitor **a situation** 1
**color** monitor, **computer** monitor, **video** monitor 3

**monk** /mʌŋk/ (**monks**) N-COUNT A **monk** is a member of a male religious community. *monje* ❑ *...Buddhist monks. ...monjes budistas.*

**mon|key** /mʌŋki/ (**monkeys**) N-COUNT A **monkey** is an animal with a long tail which lives in hot countries and climbs trees. *chango, mono*
→ see **primate**

**mon|key bars** N-PLURAL **Monkey bars** are metal or wooden bars that are joined together to form a structure for children to climb and play on. *estructura de barras para juegos infantiles*

**mono** /mɒnoʊ/ N-UNCOUNT **Mono** is the same as **mononucleosis**. *mononucleosis, enfermedad del beso, fiebre glandular* [INFORMAL]

**mono|chro|mat|ic** /mɒnəkrəmætɪk/ ADJ **Monochromatic** pictures use only one color in various shades. *monocromático*

**mono|cline** /mɒnəklaɪn/ (**monoclines**) N-COUNT A **monocline** is a rock formation in which layers of rock are folded so that they are horizontal on both sides of the fold. *pliegue monoclinal* [TECHNICAL]

**mono|lith|ic** /mɒnᵊlɪθɪk/ ADJ If you refer to an organization or system as **monolithic**, you are critical of it because it is very large and very slow to change. *monolítico* ❑ *...a monolithic system. ...un sistema monolítico.*

**Word Link** *mono ≈ one : monologue, monopoly, monotonous*

**mono|logue** /mɒnᵊlɔg/ (**monologues**) also **monolog** 1 N-COUNT If you refer to a long speech by one person during a conversation as a **monologue**, you mean it prevents other people from talking or expressing their opinions. *monólogo* ❑ *Morris continued his monologue. Morris continuó con su monólogo* 2 N-VAR A **monologue** is a long speech which is spoken by one person as an entertainment, or as part of an entertainment such as a play. *monólogo*

**mo|no|mial** /mɒnoʊmiəl/ (**monomials**) N-COUNT A **monomial** is an expression in algebra that consists of just one term, for example "5xy." Compare **binomial, polynomial**. *monomio* [TECHNICAL] • **monomial** is also an adjective *de un solo término, de un monomio* ❑ *...monomial expressions. ...expresiones de un monomio.*

**mono|nu|cleo|sis** /mɒnoʊnuklioʊsɪs/ N-UNCOUNT **Mononucleosis** is a disease which causes swollen glands, fever, and a sore throat. *mononucleosis, fiebre glandular, enfermedad del beso*

**mo|nopo|lize** /mənɒpəlaɪz/ (**monopolizes, monopolizing, monopolized**) V-T If someone **monopolizes** something, they have a very large share of it and prevent other people from having a share. *monopolizar* ❑ *One company is monopolizing the* market. Una compañía está monopolizando el mercado.

**Word Link** *mono ≈ one : monologue, monopoly, monotonous*

**mo|nopo|ly** /mənɒpəli/ (**monopolies**) 1 N-VAR If a company, person, or state has a **monopoly on** something such as an industry, they have complete control over it. monopolio [BUSINESS] ❑ *The company has a monopoly on trade with India.* *La compañía tiene el monopolio de comercio con la India.* 2 N-COUNT A **monopoly** is a company which is the only one providing a particular product or service. monopolio [BUSINESS] ❑ *The two companies joined together, creating a monopoly.* *Las dos compañías se unieron, creando un monopolio.*

**mono|theism** /mɒnəθiɪzəm/ N-UNCOUNT **Monotheism** is the belief that there is only one God. *monoteísmo* ❑ *...the monotheism of the Christian religion.* *...el monoteísmo de la religión Cristiana.*

**mono|theis|tic** /mɒnəθiɪstɪk/ ADJ **Monotheistic** religions believe that there is only one God. *monoteístas* ❑ *...all the major monotheistic religions.* *...todas las religiones monoteístas más importantes.*

**mo|noto|nous** /mənɒtᵊnəs/ ADJ Something that is **monotonous** is very boring because it has a regular, repeated pattern which never changes. *monótono* ❑ *It's monotonous work, like most factory jobs.* *Es un trabajo monótono, como la mayoría de los trabajos en las fábricas.*

**mono|treme** /mɒnətrim/ (**monotremes**) N-COUNT A **monotreme** is a mammal that gives birth by laying eggs. *monotrema* [TECHNICAL]

**mon|soon** /mɒnsun/ (**monsoons**) N-COUNT The **monsoon** is the season in southern Asia when there is a lot of very heavy rain. *monzón* ❑ *...the end of the monsoon.* *...el fin del monzón*
→ see **disaster**

**mon|ster** /mɒnstər/ (**monsters**) 1 N-COUNT A **monster** is a large imaginary creature that looks very ugly and frightening. *monstruo* ❑ *The movie is about a monster in the bedroom closet.* *La película es acerca de un monstruo en el clóset del dormitorio.* 2 ADJ **Monster** means extremely and surprisingly large. *gigante* [INFORMAL] ❑ *...a monster weapon.* *...un arma gigante.*

**month** /mʌnθ/ (**months**) N-COUNT A **month** is one of the twelve periods of time that a year is divided into, for example January or February. *mes* ❑ *The trial will begin next month.* *El juicio comenzará el próximo mes.*
→ see **year**

**month|ly** /mʌnθli/ ADJ A **monthly** event or publication happens or appears every month. *mensual* ❑ *Many people are now having trouble making their monthly payments.* *Ahora mucha gente está teniendo problemas para realizar sus pagos mensuales.* • **Monthly** is also an adverb. *mensualmente* ❑ *The magazine is published monthly.* *La revista se publica mensualmente.*

**monu|ment** /mɒnyəmənt/ (**monuments**) N-COUNT A **monument** is a large structure, usually made of stone, which is built to remind people of an event in history or of a famous person. *monumento* ❑ *This monument was built in memory of the 90,000 Indian soldiers who died in World War I.* *Este monumento fue construido en memoria de los 90,000 soldados indios quienes murieron en la primera guerra mundial.*

**monu|men|tal** /mɒnyəmɛntᵊl/ ADJ You can use **monumental** to emphasize the large size or extent of something. *monumental* ❑ *It was a monumental mistake to give him the job.* *Fue un error monumental haberle dado el trabajo.* ❑ *...his monumental work on AIDS.* *...su trabajo monumental sobre el SIDA.*

**mood** /mud/ (**moods**) 1 N-COUNT Your **mood** is the way you are feeling at a particular time. *humor* ❑ *He is in a good mood today.* *Hoy está de buen humor.* ❑ *Lily was in one of her aggressive moods.* *Lily estaba de un humor agresivo.* 2 N-COUNT If someone is **in a mood**, the way they are behaving shows that they are feeling angry and impatient. *estar de mal humor* ❑ *She was obviously in a mood.* *Obviamente estaba de mal humor.* 3 N-SING **The mood** of a group of people is the way that they think and feel about an idea, event, or question at a particular time. *humor* ❑ *The mood of the people changed.* *El humor de la gente cambió.*

**Word Partnership** Usar *mood* con:

| | |
|---|---|
| ADJ. | **bad/good** mood, **depressed** mood, **foul** mood, **positive** mood, **tense** mood 1 |
| N. | mood **change**, mood **disorder**, mood **swings** 1 |
| V. | **create a** mood, **set a** mood 3 |

**moody** /mudi/ (**moodier, moodiest**) ADJ A **moody** person often becomes depressed or angry without any warning. *voluble, temperamental* ❑ *David's mother was very moody.* *La madre de David era muy voluble.* • **moodi|ly** /mudɪli/ ADV *de mal humor* ❑ *He sat and stared moodily out the window.* *Se sentó y miró fijamente y de mal humor por la ventana.* • **moodi|ness** N-UNCOUNT *mal humor* ❑ *His poor health probably caused his moodiness.* *Su escasa salud probablemente haya causado su mal humor.*

**moon** /mun/ (**moons**) 1 N-SING **The moon** is the object in the sky that goes around the Earth once every four weeks. You often see it at night as a circle or part of a circle. *luna* ❑ *...the first man on the moon.* *...el primer hombre en la luna.* 2 N-COUNT A **moon** is an object similar to a small planet that travels around a planet. *luna* ❑ *...Neptune's large moon.* *...la gran luna de Neptuno.*
→ see Word Web: **moon**
→ see **astronomer, eclipse, satellite, solar system, tide**

**Word Link** *light ≈ shining : daylight, headlight, moonlight*

**moon|light** /munlaɪt/ (**moonlights, moonlighting, moonlighted**) 1 N-UNCOUNT **Moonlight** is the light that comes from the moon at night. *luz de (la) luna* ❑ *They walked along the road in the moonlight.* *Caminaron a lo largo del camino a la luz de la luna.* 2 V-I If someone **moonlights**, they have a second job in addition to their main job. *tener un segundo empleo* ❑ *He was a builder moonlighting as a taxi driver.* *Era un constructor y tenía un segundo empleo como taxista.*

**moon|shine** /munʃaɪn/ 1 N-UNCOUNT

m

**Word Web** **moon**

Scientists believe the **moon** is about five billion years old. They think a large asteroid hit the earth. A big piece of the earth broke off. It went flying into **space**. However, the earth's **gravity** caught it. It began to circle the earth. This piece became our moon. The moon orbits the earth once a month. It also **rotates** on its **axis** every thirty days. The moon has no **atmosphere**, so meteoroids crash into it. When a meteoroid hits the moon, it makes a **crater**. Craters cover the surface of the moon.

**Moonshine** is whiskey that is made illegally. *aguardiente casero* **2** N-UNCOUNT If you say that someone's thoughts, ideas, or comments are **moonshine**, you think they are foolish and not based on reality. *tontería, sandez, estupidez*

**moor** /mʊər/ (**moors, mooring, moored**) V-T/V-I If you **moor**, or **moor** a boat somewhere, you stop and tie the boat to the land with a rope or chain so that it cannot move away. *atracar, amarrar (un bote, un barco)* ❑ *She had moored her boat on the right bank of the river. Había amarrado su bote en la orilla derecha del río.* ❑ *I decided to moor near some small boats. Decidí atracar cerca de unos botes pequeños.*

**mop** /mɒp/ (**mops, mopping, mopped**) **1** N-COUNT A **mop** is a piece of equipment for washing floors. It consists of a sponge or many pieces of string attached to a long handle. *trapeador* **2** V-T If you **mop** a surface such as a floor, you clean it with a mop. *trapear* ❑ *There was a woman mopping the stairs. Había una mujer trapeando las escaleras.* **3** V-T If you **mop** sweat from your forehead or **mop** your forehead, you wipe it with a piece of cloth. *secarse la frente* ❑ *He mopped sweat from his forehead. Secó el sudor de su frente.*

▸ **mop up** PHR-VERB If you **mop up** a liquid, you clean it with a cloth so that the liquid is absorbed. *limpiar, secar* ❑ *A waiter mopped up the mess as well as he could. Un mesero limpió el desorden tan bien como pudo.* ❑ *If the washing machine leaks water we can mop it up. Si la lavadora tira agua la podemos secar.*

**Word Link** *ped ≈ foot : moped, pedal, pedestrian*

**mo|ped** /moʊpɛd/ (**mopeds**) N-COUNT A **moped** is a small motorcycle which you can also pedal like a bicycle. *bicimoto*

**mo|raine** /məreɪn/ (**moraines**) N-COUNT A **moraine** is a pile of rocks and soil left behind by a glacier. *morena* [TECHNICAL]

**mor|al** /mɔrᵊl/ (**morals**) **1** N-PLURAL **Morals** are principles and beliefs concerning right and wrong behavior. *moralidad, sentido moral* ❑ *...Western ideas and morals. ...la moralidad y las ideas occidentales.* **2** ADJ **Moral** means relating to beliefs about what is right or wrong. *moral* ❑ *She had to make a moral judgment about what was the right thing to do. Tenía que hacer un juicio moral sobre lo que era correcto hacer.* ● **mor|al|ly** ADV *moralmente* ❑ *It is morally wrong to kill a person. ¿Es moralmente incorrecto matar a una persona?* **3** ADJ A **moral** person behaves in a way that is believed by most people to be good and right. *moral* ❑ *The minister was a very moral man. El ministro era un hombre muy moral.* ● **mor|al|ly** ADV *moralmente* ❑ *Art is not there to improve you morally. El arte no está ahí para mejorarte moralmente.* **4** ADJ If you give someone **moral** support, you encourage them in what they are doing by expressing approval. *apoyo moral* ❑ *I'm just there to give her moral support. Sólo estoy ahí para darle apoyo moral.* **5** N-COUNT **The moral** of a story or event is what you learn from it about how you should or should not behave. *moraleja* ❑ *The moral of the story is do not trust anyone. La moraleja de la historia es que no confíes en nadie.*
→ see **philosophy**

**mo|rale** /məræl/ N-UNCOUNT **Morale** is the amount of confidence and cheerfulness that a group of people have. *ánimo* ❑ *Many teachers are suffering from low morale. El ánimo de muchos maestros es muy bajo.*

**mor|al fi|ber** N-UNCOUNT **Moral fiber** is the quality of being determined to do what you think is right. *carácter* ❑ *He was a man of strong moral fiber. Era un hombre de un gran carácter.*

**mo|ral|ity** /mərælɪti/ **1** N-UNCOUNT **Morality** is the belief that some behavior is right and acceptable and that other behavior is wrong. *moralidad* ❑ *...standards of morality in society. ...los normas morales de la sociedad.* **2** N-UNCOUNT **The morality of** something is how right or acceptable it is. *moralidad* ❑ *...arguments about the morality of nuclear weapons. ...argumentos sobre la ética del empleo de las armas nucleares.*

**more** /mɔr/

**More** is often considered to be the comparative form of **much** and **many**.

**1** DET You use **more** to indicate that there is a greater amount of something than before or than average, or than something else. You can use "a little," "a lot," "a bit," "far," and "much" in front of **more**. *más* ❑ *More and more people are surviving heart attacks. Más y más personas sobreviven a un ataque cardiaco.* ❑ *He spent more time going out with his friends. Pasaba más tiempo saliendo con sus amigos.* ● **More** is also a pronoun. *más* ❑ *As the workers worked harder, they ate more. Mientras más trabajaban, los obreros comían más.* ● **More** is also a quantifier. *más* ❑ *They're doing more of their own work. Están haciendo más de su propio trabajo.* **2** PHRASE You use **more than** before a number or amount to say that the actual number or amount is even greater. *más que, más de* ❑ *The airport had been closed for more than a year. El aeropuero había estado cerrado por más de un año.* **3** ADV You can use **more** or **some more** to indicate that something continues to happen for a further period of time. *más* ❑ *You should talk* about your problems a bit more. *Deberías hablar de tus problemas un poco más.* **4** ADV You use **more** to indicate that something is repeated. *más* ❑ *This train will stop twice more before we arrive in Baltimore. Este tren parará dos veces más antes de que lleguemos a Baltimore.* **5** DET You use **more** to refer to an additional thing or amount. *más* ❑ *They needed more time to think about what to do. Necesitaban más tiempo para pensar qué hacer.* ● **More** is also an adjective. *más* ❑ *We stayed in Danville two more days. Nos quedamos en Danville dos días más.* ● **More** is also a pronoun. *más* ❑ *We should be doing more to help people with AIDS. Deberíamos hacer más para ayudar a la gente con SIDA.* **6** PHRASE You can use **more and more** to indicate that something is becoming greater in amount, extent, or degree all the time. *más y más, cada vez más* ❑ *She began eating more and more. Empezó a comer más y más.* **7** PHRASE You use **more than** to say that something is true to a greater degree than is necessary or than average. *más que* ❑ *The company has more than enough money to pay what it owes. La compañía tiene más que suficiente dinero para pagar lo que debe.* **8** PHRASE You can use **what is more** or **what's more** to introduce an extra piece of information which supports or emphasizes the point you are making. *lo que es más* ❑ *I am able to help you, and what is more, I want to. Soy capaz de ayudarte y, lo que es más, quiero hacerlo.* **9** **all the more** → see **all** **10** **any more** → see **any**

**more|over** /mɔroʊvər/ ADV You use **moreover** to introduce a piece of information that adds to or supports the previous statement. *además* [FORMAL] ❑ *She saw that there was a man behind her. Moreover, he was looking at her. Vio que había un hombre detrás de ella y, además, que estaba mirándola.*

**morn|ing** /mɔrnɪŋ/ (**mornings**) **1** N-VAR The **morning** is the part of each day between the time that people usually wake up and 12 o'clock noon or lunchtime. *mañana* ❑ *Tomorrow morning your guide will take you around the city. Mañana por la mañana su guía los llevará por la ciudad.* ❑ *On Sunday morning the telephone woke Bill. El domingo por la mañana, el teléfono despertó a Bill.* **2** N-SING If you refer to a particular time in **the morning**, you mean a time between 12 o'clock midnight and 12 o'clock noon. *mañana* ❑ *I often stayed up until two or three in the morning. A menudo me acostaba hasta las dos o tres de la mañana.* **3** PHRASE If you say that something will happen **in the morning**, you mean that it will happen during the morning of the following day. *en la mañana* ❑ *I'll fly to St. Louis in the morning. Volaré a San Luis en la mañana.*
→ see **time**

| **Thesaurus** | *morning* | Ver también: |
|---|---|---|
| N. | dawn, light, sunrise **1** | |

**mor|tal** /mɔrtᵊl/ (**mortals**) **1** ADJ If you refer to the fact that people are **mortal**, you mean that they have to die and cannot live forever. *mortal* ❑ *A man is mortal. He grows, he becomes old, and he dies. Un hombre es mortal. Crece, envejece y muere.* ● **mor|tal|ity** /mɔrtælɪti/ N-UNCOUNT *mortalidad* ❑ *...fears about our own mortality. ...miedo de nuestra propia mortalidad.* **2** N-COUNT You can describe someone as a **mortal** when you want to say that they are an ordinary person. *mortal* ❑ *We are all mere mortals and we make mistakes. No somos sino simples mortales y cometemos errores.* **3** ADJ You can use **mortal** to show that something is very serious or may cause death. *mortal* ❑ *The police were defending people against mortal danger. La policía defendía a la gente del peligro mortal.* ● **mor|tal|ly** ADV *mortalmente* ❑ *He falls, mortally wounded. Cae, mortalmente herido.*

**mor|tar** /mɔrtər/ (**mortars**) **1** N-COUNT A **mortar** is a big gun that fires missiles high into the air over a short distance. *mortero* ❑ *Mortars were still exploding. Los morteros estaban explotando aún.* **2** N-UNCOUNT **Mortar** is a mixture of sand, water, and cement or lime which is put between bricks to hold them together. *mortero, cemento* ❑ *Bricks and mortar are basic building materials. Los ladrillos y el mortero son materiales básicos de la construcción.*

**mor|tar|board** (**mortarboards**) N-COUNT A **mortarboard** is a stiff, black cap which has a flat, square top with a bunch of threads attached to it. In the United States, mortarboards are worn by students at graduation ceremonies at high schools, colleges, and universities. *birrete*
→ see **hat**

**mort|gage** /mɔrgɪdʒ/ (**mortgages, mortgaging, mortgaged**) **1** N-COUNT A **mortgage** is a loan of money which you get from a bank or savings and loan association in order to buy a house. *hipoteca* ❑ *We go to work each day to pay the mortgage. Vamos a trabajar todos los días para poder pagar la hipoteca.* **2** V-T If you **mortgage** your house or land, you use it as a guarantee to a company in order to borrow money from them. *hipotecar* ❑ *They had to mortgage their home to pay the bills. Tuvieron que hipotecar su casa para pagar las deudas.*

**mo|sa|ic** /moʊzeɪɪk/ (**mosaics**) N-VAR A **mosaic** is a design which consists of small pieces of colored glass, pottery, or stone set in concrete or plaster. *mosaico* ❑ *The Roman house has a beautiful mosaic floor. La casa romana tiene un precioso piso de mosaico.*

**mosque** /mɒsk/ (**mosques**) N-COUNT A **mosque** is a building where Muslims go to worship. *mezquita*

**mos|qui|to** /məskitoʊ/ (**mosquitoes** or **mosquitos**) N-COUNT **Mosquitos** are small flying insects which bite people and animals in order to suck their blood. *mosquito*
→ see **insect**

**moss** /mɒs/ (**mosses**) N-VAR **Moss** is a very small, soft, green plant which grows on damp soil, or on wood or stone. *musgo* ❑ *...ground covered with moss. ...suelo cubierto de musgo.*

**most** /moʊst/

| **Most** is often considered to be the superlative form of **much** and **many**. |
|---|

**1** QUANT You use **most** to refer to the majority of a group of things or people, or the largest part of something. *casi todos, la mayoría, la mayor parte* ❑ *Most of the houses here are very old. Casi todas las casas en este lugar son muy viejas.* ❑ *I was away from home most of the time. Estaba fuera de casa la mayor parte del tiempo.* ● **Most** is also a determiner. *casi todos* ❑ *Most people think he is younger than he is. Casi todos piensan que es más joven de lo que en verdad es.* ● **Most** is also a pronoun. *la mayoría* ❑ *Seventeen*

m

people were hurt. *Most are students.* *Diecisiete personas salieron lastimadas. La mayoría son estudiantes.* **2** ADJ You use **the most** to mean a larger amount than anyone or anything else, or the largest amount possible. *la mayor* ❑ *The president won the most votes.* *El presidente ganó la mayor cantidad de votos.* • **Most** is also a pronoun. *lo más* ❑ *The most they earn in a day is fifty dollars.* *Lo más que ganan al día son cincuenta dólares.* **3** ADV You use **most** to indicate that something is true or happens to a greater degree or extent than anything else. *más* ❑ *What she feared most was becoming like her mother.* *Lo que más la asustaba era parecerse a su madre.* ❑ *...Professor Morris, the teacher he most disliked.* *...el maestro Morris, aquél al que más detestaba.* PHRASE • You use **most of all** to indicate that something happens or is true to a greater extent than anything else. *sobre todo* **4** ADV You use **most** to indicate that someone or something has a greater amount of a particular quality than most other things of its kind. *más* ❑ *Her children had the most unusual birthday parties in the neighborhood.* *Sus hijos tenían las fiestas de cumpleaños más raras del vecindario.* ❑ *He was one of the most kind men I have ever met.* *Era uno de los hombres más amables que he conocido.* **5** ADV If you do something **the most,** you do it to the greatest extent possible or with the greatest frequency. *más* ❑ *What question are you asked the most?* *¿Cuál es la pregunta que más le hacen?* **6** PHRASE You use **at most** or **at the most** to say that a number or amount is the maximum that is possible and that the actual number or amount may be smaller. *máximo, como más* ❑ *Heat the sauce for ten minutes at most.* *Caliente la salsa por diez minutos máximo.* **7** PHRASE If you **make the most of** something, you get the maximum use or advantage from it. *sacar el mayor provecho* ❑ *Happiness is the ability to make the most of what you have.* *La felicidad es la capacidad de sacar el mayor provecho de lo que se tiene.* **8** → see also **almost**

| Word Link | *most ≈ superlative degree : almost, mostly, utmost* |
|---|---|

**most|ly** /moʊstli/ ADV You use **mostly** to indicate that a statement is generally true, for example true about the majority of a group of things or people, true most of the time, or true in most respects. *principalmente, en su mayor parte* ❑ *My friends are mostly students.* *Mis amigos son principalmente estudiantes.* ❑ *Cars are mostly metal.* *Los coches son, en su mayor parte, de metal.*

**mo|tel** /moʊtɛl/ (**motels**) N-COUNT A **motel** is a hotel intended for people who are traveling by car. *motel*

**moth** /mɔθ/ (**moths**) N-COUNT A **moth** is an insect like a butterfly which usually flies around at night. *polilla*

**moth|er** /mʌðər/ (**mothers, mothering, mothered**) **1** N-COUNT Your **mother** is your female parent. *madre* ❑ *She's a mother of two children.* *Es madre de dos niños.* **2** V-T If you **mother** someone, you treat them with great care and affection, as if they were a small child. *proteger* ❑ *Stop mothering me.* *Deja de protegerme.*
→ see **family**

**moth|er coun|try** (**mother countries**) N-COUNT Someone's **mother country** is the country in which they or their ancestors were born and to which they still feel emotionally linked, even if they live somewhere else. *madre patria* ❑ *He thinks of Turkey as his mother country.* *Recuerda a Turquía como su madre patria.*

**mother-in-law** (**mothers-in-law**) N-COUNT Someone's **mother-in-law** is the mother of their husband or wife. *suegra*
→ see **family**

| Word Link | *mot ≈ moving : motion, motivate, promote* |
|---|---|

**mo|tion** /moʊʃ$^{\text{ə}}$n/ (**motions, motioning, motioned**) **1** N-UNCOUNT **Motion** is the activity or process of continually changing position or moving from one place to another. *movimiento* ❑ *...Newton's three laws of motion.* *...las tres leyes del movimiento de Newton.* ❑ *The doors will not open when the elevator is in motion.* **2** N-COUNT A **motion** is an action, gesture, or movement. *ademán, gesto* ❑ *He made a motion toward the door with his hand.* *Hizo un gesto con la mano en dirección a la puerta.* **3** N-COUNT A **motion** is a formal proposal or statement in a meeting, debate, or trial, which is discussed and then voted on or decided on. *moción* ❑ *The committee debated the motion all day.* *El comité debatió la moción todo el día.* **4** V-T/V-I If you **motion** to someone, you move your hand or head as a way of telling them to do something or telling them where to go. *indicar con un gesto, indicar con la mano* ❑ *She motioned for my father to come in.* *Le indicó con un gesto a su padre que entrara.* ❑ *He motioned Don to the door.* *Le indicó la puerta a Don con un gesto.* **5** → see also **slow motion** **6** PHRASE If you say that someone **is going through the motions,** you think they are only saying or doing something because it is expected of them without being interested, enthusiastic, or sympathetic. *hacer algo sin interés, hacer algo por pura fórmula* ❑ *"You really don't care, do you?" she said quietly. "You're just going through the motions."* *—Realmente no te importa, ¿verdad?—dijo quedamente—, lo haces por pura fórmula.* **7** PHRASE If a process or event is set **in motion,** it is happening or beginning to happen. *en movimiento, en marcha* ❑ *Big changes can be set in motion by small things.* *Las pequeñas cosas pueden poner en marcha los grandes cambios.* **8** PHRASE If someone **sets the wheels in motion,** they take the necessary action to make something start happening. *poner en marcha, echar a andar* ❑ *They have set the wheels in motion to sell their Arizona home.* *Ya echaron a andar las cosas para vender su casa de Arizona.*
→ see Word Web: **motion**

**Word Partnership** Usar *motion* con:

ADJ. **constant** motion, **full** motion, **perpetual** motion **1**
**circular** motion, **smooth** motion **1 2**
**quick** motion **2**
V. **set** *something* **in** motion **1 7 8**

**mo|tion pic|ture** (**motion pictures**) N-COUNT A **motion picture** is a movie made for movie theaters. *película, cine* [FORMAL] ❑ *...the motion picture industry.* *...la industria cinematográfica.*

**Word Web** motion

Newton's three laws of **motion** describe how **forces** affect the movement of objects. This is the first law: an object at **rest** won't move unless a force makes it move. Also, a moving object keeps its **momentum** unless something stops it. The second law is about **acceleration**. The **rate** of acceleration depends on two things: how strong the push on the object is, and how much the object weighs. The third law says that for every **action** there is an equal and opposite **reaction**. When one object **exerts** a force on another, the second object pushes back with an equal force.

**Word Link** *ate ≈ causing to be : complicate, humiliate, motivate*

**Word Link** *mot ≈ moving : motion, motivate, promote*

**mo|ti|vate** /moʊtɪveɪt/ (**motivates, motivating, motivated**) **1** V-T If you **are motivated** by something, especially an emotion, it causes you to behave in a particular way. *motivar* ❑ *They are motivated by greed. Están motivados por la avaricia.* ● **mo|ti|vat|ed** ADJ *motivado* ❑ *...highly motivated employees. ...empleados altamente motivados.* ● **mo|ti|va|tion** /moʊtɪveɪʃᵊn/ N-UNCOUNT *motivación* ❑ *His poor performance is caused by lack of motivation. Su bajo desempeño es provocado por una falta de motivación.* **2** V-T If someone **motivates** you to do something, they make you feel determined to do it. *motivar* ❑ *How do you motivate people to work hard? ¿Cómo motivas a las personas para que trabajen duro?* ● **mo|ti|va|tion** N-UNCOUNT *motivación* ❑ *Students are more likely to succeed if they have parental motivation. Es más probable que los estudiantes tengan éxito si tienen la motivación de sus padres.*

**mo|ti|va|tion** /moʊtɪveɪʃᵊn/ (**motivations**) N-COUNT Your **motivation** for doing something is what causes you to want to do it. *motivación* ❑ *Money is my motivation. El dinero es mi motivación.*

**mo|tive** /moʊtɪv/ (**motives**) N-COUNT Your **motive** for doing something is your reason for doing it. *motivo* ❑ *Police do not think robbery was a motive for the killing. La policía no cree que un robo haya sido el motivo del asesinato.*

**mo|tor** /moʊtər/ (**motors**) **1** N-COUNT The **motor** in a machine, vehicle, or boat is the part that uses electricity or fuel to produce movement, so that the machine, vehicle, or boat can work. *motor* ❑ *She got in the boat and started the motor. Se metió al bote y encendió el motor.* **2** ADJ **Motor** vehicles and boats have a gasoline or diesel engine. *motorizado* ❑ *Motor vehicles use a lot of fuel. Los vehículos motorizados usan mucho combustible.*
→ see **boat**

motorcycle

**motor|cycle** /moʊtərsaɪkᵊl/ (**motorcycles**) N-COUNT A **motorcycle** is a vehicle with two wheels and an engine. *motocicleta*

**mo|tor|ist** /moʊtərɪst/ (**motorists**) N-COUNT A **motorist** is a person who drives a car. *automovilista* ❑ *Motorists should take extra care on the roads when it is raining. Los automovilistas deben tener más cuidado en los caminos cuando llueve.*

**mo|tor neu|ron** (**motor neurons**) N-COUNT **Motor neurons** are nerve cells that carry information from the brain and spinal cord to the muscles in your body. *neurona motora* [TECHNICAL]

**mound** /maʊnd/ (**mounds**) **1** N-COUNT A **mound** of something is a large, rounded pile of it. *montículo, montón* ❑ *...huge mounds of dirt. ...enormes montones de tierra.* **2** N-COUNT In baseball, the **mound** is the raised area where the pitcher stands when he or she throws the ball. *montículo* ❑ *He went to the mound to talk with the pitcher. Fue al montículo a hablar con el lanzador.*
→ see **baseball**

**mount** /maʊnt/ (**mounts, mounting, mounted**) **1** V-T If you **mount** a campaign or event, you organize it and make it take place. *montar, realizar* ❑ *The police mounted a search of the area. La policía realizó una búsqueda del área.* **2** V-I If something **mounts,** it increases in intensity. *aumentar* ❑ *The pressure was mounting. La presión aumentaba.* **3** V-I If something **mounts,** it increases in quantity. *acumular* ❑ *The garbage mounts in city streets. La basura se acumula en las calles de la ciudad* ● To **mount up** means the same as to **mount.** *acumular* ❑ *Her medical bills mounted up. Sus facturas médicas se acumulaban.* **4** V-T If you **mount** the stairs or a platform, you go up the stairs or go up onto the platform. *subir* [FORMAL] ❑ *I mounted the steps to my room. Subí a mi cuarto.* **5** V-T If you **mount** a horse or motorcycle, you climb onto it so that you can ride it. *montar* ❑ *A man was mounting a motorcycle. El hombre montaba una motocicleta.* **6** V-T If you **mount** an object **on** something, you fix it there firmly. *montar* ❑ *Her husband mounts the work on colored paper. Su esposo monta el trabajo sobre papel de colores.* ● **-mounted** ADJ *montado* ❑ *...a wall-mounted electric fan. ...un ventilador eléctrico montado en la pared.* **7** N-COUNT **Mount** is used as part of the name of a mountain. *monte* ❑ *...Mount Everest. ...el monte Everest.* **8** → see also **mounted**

**moun|tain** /maʊntᵊn/ (**mountains**) **1** N-COUNT A **mountain** is a very high area of land with steep sides. *montaña* ❑ *Mt. McKinley is the highest mountain in North America. El monte McKinley es el más alto de Norteamérica.* **2** QUANT A **mountain of** something is a very large amount of it. *montaña* [INFORMAL] ❑ *He has a mountain of homework. Tiene un montón de tarea.*
→ see Picture Dictionary: **mountain**
→ see **landform**

m

Picture Dictionary **mountain**

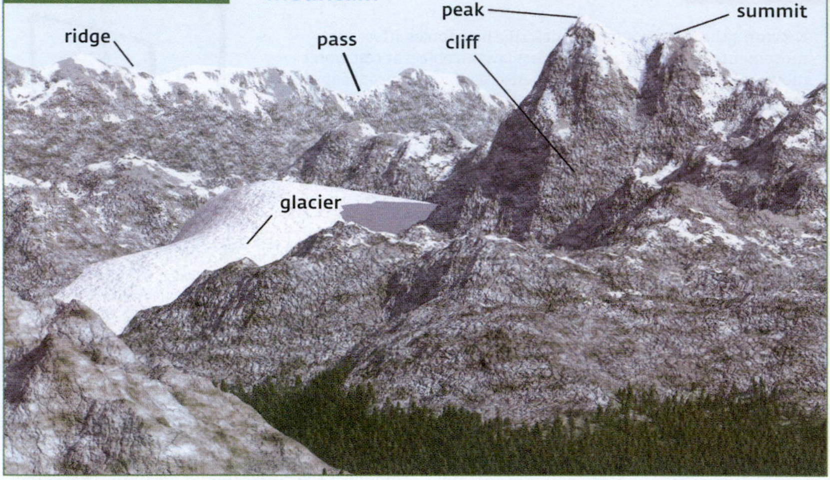


**moun|tain bike** (**mountain bikes**) N-COUNT A **mountain bike** is a type of bicycle that is suitable for riding over rough ground. It has a strong frame and thick tires. *bicicleta de montaña*
→ see **bicycle**

M

**moun|tain go|ril|la** (**mountain gorillas**) N-COUNT A **mountain gorilla** is a type of gorilla that has long, dark hair and lives in central Africa. *gorila de montaña*

**moun|tain lion** (**mountain lions**) N-COUNT A **mountain lion** is a wild animal that is a member of the cat family. Mountain lions have brownish-gray fur and live in mountain regions of North and South America. *puma, león de montaña*

**mount|ed** /maʊntɪd/ **1** ADJ **Mounted** police or soldiers ride horses when they are on duty. *policía montada* ❑ *A group of mounted police rode forward. Un grupo de la policía montada avanzó en sus caballos.* **2** → see also **mount**

**mourn** /mɔrn/ (**mourns, mourning, mourned**) **1** V-T/V-I If you **mourn** someone who has died or **mourn for** them, you are very sad that they have died and show your sorrow in the way that you behave. *llorar, enlutarse, llevar luto* ❑ *Joan still mourns her father. Joan todavía llora a su padre.* ❑ *He mourned for his dead son. Llevaba luto por su hijo muerto.* **2** V-T/V-I If you **mourn** something or **mourn for** it, you regret that you no longer have it and show your regret in the way that you behave. *lamentar* ❑ *We mourned the loss of open space and parks in our cities. Lamentamos la pérdida de los espacios abiertos y los parques en la ciudad.*

**mouse** /maʊs/ (**mice**) **1** N-COUNT A **mouse** is a small, furry animal with a long tail. *ratón* ❑ *...a mouse in a cage. ...un ratón en una jaula.* **2** N-COUNT A **mouse** is a device that you use to do things on a computer without using the keyboard. *mouse, ratón* ❑ *She clicked the mouse twice. Hizo clic dos veces con el mouse.*
→ see **computer**

**mouse pad** (**mouse pads**) also **mousepad** N-COUNT A **mouse pad** is a flat piece of plastic or some other material that you rest the mouse on while using a computer. *mousepad, cojín del mouse, cojín del ratón*
→ see **computer**

**mousse** /mus/ (**mousses**) N-VAR **Mousse** is a sweet, light food made from eggs and cream. *mousse* ❑ *...chocolate mousse. ...mousse de chocolate.*
→ see **dessert**

**mouth** (**mouths, mouthing, mouthed**)

> The noun is pronounced /maʊθ/. The verb is pronounced /maʊð/. The plural of the noun and the third person singular of the verb are both pronounced /maʊðz/.

**1** N-COUNT Your **mouth** is the area of your face where your lips are, or the space behind your lips where your teeth and tongue are. *boca* ❑ *She covered her mouth with her hand. Se cubrió la boca con la mano.* ● **-mouthed** /-maʊðd/ ADJ *boqui-* ❑ *He looked at me, open-mouthed. Me miró boquiabierto.* **2** N-COUNT The **mouth** of a cave, hole, or bottle is its entrance or opening. *boca, entrada* ❑ *He stopped at the mouth of the tunnel. Se detuvo en la boca del túnel.* **3** N-COUNT The **mouth** of a river is the place where it flows into the sea. *desembocadura* ❑ *...the town at the mouth of the River Fox. ...el pueblo que está en la desembocadura del río Fox.* **4** V-T If you **mouth** something, you form words with your lips without making any sound. *esbozar con los labios* ❑ *I mouthed a goodbye and hurried into the house. Esbocé un adiós con los labios y entré corriendo a la casa.* **5** to **live hand to mouth** → see **hand**
→ see **face, respiratory system**

**mov|able pul|ley** (**movable pulleys**) also **moveable pulley** N-COUNT A **movable pulley** is a pulley in which the axle is not attached to anything and can therefore move freely. Compare **fixed pulley**. *polea móvil* [TECHNICAL]

**move**
❶ VERB AND NOUN USES
❷ PHRASE USE
❸ PHRASAL VERBS

❶ **move** /mu̲v/ (**moves, moving, moved**) **1** V-T/V-I When you **move** something or when it **moves,** its position changes. *mover(se), quitar* ❑ *She moved her clothes off the bed. Quitó su ropa de la cama.* ❑ *A policeman asked him to move his car. Un policía le pidió que moviera su coche.* ❑ *The train began to move. El tren comenzó a moverse.* **2** V-I When you **move,** you change your position or go to a different place. *moverse* ❑ *She waited for him to get up, but he didn't move. Esperó a que se levantara, pero no se movió.* ❑ *He moved around the room, putting things in a bag. Se movió por todo el cuarto, metiendo cosas a una bolsa.* ● **Move** is also a noun. *movimiento* ❑ *The doctor made a move toward the door. El doctor hizo un movimiento hacia la puerta.* **3** N-COUNT A **move** is an action that you take in order to achieve something. *paso, jugada, movida* ❑ *Going to bed early was a sensible move. El irse a la cama temprano fue una decisión sensata.* ❑ *It may be a good move to talk to someone about your problems. Puede ser un buen paso el que hables con alguien sobre tus problemas.* **4** V-I If a person or company **moves,** they leave the building where they have been living or working, and they go to live or work in a different place, taking their possessions with them. *cambiarse, mudar* ❑ *The children don't want to move. Los niños no quieren cambiarse (de casa).* ❑ *She often considered moving to Seattle. A menudo consideró mudarse a Seattle.* ● **Move** is also a noun. *mudanza* ❑ *After his move to New York, he got a job as an actor. Después de mudarse a Nueva York, consiguió un trabajo como actor.* **5** V-I If you **move from** one job or interest **to** another, you change to it. *cambiar, pasar* ❑ *He moved from being a teacher to a college vice president. Pasó de maestro a vicerrector de una universidad.* ● **Move** is also a noun. *cambio* ❑ *His move to the chairmanship means he will have a lot more work. Su cambio a la presidencia significa que tendrá mucho más trabajo.* **6** V-I If you **move** toward a particular state, activity, or opinion, you start to be in that state, do that activity, or have that opinion. *mudar/cambiar de opinión, avanzar* ❑ *Many countries are now moving toward democracy. Muchos países están avanzando hacia la democracia.* ● **Move** is also a noun. *mudanza/cambio de opinión, avance* ❑ *...the politician's move to the left. ...la mudanza del político a la izquierda.* **7** V-I If a situation or process **is moving,** it is developing or progressing, rather than staying still. *desarrollarse, moverse* ❑ *Events are moving fast. Los sucesos se están desarrollando con rapidez.* **8** V-T If something **moves** you **to** do something, it influences you and causes you to do it. *incitar, causar* ❑ *What moved you to join a band? ¿Qué te incitó a unirte a una banda?* **9** V-T If something **moves** you, it causes you to feel sadness or sympathy for another person. *conmover(se)* ❑ *These stories surprised and moved me. Estas historias me sorprendieron y me conmovieron.* ● **moved** ADJ *conmovido* ❑ *We were moved when we heard his story. Nos conmovimos cuando escuchamos su historia.*
→ see **printing**

❷ **move** /mu̲v/ PHRASE If you are **on the move,** you are going from one place to another. *en marcha, en movimiento, de un lado para otro* ❑ *Jack never wanted to stay in one place for very long, so they were always on the move. Jack nunca quiso quedarse en un solo lugar por mucho tiempo, así que siempre anduvieron de un lado para otro.*

❸ **move** /mu̲v/ (**moves, moving, moved**)
▸ **move in** **1** PHR-VERB When you **move in** somewhere, you begin to live there as your home. *cambiarse, mudarse* ❑ *Her house was perfect when she moved in. Su casa era perfecta cuando se mudó.* ❑ *After college, Woody moved back in with Mom. Después de la universidad, Woody se mudó de vuelta con su madre.* **2** PHR-VERB If police, soldiers, or attackers **move in,** they go toward a place or person in order to deal with or attack them. *intervenir* ❑ *Police moved in to stop the fighting. La policía intervino para detener la pelea.*
▸ **move off** PHR-VERB When you **move off,** you start moving away from a place. *retirarse, alejarse* ❑ *The car moved off. El coche se alejó.*
▸ **move on** PHR-VERB When you **move on** somewhere, you leave the place where you have been staying or waiting and go there. *trasladarse* ❑ *Mr. Brooke moved on from Los Angeles to Phoenix. El Sr. Brooke se trasladó de Los Angeles a Phoenix.*
▸ **move out** PHR-VERB If you **move out,** you stop living in a particular house or place and go to live somewhere else. *mudarse* ❑ *I had a fight with my roommate and decided to move out. Tuve una pelea con quien compartía el departamento y decidí mudarme.*
▸ **move up** PHR-VERB If you **move up,** you change your position, especially in order to be nearer someone or to make room for someone else. *hacerse a un lado* ❑ *Move up, John, and let the lady sit down. Hazte a un lado, John, y deja que la señora se siente.*

| Word Link | ment ≈ state, condition : agreement, management, movement |
|---|---|

| Word Link | mov ≈ moving : movement, movie, remove |
|---|---|

**move|ment** /mu̲vmənt/ (**movements**) **1** N-COUNT A **movement** is a group of people who share the same beliefs, ideas, or aims. *movimiento* ❑ *...an Islamic political movement. ...un movimiento político islámico.* **2** N-VAR **Movement** involves changing position or going from one place to another. *movimiento, desplazamiento* ❑ *...the movement of the fish going up the river. ...el desplazamiento de los peces río arriba.* ❑ *There was movement behind the window in the back door. Había movimiento tras la ventana de la puerta trasera.* **3** N-VAR **Movement** is a gradual development or change of an attitude, opinion, or policy. *avance* ❑ *...the movement toward democracy in Latin America. ...el avance hacia la la democracia en América Latina.* **4** N-PLURAL Your **movements** are everything that you do or plan to do during a period of time. *actividades, movimiento* ❑ *What were your movements the night Mr. Gower was killed? ¿Cuáles fueron sus actividades la noche que mataron al Sr. Gower?*
→ see **brain**

**move|ment pat|tern** (**movement patterns**) N-COUNT A **movement pattern** is a series of

m

movements that involve a particular part of the body, for example the neck or head. *patrón de movimiento* [TECHNICAL]

**mov|er** /muvər/ (**movers**) N-COUNT **Movers** are people whose job is to move furniture or equipment from one building to another. *cargador o cargadora, persona que hace mudanzas*

| Word Link | *mov ≈ moving : movement, movie, remove* |
|---|---|

**movie** /muvi/ (**movies**) **1** N-COUNT A **movie** is a series of moving pictures that have been recorded so that they can be shown in a theater or on television. A movie tells a story, or shows a real situation. *película* ❑ *...the first movie Tony Curtis ever made. ...la primera película que hizo Tony Curtis.* **2** N-PLURAL You can talk about **the movies** when you are talking about seeing a movie in a movie theater. *cine* ❑ *He took her to the movies. La llevó al cine.*
→ see **genre**

**Word Partnership** Usar *movie* con:

| | |
|---|---|
| ADJ. | **bad/good** movie, **favorite** movie, **new/old** movie, **popular** movie **1** |
| V. | **go to a** movie, **see a** movie, **watch a** movie **1** |
| N. | **scene in a** movie, movie **screen**, movie **set**, movie **studio**, **television/TV** movie **1** |

M

**movie star** (**movie stars**) N-COUNT A **movie star** is a famous actor or actress who appears in movies. *estrella del cine*

**movie thea|ter** (**movie theaters**) N-COUNT A **movie theater** is a place where people go to watch movies for entertainment. *cine*

**mov|ing** /muvɪŋ/ **1** ADJ If something is **moving**, it makes you feel a strong emotion such as sadness, pity, or sympathy. *conmovedor* ❑ *It is very moving to see how much she loves her mother. Es muy conmovedor ver cuánto quiere a su madre.* • **mov|ing|ly** ADV *de manera conmovedora* ❑ *You write very movingly about your family. Escribes de manera muy conmovedora acerca de tu familia.* **2** ADJ A **moving** model or part of a machine moves or is able to move. *movible, móvil* ❑ *...a digital player with no moving parts. ...un reproductor digital sin partes móviles.*

**moz|za|rel|la** /mɑtsərɛlə, moʊt-/ N-UNCOUNT **Mozzarella** is a type of white Italian cheese, often used as a topping for pizzas. *queso mozzarella* ❑ *...layers of fresh mozzarella. ...capas de queso mozzarella fresco.*

**MP3** /ɛm pi θri/ N-COUNT An **MP3** is a type of compressed audio or video file that can be downloaded from the Internet. *MP3*

**MP3 play|er** (**MP3 players**) N-COUNT An **MP3 player** is a machine on which you can play music or videos downloaded from the Internet. *reproductor de MP3*

**mph** also **m.p.h.** **mph** is written after a number to indicate the speed of something such as a vehicle. **mph** is an abbreviation for "miles per hour." *mph, millas por hora* ❑ *On this road, you must not drive faster than 20 mph. En esta calle, no se debe manejar a más de 20 mph (32 kph).*

**Mr.** /mɪstər/ N-TITLE **Mr.** is used before a man's name when you are speaking or referring to him. *señor (Sr.)* ❑ *...Mr. Grant. ...señor Grant.* ❑ *...Mr. Bob Price. ...señor Bob Price.*

**Mrs.** /mɪsɪz/ N-TITLE **Mrs.** is used before the name of a married woman when you are speaking or referring to her. *señora (Sra.)* ❑ *Hello, Mrs. Miles. Hola, señora Miles.* ❑ *...Mrs. Anne Pritchard. ...señora Anne Pritchard.*

**Ms.** /mɪz/ N-TITLE **Ms.** is used, especially in written English, before a woman's name when you are speaking to her or referring to her. If you use **Ms.**, you are not specifying if the woman is married or not. *señorita (Srita.)* ❑ *...Ms. Brown. ...señorita Brown.*

**MS** /ɛm ɛs/ N-UNCOUNT **MS** is a serious disease of the nervous system, which gradually makes a person weaker, and sometimes affects their sight or speech. **MS** is an abbreviation for "multiple sclerosis." *esclerosis múltiple (EM)*

**m/s** **m/s** is an abbreviation for **meters per second**. *m/s, metros por segundo*

**m/s/s** **m/s/s** or **m/s per second** is a unit of acceleration in physics. **m/s/s** is an abbreviation for "meters per second per second." *m/s2, metros por segundo cuadrado* [TECHNICAL]

**much** /mʌtʃ/ **1** ADV You use **much** to indicate the great intensity, extent, or degree of something such as an action, feeling, or change. **Much** is usually used with "so," "too," and "very," and in negative clauses with this meaning. *mucho, adverbio que hace énfasis en la magnitud en combinación con otras palabras* ❑ *She laughs too much. Se ríe demasiado.* ❑ *Thank you very much. Muchísimas gracias.* **2** ADV If something does not happen **much,** it does not happen very often. *mucho, tanto* ❑ *He said that his father never talked much about the war. Dijo que su padre nunca hablaba mucho sobre la guerra.* ❑ *Gwen did not see her father all that much. Gwen no veía tanto a su padre.* **3** ADV If one thing is **much** the same as another thing, it is very similar to it. *muy similar* ❑ *The day ended much as it began. El final del día fue muy similar a su inicio.* **4** DET You use **much** to indicate that you are referring to a large amount of a substance or thing. *mucho* ❑ *These plants do not need much water. Estas plantas no necesitan mucha agua.* ❑ *He doesn't earn much money. No gana mucho dinero.* • **Much** is also a pronoun. *mucho* ❑ *You eat too much. Tú comes mucho.* • **Much** is also a quantifier. *la mayor parte* ❑ *Much of the time we do not notice that we are solving problems. La mayor parte del tiempo no nos damos cuenta de que estamos resolviendo problemas.* **5** DET You use **much** in the expression **how much** to ask questions about amounts or degrees, and also in reported clauses and statements to give information about the amount or degree of something. *¿cuánto?* ❑ *How much money can I spend? ¿Cuánto dinero puedo gastar?* • **Much** is also an adverb. *cuánto* ❑ *She knows how much this upsets me. Ella sabe cuánto me molesta esto.* • **Much** is also a pronoun. *¿cuánto?* ❑ *How much do you earn? ¿Cuánto ganas?* **6** PHRASE If you say that something is not **so much** one thing **as** another, you mean that it is more like the second thing than the first. *no tan...como /no tanto como* ❑ *I don't really think of her as a daughter so much as a very good friend. No pienso*

*tanto en ella como una hija, sino como una gran amiga.*
**7** PHRASE If a situation or action is **too much for** you, it is so difficult, tiring, or upsetting that you cannot cope with it. *demasiado* ❑ *All the traveling got too much for her. tanto viajar resultó demasiado para ella.*
**8** **a bit much** → see **bit**

**mu|cus** /myukəs/ N-UNCOUNT **Mucus** is a thick liquid that is produced in some parts of your body, for example the inside of your nose. *mucosa*

**mud** /mʌd/ N-UNCOUNT **Mud** is a sticky mixture of earth and water. *lodo, fango* ❑ *His clothes were covered with mud. Su ropa estaba cubierta de lodo.*

**mud|dle** /mʌdᵊl/ (**muddles, muddling, muddled**) **1** N-VAR If people or things are **in a muddle,** they are in a state of confusion or disorder. *lío* ❑ *My thoughts are all in a muddle. Mis pensamientos están hechos un lío.* ❑ *We are going to get into a muddle. Nos vamos a meter en un lío.* **2** V-T If you **muddle** things or people, you get them mixed up, so that you do not know which is which. *confundir* ❑ *People often muddle the two names. La gente confunde los dos nombres muy seguido.* ● **Muddle up** means the same as **muddle.** *confundir, enredar, entreverar* ❑ *The question muddles up three separate issues. La cuestión entrevera tres asuntos diferentes.* ● **mud|dled up** ADJ *enredado, hecho un lío* ❑ *I know that I am getting my words muddled up. Sé que me estoy haciendo un lío al hablar.*
▸ **muddle through** PHR-VERB If you **muddle through,** you manage to do something even though you do not have the proper equipment or do not really know how to do it. *arreglárselas* ❑ *We will muddle through until we get the right equipment. Nos las arreglaremos hasta que llegue el equipo adecuado.* ❑ *They may be able to muddle through the next five years like this. Es posible que logren arreglárselas así los próximos cinco años.*
▸ **muddle up** → see **muddle 2**

**mud|dled** /mʌdᵊld/ ADJ If someone is **muddled,** they are confused about something. *confundido, hecho un lío* ❑ *I'm afraid I'm a little muddled. I'm not exactly sure where to begin. Creo que estoy hecho un lío. No sé muy bien por dónde empezar.*

**mud|dy** /mʌdi/ (**muddier, muddiest, muddies, muddying, muddied**) **1** ADJ Something that is **muddy** contains mud or is covered in mud. *lodoso* ❑ *...a muddy track. ...un sendero lodoso.* **2** V-T If you **muddy** something, you cause it to be muddy. *enlodar(se)* ❑ *The ground was wet and they muddied their shoes. El suelo estaba mojado y se enlodaron los zapatos.* **3** V-T If someone or something **muddies** a situation or issue, they cause it to seem less clear and less easy to understand. *enredar, enmarañar* ❑ *Don't muddy the issue with religion. No enredes el asunto con la religión.*

**mud|flow** /mʌdfloʊ/ (**mudflows**) N-COUNT A **mudflow** is the same as a **mudslide.** *alud de lodo*

**mud|slide** /mʌdslaɪd/ (**mudslides**) N-COUNT A **mudslide** is a large amount of mud sliding down a mountain, usually causing damage or destruction. *alud de lodo.*
→ see **disaster, erosion**

**muf|fin** /mʌfɪn/ (**muffins**) N-COUNT **Muffins** are small, round, sweet cakes, often with fruit inside. They are usually eaten for breakfast. *panquecito, panqueque* ❑ *...blueberry muffins. ...panquecitos de arándano.*

**mug** /mʌg/ (**mugs, mugging, mugged**) **1** N-COUNT A **mug** is a large, deep cup with straight sides. *tarro* ❑ *He put sugar into two of the mugs. Puso azúcar en dos de los tarros.* **2** V-T If someone **mugs** you, they attack you in order to steal your money. *asaltar* ❑ *I was walking to my car when this guy tried to mug me. Iba hacia mi carro cuando un tipo trató de asaltarme.* ● **mug|ging** N-VAR (**muggings**) *asalto* ❑ *Muggings are unusual in this neighborhood. Los asaltos no son comunes en esta colonia.* ● **mug|ger** N-COUNT (**muggers**) *asaltante* ❑ *...hiding places for muggers and thieves. ...escondites de ladrones y asaltantes.*
→ see **crime, dish**

**multi|cel|lu|lar** /mʌltisɛlyələr/ ADJ **Multicellular** organisms are organisms such as animals and plants that consist of more than one cell. *pluricelular, multicelular*

| Word Link | *multi ≈ many : multicolored, multimedia, multinational* |
|---|---|

**multi|col|ored** /mʌltikʌlərd/ ADJ A **multicolored** object has many different colors. *multicolor* ❑ *...a multicolored shirt. ...una camisa multicolor.*

**multi|lat|er|al** /mʌltilætərᵊl/ ADJ **Multilateral** means involving at least three different groups of people or nations. *multilateral* ❑ *...multilateral trade talks. ...negociaciones de comercio multilateral.*

**multi|media** /mʌltimidiə/ **1** N-UNCOUNT You use **multimedia** to refer to computer programs and products which involve sound, pictures, and film, as well as text. *multimedia* ❑ *...teachers who use multimedia in the classroom. ...maestros que hacen uso de la multimedia en el salón.* **2** N-UNCOUNT In education, **multimedia** is the use of television and other different media in a lesson, as well as books. *multimedia* ❑ *I am making a multimedia presentation for my science project. Estoy haciendo una presentación multimedia para mi proyeto de ciencias.*

**multi|na|tion|al** /mʌltinæʃənᵊl/ (**multinationals**) **1** ADJ A **multinational** company has branches or owns companies in many different countries. *multinacional* ● **Multinational** is also a noun. *compañía multinacional* ❑ *...multinationals such as Ford and IBM. ...compañías multinacionales como Ford y la IBM.* **2** ADJ **Multinational** armies, organizations, or other groups involve people from several different countries. *multinacional* ❑ *The U.S. soldiers will be part of a multinational force. Los soldados estadounidenses formarán parte de una fuerza multinacional.*

**multi|ple** /mʌltɪpᵊl/ (**multiples**) **1** ADJ You use **multiple** to describe things that consist of many parts, involve many people, or have many uses. *múltiple* ❑ *He died of multiple injuries. Murió de heridas múltiples.* **2** N-COUNT If one number is a **multiple of** a smaller number, it can be exactly divided by that smaller number. *múltiplo* ❑ *Our system of numbers is based on multiples of the number ten. Nuestro sistema numérico se basa en múltiplos de diez.*

**multi|pli|er** /mʌltɪplaɪər/ (**multipliers**) N-COUNT When you multiply a number by another number, the second number is the

m

multiplier. multiplicador [TECHNICAL]

**multi|ply** /mʌltɪplaɪ/ (**multiplies, multiplying, multiplied**) **1** V-T/V-I When something **multiplies** or when you **multiply** it, it increases greatly in number or amount. multiplicar ❑ *Such arguments multiplied in the eighteenth and nineteenth centuries. Tales argumentos se mutiplicaron en los siglos dieciocho y diecinueve.* • **multi|pli|ca|tion** /mʌltɪplɪkeɪʃᵊn/ N-UNCOUNT multiplicación ❑ *...the multiplication of cells. ...la multiplicación de las células.* **2** V-T If you **multiply** one number by another, you add the first number to itself as many times as is indicated by the second number. multiplicar ❑ *What do you get if you multiply six by nine? ¿Cuánto obtienes al multiplicar seis por nueve?* • **multi|pli|ca|tion** N-UNCOUNT multiplicación ❑ *There will be simple tests in multiplication. Habrá exámenes sencillos de multiplicaciones.*

→ see **mathematics**

**multi|pur|pose** /mʌltipɜrpəs/ ADJ A **multipurpose** object can be used for several different purposes. multiuso ❑ *...a multipurpose tool. ...una herramienta multiusos.*

**multi|story** /mʌltistɔri/ also **multistoried** ADJ A **multistory** building has several floors at different levels above the ground. edificio de varios pisos ❑ *The store is a big multistory building. Esta tienda es un edificio de varios pisos.* ❑ *...a multistory parking garage. ...un estacionamiento de varios pisos.*

**multi|vita|min** /mʌltivaɪtəmɪn/ (**multivitamins**) also **multi-vitamin** N-COUNT **Multivitamins** are pills that contain several different vitamins. multivitamínico

M

**mu|nici|pal** /myunɪsɪpᵊl/ ADJ **Municipal** means associated with or belonging to a city or town that has its own local government. municipal ❑ *...next month's municipal elections. ...las elecciones municipales del próximo mes.*

**mu|ni|tions** /myunɪʃᵊnz/ N-PLURAL **Munitions** are military equipment and supplies, especially bombs, shells, and guns. municiones ❑ *There are not enough men and munitions. No hay hombres ni municiones suficientes.*

**mu|ral** /myʊərəl/ (**murals**) N-COUNT A **mural** is a picture painted on a wall. mural ❑ *...a mural of San Francisco Bay. ...un mural de la bahía de San Francisco.*

**mur|der** /mɜrdər/ (**murders, murdering, murdered**) **1** N-VAR **Murder** is the crime of deliberately killing a person. asesinato ❑ *The jury found him guilty of murder. El jurado lo declaró culpable de asesinato.* ❑ *The detective has worked on hundreds of murder cases. El detective ha trabajado en cientos de casos de asesinato.* **2** V-T To **murder** someone means to commit the crime of killing them deliberately. asesinar ❑ *...a movie about a woman who murders her husband. ...una película acerca de una mujer que asesina a su marido.* • **mur|der|er** /mɜrdərər/ N-COUNT (**murderers**) asesino o asesina ❑ *One of these men is the murderer. Uno de estos hombres es el asesino.*

**mur|mur** /mɜrmər/ (**murmurs, murmuring, murmured**) **1** V-T If you **murmur** something, you say it very quietly, so that not many people can hear what you are saying. susurrar, murmurar ❑ *He turned and murmured something to Karen. Volteó y le susurró algo a Karen.* ❑ *"How lovely," she murmured. —¡Qué hermoso! —murmuró.* **2** N-COUNT A **murmur** is something that is said but can hardly be heard. susurro ❑ *They spoke in low murmurs. Hablaban en susurros.* **3** N-SING A **murmur** is a continuous low sound, like the noise of a river or of voices far away. murmullo ❑ *The music mixes with the murmur of conversation. La música se mezcla con el murmullo de la conversación.*

**mus|cle** /mʌsᵊl/ (**muscles, muscling, muscled**) **1** N-VAR A **muscle** is a piece of tissue inside your body that connects two bones and which you use when you make a movement. músculo ❑ *Exercise helps to keep your muscles strong. El ejercicio ayuda a mantener fuertes los músculos.* **2** N-UNCOUNT If you say that someone has **muscle,** you mean that they have power and influence, which enables them to do difficult things. influencia ❑ *The president used his muscle to change the law. El presidente utilizó su influencia para cambiar la ley.* **3** PHRASE If a group, organization, or country **flexes** its **muscles,** it does something to impress or frighten people, in order to show them that it has power and is considering using it. demostrar poder ❑ *The government began to flex its muscles. El gobierno empezó a demostrar todo su poder.*

→ see Word Web: **muscle**

→ see **nervous system**

▸ **muscle in** PHR-VERB If someone **muscles in on** something, they force their way into a situation where they have no right to be and where they are not welcome. meterse por la fuerza, entrometerse ❑ *Cohen complained that Kravis was muscling in on his deal. Cohen se quejó de que Kravis estaba entrometiéndose en su trato.*

**Word Web** muscle

There are three types of **muscles** in the body. **Voluntary** or **skeletal** muscles make external movements. **Involuntary** or **smooth** muscles move within the body. For example, the smooth muscles in the **iris** of the eye adjust the size of the pupil. This controls how much light enters the eye. **Cardiac** muscles are in the heart. They work constantly but never get tired. When we **exercise**, voluntary muscles **contract** and then **relax**. Repeated **workouts** can **build** these muscles and increase their **strength**. If we don't exercise, these muscles can atrophy and become **weak**.

**Word Partnership** Usar *muscle* con:

N. muscle **aches**, muscle **mass**, muscle **pain**, muscle **tone** 1
V. **contract a** muscle, **flex a** muscle, **pull a** muscle 1

**mus|cle tis|sue** (**muscle tissues**) N-VAR **Muscle tissue** is tissue in animals and plants which is made of cells that can become shorter or longer. *tejido muscular*

**mus|cu|lar** /mʌskyələr/ 1 ADJ **Muscular** means involving or affecting your muscles. *muscular* ❑ *...exercises to improve muscular strength. ...ejercicios para mejorar la fuerza muscular.* 2 ADJ If a person or their body is **muscular,** they have strong, firm muscles. *musculoso* ❑ *He was tall and muscular. Era alto y musculoso.*

**mus|cu|lar sys|tem** (**muscular systems**) N-COUNT The **muscular system** is the muscles and other parts of the body that control movement. *sistema muscular*

**muse** /myuz/ (**muses, musing, mused**) V-T/V-I If you **muse** on something, you think about it, usually saying or writing what you are thinking at the same time. *cavilar, preguntarse, reflexionar* [WRITTEN] ❑ *Many of the papers muse on what will happen to the president. En muchos de los periódicos se preguntan qué será del presidente.* ❑ *"I like most of his work," she muses. —Me gusta casi todo su trabajo —reflexiona.* ● **mus|ing** N-COUNT (**musings**) *cavilación* ❑ *His mother interrupted his musings. Su madre interrumpió sus cavilaciones.*

**mu|seum** /myuziəm/ (**museums**) N-COUNT A **museum** is a building where a large number of interesting and valuable objects, such as works of art or historical items, are kept, studied, and displayed to the public. *museo* ❑ *Malcolm wanted to visit the New York art museums. Malcolm quería visitar los museos de arte de Nueva York.*

**mush|room** /mʌʃrum/ (**mushrooms, mushrooming, mushroomed**) 1 N-VAR **Mushrooms** are fungi with short stems and round tops that you can eat. *hongo* ❑ *There are many types of wild mushrooms. Hay muchos tipos de hongos silvestres.* 2 V-I If something such as an industry or a place **mushrooms,** it grows or comes into existence very quickly. *crecer como hongo* ❑ *Internet companies mushroomed very quickly. Las compañías de internet crecieron rápidamente como hongos.*
→ see **fungus**

**mu|sic** /myuzɪk/ 1 N-UNCOUNT **Music** is the pattern of sounds produced by people singing or playing instruments. *música* ❑ *...classical music. ...música clásica* 2 N-UNCOUNT **Music** is the symbols written on paper which represent musical sounds. *música* ❑ *He can't read music. No sabe leer música.*
→ see Word Web: **music**
→ see **concert, genre**

**Word Partnership** Usar *music* con:

ADJ. **live** music, **loud** music, **new** music, **pop(ular)** music 1
N. **background** music, music **business**, music **critic**, music **festival**, music **industry** 1
music **lesson** 2
V. **download** music, **hear** music, **listen to** music, **play** music 1
**compose** music, **study** music, **write** music 2

**mu|si|cal** /myuzɪkəl/ (**musicals**) 1 ADJ You use **musical** to indicate that something is connected with playing or studying music. *musical* ❑ *...a series of musical notes. ...una serie de notas musicales.* ● **mu|si|cal|ly** /myuzɪkli/ ADV *musicalmente* ❑ *Musically there is a lot to enjoy. Musicalmente, hay mucho que disfrutar.* 2 N-COUNT A **musical** is a play or movie that uses singing and dancing in the story. *musical* ❑ *...the musical, "Miss Saigon." ...el musical "Miss Saigon".* 3 ADJ Someone who is **musical** has a natural ability and interest in music. *con aptitudes para la música* ❑ *I came from a musical family. Vengo de una familia con aptitudes para la música.*
→ see **theater**

**mu|si|cal in|stru|ment** (**musical instruments**) N-COUNT A **musical instrument** is an object such as a piano, guitar, or violin which you play in order to produce music. *instrumento musical* ❑ *The drum is one of the oldest musical instruments. El tambor es uno de los intrumentos musicales más antiguos.*

**mu|si|cal|ity** /myuzɪkælɪti/ N-UNCOUNT In dance, **musicality** is the ability to interpret music artistically by dancing in a way that is appropriate for the music. *musicalidad*

**mu|si|cal thea|ter** N-UNCOUNT **Musical theater** is a form of entertainment that contains music, song, and dance, as well as spoken dialogue. *teatro musical*

**Word Web** music

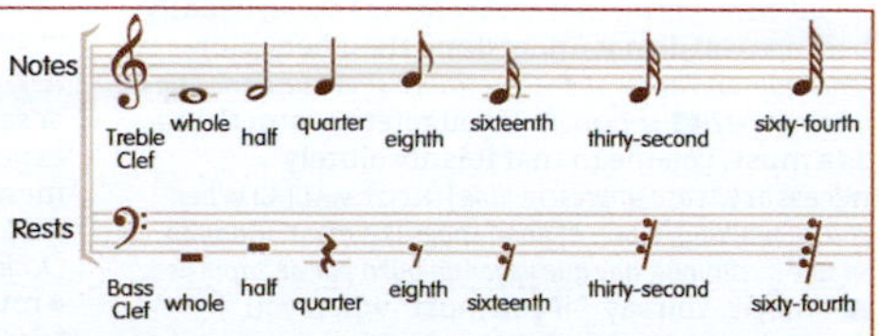


Wolfgang Amadeus Mozart lived only 35 years (1756-1791). However, he is one of the most important **musicians** in history. Mozart began playing the **piano** when he was four years old. A year later he **composed** his first **song**. Since he hadn't learned musical **notation** yet, his father wrote out the **score** for him. Mozart played for royalty across Europe. Soon Mozart became known as a gifted **composer**. He wrote more than 50 **symphonies**. He also composed **operas, concertos**, arias, and other musical works.

m

**Word Link** *ician ≈ person who works at : electrician, musician, physician*

**mu|si|cian** /myuzɪʃ°n/ (**musicians**) N-COUNT A **musician** is a person who plays a musical instrument as their job or hobby. *músico o música* ❑ *He was a brilliant musician. Era un músico brillante.*
→ see **concert, music, orchestra**

**Mus|lim** /mʌzlɪm/ (**Muslims**) **1** N-COUNT A **Muslim** is someone who believes in Islam and lives according to its rules. *musulmán o musulmana* **2** ADJ **Muslim** means relating to Islam or Muslims. *musulmán* ❑ *...Iran and other Muslim countries. ...Irán y otros países musulmanes.*

**muss** /mʌs/ (**musses, mussing, mussed**) V-T To **muss** something, especially someone's hair, or to **muss** it **up,** means to make it messy. *desordenar, despeinar* ❑ *He reached out and mussed my hair. Alargó la mano y me despeinó.* ❑ *His clothes were all mussed up. Su ropa estaba toda desordenada.*

**mus|sel** (**mussels**) N-COUNT **Mussels** are a kind of shellfish that you can eat from their shells. *mejillón*
→ see **shellfish**

**must** /məst, STRONG mʌst/ (**musts**)

The noun is pronounced /mauθ/. The verb is pronounced /mauð/. The plural of the noun and the third person singular of the verb are both pronounced /mauðz/.

**Must** is a modal verb. It is followed by the base form of a verb.

M

**1** MODAL You use **must** to indicate that you think it is very important or necessary for something to happen. *deber* ❑ *Your clothes must fit well. La ropa debe quedarte bien.* ❑ *You must tell me everything you know. Debes decirme todo lo que sabes.* **2** MODAL You use **must** to indicate that you are fairly sure that something is true. *deber* ❑ *At 20 years old, Russell must be one of the youngest company directors. A sus 20 años, Russell debe ser uno de los directores más jóvenes.* ❑ *Claire's car wasn't there, so she must have gone to her mother's. El carro de Clare no estaba allí, así que debe haber ido a casa de su madre.* **3** MODAL You use **must** to express your intention to do something. *tener que* ❑ *I must go home now. Tengo que irme a casa ahora.* ❑ *I must telephone my parents. Tengo que llamar por teléfono a mis padres.* **4** MODAL You use **must** to make suggestions or invitations very forcefully. *tener que* ❑ *You must see a doctor, Frederick. Tienes que ir a ver a un doctor, Frederick.* **5** MODAL You use **must** in questions to express your anger or irritation about something that someone has done, usually because you do not understand their behavior. *tener que* ❑ *Why must she interrupt? ¿Por qué tiene que interrumpir?* **6** N-COUNT If you refer to something as **a must,** you mean that it is absolutely necessary. *cosa imprescindible* [INFORMAL] ❑ *When you go walking, a pair of good shoes is a must. Cuando se sale a caminar, hay que llevar un buen par de zapatos.* **7** PHRASE You say **"if you must"** when you know that you cannot stop someone from doing something that you think is wrong or stupid. *si uno debe hacer algo* ❑ *If you must be in the sun, use the strongest sunscreen you can get. Si tienes que asolearte, usa el mejor protector solar que puedas conseguir.*

**mus|tache** /mʌstæʃ/ (**mustaches**) N-COUNT A man's **mustache** is the hair that grows on his upper lip. *bigote* ❑ *He has a black mustache. Tiene un bigote negro.*

**mus|tard** /mʌstərd/ (**mustards**) N-VAR **Mustard** is a yellow or brown paste usually eaten with meat. It tastes hot and spicy. *mostaza* ❑ *...a jar of mustard. ...un frasco de mostaza.*

**mustn't** /mʌs°nt/ **Mustn't** is the usual spoken form of "must not." *forma hablada usual de **must not***

**must've** /mʌstəv/ **Must've** is the usual spoken form of "must have," especially when "have" is an auxiliary verb. *forma hablada usual de **must have***

**mu|ta|gen** /myutədʒən, -dʒɛn/ (**mutagens**) N-COUNT **Mutagens** are processes or substances, for example x-rays or certain chemicals, that can cause genetic changes in cells. *mutágeno* [TECHNICAL]

**mute** /myut/ (**mutes, muting, muted**) **1** ADJ Someone who is **mute** does not speak. *mudo* ❑ *Alexander was mute for a few minutes. Alexander se quedó mudo unos minutos.* • **Mute** is also an adverb. *mudo* ❑ *He could watch her standing mute by the phone. Podía verla ahí parada, muda junto al teléfono.* **2** V-T If someone **mutes** something such as their feelings or their activities, they reduce the strength or intensity of them. *disminuir* ❑ *The problems have not muted the country's economic success. Los problemas no han disminuido el éxito ecomómico del país.* • **mut|ed** ADJ *débil* ❑ *...muted criticism. ...la débil crítica.* **3** V-T If you **mute** a noise or sound, you lower its volume or make it less distinct. *bajar el sonido o el volumen* ❑ *They begin to mute their voices. Comienzan a bajar sus voces.* • **mut|ed** ADJ *bajo* ❑ *His voice was so muted that I couldn't hear his reply. Su voz era tan baja que no pude oír su respuesta.*

**mut|ter** /mʌtər/ (**mutters, muttering, muttered**) V-T/V-I If you **mutter,** you speak very quietly so that you cannot easily be heard, often because you are complaining about something. *hablar entre dientes, mascullar* ❑ *"He's crazy," she muttered. —Está loco —dijo entre dientes.* ❑ *She can hear the old woman muttering about politeness. Puede oír a la anciana mascullar algo sobre la cortesía.* • **Mutter** is also a noun. *murmullo* ❑ *...a mutter of protest. ...un murmullo de protesta.* • **mut|ter|ing** N-VAR (**mutterings**) *murmullos, comentarios en voz baja* ❑ *He heard muttering from the front of the crowd. Escuchó algunos comentarios en voz baja entre las primeras filas de la muchedumbre.*

**mut|ton** /mʌt°n/ N-UNCOUNT **Mutton** is meat from an adult sheep. *carne de borrego/carnero* ❑ *...a leg of mutton. ...una pierna de borrego/carnero.*
→ see **meat**

**mu|tu|al** /myutʃuəl/ ADJ You use **mutual** to describe a situation, feeling, or action that is experienced, felt, or done by both of two people mentioned. *mutuo* ❑ *The East and the West can work together for their mutual benefit. Oriente y Occidente pueden trabajar juntos para beneficio mutuo.* • **mu|tu|al|ly** ADV *para ambos, para todos* ❑ *They tried to reach a mutually acceptable solution. Trataron de alcanzar una solución aceptable para todos.* → see **exclusive**

**mu|tu|al fund** (**mutual funds**) N-COUNT A **mutual fund** is an organization which invests money in many different kinds of businesses and which offers units for sale to the public as an investment. *fondo de inversión* [BUSINESS]

**mu|tu|al|ism** /myu̲tʃuəlɪzəm/ (**mutualisms**) N-VAR **Mutualism** is a relationship between two species of animals or plants from which both species benefit. *mutualismo* [TECHNICAL]

**muz|zle** /mʌ̲zᵊl/ (**muzzles, muzzling, muzzled**) **1** N-COUNT The **muzzle** of an animal such as a dog is its nose and mouth. *hocico* ❑ *The dog wanted me to scratch its muzzle. El perro quería que le rascara el hocico.* **2** N-COUNT A **muzzle** is an object that is put over a dog's nose and mouth so that it cannot bite people or make a noise. *bozal* ❑ *Some dogs have to wear a muzzle. Algunos perros deben utilizar un bozal.* **3** V-T If you **muzzle** a dog or other animal, you put a muzzle over its nose and mouth. *poner un bozal* ❑ *He refused to muzzle his dog. Se negó a ponerle un bozal a su perro.* **4** N-COUNT The **muzzle** of a gun is the end where the bullets come out when it is fired. *boca, cañón (de un arma)* ❑ *Mickey felt the muzzle of a gun press against his neck. Mickey sintió el cañón de una pistola contra su cuello.*

→ see **horse**

**MVP** /ɛm vi pi̲/ (**MVPs**) N-COUNT Journalists sometimes use **MVP** to talk about the player on a sports team who has performed best in a particular game or series of games. **MVP** is an abbreviation for "most valuable player." *jugador más valioso o jugadora más valiosa* ❑ *Brondello won the MVP award by scoring 357 points. Brondello ganó el premio al jugador más valioso por anotar 357 puntos.*

**my** /maɪ/

> **My** is the first person singular possessive determiner.

DET A speaker or writer uses **my** to indicate that something belongs or relates to himself or herself. *mi* ❑ *I invited him back to my apartment. Lo invité a mi departamento.*

**my|self** /maɪsɛ̲lf/

> **Myself** is the first person singular reflexive pronoun.

**1** PRON A speaker or writer uses **myself** to refer to himself or herself. **Myself** is used as the object of a verb or preposition when the subject refers to the same person. *yo mismo o yo misma, a mí mismo o a mí misma* ❑ *I asked myself what I should do. Me pregunté a mí mismo qué debía hacer.* **2** PRON You use **myself** to emphasize a first person singular subject. In more formal English, **myself** is sometimes used instead of "me" as the object of a verb or preposition, for emphasis. *yo mismo o yo misma, a mí mismo o a mí misma, por mi parte* ❑ *I myself enjoy movies and long walks. Por mi parte, yo disfruto las películas y las caminatas largas.* **3** PRON If you say something such as "I did it **myself,**" you are emphasizing that you did it, rather than anyone else. *yo mismo o yo misma* ❑ *"Where did you get that dress?"— "I made it myself." —¿Dónde conseguiste ese vestido?—Me lo hice yo misma.*

> **Word Link** *ous ≈ having the qualities of : dangerous, fabulous, mysterious*

**mys|teri|ous** /mɪstɪ̲əriəs/ **1** ADJ Someone or something that is **mysterious** is strange and is not known about or understood. *misterioso* ❑ *He died in mysterious circumstances. Murió en circunstanias misteriosas.* ❑ *A mysterious illness made him sick. Se enfermó de una enfermedad misteriosa* ● **mys|teri|ous|ly** ADV *misteriosamente* ❑ *Two messages mysteriously disappeared. Dos mensajes desaparecieron misteriosamente.* **2** ADJ If someone is **mysterious** about something, they deliberately do not talk much about it, sometimes because they want to make people more interested in it. *misterioso* ❑ *He was very mysterious about his job. Estaba muy misterioso acerca de su trabajo.* ● **mys|teri|ous|ly** ADV *misteriosamente* ❑ *When I asked her what she meant, she just smiled mysteriously. Cuando le pregunté qué quería decir, sólo sonrió misteriosamente.*

**mys|tery** /mɪ̲stəri, mɪ̲stri/ (**mysteries**) **1** N-COUNT A **mystery** is something that is not understood or known about. *misterio* ❑ *Who took the painting is still a mystery. Todavía es un misterio quién tomó la pintura.* **2** N-UNCOUNT If you talk about the **mystery** of someone or something, you are talking about how difficult they are to understand or know about, especially when this gives them a rather strange or magical quality. *misterio* ❑ *She's a lady of mystery. Es una mujer misteriosa.* **3** ADJ A **mystery** person or thing is one whose identity or nature is not known. *misterioso* ❑ *The mystery hero immediately called the police after seeing a bomb. El héroe misterioso llamó inmediatamente a la policía tras haber visto una bomba.* **4** N-COUNT A **mystery** is a story in which strange things happen that are not explained until the end. *novela de misterio/suspenso* ❑ *His fourth novel is a mystery set in London. Su cuarta novela es de misterio y transcurre en Londres.*

> **Word Partnership** Usar *mystery* con:
>
> V. **remain a** mystery, **unravel a** mystery **1** **solve a** mystery **1** **4**
>
> N. **murder** mystery, mystery **novel**, mystery **readers** **4**

**myth** /mɪ̲θ/ (**myths**) **1** N-VAR A **myth** is a well-known story which was made up in the past to explain natural events or to justify religious beliefs or social customs. *mito* ❑ *...a famous Greek myth. ...un famoso mito griego.* ● **mythi|cal** ADJ *mítico* Something or someone that is **mythical** exists only in myths and is therefore imaginary. *mítico* ❑ *The Hydra is a mythical beast that had seven or more heads. La Hydra es una bestia mítica que tenía siete o más cabezas.* **2** N-VAR If you describe a belief or explanation as a **myth,** you mean that many people believe it but it is actually untrue. *mito* ❑ *It is a myth that all women love spending money. Es un mito el que a todas las mujeres les guste gastar el dinero.*

→ see Word Web: **myth**

→ see **fantasy**

> **Word Partnership** Usar *myth* con:
>
> ADJ. **ancient** myth, **Greek** myth **1** **popular** myth **2**

m

**Word Web** myth

The scholar Joseph Campbell* believed that **mythologies** explain how a **culture** understands its world. **Stories**, **symbols**, **rituals**, and **myths** explain the **psychological**, **social**, **cosmological**, and **spiritual** parts of life. Campbell also believed that artists and thinkers are a culture's mythmakers. He explored **archetypal themes** in myths from many different cultures. He showed that themes are repeated in many different cultures. For example, the **hero's** journey appears in ancient Greece in *The Odyssey**. The hero's journey also appeared later in England in a story about King Arthur's* search for the Holy Grail*. The film *Star Wars* is a 20th century version of the hero's journey.

*Joseph Campbell (1904–1987): an American professor and author.*

*The Odyssey: an epic poem from ancient Greece.*

*King Arthur: a legendary king of Great Britain.*

*Holy Grail: a cup that legends say Jesus used.*

**Word Link** ***logy, ology ≈ study of : biology, geology, mythology***

**my|thol|ogy** /mɪθɒlədʒi/ (**mythologies**) N-VAR **Mythology** is a group of myths, especially all the myths from a particular country, religion, or culture. mitología ❑ *...Greek mythology. ...mitología griega.* ● **mytho|logi|cal** /mɪθəlɒdʒɪkᵊl/ ADJ *mitológico* ❑ *...mythological creatures. ...criaturas mitológicas., ...seres mitológicos.*

→ see **hero, myth**

# Nn

**na|cho** /nɑtʃoʊ/ (**nachos**) N-COUNT **Nachos** are snack, originally from Mexico, consisting of pieces of fried tortilla, usually with a topping of cheese, salsa, and chili peppers. totopos ❑ *...a plate of nachos. un plato de totopos.*

**nail** /neɪl/ (**nails, nailing, nailed**) **1** N-COUNT A **nail** is a thin piece of metal with one pointed end and one flat end. You hit the flat end with a hammer in order to push the nail into something such as a wall. *clavo* ❑ *A mirror hung on a nail above the sink. Un espejo colgaba de un clavo sobre el lavabo.* **2** V-T If you **nail** something somewhere, you fasten it there using one or more nails. *clavar* ❑ *Frank put the first board down and nailed it in place. Frank puso la primera tabla y la clavó en su lugar.* ❑ *They nailed the window shut. Condenaron la ventana con clavos.* **3** N-COUNT Your **nails** are the thin hard parts that grow at the ends of your fingers and toes. *uña* ❑ *Keep your nails short. Mantén tus uñas cortas.*

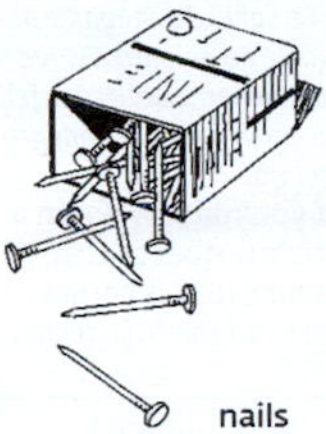

nails

▸ **nail down** **1** PHR-VERB If you **nail down** something unknown or uncertain, you find out exactly what it is. *establecer con certeza* ❑ *Try to nail down the date of the meeting. Trata de establecer con certeza la fecha de la reunión.* **2** PHR-VERB If you **nail down** an agreement, you manage to reach a firm agreement with a definite result. *concretar* ❑ *The two men tried to nail down the contract. Los dos trataron de concretar el contrato.*

**na|ive** /naɪiv/ also **naïve** ADJ If you describe someone as **naive**, you think they lack experience and so expect things to be easy or people to be honest or kind. *ingenuo* ❑ *I was naive to think they would agree. Fui muy ingenuo al creer que estarían de acuerdo.* ● **na|ive|ly** ADV *ingenuamente* ❑ *I naively thought that everything would be fine once we were married. Creí ingenuamente que todo saldría bien una vez que nos casáramos.* ● **na|ive|té** /naɪivteɪ, -ivteɪ/ N-UNCOUNT *ingenuidad* ❑ *I was alarmed by his naiveté. Me alarmó su ingenuidad.*

**na|ked** /neɪkɪd/ **1** ADJ Someone who is **naked** is not wearing any clothes. *desnudo* ❑ *She held the naked baby in her arms. Sostuvo al bebé desnudo en los brazos.* ● **na|ked|ness** N-UNCOUNT *desnudez* ❑ *He pulled the blanket over his body to hide his nakedness. Jaló la cobija para cubrir la desnudez de su cuerpo.* **2** ADJ You can describe an object as **naked** when it does not have its normal covering. *descubierto* ❑ *...a naked light bulb. ...un foco descubierto.* **3** ADJ **Naked** emotions are easily recognized because they are very strongly felt and cannot be hidden. *manifiesto* [WRITTEN] ❑ *I could see the naked hatred in her face. Pude ver el odio manifiesto en su rostro.* ● **nakedly** ADV *manifiestamente* ❑ *He nakedly desired success. Era manifiesto que deseaba tener éxito.* **4** PHRASE If you say that something cannot be seen by **the naked eye,** you mean that it cannot be seen without the help of equipment such as a telescope or microscope. *a simple vista*

**name** /neɪm/ (**names, naming, named**) **1** N-COUNT The **name** of a person, place, or thing is the word or words that you use to identify them. *nombre* ❑ *"What's his name?"— "Peter." —¿Cómo se llama? —Peter.* ❑ *They changed the name of the street. Cambiaron el nombre de la calle.* **2** V-T When you **name** someone or something, you give them a name, usually at the beginning of their life. If you **name** someone or something **after** a person or thing, you give them the same name as that person or thing. *nombrar, llamar* ❑ *...a man named John T. Benson. ...un hombre llamado John T. Benson.* ❑ *He named his first child after his brother. Le puso el nombre de su hermano a su primer hijo.* **3** V-T If you **name** someone, you identify them by stating their name. *identificar* ❑ *The victim was named as twenty-year-old John Barr. Se identificó a la víctima como John Barr, de veinte años de edad.* **4** V-T If you **name** something such as a price, time, or place, you say what you want it to be. *decir* ❑ *Call Marty, and tell him to name his price. —Llama a Marty y pídele que te diga cuánto cobra.* **5** N-COUNT You can refer to the reputation of a person or thing as their **name.** *nombre* ❑ *...the good name of the vice-president. ...el buen nombre del vicepresidente.* **6** N-COUNT You can refer to someone as, for example, a famous **name** or a great **name** when they are well known. *nombre* ❑ *...some of the most famous names in show business. ...algunos de los nombres más famosos del espectáculo/de la farándula.* **7** → see also **brand name, Christian name, first name** **8** PHRASE You can use **by name** or **by the name of** when you are saying what someone is called. *responder al nombre de* [FORMAL] ❑ *He met a young Australian by the name of Harry Busteed. Conoció a un joven australiano que respondía al nombre de Harry Busteed.* **9** PHRASE If someone **calls** you **names,** they insult you by saying unpleasant things to you or about you. *insultar, decir de todo* ❑ *At my last school they called me names because I was fat. En mi escuela anterior me decían de todo porque estaba gordo.* **10** PHRASE If something is **in** someone's **name,** it officially belongs to them or is reserved for them. *a nombre de* ❑ *The house is in my husband's name. La casa está a nombre de mi esposo.* **11** PHRASE If you do something **in the name of** an ideal or an abstract thing, you do it in order to preserve or promote that thing. *en nombre*

de, con pretexto de ❑ We all do such crazy things in the name of love. Todos cometemos locuras en nombre del amor. **12** PHRASE If you **make a name for yourself** or **make** your **name as** something, you become well known for that thing. hacerse de un nombre, hacerse de fama ❑ She is making a name for herself as a photographer. Se está haciendo de fama como fotógrafa. **13** If you say that something is **the name of the game,** you mean that it is the most important aspect of a situation. el nombre del juego [INFORMAL] ❑ Survival is the name of the game. El nombre del juego es supervivencia.
→ see **Internet**

**Word Partnership** Usar *name* con:

N. name **and address, company** name, name **and number** **1**
ADJ. **common** name, **full** name, **real** name **1** **familiar** name, **famous** name, **well-known** name **6**

**name|ly** /neɪmli/ ADV You use **namely** to introduce detailed information about the subject you are discussing, or a particular aspect of it. es decir, a saber ❑ ...the starting point of business, namely money. ...el punto de partida de los negocios, es decir, el dinero.

**nan|ny** /næni/ (**nannies**) N-COUNT A **nanny** is a woman who is paid by parents to take care of their child or children. nana, niñera

**nap** /næp/ (**naps, napping, napped**) **1** N-COUNT If you take or have a **nap,** you have a short sleep, usually during the day. siesta ❑ We had a nap after lunch. Hicimos la siesta después de comer. **2** V-I If you **nap,** you sleep for a short period of time, usually during the day. dormitar ❑ Many elderly people nap during the day. Muchos ancianos dormitan durante el día.
→ see **sleep**

N

**nap|kin** /næpkɪn/ (**napkins**) N-COUNT A **napkin** is a square of cloth or paper that you use when you are eating to protect your clothes, or to wipe your mouth or hands. servilleta ❑ I took a bite of a hot dog and wiped my lips with a napkin. Le di una mordida al perro caliente y me limpié la boca con una servilleta.

**nar|ra|tive** /nærətɪv/ (**narratives**) N-COUNT A **narrative** is a story or an account of a series of events. relato, narración ❑ ...a fast-moving narrative. ...un relato lleno de acción.

**nar|row** /næroʊ/ (**narrower, narrowest, narrows, narrowing, narrowed**) **1** ADJ Something that is **narrow** measures a very small distance from one side to the other, especially compared to its length or height. angosto, estrecho ❑ ...the town's narrow streets. ...las angostas/estrechas calles de la ciudad. ❑ She had long, narrow feet. Tenía pies largos y angostos. ● **nar|row|ness** N-UNCOUNT estrechez ❑ ...the narrowness of her waist. ...lo estrecho de su cintura. **2** V-I If something **narrows,** it becomes less wide. estrecharse, angostarse ❑ The wide track narrows before crossing a stream. El ancho sendero se estrecha antes de cruzar un riachuelo. **3** ADJ If you describe someone's ideas, attitudes, or beliefs as **narrow,** you disapprove of them because they are restricted in some way, and often ignore the more important aspects of an argument or situation. intolerante ❑ ...a narrow and outdated view of family life. ...un punto de vista intolerante y anticuado de la vida en familia. ● **nar|row|ness** N-UNCOUNT cerrado, intolerante ❑ ...the narrowness of their opinions. ...lo cerrado de sus opiniones. **4** V-T/V-I If something **narrows** or if you **narrow** it, its extent or range becomes smaller. reducir ❑ The EU and America narrowed their political differences. Estados Unidos y el resto de América redujeron sus diferencias políticas. ● **nar|row|ing** N-SING reducción ❑ ...a narrowing of the gap between rich and poor people. ...una reducción de la distancia entre ricos y pobres. **5** ADJ If you have a **narrow** victory, you succeed in winning but only by a small amount. escaso ❑ Mr Kerry won the debate by a narrow margin. El señor Kerry ganó el debate por un escaso margen. ● **nar|row|ly** ADV escasamente ❑ She narrowly failed to win enough votes. No logró obtener los votos suficientes por un escaso margen. **6** ADJ If you have a **narrow** escape, something unpleasant nearly happens to you. salvarse de milagro ❑ He had a narrow escape from drowning. Se salvó de ahogarse de milagro. ● **nar|row|ly** ADV salvarse de milagro ❑ Five firefighters narrowly escaped death when a staircase fell on them. Cinco bomberos se salvaron de morir de milagro cuando una escalera se les vino encima.
▸ **narrow down** PHR-VERB If you **narrow down** a range of things, you reduce the number of things included in it. reducir ❑ The committee has narrowed down the list to the best candidates. La comisión redujo la lista a los mejores candidatos.

**Thesaurus** *narrow* Ver también:

ADJ. close, cramped, restricted, tight; (*ant.*) broad, wide **1** **3**

**Word Partnership** Usar *narrow* con:

ADV. **relatively** narrow, **too** narrow **1**
N. narrow **band,** narrow **hallway,** narrow **opening,** narrow **path** **1**
narrow **definition,** narrow **focus,** narrow **mind,** narrow **view** **3**

**nas|ty** /næsti/ (**nastier, nastiest**) **1** ADJ Something that is **nasty** is very unpleasant or unattractive. detestable, repugnante, horripilante ❑ ...a very nasty murder. ...un asesinato horripilante. ● **nas|ti|ness** N-UNCOUNT lo repugnante ❑ ...the nastiness of war. ...lo repugnante de la guerra. **2** ADJ If you describe a person or their behavior as **nasty,** you mean that they behave in an unkind and unpleasant way. cruel ❑ She is so nasty to me. Es tan cruel conmigo. ❑ The guards looked really nasty. Los guardias tenían una apariencia realmente cruel. ● **nas|ti|ly** ADV de manera cruel ❑ Mr. Saunders looked at him nastily. El señor Saunders le lanzó una mirada llena de crueldad. **3** ADJ A **nasty** problem or situation is very worrisome and difficult to deal with. peliagudo ❑ It was a nasty problem but we solved it. Era un problema peliagudo, pero lo resolvimos. **4** ADJ If you describe an injury or a disease as **nasty,** you mean that it is serious or looks unpleasant. horrible ❑ Alison cut her knee—it was a nasty wound. Alison se cortó la rodilla y se hizo una herida horrible. ❑ She had a nasty infection. Tenía una infección horrible.

**na|tion** /neɪʃᵊn/ (**nations**) N-COUNT A **nation** is an individual country considered together with its social and political structures. nación,

país, estado ❑ *...the United States and other nations.* *...Estados Unidos y otros países.*
→ see **country**

**Thesaurus** *nation* Ver también:
N. country, democracy, population, republic, society

**na|tion|al** /næʃənᵊl/ (**nationals**) **1** ADJ **National** means relating to the whole of a country or nation rather than to part of it or to other nations. nacional ❑ *...major national and international issues.* *...importantes cuestiones nacionales e internacionales.* • **na|tion|al|ly** ADV a escala nacional ❑ *...a nationally-televised speech.* *...un discurso televisado a escala nacional.* **2** ADJ **National** means typical of the people or customs of a particular country or nation. nacional ❑ *Baseball is the national pastime.* *El béisbol es el pasatiempo nacional.* **3** N-COUNT You can refer to someone who is legally a citizen of a country as a **national** of that country. ciudadano o ciudadana ❑ *...a French national.* *...una ciudadana francesa.*

**na|tion|al debt** (**national debts**) N-COUNT A country's **national debt** is all the money that the government of the country has borrowed and still owes. deuda nacional ❑ *He talked about the importance of reducing the national debt.* *Habló sobre la importancia de reducir la deuda nacional.*

**na|tion|al holi|day** (**national holidays**) N-COUNT A **national holiday** is a day when people do not go to work or school and celebrate some special event, often a national or religious event. fiesta patria, día de fiesta nacional ❑ *Today is a national holiday in Japan.* *Hoy es un día de fiesta nacional en Japón.*

**na|tion|al|ist** /næʃənᵊlɪst/ (**nationalists**) **1** ADJ **Nationalist** means connected with the desire of a group of people within a country for political independence. nacionalista ❑ *She has strong nationalist views.* *Tiene opiniones muy nacionalistas.* • A **nationalist** is someone with nationalist views. nacionalista ❑ *...demands by nationalists for an independent state.* *...las demandas de los nacionalistas de tener un estado independiente.* **2** ADJ **Nationalist** means connected with a person's great love for their nation, or their belief that their nation is better than others. nacionalista ❑ *...nationalist beliefs.* *...creencias nacionalistas.* • A **nationalist** is someone with nationalist views. nacionalista ❑ *...the late African-American nationalist, Malcolm X.* *...el finado nacionalista estadunidense de origen africano, Malcom X.* • **nationalism** N-UNCOUNT nacionalismo ❑ *...extreme nationalism.* *...nacionalismo extremo.*

**na|tion|al|ity** /næʃənælɪti/ (**nationalities**) N-VAR If you have the **nationality** of a particular country, you were born there or have the legal right to be a citizen. nacionalidad ❑ *Mr Harris has joint British and Australian nationality.* *El señor Harris tiene la doble nacionalidad británica y australiana.*

**na|tion|al se|cu|rity** N-UNCOUNT A country's **national security** is its ability to protect itself from the threat of violence or attack. seguridad nacional ❑ *We must deal with threats to our national security.* *Debemos enfrentar las amenazas a nuestra seguridad nacional.*

**Word Link** *wide* ≈ *extending throughout* : *citywide, nationwide, worldwide*

**nation|wide** /neɪʃᵊnwaɪd/ ADJ **Nationwide** activities or situations happen or exist in all parts of a country. a escala nacional, en todo el país ❑ *Car crime is a nationwide problem.* *El robo de autos es un problema a escala nacional.* • **Nationwide** is also an adverb. a escala nacional, en todo el país ❑ *Unemployment fell nationwide last month.* *El mes pasado, el desempleo se redujo en todo el país.*

**na|tive** /neɪtɪv/ (**natives**) **1** ADJ Your **native** country or area is the country or area where you were born and brought up. natal ❑ *It was his first visit to his native country since 1948.* *Era su primera visita a su tierra natal desde 1948.* **2** N-COUNT A **native of** a particular country, region or town is someone who was born in that country, region or town. originario de u originaria de ❑ *Dr. Aubin is a native of St. Louis.* *El doctor Aubin es originario de St. Louis.* • **Native** is also an adjective. originario de ❑ *Joshua Halpern is a native Northern Californian.* *Joshua Halpern es originario del norte de California.* **3** ADJ Your **native** language or tongue is the first language that you learned to speak when you were a child. natal, materno ❑ *Her native language was Swedish.* *Su idioma materno era el sueco.* **4** ADJ Plants or animals that are **native to** a particular region live or grow there naturally and were not brought there. originario de ❑ *Many of the plants are native to Brazil.* *Muchas de las plantas son originarias del Brasil.* • **Native** is also a noun. originario de u originaria de ❑ *The coconut palm is a native of Malaysia.* *La palma de coco es originaria de Malasia.*

**Word Partnership** Usar *native* con:
N. native **country**, native **land** **1**
native **language**, native **tongue** **3**

**natu|ral** /nætʃərəl, nætʃrəl/ (**naturals**) **1** ADJ If you say that it is **natural** for someone to act in a particular way or for something to happen in that way, you mean that it is reasonable in the circumstances. natural ❑ *It is only natural for youngsters to want excitement.* *Es completamente natural que los jóvenes busquen emociones.* **2** ADJ **Natural** behavior is shared by all people or all animals of a particular type. natural ❑ *...the insect's natural instinct to feed.* *...el instinto natural de los insectos de alimentarse.* **3** ADJ Someone with a **natural** ability or skill was born with that ability and did not have to learn it. nato, innato, de nacimiento ❑ *Alan is a natural musician.* *Alan es un músico nato/innato.* **4** N-COUNT If you say that someone is **a natural,** you mean that they do something very well and very easily. talento innato ❑ *He's a natural with children.* *Tiene un talento innato para tratar a los niños.* **5** ADJ If someone's behavior is **natural,** they appear to be relaxed and are not trying to hide anything. natural ❑ *Mary's sister is as friendly and natural as the rest of the family.* *La hermana de Mary es tan amigable y natural como el resto de la familia.* • **natu|ral|ly** ADV con naturalidad ❑ *It's important to act naturally if you can.* *Es importante actuar con naturalidad, si se puede.* • **natu|ral|ness** N-UNCOUNT naturalidad ❑ *The critics praised the naturalness of the acting.* *Los críticos alabaron la*

*naturalidad de su actuación.* 6 ADJ **Natural** things exist in nature and were not created by people. *natural* ❑ *...a natural harbor. ...un puerto natural.*
● **natu|ral|ly** ADV *naturalmente* ❑ *Gas is naturally odorless. El gas es naturalmente inodoro.*

**Thesaurus** *natural* Ver también:

ADJ. normal 1
innate, instinctive 2 3
genuine, sincere, unaffected 5
wild; (*ant.*) artificial 6

**Word Partnership** Usar *natural* con:

ADV. **perfectly** natural 1 2 5
N. natural **reaction**, natural **tendency** 2
natural **beauty**, natural **disaster**, natural **food** 6

**natu|ral food** (**natural foods**) N-VAR **Natural food** is food which has not been processed much and has not had artificial ingredients added to it. *alimento natural* ❑ *Olive oil is a natural food. El aceite de oliva es un alimento natural.*

**natu|ral gas** N-UNCOUNT **Natural gas** is gas which is found underground or under the sea. It is collected and stored, and piped into people's homes to be used for cooking and heating *gas natural*
→ see **energy**

**natu|ral light** N-UNCOUNT **Natural light** is light from the sun rather than from an artificial source such as an electric light. *luz natural*

N

**natu|ral|ly** /nætʃərəli, nætʃrəli/ 1 ADV You use **naturally** to indicate that something is very obvious and not surprising under the circumstances. *naturalmente* ❑ *When things go wrong, all of us naturally feel disappointed. Naturalmente, cuando las cosas van mal, todos nos sentimos decepcionados.* 2 ADV If one thing develops **naturally** from another, it develops as a normal result of it. *de manera natural* ❑ *His love of machines led naturally to a career in engineering. Su gusto por las máquinas lo llevó de manera natural a la carrera de ingeniería.* 3 PHRASE If something **comes naturally to** you, you find it easy to do and quickly become good at it. *con toda naturalidad* ❑ *Biking comes naturally to kids. Los niños aprenden a montar en bicicleta con toda naturalidad.* 4 → see also **natural**

**natu|ral re|sources** N-PLURAL **Natural resources** are all the land, forests, energy sources and minerals existing naturally in a place that can be used by people. *recursos naturales*

**natu|ral se|lec|tion** N-UNCOUNT **Natural selection** is a process by which species of animals and plants that are best adapted to their environment survive and reproduce, while those that are less well adapted die out. *selección natural* ❑ *Natural selection ensures only the fittest survive to pass their genes on to the next generation. La selección natural asegura que sólo los más aptos sobrevivan para pasar sus genes a la siguiente generación.*

**na|ture** /neɪtʃər/ 1 N-UNCOUNT **Nature** is all the animals, plants, and other things in the world that are not made by people, and all the events and processes that are not caused by people. *naturaleza* ❑ *...the relationship between man and nature. ...la relación entre el hombre y la naturaleza.* 2 N-SING The **nature** of something is its basic quality or character. *naturaleza* ❑ *The police would not comment on the nature of the investigation. La policía no quiso hacer comentarios sobre la naturaleza de las indagaciones.* ❑ *He is quiet by nature. Es tranquilo por naturaleza.* 3 N-SING Someone's **nature** is their character, which they show by the way they behave. *naturaleza, carácter, índole* ❑ *Her nickname was "Sunny" because of her friendly nature. Lo apodan "Risueño" por su naturaleza amistosa.* ❑ *She trusted people. That was her nature. Confiaba en las personas; así era su carácter natural.* 4 → see also **human nature** 5 PHRASE If you say that something has a particular characteristic **by** its **nature** or **by** its **very nature,** you mean that things of that type always have that characteristic. *por su naturaleza* ❑ *Hockey is by its nature a violent game. Por su naturaleza, el hockey es un juego violento.* 6 PHRASE If a way of behaving is **second nature to** you, you do it almost without thinking because it is easy for you or obvious to you. *parte de la naturaleza de* ❑ *Planning ahead came as second nature to her. El planear con anticipación formaba parte de su naturaleza.*

**Word Partnership** Usar *nature* con:

V. **love** nature, **preserve** nature 1
N. **love of** nature, **wonders of** nature 1
nature **of life**, nature **of society**, nature **of work** 2

**naugh|ty** /nɔti/ (**naughtier, naughtiest**) ADJ A **naughty** child behaves badly or does not do what they are told. *travieso* ❑ *Girls, you're being very naughty. Niñas, ¡no sean tan traviesas!*

**Word Link** *nav ≈ ship : naval, navigate, navy*

**na|val** /neɪvᵊl/ ADJ **Naval** means belonging to, relating to, or involving a country's navy. *naval, de la marina* ❑ *He was a senior naval officer. Era oficial de alto rango de la marina.*

**navi|gate** /nævɪgeɪt/ (**navigates, navigating, navigated**) 1 V-T/V-I When someone **navigates** a ship or an aircraft somewhere, they decide which course to follow and steer it there. *conducir, navegar, capitanear* ❑ *Captain Cook navigated his ship without accident for 100 voyages. El capitán Cook capitaneó su barco en 100 viajes sin un solo accidente.* ❑ *I navigated for 12 or 14 hours a day on the boat. Solía navegar durante 12 o 14 horas diarias en el bote.*
● **navi|ga|tion** /nævɪgeɪʃᵊn/ N-VAR (**navigations**) *navegación* ❑ *The planes had their navigation lights on. Los aviones tenían encendidas las luces de navegación.* 2 V-T/V-I When a ship or boat **navigates** an area of water, it sails on or across it. *navegar* ❑ *Every year they navigate the Greek islands in a sailboat. Todos los años navegan por las islas griegas en un bote de vela.* ❑ *Such boats can navigate on the Hudson. Esos barcos pueden navegar por el río Hudson.*
→ see Word Web: **navigation**
→ see **star**

**navy** /neɪvi/ (**navies**) 1 N-COUNT A country's **navy** consists of the people it employs to fight at sea, and the ships they use. *marina de guerra, armada* ❑ *The operation was organized by the U.S. Navy. La operación fue organizada por la Marina de Estados*

**Word Web** **navigation**

Early explorers used the **sun** and **stars** to navigate the seas. Later navigators also used the sextant. With this tool, sailors could look at the sun or stars and accurately find their **position**. By sighting or measuring their position at noon, sailors could figure out their **latitude**. The **compass** helped sailors find their position at any time of night or day. It also worked in any weather. Today many travelers use the global positioning system (GPS) to guide their journeys. A GPS **receiver** is connected to a system of 24 **satellites** that can establish a location within a few feet.

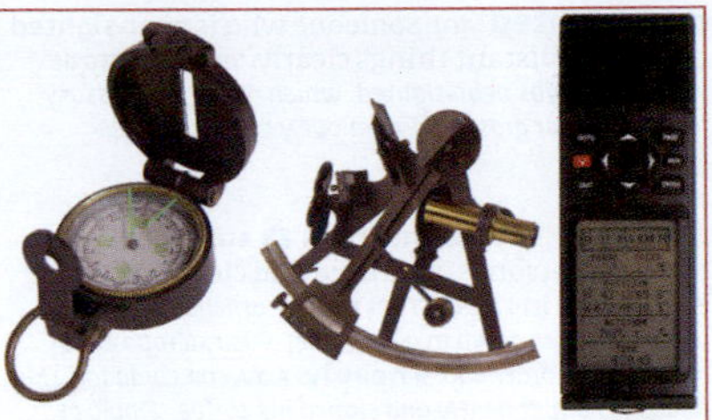

compass sextant GPS

*Unidos.* ❑ *Her own son was also in the navy.* *Su hijo también estaba en la marina.* **2** COLOR Something that is **navy** or **navy-blue** is very dark blue. *azul marino* ❑ *I mostly wore white shirts and black or navy pants.* *Casi siempre usaba camisa blanca y pantalones negros o azul marino.*

**NBA** /ɛn bi eɪ/ N-PROPER In the United States, **the NBA** is the organization responsible for professional basketball. **NBA** is an abbreviation for "National Basketball Association." *Asociación Nacional de Baloncesto/Basketball, NBA* ❑ *The Portland Trail Blazers had the best record in the NBA last year.* *El año pasado fue el mejor de los Trailblazers de Portland en la NBA.* ❑ *...the new NBA champions.* *...los nuevos campeones de la NBA.*

**Ne|an|der|thal** /niændərθɔl, -tɔl/ (**Neanderthals**) ADJ **Neanderthal** people lived in Europe between 35,000 and 70,000 years ago. *Neanderthal* • You can refer to people from the Neanderthal period as **Neanderthals.** *Se puede uno referir a los homínidos que vivieron durante el pleistoceno como el "hombre de Neanderthal".*
→ see **evolution**

**neap tide** /nip taɪd/ (**neap tides**) N-COUNT A **neap tide** is a tide with a smaller rise and fall than normal, which occurs when the moon is halfway between a new moon and a full moon. *marea muerta*

**near** /nɪər/ (**nearer, nearest, nears, nearing, neared**) **1** PREP If something is **near** a place, thing, or person, it is a short distance from them. *cerca* ❑ *Don't come near me.* *No te me acerques.* • **Near** is also an adverb. *cerca* ❑ *He stood as near to the door as he could.* *Se paró tan cerca de la puerta como pudo.* • **Near** is also an adjective. *cercano* ❑ *He sat in the nearest chair.* *Se sentó en la silla más cercana.* ❑ *The nearer of the two cars was half a mile away.* *El más cercano de los dos coches estaba a 800 metros de distancia.* **2** PHRASE If someone or something is **near to** a particular state, they have almost reached it. *a punto de* ❑ *They are near to reaching agreement.* *Están a punto de llegar a un acuerdo.* • **Near** means the same as **near to.** *al borde de, a punto de* ❑ *He was near tears.* *Estaba al borde de las lágrimas.* **3** PHRASE If something is similar to something else, you can say that it is **near to** it. *cercano* ❑ *...a feeling that was near to panic.* *...un sentimiento cercano al pánico.* • **Near** means the same as **near to.** *cercano* ❑ *Her feelings were nearer hatred than love.* *Sus sentimientos estaban más cercanos del odio que del amor.* **4** PREP If something happens **near** a particular time, it happens just before or just after that time. *cerca de* ❑ *The group stopped for lunch near midday.* *El grupo se detuvo para comer cerca del mediodía.* **5** PREP You use **near** to say that something is a little more or less than an amount or number stated. *casi* ❑ *Temperatures dropped to near zero.* *La temperatura bajó a casi cero.* **6** ADJ You use **near** to indicate that something is almost the thing mentioned. *casi* ❑ *They were sitting in near darkness.* *Estaban sentados casi en la oscuridad.* • **Near** is also an adverb. *casi* ❑ *She had near perfect eyesight.* *Tenía una vista casi perfecta.* **7** V-T When someone or something **nears** a particular place, stage or point, they will soon reach that stage or point. *cerca de* ❑ *His age is hard to guess—he must be nearing fifty.* *Es difícil determinar su edad; debe estar cerca de los cincuenta.* **8** PHRASE If you say that something will happen **in the near future,** you mean that it will happen quite soon. *en un futuro próximo* ❑ *We're hoping to visit New York in the near future.* *Esperamos ir a Nueva York en un futuro próximo.* **9** PHRASE You use **nowhere near** and **not anywhere near** to say that something is not the case. *ni siquiera cerca, para nada* ❑ *They are nowhere near good enough to win.* *No están ni siquiera cerca de poder ganar.* ❑ *It was not anywhere near as painful as David expected.* *Para nada era tan doloroso como David se lo esperaba.*

**near|by** /nɪərbaɪ/ ADV If something is **nearby,** it is only a short distance away. *cerca* ❑ *Her sister lived nearby.* *Su hermana vivía cerca.* ❑ *The helicopter crashed to earth nearby.* *El helicóptero se vino a tierra cerca de ahí.* • **Nearby** is also an adjective. *cercano* ❑ *...a nearby table.* *...una mesa cercana.*

**near|ly** /nɪərli/ **1** ADV If something is **nearly** a quantity, it is very close to that quantity but slightly less than it. If something is **nearly** a certain state, it is very close to that state but has not quite reached it. *casi* ❑ *We waited nearly half an hour for the bus.* *Esperamos el autobús durante casi media hora.* ❑ *It was already nearly eight o'clock.* *Ya casi iban a dar las ocho.* ❑ *I've nearly finished.* *Ya casi he terminado.* **2** PHRASE You use **not nearly** to emphasize that something is not the case. For example, if something is **not nearly** big enough, it is much too small. *ni con mucho* ❑ *My father's apartment isn't nearly as large as this.* *El departamento de mi padre no es ni con mucho tan grande como este.*

**Thesaurus** *nearly* Ver también:
ADV. almost, approximately **1**

n

**near-sighted** ADJ Someone who is **near-sighted** cannot see distant things clearly. miope, corto de vista ❑ *She was near-sighted, which made it necessary for her to wear glasses.* *Era miope y necesitaba usar lentes.*
→ see **eye**

**neat** /nit/ (**neater, neatest**) **1** ADJ A **neat** place, thing, or person is organized and clean, and has everything in the correct place. ordenado ❑ *She put her clothes down in a neat pile.* *Puso su ropa en un montón bien ordenado.* ● **neat|ly** ADV con cuidado ❑ *He folded his paper neatly and sipped his coffee.* *Dobló el papel con cuidado y tomó un sorbo de café.* ● **neat|ness** N-UNCOUNT pulcritud ❑ *...the neatness of her appearance.* *...la pulcritud de su apariencia.* **2** ADJ If you say that something is **neat,** you mean that it is very good. a todo dar [INFORMAL] ❑ *He thought Mike was a really neat guy.* *Pensó que Mike era un cuate a todo dar.* **3** ADJ A **neat** explanation or method is clever and convenient. ingenioso ❑ *It was such a neat, clever plan.* *Era un plan ingenioso y bien pensado.* ● **neat|ly** ADV netamente ❑ *Real people do not fit neatly into these categories.* *Las personas reales no corresponden netamente a esas categorías.*

| **Thesaurus** | *neat* | Ver también: |
|---|---|---|
| ADJ. | orderly, tidy **1** | |

**nebu|la** /nɛbyələ/ (**nebulae**) N-COUNT A **nebula** is a cloud of dust and gas in space. New stars are produced from nebulae. nebulosa

**nec|es|sari|ly** /nɛsɪsɛərɪli/ ADV If you say that something is **not necessarily** true, you mean that it may not be true or is not always true. necesariamente ❑ *Women do not necessarily have to act like men to be successful.* *Las mujeres no tienen que actuar necesariamente como hombres para alcanzar el éxito.* CONVENTION ● If you reply **"Not necessarily,"** you mean that what has just been said or suggested may not be true. necesariamente ❑ *"He was lying, of course." — "Not necessarily."* *—Estaba mintiendo, claro. —No necesariamente.*

**nec|es|sary** /nɛsɪsɛri/ **1** ADJ Something that is **necessary** is needed in order for something else to happen. necesario ❑ *It might be necessary to leave fast.* *Podría ser necesario que nos vayamos pronto.* ❑ *Make the necessary arrangements.* *Haz los arreglos necesarios.* **2** PHRASE A **necessary evil** is something unpleasant or which you do not like but which must happen in order to achieve the result you want. mal necesario ❑ *For most of us, work is a necessary evil.* *El trabajo es un mal necesario para la mayoría de nosotros.*

| **Thesaurus** | *necessary* | Ver también: |
|---|---|---|
| ADJ. | essential, mandatory, obligatory, required; (*ant.*) unnecessary **1** | |

**ne|ces|sity** /nɪsɛsɪti/ (**necessities**) **1** N-UNCOUNT The **necessity** of something is the fact that it must happen or exist. necesidad ❑ *He learned the necessity of hiding his feelings.* *Vio la necesidad de ocultar sus sentimientos.* PHRASE ● If you say that something is **of necessity** true, you mean that it is true because nothing else is possible or practical under the circumstances. por necesidad [FORMAL] ❑ *In large families, children, of necessity, shared a bed.* *En las familias numerosas, por necesidad, los niños comparten camas.* **2** N-COUNT **Necessities** are things that you must have to live. necesidad ❑ *Water is a basic necessity of life.* *El agua es una necesidad básica de la vida.*

**neck** /nɛk/ (**necks**) **1** N-COUNT Your **neck** is the part of your body which joins your head to the rest of your body. cuello ❑ *She was wearing a red scarf around her neck.* *Llevaba una bufanda roja en torno al cuello.* **2** N-COUNT The **neck** of a shirt or a dress is the part which surrounds your neck. cuello ❑ *...the low neck of her dress.* *...el escote de su vestido.* **3** N-COUNT The **neck** of something such as a bottle or a guitar is the long narrow part at one end of it. cuello ❑ *The neck of the bottle broke.* *Se rompió el cuello de la botella.* **4** PHRASE In a competition, especially an election, if two or more competitors are **neck and neck,** they are level with each other and have an equal chance of winning. a la par ❑ *The Democrats and the Republicans are neck and neck.* *Demócratas y republicanos van a la par.*
→ see **body**

| **Word Partnership** | Usar *neck* con: |
|---|---|
| N. | **back/nape of the** neck, **head and** neck, neck **injury** **1** |
| ADJ. | **broken** neck, **long** neck, **stiff** neck, **thick** neck **1** |

**neck|lace** /nɛklɪs/ (**necklaces**) N-COUNT A **necklace** is a piece of jewelry such as a chain or a string of beads which someone, usually a woman, wears around their neck. collar ❑ *...a diamond necklace.* *...un collar de diamantes.*
→ see **jewelry**

**nec|tar** /nɛktər/ N-UNCOUNT **Nectar** is a sweet liquid produced by flowers, which bees and other insects collect. néctar

**need** /nid/ (**needs, needing, needed**) **1** V-T If you **need** something, or **need to** do something, you cannot successfully achieve what you want or live properly without it. necesitar ❑ *He desperately needed money.* *Necesitaba dinero con desesperación.* ❑ *I need to make a phone call.* *Necesito hacer una llamada.* ❑ *I need you to do something for me.* *Necesito que hagas algo por mí.* ❑ *I need you here, Wally.* *Te necesito aquí, Wally.* ● **Need** is also a noun. necesidad ❑ *Charles has never felt the need to compete with anyone.* *Charles nunca ha sentido la necesidad de competir con nadie.* ❑ *...his need for attention.* *...su necesidad de atención.* **2** V-T If an object or place **needs** something done to it, that action should be done to improve the object or place. If a task **needs** doing, it should be done to improve a particular situation. necesitar ❑ *The building needs quite a few repairs.* *El edificio necesita bastantes reparaciones.* ❑ *My house needs cleaning.* *Mi casa necesita limpieza.* ❑ *Action needs to be taken quickly.* *Es necesario actuar rápidamente.* **3** N-SING If there is a **need for** something, that thing would improve a situation. necesidad ❑ *There is a need for other similar schools.* *Existe la necesidad de más escuelas similares.* ❑ *"I think you should see a doctor." — "I don't think there's any need for that."* *—Creo que deberías ver a un médico. —No creo que haya ninguna necesidad de ello.* **4** V-T If you say that someone does not **need to** do something, you are telling them not to do it, or advising or suggesting

N

that they should not do it. _necesitar_ ❑ *You don't need to apologize.* _No necesita disculparse._ **5** V-T If someone **didn't need to** do something, it wasn't necessary or useful for them to do it, although they did it. _necesitar_ ❑ *You didn't need to give me any more money, but thank you.* _No necesitabas darme más dinero, pero, gracias._ **6** PHRASE People **in need** do not have enough of essential things such as money, food, or good health. _necesitado_ ❑ *Leiter's Landing is a charity that helps children in need.* _Leiter's Landing es una institución de beneficencia que ayuda a los niños necesitados._ **7** PHRASE If you are **in need of** something, you need it or ought to have it. _necesitar, hacer falta_ ❑ *I was all right but in need of rest.* _Estaba bien, pero necesitaba descansar._ ❑ *He was badly in need of a shave.* _Le hacía mucha falta una buena rasurada._

| Thesaurus | *need* | Ver también: |
|---|---|---|
| v. | demand, require **1** | |

**nee|dle** /nidᵊl/ (**needles**) **1** N-COUNT A **needle** is a small, very thin piece of polished metal which is used for sewing. It has a sharp point at one end and a hole in the other for a thread to go through. _aguja_ ❑ *...a needle and thread.* _...hilo y aguja._ **2** N-COUNT A **needle** is a thin hollow metal tube with a sharp point. It is used to give injections. _aguja hipodérmica_ ❑ *Dirty needles spread disease.* _Las agujas hipodérmicas sucias transmiten enfermedades._

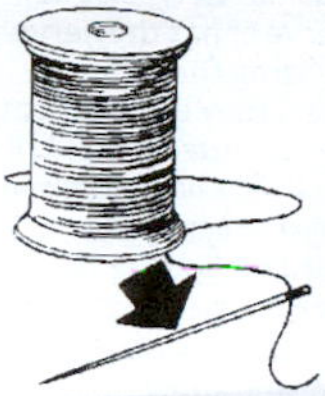
needle

**3** N-COUNT Knitting **needles** are thin metal or plastic sticks that are used for knitting. _aguja de tejer_ ❑ *...a pair of knitting needles.* _...un par de agujas de tejer._ **4** N-COUNT On an instrument which measures something such as speed or weight, the **needle** is the long strip of metal or plastic on the dial that moves backward and forward, showing the measurement. _aguja_ ❑ *The needle on the boiler had reached 200 degrees.* _La aguja de la caldera/el calentador había llegado a los 200 grados._ **5** N-COUNT The **needles** of a fir or pine tree are its thin, hard, pointed leaves. _aguja_ ❑ *Pine needles lay thickly on the ground.* _Hay una gruesa capa de agujas de pino sobre el suelo._

**nega|tive** /nɛgətɪv/ (**negatives**) **1** ADJ A fact, situation, or experience that is **negative** is unpleasant, depressing, or harmful. _desalentador_ ❑ *The news from overseas is very negative.* _Las noticias del extranjero eran muy desalentadoras._ **2** ADJ If someone is **negative** or has a **negative** attitude, they consider only the bad aspects of a situation, rather than the good ones. _negativo_ ❑ *When someone asks for your views, don't be negative.* _Cuando alguien te pida tu opinión, no seas negativo._ ● **nega|tive|ly** ADV _negativamente_ ❑ *Why do so many people think negatively?* _—¿Por qué tanta gente piensa negativamente?_ ● **nega|tiv|ity** /nɛgətɪvɪti/ N-UNCOUNT _negativismo_ ❑ *I hate negativity. I can't stand people who complain.* _Odio el negativismo. No soporto a la gente que se queja._ **3** ADJ A **negative** reply or decision indicates the answer "no." _negativo_ ❑ *Dr. Velayati gave a negative response.* _El doctor Velayati dio una respuesta negativa._ ● **nega|tive|ly** ADV _negativamente_ ❑ *Sixty percent of people answered negatively.* _El sesenta por ciento de las personas contestó negativamente._ **4** N-COUNT A **negative** is a word, expression, or gesture that means "no" or "not." _negación_ ❑ *He used five negatives in 53 words.* _Usó cinco negaciones en 53 palabras._ **5** ADJ In grammar, a **negative** clause contains a word such as "not," "never," or "no one." _oración enunciativa en forma negativa_ **6** ADJ If a medical test or scientific test is **negative,** it shows that the medical condition or substance that you are looking for is not there. _negativo_ ❑ *So far all the tests have been negative.* _Hasta ahora, todas las pruebas han sido negativas._ **7** ADJ A **negative** number, quantity, or measurement is less than zero. _negativo_ ❑ *...negative numbers such as -1.* _...números negativos, como -1._ **8** ADJ In painting and sculpture, **negative** space is the empty space that surrounds an object or form. _negativo_ [TECHNICAL]

| Word Partnership | Usar *negative* con: |
|---|---|
| N. | negative **effect**, negative **experience**, negative **image**, negative **publicity** **1**<br>negative **attitude**, negative **comment**, negative **thoughts** **1** **2**<br>negative **reaction**, negative **response** **3** |

**nega|tive ac|cel|era|tion** N-UNCOUNT **Negative acceleration** is a decrease in speed or velocity. _aceleración negativa, desaceleración_ [TECHNICAL]

**ne|glect** /nɪglɛkt/ (**neglects, neglecting, neglected**) **1** V-T If you **neglect** someone or something, you do not take care of them properly. _descuidar, abandonar, desatender_ ❑ *The woman denied neglecting her child.* _La mujer negó haber descuidado a su hijo._ ● **Neglect** is also a noun. _descuido, abandono, negligencia_ ❑ *The house has suffered years of neglect.* _La casa ha sufrido años de abandono._ **2** V-T If you **neglect** someone or something, you fail to give them the amount of attention that they deserve. _descuidar, abandonar, desatender_ ❑ *He's given too much to his career, worked long hours, neglected her.* _Ha dedicado mucho a su carrera, trabajado largas horas, y a ella la ha desatendido._ ● **ne|glect|ed** ADJ _abandonado, olvidado_ ❑ *Her grandmother feels lonely and neglected.* _Su abuela se siente sola y abandonada._ ❑ *...a neglected period of the city's history.* _...una época olvidada de la historia de la ciudad._ **3** V-T If you **neglect to** do something, you fail to do it. _descuidar_ ❑ *We often neglect to eat a healthy diet.* _Frecuentemente descuidamos comer saludablemente._

**ne|go|ti|ate** /nɪgoʊʃieɪt/ (**negotiates, negotiating, negotiated**) V-RECIP If people **negotiate with** each other or **negotiate** an agreement, they talk about a problem or a situation such as a business arrangement in order to solve the problem or complete the arrangement. _negociar_ ❑ *The president is willing to negotiate with the Democrats.* _El presidente está dispuesto a negociar con los demócratas._ ❑ *The government and the army negotiated an agreement.* _El gobierno y el ejército negociaron un acuerdo._

**ne|go|tia|tion** /nɪgoʊʃieɪʃᵊn/ (**negotiations**) N-VAR **Negotiations** are discussions between people with different aims, during which they try to reach an agreement. *negociación* ❑ *The negotiations were successful. Las negociaciones fueron exitosas.*

**neigh|bor** /neɪbər/ (**neighbors**) **1** N-COUNT Your **neighbor** is someone who lives near you. *vecino o vecina* ❑ *My neighbor is a teacher. Mi vecina es maestra.* **2** N-COUNT You can refer to the person who is standing or sitting next to you as your **neighbor.** *persona que está al lado* ❑ *The woman spoke to her neighbor. La mujer se dirigió a la persona que estaba a su lado.* **3** N-COUNT You can refer to something which stands next to something else of the same kind as its **neighbor.** *cosas que están cerca o junto a otra* ❑ *Consider each plant in your garden in relation to its neighbors. Piense en cada planta de su jardín en relación con las que estén cerca de ella.*

**neigh|bor|hood** /neɪbərhʊd/ (**neighborhoods**) N-COUNT A **neighborhood** is one of the parts of a town where people live. *vecindario, barrio* ❑ *...a wealthy Los Angeles neighborhood. ...un vecindario/barrio rico de Los Ángeles.*

**Word Partnership** Usar *neighborhood* con:

ADJ. **poor** neighborhood, **residential** neighborhood, **run-down** neighborhood

**neigh|bor|ing** /neɪbərɪŋ/ ADJ **Neighboring** places or things are near other things of the same kind. *vecino* ❑ *...Thailand and its neighboring countries. ...Tailandia y sus países vecinos.*

**neigh|bor|ly** /neɪbərli/ ADJ If the people who live near you are **neighborly,** they are friendly and helpful. *amable, con amabilidad* ❑ *They welcomed us in a very neighborly way. Nos dieron la bienvenida muy amablemente.*

**N**

**nei|ther** /niðər, naɪ-/ **1** CONJ You use **neither** in front of the first of two or more words or expressions when you are linking two or more things which are not true or do not happen. The other thing is introduced by "nor." *ni* ❑ *Professor Hisamatsu spoke neither English nor German. El profesor Hisamatsu no hablaba ni inglés ni alemán.* **2** DET You use **neither** to refer to each of two things or people, when you are making a negative statement that includes both of them. *ninguno, ni uno ni otro* ❑ *At first, neither man could speak. Al principio, ninguno (de los dos hombres) pudo hablar.* • **Neither** is also a quantifier. *ninguno* ❑ *Neither of us felt like going out. Ninguna de las dos tenía ganas de salir.* • **Neither** is also a pronoun. *ninguno o ninguna* ❑ *Neither noticed him leave the room. Ninguno de los dos lo vio salir del cuarto.* **3** CONJ If you say that one person or thing does not do something and **neither** does another, what you say is true of all the people or things that you are talking about. *tampoco* ❑ *I never learned to swim and neither did they. Jamás aprendí a nadar, y ellos tampoco.*

**nek|ton** /nɛktɒn/ N-PLURAL **Nekton** are animals such as fish and whales that are capable of swimming against a current. *necton* [TECHNICAL]

**neph|ew** /nɛfyu/ (**nephews**) N-COUNT Someone's **nephew** is the son of their sister or brother. *sobrino* ❑ *I am planning a 25th birthday party for my nephew. Estoy planeando una fiesta por los 25 años de mi sobrino.*

**Nep|tune** /nɛptun/ N-PROPER **Neptune** is the eighth planet from the sun. *Neptuno*
→ see **solar system**

**nerve** /nɜrv/ (**nerves**) **1** N-COUNT **Nerves** are long thin fibers that send messages between your brain and other parts of your body. *nervio* ❑ *...pain from a damaged nerve. ...dolor por un nervio lesionado.* **2** N-PLURAL If you refer to someone's **nerves,** you mean their ability to cope with problems such as stress, worry, and danger. *nervios* ❑ *His nerves are bad—he has a lot of depression. —Está mal de los nervios y sufre muchas depresiones.* **3** N-PLURAL You can refer to someone's feelings of worry or stress as **nerves.** *nervios* ❑ *It wasn't nerves—I just played badly. No fueron los nervios; simplemente, jugué mal.* **4** N-UNCOUNT **Nerve** is the courage that you need in order to do something difficult or dangerous. *valor, coraje* ❑ *I don't know why he lost his nerve. No sé por qué perdió el coraje.* **5** PHRASE If someone or something **gets on** your **nerves,** they annoy or irritate you. *poner los nervios de punta, crispar los nervios, sacar de quicio* [INFORMAL] ❑ *Jay loves his children, but their constant demands get on his nerves. Jay adora a sus hijos, pero sus constantes exigencias la sacan de quicio.* **6** PHRASE If you say that someone **has a nerve** or **has the nerve** to do something, you are criticizing them for doing something which you feel they had no right to do. *frescura, desvergüenza, descaro* [INFORMAL] ❑ *I can't believe you have the nerve to sit here and tell unkind stories about him. No creo que tengas el descaro/la desvergüenza de sentarte aquí a hablar mal de él.*
→ see **ear, nervous system, smell**

**nerv|ous** /nɜrvəs/ **1** ADJ If someone is **nervous,** they are frightened or worried, and show this in their behavior. *nervioso* ❑ *I was very nervous during the job interview. Estuve muy nervioso durante la entrevista de trabajo.* • **nerv|ous|ly** ADV *nerviosamente* ❑ *Beth stood up nervously as the men came into the room. Beth se paró nerviosamente cuando los hombres entraron al cuarto.* • **nerv|ous|ness** N-UNCOUNT *nerviosismo* ❑ *I smiled warmly so he wouldn't see my nervousness. Sonreí calurosamente para que no notara mi nerviosismo.* **2** ADJ A **nervous** person is very tense and easily upset. *nervioso* ❑ *She was a nervous person, easily startled by a sudden "hello." Era muy nerviosa; se sobresaltaba fácilmente si alguien la saludaba de repente.* **3** ADJ A **nervous** illness or condition is one that affects your mental state. *nervioso* ❑ *Abel has just been released from hospital where he was treated for a nervous disorder. Abel acaba de salir del hospital donde lo trataron por un trastorno nervioso.*

**Word Partnership** Usar *nervous* con:

PREP. nervous **about** ***something*** **1**
V. **become** nervous, **feel** nervous, **get** nervous, **look** nervous, **make** ***someone*** nervous **1**
ADV. **increasingly** nervous, **a little** nervous, **too** nervous, **very** nervous **1** **2**

**nerv|ous sys|tem** (**nervous systems**) N-COUNT Your **nervous system** consists of all the nerves in your body together with your brain and spinal cord. *sistema nervioso* ❑ *Multiple sclerosis is a disease of the nervous system. La esclerosis múltiple es una enfermedad del sistema nervioso.*
→ see Word Web: **nervous system**

**Word Web** nervous system

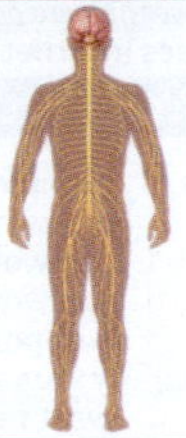

The body's **nervous system** is a two-way road which carries electrochemical messages to and from different parts of the body. **Sensory** neurons carry information from both inside and outside the body to the **central nervous system** (CNS). The CNS is made of both the **brain** and the **spinal cord**. Motor neurons carry impulses from the CNS to **organs** and to **muscles** such as the muscles in the hand, telling them how to move. **Nerves** are made of sensory and motor neurons. **Nerves** run through the whole body.

**nerv|ous tis|sue** (**nervous tissues**) N-VAR **Nervous tissue** is tissue in the bodies of animals that consists of neurons. *tejido nervioso* [TECHNICAL]

**nervy** /nɜrvi/ (**nervier, nerviest**) If you say that someone is **nervy**, you mean that their behavior is bold or daring. *valiente* ADJ ❏ *John liked him because he was a nervy guy. A John le agradaba porque era un tipo valiente.*

**nest** /nɛst/ (**nests, nesting, nested**) **1** N-COUNT A bird's **nest** is the home that it makes to lay its eggs in. *nido* ❏ *...the cuckoo's habit of laying its eggs in the nests of other birds. ...la costumbre del cuclillo de poner sus huevos en los nidos de otras aves.* **2** V-I When a bird **nests** somewhere, it builds a nest and settles there to lay its eggs. *anidar* ❏ *There are birds nesting on the cliffs. Hay aves que anidan en los acantilados.* **3** N-COUNT A **nest** is a home that a group of insects or small animals make in order to live in and give birth to their young in. *nido, colmena, avispero, hormiguero, ratonera* ❏ *Some bees make their nests in the ground. Algunas abejas hacen su colmena en el suelo.*

→ see **bird**

nest

**net**

❶ NOUN AND VERB USES

❷ ADJECTIVE AND ADVERB USES

❶ **net** /nɛt/ (**nets, netting, netted**)

**1** N-UNCOUNT **Net** is a kind of material made of threads, strings or wires woven together so that there are small equal spaces between them. *red* ❏ *...net curtains. ...visillos.* **2** N-COUNT A **net** is a piece of net which is used, for example, to cover something or to catch fish. *net* ❏ *...a mosquito net. ...un mosquitero.* ❏ *The fishermen sat fixing their nets. Los pescadores se sentaron a remendar sus redes.* **3** V-T If you **net** something, you manage to get it, especially by using skill. *producir* ❏ *Their first movie netted them an Oscar. Su primera película les produjo un Óscar.* **4** V-T If you **net** a particular amount of money, you gain it as profit after all expenses have been paid. *ganar* ❏ *He netted a profit of $1.85 billion. Obtuvo una ganancia de 1,850 millones de dólares.* **5** N-SING **The Net** is the same as the **Internet**. *Internet* ❏ *We've been on the Net since 1993. Hemos estado en Internet desde 1993.*

→ see **tennis**

❷ **net** /nɛt/ **1** ADJ A **net** amount is the amount that remains when everything that should be subtracted from it has been subtracted. *neto* ❏ *...a rise in sales and net profit. ...un aumento de las ventas y de las utilidades netas.* ● **Net** is also an adverb. *neto* ❏ *Balances of $5,000 and above will earn 8.25 percent net. Los saldos de 5,000 dólares y más ganarán el 8.25 por ciento neto.* ❏ *They pay him around $2 million net. Le pagan aproximadamente dos millones de dólares netos.* **2** ADJ The **net** weight of something is its weight without its container or the material that has been used to wrap it. *neto* ❏ *...the finest candies, net weight 1 pound. ...los dulces más finos; peso neto: 454 gramos.* **3** ADJ A **net** result is a final result after all the details have been considered or included. *neto* ❏ *...a net increase in jobs. ...un aumento neto de los empleos.*

**Word Partnership** Usar *net* con:

| | |
|---|---|
| N. | **fishing** net ❶ **2**<br>Net **users** ❶ **5** |
| V. | **access the** Net, **surf the** Net ❶ **5** |
| N. | net **earnings**, net **gain**, net **income/loss**, net **increase**, net **proceeds**, net **profit**, net **result**, net **revenue** ❷ **1** |

**net force** (**net forces**) N-COUNT A **net force** is the overall force that is acting upon an object, after all the individual forces acting on the object have been added together. *fuerza neta* [TECHNICAL]

**net|work** /nɛtwɜrk/ (**networks, networking, networked**) **1** N-COUNT A radio or television **network** is a company or group of companies that broadcast radio or television programs throughout an area. *red, cadena* ❏ *...a Spanish-language television network. ...una cadena de televisión en lengua española.* **2** N-COUNT A **network of** people or institutions is a large number of them that have a connection with each other and work together as a system. *red, grupo* ❏ *She has a strong network of friends and family to help her. Tiene un grupo muy unido de amigos y familiares que la ayudan.* **3** N-COUNT A particular **network** is a system of things which are connected and which operate together. For example, a **computer network** consists of a number of computers that are part of the same system. *red* ❏ *...a computer network with 54 machines. ...una red de 54 computadoras.* **4** N-COUNT A **network of** lines, roads, veins, or other long thin things is a large number of them which cross each other or meet at many points. *red* ❏ *Strasbourg has a network of old streets. Estrasburgo tiene una red de calles antiguas.* **5** V-I If you **network**, you try to meet new people who might be useful to you in your job. *establecer contacto* [BUSINESS] ❏ *In business, it is important to network with as many people as possible. En los negocios, es importante establecer contactos con el*

n

*mayor número posible de personas.*
→ see **Internet**

**Word Partnership** Usar *network* con:

N. **broadcast** network, **cable** network, **radio** network, **television/TV** network 1
network **administrator**, **computer** network, network **coverage**, network **support** 3
ADJ. **extensive** network, **nationwide** network, **vast** network, **worldwide** network 1 – 4
**wireless** network 3

**net|work card** (**network cards**) also **network interface card** N-COUNT A **network card** or a **network interface card** is a card that connects a computer to a network. *tarjeta de red* [COMPUTING]

**neu|ron** /nʊərɒn/ (**neurons**) N-COUNT A **neuron** is a cell which is part of the nervous system. Neurons send messages to and from the brain. *neurona* [TECHNICAL] ❑ *Information is transferred along each neuron by means of an electrical impulse. La información se transmite de una neurona a otra mediante un impulso eléctrico.*

**neu|tral** /nutrəl/ 1 ADJ A **neutral** person or country does not support anyone in a disagreement, war, or contest. *neutral* ❑ *Let's meet on neutral territory. Reunámonos en un territorio neutral.* ● **neu|tral|ity** /nutrælɪti/ N-UNCOUNT *neutralidad* ❑ *...the loss of political neutrality. ...la pérdida de la neutralidad política.* 2 ADJ If someone's facial expression or language is **neutral,** they do not show what they are thinking or feeling. *neutro* ❑ *Isabel said in a neutral voice, "You're very late, darling." —Llegas muy tarde, querido —le dijo Isabel con un tono neutro.* 3 N-UNCOUNT **Neutral** is the position between the gears of a vehicle, in which the gears are not connected to the engine. *punto muerto* ❑ *She put the truck in neutral and started it again. Puso el camión en punto muerto y volvió a arrancarlo.* 4 ADJ **Neutral** colors are colors such as black, white, and gray that are considered to combine well with other colors. *neutro*
→ see **war**

N

**neu|tron** /nutrɒn/ (**neutrons**) N-COUNT A **neutron** is an atomic particle that has no electrical charge. *neutrón*

**neu|tron star** (**neutron stars**) N-COUNT A **neutron star** is a star that has collapsed under the weight of its own gravity. *estrella de neutrones*

**nev|er** /nɛvər/ 1 ADV **Never** means at no time in the past or future. *nunca* ❑ *I have never lost the weight I put on in my teens. Nunca he logrado perder el peso que aumenté cuando era adolescente.* ❑ *That was a mistake. We'll never do it again. Fue un error. Nunca volveremos a cometerlo.* ❑ *Never say that! ¡Nunca digas eso!* 2 ADV **Never** means not in any circumstances. *nunca* ❑ *I would never do anything to hurt him. Nunca haría algo/nada que lo ofendiera.* ❑ *Losing is never easy. Nunca es fácil perder.* 3 PHRASE **Never ever** is a strong way of saying "never." *nunca jamás* ❑ *I never, ever sit around thinking, "What shall I do next?" Nunca jamás me pongo a pensar: "¿Qué voy a hacer ahora?".* 4 ADV **Never** is used to refer to the past and means "not." *nunca* ❑ *He never did anything to hurt anyone. Nunca hizo nada que ofendiera a nadie.* ❑ *I never knew him. Nunca lo conocí.* 5 **never mind** → see **mind**

**never|the|less** /nɛvərðəlɛs/ ADV You use **nevertheless** when saying something that contrasts with what has just been said. *no obstante, sin embargo* [FORMAL] ❑ *Leon had problems, but nevertheless managed to finish his most famous painting. Leon tenía problemas; sin embargo/no obstante, se las arregló para terminar su pintura más famosa.*

**new** /nu/ (**newer, newest**) 1 ADJ Something that is **new** has been recently created or invented. *nuevo* ❑ *They've just opened a new hotel. Acaban de abrir un nuevo hotel.* ❑ *These ideas are nothing new. Estas ideas no tienen nada de nuevo.* 2 ADJ Something that is **new** has not been used or owned by anyone. *nuevo* ❑ *That afternoon she went out and bought a new dress. Esa tarde salió a comprarse un vestido nuevo.* ❑ *There are many boats, new and used, for sale. Hay muchos botes en venta, nuevos y usados.* 3 ADJ You use **new** to describe something which has replaced another thing, for example because you no longer have the old one, or it no longer exists, or it is no longer useful. *nuevo* ❑ *I had to find somewhere new to live. Tuve que buscar otro/un nuevo lugar dónde vivir.* ❑ *Rachel has a new boyfriend. Rachel tiene novio nuevo.* 4 ADJ **New** is used to describe something that has only recently been discovered or noticed. *nuevo* ❑ *The new planet is about ten times the size of the Earth. El nuevo planeta es aproximadamente diez veces más grande que la Tierra.* 5 ADJ If you are **new to** a situation or place, or if the situation or place is **new to** you, you have not seen it or had any experience of it before. *nuevo* ❑ *She is new to the company. Es nueva en la compañía.* ❑ *His name was new to me. Su nombre era algo nuevo para mí.* 6 → see also **brand-new**

**Thesaurus** *new* Ver también:

ADJ. contemporary, current, latest, modern, novel; (*ant.*) existing, old, past 1

**new|comer** /nukʌmər/ (**newcomers**) N-COUNT A **newcomer** is a person who has recently arrived in a place, joined an organization, or started a new activity. *recién llegado* ❑ *...a newcomer to Salt Lake City. ...un recién llegado en Salt Lake City.*

**new|ly** /nuli/ ADV **Newly** is used before a past participle or an adjective to indicate that an action or situation is very recent. *recientemente, recién* ❑ *She was young at the time, and newly married. Era joven en la época, y estaba recién casada.*

**news** /nuz/ 1 N-UNCOUNT **News** is information about a recently-changed situation or a recent event. *noticia, nueva* ❑ *We waited and waited for news of him. Esperamos y esperamos nuevas de él.* ❑ *They still haven't had any news about when they'll be able to go home. Todavía no han recibido ninguna noticia sobre cuándo podrán volver a su casa.* 2 N-UNCOUNT **News** is information that is published in newspapers and broadcast on radio and television about recent events in the country or world or in a particular area of activity. *noticia* ❑ *Foreign News is on page 16. La Sección Internacional está en la página 16.* ❑ *Those are some of the top stories in the news. Estas son algunas de las noticias principales.* 3 N-SING **The news** is a television or radio broadcast which consists of information about recent events. *noticias* ❑ *I heard all about the bombs on the news. Oí todo sobre las bombas en las noticias.* **4** PHRASE If you say that something is **bad news,** you mean that it will cause you trouble or problems. If you say that something is **good news,** you mean that it will be useful or helpful to you. *buenas/malas nuevas* ❑ *The agreement is good news for U.S. and Japanese firms. El convenio significa buenas nuevas para las empresas estadounidenses y japonesas.* **5** PHRASE If you say that something **is news to** you, you mean that you did not already know what you have just been told, especially when you are surprised or annoyed about it. *ser nuevo para* ❑ *This is news to me. I haven't heard about it. Eso es nuevo para mí; no me había enterado.*

**Word Partnership** Usar *news* con:

ADJ. **big** news, **grim** news, **sad** news **1**
**latest** news **1** **2**
V. **spread the** news, **tell** *someone* **the** news **1**
**hear the** news **1** – **3**
**listen to the** news, **watch the** news **3**
N. news **headlines**, news **media**, news **report**, news **update** **2**

**news agen|cy** (**news agencies**) N-COUNT A **news agency** is an organization that collects news stories from a particular country or from all over the world and supplies them to journalists. *agencia de noticias* ❑ *...a correspondent for Reuters news agency. ...un corresponsal de la agencia de noticias Reuters.*

**news|cast** /nuzkæst/ (**newscasts**) N-COUNT A **newscast** is a news program that is broadcast on the radio or on television. *noticiario (formal), noticiero (informal)* ❑ *Coming up after the newscast, a review of the week's news. Después del noticiario, le presentaremos un resumen de las noticias de la semana.*

**news|caster** /nuzkæstər/ (**newscasters**) N-COUNT A **newscaster** is a person who reads the news on the radio or on television. *locutor o locutora, presentador o presentadora* ❑ *...TV newscaster Barbara Walters. ...Barbara Walters, la locutora de televisión.*

**news con|fer|ence** (**news conferences**) N-COUNT A **news conference** is a meeting held by a famous or important person in which they answer journalists' questions. *rueda de prensa, conferencia de prensa* ❑ *He is due to hold a news conference in about an hour. Tiene una rueda/conferencia de prensa en una media hora.*

**news|paper** /nuzpeɪpər, nus-/ (**newspapers**) **1** N-COUNT A **newspaper** is a publication consisting of a number of large sheets of folded paper, on which news, advertisements, and other information is printed. *periódico, diario* ❑ *They read about it in the newspaper. Lo leyeron en el periódico.* **2** N-COUNT A **newspaper** is an organization that produces a newspaper. *periódico, diario* ❑ *It is the nation's fastest-growing national daily newspaper. Es el diario nacional cuya circulación crece con mayor rapidez en el país.* **3** N-UNCOUNT **Newspaper** consists of pieces of old newspapers, especially when they are being used for another purpose such as wrapping things up. *papel periódico* ❑ *He found two pots, each wrapped in newspaper. Halló dos ollas, cada una envuelta en papel periódico.*

**news re|lease** (**news releases**) N-COUNT A **news release** is a written statement about a matter of public interest which is given to the press by an organization concerned with the matter. *comunicado de prensa* ❑ *The company made the announcement in a news release. La compañía hizo el anuncio en un comunicado de prensa.*

**new|ton** /nutᵊn/ (**newtons**) N-COUNT In physics, a **newton** is a unit of force. The abbreviation **N** is also used. *newton* [TECHNICAL]

**New Year's** N-UNCOUNT **New Year's** is the time when people celebrate the start of a year. *Año Nuevo*

**next** /nɛkst/ **1** ORD The **next** period of time, event, person, or thing is the one that comes immediately after the present one or after the previous one. *siguiente, próximo* ❑ *I got up early the next morning. Me levanté temprano a la mañana siguiente.* ❑ *...the next available flight. ...el próximo vuelo disponible.* ❑ *Who will be the next mayor? ¿Quién será el próximo presidente municipal?* **2** DET You use **next** in expressions such as **next Friday, next day,** and **next year** to refer, for example, to the first Friday, day, or year that comes after the present or previous one. *próximo* ❑ *Let's plan a night out next week. Planeemos una salida nocturna para la próxima semana.* ❑ *He retires next January. Se jubila en enero.*
● **Next** is also an adjective. *próximo* ❑ *I'll be 26 years old next Friday. Cumpliré 26 años el próximo viernes.*
● **Next** is also a pronoun. *próximo, siguiente* ❑ *John is coming the week after next. John viene dentro de dos semanas.* **3** ADJ **The next** place or person is the one that is nearest to you or that is the first one that you come to. *de al lado* ❑ *There was a party going on in the next room. Había una fiesta en el cuarto de al lado.* ❑ *The man in the next chair was asleep. El hombre en la silla de al lado estaba dormido.* **4** ADV The thing that happens **next** is the thing that happens immediately after something else. *ahora* ❑ *Next, close your eyes. Ahora, cierra los ojos.* ❑ *I don't know what to do next. No sé qué hacer ahora.* **5** ADV When you **next** do something, you do it for the first time since you last did it. *siguiente* ❑ *I next saw him at his house in Vermont. La siguiente vez que lo vi fue en su casa de Vermont.* **6** ADV You use **next** to say that something has more of a particular quality than all other things except one. For example, the thing that is **next** best is the one that is the best except for one other thing. *segundo mejor* ❑ *He doesn't have a son. I think he feels that a grandson is the next best thing. No tiene hijos varones, así que se conformaría con tener un nieto.* **7** PHRASE If one thing is **next to** another, it is at the side of it. *junto a* ❑ *She sat down next to him on the sofa. Se sentó junto a él en el sofá.* **8** PHRASE You use **next to** before a negative, or a word that suggests something negative, to mean almost, but not completely. *casi, prácticamente* ❑ *Johnson still knew next to nothing about politics. Johnson seguía sin saber prácticamente nada de política.*

**Word Partnership** Usar *next* con:

N. next **election**, next **generation**, next **level**, next **meeting**, next **move**, next **question**, next **step**, next **stop**, next **time**, next **train** 1
next **day/hour/month/week/year** 1 2
V. **come** next, **go** next, **happen** next 4

**NFL** /ɛn ɛf ɛl/ N-PROPER In the United States, **the NFL** is the organization responsible for professional football. **NFL** is an abbreviation for "National Football League." *Liga Nacional de Fútbol* ❑ *...one of the best teams in the NFL. ...uno de los mejores equipos de la Liga Nacional de Fútbol.* ❑ *...an NFL player. ...un jugador de la Liga Nacional de Fútbol.*

**NHL** /ɛn eɪtʃɛl/ N-PROPER In the United States, **the NHL** is the organization responsible for professional ice hockey. **NHL** is an abbreviation for "National Hockey League." *Liga Nacional de Hockey sobre hielo* ❑ *...the best goalkeeper in the NHL. ...el mejor portero/guardameta de la Liga Nacional de Hockey sobre hielo.*

**nice** /naɪs/ (**nicer, nicest**) 1 ADJ If you say that something is **nice,** you mean that it is attractive, pleasant, or enjoyable. *sabroso, rico, bueno* ❑ *The chocolate-chip cookies were nice. Las galletas con chispas de chocolate estaban ricas.* ❑ *It's nice to be here together again. Es bueno estar juntos aquí otra vez.* ● **nice|ly** ADV *hermosamente* ❑ *The book is nicely illustrated. El libro está hermosamente ilustrado.* 2 ADJ If someone is **nice,** they are friendly and pleasant. *amable* ❑ *I've met your father and he's very nice. Conocí a tu padre; y es muy amable.* ❑ *They were extremely nice to me. Fueron amabilísimos conmigo.* ● **nice|ly** ADV *amablemente* ❑ *He treated you nicely. Te trató amablemente.* 3 ADJ If you say that it is **nice of** someone to say or do something, you are saying that they are being kind and thoughtful. This is often used as a way of thanking someone. *amable* ❑ *It's so nice of you to come all this way to see me. Es tan amable de tu parte haber venido (de) tan lejos para verme.* ❑ *"How are your boys?"—"How nice of you to ask." —¿Cómo están sus hijos? —¡Qué amable de su parte el preguntarlo!* 4 → see also **nicely**

**Thesaurus** *nice* Ver también:

ADJ. friendly, kind, likable, pleasant, polite; (ant.) mean, unpleasant 2 3

**Word Partnership** Usar *nice* con:

ADJ. nice **and clean** 1
V. **look** nice, nice **to see *someone/something*** 1
N. nice **clothes**, nice **guy**, nice **people**, nice **place**, nice **smile** 1 2

**nice|ly** /naɪsli/ 1 ADV If something is happening or working **nicely,** it is happening or working in a satisfactory way or in the way that you want it to. *muy bien* ❑ *The computer system is now working nicely. El sistema de la computadora ya está funcionando muy bien.* 2 → see also **nice**

**nick** /nɪk/ (**nicks, nicking, nicked**) 1 V-T If you **nick** something or **nick** yourself, you accidentally make a small cut in the surface of the object or your skin. *hacer una muesca, cortar(se)* ❑ *A bullet nicked the edge of the wall. Una bala hizo una muesca en el borde del muro.* ❑ *He nicked himself on the chin when he was shaving. Se cortó el mentón/la barbilla al rasurarse.* 2 N-COUNT A **nick** is a small cut made in the surface of something, usually in someone's skin. *muesca, corte, rasguño* ❑ *I had a tiny nick just below my right eye. Tenía un ligero rasguño justo abajo del ojo derecho.* 3 PHRASE If something is achieved **in the nick of time,** it is achieved successfully, at the last possible moment. *justo a tiempo, muy a tiempo* [INFORMAL] ❑ *It seems we got here just in the nick of time. Parece que llegamos justo/muy a tiempo.*

**nick|el** /nɪkᵊl/ (**nickels**) 1 N-UNCOUNT **Nickel** is a silver-colored metal that is used in making steel. *níquel* 2 N-COUNT In the United States and Canada, a **nickel** is a coin worth five cents. *centavo, céntimo* ❑ *The large glass jar was filled with nickels, dimes, and quarters. El gran frasco de cristal estaba lleno de monedas de uno, diez y veinticinco centavos.*

**nick|name** /nɪkneɪm/ (**nicknames, nicknaming, nicknamed**) 1 N-COUNT A **nickname** is an informal name for someone or something. *apodo, sobrenombre, mote* ❑ *Red got his nickname for his red hair. A Rojillo le pusieron ese apodo por ser pelirrojo.* 2 V-T If you **nickname** someone or something, you give them an informal name. *apodar, poner (un apodo)* ❑ *When he got older, I nicknamed him Little Alf. Cuando creció, le puse Alfito.*

**niece** /nis/ (**nieces**) N-COUNT Someone's **niece** is the daughter of their sister or brother. *sobrina* ❑ *...his niece, the daughter of his eldest sister. ...su sobrina, la hija de su hermana mayor.*

**night** /naɪt/ (**nights**) 1 N-VAR The **night** is the part of each period of twenty-four hours when the sun has set and it is dark outside, especially the time when people are sleeping. *noche* ❑ *The fighting continued all night. Los combates continuaron toda la noche.* ❑ *It was one of the darkest nights I'd ever seen. Fue una de las noches más oscuras que jamás había visto.* 2 N-COUNT The **night** is the period of time between the end of the afternoon and the time that you go to bed, especially the time when you relax before going to bed. *noche, anoche* ❑ *Whose party did you go to last night? —¿A la fiesta de quién fuiste ayer por la noche?* 3 PHRASE If it is a particular time **at night,** it is during the time when it is dark and is before midnight. *de la noche* ❑ *It's eleven o'clock at night in Moscow. Son las once de la noche en punto en Moscú.* 4 PHRASE If something happens **day and night** or **night and day,** it happens all the time without stopping. *noche y día, día y noche* ❑ *The doctors and nurses have been working day and night for weeks. Los médicos y enfermeras han estado trabajando noche y día durante semanas.* 5 PHRASE If you have **an early night,** you go to bed early. If you have **a late night,** you go to bed late. *acostarse temprano/tarde* ❑ *All I want is an early night. Todo lo que quiero es acostarme temprano.*
→ see **star, time**

**Word Partnership** Usar *night* con:

ADJ. **cold** night, **cool** night, **dark** night, **rainy** night, **warm** night 1
V. **spend a/the** night 1
**sleep at** night, **stay out at** night, **stay the** night, **work at** night 1 2

**night|club** /naɪtklʌb/ (**nightclubs**) N-COUNT A **nightclub** is a place where people go late in the evening to drink and dance. club nocturno

**night|gown** /naɪtgaʊn/ (**nightgowns**) N-COUNT A **nightgown** is a sort of loose dress that a woman or girl wears in bed. camisón

**night|mare** /naɪtmɛər/ (**nightmares**) 1 N-COUNT A **nightmare** is a very frightening dream. pesadilla ❑ *She woke up during the night with a nightmare.* *Se despertó durante la noche con una pesadilla.* 2 N-COUNT If you refer to a situation as a **nightmare**, you mean that it is very unpleasant. pesadilla ❑ *The years in prison were a nightmare.* *Los años en prisión fueron una pesadilla.* 3 N-COUNT If you refer to a situation as a **nightmare**, you are saying strongly that it causes you a lot of trouble. pesadilla ❑ *New York traffic is a nightmare.* *El tránsito de Nueva York es una pesadilla.*

**night|stick** /naɪtstɪk/ (**nightsticks**) N-COUNT A **nightstick** is a short thick club that is carried by police officers in the United States. macana, porra

**nil** /nɪl/ N-UNCOUNT If you say that something **is nil**, you mean that it does not exist at all. nada, cero, nulo ❑ *Their legal rights are almost nil.* *Sus derechos legales son casi nulos.*

**nim|bus** /nɪmbəs/ N-SING A **nimbus** is a large gray cloud that brings rain or snow. nimbo [TECHNICAL] ❑ *...layers of cold nimbus clouds.* *...capas de nimbos fríos.*
→ see **cloud**

**NIMBY** /nɪmbi/ also **Nimby** ADJ If you say that someone has a **NIMBY** attitude, you are criticizing them because they do not want something such as a new road, housing development, or prison built near where they live. **NIMBY** is an abbreviation for "not in my backyard." comodino [INFORMAL] ❑ *...the usual NIMBY protests from local residents.* *...las protestas de costumbre de los vecinos comodinos.*

**nine** /naɪn/ (**nines**) NUM **Nine** is the number 9. nueve ❑ *We saw nine sailboats.* *Vimos nueve botes/barcos de vela.* ❑ *...nine hundred dollars.* *...novecientos dólares.*

**nine-eleven** /naɪn ɪlɛvᵊn/ also **nine eleven** also **9/11** N-PROPER **9/11** or **nine-eleven** is used to refer to the events that took place in the United States on September 11, 2001, when terrorists attacked the World Trade Center in New York and the Pentagon in Washington. once de septiembre ❑ *...the victims of 9/11.* *...las víctimas del once de septiembre.* ❑ *Everything changed after nine-eleven.* *Todo cambió después del once de septiembre.*

**nine|teen** /naɪntin/ (**nineteens**) NUM **Nineteen** is the number 19. diecinueve ❑ *He was in prison for nineteen years.* *Estuvo en la cárcel (durante) diecinueve años.*

**nine|teenth** /naɪntinθ/ ORD The **nineteenth** item in a series is the one that you count as number nineteen. décimonono, décimonoveno ❑ *...my nineteenth birthday.* *...mi décimonoveno cumpleaños.*

**nine|ti|eth** /naɪntiɪθ/ ORD The **ninetieth** item in a series is the one that you count as number ninety. nonagésimo ❑ *He celebrates his ninetieth birthday on Friday.* *El viernes celebra su nonagésimo cumpleaños.*

**nine-to-five** ADJ A **nine-to-five** job is one that you do during normal office hours, for example a job in a factory or an office. de nueve a cinco ❑ *She works a nine-to-five job.* *Trabaja de nueve a cinco.*, *Su jornada es de nueve a cinco.* ● **Nine to five** is also an adverb. de nueve a cinco ❑ *I wish I could go to work in a factory, nine to five.* *Quisiera poder trabajar en una fábrica con un horario (una jornada) de nueve a cinco.*

**nine|ty** /naɪnti/ (**nineties**) 1 NUM **Ninety** is the number 90. noventa ❑ *Ninety people were hurt in the accident.* *Noventa personas resultaron heridas en el accidente.* 2 N-PLURAL When you talk about the **nineties**, you are referring to numbers between 90 and 99. For example, if you are **in** your **nineties**, you are aged between 90 and 99. If the temperature is **in the nineties**, the temperature is between 90 and 99 degrees. noventa ❑ *Even in her nineties she was still appearing in public.* *Aún con más de noventa años seguía presentándose en público.* 3 N-PLURAL **The nineties** is the decade between 1990 and 1999. los años noventa ❑ *...British art in the nineties.* *...el arte británico de los años noventa.*

**ninth** /naɪnθ/ (**ninths**) 1 ORD The **ninth** item in a series is the one that you count as number nine. noveno ❑ *...January the ninth.* *...el 9 de enero.* ❑ *...students in the ninth grade.* *...estudiantes del noveno grado.* 2 FRACTION A **ninth** is one of nine equal parts of something. noveno ❑ *The area covers one-ninth of the Earth's surface.* *El área cubre la novena parte de la superficie de la Tierra.*

**nite** /naɪt/ (**nites**) N-VAR **Nite** is another spelling of **night**, used in less formal written English. noche ❑ *...$50 per nite, $350 weekly.* *...50 dólares por noche, 350 dólares semanalmente.*

**ni|trate** /naɪtreɪt/ (**nitrates**) N-COUNT A **nitrate** is a chemical compound that includes nitrogen and oxygen. Nitrates are used as fertilizers in agriculture. nitrato ❑ *...high levels of nitrates.* *...altas concentraciones de nitratos.*
→ see **firework**

**ni|tro|gen** /naɪtrədʒən/ N-UNCOUNT **Nitrogen** is a colorless element that has no smell and is usually found as a gas. It forms about 78 percent of the Earth's atmosphere, and is found in all living things. nitrógeno
→ see **air**

**nix** /nɪks/ (**nixes, nixing, nixed**) V-T If you **nix** a plan or suggestion, you reject or forbid it. rechazar [INFORMAL] ❑ *It only took a few minutes for me to nix this proposal.* *Sólo me tomó unos minutos rechazar esta propuesta.*

**no** /noʊ/ (**noes** or **no's**) 1 CONVENTION You use **no** to give a negative response to a question, to say that something is not true, to refuse an offer or a request, or to refuse permission. no ❑ *"Any problems?"— "No, I'm O.K."* *—¿Tienes algún problema? —No; estoy bien.* ❑ *"We thought you were sick."— "No, no."* *—Creímos que estabas enferma. —No, no.* ❑ *"Here, have mine."— "No, this is fine."* *—Ten; toma el mío. —No; este está bien.* ❑ *No. I forbid it.* *No. Te lo prohíbo.* 2 CONVENTION You use **no** to acknowledge a negative statement or to show that you accept and understand it. no ❑ *"We're not on the main campus."— "No."* *—No estamos en la zona principal. —No.* ❑ *"It's not my favorite kind of music."— "No."* *—No es la música que*

n

*prefiero.* —No. **3** CONVENTION You use **no** before correcting what you have just said. *no* ❑ *I was twenty-two—no, twenty-one. Tenía veintidós; no, veintiuno.* **4** EXCLAM You use **no** to express shock or disappointment at something you have just been told. *no* ❑ *Oh no, not again. ¡No! ¡Otra vez no, por favor!* **5** DET You use **no** to mean not any or not one person or thing. *no...ninguno/ninguna* ❑ *He had no intention of paying. No tenía ninguna intención de pagar.* ❑ *No letters survive from the early part of his life. No se conserva ninguna carta de los primeros años de su vida.* **6** DET You use **no** to emphasize that someone or something is not the type of thing mentioned. *no...ninguno/ninguna* ❑ *He is no singer. No es ningún cantante.* ❑ *It's no secret that people were very upset. No es ningún secreto que la gente estaba muy molesta.* **7** ADV You can use **no** to make the negative form of a comparative. *no* ❑ *...no later than the end of 2014. ...no después del/más tarde que al final de 2014.* ❑ *The game attracted no fewer than 75 million viewers. El juego atrajo a no menos de 75 millones de telespectadores.* **8** DET **No** is used in notices or instructions to say that a particular activity or thing is forbidden. *no* ❑ *Government officials have put up "no parking" signs. Los funcionarios gubernamentales pusieron letreros de "No estacionarse".* ❑ *The door was marked "NO ENTRY." Había un letrero en la puerta que decía "No entrar".* **9** N-COUNT A **no** is a person who has answered "no" to a question or who has voted against something. **No** is also used to refer to their answer or vote. *no* ❑ *According to the latest opinion polls, the noes have 50 percent, the yeses 35 percent. Según las últimas encuestas de opinión, el No tiene el 50 por ciento y el Sí el 35 por ciento.* **10** PHRASE If you say **there is no** doing a particular thing, you mean that it is very difficult or impossible to do that thing. *no hay* ❑ *There is no going back to the life she had. No hay manera de que vuelva a la vida que tuvo.* **11** **no doubt** → see **doubt** **12** **no longer** → see **long**

**No.** (**Nos**) **No.** is a written abbreviation for **number**. *No.* ❑ *That year he was named the nation's No. 1 college football star. Ese año lo nombraron como el jugador No. 1 del fútbol universitario del país.*

**no|ble** /noʊbᵊl/ (**nobler, noblest**) **1** ADJ If you say that someone is a **noble** person, you admire and respect them because they are unselfish and morally good. *noble* ❑ *He was a generous and noble man who was always willing to help. Era un hombre generoso y noble que siempre estaba dispuesto a ayudar.* • **no|bly** ADV *generosamente* ❑ *Eric's sister nobly offered to help with the gardening. La hermana de Eric se ofreció generosamente a ayudar en el jardín.* **2** ADJ **Noble** means belonging to a high social class and having a title. *aristócrata, noble* ❑ *...rich and noble families. ...familias aristócratas y ricas.*

**no|ble gas** (**noble gases**) N-COUNT The **noble gases** are chemical elements such as helium, neon, and argon, which do not generally react when mixed with other substances. *gas noble, gas inerte, gas raro* [TECHNICAL]

**no|body** /noʊbɒdi, -bʌdi/ (**nobodies**) **1** PRON **Nobody** means not a single person. *nadie* ❑ *For a long time nobody spoke. Durante un buen tiempo, nadie habló.* ❑ *Nobody realizes how bad things are. Nadie se da cuenta de lo mal que están las cosas.* **2** N-COUNT If someone says that a person is a **nobody**, they are saying in an unkind way that the person is not at all important. *don nadie* ❑ *A man in my position has nothing to fear from a nobody like you. Un hombre de mi posición no tiene hada qué temer de un don nadie como tú.*

**no-brain|er** (**no-brainers**) N-COUNT If you describe a question or decision as **a no-brainer**, you mean that it is a very easy one to answer or make. *algo muy fácil de hacer, entender o responder* [INFORMAL] ❑ *It's a no-brainer that music is part of a well-rounded education. Hasta el más ignorante sabe que la música forma parte de una educación completa.*

**noc|tur|nal** /nɒktɜrnᵊl/ **1** ADJ **Nocturnal** means occurring at night. *nocturno* ❑ *...long nocturnal walks. ...largas caminatas nocturnas.* **2** ADJ **Nocturnal** animals are active mainly at night. *nocturno, noctívago* ❑ *Rats are nocturnal creatures. Las ratas son animales nocturnos.*
→ see **bat**

**nod** /nɒd/ (**nods, nodding, nodded**) **1** V-T/V-I If you **nod**, you move your head downward and upward to show that you are answering "yes" to a question, or to show agreement, understanding, or approval. *asentir con la cabeza, hacer un gesto de aprobación con la cabeza* ❑ *"Are you okay?" I asked. She nodded and smiled. —¿Estás bien?—, le pregunté; y asintió con la cabeza.* ❑ *Jacques tasted a cookie and nodded his approval. Jacques probó la galleta y dio su aprobación con un gesto de la cabeza.* • **Nod** is also a noun. *asentir con la cabeza* ❑ *She gave a nod and said, "I see." Asintió con la cabeza y dijo: —Ya veo.* ❑ *"Probably," agreed Harry, with a slow nod of his head. —Probablemente—, concordó Harry; y asintió lentamente con la cabeza.* **2** V-I If you **nod** in a particular direction, you bend your head once in that direction in order to indicate something or to give someone a signal. *señalar con la cabeza* ❑ *"Does it work?" he asked, nodding at the piano. —¿Funciona?—, preguntó, señalando el piano con la cabeza.* ❑ *She nodded toward the dining room. "He's in there." Señaló con la cabeza hacia el comedor y dijo: —Está ahí.* **3** V-T/V-I If you **nod**, you bend your head once, as a way of saying hello or goodbye. *Saludar con (un gesto de) la cabeza.* ❑ *All the girls nodded and said "Hi." Todas las muchachas saludaron con la cabeza y dijeron: —Hola.* ❑ *Both of them smiled and nodded at friends. Ambos sonrieron y saludaron con la cabeza a los amigos.* ❑ *Tom nodded a greeting. Tom saludó con la cabeza.*
▸ **nod off** PHR-VERB If you **nod off**, you fall asleep, especially when you did not intend to. *cabecear, quedarse dormido* [INFORMAL] ❑ *The judge appeared to nod off. El juez parecía haberse quedado dormido.*

**Noh** /noʊ/ N-UNCOUNT **Noh** is a traditional form of Japanese theater which combines dance, music, and poetry, and in which the actors wear masks. *teatro no/nō*

**noise** /nɔɪz/ (**noises**) **1** N-UNCOUNT **Noise** is a loud or unpleasant sound. *ruido* ❑ *The noise from the crowd became deafening. El ruido de la multitud se hizo ensordecedor.* **2** N-COUNT A **noise** is a sound that someone or something makes. *ruido* ❑ *A noise came from behind the tent. Se oyó un ruido proveniente de atrás de la tienda.* ❑ *...animal noises. ...ruidos de animales.*

**Word Partnership** Usar *noise* con:

| | |
|---|---|
| N. | **background** noise, noise **level**, noise **pollution**, **traffic** noise 1 |
| ADJ. | **loud** noise 1 2 |
| V. | **hear a** noise, **make a** noise 2 |

**noisy** /nɔɪzi/ (**noisier, noisiest**) 1 ADJ A **noisy** person or thing makes a lot of loud or unpleasant noise. *ruidoso* ❑ *...my noisy old car.* *...mi ruidoso coche viejo.* • **noisi|ly** ADV *ruidosamente* ❑ *The students cheered noisily.* *Los estudiantes vitorearon ruidosamente.* 2 ADJ A **noisy** place is full of a lot of loud or unpleasant noise. *ruidoso* ❑ *The café is a noisy place.* *El café es un lugar ruidoso.* ❑ *The airport was crowded and noisy.* *El aeropuerto estaba atestado de gente y había mucho ruido.*

**no|mad** /noʊmæd/ (**nomads**) N-COUNT A **nomad** is a member of a group of people who travel from place to place rather than living in one place all the time. *nómada, nómade* ❑ *...a country of nomads who raise cattle and camels.* *...un país de nómadas que crían ganado y camellos.* • **no|mad|ic** /noʊmædɪk/ ADJ *nómada, mómade* ❑ *...the nomadic tribes of the Western Sahara.* *...las tribus nómadas del Sáhara occidental.*

**nomi|nal** /nɒmɪnᵊl/ 1 ADJ You use **nominal** to indicate that someone or something is supposed to have a particular identity or status, but in reality does not have it. *nominal* ❑ *His wife became the nominal head of the company.* *Su esposa se convirtió en el jefe nominal de la compañía.* • **nomi|nal|ly** ADV *nominalmente* ❑ *Both countries are nominally equal.* *Los dos países son nominalmente iguales.* 2 ADJ A **nominal** price or sum of money is very small in comparison with the real cost or value of the thing that is being bought or sold. *nominal* ❑ *I sold my car at a nominal price.* *Vendí mi coche a su valor nominal.*

**nomi|nate** /nɒmɪneɪt/ (**nominates, nominating, nominated**) V-T If someone **is nominated** for a job, a position, or a prize, their name is formally suggested for it. *nombrar, postular, nominar* ❑ *He was nominated by the Democratic Party for the presidency of the United States.* *Fue postulado por el Partido Demócrata para la presidencia de Estados Unidos.* ❑ *This year a panel of writers nominated six novels for the Booker Prize.* *Este año, un jurado de escritores nominó seis novelas para el Premio Booker.*

**nomi|na|tion** /nɒmɪneɪʃᵊn/ (**nominations**) N-COUNT A **nomination** is an official suggestion of someone as a candidate for a job, position, or prize. *nombramiento, postulación, nominación* ❑ *...his candidacy for the Republican presidential nomination.* *...su candidatura a la postulación de los republicanos para la presidencia.* ❑ *He's certain to get an Oscar nomination for best actor.* *Está seguro de que lo nominarán para el Óscar al mejor actor.*

**nomi|nee** /nɒmɪni/ (**nominees**) N-COUNT A **nominee** is someone who is nominated for a job, position, or award. *candidato* ❑ *...his nominee for vice president.* *...su candidato para vicepresidente.*

**none** /nʌn/ 1 QUANT **None of** something means not even a small amount of it. **None of** a group of people or things means not even one of them. *ninguno, ninguna* ❑ *None of us knew her.* *Ninguno de nosotros la conocía.* • **None** is also a pronoun. *ninguno, ninguna, nada* ❑ *I searched bookstores and libraries for information, but found none.* *Busqué información en las librerías y las bibliotecas, pero no encontré nada.* 2 PHRASE You use **none the** to say that someone or something does not have any more of a particular quality than they did before. *negación de un hecho (su traducción depende del contexto)* ❑ *Three months after the event, police are still none the wiser as to the motive for the attack.* *Tres meses después de los sucesos, la policía sigue sin saber nada sobre el motivo del asalto.* 3 PHRASE You use **none too** in front of an adjective or adverb in order to emphasize that the quality mentioned is not present. *no...mucho/muy* [FORMAL] ❑ *He was none too pleased to hear from me.* *No le agradó mucho saber de mí., No estaba muy complacido de saber de mí.* 4 **second to none** → see **second**

**none|the|less** /nʌnðəlɛs/ ADV **Nonetheless** means the same as **nevertheless.** *no obstante, sin embargo* [FORMAL] ❑ *There is still a long way to go. Nonetheless, some progress has been made.* *Todavía queda mucho camino por recorrer; no obstante, se ha avanzado un poco.*

**non|fo|li|at|ed** /nɒnfoʊlieɪtɪd/ ADJ **Nonfoliated** rock is rock that does not consist of regular, thin layers. *sin foliación* [TECHNICAL]

**non|liv|ing** /nɒnlɪvɪŋ/ also **non-living** ADJ **Nonliving** objects are objects that are not alive, such as rocks and minerals. *inorgánico*

**non|met|al** /nɒnmɛtᵊl/ (**nonmetals**) also **non-metal** N-COUNT **Nonmetals** are chemical elements that are not metals. *no metal*

**non|ob|jec|tive** /nɒnəbjɛktɪv/ ADJ **Nonobjective** art makes use of shapes and patterns rather than showing people or things. *abstracto* [TECHNICAL]

**nonpoint-source pol|lu|tion** /nɒnpɔɪnt sɔrs pəluʃᵊn/ N-UNCOUNT **Nonpoint-source pollution** is pollution that comes from many different sources, for example chemicals from farmland and factories that are carried into rivers by rain. *contaminación sin origen determinado* [TECHNICAL]

**Word Link** *non ≈ not : nonprescription, nonsense, nonverbal*

**non|pre|scrip|tion** /nɒnprɪskrɪpʃᵊn/ ADJ **Nonprescription** drugs are medicines that you can buy without the need for a doctor's prescription. *sin receta, sin necesidad de receta* ❑ *Aspirin is the most popular nonprescription drug on the market.* *La aspirina es la droga más popular de las que venden sin (necesidad de) receta.*

**non|profit** /nɒnprɒfɪt/ also **not-for-profit** ADJ A **nonprofit** organization is one which is not run with the aim of making a profit. *sin fines de lucro, sin fines lucrativos* [BUSINESS] ❑ *...a nonprofit foundation that brings technology into public schools.* *...una fundación sin fines de lucro que lleva la tecnología a las escuelas públicas.*

**non|re|new|able** /nɒnrɪnuəbᵊl/ (**nonrenewables**) also **non-renewable** 1 ADJ **Nonrenewable** resources are natural materials such as coal, oil and gas that exist in limited amounts and take a very long time to replace. no renovable **2** N-PLURAL You can refer to nonrenewable resources as **nonrenewables.** recursos no renovables

| Word Link | *non ≈ not : nonprescription, nonsense, nonverbal* |
|---|---|

**non|sense** /nɒnsɛns, -səns/ **1** N-UNCOUNT If you say that something spoken or written is **nonsense,** you think it is untrue or silly. tontería, disparate, desatino ❑ *Most doctors say this is complete nonsense.* *La mayoría de los médicos dicen que son puros disparates.* ❑ *...all that poetic nonsense about love.* *...todos esos desatinos poéticos sobre el amor.* **2** N-UNCOUNT; N-SING You can use **nonsense** to refer to behavior that you think is foolish or that you disapprove of. tontería, disparate, desatino ❑ *I don't think people can take much more of this nonsense.* *No creo que la gente aguante muchos desatinos más.*

**non|sense syl|la|ble** (**nonsense syllables**) N-COUNT A **nonsense syllable** is a combination of letters, for example "kak" or "mek", that does not form a proper word. Nonsense syllables are used in the teaching of reading skills. sílaba absurda [TECHNICAL]

**non|sili|cate min|er|al** /nɒnsɪlɪkɪt mɪnərəl/ (**nonsilicate minerals**) N-COUNT A **nonsilicate mineral** is a mineral that does not contain a compound of silicone and oxygen. mineral sin silicatos [TECHNICAL]

**non|stand|ard unit** (**nonstandard units**) N-COUNT **Nonstandard units** are units of measurement consisting of objects which are not normally used to measure things, for example matchsticks or paper clips. unidad no normalizada [TECHNICAL]

N

**non|vas|cu|lar plant** /nɒnvæskyələr plænt/ (**nonvascular plants**) also **non-vascular plant** N-COUNT **Nonvascular plants** are plants such as mosses and algae that are unable to move water or nutrients through themselves. planta sin sistema vascular [TECHNICAL]

**non|ver|bal** /nɒnvɜrbəl/ ADJ **Nonverbal** communication consists of things such as the expression on your face, your arm movements, or your tone of voice, which show how you feel about something without using words. no verbal

**noo|dle** /nudəl/ (**noodles**) N-COUNT **Noodles** are long, thin strips of pasta. They are used especially in Chinese and Italian cooking. fideo

**noon** /nun/ N-UNCOUNT **Noon** is twelve o'clock in the middle of the day. mediodía ❑ *The meetings started at noon.* *Las reuniones comenzaron al mediodía.*
→ see **time**

**no one** PRON **No one** means not a single person, or not a single member of a particular group or set. nadie ❑ *Everyone wants to be a hero, but no one wants to die.* *Todo el mundo quiere ser un héroe, pero nadie quiere morir.*

**noon|time** /nuntaɪm/ also **noon-time** or **noon time** N-UNCOUNT **Noontime** is the middle part of the day. mediodía ❑ *There was a demonstration at noontime yesterday at the Chinese Embassy.* *Hubo una demostración/manifestación frente a la Embajada China ayer al mediodía.* ❑ *...their noontime meal.* *...su comida del mediodía.*

**nor** /nɔr/ **1** CONJ You use **nor** after "neither" to introduce the second thing that a negative statement applies to. ni ❑ *Neither Mr. Reese nor Mr. Woodhouse was available for comment.* *Ni el señor Reese ni el señor Woodhouse estaban disponibles para hacer algún comentario.* ❑ *I can give you neither an opinion nor any advice.* *No puedo darte ni una opinión ni consejo alguno.* **2** CONJ You use **nor** after a negative statement in order to introduce another negative statement which adds information to the previous one. ni ❑ *Cooking a quick meal doesn't mean you have to sacrifice flavor. Nor does fast food have to be junk food.* *Preparar una comida rápida no significa que debas sacrificar el sabor ni la comida rápida tiene que ser una porquería.* **3** CONJ You use **nor** after a negative statement in order to indicate that the negative statement also applies to you or to someone or something else. tampoco ❑ *"None of us has any idea how long we're going to be here." — "Nor do I."* *—Ninguno tiene idea de cuánto tiempo vamos a estar aquí. —Ni yo tampoco.* ❑ *"If my husband has no future," she said, "then nor do my children."* *—Si mi esposo no tiene futuro —dijo—, entonces, tampoco mis hijos.*

**norm** /nɔrm/ (**norms**) **1** N-COUNT **Norms** are ways of behaving that are considered normal in a particular society. norma ❑ *...the professional norms of journalism.* *...las normas del periodismo profesional.* **2** N-SING If you say that a situation is **the norm,** you mean that it is usual and expected. norma ❑ *Families of six or seven are the norm in Borough Park.* *Las familias de seis o siete miembros son la norma en Borough Park.*

**nor|mal** /nɔrməl/ **1** ADJ Something that is **normal** is usual and ordinary, and is what people expect. normal ❑ *The situation has returned to normal.* *La situación ha vuelto a lo normal.* ❑ *Her height and weight are normal for her age.* *Su peso y estatura son normales para su edad.* **2** ADJ A **normal** person has no serious physical or mental health problems. normal ❑ *She gave birth to a normal, healthy baby.* *Dio a luz un niño normal y saludable.*

| Thesaurus | *normal* Ver también: |
|---|---|
| ADJ. | ordinary, regular, typical, usual **1** |

| Word Partnership | Usar *normal* con: |
|---|---|
| N. | normal **conditions**, normal **development**, normal **routine** **1** |
| V. | **return to** normal **1** |
| ADV. | **back to** normal **1** |
| | **completely** normal, **perfectly** normal **1** **2** |

**nor|mal fault** (**normal faults**) N-COUNT A **normal fault** is a fault in the surface of the Earth where the rock above the fault has moved down. falla normal [TECHNICAL]

**nor|mal|ly** /nɔrməli/ **1** ADV If you say that something **normally** happens or that you **normally** do a particular thing, you mean that it is what usually happens or what you usually do. normalmente ❑ *All airports in the country are working normally today.* *Todos los aeropuertos del país están funcionando normalmente hoy.* ❑ *Normally the bill is less than $30 a month.* *Normalmente, la factura es por menos de 30 dólares mensuales.* **2** ADV If you do something **normally,** you do it in the usual or conventional way. normalmente ❑ *She's getting better and beginning to eat normally again.* *Ya está mejorando y empezando a comer normalmente otra vez.*

**north** /nɔrθ/ also **North** 1 N-UNCOUNT The **north** is the direction which is on your left when you are looking toward the direction where the sun rises. norte ❑ *In the north snow and ice cover the ground.* *La nieve y el hielo cubren el suelo en el norte.* ❑ *Birds usually migrate from north to south.* *Las aves suelen migrar del norte al sur.* 2 N-SING **The north** of a place, country, or region is the part which is in the north. norte ❑ *He lives in the north of England.* *Vive en el norte de Inglaterra.* 3 ADV If you go **north,** you travel toward the north. norte ❑ *Anita drove north up Pacific Highway.* *Anita condujo hacia el norte por la Autopista del Pacífico.* 4 ADV Something that is **north** of a place is positioned to the north of it. norte ❑ *She lives in a village a few miles north of Portland.* *Vive en un pueblo a unos cuantos kilómetros al norte de Portland.* 5 ADJ The **north** edge, corner, or part of a place or country is the part which is toward the north. norte ❑ *...the north side of the mountain.* *...la ladera norte de la montaña.* ❑ *...North America.* *...América del Norte.* 6 ADJ A **north** wind is a wind that blows from the north. norte ❑ *...a bitterly cold north wind.* *...un viento glacial del norte.*

**north|east** /nɔrθist/ 1 N-UNCOUNT The **northeast** is the direction which is halfway between north and east. noreste/nordeste ❑ *The earthquake was felt in Jerusalem, more than 250 miles to the northeast.* *El terremoto se sintió en Jerusalén, a más de 400 kilómetros al noreste.* 2 N-SING **The northeast of** a place, country, or region is the part which is in the northeast. noreste/nordeste ❑ *Kruger Park, located in the northeast of South Africa, is the size of a small European country.* *El Parque Kruger, ubicado en el noreste de Suráfrica, es del tamaño de un país europeo pequeño.* 3 ADV If you go **northeast,** you travel toward the northeast. noreste/nordeste ❑ *I think we need to go northeast.* *Creo que tenemos que ir hacia el noreste.* 4 ADV Something that is **northeast of** a place is positioned to the northeast of it. noreste/nordeste ❑ *Payson is a small town about 70 miles northeast of Phoenix.* *Payson es un pueblito a aproximadamente 110 kilómetros al noreste de Phoenix.* 5 ADJ The **northeast** part of a place, country, or region is the part which is toward the northeast. noreste/nordeste ❑ *...rural northeast Louisiana.* *...el noreste rural de Luisiana.* ❑ *...Northeast Asia.* *...el noreste de Asia/Asia del Noreste.* 6 ADJ A **northeast** wind is a wind that blows from the northeast. noreste/nordeste ❑ *...a light northeast wind.* *...un viento ligero del noreste.*

**north|eastern** /nɔrθistərn/ ADJ **Northeastern** means in or from the northeast of a region or country. noreste/nordeste ❑ *Smith had three children and came from northeastern England.* *Smith tenía tres hijos y venían del noreste de Inglaterra.*

**north|ern** /nɔrðərn/ also **Northern** ADJ **Northern** means in or from the north of a region, state, or country. del norte ❑ *...Northern Ireland.* *...Irlanda del Norte.*

**north|ern|er** /nɔrðərnər/ (**northerners**) N-COUNT A **northerner** is a person who was born in or lives in the north of a country. norteño ❑ *He was a northerner, born in New York City.* *Era un norteño nacido en la ciudad de Nueva York.*

**nose** /noʊz/ (**noses**) 1 N-COUNT Your **nose** is the part of your face which sticks out above your mouth. You use it for smelling and breathing. nariz ❑ *She wiped her nose with a tissue.* *Se limpió la nariz con un pañuelo desechable.* 2 N-COUNT The **nose** of a vehicle such as an airplane or a boat is the front part of it. proa 3 PHRASE If you do something **under** someone's **nose,** you do it right in front of them, without trying to hide it from them. en las narices ❑ *She stole items from right under the noses of the staff.* *(Se) Robó cosas en las propias narices del personal.*

→ see **face, respiratory system, smell**

| **Word Partnership** | Usar *nose* con: |
|---|---|
| ADJ. | **big** nose, **bloody** nose, **broken** nose, **long** nose, **red** nose, **runny** nose, **straight** nose 1 |

**nosh** /nɒʃ/ N-SING A **nosh** is a snack or light meal. tentenpié, bocado [INFORMAL]

**no-show** (**no-shows**) N-COUNT If someone who is expected to go somewhere fails to go there, you can say that they are a **no-show.** alguien que no se presenta donde lo esperaban ❑ *John Henry Williams was a no-show at last week's game in Milwaukee.* *John Henry Williams no se presentó al juego de la semana pasada en Milwakee.*

**not** /nɒt/

> **Not** is often shortened to **n't** in spoken English, and added to the auxiliary or modal verb. For example, "did not" is often shortened to "didn't."

1 NEG You use **not** with verbs to form negative statements. no ❑ *Their plan was not working.* *Su plan no estaba resultando.* ❑ *I don't trust my father anymore.* *Ya no confío en mi padre.* 2 NEG You use **not** to form questions to which you expect the answer "yes." no ❑ *Haven't they got enough problems there already?* *¿No tienen ya suficientes problemas allí?* ❑ *Didn't I see you at the party last week?* *¿No te vi en la fiesta la semana pasada?* 3 NEG You use **not,** usually in the form **n't,** in questions which imply that someone should have done something, or to express surprise that something is not the case. no ❑ *Why didn't you do it months ago?* *¿Por qué no lo hiciste hace meses?* ❑ *Why couldn't he listen to her?* *¿Por qué no le hizo caso?* 4 NEG You use **not,** usually in the form **n't,** when you want to change a positive statement into a question. no ❑ *It's crazy, isn't it?* *Es una locura, ¿no?* ❑ *I've been a great husband, haven't I?* *He sido un buen esposo, ¿no?* 5 NEG You use **not,** usually in the form **n't,** in polite suggestions. no ❑ *Why don't you fill out the application?* *¿Por qué no llena la solicitud?* 6 NEG You use **not** to represent the negative of a word, group, or clause that has just been used. no ❑ *"Have you found Paula?"— "I'm afraid not."* *—¿Ya encontraste a Paula? —Me temo que no.* 7 NEG You can use **not** in front of "all" or "every" when you want to say something that applies only to some members of the group that you are talking about. no ❑ *Not all the money has been spent.* *No todo el dinero se ha gastado.* 8 NEG You can use **not** or **not even** in front of "a" or "one" to emphasize that there is none at all of what is being mentioned. no...ni ❑ *I sent report after report. But not one word was published.*

*Envié informe tras informe, pero no han publicado ni una sola palabra.* 9 NEG You use **not** when you are contrasting something that is true with something that people might wrongly believe to be true. *no* ❑ *People are working very hard, not because they have to, but because they want to. La gente está trabajando mucho; no porque tengan que hacerlo, sino porque quieren.* ❑ *Training is an investment not a cost. La capacitación es una inversión, no un gasto.* 10 NEG You use **not** in expressions such as "not only," "not just," and "not simply" to emphasize that something is true, but it is not the whole truth. *no* ❑ *These movies were not only making money; they were also very good. Las películas no sólo estaban produciendo dinero; también eran muy buenas.* ❑ *Not every applicant has a degree. No todos los solicitantes tienen un título.* 11 PHRASE You use **not that** to introduce a negative clause that contradicts something in the previous statement. *no* ❑ *He only had four hours' sleep. Not that he's complaining. Sólo pudo dormir cuatro horas; no es que se esté quejando.* 12 CONVENTION **Not at all** is a strong way of saying "No" or of agreeing that the answer to a question is "No." *claro que no* ❑ *"Sorry. I sound like Abby, don't I?"— "No. Not at all." —Discúlpame. Ya me parezco a Abby, ¿no? —No; claro que no.* 13 **more often than not** → see **often**

**no|table** /noʊtəbᵊl/ ADJ Someone or something that is **notable** is important or interesting. *notable* ❑ *The quiet little town is notable for its church. El tranquilo pueblito es notable por su iglesia.*

**no|tably** /noʊtəbli/ ADV You use **notably** to specify an important or typical example of something that you are talking about. *especialmente, particularmente* ❑ *He has apologized many times, most notably in the newspapers. Se ha disculpado muchas veces, especialmente en los periódicos.*



**no|ta|tion** /noʊteɪʃᵊn/ (**notations**) N-VAR A system of **notation** is a set of written symbols that are used to represent something such as music or mathematics. *notación*
→ see **music**

**note** /noʊt/ (**notes, noting, noted**) 1 N-COUNT A **note** is a short letter. *nota* ❑ *Steven wrote him a note asking him to come to his apartment. Steven le escribió una nota donde le pedía que fuera a su departamento.* 2 N-COUNT A **note** is something that you write down to remind yourself of something. *nota* ❑ *She didn't take notes on the lecture. No tomó notas en la conferencia.* 3 N-COUNT In a book or article, a **note** is a short piece of additional information. *nota* ❑ *See Note 16 on p. 223. Véase la nota 16 en la página 223.* 4 N-COUNT In music, a **note** is the sound of a particular pitch, or a written symbol representing this sound. *nota* ❑ *She has a deep voice and can't sing high notes. Tiene una voz grave y no alcanza las notas agudas.* 5 N-SING You can use **note** to refer to a particular feeling, impression, or atmosphere. *nota* ❑ *The movie ends on a positive note. La película termina con una nota de optimismo.* ❑ *There was a note of surprise in his voice. Había un tono de sorpresa en su voz.* 6 V-T If you **note** a fact, you become aware of it. *notar* ❑ *We noted his absence an hour ago. Notamos su ausencia hace una hora.* ❑ *Suddenly, I noted that the rain had stopped. De repente, noté que la lluvia había cesado.* 7 V-T When you **note** something, you write it down as a record of what has happened. *anotar* ❑ *"He has been very ill," she noted in her diary. —Ha estado muy enfermo—, anotó en su diario.* ❑ *An off-duty police officer noted the license plate of the car. Un policía que no estaba en servicio anotó las placas del coche.* 8 → see also **noted, promissory note** 9 PHRASE If you **compare notes with** someone or if the two of you **compare notes,** you talk to them and find out whether they have the same opinion, information, or experiences as yourself. *comparar notas* ❑ *...the chance to compare notes with other mothers. ...la oportunidad de comparar notas con otras madres.* 10 PHRASE Someone or something that is **of note** is important, worth mentioning, or well known. *de nota, digno de nota, notable* ❑ *...politicians of note. ...políticos notables.* 11 PHRASE If you **take note of** something, you pay attention to it because you think that it is important or significant. *tomar nota* ❑ *Take note of the weather conditions. Toma nota de las condiciones del tiempo.*
→ see **office**

▸ **note down** PHR-VERB If you **note down** something, you write it down quickly, so that you have a record of it. *anotar* ❑ *She noted down the names. Anotó los nombres.* ❑ *If you find a name that's on the list, note it down. Si encuentras un nombre que esté en la lista, anótalo.*

**Word Partnership** Usar *note* con:

| | |
|---|---|
| V. | **leave a** note, **send a** note 1 |
| | **find a** note, **read a** note, **scribble a** note, |
| | **write a** note 1 2 |
| | **make a** note 2 |
| | **sound a** note, **strike a** note 4 |
| | **take** note **of** *something* 11 |

**note|book** /noʊtbʊk/ (**notebooks**) 1 N-COUNT A **notebook** is a small book for writing notes in. *cuaderno (de notas)* ❑ *He took a notebook and pen from his pocket. Sacó un cuaderno y una pluma de la bolsa/del bolsillo.* 2 N-COUNT A **notebook** computer is a small personal computer. *computadora portátil* ❑ *...a new range of notebook computers. ...una nueva gama de computadoras portátiles.*

notebook

**not|ed** /noʊtɪd/ ADJ To be **noted for** something you do or have means to be well known and admired for it. *conocido* ❑ *Sanders was a man noted for his leadership skills. Sanders era conocido por su capacidad de dirección/liderazgo.*

**noth|ing** /nʌθɪŋ/ (**nothings**) 1 PRON **Nothing** means not a single thing, or not a single part of something. *nada* ❑ *I've done nothing much since this morning. No he hecho gran cosa desde esta mañana.* ❑ *There is nothing wrong with the car. El coche no tiene nada malo.* 2 PRON You use **nothing** to indicate that something or someone is not important or significant. *nada* ❑ *Because he has always had money, it means nothing to him. Como siempre ha tenido dinero, no significa nada para él.* ❑ *Do our years together mean nothing? ¿No significan nada los años que hemos pasado juntos?* 3 PHRASE You use **nothing but** in front of a noun, an infinitive without "to," or an "-ing" form to mean "only." *lo único que, solamente* ❑ *All that money brought nothing but misery. Lo único que* *produjo todo ese dinero fue sufrimiento.* ❑ *He is focused on nothing but winning.* *Solamente está empeñado en ganar.* **4** PHRASE If you say about an activity that there is **nothing to it**, you mean that it is extremely easy. *ser muy fácil* ❑ *Don't be scared—there's really nothing to it!* *—No tengas miedo; es muy fácil.* **5** to **think nothing of** → see **think**

**no|tice** /noʊtɪs/ (**notices, noticing, noticed**) **1** V-T/V-I If you **notice** something or someone, you become aware of them. *notar* ❑ *Didn't you notice anything special about him?* *—¿No notaste nada extraño en él?* ❑ *She noticed he was acting strangely.* *Notó que estaba actuando de una manera extraña.* ❑ *Luckily, I noticed where you left the car.* *Por suerte noté dónde dejaste el coche.* ❑ *If he thought no one would notice, he's wrong.* *Si creyó que nadie lo notaría, se equivocó.* **2** N-COUNT A **notice** is a written announcement in a place where everyone can read it. *letrero* ❑ *A few guest houses had "No Vacancies" notices in their windows.* *Unas cuantas casas de huéspedes tenían letreros de "Completo/Cupo agotado" en las ventanas.* **3** N-UNCOUNT If you give **notice** about something that is going to happen, you give a warning in advance that it is going to happen. *aviso* ❑ *She was moved to a different office without notice.* *La mudaron a una oficina diferente sin previo aviso.* ❑ *You have to give three months' notice if you want to leave.* *Si quiere irse, tiene que dar aviso con tres meses de antelación.* **4** PHRASE **Notice** is used in expressions such as "**on short notice,**" "**at a moment's notice,**" or "**at twenty-four hours' notice,**" to indicate that something can or must be done within a short period of time. *aviso, avisar* ❑ *There's no one available on such short notice to take her class.* *Con tan poco tiempo de aviso, no hay nadie disponible que tome su clase.* ❑ *I live just a mile away, so I can usually be available on short notice.* *Vivo a apenas un par de kilómetros, así que por lo general estoy disponible aunque me avisen con poco tiempo.* **5** PHRASE If a situation will exist **until further notice,** it will continue until someone changes it. *hasta nuevo aviso* ❑ *All flights were canceled until further notice.* *Todos los vuelos fueron cancelados hasta nuevo aviso.* **6** PHRASE If an employer **gives** an employee **notice,** the employer tells the employee that they must leave their job within a short fixed period of time. *avisar, despedir* [BUSINESS] ❑ *The next morning I gave him his notice.* *Al otro día, lo despedí/le avisé de su despido.* **7** PHRASE If you **give notice** or **hand in notice** you tell your employer that you intend to leave your job soon, within a set period of time. You can also **hand in** your **notice.** *presentar la renuncia* [BUSINESS] ❑ *He handed in his notice at the bank.* *Presentó su dimisión al banco.* **8** PHRASE If you **take notice of** a particular fact or situation, you behave in a way that shows that you are aware of it. *prestar atención* ❑ *We want the government to take notice of what we say.* *Queremos que el gobierno preste atención a lo que decimos.* **9** PHRASE If you **take no notice of** someone or something, you do not consider them to be important enough to affect what you think or what you do. *no hacer caso* ❑ *For years, society took no notice of the needs of the disabled.* *Durante años, la sociedad no hizo caso de las necesidades de los inválidos.*

| **Thesaurus** *notice* | Ver también: |
|---|---|
| V. | note, observe, perceive, see **1** |
| N. | advertisement, announcement **2** |

| **Word Partnership** | Usar *notice* con: |
|---|---|
| N. | notice **a change**, notice **a difference** **1** |
| V. | **begin to** notice, **fail to** notice, **pretend not to** notice **1**<br>**receive** notice, **serve** notice **3**<br>**give** notice **3** **6** **7** |

**no|tice|able** /noʊtɪsəbᵊl/ ADJ Something that is **noticeable** is very obvious, so that it is easy to see, hear, or recognize. *perceptible, evidente* ❑ *It was noticeable that his face and arms were red.* *Era evidente que su cara y sus brazos estaban rojos.* • **no|tice|ably** ADV *perceptiblemente* ❑ *The traffic has gotten noticeably worse.* *El tránsito ha empeorado perceptiblemente.*

**no|ti|fy** /noʊtɪfaɪ/ (**notifies, notifying, notified**) V-T If you **notify** someone of something, you officially inform them about it. *notificar* [FORMAL] ❑ *We have notified the police.* *Ya notificamos a la policía.* ❑ *They were notified that they had to leave.* *Les notificaron que tenían que irse.* • **no|ti|fi|ca|tion** /noʊtɪfɪkeɪʃən/ N-VAR (**notifications**) *notificación* ❑ *We gave them notification that we would end the agreement September 15.* *Les entregamos la notificación de que daríamos por terminado el convenio el 15 de septiembre.*

**no|tion** /noʊʃᵊn/ (**notions**) **1** N-COUNT A **notion** is an idea or belief about something. *idea* ❑ *We each have a notion of what kind of person we'd like to be.* *Todos tenemos una idea de la clase de persona que queremos ser.* **2** N-PLURAL **Notions** are small articles for sewing, such as buttons, zippers, and thread. *artículo (de la materia de que se trate)*

| **Thesaurus** *notion* | Ver también: |
|---|---|
| N. | concept, idea, opinion, thought **1** |

**no|to|ri|ous** /noʊtɔriəs/ ADJ To be **notorious** means to be well known for something bad. *notorio, de mala fama* ❑ *...an area notorious for crime and violence.* *...una zona notoria/de mala fama por el crimen y la violencia.* • **no|to|ri|ous|ly** ADV *notoriamente* ❑ *Living space in New York City is notoriously expensive.* *La vivienda es notoriamente cara en la ciudad de Nueva York.*

**noun** /naʊn/ (**nouns**) **1** N-COUNT A **noun** is a word such as "car," "love," or "Anne" which is used to refer to a person or thing. *nombre, sustantivo* **2** → see also **count noun, proper noun**

| **Word Link** | *nov ≈ new : innovation, novel, renovate* |
|---|---|

**nov|el** /nɒvᵊl/ (**novels**) **1** N-COUNT A **novel** is a long written story about imaginary people and events. *novela* ❑ *...a novel by Herman Hesse.* *...una novela por/de Herman Hesse.* **2** ADJ **Novel** things are new and different from anything that has been done, experienced, or made before. *novedoso* ❑ *...a novel way of raising money.* *...una manera novedosa de recaudar dinero.*
→ see **library**

n

**nov|el|ist** /nɒvəlɪst/ (**novelists**) N-COUNT A **novelist** is a person who writes novels. *novelista* ❑ *...a successful novelist. ...un novelista de éxito.*
→ see **fantasy**

**No|vem|ber** /noʊvɛmbər/ (**Novembers**) N-VAR **November** is the eleventh month of the year in the Western calendar. *noviembre* ❑ *He arrived in London in November 1939. Llegó a Londres en noviembre de 1939.*

**nov|ice** /nɒvɪs/ (**novices**) N-COUNT A **novice** is someone who has been doing a job or other activity for only a short time and so is not experienced at it. *novato o novata, principiante o principianta* ❑ *I'm a novice at these things. You're the professional. Yo soy un novato en esto; usted es el profesional.*

**now** /naʊ/ **1** ADV You use **now** to refer to the present time, often in contrast to a time in the past or the future. *ahora, ya/ahora/ya...ahora* ❑ *She should know that by now. Ya debería saberlo (ahora).* ❑ *I must go now. Ya tengo que irme.* ● **Now** is also a pronoun. *ahora* ❑ *Now is your chance to talk to him. Ahora es tu oportunidad de hablar con él.* **2** CONJ You use **now** or **now that** to indicate that an event has occurred and as a result something else may or will happen. *ahora* ❑ *Now our children are grown, I have time to help other people. Ahora que nuestros hijos están grandes, ya tengo tiempo para ayudar a otras personas.* **3** ADV You use **now** in statements which specify the length of time up to the present that something has lasted. *ya* ❑ *They've been married now for 30 years. Ya llevan casados 30 años.* ❑ *They have been missing for a long time now. Hace ya mucho tiempo que están perdidos.* **4** ADV You say "**Now**" or "**Now then**" to indicate to the person or people you are with that you want their attention, or that you are about to change the subject. *bueno, vamos* [SPOKEN] ❑ *"Now then," Max said, "to get back to the point." —Bueno —dijo Max—, volvamos a donde estábamos.* ❑ *Now then, what's the trouble? —Vamos a ver, ¿cuál es el problema?* **5** ADV You can say "**Now**" to introduce new information into a story or account. *ahora que* [SPOKEN] ❑ *Now I didn't tell him that, so he must have found out on his own. Ya que yo no le dije eso, debió averiguarlo por su cuenta.* **6** PHRASE If you say that something will happen **any day now, any moment now,** or **any time now,** you mean that it will happen very soon. *en cualquier momento* ❑ *We are expecting him home any day now. Lo esperamos en casa en cualquier momento.* **7** PHRASE **Just now** means a very short time ago. *hace un rato* [SPOKEN] ❑ *You looked pretty upset just now. Parecías muy enojado hace un rato.* **8** PHRASE If you say that something happens **now and then** or **every now and again,** you mean that it happens sometimes but not very often or regularly. *de vez en cuando, alguna que otra vez, de cuando en cuando* ❑ *Now and then they heard the roar of a heavy truck. Alguna que otra vez oían el estruendo de un camión pesado.*

**nowa|days** /naʊədeɪz/ ADV **Nowadays** means at the present time, in contrast with the past. *hoy en día, en la actualidad, actualmente* ❑ *Nowadays we have more career choices when we leave school. Actualmente tenemos más opciones cuando salimos de la escuela.*

**no|where** /noʊwɛər/ **1** ADV You use **nowhere** to emphasize that a place has more of a particular quality than any other place, or that it is the only place where something happens or exists. *en ningún lugar* ❑ *Nowhere is the problem worse than in Asia. No hay ningún lugar donde el problema sea peor que en Asia.* ❑ *This kind of forest exists nowhere else in the world. Este tipo de bosque no existe en ningún otro lugar del mundo.* **2** ADV You use **nowhere** when making negative statements to say that a suitable place of the specified kind does not exist. *en ningún lugar* ❑ *There was nowhere to hide and nowhere to run. No había dónde ocultarse ni a dónde correr.* ❑ *I have nowhere else to go, nowhere in the world. No tengo a dónde más ir, en ningún lugar del mundo.* **3** ADV If you say that something or someone appears **from nowhere** or **out of nowhere,** you mean that they appear suddenly and unexpectedly. *de la nada* ❑ *A car came from nowhere, and I had to jump back off the road. Salió un coche de la nada y tuve que saltar hacia un lado de la carretera.* PHRASE ● If you say that you **are getting nowhere** or that something **is getting** you **nowhere**, you mean that you are not achieving anything or having any success. *no llevar a ninguna parte/ningún lado* ❑ *Oh, stop arguing! This is getting us nowhere. ¡Deja de quejarte! Esto no nos lleva a ningún lado.* **4** PHRASE If you say that a place is **in the middle of nowhere,** you mean that it is a long way from other places. *en medio de la nada* ❑ *We put up our tent in the middle of nowhere. Levantamos la tienda en medio de la nada.* **5** PHRASE If you use **nowhere near** in front of a word or expression, you are emphasizing that the real situation is very different from, or has not reached, the state which that word or expression suggests. *ni por asomo, ni con mucho* ❑ *He's nowhere near finished yet. Ni por asomo está cerca de terminar.*

| **Word Partnership** | Usar *nowhere* con: |
|---|---|
| V. | nowhere **to be found**, nowhere **to be seen**, ***have*** nowhere **to go**, ***have*** nowhere **to hide**, ***have*** nowhere **to run** **2** **go** nowhere **3** |

**no-win situa|tion** (**no-win situations**) N-COUNT If you are in a **no-win situation,** any action you take will fail to benefit you in any way. *callejón sin salida* ❑ *They are in a no-win situation. Whatever they do, they are going to get criticized for it. Están en un callejón sin salida. Hagan lo que hagan, los van a criticar.*

**nu|clear** /nukliər/ ADJ **Nuclear** means relating to the nuclei of atoms, or to the energy released when these nuclei are split or combined. *nuclear* ❑ *...a nuclear power station. ...una central nuclear.* ❑ *...nuclear weapons. ...armas nucleares.*
→ see **energy**

**nu|clear en|er|gy** N-UNCOUNT **Nuclear energy** is energy that is released when the nuclei of atoms are split or combined. *energía nuclear*

**nu|clear fis|sion** N-UNCOUNT **Nuclear fission** is the same as **fission.** *fisión nuclear*

**nu|clear fu|sion** N-UNCOUNT → see **fusion**

**nu|cleic acid** /nukliɪk æsɪd, -kleɪ-/ (**nucleic acids**) N-COUNT **Nucleic acids** are complex chemical substances, such as DNA, which are found in living cells. *ácido nucleico* [TECHNICAL]

**nu|cleo|tide** /nukliətaɪd/ (**nucleotides**) N-COUNT **Nucleotides** are molecules that join together to form DNA and RNA. nucleótido [TECHNICAL]

**null** /nʌl/ PHRASE If an agreement, a declaration, or the result of an election is **null and void,** it is not legally valid. nulo, inválido ❑ *A spokeswoman said the agreement had been declared null and void.* *Una vocera afirmó que el convenio había sido declarado inválido.*
→ see **zero**

**numb** /nʌm/ (**numbs, numbing, numbed, number, numbest**) **1** ADJ If a part of your body is **numb,** you cannot feel anything there. entumecido, adormecido ❑ *He could feel his fingers growing numb.* *Podía sentir cómo se le iban entumeciendo los dedos.* ● **numb|ness** N-UNCOUNT entumecimiento, adormecimiento ❑ *I'm suffering from pain and numbness in my hands.* *Tengo las manos entumecidas y me duelen.* **2** ADJ If you are **numb with** shock, fear, or grief, you are so shocked, frightened, or upset that you cannot think clearly or feel any emotion. petrificado ❑ *He looked at the price label and went numb with surprise.* *Vio la etiqueta del precio y se quedó petrificado por la sorpresa.* **3** V-T If an event or experience **numbs** you, you can no longer think clearly or feel any emotion. atontar ❑ *For a while the shock of Philippe's letter numbed her.* *La impresión que le causó la carta de Philippe la dejó como atontada por un momento.* ● **numbed** ADJ atontado ❑ *We were numbed by the terrible news.* *Nos quedamos como atontados por las terribles noticias.* **4** V-T If cold weather, a drug, or a blow **numbs** a part of your body, you can no longer feel anything in it. entumecer ❑ *The cold numbed my fingers.* *Tenía los dedos entumecidos por el frío.*

**num|ber** /nʌmbər/ (**numbers, numbering, numbered**) **1** N-COUNT A **number** is a word such as "two," "nine," or "twelve," or a symbol such as 1, 3, or 47, which is used in counting something. número ❑ *I don't know the room number.* *No sé (cuál es) el número del cuarto.* ❑ *...number 3, Argyll Street.* *...calle Argyll, número 3.* **2** N-COUNT You use **number** with words such as "large" or "small" to say approximately how many things or people there are. número ❑ *We're holding a large number of interviews for this job.* *Vamos a tener un gran número de entrevistas para este puesto.* ❑ *I have received an enormous number of letters.* *He recibido un sinnúmero de cartas.* **3** N-SING If there are **a number of** things or people, there are several of them. If there are **any number of** things or people, there is a large quantity of them. vario ❑ *Sam told a number of lies.* *Sam dijo varias mentiras.* **4** V-T If a group of people or things **numbers** a particular total, that is how many there are. tener en total ❑ *Their village numbered 100 houses.* *Su pueblo tenía 100 casas en total.* **5** N-COUNT A **number** is the series of numbers that you dial when you are making a telephone call. número ❑ *...a list of names and telephone numbers.* *...una lista de nombres y números de teléfono.* ❑ *My number is 414-3925.* *Mi número (de teléfono) es el 414-3925.* **6** V-T If you **number** something, you mark it with a number, usually starting at 1. numerar ❑ *He cut the paper up into tiny squares, and he numbered each one.* *Cortó el papel en cuadritos y numeró cada uno.*
→ see also **amount**
→ see **mathematics, zero**

**nu|mer|ous** /nuːmərəs/ ADJ If people or things are **numerous,** they exist or are present in large numbers. numeroso ❑ *He made numerous attempts to lose weight.* *Hizo numerosos intentos por bajar de peso.*

**nun** /nʌn/ (**nuns**) N-COUNT A **nun** is a member of a female religious community. monja ❑ *She is studying to become a nun.* *Se metió al convento para convertirse en monja.*

**nurse** /nɜrs/ (**nurses, nursing, nursed**) **1** N-COUNT; N-TITLE; N-VOC A **nurse** is a person whose job is to care for people who are ill. enfermero o enfermera ❑ *She spent 29 years as a nurse.* *Pasó 29 años como enfermera.* **2** V-T If you **nurse** someone, you care for them when they are ill. atender, cuidar ❑ *All the years he was sick my mother nursed him.* *Mi madre lo cuidó todos los años que estuvo enfermo.* **3** V-T If you **nurse** an illness or injury, you allow it to get better by resting as much as possible. cuidar ❑ *We're going to go home and nurse our colds.* *Vamos a quedarnos en casa y cuidarnos hasta que se nos pase el catarro.* **4** V-T If you **nurse** an emotion or desire, you feel it strongly for a long time. abrigar, sufrir ❑ *Jane still nurses the pain of rejection.* *Jane sigue sufriendo por el dolor del rechazo.*

**Word Partnership** Usar *nurse* con:

| | |
|---|---|
| N. | nurse's **aide** 1 |
| ADJ. | **visiting** nurse 1 |

**nurse prac|ti|tion|er** (**nurse practitioners**) N-COUNT A **nurse practitioner** is a nurse with advanced training who provides some of the medical care usually provided by a doctor. enfermero especializado o enfermera especializada ❑ *California law allows nurse practitioners to write prescriptions.* *Las leyes de California permiten que los enfermeros especializados receten.*

**nurse|ry** /nɜrsəri/ (**nurseries**) N-COUNT A **nursery** is a place where plants are grown in order to be sold. semillero, vivero ❑ *The garden, developed over the past 35 years, includes a nursery.* *El jardín, que se ha desarrollado en los últimos 35 años, comprende un vivero.*

**nurse|ry rhyme** (**nursery rhymes**) N-COUNT A **nursery rhyme** is a poem or song for young children, especially one that is old or well known. canción infantil

**nur|ture** /nɜrtʃər/ (**nurtures, nurturing, nurtured**) **1** V-T If you **nurture** something such as a young child or a young plant, you care for it while it is growing and developing. criar, educar [FORMAL] ❑ *Parents want to know the best way to nurture and raise their child.* *Los padres quieren saber cuál es la mejor manera de criar y educar a los hijos.* **2** V-T If you **nurture** plans, ideas, or people, you encourage them or help them to develop. fomentar [FORMAL] ❑ *She always nurtured the talent of others.* *Siempre fomentó el talento de otros.*

**nut** /nʌt/ (**nuts**) **1** N-COUNT The firm shelled fruit of some trees and bushes are called **nuts.** nuez ❑ *Nuts and seeds are very good for you.* *Las nueces y semillas son muy buenas para uno.* **2** → see also **peanut** **3** N-COUNT A **nut** is a thick metal ring which you screw onto a metal rod called a bolt. Nuts and bolts are used to hold things such as pieces of machinery together. tuerca ❑ *If you want to repair the wheels, you must undo the four nuts.* *Si*

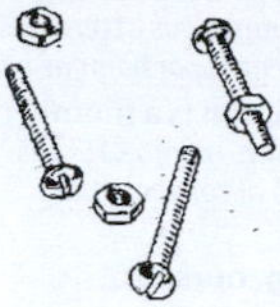
nuts and bolts

quieres reparar las ruedas, tienes que quitar las cuatro tuercas. **4** N-COUNT If you describe someone as, for example, a baseball **nut** or a health **nut,** you mean that they are extremely enthusiastic about the thing mentioned. *fanático o fanática* [INFORMAL] ❑ *I'm a football nut.* *Soy un fanático del fútbol.* **5** ADJ If you are **nuts about** something or someone, you like them very much. *loco, chiflado* [INFORMAL] ❑ *She's nuts about you and you're in love with her.* *Ella está loca por ti y tú estás enamorado de ella.* **6** ADJ If you say that someone goes **nuts** or is **nuts,** you mean that they go crazy or are very foolish. *loco* [INFORMAL] ❑ *You guys are nuts.* *Ustedes están locos.* **7** PHRASE If someone **goes nuts,** they become extremely angry. *estar hecho una fiera* [INFORMAL] ❑ *My father would go nuts if I told him.* *Mi padre se pondría como una fiera/un basilisco si le dijera.*
→ see **peanut**

**nu|tri|ent** /nuːtriənt/ (**nutrients**) N-COUNT **Nutrients** are substances that help plants and animals to grow. *nutriente* ❑ *...vitamins, minerals, and other essential nutrients.* *...vitaminas, minerales y otros nutrientes fundamentales.*
→ see **cardiovascular system, food**

**nu|tri|tion** /nuːtrɪʃᵊn/ N-UNCOUNT **Nutrition** is the process of taking and absorbing nutrients from food. *nutrición* ❑ *He offers nutrition advice to families.* *Ofrece consejos sobre nutrición a las familias.*

**nu|tri|tious** /nuːtrɪʃəs/ ADJ **Nutritious** food contains substances which help your body to be healthy. *nutritivo* ❑ *It is important to eat enjoyable, nutritious foods.* *Es importante consumir alimentos nutritivos y agradables al paladar.*

N

# Oo

**oak** /oʊk/ (**oaks**) N-VAR An **oak** or an **oak tree** is a large tree with strong, hard wood. *roble* • **Oak** is the wood of this tree. *(madera de) roble*

oar

**oar** /ɔr/ (**oars**) N-COUNT **Oars** are long poles with a wide, flat blade at one end which are used for rowing a boat. *remo*
→ see **boat**

**oasis** /oʊeɪsɪs/ (**oases** /oʊeɪsiz/) **1** N-COUNT An **oasis** is a small area in a desert where water and plants are found. *oasis* **2** N-COUNT You can refer to a pleasant place or situation as an **oasis** when it is surrounded by unpleasant ones. *oasis* ❑ *Gardens are an oasis in a busy city. Los jardines son un oasis en las ciudades agitadas.*
→ see **desert**

**oath** /oʊθ/ (**oaths**) **1** N-COUNT An **oath** is a formal promise. *juramento* ❑ *The soldiers take an oath to defend the country. Los soldados hacen el juramento de defender su país.* ❑ *We signed an oath that we would not talk about the experiment. Nos comprometimos por escrito a que no hablaríamos sobre el experimento.* **2** N-SING In a court of law, when someone takes **the oath,** they make a formal promise to tell the truth. You can say that someone is **under oath** when they have made this promise. *juramento*
→ see **medicine**

**oat|meal** /oʊtmil/ N-UNCOUNT **Oatmeal** is a thick sticky food made from oats cooked in water or milk and eaten hot, especially for breakfast. *avena, hojuelas de avena*

**oats** /oʊts/

| |
|---|
| The form **oat** is used as a modifier. |

N-PLURAL **Oats** are a cereal crop or its grains, used for making cookies or oatmeal, or for feeding animals. *avena*
→ see **grain**

**obese** /oʊbis/ ADJ If someone is **obese,** they are extremely fat. *obeso* ❑ *Obese people often have more health problems than thinner people. La gente obesa suele tener más problemas de salud que la gente delgada.* • **obesity** /oʊbisɪti/ N-UNCOUNT *obesidad* ❑ *Eating too much sugar can lead to obesity. Consumir demasiado azúcar puede provocar obesidad.*
→ see **sugar**

**obey** /oʊbeɪ/ (**obeys, obeying, obeyed**) V-T/V-I If you **obey** a person, a command, or an instruction, you do what you are told to do. *obedecer* ❑ *Most people obey the law. La mayoría de la gente obedece la ley.* ❑ *It was his duty to obey. Su deber era obedecer.*

| **Word Partnership** | Usar *obey* con: |
|---|---|
| N. | obey **a command**, obey **God**, obey **the law**, obey **orders**, obey **the rules** |
| V. | **refuse to** obey |

**ob/gyn** /oʊ bi dʒi waɪ ɛn/ (**ob/gyns**) **1** N-UNCOUNT **Ob/gyn** is the branch of medicine that deals with women's medical conditions, pregnancy, and birth. **Ob/gyn** is an abbreviation for "obstetrics/gynecology." *ginecología* [INFORMAL] **2** N-COUNT An **ob/gyn** is a doctor who specializes in women's medical conditions, pregnancy, and birth. **Ob/gyn** is an abbreviation for "obstetrician/gynecologist." *ginecólogo o ginecóloga* [INFORMAL]

**obi|tu|ary** /oʊbɪtʃuɛri/ (**obituaries**) N-COUNT Someone's **obituary** is an account of their life and achievements which is published soon after they die. *obituario, nota necrológica* ❑ *I read his obituary in the newspaper. Leí su obituario en el periódico.*

**ob|ject** (**objects, objecting, objected**)

| |
|---|
| The noun is pronounced /ɒbdʒɪkt/. The verb is pronounced /əbdʒɛkt/. |

**1** N-COUNT An **object** is anything that has a fixed shape or form, and that is not alive. *objeto* ❑ *...everyday objects such as wooden spoons. ...objetos cotidianos, como las cucharas de madera.* ❑ *...an object the shape of an orange. ...un objeto en forma de naranja.* **2** N-COUNT The **object** of what someone is doing is their aim or purpose. *objeto, propósito* ❑ *The object of the event is to raise money. El propósito del acto es recaudar dinero.* **3** N-COUNT The **object of** a particular feeling or reaction is the person or thing it is directed toward or that causes it. *objeto* ❑ *The object of her love was Bob Andrews. El objeto de su amor era Bob Andrews.* **4** N-COUNT In grammar, the **object** of a verb or a preposition is the word or phrase which completes the structure begun by the verb or preposition. *objeto* **5** → see also **direct object, indirect object** **6** V-T/V-I If you **object** to something, you express your dislike or disapproval of it. *objetar, poner objeción* ❑ *A lot of people objected to the book. Mucha gente le puso objeciones al libro.* ❑ *Cullen objected that he had too much work. Cullen objetó que tenía demasiado trabajo.* **7** PHRASE If you say that **money is no object** or **distance is no object,** you are emphasizing that you will spend as much money as necessary or travel whatever distance is required. *el dinero no preocupa* ❑ *If money was no object, would you buy this car? —Si el dinero no le preocupara, ¿compraría este automóvil?*

**Thesaurus** *object* Ver también:

N. item, thing 1
aim, goal, intent 2
V. argue, disagree, oppose, protest against 6

**Word Partnership** Usar *object* con:

ADJ. **foreign** object, **inanimate** object, **moving** object, **solid** object 1
N. object **to *someone/something*** 6

**ob|jec|tion** /əbdʒɛkʃᵊn/ (**objections**) N-VAR If you express or raise an **objection to** something, you say that you do not like it or agree with it. *objeción* ❑ *I don't have any objection to banks making money. No tengo ninguna objeción a que los bancos ganen dinero.*

**ob|jec|tive** /əbdʒɛktɪv/ (**objectives**) 1 N-COUNT Your **objective** is what you are trying to achieve. *objetivo* ❑ *Our main objective was to find the child. Nuestro principal objetivo era encontrar al niño.* 2 ADJ **Objective** information is based on facts. *objetivo* ❑ *Give me some objective evidence and I'll believe it. Dame alguna prueba objetiva y lo creeré.* ● **ob|jec|tive|ly** ADV *objetivamente* ❑ *We want to inform people objectively about events. Deseamos informar objetivamente a la gente sobre los acontecimientos.* ● **ob|jec|tiv|ity** /ɒbdʒɛktɪvɪti/ N-UNCOUNT *objetividad* ❑ *Most people worry about the objectivity of research. A la mayoría de la gente le preocupa la objetividad de la investigación.* 3 ADJ If someone is **objective,** they base their opinions on facts rather than on their personal feelings. *objetivo* ❑ *A journalist should be completely objective. Un periodista debe ser completamente objetivo.* ● **ob|jec|tive|ly** ADV *objetivamente* ❑ *Try to see things more objectively. Trata de ver las cosas más objetivamente.* ● **ob|jec|tiv|ity** N-UNCOUNT *objetividad* ❑ *Doctors must maintain objectivity. Los médicos deben mantener la objetividad.*

**ob|jec|tive lens** (**objective lenses**) N-COUNT The **objective lens** of a microscope is the lens that is closest to the object being observed and furthest from the eyepiece. *objetivo*

**ob|li|ga|tion** /ɒblɪgeɪʃᵊn/ (**obligations**) 1 N-VAR If you have an **obligation to** do something, it is your duty to do it. *obligación* ❑ *The judge has an obligation to find out the truth. El juez tiene la obligación de averiguar la verdad.* 2 N-VAR If you have an **obligation to** a person, it is your duty to take care of them. *obligación* ❑ *...the United States' obligations to its own citizens. ...las obligaciones de Estados Unidos con sus ciudadanos.*

**Thesaurus** *obligation* Ver también:

N. duty, responsibility 1 2

**Word Partnership** Usar *obligation* con:

V. obligation **to pay** 1
**feel an** obligation, **fulfill an** obligation, **meet an** obligation 1 2
ADJ. **legal** obligation, **moral** obligation 1 2
N. **sense of** obligation 1 2

**oblige** /əblaɪdʒ/ (**obliges, obliging, obliged**) 1 V-T If you **are obliged to** do something, a situation, rule, or law makes it necessary for you to do it. *obligar* ❑ *My family needed the money so I was obliged to work. Mi familia necesitaba dinero, así que me vi obligado a trabajar.* 2 V-T/V-I To **oblige** someone means to be helpful to them by doing what they have asked you to do. *ponerse a disposición, complacer* ❑ *If you ever need help, I'd be happy to oblige. Si alguna vez necesitan ayuda, con gusto me pongo a su disposición.* ❑ *They obliged with very simple answers. Complacieron con respuestas muy simples.*

**obo** In advertisements, **obo** is used after a price to indicate that the person who is selling something is willing to accept slightly less money than the sum they have mentioned. **Obo** is a written abbreviation for "or best offer." *ofrezca* ❑ *Family boat. $6,000 obo. Bote familiar. 6,000 dólares. Ofrezca.*

**ob|scure** /əbskyʊər/ (**obscurer, obscurest, obscures, obscuring, obscured**) 1 ADJ If something or someone is **obscure,** they are unknown, or are known by only a few people. *oscuro* ❑ *The origin of the word is obscure. El origen de la palabra es oscuro.* ● **ob|scu|rity** N-UNCOUNT *oscuridad* ❑ *She came from obscurity into the world of television. Salió de la oscuridad al mundo de la televisión.* 2 ADJ Something that is **obscure** is difficult to understand or deal with, usually because it involves so many parts or details. *oscuro, críptico* ❑ *The contracts are written in obscure language. Los contratos están redactados en un lenguaje obscuro.* ● **ob|scu|rity** N-UNCOUNT *oscuridad* ❑ *He was irritated by the obscurity of Henry's reply. Estaba irritado por lo críptico de la respuesta de Henry.* 3 V-T If one thing **obscures** another, it prevents it from being seen or heard properly. *tapar* ❑ *Trees obscured his view of the scene. Unos árboles le tapaban la vista de la escena.*

**Word Link** ***ation ≈ state of : elevation, humiliation, observation***

**ob|ser|va|tion** /ɒbzərveɪʃᵊn/ (**observations**) 1 N-UNCOUNT **Observation** is the action or process of carefully watching someone or something. *observación* ❑ *In the hospital she'll be under observation all the time. En el hospital estará en observación todo el tiempo.* ● **ob|ser|va|tion|al** ADJ *de observación* ❑ *...observational studies of children. ...estudios de observación de los niños.* 2 N-COUNT An **observation** is something that you have learned by seeing or watching something and thinking about it. *observación* ❑ *...observations about the causes of heart disease. ...las observaciones sobre las causas de las enfermedades cardiacas.* 3 N-COUNT If a person makes an **observation,** they make a comment about something or someone after watching how they behave. *observación* ❑ *He made the observation that life is full of difficulty. Hizo la observación de que la vida está llena de dificultades.* 4 N-UNCOUNT **Observation** is the ability to notice things that are not usually noticed. *observación* ❑ *She has good powers of observation. Tiene una buena capacidad de observación.*
→ see **experiment, forecast, science**

**Word Partnership** Usar *observation* con:

PREP. **by** observation, **through** observation, **under** observation 1
ADJ. **careful** observation 1
**direct** observation 1 2
V. **make an** observation 3

**Word Link** *serv ≈ keeping : conserve, observe, preserve*

**ob|serve** /əbzɜrv/ (**observes, observing, observed**) 1 V-T If you **observe** a person or thing, you watch them carefully, especially in order to learn something about them. *observar* ❑ *Olson studied and observed the behavior of babies.* *Olson estudió y observó el comportamiento de los bebés.* 2 V-T If you **observe** someone or something, you see or notice them. *observar* [FORMAL] ❑ *He observed a red spot on his skin.* *Observó una mancha roja en su piel.* 3 V-T If you **observe** something such as a law or custom, you obey it or follow it. *observar* ❑ *Drivers should observe speed limits.* *Los conductores deben observar los límites de velocidad.* ● **ob|ser|vance** N-VAR (**observances**) *observancia* ❑ *...strict observance of laws.* *...la estricta observancia de las leyes.*

**Thesaurus** *observe* Ver también:

V. study, watch 1
detect, notice, spot 2

**Word Partnership** Usar *observe* con:

N. observe **behavior**, **opportunity to** observe 1 2
observe **guidelines**, observe **rules** 3

**ob|serv|er** /əbzɜrvər/ (**observers**) 1 N-COUNT You can refer to someone who sees or notices something as an **observer.** *observador u observadora* ❑ *Observers say the woman stabbed him.* *Los que observaron lo que pasó dicen que la mujer lo apuñaló.* 2 N-COUNT An **observer** is someone who studies current events and situations. *observador u observadora* ❑ *Observers say the president's decision will affect his popularity.* *Los observadores dicen que la decisión del presidente afectará su popularidad.*

**ob|sess** /əbsɛs/ (**obsesses, obsessing, obsessed**) V-T/V-I If something **obsesses** you or if you **obsess about** something, you keep thinking about it and find it difficult to think about anything else. *obsesionar(se)* ❑ *The idea of space travel has obsessed me all my life.* *La idea de viajar por el espacio me ha obsesionado toda la vida.* ❑ *She was obsessing about her weight.* *Estaba obsesionándose por su peso.* ● **ob|sessed** ADJ *obsesionado* ❑ *He was obsessed with crime movies.* *Estaba obsesionado por las películas policiacas.*

**ob|ses|sion** /əbsɛʃᵊn/ (**obsessions**) N-VAR If you say that someone has an **obsession** with a person or thing, you think they are spending too much time thinking about them. *obsesión* ❑ *She tried to forget her obsession with Christopher.* *Trató de olvidar su obsesión por Christopher.*

**ob|sta|cle** /ɒbstəkᵊl/ (**obstacles**) N-COUNT An **obstacle** is an object that makes it difficult for you to go where you want to go, or to do something. *obstáculo* ❑ *We came to our first major obstacle, a fallen tree across the road.* *Nos topamos con nuestro primer obstáculo: un árbol caído atravesado en la carretera.* ❑ *The most difficult obstacle to overcome was the heavy rain.* *El obstáculo más difícil de superar fue la abundante lluvia.*

**Word Partnership** Usar *obstacle* con:

V. **be an** obstacle, **hit an** obstacle, **overcome an** obstacle
ADJ. **big/biggest** obstacle, **main** obstacle, **major** obstacle, **serious** obstacle
N. obstacle **course**, obstacle **to peace**

**ob|tain** /əbteɪn/ (**obtains, obtaining, obtained**) V-T To **obtain** something means to get it. *obtener* [FORMAL] ❑ *Evans tried to obtain a false passport.* *Evans trató de obtener un pasaporte falso.*

**Word Partnership** Usar *obtain* con:

ADJ. **able to** obtain, **difficult to** obtain, **easy to** obtain, **unable to** obtain
N. obtain **approval**, obtain **a copy**, obtain **financing**, obtain **help**, obtain **information**, obtain **insurance**, obtain **permission**, obtain **weapons**

**ob|vi|ous** /ɒbviəs/ ADJ If something is **obvious,** it is easy to see or understand. *obvio* ❑ *It's obvious he's worried about us.* *Es obvio que está preocupado por nosotros.*

**Thesaurus** *obvious* Ver también:

ADJ. noticeable, plain, unmistakable

**Word Partnership** Usar *obvious* con:

N. obvious **answer**, obvious **choice**, obvious **differences**, obvious **example**, obvious **question**, obvious **reasons**, obvious **solution**
ADV. **fairly** obvious, **immediately** obvious, **less** obvious, **most** obvious, **painfully** obvious, **quite** obvious, **so** obvious

**ob|vi|ous|ly** /ɒbviəsli/ 1 ADV You use **obviously** when you are stating something that you expect the person who is listening to know already. *obviamente* ❑ *Obviously I'll be disappointed if they don't come, but it wouldn't be a disaster.* *Obviamente, me sentiré decepcionado si no vienen, pero no sería catastrófico.* 2 ADV You use **obviously** to indicate that something is easily noticed, seen, or recognized. *evidente, claro* ❑ *He obviously likes you very much.* *Es evidente que le gustas mucho.*

**oc|ca|sion** /əkeɪʒᵊn/ (**occasions**) 1 N-COUNT An **occasion** is a time when something happens. *ocasión* ❑ *On one occasion he looked so sick that we took him to the hospital.* *En una ocasión se veía tan enfermo que lo llevamos al hospital.* 2 N-COUNT An **occasion** is an important event, ceremony, or celebration. *ocasión* ❑ *The wedding was a happy occasion.* *La boda fue una ocasión feliz.* 3 N-COUNT An **occasion for** doing something is an opportunity for doing it. *ocasión* [FORMAL] ❑ *It is an occasion for all the family to celebrate.* *Es una ocasión para que toda la familia festeje.*

**Word Partnership** Usar *occasion* con:

ADJ. **festive** occasion, **historic** occasion, **rare** occasion, **solemn** occasion, **special** occasion 1 2
V. **mark an** occasion 2

**oc|ca|sion|al** /əkeɪʒənᵊl/ ADJ **Occasional** means happening sometimes, but not regularly or often. ocasional ❑ *I get occasional headaches.* *Tengo dolores de cabeza ocasionales.* • **oc|ca|sion|al|ly** ADV ocasionalmente ❑ *He misbehaves occasionally.* *Ocasionalmente se porta mal.*

**Word Link** *ant ≈ one who does, has : defendant, immigrant, occupant*

**oc|cu|pant** /ɒkyəpənt/ (**occupants**) N-COUNT The **occupants** of a building or room are the people who live or work there. ocupante, inquilino o inquilina ❑ *Most of the occupants left the building before the fire spread.* *La mayoría de los ocupantes abandonaron el edificio antes de que el fuego se propagara.*

**oc|cu|pa|tion** /ɒkyəpeɪʃᵊn/ (**occupations**) 1 N-COUNT Your **occupation** is your job or profession. ocupación ❑ *I was looking for an occupation which was enjoyable.* *Estaba buscando una ocupación agradable.* • **oc|cu|pa|tion|al** ADJ profesional ❑ *...advertising people and other occupational groups.* *...la gente de la publicidad y otros grupos de profesionales.* 2 N-COUNT An **occupation** is something that you spend time doing, either for pleasure or because it needs to be done. ocupación, trabajo ❑ *Mining is a dangerous occupation.* *La minería es un trabajo peligroso.* 3 N-UNCOUNT The **occupation** of a country happens when it is entered and controlled by a foreign army. ocupación ❑ *...the occupation of Poland from 1939 to 1945.* *...la ocupación de Polonia de 1939 a 1945.*

O

**oc|cu|py** /ɒkyəpaɪ/ (**occupies, occupying, occupied**) 1 V-T The people who **occupy** a building or a place are the people who live or work there. ocupar ❑ *The company occupies the top floor of the building.* *La empresa ocupa el piso superior del edificio.* 2 V-T PASSIVE If a room or something such as a seat **is occupied,** someone is using it, so that it is not available for anyone else. ocupar ❑ *The chair was occupied by his wife.* *La silla estaba ocupada por su esposa.* 3 V-T If an army **occupies** a place, they move into it, using force in order to gain control of it. ocupar ❑ *U.S. forces occupy a part of the country.* *Las fuerzas estadounidenses ocupan una parte del país.* 4 V-T If someone or something **occupies** a particular place in a system, process, or plan, they have that place. ocupar ❑ *Managers occupy a position of power.* *Los directores ocupan una posición de poder.* 5 V-T If something **occupies** you, or if you **occupy** yourself, your time, or your mind with it, you are busy doing it or thinking about it. ocupar(se) ❑ *Her career occupies all of her time.* *Su carrera ocupa todo su tiempo.* ❑ *He occupied himself with loading the car.* *Se ocupó cargando las cosas en el coche.* • **oc|cu|pied** ADJ ocupado ❑ *Keep your brain occupied.* *Mantén la mente ocupada.*

**Word Partnership** Usar *occupy* con:

N. occupy **a house,** occupy **land** 1
occupy **a place** 1 3 4
occupy **an area, forces** occupy *someplace*, occupy **space, troops** occupy *someplace* 3
occupy **a position** 3 4

**oc|cur** /əkɜr/ (**occurs, occurring, occurred**) 1 V-I When something **occurs,** it happens. ocurrir ❑ *The car crash occurred at night.* *El accidente automovilístico ocurrió por la noche.* 2 V-I When something **occurs** in a particular place, it exists or is present there. haber ❑ *Snow showers will occur in the mountains today.* *Hoy caerán nevadas en las montañas.* 3 V-I If a thought or idea **occurs to** you, you suddenly think of it or realize it. ocurrirse ❑ *Suddenly it occurred to her that the door might be open.* *De repente se le ocurrió que la puerta podría estar abierta.*

**Thesaurus** *occur* Ver también:

V. come about, develop, happen 1
dawn on, strike 3

**Word Partnership** Usar *occur* con:

N. **accidents** occur, **changes** occur, **deaths** occur, **diseases** occur, **events** occur, **injuries** occur, **problems** occur 1
ADV. **frequently** occur, **naturally** occur, **normally** occur, **often** occur, **usually** occur 1 – 3

**ocean** /oʊʃᵊn/ (**oceans**) 1 N-SING **The ocean** is the salty water that covers much of the Earth's surface. océano ❑ *...the beautiful sight of the ocean.* *...la maravillosa vista del mar.* 2 N-COUNT An **ocean** is one of the five very large areas of salt water on the Earth's surface. océano ❑ *...the Pacific Ocean.* *...el Océano Pacífico.*
→ see Word Web: **ocean**
→ see **beach, earth, river, tide, whale**

**ocean-going** ADJ **Ocean-going** ships are designed for traveling on the sea rather than on rivers, canals, or lakes. trasatlántico ❑ *At the height of his shipping career he owned about 60 ocean-going vessels.* *Cuando se encontraba en la cúspide de su carrera como naviero, era propietario de aproximadamente sesenta trasatlánticos.*
→ see **ship**

**ocean|og|ra|phy** /oʊʃənɒgrəfi/ N-UNCOUNT **Oceanography** is the scientific study of sea currents, the ocean floor, and the fish and animals that live in the sea. oceanografía

**ocean trench** (**ocean trenches**) N-COUNT An **ocean trench** is a deep crack in the sea floor that forms when one section of the sea floor slides under another section. fosa oceánica, fosa submarina [TECHNICAL]

**o'clock** /əklɒk/ ADV You use **o'clock** after numbers from one to twelve to say what time it is. en punto ❑ *I went to bed at ten o'clock last night.* *Anoche me fui a la cama a las diez en punto.*

**Word Web** **ocean**

**Oceans** cover more than seventy-five percent of the earth. These huge bodies of **saltwater** are always moving. On the surface, the wind pushes the water into **waves**. At the same time, **currents** under the surface flow like rivers through the oceans. These currents are affected by the earth's rotation. It shifts them to the right in the northern hemisphere and to the left in the southern hemisphere. Other forces affect the oceans as well. For example, the gravitational pull of the moon and sun cause the **ebb** and **flow** of ocean **tides**.

**Usage** **o'clock**

Use *o'clock* for times that are exactly on the hour:" *Is it four o'clock yet?" "Not quite, it's three forty-five."*

**Oc|to|ber** /ɒktoʊbər/ (**Octobers**) N-VAR **October** is the tenth month of the year in the Western calendar. *octubre* ❑ *...in early October. ...a principios de octubre.* ❑ *They left on October 2. Partieron el 2 de octubre.*

octopus

**oc|to|pus** /ɒktəpəs/ (**octopuses**) N-VAR An **octopus** is a soft sea creature with eight long arms called tentacles. *pulpo*

**odd** /ɒd/ (**odder, oddest**) **1** ADJ If you describe someone or something as **odd**, you think that they are strange or unusual. *raro, extraño* ❑ *His behavior was odd. Su comportamiento era raro.* ● **odd|ly** ADV *de manera rara* ❑ *...an oddly shaped hill. ...una colina de forma extraña.* **2** ADJ You use **odd** before a noun to indicate that the type, size, or quality of something is not important. *ocasional, uno que otro* ❑ *We hear the odd car going by. Oímos pasar uno que otro carro.* **3** ADV You use **odd** after a number to indicate that it is only approximate. *y tantos, y tantas* [INFORMAL] ❑ *He appeared in sixty-odd movies. Apareció en sesenta y tantas películas.* **4** ADJ **Odd** numbers, such as 3 and 17, are those which cannot be divided exactly by the number two. *impar, non* **5** ADJ You say that two things are **odd** when they do not belong to the same set or pair. *impar* ❑ *I'm wearing odd socks. Tengo puestos calcetines impares.* **6** PHRASE **The odd man out,** or **the odd one out** in a particular situation is the one that is different from the others. *excepción* ❑ *Martin is becoming the odd man out in the company. Martin se está volviendo la excepción en la compañía.* **7** → see also **odds**

**Thesaurus** *odd* Ver también:

ADJ. bizarre, different, eccentric, peculiar, strange, unusual, weird; (*ant.*) normal, regular **1**

**Word Partnership** Usar *odd* con:

N. odd **combination**, odd **thing** **1**
V. **feel** odd, **look** odd, **seem** odd, **sound** odd, **strike** *someone* **as** odd, **think** *something* odd **1**
ADJ. odd **numbered** **4**

**odd jobs** N-PLURAL **Odd jobs** are various small jobs that have to be done in your home, such as cleaning or repairing things. *trabajitos*

**odds** /ɒdz/ **1** N-PLURAL You refer to how likely something is to happen as the **odds** that it will happen. *probabilidad* ❑ *What are the odds of finding a parking space right outside the door? ¿Cuáles son las probabilidades de encontrar un lugar para estacionarse justo frente a la puerta?* **2** PHRASE If someone is **at odds** with someone else, or if two people are **at odds,** they are disagreeing or arguing with each other. *en desacuerdo, enfrentado* **3** PHRASE If something happens **against** all **odds,** it happens or succeeds although it seemed impossible or very unlikely. *en contra de todo, a pesar de todo* ❑ *...families who have stayed together against all odds. ...las familias que han permanecido juntas a pesar de todo.*

**Word Partnership** Usar *odds* con:

V. **beat the** odds **1**
N. odds **in** *someone's/something's* **favor**, odds **of winning** **1**
PREP. **the** odds **of** *something* **1**
**at** odds (**with** *someone*) **2**
**against all** odds **3**

**odom|eter** /oʊdɒmɪtər/ (**odometers**) N-COUNT An **odometer** is a device in a vehicle which shows how far the vehicle has traveled. *odómetro*

**odor** /oʊdər/ (**odors**) N-VAR An **odor** is a smell. *olor* ❑ *...the odor of rotting fish. ...el olor a pescado podrido.* → see **smell, taste**

**odor|less** /oʊdərlɪs/ ADJ An **odorless** substance has no smell. *inodoro* ❑ *...an odorless gas. ...un gas inodoro.*

**od|ys|sey** /ɒdɪsi/ (**odysseys**) N-COUNT An **odyssey** is a long, exciting journey on which a lot of things happen. *odisea* [LITERARY]

**of** /əv, STRONG ʌv/ **1** PREP You use **of** to say who or what someone or something belongs to or is connected with. *de* ❑ *...the luxury homes of rich people. ...las casas lujosas de la gente rica.* ❑ *...the new*

O

mayor of Los Angeles. ...el nuevo alcalde de Los Ángeles. **2** PREP You use **of** to say what something relates to or concerns. de ❑ ...her feelings of anger. ...sus sentimientos de enojo. ❑ ...a fracture of the skull. ...una fractura del cráneo. **3** PREP You use **of** to say who or what a feeling or quality relates to. a, de ❑ I am very fond of Alec. Le tengo mucho cariño a Alec. ❑ She was guilty of lying to her mother. Era culpable de mentir a su madre. **4** PREP You use **of** to talk about someone or something else who is involved in an action. con, de ❑ He was dreaming of her. Estaba soñando con ella. ❑ People accused him of ignoring the problem. La gente lo acusó de ignorar el problema. **5** PREP You use **of** to show that someone or something is part of a larger group. de ❑ She is the youngest child of three. Es la más joven de tres niños. **6** PREP You use **of** to talk about amounts or contents. de ❑ ...a rise of 13.8%. ...un aumento del 13.8 por ciento. ❑ ...a glass of milk. ...un vaso de leche. **7** PREP You use **of** to say how old someone or something is. de ❑ She is a young woman of twenty-six. Es una mujer joven de veintiséis años. **8** PREP You use **of** to say the date when talking about what day of the month it is. de ❑ ...the 4th of July. ...el 4 de julio. **9** PREP You use **of** to say when something happened. de ❑ ...the mistakes of the past. ...los errores del pasado. ❑ Rene is retiring at the end of the month. Rene se jubila al final del mes. **10** PREP You use **of** to say what substance or materials something is formed from. de ❑ ...a mixture of flour and water. ...una mezcla de harina y agua. **11** PREP You use **of** to say what caused or is causing a person's or animal's death. de ❑ He died of a heart attack. Murió de un ataque al corazón. **12** PREP You use **of** to talk about someone's qualities or characteristics. de ❑ Andrew is a man of great intelligence. Andrew es un hombre de gran inteligencia. **13** PREP You use **of** to describe someone's behavior. de ❑ It's very kind of you to help. Es muy amable de su parte ayudarme. **14** PREP You can use **of** to say what time it is by indicating how many minutes there are before the hour mentioned. para ❑ It's a quarter of eight. Falta un cuarto para las ocho.

O

**of course** **1** ADV You say **of course** to suggest that something is not surprising because it is normal, obvious, or well-known. claro, desde luego, por supuesto [SPOKEN] ❑ Of course there were lots of interesting things to see. Claro que había muchas cosas interesantes que ver. **2** CONVENTION You use **of course** as a polite way of giving permission. claro, desde luego, por supuesto [SPOKEN] ❑ "Can I ask you something?"—"Yes, of course." —¿Puedo preguntarle algo?—Sí, claro. **3** ADV You use **of course** in order to emphasize a statement that you are making. claro, desde luego, por supuesto [SPOKEN] ❑ Of course I'm not afraid! ¡Claro que no tengo miedo! **4** CONVENTION **Of course not** is an emphatic way of saying no. claro que no, desde luego que no, por supuesto que no [SPOKEN] ❑ "You're not going to go, are you?"—"No, of course not." —No vas a ir, ¿verdad? —¡No, por supuesto que no!

**off**
❶ AWAY FROM
❷ OTHER USES

**❶ off**

The preposition is pronounced /ɔf/. The adverb is pronounced /ɔ̱f/.

**1** PREP If something is taken **off** something else or moves **off** it, it is no longer touching that thing. de ❑ He took his feet off the desk. Bajó los pies del escritorio. • **Off** is also an adverb. separando ❑ I broke off a piece of chocolate and ate it. Partí un pedazo de chocolate y me lo comí. **2** PREP When you get **off** a bus, train, or plane, you come out of it. hacia afuera de ❑ Don't get on or off a moving train! ¡No suba ni baje de un tren en movimiento! • **Off** is also an adverb. hacia afuera ❑ At the next station the man got off. El hombre se bajó en la siguiente estación. **3** PREP If you keep **off** a street or piece of land, you do not go there. fuera de ❑ The police told visitors to keep off the beach. La policía dijo a los turistas que estaba prohibido el paso a la playa. • **Off** is also an adverb. fuera ❑ A sign on the grass said "Keep Off." En el pasto había un letrero que decía "Prohibido pisar el pasto". **4** PREP If something is situated **off** a place such as a coast, room, or road, it is near to it or next to it, but not exactly in it. frente a, cerca de, a poca distancia de ❑ The boat was sailing off the northern coast. El barco navegaba frente a la costa norte. ❑ ...a house just off Park Avenue. ...una casa cerca de la Avenida Park. **5** ADV If you go **off**, you leave a place. alejándose ❑ He was just about to drive off. Estaba a punto de irse en el coche. ❑ She is off to Spain tomorrow. Se va a España mañana. **6** ADV If you have time **off** or a particular day **off**, you do not go to work or school, for example, because you are sick or it is a day when you do not usually work. libre ❑ She had the day off. Tenía el día libre. ❑ I'm off tomorrow. Estoy libre mañana. • **Off** is also a preposition. libre ❑ He could not get time off work to go on vacation. No logró que le dieran tiempo libre en el trabajo para irse de vacaciones. **7** ADV If something is a long time **off**, it will not happen for a long time. en el futuro ❑ An end to the war seems a long way off. El final de la guerra parece muy lejano.

**❷ off**

The preposition is pronounced /ɔf/. The adverb is pronounced /ɔ̱f/.

**1** ADV If something such as an agreement or a sports event is **off**, it is canceled. cancelado ❑ The deal's off. Se canceló el trato. **2** PREP If you are **off** something, you have stopped using it or liking it. sin tomar, sin usar ❑ I'm off coffee at the moment. Dejé de tomar café por el momento. ❑ The doctor took her off the medicine. El doctor le suspendió la medicina. **3** ADV When something such as a machine or electric light is **off**, it is not functioning or in use. apagado ❑ Her bedroom light was off. La luz de su recámara estaba apagada. ❑ We turned the engine off to save fuel. Apagamos el motor para ahorrar combustible. **4** PHRASE If something happens **on and off**, or **off and on**, it happens occasionally, or only for part of a period of time, not in a regular or continuous way. de vez en cuando, alguna que otra vez, de cuando en cuando ❑ I work on and off as a waitress. Trabajo de vez en cuando como mesera.

In addition to the uses shown here, **off** is used after some verbs and nouns in order to introduce extra information. **Off** is also used in phrasal verbs such as "get off," "pair off," and "sleep off."

**off-center** **1** ADJ If something is **off-center**, it is not exactly in the middle of a space or surface. descentrado, de lado ❑ ...an off-center smile. ...una sonrisa de lado. **2** ADJ If you describe someone or something as **off-center,** you mean that they are less conventional than other people or things. heterodoxo, poco convencional ❑ *David's writing is too off-center to be popular.* *La manera de escribir de David es demasiado heterodoxa para ser popular.*

**off-color** ADJ An **off-color** joke or remark is rude or offensive. impropio, atrevido, de color subido

| Word Link | *fend ≈ striking : defend, fender, offend* |
|---|---|

**of|fend** /əfɛnd/ (**offends, offending, offended**) **1** V-T/V-I If you **offend** someone, you say or do something which upsets or embarrasses them. ofender ❑ *I'm sorry if I offended you.* *Si la ofendí, le pido una disculpa.* ❑ *Do not use words that are likely to offend.* *No uses un vocabulario que podría ofender.* ● **of|fend|ed** ADJ ofendido ❑ *He was very offended by her comments.* *Estaba muy ofendido por sus comentarios.* **2** V-I If someone **offends,** they commit a crime. delinquir, infringir la ley [FORMAL] ❑ *Women are less likely to offend than men.* *Las mujeres son menos inclinadas a delinquir que los hombres.* ● **of|fend|er** N-COUNT (**offenders**) delincuente, criminal ❑ *Should the public be told when an offender leaves prison?* *¿Se debería poner sobre aviso al público cuando un criminal sale de la cárcel?*

**of|fense** /əfɛns/ (**offenses**)

Pronounced /ɔfɛns/ for meaning **3**.

**1** N-COUNT An **offense** is a crime that breaks a particular law. delito, infracción, crimen ❑ *There is a fine of $1,000 for a first offense.* *La multa por una primera infracción es de 1,000 dólares.* **2** N-VAR **Offense** or an **offense** is behavior that causes people to be upset or embarrassed. ofensa, insulto, afrenta ❑ *He didn't mean to cause offense.* *No tenía la intención de ofender.* **3** N-SING In sports such as football or basketball, **the offense** is the team which has possession of the ball and is trying to score. ofensiva **4** PHRASE If you **take offense,** you are upset by something that someone says or does. ofenderse, sentirse ofendido ❑ *Instead of taking offense, the woman smiled.* *En lugar de ofenderse, la mujer sonrió.*

| Thesaurus | *offense* | Ver también: |
|---|---|---|
| N. | crime, infraction, violation, wrongdoing **1** | |
| | assault, attack, insult, snub **2** | |

| Word Partnership | Usar *offense* con: |
|---|---|
| ADJ. | **criminal** offense **1** |
| | **serious** offense **1** **2** |
| V. | **commit an** offense **1** **2** |
| | **take** offense **4** |

**of|fen|sive** /əfɛnsɪv/ (**offensives**) **1** ADJ Something that is **offensive** upsets or embarrasses people because it is rude or insulting. ofensivo ❑ *Some people thought the play was offensive.* *Algunas personas opinaron que la obra era ofensiva.* **2** N-COUNT A military **offensive** is a carefully planned attack made by a large group of soldiers. ofensiva **3** ADJ In sports such as football or basketball, the **offensive** team is the team which has possession of the ball and is trying to score. ofensivo **4** PHRASE If you **go on the offensive,** or **take the offensive,** you begin to take strong action against people who have been attacking you. tomar la ofensiva

| Word Partnership | Usar *offensive* con: |
|---|---|
| N. | offensive **language** **1** |
| V. | **launch an** offensive, **mount an** offensive **2** |
| | **take the** offensive **4** |

**of|fer** /ɔfər/ (**offers, offering, offered**) **1** V-T If you **offer** something to someone, you ask them if they would like to have it or use it. ofrecer ❑ *He offered his seat to the young woman.* *Ofreció su asiento a la señorita.* ❑ *She offered him a cup of tea.* *Le ofreció una taza de té.* **2** V-T If you **offer to** do something, you say that you are willing to do it. ofrecerse ❑ *Peter offered to teach me to drive.* *Peter se ofreció a enseñarme a manejar.* **3** N-COUNT An **offer** is something that someone says they will give you or do for you. ofrecimiento ❑ *I hope you will accept my offer of help.* *Espero que acepte mi ofrecimiento de ayuda.* **4** N-COUNT An **offer** in a store is a specially low price for something or something extra that you get if you buy a certain product. oferta ❑ *There's a special offer on computers.* *Hay una oferta especial de computadoras.* **5** V-T If you **offer** a particular amount of money for something, you say that you will pay that much to buy it. ofrecer ❑ *He offered $5,000 for the car.* *Ofreció 5,000 dólares por el coche.*

**of|fer|ing** /ɔfərɪŋ/ (**offerings**) N-COUNT An **offering** is something that is being sold. oferta ❑ *The meal was much better than offerings in many other restaurants.* *La comida estuvo mucho mejor que lo que ofrecen en muchos otros restaurantes.*

**of|fice** /ɔfɪs/ (**offices**) **1** N-COUNT An **office** is a room or a part of a building where people work sitting at desks. oficina ❑ *Flynn arrived at his office.* *Flynn llegó a su oficina.* **2** N-COUNT An **office** is a department of an organization, especially the government, where people deal with a particular kind of administrative work. ministerio, departamento, dirección ❑ *...the Congressional Budget Office.* *...la Dirección de Presupuesto del Congreso.* **3** N-COUNT An **office** is a small building or room where people can go for information, tickets, or a service of some kind. oficina ❑ *...the tourist office.* *...la oficina de turismo.* **4** N-COUNT A doctor's or dentist's **office** is a place where a doctor or dentist sees their patients. consultorio, consulta **5** N-UNCOUNT If someone holds **office** in a government, they have an important job or position of authority. cargo ❑ *The events marked the president's four years in office.* *Los acontecimientos marcaron los cuatro años del presidente en el cargo.* **6** → see also **box office, post office** → see Picture Dictionary: **office**

**of|fice build|ing** (**office buildings**) N-COUNT An **office building** is a large building that contains offices. edificio de oficinas

**of|fic|er** /ɔfɪsər/ (**officers**) **1** N-COUNT In the armed forces, an **officer** is a person in a position of authority. oficial ❑ *...an army officer.* *...un oficial del ejército.* **2** N-COUNT; N-VOC Members of the

O

## Picture Dictionary office

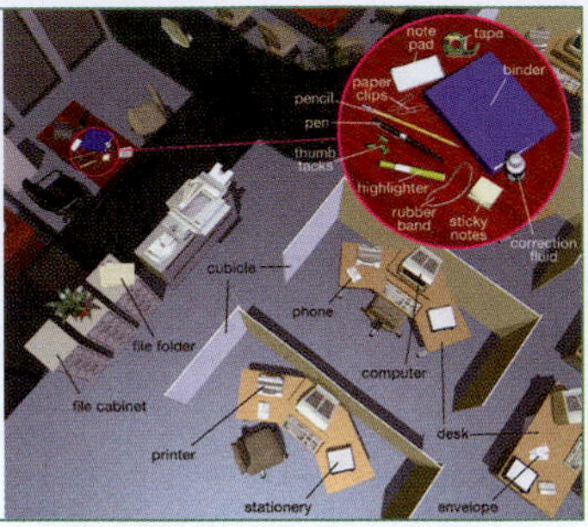


police force can be referred to as **officers.** _agente, policía_ ❑ *The officer saw no sign of a robbery.* _El agente de la policía no vio señales de robo._ ❑ *Officer Montoya was the first on the scene.* _El agente Montoya fue el primero en llegar a la escena del crimen._ **3** N-COUNT An **officer** is a person who has a responsible position in an organization, especially a government organization. _directivo_ ❑ *...chief executive officer of Boeing Commercial Airplanes.* _...presidente de Boeing Commercial Airplanes._ **4** → see also **police officer**

**of|fi|cial** /əfɪʃᵊl/ **(officials)** **1** ADJ **Official** means approved by the government or by someone in authority. _oficial_ ❑ *...the official unemployment figures.* _...las cifras oficiales de desempleo._ ● **of|fi|cial|ly** ADV _oficialmente_ ❑ *The election results have not yet been officially announced.* _Todavía no han sido anunciados oficialmente los resultados de las elecciones._ **2** ADJ **Official** activities are carried out by a person in authority as part of their job. _oficial_ ❑ *The president is in Brazil for an official visit.* _El presidente se encuentra en Brasil en visita oficial._ **3** ADJ **Official** things are used by a person in authority as part of their job. _oficial_ ❑ *...the White House, the official residence of the U.S. president.* _...la Casa Blanca, la residencia oficial del presidente de Estados Unidos._ **4** N-COUNT An **official** is a person who holds a position of authority in an organization. _funcionario o funcionaria_ ❑ *...a senior United Nations official.* _...un funcionario de alto rango (de la Organización) de las Naciones Unidas._

**Thesaurus** *official* Ver también:

ADJ. authentic, formal, legitimate, valid; (*ant.*) unauthorized, unofficial **1**
N. administrator, director, executive, manager **4**

**Word Partnership** Usar *official* con:

N. official **documents**, official **language**, official **report**, official **sources**, official **statement** **1**
official **duties**, official **visit** **2**
**administration** official, **city** official, **government** official **4**
ADJ. **elected** official, **federal** official, **local** official, **military** official, **senior** official, **top** official **4**

**off|line** /ɔflaɪn/ ADJ If a computer is **offline,** it is not connected to the Internet. Compare **online.** _fuera de línea, desconectado_ [COMPUTING] ❑ *The system was offline for a few days.* _El sistema estuvo fuera de línea unos días._ ● **Offline** is also an adverb. _fuera de línea_ ❑ *Most software programs allow you to write e-mails offline.* _Con la mayoría de los programas de computación se puede escribir mensajes electrónicos fuera de línea._

**off-peak** ADJ You use **off-peak** to describe something that happens or that is used at times when there is the least demand for it. Prices at off-peak times are often lower than at other times. _fuera de las horas pico_ ● **Off-peak** is also an adverb. _en las horas de menor demanda_ ❑ *Calls cost 36 cents per minute off-peak.* _Las llamadas cuestan 36 centavos el minuto en las horas de menor demanda._

**off-ramp** **(off-ramps)** N-COUNT An **off-ramp** is a road which cars use to drive off a highway. _vía de salida_

**off|set** /ɔfsɛt/ **(offsets, offsetting)**

The form **offset** is used in the present tense and is the past tense and past participle of the verb.

V-T If one thing **is offset** by another, the effect of the first thing is reduced by the second, so that any advantage or disadvantage is canceled out. _compensar_ ❑ *The increase in costs was offset by higher sales.* _El aumento de las ventas compensó el aumento de los costos._

**off|shore** /ɔfʃɔr/ ADJ **Offshore** means situated or happening in the ocean, near the coast. _a distancia de la costa, frente a la costa, marino_ ❑ *...the offshore oil industry.* _...la industria petrolera submarina._ ● **Offshore** is also an adverb. _a cierta distancia de la costa_ ❑ *A ship anchored offshore.* _Un barco anclado a cierta distancia de la costa._

**off|spring** /ɔfsprɪŋ/

**Offspring** is both the singular and the plural form.

N-COUNT You can refer to a person's children or to an animal's young as their **offspring.** _descendencia, progenie_ [FORMAL] ❑ *Eleanor was worried about her offspring.* _Eleanor estaba preocupada por su descendencia._

**of|ten** /ɔfᵊn/

**Often** is usually used before the verb, but it may be used after the verb when it has a word like "less" or "more" before it, or when the clause is negative.

**1** ADV If something **often** happens, it happens many times or much of the time. _frecuentemente,_ con frecuencia, a menudo ❑ *They often spend the weekend together.* Frecuentemente pasan el fin de semana juntos. ❑ *That doesn't happen very often.* Eso no ocurre con mucha frecuencia. **2** ADV You use **how often** to ask questions about frequency. You also use **often** in statements to give information about the frequency of something. con qué frecuencia, qué tan seguido ❑ *How often do you brush your teeth?* ¿Con qué frecuencia se lava los dientes? **3** PHRASE If something happens **every so often,** it happens regularly, but with fairly long periods between each occasion. de vez en cuando ❑ *She visited every so often.* Los visitaba de vez en cuando. **4** PHRASE If you say that something happens **as often as not,** or **more often than not,** you mean that it happens fairly frequently, and that this can be considered as typical. la mitad de las veces, las más de las veces ❑ *As often as not, they argue.* La mitad de las veces discuten.

| **Thesaurus** | *often* | Ver también: |
|---|---|---|
| ADV. | regularly, repeatedly, usually; (*ant.*) never, rarely, seldom **1** | |

**often|times** /ɔfᵊntaɪmz/ ADV If something **oftentimes** happens, it happens many times or much of the time. frecuentemente ❑ *Oftentimes, I didn't even return his calls.* Frecuentemente, ni siquiera le devolvía sus llamadas.

**oh** /oʊ/ **1** CONVENTION You use **oh** to introduce a response or a comment on something that has just been said. ah [SPOKEN] ❑ *"Have you spoken to her about it?"—"Oh yes."* —¿Ya hablaste con ella de esto?—Ah, sí. **2** EXCLAM You use **oh** to express a feeling such as surprise, pain, annoyance, or happiness. vaya [SPOKEN] ❑ *"Oh!" Kenny said. "Has everyone gone?"* —¡Vaya! —dijo Kenny—, ¿ya se fueron todos? **3** CONVENTION You use **oh** when you are hesitating while speaking, for example, because you are trying to estimate something, or because you are searching for the right word. este, ah [SPOKEN] ❑ *I've been here, oh, since the end of June.* Estoy aquí desde, este, desde finales de junio.

**oil** /ɔɪl/ (**oils, oiling, oiled**) **1** N-VAR **Oil** is a smooth, thick liquid that is used as a fuel and for making the parts of machines move smoothly. Oil is found underground. petróleo ❑ *The company buys and sells 600,000 barrels of oil a day.* La compañía compra y vende 600,000 barriles de petróleo al día. **2** V-T If you **oil** something, you put oil onto or into it, for example, to make it work smoothly or to protect it. aceitar ❑ *He oiled the lock on the door.* Aceitó la cerradura de la puerta. **3** N-VAR **Oil** is a smooth, thick liquid made from plants and is often used for cooking. aceite ❑ *...olive oil.* ...aceite de oliva. **4** → see also **crude oil, olive oil**
→ see Word Web: **oil**
→ see **petroleum, ship**

**oil|field** /ɔɪlfild/ (**oilfields**) also **oil field** N-COUNT An **oilfield** is an area of land or sea under which there is oil. yacimiento petrolífero

**oil paint** (**oil paints**) N-VAR **Oil paint** is a thick paint used by artists. color al óleo, pintura al óleo, óleo

**oil paint|ing** (**oil paintings**) N-COUNT An **oil painting** is a picture which has been painted using oil paints. cuadro al óleo, pintura al óleo, óleo

**oil plat|form** (**oil platforms**) N-COUNT An **oil platform** is a structure that is used when getting oil from the ground under the sea. plataforma petrolífera

**OJ** /oʊ dʒeɪ/ N-UNCOUNT **OJ** is the same as **orange juice.** jugo de naranja [INFORMAL]

**okay** /oʊkeɪ/ (**okays**) also **OK** or **O.K.** or **ok** **1** ADJ If you say that something is **okay,** you find it acceptable. bien [INFORMAL] ❑ *...Is it OK to talk now?* ...¿Te parece bien que hablemos ahora? ❑ *Is it okay if I go by myself?* ¿Tiene inconveniente en que yo vaya solo? ● **Okay** is also an adverb. bien ❑ *We seemed to manage okay.* Parece que nos las arreglamos bien. **2** ADJ If you say that someone is **okay,** you mean that they are safe and well. bien [INFORMAL] ❑ *Check that the baby's okay.* Ve que el niño esté tranquilo. **3** CONVENTION You can say **"Okay"** to show that you agree to something. de acuerdo [INFORMAL] ❑ *"Just tell him I would like to talk to him."— "OK."* —Sólo dile que me gustaría hablar con él. —Muy bien. **4** CONVENTION You can say **"Okay?"** to check whether the person you are talking to understands what you have said and accepts it. ¿te parece? [INFORMAL] ❑ *We'll meet next week, OK?* Nos vemos la semana que entra, ¿sale?

**okey do|key** /oʊki doʊki/ also **okey doke** CONVENTION **Okey dokey** is used in the same way as "OK" to show that you agree to something, or that you want to start talking about something else or doing something else. bien [INFORMAL, SPOKEN] ❑ *Okey dokey. I'll call you tomorrow.* ¡Órale! Te llamo mañana.

**old** /oʊld/ (**older, oldest**) **1** ADJ Someone who is **old** has lived for many years and is no longer young. anciano ❑ *...an old man.* ...un anciano. ● **The old** are people who are old. ancianos ❑ *...the needs of the old.* ...las necesidades de los ancianos. **2** ADJ You use **old** to talk or ask about the age of someone or something. de edad ❑ *He is three months old.* Tiene tres meses de edad. ❑ *How old are you now?* ¿Cuántos

**Word Web** oil

There is a great demand for **petroleum** in the world today. Companies are constantly **drilling oil wells** in oilfields on land and on the ocean floor. In the ocean, drilling **rigs** or **oil platforms** sit on concrete or metal foundations on man-made islands. Others float on ships. The **crude oil** from these wells goes to **refineries** through **pipelines** or in huge **tanker** ships. At the refinery, the crude oil is processed into a variety of products including **gasoline, aviation fuel,** and **plastics.**

O

*años tienes ya?* **3** ADJ Something that is **old** has existed for a long time. *viejo, antiguo* ❑ *...the big old house. ...la gran casa vieja., ...la antigua casa grande.* ❑ *These books look very old. Estos libros parecen muy antiguos.* **4** ADJ Something that is **old** is no longer in good condition because of its age or because it has been used a lot. *viejo* ❑ *...his old jeans. ...sus viejos pantalones de mezclilla.* **5** ADJ You use **old** to refer to something that is no longer used, that no longer exists, or that has been replaced by something else. *viejo* ❑ *Grass covered the old road. La hierba cubrió la carretera vieja.* **6** ADJ You use **old** to refer to something that used to belong to you, or to a person or thing that used to have a particular role in your life. *antiguo* ❑ *You can stay in your old room. Puedes quedarte en tu antiguo cuarto.* ❑ *I still remember my old school. Todavía recuerdo mi antigua escuela.* **7** ADJ An **old** friend, enemy, or rival is someone who has been your friend, enemy, or rival for a long time. *viejo* ❑ *I called my old friend John Horner. Llamé a mi viejo amigo John Horner.* **8** PHRASE You use **any old** to emphasize that the quality or type of something is not important. *cualquier* [INFORMAL] ❑ *On Sundays I wear any old thing that's comfortable. Los domingos me pongo cualquier cosa que sea cómoda.* ❑ *But not any old peanut butter is good enough for U.S. troops—it's made specially for them in Georgia. ...pero no cualquier crema de cacahuate es buena para las tropas estadounidenses; la hacen especialmente para ellas en Georgia.* **9** to **settle an old score** → see **score**

| **Thesaurus** | *old* | Ver también: |
|---|---|---|
| ADJ. | elderly, mature, senior; (*ant.*) young **1** ancient, antique, dated, old-fashioned, outdated, traditional; (*ant.*) new **5** | |

O

**old-fashioned** ADJ Something that is **old-fashioned** is no longer used, done, or believed by most people, because it has been replaced by something more modern. *anticuado, pasado de moda* ❑ *The house was old-fashioned and in bad condition. La casa era anticuada y se encontraba en mal estado.*

**Old Glo|ry** N-UNCOUNT People sometimes refer to the flag of the United States as **Old Glory**. *bandera de Estados Unidos*

**old-timer** (**old-timers**) N-COUNT An old man is sometimes referred to as an **old-timer**. *viejo* [INFORMAL] ❑ *The old-timers used to talk about their childhoods. Los viejos acostumbraban hablar de su niñez.*

**old world** also **Old World** or **old-world** ADJ **Old world** is used to describe places and things that are or seem to be from an earlier period of history, and that look interesting or attractive. *pintoresco* ❑ *The village's Old World charm attracted many visitors. El encanto pintoresco del pueblo atrajo a muchos visitantes.*

**ol|ive** /ɒlɪv/ (**olives**) **1** N-VAR **Olives** are small green or black fruits with a bitter taste. *aceituna* **2** N-COUNT An **olive tree** or an **olive** is a tree on which olives grow. *olivo* **3** COLOR Something that is **olive** is yellowish-green in color. *color aceituna, aceitunado*

**ol|ive oil** (**olive oils**) N-VAR **Olive oil** is oil used in cooking that is obtained by pressing olives. *aceite de oliva*

**Olym|pic** /əlɪmpɪk/ (**Olympics**) **1** ADJ **Olympic** means relating to the Olympic Games. *olímpico* ❑ *...the Olympic champion. ...el campeón olímpico.* **2** N-PROPER **The Olympics** are the Olympic Games. *olimpiadas, juegos olímpicos*

**Olym|pic Games** N-PROPER **The Olympic Games** are a set of international sports competitions which take place every four years, each time in a different city. *juegos olímpicos, olimpiadas*

**ome|let** /ɒmlɪt, ɒməlɪt/ (**omelets**) also **omelette** N-COUNT An **omelet** is a type of food made by beating eggs and cooking them in a frying pan. *omelet, tortilla de huevo* ❑ *...a cheese omelet. ...una tortilla de huevo con queso., ...un omelet de queso.*
→ see **egg**

**omit** /oʊmɪt/ (**omits, omitting, omitted**) **1** V-T If you **omit** something, you do not include it in an activity or piece of work. *omitir* ❑ *Omit the salt in this recipe. Omita la sal en esta receta.* **2** V-T If you **omit to** do something, you do not do it. *omitir, olvidar* [FORMAL] ❑ *He omitted to mention his friend's name. Omitió mencionar el nombre de su amigo.*

| **Thesaurus** | *omit* | Ver también: |
|---|---|---|
| V. | forget, leave out, miss; (*ant.*) add, include **1** | |

**om|ni|vore** /ɒmnɪvɔr/ (**omnivores**) N-COUNT An **omnivore** is an animal that eats all kinds of food, including both meat and plants. Compare **carnivore, herbivore**. *omnívoro u omnívora* [TECHNICAL]

**om|niv|or|ous** /ɒmnɪvərəs/ **1** ADJ An **omnivorous** person or animal eats all kinds of food, including both meat and plants. *omnívoro* [FORMAL, TECHNICAL] ❑ *Brown bears are omnivorous, eating anything that they can get their paws on. Los osos pardos son omnívoros y comen todo aquello a lo que puedan ponerle la pata encima.* **2** ADJ **Omnivorous** means liking a wide variety of things of a particular type. *voraz* [FORMAL] ❑ *As a child, Coleridge developed omnivorous reading habits. Coleridge desarrolló un voraz apetito por la lectura cuando era niño.*
→ see **carnivore, mammal**

**on**

1. DESCRIBING POSITIONS AND LOCATIONS
2. TALKING ABOUT HOW OR WHEN SOMETHING HAPPENS
3. OTHER USES
4. PHRASES

**1 on**

The preposition is pronounced /ɒn/. The adverb and the adjective are pronounced /ɒn/.

**1** PREP If someone or something is **on** a surface or object, the surface or object is immediately below them and is supporting their weight. *en* ❑ *He was sitting beside her on the sofa. Estaba sentado junto a ella en el sillón.* ❑ *On top of the cupboards are some baskets. Encima de los aparadores hay unas canastas.* **2** PREP

If something is **on** a surface or object, it is stuck to it or attached to it. de ❑ ...*the paint on the door.* ...*la pintura de la puerta.* ❑ ...*the clock on the wall.* ...*el reloj de la pared.* **3** ADV When you put a piece of clothing **on**, you place it over part of your body in order to wear it. If you have it **on**, you are wearing it. *encima* ❑ *He put his coat on.* *Se puso el abrigo.* **4** PREP You can say that you have something **on** you if you are carrying it in your pocket or in a purse. *con* ❑ *I didn't have any money on me.* *No llevaba nada de dinero.* **5** PREP If you get **on** a bus, train, or plane, you go into it in order to travel somewhere. If you are **on** it, you are traveling in it. *a* ❑ *We got on the plane.* *Nos subimos al avión.*
→ see **location**

**❷ on**

The preposition is pronounced /ɒn/. The adverb and the adjective are pronounced /ɒn/.

**1** PREP If something is done **on** an instrument or a machine, it is done using that instrument or machine. *en* ❑ *I played these songs on the piano.* *Toqué estas tonadas en el piano.* **2** PREP If something is being broadcast, you can say that it is **on** the radio or television. *en* ❑ *What's on TV?* *¿Qué hay en la televisión?* **3** ADJ When an activity is taking place, you can say that it is **on**. *ahora* ❑ *There's an exciting game on right now.* *Hay un juego muy emocionante justo ahora.* **4** ADV You use **on** in expressions such as **"have a lot going on"** and **"not have very much on"** to indicate how busy someone is. *en proceso* [SPOKEN] ❑ *I have a lot going on next week.* *Tengo mucho que hacer la próxima semana.* **5** PREP If something happens **on** a particular day or date, that is when it happens. *en* ❑ *This year's event will be on June 19th.* *El acto de este año será el 19 de junio.* ❑ *We'll see you on Tuesday.* *Te vemos el martes.* **6** PREP You use **on** when mentioning an event that was followed by another one. *a* ❑ *She waited to welcome her children on their arrival from Vancouver.* *Aguardó para recibir a sus hijos a su llegada de Vancouver.* **7** ADV You use **on** to say that someone is continuing to do something. *todavía* ❑ *They walked on for a while.* *Siguieron caminando un rato.* ❑ *We worked on into the night.* *Seguimos trabajando hasta entrada la noche.*

**❸ on**

The preposition is pronounced /ɒn/. The adverb and the adjective are pronounced /ɒn/.

**1** PREP Books, discussions, or ideas **on** a particular subject are concerned with that subject. *sobre* ❑ ...*advice on health.* ...*consejos sobre la salud.* ❑ *There was no information on the cause of the crash.* *No había información sobre las causas del accidente.* **2** ADV When something such as a machine or an electric light is **on**, it is functioning or in use. *encendido* ❑ *The light was on.* *La luz estaba encendida.* ❑ *The heat was turned off. I've turned it on again.* *La calefacción estaba apagada; ya la encendí otra vez.* **3** PREP If you are **on** a committee or council, you are a member of it. *en* ❑ *Claire and Alita were on the organizing committee.* *Claire y Alita estaban en el comité organizador.* **4** PREP Someone who is **on** a drug takes it regularly. *tomando* ❑ *She was on antibiotics for an eye infection.* *Estaba tomando antibióticos para una infección en los ojos.* **5** PREP When you spend time or energy **on** a particular activity, you spend time or energy doing it. *en* ❑ *Some children spend a lot of time on computer games.* *Algunos niños pasan mucho tiempo en los juegos de computadora.* ❑ *I won't waste time on guys like him.* *No desperdiciaré mi tiempo en tipos como él.*

**❹ on** /ɒn/ **1** **on and off** → see **off** **2** **and so on** → see **so** **3** **on top of** → see **top**

In addition to the uses shown here, **on** is used after some verbs, nouns, and adjectives in order to introduce extra information. **On** is also used in phrasal verbs such as "keep on" and "sign on."

**on board** also **onboard** or **on-board** ADJ If a person or group of people is **on board,** they support you and agree with what you are doing. *comprometido* ❑ *We want everyone to be on board for making changes.* *Queremos que todos participen para hacer los cambios.*

**once** /wʌns/ **1** ADV If something happens **once,** it happens one time only. *una vez* ❑ *I met Miquela once, briefly.* *Me encontré con Miquela una vez, brevemente.* ❑ *The baby hasn't once slept through the night.* *El niño no ha pasado la noche sin despertar una sola vez.* **2** ADV If something was **once** true, it was true at some time in the past, but is no longer true. *antes, en otro tiempo* ❑ *Her parents once owned a store.* *Sus padres tenían una tienda antes.* ❑ *I lived in Paris once.* *En otro tiempo viví en París.* **3** CONJ If something happens **once** another thing has happened, it happens immediately afterward. *una vez que* ❑ *The decision was easy once he read the letter.* *Una vez que leyó la carta, la decisión fue fácil.* **4** PHRASE If you do something **at once,** you do it immediately. *inmediatamente, ahora mismo* ❑ *I have to go at once.* *Tengo que irme ahora mismo.* **5** PHRASE If a number of different things happen **at once** or **all at once,** they all happen at the same time. *al mismo tiempo* ❑ *You can't do both things at once.* *No puedes hacer las dos cosas al mismo tiempo.* **6** PHRASE **For once** is used to emphasize that something happens on this particular occasion, that it has never happened before, and may never happen again. *por una vez siquiera* ❑ *For once, Dad is not complaining.* *Por una vez siquiera, papá no se está quejando.* **7** PHRASE If something happens **once and for all,** it happens completely or finally. *de una vez por todas* ❑ *We must solve the problem once and for all.* *Debemos resolver el problema de una vez por todas.* **8** PHRASE If something happens **once in a while,** it happens sometimes, but not very often. *de vez en cuando* ❑ *Everyone feels sad once in a while.* *Todo el mundo se siente triste de vez en cuando.*

**one**

❶ NUMBER
❷ PRONOUN AND DETERMINER USES
❸ PHRASES

**❶ one** /wʌn/ (**ones**) NUM **One** is the number 1. *un, una* ❑ *They have one daughter.* *Tienen una hija.* ❑ ...*one thousand years ago.* ...*hace mil años.*

**❷ one** /wʌn/ (**ones**) **1** DET You can use **one** to refer to the first of two or more things that you are comparing. *un, una* ❑ *Prices vary from one store to another.* *Los precios varían de una tienda a otra.* • **One** is also a pronoun. *uno, una* ❑ *The twins wore different* *clothes and one was thinner than the other.* *Los gemelos iban vestidos diferente y uno era más delgado que el otro.* **2** PRON You can use **one** or **ones** instead of a noun when it is clear what type of thing or person you are referring to and you are describing them or giving more information about them. *uno, una* ❑ *They are selling their house and moving to a smaller one.* *Están vendiendo su casa y se van a cambiar a una más chica.* **3** DET You can use **one** when referring to a time in the past or in the future. For example, if you say that you did something **one day,** you mean that you did it on a day in the past. *un, una, algún, alguno, alguna* ❑ *Would you like to go out one night?* *¿Te gustaría salir una noche de estas?* **4** **one day** → see **day** **5** PRON Speakers and writers sometimes use **one** to make statements about people in general which also apply to themselves. **One** can be used as the subject or object of a sentence. *uno* [FORMAL] ❑ *If one thinks about it, a lot of good things are happening in the world.* *Si uno lo piensa, en el mundo están pasando muchas cosas buenas.*

**Usage** **one** and **you**

Sometimes *one* is used to refer to any person or to people in general, but it sounds formal: *One has to be smart about buying a computer.* In everyday English, use *you* instead of *one*: *You should only call 911 in an emergency.*

**❸ one** /wʌn/ **1** PHRASE You use **one or other** to refer to one or more things or people in a group, when it does not matter which particular one or ones are thought of or chosen. *uno u otro, uno de los dos* ❑ *One or other of the two women was wrong.* *Una de las dos mujeres estaba equivocada.* **2** PHRASE **One or two** means a few. *uno o dos* ❑ *We made one or two changes.* *Hicimos uno o dos cambios.* **3** **one another** → see **another** **4** **one thing after another** → see **another** **5** **in one piece** → see **piece**

**one-of-a-kind** ADJ You use **one-of-a-kind** to describe something that is special because there is nothing else exactly like it. *único* ❑ *...a small one-of-a-kind publisher.* *...una pequeña editorial única en su género.*

**one-point per|spec|tive** (**one-point perspectives**) N-COUNT A **one-point perspective** is a method of drawing or painting something in which you create the appearance of three dimensions by using slanting lines that appear to meet at a point on the horizon. *perspectiva con un solo punto de fuga* [TECHNICAL]

**one's** /wʌnz/ **1** DET Speakers and writers use **one's** to indicate that something belongs or relates to people in general, or to themselves in particular. *de uno* [FORMAL] ❑ *It is natural to care for one's family and one's children.* *Es natural cuidar a la familia y a los hijos de uno.* **2** **One's** can be used as a spoken form of "one is" or "one has," especially when "has" is an auxiliary verb. *forma hablada usual de* ***one is*** *o* ***one has*** ❑ *No one's going to hurt you.* *Nadie va a hacerte daño.* → see **one**

**one|self** /wʌnsɛlf/

**Oneself** is a third person singular reflexive pronoun.

PRON A speaker or writer uses **oneself** to refer to themselves or to any person in general. *uno mismo, sí mismo* [FORMAL] ❑ *To work one must have time to oneself.* *Para trabajar, es necesario tener tiempo para sí mismo.*

**one-shot** ADJ A **one-shot** thing is made or happens only once. *excepcional* ❑ *This is not a one-shot deal.* *Este no es un arreglo excepcional.*

**one-time** also **onetime** **1** ADJ **One-time** is used to describe something which happened in the past, or something such as a job or position which someone used to have. *antiguo, el que fuera* ❑ *...Al Gore, the one-time presidential candidate.* *...Al Gore, el antiguo candidato a la presidencia.* **2** ADJ A **one-time** thing is made or happens only once. *único* ❑ *...a one-time charge.* *...un cargo único.*

**one-way** **1** ADJ In **one-way** streets or traffic systems, vehicles can only travel along in one direction. *de sentido único, de un solo sentido* **2** ADJ A **one-way** ticket or fare is for a trip from one place to another, but not back again. *de ida, sencillo* ❑ *...a one-way ticket from New York to Los Angeles.* *...un boleto sencillo de Nueva York a Los Ángeles.* ● **One-way** is also an adverb. *sencillo* ❑ *The fare is $80 one-way.* *La tarifa sencilla es de 80 dólares.*

**on|going** /ɒngoʊɪŋ/ ADJ An **ongoing** situation has been happening for quite a long time and seems likely to continue. *en curso* ❑ *There is an ongoing debate on the issue.* *Hay un debate en curso sobre la cuestión.*

**on|ion** /ʌnyən/ (**onions**) N-VAR An **onion** is a round vegetable with a light brown skin. It has a strong, sharp smell and taste. *cebolla* → see **spice, vegetable**

**on|line** /ɒnlaɪn/ also **on-line** **1** ADV If a company goes **online,** its services become available on the Internet. *en línea* [BUSINESS, COMPUTING] ● **Online** is also an adjective. *en línea* ❑ *...an online shopping center.* *...un centro comercial en línea.* **2** ADJ If you are **online,** your computer is connected to the Internet. Compare **offline.** *en línea* [COMPUTING] ❑ *You can chat to other people who are online.* *Se puede platicar con otras personas que estén en línea.* ● **Online** is also an adverb. *en línea* ❑ *...the things you can buy online.* *...las cosas que puedes comprar en línea.* **3** **on line** → see **line**

**only**

❶ ADVERB AND ADJECTIVE USES
❷ CONJUNCTION
❸ PHRASES

**❶ only** /oʊnli/

In written English, **only** is usually placed immediately before the word it qualifies. In spoken English, however, you can use stress to indicate what **only** qualifies, so its position is not so important.

**1** ADV You use **only** to indicate the one thing that is true, appropriate, or necessary in a particular situation, in contrast to all the other things that are not. *sólo, solamente* ❑ *It's a decision only the president can make.* *Es una decisión que sólo el presidente puede tomar.* ❑ *You can only start a business if you have enough money.* *Solamente se puede emprender un* negocio si se tiene suficiente dinero. **2** ADV You use **only** to introduce the thing which must happen before the thing mentioned in the main part of the sentence can happen. *sólo, solamente* ❑ *The lawyer is paid only if he wins. Sólo se le paga al abogado si gana el caso.* **3** ADJ If you talk about **the only** person or thing involved in a particular situation, you mean there are no others involved in it. *único* ❑ *She was the only woman in the department. Era la única mujer en el departamento.* **4** ADJ An **only** child is a child who has no brothers or sisters. *único* **5** ADV You use **only** to indicate that something is unimportant. *sólo, solamente* ❑ *It's only an idea. Es sólo una idea.* ❑ *I'm only a sergeant. Sólo soy sargento.* **6** ADV You use **only** to emphasize how small an amount is or how short a length of time is. *sólo, solamente* ❑ *The movie only cost $3.99 to rent. El alquiler de la película costó solamente 3.99 dólares.* **7** ADV You can use **only** in the expressions **I only wish** or **I only hope** in order to emphasize what you are hoping or wishing. *tan sólo* ❑ *I only hope he knows what he's doing. Tan sólo espero que sepa lo que está haciendo.* **8** ADV You can use **only** before an infinitive to introduce an event which happens immediately after one you have just mentioned, and which is surprising or unfortunate. *pero* ❑ *Ron called her office, only to learn that she was in a meeting. Ron llamó a su oficina, pero le dijeron que estaba en una junta.* **9** ADV You can use **only** to emphasize how appropriate a certain course of action or type of behavior is. *más que* ❑ *It's only fair to tell her you're coming. Creo que debes decirle que vas a venir.*

| **Thesaurus** *only* | Ver también: |
|---|---|
| ADJ. | alone, individual, single, solitary, unique ❶ **1** |

**❷ only** /oʊnli/ **1** CONJ **Only** can be used to add a comment which slightly changes or limits what you have just said. *sólo, solamente* [INFORMAL] ❑ *The situation is as dramatic as a movie, only it's real. La situación es tan dramática como una película, sólo que es real.* ❑ *It's like my house, only nicer. Es como mi casa, sólo que más agradable.* **2** CONJ **Only** can be used after a clause with "would" to indicate why something is not done. *pero* [SPOKEN] ❑ *I'd ask you to come with me, only it's such a long way. Te pediría que vinieras conmigo, pero está tan lejos.*

**❸ only** /oʊnli/ **1** PHRASE You can say that something has **only just** happened when you want to emphasize that it happened a very short time ago. *apenas, acabar de* ❑ *I've only just arrived. Apenas llegué., Acabo de llegar.* **2** PHRASE You use **only just** to emphasize that something is true, but by such a small degree that it is almost not true at all. *apenas* ❑ *We only just managed to get to the airport in time for the flight. Apenas nos las arreglamos para llegar al aeropuerto a tiempo para el vuelo.* ❑ *I am old enough to remember the war, but only just. Soy bastante viejo para recordar la guerra, pero apenas.* **3 if only** → see **if** **4 not only** → see **not**

**ono|mato|poeia** /ɒnəmætəpiə, -mɑtə-/ N-UNCOUNT **Onomatopoeia** refers to the use of words which sound like the noise they refer to. "Hiss," "buzz," and "rat-a-tat-tat" are examples of onomatopoeia. *onomatopeya* [TECHNICAL]

**on-ramp** (**on-ramps**) N-COUNT An **on-ramp** is a road which cars use to drive onto a highway. *vía de acceso*

**onto** /ɒntu/

> The spelling **on to** is also used, when **on** is part of a phrasal verb.

**1** PREP If something moves **onto** or is put **onto** an object or surface, it is then on that object or surface. *hasta* ❑ *I lowered myself onto the floor. Me recosté en el piso.* **2** PREP When you get **onto** a bus, train, or plane, you enter it. *a* ❑ *He got onto the plane. Abordó el avión.* **3** PREP **Onto** is used after verbs such as "hold," "hang," and "cling" to indicate what someone is holding firmly or where something is being held firmly. *a* ❑ *Nick smiled and held onto her hand tightly. Nick sonrió y se aferró a su mano firmemente.* **4** PREP If people who are talking get **onto** a different subject, they begin talking about it. *a* ❑ *Let's get on to more important things. Pasemos a asuntos más importantes.* **5** PREP If someone **is onto** something, they are about to discover something important. *sobre la pista de* [INFORMAL] ❑ *We knew we were onto something exciting when we started digging. Sabíamos que habíamos dado con algo emocionante cuando empezamos a excavar.* **6** PREP If someone **is onto** you, they have discovered that you are doing something illegal or wrong. *tras* [INFORMAL] ❑ *The police were onto him. La policía estaba tras él.*

**on|ward** /ɒnwərd/

> The form **onwards** can also be used as an adverb.

**1** ADJ **Onward** means moving forward or continuing a journey. *de conexión* ❑ *American Airlines flies to Bangkok, and there are onward flights to Phnom Penh. American Airlines vuela a Bangkok, y hay vuelos de conexión a Phnom Penh.* ● **Onward** is also an adverb. *adelante* ❑ *The bus continued onward. El autobús siguió adelante.* **2** ADJ **Onward** means developing, progressing, or becoming more important over a period of time. *hacia adelante* ❑ *...the onward march of progress in the aircraft industry. ...el progreso continuo de la industria aeronáutica.* ● **Onward** is also an adverb. *adelante* ❑ *It was onward and upward all the way. Todo el camino fue subir y seguir adelante.* **3** ADV If something happens from a particular time **onward,** it begins to happen at that time and continues to happen afterward. *en adelante* ❑ *From the age of six months onward, you should start to give babies solid food. De los seis meses de edad en adelante, se debe empezar a dar alimento sólido a los bebés.*

**Oort cloud** /ɔrt klaʊd/ (**Oort clouds**) N-COUNT The **Oort cloud** is a region of rocks, dust, and comets that surrounds our solar system. *Nube de Oort* [TECHNICAL]

**op-ed** ADJ In a newspaper, the **op-ed** page is a page containing articles in which people express their opinions about things. *artículos de opinión* [INFORMAL]

**open**
❶ DESCRIBING A POSITION OR MOVEMENT
❷ ACCESSIBLE OR AVAILABLE; NOT HIDDEN, BLOCKED, ETC.
❸ BEGIN, START
❹ PHRASES AND PHRASAL VERBS

**❶ open** /oʊpən/ (**opens, opening, opened**) **1** V-T/V-I If you **open** something such as a door, window, or lid, or if it **opens,** its position is changed so that it no longer covers a hole or gap. *abrir* ❑ *He opened the window. Abrió la ventana.* ● **Open** is also an adjective. *abierto* ❑ *...an open door. ...una puerta abierta.* **2** V-T If you **open** something such as a container or a letter, you move, remove, or cut part of it so you can take out what is inside. *abrir* ❑ *He opened the pack of cards. Abrió el paquete de cartas.* ● **Open** is also an adjective. *abierto, destapado* ❑ *...an open bottle. ...una botella destapada.* ● **Open up** means the same as **open.** *abrir* ❑ *He opened up the boxes of food. Abrió las cajas de comida.* **3** V-T/V-I If you **open** something such as a book, an umbrella, or your hand, or if it **opens,** the different parts of it move away from each other so that the inside of it can be seen. *abrir* ❑ *He opened the book. Abrió el libro.* ❑ *The flower opened and there was a bee inside. Cuando la flor abrió, tenía una abeja dentro.* ● **Open** is also an adjective. *abierto* ❑ *Barbara put the book into her open hand. Barbara puso el libro en la palma de su mano.* ● **Open out** means the same as **open.** *abrir, desplegar, extender* ❑ *Keith took a map and opened it out on his knees. Keith tomó un mapa y lo extendió sobre sus rodillas.* **4** V-T If you **open** a computer file, you give the computer an instruction to display it on the screen. *abrir* [COMPUTING] **5** V-T/V-I When you **open** your eyes or your eyes **open,** you move your eyelids upward, for example, when you wake up, so that you can see. *abrir* ● **Open** is also an adjective. *abierto* ❑ *His eyes were open and he was smiling. Estaba con los ojos abiertos y sonriendo.* **6** V-T If you **open** your shirt or coat, you undo the buttons or pull down the zipper. *abrir, desabrochar, desabotonar* ❑ *I opened my jacket to put away my pen. Me desabroché el saco para guardar la pluma.* ● **Open** is also an adjective. *abierto* ❑ *You can wear the shirt open over a T-shirt. Puedes ponerte la camisa abierta sobre una camiseta.*

**❷ open** /oʊpən/ (**opens, opening, opened**) **1** V-T/V-I If people **open** something such as a blocked road or a border, or if it **opens,** people can then pass along it or through it. *abrir* ❑ *Police opened the road two hours after the accident. La policía abrió la carretera dos horas después del accidente.* ● **Open** is also an adjective. *abierto* ❑ *We want to keep the highway open. Queremos que la autopista siga abierta.* ● **Open up** means the same as **open.** *abrir* ❑ *Workers opened up roads today, after the floods. Después de las inundaciones, los trabajadores abrieron las carreteras hoy.* **2** ADJ An **open** area is a large area that does not have many buildings or trees in it. *abierto* ❑ *Police officers continued their search of open ground. Los agentes de la policía continuaron con la búsqueda en campo abierto.* **3** ADJ An **open** structure or object is not covered or enclosed. *su traducción depende del nombre* ❑ *...a room with an open fire. ...un cuarto con una chimenea.* **4** V-T/V-I When a store, office, or public building **opens** or **is opened,** its doors are unlocked and people can go in. *abrir* ❑ *Banks don't open again until Monday morning. Los bancos no vuelven a abrir hasta el lunes por la mañana.* ● **Open** is also an adjective. *abierto* ❑ *The store is open Monday through Friday, 9 a.m. to 6 p.m. La tienda permanece abierta de lunes a viernes, de las 9 de la mañana a las 6 de la tarde.* **5** V-T/V-I When a public building, factory, or company **opens** or when someone **opens** it, it starts operating for the first time. *inaugurar, abrir* ❑ *The station opened in 1954. La estación se inauguró en 1954.* **6** ADJ If you describe a person or their character as **open,** you mean they are honest and do not want or try to hide anything or to deceive anyone. *abierto, sincero, franco* ❑ *He was always open with her. Siempre fue abierto con ella.* ● **open|ness** N-UNCOUNT *sinceridad, franqueza* ❑ *Our relationship is based on honesty and openness. Nuestra relación se basa en la honestidad y la franqueza.* **7** ADJ If you are **open to** suggestions or ideas, you are ready and willing to consider or accept them. *abierto* ❑ *They are open to suggestions on how working conditions could be improved. Siempre estaban abiertos a recibir sugerencias sobre la manera de mejorar las condiciones de trabajo.* **8** ADJ If you say that a system, person, or idea is **open to** something such as abuse or criticism, you mean they might receive abuse or criticism because of their qualities, effects, or actions. *expuesto a* ❑ *Their behavior is open to question. Su conducta es dudosa.*

**❸ open** /oʊpən/ (**opens, opening, opened**) **1** V-T/V-I When an event such as a conference **opens,** or **is opened,** it begins. *inaugurar, iniciar* ❑ *The conference will open tomorrow. La conferencia se inaugura mañana.* ● **open|ing** N-SING *comienzo, inicio* ❑ *...the opening of the talks. ...el inicio de las pláticas.* **2** V-I When a movie, play, or other public event **opens,** it begins to be shown, be performed, or to take place for a limited time. *inaugurar, dar inicio* ❑ *A photographic exhibition opens at the museum on Wednesday. El miércoles se inaugura una exposición de fotografía en el museo.* ● **open|ing** N-SING *inauguración* ❑ *...the opening of the Olympic Games. ...la inauguración de los Juegos Olímpicos.* **3** V-T If you **open** an account with a bank or a commercial organization, you begin to use their services. *abrir*

**❹ open** /oʊpən/ (**opens, opening, opened**) **1** PHRASE If you do something **in the open** or **out in the open,** you do it outdoors. *al aire libre, a la intemperie* ❑ *Many people sleep in the open because they are homeless. Mucha gente duerme a la intemperie porque no tiene casa.* **2** PHRASE If an attitude or situation is **in the open** or **out in the open,** people know about it and it is no longer kept secret. *público, a la luz* ❑ *We wanted the secret to be out in the open. Queríamos que el secreto saliera a la luz.* **3** to **keep** your **eyes open** → see **eye** **4** **an open mind** → see **mind** **5** to **keep** your **options open** → see **option**
▸ **open out** → see **open ❶ 3**
▸ **open up** **1** → see **open ❶ 2** → see **open ❷**
**1** **2** PHR-VERB If a place, economy, or area of interest **opens up,** or if someone **opens** it **up,** more people can go there or become involved in it. *abrirse* ❑ *As the market opens up, more goods will be available. A medida que el mercado se abra, habrá más bienes disponibles.* ❑ *He wanted to see how Albania was*

O

*opening up to the world.* Deseaba ver cómo se estaba abriendo Albania al mundo. **3** PHR-VERB If something **opens up** opportunities or possibilities, or if they **open up,** they are created. hacer surgir, generar ❑ *The changes have opened up new opportunities for the company.* Los cambios han hecho surgir nuevas oportunidades para la compañía. **4** PHR-VERB When you **open up** a building, you unlock and open the door so that people can get in. abrir ❑ *Several customers were waiting when I arrived to open up the store.* Cuando llegué a abrir la tienda, ya había varios clientes esperando.

**open cir|cu|la|tory sys|tem** (**open circulatory systems**) N-COUNT In animals that have an **open circulatory system,** the heart pumps blood into spaces around the body. sistema circulatorio abierto [TECHNICAL]

**open clus|ter** (**open clusters**) N-COUNT An **open cluster** is a group of stars that were all formed at the same time and are held together by gravity. cúmulo abierto [TECHNICAL]

**open|er** /oʊpənər/ (**openers**) N-COUNT An **opener** is a tool which is used to open containers such as cans or bottles. abridor, destapador ❑ *...a can opener.* ...un abrelatas.
→ see **utensil**

**open|ing** /oʊpənɪŋ/ (**openings**) **1** ADJ The **opening** event, item, day, or week in a series is the first one. inicial, primero ❑ *...the competition's opening game.* ...el juego inicial de la competencia., ...el primer juego de la competencia. **2** N-COUNT **The opening of** something such as a book, play, or concert is the first part of it. introducción, primera escena, obertura ❑ *They waited for the opening of the musical.* Aguardaron la introducción del musical. **3** N-COUNT An **opening** is a hole or empty space through which things or people can pass. abertura ❑ *He pushed through a narrow opening in the fence.* Pasó a través de una estrecha abertura en la cerca. **4** N-COUNT An **opening** in a forest is a small area where there are no trees or bushes. claro ❑ *I looked down at the beach as we passed an opening in the trees.* Vi la playa abajo cuando pasamos por un claro entre los árboles. **5** N-COUNT An **opening** is a good opportunity to do something. oportunidad ❑ *All she needed was an opening to show what she could do.* Sólo necesitaba una oportunidad para demostrar lo que sabía hacer. **6** N-COUNT An **opening** is a job that is available. vacante ❑ *We don't have any openings now.* Por ahora no tenemos vacantes. **7** → see also **open**

| **Thesaurus** | *opening* | Ver también: |
|---|---|---|
| N. | cut, door, gap, slot, space, window **3** | |
| | clearing **4** | |
| | job, position **6** | |

**open|ly** /oʊpənli/ ADV If you do something **openly,** you do it without hiding any facts or your feelings. abiertamente, francamente ❑ *She openly talked with friends about it.* Habló abiertamente al respecto con los amigos.

**open-source** also **open source** ADJ **Open-source** software is software that anyone is allowed to modify without asking permission from the company that developed it. código abierto [COMPUTING]

**open-water zone** (**open-water zones**) N-COUNT The **open-water zone** of a lake or pond is the area closest to the surface, where sunlight can reach. zona de agua superficial [TECHNICAL]

| **Word Link** | *oper ≈ work : cooperate, opera, operation* |
|---|---|

**op|era** /ɒpərə, ɒprə/ (**operas**) **1** N-VAR An **opera** is a play with music in which all the words are sung. ópera ❑ *...an opera singer.* ...una cantante de ópera. **2** → see also **soap opera** ● **op|er|at|ic** /ɒpəræt̬ɪk/ ADJ operístico ❑ *...the local amateur operatic society.* ...la sociedad local de aficionados a la ópera.
→ see **music**

**op|er|ate** /ɒpəreɪt/ (**operates, operating, operated**) **1** V-T/V-I If you **operate** a business or organization, or if it **operates,** it does the work it is supposed to. operar ❑ *Greenwood owned and operated a truck rental company.* Greenwood era propietario y operador de una empresa de alquiler de camiones. ❑ *...the first overseas bank to operate in Cambodia for more than 15 years.* ...el primer banco extranjero que opera en Camboya en más de 15 años. ● **op|era|tion** /ɒpəreɪʃən/ N-UNCOUNT operación ❑ *...the day-to-day operation of the company.* ...la operación cotidiana de la empresa. **2** V-I The way that something **operates** is the way that it works or has a particular effect. funcionar ❑ *Ceiling and wall lights can operate independently.* El alumbrado del techo y el de los muros pueden funcionar independientemente. ● **op|era|tion** N-UNCOUNT funcionamiento ❑ *...the operation of government.* ...el funcionamiento del gobierno. **3** V-T/V-I When you **operate** a machine or device, or when it **operates,** you make it work. manejar, manipular ❑ *He used to sing as he was operating the machine.* Acostumbraba cantar mientras estaba manipulando la máquina. ● **op|era|tion** N-UNCOUNT funcionamiento ❑ *...the operation of the engine.* ...el funcionamiento del motor. **4** V-I When surgeons **operate on** a patient, they cut open the patient's body in order to remove, replace, or repair a diseased or damaged part. operar, intervenir ❑ *Surgeons operated on Max to remove a brain tumor.* Los cirujanos operaron a Max para extraerle un tumor cerebral. **5** → see also **operation**

| **Word Partnership** | Usar *operate* con: |
|---|---|
| N. | operate **a business/company, schools** |
| | operate **1** |
| | **forces** operate **1 2** |
| V. | ***be* allowed to** operate, **continue to** operate **1 – 3** |
| ADV. | operate **efficiently 1 2** |
| | operate **independently 2** |

**op|er|at|ing room** (**operating rooms**) N-COUNT An **operating room** is a room in a hospital where surgeons carry out medical operations. sala de operaciones, quirófano

**op|era|tion** /ɒpəreɪʃən/ (**operations**) **1** N-COUNT An **operation** is a highly-organized activity that involves many people doing different things. operación ❑ *The rescue operation began on Friday.* La operación de rescate comenzó el viernes. ❑ *...a military operation.* ...una operación militar. **2** N-COUNT A business or company can be referred to as an **operation.** empresa, compañía [BUSINESS]

O

❑ ...an electronics operation. ...una empresa de electrónica. 3 N-COUNT When a patient has an **operation**, a surgeon cuts open their body in order to remove, replace, or repair a diseased or damaged part. *operación* ❑ *Charles had an operation on his arm. Operaron a Charles del brazo.* 4 N-UNCOUNT If a system is **in operation**, it is being used. *funcionamiento* ❑ *This banking system is currently in operation. Este sistema bancario está en funcionamiento actualmente.* 5 N-UNCOUNT If a machine or device is **in operation**, it is working. *funcionamiento* ❑ *There are three ski lifts in operation today. Hoy hay tres telesillas en funcionamiento.* 6 → see also **operative**

**Word Partnership** Usar *operation* con:

N. **relief** operation, **rescue** operation 1
V. **carry out an** operation, **plan an** operation 1
**perform an** operation 1 3
ADJ. **covert** operation, **massive** operation, **military** operation, **undercover** operation 1
**major** operation, **successful** operation 1 – 3
**emergency** operation 1 3

**op|era|tion|al** /ɒpəreɪʃənᵊl/ 1 ADJ A machine or piece of equipment that is **operational** is in use or is ready for use. *en funcionamiento, en servicio* ❑ *The new system will be fully operational by December. El nuevo sistema estará en pleno funcionamiento antes de diciembre.* 2 ADJ **Operational** factors or problems relate to the working of a system, device, or plan. *de funcionamiento* ❑ *...high operational costs. ...altos costos de funcionamiento.* • **op|era|tion|al|ly** ADV *en lo referente al funcionamiento* ❑ *Operationally, the company is performing well. En lo referente al funcionamiento, la empresa está marchando bien.*

O

**op|era|tive** /ɒpərətɪv, -əreɪtɪv/ (**operatives**) 1 ADJ A system or service that is **operative** is working or having an effect. *en vigor* [FORMAL] ❑ *The service was no longer operative. El servicio ya no se ofrecía.* 2 N-COUNT An **operative** is a worker, especially one who does work with their hands. *operario u operaria* [FORMAL] ❑ *In an automated car factory, you can't see any human operatives. En una planta automovilística automatizada no hay ningún operario.* 3 N-COUNT An **operative** is someone who works for a government agency such as the intelligence service. *agente secreto* ❑ *The CIA wants to protect its operatives. La CIA desea proteger a sus agentes secretos.* 4 PHRASE If you describe a word as **the operative word**, you want to draw attention to it because you think it is important or exactly true in a particular situation. *pertinente* ❑ *This is a good little company, but the operative word is "little." Es una pequeña empresa buena, pero la palabra pertinente es "pequeña".*

**op|era|tor** /ɒpəreɪtər/ (**operators**) 1 N-COUNT An **operator** is a person who connects telephone calls at a telephone exchange or in a place such as an office or hotel. *operador u operadora* ❑ *He called the operator. Llamó a la operadora.* 2 N-COUNT An **operator** is a person who is employed to operate or control a machine. *operario u operaria* ❑ *...computer operators. ...operarios de computadoras.* 3 N-COUNT An **operator** is a person or a company that operates a business. *empresa* [BUSINESS] ❑ *...the nation's largest cable TV operator. ...la empresa de televisión por cable más grande del país.*

**opin|ion** /əpɪnyən/ (**opinions**) 1 N-COUNT Your **opinion** about something is what you think or believe about it. *opinión* ❑ *I didn't ask for your opinion. No te pedí tu opinión.* 2 N-SING Your **opinion of** someone is your judgment of their character or ability. *opinión* ❑ *Thomas has a high opinion of himself. Thomas tiene una muy buena opinión de sí mismo.* ❑ *She held the opinion that he was a fool. Ella sostenía la opinión de que era un tonto.* 3 N-UNCOUNT You can refer to the beliefs or views that people have as **opinion**. *opinión* ❑ *The president understands the importance of world opinion. El presidente entiende la importancia de la opinión internacional.*

**Thesaurus** *opinion* Ver también:

N. feeling, judgment, thought, viewpoint 1 – 3

**Word Partnership** Usar *opinion* con:

V. **ask for an** opinion, **express an** opinion, **give an** opinion, **share an** opinion 1 2
ADJ. **favorable** opinion 1 2
**expert** opinion, **legal** opinion, **majority** opinion, **medical** opinion 3

**opin|ion poll** (**opinion polls**) N-COUNT An **opinion poll** involves asking people's opinions on a particular subject, especially one concerning politics. *encuesta de opinión, sondeo de opinión* ❑ *75% of people questioned in an opinion poll agreed with the government's decision. El 75% de las personas incluidas en un sondeo de opinión se mostró de acuerdo con la decisión del gobierno.*

**op|po|nent** /əpoʊnənt/ (**opponents**) 1 N-COUNT A politician's **opponents** are other politicians who belong to a different party or who have different aims or policies. *oponente, adversario* ❑ *...Mr. Kennedy's opponent in the contest. ...el adversario del señor Kennedy en la contienda.* 2 N-COUNT In a sports contest, your **opponent** is the person who is playing against you. *contrincante, rival* ❑ *Los Angeles will be the team's first-round opponent. Los Ángeles será el rival del equipo en la primera vuelta.* 3 N-COUNT The **opponents of** an idea or policy do not agree with it. *opositor u opositora* ❑ *...opponents of the increase in nuclear weapons. ...los opositores al incremento de las armas nucleares.*
→ see **chess**

**op|por|tu|nity** /ɒpərtunɪti/ (**opportunities**) N-VAR An **opportunity** is a situation in which it is possible for you to do something that you want to do. *oportunidad* ❑ *I had an opportunity to go to New York and study. Tuve la oportunidad de ir a Nueva York a estudiar.* ❑ *We provide opportunities for people to meet each other. Ofrecemos la oportunidad para que la gente se encuentre.*

**Word Web** orchestra

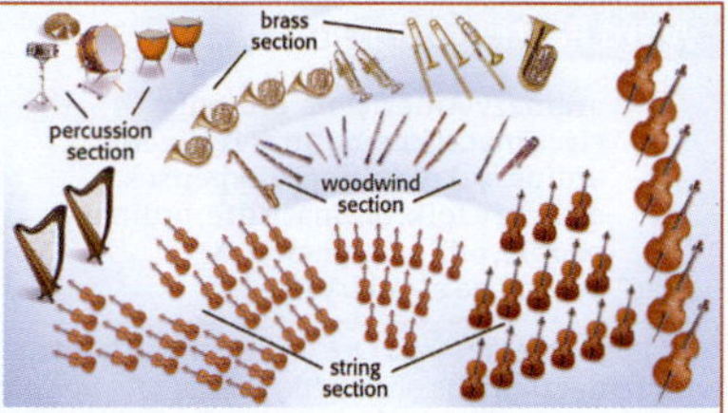


The modern **symphony orchestra** usually has between 60 and 100 **musicians.** The largest group of musicians are in the **string** section. It gives the orchestra its rich, flowing sound. String **instruments** include **violins, violas, cellos,** and usually **double basses. Flutes,** oboes, **clarinets,** and bassoons make up the woodwind section. The **brass** section is usually quite small. Too much of this sound could overwhelm the quieter strings. Brass **instruments** include the French horn, **trumpet, trombone,** and tuba. The size of the **percussion** section depends on the **composition** being performed. However, there is almost always a timpani player.

*para* ❑ *In order for the computer to find someone's records, we need the person's name and address.* *Para que la computadora encuentre el registro de alguien, necesitamos el nombre y el domicilio de la persona.*

❷ **or|der** /ɔrdər/ (**orders, ordering, ordered**) 1 V-T If a person in authority **orders** someone **to** do something, they tell them to do it. *ordenar* ❑ *Williams ordered him to leave.* *Williams le ordenó que se marchara.* 2 V-T If someone in authority **orders** something, they give instructions that it should be done. *ordenar* ❑ *The president ordered a full report of what happened.* *EL presidente ordenó un informe detallado de lo que había pasado.* 3 N-COUNT If someone in authority gives you an **order,** they tell you to do something. *orden* ❑ *The commander gave orders to move out in a few minutes.* *El comandante dio órdenes de retirarse en unos minutos.* 4 V-T/V-I When you **order** something that you are going to pay for, you ask for it to be brought to you or sent to you. *pedir* ❑ *They ordered a new washing machine.* *Hicieron un pedido por una lavadora nueva.* ❑ *The waitress asked, "Are you ready to order?"* *La mesera preguntó: "¿Ya decidieron qué van a pedir?".* 5 N-COUNT Someone's **order** is what they have asked to be brought, made, or obtained for them in return for money. *pedido* ❑ *The waiter returned with their order.* *El mesero llegó con lo que pidieron.* 6 → see also **mail order** 7 PHRASE If you are **under orders to** do something, you have been told to do it by someone in authority. *bajo órdenes de* ❑ *I am under orders not to discuss this.* *Tengo la orden de no discutirlo.* 8 **a tall order** → see **tall**

**Thesaurus** *order* Ver también:

| | |
|---|---|
| V. | charge, command, direct, tell ❷ 1<br>buy, request ❷ 4 |
| N. | command, direction, instruction ❷ 3 |

▸ **order around** PHR-VERB If you say that someone **is ordering** you **around,** you mean they are telling you what to do as if they have authority over you, and you dislike this. *mandar de acá para allá* ❑ *He started ordering me around.* *Empezó a mandarme de acá para allá.*

❸ **or|der** /ɔrdər/ (**orders**) 1 N-UNCOUNT If things are arranged or done **in** a particular **order,** one thing is put first or done first, another thing second, another thing third, and so on. *orden* ❑ *Bookstores should arrange the books in alphabetical order.* *Las librerías deberían arreglar los libros en orden alfabético.* 2 N-UNCOUNT **Order** is the situation that exists when everything is in the correct or expected place, or happens at the correct time. *orden* ❑ *I love rules. I love order.* *Me encantan las reglas; me encanta el orden.* 3 N-UNCOUNT **Order** is the situation that exists when people obey the law and do not fight or riot. *orden* ❑ *Troops were sent to the islands to restore order.* *Enviaron tropas a las islas para restaurar el orden.* 4 N-SING When people talk about a particular **order,** they mean the way society is organized at a particular time. *sistema* ❑ *He and his followers want to create a better social order.* *Él y sus seguidores quieren crear un mejor sistema social.* 5 N-COUNT A religious **order** is a group of monks or nuns who live according to a particular set of rules. *orden* ❑ *...the Benedictine order of monks.* *...la orden de los monjes benedictinos.* 6 N-COUNT In biology, an **order** of animals or plants is a group of related species. Compare **class, family.** *orden* 7 → see also **law and order** 8 PHRASE You use **in the order of** or **on the order of** when mentioning an approximate figure. *aproximadamente, del orden de* ❑ *They borrowed something in the order of $10 million.* *Pidieron un préstamo del orden de 10 millones de dólares.* 9 PHRASE A machine or device that is **in working order** is functioning properly and is not broken. *funcionar bien* ❑ *...a ten-year-old car that is in perfect working order.* *...un coche de diez años de antigüedad que funciona perfectamente.* 10 PHRASE A machine or device that is **out of order** is broken and does not work. *descompuesto* ❑ *Their phone's out of order.* *Su teléfono está descompuesto.*

**or|di|nary** /ɔrdᵊnɛri/ 1 ADJ **Ordinary** people or things are normal and not special or different in any way. *común, normal* ❑ *Most ordinary people would agree with me.* *La mayoría de la gente común estaría de acuerdo conmigo.* ❑ *It has 25 calories fewer than ordinary ice cream.* *Tiene 25 calorías menos que el helado normal.* 2 PHRASE Something that is **out of the ordinary** is unusual or different. *fuera de lo normal* ❑ *The police chief asked the public to report anything out of the ordinary.* *El jefe de la policía pidió al público que informara sobre cualquier cosa fuera de lo normal.*

**Thesaurus** *ordinary* Ver también:

| | |
|---|---|
| ADJ. | common, everyday, normal, regular, standard, typical, usual; (*ant.*) abnormal, unusual 1 |

**Word Partnership** Usar *ordinary* con:

N. ordinary **Americans**, ordinary **circumstances**, ordinary **citizens**, ordinary **day**, ordinary **expenses**, ordinary **folk**, ordinary **life**, ordinary **people**, ordinary **person** 1
PREP. **out of the** ordinary 2

**ore** /ɔr/ (**ores**) N-VAR **Ore** is rock or earth from which metal can be obtained. *mineral* ❑ *...iron ore. mineral de hierro.*

**or|gan** /ɔrgən/ (**organs**) 1 N-COUNT An **organ** is a part of your body that has a particular purpose or function, for example, your heart or lungs. *órgano* ❑ *...damage to the muscles and internal organs. ...daños a los músculos y los órganos internos.* ❑ *...human organs. ...órganos humanos.* 2 N-COUNT An **organ** is a large musical instrument with pipes of different lengths through which air is forced. It has keys and pedals like a piano. *órgano* • **or|gan|ist** N-COUNT (**organists**) *organista* ❑ *...the church organist. ...el organista de la iglesia.*
→ see **donor, keyboard, nervous system**

**or|gan|elle** /ɔrgənɛl/ (**organelles**) N-COUNT **Organelles** are structures within cells that have a specialized function, such as mitochondria or the nucleus. *orgánulo* [TECHNICAL]

**or|gan|ic** /ɔrgænɪk/ 1 ADJ **Organic** farming or gardening uses only natural animal and plant products and does not use artificial fertilizers or pesticides. *orgánico* • **or|gani|cal|ly** ADV *orgánicamente, biológicamente* ❑ *...organically grown vegetables. ...verduras cultivadas biológicamente.* 2 ADJ **Organic** substances are produced by or found in living things. *orgánico* ❑ *...organic waste such as unwanted food. ...desechos orgánicos, como la comida que no se consume.* 3 ADJ In art, **organic** shapes or designs use curved lines rather than straight lines and resemble shapes that exist in nature. *orgánico*

**or|gan|ic com|pound** (**organic compounds**) N-COUNT An **organic compound** is a chemical compound that contains carbon. *compuesto orgánico* [TECHNICAL]

**or|gan|ism** /ɔrgənɪzəm/ (**organisms**) N-COUNT An **organism** is an animal or plant, especially one that is so small that you cannot see it without using a microscope. *organismo* ❑ *...tiny organisms such as bacteria. ...organismos diminutos, como las bacterias.*

**or|gani|za|tion** /ɔrgənɪzeɪʃ^ən/ (**organizations**) 1 N-COUNT An **organization** is an official group of people, for example, a political party, a business, a charity, or a club. *organización* ❑ *She worked for the organization for six years. Trabajó para la organización durante seis años.* • **or|gani|za|tion|al** ADJ *organizativo* ❑ *...organizational change. ...cambio organizativo.* 2 N-UNCOUNT The **organization** of an event or activity involves making all the necessary arrangements for it. *organización* ❑ *I helped in the organization of the concert. Ayudé a la organización del concierto.* • **or|gani|za|tion|al** ADJ *organizativo* ❑ *...Evelyn's excellent organizational skills. ...la excelente capacidad organizativa de Evelyn.* 3 N-UNCOUNT The **organization of** something is the way in which its different parts are arranged or relate to each other. *organización, estructura* ❑ *Is the general organization of your report clear? ¿Es clara la estructura general de su informe?* • **or|gani|za|tion|al** ADJ *orgánico, organizativo* ❑ *Big organizational changes are needed. Es necesario hacer cambios organizativos profundos.*

**or|gan|ize** /ɔrgənaɪz/ (**organizes, organizing, organized**) 1 V-T If you **organize** an event or activity, you make all the arrangements for it. *organizar* ❑ *We decided to organize a concert. Decidimos organizar un concierto.* • **or|gan|iz|er** N-COUNT (**organizers**) *organizador u organizadora* ❑ *He was a great organizer and leader. Era un gran organizador y un gran líder.* 2 V-T If you **organize** something that someone wants or needs, you make sure that it is provided. *organizar* ❑ *I will organize transportation. Yo organizaré el transporte.* 3 V-T If you **organize** things, you arrange them in an ordered way or give them a structure. *organizar* ❑ *He began to organize his papers. Empezó a organizar sus papeles.*
→ see **union**

**Thesaurus** *organize* Ver también:

V. coordinate, plan, set up 1
arrange, line up, straighten out 3

**or|gan|ized** /ɔrgənaɪzd/ 1 ADJ An **organized** activity or group involves a number of people doing something together in a structured way, rather than doing it by themselves. *organizado* ❑ *...organized groups of art thieves. ...grupos organizados de ladrones de obras de arte.* ❑ *...organized religion. ...la religión institucional.* 2 ADJ Someone who is **organized** plans their work and activities efficiently. *organizado* ❑ *Managers need to be very organized. Los directivos necesitan ser muy organizados.*

**or|gan sys|tem** (**organ systems**) N-COUNT An **organ system** is a group of related organs within an organism, for example the nervous system. *sistema de órganos*

**ori|en|tal** /ɔriɛnt^əl/ ADJ **Oriental** means coming from or associated with eastern Asia, especially China and Japan. *oriental* ❑ *...oriental carpets. ...tapetes orientales.*

**Usage** **Oriental**

*Oriental* should not be used to refer to people, because it may cause offense. Instead, use either *Asian* or the person's nationality. Use *Oriental* only to describe things: *I bought an Oriental vase.*

**ori|en|ta|tion** /ɔriənteɪʃ^ən/ (**orientations**) 1 N-VAR If you talk about the **orientation** of an organization or country, you are talking about its aims and interests. *orientación, brújula* ❑ *Society has lost its orientation. La sociedad perdió la orientación.* 2 N-VAR Someone's **orientation** is their basic beliefs or preferences. *orientación, tendencia* ❑ *...the religious orientation of the school. ...la orientación religiosa de la escuela.*

**ori|ent|ed** /ɔriɛntɪd/

The form **orientated** is also used.

ADJ If someone **is oriented toward** or **oriented to** a particular thing or person, they are mainly concerned with that thing or person. *orientado a* ❑ *The town has lots of family-oriented things to do. La ciudad ofrece muchas actividades orientadas a la familia.*

**ori|gin** /ɔrɪdʒɪn/ (**origins**) **1** N-COUNT You can refer to the beginning, cause, or source of something as its **origin** or **origins**. *origen* ❑ *...theories about the origin of life. ...las teorías sobre el origen de la vida.* ❑ *The names "Gullah" and "Geechee" are African in origin. Los nombres "Gullah" y "Geechee" son de origen africano.* **2** N-COUNT Your **origin** or **origins** is the country, race, or living conditions of your parents or ancestors. *origen* ❑ *Thomas has not forgotten his humble origins. Thomas no ha olvidado su origen humilde.* ❑ *...people of Asian origin. ...gente de origen asiático.*

**Word Partnership** Usar *origin* con:

| | |
|---|---|
| N. | origin **of life, point of** origin, origin **of the universe** 1 |
| | **country of** origin, **family of** origin 2 |
| ADJ. | **unknown** origin 1 2 |
| | **ethnic** origin, **Hispanic** origin, **national** origin 2 |

**origi|nal** /ərɪdʒɪnᵊl/ (**originals**) **1** ADJ You use **original** when referring to something that existed at the beginning of a process or activity, or the characteristics that something had when it began or was made. *original* ❑ *The original plan was to go by bus. El plan original era ir en autobús.* ● **origi|nal|ly** ADV *originalmente* ❑ *They stayed longer than they originally intended. Se quedaron más tiempo de lo que tenían pensado originalmente.* **2** N-COUNT If something such as a document, a work of art, or a piece of writing is an **original**, it is not a copy or a later version. *original* ❑ *Photocopy the document and send the original to your employer. Haga una fotocopia del documento y envíe el original a su patrón.* **3** ADJ An **original** piece of writing or music was written recently and has not been published or performed before. *original* ❑ *...with original songs by Richard Warner. ...con canciones originales de Richard Warner.* **4** ADJ If you describe someone or their work as **original**, you approve of them because they are very imaginative and have new ideas. *original* ❑ *Kandinsky is arguably the most original painter of the past 100 years. Podría decirse que Kandinsky es el pintor más original de los últimos cien años.* ● **origi|nal|ity** /ərɪdʒɪnælɪti/ N-UNCOUNT *originalidad* ❑ *...a musical work of great originality. ...una obra musical de gran originalidad.*

**Thesaurus** *original* Ver también:

| | |
|---|---|
| ADJ. | early, first, initial 1 |
| | authentic, genuine 2 |
| | creative, unique 4 |
| N. | master; (*ant.*) copy 2 |

**origi|nate** /ərɪdʒɪneɪt/ (**originates, originating, originated**) V-I If something **originated** at a particular time or in a particular place, it began to happen or exist at that time or in that place. *originarse* [FORMAL] ❑ *The disease originated in Africa. La enfermedad se originó en África.*

**ori|ole** /ɔrioʊl/ (**orioles**) N-COUNT An **oriole** is a bird which has black and yellow or orange feathers. *oropéndola, oriol*

**or|nery** /ɔrnəri/ ADJ If you describe someone as **ornery**, you mean that they are bad-tempered, difficult, and often do things that are mean. *intratable, de mal genio, de malas pulgas* [INFORMAL] ❑ *The old lady was still being ornery, but she agreed to his visit. La vieja seguía teniendo malas pulgas, pero aceptó que la visitara.*

**or|phan** /ɔrfən/ (**orphans, orphaned**) **1** N-COUNT An **orphan** is a child whose parents are dead. *huérfano o huérfana* **2** V-T PASSIVE If a child **is orphaned**, their parents die, or their remaining parent dies. *quedar huérfano, dejar huérfano*

**ortho|dox** /ɔrθədɒks/

The spelling **Orthodox** is also used for meaning **2**.

**1** ADJ **Orthodox** beliefs, methods, or systems are ones which are accepted or used by most people. *ortodoxo* ❑ *...orthodox medical treatment. ...un tratamiento médico ortodoxo.* **2** ADJ If you describe someone as **orthodox**, you mean that they hold the older and more traditional ideas of their religion or party. *ortodoxo* ❑ *...Orthodox Jews. ...judíos ortodoxos.*

**or|thog|ra|phy** /ɔrθɒgrəfi/ (**orthographies**) N-VAR The **orthography** of a language is the set of rules about how to spell words in the language correctly. *ortografía* [TECHNICAL]

**ortho|pedic** /ɔrθəpidɪk/ ADJ **Orthopedic** means relating to problems affecting people's joints and spines. *ortopedista, ortopédico* [MEDICAL] ❑ *...an orthopedic surgeon. ...un (cirujano) ortopedista* ❑ *...orthopedic shoes. ...zapatos ortopédicos.*

**OS** /oʊ ɛs/ (**OS's**) N-COUNT **OS** is an abbreviation for **operating system**. *sistema operativo* [COMPUTING]

**OSHA** /oʊʃə/ N-PROPER **OSHA** is a government agency in the United States which is responsible for maintaining standards of health and safety in workplaces. **OSHA** is an abbreviation for "Occupational Safety and Health Administration." *Departamento de Salud y Seguridad en el Trabajo, Administración de la Seguridad y Salud Ocupacionales*

**os|ti|na|to** /ɒstɪnɑtoʊ/ (**ostinatos**) N-COUNT An **ostinato** is a short melody or rhythm that is repeated continually throughout a piece of music. *ostinato* [TECHNICAL]

**OT** /oʊ ti/ (**OTs**) N-VAR In sports, **OT** is an abbreviation for **overtime**. *tiempo suplementario, prórroga* ❑ *Mullin's team got a one-point victory in OT. El equipo de Mullin logró la victoria por un punto en tiempo suplementario.*

**oth|er** /ʌðər/ (**others**)

When **other** follows the determiner **an**, it is written as one word: see **another**.

**1** ADJ You use **other** to refer to an additional thing or person of the same type as one that has been mentioned or is known about. *otro* ❑ *They were just like any other young couple. Eran exactamente como cualquier otra pareja joven.* ● **Other** is also a pronoun. *otro u otra* ❑ *Four people were killed, one other was injured. Murieron cuatro personas y otra resultó herida.* **2** ADJ You use **other** to indicate that a thing or

O

person is not the one already mentioned, but a different one. *otro* ❑ *Johnson and other teachers at the school are very worried.* *Johnson y otros maestros de la escuela están muy preocupados.* ❑ *He would have to accept it; there was no other way.* *Tendría que aceptarlo; no había otra salida.* • **Other** is also a pronoun. *otro* ❑ *This issue, more than any other, has upset local people.* *Esta cuestión, más que ninguna otra, ha molestado a la gente del lugar.* **3** ADJ You use **the other** to refer to the second of two things or people when the identity of the first is already known or understood, or has already been mentioned. *otro* ❑ *William was at the other end of the room.* *William estaba en el otro extremo de la habitación.* • **The other** is also a pronoun. *otro* ❑ *He had a pen in one hand and a book in the other.* *Tenía una pluma en una mano y un libro en la otra.* **4** ADJ You use **the other** to refer to the rest of the people or things in a group, when you are talking about one particular person or thing. *otro* ❑ *The other kids went to the park but he stayed home.* *Los otros niños fueron al parque, pero él se quedó en la casa.* • **The others** is also a pronoun. *los otros o las otras* ❑ *Alison is coming here with the others.* *Alison va a venir acá con los otros.* **5** ADJ **Other** people are people in general, as opposed to yourself or a person you have already mentioned. *otro* ❑ *The suffering of other people upsets me.* *El sufrimiento de los demás me afecta.* • **Others** means the same as **other people.** *los demás* ❑ *...his hate for others.* *...su odio por los demás.* **6** ADJ You use **other** in expressions of time such as **the other day, the other evening,** or **the other week** to refer to a day, evening, or week in the recent past. *otro* ❑ *I called her the other day.* *La llamé el otro día.* **7** PHRASE If something happens, for example, **every other day** or **every other month,** there is a day or month when it does not happen between each day or month when it happens. *cada tercer día, mes, año*, *un día, semana, mes, año sí, otro no*, *en días, semanas, meses, años alternos* ❑ *I wash my hair every other day.* *Me lavo el pelo cada tercer día.* **8** PHRASE You use **nothing other than** and **no other than** to talk about a course of action, decision, or description that is the only one possible in the situation. *nada más que* ❑ *His success was due to nothing other than hard work.* *Su éxito no se debió a nada más que a su empeño en el trabajo.* **9** PHRASE You use **other than** after a negative in order to introduce an exception to what you have said. *excepto por* ❑ *She did not talk about any work other than her own.* *Únicamente hablaba de su propio trabajo.* **10** **each other** → see **each** **11** **one or other** → see **one** **12** **in other words** → see **word**

O

**Word Link** *wise ≈ in the direction or manner of: clockwise, likewise, otherwise*

**other|wise** /ʌðərwaɪz/ **1** ADV You use **otherwise** after mentioning a situation or fact, to say what the result would be if the situation or fact was not true. *de lo contrario* ❑ *I'm lucky that I enjoy school, otherwise I'd go crazy.* *Tengo suerte de que me guste la escuela; de lo contrario, me volvería loco.* **2** ADV You use **otherwise** to state the general condition or quality of something, when you are also mentioning an exception to this. *por lo demás* ❑ *He woke at about 7 a.m., very hungry but otherwise happy.* *Despertó como a las 7 de la mañana, muy hambriento, pero feliz, por lo demás.* **3** ADV You use **otherwise** to refer to actions or ways of doing something that are different from the one mentioned in your main statement. *a menos que* [WRITTEN] ❑ *Take one pill three times a day, unless told otherwise by a doctor.* *Tome una píldora tres veces al día, a menos que su médico ordene otra dosis.*

**ot|to|man** /ɒtəmən/ (**ottomans**) **1** N-COUNT An **ottoman** is a low, padded seat similar to a couch but without a back or arms. *otomana*, *diván* **2** N-COUNT An **ottoman** is a low, padded stool that you can rest your feet on when you are sitting in a chair. *reposapiés*, *cojín para los pies*

**ought** /ɔt/

**Ought to** is a phrasal modal verb. It is used with the base form of a verb.

**1** PHRASE If you say that someone **ought to** do something, you mean that it is the right or sensible thing to do. *deber* ❑ *You ought to read the book.* *Deberías leer el libro.* ❑ *He ought to say sorry.* *Debería disculparse.* **2** PHRASE You use **ought to** to indicate that you expect something to be true or to happen. *deber de* ❑ *"This party ought to be fun," he told Alex.* *—Esta fiesta debe de ser divertida —le dijo a Alex.* **3** PHRASE You use **ought to** to indicate that you expect something to have happened. *deber* ❑ *He ought to be home by now.* *Ya debería haber llegado (a casa).* **4** PHRASE If you say that someone **ought to have** done something, you mean that it would have been the right or sensible thing to do, but they did not do it. *deber* ❑ *She ought to have told him about it.* *Debió habérselo dicho.* ❑ *I ought not to have asked you. I'm sorry.* *No debí haberle preguntado. Discúlpeme.*

**Usage** **ought**

*Ought* is generally used with *to*: *We ought to go home soon. You ought to tell her the good news right away!*

**oughtn't** /ɔtᵊnt/ **Oughtn't** is a spoken form of "ought not." *forma hablada de* ***ought not***

**ounce** /aʊns/ (**ounces**) **1** N-COUNT An **ounce** is a unit of weight used in the U.S. and Britain. There are sixteen ounces in a pound and one ounce is equal to 28.35 grams. *onza* **2** N-SING You can refer to a very small amount of something, such as a quality or characteristic, as an **ounce.** *pizca* ❑ *He didn't have an ounce of business sense.* *No tenía ni una pizca de sentido para los negocios.*

**our** /aʊər/

**Our** is the first person plural possessive determiner.

**1** DET A speaker or writer uses **our** to indicate that something belongs or relates both to himself or herself and to one or more other people. *nuestro* ❑ *We're expecting our first baby.* *Estamos esperando a nuestro primer hijo.* **2** DET A speaker or writer sometimes uses **our** to indicate that something belongs or relates to people in general. *nuestro* ❑ *We are responsible for our actions.* *Todos somos responsables de nuestros propios actos.*

**ours** /aʊərz/

**Ours** is the first person plural possessive pronoun.

PRON A speaker or writer uses **ours** to refer to something that belongs or relates both to himself or herself and to one or more other people. nuestro ❑ *That car is ours.* Ese carro es nuestro.

**our|selves** /aʊərsɛlvz/

Ourselves is the first person plural reflexive pronoun.

1 PRON You use **ourselves** to refer to yourself and one or more other people as a group. nos ❑ *We sat by the fire to keep ourselves warm.* *Nos sentamos junto al fuego para mantenernos calientes.* 2 PRON A speaker or writer sometimes uses **ourselves** to refer to people in general. nosotros mismos ❑ *We all worry about ourselves and the situation we're in.* *Todos nos preocupamos por nosotros mismos y por nuestra situación.* 3 PRON You use **ourselves** to emphasize a first person plural subject. nosotros ❑ *Other people think the same as we ourselves think.* *Otros piensan lo mismo que nosotros.* 4 PRON If you say something such as "We did it **ourselves**," you are indicating that the people you are referring to did it, rather than anyone else. nosotros mismos ❑ *We built the house ourselves.* *Nosotros mismos construimos la casa.*

**oust** /aʊst/ (**ousts, ousting, ousted**) V-T If someone **is ousted** from a position of power, job, or place, they are forced to leave it. expulsar, hacer caer ❑ *The leaders were ousted from power.* *Expulsaron del poder a los dirigentes.* ❑ *The Republicans may oust him in November.* *Los republicanos pueden hacerlo caer en noviembre.* ● **oust|er** N-COUNT (**ousters**) destitución ❑ *Some groups called for the ouster of the police chief.* *Algunos grupos pidieron la destitución del jefe de la policía.* ● **oust|ing** N-UNCOUNT destitución ❑ *...the ousting of his boss.* *...la destitución de su jefe.*

**out**

1 ADVERB USES
2 ADJECTIVE AND ADVERB USES
3 PREPOSITION USES

**1 out** /aʊt/

Out is often used with verbs of movement, such as "walk" and "pull," and also in phrasal verbs such as "give out" and "run out."

1 ADV When something is in a particular place and you take it **out**, you remove it from that place. fuera ❑ *He took out his notebook.* *Sacó su cuaderno de notas.* 2 ADV If you are **out**, you are not at home or not at your usual place of work. fuera ❑ *I called you yesterday, but you were out.* *Llamé ayer, pero estaban fuera.*

**2 out** /aʊt/ 1 ADJ If a light or fire is **out** or goes **out**, it is no longer shining or burning. apagado ❑ *All the lights were out in the house.* *Todas las luces de la casa estaban apagadas.* 2 ADJ If flowers are **out**, their petals have opened. abierto ● **Out** is also an adverb. en flor ❑ *I love it when I see the spring flowers coming out.* *Me encanta ver las flores abrirse en la primavera.* 3 ADJ If something such as a book or CD is **out**, it is available for people to buy. a la venta ❑ *Their new album is out now.* *Ya salió su nuevo álbum.* ● **Out** is also an adverb. a la venta ❑ *The book came out in 2006.* *El libro salió en 2006.* 4 ADJ In a game or sport, if someone is **out**, they can no longer take part either because they are unable to or because they have been defeated. eliminado 5 ADJ In baseball, a player is **out** if they do not reach a base safely. When three players on a team are out in an inning, then the team is **out.** fuera 6 ADJ If you say that a calculation or measurement is **out,** you mean that it is incorrect. incorrecto ❑ *It was only a few inches out.* *Era incorrecto por sólo algunos centímetros.* 7 ADJ If someone is **out** to do something, they intend to do it. en busca de [INFORMAL] ❑ *Most companies are just out to make money.* *El único objetivo de la mayoría de las empresas es ganar dinero.*

**3 out** /aʊt/

**Out of** is used with verbs of movement, such as "walk" and "pull," and also in phrasal verbs such as "get out of" and "grow out of." **Out** is often used instead of **out of**, for example in "He looked out the window."

1 PHRASE If you go **out of** a place, you leave it. fuera de ❑ *She let him out of the house.* *Lo dejó salir de la casa.* 2 PHRASE If you take something **out of** the container or place where it has been, you remove it so that it is no longer there. sacar ❑ *I took the key out of my purse.* *Saqué la llave de mi bolsa.* 3 PHRASE If you look or shout **out of** a window, you look or shout from the room where you are toward the outside. hacia afuera ❑ *He was looking out of the window.* *Estaba mirando hacia afuera por la ventana.*

out

4 PHRASE If you are **out of** the sun, the rain, or the wind, you are sheltered from it. fuera de ❑ *Keep babies out of the sun.* *Proteja del sol a los recién nacidos.* 5 PHRASE If someone or something gets **out of** a situation, especially an unpleasant one, they are then no longer in it. If they keep **out of** it, they do not start being in it. fuera de ❑ *He needed his brother to get him out of trouble.* *Necesitaba que su hermano lo sacara del problema.* 6 PHRASE You use **out of** to say what feeling or reason causes someone to do something. por ❑ *He visited her out of a sense of duty.* *La visitó por su sentido del deber.* 7 PHRASE If you get something such as information or work **out of** someone, you manage to make them give it to you. sacar ❑ *I asked him where she was, but I couldn't get anything out of him.* *Le pregunté dónde estaba, pero no pude sacarle nada.* 8 PHRASE If you get pleasure or an advantage **out of** something, you get it as a result of being involved with that thing or making use of it. sacar de ❑ *I wasn't getting any fun out of tennis anymore.* *Ya no me estaba divirtiendo con el tenis.* 9 PHRASE If you are **out of** something, you no longer have any of it. acabarse, agotarse, no tener ❑ *We're out of milk.* *Se nos acabó la leche.* 10 PHRASE If something is made **out of** a particular material, it has been formed or constructed from it. de ❑ *...buildings made out of wood.* *...edificios de madera.* 11 PHRASE You use **out of** to indicate what proportion of a group of things something is true of. de cada ❑ *Three out of four people say there's too much violence on TV.* *Tres de cada cuatro personas opinan que hay mucha violencia en la televisión.*

**out|age** /aʊtɪdʒ/ (**outages**) N-COUNT An **outage** is a period of time when the electricity supply to a building or area is interrupted, for example because of damage to the cables. corte

O

*de luz, apagón* ❑ *A windstorm caused power outages throughout the region. Un vendaval provocó apagones en toda la región.*

**out|box** /aʊtbɒks/ (**outboxes**) also **out-box** **1** N-COUNT An **outbox** is a shallow container used in offices to put letters and documents in when they have been dealt with. *bandeja de salida* ❑ *He put the letter in his outbox. Puso la carta en su bandeja de salida.* **2** N-COUNT On a computer, your **outbox** is the part of your mailbox which stores e-mails that you have not yet sent. *bandeja de salida*

**out|break** /aʊtbreɪk/ (**outbreaks**) N-COUNT If there is an **outbreak of** something unpleasant, such as violence or a disease, it suddenly starts to happen. *brote* ❑ *The outbreak of violence involved hundreds of youths. Cientos de jóvenes participaron en el brote de violencia.* ❑ *...an outbreak of flu. ...un brote de gripa.*

**out|come** /aʊtkʌm/ (**outcomes**) N-COUNT The **outcome** of an activity, process, or situation is the situation that exists at the end of it. *resultado, consecuencia* ❑ *He was pleased with the outcome of the meeting. Estaba complacido por el resultado de la reunión.* ❑ *It's too early to know the outcome of her illness. Es demasiado pronto para saber cuáles serán las consecuencias de su enfermedad.*

**out|dat|ed** /aʊtdeɪtɪd/ ADJ If you describe something as **outdated**, you mean that you think it is old-fashioned and no longer useful or relevant to modern life. *anticuado, pasado de moda* ❑ *...outdated and inefficient factories. ...fábricas anticuadas e ineficaces.* ❑ *...outdated attitudes. ...actitudes anticuadas.*

**out|do** /aʊtdu/ (**outdoes, outdoing, outdid, outdone**) V-T If you **outdo** someone, you are a lot more successful than they are at a particular activity. *superar* ❑ *His cousin outdid him in everything. Su primo lo superaba en todo.*

O

**out|door** /aʊtdɔr/ ADJ **Outdoor** activities or things happen or are used outside and not in a building. *al aire libre* ❑ *If you enjoy outdoor activities, you should try rock climbing. Si le agradan las actividades al aire libre, debería probar la escalada en roca.*

**out|doors** /aʊtdɔrz/ **1** ADV If something happens **outdoors**, it happens outside rather than in a building. *al aire libre, afuera* ❑ *It was warm enough to be outdoors all afternoon. Hacía bastante calor para quedarse afuera toda la tarde.* **2** N-SING You refer to **the outdoors** when talking about activities that take place outside away from buildings. *vida al aire libre* ❑ *I love the outdoors. Me encanta la vida al aire libre.*

**out|doors|man** /aʊtdɔrzmən/ (**outdoorsmen**) N-COUNT An **outdoorsman** is a man who spends a lot of time outdoors, doing things such as camping, hunting, or fishing. *persona que gusta de la vida al aire libre*

**out|er** /aʊtər/ ADJ The **outer** parts of something are the parts which contain or enclose the other parts, and which are furthest from the center. *exterior* ❑ *He heard a voice in the outer room. Oyó una voz en la habitación exterior.*

**out|er core** N-SING The **outer core** of the Earth is the layer of the Earth's interior between the mantle and the inner core. *núcleo externo*
→ see **core**

**out|er space** N-UNCOUNT **Outer space** is the area outside the Earth's atmosphere where the other planets and stars are. *espacio exterior, espacio sideral*
→ see **satellite**

**out|fit** /aʊtfɪt/ (**outfits, outfitting, outfitted**) **1** N-COUNT An **outfit** is a set of clothes. *traje, conjunto* ❑ *William wore a green outfit with brown shoes. William vestía un traje verde con zapatos café.* **2** N-COUNT You can refer to an organization as an **outfit**. *equipo* ❑ *We are a professional outfit. Somos un equipo profesional.* **3** V-T To **outfit** someone or something means to provide them with equipment for a particular purpose. *equipar* ❑ *They outfitted me with a talking computer. Me equiparon con una computadora parlante.*

**out|going** /aʊtgoʊɪŋ/ **1** ADJ **Outgoing** things such as planes, mail, and passengers are leaving or being sent somewhere. *de salida* ❑ *All outgoing flights were canceled. Todas las salidas de vuelos fueron canceladas.* **2** ADJ Someone who is **outgoing** is very friendly and likes meeting and talking to people. *sociable, extrovertido* ❑ *He was an outgoing, fun-loving guy. Era un hombre sociable, amante de la diversión.* **3** ADJ You use **outgoing** to describe a person in charge of something who is soon going to leave that position. *saliente* ❑ *...the outgoing director of the International Music Festival. ...el director saliente del Festival Internacional de Música.*

**out|house** /aʊthaʊs/ (**outhouses**) N-COUNT An **outhouse** is an outside toilet. *excusado exterior*

**out|ing** /aʊtɪŋ/ (**outings**) N-COUNT An **outing** is a short trip, usually with a group of people, away from your home, school, or place of work. *excursión* ❑ *She went on an outing to the local movie theater. Fue con unos amigos al cine del pueblo.*

**out|law** /aʊtlɔ/ (**outlaws, outlawing, outlawed**) V-T When you **outlaw** something, or it **is outlawed**, it is made illegal. *prohibir, declarar ilegal* ❑ *Should using a cellphone while driving be outlawed? ¿Debería prohibirse el uso del teléfono portátil mientras se conduce?* ❑ *The government has outlawed some political groups. El gobierno declaró ilegales a algunos grupos políticos.*

**out|let** /aʊtlɛt, -lɪt/ (**outlets**) **1** N-COUNT An **outlet** is a store or organization which sells the goods made by a particular manufacturer at a discount price, often direct from the manufacturer. *tienda* ❑ *...the largest retail outlet in the city. ...la tienda al por menor más grande de la ciudad.* ❑ *At the factory outlet you'll find items costing 75% less than regular prices. En la tienda de la fábrica encontrará artículos que cuestan el 75 por ciento menos del precio normal.* **2** N-COUNT If someone has an **outlet for** their feelings or ideas, they have a means of expressing and releasing them. *válvula de escape* ❑ *Trevor found an outlet for his talent when he got a part in the school play. Trevor descubrió la manera de encauzar su talento cuando le dieron un papel en la obra escolar.* **3** N-COUNT An **outlet** is a hole or pipe through which liquid or air can flow away. *salida* ❑ *...a warm air outlet. ...una salida de aire caliente.* **4** N-COUNT An **outlet** is a place, usually in a wall, where you can connect electrical devices to the electricity supply. *enchufe, tomacorriente* ❑ *Just plug it into any electric outlet. Sólo conéctelo en cualquier enchufe.*

**out|line** /aʊtlaɪn/ (**outlines, outlining, outlined**) **1** V-T If you **outline** an idea or a plan, you explain it in a general way. *bosquejar* ❑ *The governor outlined his plan to improve the state's image. El gobernador bosquejó su plan para mejorar la imagen del estado.* **2** N-COUNT An **outline** is a general explanation or description of something. *bosquejo* ❑ *...an outline of the results of the study. ...un bosquejo de los resultados del estudio.* **3** V-T PASSIVE You say that an object **is outlined** when you can see its general shape because there is light behind it. *recortarse* ❑ *The hotel was outlined against the lights. El hotel se recortaba contra las luces.*

**Word Partnership** Usar *outline* con:

| | |
|---|---|
| N. | outline **a paper**, outline **a plan** 1 **chapter** outline 2 |
| ADJ. | **broad** outline, **detailed** outline, **general** outline 2 |
| V. | **write an** outline 2 |

**out|look** /aʊtlʊk/ (**outlooks**) **1** N-COUNT Your **outlook** is your general attitude toward life. *actitud* ❑ *He had a positive outlook on life. Tenía una actitud optimista ante la vida.* **2** N-SING The **outlook** for something is whether or not it is going to be positive, successful, or safe. *panorama* ❑ *The economic outlook is not good. El panorama económico no es bueno.*

**out|ma|neu|ver** /aʊtmənuvər/ (**outmaneuvers, outmaneuvering, outmaneuvered**) V-T If you **outmaneuver** someone, you gain an advantage over them in a particular situation by behaving in a clever and skillful way. *mostrarse más hábil que* ❑ *Murphy quietly outmaneuvered him. Calladamente, Murphy se mostró más hábil que él.*

**out|num|ber** /aʊtnʌmbər/ (**outnumbers, outnumbering, outnumbered**) V-T If one group of people or things **outnumbers** another, the first group has more people or things in it than the second group. *superar en número, ser más numeroso* ❑ *In this town, men outnumber women four to one. En este pueblo, los hombres son más numerosos que las mujeres cuatro a uno.*

**out-of-court** → see **court**

**out-of-state** **1** ADJ **Out-of-state** is used to describe people who do not live permanently in a particular state within a country, but have traveled there from somewhere else. *forastero, foráneo, fuereño* ❑ *95% of our students are out-of-state students. El 95 por ciento de los estudiantes son fuereños.* **2** ADJ **Out-of-state** companies are based outside a particular state but conduct business within that state. *foráneo, de fuera del lugar* ❑ *...competition from out-of-state banks. ...la competencia entre los bancos de fuera del estado.*

**out|put** /aʊtpʊt/ (**outputs**) **1** N-VAR **Output** is used to refer to the amount of something that a person or thing produces. *producción* ❑ *...a large fall in industrial output. ...una marcada reducción de la producción industrial.* **2** N-VAR The **output** of a computer is the information that it displays on a screen or prints on paper as a result of a particular program. *resultado, salida* ❑ *You run the software, then look at the output. Corra el programa y vea el resultado.*

**out|put force** (**output forces**) N-VAR The **output force** is the force that is applied to an object by a machine. *potencia de salida* [TECHNICAL]

**out|rage** (**outrages, outraging, outraged**)

The verb is pronounced /aʊtreɪdʒ/. The noun is pronounced /aʊtreɪdʒ/.

**1** V-T If you **are outraged** by something, it makes you extremely angry and shocked. *indignar, ultrajar, escandalizar* ❑ *Many people were outraged by his comments. Mucha gente estaba escandalizada por sus comentarios.* ● **out|raged** ADJ *escandalizado* ❑ *...outraged readers. ...los lectores escandalizados.* **2** N-UNCOUNT **Outrage** is an intense feeling of anger and shock. *indignación* ❑ *Several teachers wrote to the newspapers to express their outrage. Varios maestros escribieron a los periódicos para manifestar su indignación.* **3** N-COUNT You can refer to an act or event that angers and shocks you as an **outrage.** *ultraje, escándalo* ❑ *It is an outrage that he is being let out of prison so soon. Es escandaloso que lo dejen salir de la cárcel tan pronto.*

**out|ra|geous** /aʊtreɪdʒəs/ ADJ If you describe something as **outrageous,** you are emphasizing that it is unacceptable or very shocking. *escandaloso* ❑ *It was outrageous behavior. Fue una conducta escandalosa.* ● **out|ra|geous|ly** ADV *escandalosamente* ❑ *...outrageously expensive skincare items. ...productos para el cuidado de la piel escandalosamente caros.*

**out|right**

The adjective is pronounced /aʊtraɪt/. The adverb is pronounced /aʊtraɪt/.

**1** ADJ You use **outright** to describe behavior and actions that are open and direct, rather than indirect. *descarado* ❑ *He told an outright lie. Mintió descaradamente.* ● **Outright** is also an adverb. *abiertamente* ❑ *Why don't you tell me outright? ¿Por qué no me lo dices abiertamente?* **2** ADJ **Outright** means complete and total. *categórico, rotundo* ❑ *She failed to win an outright victory. No logró obtener una victoria rotunda.* ● **Outright** is also an adverb. *categóricamente, rotundamente* ❑ *The offer wasn't rejected outright. La oferta no fue rechazada categóricamente.* PHRASE ● If someone **is killed outright**, they die immediately, for example, in an accident. *en el acto, instantáneamente*

**out|set** /aʊtsɛt/ PHRASE If something happens **at the outset** of an event, process, or period of time, it happens at the beginning of it. If something happens **from the outset,** it happens from the beginning and continues to happen. *principio, comienzo* ❑ *You must decide at the outset which courses you want to take. Debe decidir desde el principio qué cursos desea seguir.*

**out|side** /aʊtsaɪd/ (**outsides**)

The form **outside of** can also be used as a preposition.

**1** N-COUNT The **outside** of something is the part which surrounds or encloses the rest of it. *exterior* ❑ *...the outside of the building. ...el exterior del edificio.* ● **Outside** is also an adjective. *exterior* ❑ *...the outside wall. ...el muro exterior.* **2** ADV If you are **outside,** you are not inside a building but are quite close to it. *fuera* ❑ *She went outside to look for Sam. Salió a buscar a Sam.* ● **Outside** is also a preposition.

O

*afuera de* ❑ *The victim was outside a store when he was attacked. La víctima estaba afuera de una tienda cuando fue asaltada.* • **Outside** is also an adjective. *exterior* ❑ *...the outside temperature. ...la temperatura exterior.* **3** PREP If you are **outside** a room, you are not in it but are in the passage or area next to it. *fuera de* ❑ *She sent him outside the classroom. Le ordenó salir del salón de clases.* • **Outside** is also an adverb. *fuera, afuera* ❑ *They heard voices coming from outside in the hall. Oyeron voces que venían de afuera del cuarto, en la entrada.* **4** ADJ When you talk about the **outside** world, you are referring to things that happen or exist in places other than your own home or community. *exterior* ❑ *The soldiers had no radios and no news of the outside world. Los soldados no tenían radio ni noticias del mundo exterior.* **5** PREP People or things **outside** a country, city, or region are not in it. *en las afueras de* ❑ *...a castle outside Budapest. ...un castillo en las afueras de Budapest.* • **Outside** is also a noun. *exterior* ❑ *We can only look at this society from the outside. Sólo podemos estudiar esta sociedad desde el exterior.* **6** ADJ **Outside** people or organizations are not part of a particular organization or group. *externo* ❑ *...outside consultants. ...asesores externos.* • **Outside** is also a preposition. *externo a* ❑ *He hired someone from outside the company. Contrató a alguien externo a la compañía.* **7** PREP Something that happens **outside** a particular period of time happens at a different time from the one mentioned. *fuera de* ❑ *The bank is open outside normal banking hours. El banco está abierto fuera del horario de oficina normal.*

| **Thesaurus** | *outside* Ver también: |
|---|---|
| ADJ. | exterior, outdoor; (*ant.*) inside, interior **1** |
| PREP. | beyond, near; (*ant.*) inside **3** |

O

| **Word Partnership** | Usar *outside* con: |
|---|---|
| N. | **the** outside **of a building** **1**<br>outside **a building**, outside **a car**, outside **a room**, outside **a store** **3**<br>**the** outside **world** **4**<br>outside **a city/town**, outside **a country** **5**<br>outside **sources** **6** |
| ADJ. | **cold** outside, **dark** outside **2** |
| V. | **gather** outside, **go** outside, **park** outside, **sit** outside, **stand** outside, **step** outside, **wait** outside **2** **3** |

**out|sid|er** /aʊtsaɪdər/ (**outsiders**) **1** N-COUNT An **outsider** is someone who does not belong to a particular group or organization. *externo, extraño* ❑ *A lot of the work went to outsiders. Una gran parte del trabajo se dio a gente externa.* **2** N-COUNT An **outsider** is someone who is not accepted by a particular group, or who feels that they do not belong in it. *extraño* ❑ *Malone felt very much an outsider. Malone se sentía como un verdadero extraño.* **3** N-COUNT In a competition, an **outsider** is a competitor who is unlikely to win. *desconocido* ❑ *He was an outsider in the race. Era un desconocido en la carrera.*

**out|skirts** /aʊtskɜrts/ N-PLURAL **The outskirts of** a city or town are the parts of it that are farthest away from its center. *las afueras, los alrededores* ❑ *...the outskirts of New York. ...las afueras de Nueva York.*

**out|spo|ken** /aʊtspoʊkən/ ADJ Someone who is **outspoken** gives their opinions about things openly and honestly, even if they are likely to shock or offend people. *directo, categórico* ❑ *He was outspoken in his support for political change. Fue franco en su apoyo al cambio político.* • **out|spo|ken|ness** N-UNCOUNT *franqueza* ❑ *The company fired her because of her outspokenness. La compañía la despidió porque era muy franca.*

**out|stand|ing** /aʊtstændɪŋ/ **1** ADJ If you describe someone or something as **outstanding,** you think that they are very remarkable and impressive. *destacado, extraordinario* ❑ *Derartu is an outstanding athlete. Derartu es un atleta excepcional.* • **out|stand|ing|ly** ADV *extraordinariamente, excepcionalmente* ❑ *Guatemala is an outstandingly beautiful place. Guatemala es un lugar excepcionalmente bello.* **2** ADJ Money that is **outstanding** has not yet been paid and is still owed to someone. *pendiente* ❑ *The total debt outstanding is $70 billion. El total de la deuda pendiente (de pago) es de 70,000 millones de dólares.* **3** ADJ **Outstanding** issues or problems have not yet been resolved. *pendiente* ❑ *There are still outstanding matters to resolve. Todavía hay asuntos pendientes que resolver.* **4** ADJ **Outstanding** means very important or obvious. *notable* ❑ *...an outstanding example of a small business that became a big one. ...un ejemplo notable de una pequeña empresa que llegó a ser grande.*

**outta** /aʊtə/ **Outta** is used in written English to represent the words "out of" when they are pronounced informally. *fuera de* ❑ *Get outta here! ¡Fuera de aquí!*

**out|ward** /aʊtwərd/

> The form **outwards** can also be used for meaning **3**.

**1** ADJ The **outward** feelings, qualities, or attitudes of someone or something are the ones they appear to have rather than the ones that they actually have. *aparente* ❑ *In spite of my outward calm, I was very scared. A pesar de mi calma aparente, estaba muy asustado.* • **out|ward|ly** ADV *aparentemente, en apariencia* ❑ *He was outwardly friendly and charming. Su apariencia era la de alguien amistoso y encantador.* **2** ADJ The **outward** features of something are the ones that you can see from the outside. *aparente, externo* ❑ *Mark had no outward sign of injury. Mark no tenía señales aparentes de estar herido.* **3** ADV If something moves or faces **outward,** it moves or faces away from the place you are in or the place you are talking about. *hacia afuera, hacia el exterior* ❑ *The top door opened outward. La puerta superior abría hacia afuera.* **4** ADJ An **outward** flight or journey is one that you make away from a place that you are intending to return to later. *de ida*

**out|wards** /aʊtwərdz/ → see **outward**

**oval** /oʊvᵊl/ (**ovals**) ADJ **Oval** things have a shape that is like a circle but is wider in one direction than the other. *ovalado, oval* • **Oval** is also a noun. *óvalo* ❑ *Cut the cheese into ovals. Corte el queso en óvalos.*
→ see **shape**

**Oval Of|fice** N-UNCOUNT **The Oval Office** is the American president's private office in the White House. You can also use **the Oval Office** to refer to the American presidency itself. *el despacho oval*

**oven** /ʌvᵊn/ (**ovens**) N-COUNT An **oven** is a device for cooking that is like a large box with a door. *horno*

**over**
❶ POSITION AND MOVEMENT
❷ AMOUNTS AND OCCURRENCES
❸ OTHER USES

❶ **over** /oʊvər/

In addition to the uses shown below, **over** is used after some verbs, nouns, and adjectives in order to introduce extra information. **Over** is also used in phrasal verbs such as "hand over" and "glaze over."

**1** PREP If one thing is **over** another thing or is moving **over** it, the first thing is directly above the second, either resting on it, or with a space between them. *sobre* ❑ *He looked at himself in the mirror over the table.* *Se miró en el espejo que estaba sobre la mesa.* ● **Over** is also an adverb. *por encima* ❑ *...planes flying over.* *...aviones que vuelan por encima.* **2** PREP If one thing is **over** another thing, it covers part or all of it. *sobre, encima de* ❑ *Pour the sauce over the mushrooms.* *Vierta la salsa sobre los hongos.* ❑ *He was wearing a gray suit over a shirt.* *Vestía traje gris y camisa blanca.* ● **Over** is also an adverb. *encima* ❑ *Heat the milk and pour it over.* *Caliente la leche y viértala encima.* **3** PREP If you lean **over** an object, you bend your body so that the top part of it is above the object. *por encima de* ❑ *They stopped to lean over a gate.* *Se detuvieron para apoyarse en una verja.* ● **Over** is also an adverb. *hacia un lado* ❑ *Sam leaned over, and opened the door of the car.* *Sam se inclinó y abrió la puerta del coche.* **4** PREP If you look **over** or talk **over** an object, you look or talk across the top of it. *por sobre* ❑ *I looked over his shoulder.* *Miré por sobre su hombro.* **5** PREP If a window has a view **over** an area of land or water, you can see the land or water through the window. *sobre, al* ❑ *The restaurant has a wonderful view over the river.* *El restaurante tiene una vista maravillosa al río.* **6** PREP If someone or something goes **over** a barrier, obstacle, or boundary, they get to the other side of it by going across it, or across the top of it. *sobre* ❑ *I stepped over a piece of wood.* *Pasé sobre un pedazo de madera.* ● **Over** is also an adverb. *sobre* ❑ *I climbed over into the back seat of the car.* *Me pasé al asiento trasero del coche.* **7** PREP If something is on the opposite side of a road or river, you can say that it is **over** the road or river. *al otro lado* ❑ *...a fashionable neighborhood, just over the river from Manhattan.* *...un barrio de moda, justo al otro lado del río, frente a Manhattan.* **8** ADV You can use **over** to indicate a particular position or place a short distance away from you. *allá* ❑ *He saw Rolfe standing over by the window.* *Vió a Rolfe de pie, allá, junto a la ventana.* **9** ADV If something rolls **over** or is turned **over**, its position changes so that the part that was facing upward is now facing downward. *al revés* ❑ *His car rolled over on an icy road.* *Su auto se volcó en una carretera cubierta de hielo.* **10** PHRASE **Over here** means near you, or in the country you are in. *acá, aquí* ❑ *Why don't you come over here tomorrow?* *¿Por qué no vienen aquí mañana?* **11** PHRASE **Over there** means in a place a short distance away from you, or in another country. *allí, ahí, allá* ❑ *The café is just over there.* *El café está justo allí.* ❑ *Ray asked me about France. He's going over there for a while.* *Ray me hizo preguntas sobre Francia. Va a ir allá por un tiempo.*
→ see **location**

❷ **over** /oʊvər/ **1** PREP If something is **over** a particular amount, measurement, or age, it is more than that amount, measurement, or age. *más de* ❑ *The disease killed over 4 million people last year.* *La enfermedad mató a más de cuatro millones de personas el año pasado.* ❑ *The house is worth well over $1 million.* *La casa vale mucho más de un millón de dólares.* ● **Over** is also an adverb. *más* ❑ *...people aged 65 and over.* *...la gente de 65 años de edad y más.* **2** PHRASE **Over and above** an amount, especially a normal amount, means more than that amount or in addition to it. *por encima de, en exceso de* ❑ *We grew vegetables in the garden over and above our own needs.* *Cultivábamos verduras en la hortaliza por encima de nuestras necesidades.* **3** ADV If you do something **over,** you do it again or start doing it again from the beginning. *otra vez, de nuevo* ❑ *He wanted a chance to come back and do it over.* *Quería la oportunidad de regresar y hacerlo otra vez.*

❸ **over** /oʊvər/ **1** ADJ If an activity is **over** or **all over,** it is completely finished. *terminado, acabado* ❑ *The war is over.* *La guerra terminó.* ❑ *I am glad it's all over.* *Me alegra que (todo) haya terminado.* **2** PREP If you are **over** an illness or an experience, it has finished and you have recovered from its effects. *del otro lado de* ❑ *I'm glad that you're over the flu.* *Me alegra que te hayas repuesto de la gripa.* **3** PREP If you have control or influence **over** someone or something, you are able to control them or influence them. *sobre* ❑ *He never had any influence over her.* *Él nunca tuvo influencia alguna sobre ella.* **4** PREP You use **over** to indicate what a disagreement or feeling relates to or is caused by. *por* ❑ *Staff are protesting over pay.* *El personal está protestando por la paga.* **5** PREP If something happens **over** a particular period of time or **over** something such as a meal, it happens during that time or during the meal. *a lo largo de, durante* ❑ *The number of attacks has gone down over the past week.* *El número de ataques se redujo a lo largo de la semana pasada.*

**over|all** (**overalls**)

The adjective and adverb are pronounced /oʊvərɔl/. The noun is pronounced /oʊvərɔl/.

**1** ADJ You use **overall** to indicate that you are talking about a situation in general or about the whole of something. *general, global, en conjunto* ❑ *...the overall rise in unemployment.* *...el aumento global del desempleo.* ● **Overall** is also an adverb. *a final de cuentas* ❑ *Overall I was disappointed.* *A final de cuentas me sentía decepcionado.* **2** N-PLURAL **Overalls** are pants that are attached to a piece of cloth which covers your chest and which has straps going over your shoulders. *overol, pantalones de peto, mameluco*

**over|came** /oʊvərkeɪm/ **Overcame** is the past tense of **overcome**. *pasado de* ***overcome***

**over|coat** /oʊvərkoʊt/ (**overcoats**) N-COUNT An **overcoat** is a thick warm coat. *abrigo, sobretodo*

**over|come** /oʊvərkʌm/ (**overcomes, overcoming, overcame**)

O

The form **overcome** is used in the present tense and is also the past participle.

**1** V-T If you **overcome** a problem or a feeling, you successfully deal with it and control it. *superar, vencer* ❑ *Molly finally overcame her fear of flying. Molly superó finalmente su miedo a volar.* **2** V-T If you **are overcome by** a feeling, you feel it very strongly. *abrumar* ❑ *The night before the test I was overcome by fear. La noche anterior al examen me sentí abrumado por el miedo.* **3** V-T If you **are overcome by** smoke or a poisonous gas, you become very ill or die from breathing it in. *vencer* ❑ *People tried to escape from the fire but were overcome by smoke. La gente trató de escapar del fuego, pero el humo los venció.*

**Word Partnership** Usar *overcome* con:

ADJ. **difficult to** overcome, **hard to** overcome **1**
N. overcome **difficulties**, overcome **a fear**, overcome **an obstacle/problem**, overcome **opposition** **1**
overcome **by emotion**, overcome **by fear** **2**

**over|do** /oʊvərdu/ (**overdoes, overdoing, overdid, overdone**) **1** V-T If someone **overdoes** something, they behave in an exaggerated or extreme way. *exagerar* ❑ *Don't overdo the praise. No exageres los elogios.* **2** V-T If you **overdo** an activity, you try to do more than you can physically manage. *excederse* ❑ *It is important not to overdo new exercises. Es importante no excederse con los ejercicios nuevos.* ❑ *It's important to study hard, but don't overdo it. Es importante estudiar con empeño, pero sin excederse.*

O

**over|dose** /oʊvərdoʊs/ (**overdoses, overdosing, overdosed**) **1** N-COUNT If someone takes an **overdose** of a drug, they take more of it than is safe. *sobredosis, dosis excesiva* ❑ *He died of an overdose of sleeping pills. Murió por una sobredosis de somníferos.* **2** V-I If someone **overdoses on** a drug, they take more of it than is safe. *tomar una sobredosis de* ❑ *He overdosed on painkillers. Tomó una sobredosis de analgésicos.*

**over|due** /oʊvərdu/ **1** ADJ If you say that a change or an event is **overdue,** you mean that you think it should have happened before now. *ya era hora* ❑ *This discussion is long overdue. Ya era hora para tener esta discusión.* **2** ADJ **Overdue** sums of money have not been paid, even though it is later than the date on which they should have been paid. *vencido, atrasado* ❑ *...a 2% interest charge on overdue accounts. ...un cargo del dos por ciento de interés en las cuentas vencidas.*

**over easy** also **over-easy** PHRASE If a fried egg is served **over easy,** it is cooked on both sides. *frito de los dos lados*

**over|flow** (**overflows, overflowing, overflowed**)

The verb is pronounced /oʊvərfloʊ/. The noun is pronounced /oʊvərfloʊ/.

**1** V-T/V-I If a liquid or a river **overflows,** it flows over the edges of the container or place it is in. *derramarse, desbordarse* ❑ *The rivers overflowed their banks. Los ríos se desbordaron.* ❑ *The bath overflowed. La tina se desbordó.* **2** V-I If a place or container **is overflowing with** people or things, it is too full of them. *rebosante de, repleto de* ❑ *...a room overflowing with journalists. ...un cuarto repleto de periodistas.*

**over|head**

The adjective is pronounced /oʊvərhɛd/. The adverb is pronounced /oʊvərhɛd/.

ADJ You use **overhead** to indicate that something is above you or above the place that you are talking about. *interior, de arriba* ❑ *She turned on the overhead light. Encendió la luz de arriba., Encendió la luz interior (del coche).* ● **Overhead** is also an adverb. *por encima* ❑ *Planes passed overhead. Pasaron unos aviones.*

**over|lap** (**overlaps, overlapping, overlapped**)

The verb is pronounced /oʊvərlæp/. The noun is pronounced /oʊvərlæp/.

**1** V-RECIP If one thing **overlaps** another, or if you **overlap** them, a part of the first thing covers a part of the other. You can also say that two things **overlap.** *superponer, sobreponer, traslapar* ❑ *When the bag is folded, the bottom overlaps one side. Cuando la bolsa está doblada, el fondo queda superpuesto a un lado.* ❑ *Overlap the tomato slices. Sobreponga las rebanadas de jitomate.* **2** V-RECIP If one idea or activity **overlaps** another, or **overlaps** with another, they involve some of the same subjects, people, or periods of time. *coincidir parcialmente* ❑ *The baseball season overlapped with the Olympics. La temporada de béisbol concidió parcialmente con los juegos olímpicos.* ● **Overlap** is also a noun. *traslape, superposición* ❑ *...the overlap between the policies of the two political parties. ...la superposición de las políticas de los dos partidos.*

**over|look** /oʊvərlʊk/ (**overlooks, overlooking, overlooked**) **1** V-T If a building or window **overlooks** a place, you can see the place clearly from the building or window. *tener vista a* ❑ *The hotel's rooms overlook a beautiful garden. Los cuartos del hotel tienen vista a un hermoso jardín.* **2** V-T If you **overlook** a fact or problem, you do not notice it, or do not realize how important it is. *pasar por alto, descuidar* ❑ *We overlook all sorts of warning signals about our own health. Pasamos por alto toda clase de señales de alerta sobre nuestra propia salud.* **3** V-T If you **overlook** someone's faults or bad behavior, you forgive them and take no action. *pasar por alto* ❑ *They're a close family who overlook each other's faults. Son una familia unida que pasa por alto las faltas de cada uno.*

**over|night** /oʊvərnaɪt/ **1** ADV **Overnight** means throughout the night or at some point during the night. *durante la noche* ❑ *The decision was reached overnight. La decisión se tomó durante la noche.* ● **Overnight** is also an adjective. *nocturno* ❑ *Travel and overnight accommodations are included in the price. El viaje y el hospedaje están incluidos en el precio.* **2** ADV You can say that something happens **overnight** when it happens very quickly and unexpectedly. *de la noche a la mañana* ❑ *The rules are not going to change overnight. Las reglas no van a cambiar de la noche a la mañana.* ● **Overnight** is also an adjective. *de la noche a la mañana* ❑ *He became an overnight success. Logró el éxito de la noche a la mañana.*

**over|pass** /oʊvərpæs/ (**overpasses**) N-COUNT An **overpass** is a structure which carries one road over the top of another one. *paso elevado, paso a desnivel, paso superior*

**over|popu|la|tion** /oʊvərpɒpyəleɪʃən/

N-UNCOUNT If there is a problem of **overpopulation** in an area, there are more people living there than can be supported properly. *sobrepoblación*
→ see **city**

**over|ride** (**overrides, overriding, overrode, overridden**)

The verb is pronounced /oʊvərraɪd/. The noun is pronounced /oʊvərraɪd/.

1 V-T If one thing in a situation **overrides** other things, it is more important than they are. *pasar por encima de* ❑ *A child's needs should always override those of its parents. Las necesidades del niño siempre deben pasar por encima de las de sus padres.* • **over|rid|ing** ADJ *primordial* ❑ *My overriding concern is to raise the standards of education. Mi preocupación primordial es elevar la calidad de la educación.* 2 V-T If someone in authority **overrides** a person or their decisions, they cancel their decisions. *invalidar, anular* ❑ *The senate failed to override his decision. El senado no logró anular su decisión.* 3 N-COUNT An **override** is an attempt to cancel a decision by using your authority over someone or by gaining more votes than they do in an election or contest. *anulación* ❑ *...the override of a decision of the Supreme Court. ...la anulación de una resolución de la Corte Suprema.*

**over|seas** /oʊvərsiz/ 1 ADJ You use **overseas** to describe things that involve or are in foreign countries. *extranjero, exterior* ❑ *...his overseas trip. ...su viaje al extranjero.* • **Overseas** is also an adverb. *en el extranjero* ❑ *He's currently working overseas. En la actualidad está trabajando en el extranjero.* 2 ADJ An **overseas** student or visitor comes from a foreign country. *extranjero* ❑ *Every year nine million overseas visitors come to the city. Cada año vienen a la ciudad nueve millones de turistas extranjeros.*

**over|see** /oʊvərsi/ (**oversees, overseeing, oversaw, overseen**) V-T If someone in authority **oversees** a job or an activity, they make sure that it is done properly. *supervisar* ❑ *As program manager, she oversaw a team of engineers working on a new line of cars. En su calidad de directora, supervisaba a un equipo de ingenieros que trabajaba en una nueva línea de autos.*

**over|take** /oʊvərteɪk/ (**overtakes, overtaking, overtook, overtaken**) V-T If a feeling **overtakes** you, it affects you very strongly. *sobrecoger* [LITERARY] ❑ *A feeling of panic overtook me. Me sobrecogió una sensación de pánico.*

**over|throw** (**overthrows, overthrowing, overthrew, overthrown**)

The verb is pronounced /oʊvərθroʊ/. The noun is pronounced /oʊvərθroʊ/.

V-T When a government or leader **is overthrown**, they are removed from power by force. *derrocar* ❑ *The government was overthrown by the army. El gobierno fue derrocado por el ejército.* • **Overthrow** is also a noun. *derrocamiento, caída* ❑ *...the overthrow of the dictator last April. ...el derrocamiento del dictador el pasado abril.*

**over|turn** /oʊvərtɜrn/ (**overturns, overturning, overturned**) 1 V-T/V-I If something **overturns** or if you **overturn** it, it turns upside down or on its side. *volcar, dar una vuelta de campana* ❑ *The car went out of control and overturned. El carro quedó fuera de control y se volcó.* ❑ *Alex jumped up so quickly that he overturned his glass of water. Alex saltó con tanta rapidez que volcó su vaso de agua.* 2 V-T If someone in authority **overturns** a legal decision, they officially decide that that decision is incorrect or not valid. *anular, invalidar, revocar* ❑ *The courts overturned his decision. Los tribunales invalidaron su decisión.*

**over|weight** /oʊvərweɪt/ ADJ Someone who is **overweight** weighs more than is considered healthy or attractive. *excedido de peso*
→ see **diet**

**over|whelm** /oʊvərwɛlm/ (**overwhelms, overwhelming, overwhelmed**) 1 V-T If you **are overwhelmed by** a feeling or event, it affects you very strongly, and you do not know how to deal with it. *abrumar, anonadar* ❑ *They were overwhelmed by the kindness of the local people. Se sentían anonadados por la amabilidad de la gente del lugar.* • **over|whelmed** ADJ *abrumado, anonadado* ❑ *She felt a little overwhelmed by the crowds. Se sentía un poco abrumada por las muchedumbres.* 2 V-T If a group of people **overwhelm** a place or another group, they gain control over them. *abrumar, arrollar* ❑ *The attack overwhelmed the weakened enemy. El ataque arrolló al debilitado enemigo.*

**over|whelm|ing** /oʊvərwɛlmɪŋ/ 1 ADJ If something is **overwhelming,** it affects you very strongly, and you do not know how to deal with it. *abrumador, inmenso* ❑ *She had an overwhelming feeling of guilt. Tenía un inmenso sentimiento de culpa.* • **over|whelm|ing|ly** ADV *extremadamente* ❑ *The others all seemed overwhelmingly confident. Los demás parecían extremadamente seguros de sí mismos.* 2 ADJ You can use **overwhelming** to emphasize that an amount or quantity is much greater than other amounts or quantities. *abrumador, inmenso* ❑ *The overwhelming majority of small businesses go bankrupt within the first twenty-four months. En su inmensa mayoría, los negocios pequeños quiebran en los primeros veinticuatro meses.* • **over|whelm|ing|ly** ADV *abrumadoramente* ❑ *The people voted overwhelmingly for change. La gente votó abrumadoramente por el cambio.*

**ovule** /ɒvyul, oʊv-/ (**ovules**) N-COUNT An **ovule** is the part of a plant that develops into a seed. *óvulo* [TECHNICAL]

**owe** /oʊ/ (**owes, owing, owed**) 1 V-T If you **owe** money **to** someone, they have lent it to you and you have not yet paid it back. *deber, adeudar* ❑ *The company owes money to more than 60 banks. La empresa debe dinero a más de 60 bancos.* ❑ *Blake owed him nearly $50. Blake le debía casi 50 dólares.* 2 V-T If someone or something **owes** a particular quality or their success **to** a person or thing, they only have it because of that person or thing. *deber* ❑ *I owe him my life. Le debo la vida.* 3 V-T If you say that you **owe** someone gratitude, respect, or loyalty, you mean that they deserve it from you. *deber* ❑ *We owe him respect and gratitude for his work. Le debemos respeto y gratitud por su trabajo.* ❑ *I owe you an apology. Te debo una disculpa.* 4 V-T If you say that you **owe it to** someone to do something, you mean that you should do that thing because they deserve it. *deber, estar obligado* ❑ *I owe it to him to stay. Estoy obligado a quedarme; se lo debo.* 5 PHRASE You use **owing to** when you are introducing the reason for something. debido a ❑ Owing to staff shortages, there was no food on the plane. Debido a la insuficiencia de personal, no había comida en el avión.

**Word Partnership** Usar *owe* con:

N. owe **a debt**, owe **money**, owe **taxes** 1
owe **a great deal to** ***someone*** 3

**owl** /aʊl/ (**owls**) N-COUNT An **owl** is a bird with a flat face, large eyes, and a small sharp beak. *tecolote, lechuza, búho*

**own** /oʊn/ (**owns, owning, owned**) 1 ADJ You use **own** to indicate that something belongs to a particular person or thing. *propio* ❑ *I wanted to have my own business. Quería tener mi propio negocio.* ❑ *He didn't trust his own judgment anymore. Ya no confiaba en su propio juicio.* • **Own** is also a pronoun. *el mío, el tuyo, el suyo, el nuestro* ❑ *The man's face was a few inches from his own. La cara del hombre estaba a unos centímetros de la suya.* 2 ADJ You use **own** to indicate that something is used by, or is characteristic of, only one person, thing, or group. *propio* ❑ *Jennifer wanted her own room. Jennifer quería su propio cuarto.* ❑ *Everyone has their own way of doing things. Cada uno tiene su propia manera de hacer las cosas.* • **Own** is also a pronoun. *propio* ❑ *She has a style that is very much her own. Tiene un estilo que le es muy propio.* 3 ADJ You use **own** to indicate that someone does something without any help from other people. *propio* ❑ *They enjoy making their own decisions. Disfrutan tomando sus propias decisiones.* • **Own** is also a pronoun. *el mío, el tuyo, el suyo, el nuestro* ❑ *There's no career structure; you have to create your own. No hay un plan para la carrera; cada uno tiene que crear el suyo.* 4 V-T If you **own** something, it is your property. *tener, ser dueño de, poseer* ❑ *His father owns a local computer store. Su padre tiene una tienda de computadoras local.* 5 PHRASE If someone or something **comes into** their **own,** they become very successful or start to perform very well because the circumstances are right. *lograr el éxito merecido* ❑ *Many women come into their own as teachers. Muchas mujeres logran como maestras el éxito merecido.* 6 PHRASE When you are **on** your **own,** you are alone. *solo* ❑ *He lives on his own. Vive solo.* ❑ *I felt pretty lonely on my own. Me sentía muy solitario estando solo.* 7 PHRASE If you do something **on** your **own,** you do it without any help from other people. *solo* ❑ *I work best on my own. Trabajo mejor solo.* 8 to **hold** your **own** → see **hold**

▸ **own up** PHR-VERB If you **own up** to something wrong that you have done, you admit that you did it. *reconocer, admitir, confesar* ❑ *The teacher is waiting for someone to own up to breaking the window. El maestro está esperando a que alguien confiese haber roto la ventana.*

O

**own|er** /oʊnər/ (**owners**) N-COUNT If you are the **owner** of something, it belongs to you. *dueño o dueña, propietario o propietaria* ❑ *...the owner of the store. ...la dueña de la tienda.*

**own|er|ship** /oʊnərʃɪp/ N-UNCOUNT **Ownership** of something is the state of owning it. *propiedad* ❑ *...the increase in home ownership. ...el aumento de la propiedad de la vivienda.*

**ox** /ɒks/ (**oxen** /ɒksən/) N-COUNT An **ox** is a bull that has been castrated. *buey*

**ox|ford** /ɑksfərd/ (**oxfords**) also **Oxford** 1 N-PLURAL **Oxfords** are low shoes with laces at the front. *zapato de estilo Oxford (zapato bajo de hombre, enlazado con cordones)* 2 N-UNCOUNT **Oxford** or **oxford cloth** is a type of cotton fabric, used especially for men's shirts. *tela de algodón especial para camisas*

**oxy|gen** /ɒksɪdʒən/ N-UNCOUNT **Oxygen** is a colorless gas in the air which is needed by all plants and animals. *oxígeno*
→ see **air, cardiovascular system, earth, ozone, photosynthesis, respiratory system**

**oys|ter** /ɔɪstər/ (**oysters**) N-COUNT An **oyster** is a large flat shellfish. *ostra, ostión*
→ see **shellfish**

**oz.** **Oz.** is a written abbreviation for **ounce.** *onza* ❑ *...1 oz. of butter. ...1 onza de mantequilla.*

**ozone** /oʊzoʊn/ N-UNCOUNT **Ozone** is a colorless gas which is a form of oxygen. There is a layer of ozone high above the Earth's surface, that protects us from harmful radiation from the sun. *ozono*
→ see Word Web: **ozone**

**ozone-friendly** ADJ **Ozone-friendly** chemicals, products, or technology do not cause harm to the ozone layer. *inocuo para la capa de ozono, que no daña la capa de ozono*

**ozone lay|er** N-SING **The ozone layer** is the part of the Earth's atmosphere that has the most ozone in it and protects living things from the harmful radiation of the sun. *capa de ozono* ❑ *...the hole in the ozone layer. ...el agujero en la capa de ozono.*

**Word Web** ozone

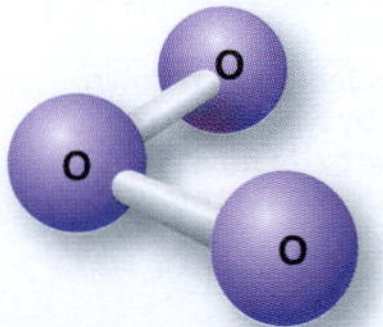


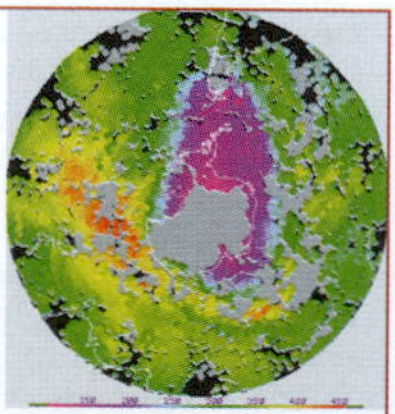

In the Earth's **atmosphere** there are small amounts of **ozone.** Ozone is a molecule that is made up of three **oxygen** atoms. Too much ozone can cause problems. Near the ground, it can be a **pollutant.** Cars and factories produce **carbon monoxide** and **carbon dioxide.** These gases mix with ozone and make **smog.** Too little ozone can also cause problems. The **ozone layer** in the upper **atmosphere** stops harmful **ultraviolet light** from reaching the Earth. Some scientists say a large hole is opening in the ozone layer. This may add to the **greenhouse effect** and **global warming.**

# Pp

**PAC** /pæk/ (**PACs**) N-COUNT A **PAC** is an organization that campaigns for particular political policies, and that gives money to political parties or candidates who support those policies. **PAC** is an abbreviation for **political action committee.** *PAC* ❑ *...$2 million of PAC money.* *...dos millones de dólares del PAC.*

**pace** /peɪs/ (**paces, pacing, paced**) **1** N-SING The **pace** of something is the speed at which it happens or is done. *ritmo* ❑ *Many people were not satisfied with the pace of change.* *Muchas personas no estaban satisfechas con el ritmo del cambio.* **2** N-SING Your **pace** is the speed at which you walk. *paso* ❑ *He moved at a fast pace.* *Avanzaba a paso veloz.* **3** N-COUNT A **pace** is the distance that you move when you take one step. *paso* ❑ *Peter walked a few paces behind me.* *Peter caminaba unos pocos pasos detrás de mí.* **4** V-T/V-I If you **pace** a small area, you keep walking up and down it, because you are anxious or impatient. *pasearse* ❑ *As they waited, Kravis paced the room nervously.* *Mientras esperaban, Kravis se paseaba nerviosamente por la habitación.* ❑ *He found John pacing around the house.* *Se encontró a John paseándose por la casa.* **5** PHRASE To **keep pace with** something that is changing means to change quickly in response to it. *mantenerse al ritmo* ❑ *We need 32,000 new homes a year to keep pace with population growth.* *Necesitamos 32,000 casas nuevas al año para mantenernos al ritmo del crecimiento poblacional.* **6** PHRASE If you do something **at** your **own pace,** you do it at a speed that is comfortable for you. *al ritmo propio* ❑ *The computer will allow students to learn at their own pace.* *La computadora les permitirá a los alumnos aprender a su propio ritmo.*

**Word Partnership** Usar *pace* con:

N. pace **of change** **1**
ADJ. **brisk** pace, **fast** pace, **record** pace, **slow** pace **1** **2**
V. **pick up the** pace, **set a** pace **1** **2**
**keep** pace **with** *something* **5**

**Pa|cif|ic Rim** N-SING *The* **Pacific Rim** is the area including the countries and regions which border the Pacific Ocean. *Cuenca del Pacífico* ❑ *...the growing need for energy in Asia and the Pacific Rim.* *...la creciente necesidad de energía en Asia y la Cuenca del Pacífico.*

**pac|ing** N-UNCOUNT The **pacing** of something such as a play, movie, or novel is the speed at which the story develops. *ritmo*

**pack** /pæk/ (**packs, packing, packed**) **1** V-T/V-I When you **pack** a bag, you put clothes and other things into it, because you are leaving. *empacar* ❑ *When I was 17, I packed my bags and left home.* *Cuando tenía 17 años empaqué mis cosas y me fui de casa.* ❑ *I began to pack for the trip.* *Comencé a empacar para el viaje.* • **pack|ing** N-UNCOUNT *hacer las maletas* ❑ *She left Frances to finish her packing.* *Dejó que Frances acabara de hacer sus maletas.* **2** V-T To **pack** things, for example, in a factory, means to put them into containers or boxes so that they can be shipped and sold. *embalar, envasar* ❑ *They offered me a job packing boxes in a warehouse.* *Me ofrecieron el empleo de embalar cajas en un almacén.* ❑ *Machines pack the olives in jars.* *Unas máquinas envasan las aceitunas en los botes.* **3** V-T/V-I If people or things **pack into** a place or if they **pack** a place, there are so many of them that the place is full. *apiñar(se)* ❑ *Hundreds of people packed into the temple.* *Cientos de personas se apiñaron en el templo.* • **packed** ADJ *abarrotado* ❑ *The place is packed at lunchtime.* *El lugar está abarrotado a la hora de la comida.* ❑ *...a packed meeting.* *...una reunión llena de gente.* **4** N-COUNT A **pack of** things is a collection of them that is sold or given together in a container, box or bag. *paquete* ❑ *...a free information pack with road travel advice.* *...un paquete informativo gratis con sugerencias para el viaje por carretera.* ❑ *...a pack of gum.* *...un paquetito de chicles.* **5** N-COUNT A **pack of** wolves or dogs is a group of them that hunt together. *jauría* ❑ *...a pack of wild dogs.* *...una jauría de perros salvajes.*

pack

**pack|age** /pækɪdʒ/ (**packages, packaging, packaged**) **1** N-COUNT A **package** is something wrapped in paper so that it can be sent to someone by mail. *paquete* ❑ *I tore open the package.* *Abrí el paquete rompiendo el papel.* **2** N-COUNT A **package** is a small bag, box, or envelope in which a quantity of something is sold. *paquete* ❑ *...a package of doughnuts.* *...un paquete de donas.* **3** N-COUNT A **package** is a set of proposals that are made by a government or organization. *paquete* ❑ *Congress passed a package of new rules for the financial markets.* *El Congreso pasó un paquete de nuevas normas para los mercados financieros.* **4** V-T When a product **is packaged,** it is put into containers to be sold. *empacar, envasar* ❑ *The coffee beans are ground and packaged for sale.* *Los granos de café son molidos y envasados para su venta.*
→ see **container**

**Thesaurus** *package* Ver también:

N. batch, bundle, container, pack **2**

**pack|ag|ing** /pækɪdʒɪŋ/ N-UNCOUNT **Packaging** is the container or covering that something is

P

sold in. *envase, empaque, presentación* ❑ *It is selling very well because the packaging is so attractive. Se está vendiendo muy bien porque el envase es muy atractivo.*

**pack|et** /pækɪt/ (**packets**) 1 N-COUNT A **packet** is a set of information about a particular subject that is given to people who are interested in it. *paquete* ❑ *Call us for a free information packet. Llámenos y le enviaremos gratis un paquete informativo.* 2 N-COUNT A **packet** is a small box, bag, or envelope in which a quantity of something is sold. *paquete* ❑ *...a packet of sugar. ...un paquete de azúcar.*
→ see **container**

**pact** /pækt/ (**pacts**) N-COUNT A **pact** is a formal agreement between two or more people, organizations, or governments. *pacto* ❑ *He signed a new pact with Germany. Firmó un nuevo pacto con Alemania.*

**pad** /pæd/ (**pads**) 1 N-COUNT A **pad** is a fairly thick, flat piece of a material such as cloth or rubber. Pads are used, for example, to clean things or for protection. *almohadilla, algodón, fibra* ❑ *He placed a pad of cotton over the spot. Colocó una almohadilla de algodón sobre el grano.* ❑ *...an oven-cleaning pad. ...una fibra para limpiar el horno.* 2 N-COUNT A **pad of** paper is a number of pieces of paper attached together along the top or the side, so that each piece can be torn off when it has been used. *bloc de notas* ❑ *Have a pad ready and write down the information. Tengan listo un bloc de notas para escribir la información.*
→ see **office**

**pad|ded** /pædɪd/ ADJ Something that is **padded** has soft material on it or inside it which makes it less hard, protects it, or changes its shape. *acolchado* ❑ *...a padded jacket. ...una chamarra acolchada.*

**pad|dle** /pædᵊl/ (**paddles**) 1 N-COUNT A **paddle** is a short pole with a wide flat part at one end or at both ends, used to move a small boat through water. *remo* ❑ *We were able to push ourselves across with the paddle. Logramos cruzar a golpe de remo.* 2 N-COUNT A **paddle** is a specially shaped piece of wood that is used for hitting the ball in table tennis. *paleta*
→ see **boat**

P

**pa|gan** /peɪgən/ ADJ **Pagan** beliefs are ones that do not belong to any of the main religions of the world, often ancient beliefs that existed before these religions developed. *pagano* ❑ *...the pagan festival of Yule. ...el festival pagano de Yule.*

**page** /peɪdʒ/ (**pages**) 1 N-COUNT A **page** is one side of one of the pieces of paper in a book, magazine, or newspaper. *página, hoja* ❑ *Turn to page 4. Pasar a la página 4.* ❑ *...the front page of USA Today. ... la portada de USA Today.* 2 N-COUNT The **pages** of a book, magazine, or newspaper are the pieces of paper it consists of. *páginas, hojas* ❑ *He turned the pages of his notebook. Dio vuelta a las hojas de su cuaderno.* 3 N-COUNT A **page** is a young person who takes messages or does small jobs for members of the United States Congress or state legislatures. *mensajero o mensajera*
→ see **printing**

**paid** /peɪd/ 1 **Paid** is the past tense and past participle of **pay**. *pasado y participio pasado de **pay*** 2 ADJ **Paid** means given money in exchange for working for an employer. *a sueldo* ❑ *...a small team of paid staff. ...un pequeño equipo de empleados a sueldo.* ❑ *...two weeks' paid vacation. ...dos semanas de vacaciones pagadas.* ❑ *...a well-paid accountant. ...un contador bien pagado.*

**pail** /peɪl/ (**pails**) N-COUNT A **pail** is a bucket, usually made of metal or wood. *cubeta, cubo, balde*

**pain** /peɪn/ (**pains, pained**) 1 N-VAR **Pain** is a feeling of great discomfort in part of your body, because of illness or an injury. *dolor* ❑ *...a bone disease that caused terrible pain. ...una enfermedad de los huesos que provocaba un dolor terrible.* ❑ *I felt a sharp pain in my lower back. Sentí un dolor agudo en la parte baja de la espalda.* PHRASE ● If you are **in pain**, you feel pain. *sufrir dolor* ❑ *She was obviously in pain. Ella evidentemente estaba sufriendo dolor.* 2 N-UNCOUNT **Pain** is the unhappiness that you feel when something very upsetting happens. *dolor* ❑ *...gray eyes that seemed filled with pain. ...ojos grises que parecían embargados de dolor.* 3 V-T If something **pains** you, it makes you feel upset or unhappy. *doler* ❑ *Sylvia shook her head as if the memory pained her. Sylvia sacudió la cabeza como si el recuerdo le doliera.* ● **pained** ADJ *afligido* ❑ *...a pained look. ...una mirada de reproche.* 4 PHRASE If you call someone or something **a pain** or **a pain in the neck**, you mean that they are very annoying or irritating. *lata* [INFORMAL] ❑ *It was a real pain having to get up at 4 a.m. every morning. Realmente era una lata tener que levantarse todas las mañanas a las 4 am.* 5 PHRASE If you **take pains to** do something, you try hard to do it successfully. *esmerarse* ❑ *He took great pains to see that he did it right. Se esmeró mucho en hacerlo bien.*

**Thesaurus** *pain* Ver también:

| | |
|---|---|
| N. | ache, agony, discomfort 1; anguish, distress, heartache, suffering 2 |
| V. | bother, distress, grieve, hurt, upset, wound 3 |

**pain|ful** /peɪnfəl/ 1 ADJ If a part of your body is **painful**, it hurts. *adolorido* ❑ *Her toe was swollen and painful. Su dedo del pie estaba hinchado y adolorido.* ● **pain|ful|ly** ADV *dolorosamente* ❑ *His tooth started to throb painfully. Empezó a sentir punzadas de dolor en la muela.* 2 ADJ If something such as an illness, injury, or operation is **painful**, it causes you a lot of physical pain. *doloroso* ❑ *...a painful back injury. ...una dolorosa lesión en la espalda.* ● **pain|ful|ly** ADV *dolorosamente* ❑ *He knocked his head painfully against the cupboard. Se lastimó la cabeza contra la alacena.* 3 ADJ Situations, memories, or experiences that are **painful** are difficult and unpleasant to deal with, and often make you feel sad and upset. *doloroso* ❑ *His unkind remarks brought back painful memories. Sus hirientes comentarios le trajeron a la memoria dolorosos recuerdos.*

**Word Partnership** Usar *painful* con:

| | |
|---|---|
| ADV. | **extremely** painful, **less/more** painful, **often** painful, **sometimes** painful, **too** painful, **very** painful 1 – 3 |
| N. | painful **death**, painful **process** 2 3; painful **experience**, painful **feelings**, painful **lesson**, painful **memory** 3 |

**pain|killer** /peɪnkɪlər/ (**painkillers**) N-COUNT A

**painkiller** is a drug that reduces or stops physical pain. *analgésico*

**paint** /peɪnt/ (**paints, painting, painted**) **1** N-VAR **Paint** is a colored liquid that you put onto a surface with a brush in order to protect the surface or to make it look nice, or that you use to produce a picture. *pintura* ❑ *...a can of red paint.* *...un bote de pintura roja.* ❑ *They saw some large letters in white paint.* *Vieron unas letras grandes hechas con pintura blanca.* ❑ *The paint was peeling on the window frames.* *la pintura se estaba levantando en los marcos de las ventanas.* **2** V-T If you **paint** a wall or an object, you cover it with paint. *pintar* ❑ *They started to paint the walls.* *Comenzaron a pintar las paredes.* **3** V-T/V-I If you **paint** something or **paint** a picture of it, you produce a picture of it using paint. *pintar* ❑ *He is painting a huge volcano.* *Está pintando un inmenso volcán.* ❑ *Why do people paint pictures?* *¿Por qué la gente pinta cuadros?* ❑ *I came here to paint.* *Vine aquí a pintar.* **4** → see also **oil paint, painting**
→ see **draw, painting, petroleum**

**Word Partnership** Usar *paint* con:

ADJ. **blue/green/red/white/yellow** paint, **fresh** paint, **peeling** paint **1**
N. **can of** paint, **coat of** paint **1**
paint **a picture**, paint **a portrait** **3**

**paint|brush** /peɪntbrʌʃ/ (**paintbrushes**) N-COUNT A **paintbrush** is a brush that you use for painting. *pincel, brocha*

**Word Link** *er, or ≈ one who does, that which does : author, painter, writer*

**paint|er** /peɪntər/ (**painters**) **1** N-COUNT A **painter** is an artist who paints pictures. *pintor o pintora* ❑ *...the French painter Claude Monet.* *...el pintor francés, Claude Monet.* **2** N-COUNT A **painter** is someone who paints walls, doors, and some other parts of buildings as their job. *pintor o pintora* ❑ *I've worked as a house painter.* *He trabajado como pintor de casas.*

**paint|ing** /peɪntɪŋ/ (**paintings**) **1** N-COUNT A **painting** is a picture that someone has painted. *cuadro* ❑ *...a large painting of Dwight Eisenhower.* *...una gran pintura de Dwight Eisenhower.* **2** N-UNCOUNT **Painting** is the activity of painting pictures or covering surfaces with paint. *pintar* ❑ *She really enjoyed painting and gardening.* *Ella realmente disfrutaba de la pintura y la jardinería.*
→ see Word Web: **painting**
→ see **art**

**pair** /pɛər/ (**pairs**) **1** N-COUNT A **pair of** things are two things of the same size and shape that are used together. *par* ❑ *...a pair of socks.* *...un par de calcetines.* ❑ *...earrings that cost $142.50 a pair.* *...aretes que cuestan 142.50 dólares el par.* **2** N-COUNT Some objects that have two main parts of the same size and shape are referred to as a **pair**, for example, **a pair of pants** or **a pair of scissors.** *par* ❑ *...a pair of faded jeans.* *...unos pantalones de mezclilla desgastados.* **3** N-SING You can refer to two people as a **pair** when they are standing or walking together. *par* ❑ *...a pair of teenage boys in private school uniforms.* *...un par de adolescentes en uniformes de escuela privada.* **4** → see also **au pair**

**Thesaurus** *pair* Ver también:

N. combination, couple, duo, match, two **1** **3**

**pais|ley** /peɪzli/ (**paisleys**) N-VAR **Paisley** is a special pattern of curving shapes and colors, used especially on fabric. *tejido fino de algodón o lana de colores y dibujos vistosos, Paisley* ❑ *He was elegantly dressed in a grey suit, blue shirt, and paisley tie.* *Vestía elegantemente, con un traje gris, una camisa azul y una corbata de Paisley.*
→ see **pattern**

**pa|jam|as** /pədʒɑməz, -dʒæm-/ N-PLURAL A pair of **pajamas** consists of loose pants and a top that people wear to bed. *pijama, piyama* ❑ *I don't want to get out of my pajamas in the morning.* *No quiero quitarme la piyama en las mañanas.*

**pal** /pæl/ (**pals**) N-COUNT Your **pals** are your friends. *cuate* [INFORMAL] ❑ *They talked like old pals.* *Hablaban como viejos cuates.*

**pal|ace** /pælɪs/ (**palaces**) N-COUNT A **palace** is a very large impressive house, especially the official home of a king, queen, or president. *palacio* ❑ *...Buckingham Palace.* *...el palacio de Buckingham.*

**pale** /peɪl/ (**paler, palest**) **1** ADJ Something that is **pale** is not strong or bright in color. *claro, pálido* ❑ *...a pale blue dress.* *...un vestido azul claro.* ❑ *Birds filled the pale sky.* *Los pájaros llenaban el claro cielo.* **2** ADJ If someone looks **pale,** their face looks a lighter color than usual, usually because they are ill, frightened, or shocked. *pálido* ❑ *She looked pale and tired.* *Se veía pálida y cansada.*

**pale|on|tol|ogy** /peɪliəntɒlədʒi/ N-UNCOUNT **Paleontology** is the study of fossils as a guide to the history of life on earth. *paleontología*
• **pale|on|tolo|gist** N-COUNT (**paleontologists**) *paleontólogo o paleontóloga*

P

**Word Web** painting

Oil **painting** uses special tools and techniques. First, artists stretch a piece of **canvas** over a wooden **frame.** Then they cover the surface with a **coat** of white **paint.** When it dries, they put it on an **easel.** Most painters use a **palette knife** on a **palette** to mix **colors** together. They paint the canvas with soft bristle **paintbrushes.** When they are finished, they use turpentine to clean up the brushes and the palette. Three common oil painting styles are the **still life,** the **landscape,** and the **portrait.**

**Paleo|zo|ic era** /peɪliəzoʊɪk ɪərə/ N-SING **The Paleozoic era** is a period in the history of the Earth that began around 550 million years ago and ended around 230 million years ago. *era paleozoica* [TECHNICAL]

**pal|ette knife** /pælɪt naɪf/ (**palette knives**) N-COUNT A **palette knife** is a knife with a broad, flat, flexible blade used in cooking, or in painting to apply oil paint to a canvas or other surface. *espátula, paleta*

**palm** /pɑm/ (**palms**) **1** N-VAR A **palm** or a **palm tree** is a tree that grows in hot countries. It has long leaves at the top, and no branches. *palmera* ❑ *...golden sands and swaying palms. ...la arena dorada y las palmeras meciéndose.* **2** N-COUNT **The palm of** your hand is the inside part of your hand, between your fingers and your wrist. *palma* ❑ *Dornberg slapped the table with the palm of his hand. Dornberg golpeó la mesa con la palma de la mano.*
→ see **desert, hand**

**Word Link** *let ≈ little : booklet, caplet, pamphlet*

**pam|phlet** /pæmflɪt/ (**pamphlets**) N-COUNT A **pamphlet** is a very thin book with a paper cover that gives information about something. *folleto* ❑ *...a pamphlet about parenting. ...un folleto sobre la paternidad.*

**pan** /pæn/ (**pans**) **1** N-COUNT A **pan** is a round metal container with a long handle, that is used for cooking things in, usually on top of a stove. *sartén* ❑ *Heat the butter and oil in a large pan. Calienta la mantequilla y el aceite en un sartén grande.* **2** N-COUNT A **pan** is a shallow metal container used for baking foods. *refractario*
→ see Word Web: **pan**

pancakes

**pan|cake** /pænkeɪk/ (**pancakes**) N-COUNT A **pancake** is a thin, flat, circular piece of cooked batter made from milk, flour, and eggs. Pancakes are usually eaten for breakfast, with butter and syrup. *hotcake*

**pan|da** /pændə/ (**pandas**) N-COUNT A **panda** is a large animal with black and white fur that lives in China. *panda*
→ see **zoo**

**pane** /peɪn/ (**panes**) N-COUNT A **pane** of glass is a flat sheet of glass in a window or door. *hoja* ❑ *I watched my reflection in a pane of glass. Vi mi reflejo en el vidrio de una ventana.*

**pan|el** /pænᵊl/ (**panels**) **1** N-COUNT A **panel** is a small group of people who are chosen to do something, for example, to discuss something in public or to make a decision. *panel* ❑ *He assembled a panel of scholars to advise him. Reunió a un panel de académicos para que lo aconsejaran.* **2** N-COUNT A **panel** is a flat rectangular piece of wood or other material that forms part of a larger object such as a door. *hoja* ❑ *...the glass panel set in the center of the door. ...la hoja de vidrio ubicada en el centro de la puerta.* **3** N-COUNT A control **panel** or instrument **panel** is a board containing switches and controls. *tablero* ❑ *The equipment was monitored from a central control panel. El equipo se monitoreaba desde el tablero de control central.*

**pan|el|ist** /pænəlɪst/ (**panelists**) N-COUNT A **panelist** is a person who is a member of a panel and speaks in public, especially on a radio or television program. *panelista*

**pan|el truck** (**panel trucks**) N-COUNT A **panel truck** is a small van, used especially for delivering goods. *camioneta de reparto*

**Pan|gaea** /pændʒiə/ N-PROPER **Pangaea** is the name given by scientists to the huge landmass that existed on the Earth millions of years ago, before it split into separate continents. *Pangaea* [TECHNICAL]
→ see **continent**

**pan|han|dle** /pænhændᵊl/ (**panhandles, panhandling, panhandled**) **1** N-COUNT A **panhandle** is a narrow strip of land joined to a larger area of land. *delgada franja de tierra* ❑ *...the Texas panhandle. ...la delgada franja de tierra de Texas localizada entre Oklahoma y Nuevo México.* **2** V-I If someone **panhandles,** they stop people in the street and ask them for food or money. *mendigar* [INFORMAL] ❑ *These people support themselves by panhandling. Estas personas se mantienen mendigando.*
• **pan|han|dler** N-COUNT (**panhandlers**) *mendigo o mendiga* [INFORMAL] ❑ *You can't walk downtown without a panhandler asking you for money. No puedes caminar por el centro sin que un mendigo llegue a pedirte dinero.*

**pan|ic** /pænɪk/ (**panics, panicking, panicked**) **1** N-VAR **Panic** is a strong feeling of anxiety or fear that makes you act without thinking carefully. *pánico* ❑ *An earthquake caused panic among the population. Un terremoto provocó pánico en la población.* ❑ *I'm in a panic about getting everything done in time. Me da pánico no tener todo listo a tiempo.* **2** V-T/V-I If you **panic** or if someone **panics** you, you suddenly feel anxious or afraid, and act without thinking carefully. *entrar en pánico* ❑ *Guests panicked and*

**Word Web** **pan**

No **saucepan** or **frying pan** is perfect. **Copper pans** conduct heat well. This makes them good for cooking on the stove. However, copper also reacts with the acid in some foods. For this reason, the best pans have a thin layer of **tin** covering the copper. **Cast iron** pans are very heavy and **heat up** slowly. But they stay hot for a long time. Some people like **stainless steel** pans because they heat up quickly and don't react with chemicals in food. However, the bottom of a stainless pan may not heat up evenly.

P

**Word Web** paper

Around 3000 BC, Egyptians began to make **paper** from the papyrus plant. They cut the stems of the plant into thin slices and pressed them into **sheets**. A very different Chinese technique developed about the same time. It was more like today's paper-making process. Chinese paper makers cooked **fiber** made of tree bark. Then they pressed it into molds and let it dry. Around 200 BC, a third paper-making process began in the Middle East. Craftsmen started using animal skins to make parchment. Today, paper manufacturing destroys millions of trees every year. This has led to **recycling** programs and paperless offices.

*screamed when the bomb exploded.* *Los invitados entraron en pánico y gritaron cuando explotó la bomba.* ❑ *The sudden memory panicked her.* *El recuerdo repentino le dio pánico.*

**Thesaurus** *panic* Ver también:

N. agitation, alarm, dread, fear, fright; (*ant.*) calm 1
V. alarm, fear, terrify, unnerve; (*ant.*) relax 2

**panties** /pæntiz/ N-PLURAL **Panties** are short, close-fitting underpants worn by women or girls. *calzones*

**pan|to|mime** /pæntəmaɪm/ (**pantomimes**) N-COUNT A **pantomime** is a performance involving acting without words through facial expression, gesture, and movement. *pantomima*

**pants** /pænts/ N-PLURAL **Pants** are a piece of clothing that covers the lower part of your body and each leg. *pantalones* ❑ *He wore brown corduroy pants and a white cotton shirt.* *Vestía unos pantalones cafés de pana y y una camiseta blanca de algodón.*
→ see **clothing**

**pant|suit** /pæntsut/ (**pantsuits**) also **pants suit** N-COUNT A **pantsuit** is women's clothing consisting of a pair of pants and a jacket which are made from the same material. *traje sastre* ❑ *She wore a red pantsuit that fit very well.* *Ella llevaba puesto un traje sastre rojo que le quedaba muy bien.*

**pan|ty|hose** /pæntihoʊz/ also **panty hose** N-PLURAL **Pantyhose** are a piece of thin nylon clothing worn by women, that cover the body from the waist downward and cover each leg separately. *medias*

**pa|pa|raz|zi** /pɑpərɑtsi/ N-PLURAL **The paparazzi** are photographers who follow famous people around, hoping to take interesting or shocking photographs of them. *paparazzi* ❑ *The paparazzi pursue Armani wherever he goes.* *Los paparazzi persiguen a Armani adondequiera que va.*

**pa|per** /peɪpər/ (**papers, papering, papered**) 1 N-UNCOUNT **Paper** is a material that you write on or wrap things with. *papel* ❑ *He wrote his name down on a piece of paper.* *Escribió su nombre en un pedazo de papel.* ❑ *...a paper bag.* *...una bolsa de papel.* 2 N-COUNT A **paper** is a newspaper. *periódico* ❑ *I might get a paper in the town.* *Quizá consiga un periódico en el pueblo.* 3 N-PLURAL **Papers** are sheets of paper with information on them. *documentos* ❑ *...papers including letters and legal documents.* *...papeles, entre ellos cartas y documentos legales.* 4 N-PLURAL Your **papers** are your official documents, such as your passport or identity card. *identificación* ❑ *The young man refused to show his papers to the police.* *El joven se negó a mostrarle su identificación a la policía.* 5 N-COUNT A **paper** is a long piece of writing on an academic subject. *artículo, ponencia* ❑ *He just published a paper in the journal "Nature."* *Acaba de publicar un artículo en la revista "Nature"* ❑ *...the ten errors that appear most frequently in student papers.* *...los diez errores que aparecen con más frecuencia en los trabajos de los estudiantes.* 6 N-COUNT A **paper** prepared by a government or a committee is a report on a question they have been considering or a set of proposals for changes in the law. *informe, propuesta* ❑ *...a new government paper on education.* *...una nueva propuesta educativa del gobierno.* 7 V-T If you **paper** a wall, you put wallpaper on it. *empapelar, tapizar* ❑ *We papered all four bedrooms.* *Empapelamos las cuatro recámaras.*
→ see Word Web: **paper**

**Word Partnership** Usar *paper* con:

ADJ. **blank** paper, **brown** paper, **colored** paper, **recycled** paper 1
**daily** paper 2
V. **fold** paper 1
**read the** paper 2
**present a** paper, **publish a** paper 5
**draft a** paper, **write a** paper 5 6
N. **morning** paper 2
**research** paper 5 6

**paper|back** /peɪpərbæk/ (**paperbacks**) N-COUNT A **paperback** is a book with a thin cardboard or paper cover. *edición de tapa blanda, edición en rústica* ❑ *She will buy the book when it comes out in paperback.* *Comprará el libro cuando salga en una edición de tapa blanda.*

**pa|per clip** (**paper clips**) also **paper-clip** or **paperclip** N-COUNT A **paper clip** is a small piece of bent wire that is used to hold papers together. *clip, sujetapapeles*
→ see **office**

**pa|per route** (**paper routes**) N-COUNT A **paper route** is the job of delivering newspapers to particular houses, often done by children. *reparto de periódicos*

**pa|per trail** N-SING Documents which provide evidence of someone's activities can be referred to as a **paper trail**. *expediente* ❑ *We are not certain of the amounts lost, as there is no paper trail.* *No estamos seguros de cuánto se perdió, puesto que no hay un expediente.*

**paper|work** /peɪpərwɜrk/ N-UNCOUNT **Paperwork** is the routine part of a job that involves dealing with letters, reports, and records. *papeleo burocrático* ❑ *There will be paperwork—forms to fill in, letters to write. Va a haber que llenar formas burocráticas y escribir cartas.*

**par** /pɑr/ **1** PHRASE If you say that two people or things are **on a par with** each other, you mean that they are equally good or bad, or equally important. *del mismo nivel* ❑ *The coffee was on a par with the one he had in Paris. El café estuvo igual de bueno que el que probó en París.* **2** PHRASE If you say that someone or something is **below par,** they are below the standard you expected. *no estar a la altura* ❑ *Duffy's guitar playing is well below par. Duffy toca la guitarra muy por debajo del estándar esperado.*

**para|chute** /pærəʃut/ (**parachutes, parachuting, parachuted**) **1** N-COUNT A **parachute** is a device that enables a person to jump from an aircraft and float safely to the ground. It consists of a large piece of thin cloth attached to your body by strings. *paracaídas* ❑ *They fell 41,000 feet before opening their parachutes. Descendieron 12,500 metros antes de abrir sus paracaídas.* **2** V-T/V-I If a person **parachutes** or someone **parachutes** them somewhere, they jump from an aircraft using a parachute. *lanzarse en paracaídas* ❑ *He parachuted into Warsaw. Se lanzó en paracaídas sobre Varsovia.*

parachute

→ see **fly**

**pa|rade** /pəreɪd/ (**parades, parading, paraded**) **1** N-COUNT A **parade** is a line of people or vehicles moving through a public place in order to celebrate an important day or event. *desfile* ❑ *A military parade marched down Pennsylvania Avenue. Un desfile militar marchó por la Pennsylvania Avenue.* **2** V-I When people **parade** somewhere, they walk together in a formal group or a line, usually with other people watching them. *desfilar* ❑ *Soldiers paraded down the Champs Élysées. Los soldados desfilaron por Champs Élysées.* **3** N-VAR **Parade** is a formal occasion when soldiers stand in lines to be seen by an officer or important person, or march in a group. *formación* ❑ *They were already on parade at six o'clock in the morning. Ya estaban formados a las seis de la mañana.* **4** V-T If someone **parades** a person or thing, they show them in public, often in order to impress people or gain some advantage. *exhibir* ❑ *She refused to parade her problems on TV. Se negó a exhibir sus problemas en la TV.* ❑ *Captured prisoners were paraded before television cameras. Los prisioneros capturados fueron exhibidos ante las cámaras de televisión.*

parade

**para|dise** /pærədaɪs/ (**paradises**) **1** N-PROPER According to some religions, **paradise** is a wonderful place where people go after they die, if they have led good lives. *paraíso* ❑ *The Koran describes paradise as a garden of delight. El Corán describe al paraíso como un jardín de delicias.* **2** N-VAR You can refer to a place or situation that seems beautiful or perfect as **paradise** or **a paradise.** *paraíso* ❑ *Bali is one of the world's natural paradises. Bali es uno de los paraísos naturales del mundo.*

**para|graph** /pærəgræf/ (**paragraphs**) N-COUNT A **paragraph** is a section of a piece of writing. A paragraph always begins on a new line and contains at least one sentence. *párrafo* ❑ *His story was only one paragraph long. Su cuento era de un solo párrafo.*

**Word Link** *para ≈ beside : paralegal, parallel, paraphrase*

**para|le|gal** /pærəligᵊl/ (**paralegals**) N-COUNT A **paralegal** is someone who helps lawyers with their work but is not completely qualified as a lawyer. *asistente de abogado*

**par|al|lax** /pærəlæks/ (**parallaxes**) N-VAR **Parallax** is when an object appears to change its position because the person or instrument observing it has changed their position. *paralaje* [TECHNICAL]

**par|al|lel** /pærəlɛl/ (**parallels, paralleling, paralleled**) **1** N-COUNT If something has a **parallel,** it is similar to something else in some way. *paralelismo* ❑ *It is impossible to draw parallels between the UK and New Zealand, a country with a population of four million. Es imposible establecer paralelismos entre el Reino Unido y Nueva Zelanda, un país con cuatro millones de habitantes.* ❑ *It's a disaster with no parallel anywhere else in the world. Es un desastre sin parangón en ninguna otra parte del mundo.* **2** V-T If one thing **parallels** another, they happen at the same time or are similar, and often seem to be connected. *asemejarse* ❑ *His remarks paralleled those of the president. Sus comentarios se asemejaban a los del presidente.* **3** ADJ **Parallel** events or situations happen at the same time, or are similar to one another. *paralelo* ❑ *...parallel talks between the two countries' foreign ministers. ...conversaciones paralelas entre los cancilleres de los dos países.* **4** ADJ If two lines, two objects, or two lines of movement are **parallel,** they are the same distance apart along their whole length. *paralelo* ❑ *...seventy-two ships, drawn up in two parallel lines. ...setenta y dos barcos formados en dos líneas paralelas.* ❑ *Remsen Street is parallel with Montague Street. Remsen Street corre paralela a Montague Street.*

**par|al|lel cir|cuit** (**parallel circuits**) N-COUNT A **parallel circuit** is an electrical circuit in which the current travels along more than one path so that it can power several devices at the same time. *circuito en paralelo* [TECHNICAL]

**par|al|lel|ism** /pærəlɛlɪzəm/ N-UNCOUNT **Parallelism** is the use of similar grammatical structures within a piece of writing so that ideas which are closely related are expressed in a similar way. The phrase "government of the people, by the people, for the people" is an example of parallelism. *paralelismo sintáctico* [TECHNICAL]

**para|lyze** /pærəlaɪz/ (**paralyzes, paralyzing,**

**paralyzed)** **1** V-T If someone **is paralyzed** by an accident or an illness, they have no feeling in their body, or in part of their body, and are unable to move. *paralizar* ❑ *She is paralyzed from the waist down. Sufre parálisis de la cintura a los pies.* • **para|lyzed** ADJ ❑ *...a guy with paralyzed legs. ...un hombre con parálisis en las piernas.* **2** V-T If a person, place, or organization **is paralyzed by** something, they become unable to act or function properly. *paralizar* ❑ *She was paralyzed by fear. Estaba paralizada por el miedo.*

**para|mecium** /pærəmiʃiəm, -si-/ (**paramecia**) N-COUNT **Paramecia** are a type of protozoa that are found in fresh water. *paramecio*

| Word Link | *para ≈ beside : paralegal, parallel, paraphrase* |
|---|---|

**para|phrase** /pærəfreɪz/ (**paraphrases, paraphrasing, paraphrased**) **1** V-T If you **paraphrase** someone or **paraphrase** something that they have said or written, you express what they have said or written in a different way. *parafrasear* ❑ *To paraphrase Oscar Wilde, acting is so much more real than life. Parafraseando a Oscar Wilde, la actuación es mucho más real que la vida.* ❑ *...a paraphrased edition of the Bible. ...una edición parafraseada de la Biblia.* **2** N-COUNT A **paraphrase** of something written or spoken is the same thing expressed in a different way. *paráfrasis* ❑ *The last two sentences were an exact quote rather than a paraphrase. Las dos últimas oraciones eran una cita exacta en vez de una paráfrasis.*

**para|site** /pærəsaɪt/ (**parasites**) **1** N-COUNT A **parasite** is a small animal or plant that lives on or inside a larger animal or plant, and gets its food from it. *parásito* ❑ *Very small parasites live in the stomach of some insects. Parásitos muy pequeños viven en el estómago de algunos insectos.* • **para|sit|ic** /pærəsɪtɪk/ ADJ *parásito* ❑ *...tiny parasitic insects. ...diminutos insectos parásitos.* **2** N-COUNT If you call someone a **parasite,** you disapprove of them because you think that they get money or other things from people but do not do anything in return. *parásito o parásita* ❑ *He was a parasite, who produced nothing, but lived on the work of others. Era un parásito que no producía nada sino que vivía del trabajo de los demás.*

**para|sit|ism** /pærəsaɪtɪzəm/ N-UNCOUNT In biology, **parasitism** is the state of being a parasite. *parasitismo*

**par|cel** /pɑrsᵊl/ (**parcels**) **1** N-COUNT A **parcel** is something wrapped in paper, usually so that it can be sent by mail. *paquete* ❑ *They sent parcels of food and clothing. Enviaron paquetes de comida y ropa.* **2** PHRASE If you say that something is **part and parcel of** something else, you are emphasizing that it is involved or included in it. *parte de* ❑ *Learning about a new culture is part and parcel of going to live abroad. Aprender sobre una nueva cultura forma parte de la experiencia de ir a vivir al extranjero.*

**par|cel post** N-UNCOUNT **Parcel post** is a mail service for the delivery of packages. *paquete postal* ❑ *It is much quicker than sending them by parcel post. Esto es mucho más rápido que si los envías por paquete postal.*

| Word Link | *don ≈ giving : donate, donor, pardon* |
|---|---|

**par|don** /pɑrdᵊn/ (**pardons, pardoning, pardoned**) **1** CONVENTION You say "**Pardon?,**" "**I beg your pardon?,**" or "**Pardon me?**" when you want someone to repeat what they have just said, either because you have not heard or understood it or because you are surprised by it. *¿Perdón?* [SPOKEN] ❑ *"Will you let me open it?" — "Pardon?" — "Can I open it?" —¿Me permite abrirlo?—¿Perdón?—¿Puedo abrirlo?* **2** CONVENTION You say "**I beg your pardon**" as a way of apologizing for accidentally doing something wrong, such as disturbing someone or making a mistake. *Disculpe* [SPOKEN] ❑ *I beg your pardon. I thought you were someone else. Disculpe. Lo confundí con otra persona.* **3** V-T If someone who has been found guilty of a crime **is pardoned,** they are officially allowed to go free and are not punished. *indultar* ❑ *Hundreds of political prisoners were pardoned and released. Cientos de prisioneros políticos fueron indultados y liberados.* • **Pardon** is also a noun. *indulto* ❑ *He received a pardon from the president. Recibió el indulto del presidente.*

**par|ent** /pɛərənt, pær-/ (**parents**) **1** N-COUNT Your **parents** are your mother and father. *padre, madre* ❑ *Children need their parents. Los niños necesitan a sus padres.* **2** → see also **single parent** • **pa|ren|tal** /pərɛntᵊl/ ADJ *de los padres* ❑ *Children must have parental permission to attend the party. Los niños deben tener el permiso de los padres para asistir a la fiesta.*
→ see **child**

**par|ent cell** (**parent cells**) N-COUNT A **parent cell** is a cell in an organism which divides to produce other cells. Compare **daughter cell**. *célula madre* [TECHNICAL]

**par|ent|hood** /pɛərənthʊd, pær-/ N-UNCOUNT **Parenthood** is the state of being a parent. *paternidad* ❑ *...the responsibilities of parenthood. ...las responsabilidades de la paternidad.*

**par|ish** /pærɪʃ/ (**parishes**) **1** N-COUNT A **parish** is part of a city or town that has its own church and priest. *parroquia* **2** N-COUNT In some parts of the United States, a **parish** is a small region within a state which has its own local government. *condado*

**park** /pɑrk/ (**parks, parking, parked**) **1** N-COUNT A **park** is a public area of land with grass and trees, usually in a town, where people go in order to relax and enjoy themselves. *parque* ❑ *...Central Park. ...Central Park.* ❑ *...a walk with the dog around the park. ...un paseo por el parque con el perro.* **2** N-COUNT A **park** is a place where baseball is played. *campo* ❑ *Jack hit the ball out of the park. Jack sacó la pelota del campo.* **3** V-T/V-I When you **park** a vehicle or **park** somewhere, you drive the vehicle into a position where it can stay for a period of time and you leave it. *estacionar(se)* ❑ *They parked in the street outside the house. Se estacionaron en la calle, frente a la casa.* ❑ *He found a place to park the car. Encontró un lugar donde estacionar el carro.* • **parked** ADJ *estacionado* ❑ *We're parked over there. Estamos estacionados allí.* • **parking** N-UNCOUNT *estacionarse* ❑ *Parking is allowed only on one side of the street. Sólo está permitido estacionarse de un lado de la calle.* **4** → see also **national park**
→ see Word Web: **park**

**Word Web** park

Central Park* was the first planned urban **park** in the United States. When it opened in 1858 only a few wealthy families lived close enough to enjoy it. Today more than 20 million visitors use the park for **recreation** each year. Children enjoy the **playgrounds**, the carousel, and the petting **zoo**. Families have **picnics** on the grass. Couples rent rowboats and row around the lake. Seniors **stroll** through the **gardens**. Players use the **tennis courts** and **baseball diamonds** all summer. **Cyclists** and **runners** use Central Park Drive* on weekends when it is closed to car traffic.

*Central Park: an 843-acre park in New York City.*
*Central Park Drive: a road in Central Park.*

**park|ing gar|age** (**parking garages**) N-COUNT A **parking garage** is a building where people can leave their cars. *estacionamiento*

**park|ing lot** (**parking lots**) N-COUNT A **parking lot** is an area of ground where people can leave their cars. *estacionamiento* ❑ *I found a parking lot one block up the street. Encontré un estacionamiento a una cuadra.*

**park|way** /pɑrkweɪ/ (**parkways**) N-COUNT A **parkway** is a wide road with trees and grass on both sides. *avenida*

**par|lia|ment** /pɑrləmənt/ (**parliaments**) also **Parliament** 1 N-COUNT; N-PROPER The **parliament** of some countries is the group of people who make or change its laws. *parlamento* ❑ *The Bangladesh Parliament today approved the policy. El día de hoy el Parlamento de Bangladesh aprobó el proyecto.* 2 → see also **Member of Parliament**

**par|lia|men|ta|ry** /pɑrləmɛntəri/ ADJ **Parliamentary** is used to describe things that are connected with a parliament. *parlamentario* ❑ *...a parliamentary debate. un debate parlamentario.*

**pa|ro|chial school** (**parochial schools**) N-COUNT A **parochial school** is a private school that is funded and controlled by a particular branch of the Christian church. *escuela religiosa*

**par|rot** /pærət/ (**parrots, parroting, parroted**) 1 N-COUNT A **parrot** is a tropical bird with a curved beak and brightly-colored or gray feathers. Parrots can be kept as pets. *perico* 2 V-T If you **parrot** what someone else says, you repeat it without really understanding what it means. *repetir como perico* ❑ *Students have learned to parrot the standard answers. Los estudiantes han aprendido a repetir como perico las respuestas válidas.*

**pars|ley** /pɑrsli/ N-UNCOUNT **Parsley** is a small plant whose leaves are used for flavoring or decorating food. *perejil*

P

**part**
❶ NOUN USES AND PHRASES
❷ VERB USES

**Word Link** *par ≈ equal : compare, part, partner*

❶ **part** /pɑrt/ (**parts**)
→ Please look at category 11 to see if the expression you are looking for is shown under another headword. 1 N-VAR **Part of** something or a **part of** it is one of the pieces, sections, or elements that it consists of. *parte* ❑ *I like that part of Cape Town. Me gusta esta parte de Ciudad del Cabo.* ❑ *Perry spent part of his childhood in Canada. Perry pasó parte de su infancia en Canadá.* 2 N-COUNT A **part** for a machine or vehicle is one of the smaller pieces that is used to make it. *pieza* ❑ *...spare parts for military equipment. ...refacciones para equipo militar.* 3 N-COUNT A **part** in a play or movie is one of the roles in it which an actor or actress can perform. *papel* ❑ *Alf offered her a part in the play he was directing. Alf le ofreció un papel en la película que estaba dirigiendo.* 4 N-SING Your **part in** something that happens is your involvement in it. *participación* ❑ *He tried to conceal his part in the accident. Trató de ocultar su participación en el accidente.* 5 N-COUNT A **part** in your hair is a line running from the front to the back of your head where your hair lies in different directions. *raya* 6 PHRASE If something or someone **plays** a large or important **part in** an event or situation, they are very involved in it and have an important effect on what happens. *jugar un papel* ❑ *Work plays an important part in our lives. El trabajo juega un papel importante en nuestras vidas.* 7 PHRASE If you **take part in** an activity, you do it together with other people. *tomar parte, participar* ❑ *Thousands of students have taken part in demonstrations. Miles de estudiantes participaron en las demostraciones.* 8 PHRASE You can say, for example, that **for** your **part** you thought or did something, to introduce what you thought or did. *por mi/su/tu, etc parte* [FORMAL] ❑ *For my part, I feel close to tears. Por mi parte, estoy al borde de las lágrimas.* 9 PHRASE If you

talk about a feeling or action **on** your **part,** you are referring to something that you feel or do. *de mi/tu/su, etc parte* ❑ *There is no need for any further instructions on my part. No hay necesidad de más instrucciones de mi parte.* **10** PHRASE You use **in part** to indicate that something exists or happens to some extent but not completely. *en parte* [FORMAL] ❑ *They're getting more visitors than before, thanks in part to the weather. Están recibiendo más visitantes que antes, en parte debido al clima.* **11** **part and parcel** → see **parcel**

| Thesaurus | *part* | Ver también: |
|---|---|---|
| N. | component, fraction, half, ingredient, piece, portion, section; (*ant.*) entirety, whole ❶ **1** | |
| | role, share ❶ **4** | |
| V. | break up, separate, split ❷ **3** | |

❷ **part** /pɑrt/ (**parts, parting, parted**) **1** V-T/V-I If things that are next to each other **part** or if you **part** them, they move away from each other. *separar, abrir* ❑ *Her lips parted in a smile. Sus labios se abrieron en una sonrisa.* ❑ *Livy parted the curtains. Livy abrió las cortinas.* **2** V-T If you **part** your hair, you comb it in two different directions so that there is a straight line from the front of your head to the back. *hacer la raya* ❑ *Picking up a brush, Joanna parted her hair. Joanna tomó un cepillo y se hizo la raya en el pelo.* **3** V-RECIP When two people **part,** or if one person **parts from** another, they leave each other. *separarse* [FORMAL] ❑ *He gave me the envelope and we parted. Me entregó el sobre y nos separamos.* • **part|ing** N-VAR (**partings**) *separación* ❑ *After her parting with Jackson, she lived in France. Después de su separación con Jackson, vivió en Francia.*

▸ **part with** PHR-VERB If you **part with** something that is valuable or that you would prefer to keep, you give it or sell it to someone else. *dejar ir* ❑ *Think carefully before parting with money. Piénsalo cuidadosamente antes de dejar ir el dinero.*

**par|tial** /pɑrʃᵊl/ **1** ADJ You use **partial** to refer to something that is not complete or whole. *parcial* ❑ *Partial agreement was all they could manage. Un acuerdo parcial fue todo lo que pudieron lograr.* ❑ *The plant enjoys partial shade. La planta está bien con un poco de sombra.* • **par|tial|ly** ADV *parcialmente* ❑ *Lisa is partially blind. Lisa es parcialmente ciega.* **2** ADJ If you are **partial to** something, you like it. *inclinarse por, tener debilidad por* ❑ *Mollie is partial to pink. Mollie tiene debilidad por el rosa.*

**par|tial eclipse** (**partial eclipses**) N-COUNT A **partial eclipse of** the sun is an occasion when the moon is between the earth and the sun, so that for a short time you cannot see part of the sun. A **partial eclipse of** the moon is an occasion when the earth is between the sun and the moon, so that for a short time you cannot see part of the moon. Compare **total eclipse.** *eclipse parcial*

**par|tici|pant** /pɑrtɪsɪpənt/ (**participants**) N-COUNT The **participants** in an activity are the people who take part in it. *participante* ❑ *40 of the course participants were offered employment. Se les ofreció empleo a 40 participantes del curso.*

**par|tici|pate** /pɑrtɪsɪpeɪt/ (**participates, participating, participated**) V-I If you **participate in** an activity, you take part in it. *participar* ❑ *Most sufferers can drive a car, participate in sports, etc. La mayoría de los que sufren la enfermedad pueden conducir un carro, realizar actividades deportivas, etc.* • **par|tici|pa|tion** /pɑrtɪsɪpeɪʃᵊn/ N-UNCOUNT *participación* ❑ *...participation in religious activities. ...participación en actividades religiosas.*

**par|ti|ci|ple** /pɑrtɪsɪpᵊl/ (**participles**) N-COUNT In grammar, a **participle** is a form of a verb that can be used in compound tenses of the verb. English verbs have a past participle, which usually ends in "-ed," and a present participle, which ends in "-ing." *participio*

| Word Link | ***cle ≈ small : article, follicle, particle*** |
|---|---|

**par|ti|cle** /pɑrtɪkᵊl/ (**particles**) N-COUNT A **particle of** something is a very small piece or amount of it. *partícula* ❑ *...a particle of hot metal. ...una partícula de metal caliente.* ❑ *There is a particle of truth in his statement. Hay una pizca de verdad en su afirmación.*
→ see **lightning**

**par|ticu|lar** /pərtɪkyələr/ **1** ADJ You use **particular** to emphasize that you are talking about one thing or one kind of thing rather than other similar ones. *específico, concreto, en particular* ❑ *Where and when did you hear that particular story? ¿Dónde y cuándo escuchaste esa historia en particular?* ❑ *I have to know exactly why I'm doing a particular job. Necesito saber exactamente por qué estoy haciendo un trabajo concreto.* **2** ADJ If a person or thing has a **particular** quality or possession, it is distinct and belongs only to them. *especial, particular* ❑ *I have a particular responsibility to make the right decision. Tengo una responsabilidad particular para tomar la decisión correcta.* **3** ADJ You can use **particular** to emphasize that something is greater or more intense than usual. *particular* ❑ *Particular emphasis will be placed on language training. Se pondrá un énfasis particular en la enseñanza de la lengua.* **4** ADJ Someone who is **particular** chooses and does things very carefully, and is not easily satisfied. *especial* ❑ *Ted was very particular about the colors he wore. Ted era muy especial con los colores que vestía.* **5** → see also **particulars** **6** PHRASE You use **in particular** to indicate that what you are saying applies especially to one thing or person. *en particular* ❑ *Why should he notice her car in particular? ¿Por qué tenía que notar el carro de ella en particular?*

**par|ticu|lar|ly** /pərtɪkyələrli/ ADV You use **particularly** to indicate that what you are saying applies especially to one thing or situation. *particularmente* ❑ *Keep your office space looking good, particularly your desk. Cuida la apariencia de tu oficina, particularmente la de tu escritorio.* ❑ *I particularly liked the wooden chairs. Me gustaron particularmente las sillas de madera.*

**par|ticu|lars** /pərtɪkyələrz/ N-PLURAL The **particulars** of something or someone are facts or details about them that are kept as a record. *detalles, pormenores* ❑ *You will find all the particulars in Chapter 9. Encontrarán todos los pormenores del tema en el capítulo 9.*

**par|ti|san** /pɑrtɪzən/ (**partisans**) ADJ Someone who is **partisan** strongly supports a particular person or cause, often without thinking carefully about the matter. *partidario* ❑ *It was an extremely*

P

*partisan crowd, and they were very enthusiastic.* *Era una multitud extremadamente fanática y estaba muy entusiasmada.*

**part|ly** /pɑ̲rtli/ ADV You use **partly** to indicate that something happens or exists to some extent, but not completely. *en parte* ❑ *It's partly my fault.* *En parte es mi culpa.* ❑ *I have not worried so much this year, partly because I have had other things to think about.* *No me he preocupado tanto este año, en parte porque he tenido otras cosas en qué pensar.*

| Word Link | par ≈ equal : compare, part, partner |
|---|---|

**part|ner** /pɑ̲rtnər/ (**partners, partnering, partnered**) **1** N-COUNT Your **partner** is the person you are married to or are having a long-term sexual relationship with. *pareja* ❑ *Wanting other friends doesn't mean you don't love your partner.* *Que quieras tener otros amigos no significa que no ames a tu pareja.* **2** N-COUNT Your **partner** in an activity such as a game or dance is the person you are playing or dancing with. *pareja* ❑ *Her partner for the doubles game was Venus Williams.* *Su pareja para el juego de dobles fue Venus Williams.* **3** N-COUNT The **partners** in a firm or business are the people who share the ownership of it. *socio o socia* [BUSINESS] ❑ *He's a partner in a Chicago law firm.* *Es socio en un bufete de abogados de Chicago.* **4** N-COUNT The **partner** of a country or organization is another country or organization with which they work or do business. *socio* ❑ *Spain has been one of Cuba's major trading partners.* *España ha sido uno de los mayores socios comerciales de Cuba.* **5** V-T If you **partner** someone, you are their partner in a game or in a dance. *ser pareja de* ❑ *He partnered a Russian ballerina.* *Él fue la pareja de baile de una bailarina rusa.*

**part|ner and group skills** N-PLURAL **Partner and group skills** are skills that require people to work together as a team. *habilidades para trabajar en equipo*

P

**part|ner|ship** /pɑ̲rtnərʃɪp/ (**partnerships**) N-VAR **Partnership** or a **partnership** is a relationship in which two or more people, organizations, or countries work together as partners. *sociedad, relación, asociación* ❑ *...the partnership between Germany's banks and its businesses.* *...la estrecha asociación entre las empresas y los bancos alemanes.*

**part-time**

| The adverb is also spelled **part time**. |
|---|

ADJ If someone is a **part-time** worker or has a **part-time** job, they work for only part of each day or week. *medio tiempo* ❑ *...lower-paid part-time workers.* *...trabajadores de medio tiempo con sueldos más bajos.* ● **Part-time** is also an adverb. *medio tiempo* ❑ *I want to work part-time.* *Quisiera trabajar medio tiempo.*

**par|ty** /pɑ̲rti/ (**parties, partying, partied**) **1** N-COUNT A **party** is a political organization whose members have similar aims and beliefs, that tries to get its members elected to the legislature of a country. *partido* ❑ *...a member of the Republican Party.* *...un miembro del Partido Republicano.* **2** N-COUNT A **party** is a social event at which people enjoy themselves doing things such as eating or dancing. *fiesta* ❑ *The couple met at a party.* *Se conocieron en una fiesta.* ❑ *We organized a huge birthday party.* *Organizamos una gran fiesta de cumpleaños.* **3** V-I If you **party,** you enjoy yourself doing things such as going out to parties and dancing. *ir de juerga, fiestear* ❑ *He partied a little just like all teenagers.* *Él fiesteó un poco, como todos los adolescentes.* **4** N-COUNT A **party of** people is a group of them doing something together, for example, traveling. *grupo* ❑ *They became separated from their party.* *Se separaron de su grupo.* ❑ *...a party of tourists.* *...un grupo de turistas.* **5** N-COUNT One of the people involved in a legal agreement or dispute can be referred to as a particular **party.** *parte* [LEGAL] ❑ *They must prove that we are the guilty party.* *Ellos deben probar que somos culpables.* **6** PHRASE Someone who **is a party to** or **is party to** an action or agreement is involved in it, and therefore partly responsible for it. *prestarse a* ❑ *I'd never be a party to such a terrible thing.* *Nunca me prestaría a hacer algo tan terrible.*

**pas|cal** /pæskæ̲l, pɑskɑ̲l/ (**pascals**) N-COUNT In physics, a **pascal** is a unit of pressure. The abbreviation "Pa" is also used. *pascal* [TECHNICAL]

**Pasca̲l's prin|ci|ple** also **Pascal's law** N-UNCOUNT **Pascal's principle** or **Pascal's law** is a rule in physics which states that, when pressure is applied to a fluid in a container, the pressure is distributed equally throughout all parts of the fluid. *ley de Pascal* [TECHNICAL]

**pass**

❶ VERB USES
❷ NOUN USES
❸ PHRASAL VERBS

❶ **pass** /pæ̲s/ (**passes, passing, passed**) **1** V-T/V-I To **pass** someone or something means to go past them. *pasar* ❑ *As she passed the library door, the telephone began to ring.* *Mientras pasaba por la puerta de la biblioteca, comenzó a sonar el teléfono.* ❑ *Jane stood aside to let her pass.* *Jane se hizo a un lado para dejarla pasar.* **2** V-I When someone or something **passes** in a particular direction, they move in that direction. *pasar, atravesar* ❑ *He passed through the doorway into the kitchen.* *Pasó por la entrada en dirección a la cocina.* ❑ *A dirt road passes through the town.* *Un camino de terracería atraviesa el pueblo.* **3** V-T If you **pass** something through, over, or around something else, you move or push it through, over, or around that thing. *pasar* ❑ *He passed a hand through his hair.* *Se pasó la mano por el pelo.* **4** V-T If you **pass** an object **to** someone, you give it to them either from your hand or by kicking or throwing it to them. *pasar* ❑ *Ken passed the books to Dr Wong.* *Ken le pasó los libros al Dr. Wong.* ❑ *Your partner should then pass the ball back to you.* *Tu compañero debe después pasarte el balón de regreso.* **5** V-T/V-I If something **passes** or **is passed from** one person **to** another, the first person gives it to the second. *pasar* ❑ *His mother's property passed to him after her death.* *Al morir su madre, sus propiedades pasaron a sus manos.* ❑ *Officials failed to pass important information to their bosses.* *Los funcionarios no supieron transmitirles información importante a sus jefes.* ● **Pass on** means the same as **pass.** *pasar* ❑ *I passed on the information.* *Transmití la información.* **6** V-I When a period of time **passes,** it happens and finishes. *pasar* ❑ *He has let so much time pass without contacting her.* *Ha dejado pasar tanto tiempo*

*sin ponerse en contacto con ella.* ❑ *As the years passed he felt trapped by marriage.* *A medida que pasaban los años, se fue sintiendo cada vez más atrapado en el matrimonio.* ● **pass|ing** N-SING *paso* ❑ *...the passing of time.* *...el paso del tiempo.* **7** V-T If you **pass** a period of time in a particular way, you spend it in that way. *pasar* ❑ *The children passed the time playing in the streets.* *Los niños se pasaban el tiempo jugando en las calles.* **8** V-T If an amount **passes** a particular total or level, it becomes greater than that total or level. *pasar, rebasar* ❑ *...the first company to pass the $2 billion mark.* *...la primera empresa en rebasar la marca de los 2 mil millones de dólares.* **9** V-T/V-I If someone or something **passes** a test or **is passed,** they are considered to be of an acceptable standard. *pasar* ❑ *Kevin has just passed his driving test.* *Kevin acaba de pasar su prueba de manejo.* ❑ *I didn't pass.* *No pasé.* **10** V-T When people in authority **pass** a new law or a proposal, they formally agree to it or approve it. *pasar* ❑ *Congress may pass a law that allows banks to sell insurance.* *El Congreso podría pasar una ley que le permita a los bancos vender seguros.* **11** V-I To **pass for** or **pass as** a particular thing means to be accepted as that thing, in spite of not having all the right qualities. *pasar* ❑ *You could pass for a high school senior.* *Tú podrías pasar por un alumno de último año de bachillerato.* ❑ *Ted, with his fluent French, passed as one of the locals.* *Ted, con su dominio del francés, pasó por uno de los lugareños.* **12** to **pass the buck** → see **buck**
→ see also **past**
→ see **mountain**

**❷ pass** /pæs/ (**passes**) **1** N-COUNT A **pass** in an examination, test, or course is a successful result in it. *aprobado* ❑ *He's been allowed to re-take the exam, and he'll probably pass.* *Se le permitió volver a dar el examen y probablemente lo pase.* **2** N-COUNT A **pass** is a document that allows you to do something. *pase* ❑ *He used his journalist's pass to enter the White House.* *Usó su pase de periodista para entrar a la Casa Blanca.* **3** N-COUNT A **pass** in a game such as football or basketball is an act of throwing the ball to someone on your team. *pase* ❑ *Bryan Randall threw a short pass to Ernest Wilford.* *Bryan Randall le hizo un pase corto a Ernest Wilford.* **4** N-COUNT A **pass** is a narrow path or route between mountains. *paso* ❑ *The village is in a mountain pass.* *La aldea está en un paso entre las montañas.*

**❸ pass** /pæs/ (**passes, passing, passed**)
▸ **pass away** PHR-VERB You can say that someone **passed away** to mean that they died, if you want to avoid using the word "die" because it might upset people. *pasar a mejor vida, fallecer* ❑ *He passed away last year.* *Pasó a mejor vida el año pasado.*
▸ **pass off as** PHR-VERB If you **pass** something **off as** something that it is not, you convince people that it is that thing. *hacer pasar* ❑ *He passed himself off as a doctor.* *Se hizo pasar por un médico.* ❑ *Some bad writers try to pass off their gossiping as reporting.* *Algunos malos escritores tratan de hacer pasar su chismerío por un reportaje.*
▸ **pass on** **1** PHR-VERB **Passed on** means the same as **pass away**. *fallecer* ❑ *He passed on at the age of 72.* *Falleció a la edad de 72 años.* **2** → see also **pass ❶ 5**
▸ **pass out** PHR-VERB If you **pass out,** you faint or collapse. *perder el conocimiento* ❑ *He felt sick and dizzy and then passed out.* *Sintió náuseas y mareo y luego perdió el conocimiento.*
▸ **pass over** PHR-VERB If someone **is passed over for** a job, they do not get the job and someone younger or less experienced is chosen instead. *pasar por alto* ❑ *She was repeatedly passed over for promotion.* *Van varias veces que la pasan por alto y le dan el ascenso a otros.*
▸ **pass up** PHR-VERB If you **pass up** an opportunity, you do not take advantage of it. *dejar pasar* ❑ *We can't pass up a chance like this.* *No podemos dejar pasar una oportunidad como esta.*

**pas|sage** /pæsɪdʒ/ (**passages**) **1** N-COUNT A **passage** is a long narrow space with walls or fences on both sides, that connects one place or room with another. *pasillo* ❑ *Harry stepped into the passage.* *Harry se introdujo al pasillo.* **2** N-COUNT A **passage** in a book, speech, or piece of music is a section of it. *pasaje* ❑ *He read a passage from Emerson.* *Leyó un pasaje de Emerson.* **3** N-UNCOUNT The **passage** of someone or something is their movement or progress from one place or stage to another. *paso* ❑ *...the passage of troops through Spain.* *...el paso de las tropas por España.* ❑ *...Russia's passage to democracy.* *...el paso de Rusia a la democracia.* **4** N-SING **The passage of** a period of time is its passing. *paso* ❑ *The painting will increase in value with the passage of time.* *La pintura incrementará su valor con el paso del tiempo.*

**pas|sen|ger** /pæsɪndʒər/ (**passengers**) N-COUNT A **passenger** in a vehicle such as a bus, boat, or plane is a person who is traveling in it, but who is not driving it or working on it. *pasajero o pasajera* ❑ *Mr. Smith was a passenger in the car when it crashed.* *El Sr. Smith era uno de los pasajeros del carro cuando éste chocó.*
→ see **fly, train**

**pass|ing** /pæsɪŋ/ **1** ADJ A **passing** feeling or action is brief and not very serious or important. *pasajero, al pasar* ❑ *...a passing remark in a television interview.* *...un comentario al pasar en una entrevista de televisión.* **2** N-SING The **passing** of a person or thing is the fact of their dying or coming to an end. *muerte, fin* ❑ *We celebrated the passing of the century.* *Celebramos el cambio de siglo.* ❑ *His passing will be mourned by many people.* *Su muerte será lamentada por muchas personas.* **3** → see also **pass** **4** PHRASE If you mention something **in passing,** you mention it briefly while you are talking or writing about something else. *de pasada, al pasar* ❑ *He mentioned the army in passing.* *Mencionó al ejército de pasada.*

**pas|sion** /pæʃᵊn/ (**passions**) **1** N-UNCOUNT **Passion** is a very strong feeling of love and sexual attraction for someone. *pasión* ❑ *I can't feel any passion for George.* *No puedo sentir ninguna pasión por George.* **2** N-UNCOUNT **Passion** is a very strong feeling about something or a strong belief in something. *pasión* ❑ *He spoke with great passion.* *Habló con mucha pasión.* **3** N-COUNT If you have a **passion for** something, you have a very strong interest in it and like it very much. *pasión* ❑ *She had a passion for gardening.* *La apasionaba la jardinería.*

| **Thesaurus** *passion* | Ver también: |
|---|---|
| N. | affection, desire, love **1**<br>enthusiasm, fondness, interest **2** **3** |

**pas|sion|ate** /pæʃənɪt/ ADJ A **passionate** person has very strong feelings about something or a strong belief in something. *apasionado* ❑ *...his passionate commitment to peace. ...su apasionado compromiso con la paz.* ❑ *He is very passionate about the project. Es muy apasionado con su proyecto.* ● **pas|sion|ate|ly** ADV *apasionadamente* ❑ *I am passionately opposed to the plans. Me opongo acaloradamente a los planes.*

**pas|sive** /pæsɪv/ **1** ADJ If you describe someone as **passive**, you disapprove of the fact that they do not take action, but instead let things happen to them. *pasivo* ❑ *...his passive attitude. ...su actitud pasiva.* ● **pas|sive|ly** ADV *pasivamente* ❑ *He sat there passively, waiting for his father to say something. Se quedó sentado pasivamente, esperando que su padre dijera algo.* **2** N-SING In grammar, **the passive** or **the passive voice** is formed using "be" and the past participle of a verb. The subject of a passive clause does not perform the action expressed by the verb but is affected by it. For example, in "He's been murdered," the verb is in the passive. Compare **active**. *pasiva*

**pas|sive so|lar heat|ing** N-UNCOUNT **Passive solar heating** is a method of heating a building by using the materials or design of the building to collect sunlight directly, for example by the use of thick walls or large windows. *calefacción solar pasiva*

**pas|sive trans|port** N-UNCOUNT In biology, **passive transport** is the movement of chemicals and other substances through the membranes of cells by a process called diffusion, which does not require the cells to use energy. Compare **active transport**. *transporte pasivo* [TECHNICAL]

**pass|port** /pæspɔrt/ (**passports**) N-COUNT Your **passport** is an official document which you have to show when you enter or leave a country. *pasaporte* ❑ *You should take your passport with you when changing money. Deberías llevar tu pasaporte cuando vas a cambiar dinero.*

P

**pass|word** /pæswɜrd/ (**passwords**) N-COUNT A **password** is a secret word or phrase that enables you to enter a place or use a computer system. *clave* ❑ *They were only allowed in if they could give the password. Sólo podían entrar si podían dar la clave.* → see **Internet**

**past** /pæst/ (**pasts**)

In addition to the uses shown below, **past** is used in phrasal verbs such as "run past."

**1** N-SING **The past** is the time before the present, and the things that have happened. *pasado* ❑ *In the past, most babies with the disease died. En el pasado, la mayoría de los bebés que padecían la enfermedad morían.* **2** N-COUNT Your **past** consists of all the things that you have done or that have happened to you. *pasado* ❑ *He was honest about his past. Fue honesto respecto de su pasado.* **3** ADJ **Past** events and things happened or existed before the present time. *anterior* ❑ *I knew from past experience that this treatment could help. Sabía por experiencias anteriores que este tratamiento podría ayudar.* ❑ *...scenes from life in past centuries. ...escenas de la vida en los siglos pasados.* **4** ADJ You use **past** to talk about a period of time that has just finished. *pasado* ❑ *Most stores have remained closed for the past three days. La mayoría de las tiendas permanecieron cerradas durante los últimos tres días.* **5** PREP You use **past** when you are stating a time that is thirty minutes or less after a particular hour. *y* ❑ *It's ten past eleven. Son las once y diez.* ● **Past** is also an adverb. *pasadas* ❑ *I have my lunch at half past. Como mi almuerzo a las ...y media.* **6** PREP If you go **past** someone or something, you go near them and keep moving, so that they are then behind you. *pasar* ❑ *I walked past him. Lo pasé caminando.* ● **Past** is also an adverb. *Past también puede usarse como adverbio.* ❑ *An ambulance drove past. Pasó una ambulancia.* **7** PREP If something is **past** a place, it is on the other side of it. *pasando* ❑ *Go north on Route I-15 to the exit just past Barstow. Diríjase hacia el norte, sobre la ruta 1-15 hasta la salida que está justo pasando Barstow.* → see **history**

**Usage** past and passed

The adverb or adjective *past* and the verb *passed* (past tense of *pass*) are often confused. They are pronounced the same and can have similar meanings: *Jack passed Jill by rolling past her down the hill. This past week, Shaya passed his history exam and his driving test!*

pasta

**pas|ta** /pɑstə/ (**pastas**) N-VAR **Pasta** is a type of food made from a mixture of flour, eggs, and water that is formed into different shapes and then boiled. Spaghetti and macaroni are types of pasta. *pasta*

**paste** /peɪst/ (**pastes, pasting, pasted**) **1** N-UNCOUNT **Paste** is a soft, wet, sticky mixture that can be spread easily. Some types of paste are used to stick things together. *pasta, engrudo* ❑ *Mix a little milk with the powder to form a paste. Mezcle un poco de leche con el polvo para formar una pasta.* ❑ *...tomato paste. ...concentrado de jitomate.* **2** V-T If you **paste** something on a surface, you put glue or paste on it and stick it on the surface. *pegar* ❑ *...pasting labels on bottles. ...pegar etiquetas a las botellas.*

**pas|try** /peɪstri/ (**pastries**) **1** N-UNCOUNT **Pastry** is a food made from flour, fat, and water that is used, for example, for making pies. *masa* **2** N-COUNT A **pastry** is a small cake made with sweet pastry. *repostería* ❑ *...a wide range of cakes and pastries. ...una gran variedad de pasteles y repostería.*

**pas|ture** /pæstʃər/ (**pastures**) N-VAR **Pasture** is land with grass growing on it for farm animals to eat. *prado, pastura* ❑ *The cows are out now, grazing in the pasture. Las vacas están afuera, pastando en el prado.* → see **barn**

**pat** /pæt/ (**pats, patting, patted**) **1** V-T If you **pat** something or someone, you tap them lightly, usually with your hand held flat. *dar palmaditas* ❑ *"Don't you worry about this," she said patting me on the knee. —No te preocupes por esto—me dijo dándome palmaditas en la rodilla.* ❑ *The lady patted her hair nervously. La mujer se dio palmaditas en la cabeza de manera nerviosa.* ● **Pat** is also a noun. *palmada* ❑ *He gave her an encouraging pat on the shoulder. Le dio una palmada alentadora en el hombro.* **2** PHRASE If you **stand pat**, you refuse to change your mind about something. *no cambiar de opinión, no dar su brazo a* *torcer.* ❑ *He seems to think that the right thing in this situation is to stand pat.* *Parece pensar que lo correcto en esta situación es no dar su brazo a torcer.*

**patch** /pætʃ/ (**patches, patching, patched**) **1** N-COUNT A **patch** on a surface is a part of it that is different in appearance from the area around it. *porción* ❑ *...the bald patch on the top of his head.* *...la calva en la parte de arriba de su cabeza.* ❑ *There was a small patch of blue in the gray clouds.* *Había una pequeña porción de azul entre las nubes grises.* **2** N-COUNT A **patch of** land is a small area of land where a particular plant or crop grows. *parcela, huerto* ❑ *...a patch of land covered with trees.* *...una parcela cubierta de árboles.* ❑ *...the little vegetable patch in her backyard.* *...el pequeño huerto en su jardín trasero.* **3** N-COUNT A **patch** is a piece of material that you use to cover a hole in something. *parche* ❑ *...jackets with patches on the elbows.* *...chamarras con parches en los codos.* **4** V-T If you **patch** something that has a hole in it, you repair it by fastening a patch over the hole. *parchar* ❑ *He and Williams patched the barn roof.* *Él y Wiliams parcharon el techo del granero.* **5** N-COUNT A **patch** is a piece of computer program code written as a temporary solution for dealing with a problem. *parche* [COMPUTING] ❑ *Older machines will need a software patch to correct the problem.* *Las computadoras más antiguas necesitarán un parche de software para corregir el problema.* **6** PHRASE If you have or go through **a rough patch,** you have a lot of problems for a time. *una mala racha* ❑ *He went through a rough patch after he lost his job.* *Pasó por una mala racha después de que perdió su trabajo.*

▸ **patch up** **1** PHR-VERB If you **patch up** an argument or relationship, you try to be friendly again and not to argue anymore. *hacer las paces* ❑ *They soon patched up their friendship.* *Pronto hicieron las paces y reanudaron su amistad.* ❑ *Robbie has patched things up with his mom.* *Robbie ha hecho las paces con su mamá.* **2** PHR-VERB If you **patch up** something that is damaged, you repair it. *arreglar, parchar* ❑ *We can patch up those holes.* *Podemos arreglar esos hoyos.*

**pa|tent** /pætᵊnt/ (**patents, patenting, patented**) **1** N-COUNT A **patent** is an official right to be the only person or company allowed to make or sell a new product for a certain period of time. *patente* ❑ *P&G applied for a patent on its cookies.* *P&G solicitó una patente para sus galletas.* ❑ *He held a number of patents for his many inventions.* *Tenía varias patentes de sus muchos inventos.* **2** V-T If you **patent** something, you obtain a patent for it. *patentar* ❑ *He patented the idea that the atom could be split.* *Patentó la idea de que el átomo era divisible.* ❑ *The invention has been patented by the university.* *El invento ha sido patentado por la universidad.* **3** ADJ You use **patent** to emphasize that something, especially something bad, is obvious. *patente, evidente* ❑ *This was patent nonsense.* *Era una tontería patente.* • **pa|tent|ly** ADV *evidentemente, de manera patente* ❑ *He made his anger patently obvious.* *Hizo que su enojo fuera patentemente obvio.*

**pa|ter|nal** /pətɜrnᵊl/ ADJ **Paternal** is used to describe feelings or actions that are typical of those of a kind father toward his child. *paternal* ❑ *...paternal love.* *...amor paternal.*

**path** /pæθ/ (**paths**) **1** N-COUNT A **path** is a strip of ground that people walk along. *sendero* ❑ *We followed the path along the cliff.* *Seguimos el sendero a lo largo del acantilado.* ❑ *Feet had worn a path in the rock.* *Las pisadas habían trazado un sendero en la roca.* **2** N-COUNT Your **path** is the space ahead of you as you move along. *camino* ❑ *A group of reporters blocked his path.* *Un grupo de reporteros le bloqueaban el camino.* **3** N-COUNT The **path** of something is the line that it moves along in a particular direction. *camino* ❑ *He stepped into the path of a moving car.* *Se puso en el camino de un coche que venía.* ❑ *...people who live under the flight path of airplanes.* *...gente que vive bajo la ruta de los aviones.* **4** N-COUNT A **path** that you take is a particular course of action or way of achieving something. *camino* ❑ *He chose the path of rock stardom.* *Escogió el camino de estrella de rock.*

→ see **golf**

| **Word Link** | *path ≈ feeling : empathy, pathetic, sympathy* |
|---|---|

**pa|thet|ic** /pəθɛtɪk/ **1** ADJ If you describe a person or animal as **pathetic,** you mean that they are sad and weak or helpless, and they make you feel very sorry for them. *patético* ❑ *...a pathetic little dog with a curly tail.* *...un perrito patético con cola rizada.* ❑ *The small group of onlookers were a pathetic sight.* *El pequeño grupo de mirones hacían una vista patética.* • **pa|theti|cal|ly** /pəθɛtɪkli/ ADV *patéticamente* ❑ *She was pathetically thin.* *Estaba patéticamente flaca.* **2** ADJ If you describe someone or something as **pathetic,** you mean that they make you feel impatient or angry, often because they are weak or not very good. *patético* ❑ *What pathetic excuses.* *Qué pretextos tan patéticos.* ❑ *Don't be so pathetic.* *No seas tan patético.* • **pa|theti|cal|ly** ADV *lastimeramente* ❑ *Five women in a group of 18 people is a pathetically small number.* *Cinco mujeres en un grupo de 18 personas es un número tan bajo que da pena.*

**path|way** /pæθweɪ/ (**pathways**) **1** N-COUNT A **pathway** is the same as a **path.** *camino, sendero* ❑ *Richard was coming up the pathway.* *Richard subía por el sendero.* ❑ *...the pathway to success.* *...el camino del éxito.* **2** N-COUNT The **pathway** of something is the line which it moves along in a particular direction. *camino*

| **Word Link** | *ence ≈ state, condition : excellence, intelligence, patience* |
|---|---|

**pa|tience** /peɪʃᵊns/ N-UNCOUNT If you have **patience,** you are able to stay calm and not get annoyed, for example, when something takes a long time. *paciencia* ❑ *He doesn't have the patience to wait.* *No tiene paciencia para esperar.*

**pa|tient** /peɪʃᵊnt/ (**patients**) **1** N-COUNT A **patient** is a person who receives medical treatment from a doctor or hospital. *paciente* ❑ *45,000 patients have been waiting more than six months for operations.* *45,000 pacientes han estado esperando más de seis meses para ser operados.* ❑ *She was tough but wonderful with her patients.* *Era dura pero maravillosa con sus pacientes.* **2** ADJ If you are **patient,** you stay calm and do not get annoyed, for example, when something takes a long time. *paciente* ❑ *Please be patient—your check will arrive.* *Por favor sea paciente—, su cheque va a llegar.* • **pa|tient|ly** ADV *pacientemente* ❑ *She waited patiently for Frances to finish.* *Esperó pacientemente a que terminara Frances.*

P

**3** → see also **customer**
→ see **diagnosis, illness**

**pa|tri|ot** /ˈpeɪtriət/ (**patriots**) N-COUNT A **patriot** is someone who loves their country and feels very loyal toward it. *patriota* ❏ *…true patriots. …verdaderos patriotas.*

**pat|ri|ot|ic** /ˌpeɪtriˈɒtɪk/ ADJ Someone who is **patriotic** loves their country and feels very loyal toward it. *patriota* ❏ *They are very patriotic guys who give everything for their country. Son muchachos muy patriotas que dan todo por su país.* ● **pat|ri|ot|ism** /ˈpeɪtriətɪzəm/ N-UNCOUNT *patriotismo* ❏ *…a boy who joined the army out of a sense of patriotism. …un niño que se enlistó al ejército por su sentido de patriotismo.*

**pa|trol** /pəˈtroʊl/ (**patrols, patrolling, patrolled**) **1** V-T When soldiers, police, or guards **patrol** an area or building, they move around it in order to make sure that there is no trouble there. *patrullar* ❏ *Prison officers continued to patrol the grounds. Los policías continuaban patrullando el terreno.* ● **Patrol** is also a noun. *patrulla* ❏ *He failed to return from a patrol. No regresó de la patrulla.* ❏ *The army is now on patrol. El ejército está de patrulla.* **2** N-COUNT A **patrol** is a group of soldiers or vehicles that are patrolling an area. *patrulla* ❏ *Police are searching for three men who attacked a patrol last night. La policía busca a tres hombres que atacaron a una patrulla ayer en la noche.*

**patrol|man** /pəˈtroʊlmən/ (**patrolmen**) N-COUNT A **patrolman** is a policeman who patrols a particular area. *patrullero*

**pa|tron** /ˈpeɪtrən/ (**patrons**) **1** N-COUNT A **patron** is a person who supports and gives money to artists, writers, or musicians. *patrocinador o patrocinadora, mecenas* ❏ *…a patron of the arts. …un mecenas.* **2** N-COUNT The **patron** of a charity, group, or campaign is an important person who allows his or her name to be used for publicity. *patrocinador o patrocinadora* ❏ *He has now become one of the patrons of the association. Se ha convertido en uno*

de los patrocinadores de la asociación. **3** N-COUNT The **patrons** of a place such as a restaurant or hotel are its customers. *cliente* ❏ *…patrons of a high-priced hotel. …los clientes de un hotel muy caro.*

**pat|tern** /ˈpætərn/ (**patterns**) **1** N-COUNT A **pattern** is the repeated or regular way in which something happens or is done. *patrón* ❏ *All three attacks followed the same pattern. Los tres ataques seguían el mismo patrón.* **2** N-COUNT A **pattern** is an arrangement of lines or shapes repeated at regular intervals. *patrón* ❏ *…a pattern of light and dark stripes. …un patrón de rayas claras y oscuras.* **3** N-COUNT A **pattern** is a diagram or shape that you can use as a guide when you are making something such as a model or a piece of clothing. *patrón* ❏ *Send for our free knitting patterns. Pida sus patrones de tejido gratis.*
→ see Picture Dictionary: **patterns**
→ see **quilt**

**pat|ty** /ˈpæti/ (**patties**) N-COUNT A **patty** is an amount of ground beef formed into a flat, round shape. *hamburguesa* ❏ *…the beef patties frying on the grill. …las hamburguesas que se freían en la parrilla.*

**pause** /pɔz/ (**pauses, pausing, paused**) **1** V-I If you **pause** while you are doing something, you stop for a short period and then continue. *detenerse, hacer una pausa* ❏ *"It's rather embarrassing," he began, and paused. —Es bastante penoso—empezó, y se detuvo.* ❏ *He talked for two hours, hardly pausing for breath. Habló durante dos horas, apenas deteniéndose para respirar.* **2** N-COUNT A **pause** is a short period when you stop doing something before continuing. *pausa* ❏ *After a pause Al said: "I'm sorry*

P

**Picture Dictionary**    **patterns**

pinstripe      polka dot      stripe      checked

plaid      paisley      solid

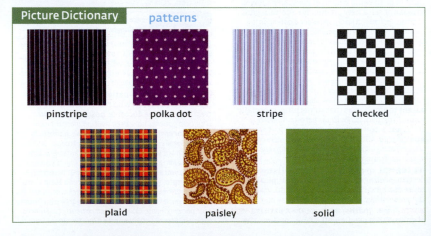

if I upset you." *Después de una pausa, Al dijo—Lamento haberte molestado.*

**Word Partnership** Usar *pause* con:

ADJ. **awkward** pause, **brief** pause, **long** pause, **short** pause, **slight** pause 2

**pave** /peɪv/ (**paves, paving, paved**) V-T If a road or an area of ground **has been paved,** it has been covered with asphalt or concrete, so that it is easy to walk or drive on. *pavimentar* ❑ *The avenue has never been paved. La avenida nunca ha sido pavimentada.*

**pave|ment** /peɪvmənt/ (**pavements**) N-COUNT The **pavement** is the hard surface of a road. *pavimento* ❑ *...the wet pavement. ...el pavimento mojado.*

**paw** /pɔ/ (**paws, pawing, pawed**) 1 N-COUNT The **paws** of an animal such as a cat, dog, or bear are its feet. *pata* ❑ *The kitten was black with white front paws. El gatito era negro con sus patas delanteras blancas.* 2 V-T If an animal **paws** something, it draws its paw or hoof over it. *tocar con la pata* ❑ *Madigan's horse pawed the ground. El caballo de Madigan tocó el suelo con la pata.*

**pawn** /pɔn/ (**pawns, pawning, pawned**) 1 V-T If you **pawn** something that you own, you leave it with a pawnbroker, who gives you money for it and who can sell it if you do not pay back the money before a certain time. *empeñar* ❑ *He is thinking about pawning his watch. Está considerando empeñar su reloj.* 2 N-COUNT In chess, a **pawn** is the smallest and least valuable playing piece. Each player has eight pawns at the start of the game. *peón* 3 N-COUNT If you say that someone is using you as a **pawn,** you mean that they are using you for their own advantage. *títere* ❑ *He is being used as a political pawn by the president. El presidente lo está utilizando como su títere político.*

**pay** /peɪ/ (**pays, paying, paid**) 1 V-T/V-I When you **pay** an amount of money **to** someone, you give it to them because you are buying something from them or because you owe it to them. When you **pay** something such as a bill or a debt, you pay the amount that you owe. *pagar* ❑ *You've already paid for the call. Ya pagó la llamada.* ❑ *The wealthier people may have to pay a little more in taxes. La gente más acaudalada puede tener que pagar más impuestos.* 2 V-T When you **are paid,** you get your wages or salary from your employer. *pagar* ❑ *The lawyer was paid a huge salary. Al abogado le pagaban un sueldo estratosférico.* ❑ *I get paid monthly. A mí me pagan mensualmente.* ● **Pay** is also a noun. *paga* ❑ *...complaints about their pay and working conditions. ...quejas sobre su paga y condiciones laborales.* 3 V-I If a course of action **pays,** it results in some advantage or benefit for you. *convenir, pagar* ❑ *As always, it pays to do some research. Como siempre, conviene investigar.* ❑ *We must show that crime does not pay. Debemos mostrar que el crimen no paga.* 4 V-T/V-I If you **pay for** something that you do or have, you suffer as a result of it. *pagar* ❑ *Lakoto paid for his beliefs with years in prison. Lakoto pagó sus creencias con años de cárcel.* ❑ *Why should I pay the penalty for somebody else's mistake? ¿Por qué debo pagar yo el castigo por un error ajeno?* 5 V-T You use **pay** with some nouns, such as in the expressions **pay a visit** and **pay attention,** to indicate that something is given or done. *prestar, hacer* ❑ *Pay us a visit next time you're in Portland. Haznos una visita la próxima vez que estés en Portland.* ❑ *He felt a heavy bump, but paid no attention to it. Sintió un golpe fuerte, pero no le prestó atención.* 6 → see also **paid** 7 to **pay dividends** → see **dividend**

▸ **pay back** PHR-VERB If you **pay back** money that you have borrowed or taken from someone, you give them an equal amount at a later time. *pagar* ❑ *He will have to pay back everything he has stolen. Va a tener que pagar todo lo que se robó.*

▸ **pay off** 1 PHR-VERB If you **pay off** a debt, you give back all the money that you owe. *terminar de pagar* ❑ *It will take him the rest of his life to pay off that loan. Le va a tomar toda la vida terminar de pagar ese préstamo.* 2 PHR-VERB If an action **pays off,** it is successful. *valer la pena* ❑ *It looks like all their hard work finally paid off. Parece que todo su trabajo finalmente valió la pena.* 3 → see also **payoff**

▸ **pay out** PHR-VERB If you **pay out** money, usually a large amount, you spend it on something. *desembolsar* ❑ *The insurance industry will pay out billions of dollars for damage caused by Hurricane Katrina. La industria de seguros desembolsará billones de dólares por los daños causados por el huracán Katrina.*

▸ **pay up** PHR-VERB If you **pay up,** you give someone money that they say you owe them. *pagar* ❑ *We asked for a refund, but they would not pay up. Pedimos un reembolso, pero no querían pagar.*

**pay|back** /peɪbæk/ N-SING A **payback** is the profit or benefit that you obtain from something that you have spent money, time, or effort on. *recuperación* ❑ *With such high costs, there would be no payback from the program. Con costos tan altos, no habría ninguna recuperación del programa.*

**pay|check** /peɪtʃɛk/ (**paychecks**) N-COUNT Your **paycheck** is the money that your employer gives you as your wages or salary. *sueldo* ❑ *I just get a small paycheck every month. Sólo recibo un pequeño sueldo cada mes.*

**pay|dirt** /peɪdɜrt/ also **pay dirt** PHRASE If you say that someone **has struck paydirt** or **has hit paydirt,** you mean that they have achieved sudden success or gained a lot of money very quickly. *encontrar una mina de oro* [INFORMAL] ❑ *Howard Hawks hit paydirt with "Rio Bravo." Howard Hawks encontró una mina de oro con "Río Bravo".*

**pay|ment** /peɪmənt/ (**payments**) 1 N-COUNT A **payment** is an amount of money that is paid to someone. *pago* ❑ *...mortgage payments. ...pagos de la hipoteca.* 2 N-UNCOUNT **Payment** is the act of paying money to someone or of being paid. *pago* ❑ *Players now expect payment for interviews. Los jugadores esperan ahora recibir un pago por entrevistas.* 3 → see also **down payment**

**Word Partnership** Usar *payment* con:

V. **accept** payment, **make a** payment, **receive** payment 1
ADJ. **late** payment, **minimum** payment, **monthly** payment 1
N. payment **in cash**, payment **by check**, **mortgage** payment 1
payment **date** 1 2
payment **method**, payment **plan** 2

**pay|off** /peɪɔf/ (**payoffs**) also **pay-off**

P

1 N-COUNT The **payoff from** an action is the advantage or benefit that you get from it. *beneficio* ❑ *The payoffs from this approach are huge. Los beneficios de este enfoque son enormes.* 2 N-COUNT A **payoff** is a payment made to someone, often secretly or illegally, so that they will not cause trouble. *soborno, mordida* ❑ *At that time, payoffs to public officials were quite usual. En esa época, los sobornos a funcionarios públicos eran muy comunes.*

**pay|roll** /peɪroʊl/ (**payrolls**) N-COUNT The people **on** the **payroll** of a company or an organization are the people who work for it and are paid by it. *nómina* [BUSINESS] ❑ *They have 87,000 employees on the payroll. Tienen a 87,000 empleados en la nómina.*

**PBS** /pi bi ɛs/ N-PROPER In the United States, **PBS** is an organization that broadcasts television programs and is not financed by advertising. **PBS** is an abbreviation for "Public Broadcasting Service." *PBS, cadena independiente de televisión, por sus siglas en inglés.*

**PC** /pi si/ (**PCs**) N-COUNT A **PC** is a computer that is used by one person at a time in a business, a school, or at home. **PC** is an abbreviation for **personal computer**. *PC (computadora personal)* ❑ *The price of a PC has fallen. Los precios de las PCs han caído.*

**PDA** /pi di eɪ/ (**PDAs**) N-COUNT A **PDA** is a handheld computer, used mainly for storing and accessing personal information such as addresses, telephone numbers, and memos. **PDA** is an abbreviation for **personal digital assistant**. *agenda electrónica, PDA por sus siglas en inglés.* ❑ *A typical PDA can function as a cell phone and a personal organizer. La típica agenda electrónica PDA puede funcionar como celular y organizador personal.*

**PDF** /pi di ɛf/ N-UNCOUNT **PDF** files are computer documents which look exactly like the original documents, regardless of which software or operating system was used to create them. **PDF** is an abbreviation for "Portable Document Format." *PDF, archivos de computadora* [COMPUTING]

**pea** /pi/ (**peas**) N-COUNT **Peas** are small, round, green seeds that are eaten as a vegetable. *chícharo, guisante*
→ see **vegetable**

**peace** /pis/ 1 N-UNCOUNT When there is **peace** in a country, it is not involved in a war. *paz* ❑ *...a shared commitment to world peace. ...un compromiso compartido por la paz mundial.* ❑ *...a peace agreement. ...un acuerdo de paz.* 2 N-UNCOUNT **Peace** is a state of undisturbed quiet and calm. *paz* ❑ *All I want is to have some peace and quiet. Todo lo que quiero es tener algo de paz y tranquilidad.* 3 N-UNCOUNT If there is **peace** among a group of people, they live or work together in a friendly way and do not argue. *paz* ❑ *Mandela called for peace among people of different races and cultures. Mandela pidió que hubiera paz entre personas de diferentes razas y culturas.*

**peace|ful** /pisfəl/ 1 ADJ **Peaceful** means not involving war or violence. *pacífico* ❑ *He has attempted to find a peaceful solution to the conflict. Ha intentado encontrar una solución pacífica al problema.*
• **peace|ful|ly** ADV *pacíficamente* ❑ *The governor asked the protestors to leave peacefully. El gobernador pidió a los manifestantes que se fueran pacíficamente.* 2 ADJ A **peaceful** place or time is quiet, calm, and free from disturbance. *tranquilo* ❑ *...a peaceful house in the Ozarks. ...una casa tranquila en Ozarks.*
• **peace|ful|ly** ADV *tranquilamente* ❑ *Except for traffic noise, the night passed peacefully. La noche transcurrió tranquilamente excepto por el ruido del tráfico.* 3 ADJ Someone who feels or looks **peaceful** feels or looks calm and free from worry or pain. *tranquilo*
• **peace|ful|ly** ADV *tranquilamente* ❑ *He was sleeping peacefully at her side. Dormía tranquilamente a su lado.*
4 → see also **peaceful**

**peach** /pitʃ/ (**peaches**) 1 N-COUNT A **peach** is a soft, round, slightly furry fruit with sweet yellow flesh and pinky-orange skin. *durazno* 2 COLOR Something that is **peach** is pale pinky-orange in color. *color durazno* ❑ *...a peach silk blouse. ...una blusa de seda color durazno.*

**peachy** /pitʃi/ ADJ If you say that something is **peachy** or **peachy keen**, you mean that it is very nice. *de perlas* [INFORMAL] ❑ *Everything in her life is just peachy. Todo en su vida va de perlas.*

**peak** /pik/ (**peaks, peaking, peaked**) 1 N-COUNT The **peak** of a process or an activity is the point at which it is at its strongest, most successful, or most fully developed. *apogeo* ❑ *His career was at its peak when he died. Su carrera estaba en su apogeo cuando murió.* 2 V-I When something **peaks**, it reaches its highest value or its highest level. *alcanzar el nivel más alto* ❑ *Temperatures have peaked at over 90 degrees. Las temperaturas alcanzaron su nivel más alto, sobre los 90 grados* 3 ADJ The **peak** level or value of something is its highest level or value. *más alto* ❑ *Today's price is 59% lower than the peak level of $1.5 million. El precio actual es 59% menor que el nivel más alto de 1.5 millones de dólares.* 4 N-COUNT A **peak** is a mountain or the top of a mountain. *cima, cumbre* ❑ *...the snow-covered peaks. ...las cumbres cubiertas de nieve.*
→ see **mountain**

**pea|nut** /pinʌt, -nət/ (**peanuts**) N-COUNT **Peanuts** are small nuts often eaten as a snack. *cacahuate, maní*
→ see Word Web: **peanut**

**pear** /pɛər/ (**pears**) N-COUNT A **pear** is a juicy fruit that is narrow at the top and wider at the bottom. Pears have white flesh and green, yellow, or brown skin. *pera*
→ see **fruit**

**pearl** /pɜrl/ (**pearls**) N-COUNT A **pearl** is a hard, white, shiny, round object that grows inside the shell of an oyster and is used for making jewelry. *perla* ❑ *She wore a string of pearls. Traía un collar de perlas.*

**peas|ant** /pɛzᵊnt/ (**peasants**) N-COUNT People refer to small farmers or farm workers in poor countries as **peasants**. *campesino* ❑ *The film describes the customs and habits of peasants in Peru. La película describe los hábitos y las costumbres de los campesinos de Perú.*

**peat** /pit/ N-UNCOUNT **Peat** is decaying plant material that is found in some cool, wet regions. *turba* ❑ *A peat fire burned smokily in the large fireplace. La turba ardía humeante en la gran chimenea.*
→ see **wetland**

**peb|ble** /pɛbᵊl/ (**pebbles**) N-COUNT A **pebble** is a small, smooth stone. *piedrita, guijarro*
→ see **beach**

P

## Word Web **peanut**

The **peanut** is not really a **nut**. It is a legume and grows under the ground. Peanuts originated in South America about 3,500 years ago. Explorers took them to Africa. Later, African slaves introduced the peanut into North America. Only poor people ate them at first. But they were a popular **snack** by 1900. You could buy **roasted** peanuts on city streets and at baseball games and the circus. Some scientists believe that roasted peanuts cause more **allergic** reactions than boiled peanuts. George Washington Carver, an African-American scientist, found 325 different uses for peanuts—including **peanut butter**.

**pec|to|ral** /pɛktərəl/ (**pectorals**) N-COUNT Your **pectorals** are the large chest muscles that help you to move your shoulders and your arms. *pectoral*

**pe|cu|liar** /pɪkyulyər/ **1** ADJ If you describe someone or something as **peculiar**, you think that they are strange or unusual, sometimes in an unpleasant way. *raro* ❑ *Mr. Kennet has a rather peculiar sense of humor.* *El Sr. Kennet tiene un raro sentido del humor.* • **pe|cu|liar|ly** ADV *peculiarmente* ❑ *His face became peculiarly expressionless.* *Su rostro se tornó peculiarmente inexpresivo.* **2** ADJ If something is **peculiar to** a particular thing, person, or situation, it belongs or relates only to that thing, person, or situation. *peculiar, característico* ❑ *This expression is peculiar to British English.* *Esta expresión sólo existe en el inglés británico.* • **pe|cu|liar|ly** ADV *típicamente* ❑ *...the peculiarly American business of making Hollywood movies.* *...el negocio, típicamente americano, de hacer películas hollywoodenses.*

**Word Link** *ped ≈ foot : moped, pedal, pedestrian*

**ped|al** /pɛdᵊl/ (**pedals, pedaling** or **pedalling, pedaled** or **pedalled**) **1** N-COUNT The **pedals** on a bicycle are the two parts that you push with your feet in order to make the bicycle move. *pedal* **2** V-T/V-I When you **pedal** a bicycle, you push the pedals around with your feet to make it move. *pedalear* ❑ *She pedaled the five miles home.* *Pedaleó las cinco millas hasta su casa.* ❑ *We pedalled slowly through the city streets.* *pedaleamos lentamente por las calles de la ciudad.* **3** N-COUNT A **pedal** in a car or on a machine is a lever that you press with your foot in order to control the car or machine. *pedal* ❑ *...the brake and the gas pedal.* *...los pedales del freno y el acelerador.*
→ see **bicycle**

**Word Link** *an, ian ≈ one of, relating to : Christian, European, pedestrian*

**pe|des|trian** /pɪdɛstriən/ (**pedestrians**) **1** N-COUNT A **pedestrian** is a person who is walking, especially in a town. *peatón, peatona* ❑ *...Los Angeles, where a pedestrian is a rare sight.* *...Los Angeles, donde los peatones no son muy comunes.* **2** ADJ If you describe something as **pedestrian**, you mean that it is ordinary and not at all interesting. *pedestre* ❑ *His writing style is so pedestrian that the book becomes boring.* *Su estilo al escribir es tan pedestre, que el libro se vuelve aburrido.*

**pe|dia|tri|cian** /pidiətrɪʃᵊn/ (**pediatricians**) N-COUNT A **pediatrician** is a doctor who specializes in treating children. *pediatra*

**pe|dom|eter** /pɪdɒmɪtər/ (**pedometers**) N-COUNT A **pedometer** is a device that measures the distance that someone has walked. *podómetro*

peek

**peek** /pik/ (**peeks, peeking, peeked**) V-I If you **peek at** something or someone, you take a quick look at them, often secretly. *mirar a hurtadillas* ❑ *She peeked at him through a crack in the wall.* *Lo miró a hurtadillas a través de una grieta en la pared.* • **Peek** is also a noun. *vistazo* ❑ *Companies have been paying huge amounts of money for a peek at the information.* *Las compañías han estado pagando grandes cantidades de dinero por darle un vistazo a la información.*

**peel** /pil/ (**peels, peeling, peeled**) **1** N-VAR The **peel** of a fruit such as a lemon or an apple is its skin. *cáscara* ❑ *...grated lemon peel.* *...cáscara de limón rallada.* ❑ *...a banana peel.* *...una cáscara de plátano.* **2** V-T When you **peel** fruit or vegetables, you remove their skins. *pelar* ❑ *She began peeling potatoes.* *Comenzó a pelar las papas.* **3** V-T/V-I If you **peel** something **off** a surface or if it **peels off**, it comes away from the surface. *despegar* ❑ *One of the kids was peeling plaster off the wall.* *Uno de los niños estaba despegando el yeso de la pared.* ❑ *It took me two days to peel off the labels.* *Me tomó dos días despegar todas las etiquetas.* ❑ *Paint was peeling off the walls.* *La pintura se estaba despegando de las paredes.*
→ see **cut, fruit**

**peer** /pɪər/ (**peers, peering, peered**) **1** V-I If you **peer at** something, you look at it very hard, usually because it is difficult to see clearly. *mirar detenidamente, escudriñar* ❑ *He found her peering at a computer print-out.* *La encontró escudriñando una hoja impresa en computadora.* **2** N-COUNT Your **peers** are the people who are the same age as you or who have the same status as you. *igual, par, compañero o compañera* ❑ *He is popular with his peers.* *Es popular entre sus compañeros.*

**peer press|ure** N-UNCOUNT If someone does something because of **peer pressure**, they do it because other people in their social group do it. *presión del grupo* ❑ *...peer pressure to be cool.* *...presión del grupo para ser "buena onda".*

**peeve** /piv/ (**peeves**) N-COUNT If something is your **peeve** or your **pet peeve**, it makes you particularly irritated or angry. *fastidio* ❑ *Ads on the computer screen are a pet peeve for many users.*

P

*Los anuncios en las pantallas de la computadora son un fastidio para muchos usuarios.*

**peg** /pɛg/ (**pegs, pegging, pegged**) **1** N-COUNT A **peg** is a small piece of wood or metal that is used for fastening something to something else. *espiga, estaquilla* ❑ *He builds furniture using wooden pegs instead of nails. Construye muebles usando estaquillas, en lugar de clavos.* **2** N-COUNT A **peg** is a small hook or knob that is attached to a wall or door and is used for hanging things on. *colgador, gancho* ❑ *His work jacket hung on the peg in the kitchen. Su chaqueta de trabajo colgaba de un gancho en la cocina.* **3** V-T If a price or amount of something **is pegged at** a particular level, it is fixed at that level. *vincular, congelar* ❑ *The peso is pegged to the dollar. El peso está vinculado al dólar.* ❑ *The bank wants to peg rates at 9%. El banco quiere congelar las tasas en el 9 por ciento.*

**pe|lag|ic en|vi|ron|ment** /pəlædʒɪk ɛnvaɪrənmənt, -vaɪərn-/ also **pelagic zone** N-SING The **pelagic environment** or **pelagic zone** is the parts of the ocean that are away from the coast and above the ocean floor, and all the organisms that live there. Compare **benthic.** *hábitat pelágico, zona pelágica* [TECHNICAL]

**pen** /pɛn/ (**pens, penning, penned**) **1** N-COUNT A **pen** is a long thin object which you use to write in ink. *pluma* **2** V-T If someone **pens** a letter, article, or book, they write it. *redactar, escribir* [FORMAL] ❑ *I really intended to pen this letter to you early this morning. Realmente tenía la intención de escribirle esta carta temprano esta mañana.* **3** N-COUNT A **pen** is also a small area with a fence around it in which farm animals are kept for a short time. *redil, corral* ❑ *...a holding pen for sheep. ...un corral para ovejas.* **4** V-T If people or animals **are penned** somewhere or **are penned up,** they are forced to remain in a very small area. *acorralar, encerrar* ❑ *The cattle were penned for the night. Se acorraló el ganado para pasar la noche.* ❑ *The animals were penned up in cages. Se encerró a los animales en jaulas.* **5** N-COUNT People sometimes refer to a prison as **the pen.** *el tanque* [INFORMAL]
→ see **office**

P

**pen|al|ty** /pɛnᵊlti/ (**penalties**) **1** N-COUNT A **penalty** is a punishment for doing something which is against a law or rule. *pena, castigo, multa* ❑ *He faces a penalty of 10 years in prison and a $500,000 fine. Enfrenta una pena de diez años de prisión y una multa de 500,000 dólares.* **2** N-COUNT In sports such as soccer, football, and hockey, a **penalty** is a disadvantage forced on the team that breaks a rule. *castigo, penalty, penalti, penal* ❑ *The team needs to work hard to avoid bad penalties. El equipo tiene que trabajar duro para evitar penaltis.*

**pen|cil** /pɛnsᵊl/ (**pencils**) N-COUNT A **pencil** is a thin wooden rod with a black or colored substance through the middle that you write or draw with. *lápiz* ❑ *I found a pencil and some blank paper. Encontré un lápiz y papel en blanco.*
→ see **office**

**pen|cil push|er** (**pencil pushers**) N-COUNT If you call someone a **pencil pusher,** you disapprove of them because you think that their work consists of writing documents rather than dealing with real people or real situations. *tinterillo* ❑ *That's a job for a pencil pusher. Ese trabajo es para un tinterillo.*

**pen|dant** /pɛndənt/ (**pendants**) N-COUNT A **pendant** is an ornament on a chain that you wear around your neck. *colgante*
→ see **jewelry**

**pend|ing** /pɛndɪŋ/ **1** ADJ If something such as a legal procedure is **pending,** it is waiting to be dealt with or settled. *pendiente* [FORMAL] ❑ *He will not be available while the case is pending. No estará disponible mientras el caso esté pendiente.* **2** PREP If something is done **pending** a future event, it is done until that event happens. *en espera de, a reserva de* [FORMAL] ❑ *The police released him pending a further investigation. La policía lo dejó en libertad a reserva de más indagaciones.*

**pen|etrate** /pɛnɪtreɪt/ (**penetrates, penetrating, penetrated**) **1** V-T If something or someone **penetrates** a physical object or an area, they succeed in getting into it or passing through it. *penetrar* ❑ *X-rays can penetrate many objects. Los rayos X pueden penetrar muchos objetos.*
• **pen|etra|tion** /pɛnɪtreɪʃᵊn/ N-UNCOUNT (**penetrations**) *penetración, filtración* ❑ *The thick walls prevented penetration by rainwater. Los gruesos muros impidieron que se filtrara el agua de lluvia.* **2** V-T If someone **penetrates** an organization, a group, or a profession, they succeed in entering it although it is difficult to do so. *introducirse, infiltrarse* ❑ *We need people who can speak foreign languages to penetrate these organizations. Necesitamos personas que sepan hablar lenguas extranjeras para infiltrarse en esas organizaciones* **3** V-T If someone **penetrates** an enemy group, they succeed in joining it in order to get information or to cause trouble. *infiltrarse* ❑ *It is not normally possible to penetrate a terrorist organization from the outside. Normalmente no es posible infiltrarse en una organización terrorista desde el exterior.*
• **pen|etra|tion** N-UNCOUNT *infiltración* ❑ *...the penetration of foreign companies to gather business information. ...la infiltración en empresas extranjeras para obtener información comercial.*

penguin

**pen|guin** /pɛŋgwɪn/ (**penguins**) N-COUNT A **penguin** is a black and white sea bird found mainly in the Antarctic. Penguins cannot fly. *pingüino*

| **Word Link** | ***insula ≈ island : insulate, insulation, peninsula*** |
| --- | --- |

**pen|in|su|la** /pənɪnsələ, -nɪnsyə-/ (**peninsulas**) N-COUNT A **peninsula** is a long narrow piece of land that sticks out from a larger piece of land and is almost completely surrounded by water. *península* ❑ *...the Iberian peninsula. ...la península Ibérica.*
→ see **landform**

**pe|nis** /pinɪs/ (**penises**) N-COUNT A man's **penis** is the part of his body that he uses when he urinates and when he has sex. *pene*

**peni|ten|tia|ry** /pɛnɪtɛnʃəri/ (**penitentiaries**) N-COUNT A **penitentiary** is a prison for criminals who have committed serious crimes. *penitenciaría* [FORMAL]

**pen|nant** /pɛnənt/ (**pennants**) N-COUNT In

baseball, a **pennant** is a flag that is given each year to the top team in a league. gallardete ❑ *The Red Sox lost the pennant to Detroit by a single game.* *Los Medias Rojas perdieron el gallardete con Detroit por un solo juego.*

**pen|ni|less** /pɛnilɪs/ ADJ Someone who is **penniless** has almost no money. pobre, indigente, en la miseria ❑ *They would soon be penniless and homeless.* *Pronto quedarían en la miseria y sin hogar.*

**pen|ny** /pɛni/ (**pennies**) N-COUNT A **penny** is one cent, or a coin worth one cent. centavo, céntimo [INFORMAL] ❑ *The price of gasoline rose by more than a penny a gallon.* *El precio de la gasolina aumentó más de un céntimo de dólar por galón.*

**pen|sion** /pɛnʃᵊn/ (**pensions**) N-COUNT A **pension** is a sum of money that a retired, widowed, or disabled person regularly receives from a former employer. pensión ❑ *He gets a $35,000 a year pension.* *Recibe una pensión de 35,000 dólares al año.*

**Pen|ta|gon** N-PROPER **The Pentagon** is the main building of the U.S. Defense Department, in Washington DC. Pentágono ❑ *...a news conference at the Pentagon.* *...una conferencia de prensa en el Pentágono.*

**pen|ta|ton|ic scale** /pɛntətɒnɪk skeɪl/ (**pentatonic scales**) N-COUNT A **pentatonic scale** is a musical scale that has five notes in each octave. escala pentatónica, escala de cinco notas [TECHNICAL]

**peo|ple** /pipᵊl/ (**peoples, peopling, peopled**) **1** N-PLURAL **People** are men, women, and children. **People** is normally used as the plural of **person**, instead of "persons." gente, personas, pueblo ❑ *Millions of people have lost their homes.* *Millones de personas han perdido su hogar.* ❑ *...the people of Angola.* *...el pueblo de Angola.* **2** N-PLURAL **The people** is sometimes used to refer to ordinary men and women, in contrast to the government or the military. pueblo ❑ *...the will of the people.* *...la voluntad del pueblo.* **3** N-COUNT A **people** is all the men, women, and children of a particular country or race. pueblo ❑ *...the native peoples of Central and South America.* *...los pueblos nativos de América del Centro y del Sur.* **4** V-T If a place or country **is peopled by** a particular group of people, that group of people live there. poblar ❑ *It was a country peopled by proud men and women.* *Era un país poblado por hombres y mujeres orgullosos.*

> **Usage** **people** and **peoples**
> *People* is plural when it refers to human beings in general or to many individual human beings together; but when *people* refers to a particular racial, ethnic, or national group, it's singular, and the plural is *peoples*: *Often, people from Europe and the United States haven't even heard of the major peoples of Africa.*

**pep|per** /pɛpər/ (**peppers, peppering, peppered**) **1** N-UNCOUNT **Pepper** or **black pepper** is a hot-tasting spice used to flavor food. pimienta ❑ *Season with salt and pepper.* *Sazone con sal y pimienta.* **2** N-COUNT A **pepper, or a bell pepper,** is a hollow green, red, or yellow vegetable with seeds inside it. pimiento, pimentón ❑ *...2 red or green peppers, sliced.* *...dos pimientos rojos o verdes, rebanados.* **3** V-T If something **is peppered with** things, there are a lot of those things in it. salpicar con, salpicar de ❑ *Readers' letters on the subject were peppered with words like "horrible" and "ugly."* *Las cartas de los lectores sobre el tema estaban salpicadas de términos como "horrible" y "feo".* **4** V-T If something **is peppered with** small objects, a lot of those objects hit it. acribillar ❑ *Houses were peppered with machine gun fire.* *Las casas fueron acribilladas con fuego de ametralladora.*
→ see **spice, vegetable**

**pep|per shak|er** (**pepper shakers**) N-COUNT A **pepper shaker** is a small container with holes at one end, used for shaking pepper onto food. pimentero
→ see **dish**

**pep|per spray** (**pepper sprays**) N-VAR A **pepper spray** is a device that releases a substance which stings the skin, used as a defense against rioters or attackers. gas pimienta ❑ *The officers blasted him with pepper spray.* *Los agentes le arrojaron gas pimienta.*

**pep ral|ly** (**pep rallies**) N-COUNT A **pep rally** at a school, college, or university is a gathering to support a sports team. reunión de apoyo

**per** /pər, STRONG pɜr/ **1** PREP You use **per** to express rates and ratios. For example, if a vehicle is traveling at 40 miles **per** hour, it travels 40 miles each hour. por ❑ *...$16 per week for lunch.* *...16 dólares por semana para la comida.* **2** **per head** → see **head**

> **Word Link** ann ≈ year : anniversary, annual, perannum

**per an|num** /pər ænəm/ ADV A particular amount **per annum** means that amount each year. por año ❑ *...a fee of $35 per annum.* *...una cuota de 35 dólares por año.*

> **Word Link** per ≈ through, thoroughly : perceive, perfect, permit

**per|ceive** /pərsiv/ (**perceives, perceiving, perceived**) **1** V-T If you **perceive** something, you see, notice, or realize it, especially when it is not obvious. percibir ❑ *A great artist teaches us to perceive reality in a different way.* *Un gran artista nos enseña a percibir la realidad de una manera diferente.* **2** V-T If you **perceive** someone or something **as** doing or being a particular thing, it is your opinion that they do this thing or that they are that thing. considerar ❑ *Stress is widely perceived as a cause of heart disease.* *Comúnmente se considera que la tensión es una de las causas de los padecimientos cardiacos.*

> **Word Link** cent ≈ hundred : cent, century, percent

**percent** /pərsɛnt/ (**percent**) N-COUNT You use **percent** to talk about amounts. For example, if an amount is 10 percent (10%) of a larger amount, it is equal to 10 hundredths of the larger amount. por ciento ❑ *Sixteen percent of children live in poverty in this country.* *El dieciséis por ciento de los niños en este país viven en la pobreza.* ❑ *Sales of new homes fell by 1.4 percent in August.* *Las ventas de casas nuevas cayeron en un 1.4 por ciento en agosto.* ● ADJ ❑ *...a 15 percent increase in border patrols.* *...un 15 por ciento de aumento en las patrullas fronterizas.* ● ADV **Percent** is also an adverb. por ciento ❑ *He predicted sales will fall 2 percent to 6 percent in the second quarter.* *Pronosticó que las ventas caerán entre un 2 y un 6 por ciento en el segundo trimestre.*

P

Picture Dictionary **percussion**

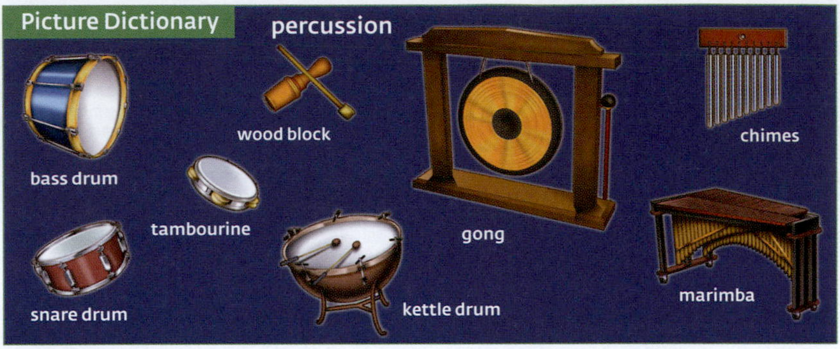


**Word Link** *age ≈ state of, related to : courage, marriage, percentage*

**per|cent|age** /pərsɛntɪdʒ/ (**percentages**) N-COUNT A **percentage** is a fraction of an amount expressed as a particular number of hundredths. *porcentaje* ❑ *...a high percentage of protein. ...un alto porcentaje de proteínas.*
→ see **fractions**

**per|cent|age point** (**percentage points**) N-COUNT A **percentage point** is one percent of something. *punto porcentual* ❑ *New home sales fell by a full percentage point in September. Las ventas de casas nuevas cayeron todo un punto porcentual en septiembre.*

**per|cen|tile** /pərsɛntaɪl/ (**percentiles**) N-COUNT A **percentile** is one of the equal divisions of an amount, expressed on a scale from 0 to 100. The 90th percentile of an amount is all amounts between zero percent and ninety percent. *percentil*

**per|cep|tion** /pərsɛpʃᵊn/ (**perceptions**) **1** N-COUNT Your **perception of** something is the way that you think about it or the impression you have of it. *idea, imagen* ❑ *Our perceptions of death affect the way we live. Nuestras ideas sobre la muerte influyen en nuestra manera de vivir.* **2** N-UNCOUNT Someone who has **perception** realizes or notices things that are not obvious. *perspicacia* ❑ *It did not require a lot of perception to realize the interview was over. No se requería mucha perspicacia para entender que la entrevista había terminado.* **3** N-COUNT **Perception** is the recognition of things using your senses, especially the sense of sight. *percepción*

**per|cep|tive** /pərsɛptɪv/ ADJ A **perceptive** person realizes or notices things that are not obvious. *perspicaz, inteligente* ❑ *...one of the finest and most perceptive sports writers. ...uno de los mejores y más perspicaces columnistas de deportes.*

**perch** /pɜrtʃ/ (**perches, perching, perched**) **1** V-I If you **perch on** something, you sit down lightly on the very edge of it. *sentarse en el borde de algo* ❑ *He perched on the corner of the desk. Se sentó en el borde de una esquina del escritorio.* **2** V-I To **perch** somewhere means to be on the top or edge of something. *encaramar* ❑ *The big mansion perches high on a hill. La enorme mansión está encaramada en lo alto de una colina.* **3** V-T If you **perch** something **on** something else, you put or balance it on the top or edge of that thing. *colgar* ❑ *He perched a pair of reading glasses low on his nose. Se colgó unos anteojos para leer en la punta de la nariz.* **4** V-I When a bird **perches on** a branch or a wall, it lands on it and stands there. *posarse* ❑ *Two doves perched on a nearby fence. Dos palomas se posaron en una valla cercana.*

**per|cus|sion** /pərkʌʃᵊn/ N-UNCOUNT **Percussion** instruments are musical instruments that you hit, such as drums. *percusión* ❑ *...the orchestra's powerful percussion section. ...la sonora sección de percusiones de la orquesta.*
→ see Picture Dictionary: **percussion**
→ see **orchestra**

**per diem** /pɜr diəm, pər/ N-SING A **per diem** is an amount of money that someone is given to cover their daily expenses while they are working. *por día, diario* ❑ *He received a per diem allowance for his travel expenses. Recibió un complemento diario para sus gastos de viaje.*

**Word Link** *enn ≈ year : bicentennial, centennial, perennial*

**per|en|nial** /pərɛniəl/ ADJ You use **perennial** to describe situations or problems that keep occurring or that seem to exist all the time. *perenne, eterno* ❑ *...the perennial problem of homelessness. ...el eterno problema de la gente sin hogar.*

**Word Link** *per ≈ through, thoroughly : perceive, perfect, permit*

**per|fect** (**perfects, perfecting, perfected**)

The adjective is pronounced /pɜrfɪkt/. The verb is pronounced /pərfɛkt/.

**1** ADJ Something that is **perfect** is as good as it could possibly be. *perfecto* ❑ *He spoke perfect English. Hablaba un inglés perfecto.* ❑ *Nobody is perfect. Nadie es perfecto.* • **per|fect|ly** ADV *perfectamente* ❑ *The system worked perfectly. El sistema funcionó perfectamente.* **2** ADJ If you say that something is **perfect for** a particular person, thing, or activity, you are emphasizing that it is very suitable for them or for that activity. *perfecto* ❑ *The pool area is perfect for entertaining. El área de la alberca es perfecta para recibir invitados.* **3** ADJ You can use **perfect** for emphasis. *perfecto, redomado, consumado* ❑ *She felt a perfect fool. Se sintió como una perfecta tonta.* • **per|fect|ly** ADV *perfectamente* ❑ *They made it perfectly clear that they didn't want us to continue. Dejaron perfectamente en claro que no querían que*

P

*continuáramos.* **4** V-T If you **perfect** something, you improve it so that it becomes as good as it can possibly be. *perfeccionar* ❑ *We perfected our recipe for vegetable stew. Perfeccionamos nuestra receta del estofado de verduras.*

**Thesaurus** *perfect* Ver también:
ADJ. flawless, ideal; (*ant.*) defective, faulty **1**

**per|fec|tion** /pərfɛkʃ<sup></sup>n/ N-UNCOUNT **Perfection** is the quality of being as good as it is possible for something of a particular kind to be. *perfección* ❑ *The meat was cooked to perfection. La carne estaba en su punto.*

**per|form** /pərfɔ̲rm/ (**performs, performing, performed**) **1** V-T When you **perform** a task or action, you do it. *ejecutar, llevar a cabo* ❑ *...people who have performed outstanding acts of bravery. ...gente que ha llevado a cabo actos de valentía excepcionales.* ❑ *You must perform this exercise correctly to avoid back pain. Debe ejecutar correctamente el ejercicio para evitar un dolor de espalda.* **2** V-T/V-I To **perform** a play, a piece of music, or a dance means to do it in front of an audience. *actuar, ejecutar, interpretar* ❑ *They will be performing works by Bach and Scarlatti. Interpretarán obras de Bach y Scarlatti.* ❑ *He began performing regularly in the early fifties. Empezó a actuar regularmente a principios de los años 1950.* ● **per|form|er** N-COUNT (**performers**) *actor o actriz, ejecutante, intérprete* ❑ *She was one of the top jazz performers in New York City. Era una de las mejores intérpretes de jazz de la ciudad de Nueva York.* **3** V-I If someone or something **performs well,** they work well or achieve a good result. *desempeñarse* ❑ *He has not performed well on his exams. No ha tenido un buen desempeño en sus exámenes.* ❑ *Those industries will always perform poorly. Esas industrias siempre tendrán malos rendimientos.* ● **per|form|er** N-COUNT *empresa cotizada en la bolsa* ❑ *...the stock-market's star performers. ...las empresas con mejores rendimientos en el mercado de valores.*

**Word Partnership** Usar *perform* con:
N. perform **miracles**, perform **tasks** **1**
ADJ. **able to** perform **1** **2**
V. **continue to** perform **1** **2**
ADV. perform **well** **3**

**Word Link** *ance ≈ quality, state : insurance, performance, resistance*

**per|for|mance** /pərfɔ̲rməns/ (**performances**) **1** N-COUNT A **performance** involves entertaining an audience by singing, dancing, or acting. *representación, función* ❑ *They were giving a performance of Bizet's "Carmen." Estaban haciendo una representación de "Carmen", de Bizet.* **2** N-VAR Someone's or something's **performance** is how successful they are or how well they do something. *desempeño, rendimiento* ❑ *The study looked at the performance of 18 surgeons. En el estudio se examinó el desempeño de dieciocho cirujanos.* ❑ *...the poor performance of the U.S. economy. ...el pobre rendimiento de la economía estadounidense.*
→ see **concert**

**per|for|mance art** N-UNCOUNT **Performance art** is a theatrical presentation that includes various art forms such as dance, music, painting, and sculpture. *arte de acción*

**per|fume** /pɜ̲rfyum, pərfyu̲m/ (**perfumes**) N-VAR **Perfume** is a pleasant-smelling liquid that women put on their skin to make themselves smell nice. *perfume* ❑ *The hall smelled of her mother's perfume. La entrada olía al perfume de su madre.*

**per|haps** /pərhæps, præps/ ADV You use **perhaps** to indicate that you are not sure whether something is true, possible, or likely. *quizá, quizás, tal vez* ❑ *In the end they lost millions, perhaps billions. Al final perdieron millones, quizá miles de millones.* ❑ *Perhaps, in time, they will understand. Tal vez lo entiendan con el tiempo.*

**Word Link** *peri ≈ around : perihelion, perimeter, periodical*

**peri|he|lion** /pɛrɪhi̲liən, -hi̲lyən/ (**perihelia**) N-COUNT The **perihelion** of a planet is the point in its orbit at which it is closest to the sun. Compare **aphelion**. *perihelio* [TECHNICAL]

**Word Link** *meter ≈ measuring : kilometer, meter, perimeter*

**pe|rim|eter** /pərɪ̲mɪtər/ (**perimeters**) N-COUNT The **perimeter** of an area of land is the whole of its outer edge or boundary. *perímetro* ❑ *...the perimeter of the airport. ...el perímetro del aeropuerto.*
→ see **area**

**pe|ri|od** /pɪ̲əriəd/ (**periods**) **1** N-COUNT A **period** is a length of time. *período, periodo* ❑ *He couldn't work for a long period of time. No pudo trabajar durante un largo período de tiempo.* ❑ *...a period of a few months. ...un período de unos cuantos meses.* ❑ *...a period of economic health. ...un periodo de salud económica.* **2** ADJ **Period** costumes, furniture, and instruments were made at an earlier time in history, or look as if they were made then. *de época* ❑ *The characters were dressed in full period costume. El vestuario de los personajes era completamente de época.* **3** N-COUNT A **period** is the punctuation mark (.) that you use at the end of a sentence when it is not a question or an exclamation. *punto* **4** N-COUNT When a woman has her **period,** she bleeds from her uterus. This usually happens once a month, unless she is pregnant. *período* **5** N-COUNT In chemistry, a **period** is one of the horizontal rows of substances in the periodic table of elements. *período* [TECHNICAL] **6** PHRASE The **period of revolution** of an object such as a planet is the time it takes to orbit another object such as a star. The Earth's period of revolution is one year. *período de revolución* **7** PHRASE The **period of rotation** of an object such as a planet is the time it takes to turn once on its axis. The Earth's period of rotation is one day. *período de rotación*
→ see **periodic table, punctuation**

**pe|ri|odi|cal** /pɪ̲əriɒ̲dɪkəl/ (**periodicals**) **1** N-COUNT A **periodical** is a magazine. *revista, publicación periódica* ❑ *...a large selection of books and periodicals. ...una amplia selección de libros y publicaciones periódicas.* **2** ADJ **Periodical** means the same as **periodic**. *periódico* ❑ *She made periodical visits to her dentist. Hacía visitas periódicas a su dentista.* ● **pe|ri|odi|cal|ly** /pɪ̲əriɒ̲dɪkli/ ADV *periódicamente* ❑ *Meetings are held periodically. Las reuniones tienen lugar periódicamente.*
→ see **library**

P

## Word Web periodic table

### The Periodic Table of Elements

| | | | | | | | | | | | | | | | | | |
|---|---|---|---|---|---|---|---|---|---|---|---|---|---|---|---|---|---|
| H | | | | | | | | | | | | | | | | | He |
| Li | Be | | | | | | | | | | | B | C | N | O | F | Ne |
| Na | Mg | | | | | | | | | | | Al | Si | P | S | Cl | Ar |
| K | Ca | Sc | Ti | V | Cr | Mn | Fe | Co | Ni | Cu | Zn | Ga | Ge | As | Se | Br | Kr |
| Rb | Sr | Y | Zr | Nb | Mo | Tc | Ru | Rh | Pd | Ag | Cd | In | Sn | Sb | Te | I | Xe |
| Cs | Ba | La | Hf | Ta | W | Re | Os | Ir | Pt | Au | Hg | Tl | Pb | Bi | Po | At | Rn |
| Fr | Ra | Ac | Rf | Db | Sg | Bh | Hs | Mt | Ds | Rg | | | | | | | |
| | | | Ce | Pr | Nd | Pm | Sm | Eu | Gd | Tb | Dy | Ho | Er | Tm | Yb | Lu | |
| | | | Th | Pa | U | Np | Pu | Am | Cm | Bk | Cf | Es | Fm | Md | No | Lr | |

Scientists started finding **elements** thousands of years ago. But it was not until 1869 that anyone understood how one element related to another. In that year, the Russian scientist Dmitri Mendeleyev created the **periodic table**. The vertical columns are called **groups**. Each group contains elements with similar **chemical** and **physical properties**. The horizontal rows are called **periods**. The elements in each row increase in **atomic mass** from left to right. Mendeleyev's original chart had many gaps. He predicted that scientists would find elements to fill these spaces. He was correct. He also predicted the properties of these new elements quite accurately.

**pe|ri|od|ic law** N-SING **The periodic law** is a law in chemistry which describes the relationship between the chemical properties of elements and their atomic numbers. *ley de periodicidad* [TECHNICAL]

**pe|ri|od|ic ta|ble** N-SING In chemistry, **the periodic table** is a table showing the chemical elements arranged according to their atomic numbers. *sistema periódico de los elementos, tabla periódica de los elementos*
→ see Word Web: **periodic table**
→ see **element**

**pe|riph|er|al ner|vous sys|tem** (**peripheral nervous system**) N-COUNT Your **peripheral nervous system** is all the nerves in your body that are outside your brain and spinal cord. Compare **central nervous system**. *sistema nervioso periférico* [TECHNICAL]

P

**per|ma|frost** /pɜrməfrɔst/ N-UNCOUNT **Permafrost** is land that is permanently frozen to a great depth. *permafrost*

**per|ma|nent** /pɜrmənənt/ (**permanents**) ADJ **Permanent** means lasting forever or occurring all the time. *permanente* ❑ *Some ear infections can cause permanent damage. Algunas infecciones del oído pueden causar daños permanentes.* ❑ *...a permanent state of tension. ...un estado de tensión permanente.* ● **per|ma|nent|ly** ADV *permanentemente* ❑ *His confidence has been permanently affected. Su confianza se ha visto afectada permanentemente.* ❑ *...the heavy, permanently locked gate. ...el pesado portón, permanentemente cerrado.* ● **per|ma|nence** N-UNCOUNT *permanencia* ❑ *...the permanence of the treaty. ...la permanencia del tratado.*

**Thesaurus** *permanent* Ver también:

ADJ. constant, continual, everlasting; (*ant.*) fleeting, temporary

**per|me|able** /pɜrmiəbᵊl/ ADJ If a substance is **permeable,** something such as water or gas can pass through it or soak into it. *permeable* ● **permeability** /pɜrmiəbɪlɪti/ N-UNCOUNT *permeabilidad* ❑ *...the permeability of the rock. ...la permeabilidad de la roca.*
→ see **amphibian**

**per|mis|sible** /pərmɪsəbᵊl/ ADJ If something is **permissible,** it is allowed because it does not break any laws or rules. *permisible, lícito* ❑ *There are times when this sort of behavior is perfectly permissible. Hay ocasiones en que esa clase de comportamiento es perfectamente permisible.*

**per|mis|sion** /pərmɪʃᵊn/ N-UNCOUNT If you give someone **permission to** do something, you tell them that they can do it. *permiso* ❑ *He asked permission to leave the room. Pidió permiso para salir de la habitación.* ❑ *They cannot leave the country without permission. No pueden salir del país sin permiso.*

**Word Partnership** Usar *permission* con:

V. **ask (for)** permission, **get** permission, permission **to leave**, **need** permission, **obtain** permission, **receive** permission, **request** permission, **seek** permission
ADJ. **special** permission, **written** permission

**Word Link** *per ≈ through, thoroughly : perceive, perfect, permit*

**per|mit** (**permits, permitting, permitted**)

The verb is pronounced /pərmɪt/. The noun is pronounced /pɜrmɪt/.

**1** V-T If someone **permits** you **to** do something, they allow you to do it. *permitir* [FORMAL] ❑ *The guards permitted me to bring my camera. Los guardias me permitieron entrar con mi cámara.* **2** N-COUNT A **permit** is an official document allowing you to do something. *permiso* ❑ *...a work permit. ...un permiso de trabajo.* **3** V-T/V-I If a situation **permits** something, it makes it possible for that thing to exist, happen, or be done. *permitir* [FORMAL] ❑ *Go out for a walk at lunchtime, if the weather permits. Si el tiempo lo permite, salga a caminar a la hora de la comida.* ❑ *This job permits me to arrange my hours around my family. Este empleo me permite organizar mi tiempo en función de mi familia.*

**per|mu|ta|tion** /pɜrmyʊteɪʃᵊn/ (**permutations**) N-COUNT A **permutation** is one of the ways in which a number of things can be ordered or arranged. *permutación, combinación, variante*

**per|pet|ual mo|tion ma|chine** (**perpetual motion machines**) N-COUNT A **perpetual motion**

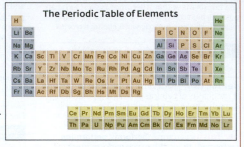

**machine** is an imaginary machine which, if it existed, would be able to continue working forever because it does not need energy from anything else. *máquina de movimiento perpetuo*

**per|secute** /pɜrsɪkyut/ (**persecutes, persecuting, persecuted**) V-T If someone **is persecuted,** they are treated cruelly and unfairly, often because of their race or beliefs. *perseguir* ❑ *They have been persecuted because of their beliefs. Los han perseguido por sus creencias.* ❑ *They began persecuting the Catholic Church. Empezaron a perseguir a la Iglesia Católica.* • **per|secu|tion** N-UNCOUNT *persecución* ❑ *...victims of political persecution. ...víctimas de la persecución política.* • **per|secu|tor** N-COUNT (**persecutors**) *perseguidor o perseguidora* ❑ *How could he forgive his persecutors? ¿Cómo podría perdonar a sus perseguidores?*

**per|sist** /pərsɪst/ (**persists, persisting, persisted**) **1** V-I If something undesirable **persists,** it continues to exist. *persistir* ❑ *Contact your doctor if the cough persists. Si la tos persiste, consulte a su médico.* **2** V-I If you **persist in** doing something, you continue to do it, even though it is difficult or other people oppose you. *persistir, insistir* ❑ *Why do people persist in ignoring the problem? ¿Por qué la gente persiste en ignorar el problema?* ❑ *He urged them to persist with their efforts to bring peace. Los urgió a persistir en sus esfuerzos por alcanzar la paz.*

**per|sis|tent** /pərsɪstənt/ **1** ADJ Something undesirable that is **persistent** continues to exist or happen for a long time. *persistente* ❑ *...persistent fears. ...temores persistentes.* ❑ *His cough grew more persistent. Su tos se volvió más persistente.* • **per|sis|tence** N-UNCOUNT *persistencia* ❑ *...the persistence of the same problems year after year. ...la persistencia de los mismos problemas año tras año.* • **per|sis|tent|ly** ADV *persistentemente* ❑ *...persistently high unemployment. ...un desempleo persistentemente alto.* **2** ADJ Someone who is **persistent** continues trying to do something, even though it is difficult or other people are against it. *persistente, tenaz* ❑ *...a persistent critic of the president. ...un crítico tenaz del presidente.* • **per|sis|tence** N-UNCOUNT *persistencia, tenacidad, perseverancia* ❑ *Skill comes only with practice, patience, and persistence. La habilidad llega con la práctica, la paciencia y la perseverancia.* • **per|sis|tent|ly** ADV *persistentemente* ❑ *He persistently refused to see a doctor. Se rehusaba persistentemente a consultar a un médico.*

**per|snick|ety** /pərsnɪkɪti/ ADJ If you describe someone as **persnickety,** you disapprove of the fact that they pay too much attention to small, unimportant details. *quisquilloso* [INFORMAL] ❑ *He has a persnickety housekeeper and never has parties. Tiene un ama de llaves quisquillosa y nunca hace fiestas.*

**per|son** /pɜrsᵊn/ (**people** or **persons**)

> The usual plural of person is **people**. The form **persons** is used as the plural in formal or legal language.

**1** N-COUNT A **person** is a man, woman, or child. *persona* ❑ *At least one person died and several others were injured. Al menos una persona murió y varias más resultaron heridas.* ❑ *They were both lovely, friendly people. Las dos eran personas encantadoras y amigables.* **2** PHRASE If you do something **in person,** you do it yourself rather than letting someone else do it for you. *en persona* ❑ *You must collect the mail in person. Debe recoger la correspondencia en persona.* **3** PHRASE If you meet, hear, or see someone **in person,** you are in the same place as them, rather than speaking to them on the telephone or writing to them. *en persona, personalmente* ❑ *She saw him in person for the first time last night. Lo vio en persona por primera vez anoche.* **4** N-COUNT In grammar, we use the term **first person** when referring to "I" and "we," **second person** when referring to "you," and **third person** when referring to "he," "she," "it," "they," and all other noun groups. **Person** is also used like this when referring to the verb forms that go with these pronouns and noun groups. *primera, segunda, tercera persona*

**per|son|al** /pɜrsənᵊl/ **1** ADJ A **personal** opinion, quality, or thing belongs or relates to a particular person. *personal* ❑ *He learned this lesson the hard way—from his own personal experience. Aprendió la lección de la manera difícil: por su propia experiencia personal.* ❑ *That's my personal opinion. Esa es mi opinión personal.* **2** ADJ If you give something your **personal** care or attention, you deal with it yourself rather than letting someone else deal with it. *personal* ❑ *...a personal letter from the president's secretary. ...una carta personal del secretario del presidente.* **3** ADJ **Personal** matters relate to your feelings, relationships, and health. *personal* ❑ *You never allow personal problems to affect your performance. Nunca permita que sus problemas personales afecten a su desempeño.* **4** ADJ **Personal** comments refer to your appearance or character in an offensive way. *personal* ❑ *I have had to face a lot of personal criticism. Tuve que enfrentar muchas críticas a mi persona.* **5** → see also **personals**

**per|son|al com|put|er** (**personal computers**) N-COUNT A **personal computer** is a computer that is used by one person at a time in a business, a school, or at home. The abbreviation **PC** is also used. *computadora personal*

**per|son|al ex|emp|tion** (**personal exemptions**) N-COUNT Your **personal exemption** is the amount of money that is deducted from your gross income before you have to start paying income tax. *exenciones para las personas físicas* ❑ *Changes for this year include an increase in the personal exemption. Las modificaciones para este año incluyen un incremento de las exenciones para las personas físicas.*

**per|son|al|ity** /pɜrsənælɪti/ (**personalities**) **1** N-VAR Your **personality** is your whole character and nature. *personalidad* ❑ *She has such a kind, friendly personality. Tiene una personalidad muy amable y amigable.* ❑ *The contest was as much about personalities as it was about politics. La contienda era tanto sobre la personalidad como sobre la política.* **2** N-COUNT You can refer to a famous person, especially in entertainment, broadcasting, or sports, as a **personality.** *personalidad* ❑ *...the radio and television personality, Johnny Carson. ...la personalidad de la radio y la televisión, Johnny Carson.*

P

**Word Partnership** Usar *personality* con:

ADJ. **strong** personality, **unique** personality 1
N. personality **trait** 1
**radio** personality, **television/TV** personality 2

**per|son|al|ly** /pɜrsənəli/ 1 ADV You use **personally** to emphasize that you are giving your own opinion. *personalmente* ❑ *Personally I think it's a waste of time. Personalmente, creo que es una pérdida de tiempo.* 2 ADV If you do something **personally,** you do it yourself rather than letting someone else do it. *personalmente* ❑ *We will personally inspect the apartment with you when you arrive. Inspeccionaremos el departamento personalmente con ustedes cuando lleguen.* 3 ADV If you meet or know someone **personally,** you meet or know them in real life, rather than knowing about them or knowing their work. *personalmente* ❑ *He did not know them personally, but he was familiar with their reputation. No los conocía personalmente, pero estaba al tanto de su reputación.*

**per|son|al pro|noun** (**personal pronouns**) N-COUNT A **personal pronoun** is a pronoun such as "I," "you," "she," or "they" which is used to refer to the speaker or the person spoken to, or to a person or thing whose identity is clear. *pronombre personal*

**per|son|als** /pɜrsənᵊlz/ N-PLURAL The section in a newspaper or magazine which contains messages or advertisements from individual people rather than businesses is called **the personals.** *anuncios clasificados*

**per|son|nel** /pɜrsənɛl/ N-PLURAL The **personnel** of an organization are the people who work for it. *personal* ❑ *...military personnel. ...el personal militar.*

**per|spec|tive** /pərspɛktɪv/ (**perspectives**) 1 N-COUNT A particular **perspective** is a particular way of thinking about something. *visión* ❑ *The death of his father has given him a new perspective on life. Gracias a la muerte de su padre, tiene una nueva visión de la vida.* ❑ *...two different perspectives on child development. ...dos visiones diferentes sobre el desarrollo infantil.* 2 N-UNCOUNT **Perspective** is the theory of representing three dimensions on a two-dimensional surface, in order to recreate the appearance of objects that are further away as smaller than those that are nearer. *perspectiva* 3 PHRASE If you get something **in perspective** or **into perspective,** you judge its real importance by considering it in relation to everything else. If you get something **out of perspective,** you fail to do this. *objetivamente* ❑ *Remember to keep things in perspective. Recuerda que debes ver las cosas objetivamente.* ❑ *I think I've let things get out of perspective. Creo que dejé de ser objetivo.*

**Thesaurus** *perspective* Ver también:

N. attitude, outlook, viewpoint 1

**per|suade** /pərsweɪd/ (**persuades, persuading, persuaded**) 1 V-T If you **persuade** someone **to** do something, you cause them to do it by giving them good reasons for doing it. *persuadir de, convencer de* ❑ *My husband persuaded me to come. Mi esposo me convenció de que viniera.* 2 V-T If you **persuade** someone that something is true, you say things that eventually make them believe that it is true. *persuadir de, convencer de* ❑ *I've persuaded her to talk to you. La persuadí de que hablara contigo.*

**Thesaurus** *persuade* Ver también:

V. cajole, convince, influence, sway, talk into, win over; (*ant.*) discourage, dissuade 1 2

**Word Partnership** Usar *persuade* con:

V. **attempt to** persuade, **be able to** persuade, **fail to** persuade, **try to** persuade 1 2

**per|sua|sion** /pərsweɪʒᵊn/ (**persuasions**) 1 N-UNCOUNT **Persuasion** is the act of persuading someone to do something or to believe that something is true. *persuasión, insistencia* ❑ *After much persuasion from Ellis, she agreed to perform. Después de que Ellis le insistiera mucho, aceptó actuar.* 2 N-COUNT If you are **of** a particular **persuasion,** you have a particular belief or set of beliefs. *creencia, convicción, credo* [FORMAL] ❑ *...people of all political persuasions. ...gente de todas las convicciones políticas.*

**pest** /pɛst/ (**pests**) 1 N-COUNT **Pests** are insects or small animals that damage crops or food supplies. *plaga, insecto nocivo* ❑ *There are very few insect pests or diseases in this country. En este país hay muy pocas enfermedades o insectos nocivos.* 2 N-COUNT You can describe someone, especially a child, as a **pest** if they keep bothering you. *fastidio, lata* [INFORMAL] ❑ *He climbed on the table, pulled my hair, and was generally a pest. Se trepó sobre la mesa, me jaló el pelo, e hizo todo lo posible por fastidiar.*
→ see **farm**

**pes|ter** /pɛstər/ (**pesters, pestering, pestered**) V-T If you say that someone **is pestering** you, you mean that they keep asking you to do something, or keep talking to you, and you find this annoying. *molestar, acosar* ❑ *I wish she would stop pestering me. Ojalá dejara de molestarme.* ❑ *He gets annoyed with people pestering him for money. Se enoja con la gente que lo molesta pidiéndole dinero.*

**Word Link** *cide ≈ killing : genocide, pesticide, suicide*

**pes|ti|cide** /pɛstɪsaɪd/ (**pesticides**) N-VAR **Pesticides** are chemicals that farmers put on their crops to kill harmful insects. *pesticida*
→ see **pollution**

**pes|tle** /pɛsᵊl/ (**pestles**) N-COUNT A **pestle** is a short rod with a thick round end. It is used for crushing things such as herbs, spices, or grain in a bowl called a mortar. *mano de mortero*
→ see **laboratory**

**pet** /pɛt/ (**pets, petting, petted**) 1 N-COUNT A **pet** is an animal that you keep in your home to give you company and pleasure. *mascota* ❑ *It is cruel to keep turtles as pets. Es cruel tener tortugas como mascotas.* ❑ *...his pet dog. ...su perro mascota.* 2 ADJ Someone's **pet** subject is one that they particularly like. *favorito* ❑ *...speeches about her pet subject of education. ...discursos sobre su tema favorito,*

P

**Word Web** pet

Americans love **pets**. They own more than 51 million **dogs**, 56 million **cats**, and 45 million **birds**. They also have more than 75 million small **mammals** and **reptiles**, and millions of **fish**. Recent studies suggest that adult pet owners are healthier than adults who don't have **companion animals**. One study (Katcher, 1982) suggests that pet owners have lower blood pressure. In 2001 the German Socio-Economic Panel Survey studied a group of people. Some of the people owned pets and some did not. The survey showed that people with pets went to the doctor less often than people without pets. And a study in the *American Journal of Cardiology* found that male dog owners were less likely to die within a year after a heart attack than men who didn't own dogs.

*la educación.* **3** V-T If you **pet** an animal, you pat or stroke it in an affectionate way. *acariciar* ❑ *He reached down and petted the dog. Se agachó y acarició al perro.*
→ see Word Web: **pet**

**pet|al** /pɛtᵊl/ (**petals**) N-COUNT The **petals** of a flower are the thin colored or white parts that together form the flower. *pétalo* ❑ *...bowls of dried rose petals. ...tazones con pétalos de rosa secos.*
→ see **flower**

**pe|ter** /pitər/ (**peters, petering, petered**)
▸ **peter out** PHR-VERB If something **peters out,** it gradually comes to an end. *decaer, apagarse, agotarse* ❑ *The strike seems to be petering out. La huelga parece estar decayendo.*

**pe|tite** /pətit/ ADJ A **petite** woman is small and slim. *pequeño, menudo* ❑ *...catalogs that supply clothes for the petite female customer. ...catálogos de ropa para mujeres menudas.*

**pe|ti|tion** /pətɪʃᵊn/ (**petitions, petitioning, petitioned**) **1** N-COUNT A **petition** is a document signed by a lot of people that asks a government or other official group to do a particular thing. *petición* ❑ *...a petition signed by 4,500 people. ...una petición firmada por 4,500 personas.* **2** V-T/V-I If you **petition** someone in authority, you make a formal request to them. *presentar una petición, presentar una demanda* [LEGAL] ❑ *...couples petitioning for divorce. ...parejas que presentan demandas de divorcio.* ❑ *All the attempts to petition Congress have failed. Todos los intentos por presentar una petición ante el Congreso han fracasado.*

**Petri dish** /pitrɪ dɪʃ/ (**Petri dishes**) N-COUNT A **Petri dish** is a shallow circular dish that is used in laboratories for producing groups of microorganisms. *cápsula o caja de Petri* [TECHNICAL]
→ see **laboratory**

**pe|tro|leum** /pətroʊliəm/ N-UNCOUNT **Petroleum** is oil that is found under the surface of the earth or under the sea bed. Gasoline and kerosene are obtained from petroleum. *petróleo*
→ see Word Web: **petroleum**
→ see **energy, oil**

**pet|ty** /pɛti/ (**pettier, pettiest**) **1** ADJ You can use **petty** to describe things such as problems, rules, or arguments that you think are unimportant. *insignificante, trivial, nimio* ❑ *Fights would start over petty things. Las peleas empezaban por nimiedades.* ❑ *...endless rules and petty regulations. ...reglas interminables y reglamentos triviales.* **2** ADJ If you describe someone as **petty,** you disapprove of them because they are willing to be unpleasant to other people because of small, unimportant things. *mezquino* ❑ *Always give your best, never be petty. Da siempre lo mejor de ti mismo; nunca seas mezquino.* • **pet|ti|ness** N-UNCOUNT *mezquindad* ❑ *...nasty pettiness. ...una mezquindad cruel.* **3** ADJ **Petty** is used of people or actions that are less important, serious, or great than others. *menor* ❑ *...petty crime, such as purse-snatching. ...delitos*

**Word Web** petroleum

Most **petroleum** is used as **fuel**. We use **gasoline** to power our cars and **heating oil** to warm our homes. About 20% of **crude oil** becomes **gas** and 10% becomes heating oil. Today 90% of the **energy** used in transport comes from petroleum. Other petroleum products include household items such as **paint**, **deodorant**, and **shampoo**. Some of our clothes are also made using petroleum. These include **shoes**, **sweaters**, and **polyester shirts** and **dresses**. Petroleum products are also important for building new houses. They are used to make water **pipes**, **shower** doors, and even **toilet** seats.

P

**Word Web** **philosophy**

Confucius

Plato

Aristotle

**Philosophy** helps us **understand** ourselves and the purpose of our lives. **Philosophers** have studied the same **issues** for thousands of years. The Chinese philosopher Confucius* wrote about personal and **political morals**. He taught that people should love others and honor their parents. They should do what is right, not what is best for themselves. He thought that a ruler who had to use force had failed. The Greek philosopher Plato* wrote about politics and science. Later, Aristotle* created a system of **logic** and **reasoning**. He wanted to be absolutely sure of what is true and what is not.

*Confucius (551-479 BC)*
*Plato (427-347 BC)*
*Aristotle (384-322 BC)*

*menores, como arrebatar la bolsa a una mujer.*

**pH** /pi eɪtʃ/ N-UNCOUNT The **pH of** a solution indicates how acid or alkaline the solution is. A pH of less than 7 indicates that it is an acid, and a pH of more than 7 indicates that it is an alkali. *valor pH, potencial de hidrógeno, índice de Sörensen*

**phar|ma|ceu|ti|cal** /fɑrməsutɪkᵊl/ (**pharmaceuticals**) **1** ADJ **Pharmaceutical** means connected with the industrial production of medicines. *farmacéutico* ❑ *...a Swiss pharmaceutical company. ...una compañía farmacéutica suiza.* **2** N-PLURAL **Pharmaceuticals** are medicines. *productos farmacéuticos*

**phar|ma|cy** /fɑrməsi/ (**pharmacies**) **1** N-COUNT A **pharmacy** is a place where medicines are sold or given out. *farmacia, botica* ❑ *Pick up the medicine from the pharmacy. Recoja la medicina en la farmacia.* **2** N-UNCOUNT **Pharmacy** is the job or the science of preparing medicines. *farmacia, química farmacéutica* ❑ *He spent four years studying pharmacy. Pasó cuatro años estudiando química farmacéutica.*

P

**phar|ynx** /færɪŋks/ (**pharynges** /fərɪndʒiz/ or **pharynxes** /færɪŋksɪz/) N-COUNT Your **pharynx** is the area at the back of your throat, which connects your mouth and nose to your windpipe. *faringe* [TECHNICAL]

**phase** /feɪz/ (**phases, phasing, phased**) N-COUNT A **phase** is a particular stage in a process or in the development of something. *fase, etapa* ❑ *6000 women will take part in the first phase of the project. 6,000 mujeres tomarán parte en la primera fase del proyecto.* ❑ *The crisis is entering a critical phase. La situación está entrando en una fase crítica.* N-COUNT *The* **phases** *of* the moon are the different stages of the moon's appearance, for example a new moon or a full moon. *fase*

▸ **phase in** PHR-VERB If a new way of doing something **is phased in,** it is introduced gradually. *introducir/aplicar paulatinamente* ❑ *The reforms will be phased in over three years. Las reformas se introducirán paulatinamente a lo largo de tres años.*

▸ **phase out** PHR-VERB If something **is phased out,** people gradually stop using it. *eliminar paulatinamente, excluir por fases, discontinuar por etapas* ❑ *They think that the present system should be phased out. Ellos opinan que el actual sistema debería eliminarse paulatinamente.*

**Ph.D.** /pi eɪtʃdi/ (**Ph.D.s**) also **PhD** N-COUNT A **Ph.D.** is a degree awarded to people who have done advanced research into a particular subject. **Ph.D.** is an abbreviation for **Doctor of Philosophy**. *doctorado* ❑ *He is highly educated and has a Ph.D. in chemistry. Es muy culto y tiene un doctorado en química.*
→ see **graduation**

**phe|nom|enon** /fɪnɒmɪnɒn/ (**phenomena**) N-COUNT A **phenomenon** is something that is observed to happen or exist. *fenómeno* [FORMAL] ❑ *...natural phenomena such as thunder and lightning. ...los fenómenos naturales, como el trueno y el rayo.*
→ see **experiment, science**

**phe|no|type** /finətaɪp/ (**phenotypes**) N-VAR The **phenotype** of an animal or plant is all the physical characteristics it has as a result of the interaction between its genes and the environment. *fenotipo* [TECHNICAL]

**phero|mone** /fɛrəmoʊn/ (**pheromones**) N-COUNT Some animals and insects produce chemicals called **pheromones** that affect the behavior of other animals and insects of the same type, for example, by attracting them sexually. *feromona* [TECHNICAL]

**phi|loso|pher** /fɪlɒsəfər/ (**philosophers**) N-COUNT A **philosopher** is a person who studies or writes about philosophy. *filósofo* ❑ *...the Greek philosopher Plato. ...el filósofo griego Platón.*
→ see **philosophy**

**philo|sophi|cal** /fɪləsɒfɪkᵊl/ **1** ADJ **Philosophical** means concerned with or relating to philosophy. *filosófico* ❑ *...philosophical discussions. ...discusiones filosóficas.* ● **philo|sophi|cal|ly** /fɪləsɒfɪkli/ ADV *filosóficamente, desde el punto de vista de la filosofía* ❑ *He's philosophically opposed to war. Se opone a la guerra por razones filosóficas.* **2** ADJ Someone who is **philosophical** does not get upset when disappointing or disturbing things happen; used to show approval. *que se toma las cosas con filosofía* ❑ *Lewis grew philosophical about life. Lewis empezó a tomar la vida con filosofía.* ● **philo|sophi|cal|ly** ADV *filosóficamente* ❑ *She says philosophically: "It could have been far worse."*

*Tomándose las cosas con filosofía, dice: "Pudo haber sido mucho peor".*

**phi|loso|phy** /fɪlɒsəfi/ (**philosophies**) **1** N-UNCOUNT **Philosophy** is the study or creation of theories about basic things such as the nature of existence or how people should live. *filosofía* ❑ *...traditional Chinese philosophy. ...la filosofía china tradicional.* **2** N-COUNT A **philosophy** is a particular theory or belief. *filosofía* ❑ *The best philosophy is to change to a low-sugar diet. Lo mejor para uno es cambiar a una dieta baja en azúcar.*
→ see Word Web: **philosophy**

**phloem** /floʊɛm/ (**phloems**) N-VAR **Phloem** is the layer of material in plants that carries food from the leaves to the rest of the plant. Compare **xylem.** *floema* [TECHNICAL]

**pho|bia** /foʊbiə/ (**phobias**) N-COUNT A **phobia** is a strong irrational fear or hatred of something. *fobia* ❑ *The man had a phobia about flying. El hombre tenía fobia a volar.*

**phone** /foʊn/ (**phones, phoning, phoned**) **1** N-SING The **phone** is an electrical system that you use to talk to someone else in another place, by dialing a number on a piece of equipment and speaking into it. *teléfono* ❑ *I told you over the phone. Te lo dije por teléfono.* ❑ *She looked forward to talking to her daughter by phone. Estaba ansiosa por hablar con su hija por teléfono.* **2** N-COUNT The **phone** is the piece of equipment that you use when you dial a phone number and talk to someone. *teléfono* ❑ *Two minutes later the phone rang. Dos minutos después, sonó el teléfono.* **3** → see also **cellular phone** **4** V-T/V-I When you **phone** someone or when you **phone** them **up,** you dial their phone number and speak to them by phone. *llamar por teléfono, telefonear* ❑ *He phoned Laura to see if she was better. Llamó a Laura por teléfono para ver cómo seguía.* ❑ *"Did anybody phone?" asked Alberg. —¿Llamó alguien?—preguntó Alberg.* **5** PHRASE If someone is **on the phone,** they are speaking to someone by phone. *al teléfono, estar hablando por teléfono* ❑ *She's always on the phone. Se la pasa hablando por teléfono.*
→ see **office**

**phone booth** (**phone booths**) N-COUNT A **phone booth** is a small shelter outdoors or in a building in which there is a public telephone. *cabina telefónica*

**phone call** (**phone calls**) N-COUNT If you make a **phone call,** you dial a phone number and speak to someone by phone. *llamada telefónica* ❑ *I have to make a phone call. Tengo que hacer una llamada telefónica.*

**phone|card** /foʊnkɑrd/ (**phonecards**) also **phone card** N-COUNT A **phonecard** is a plastic card that you can use instead of money in some telephones. *tarjeta telefónica*

**pho|neme** /foʊnim/ (**phonemes**) N-COUNT A **phoneme** is the smallest unit of significant sound in a language. *fonema* [TECHNICAL]

**pho|ne|mic aware|ness** /fənimɪk/ N-UNCOUNT **Phonemic awareness** is the ability to distinguish the small, separate sounds that spoken words consist of. *conciencia fonémica* [TECHNICAL]

**phon|ics** /fɒnɪks/ N-UNCOUNT **Phonics** is a method of teaching people to read by training them to associate written letters with their sounds. *fonética* [TECHNICAL]

**pho|no|gram** /foʊnəgræm/ (**phonograms**) N-COUNT A **phonogram** is a written letter or symbol, or a series of written letters or symbols, that represents a word or part of a word. For example, the symbol "@" is a phonogram that represents the word "at," and the letters "ake" are a phonogram that appears in words such as "make" and "take." *fonograma* [TECHNICAL]

**pho|ny** /foʊni/ (**phonier, phoniest, phonies**) also **phoney** **1** ADJ If you describe something as **phony,** you disapprove of it because it is not genuine. *falso* [INFORMAL] ❑ *He telephoned with some phony excuse. Telefoneó con un pretexto cualquiera.* **2** ADJ If you describe someone as **phony,** you disapprove of them because they are pretending to be something they are not. *farsante* [INFORMAL] ● **Phony** is also a noun. *farsante, impostor* ❑ *He's such a phony. Es tan farsante.*

**phos|pho|lip|id** /fɒsfoʊlɪpɪd, -laɪp-/ (**phospholipids**) N-COUNT **Phospholipids** are fats that form an important part of the structure of cell membranes. *fosfolípido* [TECHNICAL]

**pho|to** /foʊtoʊ/ (**photos**) N-COUNT A **photo** is the same as a **photograph.** *foto*
→ see **photography**

**photo|cell** /foʊtoʊsɛl/ (**photocells**) also **photoelectric cell** N-COUNT A **photocell** or a **photoelectric cell** is a device that measures the amount of light that is present and converts it into electricity. *fotocélula, célula fotoeléctrica, fotocelda* [TECHNICAL]

**photo|copi|er** /foʊtəkɒpiər/ (**photocopiers**) N-COUNT A **photocopier** is a machine that quickly copies documents by photographing them. *fotocopiadora*

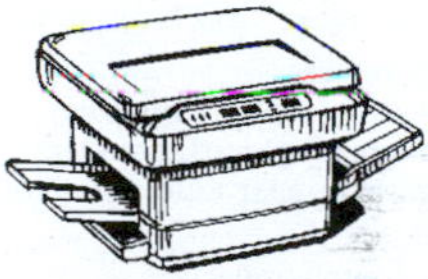
photocopier

**photo|copy** /foʊtəkɒpi/ (**photocopies, photocopying, photocopied**) **1** N-COUNT A **photocopy** is a copy of a document made using a photocopier. *fotocopia* ❑ *He was shown a photocopy of the letter. Le mostraron una fotocopia de la carta.* **2** V-T If you **photocopy** a document, you make a copy of it using a photocopier. *fotocopiar* ❑ *Staff photocopied the check before cashing it. El personal fotocopió el cheque antes de cobrarlo.*

**photo|graph** /foʊtəgræf/ (**photographs, photographing, photographed**) **1** N-COUNT A **photograph** is a picture that is made using a camera. *fotografía* ❑ *He wants to take some photographs of the house. Quiere tomar unas fotografías de la casa.* **2** V-T When you **photograph** someone or something, you use a camera to obtain a picture of them. *fotografiar* [FORMAL] ❑ *She photographed the children. Fotografió a los niños.* ❑ *They were photographed kissing. Los fotografiaron besándose.*

**pho|tog|ra|pher** /fətɒgrəfər/ (**photographers**) N-COUNT A **photographer** is someone who takes photographs as a job or hobby. *fotógrafo o fotógrafa* ❑ *...a professional photographer. ...una fotógrafa profesional.*
→ see **photography**

## Word Web photography

It's easy to **take** a **picture** with a digital **camera**. You just look through the viewfinder and push the **shutter button**. But professional **photographers** need to produce high quality **photos**. So their job is harder. First they choose the right **film** and **load** the camera. Then they check the **lighting** and carefully **focus** the camera. They usually take several **shots**, one after another. Then it's time to **develop** the film and make **prints**. Sometimes a photographer will **crop** a photo or **enlarge** it to create a more striking **image**.

**photo|graph|ic** /foʊtəgræfɪk/ ADJ **Photographic** means connected with photographs or photography. *fotográfico* ❑ *...photographic equipment. ...equipo fotográfico.*

**pho|tog|ra|phy** /fətɒgrəfi/ N-UNCOUNT **Photography** is the skill, job, or process of producing photographs. *fotografía* ❑ *Photography is one of her hobbies. La fotografía es uno de sus pasatiempos.*
→ see Word Web: **photography**

**photo|recep|tor** /foʊtoʊrɪsɛptər/ (**photoreceptors**) N-COUNT **Photoreceptors** are very small structures in the eye which can detect and respond to light. *fotorreceptor, fotorreceptora* [TECHNICAL]

**pho|to shoot** (**photo shoots**) also **photo-shoot** N-COUNT A **photo shoot** is an occasion when a photographer takes pictures, especially of models or famous people, to be used in a newspaper or magazine. *sesión de fotos* ❑ *...a long day of interviews and photo-shoots. ...un largo día de entrevistas y sesiones de fotografías.*

**photo|sphere** /foʊtəsfɪər/ (**photospheres**) N-COUNT The **photosphere** is the surface of the sun, where the sun's gases appear solid. *fotosfera* [TECHNICAL]

P

**photo|syn|the|sis** /foʊtoʊsɪnθəsɪs/ N-UNCOUNT **Photosynthesis** is the way that green plants make their food using sunlight. *fotosíntesis* [TECHNICAL]
→ see Word Web: **photosynthesis**

**pho|tot|ro|pism** /foʊtɒtrəpɪzəm/ (**phototropisms**) N-VAR **Phototropism** is the tendency of a plant to grow in the direction of a light source. *fototropismo* [TECHNICAL]

**photovoltaic** /foʊtoʊvɔlteɪɪk/ ADJ A **photovoltaic** cell or panel is a device that uses sunlight to cause a chemical reaction which produces electricity. *fotovoltaico* [TECHNICAL]
→ see **electricity**

**phras|al verb** /freɪzᵊl vɜrb/ (**phrasal verbs**) N-COUNT A **phrasal verb** is a combination of a verb and an adverb or preposition, for example, "get over" or "knock back," which together have a particular meaning. *frase verbal*

**phrase** /freɪz/ (**phrases, phrasing, phrased**) **1** N-COUNT A **phrase** is a short group of words that are used as a unit and whose meaning may not be obvious from the words contained in it. *frase hecha* ❑ *I hate the phrase: "You have to be cruel to be kind." Detesto las frases hechas como: "Para ser amable, tienes que ser cruel".* **2** V-T If you **phrase** something in a particular way, you say or write it in that way. *expresar, formular, redactar* ❑ *I would have phrased it quite differently. Yo lo hubiera expresado de una manera completamente diferente.* ❑ *The speech was carefully phrased. El discurso estaba cuidadosamente redactado.* **3** N-COUNT A **phrase** is a short section of a piece of music which expresses a musical idea. *frase* **4** PHRASE If someone has a particular **turn of phrase,** they have a particular way of expressing themselves in words. *manera de expresarse* ❑ *...an entertaining person with a delightful turn of phrase. ...una persona amena, con una encantadora manera de expresarse.*

**phras|ing** /freɪzɪŋ/ N-UNCOUNT The **phrasing** of someone who is singing, playing a piece of music, acting, dancing, or reading something aloud is the way in which they divide up the work by pausing slightly in appropriate places. *fraseo*

**phy|lum** /faɪləm/ (**phyla**) N-COUNT A **phylum**

## Word Web photosynthesis

**Plants** make their own food from **sunlight**, **water**, and **soil**. They get water and **minerals** from the ground through their roots. They also absorb **carbon dioxide** from the air through tiny holes in their leaves. The green pigment in plant leaves is called **chlorophyll**. It combines **solar energy** with water and carbon dioxide to produce **glucose**. This process is called **photosynthesis**. During the process, the plant releases **oxygen** into the atmosphere. It uses some of the glucose to grow larger. When humans and other animals eat plants, they also make use of this stored **energy**.

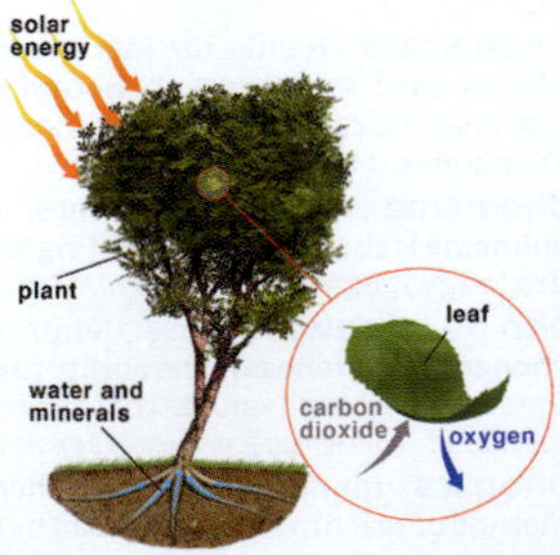

is a group of related species of animals or plants. Compare **kingdom**, **class**. filum, filo [TECHNICAL]

**phys ed** /fɪz ɛd/ N-UNCOUNT **Phys ed** is the same as **physical education**. educación física, deportes [INFORMAL] ❑ ...Don, who taught phys ed at a junior high school. ...Don, el que enseñaba educación física en una secundaria.

**Word Link** *physi ≈ of nature : physical, physician, physics*

**physi|cal** /fɪzɪkᵊl/ 1 ADJ **Physical** means connected with a person's body, rather than with their mind. físico ❑ ...physical and mental problems. ...problemas físicos y mentales. ❑ Physical activity promotes good health. La actividad física fomenta la buena salud. • **physi|cal|ly** ADV físicamente ❑ You may be physically and mentally exhausted after a long flight. Después de un vuelo largo, se puede estar física y mentalmente exhausto. En español, cuando 2 ADJ **Physical** things are real things that can be touched and seen. físico ❑ ...physical evidence to support the story. ...pruebas físicas que sustentan la historia. → see **periodic table**
→ see **diagnosis**

**physi|cal change** (**physical changes**) N-VAR When there is a **physical change** to a substance, its form or appearance changes but it does not become a different substance. cambio físico

**physi|cal ed|u|ca|tion** N-UNCOUNT **Physical education** is the school subject in which students do physical exercises or take part in physical games and sports. educación física, deportes

**physi|cal prop|er|ty** (**physical properties**) N-COUNT The **physical properties** of a substance are qualities such as its size and shape, which can be measured without changing what the substance is. propiedad física
→ see **periodic table**

**physi|cal sci|ence** (**physical sciences**) N-COUNT **The physical sciences** are branches of science such as physics, chemistry, and geology that are concerned with natural forces and with things that do not have life. ciencias físicas

**physi|cal ther|a|py** N-UNCOUNT **Physical therapy** is medical treatment given to people who have injured part of their body that involves exercise, massage, or heat treatment. fisioterapia, kinesiología, quinesiología, terapia física
→ see **illness**

**Word Link** *ician ≈ person who works at : electrician, musician, physician*

**phy|si|cian** /fɪzɪʃᵊn/ (**physicians**) N-COUNT A **physician** is a medical doctor. médico o médica [FORMAL] ❑ ...your family physician. ...su médico familiar.
→ see **diagnosis, hospital, medicine**

**phy|si|cian's as|sis|tant** (**physician's assistants**) N-COUNT A **physician's assistant** is a person who is trained to do some of the same work that a doctor does but who is not a doctor. asociado médico o asociada médica

**physi|cist** /fɪzɪsɪst/ (**physicists**) N-COUNT A **physicist** is a person who studies physics. físico o física ❑ ...a nuclear physicist. ...un físico nuclear.

**phys|ics** /fɪzɪks/ N-UNCOUNT **Physics** is the scientific study of forces such as heat, light, sound, pressure, gravity, and electricity. física ❑ ...the laws of physics. ...las leyes de la física.

**phy|sique** /fɪzik/ (**physiques**) N-COUNT Someone's **physique** is the shape and size of their body. físico ❑ He has the physique of a man half his age. Tiene el físico de un hombre de la mitad de su edad.

**phyto|plank|ton** /faɪtoʊplæŋktən/ N-PLURAL **Phytoplankton** are tiny plants such as algae that are found in plankton. fitoplancton [TECHNICAL]

**Word Link** *ist ≈ one who practices : artist, chemist, pianist*

**pia|nist** /piænɪst, piənɪst/ (**pianists**) N-COUNT A **pianist** is a person who plays the **piano**. pianista ❑ ...a concert pianist. ...pianista de concierto.

**pi|ano** /piænoʊ, pyænoʊ/ (**pianos**) N-VAR A **piano** is a large musical instrument with a row of black and white keys, which you strike with your fingers. piano ❑ I taught myself how to play the piano. Yo mismo me enseñé a tocar el piano.
→ see **keyboard, music**

**pick** /pɪk/ (**picks, picking, picked**) 1 V-T If you **pick** a particular person or thing, you choose that one. escoger, seleccionar, elegir ❑ Mr. Nowell picked ten people to interview. El señor Nowell escogió a diez personas para entrevistarlas. 2 N-SING You can refer to the best things or people in a particular group as **the pick of** that group. lo mejor ❑ The boys here are the pick of the high school's soccer players. Estos muchachos son lo mejor de los jugadores de fútbol de la secundaria. 3 V-T When you **pick** flowers, fruit, or leaves, you break them off the plant or tree and collect them. cortar, recoger ❑ I've picked some flowers from the garden. Corté unas flores del jardín. 4 V-T If you **pick** something from a place, you remove it from there with your fingers or your hand. recoger ❑ He picked the napkin from his lap. Recogió la servilleta de sus rodillas. 5 V-T If you **pick** a fight **with** someone, you deliberately cause one. buscar ❑ He picked a fight with a waiter. Le buscó pelea al mesero. 6 V-T If someone such as a thief **picks** a lock, they open it without a key, for example, by using a piece of wire. forzar ❑ She picked the lock on his door and stepped inside. Forzó la cerradura de su puerta y entró.

▸ **pick on** PHR-VERB If someone **picks on** you, they repeatedly criticize you unfairly or treat you unkindly. meterse con, agarrarla con [INFORMAL] ❑ Bullies often pick on younger children. Los bravucones acostumbran agarrarla con los niños menores.

▸ **pick out** 1 PHR-VERB If you **pick out** someone or something, you recognize them when it is difficult to see them. reconocer, distinguir ❑ I had trouble picking out the words, even with my glasses on. Tuve problemas para distinguir las palabras, aun con los lentes puestos. 2 PHR-VERB If you **pick out** someone or something, you choose them from a group of people or things. escoger, seleccionar ❑ I have been picked out to represent the whole team. Me escogieron para representar a todo el equipo.

▸ **pick up** 1 PHR-VERB When you **pick** something **up**, you lift it up. recoger, levantar ❑ He picked his cap up from the floor. Levantó su gorra del piso. 2 PHR-VERB When you **pick up** someone or something, you collect them from somewhere, often in a car. recoger, ir a buscar ❑ She was going

P

over to her parents' house to pick up some clean clothes. *Iba a pasar a la casa de sus padres a recoger ropa limpia.* 3 PHR-VERB If you **pick up** a skill or an idea, you acquire it without effort over a period of time. *aprender* [INFORMAL] ❑ *Where did you pick up your English? —¿Donde aprendió su inglés?* 4 PHR-VERB If you **pick up** an illness, you get it from somewhere or something. *adquirir* ❑ *They've picked up an infection from something they've eaten. Adquirieron una infección por algo que habían comido.* 5 PHR-VERB If a piece of equipment **picks up** a signal or sound, it receives it or detects it. *captar, recibir* ❑ *We can pick up Mexican television. Podemos recibir la televisión mexicana.* 6 PHR-VERB If trade or the economy of a country **picks up,** it improves. *repuntar* ❑ *Industrial production is beginning to pick up. La producción industrial está empezando a repuntar.*

**Thesaurus** *pick* Ver también:

V. choose, decide on, elect, select 1
collect, gather, harvest, pull 3

**pick|le** /pɪkəl/ (**pickles**) 1 N-PLURAL **Pickles** are vegetables or fruit which have been kept in vinegar or salt water for a long time to give them a strong, sharp taste. *encurtido* ❑ *...a hamburger with pickles, ketchup, and mustard. ...una hamburguesa con encurtidos, catsup y mostaza.* 2 N-VAR **Pickle** is a cold spicy sauce with pieces of vegetables and fruit in it. *escabeche, adobo, condimento a base de encurtidos en una salsa* ❑ *...jars of pickle. ...tarros de escabeche.*

**pick|led** /pɪkəld/ ADJ **Pickled** food has been kept in vinegar or salt water to preserve it. *en salmuera* ❑ *...a jar of pickled fruit. ...un tarro de fruta en salmuera.*

**pick|up** /pɪkʌp/ (**pickups**) 1 N-COUNT A **pickup** or a **pickup truck** is a small truck with low sides that can be easily loaded and unloaded. *camioneta* 2 N-SING A **pickup in** trade or **in** a country's economy is an improvement in it. *repunte, mejora* ❑ *...a pickup in the housing market. ...un repunte del mercado de la vivienda.* 3 N-COUNT A **pickup** takes place when someone picks up a person or thing that is waiting to be collected. *recogida* ❑ *The company had pickup points in most cities. La empresa tenía lugares de recogida en la mayoría de las ciudades.*
→ see **car**

P

**pic|nic** /pɪknɪk/ (**picnics, picnicking, picnicked**) 1 N-COUNT When people have a **picnic,** they eat a meal outdoors, usually in a park or a forest, or at the beach. *comida en el campo, picnic* ❑ *We're going on a picnic tomorrow. Mañana vamos a una comida en el campo.* 2 V-I When people **picnic** somewhere, they have a picnic. *comer* ❑ *Afterward, we picnicked by the river. Después comimos junto al río.*
→ see **park**

**pic|ture** /pɪktʃər/ (**pictures, picturing, pictured**) 1 N-COUNT A **picture** consists of lines and shapes that are drawn, painted, or printed on a surface and show a person, thing, or scene. *pintura, cuadro* ❑ *...a small picture drawn with colored chalk. ...un pequeño cuadro dibujado con gis(es) de color.* 2 N-COUNT A **picture** is a photograph. *fotografía* ❑ *The tourists have nothing to do but take pictures of each other. Los turistas no tienen otra cosa que hacer que tomarse fotos unos a otros.* 3 N-COUNT Television **pictures** are the scenes that you see on a television screen. *imagen* ❑ *...television pictures of human suffering. ...imágenes televisivas del sufrimiento humano.* 4 V-T If someone or something **is pictured** in a newspaper or magazine, they appear in a photograph in it. *retratar* ❑ *The golfer is pictured on many of the front pages. El golfista aparece en muchas de las primeras planas.* 5 N-COUNT You can refer to a movie as a **picture.** *película* ❑ *...a director of action pictures. ...un director de películas de acción.* 6 V-T If you **picture** something in your mind, you think of it and have such a clear memory or idea of it that you seem to be able to see it. *representarse, imaginarse* ❑ *He pictured her with long black hair. Se la imaginó con cabello largo y negro.* ❑ *He pictured Carrie sitting out in the car. Se imaginó a Carrie afuera, sentada en el coche.* ● **Picture** is also a noun. *cuadro, imagen, idea* ❑ *We do have a picture of how we'd like things to be. Sí tenemos una idea de cómo quisiéramos que fuesen las cosas.* 7 N-COUNT A **picture** of something is a description of it or an indication of what it is like. *descripción* ❑ *I'll try and give you a better picture of what the boys do. Voy a tratar de describirte mejor lo que hacen los muchachos.* 8 N-SING When you refer to the **picture** in a particular place, you are referring to the situation there. *situación, circunstancia* ❑ *It's a similar picture across the border in Ethiopia. La situación es similar al otro lado de la frontera, en Etiopía.* 9 PHRASE If you **put** someone **in the picture,** you tell them about a situation which they need to know about. *poner al tanto* ❑ *Has anyone put you in the picture? ¿Ya te puso alguien al tanto de lo que está pasando?*
→ see **photography**

**Thesaurus** *picture* Ver también:

N. drawing, illustration, image, painting 1
photograph 2
V. envision, imagine, visualize 6

**Word Partnership** Usar *picture* con:

ADJ. **pretty as a** picture 1
**mental** picture 6
**accurate** picture, **clear** picture, **complete** picture, **different** picture, **larger** picture, **overall** picture, **vivid** picture, **whole** picture 6 – 8

**pic|ture mes|sag|ing** N-UNCOUNT **Picture messaging** is the sending of photographs or pictures from one cellphone to another. *envío de fotografías o imágenes de un teléfono portátil a otro*

**pie** /paɪ/ (**pies**) N-VAR A **pie** consists of fruit, meat, or vegetables baked in pastry. *pastel, pay* ❑ *...a slice of apple pie. ...una rebanada de pay de manzana.*
→ see **dessert**

**piece** /pis/ (**pieces, piecing, pieced**) 1 N-COUNT A **piece of** something is an amount of it that has been broken off, torn off, or cut off. *trozo, pedazo* ❑ *...a piece of cake. ...una rebanada de pastel.* ❑ *Cut the ham into pieces. Corte el jamón en trocitos.* 2 N-COUNT A **piece of** something of a particular kind is an individual item of it. For example, you can refer to some advice as a **piece of advice.** *no se traduce* ❑ *This is his finest piece of work yet. Este es su mejor trabajo hasta ahora.* ❑ *...an interesting piece of information. ...una información interesante.*

**3** N-COUNT A **piece** is something that is written or created, such as an article, work of art, or musical composition. *artículo, pieza, obra, cuadro* [FORMAL] ❑ *She wrote a piece on Gwyneth Paltrow for the "New Yorker". Escribió un artículo sobre Gwyneth Paltrow para el New Yorker.* ❑ *Each piece is painted by an artist according to your design. Cada cuadro lo pinta un artista de acuerdo con su diseño.* **4** N-COUNT **A piece of** something is part of it or a share of it. *parte* ❑ *They got a small piece of the profits. Recibieron una pequeña parte de las utilidades.* **5** PHRASE If someone or something is still **in one piece** after a dangerous journey or experience, they are safe and not damaged or hurt. *sano y salvo* ❑ *The main thing is that my brother gets back in one piece. Lo principal es que mi hermano vuelva sano y salvo.* **6** PHRASE If you **go to pieces,** you are so upset or nervous that you lose control of yourself and cannot do what you should do. *quedar deshecho* [INFORMAL] ❑ *She nearly went to pieces when Arnie died. Quedó casi destrozada cuando Arnie murió.*

▸ **piece together** **1** PHR-VERB If you **piece together** the truth about something, you gradually discover it. *reconstruir* ❑ *They've pieced together his movements for the last few days. Reconstruyeron sus movimientos de los últimos días.* ❑ *I've been trying to piece together what happened. He estado tratando de reconstruir lo que ocurrió.* **2** PHR-VERB If you **piece** something **together,** you gradually make it by joining several things or parts together. *unir los pedazos de* ❑ *This process is like piecing together a jigsaw puzzle. Este proceso es como unir las piezas de un rompecabezas.*

→ see **chess**

**pie chart** (**pie charts**) N-COUNT A **pie chart** is a circle divided into sections to show the relative proportions of a set of things. *gráfica circular, gráfico circular*

→ see **chart**

**pierce** /pɪərs/ (**pierces, piercing, pierced**) **1** V-T If a sharp object **pierces** something, or if you **pierce** something **with** a sharp object, the object goes into it and makes a hole in it. *pinchar, agujerear, perforar* ❑ *Pierce the chicken with a sharp knife to check that it is cooked. Pinche el pollo con un cuchillo filoso para comprobar que esté cocido.* **2** V-T If you have your ears or another part of your body **pierced,** you have a small hole made through them so that you can wear a piece of jewelry in them. *agujerear* ❑ *I'm having my ears pierced on Saturday. El sábado voy a que me hagan agujeros en las orejas.* • **pierc|ing** N-VAR *piercing* ❑ *...health risks from needles used in piercing. ...los riesgos para la salud por las agujas que se utilizan para el piercing.* ❑ *...girls with braids and piercings. ...muchachas con trenzas y piercing.*

**pig** /pɪg/ (**pigs**) **1** N-COUNT A **pig** is a farm animal with pink, white, or black skin. Pigs are kept for their meat, which is called pork, ham, or bacon. *puerco, cerdo, chancho* ❑ *Kids can help feed the pigs. Los niños pueden ayudar a alimentar los puercos.* **2** N-COUNT If you call someone a **pig,** you are insulting them, usually because you think that they are greedy or unkind. *cerdo* [INFORMAL] ❑ *These guys destroyed the company. They're a bunch of greedy pigs. Esos tipos destruyeron la empresa. Son un montón de cerdos codiciosos.*

→ see **meat**

**pi|geon** /pɪdʒɪn/ (**pigeons**) N-COUNT A **pigeon** is a gray bird that is often seen in cities. *paloma, pichón*

**pig|ment** /pɪgmənt/ (**pigments**) N-VAR A **pigment** is a substance that gives something a particular color. *pigmento* [FORMAL] ❑ *The Romans used natural pigments on their fabrics. Los romanos empleaban pigmentos naturales en sus telas.*

**pig|pen** /pɪgpɛn/ (**pigpens**) also **pig pen** N-COUNT A **pigpen** is an enclosed place where pigs are kept on a farm. *zahúrda, pocilga, chiquero*

**pig|tail** /pɪgteɪl/ (**pigtails**) N-COUNT If someone has a **pigtail** or **pigtails,** their hair is braided into two lengths. *trenza* ❑ *...a little girl with pigtails. ...una niñita con trenzas.*

→ see **hair**

**Pilates** /pɪlɑtiz/ N-UNCOUNT **Pilates** is a type of exercise similar to yoga. *pilates* ❑ *She's never done Pilates before. Nunca antes ha hecho pilates.*

**pile** /paɪl/ (**piles, piling, piled**) **1** N-COUNT A **pile of** things is a quantity of them lying on top of one another. *montón, pila* ❑ *...a pile of boxes. ...una pila de cajas.* ❑ *The leaves have been swept into huge piles. Barrieron las hojas e hicieron enormes montones con ellas.* **2** V-T If you **pile** things somewhere, you put them there so that they form a pile. *amontonar, apilar* ❑ *He was piling clothes into the suitcase. Estaba amontonando ropa en la maleta.* **3** V-T If something **is piled with** things, it is covered or filled with piles of things. *amontonar* ❑ *Tables were piled with food. En las mesas había montones de comida.* **4** V-I If a group of people **pile into** or **out of** a place, they all get into it or out of it in a disorganized way. *entrar o salir desordenadamente* ❑ *They all piled into Jerry's car. Se metieron todos desordenadamente en el coche de Jerry.* **5** N-SING The **pile** of a carpet or of a fabric such as velvet is its soft surface. It consists of a lot of little threads standing on end. *pelo* ❑ *...the carpet's thick pile. ...el tupido pelo de la alfombra.* **6** PHRASE Someone who is **at the bottom of the pile** is low down in society or low down in an organization. Someone who is **at the top of the pile** is high up in society or high up in an organization. *ser los últimos/primeros en la lista* [INFORMAL] ❑ *These workers are at the bottom of the pile when it comes to pay. Estos trabajadores son los últimos en la lista cuando se trata del salario.*

▸ **pile up** **1** PHR-VERB If you **pile up** a quantity of things or if they **pile up,** they gradually form a pile. *apilar* ❑ *They piled up rocks to build a wall. Apilaron piedras para construir un muro.* **2** PHR-VERB If you **pile up** work, problems, or losses or if they **pile up,** you get more and more of them. *apilarse, acumularse* ❑ *Problems were piling up at work. Los problemas estaban acumulándose en el trabajo.*

**pil|grim** /pɪlgrɪm/ (**pilgrims**) N-COUNT **Pilgrims** are people who journey to a holy place for a religious reason. *peregrino* ❑ *...tourists and pilgrims visiting Rome. ...los turistas y peregrinos que visitan Roma.*

**pill** /pɪl/ (**pills**) **1** N-COUNT **Pills** are small solid round masses of medicine or vitamins that you swallow. *píldora* ❑ *Why do I have to take all these pills?—¿Por qué tengo que tomar tantas píldoras?* **2** N-SING If a woman is **on the pill,** she takes a special pill that prevents her from becoming pregnant. *píldora*

❑ *She has been on the pill for three years.* *Ha estado tomando la píldora durante tres años.*

**pil|lar** /pɪlər/ (**pillars**) 1 N-COUNT A **pillar** is a tall solid structure that is usually used to support part of a building. *pilar* ❑ *...the pillars supporting the roof.* *...los pilares que sostienen el techo.* 2 N-COUNT If you describe someone as a **pillar of** the community, you approve of them because they play an important and active part in the community. *pilar*

**pil|low** /pɪloʊ/ (**pillows**) N-COUNT A **pillow** is a rectangular cushion that you rest your head on when you are in bed. *almohada*
→ see **bed, sleep**

**pi|lot** /paɪlət/ (**pilots, piloting, piloted**) 1 N-COUNT A **pilot** is a person who is trained to fly an aircraft. *piloto* ❑ *He spent seventeen years as an airline pilot.* *Trabajó diecisiete años como piloto de una aerolínea.* 2 V-T If someone **pilots** an aircraft or ship, they act as its pilot. *pilotear, pilotar* ❑ *He piloted his own plane to Washington.* *Piloteó su propio avión hasta Washington.* 3 ADJ A **pilot** plan or a **pilot** project is one that is used to test an idea before deciding whether to introduce it on a larger scale. *piloto* ❑ *We are going to run a pilot study funded by the government.* *Vamos a hacer un estudio piloto financiado por el gobierno.* 4 V-T If a government or organization **pilots** a program or project, they test it, before deciding whether to introduce it on a larger scale. *poner a prueba* ❑ *Teachers are piloting a literature-based reading program.* *Los maestros están poniendo a prueba un programa de lectura basado en la literatura.*

**pin** /pɪn/ (**pins, pinning, pinned**) 1 N-COUNT **Pins** are very small thin pointed pieces of metal which are used to fasten things together. *alfiler* ❑ *...a box of needles and pins.* *...una caja de agujas y alfileres.* 2 V-T If you **pin** something **on** or **to** something, you attach it there with a pin. *prender con alfileres* ❑ *They pinned a notice to the door.* *Pusieron un aviso en la puerta* ❑ *Everyone was supposed to pin money on the bride's dress.* *Se suponía que todo el mundo debía prender un billete en el vestido de la novia.* 3 V-T If someone **pins** you in a particular position, they press you against a surface so that you cannot move. *inmovilizar* ❑ *I pinned him against the wall.* *Lo inmovilicé contra la pared.* ❑ *I pinned him down until the police arrived.* *Lo inmovilicé en el suelo hasta que llegó la policía.* 4 N-COUNT A **pin** is any long narrow piece of metal or wood that is not sharp, especially one that is used to fasten two things together. *perno, clavo* ❑ *...the 18-inch steel pin holding his left leg together.* *...el clavo de 45 centímetros que mantiene unida su pierna izquierda.* 5 V-T If someone tries to **pin** something bad **on** you, they say that you were responsible for it. *atribuir, echar* ❑ *They couldn't pin the blame on anyone.* *No pudieron atribuirle la culpa a nadie.* 6 V-T If you **pin** your hopes **on** someone or something, your future success or happiness depends on them. *cifrar* ❑ *The Democrats are pinning their hopes on the next election.* *Los demócratas cifran sus esperanzas en las próximas elecciones.* 7 N-COUNT A **pin** is a decorative object worn on your clothing which is fastened with a pointed piece of metal. *broche, prendedor, botón* ❑ *...necklaces, bracelets, and pins.* *...collares, pulseras y prendedores.*
▸ **pin down** 1 PHR-VERB If you try to **pin** something **down**, you try to discover exactly what, where, or when it is. *precisar* ❑ *We've been trying to pin down the exact location of the building.* *Hemos estado tratando de precisar la ubicación exacta del edificio.* ❑ *I can pin the event down to some time between 1936 and 1942.* *Sólo puedo precisar que el acontecimiento tuvo lugar en algún momento entre 1936 y 1942.* 2 PHR-VERB If you **pin** someone **down**, you force them to make a definite statement. *comprometer* ❑ *She couldn't pin him down to a date.* *No logró que se comprometiera a una cita.*
→ see **jewelry**

**pinch** /pɪntʃ/ (**pinches, pinching, pinched**) 1 V-T If you **pinch** someone, you squeeze a part of their body between your thumb and first finger. *pellizcar* ❑ *She pinched his arm as hard as she could.* *Lo pellizcó en el brazo tan fuerte como pudo.* • **Pinch** is also a noun. *pellizco* ❑ *She gave him a little pinch.* *Le dio un ligero pellizco.* 2 N-COUNT A **pinch of** an ingredient such as salt is the amount of it that you can hold between your thumb and your first finger. *pellizco, pizca* ❑ *...a pinch of cinnamon.* *...una pizca de canela.* 3 V-T To **pinch** something, especially something of little value, means to steal it. *birlar* [INFORMAL] ❑ *Do you remember when I pinched your glasses?* *—¿Te acuerdas de cuando te birlé tus anteojos?* 4 PHRASE If a person or company **is feeling the pinch,** they do not have as much money as they used to, and so they cannot buy the things they would like to buy. *estar apretado, pasar estrecheces* ❑ *American families and small businesses are feeling the pinch from rising gas prices.* *Las familias y los pequeños negocios estadounidenses están pasando estrecheces por los aumentos al precio del gas.*

**pinch-hit** /pɪntʃhɪt/ (**pinch-hits, pinch-hitting, pinch-hit**) also **pinch hit** 1 V-I If you **pinch-hit for** someone, you do something for them because they are unexpectedly unable to do it. *substituir, sustituir* ❑ *The staff here can pinch hit for each other when the hotel is busy.* *Todos los empleados pueden substituirse unos a otros cuando el hotel está concurrido.* 2 V-I In a game of baseball, if you **pinch-hit** for another player, you hit the ball instead of them. *batear de emergencia* ❑ *Davalillo goes up to pinch-hit.* *Davalillo será el bateador de emergencia.*

**pine** /paɪn/ (**pines, pining, pined**) 1 N-VAR A **pine tree** or a **pine** is a tall tree with long, thin leaves that it keeps all year round. *pino* ❑ *...high mountains covered in pine trees.* *...altas montañas cubiertas de pinos.* • **Pine** is the wood of this tree. *(madera de) pino* ❑ *...a big pine table.* *...una gran mesa de pino.* 2 V-I If you **pine for** something or someone, you feel sad because you cannot have them or cannot be with them. *suspirar por, anhelar, extrañar* ❑ *I pine for the countryside.* *Suspiro por la campiña.* ❑ *Make sure your pet doesn't pine while you're away.* *Asegúrese de que su mascota no lo extrañe mientras usted está fuera.*

**pine|apple** /paɪnæpᵊl/ (**pineapples**) N-VAR A **pineapple** is a large oval fruit with sweet, juicy, yellow flesh and thick brown skin. *piña*
→ see **fruit**

**pink** /pɪŋk/ (**pinks, pinker, pinkest**) COLOR Something that is **pink** is the color between red and white. *rosa, rosado* ❑ *...pink lipstick.* *...lápiz labial rosa.* ❑ *...white flowers edged with pink.* *...flores blancas con bordes rosados.*

**pink slip** (**pink slips**) N-COUNT If employees are given their **pink slips,** they are informed that they are no longer needed to do the job that they have been doing. aviso de despido [INFORMAL] ❑ *It was his fourth pink slip in two years.* *Era la cuarta vez que lo despedían en cuatro años.*

**pin|stripe** /pɪnstraɪp/ (**pinstripes**) also **pin-stripe** N-COUNT **Pinstripes** are very narrow vertical stripes found on certain types of clothing. Businessmen's suits often have pinstripes. raya ❑ *He wore an expensive, dark blue pinstripe suit.* *Vestía un costoso traje azul oscuro a rayas.*
→ see **pattern**

**pint** /paɪnt/ (**pints**) N-COUNT A **pint** is a unit of measurement for liquids equal to 473 cubic centimeters or one eighth of a gallon. medio litro, pinta ❑ *...a pint of ice cream.* *...un medio litro de helado.*
→ see **measurement**

**pin|to bean** /pɪntoʊ bin/ (**pinto beans**) N-COUNT **Pinto beans** are a type of bean, similar to kidney beans, that are eaten as a vegetable. frijol pinto, judía pinta

**pio|neer** /paɪənɪər/ (**pioneers, pioneering, pioneered**) **1** N-COUNT A **pioneer** in a particular area of activity is one of the first people to be involved in it. precursor o precursora ❑ *...one of the leading pioneers of the Internet.* *...uno de los principales precursores de la Internet.* **2** V-T Someone who **pioneers** a new activity, invention, or process is one of the first people to do it. ser el primero en desarrollar ❑ *...Professor Alec Jeffreys, who invented and pioneered DNA tests.* *...el profesor Alec Jeffreys, que inventó las pruebas de ADN y fue su precursor.* • **pio|neer|ing** ADJ innovador, precursor ❑ *The school has won awards for its pioneering work with the community.* *La escuela ha ganado premios por su trabajo innovador con la comunidad.* **3** N-COUNT **Pioneers** are people who leave their own country and go and live in a place that has not been lived in before. colonizador o colonizadora, pionero o pionera

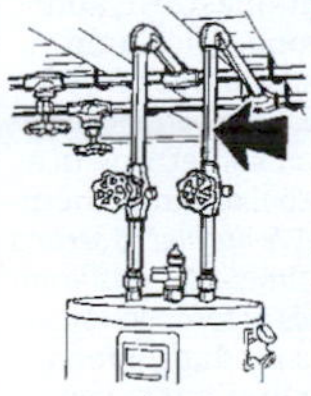
pipe

**pipe** /paɪp/ (**pipes, piping, piped**) **1** N-COUNT A **pipe** is a long, round, hollow object through which a liquid or gas can flow. tubo, tubería ❑ *...water pipes.* *...tubería de agua.* **2** N-COUNT A **pipe** is an object that is used for smoking tobacco. pipa ❑ *Do you smoke a pipe?* *—¿Fuma (en) pipa?* **3** N-COUNT **Organ pipes** are the long hollow tubes which produce musical notes from an organ. tubo de órgano, cañón de órgano **4** V-T If liquid or gas **is piped** somewhere, it is transferred from one place to another through a pipe. llevar ❑ *Clean water is piped into our homes.* *El agua potable llega a nuestras casas por tubería.*
→ see **keyboard, petroleum, tool**

**pipe|line** /paɪplaɪn/ (**pipelines**) **1** N-COUNT A **pipeline** is a large pipe that is used for carrying oil or gas over a long distance, often underground. conducto, ducto ❑ *...a natural-gas pipeline.* *...un ducto de gas natural.* **2** PHRASE If something is **in the pipeline,** it has been planned or begun. estar proyectado, estar previsto ❑ *A 2.9 percent pay increase is in the pipeline for teachers.* *Está previsto un incremento del 2.9 por ciento para los maestros.*
→ see **oil**

**pipe or|gan** (**pipe organs**) N-COUNT A **pipe organ** is a large musical instrument with pipes of different lengths through which air is forced. It has keys and pedals like a piano. órgano de tubos, órgano de cañones

**pi|rate** /paɪrɪt/ (**pirates, pirating, pirated**) **1** N-COUNT **Pirates** are sailors who attack other ships and steal property from them. pirata ❑ *In the nineteenth century, pirates sailed the seas.* *En el siglo XIX, los piratas surcaban los mares.* **2** V-T Someone who **pirates** CDs, DVDs, books, or computer programs copies and sells them when they have no right to do so. piratear ❑ *Computer crimes include data theft and pirating software.* *Los crímenes informáticos incluyen el robo de datos y el pirateo de programas de computación.* • **pi|rated** ADJ pirata ❑ *...pirated copies of music and movies.* *...copias pirata de música y películas.*

**pis|til** /pɪstᵊl/ (**pistils**) N-COUNT The **pistil** is the female part of a flower, which produces seeds. pistilo [TECHNICAL]
→ see **flower**

**pis|tol** /pɪstᵊl/ (**pistols**) N-COUNT A **pistol** is a small gun. pistola

**pit** /pɪt/ (**pits, pitting, pitted**) **1** N-COUNT A **pit** is the underground part of a mine, especially a coal mine. pozo, mina, galería **2** V-T If two opposing things or people **are pitted against** one another, they are in conflict or in competition. enfrentar ❑ *You will be pitted against people who are as good as you are.* *Te verás enfrentado a gente que es tan buena como tú.* **3** N-COUNT A **pit** is a large hole that is dug in the ground. pozo ❑ *Eric lost his footing and began to slide into the pit.* *A Eric se le fueron los pies y empezó a deslizarse dentro del pozo.* **4** N-PLURAL In auto racing, **the pits** are the areas at the side of the track where drivers go for fuel and repairs during races. pits **5** N-COUNT A **pit** is the large hard seed of a fruit or vegetable. hueso ❑ *...cherry pits.* *...huesos de cereza.* **6** → see also **pitted**

**pitch** /pɪtʃ/ (**pitches, pitching, pitched**) **1** V-T If you **pitch** something somewhere, you throw it with some force. lanzar, arrojar ❑ *Simon pitched the empty bottle into the lake.* *Simon arrojó la botella vacía al lago.* ❑ *We spent long, hot afternoons pitching a baseball.* *Pasábamos las largas y cálidas tardes lanzando una pelota de béisbol.* **2** V-I To **pitch** somewhere means to fall forward suddenly and with a lot of force. caerse de bruces, irse de bruces ❑ *The movement took him by surprise, and he pitched forward.* *El movimiento lo tomó por sorpresa y se fue de bruces.* **3** N-UNCOUNT The **pitch** of a sound is how high or low it is. tono ❑ *He raised his voice to an even higher pitch.* *Ajustó la voz a un tono aún más alto.* **4** V-T If something **is pitched at** a particular level, it is set at that level. establecer ❑ *The level of the course is pitched too high for our students.* *La dificultad del curso es demasiado grande para nuestros estudiantes.* **5** N-SING If something such as a feeling or a situation rises to a high **pitch,** it rises to a high level. grado ❑ *The game ended on a high pitch of excitement.* *El juego terminó con un alto grado de excitación.*

▸ **pitch in** PHR-VERB If you **pitch in,** you join in

P

and help with an activity. *echar la mano, arrimar el hombro* [INFORMAL] ❑ *International agencies also have pitched in. Las agencias internacionales también han echado la mano.*

**pitch|er** /pɪtʃər/ (**pitchers**) **1** N-COUNT A **pitcher** is a cylindrical container with a handle, used for holding and pouring liquids. *jarra* ❑ *...a pitcher of iced water. ...una jarra de agua helada.* **2** N-COUNT In baseball, the **pitcher** is the person who throws the ball to the batter, who tries to hit it. *lanzador o lanzadora, pítcher*
→ see **baseball**

pitcher

**pit|ted** /pɪtɪd/ **1** ADJ **Pitted** fruits have had their pits removed. *deshuesado* ❑ *...pitted olives. ...aceitunas deshuesadas.* **2** ADJ If the surface of something is **pitted,** it is covered with a lot of small, shallow holes. *salpicado, lleno de* ❑ *The walls are pitted with bullet holes. Los muros están salpicados de agujeros de bala.*

**pity** /pɪti/ (**pities, pitying, pitied**) **1** V-T If you **pity** someone, you feel very sorry for them. *lástima, pena* ❑ *I don't know whether to hate or pity him. No sé si odiarlo o sentir lástima por él.* • **Pity** is also a noun. *pena* ❑ *He felt a sudden tender pity for her. Repentinamente sintió pena y ternura por ella.* **2** N-SING If you say that it is **a pity** that something is true, you mean that you feel disappointment or regret about it. *lástima, pena* ❑ *It is a great pity that all students cannot have the same chances. Es una verdadera lástima que no todos los estudiantes tengan las mismas oportunidades.* ❑ *It's a pity you arrived so late. Es una lástima que hayas llegado tan tarde.* **3** PHRASE If you **take pity on** someone, you feel sorry for them and help them. *compadecerse* ❑ *Nobody took pity on him. Nadie se compadeció de él.*

P

**piz|za** /pitsə/ (**pizzas**) N-VAR A **pizza** is a flat, round piece of dough covered with tomatoes, cheese, and other toppings, and then baked in an oven. *pizza* ❑ *...the last piece of pizza. ...la última rebanada de pizza.*

**pjs** /pidʒeɪz/ also **pj's** N-PLURAL **Pjs** are the same as **pajamas.** *piyama* [INFORMAL] ❑ *I work from home and live in my pjs most of the time. Trabajo en la casa y me paso la mayor parte del tiempo en piyama.*

**pkg.** **Pkg.** is a written abbreviation for **package.** *paquete*

**place**
❶ NOUN USES
❷ VERB USES
❸ PHRASES

❶ **place** /pleɪs/ (**places**) **1** N-COUNT A **place** is any point, building, area, town, or country. *lugar* ❑ *...a list of museums and places of interest. ...una lista de museos y lugares de interés.* ❑ *We're going to a place called Platoro. Vamos a un lugar llamado Platoro.* ❑ *The pain is always in the same place. El dolor está siempre en el mismo lugar.* **2** N-SING **Place** can be used after "any," "no," "some," or "every" to mean "anywhere," "nowhere," "somewhere," or "everywhere." *lugar* [INFORMAL] ❑ *The poor guy didn't have any place to go for Easter. El pobre tipo no tenía ningún lugar a dónde ir en Semana Santa.* **3** N-COUNT You can refer to the position where something belongs, or where it is supposed to be, as its **place.** *lugar* ❑ *He returned the album to its place on the shelf. Volvió a poner el álbum en su lugar en el estante.* **4** N-COUNT A **place** is a seat or position that is available for someone to occupy. *lugar* ❑ *He sat at the nearest of two empty places. Se sentó en el más cercano de los dos lugares vacíos.* **5** N-COUNT Someone's or something's **place** in a society, system, or situation is their position in relation to other people or things. *lugar* ❑ *...educating the children so they can take their place in adult society... ...educar a los niños para que puedan ocupar su lugar en la sociedad adulta.* **6** N-COUNT Your **place** in a race or competition is your position in relation to the other competitors. If you are in first place, you are ahead of all the other competitors. *lugar* ❑ *He has risen to second place in the opinion polls. Subió al segundo lugar en los sondeos de opinión.* **7** N-COUNT If you get a **place** on a team, on a committee, or in an institution, for example, you are accepted as a member of the team or committee or as a resident of the institution. *lugar* ❑ *Derek has lost his place on the team. Derek perdió su lugar en el equipo.* ❑ *There are no more places available in the school this year. Ya no hay más lugares disponibles en la escuela este año.* **8** N-COUNT Your **place** is the house or apartment where you live. *casa* [INFORMAL] ❑ *Let's all go back to my place! —¡Vamos todos a mi casa!*
→ see **zero**

❷ **place** /pleɪs/ (**places, placing, placed**) **1** V-T If you **place** something somewhere, you put it in a particular position. *colocar, meter* ❑ *Brand placed the letter in the inside pocket of his jacket. Brand se metió la carta en la bolsa interior del saco.* **2** V-T You can use **place** instead of "put" or "lay" in certain expressions where the meaning is carried by the following noun. For example, if you **place emphasis on** something, you emphasize it, and if you **place the blame on** someone, you blame them. *poner* ❑ *He placed great importance on family life. La vida familiar tenía un lugar muy importante para él.* **3** V-T If you **place** someone or something in a particular class or group, you label or judge them in that way. *colocar, clasificar* ❑ *We are placed second among the state's most successful firms. Nos clasificaron en segundo lugar entre las firmas más exitosas del estado.* **4** V-T If you **place an order for** a product or **for** a meal, you ask for it to be sent or brought to you. *hacer un pedido* ❑ *It is a good idea to place your order early. Es una buena idea hacer su pedido antes.* **5** V-T If you **place an advertisement in** a newspaper, you arrange for the advertisement to appear in the newspaper. *poner* ❑ *They placed an advertisement in the local paper for a secretary. Pusieron un anuncio en el periódico local para buscar una secretaria.*

❸ **place** /pleɪs/ (**places, placing, placed**) **1** PHRASE If you have been trying to understand something puzzling and then everything **falls into place** or **clicks into place,** you suddenly understand how different pieces of information are connected and everything becomes clearer. *aclararse* ❑ *When the reasons for the decision were explained, it all fell into place. Cuando explicaron las* *razones de la decisión, todo se aclaró.* **2** PHRASE If things **fall into place,** events happen naturally to produce a situation you want. *ocupar su lugar* ❑ *Once the decision was made, things fell into place rapidly.* *Una vez que se tomó la decisión, todo se arregló en consecuencia rápidamente.* **3** PHRASE If something such as a law, a policy, or system is **in place,** it is working or able to be used. *en aplicación* ❑ *A similar program is already in place in Utah.* *En Utah ya se está aplicando un programa similar.* **4** PHRASE If one thing or person is used or does something **in place of** another, they replace the other thing or person. *en lugar de* ❑ *Cooked kidney beans can be used in place of green beans.* *Se pueden usar frijoles cocidos en lugar de ejotes.* **5** PHRASE You say **in the first place** when you are talking about the beginning of a situation or about the situation as it was before a series of events. *en primer lugar* ❑ *What brought you to Washington in the first place?* *—¿Qué lo trajo a Washington, en primer lugar?* **6** PHRASE If you **put** someone **in** their **place,** you show them that they are less important or clever than they think they are. *poner en su lugar* ❑ *In a few words she put him in his place.* *Lo puso en su lugar con unas cuantas palabras.* **7** PHRASE When something **takes place,** it happens, especially in a controlled or organized way. *tener lugar* ❑ *The discussions took place in Paris.* *Las discusiones tuvieron lugar en París.* ❑ *She wanted the wedding to take place quickly.* *Ella quería que la boda tuviera lugar rápidamente.*

**place|ment test** (**placement tests**) N-COUNT A **placement test** is a test given by a school to determine the academic or skill level of a student in order to place them in the correct class. *prueba de aptitud* ❑ *Students are required to take placement tests before registering.* *Se requiere que los estudiantes hagan el examen de aptitud antes de inscribirse*

**pla|cen|ta** /pləsɛntə/ (**placentas**) N-COUNT **The placenta** is the mass of veins and tissue inside the uterus of a pregnant woman or animal, which the unborn baby is attached to. *placenta*

**pla|cen|tal mam|mal** /pləsɛntᵊl mæməl/ (**placental mammals**) N-COUNT A **placental mammal** is an animal that has a placenta. *mamífero placentario, mamífero placentado* [TECHNICAL]

**plague** /pleɪg/ (**plagues, plaguing, plagued**) **1** N-COUNT A **plague** is an infectious disease that spreads quickly and kills large numbers of people. *plaga, peste (bubónica)* ❑ *A cough or a sneeze could spread the plague.* *La tos o un estornudo propagaban la peste.* **2** N-COUNT A **plague of** unpleasant things is a large number of them that arrive or happen at the same time. *plaga* ❑ *...a plague of rats.* *...una plaga de ratas.* **3** V-T If you **are plagued by** unpleasant things, they continually cause you a lot of trouble or suffering. *atormentado* ❑ *She was plagued by weakness and dizziness.* *La debilidad y los vahídos la atormentaban.*

**plaid** /plæd/ (**plaids**) N-MASS **Plaid** is material with a check design on it. **Plaid** is also the design itself. *cuadro* ❑ *Eddie wore blue jeans and a plaid shirt.* *Eddie vestía pantalones de mezclilla azules y una camisa a cuadros.*
→ see **pattern**

**plain** /pleɪn/ (**plainer, plainest, plains**) **1** ADJ A **plain** object, surface, or fabric is entirely in one color and has no pattern, design, or writing on it. *liso* ❑ *A plain carpet makes a room look bigger.* *Una alfombra lisa hace que un cuarto se vea más grande.* ❑ *He placed the paper in a plain envelope.* *Metió el papel en un sobre liso.* **2** ADJ Something that is **plain** is very simple in style. *simple, sencillo* ❑ *It was a plain, gray stone house.* *Era una casa sencilla de piedra gris.* ● **plain|ly** ADV *simplemente, sencillamente, con sencillez* ❑ *He was very tall and plainly dressed.* *Era muy alto y vestía con sencillez.* **3** ADJ If a fact, situation, or statement is **plain,** it is easy to recognize or understand. *claro* ❑ *It was plain to him what had to be done.* *Para él era claro lo que tenía que hacerse.* **4** ADJ If you describe someone as **plain,** you think they look ordinary and not at all beautiful. *poco atractivo* ❑ *...a shy, rather plain girl.* *...una chica tímida, más bien fea.* **5** N-COUNT A **plain** is a large flat area of land with very few trees on it. *planicie, llanura* ❑ *Once there were 70 million buffalo on the plains.* *Alguna vez hubo 70 millones de bisontes/búfalos en las planicies.* **6** **plain sailing** → see **sailing**

**Thesaurus** *plain* Ver también:

| | |
|---|---|
| ADJ. | bare, modest, simple; (*ant.*) elaborate, fancy **1** |
| | common, everyday, modest, ordinary, simple, usual; (*ant.*) elaborate, fancy **2** |
| | clear, distinct, evident, transparent **3** |

**Word Partnership** Usar *plain* con:

| | |
|---|---|
| N. | plain **style** **2** |
| | plain **English**, plain **language**, plain **speech**, plain **truth** **3** |

**plain|tiff** /pleɪntɪf/ (**plaintiffs**) N-COUNT A **plaintiff** is a person who brings a legal case against someone in a court of law. *demandante* ❑ *The government was ordered to pay $83,000 to each plaintiff.* *Se ordenó al gobierno que pagara 83,000 dólares a cada demandante.*
→ see **trial**

**plan** /plæn/ (**plans, planning, planned**) **1** N-COUNT A **plan** is a method of achieving something that you have worked out in detail beforehand. *plan* ❑ *...a peace plan.* *...un plan de paz.* ❑ *He says that everything is going according to plan.* *Dice que todo está marchando de acuerdo con el plan.* **2** V-T/V-I If you **plan** what you are going to do, you decide in detail what you are going to do. *planear, programar, hacer planes* ❑ *Plan what you're going to eat.* *Programe lo que va a comer.* ❑ *He plans to leave Baghdad on Monday.* *Sus planes son partir de Bagdad el lunes.* ❑ *Republicans gathered together to plan for the future.* *Los republicanos se reunieron para hacer planes para el futuro.* **3** N-PLURAL If you have **plans,** you are intending to do a particular thing. *planes* ❑ *"I'm sorry," she said. "I have plans for tonight."* *—Discúlpeme—dijo—, ya tengo planes para esta noche.* **4** N-COUNT A **plan of** something that is going to be built or made is a detailed diagram or drawing of it. *plano* ❑ *...a plan of the garden.* *...un plano del jardín.* **5** → see also **planning**
▸ **plan on** PHR-VERB If you **plan on** doing something, you intend to do it. *planear, pensar en* ❑ *They were planning on getting married.* *Estaban planeando casarse.*

**plane** /pleɪn/ (**planes, planing, planed**)

P

**1** N-COUNT A **plane** is a vehicle with wings and engines that can fly. *avión* ❑ *He had plenty of time to catch his plane. Tenía tiempo de sobra para tomar el avión.* **2** N-COUNT A **plane** is a flat, level surface that may be sloping at a particular angle. *plano* ❑ *...the angled plane of the propeller. ...el plano inclinado de (del aspa de) la hélice.* **3** N-COUNT A **plane** is a tool that has a flat bottom with a sharp blade in it, used for shaping and smoothing wood. *cepillo, garlopa* **4** V-T If you **plane** a piece of wood, you make it smaller or smoother by using a plane. *cepillar, desbastar* ❑ *He found his father planing wood in the shed. Encontró a su padre en el cobertizo cepillando una pieza de madera.*

**Thesaurus** *plane* Ver también:

N. aircraft, airplane, craft, jet **1**
horizontal, level, surface **2**

**plan|et** /plænɪt/ (**planets**) N-COUNT A **planet** is a large, round object in space that moves around a star. The Earth is a planet. *planeta* ❑ *...the planets in the solar system. ...los planetas del sistema solar.*
→ see **astronomer, galaxy, satellite, solar system**

**plan|etary** /plænɪtɛri/ ADJ **Planetary** means relating to or belonging to planets. *planetario* ❑ *...planetary systems. ...sistemas planetarios.*

**plan|etesi|mal** /plænɪtɛsɪməl/ (**planetesimals**) N-COUNT **Planetesimals** are small pieces of rock in space that combine to form planets. *corpúsculo (del espacio)* [TECHNICAL]

**plank|ton** /plæŋktən/ N-UNCOUNT **Plankton** is a mass of tiny animals and plants that live in the surface layer of the sea. *plancton*

**plan|ner** /plænər/ (**planners**) N-COUNT **Planners** are people whose job is to make decisions about what is going to be done in the future. *planificador o planificadora* ❑ *...city planners. ...los planificadores del ayuntamiento.*

P

**plan|ning** /plænɪŋ/ **1** N-UNCOUNT **Planning** is the process of deciding in detail how to do something before you actually start to do it. *planificación, programación* ❑ *The trip needs careful planning. Es necesario planear el viaje con cuidado.* **2** N-UNCOUNT **Planning** is control by the local government of the way that land is used in an area and of what new buildings are built there. *urbanismo* ❑ *He is an architect and a town-planning expert. Es arquitecto y experto en urbanismo.*

**plant** /plænt/ (**plants, planting, planted**) **1** N-COUNT A **plant** is a living thing that grows in the earth and has a stem, leaves, and roots. *planta, vegetal* ❑ *Water each plant as often as required. Riegue cada planta con la frecuencia necesaria.* **2** V-T When you **plant** a seed, plant, or young tree, you put it into the ground so that it will grow. *sembrar, plantar* ❑ *He plans to plant fruit trees. Piensa plantar árboles frutales.* ● **plant|ing** N-UNCOUNT *siembra* ❑ *Bad weather has delayed planting. El mal tiempo ha retrasado la siembra.* **3** V-T When someone **plants** land, they put plants, seeds, or young trees into the land to grow. *plantar de* ❑ *They plan to plant the area with grass and trees. Piensan plantar el terreno de pasto y árboles.* ❑ *We've been planting a vegetable garden. Hemos estado plantando una hortaliza.* **4** N-COUNT A **plant** is a factory or a place where power is produced. *planta* ❑ *...Ford's car assembly plants. ...las plantas armadoras de Ford.* **5** N-UNCOUNT **Plant** is large machinery that is used in industrial processes. *maquinaria pesada* ❑ *The company is planning to invest in plant and equipment abroad. La compañía está planeando invertir en maquinaria pesada y equipo en el extranjero.* **6** V-T If you **plant** something somewhere, you put it there firmly. *plantar* ❑ *She planted her feet wide apart. Se plantó con los pies muy separados.* **7** V-T To **plant** a bomb means to hide it somewhere so that it explodes there. *colocar* ❑ *So far no one has admitted planting the bomb. Hasta ahora, nadie ha admitido haber colocado la bomba.* **8** V-T If something such as a weapon or drugs **is planted** on someone, it is put among their possessions or in their house so that they will be wrongly accused of a crime. *colocar subrepticiamente* ❑ *Alexia says that she is innocent, and that the gun was planted. Alexia afirma que es inocente y que el arma fue colocada para inculparla.*
→ see Picture Dictionary: **plants**
→ see **earth, farm, food, herbivore, photosynthesis, tide, tree**

**Picture Dictionary** plants

**Plan|tae** /plænti/ N-PLURAL All the plants in the world can be referred to together as **Plantae.** *vegetales* [TECHNICAL]

**plan|ta|tion** /plænteɪʃᵊn/ (**plantations**) **1** N-COUNT A **plantation** is a large piece of land, where crops such as rubber, tea, or sugar are grown. *plantación* ❑ *...banana plantations in Costa Rica. ...plantaciones de plátano de Costa Rica.* **2** N-COUNT A **plantation** is a large number of trees that have been planted together. *plantación* ❑ *...a plantation of young trees. ...una plantación de árboles jóvenes.*

**plas|ma screen** (**plasma screens**) also **plasma display** N-COUNT A **plasma screen** is a type of thin television screen or computer screen that produces high-quality images. *pantalla de plasma*

**plas|tered** /plæstərd/ **1** ADJ If something is **plastered to** a surface, it is sticking to the surface. *pegado* ❑ *His hair was plastered down to his head. Tenía el pelo pegado a la cabeza.* **2** ADJ If a surface is **plastered with** something, it is covered with it. *cubierto* ❑ *My hands, boots, and pants were plastered with mud. Tenía las manos, las botas y los pantalones cubiertos de lodo.*

**plas|tic** /plæstɪk/ (**plastics**) N-VAR **Plastic** is a light but strong material produced by a chemical process. *plástico* ❑ *...sheets of plastic. ...hojas de plástico.* ❑ *...the plastics that carmakers use. ...los plásticos que usan los fabricantes de automóviles.*
→ see **oil**

**plas|tic wrap** N-UNCOUNT **Plastic wrap** is a thin, clear, stretchy plastic which you use to cover food to keep it fresh. *plástico adherente, película adherente*

**plate** /pleɪt/ (**plates**) **1** N-COUNT A **plate** is a round or oval flat dish that is used to hold food. *plato* ❑ *Anita pushed her plate away. Anita hizo a un lado su plato.* ❑ *...a huge plate of bacon and eggs. ...un copioso plato de huevos con tocino.* **2** N-COUNT A **plate** is a flat piece of metal, for example on part of a machine. *placa* ❑ *He has had a metal plate inserted into his broken jaw. Tiene una placa metálica en la mandíbula fracturada.* **3** N-PLURAL On a road vehicle, the **plates** are the panels on the front and back that display the license number. *placas, chapas* ❑ *...cars with New Jersey plates. ...coches con placas de Nueva Jersey.* **4** → see also **license plate** **5** N-COUNT A **plate** in a book is a picture or photograph that takes up a whole page. *ilustración, lámina* ❑ *The book has 55 color plates. El libro tiene 55 láminas a color.* **6** N-COUNT In baseball, **the plate** is the same as the **home plate.** *plato* **7** N-COUNT In geology, a **plate** is a large piece of the Earth's surface, perhaps as large as a continent, which moves very slowly. *placa* [TECHNICAL]
→ see **continent, dish, rock**

**plate bounda|ry** (**plate boundaries**) N-COUNT A **plate boundary** is a place on the Earth's surface where two or more tectonic plates meet. *frontera de placas tectónicas* [TECHNICAL]

**plat|ed** /pleɪtɪd/ ADJ If something made of metal is **plated with** a thin layer of another type of metal, it is covered with it. *(en)chapado, recubierto* ❑ *...a range of jewelry, plated with 22-carat gold. ...una variedad de joyas con chapa de oro de 22 quilates.*

**plate|let** /pleɪtlɪt/ (**platelets**) N-COUNT **Platelets** are a kind of blood cell. If you cut yourself and you are bleeding, platelets help to stop the bleeding. *plaqueta* [TECHNICAL]
→ see **cardiovascular system**

**plate tec|ton|ics** N-UNCOUNT **Plate tectonics** is the way that large pieces of the Earth's surface move slowly around. *tectónica de placas* [TECHNICAL]

**plat|form** /plætfɔrm/ (**platforms**) **1** N-COUNT A **platform** is a flat raised structure or area on which someone or something can stand. *plataforma* ❑ *He walked toward the platform to begin his speech. Caminó hacia la plataforma para dar inicio a su discurso.* ❑ *They found a rocky platform where they could put up their tents. Encontraron una plataforma rocosa donde pudieron armar sus tiendas.* **2** N-COUNT A **platform** in a train or subway station is the area beside the tracks where you wait for or get off a train. *plataforma, andén* ❑ *The train was about to leave and I was not even on the platform. El tren estaba a punto de partir y yo ni siquiera había llegado al andén.* **3** N-COUNT The **platform** of a political party is what they say they will do if they are elected. *plataforma* ❑ *...a platform of political and economic reforms. ...una plataforma de reformas políticas y económicas.*
→ see **oil**

**plati|tude** /plætɪtud/ (**platitudes**) N-COUNT A **platitude** is a statement that is considered meaningless because it has been made many times before in similar situations. *tópico, lugar común* ❑ *Why couldn't he say something original instead of just repeating the same old platitudes? ¿Por qué no pudo decir algo original en lugar de seguir repitiendo los mismos lugares comunes?*

**plat|ter** /plætər/ (**platters**) **1** N-COUNT A **platter** is a large flat plate used for serving food. *fuente, platón, bandeja* ❑ *The food was served on silver platters. Sirvieron la comida en bandejas de plata.* ❑ *...platters of cheese and fruit. ...platones de queso y fruta.* **2** PHRASE If you say that someone has things **handed to** them **on a platter,** you disapprove of them because they get good things easily. *servir en bandeja de plata* ❑ *The job was handed to him on a platter. Le sirvieron el trabajo en bandeja de plata.*
→ see **dish**

**plau|sible** /plɔzɪbᵊl/ ADJ An explanation or statement that is **plausible** seems likely to be true or valid. *verosímil, creíble, convincente* ❑ *This is a plausible explanation of what might have happened. Es una explicación creíble de lo que pudo haber pasado.* ● **plau|sibly** /plɔzɪbli/ ADV *razonablemente* ❑ *Since he has gotten in without paying, he cannot plausibly demand his money back. Dado que entró sin pagar, no es razonable pedir que le devuelvan el dinero.* ● **plau|sibil|ity** /plɔzɪbɪlɪti/ N-UNCOUNT *credibilidad, admisibilidad* ❑ *...the plausibility of the theory. ...la credibilidad de la teoría.*

**play** /pleɪ/ (**plays, playing, played**) **1** V-I When children or animals **play,** they spend time doing enjoyable things, such as using toys and taking part in games. *jugar* ❑ *They played in the little garden. Jugaron en el jardincito.* ❑ *Polly was playing with her dolls. Polly estaba jugando a las muñecas.* ● **Play** is also a noun. *juego* ❑ *...a few hours of play until the babysitter puts them to bed. ...unas horas de juego hasta que la niñera los acueste.* **2** V-T When you **play** a sport, game, or match, you take part in it. *jugar* a ❑ *The twins played cards.* *Los gemelos jugaban a las cartas.* ❑ *I used to play basketball.* *Yo acostumbraba jugar al basquetbol.* ● **Play** is also a noun. *juego* ❑ *This team has a more exciting style of play.* *Este equipo tiene un estilo de juego más emocionante.* **3** V-T/V-I When one person or team **plays** another or **plays against** them, they compete against them in a sport or game. *jugar con, jugar contra* ❑ *Dallas will play Green Bay.* *Dallas jugará con Green Bay.* **4** V-T If you **play** a joke or a trick on someone, you deceive them or give them a surprise in a way that you think is funny, but may cause problems for them or annoy them. *gastar* ❑ *Someone played a trick on her, and stretched a piece of string across the top of those steps.* *Alguien le hizo una mala jugada: puso una cuerda atravesada en el escalón superior.* **5** N-COUNT A **play** is a piece of writing performed in a theater, on the radio, or on television. *obra* ❑ *"Hamlet" is my favorite play.* *Mi obra favorita es Hamlet.* **6** V-T If an actor **plays** a role or character in a play or movie, he or she performs the part of that character. *actuar, representar un papel* ❑ *...a production of Dr. Jekyll and Mr. Hyde, in which he played Hyde.* *...una producción de El doctor Jekyll y el señor Hyde, en la que representó el papel del señor Hyde.* **7** V-T/V-I If you **play** a musical instrument or **play** a tune on it, you produce music from it. *tocar* ❑ *Nina was playing the piano.* *Nina estaba tocando el piano.* ❑ *He played for me.* *Tocó para mí.* **8** V-T/V-I If you **play** a record, a CD, or a DVD, you put it into a machine, and sound and sometimes pictures are produced. *poner* ❑ *She played her CDs too loudly.* *Ponía su música demasiado fuerte.* ❑ *There is classical music playing in the background.* *Se escucha un pasaje de música clásica en el fondo.* **9** PHRASE If something or someone **plays a part** or **plays a role in** a situation, they are involved in it and have an effect on it. *influir, tener que ver* ❑ *It appears that the weather played a role in the crash.* *Parece que el tiempo influyó en el accidente.*

P

▸**play around** **1** PHR-VERB If you **play around,** you behave in a silly way to amuse yourself or other people. *juguetear, jugar* [INFORMAL] ❑ *Stop playing around and eat!* *¡Deja de juguetear y come!* **2** PHR-VERB If you **play around with** a problem or an arrangement of objects, you try different ways of organizing it in order to find the best solution or arrangement. *jugar con* [INFORMAL] ❑ *I can play around with the pictures to make them more appealing.* *Puedo jugar con las fotos para tratar de hacerlas más interesantes.*

▸**play at** **1** PHR-VERB If you say that someone **is playing at** something, you disapprove of the fact that they are doing it casually and not very seriously. *jugar a* ❑ *It was a terrible piece of work; now I see that I was just playing at being a writer.* *Era una obra malísima: ahora veo que sólo estaba jugando a ser escritor.* **2** PHR-VERB If you ask what someone **is playing at,** you are angry because you do not understand what they are doing or why they are doing it. *jugar a* [INFORMAL] ❑ *She began to wonder what he was playing at.* *Empezó a preguntarse a qué estaba jugando.*

▸**play back** PHR-VERB When you **play back** a tape or film, you listen to the sounds or watch the pictures after recording them. *reproducir* ❑ *If you press this button, the machine plays back your messages.* *Si oprime este botón, la grabadora reproduce sus mensajes.*

▸**play down** PHR-VERB If you **play down** something, you try to make people believe that it is not particularly important. *restar importancia a* ❑ *Politicians have played down the significance of the reports.* *Los políticos han restado importancia a los informes.*

▸**play on** PHR-VERB If you **play on** someone's fears, weaknesses, or faults, you deliberately use them in order to achieve what you want. *aprovecharse de, explotar* ❑ *...new laws which play on the population's fear of change.* *...nuevas leyes que explotan el temor de la población al cambio.*

→ see **theater**

**play-by-play** N-SING A **play-by-play** is a commentary on a sports game or other event that describes every part of it in great detail. *comentario jugada a jugada* ❑ *Gene Deckerhoff does radio play-by-play for Florida State.* *Gene Duckerhoff hace la crónica por radio de los partidos del equipo estatal de Florida.*

**play|er** /pleɪər/ (**players**) **1** N-COUNT A **player** in a sport or game is a person who takes part. *jugador o jugadora* ❑ *...his greatness as a player.* *...su grandeza como jugador.* ❑ *She was a good tennis player.* *Era una buena tenista.* **2** N-COUNT You can use **player** to refer to a musician. *ejecutante, músico o música* ❑ *...a professional trumpet player.* *...un trompetista profesional.* **3** N-COUNT If a person, country, or organization is a **player in** something, they are involved in it and important in it. *protagonista* ❑ *The company has become a major player in the film world.* *La compañía ha llegado a ser un protagonista importante en el mundo cinematográfico.* **4** → see also **CD player, record player**

→ see **chess, football, soccer**

**play|ful** /pleɪfəl/ ADJ A **playful** gesture or person is friendly or humorous. *juguetón* ❑ *...a playful kiss.* *...un beso juguetón.* ❑ *...a playful fight.* *...una pelea en broma.* ● **play|ful|ly** ADV *juguetonamente* ❑ *She pushed him away playfully.* *Lo apartó juguetonamente.* ● **play|ful|ness** N-UNCOUNT *calidad de juguetón* ❑ *...the child's natural playfulness.* *...el natural carácter juguetón del niño.*

**play|ground** /pleɪgraʊnd/ (**playgrounds**) N-COUNT A **playground** is a piece of land where children can play. *patio de recreo* ❑ *...a seven-year-old boy playing in a school playground.* *...un niño de siete años jugando en el patio de recreo de una escuela.*

→ see **park**

**play|ing card** (**playing cards**) N-COUNT **Playing cards** are thin pieces of cardboard with numbers or pictures printed on them that are used to play games. *carta, naipe, baraja* ❑ *...a deck of playing cards.* *...una baraja.*, *...un mazo de naipes.*, *...un mazo de cartas.*

playing card

**play|off** /pleɪɔf/ (**playoffs**) **1** N-COUNT A **playoff** is an extra game that is played to decide the winner of a sports competition when two or more people have the same score. *final, partida decisiva* ❑ *Nick Faldo was beaten by Peter Baker in a playoff.* *Nick Faldo fue derrotado por Peter Baker en la final decisiva.* **2** N-COUNT You use **playoffs** to refer to a series of games that are played to decide the winner of a championship. *final* ❑ *It's been a long time since these two teams faced each other in the playoffs.* *Hacía mucho tiempo que esos dos equipos* *no se enfrentaban en la final.*

**play|wright** /pleɪraɪt/ (**playwrights**) N-COUNT A **playwright** is a person who writes plays. *dramaturgo o dramaturga, autor o autora*
→ see **theater**

**pla|za** /plɑzə, plæzə/ (**plazas**) **1** N-COUNT A **plaza** is an open square in a city. *plaza* ❑ *Across the busy plaza, vendors sell hot dogs. Del otro lado de la bulliciosa plaza, había vendedores de perros calientes.* **2** N-COUNT A **plaza** is a group of stores or buildings that are joined together or share common areas. *centro comercial* ❑ *...a new retail plaza. ...un nuevo centro comercial.*

**plea** /pli/ (**pleas**) **1** N-COUNT A **plea** is an appeal or request for something, made in an intense or emotional way. *llamado, petición, súplica* ❑ *...an emotional plea for help. ...una emotiva petición/súplica de ayuda.* **2** N-COUNT In a court of law, a person's **plea** is the answer that they give when they have been charged with a crime. *alegato* ❑ *The judge questioned him about his guilty plea. El juez le inquirió sobre su alegato de culpabilidad.* ❑ *We will enter a plea of not guilty. Interpondremos un alegato de inocencia.*

**plead** /plid/ (**pleads, pleading, pleaded, pled**) **1** V-I If you **plead with** someone to do something, you ask them in an intense, emotional way to do it. *suplicar* ❑ *The lady pleaded with her daughter to come back home. La mujer suplicó a su hija que retornara al hogar.* ❑ *He was kneeling on the floor pleading for mercy. Estaba arrodillado, suplicando piedad.* **2** V-I When someone charged with a crime **pleads guilty** or **not guilty** in a court of law, they officially state that they are guilty or not guilty of the crime. *declararse (culpable o inocente), confesarse (culpable)* ❑ *Morris pleaded guilty to robbery. Morris se declaró culpable del robo.* **3** V-T If you **plead the case** or **cause** of someone or something, you speak out in their support or defense. *defender* ❑ *He appeared before the committee to plead his case. Se presentó ante la comisión para defender su caso.* **4** V-T If you **plead** a particular thing as the reason for doing or not doing something, you give it as your excuse. *aducir* ❑ *Mr. Giles pleads ignorance as his excuse. El señor Giles aduce su ignorancia como excusa.*
→ see **trial**

**pleas|ant** /plɛzᵊnt/ (**pleasanter, pleasantest**) **1** ADJ Something that is **pleasant** is enjoyable or attractive. *agradable* ❑ *I've got a pleasant little apartment. Tengo un departamentito agradable.*
• **pleas|ant|ly** ADV *agradablemente* ❑ *We talked pleasantly of old times. Charlamos agradablemente de los viejos tiempos.* **2** ADJ Someone who is **pleasant** is friendly and likeable. *agradable* ❑ *The woman had a pleasant face. La mujer tenía un rostro agradable.*

| **Thesaurus** | *pleasant* Ver también: |
|---|---|
| ADJ. | agreeable, cheerful, delightful, likable, friendly, nice; (*ant.*) unpleasant **2** |

**please** /pliz/ (**pleases, pleasing, pleased**) **1** ADV You say **please** when you are politely asking or inviting someone to do something. *por favor* ❑ *Can you help us, please? ¿Puede ayudarnos, por favor?* ❑ *Please come in. Venga, por favor.* ❑ *Can we have the bill, please? ¿Nos da la cuenta, por favor?* **2** ADV You say **please** when you are accepting something politely. *por favor* ❑ *"Tea?" — "Yes, please." —¿Le sirvo té?/¿Un poco de té?—Sí, por favor.* **3** V-T/V-I If someone or something **pleases** you, they make you feel happy and satisfied. *complacer, agradar, contentar* ❑ *More than anything, I want to please you. Más que nada, lo que quiero es complacerte.* ❑ *It pleased him to talk to her. Le agradó hablar con ella., Estaba contento de hablar con ella.* ❑ *He was anxious to please. Estaba ansioso por agradar.* **4** PHRASE You use **please** in expressions such as **as she pleases, whatever you please,** and **anything he pleases** to indicate that someone can do or have whatever they want. *como guste, lo que quiera, lo que le plazca* ❑ *Women should be free to dress as they please. Las mujeres deberían ser libres de vestirse como quieran.* ❑ *He does whatever he pleases. Hace lo que quiere.*

**pleased** /plizd/ **1** ADJ If you are **pleased,** you are happy about something or satisfied with something. *contento, complacido* ❑ *Felicity seemed pleased at the suggestion. Felicity parecía contenta con la sugerencia.* ❑ *I think he's going to be pleased that we solved the problem. Creo que va a estar complacido de que hayamos resuelto el problema.* ❑ *I'm pleased with the way things have been going. Estoy contento con la manera como han estado resultando las cosas.* ❑ *I am very pleased about the result. Estoy muy contento con el resultado.* **2** CONVENTION You can say "**Pleased to meet you**" as a polite way of greeting someone who you are meeting for the first time. *encantado de conocerlo/conocerla, mucho gusto de conocerlo/conocerla*

**pleas|ing** /plizɪŋ/ ADJ Something that is **pleasing** gives you pleasure and satisfaction. *agradable* ❑ *This area of France has a pleasing climate. Esta región de Francia tiene un clima agradable.*
• **pleas|ing|ly** ADV *agradablemente* ❑ *The design is pleasingly simple. El diseño es agradablemente simple.*

**pleas|ure** /plɛʒər/ (**pleasures**) **1** N-UNCOUNT If something gives you **pleasure,** you get a feeling of happiness, satisfaction, or enjoyment from it. *placer, gusto* ❑ *Watching sports gave him great pleasure. Ver los deportes era un gran placer para él.* ❑ *Everybody takes pleasure in eating. Comer es un placer para todo el mundo.* **2** N-UNCOUNT **Pleasure** is the activity of enjoying yourself, especially rather than working. *ocio, diversión* ❑ *He mixes business and pleasure. Combina los negocios con la diversión.* **3** N-COUNT A **pleasure** is an activity or experience that you find enjoyable and satisfying. *gusto, placer* ❑ *Watching TV is our only pleasure. Ver la televisión es nuestro único gusto.* ❑ *...the pleasure of seeing a smiling face. ...el placer de ver un rostro sonriente.* **4** CONVENTION You can say "**It's a pleasure**" or "**My pleasure**" as a polite way of replying to someone who has just thanked you for doing something. *de nada, no hay de qué* ❑ *"Thanks very much anyhow." — "It's a pleasure." —Muchas gracias, de todos modos.—No hay de qué.*

**pleat|ed** /plitɪd/ ADJ A **pleated** piece of clothing has pleats in it. *plisado, tableado* ❑ *...a short white pleated skirt. ...una falda blanca corta y plisada.*

**pledge** /plɛdʒ/ (**pledges, pledging, pledged**) **1** V-T When someone **pledges to** do something, they promise in a serious way to do it. When they **pledge** something, they promise to give it. *prometer, comprometerse* ❑ *He pledged to support the group. Se comprometió a apoyar al grupo.* ❑ *The French president is pledging $150 million in aid next* year. *El presidente de Francia se comprometió a destinar 150 millones de dólares a la ayuda exterior el año próximo.* • **Pledge** is also a noun. *compromiso* ❑ *...a pledge to improve relations between the six states. ...un compromiso para mejorar las relaciones entre los seis estados.* **2** V-T If you **pledge yourself to** something, you commit yourself to following a particular course of action or to supporting a particular person, group, or idea. *comprometerse* ❑ *The president pledged himself to protect the poor. El presidente se comprometió a proteger a los pobres.*

**plen|ty** /plɛnti/ QUANT If there is **plenty of** something, there is a large amount of it, often more than is needed. *mucho, de sobra* ❑ *There was still plenty of time to take Jill out for pizza. Todavía había tiempo de sobra para llevar a Jill a comer pizza.* ❑ *Most businesses face plenty of competition. La mayoría de los negocios deben hacer frente a muchos competidores.* • **Plenty** is also a pronoun. *más que suficiente* ❑ *I don't believe in long interviews. Fifteen minutes is plenty. No creo en las entrevistas largas; quince minutos es más que suficiente.*

| **Thesaurus** | *plenty* | Ver también: |
|---|---|---|
| N. | abundance, capacity, quantity; (*ant.*) scarcity | |

**pli|ers** /plaɪərz/ N-PLURAL **Pliers** are a tool with two handles at one end and two hard, flat, metal parts at the other. Pliers are used for holding or pulling out things such as nails, or for bending or cutting wire. *alicate(s), pinza(s)*
→ see **tool**

**plight** /plaɪt/ (**plights**) N-COUNT Someone's **plight** is the difficult or dangerous situation that they are in. *apuro, aprieto, situación peligrosa* ❑ *...the plight of children living in war zones. ...la peligrosa situación de los niños que viven en las zonas de guerra.*



**plot** /plɒt/ (**plots, plotting, plotted**) **1** V-T/V-I If people **plot to** do something or **plot** something illegal or wrong, they plan secretly to do it. *conspirar* ❑ *They plotted to overthrow the government. Conspiraron para derrocar al gobierno.* ❑ *...They were accused of plotting against the state. ...fueron acusados de conspirar contra el Estado.* • **Plot** is also a noun. *conspiración, complot* ❑ *...a plot to pass secrets to the Russians. ...una conspiración para entregar secretos a los rusos.* • **plot|ter** N-COUNT (**plotters**) *conspirador o conspiradora* ❑ *The plotters used the Internet to communicate. Los conspiradores se valían de Internet para comunicarse.* **2** N-VAR The **plot** of a movie, novel, or play is the connected series of events which make up the story. *trama, argumento* ❑ *He told me the plot of his new book. Me narró la trama de su nuevo libro.* **3** N-COUNT A **plot** is a small piece of land, especially one that is intended for a purpose, such as building houses or growing vegetables. *parcela, solar, terreno* ❑ *I bought a small plot of land and built a house on it. Compré un terrenito y levanté una casa en él.* **4** V-T When people **plot** a strategy or a course of action, they carefully plan each step of it. *trazar* ❑ *The aim of the meeting was to plot a strategy for the party. El objeto de la reunión era trazar la estrategia para el partido.* **5** V-T When someone **plots** something on a graph, they mark certain points on it and then join the points up. *trazar* ❑ *We plotted about eight points on the graph. Trazamos unos ocho puntos en la gráfica.* **6** V-T When someone **plots** the position or progress of something, they follow its position or progress and show it on a map or diagram. *determinar* ❑ *We were trying to plot the course of the submarine. Estábamos tratando de determinar el rumbo del submarino.*

**plot|line** /plɒtlaɪn/ (**plotlines**) N-COUNT The **plotline** of a book, movie, or play is its plot and the way in which it develops. *argumento, trama*

**plow** /plaʊ/ (**plows, plowing, plowed**) **1** N-COUNT A **plow** is a large farming tool with sharp blades that is pulled across the soil to turn it over, usually before seeds are planted. *arado* **2** → see also **snowplow** **3** V-T When someone **plows** an area of land, they turn over the soil using a plow. *arar* ❑ *They were using horses to plow their fields. Estuvieron usando caballos para arar sus campos.*
→ see **barn**

plow

**plug** /plʌg/ (**plugs, plugging, plugged**) **1** N-COUNT A **plug** on a piece of electrical equipment is a small plastic object with two or three metal pins that fit into the holes of an electric outlet and connect the equipment to the electricity supply. *clavija, enchufe* ❑ *I used to go around and take every plug out at night. Acostumbraba hacer un recorrido en la noche y desconectar todas las clavijas.* **2** N-COUNT A **plug** is a thick, circular piece of rubber or plastic that you use to block the hole in a bathtub or sink when it is filled with water. *tapón* ❑ *She put in the plug and filled the sink with cold water. Puso el tapón y llenó el lavabo con agua fría.* **3** V-T If you **plug** a hole or a leak, you block it with something. *tapar* ❑ *Crews are working to plug a major oil leak. Las cuadrillas están trabajando para tapar una gran fuga de petróleo.* **4** V-T If someone **plugs** a product such as a book or a movie, they talk about it in order to encourage people to buy it or see it. *promover* ❑ *Most people on the show are only interested in plugging a book or movie. A la mayoría de la gente del programa sólo le interesa hacerle publicidad a un libro o una película.* • **Plug** is also a noun. *publicidad* ❑ *They managed to put in a plug for the store's new website. Se las arreglaron para hacerle publicidad al nuevo sitio en Internet de la tienda.* **5** PHRASE If someone in a position of power **pulls the plug on** a project or **on** someone's activities, they use their power to stop them from continuing. *(hacer) cancelar* ❑ *The banks have the power to pull the plug on the project. Los bancos tienen el poder para (hacer) cancelar el proyecto.*

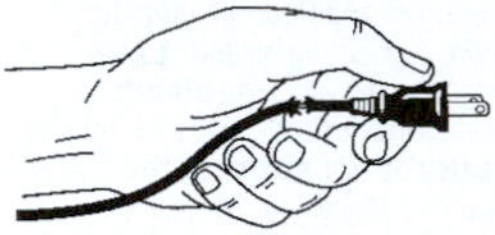

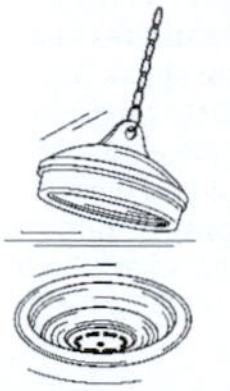
plugs

▸ **plug in** or **plug into** PHR-VERB If you **plug** a piece of electrical equipment **into** an electricity supply or if you **plug** it **in**, you push its plug into an electric outlet so that it can work. *conectar,* enchufar ❑ They plugged in their tape-recorders. Enchufaron sus grabadoras. ❑ I had a TV set but there was no place to plug it in. Tenía una televisión, pero no había dónde enchufarla.

**plugged** /plʌgd/ also **plugged up** ADJ If something is **plugged** or **plugged up,** it is completely blocked so that nothing can get through it. tapado, obstruido, atorado ❑ ...a plugged toilet. ...un excusado tapado. ❑ His ears and nose were plugged up. Tenía los oídos y la nariz tapados.

**plum** /plʌm/ (**plums**) N-COUNT A **plum** is a small, sweet fruit with a smooth purple, red, or yellow skin and a pit in the middle. ciruela

**plumb|er** /plʌmər/ (**plumbers**) N-COUNT A **plumber** is a person whose job is to connect and repair things such as water and drainage pipes, bathtubs, and toilets. plomero o plomera, fontanero o fontanera

**plumb|ing** /plʌmɪŋ/ **1** N-UNCOUNT The **plumbing** in a building consists of the water and drainage pipes, bathtubs, and toilets in it. cañería, tubería ❑ The entire building was in need of new plumbing. Todo el edificio necesitaba tuberías nuevas. **2** N-UNCOUNT **Plumbing** is the work of connecting and repairing water and drainage pipes, bathtubs, and toilets. plomería, fontanería ❑ They run a small plumbing business. Tienen un pequeño negocio de plomería.

**plunge** /plʌndʒ/ (**plunges, plunging, plunged**) **1** V-I If something or someone **plunges** in a particular direction, especially into water, they fall, rush, or throw themselves in that direction. zambullirse ❑ The bus plunged into a river. El autobús cayó en un río. **2** V-T If you **plunge** an object **into** something, you push it quickly or violently into it. clavar, hincar, hundir ❑ He plunged a fork into his dinner. Clavó el tenedor en su plato. **3** V-T/V-I If a person or thing **is plunged into** a particular state or situation, or if they **plunge into** it, they are suddenly in that state or situation. precipitar, hundir ❑ Reforms threaten to plunge the country into violence. Las reformas amenazan hundir el país en la violencia. ❑ ...a country plunging into poverty. ...un país que se hunde en la pobreza. **4** V-T/V-I If you **plunge into** an activity or **are plunged into** it, you suddenly get very involved in it. zambullirse ❑ The two men plunged into discussion. Los (dos) hombres se zambulleron en una discusión. **5** V-I If an amount or rate **plunges,** it decreases quickly and suddenly. desplomarse, irse a pique ❑ His weight began to plunge. Empezó a bajar de peso aceleradamente. ● **Plunge** is also a noun. desplome ❑ ...the stock market plunge. ...el desplome del mercado de valores. **6** PHRASE If you **take the plunge,** you decide to do something that you consider difficult or risky. arriesgarse, dar el paso ❑ She took the plunge and invited him back. Decidió dar el paso y devolverle la invitación.

**plung|er** /plʌndʒər/ (**plungers**) N-COUNT A **plunger** is a device for clearing waste pipes. It consists of a rubber cup on the end of a stick which you press down several times over the end of the pipe. desatascador, destapador, bomba (de excusado) → see **bathroom**

**plunk** /plʌŋk/ (**plunks, plunking, plunked**) **1** V-T If you **plunk** something somewhere, you put it there without great care. dejar caer, aventar [INFORMAL] ❑ Melanie plunked her case down on a chair. Melanie aventó su maleta sobre una silla. **2** V-I If you **plunk yourself** somewhere, or **plunk down,** you sit down heavily and clumsily. dejarse caer [INFORMAL] ❑ I plunked down on one of the small chairs. Me dejé caer en una de las sillas chicas.

**plu|ral** /plʊərəl/ (**plurals**) N-COUNT The **plural** of a noun is the form of it that is used to refer to more than one person or thing. plural ❑ What is the plural of "person?" ¿Cuál es el plural de "persona"? ● **Plural** is also an adjective. plural ❑ "Men" is the plural form of "man." "Hombres" es el plural de "hombre".

**plus** /plʌs/ (**pluses** or **plusses**) **1** CONJ You say **plus** to show that one number or quantity is being added to another. más ❑ ...$5 for a small locker, plus a $3 deposit. ...5 dólares por un casillero chico, más 3 dólares de depósito. **2** ADJ **Plus** before a number or quantity means that the number or quantity is greater than zero. más ❑ ...temperatures from minus 65 degrees to plus 120 degrees. ...temperaturas de menos 54 a más 49 grados. **3** CONJ You can use **plus** when mentioning an additional item or fact. más [INFORMAL] ❑ It's just the original story plus a lot of extra photographs. Es sólo el cuento original más muchas fotos más. **4** ADJ You use **plus** after a number or quantity to indicate that the actual number or quantity is greater than the one mentioned. más de ❑ There are only 35 staff to serve 30,000-plus customers. Hay sólo 35 empleados para atender a más de 30,000 clientes. **5** ADJ Teachers use **plus** in grading work. "B plus" is a better grade than "B," but it is not as good as "A." calificación intermedia (no existe en español y se traduce a la escala de calificaciones del país de que se trate) **6** N-COUNT A **plus** is an advantage or benefit. ventaja [INFORMAL] ❑ Experience in sales is a big plus. La experiencia en ventas es una gran ventaja.

**Pluto** /plutoʊ/ N-PROPER **Pluto** is the second largest dwarf planet in the Solar System. Plutón

**p.m.** /pi ɛm/ also **pm** ADV **p.m.** is used after a number to show that you are referring to a particular time between 12 noon and 12 midnight. Compare **a.m.** la tarde, pasado meridiano ❑ The pool is open from 7:00 a.m. to 9:00 p.m. every day. La alberca está abierta de las 7 de la mañana a las 9 de la noche todos los días.

**pock|et** /pɒkɪt/ (**pockets, pocketing, pocketed**) **1** N-COUNT A **pocket** is a small bag or pouch that forms part of a piece of clothing. bolsa, bolsillo ❑ ...his jacket pocket. ...la bolsa de su saco. **2** N-COUNT You can use **pocket** in expressions that refer to money that people have, get, or spend. For example, if someone gives or pays a lot of money, you can say that they **dig deep into** their **pocket.** bolsillo ❑ ...ladies' fashions to suit all shapes, sizes, and pockets. ...modas para mujer adaptadas a todos los estilos, tallas y bolsillos. **3** ADJ You use **pocket** to describe something that is small enough to fit into a pocket. de bolsillo ❑ ...a pocket calculator. ...una calculadora de bolsillo. **4** V-T If someone **pockets** something that does not belong to them, they keep it or steal it. embolsarse ❑ Banks have passed some of the savings on to customers and pocketed the rest. Los bancos pasaron parte de los ahorros a los clientes y se embolsaron el resto. **5** PHRASE If you are **out of pocket,** you have less money than you should have or than you intended. corto de dinero ❑ Make sure you claim back the money; I don't want you to be out of pocket. Asegúrate de que te devuelvan el dinero; no quiero que te quedes corto.

**pocket|book** /pɒkɪtbʊk/ (**pocketbooks**) N-COUNT A **pocketbook** is a small bag which a woman uses to carry things such as her money and keys. bolsa, monedero

**pod|cast** /pɒdkæst/ (**podcasts**) N-COUNT A **podcast** is an audio file similar to a radio broadcast, that can be downloaded and listened to on a computer or **MP3 player**. podcast, archivo de audio ❑ *There are thousands of new podcasts available every day.* *Todos los días hay miles de nuevos podcasts disponibles.*

**poem** /poʊəm/ (**poems**) N-COUNT A **poem** is a piece of writing in which the words are chosen for their beauty and sound and are carefully arranged, often in short lines. poema ❑ *...a book of love poems.* *...un libro de poemas de amor.*

**poet** /poʊɪt/ (**poets**) N-COUNT A **poet** is a person who writes poems. poeta o poetisa ❑ *He was a painter and poet.* *Era pintor y poeta.*

**po|et|ic li|cense** N-UNCOUNT If someone such as a writer or movie director uses **poetic license,** they break the usual rules of language or style, or they change the facts, in order to create a particular effect. licencia poética ❑ *Memory takes a lot of poetic license: it leaves out some details and focuses on others.* *La memoria se toma una gran licencia poética: deja fuera unos detalles y se centra en otros.*

**po|et|ry** /poʊɪtri/ N-UNCOUNT Poems, considered as a form of literature, are referred to as **poetry.** poesía ❑ *...Russian poetry.* *...poesía rusa.* → see **genre**

**point**
❶ NOUN USES
❷ VERB USES
❸ PHRASES

P

❶ **point** /pɔɪnt/ (**points**) **1** N-COUNT A **point** is an opinion or fact expressed by someone. argumento, opinión, observación ❑ *We disagree with every point she makes.* *Estamos en desacuerdo con todos sus argumentos.* **2** N-SING If you say that someone **has a point,** or if you **take** their **point,** you mean that you accept that what they have said should be considered. tener razón en algo ❑ *"You have a point there," Dave agreed.* *—Tienes razón en eso—, aceptó David.* **3** N-SING **The point** of what you are saying or discussing is the most important part. asunto ❑ *"Did I ask you to talk to me?" — "That's not the point."* *—¿Te pedí que me hablaras?—No se trata de eso.* ❑ *He came to the point at once. "You did a splendid job."* *Fue al grano de inmediato: "Hiciste un trabajo magnífico".* **4** N-SING If you ask what **the point of** something is, or say that there is **no point in** it, you are indicating that a particular action has no purpose or would not be useful. caso, sentido ❑ *What was the point of thinking about him?* *—¿Qué caso tenía pensar en él?* **5** N-COUNT A **point** is an aspect or quality of something or someone. aspecto, característica ❑ *The most interesting point about the village was its religion.* *El aspecto más interesante del pueblo era su religión.* **6** N-COUNT A **point** is a particular position or time. lugar, momento ❑ *The pain was coming from a point in his right thigh.* *El dolor venía de un lugar en su muslo derecho.* ❑ *We're all going to die at some point.* *Todos vamos a morir en algún momento.* **7** N-COUNT The **point** of something such as a needle or knife is the thin, sharp end of it. punta ❑ *...the point of a knife.* *...la punta de un cuchillo.* **8** In spoken English, you use **point** to refer to the dot or mark in a decimal number that separates the whole numbers from the fractions. punto decimal ❑ *The earthquake measured five-point-two on the Richter scale.* *El terremoto fue de cinco punto dos en la escala de Richter.* **9** N-COUNT In some sports and games, a **point** is one of the single marks that are added together to give the total score. punto ❑ *Chamberlain scored 50 points.* *Chamberlain anotó 50 puntos.* **10** N-COUNT The **points of the compass** are directions such as North, South, East, and West. puntos cardinales ❑ *People came to visit from all points of the compass.* *La gente vino de visita de todos los rincones del mundo.* **11** → see also **breaking point**

| Thesaurus | point | Ver también: |
|---|---|---|
| N. | argument, gist, topic ❶ **3** | |
| | location, place, position, spot ❶ **6** | |

❷ **point** /pɔɪnt/ (**points, pointing, pointed**) **1** V-I If you **point at** a person or thing, you hold out your finger or an object toward them in order to make someone notice them. señalar (con el dedo) ❑ *I pointed at the boy sitting nearest me.* *Señalé (con el dedo) al muchacho sentado más cerca de mí.* **2** V-T If you **point** something **at** someone, you aim the tip or end of it toward them. apuntar ❑ *A man pointed a gun at them.* *Un hombre los apuntó con una pistola.* **3** V-I If something **points to** a place or **points** in a particular direction, it shows where that place is or it faces in that direction. apuntar ❑ *An arrow pointed to the restrooms.* *Una flecha apuntaba hacia los baños.* **4** V-I If something **points to** a particular situation, it suggests that the situation exists or is likely to occur. indicar ❑ *Earlier reports pointed to improved results.* *Los anteriores informes indicaban una mejoría de los resultados.* **5** → see also **pointed**

❸ **point** /pɔɪnt/ **1** PHRASE If you **make a point of** doing something, you do it in a deliberate or obvious way. proponerse ❑ *She made a point of spending as much time as possible away from Oklahoma.* *Se proponía pasar lejos de Oklahoma tanto tiempo como fuese posible.* **2** PHRASE If you are **on the point of** doing something, you are about to do it. a punto de ❑ *He was on the point of saying something when the phone rang.* *Estaba a punto de decir algo cuando sonó el teléfono.* **3** PHRASE If you say that something is true **up to a point,** you mean that it is partly but not completely true. hasta cierto punto ❑ *It worked up to a point.* *Funcionó hasta cierto punto.* **4** **in point of fact** → see **fact** **5** to **point the finger at** someone → see **finger**

▸ **point out** **1** PHR-VERB If you **point out** an object or place to someone, you direct their attention to it. señalar ❑ *Encourage your baby to lift his head by calling to him and pointing things out.* *Anime a su bebé a levantar la cabeza llamándolo y señalándole las cosas.* **2** PHR-VERB If you **point out** a fact or mistake, you tell someone about it. señalar ❑ *I should point out that he was joking, of course.* *Debo señalar que estaba bromeando, claro.*

**point|ed** /pɔɪntɪd/ **1** ADJ Something that is **pointed** has a point at one end. *acabado en punta, puntiagudo* ❑ *...a pointed roof. ...un techo acabado en punta.* **2** ADJ **Pointed** comments or behavior express criticism in a clear and direct way. *mordaz* ❑ *...her mother's criticisms and pointed remarks. ...las críticas y observaciones mordaces de su madre.* • **point|ed|ly** ADV *deliberadamente, significativamente* ❑ *They were pointedly absent from the news conference. Faltaron deliberadamente a la conferencia de prensa.*

**point|less** /pɔɪntlɪs/ ADJ Something that is **pointless** has no sense or purpose. *vano, inútil, sin sentido* ❑ *Violence is always pointless. La violencia siempre carece de sentido.* ❑ *Without an audience the performance is pointless. Sin público, la función carece de sentido.* • **point|less|ly** ADV *innecesariamente* ❑ *The movie is pointlessly long, with a weak ending. La película es innecesariamente larga, con un final poco convincente.*

**point of view** (**points of view**) **1** N-COUNT You can refer to the opinions that you have about something as your **point of view.** *punto de vista, opinión* ❑ *Thanks for your point of view, John. Gracias por tu punto de vista, John.* **2** N-COUNT If you consider something **from** a particular **point of view,** you use one aspect of a situation in order to judge it. *punto de vista* ❑ *This is enormously important from the point of view of protecting citizens. Esto es enormemente importante desde el punto de vista de la protección de los ciudadanos.* **3** N-COUNT The **point of view** of someone who is looking at a painting or other object is the angle or position from which they are viewing it. *punto de vista*
→ see **history**

**point-source pol|lu|tion** N-UNCOUNT **Point-source pollution** is pollution that comes from one particular source, for example from a particular factory. *fuente puntual de la contaminación* [TECHNICAL]

**poised** /pɔɪzd/ **1** ADJ If a part of your body is **poised,** it is completely still but ready to move at any moment. *listo, preparado* ❑ *He studied the keyboard carefully, one finger poised. Estudió el teclado cuidadosamente, con un dedo listo.* **2** ADJ If someone is **poised to** do something, they are ready to take action at any moment. *dispuesto* ❑ *Foster looked poised to win the match when he won the first game 6 – 2. Foster parecía dispuesto a ganar el partido cuando ganó el primer juego.* **3** ADJ If you are **poised,** you are calm, dignified, and self-controlled. *sereno* ❑ *She was self-assured, poised. Era segura de sí misma y serena.*

**poi|son** /pɔɪzᵊn/ (**poisons, poisoning, poisoned**) **1** N-VAR **Poison** is a substance that harms or kills people or animals if they swallow it or absorb it. *veneno* ❑ *Poison from the fish causes swelling and nausea. El veneno del pez provoca hinchazón y náuseas.* **2** V-T To **poison** someone or something means to harm or damage them by giving them poison or putting poison into them. *envenenar* ❑ *...rumors that she had poisoned him. ...rumores de que ella lo había envenenado.* ❑ *The land was poisoned by chemicals. La tierra había sido envenenada por substancias químicas.* • **poi|son|ing** N-UNCOUNT *envenenamiento* ❑ *...imprisonment for poisoning and attempted murder. ...prisión por envenenamiento e intento de homicidio.* **3** V-T Something that **poisons** a good situation or relationship spoils it or destroys it. *envenenar* ❑ *The letter poisoned her relationship with her family forever. La carta envenenó para siempre su relación con su familia.*

**poi|son oak** N-UNCOUNT **Poison oak** is a plant that causes a rash or skin problems if you touch it. *zumaque venenoso*

**poi|son|ous** /pɔɪzᵊnəs/ **1** ADJ Something that is **poisonous** will kill you or harm you if you swallow or absorb it. *venenoso* ❑ *All parts of the yew tree are poisonous. Todas las partes del tejo son venenosas.* **2** ADJ An animal that is **poisonous** produces a poison that will kill you or make you ill if the animal bites you. *venenoso* ❑ *...poisonous spiders and snakes. ...arañas y serpientes venenosas.*

**poke** /poʊk/ (**pokes, poking, poked**) **1** V-T If you **poke** someone or something, you quickly push them with your finger or with a sharp object. *meter* ❑ *Lindy poked him in the ribs. Linda le metió el dedo en las costillas.* • **Poke** is also a noun. *golpe* ❑ *John gave Richard a playful poke. John dio a Richard un golpe juguetón.* **2** V-T If you **poke** one thing **into** another, you push the first thing into the second thing. *meter* ❑ *He poked his finger into the hole. Metió un dedo en el agujero.* **3** V-I If something **pokes out of** or **through** another thing, or if someone **pokes** it there, you can see part of it appearing from behind or underneath the other thing. *asomar, meter* ❑ *He saw the dog's nose poke out of the basket. Vio que la nariz del perro asomaba en la canasta.* ❑ *Julie tapped on my door and poked her head in. Julie llamó a mi puerta y metió la cabeza.* **4** to **poke fun at** → see **fun**

**po|lar** /poʊlər/ ADJ **Polar** means near the North Pole or South Pole. *polar* ❑ *...life in the polar regions. ...la vida en las regiones polares.*
→ see **glacier**

**po|lar co|or|di|nate** (**polar coordinates**) N-COUNT **Polar coordinates** are a set of two numbers that are used in mathematics to describe the position of something by measuring its distance and angle from a particular point. *coordenadas polares* [TECHNICAL]

**po|lar east|er|lies** N-PLURAL The **polar easterlies** are winds that blow from the north and south poles towards the equator. *viento polar de levante* [TECHNICAL]

**po|lar equa|tion** (**polar equations**) N-COUNT A **polar equation** is a mathematical equation that uses polar coordinates. *ecuación de coordenadas polares* [TECHNICAL]

**po|lar zone** (**polar zones**) N-COUNT The **polar zones** are the areas of the Earth around the north and south poles. *zona polar*

**pole** /poʊl/ (**poles**) **1** N-COUNT A **pole** is a long thin piece of wood or metal, used especially for supporting things. *poste* ❑ *...a telephone pole. ...un poste de teléfono.* **2** N-COUNT The Earth's **poles** are the two opposite ends of its axis, its most northern and southern points. *polo* ❑ *For six months of the year, there is hardly any light at the poles. Durante seis meses del año, casi no hay nada de luz en los polos.*
→ see **magnet**

| Word Link | *poli ≈ city : metropolitan, politics, police* |
|---|---|

**po|lice** /pəlis/ (**polices, policing, policed**) **1** N-PLURAL The **police** are the official organization that is responsible for making sure that people obey the law. *policía* ❑ *The police are* *looking for the car. La policía está buscando el coche.* ❑ *Police say they have arrested twenty people. La policía dice que arrestó a veinte personas.* 2 N-PLURAL **Police** are men and women who are members of the police. *policías* ❑ *More than one hundred police are in the area. Hay más de cien policías en la zona.* 3 V-T To **police** an area, event, or activity means to make sure that the law or rules are followed within it. *patrullar, vigilar, supervisar* ❑ *...It is difficult to police the border effectively. ...es difícil patrullar la frontera con efectividad.* ❑ *...the committee that polices senators' behavior. ...la comisión que supervisa la conducta de los senadores.*

**po|lice de|part|ment** (**police departments**) N-COUNT A **police department** is an official organization which is responsible for making sure that people obey the law. *departamento de policía* ❑ *...the Los Angeles Police Department. ...el Departamento de Policía de Los Ángeles.*

**po|lice force** (**police forces**) N-COUNT A **police force** is the police organization in a particular country or area. *policía, fuerzas del orden* ❑ *...the Wichita police force. ...la policía de Wichita.*

**police|man** /pəliːsmən/ (**policemen**) N-COUNT A **policeman** is a man who is a member of the police force. *policía*

**po|lice of|fic|er** (**police officers**) N-COUNT A **police officer** is a member of the police force. *oficial de policía* ❑ *...a meeting of senior police officers. ...una reunión de los oficiales de alto grado de la policía.*

**po|lice sta|tion** (**police stations**) N-COUNT A **police station** is the local office of a police force in a particular area. *comisaría* ❑ *Two police officers arrested him and took him to Gettysburg police station. Lo arrestaron dos policías y lo llevaron a la comisaría de Gettysburg.*

**police|woman** /pəliːswʊmən/ (**policewomen**) N-COUNT A **policewoman** is a woman who is a member of the police force. *mujer policía*

P

**poli|cy** /pɒlɪsi/ (**policies**) 1 N-VAR A **policy** is a set of ideas or plans that is used as a basis for making decisions, especially in politics, economics, or business. *política* ❑ *...changes in foreign policy. ...cambios en la política exterior.* ❑ *...the government's policy on housing. ...la política gubernamental sobre la vivienda.* 2 N-COUNT An insurance **policy** is a document that shows an agreement that you have made with an insurance company. *póliza de seguro* [BUSINESS] ❑ *...car insurance policies. ...pólizas de seguro sobre automóviles.*

**po|lio** /poʊlioʊ/ N-UNCOUNT **Polio** is a serious infectious disease that can cause paralysis. *poliomielitis, polio* ❑ *Their first child died of polio at the age of 3. Su primer hijo murió de poliomielitis cuando tenía tres años.*

→ see **hospital**

**pol|ish** /pɒlɪʃ/ (**polishes, polishing, polished**)

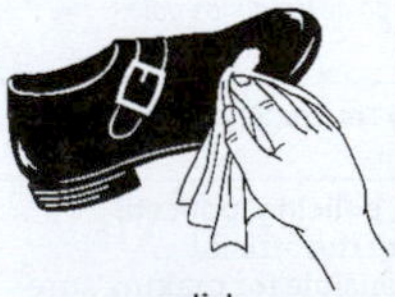

polish

1 N-VAR **Polish** is a substance that you put on the surface of an object in order to clean it, protect it, and make it shine. *cera, betún* ❑ *...furniture polish. ...cera para muebles.* 2 V-T If you **polish** something, you put polish on it or rub it with a cloth to make it shine. *pulir, lustrar, sacar brillo* ❑ *He polished his shoes. Sacó brillo a sus zapatos.* ● **pol|ished** ADJ *pulido* ❑ *...a highly polished floor. ...un piso muy pulido.* 3 N-UNCOUNT If you say that a performance or piece of work has **polish**, you mean that it is of a very high standard. *brillo* ❑ *The opera lacks the polish of his later work. La ópera carece del brillo de su último trabajo.* ● **pol|ished** ADJ *pulido* ❑ *...a very polished performance. ...una actuación muy pulida.* 4 V-T If you **polish** your technique, performance, or skill at doing something, you work on improving it. *pulir* ❑ *They need to polish their technique. Necesitan pulir su técnica.* ● **Polish up** means the same as **polish**. *pulir, perfeccionar* ❑ *Polish up your writing skills. Perfeccione su habilidad para redactar.*

**po|lite** /pəlaɪt/ (**politer, politest**) ADJ A **polite** person has good manners and is not rude to other people. *cortés* ❑ *...a quiet and very polite young man. ...un joven tranquilo y muy cortés.* ● **po|lite|ly** ADV *cortésmente* ❑ *"Your home is beautiful," I said politely. —Su casa es hermosa—dije cortésmente.* ● **po|lite|ness** N-UNCOUNT *cortesía* ❑ *She listened to him, but only out of politeness. Le prestó atención, pero sólo por cortesía.*

| Thesaurus | *polite* | Ver también: |
|---|---|---|
| ADJ. | considerate, courteous, gracious, respectful; (*ant.*) brash, rude | |

**po|liti|cal** /pəlɪtɪkᵊl/ 1 ADJ **Political** means relating to the way power is achieved and used in a country or society. *político* ❑ *All other political parties there have been completely banned. Todos los demás partidos políticos han sido prohibidos totalmente.* ● **po|liti|cal|ly** /pəlɪtɪkli/ ADV *políticamente* ❑ *The news was politically damaging for the Republicans. La noticia fue políticamente perjudicial para los republicanos.* 2 ADJ Someone who is **political** is interested in politics and holds strong beliefs about it. *referente a la política* ❑ *I'm not political, I take no interest in politics. No me interesa la política.*

→ see **empire, philosophy**

**po|liti|cal ac|tion com|mit|tee** (**political action committees**) N-COUNT A **political action committee** is an organization which campaigns for particular political policies, and that gives money to political parties or candidates who support those policies. The abbreviation **PAC** is also used. *comité de acción política*

**poli|ti|cian** /pɒlɪtɪʃᵊn/ (**politicians**) N-COUNT A **politician** is a person whose job is in politics, especially a member of the government. *político* ❑ *They have arrested a number of politicians. Arrestaron a varios políticos.*

| Word Link | *poli ≈ city : metropolitan, politics, police* |
|---|---|

**poli|tics** /pɒlɪtɪks/ 1 N-UNCOUNT **Politics** is the actions or activities concerned with achieving and using power in a country or organization. *política* ❑ *He was involved in local politics. Participaba en la política del lugar.* 2 N-PLURAL Your **politics** are your beliefs about how a country ought to be governed. *ideas políticas* ❑ *His politics are extreme and often confused. Sus ideas políticas son extremistas y a menudo confusas.*

**pol|ka dots**

The spelling **polka-dot** is also used, especially as a modifier. The word **polka** is pronounced /poʊkə/ when it is part of this compound.

N-PLURAL **Polka dots** are small spots printed on a piece of cloth. *lunares* ❑ *...a yellow bikini with polka dots.* *...un bikini amarillo con lunares.* ❑ *...a tight-fitting polka-dot blouse.* *...una estrecha blusa con lunares.*
→ see **pattern**

**poll** /poʊl/ (**polls**) **1** N-COUNT A **poll** is a survey in which people are asked their opinions about something. *encuesta, sondeo* ❑ *Polls show that 70% of the time it is women who decide which movie to see on a date.* *Las encuestas indican que, el 70 por ciento de las veces, las mujeres deciden qué película ver cuando salen con alguien.* **2** → see also **opinion poll** **3** N-PLURAL **The polls** means an election for a country's government, or the place where people go to vote in an election. *votación, urna* ❑ *Voters go to the polls on Sunday to elect a new president.* *Los votantes irán a las urnas el domingo para elegir a un nuevo presidente.* **4** → see also **polling place**

**pol|li|nate** /pɒlɪneɪt/ (**pollinates, pollinating, pollinated**) V-T To **pollinate** a plant or tree means to fertilize it with pollen. This is often done by insects. *polinizar* ❑ *Many of the indigenous insects are needed to pollinate the local plants.* *Muchos de los insectos endémicos son necesarios para polinizar las plantas de la región.* ● **pol|li|na|tion** /pɒlɪneɪʃᵊn/ N-UNCOUNT *polinización* ❑ *Without sufficient pollination, the growth of the corn is stunted.* *Sin la suficiente polinización, el desarrollo del maíz se atrofia.*

**poll|ing place** (**polling places**) N-COUNT A **polling place** is a place where people go to vote in an election. *centro electoral, casilla de votación* ❑ *Voters were lining up at polling places as early as 6:00 this morning.* *Los votantes ya estaban haciendo cola en las casillas de votación desde las seis de la mañana.*
→ see **election, vote**

**pol|lu|tant** /pəlutᵊnt/ (**pollutants**) N-VAR **Pollutants** are substances that pollute the environment, especially poisonous chemicals produced as waste by vehicles and by industry. *contaminante*
→ see **ozone**

**pol|lute** /pəlut/ (**pollutes, polluting, polluted**) V-T To **pollute** water, air, or land means to make it dirty and dangerous to live in or to use, especially with poisonous chemicals or sewage. *contaminar* ❑ *Industry pollutes our rivers with chemicals.* *La industria contamina nuestros ríos con substancias químicas.* ● **pol|lut|ed** ADJ *contaminado* ❑ *...the polluted river.* *...el río contaminado.*

**pol|lu|tion** /pəluʃᵊn/ **1** N-UNCOUNT **Pollution** is the process of polluting water, air, or land. *contaminación* ❑ *...measures to stop pollution of the air, sea, rivers, and soil.* *...medidas para detener la contaminación del aire, el mar, los ríos y el suelo.* **2** N-UNCOUNT **Pollution** is poisonous substances that are polluting water, air, or land. *contaminación* ❑ *The level of pollution in the river was falling.* *El nivel de contaminación en el río estaba decayendo.*
→ see Word Web: **pollution**
→ see **air, factory, solar**

**poly|es|ter** /pɒliɛstər/ (**polyesters**) N-UNCOUNT **Polyester** is a type of synthetic cloth used especially to make clothes. *poliéster* ❑ *...a green polyester shirt.* *...una camisa verde de poliéster.*
→ see **petroleum**

**poly|no|mial** /pɒlɪnoʊmiəl/ (**polynomials**) N-COUNT A **polynomial** is an expression in algebra that is the sum of several terms. Compare **binomial, monomial.** *polinomio* [TECHNICAL] ● **Polynomial** is also an adjective. *polinomio* ❑ *...a polynomial expression* *...una expresión en polinomio*

**pol|yp** /pɒlɪp/ (**polyps**) N-COUNT A **polyp** is a small animal that lives in the sea. It has a hollow body like a tube and long parts called tentacles around its mouth. *pólipo*

**pom|mel horse** (**pommel horses**) N-COUNT A **pommel horse** is a tall piece of gymnastic equipment for jumping over. *caballo con arzones*

**pond** /pɒnd/ (**ponds**) N-COUNT A **pond** is a small, usually artificially made, area of water. *estanque* ❑ *We sat on a bench beside the duck pond.* *Nos sentamos en una banca al lado del estanque de los patos.*

**pon|der** /pɒndər/ (**ponders, pondering, pondered**) V-T If you **ponder** something, you think about it carefully. *ponderar* ❑ *I found myself constantly pondering the question.* *A menudo me hallaba a mí mismo ponderando la pregunta.*

**pony** /poʊni/ (**ponies, ponying, ponied**) N-COUNT A **pony** is a small or young horse. *pony* ▸ **pony up** PHR-VERB If you **pony up** a sum of money, you pay the money that is needed for something, often unwillingly. *pagar, apoquinar* [INFORMAL] ❑ *They are not prepared to pony up the $4 billion that we need.* *No están dispuestos a pagar los $4 mil millones que necesitamos.*

**pony|tail** /poʊniteɪl/ (**ponytails**) N-COUNT A **ponytail** is a hairstyle in which your hair is tied up at the back of your head and hangs down like a tail. *cola de caballo, coleta* ❑ *Her long, fine hair was tied*

P

**Word Web** pollution

**Pollution** affects the whole **environment**. **Airborne emissions** from factories and car **exhaust** cause air pollution. These smoky **emissions** combine with fog and make **smog**. Pollutants in the air can travel long distances. **Acid rain** caused by factories in the Midwest falls on states to the east. There it damages trees and kills fish in lakes. Chemicals from factories, **sewage**, and **garbage** pollute the water and land in many areas. Too many **pesticides** and **fertilizers** make the problem worse. These chemicals build up in the soil and poison the earth.

back in a ponytail. *Llevaba el largo y delgado pelo atado en forma de cola de caballo.*
→ see **hair**

**pool** /pul/ (**pools, pooling, pooled**) **1** N-COUNT A **pool** is the same as a **swimming pool**. *alberca, piscina, pileta* ❑ *...a heated indoor pool. ...una alberca techada con calefacción.* **2** N-COUNT A **pool** is a small area of still water. *estanque* ❑ *The pool has dried up. El estanque se secó.* **3** N-COUNT A **pool of** liquid or light is a small area of it. *charco* ❑ *...the pool of light cast from his desk lamp. ...el charco de luz que brotaba de la lámpara de su escritorio.* **4** N-COUNT A **pool of** people, money, or things is a quantity or number of them that is available for use. *cantidad, grupo* ❑ *The population is quite small and the available pool of talent is limited. La población es bastante pequeña y la cantidad de talento disponible es limitado.* **5** → see also **carpool** **6** V-T If people **pool** their money, knowledge, or equipment, they share it or put it together so that it can be used for a particular purpose. *juntar* ❑ *We pooled ideas and information. Juntamos ideas e información.* **7** N-UNCOUNT **Pool** is a game played on a special table. Players use a long stick called a cue to hit a white ball so that it knocks colored balls into six holes around the edge of the table. *billar*

**pool hall** (**pool halls**) N-COUNT A **pool hall** is a building where you can play pool. *billar*

**pooped** /pupt/ ADJ If you are **pooped**, you are very tired. *muerto* [INFORMAL]

**poor** /pʊər/ (**poorer, poorest**) **1** ADJ Someone who is **poor** has very little money and few possessions. *pobre* ❑ *"We were very poor in those days," he says. —Éramos muy pobres en aquel entonces—dice.* ● **The poor** are people who are poor. *Los pobres* ❑ *...huge differences between the rich and the poor. ...enormes diferencias entre los ricos y los pobres.* **2** ADJ A **poor** country or area is inhabited by people who are poor. *pobre* ❑ *The country is poor, and many people are unemployed. El país es pobre, y muchas personas están desempleadas.* **3** ADJ You use **poor** to express your sympathy for someone. *pobre* ❑ *I feel sorry for that poor child. Me siento mal por ese pobre niño.* **4** ADJ If you describe something as **poor**, you mean that it is of a low quality or standard. *pobre, mal* ❑ *...the poor state of the economy. El pobre estado de la economía.* ● **poor|ly** ADV *pobremente* ❑ *They are living in poorly built apartments. Viven en departamentos pobremente construidos.* **5** ADJ If you describe an amount, rate, or number as **poor**, you mean that it is less than expected or less than is considered reasonable. *pobre, bajo* ❑ *...poor wages and working conditions. ...salarios bajos y malas condiciones de trabajo.* ● **poor|ly** ADV *pobremente* ❑ *The evening meetings were poorly attended. Poca gente asistió a las juntas de la tarde.* **6** ADJ You use **poor** to describe someone who is not very skillful in a particular activity. *mal* ❑ *He was a poor actor. Era un mal actor.* ● **poor|ly** ADV *mal* ❑ *"We played poorly in the first game," Mendez said. —Jugamos mal el primer juego—dijo Méndez.* **7** ADJ If something is **poor in** a particular quality or substance, it contains very little of the quality or substance. *bajo en* ❑ *Fat and sugar are very rich in energy, but poor in vitamins. La grasa y el azúcar son altos en energía, pero bajos en vitaminas.*

P

**Thesaurus** *poor* Ver también:
ADJ. impoverished, penniless; (*ant.*) rich, wealthy **1** **2**
inferior **4**

**pop** /pɒp/ (**pops, popping, popped**) **1** N-UNCOUNT **Pop** is modern music that usually has a strong rhythm and uses electronic equipment. *pop, música popular* ❑ *...the perfect combination of Caribbean rhythms and European pop. ...la combinación perfecta entre ritmos caribeños y el pop europeo.* ❑ *...a poster of a pop star. ...un poster de una estrella del pop.* **2** V-I If something **pops,** it makes a short sharp sound. *estallar, reventar, chasquear* ❑ *He heard a balloon pop behind his head. Escuchó un globo reventar detrás de él.* ● **Pop** is also a noun. *chasquido* ❑ *Each corn kernel will make a loud pop when cooked. Cada grano de maíz dará un chasquido al cocinarse.* **3** V-I If your eyes **pop,** you look very surprised or excited when you see something. *salírsele o saltársele a uno* [INFORMAL] ❑ *My eyes popped at the sight of the food. Se me salieron los ojos al ver la comida.* **4** V-T If you **pop** something somewhere, you put it there quickly. *echar de repente* [INFORMAL] ❑ *He popped some gum into his mouth. Se echó un chicle dentro de la boca de repente.* **5** N-COUNT Some people call their father **pop.** *pa* [INFORMAL] ❑ *I looked at Pop and he had big tears in his eyes. Miré a mi pa y tenía grandes lágrimas en los ojos.*

▸ **pop off** PHR-VERB If someone **pops off,** they say or write something very angrily or in a very emotional way. *vociferar, clamar* [INFORMAL] ❑ *He made the mistake of popping off about his boss to one of his colleagues. Cometió el error de vociferar acerca de su jefe con uno de sus colegas.*

▸ **pop up** PHR-VERB If someone or something **pops up,** they appear in a place or situation unexpectedly. *aparecer* [INFORMAL] ❑ *She was startled when Lisa popped up. Se sobrasaltó cuando apareció Lisa.*

**pop|corn** /pɒpkɔrn/ N-UNCOUNT **Popcorn** is a snack that consists of grains of corn that have been heated until they have burst and become large and light. *palomitas*

**pop|over** /pɒpoʊvər/ (**popovers**) N-COUNT A **popover** is a light, hollow muffin. *panecillo* ❑ *...blueberry popovers. ...panecillos de arándano.*

**pop|per** /pɒpər/ N-COUNT A **popper** is a pan or basket that you use when making popcorn. *utensilio para hacer palomitas*

**Word Link** *popul ≈ people : popular, population, unpopular*

**popu|lar** /pɒpyələr/ **1** ADJ Something or someone that is **popular** is liked by a lot of people. *popular* ❑ *He was the most popular politician in Arkansas. Era el político más popular en Arkansas.* ❑ *Chocolate sauce is always popular with youngsters. La salsa de chocolate siempre es popular entre los jóvenes.* ● **popu|lar|ity** /pɒpyəlærɪti/ N-UNCOUNT *popularidad* ❑ *...the growing popularity of Polish sausage among consumers. ...la creciente popularidad de las salchichas polacas entre los consumidores.* ❑ *...his popularity with ordinary people. ...su popularidad entre el común de la gente.* **2** ADJ **Popular** newspapers, television programs, or forms of art are aimed at

ordinary people and not at experts or intellectuals. *popular* ❑ *...the popular press in Britain. ...la prensa popular en el Reino Unido.* ❑ *...one of the classics of modern popular music. ...uno de los clásicos de la música popular moderna.* **3** ADJ **Popular** ideas or attitudes are approved of or held by most people. *común, generalizado* ❑ *...the popular belief that unemployment causes crime. ...la creencia generalizada que el desempleo causa el crimen.* ● **popu|lar|ity** N-UNCOUNT *popularidad* ❑ *Over time, Watson's views gained in popularity. Conforme pasaba el tiempo, las opiniones de Watson ganaron en popularidad.* **4** ADJ **Popular** is used to describe political activities that involve the ordinary people of a country. *popular* ❑ *They are trying to build popular support for military action. Están tratando de crear apoyo popular para la acción militar.*
→ see **genre**

**Word Partnership** Usar *popular* con:

ADV. **extremely** popular, **increasingly** popular, **more** popular, **most** popular, **wildly** popular **1**
N. popular **movie**, popular **restaurant**, popular **show**, popular **song** **1** popular **magazine**, popular **novel** **1** **2** popular **culture**, popular **music** **2**

**Word Link** *popul ≈ people : popular, population, unpopular*

**popu|la|tion** /pɒpyəleɪʃᵊn/ (**populations**) **1** N-COUNT The **population** of a country or area is all the people who live in it. *población* ❑ *Bangladesh now has a population of about 150 million. Bangladesh tiene una población que ahora ronda los 150 millones.* ❑ *...the annual rate of population growth. ...la tasa anual de crecimiento de población.* **2** N-COUNT If you refer to a particular type of **population** in a country or area, you are referring to all the people or animals of that type there. *población* [FORMAL] ❑ *...75.6 percent of the male population. ...75.6 porciento de la población masculina.*
→ see **country**

**porce|lain** /pɔrsəlɪn, pɔrslɪn/ N-UNCOUNT **Porcelain** is a hard, shiny substance made by heating clay. It is used to make cups, plates, and ornaments. *porcelana* ❑ *...tall white porcelain vases. ...altos jarrones de porcelana blanca.*
→ see **pottery**

porch

**porch** /pɔrtʃ/ (**porches**) N-COUNT A **porch** is a raised platform built along the outside wall of a house and often covered with a roof. *porche* ❑ *He was standing on the porch, waving as we drove away. Estaba de pie en el porche, despidiéndose mientras nos alejábamos en el coche.*

**pork** /pɔrk/ N-UNCOUNT **Pork** is meat from a pig, usually fresh and not smoked or salted. *cerdo, puerco* ❑ *...fried pork chops. ...chuletas de cerdo fritas.*
→ see **meat**

**pork bar|rel** also **pork-barrel** N-SING If you say that someone is using **pork barrel** politics, you disapprove of the fact that they are spending a lot of government money on a local project in order to win the votes of the people who live in that area. *partida del presupuesto público que usan los políticos para su propio beneficio; corrupción* ❑ *...useless billion dollar pork barrel projects. ...proyectos corruptos e inútiles por miles de millones de dólares.*

**po|ros|ity** /pɔrɒsɪti/ N-UNCOUNT **Porosity** is the amount of open space between individual rock particles. *porosidad*

**po|rous** /pɔrəs/ ADJ Something that is **porous** has many small holes in it that water and air can pass through. *poroso* ❑ *...a porous material like sand. ...un material poroso como la arena.*
→ see **pottery**

**port** /pɔrt/ (**ports**) **1** N-COUNT A **port** is a town or a harbor area where ships load and unload goods or passengers. *puerto* ❑ *...the Mediterranean port of Marseilles. ...el puerto mediterráneo de Marsella.* **2** N-COUNT A **port** on a computer is a place where you can attach another piece of equipment such as a printer. *puerto* [COMPUTING] ❑ *The scanner plugs into the printer port of your computer. El escáner se conecta al puerto de la impresora de tu computadora.* **3** ADJ The **port** side of a ship is the left side when you are on it and facing toward the front. *babor* [TECHNICAL] ● **Port** is also a noun. *babor* ❑ *The ship turned to port. El barco viró a babor.* **4** N-VAR **Port** is a type of strong, sweet red wine. *oporto* ❑ *...a glass of port. ...un vaso de oporto.*
→ see **ship**

**Word Link** *able ≈ able to be : acceptable, incurable, portable*

**Word Link** *port ≈ carrying : export, import, portable*

**port|able** /pɔrtəbᵊl/ (**portables**) **1** ADJ A **portable** machine or device is designed to be easily carried or moved. *portátil* ❑ *...a little portable television. ...una pequeña televisión portátil.* **2** N-COUNT A **portable** is something such as a television, radio, or computer that can be easily carried or moved. *portátil* ❑ *We bought a portable for the bedroom. Compramos un portátil para el cuarto.*

**por|ter** /pɔrtər/ (**porters**) N-COUNT A **porter** is a person whose job is to carry things, for example, people's luggage at a train station or in a hotel. *maletero, cargador* ❑ *Our taxi arrived at the station and a porter came to the door. Nuestro taxi llegó a la estación y un maletero vino a nuestro encuentro.*

**port|fo|lio** /pɔrtfoʊlioʊ/ (**portfolios**) **1** N-COUNT A **portfolio** is a set of pictures or photographs of someone's work, which they show when they are trying to get a job. *carpeta, colección* ❑ *Edith showed them a portfolio of her drawings. Edith les mostró una colección de sus dibujos.* **2** N-COUNT A **portfolio** is an organized collection of student work. *carpeta, colección*

**por|tion** /pɔrʃᵊn/ (**portions**) **1** N-COUNT A **portion of** something is a part of it. *porción, parte* ❑ *Only a small portion of the castle was damaged. Sólo una pequeña parte del castillo fue dañada.* ❑ *I have spent a large portion of my life here. He pasado buena parte de mi vida aquí.* **2** N-COUNT A **portion** is the amount of food that is given to one person at a meal. *porción* ❑ *The portions were generous. Las porciones eran generosas.*

P

**por|trait** /pɔrtrɪt, -treɪt/ (**portraits**) N-COUNT A **portrait** is a painting, drawing, or photograph of a particular person. *retrato* ❑ *...family portraits. ...retratos de la familia.*
→ see **painting**

**por|tray** /pɔrtreɪ/ (**portrays, portraying, portrayed**) **1** V-T When an actor or actress **portrays** someone, he or she plays that person in a play or movie. *representar* ❑ *He portrayed the king in "Camelot." Representó al rey en "Camelot".* **2** V-T To **portray** someone or something means to represent them, for example in a book or movie. *retratar* ❑ *The film portrays a group of young people who live in lower Manhattan. La película retrata a un grupo de jóvenes que viven en el centro de Manhattan.*

**pose** /poʊz/ (**poses, posing, posed**) **1** V-T If something **poses** a problem or a danger, it is the cause of that problem or danger. *plantear* ❑ *New shopping malls pose a threat to independent stores. Los nuevos centros comerciales plantean una amenaza a las tiendas independientes.* **2** V-T If you **pose** a question, you ask it. *formular* [FORMAL] ❑ *I finally posed the question, "Why?" Finalmente formulé la pregunta,—¿Por qué?* **3** V-I If you **pose as** someone, you pretend to be that person in order to deceive people. *hacerse pasar por* ❑ *...people employed to pose as customers. ...las personas empleadas para hacerse pasar por clientes.* **4** V-I If you **pose for** a photograph or painting, you stay in a particular position so that someone can photograph you or paint you. *posar* ❑ *The six foreign ministers posed for photographs. Los seis ministros de relaciones exteriores posaron para las fotografías.* **5** N-COUNT A **pose** is a particular position that you stay in when you are being photographed or painted. *pose* ❑ *We tried various poses. Intentamos varias poses.*

**po|si|tion** /pəzɪʃᵊn/ (**positions, positioning, positioned**) **1** N-COUNT The **position** of someone or something is the place where they are in relation to other things. *posición* ❑ *...a device for planning your route and locating your position. ...un dispositivo para planear tu ruta y localizar tu posición.* **2** N-COUNT When someone or something is in a particular **position,** they are sitting, lying, or arranged in that way. *posición* ❑ *Mr. Dambar raised himself to a sitting position. El señor Dambar se irguió hasta quedar sentado.* **3** V-T If you **position** something somewhere, you put it there carefully, so that it is in the right place or position. *colocar* ❑ *Position the table in an open area where a cat can't jump onto it. Coloca la mesa en un área despejada en donde un gato no pueda brincar hasta ella.* **4** N-COUNT Your **position** in society is the role and the importance that you have in it. *posición* ❑ *...their changing role and position in society. ...su cambiante papel y posición en la sociedad.* **5** N-COUNT A **position** in a company or organization is a job. *puesto* [FORMAL] ❑ *He left a career in teaching to take a position with IBM. Dejó una carrera en la enseñanza para tomar un puesto en IBM.* **6** N-COUNT Your **position** in a race or competition is how well you did in relation to the other competitors or how well you are doing. *posición, puesto* ❑ *The car was running in eighth position. El auto corría en la octava posición.* **7** N-COUNT You can describe your situation at a particular time by saying that you are in a particular **position.** *posición* ❑ *He's going to be in a very difficult position if things go badly. Va a quedar en una posición muy difícil si las cosas salen mal.* ❑ *The club's financial position is still uncertain. La posición financiera del club es aún incierta.* **8** N-COUNT Your **position on** a particular matter is your attitude toward it or your opinion of it. *posición* [FORMAL] ❑ *What is your position on this issue? ¿Cuál es tu posición en este tema?* **9** N-SING If you are **in a position to** do something, you are able to do it. *en posición de* ❑ *I am not in a position to comment. No estoy en posición de hacer comentarios.*
→ see **navigation**

**Word Partnership** Usar *position* con:

ADJ. **better** position **1** **2** **4**–**7**
**fetal** position **2**
**(un)comfortable** position **2** **7**
**difficult** position, **financial** position **7**
**official** position **8**

**posi|tive** /pɒzɪtɪv/ **1** ADJ If you are **positive,** you are hopeful and confident, and think of the good aspects of a situation rather than the bad ones. *positivo, optimista* ❑ *Be positive about your future. Sé positivo acerca de tu futuro.* • **posi|tive|ly** ADV *positivamente* ❑ *You really must try to start thinking positively. En verdad debes de empezar a pensar positivamente.* **2** ADJ A **positive** situation or experience is pleasant and helpful to you in some way. *positivo* ❑ *I've got two grandchildren now, and I want to have a positive effect on their lives. Tengo dos nietos ahora, y quiero tener un efecto positivo en sus vidas.* • **The positive** in a situation is the good and pleasant aspects of it. *lo positivo* ❑ *He prefers to focus on the positive. Prefiere enfocarse en lo positivo.* **3** ADJ If you make a **positive** decision or take **positive** action, you do something definite in order to deal with a task or problem. *positivo* ❑ *I wanted to do something positive and creative, for myself and the country. Quería hacer algo positivo y creativo, por mí mismo y por mi país.* **4** ADJ A **positive** response to something indicates agreement, approval, or encouragement. *positivo* ❑ *There's been a positive response to the UN's recent peace efforts. Ha habido una respuesta positiva a los recientes esfuerzos de paz por parte de la ONU.* • **posi|tive|ly** ADV *positivamente* ❑ *He responded positively and accepted the idea. Respondió positivamente y aceptó la idea.* **5** ADJ If you are **positive** about something, you are completely sure about it. *seguro* ❑ *"Judith's never late. You sure she said eight?"— "Positive." —Judith nunca se retrasa. ¿Estás seguro que dijo a las ocho?—Seguro.* **6** ADJ **Positive** evidence gives definite proof of something. *cierto* ❑ *There is some positive evidence that the economy is improving. Hay evidencias ciertas de que la economía está mejorando.* • **posi|tive|ly** ADV *de forma definitva* ❑ *He has positively identified the body as that of his wife. Ha hecho una identificación definitiva del cadáver de su esposa.* **7** ADJ If a medical or scientific test is **positive,** it shows that something has happened or is present. *positivo* ❑ *If the test is positive, treatment will start immediately. Si la prueba sale positiva, el tratamiento empezará de inmediato.* **8** **HIV positive** → see **HIV** **9** ADJ In art and sculpture, **positive** space is the parts of a painting that represent solid objects or the parts of a sculpture that are made of solid material.

P

Compare **negative**. *positivo* [TECHNICAL]

**pos|i|tive ac|cel|er|a|tion** N-UNCOUNT **Positive acceleration** is an increase in speed or velocity. Compare **negative acceleration**. *aceleración positiva* [TECHNICAL]

**pos|sess** /pəzɛs/ (**possesses, possessing, possessed**) V-T If you **possess** something, you have it or own it. *poseer* ❑ *He possessed charm and diplomatic skills. Poseía carisma y aptitudes diplomáticas.*

**pos|ses|sion** /pəzɛʃᵊn/ (**possessions**) **1** N-UNCOUNT If you are **in possession of** something, you have it, because you have obtained it or because it belongs to you. *posesión* [FORMAL] ❑ *Those documents are now in the possession of the Washington Post. Esos documentos están ahora en posesión del Washington Post* ❑ *...the possession of private property. ...la posesión de la propiedad privada.* **2** N-COUNT Your **possessions** are the things that you own or have with you at a particular time. *posesiones* ❑ *People have lost their homes and all their possessions. La gente ha perdido sus casas y todas sus posesiones.*

**Word Partnership** Usar *possession* con:

N. **cocaine** possession, **drug** possession, possession **of a firearm**, possession **of property**, **weapons** possession **1**

**pos|ses|sive** /pəzɛsɪv/ **1** ADJ Someone who is **possessive about** another person wants all that person's love and attention. *posesivo* ❑ *Danny could be very jealous and possessive about me. Danny podía llegar a ser muy celoso y posesivo conmigo.*
● **pos|ses|sive|ness** N-UNCOUNT *posesividad, celos* ❑ *I've ruined every relationship with my possessiveness. He arruinado todas mis relaciones con mi posesividad.* **2** ADJ In grammar, a **possessive determiner** or **possessive adjective** is a word such as "my" or "his" that shows who or what something belongs to or is connected with. The **possessive** form of a name or noun has **'s** added to it, as in "Jenny's" or "cat's." *adjetivo o pronombre posesivo*

**pos|sibil|ity** /pɒsɪbɪlɪti/ (**possibilities**) **1** N-COUNT If you say there is a **possibility that** something is true or **that** something will happen, you mean that it might be true or it might happen. *posibilidad* ❑ *Be prepared for the possibility that he may never answer. Debes estar preparado para la posibilidad de que nunca te conteste.* **2** N-COUNT A **possibility** is one of several different things that could be done. *posibilidad* ❑ *There were several possibilities open to us. Había varias posibilidades ante nosotros.*

**Word Link** *ible = able to be : audible, flexible, possible*

**pos|sible** /pɒsɪbᵊl/ (**possibles**) **1** ADJ If it is **possible** to do something, it can be done. *posible* ❑ *If it is possible to find out where your brother is, we will. Si es posible averiguar dónde está tu hermano, lo haremos.* ❑ *Anything is possible if you want it enough. Cualquier cosa es posible si lo deseas lo suficiente.* **2** ADJ A **possible** event is one that might happen. *posible* ❑ *The army is prepared for possible military action. El ejército está preparado para una posible acción militar.* **3** ADJ If you say that it is **possible that** something is true or correct, you mean that although you do not know whether it is true or correct, you accept that it might be. *posible* ❑ *It is possible that he's telling the truth. Es posible que esté diciendo la verdad.* **4** ADJ If you do something **as soon as possible**, you do it as soon as you can. If you get **as** much **as possible** of something, you get as much of it as you can. *tan ...como sea posible* ❑ *Please make your decision as soon as possible. Por favor tome la decisión tan pronto sea posible.* ❑ *Mrs. Pollard decided to learn as much as possible about the country before going there. La señora Pollard decidió aprender tanto como le fuera posible acerca del país antes de ir.* **5** ADJ You use **possible** with superlative adjectives to emphasize that something has more or less of a quality than anything else of its kind. *posible* ❑ *They joined the company at the worst possible time. Se unieron a la compañía en el peor momento posible.* ❑ *He is doing the best job possible. Está haciendo el mejor trabajo posible.* **6** N-SING **The possible** is everything that can be done in a situation. *lo posible* ❑ *Politics is the art of the possible. La política es el arte de lo posible.*

**Thesaurus** *possible* Ver también:

ADJ. feasible, likely; (*ant.*) impossible, unlikely **1**

**pos|sibly** /pɒsɪbli/ **1** ADV You use **possibly** to indicate that you are not sure whether something is true or might happen. *posiblemente* ❑ *Exercise will possibly protect against heart attacks. El ejercicio puede tal vez proteger al corazón de infartos.* ❑ *They were casually dressed; possibly students. Estaban vestidos de manera informal; posiblemente eran estudiantes.* **2** ADV You use **possibly** to emphasize that you are surprised or puzzled. *es posible* ❑ *How could they possibly eat that stuff? ¿Cómo es posible que puedan comer esa cosa?* **3** ADV You use **possibly** to emphasize that something is possible, or with a negative to emphasize that it is not possible. *posiblemente* ❑ *They've done everything they can possibly think of. Han hecho todo lo que se les ha ocurrido.* ❑ *I can't possibly answer that! ¡No puedo contestar eso!*

**post**
❶ INFORMATION AND COMMUNICATION
❷ JOBS AND PLACES
❸ POLE

❶ **post** /poʊst/ (**posts, posting, posted**) **1** V-T If you **post** notices, signs, or other pieces of information somewhere, you attach them to a wall or board so that everyone can see them. *fijar, colgar* ❑ *Officials began posting warning notices. Los oficiales empezaron a colgar carteles de advertencia.*
● **Post up** means the same as **post**. *colgar, fijar* ❑ *He has posted a sign up that says "No Fishing." Ha colgado un letrero que dice "No pescar".* **2** V-T If you **post** information on the Internet, you make the information available to other people on the Internet. *colgar, subir, poner* [COMPUTING] ❑ *...a statement posted on the Internet. ...una declaración colgada en el internet.*

❷ **post** /poʊst/ (**posts, posting, posted**) **1** N-COUNT A **post** in a company or organization

P

is a job or official position in it. *puesto* [FORMAL] ❑ *She took up a post as President Menem's assistant. Tomo un puesto como asisitente del presidente Menem.* **2** V-T If you **are posted** somewhere, you are sent there by your employers to work. *asignar a un puesto* ❑ *After her training she was posted to Biloxi. Después de su entrenamiento fue asignada a un puesto en Biloxi.*

**❸ post** /poʊst/ (**posts**) N-COUNT A **post** is a strong upright pole fixed into the ground. *poste* ❑ *The device is fixed to a post. El dispositivo se coloca en un poste.*

**post|age** /poʊstɪdʒ/ N-UNCOUNT **Postage** is the money that you pay for sending letters and packages by mail. *gastos de envío, franqueo* ❑ *All prices include postage. Todos los precios incluyen gastos de envío.*

**post|card** /poʊstkɑrd/ (**postcards**) also **post card** N-COUNT A **postcard** is a thin card, often with a picture on one side, which you can write on and mail to someone without using an envelope. *postal*

**post|er** /poʊstər/ (**posters**) N-COUNT A **poster** is a large notice or picture that you stick on a wall or board, often in order to advertise something. *póster, cartel* ❑ *...a poster for the jazz festival in Monterey. ...un cartel anunciando el festival de jazz de Monterey.*

**post|er child** also **poster boy** also **poster girl** N-COUNT If someone or something is a **poster child for** a particular cause, characteristic, or activity, they are seen as a very good or typical example of it. *perfecto ejemplo* ❑ *He called Coleman a "poster child for what is wrong in politics." Llamó a Coleman el "perfecto ejemplo de lo que anda mal en la política".*

**post|mod|ern dance** also **post-modern dance** N-UNCOUNT **Postmodern dance** is a form of dance that began in the 1960s as a reaction against modern dance. *danza posmoderna*

P

| Word Link | post ≈ after : postmortem, postpone, postwar |
|---|---|

**post|mor|tem** /poʊstmɔrtəm/ (**postmortems**) **1** N-COUNT A **postmortem** is a medical examination of a dead person's body to find out how they died. *autopsia* ❑ *The body was taken to hospital for a postmortem. El cuerpo fue llevado al hospital para una autopsia.* **2** N-COUNT A **postmortem** is an examination of something that has recently happened, especially something that has failed or gone wrong. *autopsia* ❑ *The postmortem on the presidential campaign is under way. La autopsia de la campaña presidencial se está llevando a cabo.*

**post of|fice** (**post offices**) **1** N-COUNT A **post office** is a building where you can buy stamps, mail letters and packages, and use other services provided by the national postal service. *correo* ❑ *She needed to get to the post office before it closed. Necesitaba llegar al correo antes de que cerraran.* **2** N-SING **The Post Office** is sometimes used to refer to the U.S. Postal Service. *correo*

**post|partum de|pres|sion** /poʊstpɑrtəm dɪprɛʃᵊn/ N-UNCOUNT **Postpartum depression** is a mental state involving feelings of anxiety and sudden mood swings which some women experience after they have given birth. *depresión posparto*

**post|pone** /poʊstpoʊn, poʊspoʊn/ (**postpones, postponing, postponed**) V-T If you **postpone** an event, you delay it or arrange for it to take place at a later time than was originally planned. *posponer, aplazar* ❑ *He decided to postpone the trip until the following day. Decidió posponer su viaje hasta el día siguiente.* ● **post|pone|ment** N-VAR (**postponements**) *posposición, aplazamiento* ❑ *...the postponement of yesterday's match. ...la posposición del partido de ayer.*

**pos|ture** /pɒstʃər/ (**postures**) **1** N-VAR Your **posture** is the position in which you stand or sit. *postura* ❑ *You can make your stomach look flatter by improving your posture. Puedes hacer que tu estómago parezca más plano si mejoras tu postura.* **2** N-COUNT A **posture** is an attitude that you have or a way that you behave toward a person or thing. *posición* [FORMAL] ❑ *Mr Bush's new posture helped open the way for the next proposal. La posición del señor Bush ayudó a abrir el camino para la siguiente propuesta.*
→ see **brain**

**post|war** /poʊstwɔr/ ADJ **Postwar** is used to describe things that happened, existed, or were made in the period immediately after a war, especially World War II, 1939–45. *de posguerra* ❑ *Bottle feeding babies was popular in the early postwar years. Dar a los bebés de comer de una mamila estuvo de moda en tiempos de posguerra.*

**pot** /pɒt/ (**pots, potting, potted**) **1** N-COUNT A **pot** is a deep round container used for cooking food. *olla* ❑ *...metal cooking pots. ...ollas de metal.* **2** N-COUNT A **pot** is a teapot or coffee pot. *tetera, cafetera* ❑ *There's tea in the pot. Hay té en la tetera.* **3** V-T If you **pot** a plant, you put it into a container filled with soil. *plantar en maceta* ❑ *Pot the plants individually. Plántalas en macetas individuales.* **4** N-SING You can refer to a fund consisting of money from several people as **the pot.** *fondo común, vaca, pozo* ❑ *I've taken some money from the pot to buy wrapping paper. Tomé un poco de dinero del pozo para comprar papel para envolver.* **5** N-COUNT Someone who has a **pot** has a round, fat stomach which sticks out. *barriga*

**po|table** /poʊtəbᵊl/ ADJ **Potable** water is clean and safe for drinking. *potable*

**po|ta|to** /pəteɪtoʊ/ (**potatoes**) N-VAR **Potatoes** are round vegetables with brown or red skins and white insides. They grow under the ground. *papa*
→ see **vegetable**

**po|ta|to chip** (**potato chips**) N-COUNT **Potato chips** are very thin slices of potato that have been fried until they are hard, dry, and crisp. *papa*

| Word Link | potent ≈ ability, power : impotent, potent, potential |
|---|---|

**po|tent** /poʊtᵊnt/ ADJ Something that is **potent** is very effective and powerful. *potente* ❑ *Their most potent weapon was the Exocet missile. Su arma más potente era el misil Exocet.* ● **po|ten|cy** /poʊtᵊnsi/ N-UNCOUNT *potencia* ❑ *Sunscreen can lose its potency if left over winter in the bathroom cabinet. El filtro solar puede perder su potencia si se deja todo el invierno dentro del botiquín del baño.*

**po|ten|tial** /pətɛnʃᵊl/ **1** ADJ You use **potential** to say that someone or something is capable

**Word Web** pottery

There are three basic types of **pottery**. Earthenware **dishes** are made from **clay** and **fired** at a relatively low temperature. They are **porous** and must be **glazed** in order to hold water. Potters first created earthenware objects about 15,000 years ago. Stoneware pieces are heavier and are fired at a higher temperature. They are impermeable even without a glaze. **Porcelain ceramics** are fragile. They have thin walls and are **translucent**. Stoneware and porcelain are not as old as earthenware. They appeared about 2,000 years ago when the Chinese started building high-temperature kilns. Another name for porcelain is **china**.

of developing into a particular kind of person or thing. *potencial, posible* ❑ *The company has identified 60 potential customers. La compañía ha identificado a 60 posibles clientes.* ❑ *We are aware of the potential problems. Conocemos los posibles problemas.* • **po|ten|tial|ly** ADV *potencialmente, posiblemente* ❑ *This is a potentially dangerous situation. Ésta es una situación potencialmente péligrosa.* **2** N-UNCOUNT If you say that someone or something has **potential,** you mean that they have the necessary abilities or qualities to become successful or useful in the future. *potencial* ❑ *The boy has great potential. El niño tiene mucho potencial.* **3** N-UNCOUNT If you say that someone or something has **potential for** doing a particular thing, you mean that it is possible they may do it. If there is **the potential for** something, it may happen. *posibilidad* ❑ *The potential for conflict is great. La posibilidad de un conflicto es alta.*

**po|ten|tial dif|fer|ence** /pətɛnʃᵊl dɪfərəns, dɪfrəns/ N-VAR **Potential difference** is the difference in voltage between two points on an electrical circuit. *diferencia potencial* [TECHNICAL]

**po|ten|tial en|er|gy** N-UNCOUNT **Potential energy** is the energy that an object has because of its position or condition, for example because it is raised above the ground. Compare **kinetic energy**. *energía potencial*

**pot|tery** /pɒtəri/ (**potteries**) **1** N-UNCOUNT **Pottery** is pots, dishes, and other objects made from clay. *cerámica* ❑ *...a fine range of pottery. ...una magnífica variedad de cerámica.* **2** N-UNCOUNT **Pottery** is the craft or activity of making objects out of clay. *alfarería* ❑ *He became interested in sculpting and pottery. Se interesó en la escultura y la alfarería.*
→ see Word Web: **pottery**

**pouch** /paʊtʃ/ (**pouches**) **1** N-COUNT A **pouch** is a flexible container like a small bag. *bolsa pequeña* ❑ *...a pouch of silver coins. ...una pequeña bolsa con monedas de plata.* **2** N-COUNT The **pouch** of an animal such as a kangaroo or a koala bear is the pocket of skin on its stomach in which its baby grows. *bolsa* ❑ *...a kangaroo with a baby in its pouch. ...un canguro con un bebé en su bolsa.*

**poul|try** /poʊltri/ N-PLURAL You can refer to chickens, ducks, and other birds that are kept for their eggs and meat as **poultry.** *aves de corral* ❑ *...methods of raising poultry. ...métodos para criar aves de corral.* • Meat from these birds is also referred to as **poultry**. *carne de ave, volatería, aves* ❑ *The menu offers roast meats and poultry. El menú incluye carnes asadas y aves.*
→ see **meat**

**pound** /paʊnd/ (**pounds, pounding, pounded**) **1** N-COUNT A **pound** is a unit of weight used mainly in the U.S., Britain, and other countries where English is spoken. One pound is equal to 0.454 kilograms. *libra* ❑ *Her weight was under ninety pounds. Su peso era inferior a las noventa libras.* ❑ *...a pound of cheese. ...una libra de queso.* **2** N-COUNT The **pound** is the unit of money which is used in Britain. It is represented by the symbol £. Some other countries, for example, Egypt, also have a unit of money called a **pound.** *libra esterlina* **3** V-T/V-I If you **pound** something or **pound on** it, you hit it with great force, usually loudly and repeatedly. *golpear* ❑ *He pounded the table with his fist. Golpeó la mesa con su puño.* ❑ *Somebody began pounding on the front door. Alguien comenzó a golpear en la puerta de entrada.* **4** V-I If your heart **is pounding,** it is beating with an unusually strong and fast rhythm, usually because you are afraid. *latir con fuerza* ❑ *I'm sweating, my heart is pounding. Estoy sudando, mi corazón late con fuerza.*

**pound cake** (**pound cakes**) N-VAR A **pound cake** is a very rich cake, originally made using a pound of butter, a pound of sugar, and a pound of flour. *bizcocho*

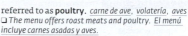

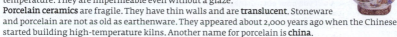

pour

**pour** /pɔr/ (**pours, pouring, poured**) **1** V-T If you **pour** a liquid or other substance, you make it flow steadily out of a container by holding the container at an angle. *verter, vaciar* ❑ *She poured some water into a bowl. Vertió un poco de agua a un tazón.* **2** V-T If you **pour** someone a drink, you put some of the drink in a cup or glass so that they can drink it. *servir* ❑ *She asked Tillie to pour her a cup of coffee. Le pidió a Tillie que le sirviera una taza de café.* **3** V-I When a liquid or other substance **pours** somewhere, it flows there quickly and in large quantities. *brotar, salir a borbotones* ❑ *Blood was pouring from his broken nose. Le brotaba sangre de la nariz rota.* ❑ *Tears poured down our faces. Lágrimas brotaron de nuestros ojos.* **4** V-I When it rains very heavily, you can say that **it is pouring.** *diluviar* ❑ *It was still pouring outside. Estaba diluviando afuera.* ❑ *The rain was pouring down. Diluviaba.* **5** V-I

If people **pour** into or out of a place, they go there quickly and in large numbers. *llegar/salir en cantidades grandes* ❑ *At six p.m. workers poured from the offices. A las seis de la tarde grandes cantidades de trabajadores salían de sus oficinas.* **6** V-I If something such as information **pours** into a place, a lot of it is obtained or given. *entrar a montones en, llegar a montones* ❑ *Thousands of get-well messages poured in from all over the world. Miles de mensajes de todo el mundo que deseaban su pronta recuperación llegaron a montones.*

▸ **pour out** PHR-VERB If you **pour out** a drink, you put some of it in a cup or glass. *llenar* ❑ *Larry poured out four glasses of water. Larry llenó cuatro vasos de agua.*

**Word Partnership** Usar *pour* con:

N. pour **a liquid,** pour **a mixture,** pour **water** **1** pour **coffee,** pour **a drink** **2**

**pov|er|ty** /pɒvərti/ N-UNCOUNT **Poverty** is the state of being very poor. *pobreza* ❑ *...people living in poverty. ...gente viviendo en la pobreza.*

**pow|der** /paʊdər/ (**powders**) N-VAR **Powder** consists of many tiny particles of a solid substance. *polvo* ❑ *Put a small amount of the powder into a container and mix with water. Pon un poco del polvo en un frasco y mézclalo con agua.* ❑ *...cocoa powder. ...polvo de chocolate.*
→ see **makeup**

**pow|dered** /paʊdərd/ ADJ A **powdered** substance is one that is in the form of a powder although it can come in a different form. *en polvo* ❑ *...powdered milk. ...leche en polvo.*

**pow|er** /paʊər/ (**powers, powering, powered**) **1** N-UNCOUNT If someone has **power,** they have a lot of control over people and activities. *poder* ❑ *When your children are young you still have a lot of power; you shape your child's world. Cuando tus hijos son pequeños todavía tienes mucho poder; moldeas el mundo de tus hijos.* **2** N-UNCOUNT Your **power to** do something is your ability to do it. *capacidad* ❑ *She has the power to charm anyone. Tiene la capacidad de encantar a cualquiera.* **3** N-UNCOUNT If it is **in** or **within** your **power to** do something, you are able to do it or you have the resources to deal with it. *en su poder* ❑ *It is within your power to change your life if you are not happy. Está en tu poder el cambiar tu vida si no estás a gusto.* **4** N-UNCOUNT If someone in authority has the **power** to do something, they have the legal right to do it. *facultad* ❑ *The police have the power to arrest people carrying knives. La policía tiene la facultad de arrestar a la gente que porta cuchillos.* **5** N-UNCOUNT If people take **power** or come to **power,** they take charge of a country's affairs. If a group of people are **in power,** they are in charge of a country's affairs. *poder* ❑ *Amin came into power several years later. Amin tomó el poder unos años más tarde.* **6** N-UNCOUNT The **power** of something is its physical strength or the ability that it has to move or affect things. *potencia* ❑ *The vehicle had better power and better brakes. El vehículo tenía más potencia y mejores frenos.* **7** N-UNCOUNT **Power** is energy, especially electricity, that is obtained in large quantities from a fuel source. *energía* ❑ *Nuclear power is cleaner than coal. La energía nuclear es más limpia que el carbón.* ❑ *Power has been restored to most areas that were affected by the high winds. El suministro de energía se ha restablecido en la mayoría de las áreas afectadas por los fuertes vientos.* **8** V-T The device or fuel that **powers** a machine provides the energy that the machine needs in order to work. *dar energía a* ❑ *The battery could power an electric car. La batería podría dar energía a un auto eléctrico.* **9** N-UNCOUNT In physics, **power** is a measure of the amount of work that is done in a particular time. *fuerza* [TECHNICAL]
→ see **electricity, energy, solar**

P

**pow|er|ful** /paʊərfəl/ **1** ADJ A **powerful** person or organization is able to control or influence people and events. *poderoso* ❑ *You're a powerful man—people will listen to you. Eres un hombre poderoso—la gente te escuchará.* ❑ *...Russia and India, two large, powerful countries. ...Rusia e India, dos países grandes y poderosos.* **2** ADJ You say that someone's body is **powerful** when it is physically strong. *poderoso* ❑ *...his powerful muscles. ...sus poderosos músculos.* ● **pow|er|ful|ly** ADV *poderosamente* ❑ *...a strong, powerfully built man of 60. ...un hombre de 60 años fuerte y poderosamente constituído.* **3** ADJ A **powerful** machine or substance is effective because it is very strong. *potente* ❑ *The more powerful the car the more difficult it is to control. Mientras más potente sea el coche será más difícil de controlar.* ❑ *...powerful computer systems. ...poderosos sistemas computacionales.* ● **pow|er|ful|ly** ADV *potentemente* ❑ *The SC430 model has a powerfully smooth engine. El modelo SC430 tiene un motor potentemente suave.* **4** ADJ A **powerful** smell is very strong. *fuerte* ❑ *There's a powerful smell of cooking. Hay un fuerte olor a comida.* **5** ADJ A **powerful** voice is loud and can be heard from a long way away. *potente* ❑ *Mrs. Jones's powerful voice interrupted them. La potente voz de la señora Jones los interrumpió.* **6** ADJ You describe a piece of writing, speech, or work of art as **powerful** when it has a strong effect on people's feelings or beliefs. *poderoso* ❑ *...a powerful drama about the effects of racism. ...una poderosa obra de teatro acerca de los efectos del racismo.* ● **pow|er|ful|ly** ADV *poderosamente* ❑ *The play is painful, funny, and powerfully acted. La obra es dolorosa, divertida y está poderosamente actuada.*

**pow|er plant** (**power plants**) N-COUNT A **power plant** is the same as a **power station.** *central eléctrica*

**pow|er sta|tion** (**power stations**) N-COUNT A **power station** is a place where electricity is produced. *central eléctrica*
→ see **electricity**

**pow|er walk|ing** also **power-walking** N-UNCOUNT **Power walking** is the activity of walking very fast, as a means of keeping fit. *caminata rápida*

**PPO** /pi pi oʊ/ (**PPOs**) N-COUNT A **PPO** is an organization whose members receive medical care at a greatly reduced cost only if they use doctors and hospitals which belong to the organization. **PPO** is an abbreviation for **Preferred Provider Organization.** *PPO, organización que ofrece descuentos médicos*

**PR** /pi ɑr/ N-UNCOUNT **PR** is an abbreviation for **public relations.** *RR.PP.* ❑ *...a PR firm. ...una empresa de RR.PP.*

**prac|ti|cal** /prǽktɪkəl/ **1** ADJ **Practical** means involving real situations and events, rather than ideas and theories. práctico ❑ *...practical suggestions on how to eat more fiber.* *...sugerencias prácticas acerca de cómo comer más fibra.* **2** ADJ You describe people as **practical** when they make sensible decisions and deal effectively with problems. práctico ❑ *You were always so practical, Maria.* *Siempre fuiste tan práctica, María.* **3** ADJ **Practical** ideas and methods are likely to be effective or successful in a real situation. práctico ❑ *Our system is the most practical way of preventing crime.* *Nuestro sistema es la forma más práctica de prevenir el crimen.* **4** ADJ You can describe clothes and things in your house as **practical** when they are useful rather than just being fashionable or attractive. práctico ❑ *...lightweight, practical clothes.* *...ropa ligera y práctica.*

| **Thesaurus** | *practical* Ver también: |
|---|---|
| ADJ. | businesslike, pragmatic, reasonable, sensible, systematic; (*ant.*) impractical **2** **3** |

**prac|ti|cal|ly** /prǽktɪkli/ **1** ADV **Practically** means almost. prácticamente ❑ *He's known the old man practically all his life.* *Ha conocido al viejo prácticamente toda su vida.* **2** ADV You use **practically** to describe something that involves real actions or events rather than ideas or theories. en la práctica ❑ *The course is practically based.* *El curso está basado en la práctica.*

**prac|tice** /prǽktɪs/ (**practices, practicing, practiced**) **1** N-COUNT You can refer to something that people do regularly as a **practice.** práctica ❑ *...the practice of using chemicals to color the hair.* *...la práctica de usar químicos para teñirse el cabello.* **2** N-VAR **Practice** means doing something regularly in order to be able to do it better. A **practice** is one of these periods of doing something. práctica ❑ *...the hard practice necessary to become a good musician.* *...la difícil práctica que se necesita para convertirse en un buen músico.* ❑ *...a basketball practice.* *...una práctica de beisbol.* **3** N-UNCOUNT The work done by doctors and lawyers is referred to as the **practice** of medicine and law. People's religious activities are referred to as the **practice** of a religion. ejercicio ❑ *...the practice of modern medicine.* *...el ejercicio de la medicina moderna.* **4** N-COUNT A doctor's or lawyer's **practice** is his or her business, often shared with other doctors or lawyers. despacho, clientela ❑ *The new doctor's practice was miles away from where I lived.* *El despacho del nuevo doctor estaba a kilómetros de donde vivía.* **5** V-T/V-I If you **practice** something, you keep doing it regularly in order to do it better. practicar ❑ *She practiced the piano in the school basement.* *Practicaba el piano en el sótano de la escuela.* ❑ *Keep practicing, and maybe next time you'll do better* *Sigue practicando y tal vez a la siguiente vez lo hagas mejor.* **6** → see also **practiced** **7** V-T When people **practice** something such as a custom, craft, or religion, they take part in the activities associated with it. practicar ❑ *...a family that practiced traditional Judaism.* *...una familia que practicaba el judaísmo tradicional.* ● **prac|tic|ing** ADJ practicante ❑ *He was a practicing Muslim throughout his life.* *Fue un practicante musulmán toda su vida.* **8** V-T/V-I Someone who **practices** medicine or law works as a doctor or a lawyer. ejercer ❑ *He doesn't practice medicine for the money.* *No ejerce la medicina por dinero.* ❑ *...my license to practice as a lawyer.* *...mi cédula para ejercer la abogacía.* **9** PHRASE What happens **in practice** is what actually happens, in contrast to what is supposed to happen. en la práctica ❑ *Let's review the plan when we've seen how it works in practice.* *Revisemos el plan cuando hayamos visto cómo funciona en la práctica.* **10** PHRASE If you **put** a belief or method **into practice,** you behave or act in accordance with it. poner en práctica ❑ *The mayor has another chance to put his new ideas into practice.* *el alcalde tiene otra oportunidad de poner sus ideas en práctica.*

| **Thesaurus** | *practice* Ver también: |
|---|---|
| N. | custom, habit, method, procedure, system, way **1** exercise, rehearsal, training, workout **2** |

**prac|ticed** /prǽktɪst/ ADJ Someone who is **practiced at** doing something is good at it because they have had experience and have developed their skill at it. experto ❑ *She's well practiced at appearing happy.* *Es experta en aparentar estar contenta.* ❑ *...a practiced and experienced surgeon.* *...un experto y experimentado cirujano.*

**prac|ti|tion|er** /prækt<u>ɪ</u>ʃənər/ (**practitioners**) N-COUNT Doctors are sometimes referred to as **practitioners.** médico o médica [FORMAL]

**prai|rie** /prɛəri/ (**prairies**) N-VAR A **prairie** is a large area of flat, grassy land in North America where very few trees grow. pradera, llanura → see **grassland, habitat**

**praise** /pr<u>eɪ</u>z/ (**praises, praising, praised**) V-T If you **praise** someone or something, you express approval for their achievements or qualities. alabar ❑ *The American president praised Turkey for its courage.* *El presidente estadounidense alabó a Turquía por su valentía.* ❑ *The passengers praised John for saving their lives.* *Los pasajeros alabaron a John por haberles salvado la vida.* ● **Praise** is also a noun. elogio ❑ *The ladies are full of praise for the staff.* *Las señoritas están llenas de elogios para el personal.* ❑ *I have nothing but praise for the police.* *No tengo más que elogios para la policía.*

**pray** /pr<u>eɪ</u>/ (**prays, praying, prayed**) **1** V-T/V-I When people **pray,** they speak to God in order to give thanks or to ask for help. rezar ❑ *He spent his time in prison praying and studying.* *Pasó su tiempo en prisión rezando y estudiando.* ❑ *Now all we can do is to pray to God.* *Todo lo que nos queda hacer ahora es rezarle a Dios.* ❑ *We pray that Billy's family will now find peace.* *Rezamos porque la familia de Billy encuentre ahora la paz.* **2** V-T/V-I When someone is hoping very much that something will happen, you can say that they **are praying** that it will happen. rezar ❑ *I'm praying for good weather.* *Estoy rezando para que haga buen tiempo.* ❑ *I'm praying that somebody in Congress will do something before it's too late.* *Estoy rezando porque alguien en el congreso haga algo antes de que sea demasiado tarde.*

**prayer** /prɛər/ (**prayers**) **1** N-UNCOUNT **Prayer** is the activity of speaking to God. oración ❑ *They dedicated their lives to prayer.* *Dedicaron sus vidas a la oración.* **2** N-COUNT A **prayer** is the words a person says when they speak to God. oración

P

**Word Web** **precipitation**

**Clouds** are made of tiny **droplets** of **water vapor**. When the droplets fall to earth, they are called **precipitation**. Tiny droplets fall as **drizzle**. Larger droplets fall as **rain**. **Snow** is falling **ice crystals**. **Freezing rain** begins as snow. The **snowflakes** melt and then freeze again when they hit an object. **Sleet** is frozen **raindrops** that bounce when they hit the ground. **Hail** is made of frozen raindrops that travel up and down within a cloud. Each time they move downward, more water freezes on their surfaces. Finally they strike the earth as balls of ice.

❑ *They should say a prayer for the people on both sides.* *Deberían decir una oración por las personas en ambos lados.* **3** N-COUNT You can refer to a strong hope that you have as your **prayer.** *oración* ❑ *This drug could be the answer to our prayers.* *Esta medicina podría ser la respuesta a nuestras oraciones.* **4** N-PLURAL A short religious service at which people gather to pray can be referred to as **prayers.** *rezos* ❑ *...evening prayers.* *...rezos vespertinos.*

**preach** /pritʃ/ (**preaches, preaching, preached**) **1** V-T/V-I When a member of the clergy **preaches** a sermon, he or she gives a talk on a religious or moral subject during a religious service. *pronunciar un sermón, dar un sermón* ❑ *The priest preached a sermon on the devil.* *El sacerdote pronunció un sermón sobre el demonio.* ❑ *The bishop will preach to a crowd of several hundred people.* *El obispo dará un sermón para una multitud de cientos de personas.* ● **preach|er** N-COUNT (**preachers**) *sacerdote* ❑ *...acceptance of women preachers.* *...la aceptación de sacerdotes mujeres.* **2** V-T/V-I When people **preach,** or **preach** a belief or a course of action, they try to persuade other people to accept the belief or to take the course of action. *predicar, aconsejar* ❑ *He was trying to preach peace.* *Estaba tratando de predicar la paz.* ❑ *Experts are preaching that even a little exercise is better than none at all.* *Los expertos aconsejan que incluso un poco de ejercicio es mejor que ninguno.*

**Pre|cam|brian** /prikæmbriən/ also **Pre-Cambrian** ADJ **Precambrian** time is the period of the Earth's history from the time the Earth formed until around 600 million years ago. *precámbrico* [TECHNICAL]

**Word Link** *caut ≈ taking care : caution, cautious, precaution*

**Word Link** *pre ≈ before : precaution, precede, predict*

**pre|cau|tion** /prɪkɔʃən/ (**precautions**) N-COUNT A **precaution** is an action that is intended to prevent something dangerous or unpleasant from happening. *precaución* ❑ *Just as a precaution, couldn't he move to a place of safety?* *Sólo como precaución, ¿no podría moverse a un lugar seguro?*

**pre|cede** /prɪsid/ (**precedes, preceding, preceded**) V-T If one event or period of time **precedes** another, it happens before it. *preceder* [FORMAL] ❑ *Discussions between the main parties preceded the vote.* *Discusiones entre las partes principales precedieron al voto.* ❑ *The earthquake was preceded by a loud roar.* *El terremoto fue precedido de un fuerte rugido.*

**prec|edent** /prɛsɪdənt/ (**precedents**) N-VAR If there is a **precedent for** an action or event, it has happened before, and this can be regarded as an argument for doing it again. *precedente* [FORMAL] ❑ *The trial could set an important precedent for dealing with similar cases.* *El juicio podría sentar un importante precedente para resolver casos similares.*

**pre|cious** /prɛʃəs/ **1** ADJ If something such as a resource is **precious,** it is valuable and should not be wasted or used badly. *precioso* ❑ *After four months of being abroad, every hour at home was precious.* *Después de esta cuatro meses en el extranjero, cada hora pasada en casa era tiempo precioso.* **2** ADJ **Precious** objects and materials are worth a lot of money because they are rare. *precioso* ❑ *...precious metals.* *...metales preciosos.* **3** ADJ If something is **precious** to you, you regard it as important and do not want to lose it. *preciado* ❑ *Her family's support is particularly precious to Josie.* *El apoyo de su familia es particularmente preciado para Josie.*

**pre|cipi|ta|tion** /prɪsɪpɪteɪʃən/ **1** N-UNCOUNT **Precipitation** is rain, snow, or hail. *precipitación* [TECHNICAL] **2** N-UNCOUNT **Precipitation** is a process in a chemical reaction that causes solid particles to become separated from a liquid. *precipitación* [TECHNICAL]
→ see Word Web: **precipitation**
→ see **climate**

**pre|cise** /prɪsaɪs/ **1** ADJ You use **precise** to emphasize that you are referring to an exact thing, rather than something vague. *preciso, exacto* ❑ *I can remember the precise moment when my daughter came to see me.* *Puedo recordar el momento preciso en el que mi hija vino a verme.* ❑ *The equipment sent back information on the precise distance between the moon and the Earth.* *El equipo envió información acerca de la distancia precisa entre la tierra y la luna.* **2** ADJ Something that is **precise** is exact and accurate in all its details. *preciso* ❑ *They speak very precise English.* *Hablan un inglés muy preciso.*

**pre|cise|ly** /prɪsaɪsli/ **1** ADV **Precisely** means accurately and exactly. *precisamente* ❑ *Nobody knows precisely how many people are still living there.*

*Nadie sabe precisamente cuántas personas viven aún ahí.* ❑ *The first bell rang at precisely 10:29 a.m.* *La primera campanada sonó precisamente a las 10:29 de la mañana.* **2** ADV You can use **precisely** to emphasize that a reason or fact is the only important one there is, or that it is obvious. *precisamente* ❑ *Children come to zoos precisely to see captive animals.* *Los niños vienen al zoológico precisamente para ver a los animales cautivos.*

**pre|ci|sion** /prɪsɪʒᵊn/ N-UNCOUNT If you do something **with precision,** you do it exactly as it should be done. *precisión* ❑ *The choir sang with precision.* *El coro cantó con precisión.*

**pre|co|cial** /prɪkoʊʃᵊl/ ADJ A **precocial** chick is a young bird that is relatively well-developed when it is born and requires little parental care. Compare **altricial.** *precocial* [TECHNICAL]

**preda|tor** /prɛdətər/ (**predators**) N-COUNT A **predator** is an animal that kills and eats other animals. *depredador* ❑ *With no natural predators on the island, the herd increased rapidly.* *Sin depredadores naturales en la isla, el rebaño creció rápidamente.*
→ see **carnivore, food, shark**

**pre|de|ces|sor** /prɛdɪsɛsər/ (**predecessors**) **1** N-COUNT Your **predecessor** is the person who had your job before you. *predecesor o predecesora* ❑ *He learned everything he knew from his predecessor.* *Aprendió todo lo que sabía de su predecesor.* **2** N-COUNT The **predecessor** of an object or machine is the object or machine that came before it in a sequence or process of development. *antecesor* ❑ *The car is 2 inches shorter than its predecessor.* *El coche es dos pulgadas más corto que su antecesor.*

| Word Link | *dict ≈ speaking : contradict, dictate, predict* |
|---|---|

| Word Link | *pre ≈ before : precaution, precede, predict* |
|---|---|

**pre|dict** /prɪdɪkt/ (**predicts, predicting, predicted**) V-T If you **predict** an event, you say that it will happen. *predecir* ❑ *The latest opinion polls are predicting a very close contest.* *Las últimas encuestas de opinión predicen que será una contienda cerrada.* ❑ *He predicted that my hair would grow back quickly.* *Predijo que mi cabello volvería a crecer rápidamente.*
→ see **experiment, forecast**

**pre|dict|able** /prɪdɪktəbᵊl/ ADJ If you say that an event is **predictable,** you mean that it is obvious in advance that it will happen. *previsible, predecible* ❑ *This was a predictable reaction.* *Era una reacción previsible.* ● **pre|dict|ably** ADV *previsiblemente, predeciblemente* ❑ *His article is, predictably, an attack on capitalism.* *Su artículo, predeciblemente, es un ataque al capitalismo.* ● **pre|dict|abil|ity** /prɪdɪktəbɪlɪti/ N-UNCOUNT *previsibilidad, predecibilidad, predictabilidad* ❑ *Your mother values the predictability of your Sunday calls.* *Tu madre aprecia la predecibilidad de tus llamadas los domingos.*

**pre|dic|tion** /prɪdɪkʃᵊn/ (**predictions**) N-VAR If you make a **prediction,** you say what you think will happen. *predicción* ❑ *Weather prediction has never been a perfect science.* *La predicción del clima nunca ha sido una ciencia perfecta.*
→ see **science**

**preen** /prin/ (**preens, preening, preened**) V-T When birds **preen** their feathers, they clean them and arrange them neatly using their beaks. *limpiar y arreglar* ● **preening** N-UNCOUNT *limpieza y arreglado* ❑ *Preening of the feathers keeps them waterproof and in good condition.* *La limpieza y arreglado de las plumas mantiene a los pájaros a prueba de agua y en buenas condiciones.*

**pref|ace** /prɛfɪs/ (**prefaces, prefacing, prefaced**) **1** N-COUNT A **preface** is an introduction at the beginning of a book. *prefacio* ❑ *...the preface to Kelman's novel.* *...el prefacio a la novela de Kelman.* **2** V-T If you **preface** an action or speech **with** something else, you do or say this other thing first. *prologar, escribir un prefacio* ❑ *I will preface what I am going to say with a few lines from Shakespeare.* *Voy a hacer mi introducción con unas líneas de Shakespeare.*

**pre|fer** /prɪfɜr/ (**prefers, preferring, preferred**) V-T If you **prefer** someone or something, you like that person or thing better than another. *preferir* ❑ *Does he prefer a particular sort of music?* *¿Prefiere algún tipo de música en particular?* ❑ *I preferred books and people to politics.* *Prefería los libros y las personas que la política.* ❑ *I prefer to think of peace not war.* *Prefiero pensar en la paz en vez de en la guerra.* ❑ *He would prefer to be in Philadelphia.* *Preferiría estar en Filadelfia.*

**pref|er|able** /prɛfərəbᵊl, prɛfrə-, prɪfɜrə-/ ADJ If you say that one thing is **preferable to** another, you mean that it is more desirable or suitable. *preferible* ❑ *A big earthquake a long way off is preferable to a smaller one nearby.* *Un gran temblor a mucha distancia es preferible a uno pequeño más cerca.* ❑ *Prevention of a problem is preferable to trying to cure it.* *Prevenir un problema es preferible a tratar de arreglarlo.* ● **pref|er|ably** /prɛfərəbli,, prɛfrə-, prɪfɜrə-/ ADV *preferiblemente, de preferencia* ❑ *Get exercise, preferably in the fresh air.* *Haz ejercicio, preferiblemente al aire libre.*

**pref|er|ence** /prɛfərəns/ (**preferences**) **1** N-VAR If you have a **preference for** something, you would like to have or do that thing rather than something else. *predilección, preferencia* ❑ *...a preference for salty snacks over cookies.* *...una predilección por tentempiés salados en vez de galletas.* **2** N-UNCOUNT If you **give preference to** someone with a particular qualification or feature, you choose them rather than someone else. *dar preferencia a*

| Word Link | *fix ≈ fastening : fixture, prefix, suffix* |
|---|---|

**pre|fix** /prifɪks/ (**prefixes**) N-COUNT A **prefix** is a letter or group of letters that is added to the beginning of a word in order to form a different word. For example, the prefix "un-" is added to "happy" to form "unhappy." *prefijo*

**pre|game** /prigeɪm/ also **pre-game** ADJ **Pregame** activities take place before a sports game. *previo al juego o al partido, realizado antes del juego o partido* ❑ *...pregame ceremonies.* *...las ceremonias previas al partido.*

**preg|nant** /prɛgnənt/ ADJ If a woman or female animal is **pregnant,** she has a baby or babies developing in her body. *embarazada* ❑ *I'm seven months pregnant.* *Estoy embarazada de siete meses.* ● **preg|nan|cy** /prɛgnənsi/ N-VAR (**pregnancies**) *embarazo* ❑ *...weight gain during pregnancy.* *...ganar peso durante el embarazo.*
→ see **reproduction**

**Word Partnership** Usar *pregnant* con:

N. pregnant **with a baby/child**, pregnant **mother**, pregnant **wife**, pregnant **woman**
V. **be** pregnant, **become** pregnant, **get** pregnant

**preju|dice** /prɛdʒədɪs/ (**prejudices, prejudicing, prejudiced**) **1** N-VAR **Prejudice** is an unreasonable dislike of a particular group of people or things, or an unreasonable preference for one group over another. *prejuicio* ❑ *...racial prejudice.* *...prejuicio racial.* ❑ *There seems to be some prejudice against workers over 45.* *Parece que hay algunos prejuicios contra los trabajadores mayores de 45 años.* **2** V-T If you **prejudice** someone or something, you influence them so that they are unfair in some way. *predisponer* ❑ *Words like "mankind" and "manpower" may prejudice us against women.* *Palabras como "mankind" y "manpower" pueden predisponernos en contra de las mujeres.* ❑ *The report was held back for fear of prejudicing his trial.* *El reporte fue detenido por miedo a predisponer el juicio en su contra.* **3** V-T If someone **prejudices** another person's situation, they do something that makes it worse than it should be. *perjudicar* [FORMAL] ❑ *Her report was not intended to prejudice the future of the college.* *Su reporte no tenía la intención de perjudicar el futuro del colegio.*

**Thesaurus** *prejudice* Ver también:

N. bias, bigotry, disapproval, intolerance; (*ant.*) tolerance **1**

**pre|limi|nary** /prɪlɪmɪnɛri/ ADJ **Preliminary** activities or discussions take place at the beginning of an event, often as a form of preparation. *preliminar* ❑ *Preliminary results show the Republican Party with 11 percent of the vote.* *Los resultados preliminares muestran que el Partido Republicano tiene el 11 por ciento de los votos.*

**prema|ture** /primətʃʊər/ **1** ADJ Something that is **premature** happens too early or earlier than people expect. *prematuro* ❑ *...the commonest cause of premature death.* *...la causa más común de muerte prematura.* ❑ *His career was brought to a premature end.* *Su carrera llegó a un final prematuro.* • **prema|ture|ly** ADV *prematuramente* ❑ *The years in the harsh mountains have prematurely aged him.* *Los años en lo inhóspito de la montaña lo han envejecido prematuramente.* **2** ADJ A **premature** baby is one that was born before the date when it was expected to be born. *prematuro* ❑ *Even very young premature babies respond to their mother's presence.* *Incluso los bebés prematuros muy jóvenes responden a la presencia de sus madres.* • **prema|ture|ly** ADV *prematuramente* ❑ *Danny was born prematurely, weighing only 3 lb 3 oz.* *Danny nació prematuro, y pesó sólo kilo y medio.*

**pre|med** /primɛd/ also **pre-med** ADJ A **premed** student is a student who is taking courses that are required in order for the student to study at medical school. *premédico* [INFORMAL] ❑ *Tim is a premed student at MSU.* *Tim estudia un curso premédico en la Universidad Estatal de Michigan.*

**prem|ier** /prɪmɪər/ (**premiers**) **1** N-COUNT The leader of the government of a country is sometimes referred to as the country's **premier.** *primer ministro o primera ministro o primera ministra* ❑ *...Australian premier John Howard.* *...el primer ministro australiano John Howard.* **2** ADJ **Premier** is used to describe something that is considered to be the best or most important thing of a particular type. *primero* ❑ *...the country's premier opera company.* *...la primera compañía de ópera del país.*

**premi|ere** /prɪmɪər, prɪmyɛər/ (**premieres**) N-COUNT The **premiere** of a new play or movie is the first public performance of it. *estreno* ❑ *...last week's premiere of his new movie.* *...el estreno de su nueva película la semana pasada.*

**prem|ise** /prɛmɪs/ (**premises**) **1** N-PLURAL The **premises** of a business or an institution are all the buildings and land that it occupies. *edificio* ❑ *There is a kitchen on the premises.* *Hay una cocina en el edificio.* **2** N-COUNT A **premise** is something that you suppose is true and that you use as a basis for developing an idea. *premisa* [FORMAL] ❑ *The premise is that schools will work harder to improve if they must compete.* *La premisa es que las escuelas trabajarán más duro por mejorar si son obligadas a competir.*

**pre|mium** /primiəm/ (**premiums**) **1** N-COUNT A **premium** is a sum of money that you pay regularly to an insurance company for an insurance policy. *prima* ❑ *...insurance premiums.* *...las primas del seguro.* **2** N-COUNT A **premium** is a sum of money that you have to pay for something in addition to the normal cost. *extra* ❑ *People will normally pay a premium for a good house in a good area.* *Las personas a menudo pagarán extra por una buena casa en una buena zona.* **3** PHRASE If something is **at a premium,** it is wanted or needed, but is difficult to get or achieve. *escasea* ❑ *If space is at a premium, choose furniture that folds away.* *Si el espacio escasea, elija muebles que se puedan doblar.*

**pre|nup** /prinʌp/ (**prenups**) also **pre-nup** N-COUNT A **prenup** is the same as a **prenuptial agreement**. *acuerdo prenupcial* [INFORMAL]

**pre|nup|tial agree|ment** /prinʌpʃᵊl əgrimənt, -nʌptʃᵊl/ (**prenuptial agreements**) also **pre-nuptial agreement** N-COUNT A **prenuptial agreement** is a written contract made between a man and a woman before they marry, in which they state how their assets such as property and money should be divided if they get divorced. *acuerdo prenupcial* ❑ *We signed a prenuptial agreement.* *Firmamos un acuerdo prenupcial.*

**pre-owned** ADJ Something that is **pre-owned** has been owned by someone else and is now for sale. *usado* ❑ *...pre-owned vehicles.* *...coches usados.*

**prep** /prɛp/ (**prepping, prepped**) **1** V-T If you **prep** something, you prepare it. *preparar* [INFORMAL] ❑ *After prepping the boat, they sailed it down to Carloforte.* *Después de preparar el bote, navegaron hasta Carloforte.* **2** V-T If a doctor or nurse **preps** a patient, they get them ready for surgery or another procedure. *preparar* [INFORMAL] ❑ *I was already prepped for surgery.* *Ya me habían preparado para la cirugía.*

**prepa|ra|tion** /prɛpəreɪʃᵊn/ (**preparations**) **1** N-UNCOUNT **Preparation** is the process of getting something ready for use or for a particular purpose. *preparación* ❑ *Todd put the papers in his*

P

*briefcase in preparation for the meeting.* Todd puso los papeles en su portafolio en preparación para la junta. ❑ *...the preparation of his weekly sermons.* ...la preparación de sus sermones semanales. **2** N-PLURAL **Preparations** are all the arrangements that are made for a future event. preparativos ❑ *We were making preparations for our wedding.* Estábamos haciendo preparativos para nuestra boda.

**pre|pare** /prɪpɛər/ (**prepares, preparing, prepared**) **1** V-T If you **prepare** something, you make it ready for something that is going to happen. preparar ❑ *They were preparing a recording of last week's program.* Preparaban una grabación de los programas de la semana pasada. ❑ *We will need 1,000 hours to prepare the report.* Necesitaremos de mil horas para preparar el reporte. **2** V-T/V-I If you **prepare for** an event or action that will happen soon, you get yourself ready for it or make the necessary arrangements. preparar para ❑ *...to prepare for the cost of your child's education.* ...prepararse para el costo de la educación de los hijos. ❑ *He went back to his hotel and prepared to catch a train.* Regresó a su hotel y se preparó para tomar el tren. **3** V-T When you **prepare** food, you get it ready to be eaten. preparar ❑ *She entered the kitchen, hoping to find someone preparing dinner.* Entró a la cocina, esperando encontrar a alguien preparando la cena.

**Word Partnership** Usar *prepare* con:

N. prepare **a list**, prepare **a plan**, prepare **a report** **1**
prepare **for battle/war**, prepare **for the future**, prepare **for the worst** **2**
prepare **dinner**, prepare **food**, prepare **a meal** **3**

**pre|pared** /prɪpɛərd/ **1** ADJ If you are **prepared to** do something, you are willing to do it if necessary. preparado, listo ❑ *Are you prepared to take action?* ¿Estás listo para hacer algo? **2** ADJ If you are **prepared for** something that you think is going to happen, you are ready for it. listo para, preparado para ❑ *Police are prepared for large numbers of demonstrators.* La policía está preparada para un gran número de manifestantes. ● **pre|par|ed|ness** /prɪpɛərɪdnɪs/ N-UNCOUNT preparación ❑ *...the need for military preparedness.* ...la necesidad de la preparación militar. **3** ADJ You can describe something as **prepared** when it has been done or made beforehand, so that it is ready when it is needed. preparado ❑ *He ended his prepared statement by thanking the police.* Terminó la declaración que había preparado agradeciendo a la policía.

**pre-pay** (**pre-pays, pre-paying, pre-paid**) also **prepay** V-T/V-I If you **pre-pay** something or **pre-pay for** it, you pay for it before you receive it or use it. pagar por adelantado, prepagar ❑ *...electricity customers who prepay for their energy.* ...los clientes de la compañía eléctrica que pagan su consumo por adelantado.

**Word Link** *pos ≈ placing : deposit, preposition, repository*

**prepo|si|tion** /prɛpəzɪʃᵊn/ (**prepositions**) N-COUNT A **preposition** is a word such as "by," "for," "into," or "with" that usually has a noun group as its object. preposición

**prep|py** /prɛpi/ (**preppies**) **1** N-COUNT In the United States, **preppies** are young people who are conventional and conservative in their attitudes and dress, usually young people who have been to an expensive private school. fresa **2** ADJ If you describe someone or their clothes, attitudes, or behavior as **preppy**, you mean that they are like a preppy. fresa ❑ *...preppy students.* ...estudiantes fresas. ❑ *...a preppy shirt and tie.* ...una camisa y corbata fresas.

**pre|school|er** /priskulər/ (**preschoolers**) also **pre-schooler** N-COUNT Children who are no longer babies but are not yet old enough to go to school are sometimes referred to as **preschoolers**. niño en edad preescolar [WRITTEN]

**pre|scribe** /prɪskraɪb/ (**prescribes, prescribing, prescribed**) **1** V-T If a doctor **prescribes** medicine or treatment for you, he or she tells you what medicine or treatment to have. recetar ❑ *The physician examines the patient and prescribes medication.* El médico examina al paciente y receta medicamentos. ❑ *...the prescribed dose of sleeping tablets.* ...la dosis recetada de pastillas para dormir. **2** V-T If a person or set of laws or rules **prescribes** an action or duty, they state that it must be carried out. prescribir [FORMAL] ❑ *...Article II of the Constitution, which prescribes the method of electing a president.* ...el artículo II de la Constitución, que prescribe el método de elección del presidente.

**Word Link** *script ≈ writing : manuscript, prescription, transcript*

**pre|scrip|tion** /prɪskrɪpʃᵊn/ (**prescriptions**) N-COUNT A **prescription** is a medicine that a doctor has told you to take, or the piece of paper on which the doctor writes an order for the prescription. receta ❑ *He gave me a prescription for some cream.* Me dio una receta para una crema. PHRASE ● If a medicine is available **by prescription**, you can only get it from a pharmacist if a doctor gives you a prescription for it. con receta

**pre|sea|son** /prisizᵊn/ also **pre-season** ADJ **Preseason** activities take place before the start of a sports season. pretemporada ❑ *...a preseason game against Phoenix.* ...un juego de pretemporada contra Phoenix.

**pres|ence** /prɛzᵊns/ (**presences**) **1** N-SING Someone's **presence** in a place is the fact that they are there. presencia ❑ *His presence causes too much trouble.* Su presencia causa demasiados problemas. **2** N-UNCOUNT If you say that someone has **presence**, you mean that they impress people by their appearance and manner. porte ❑ *...the authoritative presence of those great men.* ...el porte autoritario de aquellos grandes hombres. **3** PHRASE If you are **in** someone's **presence**, you are in the same place as that person, and are close enough to them to be seen or heard. en presencia de ❑ *Doing homework in the presence of parents was related to higher achievement in school.* El hacer la tarea en presencia de los padres se relacionó directamente con un mejor aprovechamiento en la escuela.

P

**present**
❶ EXISTING OR HAPPENING NOW
❷ BEING SOMEWHERE
❸ GIFT
❹ VERB USES

❶ **pres|ent** /prɛzᵊnt/ **1** ADJ You use **present** to describe things and people that exist now, rather than those that existed in the past or those that may exist in the future. actual ❑ *...the present crisis.* *...la crisis actual.* ❑ *...the present owners of the property.* *...los dueños actuales de la propiedad.* **2** N-SING **The present** is the period of time that we are in now and the things that are happening now. el presente ❑ *...the story of my life from my childhood up to the present.* *...la historia de mi vida desde mi infancia hasta el presente.* **3** PHRASE A situation that exists **at present** exists now, although it may change. por el momento ❑ *At present, there is no way of knowing which people will develop the disease.* *Por el momento, no hay modo de saber quienes desarrollarán la enfermedad.* **4** PHRASE **The present day** is the period of history that we are in now. el día de hoy ❑ *...Western European art from the period of Giotto to the present day.* *...arte de Europa occidental desde la época de Giotto hasta el día de hoy.*

❷ **pres|ent** /prɛzᵊnt/ **1** ADJ If someone is **present at** an event, they are there. presente ❑ *Nearly 85 percent of men are present at the birth of their children.* *Casi el 85 por ciento de los hombres están presentes en el nacimiento de sus hijos.* **2** ADJ If something, especially a substance or disease, is **present in** something else, it exists within that thing. presente en ❑ *Vitamin D is naturally present in breast milk.* *La leche de pecho contiene vitamina D de manera natural.*

❸ **pres|ent** /prɛzᵊnt/ (**presents**) N-COUNT A **present** is something that you give to someone, for example, on their birthday or when you visit them. regalo ❑ *The carpet was a wedding present from Jack's parents.* *La alfombra fue un regalo de bodas de parte de los papás de Jack.* ❑ *She bought a birthday present for her mother.* *Le compró un regalo de cumpleaños a su madre.*

**Usage** **present**
Make sure you pronounce *present* correctly—the noun or adjective has stress on the first syllable, while the verb has stress on the second syllable: *At the present moment, Timmy has two birthday presents hidden in his closet, ready to present to Abby when she comes home.*

❹ **pre|sent** /prɪzɛnt/ (**presents, presenting, presented**) **1** V-T If you **present** someone **with** something such as a prize or document, or if you **present** it **to** them, you formally give it to them. hacer entrega de ❑ *The mayor presented him with a gold medal.* *El alcalde le hizo entrega de una medalla de oro.* ❑ *Betty will present the prizes to the winners.* *Betty hará entrega de los premios a los ganadores.* • **pres|en|ta|tion** N-UNCOUNT entrega ❑ *Then came the presentation of the awards.* *Después vino la entrega de los reconocimientos.* **2** V-T If something **presents** a difficulty or challenge, it causes or provides it. presentar ❑ *This presents a problem for many customers.* *Esto presenta un problema para muchos clientes.* ❑ *The future presents many challenges.* *El futuro presenta muchos desafíos.* **3** V-T If you **present** someone or something in a particular way, you describe them in that way. presentar, aparentar ❑ *Many false statements were presented as facts.* *Muchas declaraciones falsas fueron presentadas como hechos.* ❑ *...tricks to help him present himself in a more confident way.* *...trucos que usaba para aparentar tener más confianza.*

**pres|en|ta|tion** /prɪzɛnteɪʃᵊn/ (**presentations**) **1** N-UNCOUNT **Presentation** is the appearance of something that someone has worked to create. presentación ❑ *Keep the presentation of food attractive but simple.* *Mantén la presentación de la comida atractiva pero sencilla.* **2** N-COUNT A **presentation** is a formal event at which someone is given a prize or award. presentación ❑ *He received his award at a presentation in Kansas City.* *Recibió su premio durante una presentación en Kansas City.* **3** N-COUNT When someone gives a **presentation**, they give a formal talk. presentación ❑ *Philip and I gave a video presentation.* *Philip y yo dimos una presentación en video.* **4** → see also **present**

**Word Link** *serv ≈ keeping : conserve, observe, preserve*

**pre|serve** /prɪzɜrv/ (**preserves, preserving, preserved**) **1** V-T If you **preserve** a situation or condition, you make sure that it remains as it is, and does not change or end. preservar, conservar ❑ *We will do everything to preserve peace.* *Haremos todo para preservar la paz.* • **pres|er|va|tion** /prɛzərveɪʃᵊn/ N-UNCOUNT preservación ❑ *...the preservation of political freedom.* *...la preservación de la libertad política.* **2** V-T If you **preserve** something, you take action to save it or protect it. preservar, conservar ❑ *We need to preserve the forest.* *Necesitamos preservar el bosque.* • **pres|er|va|tion** N-UNCOUNT preservación ❑ *...the preservation of historic buildings.* *...la preservación de edificios históricos.* **3** V-T If you **preserve** food, you treat it in order to prevent it from decaying. conservar ❑ *Use only enough sugar to preserve the plums.* *Usa solo la cantidad suficiente de azúcar para conservar las ciruelas.* **4** N-COUNT A nature **preserve** is an area of land or water where animals are protected from hunters. reserva ❑ *...Pantanal, one of the world's great wildlife preserves.* *...Pantanal, una de las más grandes reservas de vida salvaje del mundo.*

**Word Link** *sid ≈ sitting : preside, president, residence*

**pre|side** /prɪzaɪd/ (**presides, presiding, presided**) V-I If you **preside over** a meeting or an event, you are in charge. presidir ❑ *Rumsfeld presided over a ceremony at the Pentagon.* *Rumsfeld presidió una ceremonia en el Pentágono.*

**presi|den|cy** /prɛzɪdənsi/ (**presidencies**) N-COUNT The **presidency** of a country or organization is the position of being the president or the period of time during which someone is president. presidencia ❑ *He was offered the presidency of the University of Saskatchewan.* *Le ofrecieron la presidencia de la Universidad de Saskatchewan.*

**presi|dent** /prɛzɪdənt/ (**presidents**) **1** N-TITLE; N-COUNT The **president** of a country that has no king or queen is the person who is the head of state of that country. presidente ❑ *...President*

P

Mubarak. *...el presidente Mubarak* ❑ *...the president's ability to act quickly. ...la habilidad del presidente para actuar rápido.* **2** N-COUNT The **president** of an organization is the person who has the highest position in it. *presidente* ❑ *...the president of the medical commission. ...el presidente de la comisión médica.*
→ see **election**

**presi|den|tial** /prɛzɪdɛnʃ^əl/ ADJ **Presidential** activities or things relate or belong to a president. *presidencial* ❑ *...Peru's presidential election. ...la elección presidencial de Perú.*
→ see **election**

**Presi|dents' Day** N-UNCOUNT In the United States, **Presidents' Day** is a public holiday held in commemoration of the birthdays of George Washington and Abraham Lincoln. It is the third Monday in February. *el Día del Presidente* ❑ *Today is Presidents' Day, a federal holiday. Hoy se celebra el Día del Presidente, día festivo federal en Estados Unidos.*

**press** /prɛs/ (**presses, pressing, pressed**) **1** V-T If you **press** something somewhere, you push it firmly against something else. *presionar, empujar* ❑ *He pressed his back against the door. Presionó su espalda contra la puerta.* **2** V-T If you **press** a button or switch, you push it with your finger in order to make a machine or device work. *apretar, presionar* ❑ *Drago pressed a button and the door closed. Drago presionó un botón y la puerta se cerró.* ● **Press** is also a noun. *presión* ❑ *...a TV that rises from a table at the press of a button. ...una televisión que surge de una mesa a la presión de un botón.* **3** V-T/V-I If you **press** something or **press down on** it, you push hard against it with your foot or hand. *presionar, pisar* ❑ *He pressed the gas pedal hard. Pisó el pedal de la gasolina con fuerza.* **4** V-I If you **press for** something, you try hard to persuade someone to give it to you or to agree to it. *pedir, insistir* ❑ *Police might now press for changes in the law. La policía podría ahora insistir que se hagan cambios a la ley.* **5** V-T If you **press** someone, you try hard to persuade them to do something. *presionar* ❑ *They pressed him to have something to eat. Lo presionaron para que comiera algo.* ❑ *It is certain they will press Mr. King for more details. Es una certeza que presionarán al señor King para obtener más detalles.* **6** V-T If you **press** clothes, you iron them. *planchar* ❑ *Vera pressed his shirt. Vera planchó su camisa.* **7** N-SING Newspapers and the journalists and reporters who write for them are referred to as **the press**. *la prensa* ❑ *...interviews in the local and foreign press. ...entrevistas para la prensa local y la extranjera.* ❑ *Christie looked relaxed and calm as she faced the press. Christie se veía calmada mientras se enfrentaba a la prensa.* **8** N-COUNT A **press** or a **printing press** is a machine used for printing things such as books and newspapers. *imprenta* **9** **10** PHRASE If you **press charges against** someone, you make an official accusation against them that has to be decided in a court of law. *levantar cargos* ❑ *I could have pressed charges against him. Pude haber levantado cargos en su contra.* **11** PHRASE When substances such as sand or gravel **press together** or when they **are pressed together,** they are pushed hard against each other so that they form a single layer. *fusionar*
→ see **printing**

**Word Partnership** Usar *press* con:

N. press **a button, at the** press **of a button** **2**
press **accounts,** press **coverage, freedom of the** press, press **reports** **7**
press **charges** **10**

**press con|fer|ence** (**press conferences**) N-COUNT A **press conference** is a meeting held by a famous or important person in which they answer reporters' questions. *conferencia de prensa* ❑ *She gave her reaction at a press conference. Habló de su reacción en una conferencia de prensa.*

**pres|sure** /prɛʃər/ (**pressures, pressuring, pressured**) **1** N-UNCOUNT **Pressure** is force that you produce when you press hard on something. *presión* ❑ *She pushed the door with her foot, and the pressure was enough to open it. Empujó la puerta con su pie y la presión fue suficiente para abrirla.* ❑ *The pressure of his fingers on her arm relaxed. La presión de sus dedos en su brazo se redujo.* **2** N-UNCOUNT The **pressure** in a place or container is the force produced by the quantity of gas or liquid in that place or container. *presión* ❑ *If the pressure falls in the cabin, an oxygen mask will drop in front of you. Si la presión de aire en la cabina llegase a descender, una máscara de oxigeno caerá del techo frente a usted.* **3** N-UNCOUNT If there is **pressure on** a person, someone is trying to persuade or force them to do something. *presión* ❑ *He may have put pressure on her to agree. Puede que le haya puesto presión para que accediera.* ❑ *The director was under pressure to leave the company. El director estaba bajo presión para que abandonara la empresa.* **4** N-UNCOUNT If you are experiencing **pressure,** you feel that you must do a lot of tasks or make a lot of decisions in very little time, or that people expect a lot from you. *presión* ❑ *Can you work under pressure? ¿Puedes trabajar bajo presión?* ❑ *Even if I had the talent to play tennis professionally, I couldn't stand the pressure. Aunque tuviera el talento para jugar tenis de manera profesional, no podría soportar la presión.* **5** V-T If you **pressure** someone **to** do something, you try forcefully to persuade them to do it. *presionar* ❑ *He will never pressure you to get married. Nunca te presionará para que te cases.* ❑ *He was pressured into making a decision. Estaba siendo presionado para tomar una decisión.* ● **pres|sured** ADJ *presionado* ❑ *You're likely to feel anxious and pressured. Lo más probable es que te sientas presionado y nervioso.* **6** → see also **blood pressure**
→ see **forecast, weather**

**pres|sur|ized** /prɛʃəraɪzd/ ADJ In a **pressurized** container or area, the pressure inside is different from the pressure outside. *presurizado* ❑ *...a pipe carrying highly pressurized gas. ...una tubería que lleva gas altamente presurizado.*

**pres|tige** /prɛstiʒ, -stidʒ/ N-UNCOUNT If a person, a country, or an organization has **prestige,** they are admired and respected because they are important or successful. *prestigio* ❑ *...efforts to build up the prestige of the United Nations. ...esfuerzos para aumentar el prestigio de las Naciones Unidas.* ❑ *His position in the company brought him prestige. Su posición en la empresa le trajo prestigio.*

**pres|tig|ious** /prɛstɪdʒəs, -stidʒəs/ ADJ A **prestigious** institution, job, or activity is respected and admired by people. prestigioso ❑ ...one of the most prestigious schools in the country. ...una de las escuelas más prestigiosas en el país.

**pre|sum|ably** /prɪzuməbli/ ADV If you say that something is **presumably** the case, you mean that you think it is very likely to be the case, although you are not certain. probablemente, presumiblemente ❑ *He's not going this year, presumably because of his age.* *No va a acudir este año, presumiblemente debido a su edad.*

**Word Link** *sume ≈ taking : assume, consume, presume*

**pre|sume** /prɪzum/ (**presumes, presuming, presumed**) **1** V-T If you **presume that** something is the case, you think that it is the case, although you are not certain. imaginarse, suponer, presumir ❑ *I presume that you're here on business.* *Me imagino que está usted aquí por negocios.* ❑ *"Has he been home all week?" — "I presume so."* *—¿Ha estado en casa toda la semana?—Lo supongo.* **2** V-T If you say that someone **presumes to** do something, you mean that they do it even though they have no right to do it. atreverse a [FORMAL] ❑ *I would not presume to advise you on such matters.* *No me atrevería a aconsejarte en un caso así.*

**pre|tend** /prɪtɛnd/ (**pretends, pretending, pretended**) **1** V-T If you **pretend that** something is true, you try to make people believe that it is true, although in fact it is not. aparentar, fingir ❑ *I pretend that things are really okay when they're not.* *Aparento que las cosas están bien cuando no lo están.* ❑ *He pretended to be asleep.* *Fingió estar dormido.* **2** V-T If you **pretend that** you are doing something, you imagine that you are doing it, for example, as part of a game. imaginarse ❑ *She can sunbathe and pretend she's in Cancun.* *Puede asolearse e imaginarse que está en Cancún.*

P

**pret|ty** /prɪti/ (**prettier, prettiest**) **1** ADJ If you describe someone, especially a girl, as **pretty**, you mean that they look nice and are attractive in a delicate way. bonito ❑ *She's a very charming and very pretty girl.* *Es una muchacha encantadora y muy bonita.* • **pret|ti|ly** /prɪtɪli/ ADV hermosamente ❑ *She smiled again, prettily.* *Sonrió de nuevo, hermosamente.* **2** ADJ A place or a thing that is **pretty** is attractive and pleasant, in a charming but not particularly unusual way. lindo ❑ *...a very pretty little town.* *...un lindo pueblito.* • **pret|ti|ly** ADV lindamente ❑ *The living-room was prettily decorated.* *La sala estaba lindamente decorada.* **3** ADV You can use **pretty** before an adjective or adverb to mean "fairly" or "quite". bastante [INFORMAL] ❑ *I had a pretty good idea what she was going to do.* *Tenía una idea bastante buena de lo que iba a hacer.*

**Thesaurus** *pretty* Ver también:

ADJ. beautiful, cute, lovely **1**
beautiful, charming, pleasant **2**

**pre|vail** /prɪveɪl/ (**prevails, prevailing, prevailed**) **1** V-I If a proposal, principle, or opinion **prevails,** it gains influence or is accepted. prevalecer ❑ *We hoped that common sense would prevail.* *Esperábamos que prevaleciera el sentido común.* ❑ *Rick still believes that justice will prevail.* *Rick aún cree que la justicia prevalecerá.* **2** V-I If a situation or attitude **prevails** in a particular place at a particular time, it is normal or most common in that place at that time. prevalecer, existir ❑ *A similar situation prevails in Canada.* *Una situación similar existe en Canadá.* ❑ *...the confusion which prevailed at the time of the revolution.* *...la confusión que existió en tiempos de la revolución.*

**pre|vail|ing** /prɪveɪlɪŋ/ ADJ The **prevailing** wind in an area is the type of wind that blows over that area most of the time. predominante

**pre|vent** /prɪvɛnt/ (**prevents, preventing, prevented**) V-T To **prevent** something means to ensure that it does not happen. evitar, impedir ❑ *The best way to prevent injury is to wear a seat belt.* *La mejor manera de evitar el salir lastimado es usar el cinturón de seguridad.* ❑ *The new law may prevent companies from creating new jobs.* *La nueva ley podría impedir que las compañías crearan nuevos empleos.* • **pre|ven|tion** N-UNCOUNT prevención ❑ *...the prevention of heart disease.* *...la prevención de enfermedades del corazón.*

**Word Partnership** Usar *prevent* con:

N. prevent **attacks**, prevent **cancer**, prevent **damage**, prevent **disease**, prevent **infection**, prevent **injuries**, prevent **loss**, prevent **pregnancy**, prevent **problems**, prevent **violence**, prevent **war**

**pre|view** /privyu/ (**previews**) N-COUNT A **preview** is an opportunity to see something such as a movie or invention before it is open or available to the public. avance, preestreno ❑ *He went to a preview of the play.* *Fue a ver un avance de la obra.*

**pre|vi|ous** /priviəs/ ADJ A **previous** event or thing is one that happened or existed before the one that you are talking about. anterior, previo ❑ *She has a teenage daughter from a previous marriage.* *Tiene una hija adolescente de un matrimonio anterior.*

**pre|vi|ous|ly** /priviəsli/ **1** ADV **Previously** means at some time before the period that you are talking about. previamente, antes, hasta entonces ❑ *Guyana's railroads were previously owned by private companies.* *Antes los ferrocarriles de Guyana eran propiedad de compañías privadas.* ❑ *They gave the contract to a previously unknown company.* *Le dieron el contrato a una compañía hasta entonces desconocida.* **2** ADV You can use **previously** to say how much earlier one event was than another event. antes ❑ *Ingrid had moved to San Diego two weeks previously.* *Ingrid se había mudado a San Diego dos semanas antes.*

**pre|writ|ing** /priraɪtɪŋ/ also **pre-writing** N-UNCOUNT **Prewriting** is the thinking and planning that a writer does before beginning to write something. ejercicios o preparación previa a la escritura

**prey** /preɪ/ (**preys, preying, preyed**) **1** N-UNCOUNT A creature's **prey** are the creatures that it hunts and eats in order to live. presa ❑ *They may not eat their prey until much later.* *Muchas veces no se comen a su presa hasta mucho más tarde.* **2** V-I A creature that **preys on** other creatures lives by catching and eating them. alimentarse de ❑ *...mountain lions and bears that prey on sheep.* *...pumas y osos que se alimentan de ovejas.*
→ see **carnivore, shark**

**price** /praɪs/ (**prices, pricing, priced**) **1** N-COUNT

**Word Web** primate

**Monkeys, apes,** and **humans** are all primates. Humans and other primates are alike in surprising ways. We used to believe that only humans were right-handed or left-handed. But when researchers studied a group of 66 **chimpanzees**, they found that chimps are also right-handed and left-handed. Other researchers learned that chimpanzee groups have different cultures. In 1972 a female **gorilla** named Koko began to learn sign language from a college student. Today Koko understands about 2,000 words and can sign about 500 of them. She makes up sentences using three to six words.

The **price** of something is the amount of money that you have to pay in order to buy it. precio, costo ❑ *...the price of gas.* *...el precio de la gasolina.* ❑ *They expect home prices to rise.* *Esperan que los precios de las casas suban.* **2** N-SING The **price** that you pay for something that you want is an unpleasant thing that you have to do or suffer in order to get it. *precio, costo* ❑ *These stars often pay a high price for their success.* *Estas estrellas a menudo pagan un alto precio por su éxito.* **3** V-T If something **is priced at** a particular amount, the price is set at that amount. *costar, tener precio de* ❑ *The software is priced at $90.* *El software cuesta $90.* • **pric|ing** N-UNCOUNT *poner precio* ❑ *We need a change in the rules on car pricing.* *Necesitamos cambiar la forma en la que ponemos precio a los coches.* **4** PHRASE If you want something **at any price,** you are determined to get it, even if unpleasant things happen as a result. *a cualquier precio* ❑ *They wanted fame at any price.* *Querían ser famosos a cualquier precio.*

**pride** /praɪd/ (**prides, priding, prided**) **1** N-UNCOUNT **Pride** is a feeling of satisfaction that you have because you or people close to you have done something good or possess something good. *orgullo* ❑ *...the sense of pride in a job well done.* *...la sensación de orgullo que da un trabajo bien hecho.* ❑ *We take pride in offering you the highest standards.* *Nos orgullecemos de ofrecerle los estándares más altos.* **2** N-UNCOUNT **Pride** is a sense of dignity and self-respect. *orgullo* ❑ *His pride wouldn't allow him to ask for help.* *Su orgullo no lo dejaba pedir ayuda.* **3** N-UNCOUNT Someone's **pride** is the feeling that they have that they are better or more important than other people. *orgullo* ❑ *His pride may still be his downfall.* *Su orgullo aún puede ser su ruina.* **4** V-T If you **pride** yourself **on** a quality or skill that you have, you are very proud of it. *enorgullecerse* ❑ *He prides himself on being a good listener.* *Se enorgullece de ser buen escuchador.*

**priest** /prist/ (**priests**) **1** N-COUNT A **priest** is a member of the Christian clergy in the Catholic, Anglican, or Orthodox church. *sacerdote* ❑ *He trained to be a Catholic priest.* *Se preparó para ser un sacerdote católico.* **2** N-COUNT In many non-Christian religions a **priest** is a man who has particular duties and responsibilities in a place where people worship. *sacerdote* ❑ *...a New Age priest or priestess.* *...un sacerdote o sacerdotisa New Age.*

**pri|mari|ly** /praɪmɛrɪli/ ADV You use **primarily** to say what is mainly true in a particular situation. *primordialmente* ❑ *These reports come primarily from passengers on the plane.* *Estos reportes provienen primordialmente de pasajeros del avión.*

**Word Link** *prim ≈ first : primary, prime, primitive*

**pri|ma|ry** /praɪmɛri, -məri/ (**primaries**) **1** ADJ You use **primary** to describe something that is very important or most important for someone or something. *primordial* [FORMAL] ❑ *His difficulty with language was the primary cause of his problems.* *Su dificultad con el lenguaje era la causa primordial de sus problemas.* **2** ADJ **Primary** education is the first few years of formal education for children. *primaria* ❑ *Ninety-nine percent of primary students now have experience with computers.* *Hoy en día, el noventa por ciento de los estudiantes de primaria tiene experiencia con computadoras.* **3** N-COUNT A **primary** or a **primary election** is an election in an American state in which people vote for someone to become a candidate for a political office. *elección primaria* ❑ *...the 1968 New Hampshire primary.* *...las elecciones primarias de 1968 en New Hampshire.*
→ see **diary**

**pri|ma|ry col|or** (**primary colors**) N-COUNT **Primary colors** are basic colors that can be mixed together to produce other colors. They are usually considered to be red, yellow, and blue. *color primario* ❑ *...bright primary colors that kids will love.* *...colores primarios brillantes que les encantarán a los niños.*
→ see **color**

**pri|ma|ry pol|lu|tant** (**primary pollutants**) N-COUNT **Primary pollutants** are substances that are released into the atmosphere and cause pollution. Compare **secondary pollutant**. *principal contaminante* [TECHNICAL]

**pri|mate** /praɪmeɪt/ (**primates**) N-COUNT A **primate** is a member of the group of mammals that includes humans, monkeys, and apes. *primate* ❑ *The woolly spider monkey is the largest primate in the Americas.* *El mono araña es el primate más grande del Continente Americano.*
→ see Word Web: **primate**

**prime** /praɪm/ (**primes, priming, primed**) **1** ADJ You use **prime** to describe something that is most important in a situation. *principal* ❑ *Your happiness is my prime concern.* *Tu felicicdad es mi preocupación principal.* ❑ *It could be a prime target for attack.* *Podría ser un blanco principal en un ataque.* **2** ADJ You use **prime** to describe something that is of the best possible quality. *excelente, de primera* ❑ *These*

P

*beaches are prime sites for development.* *Estas playas son excelentes sitios para los desarrollos.* **3** ADJ You use **prime** to describe an example of a particular kind of thing that is absolutely typical. *mejor* ❑ *Jodie Foster: the prime example of a child actor who became a respected adult star.* *Jodie Foster es el mejor ejemplo de una actriz infantil que se convierte en una estrella adulta reconocida.* **4** N-UNCOUNT Your **prime** is the stage in your life when you are strongest, most active, or most successful. *plenitud* ❑ *I'm just coming into my prime now.* *Hasta ahora estoy entrando en mi plenitud.* ❑ *Some of these athletes are well past their prime.* *Algunos de estos atletas ya dejaron atrás la plenitud.* **5** V-T If you **prime** someone **to** do something, you prepare them to do it, for example, by giving them information about it beforehand. *preparar* ❑ *Arnold primed her for her duties.* *Arnold la preparó para sus tareas.* **6** N-COUNT A **prime** is the same as a **prime number**. *número primo* [TECHNICAL]

**prime me|rid|ian** N-SING **The prime meridian** is the line of longitude, corresponding to zero degrees and passing through Greenwich, England, from which all the other lines of longitude are calculated. *primer meridiano* [TECHNICAL]

**prime min|is|ter** (**prime ministers**) N-COUNT; N-TITLE The leader of the government in some countries is called **the prime minister.** *primer ministro o primera ministro o primera ministra* ❑ *...the former prime minister of Pakistan, Miss Benazir Bhutto.* *...la ex primer ministro de Pakistán, la señorita Benazir Bhutto.*

**Word Link** *prim ≈ first : primary, prime, primitive*

**primi|tive** /prɪmɪtɪv/ **1** ADJ **Primitive** means belonging to a society in which people live in a very simple way, usually without industries or a writing system. *primitivo* ❑ *...studies of primitive societies.* *...estudios sobre sociedades primitivas.* **2** ADJ **Primitive** means belonging to a very early period in the development of an animal or plant. *primitivo* ❑ *...primitive whales.* *...ballenas primitivas.* **3** ADJ If you describe something as **primitive,** you mean that it is very simple in style or very old-fashioned. *rudimentario* ❑ *The conditions are primitive.* *Las condiciones son rudimentarias.*

**prince** /prɪns/ (**princes**) N-TITLE; N-COUNT A **prince** is a male member of a royal family, especially the son of the king or queen of a country. *príncipe*

**prin|cess** /prɪnsɪs, -sɛs/ (**princesses**) N-TITLE; N-COUNT A **princess** is a female member of a royal family, usually the daughter of a king or queen or the wife of a prince. *princesa*

**prin|ci|pal** /prɪnsɪpᵊl/ (**principals**) **1** ADJ **Principal** means first in order of importance. *principal* ❑ *Money was not the principal reason for his action.* *El dinero no fue la razón principal por la que actuó así.* ❑ *Newspapers were the principal source of information.* *Los periódicos eran la fuente principal de información.* **2** N-COUNT The **principal** of a school is the person in charge of the school. *director o directora* ❑ *Donald King is the principal of Dartmouth High School.* *Donald King es el director de la Preparatoria Dartmouth.*

**prin|ci|pal parts** N-PLURAL In grammar, the **principal parts** of a verb are the main inflected forms of the verb. The principal parts of the verb "to sing" are "sings", "singing", "sang", and "sung". *formas principales del verbo* [TECHNICAL]

**prin|ci|ple** /prɪnsɪpᵊl/ (**principles**) **1** N-VAR A **principle** is a belief that you have about the way you should behave. *principio* ❑ *These changes go against my principles.* *Estos cambios van en contra de mis principios.* ❑ *...a matter of principle.* *...una cuestión de principios.* **2** N-COUNT The **principles of** a particular theory or philosophy are its basic rules or laws. *principios* ❑ *...the basic principles of democracy.* *...los principios básicos de la democracia.* **3** PHRASE If you agree with something **in principle,** you agree in general terms to the idea of it, although you do not yet know the details or know if it will be possible. *en principio* ❑ *I agree with it in principle but I doubt if it will happen in practice.* *Estoy de acuerdo con ello en principio, pero dudo que suceda en la práctica.* **4** PHRASE If you refuse to do something **on principle,** you refuse to do it because of your beliefs. *por principio* ❑ *He would vote against the proposal on principle.* *Votaría en contra de la propuesta por principio.* **5** PHRASE The **principles of composition** are the rules used by choreographers, writers, and other artists to produce good dance, writing, and other art forms. *principios de composición* **6** PHRASE The **principles of design** are the rules used by painters and other visual artists to create a work of art, involving concepts such as balance, contrast, and emphasis. *principios de diseño*

**Usage** **principle** and **principal**

*Principal* and *principle* are often confused because they are pronounced exactly alike. A *principle* is a rule, whereas a *principal* is a person in charge of a school: *The principal handed out a list of principles for student behavior in class.* The adjective *principal* means "most important": *The principal reason for going to school is to become educated.*

**print** /prɪnt/ (**prints, printing, printed**) **1** V-T If someone **prints** something such as a book or newspaper, they produce it in large quantities using a machine. *imprimir* ❑ *He started to print his own posters.* *Empezó a imprimir sus propios carteles.* ❑ *The new calendar is printed on high quality paper.* *El nuevo calendario está impreso en papel de alta calidad.* ● **Print up** means the same as **print.** *imprimir en* ❑ *We're printing up shirts and caps, trying to get everybody involved.* *Estábamos imprimiendo en camisetas y gorras, tratando de involucrar a todos.* ● **print|ing** N-UNCOUNT *imprenta* ❑ *...a printing and publishing company.* *...una imprenta y editorial.* **2** V-T If a newspaper or magazine **prints** a piece of writing, it includes it or publishes it. *publicar* ❑ *We can only print letters that have the writer's name and address on them.* *Sólo podemos publicar las cartas que traigan el nombre y dirección del autor.* **3** V-T If numbers, letters, or designs **are printed on** a surface, they appear on it. *imprimir* ❑ *...the number printed on the receipt.* *...el número impreso en el recibo.* ❑ *The company prints its phone number on all of its products.* *La compañía imprime su número de teléfono en todos sus productos.* **4** N-UNCOUNT **Print** is used to refer to letters and numbers as they appear on the

P

**Word Web** printing

Before **printing** was invented, scribes wrote **documents** by hand. The first **printers** were the Chinese. They used pieces of wood with rows of **characters** carved into them. Later, they started using **movable type** made of baked clay. They created full **pages** by lining up rows of type. A German named Gutenberg made the first metal type. He also introduced the **printing press**. The idea came from the wine press, which was hundreds of years old. In the 1500s, printed advertisements were handbills. The earliest newspapers were **published** in the 1600s.

pages of a printed document. texto ❑ *...columns of tiny print.* *...columnas de texto diminuto.* **5** V-T If you **print** words, you write in letters that are not joined together. escribir con letra de molde ❑ *Print your name and address on a postcard and send it to us.* *Escriba su nombre y dirección con letra de molde en una postal y envíenosla.* **6** PHRASE If you appear **in print,** or get **into print,** what you say or write is published in a book or newspaper. ser publicado ❑ *These poets appeared in print long after their deaths.* *Estos poetas fueron publicados mucho después de fallecidos.*
→ see Word Web: **printing**
→ see **photography**
▸ **print out** PHR-VERB If a computer or a machine attached to a computer **prints** something **out,** it produces a copy of it on paper. imprimir ❑ *You enter measurements and the computer will print out the pattern.* *Si le das las medidas, la computadora te mostrará el patrón a seguir.*

**print|er** /prɪntər/ (**printers**) **1** N-COUNT A **printer** is a machine that can be connected to a computer in order to make copies on paper of information held by the computer. impresora **2** N-COUNT A **printer** is a person or company whose job is printing things such as books. imprenta ❑ *The manuscript has been sent off to the printer.* *El manuscrito ha sido enviado a la imprenta.*
→ see **computer, office, printing**

**print|mak|ing** /prɪntmeɪkɪŋ/ N-UNCOUNT **Printmaking** is an artistic technique that consists of making a series of pictures from an original, or from a specially prepared surface. estampar, hacer grabados, grabar

**pri|or** /praɪər/ **1** ADJ You use **prior** to indicate that something has already happened, or must happen, before another event takes place. previo, anterior ❑ *He claimed he had no prior knowledge of the protest.* *Dijo que no tenía conocimiento previo de la protesta.* **2** PHRASE If something happens **prior to** a particular time or event, it happens before that time or event. antes de [FORMAL] ❑ *Prior to his trip to Japan, he went to New York.* *Antes de su viaje a Japón, fue a Nueva York.*

**pri|or|ity** /praɪɒrɪti/ (**priorities**) **1** N-COUNT If something is a **priority,** it is the most important thing you have to achieve or deal with before everything else. prioridad ❑ *Being a parent is her first priority.* *Ser madre es su prioridad.* ❑ *The government's priority is to build more schools.* *La prioridad del gobierno es construir más escuelas.* **2** PHRASE If you **give priority to** something or someone, you treat them as more important than anything or anyone else. dar prioridad ❑ *Most schools give priority to children who live nearby.* *La mayoría de las escuelas dan prioridad a los niños que viven cerca.* **3** PHRASE If something **takes priority** or **has priority over** other things, it is regarded as being more important than them and is dealt with first. ser prioritario ❑ *The needs of the poor must take priority over the desires of the rich.* *Las necesidades de los pobres deben ser prioritarias por encima de los deseos de los ricos.*

**prism** /prɪzəm/ (**prisms**) N-COUNT A **prism** is a block of clear glass or plastic that separates the light passing through it into different colors. prisma
→ see **color, solid**

**pris|on** /prɪzᵊn/ (**prisons**) N-VAR A **prison** is a building where criminals are kept as punishment. cárcel, prisión ❑ *He went to prison for robbery.* *Fue a la cárcel por robo.*

**Word Partnership** Usar *prison* con:

| | |
|---|---|
| V. | **die in** prison, **escape from** prison, **face** prison, **go to** prison, **release** ***someone*** **from** prison, **send** ***someone*** **to** prison, **serve/spend time in** prison |
| N. | **life in** prison, prison **officials**, prison **population**, prison **reform**, prison **sentence**, prison **time** |

**pris|on|er** /prɪzənər/ (**prisoners**) N-COUNT A **prisoner** is a person who is kept in a prison as a punishment or because they have been captured by an enemy. prisionero o prisionera ❑ *...the large number of prisoners sharing cells.* *...el gran número de prisioneros que comparten celdas.* ❑ *...a former Vietnam war prisoner.* *...un antiguo prisionero de la guerra de Vietnam.*
→ see **war**

**pri|va|cy** /praɪvəsi/ N-UNCOUNT If you have **privacy,** you are in a private place or situation where you can do things without being seen or disturbed. privacidad, privacía ❑ *...exercises you can do in the privacy of your own home.* *...ejercicios que puede hacer en la privacidad de su hogar.* ❑ *...relaxing and reading in privacy.* *...relajándose y leyendo en privado.*

**pri|vate** /praɪvɪt/ (**privates**) **1** ADJ **Private** companies, industries, and services are owned or controlled by individuals or stockholders, rather than by the government or an official organization. privado, particular [BUSINESS] ❑ *...research facilities in private industry.* *...instalaciones para investigación en la industria privada.* ❑ *...the cost of private education.* *...el costo* de la educación privada. • **pri|vate|ly** ADV *privado* ❑ *...privately owned businesses. ...negocios privados.* **2** ADJ If something is **private,** it is for the use of one person or group, and not for the general public. *privado* ❑ *...private golf clubs. ...clubes de golf privados.* ❑ *The door is marked "Private." La puerta dice "privado".* **3** ADJ **Private** meetings, discussions, and other activities involve only a small number of people, who do not discuss them with other people. *privado* ❑ *...private conversations. ...conversaciones privadas.* • **pri|vate|ly** ADV *en privado* ❑ *Privately her resignation has been welcomed. Su renuncia ha sido bien recibida en privado.* **4** ADJ Your **private life** is that part of your life that is concerned with your personal relationships and activities, rather than with your work or business. *vida privada* ❑ *I've always kept my private and professional life separate. Siempre he mantenido mi vida privada separada de la profesional.* **5** ADJ Your **private** thoughts or feelings are ones that you do not talk about to other people. *íntimo* ❑ *...his private grief. ...su duelo íntimo.* • **pri|vate|ly** ADV *íntimamente* ❑ *Privately, she worries about whether she's really good enough. Íntimamente, se pregunta si en verdad es suficientemente buena.* **6** ADJ If you describe a place as **private,** you mean that it is a quiet place and you can be alone there without being disturbed. *privado* ❑ *It was the only private place they could find. Fue el único lugar privado que encontraron.* **7** N-COUNT; N-TITLE; N-VOC A **private** is a soldier of the lowest rank in an army or the marines. *soldado raso o soldado rasa* ❑ *He was a private in the U.S. Army. Era un soldado en el ejército de Estados Unidos.* **8** PHRASE If you do something **in private,** you do it without other people being present, often because it is something that you want to keep secret. *en privado* ❑ *This should be discussed in private. Esto debe discutirse en privado.*

P

**privately held corporation** (**privately held corporations**) N-COUNT A **privately held corporation** is a company whose shares cannot be bought by the general public. *corporación privada*

**pri|vat|ize** /praɪvətaɪz/ (**privatizes, privatizing, privatized**) V-T If a company, industry, or service that is owned by the state **is privatized,** the government sells it and makes it a private company. *privatizar* [BUSINESS] ❑ *Many state-owned companies were privatized. Muchas empresas paraestatales fueron privatizadas.* • **pri|vati|za|tion** /praɪvətɪzeɪʃᵊn/ N-VAR (**privatizations**) *privatización* ❑ *...the privatization of government services. ...la privatización de los servicios gubernamentales.*

**privi|lege** /prɪvɪlɪdʒ, prɪvlɪdʒ/ (**privileges**) **1** N-COUNT A **privilege** is a special right or advantage that only one person or group has. *privilegio* ❑ *...special privileges for government officials. ...privilegios especiales para los funcionarios públicos.* **2** N-UNCOUNT **Privilege** is the power and advantages that belong to a small group of people, usually because of their wealth or their connections with powerful people. *privilegios* ❑ *...a life of privilege. ...una vida de privilegios.*

**Word Partnership** Usar *privilege* con:

ADJ. **executive** privilege, **special** privilege **1**
N. **attorney-client** privilege **1**
**power and** privilege **2**

**privi|leged** /prɪvɪlɪdʒd, prɪvlɪdʒd/ ADJ Someone who is **privileged** has an advantage or opportunity that most other people do not have, often because of their wealth or connections with powerful people. *privilegiado* ❑ *...wealthy, privileged young women. ...mujeres jóvenes, ricas y privilegiadas.*

**prize** /praɪz/ (**prizes, prizing, prized**) **1** N-COUNT A **prize** is money or something valuable, such as money or a trophy, that is given to the winner of a game or competition. *premio* ❑ *He won first prize. Obtuvo el primer lugar.* ❑ *He was awarded the Nobel Prize for Physics. Le otorgaron el Premio Nobel de Física.* **2** ADJ You use **prize** to describe things that are of such good quality that they win prizes or deserve to win prizes. *premiado, digno de premio* ❑ *...a prize bull. ...un toro digno de premio.* **3** V-T Something that **is prized** is wanted and admired because it is considered to be very valuable or very good quality. *apreciar* ❑ *These colorful baskets are prized by collectors. Estas canastas coloridas son apreciadas por los coleccionistas.* **4** V-T If you **prize** something **open** or **prize** it away from a surface, you force it open or away from a surface. *forzar* ❑ *The drawer has been prized open with a screwdriver. El cajón ha sido forzado con un desarmador.*

**Word Partnership** Usar *prize* con:

V. **award a** prize, **claim a** prize, **receive a** prize, **share a** prize, **win a** prize **1**
ORD. **first** prize **1**
ADJ. **grand** prize, **top** prize **1**

**pro** /proʊ/ (**pros**) **1** N-COUNT A **pro** is a professional, especially a professional athlete. *profesional* [INFORMAL] ❑ *Langer was a pro for 29 years, and competed in nearly 80 championships. Langer fue profesional durante 29 años, y compitió en casi 80 campeonatos.* ❑ *...a former college and pro basketball player. ...un ex jugador de baloncesto a nivel universitario y profesional.* **2** PHRASE The **pros and cons** of something are its advantages and disadvantages. *el pro y contra* ❑ *Motherhood has its pros and cons. Ser madre tiene sus pros y sus contras.*

**Word Link** *prob ≈ testing : probably, probe, problem*

**prob|ably** /prɒbəbli/ ADV If you say that something is **probably** the case, you think that it is likely to be the case, although you are not sure. *probablemente* ❑ *The White House probably won't make this plan public until July. La Casa Blanca probablemente no haga público este plan hasta julio.* ❑ *Van Gogh is probably the best-known painter in the world. Probablemente Van Gogh sea el pintor más conocido en el mundo.*

**probe** /proʊb/ (**probes, probing, probed**) **1** V-I If you **probe into** something, you ask questions or try to discover facts about it. *investigar* ❑ *The more they probed into his background, the more suspicious they became. Mientras más investigaban* *sus antecedentes, tenían más sospechas.* • **Probe** is also a noun. *investigación* ❑ *Officials have opened a probe into Monday's crash. Los oficiales han abierto una investigación acerca del choque del lunes.* **2** V-T If you **probe** a place, you search it in order to find someone or something that you are looking for. *escudriñar* ❑ *A flashlight beam probed the bushes. El haz de una linterna escudriñó los arbustos.*

**Word Link** *prob ≈ testing : probably, probe, problem*

**prob|lem** /prɒbləm/ (**problems**) **1** N-COUNT A **problem** is a situation that is unsatisfactory and causes difficulties for people. *problema* ❑ *...the economic problems of the city. ...los problemas económicos de la ciudad.* ❑ *I do not have a simple solution to the garbage problem. No tengo una solución sencilla al problema de la basura.* **2** N-COUNT A **problem** is a puzzle that requires logical thought or mathematics to solve it. *problema* ❑ *...geometry problems. ...problemas de geometría.*
→ see **fractions**

**Thesaurus** *problem* Ver también:

N. complication, difficulty, hitch **1**
puzzle, question, riddle **2**

**pro|cedure** /prəsidʒər/ (**procedures**) N-VAR A **procedure** is a way of doing something, especially the usual or correct way. *procedimiento* ❑ *...a minor surgical procedure. ...un procedimiento quirúrgico sencillo.* ❑ *...the correct procedure in applying for a visa. ...el procedimiento correcto para solicitar una visa.*

**Word Partnership** Usar *procedure* con:

V. **follow a** procedure, **perform a** procedure, **use a** procedure
ADJ. **simple** procedure, **standard (operating)** procedure, **surgical** procedure

**Word Link** *pro ≈ in front, before : proceed, produce, propose*

**pro|ceed** (**proceeds, proceeding, proceeded**)

The verb is pronounced /prəsid/. The plural noun in meaning **3** is pronounced /proʊsidz/.

**1** V-T If you **proceed to** do something, you do it after doing something else. *proceder a* ❑ *He proceeded to tell me the real story. Procedió a contarme la verdadera historia.* **2** V-I To **proceed** means to continue. *proceder, seguir adelante* [FORMAL] ❑ *The group proceeded with a march despite the warning. El grupo procedió con la marcha a pesar de la advertencia.* ❑ *Their development has proceeded steadily since the war. No ha dejado de avanzar desde la guerra.* **3** N-PLURAL **The proceeds** of an event or activity are the money that has been obtained from it. *ganancias* ❑ *The proceeds of the concert went to charity. Las ganancias del concierto fueron donadas a la caridad.*

**pro|cess** /prɒsɛs/ (**processes, processing, processed**) **1** N-COUNT A **process** is a series of actions or events which have a particular result. *proceso* ❑ *...agreement to start the peace process as soon as possible. ...un acuerdo para comenzar el proceso de paz tan pronto sea posible.* ❑ *It occurs as part of the aging process. Ocurre como parte del proceso de envejecimiento.* **2** V-T When raw materials or foods **are processed,** they are prepared in factories before they are used or sold. *procesar* ❑ *The fish are processed by freezing, canning, and smoking. El pescado es procesado mediante congelamiento, enlatado y ahumado.* ❑ *The material will be processed into plastic pellets. Este material será procesado para convertirlo en balines de plástico.* • **pro|cess|ing** N-UNCOUNT *procesamiento* ❑ *America sent cotton to England for processing. Los Estados Unidos enviaban algodón a Inglaterra para su procesamiento.* **3** V-T When people **process** information, they put it through a system or into a computer in order to deal with it. *procesar* ❑ *...facilities to process the data. ...instalaciones para procesar los datos.* • **pro|cess|ing** N-UNCOUNT *procesamiento* ❑ *...data processing. ...procesamiento de los datos.* **4** → see also **word processing**
**5** N-COUNT A **process** is a series of things that happen naturally and result in a biological or chemical change. *proceso* **6** PHRASE If you are **in the process of** doing something, you have started to do it and are still doing it. *en proceso de* ❑ *We are in the process of working out the details. Estamos en proceso de afinar los detalles.* **7** PHRASE If you are doing something and you do something else **in the process,** you do the second thing as part of doing the first thing. *mientras, al mismo tiempo* ❑ *We attend the meetings and in the process, we learn new words and phrases. Vamos a las juntas y, al mismo tiempo, aprendemos nuevas palabras y frases.*

**pro|ces|sion** /prəsɛʃən/ (**processions**) N-COUNT A **procession** is a group of people who are walking, riding, or driving in a line as part of a public event. *procesión* ❑ *...a funeral procession. ...una procesión fúnebre.*

**pro|ces|sor** /prɒsɛsər/ (**processors**) N-COUNT A **processor** is the part of a computer that interprets commands and performs the processes the user has requested. *procesador* [COMPUTING]

**pro|claim** /proʊkleɪm/ (**proclaims, proclaiming, proclaimed**) V-T If people **proclaim** something, they formally make it known. *proclamar* ❑ *The new government proclaimed its independence. El nuevo gobierno proclamó su independencia.* ❑ *Britain proudly proclaims that it is a nation of animal lovers. Gran Bretaña orgullosamente proclama que es una nación de amantes de animales.*

**pro|duce** (**produces, producing, produced**)

The verb is pronounced /prədus/. The noun is pronounced /prɒdus/ or /proʊdus/.

**1** V-T To **produce** something means to cause it to happen. *producir, ocasionar* ❑ *The drug can produce side-effects. La medicina puede producir efectos secundarios.* **2** V-T If you **produce** something, you make or create it. *producir* • **pro|duc|er** N-COUNT (**producers**) *productor* ❑ *...Saudi Arabia, the world's leading oil producer. ...Arabia Saudita, el primer productor de petróleo del mundo.* **3** V-T If you **produce** evidence or an argument, you show it or explain it to people. *mostrar* ❑ *He had to produce evidence of where he would be staying. Tuvo que mostrar evidencia de dónde se iba a hospedar.* **4** V-T If you **produce** an object from somewhere, you show it or bring it out so that it can be seen. *presentar* ❑ *To rent a car you must produce a passport. Para rentar un coche debe*

P

*presentar un pasaporte.* **5** V-T If someone **produces** something such as a movie, a magazine, or a CD, they organize it and decide how it should be made. *producir* ❑ *He has produced his own sports magazine. Ha producido su propia revista deportiva.* • **pro|duc|er** N-COUNT (**producers**) *productor o productora* ❑ *...a film producer. ...un productor de cine.* **6** N-UNCOUNT **Produce** is fruit and vegetables that are grown in large quantities to be sold. *producto agrícola* ❑ *We manage to get most of our produce in farmers' markets. Logramos comprar la mayor parte de nuestras frutas y verduras en los mercados de granjeros.*

**pro|duc|er** /prədusər/ (**producers**) N-COUNT In biology, **producers** are plants or bacteria that can produce their own food, especially by means of photosynthesis. *productor* [TECHNICAL]
→ see **theater**

**prod|uct** /prɒdʌkt/ (**products**) **1** N-COUNT A **product** is something that is produced and sold in large quantities. *producto* ❑ *Try to get the best product at the lowest price. Trata de conseguir el mejor producto al menor precio.* **2** N-COUNT If you say that someone or something is a **product of** a situation or process, you mean that the situation or process has had a significant effect in making them what they are. *producto de* ❑ *We are all products of our time. Todos somos producto de nuestro tiempo.* **3** N-COUNT The **product** of a chemical reaction is the substance that is formed as a result of the chemical reaction. *producto, resultado*
→ see **industry**

**pro|duc|tion** /prədʌkʃ^ən/ (**productions**) **1** N-UNCOUNT **Production** is the process of manufacturing or growing something in large quantities, or the amount of goods manufactured or grown. *producción* ❑ *That model won't go into production before late 2009. Ese modelo no se irá a producción antes de finales de 2009.* ❑ *We needed to increase production. Necesitábamos incrementar la producción.* **2** N-UNCOUNT The **production of** something is its creation as the result of a natural process. *producción* ❑ *These proteins stimulate the production of blood cells. Estas proteínas estimulan la producción de células sanguíneas.* **3** N-UNCOUNT **Production** is the process of organizing and preparing a play, movie, program, or CD, in order to present it to the public. *producción* ❑ *She is head of the production company. Ella dirige la productora.* **4** N-COUNT A **production** is a play, opera, or other show that is performed in a theater. *producción* ❑ *...a production of "Othello." ...una producción de "Otelo".*
→ see **theater**

**pro|duc|tion values** N-PLURAL The **production values** of a movie or play are the quality of its technical aspects, such as the lighting, sets, makeup, and special effects. *valores de producción*

**pro|duc|tive** /prədʌktɪv/ **1** ADJ Someone or something that is **productive** produces or does a lot for the amount of resources used. *productivo* ❑ *Training makes workers more productive. La capacitación hace más productivos a los trabajadores.* ❑ *The more productive farmers can provide cheaper food. Los agricultores más productivos pueden ofrecer alimentos a menor costo.* **2** ADJ If you say that a relationship between people is **productive,** you mean that a lot of good or useful things happen as a result of it. *fructífero, productivo* ❑ *He was hopeful that the talks would be productive. Tenía la esperanza de que las pláticas resultaran productivas.*

**prod|uc|tiv|ity** /prɒdʊktɪvɪti/ N-UNCOUNT **Productivity** is the rate at which goods are produced. *productividad* ❑ *...continued improvements in productivity. ...incrementos constantes de la productividad.*

**pro|fes|sion** /prəfɛʃ^ən/ (**professions**) **1** N-COUNT A **profession** is a type of job that requires advanced education or training. *profesión* ❑ *Harper was a teacher by profession. Harper era maestro de profesión.* **2** N-COUNT You can use **profession** to refer to all the people who have the same profession. *profesión* ❑ *...the medical profession. ...la profesión médica.*

**pro|fes|sion|al** /prəfɛʃən^əl/ (**professionals**) **1** ADJ **Professional** means relating to a person's work, especially work that requires special training. *profesional* ❑ *His professional career started at Colgate University. Empezó su carrera profesional en la Colgate University.* • **pro|fes|sion|al|ly** ADV *profesionalmente, con profesionalismo* ❑ *...a professionally qualified architect. ...un arquitecto profesionalmente calificado.* **2** ADJ **Professional** people have jobs that require advanced education or training. *profesional* ❑ *...highly qualified professional people like doctors and engineers. ...personas con una profesión, altamente calificadas, como médicos e ingenieros.* • **Professional** is also a noun. *profesional, con carrera* ❑ *My father wanted me to become a professional. Mi padre quería que yo hiciera una carrera.* **3** ADJ You use **professional** to describe people who do a particular thing to earn money rather than as a hobby. *profesional* ❑ *...a professional athlete. ...un atleta profesional.* • **Professional** is also a noun. *profesional* ❑ *He has been a professional since March 1985. Ha sido profesional desde marzo de 1985.* • **pro|fes|sion|al|ly** ADV *profesionalmente* ❑ *By age 16 he was playing professionally with bands. Como a los 16 ya tocaba profesionalmente en algunas bandas.* **4** ADJ If you say something that someone does or produces is **professional,** you approve of it because you think that it is of a very high standard. *profesional* ❑ *They run it with a truly professional but personal touch. Lo hacen de forma verdaderamente profesional, pero con un toque personal.* • **Professional** is also a noun. *profesional* ❑ *...a dedicated professional who worked well with others. ...un profesional dedicado que trabajaba bien en equipo.* • **pro|fes|sion|al|ism** N-UNCOUNT *profesionalismo* ❑ *She did her job with supreme professionalism. HIzo su trabajo con gran profesionalismo.* • **pro|fes|sion|al|ly** ADV *profesionalmente* ❑ *...very professionally designed invitations. ...invitaciones diseñadas muy profesionalmente.*

**pro|fes|sor** /prəfɛsər/ (**professors**) **1** N-COUNT; N-TITLE; N-VOC A **professor** in an American or Canadian university or college is a teacher of the highest rank. *profesor universitario o profesora universitaria, catedrático o catedrática* ❑ *...a professor of economics at George Washington University. ...un profesor de economía de la George Washington University.* **2** N-TITLE; N-COUNT; N-VOC A **professor** in a British university is the most senior teacher in a department. *profesor o profesora, doctor o doctora* ❑ *...Professor Cameron. ...el doctor Cameron.*
→ see **graduation**

**pro|file** /proʊfaɪl/ (**profiles**) **1** N-COUNT Your **profile** is the outline of your face seen from the side. perfil ❑ *He was young and slim, with black hair and a handsome profile.* *Era joven y delgado, de cabello negro y perfil agraciado.* **2** PHRASE If someone has a **high profile,** people notice them and what they do. If you **keep a low profile,** you avoid doing things that will make people notice you. papel destacado ❑ *Indians make up only 2% of South Africa's population but they have a high profile.* *Los indios representan sólo el 2% de la población de Sudáfrica, pero tienen un papel preponderante.*

profile

**prof|it** /prɒfɪt/ (**profits, profiting, profited**) **1** N-VAR A **profit** is an amount of money that you gain when you are paid more for something than it cost you. ganancia, utilidad, beneficio ❑ *The bank made profits of $6.5 million.* *Las utilidades del banco fueron de 6.5 millones de dólares.* **2** V-I If you **profit from** something, you earn a profit or gain some advantage from it. sacar provecho, beneficiarse con algo ❑ *No one was profiting from the war effort.* *Nadie está sacando provecho de la guerra.* ❑ *She would profit from a more relaxed lifestyle.* *Le convendría un estilo de vida más relajado.*

**prof|it|able** /prɒfɪtəbəl/ **1** ADJ A **profitable** organization or practice makes a profit. rentable, redituable, lucrativo ❑ *...the most profitable business in the U.S.* *...los negocios más redituables de los Estados Unidos.* • **prof|it|ably** /prɒfɪtəbli/ ADV de manera rentable, lucrativamente ❑ *The 28 French stores are trading profitably.* *Las 28 tiendas francesas están produciendo utilidades.* • **prof|it|abil|ity** /prɒfɪtəbɪlɪti/ N-UNCOUNT rentabilidad ❑ *Changes were made to increase profitability.* *Se hicieron cambios para incrementar la rentabilidad.* **2** ADJ Something that is **profitable** results in some benefit for you. rentable, redituable ❑ *...a profitable exchange of ideas.* *...un fructífero intercambio de ideas.* • **prof|it|ably** ADV provechosamente ❑ *He could have spent his time more profitably.* *Podía haber dispuesto de su tiempo de manera más provechosa.*

| **Word Link** | *found ≈ base : foundation, founder, profound* |
|---|---|

**pro|found** /prəfaʊnd/ (**profounder, profoundest**) **1** ADJ You use **profound** to emphasize that something is very great or intense. profundo, intenso ❑ *...discoveries which had a profound effect on many areas of medicine.* *...descubrimientos que dejaron huella en muchas áreas de la medicina.* ❑ *...profound disagreement.* *...profundo desacuerdo.* • **pro|found|ly** ADV profundamente ❑ *This has profoundly affected my life.* *Esto ha afectado profundamente mi vida.* **2** ADJ A **profound** idea, work, or person shows great intellectual depth and understanding. profundo ❑ *...this tender and profound love poem.* *...este tierno e intenso poema de amor.*

**pro|grade ro|ta|tion** /proʊgreɪd roʊteɪʃən/ N-UNCOUNT Planets that have **prograde rotation** spin on their axis in the same direction that they orbit the sun. Compare **retrograde rotation.** rotación prógrada [TECHNICAL]

| **Word Link** | *gram ≈ writing : diagram, grammar, program* |
|---|---|

**pro|gram** /proʊgræm, -grəm/ (**programs, programming, programmed**) **1** N-COUNT A **program** of actions or events is a series of actions or events that are planned to be done. programa ❑ *...the nation's largest training and education program for adults.* *...el programa de capacitación y educación para adultos más extenso del país.* **2** N-COUNT A television or radio **program** is something that is broadcast on television or radio. programa ❑ *...a network television program.* *...un programa de la red televisiva.* **3** N-COUNT A theater or concert **program** is a small book or sheet of paper that gives information about the play or concert. programa ❑ *When you go to concerts, it's helpful to read the program.* *Cuando vas a un concierto, conviene leer el programa.* **4** V-T When you **program** a machine or system, you set its controls so that it will work in a particular way. programar ❑ *Parents can program the machine not to turn on at certain times.* *Los padres pueden programar el aparato para que no se encienda a ciertas horas.* **5** N-COUNT A **program** is a set of instructions that a computer follows in order to perform a particular task. programa [COMPUTING] ❑ *...an error in a computer program.* *...un error en un programa de computadora.* **6** V-T When you **program** a computer, you give it a set of instructions to make it able to perform a particular task. programar [COMPUTING] ❑ *He programmed his computer to compare the 1,431 possible combinations.* *Programó su computadora para comparar las 1,431 combinaciones posibles.* • **pro|gram|ming** N-UNCOUNT programación ❑ *...programming skills.* *...habilidades de programación.* • **pro|gram|mer** N-COUNT (**programmers**) programador o programadora ❑ *...a computer programmer.* *...un programador de computadoras.*
→ see **radio**

| **Word Partnership** | Usar *program* con: |
|---|---|
| V. | **create a** program, **expand a** program, **implement a** program, **launch a** program, **run a** program **1** **5** program **a computer** **6** |
| N. | **computer** program, **software** program **5** |

**pro|gress** (**progresses, progressing, progressed**)

| The noun is pronounced /prɒgrɛs/. The verb is pronounced /prəgrɛs/. |
|---|

**1** N-UNCOUNT **Progress** is the process of gradually improving or getting nearer to achieving or completing something. progreso, avance, desarrollo, evolución ❑ *We are making progress in the fight against cancer.* *Estamos haciendo progresos en la lucha contra el cáncer.* **2** N-SING **The progress of** a situation or action is the way in which it develops. avance, desarrollo ❑ *The president was delighted with the progress of the first day's talks.* *El presidente estaba feliz con el avance del primer día de pláticas.* **3** V-I To **progress** means to improve or to become more advanced or successful. progresar, avanzar ❑ *He will visit regularly to see how his new employees are progressing.* *Hará visitas frecuentes para ver cómo van* *progresando sus nuevos empleados.* **4** V-I If events **progress,** they continue to happen gradually over a period of time. *desarrollar, avanzar* ❑ *As the evening progressed, sadness turned to anger. Conforme avanzaba la tarde, la tristeza se tornaba en ira.* **5** PHRASE If something is **in progress,** it has started and is still continuing. *en proceso* ❑ *The game was already in progress when we arrived. El juego ya había empezado cuando llegamos.*

**pro|gres|sive** /prəgrɛsɪv/ (**progressives**) **1** ADJ Someone who is **progressive** has modern ideas about how things should be done, rather than traditional ones. *progresista* ❑ *...a progressive businessman who fought for the rights of consumers. ...un hombre de negocios progresista que luchó por los derechos de los consumidores.* ● A **progressive** is someone who is progressive. *progresista* ❑ *The Republicans were split between progressives and conservatives. Los Republicanos estaban divididos en progresistas y conservadores.* **2** ADJ A **progressive** change happens gradually over a period of time. *progresivo* ❑ *One symptom of the disease is progressive loss of memory. Un síntoma de la enfermedad es la pérdida progresiva de la memoria.* ● **pro|gres|sive|ly** ADV *progresivamente, cada vez más* ❑ *Her symptoms became progressively worse. Sus síntomas empeoraban progresivamente.*

**pro|hib|it** /proʊhɪbɪt/ (**prohibits, prohibiting, prohibited**) V-T If a law or someone in authority **prohibits** something, they forbid it or make it illegal. *prohibir* [FORMAL] ❑ *...a school that prohibits calculators. ...una escuela en que se prohibe el uso de calculadoras.* ❑ *Fishing is prohibited. Prohibido pescar.* ● **pro|hi|bi|tion** /proʊɪbɪʃᵊn/ N-UNCOUNT *prohibición* ❑ *...the prohibition of slavery. ...la prohibición de la esclavitud.*

**proj|ect** (**projects, projecting, projected**)

The noun is pronounced /prɒdʒɛkt/. The verb is pronounced /prədʒɛkt/.

**1** N-COUNT A **project** is a task that requires a lot of time and effort. *proyecto* ❑ *Money will go into local development projects. El dinero irá a proyectos de desarrollo local.* ❑ *...an international science project. ...un proyecto científico internacional.* **2** N-COUNT A **project** is a detailed study of a subject by a student. *trabajo, proyecto* ❑ *The kids in my class have just finished a project on ancient Greece. Los niños de mi clase acaban de terminar un trabajo sobre la antigua Grecia.* **3** V-T If something **is projected**, it is planned or expected. *proyectar* ❑ *13% of Americans are over 65; this number is projected to reach 22% by the year 2030. El 13% de los estadounidenses tiene más de 65; se proyecta que esta cifra llegará al 22% para el 2030.* ❑ *The government has projected a 5% price increase for the year. El gobierno ha proyectado un incremento del 5% en los precios para este año.* **4** V-T If you **project** a particular feeling or quality, you show it in your behavior. If you **project** yourself in a particular way, you try to make people see you in that way. *proyectar, reflejar* ❑ *Bradley projects a natural warmth and sincerity. Bradley refleja calidez y sinceridad naturales.* ❑ *He hasn't been able to project himself as a strong leader. No ha sido capaz de proyectarse como un verdadero líder.* **5** V-T If you **project** a film or picture **onto** a screen or wall, you make it appear there. *proyectar* ❑ *We tried projecting the maps onto the screen. Intentamos proyectar los mapas en la pantalla.* **6** V-I If something **projects,** it sticks out above or beyond a surface or edge. *proyectarse* [FORMAL] ❑ *...a narrow ledge that projected out from the bank of the river. ...un estrecho reborde que se proyectaba de la orilla del río.*

**Word Partnership** Usar *project* con:

| | |
|---|---|
| V. | **approve a** project, **launch a** project **1** **complete a** project, **start a** project **1** **2** |
| N. | **construction** project, **development** project, project **director/manager** **1** **research** project, **science** project, **writing** project **1** **2** |
| ADJ. | **involved in a** project, **latest** project, **new** project, **special** project **1** **2** |

**pro|jec|tile mo|tion** N-UNCOUNT **Projectile motion** is the curved path of an object which has been propelled into the air at an angle, for example a ball that is kicked or thrown. *trayectoria del proyectil* [TECHNICAL]

**pro|jec|tion** /prədʒɛkʃᵊn/ (**projections**) **1** N-COUNT A **projection** is an estimate of a future amount. *proyección, pronóstico, extrapolación* ❑ *...the company's projection of 11 million visitors for the first year. ...el pronóstico de la empresa de 11 millones de visitantes para el primer año.* **2** N-UNCOUNT The **projection** of a film or picture is the act of projecting it onto a screen or wall. *proyección* ❑ *They took me into a projection room to see the picture. Me llevaron a una sala de proyección a ver la película.* **3** N-UNCOUNT A speaker or performer who has good **projection** is skillful at speaking to an audience or communicating with an audience in a clear and confident way. *voz y presencia*

**pro|karyo|tic cell** /proʊkærinɒtɪk/ (**prokaryotic cells**) also **prokaryote** /proʊkærioʊt/ N-COUNT **Prokaryotic cells** or **prokaryotes** are cells or organisms such as bacteria that do not have a nucleus. Compare **eukaryotic cell** *célula procariota, célula procariótica* [TECHNICAL]

**pro|lif|er|ate** /prəlɪfəreɪt/ (**proliferates, proliferating, proliferated**) V-I If things **proliferate,** they increase in number very quickly. *proliferar* [FORMAL] ❑ *Computerized databases are proliferating fast. Las bases de datos computarizadas están proliferando con rapidez.* ● **pro|lif|era|tion** /prəlɪfəreɪʃᵊn/ N-UNCOUNT *proliferación* ❑ *...the proliferation of nuclear weapons. ...la proliferación de las armas nucleares.*

**pro|longed** /prəlɔŋd/ ADJ A **prolonged** event or situation continues for a long time, or for longer than expected. *prolongado* ❑ *...a prolonged period of peace. ...un prolongado periodo de paz.*

**prom** /prɒm/ (**proms**) N-COUNT A **prom** is a formal dance at a school or college which usually takes place at the end of the academic year. *baile de graduación, baile de la escuela* ❑ *I didn't want to go to the prom with Craig. Yo no quería ir al baile de graduación con Craig.* ❑ *...my senior prom. ...mi baile de graduación de la universidad.*

**promi|nent** /prɒmɪnənt/ **1** ADJ Someone who is **prominent** is important and well-known. *destacado, prominente, importante* ❑ *...the children of very prominent or successful parents. ...los hijos de padres muy destacados o exitosos.* ● **promi|nence**

P

N-UNCOUNT *prominencia, importancia* ❑ *Crime prevention needs to have more prominence. Es necesario dar más importancia a la prevención del delito.* **2** ADJ Something that is **prominent** is very noticeable. *prominente* ❑ *...a prominent nose. ...una nariz prominente.* ● **promi|nent|ly** ADV *prominentemente* ❑ *The poster is prominently displayed in the hall. El póster está muy a la vista en el vestíbulo.*

**prom|ise** /prɒmɪs/ (**promises, promising, promised**) **1** V-T/V-I If you **promise that** you will do something, you say to someone that you will definitely do it. *prometer* ❑ *The post office has promised to resume mail delivery to the area on Friday. En la oficina de correos prometieron que el viernes se reanudaría la entrega de correspondencia en el área.* ❑ *He promised that the rich would no longer get special treatment. Prometió que los ricos ya no recibirían trato especial.* ❑ *Promise me you will not waste your time. Prométeme que no perderás el tiempo.* ● **Promise** is also a noun. *promesa* ❑ *If you make a promise, you should keep it. Si haces una promesa, tienes que cumplirla.* **2** V-T If you **promise** someone something, you tell them that you will definitely give it to them or make sure that they have it. *prometer* ❑ *I've promised them a house in the country. Les prometí una casa en el campo.* **3** V-T If a situation or event **promises to** have a particular quality or **to** be a particular thing, it shows signs that it will have that quality or be that thing. *presagiar* ❑ *Thursday promises to be a busy day. Parece que el jueves habrá mucho trabajo.* **4** N-UNCOUNT If someone or something shows **promise,** they seem likely to be very good or successful. *que promete* ❑ *The boy showed promise as an athlete. El muchacho prometía como atleta.*

**Word Partnership** Usar *promise* con:

N. **campaign** promise **1**
V. **break a** promise, **deliver on a** promise, **keep a** promise, **make a** promise **1**
**hold** promise, **show** promise **4**
ADJ. **broken** promise, **empty** promise, **false** promise **1**
**enormous** promise, **great** promise, **real** promise **4**

**prom|is|ing** /prɒmɪsɪŋ/ ADJ Someone or something that is **promising** seems likely to be very good or successful. *prometedor* ❑ *...one of the most promising poets of his generation. ...uno de los poetas más prometedores de su generación.*

**prom|is|sory note** /prɒmɪsɔri noʊt/ (**promissory notes**) N-COUNT A **promissory note** is a written promise to pay a specific sum of money to a particular person. *pagaré* [BUSINESS] ❑ *...a $36.4 million, five-year promissory note. ...un pagaré a cinco años por 36.4 millones de dólares.*

**Word Link** *mot ≈ moving : motion, motivate, promote*

**pro|mote** /prəmoʊt/ (**promotes, promoting, promoted**) **1** V-T If people **promote** something, they help it to happen, increase, or become more popular. *promover, fomentar, impulsar* ❑ *...trying to promote the idea that war is a bad thing. ...tratando de promover la idea de que la guerra no es buena.* ● **pro|mo|tion** N-VAR (**promotions**) *promoción, fomento* ❑ *...the promotion of democracy. ...el fomento de la democracia.* ❑ *...TV commercials and other promotions. ...comerciales en televisión y otras promociones.* **2** V-T If someone **is promoted,** they are given a more important job or rank in the organization that they work for. *ascender* ❑ *He was promoted to general manager. Lo ascendieron a gerente general.* ● **pro|mo|tion** N-VAR *ascenso* ❑ *Consider changing jobs or trying for promotion. Piensa en cambiar de trabajo o buscar un ascenso.*
→ see concert

**pro|mot|er** /prəmoʊtər/ (**promoters**) **1** N-COUNT A **promoter** is a person who helps organize and finance an event, especially a sports event. *promotor o promotora, hombre de negocios o mujer de negocios* ❑ *...one of the top boxing promoters in Las Vegas. ...uno de los principales promotores de las peleas de box en Las Vegas.* **2** N-COUNT The **promoter of** a cause or idea tries to make it become popular. *promotor* ❑ *His father is a publisher and promoter of classical music. Su padre es editor y promotor de música clásica.*

**pro|mo|tion|al** /prəmoʊʃənᵊl/ ADJ **Promotional** material, events, or ideas are designed to increase the sales of a product or service. *promocional, publicitario* ❑ *The hotel's promotional material shows a couple in the pool. El material publicitario del hotel muestra a una pareja en la alberca.*

**prompt** /prɒmpt/ (**prompts, prompting, prompted**) **1** V-T To **prompt** someone **to** do something means to make them decide to do it. *provocar, inducir, incitar, sugerir* ❑ *The article prompted readers to complain. El artículo instaba a los lectores a quejarse.* **2** V-T If you **prompt** someone, you encourage or remind them to do something or to continue doing something. *inducir* ❑ *"Well, Daniel?" Wilson prompted. —¿Y bien, Daniel?—le preguntó Wilson.* ● **prompt|ing** N-VAR (**promptings**) *recordatorio, sugerencia, estímulo* ❑ *The team needed little prompting from their coach. El equipo poco necesitaba el impulso del entrenador.* **3** ADJ A **prompt** action is done without any delay. *pronto, inmediato* ❑ *It is not too late, but prompt action is needed. No es demasiado tarde, pero se necesitan medidas inmediatas.*

**prompt|ly** /prɒmptli/ **1** ADV If you do something **promptly,** you do it immediately. *prontamente, sin demora* ❑ *She entered the room, took her seat, and promptly fell asleep. Entró en el salón, se sentó y pronto estaba dormida.* **2** ADV If you do something **promptly at** a particular time, you do it at exactly that time. *puntualmente* ❑ *Promptly at a quarter past seven, we left the hotel. Salimos del hotel puntualmente, a las siete y cuarto.*

**prone** /proʊn/ ADJ To be **prone to** something, usually something bad, means to have a tendency to be affected by it or to do it. *propenso a, proclive a* ❑ *They are prone to errors and accidents. Son propensos a errores y accidentes.* ● **Prone** combines with nouns to make adjectives that describe people who are frequently affected by something bad. *propenso, proclive* ❑ *...the most injury-prone rider. ...los jinetes más propensos a lesiones*

**pro|noun** /proʊnaʊn/ (**pronouns**) N-COUNT A **pronoun** is a word that you use instead of a noun group to refer to someone or something. "It," "she," "something," and "myself" are pronouns. *pronombre*

P

**Word Link** *nounce ≈ repoting : announce, denounce, pronounce*

**pro|nounce** /prənaʊns/ (**pronounces, pronouncing, pronounced**) **1** V-T To **pronounce** a word means to say it using particular sounds. *pronunciar* ❑ *Have I pronounced your name correctly? ¿Pronuncié correctamente su nombre?* **2** V-T If you **pronounce** something, you state it formally or publicly. *pronunciarse, declarar* [FORMAL] ❑ *A specialist has pronounced him fully fit. Un especialista dictaminó que es perfectamente apto.*
→ see **trial**

**pro|nun|cia|tion** /prənʌnsieɪʃᵊn/ (**pronunciations**) N-VAR The **pronunciation** of a word or language is the way it is pronounced. *pronunciación* ❑ *She gave the word its French pronunciation. Pronunció la palabra como si fuera francés.*

**proof** /pruf/ (**proofs**) N-VAR **Proof** is a fact, argument, or piece of evidence showing that something is true or exists. *prueba, acreditación* ❑ *You have to have proof of residence in the state. Necesita acreditar que reside en el estado* ❑ *This is proof that he is wrong. Es prueba de que está equivocado.*

**Word Partnership** Usar *proof* con:

ADJ. **convincing** proof, **final** proof, **living** proof, proof **positive**
V. **have** proof, **need** proof, **offer** proof, **provide** proof, **require** proof, **show** proof

**prop** /prɒp/ (**props, propping, propped**) **1** V-T If you **prop** an object **on** or **against** something, you support it by putting something underneath it or by resting it somewhere. *apoyar* ❑ *He propped his feet on the desk. Apoyó los pies en el escritorio.* ● **Prop up** means the same as **prop**. *apoyar* ❑ *Sam propped his elbows up on the bench behind him. Sam apoyó los codos en la banca que tenía detrás.* **2** N-COUNT A **prop** is a stick or other object that you use to support something. *puntal, soporte* ❑ *Using the table as a prop, he dragged himself to his feet. Usando la mesa como apoyo, se puso de pie.* **3** N-COUNT The **props** in a play or movie are the objects and pieces of furniture that are used in it. *utilería* ❑ *...the props for a stage show. ...la utilería para una puesta en escena.*
▸ **prop up** PHR-VERB To **prop up** something means to support it or help it to survive. *apoyar* ❑ *Investments in the U.S. money market have propped up the dollar. Las inversiones en el mercado de dinero de los Estados Unidos han apoyado al dólar.* → see **prop 1**
→ see **theater**

**propa|gan|da** /prɒpəgændə/ N-UNCOUNT **Propaganda** is information, often inaccurate information, that a political organization publishes or broadcasts in order to influence people. *propaganda* ❑ *A huge propaganda campaign was mounted by the state media. Los medios estatales hicieron intensa propaganda.*

**Word Link** *pel ≈ driving, forcing : compel, expel, propeller*

**pro|pel|ler** /prəpɛlər/ (**propellers**) N-COUNT A **propeller** is a device with blades attached to a boat or aircraft, that spins around and causes the boat or aircraft to move. *hélice, impulsor, propulsor* ❑ *...a three-bladed propeller. ...una hélice de tres aspas.*

**prop|er** /prɒpər/ **1** ADJ You use **proper** to describe things that you consider to be real and satisfactory rather than inadequate in some way. *apropiado, verdadero* ❑ *Two out of five people lack a proper job. Dos de cada cinco personas carecen de un trabajo decoroso.* ● **prop|er|ly** ADV *con propiedad, correctamente* ❑ *You're not eating properly. No estás comiendo como es debido.* **2** ADJ The **proper** thing is the one that is correct or most suitable. *adecuado, apropiado, correcto* ❑ *The proper procedures have been followed. Se han aplicado los procedimientos adecuados.* **3** ADJ If you say that a way of behaving is **proper,** you mean that it is considered socially acceptable and right. *propio, correcto* ❑ *It was not thought proper for a woman to be on the stage. No se consideraba adecuado que una mujer se presentara en el escenario.* ● **prop|er|ly** ADV *adecuadamente, con propiedad* ❑ *It's about time he learned to behave properly. Es tiempo de que aprenda a comportarse propiamente.*

**prop|er noun** (**proper nouns**) N-COUNT A **proper noun** is the name of a particular person, place, organization, or thing. Proper nouns begin with a capital letter. *nombre propio*

**prop|er|ty** /prɒpərti/ (**properties**) **1** N-UNCOUNT Someone's **property** is all the things that belong to them or something that belongs to them. *propiedad* [FORMAL] ❑ *...her personal property. ...sus pertenencias personales.* **2** N-VAR A **property** is a building and the land belonging to it. *propiedad, inmueble* [FORMAL] ❑ *Get out of here—this is a private property! ¡Salga de aquí—es propiedad privada!* **3** N-COUNT The **properties** of a substance or object are the ways in which it behaves in particular conditions. *propiedad* ❑ *A radio signal has both electrical and magnetic properties. Una señal de radio tiene propiedades tanto eléctricas como magnéticas.*
→ see **element, periodic table**

**prop|er|ty tax** (**property taxes**) N-VAR **Property tax** is tax that you pay on buildings and land that you own. *impuesto predial, impuesto sobre la propiedad inmobiliaria.* ❑ *We've got the highest property taxes in the United States. Pagamos los impuestos prediales más altos de los Estados Unidos.*

**pro|phase** /proʊfeɪz/ (**prophases**) N-VAR **Prophase** is the first stage of cell division, in which the DNA inside a cell forms into chromosomes. *profase* [TECHNICAL]

**proph|et** /prɒfɪt/ (**prophets**) N-COUNT A **prophet** is a person who is believed to be chosen by God to say the things that God wants to tell people. *profeta* ❑ *...the Holy Prophet of Islam. ...el Sagrado Profeta del Islam.*

**pro|por|tion** /prəpɔrʃᵊn/ (**proportions**) **1** N-COUNT A **proportion of** a group or an amount is a part of it. *parte, proporción* [FORMAL] ❑ *A large proportion of the dolphins in that area will die. Gran parte de los delfines en esa área morirán.* **2** N-COUNT The **proportion of** one kind of person or thing in a group is the number of people or things of that kind compared to the total number of people or things in the group. *proporción, porcentaje* ❑ *The proportion of women in the profession is now 17.3%. El porcentaje de mujeres en la profesión es ahora de 17.3%.* **3** N-PLURAL If you refer to the **proportions** of

P

something, you are referring to its size, usually when this is extremely large. *tamaño, dimensiones* [WRITTEN] ❑ *In the tropics plants grow to huge proportions. En los trópicos, las plantas adquieren dimensiones enormes.* **4** N-PLURAL If you refer to the **proportions** in a work of art or design, you are referring to the relative sizes of its different parts. *proporciones* ❑ *This computer program lets you change the proportions of things in your picture very simply. Con este programa de computadora se pueden modificar muy fácilmente las proporciones de la imagen.* **5** PHRASE If one thing increases or decreases **in proportion to** another thing, it increases or decreases to the same degree as that thing. *Han acordado incrementar los salarios en proporción con los incrementos de precios.* **6** PHRASE If something is small or large **in proportion to** something else, it is small or large when compared with that thing. *respecto de, comparado con* ❑ *His head was large in proportion to the rest of his body. Su cabeza era grande respecto del resto del cuerpo.* **7** PHRASE If you say that something is **out of proportion to** something else, you think that it is far greater or more serious than it should be. *desproporcionado* ❑ *The punishment was out of all proportion to the crime. El castigo fue exagerado respecto del delito.*

**pro|por|tion|al** /prəpɔrʃənᵊl/ ADJ If one amount is **proportional to** another, the two amounts increase and decrease at the same rate so there is always the same relationship between them. *proporcional* [FORMAL] ❑ *Loss of weight is directly proportional to taking more exercise and eating carefully. La disminución del peso es directamente proporcional al incremento del ejercicio y una alimentación cuidadosa.*

**pro|po|sal** /prəpoʊzᵊl/ (**proposals**) **1** N-COUNT A **proposal** is a suggestion or plan, often a formal or written one. *propuesta, oferta* ❑ *...the details of their new proposals. ...los detalles de sus nuevas propuestas.* ❑ *...a UN proposal to grant the colony independence. ...una propuesta de Naciones Unidas para conceder su independencia a la colonia.* **2** N-COUNT A **proposal** is the act of asking someone to marry you. *propuesta* ❑ *Pam accepted Randy's proposal of marriage. Pam aceptó la propuesta de matrimonio de Randy.*

**Word Partnership** Usar *proposal* con:

ADJ. **new** proposal, **original** proposal **1**
V. **adopt a** proposal, **approve a** proposal, **support a** proposal, **vote on a** proposal **1** **accept a** proposal, **make a** proposal, **reject a** proposal **1** **2**
N. **budget** proposal, **peace** proposal **1** **marriage** proposal **2**

**Word Link** *pro ≈ in front, before : proceed, produce, propose*

**pro|pose** /prəpoʊz/ (**proposes, proposing, proposed**) **1** V-T If you **propose** a plan or an idea, you suggest it. *proponer, sugerir* ❑ *Morris proposed a change in the law. Morris sugirió un cambio en la ley.* **2** V-T If you **propose** to do something, you intend to do it. *proponer* **3** V-I If you **propose to** someone, or **propose marriage to** them, you ask them to marry you. *proponer matrimonio* ❑ *He proposed to his girlfriend. Le propuso matrimonio a su novia.*

**Word Partnership** Usar *propose* con:

N. propose **changes**, propose **legislation**, propose **a plan**, propose **a solution**, propose **a tax**, propose **a theory**, propose **a toast** **1** propose **marriage** **2**

**propo|si|tion** /prɒpəzɪʃᵊn/ (**propositions**) **1** N-COUNT If you describe something such as a task or an activity as, for example, a difficult **proposition** or an attractive **proposition,** you mean that it is difficult or pleasant to do. *propuesta, proposición, oferta* ❑ *Making money easily has always been an attractive proposition. Hacer dinero fácilmente siempre ha sido una propuesta atractiva.* **2** N-COUNT A **proposition** is a statement or an idea that people can consider or discuss to decide whether it is true. *propuesta, argumento* [FORMAL] ❑ *...the proposition that democracies do not fight each other. ...el argumento de que las democracias no pelean entre ellas.* **3** N-COUNT A **proposition** is an offer or a suggestion. *propuesta* ❑ *I went to see him at his office the other day with a business proposition. Fui a verlo a su oficina el otro día con una propuesta de negocio.*

**pro|pri|etor** /prəpraɪətər/ (**proprietors**) N-COUNT The **proprietor** of a hotel, store, newspaper, or other business is the person who owns it. *propietario o propietaria, dueño o dueña* [FORMAL] ❑ *...the proprietor of a local restaurant. ...el propietario de un restaurante de la localidad.*

**pro|rate** /proʊreɪt/ (**prorates, prorating, prorated**) also **pro-rate** V-T If a cost **is prorated,** it is divided or assessed in a proportional way. *prorratear* ❑ *If sea conditions cause your trip to return early, the boat fare will be prorated. Si por las condiciones del mar el recorrido termina antes, la tarifa del bote se prorratea.*

**pro|scenium** /proʊsiniəm, prə-/ (**prosceniums**) N-COUNT A **proscenium** or a **proscenium arch** is an arch in a theater that separates the stage from the audience. *arco del proscenio, proscenio*

**prose** /proʊz/ N-UNCOUNT **Prose** is ordinary written language, in contrast to poetry. *prosa*

**pros|ecute** /prɒsɪkyut/ (**prosecutes, prosecuting, prosecuted**) V-T/V-I If the authorities **prosecute** someone, they charge them with a crime and put them on trial. *procesar, enjuiciar* ❑ *The police have decided not to prosecute. La policía decidió no llevarlo a juicio.* ❑ *Photographs taken by roadside cameras are used to prosecute drivers for speeding. Las fotografías tomadas por las cámaras que están en los caminos sirven para llevar a juicio a conductores que rebasan el límite de velocidad.* • **pros|ecu|tion** N-VAR (**prosecutions**) *proceso, juicio* ❑ *The government called for the prosecution of those responsible. El gobierno solicitó el enjuiciamiento de los responsables.*

**pros|ecu|tion** /prɒsɪkyuʃᵊn/ N-SING The lawyers who try to prove that a person on trial is guilty are called **the prosecution.** *parte acusadora* ❑ *...a witness for the prosecution. ...un testigo de la parte acusadora.*

**pros|ecu|tor** /prɒsɪkyutər/ (**prosecutors**)

p

N-COUNT In some countries, a **prosecutor** is a lawyer or official who brings charges against someone or tries to prove in a trial that they are guilty. *fiscal, querellante, demandante*

**pro|sim|ian** /proʊsɪmiən/ (**prosimians**) also **pro-simian** N-COUNT **Prosimians** are animals such as lemurs and other primates who resemble the early ancestors of apes and humans. *prosimio* [TECHNICAL] ● **prosimian** is also an adjective. *prosimio* ❑ *...a prosimian species. ...una especie de prosimios.*

**pros|pect** /prɑspɛkt/ (**prospects, prospecting, prospected**) **1** N-VAR A **prospect** is a possibility or possible event. *posibilidad, perspectiva* ❑ *There is little prospect of getting an answer to these questions. Hay pocas posibilidades de recibir una respuesta para estas preguntas.* ❑ *The prospects for peace are becoming brighter. Las perspectivas de paz son cada vez más alentadoras.* **2** N-PLURAL Someone's **prospects** are their chances of being successful. *perspectivas* ❑ *I chose to work abroad to improve my career prospects. Decidí trabajar en el extranjero para mejorar mis perspectivas profesionales.* **3** V-I To **prospect for** a substance such as oil or gold means to look for it in the ground or under the sea. *buscar, explorar* ❑ *He has prospected for minerals everywhere. Ha buscado minerales por todas partes.*

**pro|spec|tive** /prəspɛktɪv/ ADJ You use **prospective** to describe someone who wants to be the thing mentioned or who is likely to be the thing mentioned. *potencial, posible* ❑ *The story should act as a warning to prospective buyers. La historia debe poner en alerta a posibles compradores.*

**pros|per|ity** /prɒspɛrɪti/ N-UNCOUNT **Prosperity** is a condition in which a person or community is doing well financially. *prosperidad* ❑ *...a long period of peace and prosperity. ...un largo periodo de paz y prosperidad.*

P

**pros|per|ous** /prɒspərəs/ ADJ **Prosperous** people, places, and economies are rich and successful. *próspero, floreciente* [FORMAL] ❑ *...a relatively prosperous family. ...una familia relativamente próspera.*

**pros|ti|tute** /prɒstɪtut/ (**prostitutes**) N-COUNT A **prostitute** is a person, usually a woman, who has sex with men in exchange for money. *prostituta*

| Word Link | *tect ≈ covering : detect, protect, protective* |
|---|---|

**pro|tect** /prətɛkt/ (**protects, protecting, protected**) V-T To **protect** someone or something means to prevent them from being harmed or damaged. *proteger, defender, custodiar* ❑ *What can women do to protect themselves from heart disease? ¿Qué pueden hacer las mujeres para protegerse de las enfermedades cardíacas?* ❑ *We are committed to protecting the interests of children. Nos hemos comprometido a proteger los intereses de los niños.*
● **pro|tec|tor** N-COUNT (**protectors**) *protector o protectora, defensor o defensora* ❑ *I always saw my father as a protector. Siempre consideré a mi padre como un protector.*
→ see **hero**

| Word Partnership | Usar *protect* con: |
|---|---|
| N. | protect **against attacks**, protect **children**, protect **citizens**, **duty to** protect, **efforts to** protect, protect **the environment**, **laws** protect, protect **people**, protect **privacy**, protect **property**, protect **women**, protect **workers** |
| ADJ. | **designed to** protect, **necessary to** protect, **supposed to** protect |

**pro|tec|tion** /prətɛkʃᵊn/ (**protections**) N-VAR If something gives **protection** against something unpleasant, it prevents people or things from being harmed or damaged by it. *protección, resguardo, defensa* ❑ *The diet is believed to offer protection against cancer. Se supone que la dieta sirve como protección contra el cáncer.* ❑ *The primary duty of parents is to provide protection for our children. El principal deber de los padres es dar protección a nuestros hijos.*

**pro|tec|tive** /prətɛktɪv/ **1** ADJ **Protective** means designed or intended to protect something or someone from harm. *protector* ❑ *You should wear protective gloves. Debes usar guantes de seguridad.* **2** ADJ If someone is **protective toward** you, they look after you and show a strong desire to keep you safe. *protector* ❑ *He is very protective toward his mother. Es muy protector con su madre.*

**pro|tein** /proʊtin/ (**proteins**) N-VAR **Protein** is a substance which the body needs and which is found in meat, eggs, and milk. *proteína* ❑ *Fish is a major source of protein. El pescado es una fuente importante de proteínas.*
→ see **calorie, diet**

**pro|test** (**protests, protesting, protested**)

> The verb is usually pronounced /prətɛst/. The noun, and sometimes the verb, is pronounced /proʊtɛst/.

**1** V-T/V-I To **protest** means to say or show publicly that you object to something. *protestar, quejarse* ❑ *They were protesting high prices. Estaban protestando contra los precios altos.* ❑ *...demonstrators protesting against food price rises. ...manifestantes que protestan contra el incremento de los precios de los alimentos.* ● **pro|test|er** also **protestor** N-COUNT (**protesters**) *manifestante* ❑ *The protesters say the government is corrupt. Los manifestantes dicen que el gobierno es corrupto.* **2** N-VAR A **protest** is the act of saying or showing publicly that you object to something. *protesta, manifestación* ❑ *...the start of protests against the war. ...el inicio de las manifestaciones contra la guerra.* ❑ *The Mexican president canceled a trip to Texas in protest. Como protesta, el presidente de México canceló un viaje a Texas.* **3** V-T If you **protest** that something is the case, you insist that it is the case, when other people think that it may not be. *protestar, quejarse* ❑ *We tried to protest that Mo was beaten up. Tratamos de quejarnos porque habían golpeado a Mo.* ❑ *"I never said any of that to her," he protested. —Nunca le dije nada de eso a ella—protestó.*

**Word Partnership** Usar *protest* con:

N. **workers** protest 1
protest **demonstrations**, protest **groups**, protest **march**, protest **rally** 2
ADJ. **anti-government** protest, **anti-war** protest, **organized** protest, **peaceful** protest, **political** protest 2

**Prot|es|tant** /prɒtɪstənt/ (**Protestants**) N-COUNT A **Protestant** is a Christian who belongs to the branch of the Christian church that separated from the Catholic church in the sixteenth century. *protestante*

**pro|tist** /proʊtɪst/ (**protists**) N-COUNT **Protists** are organisms such as algae and molds that are not animals, plants or fungi. *protisto* [TECHNICAL]

**Pro|tis|ta** /proʊtɪstə/ N-UNCOUNT **Protista** is the biological group to which organisms called protists belong. *protista*, *protoctista* [TECHNICAL]

**pro|ton** /proʊtɒn/ (**protons**) N-COUNT A **proton** is an atomic particle that has a positive electrical charge. *protón* [TECHNICAL]

**proto|type** /proʊtətaɪp/ (**prototypes**) N-COUNT A **prototype** is the first model or example of a new type of thing. *prototipo* ❑ *...a prototype of a pollution-free car.* *...un prototipo de auto que no contamina.*

**proto|zoan** /proʊtəzoʊən/ (**protozoa** or **protozoans**) N-COUNT **Protozoa** are very small organisms that often live inside larger animals. *protozoario*, *protozoo* [TECHNICAL]

**proud** /praʊd/ (**prouder**, **proudest**) 1 ADJ If you feel **proud**, you feel pleased and satisfied about something good that you own, have done, or are connected with. *orgulloso*, *satisfecho*, *ufano* ❑ *I felt proud of his efforts.* *Me sentía orgulloso de sus esfuerzos.* ❑ *They are proud that she is doing well at school.* *Están satisfechos porque le va bien en la escuela.* • **proud|ly** ADV *orgullosamente* ❑ *"That's the first part finished," he said proudly.* *—Esta es la primera parte, ya terminada —dijo con orgullo.* 2 ADJ Someone who is **proud** has a lot of dignity and self-respect. *orgulloso* ❑ *He was too proud to ask his family for help and support.* *Era demasiado orgulloso como para pedir ayuda y apoyo a su familia.* 3 ADJ Someone who is **proud** feels that they are better or more important than other people. *arrogante*, *altanero* ❑ *He described Sir Terence as "vain, proud and selfish."* *Describió a Sir Terence como "vanidoso, altanero y egoísta".*

proud

**prove** /pruv/ (**proves**, **proving**, **proved**, **proven**)

The forms **proved** and **proven** can both be used as a past participle.

1 V-LINK If something **proves to** be true or **to** have a particular quality, it becomes clear after a period of time that it is true or has that quality. *resultar* ❑ *All our reports proved to be true.* *Todos nuestros informes resultaron ciertos.* ❑ *This process has often proven difficult.* *Este proceso muchas veces resulta problemático.* 2 V-T If you **prove that** something is true, you show by means of argument or evidence that it is definitely true. *demostrar*, *probar* ❑ *My theory has been proved!* *¡Mi teoría ha sido demostrada!* ❑ *These results prove that we were right.* *Estos resultados prueban que teníamos razón.* ❑ *I was determined to prove him wrong.* *Estaba decidida a demostrar que estaba equivocado.* 3 V-T If you **prove yourself**, you show by your actions that you have a certain good quality. *demostrar la propia valía* ❑ *I had two injuries, but I felt I had to come back and prove myself.* *Tenía dos heridas, pero sentí que tenía que regresar y ponerme a prueba.*
→ see **science**

**Word Partnership** Usar *prove* con:

ADJ. prove **(to be) difficult**, prove **helpful**, prove **useful**, prove **worthy** 1
**difficult to** prove, **hard to** prove 2
V. **be able to** prove, **have (*something*) to** prove, **try to** prove 2

**Word Link** *verb ≈ word : adverb, proverb, verbal*

**prov|erb** /prɒvɜrb/ (**proverbs**) N-COUNT A **proverb** is a short sentence that people often quote, because it gives advice or tells you something about life. *proverbio*, *refrán* ❑ *An old Arab proverb says, "The enemy of my enemy is my friend."* *Un antiguo proverbio árabe reza que "el enemigo de mi enemigo es mi amigo".*

**pro|vide** /prəvaɪd/ (**provides**, **providing**, **provided**) 1 V-T If you **provide** something that someone needs or wants, or if you **provide** them **with** it, you give it to them or make it available to them. *proporcionar*, *proveer* ❑ *They would not provide any details.* *No darían ningún detalle.* ❑ *They provided him with a car and a driver.* *Le proporcionaron un auto con chofer.* 2 V-T If a law or agreement **provides that** something will happen, it states that it will happen. *estipular*, *disponer* [FORMAL] ❑ *Muslim law provides that women must dress modestly.* *La ley musulmana estipula que las mujeres deben vestir con modestia.* 3 → see also **provided**
▸ **provide for** 1 PHR-VERB If you **provide for** someone, you support them financially and make sure that they have the things that they need. *mantener*, *sostener* ❑ *Elaine wouldn't let him provide for her.* *Elaine no lo dejaría mantenerla.* 2 PHR-VERB If you **provide for** something that might happen or that might need to be done, you make arrangements to deal with it. *prever* ❑ *Jim has provided for just such an emergency.* *Jim ha tomado medidas para ese tipo de emergencias.*

**pro|vid|ed** /prəvaɪdɪd/ CONJ If you say that something will happen **provided** or **providing** that something else happens, you mean that the first thing will happen only if the second thing also happens. *siempre que*, *siempre y cuando* ❑ *The banks are prepared to help, provided that he has a specific plan.* *Los bancos están listos para ayudar, siempre que él tenga un plan específico.*

**prov|ince** /prɒvɪns/ (**provinces**) 1 N-COUNT A **province** is a large section of a country that has its own administration. *provincia*, *estado* ❑ *...the Algarve, Portugal's southernmost province.* *...Algarve, la provincia portuguesa situada más al sur.* 2 N-PLURAL **The provinces** are all the parts of a country except

P

the part where the capital is situated. provincia ❑ *...plans to transfer 30,000 government jobs from Paris to the provinces.* *...planes de trasladar 20,000 puestos públicos de París a la provincia.*

**pro|vin|cial** /prəvɪnʃᵊl/ **1** ADJ **Provincial** means connected with the parts of a country away from the capital city. provincial, de la provincia ❑ *...the Quebec and Ontario provincial police.* *...la policía provincial de Quebec y Ontario.* **2** ADJ If you describe someone or something as **provincial,** you disapprove of them because you think that they are old-fashioned and boring. provinciano, pueblerino ❑ *...the company's provincial image.* *...la imagen provinciana de la compañía.*

**pro|vi|sion** /prəvɪʒᵊn/ (**provisions**) **1** N-UNCOUNT The **provision of** something is the act of giving it or making it available to people who need or want it. provisión, aprovisionamiento ❑ *The department is responsible for the provision of services.* *El departamento es responsable de la provisión de servicios.* **2** N-VAR If you make **provision for** something that might happen or that might need to be done, you make arrangements to deal with it. medidas, previsiones ❑ *Has she made provision for her retirement?* *¿Ya tomó medidas para cuando se jubile?* **3** N-COUNT A **provision** in a law or an agreement is an arrangement which is included in it. disposición ❑ *...a provision that allows the president to decide how to spend the money.* *...una medida que permite al presidente decidir cómo gastar el dinero.*

**pro|vi|sion|al** /prəvɪʒənᵊl/ ADJ You use **provisional** to describe something that has been arranged or appointed for the present, but may be changed in the future. provisional, transitorio ❑ *...a provisional government.* *...un gobierno provisional.* • **pro|vi|sion|al|ly** ADV de manera provisional ❑ *We've provisionally booked seats for Thursday.* *Provisionalmente reservamos lugares para el jueves.*

P

**pro|voke** /prəvoʊk/ (**provokes, provoking, provoked**) **1** V-T If you **provoke** someone, you deliberately annoy them and try to make them behave aggressively. provocar, irritar ❑ *I didn't do anything to provoke him.* *Yo no hice nada para provocarlo.* **2** V-T If something **provokes** a reaction, it causes it. provocar, suscitar ❑ *The election result provoked an angry reaction from some students.* *Los resultados de la elección provocaron una airada reacción de algunos estudiantes.*

**pro|vo|lo|ne** /proʊvəloʊni/ also **provolone cheese** N-UNCOUNT **Provolone** is a type of cream-colored, smoked cheese, originally made in Italy. provolone, queso provolone ❑ *...a slice of provolone.* *...una rebanada de provolone.*

**prune** /prun/ (**prunes, pruning, pruned**) **1** N-COUNT A **prune** is a dried plum. ciruela pasa **2** V-T When you **prune** a tree or bush, you cut off some of the branches so that it will grow better the next year. podar ❑ *You have to prune a bush if you want fruit.* *Tienes que podar los arbustos si quieres que den fruto.* • **Prune back** means the same as **prune.** podar ❑ *Cherry trees can be pruned back when they've lost their leaves.* *Los cerezos pueden podarse una vez que pierden las hojas.*

**prun|ing shears** N-PLURAL **Pruning shears** are a gardening tool that look like a pair of strong, heavy scissors, used for cutting the stems of plants. tijeras de podar

**pry** /praɪ/ (**pries, prying, pried**) **1** V-I If someone **pries,** they try to find out about someone else's private affairs, or look at their personal possessions. husmear, fisgonear, curiosear ❑ *We do not want people prying into our affairs.* *No queremos que la gente se meta en nuestros asuntos.* ❑ *She worried that Imelda might think she was prying.* *Le preocupaba que Imelda pensara que la estaba espiando.* **2** V-T If you **pry** something **open** or **pry** it away from a surface, you force it open or away from a surface. forzar ❑ *They pried open a can of blue paint.* *Abrieron a fuerza una lata de pintura azul.* ❑ *They pried the bars apart to free the dog.* *Forzaron los barrotes para soltar al perro.* **3** V-T If you **pry** something such as information **out of** someone, you persuade them to tell you although they may be very unwilling to. sacarle algo a alguien ❑ *She finally managed to pry the news out of me.* *Por fin logró sacarme la noticia.*

**P.S.** /pi ɛs/ also **PS** You write **P.S.** to introduce something that you add at the end of a letter after you have signed it. posdata ❑ *P.S. Please show your friends this letter.* *P.S. Por favor enséñales a tus amigos esta carta.*

**pseudo|pod** /sudəpɒd/ (**pseudopods** or **pseudopodia**) N-COUNT **Pseudopods** are the tiny extensions of cells within some microorganisms that are used for movement and feeding. pseudópodo, seudópodo [TECHNICAL]

| Word Link | psych ≈ mind : psychic, psychology, psychotherapy |
|---|---|

**psy|chic** /saɪkɪk/ (**psychics**) **1** ADJ If you believe that someone is **psychic,** you believe that they have strange mental powers, such as being able to read the minds of other people or to see into the future. psíquico, síquico ❑ *The woman helped police by using her psychic powers.* *La mujer ayudó a la policía gracias a sus poderes psíquicos.* • A **psychic** is someone who seems to be psychic. psíquico, médium, síquico ❑ *...a psychic who can see the future.* *...un psíquico que puede ver el futuro.* **2** ADJ **Psychic** means relating to ghosts and the spirits of the dead. psíquico, síquico ❑ *...his total disbelief in psychic phenomena.* *...su total incredulidad respecto de los fenómenos psíquicos.*

**psycho|logi|cal** /saɪkəlɒdʒɪkᵊl/ ADJ **Psychological** means concerned with a person's mind and thoughts. psicólogico, sicológico ❑ *...physical and psychological abuse.* *...abuso físico y psicológico.* • **psycho|logi|cal|ly** /saɪkəlɒdʒɪkli/ ADV psicológicamente, sicológicamente ❑ *It was very important psychologically for us to succeed.* *Psicológicamente, para nosotros era muy importante lograr el éxito.*

→ see **myth**

**psy|chol|ogy** /saɪkɒlədʒi/ **1** N-UNCOUNT **Psychology** is the scientific study of the human mind and the reasons for people's behavior. psicología, sicología ❑ *...Professor of Psychology at Haverford College.* *...profesor de psicología en el Haverford College.* • **psy|cholo|gist** N-COUNT (**psychologists**) psicólogo o psicóloga, sicólogo o sicóloga ❑ *She is seeing a psychologist.* *Está viendo a un psicólogo.* **2** N-UNCOUNT The **psychology of** a person is the kind of mind that they have, which makes them think or behave in the way that they do. psicología, sicología ❑ ...the psychology of murderers. ...la psicología de los asesinos

**Word Link** psych ≈ mind : psychic, psychology, psychotherapy

**psycho|thera|py** /saɪkoʊθɛrəpi/ N-UNCOUNT **Psychotherapy** is the use of psychological methods in treating people who are mentally ill. psicoterapia, sicoterapia ❑ For milder depressions, certain forms of psychotherapy work well. Ciertas formas de psicoterapia resultan efectivas para depresiones leves. • **psycho|thera|pist** N-COUNT (**psychotherapists**) psicoterapeuta, sicoterapeuta ❑ He arranged for Jim to see a psychotherapist. Arregló que Jim viera a un psicoterapeuta.

**psy|chrom|eter** /saɪkrɒmɪtər/ (**psychrometers**) N-COUNT A **psychrometer** is an instrument that is used to measure the amount of water vapor in the air. psicrómetro [TECHNICAL]

**pub|lic** /pʌblɪk/ **1** N-SING You can refer to people in general as **the public.** público, gente ❑ The park is now open to the public. El parque ya está abierto al público. ❑ The car is not yet for sale to the general public. El auto todavía no está a la venta para el público en general. **2** ADJ **Public** means relating to all the people in a country or community. público ❑ Their policies enjoy strong public support. Sus políticas gozan de un gran apoyo público. **3** ADJ **Public** means relating to the government or state, or things that are done for the people by the state. público ❑ More public spending cuts were announced this week. Esta semana se anunciaron más recortes al gasto público. • **pub|lic|ly** ADV públicamente ❑ ...publicly funded legal services. ...servicios legales financiados con fondos públicos. **4** ADJ **Public** buildings and services are provided for everyone to use. público ❑ ...the New York Public Library. ...la biblioteca pública de Nueva York. ❑ ...public transportation. ...transporte público. **5** ADJ If someone is a **public figure** or in **public life,** many people know who they are because they are often mentioned in newspapers and on television. figura pública, de la vida pública ❑ ...politicians and other public figures. ...políticos y otras figuras públicas. **6** ADJ **Public** is used to describe statements, actions, and events that are made or done in such a way that any member of the public can see them or be aware of them. público ❑ ...a public inquiry. ...una investigación pública. ❑ ...the governor's first public statement on the subject. ...la primera declaración pública del gobernador al respecto. • **pub|lic|ly** ADV públicamente ❑ He never spoke publicly about the incident. Nunca habló en público del incidente. **7** ADJ If a fact is made **public** or becomes **public,** it becomes known to everyone rather than being kept secret. público ❑ The news finally became public. Las noticias acabaron por hacerse públicas. **8** PHRASE If you say or do something **in public,** you say or do it when a group of people are present. en público ❑ He hasn't performed in public in more than 40 years. No se ha presentado en público en más de 40 años.
→ see **library**

**pub|lic as|sis|tance** N-UNCOUNT In the United States, **public assistance** is money that is paid by the government to people who are poor, unemployed, or sick. asistencia pública ❑ More than 70 percent of the citizens are on public assistance. Más del 70 por ciento de los ciudadanos vive de la asistencia pública.

**pub|li|ca|tion** /pʌblɪkeɪʃən/ (**publications**) **1** N-UNCOUNT The **publication** of a book or magazine is the act of printing it and sending it to stores to be sold. publicación ❑ The guide will be ready for publication near Christmas. La guía estará lista para publicación para navidad. **2** N-COUNT A **publication** is a book or magazine that has been published. publicación ❑ He has written for several local New York publications. Ha escrito para varias publicaciones neoyorkinas locales.

**pub|lic de|fend|er** (**public defenders**) N-COUNT A **public defender** is a lawyer who is employed by a city or county to represent people who are accused of crimes but cannot afford to pay for a lawyer themselves. abogado de oficio o abogada de oficio

**pub|lic hous|ing** N-UNCOUNT **Public housing** is apartments or houses that are rented to poor people, usually at a low cost, by the government. vivienda subvencionada ❑ ...the construction of more public housing. ...la construcción de más viviendas subvencionadas.

**pub|lic|ity** /pʌblɪsɪti/ **1** N-UNCOUNT **Publicity** is information or actions that are intended to attract the public's attention to someone or something. publicidad, propaganda ❑ A lot of publicity was given to the talks. Se hizo mucha publicidad a las pláticas. ❑ ...government publicity campaigns. ...campañas publicitarias del gobierno. **2** N-UNCOUNT When the news media and the public show a lot of interest in something, you can say that it is receiving **publicity.** publicidad ❑ The case has generated enormous publicity in Brazil. El caso ha generado mucha publicidad en Brasil.

**Word Partnership** Usar publicity con:

| | |
|---|---|
| V. | **generate** publicity **1** **2**<br>**get** publicity, **receive** publicity, publicity **surrounding** *someone/something* **2** |
| ADJ. | **bad** publicity, **negative** publicity **2** |

**Word Link** ize ≈ making : finalize, modernize, publicize

**pub|li|cize** /pʌblɪsaɪz/ (**publicizes, publicizing, publicized**) V-T If you **publicize** a fact or event, you make it widely known to the public. hacer público, divulgar ❑ The author appeared on television to publicize her latest book. El autor apareció en televisión para promover su último libro.

**pub|lic of|fice** N-UNCOUNT Someone who is in **public office** is in a job that they have been elected to do by the public. puesto público, puesto de elección popular ❑ He has held public office for twenty years. Ha ocupado puestos públicos desde hace veinte años.

**pub|lic re|la|tions** **1** N-UNCOUNT **Public relations** is the part of an organization's work that is concerned with obtaining the public's approval for what it does. The abbreviation **PR** is often used. relaciones públicas, PR [BUSINESS] ❑ Mr. MacGregor runs a public relations firm in London. El Sr. MacGregor dirige una agencia de relaciones públicas en Londres. **2** N-PLURAL You can refer to the opinion that the public has of an organization as **public relations.** relaciones públicas ❑ Cutting costs is important for public relations. Reducir los costos es importante para las relaciones públicas.

P

**pub|lic school** (public schools) 1 N-VAR In the United States, Australia, and many other countries, a **public school** is a school that is supported financially by the government and usually provides free education. *escuela pública, escuela de gobierno, escuela oficial* ❑ *...Milwaukee's public school system. ...el sistema de escuelas públicas de Milwaukee.* 2 N-VAR In Britain, a **public school** is a private school that provides secondary education that parents have to pay for. The students often live at the school during the school term. *colegio privado, internado privado* ❑ *He was headmaster of a public school in the West of England. Era director de un colegio privado en el oeste de Inglaterra.*

**pub|lic sec|tor** N-SING **The public sector** is the part of a country's economy which is controlled or supported financially by the government. *sector público* [BUSINESS] ❑ *...Menem's policy of reducing the public sector. ...la política de Menem de reducir el sector público.*

**pub|lic tele|vi|sion** also **public TV** N-UNCOUNT **Public television** is television that is funded by the government, businesses, and viewers, rather than by advertising. *televisión oficial* ❑ *...the kind of program you only find on public television. ...el tipo de programas que sólo encuentras en la televisión oficial.*

**pub|lic trans|por|ta|tion** N-UNCOUNT **Public transportation** is a system for taking people from one place to another, for example, using buses or trains. *transporte público* ❑ *There is no electricity, no water, no public transportation. No hay electricidad, ni agua, ni transporte público.*

**pub|lish** /pʌblɪʃ/ (publishes, publishing, published) 1 V-T When a company **publishes** a book or magazine, it prints copies of it, which are sent to stores to be sold. *publicar* ❑ *They publish reference books. Publican obras de referencia.* 2 V-T When the people in charge of a newspaper or magazine **publish** a piece of writing or a photograph, they print it in their newspaper or magazine. *publicar, publicarse, sacar* ❑ *The magazine no longer publishes articles about losing weight. En la revista ya no se publican artículos sobre cómo bajar de peso.* 3 V-T If someone **publishes** a book or an article that they have written, they arrange to have it published. *publicar* ❑ *Walker has published four books of her poetry. Walker ha publicado cuatro libros de su poesía.*
→ see **laboratory, printing**

P

**pub|lish|er** /pʌblɪʃər/ (publishers) N-COUNT A **publisher** is a person or a company that publishes books, newspapers, or magazines. *editor o editora* ❑ *The publishers plan to produce a new weekly journal. Los editores piensan producir una nueva revista semanal.*

**pub|lish|ing** /pʌblɪʃɪŋ/ N-UNCOUNT **Publishing** is the profession of publishing books. *edición* ❑ *I had a job in publishing. Tenía un trabajo en una editorial.*

**pud|ding** /pʊdɪŋ/ (puddings) N-VAR A **pudding** is a cooked sweet food made from ingredients such as milk, sugar, flour, and eggs, and is served either hot or cold. *budín, natilla* ❑ *...a banana vanilla pudding. ...una natilla de plátano y vainilla.*
→ see **dessert**

**pud|dle** /pʌdᵊl/ (puddles) N-COUNT A **puddle** is a small, shallow pool of liquid on the ground. *charco* ❑ *The road was shiny with puddles. La carretera brillaba por los charcos.*

**pudgy** /pʌdʒi/ ADJ If you describe someone as **pudgy,** you mean that they are rather fat in an unattractive way. *gordinflón, rechoncho* ❑ *He put a pudgy arm around Harry's shoulder. Puso su brazo bofo en los hombros de Harry.*

**pueb|lo** /pwɛbloʊ/ (pueblos) N-COUNT A **pueblo** is a village, especially in the southwestern United States. *aldea de indios* ❑ *There are several Indian pueblos near Santa Fe. Hay varios pueblos indios cerca de Santa Fe.*

**puff** /pʌf/ (puffs, puffing, puffed) 1 V-T If someone **puffs on** or **at** a cigarette, cigar, or pipe, they smoke it. *dar una fumada, dar una calada, fumar* ❑ *He lit his pipe and puffed on it twice. Prendió su pipa y le dio dos fumadas.* ● **Puff** is also a noun. *fumada, calada* ❑ *I took a puff on the cigarette and started coughing. Le di una fumada al cigarro y empecé a toser.* 2 N-COUNT A **puff of** air or smoke is a small amount of it that is blown out from somewhere. *bocanada, nube* ❑ *The wind caught a sudden puff of dust. El viento levantó una repentina nube de polvo.* 3 V-I If you **are puffing,** you are breathing loudly and quickly with your mouth open because you are out of breath after a lot of physical effort. *resoplar, jadear* ❑ *I could see he was unfit, because he was puffing. Me di cuenta de que no tenía condición física porque jadeaba.* 4 N-COUNT A **puff for** a book, movie, or product is something that is done or said in order to attract people's attention and tell them how good it is. *comentario favorable* [INFORMAL] ❑ *The interview was just a puff for his latest work. La entrevista no fue más que publicidad para su última obra.*

**Pu|lit|zer Prize** /pʊlɪtsər praɪz/ (Pulitzer Prizes) N-COUNT A **Pulitzer Prize** is one of a series of prizes awarded each year in the United States for outstanding achievement in the fields of journalism, literature, and music. *Premio Pulitzer* ❑ *He won the Pulitzer Prize for Poetry. Ganó el Premio Pulitzer de poesía.*

**pull** /pʊl/ (pulls, pulling, pulled) 1 V-T/V-I When you **pull** something, you hold it firmly and use force in order to move it toward you or away from its previous position. *jalar, tirar de, extraer, arrancar* ❑ *The dentist pulled out all his teeth. El dentista le sacó todos los dientes.* ❑ *Erica was pulling at her blonde curls. Erica se jalaba los rizos rubios.* ❑ *I helped pull him out of the water. Ayudé a sacarlo del agua.* ❑ *Someone pulled her hair. Alguien le jaló el pelo.* ● **Pull** is also a noun. *jalón* ❑ *The feather must be removed with a straight, firm pull. La pluma se arranca con un jalón enérgico y firme.* 2 V-T When a vehicle, animal, or person **pulls** a cart or piece of machinery, they are attached to it or hold it, so that it moves along behind them when they move forward. *jalar, arrastrar, tirar de* ❑ *The beast pulled the cart. El animal tiraba del carro.* 3 V-T If you **pull yourself** or **pull** a part of your body in a particular direction, you move your body or a part of your body with effort or force. *estirarse, ponerse* ❑ *Hughes pulled himself*

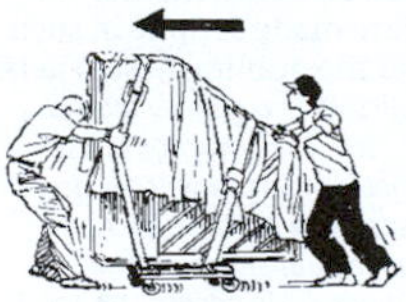

pull

*slowly to his feet. Hughes se puso lentamente de pie.* ❑ *He pulled his arms out of the sleeves. Sacó los brazos de las mangas.* **4** N-COUNT A **pull** is a strong physical force that causes things to move in a particular direction. *fuerza* ❑ *...the pull of gravity. ...la fuerza de la gravedad.* **5** to **pull** your **weight** → see **weight**

▸ **pull away** **1** PHR-VERB When a vehicle or driver **pulls away,** the vehicle starts moving forward. *arrancar(se)* ❑ *I watched him back out of the driveway and pull away. Lo vi sacar el coche y arrancarse.* **2** PHR-VERB If you **pull away from** someone that you have had close links with, you deliberately become less close to them. *separarse, alejarse* ❑ *The Soviet Union began to pull away from Cuba. La Unión Soviética empezó a alejarse de Cuba.*

▸ **pull back** PHR-VERB If someone **pulls back from** an action, they decide not to do it or continue with it, because it could have bad consequences. *echarse para atrás, retirarse* ❑ *He encouraged both sides to pull back from the violence. Instó a ambas partes a no hacer eco de la violencia.*

▸ **pull down** PHR-VERB To **pull down** a building or statue means to deliberately destroy it. *demoler* ❑ *They pulled the offices down, leaving a large open space. Tiraron las oficinas y dejaron un enorme espacio vacío.*

▸ **pull in** PHR-VERB When a vehicle or driver **pulls in** somewhere, the vehicle stops there. *detenerse* ❑ *He pulled in at the side of the road. Se detuvo a un lado de la carretera.*

▸ **pull into** PHR-VERB When a vehicle or driver **pulls into** a place, the vehicle moves into the place and stops there. *estacionarse* ❑ *He pulled into the driveway in front of her garage. Se estacionó frente a la entrada de su garage.*

▸ **pull off** PHR-VERB If you **pull off** something very difficult, you succeed in achieving it. *lograr* ❑ *The National League for Democracy pulled off a victory. La Liga Nacional para la Democracia consiguió una victoria.*

▸ **pull out** **1** PHR-VERB When a vehicle or driver **pulls out,** the vehicle moves out into the road or nearer the center of the road. *arrancar* ❑ *She pulled out into the street. Se incorporó a la circulación.* **2** PHR-VERB If you **pull out of** an agreement, a contest, or an organization, you withdraw from it. *salirse, retirarse* ❑ *The World Bank should pull out of the project. El Banco Mundial debe retirarse del proyecto.* **3** PHR-VERB If troops **pull out of** a place, they leave it. *retirarse, irse* ❑ *Israeli forces agreed to pull out of Ramallah last night. Las fuerzas israelíes aceptaron retirarse de Ramallah anoche.*

▸ **pull over** PHR-VERB When a vehicle or driver **pulls over,** the vehicle moves closer to the side of the road and stops there. *estacionarse* ❑ *I had to pull over and force him to get out. Tuve que estacionarme y obligarlo a bajarse.*

▸ **pull through** PHR-VERB If someone with a serious illness or someone in a very difficult situation **pulls through,** they recover. *reponerse, recuperarse* ❑ *Everyone was very concerned whether he would pull through or not. A todos les preocupaba mucho saber si se recuperaría o no.*

▸ **pull together** **1** PHR-VERB If people **pull together,** they cooperate with each other. *unirse, trabajar en conjunto* ❑ *The nation was urged to pull together to avoid complete chaos. A la nación le urgía hacer un esfuerzo común para evitar el caos absoluto.* **2** PHR-VERB If you are upset or depressed and someone tells you to **pull yourself together,** they are telling you to control your feelings and behave calmly again. *calmarse, recobrar la compostura* ❑ *Pull yourself together, boy! ¡Tranquilízate, muchacho!*

▸ **pull up** PHR-VERB When a vehicle or driver **pulls up,** the vehicle slows down and stops. *parar, detenerse* ❑ *The cab pulled up and the driver jumped out. El taxi se detuvo y el chofer se bajó de un salto.*

**pul|ley** /pʊli/ (**pulleys**) N-COUNT A **pulley** is a device consisting of a wheel over which a rope or chain is pulled in order to lift heavy objects. *polea*

**Pull|man** /pʊlmən/ N-COUNT A **Pullman** or a **Pullman car** on a train is a railway car that has beds for passengers to sleep in. *pullman, carro dormitorio*

**pul|mo|nary cir|cu|la|tion** N-UNCOUNT **Pulmonary circulation** is the flow of blood between the heart and lungs. *circulación pulmonar* → see **cardiovascular system**

**pul|sar** /pʌlsɑr/ (**pulsars**) N-COUNT A **pulsar** is a star that spins very fast and cannot be seen but produces regular radio signals. *pulsar*

**pulse** /pʌls/ (**pulses**) **1** N-COUNT Your **pulse** is the regular beating of blood through your body, which you can feel when you touch particular parts of your body, especially your wrist. *pulso* ❑ *Mahoney's pulse was racing, and he felt confused. A Mahoney se le aceleró el pulso y se sentía confundido.* **2** N-COUNT A **pulse of** electrical current, light, or sound is a temporary increase in its level. *pulsación, impulso* ❑ *...a pulse of radio waves. ...un impulso de ondas radioeléctricas.*

**pump** /pʌmp/ (**pumps, pumping, pumped**) **1** N-COUNT A **pump** is a machine that is used to force a liquid or gas to flow in a particular direction. *bomba* ❑ *...pumps that circulate the fuel around the engine. ...bombas que hacen circular el combustible por el motor.* ❑ *...a gas pump. ...una bomba de gasolina.* **2** V-T To **pump** a liquid or gas in a particular direction means to force it to flow in that direction using a pump. *bombear* ❑ *They've been getting rid of sewage by pumping it out to sea. Se han estado quitando de encima las aguas negras bombeándolas al mar.* **3** V-T If someone **has** their stomach **pumped,** doctors remove the contents of their stomach, for example, because they have swallowed poison or drugs. *lavar el estómago, hacer un lavado de estómago* ❑ *One woman was rushed to the emergency room to have her stomach pumped. Llevaron a una mujer a emergencias para lavarle el estómago.* **4** N-COUNT **Pumps** are women's shoes that do not cover the top part of the foot and are usually made of plain leather. *zapatilla escotada* → see **shoe**

▸ **pump out** PHR-VERB To **pump out** something means to produce or supply it continually and in large amounts. *producir intensivamente* ❑ *Japanese companies have been pumping out plenty of new products. Los productores japoneses han estado sacando muchos productos nuevos.*

▸ **pump up** PHR-VERB If you **pump up** something such as a tire, you fill it with air using a pump. *inflar* ❑ *Pump all the tires up. Infla todas las llantas.*

**pump|kin** /pʌmpkɪn/ (**pumpkins**) N-VAR A **pumpkin** is a large, round, orange vegetable with a thick skin. *calabaza* ❑ *Cut the pumpkin into four and*

P

**Picture Dictionary** punctuation

A: I want to learn to drive; however, cars scare me.
semi-colon period

B: Why not take a driver-training course?
hyphen question mark

A: I'm not ready.
apostrophe

B: I know! If you want, I'll teach you to drive.
exclamation mark comma

A: OK, but remember this: it was your idea, not mine.
colon

*remove the seeds.* *Corta la calabaza en cuatro y quítale las semillas.*

**punch** /pʌntʃ/ (**punches, punching, punched**) **1** V-T If you **punch** someone or something, you hit them hard with your fist. *dar puñetazos, dar trompadas* ❑ *After punching him on the chin she hit him over the head.* *Después de darle un puñetazo en la barbilla, le pegó en la cabeza.* • **Punch** is also a noun. *puñetazo, trompada* ❑ *He was hurting Johansson with body punches in the fourth round.* *En el cuarto round estaba acabando con Johansson, yéndosele al cuerpo.* • **Punch out** means the same as **punch**. *dar puñetazos, dar trompadas* ❑ *I punched out this guy.* *Le di de trompadas a ese fulano.* **2** V-T If you **punch** something such as the buttons on a keyboard, you press them in order to store information on a machine such as a computer or to give the machine a command to do something. *presionar, oprimir, picar* ❑ *Lianne punched the button to call the elevator.* *Lianne oprimió el botón para llamar al elevador.* **3** V-T If you **punch** holes **in** something, you make holes in it by pushing or pressing it with something sharp. *perforar, picar* ❑ *I took a pen and punched a hole in the box.* *Con una pluma le hice un agujero a la caja.* **4** N-COUNT A **punch** is a tool that you use for making holes in something. *perforadora* ❑ *...a three-hole punch.* *...una perforadora de tres hoyos.* **5** N-VAR **Punch** is a drink made from wine, spirits, or fruit juice, mixed with things such as sugar and spices. *ponche* ❑ *...a bowl of punch.* *...una jarra de ponche.*

punch

▸ **punch in** PHR-VERB If you **punch in** a number on a machine or **punch** numbers **into** it, you push the machine's buttons or keys in order to give it a command to do something. *teclear, marcar* ❑ *Punch in your account number on the phone.* *Marca tu número de cuenta en el teléfono.*

**punch|ing bag** (**punching bags**) N-COUNT A **punching bag** is a heavy leather bag, filled with firm material, that hangs on a rope and is used for training by boxers and other athletes. *punching bag, costal de boxeo, costal*

**punc|tu|al** /pʌŋktʃuəl/ ADJ If you are **punctual**, you do something or arrive somewhere at the right time and are not late. *puntual* ❑ *He's always very punctual.* *Siempre es muy puntual.* • **punc|tu|al|ly** ADV *puntualmente, en punto* ❑ *My guest arrived punctually.* *Mi invitado llegó en punto.*

**punc|tu|ate** /pʌŋktʃueɪt/ (**punctuates, punctuating, punctuated**) V-T If an activity or situation **is punctuated by** particular things, it is interrupted by them at intervals. *interrumpir* [WRITTEN] ❑ *The game was punctuated by a series of injuries.* *El juego se vio interrumpido por una serie de lesiones.*

**punc|tua|tion** /pʌŋktʃueɪʃən/ N-UNCOUNT **Punctuation** is the system of signs such as periods, commas, or question marks that you use in writing to divide words into sentences and clauses. *puntuación* ❑ *He was known for his poor grammar and punctuation.* *Se distinguía por su deficiente gramática y puntuación.*
→ see Picture Dictionary: **punctuation**

**punc|tua|tion mark** (**punctuation marks**) N-COUNT A **punctuation mark** is a symbol such as a period, comma, or question mark. *signo de puntuación*

**pun|ish** /pʌnɪʃ/ (**punishes, punishing, punished**) **1** V-T To **punish** someone means to make them suffer in some way because they have done something wrong. *castigar, sancionar* ❑ *I don't think George ever had to punish the children.* *Creo que George nunca tuvo que castigar a los niños.* **2** V-T To **punish** a crime means to punish anyone who commits that crime. *castigar* ❑ *...federal laws to punish crimes such as murder.* *...leyes federales en contra de delitos como el asesinato.*

**pun|ish|ment** /pʌnɪʃmənt/ (**punishments**) **1** N-UNCOUNT **Punishment** is the act of punishing someone or of being punished. *castigo, sanción* ❑ *...the physical punishment of children.* *...el castigo físico en el caso de los niños.* **2** N-VAR A **punishment** is a particular way of punishing someone. *sanción* ❑ *There will be tougher punishments for crimes of violence.* *Habrá sanciones más fuertes para los delitos violentos.* **3** → see also **capital punishment, corporal punishment**

**punk** /pʌŋk/ (**punks**) **1** N-UNCOUNT **Punk** or **punk rock** is rock music that is played in a fast, loud, and aggressive way and is often a protest against conventional attitudes and behavior. Punk rock was particularly popular in the late 1970s. *música punk* **2** N-COUNT A **punk** or a **punk rocker** is a young person who likes punk music and dresses in a very noticeable and unconventional way, for example, by having brightly colored hair and wearing metal chains.

punk ❑ In the 1970s, punks wore safety pins through their cheeks. En los años setenta, los punks se ponían alfileres de seguridad en las mejillas. **3** N-COUNT A **punk** is a young person who behaves in a rude, aggressive, or violent way. *hooligan, vándalo* [INFORMAL] ❑ *Brad Pitt stars as a young punk living in New York's Lower East Side. Brad Pitt representa a un joven vándalo del lado este de Nueva York.*

**Pun|nett square** /pʌnɪt skwɛər/ (**Punnett squares**) N-COUNT A **Punnett square** is a diagram used by biologists to predict the genetic makeup of an organism. *rejilla de Punnett* [TECHNICAL]

**pu|pil** /pyupɪl/ (**pupils**) **1** N-COUNT A **pupil** of a painter, musician, or other expert is someone who studies under that expert and learns his or her skills. *discípulo* ❑ *Goldschmidt became a pupil of the composer Franz Schreker. Goldschmidt llegó a ser discípulo del compositor Franz Schreker.* **2** N-COUNT The **pupils** of a school are the children who go to it. *alumno* ❑ *...schools with over 1,000 pupils. ...escuelas con más de 1,000 alumnos.* **3** N-COUNT The **pupils** of your eyes are the small, round, black holes in the center of them. *pupila* ❑ *The pupils of her eyes widened. Se le dilataron las pupilas.*
→ see **eye**

**pup|pet** /pʌpɪt/ (**puppets**) **1** N-COUNT A **puppet** is a doll that you can move, either by pulling strings that are attached to it or by putting your hand inside its body and moving your fingers. *marioneta, títere* **2** N-COUNT You can refer to a person or country as a **puppet** when you mean that their actions are controlled by a more powerful person or government, even though they may appear to be independent. *títere, instrumento* ❑ *They accused his government of being a puppet of Moscow. Acusaron a su gobierno de ser un títere de Moscú.*

**pup|pet|ry** /pʌpɪtri/ N-UNCOUNT **Puppetry** is the art of entertaining people with puppets. *teatro de títeres, teatro de marionetas*

**pup|py** /pʌpi/ (**puppies**) N-COUNT A **puppy** is a young dog. *perrito, cachorro*

**pur|chase** /pɜrtʃɪs/ (**purchases, purchasing, purchased**) **1** V-T When you **purchase** something, you buy it. *comprar, adquirir* [FORMAL] ❑ *He purchased a ticket. Compró un boleto.* • **pur|chas|er** N-COUNT (**purchasers**) *comprador o compradora* ❑ *The broker will get 5% if he finds a purchaser. El agente recibirá el 5% si encuentra un comprador.* **2** N-UNCOUNT The **purchase of** something is the act of buying it. *compra, adquisición* [FORMAL] ❑ *The company will today announce the purchase of two radio stations. La compañía va a anunciar hoy la adquisición de dos estaciones de radio.* **3** N-COUNT A **purchase** is something that you buy. *compra, lo comprado* [FORMAL] ❑ *She opened the box and looked at her purchase. Abrió la caja y miró su compra.*

**pure** /pyʊər/ (**purer, purest**) **1** ADJ A **pure** substance is not mixed with anything else. *puro, sin mezcla* ❑ *...a carton of pure orange juice. ...un envase de jugo de naranja puro.* • **pu|rity** /pyʊərɪti/ N-UNCOUNT *pureza* ❑ *...their obsession with moral purity. ...su obsesión por la pureza moral.* **2** ADJ Something that is **pure** is clean and does not contain any harmful substances. *puro* ❑ *The air is pure and the crops are free of chemicals. El aire es puro y los cultivos no tienen sustancias químicas.* • **pu|rity** N-UNCOUNT *pureza* ❑ *They worried about the purity of the tap water. Les preocupaba la calidad del agua de la llave.* **3** ADJ **Pure** science or **pure** research is concerned only with theory and not with how this theory can be used in practical ways. *puro* ❑ *Physics isn't just pure science; it has uses. La física no es nada más una ciencia pura, tiene sus aplicaciones.* **4** ADJ **Pure** means complete and total. *genuino* ❑ *...a look of pure surprise. ...una mirada de genuina sorpresa.*
→ see **science**

**pure|ly** /pyʊərli/ ADV You use **purely** to emphasize that the thing you are mentioning is the most important feature or that it is the only thing which should be considered. *únicamente, estrictamente* ❑ *It is a racing machine, designed purely for speed. Es un motor de carreras, diseñado estrictamente para la velocidad.*

**pur|ple** /pɜrpəl/ (**purples**) COLOR Something that is **purple** is of a reddish-blue color. *púrpura, morado, violeta* ❑ *She wore purple and green silk. Iba vestida de seda púrpura y verde.*

**pur|pose** /pɜrpəs/ (**purposes**) **1** N-COUNT The **purpose** of something is the reason for which it is made or done. *objetivo, propósito, fin* ❑ *The purpose of the occasion was to raise money for medical supplies. El objetivo del evento era recaudar fondos para artículos médicos.* ❑ *...the use of nuclear energy for military purposes. ...el uso de la energía nuclear con fines militares.* **2** N-COUNT Your **purpose** is the thing that you want to achieve. *objetivo* ❑ *They might be prepared to harm you in order to achieve their purpose. Podrían incluso hacerte daño con tal de lograr su objetivo.* **3** N-UNCOUNT **Purpose** is the feeling of having a definite aim and of being determined to achieve it. *propósito, objetivo* ❑ *Our teachers have a sense of purpose. Nuestros maestros tienen claro hacia dónde van.* **4** PHRASE If you do something **on purpose,** you do it intentionally. *intencionalmente, a propósito* ❑ *Was it an accident or did David do it on purpose? ¿Fue un accidente o David lo hizo a propósito?*

**Word Partnership** Usar *purpose* con:

| | |
|---|---|
| V. | **serve a** purpose **1**<br>**accomplish a** purpose, **achieve a** purpose **2** |
| ADJ. | **main** purpose, **original** purpose, **primary** purpose, **real** purpose, **sole** purpose **1** **2** |

**purse** /pɜrs/ (**purses, pursing, pursed**) **1** N-COUNT A **purse** is a small bag or a handbag that women carry. *bolso, bolsa, cartera* ❑ *She reached in her purse for her keys. Sacó sus llaves de la bolsa.* **2** V-T If you **purse** your **lips,** you move them into a small, rounded shape. *fruncir* ❑ *She pursed her lips in disapproval. Frunció los labios con desaprobación.*

**pur|sue** /pərsu/ (**pursues, pursuing, pursued**) **1** V-T If you **pursue** a particular aim or result, you make efforts to achieve it, often over a long period of time. *buscar, luchar por, continuar con* [FORMAL] ❑ *He will pursue a trade policy that protects American workers. Luchará por una política comercial que proteja a los trabajadores americanos.* **2** V-T If you **pursue** a particular topic, you try to find out more about it by asking questions. *continuar con, proseguir*

[FORMAL] ❑ *If there has been a mistake, you should pursue the matter with our customer service department.* *Si hubo un error, debe continuar con el asunto con nuestro departamento de servicio al cliente.* **3** V-T If you **pursue** a person, vehicle, or animal, you follow them, usually in order to catch them. *perseguir* [FORMAL] ❑ *She pursued the man who stole the woman's bag.* *Ella persiguió al hombre que robó la bolsa de la mujer.* ● **pur|su|er** N-COUNT (**pursuers**) *perseguidor o perseguidora* ❑ *They could hear the voices of their pursuers.* *Podían oir las voces de sus perseguidores.*

**pur|suit** /pərsu̲t/ (**pursuits**) **1** N-UNCOUNT Your **pursuit of** something is your attempts at achieving it. *búsqueda* ❑ *...his pursuit of excellence.* *...su búsqueda de la excelencia.* ❑ *They frequently move around the country in pursuit of a medical career.* *Frecuentemente se mudan de un lado al otro del país en su lucha por hacer carrera en la medicina.* **2** N-UNCOUNT If you are **in pursuit of** a person, vehicle, or animal, you are chasing them. *en persecución de, a la caza de* ❑ *...a police patrol car in pursuit of a motorcycle.* *...una patrulla de la policía tras un motociclista.* **3** N-COUNT Your **pursuits** are your activities, usually activities that you enjoy when you are not working. *actividad, pasatiempo, recreación* ❑ *They both love outdoor pursuits.* *Ambos disfrutan las actividades al aire libre.*

**push** /pʊ̲ʃ/ (**pushes, pushing, pushed**) **1** V-T/V-I When you **push** something, you use force to make it move away from you or away from its previous position. *empujar, impulsar, mover* ❑ *The woman pushed back her chair and stood up.* *La mujer echó para atrás su silla y se puso de pie.* ❑ *They pushed him into the car.* *Lo empujaron dentro del auto.* ❑ *...a pregnant woman pushing a stroller.* *...una mujer embarazada empujando una carriola.* ❑ *He put both hands on the door and pushed as hard as he could.* *Puso ambas manos en la puerta y empujó con todas sus fuerzas.* ● **Push** is also a noun. *empujón, impulso* ❑ *He gave me a sharp push.* *Me dio un brusco empujón.* **2** V-T/V-I If you **push through** things that are blocking your way or **push** your **way through** them, you use force in order to move past them. *abrirse paso a empujones* ❑ *I pushed through the crowds and on to the escalator.* *Empujé a la gente y llegué a la escalera eléctrica.* ❑ *He pushed his way toward her, laughing.* *Avanzó a fuerza hacia ella, riéndose.* **3** V-T To **push** a value or amount **up** or **down** means to cause it to increase or decrease. *presionar* ❑ *Any shortage could push up grain prices.* *Cualquier escasez presionaría hacia arriba los precios de los granos.* **4** V-T If you **push** someone **to** do something or **push** them **into** doing it, you encourage or force them to do it. *impulsar, obligar* ❑ *She thanked her parents for pushing her to study.* *Agradeció a sus padres haberla impulsado a estudiar.* ❑ *Jason did not push her into stealing the money.* *Jason no la obligó a robar el dinero.* ● **Push** is also a noun. *empujón, impulso* ❑ *We need a push to take the first step.* *Necesitamos un impulso para dar el primer paso.* **5** V-I If you **push for** something, you try very hard to achieve it or to persuade someone to do it. *luchar por, impulsar* ❑ *Consumer groups are pushing for health care changes.* *Los grupos de consumidores están luchando por que se hagan cambios en los servicios de salud.* ● **Push** is also a noun. *impulso, lucha* ❑ *...a push for economic growth.* *...una lucha para que crezca la economía* **6** V-T If someone **pushes** an idea, a point, or a product, they try in a forceful way to convince people to accept it or buy it. *impulsar, empujar, promocionar* ❑ *...an advertising campaign to push a product.* *...una campaña de publicidad para promocionar un producto.* **7** V-T When someone **pushes** drugs, they sell them illegally. *vender ilegalmente* [INFORMAL]

▸ **push ahead** or **push forward** If you **push ahead** or **push forward with** something, you make progress with it. *seguir adelante con* ❑ *The government intends to push ahead with the changes.* *El gobierno pretende seguir con los cambios.*

▸ **push on** PHR-VERB When you **push on**, you continue with a trip or task. *seguir adelante* ❑ *Although the journey was a long and lonely one, Tumalo pushed on.* *Aunque la jornada fuera larga y solitaria, Tumalo seguía adelante.*

▸ **push over** PHR-VERB If you **push** someone or something **over**, you push them so that they fall onto the ground. *derribar, tumbar* ❑ *...people damaging hedges, uprooting trees and pushing over walls.* *...gente que dañaba setos, desarraigaba árboles y derribaba muros.*

▸ **push through** PHR-VERB If someone **pushes through** a law, they succeed in getting it accepted although some people oppose it. *hacer aprobar* ❑ *He tried to push the law through.* *Trató de que la ley fuera aprobada.*

**Thesaurus** *push* Ver también:

v. drive, force, move, pressure, propel, shove, thrust; (*ant.*) pull **1** **2**
encourage, urge **4** **5** **6**

**Word Partnership** Usar *push* con:

N. push **a button, at the** push **of a button,** push **a door** **1**
push **prices,** push **rates** **3**
push **an agenda,** push **legislation** **6**

**push|cart** /pʊ̲ʃkɑrt/ (**pushcarts**) N-COUNT A **pushcart** is a cart from which fruit or other goods are sold in the street. *carretilla, carrito*

**pu̲sh-up** (**push-ups**) N-COUNT **Push-ups** are exercises to strengthen your arms and chest muscles. They are done by lying with your face towards the floor and pushing with your hands to raise your body until your arms are straight. *lagartija, plancha, flexión de brazos*

**put** /pʊ̲t/ (**puts, putting**)

The form **put** is used in the present tense and is the past tense and past participle.

**Put** is used in a large number of expressions that are explained under other words in this dictionary. For example, the expression **to put someone in the picture** is explained at **picture**.

**1** V-T When you **put** something in a particular place or position, you move it into that place or position. *poner, colocar, situar, acomodar* ❑ *Leaphorn put the photograph on the desk.* *Leaphorn acomodó la fotografía en el escritorio.* ❑ *She put her hand on Grace's arm.* *Puso la mano en el brazo de Grace.* **2** V-T If you **put** someone somewhere, you cause them to go there and to stay there for a period of time. *internar, encerrar* ❑ *Rather than put him in the hospital, she is caring for him at home.* *En vez de internarlo en el* *hospital, ella lo está atendiendo en casa.* **3** V-T To **put** someone or something in a particular state or situation means to cause them to be in that state or situation. *poner(se)* ❑ *This is going to put them out of business. Esto los va a sacar del negocio.* ❑ *He was putting himself at risk. Se estaba poniendo en riesgo.* **4** V-T If you **put** your trust, faith, or confidence **in** someone or something, you trust them or have faith or confidence in them. *depositar* ❑ *Are we right to put our confidence in computers? ¿No nos equivocaremos depositando nuestra confianza en las computadoras?* **5** V-T If you **put** time, strength, or energy **into** an activity, you use it in doing that activity. *dedicar, invertir* ❑ *She did not put much energy into the discussion. No le puso muchas ganas a la discusión.* **6** V-T When you **put** an idea or remark in a particular way, you express it in that way. You can use expressions like **to put it simply** and **to put it bluntly** before saying something when you want to explain how you are going to express it. *expresar(se)* ❑ *You can't put that sort of fear into words. No se puede expresar con palabras ese tipo de miedo.* ❑ *He admitted the security forces might have made some mistakes, as he put it. Por como lo dijo, aceptó que las fuerzas de seguridad habían cometido algunos errores.* **7** V-T When you **put a question to** someone, you ask them the question. *preguntar a, hacer una pregunta a, interrogar a* ❑ *Is this fair? Well, I put that question today to the mayor. ¿Es esto justo? Bueno, yo le hice esa pregunta hoy al alcalde.* **8** V-T If you **put** something **at** a particular value or **in** a particular category, you consider that it has that value or that it belongs in that category. *estimar, calcular* ❑ *I would put her age at about 50. Yo diría que tiene unos 50 años.* ❑ *The more technically advanced countries put a high value on science. Los países con mayor avance técnico dan gran valor a la ciencia.* **9** V-T If you **put** written information somewhere, you write, type, or print it there. *poner por escrito* ❑ *They put an announcement in the local paper. Pusieron un anuncio en el periódico local.*

▸ **put across** or **put over** PHR-VERB When you **put** something **across** or **put** it **over,** you succeed in describing or explaining it to someone. *hacer entender* ❑ *If you don't put your point across, you can't expect people to understand. Si no explicas tu punto, no esperes que la gente entienda.*

▸ **put aside** PHR-VERB If you **put** something **aside,** you keep it to be dealt with or used at a later time. *guardar, reservar* ❑ *Encourage children to put aside some money to buy Christmas presents. Impulse a los niños a que ahorren algo de dinero para comprar regalos de navidad.*

▸ **put away** PHR-VERB If you **put** something **away,** you put it into the place where it is normally kept when it is not being used. *guardar* ❑ *She finished putting the milk away. Terminó de guardar la leche en su lugar.* ❑ *She slowly put away her doll. Lentamente guardó su muñeca.*

▸ **put back** PHR-VERB To **put** something **back** means to delay it or arrange for it to happen later than you previously planned. *posponer, retrasar* ❑ *There are always problems which put the opening date back further. Siempre hay problemas que retrasan aún más la fecha de la inauguración.*

▸ **put down** **1** PHR-VERB If you **put** something **down** somewhere, you write or type it there. *anotar, escribir, apuntar* ❑ *Never put anything down on paper which might be used against you. Nunca ponga en papel nada que pueda incriminarlo.* ❑ *The journalists simply put down what they thought they heard. Los periodistas simplemente escribieron lo que creyeron haber oído.* **2** PHR-VERB If you **put down** some money, you pay part of the price of something, and will pay the rest later. *dar un anticipo, dejar un depósito* ❑ *He bought a property for $100,000 and put down $20,000. Compró una propiedad en 100,000 dólares y dio 20,000 de enganche.* **3** PHR-VERB When soldiers, police, or the government **put down** a riot or rebellion, they stop it by using force. *sofocar, aplastar* ❑ *Soldiers went in to put down a riot. Llegaron los soldados para sofocar una revuelta.* **4** PHR-VERB If someone **puts** you **down,** they treat you in an unpleasant way by criticizing you in front of other people or making you appear foolish. *humillar, rebajar* ❑ *I know that I sometimes put people down. Sé que algunas veces humillo a las personas.* **5** PHR-VERB When an animal **is put down,** it is killed because it is dangerous or very ill. *sacrificar, matar* ❑ *The judge ordered the dog to be put down immediately. El juez ordenó que el perro fuera sacrificado de inmediato.*

▸ **put down to** PHR-VERB If you **put** something **down to** a particular thing, you believe that it is caused by that thing. *atribuir* ❑ *He first felt the pain in January, but put it down to tiredness. En enero sintió el dolor por primera vez, pero se lo achacó al cansancio.*

▸ **put forward** PHR-VERB If you **put forward** a plan, proposal, or name, you suggest that it should be considered for a particular purpose or job. *presentar, proponer* ❑ *He has put forward new peace proposals. Presentó nuevas propuestas de paz.*

▸ **put in** **1** PHR-VERB If you **put in** time or effort doing something, you spend that time or effort doing it. *dedicar* ❑ *They've put in time and effort to keep the strike going. Han invertido tiempo y esfuerzo para que la huelga siga.* **2** PHR-VERB If you **put in** a request or **put in for** something, you make a formal request or application. *solicitar, presentar* ❑ *I put in a request for some overtime. Metí mi solicitud de tiempo extra.*

▸ **put off** **1** PHR-VERB If you **put** something **off,** you delay doing it. *posponer, postergar* ❑ *He frequently puts off making difficult decisions. Frecuentemente aplaza las decisiones difíciles.* **2** PHR-VERB If you **put** someone **off,** you make them wait for something that they want. *desalentar* ❑ *He tried to put them off, saying that it was late. Trató de desanimarlos con el pretexto de que era tarde.* **3** PHR-VERB To **put** someone **off** something means to cause them to dislike it or not want it. *provocar rechazo* ❑ *That cake put me off chocolate for life. Ese pastel me quitó para siempre las ganas de comer chocolate.* ❑ *His personal habits put them off. Sus hábitos personales provocaban rechazo.* **4** PHR-VERB If someone or something **puts** you **off,** they take your attention from what you are trying to do and make it more difficult for you to do it. *distraer* ❑ *She said it put her off if I laughed. Dijo que se desconcentraba si me reía.*

▸ **put on** **1** PHR-VERB When you **put on** clothing or makeup, you place it on your body in order to wear it. *poner(se)* ❑ *She put her coat on and went out. Se puso el abrigo y salió.* ❑ *Maximo put on a pair of glasses. Máximo se puso unos anteojos.* **2** PHR-VERB When people **put on** a show, exhibition, or service, they perform it or organize it. *montar, presentar,* organizar ❑ *The band is hoping to put on a show before the end of the year.* *La banda espera presentarse antes de que termine el año.* **3** PHR-VERB If someone **puts on** weight, they become heavier. *engordar* ❑ *I can eat what I want but I never put on weight.* *Coma lo que coma, nunca subo de peso.* **4** PHR-VERB If you **put on** a piece of equipment or a device, you make it start working, for example, by pressing a switch or turning a knob. *prender, encender* ❑ *I put the radio on.* *Prendí el radio.* **5** PHR-VERB If you **put** a record, tape, or CD **on,** you place it in a record, tape, or CD player and listen to it. *poner*

▸ **put out** **1** PHR-VERB If you **put out** an announcement or story, you make it known to a lot of people. *sacar, publicar* ❑ *Thomson put out a statement saying there was no problem between the two men.* *Thomson publicó una declaración para hacer saber que no había ningún problema entre los dos hombres.* **2** PHR-VERB If you **put out** a fire, candle, or cigarette, you make it stop burning. *apagar, extinguir* ❑ *Firemen tried to put out the blaze.* *Los bomberos intentaron apagar el incendio.* **3** PHR-VERB If you **put out** an electric light, you make it stop shining by pressing a switch. *apagar* ❑ *He went to the table and put out the light.* *Se acercó a la mesa y apagó la luz.* **4** PHR-VERB If you **put out** things that will be needed, you place them somewhere ready to be used. *sacar* ❑ *Paula put out her luggage for the bus.* *Paula sacó su equipaje para que lo subieran al camión.* **5** PHR-VERB If you **put out** your **hand,** you move it forward, away from your body. *extender, dar* ❑ *He put out his hand to Alfred.* *Le dio la mano a Alfred.* **6** PHR-VERB If you **put** someone **out,** you cause them trouble because they have to do something for you. *causar molestia* ❑ *"I can give you a lift." — "No, no. I can't put you out like that."* *—Te puedo llevar.—No, no quiero molestarte con eso.*

▸ **put over** → see **put across**

▸ **put through** **1** PHR-VERB When someone **puts through** someone who is making a telephone call, they make the connection that allows the telephone call to take place. *comunicar, pasar la comunicación* ❑ *The operator will put you through.* *La operadora te comunicará.* **2** PHR-VERB If someone **puts** you **through** an unpleasant experience, they make you experience it. *someter* ❑ *We've put them through a lot. Now it's time we let them have a rest.* *Ya les hicimos pasar un mal rato, es tiempo de dejarlos descansar.*

▸ **put together** **1** PHR-VERB If you **put** something **together,** you join its different parts to each other so that it can be used. *armar, montar* ❑ *He took it apart brick by brick, and put it back together again.* *Lo desarmó, pieza por pieza, y lo volvió a armar.* **2** PHR-VERB If you **put together** a group of people or things, you form them into a team or collection. *reunir* ❑ *I put together a group of 125 volunteers.* *Reuní un grupo de 125 voluntarios.* **3** PHR-VERB If you **put together** an agreement, plan, or product, you design and create it. *hacer, preparar* ❑ *We wouldn't have time to put together an agreement.* *No tendríamos tiempo de redactar un convenio.*

▸ **put up** **1** PHR-VERB If people **put up** a wall, building, tent, or other structure, they construct it. *construir, levantar* ❑ *He put up a new office building.* *Construyó un nuevo edificio de oficinas.* **2** PHR-VERB If you **put up** a poster or notice, you attach it to a wall or board. *poner, colgar* ❑ *They're putting new street signs up.* *Están poniendo letreros nuevos en las calles.* **3** PHR-VERB To **put up** resistance to something means to resist it. *oponer* ❑ *The man put up no resistance as they took him from his car.* *El hombre no opuso resistencia cuando lo bajaron del auto.* **4** PHR-VERB If you **put up** money for something, you provide the money that is needed to pay for it. *poner* ❑ *The state agreed to put up $69,000 to start his company.* *El estado aceptó aportar 69,000 dólares para que iniciara su compañía.* **5** PHR-VERB To **put up** the price of something means to cause it to increase. *elevar, incrementar* ❑ *Their friends told them they should put up their prices.* *Sus amigos les dijeron que debían subir sus precios.* **6** PHR-VERB If a person or hotel **puts** you **up,** you stay there for one or more nights. *alojar* ❑ *I wanted to know if she could put me up for a few days.* *Quería saber si ella podría alojarme durante unos días.*

▸ **put up with** PHR-VERB If you **put up with** something, you tolerate or accept it, even though you find it unpleasant or unsatisfactory. *aguantar, soportar* ❑ *They put up with terrible behavior from their son.* *Toleraron el terrible comportamiento de su hijo.*

**putt** /pʌt/ (**putts, putting, putted**) V-T/V-I In golf, when you **putt,** or **putt** the ball, you hit it a short distance on the green. *potear, golpear (la pelota)* ❑ *Turner putted superbly.* *Turner poteó de maravilla.*

**putt|er** /pʌtər/ (**putters, puttering, puttered**) **1** N-COUNT A **putter** is a club used for hitting a golf ball a short distance on the green. *putter* **2** V-I If you **putter around,** you do unimportant but quite enjoyable things, without hurrying. *entretenerse* ❑ *I started puttering around outside.* *Me puse a hacer esto y aquello en el jardín.*

**puz|zle** /pʌzəl/ (**puzzles**) **1** V-T If something **puzzles** you, you do not understand it and feel confused. *confundir* ❑ *My sister puzzles me.* *No entiendo a mi hermana.* • **puz|zled** /pʌzəld/ ADJ *confundido, perplejo* ❑ *Critics remain puzzled by the election results.* *Los críticos siguen desconcertados por los resultados de la elección.* • **puz|zling** ADJ *preocupante, curioso, desconcertante* ❑ *His letter poses a number of puzzling questions.* *Su carta plantea varios problemas difíciles de resolver.* **2** V-I If you **puzzle over** something, you try hard to think of the answer to it or the explanation for it. *reflexionar, pensar* ❑ *In reading Shakespeare, I puzzle over his verse and prose.* *Al leer a Shakespeare, me hago preguntas sobre su poesía y su prosa.* **3** N-COUNT A **puzzle** is a question, game, or toy that you have to think about carefully in order to answer it correctly or put it together properly. *acertijo, juego, adivinanza* ❑ *...a word puzzle.* *...un juego de palabras.* **4** → see also **crossword, jigsaw** **5** N-SING You can describe a person or thing that is hard to understand as **a puzzle.** *enigma, misterio* ❑ *The rise in accidents remains a puzzle.* *El incremento en el número de accidentes sigue siendo inexplicable.*

puzzle

P

**P wave** /pi weɪv/ (**P waves**) also **P-wave** N-COUNT **P waves** are rapid waves of energy that are released in an earthquake. **P wave** is an abbreviation for "pressure wave" or "primary wave". *onda (primaria)* [TECHNICAL]

**pyra|mid** /pɪrəmɪd/ (**pyramids**) N-COUNT A **pyramid** is a three-dimensional shape with a flat base and flat triangular sides that slope upward to a point. *pirámide*

→ see **solid, volume**

**pyro|clas|tic ma|terial** /paɪrəklæstɪk mətɪəriəl/ N-UNCOUNT **Pyroclastic material** is fragments of rock and other substances that are released into the air when a volcano erupts. *material piroclástico* [TECHNICAL]

# Qq

**qt.** **qt.** is a written abbreviation for **quart.** *abreviatura de "quart" (un cuarto de galón), medida equivalente a 0.9463529 litros*

**quad|rat|ic func|tion** /kwɒdrætɪk fʌŋkʃᵊn/ (**quadratic functions**) N-COUNT A **quadratic function** is a mathematical expression that is used in calculating the area within a square. *función cuadrática* [TECHNICAL]

**quad|ru|ple** /kwɒdrʌpəl, -druːpᵊl, kwɒdrʊpᵊl/ (**quadruples, quadrupling, quadrupled**) **1** V-T/V-I If someone **quadruples** an amount or if it **quadruples,** it becomes four times bigger. *cuadruplicar* ❑ *The new system will quadruple the number of phone lines. El nuevo sistema cuadruplicará el número de líneas telefónicas.* **2** PREDET If one amount is **quadruple** another amount, it is four times bigger. *cuádruple, cuádruplo* ❑ *There are about 60 cases of the disease a year; that's quadruple the number we had five years ago. Este año hay aproximadamente 60 casos de la enfermedad, el cuádruple de los que tuvimos hace cinco años.* **3** ADJ You use **quadruple** to indicate that something has four parts or happens four times. *cuádruple, cuádruplo* ❑ *She's a quadruple gold medal winner. Ha ganado cuatro medallas de oro.*

**quad|ru|plet** /kwɒdrʌplɪt, -druːplɪt, kwɒdrʊplɪt/ (**quadruplets**) N-COUNT **Quadruplets** are four children who are born to the same mother at the same time. *cuádruple*

**quag|ga** /kwægə/ (**quaggas**) N-COUNT A **quagga** was a type of zebra that is now extinct. *cuaga (mamífero africano extinto)*

Q

**quail** /kweɪl/ (**quails** or **quail**) N-COUNT A **quail** is a small bird that lives on the ground and is sometimes hunted for sport and eaten. *codorniz*

quail

**quaint** /kweɪnt/ (**quainter, quaintest**) ADJ Something that is **quaint** is attractive because it is old-fashioned. *pintoresco, extraño, curioso* ❑ *It's a small, quaint town with narrow streets. Es un pueblito pintoresco, con callejuelas angostas.*

**quake** /kweɪk/ (**quakes, quaking, quaked**) **1** N-COUNT A **quake** is the same as an **earthquake.** *terremoto, sismo, temblor (de tierra)* [INFORMAL] **2** V-I If you **quake,** you shake, usually because you are very afraid. *temblar, estremecerse* ❑ *I stood there, quaking with fear. Me quedé ahí parado, temblando de miedo.*

**quali|fi|ca|tion** /kwɒlɪfɪkeɪʃᵊn/ (**qualifications**) **1** N-COUNT The **qualifications** you need for an activity or task are the qualities and skills that you need to be able to do it. *calificación, requisito, condición* ❑ *I believe I have all the qualifications to be a good teacher. Creo que cumplo con todos los requisitos para ser un buen maestro.* **2** N-VAR A **qualification** is a detail or explanation that you add to a statement to make it less strong or less general. *limitación, salvedad, reserva* ❑ *The president accepted the peace plan without qualification. El presidente aceptó el plan de paz sin reservas.*

| **Word Partnership** | Usar *qualification* con: |
|---|---|
| N. | qualification **for a job, standards for** qualification **1** |
| ADJ. | **necessary** qualification **1** |
| PREP. | **without** qualification **2** |

**quali|fied** /kwɒlɪfaɪd/ ADJ If you give someone or something **qualified** support or approval, your support or approval is not total because you have some doubts. *con reservas, con salvedad* ❑ *William answered the question with a qualified "yes." William contestó la pregunta afirmativamente, pero con reservas.*

**quali|fi|er** /kwɒlɪfaɪər/ (**qualifiers**) **1** N-COUNT A **qualifier** is an early round or stage in some competitions. *eliminatoria* ❑ *Wang quickly won her three qualifiers. Wang ganó rápidamente sus tres eliminatorias.* **2** → see also **qualify**

**quali|fy** /kwɒlɪfaɪ/ (**qualifies, qualifying, qualified**) **1** V-I If you **qualify** in a competition, you are successful in one part of it and go on to the next stage. *clasificar(se)* ❑ *We qualified for the final by beating Stanford. Nos clasificamos para la final ganándole a Stanford.* • **quali|fi|er** N-COUNT (**qualifiers**) *clasificado* ❑ *Kenya's Robert Kibe was the fastest qualifier for the 800 meters final. Robert Kibe, de Kenia, fue el mejor clasificado para la final de los 800 metros.* **2** V-T If you **qualify** a statement, you make it less strong or less general by adding a detail or explanation to it. *moderar, suavizar* ❑ *He later qualified his remarks by agreeing that the movie was successful. Más tarde moderó sus observaciones, al admitir que la película era exitosa.* **3** V-T/V-I If you **qualify** for something or if something **qualifies** you for it, you have the right to do it or have it. *habilitar, capacitar* ❑ *This course does not qualify you to practice as a therapist. Este curso no lo habilita para ejercer como terapeuta.* **4** V-I When someone **qualifies,** they receive the certificate or license that they need to be able to work in a particular profession. *titularse, recibirse* ❑ *I qualified and started teaching last year. Me titulé y empecé a enseñar el año pasado.* **5** → see also **qualified**

**Word Partnership** Usar *qualify* con:

PREP. qualify **as** ***something*** 1
qualify **for** ***something*** 3
V. **chance to** qualify, **fail to** qualify 1 3 4

**quali|ta|tive** /kwɒlɪteɪtɪv/ ADJ **Qualitative** means relating to the quality of things. *cualitativo* [FORMAL] ❑ *It is impossible to make qualitative choices about the best movies of the year. Es imposible hacer una elección cualitativa de las mejores películas del año.*

**qual|ity** /kwɒlɪti/ (**qualities**) 1 N-UNCOUNT The **quality** of something is how good or bad it is. *calidad* ❑ *The quality of the food here is excellent. La calidad de la comida es excelente aquí.* 2 N-UNCOUNT Something of **quality** is of a high standard. *calidad* ❑ *This is a college of quality. Este es un colegio de calidad.* 3 N-COUNT Someone's **qualities** are their good characteristics. *cualidad* ❑ *Where do your kids get their lovable qualities from? ¿De dónde sacaron sus hijos sus adorables cualidades?* 4 N-COUNT You can describe a particular characteristic of a person or thing as a **quality.** *característica, naturaleza* ❑ *He has a childlike quality. Tiene cierto aire de niño.*

**Word Partnership** Usar *quality* con:

N. **air** quality, quality **of life**, quality **of service**, **water** quality, quality **of work** 1
ADJ. **best/better/good** quality, **high/higher/highest** quality, **low** quality, **poor** quality, **top** quality 1 2

**qual|ity of life** N-SING Someone's **quality of life** is the extent to which their life is comfortable or satisfying. *calidad de vida* ❑ *Before the operation, the patient did not have a very high quality of life. Antes de la operación, la calidad de la vida del paciente no era muy buena.*

**qualm** /kwɑm/ (**qualms**) N-COUNT If you have no **qualms** about doing something, you are not worried that it may be wrong. *escrúpulo (de conciencia)* ❑ *She had no qualms about taking the money. No tuvo escrúpulos (de conciencia) para tomar el dinero.*

**quan|tity** /kwɒntɪti/ (**quantities**) 1 N-VAR A **quantity** is an amount. *cantidad* ❑ *Pour a small quantity of water into a pan. Vierta una pequeña cantidad de agua en un sartén.* 2 N-UNCOUNT Things that are produced or available in **quantity** are produced or available in large amounts. *cantidad* ❑ *These toys are sold in quantity and the quality doesn't seem to matter. Esos juguetes se venden en grandes cantidades y la calidad no parece importar.*
→ see **mathematics**

**quan|tum** /kwɒntəm/ 1 ADJ In physics, **quantum** theory and **quantum** mechanics are concerned with the behavior of atomic particles. *quántum* 2 ADJ A **quantum leap** or **quantum jump** in something is a very great and sudden increase in its size, amount, or quality. *avance espectacular* ❑ *We haven't had a quantum leap in aircraft technology for a few years. En los últimos años no ha habido ningún avance espectacular en la tecnología aeronáutica.*

**quar|an|tine** /kwɔrəntin/ N-UNCOUNT If a person or animal is **in quarantine,** they are kept separate from other people or animals for a period of time, because they have or may have a disease that could spread. *cuarentena*
→ see **illness**

**quar|rel** /kwɔrəl/ (**quarrels, quarreling, quarreled**) 1 N-COUNT A **quarrel** is an angry argument between two or more friends or family members. *pelea, riña* ❑ *I had a terrible quarrel with my brothers. Tuve una riña terrible con mis hermanos.* 2 V-RECIP When two or more people **quarrel,** they have an angry argument. *pelearse, reñir* ❑ *Yes, we quarreled over something silly. Sí, reñimos por una tontería.* 3 N-SING If you say that you have no **quarrel** with someone or something, you mean that you do not disagree with them. *no tener nada contra*

**Word Link** *quart* ≈ *four* : *quart, quarter, quarterback*

**quart** /kwɔrt/ (**quarts**) N-COUNT A **quart** is a unit of volume that is equal to two pints. *cuarto (de galón), medida equivalente a 0.9463529 litros* ❑ *Use a quart of milk. Utilice un cuarto de leche.*
→ see **measurement**

**quar|ter** /kwɔrtər/ (**quarters**) 1 N-COUNT A **quarter** is one of four equal parts of something. *cuarto, cuarta parte* ❑ *A quarter of the residents are over 55 years old. La cuarta parte de los residentes es mayor de 55 años de edad.* ❑ *Prices have fallen by a quarter since January. Los precios han caído el 25 por ciento desde enero.* ● **Quarter** is also a predeterminer. *cuarto, cuarta parte* ❑ *The planet is about a quarter the size of the moon. El planeta es aproximadamente una cuarta parte del tamaño de la luna.* ● **Quarter** is also an adjective. *cuarto, cuarta parte* ❑ *...the past quarter century. ...el último cuarto de siglo.* 2 N-COUNT A **quarter** is an American or Canadian coin that is worth 25 cents. *moneda de veinticinco centavos* 3 N-COUNT A **quarter** is a fixed period of three months. *trimestre* ❑ *Results for the third quarter are due on October 31. Los resultados del tercer trimestre deben estar listos el 31 de octubre.* 4 N-UNCOUNT; N-SING When you are telling the time, you use **quarter** to talk about the fifteen minutes before or after an hour. For example, 8:15 is **quarter after** eight and 8:45 is a **quarter of** nine. You can also say that 8:15 is **quarter past** eight, and 8:45 is **quarter to** nine. *cuarto* 5 N-COUNT A particular **quarter** of a town is a part of the town where a particular group of people traditionally live or work. *barrio* ❑ *I work in the Chinese quarter. Trabajo en el barrio chino.* 6 PHRASE If you do something **at close quarters,** you do it very near to a particular person or thing. *desde cerca* ❑ *You can watch aircraft take off or land at close quarters. Se puede ver despegar y aterrizar los aviones desde cerca.*
→ see **time**

**Word Partnership** Usar *quarter* con:

N. quarter **(of a) century**, quarter **(of a) pound** 1
ADJ. **first/fourth/second/third** quarter 3
PREP. **for the** quarter, **in the** quarter 3
quarter **after**, quarter **of**, quarter **past**, quarter **to** 4

**quarter|back** /kwɔrtərbæk/ (**quarterbacks**) N-COUNT In football, a **quarterback** is the player on the attacking team who begins each play and

q

who decides which play to use. mariscal de campo, quarterback

**quar|ter|final** /kwɔrtərfaɪnᵊl/ (**quarterfinals**) N-COUNT A **quarterfinal** is one of the four games in a competition which decides which four players or teams will compete in the semifinals. *cuarto de final*

**quar|ter|ly** /kwɔrtərli/ ADJ A **quarterly** event happens four times a year, at intervals of three months. *trimestral* ❑ *...the latest Bank of Japan quarterly report. ...el último informe trimestral del Banco de Japón.* • **Quarterly** is also an adverb. *trimestralmente* ❑ *Your money can be paid quarterly or annually. Se le puede pagar su dinero trimestral o anualmente.*

**quar|ter note** (**quarter notes**) N-COUNT A **quarter note** is a musical note that has a time value equal to two eighth notes. *negra, semínima*

**quar|tet** /kwɔrtɛt/ (**quartets**) **1** N-COUNT A **quartet** is a group of four people who play musical instruments or sing together. *cuarteto* **2** N-COUNT A **quartet** is a piece of music for four instruments or four singers. *cuarteto*

**qua|sar** /kweɪzɑr/ (**quasars**) N-COUNT A **quasar** is an object far away in space that produces bright light and radio waves. *quasar*

**queen** /kwin/ (**queens**) **1** N-TITLE; N-COUNT A **queen** is a woman who rules a country as its monarch. *reina* ❑ *...Queen Elizabeth. ...la reina Elizabeth.* **2** N-COUNT In chess, the **queen** is the most powerful piece, which can be moved in any direction. *reina* **3** N-COUNT A **queen** is a playing card with a picture of a queen on it. *reina* ❑ *...the queen of spades. ...la reina de espadas.*
→ see **chess**

**que|ry** /kwɪəri/ (**queries, querying, queried**) **1** N-COUNT A **query** is a question, especially one that you ask an organization, publication, or expert. *duda* ❑ *If you have any queries, please do not hesitate to contact us. Si tiene alguna duda, por favor, comuníquese con nosotros.* **2** V-T If you **query** something, you check it by asking about it because you are not sure if it is correct. *preguntar por, consultar* ❑ *There's a number you can call to query your bill. Hay un número al que puedes llamar para consultar sobre tu factura.* **3** V-T To **query** means to ask a question. *preguntar, inquirir* ❑ *"Is there something else?" Ray queried. —¿Algo más?—inquirió Ray.*

Q

**quest** /kwɛst/ (**quests**) N-COUNT A **quest** is a long and difficult search for something. *búsqueda* [LITERARY] ❑ *My quest for a better bank continues. Sigo buscando un mejor banco.*

**ques|tion** /kwɛstʃᵊn/ (**questions, questioning, questioned**) **1** N-COUNT A **question** is something that you say or write in order to ask a person about something. *pregunta* ❑ *They asked a lot of questions about her health. Hicieron muchas preguntas sobre su salud.* **2** V-T If you **question** someone, you ask them a lot of questions about something. *preguntar, hacer preguntas, interrogar* ❑ *The doctor questioned Jim about his parents. El médico interrogó a Jim sobre sus padres.* • **ques|tion|er** N-COUNT (**questioners**) *interrogador o interrogadora* ❑ *He agreed with the questioner. Estuvo de acuerdo con el interrogador.* • **ques|tion|ing** N-UNCOUNT *interrogatorio* ❑ *The police want thirty-two people for questioning. La policía busca a treinta y dos personas para someterlas a interrogatorio.* **3** V-T If you **question** something, you have or express doubts about it. *dudar de, poner en duda, poner en tela de juicio* ❑ *They never question the doctor's decisions. Nunca ponen en duda las decisiones del médico.* **4** N-SING If you say that there is some **question** about something, you mean that there is doubt or uncertainty about it. If something is **in question** or has been **called into question,** doubt or uncertainty has been expressed about it. *duda* ❑ *There's no question about their success. No hay duda sobre su éxito.* **5** N-COUNT A **question** is a problem, matter, or point which needs to be considered. *cuestión* ❑ *The question of nuclear energy is complex. La cuestión de la energía nuclear es compleja.* **6** N-COUNT The **questions** on an examination are the problems that test your knowledge or ability. *pregunta* ❑ *That question came up on the test. Esa pregunta venía en el examen.* **7** PHRASE The person, thing, or time **in question** is one which you have just been talking about. *(cosa) en cuestión, (cosa) de que se trate* ❑ *Add up all your income over the time in question. Sume todos sus ingresos durante el periodo en cuestión.* **8** PHRASE If you say that something is **out of the question,** it is completely impossible or unacceptable. *imposible, inaceptable, impensable* ❑ *An expensive vacation is out of the question for him. Unas vacaciones caras son impensables para él.* **9** PHRASE If you say **there is no question of** something happening, you are emphasizing that it is not going to happen. *no hay posibilidad de hacer algo* ❑ *There was no question of visiting her school friends. "Ni pensar en que visitara a sus amigas de la escuela.*

**Word Partnership** Usar *question* con:

| | |
|---|---|
| V. | **answer a** question, **ask a** question, **beg the** question, **pose a** question, **raise a** question **1** |
| N. | **answer/response to a** question **1** |
| ADJ. | **difficult** question, **good** question, **important** question **1** |

**ques|tion|able** /kwɛstʃənəbᵊl/ ADJ If you say that something is **questionable,** you mean that it is not completely honest or reasonable. *discutible, dudoso, sospechoso* [FORMAL] ❑ *These are questionable business practices. Estas prácticas comerciales son discutibles.*

**ques|tion mark** (**question marks**) N-COUNT A **question mark** is the punctuation mark ? which is used in writing at the end of a question. *signo de interrogación* ❑ *Why does the title of the show "Who Wants To Be A Millionaire" not have a question mark at the end? ¿Por qué el título del espectáculo "Quién quiere ser millonario" no está entre signos de interrogación?*
→ see **punctuation**

**ques|tion|naire** /kwɛstʃənɛər/ (**questionnaires**) N-COUNT A **questionnaire** is a written list of questions which are answered by a lot of people in order to provide information for a report or a survey. *cuestionario* ❑ *Each person will fill out a five-minute questionnaire. Cada persona llenará un cuestionario de cinco minutos.*

**quick** /kwɪk/ (**quicker, quickest**) **1** ADJ

## Word Web quilt

The Hmong* tribes are famous for their colorful **quilts**. Many people think of a quilt as a bed covering. But these **textiles** feature pictures that tell stories about the people who made them. A favorite story shows how the Hmong fled from China to southeast Asia in the early 1800s. The story sometimes shows the quiltmaker arriving in a new country. The seamstress **sews** small pieces of colorful **fabric** together to make the **design**. The needlework is very complicated. It includes cross-stitching, **embroidery**, and appliqué. A common border **pattern** is a design that represents mountains—the Hmong's original home.

*Hmong: a group of people who live in the mountains of China, Vietnam, Laos, and Thailand.*

Someone or something that is **quick** moves or does things with great speed. *rápido, veloz* ❑ *You'll have to be quick. Tienes que ser rápido.* ● **quick|ly** ADV *rápidamente, rápido, velozmente* ❑ *Cussane worked quickly. Cussane trabajó rápidamente.* ● **quick|ness** N-UNCOUNT *rapidez* ❑ *The program is for athletes who want to improve their speed, agility, and quickness. El programa es para los atletas que quieran mejorar su velocidad, agilidad y rapidez.* **2** ADJ Something that is **quick** takes or lasts only a short time. *rápido* ❑ *He took a quick look around the room. Echó una rápida mirada por el cuarto.* ● **quick|ly** ADV *rápidamente, rápido* ❑ *You can get fit quite quickly if you exercise. Puede ponerse en forma muy rápidamente si hace ejercicio.* **3** ADJ **Quick** means happening with very little delay. *rápido* ❑ *We are hoping for a quick end to the strike. Esperamos que la huelga tenga un fin rápido.* ● **quick|ly** ADV *rápidamente, rápido* ❑ *We need to get it back as quickly as possible. Es necesario que lo recuperemos tan rápido como sea posible.*

**Thesaurus** *quick* Ver también:

ADJ. brisk, fast, rapid, speedy, swift; (*ant.*) slow **1**

**Word Partnership** Usar *quick* con:

N. quick **learner** **1**
quick **glance**, quick **kiss**, quick **look**, quick **question**, quick **smile** **2**
quick **action**, quick **profit**, quick **response**, quick **start**, quick **thinking** **3**

**quick study** (**quick studies**) N-COUNT If you describe someone as a **quick study**, you mean that they are able to learn or memorize things very quickly. *perspicaz* ❑ *She's a quick study. She sees a thing once and remembers it. Es muy perspicaz. Ve algo una sola vez y lo memoriza de inmediato.*

**qui|et** /kwaɪɪt/ (**quieter, quietest, quiets, quieting, quieted**) **1** ADJ Someone or something that is **quiet** makes only a small amount of noise. *callado* ❑ *Tania kept the children reasonably quiet. Tania mantuvo a los niños razonablemente callados.* ● **qui|et|ly** ADV *calladamente, discretamente* ❑ *The officers spoke so quietly that we couldn't hear anything they said. Los policías hablaron tan calladamente que no pudimos oír nada de lo que decían.* ● **qui|et|ness** N-UNCOUNT *silencio, tranquilidad* ❑ *I liked the smoothness and quietness of the flight. Me gustó la suavidad y el silencio del vuelo.* **2** ADJ If a place, situation, or time is **quiet**, there is no excitement, activity, or trouble. *tranquilo* ❑ *It's in a quiet little village. Está en un pueblito tranquilo.* ● **qui|et|ly** ADV *tranquilamente* ❑ *He spends his free time quietly on his farm. Pasa su tiempo libre tranquilamente en su rancho.* ● **qui|et|ness** N-UNCOUNT *tranquilidad, quietud* ❑ *He read the letter in the quietness of the morning. Leyó la carta en la tranquilidad de la mañana.* **3** ADJ If you are **quiet**, you are not saying anything. *callado* ❑ *I told them to be quiet and go to sleep. Les dije que se callaran y se fueran a dormir.* ● **qui|et|ly** ADV *silenciosamente, en silencio* ❑ *Amy stood quietly in the doorway. Amy se quedó parada en silencio en la entrada.* **4** V-T/V-I If someone or something **quiets** or if you **quiet** them, they become less noisy, less active, or silent. *callar(se)* ❑ *The group of people quieted as Derek and Billy walked past. El grupo se calló cuando Derek y Billy pasaron junto a ellos.* **5** V-T To **quiet** fears or complaints means to persuade people that there is no good reason for them. *tranquilizar, calmar* ❑ *Music seemed to quiet her worries. La música pareció calmar su preocupación.* **6** PHRASE If you **keep quiet about** something or **keep** something **quiet**, you do not say anything about it. *callar, guardar silencio* ❑ *I told her to keep quiet about it. Le dije que guardara silencio al respecto.*

**Word Partnership** Usar *quiet* con:

V. **be** quiet, **keep** quiet **1**
ADV. **really** quiet, **relatively** quiet, **too** quiet, **very** quiet **1**–**3**
N. quiet **day/evening/night**, quiet **life**, quiet **neighborhood/street**, **peace and** quiet, quiet **place/spot** **2**

**quilt** /kwɪlt/ (**quilts**) **1** N-COUNT A **quilt** is a bed cover made by sewing layers of cloth together, usually with different colors sewn together to make a design. *colcha* ❑ *An old quilt was on the bed. Había una colcha vieja sobre la cama.* **2** N-COUNT A **quilt** is the same as a **comforter**. *colcha, edredón* → see Word Web: quilt

**quilt|ing** /kwɪltɪŋ/ N-UNCOUNT **Quilting** is the activity of making a quilt. *acolchar, hacer colchas* ❑ *She does a lot of quilting. Hace muchas colchas.*

**quin|tu|plet** /kwɪntʌplɪt, -tuplɪt, kwɪntʊplɪt/

q

(**quintuplets**) N-COUNT **Quintuplets** are five children who are born to the same mother at the same time. quíntuple

**quit** /kwɪt/ (**quits, quitting**)

The form **quit** is used in the present tense and is the past tense and past participle.

**1** V-T/V-I If you **quit**, or **quit** your job, you choose to leave it. dejar [INFORMAL] ❑ *Christina quit her job last year to stay home with her young son.* *Christina dejó su trabajo el año pasado para quedarse en la casa con su hijo menor.* **2** V-T If you **quit** an activity or **quit** doing something, you stop doing it. dejar de ❑ *Quit acting like you don't know.* *Deja de actuar como si no lo supieras.* **3** V-T If you **quit** a place, you leave it completely and do not go back to it. dejar ❑ *He quit school at the age of 16.* *Dejó la escuela a los 16.* **4** PHRASE If you say that you are going to **call it quits**, you mean that you have decided to stop doing something or being involved in something. darse por satisfecho ❑ *They raised $630,000 from supporters, and then called it quits.* *Recaudaron 630,000 dólares entre sus seguidores y se dieron por satisfechos.*

**quite** /kwaɪt/ **1** ADV You use **quite** to indicate that something is true to a fairly great extent. **Quite** is not as strong as "very." bastante ❑ *I felt quite bad about it at the time.* *Me sentí medio mal por eso en el momento.* ❑ *You need to do quite a bit of work.* *Necesitas trabajar muchísimo.* **2** ADV You use **quite** to emphasize what you are saying. totalmente, muy ❑ *I made it quite clear again and again.* *Se lo dije muy claramente una y otra vez.* ❑ *My position is quite different.* *Mi posición es totalmente diferente.* **3** ADV You use **quite** after a negative to make what you are saying weaker or less definite. muy ❑ *Something here is not quite right.* *Algo no anda muy bien aquí.* **4** PREDET You use **quite** in front of a noun group to emphasize that a person or thing is very impressive or unusual. todo un ❑ *He's quite a character.* *Es todo un personaje.*

**quiz** /kwɪz/ (**quizzes, quizzing, quizzed**) **1** N-COUNT A **quiz** is a test, game, or competition in which someone tests your knowledge by asking you questions. serie de preguntas, concurso ❑ *We'll have a quiz after we visit the museum.* *Haremos un concurso después de visitar el museo.* **2** N-COUNT A **quiz** is a short test that a teacher gives to a class. examen ❑ *We had a vocabulary quiz today in English class.* *Hoy tuvimos un examen de vocabulario en la clase de inglés.* **3** V-T If you **are quizzed** by someone about something, they ask you questions about it. preguntar, interrogar ❑ *I quizzed him about his income.* *Le pregunté por sus ingresos.*

Q

**quo|ta** /kwoʊtə/ (**quotas**) **1** N-COUNT A **quota** is the limited number or quantity of something which is officially allowed. cuota ❑ *There's a quota of four tickets per person.* *Hay una cuota de cuatro boletos por persona.* **2** N-COUNT Someone's **quota of** something is their expected or deserved share of it. cuota, parte ❑ *She's had the usual quota of teenage problems.* *Tuvo su cuota normal de problemas de adolescencia.*

**quo|ta|tion** /kwoʊteɪʃᵊn/ (**quotations**) **1** N-COUNT A **quotation** is a sentence or phrase taken from a book, poem, speech, or play, which is repeated by someone else. cita ❑ *He used quotations from Martin Luther King Jr. in his lecture.* *Empleó citas de Martin Luther King hijo en su conferencia.* **2** N-COUNT When someone gives you a **quotation,** they tell you how much they will charge to do a particular piece of work. presupuesto, cotización ❑ *Get several written quotations before you agree on a price.* *Solicite varios presupuestos por escrito antes de acordar el precio.*

**quo|ta|tion mark** (**quotation marks**) N-COUNT **Quotation marks** are punctuation marks that are used in writing to show where speech or a quotation begins and ends. They are usually written or printed as "...". comillas

**quote** /kwoʊt/ (**quotes, quoting, quoted**) **1** V-T/V-I If you **quote** someone as saying something or **quote** from something, you repeat what someone has written or said. citar ❑ *I gave the letter to the reporter and he quoted from it.* *Le di la carta al periodista y él citó algunos pasajes.* **2** N-COUNT A **quote from** a book, poem, play, or speech is a passage or phrase from it. cita **3** V-T If you **quote** something such as a law or a fact, you state it because it supports what you are saying. citar ❑ *The congresswoman quoted figures to prove her point.* *La legisladora citó algunas cifras para probar su dicho.* **4** V-T If someone **quotes** a price **for** doing something, they say how much money they would charge you for it. presupuestar, cotizar ❑ *A travel agent quoted her $260 for a flight from Boston to New Jersey.* *Un agente de viajes le presupuestó 260 dólares por un vuelo de Boston a Nueva Jersey.* **5** N-COUNT A **quote for** a piece of work is the price that someone says they will charge you for it. presupuesto, cotización ❑ *Always get a written quote for any repairs needed.* *Solicite siempre un presupuesto de toda reparación que necesite.* **6** N-PLURAL **Quotes** are the same as **quotation marks.** comillas [INFORMAL] ❑ *The word "remembered" is in quotes.* *La palabra "recordado" está entre comillas.*

**Thesaurus** *quote* Ver también:

V. cite, recite, repeat **1** **3**
N. estimate, price **5**

# Rr

**rab|bi** /ræbaɪ/ (**rabbis**) N-COUNT; N-TITLE A **rabbi** is a Jewish religious leader. *rabino*

rabbit

**rab|bit** /ræbɪt/ (**rabbits**) N-COUNT A **rabbit** is a small, furry animal with long ears. Rabbits are sometimes kept as pets, or live wild in holes in the ground. *conejo*

**race** /reɪs/ (**races, racing, raced**) **1** N-COUNT A **race** is a competition to see who is the fastest, for example in running, swimming, or driving. *carrera* **2** V-T/V-I If you **race,** you take part in a race. *correr, jugar una carrera, echar(se) una carrera* ❑ *In the 10 years I raced in Europe, 30 drivers were killed. En los diez años que corrí en Europa, murieron treinta pilotos.* ❑ *We raced them to the top of the hill. Nos echamos una carrera a la cima del cerro.* **3** N-COUNT A **race** is a situation in which people or organizations compete with each other for power or control. *contienda* ❑ *He's in the race for the governor of Oregon. Participa en la contienda para gobernador de Oregon.* **4** N-VAR A **race** is one of the major groups which human beings can be divided into according to their physical features, such as the color of their skin. *raza* ❑ *The college welcomes students of all races. El colegio da la bienvenida a estudiantes de todas las razas.* **5** V-I If you **race** somewhere, you go there as quickly as possible. *correr* ❑ *He raced across town to the hospital. Corrió a través del pueblo hasta el hospital.* **6** V-I If your mind **races,** or if thoughts **race** through your mind, you think very fast about something, especially when you are in a difficult or dangerous situation. *agolparse las ideas en la cabeza* ❑ *I sounded calm but my mind was racing. Parecía calmado, pero las ideas se me agolpaban en la cabeza.* **7** V-I If your heart **races,** it beats very quickly because you are excited or afraid. *latir apresuradamente* ❑ *Kate felt her heart racing. Kate sentía latir su corazón apresuradamente.* **8** → see also **racing** **9** PHRASE You describe a situation as a **race against time** when you have to work very fast in order to do something before a particular time. *una carrera contra el tiempo* ❑ *The rescue operation was a race against time. La operación de rescate fue una carrera contra el tiempo.*

**race|way** /reɪsweɪ/ (**raceways**) N-COUNT A **raceway** is a racetrack. *autódromo, pista de carreras*

**ra|cial** /reɪʃᵊl/ ADJ **Racial** describes things relating to people's race. *racial* ❑ *...the protection of racial minorities. ...la protección de las razas minoritarias.* ● **ra|cial|ly** ADV *racialmente* ❑ *...children of racially mixed marriages. ...hijos de matrimonios mixtos (matrimonios de razas diferentes).*

| **Word Partnership** | Usar *racial* con: |
| --- | --- |
| N. | racial **differences**, racial **discrimination**, racial **diversity**, racial **equality**, racial **groups**, racial **minorities**, racial **prejudice**, racial **tensions** |

**rac|ing** /reɪsɪŋ/ N-UNCOUNT **Racing** refers to races between animals, especially horses, or between vehicles. *carreras*
→ see **bicycle**

**rac|ist** /reɪsɪst/ (**racists**) ADJ If you describe people, things, attitudes, or behavior as **racist,** you disapprove of them because they are influenced by the belief that some people are inferior because they belong to a particular race. *racista* ❑ *We live in a racist society. Vivimos en una sociedad racista.* ● A **racist** is someone who is racist. *racista* ❑ *...white racists. ...racistas blancos.* ● **rac|ism** N-UNCOUNT *racismo* ❑ *The level of racism is increasing. El racismo está aumentando.*

**rack** /ræk/ (**racks, racking, racked**)

The spelling **wrack** is also used for meaning **2**.

**1** N-COUNT A **rack** is a frame or shelf, usually with bars or hooks, that is used for holding things or for hanging things on. *estante* ❑ *...a luggage rack. ...un portaequipaje.* **2** V-T If someone **is racked by** something such as illness or anxiety, it causes them great suffering or pain. *sufrir dolores atroces* ❑ *His body was racked by pain. Sufría dolores atroces en todo el cuerpo.* **3** PHRASE **Off-the-rack** clothes or goods are made in large numbers, rather than being made specially for a particular person. *de confección* ❑ *...an off-the-rack dress. ...un vestido de confección.*

**rack|et** /rækɪt/ (**rackets**)

The spelling **racquet** is also used for meaning **3**.

**1** N-SING A **racket** is a loud, unpleasant noise. *jaleo, bulla* ❑ *The children were making a racket. Los niños estaban armando un jaleo.* **2** N-COUNT You can refer to an illegal activity used to make money as a **racket.** *fraude organizado, tinglado, intriga* [INFORMAL] ❑ *...an international smuggling racket. ...una intriga internacional de contrabando.* **3** N-COUNT A **racket** is an oval-shaped bat with strings across it, which is used in games such as tennis. *raqueta*

racket

**rac|quet|ball** /rækɪtbɔl/ N-UNCOUNT **Racquetball** is a game which is similar to squash but which uses a different ball and court

## Word Web radio

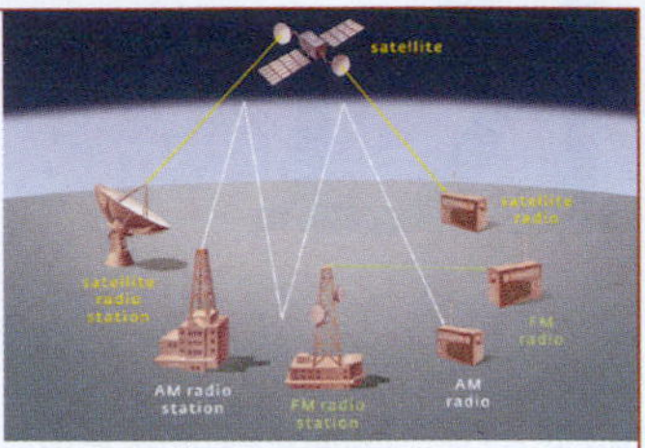


**Radio's** first use was for **communication** between ships. Ships also radioed **stations** on land. In 1912, the *Titanic* sank in the North Atlantic with more than 2,000 people on board. A radio call to a nearby ship helped save a third of the passengers. What we call a radio is actually a **receiver**. The **waves** it receives come from a **transmitter**. Radio is an important source of **entertainment**. AM radio carries all kinds of radio **programs**. **Listeners** often prefer musical programs on the FM waveband or from **satellites** because the sound quality is better.

size. *juego parecido al frontenis*

**Word Link** *rad ≈ ray : radar, radiation, radio*

**ra|dar** /reɪdɑr/ (**radars**) N-VAR **Radar** is a way of discovering the position or speed of objects such as aircraft or ships when they cannot be seen, by using radio signals. *radar* ❑ *...a ship's radar screen. ...la pantalla de radar de un barco.*
→ see **bat, forecast**

**ra|dial sym|me|try** N-UNCOUNT An organism that has **radial symmetry** has a body that resembles the pattern you get when straight lines are drawn from the center of a circle to a number of points around the edge. Compare **bilateral symmetry**. *simetría radial* [TECHNICAL]

**ra|dia|tion** /reɪdieɪʃᵊn/ **1** N-UNCOUNT **Radiation** consists of very small particles of a radioactive substance. Large amounts of radiation can cause illness and death. *radiación* ❑ *...the effects of radiation. ...los efectos de la radiación.* **2** N-UNCOUNT **Radiation** is energy, especially heat, that comes from a particular source. *radiación* ❑ *...energy radiation from the stars. ...la radiación de energía de las estrellas.*
→ see **cancer, greenhouse effect, wave**

**Word Partnership** Usar *radiation* con:

ADJ. **nuclear** radiation **1**
N. radiation **levels**, radiation **therapy/treatment** **1**
radiation **damage**, **effects of** radiation, **exposure to** radiation **1** **2**

**ra|dia|tive zone** /reɪdieɪtɪv zoʊn/ (**radiative zones**) N-COUNT The **radiative zone** is the area of the sun around the core, where energy travels in the form of radiation. *zona de radiación* [TECHNICAL]

**radi|cal** /rædɪkᵊl/ (**radicals**) **1** ADJ **Radical** changes and differences are very important and great in degree. *radical* ❑ *...radical economic reforms. ...reformas económicas radicales.* ● **radi|cal|ly** /rædɪkli/ ADV *radicalmente* ❑ *...people with radically different beliefs. ...gente con creencias radicalmente distintas.* **2** ADJ **Radical** people believe that there should be great changes in society and try to bring about these changes. *radical* ❑ *...a radical leader. ...un dirigente radical.* ● A **radical** is someone who has radical views. *radical* ❑ *...student radicals. ...estudiantes radicales.*

**ra|dio** /reɪdioʊ/ (**radios, radioing, radioed**) **1** N-UNCOUNT **Radio** is the broadcasting of programs for the public to listen to, by sending out signals from a transmitter. *radio* ❑ *The event was broadcast on local radio. El acto fue transmitido por la radio local.* **2** N-SING You can refer to the programs broadcast by radio stations as **the radio**. *radio* ❑ *A lot of people listen to the radio. Mucha gente escucha la radio.* **3** N-COUNT A **radio** is the piece of equipment that you use in order to listen to radio programs. *radio* ❑ *He turned on the radio. Encendió el radio.* **4** N-UNCOUNT **Radio** is a system of sending and receiving sound using electronic signals. *radio* ❑ *They are in radio contact with the leader. Están en contacto por radio con el dirigente.* **5** N-COUNT A **radio** is a piece of equipment that is used for sending and receiving spoken messages. *radio* ❑ *The policeman called for extra officers on his radio. El policía solicitó más agentes por su radio.* **6** V-T/V-I If you **radio** someone, you send a spoken message to them by radio. *transmitir por radio, llamar por radio* ❑ *The officer radioed for advice. El agente llamó por radio para pedir consejo.* ❑ *Martin radioed his team to tell them he was OK. Martin llamó por radio a su equipo para decirles que estaba bien.*
→ see Word Web: **radio**

**radio|ac|tive** /reɪdioʊæktɪv/ ADJ Something that is **radioactive** contains a substance that produces energy in the form of powerful and harmful rays. *radioactivo* ❑ *...radioactive waste. ...residuos radioactivos.* ● **radio|ac|tiv|ity** /reɪdioʊæktɪvɪti/ N-UNCOUNT *radioactividad* ❑ *...a harmful release of radioactivity. ...una fuga de radioactividad nociva.*

**radio|act|ive sym|bol** (**radioactive symbols**) N-COUNT A **radioactive symbol** is a printed sign which shows that a place or an object contains dangerous amounts of radiation. *símbolo de radioactividad*

**ra|dio tele|scope** (**radio telescopes**) N-COUNT A **radio telescope** is an instrument that receives radio waves from space and finds the position of stars and other objects in space. *radiotelescopio, radiorreceptor*
→ see **telescope**

**ra|dio wave** (**radio waves**) N-COUNT **Radio waves** are the form in which radio signals travel. *onda de radio, onda radioeléctrica*
→ see **wave**

**ra|dius** /reɪdiəs/ (**radii** /reɪdiaɪ/) **1** N-SING The **radius** around a particular point is the distance from it in any direction. *radio* ❑ *Nick searched for work in a ten-mile radius around his home. Nick buscó trabajo en un radio de 15 kilómetros a partir de su casa.* **2** N-COUNT The **radius** of a circle is the distance

from its center to its outside edge. radio ❑ *...a circle with a radius of about thirty miles.* *...un círculo con un radio de aproximadamente 48 kilómetros.*
→ see **area**

**raft** /ræft/ (**rafts**) **1** N-COUNT A **raft** is a floating platform made from large pieces of wood or other materials tied together. *balsa* ❑ *...a river trip on bamboo rafts.* *...un viaje por río en balsas de bambú.* **2** N-COUNT A **raft** is a small rubber or plastic boat that you blow air into to make it float. *balsa* ❑ *The crew spent two days and nights in their raft.* *La tripulación pasó dos días con sus noches en su balsa.*
→ see **boat**

**rag** /ræg/ (**rags**) **1** N-VAR A **rag** is a piece of old cloth which you can use to clean or wipe things. *trapo* ❑ *He was wiping his hands on an oily rag.* *Se estaba limpiando las manos con un trapo grasiento.* **2** N-PLURAL **Rags** are old torn clothes. *andrajos, harapos* ❑ *...children dressed in rags.* *...niños cubiertos de harapos.*

**rage** /reɪdʒ/ (**rages, raging, raged**) **1** N-VAR **Rage** is strong anger that is difficult to control. *ira, rabia, cólera* ❑ *His face was red with rage.* *Tenía el rostro rojo por la ira.* **2** V-I You say that something powerful or unpleasant **rages** when it continues with great force or violence. *rugir, enfurecer, embravecer* ❑ *The fire raged for four hours.* *El fuego ardió furiosamente durante cuatro horas.* ● **rag|ing** ADJ *rugiente, enfurecido* ❑ *The raging river flooded many villages.* *El río embravecido inundó muchos pueblos.* **3** V-I If you **rage** about something, you speak or think very angrily about it. *expresar ira* ❑ *She was raging about her unfair treatment.* *Estaba airada por el trato injusto que le dieron.*
→ see **anger**

**Thesaurus** *rage* Ver también:
N. anger, frenzy, madness, tantrum **1**
V. fume, scream, yell **3**

**raid** /reɪd/ (**raids, raiding, raided**) **1** V-T When soldiers **raid** a place, they make a sudden armed attack against it, with the aim of causing damage. *asaltar* ● **Raid** is also a noun. *asalto* ❑ *The soldiers attempted a raid on the camp.* *Los soldados intentaron lanzar un asalto contra el campo.* **2** → see also **air raid** **3** V-T If the police **raid** a building, they enter it suddenly and by force in order to look for someone or something. *allanar, registrar* ❑ *Police raided the company's offices.* *La policía allanó las oficinas de la compañía.* ● **Raid** is also a noun. *allanamiento, registro* ❑ *They were arrested after a raid on a house by police.* *Los arrestaron después de que la policía hiciera el registro de una casa.*

**rail** /reɪl/ (**rails**) **1** N-COUNT A **rail** is a horizontal bar around or along something that you hold on to for support. *riel, barra* ❑ *She gripped the hand rail.* *Se aferró al pasamanos.* **2** N-COUNT A **rail** is a horizontal bar that you hang things on. *barra, cortinero* ❑ *These curtains will fit a rail that is 6 feet wide.* *Estas cortinas están hechas para un cortinero de 1.80 metros de largo.* **3** N-COUNT **Rails** are the steel bars which trains run on. *vía, carril, raíl* ❑ *The train left the rails.* *El tren se salió de la vía.* **4** N-UNCOUNT If you travel or send something **by rail,** you travel or send it on a train. *en tren* ❑ *The president traveled by rail.* *El presidente viajó por ferrocarril.*
→ see **train, transportation**

**rail|road** /reɪlroʊd/ (**railroads**) **1** N-COUNT A **railroad** is a route between two places along which trains travel on steel rails. *ferrocarril, vía* ❑ *...railroad tracks.* *...la vía del tren.* **2** N-COUNT A **railroad** is a company or organization that operates railroad routes. *ferrocarril* ❑ *...the Chicago and Northwestern Railroad.* *...el Ferrocarril Chicago y Northwestern.*

**rail|road cross|ing** (**railroad crossings**) N-COUNT A **railroad crossing** is a place where a railroad track crosses a road at the same level. *paso a nivel, crucero* ❑ *His van was hit by a train at a railroad crossing.* *El tren embistió su camioneta en un crucero.*

**rain** /reɪn/ (**rains, raining, rained**) **1** N-UNCOUNT **Rain** is water that falls from the clouds in small drops. *lluvia* ❑ *We got very wet in the rain.* *Nos empapamos con la lluvia.* **2** V-I When rain falls, you can say that **it is raining.** *llover* ❑ *It was raining hard.* *Estaba lloviendo a cántaros.*
→ see **disaster, hurricane, precipitation, storm, water**
▶ **rain out** PHR-VERB If a sports game **is rained out,** it has to stop, or it is not able to start, because of rain. *suspenderse, cancelarse*

**Thesaurus** *rain* Ver también:
N. drizzle, shower, sleet **1**

**rain|bow** /reɪnboʊ/ (**rainbows**) N-COUNT A **rainbow** is an arch of different colors that you can sometimes see in the sky when it rains or after it rains. *arco iris*
→ see Word Web: **rainbow**

**rain check** (**rain checks**) N-COUNT A **rain check**

**Word Web** rainbow

**Sunlight** contains all of the colors. When a **ray** of sunlight passes through a prism, it splits into different colors. This is also what happens when light passes through the drops of water in the air. The light is refracted, and we see a **rainbow**. The colors of the rainbow are **red**, **orange**, **yellow**, **green**, **blue**, indigo, and **violet**. One tradition says that there is a pot of gold at the end of the rainbow. Other myths say that the rainbow is a bridge between Earth and the land of the gods.

r

is a free ticket that is given to people when an outdoor game or event is stopped because of rain or bad weather, so that they can go to it when it is held again. vale por suspensión o cancelación de un espectáculo

**rain|drop** /reɪndrɒp/ (**raindrops**) N-COUNT A **raindrop** is a single drop of rain. gota de lluvia
→ see **precipitation**

**rain|fall** /reɪnfɔl/ N-UNCOUNT **Rainfall** is the amount of rain that falls in a place during a particular period. precipitación pluvial ❑ *...below average rainfall.* *...inferior a la precipitación pluvial media.*
→ see **erosion, habitat, storm**

**rain for|est** (**rain forests**) also **rainforest** N-VAR A **rain forest** is a thick forest of tall trees which is found mainly in tropical areas where there is a lot of rain. selva (tropical), bosque (ecuatorial o pluvial) ❑ *...the destruction of the Amazon rain forest.* *...la destrucción de la selva amazónica.*
→ see **habitat**

**rainy** /reɪni/ (**rainier, rainiest**) ADJ If it is **rainy** it is raining a lot. lluvioso ❑ *...a rainy day.* *...un día lluvioso.*

**raise** /reɪz/ (**raises, raising, raised**) **1** V-T If you **raise** something, you move it so that it is in a higher position. levantar, alzar, llevarse a ❑ *He raised his hand to wave.* *Alzó la mano para saludar.* ❑ *Milton raised the glass to his lips.* *Milton se llevó el vaso a la boca.* **2** V-T If you **raise** the rate or level of something, you increase it. aumentar, incrementar ❑ *Many stores have raised their prices.* *Muchas tiendas han aumentado sus precios.* **3** V-T To **raise** the standard of something means to improve it. mejorar ❑ *...a new program to raise standards in schools.* *...un nuevo programa para mejorar la calidad en las escuelas.* **4** V-T If you **raise** your **voice**, you speak more loudly. alzar, levantar **5** N-COUNT A **raise** is an increase in your wages or salary. aumento ❑ *Kelly got a raise.* *Kelly recibió un aumento.* **6** V-T If you **raise** money **for** a charity or an institution, you ask people for money which you collect on its behalf. recaudar ❑ *The event is to raise money for the school.* *El acto es para recaudar dinero para la escuela.* **7** V-T If an event **raises** a particular emotion or question, it makes people feel the emotion or consider the question. alimentar ❑ *The agreement raised hopes that the war would end soon.* *El acuerdo alimentó la esperanza de que la guerra terminaría pronto.* **8** V-T If you **raise** a subject, an objection, or a question, you mention it or bring it to someone's attention. poner ❑ *They asked him to help and he raised no objections.* *Le pidieron que ayudara y no puso objeciones.* **9** V-T To **raise** children means to take care of them until they are grown up. criar, educar ❑ *She raised four children on her own.* *Crió a cuatro hijos por sí sola.* **10** V-T To **raise** a particular type of animal or crop means to breed that animal or grow that crop. criar, cultivar **11** to **raise** your **eyebrows** → see **eyebrow**
→ see **union**

R

**Usage** **raise** and **rise**

*Raise* is often confused with *rise*, but it has a different meaning. *Raise* means "to move something to a higher position": *Students raise their hand when they want to speak in class.* *Rise* means that something moves upward: *When steam rises from the pot, add the pasta.*

**rai|sin** /reɪzᵊn/ (**raisins**) N-COUNT **Raisins** are dried grapes. pasa

**rake** /reɪk/ (**rakes, raking, raked**) **1** N-COUNT A **rake** is a garden tool consisting of a row of metal or wooden teeth attached to a long handle. rastrillo **2** V-T If you **rake** a surface, you move a rake across it in order to make it smooth and level. rastrillar ❑ *Rake the soil and plant the seeds.* *Rastrille el suelo y plante las semillas.* **3** V-T If you **rake** leaves or ashes, you move them somewhere using a rake. recoger con rastrillo ❑ *The men raked the leaves into piles.* *Los hombres amontonaron las hojas con rastrillos.*

rake

▸ **rake in** PHR-VERB If you say that someone **is raking in** money, you mean that they are making a lot of money. forrarse con, embolsarse [INFORMAL] ❑ *The company raked in more than $500 million last year.* *La compañía se embolsó más de 500 millones de dólares el año pasado.*
→ see **garden**

**ral|ly** /ræli/ (**rallies, rallying, rallied**) **1** N-COUNT A **rally** is a large public meeting that is held in order to show support for something such as a political party. concentración, manifestación ❑ *...a rally to demand better working conditions.* *...una manifestación para exigir mejores condiciones de trabajo.* **2** V-T/V-I When people **rally to** something or when something **rallies** them, they unite to support it. unirse en apoyo de ❑ *Her colleagues rallied to her support.* *Sus colegas se unieron en su apoyo.* **3** V-I When someone or something **rallies,** they begin to recover or improve after having been weak. recuperarse, reponerse ❑ *He rallied enough to thank his doctors.* *Se recuperó lo suficiente para agradecer a sus médicos.* **4** N-COUNT A **rally** is a competition in which vehicles are driven over public roads. carrera ❑ *Rally driver John Crawford won titles from 1982 to 1987.* *El piloto de carreras John Crawford ganó títulos de 1982 a 1987.*

▸ **rally around** PHR-VERB When people **rally around,** they work as a group in order to support someone or something at a difficult time. acudir en apoyo de ❑ *Many people rallied around the family to help them.* *Mucha gente acudió en apoyo de la familia.*

**Word Partnership** Usar *rally* con:

ADJ. **political** rally **1**
N. **campaign** rally, **protest** rally, rally **in support of** *someone/something* **1**
**prices/stocks** rally **3**
PREP. rally **behind** *someone/something* **2**

**ram|bunc|tious** /ræmbʌŋkʃəs/ ADJ A **rambunctious** person is energetic in a cheerful, noisy way. *revoltoso* ❑ *...a very rambunctious and energetic class.* *...un grupo muy revoltoso y lleno de energía.*

**ramp** /ræmp/ (**ramps**) **1** N-COUNT A **ramp** is a sloping surface between two places that are at different levels. *rampa* ❑ *Lillian was coming down the ramp from the museum.* *Lillian venía descendiendo por la rampa del museo.* **2** N-COUNT An entrance **ramp** is a road which cars use to drive onto a major road, and an exit **ramp** is a road which cars use to drive off a major road. *rampa*
→ see **disability, traffic**

**ran** /ræn/ **Ran** is the past tense of **run**. *pasado de* ***run***

**ranch** /ræntʃ/ (**ranches**) N-COUNT A **ranch** is a large farm used for raising animals. *rancho* ❑ *...a cattle ranch in Texas.* *...un rancho ganadero en Texas.*

**ranch house** (**ranch houses**) **1** N-COUNT A **ranch house** is a single-story house, usually with a low roof. *casa de una sola planta* ❑ *...streets full of treeless lawns and one-story ranch houses.* *...calles llenas de prados sin árboles y de casas de una sola planta.* **2** N-COUNT A **ranch house** is the main house on a ranch. *casa (principal)*

**ran|dom** /rændəm/ **1** ADJ A **random** sample or method is one in which all the people or things involved have an equal chance of being chosen. *aleatorio* ❑ *The survey used a random sample of two thousand people.* *Para la encuesta, se tomó una muestra aleatoria de dos mil personas.* ● **ran|dom|ly** ADV *al azar* ❑ *...interviews with a randomly chosen sample of 30 girls.* *...entrevistas con una muestra de treinta muchachas seleccionadas al azar.* **2** ADJ If you describe events as **random,** you mean that they do not seem to follow a definite plan or pattern. *fortuito, aleatorio* ❑ *...random violence against innocent victims.* *...violencia fortuita contra víctimas inocentes.* ● **ran|dom|ly** ADV *al azar* ❑ *Pictures were placed randomly on the walls.* *Había cuadros colgados al azar en los muros.* **3** PHRASE If something happens **at random,** it happens without a definite plan or pattern. *al azar* ❑ *The gunman fired at random.* *El pistolero disparó al azar.*

**ran|dom vari|able** (**random variables**) N-COUNT In statistics, a **random variable** is a quantity whose value depends on a set of probabilities. *variable aleatoria* [TECHNICAL]

**R & R** /ɑr ən ɑr/ also **R and R** N-UNCOUNT **R&R** refers to time that you spend relaxing, when you are not working. **R&R** is an abbreviation for "rest and relaxation." *abreviatura de "descanso y esparcimiento"* ❑ *Our vacation homes are just the thing for serious R&R.* *Nuestras casas de campo son justo lo necesario para descansar y recuperarnos en serio.*

**range** /reɪndʒ/ (**ranges, ranging, ranged**) **1** N-COUNT A **range of** things is a number of different things of the same general kind. *gama, variedad* ❑ *...a wide range of colors.* *...una amplia gama de colores.* **2** N-COUNT A **range** is the complete group that is included between two points on a scale of measurement or quality. *intervalo* ❑ *The average age range is between 35 and 55.* *El intervalo promedio de edad es de 35 a 55 años* **3** N-COUNT The **range of** something is the maximum area in which it can reach things or detect things. *alcance* ❑ *The weapon has a range of 18,000 yards.* *El arma tiene un alcance de 16,460 metros.* **4** V-I If things **range between** two points or **range from** one point **to** another, they vary within these points on a scale of measurement or quality. *variar de...a, ir de...a* ❑ *They range in price from $3 to $15.* *Su precio varía de 3 a 5 dólares.* **5** N-COUNT A **range** of mountains or hills is a line of them. *sierra, cordillera, cadena* ❑ *...snowy mountain ranges.* *...cadenas montañosas nevadas.* **6** N-COUNT A rifle **range** or a shooting **range** is a place where people can practice shooting at targets. *campo de tiro* **7** N-COUNT The **range** of a set of numbers is the difference between the biggest number and the smallest number. *escala*
→ see **graph**

**Word Partnership** Usar *range* con:

ADJ. **broad** range, **limited** range, **narrow** range, **wide** range **1**
**full** range, **normal** range, **whole** range **2**
N. range **of emotions**, range **of possibilities** **1**
**age** range, **price** range, **temperature** range **2**

**rank** /ræŋk/ (**ranks, ranking, ranked**) **1** N-VAR Someone's **rank** is the position or grade that they have in an organization. *grado (militar), categoría* ❑ *He rose to the rank of captain.* *Ascendió al grado de capitán.* **2** V-T/V-I If an official organization **ranks** someone or something 1st, 5th, or 50th, for example, they calculate that the person or thing has that position on a scale. You can also say that someone or something **ranks** 1st, 5th, or 50th, for example. *clasificar* ❑ *The report ranks the U.S. 20th out of 22 countries.* *El informe clasifica a EE.UU. como el vigésimo de 22 países.* ❑ *She doesn't even rank in the world's top ten.* *Ni siquiera clasifica entre las diez mejores del mundo.* **3** N-PLURAL **The ranks** are the ordinary members of an organization, especially of the armed forces. *filas* ❑ *He rose through the ranks from researcher to professor.* *Se abrió paso de las categorías más bajas de investigador a catedrático.* **4** PHRASE If a member of a group or organization **breaks rank,** they disobey the instructions of their group or organization. *romper filas* ❑ *The senator broke ranks with the rest of his party.* *El senador rompió filas con el resto de su partido.* **5** PHRASE If the members of a group **close ranks,** they are supporting each other only because their group is being criticized. *cerrar filas* ❑ *The party closed ranks to support their leader.* *El partido cerró filas para apoyar a su dirigente.*

**Word Partnership** Usar *rank* con:

ADJ. **high** rank, **top** rank **1**
PREP. rank **above**, rank **below** **2**

**rank|ing** /ræŋkɪŋ/ ADJ The **ranking** member of a group, usually a political group, is the most senior person in it. *de más alto grado, de mayor jerarquía* ❑ *...the ranking American diplomat in Baghdad.* *...el diplomático estadounidense de mayor jerarquía en Baghdad.*

**rap** /ræp/ (**raps, rapping, rapped**) **1** N-UNCOUNT **Rap** is a type of music in which the words are not sung but are spoken in a rapid, rhythmic way. *rap* ❑ *...a rap group.* *...un grupo de rap.* ● **rap|per** N-COUNT (**rappers**) *cantante de rap* ❑ *...a talented*

rapper. *...un cantante de rap talentoso.* **2** V-I Someone who **raps** performs rap music. *intérprete de música rap* **3** V-T/V-I If you **rap on** something or **rap** it, you hit it with a series of quick blows. *golpetear, llamar* ❑ *Mary rapped on Charlie's door. Mary llamó a la puerta de Charlie.* ● **Rap** is also a noun. *golpe, golpeteo* ❑ *There was a loud rap on the door. Se oyó un fuerte golpe en la puerta.*
→ see **genre**

**rape** /reɪp/ (**rapes, raping, raped**) **1** V-T If someone **is raped,** they are forced to have sex, usually by violence. *violar* ❑ *A young woman was raped. Violaron a una muchacha.* ● **rapist** N-COUNT (**rapists**) *violador o violadora* ❑ *...information that led to the rapist's arrest. ...información que llevó al arresto del violador.* **2** N-VAR **Rape** is the crime of forcing someone to have sex. *violación*

**rap|id** /ræpɪd/ **1** ADJ A **rapid** change is one that happens very quickly. *rápido* ❑ *...the country's rapid economic growth. ...el rápido desarrollo económico del país.* ● **rap|id|ly** ADV *rápidamente, rápido* ❑ *...countries with rapidly growing populations. ...países con una población en rápido aumento.* ● **ra|pid|ity** /rəpɪdɪti/ N-UNCOUNT *rapidez* ❑ *...the rapidity with which the weather can change. ...la rapidez con que puede cambiar el clima.* **2** ADJ A **rapid** movement is one that is very fast. *rápido* ❑ *He walked at a rapid pace. Caminó con paso rápido.* ● **rap|id|ly** ADV *rápidamente, rápido* ❑ *He was moving rapidly around the room. Se movía rápidamente por el cuarto.* ● **ra|pid|ity** N-UNCOUNT *rapidez* ❑ *The water rushed through the tunnel with great rapidity. El agua corría por el túnel con una gran rapidez.*

**Thesaurus** *rapid* Ver también:
ADJ. fast, speedy, swift; (*ant.*) slow **1** **2**

**Word Partnership** Usar *rapid* con:
N. rapid **change**, rapid **decline**, rapid **development**, rapid **expansion**, rapid **growth**, rapid **increase**, rapid **progress** **1** rapid **pace**, rapid **pulse** **2**

R

**rapid-fire** ADJ A **rapid-fire** economic activity or development is one that takes place very quickly. *rápido, veloz* [JOURNALISM] ❑ *...the rapid-fire buying and selling of shares. ...la veloz compraventa de acciones.*

**rap|pel** /ræpɛl, rə-/ (**rappels, rappelling, rappelled**) V-I To **rappel** down a cliff or rock face means to slide down it in a controlled way using a rope, with your feet against the cliff or rock. *practicar rappel*

**rap sheet** (**rap sheets**) N-COUNT A **rap sheet** is a legal document which records someone's arrests and crimes. *antecedentes penales*

**rare** /rɛər/ (**rarer, rarest**) **1** ADJ Something that is **rare** is not common and is therefore interesting or valuable. *raro* ❑ *...one of the rarest birds in the world. ...una de las aves más raras del mundo.* **2** ADJ An event or situation that is **rare** does not occur very often. *raro* ❑ *...on the rare occasions when he sees her. ...en las raras ocasiones en que la ve.* **3** ADJ Meat that is **rare** is cooked very lightly so that the inside is still red. *poco asado, casi crudo, a la inglesa*

**rar|efac|tion** /rɛərɪfækʃən/ N-UNCOUNT **Rarefaction** is a reduction in the density of something, especially the density of the atmosphere. *rarefacción, enrarecimiento* [TECHNICAL]

**rare|ly** /rɛərli/ ADV If something **rarely** happens, it does not happen very often. *raramente, pocas veces, raro*

**rash** /ræʃ/ (**rashes**) **1** ADJ If someone is **rash** or does **rash** things, they act without thinking carefully first. *precipitado, irreflexivo* ❑ *You might regret a rash decision like that for years. Podrías arrepentirte durante años de esa decisión tan precipitada.* ● **rash|ly** ADV *imprudentemente, irreflexivamente* ❑ *I made a lot of money, but I rashly spent most of it. Gané mucho dinero, pero gasté imprudentemente la mayor parte de él.* **2** N-COUNT A **rash** is an area of red spots that appears on your skin when you are ill or have a bad reaction to something that you have eaten or touched. *salpullido, sarpullido, erupción, roncha* ❑ *I always get a rash when I've eaten nuts. Siempre me salen ronchas cuando como nueces.* **3** N-SING A **rash of** events or things is a large number of them that all happen or appear within a short period of time. *proliferación* ❑ *...a rash of burglaries. ...proliferación de los robos con allanamiento de morada.*

**rasp|berry** /ræzbɛri/ (**raspberries**) N-COUNT **Raspberries** are small, soft, red fruit that grow on bushes. *frambuesa*

**rat** /ræt/ (**rats**) N-COUNT A **rat** is an animal which has a long tail and looks like a large mouse. *rata* ❑ *...experiments with rats. ...experimentos con ratas.*

**rate** /reɪt/ (**rates, rating, rated**) **1** N-COUNT The **rate** at which something happens is the speed with which it happens. *velocidad, ritmo* ❑ *...the rate at which hair grows. ...la velocidad de crecimiento del pelo.* **2** N-COUNT The **rate** at which something happens is the number of times it happens over a period of time. *ritmo* ❑ *New diet books appear at a rate of one a week. Los libros sobre dietas aparecen al ritmo de uno nuevo por semana.* **3** N-COUNT A **rate** is the amount of money that is charged for goods or services. *tarifa* ❑ *The hotel offers a special weekend rate. El hotel ofrece una tarifa especial de fin de semana.* **4** → see also **exchange rate** **5** N-COUNT The **rate** of taxation or interest is the amount of tax or interest that needs to be paid, expressed as a percentage. *tasa* [BUSINESS] ❑ *...interest rate cuts. ...reducciones de la tasa de interés.* **6** V-T/V-I If you **rate** someone or something as good or bad, you consider them to be good or bad. *considerar, clasificar* ❑ *We rate him as one of the best. Lo consideramos como uno de los mejores.* ❑ *This small shop rated well in our survey. Esta pequeña tienda logró una buena clasificación en nuestro sondeo.* **7** → see also **rating** **8** PHRASE You use **at any rate** to indicate that what you have just said might be incorrect or unclear in some way, and that you are now being more precise. *en todo caso* ❑ *His friends liked her—well, most of them at any rate. Sus amigos la querían mucho; bueno, la mayoría, en todo caso.* **9** PHRASE If you say that **at this rate** something bad or extreme will happen, you mean that it will happen if things continue to develop as they have been doing. *a este paso, a este ritmo* ❑ *At this rate we'll never get home. A este paso, nunca llegaremos a casa.*
→ see **motion**

**Word Partnership** Usar *rate* con:

N. rate **of change** 1
**birth** rate, **crime** rate, **dropout** rate, **heart** rate, **pulse** rate, **survival** rate, **unemployment** rate 2
**interest** rate 5
ADJ. **average** rate, **faster** rate, **slow** rate, **steady** rate 1 2
**high** rate, **low** rate 1 – 4

**ra|ther** /rædər/ 1 PHRASE You use **rather than** when you are contrasting two things or situations. **Rather than** introduces the thing or situation that is not true or that you do not want. *antes que, más bien que* ❑ *I use the bike when I can rather than the car. Cuando puedo, prefiero usar la bici al carro.* ● **Rather than** is also a conjunction. *antes que, en lugar de* ❑ *Use glass bottles again rather than throw them away. Vuelva a usar las botellas de vidrio, en lugar de tirarlas.* 2 ADV You use **rather** when you are correcting something that you have just said, especially when you are describing a particular situation after saying what it is not. *más bien* ❑ *This is not a solution, but rather will create new problems. Ésta no es la solución; más bien, va a traer más problemas.* 3 PHRASE If you **would rather** do something, you would prefer to do it. *preferir hacer una cosa a otra* ❑ *Kids would rather play than study. Los niños prefieren jugar a estudiar.* 4 ADV You use **rather** to indicate that something is true to a fairly great extent. *más bien* ❑ *...rather unusual circumstances. ...circunstancias más bien inusuales.*

**rati|fy** /rætɪfaɪ/ (**ratifies, ratifying, ratified**) V-T When national leaders or organizations **ratify** a treaty or written agreement, they make it official by giving their formal approval to it, usually by signing it or voting for it. *ratificar* ● **rati|fi|ca|tion** /rætɪfɪkeɪʃən/ N-VAR (**ratifications**) *ratificación* ❑ *We hope for early ratification of the treaty. Esperamos una pronta ratificación del tratado.*

**rat|ing** /reɪtɪŋ/ (**ratings**) N-COUNT A **rating** of something is a score or measurement of how good or popular it is. *renombre, reputación, índice* ❑ *The president's popularity rating is at its lowest point. El índice de popularidad del presidente está en su punto más bajo.*

**Word Partnership** Usar *rating* con:

N. **approval** rating
ADJ. **high** rating, **low** rating, **poor** rating, **top** rating

**Word Link** *ratio ≈ reasoning : irrational, ratio, rational*

**ra|tio** /reɪʃoʊ, -ʃioʊ/ (**ratios**) N-COUNT A **ratio** is a relationship between two things when it is expressed in numbers or amounts. *proporción* ❑ *The adult to child ratio is one to six. La proporción entre el número de niños y el de adultos es de uno a seis.*

**ra|tion|al** /ræʃənəl/ 1 ADJ **Rational** decisions and thoughts are based on reason rather than on emotion. *racional, inteligente* ❑ *They discussed it in a rational manner. Lo discutieron de una manera racional.* ● **ra|tion|al|ly** ADV *racionalmente* ❑ *It is difficult to think rationally when you're worried. Es difícil pensar racionalmente cuando se está preocupado.* ● **ra|tion|al|ity** /ræʃənælɪti/ N-UNCOUNT *racionalidad, racionalismo* ❑ *We live in a time of rationality. Vivimos en una época de racionalidad.* 2 ADJ A **rational** person is someone who is sensible and is able to make decisions based on intelligent thinking rather than on emotion. *razonable, en su (sano) juicio* ❑ *Rachel looked calmer and more rational now. Rachel parecía estar ya más calmada y en su sano juicio.*

**Word Partnership** Usar *rational* con:

N. rational **approach**, rational **choice**, rational **decision**, rational **explanation** 1
rational **human being**, rational **person** 2

**ra|tion|al num|ber** (**rational numbers**) N-COUNT **Rational numbers** are numbers that can be expressed as whole numbers, fractions, or decimals. *número racional* [TECHNICAL]

**rat|tle** /rætəl/ (**rattles, rattling, rattled**) 1 V-T/V-I When something **rattles** or when you **rattle** it, it makes short, sharp, knocking sounds because it is being shaken or it keeps hitting against something hard. *traquetear* ❑ *A train rattled by. Un tren pasó traqueteando.* ● **Rattle** is also a noun. *traqueteo, ruido* ❑ *...a rattle of the door handle. ...el ruido del picaporte.* 2 N-COUNT A **rattle** is a baby's toy with small, loose objects inside which make a noise when the baby shakes it. *sonaja, sonajero* 3 V-T If something or someone **rattles** you, they make you nervous. *inquietar, poner nervioso* ❑ *The meeting with her boss rattled her. La reunión con su jefe la puso nerviosa.* ● **rat|tled** ADJ *inquieto, nervioso* ❑ *His expression showed that he was rattled. Su expresión indicaba que estaba inquieto.*

**rat|ty** /ræti/ (**rattier, rattiest**) ADJ **Ratty** clothes and objects are torn or in bad condition, especially because they are old. *raído, andrajoso* ❑ *...my ratty old pajamas. ...mi raída piyama.*

**rave** /reɪv/ (**raves, raving, raved**) 1 V-T/V-I If someone **raves,** they talk in an excited and uncontrolled way. *desvariar, disparatar, despotricar* ❑ *"What is wrong with you?" she raved. —¡Qué te pasa! —le dijo furiosa.* ❑ *She cried and raved for hours. Lloró y despotricó por horas.* 2 V-T/V-I If you **rave about** something, you speak or write about it with great enthusiasm. *deshacerse en elogios por, hablar de algo con entusiasmo* ❑ *Rachel raved about the movie. Rachel se deshizo en elogios de la película.* ❑ *"I didn't know Italy was so beautiful!" she raved. —¡No sabía que Italia fuese tan bella!—, dijo entusiasmada.* 3 N-COUNT A **rave** is a big event at which young people dance to electronic music in a large building or in the open air. *fiesta con música electrónica* ❑ *...an all-night rave. ...una fiesta de toda la noche (con música electrónica).* 4

**raw** /rɔ/ (**rawer, rawest**) 1 ADJ **Raw** materials or substances are in their natural state before being processed. *prima* ❑ *We import raw materials. Importamos materias primas.* 2 ADJ **Raw** food is eaten uncooked, has not yet been cooked, or has not been cooked enough. *crudo* ❑ *...a dish made of raw fish. ...un platillo de pescado crudo.* 3 ADJ If a part of your body is **raw,** it is red and painful, perhaps because the skin has come off or has been

r

burned. carne viva ❑ *Her skin was raw where the ropes had rubbed it.* *Tenía la carne viva donde la cuerda la había rozado.* **4** ADJ If you describe someone in a new job as **raw,** or as a **raw** recruit, you mean that they lack experience in that job. novato, inexperto, bisoño **5** PHRASE If you say that you are getting **a raw deal,** you mean that you are being treated unfairly. mala pasada, tratamiento severo o injusto [INFORMAL] ❑ *I think the man who lost his job got a raw deal.* *Creo que le jugaron una mala pasada al hombre que perdió su trabajo.*

→ see **industry**

| Thesaurus | *raw* | Ver también: |
|---|---|---|
| ADJ. | natural **1** | |
| | fresh; (*ant.*) cooked **2** | |

**raw|hide** /rɔhaɪd/ N-UNCOUNT **Rawhide** is leather that comes from cattle, and has not been treated or tanned. cuero crudo o sin curtir

**ray** /reɪ/ (**rays**) **1** N-COUNT **Rays** of light are narrow beams of light. rayo ❑ *...the sun's rays.* *...los rayos del sol.* **2** → see also **X-ray** **3** N-COUNT A **ray of** hope, comfort, or other positive quality is a small amount of it that makes a bad situation seem less bad. rayo ❑ *The research provides a ray of hope for sufferers of the disease.* *La investigación ofrece un rayo de esperanza a los que padecen la enfermedad.*

→ see **rainbow, telescope**

**ra|zor** /reɪzər/ (**razors**) N-COUNT A **razor** is a tool that people use for shaving. rasuradora, rastrillo para rasurarse, navaja para rasurarse

**razz** /ræz/ (**razzes, razzing, razzed**) V-T To **razz** someone means to tease them, especially in an unkind way. tomar el pelo, reírse de, vacilar a [INFORMAL] ❑ *Molly razzed me about dropping the ball.* *Molly se burló de mí porque dejé caer la pelota.*

**r-controlled sound** /ɑrkəntroʊld saʊnd/ (**r-controlled sounds**) N-COUNT In language teaching, an **r-controlled sound** is a vowel that is pronounced differently when it comes before the letter "r," such as the vowel sound represented by the letters "ai" in "air." vocal cuyo sonido varía por influencia de la "r" [TECHNICAL]

R

**reach** /ritʃ/ (**reaches, reaching, reached**) **1** V-T When someone or something **reaches** a place, they arrive there. llegar ❑ *He did not stop until he reached the door.* *No se detuvo hasta llegar a la puerta.* **2** V-T If someone or something has **reached** a certain stage, level, or amount, they are at that stage, level, or amount. alcanzar ❑ *The figure could reach 100,000 next year.* *La cifra podría alcanzar los 100,000 el próximo año.* **3** V-I If you **reach** somewhere, you move your arm and hand to take or touch something. meter la mano ❑ *Judy reached into her bag.* *Judy metió la mano en su bolsa.* **4** V-T If you can **reach** something, you are able to touch it by stretching out your arm or leg. alcanzar(se) ❑ *Can you reach your toes with your fingertips?* *¿Puede alcanzarse los dedos de los pies con los de las manos?* **5** V-T If you try to **reach** someone, you try to contact them, usually by telephone. comunicarse ❑ *You can reach me at this phone number.* *Puede comunicarse conmigo a este número telefónico.* **6** V-T/V-I If something **reaches** a place, point, or level, it extends as far as that place, point, or level. llegar ❑ *...a shirt that reached to his knees.* *...una camisa que le llegaba a las rodillas.* **7** V-T When people **reach** an agreement or a decision, they succeed in achieving it. llegar, alcanzar ❑ *They failed to reach agreement over the issue.* *No lograron llegar a un acuerdo sobre la cuestión.*

| Word Partnership | Usar *reach* con: |
|---|---|
| N. | reach **a destination** **1** |
| | reach **a goal**, reach ***one's* potential** **2** |
| | reach **(an) agreement**, reach **a compromise**, reach **a conclusion**, reach **a consensus**, reach **a decision** **7** |

**re|act** /riækt/ (**reacts, reacting, reacted**) **1** V-I When you **react to** something that has happened to you, you behave in a particular way because of it. reaccionar ❑ *They reacted violently to the news.* *Reaccionaron violentamente a las noticias.* **2** V-I If you **react against** someone's way of behaving, you deliberately behave in a different way because you do not like the way he or she behaves. actuar de manera distinta ❑ *My father never saved money and I reacted against that.* *Mi padre nunca ahorró dinero y yo actué de manera distinta.* **3** V-I If you **react to** a substance such as a drug, or **to** something you have touched, you are affected unpleasantly or made ill by it. reaccionar ❑ *Someone who is allergic to milk will also react to cheese.* *Alguien que es alérgico a la leche también tendrá reacciones con el queso.* **4** V-RECIP When one chemical substance **reacts with** another, or when two chemical substances **react,** they combine chemically to form another substance. reaccionar ❑ *Calcium reacts with water.* *El calcio reacciona con el agua.*

| Word Partnership | Usar *react* con: |
|---|---|
| ADJ. | **slow to** react **1** |
| N. | react **to news**, react **to a situation** **1** |
| ADV. | react **differently**, react **emotionally**, **how to** react, react **negatively**, react **positively**, react **quickly** **1** |
| | react **strongly**, react **violently** **1**–**4** |

**re|ac|tant** /riæktənt/ (**reactants**) N-COUNT In a chemical reaction, the **reactants** are the substances that are present at the start of the reaction. reactivo, cuerpo que entra en una reacción química [TECHNICAL]

**re|ac|tion** /riækʃᵊn/ (**reactions**) **1** N-VAR Your **reaction to** something that has happened or something that you have experienced is what you feel, say, or do because of it. reacción ❑ *He showed no reaction to the news.* *No mostró reacción alguna a las noticias.* **2** N-COUNT A **reaction against** something is a way of behaving or doing something that is deliberately different from what has been done before. reacción contra ❑ *...a reaction against this type of progress.* *...una reacción contra ese tipo de progreso.* **3** N-PLURAL Your **reactions** are your ability to move quickly in response to something. reacción, reflejo ❑ *The sport requires very fast reactions.* *El deporte exige reflejos muy rápidos.* **4** N-COUNT A chemical **reaction** is a process in which two substances combine together chemically to form another substance. reacción ❑ *...a chemical reaction between oxygen and hydrogen.* *...una reacción química entre el oxígeno y el hidrógeno.* **5** N-COUNT If you have a **reaction to** a substance such as a

drug, or **to** something you have touched, you are affected unpleasantly or made ill by it. reacción ❑ *He suffered a serious reaction to the drug.* *La droga le provocó una reacción muy grave.*
→ see **motion**

**Word Partnership** Usar *reaction* con:

ADJ. **mixed** reaction, **negative** reaction, **positive** reaction 1
**emotional** reaction, **initial** reaction 1 2
**chemical** reaction 4
**allergic** reaction 5

**re|ac|tor** /riæktər/ (**reactors**) N-COUNT A **reactor** is the same as a **nuclear reactor**. reactor nuclear

**read** (**reads, reading, read**)

The form **read** is pronounced /rid/ when it is the present tense, and /rɛd/ when it is the past tense and past participle.

1 V-T/V-I When you **read** something such as a book or article, you look at and understand the words that are written there. leer ❑ *Have you read this book?* *¿Ya leyó este libro?* ❑ *I read about it in the paper.* *Lo leí en el periódico.* ❑ *She spends all her time reading.* *Se pasa todo el tiempo leyendo.* ● **Read** is also a noun. lectura ❑ *I sat down to have a good read.* *Me senté para leer a placer.* 2 V-T If you can **read** music, you have the ability to look at and understand the symbols that are used in written music to represent musical sounds. leer 3 V-T You can use **read** when saying what is written on something or in something. decir ❑ *The sign on the door read "Private."* *El letrero sobre la puerta decía "Privado".* 4 V-I If you refer to how a piece of writing **reads,** you are referring to its style. sonar ❑ *The book reads very awkwardly.* *El estilo de este libro es muy poco fluido.* 5 N-COUNT If you say that a book or magazine is a good **read,** you mean that it is very enjoyable to read. lectura ❑ *Ben Okri's novel is a good read.* *La novela de Ben Okri es una lectura amena.* 6 V-T If someone **reads** your mind or thoughts, he or she knows exactly what you are thinking without you telling him or her. leer 7 V-T When you **read** a measuring device, you look at it to see what the figure or measurement on it is. leer ❑ *He was able to read a thermometer.* *Podía leer el termómetro.* 8 → see also **reading**

▸ **read into** PHR-VERB If you **read** a meaning **into** something, you think it is there although it may not actually be there. buscar significado ❑ *Don't read too much into his comments.* *No pienses que sus comentarios son muy profundos.*

▸ **read out** PHR-VERB If you **read out** a piece of writing, you say it aloud. leer en voz alta ❑ *The evidence was read out in court.* *El documento probatorio fue leído en voz alta en el tribunal.*

▸ **read up on** PHR-VERB If you **read up on** a subject, you read a lot about it so that you become informed about it. estudiar, investigar ❑ *I've read up on the subject.* *He investigado sobre el tema.*

**Thesaurus** *read* Ver también:

V. scan, skim, study 1
comprehend; (*ant.*) sense 1 2

**Word Partnership** Usar *read* con:

N. **ability to** read, read **a book/magazine/ (news)paper**, read **a sentence**, read **a sign**, read **a statement** 1
ADV. read **carefully**, read **silently** 1
V. **learn (how)** to read, **like to** read, **listen to** *someone* read, **want to** read 1

**read|er** /ridər/ (**readers**) N-COUNT The **readers** of a newspaper, magazine, or book are the people who read it. lector o lectora ❑ *The book gives the reader an interesting view of life in Spain.* *El libro ofrece al lector una visión interesante de la vida en España.*

**read|er's thea|ter** N-UNCOUNT **Reader's theater** is a form of theater, used especially in teaching, in which the performers read from scripts and which does not involve costumes, stage sets, or special lighting. teatro de lectura

**read|ily** /rɛdɪli/ 1 ADV If you do something **readily,** you do it in a way which shows that you are very willing to do it. inmediatamente ❑ *I asked her to help, and she readily agreed.* *Le pedí que me ayudara y aceptó inmediatamente.* 2 ADV You also use **readily** to say that something can be done or obtained quickly and easily. For example, if you say that something can be readily understood, you mean that people can understand it quickly and easily. sin dificultad ❑ *The parts are readily available in hardware stores.* *Las piezas se encuentran disponibles sin dificultad en las ferreterías.*

**Word Partnership** Usar *readily* con:

V. readily **accept**, readily **admit**, readily **agree** 1
ADJ. readily **apparent** 1
*be* readily **available**, **make** readily **available** 2

**read|ing** /ridɪŋ/ (**readings**) 1 N-UNCOUNT **Reading** is the activity of reading books. lectura ❑ *I love reading.* *Me encanta la lectura.* 2 N-COUNT A **reading** is an event at which poetry or extracts from books are read to an audience. recital ❑ *...a poetry reading.* *...un recital de poesía.* 3 N-COUNT The **reading** on a measuring device is the figure or measurement that it shows. lectura ❑ *The thermometer gave a faulty reading.* *El termómetro marcaba una temperatura errónea.*

**ready** /rɛdi/ (**readier, readiest, readies, readying, readied**) 1 ADJ If someone is **ready,** they are properly prepared for something. If something is **ready,** it has been properly prepared and is now able to be used. listo, preparado ❑ *It took her a long time to get ready for school.* *Le llevó mucho tiempo prepararse para ir a la escuela.* ● **readi|ness** N-UNCOUNT preparación ❑ *We keep the room neat and clean in readiness for visitors.* *Mantenemos el cuarto ordenado y limpio por si llegan visitas.* 2 ADJ If you are **ready to** do something, you are willing to do it. dispuesto ❑ *They were ready to help.* *Estaban dispuestas a ayudar.* ● **readiness** N-UNCOUNT disposición ❑ *...their readiness to cooperate.* *...su disposición para cooperar.* 3 ADJ If you are **ready for** something, you need it or want it. listo, a punto ❑ *I'm ready for bed.* *Estoy listo para irme a la cama.* 4 ADJ To be **ready to**

do something means to be about to do it or likely to do it. a punto de ❑ *She looked ready to cry.* Parecía a punto de llorar. **5** ADJ You use **ready** to describe things that are able to be used very quickly and easily. *a la mano, fácil* ❑ *I didn't have a ready answer for this question.* No tenía una respuesta a la mano para la cuestión. **6** V-T When you **ready** something, you prepare it for a particular purpose. *prepararse* [FORMAL] ❑ *Soldiers were readying themselves for the attack.* Los soldados estaban preparándose para el ataque.

**Word Partnership** Usar *ready* con:

N. ready **for bed**, ready **for dinner** **1**
ADV. **always** ready, **not quite** ready, **not** ready **yet** **1**–**4**
V. **get** ready **1**
ready **to begin**, ready **to fight**, ready **to go/leave**, ready **to play**, ready **to start** **1** **2** **4**
ready **to burst** **4**

**ready-made** **1** ADJ If something that you buy is **ready-made,** you can use it immediately. *de confección, preparado, precocido* ❑ *...ready-made meals.* ...alimentos preparados. **2** ADJ **Ready-made** means extremely convenient or useful for a particular purpose. *tópico* ❑ *...a ready-made topic of conversation.* ...un tópico.

**real** /ri̱l/ **1** ADJ Something that is **real** actually exists and is not imagined or theoretical. *real* ❑ *No, it wasn't a dream. It was real.* No, no fue un sueño; fue real. **2** ADJ A material or object that is **real** is natural or functioning, and not artificial or an imitation. *real, verdadero* ❑ *...the smell of real leather.* ...el olor de la verdadera piel. **3** ADJ You can use **real** to describe someone or something that has all the characteristics or qualities that such a person or thing typically has. *verdadero* ❑ *...his first real girlfriend.* ...su verdadera primera novia. **4** ADJ You can use **real** to describe something that is the true or original thing of its kind, rather than what someone wants you to believe. *verdadero* ❑ *This was the real reason for her call.* Esa fue la verdadera razón de su llamada. **5** ADV You can use **real** to emphasize an adjective or adverb. *realmente, verdaderamente* [INFORMAL] ❑ *He is finding prison life "real tough."* La vida en prisión le parece "realmente difícil". **6** PHRASE If you say that someone does something **for real,** you mean that they actually do it and do not just pretend to do it. *en serio, de verdad* [INFORMAL] ❑ *I dreamed about becoming an actor but I never thought I'd do it for real.* Soñaba con ser actor, pero nunca pensé que lo haría en serio.

**real es|tate** **1** N-UNCOUNT **Real estate** is property in the form of land and buildings. *bien raíz* ❑ *...investing in real estate.* ...inversión en bienes raíces. **2** N-UNCOUNT **Real estate** businesses or **real estate** agents sell houses, buildings, and land. *agente inmobiliario, inmobiliaria*

**re|al|is|tic** /ri̱əlɪstɪk/ **1** ADJ If you are **realistic** about a situation, you recognize and accept its true nature and try to deal with it in a practical way. *realista* ❑ *Police must be realistic about violent crime.* La policía debe ser realista acerca de los crímenes con violencia. ● **re|al|is|ti|cal|ly** ADV *realistamente* ❑ *As an adult, you can think about the situation realistically.* Cuando se es adulto, se puede pensar en la situación realistamente. **2** ADJ You say that a painting, story, or movie is **realistic** when the people and things in it are like people and things in real life. *realista* ● **re|al|is|ti|cal|ly** ADV *realistamente* ❑ *The movie begins realistically and then turns into a fantasy.* La película comienza realistamente y luego se vuelve una fantasía.
→ see **art, fantasy**

**Word Partnership** Usar *realistic* con:

N. realistic **assessment**, realistic **expectations**, realistic **goals**, realistic **view** **1**
ADV. **more** realistic, **very** realistic **1**
V. **be** realistic **1** **2**

**Word Link** *real ≈ actual : reality, realize, really*

**re|al|ity** /riæ̱lɪti/ (**realities**) **1** N-UNCOUNT You use **reality** to refer to real things or the real nature of things rather than imagined, invented, or theoretical ideas. *realidad* ❑ *Her dream ended and she had to return to reality.* Su sueño terminó y tuvo que volver a la realidad. **2** → see also **virtual reality** **3** N-COUNT **The reality of** a situation is the truth about it, especially when it is unpleasant. *realidad* ❑ *...the harsh reality of life.* ...la dura realidad de la vida. **4** N-SING If something becomes a **reality,** it actually exists or is actually happening. *realidad* ❑ *The reality is that they are poor.* La realidad es que son pobres. **5** PHRASE You can use **in reality** to introduce a statement about the real nature of something, when it contrasts with something incorrect that has just been described. *en realidad* ❑ *He promised a lot, but in reality nothing changed.* Le prometió mucho, pero nada cambió en realidad.
→ see **fantasy**

**Word Partnership** Usar *reality* con:

V. **distort** reality **1**
**become** a reality **4**
ADJ. **virtual** reality **1** **2**
N. reality **of life**, reality **of war** **3**
PREP. **in** reality **5**

**re|al|ity check** (**reality checks**) N-COUNT If you say that something is a **reality check** for someone, you mean that it makes them recognize the truth about a situation, especially about the difficulties involved. *toma de conciencia* ❑ *It's time for a reality check on what's happening.* Ya es hora de revisar realmente lo que está pasando.

**re|al|ity show** (**reality shows**) N-COUNT A **reality show** is a type of television program that aims to show how ordinary people behave in everyday life or in situations which are intended to represent everyday life. *programa televisivo que presenta con toda crudeza conflictos de la vida privada de las personas o sucesos, espectáculo realista*

**re|al|ity TV** N-UNCOUNT **Reality TV** is a type of television programming that aims to show how ordinary people behave in everyday life or in situations which are intended to represent everyday life. *televisión realista*

**Word Link** real ≈ actual : **real**ity, **real**ize, **real**ly

**re|al|ize** /riəlaɪz/ (**realizes, realizing, realized**) **1** V-T/V-I If you **realize** that something is true, you become aware of that fact or understand it. *darse cuenta de, comprender, caer en la cuenta de* ❑ *As soon as we realized that something was wrong, we rushed to help. Tan pronto como nos dimos cuenta de que algo andaba mal, corrimos a ayudar.* ❑ *People don't realize how serious the situation is. La gente no se da cuenta de lo grave que es la situación.* • **re|ali|za|tion** /riəlɪzeɪʃᵊn/ N-VAR (**realizations**) *comprensión* ❑ *There was a growing realization that something must change. Cada vez se comprendía más que algo debía cambiar.* **2** V-T If your hopes, desires, or fears **are realized,** the things that you hope for, desire, or fear actually happen. *hacerse realidad, convertirse en realidad, cumplirse* ❑ *All his worst fears were realized. Sus peores temores se hicieron realidad.* • **re|ali|za|tion** N-UNCOUNT *cumplimiento* ❑ *...the realization of his hopes. ...el cumplimiento de sus esperanzas.* **3** V-T When someone **realizes** a design or an idea, they make or organize something based on that design or idea. *hacer* [FORMAL] ❑ *...the method that I used in order to realize the sculpture. ...el método que empleé para hacer la escultura.*

**Word Partnership** Usar *realize* con:

| | |
|---|---|
| ADV. | **suddenly** realize **1** |
| | **finally** realize, **fully** realize **1**–**3** |
| V. | **come to** realize, **make** ***someone*** realize **1** |
| | **begin to** realize, **fail to** realize **1** **3** |
| N. | realize **a dream** **2** |
| | realize ***your*** **potential** **3** |

**re|al|ly** /riəli/ **1** ADV You can use **really** to emphasize a statement. *de veras, de verdad* [SPOKEN] ❑ *I'm very sorry. I really am. De verdad lo siento.* **2** ADV You use **really** when you are discussing the real facts about something, in contrast to the ones someone wants you to believe. *realmente* ❑ *My father didn't really have a wooden leg. Mi padre no tenía realmente una pata de palo.* **3** ADV People sometimes use **really** to slightly reduce the force of a negative statement. *realmente* [SPOKEN] ❑ *I'm not really surprised. Realmente no me sorprende.* **4** CONVENTION You can say **really** to express surprise or disbelief at what someone has said. *de veras, de verdad* [SPOKEN] ❑ *"I once met the president." —"Really?" —Una vez hablé con el presidente.—¿De veras?*

**realm** /rɛlm/ (**realms**) N-COUNT You can use **realm** to refer to any area of activity, interest, or thought. *campo, esfera, terreno* [FORMAL] ❑ *...the realm of politics. ...el campo de la política.*

**real num|ber** (**real numbers**) N-COUNT In mathematics, rational numbers and irrational numbers can be referred to collectively as **real** numbers. *número real* [TECHNICAL]

**real prop|er|ty** N-UNCOUNT **Real property** is property in the form of land and buildings, rather than personal possessions. *bien raíz, inmueble*

**real world** N-SING If you talk about **the real world,** you are referring to the world and life in general, in contrast to a particular person's own life, experience, and ideas. *realidad, mundo real* ❑ *I'm not sure whether the plan will work in the real world. No estoy seguro de que el plan funcione en la realidad.*

**rear** /rɪər/ (**rears, rearing, reared**) **1** N-SING The **rear** of something is the back part of it. *parte trasera* ❑ *He settled back in the rear of the taxi. Se acomodó en la parte trasera del taxi.* • **Rear** is also an adjective. *trasero* ❑ *...rear seat belts. ...cinturones de los asientos traseros.* **2** V-T If you **rear** children, you take care of them until they are old enough to take care of themselves. *criar* ❑ *I was reared in Texas. Me crié en Texas.* **3** V-T If you **rear** a young animal, you keep and take care of it until it is old enough to be used for work or food, or until it can look after itself. *criar* ❑ *She spends a lot of time rearing animals. Pasa mucho tiempo criando animales.* **4** V-I When a horse **rears,** it moves the front part of its body upward, so that its front legs are high in the air and it is standing on its back legs. *encabritarse, empinarse, pararse en dos patas* ❑ *The horse reared and threw off its rider. El caballo se paró en dos patas y derribó a su jinete.*

**re|arrange** /riəreɪndʒ/ (**rearranges, rearranging, rearranged**) V-T If you **rearrange** things, you change the way in which they are organized or ordered. *cambiar de orden, volver a arreglar o disponer, reorganizar* ❑ *Malcolm rearranged all the furniture. Malcolm cambió de lugar todos los muebles.* • **re|arrange|ment** N-VAR (**rearrangements**) *reorganización* ❑ *...a rearrangement of the company structure. ...una reorganización de la estructura empresarial.*

**rea|son** /rizᵊn/ (**reasons, reasoning, reasoned**) **1** N-COUNT The **reason for** something is a fact or situation which explains why it happens. *razón, motivo, causa* ❑ *There is a reason for every important thing that happens. Hay una razón para todas las cosas importantes que ocurren.* **2** N-UNCOUNT If you say that you have **reason to** believe something or **to** have a particular emotion, you mean that you have evidence for your belief or there is a definite cause of your feeling. *motivos* ❑ *They had reason to believe that he was not telling the truth. Tenían motivos para creer que no estaba diciendo la verdad.* **3** N-UNCOUNT The ability that people have to think and to make sensible judgments can be referred to as **reason.** *razón* ❑ *...a conflict between emotion and reason. ...un conflicto entre los sentimientos y la razón.* **4** V-T If you **reason that** something is true, you decide that it is true after thinking carefully about all the facts. *razonar, pensar, reflexionar* ❑ *I reasoned that if he could do it, so could I. Pensé que, si él podía hacerlo, yo también.* **5** PHRASE If one thing happens **by reason of** another, it happens because of it. *en virtud de* [FORMAL] ❑ *The boss has enormous influence by reason of his position. El jefe tiene una gran influencia en virtud de su posición.*
→ see **philosophy**
▸ **reason with** PHR-VERB If you try to **reason with** someone, you try to persuade them to do or accept something by using sensible arguments. *razonar con* ❑ *He never listens. I can't reason with him. Nunca escucha. No puedo razonar con él.*

**Word Partnership** Usar *reason* con:

ADJ. **main** reason, **major** reason, **obvious** reason, **only** reason, **primary** reason, **real** reason, **same** reason, **simple** reason 1
**compelling** reason, **good** reason, **sufficient** reason 1 2

**rea|son|able** /ri̲zənəbᵊl/ 1 ADJ If you think that someone is fair and sensible you can say that they are **reasonable.** *razonable* ❑ *He's a reasonable person. Es una persona razonable.* ● **rea|son|ably** /ri̲zənəbli/ ADV *sensatamente* ❑ *"Can I think about it?" she asked reasonably. —¿Puedo pensarlo?—preguntó sensatamente.* ● **rea|son|able|ness** N-UNCOUNT *sensatez* ❑ *"I can understand how you feel," Dan said with great reasonableness. —Entiendo cómo te sientes—dijo Dan con gran sensatez.* 2 ADJ If you say that a decision or action is **reasonable,** you mean that it is fair and sensible. *razonable* ❑ *...a perfectly reasonable decision. ...una decisión completamente razonable.* 3 ADJ If you say that an expectation or explanation is **reasonable,** you mean that there are good reasons why it may be correct. *razonable* ❑ *It seems reasonable to think that cities will increase in size. Parece razonable pensar que las ciudades se extenderán.* ● **rea|son|ably** ADV *razonablemente, con seguridad* ❑ *You can reasonably expect your goods to arrive within six weeks. Puede esperar que, con seguridad, sus mercancías llegarán en un plazo máximo de seis semanas.* 4 ADJ If you say that the price of something is **reasonable,** you mean that it is fair and not too high. *razonable* ● **rea|son|ably** ADV *razonablemente* ❑ *...reasonably priced hotels. ...hoteles con precios razonables.* 5 ADJ You can use **reasonable** to describe something that is fairly good, but not very good. *aceptable* ❑ *The boy spoke reasonable French. El niño hablaba un francés aceptable.* ● **rea|son|ably** ADV *aceptablemente* ❑ *I can dance reasonably well. Sé bailar aceptablemente bien.* 6 ADJ A **reasonable** amount of something is a fairly large amount of it. *bastante* ❑ *They will need a reasonable amount of space. Necesitarán bastante espacio.* ● **rea|son|ably** ADV *bastante* ❑ *Things happened reasonably quickly. Las cosas pasaron bastante rápidamente.*

R

**Thesaurus** *reasonable* Ver también:

ADJ. rational 1
acceptable, fair, sensible; (*ant.*) unreasonable 2
likely, probable, right 3
fair, inexpensive 4

**Word Partnership** Usar *reasonable* con:

N. reasonable **person** 1
**beyond a** reasonable **doubt**, reasonable **expectation**, reasonable **explanation** 3
reasonable **cost**, reasonable **price**, reasonable **rates** 4
reasonable **amount** 6

**re|assure** /ri̲əʃʊər/ (**reassures, reassuring, reassured**) V-T If you **reassure** someone, you say or do things to make them stop worrying about something. *tranquilizar* ● **re|assur|ance** N-UNCOUNT *seguridad* ❑ *He needed reassurance that she loved him. Necesitaba tener la seguridad de que ella lo quería.*

**Word Partnership** Usar *reassure* con:

N. reassure **citizens**, reassure **customers**, reassure **investors**, reassure **the public**
V. **seek to** reassure, **try to** reassure

**re|bel** (**rebels, rebelling, rebelled**)

The noun is pronounced /rɛ̲bəl/. The verb is pronounced /rɪbɛ̲l/.

1 N-COUNT **Rebels** are people who are fighting against their own country's army in order to change the political system there. *rebelde* ❑ *...fighting between rebels and government forces. ...los combates entre los rebeldes y las fuerzas gubernamentales.* 2 N-COUNT You can say that someone is a **rebel** if you think that they behave differently from other people and have rejected the values of society or of their parents. *rebelde* ❑ *She was a rebel at school. Era una rebelde en la escuela.* 3 V-I When someone **rebels,** they start to behave differently from other people and reject the values of society or of their parents. *rebelarse* ❑ *Teenagers often rebel. Los adolescentes se rebelan con frecuencia.*

**re|bel|lion** /rɪbɛ̲lyən/ (**rebellions**) N-VAR A **rebellion** is a violent organized action by a large group of people who are trying to change their country's political system. *rebelión* ❑ *...the government's response to the rebellion. ...la respuesta del gobierno a la rebelión.*

**re|boot** /ri̲bu̲t/ (**reboots, rebooting, rebooted**) V-T/V-I If you **reboot** a computer, or if you **reboot,** you shut it down and start it again. *reiniciar* [COMPUTING] ❑ *When you reboot your computer, the software is ready to use. Cuando reinicie la computadora, el programa estará listo para usarlo.* ● **Reboot** is also a noun. *reinicio* ❑ *...the time spent waiting for a reboot. ...el tiempo perdido esperando el reinicio.*

**re|bound** /rɪbaʊ̲nd/ (**rebounds, rebounding, rebounded**) 1 V-I If something **rebounds** from a solid surface, it bounces or springs back from it. *rebotar* ❑ *The ball rebounded from a post. La pelota rebotó en un poste.* 2 V-I If an action or situation **rebounds on** you, it has an unpleasant effect on you, especially when this effect was intended for someone else. *salir el tiro por la culata* ❑ *Her trick rebounded on her. Le salió el tiro por la culata.*

**re|build** /ri̲bɪ̲ld/ (**rebuilds, rebuilding, rebuilt**) 1 V-T When people **rebuild** something such as a building, they build it again after it has been damaged or destroyed. *reconstruir* ❑ *The house must be rebuilt. Es necesario reconstruir la casa.* 2 V-T When people **rebuild** something such as an institution, a system, or an aspect of their lives, they take action to bring it back to its previous condition. *reconstruir, restablecer* ❑ *Everyone worked hard to rebuild the economy. Todo el mundo trabajó mucho para restablecer la economía.*

**re|call** (**recalls, recalling, recalled**)

The verb is pronounced /rɪkɔ̲l/. The noun is pronounced /ri̲kɔl/.

1 V-T/V-I When you **recall** something, you remember it. *recordar* ❑ *He recalled that he met*

*Pollard during a business trip.* *Recordó que había conocido a Pollard durante un viaje de negocios.* ❑ *"What was his name?" — "I don't recall."* *—¿Cómo se llama?—No recuerdo.* **2** V-T If you **are recalled** to your home, country, or the place where you work, you are ordered to return there. *llamar* ❑ *The U.S. representative was recalled to Washington.* *El representante de Estados Unidos fue llamado a Washington.*

**re|cede** /rɪsid/ (**recedes, receding, receded**) **1** V-I If something **recedes** from you, it moves away into the distance. *retroceder, alejarse, desvanecerse* ❑ *Luke's footsteps receded.* *Los pasos de Luke se desvanecieron.* **2** V-I When something such as a quality, problem, or illness **recedes,** it becomes weaker, smaller, or less intense. *ceder* **3** V-I If a man's hair starts to **recede,** it no longer grows on the front of his head. *tener entradas*

**re|ceipt** /rɪsit/ (**receipts**) **1** N-COUNT A **receipt** is a piece of paper that you get from someone as proof that they have received money or goods from you. *recibo* ❑ *I gave her a receipt for the money.* *Le di un recibo por el dinero.* **2** N-PLURAL **Receipts** are the amount of money received during a particular period, for example by a store or theater. *ingresos, entradas* ❑ *He was adding up the day's receipts.* *Estaba sumando las entradas del día.* **3** N-UNCOUNT The **receipt** of something is the act of receiving it. *recibo, recepción* [FORMAL] ❑ *Goods are sent within 28 days after the receipt of your order.* *La mercancía le será enviada dentro de los 28 días posteriores a la recepción de su pedido.*

**re|ceive** /rɪsiv/ (**receives, receiving, received**) **1** V-T When you **receive** something, you get it after someone gives it to you or sends it to you. *recibir* ❑ *They received their awards at a ceremony in San Francisco.* *Recibieron sus premios en una ceremonia efectuada en San Francisco.* **2** V-T You can use **receive** to say that certain kinds of things happen to someone. *ser objeto de* ❑ *He received most of the blame.* *Le echaron casi toda la culpa.* **3** V-T If you say that something **is received** in a particular way, you mean that people react to it in that way. *recibir, acoger* ❑ *The decision was received with great disappointment.* *La decisión fue recibida con una gran decepción.*

**re|ceiv|er** /rɪsivər/ (**receivers**) **1** N-COUNT A telephone's **receiver** is the part that you hold near to your ear and speak into. *auricular* ❑ *She picked up the receiver and started to dial.* *Descolgó el teléfono y empezó a marcar.* **2** N-COUNT A **receiver** is the part of a radio or television that picks up signals and converts them into sound or pictures. *receptor* **3** N-COUNT **The receiver** is someone who is appointed by a court of law to manage the affairs of a business, usually when it is facing financial failure. *síndico* [BUSINESS]
→ see **navigation, radio, television**

**re|cent** /risᵊnt/ ADJ A **recent** event or period of time happened only a short while ago. *reciente* ❑ *...the recent murder of an American journalist.* *...el reciente asesinato de un periodista estadounidense.*

**re|cent|ly** /risᵊntli/ ADV If something happened **recently,** it happened only a short time ago. *recientemente* ❑ *The bank recently opened a branch in Miami.* *El banco abrió recientemente una sucursal en Miami.*

**Usage** **recently**

*Recently* and *lately* can both be used to express that something began in the past and continues into the present: *Recently/Lately I've been considering going back to school to get a master's degree.* *Recently*, but not *lately*, is also used to describe a completed action: *I recently graduated from high school.*

**re|cep|tion** /rɪsɛpʃᵊn/ (**receptions**) **1** N-COUNT A **reception** is a formal party which is given to welcome someone or to celebrate a special event. *recepción* ❑ *...a wedding reception.* *...una recepción de bodas.* **2** N-UNCOUNT **Reception** in a hotel is the desk or office that books rooms for people and answers their questions. *recepción* ❑ *She was waiting at reception.* *Estaba esperando en la recepción.* **3** N-COUNT If someone or something has a particular kind of **reception,** that is the way that people react to them. *acogida* ❑ *They gave Mr. Mandela a friendly reception.* *Le dieron al señor Mandela una acogida cordial.* **4** N-UNCOUNT If you get good **reception** from your radio or television, the sound or picture is clear because the signal is strong. If the **reception** is poor, the sound or picture is unclear because the signal is weak. *recepción*
→ see **wedding**

**re|cep|tion|ist** /rɪsɛpʃənɪst/ (**receptionists**) **1** N-COUNT In an office or hospital, the **receptionist** is the person whose job is to answer the telephone, arrange appointments, and deal with people when they first arrive. *recepcionista* **2** N-COUNT In a hotel, the **receptionist** is the person whose job is to reserve rooms for people and answer their questions. *recepcionista*

**re|cep|tor** /rɪsɛptər/ (**receptors**) N-COUNT **Receptors** are nerve endings in your body which react to changes and stimuli and make your body respond in a particular way. *receptor, órgano sensorio* [TECHNICAL]

**re|ces|sion** /rɪsɛʃᵊn/ (**recessions**) N-VAR A **recession** is a period when the economy of a country is doing badly. *recesión* ❑ *The oil price increases sent Europe into recession.* *Los aumentos del precio del petróleo provocaron recesión en Europa.*

**re|ces|sive** /rɪsɛsɪv/ ADJ A **recessive** gene produces a particular characteristic only if a person has two of these genes, one from each parent. Compare **dominant.** *recesivo* [TECHNICAL]

**reci|pe** /rɛsɪpi/ (**recipes**) **1** N-COUNT A **recipe** is a list of ingredients and a set of instructions that tell you how to cook something. *receta* ❑ *...a recipe for chocolate cake.* *...una receta de pastel de chocolate.* **2** N-SING If you say that something is **a recipe for** a particular situation, you mean that it is likely to result in that situation. *fórmula* ❑ *Having no smoke alarm is a recipe for disaster.* *La falta de un detector de humo es la fórmula para el desastre.*

**re|cipi|ent** /rɪsɪpiənt/ (**recipients**) N-COUNT The **recipient** of something is the person who receives it. *destinatario o destinataria, receptor o receptora, ganador o ganadora* [FORMAL] ❑ *...the recipient of the prize.* *...el ganador del premio.*
→ see **donor**

**re|cite** /rɪsaɪt/ (**recites, reciting, recited**) **1** V-T When someone **recites** a poem or other piece of writing, they say it aloud after they have learned it. recitar ❑ *They recited poetry.* *Recitaron poesía.* **2** V-T If you **recite** something such as a list, you say it aloud. recitar, enumerar ❑ *He recited a list of government failings.* *Enumeró una lista de fracasos del gobierno.*

**reck|on** /rɛkən/ (**reckons, reckoning, reckoned**) **1** V-T If you **reckon** that something is true, you think that it is true. suponer [INFORMAL] ❑ *I reckon it's about three o'clock.* *Supongo que son las tres aproximadamente.* **2** V-T If something **is reckoned** to be a particular figure, it is calculated to be roughly that amount. calcular, estimar ❑ *The business is reckoned to be worth $1.4 billion.* *Se calcula que el negocio vale 1,400 millones de dólares.*

▸ **reckon with** **1** PHR-VERB If you say that you had not **reckoned with** something, you mean that you had not expected it and so were not prepared for it. tener o tomar en cuenta, contar con ❑ *Gary had not reckoned with the strength of Sally's feelings.* *Gary no había contado con la profundidad de los sentimientos de Sally.* **2** PHRASE If you say that there is someone or something **to be reckoned with,** you mean that they must be dealt with and it will be difficult. vérselas con, habérselas con ❑ *He was someone to be reckoned with.* *Tendrían que vérselas con él.*

**re|claim** /rɪkleɪm/ (**reclaims, reclaiming, reclaimed**) **1** V-T If you **reclaim** something that you have lost or that has been taken away from you, you succeed in getting it back. reivindicar, recuperar ❑ *It was difficult for him to reclaim his authority.* *Era difícil para él recuperar su autoridad.* **2** V-T When people **reclaim** land, they make it suitable for a purpose such as farming or building, for example by draining it or by building a barrier against the sea. recuperar ❑ *They are reclaiming farmland from water.* *Están ganando tierras de cultivo al agua.*

**rec|la|ma|tion** /rɛkləmeɪʃᵊn/ N-UNCOUNT **Reclamation** is the process of changing land that is unsuitable for farming or building into land that can be used. rescate, recuperación

| Word Link | *clin ≈ leaning : decline, incline, recline* |
|---|---|

R

**re|cline** /rɪklaɪn/ (**reclines, reclining, reclined**) **1** V-I If you **recline on** something, you sit or lie on it with the upper part of your body supported at an angle. reclinar(se), recostar(se), apoyar(se) ❑ *She was reclining on the sofa.* *Estaba recostada en el sillón.* **2** V-T/V-I When a seat **reclines** or when you **recline** it, you lower the back so that it is more comfortable to sit in. reclinar, recostar, abatir ❑ *First-class seats on the plane recline almost like beds.* *Los asientos de primera clase del avión se reclinan hasta casi convertirse en cama.*

**re|clin|er** /rɪklaɪnər/ (**recliners**) N-COUNT A **recliner** is a type of armchair with a back which can be adjusted to slope at different angles. sillón reclinable

**rec|og|ni|tion** /rɛkəgnɪʃᵊn/ **1** N-UNCOUNT **Recognition** is the act of recognizing someone or identifying something when you see it. reconocimiento ❑ *There was no sign of recognition on her face.* *Su rostro no indicaba que lo hubiese reconocido.* **2** N-UNCOUNT **Recognition of** something is an understanding and acceptance of it. reconocimiento ❑ *...recognition of the importance of exercise.* *...reconocimiento de la importancia del ejercicio.* **3** N-UNCOUNT When a person receives **recognition** for the things that they have done, people acknowledge the value or skill of their work. reconocimiento, aceptación ❑ *His work received public recognition.* *Su obra contó con el reconocimiento del público.* **4** PHRASE If something is done **in recognition of** someone's achievements, it is done as a way of showing official appreciation of him or her. en reconocimiento por ❑ *...a small gift in recognition of her contribution to the university.* *...un pequeño obsequio en reconocimiento por su contribución a la universidad.*

**rec|og|nize** /rɛkəgnaɪz/ (**recognizes, recognizing, recognized**) **1** V-T If you **recognize** someone or something, you know who that person is or what that thing is because you have seen or heard them before. reconocer ❑ *She recognized him immediately.* *Lo reconoció inmediatamente.* **2** V-T If someone says that they **recognize** something, they acknowledge that it exists or that it is true. reconocer ❑ *I recognize my own faults.* *Reconozco mis propias faltas.* **3** V-T If people or organizations **recognize** something as valid, they officially accept it or approve of it. reconocer ❑ *They recognized the independence of Slovenia.* *Reconocieron la independencia de Eslovenia.* **4** V-T When people **recognize** the work that someone has done, they show their appreciation of it, often by giving that person an award. reconocer, apreciar

**re|com|bi|nant DNA** /rikɒmbɪnənt di ɛn eɪ/ N-UNCOUNT **Recombinant DNA** is DNA that contains genes from different sources, which have been combined using genetic engineering. ADN recombinante [TECHNICAL]

**rec|om|mend** /rɛkəmɛnd/ (**recommends, recommending, recommended**) **1** V-T If someone **recommends** a person or thing to you, they suggest that you would find that person or thing good or useful. recomendar ❑ *I recommend Barbados as a place for a vacation.* *Recomiendo Barbados para pasar las vacaciones.* ❑ *I'll recommend you for the job.* *Te recomendaré para el puesto.* • **rec|om|mend|ed** ADJ recomendado, recomendable ❑ *This book is highly recommended.* *Este libro es muy recomendable.* • **rec|om|men|da|tion** N-COUNT recomendación (**recommendations**) ❑ *The best way of finding a lawyer is through personal recommendation.* *La mejor manera de encontrar abogado es por medio de una recomendación personal.* **2** V-T If you **recommend** that something is done, you suggest that it should be done. recomendar, aconsejar ❑ *The doctor recommended that I lose some weight.* *El doctor me aconsejó que bajara de peso.* • **recommendation** N-COUNT recomendación ❑ *...the committee's recommendations.* *...las recomendaciones de la comisión.* **3** V-T If something or someone has a particular quality to **recommend** them, that quality makes them attractive or gives them an advantage over similar things or people. recomendar ❑ *The restaurant has much to recommend it.* *Existen muchas razones para recomendar el restaurante.*

**Word Partnership** Usar *recommend* con:

N. **doctors** recommend, **experts** recommend 1 2
recommend **changes** 2
ADV. **highly** recommend, **strongly** recommend 1 2

**rec|on|cile** /rɛkənsaɪl/ (**reconciles, reconciling, reconciled**) 1 V-T If you **reconcile** two beliefs, facts, or demands that seem to be opposed or completely different, you find a way in which they can both be true or both be successful. *reconciliar con* ❑ *It's difficult to reconcile the demands of my job and the wish to be a good father.* *Es difícil reconciliar las exigencias de mi trabajo con el deseo de ser un buen padre.* 2 V-I/V-RECIP-PASSIVE If you **reconcile** or **are reconciled with** someone, you become friendly with them again after a disagreement. *reconciliarse (con)* ❑ *I don't think Susan and I will be reconciled.* *No creo que Susan y yo nos reconciliemos.* ❑ *You must reconcile with your partner.* *Debes reconciliarte con tu pareja.* • **rec|on|cilia|tion** /rɛkənsɪlieɪʃᵊn/ N-VAR (**reconciliations**) *reconciliación* ❑ *...an appeal for reconciliation between the two religious groups.* *...llamamiento a la reconciliación entre los dos grupos religiosos.* 3 V-T If you **reconcile yourself to** an unpleasant situation, you accept it. *resignarse* ❑ *She reconciled herself to never seeing him again.* *Se resignó a no volver a verlo nunca.* • **rec|on|ciled** ADJ *resignado* ❑ *He seemed reconciled to defeat.* *Parecía resignado a la derrota.*

**rec|ord** (**records, recording, recorded**)

The noun is pronounced /rɛkərd/. The verb is pronounced /rɪkɔrd/.

1 N-COUNT If you keep a **record of** something, you keep a written account or photographs of it so that it can be referred to later. *registro* ❑ *Keep a record of all the payments.* *Lleve un registro de todos los pagos.* 2 V-T If you **record** a piece of information or an event, you write it down, photograph it, or put it into a computer so that in the future people can refer to it. *registrar* ❑ *Her letters record the details of her life in China.* *Sus cartas registran los detalles de su vida en China.* 3 V-T If you **record** something such as a speech or performance, you put it on tape or film so that it can be heard or seen again later. *grabar* ❑ *Viewers can record the films.* *Los televidentes pueden grabar las películas.* 4 N-COUNT A **record** is a round, flat piece of black plastic on which sound, especially music, is stored, and which can be played on a record player. *disco* 5 N-COUNT A **record** is the best result that has ever been achieved in a particular sport or activity, for example the fastest time or the farthest distance. *registro, marca, récord* ❑ *He set the world record of 12.92 seconds.* *Impuso el récord mundial de 12.92 segundos.* 6 → see also **recording, track record** 7 PHRASE If something that you say is **off the record,** you do not intend it to be considered as official, or published with your name attached to it. *extraoficial* 8 PHRASE If you keep information **on record,** you write it down or store it in a computer so that it can be used later. *en disco*
→ see **history**

**Word Partnership** Usar *record* con:

N. record **a song** 3
record **album**, record **club**, record **company**, **hit** record, record **industry**, record **label**, record **producer**, record **store** 4
record **earnings**, record **high**, record **low**, record **numbers**, record **temperatures**, record **time**, **world** record 5
V. **break a** record, **set a** record 5

**re|cord|er** /rɪkɔrdər/ (**recorders**) N-VAR A **recorder** is a wooden or plastic musical instrument in the shape of a pipe that you play by blowing down one end and covering holes with your fingers. *flauta dulce*

**re|cord|ing** /rɪkɔrdɪŋ/ (**recordings**) 1 N-COUNT A **recording of** something is a record, CD, tape, video, or DVD of it. *grabación* ❑ *...a video recording of a police interview.* *...una grabación en video de un interrogatorio policial.* 2 N-UNCOUNT **Recording** is the process of making records, CDs, tapes, videos, or DVDs. *grabación* ❑ *...the recording industry.* *...la industria de la grabación.*

**rec|ord play|er** (**record players**) N-COUNT A **record player** is a machine on which you play records. *tocadiscos, fonógrafo, gramófono*

**re|cov|er** /rɪkʌvər/ (**recovers, recovering, recovered**) 1 V-I When you **recover from** an illness or an injury, you become well again. *recuperarse* ❑ *He is recovering from a knee injury.* *Se está recuperando de una herida en la rodilla.* 2 V-I If you **recover from** an unhappy or unpleasant experience, you stop being upset by it. *recuperarse* ❑ *...a tragedy from which he never fully recovered.* *...una tragedia de la que nunca se recuperó completamente.* 3 V-T If you **recover** something that has been lost or stolen, you find it or get it back. *recuperar, recobrar* ❑ *Police raided five houses and recovered stolen goods.* *La policía allanó cinco casas y recuperó algunas mercancías robadas.* 4 V-T If you **recover** your former mental or physical state, it comes back again. *recobrar, recuperar* ❑ *She never recovered consciousness.* *Nunca recobró el conocimiento.*

**re|cov|ery** /rɪkʌvəri/ (**recoveries**) 1 N-VAR If a sick person makes a **recovery,** he or she becomes well again. *recuperación, restablecimiento* ❑ *He made a remarkable recovery from his injuries.* *Su restablecimiento después de las heridas fue sorprendente.* 2 N-VAR When there is a **recovery** in a country's economy, it improves. *recuperación, reactivación* ❑ *The measures have failed to bring about economic recovery.* *Las medidas para lograr la recuperación de la economía han fracasado.* 3 N-UNCOUNT You talk about the **recovery of** something when you get it back after it has been lost or stolen. *recuperación* ❑ *The museum is offering a reward for the recovery of the painting.* *El museo ofrece una recompensa por la recuperación del cuadro.* 4 N-UNCOUNT You talk about the **recovery of** someone's physical or mental state when he or she returns to this state. *recuperación* ❑ *...the sudden loss and recovery of consciousness.* *...la pérdida y recuperación repentinas del conocimiento.*

**re|cov|ery room** (**recovery rooms**) N-COUNT A

r

**recovery room** is a room where patients who have just had an operation are placed, so that they can be watched while they recover. *sala de recuperación, sala de restablecimiento*

**rec|rea|tion** /rɛkrieɪʃən/ (**recreations**) N-VAR **Recreation** consists of things that you do in your spare time to relax. *esparcimiento, diversión, entretenimiento* ❑ *Saturday afternoon is for recreation. La tarde del sábado es para la diversión.* • **rec|rea|tion|al** ADJ *recreativo* ❑ *...parks and other recreational facilities. ...parques y otros centros recreativos.*
→ see **park**

**rec|rea|tion|al ve|hi|cle** (**recreational vehicles**) N-COUNT A **recreational vehicle** is a large vehicle that you can live in. The abbreviation **RV** is also used. *caravana, cámper, vehículo de recreo*

**re|cruit** /rɪkrut/ (**recruits, recruiting, recruited**) **1** V-T If you **recruit** people for an organization, you select them and persuade them to join it or work for it. *reclutar* ❑ *We need to recruit and train more teachers. Necesitamos reclutar y capacitar a más maestros.* • **re|cruit|ing** N-UNCOUNT *reclutamiento* ❑ *...an army recruiting office. ...una oficina de reclutamiento del ejército.* • **re|cruit|ment** N-UNCOUNT *reclutamiento* ❑ *...the recruitment of soldiers. ...el reclutamiento de soldados.* **2** N-COUNT A **recruit** is a person who has recently joined an organization or an army. *recluta* ❑ *...a new recruit to the police department. ...un recluta para el departamento de policía.*

| Word Link | *rect ≈ right, straight : correct, rectangle, rectify* |
|---|---|

**rec|tan|gle** /rɛktæŋgəl/ (**rectangles**) N-COUNT A **rectangle** is a four-sided shape whose corners are all ninety-degree angles. Each side of a rectangle is the same length as the one opposite to it. *rectángulo*
→ see **shape, volume**

**rec|ti|fy** /rɛktɪfaɪ/ (**rectifies, rectifying, rectified**) V-T If you **rectify** something that is wrong, you change it so that it becomes correct or satisfactory. *rectificar* ❑ *Only a new law will rectify the situation. Solamente una nueva ley rectificaría la situación.*

**rec|ti|lin|ear** /rɛktɪlɪniər/ ADJ A **rectilinear** shape has straight lines. Compare **curvilinear**. *rectilíneo*

**re|cu|per|ate** /rɪkupəreɪt/ (**recuperates, recuperating, recuperated**) V-I When you **recuperate**, you recover your health or strength after you have been ill or injured. *recuperarse, recobrarse, restablecerse* ❑ *I went away to the country to recuperate. Fui al campo para restablecerme.* • **re|cu|pera|tion** /rɪkupəreɪʃən/ N-UNCOUNT *recuperación, restablecimiento* ❑ *Sleep is necessary for recuperation. Dormir es necesario para el restablecimiento.*

**re|cur** /rɪkɜr/ (**recurs, recurring, recurred**) V-I If something **recurs**, it happens more than once. *recurrir, volver a ocurrir, repetirse* ❑ *...a theme that recurs frequently in his work. ...un tema muy recurrente en su trabajo.* • **re|cur|rence** /rɪkɜrəns/ N-VAR (**recurrences**) *repetición, reaparición* ❑ *Police want to prevent a recurrence of the violence. La policía quiere prevenir la reaparición de la violencia.*

**re|cuse** /rɪkyuz/ (**recuses, recusing, recused**) V-T If a judge **recuses himself** or **herself from** a legal case, they state that they will not be involved in making decisions about the case, for example because they think they are biased. *declinar, eximirse* ❑ *The judge himself must decide which cases to recuse himself from. El propio juez debe decidir de qué casos eximirse.*

**re|cy|cle** /risaɪkəl/ (**recycles, recycling, recycled**) V-T If you **recycle** things that have already been used, such as bottles or sheets of paper, you process them so that they can be used again. *reciclar*
→ see **dump, paper**

**red** /rɛd/ (**reds, redder, reddest**) **1** COLOR Something that is **red** is the color of blood or a tomato. *rojo* ❑ *...a bunch of red roses. ...un ramo de rosas rojas.* ❑ *She was dressed in red. Iba vestida de rojo.* **2** COLOR **Red** hair is between red and brown in color. *pelirrojo* **3** PHRASE If a person or company is **in the red** or if their bank account is **in the red,** they have spent more money than they have in their account and therefore they owe money to the bank. *en números rojos* **4** PHRASE If you **see red,** you suddenly become very angry. *enfurecerse, ponerse furioso* ❑ *I didn't mean to hit him. I just saw red. No tenía la intención de pegarle, pero me enfurecí.*
→ see **color, hair, rainbow**

**red blood cell** (**red blood cells**) N-COUNT Your **red blood cells** are the cells in your blood which carry oxygen around your body. Compare **white blood cell**. *glóbulo rojo*
→ see **cardiovascular system**

**red card** (**red cards**) N-COUNT In soccer, if a player is shown the **red card,** the referee holds up a red card to indicate that the player must leave the field for breaking the rules. *tarjeta roja* ❑ *He received a red card for arguing with the referee. Le mostraron la tarjeta roja por discutir con el árbitro.*

**red gi|ant** (**red giants**) N-COUNT A **red giant** is a very large, relatively cool star that is in the final stages of its life. *gigante roja*

**red her|ring** (**red herrings**) N-COUNT If you say that something is a **red herring,** you mean that it is not important and it takes your attention away from the main subject or problem you are considering. *indicio falso, pista falsa*

**red-hot** ADJ Something that is **red-hot** is extremely hot. *al rojo (vivo)* ❑ *...red-hot radiators. ...radiadores al rojo (vivo).*

**re|dis|trict|ing** /ridɪstrɪktɪŋ/ N-UNCOUNT **Redistricting** is the division of an area into new administrative or election districts. *volver a dividir en distritos* ❑ *A redistricting committee will redraw the City Council district lines. Una comisión de demarcación fijará los nuevos límites del ayuntamiento.*

**red tape** N-UNCOUNT You refer to official rules and procedures as **red tape** when they seem unnecessary and cause delay. *papeleo, burocracia, trámites burocráticos* ❑ *...promises to reduce educational red tape in their states. ...promesas de reducir la burocracia educativa en sus estados.*

**re|duce** /rɪdus/ (**reduces, reducing, reduced**) **1** V-T If you **reduce** something, you make it smaller. *reducir, achicar* ❑ *Exercise reduces the risks*

*of heart disease.* *El ejercicio reduce los riesgos de contraer enfermedades cardíacas.* **2** V-T If someone **is reduced to** a weaker or inferior state, they become weaker or inferior as a result of something that happens to them. *reducir a, sumir en* ❑ *They were reduced to extreme poverty.* *Se vieron reducidos a la extrema pobreza.* **3** V-T If you say that someone **is reduced to** doing something, you mean that they have to do it, although it is unpleasant or embarrassing. *reducir a* ❑ *He was reduced to begging on the streets.* *Se vio reducido a mendigar en la calle.* **4** V-T If something is changed to a different or less complicated form, you can say that it **is reduced to** that form. *reducir a* ❑ *The buildings were reduced to rubble by the earthquake.* *Los edificios fueron reducidos a escombros por el terremoto.*
→ see **mineral**

**Word Partnership** Usar *reduce* con:

N. reduce **anxiety**, reduce **costs**, reduce **crime**, reduce **debt**, reduce **pain**, reduce **spending**, reduce **stress**, reduce **taxes**, reduce **violence**, reduce **waste** **1**
ADV. **dramatically** reduce, **greatly** reduce, **significantly** reduce, **substantially** reduce **1**
V. **help** reduce, **plan to** reduce, **try to** reduce **1**

**re|duc|tion** /rɪdʌkʃᵊn/ (**reductions**) N-VAR When there is a **reduction in** something, it is made smaller. *reducción, disminución* ❑ *...a reduction in prices.* *...una reducción de precios.*
→ see **dump**

**re|dun|dant** /rɪdʌndənt/ ADJ Something that is **redundant** is unnecessary, for example, because it has been replaced by something else. *redundante, superfluo* ❑ *Changes in technology mean that many skills are now redundant.* *Los cambios tecnológicos implican que muchas habilidades ahora son redundantes.*

**reek** /ri̱k/ (**reeks, reeking, reeked**) **1** V-I To **reek of** something, usually something unpleasant, means to smell very strongly of it. *apestar, oler* ❑ *Your breath reeks of garlic.* *La boca te huele a ajo.* ● **Reek** is also a noun. *hedor, peste* ❑ *...the reek of dead fish.* *...la peste del pescado muerto.* **2** V-I If you say that something **reeks of** unpleasant ideas, feelings, or practices, you disapprove of it because it involves those ideas, feelings, or practices. *oler a algo* ❑ *The whole thing reeks of stupidity.* *Todo el asunto me huele a tontería.*

**reel** /ri̱l/ (**reels, reeling, reeled**) **1** N-COUNT A **reel** is a cylindrical object around which you wrap something such as movie film, magnetic tape, or fishing line. *carrete, rollo* ❑ *...a 30-meter reel of cable.* *...un carrete de 30 metros de cable.* **2** V-I If someone **reels,** they move about in an unsteady way as if they are going to fall. *tambalearse, flaquear* ❑ *She was reeling with tiredness.* *Se tambaleaba de cansancio.* **3** V-I If you **are reeling** from a shock, you are feeling extremely surprised or upset because of it. *impactarse* ❑ *I'm still reeling from the shock of his death.* *Todavía no me recupero del golpe de su muerte.* **4** V-I If you say that your brain or your mind **is reeling,** you mean that you are very confused because you have too many things to think about. *aturdirse*

▸ **reel off** PHR-VERB If you **reel off** information, you repeat it from memory quickly and easily. *recitar* ❑ *She reeled off a list of things she was going to do.* *Repasó la lista de cosas que iba a hacer.*

**re|elect** /ri̱ɪlɛ̱kt/ (**reelects, reelecting, reelected**) also **re-elect** V-T When someone such as a politician or an official who has been elected **is reelected,** they win another election and are therefore able to continue in their position. *reelegir* ❑ *He was reelected five times.* *Lo reeligieron cinco veces.* ● **re|elec|tion** /ri̱ɪlɛkʃᵊn/ N-UNCOUNT *reelección* ❑ *He will run for reelection next year.* *El próximo año se postulará para la reelección.*

**re|evalu|ate** /ri̱ɪvælyueɪt/ (**reevaluates, reevaluating, reevaluated**) V-T If you **reevaluate** something or someone, you consider them again in order to reassess your opinion of them. *reconsiderar, volver a evaluar* ❑ *This is the time to reevaluate the whole issue.* *Es el momento de reconsiderar todo el asunto.* ● **re|evalu|ation** /ri̱ɪvælyue̱ɪʃᵊn/ N-VAR (**reevaluations**) *revaluación* ❑ *...a period of reevaluation.* *...un periodo de revaluación.*

**re|fer** /rɪfɜ̱r/ (**refers, referring, referred**) **1** V-I If you **refer to** a particular subject or person, you mention them. *referirse a, hacer referencia a* ❑ *He referred to his trip to Canada.* *Se refirió a su viaje a Canadá.* ● **ref|er|ence** /rɛ̱fərəns, rɛ̱frəns/ N-VAR (**references**) *referencia* ❑ *He made no reference to any agreement.* *No hizo referencia a ningún acuerdo.* **2** V-I If a word **refers to** a particular thing, situation, or idea, it describes it. *referir, remitir* ❑ *The word "man" refers most clearly to an adult male.* *La palabra "hombre" remite muy claramente a un varón adulto.* **3** V-T If a person who is ill **is referred to** a hospital or a specialist, they are sent there by a doctor in order to be treated. *remitir* ❑ *She was referred to the hospital by her doctor.* *Su médico la remitió al hospital.* **4** V-T If you **refer** a task or a problem **to** a person or an organization, you formally tell them about it, so that they can deal with it. *remitir* ❑ *He could refer the matter to the high court.* *Pudo remitir el asunto a la corte suprema.* **5** V-I If you **refer to** a book or other source of information, you look at it in order to find something out. *consultar* ❑ *He referred briefly to his notebook.* *Consultó brevemente su cuaderno.* ● **ref|er|ence** N-UNCOUNT *referencia, consulta* ❑ *Keep this book in a safe place for reference.* *Conserva este libro en lugar seguro, para consultas.*

**ref|eree** /rɛ̱fəri̱/ (**referees, refereeing, refereed**)

referee

**1** N-COUNT The **referee** is the official who controls a sports event such as a football game or a boxing match. *árbitro o árbitra, réferi* **2** V-I When someone **referees** a sports event, they act as referee. *arbitrar, hacer de árbitro* ❑ *Vautrot refereed in two soccer games.* *Vautrot arbitró dos juegos de futbol.*
→ see **basketball, football**

**ref|er|ence** /rɛ̱fərəns, rɛ̱frəns/ (**references**) **1** ADJ **Reference** books are ones that you look at when you need specific information or facts about a subject. *de referencia* **2** N-COUNT A **reference** is something such as a number or a name that tells you where you can obtain the information.

r

*referencia* ❑ *...the reference number on the form. ...el número de referencia que viene en la forma.* **3** N-COUNT A **reference** is a letter that is written by someone who knows you and which describes your character and abilities. *referencia, recomendación* ❑ *The firm offered to give her a reference. La empresa le ofreció darle una carta de recomendación.* **4** PHRASE You use **with reference to** or **in reference to** in order to indicate what something relates to. *respecto de, en relación con* ❑ *I am writing with reference to your article on trees. Le escribo respecto de su artículo sobre los árboles.*

**Word Partnership** Usar *reference* con:

N. reference **books**, reference **materials** **1**
reference **number** **2**
ADJ. **clear** reference, **quick** reference, **specific** reference **2**

**ref|er|ence point** (**reference points**) N-COUNT A **reference point** is a fixed point, for example on the surface of the Earth, that is used in order to measure the motion of a moving object. *punto de referencia*

**ref|er|en|dum** /rɛfərɛndəm/ (**referendums** or **referenda** /rɛfərɛndə/) N-COUNT A **referendum** is a vote in which all the people in a country are asked whether they agree or disagree with a particular policy. *referéndum, referendo, plebiscito* ❑ *The country held a referendum on independence. En el país se llevó a cabo un referéndum sobre la independencia.*

**re|fer|ral** /rɪfɜrəl/ (**referrals**) N-VAR **Referral** is the act of officially sending someone to a person or authority that is qualified to deal with them. *referencia* ❑ *...an increase in referrals to the hospital. ...un aumento en el número de referencias al hospital.*

**re|fine** /rɪfaɪn/ (**refines, refining, refined**) **1** V-T When a substance **is refined,** it is made pure by having all other substances removed from it. *refinar* ❑ *Oil is refined to remove impurities. El petróleo se refina para eliminar las impurezas.* • **re|fin|ing** N-UNCOUNT *refinación* ❑ *...oil refining. ...refinación del petróleo.* **2** V-T If something such as a process, theory, or machine **is refined,** it is improved by having small changes made to it. *pulir, mejorar, perfeccionar* ❑ *Medical techniques are constantly being refined. Las técnicas médicas se perfeccionan constantemente.* • **re|fine|ment** N-VAR (**refinements**) *refinamiento, refinación, mejoramiento* ❑ *Older cars lack the latest safety refinements. A los coches viejos les faltan las últimas mejoras en cuanto a seguridad.*
→ see **industry, sugar**

R

**re|fin|ery** /rɪfaɪnəri/ (**refineries**) N-COUNT A **refinery** is a factory where a substance such as oil or sugar is refined. *refinería* ❑ *...an oil refinery. ...una refinería de petróleo.*

**Word Link** *re ≈ back, again : reflect, refuel, restore*

**re|flect** /rɪflɛkt/ (**reflects, reflecting, reflected**) **1** V-T If something **reflects** an attitude or situation, it shows that the attitude or situation exists. *reflejar* ❑ *The agreement was changed to reflect the views of Russia and France. El convenio se modificó de modo que reflejara los puntos de vista de Rusia y Francia.* **2** V-T/V-I When light, heat, or other rays **reflect** off a surface or when a surface **reflects** them, they are sent back from the surface and do not pass through it. *reflejarse* ❑ *The sun reflected off the snow-covered mountains. El sol se reflejaba en las montañas cubiertas de nieve.* **3** V-T When something **is reflected** in a mirror or in water, you can see its image in the mirror or in the water. *reflejar* ❑ *His face was reflected in the mirror. Su cara se reflejaba en el espejo.* **4** V-I When you **reflect on** something, you think deeply about it. *reflexionar, pensar* ❑ *We need some time to reflect. Necesitamos tiempo para reflexionar.* **5** V-I If an action or situation **reflects** in a particular way **on** someone or something, it gives people a good or bad impression of them. *verse* ❑ *It will reflect badly on me if I don't tell the police. Me desprestigiaré si no se lo digo a la policía.*
→ see **echo, telescope**

reflection

**re|flec|tion** /rɪflɛkʃᵊn/ (**reflections**) **1** N-COUNT A **reflection** is an image that you can see in a mirror or in glass or water. *reflejo* ❑ *Meg stared at her reflection in the mirror. Meg observó su reflejo en el espejo.* **2** N-COUNT If you say that something is a **reflection of** a particular person's attitude or **of** a situation, you mean that it shows that attitude or situation exists. *reflejo* ❑ *His drawings are a reflection of his own unhappiness. Sus dibujos son reflejo de su propia infelicidad.* **3** N-SING If something is a **reflection** or a **sad reflection on** a person or thing, it gives a bad impression of them. *reflejo* ❑ *The increase in crime is a sad reflection on society. El aumento de los delitos es un triste reflejo de la sociedad.* **4** N-UNCOUNT **Reflection** is careful thought about a particular subject. *reflexión* ❑ *After days of reflection she decided to write to him. Después de días de reflexión, decidió escribirle.* **5** N-COUNT A **reflection** produces a mirror image of a geometric figure. For example, a **reflection** of the letter "d" would look like the letter "b." *imagen en espejo* **6** N-UNCOUNT **Reflection** is the process by which light and heat are sent back from a surface and do not pass through it. *reflexión* **7** N-SING The **law of reflection** is a principle in physics which states that, when a light wave strikes a flat surface, it is returned at the same angle at which it struck the surface. *ley de la reflexión de la luz* [TECHNICAL]
→ see **echo**

**Word Link** *flex ≈ bending : flexible, flextime, reflex*

**re|flex** /riflɛks/ (**reflexes**) **1** N-COUNT A **reflex** or a **reflex action** is a normal, uncontrollable reaction of your body to something that you feel, see, or experience. *reflejo, acción refleja, acto reflejo* ❑ *Blushing is a reflex action. Sonrojarse es una acción refleja.* **2** N-PLURAL Your **reflexes** refer to your ability to react quickly with your body when something unexpected happens. *reflejos* ❑ *...the reflexes of an athlete. ...los reflejos de un atleta.*

**re|flex|ive pro|noun** (**reflexive pronouns**) N-COUNT A **reflexive pronoun** is a pronoun such as "myself" which refers back to the subject of a sentence or clause. *pronombre reflexivo*

**re|flex|ive verb** (**reflexive verbs**) N-COUNT A **reflexive verb** is a transitive verb whose subject and object always refer to the same person or thing, so the object is always a reflexive pronoun. An example is "to enjoy yourself." *verbo reflexivo*

**re|form** /rɪfɔrm/ (**reforms, reforming, reformed**) **1** N-VAR **Reform** consists of changes and improvements to a law, social system, or institution. A **reform** is an instance of such a change or improvement. *reforma* ❑ *...a program of economic reform.* *...un programa de reformas económicas.* **2** V-T If someone **reforms** something such as a law, social system, or institution, they change or improve it. *modificar, reformar* ❑ *...his plans to reform the country's economy.* *...sus planes para reformar la economía del país.* ● **re|form|er** N-COUNT (**reformers**) *reformador o reformadora* ❑ *...prison reformers.* *...reformadores de las prisiones.* **3** V-T/V-I When someone **reforms** or when something **reforms** them, they stop doing things that society does not approve of. *reformar(se), corregir(se)* ❑ *After his time in prison, James promised to reform.* *Después de cumplir su sentencia, James prometió corregirse.* ● **re|formed** ADJ *reformado* ❑ *...a reformed criminal.* *...un delincuente reformado.*

**Word Partnership** Usar *reform* con:

ADJ. **economic** reform, **political** reform **1**
N. **education** reform, **election** reform, **health care** reform, reform **movement**, **party** reform, **prison** reform, **tax** reform **1**

**re|form school** (**reform schools**) N-VAR A **reform school** is a prison for young criminals who are not old enough to be sent to ordinary prisons. *reformatorio, centro de readaptación social para menores*

**re|fract** /rɪfrækt/ (**refracts, refracting, refracted**) V-T/V-I When a ray of light or a sound wave **refracts** or **is refracted,** the path it follows bends at a particular point, for example when it enters water or glass. *refractar(se)* ❑ *As we age, the lenses of the eyes thicken, and thus refract light differently.* *Con la edad, el cristalino del ojo se engruesa y refracta la luz de manera diferente.* ❑ *...surfaces that cause the light to reflect and refract.* *...superficies que reflejan y refractan la luz.* ● **re|frac|tion** /rɪfrækʃᵊn/ N-UNCOUNT *refracción* ❑ *...the refraction of the light on the dancing waves.* *...la refracción de la luz en las olas danzarinas.*

**re|fract|ing tele|scope** (**refracting telescopes**) N-COUNT A **refracting telescope** is a telescope that uses lenses to focus light rays and produce a clear image. *telescopio de refracción*
→ see **telescope**

**re|frain** /rɪfreɪn/ (**refrains, refraining, refrained**) **1** V-I If you **refrain from** doing something, you deliberately do not do it. *abstenerse de, refrenarse de* ❑ *Mrs. Hardie refrained from making any comment.* *La Sra. Hardie se abstuvo de hacer comentarios.* **2** N-COUNT A **refrain** is a short, simple part of a song, which is repeated many times. *estribillo* ❑ *...a refrain from an old song.* *...el estribillo de una vieja canción.*

**re|fresh** /rɪfrɛʃ/ (**refreshes, refreshing, refreshed**) **1** V-T If something **refreshes** you when you are hot, tired, or thirsty, it makes you feel cooler or more energetic. *refrescar* ❑ *The lotion cools and refreshes the skin.* *La crema refresca la piel.* ● **re|freshed** ADJ *fresco, como nuevo* ❑ *He awoke feeling completely refreshed.* *Despertó sintiéndose totalmente renovado.* ● **re|fresh|ing** ADJ *refrescante* ❑ *...refreshing drinks.* *...bebidas refrescantes.* **2** V-T If someone **refreshes** your memory, they tell you something that you had forgotten. *refrescar, ayudar a recordar* ❑ *Can you refresh my memory and tell me what I need to do?* *¿Me recuerdas qué necesito hacer?*

**re|fresh|ing** /rɪfrɛʃɪŋ/ ADJ You say that something is **refreshing** when it is pleasantly different from what you are used to. *refrescante, alentador* ❑ *It's refreshing to hear somebody speaking so honestly.* *Es alentador oír a alguien que se expresa con tanta honestidad.* ● **re|fresh|ing|ly** ADV *refrescantemente* ❑ *He was refreshingly honest.* *Era refrescante su honestidad.*

**re|fried beans** /rifraɪd binz/ N-PLURAL **Refried beans** are beans that have been boiled and crushed before being fried, used especially in Mexican cooking. *frijoles refritos*

**re|frig|era|tor** /rɪfrɪdʒəreɪtər/ (**refrigerators**) N-COUNT A **refrigerator** is a large container which is kept cool inside, usually by electricity, so that the food and drink in it stays fresh. *refrigerador, nevera*

**Word Link** *re ≈ back, again : reflect, refuel, restore*

**re|fu|el** /rifyuəl/ (**refuels, refueling** or **refuelling, refueled** or **refuelled**) V-T/V-I When an aircraft or other vehicle **refuels** or when someone **refuels** it, it is filled with more fuel so that it can continue its journey. *reabastecer, repostar, poner gasolina, llenar el tanque* ● **re|fu|el|ing** N-UNCOUNT *reabastecimiento de combustible* ❑ *...refueling of vehicles.* *...reabastecer de combustible a los vehículos.*

**ref|uge** /rɛfyudʒ/ (**refuges**) **1** N-UNCOUNT If you take **refuge** somewhere, you try to protect yourself from physical harm by going there. *refugio* ❑ *They took refuge in a shelter.* *Acudieron a un refugio.* **2** N-COUNT A **refuge** is a place where you go for safety and protection. *refugio* ❑ *...a refuge for homeless people.* *...un refugio para personas sin hogar.*

**refu|gee** /rɛfyudʒi/ (**refugees**) N-COUNT **Refugees** are people who have been forced to leave their homes or their country, either because there is a war there or because of their political or religious beliefs. *refugiado o refugiada*

**re|fund** (**refunds, refunding, refunded**)

The noun is pronounced /rifʌnd/. The verb is pronounced /rɪfʌnd/.

**1** N-COUNT A **refund** is a sum of money that is returned to you, for example because you have paid too much or because you have returned goods to a store. *devolución, rembolso, reembolso* ❑ *He took the boots back to the store and asked for a refund.* *Regresó las botas a la tienda y solicitó la devolución.* **2** V-T If someone **refunds** your money, they return it to you, for example because you have paid too much or because you have returned goods to a store. *devolver, rembolsar, reembolsar*

**Thesaurus** *refund* Ver también:

N. payment, reimbursement 1
V. give back, pay back, reimburse 2

**re|fur|bish** /rifɜrbɪʃ/ (**refurbishes, refurbishing, refurbished**) V-T To **refurbish** a building or room means to clean it and decorate it and make it more attractive or better equipped. renovar, retocar ❑ *We refurbished the offices.* *Renovamos las oficinas.*
● **re|fur|bish|ment** N-VAR (**refurbishments**) renovación ❑ *The restaurant is closed for refurbishment.* *El restaurante está cerrado por renovación.*

**re|fus|al** /rɪfyuzᵊl/ (**refusals**) N-VAR Someone's **refusal to** do something is the fact of them showing or saying that they will not do it, allow it, or accept it. negativa, rechazo ❑ *...her refusal to accept change.* *...su negativa a aceptar cambios.*

**re|fuse** (**refuses, refusing, refused**)

The verb is pronounced /rɪfyuz/. The noun is pronounced /rɛfyus/ and is hyphenated ref|use.

1 V-I If you **refuse to** do something, you deliberately do not do it, or you say firmly that you will not do it. rehusar, negarse, rechazar ❑ *He refused to comment.* *Se negó a hacer comentarios.* ❑ *I couldn't refuse, could I?* *No podía negarme, ¿o sí?* 2 V-T If someone **refuses** you something, they do not give it to you or do not allow you to have it. negar ❑ *The United States has refused him a visa.* *Los Estados Unidos le negaron la visa.* 3 V-T If you **refuse** something that is offered to you, you do not accept it. rechazar ❑ *The patient has the right to refuse treatment.* *El paciente tiene derecho a rechazar el tratamiento.* 4 N-UNCOUNT **Refuse** consists of the trash and all the things that are not wanted in a house, store, or factory, and that are regularly thrown away. basura, residuos, desperdicio ❑ *...a weekly collection of refuse.* *...recolección semanal de los desechos.*
→ see **dump**

**Thesaurus** *refuse* Ver también:

V. decline, reject, turn down; (*ant.*) accept 1 3
N. garbage, rubbish, trash 4

**Word Partnership** Usar *refuse* con:

V. refuse **to answer**, refuse **to cooperate**, refuse **to go**, refuse **to participate**, refuse **to pay** 1
refuse **to allow**, refuse **to give** 1 2
refuse **to accept** 1 3

**re|fute** /rɪfyut/ (**refutes, refuting, refuted**) 1 V-T If you **refute** an argument, accusation, or theory, you prove that it is wrong. refutar, rebatir [FORMAL] ❑ *It was the kind of rumor that is impossible to refute.* *Era el tipo de rumor imposible de rebatir.* 2 V-T If you **refute** an argument or accusation, you say that it is not true. refutar [FORMAL] ❑ *He angrily refuted the accusation.* *Rebatió, enojado, la acusación.*

**re|gain** /rɪgeɪn/ (**regains, regaining, regained**) V-T If you **regain** something that you have lost, you get it back again. recuperar, recobrar ❑ *Troops have regained control of the city.* *Las tropas recuperaron el control de la ciudad.*

R

**re|gard** /rɪgɑrd/ (**regards, regarding, regarded**) 1 V-T If you **regard** someone or something **as** being a particular thing or **as** having a particular quality, you believe that they are that thing or have that quality. considerar ❑ *He was regarded as the most successful president of modern times.* *Era considerado como el presidente más exitoso de la época moderna.* 2 V-T If you **regard** something or someone **with** a feeling such as dislike or respect, you have that feeling about them. mirar con ❑ *He regarded her with suspicion.* *La miró con recelo.* 3 N-UNCOUNT If you have **regard for** someone or something, you respect them. respeto, consideración ❑ *I have a very high regard for him and his achievements.* *Siento mucho respeto por él y por sus logros.* 4 N-PLURAL **Regards** are greetings. You use **regards** in expressions such as **best regards** and **with kind regards** as a way of expressing friendly feelings toward someone. saludos ❑ *Give my regards to your family.* *Saludos a tu familia.* 5 PHRASE You can use **as regards** to indicate the subject that is being talked or written about. en cuanto a, en relación con, respecto de ❑ *As regards the future of the business, we are discussing a deal.* *En cuanto al futuro del negocio, estamos discutiendo un arreglo.* 6 PHRASE You can use **with regard to** or **in regard to** to indicate the subject that is being talked or written about. en relación con, respecto de, en cuanto a ❑ *...his opinions with regard to the law.* *...sus opiniones respecto de la ley.*

**re|gard|ing** /rɪgɑrdɪŋ/ PREP You can use **regarding** to indicate the subject that is being talked or written about. respecto de, en cuanto a, en relación con ❑ *He refused to give any information regarding the man's financial situation.* *Se negó a dar información sobre la situación financiera del hombre.*

**re|gard|less** /rɪgɑrdlɪs/ 1 PHRASE If something happens **regardless of** something else, it is not affected or influenced at all by that other thing. independientemente, a pesar de ❑ *The organization helps anyone regardless of their age.* *La organización ayuda a cualquiera, sin importar su edad.* 2 ADV If you say that someone did something **regardless,** you mean that they did it even though there were problems or factors that could have stopped them. a pesar de ❑ *Her knee was painful but she continued walking regardless.* *Le dolía la rodilla, pero a pesar de ello, siguió caminando.*

**reg|gae** /rɛgeɪ/ N-UNCOUNT **Reggae** is a kind of West Indian popular music with a very strong beat. reggae

**re|gime** /rəʒim, reɪ-/ (**regimes**) N-COUNT If you refer to a government or system of running a country as a **regime,** you are critical of it because you think it is not democratic and uses unacceptable methods. régimen, sistema ❑ *...the collapse of the regime.* *...el colapso del régimen.*

**regi|ment** /rɛdʒɪmənt/ (**regiments**) N-COUNT A **regiment** is a large group of soldiers that is commanded by a colonel. regimiento ● **regi|men|tal** /rɛdʒɪmɛntᵊl/ ADJ de regimiento ❑ *...a regimental commander.* *...un comandante de regimiento.*

**re|gion** /ridʒᵊn/ (**regions**) 1 N-COUNT A **region** is an area of a country or of the world. región, zona, área ❑ *...the coastal region of South Carolina.* *...la región costera de Carolina del Sur.* ● **re|gion|al** ADJ regional ❑ *...Hawaiian regional cooking.* *...la cocina* *regional hawaiana.* **2** PHRASE You say **in the region of** to indicate that an amount that you are stating is approximate. *alrededor de* ❑ *The plan will cost in the region of six million dollars. El plan costará más o menos seis millones de dólares.*

**reg|is|ter** /rɛdʒɪstər/ (**registers, registering, registered**) **1** N-COUNT A **register** is an official list or record of people or things. *registro, lista, padrón* ❑ *...registers of births, deaths, and marriages. ...padrones de nacimientos, muertes y matrimonios.* **2** V-T/V-I If you **register,** or **register** to do something, you put your name on an official list, in order to be able to do that thing. *registrarse, inscribirse* ❑ *Thousands of people registered to vote. Miles de personas se empadronaron para votar.* ❑ *He is not registered to practice law in Virginia. No está autorizado para fungir como abogado en Virginia.* **3** V-T If you **register** something, you have it recorded on an official list. *registrar* ❑ *The boy's mother never registered his birth. La madre del niño nunca lo registró.* **4** V-T/V-I When something **registers on** a scale or measuring instrument, it shows a particular value. You can also say that something **registers** a certain amount **on** a scale or measuring instrument. *registrar* ❑ *The earthquake registered 5.7 on the Richter scale. El terremoto marcó 5.7 en la escala de Richter.* **5** V-T If you **register** your feelings or opinions about something, you do something that makes them clear to other people. *demostrar* ❑ *Voters registered their dissatisfaction with the government. Los votantes demostraron su insatisfacción con el gobierno.*

**Word Partnership** Usar *register* con:

V. register **to vote** **2**
N. **voters** register **2**

**reg|is|tered nurse** (**registered nurses**) N-COUNT A **registered nurse** is someone who is qualified to work as a nurse. *enfermera titulada o enfermero titulado*

**Word Link** *ar, er ≈ one who acts as : buyer, registrar, seller*

**reg|is|trar** /rɛdʒɪstrɑr/ (**registrars**) N-COUNT A **registrar** is an administrative official in a college or university who is responsible for student records. *secretario de admisiones o secretaria de admisiones*

**reg|is|tra|tion** /rɛdʒɪstreɪʃən/ N-UNCOUNT The **registration** of something is the recording of it in an official list. *registro, padrón* ❑ *...voter registration. ...padrón de votantes.*

**re|gret** /rɪgrɛt/ (**regrets, regretting, regretted**) **1** V-T If you **regret** something that you have done, you wish that you had not done it. *arrepentirse, lamentar* ❑ *I lied to him, and I've regretted it ever since. Le mentí, y me he arrepentido siempre.* ❑ *Ellis regretted that he had asked the question. Ellis se arrepintió de haber hecho la pregunta.* **2** N-VAR **Regret** is a feeling of sadness or disappointment, which is caused by something that has happened or something that you have done or not done. *arrepentimiento, pesar, remordimiento* ❑ *He had no regrets about leaving. No sentía remordimiento por irse.* **3** V-T You use **regret** in expressions such as **I regret to say** or **I regret to inform you** to show that you are sorry about something. *lamentar*

**Word Partnership** Usar *regret* con:

N. regret **a decision,** regret **a loss** **1**
V. **come to** regret **1**
**express** regret **2**

**regu|lar** /rɛgyələr/ (**regulars**) **1** ADJ **Regular** events have equal amounts of time between them, so that they happen, for example, at the same time each day or each week. *regular, sistemático, habitual* ❑ *Get regular exercise. Haz ejercicio con regularidad.* • **regu|lar|ly** ADV *regularmente, con regularidad* ❑ *He writes regularly for the magazine. Escribe regularmente para la revista.* • **regu|lar|ity** N-UNCOUNT *regularidad* ❑ *...the regularity of the payments. ...la regularidad de los pagos.* **2** ADJ **Regular** events happen often. *regular, común, constante* ❑ *We meet on a regular basis. Nos reunimos de manera regular.* • **regu|lar|ly** ADV *regularmente, frecuentemente* ❑ *...if you regularly take snacks instead of eating properly. ...si frecuentemente te comes un bocadillo en vez de comer bien.* • **regu|lar|ity** N-UNCOUNT *regularidad* ❑ *Job losses were announced with regularity. Se hablaba con regularidad de la pérdida de empleos.* **3** ADJ If you are, for example, a **regular** customer at a store or a **regular** visitor to a place, you go there often. *regular, habitual, asiduo* ❑ *She was a regular visitor to the museum. Era de los visitantes habituales del museo.* **4** N-COUNT The **regulars** at a place or on a team are the people who often go to the place or are often on the team. *asiduo o asidua* ❑ *...regulars at the club. ...los asiduos del club.* **5** ADJ **Regular** means normal or ordinary. *común, normal* ❑ *They were just regular trucks. Eran camiones normales.* **6** ADJ If something has a **regular** shape, both halves are the same and it has straight edges or a smooth outline. *regular* ❑ *...a man of average height with regular features. ...un hombre de estatura promedio y facciones regulares.* **7** ADJ In grammar, a **regular** verb, noun, or adjective inflects in the same way as most verbs, nouns, or adjectives in the language. *regular*

**Word Partnership** Usar *regular* con:

N. regular **basis,** regular **checkups,** regular **exercise,** regular **meetings,** regular **schedule,** regular **visits** **1** **2**
regular **customer,** regular **visitor** **3**
regular **coffee,** regular **guy,** regular **hours,** regular **mail,** regular **season** **5**
regular **verbs** **7**

**regu|late** /rɛgyəleɪt/ (**regulates, regulating, regulated**) V-T To **regulate** an activity or process means to control it, especially by means of rules. *regular, reglamentar* ❑ *The plan will regulate competition among insurance companies. El plan regulará la competencia entre compañías de seguros.*

**regu|la|tion** /rɛgyəleɪʃən/ (**regulations**) N-COUNT **Regulations** are rules made by a government or other authority in order to control the way something is done or the way people behave. *regla, reglamento* ❑ *...new safety regulations. ...nuevas normas de seguridad.*
→ see **factory**

**regu|la|tor** /rɛgyəleɪtər/ (**regulators**) N-COUNT A **regulator** is a person or organization appointed by a government to regulate an area of activity such as banking or industry. *regulador o reguladora* ❑ *Regulators took control of the $22 billion banking company on Sunday. El domingo, los reguladores tomaron el control de la institución bancaria de 22 mil millones de dólares.* • **regu|la|tory** /rɛgyələtɔri/ ADJ *regulador, reglamentario* ❑ *...the U.S.'s financial regulatory system. ...el sistema regulador de las finanzas en los Estados Unidos.*

**re|ha|bili|tate** /rihəbɪlɪteɪt/ (**rehabilitates, rehabilitating, rehabilitated**) V-T To **rehabilitate** someone who has been ill or in prison means to help them to live a normal life again. *rehabilitar* • **re|ha|bili|ta|tion** /rihəbɪlɪteɪʃən/ N-UNCOUNT *rehabilitación* ❑ *...the rehabilitation of prisoners. ...la rehabilitación de los presos.*

**re|hears|al** /rɪhɜrsəl/ (**rehearsals**) N-VAR A **rehearsal** of a play, dance, or piece of music is a practice of it in preparation for a performance. *ensayo* ❑ *...rehearsals for the concert. ...los ensayos para el concierto.*
→ see **theater**

**reign** /reɪn/ (**reigns, reigning, reigned**) **1** V-I If you say, for example, that silence **reigns** in a place or confusion **reigns** in a situation, you mean that the place is silent or the situation is confused. *reinar* [WRITTEN] **2** V-I When a king or queen **reigns**, he or she rules a country. *reinar* ❑ *...Henry II, who reigned in England from 1154 to 1189. ...Enrique II, que reinó en Inglaterra de 1154 a 1189.* • **Reign** is also a noun. *reino* ❑ *...Queen Victoria's reign. ...el reino de la reina Victoria.*

**re|im|burse** /riɪmbɜrs/ (**reimburses, reimbursing, reimbursed**) V-T If you **reimburse** someone **for** something, you pay them back the money that they have spent or lost because of it. *reembolsar* [FORMAL] ❑ *I'll reimburse you for any expenses you have. Le reembolsaré todos los gastos que haga.* • **re|im|burse|ment** N-VAR (**reimbursements**) *reembolso* ❑ *She wants reimbursement for medical expenses. Quiere el reembolso de sus gastos médicos.*

**rein** /reɪn/ (**reins, reining, reined**) **1** N-PLURAL **Reins** are the thin leather straps attached around a horse's neck which are used to control the horse. *rienda* ❑ *She held the reins while the horse pulled. Sostuvo las riendas mientras el caballo tiraba.* **2** PHRASE If you **give free rein to** someone, you give them a lot of freedom to do what they want. *dar rienda suelta, dar carta blanca, dejar las manos libres* ❑ *Horrigan was given free rein to run the company. Horrigan recibió carta blanca para dirigir la compañía.*
▸ **rein in** PHR-VERB To **rein in** something means to control it. *frenar* ❑ *We need to rein in spending. Necesitamos frenar los gastos.*
→ see **horse**

R

**re|inforce** /riɪnfɔrs/ (**reinforces, reinforcing, reinforced**) **1** V-T If something **reinforces** a feeling, situation, or process, it makes it stronger. *reforzar, fortalecer* ❑ *This reinforced our determination to deal with the problem. Esto reforzó nuestra determinación para enfrentar el problema.* • **re|inforce|ment** N-VAR (**reinforcements**) *refuerzo, fortalecimiento* ❑ *...the reinforcement of peace. ...el fortalecimiento de la paz.* **2** V-T To **reinforce** an object means to make it stronger or harder. *reforzar* ❑ *They had to reinforce the floor with concrete. Tuvieron que reforzar el piso con concreto.*

**re|install** /riɪnstɔl/ (**reinstalls, reinstalling, reinstalled**) V-T If you **reinstall** something such as software on your computer, you set it up again, usually because you have been having problems with it. *reinstalar* ❑ *You need to reinstall all the software. Necesita reinstalar todos los programas.*

**re|instate** /riɪnsteɪt/ (**reinstates, reinstating, reinstated**) V-T If you **reinstate** someone, you give them back a job or position that was taken away from them. *restituir, rehabilitar* ❑ *The governor will reinstate the five workers who were fired. El gobernador restituirá a los cinco trabajadores que fueron despedidos.* • **re|instate|ment** N-UNCOUNT *rehabilitación* ❑ *The former officers will now apply for reinstatement. Ahora, los ex policías solicitarán la rehabilitación.*

**re|it|er|ate** /riɪtəreɪt/ (**reiterates, reiterating, reiterated**) V-T If you **reiterate** something, you say it again to emphasize it. *reiterar* [FORMAL] ❑ *He reiterated his opposition to the plan. Reiteró su oposición al plan.*

**re|ject** (**rejects, rejecting, rejected**)

> The verb is pronounced /rɪdʒɛkt/. The noun is pronounced /ridʒɛkt/.

**1** V-T If you **reject** something such as a proposal or a request, you do not accept it or agree to it. *rechazar* ❑ *The president rejected the offer. El presidente rechazó el ofrecimiento.* • **re|jec|tion** /rɪdʒɛkʃən/ N-VAR (**rejections**) *rechazo* ❑ *...his rejection of our values. ...su rechazo de nuestros valores.* **2** V-T If someone **is rejected** for a job or course of study, it is not offered to them. *rechazar* ❑ *He was rejected by another university. Fue rechazado por otra universidad.* • **re|jec|tion** N-COUNT *rechazo* ❑ *Be prepared for lots of rejections before you get a job. Prepárate para recibir muchos rechazos antes de que consigas trabajo.* **3** V-T If someone **rejects** another person who expects affection from them, they are cold and unfriendly toward them. *rechazar* ❑ *...people who were rejected by their parents. ...gente que sufrió el rechazo de sus padres.* • **re|jec|tion** N-VAR *rechazo* ❑ *...feelings of rejection and hurt. ...sentimientos de rechazo y dolor.* **4** N-COUNT A **reject** is a product that has not been accepted for use or sale, because there is something wrong with it. *producto defectuoso* ❑ *The shirt is a reject—all the buttons are missing. La camisa es defectuosa; le faltan todos los botones.*

**Word Partnership** Usar *reject* con:

| | |
|---|---|
| N. | reject **an application**, reject **an idea**, reject **an offer**, reject **a plan**, reject **a proposal**, **voters** reject **1** |
| V. | **vote to** reject **1** |

**re|late** /rɪleɪt/ (**relates, relating, related**) **1** V-I If something **relates to** a particular subject, it concerns that subject. *relacionarse* ❑ *...information relating to the crime. ...información que se relaciona con el crimen.* **2** V-RECIP The way that two things **relate**, or the way that one thing **relates to** another, is the sort of connection that exists between them. *relacionar(se)* ❑ *...new thinking about how the two sciences relate. ...nuevas ideas sobre la manera en que se relacionan las dos ciencias.* ❑ *He tried to relate new ideas to his past experiences. Trató de relacionar las nuevas ideas con sus pasadas* *experiencias.* • **re|lat|ed** ADJ *relacionado* ❑ *Crime and poverty are closely related. El crimen y la pobreza están íntimamente relacionados.* **3** V-RECIP If you can **relate to** someone, you can understand how they feel or behave so that you are able to communicate with them or deal with them easily. *relacionarse* ❑ *He is unable to relate to other people. Es incapaz de relacionarse con los demás.*

**re|lat|ed** /rɪleɪtɪd/ ADJ People who are **related** belong to the same family. *emparentado, pariente de* ❑ *The boys have the same last name but are not related. Los niños tienen el mismo apellido, pero no son parientes.*

**re|la|tion** /rɪleɪʃᵊn/ (**relations**) **1** N-COUNT **Relations** between people, groups, or countries are contacts between them and the way in which they behave toward each other. *relación* ❑ *The country has good relations with Israel. El país tiene buenas relaciones con Israel.* **2** → see also **public relations** **3** N-COUNT The **relation of** one thing **to** another is the connection between them. *relación* ❑ *...the relation of his job to his lifestyle. ...la relación de su trabajo con su estilo de vida.* **4** N-COUNT Your **relations** are the members of your family. *pariente* ❑ *...visits to friends and relations. ...visitas a los amigos y parientes.* **5** PHRASE You can talk about something **in relation to** something else when you want to compare the size, condition, or position of the two things. *en relación con, con relación a* ❑ *The cost was small in relation to his salary. El costo fue reducido en relación con su salario.*

**re|la|tion|ship** /rɪleɪʃᵊnʃɪp/ (**relationships**) **1** N-COUNT The **relationship** between two people or groups is the way in which they feel and behave toward each other. *relación* ❑ *...the friendly relationship between France and Britain. ...la relación amistosa entre Francia y la Gran Bretaña.* **2** N-COUNT A **relationship** is a close friendship between two people, especially one involving romantic or sexual feelings. *relación* ❑ *She felt their relationship was developing too quickly. Pensaba que su relación estaba yendo muy rápido.* **3** N-COUNT The **relationship** between two things is the way in which they are connected. *relación* ❑ *...a relationship between diet and cancer. ...una relación entre la alimentación (el régimen alimenticio) y el cáncer.* **4** N-COUNT The **relationship** between an organism and its environment is the way that the organism and its environment interact and the effect they have on each other. *relación*

**rela|tive** /rɛlətɪv/ (**relatives**) **1** N-COUNT Your **relatives** are the members of your family. *pariente* ❑ *Ask a relative to look after the children. Pídale a un pariente que cuide a los niños.* **2** ADJ You use **relative** to say that something is true to a certain degree, especially when compared with other things of the same kind. *relativo* ❑ *The fighting started again after a period of relative calm. Los combates se reiniciaron después de un lapso de calma relativa.* **3** ADJ You use **relative** when you are comparing the quality or size of two things. *relativo* ❑ *...the relative advantages of New York and Washington as places to live. ...las ventajas relativas de Nueva York y Washington como lugares para vivir.* • **rela|tive|ly** ADV *relativamente* ❑ *The amount of money that you need is relatively small. La cantidad de dinero que necesita es relativamente pequeña.* **4** PHRASE **Relative to** something means with reference to it or in comparison with it. *en relación con, con relación a, en comparación con* ❑ *Japanese interest rates rose relative to France's. Las tasas de interés del Japón aumentaron en comparación con las de Francia.*

**Word Partnership** Usar *relative* con:

ADJ. **close** relative, **distant** relative **1**
N. **friend and** relative **1**
relative **calm**, relative **ease**, relative **safety**, relative **stability** **2**

**rela|tive clause** (**relative clauses**) N-COUNT A **relative clause** is a subordinate clause that gives information about a person or thing. Relative clauses come after a noun or pronoun and often begin with "who," "which," or "that." *oración adjetiva, oración de relativo*

**rela|tive da|ting** N-UNCOUNT **Relative dating** is a technique used by archaeologists to determine whether an object such as a fossil is older or younger than other objects. *fechamiento relativo, datación relativa*

**rela|tive hu|mid|ity** (**relative humidities**) N-VAR **Relative humidity** is a measure of the amount of water vapor contained in the air, compared with the maximum amount of water vapor that the air is able to hold. *humedad relativa*

**rela|tive pro|noun** (**relative pronouns**) N-COUNT A **relative pronoun** is a word such as "who," "that," or "which" that is used to introduce a relative clause. *pronombre relativo*

**re|lax** /rɪlæks/ (**relaxes, relaxing, relaxed**) **1** V-T/V-I If you **relax** or if something **relaxes** you, you feel more calm and less worried or tense. *descansar, relajarse* ❑ *I should relax and stop worrying. Debería relajarme y dejar de preocuparme.* • **re|laxa|tion** /rilækseɪʃᵊn/ N-UNCOUNT *relajamiento, relajación* ❑ *...relaxation techniques. ...técnicas de relajamiento.* • **re|laxed** ADJ *informal* ❑ *The atmosphere at lunch was relaxed. El ambiente durante la comida fue informal.* • **re|lax|ing** ADJ *relajante* ❑ *I find cooking very relaxing. Cocinar es muy relajante para mí.* **2** V-T/V-I When a part of your body **relaxes**, or when you **relax** it, it becomes less stiff or firm. *relajar(se)* ❑ *Have a massage to relax your muscles. Hágase dar un masaje para relajar los músculos.* **3** V-T If you **relax** your grip or hold on something, you hold it less tightly than before. *aflojar* **4** V-T/V-I If you **relax** a rule or your control over something, or if it **relaxes**, it becomes less firm or strong. *relajar* ❑ *The rules have relaxed in recent years. Las reglas se han relajado en los últimos años.*
→ see **muscle**

**Thesaurus** *relax* Ver también:

V. calm down, rest; (*ant.*) easy, unwind **2**
loosen **3** **4**

**Word Partnership** Usar *relax* con:

V. **sit back and** relax **1**
**begin to** relax, **try to** relax **1** **2**
N. **time to** relax **1**
relax ***your*** **body, muscles** relax **2**

r

**re|lay** (**relays, relaying, relayed**)

> The noun is pronounced /rileɪ/. The verb is pronounced /rɪleɪ/.

1 N-COUNT A **relay** or a **relay race** is a race between two or more teams in which each member of the team runs or swims one section of the race. *carrera de relevos, carrera de postas* ❑ *Britain's chances of winning the relay were good. Las probabilidades de que Gran Bretaña ganara la carrera de relevos eran buenas.* 2 V-T To **relay** television or radio signals means to send them or broadcast them. *transmitir por repetidor, retransmitir* ❑ *The satellite relays television programs. El satélite retransmite programas de televisión.*

**re|lease** /rɪlis/ (**releases, releasing, released**) 1 V-T If a person or animal **is released,** they are set free. *poner en libertad, soltar* ❑ *He was released from prison the next day. Lo pusieron en libertad al día siguiente.* 2 V-T If someone or something **releases** you **from** a duty, task, or feeling, they free you from it. *liberar, eximir, aliviar* [FORMAL] ❑ *Finally the record company released him from his contract. Finalmente, la (compañía) disquera lo liberó de su contrato.* ● **Release** is also a noun. *alivio* ❑ *...release from stress. ...alivio de la tensión.* 3 V-T If someone in authority **releases** something such as a document or information, they make it available. *divulgar* ❑ *Police are not releasing any more details yet. La policía no va a divulgar todavía ningún otro detalle.* ● **Release** is also a noun. *divulgación* ❑ *...the release of the names of those who died. ...la divulgación de los nombres de los que murieron.* 4 V-T If you **release** someone or something, you stop holding them. *soltar* [FORMAL] ❑ *He released her hand and they walked on in silence. Le soltó la mano y caminaron en silencio.* 5 V-T When a form of energy or a substance such as a gas **is released** from something, it enters the surrounding atmosphere or area. *despedir, liberar* ❑ *...a weapon that releases poisonous gas. ...un arma que despide gas venenoso.* ● **Release** is also a noun. *liberación* ❑ *...the release of radioactive materials into the environment. ...la liberación de materiales radioactivos al medio ambiente.* 6 V-T When an entertainer or company **releases** a new CD, DVD, or movie, it becomes available so that people can buy it or see it. *lanzar, poner en circulación* ❑ *He is releasing a CD of love songs. Va a lanzar un disco compacto con canciones de amor.* 7 N-COUNT A new **release** is a new CD, DVD, or movie that has just become available for people to buy or see. *novedad* ❑ *A movie—generally a new release—is shown each night. Todas las noches transmiten una película diferente, una novedad, por lo general.* 8

**rel|egate** /rɛlɪgeɪt/ (**relegates, relegating, relegated**) V-T If you **relegate** someone or something **to** a less important position, you give them this position. *relegar* ❑ *The coach relegated him to a place on the second team. El entrenador lo relegó al segundo equipo.*

**re|lent|less** /rɪlɛntlɪs/ ADJ Something bad that is **relentless** never stops or never becomes less intense. *incesante* ❑ *The pressure was relentless. La presión era incesante.* ● **re|lent|less|ly** ADV *incesantemente* ❑ *It rained relentlessly. Llovió incesantemente.*

**rel|evant** /rɛləvᵊnt/ ADJ Something that is **relevant to** a situation or person is important or significant in that situation or to that person. *importante, relevante* ❑ *Is religion still relevant to people's lives? ¿Todavía es importante la religión en la vida de la gente?* ● **rel|evance** /rɛləvᵊns/ N-UNCOUNT *relevancia* ❑ *Politicians' private lives have no relevance to their public roles. La vida privada de los políticos no tiene nada qué ver con su función pública.*

**re|li|able** /rɪlaɪəbᵊl/ 1 ADJ People or things that are **reliable** can be trusted to work well or to behave in the way that you want them to. *confiable* ❑ *She was efficient and reliable. Era eficiente y confiable.* ● **re|li|ably** /rɪlaɪəbli/ ADV *confiablemente, con seguridad, con confianza* ❑ *The washing machine worked reliably for years. La lavadora funcionó sin problemas durante años.* ● **re|li|abil|ity** /rɪlaɪəbɪlɪti/ N-UNCOUNT *seguridad de funcionamiento, fiabilidad* ❑ *He's worried about his car's reliability. Le preocupa la fiabilidad de su automóvil.* 2 ADJ Information that is **reliable** or that is from a **reliable** source is very likely to be correct. *fidedigno* ❑ *There is no reliable information about how many people have died. No hay información fidedigna acerca del número de muertes.* ● **re|li|ably** ADV *de fuente fidedigna, con seguridad* ❑ *We are reliably informed that he is here. Sabemos con seguridad que está aquí.* ● **re|li|abil|ity** N-UNCOUNT *fiabilidad* ❑ *We questioned the reliability of the research. Pusimos en duda la fiabilidad de la investigación.*

**Word Partnership** Usar *reliable* con:

| | |
|---|---|
| N. | reliable **service** 1<br>reliable **data**, reliable **information**, reliable **source** 2 |
| ADV. | **highly** reliable, **less/more/most** reliable, **usually** reliable, **very** reliable 1 2 |

**re|lief** /rɪlif/ 1 N-UNCOUNT; N-SING If you feel a sense of **relief,** you feel happy because something unpleasant has not happened or is no longer happening. *alivio* ❑ *I breathed a sigh of relief. Suspiré de alivio.* 2 N-UNCOUNT If something provides **relief from** pain or distress, it stops the pain or distress. *alivio* ❑ *...relief from the pain. ...alivio del dolor.* 3 N-UNCOUNT **Relief** is money, food, or clothing that is provided for people who are very poor, or who have been affected by war or a natural disaster. *ayuda, auxilio* ❑ *Relief agencies are increasing efforts to provide food and shelter. Las agencias de ayuda se están esforzando más por proporcionar alimentos y abrigo.* 4 N-UNCOUNT The **relief** on a map is the difference in height between the highest area on the map and the lowest area. *relieve*

**Word Partnership** Usar *relief* con:

| | |
|---|---|
| V. | **express** relief 1<br>**feel** relief, **seek** relief 1 2<br>**bring** relief, **get** relief, **provide** relief 1 – 3<br>**supply** relief 2 3 |
| N. | **sense of** relief, **sigh of** relief 1<br>**pain** relief, relief **from symptoms**, relief **from tension** 2<br>**disaster** relief, **emergency** relief 3 |

**re|lief map** (**relief maps**) N-COUNT A **relief map** is a map that shows the height of the land, usually by using different colors or by raising some parts. *mapa en relieve*

**re|lieve** /rɪliv/ (**relieves, relieving, relieved**) **1** V-T If something **relieves** an unpleasant feeling or situation, it makes it less unpleasant or causes it to disappear completely. aliviar ❑ *Drugs can relieve the pain.* *Las drogas pueden aliviar el dolor.* **2** V-T If someone or something **relieves** you **of** an unpleasant feeling or difficult task, they take it from you. aliviar, tranquilizar ❑ *Receiving the check relieved me of a lot of worry.* *Cuando recibí el cheque me tranquilicé mucho., El cheque me alivió de muchos dolores de cabeza.* **3** V-T If you **relieve** someone, you take their place and continue to do the job or duty that they have been doing. relevar ❑ *At seven o'clock another nurse arrived to relieve her.* *A las siete en punto llegó otra enfermera para relevarla.*

**re|lieved** /rɪlivd/ ADJ If you are **relieved**, you feel happy because something unpleasant has not happened or is no longer happening. aliviado ❑ *We are relieved to be back home.* *Es un alivio estar de vuelta en casa.*

**re|li|gion** /rɪlɪdʒ$^{ə}$n/ (**religions**) **1** N-UNCOUNT **Religion** is belief in a god or gods and the activities that are connected with this belief. religión ❑ *...Indian philosophy and religion.* *...la filosofía y la religión de la India.* **2** N-COUNT A **religion** is a particular system of belief in a god or gods and the activities that are connected with this system. religión ❑ *...the Christian religion.* *...la religión cristiana.*

**re|li|gious** /rɪlɪdʒəs/ **1** ADJ **Religious** means connected with religion or with one particular religion. religioso ❑ *Religious groups are able to meet quite freely.* *Los grupos religiosos pueden reunirse libremente.* **2** ADJ Someone who is **religious** has a strong belief in a god or gods. religioso

**rel|ish** /rɛlɪʃ/ (**relishes, relishing, relished**) **1** V-T If you **relish** something, you get a lot of enjoyment from it. saborearse ❑ *I relish the challenge of doing the job.* *Me saboreo el reto de hacer el trabajo.* ● **Relish** is also a noun. fruición, deleite ❑ *The men ate with relish.* *Los hombres comieron con placer* **2** N-VAR **Relish** is a thick sauce made from fruit or vegetables that is eaten with meat, often with hot dogs. salsa (de frutas o verduras)

**re|lo|cate** /riloʊkeɪt/ (**relocates, relocating, relocated**) V-T/V-I If people or businesses **relocate** or if someone **relocates** them, they move to a different place. trasladar(se), establecerse en un nuevo lugar ❑ *The company relocated, and many employees were forced to move.* *La compañía se estableció en un nuevo lugar y muchos empleados se vieron obligados a mudarse.* ● **re|lo|ca|tion** /riloʊkeɪʃ$^{ə}$n/ N-VAR (**relocations**) traslado, mudanza ❑ *...the cost of relocation.* *...el costo del traslado.*

**re|luc|tant** /rɪlʌktənt/ ADJ If you are **reluctant to** do something, you are unwilling to do it and hesitate before doing it, or do it slowly and without enthusiasm. renuente, reacio ❑ *Mr. Spero was reluctant to ask for help.* *El señor Spero era reacio a pedir ayuda.* ● **re|luc|tant|ly** ADV con renuencia, a regañadientes ❑ *We have reluctantly agreed to let him go.* *Aceptamos de mala gana dejarlo ir.* ● **re|luc|tance** N-UNCOUNT renuencia, a regañadientes, de mala gana ❑ *Frank boarded his train with great reluctance.* *Frank abordó su tren de muy mala gana.*

**rely** /rɪlaɪ/ (**relies, relying, relied**) **1** V-I If you **rely on** someone or something, you need them and depend on them in order to live or work properly. depender de ❑ *They relied heavily on the advice of their professional advisers.* *Dependían en una gran medida (del consejo) de sus asesores profesionales.* **2** V-I If you can **rely on** someone to work well or to behave as you want them to, you can trust them to do this. confiar en, contar con ❑ *I know I can rely on you to deal with the problem.* *Sé que puedo contar contigo para resolver el problema.*

**re|main** /rɪmeɪn/ (**remains, remaining, remained**) **1** V-LINK To **remain** in a particular state or condition means to stay in that state or condition and not change. permanecer ❑ *The men remained silent.* *Los hombres permanecieron en silencio.* ❑ *The government remained in control.* *El gobierno permaneció en control.* **2** V-I If you **remain** in a place, you stay there and do not move away. quedarse ❑ *Police asked people to remain in their homes.* *La policía pidió a la gente que se quedara en su casa.* **3** V-I You can say that something **remains** when it still exists. persistir, perdurar, subsistir ❑ *The wider problem remains.* *El problema global subsiste.* **4** V-LINK If something **remains to be** done, it still needs to be done. quedar ❑ *Questions remain to be answered about his work.* *Todavía quedan dudas sin aclarar sobre su trabajo.* **5** N-PLURAL **The remains of** something are the parts of it that are left after most of it has been taken away or destroyed. restos ❑ *They were cleaning up the remains of their picnic.* *Estaban recogiendo los restos de su comida campestre.* **6** N-PLURAL The **remains** of a person or animal are the parts of their body that are left after they have died, sometimes after they have been dead for a long time. restos ❑ *...human remains.* *...restos humanos.* **7** → see also **remaining**

**re|main|der** /rɪmeɪndər/ QUANT **The remainder of** a group are the things or people that still remain after the other things or people have gone or have been dealt with. resto ❑ *He drank the remainder of his coffee.* *Bebió el resto de su café.*

**re|main|ing** /rɪmeɪnɪŋ/ **1** ADJ The **remaining** things or people out of a group are the things or people that still exist, are still present, or have not yet been dealt with. restante ❑ *...his few remaining supporters.* *...sus pocos partidarios restantes.* **2** → see also **remain**

**re|mark** /rɪmɑrk/ (**remarks, remarking, remarked**) **1** V-T/V-I If you **remark** that something is true, you say that it is true. observar, comentar, hacer observaciones ❑ *Many people remarked that the president had not been tough enough.* *Mucha gente comentó que el presidente no había sido lo bastante enérgico.* ❑ *She remarked on how tired I looked.* *Me hizo la observación de lo cansado que me veía.* **2** N-COUNT If you make a **remark** about something, you say something about it. comentario, observación ❑ *She made rude remarks about his weight.* *Hizo comentarios muy descorteses sobre su peso.*

| **Word Partnership** | Usar *remark* con: |
|---|---|
| ADJ. | **casual** remark, **offhand** remark **2** |
| V. | **hear a** remark, **make a** remark **2** |

**re|mark|able** /rɪmɑrkəb$^{ə}$l/ ADJ Someone or something that is **remarkable** is very impressive or unusual. extraordinario, admirable

r

❑ *He was a remarkable man.* *Era un hombre notable.* • **re|mark|ably** /rɪmɑrkəbli/ ADV *extraordinariamente* ❑ *The book was remarkably successful.* *El libro tuvo un éxito extraordinario.*

**re|match** /rimætʃ/ (**rematches**) N-COUNT A **rematch** is a second game or contest between two people or teams who have already faced each other. *partido de desquite, partido de revancha* ❑ *Stanford will play in a rematch.* *Stanford jugará un partido de revancha.*

**rem|edy** /rɛmədi/ (**remedies, remedying, remedied**) **1** N-COUNT A **remedy** is a successful way of dealing with a problem. *remedio* ❑ *The government's remedy involved tax increases.* *El remedio del gobierno implicó el aumento de impuestos.* **2** N-COUNT A **remedy** is something that is intended to cure you when you are ill or in pain. *remedio* ❑ *...natural remedies for infections.* *...remedios naturales para las infecciones.* **3** V-T If you **remedy** something that is wrong or harmful, you correct it or improve it. *remediar* ❑ *They worked hard to remedy the situation.* *Trabajaron con empeño para remediar la situación.*

**re|mem|ber** /rɪmɛmbər/ (**remembers, remembering, remembered**) **1** V-T/V-I If you **remember** people or events from the past, you still have an idea of them in your mind and you are able to think about them. *recordar, acordarse de* ❑ *I remember the first time I met him.* *Recuerdo cuando lo conocí.* ❑ *I remember that we went to his wedding.* *Recuerdo que fuimos a su boda.* ❑ *The weather was terrible, do you remember?* *El tiempo era espantoso, ¿te acuerdas?* **2** V-T If you **remember** that something is true, you become aware of it again after a time when you did not think about it. *recordar, acordarse de* ❑ *She remembered that she was going to the club that evening.* *Se acordó de que iba a ir al club esa noche.* **3** V-T If you **remember to** do something, you do it when you intend to. *recordar, acordarse de* ❑ *Please remember to mail the letter.* *Por favor, acuérdese de echar la carta al buzón.*

**Thesaurus** *remember* Ver también:

V. look back, recall, think back; (*ant.*) forget **1** **3**

**Word Partnership** Usar *remember* con:

ADV. remember **clearly**, remember **correctly**, remember **exactly**, **still** remember, remember **vividly** **1**
**always** remember **1** – **3**

ADJ. **easy to** remember, **important to** remember **1** – **3**

CONJ. remember **what**, remember **when**, remember **where**, remember **why** **1** – **3**

**re|mind** /rɪmaɪnd/ (**reminds, reminding, reminded**) **1** V-T If someone **reminds** you **of** a fact or event that you already know about, they say something which makes you think about it. *recordar a, hacer acordarse a* ❑ *She reminded Tim of the last time they met.* *Le recordó a Tim la última vez que se vieron.* **2** V-T If someone **reminds** you **to** do a particular thing, they say something which makes you remember to do it. *recordar a, acordar de* ❑ *Can you remind me to buy some milk?* *Recuérdame que compre leche, ¿sí?* **3** V-T If you say that someone or something **reminds** you **of** another person or thing, you mean that they are similar to the other person or thing and that they make you think about them. *recordar a* ❑ *She reminds me of your sister.* *Ella me recuerda a tu hermana.*

**Word Partnership** Usar *remind* con:

PREP. remind ***someone of something*** **1**
remind ***you of someone/something*** **3**

**re|mind|er** /rɪmaɪndər/ (**reminders**) **1** N-COUNT Something that serves as a **reminder of** another thing makes you think about the other thing. *recordatorio* [WRITTEN] ❑ *...a constant reminder of a bad experience.* *...un recordatorio constante de una mala experiencia.* **2** N-COUNT A **reminder** is a letter or note that is sent to tell you that you have not done something such as pay a bill or return library books. *recordatorio* ❑ *...the final reminder for the gas bill.* *...el último recordatorio de la factura del gas.*

**remi|nisce** /rɛmɪnɪs/ (**reminisces, reminiscing, reminisced**) V-I If you **reminisce** about something from your past, you write or talk about it, often with pleasure. *rememorar, recordar* [FORMAL] ❑ *I don't like reminiscing because it makes me feel old.* *No me gusta recordar porque me hace sentirme viejo.*

**remi|nis|cent** /rɛmɪnɪsənt/ ADJ If you say that one thing is **reminiscent of** another, you mean that it reminds you of it. *que recuerda* [FORMAL] ❑ *His voice was reminiscent of her son's.* *Su voz recordaba la de su hijo.*

**re|mold** /rimoʊld/ (**remolds, remolding, remolded**) V-T To **remold** something such as an idea or an economy means to change it so that it has a new structure or is based on new principles. *cambiar* ❑ *...our ability to remold our lives after a severe loss.* *...nuestra aptitud para cambiar nuestra vida después de una pérdida grave.*

**re|mote** /rɪmoʊt/ (**remoter, remotest**) **1** ADJ **Remote** areas are far away from cities and places where most people live. *remoto* ❑ *...villages in remote areas.* *...pueblos en regiones remotas.* **2** ADJ If something is **remote from** what people want or need, it is not relevant to it because it is so different from it or has no connection with it. *remoto, alejado* ❑ *Teenagers have to study subjects that seem remote from their daily lives.* *Los adolescentes tienen que estudiar materias que parecen alejadas de su vida cotidiana.* **3** ADJ If there is a **remote** possibility that something will happen, there is only a very small chance that it will happen. *remoto* ❑ *I use sunscreen when there is a remote possibility that I will be in the sun.* *Uso protector solar cuando hay una remota posibilidad de que vaya a exponerme al sol.* **4** ADJ If you describe someone as **remote,** you mean that they behave as if they do not want to be friendly or closely involved with other people. *distante*

**re|mote con|trol** (**remote controls**) **1** N-UNCOUNT **Remote control** is a system of controlling a machine or a vehicle from a distance by using radio or electronic signals. *control remoto* ❑ *The bomb was exploded by remote control.* *La bomba fue explotada por control remoto.* **2** N-COUNT The **remote control** for a television or other equipment

R

is the device that you use to control the machine from a distance, by pressing the buttons on it. *control remoto* ❑ *Richard picked up the remote control and turned on the television.* *Richard tomó el control remoto y encendió la televisión.*

**re|mote sens|ing** N-UNCOUNT **Remote sensing** is the gathering of information about something by observing it from space or from the air. *detección a distancia*

**re|mov|al** /rɪmuvᵊl/ (**removals**) N-UNCOUNT The **removal** of something is the act of removing it. *remoción, extirpación* ❑ *...the removal of a tumor.* *...la extirpación de un tumor.*

**Word Link** *mov ≈ moving : movement, movie, remove*

**re|move** /rɪmuv/ (**removes, removing, removed**) **1** V-T If you **remove** something from a place, you take it away. *retirar, sacar* [WRITTEN] ❑ *Remove the cake from the oven when it is cooked.* *Saque el pastel del horno cuando ya esté cocido.* **2** V-T If you **remove** clothing, you take it off. *quitarse* [WRITTEN] ❑ *He removed his jacket.* *Se quitó el saco.* **3** V-T If you **remove** an obstacle, a restriction, or a problem, you get rid of it. *remover* ❑ *Yesterday they removed the last remaining obstacle for peace.* *Ayer removieron el último obstáculo que quedaba para la paz.*

**Thesaurus** *remove* Ver también:
V. take away, take out **1**
take off, undress **2**

**re|moved** /rɪmuvd/ ADJ If you say that an idea or situation is far **removed from** something, you mean that it is very different from it. *distante* ❑ *The story was far removed from the truth.* *El relato estaba muy distante de la verdad.*

**re|nais|sance** /rɛnɪsɑns/ N-SING If something experiences a **renaissance**, it becomes popular or successful again after a time when people were not interested in it. *renacimiento* ❑ *The jazz trumpet is experiencing a renaissance.* *La trompeta de jazz está pasando por un renacimiento.*

**ren|der** /rɛndər/ (**renders, rendering, rendered**) V-T You can use **render** to say that something is changed into a different state. *hacer* ❑ *...a problem with the phone which rendered it unusable.* *...un problema con el teléfono que lo hizo inservible.*

**re|new** /rɪnu/ (**renews, renewing, renewed**) **1** V-T If you **renew** an activity, you begin it again. *renovar* ❑ *He renewed his attack on government policy.* *Renovó sus ataques contra la política gubernamental.* **2** V-T If you **renew** a relationship **with** someone, you start it again after you have not seen them or have not been friendly with them for some time. *renovar* ❑ *When the men met again after the war they renewed their friendship.* *Cuando los hombres se volvieron a encontrar después de la guerra, renovaron su amistad.* **3** V-T When you **renew** something such as a license or a contract, you extend the period of time for which it is valid. *renovar* ❑ *Larry's landlord refused to renew his lease.* *El casero de Larry se rehusó a renovarle el contrato (de arrendamiento).* **4** V-T You can say that something **is renewed** when it grows again or is replaced after it has been destroyed or lost. *renovar* ❑ *Cells in the body are being constantly renewed.* *Las células del cuerpo se renuevan constantemente.*

**Thesaurus** *renew* Ver también:
V. continue, resume, revive **1** – **3**

**re|new|al** /rɪnuəl/ (**renewals**) **1** N-SING If there is a **renewal of** an activity or a situation, it starts again. *renovación* ❑ *...the renewal of fighting in the area.* *...la renovación de los combates en el área.* **2** N-VAR The **renewal** of a document such as a license or a contract is an official extension of the period of time for which it remains valid. *renovación* ❑ *His contract is due for renewal.* *Debe hacer la renovación de su contrato.*

**Word Link** *nov ≈ new : innovation, novel, renovate*

**reno|vate** /rɛnəveɪt/ (**renovates, renovating, renovated**) V-T If someone **renovates** an old building, they repair and improve it and get it back into good condition. *renovar, restaurar* ❑ *They spent a lot of money renovating the house.* *Gastaron mucho dinero en la renovación de la casa.* ● **reno|va|tion** /rɛnəveɪʃᵊn/ N-VAR (**renovations**) *renovación, restauración* ❑ *...a house which needs extensive renovation.* *...una casa que necesita muchos trabajos de renovación.*

**re|nowned** /rɪnaʊnd/ ADJ A person or place that is **renowned for** something, usually something good, is well known because of it. *renombrado, famoso, conocido* ❑ *The area is renowned for its beautiful churches.* *La zona es renombrada por sus bellas iglesias.*

**rent** /rɛnt/ (**rents, renting, rented**) **1** V-T If you **rent** something, such as a car or property, you regularly pay its owner a sum of money in order to be able to have it or use it yourself. *alquilar, rentar* ❑ *She rents a house with three other women.* *Alquila una casa junto con otras tres mujeres.* **2** V-T If you **rent** something **to** someone, you let them have it and use it in exchange for a sum of money which they pay you regularly. *alquilar, rentar* ❑ *She rented rooms to university students.* *Alquilaba cuartos a estudiantes universitarios.* ● **Rent out** means the same as **rent**. *alquilar, rentar* ❑ *Last summer Brian Williams rented out his house and went camping.* *Brian Williams alquiló su casa el verano pasado y se fue de campamento.* **3** N-VAR **Rent** is the amount of money that you pay regularly to use a house, apartment, or piece of land. *alquiler, renta* ❑ *She worked to pay the rent.* *Trabajaba para pagar la renta.*

**rent|al** /rɛntᵊl/ (**rentals**) **1** N-UNCOUNT The **rental** of something such as a car or piece of equipment is the activity or process of renting it. *alquiler* ❑ *We can arrange car rental from the airport.* *Podemos alquilar un coche en el aeropuerto.* **2** N-COUNT The **rental** is the amount of money that you pay when you rent something such as a car, property, or piece of equipment. *alquiler, renta* ❑ *We pay a yearly rental of $393,000.* *Pagamos un alquiler anual de 393,000 dólares.* **3** ADJ You use **rental** to describe things that are connected with the renting of goods, properties, and services. *de alquiler* ❑ *...a rental car.* *...un coche de alquiler.*

**re|or|gan|ize** /riɔrgənaɪz/ (**reorganizes, reorganizing, reorganized**) V-T/V-I To **reorganize** something means to change the way in which it is organized, arranged, or done. *reorganizar* ❑ *She wanted to reorganize her life. Quería reorganizar su vida.* • **re|or|gani|za|tion** /riɔrgənɪzeɪʃən/ N-VAR (**reorganizations**) *reorganización* ❑ *...the reorganization of the legal system. ...la reorganización del sistema legal.*

**rep** /rɛp/ (**reps**) **1** N-COUNT A **rep** is a person whose job is to sell a company's products or services, especially by traveling around and visiting other companies. *representante comercial, agente comercial* ❑ *...a sales rep for a photographic company. ...un agente de ventas de una compañía de fotografía.* **2** N-COUNT A **rep** is a person who acts as a representative for a group of people, usually a group of people who work together. *representante* ❑ *...a labor union rep. ...un representante sindical.*

**Rep.** **Rep.** is a written abbreviation for **Representative**. *miembro de la Cámara de Representantes de Estados Unidos*

**re|pair** /rɪpɛər/ (**repairs, repairing, repaired**) **1** V-T If you **repair** something that has been damaged or is not working properly, you fix it. *reparar* ❑ *Goldman has repaired the roof. Goldman reparó el techo.* **2** N-VAR A **repair** is something that you do to mend a machine, building, piece of clothing, or other thing that has been damaged or is not working properly. *reparación* ❑ *Many people do not know how to make repairs on their cars. Mucha gente no sabe cómo reparar su automóvil.*

**Word Partnership** Usar *repair* con:

N. repair **a chimney**, repair **damage**, repair **equipment**, repair **a roof** **1**
**auto** repair, **car** repair, **home** repair, repair **parts**, **road** repair, repair **service**, repair **shop** **2**

**re|pat|ri|ate** /ripeɪtrieɪt/ (**repatriates, repatriating, repatriated**) V-T If a country **repatriates** someone, it sends them back to their home country. *repatriar* ❑ *The government does not repatriate genuine refugees. El gobierno no repatria a los verdaderos refugiados.* • **re|pat|ria|tion** /ripeɪtrieɪʃən/ N-VAR (**repatriations**) *repatriación* ❑ *...the forced repatriation of immigrants. ...la repatriación forzada de los inmigrantes.*

**R**

**re|pay** /rɪpeɪ/ (**repays, repaying, repaid**) **1** V-T If you **repay** a debt, you pay back the money that you owe to someone. *pagar* **2** V-T If you **repay** a favor that someone once did for you, you do something for them in return. *pagar, corresponder* ❑ *It was very kind. I don't know how I can ever repay you. Fue muy amable de su parte. No sé cómo podré corresponderle.*

**re|pay|ment** /rɪpeɪmənt/ (**repayments**) N-UNCOUNT The **repayment of** money is the act or process of paying it back to the person you owe it to. *pago* ❑ *...the repayment of a $114 million loan. ...el pago de un préstamo de 114 millones de dólares.*

**re|peat** /rɪpit/ (**repeats, repeating, repeated**) **1** V-T If you **repeat** something, you say or write it again. *repetir* ❑ *He repeated that he was innocent. Repitió que era inocente.* ❑ *She repeated her request for more money. Repitió su solicitud de más dinero.* **2** V-T If you **repeat** something that someone else has said or written, you say or write the same thing. *repetir* ❑ *She had a habit of repeating everything I said to her. Tenía la costumbre de repetir todo lo que yo le decía.* **3** V-T If you **repeat** an action, you do it again. *repetir* ❑ *The next day I repeated the task. Al día siguiente repetí la tarea.* **4** V-T If an event or series of events **repeats itself**, it happens again. *repetirse* ❑ *They say sometimes history repeats itself. Dicen que a veces la historia se repite.* **5** N-COUNT If there is a **repeat of** an event, usually an undesirable event, it happens again. *repetición* ❑ *...a repeat of last year's strikes. ...la repetición de las huelgas del año pasado.* **6** N-COUNT A **repeat** is a television or radio program that has been broadcast before. *repetición*

**Thesaurus** *repeat* Ver también:

V. reiterate, restate **1** **2**
N. encore **6**

**re|peat|ed** /rɪpitɪd/ ADJ **Repeated** actions or events are ones that happen many times. *repetido, reiterado* ❑ *He did not return the money, despite repeated reminders. No devolvió el dinero, a pesar de los repetidos recordatorios.* • **re|peat|ed|ly** ADV *repetidamente, reiteradamente* ❑ *Both men have repeatedly denied doing anything wrong. Ambos niegan reiteradamente haber hecho algo malo.*

**re|pel** /rɪpɛl/ (**repels, repelling, repelled**) **1** V-T When an army **repels** an attack, they successfully fight and drive back soldiers from another army who have attacked them. *rechazar, repeler* [FORMAL] **2** V-T If something **repels** you, you find it horrible and disgusting. *repugnar, rechazar* ❑ *Politics both fascinated and repelled him. La política lo fascinaba y, al mismo tiempo, le repugnaba.* • **re|pelled** ADJ *repulsado* ❑ *She was very beautiful but in some way I felt repelled. Era muy bella, pero de alguna manera me sentí repulsado.*

**rep|eti|tion** /rɛpɪtɪʃən/ (**repetitions**) **1** N-VAR If there is a **repetition of** an event, usually an undesirable event, it happens again. *repetición* ❑ *The city government wants to prevent a repetition of last year's violence. El gobierno de la ciudad quiere evitar la repetición de la violencia del año pasado.* **2** N-VAR In dance, **repetition** means performing the same movement again or doing it several times. *repetición*

**re|place** /rɪpleɪs/ (**replaces, replacing, replaced**) **1** V-T To **replace** a person or thing means to put another person or thing in their place. *reemplazar* ❑ *...the lawyer who replaced Robert as chairman. ...el abogado que reemplazó a Robert como presidente.* **2** V-T If you **replace** something that is broken, damaged, or lost, you get a new one to use instead. *reemplazar, cambiar* ❑ *The shower has broken and we cannot afford to replace it. La regadera está rota y no tenemos para reemplazarla.* • **re|place|ment** N-UNCOUNT *reemplazo, reposición* ❑ *...the replacement of damaged books. ...el reemplazo de los libros dañados.* **3** V-T If you **replace** something, you put it back where it was before. *volver a poner* ❑ *Replace the caps on the bottles. Vuelva a tapar las botellas.*

**re|place|ment** /rɪpleɪsmənt/ (**replacements**) N-COUNT One thing or person that replaces another can be referred to as their **replacement**. *reemplazo, substituto* ❑ *Taylor has suggested Adams as his replacement. Taylor sugirió a Adams como su substituto.*

**re|play** (**replays, replaying, replayed**)

The verb is pronounced /ripleɪ/. The noun is pronounced /ripleɪ/.

**1** V-T If a game or match between two sports teams **is replayed,** the two teams play it again, because neither team won the first time, or because the game was stopped because of bad weather. *volver a jugar, repetir* **2** N-COUNT *repetición* ❑ *They won the replay 2–1. Ganaron la repetición 2 a 1.* **3** N-COUNT A **replay** of something which has been recorded on film or tape is another showing of it. *repetición* ❑ *...a slow-motion replay of his fall. ...la repetición de su caída en cámara lenta.*

**re|ply** /rɪplaɪ/ (**replies, replying, replied**) **1** V-T/V-I When you **reply to** something that someone has said or written to you, you say or write an answer to them. *responder, reponer, contestar* ❑ *"That's a nice dress," said Michael. "Thanks," she replied. —¡Qué bonito vestido!—dijo Michael. —Gracias—repuso ella.* ❑ *He replied that this was absolutely impossible. Replicó que era absolutamente imposible.* ❑ *He never replied to the letters. Nunco respondió a las cartas.* **2** N-COUNT A **reply** is something that you say or write when you answer someone or answer a letter or advertisement. *respuesta* ❑ *I called out, but there was no reply. Llamé, pero no hubo respuesta.* **3** V-I If you **reply to** something such as an attack **with** violence or **with** another action, you do something in response. *responder* ❑ *The soldiers replied with an offer of peace. Los soldados respondieron con una oferta de paz.*

**Thesaurus** *reply* Ver también:

V. acknowledge, answer, respond, return **1**
N. acknowledgement, answer, response **2**

**Word Partnership** Usar *reply* con:

N. reply **card,** reply **envelope,** reply **form** **2**
V. **make a** reply, **receive a** reply **2**

**re|port** /rɪpɔrt/ (**reports, reporting, reported**) **1** V-T If you **report** something that has happened, you tell people about it. *informar, denunciar, dar parte de* ❑ *I reported the theft to the police. Denuncié el robo a la policía.* ❑ *Officials reported that the ships were heading for Malta. Los funcionarios informaron que los barcos se dirigían a Malta.* ❑ *"He seems to be all right now," he reported. —Parece ya estar bien ahora—informó.* ❑ *She reported him missing the next day. Dio parte de su desaparición al día siguiente.* **2** V-I If you **report on** an event or subject, you tell people about it, because it is your job or duty to do so. *informar* ❑ *...journalists reporting on politics. ...los periodistas que cubren la fuente de política.* **3** N-COUNT A **report** is a news article or broadcast which gives information about something that has just happened. *noticia, informe* ❑ *According to a newspaper report, the couple are getting married. Según una noticia periodística, la pareja va a casarse.* **4** N-COUNT If you give someone a **report** on something, you tell them what has been happening. *informe* ❑ *She gave us a progress report on the project. Nos dio un informe de avances del proyecto.* **5** V-T If someone **reports** you **to** a person in authority, they tell that person about something wrong that you have done. *denunciar* ❑ *His boss reported him to police. Su jefe lo denunció a la policía.* **6** V-I If you **report to** a person or place, you go to them and say that you are ready to start work. *presentarse* **7** → see also **reporting**

**re|port card** (**report cards**) N-COUNT A **report card** is an official written account of how well or how badly a student has done during the term or year that has just finished. *boleta de calificaciones* ❑ *I brought home straight "A"s on my report card. Llevé a casa mi boleta de calificaciones llena de dieces.*

**re|port|ed|ly** /rɪpɔrtɪdli/ ADV If you say that something is **reportedly** true, you mean that someone has said that it is true, but you have no direct evidence of it. *según se informa, según se dice* [FORMAL] ❑ *More than two hundred people were reportedly killed. Según se informa, murieron más de doscientas personas.*

**re|port|ed speech** N-UNCOUNT **Reported speech** is speech which tells you what someone said, but does not use the person's actual words: for example, "They said you didn't like it," and "I asked him what his plans were." *discurso indirecto, estilo indirecto*

**re|port|er** /rɪpɔrtər/ (**reporters**) N-COUNT A **reporter** is someone who writes news articles or who broadcasts news reports. *reportero o reportera* ❑ *...a TV reporter. ...un reportero de televisión.*

**re|port|ing** /rɪpɔrtɪŋ/ N-UNCOUNT **Reporting** is the presenting of news in newspapers, on radio, and on television. *reportajes, cobertura* ❑ *...political reporting. ...reportajes políticos.*

**Word Link** *pos ≈ placing : deposit, preposition, repository*

**re|posi|tory** /rɪpɒzɪtɔri/ (**repositories**) N-COUNT A **repository** is a place where something is kept safely. *depósito, almacén, museo* [FORMAL] ❑ *The nation's giant historical repository is called the Smithsonian Institution. El museo histórico más grande de Estados Unidos se llama Instituto Smithsoniano.*

**re|pos|sess** /ripəzɛs/ (**repossesses, repossessing, repossessed**) V-T If your car or house **is repossessed,** it is taken away from you because you have not paid what you owe for it. *recuperar la posesión de*

**rep|re|sent** /rɛprɪzɛnt/ (**represents, representing, represented**) **1** V-T If someone such as a lawyer or a politician **represents** a person, a group of people, or a place, they act on behalf of that person, group, or place. *representar* ❑ *...the politicians we elect to represent us. ...los políticos que elegimos para representarnos.* **2** V-T If a sign or symbol **represents** something, it is accepted as meaning that thing. *representar* ❑ *A cross on the map represents a church. Una cruz en el mapa representa una iglesia.* **3** V-T To **represent** an idea or quality means to be a symbol or an expression of that idea or quality. *representar* ❑ *New York represents everything that's great about America. Nueva York representa toda la grandeza de Estados Unidos.* **4** V-T If you **represent** a person or thing **as** a particular thing, you describe them as being that thing. *presentar* ❑ *The newspaper represented him as a hero. El periódico lo presentó como un héroe.*

**rep|re|sen|ta|tion** /rɛprɪzɛnteɪʃᵊn/ (**representations**) **1** N-UNCOUNT If a group or

**Word Web** **reproduction**

Human **reproduction** requires a **sperm** from the **male** and an **egg** from the **female**. These two cells come together to begin the new life. This process is called **fertilization**. It is the beginning of the woman's **pregnancy**. From fertilization to eight weeks of development, we call the fertilized egg a **zygote**. From eight to twelve weeks, it is called an **embryo**. After three months of development, we call it a **foetus**. **Birth** usually takes place after nine months of pregnancy.

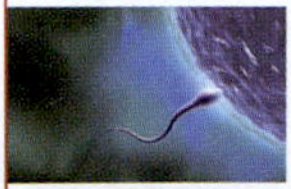
egg and sperm

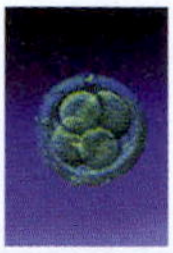
zygote

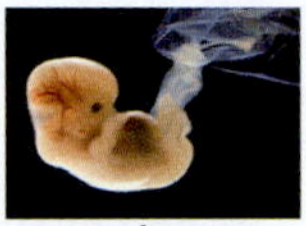
embryo

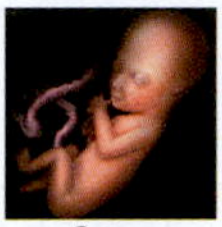
fetus

mother, father, and baby

person has **representation** in a legislature or on a committee, someone in the legislature or on the committee supports them and makes decisions on their behalf. *representación* ❑ *Puerto Ricans are U.S. citizens but they have no representation in Congress. Los portorriqueños son ciudadanos estadounidenses, pero no tienen representación en el Congreso.* **2** N-COUNT You can describe a picture, model, or statue of a person or thing as a **representation of** them. *representación* [FORMAL] ❑ *...a lifelike representation of Bill Clinton. ...una representación muy vívida de Bill Clinton.*

**rep|re|senta|tive** /rɛprɪzɛntətɪv/ (**representatives**) **1** N-COUNT A **representative** is a person who has been chosen to act or make decisions on behalf of another person or a group of people. *representante* ❑ *...labor union representatives. ...representantes sindicales.* **2** N-COUNT In the United States, a **representative** is a member of the House of Representatives, the less powerful of the two parts of Congress. *representante* ❑ *...a Republican representative from Wyoming. ...un representante republicano de Wyoming.* **3** ADJ A **representative** group consists of a small number of people who have been chosen to make decisions on behalf of a larger group. *representante* ❑ *The new chairman was chosen by a representative council. El nuevo presidente fue elegido por un consejo de representantes.* **4** ADJ If someone or something is **representative** of a group, he, she or it is typical of it. *representativo* ❑ *He was in no way representative of teachers in general. No era representativo en modo alguno de los maestros en general.*

**re|pro|duce** /ri̱prədu̱s/ (**reproduces, reproducing, reproduced**) **1** V-T If you try to **reproduce** something, you copy it. *reproducir* ❑ *The effect was hard to reproduce. Era difícil reproducir el efecto.* **2** V-I When people, animals, or plants **reproduce,** they produce young. *reproducirse* ❑ *...people's ability to reproduce. ...la capacidad de reproducción de los seres humanos.* • **re|pro|duc|tion** /ri̱prədʌ̱kʃᵊn/ N-UNCOUNT *reproducción* ❑ *...human reproduction. ...reproducción humana.*

**re|pro|duc|tion** /riprədʌ̱kʃᵊn/ (**reproductions**) **1** N-COUNT A **reproduction** is a copy of something such as a piece of furniture or a work of art. *reproducción* ❑ *...a reproduction of a religious painting. ...una reproducción de una pintura religiosa.* **2** → see also **reproduce**
→ see Word Web: **reproduction**

**rep|tile** /rɛ̱ptaɪl, -tɪl/ (**reptiles**) N-COUNT **Reptiles** are a group of cold-blooded animals which lay eggs and have skins covered with small, hard plates called scales. Snakes, lizards, and crocodiles are reptiles. *reptil*
→ see **pet**

**re|pub|lic** /rɪpʌ̱blɪk/ (**republics**) N-COUNT A **republic** is a country that has a president or whose system of government is based on the idea that every citizen has equal status. *república* ❑ *In 1918, Austria became a republic. Austria se hizo república en 1918.* ❑ *...the Baltic republics. ...las repúblicas bálticas.*

**re|pub|li|can** /rɪpʌ̱blɪkən/ (**republicans**) **1** ADJ A **republican** government has a president or is based on the idea that every citizen has equal status. You can also say that someone has **republican** views. *republicano* ❑ *...the republican side in the Spanish Civil War. ...el bando republicano en la guerra civil española.* **2** ADJ If someone is **Republican,** they belong to or support the Republican Party. *republicano* ❑ *Lower taxes made Republican voters happier with their party. Los votantes republicanos estaban felices con su partido por la reducción de impuestos.* • A **Republican** is someone who supports or belongs to the Republican Party. *republicano* ❑ *What made you decide to become a Republican? —¿Qué fue lo que lo decidió a hacerse republicano?*

**Word Link** *put ≈ thinking : computer, dispute, reputation*

**repu|ta|tion** /rɛpyəteɪʃᵊn/ (**reputations**) **1** N-COUNT To have a **reputation for** something means to be known or remembered for it. *reputación* ❑ *...his reputation for honesty. ...su reputación de persona honesta.* **2** N-COUNT Your **reputation** is the opinion that people have about you. *reputación* ❑ *This college has a good reputation. Este colegio tiene una buena reputación.*

**Word Partnership** Usar *reputation* con:

V. **acquire a** reputation, **build a** reputation, **damage** ***someone's*** reputation, **earn a** reputation, **establish a** reputation, **gain a** reputation, **have a** reputation, **ruin** ***someone's*** reputation, **tarnish** ***someone's*** reputation 1 2
ADJ. **bad** reputation, **good** reputation 1 2

**re|quest** /rɪkwɛ̲st/ (**requests, requesting, requested**) 1 V-T If you **request** something, you ask for it politely or formally. solicitar [FORMAL] ❑ *He requested the use of a telephone.* *Solicitó usar el teléfono.* 2 N-COUNT If you make a **request,** you politely or formally ask someone to do something. solicitud, petición ❑ *They agreed to his request for more money.* *Aceptaron su solicitud de más dinero.* 3 PHRASE If you do something **at** someone's **request,** you do it because he or she has asked you to. a petición de ❑ *No one sent flowers for his funeral at the request of his family.* *A petición de su familia, nadie envió flores a su funeral.* 4 PHRASE If something is given or done **on request,** it is given or done whenever you ask for it. a solicitud de ❑ *Details are available on request.* *Si necesita más información, comuníquese con nosotros, por favor.*

**re|quire** /rɪkwa̲ɪər/ (**requires, requiring, required**) 1 V-T To **require** something means to need it. requerir, necesitar [FORMAL] ❑ *If you require further information, please write to this address.* *Si requiere más información, escriba a esta dirección, por favor.* ❑ *...the kind of problem that requires us to act immediately.* *...la clase de problema que requiere que actuemos inmediatamente.* 2 V-T If a law or rule **requires** you **to** do something, you have to do it. obligar [FORMAL] ❑ *The rules require employers to provide safety training.* *El reglamento obliga a los empleadores a proporcionar capacitación sobre seguridad.* ❑ *...a law requiring immediate reporting of faults.* *...una ley que obliga a la denuncia inmediata de las faltas.*

**re|quire|ment** /rɪkwa̲ɪərmənt/ (**requirements**) 1 N-COUNT A **requirement** is a quality or qualification that you must have in order to be allowed to do something or to be suitable for something. requisito ❑ *Its products met all legal requirements.* *Sus productos cumplieron con todos los requisitos legales.* 2 N-COUNT Your **requirements** are the things that you need. necesidad [FORMAL] ❑ *We can provide various programs to suit your requirements.* *Podemos ofrecerle varios programas adecuados a sus necesidades.*

**Word Partnership** Usar *requirement* con:

ADJ. **legal** requirement, **minimum** requirement 1
V. **meet a** requirement 1

**res|cue** /rɛ̲skyu/ (**rescues, rescuing, rescued**) 1 V-T If you **rescue** someone, you get them out of a dangerous or unpleasant situation. rescatar ❑ *Helicopters rescued 20 people from the roof of the building.* *Los helicópteros rescataron a 20 personas del techo del edificio.* ● **res|cu|er** N-COUNT (**rescuers**) rescatador ❑ *It took rescuers 90 minutes to reach the trapped men.* *Los rescatadores tardaron 90 minutos en llegar al hombre atrapado.* 2 N-VAR A **rescue** is an attempt to save someone from a dangerous or unpleasant situation. rescate ❑ *A major rescue is taking place.* *Se está llevando a cabo un importante rescate.* ❑ *...a big rescue operation.* *...una gran operación de rescate.* 3 PHRASE If someone **goes to** your **rescue** or **comes to** your **rescue,** he or she helps you when you are in danger or difficulty. ir en auxilio de ❑ *Her screams were heard by a neighbor who went to her rescue.* *Un vecino que oyó sus gritos fue a auxiliarla.*

**Word Partnership** Usar *rescue* con:

N. **firefighters** rescue, rescue **a hostage**, rescue **miners**, rescue **people**, **police** rescue, **volunteers** rescue, rescue **wildlife** 1
rescue **attempt**, rescue **crews**, rescue **effort**, rescue **mission**, rescue **operation**, rescue **teams**, rescue **workers** 2

**re|search** /rɪsɜ̲rtʃ, ri̲sɜrtʃ/ (**researches, researching, researched**) 1 N-UNCOUNT **Research** is work that involves studying something and trying to discover facts about it. investigación ❑ *...scientific research.* *...investigación científica.* 2 V-T If you **research** something, you try to discover facts about it. investigar ❑ *She spent two years in Florida researching her book.* *Pasó dos años en Florida investigando para escribir su libro.* ● **re|search|er** N-COUNT (**researchers**) investigador o investigadora ❑ *...a market researcher.* *...un investigador de mercado.*
→ see **hospital, laboratory, medicine, science, zoo**

**Word Partnership** Usar *research* con:

N. **animal** research, **cancer** research, research **and development**, research **facility**, research **findings**, **laboratory** research, research **methods**, research **paper**, research **project**, research **report**, research **results**, research **scientist** 1
ADJ. **biological** research, **clinical** research, **current** research, **experimental** research, **medical** research, **recent** research, **scientific** research 1

**re|sem|blance** /rɪzɛ̲mbləns/ (**resemblances**) N-VAR If there is a **resemblance** between two people or things, they are similar to each other. parecido ❑ *There was a remarkable resemblance between him and Pete.* *Había un parecido asombroso entre él y Pete.*

**re|sem|ble** /rɪzɛ̲mbᵊl/ (**resembles, resembling, resembled**) V-T If one thing or person **resembles** another, they are similar to each other. parecerse ❑ *She resembles her mother.* *Se parece a su madre.*

**re|sent** /rɪzɛ̲nt/ (**resents, resenting, resented**) V-T If you **resent** someone or something, you feel bitter and angry about them. resentir ❑ *She resents her mother for leaving.* *Está resentida con su madre por haberse ido.*

**re|sent|ment** /rɪzɛ̲ntmənt/ (**resentments**) N-VAR **Resentment** is bitterness and anger that someone feels about something. resentimiento ❑ *She felt resentment at his behavior.* *Le guardaba resentimiento por su conducta.*

**res|er|va|tion** /rɛ̲zərveɪ̲ʃᵊn/ (**reservations**) 1 N-VAR If you have **reservations about**

r

something, you are not sure that it is entirely good or right. *reserva* ❑ *He had no reservations at all about leaving home. No tenía reserva alguna respecto a irse de casa.* **2** N-COUNT If you make a **reservation,** you arrange for something such as a table in a restaurant or a room in a hotel to be kept for you. *reservación* ❑ *He went to the desk to make a reservation. Fue a la recepción a hacer una reservación.*
→ see **hotel**

**re|serve** /rɪzɜrv/ (**reserves, reserving, reserved**) **1** V-T If something **is reserved for** a particular person or purpose, it is kept specially for that person or purpose. *reservar* ❑ *A room was reserved for him. Le reservaron un cuarto.* **2** N-COUNT A **reserve** is a supply of something that is available for use when it is needed. *reserva* ❑ *...the world's oil reserves. ...las reservas mundiales de petróleo.* **3** N-UNCOUNT If someone shows **reserve,** they keep their feelings hidden. *reserva* ❑ *He lost his reserve and told her what he thought. Dejó a un lado sus reservas y le dijo lo que pensaba.* **4** PHRASE If you have something **in reserve,** you have it available for use when it is needed. *en reserva* ❑ *...the money that he kept in reserve. ...el dinero que tenía en reserva.*

**re|served** /rɪzɜrvd/ ADJ Someone who is **reserved** keeps their feelings hidden. *reservado* ❑ *He was quiet and reserved. Era callado y reservado.*

**res|er|voir** /rɛzərvwɑr/ (**reservoirs**) **1** N-COUNT A **reservoir** is a lake that is used for storing water before it is supplied to people. *embalse, presa, represa* **2** N-COUNT A **reservoir of** something is a large quantity of it that is available for use when needed. *reserva* ❑ *...the huge oil reservoir beneath the desert. ...las cuantiosas reservas de petróleo en el subsuelo del desierto.*
→ see **dam**

| Word Link | *sid ≈ sitting : preside, president, residence* |
|---|---|

**resi|dence** /rɛzɪdəns/ (**residences**) **1** N-COUNT A **residence** is a house where people live. *residencia* [FORMAL] ❑ *...a private residence. ...una residencia privada.* **2** N-UNCOUNT Your place of **residence** is the place where you live. *residencia* [FORMAL] **3** PHRASE If someone is **in residence** in a particular place, they are living there. *tener su residencia en, residir en*

**resi|dence hall** (**residence halls**) N-COUNT **Residence halls** are buildings with rooms or apartments, usually built by universities or colleges, in which students live during the school year. *residencia de estudiantes* ❑ *A freshman adviser lives in each residence hall. En cada residencia de estudiantes vive un consejero de alumnos de primer grado.*

**resi|den|cy** /rɛzɪdənsi/ (**residencies**) N-COUNT A doctor's **residency** is the period of specialized training in a hospital that he or she receives after completing an internship. *internado, residencia* ❑ *He completed his residency at Stanford University Hospital. Hizo su residencia en el Hospital de la Universidad de Stanford.*

| Word Link | *ent ≈ one who does, has : dependent, resident, superintendent* |
|---|---|

**resi|dent** /rɛzɪdənt/ (**residents**) **1** N-COUNT The **residents** of a house or area are the people who live there. *residente* ❑ *Local residents complained that the road was dangerous. Los residentes del lugar se quejaron de que la carretera era peligrosa.* **2** N-COUNT Someone who is a **resident of** a country or a city lives there. *residente, vecino, habitante* ❑ *He has been a resident of Baltimore since 1967. Ha vivido en Baltimore desde 1967.* **3** N-COUNT A **resident** or a **resident** doctor is a doctor who is receiving a period of specialized training in a hospital after completing his or her internship. *médico interno o médica interna*
→ see **country, hospital**

**resi|dent al|ien** (**resident aliens**) N-COUNT A **resident alien** is a person who was born in one country but has moved to another country and has official permission to live there. *residente extranjero*

**resi|den|tial** /rɛzɪdɛnʃᵊl/ **1** ADJ A **residential** area contains houses rather than offices or factories. *residencial* ❑ *...a residential area of Maryland. ...un barrio residencial de Maryland.* **2** ADJ A **residential** institution is one where people live while they are studying there or being cared for there. *internado* ❑ *...a two-year residential college. ...un internado de dos años.*

**re|sign** /rɪzaɪn/ (**resigns, resigning, resigned**) **1** V-T/V-I If you **resign** from a job or position, you formally announce that you are leaving it. *renunciar* ❑ *He was forced to resign. Lo obligaron a renunciar.* ❑ *Mr. Robb resigned his position last month. El señor Robb renunció a su puesto el mes pasado.* **2** V-T If you **resign yourself to** an unpleasant situation or fact, you accept it because you realize that you cannot change it. *resignarse* ❑ *Pat and I resigned ourselves to another summer without a boat. Pat y yo nos resignamos a pasar otro verano sin bote.* **3** → see also **resigned**

| Thesaurus | *resign* | Ver también: |
|---|---|---|
| v. | leave, quit, step down **1** | |

**res|ig|na|tion** /rɛzɪgneɪʃᵊn/ (**resignations**) **1** N-VAR Your **resignation** is a formal statement of your intention to leave a job or position. *renuncia* ❑ *Bob Morgan offered his resignation and it was accepted. Bob Morgan presentó su renuncia y le fue aceptada.* **2** N-UNCOUNT **Resignation** is the acceptance of an unpleasant situation or fact because you realize that you cannot change it. *resignación* ❑ *He sighed with resignation. Suspiró con resignación.*

**re|signed** /rɪzaɪnd/ ADJ If you are **resigned to** an unpleasant situation or fact, you accept it without complaining because you realize that you cannot change it. *resignado* ❑ *He is resigned to the noise and the mess. Está resignado al ruido y el desorden.*

**re|sist** /rɪzɪst/ (**resists, resisting, resisted**) **1** V-T If you **resist** something such as a change, you refuse to accept it and try to prevent it. *resistirse* ❑ *They resisted our attempts to change things. Se resistieron a nuestros intentos por cambiar las cosas.* **2** V-T/V-I If you **resist** someone or **resist** an attack by them, you fight back against them. *resistirse* ❑ *The man tried to resist arrest. El sujeto trató de resistirse al arresto.* ❑ *When she attempted to cut his nails he resisted. Cuando intentó cortarle las uñas, se resistió.* **3** V-T If you **resist** doing something, or **resist** the temptation to do it, you stop yourself from doing it although you would like to do it. resistir ❑ *She resisted the urge to laugh.* *Resistió las ganas de reír.* **4** V-T If someone or something **resists** damage, they are not damaged. resistir ❑ *This leather resists water, oil, grease and even acids.* *Esta piel es resistente al agua, el aceite, la grasa y aun a los ácidos.*

**Word Link** *ance ≈ quality, state : insurance, performance, resistance*

**re|sist|ance** /rɪzɪstəns/ (**resistances**) **1** N-UNCOUNT **Resistance** to something such as a change or a new idea is a refusal to accept it. resistencia ❑ *...his resistance to anything new.* *...su resistencia a todo lo nuevo.* **2** N-UNCOUNT **Resistance** to an attack consists of fighting back against the people who have attacked you. resistencia ❑ *The soldiers are facing strong resistance.* *Los soldados enfrentan una fuerte resistencia.* **3** N-UNCOUNT The **resistance** of your body **to** germs or diseases is its power to remain unharmed or unaffected by them. resistencia ❑ *Most people have a natural resistance to the disease.* *La mayoría de la gente posee una resistencia natural a esta enfermedad.* **4** N-VAR In electrical engineering or physics, **resistance** is the ability of a substance or an electrical circuit to stop the flow of an electrical current through it. resistencia
→ see **bicycle**

**re|sist|ant** /rɪzɪstənt/ **1** ADJ Someone who is **resistant to** something is opposed to it and wants to prevent it. renuente ❑ *Some people are very resistant to the idea of exercise.* *Algunas personas son muy renuentes a la idea de hacer ejercicio.* **2** ADJ If something is **resistant to** a particular thing, it is not harmed by it. resistente ❑ *...how to make plants more resistant to disease.* *...la manera de hacer que las plantas sean más resistentes a las enfermedades.*

**reso|lu|tion** /rɛzəluʃən/ (**resolutions**) **1** N-COUNT A **resolution** is a formal decision made at a meeting by means of a vote. resolución ❑ *He was not satisfied with the resolution.* *No estaba satisfecho con la resolución.* **2** N-COUNT If you make a **resolution,** you decide to try very hard to do something. propósito ❑ *They made a resolution to get more exercise.* *Se hicieron el propósito de hacer más ejercicio.* **3** N-UNCOUNT **Resolution** is determination to do something or not do something. decisión ❑ *"I think I'll look for a new job," I said with sudden resolution.* *—Creo que voy a buscar otro empleo—dije, con repentina decisión.* **4** N-SING The **resolution** of a problem or difficulty is the final solving of it. solución [FORMAL] ❑ *...the successful resolution of an argument.* *...la solución exitosa de una polémica.*

**re|solve** /rɪzɒlv/ (**resolves, resolving, resolved**) **1** V-T To **resolve** a problem, argument, or difficulty means to find a solution to it. resolver [FORMAL] ❑ *We must resolve these problems.* *Debemos resolver estos problemas.* **2** V-T If you **resolve to** do something, you make a firm decision to do it. resolver [FORMAL] ❑ *Judy resolved to be a better mother.* *Judy resolvió ser mejor madre.* **3** N-VAR **Resolve** is determination to do what you have decided to do. resolución [FORMAL] ❑ *...the American public's resolve to go to war if necessary.* *...la resolución del pueblo estadounidense de ir a la guerra si es necesario.*

**reso|nance** /rɛzənəns/ (**resonances**) N-VAR A **resonance** is the sound that is produced by an object when it vibrates at the same rate as the sound waves from another object. resonancia [TECHNICAL]

**re|sort** /rɪzɔrt/ (**resorts, resorting, resorted**) **1** V-I If you **resort to** a course of action that you do not really approve of, you adopt it because you cannot see any other way of achieving what you want. recurrir ❑ *The two men resorted to shouting.* *Los hombres recurrieron a gritar.* **2** PHRASE If you do something **as a last resort,** you do it because you can find no other way of getting out of a difficult situation or of solving a problem. como último recurso ❑ *As a last resort, we hired a private detective.* *Como último recurso, contratamos a un detective privado.* **3** N-COUNT A **resort** is a place where a lot of people spend their vacation. centro vacacional ❑ *...ski resorts.* *...centros de esquí.*

**re|source** /risɔrs/ (**resources**) N-COUNT The **resources** of a country, organization, or person are the materials, money, and other things that they have and can use. recurso ❑ *Some families don't even have the resources to feed themselves.* *Algunas familias ni siquiera tienen los recursos para alimentarse.*

**re|source re|cov|ery** N-UNCOUNT **Resource recovery** is the process of obtaining useful materials or energy from things that are thrown away, such as paper or glass. recuperación de recursos

**re|spect** /rɪspɛkt/ (**respects, respecting, respected**) **1** V-T If you **respect** someone, you have a good opinion of their character or ideas. respetar ❑ *I want her to respect me for my work.* *Quiero que me respete por mi trabajo.* **2** N-UNCOUNT If you have **respect for** someone, you have a good opinion of them. respeto ❑ *I have tremendous respect for Dean.* *Tengo un enorme respeto por Dean.* **3** → see also **self-respect** **4** V-T If someone **respects** your wishes, rights, or customs, he or she avoids doing things that you would dislike or regard as wrong. respetar ❑ *I tried to respect her wishes.* *Traté de respetar sus deseos.* **5** N-UNCOUNT If someone shows **respect for** your wishes, rights, or customs, he or she avoids doing anything you would dislike or regard as wrong. respeto ❑ *...respect for people's rights and customs.* *...el respeto a los derechos y costumbres de la gente.* **6** PHRASE If you **pay** your **respects to** someone, you go to see them or speak to them in order to be polite. presentar respetos [FORMAL] ❑ *I have come to pay my respects to the princess.* *He venido a presentarle mis respetos a la princesa.* **7** PHRASE You use expressions like **in this respect** and **in many respects** to indicate that what you are saying applies to the thing or things you have just mentioned. en este sentido/en muchos sentidos ❑ *The brothers were different from each other in many respects.* *Los hermanos eran diferentes uno del otro en muchos sentidos.* **8** PHRASE You use **with respect to** to say what something relates to. con respecto a [FORMAL] ❑ *The decision was legal with respect to Swiss law.* *La decisión fue legal con respecto a la ley suiza.* **9** → see also **respected**

**Thesaurus** *respect* Ver también:
V. admire **1**
N. consideration, courtesy, esteem **5**

r

**re|spect|able** /rɪspɛktəbᵊl/ **1** ADJ Someone or something that is **respectable** is approved of by society and considered to be morally correct. respetable ❑ *...a respectable family. ...una familia respetable.* • **re|spect|abil|ity** /rɪspɛktəbɪlɪti/ N-UNCOUNT respetabilidad ❑ *A single house with a yard became the sign of respectability. Una casa simple con patio llegó a ser símbolo de respetabilidad.* **2** ADJ **Respectable** means good enough or acceptable. aceptable, digno ❑ *The team scored a respectable 68. El equipo logró una digna puntuación de 68.*

**re|spect|ed** /rɪspɛktɪd/ ADJ Someone or something that is **respected** is admired and considered important by many people. respetado ❑ *He is highly respected for his art. Se le respeta mucho por su arte.*

**re|spec|tive|ly** /rɪspɛktɪvli/ ADV **Respectively** means in the same order as the items that you have just mentioned. respectivamente ❑ *Their sons, Ben and Jonathan, were three and six respectively. Sus hijos, Ben y Jonathan, tenían tres y seis años de edad, respectivamente.*

**res|pi|ra|tion** /rɛspɪreɪʃᵊn/ N-UNCOUNT **Respiration** is the exchange of gases between living cells and their environment. In humans and animals, **respiration** is breathing. respiración [MEDICAL]

**Word Link** *spir ≈ breath : aspiration, inspire, respiratory*

**res|pira|tory** /rɛspərətɔri/ ADJ **Respiratory** means relating to breathing. respiratorio [MEDICAL] ❑ *...people with respiratory problems. ...gente con problemas respiratorios.*

**res|pira|tory sys|tem** (**respiratory systems**) N-COUNT Your body's **respiratory system** is the group of organs that are involved in breathing, including the nose, mouth, and lungs. vías respiratorias, aparato respiratorio, sistema respiratorio
→ see Word Web: **respiratory system**

**re|spond** /rɪspɒnd/ (**responds, responding, responded**) V-T/V-I When you **respond** to something that is done or said, you react to it by doing or saying something yourself. responder ❑ *They responded positively to the president's request for financial help. Respondieron positivamente a la petición de ayuda económica del presidente.* ❑ *The army responded with gunfire. El ejército respondió abriendo fuego.* ❑ *"I have no idea," she responded. —No tengo idea—respondió.*

**re|sponse** /rɪspɒns/ (**responses**) **1** N-COUNT Your **response** to an event or to something that is said is your reply or reaction to it. reacción ❑ *There has been no response to his remarks. No ha habido reacción a sus comentarios.* **2** N-COUNT The **response** of an organism to a stimulus is the way that the organism reacts to it. reacción

**Word Partnership** Usar *response* con:

ADJ. **correct** response, **enthusiastic** response, **military** response, **overwhelming** response, **written** response **1**
**immediate** response, **negative/positive** response, **quick** response **1** **2**

**re|spon|sibil|ity** /rɪspɒnsɪbɪlɪti/ (**responsibilities**) **1** N-UNCOUNT If you have **responsibility** for something or someone, or if they are your **responsibility,** it is your job or duty to deal with them. responsabilidad ❑ *Each manager had responsibility for ten people. Cada director tenía bajo su responsabilidad a diez personas.* **2** N-UNCOUNT If you accept **responsibility for** something that has happened, you agree that you were to blame for it. responsabilidad ❑ *No one admitted responsibility for the attacks. Nadie se ha hecho responsable de los ataques.* **3** N-PLURAL Your **responsibilities** are the duties that you have because of your job or position. responsabilidades ❑ *...work and family responsibilities. ...responsabilidades laborales y familiares.* **4** N-SING If you think that you have a **responsibility to** do something, you feel that you ought to do it because it is morally right to do it. responsabilidad ❑ *We have a responsibility to help older people in our community. Tenemos la responsabilidad de ayudar a los ancianos de nuestra comunidad.*

**Word Partnership** Usar *responsibility* con:

V. **be given** responsibility **1**
**assume** responsibility, **bear** responsibility, **share** responsibility, **take** responsibility **1** **2** **4**
**have (a)** responsibility **1** **4**
**accept** responsibility, **claim** responsibility **2**
ADJ. **financial** responsibility, **moral** responsibility, **personal** responsibility **1** **2** **4**

**re|spon|sible** /rɪspɒnsɪbᵊl/ **1** ADJ If someone or something is **responsible for** a particular event or situation, they are the cause of it or they can be blamed for it. responsable ❑ *He still felt responsible for her death. Todavía se sentía responsable de su muerte.*

R

**Word Web** respiratory system

Respiration moves **air** into and out of the **lungs**. Air enters through the **nose** or **mouth**. Then it travels down the windpipe and into the **lungs**. In the lungs **oxygen** absorbs into the bloodstream. Blood carries oxygen to the heart and other organs. The lungs also remove **carbon dioxide** from the blood. This gas is then **exhaled** through the mouth. During inhalation the **diaphragm** moves downward and the lungs fill with air. During **exhalation** the diaphragm relaxes and air flows out. Adult humans **breathe** about six liters of air each minute.

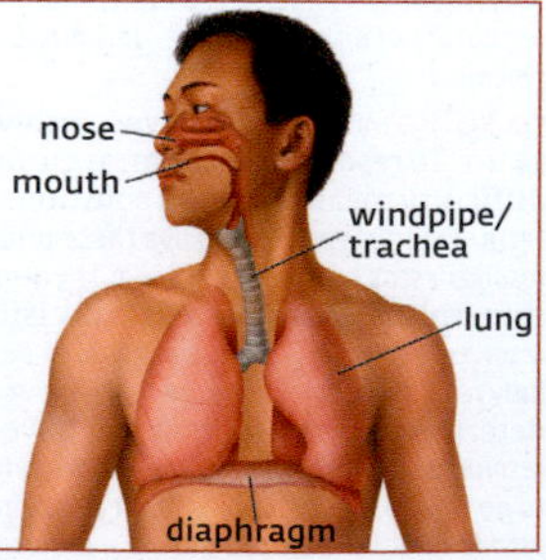

**2** ADJ If you are **responsible for** something, it is your job or duty to deal with it. *responsable* ❑ *...the people responsible for sales and marketing.* *...los responsables de las ventas y el mercadeo.* **3** ADJ If you are **responsible to** a person or group, they have authority over you and you have to report to them about what you do. *responsable* ❑ *The President of the Republic is responsible to the French people.* *El presidente de la república es responsable ante el pueblo francés.* **4** ADJ **Responsible** people behave properly and sensibly, without needing to be supervised. *responsable* ❑ *The media should be more responsible in what they report.* *Los medios de comunicación deberían ser más responsables respecto a lo que informan.* ● **re|spon|sibly** ADV *responsablemente* ❑ *He urged everyone to behave responsibly.* *Instó a todos a actuar responsablemente.*

**rest**
❶ QUANTIFIER USES
❷ VERB AND NOUN USES

❶ **rest** /rɛst/ **1** QUANT **The rest** is used to refer to all the parts of something or all the things in a group that remain or that you have not already mentioned. *resto* ❑ *...an experience I will remember for the rest of my life.* *...una experiencia que recordaré el resto de mi vida.* ● **Rest** is also a pronoun. *resto* ❑ *I ate two cakes and saved the rest.* *Me comí dos pasteles y guardé el resto.* **2** PHRASE You can add **and the rest** or **all the rest of it** to the end of a statement or list when you want to refer in a vague way to other things that are associated with the ones you have already mentioned. *etcétera* [SPOKEN] ❑ *...a man with nice clothes, a nice car and the rest.* *...un hombre con ropa bonita, un coche bonito, etcétera, etcétera.*

| **Thesaurus** | *rest* | Ver también: |
|---|---|---|
| v. | lie down, relax ❷ **1** | |

❷ **rest** /rɛst/ (**rests, resting, rested**) **1** V-T/V-I If you **rest** or if you **rest** your body, you do not do anything active for a time. *descansar* ❑ *He's tired and the doctor advised him to rest.* *Está cansado y el médico le aconsejó descansar.* ● **rest|ed** ADJ *descansado* ❑ *He looked well rested after his vacation.* *Se veía muy descansado después de sus vacaciones.* **2** N-VAR If you get some **rest** or have a **rest**, you do not do anything active for a time. *descanso* ❑ *You're exhausted—go home and get some rest.* *—Te ves agotado; vete a casa y descansa.* **3** V-I If something such as a theory or your success **rests on** a particular thing, it depends on that thing. *depender* [FORMAL] ❑ *My whole future rests on his decision.* *Todo mi futuro depende de su decisión.* **4** V-T If you **rest** something somewhere, you put it there so that its weight is supported. *apoyar* ❑ *He rested his arms on the back of the chair.* *Apoyó los brazos en el respaldo de la silla.* **5** V-T/V-I If something **is resting** somewhere, or if you **are resting** it there, it is in a position where its weight is supported. *descansar, apoyar* ❑ *His head was resting on her shoulder.* *Su cabeza descansaba en su hombro.*, *Tenía la cabeza apoyada en su hombro.* **6** V-I If you **rest** on or against someone or something, you lean on them so that they support the weight of your body. *apoyarse* ❑ *He rested on his shovel.* *Se apoyó en la pala.* **7** PHRASE When an object that has been moving **comes to rest**, it finally stops. *detenerse* [FORMAL] ❑ *The car skidded off the road and came to rest in a field.* *El coche derrapó, se salió del camino y se detuvo en un campo.*
→ see **motion, sleep**

**rest area** (**rest areas**) N-COUNT A **rest area** is a place beside a highway where you can buy gasoline and other things, or have a meal. *parada de descanso, área de descanso, área de reposo*

**res|tau|rant** /rɛstərənt, -tərɑnt, -trɑnt/ (**restaurants**) N-COUNT A **restaurant** is a place where you can buy and eat a meal and pay for it. In restaurants, your food is usually served to you at your table by a waiter or waitress. *restaurante* ❑ *...an Italian restaurant.* *...un restaurante italiano.*
→ see **city**

**rest|less** /rɛstlɪs/ **1** ADJ If you are **restless**, you are bored, impatient, or dissatisfied, and you want to do something else. *impaciente* ❑ *I got restless and moved to San Francisco.* *Me impacienté y me cambié a San Francisco.* ● **rest|less|ness** N-UNCOUNT *inquietud* ❑ *Many fears and anxieties cause a feeling of restlessness.* *Muchos temores y ansiedades provocan un sentimiento de inquietud.* **2** ADJ If someone is **restless**, they keep moving around because they find it difficult to keep still. *inquieto, nervioso, impaciente* ❑ *My father seemed very restless and excited.* *Mi padre parecía muy inquieto y emocionado.* ● **rest|less|ly** ADV *nerviosamente* ❑ *He walked up and down restlessly.* *Caminaba nerviosamente de un lado a otro.*

| **Word Link** | *re ≈ back, again : reflect, refuel, restore* |
|---|---|

**re|store** /rɪstɔr/ (**restores, restoring, restored**) **1** V-T To **restore** something means to cause it to exist again. *restablecer* ❑ *The army was brought in to restore order.* *Llamaron al ejército para restablecer el orden.* ● **res|to|ra|tion** /rɛstəreɪʃən/ N-UNCOUNT *restablecimiento* ❑ *...the restoration of law and order.* *...el restablecimiento de la ley y el orden.* **2** V-T To **restore** someone or something **to** a previous condition or place means to cause them to be in that condition or place again. *devolver, restituir* ❑ *We will restore her to health.* *Nosotros le restituiremos la salud.* **3** V-T To **restore** an old building, painting, or piece of furniture means to repair and clean it, so that it looks like it did when it was new. *restaurar* ❑ *...experts who specialize in restoring old buildings.* *...expertos especializados en la restauración de edificios antiguos.* ● **res|to|ra|tion** N-VAR (**restorations**) *restauración* ❑ *...the restoration of old houses.* *...la restauración de casas antiguas.*

**re|strain** /rɪstreɪn/ (**restrains, restraining, restrained**) **1** V-T If you **restrain** someone, you stop them from doing what they intended or wanted to do, usually by using your physical strength. *contener* ❑ *Wally gripped my arm to restrain me.* *Wally me asió del brazo para contenerme.* **2** V-T If you **restrain** an emotion or you **restrain yourself from** doing something, you prevent yourself from showing that emotion or doing what you wanted or intended to do. *contener* ❑ *She was unable to restrain her anger.* *Era incapaz de contener su cólera.* ● **re|strained** ADJ *moderado* ❑ *He was very restrained in the circumstances.* *Dadas las circunstancias, fue muy moderado.* **3** V-T To **restrain** something that is

r

growing or increasing means to prevent it from getting too large. *moderar, contener* ❑ *The speech is about economic growth and restrained spending. El discurso es sobre el crecimiento económico y la contención del gasto.*

**re|strain|ing or|der** (**restraining orders**) N-COUNT A **restraining order** is an order by a court of law that someone should stop doing something until a court decides whether they are legally allowed to continue doing it. *orden restrictiva* [LEGAL] ❑ *She took out a restraining order against him. Pidió una orden restrictiva en su contra.*

**re|straint** /rɪstreɪnt/ (**restraints**) **1** N-VAR **Restraints** are rules or conditions that limit or restrict someone or something. *restricción, limitación* ❑ *...the need for spending restraints in some areas. ...la necesidad de restricciones al gasto en algunas áreas.* **2** N-UNCOUNT **Restraint** is calm, controlled, and unemotional behavior. *compostura, circunspección* ❑ *They behaved with great restraint. Actuaron con gran circunspección.*

**re|strict** /rɪstrɪkt/ (**restricts, restricting, restricted**) **1** V-T If you **restrict** something, you put a limit on it to prevent it from becoming too great. *restringir, limitar* ❑ *...restricting the number of students. ...limitar el número de estudiantes.* • **re|strict|ed** ADJ *restringido, limitado* ❑ *...a carefully restricted diet. ...una dieta cuidadosamente restringida.* • **re|stric|tion** /rɪstrɪkʃᵊn/ N-VAR (**restrictions**) *restricción, límite* ❑ *...restrictions on spending. ...restricciones al gasto.* **2** V-T To **restrict** the movement or actions of someone or something means to prevent them from moving or acting freely. *restringir* ❑ *The government restricted the media. El gobierno restringió a los medios de comunicación.* • **re|strict|ed** ADJ *restringido* ❑ *...a highly restricted area. ...una zona muy restringida.* • **re|stric|tion** N-VAR *restricción* ❑ *...this restriction of individual freedom. ...esta restricción de la libertad individual.* ❑ *...the restrictions of city living. ...las restricciones de la vida en la ciudad.* **3** V-T If you **restrict** someone or their activities **to** one thing, they can only do, have, or deal with that thing. If you **restrict** them **to** one place, they cannot go anywhere else. *restringir* ❑ *Patients are restricted to the grounds of the hospital. Los pacientes tienen prohibido salir de los terrenos del hospital.* **4** V-T If you **restrict** something **to** a particular group, only that group can do it or have it. If you **restrict** something **to** a particular place, it is allowed only in that place. *restringir, limitar* ❑ *They decided to restrict acceptance to 30 percent of applicants. Decidieron restringir la admisión al 30 por ciento de los solicitantes.*

**restroom** (**restrooms**) also **rest room** N-COUNT In a restaurant, theater, or other public place, a **restroom** is a room with a toilet for people to use. *baños, sanitarios, servicios*

**re|struc|ture** /ristrʌktʃər/ (**restructures, restructuring, restructured**) V-T To **restructure** an organization or system means to change the way it is organized, usually in order to make it work more effectively. *reestructurar* ❑ *...plans to restructure American education. ...planes para reestructurar la educación en Estados Unidos.* • **re|struc|tur|ing** N-VAR (**restructurings**) *reestructuración* ❑ *The company got rid of 1,520 workers as part of a restructuring. La empresa se deshizo de 1,520 trabajadores como parte de la reestructuración.*

**rest stop** (**rest stops**) N-COUNT On a long journey by road, a **rest stop** is a short period when you stop and leave your vehicle, for example to eat or use the restroom. *parada de descanso*

**re|sult** /rɪzʌlt/ (**results, resulting, resulted**) **1** N-COUNT A **result** is something that happens or exists because of something else that has happened. *resultado* ❑ *...people who developed the disease as a direct result of their work. ...gente que contrajo la enfermedad como resultado directo de su trabajo.* **2** V-I If something **results in** a particular situation or event, it causes that situation or event to happen. *resultar* ❑ *Fifty percent of road accidents result in head injuries. El cincuenta por ciento de los accidentes en carretera tienen como resultado traumatismos craneanos.* **3** V-I If something **results from** a particular event or action, it is caused by that event or action. *resultar* ❑ *Many hair problems result from what you eat. Muchos problemas del pelo son el resultado de lo que se come.* **4** N-COUNT A **result** is the situation that exists at the end of a contest. *resultado* ❑ *...election results. ...los resultados de las elecciones.* **5** N-COUNT A **result** is the number that you get when you do a calculation. *resultado* ❑ *Our computers made the same calculation but got different results. Nuestras computadoras hicieron el mismo cálculo pero arrojaron resultados diferentes.*

**re|sult|ant ve|loc|ity** (**resultant velocities**) N-COUNT The **resultant velocity** of a moving object is its total speed in a particular direction once all the different forces acting on it have been taken into account. *velocidad resultante* [TECHNICAL]

| Word Link | *sumpt ≈ taking : assumption, consumption, resumption* |
|---|---|

**re|sume** /rɪzum/ (**resumes, resuming, resumed**) V-T/V-I If you **resume** an activity or if it **resumes,** it begins again. *reasumir, reanudar* [FORMAL] ❑ *After the war he resumed his job at Wellesley College. Después de la guerra, reasumió su trabajo en el Colegio Wellesley.* • **re|sump|tion** /rɪzʌmpʃᵊn/ N-UNCOUNT *reanudación* ❑ *...the resumption of discussions. ...la reanudación de las negociaciones.*

**ré|su|mé** /rɛzʊmeɪ/ (**résumés**) also **resume** **1** N-COUNT A **résumé** is a short account, either spoken or written, of something that has happened or that someone has said or written. *resumen, reseña* ❑ *...a résumé of his speech. ...una reseña de su discurso.* **2** N-COUNT Your **résumé** is a brief account of your personal information, your education, and the jobs you have had. *currículum vítae*

**re|tail** /riteɪl/ (**retails, retailing, retailed**) **1** N-UNCOUNT **Retail** is the activity of selling products directly to the public. *por menor, minorista* [BUSINESS] ❑ *...retail stores. ...tiendas minoristas.* **2** V-I If an item in a store **retails at** or **for** a particular price, it is for sale at that price. *vender al por menor* [BUSINESS] ❑ *It originally retailed for $23.50. Originalmente su precio al por menor era de 23.50 dólares.* → see **city**

**re|tail|er** /riteɪlər/ (**retailers**) N-COUNT A **retailer** is a person or business that sells goods to the public. *minorista* [BUSINESS] ❑ *...carpet retailers. ...minoristas de alfombras y tapetes.*

R

**re|tain** /rɪteɪn/ (**retains, retaining, retained**) V-T To **retain** something means to continue to have that thing. *conservar* [FORMAL] ❑ *The inside of the shop still retains a nineteenth-century atmosphere. El interior de la tienda todavía conserva un ambiente decimonónico.*

| **Thesaurus** | *retain* | Ver también: |
|---|---|---|
| v. | hold, keep, maintain, remember, save; (*ant.*) give up, lose | |

**re|tali|ate** /rɪtælieɪt/ (**retaliates, retaliating, retaliated**) V-I If you **retaliate** when someone harms or annoys you, you do something which harms or annoys them in return. *vengarse, desquitarse, tomar represalias* ❑ *I was tempted to retaliate. Estuve tentado a desquitarme.* ❑ *...actions designed to retaliate against the government. ...actos destinados a ejercer represalias contra el gobierno.*
● **re|talia|tion** /rɪtælieɪʃᵊn/ N-UNCOUNT *venganza* ❑ *The attack was in retaliation for his death. El ataque fue en venganza de su muerte.*

**reti|na** /rɛtɪnə/ (**retinas**) N-COUNT Your **retina** is the area at the back of your eye that sends images to your brain. *retina*
→ see **eye**

**re|tire** /rɪtaɪər/ (**retires, retiring, retired**) V-I When older people **retire,** they leave their job and usually stop working completely. *jubilarse* ❑ *He planned to retire at 65. Hizo planes para jubilarse a los 65 años de edad.* ● **re|tired** ADJ *jubilado* ❑ *...a seventy-three-year-old retired teacher. ...un maestro jubilado de 73 años de edad.*

**re|tiree** /rɪtaɪəri/ (**retirees**) N-COUNT A **retiree** is a retired person. *jubilado* ❑ *...a city suitable for retirees and young families. ...una ciudad apropiada para jubilados y familias jóvenes.*

**re|tire|ment** /rɪtaɪərmənt/ (**retirements**) **1** N-VAR **Retirement** is the time when a worker retires. *jubilación* ❑ *...the proportion of people who are over retirement age. ...la proporción de personas que han superado la edad de jubilación.* **2** N-UNCOUNT A person's **retirement** is the period in their life after they have retired. *jubilación* ❑ *...financial support during retirement. ...apoyo económico posterior a la jubilación.*

**re|tire|ment fund** (**retirement funds**) N-COUNT A **retirement fund** is a special fund which people pay money into so that, when they retire from their job, they will receive money regularly as a pension. *fondo de jubilación, fondo de retiro*

**re|tire|ment plan** (**retirement plans**) N-COUNT A **retirement plan** is a savings plan in which part of the money that you earn is invested in the plan for you to use when you retire. *plan de jubilación, plan de retiro* [BUSINESS]

**re|tort** /rɪtɔrt/ (**retorts, retorting, retorted**) V-T To **retort** means to reply angrily to someone. *replicar* [WRITTEN] ❑ *"I did not!" Sherrie retorted. —¡Claro que no!—replicó enojada Sherrie.* ● **Retort** is also a noun. *réplica* ❑ *She was trying to think of some smart retort. Estaba pensando cómo replicarle.*

**re|treat** /rɪtrit/ (**retreats, retreating, retreated**) **1** V-I If you **retreat,** you move away from something or someone. *retirarse* ❑ *I retreated from the room. Me retiré del cuarto.* **2** V-I When an army **retreats,** it moves away from enemy forces in order to avoid fighting them. *retirarse* ❑ *The French were forced to retreat. Los franceses se vieron forzados a retirarse.* ● **Retreat** is also a noun. *retirada* ❑ *The British Army was in full retreat. El ejército británico se batía en plena retirada.* **3** N-COUNT A **retreat** is a quiet, isolated place that you go to in order to rest or to do things in private. *retiro* ❑ *He spent yesterday hidden away in his country retreat. Pasó el día de ayer oculto en su retiro en el campo.*

**re|triev|al** /rɪtrivᵊl/ N-UNCOUNT The **retrieval** of something is the process of getting it back from a particular place. *recuperación* ❑ *Data is stored in a computer so that retrieval is very easy. Los datos están almacenados en una computadora, por lo que su recuperación es muy fácil.*

**re|trieve** /rɪtriv/ (**retrieves, retrieving, retrieved**) V-T If you **retrieve** something, you get it back from the place where you left it. *ir por* ❑ *Alexander went into the bedroom to retrieve his hat. Alexander fue a la recámara por su sombrero.*

**retro|grade** /rɛtrəgreɪd/ (**retrogrades**) N-VAR A **retrograde** is a section of dance or music in which the usual order is reversed, by beginning at the end and ending at the beginning. *inversión* [TECHNICAL]

**retro|grade or|bit** (**retrograde orbits**) N-VAR Planets that have a **retrograde orbit** move around the sun in the opposite direction to the direction in which they spin on their own axis. *órbita retrógrada* [TECHNICAL]

**retro|grade ro|ta|tion** N-UNCOUNT Planets that have **retrograde rotation** spin on their axis in the opposite direction to the direction that they move around the sun. Compare **prograde rotation.** *rotación retrógrada* [TECHNICAL]

**retro|spect** /rɛtrəspɛkt/ PHRASE When you consider something **in retrospect,** you think about it afterward, and often have a different opinion about it from the one that you had at the time. *en retrospectiva* ❑ *The decision was not a very good one in retrospect. En retrospectiva, la decisión no fue muy buena.*

**re|turn** /rɪtɜrn/ (**returns, returning, returned**) **1** V-I When you **return to** a place, you go back there after you have been away. *volver, regresar, retornar* ❑ *He will return to Moscow tomorrow. Mañana regresará a Moscú.* **2** N-SING Your **return** is your arrival back at a place where you were before. *vuelta, regreso, retorno* ❑ *Kenny explained the reason for his sudden return to Dallas. Kenny explicó las razones de su repentino regreso a Dallas.* **3** V-T If you **return** something that you have borrowed or taken, you give it back or put it back. *devolver* ❑ *I enjoyed the book and said so when I returned it. Disfruté el libro; y así lo dije cuando lo devolví.* ● **Return** is also a noun. *devolución* ❑ *...Japan's demand for the return of the islands. ...la exigencia de Japón de la devolución de las islas.* **4** V-T If you **return** someone's action, you do the same thing to him or her as he or she has just done to you. If you **return** someone's feelings, you feel the same way toward him or her as he or she feels toward you. *devolver* ❑ *Harry returned my phone call. Harry me devolvió la llamada.* **5** V-I If you **return to** a state that you were in before, you start being in that state again. *volver a* ❑ *Life has improved and*

r

returned to normal. La vida ha mejorado y vuelto a la normalidad. • **Return** is also a noun. recuperación ❑ *He made a return to normal health.* Recuperó la salud. **6** V-I If you **return to** a subject that you have mentioned before, you begin talking about it again. volver a, regresar a ❑ *Reporters returned to the subject of baseball.* Los reporteros volvieron al tema del béisbol. **7** V-I If you **return to** an activity that you were doing before, you start doing it again. volver a, regresar a ❑ *At 52, he is young enough to return to politics.* A los 52 años todavía es bastante joven para volver a la política. • **Return** is also a noun. vuelta, regreso, retorno ❑ *He has not ruled out the possibility of a return to football.* No ha descartado la posibilidad de su regreso al fútbol. **8** V-T When a judge or jury **returns** a verdict, they announce whether they think the person on trial is guilty or not. emitir ❑ *They returned a verdict of not guilty.* Emitieron un veredicto de inocencia. **9** N-COUNT The **return on** an investment is the profit that you get from it. rendimiento [BUSINESS] ❑ *The return on the money remains tiny.* Los rendimientos del dinero siguen siendo minúsculos. **10** PHRASE If you do something **in return for** what someone else has done for you, you do it because they did that thing for you. a su turno, corresponder ❑ *He nodded at Alison and she nodded in return.* Saludó a Alison con un movimiento de cabeza y ella le devolvió el saludo.
→ see **library**

| **Thesaurus** | *return* | Ver también: |
|---|---|---|
| V. | come back, go back, reappear **1**<br>give back, hand back, pay back; (*ant.*) keep **3** | |
| N. | arrival, homecoming; (*ant.*) departure **2** | |

| **Word Partnership** | Usar *return* con: |
|---|---|
| V. | **decide to** return, **plan to** return, **want to** return **1 3 4 – 7** |
| N. | return **trip 2**<br>return **a (phone) call 4**<br>return **to work 7** |

R

**re|union** /riyuniən/ (**reunions**) **1** N-COUNT A **reunion** is a party attended by members of the same family, school, or other group who have not seen each other for a long time. reunión ❑ *The school holds an annual reunion.* La escuela celebra una reunión anual. **2** N-VAR A **reunion** is a meeting between people who have been separated for some time. reencuentro ❑ *It was a very emotional reunion.* Fue un reencuentro muy emotivo.

**re|use** (**reuses, reusing, reused**)

> The verb is pronounced /riyuz/. The noun is pronounced /riyus/.

V-T When you **reuse** something, you use it again instead of throwing it away. reutilizar, volver a utilizar ❑ *Try where possible to reuse paper.* Siempre que sea posible, trate de volver a usar el papel. • **Reuse** is also a noun. reutilización ❑ *Copper, brass, and aluminium are separated and remelted for reuse.* El cobre, el latón y el aluminio se separan y vuelven a fundir para su reutilización.
→ see **dump**

**re|veal** /rɪvil/ (**reveals, revealing, revealed**) **1** V-T To **reveal** something means to make people aware of it. revelar ❑ *She has refused to reveal any more details.* Se ha rehusado a revelar más detalles. ❑ *A survey revealed that a growing number of people are overweight.* Un sondeo reveló que cada vez hay más personas con sobrepeso. **2** V-T If you **reveal** something that has been out of sight, you uncover it so that people can see it. descubrir, dejar ver ❑ *We removed the carpet to reveal the wooden floor beneath.* Quitamos el tapete para dejar ver el piso de madera.

**re|veal|ing** /rɪvilɪŋ/ ADJ A **revealing** statement, account, or action tells you something that you did not know, especially about the person doing it or making it. revelador ❑ *...a revealing interview.* ...una entrevista reveladora.

**rev|ela|tion** /rɛvəleɪʃ^ə^n/ (**revelations**) **1** N-COUNT A **revelation** is a surprising or interesting fact that is made known to people. revelación ❑ *...revelations about his private life.* ...revelaciones sobre su vida privada. **2** N-VAR The **revelation of** something is the act of making it known. revelación ❑ *...the revelation of his true identity.* ...la revelación de su verdadera identidad. **3** N-SING If you say that something you experienced was **a revelation,** you are saying that it was very surprising or very good. revelación ❑ *Degas's work was a revelation to her.* La obra de Degas fue una revelación para ella.

**rev|el|er** /rɛvələr/ (**revelers**) also **reveller** N-COUNT **Revelers** are people who are enjoying themselves in a noisy way. juerguista, parrandero o parrandera, jaranero o jaranera [LITERARY] ❑ *...a crowd of revelers.* ...una multitud de jaraneros.

**re|venge** /rɪvɛndʒ/ N-UNCOUNT **Revenge** involves hurting or punishing someone who has hurt or harmed you. venganza ❑ *The attackers took revenge on the boy, claiming he was a school bully.* Los atacantes se vengaron del muchacho, afirmando que era un bravucón.

**rev|enue** /rɛvənyu/ (**revenues**) **1** N-VAR **Revenue** is money that a company, organization, or government receives from people. ingreso [BUSINESS] ❑ *One butcher shop saw a 50 percent drop in revenue.* Los ingresos de una carnicería cayeron el 50 por ciento. **2** → see also **Internal Revenue Service**

**rev|enue stream** (**revenue streams**) N-COUNT A company's **revenue stream** is the amount of money that it receives from selling a particular product or service. ingreso [BUSINESS] ❑ *This unexpected revenue stream provided them with cash.* Esos ingresos inesperados los proveyeron de dinero en efectivo.

**Rev|er|end** /rɛvərənd/ N-TITLE **Reverend** is a title used before the name or rank of an officially appointed Christian religious leader. clérigo, religioso, sacerdote ❑ *...the Reverend Jim Simons.* ...el reverendo pastor Jim Simons.

**re|verse** /rɪvɜrs/ (**reverses, reversing, reversed**) **1** V-T To **reverse** a decision, policy, or trend means to change it to the opposite decision, policy, or trend. revocar (legal), anular (legal), cambiar, dar marcha atrás ❑ *They will not reverse the decision to increase prices.* No darán marcha atrás en la decisión de aumentar los precios. **2** V-T If you **reverse** the order of a set of things, you arrange them in the opposite order, so that the first thing comes last.

*invertir* ❑ *In German, you sometimes have to reverse the normal word order.* *En alemán, en ocasiones se debe invertir el orden normal de las palabras.* 3 N-UNCOUNT If your car is **in reverse,** you have changed gears so that you can drive it backward. *en reversa, en marcha atrás* 4 ADJ **Reverse** means opposite from what you expect or to what has just been described. *inverso, contrario* ❑ *The wrong attitude will have exactly the reverse effect.* *Una mala actitud provocará exactamente el efecto contrario.* 5 N-SING If you say that one thing is **the reverse** of another, you are emphasizing that the first thing is the complete opposite of the second thing. *contrario, opuesto* ❑ *He was not at all happy. Quite the reverse.* *No estaba feliz en absoluto; todo lo contrario.* 6 PHRASE If something happens **in reverse** or goes **into reverse,** things happen in the opposite way from what usually happens or from what has been happening. *a la inversa, al revés* ❑ *Amis tells the story in reverse, from the moment the man dies.* *Amis narra la historia al revés, a partir del momento en que el hombre muere.*

**re|verse fault** (**reverse faults**) N-COUNT A **reverse fault** is a fault in the surface of the Earth where the rock above the fault has moved up. Compare **normal fault.** *falla inversa, falla invertida* [TECHNICAL]

**re|verse psy|chol|ogy** N-UNCOUNT If you use **reverse psychology** on someone, you try to get them to do something by saying or doing the opposite of what they expect. *decir o hacer lo opuesto de lo que alguien espera para tratar de que haga lo que uno quiere* ❑ *He was trying some reverse psychology, pretending he wasn't interested, when really he was.* *Estaba tratando de hacer creer que no le interesaba, cuando en realidad sí estaba interesado.*

**re|vert** /rɪvɜrt/ (**reverts, reverting, reverted**) V-I When people or things **revert to** a previous state, system, or type of behavior, they go back to it. *volver a, revertir* ❑ *He made a few comments and then reverted to silence.* *Hizo unos cuantos comentarios y después volvió a guardar silencio.*

**re|view** /rɪvyu/ (**reviews, reviewing, reviewed**) 1 N-COUNT A **review of** a situation or system is an examination of it by people in authority, to see if changes are needed. *revisión, estudio, examen* ❑ *The president ordered a review of the situation.* *El presidente ordenó una revisión de la situación.* 2 V-T If you **review** a situation or system, you consider it carefully to see if changes are needed. *revisar, estudiar, examinar* ❑ *The new proposal will be reviewed by the city council on Monday.* *El ayuntamiento revisará la nueva propuesta el lunes.* 3 N-COUNT A **review** is a report in the media in which someone gives their opinion of something such as a new book or movie. *crítica, reseña* ❑ *The movie had a good review in the magazine.* *La película tuvo una buena reseña en la revista.* 4 V-T If someone **reviews** something such as a new book or movie, they write a report or give a talk on television or radio in which they express their opinion of it. *reseñar* ❑ *Richard Coles reviews all the latest DVD releases.* *Richard Coles hace la reseña de todas las novedades en DVD.* • **re|view|er** N-COUNT (**reviewers**) *crítico o crítica* ❑ *...the reviewer for Atlantic Monthly.* *...el crítico del Atlantic Monthly.* 5 V-T/V-I When you **review for** an exam, or when you **review** your work, you read things again and make notes in order to be prepared for the exam. *repasar* ❑ *Review all the notes for each course.* *Repasa todas las notas de cada curso.* • **Review** is also a noun. *repaso* ❑ *...three two-hour reviews.* *...tres repasos de dos horas.*

**Word Partnership** Usar *review* con:

N. **performance** review 1
review **a case**, review **evidence** 2
**book** review, **film/movie** review, **restaurant** review 3
review **questions** 5

**re|vise** /rɪvaɪz/ (**revises, revising, revised**) V-T If you **revise** something, you alter it in order to make it better or more accurate. *reconsiderar, cambiar, revisar* ❑ *He revised his opinion of the professor.* *Reconsideró la opinión que tenía del profesor.* ❑ *They revised their prices to make them equal with their competitors' prices.* *Revisaron sus precios para igualarlos con los de sus competidores.* • **re|vi|sion** /rɪvɪʒᵊn/ N-VAR (**revisions**) *revisión* ❑ *The phase of writing that is most important is revision.* *La fase más importante de la redacción es su revisión.*

**re|vis|it** /rivɪzɪt/ (**revisits, revisiting, revisited**) V-T If you **revisit** a place, you return there for a visit after you have been away for a long time. *volver a visitar* ❑ *When we returned to Canada, we revisited this lake.* *Cuando regresamos a Canadá, volvimos a ir a ese lago.*

**Word Link** viv ≈ living : revival, survive, vivid

**re|viv|al** /rɪvaɪvᵊl/ (**revivals**) 1 N-COUNT When there is a **revival of** something, it becomes active or popular again. *renovación* ❑ *...a revival of interest in a number of artists.* *...la renovación del interés por varios artistas.* 2 N-COUNT A **revival** is a new production of a play, an opera, or a ballet. *reposición, reestreno* ❑ *...John Clement's revival of Chekhov's "The Seagull."* *...la reposición de "La Gaviota" de Chéjov por John Clement.*

**re|vive** /rɪvaɪv/ (**revives, reviving, revived**) 1 V-T/V-I When something such as the economy, a business, a trend, or a feeling **is revived** or when it **revives,** it becomes active, popular, or successful again. *reactivar* ❑ *...an attempt to revive the economy.* *...un intento por reactivar la economía.* 2 V-T When someone **revives** a play, opera, or ballet, they present a new production of it. *reponer, reestrenar* ❑ *His plays were revived both here and abroad.* *Sus obras fueron repuestas tanto aquí como en el extranjero.* 3 V-T/V-I If you **revive** someone who has fainted or if they **revive,** they become conscious again. *reanimar* ❑ *She tried to revive him.* *Trató de reanimarlo.*

**re|volt** /rɪvoʊlt/ (**revolts, revolting, revolted**) 1 N-VAR A **revolt** is an illegal and often violent attempt by a group of people to change their country's political system. *revuelta, levantamiento, sublevación* ❑ *...a revolt by ordinary people against their leaders.* *...una revuelta de la gente común en contra de sus dirigentes.* 2 V-I When people **revolt,** they make an illegal and often violent attempt to change their country's political system. *sublevarse, rebelarse, alzarse* ❑ *In 1375 the people revolted.* *El pueblo se sublevó en 1375.* 3 N-VAR A **revolt** by a person or group against someone or something is a refusal to accept the authority of that person

r

or thing. rechazo ❑ *Conservative Republicans led the revolt against the policy.* *Los republicanos conservadores encabezaron el rechazo de la política.* **4** V-I When people **revolt against** someone or something, they reject the authority of that person or reject that thing. rebelarse ❑ *California taxpayers revolted against higher taxes.* *Los contribuyentes de California se rebelaron en contra del alza a los impuestos.*

**revo|lu|tion** /rɛvəluʃᵊn/ (**revolutions**) **1** N-COUNT A **revolution** is a successful attempt by a large group of people to change the political system of their country by force. revolución ❑ *The period since the revolution has been very unsettled.* *El período posterior a la revolución ha sido muy agitado.* **2** N-COUNT A **revolution** in a particular area of human activity is an important change in that area. revolución ❑ *There was a revolution in ship design in the nineteenth century.* *En el siglo XIX tuvo lugar una revolución del diseño naval.* **3** N-COUNT A **revolution** of an object such as a planet is one complete circle that it makes around a central point such as a star. revolución

**revo|lu|tion|ary** /rɛvəluʃənɛri/ (**revolutionaries**) **1** ADJ **Revolutionary** activities, organizations, or people have the aim of causing a political revolution. revolucionario ❑ *Do you know anything about the revolutionary movement?* *¿Sabes algo acerca del movimiento revolucionario?* **2** N-COUNT A **revolutionary** is a person who tries to cause a revolution or who takes an active part in one. revolucionario o revolucionaria **3** ADJ **Revolutionary** ideas and developments involve great changes in the way that something is done or made. revolucionario ❑ *...a revolutionary new product.* *...un producto nuevo revolucionario.*

**re|volve** /rɪvɒlv/ (**revolves, revolving, revolved**) **1** V-I If one thing **revolves around** another thing, the second thing is the main feature or focus of the first thing. girar en torno a ❑ *Since childhood, her life has revolved around tennis.* *Su vida ha girado en torno al tenis desde la niñez.* **2** V-I If a discussion or conversation **revolves around** a particular topic, it is mainly about that topic. girar en torno a ❑ *Most of the conversation revolved around Daniel's trip to New York.* *La mayor parte de la conversación giró en torno al viaje de Daniel a Nueva York.* **3** V-T/V-I When something **revolves** or when you **revolve** it, it moves or turns in a circle around a central point or line. girar, dar vueltas ❑ *The fan revolved slowly.* *El ventilador giraba lentamente.*

R

**re|volv|er** /rɪvɒlvər/ (**revolvers**) N-COUNT A **revolver** is a kind of hand gun. revólver

**re|ward** /rɪwɔrd/ (**rewards, rewarding, rewarded**) **1** N-COUNT A **reward** is something that you are given, for example because you have behaved well, worked hard, or provided a service to the community. premio, prima ❑ *The school gives rewards for good behavior.* *La escuela premia la buena conducta.* **2** N-COUNT A **reward** is a sum of money offered to anyone who can give information about lost or stolen property, a missing person, or someone who is wanted by the police. recompensa ❑ *The firm offered a $10,000 reward for information leading to the arrest of the killer.* *La firma ofreció una recompensa de 10,000 dólares por cualquier información que lleve al arresto del asesino.* **3** V-T If you do something and **are rewarded** with a particular benefit, you receive that benefit as a result of doing that thing. recompensar, premiar ❑ *He thanked her and was rewarded with a smile.* *Le dio las gracias y ella lo premió con una sonrisa.*

| **Thesaurus** | *reward* | Ver también: |
|---|---|---|
| N. | bonus, prize; (*ant.*) punishment **1** | |

**re|ward|ing** /rɪwɔrdɪŋ/ ADJ An experience or action that is **rewarding** gives you satisfaction or brings you benefits. gratificante ❑ *...a career that is very rewarding.* *...una carrera muy gratificante.*

**re|write** /rɪraɪt/ (**rewrites, rewriting, rewrote, rewritten**) V-T If someone **rewrites** a piece of writing such as a book, an article, or a law, they write it in a different way in order to improve it. volver a redactar, volver a dictar ❑ *She decided to rewrite her will.* *Decidió volver a redactar su testamento.*

**rheto|ric** /rɛtərɪk/ N-UNCOUNT If you refer to speech or writing as **rhetoric,** you disapprove of it because it is intended to convince and impress people but may not be sincere or honest. retórica ❑ *...political rhetoric rather than reality.* *...retórica política, en lugar de realidad.*

**rhe|tori|cal strat|egy** (**rhetorical strategies**) N-COUNT A **rhetorical strategy** is one of the traditional methods used to communicate meaning in a speech or piece of writing, for example exposition or description. estrategia retórica

**rhi|zoid** /raɪzɔɪd/ (**rhizoids**) N-COUNT **Rhizoids** are thin structures that grow downward from plants such as mosses and fungi and have a similar function to roots. rizoide [TECHNICAL]

**rhi|zome** /raɪzoʊm/ (**rhizomes**) N-COUNT **Rhizomes** are the horizontal stems from which some plants, such as irises, grow. Rhizomes are found on or just under the surface of the earth. rizoma

**rhom|bus** /rɒmbəs/ (**rhombuses**) N-COUNT A **rhombus** is a geometric shape which has four equal sides but is not a square. rombo [TECHNICAL] → see **shape**

**rhyme** /raɪm/ (**rhymes, rhyming, rhymed**) **1** V-RECIP If one word **rhymes with** another or if two words **rhyme,** they have a very similar sound. rimar ❑ *June rhymes with moon.* *Tuna rima con luna.* ❑ *...names that rhyme: Donnie, Ronnie, Connie.* *...nombres que riman: Aura, Laura, Isaura.* **2** N-COUNT A **rhyme** is a short poem which has rhyming words at the ends of its lines. poema ❑ *He was teaching Helen a rhyme.* *Estaba enseñándole un poema a Helen.* **3** N-UNCOUNT **Rhyme** is the use of rhyming words as a technique in poetry. rima ❑ *The plays are in rhyme.* *Las obras están escritas con rima.*

**rhythm** /rɪðəm/ (**rhythms**) **1** N-VAR A **rhythm** is a regular series of sounds or movements. ritmo ❑ *...the rhythms of jazz.* *...el ritmo del jazz.* **2** N-COUNT A **rhythm** is a regular pattern of changes, for example changes in your body, in the seasons, or in the tides. ritmo **3** N-COUNT A **rhythm** is a regular repetition of lines of shapes to achieve a specific effect or pattern. ritmo

**rib** /rɪb/ (**ribs**) N-COUNT Your **ribs** are the 12 pairs of curved bones that surround your chest. costilla ❑ *Her heart was thumping against her ribs.* *El corazón le*

**Word Web** rice

An old Chinese myth says that an animal gave **rice** to humans. A large flood destroyed all the crops. When the people returned from the hills, they saw a dog. It had rice **seeds** in its tail. They planted this new **grain** and were never hungry again. In many Asian countries the words for rice and **food** are the same. Rice has many other uses. It is the main ingredient in some kinds of laundry **starch**. In Thailand, rice **straw** is made into hats and shoes.

*latía contra las costillas.*

**rib|bon** /rɪbən/ (**ribbons**) N-VAR A **ribbon** is a long, narrow piece of cloth that you use for tying things together or as a decoration. *cinta, listón* ❑ *She tied back her hair with a ribbon. Se ató el pelo con un listón.*

**ribo|some** /raɪbəsoʊm/ (**ribosomes**) N-COUNT **Ribosomes** are structures within the cells of an organism that produce proteins. *ribosoma*

**rice** /raɪs/ (**rices**) N-VAR **Rice** consists of white or brown grains taken from a cereal plant. *arroz* ❑ *...a meal consisting of chicken, rice, and vegetables. ...un platillo de pollo, arroz y verduras.*
→ see Word Web: **rice**
→ see **dessert, grain**

**rich** /rɪtʃ/ (**richer, richest, riches**) **1** ADJ A **rich** person has a lot of money or valuable possessions. *rico* ❑ *He was a very rich man. Era un hombre muy rico.* ● **The rich** are rich people. *los ricos* ❑ *Only the rich can afford to live there. Sólo los ricos pueden darse el lujo de vivir ahí.* **2** N-PLURAL **Riches** are valuable possessions or large amounts of money. *riqueza* ❑ *He starred in a movie that led to success and riches. Protagonizó una película que le produjo éxito y riquezas.* **3** ADJ If something is **rich in** a useful or valuable substance or is a **rich source of** it, it contains a lot of it. *rico en* ❑ *Oranges are rich in vitamin C. Las naranjas son ricas en vitamina C.* **4** ADJ **Rich** food contains a lot of fat or oil. *grasoso, pesado, indigesto* ❑ *More cream would make it too rich. Más crema lo haría demasiado pesado.* **5** ADJ A **rich** life or history is one that is interesting because it is full of different events and activities. *rico* ❑ *...a rich and interesting life. ...una vida rica e interesante.* ● **rich|ness** N-UNCOUNT *riqueza* ❑ *...the richness of human life. ...la riqueza de la vida humana.*

**Thesaurus** *rich* Ver también:

ADJ. affluent, wealthy; (*ant.*) poor **1**

**Word Partnership** Usar *rich* con:

ADJ. rich **and beautiful**, rich **and famous**, rich **and powerful** **1**
V. **become** rich, **get** rich (**quick**) **1**
N. rich **kids**, rich **man/people**, rich **and poor** **1**
rich **in natural resources** **3**
rich **diet**, rich **food** **4**
rich **culture**, rich **heritage**, rich **history**, rich **tradition** **5**

**ri|cot|ta** /rɪkɒtə/ also **ricotta cheese** N-UNCOUNT **Ricotta** is a soft, white, unsalted cheese made from sheep's milk. *queso ricota, requesón*

**rid** /rɪd/ (**rids, ridding**)

The form **rid** is used in the present tense and is the past tense and past participle of the verb.

**1** PHRASE When you **get rid of** something that you do not want or do not like, you take action so that you no longer have it. *deshacerse de* ❑ *The owner needs to get rid of the car for financial reasons. El propietario necesita deshacerse del automóvil por motivos económicos.* **2** PHRASE If you **get rid of** someone who is causing problems for you or who you do not like, you make them leave. *deshacerse de* ❑ *He believed that his manager wanted to get rid of him. Creía que su jefe quería deshacerse de él.* **3** V-T If you **rid** a place or person **of** something undesirable, you succeed in removing it completely from that place or person. *librar de* ❑ *...an attempt to rid the country of political corruption. ...un intento por librar al país de la corrupción política.* **4** ADJ If you **are rid of** someone or something that you did not want or that caused problems for you, they are no longer with you or causing problems for you. *deshacerse de* ❑ *The family wanted a way to be rid of her. La familia buscaba la manera de deshacerse de ella.*

**rid|dle** /rɪdᵊl/ (**riddles**) **1** N-COUNT A **riddle** is a puzzle or joke in which you ask a question that seems to be nonsense but which has a clever or amusing answer. *adivinanza, acertijo* **2** N-COUNT You can describe something that is puzzling as a **riddle**. *enigma, misterio* ❑ *Police are trying to solve the riddle of Tina's murder. La policía trata de resolver el enigma del asesinato de Tina.*

**ride** /raɪd/ (**rides, riding, rode, ridden**) **1** V-T/V-I When you **ride** a horse, you sit on it and control its movements. *montar* ❑ *I saw a girl riding a horse. Vi a una muchacha montando a caballo.* ❑ *Can you ride? ¿Sabes montar (a caballo)?* **2** V-T/V-I When you **ride** a bicycle or a motorcycle, you sit on it, control it, and travel along on it. *montar en, andar en* ❑ *Riding a bike is great exercise. Andar en bicicleta es un gran ejercicio.* ❑ *...men riding on motorcycles. ...hombres en motocicleta.* **3** V-I When you **ride in** a vehicle such as a car, you travel in it. *viajar* ❑ *He prefers traveling on the subway to riding in a car. Prefiere viajar en el metro que en coche.* **4** N-COUNT A **ride** is a trip on a horse or bicycle, or in a vehicle. *paseo, vuelta* ❑ *She took some friends for a ride in the car. Llevó a unos amigos a dar una vuelta en el coche.* **5** → see also **riding**
**6** PHRASE If you say that someone faces **a rough**

r

**ride,** you mean that things are going to be difficult for them because people will criticize them a lot or treat them badly. mal rato [INFORMAL] ❑ *The president will face a rough ride unless the plan works.* *El presidente pasará un mal rato, a menos que el plan dé resultado.* **7** PHRASE If someone **rides herd on** other people or their actions, they supervise them or watch them closely. *supervisar, vigilar* ❑ *Hank often stayed late at the office, riding herd on the day-to-day business of the magazine.* *Hank se quedaba hasta tarde en la oficina frecuentemente, supervisando los asuntos cotidianos de la revista.*

| Word Partnership | Usar *ride* con: |
|---|---|
| N. | **bus/car/subway/train** ride **4** |
| V. | **give *someone* a** ride, **go for a** ride, **offer *someone* a** ride **4** |
| ADV. | ride **home 4** |
| ADJ. | **long** ride, **scenic** ride, **short** ride, **smooth** ride **4** |

**rid|er** /raɪdər/ (**riders**) N-COUNT A **rider** is someone who rides a horse, a bicycle, or a motorcycle. *jinete o amazona, ciclista, motociclista* ❑ *She is a very good rider.* *Es una jinete muy buena.*
→ see **horse**

**ridge** /rɪdʒ/ (**ridges**) **1** N-COUNT A **ridge** is a long, narrow piece of raised land. *cresta* ❑ *...a high road along a mountain ridge.* *...una carretera en lo alto que sigue una cresta montañosa.* **2** N-COUNT A **ridge** is a raised line on a flat surface. *protuberancia* ❑ *...the bony ridge of his nose.* *...la protuberancia huesuda de su nariz.*
→ see **mountain**

**ri|dicu|lous** /rɪdɪkyələs/ ADJ If you say that something or someone is **ridiculous,** you mean that they are very foolish. *ridículo* ❑ *It is ridiculous to suggest we are having a romance.* *Es ridículo sugerir que tenemos un romance.*

**rid|ing** /raɪdɪŋ/ N-UNCOUNT **Riding** is the activity or sport of riding horses. *monta, equitación* ❑ *The next morning we went riding.* *La mañana siguiente fuimos a montar.*

**rife** /raɪf/ ADJ If you say that something, usually something bad, is **rife** in a place or that the place is **rife with** it, you mean that it is very common. *extendido* ❑ *Disease was rife in the prison.* *Las enfermedades hacían estragos en la cárcel.*

R

**ri|fle** /raɪfᵊl/ (**rifles, rifling, rifled**) **1** N-COUNT A **rifle** is a gun with a long barrel. *rifle* ❑ *They shot him with an automatic rifle.* *Lo mataron con un rifle automático.* **2** V-T/V-I If you **rifle through** things or **rifle** them, you make a quick search among them in order to find something or steal something. *buscar, hojear* ❑ *She was rifling though her files.* *Estaba hojeando sus archivos.*

**rift val|ley** (**rift valleys**) N-COUNT A **rift valley** is a valley formed as the result of a crack in the Earth's surface. *valle producto de una fisura o grieta en la superficie de la tierra*

**rig** /rɪg/ (**rigs, rigging, rigged**) **1** V-T If someone **rigs** an election, a job appointment, or a game, they dishonestly arrange it to get the result they want or to give someone an unfair advantage. *amañar, arreglar, manipular* ❑ *She accused her opponents of rigging the vote.* *Acusó a sus opositores de haber amañado la votación.* ● **rig|ging** N-UNCOUNT *fraude* ❑ *...vote rigging.* *...fraude electoral.* **2** N-COUNT A **rig** is a large structure that is used for looking for oil or gas and for taking it out of the ground or the bottom of the ocean. *plataforma* ❑ *...oil rigs.* *...plataformas petroleras.* **3** N-COUNT A **rig** is a truck that is made in two or more sections which are jointed together by metal bars, so that the vehicle can turn more easily. *camión de remolque*
→ see **oil**

**right**

1. CORRECT, APPROPRIATE, OR ACCEPTABLE
2. DIRECTION AND POLITICAL GROUPINGS
3. ENTITLEMENT
4. DISCOURSE USES
5. USED FOR EMPHASIS

**❶ right** /raɪt/ (**rights, righting, righted**) **1** ADJ If something is **right,** it is correct and agrees with the facts. *correcto* ❑ *That's absolutely right.* *Es absolutamente correcto.* ❑ *That clock never told the right time.* *El reloj nunca marcaba la hora correcta.* ● **Right** is also an adverb. *correctamente* ❑ *He guessed right about some things.* *Adivinó correctamente algunas cosas.* **2** ADJ If you do something in the **right** way or in the **right** place, you do it as or where it should be done or was planned to be done. *correcto, bien, indicado* ❑ *Walking, done in the right way, is a good form of exercise.* *La caminata es una buena forma de ejercicio, si se hace como debe ser.* ❑ *...delivery of the right pizza to the right place.* *...entrega de la piza indicada en el lugar indicado.* ● **Right** is also an adverb. *correctamente, bien* ❑ *To make sure I did everything right, I bought an instruction book.* *Compré un manual para asegurarme de que todo lo hacía bien.* **3** ADJ If you say that someone is seen in **all the right** places or knows **all the right** people, you mean that they go to places that are socially acceptable or know people who are socially acceptable. *adecuado, indicado* **4** ADJ If someone is **right about** something, they are correct in what they say or think about it. *tener razón* ❑ *Ron was right about the result of the election.* *Ron tenía razón sobre el resultado de las elecciones.* **5** ADJ If something such as a choice, action, or decision is the **right** one, it is the best or most suitable one. *adecuado* ❑ *She made the right choice in leaving New York.* *Tomó la decisión adecuada de irse de Nueva York.* **6** ADJ **Right** is used to refer to activities or actions that are considered to be morally good and acceptable. *bien* ❑ *It's not right, leaving her like this.* *No está bien dejarla así.* ● **Right** is also a noun. *bien* ❑ *He knew right from wrong.* *Sabía distinguir entre el bien y el mal.* ● **right|ness** N-UNCOUNT *rectitud* ❑ *...an offense against rightness.* *...una ofensa a la rectitud.* **7** V-T If you **right** a wrong, you do something to make up for a mistake or something bad that you did in the past. *rectificar* **8** V-T If you **right** something that has fallen or rolled over, or if it **rights itself,** it returns to its normal upright position. *enderezar* ❑ *He righted the boat and continued the race.* *Enderezó el bote y continuó la carrera.* **9** ADJ The **right** side of a material is the side that is intended to be seen and that faces outward when it is made into something. *derecho* ❑ *Turn*

*the pants right side out.* *Voltee los pantalones al derecho.*
**10** **it serves** you **right** → see **serve**

**❷ right** /raɪt/

The spelling **Right** is also used for meaning **3**.

**1** N-SING The **right** is one of two opposite directions, sides, or positions. If you are facing north and you turn to the right, you will be facing east. *derecha* ❑ *On the right is a lovely garden.* *A la derecha hay un hermoso jardín.* • **Right** is also an adverb. *derecha* ❑ *Turn right into the street.* *Dé vuelta a la derecha en la calle.* **2** ADJ Your **right** arm, leg, or ear, for example, is the one which is on the right side of your body. *derecho* **3** N-SING You can refer to people who support the political ideals of capitalism and conservatism as **the right.** *derecha* ❑ *This man is the best hope of the Republican Right.* *Este hombre es la gran esperanza de la derecha republicana.*

**❸ right** /raɪt/ (**rights**) **1** N-PLURAL Your **rights** are what you are morally or legally entitled to do or to have. *derecho* ❑ *They don't know their rights.* *No conocen sus derechos.* **2** N-SING If you have a **right to** do or to have something, you are morally or legally entitled to do it or to have it. *derecho a* ❑ *We have the right to protest.* *Tenemos el derecho a protestar.* **3** PHRASE If something is not true but you think that it should be, you can say that **by rights** it should be true. *por derecho, propiamente* ❑ *She did work which by rights should be done by someone else.* *Hacía el trabajo que, propiamente, debería hacer alguien más.* **4** PHRASE If someone is a successful or respected person **in** their **own right**, they are successful or respected because of their own efforts and talents rather than those of the people they are connected with. *por derecho propio* ❑ *The president's daughter is famous in her own right.* *La hija del presidente es famosa a título propio.*

**❹ right** /raɪt/ CONVENTION You can use **right** to check whether what you have just said is correct. *¿verdad?* [SPOKEN] ❑ *They have a small plane, right?* *Tienen un avión chico, ¿verdad?* → see also **all right**

**❺ right** /raɪt/ **1** ADV You can use **right** to emphasize the exact place, position, or time of something. *justo* ❑ *A car appeared right in front of him.* *Un coche apareció justo frente a él.* **2** ADV If you say that something happened **right after** a particular time or event or **right before** it, you mean that it happened immediately after or before it. *justo después* ❑ *All of a sudden, right after the summer, Mother got married.* *Repentinamente, justo después del verano, mamá se casó.* **3** ADV If you say **I'll be right there** or **I'll be right back,** you mean that you will get to a place or get back to it in a very short time. *vuelvo enseguida* ❑ *I'm going to get some water. I'll be right back.* *Voy por un poco de agua. Vuelvo enseguida.* **4** PHRASE If you do something **right away,** you do it immediately. *de inmediato, inmediatamente* [INFORMAL] ❑ *He wants to see you right away.* *Quiere verte inmediatamente.* **5** PHRASE You can use **right now** to emphasize that you are referring to the present moment. *justo ahora, en este preciso momento* [INFORMAL] ❑ *Right now I'm feeling very excited.* *En este preciso momento, me siento muy emocionado.*

**right an|gle** (**right angles**) **1** N-COUNT A **right angle** is an angle of ninety degrees. *ángulo recto* **2** PHRASE If two things are **at right angles,** they form an angle of 90° where they touch each other. You can also say that one thing is **at right angles to** another. *en ángulo recto* ❑ *...two lines at right angles.* *...dos líneas en ángulo recto.*

**right|ful** /raɪtfəl/ ADJ If you say that someone or something has returned to its **rightful** place or position, they have returned to the place or position that you think they should have. *legítimo* ❑ *The stolen goods were returned to their rightful owner.* *Los bienes robados fueron devueltos a su legítimo dueño.* • **right|ful|ly** ADV *legítimamente, por legítimo derecho* ❑ *Jealousy is the feeling that someone else has something that rightfully belongs to you.* *Los celos son el sentimiento de que alguien tiene algo que nos pertenece por legítimo derecho.*

**right-hand** ADJ If something is on the **right-hand** side of something, it is positioned on the right of it. *a la derecha, al lado derecho* ❑ *...a church on the right-hand side of the road.* *...una iglesia a la derecha del camino.*

**right-handed** ADJ Someone who is **right-handed** uses their right hand rather than their left hand for activities such as writing and sports, and for picking things up. *diestro, derecho* • **Right-handed** is also an adverb. *con la derecha* ❑ *I batted left-handed and bowled right-handed.* *Bateaba con la izquierda y lanzaba la pelota con la derecha.*

**right-of-center** ADJ A **right-of-center** person or political party has political views which are closer to capitalism and conservatism than to socialism but which are not very extreme. *centro-derecha* ❑ *...the right-of-center candidate.* *...el candidato de centro-derecha.*

**right of way** (**rights of way**) N-COUNT A **right of way** is a public path across private land. *servidumbre, derecho de paso*
→ see **transportation**

**right tri|an|gle** (**right triangles**) N-COUNT A **right triangle** has one angle that is a right angle. *triángulo rectángulo*
→ see **shape**

**right-wing**

The spelling **right wing** is used for meaning **2**.

**1** ADJ A **right-wing** person or group has conservative or capitalist views. *de derecha, derechista* ❑ *...a right-wing government.* *...un gobierno derechista.* • **right-winger** N-COUNT (**right-wingers**) *derechista* ❑ *Across Europe, right-wingers are gaining power.* *Los derechistas están ganando el poder en toda Europa.* **2** N-SING **The right wing** of a political party consists of the members who have the most conservative or the most capitalist views. *ala derecha* ❑ *...the right wing of the Republican Party.* *...el ala derecha del Partido Republicano.*

**rig|id** /rɪdʒɪd/ **1** ADJ Laws, rules, or systems that are **rigid** cannot be changed or varied, and are therefore considered to be rather severe. *riguroso, rígido* ❑ *...rigid rules about student behavior.* *...reglas estrictas sobre la conducta estudiantil.* • **ri|gid|ity** /rɪdʒɪdɪti/ N-UNCOUNT *severidad, rigidez* ❑ *...the rigidity of government policy.* *...la rigidez de la política gubernamental.* • **rig|id|ly** ADV *rigurosamente* ❑ *The law was rigidly enforced.* *La ley fue aplicada rigurosamente.* **2** ADJ A **rigid** substance or object is stiff and does not bend, stretch, or twist easily.

rígido ❑ ...rigid plastic containers. ...recipientes de plástico rígido. • **ri|gid|ity** N-UNCOUNT rigidez ❑ ...the strength and rigidity of glass. ...la resistencia y rigidez del vidrio.

**rig|id mo|tion** (**rigid motions**) N-VAR **Rigid motion** is a change to the position of a geometric figure such as a triangle in which the distances and angles between points in the figure remain the same. *movimiento rígido* [TECHNICAL]

**rig|or|ous** /rɪgərəs/ ADJ A test, system, or procedure that is **rigorous** is very thorough and strict. *riguroso* ❑ *...rigorous tests. ...pruebas rigurosas.* • **rig|or|ous|ly** ADV *rigurosamente* ❑ *...rigorously conducted research. ...una investigación llevada a cabo rigurosamente.*

**rim** /rɪm/ (**rims**) N-COUNT The **rim** of a container or a circular object is the edge that goes all the way around the top or around the outside. *borde* ❑ *She looked at him over the rim of her glass. Lo miró por sobre el borde de su vaso.*

**ring**
❶ TELEPHONING OR MAKING A SOUND
❷ SHAPES AND GROUPS

❶ **ring** /rɪŋ/ (**rings, ringing, rang, rung**) **1** V-I When a telephone **rings,** it makes a sound to let you know that someone is phoning you. *sonar, repicar, repiquetear* • **Ring** is also a noun. *sonido, repique* ❑ *After eight rings, someone answered the phone. Después de ocho repiques, alguien contestó el teléfono.* **2** V-T/V-I When you **ring** a bell or when a bell **rings,** it makes a sound. *sonar, repiquetear* ❑ *He heard the school bell ring. Oyó repiquetear la campana de la escuela.* • **Ring** is also a noun. *timbrazo, repique* ❑ *There was a ring of the bell. Sonó un timbrazo.* **3** N-SING You can use **ring** to describe a quality that something such as a statement, discussion, or argument seems to have. For example, if an argument **has a familiar ring,** it seems familiar. *sonido* **4** PHRASE If a statement **rings true,** it seems to be true or genuine. If it **rings hollow,** it does not seem to be true or genuine. *suena convincente/hueco*

▸ **ring up** → see **ring** ❶ **2**

❷ **ring** /rɪŋ/ (**rings, ringing, ringed**) **1** N-COUNT A **ring** is a small circle of metal that you wear on your finger. *anillo, alianza, sortija* ❑ *...a gold wedding ring. ...un anillo de bodas.* **2** N-COUNT An object or substance that is in the shape of a circle can be described as a **ring.** *aro* ❑ *...a large ring of keys. ...un gran aro de llaves.* **3** N-COUNT At a boxing or wrestling match or a circus, the **ring** is the place where the contest or performance takes place. *cuadrilátero, ring* ❑ *...a boxing ring. ...un cuadrilátero de box.* **4** N-COUNT You can refer to an organized group of people who are involved in an illegal activity as a **ring.** *red, banda* ❑ *...an art theft ring. ...una banda de ladrones de arte.* **5** V-T If a building or place **is ringed with** or **by** something, it is surrounded by it. *cercar, rodear* ❑ *The areas are ringed by soldiers. Las áreas están cercadas por los soldados.*
→ see **jewelry**

**ringtone** (**ringtones**) N-COUNT The **ringtone** is the sound made by a telephone, especially a cellphone, when it rings. *melodía*

**rinky-dink** /rɪŋkidɪŋk/ ADJ **Rinky-dink** things are small or unimportant. *de mala muerte* [INFORMAL] ❑ *I moved to this rinky-dink little place in Massachusetts. Me vine a vivir a este pueblito de mala muerte en Massachusetts.*

**rinse** /rɪns/ (**rinses, rinsing, rinsed**) V-T When you **rinse** something, you wash it in clean water in order to remove dirt or soap from it. *enjuagar* ❑ *Rinse the rice. Enjuague el arroz.* • **Rinse** is also a noun. *enjuague* ❑ *...a rinse with water. ...un enjuague.*

**riot** /raɪət/ (**riots, rioting, rioted**) **1** N-COUNT When there is a **riot,** a crowd of people behave violently in a public place. *disturbio* ❑ *Twelve people were killed during a riot at the prison. Doce personas resultaron muertas durante un motín en la cárcel.* **2** V-I If people **riot,** they behave violently in a public place. *causar disturbios, amotinarse* ❑ *They rioted in protest against the government. Causaron desórdenes en protesta contra el gobierno.* • **ri|ot|er** N-COUNT (**rioters**) *alborotador o alborotadora* ❑ *The police held the rioters back. La policía contuvo a los alborotadores.* • **ri|ot|ing** N-UNCOUNT *disturbio, desorden* ❑ *...three days of rioting. ...tres días de disturbios.*

**rip** /rɪp/ (**rips, ripping, ripped**) **1** V-T/V-I When something **rips** or when you **rip** it, you tear it forcefully with your hands or with a tool such as a knife. *rasgar, romper* ❑ *She ripped the photographs to pieces. Rompió las fotografías.* **2** N-COUNT A **rip** is a long cut or split in something made of cloth or paper. *rasgadura* ❑ *...the rip in her new dress. ...la rasgadura de su vestido nuevo.* **3** V-T If you **rip** something away, you remove it quickly and forcefully. *arrancar(se)* ❑ *Tatiana ripped the ring off her finger. Tatiana se arrancó el anillo del dedo.*

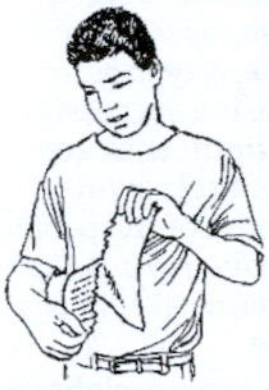
rip

▸ **rip off** PHR-VERB If someone **rips** you **off,** they cheat you by charging you too much money for something. *timar, tracalear* [INFORMAL] ❑ *Make sure the taxi driver doesn't rip you off. Asegúrate de que el taxista no te time.*

▸ **rip up** PHR-VERB If you **rip** something **up,** you tear it into small pieces. *romper en pedazos* ❑ *He ripped up the letter. Rompió la carta en pedazos.*
→ see **cut**

**ripe** /raɪp/ (**riper, ripest**) **1** ADJ **Ripe** fruit or grain is fully grown and ready to eat. *maduro* ❑ *...firm, but ripe fruit. ...fruta consistente, pero madura.* **2** ADJ If a situation is **ripe for** a particular development or event, that development or event is likely to happen soon. *oportuno, propicio* ❑ *The time was ripe for change. Era el momento propicio para cambiar.*

**rip|en** /raɪpən/ (**ripens, ripening, ripened**) V-T/V-I When crops **ripen** or when the sun **ripens** them, they become ripe. *madurar* ❑ *I'm waiting for the apples to ripen. Estoy aguardando a que maduren las manzanas.*

**rise** /raɪz/ (**rises, rising, rose, risen**) **1** V-I If something **rises,** it moves upward. *subir, elevarse* ❑ *Wilson watched the smoke rise from the chimney. Wilson vio el humo que subía de la chimenea.* • **Rise up** means the same as **rise.** *subir, elevarse* ❑ *The*

R

bubbles rose up to the surface of the water. Las burbujas subieron a la superficie del agua. **2** V-I When you **rise,** you stand up. ponerse de pie, levantarse [FORMAL] ❑ Luther rose slowly from the chair. Luther se puso lentamente de pie., Luther se levantó lentamente de la silla. **3** V-I When you **rise,** you get out of bed. levantarse [FORMAL] ❑ Tony rose early. Tony se levantó temprano. **4** V-I When the sun or moon **rises,** it appears in the sky. levantarse, salir **5** V-I If land **rises,** it slopes upward. subir ❑ ...the slope of land that rose from the house. ...la cuesta que subía de la casa. **6** V-T/V-I If an amount **rises,** it increases. aumentar, subir ❑ Interest rates rose from 4% to 5%. Las tasas de interés subieron del 4 al 5 por ciento. ❑ Exports rose 23%. Las exportaciones aumentaron el 23 por ciento. **7** N-COUNT A **rise in** the amount of something is an increase in it. aumento ❑ ...another rise in interest rates. ...otro aumento de las tasas de interés. **8** V-I If a sound **rises** or if your voice **rises,** it becomes louder or higher. aumentar de volumen, subir de tono ❑ Her voice rose angrily. Su voz subió de tono, reflejando su enojo. **9** V-I If someone **rises to** a higher position or status, they become more important, successful, or powerful. ascender ❑ She was an intelligent woman who rose to the top of the organization. Era una mujer inteligente que ascendió a la cima de la organización. **10** N-SING The **rise** of someone is the process by which they become more important, successful, or powerful. ascensión ❑ His rise at the company was very quick. Su ascensión en la compañía fue muy rápida. **11** PHRASE If something **gives rise to** an event or situation, it causes that event or situation to happen. dar origen a, dar lugar a, ocasionar ❑ ...problems in communities which give rise to crime. ...problemas en la comunidad que dan lugar al crimen. **12** to **rise to the challenge** → see **challenge**

→ see also **raise**

▸ **rise above** PHR-VERB If you **rise above** a difficulty or problem, you manage not to let it affect you. sobreponerse, superar ❑ You must rise above personal feeling. Debes sobreponerte a los sentimientos personales.

▸ **rise up** PHR-VERB When the people in a country **rise up,** they rebel against the people in authority and start fighting them. levantarse, rebelarse, alzarse ❑ People have risen up against their leader. La gente se alzó contra su dirigente.

**ris|ing ac|tion** N-UNCOUNT The **rising action** in the plot of a play or story is the events that lead to the climax of the plot. acción creciente [TECHNICAL]

**risk** /rɪsk/ (**risks, risking, risked**) **1** N-VAR If there is a **risk of** something unpleasant, there is a possibility that it will happen. riesgo ❑ There is a small risk of brain damage from the operation. Existe un pequeño riesgo de que la operación cause daños cerebrales. **2** N-COUNT If something that you do is a **risk,** it might have unpleasant or undesirable results. riesgo ❑ You're taking a big risk showing this to Kravis. Corres un gran riesgo mostrándoselo a Kravis. **3** N-COUNT If you say that something or someone is a **risk,** you mean they are likely to cause harm. riesgo ❑ Being very fat is a health risk. Estar obeso es un riesgo para la salud. **4** V-T If you **risk** something unpleasant, you do something knowing that the unpleasant thing might happen as a result. arriesgarse ❑ He risked breaking his leg when he jumped. Se arriesgó a romperse una pierna al saltar. **5** V-T If you **risk** doing something, you do it, even though you know that it might have undesirable consequences. arriesgarse ❑ I risked going back. Me arriesgué a volver. **6** V-T If you **risk** your life or something else important, you behave in a way that might result in it being lost or harmed. arriesgar ❑ She risked her own life to help him. Arriesgó su propia vida para ayudarlo. **7** PHRASE To be **at risk** means to be in a situation where something unpleasant might happen. correr riesgos ❑ Overweight people are more at risk from heart disease. Las personas con exceso de peso corren más riesgos de sufrir una enfermedad cardiaca. **8** PHRASE If you tell someone that they are doing something **at** their **own risk,** you are warning them that, if they are harmed, it will be their own responsibility. por cuenta y riesgo propios ❑ People who wish to come here do so at their own risk. Las personas que deseen venir lo hacen por su cuenta y riesgo. **9** PHRASE If you **run** the **risk of** doing or experiencing something undesirable, you do something knowing that the undesirable thing might happen as a result. correr el riesgo ❑ The officers ran the risk of losing their jobs. Los oficiales corrían el riesgo de perder su empleo.

| Thesaurus | risk | Ver también: |
|---|---|---|
| N. | accident, danger, gamble, hazard; (ant.) safety **1** **2** | |
| V. | chance, endanger, gamble, jeopardize **4** **6** | |

**risky** /rɪski/ (**riskier, riskiest**) ADJ If an activity or action is **risky,** it is dangerous or likely to fail. aventurado, peligroso, riesgoso ❑ ...risky projects. ...proyectos arriesgados.

**rite** /raɪt/ (**rites**) N-COUNT A **rite** is a traditional ceremony that is carried out by a particular group or society. rito ❑ ...a religious rite. ...un rito religioso.

**ritu|al** /rɪtʃuəl/ (**rituals**) **1** N-VAR A **ritual** is a religious service or other ceremony which involves a series of actions performed in a fixed order. ritual ❑ ...the holiest of their rituals. ...el más sagrado de sus rituales. **2** ADJ **Ritual** activities happen as part of a ritual or tradition. ritual ❑ ...ritual dancing. ...danzas rituales. **3** N-VAR A **ritual** is a way of behaving or a series of actions that people regularly carry out in a particular situation. costumbre ❑ It was a ritual that Lisa and Sarah had lunch together once a week. Era costumbre que Lisa y Sarah comieran juntas una vez a la semana.

→ see **myth**

**ri|val** /raɪvᵊl/ (**rivals, rivaling** or **rivalling, rivaled** or **rivalled**) **1** N-COUNT If people or groups are **rivals,** they are competing against each other for the same thing. rival ❑ He is well ahead of his nearest rival. Va muy adelante de su rival más cercano. **2** V-T If you say that one thing **rivals** another, you mean that they are both of the same standard or quality. rivalizar ❑ In my opinion, Chinese cooking rivals that of the French. En mi opinión, la cocina china rivaliza con la francesa.

**ri|val|ry** /raɪvᵊlri/ (**rivalries**) N-VAR **Rivalry** is competition or conflict between people or groups who want the same things. rivalidad ❑ What causes rivalry between brothers? ¿Qué causa la rivalidad entre hermanos?

Picture Dictionary

**riv|er** /rɪvər/ (**rivers**) N-COUNT A **river** is a large amount of fresh water flowing continuously in a long line across the land. *río*
→ see Picture Dictionary: **river**
→ see **landform**

**RNA** /ɑr ɛn eɪ/ N-UNCOUNT **RNA** is an acid in the chromosomes of the cells of living things which plays an important part in passing information about protein structure between different cells. **RNA** is an abbreviation for "ribonucleic acid." *ARN (ácido ribonucleico)* [TECHNICAL]

**roach** /roʊtʃ/ (**roaches**) N-COUNT A **roach** is the same as a **cockroach**. *cucaracha* ❑ *...a damp, roach-infested apartment. ...un departamento húmedo e infestado de cucarachas.*

**road** /roʊd/ (**roads**) N-COUNT A **road** is a long piece of hard ground that is built between two places so that people can drive or ride easily from one place to the other. *camino, carretera, calle* ❑ *There was very little traffic on the roads. Había muy poco tránsito en las carreteras.*
→ see **traffic**

**road|kill** /roʊdkɪl/ also **road kill** N-UNCOUNT **Roadkill** refers to the remains of animals that have been killed on the road by vehicles. *restos de animales muertos en las carreteras*

**road rage** N-UNCOUNT **Road rage** is anger or violent behavior by a driver toward another driver. *violencia vial* ❑ *...a road rage attack on a motorist. ...violencia vial contra un automovilista.*

**road|runner** /roʊdrʌnər/ (**roadrunners**) N-COUNT A **roadrunner** is a bird with a long tail, found mainly in the southwestern United States, that is able to run very quickly. *correcaminos*

**road|side** /roʊdsaɪd/ (**roadsides**) N-COUNT **The roadside** is the area at the edge of a road. *borde del camino, orilla del camino* ❑ *Bob left the car at the roadside and ran for help. Bob dejó el coche en la orilla de la carretera y corrió a buscar ayuda.*

**road test** (**road tests, road testing, road tested**) also **road-test** **1** V-T If you **road test** a car or other vehicle, you drive it on roads in order to make sure that it is working properly. *someter a una prueba de carretera* • **Road test** is also a noun *prueba de carretera* ❑ *...a road test of the car. ...una prueba del automóvil en carretera.* **2** N-COUNT A **road test** is a driving test that you must pass in order to get a driver's license. *prueba de carretera* **3** V-T If someone **road tests** a new product, they use it in order to make sure that it works properly. *probar* ❑ *Catherine Young road tests waterproof jackets. Catherine Young prueba chamarras impermeables.* • **Road test** is also a noun. *prueba* ❑ *The kids gave all three toys thorough road tests. Los niños sometieron los tres juguetes a pruebas rigurosas.*

**road|work** /roʊdwɜrk/ N-UNCOUNT **Roadwork** refers to repairs or other work being done on a road. *obras viales* ❑ *The traffic was not moving due to roadwork. El tránsito no avanzaba debido a unas obras viales.*

**roam** /roʊm/ (**roams, roaming, roamed**) V-T/V-I If you **roam** an area or **roam around** it, you wander around it without having a particular purpose. *vagar* ❑ *Children roamed the streets. Unos niños vagaban por las calles.*

**roar** /rɔr/ (**roars, roaring, roared**) **1** V-I If something, usually a vehicle, **roars** somewhere, it goes there very fast, making a loud noise. *zumbar* [WRITTEN] ❑ *A police car roared past. Una patrulla de la policía pasó zumbando.* **2** V-I If something **roars**, it makes a very loud noise. *zumbar* [WRITTEN] ❑ *The engine roared, and the vehicle moved forward. El motor zumbó y el vehículo avanzó.* • **Roar** is also a noun. *ruido, estrépito* ❑ *...the roar of traffic. ...el ruido del tránsito.* **3** V-I If someone **roars with** laughter, they laugh in a very noisy way. *reír(se) a carcajadas* **4** V-T/V-I If someone **roars**, they shout something in a very loud voice. *rugir, bramar* [WRITTEN] ❑ *"I'll kill you for that," he roared. —Voy a matarte—bramó.* **5** V-I When a lion **roars**, it makes the loud sound that lions typically make. *rugir* • **Roar** is also a noun. *rugido* ❑ *...the roar of lions. ...el rugido de los leones.*

**roast** /roʊst/ (**roasts, roasting, roasted**) **1** V-T When you **roast** meat or other food, you cook it by dry heat in an oven or over a fire. *asar* ❑ *He roasted the chicken. Asó el pollo.* **2** ADJ **Roast** meat has been

**Word Web** rock

igneous sedimentary metamorphic

**Rocks** are made of **minerals**. Sometimes they may contain only one **element**. Usually they contain **compounds** of several elements. Each type of rock also has a unique **crystal** structure. Rock is always changing. When **lava erupts** from a **volcano**, it forms **igneous** rock. Wind, water, and ice **erode** this type of rock. The resulting **sediment** collects in rivers. Layers of sediment build up and form **sedimentary** rock. When tectonic **plates** move around, they create heat and pressure. This melting and crushing changes sedimentary rock into **metamorphic** rock.

cooked by roasting. asado ❏ *...roast beef.* *...carne asada.*
→ see **cook, peanut**

**rob** /rɒb/ (**robs, robbing, robbed**) 1 V-T If someone **is robbed,** they have money or property stolen from them. robar, asaltar ❏ *Mrs. Yacoub was robbed of her watch.* *Le robaron el reloj a la señora Yacoub.* ● **rob|ber** N-COUNT (**robbers**) ladrón o ladrona ❏ *Armed robbers broke into a jeweler's.* *Unos ladrones armados entraron a robar en una joyería.* 2 V-T If someone **is robbed of** something that they deserve, have, or need, it is taken away from them. privar ❏ *A knee injury robbed him of his place on the football team.* *Una lesión en la rodilla lo privó de su lugar en el equipo de fútbol.*

**rob|bery** /rɒbəri/ (**robberies**) N-VAR **Robbery** is the crime of stealing money or property from a place, often by using force. robo, asalto ❏ *The gang committed several armed robberies.* *La pandilla cometió varios robos a mano armada.*

**robe** /roʊb/ (**robes**) 1 N-COUNT A **robe** is a loose piece of clothing, usually worn in official or religious ceremonies. toga [FORMAL] ❏ *...the Pope's white robes.* *...las vestiduras blancas del papa.* 2 N-COUNT A **robe** is a piece of clothing, often made of toweling, which people wear in the house, especially when they have just gotten up or taken a bath or shower. bata ❏ *Kyle put on a robe and went down to the kitchen.* *Kyle se puso una bata y bajó a la cocina.*

**rob|in** /rɒbɪn/ (**robins**) N-COUNT A **robin** is a brown bird with an orangey red neck and breast. European robins are smaller than North American ones, and are a completely different species of bird. petirrojo, tordo norteamericano

**ro|bot** /roʊbət, -bɒt/ (**robots**) N-COUNT A **robot** is a machine that is programmed to move and perform tasks automatically. robot ❏ *...very lightweight robots that we could send to the moon.* *...robots muy ligeros que podríamos enviar a la luna.*

**ro|bust** /roʊbʌst, roʊbʌst/ ADJ Someone or something that is **robust** is very strong or healthy. robusto ❏ *He was young and physically robust.* *Era joven y robusto.*

**rock** /rɒk/ (**rocks, rocking, rocked**) 1 N-UNCOUNT **Rock** is the hard substance which the Earth is made of. roca ❏ *The hills above the valley are bare rock.* *Las colinas sobre el valle son de roca desnuda.* 2 N-COUNT A **rock** is a large piece of rock that sticks up out of the ground or the sea, or that has broken away from a mountain or a cliff. peñasco, peñón ❏ *She sat on the rock.* *Se sentó en el peñasco.* 3 N-COUNT A **rock** is a piece of rock that is small enough for you to pick up. piedra ❏ *She picked up a rock and threw it into the water.* *Recogió una piedra y la arrojó al agua.* 4 V-T/V-I When something **rocks** or when you **rock** it, it moves slowly and regularly backward and forward or from side to side. mecer(se) ❏ *His body rocked from side to side with the train.* *Su cuerpo se mecía con el movimiento del tren.* 5 V-T If an event or a piece of news **rocks** a group or society, it shocks them or makes them feel less secure. sacudir, estremecer ❏ *His death rocked the fashion business.* *Su muerte estremeció al mundo de la moda.* 6 N-UNCOUNT **Rock** is loud music with a strong beat that is usually played and sung by a small group of people using instruments such as electric guitars and drums. rock ❏ *...a rock concert.* *...un concierto de rock.*
→ see Word Web: **rock**
→ see **concert, crystal, earth, fossil, genre**

**rock cy|cle** (**rock cycles**) N-COUNT The **rock cycle** is the continuous process in which a particular type of rock, such as igneous rock, slowly changes into other types of rock, such as sedimentary or metamorphic rock. ciclo de las rocas [TECHNICAL]

**rock|et** /rɒkɪt/ (**rockets, rocketing, rocketed**) 1 N-COUNT A **rocket** is a space vehicle that is shaped like a long tube. cohete espacial ❏ *...the rocket that took astronauts to the moon.* *...el cohete espacial que llevó a los astronautas a la luna.* 2 N-COUNT A **rocket** is a missile containing explosives that is powered by gas. cohete, misil ❏ *There was another rocket attack on the city.* *Hubo otro ataque con misiles sobre la ciudad.* 3 V-I If things such as prices or social problems **rocket,** they increase very quickly and suddenly. dispararse ❏ *Prices for fresh food have rocketed.* *Los precios de los alimentos perecederos se dispararon.*

**rock fall** (**rock falls**) N-COUNT A **rock fall** is the movement of a group of loose rocks down a steep slope such as the side of a mountain. alud de rocas, desprendimiento de rocas

**rod** /rɒd/ (**rods**) 1 N-COUNT A **rod** is a long, thin, metal or wooden bar. barra, varilla ❏ *The roof was strengthened with steel rods.* *Reforzaron el techo con varillas de acero.* 2 N-COUNT **Rods** are cells in the retina of the eye that help you to see in dim light. Compare **cone.** bastoncillo [TECHNICAL]

**ro|dent** /roʊdənt/ (**rodents**) N-COUNT **Rodents** are small mammals which have sharp front teeth. Rats, mice, and squirrels are rodents. roedor
→ see **herbivore**

**rogue state** (**rogue states**) N-COUNT When

r

politicians or journalists talk about a **rogue state,** they mean a country that they regard as a threat to their own country's security, for example, because it supports terrorism. *estado malhechor* ❑ *...possible attacks from rogue states and terrorists. ...posibles ataques de estados malhechores y terroristas.*

**roil** /rɔɪl/ (**roils, roiling, roiled**) V-I If water **roils,** it is rough and disturbed. *arremolinarse, revolverse* ❑ *The water roiled as he climbed at the edge of the waterfall. El agua se revolvía mientras trepaba por el borde de la cascada.*

**role** /roʊl/ (**roles**) **1** N-COUNT The **role** of someone or something in a situation is their position and function in it. *función, papel* ❑ *...the role of parents in raising their children. ...la función de los padres en la cría de los hijos.* **2** N-COUNT A **role** is one of the characters that an actor or singer can play in a movie, play, or opera. *papel* ❑ *She got the lead role in the movie. Le dieron el papel principal en la película.*
→ see **theater**

**Word Partnership** Usar *role* con:

ADJ. **active** role, **key** role, **parental** role, **positive** role, **significant** role, **traditional** role, **vital** role **1**
**bigger/larger** role, **leading** role, **major** role **1** **2**
**starring** role **2**
N. **leadership** role, role **reversal** **1**
**lead** role **1** **2**
V. **play** a role, **take on a** role **1** **2**

**role mod|el** (**role models**) N-COUNT A **role model** is someone you admire and try to imitate. *modelo de conducta* ❑ *Anne is my role model, who I look up to. Anne es mi modelo de conducta, a quien admiro.*

**roll** /roʊl/ (**rolls, rolling, rolled**) **1** V-T/V-I When something **rolls** or when you **roll** it, it moves along a surface, turning over many times. *rodar* ❑ *The ball rolled into the net. La pelota rodó a la red.* **2** V-I When vehicles **roll** along, they move along slowly. *rodar* ❑ *The truck rolled forward. El camión siguió adelante.* **3** V-I If drops of liquid **roll** down a surface, they move quickly down it. *rodar* ❑ *Tears rolled down her cheeks. Las lágrimas le corrían por las mejillas.* **4** V-T If you **roll** something flexible **into** a cylinder or a ball, you form it into a cylinder or a ball by wrapping it several times around itself or by shaping it between your hands. *enrollar, hacer bola de* ❑ *He took off his sweater, rolled it into a pillow, and lay down. Se quitó el suéter, lo enrolló para apoyar la cabeza y se recostó.* ● **Roll up** means the same as **roll.** *enrollar* ❑ *Stein rolled up the paper bag. Stein enrolló la bolsa de papel.* **5** N-COUNT A **roll of** paper, plastic, cloth, or wire is a long piece of it that has been wrapped many times around itself or around a tube. *rollo* ❑ *...twelve rolls of film. ...doce rollos de película.* **6** N-COUNT A **roll** is a small piece of bread that is round or long and is made to be eaten by one person. *bolillo, pancito* ❑ *He spread butter on a roll. Le puso mantequilla a un bolillo.* **7** N-COUNT A **roll** is an official list of people's names. *lista, padrón* ❑ *...a roll of people who can vote. ...el padrón de votantes.* **8** PHRASE If something is several things **rolled into one,** it combines the main features or qualities of those things. *todo en uno* ❑ *This is our kitchen, living room, and dining room all rolled into one. Esta es nuestra cocina, sala y comedor, todo en uno.*
▸**roll in** PHR-VERB If something such as money **is rolling in,** it is appearing or being received in large quantities. *entrar a raudales* [INFORMAL] ❑ *The money was rolling in. Estaba entrando dinero a raudales.*
▸**roll up** **1** PHR-VERB If you **roll up** your sleeves or pant legs, you fold the ends back several times, making them shorter. *enrollar(se)* ❑ *The jacket was too big so he rolled up the cuffs. El saco era demasiado grande, así que le enrolló los puños., Se enrolló las mangas del saco porque era demasiado grande.* **2** → see also **roll 4**
→ see **bread**

**roll|back** /roʊlbæk/ (**rollbacks**) N-COUNT A **rollback** is a reduction in price or some other change that makes something like it was before. *reducción* ❑ *The tax rollback would destroy basic services. La reducción de impuestos arruinaría los servicios básicos.*

**roll|er** /roʊlər/ (**rollers**) N-COUNT A **roller** is a cylinder that turns around in a machine or device. *rodillo*

**roll|ing pin** (**rolling pins**) N-COUNT A **rolling pin** is a cylinder that you roll backward and forward over uncooked pastry in order to make the pastry flat. *rodillo, palote*
→ see **utensil**

**ROM** /rɒm/ **1** N-UNCOUNT **ROM** is the permanent part of a computer's memory. The information stored there can be read but not changed. **ROM** is an abbreviation for "read-only memory." *ROM (memoria de lectura únicamente)* [COMPUTING] **2** → see also **CD-ROM**

**Ro|man** /roʊmən/ (**Romans**) **1** ADJ **Roman** means related to or connected with ancient Rome and its empire. *romano* ❑ *...the Roman Empire. ...el Imperio Romano.* ● A **Roman** was a citizen of ancient Rome or its empire. *romano o romana* ❑ *The Romans brought this custom to Britain. Los romanos trajeron esta costumbre a Gran Bretaña.* **2** ADJ **Roman** means related to or connected with modern Rome. *romano* ❑ *...a Roman hotel room. ...un cuarto de hotel en Roma.* ● A **Roman** is someone who lives in or comes from Rome. *romano o romana* ❑ *...soccer-mad Romans. ...romanos fanáticos del fútbol.*
→ see Picture Dictionary: **Roman numeral**

**Ro|man Catho|lic** (**Roman Catholics**) **1** ADJ The **Roman Catholic** Church is the same as the **Catholic** Church. *católico romano* ❑ *...a Roman Catholic priest. ...un sacerdote católico.* **2** N-COUNT A **Roman Catholic** is the same as a **Catholic.** *católico* ❑ *Maria was a Roman Catholic. María era católica.*

**ro|mance** /roʊmæns, roʊmæns/ (**romances**) **1** N-COUNT A **romance** is a relationship between two people who are in love with each other but who are not married to each other. *romance, idilio* ❑ *After a short romance the couple got married. Después de un breve idilio, la pareja se casó.* **2** N-UNCOUNT **Romance** refers to the actions and feelings of people who are in love, especially behavior that is very caring or affectionate. *romance* ❑ *He still finds time for romance by cooking romantic dinners for his girlfriend. Aún tiene tiempo para el romance: prepara cenas románticas para su novia.* **3** N-UNCOUNT You can refer to the pleasure and excitement of

R

Picture Dictionary

## Roman numerals

| | | | | | | | |
|---|---|---|---|---|---|---|---|
| I | 1 | XI | 11 | XXI | 21 | XL | 40 |
| II | 2 | XII | 12 | XXII | 22 | L | 50 |
| III | 3 | XIII | 13 | XXIII | 23 | LX | 60 |
| IV | 4 | XIV | 14 | XXIV | 24 | LXX | 70 |
| V | 5 | XV | 15 | XXV | 25 | LXXX | 80 |
| VI | 6 | XVI | 16 | XXVI | 26 | XC | 90 |
| VII | 7 | XVII | 17 | XXVII | 27 | C | 100 |
| VIII | 8 | XVIII | 18 | XXVIII | 28 | D | 500 |
| IX | 9 | XIX | 19 | XXIX | 29 | M | 1000 |
| X | 10 | XX | 20 | XXX | 30 | MMIX | 2009 |

doing something new or exciting as **romance.** romanticismo ❑ *...the romance and excitement that used to be part of train trips.* *...el romanticismo y la emoción que solían formar parte de los viajes en tren.* **4** N-COUNT A **romance** is a novel or movie about a love affair. *novela romántica, novela rosa* ❑ *...historical romances.* *...novelas románticas históricas.*
→ see **love**

**ro|man|tic** /roʊmæntɪk/ (**romantics**) **1** ADJ Someone who is **romantic** or does **romantic** things says and does things that make their partner feel special and loved. *romántico* ❑ *...a romantic dinner for two people.* *...una cena romántica para dos personas.* **2** ADJ **Romantic** means connected with sexual love. *romántico* ❑ *He was not interested in a romantic relationship with Ingrid.* *No le interesaba tener una relación romántica con Ingrid.* ● **ro|man|ti|cal|ly** ADV *de manera romántica* ❑ *We are not romantically involved.* *No tenemos una relación romántica.* **3** ADJ A **romantic** play, movie, or story describes or represents a love affair. *romántico* ❑ *...a lovely romantic comedy.* *...una bonita comedia romántica.* **4** ADJ If you say that someone has a **romantic** view or idea of something, you are critical of them because they think that thing is better or more exciting than it really is. *romántico* ❑ *He has a romantic view of society.* *Tiene una visión romántica de la sociedad.* ● A **romantic** is a person who has romantic views. *romántico o romántica* ❑ *You're a romantic.* *Eres una romántica.*
→ see **love**

**ron|do** /rɒndoʊ/ (**rondos**) N-COUNT A **rondo** is a piece of music in which the main theme is repeated several times, with other themes or sections between each repetition. *rondó*

**roof** /ruf/ (**roofs**)

The plural can be pronounced /rufs/ or /ruvz/.

**1** N-COUNT The **roof** of a building is the covering on top of it. *techo, tejado* ❑ *...a cottage with a red roof.* *...una cabaña con tejado rojo.* **2** N-COUNT The **roof** of a car or other vehicle is the top part of it. *techo* ❑ *The car rolled onto its roof, trapping him.* *El coche se volteó y él quedó atrapado.* **3** N-COUNT **The roof of** your mouth is the highest part of the inside of your mouth. *paladar* ❑ *She put her tongue against the roof of her mouth.* *Puso la lengua contra el paladar.* **4** PHRASE If the level or price of something **goes through the roof,** it suddenly increases very rapidly. *irse a las nubes* [INFORMAL] ❑ *Prices have gone through the roof.* *Los precios se fueron a las nubes.* **5** PHRASE If you **hit the roof** or **go through the roof,** you become very angry, and usually show your anger by shouting at someone. *poner el grito en el cielo* [INFORMAL] ❑ *Dad will hit the roof when I tell him what you did.* *Papá va a poner el grito en el cielo cuando le diga lo que hiciste.*

roof

**Word Partnership** Usar *roof* con:

| | |
|---|---|
| N. | roof **of a building/house, metal** roof, **rain on a** roof, **slate** roof, **tin** roof **1** |
| V. | roof **collapses,** roof **leaks, repair a** roof **1** |
| ADJ. | **retractable** roof **1 2** |

**rookie** /rʊki/ (**rookies**) N-COUNT A **rookie** is someone who has just started doing a job and does not have much experience, especially someone who has just joined a professional sports team or the police force. *novato o novata* [INFORMAL] ❑ *I don't want another rookie to train.* *No quiero tener que entrenar a más novatos.*

**room** /rum/ (**rooms**) **1** N-COUNT A **room** is one of the separate parts of the inside of a building. Rooms have their own walls, ceilings, floors, and doors. *cuarto, habitación, sala* ❑ *A minute later he left the room.* *Un minuto después, salió del cuarto.* ❑ *The largest conference room seats 5,000 people.* *En la sala de conferencias más grande caben 5,000 personas.* **2** N-COUNT If you talk about your **room,** you are referring to the room that you alone use, especially your bedroom at home. *cuarto, habitación* ❑ *Go to my room and bring down my sweater, please.* *Suba a mi cuarto y tráigame mi suéter, por favor.* **3** N-UNCOUNT If there is **room** somewhere, there is enough empty space there for people or things to be fitted in. *lugar, espacio* ❑ *There is room for 80 visitors.* *Hay lugar para 80 personas.* **4** N-UNCOUNT If there is **room for** a particular kind of behavior or

r

action, people are able to behave in that way or to take that action. *margen* ❑ *The amount of work left little room for worrying.* *La cantidad de trabajo dejaba poco margen para preocuparse.* 5 → see also **chat room, dining room, emergency room, living room, restroom**
→ see **hotel**

**room and board** N-UNCOUNT If you are provided with **room and board,** you are provided with food and a place to sleep, especially as part of the conditions of a job or a course of study. *pensión completa* ❑ *Students receive free room and board.* *Los estudiantes cuentan con pensión completa gratuita.*

**room|ing house** (**rooming houses**) N-COUNT A **rooming house** is a building that is divided into small apartments or single rooms which people rent to live in. *pensión*

**room|mate** /rumeɪt/ (**roommates**) N-COUNT Your **roommate** is the person you share a room, apartment, or house with, for example when you are in college. *compañero de cuarto* ❑ *Derek and I were roommates for two years.* *Derek y yo fuimos compañeros de cuarto por dos años.*

**roost** /rust/ (**roosts, roosting, roosted**) 1 N-COUNT A **roost** is a place where birds or bats rest or sleep. *percha* 2 V-I When birds or bats **roost** somewhere, they rest or sleep there. *posarse* ❑ *The birds roost in nearby bushes.* *Los pájaros se posan en los matorrales cercanos para pasar la noche.*
→ see **bat**

rooster

**roost|er** /rustər/ (**roosters**) N-COUNT A **rooster** is an adult male chicken. *gallo*

**root** /rut/ (**roots, rooting, rooted**) 1 N-COUNT The **roots** of a plant are the parts of it that grow under the ground. *raíz* ❑ *...the twisted roots of an apple tree.* *...las raíces torcidas de un manzano.* 2 N-COUNT The **root** of a hair or tooth is the part of it that is underneath the skin. *raíz* 3 N-PLURAL You can refer to the place or culture that a person or their family comes from as their **roots.** *raíces* ❑ *I am proud of my Brazilian roots.* *Estoy orgulloso de mis raíces brasileñas.* 4 N-COUNT You can refer to the cause of a problem or of an unpleasant situation as **the root of** it or **the roots of** it. *raíz* ❑ *We got to the root of the problem.* *Llegamos a la raíz del problema.* 5 V-I If you **root through** or **in** something, you search for something by moving other things around. *hurgar* ❑ *She rooted through the bag and found what she wanted.* *Hurgó en la bolsa y encontró lo que buscaba.* 6 → see also **grassroots** 7 PHRASE If an idea, belief, or custom **takes root,** it becomes established among a group of people. *echar raíz* ❑ *Time was needed for democracy to take root.* *Se requería tiempo para que la democracia echara raíces.*
▸ **root out** 1 PHR-VERB If you **root out** a person, you find them and force them from the place they are in, usually in order to punish them. *hacer una limpia de* ❑ *They tried to root out corrupt officials.* *Trataron de hacer una limpia de oficiales corruptos.* 2 PHR-VERB If you **root out** a problem or an unpleasant situation, you find out who or what is the cause of it and put an end to it. *extirpar, erradicar* ❑ *There was a campaign to root out corruption.* *Hubo una campaña para extirpar la corrupción.*
→ see **flower**

| **Word Partnership** | Usar *root* con: |
|---|---|
| N. | **tree** root 1 |
| | root **cause of *something***, root **of a problem** 4 |
| V. | **take** root 7 |

**root ex|trac|tion** (**root extractions**) N-VAR In mathematics, **root extraction** is a method of using a particular number to find another number which, when it is multiplied by itself a certain number of times, produces the original number. *extraer la raíz de un número*

**root hair** (**root hairs**) N-COUNT A plant's **root hairs** are the thin extensions that grow from its roots and take in water and minerals from the soil. *rizoma, rizoide, pelo absorbente o radical*

**root sys|tem** (**root systems**) N-COUNT A plant's **root system** is the part of the plant that contains the roots. Compare **shoot system.** *raíces*

**root word** (**root words**) N-COUNT A **root word** is a word or part of a word to which other letters can be added in order to form new words. *raíz* [TECHNICAL]

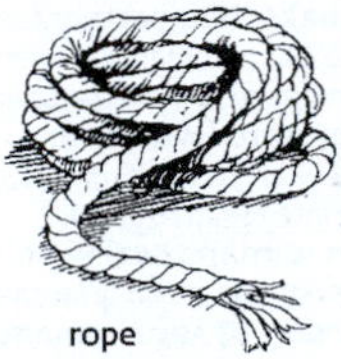
rope

**rope** /roʊp/ (**ropes, roping, roped**) 1 N-VAR A **rope** is a thick cord or wire that is made by twisting together several thinner cords or wires. *cuerda, soga* ❑ *He tied the rope around his waist.* *Ató la cuerda en torno a su cintura.* 2 V-T If you **rope** one thing **to** another, you tie the two things together with a rope. *amarrar, atar* ❑ *They roped their horses to a branch of the tree.* *Amarraron los caballos a una rama del árbol.*
▸ **rope in** PHR-VERB If you say that you **were roped in to** do a particular task, you mean that someone persuaded you to help them do that task. *agarrar* [INFORMAL] ❑ *Visitors were roped in to help pick tomatoes.* *Agarraron a los visitantes para que ayudaran a cosechar jitomates.*

**rose** /roʊz/ (**roses**) 1 **Rose** is the past tense of **rise.** *pasado de* ***rise*** 2 N-COUNT A **rose** is a flower with a pleasant smell, which grows on a bush with thorns. *rosa*

**rose-colored** PHRASE If you look at a person or situation through **rose-colored glasses** or **rose-tinted glasses,** you see only their good points and therefore your view of them is unrealistic. *ver las cosas color de rosa* ❑ *She looks at the world through rose-colored glasses.* *Ve las cosas color de rosa.*

**rosy** /roʊzi/ (**rosier, rosiest**) 1 ADJ If you say that someone has a **rosy** face, you mean that they have pink cheeks and look very healthy. *sonrosado* 2 ADJ If you say that a situation looks **rosy** or that the picture looks **rosy,** you mean that the situation seems likely to be good or successful. *halagüeño*

R

❑ *The job prospects for engineers are less rosy now than they used to be.* *El panorama laboral de los ingenieros es menos halagüeño de lo que solía ser.*

**rot** /rɒt/ (**rots, rotting, rotted**) **1** V-T/V-I When food, wood, or another substance **rots,** or when something **rots** it, it becomes softer and is gradually destroyed. *pudrirse, descomponerse* ❑ *The grain will start to rot after the rain.* *El cereal empezará a pudrirse después de la lluvia.* **2** N-UNCOUNT If there is **rot** in something, especially something that is made of wood, parts of it have decayed and fallen apart. *podredumbre, putrefacción* ❑ *Investigations showed extensive rot in the doors.* *Los estudios indicaban que las puertas estaban muy carcomidas.* **3** N-SING You can use **the rot** to refer to the way something gradually gets worse. *podredumbre, putrefacción* ❑ *The newspaper said "Don't wait until the next election to stop the rot."* *El periódico dice que no hay que aguardar hasta las próximas elecciones para parar la podredumbre.*

**ro|tate** /roʊteɪt/ (**rotates, rotating, rotated**) **1** V-T/V-I When something **rotates** or when you **rotate** it, it turns with a circular movement. *girar, rotar* ❑ *The earth rotates around the sun.* *La Tierra gira alrededor del Sol.* • **ro|ta|tion** /roʊteɪʃᵊn/ N-COUNT (**rotations**) *rotación, giro* ❑ *...the daily rotation of the earth.* *...la rotación diaria de la Tierra.* **2** V-T/V-I If people or things **rotate,** or if someone **rotates** them, they take turns to do something. *rotar(se), turnar(se)* ❑ *The men rotated frequently.* *Los hombres se turnaban frecuentemente.* • **ro|ta|tion** N-COUNT *turno* ❑ *The men will play in rotation.* *Los hombres jugarán por turnos.*
→ see **moon**

**ro|ta|tion** /roʊteɪʃᵊn/ (**rotations**) **1** N-VAR **Rotation** is circular movement. A **rotation** is the movement of something through one complete circle. *rotación, giro* **2** N-VAR In geometry, a **rotation** is a transformation in which the coordinate axes are rotated by a fixed angle about the origin. *rotación*

**ROTC** /ɑr oʊ ti si/ N-PROPER **The ROTC** is a military organization that trains college students to become officers in the armed forces, so that they are ready to join a military operation if they are needed. **ROTC** is an abbreviation for "Reserve Officers Training Corps." *Centro de Entrenamiento de Oficiales de la Reserva* ❑ *...the Army ROTC program at Fresno State University.* *...el programa del Centro de Entrenamiento de Oficiales de la Reserva del ejército en la Universidad Estatal de Fresno.*

**rot|ten** /rɒtᵊn/ **1** ADJ If food, wood, or another substance is **rotten,** it has decayed and can no longer be used. *podrido* ❑ *The smell was very strong—like rotten eggs.* *El olor era muy fuerte, como a huevos podridos.* **2** ADJ If you describe something as **rotten,** you think it is very unpleasant or of very poor quality. *pésimo* [INFORMAL] ❑ *I think it's a rotten idea.* *Me parece una pésima idea.*

**rott|wei|ler** /rɒtwaɪlər/ (**rottweilers**) also **Rottweiler** N-COUNT A **rottweiler** is a large black and brown breed of dog which is often used as a guard dog. *rottweiler (raza de perros)*

**rough** /rʌf/ (**rougher, roughest**) **1** ADJ If a surface is **rough,** it is uneven and not smooth. *áspero* ❑ *His hands were rough.* *Tenía las manos ásperas.* • **rough|ness** N-UNCOUNT *aspereza* ❑ *...the roughness of his jacket.* *...la aspereza de su saco.* **2** ADJ You say that people or their actions are **rough** when they use too much force and not enough care or gentleness. *brusco* ❑ *Football's a rough game.* *El fútbol es un juego brusco.* • **rough|ly** ADV *bruscamente* ❑ *They roughly pushed past him.* *Lo empujaron bruscamente al pasar junto a él.* **3** ADJ A **rough** area, city, school, or other place is unpleasant and dangerous because there is a lot of violence or crime there. *peligroso* ❑ *It was a rough part of town.* *Era una zona peligrosa de la ciudad.* **4** ADJ If you say that someone has had a **rough** time, you mean that they have had some difficult or unpleasant experiences. *difícil* ❑ *Old people have a rough time in our society.* *La vida es difícil para los ancianos en nuestra sociedad.* **5** ADJ A **rough** calculation or guess is approximately correct, but not exact. *aproximado* ❑ *...a rough estimate of how much fuel we need.* *...un cálculo aproximado del combustible que necesitamos.* • **rough|ly** ADV *aproximadamente* ❑ *Cancer was killing roughly half a million people a year.* *El cáncer estaba matando a aproximadamente medio millón de personas al año.*

**round**

❶ PREPOSITION AND ADVERB USES
❷ NOUN USES
❸ ADJECTIVE USES
❹ VERB USES

❶ **round** /raʊnd/

**Round** is used mainly in British English. See **around**.

PHRASE If something happens **all year round,** it happens throughout the year. *todo el año* ❑ *Many of these plants are evergreen, so you can enjoy them all year round.* *Muchas de estas plantas son de hojas perennes, por lo que puede disfrutarlas todo el año.*

❷ **round** /raʊnd/ (**rounds**) **1** N-COUNT A **round of** events is a series of related events, especially one which comes after or before a similar series of events. *ronda* ❑ *They held another round of talks.* *Celebraron otra ronda de pláticas.* **2** N-COUNT In sports, a **round** is a series of games in a competition in which the winners go on to play in the next round. *ronda eliminatoria* ❑ *...in the third round of the competition.* *...en la tercera (ronda) eliminatoria de la competencia.* **3** N-COUNT In a boxing or wrestling match, a **round** is one of the periods during which the boxers or wrestlers fight. *asalto, vuelta, round* **4** N-COUNT A **round of** golf is one game, usually including 18 holes. *vuelta, recorrido* **5** N-COUNT A person's **rounds** are a series of visits he or she makes as part of his or her job. *ronda* ❑ *The doctors did their morning rounds.* *Los médicos hicieron sus rondas matinales.* **6** N-COUNT If you buy a **round of** drinks, you buy a drink for each member of the group of people that you are with. *ronda, vuelta* **7** N-COUNT A **round of** ammunition is the bullet or bullets released when a gun is fired. *disparo (uno), andanada (varios)*

❸ **round** /raʊnd/ (**rounder, roundest**) ADJ Something that is **round** is shaped like a circle or ball. *redondo* ❑ *She had a round face.* *Tenía la cara redonda.*

r

**④ round** /raʊnd/ (**rounds, rounding, rounded**) **1** V-T If you **round** a place or obstacle, you move in a curve past the edge or corner of it. *rodear, dar vuelta, doblar* ❑ *The house disappeared from sight as we rounded a corner. La casa se perdió de vista cuando dimos vuelta en la esquina.* **2** V-T If you **round** an amount **up** or **down**, or if you **round** it **off**, you change it to the nearest whole number or nearest multiple of 10, 100, 1000, and so on. *redondear* ❑ *We needed to round up and round down numbers. Necesitábamos redondear las cifras.*

▸ **round up** **1** PHR-VERB If the police or army **round up** a number of people, they arrest or capture them. *hacer una redada de* ❑ *The police rounded up a number of suspects. La policía hizo una redada de varios sospechosos.* **2** PHR-VERB If you **round up** animals or things, you gather them together. *reunir* ❑ *He wanted a job as a cowboy, rounding up cattle. Quería un trabajo de vaquero, para reunir ganado.* **3** → see also **round④ 2** → see also **roundup**

**round|about** /raʊndəbaʊt/ **1** ADJ If you go somewhere by a **roundabout** route, you do not go there by the shortest and quickest route. *indirecto* ❑ *He left today on a roundabout route for Jordan. Partió hoy a Jordania por una ruta indirecta.* **2** ADJ If you do or say something in a **roundabout** way, you do not do or say it in a simple, clear, and direct way. *con rodeos, con ambages* ❑ *She was telling him in a roundabout way that she was getting married. Estaba diciéndole con rodeos que iba a casarse.*

**round trip** (**round trips**) N-COUNT If you make a **round trip**, you travel to a place and then back again. *viaje redondo, viaje de ida y vuelta* ❑ *The train makes the 2,400-mile round trip every week. El tren hace el viaje de ida y vuelta de 3,862 kilómetros todas las semanas.*

**round|up** /raʊndʌp/ (**roundups**) N-COUNT A **roundup** is an occasion when cattle, horses, or other animals are collected together so that they can be counted or sold. *rodeo*

**roust** /raʊst/ (**rousts, rousting, rousted**) V-T If you **roust** someone, you disturb, upset, or hit them, or make them move from their place. *provocar* ❑ *We're not trying to roust you. We just want some information. No buscamos provocarlo. Sólo buscamos información.*

R

**route** /rut, raʊt/ (**routes, routing, routed**) **1** N-COUNT A **route** is a way from one place to another. *ruta, camino* ❑ *...the most direct route to the center of town. ...la ruta más directa al centro de la ciudad.* **2** N-COUNT In the United States, **Route** is used in front of a number in the names of main roads between major cities. *carretera* ❑ *...the next exit on Route 580. ...la siguiente salida sobre la Carretera 580.* **3** N-COUNT You can refer to a way of achieving something as a **route**. *vía* ❑ *Researchers are trying to get the information through an indirect route. Los investigadores están tratando de obtener la información por una vía indirecta.* **4** V-T If vehicles, goods, or passengers **are routed** in a particular direction, they are made to travel in that direction. *encaminar, enviar, dirigir* **5** PHRASE **En route to** a place means on the way to that place. *en camino a, de camino a* ❑ *They arrived in London en route to the United States. Llegaron a Londres de camino a Estados Unidos.*

**Word Partnership** Usar *route* con:

N. **escape** route, **parade** route **1**
ADJ. **main** route, **scenic** route **1**
**alternative** route, **different** route, **direct** route, **shortest** route **1 3**

**rou|tine** /rutin/ (**routines**) **1** N-VAR A **routine** is the usual series of things that you do at a particular time in a particular order. *rutina* ❑ *The players changed their daily routine. Los jugadores cambiaron su rutina diaria.* **2** ADJ You use **routine** to describe activities that are done as a normal part of a job or process. *rutinario* ❑ *...a series of routine medical tests. ...una serie de exámenes médicos rutinarios.* • **rou|tine|ly** ADV *rutinariamente* ❑ *Doctors routinely wash their hands before examining a patient. Los médicos se lavan las manos rutinariamente antes de examinar a un paciente.*

**Word Partnership** Usar *routine* con:

ADJ. **daily** routine, **normal** routine, **regular** routine, **usual** routine **1**
N. **exercise** routine, **morning** routine, **work** routine **1**
routine **maintenance**, routine **tests** **2**

**row**
① ARRANGEMENT OR SEQUENCE
② MAKING A BOAT MOVE

**① row** /roʊ/ (**rows**) **1** N-COUNT A **row of** things or people is a number of them arranged in a line. *hilera, fila* ❑ *...a row of pretty little cottages. ...una hilera de lindas cabañas.* **2** → see also **death row** **3** PHRASE If something happens several times **in a row,** it happens that number of times without a break. If something happens several days **in a row,** it happens on each of those days. *seguidos* ❑ *They won five championships in a row. Ganaron cinco campeonatos seguidos.*

**② row** /roʊ/ (**rows, rowing, rowed**) V-T/V-I When you **row,** you sit in a boat and make it move through the water by using oars. *remar, bogar* ❑ *He rowed as quickly as he could to the shore. Remó tan rápidamente como pudo hasta la orilla.* ❑ *The boatman refused to row him back. El barquero se rehusó a llevarlo de vuelta.* • **row|ing** N-UNCOUNT *remo* ❑ *...competitions in rowing, swimming, and water skiing. ...competencias de remo, natación y esquí acuático.*

**row|boat** /roʊboʊt/ (**rowboats**) N-COUNT A **rowboat** is a small boat that you move through the water by using oars. *bote de remos*
→ see **boat**

**row house** (**row houses**) also **rowhouse** N-COUNT A **row house** is one of a row of similar houses that are joined together by both of their side walls. *casa adosada*

**roy|al** /rɔɪəl/ ADJ **Royal** means connected with a king, queen, or emperor, or their family. *real* ❑ *...an invitation to a royal garden party. ...una invitación a una recepción real al aire libre.*

**roy|al|ty** /rɔɪəlti/ (**royalties**) **1** N-UNCOUNT The members of royal families are sometimes referred to as **royalty.** *realeza* ❑ *...royalty and government leaders from around the world.* *...la realeza y los jefes de gobierno de todo el mundo.* **2** N-PLURAL **Royalties** are payments made to authors and musicians when their work is sold or performed. *regalías*

**Rte.** **Rte.** is used in front of a number in the names of main roads between major cities. **Rte.** is a written abbreviation for **route.** *carretera* ❑ *Winterthur is on Rte. 52 in Delaware.* *Winterthur está en la carretera 52, en Delaware.*

**rub** /rʌb/ (**rubs, rubbing, rubbed**) **1** V-T/V-I If you **rub** a part of your body or if you **rub at** it, you move your hand or fingers backward and forward over it while pressing firmly. *frotar(se)* ❑ *He rubbed his arms and stiff legs.* *Se frotó los brazos y las piernas entumecidas.* **2** V-T/V-I If you **rub against** a surface or **rub** a part of your body **against** a surface, you move it backward and forward while pressing it against the surface. *frotar(se) contra* ❑ *A cat was rubbing against my leg.* *Un gato estaba frotándose contra mi pierna.* **3** V-T/V-I If you **rub** something or you **rub at** it, you move a cloth backward and forward over it in order to clean or dry it. *frotar, restregar* ❑ *She took off her glasses and rubbed them hard.* *Se quitó los lentes y los frotó con fuerza.* **4** V-T If you **rub** a substance **into** a surface or **rub** something such as dirt **from** a surface, you spread it over the surface or remove it from the surface using your hand or a cloth. *frotar* ❑ *He rubbed oil into my back.* *Me frotó la espalda con aceite.* **5** V-T/V-I If you **rub** two things **together** or if they **rub together**, they move backward and forward, pressing against each other. *frotar(se)* ❑ *He rubbed his hands together.* *Se frotó las manos.* **6** PHRASE If you **rub shoulders with** famous people, you meet them and talk to them. You can also say that you **rub elbows with** someone. *codearse* ❑ *He regularly rubbed shoulders with famous people.* *Solía codearse con gente famosa.*

**Word Partnership** Usar *rub* con:

| | |
|---|---|
| PREP. | rub **against** 2 |
| | rub **off**, rub **with** 4 |
| ADV. | rub **together** 5 |

**rub|ber** /rʌbər/ (**rubbers**) N-UNCOUNT **Rubber** is a strong, waterproof, elastic substance used for making tires, boots, and other products. *goma, hule, caucho* ❑ *...the smell of burning rubber.* *...el olor a hule quemado.*

**rub|ber band** (**rubber bands**) N-COUNT A **rubber band** is a thin circle of very elastic rubber. You put it around things such as papers in order to keep them together. *banda elástica, liga*
→ see **office**

**rub|ber boot** (**rubber boots**) N-COUNT **Rubber boots** are long boots made of rubber that you wear to keep your feet dry. *bota de hule, bota de goma*

**rub|bing al|co|hol** N-UNCOUNT **Rubbing alcohol** is a liquid which is used to clean wounds or surgical instruments. *alcohol para usos médicos*

**rub|down** /rʌbdaʊn/ (**rubdowns**) N-COUNT If you give someone a **rubdown,** you dry them or massage them with something such as a towel or cloth. *fricción, friega, masaje* ❑ *He found a towel and gave his body a rubdown.* *Encontró una toalla y se masajeó el cuerpo.*

**ru|bric** /rubrɪk/ (**rubrics**) **1** N-COUNT A **rubric** is a title or heading under which something operates or is studied. *rúbrica* [FORMAL] **2** N-COUNT A **rubric** is a set of rules or instructions, for example the rules at the beginning of an examination paper. *reglas impresas en un examen* [FORMAL]

**ruck|us** /rʌkəs/ N-SING If someone or something causes a **ruckus,** they cause a great deal of noise, argument, or confusion. *jaleo* [INFORMAL] ❑ *This caused such a ruckus that they had to change their mind.* *Causó tanto jaleo que tuvieron que cambiar de opinión.*

**rude** /rud/ (**ruder, rudest**) **1** ADJ When people are **rude,** they behave in an impolite way. *grosero, maleducado* ❑ *He's rude to her friends.* *Es grosero con sus amigas.* ● **rude|ly** ADV *groseramente* ❑ *...hotel guests who treat staff rudely.* *...huéspedes de los hoteles que tratan groseramente al personal.* ● **rude|ness** N-UNCOUNT *grosería, mala educación* ❑ *Mother is annoyed at Caleb's rudeness.* *Mamá está enojada por lo grosero que es Caleb.* **2** ADJ **Rude** words and behavior are likely to embarrass or offend people because they relate to sex or to body functions. *grosero* ❑ *Fred keeps telling rude jokes.* *Fred sigue contando chistes groseros.* **3** ADJ If someone receives a **rude** shock, something unpleasant happens unexpectedly. *desagradable* ❑ *My first day at work was a rude shock.* *Mi primer día de trabajo me dejó una impresión desagradable.* ● **rude|ly** ADV *bruscamente* ❑ *People were rudely awakened by a siren.* *Una sirena despertó bruscamente a la gente.*

**Thesaurus** *rude* Ver también:

ADJ. vulgar; (*ant.*) polite 1

**ruf|fled** /rʌfəld/ ADJ Something that is **ruffled** is no longer smooth or neat. *encrespado, erizado* ❑ *Her short hair was ruffled.* *Su pelo corto estaba erizado.*

**rug** /rʌg/ (**rugs**) N-COUNT A **rug** is a piece of thick material that you put on a floor. It is like a carpet but covers a smaller area. *alfombra, tapete* ❑ *...a Persian rug.* *...una alfombra persa.*

**rug|by** /rʌgbi/ N-UNCOUNT **Rugby** or **rugby football** is a game played by two teams, who try to get an oval ball past a line at their opponents' end of the field. *rugby*

**ruin** /ruɪn/ (**ruins, ruining, ruined**) **1** V-T To **ruin** something means to severely harm, damage, or spoil it. *arruinar* ❑ *My wife was ruining her health through worry.* *Las preocupaciones estaban arruinando la salud de mi esposa.* **2** V-T To **ruin** someone means to cause them to no longer have any money. *arruinar* ❑ *He ruined her financially with his love of expensive things.* *La arruinó con su gusto por las cosas caras.* **3** N-UNCOUNT **Ruin** is the state of no longer having any money. *ruina* ❑ *...a country on the edge of ruin.* *...un país al borde de la ruina.* **4** N-PLURAL **The ruins of** something are the parts of it that remain after it has been severely damaged or weakened. *ruinas* ❑ *He bought the ruins of other people's failed businesses.* *Compraba las ruinas de negocios fracasados de otra gente.* **5** N-PLURAL **The ruins** of a building are the parts of it that remain after the rest has fallen down or been destroyed. *ruinas* ❑ *Police found* two bodies in the ruins of the house. *La policía encontró dos cadáveres en las ruinas de la casa.* **6** PHRASE If something is **in ruins,** it is completely spoiled. *en ruinas* ❑ *The economy is in ruins. La economía está en ruinas.* **7** PHRASE If a building or place is **in ruins,** most of it has been destroyed and only parts of it remain. *en ruinas* ❑ *The church was in ruins. La iglesia estaba en ruinas.*

**rule** /rul/ (**rules, ruling, ruled**) **1** N-COUNT **Rules** are instructions that tell you what you are allowed to do and what you are not allowed to do. *regla* ❑ *...a book explaining the rules of basketball. ...un libro que explica las reglas del básquetbol.* **2** N-COUNT The **rules of** something such as a language or a science are statements that describe the way that things usually happen in a particular situation. *regla* ❑ *...the rules of the language. ...las reglas del lenguaje.* **3** N-SING If something is **the rule,** it is normal or usual. *norma* ❑ *For many Americans, weekend work has become the rule. Para muchos estadounidenses, trabajar el fin de semana se ha vuelto la norma.* **4** V-T/V-I The person or group that **rules** a country controls its affairs. *gobernar* ❑ *For four centuries, foreigners have ruled Angola. Los extranjeros han gobernado Angola durante cuatro siglos.* ❑ *He ruled for eight months. Gobernó durante ocho meses.* **5** → see also **ruling** **6** PHRASE If you say that something happens **as a rule,** you mean that it usually happens. *por regla general, por lo general* ❑ *As a rule, I walk to work rather than drive. Por lo general, voy al trabajo caminando, en lugar de ir en coche.* **7** PHRASE If someone in authority **bends the rules** or **stretches the rules,** they do something even though it is against the rules. *hacer la vista gorda* ❑ *Surely you can bend the rules in this case? ¿Seguro que puede hacer la vista gorda en este caso?*

▸ **rule out** **1** PHR-VERB If you **rule out** a course of action, an idea, or a solution, you decide that it is impossible or unsuitable. *descartar* **2** PHR-VERB If something **rules out** a situation, it prevents it from happening or from being possible. *impedir, imposibilitar* ❑ *A serious car accident ruled out a career in soccer. Un grave accidente automovilístico le impidió hacer una carrera en el fútbol.*

R

**Thesaurus** *rule* Ver también:

| | |
|---|---|
| N. | guideline, law, standard **1** **2** |
| V. | command, dictate, govern **4** |

**Word Partnership** Usar *rule* con:

| | |
|---|---|
| V. | **break a** rule, **change a** rule, **follow a** rule **1** |
| N. | **gag** rule **1** |
| | **exception to a** rule **1** – **3** |
| PREP. | **against a** rule, **under a** rule **1** **2** |

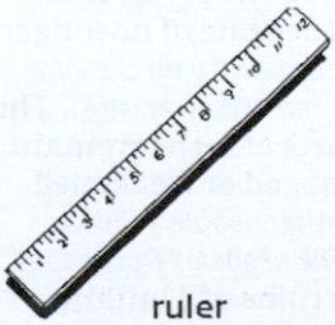
ruler

**rul|er** /rulər/ (**rulers**) **1** N-COUNT The **ruler** of a country is the person who rules the country. *gobernante, rey o reina, soberano o soberana* ❑ *...the ruler of Lesotho. ...el rey de Lesotho.* **2** N-COUNT A **ruler** is a long, flat object with straight edges, for measuring things and drawing straight lines. *regla*
→ see **measurement**

**rul|ing** /rulɪŋ/ (**rulings**) **1** ADJ The **ruling** group of people in a country or organization is the group that controls its affairs. *en el poder* ❑ *...a ruling party politician. ...un político del partido en el poder.* **2** N-COUNT A **ruling** is an official decision made by a judge or court. *fallo, resolución* ❑ *He was angry at the court's ruling. Estaba enojado por el fallo del tribunal.*

**rum|mage sale** (**rummage sales**) N-COUNT A **rummage sale** is a sale of cheap used goods that is usually held to raise money for charity. *venta de artículos donados con fines caritativos*

**ru|mor** /rumər/ (**rumors**) N-VAR A **rumor** is a story or piece of information that may or may not be true, but that people are talking about. *rumor* ❑ *U.S. officials denied the rumor. Unos funcionarios estadounidenses negaron el rumor.*

**Word Partnership** Usar *rumor* con:

| | |
|---|---|
| ADJ. | **false** rumor |
| V. | **hear a** rumor, **spread a** rumor, **start a** rumor |

**ru|mor mill** (**rumor mills**) N-COUNT You can refer to the people in a particular place or profession who spread rumors as the **rumor mill.** *personas de un lugar o profesión que hacen correr rumores, fábrica de rumores* ❑ *The Hollywood rumor mill is already talking about a marriage between the two stars. En la fábrica de rumores de Hollywood ya se está hablando del matrimonio entre los dos astros.*

**rumor|monger** /rumərmʌŋgər, -mɒŋgər/ (**rumormongers**) N-COUNT If you call someone a **rumormonger,** you disapprove of the fact that they spread rumors. *chismoso o chismosa*

**run**
1 VERB USES
2 NOUN USES
3 PHRASES
4 PHRASAL VERBS

**1 run** /rʌn/ (**runs, running, ran**)

The form **run** is used in the present tense and is also the past participle of the verb.

**1** V-T/V-I When you **run,** you move quickly, leaving the ground during each stride. *correr* ❑ *I ran back to the telephone. Volví corriendo al teléfono.* ❑ *He ran the last block. Corrió la última calle.* • **run|ning** N-UNCOUNT *correr* ❑ *We did some running. Corrimos un poco.* **2** V-I If you say that something long, such as a road, **runs** in a particular direction, you are describing its course or position. *correr* ❑ *...the path which ran through the forest. ...el sendero que corría a través del bosque.* **3** V-T If you **run** your hand or an object **through** something, you move your hand or the object through it. *pasar* ❑ *He ran his fingers through his hair. Pasó los dedos entre su pelo.* **4** V-I If someone **runs for** office in an election, they take part as a candidate. *presentarse, contender* ❑ *He announced he was running for president. Anunció que se presentaría para presidente.* ❑ *I intend to run* *against him in the next election.* *Tengo la intención de contender con él en las próximas elecciones.* 5 V-T If you **run** something such as a business or an activity, you are in charge of it or you organize it. *dirigir* ❑ *His father ran a paint business.* *Su padre dirigía un negocio de pintura.* ❑ *...a well-run, successful organization.* *...una organización exitosa, bien dirigida.* • **run|ning** N-UNCOUNT *dirección* ❑ *...the day-to-day running of the business.* *...la dirección cotidiana del negocio.* 6 V-I If you talk about how a system, an organization, or your life **is running,** you are saying how well it is operating or progressing. *funcionar* ❑ *The system is now running smoothly.* *El sistema ya está funcionando sin contratiempos.* 7 V-T/V-I If you **run** an experiment, computer program, or other process, or start it **running,** you start it and let it continue. *hacer* ❑ *The doctor ran some tests and found that I had an infection.* *El médico hizo unos análisis y descubrió que tenía una infección.* 8 V-T/V-I When a machine **is running** or when you **are running** it, it is switched on and is working. *funcionar, andar* ❑ *We told him to wait outside the house with the engine running.* *Le dijimos que esperara afuera de la casa con el motor encendido.* 9 V-I A machine or equipment that **runs on** or **off** a particular source of energy functions by using that source of energy. *funcionar con, consumir, usar* ❑ *The buses run on diesel.* *Los autobuses funcionan con diesel.* 10 V-I When vehicles such as trains and buses **run** from one place to another, they regularly travel along that route. *ir, operar* ❑ *A bus runs frequently between the station and downtown.* *Hay un servicio frecuente de autobuses entre la estación y el centro.* 11 V-T If you **run** someone somewhere in a car, you drive them there. *llevar* [INFORMAL] ❑ *Could you run me up to Baltimore?* *¿Podrías llevarme a Baltimore?* 12 V-I If you **run** over or down to a place that is quite near, you drive there. *ir* [INFORMAL] ❑ *I'll run over to the village and check on Mrs. Adams.* *Voy a ir al pueblo a ver cómo está la señora Adams.* 13 V-I If a liquid **runs** in a particular direction, it flows in that direction. *correr* ❑ *Tears were running down her cheeks.* *Las lágrimas le corrían por las mejillas.* 14 V-T If you **run** water, or if you **run** a faucet or a bath, you cause water to flow from a faucet. *abrir la llave, abrirle al agua, dejar/hacer correr el agua* ❑ *She went to the sink and ran water into her empty glass.* *Fue al lavabo y abrió la llave para llenar su vaso.* • **run|ning** ADJ *corriente* ❑ *...the sound of running water.* *...el sonido del agua corriente.* 15 V-I If the dye in some cloth or the ink on some paper **runs,** it comes off or spreads when the cloth or paper gets wet. *correrse* 16 V-I If a play, event, or legal contract **runs** for a particular period of time, it lasts for that period of time. *durar, tener validez* ❑ *The play ran for only three months.* *La obra duró en cartelera sólo tres meses.* ❑ *The contract runs from 1992 to 2020.* *El contrato tiene validez de 1992 a 2020.* 17 V-I If someone or something **is running** late, they have taken more time than was planned. If they **are running** on time or ahead of time, they have taken the time planned or less than the time planned. *atrasarse, ir con tiempo* ❑ *I'll call you back later, I'm running late.* *Te llamo después; ya se me hizo tarde.* 18 → see also **running**

| **Thesaurus** | *run* | Ver también: |
|---|---|---|
| v. | dash, jog, sprint ❶ 1 | |
| | follow, go ❶ 2 | |
| | administer, conduct, manage ❶ 5 | |

❷ **run** /rʌn/ (**runs**) 1 N-COUNT A **run** is a time when you move quickly, leaving the ground with each stride, usually for exercise. *carrera* ❑ *After a six-mile run, Jackie went home for breakfast.* *Después de correr 10 kilómetros, Jackie se fue a casa a desayunar.* 2 N-COUNT A **run** of a play or television program is the period of time during which performances are given or programs are shown. *temporada* ❑ *The show had a month's run in Philadelphia.* *El espectáculo tuvo una temporada de un mes en Filadelfia.*

❸ **run** /rʌn/ (**runs, running, ran**)

> The form **run** is used in the present tense and is also the past participle of the verb.

1 PHRASE If you talk about what will happen **in the long run,** you are saying what you think will happen over a long period of time in the future. If you talk about what will happen **in the short run,** you are saying what you think will happen in the near future. *a la larga/en el corto plazo* ❑ *Spending more on education will save money in the long run.* *Gastar más en educación ahorraría dinero a la larga.* 2 PHRASE If someone is **on the run,** they are trying to escape or hide from someone such as the police or an enemy. *fugado*

❹ **run** /rʌn/ (**runs, running, ran**)

> The form **run** is used in the present tense and is also the past participle of the verb.

▸ **run across** PHR-VERB If you **run across** someone or something, you meet them or find them unexpectedly. *toparse con, tropezarse con, encontrarse con* ❑ *We ran across some old friends.* *Nos topamos con unos viejos amigos.*

▸ **run away** 1 PHR-VERB If you **run away** from a place, you leave it because you are unhappy there. *huir, escapar(se)* ❑ *I ran away from home when I was sixteen.* *Huí de casa cuando tenía dieciséis años.* ❑ *After the attack, Stewart ran away.* *Después del ataque, Stewart huyó.* 2 → see also **runaway**

▸ **run away with** PHR-VERB If you let your imagination or your emotions **run away with** you, you fail to control them and cannot think sensibly. *dejarse llevar por, dejar correr* ❑ *You're letting your imagination run away with you.* *Estás dejándote llevar por tu imaginación.*

▸ **run down** 1 PHR-VERB If you **run** people or things **down,** you criticize them strongly. *hablar mal de, sobajar(se)* ❑ *I'm always running myself down.* *Siempre estoy sobajándome a mí mismo.* 2 PHR-VERB If a vehicle or its driver **runs** someone **down,** the vehicle hits them and injures them. *atropellar* ❑ *The motorcycle driver tried to run him down.* *El motociclista trató de atropellarlo.*

▸ **run into** 1 PHR-VERB If you **run into** problems or difficulties, you unexpectedly begin to experience them. *tropezar con* ❑ *...companies that have run into trouble.* *...compañías que han tropezado con problemas.* 2 PHR-VERB If you **run into** someone, you meet them unexpectedly. *tropezarse con, toparse con, encontrarse con* ❑ *He ran into Krettner in the hall.* *Se topó con Krettner en el vestíbulo.*

**3** PHR-VERB If a vehicle **runs into** something, it accidentally hits it. *chocar contra* ❑ *The driver was going too fast and ran into a tree. El conductor iba demasiado rápido y chocó contra un árbol.* **4** PHR-VERB You use **run into** when indicating that the cost or amount of something is very great. *llegar a, alcanzar* ❑ *...costs running into millions of dollars. ...los costos alcanzan millones de dólares.*

▶ **run off** **1** PHR-VERB If you **run off** with someone, you secretly go away with them in order to live with them or marry them. *huir, fugarse* ❑ *His secretary just ran off with the mailman. Su secretaria se acaba de fugar con el cartero.* **2** PHR-VERB If you **run off** copies of a piece of writing, you produce them using a machine. *sacar*

▶ **run out** **1** PHR-VERB If you **run out of** something, you have no more of it left. *agotarse, acabarse* ❑ *They have run out of ideas. Se les agotaron las ideas.* **2** to **run out of steam** → see **steam** **3** PHR-VERB If something **runs out,** it becomes used up so that there is no more left. *agotarse, acabarse* ❑ *Supplies are running out. Las provisiones se están agotando.* **4** PHR-VERB When a legal document **runs out,** it stops being valid. *vencer, caducar* ❑ *When the lease ran out the family moved to Cleveland. Cuando el contrato de arrendamiento venció, la familia se mudó a Cleveland.*

▶ **run over** PHR-VERB If a vehicle or its driver **runs** a person or animal **over,** it knocks them down or drives over them. *atropellar* ❑ *He nearly ran me over. Estuvo a punto de atropellarme.*

▶ **run through** **1** PHR-VERB If you **run through** a list of items, you read or mention all the items quickly. *leer, repasar* ❑ *I ran through the choices with him. Repasé las opciones con él.* **2** PHR-VERB If you **run through** a performance or a series of actions, you practice it. *ensayar* ❑ *The dance instructor ran through a few moves. El maestro de danza ensayó algunos pasos.*

▶ **run up** PHR-VERB If someone **runs up** bills or debts, they acquire them by buying a lot of things or borrowing money. *acumular* ❑ *She managed to run up a debt of $60,000. Se las arregló para acumular una deuda de 60,000 dólares.*

▶ **run up against** PHR-VERB If you **run up against** problems, you suddenly begin to experience them. *tropezarse con, toparse con, encontrarse con* ❑ *I ran up against several problems. Me topé con varios problemas.*

R

**run|away** /rʌnəweɪ/ (**runaways**) **1** ADJ You use **runaway** to describe a situation in which something increases or develops very quickly and cannot be controlled. *arrollador* ❑ *Our sale was a runaway success. Nuestra venta fue un éxito arrollador.* **2** N-COUNT A **runaway** is someone, especially a child, who leaves home without telling anyone or without permission. *niño o muchacho que se fuga temporal o definitivamente de su casa* ❑ *...a teenage runaway. ...un adolescente que se fugó de su casa.* **3** ADJ A **runaway** vehicle or animal is moving forward quickly, and its driver or rider has lost control of it. *fugitivo, que se fuga* ❑ *The runaway car hit a tree. El coche en fuga chocó contra un árbol.*

**run-in** (**run-ins**) N-COUNT A **run-in** is an argument or quarrel with someone. *roce* [INFORMAL] ❑ *I had a run-in with him. Tuve un roce con él.*

**run|ner** /rʌnər/ (**runners**) **1** N-COUNT A **runner** is a person who runs, especially for sport or pleasure. *corredor o corredora* ❑ *...a marathon runner. ...un corredor de maratón.* **2** N-COUNT **Runners** are thin strips of wood or metal underneath something which help it to move smoothly. *guía, riel, patín* ❑ *...the runners of his sled. ...los patines de su trineo.* **3** N-COUNT On a plant, **runners** are long shoots that grow from the main stem and put down roots to form a new plant. *estolón*
→ see **park**

**runner-up** (**runners-up**) N-COUNT A **runner-up** is someone who has finished in second place in a race or competition. *subcampeón* ❑ *The runner-up will receive $500. El subcampeón recibirá 500 dólares.*

**run|ning** /rʌnɪŋ/ **1** ADJ You use **running** to describe things that continue or keep occurring over a period of time. *interminable* ❑ *He began a running argument with Dean. Se metió en una discusión interminable con Dean.* **2** ADJ A **running** total is a total which changes because numbers keep being added to it as something progresses. *actualizado* ❑ *He kept a running total of who called him. Llevaba la cuenta de los que lo llamaban.* **3** ADV You can use **running** when indicating that something keeps happening. *consecutivo, seguido* ❑ *A lack of rain caused crop failure for the second year running. La falta de lluvia provocó que la cosecha se echara a perder por segundo año consecutivo.* **4** PHRASE If someone is **in the running for** something, they have a good chance of winning or obtaining it. If they are **out of the running for** something, they have no chance of winning or obtaining it. *en/fuera de la carrera* ❑ *Four people are in the running for managing director. Hay cuatro personas en la carrera para director ejecutivo.*
**5** → see also **run**

**run|ning mate** (**running mates**) N-COUNT In an election campaign, a candidate's **running mate** is the person that they have chosen to help them in the election. If the candidate wins, the running mate will become the second most important person after the winner. *compañero de candidatura o compañera de candidatura* ❑ *...Clinton's selection of Al Gore as his running mate. ...Clinton escogió a Al Gore como su compañero de fórmula.*

**run|ny** /rʌni/ (**runnier, runniest**) **1** ADJ Something that is **runny** is more liquid than usual or than was intended. *líquido, que haya perdido consistencia* ❑ *Warm the honey until it is runny. Caliente la miel hasta que pierda consistencia.* **2** ADJ If someone has a **runny** nose or **runny** eyes, liquid is flowing from their nose or eyes. *que gotea, lloroso*

**run|off** /rʌnɔf/ N-UNCOUNT **Runoff** is rainwater that forms a stream rather than being absorbed by the ground. *escurrimiento, aflujo*

**run-through** (**run-throughs**) N-COUNT A **run-through** for a show or event is a practice for it. *ensayo*

**run|way** /rʌnweɪ/ (**runways**) N-COUNT At an airport, the **runway** is the long strip of ground with a hard surface which an airplane takes off from or lands on. *pista de aterrizaje*

**rup|ture** /rʌptʃər/ (**ruptures, rupturing, ruptured**) **1** N-COUNT A **rupture** is a severe injury in which an internal part of your body tears or bursts open. *ruptura, rotura, hernia* ❑ *He died after* a rupture in a blood vessel in his head. Murió debido a la ruptura de un vaso sanguíneo en el cerebro. 2 V-T/V-I If a person or animal **ruptures** a part of their body or if it **ruptures,** it tears or bursts open. herniar(se), romper(se) ❑ His stomach might rupture. Su estómago podría sufrir una ruptura. ❑ I ruptured a tendon in my knee. Se me rompió un tendón de la rodilla. 3 N-COUNT If there is a **rupture** between people, relations between them get much worse or end completely. ruptura ❑ ...a rupture in the political relations between countries. ...una ruptura de las relaciones políticas entre los países. 4 V-T If someone or something **ruptures** relations between people, they damage them, causing them to become worse or to end. romper, reventar ❑ Fights between protesters and police ruptured the city's government. Los enfrentamientos entre los manifestantes y la policía reventaron al gobierno de la ciudad.

**ru|ral** /rʊərəl/ 1 ADJ **Rural** places are in the country, away from cities or large towns. rural ❑ ...rural areas. ...áreas rurales. 2 ADJ **Rural** means having features which are typical of country areas away from cities or large towns. campestre, rural, del campo ❑ ...the old rural way of life. ...el viejo estilo de vida del campo.

**rush** /rʌʃ/ (**rushes, rushing, rushed**) 1 V-I If you **rush** somewhere, you go there quickly. correr ❑ Emma rushed into the room. Emma corrió al cuarto. ❑ I've got to rush. I have a meeting in a few minutes. Tengo que correr. Tengo una reunión dentro de un rato. ❑ I rushed for the 7:00 a.m. train. Corrí para alcanzar el tren de las 7 de la mañana. 2 V-T If people **rush to** do something, they do it as soon as they can, because they are very eager to do it. apresurarse ❑ Russian banks rushed to buy as many dollars as they could. Los bancos rusos se apresuraron a comprar tantos dólares como pudieron. 3 N-SING A **rush** is a situation in which you need to go somewhere or do something very quickly. prisa ❑ The men left in a rush. Los hombres se fueron de prisa. 4 N-SING If there is a **rush for** something, many people suddenly try to get it or do it. torrente ❑ Record stores are expecting a huge rush for the CD. Las tiendas de discos esperan un gran torrente por el disco compacto. 5 V-T/V-I If you **rush** something, or if you **rush** at it, you do it in a hurry, often too quickly. apresurar, acelerar, precipitar ❑ You can't rush a search. No se puede apresurar una investigación. • **rushed** ADJ precipitado ❑ ...a rushed job. ...un trabajo precipitado. 6 V-T If you **rush** someone or something to a place, you take them there quickly. llevar rápidamente ❑ They rushed him to a hospital. Lo llevaron a toda prisa al hospital. 7 V-T/V-I If you **rush into** something or **are rushed into** it, you do it without thinking about it for long enough. precipitarse ❑ He will not rush into any decisions. No se precipitará para tomar una decisión. ❑ They rushed in without knowing enough about the task. Se precipitaron sin saber bien lo que tenían que hacer. • **rushed** ADJ apresurado ❑ I didn't feel rushed or under pressure. No me sentí apresurado ni presionado. 8 N-COUNT If you experience a **rush of** a feeling, you suddenly experience it very strongly. torrente, torbellino ❑ A rush of love swept over him. Un torbellino de amor se apoderó de él.

| Word Partnership | Usar *rush* con: |
|---|---|
| N. | **evening** rush, **morning** rush 3<br>rush **of adrenaline** 8 |
| ADJ. | **mad** rush 3 4<br>**sudden** rush 3 4 8 |

**rush hour** (**rush hours**) N-COUNT The **rush hour** is one of the periods of the day when most people are traveling to or from work. hora pico, hora del tránsito pesado ❑ During the evening rush hour there was a lot of traffic. Había muchísimos automóviles durante la hora del tránsito pesado en la tarde.

**Rus|sian dress|ing** N-UNCOUNT **Russian dressing** is a salad dressing made from mayonnaise mixed with a spicy sauce and chopped pickles. salsa rusa

**rust** /rʌst/ (**rusts, rusting, rusted**) 1 N-UNCOUNT **Rust** is a reddish-brown substance that forms on iron or steel when it comes into contact with water. óxido, herrumbre, orín ❑ The old car was red with rust. El viejo coche estaba lleno de herrumbre. 2 V-I When a metal object **rusts,** it becomes covered in rust. oxidarse, herrumbrarse ❑ Iron rusts. El hierro se oxida.

**rus|tler** /rʌslər/ (**rustlers**) N-COUNT **Rustlers** are people who steal farm animals, especially cattle, horses, and sheep. abigeo, cuatrero o cuatrera ❑ ...cattle rustlers. ...abigeos.

**ru|ta|ba|ga** /ru̲təbeɪgə/ (**rutabagas**) N-VAR A **rutabaga** is a round yellow root vegetable with a pale yellow or purple skin. nabo de Suecia, rutabaga

**ruth|less** /ru̲θlɪs/ ADJ If you say that someone is **ruthless,** you mean that you disapprove of them because they are very harsh or cruel, and will do anything that is necessary to achieve what they want. despiadado, cruel ❑ Was she a ruthless murderer or an innocent woman? ¿Era una asesina despiadada o una mujer inocente? • **ruth|less|ly** ADV despiadadamente ❑ The party has ruthlessly crushed any opposition. El partido aplastó despiadadamente toda oposición. • **ruth|less|ness** N-UNCOUNT crueldad ❑ ...a mixture of ambition and ruthlessness. ...una mezcla de ambición y crueldad.

**RV** /ɑr vi̲/ (**RVs**) N-COUNT An **RV** is a van which is equipped with such things as beds and cooking equipment, so that people can live in it, usually while they are on vacation. **RV** is an abbreviation for "recreational vehicle." caravana, cámper, vehículo de recreo

**Rx** /ɑr ɛks/ (**Rxs**) 1 N-COUNT An **Rx** is a doctor's prescription. receta, prescripción ❑ ...an Rx for a painkiller. ...una receta de analgésicos. 2 N-COUNT An **Rx** is a solution to a problem. receta ❑ ...an Rx for America's health-care problems. ...una receta para los problemas de la asistencia médica en Estados Unidos.

**rye** /raɪ/ 1 N-UNCOUNT **Rye** is a cereal grown in cold countries. Its grains can be used to make flour, bread, or other foods. centeno 2 N-UNCOUNT **Rye** is bread made from rye. pan de centeno ❑ ...Swiss cheese on rye. ...queso suizo en pan de centeno.

→ see **bread**

r

# Ss

**sa|ber** /seɪbər/ (**sabers**) N-COUNT A **saber** is a heavy sword with a curved blade that was used in the past by soldiers on horseback. sable

**saber-rattling** N-UNCOUNT If you describe a threat, especially a threat of military action, as **saber-rattling,** you do not believe that the threat will actually be carried out. bravuconería, fanfarronada ❑ *We can't say if these threats are just saber-rattling.* *No podemos saber si estas amenazas son sólo fanfarronadas.*

**sack** /sæk/ (**sacks**) N-COUNT A **sack** is a large bag made of thick paper or rough material. costal ❑ *...a sack of potatoes.* *...un costal de papas.*

**sa|cred** /seɪkrɪd/ **1** ADJ Something that is **sacred** is believed to be holy and to have a special connection with God. sagrado ❑ *The eagle is sacred to Native Americans.* *El águila es sagrada para los indígenas americanos.* • **sac|red|ness** N-UNCOUNT lo sagrado, lo sacro ❑ *...the sacredness of the place.* *...lo sagrado del lugar.* **2** ADJ You can describe something as **sacred** when it is regarded as too important to be changed or interfered with. sagrado ❑ *My memories are sacred to me.* *Mis recuerdos son sagrados para mí.* • **sac|red|ness** N-UNCOUNT lo sagrado, lo sacro ❑ *...the sacredness of life.* *...lo sagrado de la vida.*

**sac|ri|fice** /sækrɪfaɪs/ (**sacrifices, sacrificing, sacrificed**) **1** V-T To **sacrifice** an animal or person means to kill them in a special religious ceremony as an offering to a god. sacrificar ❑ *The priest sacrificed a chicken.* *El sacerdote sacrificó un pollo.* • **Sacrifice** is also a noun. sacrificio ❑ *...animal sacrifices to the gods.* *...sacrificios de animales para los dioses.* • **sac|ri|fi|cial** /sækrɪfɪʃəl/ ADJ expiatorio ❑ *...a sacrificial lamb.* *...un cordero expiatorio.* **2** V-T If you **sacrifice** something that is valuable or important, you give it up, usually to obtain something else for yourself or for other people. sacrificar ❑ *She sacrificed family life to her career.* *Sacrificó la vida familiar por su carrera.* ❑ *Kitty Aldridge sacrificed everything for her movie.* *Kitty Aldridge sacrificó todo por su película.* • **Sacrifice** is also a noun. sacrificio ❑ *She made many sacrifices for Anita's education.* *Hizo muchos sacrificios por la educacón de Anita.*

**sad** /sæd/ (**sadder, saddest**) **1** ADJ If you are **sad,** you feel unhappy, usually because something has happened that you do not like. triste ❑ *The end of the relationship made me feel sad and empty.* *El fin de la relación me hizo sentir triste y vacío.* ❑ *I'm sad that Julie's going away.* *Estoy triste de que Julia se vaya.* • **sad|ly** ADV con tristeza ❑ *This man will be sadly missed by all his friends.* *A este hombre, todos sus amigos lo extrañarán con tristeza.* • **sad|ness** N-UNCOUNT tristeza ❑ *I left with a mixture of sadness and joy.* *Me fui con una mezcla de tristeza y alegría.* **2** ADJ **Sad** stories and **sad** news make you feel sad. triste ❑ *It's a terribly sad novel.* *Es una novela tristísima.* **3** ADJ A **sad** event or situation is unfortunate or undesirable. triste ❑ *The sad truth is that I never opened that present.* *La triste realidad es que nunca abrí ese regalo.* • **sad|ly** ADV tristemente ❑ *Sadly, these plants die after they flower.* *Tristemente, estas plantas se mueren después de florear.*
→ see **cry, emotion**

**Thesaurus** *sad* Ver también:

ADJ. depressed, down, gloomy, unhappy; *(ant.)* cheerful, happy **1**
miserable, tragic, unhappy **3**

**Word Partnership** Usar *sad* con:

V. **feel** sad, **look** sad, **seem** sad **1**
N. sad **eyes** **1**
sad **news**, sad **story** **2**
sad **day**, sad **fact**, sad **truth** **3**
ADV. **kind of** sad, **a little** sad, **really** sad, **so** sad, **too** sad, **very** sad **1** – **3**

**sad|dle** /sædəl/ (**saddles, saddling, saddled**) **1** N-COUNT A **saddle** is a leather seat that you put on the back of an animal so that you can ride the animal. silla de montar, montura **2** V-T If you **saddle** a horse, you put a saddle on it so that you can ride it. ensillar ❑ *Let's saddle some horses and go for a ride!* *¡Ensillemos los caballos y vamos a pasear!* • **Saddle up** means the same as **saddle.** ensillar ❑ *I want to leave as soon as we can saddle up.* *Quiero irme en cuanto ensillemos los caballos.* **3** N-COUNT A **saddle** is a seat on a bicycle or motorcycle. asiento
→ see **horse**

**sa|fa|ri** /səfɑri/ (**safaris**) N-COUNT A **safari** is a trip to observe or hunt wild animals, especially in East Africa. safari ❑ *Most visitors arrive at the park the night before their safari.* *La mayoría de los visitantes llegan al parque la noche anterior a su safari.*

**safe** /seɪf/ (**safer, safest, safes**) **1** ADJ Something that is **safe** does not cause physical harm or danger. seguro ❑ *Is it safe yet to bring emergency food supplies into the city?* *¿Ya es seguro traer alimentos de emergencia a la ciudad?* • **safe|ly** ADV con seguridad ❑ *The smashed car was safely moved to one side of the road.* *El coche chocado fue llevado al otro lado del camino con seguridad.* ❑ *"Drive safely," he said, waving goodbye.* *—Maneje con seguridad —dijo, diciendo adiós con la mano.* **2** ADJ If a person or thing is **safe from** something, they cannot be harmed or damaged by it. a salvo de ❑ *They are safe from the fighting here.* *Aquí están a salvo de la batalla.* **3** ADJ If you are **safe,** you have not been harmed, or you are not in danger of being harmed. a salvo ❑ *Where is Sophy? Is she safe?* *¿Dónde está Sophy? ¿Está a salvo?*

• **safe|ly** ADV *sin peligro* ❑ *All 140 guests were brought out of the building safely. Los 140 huéspedes fueron evacuados del edificio sin peligro.* **4** ADJ A **safe** place is one where it is unlikely that any harm, damage, or unpleasant things will happen to the people or things that are there. *seguro* ❑ *This plan will make the workplace safer for everyone. Este plan hará más seguro el lugar de trabajo para todos.* • **safe|ly** ADV *seguro* ❑ *The manager keeps the money safely under his bed. El gerente mantiene el dinero seguro bajo su cama.* **5** ADJ If people or things have a **safe** trip, they reach their destination without harm, damage, or unpleasant things happening to them. *seguro* ❑ *I hope you have a safe trip home. Que tengas un viaje seguro a casa.* • **safe|ly** ADV *a salvo* ❑ *The space shuttle returned safely today. El transbordador espacial regresó a salvo hoy.* **6** ADJ If **it is safe to** say or assume something, you can say it with very little risk of being wrong. *con seguridad* ❑ *It's probably safe to say that it will be difficult for everyone. Podemos decir con seguridad que será difícil para todos.* • **safe|ly** ADV *con seguridad* ❑ *I think you can safely say she will not appear in another of my movies. Sin temor a equivocarnos, podríamos decir que ella no saldrá en otra de mis películas.* **7** N-COUNT A **safe** is a strong metal cabinet with special locks, in which you keep money, jewelry, or other valuable things. *caja fuerte* ❑ *He's the only one with a key to the safe. El es el único que tiene la llave de la caja fuerte.* **8** PHRASE If you say that a person or thing is **in safe hands,** you mean that they are being taken care of by a reliable person and will not be harmed. *en buenas manos* ❑ *I made sure the package remained in safe hands. Me aseguré de que el paquete estuviera en buenas manos.* **9** PHRASE If you say you are doing something **to be on the safe side,** you mean that you are doing it in case something undesirable happens, even though this may be unnecessary. *para mayor seguridad* ❑ *Do you still want to go for an X-ray, just to be on the safe side? ¿De todas formas quieres tomarte la radiografía, para mayor seguridad?*

**Word Partnership** Usar *safe* con:

N. safe **drinking water**, safe **operation** **1**
**children/kids are** safe, safe **at home** **3**
safe **environment**, safe **neighborhood**, safe **place**, safe **streets** **4**
ADV. **completely** safe, **perfectly** safe, **reasonably** safe, **relatively** safe **1**

**safe|guard** /seɪfgɑrd/ (**safeguards, safeguarding, safeguarded**) **1** V-T To **safeguard** something or someone means to protect them from being harmed, lost, or badly treated. *salvaguardar* [FORMAL] ❑ *We must act now to safeguard the planet. Debemos actuar ahora para salvaguardar el planeta.* **2** N-COUNT A **safeguard** is a law, rule, or measure intended to prevent someone or something from being harmed. *salvaguarda* ❑ *There are no safeguards to protect people from harm. No hay salvaguarda que proteja a la gente del daño.*

**safe ha|ven** N-UNCOUNT If a country provides **safe haven** for people from another country who have been in danger, it allows them to stay there under its official protection. *refugio* ❑ *Should these people have temporary safe haven in the U.S.? ¿Esta gente debería tener refugio temporal en los EE.UU.?*

**safe sex** N-UNCOUNT **Safe sex** is sexual activity in which people protect themselves against the risk of AIDS and other diseases, usually by using condoms. *sexo seguro*

**safe|ty** /seɪfti/ **1** N-UNCOUNT **Safety** is the state of being safe from harm or danger. *seguridad* ❑ *The report recommends improving safety on aircraft. El reporte recomienda mejorar la seguridad en las aeronaves.* **2** N-SING If you are concerned about the **safety** of something, you are concerned that it might be harmful or dangerous. *seguridad* ❑ *We're worried about the safety of the food we buy. Estamos preocupados por la seguridad de la comida que compramos.* **3** N-SING If you are concerned for someone's **safety,** you are concerned that they might be in danger. *seguridad* ❑ *There is serious concern for their safety. Hay seria preocupación por su seguridad.* **4** ADJ **Safety** features or measures are intended to make something less dangerous. *seguridad* ❑ *A smoke alarm is an important safety feature of any home. La alarma de humo es una medida de seguridad importante en cualquier hogar.*
→ see **glass**

**Word Partnership** Usar *safety* con:

V. **improve** safety, **provide** safety **1**
**ensure** safety **1**
**fear for** ***someone's*** safety **3**
N. **child** safety, **fire** safety, **health and** safety, **highway/traffic** safety, safety **measures**, **public** safety, safety **regulations**, safety **standards**, **workplace** safety **1**
safety **concerns**, **food** safety **2**
safety **device**, safety **equipment** **4**

**sag** /sæg/ (**sags, sagging, sagged**) V-I When something **sags,** it hangs down loosely or sinks downward in the middle. *caer, colgar* ❑ *The dress won't sag or lose its shape after washing. El vestido no se colgará ni perderá su forma al lavarse.*

**said** /sɛd/ **Said** is the past tense and past participle of **say**. *pasado y participio pasado de* ***say***

**sail** /seɪl/ (**sails, sailing, sailed**) **1** N-COUNT **Sails** are large pieces of material attached to the mast of a ship. *vela* ❑ *I watched the sails disappear in the distance. Vi las velas desaparecer en la distancia.* **2** V-I You say a ship **sails** when it moves over the sea. *navegar, zarpar* ❑ *The ferry sailed from the port of Zeebrugge. El ferry zarpó del puerto de Zeebrugge.* **3** V-T/V-I If you **sail** a boat or if a boat **sails,** it moves across water using its sails. *navegar a vela, velear* ❑ *The crew's job is to sail the boat. La obligación de la tripulación es hacer navegar el barco a vela.* ❑ *I'd buy a big boat and sail around the world. Compraría un barco grande y navegaría alrededor del mundo.* **4** → see also **sailing** **5** PHRASE When a ship **sets sail,** it leaves a port. *zarpar, hacerse a la mar* ❑ *Some ship captains won't set sail on Friday the 13th. A algunos capitanes de barco no les gusta hacerse a la mar en viernes 13.*

sail

▸ **sail through** PHR-VERB If someone or

S

something **sails through** a difficult situation or experience, they deal with it easily and successfully. *muy fácilmente* ❑ *She sailed through her exams, but he didn't.* *Ella pasó sus exámenes muy fácilmente, pero él no.*

**sail|boat** /seɪlboʊt/ (**sailboats**) N-COUNT A **sailboat** is a boat with sails. *velero*

**sail|ing** /seɪlɪŋ/ (**sailings**) **1** N-UNCOUNT **Sailing** is the activity or sport of sailing boats. *veleo* ❑ *There was swimming and sailing on the lake.* *En el lago había nado y veleo.* **2** N-COUNT **Sailings** are trips made by a ship carrying passengers. *salida* ❑ *Ferry companies are providing extra sailings.* *Las compañías de transbordadores están ofreciendo salidas extras.*
→ see **boat**

**sail|or** /seɪlər/ (**sailors**) N-COUNT A **sailor** is someone who works on a ship or sails a boat. *marinero*

**saint** /seɪnt/ (**saints**) **1** N-COUNT; N-TITLE A **saint** is someone who has died and been officially recognized and honored by the Christian church because his or her life was a perfect example of the way Christians should live. *santo* ❑ *Every church here was named after a saint.* *A cada iglesia de aquí se le daba el nombre de un santo.* **2** N-COUNT If you refer to a living person as a **saint,** you mean that they are extremely kind, patient, and unselfish. *santo* ❑ *My girlfriend is a saint to stay with me.* *Mi novia es una santa por quedarse conmigo.* • **saint|ly** ADJ *piadoso* ❑ *The main story is about a saintly priest.* *La historia principal se trata de un sacerdote piadoso.*

**sake** /seɪk/ (**sakes**) **1** PHRASE If you do something **for the sake of** something, you do it for that purpose or in order to achieve that result. You can also say that you do it **for** something's **sake.** *pongamos que, por el bien de* ❑ *Let's say for argument's sake that we manage to build the database.* *Pongamos por caso que logramos construir la base de datos.* ❑ *For the sake of peace, I am willing to forgive them.* *Por tener paz, estoy dispuesta a perdonarlos.* **2** PHRASE If you do something **for** its **own sake,** you do it because you want to, or because you enjoy it, and not for any other reason. *por sí mismo* ❑ *Change for its own sake cannot be good.* *El cambio por sí mismo no puede ser bueno.* **3** PHRASE When you do something **for** someone's **sake,** you do it in order to help them or make them happy. *por el bien de alguien* ❑ *Please do a good job, for Stan's sake.* *Por favor haz un buen trabajo, por el bien de Stan.*

**S**

**sal|ad** /sæləd/ (**salads**) N-VAR A **salad** is a mixture of cold foods such as lettuce, tomatoes, or cold cooked potatoes, cut up and mixed with a dressing. It is often served with other food as part of a meal. *ensalada* ❑ *...a salad of tomato, onion, and cucumber.* *...una ensalada de jitomate, cebolla y pepino.*
→ see **dessert, dish**

**sala|man|der** /sæləmændər/ (**salamanders**) N-COUNT A **salamander** is an animal that looks rather like a lizard, and that can live both on land and in water. *salamandra*

**sala|ry** /sæləri/ (**salaries**) N-VAR A **salary** is the money that someone earns each month or year from their employer. *salario, sueldo* [BUSINESS] ❑ *The lawyer was paid a huge salary.* *Al abogado se le pagaba un sueldo estratosférico.*

**sale** /seɪl/ (**sales**) **1** N-SING The **sale** of goods is the act of selling them for money. *venta* ❑ *Their advice was to stop the sale of milk from these cows.* *Su consejo era detener la venta de la leche de estas vacas.* ❑ *He is learning the best way to make a sale.* *Está aprendiendo la mejor forma de hacer una venta.* **2** N-PLURAL The **sales** of a product are the quantity of it that is sold. *ventas* ❑ *The newspaper has sales of 1.72 million.* *El periódico tiene 1.72 millones de ventas.* ❑ *...huge Christmas sales of computer games.* *...descomunales ventas de juegos de computadoras por la Navidad.* **3** N-PLURAL The part of a company that deals with **sales** deals with selling the company's products. *ventas* ❑ *Until 1983 he worked in sales and marketing.* *Trabajó en ventas y mercadotecnia hasta 1983.* **4** N-COUNT A **sale** is an occasion when a store sells things at less than their normal price. *barata, temporada de rebajas* ❑ *I got my jeans half-price in a sale.* *Conseguí mis jeans a mitad de precio en una barata.* **5** PHRASE If something is **for sale,** it is being offered to people to buy. *en venta* ❑ *The yacht is for sale for 1.7 million dollars.* *El yate está en venta por 1.7 millones de dólares.* **6** PHRASE Products that are **on sale** can be bought. *a la venta* ❑ *Tickets go on sale this week.* *Los boletos estarán a la venta esta semana.* **7** PHRASE Products that are **on sale** are for sale at a reduced price. *en rebaja* ❑ *At many stores, everything is on sale.* *Todo está en rebaja en muchas tiendas.* **8** PHRASE If a property or company is **up for sale,** its owner is trying to sell it. *en venta* ❑ *The house has been put up for sale.* *La casa ha sido puesta en venta.*

**sales clerk** (**sales clerks**) also **salesclerk** N-COUNT A **sales clerk** is a person who works in a store selling things to customers. *vendedor*

**sales|man** /seɪlzmən/ (**salesmen**) N-COUNT A **salesman** is a man whose job is to sell things, especially directly to stores or other businesses on behalf of a company. *vendedor* ❑ *He's an insurance salesman.* *Es vendedor de seguros.*

**sales slip** (**sales slips**) N-COUNT A **sales slip** is a piece of paper that you are given when you buy something in a store, which shows when you bought it and how much you paid. *recibo*

**sa|lin|ity** /səlɪnɪti/ N-UNCOUNT The **salinity** of water is the amount of salt it contains. *salinidad*

**sa|li|va** /səlaɪvə/ N-UNCOUNT **Saliva** is the watery liquid that forms in your mouth. *saliva*

**salm|on** /sæmən/ (**salmon**) N-COUNT A **salmon** is a large silver-colored fish. *salmón* • **Salmon** is the flesh of this fish eaten as food. *salmón* ❑ *He gave them a plate of salmon.* *Les dio un plato de salmón.*

**sa|lon** /səlɑn/ (**salons**) N-COUNT A **salon** is a place where people have their hair cut or colored, or have beauty treatments. *salón de belleza, estética* ❑ *...a new hair salon.* *...un nuevo salón de belleza.*

**salt** /sɔlt/ (**salts, salting, salted**) **1** N-UNCOUNT **Salt** is a strong-tasting substance, in the form of white powder or crystals, which is used to improve the flavor of food or to preserve it. *sal* ❑ *Now add salt and pepper.* *Ahora añada sal y pimienta.* **2** V-T When you **salt** food, you add salt to it. *salar* ❑ *Salt the soup and cook it very gently.* *Póngale sal a la sopa y déjela a fuego bajo.* • **salt|ed** ADJ *salado* ❑ *Boil a pan of salted water.* *Ponga a hervir agua con sal en un recipiente.* **3** N-COUNT **Salts** are substances that are formed when an acid reacts with an alkali. *sales* ❑ *The rock*

*is rich in mineral salts. La roca es rica en sales minerales.*
→ see **crystal**

**sal|ta|tion** /sælteɪʃᵊn/ N-UNCOUNT **Saltation** is the movement of sand and other particles as a result of being blown by the wind. *saltación* [TECHNICAL]

**salt|ine** /sɔltin/ (**saltines**) N-COUNT A **saltine** is a thin square cracker with salt baked into its surface. *galleta salada*

**salt shak|er** (**salt shakers**) N-COUNT A **salt shaker** is a small container for salt with a hole or holes in the top. *salero*
→ see **dish**

**salt|water** /sɔltwɔtər/ also **salt water**
**1** N-UNCOUNT **Saltwater** is water, especially from the ocean, which has salt in it. *agua salada*
**2** ADJ **Saltwater** fish live in water which is salty. **Saltwater** lakes contain salty water. *de agua salada* ❑ *...useful information for owners of saltwater fish. ...información útil para dueños de peces de agua salada.*
→ see **ocean**

**salty** /sɔlti/ (**saltier, saltiest**) ADJ Something that is **salty** contains salt or tastes of salt. *salado* ❑ *Ham and bacon are salty foods. El jamón y el tocino son alimentos salados.*
→ see **taste**

**sa|lute** /səlut/ (**salutes, saluting, saluted**)
**1** V-T/V-I If you **salute** someone, you greet them or show your respect with a formal sign. Soldiers usually salute officers by raising their right hand so that their fingers touch their forehead. *saludar* ❑ *I saluted as the captain entered the room. Saludé al capitán cuando entró al cuarto.* ❑ *I stood to attention and saluted. Me puse en firmes y saludé.* ● **Salute** is also a noun. *saludo* ❑ *He gave his salute and left. Hizo un saludo y se fue.* **2** V-T To **salute** a person or their achievements means to publicly show or state your admiration for them. *rendir homenaje a* ❑ *I salute the governor for his strong leadership. Rindo homenaje al gobernador por su gran liderazgo.*

**sal|vage** /sælvɪdʒ/ (**salvages, salvaging, salvaged**) **1** V-T If something **is salvaged**, someone manages to save it, for example, from a ship that has sunk, or from a building that has been damaged. *rescatar* ❑ *The team had to decide what equipment could be salvaged. El grupo tuvo que decidir qué parte del equipo podía rescatarse.*
**2** N-UNCOUNT **Salvage** is the act of salvaging things from somewhere such as a damaged ship or building. *rescate* ❑ *The salvage operation went on. La operación de rescate continuó.* **3** N-UNCOUNT The **salvage** from somewhere such as a damaged ship or building is the things that are saved from it. *objetos salvados* ❑ *They climbed up the hill with their salvage. Subieron la colina con los objetos salvados.*
**4** V-T If you manage to **salvage** a difficult situation, you manage to get something useful from it so that it is not a complete failure. *salvar* ❑ *We tried hard to salvage the situation. Intentamos seriamente salvar la situación.*

**sal|va|tion** /sælveɪʃᵊn/ **1** N-UNCOUNT In Christianity, **salvation** is the fact that Christ has saved a person from evil. *salvación* ❑ *The church's message of salvation has changed many lives. El mensaje de salvación de la iglesia ha cambiado muchas vidas.* **2** N-UNCOUNT The **salvation** of someone or something is the act of saving them from harm, destruction, or an unpleasant situation. *salvación* ❑ *She felt that writing was her salvation. Sentía que escribir era su salvación.*

**same** /seɪm/ **1** ADJ If two or more things, actions, or qualities are **the same,** or if one is **the same as** another, they are very like each other in some way. *igual* ❑ *The houses are all the same. Las casas son todas iguales.* ❑ *All these people have the same experience in the job. Toda esta gente tiene la misma experiencia en el trabajo.* **2** ADJ You use **same** to indicate that you are referring to only one place, time, or thing, and not to different ones. *mismo* ❑ *Bernard works at the same institute as Arlette. Bernard trabaja en el mismo instituto que Arlette.* ❑ *Can we get everybody together at the same time? ¿Podemos reunir a todos al mismo tiempo?* **3** ADJ Something that is still **the same** has not changed in any way. *igual* ❑ *If prices rise and your income stays the same, you have to buy less. Si los precios suben pero los ingresos siguen igual, compraremos menos.* **4** PRON You use **the same** to refer to something that has previously been mentioned or suggested. *lo mismo* ❑ *I breathed deeply and watched Terry do the same. Respiré hondo y observé a Terry hacer lo mismo.* ❑ *We made the decision which was right for us. Other parents must do the same. Tomamos la decisión más adecuada para nosotros. Otros padres deberían hacer lo mismo.* ● **Same** is also an adjective. *mismo* ❑ *He's so brave. I admire Ginny for the same reason. Es tan valiente. Admiro a Ginny por la misma razón.* **5** PHRASE You can say **all the same** or **just the same** to introduce a statement which indicates that a situation or your opinion has not changed, in spite of what has happened or what has just been said. *de todas formas* ❑ *It was a private arrangement. All the same, it was illegal. Aunque fue un arreglo privado, de todas formas fue ilegal.* **6** **at the same time** → see **time**

| **Thesaurus** | *same* | Ver también: |
|---|---|---|
| ADJ. | alike, equal, identical; (*ant.*) different **1** | |

**sam|ple** /sæmpᵊl/ (**samples, sampling, sampled**) **1** N-COUNT A **sample** of a substance or product is a small quantity of it that shows you what it is like. *muestra* ❑ *You'll receive samples of paint on cards. Recibirá muestras de pintura en tarjetas.* ❑ *We're giving away 2,000 free samples. Repartiremos 2,000 muestras gratis.* **2** N-COUNT A **sample** of a substance is a small amount of it that is examined and analyzed scientifically. *muestra* ❑ *They took samples of my blood. Tomó muestras de mi sangre.*
**3** N-COUNT A **sample** of people or things is a number of them chosen out of a larger group and then used in tests or used to provide information about the whole group. *muestra* ❑ *We tested a sample of more than 200 males. Sometimos a la prueba una muestra de más de 200 machos.* **4** V-T If you **sample** food or drink, you taste a small amount of it in order to find out if you like it. *degustar* ❑ *We sampled several different bottled waters. Degustamos varias aguas embotelladas diferentes.* **5** V-T If you **sample** a place or situation, you experience it for a short time in order to find out about it. *probar* ❑ *It was a chance to sample a different way of life. Fue una oportunidad de probar una forma de vida diferente.*
→ see **laboratory**

**Thesaurus** *sample* Ver también:

N. bit, piece, portion 1 2
V. experience, taste, try 4 5

**sanc|tion** /sæŋkʃᵊn/ (**sanctions, sanctioning, sanctioned**) 1 V-T If someone in authority **sanctions** an action or practice, they officially approve of it and allow it to be done. *aprobar, consentir* ❑ *He may now sanction the use of force. Puede ser que ahora apruebe el uso de la fuerza.* ● **Sanction** is also a noun. *aprobación, consentimiento* ❑ *The newspaper is run by citizens without the sanction of the government. El periódico es dirigido por ciudadanos sin el consentimiento del gobierno.* 2 N-PLURAL **Sanctions** are measures taken by countries to restrict trade and official contact with a country that has broken international law. *sanciones* ❑ *Unfortunately, they have no power to impose sanctions on countries that break the rules. Desafortunadamente, no tienen el poder para imponer sanciones a los países que rompen las reglas.*

**Word Partnership** Usar *sanction* con:

PREP. **without** sanction 1
sanction **against** 2
ADJ. **legal** sanction, **official** sanction, **proposed** sanction 1 2
V. **impose a** sanction, **lift a** sanction 2

**sanc|tu|ary** /sæŋktʃuɛri/ (**sanctuaries**) 1 N-VAR A **sanctuary** is a place where people who are in danger from other people can go to be safe. *santuario, refugio* ❑ *His church became a sanctuary for homeless people. Su iglesia se convirtió en un refugio para la gente sin hogar.* 2 N-COUNT A **sanctuary** is a place where birds or animals are protected and allowed to live freely. *santuario* ❑ *...a bird sanctuary. ...un santuario de aves.*

**sand** /sænd/ (**sands, sanding, sanded**) 1 N-UNCOUNT **Sand** is a substance that looks like powder, and consists of extremely small pieces of stone. Some deserts and most beaches are made up of sand. *arena* ❑ *They walked across the sand to the water's edge. Caminaron por la arena a la orilla del agua.* 2 N-PLURAL **Sands** are a large area of sand, for example, a beach. *arenas* ❑ *There are miles of golden sands. Son kilómetros de arenas doradas.* 3 V-T If you **sand** a wood or metal surface, you rub sandpaper over it in order to make it smooth or clean. *lijar* ❑ *Sand the surface carefully. Lije cuidadosamente la superficie.*
→ see **beach, desert, erosion, glass**

**san|dal** /sændᵊl/ (**sandals**) N-COUNT **Sandals** are light shoes that you wear in warm weather, which have straps instead of a solid part over the top of your foot. *sandalias* ❑ *...a pair of old sandals. ...un par de viejas sandalias.*
→ see **shoe**

**sand|box** /sændbɒks/ (**sandboxes**) N-COUNT A **sandbox** is a shallow hole or box in the ground with sand in it where children can play. *arenero*

**sand dune** (**sand dunes**) N-COUNT A **sand dune** is a hill of sand near the sea or in a sand desert. *duna, colina de arena, médano*
→ see **beach, desert**

**sand trap** (**sand traps**) N-COUNT On a golf course, a **sand trap** is a hollow area filled with sand, which is put there as an obstacle that players must try to avoid. *trampa de arena*
→ see **golf**

**sand|wich** /sænwɪtʃ, sænd-/ (**sandwiches, sandwiching, sandwiched**) 1 N-COUNT A **sandwich** usually consists of two slices of bread with a layer of food such as cheese or meat between them. *sándwich, emparedado* ❑ *...a ham sandwich. ...un sándwich de jamón.* 2 V-T If you **sandwich** two things **together** with something else, you put that other thing between them. If one thing **is sandwiched** between two other things, it is in a narrow space between them. *intercalar, insertar* ❑ *Cut the cake open, then sandwich the two halves together with cream. Corte el pastel en dos, y ponga crema entre ambas partes.*
→ see **meal**

**sandy** /sændi/ (**sandier, sandiest**) ADJ A **sandy** area is covered with sand. *arenoso* ❑ *...long, sandy beaches. ...largas playas arenosas.*

**Word Link** *san ≈ health : insane, sane, sanitary*

**sane** /seɪn/ (**saner, sanest**) 1 ADJ Someone who is **sane** is able to think and behave normally and reasonably, and is not mentally ill. *cuerdo* ❑ *He seemed perfectly sane. Parecía perfectamente cuerdo.* 2 ADJ A **sane** action or idea is reasonable and sensible. *sensato* ❑ *...extremely sane advice. ...un consejo extremadamente sensato.*

**sani|tary** /sænɪtɛri/ ADJ **Sanitary** means concerned with keeping things clean and healthy. *sanitario* ❑ *Sanitary conditions in the camp are very bad. Las condiciones sanitarias en el campamento son muy malas.*

**sani|tary nap|kin** (**sanitary napkins**) N-COUNT A **sanitary napkin** is a pad of thick soft material which women wear to absorb the blood during their period. *toalla sanitaria*

**san|ity** /sænɪti/ N-UNCOUNT A person's **sanity** is their ability to think and behave normally and reasonably. *cordura, sensatez* ❑ *Nobody with any sanity wants this job. Nadie que tenga un poco de cordura quiere este trabajo.*

**sap|py** /sæpi/ ADJ If you describe someone or something as **sappy**, you think they are foolish. *bobo* [INFORMAL] ❑ *I wrote this sappy love song. Escribí esta boba canción de amor.*

**sar|cas|tic** /sɑrkæstɪk/ ADJ Someone who is **sarcastic** says or does the opposite of what they really mean in order to mock or insult someone. *sarcástico* ❑ *...sarcastic remarks. ...comentarios sarcásticos.* ● **sar|cas|ti|cal|ly** /sɑrkæstɪkli/ ADV *de manera sarcástica* ❑ *"What a surprise!" Caroline said sarcastically. —¡Qué sorpresa! —dijo Carolina de manera sarcástica.*

**sar|gas|sum** /sɑrgæsəm/ N-UNCOUNT **Sargassum** is seaweed and other plant material that has formed into a large floating mass. *sargassum* [TECHNICAL]

**sass** /sæs/ (**sasses, sassing, sassed**) 1 N-UNCOUNT **Sass** is disrespectful talk. *hablar con descaro* [INFORMAL] ❑ *We're going, and I want no sass from you. Nos vamos, y no quiero que me hables con descaro.* 2 V-T If someone **sasses** you, they speak to you in a disrespectful way. *hablar irrespetuosamente* [INFORMAL] ❑ *The girl sassed the teacher all day. La niña le habló irrespetuosamente al maestro todo el día.*

**sas|sa|fras** /sæsəfræs/ (**sassafras**) **1** N-VAR **Sassafras** is an herb which is produced from the dried roots of the sassafras tree. *sasafrás* **2** N-COUNT A **sassafras** or a **sassafras tree** is a tree, found mainly in North America, the roots of which are used to make the herb sassafras. *sasafrás*

**sas|sy** /sæsi/ **1** ADJ If an older person describes a younger person as **sassy**, they mean that they are disrespectful in a lively, confident way. *fresco, respondón* [INFORMAL] ❑ *Are you that sassy with your parents, young lady? ¿Así de respondona eres con tus padres, jovencita?* **2** ADJ **Sassy** is used to describe things that are smart and stylish. *llamativo y elegante* [INFORMAL] ❑ *...his sassy hairstyle. ...su peinado llamativo y elegante.* ❑ *We sell colorful and sassy fashion accessories. Vendemos coloridos y elegantes accesorios de moda.*

**SAT** /ɛs eɪ ti/ (**SATs**) N-PROPER The **SAT** is an examination which is often taken by students who wish to enter a college or university. **SAT** is an abbreviation for "Scholastic Aptitude Test." *examen SAT, para entrar a la universidad*

**sat|el|lite** /sætᵊlaɪt/ (**satellites**) **1** N-COUNT A **satellite** is an object which has been sent into space in order to collect information or to be part of a communications system. *satélite* ❑ *The rocket carried two communications satellites. El cohete llevaba dos satélites de comunicaciones.* **2** ADJ **Satellite** television is broadcast using a satellite. *por satélite* ❑ *They have four satellite channels. Tienen cuatro canales de televisión por satélite.* **3** N-COUNT A **satellite** is a natural object in space that moves around a planet or star. *satélite* ❑ *...the satellites of Jupiter. ...los satélites de Júpiter.*
→ see Word Web: **satellite**
→ see **astronomer, forecast, navigation, radio, television**

**sat|el|lite dish** (**satellite dishes**) N-COUNT A **satellite dish** is a piece of equipment which people have on their house in order to receive satellite television. *antena de satélite*

**sat|in** /sætᵊn/ (**satins**) N-VAR **Satin** is a smooth, shiny kind of cloth, usually made from silk. *satín* ❑ *...a satin dress. ...un vestido de satín.*

**sat|ire** /sætaɪər/ (**satires**) **1** N-UNCOUNT **Satire** is the use of humor or exaggeration in order to mock or criticize people's behavior or ideas. *sátira* ❑ *Politicians are an easy target for satire. Los políticos son un blanco fácil para la sátira.* **2** N-COUNT A **satire** is a play, movie, or novel in which humor or exaggeration is used to criticize something. *sátira* ❑ *...a satire on the American political process. ...una sátira sobre el proceso político estadounidense.*

**sat|is|fac|tion** /sætɪsfækʃᵊn/ **1** N-UNCOUNT **Satisfaction** is the pleasure that you feel when you do something or get something that you wanted or needed to do or get. *satisfacción* ❑ *She felt a sense of satisfaction. Sintió satisfacción.* ❑ *Both sides expressed satisfaction with the progress so far. Ambas partes expresaron su satisfacción con los progresos hechos hasta ahora.* **2** N-UNCOUNT If you get **satisfaction** from someone, you get money or an apology from them because you have been treated badly. *reparación, satisfacción* ❑ *If you can't get any satisfaction, complain to the park owner. Si no obtienes reparación alguna, quéjate con el dueño del parque.*

**sat|is|fac|tory** /sætɪsfæktəri/ ADJ Something that is **satisfactory** is acceptable to you or fulfills a particular need or purpose. *satisfactorio* ❑ *I never got a satisfactory answer. Nunca recibí una respuesta satisfactoria.* • **sat|is|fac|to|ri|ly** /sætɪsfæktərɪli/ ADV *de manera satisfactoria* ❑ *How she died was never satisfactorily explained. Nunca se explicó de manera satisfactoria cómo había muerto.*

**sat|is|fied** /sætɪsfaɪd/ ADJ If you are **satisfied with** something, you are happy because you have gotten what you wanted or needed. *satisfecho* ❑ *We are not satisfied with these results. No estamos satisfechos con estos resultados.*

**Word Link** *sat, satis ≈ enough : insatiable, satisfy, unsatisfactory*

**sat|is|fy** /sætɪsfaɪ/ (**satisfies, satisfying, satisfied**) **1** V-T If someone or something **satisfies** you, they give you enough of what you want or need to make you pleased or contented. *satisfacer* ❑ *He will satisfy all his fans with this CD. Dejará satisfecho a todos sus fans con este CD.* **2** V-T To **satisfy** someone **that** something is true or has

S

**Word Web** **satellite**

The **moon** is the earth's best-known **satellite**. In 1957 humans began **launching** objects into **space**. That's when the first man-made satellite, Sputnik, began to **orbit** the earth. Today, hundreds of satellites circle the **planet**. The largest satellite is the International **Space Station**. It completes an orbit about every 90 minutes and sometimes can be seen from the earth. Others, such as the Hubble Telescope, help us learn more about **outer space**. The NOAA 12 monitors the earth's climate. TV weather forecasts often use pictures taken from satellites. Today, many TV programs are also broadcast by satellite.

been done properly means to convince them by giving them more information or by showing them what has been done. convencer ❑ *He has to satisfy the public that he is making real progress.* *Tiene que convencer al público de que realmente está progresando.* **3** V-T If you **satisfy** the requirements for something, you are good enough or have the right qualities to fulfill these requirements. satisfacer ❑ *Private companies have to satisfy the needs of their workers.* *Las compañías privadas tienen que satisfacer las necesidades de sus trabajadores.*

**Word Partnership** Usar *satisfy* con:

N. satisfy **an appetite**, satisfy **demands**, satisfy **a desire** **1** satisfy **a need** **1** **3** satisfy **critics**, satisfy ***someone's*** **curiosity** **2**

**sat|is|fy|ing** /sætɪsfaɪɪŋ/ ADJ Something that is **satisfying** makes you feel happy, especially because you feel you have achieved something. satisfactorio ❑ *It was a very satisfying experience.* *Fue una experiencia muy satisfactoria.*

**satu|rat|ed hydro|car|bon** /sætʃəreɪtɪd haɪdroʊkɑrbᵊn/ (**saturated hydrocarbons**) N-COUNT A **saturated hydrocarbon** is a compound of hydrogen and carbon which contains the maximum number of hydrogen atoms. hidrocarburo saturado [TECHNICAL]

**satu|rat|ed so|lu|tion** (**saturated solutions**) N-COUNT A **saturated solution** is a liquid that contains so much of a dissolved substance that it is unable to contain any more of it. solución saturada

**Sat|ur|day** /sætərdeɪ, -di/ (**Saturdays**) N-VAR **Saturday** is the day after Friday and before Sunday. sábado ❑ *He called her on Saturday morning.* *Le habló el sábado en la mañana.* ❑ *Every Saturday, Dad made soup.* *Papá hacía sopa todos los sábados.*

**Sat|urn** /sætərn/ N-PROPER **Saturn** is the sixth planet from the sun. It is surrounded by rings made of ice and dust. Saturno
→ see **solar system**

**sauce** /sɔs/ (**sauces**) N-VAR A **sauce** is a thick liquid which is served with other food. salsa ❑ *This pasta is cooked in a garlic and tomato sauce.* *Esta pasta se cuece en una salsa de ajo y jitomate.*

S

**sauce|pan** /sɔspæn/ (**saucepans**) N-COUNT A **saucepan** is a deep metal cooking pot, usually with a long handle and a lid. cacerola ❑ *Place the potatoes in a saucepan and boil them.* *Ponga a cocer las papas en una cacerola.*
→ see **pan**

**sau|cer** /sɔsər/ (**saucers**) N-COUNT A **saucer** is a small curved plate on which you stand a cup. platito para la taza ❑ *Rae's coffee splashed in the saucer as she picked it up.* *Cuando Rae levantó la taza, el café se derramó en el platito.*
→ see **dish**

**sau|sage** /sɔsɪdʒ/ (**sausages**) N-VAR A **sausage** consists of minced meat, usually pork, mixed with other ingredients, inside a long thin skin. salchicha ❑ *...sausages and fries.* *...salchichas y papas fritas.*

**sav|age** /sævɪdʒ/ (**savages, savaging, savaged**) **1** ADJ Someone or something that is **savage** is extremely cruel, violent, and uncontrolled. salvaje ❑ *This was a savage attack on a young girl.* *Fue un salvaje ataque contra una niñita.* • **sav|age|ly** ADV salvajemente ❑ *He was savagely beaten.* *Lo golpearon salvajemente.* **2** N-COUNT If you refer to people as **savages**, you dislike them because you think that they do not have an advanced society and are violent. salvaje ❑ *The Dutch and British who settled there thought the people were savages.* *Los holandeses y los británicos que se establecieron allí pensaban que los nativos eran salvajes.* **3** V-T If someone **is savaged** by a dog or other animal, the animal attacks them violently. atacar salvajemente ❑ *The animal then turned on him and he was badly savaged.* *El animal se volvió entonces contra él y lo atacó salvajemente.*

**sa|van|na** /səvænə/ (**savannas**) also **savannah** N-VAR A **savanna** is a large area of flat, grassy land, usually in Africa. sabana
→ see **grassland**

**save** /seɪv/ (**saves, saving, saved**) **1** V-T If you **save** someone or something, you help them to avoid harm or to escape from a dangerous or unpleasant situation. salvar ❑ *The program will save the country's failing economy.* *El programa salvará la declinante economía del país.* ❑ *We must save these children from disease and death.* *Debemos salvar a estos niños de la enfermedad y la muerte.* **2** V-T/V-I If you **save,** you gradually collect money by spending less than you get, usually in order to buy something that you want. ahorrar ❑ *Most people intend to save, but find it difficult.* *La mayoría de la gente tiene la intención de ahorrar, pero se le hace muy difícil.* ❑ *Tim and Barbara are now saving for a house.* *Tim y Bárbara están ahorrando para una casa.* ❑ *I was saving money to go to college.* *Estaba ahorrando para ir a la universidad.* • **Save up** means the same as **save.** ahorrar ❑ *Julie was saving up for something special.* *Julie estaba ahorrando para algo especial.* • **sav|er** N-COUNT (**savers**) ahorrador ❑ *They aren't big savers and don't have bank accounts.* *No son grandes ahorradores y no tienen cuentas de banco.* **3** V-T/V-I If you **save** something such as time or money, you prevent the loss or waste of it. ahorrar ❑ *The drivers believe going through the city saves time.* *Los conductores creen que atravesar la ciudad les ahorra tiempo.* ❑ *I'll try to save him the cost of a flight from Perth.* *Trataré de ahorrarle el costo del vuelo desde Perth.* ❑ *Families move in together to save on rent.* *Las familias se mudan a una misma casa para pagar menos renta.* **4** V-T If you **save** something, you keep it because it will be needed later. guardar ❑ *Don't tell her now. Save the news for later.* *No le cuentes ahora. Guarda las noticias para después.* **5** V-T If someone or something **saves** you **from** an unpleasant action or experience, they change the situation so that you do not have to do it or experience it. ahorrarle a alguien, salvar ❑ *This information will save you many hours of searching later.* *Esta información te ahorrará muchas horas de búsqueda más adelante.* ❑ *We must act to save people from starvation.* *Debemos hacer algo para salvar a la gente de morirse de hambre.* **6** V-T/V-I If you **save** data in a computer, you give the computer an instruction to store the data on a tape or disk. guardar [COMPUTING] ❑ *Save your work regularly.* *Guarda tu trabajo regularmente.* ❑ *It's important to save frequently when you are working on a document.* *Es importante guardar la información frecuentemente*

*al trabajar en algún documento.* **7** V-T/V-I If a goalkeeper **saves,** or **saves** a shot, they succeed in preventing the ball from going into the goal. *parar el gol* ❑ *He saved one shot when the ball hit him on the head. Paró el gol cuando el balón le pegó en la cabeza.*
● **Save** is also a noun. *parada* ❑ *The goalkeeper made some great saves. El portero hizo grandes paradas.*
▸ **save up** → see **save 2**

**sav|ings** /seɪvɪŋz/ N-PLURAL Your **savings** are the money that you have saved, especially in a bank. *ahorros* ❑ *Her savings were in the First National Bank. Sus ahorros estaban en el First National Bank.*

**sav|ings and loan** (**savings and loans**) N-COUNT A **savings and loan** is a business where people save money to earn interest, and which lends money to savers to buy houses. *sociedad de ahorro y préstamo* [BUSINESS]

**saw** /sɔ/ (**saws, sawing, sawed, sawed** or **sawn**) **1** **Saw** is the past tense of **see.** *pasado de see* **2** N-COUNT A **saw** is a tool for cutting wood, which has a blade with sharp teeth along one edge. *serrucho, sierra* **3** V-T/V-I If you **saw** something, you cut it with a saw. *aserrar* ❑ *He escaped by sawing through the bars of his jail cell. Se escapó aserrando los barrotes de su celda.* ❑ *Father sawed the dead branches off the tree. Papá aserró las ramas secas del árbol.*
→ see **cut, tool**

**say**
❶ VERB AND NOUN USES
❷ PHRASES AND CONVENTIONS

❶ **say** /seɪ/ (**says** /sɛz/ (**saying, said** /sɛd/) **1** V-T When you **say** something, you speak words. *decir* ❑ *"I'm sorry," he said. —Lo lamento —dijo.* ❑ *She said that they were very pleased. Dijeron que estaban encantados.* ❑ *Forty people are said to have died. Se dice que murieron cuarenta personas.* ❑ *I packed and said goodbye to Charlie. Empaqué y le dije adiós a Charlie.* **2** V-T You use **say** to show that you are expressing an opinion or stating a fact. *decir* ❑ *I would say this is probably illegal. Yo diría que esto probablemente es ilegal.* ❑ *I must say that rather shocked me, too. Debo decir que eso también me sorprendió.* **3** V-T You can mention the contents of a piece of writing by mentioning what it **says** or what someone **says** in it. *decir* ❑ *Our report says six people were injured. El reporte que tenemos dice que seis personas resultaron heridas.* ❑ *As the song says, "You can't have one without the other." Como dice la canción, "no puedes tener uno sin el otro".* **4** V-T If you **say** something **to yourself**, you think it. *decirse a sí mismo* ❑ *"I'm still dreaming," I said to myself. —Sigo soñando —me dije.* **5** N-SING If you have **a say in** something, you have the right to give your opinion and influence decisions relating to it. *tener voz y voto* ❑ *We want to have a say in the decision. Queremos tener voz y voto en esta decisión.* **6** V-T You indicate the information given by something such as a clock, dial, or map by mentioning what it **says.** *marcar* ❑ *The clock said four minutes past eleven. El reloj marcaba las once y cuatro minutos.* **7** V-T If something **says** something **about** a person, situation, or thing, it gives important information about them. *decir* ❑ *The fact that he is still popular says a lot about his music. El hecho de que aún sea popular dice mucho de su música.* **8** PHRASE You can use **say** or **let's say** when you mention something as an example. *por ejemplo* ❑ *...a painting by, say, Picasso. ...por ejemplo, una pintura de Picasso.*

❷ **say** /seɪ/ (**says** /sɛz/ (**saying, said** /sɛd/) **1** EXCLAM **Say** is used to attract someone's attention or to express surprise, pleasure, or admiration. *oye* [INFORMAL] ❑ *Say, Leo, how would you like to have dinner one night? Oye Leo, ¿te gustaría ir a cenar una noche?* **2** PHRASE If you say that something **says it all,** you mean that it shows you very clearly the truth about a situation or someone's feelings. *decir todo* ❑ *This is my third visit in a week, which says it all. Esta es mi tercera visita en una semana; eso dice todo.* **3** PHRASE If you say there is a lot **to be said for** something, you mean you think it has a lot of good qualities or aspects. *que decir en pro de* ❑ *There's a lot to be said for working in the country. Hay mucho que decir en pro de trabajar en el campo.* **4** PHRASE If something **goes without saying,** it is obvious. *ni falta hace decirlo, es evidente* ❑ *It goes without saying that the spices must be fresh. No hace falta decir que las especias deben estar frescas.* **5** PHRASE You use **that is to say** or **that's to say** to indicate that you are about to express the same idea more clearly or precisely. *es decir* [FORMAL] ❑ *They work with world music, that is to say, non-American, non-European music. Trabajan con música del mundo, es decir, ni estadounidense ni europea.* **6** CONVENTION You can use **"You can say that again"** to express strong agreement with what someone has just said. *¡y que lo digas!* [INFORMAL] ❑ *"You are in trouble already." — "You can say that again," sighed Richard. —Ya te metiste en problemas de nuevo —¡y que lo digas! —suspiró Richard.*

**say|ing** /seɪɪŋ/ (**sayings**) N-COUNT A **saying** is a sentence that people often say and that gives advice or information about human life and experience. *dicho* ❑ *The saying goes, "Be careful what you ask for, you might just get it." El dicho dice: "Ten cuidado con lo que pides, porque te puede ser concedido".*

**scaf|fold|ing** /skæfəldɪŋ/ N-UNCOUNT **Scaffolding** consists of poles and boards made into a temporary framework that is used by workers when they are working on the outside of a building. *andamio, andamiaje* ❑ *Workers have put up scaffolding around the tower. Los trabajadores colocaron un andamio alrededor de la torre.*

**sca|lar ma|trix** /skeɪlər meɪtrɪks/ (**scalar matrices**) N-COUNT A **scalar matrix** is a mathematical arrangement of numbers, symbols, or letters in which all of the diagonal elements are equal. *matriz escalar* [TECHNICAL]

**Word Link** *scal, scala ≈ ladder, stairs : escalate, escalator, scale*

**scale** /skeɪl/ (**scales, scaling, scaled**) **1** N-SING If you refer to the **scale** of something, you are referring to its size or extent, especially when it is very big. *escala* ❑ *He doesn't realize the scale of the problem. No se da cuenta del tamaño del problema.* ❑ *Our business now operates on a greatly reduced scale. Nuestro negocio opera ahora en una escala muy reducida.* **2** → see also **full-scale, large-scale, small-scale** **3** N-COUNT A **scale** is a set of levels or numbers which are used in a particular system of measuring things or are used when comparing

S

things. escala ❑ *The earthquake measured 5.5 on the Richter scale.* *El terremoto fue de 5.5 grados en la escala de Richter.* ❑ *He's on the high end of the pay scale.* *Está en la parte superior de la escala de pagos.* **4** N-COUNT The **scale** of a map, plan, or model is the relationship between the size of something in the map, plan, or model and its size in the real world. escala ❑ *The map is on a scale of 1:10,000.* *El mapa está en una escala de 1:10,000.* **5** → see also **full-scale, large-scale** **6** ADJ A **scale** model or **scale** replica of a building or object is a model of it which is smaller than the real thing but has all the same parts and features. modelo a escala ❑ *Frank made his mother a scale model of the house.* *Frank le hizo a su madre un modelo a escala de la casa.* **7** N-COUNT In music, a **scale** is a fixed sequence of musical notes, each one higher than the next, which begins at a particular note. escala ❑ *Play a scale of C major.* *Toca la escala de do mayor.* **8** N-COUNT The **scales** of a fish or reptile are the small, flat pieces of hard skin that cover its body. escama ❑ *Remove the scales from the fish skin.* *Quite las escamas de la piel del pescado.* **9** N-COUNT A **scale** is a piece of equipment used for weighing things, for example, for weighing amounts of food that you need in order to make a particular meal. báscula ❑ *I have new kitchen scales.* *Tengo una nueva báscula para la cocina.* ❑ *...a bathroom scale.* *...la báscula del baño.* **10** V-T If you **scale** something such as a mountain or a wall, you climb up it or over it. escalar [WRITTEN] ❑ *Rebecca Stephens was the first British woman to scale Everest.* *Rebecca Stephens fue la primera mujer británica en escalar el Everest.*
→ see **fish, graph, shark, thermometer**

▸ **scale back** PHR-VERB To **scale back** means the same as to **scale down**. reducir ❑ *Manufacturers are scaling back production.* *Los fabricantes están reduciendo la producción.*

▸ **scale down** PHR-VERB If you **scale down** something, you make it smaller in size, amount, or extent than it used to be. reducir ❑ *One factory scaled down its workforce from six hundred to only six.* *Una fábrica redujo su mano de obra de seiscientos a sólo seis.*

**scal|lion** /skælyən/ (**scallions**) N-COUNT A **scallion** is a small onion with long green leaves. cebollín, cebollita (cambray)

S

**scal|lop** /skɒləp, skæl-/ (**scallops**) N-COUNT **Scallops** are large shellfish with two flat fan-shaped shells. Scallops can be eaten. callo de hacha
→ see **shellfish**

**scalp|er** /skælpər/ (**scalpers**) N-COUNT A **scalper** is someone who sells tickets outside a sports stadium or theater, usually for more than their original value. revendedor o revendedora ❑ *A scalper charged $1000 for a $125 ticket.* *Un revendedor pedía 1,000 dólares por un boleto de 125.*

**scan** /skæn/ (**scans, scanning, scanned**) **1** V-T/V-I When you **scan** written material, you look through it quickly in order to find important or interesting information. echar un vistazo ❑ *She scanned the front page of the newspaper.* *Echó un vistazo a la primera página del periódico.* • **Scan** is also a noun. vistazo ❑ *I had a quick scan through your book again.* *Eché un vistazo de nuevo a tu libro.* **2** V-T/V-I When you **scan** a place or group of people, you look at it carefully, usually because you are looking for something or someone. recorrer con la vista, escudriñar ❑ *The officer scanned the room.* *El oficial recorrió el cuarto con la mirada.* ❑ *She nervously scanned the crowd for Paul.* *Nerviosamente, escudriñó a la multitud buscando a Paul.* **3** V-T If people **scan** something such as luggage, they examine it using a machine that can show or find things inside it that cannot be seen from the outside. escrutar ❑ *They scan every bag with an X-ray machine.* *Revisan cada maleta con una máquina de rayos X.* **4** N-COUNT A **scan** is a medical test in which a machine sends a beam of X-rays over a part of your body in order to check that it is healthy. ecografía ❑ *A brain scan showed a strange shadow.* *Una ecografía cerebral mostraba una sombra extraña.*

**scan|dal** /skændᵊl/ (**scandals**) **1** N-COUNT A **scandal** is a situation or event that is thought to be shocking and immoral and that everyone knows about. escándalo ❑ *It was a financial scandal.* *Fue un escándalo financiero.* **2** N-UNCOUNT **Scandal** is talk about the shocking and immoral aspects of someone's behavior or something that has happened. escándalo ❑ *He loved gossip and scandal.* *Le encantaba el chisme y el escándalo.*

**scan|ner** /skænər/ (**scanners**) N-COUNT A **scanner** is a machine which is used to examine, identify, or record things, for example by using a beam of light, sound, or X-rays. escáner, ecógrafo ❑ *...brain scanners.* *...ecógrafos cerebrales.*
→ see **laser**

**scape|goat** /skeɪpgoʊt/ (**scapegoats**) N-COUNT If someone is made a **scapegoat for** something bad that has happened, people blame them and may punish them for it although it may not be their fault. chivo expiatorio ❑ *Don't make me a scapegoat because of a couple of bad results.* *No quiero ser el chivo expiatorio por un par de malos resultados.*

**scar** /skɑr/ (**scars, scarring, scarred**) **1** N-COUNT A **scar** is a mark on the skin which is left after a wound has healed. cicatriz ❑ *He had a scar on his forehead.* *Tenía una cicatriz en la frente.* **2** V-T If your skin **is scarred,** it is badly marked as a result of a wound. cubierto de cicatrices ❑ *He was scarred for life during a fight.* *Quedó cubierto de cicatrices de por vida durante una pelea.* **3** V-T If a surface **is scarred,** it is damaged and there are ugly marks on it. marcar ❑ *The land is scarred by huge holes.* *El terreno está afeado por grandes hoyos.* **4** N-COUNT If an unpleasant physical or emotional experience leaves a **scar** on someone, it has a permanent effect on their mind. marca, huella ❑ *The years of fear left a deep scar on the young boy.* *Los años de miedo dejaron profunda huella en el joven.* **5** V-T If an unpleasant physical or emotional experience **scars** you, it has a permanent effect on your mind. dejar marcado ❑ *This will scar him forever.* *Esto lo dejará marcado para siempre.*

**scarce** /skɛərs/ (**scarcer, scarcest**) ADJ If something is **scarce,** there is not enough of it. escaso ❑ *Food was scarce and expensive.* *La comida era escasa y cara.* ❑ *Jobs are becoming scarce.* *Los empleos se están volviendo escasos.*

**scarce|ly** /skɛərsli/ **1** ADV You use **scarcely** to emphasize that something is only just true. apenas ❑ *He could scarcely breathe.* *Apenas podía respirar.* ❑ *I scarcely knew him.* *Apenas lo conocía.* **2** ADV You can use **scarcely** to say that something is not true, in a humorous or critical way. apenas ❑ *I would scarcely expect them to say anything else.* *Apenas esperaría que dijeran otra cosa.* **3** ADV If you say **scarcely had** one thing happened when something else happened, you mean that the first event was followed immediately by the second. apenas ❑ *Scarcely had they counted the votes when the telephone rang.* *Apenas habían contado los votos, cuando sonó el teléfono.*

**scare** /skɛər/ (**scares, scaring, scared**) **1** V-T If something **scares** you, it frightens or worries you. asustar ❑ *You're scaring me.* *Me estás asustando.* ❑ *The thought of failure scares me.* *Me asusta pensar en el fracaso.* **2** N-SING If a sudden unpleasant experience gives you a **scare,** it frightens you. susto ❑ *Don't you realize what a scare you gave us?* *¿Te das cuenta del susto que nos diste?* **3** N-COUNT A **scare** is a situation in which many people are afraid or worried because they think something dangerous is happening which will affect them all. temor ❑ *The airport has reopened after a natural gas scare this morning.* *El aeropuerto ha vuelto a operar después del gran susto de esta mañana por el gas natural.* **4** N-COUNT A bomb **scare** or a security **scare** is a situation in which there is believed to be a bomb in a place. amenaza de bomba ❑ *There have been many bomb scares, but no one has yet been hurt.* *Ha habido muchas amenazas de bomba, pero nadie ha sido herido.* **5** → see also **scared**

▸ **scare away** → see **scare off**

▸ **scare off** PHR-VERB If you **scare off** or **scare away** a person or animal, you frighten them so that they go away. ahuyentar ❑ *The alarm will scare off an attacker.* *La alarma ahuyentará al atacante.*

**scared** /skɛərd/ **1** ADJ If you are **scared of** someone or something, you are frightened of them. tener miedo ❑ *I'm not scared of him.* *No le tengo miedo.* ❑ *I was too scared to move.* *Tenía demasiado miedo como para moverme.* **2** ADJ If you are **scared that** something unpleasant might happen, you are nervous and worried because you think that it might happen. temer ❑ *I was scared that I might be sick.* *Tenía miedo de vomitar.*

**scarf** /skɑrf/ (**scarfs** or **scarves**) N-COUNT A **scarf** is a piece of cloth that you wear around your neck or head, usually to keep yourself warm. bufanda, mascada ❑ *He loosened the scarf around his neck.* *Se aflojó la bufanda que traía en el cuello.*

**scary** /skɛəri/ (**scarier, scariest**) ADJ Something that is **scary** is rather frightening. de miedo, que da miedo [INFORMAL] ❑ *I think prison will be scary for Harry.* *Creo que la cárcel le dará miedo a Harry.* ❑ *There's something very scary about him.* *Hay algo en él que da mucho miedo.*

**scat|ter** /skætər/ (**scatters, scattering, scattered**) **1** V-T If you **scatter** things over an area, you throw or drop them so that they spread all over the area. esparcir ❑ *She scattered the flowers over the grave.* *Esparció flores sobre su tumba.* ❑ *They've scattered toys everywhere.* *Regaron los juguetes por todos lados.* **2** V-T/V-I If a group of people **scatter** or if you **scatter** them, they suddenly separate and move in different directions. esparcirse ❑ *After dinner, everyone scattered.* *Después de cenar, todos se separaron.* **3** → see also **scattered**

**scat|tered** /skætərd/ **1** ADJ **Scattered** things are spread over an area in a messy or irregular way. regado, disperso, desparramado ❑ *He picked up the scattered toys.* *Recogió los juguetes que estaban regados.* ❑ *Tomorrow there will be a few scattered showers.* *Mañana habrá lluvias aisladas.* **2** ADJ If something is **scattered with** a lot of small things, they are spread all over it. esparcido, desperdigado ❑ *Every surface is scattered with photographs.* *Hay fotografías desperdigadas por todas las superficies.*

**scatter|plot** /skætərplɒt/ (**scatterplots**) N-COUNT A **scatterplot** is a type of graph used in statistics to compare two sets of data. scatterplot, gráfica de dispersión [TECHNICAL]

**scav|en|ger** /skævɪndʒər/ (**scavengers**) N-COUNT A **scavenger** is an animal that feeds on the bodies of dead animals. carroñero [TECHNICAL] ❑ *...scavengers such as rats.* *...carroñeros como las ratas.*

**scav|en|ger hunt** (**scavenger hunts**) N-COUNT A **scavenger hunt** is a game, usually played outdoors, in which the players must collect various objects from a list of things they have been given. búsqueda del tesoro, rally ❑ *On scavenger hunts I always asked Mrs. Martin for empty coffee cans.* *Siempre le pedía a la Sra. Martin latas de café vacías para los rallies.*

**sce|nario** /sɪnɛərioʊ/ (**scenarios**) N-COUNT If you talk about a likely or possible **scenario,** you are talking about the way in which a situation may develop. escenario, perspectiva ❑ *The only reasonable scenario is that he will resign.* *El único escenario razonable es que él renuncie.*

**scene** /sin/ (**scenes**) **1** N-COUNT A **scene** in a play, movie, or book is part of it in which a series of events happens in the same place. escena ❑ *This is the opening scene of "Tom Sawyer."* *Esta es la escena inicial de "Tom Sawyer".* ❑ *...Act I, scene 1.* *...Acto I, escena 1.* **2** N-COUNT You refer to a place as a **scene** when you are describing its appearance and indicating what impression it makes on you. escena, escenario, situación ❑ *It's a scene of complete horror.* *Es una escena aterradora.* **3** N-COUNT The **scene of** an event is the place where it happened. escenario ❑ *The area has been the scene of fierce fighting for three months.* *El área ha sido el escenario de feroces batallas durante tres meses.* **4** N-SING You can refer to an area of activity as a particular type of **scene.** escenario, ámbito, escena ❑ *...the local music scene.* *...el escenario de la música local.* **5** N-COUNT If you make a **scene,** you embarrass people by publicly showing your anger about something. escena ❑ *I'm sorry I made such a scene.* *Discúlpame por haber dado ese espectáculo.* **6** PHRASE If something is done **behind the scenes,** it is done secretly rather than publicly. entre bastidores, tras bastidores ❑ *Mr. Cain worked quietly behind the scenes to get a deal done.* *El Sr. Cain trabajó calladamente tras bastidores para llegar a un acuerdo.* **7** to **set the scene for** something → see **set** → see **animation**

**scen|ery** /sinəri/ **1** N-UNCOUNT The **scenery** in a country area is the land, water, or plants that you can see around you. paisaje, alrededores, panorama ❑ *...the island's beautiful scenery.* *...el hermoso paisaje de la isla.* **2** N-UNCOUNT In a theater, the **scenery** consists of the structures and painted backgrounds that show where the action in the play takes place. escenografía, decorado ❑ *The actors will move the scenery themselves.* *Los mismos actores*

S

*moverán la escenografía.*

**sce|nic** /si̲nɪk/ ADJ A **scenic** place has attractive scenery. *pintoresco* ❑ *This is an extremely scenic part of America. Esta zona de los Estados Unidos es muy pintoresca.*

**scent** /sɛ̲nt/ (**scents, scenting, scented**) **1** N-COUNT The **scent** of something is the pleasant smell that it has. *aroma, fragancia, perfume* ❑ *Flowers are chosen for their scent. Las flores se escogen por su aroma.* **2** N-UNCOUNT **Scent** is a liquid which women put on their necks and wrists to make themselves smell nice. *perfume* ❑ *She opened her bottle of scent. Abrió su botella de perfume.* **3** N-VAR The **scent** of a person or animal is the smell that they leave and that other people sometimes follow when looking for them. *olor, rastro* ❑ *A police dog picked up the murderer's scent. Un perro de la policía encontró el rastro del asesino.* **4** V-T When an animal **scents** something, it becomes aware of it by smelling it. *oler, rastrear, olfatear* ❑ *The dogs scent the hidden birds. Los perros huelen a las aves escondidas.*

**sched|ule** /skɛ̲dʒul, -uəl/ (**schedules, scheduling, scheduled**) **1** N-COUNT A **schedule** is a plan that gives a list of events or tasks and the times at which each one should happen or be done. *programa, horario, plan* ❑ *He had to adjust his schedule. Tuvo que cambiar su plan.* **2** N-UNCOUNT You can use **schedule** to refer to the time or way something is planned to be done. For example, if something is completed **on schedule,** it is completed at the time planned. *lo programado* ❑ *The plane arrived two minutes ahead of schedule. El avión llegó dos minutos adelantado.* ❑ *Everything went according to schedule. Todo se hizo según lo previsto.* **3** V-T If something **is scheduled** to happen at a particular time, arrangements are made for it to happen at that time. *programar* ❑ *The space shuttle was scheduled to lift off at 04:38. El despegue del transbordador espacial se programó para las 04:38.* ❑ *The next meeting is scheduled for tomorrow morning. La siguiente reunión está programada para mañana por la mañana.* **4** N-COUNT A **schedule** is a written list of things, for example, a list of prices, details, or conditions. *lista, catálogo, inventario* ❑ *We will issue a pricing schedule for tickets later this year. Publicaremos una lista de precios de los boletos más adelante.* **5** N-COUNT A **schedule** is a list of all the times when trains, boats, buses, or aircraft are supposed to arrive at or leave a particular place. *horario* ❑ *...a bus schedule. ...un horario de los autobuses.*

**Word Partnership** Usar *schedule* con:

ADJ. **busy** schedule, **hectic** schedule **1**
**regular** schedule **1** **5**
N. **change of** schedule, schedule **of events**, **payment** schedule, **playoff** schedule, **work** schedule **1** **4**
**bus** schedule, **train** schedule **5**
PREP. **according to** schedule, **ahead of** schedule, **behind** schedule, **on** schedule **2**

**scheme** /ski̲m/ (**schemes, scheming, schemed**) **1** N-COUNT A **scheme** is a plan for achieving something, especially something that will bring you some benefit. *esquema, proyecto, plan, programa* ❑ *...a quick money-making scheme. ...un plan para hacer dinero rápido.* ❑ *First they had to work out some scheme for breaking the lock. Primero tuvieron que idear la manera de violar la cerradura.* **2** V-T/V-I If you say that people **are scheming,** you disapprove of the fact that they are making secret plans in order to gain something for themselves. *conspirar, intrigar, tramar* ❑ *Everyone's always scheming. Siempre hay alguien conspirando.* ❑ *The family was scheming to prevent the wedding. La familia tramaba la forma de evitar la boda.* **3** PHRASE When people talk about **the scheme of things** or **the grand scheme of things,** they are referring to the way that everything in the world seems to be organized. *orden del universo* ❑ *When you look at the sea, you realize how small you are in the scheme of things. Cuando ves el mar, te das cuenta de lo poco que eres en el orden del universo.*

**Thesaurus** *scheme* Ver también:

N. design, plan, strategy **1**

**schlep** /ʃlɛ̲p/ (**schleps, schlepping, schlepped**) also **schlepp** **1** V-T If you **schlep** something somewhere, you take it there although this is difficult or inconvenient. *cargar con* [INFORMAL] ❑ *You didn't just schlep your guitar around from club to club. No cargaste con tu guitarra nada más para ir de bar en bar.* **2** V-I If you **schlep** somewhere, you go there. *andar de un lugar a otro* [INFORMAL] ❑ *It's too cold to schlep around looking at property. Hace demasiado frío como para andar nada más viendo terrenos.*

**schmooze** /ʃmu̲z/ (**schmoozes, schmoozing, schmoozed**) V-I If you **schmooze,** you talk casually and socially with someone. *cotorrear, platicar, chismear* [INFORMAL] ❑ *There are coffee houses where you can schmooze for hours. Hay cafeterías en las que puedes cotorrear durante horas.*

**schmuck** /ʃmʌ̲k/ (**schmucks**) N-COUNT If you call someone a **schmuck,** you mean that they are stupid or you do not like them. *estúpido o estúpida* [INFORMAL] ❑ *I played like a schmuck. Jugué como un estúpido.*

**schol|ar** /skɒ̲lər/ (**scholars**) N-COUNT A **scholar** is a person who studies an academic subject and knows a lot about it. *erudito o erudita, estudioso o estudiosa, sabio o sabia* [FORMAL] ❑ *The library is full of scholars and researchers. La biblioteca está llena de estudiosos e investigadores.*
→ see **history**

**schol|ar|ship** /skɒ̲lərʃɪp/ (**scholarships**) **1** N-COUNT If you get a **scholarship** to a school or university, your studies are paid for by the school or university or by some other organization. *beca* ❑ *He got a scholarship to the Pratt Institute of Art. Consiguió una beca para el Pratt Institute of Art.* **2** N-UNCOUNT **Scholarship** is serious academic study and the knowledge that is obtained from it. *erudición, saber* ❑ *Can I ask you about your lifetime of scholarship? ¿Puedo preguntarle sobre su vida dedicada al estudio?*

**school** /sku̲l/ (**schools**) **1** N-VAR A **school** is a place where children are educated. You usually refer to this place as **school** when you are talking about the time that children spend there. *escuela, colegio* ❑ *That boy was in my class at school. Ese niño estaba en mi grupo de la escuela.* ❑ *Homework is what*

S

**Word Web** science

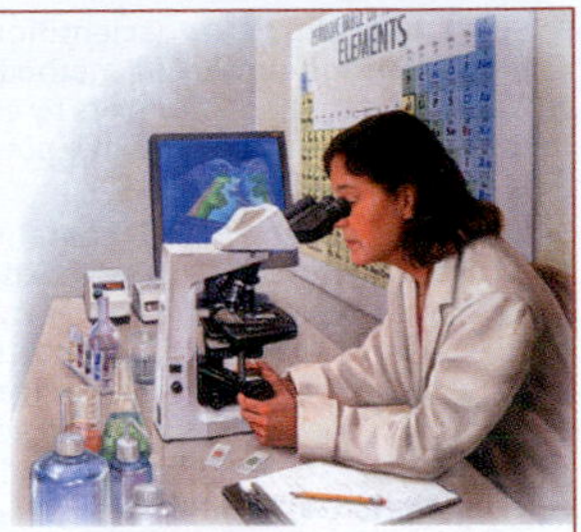

**Science** is the study of physical laws. These laws govern the natural world. Science uses **research** and **experiments** to explain various **phenomena**. Scientists follow the **scientific method** which begins with **observation** and measurement. Then they state a **hypothesis**, which is a possible explanation for the observations and measurements. Next, scientists make a **prediction**, which is a logical **deduction** based on the hypothesis. The last step is to conduct experiments which **prove** or **disprove** the hypothesis. Scientists construct and modify **theories** based on **empirical findings**. **Pure** science deals only with theories. When people use science to do something, that is **applied** science.

*we all disliked about school.* *La tarea es lo que no nos gustaba de la escuela.* ❑ *The school was built in the 1960s.* *La escuela fue construida en los años sesenta.* 2 N-COUNT A **school** is the students or staff at a school. *escuela* ❑ *Deirdre, the whole school will hate you.* *Deirdre, toda la escuela te va a odiar.* 3 N-COUNT A privately-run place where a particular skill or subject is taught can be referred to as a **school**. *escuela* ❑ *He owns a riding school.* *Tiene una escuela de equitación.* 4 N-VAR A university, college, or university department specializing in a particular subject can be referred to as a **school**. *escuela, facultad* ❑ *She's a professor in the school of medicine at the University of Pennsylvania.* *Es profesora de la facultad de medicina de la Universidad de Pensilvania.* 5 N-UNCOUNT **School** is used to refer to college. *escuela, universidad* ❑ *Jack eventually graduated from school in 1998.* *Jack acabó por graduarse de la universidad en 1998.* 6 → see also **boarding school, high school, public school, schooling, state school**

**school board** (**school boards**) N-COUNT A **school board** is a committee in charge of education in a particular city or area, or in a particular school, especially in the United States. *junta de educación* ❑ *Mr. Nelson served on the school board.* *El Sr. Nelson formó parte de la junta de educación.*

**school|boy** /skulbɔɪ/ (**schoolboys**) N-COUNT A **schoolboy** is a boy who goes to school. *colegial, estudiante, alumno* ❑ *There was a group of about ten schoolboys.* *Había un grupo de unos diez niños de escuela.*

**school dis|trict** (**school districts**) N-COUNT A **school district** is an area which includes all the schools that are situated within that area and are governed by a particular authority. *distrito escolar* ❑ *The San Francisco school district is one of the largest in the state.* *El distrito escolar de San Francisco es de los más grandes del estado.*

**school|girl** /skulgɜrl/ (**schoolgirls**) N-COUNT A **schoolgirl** is a girl who goes to school. *colegiala, estudiante, alumna* ❑ *There were half a dozen laughing schoolgirls.* *Media docena de niñas de escuela se estaban riendo.*

**school|house** /skulhaʊs/ (**schoolhouses**) N-COUNT A **schoolhouse** is a small building used as a school. *escuela (edificio)*

**school|ing** /skulɪŋ/ N-UNCOUNT **Schooling** is education that children receive at school. *formación, educación, estudios* ❑ *His formal schooling continued only until he was eleven.* *Su educación formal terminó a los once años.*

**schtick** /ʃtɪk/ (**schticks**) N-VAR An entertainer's **schtick** is a series of funny or entertaining things that they say or do. *sketch, número* [INFORMAL] ❑ *His schtick is perfect for the show.* *Su número es perfecto para el espectáculo.*

**Word Link** *sci ≈ knowing : conscience, conscious, science*

**sci|ence** /saɪəns/ (**sciences**) 1 N-UNCOUNT **Science** is the study of the nature and behavior of natural things and the knowledge that we obtain about them. *ciencia* ❑ *The best discoveries in science are very simple.* *Los mejores descubrimientos de la ciencia son muy sencillos.* 2 N-COUNT A **science** is a particular branch of science such as physics, chemistry, or biology. *ciencia* ❑ *He taught music as if it were a science.* *Enseñaba la música como si fuera una ciencia.* 3 N-COUNT A **science** is the study of some aspect of human behavior, for example, sociology or anthropology. *ciencia* ❑ *Psychology is a modern science.* *La psicología es una ciencia moderna.* 4 → see also **social science**
→ see Word Web: **science**

**sci|ence fic|tion** N-UNCOUNT **Science fiction** consists of stories in books, magazines, and movies about events that take place in the future or in other parts of the universe. *ciencia ficción*

**sci|en|tif|ic** /saɪəntɪfɪk/ 1 ADJ **Scientific** is used to describe things that relate to science or to a particular science. *científico* ❑ *This is scientific research.* *Esto es investigación científica.* • **sci|en|tifi|cal|ly** /saɪəntɪfɪkli/ ADV *científicamente* ❑ *...scientifically advanced countries.* *...países científicamente avanzados.* 2 ADJ If you do something in a **scientific** way, you do it carefully and thoroughly, using experiments or tests. *científico* ❑ *It's not a scientific way to test their opinions.* *No es una forma científica de poner a prueba las opiniones de ellos.* • **sci|en|tifi|cal|ly** ADV *científicamente, de forma científica* ❑ *It must be researched scientifically.* *Se debe investigar de forma científica.*

**sci|en|tif|ic meth|od** N-SING The **scientific method** is the set of rules and procedures followed by scientists, especially the use of experiments to test hypotheses. *método científico*
→ see **experiment, science**

**sci|en|tif|ic no|ta|tion** (**scientific notations**) N-VAR **Scientific notation** is a method of writing very large or very small numbers by expressing them as numbers multiplied by a power of ten. *notación científica* [TECHNICAL]

**sci|en|tist** /saɪəntɪst/ (**scientists**) N-COUNT A **scientist** is someone who has studied science and whose job is to teach or do research in science. *científico o científica* ❑ *Scientists say they've already collected more data than they expected. Los científicos dicen que ya han reunido más datos de lo que esperaban.*
→ see **evolution, experiment**

**sci-fi** /saɪ faɪ/ N-UNCOUNT **Sci-fi** is short for **science fiction**. *ciencia ficción, sci-fi* [INFORMAL] ❑ *It's a two hour sci-fi movie. Es una película de ciencia ficción que dura dos horas.*

**scis|sors** /sɪzərz/ N-PLURAL **Scissors** are a small cutting tool with two sharp blades that are screwed together. You use scissors for cutting things such as paper and cloth. *tijeras, tijera* ❑ *He told me to get some scissors. Me pidió que buscara unas tijeras.*
→ see **office**

**scold** /skoʊld/ (**scolds, scolding, scolded**) V-T If you **scold** someone, you speak angrily to them because they have done something wrong. *regañar, reprender, reñir, reconvenir, sermonear, amonestar* [FORMAL] ❑ *If he finds out, he'll scold me. Si se entera, me regaña.* ❑ *I scolded myself for talking so much. Me reprendí a mí mismo por hablar tanto.*

**scoop** /skup/ (**scoops, scooping, scooped**) **1** V-T If you **scoop** something from a container, you remove it with something such as a spoon. *sacar con cuchara* ❑ *I heard him scooping dog food out of a can. Lo oí sacando de la lata con una cuchara la comida del perro.* **2** N-COUNT A **scoop** is an object like a spoon which is used for picking up a quantity of a food such as ice cream or an ingredient such as flour. *pala, cuchara, cucharón* ❑ *Here, use the ice-cream scoop. Toma, usa la cuchara para helado.* **3** N-COUNT You can use **scoop** to refer to an exciting news story which is reported in one newspaper or on one television program before it appears anywhere else. *primicia, exclusiva* ❑ *It was one of the biggest scoops in the history of newspapers. Fue una de las exclusivas más impactantes en la historia de los periódicos.* **4** V-T If you **scoop** a person or thing somewhere, you put your hands or arms under or around them and quickly move them there. *levantar, coger* ❑ *Michael scooped her into his arms. Michael la levantó en brazos.*

S

▸ **scoop up** PHR-VERB If you **scoop** something **up**, you put your hands or arms under it and lift it in a quick movement. *levantar, recoger* ❑ *Use both hands to scoop up the leaves. Levanta las hojas con ambas manos.*

**scope** /skoʊp/ **1** N-UNCOUNT If there is **scope** for a particular kind of behavior or activity, people have the opportunity to behave in this way or do that activity. *oportunidad, posibilidad* ❑ *There's not a lot of scope for change here. No hay muchas opciones de cambio aquí.* **2** N-SING The **scope of** an activity, topic, or piece of work is the whole area which it deals with or includes. *alcance, campo, ámbito* ❑ *The scope of the project is too large for us to manage alone. El alcance del proyecto es demasiado amplio como para abarcarlo solos.*

**score** /skɔr/ (**scores, scoring, scored**) **1** V-T/V-I In a sport or game, if a player **scores** a goal or a point, they gain a goal or point. *anotar, marcar, meter* ❑ *Patten scored his second touchdown of the game. Patten anotó su segundo touchdown del partido.* ❑ *He scored late in the third quarter. Anotó tarde, en el tercer cuarto.* • **scor|er** N-COUNT (**scorers**) *anotador o anotadora* ❑ *David Hirst is the scorer of 11 goals this season. David Hirst es el anotador de 11 goles en esta temporada.* **2** V-T/V-I If you **score** a particular number or amount, for example, as a mark on a test, you achieve that number or amount. *sacar, obtener* ❑ *Kelly scored 147 on the test. Kelly se sacó 147 en la prueba.* ❑ *Congress scores low in public opinion polls. El congreso no destacó en las encuestas de opinión.* **3** N-COUNT Someone's **score** in a game or on a test is a number, for example, a number of points or runs, which shows what they have achieved or what level they have reached. *score, puntuación* ❑ *The U.S. Open golf tournament was won by Ben Hogan, with a score of 287. El Abierto de golf de Estados Unidos lo ganó Ben Hogan, con 287 golpes.* **4** N-COUNT The **score** in a game is the result of it up to a particular time, as indicated by the number of goals, runs, or points obtained by the two teams or players. *marcador* ❑ *4–1 was the final score. El marcador final fue de 4 a 1.* **5** V-T If you **score** a success, a victory, or a hit, you are successful in what you are doing. *lograr, conseguir* [WRITTEN] ❑ *The play scored a success on Broadway, winning a couple of awards. La obra fue un éxito en Broadway, se sacó dos premios.* **6** N-COUNT The **score** of a piece of music is the written version of it. *partitura* ❑ *He knows enough music to be able to follow a score. Sabe suficiente música como para interpretar una partitura.* **7** QUANT If you refer to **scores of** things or people, you are emphasizing that there are very many of them. *gran cantidad* [WRITTEN] ❑ *Scores of buses transported the elderly from a nearby hospital. Los ancianos fueron evacuados del hospital cercano en muchos autobuses.* **8** V-T If you **score** a surface with something sharp, you cut a line or number of lines in it. *hacer cortes* ❑ *Score the surface of the steaks with a sharp knife. Haz algunos cortes en los bisteces con un cuchillo filoso.* **9** PHRASE You can use **on that score** or **on this score** to refer to something that has just been mentioned, especially an area of difficulty or concern. *a ese respecto, en cuanto a eso* ❑ *On that score I can say very little. Muy poco tengo que decir al respecto.* **10** PHRASE If you **settle a score** or **settle an old score with** someone, you take revenge on them for something they have done in the past. *ajustar cuentas pendientes, saldar cuentas* ❑ *The groups had old scores to settle with each other. Los grupos tenían cuentas pendientes que saldar.*
→ see **music**

**scout** /skaʊt/ (**scouts, scouting, scouted**) **1** N-COUNT A **scout** is someone who is sent to an area of countryside to find out the position of an enemy army. *avanzada, patrulla de reconocimiento* ❑ *They set off, with two men out in front as scouts. Emprendieron camino, con dos hombres de avanzada.* **2** V-T/V-I If you **scout** somewhere **for** something, you go through that area searching for it. *buscar algo, reconocer el terreno* ❑ *The girls scouted the site for* *materials people had left behind.* *Las niñas revisaron el sitio para recoger lo que la gente olvida.* ❑ *A team was sent to scout for a nuclear test site.* *Se envió un equipo a buscar un sitio para pruebas nucleares.*

**scrag|gly** /skrægli/ (**scragglier, scraggliest**) ADJ **Scraggly** hair or plants are thin and messy. *ralo* ❑ *He had a scraggly mustache.* *Su bigote era ralo.*

**scram|ble** /skræmbəl/ (**scrambles, scrambling, scrambled**) **1** V-I If you **scramble** over rocks or up a hill, you move quickly over them or up it using your hands to help you. *abrirse paso con dificultad, trepar* ❑ *Tourists were scrambling over the rocks to the beach.* *Los turistas se trepaban por las rocas para llegar a la playa.* **2** V-I If you **scramble** to a different place or position, you move there in a hurried, awkward way. *apresurarse* ❑ *Ann scrambled out of bed.* *Ann saltó de la cama.* **3** V-T/V-I If a number of people **scramble for** something, they compete energetically with each other for it. *amontonarse, pelear por algo, andar a la rebatiña* ❑ *More than a million fans scrambled for tickets.* *Más de un millón de admiradores se arrebataban los boletos.* ● **Scramble** is also a noun. *rebatiña, relajo, confusión, prisa* ❑ *Then it's a scramble for jobs.* *Después viene la rebatiña por los puestos.* **4** V-T If you **scramble** eggs, you break them, mix them together, and then cook them in butter. *revolver, batir* ❑ *Make the toast and scramble the eggs.* *Tuesta el pan y revuelve los huevos.* ● **scram|bled** ADJ *revuelto* ❑ *It's just scrambled eggs and bacon.* *No son más que huevos revueltos y tocino.*
→ see **egg**

**scrap** /skræp/ (**scraps, scrapping, scrapped**) **1** N-COUNT A **scrap of** something is a very small piece or amount of it. *pedacito, pizca* ❑ *A scrap of red paper was found in her handbag.* *En su bolsa encontraron un pedacito de papel rojo.* **2** N-PLURAL **Scraps** are pieces of unwanted food which are thrown away or given to animals. *restos, desechos, sobras* **3** V-T If you **scrap** something, you get rid of it or cancel it. *descartar, deshacerse de algo, desechar, abandonar* ❑ *The president called on Middle Eastern countries to scrap nuclear weapons.* *El presidente pidió a los países de Medio Oriente que desechen las armas nucleares.* **4** N-UNCOUNT **Scrap** is metal from old or damaged machinery or cars. *chatarra, desperdicio* ❑ *...a truck piled with scrap metal.* *...un camión cargado de chatarra.*

**scrape** /skreɪp/ (**scrapes, scraping, scraped**) **1** V-T If you **scrape** something from a surface, you remove it, especially by pulling a sharp object over the surface. *rascar, raspar* ❑ *She scraped the frost off the car windows.* *Raspó el hielo de las ventanillas del carro.* **2** V-T/V-I If something **scrapes** against something else, it rubs against it, making a noise or causing slight damage. *rozar, raspar, rayar* ❑ *The only sound is knives and forks scraping against plates.* *Lo único que se oía eran los cubiertos chocando con los platos.* ❑ *The car passed us, scraping the wall as it went.* *El auto nos rebasó, raspando la pared.* ● **scrap|ing** N-SING *arrastrar* ❑ *...the scraping of a chair across the floor.* *...el chirrido de la silla al arrastrarla.* **3** V-T If you **scrape** a part of your body, you accidentally rub it against something hard and rough, and damage it slightly. *raspar(se)* ❑ *She fell, scraping her hands and knees.* *Se cayó y se raspó las manos y las rodillas.*
▸ **scrape through** PHR-VERB If you **scrape through** an examination, you just succeed in passing it. *pasar de panzazo, pasar a duras penas, pasar apenas* ❑ *He only just scraped through his final year.* *A duras penas acabó el último año.*
▸ **scrape together** PHR-VERB If you **scrape together** an amount of money or a number of things, you succeed in obtaining it with difficulty. *juntar a duras penas, conseguir con trabajos* ❑ *They just managed to scrape the money together.* *Se las arreglaron para reunir el dinero.*

**scratch** /skrætʃ/ (**scratches, scratching, scratched**) **1** V-T/V-I If you **scratch yourself**, you rub your fingernails against your skin because it is itching. *rascar(se), arañar(se), rasguñar(se)* ❑ *He scratched himself under his arm.* *Se rascó abajo del brazo.* ❑ *She scratched her nose.* *Se rasguñó la nariz.*

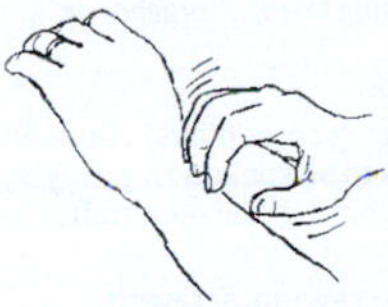
scratch

**2** V-T If a sharp object **scratches** someone or something, it makes small shallow cuts on their skin or surface. *rasguñar* ❑ *The branches scratched my face.* *Me rasguñé la cara con las ramas.* **3** N-COUNT **Scratches** on someone or something are small shallow cuts. *rasguño, arañazo* ❑ *He was found with scratches on his face and neck.* *Lo encontraron con rasguños en la cara y el cuello.* **4** PHRASE If you do something **from scratch**, you do it without making use of anything that has been done before. *de cero, desde cero* ❑ *Building a home from scratch can be very exciting.* *Puede ser muy emocionante construir su propia casa desde cero.*

**scratch card** (**scratch cards**) also **scratchcard** N-COUNT A **scratch card** is a card with hidden words or symbols on it. You scratch the surface off to reveal the words or symbols and find out if you have won a prize. *tarjeta para raspar*

**scream** /skrim/ (**screams, screaming, screamed**) **1** V-I When someone **screams**, they make a very loud, high-pitched cry, for example, because they are in pain or are very frightened. *gritar, berrear, dar alaridos, vociferar* ❑ *Women were screaming in the houses nearest the fire.* *Las mujeres de las casas vecinas al incendio daban de gritos.* ● **Scream** is also a noun. *grito, alarido, chillido* ❑ *Hilda let out a scream.* *Hilda lanzó un grito.* **2** V-T If you **scream** something, you shout it in a loud, high-pitched voice. *gritar* ❑ *"Brigid!" she screamed.* *—¡Brigid! —gritó.*

**screen** /skrin/ (**screens, screening, screened**) **1** N-COUNT A **screen** is a flat vertical surface on which pictures or words are shown. Television sets and computers have screens, and movies are shown on a screen in movie theaters. *pantalla* **2** → see also **widescreen** **3** V-T When a movie or a television program **is screened,** it is shown in the movie theater or broadcast on television. *pasar, proyectar* ❑ *The series will be screened in January.* *En enero van a pasar la serie.* ● **screen|ing** N-COUNT (**screenings**) *proyección, emisión* ❑ *The movie-makers will be at the screenings to introduce their works.* *Quienes hicieron la película van a estar el día de la proyección para presentar su trabajo.* **4** N-COUNT A **screen** is a vertical panel which can be used to separate different parts of a room. *mampara, biombo* ❑ *There was a screen in front of me so I couldn't*

see what was going on. Había un biombo frente de mí, así que no pude ver lo que estaba pasando. **5** V-T If something **is screened by** another thing, it is behind it and hidden by it. *ocultar, tapar* ❑ *The road was screened by an apartment building. Un edificio de departamentos tapaba el camino.* **6** V-T/V-I To **screen** people **for** a disease means to examine people to make sure that they do not have it. *someter a revisión médica* ❑ *All states now screen for the condition. Ahora en todos los estados se hacen exámenes médicos para detectar la enfermedad.* • **screen|ing** N-VAR *detección* ❑ *...cancer-screening tests. ...pruebas de detección del cáncer.*
→ see **computer, television**

**screen|play** /skrinpleɪ/ (**screenplays**) N-COUNT A **screenplay** is the words to be spoken in a movie, and instructions about what will be seen in it. *guión*

**screw** /skru/ (**screws, screwing, screwed**) **1** N-COUNT A **screw** is a metal object similar to a nail, with a raised spiral line around it. You turn a screw using a screwdriver so that it goes through two things, for example, two pieces of wood, and fastens them together. *tornillo* ❑ *Each shelf is fixed to the wall with screws. Los anaqueles se fijan al muro con tornillos.* **2** V-T/V-I If you **screw** something somewhere or if it **screws** somewhere, you fix it in place by means of a screw or screws. *atornillar, instalar con tornillos* ❑ *I screwed the shelf on the wall myself. Yo mismo atornillé el estante a la pared.* ❑ *Screw down any loose floorboards. Atornilla las tablas del piso que estén sueltas.* **3** V-T/V-I If you **screw** something somewhere or if it **screws** somewhere, you fix it in place by twisting it around and around. *apretar, enroscar, atornillar* ❑ *"Ready?" asked Kelly, screwing the lens on the camera. —¿Listos?—preguntó Kelly, mientras le ponía el lente a la cámara.* ❑ *Screw down the lid tightly. Enrosca firmemente la tapa.* **4** V-T If you **screw** your face or your eyes **into** a particular expression, you tighten the muscles of your face to form that expression, for example, because you are in pain or because the light is too bright. *hacer muecas, torcer el gesto* ❑ *He screwed his face into an expression of pain. Hizo una mueca de dolor.*
▸ **screw up** PHR-VERB To **screw** something **up,** or to **screw up,** means to cause something to fail or be spoiled. *fastidiar algo, echar a perder* [INFORMAL] ❑ *Don't open the window because it screws up the air conditioning. No abras la ventana porque se arruina el aire acondicionado.* ❑ *Get out! You've screwed things up enough already! ¡Vete! ¡Ya complicaste bastante las cosas!*

S

**screw|driver** /skrudraɪvər/ (**screwdrivers**) N-COUNT A **screwdriver** is a tool that is used for turning screws. *desarmador, desatornillador*
→ see **tool**

**scrim|mage** /skrɪmɪdʒ/ (**scrimmages**) **1** N-COUNT In football, **scrimmage** is the action during a single period of play. *partido, juego* ❑ *Bloom scored two touchdowns Saturday in a scrimmage. Bloom logró dos anotaciones de seis puntos en el partido del sábado.* **2** N-COUNT In sports such as football and hockey, a **scrimmage** is a session of practice that consists of an actual game. *sesión de entrenamiento, partido de práctica* ❑ *It was the first full scrimmage in Flyers training camp. Fue el primer partido de práctica completo que jugaron en el campo de los Flyers.*

**script** /skrɪpt/ (**scripts**) **1** N-COUNT The **script** of a play, movie, or television program is the written version of it. *guión* ❑ *Jenny's writing a movie script. Jenny está escribiendo el guión para una película.* **2** N-VAR You can refer to a particular system of writing as a particular **script.** *letra, caligrafía, escritura* ❑ *The text is in Arabic script. El texto está en caracteres arábigos.*
→ see **animation**

**scroll bar** (**scroll bars**) N-COUNT On a computer screen, a **scroll bar** is a long thin box along one edge of a window, which you click on with the mouse to move the text up, down, or across the window. *barra deslizable, scroll bar* [COMPUTING]

**scro|tum** /skroutəm/ (**scrotums**) N-COUNT A man's **scrotum** is the bag of skin that contains his testicles. *escroto*

**scrub** /skrʌb/ (**scrubs, scrubbing, scrubbed**) **1** V-T If you **scrub** something, you rub it hard in order to clean it, using a stiff brush and water. *restregar, tallar, fregar* ❑ *Surgeons must scrub their hands and arms with soap and water. Los cirujanos deben tallarse las manos y los brazos con jabón y agua.* • **Scrub** is also a noun. *tallada, restregada* ❑ *The walls needed a good scrub. Las paredes necesitaban una buena tallada.* **2** N-UNCOUNT **Scrub** consists of low trees and bushes, especially in an area that has very little rain. *maleza, matorral* ❑ *There is an area of scrub beside the railroad. Al lado de las vías del tren hay un área de matorrales.* **3** N-PLURAL **Scrubs** are the protective clothes that surgeons and other hospital staff wear in operating rooms. *bata* [INFORMAL] ❑ *The men wore blue hospital scrubs. Los hombres llevaban batas de cirujano de color azul.*

**scrub|ber** /skrʌbər/ (**scrubbers**) N-COUNT A **scrubber** is a device that removes pollution from gases that are released into the atmosphere, for example from a factory furnace. *depurador de gases*

**scrunchie** /skrʌntʃi/ (**scrunchies**) also **scrunchy** N-COUNT A **scrunchie** is an elastic band that is covered with material and is used to tie back your hair, for example in a ponytail. *dona, liga*

**scru|ti|ny** /skrutᵊni/ N-UNCOUNT If a person or thing is under **scrutiny,** they are being studied or observed very carefully. *observación* ❑ *His private life came under public scrutiny. Su vida privada llegó a ser del dominio público.*

**sculp|ture** /skʌlptʃər/ (**sculptures**) **1** N-VAR A **sculpture** is a three-dimensional work of art that is produced by carving or shaping stone, wood, clay, or other materials. *escultura, estatua* ❑ *There were stone sculptures of different animals. Había esculturas de piedra de diferentes animales.* **2** N-UNCOUNT **Sculpture** is the art of creating sculptures. *escultura* ❑ *Both of them studied sculpture. Ambos estudiaron escultura.*

**scut|tle** /skʌtᵊl/ (**scuttles, scuttling, scuttled**) V-I When people or small animals **scuttle** somewhere, they run there with short quick steps. *escabullirse* ❑ *Two small children scuttled away in front of them. Dos niñitos se echaron a correr frente a ellos.*

**sea** /si/ (**seas**) **1** N-SING **The sea** is the salty water that covers about three-quarters of the Earth's surface. *mar, océano* ❑ *The kids have never seen the sea. Los niños nunca han visto el mar.* **2** N-PLURAL You use **seas** when you are describing the sea at a particular time or in a particular area. *mares, aguas del mar* [LITERARY] ❑ *The seas are warm further south. Más al sur, las aguas del mar son tibias.* **3** N-COUNT A **sea** is a large area of salty water that is part of an ocean or is surrounded by land. *mar* ❑ *...the North Sea. ...el Mar del Norte.* **4** PHRASE **At sea** means on or under the sea, far away from land. *en el mar, en alta mar* ❑ *The boats are at sea for ten days at a time. Los botes están en alta mar diez días cada vez.*

**Word Partnership** Usar *sea* con:

| | |
|---|---|
| PREP. | **above the** sea, **across the** sea, **below the** sea, **beneath the** sea, **by** sea, **from the** sea, **into the** sea, **near the** sea, **over the** sea **1** |
| N. | sea **air**, sea **coast**, **land and** sea, sea **voyage** **1** |
| ADJ. | **calm** sea, **deep** sea **1** |

**sea-floor spread|ing** N-UNCOUNT **Sea-floor spreading** is the expansion of the ocean floor that occurs when two tectonic plates move apart and new rock is formed. *expansión del fondo del mar, expansión del fondo oceánico* [TECHNICAL]

**sea|food** /si̲fud/ (**seafoods**) N-VAR **Seafood** is shellfish and other sea creatures that you can eat. *marisco* ❑ *Let's find a seafood restaurant. Busquemos un restaurante de mariscos.*

**sea|gull** /si̲gʌl/ (**seagulls**) N-COUNT A **seagull** is a common kind of bird with white or gray feathers that lives near the ocean. *gaviota*

**sea|horse** /si̲hɔrs/ (**seahorses**) also **sea horse** N-COUNT A **seahorse** is a type of small fish which appears to swim in a vertical position and whose head looks a little like the head of a horse. *caballito de mar, hipocampo, caballo marino*

**seal**
❶ CLOSING
❷ ANIMAL

❶ **seal** /si̲l/ (**seals, sealing, sealed**) **1** V-T When you **seal** an envelope, you close it by folding part of it over and sticking it down. *sellar, cerrar* ❑ *He sealed the envelope and put on a stamp. Pegó el sobre y le puso un timbre.* ❑ *Write your letter and seal it in a new envelope. Escribe tu carta y guárdala en otro sobre sellado.* **2** V-T If you **seal** a container or an opening, you cover it with something in order to prevent air, liquid, or other material from getting in or out. If you **seal** something **in** a container, you put it inside and then close the container tightly. *sellar* ❑ *She filled the containers, sealed them, and stuck on labels. Llenó los envases, los tapó herméticamente y les pegó las etiquetas.* ❑ *A woman picks the parts up and seals them in plastic bags. Una mujer escoge las piezas y las pone en bolsas de plástico con cierre hermético.* **3** N-COUNT The **seal** on a container or opening is the part where it has been sealed. *sello* ❑ *Wet the edges of the pie and join them to form a seal. Humedece las orillas del pay y únelas, para que no se salga el relleno.* **4** N-COUNT A **seal** is a device or a piece of material, for example, in a machine, which closes an opening tightly so that air, liquid, or other substances cannot get in or out. *sello hermético* ❑ *Check the seal on the fridge regularly. Revisa regularmente el sello del refrigerador.* **5** N-COUNT A **seal** is a special mark or design, for example, on a document, representing someone or something. It may be used to show that something is genuine or officially approved. *sello* ❑ *The notepaper carries the presidential seal. El papel membretado lleva el sello presidencial.* **6** V-T If someone in authority **seals** an area, they stop people from entering or passing through it, for example, by placing barriers in the way. *cerrar* ❑ *The soldiers were told to seal the border. Las instrucciones de los soldados eran cerrar la frontera.* • **Seal off** means the same as **seal**. *sellar, cerrar* ❑ *Police sealed off the area after the attack. La policía acordonó el área después del ataque.*

❷ **seal** /si̲l/ (**seals**) N-COUNT A **seal** is a large animal with a rounded body and flat legs called flippers. Seals eat fish and live in and near the ocean. *foca*

**sea lev|el** also **sea-level** N-UNCOUNT **Sea level** is the average level of the ocean with respect to the land. The height of mountains or other areas is calculated in relation to **sea level**. *nivel del mar* ❑ *The stadium was 5,000 feet above sea level. El estadio estaba a 2,000 metros sobre el nivel del mar.* ❑ *The whole place is at sea level. Toda la zona está al nivel del mar.*
→ see **glacier**

**seam** /si̲m/ (**seams**) **1** N-COUNT A **seam** is a line of stitches which joins two pieces of cloth together. *costura* ❑ *The skirt tore open along a seam. A la falda se le abrió una costura.* **2** N-COUNT A **seam** of coal is a long, narrow layer of it underneath the ground. *filón* ❑ *The average coal seam here is three feet thick. Aquí, el grosor promedio de los filones de carbón es un metro.* **3** PHRASE If a place is very full, you can say that it **is bursting at the seams.** *estar a punto de estallar, retacado* ❑ *The hotels of Warsaw were bursting at the seams. Los hoteles de Varsovia estaban llenos a reventar.*

**sea|mount** /si̲maʊnt/ (**seamounts**) N-COUNT A **seamount** is a mountain that lies beneath the surface of the ocean. *montaña submarina* [TECHNICAL]

**search** /sɜ̲rtʃ/ (**searches, searching, searched**) **1** V-I If you **search for** something or someone, you look carefully for them. *buscar* ❑ *Police are already searching for the men. La policía ya está buscando a los hombres.* ❑ *They searched for a space to sit on the floor. Buscaban un lugar para sentarse en el piso.* **2** V-T/V-I If you **search** a place, you look carefully for something or someone there. *registrar, catear* ❑ *The police are searching for the missing men. La policía está buscando a los hombres que faltan.* ❑ *She searched for the papers but couldn't find them. Buscó los papeles, pero no pudo encontrarlos.* **3** N-COUNT A **search** is an attempt to find something or someone by looking for them carefully. *búsqueda* ❑ *The search is being stopped because of the heavy snow. La búsqueda se interrumpió por lo intenso de la nevada.* **4** V-T If a police officer or someone else in authority **searches** you, they look carefully to see whether you have something hidden on you. *registrar, catear* ❑ *Of course the police searched her. Por supuesto la policía la registró.* **5** PHRASE If you go **in search of** something or someone, you try to find them. *en busca de* ❑ *She went in search of Jean-Paul. Se fue en busca de Jean-Paul.*

S

**Word Partnership** Usar *search* con:

N. search **for clues, police** search 1–4
search **for information** 1 3
**investigators** search 1 2 4
search **for a job,** search **for the truth** 1 3
search **an area** 2
**talent** search 3
search **suspects** 4
V. **conduct a** search 3

**search and res|cue** also **search-and-rescue** N-UNCOUNT **Search and rescue** operations involve looking for people who are lost or in danger and bringing them back safely. *búsqueda y rescate* ❑ *A search and rescue team found the man about 12:30 p.m. Un equipo de búsqueda y rescate encontró al hombre como a las 12:30 pm.*

**search en|gine** (**search engines**) N-COUNT A **search engine** is a computer program that searches for documents containing a particular word or words on the Internet. *máquina de búsqueda, herramienta de búsqueda* [COMPUTING]

**sea|side** /sisaɪd/ N-SING You can refer to an area that is close to the ocean, especially one where people go for their vacation, as **the seaside.** *costa, playa, balneario* ❑ *I spent a few days at the seaside. Pasé unos días a la orilla del mar.*

**sea|son** /sizᵊn/ (**seasons, seasoning, seasoned**) 1 N-COUNT The **seasons** are the periods into which a year can be divided and which each have their own typical weather conditions. *estación, estación del año* ❑ *Fall is my favorite season. El otoño es mi estación favorita.* 2 N-COUNT You can use **season** to refer to the period during each year when something happens. *estación, temporada* ❑ *Then the birds arrive for the nesting season. Entonces llegan los pájaros a anidar.* ❑ *...the baseball season. ...la temporada de béisbol.* 3 V-T If you **season** food with salt, pepper, or spices, you add them to it in order to improve its flavor. *sazonar, aderezar, condimentar* ❑ *Season the meat with salt and pepper. Ponle sal y pimienta a la carne.*

**sea|son|al** /sizənᵊl/ ADJ A **seasonal** factor, event, or change occurs during one particular time of the year. *de temporada, estacional* ❑ *The seasonal workers will return from Mexico in the next few months. Los trabajadores temporales regresarán de México en los próximos meses.* • **sea|son|al|ly** ADV *en cada estación, cada temporada* ❑ *Restaurant menus change seasonally here. Aquí los menús de los restaurantes cambian con la temporada.*

S

**sea star** (**sea stars**) also **seastar** N-COUNT A **sea star** is a flat, star-shaped creature, usually with five arms, that lives in the sea. *estrella de mar*

**seat** /sit/ (**seats, seating, seated**) 1 N-COUNT A **seat** is an object that you can sit on, for example, a chair. *asiento* ❑ *Stephen returned to his seat. Stephen volvió a su asiento.* 2 N-COUNT The **seat** of a chair is the part that you sit on. *asiento* ❑ *The sofa had a red plastic seat. El asiento del sofá era de plástico rojo.* 3 V-T If you **seat yourself** somewhere, you sit down. *sentar(se)* [WRITTEN] ❑ *He seated himself at his desk. Se sentó ante su escritorio.* 4 V-T A building or vehicle that **seats** a particular number of people has enough seats for that number. *tener cupo para* ❑ *The theater seats 570 people. El teatro tiene 570 localidades.* 5 N-COUNT When someone is elected to a legislature you can say that they, or their party, have won a **seat.** *escaño, curul* ❑ *Men won the majority of seats on the council. La mayoría de los escaños fueron para hombres.* 6 N-COUNT If someone has a **seat** on the board of a company or on a committee, they are a member of it. *ser miembro de* ❑ *He has been trying to win a seat on the board of the company. Ha estado tratando de ganarse un lugar en el consejo de directores de la compañía.* 7 → see also **deep-seated** 8 PHRASE If you **take a back seat,** you allow other people to have all the power and to make all the decisions. *mantenerse al margen* ❑ *You need to take a back seat and think about the future. Tienes que mantenerte al margen y pensar en el futuro.* 9 PHRASE If you **take a seat,** you sit down. *sentar(se)* [FORMAL] ❑ *"Take a seat," he said. —Siéntate —le dijo.*

**Word Partnership** Usar *seat* con:

ADJ. **back** seat, **empty** seat, **front** seat 1
**vacant** seat, **vacated** seat 1 6
**congressional** seat 5
N. **car** seat, **child** seat, **driver's** seat, **passenger** seat, seat **at a table, theater** seat, **toilet** seat 1
seat **in the House/Senate** 5
seat **on the board** 6

seat belt

**seat belt** (**seat belts**) N-COUNT A **seat belt** is a strap attached to a seat in a car or airplane. You fasten it around your body and it stops you from being thrown forward if there is an accident. *cinturón de seguridad* ❑ *Please fasten your seat belts. Favor de abrocharse el cinturón de seguridad.* → see **car**

**sea tur|tle** (**sea turtles**) N-COUNT A **sea turtle** is a large reptile which has a thick shell covering its body and which lives in the ocean most of the time. *tortuga marina*

**sea|weed** /siwid/ (**seaweeds**) N-VAR **Seaweed** is a plant that grows in the ocean. *alga marina, alga* ❑ *Seaweed is washed up on the beach. La corriente lleva las algas a la playa.*

**SEC** /ɛs i si/ N-PROPER In the United States, **the SEC** is a government agency that regulates the buying and selling of stocks and bonds. **SEC** is an abbreviation for "Securities and Exchange Commission." *SEC, Comisión Controladora de Acciones y Valores* ❑ *The President believes the SEC is doing an excellent job. El Presidente piensa que la SEC está haciendo un excelente trabajo.*

**second**
❶ PART OF A MINUTE
❷ COMING AFTER SOMETHING ELSE

❶ **sec|ond** /sɛkənd/ (**seconds**) N-COUNT A **second** is one of the sixty parts that a minute

is divided into. People often say "**a second**" or "**seconds**" when they simply mean a very short time. *segundo* ❑ *For a few seconds nobody spoke. Nadie habló durante unos segundos.* ❑ *It only takes forty seconds. No tarda más que cuarenta segundos.*
→ see **time**

❷ **sec|ond** /sɛkənd/ (**seconds, seconding, seconded**)
→ Please look at category 7 to see if the expression you are looking for is shown under another headword. 1 ORD The **second** item in a series is the one that you count as number two. *segundo* ❑ *It was the second day of his visit to Florida. Era el segundo día de su visita a Florida.* ❑ *He is their second child. Es su segundo hijo.* ❑ *...the Second World War. ...la Segunda Guerra Mundial.* ❑ *The party is the second strongest in Italy. El partido es el segundo más fuerte de Italia.* ❑ *First, all children must start school ready to learn; and second, the high school graduation rate must increase. Primero, los niños deben empezar la escuela cuando estén listos para aprender, y segundo, debe incrementarse el porcentaje de graduados de secundaria.* 2 N-COUNT **Seconds** are goods that are sold cheaply in stores because they have slight faults. *segundas* ❑ *These are not seconds, but first-quality products. No son segundas, sino productos de primera calidad.* 3 V-T If you **second** a proposal in a meeting or debate, you formally express your agreement with it so that it can then be discussed or voted on. *secundar, apoyar* ❑ *The members proposed and seconded his nomination. Los miembros propusieron y secundaron su nominación.* 4 V-T If you **second** what someone has said, you say that you agree with them or say the same thing yourself. *apoyar, favorecer* ❑ *All the other girls seconded her idea. Todas las demás niñas estuvieron de acuerdo con su idea.* 5 PHRASE If you say that something is **second to none,** you are emphasizing that it is very good indeed or the best that there is. *sin comparación, sin par* ❑ *Our scientific research is second to none. Nuestra investigación científica es insuperable.* 6 PHRASE If you say that something is **second only to** something else, you mean that only that thing is better or greater than it. *sólo superado por* ❑ *India is second only to China with a population of 1.1 billion. Con una población de 1.1 miles de millones, a la India sólo la supera China.* 7 **second nature** → see **nature**

**sec|ond|ary** /sɛkənderi/ 1 ADJ If you describe something as **secondary,** you mean that it is less important than something else. *secundario, de menor importancia* ❑ *After the bomb fell there were secondary explosions in other buildings. Después de que cayó la bomba, hubo explosiones más pequeñas en otros edificios.* ❑ *Money is of secondary importance to them. Para ellos el dinero es menos importante.* 2 ADJ **Secondary** education is given to students between the ages of 11 or 12 and 17 or 18. *secundaria, segunda enseñanza* ❑ *They take examinations after five years of secondary education. Se examinan después de cinco años de educación secundaria.*

**sec|ond|ary col|or** (**secondary colors**) N-COUNT **Secondary colors** are colors such as orange and violet that are a mixture of two primary colors. *color secundario*
→ see **color**

**sec|ond|ary pol|lu|tant** (**secondary pollutants**) N-COUNT **Secondary pollutants** are pollutants that are created by chemical reactions in the atmosphere. Compare **primary pollutant**. *contaminante secundario, contaminante derivado* [TECHNICAL]

**second-class** also **second class** ADJ **Second-class** things are regarded as less valuable and less important than others of the same kind. *de segunda, de menor calidad* ❑ *The airlines treat children as second-class citizens. En las líneas aéreas tratan a los niños como a ciudadanos de segunda.* ❑ *...a second-class education. ...educación de menor calidad.*

**second|hand** /sɛkəndhænd/ also **second-hand** 1 ADJ **Secondhand** things are not new and have been owned by someone else. *de segunda mano, usado* ❑ *They could just afford a secondhand car. Apenas les alcanzó para comprarse un coche usado.* • **Secondhand** is also an adverb. *de segunda mano* ❑ *They bought the furniture secondhand. Compraron los muebles de segunda mano.* 2 ADJ A **secondhand** store sells secondhand goods. *de segunda mano, cosas usadas* ❑ *These are old pieces bought from a secondhand store. Estas cosas viejas se compraron en una tienda de segunda mano.* 3 ADJ **Secondhand** stories, information, or opinions are those you learn about from other people rather than directly or from your own experience. *de segunda mano, a través de terceros* ❑ *The progress reports are based on secondhand information. Los reportes de avance están basados en información de terceros.* • **Secondhand** is also an adverb. *segunda mano* ❑ *I heard about it secondhand. Me enteré de segunda mano.*

**second|hand smoke** also **second-hand smoke** N-UNCOUNT **Secondhand smoke** is tobacco smoke that people breathe in because other people around them are smoking. *humo de terceros*

**sec|ond|ly** /sɛkəndli/ ADV You say **secondly** when you want to make a second point or give a second reason for something. *en segundo lugar* ❑ *Think firstly how you're treated and secondly how you treat everybody else. Piensa primero en cómo te tratan, y después, en cómo tratas a todos los demás.*

**se|cre|cy** /sikrəsi/ N-UNCOUNT **Secrecy** is the act of keeping something secret, or the state of being kept secret. *secreto, reserva, sigilo* ❑ *They met in complete secrecy. Se reunieron en secreto.*

**se|cret** /sikrɪt/ (**secrets**) 1 ADJ If something is **secret,** it is known about by only a small number of people, and is not told or shown to anyone else. *secreto* ❑ *They tried to keep their marriage secret. Trataron de mantener su matrimonio en secreto.* • **se|cret|ly** ADV *secretamente, en secreto* ❑ *He wore a microphone to secretly record conversations. Llevaba un micrófono para grabar las conversaciones sin que se dieran cuenta.* 2 N-COUNT A **secret** is a fact that is known by only a small number of people, and is not told to anyone else. *secreto* ❑ *I think he enjoyed keeping our secret. Creo que disfrutaba guardando nuestro secreto.* 3 N-SING If a particular way of doing things is **the secret of** achieving something, it is the best or only way to achieve it. *secreto* ❑ *The secret of success is honesty. El secreto del éxito es la honestidad.* 4 PHRASE If you do something **in secret,** you do it without anyone else knowing. *en secreto* ❑ *Dan found out that we were meeting in secret. Dan se enteró de que nos estábamos viendo a escondidas.*

S

**Thesaurus** *secret* Ver también:

ADJ. hidden, private, unknown; (*ant.*) known 1

**sec|re|tary** /sɛkrɪtɛri/ (**secretaries**) 1 N-COUNT A **secretary** is a person who is employed to do office work, such as typing letters, answering phone calls, and arranging meetings. *secretaria o secretario* 2 N-COUNT The **secretary** of a company is the person who has the legal duty of keeping the company's records. *secretario o secretaria* 3 N-COUNT; N-TITLE **Secretary** is used in the titles of high officials who are in charge of main government departments. *secretario o secretaria, ministro o ministra* ❑ *...the Venezuelan foreign secretary. ...el ministro de relaciones exteriores de Venezuela.*

**Sec|re|tary of State** (**Secretaries of State**) N-COUNT In the United States, **the Secretary of State** is the head of the government department which deals with foreign affairs. *Secretario de Estado o Secretaria de Estado, Ministro de Relaciones Exteriores o Ministra de Relaciones Exteriores*

**se|cret ser|vice** (**secret services**) 1 N-COUNT A country's **secret service** is a secret government department whose job is to find out enemy secrets and to prevent its own government's secrets from being discovered. *servicio secreto, servicios de inteligencia* ❑ *...French secret service agents. ...agentes del servicio secreto francés.* 2 N-COUNT **The Secret Service** is the government department in the United States which protects the president, the vice president, and their families. *Servicio Secreto* ❑ *The Secret Service arrested 19 people outside the White House today. El Servicio Secreto arrestó hoy a 19 personas en los alrededores de la Casa Blanca.*

**sect** /sɛkt/ (**sects**) N-COUNT A **sect** is a group of people that has separated from a larger group and has a particular set of religious or political beliefs. *secta*

**Word Link** *arian* ≈ *believing in, having* : *humanitarian, sectarian, vegetarian*

**Word Link** *sect* ≈ *cutting* : *sectarian, section, sector*

S

**sec|tar|ian** /sɛktɛəriən/ ADJ **Sectarian** means resulting from the differences between different religions. *sectario, confesional* ❑ *He was killed in sectarian violence. Lo mataron en actos de violencia sectaria.* ❑ *The police said the murder was sectarian. La policía dijo que lo asesinaron por motivos religiosos.*

**sec|tion** /sɛkʃᵊn/ (**sections**) 1 N-COUNT A **section** of something is one of the parts into which it is divided or from which it is formed. *sección, parte, porción, sector* ❑ *He said it was wrong to blame one section of society. Dijo que no había razón para culpar a una parte de la sociedad.* ❑ *...the Georgetown section of Washington, D.C. ...la sección de Georgetown de Washington, D.C.* 2 → see also **cross-section**

**Word Partnership** Usar *section* con:

ADJ. **main** section, **new** section, **special** section, **thin** section 1
N. section **of a city**, section **of a coast**, **rhythm** section, **sports** section 1

**sec|tor** /sɛktər/ (**sectors**) N-COUNT A **sector** of something, especially a country's economy, is one of the parts that it is divided into. *sector, industria* ❑ *...the nation's manufacturing sector. ...el sector manufacturero del país.* ❑ *These workers came from the poorest sectors of society. Estos trabajadores provienen de los sectores más pobres de la sociedad.*

**Word Partnership** Usar *sector* con:

N. **banking** sector, **business** sector, **government** sector, **growth in a** sector, **job in a** sector, **manufacturing** sector, **technology** sector, **telecommunications** sector

**secu|lar** /sɛkyələr/ ADJ You use **secular** to describe things that have no connection with religion. *seglar, laico, secular* ❑ *He spoke about keeping the country as a secular state. Habló de que el país debe seguir siendo un estado laico.*

**se|cure** /sɪkyʊər/ (**secures, securing, secured**) 1 V-T If you **secure** something that you want or need, you obtain it, often after a lot of effort. *asegurar(se), garantizar* [FORMAL] ❑ *Western lawyers are trying to secure his release. Los abogados occidentales están intentando asegurar su liberación.* 2 V-T If you **secure** a place, you make it safe from harm or attack. *asegurar, proteger* [FORMAL] ❑ *Their mission is to secure the city's airport. Su misión es proteger el aeropuerto de la ciudad.* 3 ADJ A **secure** place is tightly locked or well protected, so that people cannot enter it or leave it. *seguro* ❑ *We'll make our home as secure as possible. Haremos de nuestra casa el lugar más seguro posible.* • **se|cure|ly** ADV *bien* ❑ *He locked the heavy door securely. Cerró muy bien la pesada puerta.* 4 V-T If you **secure** an object, you fasten it firmly to another object. *asegurar* ❑ *He secured the rope to the front of the boat. Amarró la cuerda al frente del bote.* 5 ADJ If an object is **secure,** it is fixed firmly in position. *asegurado, fijo* ❑ *Check that the wooden joints are secure. Asegúrese de que las juntas de la madera estén firmes.* • **se|cure|ly** ADV *adecuadamente* ❑ *He fastened his belt securely. Se abrochó el cinturón como debe ser.* 6 ADJ If you describe something such as a job as **secure,** it is certain not to change or end. *seguro* ❑ *For the moment, his job is secure. Por el momento, su empleo está asegurado.* 7 ADJ If you feel **secure,** you feel safe and happy and are not worried about life. *seguro* ❑ *She felt secure when she was with him. Cuando estaba con él se sentía segura.*

**Thesaurus** *secure* Ver también:

V. catch, get, obtain; (*ant.*) lose 1
attach, fasten 4
ADJ. safe, sheltered 3
locked, tight 5

**Word Partnership** Usar *secure* con:

N. secure **a job/place/position**, secure **a loan**, secure **peace**, secure ***your* rights** 1
secure **borders** 3
secure **future**, secure **jobs** 6
ADV. **less** secure, **more** secure 3 5 6 7
**financially** secure 6

**se|cu|rity** /sɪkyʊərɪti/ 1 N-UNCOUNT **Security** refers to all the measures that are taken to protect a place. seguridad ❑ *They are tightening their airport security.* *Están reforzando la seguridad del aeropuerto.* ❑ *Strict security measures are in force in the capital.* *En la capital rigen estrictas medidas de seguridad.* 2 N-UNCOUNT A feeling of **security** is a feeling of being safe and free from worry. seguridad, certeza ❑ *He loves the security of a happy home life.* *Le encanta la estabilidad de una vida doméstica feliz.* 3 N-UNCOUNT If something is **security** for a loan, you promise to give that thing to the person who lends you money, if you fail to pay the money back. garantía [BUSINESS] ❑ *She's using her own home as security for a business loan.* *Está ofreciendo su propia casa como garantía de un préstamo para su negocio.* 4 → see also **Social Security**

**se|cu|rity cam|era** (**security cameras**) N-COUNT A **security camera** is a video camera that records people's activities in order to detect and prevent crime. cámara de seguridad

**se|dan** /sɪdæn/ (**sedans**) N-COUNT A **sedan** is a car with seats for four or more people, a fixed roof, and a trunk that is separate from the part of the car that you sit in. sedán
→ see **car**

**sedi|ment** /sɛdɪmənt/ (**sediments**) N-VAR **Sediment** is solid material that settles at the bottom of a liquid. sedimento ❑ *At the bottom of the ocean, over time, the sediment forms into rock.* *Con el tiempo, los sedimentos forman rocas en el fondo del océano.*
→ see **rock**

**sedi|men|tary** /sɛdɪmɛntəri/ ADJ **Sedimentary** rocks are formed from sediment left by water, ice, or wind. sedimentario
→ see **rock**

**se|duce** /sɪdus/ (**seduces, seducing, seduced**) V-T If something **seduces** you, it is so attractive that it makes you do something that you would not otherwise do. seducir, atraer ❑ *The fabulous view always seduces visitors.* *Los visitantes siempre se sienten atraídos por la fabulosa vista.* • **se|duc|tion** /sɪdʌkʃ^ən/ N-VAR (**seductions**) seducción ❑ *...the seduction of words.* *...la seducción de las palabras.*

**see**
1 VERB USES
2 EXPRESSIONS, PHRASES AND CONVENTIONS
3 PHR-VERBS

1 **see** /si/ (**sees, seeing, saw, seen**) 1 V-T/V-I When you **see** something, you notice it using your eyes. ver ❑ *You can't see colors at night.* *En la noche no se ven los colores.* ❑ *She can see, hear, touch, smell, and taste.* *Es capaz de ver, oír, tocar, oler y gustar.* 2 V-T If you **see** someone, you visit them or meet them. ver, visitar, reunirse con ❑ *I saw him yesterday.* *Lo vi ayer.* ❑ *Mick wants to see you in his office now.* *Mick quiere verte en su oficina ahora.* 3 V-T If you **see** an entertainment such as a play, movie, concert, or sports game, you watch it. ver, asistir, ir ❑ *I haven't seen a movie for ages.* *Hace años que no voy al cine.* 4 V-T/V-I If you **see** that something is true or exists, you realize by observing it that it is true or exists. percatarse, ver ❑ *I could see she was lonely.* *Pude darme cuenta de que se sentía sola.* ❑ *A lot of people saw what happened.* *Mucha gente vio lo que pasó.* ❑ *My taste has changed a bit, as you can see.* *Como ves, mis gustos han cambiado un poco.* 5 V-T If you **see** what someone means or **see** why something happened, you understand what they mean or understand why it happened. entender, percatarse ❑ *Oh, I see what you're saying.* *Sí, me doy cuenta de lo que dices.* ❑ *I really don't see any reason for changing it.* *No veo por qué habría que cambiarlo.* ❑ *"He came home in my car." — "I see."* *—Llegó a la casa en mi coche. —Ya veo.* 6 V-T If you **see** someone or something **as** a certain thing, you have the opinion that they are that thing. considerar, pensar ❑ *They saw him as a boy, not a man.* *Lo veían como a un niño, no como a un hombre.* ❑ *He saw it as an opportunity.* *Se dio cuenta de que era una oportunidad.* ❑ *As I see it, Steve has three choices.* *Desde mi punto de vista, Steve tiene tres opciones.* 7 V-T If you **see** a particular quality **in** someone, you believe they have that quality. If you ask what someone **sees in** a particular person or thing, you want to know what they find attractive about that person or thing. ver ❑ *Frankly, I don't know what Paul sees in her.* *Francamente no sé que le ve Paul a ella.* 8 V-T If you **see** something happening in the future, you imagine it, or predict that it will happen. pronosticar, imaginarse ❑ *It's a good idea, but can you see Taylor trying it?* *Es buena idea, ¿pero te imaginas a Taylor intentándolo?* 9 V-T If a period of time or a person **sees** a particular change or event, it takes place during that period of time or while that person is alive. experimentar, sufrir ❑ *Yesterday saw heavy fighting in the city.* *Ayer la ciudad vivió intensas batallas.* ❑ *He worked well with the general and was sorry to see him go.* *Trabajaba a gusto con el general y le dio tristeza que se fuera.* 10 V-T If you **see that** something is done or if you **see to it that** it is done, you make sure that it is done. atender, encargarse de ❑ *See that you take care of him.* *Asegúrate de ocuparte de él.* 11 V-T If you **see** someone to a particular place, you accompany them to make sure that they get there safely, or to show politeness. llevar a alguien, ir con alguien ❑ *He didn't offer to see her to her car.* *No le ofreció acompañarla a su coche.* 12 V-T **See** is used in books to indicate to readers that they should look at another part of the book, or at another book, because more information is given there. ver, consultar ❑ *See chapter 7 for more information.* *Para mayor información, remítase al capítulo 7.*
→ see also **look**

**Thesaurus** *see* Ver también:

V. glimpse, look, observe, watch 1 1
grasp, observe, understand 1 5

2 **see** /si/ (**sees, seeing, saw, seen**)
1 CONVENTION People say **"I'll see"** or **"We'll**

S

**see"** to indicate that they do not intend to make a decision immediately, and will decide later. *ya veremos* ❑ *We'll see. It's a possibility. Ya veremos, es una posibilidad.* **2** CONVENTION People say **"let me see"** or **"let's see"** when they are trying to remember something, or are trying to find something. *vamos a ver* ❑ *Let's see, they're six—no, five hours ahead of us. Vamos a ver, nos llevan seis —no, cinco horas de ventaja.* **3** PHRASE You can use **seeing that** or **seeing as** to introduce a reason for what you are saying. *dado que* [INFORMAL, SPOKEN] ❑ *Seeing as you're part of the family, I'll let you borrow it. Dado que eres parte de la familia, te lo presto.* **4** CONVENTION **"See you," "be seeing you,"** and **"see you later"** are ways of saying goodbye to someone when you expect to meet them again soon. *nos vemos* [INFORMAL, SPOKEN] ❑ *"Talk to you later." — "All right. See you." —Te hablo después. —Bueno, nos vemos.* **5** to **see red** → see **red**

**❸ see** /si/ (**sees, seeing, saw, seen**)

▸ **see about** PHR-VERB When you **see about** something, you arrange for it to be done or provided. *ocuparse de algo* ❑ *It was time to see about lunch. Era hora de ver qué íbamos a comer.*

▸ **see off** PHR-VERB When you **see** someone **off,** you go with them to the station, airport, or port that they are leaving from, and say goodbye to them there. *despedir(se)* ❑ *Ben had an early night after seeing Jackie off on her plane. Ben se acostó temprano después de acompañar a Jackie al aeropuerto.*

▸ **see through** PHR-VERB If you **see through** someone or their behavior, you realize what their intentions are, even though they are trying to hide them. *no dejarse engañar* ❑ *I saw through your plan from the start. Desde el principio supe cuál era tu plan.*

▸ **see to** PHR-VERB If you **see to** something that needs attention, you deal with it. *ocuparse de* ❑ *While Frank saw to the luggage, Sara took Ellie home. Mientras Frank se encargaba del equipaje, Sara llevó a Ellie a casa.*

**seed** /si̲d/ (**seeds**) **1** N-VAR A **seed** is the small, hard part of a plant from which a new plant grows. *semilla, simiente* ❑ *I planted the seeds in small plastic pots. Planté las semillas en macetas de plástico pequeñas.* **2** N-PLURAL You can refer to the **seeds of** something when you want to talk about the beginning of a feeling or process that gradually develops and becomes stronger or more important. *germen, semilla* [LITERARY] ❑ *His questions planted seeds of doubt in my mind. Sus preguntas sembraron la duda en mi mente.*
→ see **fruit, herbivore, rice**

S

**seed fern** (**seed ferns**) N-COUNT A **seed fern** was a plant, with leaves resembling those of a fern, that is now extinct. *pteridosperma*

**seed|less** /si̲dlɪs/ ADJ A **seedless** fruit has no seeds in it. *sin semilla* ❑ *...seedless grapes. ...uvas sin semilla.*

**seek** /si̲k/ (**seeks, seeking, sought**) **1** V-T If you **seek** something, you try to find it or obtain it. *buscar, pedir* [FORMAL] ❑ *They are seeking work in hotels and bars. Están buscando trabajo en hoteles y bares.* ❑ *The Baltic states sought help from the United Nations. Los estados del Báltico pidieron ayuda a las Naciones Unidas.* • **seek|er** N-COUNT (**seekers**) *buscador o buscadora, que busca* ❑ *I am a seeker after truth. Voy en busca de la verdad.* **2** V-T If you **seek to** do something, you try to do it. *tratar, buscar, intentar* [FORMAL] ❑ *The U.S. should not seek to be the world's policeman. Los Estados Unidos no tienen por qué ser policías del mundo.*

▸ **seek out** PHR-VERB If you **seek out** someone or something or **seek** them **out,** you keep looking for them until you find them. *buscar* ❑ *Local companies are seeking out business opportunities in Europe. Empresas locales están buscando oportunidades de negocio en Europa.*

**Word Partnership** Usar *seek* con:

N. seek **advice**, seek **approval**, seek **assistance/help**, seek **asylum**, seek **counseling**, seek **election**, seek **employment**, seek **justice**, seek **permission**, seek **protection**, seek **revenge**, seek **shelter**, seek **support** **1**

**seem** /si̲m/ (**seems, seeming, seemed**) **1** V-LINK You use **seem** to say that someone or something gives the impression of having a particular quality, or of happening in the way you describe. *parecer, dar la impresión* ❑ *The thunder seemed quite close. El trueno pareció muy cercano.* ❑ *They seemed an ideal couple to everyone who knew them. Quienes los conocían pensaban que era la pareja ideal.* ❑ *The calming effect seemed to last for about ten minutes. El efecto calmante pareció durar unos diez minutos.* ❑ *It seems that the attack was carefully planned. Parece que el ataque fue cuidadosamente planeado.* ❑ *It seems as if she's never coming back. Parece que nunca fuera a volver.* **2** V-LINK You use **seem** when you are describing your own feelings or thoughts, or describing something that has happened to you, in order to make your statement less forceful. *parecer a uno, darle a uno la impresión* ❑ *I seem to have lost all my self-confidence. Me siento como si hubiera perdido toda la confianza en mí.* ❑ *I seem to remember giving you very clear instructions. Me parece que las instrucciones que te di fueron muy claras.* **3** PHRASE If you say that you **cannot seem** or **could not seem to** do something, you mean that you have tried to do it and were unable to. *parecer* ❑ *As a society, we cannot seem to look honestly at ourselves. Como sociedad, parece que no podemos analizarnos con honestidad.*

**seg|ment** /sɛ̲gmənt/ (**segments**) **1** N-COUNT A **segment of** something is one part of it. *segmento, sector, sección* ❑ *They come from the poorer segments of society. Provienen de los segmentos más pobres de la sociedad.* **2** N-COUNT The **segments** of an animal's body are its different sections, especially the sections between two joints. *parte*
→ see **fruit**

**seis|mic** /sa̲ɪzmɪk/ **1** ADJ **Seismic** means caused by or relating to an earthquake. *sísmico* ❑ *Earthquakes produce two types of seismic waves. Los terremotos producen dos tipos de ondas sísmicas.* **2** ADJ A **seismic** shift or change is a very sudden or dramatic change. *radical* ❑ *I have never seen such a seismic shift in public opinion in such a short period of time. Nunca había visto un cambio tan radical de la opinión pública en tan poco tiempo.*
→ see **earthquake**

**seis|mic gap** (**seismic gaps**) N-COUNT A **seismic gap** is a section of a geological fault where there has not been an earthquake for a relatively long time. *hiato sísmico* [TECHNICAL]

**seis|mo|gram** /saɪzməgræm/ (**seismograms**) N-COUNT A **seismogram** is a graph produced by a seismograph which shows the strength of an earthquake. *sismograma* [TECHNICAL]

**seis|mo|graph** /saɪzməgræf/ (**seismographs**) N-COUNT A **seismograph** is an instrument for recording and measuring the strength of earthquakes. *sismógrafo*
→ see **earthquake**

**seis|mol|ogy** /saɪzmɒlədʒi/ N-UNCOUNT **Seismology** is the scientific study of earthquakes. *sismología* • **seis|molo|gist** N-COUNT (**seismologists**) *sismólogo o sismóloga*
→ see **earthquake**

**seize** /siz/ (**seizes, seizing, seized**) **1** V-T If you **seize** something, you take hold of it quickly, firmly, and forcefully. *agarrar, coger, tomar, asir* ❑ *He seized my arm to hold me back. Me agarró del brazo para detenerme.* **2** V-T When a group of people **seize** a place or **seize** control of it, they take control of it quickly and suddenly, using force. *capturar, secuestrar* ❑ *Guards were ordered to seize him. Se ordenó a los guardias que lo capturaran.* **3** V-T When someone **is seized,** they are arrested or captured. *secuestrar* ❑ *U.N. officials say two military observers were seized yesterday. Funcionarios de la ONU dicen que dos observadores militares fueron secuestrados ayer.* **4** V-T When you **seize** an opportunity, you take advantage of it and do something that you want to do. *aprovechar* ❑ *They seized the opportunity to study his pictures during their visits. Durante sus visitas aprovecharon la oportunidad de estudiar sus cuadros.*

▸ **seize on** PHR-VERB If you **seize on** something or **seize upon** it, you show great interest in it, often because it is useful to you. *aprovechar* ❑ *Steve seized on the idea and I was interested too. Steve sacó partido de la idea y a mí también me interesó.*

▸ **seize up** PHR-VERB If an engine or a part of your body **seizes up,** it stops working. *atorarse, engarrotarse, agarrotarse, paralizarse, atascarse* ❑ *After that exercise, it's your arms that seize up, not your legs. Después de ese ejercicio lo que se engarrota son los brazos, no las piernas.*

**sel|dom** /sɛldəm/ ADV If something **seldom** happens, it happens only occasionally. *rara vez* ❑ *They seldom speak. Casi nunca hablan.* ❑ *I've seldom felt so happy. Pocas veces me he sentido tan feliz.*

**se|lect** /sɪlɛkt/ (**selects, selecting, selected**) **1** V-T If you **select** something, you choose it from a number of things of the same kind. *seleccionar, escoger* ❑ *Please select 5 out of the 10 events. Por favor, seleccione 5 de los 10 eventos.* ❑ *You can select a 6th book for only $4.95. Puede escoger un sexto libro por sólo 4.95 dólares.* • **se|lec|tion** N-UNCOUNT *selección, opción, elección, surtido* ❑ *Dr. Sullivan's selection was very popular. La selección del Dr. Sullivan fue muy popular.* **2** ADJ A **select** group is a small group of some of the best people or things of their kind. *selecto, escogido, distinguido* ❑ *Then select voters got a letter from the Commissioner. Después, ciertos votantes recibieron una carta del Comisionado.* ❑ *It was a select party. Fue una fiesta muy exclusiva.*

| **Thesaurus** | *select* | Ver también: |
|---|---|---|
| V. | choose, pick out, take **1** | |
| ADJ. | best, exclusive **2** | |

**se|lec|tion** /sɪlɛkʃᵊn/ (**selections**) **1** N-COUNT A **selection of** people or things is a set of them that has been selected from a larger group. *selección, surtido* ❑ *...this selection of popular songs. ...esta selección de canciones populares.* **2** N-COUNT The **selection of** goods in a store is the particular range of goods that it has available and from which you can choose what you want. *surtido* ❑ *It offers the widest selection of antiques in a one day market. Ofrece el más amplio surtido de antigüedades en una venta que dura un día.*

**se|lec|tive** /sɪlɛktɪv/ **1** ADJ A **selective** process applies only to a few things or people. *selectivo* ❑ *They put together a selective list of people to invite to the party. Hicieron una lista de las personas que invitarían a la fiesta.* • **se|lec|tive|ly** ADV *de manera selectiva* ❑ *Within the project, trees are selectively cut down. En el proyecto se seleccionan los árboles que serán derribados.* **2** ADJ When someone is **selective,** they choose things carefully, for example, the things that they buy or do. *selectivo* ❑ *Sales still happen, but buyers are more selective. Se sigue vendiendo, pero los compradores son más selectivos.* • **se|lec|tive|ly** ADV *con criterio selectivo* ❑ *People on small incomes want to shop selectively. Las personas de bajos ingresos gustan de ser selectivos en sus compras.*

**se|lec|tive breed|ing** N-UNCOUNT **Selective breeding** is the process of breeding certain traits in animals in preference to others. *cría selectiva*

**self** /sɛlf/ (**selves**) N-COUNT Your **self** is your basic personality or nature. *persona, personalidad, identidad propia* ❑ *You're looking like your usual self again. Ya pareces tú otra vez.*

**self-centered** ADJ Someone who is **self-centered** is only concerned with their own wants and needs and never thinks about other people. *egocéntrico, egoísta* ❑ *It's very self-centered to think that people are talking about you. Es egoísta pensar que la gente está hablando de uno.*

**self-confident** ADJ Someone who is **self-confident** behaves confidently because they feel sure of their abilities or value. *seguro de sí mismo* ❑ *She's become a very self-confident young woman. Se ha convertido en una joven con mucha seguridad en sí misma* • **self-confidence** N-UNCOUNT *confianza en sí mismo* ❑ *I lost all my self-confidence. Perdí toda la confianza en mí.*

**self-conscious** ADJ Someone who is **self-conscious** is easily embarrassed and nervous because they feel that everyone is looking at them and judging them. *tímido, falto de naturalidad* ❑ *I felt a bit self-conscious in my bikini. Me sentía algo cohibida en bikini.*

**self-control** N-UNCOUNT **Self-control** is the ability to not show your feelings or not do the things that your feelings make you want to do. *dominio de sí mismo* ❑ *She was told she must learn self-control. Le dijeron que tenía que aprender a controlarse.*

**self-defense** N-UNCOUNT **Self-defense** is the use of force to protect yourself against someone who is attacking you. *defensa propia, legítima defensa*

S

❑ *The women acted in self-defense.* *La mujer actuó en defensa propia.*

**self-determination** N-UNCOUNT **Self-determination** is the right of a country to be independent, instead of being controlled by a foreign country, and to choose its own form of government. *autodeterminación* ❑ *...Lithuania's right to self-determination.* *...el derecho de Lituania a la autodeterminación.*

**self-employed** ADJ If you are **self-employed,** you organize your own work and taxes and are paid by people for a service you provide, rather than being paid a regular salary by a person or a company. *que trabaja por cuenta propia* [BUSINESS] ❑ *You can change the time you start work easily if you are self-employed.* *Fácilmente cambias tu horario de trabajo si eres independiente.* ● **The self-employed** are people who are self-employed. *trabajador independiente o trabajadora independiente* ❑ *We want more support for the self-employed.* *Queremos más apoyo para los trabajadores independientes.*

**self-esteem** N-UNCOUNT Your **self-esteem** is how you feel about yourself and whether you have a good opinion of yourself. *amor propio* ❑ *Harry was a man of low self-esteem.* *Harry era un hombre con poca autoestima.*

**self-image** (**self-images**) N-COUNT Your **self-image** is the set of ideas you have about your own qualities and abilities. *imagen de sí mismo* ❑ *He seems to have a very healthy self-image right now.* *Parece que en este momento tiene una imagen saludable de sí mismo.*

**self-indulgent** ADJ If you say that someone is **self-indulgent,** you mean that they allow themselves to have or do the things that they enjoy very much. *indulgente consigo mismo* ❑ *We live in a world full of self-indulgent people.* *Vivimos en un mundo lleno de personas que no se exigen.* ● **self-indulgence** N-VAR (**self-indulgences**) *indulgencia consigo mismo* ❑ *He prayed to be saved from self-indulgence.* *Oraba por que lo libraran de la propia complacencia.*

**self-interest** N-UNCOUNT If you accuse someone of **self-interest,** you disapprove of them because they always want to do what is best for themselves rather than for anyone else. *interés propio, egoísmo* ❑ *It's good to find people who have no self-interest.* *Consuela encontrarse con personas que no piensan sólo en ellas.*

S

**self|ish** /sɛlfɪʃ/ ADJ If you say that someone is **selfish,** you disapprove of them because they care only about themselves, and not about other people. *egoísta* ❑ *I think I've been very selfish.* *Creo que he sido muy egoísta.* ● **self|ish|ly** ADV *de manera egoísta* ❑ *Someone has selfishly emptied the cookie jar.* *Alguien que no piensa en los demás se acabó las galletas.* ● **self|ish|ness** N-UNCOUNT *egoísmo* ❑ *Julie's selfishness made us sad.* *Nos dio tristeza el egoísmo de Julie.*

**self|less** /sɛlflɪs/ ADJ If you say that someone is **selfless,** you approve of them because they care about other people more than themselves. *desinteresado, desprendido* ❑ *Her kindness was entirely selfless.* *Su gentileza fue totalmente desinteresada.*

**self-pollinating** ADJ If a plant is **self-pollinating,** the female part of the plant is fertilized by pollen from the male part of the same plant. *autopolinizado, autofecundado*

**self-promotion** N-UNCOUNT If you accuse someone of **self-promotion,** you disapprove of them because they are trying to make themselves seem more important than they actually are. *que se hace promoción a sí mismo* ❑ *His self-promotion has not made him popular among his co-workers.* *La autopromoción no lo ha hecho popular entre sus colegas.*

**self-respect** N-UNCOUNT **Self-respect** is a feeling of confidence and pride in your own ability and worth. *dignidad, respeto por sí mismo* ❑ *They have lost their jobs, their homes and their self-respect.* *Perdieron su empleo, su hogar y el respeto por sí mismos.*

**self-righteous** ADJ If you describe someone as **self-righteous,** you disapprove of them because they are convinced that they are right in their beliefs, attitudes, and behavior and that other people are wrong. *pretencioso* ❑ *He thinks they are narrow-minded and self-righteous.* *Él cree que son de criterio estrecho y que se sienten superiores.* ● **self-righteousness** N-UNCOUNT *con pretensiones* ❑ *Her self-righteousness made him very angry.* *Sus pretensiones lo enojaron muchísimo.*

**self-rising flour** N-UNCOUNT **Self-rising flour** is flour that makes cakes rise as you bake them because it has chemicals added to it. *harina que no necesita levadura*

**self-study** N-UNCOUNT **Self-study** is study that you do on your own, without a teacher. *autoestudio* ❑ *...self-study courses.* *...cursos sin maestro.*

**self-sufficient** ADJ If a country or group is **self-sufficient,** it is able to produce or make everything that it needs. *autosuficiente* ❑ *Now the country is self-sufficient in sugar.* *Ahora el país es autosuficiente en azúcar.* ● **self-sufficiency** /sɛlf səfɪʃᵊnsi/ N-UNCOUNT *autosuficiencia* ❑ *We dreamed of self-sufficiency.* *Soñábamos con la autosuficiencia.*

**sell** /sɛl/ (**sells, selling, sold**) **1** V-T/V-I If you **sell** something that you own, you let someone have it in return for money. *vender* ❑ *Catlin sold the paintings to Joseph Harrison.* *Catlin le vendió las pinturas a Joseph Harrison.* ❑ *The directors sold the business for $14.8 million.* *Los directores vendieron el negocio en 14.8 millones de dólares.* ❑ *When is the best time to sell?* *¿Cuándo es la mejor época para vender?* **2** V-T If a store **sells** a particular thing, it is available for people to buy there. *vender* ❑ *It sells everything from hair ribbons to carpets.* *Venden de todo, desde listones para el cabello hasta alfombras.* **3** V-I If something **sells for** a particular price, that price is paid for it. *venderse* ❑ *The candy usually sells for $5.* *El dulce se vende normalmente en 5 dólares.* **4** V-I If something **sells,** it is bought by the public, usually in fairly large quantities. *venderse* ❑ *Even if this album doesn't sell, we won't change our style.* *Incluso si este álbum no se vende, no cambiaremos nuestro estilo.*

▸ **sell out** **1** PHR-VERB If a store **sells out** of something, it sells all its supply of it. *venderse todo, agotarse* ❑ *The supermarket sold out of flour in a single day.* *En el supermercado se quedaron sin harina en un día.* **2** PHR-VERB If a performance, sports event, or other entertainment **sells out,** all the tickets for it are sold. *agotarse* ❑ *Football games often sell out fast.* *Los boletos para el fútbol suelen agotarse rápidamente.* **3** PHR-VERB If you accuse someone of **selling out,** you disapprove of the fact that they do something which used to be against their principles, or give in to an opposing group. *vendarse* ❑ *You don't have to sell out and work for some corporation.* *No tienes que venderte e irte a trabajar a alguna empresa.* **4** → see also **sell-out**

**Word Link** *ar, er ≈ one who acts as : buyer, registrar, seller*

**sell|er** /sɛlər/ (**sellers**) **1** N-COUNT A **seller** of a type of thing is a person or company that sells that type of thing. *vendedor o vendedora* ❑ *She's a flower seller.* *Es florista.* **2** N-COUNT In a business deal, the **seller** is the person who is selling something to someone else. *vendedor o vendedora* ❑ *The seller is responsible for collecting the tax.* *El vendedor se responsabiliza de retener los impuestos.* **3** N-COUNT If you describe a product as, for example, a big **seller,** you mean that large numbers of it are being sold. *que se vende* ❑ *I think our new phone is going to be a big seller.* *Pienso que nuestro nuevo teléfono se va a vender muy bien.* **4** → see also **bestseller**

**sell-out** (**sell-outs**) also **sellout** **1** N-COUNT If a play, sports event, or other entertainment is a **sell-out,** all the tickets for it are sold. *lleno, éxito de taquilla* ❑ *Their concert there was a sell-out.* *Para su concierto de allá se agotaron las localidades.* **2** N-COUNT If you describe someone's behavior as a **sell-out,** you disapprove of the fact that they have done something which used to be against their principles. *traición* ❑ *For some, his decision to become a Socialist was simply a sell-out.* *Para algunos, su decisión de hacerse socialista fue simplemente una traición.*

**selt|zer** /sɛltsər/ (**seltzers**) also **seltzer water** N-VAR **Seltzer** is carbonated water with a lot of minerals in. *agua mineral, agua de Seltz* ❑ *...a bottle of seltzer.* *...una botella de agua mineral.*

**se|mes|ter** /sɪmɛstər/ (**semesters**) N-COUNT In colleges and universities in some countries, a **semester** is one of the two main periods into which the year is divided. *semestre* ❑ *February 22nd is when most of their students begin their spring semester.* *El 22 de febrero es cuando la mayoría de sus estudiantes empiezan el semestre de primavera.*

**semiannual** ADJ A **semiannual** event happens twice a year. *semestral* ❑ *We hold our semiannual meeting in September.* *Tenemos nuestra reunión semestral en septiembre.*

**Word Link** *semi ≈ half : semicolon, semiconductor, semifinal*

**semi|co|lon** /sɛmikoʊlən/ (**semicolons**) N-COUNT A **semicolon** is the punctuation mark ; which is used in writing to separate different parts of a sentence or list or to indicate a pause. *punto y coma*
→ see **punctuation**

**semi|con|duc|tor** /sɛmikəndʌktər, sɛmaɪ-/ (**semiconductors**) N-COUNT A **semiconductor** is a substance used in electronics whose ability to conduct electricity increases with greater heat. *semiconductor*
→ see **solar**

**semi|fi|nal** /sɛmifaɪnᵊl, sɛmaɪ-/ (**semifinals**) N-COUNT A **semifinal** is one of the two games or races in a competition that are held to decide who will compete in the final. *semifinal* ❑ *The basketball team lost in their semifinal yesterday.* *El equipo de basketball perdió la semifinal ayer.*

**semi|nar** /sɛmɪnɑr/ (**seminars**) N-COUNT A **seminar** is a class at a college or university in which the teacher and a small group of students discuss a topic. *seminario* ❑ *Students are asked to prepare material for the weekly seminars.* *Se pide a los estudiantes que preparen material para los seminarios de cada semana.*

**semi|nif|er|ous tu|bule** /sɛmɪnɪfərəs tubyul/ (**seminiferous tubules**) N-COUNT **Seminiferous tubules** are tubes inside the testes of male animals where sperm is produced. *túbulo seminífero* [TECHNICAL]

**Se|mit|ic** /sɪmɪtɪk/ **1** ADJ **Semitic** languages are a group of languages that include Arabic and Hebrew. *semítico* **2** ADJ **Semitic** people belong to one of the groups of people who speak a Semitic language. *semítico* ❑ *...an ancient Semitic religion.* *...una antigua religión semítica.* **3** ADJ **Semitic** is sometimes used to mean Jewish. *semítico*

**Sen|ate** /sɛnɪt/ (**Senates**) N-PROPER **The Senate** is the smaller and more important of the two parts of the legislature in some U.S. states and in some countries, for example, the United States and Australia. *senado* ❑ *That year the Republicans gained two Senate seats.* *Ese año, los Republicanos ganaron dos escaños en el Senado.*

**Word Link** *sen ≈ old : senator, senile, senior*

**sena|tor** /sɛnɪtər/ (**senators**) N-COUNT; N-TITLE A **senator** is a member of a Senate, for example, in the United States or Australia. *senador o senadora*

**send** /sɛnd/ (**sends, sending, sent**) **1** V-T When you **send** someone something, you arrange for it to be taken and delivered to them, for example, by mail. *mandar, enviar, remitir, expedir* ❑ *Myra Cunningham sent me a note thanking me for dinner.* *Myra Cunningham me mandó una nota de agradecimiento por la cena.* ❑ *I sent a copy to the school principal.* *Le mandé una copia al director de la escuela.* ● **send|er** N-COUNT (**senders**) *remitente, que manda* ❑ *The sender of the best letter will win a check for $50.* *El remitente de la mejor carta ganará un cheque por 50 dólares.* **2** V-T If you **send** someone somewhere, you arrange for them to go there or stay there. *mandar, echar, despedir* ❑ *The Inspector came to see her, but she sent him away.* *El Inspector fue a verla, pero ella no lo recibió.* ❑ *The government has decided to send troops to the region.* *El gobierno ha decidido mandar tropas a la región.* ❑ *I sent him for an X-ray.* *Lo mandé por una radiografía.* ❑ *His parents have chosen to send him to a boarding school.* *Sus padres prefirieron mandarlo a un internado.* **3** V-T To **send** a signal means to cause it to go to a place by means of radio waves or electricity. *mandar, enviar, emitir* ❑ *The transmitters will send a signal to a local base station.* *Los transmisores enviarán una señal a la estación de la base local.* **4** V-T If something **sends** things or people in a particular direction, it causes them to move in that direction. *lanzar* ❑ *The explosion sent bits of metal flying across the crowded highway.* *La explosión lanzó pedazos de metal al otro lado de la concurrida autopista.* ❑ *The gunshot sent him running off through* the woods. El disparo lo hizo huir por el bosque. **5** V-T To **send** someone or something **into** a particular state means to cause them to go into or be in that state. poner en cierto estado a ❑ *Something about the men sent him into a panic.* Algo en esos hombres lo hizo entrar en pánico. ❑ *Civil war sent the country plunging into chaos.* La guerra civil sumió al país en el caos.

▸ **send for** **1** PHR-VERB If you **send for** someone, you send them a message asking them to come and see you. mandar por ❑ *I've sent for the doctor.* Mandé por el doctor. **2** PHR-VERB If you **send for** something, or **send away for** it, or **send off for** it, you write and ask for it to be sent to you. mandar por algo, pedir ❑ *Send for your free catalog today.* Pida su catálogo de cortesía hoy mismo.

▸ **send off** PHR-VERB When you **send off** a letter or package, you send it somewhere by mail. mandar, enviar, despachar ❑ *He sent off copies to various people.* Mandó copias a varias personas.

▸ **send off for** → see **send for 2**

▸ **send out** **1** PHR-VERB If you **send out** things such as letters or bills, you send them to a large number of people at the same time. mandar, enviar ❑ *She sent out four hundred invitations that afternoon.* Esa tarde envió cuatrocientas invitaciones. **2** PHR-VERB To **send out** a signal, sound, light, or heat means to produce it. mandar, emitir ❑ *The crew did not send out any emergency signals.* La tripulación no emitió señales de emergencia.

▸ **send out for** PHR-VERB If you **send out for** food, for example, pizza or sandwiches, you phone and ask for it to be delivered to you. mandar por, mandar a por, encargar ❑ *Let's send out for a pizza.* Vamos a mandar por una pizza.

**Word Link** *sen ≈ old : senator, senile, senior*

**se|nile** /sinaɪl/ ADJ If old people become **senile,** they become confused, can no longer remember things, and are unable to take care of themselves. senil ❑ *He's ninety years old and a bit senile.* Tiene noventa años y está ligeramente senil. ● **se|nil|ity** /sɪnɪlɪti/ N-UNCOUNT senilidad ❑ *The old man was showing signs of senility.* El viejo mostraba signos de senilidad.

**sen|ior** /sinyər/ (**seniors**) **1** ADJ The **senior** people in an organization or profession have the highest and most important jobs. de más alto rango ❑ *These were senior officials in the Israeli government.* Eran funcionarios de alto rango del gobierno de Israel. ❑ *...the company's senior management.* ...los mandos superiores de la empresa. **2** ADJ If someone is **senior to** you, they have a higher and more important job than you. superior ❑ *The job had to be done by an officer senior to Haig.* El trabajo tenía que hacerlo un funcionario de rango superior al de Haig. ● Your **seniors** are the people who are senior to you. superiores ❑ *His seniors described him as an excellent officer.* Sus superiores dijeron que era un oficial excelente. **3** N-SING **Senior** is used when indicating how much older one person is than another. mayor ❑ *Her brother was in fact many years her senior.* De hecho su hermano era muchos años mayor que ella. **4** N-COUNT **Seniors** are students in a high school, university, or college who are in their fourth year of study. estudiante del último año ❑ *How many high school seniors go on to college?* ¿Cuántos estudiantes del último año de preparatoria van a la universidad?

S

**sen|ior citi|zen** (**senior citizens**) N-COUNT A **senior citizen** is an older person, especially someone over 65. **Senior citizens** have often retired and often receive social security benefits. persona de la tercera edad ❑ *...services for senior citizens.* ...servicios para los jubilados.

→ see **age**

**sen|ior high school** (**senior highs schools**) also **senior high** N-VAR A **senior high school** or a **senior high** is a school for students between the ages of 14 or 15 and 17 or 18. preparatoria, prepa ❑ *Our children are in senior high school.* Nuestros hijos están en prepa. ❑ *This is a daily news program for middle and senior high schools.* Es un programa noticioso para estudiantes de secundaria y preparatoria que se transmite todos los días. ❑ *...Mount Pearl Senior High.* ...Escuela Preparatoria de Mount Pearl.

**sen|ior mo|ment** (**senior moments**) N-COUNT If an elderly person has a **senior moment,** he or she forgets something or makes a mistake. mal momento [INFORMAL] ❑ *He is 69 in February and sometimes has a senior moment.* Cumple 69 en febrero y de repente se le nota.

**Word Link** *sens ≈ feeling : sensation, senseless, sensitive*

**sen|sa|tion** /sɛnseɪʃᵊn/ (**sensations**) **1** N-COUNT A **sensation** is a physical feeling. sensación ❑ *Floating can be a pleasant sensation.* Flotar puede ser una sensación muy placentera. **2** N-UNCOUNT **Sensation** is your ability to feel things physically. sensibilidad ❑ *The pain was so bad that she lost all sensation.* El dolor era tan intenso que perdió toda sensibilidad. **3** N-COUNT You can use **sensation** to refer to the general feeling or impression caused by a particular experience. sensación ❑ *It's a funny sensation to know someone's talking about you in another language.* Es curiosa la sensación de saber que alguien habla de uno en otra lengua. **4** N-COUNT If a person, event, or situation is a **sensation,** it causes great excitement or interest. sensación, éxito ❑ *This movie turned her into an overnight sensation.* Esta película se convirtió en éxito de la noche a la mañana.

→ see **taste**

**sen|sa|tion|al** /sɛnseɪʃənᵊl/ **1** ADJ A **sensational** result, event, or situation is so remarkable that it causes great excitement and interest. que causa sensación ❑ *The world champions suffered a sensational defeat.* Los campeones mundiales sufrieron una derrota que causó sensación. ● **sen|sa|tion|al|ly** ADV sensacionalmente, de manera sensacional ❑ *The judge sensationally stopped the trial yesterday.* El juez detuvo el juicio de manera sensacional ayer. **2** ADJ You can describe something as **sensational** when you think that it is extremely good. sensacional ❑ *Her voice is sensational.* Tiene una voz sensacional. ● **sen|sa|tion|al|ly** ADV sensacionalmente ❑ *This is sensationally good food.* Esta comida es sensacionalmente buena.

**sense** /sɛns/ (**senses, sensing, sensed**) **1** N-COUNT Your **senses** are the physical abilities of sight, smell, hearing, touch, and taste. sentido ❑ *She stared at him, unable to believe her senses.* Lo miró fijamente, incapaz de creer en sus sentidos. **2** V-T If you **sense** something, you become aware of it or you realize it, although it is not very obvious. sentir, intuir ❑ *She probably sensed that I wasn't telling the*

truth. *Probablemente sintió que yo no estaba diciendo la verdad.* ❑ *He looked around him, sensing danger. Miró a su alrededor, intuyendo peligro.* **3** N-SING If you have a **sense of** guilt or relief, for example, you feel guilty or relieved. *sensación* ❑ *When your child is unhappy, you feel this terrible sense of guilt. Cuando tu hijo es infeliz, tienes una terrible sensación de culpa.* **4** N-UNCOUNT **Sense** is the ability to make good judgments and to behave sensibly. *sentido común, sensatez* ❑ *When he was younger, he had a bit more sense. Cuando era más joven, tenía un poco más de sentido común.* ❑ *If that doesn't work, they sometimes have the sense to ask for help. Si eso no funciona, a veces tienen la sensatez de pedir ayuda.* **5** → see also **common sense** **6** N-COUNT A **sense** of a word or expression is one of its possible meanings. *sentido, significado* ❑ *This noun has four senses. Este sustantivo tiene cuatro significados.* **7** PHRASE If you say that someone **has come to** their **senses** or **has been brought to** their **senses,** you mean that they have stopped being foolish and are being sensible again. *entrar en razón* ❑ *Eventually the world will come to its senses. Con el tiempo el mundo entrará en razón.* **8** PHRASE If something **makes sense,** you can understand it. *tener sentido* ❑ *He sat there saying, "Yes, the figures make sense." Se sentó ahí diciendo —Sí, las cifras tienen sentido.* **9** PHRASE When you **make sense of** something, you succeed in understanding it. *entender* ❑ *If you don't try to make sense of it, it sounds beautiful. Si no tratas de entenderlo, suena hermoso.* **10** PHRASE If a course of action **makes sense,** it seems sensible. *ser razonable /sensato* ❑ *It makes sense to take care of yourself. Es razonable que te cuides.* ❑ *Does this project make good economic sense? ¿Este proyecto es razonable desde el punto de vista económico?*
→ see **smell**

| Word Link | *sens ≈ feeling : sensation, senseless, sensitive* |
|---|---|

**sense|less** /sɛnslɪs/ **1** ADJ A **senseless** action seems to have no purpose and produce no benefit. *sin sentido* ❑ *People's lives are destroyed by acts of senseless violence. La vida de las personas es destruida por actos de violencia sin sentido.* **2** ADJ If someone is **senseless,** they are unconscious. *inconsciente* ❑ *They knocked him to the ground and beat him senseless. Lo tiraron al suelo y lo golpearon hasta dejarlo inconsciente.*

**sense memo|ry** (**sense memories**) N-VAR **Sense memory** is the memory of physical sensations such as sounds and smells, which actors sometimes use in order to gain a better understanding of the character they are playing. *memoria sensorial*

**sense of hu|mor** N-SING Someone who has a **sense of humor** often finds things amusing, rather than being serious all the time. *sentido del humor* ❑ *She has a good sense of humor. Tiene muy buen sentido del humor.*

**sen|sible** /sɛnsɪbᵊl/ **1** ADJ **Sensible** actions or decisions are good because they are based on reasons rather than emotions. *sensato* ❑ *It might be sensible to get a lawyer. Sería sensato conseguir un abogado.* ❑ *The sensible thing is to leave them alone. Lo sensato es dejarlos solos.* ● **sen|sibly** /sɛnsɪbli/ ADV *con sensatez* ❑ *He sensibly decided to hide for a while. Decidió con sensatez esconderse por un tiempo.* **2** ADJ **Sensible** people behave in a sensible way. *sensato* ❑ *She was a sensible girl and did not panic. Era una chica sensata y no entró en pánico.* ❑ *Oh come on, let's be sensible about this. Ay, vamos, seamos sensatos.*

**sen|si|tive** /sɛnsɪtɪv/ **1** ADJ If you are **sensitive to** other people's needs, problems, or feelings, you show understanding and awareness of them. *sensible* ❑ *The classroom teacher must be sensitive to a child's needs. En el salón de clases, la maestra debe ser sensible a las necesidades del niño.* ● **sen|si|tive|ly** ADV *con sensibilidad* ❑ *The investigation should be done carefully and sensitively. La investigación se debe hacer con cuidado y sensibilidad.* ● **sen|si|tiv|ity** /sɛnsɪtɪvɪti/ N-UNCOUNT *sensibilidad* ❑ *A good relationship involves sensitivity for each other's feelings. Una buena relación implica demostrar sensibilidad ante los sentimientos del otro.* **2** ADJ If you are **sensitive about** something, you are easily worried and offended when people talk about it. *susceptible* ❑ *Young people are sensitive about their appearance. Los jóvenes son susceptibles a su apariencia.* ● **sen|si|tiv|ity** N-VAR (**sensitivities**) *susceptibilidad* ❑ *Some people suffer extreme sensitivity about what others think. Algunas personas sufren de una extrema susceptibilidad a lo que los otros piensan.* **3** ADJ A **sensitive** subject or issue needs to be dealt with carefully because it is likely to cause disagreement or make people angry or upset. *delicado* ❑ *Employment is a very sensitive issue. El empleo es un tema muy delicado.* ● **sen|si|tiv|ity** N-UNCOUNT *lo delicado* ❑ *He could not give any details because of the sensitivity of the subject. No pudo dar detalles por lo delicado del asunto.* **4** ADJ Something that is **sensitive to** a physical force, substance, or treatment is easily affected by it and often harmed by it. *sensible* ❑ *This chemical is sensitive to light. Este producto químico es sensible a la luz.* ● **sen|si|tiv|ity** N-UNCOUNT *sensibilidad* ❑ *We measure the sensitivity of cells to damage. Evaluamos la sensibilidad de las células al daño.* **5** ADJ A **sensitive** piece of scientific equipment is capable of measuring or recording very small changes. *sensible* ❑ *We need an extremely sensitive microscope. Necesitamos un microscopio sumamente sensible.*

| Word Partnership | Usar *sensitive* con: |
|---|---|
| ADV. | **overly** sensitive, **so** sensitive, **too** sensitive **1** **2** |
| | **highly** sensitive, **very** sensitive **1** – **5** |
| | **politically** sensitive **3** |
| | **environmentally** sensitive **4** |
| N. | sensitive **areas**, sensitive **information**, sensitive **issue**, sensitive **material** **3** |
| | **heat** sensitive, **light** sensitive, sensitive **skin** **4** |
| | sensitive **equipment** **5** |

**sen|sor** /sɛnsər/ (**sensors**) N-COUNT A **sensor** is an instrument which reacts to certain physical conditions such as heat or light. *sensor* ❑ *This data was collected from sensors aboard the space shuttle. Estos datos se recabaron de sensores a bordo del transbordador espacial.*

| Word Link | *ory ≈ relating to : advisory, contradictory, sensory* |
|---|---|

**sen|so|ry** /sɛnsəri/ ADJ **Sensory** means relating

S

to the physical senses. sensorial [FORMAL] ❑ *A number of sensory changes can be expected with age. Un número de cambios sensoriales se pueden esperar con la edad.*
→ see **nervous system, smell**

**sen|so|ry neu|ron** (**sensory neurons**) N-COUNT **Sensory neurons** are nerve cells that respond to stimuli such as light or sound and send the information to the central nervous system. neurona sensorial [TECHNICAL]

**sen|tence** /sɛntəns/ (**sentences, sentencing, sentenced**) **1** N-COUNT A **sentence** is a group of words which, when they are written down, begin with a capital letter and end with a period, question mark, or exclamation mark. Most sentences contain a subject and a verb. oración ❑ *Here we have several sentences wrongly joined by commas. Aquí tenemos varias oraciones unidas incorrectamente por comas.* **2** N-VAR In a law court, a **sentence** is the punishment that a person receives after they have been found guilty of a crime. sentencia ❑ *They are already serving prison sentences for their crimes. Ya están cumpliendo su sentencia en prisión por los crímenes que cometieron.* ❑ *He was given a four-year sentence. Su sentencia fue de cuatro años.* **3** V-T When a judge **sentences** someone, he or she states in court what their punishment will be. sentenciar ❑ *The court sentenced him to five years in prison. La corte lo sentenció a cinco años en prisión.*
→ see **trial**

**sen|ti|ment** /sɛntɪmənt/ (**sentiments**) **1** N-VAR A **sentiment** is an attitude, feeling, or opinion. sentimiento, opinión ❑ *Public sentiment was turning against him. La opinión pública se estaba volviendo en su contra.* **2** N-UNCOUNT **Sentiment** is feelings such as pity or love, especially for things in the past, and may be considered exaggerated and foolish. sentimentalismo ❑ *Laura kept that letter out of sentiment. Laura guardó esa carta por sentimentalismo.*

**sen|ti|ment|al** /sɛntɪmɛntᵊl/ **1** ADJ Someone or something that is **sentimental** feels or shows pity or love, sometimes to an extent that is considered exaggerated and foolish. sentimental ❑ *I'm trying not to be sentimental about the past. Estoy tratando de no ser sentimental por el pasado.* ● **sen|ti|men|tal|ly** ADV de manera sentimental ❑ *We look back sentimentally to our childhood. Recordamos nuestra infancia de una manera sentimental.* ● **sen|ti|men|tal|ity** /sɛntɪmɛntælɪti/ N-UNCOUNT sentimentalismo ❑ *In this book there is no sentimentality. En este libro no hay sentimentalismo.* **2** ADJ **Sentimental** means relating to or involving feelings such as pity or love, especially for things in the past. sentimental ❑ *Our photographs are only of sentimental value. Nuestras fotografías sólo tienen valor sentimental.*

**se|pal** /sipəl/ (**sepals**) N-COUNT **Sepals** are a part of the outer structure of a flower, which resemble leaves and protect the bud while it is growing. sépalo [TECHNICAL]

**sepa|rate** (**separates, separating, separated**)

> The adjective and noun are pronounced /sɛpərɪt/. The verb is pronounced /sɛpəreɪt/.

**1** ADJ If one thing is **separate from** another, the two things are apart and are not connected. diferente, separado, aparte ❑ *They are now making plans to form their own separate organization. Ahora están haciendo planes para formar su propia organización diferente.* ❑ *Use separate surfaces for cutting raw meats and cooked meats. Utiliza diferentes superficies para cortar la carne cruda y la cocida.* ❑ *Men and women have separate exercise rooms. Hombres y mujeres tienen sitios diferentes para ejercitarse.* ● **sepa|rate|ly** /sɛpərɪtli/ ADV por separado ❑ *Cook each vegetable separately. Cocina cada verdura por separado.* **2** V-T/V-I If you **separate** people or things that are together, or if they **separate,** they move apart. separar ❑ *Police moved in to separate the two groups. La policía se acercó para separar a los dos grupos.* ❑ *They separated and Stephen went home. Se separaron y Stephen se fue a casa.* ● **sepa|ra|tion** /sɛpəreɪʃᵊn/ N-VAR (**separations**) separación ❑ *She wondered if Harry would remember her after this long separation. Se preguntaba si Harry la recordaría después de esta larga separación.* **3** V-T/V-I If you **separate** people or things that have been connected, or if one **separates from** another, the connection between them is ended. separar ❑ *We want to separate teaching from research. Queremos separar la enseñanza de la investigación.* **4** V-RECIP If a couple who are married or living together **separate,** they decide to live apart. separarse ❑ *Her parents separated when she was very young. Sus padres se separaron cuando era muy joven.* ● **sepa|rat|ed** /sɛpəreɪtɪd/ ADJ separado ❑ *Most single parents are either divorced or separated. La mayoría de los padres solteros son divorciados o separados.* ● **sepa|ra|tion** /sɛpəreɪʃᵊn/ N-VAR (**separations**) separación ❑ *They agreed to try a separation. Acordaron intentar una separación.* **5** V-T An object, obstacle, distance, or period of time which **separates** two people, groups, or things exists between them. separar ❑ *The white fence separated the yard from the field. La cerca blanca separaba el patio del campo.* ❑ *Six years separated these two important events. Seis años separaban esos dos importantes acontecimientos.* **6** V-T If you **separate** one idea or fact **from** another, you clearly see or show the difference between them. separar ❑ *It is difficult to separate these two aims. Es difícil separar estos dos objetivos.* ❑ *We learn how to separate real problems from imaginary illnesses. Aprendemos cómo separar los problemas reales de las enfermedades imaginarias.* ● **Separate out** means the same as **separate.** separar ❑ *In adult speech it is often difficult to separate out individual words. En el habla adulta con frecuencia es difícil separar cada palabra.* ● **sepa|ra|tion** /sɛpəreɪʃᵊn/ N-VAR (**separations**) separación ❑ *...the separation of the body and the soul. ...la separación del cuerpo y el alma.* **7** V-T A quality or factor that **separates** one thing **from** another is the reason why the two things are different from each other. distinguir ❑ *It is the lighting that separates ordinary photographs from good photographs. La buena fotografía se distingue de la ordinaria por la iluminación.* **8** V-T/V-I If you **separate** a group of people or things **into** smaller elements, or if a group **separates,** it is divided into smaller elements. separar ❑ *The police wanted to separate them into smaller groups. La policía los quería separar en grupos más pequeños.* ❑ *Let's separate into small groups. Separémonos en grupos pequeños.* ● **Separate out** means the same as **separate.** separarse ❑ *If you do it too soon, the mixture may separate out. Si lo haces demasiado pronto, la mezcla se podría separar.*

**9** N-PLURAL **Separates** are clothes such as skirts, pants, and shirts which cover just the top half or the bottom half of your body. *prendas combinables* ❑ *She wears matching separates instead of a suit. Ella usa prendas combinables en vez de traje sastre.*
**10** PHRASE When two or more people who have been together for some time **go** their **separate ways,** they go to different places or end their relationship. *tomar caminos distintos* ❑ *Sue and her husband decided to go their separate ways. Sue y su esposo decidieron tomar caminos distintos.*
▸ **separate out** PHR-VERB If you **separate out** something from the other things it is with, you take it out. *separar* ❑ *If you beat it too much, the mixture may separate out. Si lo bates demasiado, la mezcla podría separarse.*

**Thesaurus** *separate* Ver también:
ADJ. disconnected, divided **1**
V. divide, split **2** **5**

**sepa|ra|tist** /sɛpərətɪst/ (**separatists**) N-COUNT **Separatists** are people of an ethnic or cultural group within a country who want their own separate government. *separatista* ❑ *A group of separatists wants independence from the government. Un grupo de separatistas quiere la independencia de su gobierno.* ● **sepa|ra|tism** N-UNCOUNT *separatismo* ❑ *He promised to fight separatism. Prometió combatir el separatismo.*

**Sep|tem|ber** /sɛptɛmbər/ (**Septembers**) N-VAR **September** is the ninth month of the year in the Western calendar. *septiembre* ❑ *Her son was born in September. Su hijo nació en septiembre.* ❑ *We didn't meet the September 30 deadline. No cumplimos con la fecha límite del 30 de septiembre.*

**sep|tic tank** (**septic tanks**) N-COUNT A **septic tank** is an underground tank where feces, urine, and other waste matter is made harmless using bacteria. *fosa séptica*

**Word Link** *sequ ≈ following : consequence, sequel, sequence*

**se|quel** /sikwəl/ (**sequels**) N-COUNT A book or movie which is a **sequel to** an earlier one continues the story of the earlier one. *secuela* ❑ *She is writing a sequel to Daphne du Maurier's "Rebecca." Está escribiendo la secuela de "Rebecca", de Daphne du Maurier.*

**se|quence** /sikwəns/ (**sequences**) **1** N-COUNT A **sequence of** events or things is a number of events or things that come one after another in a particular order. *secuencia* ❑ *This is the sequence of events which led to the murder. Esta es la secuencia de eventos que condujeron al asesinato.* **2** N-COUNT A particular **sequence** is a particular order in which things happen or are arranged. *secuencia, orden* ❑ *The color sequence is yellow, orange, purple, blue, green, and white. El orden de los colores es amarillo, naranja, morado, azul, verde y blanco.*

**se|quined** /sikwɪnd/ also **sequinned** ADJ A **sequined** piece of clothing is decorated or covered with sequins. *con lentejuelas* ❑ *She wore a sequined evening gown. Traía un vestido de noche de lentejuelas.*

**se|quoia** /sɪkwɔɪə/ (**sequoias**) N-COUNT A **sequoia** is a very tall tree which grows in California. *secoya*

**ser|geant** /sɑrdʒənt/ (**sergeants**) **1** N-COUNT; N-TITLE; N-VOC A **sergeant** is an officer of low rank in the army, marines, or air force. *sargento* ❑ *A sergeant with four men came into view. Apareció un sargento con cuatro hombres.* **2** N-COUNT; N-TITLE; N-VOC A **sergeant** is a police officer with the rank immediately below a captain. *sargento* ❑ *A police sergeant patrolling the area noticed the fire. Un sargento de la policía que patrullaba el área se dio cuenta del incendio.*

**ser|geant ma|jor** (**sergeant majors**) also **sergeant-major** N-COUNT; N-TITLE; N-VOC A **sergeant major** is an officer of the middle rank in the army or the marines. *sargento mayor*

**se|rial** /sɪəriəl/ (**serials**) **1** N-COUNT A **serial** is a story which is broadcast on television or radio or is published in a magazine or newspaper in a number of parts over a period of time. *serie* ❑ *This is one of television's most popular serials. Esta es una de las series más populares de la televisión.* **2** ADJ **Serial** killings or attacks are a series of killings or attacks committed by the same person. This person is known as a **serial** killer or attacker. *serial* ❑ *...serial murders. ...asesinatos seriales.*

**se|rial mu|sic** N-UNCOUNT **Serial music** is a type of music that uses a particular set of notes, usually twelve, and organizes them in a particular way. *música serial* [TECHNICAL]

**se|ries** /sɪəriz/ (**series**) **1** N-COUNT A **series of** things or events is a number of them that come one after the other. *serie* ❑ *There will be a series of meetings with political leaders. Habrá una serie de reuniones con líderes políticos.* **2** N-COUNT A radio or television **series** is a set of programs of a particular kind which have the same title. *serie* ❑ *I love the TV series "Star Trek." Me encanta la serie de televisión "Star Trek."*

**se|ries cir|cuit** (**series circuits**) N-COUNT A **series circuit** is an electrical circuit in which there is only one possible path that the electricity can follow. *circuito en serie* [TECHNICAL]

**se|ri|ous** /sɪəriəs/ **1** ADJ **Serious** problems or situations are very bad and cause people to be worried or afraid. *serio* ❑ *Crime is a serious problem in Russian society. El crimen es un problema serio en la sociedad rusa.* ❑ *The government faces very serious difficulties. El gobierno enfrenta dificultades muy serias.* ● **se|ri|ous|ly** ADV *seriamente, con seriedad* ❑ *This law could seriously damage my business. Esta ley podría dañar seriamente mi negocio.* ● **se|ri|ous|ness** N-UNCOUNT *seriedad* ❑ *They don't realize the seriousness of the crisis. No se dan cuenta de la gravedad de la crisis.* **2** ADJ **Serious** matters are important and deserve careful thought. *serio* ❑ *I regard this as a serious matter. Considero que este es un problema serio.* ❑ *It is a question that deserves serious consideration. Es un asunto que merece ser considerado seriamente.* ● **se|ri|ous|ly** ADV *seriamente* ❑ *The management will have to think seriously about their positions. La administración tendrá que pensar seriamente sobre sus posturas.* **3** ADJ If you are **serious about** something, you are sincere about it. *en serio* ❑ *You really are serious about this, aren't you? Lo estás diciendo en serio, ¿verdad?* ● **se|ri|ous|ly** ADV *en serio* ❑ *Are you seriously jealous of Erica? ¿En serio estás celosa de*

S

*Erica?* • **se|ri|ous|ness** N-UNCOUNT *seriedad* ❑ *In all seriousness, what else can I do? Con toda seriedad, ¿qué más puedo hacer?* **4** ADJ **Serious** people are thoughtful and quiet, and do not laugh very often. *serio* ❑ *He's quite a serious person. Él es una persona muy seria.* • **se|ri|ous|ly** ADV *seriamente* ❑ *They spoke to me very seriously. Hablaron conmigo muy seriamente.*

**se|ri|ous|ly** /sɪəriəsli/ **1** ADV You use **seriously** to indicate that you really mean what you say, or to ask someone if they really mean what they have said. *en serio, en verdad* ❑ *Seriously, I only watch TV in the evenings. En serio, sólo veo televisión en las noches.* ❑ *"I followed him home," he said. "Seriously?" —Lo seguí hasta su casa —dijo. —¿En serio?* **2** → see also **serious** **3** PHRASE If you **take** someone or something **seriously,** you believe that they are important and deserve attention. *tomar en serio* ❑ *It's hard to take them seriously in their pretty uniforms. Es difícil tomarlos en serio con sus bonitos uniformes.*

**ser|mon** /sɜrmən/ (**sermons**) N-COUNT A **sermon** is a talk on a religious or moral subject that is given by a member of the clergy as part of a religious service. *sermón* ❑ *Cardinal Murphy will deliver the sermon on Sunday. El cardenal Murphy dará un sermón el domingo.*

**serv|ant** /sɜrvᵊnt/ (**servants**) **1** N-COUNT A **servant** is someone who is employed to work at another person's home, for example, as a cleaner or a gardener. *sirviente o sirvienta* ❑ *It was a large Victorian family with several servants. Era una familia victoriana grande con muchos sirvientes.* **2** → see also **civil servant**

**serve** /sɜrv/ (**serves, serving, served**) **1** V-T If you **serve** your country, an organization, or a person, you do useful work for them. *servir* ❑ *This decision is unfair to soldiers who have served their country well. Esta decisión es injusta para los soldados que han servido bien a su país.* ❑ *During the second world war he served with the army. Prestó servicio en el ejército durante la segunda guerra mundial.* ❑ *They have both served on the school board. Ambos han sido miembros del consejo escolar.* **2** V-T/V-I If something **serves as** a particular thing or **serves** a particular purpose, it performs a particular function, which is often not its intended function. *servir* ❑ *She showed me into the front room, which served as her office. Me pasó al salón, que hacía las veces de su oficina.* ❑ *I do not think an investigation would serve any useful purpose. No creo que una investigación sirva un propósito útil.* **3** V-T If something **serves** people or an area, it provides them with something that they need. *servir* ❑ *There are thousands of small businesses which serve the community. Hay miles de negocios pequeños que sirven a la comunidad.* **4** V-T/V-I When you **serve** food and drinks, you give people food and drinks. *servir* ❑ *Serve the cakes warm. Sirve los pasteles calientes.* ❑ *Refrigerate until ready to serve. Refrigerar hasta que esté listo para servirse.* • **Serve up** means the same as **serve.** *servir* ❑ *It is no use serving up delicious meals if the kids won't eat them. No tiene sentido servir comida deliciosa si los niños no se la van a comer.* **5** V-T/V-I Someone who **serves** customers in a store or a bar helps them and provides them with what they want to buy. *servir* ❑ *Maggie served me coffee and pie. Maggie me sirvió café y pastel.* **6** V-T If you **serve** something such as a prison sentence or an apprenticeship, you spend a period of time doing it. *cumplir* ❑ *Leo is serving a life sentence for murder. Leo está cumpliendo una condena a cadena perpetua por asesinato.* **7** V-T/V-I When you **serve** in games such as tennis and badminton, you throw up the ball or shuttlecock and hit it to start play. *sacar, servir* ❑ *She served again and eventually won the game. Ella sacó de nuevo y finalmente ganó el partido.* • **Serve** is also a noun. *servicio, saque* ❑ *His second serve hit the net. Su segundo servicio golpeó la red.* **8** → see also **serving** **9** PHRASE If you say **it serves** someone **right** when something unpleasant happens to them, you mean that it is their own fault and you have no sympathy for them. *se lo tiene bien merecido* ❑ *It serves her right for being so difficult. Se lo tiene bien merecido por ser tan difícil.*

▸ **serve up** → see **serve 4**

**Word Partnership** Usar *serve* con:

| | |
|---|---|
| N. | serve **a community**, serve **the public** **1** **3** |
| | serve **a purpose** **2** |
| | serve **cake**, serve **food** **4** |

**serv|er** /sɜrvər/ (**servers**) **1** N-COUNT In computing, a **server** is part of a computer network which does a particular task, such as storing or processing information, for all or part of the network. *servidor* [COMPUTING] **2** N-COUNT A **server** is a person who works in a restaurant, serving people with food and drink. *mesero o mesera* ❑ *A server came by with a tray of coffee cups. Se acercó un mesero con una charola de tazas de café.*
→ see **Internet**

**service**

❶ NOUN AND ADJECTIVE USES
❷ VERB USES
❸ PHRASES

❶ **ser|vice** /sɜrvɪs/ (**services**) **1** N-COUNT A **service** is something that the public needs, such as transportation, communications facilities, hospitals, or energy supplies. *servicio* ❑ *The postal service has been trying to cut costs. El servicio postal ha estado tratando de reducir costos.* **2** N-COUNT A **service** is a job that an organization or business can do for you. *servicio* ❑ *The hotel kitchen has a twenty-four hour service. La cocina del hotel da servicio las 24 horas.* **3** N-UNCOUNT The level or standard of **service** provided by an organization or company is the amount or quality of the work it can do for you. *servicio* ❑ *We try to provide effective and efficient customer service. Tratamos de ofrecer un servicio al cliente eficaz y eficiente.* **4** N-UNCOUNT **Service** is the state or activity of working for a particular person or organization. *servicio* ❑ *He's given a lifetime of service to athletics. Ha entregado su vida al deporte.* ❑ *Most employees had long service with the company. La mayoría de los empleados han prestado sus servicios a la compañía durante largo tiempo.* **5** N-COUNT **The services** are the army, the navy, the air force, and the marines. *fuerzas armadas* ❑ *Some of the money should be spent on training in the services. Parte del dinero se debería destinar al entrenamiento de las fuerzas armadas.* **6** N-UNCOUNT When you receive **service** in a restaurant, hotel, or store, an employee asks you what you want or gives you what you have ordered. *servicio* ❑ *The service was fast and polite. El*

*servicio fue rápido y bueno.* **7** N-COUNT A **service** is a religious ceremony that takes place in a church or synagogue. *oficio religioso* ❑ *After the service, his body was taken to a cemetery. Después del funeral, su cuerpo fue llevado al cementerio.* **8** N-COUNT If a vehicle or machine has a **service,** it is examined, adjusted, and cleaned so that it will keep working efficiently and safely. *servicio* ❑ *The car needs a service. El auto necesita servicio.* **9** → see also **civil service, community service**
→ see **hotel, industry, library**

❷ **ser|vice** /sɜrvɪs/ (**services, servicing, serviced**) V-T If you have a vehicle or machine **serviced,** you arrange for someone to examine, adjust, and clean it so that it will keep working efficiently and safely. *dar servicio, revisar* ❑ *I have my car serviced at the local garage. Me hacen el servicio a mi carro en el taller de la zona.*

❸ **ser|vice** /sɜrvɪs/ PHRASE If a piece of equipment or type of vehicle is **in service,** it is being used or is able to be used. If it is **out of service,** it is not being used, usually because it is not working properly. *en servicio /fuera de servicio* ❑ *Most of the planes should be back in service by the end of the week. La mayoría de los aviones deben estar de nuevo en servicio al terminar la semana.* ❑ *The elevator was out of service so she took the stairs. El elevador estaba fuera de servicio así que usó las escaleras.*

**ser|vice|man** /sɜrvɪsmən/ (**servicemen**) N-COUNT A **serviceman** is a man who is in the army, navy, air force, or marines. *militar* ❑ *He was an American serviceman in Vietnam. Fue un militar estadounidense en Vietnam.*

**ser|vice pro|vid|er** (**service providers**) N-COUNT A **service provider** is a company that provides a service, especially an Internet service. *proveedor de servicios* [COMPUTING]

**serv|ing** /sɜrvɪŋ/ (**servings**) N-COUNT A **serving** is an amount of food that is given to one person at a meal. *porción, ración* ❑ *How many servings do you want to prepare? ¿Cuántas porciones desea preparar?*

**ses|sion** /sɛʃᵊn/ (**sessions**) **1** N-COUNT A **session** is a meeting or series of meetings of a court, legislature, or other official group. *sesión* ❑ *After two late night sessions, they failed to reach agreement. Después de dos sesiones nocturnas, no lograron llegar a un acuerdo.* ❑ *The Arab League is meeting in emergency session today. Hoy la Liga Árabe tendrá una sesión de emergencia.* ❑ *Congress remained in session from September until December. El Congreso permaneció en sesión desde septiembre hasta diciembre.* **2** N-COUNT A **session** of a particular activity is a period of that activity. *sesión* ❑ *The two leaders arrived for a photo session. Ambos líderes llegaron a una sesión fotográfica.*

**set**
❶ NOUN USES
❷ VERB AND ADJECTIVE USES

❶ **set** /sɛt/ (**sets**) **1** N-COUNT A **set of** things is a number of things that belong together or that are thought of as a group. *conjunto* ❑ *There must be one set of laws for the whole country. Todo el país debe regirse por las mismas leyes.* ❑ *The table and chairs are normally bought as a set. La mesa y las sillas normalmente se compran en conjunto.* ❑ *...a chess set. ...juego de ajedrez.* **2** N-COUNT In tennis, a **set** is one of the groups of six or more games that form part of a match. *set* ❑ *Williams was leading 5-1 in the first set. Williams llevaba la delantera 5-1 en el primer set.* **3** N-COUNT The **set** for a play, movie, or television show is the furniture and scenery that is on the stage when the play is being performed or in the studio where filming takes place. *set* ❑ *From the moment he got on the set, he wanted to be a director. Desde el momento en que puso un pie en el set, quería ser director.* ❑ *Across the street, the buildings look like stage sets. Cruzando la calle, los edificios se ven como escenarios.* **4** N-COUNT A television **set** is a television. *televisión* ❑ *Children spend too much time in front of the television set. Los niños pasan demasiado tiempo frente a la televisión.*
→ see **drama, theater**

❷ **set** /sɛt/ (**sets, setting**)

The form **set** is used in the present tense and is the past tense and past participle of the verb.

→ Please look at category **17** to see if the expression you are looking for is shown under another headword. **1** V-T If you **set** something somewhere, you put it there, especially in a careful or deliberate way. *poner, colocar* ❑ *He set the case carefully on the floor. Puso con cuidado la maleta en el piso.* **2** ADJ If something is **set** in a particular place or position, it is in that place or position. *ubicado* ❑ *The castle is set in 25 acres of park land. El castillo está ubicado en 10 hectáreas de jardines.* **3** ADJ If something is **set into** a surface, it is fixed there and does not stick out. *fijo, colocado* ❑ *The man unlocked a gate set in a high wall. El hombre abrió una reja que daba paso a través de un muro alto.* **4** V-T You can use **set** to say that a person or thing causes another person or thing to be in a particular condition or situation. For example, to **set** someone free means to cause them to be free. *dejar* ❑ *His words set my mind wandering. Sus palabras me dejaron pensando.* ❑ *Many vehicles were set on fire. Le prendieron fuego a muchos vehículos.* **5** V-T When you **set** a clock or control, you adjust it to a particular point or level. *poner* ❑ *Set the volume as high as possible. Pon el volumen lo más alto que se pueda.* **6** V-T If you **set** a date, price, goal, or level, you decide what it will be. *fijar, acordar* ❑ *The conference chairman has set a deadline of noon tomorrow. El presidente del congreso fijó como fecha límite mañana a mediodía.* ❑ *A date will be set for a future meeting. Se fijará una fecha para una próxima reunión.* **7** V-T If you **set** something such as a record, or an example, you do something that people will want to copy or try to achieve. *establecer* ❑ *The new world record was set by Stephen Jones of Great Britain. Stephen Jones de Gran Bretaña estableció el nuevo récord mundial.* **8** V-T If someone **sets** you a task or aim or if you **set yourself** a task or goal, you need to succeed in doing it. *asignar, plantear* ❑ *I have to plan my work and set myself clear targets. Tengo que planear mi trabajo y asignarme objetivos claros.* **9** ADJ You use **set** to describe something which is fixed and cannot be changed. *establecido* ❑ *I wrote music during a set period every morning. Todas las mañanas escribía música durante determinado número de horas.* **10** ADJ If a play,

S

movie, or story is **set** in a particular place or period of time, the events in it take place in that place or period. *desarrollarse* ❑ *The play is set in a small Midwestern town. La obra se desarrolla en un pequeño pueblo de la región central de Estados Unidos.* **11** ADJ If you are **set to** do something, you are ready to do it or are likely to do it. If something is **set to** happen, it is about to happen or likely to happen. *listo para* ❑ *Roberto Baggio was set to become one of the greatest players of all time. Roberto Baggio estaba listo para convertirse en uno de los mejores jugadores de todos los tiempos.* **12** ADJ If you are **set on** something, you are strongly determined to do or have it. *decidido a* ❑ *She was set on going to an all-girls school. Estaba decidida a ir a una escuela sólo para niñas.* **13** V-I When something such as jelly, glue, or cement **sets,** it becomes firm or hard. *cuajar, fraguar* ❑ *You can add fruit to these desserts as they begin to set. Puedes añadir fruta a estos postres cuando comienzan a cuajar.* **14** V-I When the sun **sets,** it goes below the horizon. *ponerse* ❑ *They watched the sun set behind the distant hills. Vieron ponerse el sol tras las distantes colinas.* **15** → see also **setting** **16** PHRASE If someone **sets the scene** or **sets the stage for** an event to take place, they make preparations so that it can take place. *situar la escena* ❑ *Today's opening will set the scene for next week's meeting of world leaders. La inauguración de hoy situará la escena para la reunión de líderes mundiales de la próxima semana.* **17** to **set fire to** something → see **fire** **18** to **set sail** → see **sail** → see also **sit**

▶ **set aside** **1** PHR-VERB If you **set** something **aside for** a special use or purpose, you keep it available for that use or purpose. *apartar, reservar* ❑ *Try to set aside time each day to relax. Trata de dedicar algo de tiempo al descanso todos los días.* **2** PHR-VERB If you **set aside** a belief, principle, or feeling, you decide that you will not be influenced by it. *dejar de lado* ❑ *At this dinner party, politics are set aside. En esta cena, la política se deja de lado.*

▶ **set back** **1** PHR-VERB If something **sets** you **back** or **sets back** a project or plan, it causes a delay. *retrasar* ❑ *We have been set so far back that I'm not sure how long it will take for us to catch up. Nos hemos retrasado tanto que no estoy seguro de cuánto tiempo nos llevará ponernos al día.* **2** PHR-VERB If something **sets** you **back** a certain amount of money, it costs you that much money. *costar* [INFORMAL] ❑ *A bottle of olive oil could set you back $7. Una botella de aceite de oliva te podría costar $7.* **3** → see also **setback**

S

▶ **set down** PHR-VERB If a committee or organization **sets down** rules for doing something, it decides what they should be and officially records them. *establecer* ❑ *I like to make suggestions rather than setting down laws. Me gusta hacer sugerencias más que establecer leyes.*

▶ **set in** PHR-VERB If something unpleasant **sets in,** it begins and seems likely to continue or develop. *llegar* ❑ *Winter is setting in and the population is facing food shortages. Llegó el invierno y la población enfrenta escasez de alimentos.*

▶ **set off** **1** PHR-VERB When you **set off,** you start a journey. *salir, partir* ❑ *Nick set off for his farmhouse in Connecticut. Nick salió a su granja de Connecticut.* **2** PHR-VERB If something **sets off** something such as an alarm or a bomb, it makes it start working so that the alarm rings or the bomb explodes. *hacer sonar, hacer explotar* ❑ *Any escape sets off the alarm. Cualquier fuga hace sonar la alarma.*

▶ **set out** **1** PHR-VERB When you **set out,** you start a journey. *salir* ❑ *When setting out on a long walk, always wear suitable shoes. Si vas a dar una larga caminata, lleva siempre zapatos apropiados.* **2** PHR-VERB If you **set out to** do something, you start trying to do it. *proponerse* ❑ *He did what he set out to do. Hizo lo que se propuso.* **3** PHR-VERB If you **set** things **out,** you arrange or display them somewhere. *colocar* ❑ *Set out the cakes attractively. Acomoda bonito los pasteles.* **4** PHR-VERB If you **set out** a number of facts, beliefs, or arguments, you explain them in writing or speech in a clear, organized way. *exponer* ❑ *He has written a letter to The New York Times setting out his views. Ha escrito una carta al New York Times exponiendo sus puntos de vista.*

▶ **set up** **1** PHR-VERB If you **set** something **up,** you create or arrange it. *crear, abrir* ❑ *The two sides agreed to set up an investigation. Ambas partes acordaron abrir una investigación.* ❑ *We set up meetings about issues of interest to women. Creamos reuniones sobre asuntos de interés para las mujeres.* ● **set|ting up** N-UNCOUNT *creación* ❑ *The government announced the setting up of a special fund. El gobierno anunció la creación de un fondo especial.* **2** PHR-VERB If you **set up** a temporary structure, you place it or build it somewhere. *montar, armar* ❑ *Brian set up a tent on the lawn. Brian armó una tienda de campaña en el jardín.* **3** PHR-VERB If you **set up** somewhere or **set yourself up** somewhere, you establish yourself in a new business or new area. *establecerse* ❑ *The mayor offered to help companies setting up in lower Manhattan. El alcalde ofreció ayudar a las compañías a establecerse al sur de Manhattan.* **4** → see also **setup**

**set|back** /sɛtbæk/ (**setbacks**) N-COUNT A **setback** is an event that delays your progress or reverses some of the progress that you have made. *contratiempo* ❑ *He suffered a serious setback in his career. Tuvo un serio contratiempo en su carrera.*

**set|ting** /sɛtɪŋ/ (**settings**) **1** N-COUNT A particular **setting** is a particular place or type of surroundings where something is or takes place. *escenario* ❑ *Rome is the perfect setting for romance. Roma es el escenario perfecto para el romance.* **2** N-COUNT A **setting** is one of the positions to which the controls of a device such as a stove or heater can be adjusted. *posición* ❑ *Bake the fish on a high setting. Hornee el pescado a una temperatura alta.*

**set|tle** /sɛtᵊl/ (**settles, settling, settled**) **1** V-T If people **settle** an argument or problem, or if something **settles** it, they solve it by making a decision about who is right or about what to do. *resolver* ❑ *They agreed to try again to settle the dispute. Acordaron tratar una vez más de resolver el conflicto.* **2** V-T/V-I If you **settle** a bill or debt, you pay the amount that you owe. *pagar, liquidar* ❑ *I settled the bill for my coffee and left. Pagué la cuenta de mi café y me fui.* **3** V-T If something **is settled,** it has all been decided and arranged. *decidido, arreglado* ❑ *We feel the matter is now settled. Creemos que el problema ahora está arreglado.* **4** V-I When people **settle** a place or in a place, they start living there permanently. *establecerse* ❑ *He visited Paris and eventually settled there. Visitó París y con el tiempo se estableció allí.* **5** V-T/V-I If you **settle yourself** somewhere or **settle** somewhere, you sit down or make yourself comfortable. *ponerse cómodo* ❑ *Albert* settled himself on the sofa. Albert se puso cómodo en el sofá. **6** V-I If something **settles,** it sinks slowly down and becomes still. asentar, quedarse ❑ A fly settled on the wall. Una mosca se paró en la pared. ❑ The fog blows over the mountains and settles in the valley. La niebla pasa por encima de las montañas y se queda en el valle. **7** → see also **settled** **8** **when the dust settles** → see **dust** **9** to **settle a score** → see **score**

▸ **settle down** **1** PHR-VERB When someone **settles down,** they start living a quiet life in one place, especially when they get married or buy a house. sentar cabeza ❑ One day I'll settle down and have a family. Un día sentaré cabeza y tendré una familia. **2** PHR-VERB If a situation or a person that has been going through a lot of problems or changes **settles down,** they become calm. calmarse, arreglarse ❑ The situation in Europe will soon settle down. La situación en Europa se arreglará pronto. **3** PHR-VERB If you **settle down to** do something or **to** something, you prepare to do it and concentrate on it. ponerse a ❑ He settled down to listen to the music. Se puso a escuchar música.

▸ **settle for** PHR-VERB If you **settle for** something, you choose or accept it, especially when it is not what you really want but there is nothing else available. conformarse con ❑ Virginia would never settle for anything less than perfection. Virginia jamás se conformaría con algo menos que perfecto.

▸ **settle in** PHR-VERB If you **settle in,** you become used to living in a new place, doing a new job, or going to a new school. adaptarse a ❑ I enjoyed school once I settled in. Disfruté la escuela una vez que me adapté.

▸ **settle on** PHR-VERB If you **settle on** a particular thing, you choose it after considering other possible choices. decidirse por ❑ I finally settled on a Mercedes. Finalmente me decidí por un Mercedes.

▸ **settle up** PHR-VERB When you **settle up,** you pay a bill or a debt. arreglar cuentas, pagar ❑ I'll have to settle up before I leave. Tendré que arreglar cuentas antes de irme.

**Word Partnership** Usar *settle* con:

N. settle **differences**, settle **a dispute**, settle **a matter**, settle **things** **1**
V. **agree to** settle, **decide to** settle **1** **2**

**set|tled** /sɛtᵊld/ **1** ADJ If you have a **settled** way of life, you stay in one place, in one job, or with one person, rather than moving around or changing. ordenado, estable ❑ He decided to lead a more settled life. Decidió llevar una vida más estable. **2** ADJ A **settled** situation or system stays the same all the time. estable ❑ The weather will be more settled tomorrow. El clima será más estable mañana.

**set|tle|ment** /sɛtᵊlmənt/ (**settlements**) **1** N-COUNT A **settlement** is an official agreement between two sides who were involved in a conflict or argument. acuerdo, convenio ❑ Officials are hoping for a peaceful settlement of the crisis. Los oficiales esperan que la crisis se resuelva por la vía pacífica. **2** N-COUNT A **settlement** is a place where people have come to live and have built homes. asentamiento ❑ The village is a settlement of just fifty houses. La aldea es un asentamiento de sólo cincuenta casas.

**set|tler** /sɛtlər, sɛtᵊl-/ (**settlers**) N-COUNT **Settlers** are people who go to live in a new country. colono, colona ❑ ...the early settlers in North America. ...los primeros colonos de Norteamérica.

**set|up** /sɛtʌp/ (**setups**) also **set-up** N-COUNT A particular **setup** is a particular system or way of organizing something. sistema, arreglo, organización [INFORMAL] ❑ It appears to be the ideal domestic setup. Parece ser el sistema doméstico ideal.

**sev|en** /sɛvᵊn/ (**sevens**) NUM **Seven** is the number 7. siete ❑ Sarah and Ella have been friends for seven years. Sarah y Ella han sido amigas por siete años.

**Word Link** *teen ≈ plus ten, from 13–19 : eighteen, seventeen, teenager*

**sev|en|teen** /sɛvᵊntin/ (**seventeens**) NUM **Seventeen** is the number 17. diecisiete ❑ Jenny is seventeen years old. Jenny tiene diecisiete años.

**sev|en|teenth** /sɛvᵊntinθ/ (**seventeenths**) ORD The **seventeenth** item in a series is the one that you count as number seventeen. decimoséptimo ❑ She got the job just after her seventeenth birthday. Consiguió el empleo justo después de su decimoséptimo cumpleaños.

**sev|enth** /sɛvᵊnθ/ (**sevenths**) **1** ORD The **seventh** item in a series is the one that you count as number seven. séptimo ❑ I was the seventh child in the family. Fui el séptimo hijo. **2** N-COUNT A **seventh** is one of seven equal parts of something. séptima parte ❑ A million people died, a seventh of the population. Un millón de personas murieron, una séptima parte de la población.

**sev|en|ti|eth** /sɛvᵊntiəθ/ (**seventieths**) ORD The **seventieth** item in a series is the one that you count as number seventy. septuagésimo ❑ It was my grandmother's seventieth birthday last week. Mi abuela cumplió setenta años la semana pasada.

**sev|en|ty** /sɛvᵊnti/ (**seventies**) **1** NUM **Seventy** is the number 70. setenta ❑ Seventy people were killed in the fire. Setenta personas murieron en el incendio. **2** N-PLURAL The **seventies** is the decade between 1970 and 1979. los setenta ❑ In the early Seventies, he wanted to direct. A principios de los setenta, quería dirigir.

**sev|er|al** /sɛvrəl/ DET **Several** is used to refer to a number of people or things that is not large but is greater than two. varios ❑ I lived two doors away from this family for several years. Viví a dos puertas de esta familia por varios años. ❑ There were several blue plastic boxes under the window. Había varias cajas de plástico azul bajo la ventana. ● **Several** is also a quantifier. varios ❑ He was with his sons, several of whom work in the business with him. Estaba con sus hijos, varios de los cuales trabajan con él en el negocio. ● **Several** is also a pronoun. varios ❑ Sometimes several different treatments have to be tried. A veces se debe intentar con varios tratamientos diferentes.

**se|vere** /sɪvɪər/ (**severer, severest**) **1** ADJ You use **severe** to indicate that something bad or undesirable is great or intense. grave, serio ❑ The business has severe financial problems. El negocio tiene serios problemas financieros. ● **se|vere|ly** ADV gravemente ❑ An aircraft crashed on the runway and was severely damaged. Un avión se estrelló en la pista y tuvo graves daños. ● **se|ver|ity** /sɪvɛrɪti/ N-UNCOUNT gravedad ❑ Not everyone agrees about the severity of the

S

problem. No todos están de acuerdo con la gravedad del problema. **2** ADJ **Severe** punishments or criticisms are very strong or harsh. *severo* ❑ *A severe sentence is necessary for such a crime.* *Se necesita una sentencia severa para un crimen así.* ● **se|vere|ly** ADV *con severidad* ❑ *They want to change the law and punish dangerous drivers more severely.* *Quieren cambiar la ley y castigar a los conductores peligrosos con más severidad.* ● **se|ver|ity** N-UNCOUNT *severidad* ❑ *They were surprised by the severity of the criticism.* *Se sorpendieron por la severidad de la crítica.*

**Thesaurus** *severe* Ver también:

ADJ. critical, extreme, intense, tough **1** **2**

**Word Partnership** Usar *severe* con:

N. severe **consequences**, severe **depression**, severe **disease/illness**, severe **drought**, severe **flooding**, severe **injuries**, severe **pain**, severe **problem**, severe **symptoms**, severe **weather** **1**
severe **penalty**, severe **punishment** **2**

ADV. **less/more/most** severe, **very** severe **1** **2**

**sew** /soʊ/ (**sews, sewing, sewed, sewn**) V-T/V-I When you **sew** something such as clothes, you make them or repair them by joining pieces of cloth together by passing thread through them with a needle. *coser* ❑ *She sewed the dresses on the sewing machine.* *Cosió los vestidos en la máquina de coser.* ❑ *Anyone can sew on a button.* *Cualquiera puede coser un botón.* ● **sew|ing** N-UNCOUNT *costura* ❑ *Her mother always did all the sewing.* *Su madre siempre hizo todo lo de costura.*
→ see **quilt**

**sew|age** /suɪdʒ/ N-UNCOUNT **Sewage** is waste matter such as feces or dirty water from homes and factories, which flows away through sewers. *aguas residuales* ❑ *...treatment of raw sewage.* *...tratamiento de aguas residuales.*
→ see **pollution**

**sew|age treat|ment plant** (**sewage treatment plants**) N-COUNT A **sewage treatment plant** is a factory that removes waste materials from water that comes from sewers and drains. *planta de tratamiento de aguas residuales*

S

**sew|er** /suər/ (**sewers**) N-COUNT A **sewer** is a large underground channel that carries waste matter and rain water away. *alcantarilla* ❑ *...the city's sewer system.* *...el sistema de alcantarillado de la ciudad.*

**sewn** /soʊn/ **Sewn** is the past participle of **sew**. *pasado de* ***sew***

**sex** /sɛks/ (**sexes, sexing, sexed**) **1** N-COUNT The two **sexes** are the two groups, male and female, into which people and animals are divided. *sexo* ❑ *This movie appeals to both sexes.* *Esta película atrae a ambos sexos.* **2** → see also **opposite sex** **3** N-COUNT The **sex** of a person or animal is their characteristic of being either male or female. *sexo* ❑ *We can identify the sex of your unborn baby.* *Podemos identificar el sexo de tu bebé aunque no haya nacido.* **4** N-UNCOUNT **Sex** is the physical activity by which people can produce children. *sexo* ❑ *He was very open in his attitudes about sex.* *Era muy abierto en sus actitudes hacia el sexo.* **5** PHRASE If two people **have sex,** they perform the act of sex. *tener relaciones sexuales*

**sex cell** (**sex cells**) N-COUNT **Sex cells** are the two types of male and female cells that join together to make a new creature. *célula sexual*

**sex chro|mo|some** (**sex chromosomes**) N-COUNT **Sex chromosomes** are the chromosomes that carry the genes which determine whether an individual will be male or female. *cromosoma sexual* [TECHNICAL]

**sex|ist** /sɛksɪst/ (**sexists**) ADJ If you describe people or their behavior as **sexist,** you disapprove of them because they show prejudice and discrimination against the members of one sex, usually women. *sexista* ❑ *Old-fashioned sexist attitudes are still common.* *Las actitudes sexistas pasadas de moda aún son comunes.* ● A **sexist** is someone with sexist views or behavior. *sexista* ❑ *You know I'm not a sexist.* *Sabes que no soy sexista.* ● **sex|ism** /sɛksɪzəm/ N-UNCOUNT *sexismo* ❑ *Students here can live in a community free of sexism.* *Aquí los estudiantes pueden vivir en una comunidad libre de sexismo.*

**sex of|fend|er** (**sex offenders**) N-COUNT A **sex offender** is a person who has been found guilty of a sexual crime such as rape or sexual assault. *delincuente sexual*

**sex|ual** /sɛkʃuəl/ **1** ADJ **Sexual** feelings or activities are connected with the act of sex or with people's desire for sex. *sexual* ❑ *The use of sexual images in advertising is not new.* *El uso de imágenes sexuales en la publicidad no es nuevo.* **2** ADJ **Sexual** means relating to the differences between male and female people. *sexual* ❑ *...sexual discrimination.* *...discriminación sexual* **3** ADJ **Sexual** means relating to the biological process by which people and animals produce young. *sexual* ❑ *Girls usually reach sexual maturity earlier than boys.* *Normalmente las niñas alcanzan la madurez sexual antes que los niños.* ● **sex|ual|ly** ADV *sexualmente* ❑ *...organisms that reproduce sexually.* *...organismos que se reproducen sexualmente.*

**sexu|al|ity** /sɛkʃuælɪti/ **1** N-UNCOUNT A person's **sexuality** is their sexual feelings. *sexualidad* ❑ *The program focuses on the scientific aspects of sexuality.* *El programa se centra en los aspectos científicos de la sexualidad.* **2** N-UNCOUNT You can refer to a person's **sexuality** when you are talking about whether they are sexually attracted to people of the same sex or a different sex. *sexualidad* ❑ *...information about sexuality, reproduction, and the human body.* *...información sobre la sexualidad, la reproducción y el cuerpo humano.*

**sex|ual|ly trans|mit|ted dis|ease** (**sexually transmitted diseases**) N-COUNT A **sexually transmitted disease** is a disease such as syphilis or herpes that can be passed from one person to another as a result of sexual activity. The abbreviation **STD** is also used. *enfermedad de transimisión sexual*

**sex|ual re|pro|duc|tion** N-UNCOUNT **Sexual reproduction** is the creation of new people, animals, or plants as a result of sexual activity. *reproducción sexual*

**sexy** /sɛksi/ (**sexier, sexiest**) ADJ You can

describe people and things as **sexy** if you think they are sexually exciting or sexually attractive. *sexy, sensual* ❑ *She is the sexiest woman I have ever seen. Es la mujer más sexy que he visto en mi vida.*

**shab|by** /ʃæbi/ (**shabbier, shabbiest**) ADJ **Shabby** things or places look old and in bad condition. *gastado* ❑ *His clothes were old and shabby. Su ropa era vieja y gastada.*

**shack** /ʃæk/ (**shacks**) N-COUNT A **shack** is a simple hut built from tin, wood, or other materials. *choza*

**shade** /ʃeɪd/ (**shades, shading, shaded**) **1** N-COUNT A **shade of** a particular color is one of its different forms. *tono* ❑ *The sky was a heavy shade of gray. El cielo tenía un tono gris oscuro.* ❑ *The walls were painted in two shades of green. Las paredes se pintaron de dos tonos de verde.* **2** N-UNCOUNT **Shade** is an area of darkness under or next to an object such as a tree, where sunlight does not reach. *sombra* ❑ *Temperatures in the shade can reach eighty degrees Fahrenheit here. La temperatura a la sombra puede alcanzar los 80 grados Fahrenheit aquí.* ❑ *Alexis was reading in the shade of a high cliff. Alexis estaba leyendo a la sombra de un gran acantilado.* **3** V-T If a place **is shaded** by something, that thing prevents light from falling on it. *dar sombra* ❑ *The beach was shaded by palm trees. Las palmeras daban sombra a la playa.* **4** N-UNCOUNT **Shade** is darkness or shadows as they are shown in a picture. *sombra* ❑ *...Rembrandt's skillful use of light and shade. ...el hábil uso de luz y sombra de Rembrandt.* **5** N-COUNT The **shades of** something abstract are its many, slightly different forms. *matiz* ❑ *In this poem we find many shades of meaning. El significado de este poema tiene muchos matices.* **6** N-COUNT A **shade** is a piece of stiff cloth or heavy paper that you can pull down over a window as a covering. *persiana* ❑ *Nancy left the shades down. Nancy dejó las persianas abajo.* **7** N-COUNT A **shade** is color with black added to it. *sombra*

**shad|ow** /ʃædoʊ/ (**shadows, shadowing, shadowed**) **1** N-COUNT A **shadow** is a dark shape on a surface that is made when something stands between a light and the surface. *sombra* ❑ *A tree threw its shadow over the pool. Un árbol proyectaba su sombra en el estanque.* **2** N-UNCOUNT **Shadow** is darkness in a place caused by something preventing light from reaching it. *sombra* ❑ *Most of the lake was in shadow. Casi todo el lago estaba en la sombra.* **3** V-T If something **shadows** a thing or place, it covers it with a shadow. *emsombrecer, dar sombra* ❑ *The hat shadowed her face. El sombrero ensombrecía su rostro.* **4** V-T If someone **shadows** you, they follow you very closely wherever you go. *seguir de cerca* ❑ *The president is shadowed by bodyguards. Los guardaespaldas siguen de cerca al presidente.*

**shad|ow zone** (**shadow zones**) N-COUNT A **shadow zone** is an area on the Earth's surface where seismic waves from an earthquake cannot be detected because they are unable to pass through the Earth's core. *zona de sombra* [TECHNICAL]

**shaft** /ʃæft/ (**shafts**) **1** N-COUNT A **shaft** is a long vertical passage, for example, for an elevator. *pozo* ❑ *The fire began in an elevator shaft. El incendio comenzó en un pozo de elevador.* **2** N-COUNT In a machine, a **shaft** is a rod that turns around continually in order to transfer movement in the machine. *árbol* ❑ *...a drive shaft. ...un árbol de levas.* **3** N-COUNT A **shaft of** light is a beam of light, for example, sunlight shining through an opening. *rayo* ❑ *A shaft of sunlight fell through the doorway. Un rayo de sol entró por la puerta.*

**shag|gy** /ʃægi/ (**shaggier, shaggiest**) ADJ **Shaggy** hair or fur is long and messy. *enmarañado* ❑ *Tim still has shaggy hair. Tim todavía tiene el cabello enmarañado.*

**shake** /ʃeɪk/ (**shakes, shaking, shook, shaken**) **1** V-T If you **shake** something or someone, you hold them and move them quickly backward and forward or up and down. *agitar* ❑ *The nurse took the thermometer and shook it. La enfermera tomó el termómetro y lo sacudió.* • **Shake** is also a noun. *sacudida* ❑ *She picked up the bag and gave it a shake. Tomó la bolsa y le dio una sacudida.* **2** V-T If you **shake** your **head**, you turn it from side to side in order to say "no" or to show disbelief or sadness. *negar con la cabeza* ❑ *Kathryn shook her head wearily. Kathryn negó con la cabeza mostrando cansancio.* • **Shake** is also a noun. *negando con la cabeza* ❑ *"The trees are dying," said Palmer, with a sad shake of his head. —Los árboles se están muriendo —dijo Palmer, con un movimiento triste de la cabeza.* **3** V-T/V-I If a force **shakes** something, or if something **shakes,** it moves from side to side or up and down with quick, small, but sometimes violent movements. *sacudir* ❑ *An explosion shook buildings several miles away. Una explosión sacudió los edificios a varios kilómetros.* **4** V-T If an event or a piece of news **shakes** you, it makes you feel upset and unable to think calmly. *impresionar, afectar* ❑ *The news of Tandy's escape shook them all. La noticia de la fuga de Tandy los impresionó a todos.* **5** PHRASE If you **shake hands with** someone, you take their right hand in your own for a few moments, often moving it up and down slightly, when you are saying hello or goodbye to them, congratulating them, or agreeing on something. You can also say that two people **shake hands.** *dar la mano* ❑ *Michael shook hands with Burke. Michael le dio la mano a Burke.*

▸ **shake off** PHR-VERB If you **shake off** someone or something that you do not want, you manage to get rid of them. *deshacerse de* ❑ *Jimmy still could not shake off his doubts. Jimmy aún no podía deshacerse de sus dudas.* ❑ *I could not shake him off. No me podía deshacer de él.*

▸ **shake out** PHR-VERB If you wonder how something will **shake out,** you wonder how it will develop and what the outcome will be. *acabar* ❑ *We don't know how this situation will shake out. No sabemos en qué va a acabar esto.*

**shaky** /ʃeɪki/ (**shakier, shakiest**) **1** ADJ If you describe a situation as **shaky,** you mean that it is weak or unstable, and seems unlikely to last long or be successful. *precario* ❑ *The president's position became increasingly shaky. La posición del presidente se volvió cada vez más precaria.* **2** ADJ If your body or your voice is **shaky,** you cannot control it properly and it shakes, for example, because you are ill or nervous. *tembloroso* ❑ *Even small operations can leave you feeling a bit shaky. Incluso las operaciones menores pueden dejarte un poco tembloroso.* • **shak|ily** ADV *de manera temblorosa* ❑ *"I'm OK," she said shakily. —Estoy bien —dijo de manera temblorosa.*

S

**shall** /ʃəl, STRONG ʃæl/

> **Shall** is a modal verb. It is used with the base form of a verb.

**1** MODAL You use **shall** with "I" and "we" in questions in order to make offers or suggestions, or to ask for advice. *Indica ofrecimientos o sugerencias, expresadas normalmente en primera persona.* ❑ *Shall I get the keys? ¿Quieres que vaya por las llaves?* ❑ *Well, shall we go? Bueno, ¿nos vamos?* ❑ *Let's go for a walk, shall we? Vamos a caminar, ¿quieren?* **2** MODAL You use **shall,** usually with "I" and "we," when you are referring to something that you intend to do, or when you are referring to something that you are sure will happen to you in the future. *Indica intención de hacer algo, normalmente usado en primera persona, en lenguaje formal* [FORMAL] ❑ *We shall be landing in Paris in sixteen minutes. Estaremos aterrizando en París en dieciséis minutos.* ❑ *I shall know more next month. Sabré más el mes que entra.* **3** MODAL You use **shall** to indicate that something must happen, usually because of a rule or law. You use **shall not** to indicate that something must not happen. *Indica certeza de que algo tiene que suceder, normalmente porque así está establecido; en negativo, indica que las cosas no deben suceder.* ❑ *The president shall hold office for five years. El presidente estará en su cargo durante cinco años.*

> **Usage** **shall** and **will**
>
> *Shall* is mainly used in the most formal writing and speech; in everyday English, use *will*. *We shall overcome all obstacles to achieve victory. We will be home later.*

**shal|low** /ʃæloʊ/ (**shallower, shallowest**) **1** ADJ A **shallow** container, hole, or area of water measures only a short distance from the top to the bottom. *poco profundo* ❑ *The water is quite shallow. El agua es poco profunda.* **2** ADJ If you describe a person, piece of work, or idea as **shallow,** you disapprove of them because they do not show or involve any serious or careful thought. *superficial* ❑ *I think he is shallow and dishonest. Creo que es superficial y deshonesto.* **3** ADJ If your breathing is **shallow,** you take only a very small amount of air into your lungs at each breath. *superficial* ❑ *She could hear her own shallow breathing. Podía escuchar su propia respiración superficial.*

S

**shame** /ʃeɪm/ (**shames, shaming, shamed**) **1** N-UNCOUNT **Shame** is an uncomfortable feeling that you get when you have done something wrong or embarrassing, or when someone close to you has. *vergüenza* ❑ *She felt a deep sense of shame. Se sintió muy avergonzada.* ❑ *At first, to my shame, I thought it was a joke. Al principio, para vergüenza mía, pensé que era una broma.* **2** N-UNCOUNT If someone brings **shame on** you, they make other people lose their respect for you. *deshonrar* ❑ *I don't want to bring shame on the family name. No quiero deshonrar el nombre de la familia.* **3** V-T If something **shames** you, it causes you to feel shame. *avergonzar* ❑ *Her son's behavior shamed her. El comportamiento de su hijo la avergonzaba.* **4** V-T If you **shame** someone **into** doing something, you force them to do it by making them feel ashamed not to. *avergonzar* ❑ *He would not let neighbors shame him into silence. No dejó que los vecinos lo avergonzaran de tal forma que tuviera que guardar silencio.* **5** N-SING If you say that something is **a shame,** you are expressing your regret about it and indicating that you wish it had happened differently. *pena* ❑ *What a shame the weather is so bad. Qué pena que el clima esté tan malo.*
→ see **emotion**

> **Word Partnership** Usar *shame* con:
>
> V. **experience** shame, **feel** shame **1**
> N. **feelings of** shame, **sense of** shame **1**

**sham|poo** /ʃæmpu/ (**shampoos, shampooing, shampooed**) **1** N-VAR **Shampoo** is a soapy liquid that you use for washing your hair. *shampoo, champú* ❑ *...a bottle of shampoo. ...una botella de shampoo.* **2** V-T When you **shampoo** your hair, you wash it using shampoo. *lavar el cabello con shampoo.* ❑ *Shampoo your hair and dry it. Lave el cabello con shampoo y séquelo.*
→ see **petroleum**

**shan't** /ʃænt/ **Shan't** is the usual spoken form of "shall not." *forma hablada de* ***shall not***

**shape** /ʃeɪp/ (**shapes, shaping, shaped**) **1** N-COUNT The **shape of** an object, a person, or an area is the appearance of their outside edges or surfaces. *forma* ❑ *Each mirror can be designed to almost any shape or size. El diseño del espejo puede ser de casi cualquier forma o tamaño.* ❑ *They sold little pens in the shape of baseball bats. Vendían unas plumas pequeñas en forma de bate de béisbol.* ❑ *We had sofas and chairs of different shapes and colors. Teníamos sofás y sillas de diferentes formas y colores.* **2** N-COUNT A **shape** is a space enclosed by an outline, for example, a circle, a square, or a triangle. *figura* ❑ *Imagine a sort of a heart shape. Imagina una suerte de figura de corazón.* **3** N-SING The **shape of** something that is planned or organized is its structure and character. *conformación* ❑ *The article outlines the shape of the changes we are planning. El artículo esboza la conformación de los cambios que planeamos.* **4** V-T Someone or something that **shapes** a situation or an activity has a very great influence on the way it develops. *forjar* ❑ *Our families shape our lives and make us what we are. Nuestras familias forjan nuestras vidas y nos hacen lo que somos.* **5** V-T If you **shape** an object, you give it a particular shape, using your hands or a tool. *moldear* ❑ *Shape the mixture into 24 meatballs. Moldee la mezcla para hacer 24 albóndigas.* **6** → see also **shaped** **7** PHRASE If someone or something is **in shape,** or **in good shape,** they are in a good state of health or in a good condition. If they are **in bad shape,** they are in a bad state of health or in a bad condition. *en buena forma* ❑ *He was in better shape than many young men. Estaba en mejor forma que muchos hombres jóvenes.* **8** PHRASE If you are **out of shape,** you are unhealthy and unable to do a lot of physical activity without getting tired. *fuera de condición* ❑ *I weighed 245 pounds and was out of shape. Pesaba 245 libras y estaba fuera de condición.*
→ see **mathematics**

▸ **shape up** PHR-VERB If something **is shaping up,** it is starting to develop or seems likely to happen. *tomar forma* ❑ *A real battle is shaping up for tonight. Esta noche habrá una verdadera batalla.* ❑ *The accident is already shaping up as a major disaster. El accidente se está convirtiendo en un gran desastre.*
→ see Picture Dictionary: **shapes**

## Picture Dictionary shapes

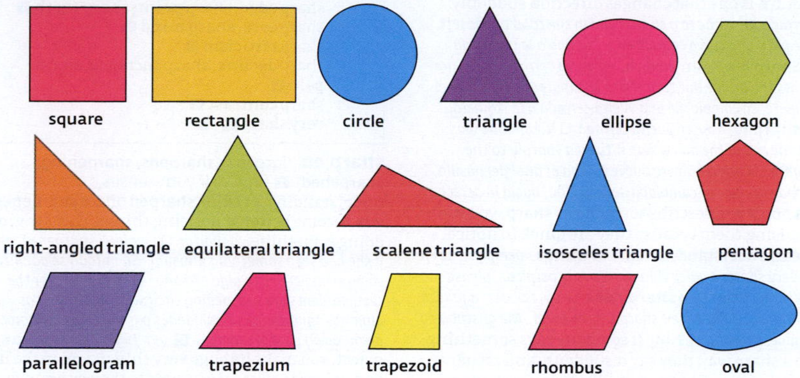


**Word Partnership** Usar *shape* con:

V. **change** shape 1
**change the** shape **of** ***something*** 1 3
**get in** shape 7
ADJ. **dark** shape 2
**(pretty) bad/good/great** shape, **better/ worse** shape, **physical** shape, **terrible** shape 7

**shaped** /ʃeɪpt/ ADJ Something that is **shaped** like a particular object or in a particular way has the shape of that object or a shape of that type. *con forma de* ❑ *The perfume was in a bottle shaped like a flower.* *El perfume estaba en una botella con forma de flor.* ❑ *...large heart-shaped leaves.* *...grandes hojas en forma de corazón.*

**share** /ʃɛər/ (**shares, sharing, shared**) 1 N-COUNT A company's **shares** are the many equal parts into which its ownership is divided. Shares can be bought by people as an investment. *acción* [BUSINESS] ❑ *People in China want to buy shares in new businesses.* *La gente en China quiere comprar acciones de compañías nuevas.* 2 V-RECIP If you **share** something **with** another person, you both have it, use it, do it, or experience it. *compartir* ❑ *He shared his food with the family.* *Compartió su comida con la familia.* ❑ *Two Americans will share this year's Nobel Prize for Medicine.* *Este año, dos estadounidenses compartirán el Premio Nóbel de Medicina.* 3 N-COUNT If you have or do your **share of** something, you have or do an amount that seems reasonable to you, or to other people. *parte* ❑ *Women must receive their fair share of job training.* *Las mujeres deben recibir la parte de capacitación laboral que en justicia les corresponde.*
▸ **share out** PHR-VERB If you **share out** an amount of something, you give each person in a group an equal or fair part of it. *dividir por partes iguales*

**share|holder** /ʃɛərhoʊldər/ (**shareholders**) N-COUNT A **shareholder** is a person who owns shares in a company. *accionista* [BUSINESS] ❑ *...a shareholders' meeting.* *...una junta de accionistas.*

**shark** /ʃɑrk/ (**sharks**) N-COUNT A **shark** is a very large fish. Some sharks have very sharp teeth and may attack people. *tiburón*
→ see Word Web: **shark**

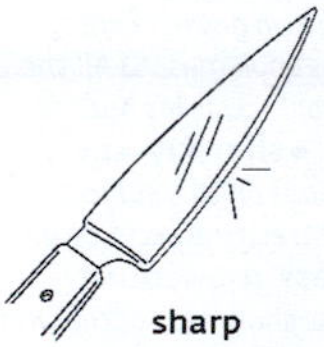

sharp

**sharp** /ʃɑrp/ (**sharps, sharper, sharpest**) 1 ADJ A **sharp** point or edge is very thin and can cut through things very easily. *afilado* ❑ *With a sharp knife, cut*



**Word Web** shark

**Sharks** are different from other **fish**. The **skeleton** of a shark is made of **cartilage**, not bone. The flexibility of cartilage allows this **predator** to maneuver around its **prey** easily. Sharks also have several gill **slits** with no flap covering them. Its **scales** are also much smaller and harder than fish scales. And its teeth are special too. Sharks grow new teeth when they lose old ones. It's almost impossible to escape from a shark. Some of them can swim up to 44 miles per hour. But sharks only kill 50 to 75 people each year worldwide.

the skin off the chicken breast. Con un cuchillo afilado despelleje la pechuga del pollo. 2 ADJ A **sharp** bend or turn is one that changes direction suddenly. cerrado ❑ I came to a sharp bend in the road to the left. Llegué a una curva cerrada en el camino a la izquierda. ● **Sharp** is also an adverb. en curva cerrada ❑ Do not cross the bridge but turn sharp left instead. No cruce el puente; en cambio, dé una vuelta cerrada a la izquierda. ● **sharp|ly** ADV en vuelta cerrada ❑ Room nine was at the end of the hall where it turned sharply to the right. El cuarto número nueve estaba al final del pasillo, donde de repente cambiaba de dirección, hacia la derecha. 3 ADJ If you describe someone as **sharp**, you are praising them because they are quick to notice, hear, understand, or react to things. perspicaz ❑ He is very sharp, a quick thinker. Es muy perpicaz, piensa muy rápidamente. ● **sharp|ness** N-UNCOUNT agudeza, claridad ❑ I liked their sharpness of mind. Me gustaba su agudeza mental. 4 ADJ If someone says something in a **sharp** way, they say it suddenly and rather firmly or angrily, for example, because they are warning or criticizing you. severo, duro ❑ His sharp reply clearly surprised her. No hay duda de que su cortante respuesta la sorprendió. ● **sharp|ly** ADV duramente, severamente ❑ "You knew," she said sharply, "and you didn't tell me?" —Tú sabías, —dijo con aspereza —¿y no me dijiste nada? ● **sharp|ness** N-UNCOUNT severidad, dureza ❑ Malone was surprised at the sharpness in his voice. Malone se sorprendió ante la dureza de su voz. 5 ADJ A **sharp** change, movement, or feeling occurs suddenly, and is great in amount, force, or degree. súbito, repentino ❑ There's been a sharp rise in the rate of inflation. Ha habido un súbito aumento en los índices inflacionarios. ❑ Tennis requires a lot of short sharp movements. El tenis requiere muchos movimentos cortos y repentinos. ● **sharp|ly** ADV súbitamente, repentinamente ❑ Unemployment rose sharply last year. El desempleo subió repentinamente el año pasado. 6 ADJ A **sharp** difference, image, or sound is very easy to see, hear, or distinguish. claro, nítido ❑ There are sharp differences between the two governments. Hay claras diferencias entre los dos gobiernos. ❑ All the footprints are quite sharp and clear. Todas las huellas son nítidas y están bien marcadas. ● **sharp|ly** ADV nítidamente, claramente ❑ Opinions on this subject are sharply divided. Las opiniones a este respecto están claramente divididas. ● **sharp|ness** N-UNCOUNT nitidez ❑ They were amazed at the sharpness of the first picture. Estaban sorprendidos ante la nitidez de la primera imagen. 7 ADJ A **sharp** taste or smell is rather strong or bitter, but is often also clear and fresh. ácido ❑ The apple tasted sharp, yet sweet. El sabor de la manzana era agridulce. 8 ADV **Sharp** is used after stating a particular time to show that something happens at exactly the time stated. en punto ❑ She unlocked the store at 8:00 sharp this morning. Abrió la tienda a las 8 en punto esta mañana. 9 N-COUNT **Sharp** is used after a letter representing a musical note to show that the note should be played or sung half a tone higher. **Sharp** is often represented by the symbol ♯. sostenido ❑ The viola played a soft F sharp. La viola tocaba en un suave tono fa sostenido.

S

**Word Partnership** Usar *sharp* con:

N. sharp **edge**, sharp **point**, sharp **teeth** 1
sharp **eyes**, sharp **mind** 3
sharp **criticism** 4
sharp **decline**, sharp **increase**, sharp **pain** 5
sharp **contrast** 6
ADV. **very** sharp 1 – 7

**sharp|en** /ʃɑrpən/ (**sharpens, sharpening, sharpened**) 1 V-T/V-I If your senses, understanding, or skills **sharpen** or **are sharpened,** you become better at noticing things, thinking, or doing something. agudizar ❑ Her look sharpened, as if she had seen something unusual. Su mirada se agudizó, como si hubiera visto algo extraño. ❑ To prepare for the test, students are sharpening their writing skills. Los alumnos agudizan sus habilidades para la escritura como preparación para el examen. 2 V-T If you **sharpen** an object, you make its edge very thin or you make its end pointed. afilar ❑ He started to sharpen his knife. Comenzó a afilar su cuchillo.

**shat|ter** /ʃætər/ (**shatters, shattering, shattered**) 1 V-T/V-I If something **shatters** or **is shattered,** it breaks into a lot of small pieces. hacerse añicos ❑ Safety glass won't shatter if it's broken. El cristal de seguridad no se hará añicos al romperse. ❑ The car shattered into a thousand burning pieces. El carro se hizo añicos, con mil pedazos en llamas. ● **shat|ter|ing** N-UNCOUNT destrozo ❑ ...the shattering of glass. ...el destrozo de los vidrios. 2 V-T If something **shatters** your dreams, hopes, or beliefs, it completely destroys them. destrozar ❑ Just one incident can shatter the trust of the people. Un solo incidente puede destrozar la confianza de la gente. 3 V-T If someone **is shattered** by an event, it shocks and upsets them very much. destrozar ❑ He was shattered by his son's death. Estaba destrozado por la muerte de su hijo. ● **shat|ter|ing** ADJ devastador ❑ Yesterday's decision was shattering. La decisión de ayer fue devastadora. 4 → see also **shattered**
→ see **crash, glass**

**shat|tered** /ʃætərd/ ADJ If you are **shattered,** you are extremely shocked and upset. devastado ❑ I was shattered to hear the news. Me sentí devastado al escuchar las noticias.

**shave** /ʃeɪv/ (**shaves, shaving, shaved**) 1 V-T/V-I To **shave** means to remove hair from your face or body using a razor or shaver. rasurar(se) ❑ He took a bath and shaved. Se dio un baño y se rasuró. ❑ Many women shave their legs. Muchas mujeres se rasuran las piernas. ● **Shave** is also a noun. afeitada, rasurada ❑ He never seemed to need a shave. Parecía que nunca necesitaba una afeitada. ● **shav|ing** N-UNCOUNT rasurarse ❑ We sell a range of shaving products. Vendemos una variedad de productos para rasurarse. 2 V-T If you **shave off** part of a piece of wood or other material, you cut very thin pieces from it. cepillar ❑ I put the log on the ground and shaved off the bark. Puse el tronco en el suelo y cepillé la corteza.

**shav|er** /ʃeɪvər/ (**shavers**) N-COUNT A **shaver** is an electric device, used for shaving hair from the face and body. rasuradora ❑ ...men's electric shavers. ...rasuradoras eléctricas para hombres.

**shawl** /ʃɔl/ (**shawls**) N-COUNT A **shawl** is a large

piece of woolen cloth which a woman wears over her shoulders or head, or which is wrapped around a baby to keep it warm. *chal, mantón*
→ see **clothing**

**she** /ʃɪ, STRONG ʃi/

> **She** is a third person singular pronoun. **She** is used as the subject of a verb.

PRON You use **she** to refer to a woman, girl, or female animal who has already been mentioned or whose identity is clear. *ella* ❑ *When Ann arrived home she found Brian watching TV. Cuando Ana llegó a casa, encontró a Brian viendo la televisión.* ❑ *She's seventeen years old. Tiene diecisiete años.*

**shed** /ʃɛd/ (**sheds, shedding**)

> The form **shed** is used in the present tense and in the past tense and past participle of the verb.

**1** N-COUNT A **shed** is a small building that is used for storing things such as garden tools. *cobertizo* ❑ *It's in the garden shed. Está en el cobertizo del jardín.* **2** V-T When a tree **sheds** its leaves, its leaves fall off in the fall. When an animal **sheds** hair or skin, some of its hair or skin drops off. *mudar, perder* ❑ *The trees were beginning to shed their leaves. Los árboles comenzaban a perder sus hojas.* **3** V-T To **shed** something means to get rid of it. *despojarse de* [FORMAL] ❑ *The firm is going to shed 700 jobs. La compañía se va a deshacer de 700 empleados.* **4** V-T If you **shed** tears, you cry. *derramar* ❑ *They will shed a few tears at their daughter's wedding. Derramarán algunas lágrimas en la boda de su hija.* **5** V-T To **shed** blood means to kill people in a violent way. If someone **sheds** their blood, they are killed in a violent way, usually when they are fighting in a war. *derramar* [FORMAL] ❑ *Britain was prepared to shed blood in support of the United States. Gran Bretaña estaba dispuesta a derramar sangre en apoyo a los Estados Unidos.* **6** to **shed light on** something → see **light**
→ see **cry**

**Word Partnership** Usar *shed* con:

N. **storage** shed **1**
shed ***your* clothes**, shed ***your* image**, shed **pounds** **3**
shed **a tear**, shed **tears** **4**
shed **blood** **5**

**she'd** /ʃid, ʃɪd/ **1** **She'd** is the usual spoken form of "she had," especially when "had" is an auxiliary verb. *forma hablada usual de she had* ❑ *She'd been all over the world. Ella había estado en todo el mundo.* **2** **She'd** is a spoken form of "she would." *forma hablada usual de **she would*** ❑ *She'd do anything for a bit of money. Ella haría lo que fuera por un poco de dinero.*

**sheep** /ʃip/ (**sheep**) N-COUNT A **sheep** is a farm animal which is covered with thick hair called wool. Sheep are kept for their wool or for their meat. *borrego, oveja*
→ see **meat**

**sheer** /ʃɪər/ (**sheerer, sheerest**) **1** ADJ You can use **sheer** to emphasize that a state or situation is complete and does not involve or is not mixed with anything else. *puro* ❑ *His music is sheer delight. Su música es un verdadero placer.* ❑ *By sheer chance he was there. Estaba ahí de pura casualidad.* **2** ADJ A **sheer** cliff or drop is extremely steep or completely vertical. *escarpado, vertical* ❑ *There was a sheer drop just outside my window. Había una caída vertical justo debajo de mi ventana.* **3** ADJ **Sheer** material is very thin, light, and delicate. *muy fino* ❑ *She wore sheer black stockings. Llevaba unas medias negras totalmente transparentes.*

**Word Partnership** Usar *sheer* con:

N. sheer **delight**, sheer **force**, sheer **luck**, sheer **number**, sheer **pleasure**, sheer **power**, sheer **size**, sheer **strength**, sheer **terror**, sheer **volume** **1**

**sheet** /ʃit/ (**sheets**) **1** N-COUNT A **sheet** is a large rectangular piece of cotton or other cloth that you sleep on or cover yourself with in a bed. *sábana* ❑ *Once a week, we change the sheets. Cambiamos las sábanas una vez a la semana.* **2** N-COUNT A **sheet of** paper is a rectangular piece of paper. *hoja* ❑ *Use a sheet of newspaper. Usa una hoja de periódico.* **3** N-COUNT A **sheet of** glass, metal, or wood is a large, flat, thin piece of it. *lámina* ❑ *The cranes were lifting giant sheets of steel. Las grúas estaban levantando láminas inmensas de acero.*
→ see **bed, glass, paper**

**sheikh** /ʃik, ʃeɪk/ (**sheikhs**) also **sheik** N-TITLE; N-COUNT A **sheikh** is a male Arab chief or ruler. *jeque* ❑ *...Sheikh Khalifa. ...el jeque Khalifa.*

**shelf** /ʃɛlf/ (**shelves**) N-COUNT A **shelf** is a flat piece of wood, metal, or glass which is attached to a wall or to the sides of a cabinet. Shelves are used for keeping things on. *estante* ❑ *He took a book from the shelf. Tomó un libro del estante.*

**shell** /ʃɛl/ (**shells, shelling, shelled**) **1** N-COUNT The **shell** of a nut or egg is the hard covering which surrounds it. *cáscara* ❑ *They cracked the nuts and removed their shells. Cascaron las nueces y quitaron las cáscaras.* ● **Shell** is the substance that a shell is made of. *cáscara* ❑ *It was a necklace made from bits of walnut shell. Era un collar hecho de pedazos de cáscara de nuez.* **2** N-COUNT The **shell** of an animal such as a tortoise, snail, or crab is the hard protective covering that it has around its body or on its back. *concha* ❑ *The snail's shell forms a spiral. La concha del caracol forma una espiral.* **3** N-COUNT **Shells** are hard objects found on beaches. They are usually pink, white, or brown and are the coverings which used to surround small sea creatures. *conchita* ❑ *I collect shells and interesting seaside items. Colecciono conchitas y cosas interesantes de la orilla del mar.* **4** V-T If you **shell** nuts, peas, shrimp, or other food, you remove their natural outer covering. *pelar* ❑ *She shelled and ate a few nuts. Peló las nueces y se comió algunas.* **5** N-COUNT A **shell** is a weapon consisting of a metal container filled with explosives that can be fired from a large gun over long distances. *proyectil* ❑ *Tanks fired shells at the house. Los tanques lanzaron proyectiles a la casa.* **6** V-T To **shell** a place means to fire explosive shells at it. *bombardear* ❑ *The army shelled the port. El ejército bombardeó el puerto.* ● **shell|ing** N-VAR (**shellings**) *bombardeo* ❑ *Out on the streets, the shelling continued. Afuera, en las calles, el bombardeo continuaba.*
▸ **shell out** PHR-VERB If you **shell out for** something, you spend a lot of money on it. *soltar, apoquinar* [INFORMAL] ❑ *He shelled out $950 for his*

**Picture Dictionary** **shellfish**

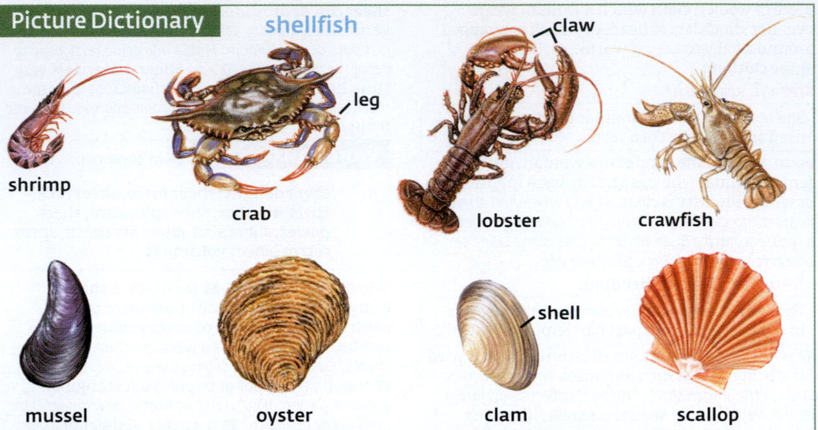


trip. Soltó 950 dólares para su viaje. ❑ *We didn't have to shell out for taxis because we had our own driver.* *No tuvimos que apoquinar lana para los taxis porque traíamos quién nos llevara.*
→ see **shellfish**

**she'll** /ʃil, ʃɪl/ **She'll** is the usual spoken form of "she will." *forma hablada usual de **she will*** ❑ *Sharon was wonderful; I know she'll be greatly missed.* *Sharon fue maravillosa. Sé que se le extrañará mucho.*

**shell|fish** /ʃɛlfɪʃ/ (**shellfish**) N-VAR **Shellfish** are small creatures that live in the sea and have a shell. *marisco* ❑ *Fish and shellfish are our specialties.* *Nuestra especialidad es el pescado y los mariscos.*
→ see Picture Dictionary: **shellfish**

**shel|ter** /ʃɛltər/ (**shelters, sheltering, sheltered**) **1** N-COUNT A **shelter** is a small building or covered place which is made to protect people from bad weather or danger. *refugio* ❑ *...a bus shelter.* *...un refugio de autobús.* **2** N-UNCOUNT If a place provides **shelter,** it provides you with a place to stay or live, especially when you need protection from bad weather or danger. *refugio* ❑ *The number of families needing shelter rose by 17 percent.* *El número de familias que necesitan refugio aumentó un 17 por ciento.* ❑ *Horses don't mind the cold but shelter from rain and wind is important.* *A los caballos no les importa el frío, pero necesitan un refugio contra la lluvia y el viento.* **3** V-I If you **shelter** in a place, you stay there and are protected from bad weather or danger. *refugiarse* ❑ *A man sheltered in a doorway.* *Un hombre se refugió en el umbral de una puerta.* **4** V-T If a place or thing **is sheltered** by something, it is protected by that thing from wind and rain. *proteger* ❑ *The house was sheltered from the sun by huge trees.* *La casa estaba protegida del sol gracias a unos enormes árboles.* **5** V-T If you **shelter** someone, usually someone who is being hunted by police or other people, you provide them with a place to stay or live. *dar refugio* ❑ *A neighbor sheltered the boy for seven days.* *Un vecino dio refugio al niño durante siete días.*
→ see **habitat**

S

**Word Partnership** Usar *shelter* con:

| | |
|---|---|
| N. | **bomb** shelter **1**<br>**emergency** shelter **1** **2**<br>shelter **and clothing, food and** shelter **2** |
| ADJ. | **temporary** shelter **1** **2** |
| V. | **find** shelter, **provide** shelter, **seek** shelter **2** |

**shelve** /ʃɛlv/ (**shelves, shelving, shelved**) **1** V-T If someone **shelves** a plan or project, they decide not to continue with it, either for a while or permanently. *dar carpetazo* ❑ *He has shelved plans for a hotel and club.* *Le dio carpetazo a sus planes de un hotel y un club.* **2** **Shelves** is the plural of **shelf**. *plural de shelf*

**shep|herd** /ʃɛpərd/ (**shepherds, shepherding, shepherded**) **1** N-COUNT A **shepherd** is a person, especially a man, whose job is to take care of sheep. *pastor o pastora* **2** V-T If you **are shepherded** somewhere, someone takes you there to make sure that you arrive at the right place safely. *conducir* ❑ *She was shepherded up the steps of the aircraft.* *Fue conducida por los escalones del avión.*

**sher|bet** /ʃɜrbɪt/ (**sherbets**) N-VAR **Sherbet** is like ice cream but made with fruit juice, sugar, and water. *nieve* ❑ *...lemon sherbet.* *...nieve de limón.*

**sher|iff** /ʃɛrɪf/ (**sheriffs**) N-COUNT; N-TITLE In the United States, a **sheriff** is a person who is elected to make sure that the law is obeyed in a particular county. *alguacil* ❑ *He's the local sheriff.* *Es el alguacil del lugar.*

**she's** /ʃiz, ʃɪz/ **1** **She's** is the usual spoken form of "she is." *forma hablada de **she is*** ❑ *She's a really good cook.* *Ella es muy buena cocinera.* **2** **She's** is a spoken form of "she has," especially when "has" is an auxiliary verb. *forma hablada de **she has*** ❑ *She's been married for seven years.* *Tiene siete años de casada.*

**shield** /ʃild/ (**shields, shielding, shielded**) **1** V-T If something or someone **shields** you **from** a danger or risk, they protect you from it. *proteger* ❑ *He shielded his eyes from the sun.* *Se protegió los ojos del sol.* **2** N-COUNT A **shield** is a large piece of metal

or leather which soldiers used to carry to protect their bodies while they were fighting. *escudo*
→ see **army**

**shield vol|ca|no** (**shield volcanoes**) N-COUNT A **shield volcano** is a broad volcano with low, sloping sides that is formed from lava that has erupted and become solid. *volcán en escudo* [TECHNICAL]

**shift** /ʃɪft/ (**shifts, shifting, shifted**) **1** V-T/V-I If you **shift** something or if it **shifts,** it moves slightly. *mover* ❑ *He stopped, shifting his bag to his left hand. Se detuvo y se cambió la bolsa a la mano izquierda.* ❑ *He shifted from foot to foot. Se apoyaba ya en un pie, ya en el otro.* **2** V-T/V-I If your opinion, a situation, or a policy **shifts** or **is shifted,** it changes slightly. *cambiar* ❑ *Attitudes to mental illness have shifted in recent years. La actitud hacia las enfermedades mentales ha cambiado en los últimos años.* • **Shift** is also a noun. *cambio* ❑ *There's been a shift in government policy. Ha habido un viraje en la política gubernamental.* **3** V-T If you **shift** gears in a car, you put the car into a different gear. *cambiar* ❑ *He shifted gears and pulled away slowly. Cambió la velocidad y avanzó lentamente.* **4** N-COUNT A **shift** is a set period of work in a place like a factory or a hospital. *turno* ❑ *His father worked shifts in a steel mill. Su papá trabajaba por turnos en una fundidora.*

**Word Partnership** Usar *shift* con:

N. shift *your* **weight** **1**
shift *your* **position** **1** **2**
shift *your* **attention**, shift **in focus**, **policy** shift, shift **in/of power**, shift **in priorities** **2**
shift **gears** **3**
shift **change**, **night** shift **4**
ADJ. **dramatic** shift, **major** shift, **significant** shift **2**

**Shi|ite** /ʃiaɪt/ (**Shiites**) also **Shi'ite** **1** N-COUNT **Shiites** are members of a branch of Islam which regards Mohammed's cousin Ali and his successors, rather than Mohammed himself, as the final authority on religious matters. *chiita* ❑ *...the Shiites in southern Iraq. ...los chiitas del sur de Irak.* **2** ADJ **Shiite** means relating to Shiites and their religious beliefs or practises. *chiita* ❑ *...Shiite Muslims. ...musulmanes chiitas.* ❑ *Iraq's population is roughly half Shiite. Aproximadamente la mitad de la población de Irak es chiita.*

**shin** /ʃɪn/ (**shins**) N-COUNT Your **shins** are the front parts of your legs between your knees and your ankles. *espinilla* ❑ *She kicked him in the shins. Le dio una patada en la espinilla.*
→ see **soccer**

**shine** /ʃaɪn/ (**shines, shining, shined** or **shone**) **1** V-I When the sun or a light **shines,** it gives out bright light. *brillar* ❑ *It is warm and the sun is shining. Hace calor y brilla el sol.* **2** V-T If you **shine** a flashlight or other light somewhere, you point it there. *alumbrar* ❑ *A man shone a light in his face. Un hombre le alumbró la cara con una linterna.* ❑ *The man walked toward her, shining a flashlight. EL hombre caminó hacia ella, alumbrando con una lámpara.* **3** V-I Something that **shines** is very bright and clear because it is reflecting light. *brillar* ❑ *Her blue eyes shone. Sus ojos azules brillaban.* **4** N-SING Something that has a **shine** is bright and clear because it is reflecting light. *brillo* ❑ *This gel gives a beautiful shine to the hair. Este gel le da un hermoso brillo al cabello.* **5** V-I Someone who **shines** at a skill or activity does it extremely well. *destacar* ❑ *Did you shine at school? ¿Destacabas en la escuela?* **6** → see also **shining**
→ see **light**

**Thesaurus** *shine* Ver también:

V. glare, gleam, illuminate, shimmer **1** **3**
N. light, radiance, sheen **4**

**shin|ing** /ʃaɪnɪŋ/ **1** ADJ A **shining** achievement or quality is a very good one which should be greatly admired. *magnífico* ❑ *She is a shining example to us all. Ella es un magnífico ejemplo para todos nosotros.* **2** → see also **shine**

**shiny** /ʃaɪni/ (**shinier, shiniest**) ADJ **Shiny** things are bright and reflect light. *brillante* ❑ *Her blonde hair was shiny and clean. Su rubio cabello estaba limpio y brillante.*
→ see **metal**

**ship** /ʃɪp/ (**ships, shipping, shipped**) **1** N-COUNT A **ship** is a large boat which carries passengers or cargo. *barco, buque* ❑ *The ship was ready for departure. El barco estaba listo para zarpar.* ❑ *We went by ship over to Europe. Fuimos a Europa en barco.* **2** V-T If people, supplies, or goods **are shipped** somewhere, they are sent there on a ship or by some other means of transportation. *embarcar, enviar por barco* ❑ *We'll ship your order to the address on your checks. Enviaremos su pedido al domicilio que aparece en los cheques.* ❑ *Food is being shipped to Southern Africa. Los alimentos se están enviando por barco al sur de África.* • **ship|ment** N-UNCOUNT *embarque, envío, remesa* ❑ *We ask for payment before shipment of the goods. Deberá hacer su pago antes del embarque de las mercancías.* **3** → see also **shipping**
→ see Word Web: **ship**

**Word Partnership** Usar *ship* con:

V. **board a** ship, **build a** ship, ship **docks**, **jump** ship, **sink a** ship **1**
N. **bow of a** ship, **captain of a** ship, **cargo** ship, ship's **crew** **1**

**ship|building** /ʃɪpbɪldɪŋ/ N-UNCOUNT **Shipbuilding** is the industry of building ships. *construcción naval*
→ see **industry**

**ship|ment** /ʃɪpmənt/ (**shipments**) N-COUNT A **shipment** is an amount of a particular kind of cargo that is sent to another country on a ship, train, airplane, or other vehicle. *envío, embarque* ❑ *Food shipments to the port could begin in a few weeks. Los envíos de alimentos al puerto podrían empezar en unas semanas.*

**ship|ping** /ʃɪpɪŋ/ N-UNCOUNT **Shipping** is the transportation of cargo or goods as a business, especially on ships. *embarque, envío* ❑ *...the international shipping industry. ...la industria naviera internacional.* ❑ *Here's a coupon for free shipping of your catalog order. Este es un cupón para el envío gratuito de su pedido por catálogo.*

**shirt** /ʃɜrt/ (**shirts**) **1** N-COUNT A **shirt** is a piece of clothing that you wear on the upper part of your

**Word Web** ship

Large **ocean-going vessels** are an important way of carrying people and **cargo. Oil tankers** and container ships are common in many **ports. Ocean liners** carry tourists and give them a place to stay. Some of these **ships** are several storeys tall. The **captain** steers a **cruise ship** from the **bridge**, while passengers enjoy themselves on the promenade **deck**. Huge **warships** carry thousands of soldiers to battlefields around the world. **Aircraft carriers** include a flight **deck** where planes can take off and land. **Ferries, barges**, fishing **craft**, and research **boats** are also an important part of the **marine** industry.

body. Shirts have a collar, sleeves, and buttons down the front. camisa, blusa **2** → see also **sweatshirt, T-shirt**
→ see **clothing, petroleum**

**Usage** **shirt** and **blouse**

Be careful not to use *blouse* when you should use *shirt*. Both men and women wear shirts, but only women wear blouses, which are usually thought of as more loose fitting and a little fancier than shirts: *Reynaldo put on a fancy shirt to go to the party, but Alma was afraid she'd get her new blouse dirty, so she put on one of the shirts she often wore to work.*

**shiv|er** /ʃɪvər/ (**shivers, shivering, shivered**) V-I When you **shiver,** your body shakes slightly because you are cold or frightened. temblar, tiritar ❑ *He shivered in the cold.* *Tiritó de frío.* • **Shiver** is also a noun. escalofrío ❑ *The emptiness here sent shivers down my spine.* *La desolación del lugar me produjo escalofríos.*

**Word Partnership** Usar *shiver* con:

V. **feel a** shiver, shiver **goes/runs down** ***your*** spine, ***something* makes *you*** shiver, ***something* sends a** shiver **down *your* spine**

S

**shock** /ʃɒk/ (**shocks, shocking, shocked**) **1** N-COUNT If you have a **shock,** something suddenly happens which is unpleasant, upsetting, or very surprising. conmoción ❑ *The city violence came as a shock.* *La violencia de la ciudad causó una conmoción.* ❑ *He never recovered from the shock of his brother's death.* *Nunca se recuperó de la conmoción que le produjera la muerte de su hermano.* **2** N-UNCOUNT **Shock** is a person's emotional and physical condition when something very frightening or upsetting has happened to them. impresión, susto ❑ *The boy was speechless with shock.* *El niño se quedó mudo de la impresión.* **3** N-UNCOUNT If someone is **in shock,** they are suffering from a serious physical condition in which their blood is not flowing around their body properly, for example, because they have had a bad injury. conmocionado ❑ *He was in shock when we found him.* *Estaba conmocionado cuando lo encontramos.* **4** V-T If something **shocks** you, it makes you feel very upset, because it involves death or suffering and because you did not expect it. escandalizar, impresionar ❑ *After forty years in the police, nothing much shocks me.* *Después de cuarenta años en la policía, ya casi nada me impresiona.* • **shocked** ADJ conmocionado, horrorizado, en estado de shock ❑ *It was a bad attack and the woman is still very shocked.* *Fue un ataque artero y la mujer todavía está en estado de shock.* **5** V-T/V-I If someone or something **shocks** you, it upsets or offends you because you think it is vulgar or morally wrong. escandalizar(se), impresionar, indignar(se) ❑ *You can't shock me.* *No me impresionas.* ❑ *We were easily shocked in those days.* *En aquella época nos escandalizábamos fácilmente.* ❑ *Their story still has the power to shock.* *Su historia todavía escandaliza.* • **shocked** ADJ escandalizado, impresionado, indignado ❑ *Don't look so shocked.* *No te escandalices tanto.* **6** N-VAR A **shock** is the force of something suddenly hitting or pulling something else. impacto, choque ❑ *The steel bars will absorb the shock.* *Las barras de acero absorberán el impacto.* **7** N-COUNT A **shock** is the same as an **electric shock.** electrochoque, descarga eléctrica
→ see **sound**

**Word Partnership** Usar *shock* con:

V. **come as a** shock **1**
**send a** shock **1 6 7**
**express** shock, **feel** shock **2**
N. **in a state of** shock, shock **value** **2**

**shock|ing** /ʃɒkɪŋ/ **1** ADJ You can say that something is **shocking** if you think that it is very bad. escandaloso, horroroso, espeluznante [INFORMAL] ❑ *The newspaper story was shocking.* *El artículo del periódico era espeluznante.* • **shock|ing|ly** ADV terriblemente ❑ *His memory became shockingly bad.* *Su memoria llegó a ser terriblemente mala.* **2** ADJ You can say that something is **shocking** if you think that it is morally wrong. escandaloso ❑ *It is shocking that nothing was said.* *Es escandaloso que no se dijera nada.* • **shock|ing|ly** ADV escandalosamente ❑ *Shockingly, this dangerous treatment did not end until the 1930s.* *Lo terrible es que tan peligroso tratamiento no dejara de aplicarse hasta el decenio de 1930.* **3** → see also **shock**

**shock wave** (**shock waves**) also **shockwave** **1** N-COUNT A **shock wave** is an area of very high pressure moving through the air, earth, or water. It is caused by an explosion or an earthquake, or by an object traveling faster than sound. onda expansiva ❑ *The shock waves were felt from Las Vegas* *to San Diego.* *Las ondas expansivas se sintieron desde Las Vegas hasta San Diego.* 2 N-COUNT A **shock wave** is the effect of something surprising, such as a piece of unpleasant news, that causes strong reactions when it spreads through a place. *conmoción* ❑ *The crime sent shock waves through the country.* *El crimen causó conmoción en todo el país.*

**shoe** /ʃu/ (**shoes, shoeing, shoed** or **shod**) 1 N-COUNT **Shoes** are objects which you wear on your feet. They cover most of your foot but not your ankles. *zapato* ❑ *...a pair of shoes.* *...un par de zapatos.* ❑ *Low-heeled comfortable shoes are best.* *Los zapatos cómodos de tacón bajo son mejores.* 2 V-T When a blacksmith **shoes** a horse, they attach horseshoes onto their feet. *herrar* ❑ *Blacksmiths spent most of their time shoeing horses.* *Los herreros pasaban la mayor parte del tiempo herrando caballos.* 3 PHRASE If you talk about being **in** someone's **shoes,** you talk about what you would do or how you would feel if you were in their situation. *en el pellejo de, en el lugar de* ❑ *I wouldn't like to be in his shoes.* *No me gustaría estar en su pellejo.*
→ see Picture Dictionary: **shoe**
→ see **clothing, petroleum**

**shoe|string** /ʃustrɪŋ/ (**shoestrings**) 1 N-COUNT **Shoestrings** are long, narrow pieces of material like pieces of string that you use to fasten your shoes. *agujeta, cordón* 2 PHRASE If you do something or make something **on a shoestring,** you do it using very little money. *con muy pocos recursos, con muy poco dinero* ❑ *We run the theater on a shoestring.* *Hacemos funcionar el teatro con muy pocos recursos.*

**shoo-in** /ʃu ɪn/ (**shoo-ins**) N-COUNT A **shoo-in** is a person who seems sure to win. *seguro y fácil ganador* [INFORMAL] ❑ *He's a shoo-in to win the award this season.* *Tiene amarrado el premio en esta temporada.*

**shook** /ʃʊk/ **Shook** is the past tense of **shake.** *pasado de* ***shake***

**shoot** /ʃut/ (**shoots, shooting, shot**) 1 V-T If someone **shoots** a person or an animal, they kill them or injure them by firing a bullet or arrow at them. *disparar* ❑ *The police had orders to shoot anyone who attacked them.* *Los policías tenían órdenes de disparar a cualquiera que los atacara.* ❑ *A man was shot dead during the robbery.* *Mataron a un hombre de un disparo durante el atraco.* • **shoot|ing** N-COUNT (**shootings**) *tiroteo, balacera* ❑ *Two bodies were found after the shooting.* *Después del tiroteo/de la balacera, encontraron dos cadáveres.* 2 V-I To **shoot** means to fire a bullet from a weapon such as a gun. *disparar, tirar* ❑ *He raised his arms above his head, shouting, "Don't shoot!"* *Alzó las manos, gritando —¡No disparen!* ❑ *The police started shooting at us.* *Los policías empezaron a dispararnos.* 3 V-I If someone or something **shoots** in a particular direction, they move in that direction quickly and suddenly. *salir disparado* ❑ *A car shot out of the driveway and crashed into them.* *Un coche salió disparado de la entrada y chocó con ellos.* 4 V-T When people **shoot** a movie or **shoot** photographs, they make a movie or take photographs using a camera. *filmar, rodar* ❑ *He wants to shoot his movie in Mexico.* *Quiere filmar su película en México.* • **Shoot** is also a noun. *filmación, rodaje* ❑ *The farm is being used for a video shoot.* *En la granja están haciendo una película para televisión.* 5 V-T When someone **shoots** pool or **shoots** craps, they play a game of pool or the dice game called craps. *jugar a* ❑ *People are still here shooting pool.* *Todavía hay gente aquí jugando al billar.* 6 N-COUNT **Shoots** are plants that are beginning to grow, or new parts growing from a plant or tree. *brote, retoño* ❑ *New shoots appear every year.* *Todos los años hay nuevos retoños.* 7 V-I In sports such as soccer or basketball, when someone **shoots,** they try to score by kicking or throwing the ball toward the goal or hoop. *patear, tirar, lanzar* ❑ *Spencer shot wide when he should have scored.* *Spencer echó la pelota fuera, cuando debió haber anotado.* 8 → see also **shot**

▸**shoot down** PHR-VERB If someone **shoots down** an airplane, a helicopter, or a missile, they make it fall to the ground by hitting it with a bullet or missile. *derribar, abatir* ❑ *They claim they shot down a missile.* *Afirman haber derribado un misil.*

▸**shoot up** PHR-VERB If something **shoots up,** it grows or increases very quickly. *dispararse* ❑ *Sales shot up by 9% last month.* *Las ventas se dispararon el 9 por ciento el mes pasado.*

**Picture Dictionary** shoe

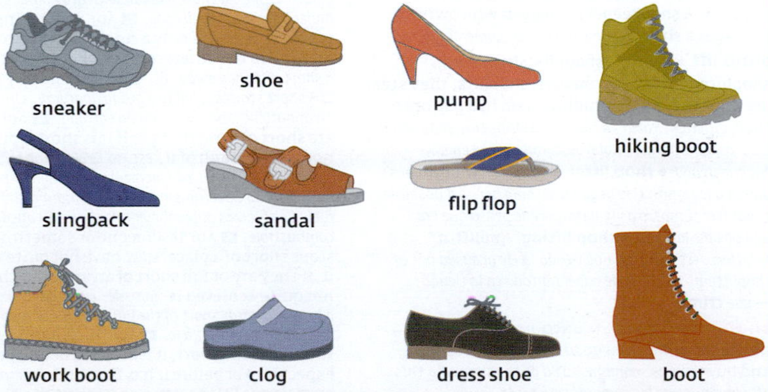

**shoot sys|tem** (**shoot systems**) N-COUNT A plant's **shoot system** is the part of the plant that is above the ground, including the stem and leaves. Compare **root system.** *parte de una planta expuesta al aire*

**shop** /ʃɒp/ (**shops, shopping, shopped**) **1** N-COUNT A **shop** is a small store that sells one type of merchandise. *tienda* ❑ *Try the gift shop. Busque en la tienda de novedades y artículos para regalo.* ❑ *He and his wife run a flower shop. Él y su esposa tienen una florería.* **2** V-I When you **shop,** you go to stores or shops and buy things. *comprar, hacer las compras, ir de compras* ❑ *He always shopped on Saturday mornings. Siempre hacía sus compras el sábado por la mañana.* ❑ *Here's some advice for when you're shopping for a new carpet. Algunos consejos para cuando vaya a comprar una alfombra nueva.* • **shop|per** N-COUNT (**shoppers**) *comprador o compradora* ❑ *There were crowds of shoppers on the streets. Había multitudes de compradores en las calles.* **3** → see also **coffee shop, shopping**

▸ **shop around** PHR-VERB If you **shop around,** you go to different stores or companies in order to compare the prices and quality of goods or services before you decide to buy them. *recorrer tiendas para comparar precios* ❑ *Prices vary so it's worth shopping around. Los precios varían, así que vale la pena recorrer varias tiendas para compararlos.*

| Word Partnership | Usar *shop* con: |
| --- | --- |
| N. | **antique** shop, **auto** shop, **barber** shop, **beauty** shop, shop **owner**, **pet** shop, **repair** shop, **souvenir** shop **1** |

**shop floor** also **shop-floor** or **shopfloor** N-SING The **shop floor** is used to refer to all the ordinary workers in a factory or the area where they work, especially in contrast to the people who are in charge. *taller, planta de producción, los obreros* ❑ *A sign at the entrance to the shop floor says "Employees Only." En la entrada de la planta hay un letrero que dice "Sólo personal autorizado".*

**shop|keeper** /ʃɒpkipər/ (**shopkeepers**) N-COUNT A **shopkeeper** is a person who owns or manages a shop. *tendero o tendera, comerciante*

**shop|lift** /ʃɒplɪft/ (**shoplifts, shoplifting, shoplifted**) V-T/V-I If someone **shoplifts,** they steal goods from a store by hiding them in a bag or in their clothes. *robar en tiendas* ❑ *He openly shoplifted from a supermarket. Robó descaradamente en un supermercado.* • **shop|lifter** N-COUNT (**shoplifters**) *ladrón o ladrona* ❑ *He began watching her as a possible shoplifter. Empezó a vigilarla, porque pensó que era una posible ladrona.* • **shop|lifting** /ʃɒplɪftɪŋ/ N-UNCOUNT *hurto en una tienda* ❑ *He accused her of shoplifting. La acusó de haber hurtado en la tienda.* → see **crime**

**shop|ping** /ʃɒpɪŋ/ N-UNCOUNT When you do **the shopping,** you go to the stores or shops and buy things. *compras* ❑ *I'll do the shopping this afternoon. Haré las compras esta tarde.*

| Word Partnership | Usar *shopping* con: |
| --- | --- |
| N. | shopping **bag**, shopping **district**, **food** shopping, **grocery** shopping, **holiday** shopping, **online** shopping, shopping **spree** |

**shop|ping cart** (**shopping carts**) N-COUNT A **shopping cart** is a large metal basket on wheels which is provided by stores such as supermarkets for customers to use while they are in the store. *carrito, carrito del súper*

**shop|ping cen|ter** (**shopping centers**) N-COUNT A **shopping center** is a specially built area containing a lot of different stores. *centro comercial* ❑ *They met in the parking lot at the shopping center. Se conocieron/encontraron en el estacionamiento del centro comercial.*

**shore** /ʃɔr/ (**shores, shoring, shored**) N-COUNT The **shores** or the **shore** of an ocean, lake, or wide river is the land along the edge of it. Someone who is **on shore** is on the land rather than on a ship. *costa, ribera, orilla* ❑ *They walked down to the shore. Se fueron caminando hacia la orilla.*

▸ **shore up** PHR-VERB If you **shore up** something that is weak or about to fail, you do something in order to strengthen it or support it. *apuntalar, fortalecer* ❑ *We need to shore up public confidence in this process. Necesitamos fortalecer la confianza del público en el proceso.*

**short**
❶ ADJECTIVE AND ADVERB USES
❷ NOUN USES

❶ **short** /ʃɔrt/ (**shorter, shortest**)
→ Please look at category **11** to see if the expression you are looking for is shown under another headword. **1** ADJ If something is **short** or lasts for a **short** time, it does not last very long. *corto, poco, ligero* ❑ *The announcement was made a short time ago. El anuncio se hizo hace poco tiempo.* ❑ *Kemp gave a short laugh. Kemp apenas se rió.* **2** ADJ Someone who is **short** is not as tall as most people are. *bajo, de corta estatura, chaparro* ❑ *I'm tall and thin and he's short and fat. Yo soy alta y delgada y él es chaparro y gordo.* ❑ *She's a short woman with gray hair. Es una mujer baja, de cabello cano.* **3** ADJ Something that is **short** measures only a small amount from one end to the other. *corto* ❑ *The restaurant is only a short distance away. El restaurante está muy cerca.* ❑ *A short staircase led to a grand doorway. Una corta escalinata llevaba a una amplia entrada.* **4** ADJ If you are **short of** something or if it is **short,** you do not have enough of it. *escaso* ❑ *Now the family is short of money. En este momento, la familia está escasa de dinero.* ❑ *Government forces are running short of fuel. Las fuerzas gubernamentales se están quedando sin combustible.* **5** ADJ If someone or something is or stops **short of** a place, they have not quite reached it. If they are or fall **short of** an amount, they have not quite achieved it. *falto de, corto de* ❑ *He stopped a hundred yards short of the building. Se detuvo cien metros antes del edificio.* **6** ADV If something is **cut short** or **stops short,** it is stopped before people expect it to or before it has finished. *interrumpir(se) bruscamente* ❑ *His career was cut short by a heart*

S

attack. *Su carrera fue interrumpida bruscamente por un ataque al corazón.* **7** ADJ If a name or abbreviation is **short for** another name, it is the short version of that name. *diminutivo* ❑ *Her friend Kes (short for Kesewa) was in tears. Su amiga Kes (diminutivo de Kesewa) estaba llorando.* **8** ADJ If you have a **short** temper, you get angry very easily. *irritable, irritarse con facilidad, tener mal genio* ❑ *She was an impatient woman with a short temper. Era una mujer impaciente e irritable.* **9** PHRASE You use **in short** when you have been giving a lot of details and you want to give a conclusion or summary. *en resumen, en suma, es decir* ❑ *Try running or swimming. In short, anything active. Pruebe a correr o nadar, es decir, cualquier actividad física.* **10** PHRASE If someone **stops short of** doing something, they come close to doing it but do not actually do it. *estar a punto de* ❑ *She stopped short of calling me a liar. Estuvo a punto de llamarme mentiroso.* **11** **in short supply** → see **supply** **12** **in the short term** → see **term**

| **Thesaurus** | *short* | Ver también: |
|---|---|---|
| ADJ. | brief, quick; (*ant.*) long ❶ **1** | |
| | petite, slight, small; (*ant.*) tall ❶ **2** | |

**❷ short** /ʃɔrt/ (**shorts**) **1** N-PLURAL **Shorts** are pants with very short legs. *pantalones cortos, cortos, short* ❑ *Two women arrived in bright cotton shorts. Llegaron dos mujeres en shorts de algodón, de colores vivos.* **2** N-PLURAL **Shorts** are men's underpants with short legs. *calzoncillos, bóxer*

**short|age** /ʃɔrtɪdʒ/ (**shortages**) N-VAR If there is a **shortage of** something, there is not enough of it. *escasez* ❑ *Officials are worried about the shortage of cheap housing. Los funcionarios están preocupados por la escasez de vivienda barata.* ❑ *Vietnam is suffering from food shortages. Vietnam está sufriendo por la falta de alimentos.*

**short|cake** /ʃɔrtkeɪk/ (**shortcakes**) N-VAR **Shortcake** is a cake or dessert which consists of a biscuit or cake with layers of fruit and whipped cream. *pastel de frutas, shortcake* ❑ *It's strawberry shortcake for dessert. De postre tenemos shortcake de fresas.*

**short|en** /ʃɔrt$^{ə}$n/ (**shortens, shortening, shortened**) **1** V-T/V-I If you **shorten** an event or the length of time that something lasts, or if it **shortens,** it does not last as long as it would usually last. *reducir, acortar, abreviar* ❑ *Eating too much can shorten your life. Comer demasiado puede acortar la vida.* ❑ *The days shorten in winter. Los días se acortan en invierno.* **2** V-T/V-I If you **shorten** an object or if it **shortens,** it becomes smaller in length. *reducir* ❑ *She paid $5,000 for an operation to shorten her nose. Pagó 5,000 dólares por la operación para reducirse la nariz.*

**short|en|ing** /ʃɔrtnɪŋ/ (**shortenings**) N-VAR **Shortening** is cooking fat that you use with flour in order to make pastry or dough. *mantequilla, manteca, margarina*

**short|hand** /ʃɔrthænd/ N-UNCOUNT **Shorthand** is a quick way of writing and uses signs to represent words or syllables. *taquigrafía* ❑ *Ben took notes in shorthand. Ben tomó notas en taquigrafía.*

**short|ly** /ʃɔrtli/ ADV If something happens **shortly** after or before something else, it happens not long after or before it. If something is going to happen **shortly,** it is going to happen soon. *en breve, dentro de poco, poco después* ❑ *Their trial will shortly begin. Su juicio empezará dentro de poco.* ❑ *Shortly after moving into her apartment, she found a job. Poco después de mudarse a su departamento, encontró trabajo.*

**short-order** ADJ A **short-order** cook is a person who is employed in a small restaurant such as a diner to cook food that is easily and quickly prepared. *plato rápido* ❑ *They employed short-order cooks to make the burgers. Emplearon cocineros de platos rápidos para hacer las hamburguesas.*

**short-term** ADJ **Short-term** is used to describe things that will last for a short time, or things that will have an effect soon rather than in the distant future. *corto plazo* ❑ *We have a short-term oil crisis facing us. Enfrentamos una crisis petrolera en el corto plazo.* ❑ *The company has 90 staff on short-term contracts. La compañía tiene a 90 empleados con contratos de corto plazo.*

**shot** /ʃɒt/ (**shots**) **1** **Shot** is the past tense and past participle of **shoot.** *pasado y participio pasado de* ***shoot*** **2** N-COUNT A **shot** is an act of firing a gun. *disparo, tiro, balazo* ❑ *He murdered Perceval with a single shot. Asesinó a Perceval de un solo disparo.* **3** N-COUNT Someone who is a good **shot** can shoot well. Someone who is a bad **shot** cannot shoot well. *buen/mal tirador o buena/mala tiradora* ❑ *He was not a very good shot. No era un tirador muy bueno.* **4** N-COUNT In sports, a **shot** is an act of kicking, hitting, or throwing the ball, especially in an attempt to score a point. *patada, disparo, lanzamiento* ❑ *He had only one shot at the goal. Sólo hizo un tiro a gol.* **5** N-COUNT A **shot** is a photograph or a particular sequence of pictures in a movie. *fotografía, toma* ❑ *A film crew was taking shots of the street. Un equipo de filmación estaba haciendo tomas de la calle.* **6** N-COUNT If you have a **shot at** something, you attempt to do it. *oportunidad* [INFORMAL] ❑ *The Olympic champion will get a shot at the world title. El campeón olímpico tendra la oportunidad de obtener el título mundial.* **7** N-COUNT A **shot of** a drug is an injection of it. *inyección* ❑ *The doctor gave me a shot of Nembutal. El médico me puso una inyección de nembutal.* **8** PHRASE If you **give** something your **best shot,** you do it as well as you possibly can. *hacer su mejor esfuerzo, lo mejor que se puede* [INFORMAL] ❑ *I don't expect to win, but I'm going to give it my best shot. No espero ganar, pero haré mi mejor esfuerzo por lograrlo.* **9** PHRASE The person who **calls the shots** is in a position to tell others what to do. *tener la última palabra, ser el que manda* ❑ *The directors here call the shots. Aquí, los directores son los que mandan.* **10** PHRASE If you describe something as **a long shot,** you mean that it is unlikely to succeed, but is worth trying. *improbable* ❑ *It was a long shot that she'd find him in the park, but it wasn't impossible. Era improbable que lo encontrara en el parque, pero no imposible.*
→ see **photography**

**Word Partnership** Usar *shot* con:

V. **fire a** shot, **hear a** shot 2
**miss a** shot 2 4
**take a** shot 2 4 5
**block a** shot, **hit a** shot 4
**get a** shot, **give** ***someone*** **a** shot 7
ADJ. **single** shot, **warning** shot 2
**good** shot 2–5
**winning** shot 4

**shot|gun** /ʃɒtgʌn/ (**shotguns**) N-COUNT A **shotgun** is a gun used for shooting birds and animals which fires a lot of small metal balls at one time. *escopeta*

**should** /ʃəd, STRONG ʃʊd/

**Should** is a modal verb. It is used with the base form of a verb.

1 MODAL You use **should** when you are saying what would be the right thing to do or the right state for something to be in. *forma modal del verbo deber* ❑ *I should exercise more. Debería hacer más ejercicio* ❑ *I don't think he should ever forget this. Creo que nunca debería olvidar esto.* 2 MODAL You use **should** to give someone an order to do something, or to report an official order. *deber* ❑ *18-year-olds should remember to register to vote. Los jóvenes de 18 años de edad deben recordar registrarse para votar.* 3 MODAL If you say that something **should have** happened, you mean that it did not happen, but that you wish it had. *deber* ❑ *I should have gone this morning but I was feeling ill. Debería haber ido esta mañana, pero me sentía enfermo.* ❑ *You shouldn't have said what you did. No deberías haber dicho lo que dijiste.* 4 MODAL You use **should** when you are saying that something is probably true or will probably happen in the way you are describing. If you say that something **should have** happened by a particular time, you mean that it will probably have happened by that time. *deber* ❑ *You should have no problem reading this. No debe de tener problemas para leer esto.* ❑ *The doctor said I should be fine by next week. El médico me dijo que ya debería de estar bien para la semana próxima.* 5 MODAL You use **should** in questions when you are asking someone for advice, permission, or information. *deber* ❑ *Should I ask for more help? ¿Debería pedir más ayuda?* ❑ *What should I do? ¿Qué debo hacer?* 6 MODAL You use **should** in "that" clauses after certain verbs, nouns, and adjectives when you are talking about a future event or situation. *deber* ❑ *He suggested that I should take a break. Me sugirió que debería de tomarme un descanso.* ❑ *I thought that we should look at every car. Pensé que deberíamos de buscar en cada automóvil.* 7 MODAL You use **should** in expressions such as **I should think** and **I should imagine** to indicate that you think something is true but you are not sure. *parecerle a uno, creer que* ❑ *I should think it will rain soon. Me parece que va a llover pronto.*

S

**shoul|der** /ʃoʊldər/ (**shoulders, shouldering, shouldered**) 1 N-COUNT Your **shoulders** are between your neck and the tops of your arms. *hombro* ❑ *She put her arm round his shoulders. Pasó su brazo sobre sus hombros.* 2 N-PLURAL When you talk about someone's problems or responsibilities, you can say that they carry them **on** their **shoulders**. *espaldas* ❑ *No one understood how much he carried on his shoulders. Nadie entendió la carga que llevaba sobre las espaldas.* 3 V-T If you **shoulder** the responsibility or the blame for something, you accept it. *echarse al hombro* ❑ *After Theresa died, John shouldered the full responsibility of continuing her work. Después de la muerte de Teresa, John se echó al hombro la responsabilidad absoluta de continuar su obra.* 4 N-COUNT On a busy road such as a highway, the **shoulder** is the area at the side of the road where vehicles are allowed to stop in an emergency. *acotamiento, banquina* 5 to **rub shoulders with** → see **rub**
→ see **body, horse**

**Word Partnership** Usar *shoulder* con:

ADJ. **bare** shoulder, **broken** shoulder, **dislocated** shoulder, **left/right** shoulder 1
V. **look over** ***your*** shoulder, **tap** ***someone*** **on the** shoulder 1
N. **head on** ***someone's*** shoulder 1
shoulder **a burden** 3

**shouldn't** /ʃʊdᵊnt/ **Shouldn't** is the usual spoken form of "should not." *forma hablada usual de* ***should not***

**should've** /ʃʊdəv/ **Should've** is the usual spoken form of "should have," especially when "have" is an auxiliary verb. *forma hablada usual de* ***should have***

**shout** /ʃaʊt/ (**shouts, shouting, shouted**) V-T/V-I If you **shout**, you say something very loudly. *gritar* ❑ *He had to shout over the noise of the wind. Tuvo que gritar por el ruido que hacía el viento.* ❑ *"She's alive!" he shouted. —¡Está viva!— gritó.* ❑ *Andrew ran out of the house, shouting for help. Andrew salió corriendo de la casa, pidiendo ayuda a gritos.* ● **Shout** is also a noun. *grito* ❑ *There were shouts from the crowd. Se oyeron los gritos de la multitud.* ● **shout|ing** N-UNCOUNT *gritería, grito* ❑ *My grandchildren heard the shouting first. Los primeros en oír los gritos fueron mis nietos.*

▸ **shout out** PHR-VERB If you **shout** something **out**, you say it very loudly so that people can hear you clearly. *gritar* ❑ *They shouted out the names of the winners. Nombraron a gritos a los ganadores.* ❑ *I shouted out "I'm OK!" —Grité: "¡Estoy bien!"*

**shove** /ʃʌv/ (**shoves, shoving, shoved**) V-T/V-I If you **shove** someone or something, you push them with a quick, violent movement. *empujar, dar empujones* ❑ *She shoved the other customers out of the way. Hizo a un lado a empujones a los otros clientes.* ❑ *He's the one who shoved me. Él fue quien me empujó.* ● **Shove** is also a noun. *empujón* ❑ *She gave Gracie a shove toward the house. Empujó a Gracie hacia la casa.*

**shov|el** /ʃʌvᵊl/ (**shovels, shoveling** or **shovelling, shoveled** or **shovelled**) 1 N-COUNT A **shovel** is a tool with a long handle that is used for lifting and moving earth, coal, or snow. *pala* ❑ *I'll need the snow shovel. Voy a necesitar la pala para nieve.* 2 V-T If you **shovel** earth, coal, or snow, you lift and move it with a shovel. *palear* ❑ *He has to go and shovel snow. Tiene que ir a palear la nieve.*
→ see **garden**

**show**
❶ VERB USES
❷ NOUN AND ADJECTIVE USES
❸ PHR-VERBS

❶ **show** /ʃoʊ/ (**shows, showing, showed, shown**) **1** V-T If something **shows that** a situation exists, it gives information that proves it or makes it clear to people. *indicar, mostrar, demostrar* ❑ *Research shows that certain foods can help prevent headaches. Las investigaciones indican que ciertos alimentos pueden ayudar a prevenir las jaquecas.* ❑ *These figures show an increase of over one million in unemployment. Estas cifras muestran un aumento de mas de un millón de desempleados.* **2** V-T If a picture, chart, movie, or piece of writing **shows** something, it represents it or gives information about it. *mostrar, ilustrar, tratar sobre* ❑ *Figure 4.1 shows the lower leg. La Figura 4.1 muestra la parte inferior de la pierna.* ❑ *The mirror, shown left, measures 20 x 12 inches. El espejo ilustrado a la izquierda mide 40 por 30 centímetros.* ❑ *The movie shows a boy trying to become a ballet dancer. La película trata sobre un niño que quiere llegar a ser bailarín de ballet.* **3** V-T If you **show** someone something, you give it to them, take them to it, or point to it, so that they can see it or know what you are referring to. *enseñar, mostrar* ❑ *Go and show this to your boss. Vaya y muéstrele esto a su jefe.* ❑ *He showed me the apartment he shares with Esther. Me enseñó el departamento que comparte con Esther.* **4** V-T If you **show** someone to a room or seat, you lead them there. *mostrar, acompañar, llevar* ❑ *Let me show you to your seat. Permítame acompañarlo a su asiento.* ❑ *Milton was shown into the office. Llevaron a Milton a la oficina.* **5** V-T If you **show** someone how to do something, you do it yourself so that they can watch you and learn how to do it. *enseñar, mostrar* ❑ *Claire showed us how to make a cake. Claire nos enseñó cómo hacer un pastel.* **6** V-T/V-I If something **shows** or if you **show** it, it is visible or noticeable. *enseñar, verse* ❑ *He smiled and showed a row of strong white teeth. Sonrió y enseñó una hilera de robustos dientes blancos.* ❑ *The sky was showing through the light cloud. El cielo se veía a través de las ligeras nubes.* **7** V-T If something **shows** a quality or characteristic or if that quality or characteristic **shows itself,** that quality or characteristic can be noticed or observed. *revelar, dar muestras* ❑ *The story shows a strong imagination and plenty of humor too. La historia revela una gran imaginación y también un gran sentido del humor.* ❑ *Rouse's career shows no sign of slowing down. La carrera de Rouse no da muestras de perder impulso.* **8** V-I If a person you are expecting to meet does not **show,** they do not arrive at the place where you expect to meet them. *presentarse, aparecerse* ❑ *There was a possibility he wouldn't show. Había la posibilidad de que no apareciera.* • **Show up** means the same as **show.** *presentarse, aparecerse* ❑ *We waited until five, but he didn't show up. Esperamos hasta las cinco, pero no se presentó.* **9** V-T/V-I If someone **shows** a movie or television program, it is broadcast or appears on television or in the movie theater. *mostrar/pasar, proyectar, estar en cartelera* ❑ *The TV news showed the same bit of film all day. Todo el día estuvieron pasando en la tele el mismo pedazo de la película.* ❑ *The movie is now showing at theaters around the country. La película está en cartelera en los cines de todo el país.* **10** PHRASE If you **have** something **to show for** your efforts, you have achieved something as a result of what you have done. *tener un beneficio* ❑ *I wish I had something to show for my time in my job. Ojalá tuviera algún beneficio después de tantos años en este trabajo.*

❷ **show** /ʃoʊ/ (**shows**) **1** N-COUNT **A show of** a feeling or quality is an attempt by someone to make it clear that they have that feeling or quality. *despliegue, demostración* ❑ *Workers gathered in the city center in a show of support for the government. Los trabajadores se reunieron en el centro de la ciudad en un despliegue de apoyo al gobierno.* **2** N-UNCOUNT If you say that something is **for show,** you mean that it has no real purpose and is done just to give a good impression. *actitud para darse tono* ❑ *Is this all for show or are you serious? ¿Dices todo esto para darte tono o hablas en serio?* **3** N-COUNT A television or radio **show** is a program on television or radio. *programa* ❑ *I had my own TV show. Tenía mi propio programa de televisión.* ❑ *It's a popular talk show on a Cuban radio station. Es un popular programa de entrevistas en una estación radiofónica cubana.* **4** N-COUNT A **show** in a theater is an entertainment or concert, especially one that includes different items such as music, dancing, and comedy. *espectáculo* ❑ *How about going to see a show? ¿Qué tal si vamos a ver un espectáculo?* **5** N-COUNT A **show** is a public exhibition of things. *exposición, desfile* ❑ *The show is in Boston now. La exposición está en Boston ahora.* ❑ *About 30 fashion shows are planned for this fall. Para este otoño están programados aproximadamente treinta desfiles de modas.*
→ see **concert, laser**

❸ **show** /ʃoʊ/ (**shows, showing, showed, shown**)
▶ **show off** **1** PHR-VERB If you say that someone **is showing off,** you are criticizing them for trying to impress people by showing in a very obvious way what they can do or what they own. *alardear, presumir* ❑ *All right, there's no need to show off. Está bien; no tienes que alardear.* **2** PHR-VERB If you **show off** something that you have, you show it to a lot of people or make it obvious that you have it, because you are proud of it. *hacer alarde* ❑ *Naomi was showing off her engagement ring. Naomi estaba haciendo alarde de su anillo de compromiso.*

**show and tell** also **show-and-tell** N-UNCOUNT **Show and tell** is a school activity in which children present an object to their class and talk about it. *exposición* ❑ *She can bring her dog to school for show-and-tell. El día que le toque exponer, puede traer su perro a la escuela.*

**show busi|ness** N-UNCOUNT **Show business** is the entertainment industry of movies, theater, and television. *farándula, mundo del espectáculo* ❑ *He started his career in show business by playing the piano. Inició su carrera en la farándula tocando el piano.*

**show|er** /ʃaʊər/ (**showers, showering, showered**) **1** N-COUNT A **shower** is a device which sprays you with water so you can wash yourself. *ducha, regadera* ❑ *She heard him turn on the shower. Lo oyó que hacía correr el agua de la regadera.* **2** N-COUNT If you take a **shower,** you wash yourself by standing under a spray of water from a shower. *baño, ducha* ❑ *I think I'll take a shower. Creo que voy a darme un baño.* **3** V-I If you **shower,** you wash yourself by standing under a spray of water from a shower. *bañarse, ducharse* ❑ *There wasn't time to*

*shower.* *No había tiempo para bañarse.* **4** N-COUNT A **shower** is a short period of rain, especially light rain. *chubasco, chaparrón* ❑ *There'll be scattered showers this afternoon.* *Pronostican lluvias aisladas para esta tarde.* **5** N-COUNT You can refer to a lot of things that are falling as a **shower of** them. *lluvia* ❑ *The suitcase fell open and a shower of banknotes fell out.* *Se abrió la maleta y cayó una lluvia de billetes.* **6** V-T If you **are showered with** a lot of small objects or pieces, they are scattered over you. *cubrir de, colmar de* ❑ *The bride and groom were showered with rice in the traditional manner.* *Como es tradicional, una lluvia de arroz cubrió a los novios.* **7** N-COUNT A **shower** is a party, usually for a woman who is getting married or having a baby, at which the guests bring gifts. *fiesta de regalos para la novia o para la mujer que va a tener un hijo* ❑ *...a baby shower.* *...una fiesta de regalos para el futuro bebé.*
→ see **bathroom, petroleum, soap, wedding**

**show|er gel** (**shower gels**) N-VAR **Shower gel** is a type of liquid soap designed for use in the shower. *gel de baño*

**shown** /ʃoʊn/ **Shown** is the past participle of **show**. *participio pasado de **show***

**shrank** /ʃræŋk/ **Shrank** is a past tense of **shrink**. *pasado de **shrink***

**shred** /ʃrɛd/ (**shreds, shredding, shredded**)
**1** V-T If you **shred** something such as food or paper, you cut it or tear it into very small, narrow pieces. *destruir* ❑ *They are shredding documents.* *Están destruyendo documentos.* **2** N-COUNT If you cut or tear food or paper **into shreds,** you cut or tear it into small, narrow pieces. *desmenuzar, cortar* ❑ *Cut the cabbage into long shreds.* *Corte la col en tiritas delgadas.*

**shrimp** /ʃrɪmp/ (**shrimp**)

> The plural can also be **shrimps**.

N-COUNT **Shrimp** are small shellfish with long tails and many legs. *camarón* ❑ *Add the shrimp and cook for 30 seconds.* *Añada los camarones y cocine durante 30 segundos.*
→ see **shellfish**

**shrimp cock|tail** (**shrimp cocktails**) N-VAR A **shrimp cocktail** is a dish that consists of shrimp, and a sauce. It is usually eaten at the beginning of a meal. *coctel de camarones*

S

**shrink** /ʃrɪŋk/ (**shrinks, shrinking, shrank** or **shrunk**) **1** V-I If cloth or clothing **shrinks,** it becomes smaller in size, usually as a result of being washed. *encogerse* ❑ *A cotton shirt shrank so much after one wash that she couldn't wear it.* *La camisa de algodón se encogió tanto después de lavarla que ya no pudo usarla.* **2** V-T/V-I If something **shrinks** or something else **shrinks** it, it becomes smaller. *reducir(se), retroceder* ❑ *The forests of West Africa have shrunk.* *Los bosques del África occidental se han reducido.* **3** V-I If you **shrink away from** someone or something, you move away from them because you are frightened, shocked, or disgusted by them. *rehuir, evitar* ❑ *One child shrinks away from me when I try to talk to him.* *Un niño me rehúye cuando trato de hablar con él.* **4** N-COUNT A **shrink** is a psychiatrist. *loquero* [INFORMAL] ❑ *I've seen a shrink already.* *Ya fui a ver a un loquero.*

**shrub** /ʃrʌb/ (**shrubs**) N-COUNT **Shrubs** are plants that have several woody stems. *arbusto, mata* ❑ *...flowering shrubs.* *...arbustos en flor.*
→ see **plant**

**shrug** /ʃrʌg/ (**shrugs, shrugging, shrugged**) V-I If you **shrug,** you raise your shoulders to show that you are not interested in something or that you do not know or care about something. *encogerse de hombros* ❑ *I shrugged, as if to say, "Why not?"* *Me encogí de hombros como diciendo: "¿por qué no?".* ● **Shrug** is also a noun. *encogerse de hombros* ❑ *"I suppose so," said Anna with a shrug.* *—Supongo —dijo Anna, encogiéndose de hombros.*
▸ **shrug off** PHR-VERB If you **shrug** something **off,** you ignore it or treat it as if it is not really important or serious. *hacer caso omiso de* ❑ *He shrugged off the criticism.* *Hizo caso omiso de las críticas.*

**shrunk** /ʃrʌŋk/ **Shrunk** is the past participle of **shrink**. *participio pasado de **shrink***

**shuck** /ʃʌk/ (**shucks, shucking, shucked**)
**1** V-T If you **shuck** something such as corn or shellfish, you remove it from its outer covering. *pelar (verduras), abrir (mariscos)* ❑ *She went outside to pick peas and to shuck them in the sunlight.* *Salió a recoger chícharos y pelarlos a la luz del sol.* **2** EXCLAM **Shucks** is an exclamation that is used to express embarrassment, disappointment, or annoyance. *¡caray!, ¡caramba!* [INFORMAL] ❑ *Terry said "Oh, shucks!" when they complimented her on her singing.* *Terry dijo —¡caray! cuando la felicitaron por su manera de cantar.*

**shuf|fle** /ʃʌfᵊl/ (**shuffles, shuffling, shuffled**)
**1** V-I If you **shuffle** somewhere, you walk there without lifting your feet properly off the ground. *arrastrar los pies* ❑ *Moira shuffled across the kitchen.* *Moira cruzó la cocina arrastrando los pies.* ● **Shuffle** is also a noun. *andar pesado* ❑ *Her walk has become a shuffle.* *Su paso se volvió un andar pesado.* **2** V-T/V-I If you **shuffle around**, you move your feet about while standing or you move your bottom about while sitting, often because you feel uncomfortable or embarrassed. *revolverse* ❑ *He shuffled around in his chair.* *Se movió incómodo en la silla.* ❑ *He smiled and shuffled his feet.* *Sonrió y cambió de pie.* **3** V-T If you **shuffle** playing cards, you mix them up before you begin a game. *barajar* ❑ *There are different ways of shuffling the cards.* *Hay diferentes modos de barajar las cartas.* **4** V-T If you **shuffle** things such as pieces of paper, you move them around so that they are in a different order. *revolver*

**shut** /ʃʌt/ (**shuts, shutting**)

> The form **shut** is used in the present tense and is the past tense and past participle.

**1** V-T/V-I If you **shut** something such as a door or if it **shuts,** it moves so that it fills a hole or a space. *cerrar(se)* ❑ *Please shut the gate.* *Por favor, cierre el portón.* ❑ *The door shut gently.* *La puerta se cerró suavemente.* ● **Shut** is also an adjective. *cerrado* ❑ *They have warned us to keep our doors and windows shut.* *Nos advirtieron que mantuviéramos cerradas las puertas y ventanas.* **2** V-T If you **shut** your eyes, you lower your eyelids so that you cannot see anything. *cerrar* ❑ *Lucy shut her eyes so she wouldn't see it happen.* *Lucy cerró los ojos para no ver lo que pasaba.* ● **Shut** is also an adjective. *cerrado* ❑ *His eyes were shut and he seemed to be asleep.* *Tenía los ojos cerrados y parecía estar dormido.* **3** V-T/V-I If your mouth **shuts** or if you **shut** your mouth, you place your lips firmly together. *cerrar* ❑ *Daniel's mouth opened, and then shut again. Daniel abrió la boca y luego la cerró nuevamente.* ● **Shut** is also an adjective. *cerrado* ❑ *She was silent for a moment, her lips tight shut. Guardó silencio por un momento, apretando los labios.* **4** V-T/V-I When a store or other public building **shuts** or when someone **shuts** it, it is closed and you cannot use it until it is open again. *cerrar* ❑ *They shut the museum without giving any notice. Cerraron el museo sin aviso previo.* ❑ *Stores usually shut from noon to 3 p.m. Por lo general, las tiendas cierran de mediodía a las 3 de la tarde.* ● **Shut** is also an adjective. *cerrado* ❑ *Make sure you have food when the local store may be shut. Asegúrese de tener alimentos cuando la tienda de su vecindario pueda estar cerrada.*

▸ **shut down** PHR-VERB If a factory or business **shuts down** or if someone **shuts** it **down,** work there stops or it is no longer in business. *cerrar* ❑ *The factory is shutting down for two weeks. La fábrica va a cerrar durante dos semanas.*

▸ **shut in** PHR-VERB If you **shut** a person or animal **in** a room, you close the door so that they cannot leave it. *encerrar* ❑ *We shut the animals in the shelter in bad weather. Encerramos los animales en el refugio cuando hace mal tiempo.*

▸ **shut off** PHR-VERB If you **shut off** something such as an engine or an electrical appliance, you turn it off to stop it from working. *apagar* ❑ *He shut off the car engine. Apagó el motor del coche.*

▸ **shut out** **1** PHR-VERB If you **shut** something or someone **out,** you prevent them from getting into a place. *echar, dejar afuera* ❑ *"I shut him out of the house," said Maureen. —Lo dejé afuera de la casa—dijo Maureen.* **2** PHR-VERB If you **shut out** a thought or a feeling, you prevent yourself from thinking or feeling it. *ahuyentar* ❑ *I tried to shut out the memory. Traté de ahuyentar el recuerdo.* **3** PHR-VERB In sports such as football and hockey, if one team **shuts out** the team they are playing against, they win and prevent the opposing team from scoring. *ganar sin conceder puntos en contra* ❑ *Harvard shut out Yale, 14 – 0. Harvard le ganó a Yale 14 a 0.* **4** → see also **shutout**

▸ **shut up** PHR-VERB If someone **shuts up** or if someone **shuts** them **up,** they stop talking. You can say" **shut up"** as an impolite way to tell a person to stop talking. *callar(se)* ❑ *Just shut up, will you? —¡Ya cállate!, ¿quieres?*

| **Word Partnership** | Usar *shut* con: |
|---|---|
| N. | shut **a door,** shut **a gate,** shut **a window** **1** |
| V. | **force** *something* shut, **pull** *something* shut, **push** *something* shut, **slam** *something* shut **1** |
| ADV. | shut **tight/tightly** **1** – **3**<br>shut **temporarily** **4** |

**shut|down** /ʃʌtdaʊn/ (**shutdowns**) N-COUNT A **shutdown** is the closing of a factory, store, or other business. *cierre, paro* ❑ *People had to walk home during the shutdown of subways and trains. La gente tuvo que caminar para ir a su casa durante el paro del metro y los trenes.*

**shut|out** /ʃʌtaʊt/ (**shutouts**) also **shut-out** N-COUNT In sports such as football and hockey, a **shutout** is a game or part of a game in which one of the teams wins and prevents the opposing team from scoring. *triunfo o partido en el que el equipo perdedor no marca tantos, derrota en cero* ❑ *It was the Mariners' 10th shutout. Fue la décima derrota en cero de los Marineros.*

**shut|ter** /ʃʌtər/ (**shutters**) **1** N-COUNT **Shutters** are wooden or metal covers fitted on the outside of a window. They can be opened to let in the light, or closed to keep out the sun or the cold. *contraventana, postigo* ❑ *She opened the shutters and looked out of the window. Abrió los postigos y se asomó por la ventana.* **2** N-COUNT The **shutter** in a camera is the part which opens to allow light through the lens when a photograph is taken. *obturador* ❑ *He pointed the camera at them and pressed the shutter. Los enfocó con la cámara y oprimió el obturador.*
→ see **photography**

**shut|tle** /ʃʌtᵊl/ (**shuttles, shuttling, shuttled**) **1** N-COUNT A **shuttle** is the same as a **space shuttle.** *transbordador espacial* **2** N-COUNT A **shuttle** is a plane, bus, or train which makes frequent trips between two places. *transbordador, avión, autobús o tren de enlace* ❑ *There is a free shuttle between the airport terminals. Hay un autobús de enlace gratis entre las terminales del aeropuerto.* **3** V-T/V-I If someone or something **shuttles** or **is shuttled** from one place to another place, they frequently go from one place to the other. *ir y venir* ❑ *He has to shuttle between Boston and New York for his work. Tiene que ir y venir entre Boston y Nueva York por su trabajo.*

**shy** /ʃaɪ/ (**shyer, shyest, shies, shying, shied**) **1** ADJ A **shy** person is nervous and uncomfortable in the company of other people. *tímido* ❑ *She was a shy, quiet girl. Era una muchacha tímida y callada.* ❑ *I was too shy to say anything. Soy muy tímido y no dije nada.* ● **shy|ly** ADV *tímidamente, con timidez* ❑ *The children smiled shyly. Los niños sonrieron tímidamente.* ● **shy|ness** N-UNCOUNT *timidez* ❑ *His shyness made it difficult for him to make friends. Su timidez le dificultaba hacer amigos.* **2** ADJ If you are **shy about** or **shy of** doing something, you are unwilling to do it because you are afraid of what might happen. *dar vergüenza, avergonzar* ❑ *They feel shy about showing their feelings. Les daba vergüenza mostrar sus sentimientos.*

▸ **shy away from** PHR-VERB If you **shy away from** doing something, you avoid doing it, often because you are afraid or not confident enough. *rehuir* ❑ *We shy away from making decisions. Rehuimos tomar decisiones.*

| **Thesaurus** | *shy* Ver también: |
|---|---|
| ADJ. | nervous, quiet, sheepish, uncomfortable; (*ant.*) confident **1** |

**Si|berian ti|ger** (**Siberian tigers**) N-COUNT A **Siberian tiger** is a species of large tiger that lives in parts of Russia. *tigre de Siberia, tigre siberiano*

**sib|ling** /sɪblɪŋ/ (**siblings**) N-COUNT Your **siblings** are your brothers and sisters. *hermano* [FORMAL] ❑ *His siblings are older than him. Sus hermanos son mayores que él.*

**sick** /sɪk/ (**sicker, sickest**) **1** ADJ If you are **sick,** you are ill. *enfermo* ❑ *He's very sick. He needs a doctor. Está muy enfermo. Necesita un médico.* ❑ *She had two small children, a sick husband, and no money. Tenía* *dos hijos pequeños, un esposo enfermo y nada de dinero.* • **The sick** are people who are sick. *los enfermos* ❑ *There are no doctors to treat the sick.* *No hay médicos para atender a los enfermos.* **2** ADJ If you are **sick,** the food that you have eaten comes up from your stomach and out of your mouth. If you **feel sick,** you feel as if you are going to be sick. *tener náuseas, tener ganas de vomitar, vomitar* ❑ *She was sick over the side of the ship.* *Estaba vomitando por la borda del barco.* ❑ *The smell of food made him feel sick.* *El olor de comida le provocó náuseas.* **3** ADJ If you are **sick of** something, you are very annoyed by it and want it to stop. *harto de, hasta la coronilla de* [INFORMAL] ❑ *I am sick of hearing these people complain.* *Estoy hasta la coronilla de oír quejarse a esa gente.* **4** ADJ If you describe something such as a joke or story as **sick,** you mean that it deals with death or suffering in an unpleasantly humorous way. *de muy mal gusto, morboso* ❑ *He told a sick joke about a cat.* *Contó un chiste de muy mal gusto sobre un gato.* **5** PHRASE If you say that something or someone **makes** you **sick,** you mean that they make you feel angry or disgusted. *dar rabia, enfermar* [INFORMAL] ❑ *It makes me sick that he lied like that.* *Me enferma que haya mentido así.* **6** PHRASE If you are **out sick,** you are not at work because you are sick. *ausente por enfermedad* ❑ *Tom is out sick today.* *Tom está enfermo, por eso no vino hoy.*

**Word Partnership** Usar *sick* con:

| | |
|---|---|
| N. | sick **children**, sick **mother**, sick **patients**, sick **people**, sick **person** 1 |
| V. | **care for the** sick 1<br>**become** sick, **feel** sick, **get** sick 1 2 |
| ADV. | **really** sick, **very** sick 1 2 |

**Word Link** *ness ≈ state, condition : consciousness, sickness, weakness*

**sick|ness** /sɪknɪs/ (**sicknesses**) **1** N-UNCOUNT **Sickness** is the state of being ill or unhealthy. *enfermedad* ❑ *He had one week of sickness in fifty-two years of working.* *Estuvo enfermo una semana en los cincuenta y dos años que trabajó.* **2** N-UNCOUNT **Sickness** is the uncomfortable feeling that you are going to vomit. *náuseas* ❑ *She suffered terribly with sickness when she was pregnant.* *Sufrió terriblemente por las náuseas cuando estuvo embarazada.* **3** N-VAR A **sickness** is a particular illness. *enfermedad* ❑ *She became ill with a mysterious sickness.* *Contrajo una enfermedad desconocida.*

S

**side**

❶ A SURFACE, POSITION, OR PLACE
❷ ONE ASPECT OR ONE POINT OF VIEW
❸ PHRASES

**❶ side** /saɪd/ (**sides**) **1** N-COUNT **The side of** something is a position to the left or right of it, rather than in front of it, behind it, or on it. *lado, costado* ❑ *On the left side of the door there's a door bell.* *A la izquierda de la puerta hay un timbre.* ❑ *Joe and Ken stood one on each side of me.* *Joe y Ken se pararon a mis lados.* **2** N-COUNT The **side** of an object, building, or vehicle is any of its flat surfaces which is not considered to be its front, its back, its top, or its bottom. *lado* ❑ *We put a label on the side of the box.* *Pusimos una etiqueta en un lado de la caja.* ❑ *The carton of milk lay on its side.* *El cartón de leche yacía de costado.* **3** N-COUNT The **sides** of a hollow place or a container are its inside vertical surfaces. *ladera* ❑ *The sides of the valley are very steep.* *Las laderas que rodean el valle son muy abruptas.* ❑ *Grease the bottom and sides of the dish.* *Engrase el fondo y los lados del platón.* **4** N-COUNT The **sides of** an area or surface are its edges. *costado, lado* ❑ *We parked on the side of the road.* *Nos estacionamos a un lado del camino.* ❑ *...a beach on the north side of the island.* *...una playa en el lado norte de la isla.* **5** N-COUNT The two **sides of** an area, surface, or object are its two halves or surfaces. *lado, cara* ❑ *She lay on the other side of the bed.* *Se acostó en el otro lado de la cama.* ❑ *You should only write on one side of the paper.* *Sólo debe escribir en un lado del papel.* **6** N-COUNT Your **sides** are the parts of your body between your front and your back, from under your arms to your hips. *costado, lado* ❑ *His arms were hanging by his sides.* *Los brazos le colgaban a los lados.* **7** N-COUNT If someone is **by** your **side** or **at** your **side,** they stay near you and give you comfort or support. *lado* ❑ *He was at his wife's side the whole time she was sick.* *Permaneció al lado de su esposa todo el tiempo que estuvo enferma.* **8** ADJ **Side** is used to describe things that are not the main or most important ones of their kind. *lateral* ❑ *She left the theater by a side door.* *Salió del teatro por una puerta lateral.* **9** N-COUNT A **side** is a small plate of food, such as French fries or salad, that you eat at the same time as the main course of a meal. *guarnición, acompañamiento*

**❷ side** /saɪd/ (**sides, siding, sided**) **1** N-COUNT The different **sides** in a war, argument, or negotiation are the groups of people who are opposing each other. *lado, parte* ❑ *Both sides want the war to end.* *Los dos lados quieren que la guerra termine.* ❑ *We have to find a solution that all sides agree with.* *Debemos encontrar una solución que acepten todas las partes.* **2** N-COUNT The different **sides of** an argument or deal are the different points of view or positions involved in it. *lado* ❑ *People on both sides of the issue are angry.* *Los partidarios de uno y otro lado están enojados.* **3** V-I If one person or country **sides with** another, they support them in an argument or a war. If people or countries **side against** another person or country, they support each other against them. *tomar partido por, ponerse de parte de* ❑ *Kentucky eventually sided with the Union.* *Finalmente, Kentucky se puso de parte de la Unión.* **4** N-COUNT A particular **side** of something such as a situation or someone's character is one aspect of it. *aspecto* ❑ *He showed a kind, gentle side of his character.* *Mostró un aspecto amable y delicado de su carácter.*

**❸ side** /saɪd/ (**sides**) **1** PHRASE If something moves **from side to side,** it moves repeatedly to the left and to the right. *de un lado a(l) otro* ❑ *She shook her head from side to side.* *Sacudió la cabeza de un lado a otro* **2** PHRASE If you are **on** someone's **side,** you are supporting them in an argument or a war. *del lado de, tomar partido por, ponerse de parte de* ❑ *He has his manager on his side.* *Tiene a su entrenador de su lado.* **3** PHRASE If someone does something **on the side,** they do it in addition to their main work. *extra* ❑ *She babysits to make a little money on the side.* *Cuida* *niños para ganar un poco de dinero extra.* **4** PHRASE If you have one type of food with another food **on the side,** you have an amount of the second food served with the first. *guarnición, acompañamiento* ❑ *Serve a bowl of warm tomato sauce on the side. Sirva un tazón de salsa de jitomate caliente como guarnición.* **5** PHRASE If you **put** something **to one side** or **put** it **on one side,** you temporarily ignore it in order to concentrate on something else. *dejar a un lado/dejar de lado* ❑ *He put the project to one side so he could spend more time with his family. Dejó el proyecto de lado para poder pasar más tiempo con su familia.* **6** PHRASE If two people or things are **side by side,** they are next to each other. *al lado, codo con codo* ❑ *We sat side by side on the beach. Nos sentamos uno al lado del otro en la playa.* **7** to **err on the side of** something → see **err** **8** to **be on the safe side** → see **safe** **9** someone's **side of the story** → see **story**

**side|burns** /saɪdbɜrnz/ N-PLURAL If a man has **sideburns,** he has a strip of hair growing down the side of each cheek. *patillas* ❑ *...a young man with long sideburns. ...un hombre joven con largas patillas.* → see **hair**

**side effect** (**side effects**) also **side-effect** N-COUNT The **side effects** of a drug are the effects, usually bad ones, that the drug has on you in addition to its function of curing illness or pain. *efecto secundario, efecto colateral* ❑ *The main side effect of the drug is tiredness. El principal efecto secundario del medicamento es el cansancio.*

**side|line** /saɪdlaɪn/ (**sidelines**) **1** N-COUNT A **sideline** is something that you do in addition to your main job in order to earn extra money. *actividad suplementaria* ❑ *Many musicians teach music as a sideline. Muchos músicos dan clases como actividad suplementaria.* **2** N-PLURAL The **sidelines** are the lines marking the long sides of the playing area, for example, on a football field or tennis court. *línea lateral* **3** N-PLURAL If you are **on the sidelines** in a situation, you do not influence events at all, either because you have chosen not to be involved, or because other people have not involved you. *al margen* ❑ *They always leave me on the sidelines when important decisions are made. Siempre me dejan al margen cuando hay que tomar decisiones importantes.*
→ see **basketball, football, soccer, tennis**

**side road** (**side roads**) N-COUNT A **side road** is a road which leads off a busier, more important road. *camino secundario*

**side sal|ad** (**side salads**) N-COUNT A **side salad** is a bowl of salad for one person which is served with a main meal. *plato de ensalada*

**side|step** /saɪdstɛp/ (**sidesteps, sidestepping, sidestepped**) also **side-step** V-T If you **sidestep** a problem, you avoid discussing it or dealing with it. *eludir, dejar de lado* ❑ *The mayor sidestepped the question. El alcalde eludió la pregunta.*

**side street** (**side streets**) N-COUNT A **side street** is a quiet, often narrow street which leads off a busier street. *calle lateral*

**side|walk** /saɪdwɔk/ (**sidewalks**) N-COUNT A **sidewalk** is a path with a hard surface by the side of a road. *acera, banqueta* ❑ *She was walking down the sidewalk toward him. Caminaba hacia él por la banqueta.*

**side|ways** /saɪdweɪz/ ADV **Sideways** means from or toward the side of something or someone. *de reojo, de soslayo* ❑ *Pete looked sideways at her. Pete la miró de soslayo.* • **Sideways** is also an adjective. *de reojo, de soslayo* ❑ *Alfred gave him a sideways glance. Alfred le echó una mirada de reojo.*

**siege** /sidʒ/ (**sieges**) N-COUNT A **siege** is a military or police operation in which soldiers or police surround a place in order to force the people there to come out or give up control of the place. *sitio* ❑ *The siege has been going on for three days. El sitio lleva ya tres días.*

| Word Partnership | Usar *siege* con: |
| --- | --- |
| PREP. | **after a** siege, **during a** siege, **under** siege |
| V. | **end a** siege, **lift a** siege |

**si|er|ra** /siɛrə/ (**sierras**) N-COUNT A **sierra** is a range of mountains with jagged peaks. *sierra*

**sigh** /saɪ/ (**sighs, sighing, sighed**) V-I When you **sigh,** you let out a deep breath, as a way of expressing feelings such as disappointment, tiredness, or pleasure. *suspirar* ❑ *Michael sighed and sat down slowly. Michael suspiró y se sentó lentamente.* ❑ *Roberta sighed with relief. Roberta suspiró aliviada.* • **Sigh** is also a noun. *suspiro* ❑ *She kicked off her shoes with a sigh. Se sacudió los zapatos de los pies y exhaló un suspiro.*

| Word Partnership | Usar *sigh* con: |
| --- | --- |
| V. | **breathe a** sigh, **give a** sigh, **hear a** sigh, **heave a** sigh, **let out a** sigh |
| ADJ. | **collective** sigh, **deep** sigh, **long** sigh |

**sight** /saɪt/ (**sights, sighting, sighted**) **1** N-UNCOUNT Your **sight** is your ability to see. *vista* ❑ *My sight is not as good as my son's. Mi vista no es tan buena como la de mi hijo.* **2** N-SING **The sight of** something is the act of seeing it or an occasion on which you see it. *al ver* ❑ *I feel ill at the sight of blood. Me siento mal al ver sangre.* **3** V-T If you **sight** someone or something, you suddenly see them, often briefly. *ver* ❑ *Police sighted a man entering the building. La policía vio a un hombre que entraba al edificio.* **4** N-PLURAL **The sights** are the places that are interesting to see and that are often visited by tourists. *lugar de interés* ❑ *We saw the sights of Paris. Vimos los lugares de interés de París.* **5** PHRASE If you **catch sight of** someone, you suddenly see them, often briefly. *descubrir* ❑ *He caught sight of her in the crowd. La descubrió entre la multitud.* **6** PHRASE If something is **in sight** or **within sight,** you can see it. If it is **out of sight,** you cannot see it. *a la vista/fuera de la vista* ❑ *At last the beach was in sight. La playa estaba por fin a la vista.* **7** PHRASE If a result or a decision is **in sight** or **within sight,** it is likely to happen within a short time. *ver venir* ❑ *An agreement was in sight. Se veía venir un acuerdo.* **8** PHRASE If you **lose sight of** an important aspect of something, you no longer pay attention to it because you are worrying about less important things. *perder de vista* ❑ *It is important not to lose sight of what really matters: your family. Es importante no perder de vista lo que realmente importa: la familia.* **9** PHRASE If someone does something **on sight,** they do it without delay, as soon as a person or thing is seen. *a la vista* ❑ *He disliked her on sight. Le desagradó a la vista.* **10** PHRASE If you **set** your **sights**

**on** something, you decide that you want it and try hard to get it. tener la vista puesta en ❑ *They set their sights on the world record.* *Tienen la mira puesta en la marca mundial.*

**Word Partnership** Usar *sight* con:

| | |
|---|---|
| V. | **catch** sight **of** ***someone/something*** 6 |
| | **come into** sight, **keep** ***someone/something*** **in** sight 7 |
| N. | **the end is in** sight 8 |

**sight|see|ing** /saɪtsiɪŋ/ N-UNCOUNT If you go **sightseeing** or do some **sightseeing,** you travel around visiting the interesting places that tourists usually visit. visita a lugares de interés ❑ *...a day's sightseeing in Venice.* *...un día recorriendo los lugares de interés de Venecia.*
→ see **city**

**sight word** (**sight words**) N-COUNT A **sight word** is a word that most readers of a language can recognize immediately without needing to analyze its separate parts. palabra de fácil reconocimiento para un lector sin análisis de sus partes [TECHNICAL]

**sign** /saɪn/ (**signs, signing, signed**) 1 N-COUNT A **sign** is a mark or shape that always has a particular meaning, for example, in mathematics or music. signo ❑ *This = is an equals sign.* *Este es el signo igual: =.* 2 N-COUNT A **sign** is a movement of your arms, hands, or head which is intended to have a particular meaning. señal ❑ *They gave me a thumbs-up sign to show that everything was OK.* *Me hicieron una señal con el pulgar levantado para indicarme que todo iba bien.* 3 N-COUNT A **sign** is a piece of wood, metal, or plastic with words or pictures on it. Signs give you information about something, or give you a warning or an instruction. letrero, señal ❑ *There was a sign saying that the highway was closed because of snow.* *Había un letrero que decía que la carretera estaba cerrada por la nieve.* 4 N-VAR If there is a **sign of** something, there is something which shows that it exists or is happening. señal, muestra ❑ *Some people see crying as a sign of weakness.* *Algunas personas consideran el llanto como una señal de debilidad.* ❑ *His face rarely showed any sign of fear.* *Casi nunca daba muestras de tener miedo.* 5 V-T When you **sign** a document, you write your name on it. firmar, subscribir ❑ *World leaders have signed an agreement to protect the environment.* *Los dirigentes mundiales firmaron un convenio para proteger el medio ambiente.* ● **sign|ing** N-UNCOUNT firma ❑ *The signing of the treaty will take place today.* *La firma del tratado tendrá lugar hoy.* 6 V-T/V-I If an organization **signs** someone or if someone **signs** for an organization, they sign a contract agreeing to work for that organization for a specified period of time. contratar, fichar ❑ *The Minnesota Vikings signed Walker to play for them for the next three years.* *Los Vikingos de Minesota ficharon a Walker para jugar con ellos los próximos tres años.* 7 N-COUNT In astrology, a **sign** or a **sign of the zodiac** is one of the twelve areas into which the heavens are divided. signo ❑ *She was born under the sign of Libra.* *Nació bajo el signo de Libra.* 8 PHRASE If you say that there is **no sign of** someone, you mean that they have not yet arrived, although you are expecting them to come. no haber señales de ❑ *I arrived at the meeting place, but there was no sign of Laura.* *Llegué al lugar de la cita, pero no había señales de Laura.*

▸ **sign for** PHR-VERB If you **sign for** something, you officially state that you have received it, by signing a form or book. firmar (por algo) ❑ *A package arrived and I signed for it.* *Llegó un paquete y yo firmé por él.*

▸ **sign in** PHR-VERB If you **sign in,** you officially indicate that you have arrived at a hotel or club by signing a book or form. registrarse ❑ *I signed in and went straight to my room.* *Firmé el registro y me fui directamente al cuarto.*

▸ **sign up** PHR-VERB If you **sign up** for an organization or if an organization **signs** you **up,** you sign a contract officially agreeing to do a job or course of study. contratar ❑ *He signed up as a flight attendant with American Airlines.* *Firmó un contrato de sobrecargo/auxiliar de vuelo con American Airlines.*

**Thesaurus** *sign* Ver también:

| | |
|---|---|
| N. | nod, signal, wave 2 |
| V. | authorize, autograph, endorse 5 |

**sig|nal** /sɪgnəl/ (**signals, signaling** or **signalling, signaled** or **signalled**) 1 N-COUNT A **signal** is a gesture, sound, or action which is intended to give a particular message to the person who sees or hears it. señal ❑ *The captain gave the signal to attack.* *El capitán dio la señal de ataque.* 2 V-T/V-I If you **signal to** someone, you make a gesture or sound in order to send them a particular message. hacer señas ❑ *Mandy signaled to Jesse to follow her.* *Mandy le hizo señas a Jesse de que la siguiera.* ❑ *She signaled that she was leaving.* *Hizo señas de que se iba.* 3 N-COUNT If an event or action is a **signal of** something, it suggests that this thing exists or is going to happen. señal ❑ *His visit seemed to be a signal of support.* *Su visita parecía ser una señal de apoyo.* 4 V-T If someone or something **signals** an event, they suggest that the event is happening or likely to happen. sugerir ❑ *In her speech, she signaled important changes in government policy.* *En su discurso sugirió que habría cambios importantes en la política gubernamental.* 5 N-COUNT A **signal** is a piece of equipment beside a railroad, which indicates to engineers whether they should stop the train or not. señal ❑ *The crash was caused by a broken signal.* *El accidente fue provocado por una señal caída (rota).* 6 N-COUNT A **signal** is a series of radio waves, light waves, or changes in electrical current which may carry information. señal ❑ *...high-frequency radio signals.* *...señales de radio de alta frecuencia.*
→ see **cellphone, television**

**Word Partnership** Usar *signal* con:

| | |
|---|---|
| V. | **give a** signal 1 3 |
| | **send a** signal 1 3 6 |
| ADJ. | **wrong** signal 1 3 |
| | **clear** signal, **strong** signal 1 3 6 |
| | **important** signal 3 |

**sig|na|ture** /sɪgnətʃər, -tʃʊər/ (**signatures**) N-COUNT Your **signature** is your name, written in your own characteristic way. firma ❑ *I put my signature at the bottom of the page.* *Puse mi firma al pie de la hoja/página.*

**sig|nifi|cance** /sɪɡnɪfɪkəns/ N-UNCOUNT The **significance** of something is the importance that it has. *importancia* ❑ *What do you think is the significance of this event? ¿Qué importancia cree que tenga este acto?*

**Word Partnership** Usar *significance* con:

ADJ. **cultural** significance, **great** significance, **historic/historical** significance, **political** significance, **religious** significance
V. **downplay the** significance **of** *something*, **explain the** significance **of** *something*, **understand the** significance **of** *something*

**sig|nifi|cant** /sɪɡnɪfɪkənt/ **1** ADJ A **significant** amount or effect is large enough to be important or noticeable. *importante* ❑ *A small but significant number of 11-year-olds cannot read. Un número reducido pero importante de niños de 11 años de edad no sabe leer.* ● **sig|nifi|cant|ly** ADV *considerablemente, significativamente* ❑ *The number of Senators who agreed with him increased significantly. El número de senadores que concordaron con él aumentó considerablemente.* **2** ADJ A **significant** fact, event, or thing is one that is important or shows something. *significativo* ❑ *I think it was significant that he never knew his own father. Creo que era significativo que nunca haya conocido a su propio padre.* ● **sig|nifi|cant|ly** ADV *significativamente* ❑ *Significantly, the company recently opened a huge store in Atlanta. Significativamente, la compañía abrió hace poco una enorme tienda en Atlanta.*

**Thesaurus** *significant* Ver también:

ADJ. big, important, large; (*ant.*) insignificant, minor, small **1**

**Sikh** /sik/ (**Sikhs**) N-COUNT A **Sikh** is a person who follows the Indian religion of Sikhism. Sihkism is an Indian religion which separated from Hinduism in the sixteenth century and which teaches that there is only one God. *sij* ❑ *Her husband is a Sikh. Su esposo es sij.* ❑ *...a Sikh temple. ...un templo sij.*

**si|lence** /saɪləns/ (**silences, silencing, silenced**) **1** N-VAR If there is **silence,** nobody is speaking. *silencio* ❑ *They stood in silence. Permanecieron en silencio.* ❑ *There was a long silence. Hubo un prolongado silencio.* **2** N-UNCOUNT Someone's **silence** about something is their failure or refusal to speak to other people about it. *silencio* ❑ *His silence on the subject doesn't mean he is guilty. Su silencio sobre el asunto no significa que sea culpable.* PHRASE ● If someone **breaks** their **silence** about something, they talk about something that they have not talked about before or for a long time. *romper el silencio* **3** V-T If someone **silences** you, they stop you from expressing opinions that they do not agree with. *silenciar, callar* ❑ *He tried to silence anyone who spoke out against him. Trató de callar a todos los que hablaron en su contra.*

**Word Partnership** Usar *silence* con:

ADJ. **awkward** silence, **complete** silence, **long** silence, **sudden** silence, **total** silence **1**
V. silence **falls, listen in** silence, **observe a** silence, **sit in** silence, **watch** *something* **in** silence **1**
**break a/*your*** silence **2**

**si|lent** /saɪlənt/ **1** ADJ Someone who is **silent** is not speaking. *callado* ❑ *Trish was silent because she did not know what to say. Trish estaba callada porque no sabía qué decir.* ❑ *He spoke no English and stayed completely silent. Como no hablaba inglés, no dijo ni media palabra.* ● **si|lent|ly** ADV *silenciosamente, en silencio* ❑ *She and Ned sat silently, enjoying the peace of the lake. Ella y Ned estaban sentados en silencio, disfrutando de la paz del lago.* **2** ADJ A place that is **silent** is completely quiet, with no sound at all. Something that is **silent** makes no sound at all. *silencioso, en silencio* ❑ *The room was silent except for the TV. El cuarto estaba en silencio, excepto por la televisión.* ● **si|lent|ly** ADV *silenciosamente, en silencio* ❑ *He moved silently across the room. Cruzó silenciosamente el cuarto.*

**Word Partnership** Usar *silent* con:

V. **go** silent, **keep** silent, **remain** silent, **sit** silent **1**
N. silent **prayer,** silent **reading** **1**
silent **auction** **2**

**si|lent part|ner** (**silent partners**) N-COUNT A **silent partner** is a person who provides some of the capital for a business but who does not take an active part in managing the business. *socio capitalista* [BUSINESS]

**sili|ca** /sɪlɪkə/ N-UNCOUNT **Silica** is silicon dioxide, a compound of silicon which is found in sand, quartz, and flint, and which is used to make glass *sílice*
→ see **glass**

**sili|cate min|er|al** /sɪlɪkɪt mɪnərəl/ (**silicate minerals**) N-COUNT **Silicate minerals** are minerals that are made mostly of a substance called silica. *silicato*

**sili|con** /sɪlɪkən, -kɒn/ N-UNCOUNT **Silicon** is an element that is found in sand and in minerals such as quartz and granite. Silicon is used to make parts of computers and other electronic equipment. *silicio* ❑ *...a silicon chip. ...un circuito integrado.*

**sili|cone** /sɪlɪkoʊn/ N-UNCOUNT **Silicone** is a tough artificial substance made from silicon, which is used to make polishes, and also used in cosmetic surgery and plastic surgery. *silicona* ❑ *Regular silicone treatments will keep these boots waterproof. Un tratamiento regular con siliconas conservará la impermeabilidad de las botas.*

**silk** /sɪlk/ (**silks**) N-VAR **Silk** is a substance which is made into smooth fine cloth and sewing thread. You can also refer to this cloth or thread as **silk**. *seda* ❑ *They bought silks from China. Compraron sedas en China.* ❑ *Pauline wore a silk dress. Pauline llevaba un vestido de seda.*

**sill** /sɪl/ (**sills**) N-COUNT A **sill** is a shelf along the bottom edge of a window, either inside or outside a building. *antepecho, alféizar* ❑ *Whitlock sat on the sill by the desk. Whitlock se sentó en el antepecho, junto al escritorio.*

**sil|ly** /sɪli/ (**sillier, silliest**) ADJ If you say that someone or something is **silly,** you mean that they are foolish, childish, or ridiculous. *tonto* ❑ *She thinks that I am silly. Cree que soy un tonto.* ❑ *I thought it would be silly to say no. Pensé que sería tonto decir no.* • **sil|li|ness** N-UNCOUNT *tontería* ❑ *Let's stop this silliness. Dejémonos de tonterías.*

**silt** /sɪlt/ N-UNCOUNT **Silt** is fine sand, soil, or mud which is carried along by a river. *cieno, limo* ❑ *The lake was full of silt. El lago estaba lleno de cieno.*
→ see **erosion**

**sil|ver** /sɪlvər/ **1** N-UNCOUNT **Silver** is a valuable pale gray metal that is used for making jewelry and ornaments. *plata* ❑ *...a bracelet made from silver. ...un brazalete de plata.* **2** N-UNCOUNT **Silver** consists of coins that are made from silver or that look like silver. *monedas de plata* ❑ *The thieves took $150,000 in silver. Los ladrones se llevaron 150,000 dólares en monedas de plata.* **3** N-UNCOUNT You can use **silver** to refer to all the things in a house that are made of silver, especially the flatware and dishes. *platería, plata* ❑ *He polished the silver. Pulió la platería/plata.* **4** COLOR **Silver** is used to describe things that are shiny and pale gray in color. *plateado* ❑ *He had thick silver hair. Tenía el pelo/cabello grueso y plateado.*
→ see **mineral, money**

**SIM card** /sɪm kɑrd/ (**SIM cards**) N-COUNT A **SIM card** is a microchip in a cell phone that connects it to a particular phone network. **SIM** is an abbreviation for "Subscriber Identity Module." *tarjeta sim (módulo de identificación del suscriptor)*

**simi|lar** /sɪmɪlər/ **1** ADJ If one thing is **similar to** another, or if two things are **similar,** they have features that are the same. *similar, semejante, parecido* ❑ *The cake tastes similar to carrot cake. Sabe parecido al pastel de zanahoria.* ❑ *The accident was similar to one that happened in 2003. EL accidente fue similar a otro que ocurrió en 2003.* **2** ADJ In geometry, two figures, such as triangles, are **similar** if they have the same shape, although they may not be the same size. *semejante* [TECHNICAL]

S

**simi|lar|ity** /sɪmɪlærɪti/ (**similarities**) **1** N-UNCOUNT If there is a **similarity between** two or more things, they are similar to each other. *parecido* ❑ *I was amazed at the similarity between the brothers. Me asombró el parecido entre los hermanos.* **2** N-COUNT **Similarities** are features that things have which make them similar to each other. *similitud, semejanza* ❑ *There are some similarities between the two machines. Hay cierta semejanza/similitud entre las dos máquinas.* **3** N-UNCOUNT In geometry, **similarity** is the relationship between two figures such as triangles that have the same shape, although they may not be the same size. *semejanza* [TECHNICAL]

**simi|lar|ly** /sɪmɪlərli/ **1** ADV You use **similarly** to say that something is similar to something else. *de manera parecida* ❑ *Most of the men were similarly dressed. La mayoría de los hombres estaban vestidos de manera parecida.* **2** ADV You use **similarly** when mentioning a fact or situation that is similar to the one you have just mentioned. *de manera similar/semejante* ❑ *Young babies prefer faces to other shapes. Similarly, they prefer familiar faces to ones they don't know. Los recién nacidos prefieren los rostros a otras formas; de manera similar, prefieren las caras conocidas a las desconocidas.*

**sim|mer** /sɪmər/ (**simmers, simmering, simmered**) V-T/V-I When you **simmer** food or when it **simmers,** you cook it by keeping it at boiling point or just below boiling point. *hervir a fuego lento* ❑ *Simmer the fruit and sugar together. Hierva juntas la fruta y el azúcar a fuego lento.*

**sim|ple** /sɪmpᵊl/ (**simpler, simplest**) **1** ADJ If something is **simple,** it is not complicated, and is therefore easy to understand. *simple* ❑ *...simple pictures and diagrams. ...ilustraciones/dibujos y diagramas simples.* ❑ *...some simple advice on filling in forms. ...unos consejos simples sobre el llenado de formularios.* • **simp|ly** ADV *simplemente, con simplicidad* ❑ *He explained his views simply and clearly. Explicó sus puntos de vista con simplicidad y claridad.* **2** ADJ If you describe people or things as **simple,** you mean that they have all the basic or necessary things they require, but nothing extra. *simple* ❑ *He ate a simple dinner of rice and beans. Tomó una cena simple de arroz con/y frijoles.* ❑ *...the simple pleasures of childhood. ...los placeres simples de la niñez.* • **simp|ly** ADV *con sencillez* ❑ *She decorated her house simply. Adornó su casa con sencillez.* **3** ADJ You use **simple** to emphasize that the thing you are referring to is the only important or relevant reason for something. *simple* ❑ *One reason why he found his new life difficult was simple boredom. Una de las razones por las que su nueva vida le parecía difícil era el simple aburrimiento.* **4** ADJ In grammar, **simple** tenses are ones which are formed without an auxiliary verb "be," for example, "I dressed and went for a walk" and "This tastes nice." Compare **continuous.** *simple* **5** → see also **simply**

| **Thesaurus** | *simple* | Ver también: |
|---|---|---|
| ADJ. | clear, easy, understandable; (*ant.*) complicated **1** plain **2** | |

**Word Partnership** Usar *simple* con:

| | |
|---|---|
| N. | simple **concept**, simple **explanation**, simple **instructions**, simple **language**, simple **message**, simple **procedure**, simple **steps** **1** |
| | simple **life**, simple **pleasure** **2** |
| | simple **answer**, simple **matter**, simple **question**, simple **task**, simple **test** **3** |
| ADV. | simple **enough**, **so** simple **1** **3** |
| | **fairly** simple, **quite** simple, **pretty** simple, **really** simple, **relatively** simple, **very** simple **1**–**3** |

**sim|ple ma|chine** (**simple machines**) N-COUNT A **simple machine** is a device such as a lever, wheel, or screw that forms a part of other, more complex machines. Compare **compound machine.** *máquina simple, pieza simple, mecanismo elemental*

**sim|pli|fy** /sɪmplɪfaɪ/ (**simplifies, simplifying, simplified**) V-T If you **simplify** something, you make it easier to understand. simplificar ❑ *We want to simplify the education system.* *Queremos simplificar el sistema de educación.* • **sim|pli|fied** ADJ simplificado ❑ *...a short, simplified version of his speech.* *...una versión breve y simplificada de su discurso.* • **sim|pli|fi|ca|tion** /sɪmplɪfɪkeɪʃᵊn/ N-VAR (**simplifications**) simplificación ❑ *...the simplification of legal language.* *...la simplificación del lenguaje legal.*

**simp|ly** /sɪmpli/ **1** ADV You use **simply** to emphasize that something consists of only one thing, happens for only one reason, or is done in only one way. simplemente, solamente ❑ *The table is simply a circle of wood.* *La mesa es simplemente una tabla redonda.* ❑ *Most of the damage was simply caused by falling trees.* *La mayor parte del daño fue causado solamente por los árboles que cayeron.* **2** ADV You use **simply** to emphasize what you are saying. simplemente ❑ *This behavior is simply unacceptable.* *Esta conducta es simplemente inaceptable.* **3** → see also **simple**

**sim|ul|ta|neous** /saɪməlteɪniəs/ ADJ Things which are **simultaneous** happen or exist at the same time. simultáneo ❑ *...the simultaneous release of the book and the CD.* *...la publicación simultánea del libro y el disco compacto.* • **sim|ul|ta|neous|ly** ADV simultáneamente ❑ *They began to speak simultaneously.* *Empezaron a hablar simultáneamente.*

**sin** /sɪn/ (**sins, sinning, sinned**) **1** N-VAR **Sin** or a **sin** is an action or type of behavior which is believed to break the laws of God. pecado ❑ *Lying is a sin.* *Mentir es pecado.* **2** V-I If you **sin**, you do something that is believed to break the laws of God. pecar ❑ *She believes she has sinned.* *Cree haber pecado.* • **sin|ner** /sɪnər/ N-COUNT (**sinners**) pecador, pecadora ❑ *Her mother thinks she's a sinner.* *Su madre cree que es una pecadora.*

**since** /sɪns/ **1** PREP You use **since** when you are mentioning a time or event in the past and indicating that a situation has continued from then until now. desde, hasta ahora ❑ *He's lived in India since 1995.* *Ha vivido en la India desde 1995.* ❑ *They met ten years ago, and since then they have had three children.* *Se conocieron hace diez años y hasta ahora han tenido tres hijos.* • **Since** is also an adverb. desde ❑ *They worked together in the 1980s, and have kept in contact ever since.* *Trabajaron junto en los años 1980 y desde entonces se han mantenido en contacto.* • **Since** is also a conjunction. desde ❑ *I've earned my own living since I was seventeen.* *Me he ganado la vida desde que tenía diecisiete años.* **2** PREP You use **since** to mention a time or event in the past when you are describing an event or situation that has happened after that time. desde ❑ *I haven't seen him since the war.* *No he vuelto a verlo desde la guerra.* • **Since** is also a conjunction. desde ❑ *So much has changed since I was a teenager.* *Han cambiado tantas cosas desde que yo era adolescente.* **3** ADV When you are talking about an event or situation in the past, you use **since** to indicate that another event happened at some point later in time. después ❑ *Five people were arrested, but have since been released.* *Arrestaron a cinco personas, pero después las liberaron a todas.* **4** CONJ You use **since** to introduce reasons or explanations. porque ❑ *I'm always on a diet, since I put on weight easily.* *Siempre estoy a dieta, porque subo de peso fácilmente.*

> **Usage** since
>
> Use *since* to say when something started. *Manuel and Alma have been married since 2000. They have been friends since 1998 and decided to marry on Alma's birthday.*

**sin|cere** /sɪnsɪər/ ADJ If you say that someone is **sincere**, you approve of them because they really mean the things they say. sincero ❑ *He's sincere in his views.* *Sus opiniones son sinceras.* • **sin|cer|ity** /sɪnsɛrɪti/ N-UNCOUNT sinceridad ❑ *I like his sincerity.* *Me agrada su sinceridad.*

**sin|cere|ly** /sɪnsɪərli/ **1** ADV If you say or feel something **sincerely**, you really mean or feel it, and are not pretending. sinceramente ❑ *"Congratulations," he said sincerely.* *—¡Felicidades! —dijo sinceramente.* **2** CONVENTION People write **"Sincerely yours"** or **"Sincerely"** before their signature at the end of a formal letter when they have addressed it to someone by name. People sometimes write **"Yours sincerely"** instead. atentamente, sinceramente ❑ *Sincerely yours, Robbie Weinz.* *Atentamente/Sinceramente suya, Robbie Weinz.*

**sine** /saɪn/ (**sines**) N-COUNT A **sine** is a mathematical calculation that is used especially in the study of triangles. In a right triangle, the sine is the ratio between the hypotenuse and the side opposite a particular angle. The abbreviation **sin** is also used. seno [TECHNICAL]

**sing** /sɪŋ/ (**sings, singing, sang, sung**) V-T/V-I When you **sing**, you make musical sounds with your voice, usually producing words that fit a tune. cantar ❑ *I love singing.* *Me encanta/gusta cantar.* ❑ *He sings about love most of the time.* *Casi siempre canta sobre el amor.* ❑ *They were all singing the same song.* *Todos estaban cantando la misma canción.* • **sing|ing** N-UNCOUNT canto ❑ *...a carnival, with singing and dancing in the streets.* *...un carnaval, con canto y baile en las calles.* ❑ *...the singing of a traditional hymn.* *...el canto de un himno tradicional.*

▸ **sing along** PHR-VERB If you **sing along with** a piece of music, you sing it while you are listening to someone else perform it. hacer coro, cantar a coro ❑ *The children can sing along with all the tunes.* *Los niños pueden hacerle coro a todas las canciones.* ❑ *Fifteen hundred people all sang along.* *Mil quinientas personas cantaron a coro.*

> **Word Partnership** Usar *sing* con:
>
> V. **begin to** sing, **can/can't** sing, **dance and** sing, **hear** *someone* sing, **like to** sing
> N. **birds** sing, sing *someone's* **praises**, sing **a song**

**sing|er** /sɪŋər/ (**singers**) N-COUNT A **singer** is a person who sings, especially as a job. cantante ❑ *My mother was a singer in a band.* *Mi madre era cantante de una banda.* → see **concert**

**sin|gle** /sɪŋgᵊl/ (**singles, singling, singled**) **1** ADJ You use **single** to emphasize that you are referring to one thing, and no more than one thing. solo

❑ *She hasn't said a single word.* *No ha dicho una sola palabra.* ❑ *We sold over two hundred pizzas in a single day.* *Vendimos más de doscientas pizzas en un solo día.* **2** ADJ You use **single** to indicate that you are considering something on its own and separately from other things like it. *(no se traduce en este caso)* ❑ *It is the single most important decision I have ever made.* *Es la decisión más importante que haya hecho en mi vida.* **3** ADJ Someone who is **single** is not married. *soltero* ❑ *When I was single, I never worried about money.* *Cuando era soltero, nunca me procupé por el dinero.* **4** ADJ A **single** room is a room intended for one person to stay or live in. *individual* ❑ *Each guest has her own single room.* *Cada huésped/invitada tiene su propio cuarto individual.* **5** ADJ A **single** bed is wide enough for one person to sleep in. *individual* ❑ *...his bedroom with its single bed.* *...su recámara/cuarto con una cama individual.* **6** N-COUNT A **single** is a CD which has one main song or a few songs on it. *sencillo* ❑ *...the band's new single.* *...el nuevo sencillo de la banda.* **7** N-UNCOUNT **Singles** is a game of tennis or badminton in which one player plays another. The plural **singles** can be used to refer to one or more of these matches. *individuales* ❑ *Roger Federer won the men's singles.* *Roger Federer ganó los individuales masculinos.* **8** **in single file** → see **file**

→ see **hotel, tennis**

▸ **single out** PHR-VERB If you **single** someone **out** from a group, you choose them and give them special attention or treatment. *señalar, distinguir* ❑ *She always singles me out and criticizes me.* *Siempre me señala y me critica.* ❑ *His boss singled him out for special praise.* *Su jefe lo distinguió con un elogio especial.*

**single-handed** also **single-handedly** ADV If you do something **single-handed,** you do it on your own, without help from anyone else. *sin ayuda, solo* ❑ *I brought up my seven children single-handed.* *Crié a mis siete hijos sin ayuda de nadie.*

**single-minded** ADJ Someone who is **single-minded** has only one aim or purpose and is determined to achieve it. *resuelto, con un solo/único propósito* ❑ *They were single-minded in their desire to win.* *Su deseo de ganar era su único propósito.* • **single-mindedness** N-UNCOUNT *resolución* ❑ *...the single-mindedness of the athletes as they train.* *...la resolución de los atletas cuando entrenan.*

S

**sin|gle par|ent** (**single parents**) N-COUNT A **single parent** is someone who is bringing up a child on their own, because the other parent is not living with them. *padre soltero, madre soltera* ❑ *I raised my three children as a single parent.* *Crié a mis tres hijos yo solo.* ❑ *...single-parent families.* *...familias monoparentales.*

**sin|gle-re|place|ment re|ac|tion** (**single-replacement reactions**) N-COUNT A **single-replacement reaction** is a chemical reaction between an element and a compound in which the atoms of the element switch places with some of the atoms of the compound. Compare **double-replacement reaction.** *reacción de desplazamiento, reacción de reemplazo simple* [TECHNICAL]

**sin|gu|lar** /sɪŋgyələr/ **1** ADJ The **singular** form of a word is the form that is used when referring to one person or thing. *singular* ❑ *The singular form of "mice" is "mouse."* *El singular de "mice" es "mouse".* **2** N-SING **The singular** of a noun is the form of it that is used to refer to one person or thing. *singular* ❑ *What is the singular of "geese?"* *¿Cuál es el singular de "geese"?*

**sin|is|ter** /sɪnɪstər/ ADJ Something that is **sinister** seems evil or harmful. *siniestro* ❑ *There was something sinister about him.* *Había algo siniestro en él.*

**sink** /sɪŋk/ (**sinks, sinking, sank, sunk**) **1** N-COUNT A **sink** is a large fixed container in a kitchen or bathroom, with faucets to supply water. *fregadero (cocina), lavaplatos (cocina), pileta, lavabo (baño), lavamanos (baño)* ❑ *There were dirty dishes in the sink.* *Había platos sucios en el fregadero.* ❑ *The bathroom has a toilet, a shower, and a sink.* *El baño tiene excusado, regadera y lavabo.* **2** V-T/V-I If a boat **sinks** or if someone or something **sinks** it, it disappears below the surface of a mass of water. *hundir(se)* ❑ *The boat was beginning to sink.* *El barco empezaba a hundirse.* ❑ *A torpedo from a submarine sank the ship.* *Un torpedo disparado por un submarino hundió el barco.* **3** V-I If something **sinks,** it disappears below the surface of a mass of water. *hundirse* ❑ *A fresh egg will sink and an old egg will float.* *Un huevo fresco se hunde y uno pasado/podrido, flota.* **4** V-I If something **sinks,** it moves slowly downward. *ponerse* ❑ *In the west the sun was sinking.* *Por el oeste, el Sol se estaba poniendo.* **5** V-I If something **sinks to** a lower level or standard, it falls to that level or standard. *caer* ❑ *Pay increases have sunk to around three percent.* *Los aumentos al salario cayeron a aproximadamente el tres por ciento.* **6** V-I If your heart or your spirits **sink,** you become depressed or lose hope. *caerse* ❑ *My heart sank because I thought he didn't like me.* *Se me cayó el alma a los pies porque pensé que no le gustaba.* **7** V-T/V-I If something sharp **sinks** or **is sunk into** something solid, it goes deeply into it. *hincar, hundir* ❑ *I sank my teeth into an apple.* *Le clavé los dientes a una manzana.* **8** → see also **sunk**

→ see **bathroom**

▸ **sink in** PHR-VERB When a statement or fact **sinks in,** you finally understand or realize it fully. *calar, comprender* ❑ *The news took a while to sink in.* *Pasó algún tiempo antes de que la noticia calara/se comprendiera.*

**Word Partnership** Usar *sink* con:

N. **bathroom** sink, **dishes in a** sink, **kitchen** sink **1**
sink **a ship** **2**

**sip** /sɪp/ (**sips, sipping, sipped**) **1** V-T/V-I If you **sip** a drink or **sip at** it, you drink by taking just a small amount at a time. *sorber, tomar/beber a sorbos* ❑ *Jessica sipped her drink slowly.* *Jessica tomó su bebida a sorbos lentos.* ❑ *He sipped at the lemonade.* *Tomó un sorbo de su limonada.* **2** N-COUNT A **sip** is a small amount of drink that you take into your mouth. *sorbo* ❑ *Harry took a sip of tea.* *Harry tomó un sorbo de té.*

**sir** /sɜr/ (**sirs**) **1** N-VOC People sometimes say **sir** as a polite way of addressing a man whose name they do not know, or an older man. *señor* ❑ *Excuse me sir, is this your car?* *—Discúlpeme, señor, ¿es su coche?* **2** N-TITLE **Sir** is the title used in front of the name of a knight. *Sir* ❑ *She introduced me to Sir Tobias and Lady Clarke.* *Me presentó con Sir Tobias y Lady Clarke.* **3** CONVENTION You use the expression **Dear Sir**

at the beginning of a formal letter or a business letter when you are writing to a man. *Estimado Señor* ❑ *Dear Sir, Enclosed is a copy of my résumé for your consideration. Estimado Señor, le anexo una copia de mi currículum vitae, que someto a su consideración.*

**si|ren** /saɪrən/ (**sirens**) N-COUNT A **siren** is a warning device which makes a long, loud noise. Most fire engines, ambulances, and police cars have sirens. *sirena* ❑ *We heard a police siren. Oímos una sirena de la policía.*

**sis|ter** /sɪstər/ (**sisters**) **1** N-COUNT Your **sister** is a girl or woman who has the same parents as you. *hermana* ❑ *This is my sister Sarah. Ella es mi hermana Sarah.* ❑ *...Vanessa Bell, the sister of Virginia Woolf. ...Vanessa Bell, la hermana de Virginia Woolf.* **2** N-TITLE; N-COUNT; N-VOC **Sister** is a title given to a woman who belongs to a religious community, such as a nun. *hermana, sor* ❑ *Sister Francesca went into the chapel. Sor Francesca (La hermana Francesca) entró a la capilla.* **3** N-COUNT You can describe a woman as your **sister** if you feel a connection with her, for example, because she belongs to the same race, religion, country, or profession. *hermana* ❑ *...our Jewish brothers and sisters. ...nuestros hermanos judíos.*
→ see **family**

**sister-in-law** (**sisters-in-law**) N-COUNT Your **sister-in-law** is the sister of your husband or wife, or the woman who is married to your brother. *cuñada*
→ see **family**

**sit** /sɪt/ (**sits, sitting, sat**) **1** V-I If you **are sitting** somewhere, for example, in a chair, your bottom is resting on the chair and the upper part of your body is upright. *estar sentado, sentarse* ❑ *Mother was sitting in her chair in the kitchen. Mamá estaba sentada en su (una) silla de la cocina.* ❑ *They sat watching television. Se quedaron viendo la televisión.* **2** V-I When you **sit** somewhere, you lower your body until you are sitting on something. *sentarse* ❑ *He put down the box and sat on it. Puso la caja en el suelo y se sentó en ella.* ❑ *Eva got a chair and sat beside her husband. Eva tomó una silla y se sentó junto a su marido/esposo.* ● **Sit down** means the same as **sit**. *sentarse* ❑ *I sat down, shocked. Me senté, horrorizado.* **3** V-T If you **sit** someone somewhere, you tell them to sit there or put them in a sitting position. *sentar* ❑ *Dad sat me on his lap. Papá me sentó sobre sus rodillas.* ● To **sit** someone **down** somewhere means to **sit** them there. *sentar* ❑ *She sat the baby down on the floor. Sentó al bebé en el suelo.* **4** V-I If you **sit on** a committee or other official group, you are a member of it. *formar parte de* ❑ *They asked him to sit on the committee. Le pidieron que formara parte de la comisión.* **5** V-I When a legislature, court, or other official body **sits,** it officially carries out its work. *sesionar* [FORMAL] ❑ *We will discuss this next time the Parliament sits. Lo discutiremos la próxima vez que sesione el parlamento.* **6** PHRASE If you **sit tight,** you remain in the same place or situation and do not take any action, usually because you are waiting for something to happen. *no te muevas/no se mueva* ❑ *Sit tight. I'll be right back. No te muevas. Vuelvo enseguida.* **7** to **sit on the fence** → see **fence**
▶ **sit back** PHR-VERB If you **sit back** while something is happening, you relax and do not become involved in it. *ponerse cómodo* [INFORMAL] ❑ *Just sit back and enjoy the show. Póngase cómodo y disfrute del espectáculo.*
▶ **sit in on** PHR-VERB If you **sit in on** a lesson, meeting, or discussion, you are present while it is taking place but do not take part in it. *asistir, estar presente* ❑ *I sat in on a few classes. Asistí a unas cuantas clases.*
▶ **sit on** PHR-VERB If you say that someone **is sitting on** something, you mean that they are delaying dealing with it. *dar largas* [INFORMAL] ❑ *He sat on my job application for weeks. Le dio largas a mi solicitud de empleo durante semanas.*
▶ **sit out** PHR-VERB If you **sit** something **out,** you wait for it to finish, without taking any action. *esperar a que algo termine* ❑ *I decided to keep quiet and sit the argument out. Decidí guardar silencio y esperar hasta que terminara la discusión.*
▶ **sit through** PHR-VERB If you **sit through** something such as a movie, lecture, or meeting, you stay until it is finished although you are not enjoying it. *aguantar* ❑ *The movie was so bad I couldn't sit through it. La película era tan mala que no pude aguantarla toda.*
▶ **sit up** **1** PHR-VERB If you **sit up,** you move into a sitting position when you have been leaning back or lying down. *incorporarse, enderezarse* ❑ *She felt dizzy when she sat up. Se sintió mareada cuando se incorporó/enderezó.* **2** PHR-VERB If you **sit up,** you do not go to bed although it is very late. *velar, quedarse en vela* ❑ *We sat up talking. Nos quedamos en vela platicando.*

**Usage** sit and set

Be careful not to confuse the verbs *sit* and *set*. *Sit* means "to be seated," and is generally used intransitively. *Sit down and let's get started*. *Set* means "to place something down somewhere," and is generally used transitively: *Terence took off his glasses and set them on the table*

**Word Partnership** Usar **sit** con:

| | |
|---|---|
| ADV. | sit **alone**, sit **back**, sit **comfortably**, sit **quietly**, sit **still** **1** |
| PREP. | sit **in a circle**, sit **on the porch**, sit **on the sidelines** **1** |
| | sit **on a bench**, sit **in a chair**, sit **down to dinner**, sit **on the floor**, sit **on *someone's* lap**, sit **around/at a table** **1** **2** |
| V. | sit **and eat**, sit **and enjoy**, sit **and listen**, sit **and talk**, sit **and wait**, sit **and watch** (**or** sit **watching**) **1** |
| | sit **down to eat**, sit **down and relax** **1** **2** |

**site** /saɪt/ (**sites, siting, sited**) **1** N-COUNT A **site** is a piece of ground that is used for a particular purpose or where a particular thing happens. *lugar, obra en construcción* ❑ *I worked on a building site. Trabajé en una obra en construcción.* ❑ *This city was the site of a terrible earthquake. En esta ciudad hubo un terremoto terrible.* **2** N-COUNT A **site** is the same as a **website**. *sitio* ❑ *Here are some of the best sites for online shopping. Estos son algunos de los mejores sitios para comprar en línea.* **3** V-T If something **is sited** in a particular place or position, it is put there or built there. *emplazar* ❑ *These weapons have never been sited in Germany. Estas armas nunca*

S

*han sido emplazadas en Alemania.* ● **sit|ing** N-SING *emplazamiento* ❑ *...the siting of a new power plant. ...el emplazamiento de una nueva central nuclear.*

> **Word Link** *site, situ ≈ position, location : situated, situation, website*

**situ|at|ed** /sɪtʃueɪtɪd/ ADJ If something is **situated** in a particular place or position, it is in that place or position. *situado* ❑ *His hotel is situated in the Loire Valley. Su hotel está situado en el valle del Loira.*

**situa|tion** /sɪtʃueɪʃən/ (**situations**) N-COUNT You use **situation** to refer generally to what is happening in a particular place at a particular time, or to refer to what is happening to you. *situación* ❑ *His situation is very difficult, because he has no job or home. Su situación es muy difícil, porque no tiene empleo ni casa.* ❑ *Army officers said the situation was under control. Unos oficiales del ejército afirmaron que la situación estaba controlada.*

> **Word Partnership** Usar *situation* con:
>
> ADJ. **bad** situation, **complicated** situation, **current** situation, **dangerous** situation, **difficult** situation, **economic** situation, **financial** situation, **political** situation, **present** situation, **same** situation, **tense** situation, **terrible** situation, **unique** situation, **unusual** situation, **whole** situation
>
> V. **describe a** situation, **discuss a** situation, **handle a** situation, **improve a** situation, **understand a** situation

**six** /sɪks/ (**sixes**) NUM **Six** is the number 6. *seis*

**six king|doms** N-PLURAL The **six kingdoms** are the six general types of organism that make up all living things: Animalia, Plantae, Fungi, Protista, Archaebacteria and Eubacteria. *los seis reinos orgánicos* [TECHNICAL]

**six|teen** /sɪkstiːn/ (**sixteens**) NUM **Sixteen** is the number 16. *dieciséis*

**six|teenth** /sɪkstiːnθ/ (**sixteenths**) **1** ORD The **sixteenth** item in a series is the one that you count as number sixteen. *decimosexto* ❑ *...the sixteenth century AD. ...el siglo XVI (decimosexto siglo) de nuestra era.* **2** N-COUNT A **sixteenth** is one of sixteen equal parts of something. *dieciseisavo* ❑ *...a sixteenth of a second. ...un dieciseisavo de segundo.*

S

**sixth** /sɪksθ/ (**sixths**) **1** ORD The **sixth** item in a series is the one that you count as number six. *sexto* ❑ *...the sixth round of the competition. ...la sexta vuelta/tanda de la competencia.* **2** N-COUNT A **sixth** is one of six equal parts of something. *sexto* ❑ *A sixth of the workforce lost their jobs. La sexta parte de los trabajadores perdieron el empleo.*

**six|ti|eth** /sɪkstiəθ/ (**sixtieths**) ORD The **sixtieth** item in a series is the one that you count as number sixty. *sexagésimo* ❑ *...his sixtieth birthday. ...su sexagésimo cumpleaños.*

**six|ty** /sɪksti/ (**sixties**) **1** NUM **Sixty** is the number 60. *sesenta* **2** N-PLURAL **The sixties** is the decade between 1960 and 1969. *el decenio/la década de 1960, los años 1960* ❑ *He came to Britain in the sixties to work as a doctor. Llegó a Gran Bretaña en el decenio de 1960 a trabajar como médico.*

**siz|able** /saɪzəbəl/ also **sizeable** ADJ **Sizable** means fairly large. *considerable* ❑ *Harry bought a sizable piece of land. Harry compró un terreno de proporciones considerables.*

**size** /saɪz/ (**sizes, sizing, sized**) **1** N-VAR **The size of** something is how big or small it is. *tamaño* ❑ *The size of the room was about 10 feet by 15 feet. El tamaño del cuarto era de aproximadamente 3 por 4.5 metros.* ❑ *...shelves containing books of various sizes. ...estantes que contienen libros de varios tamaños.* ● **-sized** ADJ *de cierto tamaño* ❑ *...a medium-sized company. ...una compañía de mediano tamaño.* **2** N-UNCOUNT **The size of** something is the fact that it is very large. *magnitud* ❑ *He understands the size of the task. Entiende la magnitud de la tarea.* **3** N-COUNT A **size** is one of a series of graded measurements, especially for things such as clothes or shoes. *talla, número* ❑ *My sister is a size 8. Mi hermana es talla 8.* ❑ *What size are your feet? ¿De qué número/talla calza?*

▸ **size up** PHR-VERB If you **size up** a person or situation, you carefully look at the person or think about the situation, so that you can decide how to act. *medir(se)* [INFORMAL] ❑ *The two groups of men looked at each other, sizing one another up. Los dos grupos de hombres se miraron, midiéndose unos a otros.*

> **Word Partnership** Usar *size* con:
>
> ADJ. **average** size, **full** size **1**
> **sheer** size **2**
> size **large/medium/small**, **mid** size, **right** size **3**
>
> N. **bite** size, **class** size, **family** size, **life** size, **pocket** size **1**
> size **chart**, **king/queen** size **3**
>
> V. **double in** size, **increase in** size, **vary in** size **1**
> **a** size **fits** **3**

**skate** /skeɪt/ (**skates, skating, skated**) **1** N-COUNT **Skates** are ice-skates. *patines de hielo* **2** N-COUNT **Skates** are roller-skates. *patines de ruedas* **3** V-I If you **skate,** you move around wearing ice-skates or roller-skates. *patinar* ❑ *When the pond freezes you can skate on it. Cuando el estanque se congela, se puede patinar ahí.* ● **skat|ing** N-UNCOUNT *patinaje, patinar* ❑ *They all went skating together in the winter. Todos fueron a patinar juntos en invierno.* ● **skat|er** N-COUNT (**skaters**) *patinador o patinadora* ❑ *The ice-rink was full of skaters. La pista (de hielo/patinaje) estaba llena de patinadores.*

**ske|dad|dle** /skɪdædəl/ (**skedaddles, skedaddling, skedaddled**) V-I If you tell someone to **skedaddle,** you are telling them to run away or to leave a place quickly. *largarse* [INFORMAL] ❑ *Now you children skedaddle. Go outside and play. —¡Anden, niños, largo! Vayan a jugar afuera.*

**skel|etal** /skɛlɪtəl/ ADJ **Skeletal** means relating to the bones in your body. *óseo* ❑ *...the skeletal remains of a large animal. ...los restos óseos de un animal grande.*
→ see **muscle**

**skel|etal mus|cle** (**skeletal muscles**) N-VAR **Skeletal muscle** is muscle that is attached to a bone and can therefore move parts of your body. *músculo esquelético* [TECHNICAL]

**skel|eton** /skɛlɪtᵊn/ (**skeletons**) **1** N-COUNT Your **skeleton** is the framework of bones in your body. esqueleto ❑ *...a human skeleton. ...un esqueleto humano.* **2** ADJ A **skeleton** staff is the smallest number of staff necessary in order to run an organization or service. mínimo, básico ❑ *We have just a skeleton staff working here over the holiday period. Durante el período de vacaciones, sólo tenemos trabajando al personal mínimo/básico.*
→ see **shark**

**skep|ti|cal** /skɛptɪkᵊl/ ADJ If you are **skeptical about** something, you have doubts about it. escéptico ❑ *We are skeptical about whether he has made the right decision. Dudamos que haya tomado una buena decisión.*

**sketch** /skɛtʃ/ (**sketches, sketching, sketched**) **1** N-COUNT A **sketch** is a drawing that is done quickly without a lot of details. bosquejo, esbozo ❑ *He did a quick sketch of the building. Hizo un rápido bosquejo/esbozo del edificio.* **2** V-T/V-I If you **sketch** something, you make a quick, rough drawing of it. bosquejar, esbozar, hacer bosquejos ❑ *I always sketch with a pen. Siempre hago mis bosquejos/esbozos con una pluma.* ❑ *She sketched a view of the hills. Hizo un bosquejo/esbozo de una vista de las colinas.* **3** N-COUNT A **sketch of** a situation, person, or incident is a brief description of it without many details. reseña, escena ❑ *He writes amusing sketches about politicians. Escribe reseñas/escenas divertidas sobre los políticos.* **4** V-T If you **sketch** a situation or incident, you give a short description of it, including only the most important facts. reseñar, resumir ❑ *Smith sketched the story briefly. Smith reseñó/resumió la historia brevemente.* ● **Sketch out** means the same as **sketch**. esbozar ❑ *He sketched out his plans for the future. Esbozó/Resumió sus planes para el futuro.* **5** N-COUNT A **sketch** is a short humorous piece of acting, usually forming part of a comedy show. escena ❑ *They performed a very funny sketch about the president. Representaron una escena muy cómica sobre el presidente.*
→ see **animation, draw**

**ski** /ski/ (**skis, skiing, skied**) **1** N-COUNT **Skis** are long, flat, narrow pieces of wood, metal, or plastic that are fastened to boots so that you can move easily on snow or water. esquí ❑ *...a pair of skis. ...un par de esquís.* **2** V-I When people **ski,** they move over snow or water on skis. esquiar ❑ *They love to ski. Les encanta esquiar.* ● **ski|er** /skiər/ N-COUNT (**skiers**) esquiador o esquiadora ❑ *He is a good skier. Es un buen esquiador.* ● **ski|ing** N-UNCOUNT esquí ❑ *My hobbies are skiing and swimming. Mis pasatiempos son el esquí y la natación.* **3** ADJ You use **ski** to refer to things that are concerned with skiing. esquí ❑ *...a Canadian ski resort. ...un centro de esquí canadiense.* ❑ *...a ski instructor. ...un instructor de esquí.*

**skid** /skɪd/ (**skids, skidding, skidded**) V-I If a vehicle **skids,** it slides sideways or forward while moving, for example, when you are trying to stop it suddenly on a wet road. patinar, derrapar ❑ *The car skidded on the dusty road. El auto derrapó/patinó en el camino (lleno) de tierra.* ● **Skid** is also a noun. patinazo, derrape ❑ *I braked too suddenly and went into a skid. Frené repentinamente y el coche derrapó/patinó.*

**skill** /skɪl/ (**skills**) **1** N-COUNT A **skill** is a type of work or activity which requires special training and knowledge. habilidad ❑ *It's good to learn new skills, whatever your age. Es bueno adquirir habilidades nuevas, sin importar la edad.* **2** N-UNCOUNT **Skill** is the knowledge and ability that enables you to do something well. habilidad, destreza ❑ *He showed great skill on the football field. Mostró una gran habilidad en el campo de fútbol.*

| Thesaurus | *skill* | Ver también: |
|---|---|---|
| N. | ability, proficiency, talent **1** **2** | |

**skilled** /skɪld/ **1** ADJ Someone who is **skilled** has the knowledge and ability to do something well. hábil ❑ *She is skilled in explaining difficult ideas to her students. Es muy hábil para explicar las ideas difíciles a sus estudiantes.* **2** ADJ **Skilled** work can only be done by people who have had some training. especializado ❑ *There was a shortage of skilled labor in the area. Había escasez de mano de obra especializada en la zona.*

**skill|ful** /skɪlfəl/ ADJ Someone who is **skillful** at something does it very well. hábil, diestro, habilidoso ❑ *He is a skillful craftsman. Es un artesano habilidoso.* ● **skill|ful|ly** ADV hábilmente ❑ *The story is skillfully written from a child's point of view. Desde el punto de vista de un niño, la historia está hábilmente escrita.*

**skim milk** N-UNCOUNT **Skim milk** is milk from which the cream has been removed. leche descremada, leche desnatada

**skin** /skɪn/ (**skins, skinning, skinned**) **1** N-VAR Your **skin** is the natural covering of your body. piel ❑ *His skin is smooth. Su piel es suave.* **2** N-VAR An animal **skin** is skin which has been removed from a dead animal. piel ❑ *Is that real crocodile skin? ¿Realmente es piel de cocodrilo?* **3** N-VAR The **skin** of a fruit or vegetable is its outer layer or covering. piel, cáscara ❑ *...banana skins. ...cáscaras de plátano.* **4** N-SING If a **skin** forms on the surface of a liquid, a thin, fairly solid layer forms on it. nata ❑ *Stir the sauce to stop a skin from forming. Revuelva la salsa para evitar que se le forme nata.* **5** V-T If you **skin** a dead animal, you remove its skin. despellejar, desollar ❑ *The chef showed her how to skin a rabbit. El cocinero le enseñó a despellejar un conejo.*
→ see Word Web: **skin**
→ see **fruit**

| Word Partnership | Usar *skin* con: |
|---|---|
| ADJ. | **dark** skin, **dry** skin, **fair** skin, **oily** skin, **pale** skin, **sensitive** skin, **smooth** skin, **soft** skin **1** |
| N. | skin **and bones**, skin **cancer**, skin **cells**, skin **color (or color of** *someone's* skin), skin **cream**, skin **problems**, skin **type** **1** **leopard** skin **2** |

**skin|ny** /skɪni/ (**skinnier, skinniest**) ADJ A **skinny** person is extremely thin, often in a way that you find unattractive. flaco, flacucho [INFORMAL] ❑ *He was a skinny little boy. Era un niñito flacucho.*

**skip** /skɪp/ (**skips, skipping, skipped**) **1** V-I If you **skip** along, you move with a series of little jumps from one foot to the other. saltar, brincar ❑ *They saw a little girl skipping along. Vieron a una niña (que pasó) brincando/saltando.* ❑ *We skipped down*

**Word Web** skin

What is the best thing you can do for your **skin**? Stay out of the sun. When skin **cells** grow normally, the skin remains smooth and firm. However, the sun's **ultraviolet** rays sometimes cause damage. This can lead to **sunburn**, **wrinkles**, and skin cancer. The damage may not be apparent for several years. However, doctors have discovered that even a light **suntan** can be dangerous. **Sunlight** makes the melanin in skin turn dark. This is the body's attempt to protect itself from the ultraviolet radiation. **Dermatologists** recommend limiting exposure to the sun and always using a **sunscreen**.

*the street.* *Saltamos/Brincamos calle abajo.* ● **Skip** is also a noun. *salto, brinco* ❑ *He gave a little skip as he left the room.* *Dio un saltito/brinquito al salir del cuarto.* **2** V-T When someone **skips rope,** they jump up and down over a rope which they or two other people are holding at each end and turning around and around. *saltar la cuerda, saltar la reata* ❑ *They skip rope in the school yard.* *Saltan la reata en el patio de la escuela.* ● **skip|ping** N-UNCOUNT *saltar la cuerda, saltar la reata* ❑ *We did rope skipping and things like that.* *Saltábamos la reata y cosas así.* **3** V-T If you **skip** something that you usually do or something that most people do, you decide not to do it. *omitir, saltarse* ❑ *It is important not to skip meals.* *Es importante no omitir/saltarse comidas.* **4** V-T/V-I If you **skip** or **skip over** a part of something you are reading or a story you are telling, you omit it or skim over it and move on to something else. *omitir, saltarse* ❑ *You might want to skip this chapter.* *Tal vez quieras saltarte/omitir este capítulo.*

**skip|per** /skɪpər/ (**skippers**) N-COUNT; N-VOC You can use **skipper** to refer to the captain of a ship or boat. *capitán, patrón, patrona* ❑ *...the skipper of a fishing boat.* *...el capitán de un barco/bote pesquero.*

**skip rope** (**skip ropes**) N-COUNT A **skip rope** is a piece of rope, usually with handles at each end. You exercise or play with it by turning it around and around and jumping over it. *cuerda para/de saltar, reata para/de saltar*

S

**skirt** /skɜrt/ (**skirts, skirting, skirted**) **1** N-COUNT A **skirt** is a piece of clothing worn by women and girls. It fastens at the waist and hangs down around the legs. *falda* **2** V-T Something that **skirts** an area is situated around the edge of it. *bordear* ❑ *The path skirted the main lawn.* *El sendero bordeaba el prado principal.* **3** V-T/V-I If you **skirt** a problem or question, you avoid dealing with it. *eludir, dar la vuelta* ❑ *They skirted around the problem.* *Le dieron la vuelta al problema.* ❑ *He skirted the most difficult issues.* *Eludió los temas más espinosos/difíciles.*
→ see **clothing**

**skull** /skʌl/ (**skulls**) N-COUNT Your **skull** is the bony part of your head which encloses your brain. *cráneo* ❑ *They X-rayed his skull.* *Le hicieron una radiografía craneal/del cráneo.*

**sky** /skaɪ/ (**skies**) N-VAR **The sky** is the space around the Earth which you can see when you stand outside and look upward. *cielo* ❑ *The sun was shining in the sky.* *El sol brillaba en el cielo.* ❑ *Today we have clear blue skies.* *Hoy tenemos un cielo azul despejado.*
→ see **star**

**Word Partnership** Usar *sky* con:

| | |
|---|---|
| ADV. | sky **above, the** sky **overhead, up in the** sky |
| ADJ. | **black** sky, **blue** sky, **bright** sky, **clear** sky, **cloudless** sky, **dark** sky, **empty** sky, **high in the** sky |

**sky|line** /skaɪlaɪn/ (**skylines**) N-COUNT **The skyline** is the line or shape that is formed where the sky meets buildings or the land. *horizonte* ❑ *The church is clear on the skyline.* *La iglesia se recorta claramente contra el horizonte.*

**sky|scraper** /skaɪskreɪpər/ (**skyscrapers**) N-COUNT A **skyscraper** is a very tall building in a city. *rascacielos*
→ see **city**

**slam** /slæm/ (**slams, slamming, slammed**) **1** V-T/V-I If you **slam** a door or window or if it **slams,** it shuts noisily and with great force. *cerrar de golpe, azotar* ❑ *She slammed the door behind her.* *Azotó la puerta tras de sí.* ❑ *I heard the front door slam.* *Oí que la puerta del frente se cerraba de golpe.* **2** V-T If you **slam** something **down**, you put it there quickly and with great force. *azotar* ❑ *She slammed the phone down angrily.* *Muy enojada, colgó el teléfono de golpe.* **3** V-T/V-I If one thing **slams** into or against another, it crashes into it with great force. *golpear, chocar, embestir* ❑ *He slammed his fist against the wall.* *Golpeó la pared/el muro con el puño., Dio un puñetazo contra la pared/el muro.* ❑ *The car slammed into a tree.* *El automóvil chocó/embistió contra un árbol.*

**Word Partnership** Usar *slam* con:

| | |
|---|---|
| N. | slam **a door** **1** |
| V. | **hear** ***something*** slam **1** |
| ADJ. | slam ***(something)*** **shut** **1** |

**slam dunk** (**slam dunks**) also **slam-dunk** **1** N-COUNT If you say that something is a **slam dunk,** you mean that a success or victory will be easily achieved. *fácil* [INFORMAL] ❑ *The movie was a financial slam dunk.* *La película fue un fácil éxito de taquilla.* **2** N-COUNT In basketball, a **slam dunk** is a shot in which a player jumps up and forces the ball through the basket. *clavada* ❑ *He is famous for his slam dunks.* *Es famoso por sus clavadas.*

**slang** /slæŋ/ N-UNCOUNT **Slang** consists of words, expressions, and meanings that are very informal and are used by people who know each other very well or who have the same interests. *jerga, argot* ❑ *Soldiers have their own slang. Los soldados tienen su propia jerga/su propio argot.*

**slant** /slænt/ (**slants, slanting, slanted**) **1** V-I Something that **slants** is sloping, rather than horizontal or vertical. *inclinar(se), sesgar(se)* ❑ *The morning sun slanted through the glass roof. Los rayos del sol caían sesgados a través del techo de cristal.* **2** N-SING If something is **on a slant,** it is in a slanting position. *inclinación, sesgo, declive* ❑ *Her hair was cut on a slant. Tenía el cabello cortado en sesgo.* **3** V-T If information or a system **is slanted,** it is made to show favor toward a particular group or opinion. *presentar con parcialidad* ❑ *The program was slanted to make the home team look good. El programa estaba presentado con parcialidad para hacer ver bien al equipo local.* **4** N-SING A particular **slant** on a subject is a particular way of thinking about it, especially one that is unfair. *inclinación* ❑ *The political slant of the newspaper is liberal. La tendencia política del periódico es liberal.*

**slap** /slæp/ (**slaps, slapping, slapped**) **1** V-T If you **slap** someone, you hit them with the palm of your hand. *abofetear, cachetear* ❑ *I slapped him hard across the face. Lo abofeteé con fuerza.* ● **Slap** is also a noun. *bofetada, cachetada* ❑ *She gave him a slap. Le dio una bofetada.* **2** V-T If you **slap** something **onto** a surface, you put it there quickly, roughly, or carelessly. *arrojar con violencia, arrojar violentamente* ❑ *He slapped some money on the table. Aventó el dinero sobre la mesa.*

**Word Partnership** Usar *slap* con:

N. a slap **on the back,** a slap **in the face,** a slap **on the wrist** **1**

**slash** /slæʃ/ (**slashes, slashing, slashed**) **1** V-T If you **slash** something, you make a long, deep cut in it. *acuchillar, tajar, mechar* ❑ *Four cars had their tires slashed. A cuatro coches les rajaron las llantas con cuchillo.* ● **Slash** is also a noun. *cuchillada, tajo, corte* ❑ *Make deep slashes in the fish and push in the herbs. Meche el pescado con las hierbas.* **2** V-I If you **slash at** a person or thing, you quickly hit at them with something such as a knife. *acuchillar* ❑ *He slashed wildly at them. Les lanzó cuchilladas como loco.* **3** V-T To **slash** something such as costs or jobs means to reduce them by a large amount. *rebajar drásticamente* ❑ *Car makers are slashing prices. Los fabricantes de automóviles están rebajando drásticamente los precios.*

**slate** /sleɪt/ (**slates**) **1** N-UNCOUNT **Slate** is a dark gray rock that can be easily split into thin layers. Slate is often used for covering roofs. *pizarra* ❑ *They lived in a cottage with a traditional slate roof. Vivían en una cabaña con un tradicional techo de pizarra.* **2** N-COUNT A **slate** is one of the small flat pieces of slate that are used for covering roofs. *pizarra, teja de pizarra* ❑ *Thieves also stole the slates from the roof. Los ladrones también robaron las pizarras del techo.*

**slaugh|ter** /slɔtər/ (**slaughters, slaughtering, slaughtered**) **1** V-T If large numbers of people or animals **are slaughtered,** they are killed in a way that is cruel or unnecessary. *masacrar* ❑ *Innocent people have been slaughtered. Masacraron a gente inocente.* ● **Slaughter** is also a noun. *carnicería, matanza* ❑ *In this war the slaughter of civilians was common. En esa guerra, la matanza de civiles fue común.* **2** V-T To **slaughter** animals such as cows and sheep means to kill them for their meat. *matar, sacrificar* ❑ *The farmers slaughter their own cows. Los granjeros sacrificaron a sus propias vacas.* ● **Slaughter** is also a noun. *carnicería, matanza* ❑ *The sheep were taken away for slaughter. Llevaron las ovejas al matadero.*

**slave** /sleɪv/ (**slaves**) **1** N-COUNT A **slave** is someone who is the property of another person and has to work for that person. *esclavo o esclava* ❑ *They had to work as slaves. Tenían que trabajar como esclavos.* **2** N-COUNT You can describe someone as a **slave** when they are completely under the control of another person or of a powerful influence. *esclavo, esclava* ❑ *She is a slave to her job. Es esclava de su trabajo.*

**slave la|bor** **1** N-UNCOUNT **Slave labor** refers to slaves or to work done by slaves. *trabajo de esclavos* ❑ *...a campaign to end slave labor. ...una campaña para poner fin al trabajo de esclavos.* **2** N-UNCOUNT If people work very hard for long hours for very little money, you can refer to it as **slave labor.** *trabajo de esclavos* ❑ *Working in the kitchen here is slave labor. Trabajar en la cocina aquí es un trabajo de esclavos.*

**slav|ery** /sleɪvəri, sleɪvri/ N-UNCOUNT **Slavery** is the system by which people are owned by other people as slaves. *esclavitud* ❑ *My people survived 400 years of slavery. Mi pueblo sobrevivió a 400 años de esclavitud.*

**slaw** /slɔ/ N-UNCOUNT **Slaw** is a salad of chopped raw carrot and cabbage in mayonnaise. *ensalada de col/repollo, zanahoria, cebolla y mayonesa.*

**slay|ing** /sleɪɪŋ/ (**slayings**) N-COUNT A **slaying** is a murder. *asesinato* ❑ *...the slaying of nine people. ...el asesinato de nueve personas.*

**slea|zy** /slizi/ (**sleazier, sleaziest**) **1** ADJ If you describe a place as **sleazy,** you dislike it because it looks dirty and badly cared for, and not respectable. *sórdido* [INFORMAL] ❑ *...sleazy bars. ...cantinas sórdidas.* **2** ADJ If you describe something or someone as **sleazy,** you disapprove of them because you think they are not respectable or honest. *vil, ruin, mezquino* [INFORMAL] ❑ *...a sleazy salesman. ...un vendedor vil.*

**sled** /slɛd/ (**sleds, sledding, sledded**) **1** N-COUNT A **sled** is an object used for traveling over snow. It consists of a framework which slides on two strips of wood or metal. *trineo* ❑ *We pulled the children across the snow on a sled. Paseamos a los niños en trineo por la nieve.* **2** V-I If you **sled** or go **sledding,** you ride on a sled. *ir en trineo, deslizarse en trineo* ❑ *We went sledding on the small hill near our house. Fuimos a deslizarnos en trineo desde la loma cercana a la casa.*

**sleep** /slip/ (**sleeps, sleeping, slept**) **1** N-UNCOUNT **Sleep** is the natural state of rest in which your eyes are closed, your body is inactive, and your mind does not think. *sueño* ❑ *They were exhausted from lack of sleep. Estaban agotadas por la falta de sueño.* ❑ *Be quiet and go to sleep. —¡Cállate y vete a dormir!* **2** V-I When you **sleep,** you rest with your eyes closed and your mind and body inactive. *dormir* ❑ *I couldn't sleep last night. No pude dormir anoche.* **3** N-COUNT A **sleep** is a period of sleeping.

**Word Web** sleep

Do you ever go to **bed** and then discover you can't **fall asleep**? You **yawn**. You feel **tired**. But your body isn't ready for **rest**. You **toss** and **turn** and pound the **pillow** for hours. After a while you may **doze**, but then a few minutes later you're **wide awake**. The scientific name for this condition is **insomnia**. There are many causes for **sleeplessness**. If you **nap** too late in the day it may change your normal sleep cycle. Worrying can also affect sleep patterns.

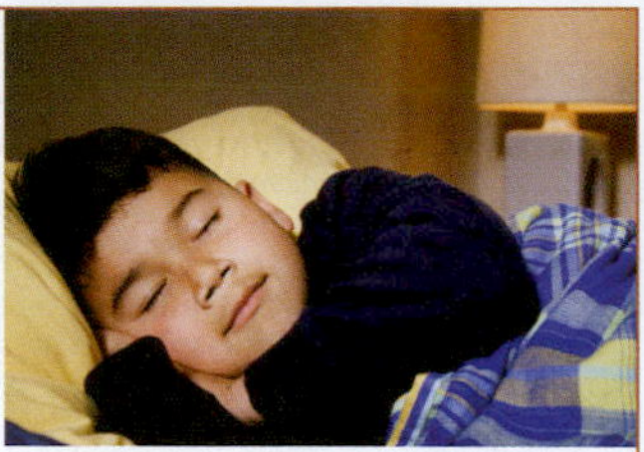

dormida, siesta ❑ *I think he needs a sleep.* Creo que necesita dormir. **4** V-T If a building or room **sleeps** a particular number of people, it has beds for that number of people. alojar, tener espacio para ❑ *The house sleeps 10.* En la casa se pueden alojar 10 personas. **5** PHRASE If you say that you didn't **lose** any **sleep over** something, you mean that you did not worry about it at all. perder el sueño ❑ *I didn't lose much sleep over his criticism.* Sus críticas no me quitaron el sueño. **6** PHRASE If a sick or injured animal **is put to sleep**, it is killed by a vet in a way that does not cause it pain. sacrificar ❑ *We had to have the dog put to sleep.* Tuvimos que sacrificar al perro.
→ see Word Web: **sleep**

▸ **sleep off** PHR-VERB If you **sleep off** the effects of too much traveling, drink, or food, you recover from it by sleeping. dormir para reponerse ❑ *She needs to sleep off her jet lag.* Necesita dormir para reponerse del desfase horario.

**Thesaurus** *sleep* Ver también:

N. nap, rest, slumber **1**
V. doze, rest; (*ant.*) awaken, wake **2**

**Word Partnership** Usar *sleep* con:

N. sleep **deprivation**, sleep **disorder**, **hours of** sleep, **lack of** sleep **1**
sleep **on the floor**, sleep **nights** **2**
V. **drift off to** sleep, **get enough** sleep, **get some** sleep, **go to** sleep, **need** sleep **1**
**can't/couldn't** sleep **2**
ADJ. **deep** sleep **1**
**good** sleep **3**

**sleep|ing bag** (**sleeping bags**) N-COUNT A **sleeping bag** is a large deep bag with a warm lining, used for sleeping in, especially when you are camping. bolsa de dormir, saco de dormir

**sleep|less** /slipləs/ **1** ADJ A **sleepless** night is one during which you do not sleep. en blanco (noche) ❑ *I have sleepless nights worrying about her.* Me paso las noches en blanco, preocupado por ella. **2** ADJ Someone who is **sleepless** is unable to sleep. desvelado, sin poder dormir ❑ *She lay there for hours, sleepless.* Estuvo acostada durante horas, sin poder dormir. • **sleep|less|ness** N-UNCOUNT insomnio ❑ *He suffers from sleeplessness.* Padece de insomnio.
→ see **sleep**

**sleepy** /slipi/ (**sleepier, sleepiest**) **1** ADJ If you are **sleepy**, you are very tired and are almost asleep. adormilado, somnoliento, soñoliento ❑ *I was feeling sleepy.* Me sentía somnoliento. • **sleepi|ly** ADV con/de sueño ❑ *Joanna sat up, blinking sleepily.* Joanna se incorporó, parpadeando soñolienta. **2** ADJ A **sleepy** place is quiet and does not have much activity or excitement. somnoliento/soñoliento ❑ *...a sleepy little town out in the countryside.* ...un pueblito somnoliento/soñoliento en el campo.

**sleet** /slit/ N-UNCOUNT **Sleet** is rain that is partly frozen. aguanieve ❑ *Today we expect rain, sleet, and snow.* Hoy esperamos lluvia, aguanieve y nieve.
→ see **precipitation, water**

**sleeve** /sliv/ (**sleeves**) **1** N-COUNT The **sleeves** of a coat, shirt, or other item of clothing are the parts that cover your arms. manga ❑ *She wore a dress with long sleeves.* Llevaba un vestido de manga larga. **2** PHRASE If you have something **up** your **sleeve**, you have an idea or plan which you have not told anyone about. You can also say that someone has **an ace, card,** or **trick up** their **sleeve**. tener bajo la manga ❑ *He wondered what tricks she had up her sleeve.* Se preguntaba qué trucos tendría ella bajo la manga.

**slice** /slaɪs/ (**slices, slicing, sliced**) **1** N-COUNT A **slice of** bread, meat, fruit, or other food is a thin piece that has been cut from a larger piece. rebanada ❑ *Would you like a slice of bread?* ¿Gusta una rebanada de pan? **2** V-T If you **slice** bread, meat, fruit, or other food, you cut it into thin pieces. rebanar ❑ *Helen sliced the cake.* Helen rebanó el pastel. **3** N-COUNT You can use **slice** to refer to a part of a situation or activity. parte ❑ *Housework takes up a large slice of my time.* El quehacer consume una gran parte de mi tiempo.
→ see **bread, cut**

**Word Partnership** Usar *slice* con:

ADJ. **small** slice, **thin** slice **1**
N. slice **of bread**, slice **of pie**, slice **of pizza** **1**
slice **a cake** **2**
slice **of life** **3**
PREP. slice **into**, slice **off**, slice **through** **2**

**slick** /slɪk/ (**slicker, slickest**) **1** ADJ A **slick** performance, production, or advertisement is skillful and impressive. ingenioso, logrado, pulido ❑ *They could afford slick TV ads for their product.* Podían pagarse anuncios de televisión ingeniosos sobre su producto. **2** ADJ A **slick** action is done quickly and smoothly, and without any obvious effort. hábil ❑ *...the slick way he passed the ball.* ...la manera tan hábil como pasó el balón. **3** ADJ If you describe a person as **slick**, you dislike them because they speak easily in a way that is likely to convince

S

people, but is not sincere. embaucador ❑ *Don't be fooled by slick politicians.* *No se deje engañar por los políticos embaucadores.* **4** N-COUNT A **slick** is the same as an **oil slick**. derrame de petróleo, marea negra ❑ *Experts are trying to clean up the huge slick.* *Los expertos están tratando de limpiar la enorme marea negra.*

**slick|er** /slɪkər/ (**slickers**) N-COUNT A **slicker** is a long, loose, waterproof coat. impermeable

**slide** /slaɪd/ (**slides, sliding, slid**) **1** V-T/V-I When something **slides** somewhere or when you **slide** it there, it moves there smoothly over or against something. deslizar ❑ *She slid the door open.* *Deslizó la puerta para abrirla.* ❑ *I slid the cellphone into my pocket.* *Deslicé el celular en mi bolsillo.* **2** V-I If you **slide** somewhere, you move there smoothly and quietly. deslizarse ❑ *He slid into the car.* *Se subió sigilosamente al auto.* **3** V-I To **slide into** a particular mood, attitude, or situation means to gradually start to have that mood, attitude, or situation often without intending to. caer ❑ *She slid into a depression.* *Cayó en la depresión.* **4** N-COUNT A **slide** is a small piece of photographic film which you project onto a screen so that you can see the picture. diapositiva, transparencia ❑ *...a slide show.* *...una proyección de transparencias.* **5** N-COUNT A **slide** is a piece of playground equipment that has a steep slope for children to go down for fun. tobogán, resbaladilla ❑ *Two young children were playing on a slide.* *Dos niños estaban jugando en las resbaladillas.* **6** N-COUNT A glass **slide** is a piece of glass on which you put something that you want to examine through a microscope. platina, portaobjetos

→ see **laboratory equipment**

**Word Partnership** Usar *slide* con:

V. **begin to** slide, **continue to** slide **1** – **3**

**slight** /slaɪt/ (**slighter, slightest, slights, slighting, slighted**) **1** ADJ Something that is **slight** is very small in degree or quantity. ligero, mínimo ❑ *...a slight change in temperature.* *...un ligero cambio de temperatura.* ❑ *He's not the slightest bit worried.* *...no está preocupado en lo más mínimo.* **2** ADJ A **slight** person has a fairly thin and delicate looking body. ligero, liviano ❑ *She is smaller and slighter than me.* *Es más pequeña y ligera que yo.* ● **slight|ly** ADV ligeramente ❑ *...a slightly built man.* *...un hombre de complexión delgada.* **3** V-T If you **are slighted,** someone does or says something that insults you by treating you as if your views or feelings are not important. sentirse ofendido, sentirse desairado, desairar ❑ *His grandson was slighted by the football coach.* *Su nieto se sintió ofendido por el entrenador de fútbol.* ● **Slight** is also a noun. desprecio, ofensa ❑ *It's not a slight on you that I enjoy being alone sometimes.* *El que yo disfrute estar solo en ocasiones no significa que te desprecie.* **4** PHRASE You use **in the slightest** to emphasize a negative statement. en lo más mínimo, en absoluto ❑ *That doesn't interest me in the slightest.* *Eso no me interesa en lo más mínimo.*

**slight|ly** /slaɪtli/ ADV **Slightly** means to some degree but not to a very large degree. ligeramente ❑ *His family moved to a slightly larger house.* *Su familia se mudó a una casa ligeramente más grande.* ❑ *Each person learns in a slightly different way.* *Cada persona aprende de una manera ligeramente diferente.*

**slim** /slɪm/ (**slimmer, slimmest, slims, slimming, slimmed**) **1** ADJ A **slim** person has an attractively thin and well-shaped body. delgado, esbelto ❑ *The young woman was tall and slim.* *La joven era alta y esbelta.* **2** ADJ A **slim** book, wallet, or other object is thinner than usual. delgado ❑ *...a slim book of poetry.* *...un delgado libro de poesía.* **3** ADJ A **slim** chance or possibility is a very small one. escaso ❑ *There's a slim chance that he may become president.* *Las posibilidades de que llegue a ser presidente son escasas.*

▸ **slim down** **1** PHR-VERB If you **slim down,** you lose weight and become thinner. adelgazar ❑ *People lose more weight when they slim down with a friend.* *Las personas adelgazan más cuando hacen ejercicio con un amigo.* **2** PHR-VERB If a company or other organization **slims down** or **is slimmed down,** it employs fewer people, in order to save money or become more efficient. reducir el personal [BUSINESS] ❑ *Many firms had to slim down.* *Muchas firmas tuvieron que hacer reducciones de personal.*

**Word Partnership** Usar *slim* con:

| | |
|---|---|
| ADJ. | **tall and** slim **1** |
| ADV. | **pretty** slim, **very** slim **1** – **3** |
| N. | slim **chance**, slim **lead**, slim **margin** **3** |

**sling|shot** /slɪŋʃɒt/ (**slingshots**) N-COUNT A **slingshot** is a device for shooting small stones. It is made of a Y-shaped stick with a piece of elastic tied between the two top posts. honda, resortera

**slip** /slɪp/ (**slips, slipping, slipped**) **1** V-I If you **slip,** you accidentally slide and lose your balance. resbalar ❑ *He slipped on the wet grass.* *Resbaló en el pasto húmedo.* **2** V-I If something **slips,** it slides out of place or out of your hand. resbalar ❑ *His glasses slipped down his nose.* *Los anteojos resbalaron por su nariz.* **3** V-I If you **slip** somewhere, you go there quickly and quietly. deslizarse ❑ *Amy slipped out of the house without being seen.* *Amy se deslizó fuera de la casa sin que la vieran.* **4** V-T If you **slip** something somewhere, you put it there quickly in a way that does not attract attention. deslizar, pasar ❑ *I slipped a note under Louise's door.* *Deslicé una nota bajo la puerta de Louise.* **5** V-T If you **slip** something **to** someone, or if you **slip** someone something, you give it to them secretly. deslizar, pasar ❑ *Robert slipped her a note in class.* *Robert le pasó una nota en clase sin que lo vieran.* **6** V-I To **slip into** a particular state or situation means to pass gradually into it, in a way that is hardly noticed. caer ❑ *You soon slip into a routine.* *Pronto se cae en la rutina.* **7** V-I If you **slip into** or **out of** clothes or shoes, you put them on or take them off quickly and easily. quitarse ❑ *She slipped out of her shoes and lay down.* *Se quitó los zapatos y se recostó.* **8** N-COUNT A **slip** is a small or unimportant mistake. desliz ❑ *We can't make any slips.* *No podemos cometer ningún desliz.* **9** N-COUNT A **slip of** paper is a small piece of paper. trozo ❑ *He wrote our names on slips of paper.* *Escribió nuestros nombres en trozos de papel.*

▸ **slip up** PHR-VERB If you **slip up,** you make a small or unimportant mistake. cometer un desliz ❑ *We slipped up a few times.* *Cometimos varios deslices.*

**Thesaurus** *slip* Ver también:

V. fall, slide, trip 1
N. blunder, failure, flub, mistake 8
leaf, page, paper, sheet 9

**Word Partnership** Usar *slip* con:

ADJ. slip **resistant** 1
N. slip **of paper, sales** slip 9

**slip|cover** /slɪpkʌvər/ (**slipcovers**) also **slip cover** N-COUNT A **slipcover** is a piece of cloth that fits over a chair or sofa and can easily be removed. *funda* ❑ *...the slipcovers on the dining room chairs. ...las fundas de las sillas del comedor.*

**slip|per** /slɪpər/ (**slippers**) N-COUNT **Slippers** are loose, soft shoes that you wear at home. *pantufla, chancla* ❑ *...a pair of old slippers. ...un par de pantuflas viejas.*

**slip|pery** /slɪpəri/ 1 ADJ Something that is **slippery** is smooth, wet, or oily and is therefore difficult to walk on or to hold. *resbaladizo, resbaloso* ❑ *The kitchen floor was wet and slippery. El piso de la cocina estaba mojado y resbaladizo.* 2 PHRASE If someone is on a **slippery slope,** they are involved in a course of action that is difficult to stop and that will eventually lead to failure or trouble. *pendiente resbaladiza* ❑ *We started on the slippery slope of borrowing money. Empezamos a deslizarnos por la pendiente del endeudamiento.*

**slit** /slɪt/ (**slits, slitting**)

The form **slit** is used in the present tense and is the past tense and past participle.

1 V-T If you **slit** something, you make a long narrow cut in it. *cortar* ❑ *Slit the pea pod and take out the peas. Abra la vaina y saque los chícharos.* ❑ *He slit open the envelope. Abrió el sobre con un abrecartas.* 2 N-COUNT A **slit** is a long narrow cut or opening in something. *corte, rasgadura, abertura* ❑ *Make a slit about half an inch long. Haga un corte de aproximadamente un centímetro de largo.* ❑ *She watched them through a slit in the curtains. Los observó por entre las cortinas.*
→ see **shark**

S

**slo|gan** /sloʊgən/ (**slogans**) N-COUNT A **slogan** is a short phrase that is easy to remember. Slogans are used in advertisements and by political parties. *lema, consigna* ❑ *They campaigned on the slogan "We'll take less of your money." Hicieron campaña con el lema "Nos llevaremos menos de su dinero".*

**slope** /sloʊp/ (**slopes, sloping, sloped**) 1 N-COUNT A **slope** is the side of a mountain, hill, or valley. *ladera* ❑ *The village is high on a mountain slope. La aldea está en lo alto de la ladera de una montaña.* 2 N-COUNT A **slope** is a surface that is at an angle, so that one end is higher than the other. *inclinación* ❑ *The table was on a slope. La mesa estaba inclinada.* 3 V-I If a surface **slopes,** it is at an angle, so that one end is higher than the other. *descender* ❑ *The land sloped down sharply to the river. La ladera descendía bruscamente hacia el río.* • **slop|ing** ADJ *inclinado, en declive* ❑ *...a building with a sloping roof. ...un edificio con un techo en declive.* 4 V-I If something **slopes,** it leans to the right or to the left rather than being upright. *inclinarse* ❑ *The writing sloped backwards. La letra se inclinaba hacia atrás.* 5 N-COUNT The **slope** of something is the angle at which it slopes. *pendiente* ❑ *The slope of the ground was very steep. La pendiente del terreno era muy pronunciada.* 6 **slippery slope** → see **slippery**

**slop|py** /slɒpi/ (**sloppier, sloppiest**) ADJ Something that is **sloppy** has been done in a careless and lazy way. *descuidado* ❑ *He hates sloppy work. Detesta el trabajo descuidado.* • **slop|pi|ness** N-UNCOUNT *descuido, dejadez* ❑ *Her sloppiness has caused a lot of problems. Su dejadez ha causado un montón de problemas.*

**slop|py joe** /slɒpi dʒoʊ/ (**sloppy joes**) N-COUNT A **sloppy joe** is a sandwich consisting of a bun filled with sauce and cooked meat. *sándwich de carne guisada en salsa* [INFORMAL]

**slot** /slɒt/ (**slots, slotting, slotted**) 1 N-COUNT A **slot** is a narrow opening in a machine or container, for example, a hole that you put coins in to make a machine work. *ranura* ❑ *He dropped a coin into the slot and dialed the number. Metió una moneda en la ranura y marcó el número.* 2 V-T/V-I If you **slot** something into something else, or if it **slots** into it, you put it into a space where it fits. *meter* ❑ *He slotted a CD into the CD player. Metió un disco compacto en el tocadiscos.* ❑ *The seat belt slotted into place easily. El broche del cinturón de seguridad del asiento cerró con facilidad.* 3 N-COUNT A **slot** in a schedule or program is a place in it where an activity can take place. *intervalo, lapso* ❑ *...a regular time slot when parents can meet with teachers. ...un horario fijo en el que los padres pueden reunirse con los maestros.*

**slow** /sloʊ/ (**slower, slowest, slows, slowing, slowed**) 1 ADJ Something that is **slow** moves, happens, or is done without much speed. *lento* ❑ *His bike was heavy and slow. Su bici/moto era pesada y lenta.* ❑ *He had a slow way of talking. Su hablar era lento.* ❑ *Cleaning up the city has been a slow process. La limpieza de la ciudad ha sido un proceso lento.* • **slow|ly** ADV *lentamente* ❑ *He spoke slowly and clearly. Habló lenta y claramente.* • **slow|ness** N-UNCOUNT *lentitud* ❑ *The slowness of our progress was very frustrating. La lentitud de nuestro avance era muy frustrante.* 2 ADJ If someone is **slow** to do something, they do it after a delay. *lento* ❑ *The government was slow to respond to the crisis. El gobierno fue lento para responder a la crisis.* 3 V-T/V-I If something **slows** or if you **slow** it, it starts to move or happen more slowly. *aminorar la velocidad* ❑ *She slowed the car and turned the corner. Aminoró la velocidad del automóvil y dobló la esquina.* 4 ADJ Someone who is **slow** is not very clever and takes a long time to understand things. *lento* ❑ *She thought he was a bit slow. Ella creía que era un poco lento.* 5 ADJ If you describe a situation, place, or activity as **slow,** you mean that it is not very exciting. *lento* ❑ *Some parts of the movie are a little slow. Algunos pasajes de la película son un poco lentos.* 6 ADJ If a clock or watch is **slow,** it shows a time that is earlier than the correct time. *atrasado* ❑ *The clock is about two minutes slow. El reloj está atrasado unos dos minutos.* 7 **slowly but surely** → see **surely**
▸ **slow down** 1 PHR-VERB If something **slows down** or if something **slows** it **down,** it starts to move or happen more slowly. *aminorar la velocidad, retardar, aminorar* ❑ *The bus slowed down for the next stop. El autobús aminoró la velocidad al acercarse a la*

*siguiente parada.* ❑ *There is no cure for the disease, although drugs can slow it down.* *La enfermedad no tiene cura, aunque los medicamentos pueden retardarla/aminorarla.* **2** PHR-VERB If someone **slows down** or if something **slows** them **down,** they become less active. *tomarse las cosas con calma* ❑ *He needs to slow down or he will get sick.* *Necesita tomarse las cosas con calma, si no, va a enfermarse.*
▸ **slow up** PHR-VERB **Slow up** means the same as **slow down** 1. *disminuir* ❑ *Sales are slowing up.* *Las ventas están disminuyendo.*

**Word Partnership** Usar *slow* con:

ADJ. slow **acting**, slow **moving** **1**
N. slow **death**, slow **growth**, slow **movements**, slow **pace**, slow **process**, slow **progress**, slow **recovery**, slow **response**, slow **speed**, slow **start**, slow **stop**, slow **traffic** **1**

**slow mo|tion** also **slow-motion** N-UNCOUNT When film or television pictures are shown **in slow motion,** they are shown much more slowly than normal. *cámara lenta* ❑ *They played it again in slow motion.* *Volvieron a proyectarla en cámara lenta.*

**slow|poke** /sloʊpoʊk/ (**slowpokes**) N-COUNT If you call someone a **slowpoke,** you are criticizing the fact that they do something slowly. *torpe* [INFORMAL] ❑ *Come on, slowpoke.* *—¡Apúrate, torpe!*

**slug|ger** /slʌgər/ (**sluggers**) N-COUNT In baseball, a **slugger** is a player who hits the ball very hard. *bateador o bateadora que golpea fuerte la pelota*

**slum** /slʌm/ (**slums**) N-COUNT A **slum** is an area of a city where living conditions are very bad. *barriada, barrio bajo* ❑ *...a slum area of St. Louis.* *...un barrio bajo de San Luis.*

**slum|ber par|ty** (**slumber parties**) N-COUNT A **slumber party** is an occasion when a group of young friends spend the night together at the home of one of the group. *piyamada* ❑ *I'm having a slumber party for my birthday.* *Voy a festejar mi cumpleaños con una piyamada.*

**slump** /slʌmp/ (**slumps, slumping, slumped**) **1** V-I If something such as the value of something **slumps,** it falls suddenly and by a large amount. *desplomarse* ❑ *Profits slumped by 41%.* *Las utilidades se desplomaron el 41 por ciento.* • **Slump** is also a noun. *desplome* ❑ *There has been a slump in house prices.* *Los precios de la vivienda sufrieron un desplome.* **2** N-COUNT A **slump** is a time when many people in a country are unemployed and poor. *depresión* ❑ *...the slump of the early 1980s.* *...la depresión de principios de la década de 1980.* **3** V-I If you **slump** somewhere, you fall or sit down there heavily. *desplomarse* ❑ *She slumped into a chair.* *Se desplomó en una silla.*

**smack** /smæk/ (**smacks, smacking, smacked**) **1** V-T If you **smack** someone, you hit them with your hand. *dar un manotazo* ❑ *She smacked me on the side of the head.* *Me dio un manotazo en la cabeza.* • **Smack** is also a noun. *manotazo* ❑ *She gave him a smack.* *Le dio un manotazo.* **2** V-T If you **smack** something somewhere, you put it or throw it there so that it makes a loud, sharp noise. *dar palmadas, palmearse* ❑ *He smacked his hands down on his knees.* *Se palmeó las rodillas.* **3** V-I If one thing **smacks of** another thing that you consider bad, it reminds you of it or is like it. *oler a* ❑ *She said their comments smacked of racism.* *Dijo que sus comentarios olían a racismo.*

**smack dab** ADV **Smack dab** is used in expressions such as "smack dab in the middle" of somewhere to mean exactly in that place. *exactamente, directamente* [INFORMAL] ❑ *...an old brick building smack dab in the middle of downtown.* *...un antiguo edificio de ladrillo exactamente en el centro.*

**small** /smɔl/ (**smaller, smallest**) **1** ADJ A **small** person, thing, or amount of something is not large in physical size. *pequeño, chico* ❑ *She is small for her age.* *Es pequeña para su edad.* ❑ *Use a small amount of glue.* *Ponga poco pegamento.* **2** ADJ A **small** group or quantity consists of only a few people or things. *pequeño* ❑ *A small group of students sat in the cafeteria.* *En la cafetería estaba sentado un pequeño grupo de estudiantes.* **3** ADJ A **small** child is a young child. *chico* ❑ *I have two small children.* *Tengo dos hijos chicos.* **4** ADJ You use **small** to describe something that is not significant or great in degree. *pequeño* ❑ *It's easy to make quite small changes to the way that you work.* *Es fácil hacer cambios muy pequeños en la manera de trabajar.* ❑ *These details are small and unimportant.* *Esos detalles son pequeños e insignificantes.* **5** ADJ **Small** businesses or companies employ a small number of people and do business with a small number of clients. *pequeña empresa* ❑ *...shops, restaurants and other small businesses.* *...tiendas, restaurantes y otras pequeñas empresas.* **6** ADJ If someone makes you look or feel **small,** they make you look or feel stupid or ashamed. *insignificante* ❑ *I felt very small when I realized what I'd said.* *Me sentí insignificante cuando me di cuenta de lo que había dicho.* **7** N-SING **The small of** your **back** is the bottom part of your back that curves in slightly. *región baja* ❑ *Place your hands on the small of your back and breathe in.* *Colóquese las manos en la región lumbar y aspire.* **8** **small wonder** → see **wonder**

**Thesaurus** *small* Ver también:

ADJ. little, petite, slight; (*ant.*) big, large **1**
minute **2**
young **3**
insignificant, minor; (*ant.*) important, major, significant **4**

**small claims court** (**small claims courts**) also **small-claims court** N-VAR **Small claims court** is a local law court which settles disputes between people that involve relatively small amounts of money. *tribunal de causas de poca monta* ❑ *They have the option of taking their case to small claims court.* *Tienen la opción de llevar su caso ante un tribunal de causas de poca monta.*

**small po|ta|toes** N-UNCOUNT If you say that something is **small potatoes,** you mean that it is unimportant in comparison with something else. *bagatelas, fruslería* [INFORMAL] ❑ *Our everyday worries are usually small potatoes.* *Por lo general, nuestras preocupaciones cotidianas no tienen importancia.*

**small-scale** ADJ A **small-scale** activity or organization is small in size and limited in extent. *pequeña escala* ❑ *...the small-scale production of cheese.* *...la producción de queso a pequeña escala.*

**small town** ADJ **Small town** is used when

S

referring to small places, usually in the United States, where people are friendly, honest, and polite, or to the people there. **Small town** is also sometimes used to suggest that someone has old-fashioned ideas. pueblerino ❑ *...a small-town America of neat, middle-class homes. ...un Estados Unidos pueblerino de cuidadas casas de clase media.*

**smart** /smart/ (**smarter, smartest, smarts, smarting, smarted**) **1** ADJ You can describe someone who is clever or intelligent as **smart.** *listo* ❑ *He's very smart and he knows exactly what he's doing. Es muy listo y sabe exactamente lo que está haciendo.* **2** V-I If a part of your body or a wound **smarts,** you feel a sharp stinging pain in it. *escocer, picar, arder* ❑ *My eyes smarted from the smoke. Los ojos me ardían por el humo.* **3** V-I If you **are smarting from** something such as criticism or failure, you feel upset about it. *estar resentido* ❑ *The Americans were still smarting from their defeat in the World Cup. Los estadounidenses todavía estaban resentidos por su derrota en la Copa Mundial.*

**smart aleck** (**smart alecks**) also **smart alec** N-COUNT If you describe someone as a **smart aleck,** you dislike the fact that they think they are very clever and always have an answer for everything. *sabiondo* [INFORMAL] ❑ *...a smart-aleck TV reporter. ...un periodista de televisión que cree saberlo todo.*

**smart growth** N-UNCOUNT People such as architects and environmentalists use **smart growth** to refer to the construction of new buildings and roads within a town or city so that they are close to people's workplaces and mass transit systems and so that open spaces are not built on. *urbanismo funcional, urbanismo orgánico*

**smart phone** (**smart phones**) N-COUNT A **smart phone** is a type of cellphone that can perform many of the operations that a computer does, such as accessing the Internet. *smartphone, teléfono celular versátil, celular inteligente*

**smarts** /smarts/ **1** N-PLURAL You can use **smarts** to mean the skill and intelligence that people need in order to be successful in difficult situations. *madera* [INFORMAL] ❑ *I didn't think he had the smarts to do something like that. No creí que fuera tan astuto como para hacer algo así.* **2** → see also **street smarts**

S

**smash** /smæʃ/ (**smashes, smashing, smashed**) **1** V-T/V-I If you **smash** something or if it **smashes,** it breaks into many pieces, for example, when it is hit or dropped. *romper, hacer(se) añicos* ❑ *The boys started smashing windows. Los muchachos empezaron a romper ventanas.* ❑ *Someone dropped a bottle and it smashed. Alguien dejó caer una botella que se hizo añicos.* **2** V-I If you **smash** through a wall, gate, or door, you get through it by hitting and breaking it. *abrirse paso a golpes* ❑ *They used a car to smash through the gates. Se valieron de un automóvil para abrir las puertas de un golpe.* **3** V-T/V-I If something **smashes** or **is smashed** against something solid, it moves very fast and with great force against it. *golpear* ❑ *He smashed his fist down on the table. Dio un fuerte puñetazo sobre la mesa.* **4** V-T To **smash** a political group or system means to deliberately destroy it. *hacer pedazos* [INFORMAL] ❑ *They want to smash our system of government. Quieren acabar con nuestro sistema de gobierno*

▸ **smash up** PHR-VERB If you **smash** something **up,** you completely destroy it by hitting it and breaking it into many pieces. *destrozar* ❑ *Someone smashed up the bus stop during the night. Alguien destrozó la parada de autobuses durante la noche.*

**smear** /smɪər/ (**smears, smearing, smeared**) **1** V-T If you **smear** a surface **with** an oily or sticky substance or **smear** the substance onto the surface, you spread a layer of the substance over the surface. *embadurnar* ❑ *My sister smeared herself with suntan oil. Mi hermana se embadurnó con bronceador.* ● **smeared** ADJ *embadurnado* ❑ *The child's face was smeared with dirt. La cara del niño estaba embadurnada de lodo.* **2** N-COUNT A **smear** is a dirty or oily mark. *mancha* ❑ *There was a smear of gravy on his chin. Tenía una mancha de salsa en el mentón/la barbilla.* **3** V-T To **smear** someone means to spread unpleasant and untrue rumors or accusations about them in order to damage their reputation. *difamar* ❑ *They planned to smear him by spreading rumors about his private life. Planeaban difamarlo difundiendo rumores sobre su vida íntima.* **4** N-COUNT A **smear** is an unpleasant and untrue rumor or accusation that is intended to damage someone's reputation. *calumnia* ❑ *...a smear campaign by another candidate. ...una campaña de calumnias de otro candidato.*

**smell** /smɛl/ (**smells, smelling, smelled**) **1** N-COUNT The **smell** of something is a quality it has which you become aware of when you breathe in through your nose. *olor* ❑ *...the smell of freshly baked bread. ...el olor a pan recién horneado.* ❑ *...horrible smells. ...olores nauseabundos.* **2** N-UNCOUNT Your sense of **smell** is the ability that your nose has to detect things. *olfato* ❑ *She has lost her sense of smell. Perdió el olfato.* **3** V-LINK If something **smells** a particular way, it has a quality which you become aware of through your nose. *oler* ❑ *The room smelled of lemons. La pieza olía a limón.* ❑ *It smells delicious. Huele delicioso.* **4** V-I If you say that something **smells,** you mean that it smells unpleasant. *apestar, oler* ❑ *The fish was old and starting to smell. El pescado no era fresco y ya empezaba a oler mal.* **5** V-T If you **smell** something, you become aware of it when you breathe in through your nose. *oler* ❑ *As soon as we opened the door we could smell the gas. En cuanto abrimos la puerta, olimos el gas.* **6** V-T If you **smell** something, you put your nose near it and breathe in, so that you can discover its smell. *oler* ❑ *I picked a flower, and smelled it. Corté una flor y la olí.*
→ see Word Web: **smell**
→ see **taste**

| **Thesaurus** | *smell* | Ver también: |
|---|---|---|
| N. | aroma, fragrance, odor, scent **1** | |
| V. | reek, stink **4** | |
| | breathe, inhale, sniff **5** | |

**smile** /smaɪl/ (**smiles, smiling, smiled**) **1** V-I When you **smile,** the corners of your mouth curve up, usually because you are pleased or amused. *sonreír* ❑ *When he saw me, he smiled. Cuando me vio, sonrió.* ❑ *The children were all smiling at her. Todos los niños le estaban sonriendo.* **2** N-COUNT A **smile** is the expression that you have on your face when you smile. *sonrisa* ❑ *She gave a little smile. Sonrió*

## Word Web smell

Scientists say that the average person can recognize about 10,000 different **odors**. Until recently we did not understand the **sense** of **smell**. Now we now know that most substances send odor molecules into the air. They enter the body through the **nose**. When they reach the **nasal cavity**, they attach to **sensory** cells. The olfactory **nerve** carries the information to the brain. The brain identifies the smell. The eyes, mouth, and throat also contain receptors that add to the olfactory experience. Interestingly, our sense of smell is better later in the day than in the morning.

*ligeramente.* ❑ *"Come in," she said with a smile. —Entra —le dijo con una sonrisa.*

**Word Partnership** Usar **smile** con:

V. smile **and laugh, make** ***someone*** smile, smile **and nod, see** ***someone*** smile, **try to** smile 1
smile **fades, flash a** smile, **give** ***someone*** **a** smile 2

ADJ. **big/little/small** smile, **broad** smile, **friendly** smile, **half** smile, **sad** smile, **shy** smile, **warm** smile, **wide** smile, **wry** smile 2

**smog** /smɒg/ (**smogs**) N-VAR **Smog** is a mixture of fog and smoke which occurs in some busy industrial cities. *esmog* ❑ *The smog in London killed 4,000 people. En Londres, el esmog mató a 4,000 personas.*
→ see **ozone, pollution**

**smoke** /smoʊk/ (**smokes, smoking, smoked**) 1 N-UNCOUNT **Smoke** consists of gas and small bits of solid material that are sent into the air when something burns. *humo* ❑ *A cloud of black smoke blew over the city. Una negra nube de humo se extendió sobre la ciudad.* 2 V-I If something **is smoking,** smoke is coming from it. *humear* ❑ *The chimney was smoking. La chimenea estaba humeando.* 3 V-T/V-I When someone **smokes** a cigarette, cigar, or pipe, they suck the smoke from it into their mouth and blow it out again. If you **smoke,** you regularly smoke cigarettes, cigars, or a pipe. *fumar* ❑ *He was smoking a big cigar. Estaba fumando un gran puro.* ❑ *You must quit smoking. Debes dejar de fumar.* ● **smok|er** N-COUNT (**smokers**) *fumador o fumadora* ❑ *...a 64-year-old smoker. ...un fumador de 64 años de edad.* ● **smok|ing** N-UNCOUNT *fumar* ❑ *Smoking is banned in many places of work. En muchos lugares de trabajo está prohibido fumar.* 4 V-T If fish or meat **is smoked,** it is hung over burning wood so that the smoke preserves it and gives it a special flavor. *ahumar* ❑ *The fish are smoked over a wood fire. El pescado se ahúma con leña.*
→ see **fire**

**smoke de|tec|tor** (**smoke detectors**) N-COUNT A **smoke detector** is a device fixed to the ceiling which makes a loud noise if there is smoke in the air, to warn people. *detector de humo*

**smol|der** /smoʊldər/ (**smolders, smoldering, smoldered**) 1 V-I If something **smolders,** it burns slowly, producing smoke but not flames. *arder (sin llamas)* ❑ *The fire was still smoldering the next morning. El fuego seguía ardiendo al día siguiente.* 2 V-I If a feeling such as anger or hatred **smolders** inside you, you continue to feel it but do not show it. *arder* ❑ *Anger smoldered in her heart for many years. La ira siguió ardiendo en su corazón durante muchos años.*
→ see **fire**

**smooth** /smuð/ (**smoother, smoothest, smooths, smoothing, smoothed**) 1 ADJ A **smooth** surface has no roughness, lumps, or holes. *terso, liso, suave* ❑ *The baby's skin was soft and smooth. La piel del bebé era suave y tersa.* ❑ *...a smooth surface such as glass. ...una superficie lisa, como el vidrio.* ● **smooth|ness** N-UNCOUNT *suavidad, tersura* ❑ *...the smoothness of her hands. ...la tersura de sus manos.* 2 ADJ A **smooth** liquid or mixture has been mixed well so that it has no lumps. *homogéneo, sin grumos* ❑ *Stir the mixture until it is smooth. Revuelva la mezcla hasta hacerla homogénea.* 3 ADJ If you describe a drink as **smooth,** you mean that it is not bitter and is pleasant to drink. *suave* ❑ *This coffee is really smooth. Este café es realmente suave.* 4 ADJ A **smooth** line or movement has no sudden breaks or changes in direction or speed. *suave* ❑ *Do the exercise in one smooth motion. Haga el ejercicio con un movimiento suave.* ● **smooth|ly** ADV *suavemente* ❑ *Move your body smoothly, without jerking. Mueva su cuerpo suavemente, sin sacudidas.* 5 ADJ You use **smooth** to describe something that is going well and is free of problems or trouble. *sin problemas* ❑ *We hope for a smooth move to our new home. Esperamos que la mudanza a nuestra nueva casa se haga sin problemas.* ● **smooth|ly** ADV *sin contratiempos* ❑ *So far, our discussions have gone smoothly. Hasta ahora, nuestras discusiones han avanzado sin contratiempos.* 6 ADJ If you describe a man as **smooth,** you mean that he is extremely smart, confident, and polite, often in a way that you find rather unpleasant. *desenvuelto y seguro de sí mismo* ❑ *A smooth young salesman came to talk to us. Un joven vendedor, desenvuelto y seguro de sí mismo, se dirigió a nosotros.* 7 V-T If you **smooth** something, you move your hands over its surface to make it smooth and flat. *alisar* ❑ *She stood up and smoothed down her skirt. Se puso de pie y se alisó la falda.*
▸ **smooth out** PHR-VERB If you **smooth out** a problem or difficulty, you solve it, especially by talking to the people concerned. *allanar* ❑ *He tried to smooth out the problem with his friends. Trató de allanar el problema con sus amigos.*
▸ **smooth over** PHR-VERB If you **smooth over** a problem or difficulty, you make it less serious and easier to deal with, especially by talking to the people concerned. *suavizar* ❑ *The president is trying*

S

*to smooth things over.* *El presidente está tratando de suavizar las cosas.*
→ see **muscle**

**smooth mus|cle** (**smooth muscles**) N-VAR **Smooth muscle** is muscle that is mainly found inside the organs of your body and that cannot be controlled voluntarily. *músculo liso, músculo involuntario* [TECHNICAL]

**smoth|er** /smʌðər/ (**smothers, smothering, smothered**) **1** V-T If you **smother** a fire, you cover it with something in order to put it out. *sofocar* ❑ *She tried to smother the flames with a blanket.* *Trató de sofocar las llamas con una manta.* **2** V-T To **smother** someone means to kill them by covering their face with something so that they cannot breathe. *asfixiar* ❑ *She tried to smother him with a pillow.* *Trató de asfixiarlo con una almohada.* **3** V-T To **smother** something **with** or **in** something means to cover it completely. *bañar* ❑ *He smothered his food with ketchup.* *Bañó su comida de catsup.* **4** V-T If you **smother** someone, you show your love for them too much and protect them too much. *asfixiar, ahogar* ❑ *You can love your children without smothering them.* *Se puede querer a los hijos sin asfixiarlos.*

**smug|gle** /smʌgᵊl/ (**smuggles, smuggling, smuggled**) V-T If someone **smuggles** things or people into a place or out of it, they take them there illegally or secretly. *contrabandear, meter de contrabando* ❑ *They smuggled goods into the country.* *Metieron al país mercancías de contrabando.* ● **smug|gler** N-COUNT (**smugglers**) *contrabandista* ❑ *...diamond smugglers.* *...contrabandistas de diamantes.* ● **smug|gling** N-UNCOUNT *contrabando* ❑ *A pilot was arrested and charged with smuggling.* *Arrestaron a un piloto y lo acusaron de contrabando.*

**snack** /snæk/ (**snacks**) **1** N-COUNT A **snack** is a simple meal that is quick to cook and to eat. *tentempié, refrigerio* ❑ *The kids have a snack when they come in from school.* *Los niños toman un tentempié cuando regresan de la escuela.* **2** N-COUNT A **snack** is something such as a chocolate bar that you eat between meals. *tentempié* ❑ *Do you eat sugary snacks?* *¿Comes dulces entre comidas?*
→ see **peanut**

**sna|fu** /snæfu/ (**snafus**) N-COUNT If you describe a situation as a **snafu,** you mean that it is disorderly or disorganized and that it is usually like this. *metedura de pata* [INFORMAL] ❑ *The project was cut short because of a technical snafu.* *Se interrumpió el proyecto debido a una metedura de pata técnica.*

S

**snag** /snæg/ (**snags, snagging, snagged**) **1** N-COUNT A **snag** is a small problem or disadvantage. *inconveniente* ❑ *We hit a snag when we disagreed about money.* *Cuando discrepamos sobre el dinero, fue un inconveniente.* **2** V-T/V-I If you **snag** part of your clothing **on** a sharp or rough object or if it **snags,** it gets caught on the object and tears. *engancharse* ❑ *She snagged her heel on a root and fell.* *Se cayó porque se le atoró el tacón en una raíz.* ❑ *Thorns snagged his suit.* *Las espinas se engancharon en su traje.*

**snail** /sneɪl/ (**snails**) N-COUNT A **snail** is a small animal with a long, soft body, no legs, and a spiral-shaped shell. Snails move very slowly. *caracol*

**snake** /sneɪk/ (**snakes, snaking, snaked**) **1** N-COUNT A **snake** is a long, thin reptile without legs. *culebra, serpiente* **2** V-I Something that **snakes** in a particular direction goes in that direction in a line with a lot of bends. *serpentear* [LITERARY] ❑ *The road snaked up the mountainside.* *El camino subía serpenteando por la ladera de la montaña.*
→ see **desert**

**snap** /snæp/ (**snaps, snapping, snapped**) **1** V-T/V-I If something **snaps** or if you **snap** it, it breaks suddenly, usually with a sharp cracking noise. *romper(se), quebrar(se)* ❑ *A twig snapped.* *Se quebró una ramita.* ● **Snap** is also a noun. *chasquido* ❑ *I heard a snap and a crash as a tree fell down.* *Oí un chasquido y luego un estrépito al caer un árbol.* **2** V-T/V-I If you **snap** something into a particular position, or if it **snaps** into that position, it moves quickly into that position, with a sharp sound. *cerrar con un chasquido, cerrar con un golpe seco* ❑ *He snapped the notebook shut.* *Cerró el cuaderno de golpe.* ❑ *She snapped the cap on her pen.* *Le puso la tapa a la pluma con un chasquido.* ● **Snap** is also a noun. *chasquido* ❑ *He shut the book with a snap.* *Cerró el libro de un golpe seco.* **3** V-T/V-I If someone **snaps at** you, they speak to you in a sharp, unfriendly way. *hablar con brusquedad* ❑ *Sorry, I didn't mean to snap at you.* *Discúlpame, no era mi intención hablarte bruscamente.* ❑ *"Of course I don't know," Roger snapped.* *—¡Claro que no sé!—, dijo Roger con brusquedad.* **4** V-I If an animal such as a dog **snaps at** you, it opens and shuts its jaws quickly near you, as if it were going to bite you. *tratar de morder* ❑ *The dog snapped at my ankle.* *El perro trató de morderme el tobillo.* **5** ADJ A **snap** decision or action is one that is taken suddenly, often without careful thought. *repentino* ❑ *I think this is too important for a snap decision.* *Creo que es demasiado importante como para tomar una decisión apresurada.* **6** N-COUNT A **snap** is a photograph. *instantánea, foto* [INFORMAL] ❑ *They showed us some snaps of their vacation.* *Nos enseñaron unas fotos de sus vacaciones.*

▶ **snap up** PHR-VERB If you **snap** something **up,** you buy it quickly because it is cheap or is just what you want. *no dejar escapar* ❑ *People rushed to the sales to snap up bargains.* *La gente se lanzó a las tiendas para aprovechar las ofertas.*

**snap|shot** /snæpʃɒt/ (**snapshots**) N-COUNT A **snapshot** is a photograph that is taken quickly and casually. *instantánea, foto* ❑ *Let me take a snapshot of you guys.* *Déjenme tomarles una foto, muchachos.*

**snare drum** (**snare drums**) N-COUNT A **snare drum** is a small drum used in orchestras and bands. Snare drums are usually played with wooden sticks, and make a continuous sound. *tambor*
→ see **percussion**

**snatch** /snætʃ/ (**snatches, snatching, snatched**) **1** V-T/V-I If you **snatch** something or **snatch at** something, you take it or pull it away quickly. *arrebatar* ❑ *Mick snatched the cards from Archie's hand.* *Mick le arrebató las cartas de la mano a Archie.* ❑ *He snatched up the telephone.* *Arrebató el teléfono.* **2** V-T If you **snatch** an opportunity, you take it quickly. If you **snatch** something to eat or **snatch** a rest, you have it quickly in between doing other things. *tomarse* ❑ *He snatched a few hours to sleep and to read.* *Se robó unas horas para dormir y leer.* **3** N-COUNT A **snatch of** a conversation or a song is a very small piece of it. *fragmento* ❑ *I heard snatches of the*

**Word Web** snow

Some people love winter. They like to watch **snowflakes** falling softly from the sky. The **snow** forms beautiful **drifts** on the ground and trees. A house with **icicles** hanging from the roof and **frost** on the windows looks warm and cosy. But winter has a dangerous side as well. **Ice** and snow on streets and roads causes many accidents. And a **blizzard** can leave behind large amounts of snow in a single day. In the mountains, large amounts of snow can cause **avalanches**. They usually happen when light, new snow falls on top of older, heavy snow.

*conversation. Oía fragmentos de la conversación.*

**sneak** /snik/ (**sneaks, sneaking, sneaked** or **snuck**)

The form **snuck** is informal.

**1** V-I If you **sneak** somewhere, you go there very quietly on foot, trying to avoid being seen or heard. *escabullirse, escurrirse* ❑ *He sneaked out of his house late at night. Se escabulló de su casa ya tarde por la noche.* **2** V-T If you **sneak** something somewhere, you take it there secretly. *hacer algo a hurtadillas* ❑ *He smuggled papers out, photocopied them, and snuck them back. Sacó algunos papeles a escondidas, los fotocopió y los devolvió a hurtadillas.* **3** V-T If you **sneak** a look at someone or something, you secretly have a quick look at them. *hacer algo con disimulo* ❑ *She sneaked a look at her watch. Echó una mirada a su reloj con disimulo.*

**sneak|er** /snikər/ (**sneakers**) N-COUNT **Sneakers** are casual shoes with rubber soles that people wear especially for sports. *tenis, zapatillas de deporte* ❑ *...a new pair of sneakers. ...un par de tenis nuevos.*
→ see **clothing, shoe**

**sneeze** /sniz/ (**sneezes, sneezing, sneezed**) V-I When you **sneeze,** you suddenly take in your breath and then blow it down your nose noisily without being able to stop yourself, for example, because you have a cold. *estornudar* ❑ *What exactly happens when we sneeze? ¿Qué pasa exactamente cuando estornudamos?* ● **Sneeze** is also a noun. *estornudo* ❑ *The disease is passed from person to person by a sneeze. La enfermedad pasa de una persona a otra con los estornudos.*

**sniff** /snɪf/ (**sniffs, sniffing, sniffed**) **1** V-I When you **sniff,** you breathe in air through your nose hard enough to make a sound, for example, when you are trying not to cry, or in order to show disapproval. *resollar, olfatear* ❑ *She dried her eyes and sniffed loudly. Se secó las lágrimas y resolló con fuerza.* ❑ *He sniffed. There was a smell of burning. Olfateó y le llegó el olor de algo que se quemaba.* ● **Sniff** is also a noun. *resuello* ❑ *I could hear quiet sobs and sniffs. Podía oír unos sollozos y resuellos apagados.* **2** V-T/V-I If you **sniff** something or **sniff at** it, you smell it by sniffing. *oler, olfatear* ❑ *Suddenly, he stopped and sniffed the air. Repentinamente, se detuvo y olfateó el aire.*

**snippy** /snɪpi/ ADJ A **snippy** person is often bad-tempered and speaks rudely to people. *atrevido* [INFORMAL] ❑ *Don't be snippy with me! —¡No seas atrevido conmigo!*

**snob** /snɒb/ (**snobs**) N-COUNT If you call someone a **snob,** you disapprove of them because they behave as if they are superior to other people because of their intelligence, taste, or social status. *presumido, esnob* ❑ *Her parents did not like him because they were snobs. No les caía bien a sus padres porque eran unos presumidos.*

**snore** /snɔr/ (**snores, snoring, snored**) V-I When someone who is asleep **snores,** they make a loud noise each time they breathe. *roncar* ❑ *His mouth was open, and he was snoring. Tenía la boca abierta y estaba roncando.* ● **Snore** is also a noun. *ronquido* ❑ *Uncle Arthur, after a loud snore, woke suddenly. Después de un sonoro ronquido, el tío Arthur se despertó repentinamente.*

**snow** /snoʊ/ (**snows, snowing, snowed**) **1** N-UNCOUNT **Snow** consists of a lot of soft white pieces of frozen water that fall from the sky in cold weather. *nieve* ❑ *Six inches of snow fell. Cayeron 15 centímetros de nieve.* **2** V-I When **it snows,** snow falls from the sky. *nevar* ❑ *It snowed all night. Nevó toda la noche.* **3** V-T If someone **snows** you, they persuade you to do something or convince you of something by flattering or deceiving you. *embaucar* [INFORMAL] ❑ *I let him snow me with his big ideas. Me dejé embaucar con lo que estaba tramando.*
→ see Word Web: **snow**
→ see **precipitation, storm, water**

**snow|ball** /snoʊbɔl/ (**snowballs, snowballing, snowballed**) **1** N-COUNT A **snowball** is a ball of snow. *bola de nieve* **2** V-I If something such as a project or campaign **snowballs,** it rapidly increases and grows. *crecer rápidamente, aumentar rápidamente* ❑ *From those early days the business has snowballed. Desde aquellos primeros días, el negocio ha crecido rápidamente.*

**snow|board** /snoʊbɔrd/ (**snowboards**) N-COUNT A **snowboard** is a narrow board that you stand on in order to slide quickly down snowy hills as a sport or for fun. *snowboard, tabla para deslizarse en la nieve*

**snow|board|ing** /snoʊbɔrdɪŋ/ N-UNCOUNT **Snowboarding** is the sport or activity of traveling down snowy slopes using a snowboard. *hacer snowboard, deslizarse en la nieve en una tabla* ❑ *He loves skiing and snowboarding. Le encanta esquiar y hacer snowboard.* ● **snow|board|er** N-COUNT *snowboarder, deslizador o deslizadora* ❑ *Snowboarders whizzed past us. Los snowboarders pasaron zumbando junto a nosotros.*

**snow|flake** /snoʊfleɪk/ (**snowflakes**) N-COUNT A **snowflake** is one of the soft, white pieces of frozen water that fall as snow. *copo de nieve*
→ see **precipitation, snow**

S

**snow pea** (**snow peas**) N-COUNT **Snow peas** are a type of pea whose pods are eaten as well as the peas inside them. *chícharo (chino), arveja*

**snow|plow** /snoʊplaʊ/ (**snowplows**) N-COUNT A **snowplow** is a vehicle which is used to push snow off roads or railroad tracks. *quitanieve, limpianieve*

**snowy** /snoʊi/ (**snowier, snowiest**) ADJ A **snowy** place is covered in snow. A **snowy** day is a day when a lot of snow has fallen. *nevado* ❑ *...snowy mountains. ...las nevadas montañas.*

**snub** /snʌb/ (**snubs, snubbing, snubbed**) **1** V-T If you **snub** someone, you deliberately insult them by ignoring them or by behaving or speaking rudely toward them. *desairar* ❑ *He snubbed her in public and made her feel an idiot. La desairó en público y la hizo sentirse una idiota.* **2** N-COUNT If you snub someone, your behavior or your remarks can be referred to as a **snub.** *desaire* ❑ *They didn't invite her and she took this as a snub. No la invitaron y lo tomó como un desaire.*

**snug** /snʌg/ (**snugger, snuggest**) **1** ADJ If you feel **snug** or are in a **snug** place, you are very warm and comfortable, especially because you are protected from cold weather. *cómodo* ❑ *They were snug and warm under the blankets. Estaban cómodos y calientes bajo las cobijas.* **2** ADJ Something such as a piece of clothing that is **snug** fits very closely or tightly. *ceñido* ❑ *He wore a snug black T-shirt and tight jeans. Llevaba una camiseta ceñida y unos pantalones de mezclilla ajustados.* ● **snug|ly** ADV *cómodamente* ❑ *The shoes fitted snugly. Los zapatos le ajustaban perfectamente.*

**so** /soʊ/

> Usually pronounced /soʊ/ for meanings **1**, **4**, **5**, **6**, **12**, and **14**.

**1** ADV You use **so** to refer back to something that has just been mentioned. *así, eso, lo* ❑ *"Do you think they will stay together?"— "I hope so." —¿Crees que seguirán juntos?—Eso espero.* ❑ *If you don't like it, then say so. —Si no te gusta, entonces dilo.* **2** ADV You use **so** when you are saying that something which has just been said about one person or thing is also true of another one. *también* ❑ *I enjoy Ann's company and so does Martin. Disfruto la compañía de Ann, igual que Martin.* ❑ *They had a wonderful time and so did I. Se la pasaron de maravilla; y yo también.* **3** CONJ You use the structures **as...so** and **just as...so** when you want to indicate that two events or situations are similar in some way. *también* ❑ *As computers become more sophisticated, so too do their users. A medida que las computadoras se vuelven más complejas, también lo hacen quienes las usan.* ❑ *Just as John has changed, so has his wife. Así como John ha cambiado, también su esposa lo ha hecho.* **4** CONJ You use **so** and **so that** to introduce the result of the situation you have just mentioned. *por eso* ❑ *I am shy and so I find it hard to talk about my feelings. Soy tímido, por eso me es difícil hablar de mis sentimientos.* ❑ *People are living longer, so that even people who are 65 or 70 feel young. La gente vive más tiempo, por eso incluso los que tienen 65 o 70 años de edad se sienten jóvenes.* **5** CONJ You use **so, so that,** and **so as** to introduce the reason for doing the thing that you have just mentioned. *para que* ❑ *Come to dinner so we can talk about what happened. Ven a cenar para que podamos hablar de lo que pasó.* ❑ *They moved to the corner of the room so that nobody would hear them. Se dirigieron a un rincón del cuarto para que nadie los oyera.* **6** ADV You can use **so** in conversations to introduce a new topic, or to introduce a question or comment about something that has been said. *entonces, así que* ❑ *So how was your day? —Entonces, ¿cómo te fue hoy?* ❑ *So you're a teacher, huh? —Así que es maestra, ¿eh?* ❑ *So as for your question, Miles, the answer is no. —Así que, en cuanto a su pregunta, Miles, la respuesta es no.* **7** CONVENTION You say **"So?"** and **"So what?"** to indicate that you think something that someone has said is unimportant. *¿Y?, ¿Y qué?* [INFORMAL] ❑ *"I don't like it."— "So?" —No me gusta. —¿Y?* **8** ADV You can use **so** in front of adjectives and adverbs to emphasize the quality that they are describing. *tan* ❑ *He was surprised they got married—they seemed so different. Estaba sorprendido de que se hubiesen casado; parecían tan diferentes.* **9** ADV You can use **so...that** and **so...as** to emphasize the degree of something by mentioning the result or consequence of it. *tan/tanto...que, tan...como para* ❑ *The tears were falling so fast that she could not see. El llanto era tanto que no podía ver.* ❑ *He's not so stupid as to listen to rumors. No es tan tonto como para hacer caso de los rumores.* **10** → see also **insofar as** **11** PHRASE You use **and so on** or **and so forth** at the end of a list to indicate that there are other items that you could also mention. *etcétera* ❑ *...important issues such as health, education, and so on. ...cuestiones importantes, como la salud, la educación, etcétera, etcétera.* **12** PHRASE You use the structures **not...so much** and **not so much...as** to say that something is one kind of thing rather than another kind. *tanto...como* ❑ *I don't object to Will's behavior so much as his personality. No tengo tantas objeciones a la conducta de Will como a su personalidad.* **13** PHRASE You use **or so** when you are giving an approximate amount. *más o menos* ❑ *A ticket will cost you $20 or so. Un boleto le costará 20 dólares más o menos.* **14** PHRASE You use **so much** and **so many** when you are saying that there is a definite limit to something but you are not saying what this limit is. *hasta cierto punto, cierta cantidad* ❑ *You can only do something so many times before you get bored. Sólo se puede hacer algo hasta cierto punto antes de aburrirse.* ❑ *There is only so much fuel in the tank. El tanque sólo tiene espacio para cierta cantidad de combustible.* **15** **so far** → see **far** **16** **every so often** → see **often**

**soak** /soʊk/ (**soaks, soaking, soaked**) **1** V-T/V-I If you **soak** something or leave it **to soak,** you put it into a liquid and leave it there. *remojar, dejar en remojo* ❑ *Soak the beans for 2 hours. Deje remojar los frijoles dos horas.* **2** V-T If a liquid **soaks** something or if you **soak** something **with** a liquid, the liquid makes the thing very wet. *empapar* ❑ *The water soaked his jacket. El agua empapó su saco.* ● **soaked** /soʊkt/ ADJ *empapado* ❑ *The tent got completely soaked in the storm. La tienda quedó completamente empapada con la tormenta.* ● **soak|ing** ADJ *empapado* ❑ *My raincoat was soaking wet. Mi impermeable estaba empapado.* **3** V-I If a liquid **soaks through** something, it passes through it. *filtrarse* ❑ *Blood soaked through the bandages. La sangre se había filtrado a través de las vendas.* **4** V-I If someone **soaks,** they spend a long time in a hot bath, because they enjoy it. *bañarse con agua caliente* ❑ *I need to soak in*

S

**Word Web** soap

**Soap** is important in everyday life. We **wash** our hands before we eat. We lather up with a **bar** of soap in the **shower** or **tub**. We use liquid **detergent** to **clean** our dishes. We use **laundry** detergent to get our clothes clean. But why do we use soap? How does it work? It works almost like a magnet. But soap doesn't attract metal. It attracts dirt and grease. It makes a **bubble** around the dirt, and water washes it all away.

*a hot tub. Necesito un buen baño de agua caliente en la tina.* • **Soak** is also a noun. *baño con agua caliente* ❑ *I had a long soak in the bath. Me quedé un buen rato en la tina.*

▸ **soak up** PHR-VERB If a soft or dry material **soaks up** a liquid, the liquid goes into the substance. *absorber* ❑ *The cotton will soak up the water. El algodón absorberá el agua.*

**soap** /soʊp/ (**soaps**) **1** N-VAR **Soap** is a substance that you use with water for washing yourself or for washing clothes. *jabón* ❑ *...a bar of soap. ...una pastilla de jabón.* ❑ *...a large box of soap powder. ...una caja grande de jabón en polvo.* **2** N-COUNT A **soap** is the same as a **soap opera.** *telenovela, culebrón, comedia* [INFORMAL]
→ see Word Web: **soap**

**soap op|era** (**soap operas**) N-COUNT A **soap opera** is a popular television drama series about the daily lives and problems of a group of people who live in a particular place. *telenovela, culebrón, comedia*

**soar** /sɔr/ (**soars, soaring, soared**) **1** V-I If the amount, value, level, or volume of something **soars,** it quickly increases by a great deal. *dispararse* ❑ *Prices have soared. Los precios se dispararon.* **2** V-I If something such as a bird **soars** into the air, it goes quickly up into the air. *elevarse, remontar el vuelo, planear* [LITERARY] ❑ *A golden eagle soared overhead. Un águila real se cernía en lo alto.*

**sob** /sɒb/ (**sobs, sobbing, sobbed**) **1** V-I When someone **sobs,** they cry in a noisy way, breathing in short breaths. *sollozar* ❑ *She began to sob. Empezó a sollozar.* • **sob|bing** N-UNCOUNT *sollozo* ❑ *The room was silent except for her sobbing. La habitación estaba en silencio, salvo por sus sollozos.* **2** N-COUNT A **sob** is one of the noises that you make when you are crying. *sollozo* ❑ *His sobs grew louder. Empezó a sollozar más fuertemente.*

**so|ber** /soʊbər/ (**sobers, sobering, sobered**) **1** ADJ When you are **sober,** you are not drunk. *sobrio* ❑ *He was completely sober. Estaba completamente sobrio.* **2** ADJ A **sober** person is serious and thoughtful. *serio* ❑ *He is very sober and realistic. Es muy serio y realista.* ❑ *Everyone had sad, sober faces. Los rostros de todos estaban tristes y serios.* • **so|ber|ly** ADV *seriamente, gravemente* ❑ *"There's a problem," he said soberly. —Tenemos un problema —dijo gravemente.* **3** ADJ **Sober** colors and clothes are plain and rather dull. *sobrio* ❑ *He dresses in sober gray suits. Viste sobrios trajes grises.* • **so|ber|ly** ADV *sobriamente* ❑ *She was soberly dressed in a dark suit. Estaba sobriamente vestida con un traje oscuro.*

▸ **sober up** PHR-VERB If someone **sobers up,** or if something **sobers** them **up,** they become sober after being drunk. *pasarse la embriaguez* ❑ *He was put in a police cell to sober up. Lo metieron en una celda de la policía para que se le pasara la embriaguez.*

**so-called** also **so called** **1** ADJ You use **so-called** to indicate that you think a word or expression used to describe someone or something is in fact wrong. *supuesto* ❑ *This so-called miracle never actually happened. El supuesto milagro nunca ocurrió realmente.* **2** ADJ You use **so-called** to indicate that something is generally referred to by the name that you are about to use. *llamado* ❑ *...the world's eight largest economies, the so-called G-8. ...las ocho economías más grandes del mundo, el llamado Grupo de los 8.*

**soc|cer** /sɒkər/ N-UNCOUNT **Soccer** is a game played by two teams of eleven players using a round ball. Players kick the ball to each other and try to score goals by kicking the ball into a large net. Outside the United States, this game is also referred to as **football.** *fútbol* ❑ *She plays soccer. Juega fútbol.*
→ see Picture Dictionary: **soccer**

**soc|cer play|er** /sɒkər pleɪər/ (**soccer players**) N-COUNT A **soccer player** is a person who plays soccer, especially as a profession. *jugador de fútbol o jugadora de fútbol*

**so|cia|ble** /soʊʃəbᵊl/ ADJ **Sociable** people are

S

**Picture Dictionary** soccer

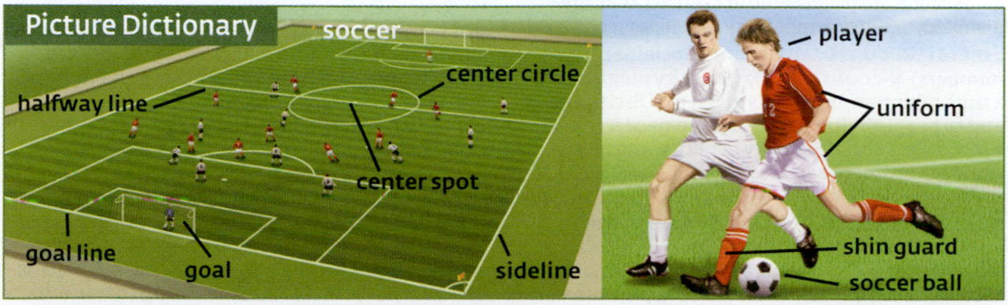

friendly and enjoy talking to other people. *sociable* ❑ *She was extremely sociable. Era sumamente sociable.*

**Word Link** *soci ≈ companion : associate, social, sociology*

**so|cial** /soʊʃᵊl/ **1** ADJ **Social** means relating to society. *social* ❑ *...unemployment, and other social problems. ...el desempleo y otros problemas sociales.* ❑ *...changing social attitudes. ...el cambio de las actitudes sociales.* ● **so|cial|ly** ADV *socialmente* ❑ *It wasn't socially acceptable to eat in the street. No era socialmente aceptable comer en la calle.* **2** ADJ **Social** means relating to leisure activities that involve meeting other people. *social* ❑ *We should organize more social events. Deberíamos organizar más actos sociales.* ● **so|cial|ly** ADV *socialmente* ❑ *We have known each other socially for a long time. Tenemos trato social desde hace mucho tiempo.*
→ see **kiss, myth**

**so|cial be|hav|ior** N-UNCOUNT **Social behavior** is the interaction between animals of the same species or between people. *conducta social*

**so|cial dance** (**social dances**) N-VAR **Social dance** is any form of dance that is done in a social setting, for example ballroom dancing or line dancing. *baile social*

**so|cial|ism** /soʊʃəlɪzəm/ N-UNCOUNT **Socialism** is a set of political principles whose general aim is to create a system in which everyone has an equal opportunity to benefit from a country's wealth. Under socialism, the country's main industries are usually owned by the state. *socialismo*

**so|cial|ist** /soʊʃəlɪst/ (**socialists**) **1** ADJ **Socialist** means based on socialism or relating to socialism. *socialista* ❑ *...members of the Socialist Party. ...miembros del Partido Socialista.* **2** N-COUNT A **socialist** is a person who believes in socialism or who is a member of a socialist party. *socialista* ❑ *His grandparents were socialists. Sus abuelos eran socialistas.*

**so|cial|ize** /soʊʃəlaɪz/ (**socializes, socializing, socialized**) V-I If you **socialize,** you meet other people socially, for example at parties. *socializar, alternar* ❑ *It is an opportunity to socialize and make new friends. Es una oportunidad para alternar y hacer nuevos amigos.*

S

**so|cial sci|ence** (**social sciences**) N-VAR **Social science** is the scientific study of society. *ciencias sociales* ❑ *...a degree in a social science. ...un título en ciencias sociales.*

**So|cial Se|cu|rity** N-UNCOUNT **Social Security** is a system by which workers and employers in the U.S. have to pay money to the government, which gives money to people who are retired, who are disabled, or who cannot work. *seguridad social*

**So|cial Se|cu|rity num|ber** (**Social Security numbers**) N-COUNT A **Social Security number** is a nine digit number that is given to U.S. citizens and to people living in the U.S. You need it to get a job, collect Social Security benefits, and receive some government services. *número de la Seguridad Social*

**so|cial ser|vices** N-PLURAL **Social services** in a district are the services provided by the local authority or government to help people who have serious family problems or financial problems. *servicios sociales* ❑ *Social services are trying to help these children. Los de servicios sociales están tratando de ayudar a estos niños.*

**so|cial work** N-UNCOUNT **Social work** is work which involves giving help and advice to people with serious family problems or financial problems. *trabajo social*

**so|cial work|er** (**social workers**) N-COUNT A **social worker** is a person whose job is to do social work. *trabajador social o trabajadora social*

**so|ci|ety** /səsaɪɪti/ (**societies**) **1** N-VAR **Society** consists of all the people in a country or region, thought of as a large organized group. *sociedad* ❑ *...common problems in society. ...los problemas comunes de la sociedad.* ❑ *We live in an unequal society. Vivimos en una sociedad desigual.* **2** N-COUNT A **society** is an organization for people who have the same interest or aim. *sociedad, asociación* ❑ *...the American Historical Society. ...la Asociación de Historia Estadounidense.* **3** N-UNCOUNT **Society** is the rich, fashionable people in a particular place who meet on social occasions. *sociedad* ❑ *The couple were well-known in society. La pareja era bien conocida en sociedad.*
→ see **culture**

**so|ci|ol|ogy** /soʊsiɒlədʒi/ N-UNCOUNT **Sociology** is the study of society or of the way society is organized. *sociología* ● **so|cio|logi|cal** /soʊsiəlɒdʒɪkᵊl/ ADJ *sociológico* ❑ *...a sociological study on the importance of the family. ...un estudio sociológico sobre la importancia de la familia.* ● **so|ci|olo|gist** N-COUNT (**sociologists**) *sociólogo, socióloga* ❑ *As a sociologist she is interested in the role of women. En cuanto socióloga, le interesa el papel de la mujer.*

**sock** /sɒk/ (**socks**) N-COUNT **Socks** are pieces of clothing which cover your foot and ankle and are worn inside shoes. *calcetín, media* ❑ *...a pair of red socks. ...un par de calcetines rojos.*
→ see **clothing**

**sock|et** /sɒkɪt/ (**sockets**) **1** N-COUNT A **socket** is a device on a piece of electrical equipment into which you can put a bulb or plug. *enchufe, tomacorriente* ❑ *He took the light bulb out of the socket. Quitó el foco del portalámparas.* **2** N-COUNT You can refer to any hollow part or opening in a structure which another part fits into as a **socket.** *alvéolo, cuenca* ❑ *His tooth was loose in its socket. Tenía el diente flojo.*

**soda pop** (**soda pops**) N-VAR **Soda pop** is the same as **soda** 1. *refresco*

**so|dium** /soʊdiəm/ N-UNCOUNT **Sodium** is a silvery white chemical element which combines with other chemicals. Salt is a sodium compound. *sodio*

**sofa** /soʊfə/ (**sofas**) N-COUNT A **sofa** is a long, comfortable seat with a back and usually with arms, which two or three people can sit on. *sillón, sofá*

**soft** /sɔft/ (**softer, softest**) **1** ADJ Something that is **soft** is pleasant to touch, and not rough or hard. *suave* ❑ *Body lotion will keep your skin soft. La crema para el cuerpo mantiene su piel suave.* ❑ *She wiped the baby's face with a soft cloth. Le limpió la cara al bebé con un trapo suave.* ● **soft|ness** N-UNCOUNT *suavidad* ❑ *He loved the softness of her hair. Adoraba la suavidad de su pelo.* **2** ADJ Something that is **soft**

**Word Web** solar

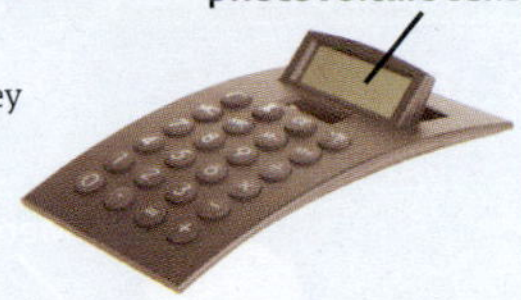


Sources of **fossil fuel energy** are becoming scarce and expensive. They also cause environmental **pollution.** Scientists are studying alternative sources of energy such as **solar power.** There are two ways to use the **sun**'s **energy. Thermal** systems produce heat. Photovoltaic systems generate electricity. Thermal systems use a **solar collector.** This is an insulated box with a clear cover. It stores the sun's energy for use in household air or water heating systems. Photovoltaic systems have thin layers of **semiconductor** materials to change the sun's heat into electricity. They are often used in calculators and solar-powered watches.

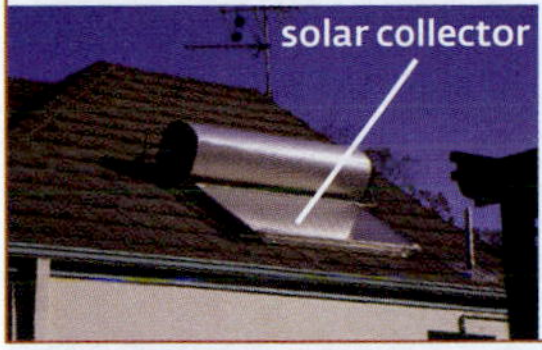


changes shape or bends easily when you press it. *suave* ❑ *Add milk to form a soft dough.* *Añada leche para formar una masa suave.* **3** ADJ Something that is **soft** is very gentle and has no force. For example, a **soft** sound or voice is quiet and not harsh. A **soft** light or color is pleasant to look at because it is not bright. *suave* ❑ *There was a soft tapping on my door.* *Oí un golpe suave en la puerta.* ● **soft|ly** ADV *suavemente, tenuemente* ❑ *She walked into the softly lit room.* *Entró en la habitación tenuemente iluminada.* **4** ADJ If you are **soft on** someone, you do not treat them as strictly or severely as you should. *indulgente* ❑ *The law is too soft on criminals.* *La ley es demasiado indulgente con los criminales.*

**Thesaurus** *soft* Ver también:

ADJ. fluffy, silky; (*ant.*) firm, hard, rough **1**
faint, gentle, light, low; (*ant.*) clear, strong **3**

**soft|cover** /sɒftkʌvər/ (**softcovers**) also **soft-cover** N-COUNT A **softcover** is a book with a thin cardboard, paper, or plastic cover. *rústica, pasta blanda* ❑ *...a set of 6 softcover books.* *...un conjunto de seis libros en rústica.* ❑ *Her cookbook is published in soft cover this month.* *Su libro de cocina será publicado en rústica este mes.*

**soft drink** (**soft drinks**) N-COUNT A **soft drink** is a cold, nonalcoholic drink such as lemonade or fruit juice, or a carbonated drink. *refresco*

**sof|ten** /sɔfᵊn/ (**softens, softening, softened**) **1** V-T/V-I If you **soften** something or if it **softens**, it becomes less hard, stiff, or firm. *ablandar* ❑ *Soften the butter in a small saucepan.* *Ablande la mantequilla en una cacerola pequeña.* **2** V-T If one thing **softens** the damaging effect of another thing, it makes the effect less severe. *amortiguar* ❑ *He wanted to soften the impact of the new tax on the poor.* *Quería amortiguar el impacto del nuevo impuesto sobre los pobres.* **3** V-T/V-I If you **soften** your position, if your position **softens,** or if you **soften,** you become more sympathetic and less hostile or critical. *moderar* ❑ *The letter shows that they have softened their position.* *La carta demuestra que ya han moderado su posición.* ❑ *His views have softened a lot in recent years.* *Sus puntos de vistas se han moderado mucho en los años recientes.*

**Word Link** *ware ≈ merchandise : hardware, software, warehouse*

**soft|ware** /sɔftwɛər/ N-UNCOUNT Computer programs are referred to as **software.** Compare **hardware.** *software* [COMPUTING] ❑ *He writes software.* *Escribe software.*
→ see **computer**

**soil** /sɔɪl/ (**soils**) N-VAR **Soil** is the substance on the surface of the earth in which plants grow. *suelo* ❑ *The soil here is good for growing vegetables.* *El suelo de aquí es bueno para el cultivo de verduras.*
→ see **erosion, farm, grassland, photosynthesis**

**so|lar** /soʊlər/ **1** ADJ **Solar** is used to describe things relating to the sun. *solar* ❑ *...solar gases.* *...gases solares.* ❑ *...solar wind.* *...viento solar.* **2** ADJ **Solar** power is obtained from the sun's light and heat. *solar* ❑ *...the advantages of solar power.* *...las ventajas de la energía solar.* ❑ *...the financial savings from solar energy.* *...el ahorro de recursos económicos derivado de la energía solar.*
→ see Word Web: **solar**
→ see **energy, greenhouse effect, photosynthesis**

**so|lar col|lec|tor** (**solar collectors**) N-COUNT A **solar collector** is a device that collects heat from the sun and converts it into electricity. *panel solar* ❑ *Large homes should have solar collectors.* *Las casas grandes deberían tener paneles solares.*
→ see **solar**

**so|lar eclipse** (**solar eclipses**) N-COUNT A **solar eclipse** is an occasion when the moon is between the Earth and the sun, so that for a short time you cannot see part or all of the sun. Compare **lunar eclipse.** *eclipse solar*
→ see **eclipse**

**so|lar neb|ula** (**solar nebulae** or **solar nebulas**) N-COUNT The **solar nebula** is the cloud of gas from which our solar system is believed to have developed. *nebulosa solar* [TECHNICAL]

**so|lar sys|tem** (**solar systems**) N-COUNT **The solar system** is the sun and all the planets that go around it. *sistema solar* ❑ *Saturn is the second biggest planet in the solar system.* *Saturno es el segundo más grande de los planetas del sistema solar.*
→ see Picture Dictionary: **solar system**
→ see **galaxy**

**sol|dier** /soʊldʒər/ (**soldiers**) N-COUNT A **soldier**

Picture Dictionary

solar system

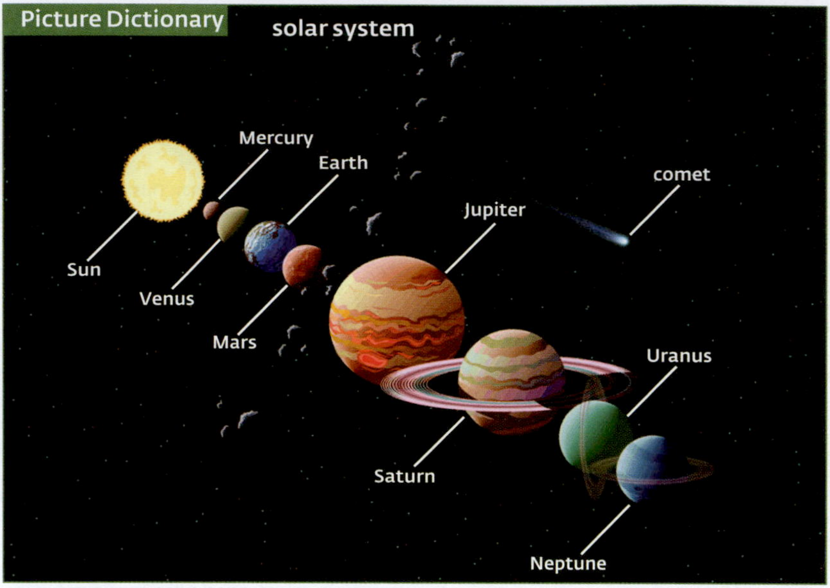


is a member of an army, especially one who is not an officer. soldado

→ see **war**

**sole** /soʊl/ (**soles**) 1 ADJ The **sole** thing or person of a particular type is the only one of that type. único ❑ *Their sole aim is to win.* *Su único objetivo es ganar.* ● **sole|ly** ADV únicamente ❑ *Doctors do not rely solely on what a patient tells them.* *Los médicos no se basan únicamente en lo que el paciente les dice.* 2 ADJ If you have **sole** charge or ownership of something, you are the only person in charge of it or who owns it. único ❑ *She was the sole caregiver for her sick mother.* *Fue la única que estuvo atendiendo a su madre enferma.* 3 N-COUNT The **sole** of your foot or of a shoe or sock is the underneath surface of it. suela, planta ❑ *...shoes with thick soles.* *...zapatos de suela gruesa.*

→ see **foot**

S

**sol|emn** /sɒləm/ 1 ADJ Someone or something that is **solemn** is very serious rather than cheerful or humorous. solemne ❑ *His face looked solemn.* *Tenía una expresión solemne.* ● **sol|emn|ly** ADV solemnemente, con solemnidad ❑ *Her listeners nodded solemnly.* *Su auditorio hizo un gesto de asentimiento con solemnidad.* ● **so|lem|nity** /səlɛmnɪti/ N-UNCOUNT solemnidad ❑ *...the solemnity of the event.* *...la solemnidad del acto.* 2 ADJ A **solemn** promise or agreement is one that you make in a very formal, sincere way. solemne ❑ *She made a solemn promise not to tell anyone.* *Hizo la promesa solemne de no decirlo a nadie.* ● **sol|emn|ly** ADV solemnemente ❑ *Her husband solemnly promised to keep it a secret.* *Su esposo le prometió solemnemente mantener el secreto.*

**sol|fege** /sɒlfɛʒ, soʊl-/ N-UNCOUNT **Solfege** is a system used in the teaching of music and singing, in which the steps of the musical scale are given the names Do, Re, Me, Fa, Sol, La, Ti, and Do. solfeo [TECHNICAL]

**so|lici|tor** /səlɪsɪtər/ (**solicitors**) N-COUNT In the United States, a **solicitor** is the chief lawyer in a government or city department. procurador o procuradora abogado o abogada, procurador o procuradora

**sol|id** /sɒlɪd/ (**solids**) 1 ADJ A **solid** substance or object stays the same shape whether it is in a container or not. sólido ❑ *He did not eat solid food for several weeks.* *No tomó alimentos sólidos durante varias semanas.* 2 N-COUNT A **solid** is a substance that stays the same shape whether it is in a container or not. sólido ❑ *Solids turn to liquids at certain temperatures.* *Los sólidos se tornan líquidos a cierta temperatura.* 3 ADJ A substance that is **solid** is very hard or firm. sólido ❑ *The lake was frozen solid.* *El lago estaba completamente congelado.* 4 ADJ A **solid** object or mass does not have a space inside it, or holes or gaps in it. sólido ❑ *...50 feet of solid rock.* *...15 metros de roca sólida.* 5 ADJ A structure that is **solid** is strong and is not likely to collapse or fall over. sólido ❑ *Only the most solid buildings were still standing after the earthquake.* *Después del terremoto, sólo los edificios más sólidos estaban en pie todavía.* ● **sol|id|ly** ADV sólidamente ❑ *Their house was solidly built.* *Su casa estaba sólidamente construida.* ● **so|lid|ity** /səlɪdɪti/ N-UNCOUNT solidez ❑ *...the solidity of the walls.* *...la solidez de las murallas.* 6 ADJ If you describe someone as **solid,** you mean that they are very reliable and respectable. serio ❑ *Her husband is solid and stable.* *Su esposo es serio y estable.* ● **sol|id|ly** ADV firmemente ❑ *Graham is so solidly consistent.* *Graham es siempre tan constante.* ● **so|lid|ity** N-UNCOUNT constancia ❑ *The British are known for their solidity.* *Los británicos son conocidos por su constancia.* 7 ADJ

You use **solid** to describe something such as advice or information which is reliable and useful. bueno, confiable ❑ *She always gives me solid advice. Siempre me da buenos consejos.* ❑ *We don't have any solid information on where he is. No tenemos información confiable sobre su paradero.* ● **sol|id|ly** ADV firmemente ❑ *Their claims are solidly based in good research. Sus afirmaciones están sólidamente respaldadas por investigaciones concienzudas.* **8** ADJ If you do something for a **solid** period of time, you do it without any pause or interruption throughout that time. seguido ❑ *We worked together for two solid years. Trabajamos juntos durante dos años seguidos.* ● **sol|id|ly** ADV sin parar ❑ *I've worked solidly since last summer and I need a break. He trabajado sin parar desde el verano pasado y necesito un descanso.*
→ see Picture Dictionary: **solids**
→ see **matter**

**soli|dar|ity** /sɒlɪdærɪti/ N-UNCOUNT If a group of people show **solidarity**, they show support for each other or for another group, especially in political or international affairs. solidaridad ❑ *People marched to show solidarity with their leaders. La gente marchó por solidaridad con sus dirigentes.*

**soli|taire** /sɒlɪtɛər/ N-UNCOUNT **Solitaire** is a card game for only one player. solitario

**solo** /soʊloʊ/ (**solos**) **1** ADJ You use **solo** to indicate that someone does something alone rather than with other people. solista ❑ *He has just recorded his first solo album. Acaba de grabar su primer álbum como solista.* ● **Solo** is also an adverb. a solas ❑ *Lindbergh was the first person to fly solo across the Atlantic. Lindbergh fue el primero en volar solo a través del Atlántico.* **2** N-COUNT A **solo** is a piece of music or a dance performed by one person. solo ❑ *The song featured a guitar solo. La canción incluía un solo de guitarra.*

**sol|stice** /sɒlstɪs, soʊl-/ (**solstices**) N-COUNT **The summer solstice** is the day of the year with the most hours of daylight, and **the winter solstice** is the day of the year with the fewest hours of daylight. solsticio

**sol|ubil|ity** /sɒlyəbɪlɪti/ N-UNCOUNT A substance's **solubility** is its ability to dissolve in another substance or the amount of it that will dissolve in another substance. solubilidad

**sol|uble** /sɒlyəbəl/ ADJ A substance that is **soluble** will dissolve in a liquid. soluble ❑ *The red dye is soluble in hot water. El tinte rojo es soluble en agua caliente.*

**so|lute** /sɒlyut, soʊlut/ (**solutes**) N-COUNT A **solute** is any substance that dissolves in another substance. soluto [TECHNICAL]

**so|lu|tion** /səluʃən/ (**solutions**) **1** N-COUNT A **solution to** a problem is a way of dealing with it so that the difficulty is removed. solución ❑ *They both want to find a peaceful solution. Ambos quieren encontrar una solución pacífica.* **2** N-COUNT The **solution to** a puzzle is the answer to it. solución ❑ *We asked readers who completed the puzzle to send in their solutions. Pedimos a los lectores que completaron el crucigrama que nos enviaran sus soluciones.* **3** N-COUNT A **solution** is a liquid in which a solid substance has been dissolved. solución ❑ *...a soapy solution. ...una solución jabonosa.*
→ see **fraction**

**Word Partnership** Usar *solution* con:

ADJ. **best** solution, **peaceful** solution, **perfect** solution, **possible** solution, **practical** solution, **temporary** solution **1**
**easy** solution, **obvious** solution, **simple** solution **1** **2**
PREP. solution **to a conflict**, solution **to a crisis** **1**
solution **to a problem** **1** **2**
V. **propose a** solution, **reach a** solution, **seek a** solution **1**
**find a** solution **1** **2**

**solve** /sɒlv/ (**solves, solving, solved**) V-T If you **solve** a problem or a question, you find a solution or an answer to it. resolver ❑ *They have not solved the problem of unemployment. No han resuelto el problema del desempleo.*

**Word Partnership** Usar *solve* con:

N. **ability to** solve ***something***, solve **a crisis**, solve **a mystery**, solve **a problem**, solve **a puzzle**, **way to** solve ***something***
V. **attempt/try to** solve ***something***, **help** solve ***something***

S

**Picture Dictionary** solids

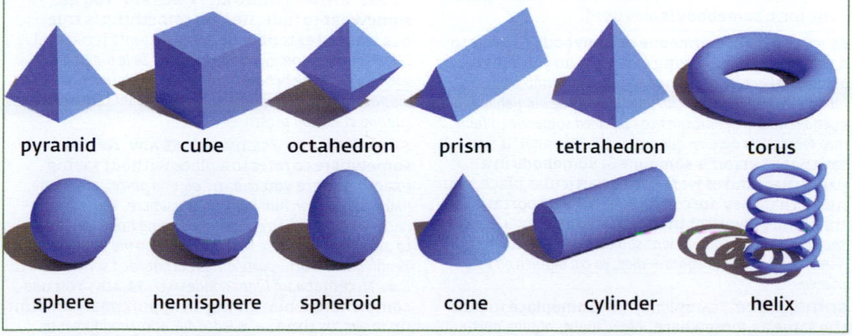

**some** /səm, STRONG sʌm/ **1** DET You use **some** to refer to a quantity of something or to a number of people or things, when you are not stating the quantity or number precisely. *un (uno, unos, una, unas), un poco de, algo de* ❑ *Would you like some orange juice? ¿Quiere un poco de jugo de naranja?* ❑ *He went to fetch some books. Fue a traer unos libros.* • **Some** is also a pronoun. *uno, una, unos, unas* ❑ *The apples are ripe, and we picked some today. Las manzanas ya están maduras y cortamos unas hoy.* **2** DET You use **some** to emphasize that a quantity or number is fairly large. For example, if an activity takes **some** time, it takes quite a lot of time. *cierto, un poco de* ❑ *We have discussed this in some detail. Lo hemos discutido con cierto detalle.* ❑ *He was silent for some time. Guardó silencio durante un rato.* **3** QUANT If you refer to **some of** the people or things in a group, you mean a few of them but not all of them. If you refer to **some of** a particular thing, you mean a part of it but not all of it. *algún (alguno, algunos, alguna, algunas), un poco de* ❑ *Some of the workers will lose their jobs. Algunos de los obreros perderán su empleo.* ❑ *Put some of the sauce onto a plate. Ponga un poco de la salsa en un plato.* • **Some** is also a pronoun. *un poco* ❑ *When the chicken is cooked I'll freeze some. Cuando el pollo esté cocido, congelaré un poco.* **4** DET If you refer to **some** person or thing, you are referring to that person or thing but in a vague way, without stating precisely which person or thing you mean. *alguno (algún, algunos, alguna, algunas)* ❑ *If you are worried about some aspect of your child's health, call us. Si le preocupa algún aspecto de la salud de su hijo, llámenos.* **5** ADV You can use **some** in front of a number to indicate that it is approximate. *unos, unas, alrededor de* ❑ *I have kept birds for some 30 years. He tenido pájaros durante unos 30 años.* **6** ADV **Some** is used to mean to a small extent or degree. *un poco* ❑ *I'll look around some to pass the time. Echaré un vistazo por ahí un rato para pasar el tiempo.*

**some|body** /sʌmbɒdi, -bʌdi/ PRON **Somebody** means the same as **someone**. *alguien*

**some|how** /sʌmhaʊ/ ADV You use **somehow** to say that you do not know or cannot say how something was done or will be done. *de alguna manera, de algún modo, de una u otra manera* ❑ *We'll manage somehow, I know we will. Nos las arreglaremos de alguna manera; lo sé.* ❑ *Somehow Karin managed to cope after he left. De alguna manera, Karin se las arregló después de su partida.*

S

**some|one** /sʌmwʌn/

The form **somebody** is also used.

**1** PRON You use **someone** or **somebody** to refer to a person without saying exactly who you mean. *alguien* ❑ *I got a call from someone who wanted to rent the apartment. Recibí una llamada de alguien que quería rentar el departamento.* ❑ *I need someone to help me. Necesito a alguien que me ayude.* **2** PRON If you say that a person is **someone** or **somebody in** a particular kind of work or **in** a particular place, you mean that they are considered to be important in that kind of work or in that place. *alguien* ❑ *"Before she arrived," she says, "I was somebody in this town." —Antes de que ella llegara —dice, yo era alguien en este pueblo.*

**some|place** /sʌmpleɪs/ ADV **Someplace** means the same as **somewhere**. *algún lugar, alguna parte* ❑ *Maybe we could go someplace together. Tal vez podríamos ir juntos a alguna parte.*

**some|thing** /sʌmθɪŋ/ **1** PRON You use **something** to refer to a thing, situation, event, or idea, without saying exactly what it is. *algo* ❑ *He knew that there was something wrong. Sabía que algo andaba mal.* ❑ *There was something funny about him. Había algo raro en él.* ❑ *Was there something you wanted to ask me? —¿Quería usted preguntarme algo?* **2** PRON You can use **something** in expressions like **"that's something"** when you think that a situation is not very good but is better than it might have been. *algo* ❑ *Well, at least he called. That was something. Bueno, al menos llamó. Eso ya es algo.* **3** PRON If you say that a thing is **something of** a disappointment, you mean that it is quite disappointing. If you say that a person is **something of** an artist, you mean that they are quite good at art. *verdadero* ❑ *The vacation was something of a disappointment. Las vacaciones fueron una verdadera decepción.* **4** PRON If you say that there is **something in** an idea or suggestion, you mean that it is quite good and should be considered seriously. *algo* ❑ *There could be something in what he said. Puede ser que tenga algo de razón.* **5** **something like** → see **like**

**some|time** /sʌmtaɪm/ ADV You use **sometime** to refer to a time in the future or the past that is unknown or that has not yet been decided. *algún día* ❑ *We will finish sometime next month. Terminaremos algún día del próximo mes.* ❑ *Why don't you come and see me sometime? ¿Por qué no vienes a verme algún día?*

> **Usage** **sometime, sometimes,** and **some time**
>
> *Sometime, sometimes,* and *some time* are easy to confuse. *Sometime* means "at some unknown time"; *sometimes* means "occasionally, from time to time"; *some time* means "some amount of time": *Sometimes Ilya enjoys spending some time catching up on his favorite soap operas; the last time he did that was sometime in August.*

**some|times** /sʌmtaɪmz/ ADV You use **sometimes** to say that something happens on some occasions rather than all the time. *a veces* ❑ *I sometimes sit out in the garden and read. A veces me siento en el jardín a leer.* ❑ *Sometimes he's a little rude. A veces es un poco grosero.*
→ see also **sometime**

**some|what** /sʌmwʌt, -wɒt/ ADV You use **somewhat** to indicate that something is true to a limited extent or degree. *un tanto* [FORMAL] ❑ *He sounded somewhat uncertain. Se le oía un tanto vacilante.* ❑ *She behaved somewhat differently when he was around. Se comportaba de manera un tanto diferente cuando él estaba presente.*

**some|where** /sʌmwɛər/ **1** ADV You use **somewhere** to refer to a place without saying exactly where you mean. *alguna parte, otra parte, lugar* ❑ *I've seen him before somewhere. Lo he visto antes en alguna parte.* ❑ *I'm not going home yet. I have to go somewhere else first. Todavía no me voy a casa. Tengo que ir a otra parte antes.* ❑ *I needed somewhere to live. Necesitaba un lugar dónde vivir.* **2** ADV You use **somewhere** when giving an approximate amount, number, or time. *alrededor de, aproximadamente*

❑ *The house is worth somewhere between $7 million and $10 million.* *La casa vale entre 7 y 10 millones de dólares, aproximadamente.* ❑ *Caray is somewhere between 73 and 80 years of age.* *Caray tiene entre 73 y 80 años de edad, aproximadamente.* 3 PHRASE If you say that you **are getting somewhere,** you mean that you are making progress toward achieving something. *avanzar, adelantar* ❑ *If we can agree on this, we'll be getting somewhere.* *Si logramos ponernos de acuerdo en esto, habremos adelantado.*

**son** /sʌn/ (**sons**) N-COUNT Someone's **son** is their male child. *hijo* ❑ *He shared a pizza with his son Laurence.* *Compartió una pizza con su hijo Laurence.* ❑ *Sam is the seven-year-old son of Eric Davies.* *Sam es el hijo de siete años de Eric Davies.*
→ see **child**

**sonata-allegro form** /sənɑtəəlɛgroʊ fɔrm/ (**sonata-allegro forms**) also **sonata form** N-VAR A **sonata-allegro form** is a piece of classical music that consists of three main sections in which musical themes are introduced, developed, and then repeated. *sonata-allegro* [TECHNICAL]

**song** /sɔŋ/ (**songs**) 1 N-COUNT A **song** is words and music sung together. *canción* ❑ *She sang a Spanish song.* *Cantó una canción española.* 2 N-UNCOUNT **Song** is the art of singing. *canto* ❑ *...a festival of dance, music, and song.* *...un festival de baile, música y canto.* 3 N-COUNT A bird's **song** is the pleasant, musical sounds that it makes. *canto, trino* ❑ *It's lovely to hear a blackbird's song in the evening.* *Es hermoso oír el canto del mirlo por la tarde.*
→ see **concert, music**

**Word Partnership** Usar *song* con:

ADJ. **beautiful** song, **favorite** song, **old** song, **popular** song 1
V. **hear a** song, **play a** song, **record a** song, **sing a** song, **write a** song 1
N. **hit** song, **love** song, song **lyrics**, song **music**, **pop** song, **rap** song, song **title**, **theme** song, **words of a** song 1
**bird's** song 3

**song|book** /sɔŋbʊk/ (**songbooks**) 1 N-COUNT A songwriter's **songbook** is all the songs that he or she has written. You can also refer to the songs that a singer performs as their **songbook.** *cancionero* ❑ *...hits from the songbook of Bob Dylan.* *...éxitos del cancionero de Bob Dylan.* 2 N-COUNT A **songbook** is a book containing the words and music of a lot of songs. *cancionero* ❑ *...a pop songbook.* *...un cancionero de música pop.*

**song form** (**song forms**) N-VAR **Song form** is a way of describing the structure of a song in which different sections of the song are represented by different letters of the alphabet. *estructura de una canción*

**son|ic** /sɒnɪk/ ADJ **Sonic** is used to describe things related to sound. [TECHNICAL] *sónico, del sonido* ❑ *...the sonic and visual effects in the show.* *...los efectos de sonido y visuales del espectáculo.*
→ see **sound**

**son-in-law** (**sons-in-law**) N-COUNT Someone's **son-in-law** is the husband of their daughter. *yerno*

**soon** /sun/ (**sooner, soonest**) 1 ADV If something is going to happen **soon,** it will happen after a short time. If something happened **soon** after a particular time or event, it happened a short time after it. *pronto* ❑ *I'll call you soon.* *Te llamo pronto.* ❑ *He arrived sooner than I expected.* *Llegó más pronto de lo que yo esperaba.* 2 PHRASE If you say that something happens **as soon as** something else happens, you mean that it happens immediately after the other thing. *tan pronto como* ❑ *As soon as the weather improves we will go.* *Iremos tan pronto como mejore el tiempo.* 3 PHRASE If you say that you **would just as soon** do something or you**'d just as soon** do it, you mean that you would prefer to do it. *preferir* ❑ *These people could afford to retire to Florida but they'd just as soon stay here.* *Estas personas podrían vivir en Florida al jubilarse, pero preferirían permanecer aquí.* ❑ *I'd just as soon not tell anyone about this.* *Preferiría no contarle esto a nadie.*

**soothe** /suð/ (**soothes, soothing, soothed**) 1 V-T If you **soothe** someone who is angry or upset, you make them feel calmer. *calmar, tranquilizar* ❑ *He sang to her to soothe her.* *Le cantó para tranquilizarla.* • **sooth|ing** ADJ *tranquilo, relajante* ❑ *Put on some nice soothing music.* *Pon un poco de música tranquila.* 2 V-T Something that **soothes** a part of your body where there is pain or discomfort makes the pain or discomfort less severe. *aliviar* ❑ *...lotion to soothe dry skin.* *...loción para aliviar la piel seca.* • **sooth|ing** ADJ *calmante* ❑ *Cold tea is very soothing for burns.* *El té frío es un buen calmante para las quemaduras.*

**so|phis|ti|cat|ed** /səfɪstɪkeɪtɪd/ 1 ADJ A **sophisticated** machine, device, or method is more advanced or complex than others. *complejo* ❑ *Bees use a very sophisticated communication system.* *Las abejas tienen un sistema de comunicación muy complejo.* 2 ADJ Someone who is **sophisticated** is comfortable in social situations and knows about culture, fashion, and other matters that are considered socially important. *mundano, sofisticado* ❑ *Claude was a charming, sophisticated man.* *Claude era un hombre mundano encantador.*

**Thesaurus** *sophisticated* Ver también:

ADJ. advanced, complex, elaborate, intricate 1
cultured, experienced, refined, worldly; (ant.) backward, crude 2

**sopho|more** /sɒfəmɔr/ (**sophomores**) N-COUNT A **sophomore** is a student in the second year of college or high school. *estudiante de segundo año de bachillerato o de universidad*

**sore** /sɔr/ (**sorer, sorest, sores**) 1 ADJ If part of your body is **sore,** it causes you pain and discomfort. *adolorido* ❑ *I had a sore throat and a cough.* *Tenía la garganta adolorida y tos.* 2 ADJ If you are **sore** about something, you are angry and upset about it. *disgustado* [INFORMAL] ❑ *Her friends are very sore at her.* *Sus amigos están muy disgustados con ella.* 3 N-COUNT A **sore** is a painful place on the body where the skin is infected. *llaga* ❑ *Our hands were covered with sores from the ropes.* *Teníamos las manos cubiertas de llagas por las sogas.*

**sor|row** /sɒroʊ/ (**sorrows**) 1 N-UNCOUNT **Sorrow** is a feeling of deep sadness or regret. *pesar* ❑ *Words cannot express my sorrow.* *Las palabras no bastan para expresar mi pesar.* 2 N-PLURAL **Sorrows** are events or situations that cause deep sadness.

S

*pesar* ❑ *...the joys and sorrows of everyday living.* *...las alegrías y pesares de la vida cotidiana.*

**sor|ry** /sɒri/ (**sorrier, sorriest**) **1** CONVENTION You say **"Sorry"** or **"I'm sorry"** as a way of apologizing to someone for something that you have done which has upset them or caused them difficulties, or when you bump into them accidentally. *sentir(lo), disculparse, lamentar* ❑ *"You're making too much noise." — "Sorry."* *—¡Estás haciendo mucho ruido! —Discúlpame.* ❑ *Sorry I took so long.* *Siento haberme tardado tanto.* ❑ *I'm really sorry if I said anything wrong.* *Lo lamento mucho si dije algo que no debí.* **2** ADJ If you are **sorry** about a situation, you feel regret, sadness, or disappointment about it. *apenar, lamentar* ❑ *She was very sorry about all the trouble she'd caused.* *Estaba muy apenada por todos los problemas que causó.* ❑ *I'm sorry he's gone.* *Lamento que haya muerto.* **3** CONVENTION You say **"I'm sorry"** to express your regret and sadness when you hear sad or unpleasant news. *qué pena* ❑ *"He can't come because he's ill." — "I'm sorry to hear that."* *—No puede ir porque está enfermo. —Qué pena me da saberlo.* **4** ADJ If you feel **sorry for** someone who is unhappy or in an unpleasant situation, you feel sympathy and sadness for them. *pena por* ❑ *I felt sorry for him because nobody listened to him.* *Sentí pena por él porque nadie lo escuchaba.* **5** CONVENTION You say **"Sorry?"** when you have not heard something that someone has said and you want them to repeat it. *¿Perdón?, ¿Cómo?* ❑ *Sorry? What did you say?* *¿Cómo? ¿Qué dijiste?* **6** ADJ If someone or something is in a **sorry** state, they are in a bad state, mentally or physically. *lamentable, lastimoso* ❑ *After the fire, the building was in a sorry state.* *Después del incendio, el edificio quedó en un estado lamentable.*

**sort** /sɔrt/ (**sorts, sorting, sorted**) **1** N-COUNT If you talk about a particular **sort of** something, you are talking about a class of things that have particular features in common and that belong to a larger group of related things. *tipo, clase, género* ❑ *What sort of school did you go to?* *¿A qué tipo de escuela fuiste?* ❑ *There are so many different sorts of mushrooms available these days.* *¡Hay tantos tipos diferentes de hongos hoy en día!* ❑ *A dozen trees of various sorts were planted.* *Se plantó una docena de árboles de diferentes clases.* **2** N-SING You describe someone as a particular **sort** when you are describing their character. *tipo* ❑ *He seemed to be just the right sort for the job.* *Parecía del tipo exacto para el puesto.* ❑ *She was a very lively sort of person.* *Era un tipo de persona muy vital.* **3** V-T/V-I If you **sort** things, you separate them into different classes, groups, or places. *organizar, clasificar, ordenar, dividir* ❑ *He sorted the materials into their folders.* *Clasificó los materiales en sus carpetas.* ❑ *He opened the box and sorted through the papers.* *Abrió la caja y rebuscó entre los papeles.* **4** PHRASE If you describe something as a thing **of sorts** or as a thing **of a sort,** you are suggesting that the thing is of a rather poor quality or standard. *una especie de* ❑ *He made a living of sorts selling books door-to-door.* *Vivía, por así decirlo, de vender libros de puerta en puerta.* **5** PHRASE You use **sort of** when you want to say that your description of something is not very accurate. *en cierto modo* [INFORMAL] ❑ *They treated us sort of like house pets.* *Nos trataban casi como si fuéramos las mascotas de la casa.*

▸**sort out** **1** PHR-VERB If you **sort out** a group of things, you separate them into different classes, groups, or places. *arreglar, separar* ❑ *Sort out all your bills as quickly as possible.* *Arregla tus cuentas lo más pronto posible.* ❑ *Davina was sorting out scraps of material.* *Davina estaba separando retazos de tela.* **2** PHR-VERB If you **sort out** a problem or the details of something, you do what is necessary to solve the problem or organize the details. *resolver, aclarar* ❑ *India and Nepal have sorted out their disagreement on trade.* *India y Nepal ya aclararon sus desavenencias comerciales.*

**soul** /soʊl/ (**souls**) **1** N-COUNT Your **soul** is the part of you that consists of your mind, character, thoughts, and feelings. Many people believe that your soul continues existing after your body is dead. *alma, espíritu* ❑ *She went to pray for the soul of her late husband.* *Fue a rezar por el alma de su difunto marido.* **2** N-SING You use **soul** in negative statements like **not a soul** to mean nobody at all. *persona* ❑ *I've never harmed a soul in my life.* *En mi vida he lastimado a nadie.* **3** N-UNCOUNT **Soul** is the same as **soul music.** *música soul, soul* ❑ *...American soul singer Anita Baker.* *...Anita Baker, cantante estadounidense de soul.*

**soul food** N-UNCOUNT **Soul food** is used to refer to the kind of food, for example corn bread, ham, and yams, that was traditionally eaten by African-Americans in the southern United States. *soul food*

**soul music** N-UNCOUNT **Soul music** is a type of pop music performed mainly by African-American musicians. It often expresses deep emotions. *soul music, soul*

**sound**

❶ NOUN AND VERB USES
❷ ADJECTIVE USES

❶ **sound** /saʊnd/ (**sounds, sounding, sounded**) **1** N-COUNT A **sound** is something that you hear. *sonido, ruido* ❑ *Peter heard the sound of gunfire.* *Peter oyó disparos.* ❑ *Liza was so frightened she couldn't make a sound.* *Liza estaba tan asustada que ni podía hablar.* **2** N-UNCOUNT **Sound** is energy that travels in waves through air, water, or other substances, and can be heard. *sonido* ❑ *The airplane will travel at twice the speed of sound.* *El avión volará al doble de la velocidad del sonido.* **3** V-T/V-I If something such as a horn or a bell **sounds** or if you **sound** it, it makes a noise. *sonar, tocar* ❑ *The buzzer sounded in Daniel's office.* *En la oficina de Daniel sonó el timbre.* **4** V-LINK When you are describing a noise, you can talk about the way it **sounds.** *sonar, oírse* ❑ *They heard what sounded like a huge explosion.* *Oyeron lo que les pareció una gran explosión.* ❑ *The creaking of the floorboards sounded very loud in that silence.* *Los crujidos de las duelas se oían muy fuerte en ese silencio.* **5** V-LINK When you talk about the way someone **sounds,** you are describing the impression you have of them when they speak. *sonar, comportarse, dar la impresión* ❑ *She sounded a bit worried.* *Daba la impresión de estar un poco preocupada.* ❑ *Murphy sounds like a child.* *Murphy se comporta como niño.* **6** V-LINK When you are describing your impression or opinion of something you have heard about or read about, you can talk about the way it **sounds.** *parecer, sonar* ❑ *It sounds like a wonderful idea to me.* *Me suena como una magnífica*

## Word Web **sound**

**Sound** is the only form of energy we can hear. The energy makes the molecules in the air **vibrate.** Fast vibrations called high **frequencies** produce high-pitched sounds. Slower vibrations produce lower frequencies. Sound vibrations travel in waves, just like **waves** in water. Each wave has a **crest** and a **trough.** Amplitude measures the size of a wave. It is the vertical distance between the middle of a wave and its crest. When a **sound wave** bounces off something, it creates an **echo.** When an airplane reaches **supersonic** speed, it generates **shock waves.** As these waves move toward the ground, a **sonic boom** occurs.

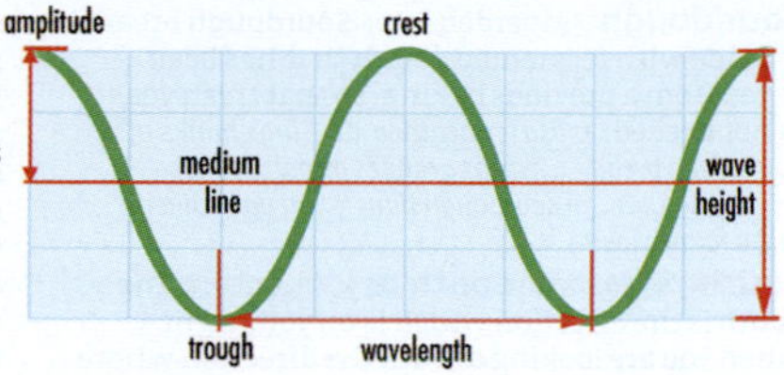


*idea.* ❑ *It sounds as if they made a mistake.* *Parece que hubieran cometido un error.* **7** N-SING You can describe your impression of something you have heard about or read about by talking about **the sound of** it. *impresión* ❑ *Here's a new idea we liked the sound of.* *Esta nueva idea nos dio buena impresión.* ❑ *I don't like the sound of Toby Osborne.* *No me gusta cómo suena Toby Osborne.*
→ see Word Web: **sound**
→ see **concert, echo**

▸ **sound out** PHR-VERB If you **sound** someone **out,** you question them in order to find out what their opinion is about something. *tantear, sondear* ❑ *The management will sound out the views of the employees.* *La administración va a sondear el punto de vista de los empleados.*

❷ **sound** /saʊnd/ (**sounder, soundest**) **1** ADJ If a structure, part of your body, or your mind is **sound,** it is in good condition or healthy. *sano, saludable, sólido, estable* ❑ *When we bought the house, it was structurally sound.* *Cuando compramos la casa, la estructura era sólida.* ❑ *The car is basically sound.* *El auto está básicamente en buenas condiciones.* **2** ADJ **Sound** advice, reasoning, or evidence is reliable and sensible. *sensato, confiable, responsable* ❑ *They are professionals who can give sound advice.* *Son profesionales que pueden dar consejos sensatos.* ❑ *Only buy from a company that is financially sound.* *Sólo compra en empresas financieramente sólidas.* **3** ADJ If someone is in a **sound** sleep, they are sleeping very deeply. *profundo* ❑ *She woke me out of a sound sleep.* *Me despertó de un profundo sueño.* • **Sound** is also an adverb. *profundamente* ❑ *He was lying in bed, sound asleep.* *Estaba acostado en la cama, profundamente dormido.*

**Thesaurus** *sound* Ver también:
ADJ. safe, sturdy, whole ❷ **1**
logical, valid, wise; (*ant.*) illogical, unreliable ❷ **2**

**sound en|er|gy** N-UNCOUNT **Sound energy** is energy in the form of sound waves. *energía sonora*

**sound|track** /saʊndtræk/ (**soundtracks**) also **sound track** N-COUNT The **soundtrack** of a movie is its sound, speech, and especially the music. *banda sonora* ❑ *...the soundtrack to a movie called "Casino Royale."* *...la banda sonora de una película llamada Casino Royale.*

**sound wave** (**sound waves**) also **soundwave** N-COUNT **Sound waves** are the waves of energy that we hear as sound. *onda sonora*
→ see **ear, sound**

**soup** /sup/ (**soups**) N-VAR **Soup** is liquid food made by boiling meat, fish, or vegetables in water. *sopa, caldo, consomé* ❑ *...homemade chicken soup.* *...sopa de pollo hecha en casa.*

**sour** /saʊər/ (**sours, souring, soured**) **1** ADJ Something that is **sour** has a sharp, unpleasant taste like the taste of a lemon. *ácido, agrio* ❑ *The stewed apple was sour.* *La compota de manzana estaba ácida.* **2** ADJ **Sour** milk is milk that has an unpleasant taste because it is no longer fresh. *agrio, cortado, acedo* ❑ *The milk has gone sour.* *La leche está cortada.* **3** ADJ Someone who is **sour** is bad-tempered and unfriendly. *desagradable* ❑ *She made a sour face in his direction.* *Lo miró y le puso cara.* • **sour|ly** ADV *agriamente* ❑ *"Leave my mother out of it," he said sourly.* *—No metas a mi madre en esto —le dijo con amargura.* **4** ADJ If a situation or relationship **turns sour** or **goes sour,** it stops being enjoyable or satisfactory. *amargado, avinagrado* ❑ *Everything turned sour for me there.* *Todo se volvió desagradable para mí allá.* ❑ *Our friendship slowly began to turn sour.* *Nuestra amistad empezó a amargarse poco a poco.* **5** V-T/V-I If a friendship, situation, or attitude **sours** or if something **sours** it, it becomes less friendly, enjoyable, or hopeful. *amargar, echar a perder* ❑ *The differences in their world views is likely to sour their relationship.* *Quizá las diferencias en su forma de ver el mundo echen a perder su relación.*
→ see **taste**

**source** /sɔrs/ (**sources**) **1** N-COUNT The **source of** something is the person, place, or thing which you get it from. *origen, fuente, principio* ❑ *Many adults use television as their major source of information.* *Muchos adultos se sirven de la televisión como principal fuente de información.* ❑ *...renewable sources of energy.* *...fuentes renovables de energía.* **2** N-COUNT A **source** is a person or book that provides information for a news story or for a piece of research. *fuente* ❑ *Military sources say the boat was heading south.* *Fuentes militares dicen que el bote iba hacia el sur.* **3** N-COUNT The **source** of a river or stream is the

place where it begins. *origen* ❑ *...the source of the Tiber.* *...el nacimiento del Tíber.*
→ see **diary**

**sour|dough** /saʊərdoʊ/ ADJ **Sourdough** bread is made with fermented dough that has been saved from a previous baking, so that fresh yeast is not needed. *masa fermentada* ❑ *...big chunks of sourdough bread.* *...trozos grandes de pan de masa fermentada.* ❑ *...a sourdough bun.* *...un panecillo de masa fermentada.*

**south** /saʊθ/ also **South** 1 N-UNCOUNT **The south** is the direction which is on your right when you are looking toward the direction where the sun rises. *sur* ❑ *The town lies ten miles to the south of here.* *El pueblo está a diez millas hacia el sur de aquí.* 2 N-SING **The south of** a place, country, or region is the part which is in the south. *sur* ❑ *...vacations in the south of Mexico.* *...vacaciones en el sur de México.* 3 ADV If you go **south,** you travel toward the south. *sur* ❑ *I drove south on Highway 9.* *Me dirigí al sur por la carretera 9.* 4 ADV Something that is **south of** a place is positioned to the south of it. *al sur* ❑ *They now live on a farm 50 miles south of Rochester.* *Ahora viven en una granja, 50 millas al sur de Rochester.* 5 ADJ The **south** edge, corner, or part of a place or country is the part which is toward the south. *sur* ❑ *...the south coast of Long Island.* *...la costa sur de Long Island.* 6 ADJ A **south** wind is a wind that blows from the south. *del sur* ❑ *...a mild south wind.* *...un suave viento del sur.*

**south|east** /saʊθist/ 1 N-UNCOUNT The **southeast** is the direction which is halfway between south and east. *sureste, sudeste* ❑ *The train left Colombo for Galle, 70 miles to the southeast.* *El tren salió de Colombo hacia Galle, 80 kilómetros hacia el sureste.* 2 N-SING **The southeast of** a place, country, or region is the part which is in the southeast. *sureste, sudeste* ❑ *There has been a lot of rain in the southeast of the country.* *Ha llovido mucho en el sureste del país.* 3 ADV If you go **southeast,** you travel toward the southeast. *al sureste, al sudeste* ❑ *I know we have to go southeast, more or less.* *Sé que tenemos que ir más o menos hacia el sudeste.* 4 ADV Something that is **southeast of** a place is positioned to the southeast of it. *sureste, sudeste* ❑ *The ship sank 500 miles southeast of Nova Scotia.* *El barco se hundió a 700 kilómetros al sureste de Nova Scotia.* 5 ADJ The **southeast** part of a place, country, or region is the part which is toward the southeast. *sureste, sudeste* ❑ *...rural southeast Kansas.* *...la zona rural del sureste de Kansas.* ❑ *...Southeast Asia.* *...el sudeste asiático.* 6 ADJ A **southeast** wind is a wind that blows from the southeast. *del sureste, del sudeste*

**south|eastern** /saʊθistərn/ ADJ **Southeastern** means in or from the southeast of a region or country. *del sureste, del sudeste* ❑ *...this city on the southeastern edge of the United States.* *...esta ciudad del extremo sureste de los Estados Unidos.*

**south|ern** /sʌðərn/ also **Southern** ADJ **Southern** means in or from the south of a region, state, or country. *del sur, sureño, sureña, meridional* ❑ *The Everglades National Park stretches across southern Florida.* *El parque nacional de los pantanos abarca la zona sur de Florida.*

**South|ern|er** /sʌðərnər/ (**Southerners**) N-COUNT A **Southerner** is a person who was born in or lives in the south of a country. *sureño, sureña* ❑ *Bob Wilson is a Southerner, from Texas.* *Bob Wilson es sureño, de Texas.*

**south|west** /saʊθwɛst/ 1 N-UNCOUNT **The southwest** is the direction which is halfway between south and west. *suroeste, sudoeste* ❑ *...about 500 kilometers to the southwest of Johannesburg.* *...unos 500 kilómetros al suroeste de Johannesburgo.* 2 N-SING **The southwest of** a place, country, or region is the part which is toward the southwest. *sudoeste, suroeste* ❑ *...the southwest of France.* *...el suroeste de Francia.* 3 ADV If you go **southwest,** you travel toward the southwest. *al suroeste, al sudoeste* ❑ *We took a plane southwest to Cappadocia.* *Tomamos un avión hacia el suroeste, a Capadocia.* 4 ADV Something that is **southwest of** a place is positioned to the southwest of it. *al suroeste, al sudoeste* ❑ *It's about 65 miles southwest of Houston.* *Está a unas 65 millas al suroeste de Houston.* 5 ADJ The **southwest** part of a place, country, or region is the part which is toward the southwest. *suroeste, sudoeste* ❑ *...a Labor Day festival in southwest Louisiana.* *...un festival del día del trabajo en el suroeste de Louisiana.* 6 ADJ A **southwest** wind is a wind that blows from the southwest. *del suroeste, del sudoeste* ❑ *Then the southwest wind began to blow.* *Entonces empezó a soplar el viento del sudoeste.*

**south|western** /saʊθwɛstərn/ ADJ **Southwestern** means in or from the southwest of a region or country. *suroeste, sudoeste* ❑ *...small towns in the southwestern part of the country.* *...poblaciones pequeñas en la parte suroeste del país.*

**sou|venir** /suvənɪər/ (**souvenirs**) N-COUNT A **souvenir** is something which you buy or keep to remind you of a vacation, place, or event. *souvenir, recuerdo* ❑ *...a souvenir of the summer of 1992.* *...un recuerdo del verano de 1992.*

**sov|er|eign** /sɒvrɪn/ (**sovereigns**) 1 ADJ A **sovereign** state or country is independent and not under the authority of any other country. *soberano* ❑ *They are now independent sovereign states.* *Ahora son estados soberanos, independientes.* 2 ADJ **Sovereign** is used to describe the person or institution that has the highest power in a country. *soberano* ❑ *Every organized society needs a sovereign power.* *Toda sociedad organizada necesita un poder soberano.* 3 N-COUNT A **sovereign** is a king, queen, or other royal ruler of a country. *soberano, soberana* ❑ *In March 1889, she became the first British sovereign to travel to Spain.* *En marzo de 1889 se convirtió en la primera soberana británica en viajar a España.*

**sov|er|eign|ty** /sɒvrɪnti/ N-UNCOUNT **Sovereignty** is the power that a country has to govern itself or another country or state. *soberanía* ❑ *It is vital to protect our national sovereignty.* *Es vital proteger la soberanía nacional.*

**sow**
1 VERB USES
2 NOUN USE

1 **sow** /soʊ/ (**sows, sowing, sowed, sown**) 1 V-T If you **sow** seeds or **sow** an area of land **with** seeds, you plant the seeds in the ground. *plantar, sembrar* ❑ *Sow the seed in a warm place in February/March.* *En febrero o marzo siembra las semillas en un lugar cálido.*

**2** V-T If someone **sows** an undesirable feeling or situation, they cause it to begin and develop. *sembrar* ❑ *...an attempt to sow confusion and terror among the people. ...un intento por sembrar la confusión y el terror entre la gente.*

**❷ sow** /saʊ/ (**sows**) N-COUNT A **sow** is an adult female pig. *cerda, puerca, cochina, marrana*

**soy** /sɔɪ/ N-UNCOUNT **Soy** flour, butter, or other food is made from soybeans. *soya*

**soy|bean** /sɔɪbin/ (**soybeans**) also **soy bean** N-COUNT **Soybeans** are beans that can be eaten or used to make flour, oil, or soy sauce. *frijol de soya*

**soy sauce** N-UNCOUNT **Soy sauce** is a dark brown liquid made from soybeans and is used as a flavoring, especially in Asian cooking. *salsa de soya*

**spa** /spɑ/ (**spas**) N-COUNT A **spa** is a place where water with minerals in it comes out of the ground. *spa, balneario de aguas termales* ❑ *...Fiuggi, a spa town famous for its water. ...Fiuggi, balneario famoso por sus aguas termales.*

**space** /speɪs/ (**spaces, spacing, spaced**) **1** N-VAR You use **space** to refer to an area of any size that is empty or available. *espacio, lugar, sitio* ❑ *They cut down more trees to make space for houses. Derribaron más árboles para hacer lugar a las casas.* ❑ *I had plenty of space to write. Tenía mucho espacio para escribir.* ❑ *The space underneath could be used as a storage area. El espacio de abajo puede utilizarse para almacenar cosas.* **2** N-SING A **space of** time is a period of time. *espacio, lapso* ❑ *They've come a long way in a short space of time. Han recorrido mucho camino en un lapso corto.* **3** N-UNCOUNT **Space** is the area beyond the Earth's atmosphere, where the stars and planets are. *espacio* ❑ *The six astronauts will spend ten days in space. Los seis astronautas pasarán diez días en el espacio.* **4** V-T If you **space** a series of things, you arrange them so that they are not all together but have gaps or intervals of time between them. *espaciar, separar* ❑ *Women are having fewer children and spacing them further apart. Las mujeres tienen menos hijos ahora, y más separados uno de otro.* ● **Space out** means the same as **space**. *espaciar, separar* ❑ *He talks quite slowly and spaces his words out. Habla más bien despacio, y separa las palabras.* ● **spac|ing** N-UNCOUNT *distancia, separación* ❑ *We felt the size of the yards and the spacing between the homes was better here than elsewhere. Pensamos que el tamaño del jardín y la distancia entre una y otra casa son mejores aquí.* **5** N-VAR In dance, **space** refers to the immediate space around the body in all directions. **Space** is also the place where a dance takes place. *espacio* **6** → see also **airspace, breathing space, outer space**
→ see **moon, satellite**

**space|craft** /speɪskræft/ (**spacecraft**) N-COUNT A **spacecraft** is a rocket or other vehicle that can travel in space. *nave espacial* ❑ *...the world's largest and most expensive spacecraft. ...la nave espacial más grande y más costosa del mundo.*

**space probe** (**space probes**) N-COUNT A **space probe** is a spacecraft with no people in it which is sent into space in order to study the planets and send information about them back to Earth. *sonda espacial*

**space|ship** /speɪsʃɪp/ (**spaceships**) N-COUNT A **spaceship** is the same as a **spacecraft**. *nave espacial*

**space shut|tle** (**space shuttles**) N-COUNT A **space shuttle** is a spacecraft that is designed to travel into space and back to Earth several times. *transbordador espacial*

**space sta|tion** (**space stations**) N-COUNT A **space station** is a place built for astronauts to live and work in, which is sent into space and then keeps going around the Earth. *estación espacial*
→ see **satellite**

**space suit** (**space suits**) also **space-suit** N-COUNT A **spacesuit** is a special protective suit that is worn by astronauts in space. *traje espacial*

**spa|cious** /speɪʃəs/ ADJ A **spacious** room or other place is large in size or area, so that you can move around freely in it. *espacioso, amplio* ❑ *The house has a spacious kitchen and dining area. La cocina y el área de comedor de la casa son amplios.*

**spade** /speɪd/ (**spades**) **1** N-COUNT A **spade** is a tool used for digging, with a flat metal blade and a long handle. *pala* ❑ *...a garden spade. ...una pala de jardinería.* **2** N-UNCOUNT **Spades** is one of the four suits in a deck of playing cards. Each card in the suit is marked with one or more black symbols: ♠. *espada* ❑ *...the ace of spades. ...el as de espadas.* ● A **spade** is a playing card of this suit. *espada* ❑ *He should play a spade now. Ahora debería tirar una espada.*
→ see **garden**

**spa|ghet|ti** /spəgɛti/ N-UNCOUNT **Spaghetti** is a type of pasta which looks like long pieces of string. *spaghetti, espagueti*

**spam** /spæm/ (**spams, spamming, spammed**) V-T In computing, to **spam** people or organizations means to send unwanted e-mail to a large number of them, usually as advertising. *enviar spam, correspondencia electrónica no deseada* [COMPUTING] ❑ *...programs that let you spam the newspapers. ...programas que permiten enviar publicidad no deseada a los periódicos.* ● **Spam** is also a noun. *spam* ❑ *People are sick of spam. La gente está cansada de los correos electrónicos no deseados.* ● **spam|mer** /spæmər/ N-COUNT (**spammers**) *spammer* ❑ *We want to stop the spammers. Queremos detener a los spammers.*

**span** /spæn/ (**spans, spanning, spanned**) **1** N-COUNT A **span** is the period of time between two dates or events during which something exists, functions, or happens. *distancia, lapso, periodo* ❑ *The batteries had a life span of six hours. Las baterías duran seis horas.* **2** N-COUNT Your concentration **span** or your attention **span** is the length of time you are able to concentrate on something or be interested in it. *periodo de atención* ❑ *His concentration span was short. No podía mantener la concentración por mucho tiempo.* **3** V-T If something **spans** a long period of time, it lasts throughout that period of time or relates to that whole period of time. *durar, extenderse, cubrir, abarcar* ❑ *His professional career spanned 16 years. Su carrera profesional se prolongó por 16 años.* **4** N-COUNT The **span** of something that extends or is spread out sideways is the total width of it from one end to the other. *envergadura* ❑ *The butterfly has a 2-inch wing span. La envergadura alar de la mariposa es de 5 centímetros* **5** V-T A bridge or other structure that **spans** something such as a river or a valley stretches right across it. *atravesar* ❑ *There is a footbridge that spans the little stream. Hay un puente*

*peatonal que atraviesa el riachuelo.*
→ see **bridge**

**Word Partnership** Usar *span* con:

ADJ. **brief** span 1
**short** span 1 4
N. **life** span, **time** span 1
**attention** span 2
span **years** 3

**spare** /spɛər/ (**spares, sparing, spared**) 1 ADJ You use **spare** to describe something that is the same as things that you are already using, but that you do not need yet and are keeping ready in case another one is needed. *de más, adicional* ❑ *It's useful to have a spare pair of glasses. Es conveniente tener un par de anteojos de repuesto.* ❑ *I'll give you the spare key. Te doy el duplicado de la llave.* ● **Spare** is also a noun. *repuesto, refacción, reserva* ❑ *In case you get a flat tire, you should always carry a spare. Siempre debes traer una llanta de refacción, por si se te ponchara alguna.* 2 ADJ You use **spare** to describe something that is not being used by anyone, and is therefore available for someone to use. *de más, de sobra* ❑ *They don't have a lot of spare cash. No les sobra mucho dinero.* ❑ *You can stay in the spare bedroom. Te puedes quedar en el cuarto de visitas.* 3 V-I If you have something such as time, money, or space **to spare,** you have some extra time, money, or space that you have not used or which you do not need. *sobrar, tener disponible* ❑ *We got to the airport with three hours to spare. Llegamos al aeropuerto tres horas antes.* 4 V-T If you **spare** time or another resource **for** a particular purpose, you make it available for that purpose. *contar con* ❑ *I can only spare 35 minutes for this meeting. Sólo tengo 35 minutos para esta reunión.* 5 V-T If you **spare** someone an unpleasant experience, you prevent them from suffering it. *evitar algo a alguien* ❑ *I wanted to spare her the embarrassment of talking about it. Quería ahorrarle la vergüenza de hablar de eso.*

**Thesaurus** *spare* Ver también:

ADJ. additional, backup, emergency, extra, reserve 1 2

**Word Partnership** Usar *spare* con:

N. spare **change**, spare **equipment** 1
spare **bedroom** 2
**a moment to** spare, **time to** spare 3

**spare part** (**spare parts**) N-COUNT **Spare parts** are parts that you can buy separately to replace old or broken parts in a piece of equipment. *repuesto, refacción* ❑ *They sell spare parts for washing machines. Venden refacciones para lavadoras.*

**spare time** N-UNCOUNT Your **spare time** is the time during which you do not have to work and you can do whatever you like. *tiempo libre, ratos libres* ❑ *In her spare time she read books on cooking. En su tiempo libre lee libros de cocina.*

**spare tire** (**spare tires**) 1 N-COUNT A **spare tire** is a wheel with a tire on it that you keep in your car in case you get a flat tire and need to replace one of your wheels. *llanta de refacción, rueda de recambio, rueda de repuesto* 2 N-COUNT If you describe someone as having a **spare tire,** you mean that they are fat around the waist. *llanta, llantita, lonja* [INFORMAL]

**spark** /spɑrk/ (**sparks, sparking, sparked**) 1 N-COUNT A **spark** is a tiny bright piece of burning material that flies up from something that is burning. *chispa* ❑ *Sparks flew out of the fire in all directions. Del fuego volaron chispas en todas direcciones.* 2 N-COUNT A **spark** is a flash of light caused by electricity. *chispa* ❑ *I saw a spark when I connected the wires. Vi una chispa cuando conecté los cables.* 3 N-COUNT A **spark of** a quality or feeling, especially a desirable one, is a small but noticeable amount of it. *chispa, gracia* ❑ *His music does not have that vital spark of imagination. Su música no tiene ni pizca de imaginación.* 4 V-T If one thing **sparks** another, the first thing causes the second thing to start happening. *desatar, desencadenar, provocar* ❑ *We had a class on space exploration that really sparked my interest. Tuvimos una clase sobre la exploración del espacio que de veras despertó mi interés.* ● **Spark off** means the same as **spark.** *desatar, desencadenar, provocar* ❑ *What sparked off their quarrel? ¿Qué desató la pelea?*
→ see **fire**

**Word Partnership** Usar *spark* con:

PREP. spark **from a fire** 1
V. **ignite a** spark, **provide a** spark 2 3
N. spark **conflict**, spark **debate**, spark **interest**, spark **a reaction** 4

**spar|kle** /spɑrkəl/ (**sparkles, sparkling, sparkled**) V-I If something **sparkles,** it is clear and bright and shines with a lot of very small points of light. *brillar, chispear, destellar* ❑ *The jewels on her fingers sparkled. Las joyas de sus dedos brillaban.* ❑ *His bright eyes sparkled. Sus brillantes ojos chispeaban.* ● **Sparkle** is also a noun. *destello, brillo, chispa* ❑ *...the sparkle of colored glass. ...el brillo del vidrio de colores.*

**spark plug** (**spark plugs**) N-COUNT A **spark plug** is a device in the engine of a motor vehicle, which produces electric sparks to make the gasoline burn. *bujía*
→ see **engine**

**spar|row** /spæroʊ/ (**sparrows**) N-COUNT A **sparrow** is a small brown bird that is very common in the United States. *gorrión*

**spa|tial** /speɪʃəl/ ADJ **Spatial** is used to describe things relating to the position of things in space. *espacial* ❑ *...a diagram showing the spatial distribution of the population. ...un diagrama que muestra la distribución espacial de la población.* ● **spa|tial|ly** ADV *desde la perspectiva espacial* ❑ *...spatially remote cultures. ...culturas muy alejadas en el espacio.*

**speak** /spik/ (**speaks, speaking, spoke, spoken**) 1 V-I When you **speak,** you use your voice in order to say something. *hablar* ❑ *He opened his mouth to speak. Abrió la boca para decir algo.* ❑ *I rang the hotel and spoke to Louie. Llamé al hotel y hablé con Louie.* ❑ *He often speaks about his mother. Habla con frecuencia de su madre.* ● **speak|er** N-COUNT (**speakers**) *hablante, el que habla o la que habla* ❑ *You can understand a lot from the speaker's tone of voice. Puedes entender mucho por el tono de voz del que habla.* ● **spo|ken** ADJ *hablado, oral* ❑ *They took tests in written and spoken English. Les hicieron pruebas de inglés escrito y hablado.* 2 V-I When someone **speaks to** a group of people, they make a speech. *hablar, pronunciar un discurso* ❑ *He spoke to an audience at the Denver International Film Festival. Pronunció un discurso en el Festival Internacional de Cine de Denver.* ❑ *He will speak at the Democratic Convention. Hablará en la Convención de los Demócratas.* ● **speak|er** N-COUNT *orador u oradora* ❑ *Bruce Wyatt will be the guest speaker at next month's meeting. Bruce Wyatt será el orador huésped de la reunión del mes próximo.* **3** V-I If you **speak for** a group of people, you make their views and demands known, or represent them. *hablar por* ❑ *It is the job of the Church to speak for the poor. Es tarea de la iglesia hablar en favor de los pobres.* ❑ *I speak for all 7,000 members of our organization. Hablo por los 7,000 miembros de nuestra organización.* **4** V-T If you **speak** a foreign language, you know the language and are able to have a conversation in it. *hablar* ❑ *He speaks English. Habla inglés.* ● **speak|er** N-COUNT *hablante* ❑ *A fifth of the population are Russian speakers. Una quinta parte de la población está conformada por hablantes de ruso.* **5** V-RECIP If two people **are not speaking,** they no longer talk to each other because they have argued. *dejarse de hablar, retirar la palabar* ❑ *He is not speaking to his mother because she threw away his TV. No le habla a su madre porque le tiró su televisión.* **6** V-I If you say that something **speaks for itself**, you mean that its meaning or quality is so obvious that it does not need explaining or pointing out. *hablar por sí mismo* ❑ *The facts speak for themselves in this case. En este caso, los hechos hablan por sí solos.* **7** PHRASE If you **speak well of** someone or **speak highly of** someone, you say good things about them. If you **speak ill of** someone, you criticize them. *hablar de alguien, decir algo de alguien* ❑ *Everyone speaks highly of him. Todos hablan muy bien de él.* **8** PHRASE You use **so to speak** to draw attention to the fact that you are describing or referring to something in a way that may be amusing or unusual rather than completely accurate. *por así decir* ❑ *He was, so to speak, one of the family. Como quien dice, era de la familia.*

▸ **speak out** PHR-VERB If you **speak out** against something or in favor of something, you say publicly that you think it is bad or good. *dar la propia opinión* ❑ *He spoke out strongly against the company's plans. Habló muy claro en contra de los planes de la compañía.*

▸ **speak up** PHR-VERB If you ask someone to **speak up,** you are asking them to speak more loudly. *hablar más fuerte* ❑ *I'm quite deaf—you'll have to speak up. Estoy medio sorda —tendrá que hablar más fuerte.*

| **Thesaurus** | *speak* Ver también: |
|---|---|
| V. | articulate, communicate, declare, talk **1** |

| **Word Partnership** | Usar *speak* con: |
|---|---|
| ADV. | speak **clearly**, speak **directly**, speak **louder**, speak **slowly** **1**<br>speak **freely**, speak **publicly** **1** **2** |
| N. | **chance to** speak, **opportunity to** speak, speak **the truth** **1** **2**<br>speak **English/French/Spanish**, speak **a (foreign) language** **4** |

**speak|er** /spikər/ (**speakers**) **1** N-PROPER; N-VOC In the legislature or parliament of many countries, the **Speaker** is the person who is in charge of meetings. *presidente* ❑ *He used to be the speaker of the California Assembly. Solía ser el presidente de la Asamblea de California.* **2** N-COUNT A **speaker** is a piece of electrical equipment, for example part of a radio or set of equipment for playing CDs or tapes, through which sound comes out. *bocina, bafle* ❑ *I bought a pair of speakers for my computer. Compré un par de bocinas para mi computadora.*

**spear** /spɪər/ (**spears, spearing, speared**) **1** N-COUNT A **spear** is a weapon consisting of a long pole with a sharp metal point attached to the end. *lanza, arpón* **2** V-T If you **spear** something, you push or throw a pointed object into it. *alancear, arponear, pinchar* ❑ *He speared a piece of chicken with his fork. Pinchó una pieza de pollo con el tenedor.*
→ see **army**

**spe|cia|tion** /spiʃieɪʃᵊn/ N-UNCOUNT **Speciation** is the development of new species of animals or plants, which occurs when two populations of the same species develop in different ways. *especiación, evolución de las especies* [TECHNICAL]

**spe|cif|ic grav|ity** (**specific gravities**) N-VAR The **specific gravity** of a substance is a measure of its weight, compared to the weight of an equal amount of water. *gravedad específica, peso específico* [TECHNICAL]

**spe|cif|ic heat ca|pac|ity** (**specific heat capacities**) N-VAR The **specific heat capacity** of a substance is the amount of heat that is needed in order to change the temperature of the substance by one degree Celsius. *calor específico* [TECHNICAL]

**spe|cial** /spɛʃᵊl/ (**specials**) **1** ADJ Someone or something that is **special** is better or more important than other people or things. *especial* ❑ *You're very special to me. Eres muy especial para mí.* ❑ *My special guest will be Jerry Seinfeld. Mi invitado especial será Jerry Seinfeld.* **2** ADJ **Special** means different from normal. *especial* ❑ *In special cases, a child can be educated at home. En casos especiales, se puede educar al niño en casa.* ❑ *Did you notice anything special about him? ¿Notaste algo especial en él?* **3** ADJ You use **special** to describe something that relates to one particular person, group, or place. *especial, específico* ❑ *Every person has his or her own special problems. Cada cual tiene sus propios problemas específicos.*

| **Thesaurus** | *special* Ver también: |
|---|---|
| ADJ. | distinctive, exceptional, unique; (*ant.*) ordinary **1** **2** |

**spe|cial ef|fect** (**special effects**) N-COUNT In a movie, **special effects** are unusual pictures or sounds that are created by using special techniques. *efectos especiales* ❑ *...a horror film with amazing special effects. ...una película de horror con efectos especiales asombrosos.*

**spe|cial|ist** /spɛʃəlɪst/ (**specialists**) N-COUNT A **specialist** is a person who has a particular skill or knows a lot about a particular subject. *especialista* ❑ *Peckham is a cancer specialist. Peckham es especialista en cáncer.*

**spe|cial|ize** /spɛʃəlaɪz/ (**specializes, specializing, specialized**) V-I If you **specialize in** a thing, you know a lot about it and concentrate a

S

great deal of your time and energy on it, especially in your work or when you are studying or training. *especializarse* ❑ *...a professor who specializes in Russian history. ...un profesor que se especializa en la historia rusa.* • **spe|ciali|za|tion** /spɛʃəlɪzeɪʃᵊn/ N-VAR (**specializations**) *especialización* ❑ *We encourage broad general knowledge rather than specialization. Estimulamos la adquisición del conocimiento en general, antes bien que la especialización.*

**spe|cial|ized** /spɛʃəlaɪzd/ ADJ Someone or something that is **specialized** is trained or developed for a particular purpose or area of knowledge. *especializado* ❑ *Children with learning difficulties need specialized support. Los niños con dificultades para el aprendizaje necesitan un apoyo especializado.*

**spe|cial|ly** /spɛʃəli/ **1** ADV If something has been done **specially for** a particular person or purpose, it has been done only for that person or purpose. *especialmente* ❑ *...a soap specially designed for sensitive skin. ...un jabón diseñado especialmente para la piel sensible.* ❑ *Patrick needs to use specially adapted computer equipment. Patrick necesita un equipo de computación adaptado especialmente para él.* **2** ADV **Specially** is used to mean more than usually or more than other things. *particularmente* [INFORMAL] ❑ *On his birthday I got up specially early. El día de su cumpleaños me levanté particularmente temprano.*

**spe|cial|ty** /spɛʃᵊlti/ (**specialties**) **1** N-COUNT Someone's **specialty** is a particular type of work that they do most or do best, or a subject that they know a lot about. *especialidad* ❑ *His specialty is international law. Su especialidad es el derecho internacional.* **2** N-COUNT A **specialty** of a particular place is a special food or product that is always very good there. *especialidad* ❑ *...seafood and other specialties. ...mariscos y otras especialidades.*

**spe|cies** /spiʃiz/ (**species**) N-COUNT A **species** is a class of plants or animals whose members have the same main characteristics and are able to breed with each other. *especie* ❑ *Many species could disappear from our earth. Muchas especies podrían desaparecer de la Tierra.*

→ see **amphibian, evolution**

**spe|cif|ic** /spɪsɪfɪk/ **1** ADJ You use **specific** to refer to a particular exact area, problem, or subject. *específico* ❑ *Do you have pain in any specific part of your body? ¿Siente dolor en alguna parte específica del cuerpo?* ❑ *There are several specific problems. Hay varios problemas específicos.* **2** ADJ If someone is **specific**, they give a description that is precise and exact. You can also use **specific** to describe their description. *específico* ❑ *She refused to be more specific about why they left the country. Se rehusó a ser más específico sobre la razón de que hayan salido del país.* **3** ADJ Something that is **specific to** a particular thing is connected with that thing only. *específico* ❑ *Some problems are specific to a particular job, but some are experienced by everyone. Algunos problemas son específicos de un trabajo en particular, pero otros los tiene todo el mundo.*

S

**spe|cifi|cal|ly** /spɪsɪfɪkli/ **1** ADV You use **specifically** to emphasize that something is given special attention and considered separately from other things of the same kind. *específicamente* ❑ *...a nursing home designed specifically for people with cancer. ...una clínica destinada específicamente a la gente con cáncer.* ❑ *The show is aimed specifically at children. El espectáculo está dirigido específicamente a los niños.* **2** ADV You use **specifically** to add something more precise or exact to what you have already said. *concretamente* ❑ *Death frightens me, specifically my own death. La muerte me atemoriza, concretamente, mi propia muerte.* ❑ *...the Christian, and specifically Protestant, religion. ...la religión cristiana, concretamente, la protestante.* **3** ADV If you state or describe something **specifically,** you state or describe it precisely and clearly. *expresamente* ❑ *I specifically asked you to come at 8 o'clock. Te pedí expresamente que vinieras a las ocho en punto.*

**spe|cif|ics** /spɪsɪfɪks/ N-PLURAL The **specifics** of a subject are the details of it that need to be considered. *detalles (específicos)* ❑ *Can you tell me more about the specifics of the project? ¿Puede darme más detalles (específicos) del proyecto?*

**speci|fy** /spɛsɪfaɪ/ (**specifies, specifying, specified**) V-T If you **specify** what should happen or be done, you explain it in an exact and detailed way. *especificar* ❑ *Each recipe specifies the size of egg to be used. Cada receta especifica el tamaño de los huevos que lleva.* ❑ *A new law specified that houses must be a certain distance from one another. Una nueva ley especificó que las casas deben estar a cierta distancia unas de otras.*

**speci|men** /spɛsɪmɪn/ (**specimens**) N-COUNT A **specimen of** something is an example or a small amount of it which gives an idea of what the whole of it is like. *espécimen, muestra* ❑ *Job applicants have to give a specimen of handwriting. Los solicitantes de empleo deben entregar una muestra de su escritura.*

| Word Link | *spect ≈ looking : spectacle, spectacular, spectator* |
|---|---|

**spec|ta|cle** /spɛktəkᵊl/ (**spectacles**) N-COUNT A **spectacle** is an interesting or impressive sight or event. *espectáculo* ❑ *The fireworks were an amazing spectacle. Los fuegos artificiales fueron un espectáculo asombroso.*

**spec|tacu|lar** /spɛktækyələr/ (**spectaculars**) **1** ADJ Something that is **spectacular** is very impressive or dramatic. *espectacular* ❑ *...spectacular views of Sugar Loaf Mountain. ...vistas espectaculares del Pan de Azúcar.* • **spec|tacu|lar|ly** ADV *espectacularmente* ❑ *Our sales increased spectacularly. Nuestras ventas aumentaron espectacularmente.* **2** N-COUNT A **spectacular** is a show or performance which is very grand and impressive. *gran espectáculo* ❑ *...a television spectacular. ...un gran espectáculo para la televisión.*

| Word Link | *ator ≈ one who does : educator, investigator, spectator* |
|---|---|

**spec|ta|tor** /spɛkteɪtər/ (**spectators**) N-COUNT A **spectator** is someone who watches something, especially a sports event. *espectador* ❑ *Thirty thousand spectators watched the game. Treinta mil espectadores presenciaron el juego.*

**spec|trum** /spɛktrəm/ (**spectra** or **spectrums**) **1** N-SING **The spectrum** is the range of different colors which is produced when light passes through a glass prism or through a drop of water.

*espectro* **2** N-COUNT A **spectrum** is a range of a particular type of thing. *gama, espectro* ❑ *His moods covered the entire emotional spectrum. Sus estados de humor cubrían toda la gama de estados emocionales.* ❑ *Politicians across the political spectrum have criticized her. Los políticos de todo el espectro político la han criticado.*

**specu|late** /spɛkyəleɪt/ (**speculates, speculating, speculated**) **1** V-T/V-I If you **speculate** about something, you make guesses about its nature or identity, or about what might happen. *especular, conjeturar* ❑ *There is no point speculating about why she left. No tiene sentido especular sobre la razón de que se haya ido.* ❑ *Doctors speculate that his death was caused by a blow on the head. Los médicos conjeturan que su muerte fue provocada por un golpe en la cabeza.* ● **specu|la|tion** /spɛkyəleɪʃən/ N-VAR (**speculations**) *especulación* ❑ *There has been a lot of speculation in the press about their marriage. Ha habido muchas especulaciones en la prensa sobre su matrimonio.* **2** V-I If someone **speculates** financially, they buy property, stocks, or shares, in the hope of being able to sell them again at a higher price and make a profit. *especular* ❑ *The banks speculated in property. Los bancos especularon con las propiedades.* ● **specu|la|tor** N-COUNT (**speculators**) *especulador, especuladora* ❑ *He sold the contracts to another speculator for a profit. Vendió los contratos a otro especulador con una utilidad.*

**speech** /spitʃ/ (**speeches**) **1** N-UNCOUNT **Speech** is the ability to speak or the act of speaking. *habla* ❑ *...the development of speech in children. ...el desarrollo del habla en el niño.* ❑ *The medication can affect speech. El medicamento puede afectar al habla.* **2** N-SING Your **speech** is the way in which you speak. *habla* ❑ *His speech became slow and unclear. Su hablar se volvió lento y poco claro.* **3** N-UNCOUNT **Speech** is spoken language. *lenguaje hablado* ❑ *She understands written Spanish very well, but not speech. Entiende muy bien el español escrito, pero no el hablado.* **4** N-COUNT A **speech** is a formal talk which someone gives to an audience. *discurso* ❑ *She made a speech on the economy. Pronunció un discurso sobre la economía.* ❑ *He delivered his speech in French. Pronunció su discurso en francés.* **5** → see also **indirect speech**
→ see **election**

**Word Partnership** Usar *speech* con:

| | |
|---|---|
| ADJ. | **slurred** speech **1** **famous** speech, **major** speech, **political** speech, **recent** speech **4** |
| N. | **acceptance** speech, **campaign** speech, **keynote** speech, speech **writing** **4** |
| V. | **deliver a** speech, **give a** speech, **make a** speech, **prepare a** speech **4** |

**speed** /spid/ (**speeds, speeding, sped** or **speeded**)

The form of the past tense and past participle is **sped** in meaning **3** but **speeded** for the phrasal verb.

**1** N-VAR The **speed** of something is the rate at which it moves, happens or is done. *velocidad, rapidez* ❑ *He drove off at high speed. Se fue en el coche a toda velocidad.* ❑ *...a way to measure wind speeds. ...un método para medir la velocidad del viento.* ❑ *The speed of technological change has increased. La rapidez del cambio tecnológico ha aumentado.* **2** N-UNCOUNT **Speed** is very fast movement or travel. *velocidad* ❑ *Speed is essential for all athletes. La velocidad es fundamental para todos los atletas.* **3** V-I If you **speed** somewhere, you move or travel there quickly, usually in a vehicle. *ir a gran velocidad* ❑ *Trains speed through the tunnel at 186 mph. Los trenes pasan por el túnel a 300 kilómetros por hora.* **4** V-I Someone who **is speeding** is driving a vehicle faster than the legal speed limit. *exceder el límite de velocidad* ❑ *Police stopped him because he was speeding. La policía lo detuvo por exceder el límite de velocidad.* ● **speed|ing** N-UNCOUNT *exceso de velocidad* ❑ *He was fined for speeding. Lo multaron por exceso de velocidad.*
▸ **speed up** PHR-VERB When something **speeds up** or when you **speed** it **up**, it moves, happens, or is done more quickly. *acelerarse, darse prisa* ❑ *My breathing speeded up a bit. Mi respiración se aceleró un poco.* ❑ *We need to speed up a solution to the problem. Necesitamos darnos prisa con la solución del problema.*

**speed bump** (**speed bumps**) **1** N-COUNT A **speed bump** is a raised part in a road that is designed to make the traffic travel more slowly. *tope* **2** N-COUNT A **speed bump** is something that stops a person or thing from progressing. *obstáculo* ❑ *It was just a minor speed bump in Anglo-American relations. Fue sólo un obstáculo menor en las relaciones anglo-estadounidenses.*

**speed da|ting** N-UNCOUNT **Speed dating** is a method of introducing single people to potential partners by arranging for them to meet a series of people on a single occasion. *sesión de contactos rápidos*

**speed lim|it** (**speed limits**) N-COUNT The **speed limit** on a road is the maximum speed at which you are legally allowed to drive. *límite de velocidad* ❑ *I was fined $158 for breaking the speed limit. Me multaron con 158 dólares por rebasar el límite de velocidad.*

**speed|way** /spidweɪ/ (**speedways**) **1** N-UNCOUNT **Speedway** is the sport of racing motorcycles on special tracks. *carrera de motocicletas* **2** N-COUNT A **speedway** is a special track for car or motorcycle racing. *pista para carreras de motocicletas*

**speedy** /spidi/ (**speedier, speediest**) ADJ A **speedy** process, event, or action happens or is done very quickly. *rápido, pronto* ❑ *We wish Bill a speedy recovery. Le deseamos a Billy una pronta recuperación.*

**spell** /spɛl/ (**spells, spelling, spelled** **1** V-T When you **spell** a word, you write or speak each letter in the word in the correct order. *deletrear* ❑ *He spelled his name. Deletreó su nombre.* ❑ *How do you spell "potato?" ¿Cómo se deletrea patata?* ● **Spell out** means the same as **spell**. *deletrear* ❑ *If I don't know a word, I ask them to spell it out for me. Si no conozco una palabra, les pido que me la deletreen.* **2** V-T/V-I Someone who can **spell** knows the correct order of letters in words. *deletrear* ❑ *Many of the students can't spell. Muchos de los estudiantes no saben deletrear.* ❑ *He can't even spell his own name. Ni siquiera sabe deletrear su propio nombre.* **3** V-T If something **spells** a particular outcome, often an unpleasant one, it suggests that this will be the result. *significar* ❑ *This plan could spell disaster for local people. Este plan podría significar un desastre para la gente del lugar.* **4** N-COUNT A **spell of** a particular type of weather or a particular activity is a short period of time during which this type of weather or activity occurs. *período* ❑ *There has been a long spell of dry weather. Ha habido un largo período de secas.* **5** N-COUNT A **spell** is a situation in which events are controlled by a magical power. *encanto, encantamiento, hechizo* ❑ *They say a witch cast a spell on her. Dicen que una bruja la hechizó.* **6** → see also **spelling**

▶ **spell out** **1** PHR-VERB If you **spell** something **out**, you explain it in detail or in a very clear way. *explicar con detalle* ❑ *You need to spell out exactly how you feel. Necesita explicar con detalle cómo se siente exactamente.* **2** → see **spell 1**

**Word Partnership** Usar *spell* con:

| | |
|---|---|
| N. | spell **a name/word** **1**<br>spell **the end of *something***, spell **trouble** **3** |
| V. | **can/can't** spell ***something*** **2**<br>**break a** spell, **cast a** spell **5** |

**spell-check** (**spell-checks, spell-checking, spell-checked**) also **spell check** V-T If you **spell-check** something you have written on a computer, you use a special program to check whether you have made any spelling mistakes. *corregir la ortografía* [COMPUTING] ❑ *This program allows you to spell-check over 100,000 different words. Este programa le permite corregir la ortografía de más de 100,000 palabras diferentes.*

**spell-checker** (**spell-checkers**) also **spell checker** N-COUNT A **spell-checker** is a special program on a computer which you can use to check whether something you have written contains any spelling mistakes. *corrector ortográfico* [COMPUTING]

**spell|ing** /spɛlɪŋ/ (**spellings**) **1** N-COUNT A **spelling** is the correct order of the letters in a word. *ortografía* ❑ *I'm not sure about the spelling of his name. No estoy seguro de cómo se escribe su nombre.* **2** N-UNCOUNT **Spelling** is the ability to spell words in the correct way. It is also an attempt to spell a word in the correct way. *deletreo* ❑ *His spelling is very bad. Su deletreo es muy malo.* **3** → see also **spell**

**spell|ing bee** (**spelling bees**) N-COUNT A **spelling bee** is a competition in which children try to spell words correctly. Anyone who makes a mistake is out and the competition continues until only one person is left. *concurso de ortografía*

S

**spe|lunk|er** /spɪlʌŋkər/ (**spelunkers**) N-COUNT A **spelunker** is someone who goes into underground caves and tunnels as a leisure activity. *espeleólogo aficionado o espeleóloga aficionada*
→ see **cave**

**spend** /spɛnd/ (**spends, spending, spent**) **1** V-T When you **spend** money, you pay money for things that you want or need. *gastar* ❑ *I have spent all my money. Gasté todo mi dinero.* ❑ *Companies spend millions advertising their products. Las empresas gastan millones en la publicidad de sus productos.* **2** V-T If you **spend** time or energy doing something, you use your time or effort doing it. *dedicar* ❑ *She spends a lot of time working on her garden. Le dedica mucho tiempo a su jardín.* **3** V-T If you **spend** a period of time in a place, you stay there for a period of time. *pasar* ❑ *We spent the night in a hotel. Pasamos la noche en un hotel.*

**Word Partnership** Usar *spend* con:

| | |
|---|---|
| N. | spend **billions/millions, companies** spend, **consumers** spend, spend **money** **1**<br>spend **an amount** **1** **2**<br>spend **energy**, spend **time** **2**<br>spend **a day**, spend **hours/minutes**, spend **months/weeks/years**, spend **a night**, spend **a weekend** **3** |
| V. | **afford to** spend, **expect to** spend, **going to** spend, **plan to** spend **1** – **3** |

**sperm** /spɜrm/ (**sperms**)

Sperm can also be used as the plural form.

**1** N-COUNT A **sperm** is a cell which is produced in the sex organs of a male animal and can enter a female animal's egg and fertilize it. *espermatozoide* ❑ *A baby is conceived when a sperm joins with an egg. El niño es concebido cuando el espermatozoide se introduce en el óvulo.* **2** N-UNCOUNT **Sperm** is used to refer to the liquid that contains sperm when it is produced. *semen, esperma* ❑ *...a test tube of sperm. ...una probeta de semen.*
→ see **reproduction**

**sperm bank** (**sperm banks**) N-COUNT A **sperm bank** is a place where sperm is frozen and stored so that it can be used to help women become pregnant. *banco de semen, banco de esperma*

**SPF** /ɛs pi ɛf/ (**SPFs**) N-COUNT **SPF** is used before a number to indicate the degree of protection from the sun's rays that is provided by a sunscreen or similar product. The higher a product's SPF, the more protection it provides. **SPF** is an abbreviation for "sun protection factor." *FPS (factor de protección solar)* ❑ *Always use sunscreen of at least SPF 15. Use siempre una crema de protección solar con un factor de al menos 15.*

**sphere** /sfɪər/ (**spheres**) **1** N-COUNT A **sphere** is an object that is completely round in shape like a ball. *esfera* ❑ *The Earth is not a perfect sphere. La Tierra no es una esfera perfecta.* **2** N-COUNT A **sphere of** activity or interest is a particular area of activity or interest. *esfera, ámbito* ❑ *...the sphere of international politics. ...la esfera de la política internacional.*
→ see **solid, volume**

**spice** /spaɪs/ (**spices**) N-VAR A **spice** is a part of a plant, or a powder made from that part, which you put in food to give it flavor. Cinnamon, ginger, and paprika are spices. *especia* ❑ *...herbs and spices. ...hierbas y especias.*
→ see Word Web: **spice**

**spicy** /spaɪsi/ (**spicier, spiciest**) ADJ **Spicy** food is strongly flavored with spices. *picante, muy condimentado* ❑ *Thai food is hot and spicy. La comida tailandesa es muy condimentada y picante.*
→ see **spice**

**spi|der** /spaɪdər/ (**spiders**) N-COUNT A **spider** is a small creature with eight legs. *araña*

**spif|fy** /spɪfi/ (**spiffier, spiffiest**) ADJ Something that is **spiffy** is stylish and attractive and often new. Someone who looks **spiffy** is stylishly and attractively dressed. *elegante* ❑ *He bought a spiffy new car. Compró un elegante coche nuevo.*

**spig|ot** /spɪgət/ (**spigots**) N-COUNT A **spigot** is a

**Word Web** spice

While studying the use of **spices** in cooking, scientists found that many spices can help prevent disease. Bacteria can grow quickly on food and cause serious illnesses in humans. The researchers found that many spices kill bacteria. For example, **garlic**, **onion**, allspice, and oregano kill almost all common **germs**. **Cinnamon**, tarragon, cumin, and **chili peppers** also stop about 75% of bacteria. And even common, everyday **black pepper** kills about 25% of all germs. The scientists also found that food is connected to climate. **Spicy** food is common in hot climates. **Bland** food is common in cold climates.

faucet or tap. *llave, canilla, espita*

**spike** /spaɪk/ (**spikes**) N-COUNT A **spike** is a long piece of metal with a sharp point. *punta* ❑ *...a high wall with iron spikes at the top. ...un alto muro con puntas de hierro encima.*

**spike heels** N-PLURAL **Spike heels** are women's shoes with very high narrow heels. *zapatos con tacón de aguja*

**spill** /spɪl/ (**spills, spilling, spilled** or **spilt**) **1** V-T/V-I If a liquid **spills** or if you **spill** it, it accidentally flows over the edge of a container. *derramar(se)* ❑ *Oil spilled into the sea. El petróleo se derramó en el mar.* ❑ *He always spilled the drinks. Siempre derramaba las bebidas.* **2** V-I If people or things **spill** out of a place, they come out of it in large numbers. *rebosar* ❑ *Tears spilled out of the boy's eyes. Los ojos del niño rebosaban de lágrimas.*

spill

**spin** /spɪn/ (**spins, spinning, spun**) **1** V-T/V-I If something **spins** or if you **spin** it, it turns quickly around a central point. *girar, dar vuelta* ❑ *The disk spins 3,600 times a minute. El disco gira 3,600 veces por minuto.* ❑ *He spun the steering wheel and turned the car around. Dio vuelta al volante y regresó por donde venía.* • **Spin** is also a noun. *vuelta* ❑ *He gave the wheel a spin. Le dio una vuelta a la rueda.* **2** N-SING If someone puts a certain **spin** on an event or situation, they interpret it and try to present it in a particular way. *giro* [INFORMAL] ❑ *Even when they lose, they try to put a positive spin on it. Incluso cuando pierden tratan de darle un giro favorable a la derrota.* **3** V-T/V-I When people **spin**, they make thread by twisting together pieces of a fiber such as wool or cotton using a device or machine. *hilar, tejer* ❑ *...a machine for spinning wool. ...una maquina para hilar lana.* ❑ *She never learned how to spin. Nunca aprendió a tejer.*

▸ **spin out** PHR-VERB If you **spin** something **out**, you make it last longer than it normally would. *alargar* ❑ *It seemed that the lawyers were spinning the case out for as long as possible. Parecía que los abogados estaban alargando el caso tanto como fuese posible.*

**spin|ach** /spɪnɪtʃ/ N-UNCOUNT **Spinach** is a vegetable with large dark green leaves. *espinaca*
→ see **vegetable**

**spi|nal** /spaɪnᵊl/ ADJ **Spinal** means relating to your spine. *espinal* ❑ *...spinal fluid. ...líquido espinal, líquido raquídeo*

**spi|nal cord** (**spinal cords**) N-COUNT Your **spinal cord** is a thick cord of nerves inside your spine which connects your brain to nerves in all parts of your body. *médula espinal*
→ see **brain, nervous system**

**spine** /spaɪn/ (**spines**) N-COUNT Your **spine** is the row of bones down your back. *columna vertebral* ❑ *He suffered injuries to his spine. Sufrió varias heridas en la columna vertebral.*

**spin|ning wheel** (**spinning wheels**) also **spinning-wheel** N-COUNT A **spinning wheel** is a wooden machine that people used in their homes to make thread from wool, in former times. *rueca*
→ see **wheel**

**spin|off** /spɪnɔf/ (**spinoffs**) **1** N-COUNT A **spinoff** is an unexpected but useful or valuable result of an activity that was designed to achieve something else. *beneficio indirecto* ❑ *The research could have valuable commercial spinoffs. La investigación podría tener valiosos beneficios comerciales indirectos.* **2** N-COUNT A **spinoff** is a book, film, or television series that comes after and is related to a successful book, film, or television series. *resultado benéfico* ❑ *The movie is a spinoff from the TV series. La película es resultado del éxito de la serie de televisión.*

**spi|ral** /spaɪrəl/ (**spirals, spiraling** or **spiralling, spiraled** or **spiralled**) **1** N-COUNT A **spiral** is a shape which winds around and around, with each curve above or outside the previous one. *espiral* ❑ *The leaves are in the shape of a spiral. Las hojas tienen forma de espiral.* • **Spiral** is also an adjective. *espiral, en forma de caracol* ❑ *...a spiral staircase. ...una escalera de caracol.* **2** V-I If something **spirals** somewhere, it grows or moves in a spiral curve. *torcerse en espiral, volar en espiral* ❑ *Vines spiraled upward toward the roof. Las vides subían hacía el techo, torciéndose en espiral.* ❑ *The aircraft began spiraling out of control. El avión empezó a volar en espiral, fuera*

S

*de control.* • **Spiral** is also a noun. *espiral, voluta* ❑ *A spiral of smoke rose from the chimney. Una espiral de humo salió de la chimenea.* **3** V-I If an amount or level **spirals,** it rises quickly and at an increasing rate. *dispararse, ascender* ❑ *Prices began to spiral. Los precios empezaron a dispararse.* ❑ *...the spiraling crime rate. ...la tasa de crimen ascendente.* • **Spiral** is also a noun. *curva ascendente* ❑ *...a spiral of debt. ...una curva ascendente de endeudamiento.*

**spi|ral gal|axy** (**spiral galaxies**) N-COUNT A **spiral galaxy** is a galaxy consisting of a flat disk at the center and spiral arms that contain many young stars. *galaxia espiral*

**spir|it** /spɪrɪt/ (**spirits**) **1** N-SING Your **spirit** is the part of you that is not physical and that consists of your character and feelings. *espíritu* ❑ *The human spirit is hard to destroy. Es difícil destruir el espíritu humano.* **2** N-COUNT A person's **spirit** is the non-physical part of them that is believed to remain alive after their death. *espíritu* ❑ *He is gone, but his spirit is still with us. Se ha ido, pero su espíritu sigue con nosotros.* **3** N-COUNT A **spirit** is a ghost or supernatural being. *espíritu* ❑ *These plants protect us against evil spirits. Estas plantas nos protegen contra los malos espíritus.* **4** N-UNCOUNT **Spirit** is the courage and determination that helps people to survive in difficult times and to keep their way of life and their beliefs. *temple* ❑ *She was very brave and everyone admired her spirit. Era muy valiente y todo el mundo admiraba su temple.* **5** N-SING The **spirit** in which you do something is the attitude you have when you are doing it. *espíritu* ❑ *She took part in the game in a spirit of fun. Tomó parte en el juego por espíritu de diversión.* **6** N-SING **The spirit of** something such as a law or an agreement is the way that it was intended to be interpreted or applied. *espíritu* ❑ *These ads go against the spirit of the law. Estos anuncios van contra el espíritu de la ley.* **7** N-PLURAL Your **spirits** are your feelings at a particular time, especially feelings of happiness or unhappiness. *estado de ánimo* ❑ *At supper, everyone was in high spirits. Durante la cena, todo el mundo estaba muy animado.*

**spir|itu|al** /spɪrɪtʃuəl/ **1** ADJ **Spiritual** means relating to people's thoughts and beliefs, rather than to their bodies and physical surroundings. *espiritual* ❑ *She is a very spiritual person, and does not really care about material things. Es una persona muy espiritual y realmente no le interesan las cosas materiales.* • **spir|itu|al|ly** ADV *espiritualmente* ❑ *We need to feed children spiritually as well as physically. Necesitamos alimentar a los niños tanto física como espiritualmente.* • **spir|itu|al|ity** /spɪrɪtʃuælɪti/ N-UNCOUNT *espiritualidad* ❑ *...the spirituality of Japanese culture. ...la espiritualidad de la cultura japonesa.* **2** ADJ **Spiritual** means relating to people's religious beliefs. *espiritual* ❑ *He is the spiritual leader of the world's Catholics. Es el líder espiritual de los católicos del mundo.*
→ see **myth**

S

**spit** /spɪt/ (**spits, spitting, spit** or **spat**) **1** N-UNCOUNT **Spit** is the watery liquid produced in your mouth. *saliva* ❑ *Spit collected in her mouth. Se le llenó la boca de saliva.* **2** V-I If someone **spits,** they force an amount of liquid out of their mouth, often to show hatred or lack of respect. *escupir* ❑ *He turned and spat in disgust. Se volvió y escupió con disgusto.* ❑ *They spat at me. Me escupieron.* **3** V-T If you **spit** liquid or food somewhere, you force a small amount of it out of your mouth. *escupir* ❑ *Spit out that gum. —¡Escupe ese chicle!*

**spite** /spaɪt/ **1** PHRASE You use **in spite of** to introduce a fact which makes the rest of the statement you are making seem surprising. *a pesar de* ❑ *He hired her in spite of the fact that she had no experience. La contrató a pesar de que no tenía experiencia.* **2** PHRASE If you do something **in spite of yourself**, you do it although you did not really intend to or expect to. *en contra de nuestra voluntad* ❑ *The comment made Richard laugh in spite of himself. El comentario hizo reír a Richard en contra de su voluntad.* **3** N-UNCOUNT If you do something cruel out of **spite,** you do it because you want to hurt or upset someone. *maldad* ❑ *I didn't help him, out of spite I suppose. No lo ayudé; por maldad, supongo.* **4** V-T If you do something cruel **to spite** someone, you do it in order to hurt or upset them. *molestar* ❑ *He left all his money to his brother, to spite his wife. Le dejó todo su dinero a su hermano, para molestar a su esposa.*

**splash** /splæʃ/ (**splashes, splashing, splashed**) **1** V-I If you **splash** around or **splash** about in water, you hit or disturb the water in a noisy way. *chapotear* ❑ *People were splashing around in the water. Había gente chapoteando en el agua.* ❑ *Children love to splash in puddles. A los niños les encanta chapotear en los charcos.* **2** V-T/V-I If you **splash** a liquid somewhere or if it **splashes,** it hits someone or something and scatters in a lot of small drops. *salpicar* ❑ *He splashed water on his face. Le salpicó la cara con agua.* ❑ *A little wave splashed in my face. Una olita me salpicó la cara.* **3** N-SING A **splash** is the sound made when something hits water or falls into it. *chapoteo* ❑ *There was a splash and something fell into the water. Se oyó el chapoteo de algo que cayó al agua.* **4** N-COUNT A **splash** of a liquid is a small quantity of it that falls on something or is added to something. *salpicadura* ❑ *There were splashes on the table cloth. El mantel tenía salpicaduras.* **5** PHRASE If you **make a splash,** you become noticed or become popular because of something that you have done. *causar un revuelo* ❑ *She first made a splash in the television show "Civil Wars." Primero causó un revuelo en el programa de televisión "Guerras civiles".*

**splat|ter** /splætər/ (**splatters, splattering, splattered**) V-T/V-I If a thick wet substance **splatters** on something or is **splattered** on it, it drops or is thrown over it. *salpicar* ❑ *Rain splattered against the windows. La lluvia salpicaba contra las ventanas.* ❑ *He splattered the cloth with jam. Salpicó el trapo de mermelada.*

**splen|did** /splɛndɪd/ ADJ If you say that something is **splendid,** you mean that it is very good. *espléndido, magnífico* ❑ *The book includes some splendid photographs. El libro tiene unas fotografías magníficas.* • **splen|did|ly** ADV *de maravilla* ❑ *We get along splendidly. Nos llevamos de maravilla.*

**split** /splɪt/ (**splits, splitting**)

> The form **split** is used in the present tense and is the past tense and past participle of the verb.

**1** V-T/V-I If something **splits** or if you **split** it, it is divided into two or more parts. *partir(se), romper(se), cortar* ❑ *The ship split in two during a storm. El barco se partió en dos durante la tormenta.* ❑ *Split* *the chicken in half.* Corte el pollo en dos. **2** V-T/V-I If an organization **splits** or **is split,** one group of members disagree strongly with the other members, and may form a group of their own. *dividir(se), escindir(se)* ❑ *The party could split over this.* *El partido podría escindirse por esto.* ● **Split** is also an adjective. *dividido* ❑ *The government is deeply split over foreign policy.* *El gobierno está muy dividido respecto a la política exterior.* **3** N-COUNT A **split in** an organization is a disagreement between its members. *división, escisión, cisma* ❑ *There are rumours of a split in the military.* *Hay rumores de un cisma entre los militares.* **4** N-SING A **split between** two things is a division or difference between them. *abismo* ❑ *There is a split between what he says and what he feels.* *Hay un abismo entre lo que dice y lo que siente.* **5** V-T/V-I If something such as wood or a piece of clothing **splits** or **is split,** a long crack or tear appears in it. *rasgarse, cortar* ❑ *The seat of his pants split.* *Los fondillos de su pantalón se rasgaron.* ❑ *He split the log with an ax.* *Cortó el tronco con un hacha.* **6** V-T If two or more people **split** something, they share it between them. *dividirse* ❑ *Let's split the bill.* *Vamos a dividirnos la cuenta.*

▸ **split up** **1** PHR-VERB If two people **split up,** or if someone or something **splits** them **up,** they end their relationship or marriage. *separar(se)* ❑ *His parents split up when he was ten.* *Sus padres se separaron cuando él tenía diez años.* ❑ *I thought that nothing could ever split us up.* *Creí que nada podría separarnos nunca.* **2** PHR-VERB If a group of people **split up** or **are split up,** they go away in different directions. *separar(se)* ❑ *We split up and searched different parts of the forest.* *Nos separamos y buscamos en diferentes partes del bosque.* ❑ *The war has split up many families.* *La guerra ha separado a muchas familias.* **3** PHR-VERB If you **split** something **up,** or if it **splits up,** you divide it so that it is in a number of smaller separate sections. *dividir, dispersar* ❑ *We are not planning to split up the company.* *No estamos pensando en dividir la empresa.* ❑ *Museums have asked to borrow her collection, but she refuses to split it up.* *Varios museos le pidieron prestada su colección, pero ella se rehúsa a dispersarla.*

| **Thesaurus** | *split* | Ver también: |
|---|---|---|
| V. | break, divide, part, separate; (*ant.*) combine **1** **2** **5** | |

| **Word Partnership** | Usar *split* con: |
|---|---|
| PREP. | split **into** **1** |
| | split **over** ***something*** **2** |
| | split **between** **4** |
| N. | split **shares,** split **wood** **1** |
| | split **in a party** **3** |
| ADV. | split **apart** **1** **2** |

**spoil** /spɔɪl/ (**spoils, spoiling, spoiled** or **spoilt**) **1** V-T If you **spoil** something, you prevent it from being successful or satisfactory. *echar a perder* ❑ *Don't let mistakes spoil your life.* *No deje que los errores le echen a perder la vida.* **2** V-T If you **spoil** children, you give them everything they want or ask for. *consentir* ❑ *Grandparents often like to spoil their grandchildren.* *A los abuelos suele gustarles consentir a sus nietos.* **3** V-T If you **spoil yourself** or **spoil** another person, you give yourself or them something nice as a treat or do something special for them. *consentirse* ❑ *Spoil yourself with a new perfume.* *Consiéntase con un nuevo perfume.*

**spoke** /spoʊk/ (**spokes**) **1** **Spoke** is the past tense of **speak.** *pasado de **speak*** **2** N-COUNT The **spokes** of a wheel are the bars that connect the outer ring to the center. *rayo*
→ see **bicycle, wheel**

**spo|ken** /spoʊkən/ **Spoken** is the past participle of **speak.** *participio pasado de **speak***

**spokes|man** /spoʊksmən/ (**spokesmen**) N-COUNT A **spokesman** is a male spokesperson. *vocero, portavoz* ❑ *A spokesman said that food is on its way.* *Un vocero dijo que los alimentos estaban en camino.*

**spokes|person** /spoʊkspɜrsᵊn/ (**spokespersons** or **spokespeople**) N-COUNT A **spokesperson** is a person who speaks as the representative of a group or organization. *vocero o vocera, portavoz* ❑ *...a White House spokesperson.* *...un vocero de la Casa Blanca.*

**spokes|woman** /spoʊkswʊmən/ (**spokeswomen**) N-COUNT A **spokeswoman** is a female spokesperson. *vocera, portavoz* ❑ *A United Nations spokeswoman said the request would be considered.* *Una portavoz de las Naciones Unidas afirmó que la solicitud sería considerada.*

**sponge** /spʌndʒ/ (**sponges, sponging, sponged**) **1** N-UNCOUNT **Sponge** is a very light soft substance with lots of little holes in it, which can be either artificial or natural. It is used to clean things or as a soft layer. *esponja, hule espuma* ❑ *...a sponge mattress.* *...un colchón de hulespuma.* **2** N-COUNT A **sponge** is a piece of sponge that you use for washing yourself or for cleaning things. *esponja* ❑ *He wiped the table with a sponge.* *Limpió la mesa con una esponja.* **3** V-T If you **sponge** something, you clean it by wiping it with a wet sponge. *limpiar con una esponja* ❑ *She gently sponged the baby's face.* *Le limpió suavemente la cara al bebé con una esponja.* **4** V-I If you say that someone **sponges off** other people or **sponges on** them, you disapprove of them because they regularly get money from other people when they should be trying to support themselves. *vivir a costa de otros* [INFORMAL] ❑ *He should get a job and stop sponging off the rest of us!* *¡Debería conseguirse un trabajo y dejar de vivir a costa de todos nosotros!* **5** N-COUNT A **sponge** is a sea animal with a soft round body made of natural sponge. *esponja*

**spon|gy bone** N-UNCOUNT **Spongy bone** is a type of bone that consists of many small pieces with spaces between them. It forms the interior of other bones. *hueso reticulado, hueso esponjoso* [TECHNICAL]

**spon|sor** /spɒnsər/ (**sponsors, sponsoring, sponsored**) **1** V-T If an organization or an individual **sponsors** something such as an event, they pay for it, often in order to get publicity for themselves. *patrocinar* ❑ *A local bank is sponsoring the race.* *Un banco del lugar patrocina la carrera.* **2** V-T If you **sponsor** someone who is doing something to raise money for charity, for example trying to walk a certain distance, you agree to give them money for the charity if they succeed in doing it. *patrocinar* ❑ *The children asked friends and family*

S

*to sponsor them.* *Los niños les pidieron a sus amigos y sus familias que los patrocinaran.* **3** V-T If you **sponsor** a proposal or suggestion, you officially introduce it and support it. *apoyar* ❑ *An animal rights group is sponsoring the proposal to stop animal testing.* *Un grupo pro derechos de los animales apoya la propuesta de poner fin a los experimentos con animales.* **4** N-COUNT A **sponsor** is a person or organization that sponsors something or someone. *patrocinador, patrocinadora* ❑ *Our company is proud to be the sponsor of this event.* *Nuestra empresa se siente orgullosa de ser la patrocinadora de este acto.*

**spon|sor|ship** /spɒnsərʃɪp/ N-UNCOUNT **Sponsorship** is financial support given by a sponsor. *patrocinio* ❑ *Athletes can make a lot of money out of sponsorship.* *Los atletas pueden ganar mucho dinero con el patrocinio.*

**spon|ta|neous** /spɒnteɪniəs/ **1** ADJ **Spontaneous** acts are not planned or arranged, but are done because someone suddenly wants to do them. *espontáneo* ❑ *He gave her a spontaneous hug.* *Le dio un abrazo espontáneo.* ● **spon|ta|neous|ly** ADV *espontáneamente* ❑ *People spontaneously stood up and cheered.* *La gente se puso de pie y lanzó vivas espontáneamente.* **2** ADJ A **spontaneous** event happens because of processes within something, rather than being caused by things outside it. *espontáneo* ❑ *...a spontaneous explosion.* *...una explosión espontánea.* ● **spon|ta|neous|ly** ADV *espontáneamente* ❑ *The memories arrived in his head spontaneously.* *Los recuerdos le vinieron espontáneamente a la mente.*

**spool** /spul/ (**spools**) N-COUNT A **spool** is a round object onto which thread, tape, or film can be wound, especially before it is put into a machine. *carrete* ❑ *...a spool of film.* *...un carrete de película.*

**spoon** /spun/ (**spoons, spooning, spooned**) **1** N-COUNT A **spoon** is an object used for eating, stirring, and serving food. One end of it is shaped like a shallow bowl and it has a long handle. *cuchara* ❑ *He stirred his coffee with a spoon.* *Removió su café con una cuchara.* **2** V-T If you **spoon** food into something, you put it there with a spoon. *cucharear, poner con cuchara* ❑ *He spooned sugar into the mug.* *Puso azúcar en el tarro con una cuchara.*
→ see **utensil**

S

**spo|ro|phyte** /spɔrəfaɪt/ (**sporophytes**) N-COUNT The **sporophyte** is the stage in the life of a plant when it produces spores. *esporofito, esporófito* [TECHNICAL]

**sport** /spɔrt/ (**sports**) N-VAR **Sports** are games such as football and basketball and other competitive leisure activities which need physical effort and skill. *deporte* ❑ *Basketball is my favorite sport.* *El básquetbol es mi deporte favorito.* ❑ *She is very good at sports.* *Es muy buena para los deportes.*

**sport coat** (**sport coats**) also **sports coat** N-COUNT A **sport coat** is a man's jacket. It is worn on informal occasions with pants of a different material. *saco deportivo, saco informal* ❑ *He wore a sport coat and a blue shirt.* *Vestía un saco informal y una camisa azul.*

**sport|ing** /spɔrtɪŋ/ ADJ **Sporting** means relating to sports or used for sports. *deportivo* ❑ *...major sporting events, such as the U.S. Open.* *...las principales pruebas deportivas, como el Abierto de Estados Unidos.*

**sport jack|et** (**sport jackets**) N-COUNT A **sport jacket** is the same as a **sport coat**. *saco deportivo, saco informal*

**sports car** (**sports cars**) N-COUNT A **sports car** is a low, fast car, usually with room for only two people. *auto/coche/carro deportivo*
→ see **car**

**sports|cast** /spɔrtskæst/ (**sportscasts**) N-COUNT A **sportscast** is a radio or television broadcast of a sporting event. *emisión deportiva*

**sports|caster** /spɔrtskæstər/ (**sportscasters**) N-COUNT A **sportscaster** is a radio or television broadcaster who describes or comments on sporting events. *comentarista de deportes*

**sports|man** /spɔrtsmən/ (**sportsmen**) N-COUNT A **sportsman** is a man who takes part in sports. *deportista*

**sports|woman** /spɔrtswʊmən/ (**sportswomen**) N-COUNT A **sportswoman** is a woman who takes part in sports. *deportista*

**spot** /spɒt/ (**spots, spotting, spotted**) **1** N-COUNT **Spots** are small, round, colored areas on a surface. *mancha* ❑ *The leaves are yellow with orange spots.* *Las hojas son amarillas con manchas anaranjadas.* **2** N-COUNT **Spots** on a person's skin are small lumps or marks. *espinilla, grano* [AM usually **pimples**] **3** N-COUNT You can refer to a particular place as a **spot**. *lugar* ❑ *This is one of the country's top tourist spots.* *Este es uno de los principales lugares turísticos del país.* **4** V-T If you **spot** something or someone, you notice them. *notar* ❑ *I didn't spot the mistake in his essay.* *No noté el error en su ensayo.* **5** PHRASE If you do something **on the spot**, you do it immediately. *de inmediato, sin demora* ❑ *They offered him the job on the spot.* *Le ofrecieron el empleo de inmediato.*
→ see **soccer**

**Word Partnership** Usar *spot* con:

ADJ. **good** spot, **perfect** spot, **popular** spot, **quiet** spot, **the right** spot **3**
N. **parking** spot, **vacation** spot **3**

**spot|light** /spɒtlaɪt/ (**spotlights, spotlighting, spotlighted**) **1** N-COUNT A **spotlight** is a powerful light, for example in a theater, which can be directed so that it lights up a small area. *reflector* **2** V-T If something **spotlights** a particular problem or situation, it makes people notice it and think about it. *poner de relieve* ❑ *Her comments spotlight the problem of racism.* *Sus comentarios ponen de relieve el problema del racismo.*

spotlight

→ see **concert**

**spot|ty** /spɒti/ ADJ Something that is **spotty** does not stay the same but is sometimes good and sometimes bad. *irregular* ❑ *His attendance record was spotty.* *Su historial de asistencias era irregular.*

**spous|al** /spaʊzəl/ ADJ **Spousal** means relating

to someone's husband or wife. marital [FORMAL] ❑ *...spousal benefits.* *...beneficios maritales.*

**spouse** /spaʊs/ (**spouses**) N-COUNT Someone's **spouse** is the person they are married to. esposo, esposa, cónyuge ❑ *You and your spouse must both sign the contract.* *Tanto usted como su esposo deben firmar el contrato.*

→ see **love**

**sprawl** /sprɔl/ (**sprawls, sprawling, sprawled**) **1** V-I If you **sprawl** somewhere, you sit or lie down with your legs and arms spread out in a careless way. despatarrarse ❑ *She sprawled on the sofa.* *Se despatarró en el sillón.* • **Sprawl out** means the same as **sprawl**. despatarrarse ❑ *He sprawled out on his bed.* *Se despatarró en su cama.* **2** V-I If you say that a place **sprawls**, you mean that it covers a large area of land. extenderse ❑ *The park sprawls over 900 acres.* *El parque se extiende sobre 365 hectáreas.* **3** N-UNCOUNT You can use **sprawl** to refer to an area where a city has grown outward in an uncontrolled way. expansión ❑ *The urban sprawl of Ankara contains over 2.6 million people.* *El área urbana de Ankara ha crecido sin control y ya alberga a más de 2.6 millones de habitantes.*

**spray** /spreɪ/ (**sprays, spraying, sprayed**) **1** N-VAR **Spray** is a lot of small drops of water which are being thrown into the air. rocío ❑ *We were hit by spray from the waterfall.* *Nos cayó el rocío de la cascada.* **2** N-VAR A **spray** is a liquid kept under pressure in a can or other container, which you can force out in very small drops. aerosol ❑ *...hair spray.* *...fijador para el pelo.* **3** V-T/V-I If you **spray** a liquid somewhere or if it **sprays** somewhere, drops of the liquid cover a place or shower someone. rociar, arrojar chorros de agua ❑ *A plane was spraying chemicals over the fields.* *Un avión estaba rociando los campos con sustancias químicas.* ❑ *Police sprayed the crowd with water.* *La policía arrojó chorros de agua contra la multitud.* **4** V-T/V-I If a lot of small things **spray** somewhere or if something **sprays** them, they are scattered somewhere with a lot of force. esparcirse ❑ *A shower of crumbs sprayed into the air.* *Una lluvia de migajas se esparció en el aire.* ❑ *The window broke, spraying glass on the street below.* *La ventana se rompió y los pedazos de vidrio se esparcieron por la calle.*

**Word Partnership** Usar *spray* con:

| | |
|---|---|
| N. | spray **bottle**, **bug** spray, spray **can**, **hair** spray, **pepper** spray **2** |
| PREP. | spray **with water** **3** |

**spread** /sprɛd/ (**spreads, spreading, spread**) **1** V-T If you **spread** something somewhere, you open it out or arrange it over a place or surface, so that all of it can be seen or used easily. extender ❑ *She spread a towel on the sand and lay on it.* *Extendió una toalla sobre la arena y se recostó en ella.* • **Spread out** means the same as **spread**. extender ❑ *He spread the papers out on a table.* *Extendió los papeles sobre una mesa.* **2** V-T If you **spread** your arms, hands, fingers, or legs, you stretch them out until they are far apart. extender ❑ *Sitting on the floor, spread your legs as far as they will go.* *Siéntese en el piso y extienda completamente las piernas.* • **Spread out** means the same as **spread**. extender ❑ *David spread out his hands.* *David extendió las manos.* **3** V-T If you **spread** a substance on a surface or **spread** the surface **with** the substance, you put a thin layer of the substance over the surface. untar ❑ *She was spreading butter on the bread.* *Estaba untando el pan con mantequilla.* **4** V-T/V-I If something **spreads** or **is spread** by people, it gradually reaches or affects a larger and larger area or more and more people. difundir(se), diseminar(se) ❑ *Information technology has spread across the world.* *La tecnología de la información se ha difundido por todo el mundo.* ❑ *Fear is spreading in the neighborhood.* *El miedo se está diseminando por el vecindario.* • **Spread** is also a noun. difusión ❑ *...the slow spread of information.* *...la lenta difusión de la información.* **5** V-T If you **spread** something **over** a period of time, it takes place regularly or continuously over that period, rather than happening at one time. diferir, pagar a plazos ❑ *You can pay the whole amount, or spread your payments over several months.* *Puede pagar el total o pagar a plazos en varios meses.* **6** V-T If you **spread** something such as wealth or work, you distribute it evenly or equally. distribuir ❑ *...policies that spread the wealth more evenly.* *...políticas que permiten distribuir la riqueza más equitativamente.* • **Spread** is also a noun. distribución ❑ *We need to encourage the even spread of wealth.* *Necesitamos estimular la distribución equitativa de la riqueza.* **7** N-SING A **spread of** ideas, interests, or other things is a wide variety of them. gama ❑ *The school has students with a wide spread of ability.* *La escuela tiene estudiantes con una amplia gama de habilidades.*

▶ **spread out** **1** PHR-VERB If people, animals, or vehicles **spread out**, they move apart from each other. dispersarse ❑ *They spread out to search the area.* *Se dispersaron para registrar la zona.* **2** → see **spread 1, 2**

**Word Partnership** Usar *spread* con:

| | |
|---|---|
| ADV. | spread **evenly** **1** **3** **5**<br>spread **quickly**, spread **rapidly**, spread **widely** **1** **4** **5** |
| PREP. | spread **of an epidemic**, spread **of technology**, spread **of a virus** **4** |
| N. | spread **fear**, **fires** spread, spread **an infection**, spread **a message**, spread **news**, spread **rumors** **4** |
| V. | **continue to** spread, **prevent/stop the** spread **of *something*** **4** **6** |

**spring** /sprɪŋ/ (**springs, springing, sprang, sprung**) **1** N-VAR **Spring** is the season between winter and summer when the weather becomes warmer and plants start to grow again. primavera ❑ *They are getting married next spring.* *Van a contraer matrimonio la próxima primavera.* **2** N-COUNT A **spring** is a spiral of wire which returns to its original shape after it is pressed or pulled. resorte ❑ *The springs in the bed were old and soft.* *Los resortes de la cama eran viejos y blandos.* **3** N-COUNT A **spring** is a place where water comes up through the ground. manantial, fuente ❑ *The town is famous for its hot springs.* *El pueblo es famoso por sus manantiales de aguas termales.* **4** V-I When a person or animal **springs**, they jump upward or forward suddenly or quickly. saltar, brincar ❑ *He sprang to his feet.* *Se puso de pie como impulsado por un resorte.* **5** V-I If something **springs** in a particular direction, it moves suddenly and quickly. abrirse de golpe ❑ *The lid of the box sprang open.* *La tapa de la caja se abrió* *de golpe.* **6** V-I If one thing **springs from** another thing, it is the result of it. *ser producto de* ❑ *His anger sprang from shock and surprise. Su ira fue producto de la conmoción y la sorpresa.* **7** V-T If you **spring** some news or a surprise **on** someone, you tell them something that they did not expect to hear, without warning them. *sorprender* ❑ *Mike sprang a new idea on him. Mike lo sorprendió con otra idea.*

▸ **spring up** PHR-VERB If something **springs up,** it suddenly appears or begins to exist. *surgir* ❑ *New theaters sprang up all over the country. Por todo el país surgieron nuevos teatros.*

→ see **river**

**Word Partnership** Usar *spring* con:

ADJ. **early** spring, **last** spring, **late** spring, **next** spring **1**
**cold** spring, **hot** spring, **warm** spring **1** **3**

N. spring **day**, spring **flowers**, spring **rains**, spring **semester**, spring **training**, spring **weather** **1**
spring **water** **3**

**spring-cleaning** N-UNCOUNT; N-SING **Spring-cleaning** is the process of thoroughly cleaning a place, especially your home. You can also say that you give a place a **spring-cleaning.** *limpieza completa* ❑ *They were giving the house a good spring-cleaning. Le estaban haciendo a la casa una buena limpieza completa.*

**spring tide** (**spring tides**) N-COUNT A **spring tide** is an unusually high tide that happens at the time of a new moon or a full moon. *marea viva*

**sprin|kle** /sprɪŋkəl/ (**sprinkles, sprinkling, sprinkled**) **1** V-T If you **sprinkle** a thing **with** something such as a liquid or powder, you scatter the liquid or powder over it. *rociar, espolvorear* ❑ *Sprinkle the meat with salt before you cook it. Espolvoree la carne con sal antes de cocerla.* **2** V-I If **it is sprinkling,** it is raining very lightly. *lloviznar, chispear*

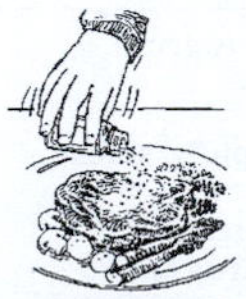
sprinkle

**sprin|kler** /sprɪŋklər/ (**sprinklers**) N-COUNT A **sprinkler** is a device used to spray water. Sprinklers are used to water plants or grass, or to put out fires in buildings. *aspersor, rociador*

→ see **garden**

**sprint** /sprɪnt/ (**sprints, sprinting, sprinted**) **1** N-SING **The sprint** is a short, fast race. *carrera de velocidad* ❑ *Rob Harmeling won the sprint. Rob Harmeling ganó la carrera de velocidad.* **2** N-SING **A sprint** is a fast run that someone does, either at the end of a race or because they are in a hurry. *carrera* ❑ *She made a sprint for the bus. Pegó una carrera para alcanzar el autobús.* **3** V-I If you **sprint,** you run or ride as fast as you can over a short distance. *correr rápidamente* ❑ *Sergeant Horne sprinted to the car. El sargento Horne corrió rápidamente hacia el auto.*

**sprout** /spraʊt/ (**sprouts, sprouting, sprouted**) **1** V-I When plants, vegetables, or seeds **sprout,** they produce new shoots or leaves. *echar brotes, echar retoños* ❑ *It only takes a few days for beans to sprout. Los frijoles sólo tardan unos cuantos días en echar brotes.* **2** V-I When leaves, shoots, or plants **sprout** somewhere, they grow there. *retoñar* ❑ *Leaves were beginning to sprout on the trees. Las hojas estaban empezando a retoñar en los árboles.* **3** V-T/V-I If something such as hair **sprouts** from a person or animal, or if they **sprout** it, it grows on them. *salir* ❑ *Hair sprouted from his chin. Le salieron vellos en el mentón.* **4** N-COUNT **Sprouts** are vegetables that look like tiny cabbages. They are also called **Brussels sprouts.** *colecita de Bruselas, repollito de Bruselas*

→ see **tree**

**spur** /spɜr/ (**spurs, spurring, spurred**) **1** V-T If one thing **spurs** you **to** do another, it encourages you to do it. *acicatear, estimular* ❑ *Money spurs these men to risk their lives. El dinero impulsa a esos hombres a arriesgar su vida.* ● **Spur on** means the same as **spur.** *alentar* ❑ *The applause seemed to spur him on. Los aplausos parecieron alentarlo.* **2** V-T If something **spurs** a change or event, it makes it happen faster or sooner. *estimular* ❑ *Our aim is to spur economic growth. Nuestro objetivo es estimular el crecimiento económico.* **3** N-COUNT Something that acts as a **spur to** something else encourages a person or organization to do that thing or makes it happen more quickly. *estímulo* ❑ *Financial profit can be a spur to progress. La ganancia económica puede ser un estímulo para el progreso.* **4** PHRASE If you do something **on the spur of the moment,** you do it suddenly, without planning it beforehand. *impulsivamente, sin pensarlo* ❑ *They went to the beach on the spur of the moment. Fueron a la playa impulsivamente.*

**Word Partnership** Usar *spur* con:

N. spur **demand**, spur **development**, spur **economic growth**, spur **the economy**, spur **interest**, spur **investment**, spur **sales** **2**

**spy** /spaɪ/ (**spies, spying, spied**) **1** N-COUNT A **spy** is a person whose job is to find out secret information about another country or organization. *espía* ❑ *He used to be a spy. Solía ser espía.* **2** V-I Someone who **spies for** a country or organization tries to find out secret information about another country or organization. *espiar* ❑ *He spied for the Soviet Union for more than twenty years. Espió para la Unión Soviética durante más de veinte años.* ❑ *The two countries are still spying on one another. Los dos países siguen espiándose todavía.* ● **spy|ing** N-UNCOUNT *espionaje* ❑ *He spent ten years in jail for spying. Estuvo diez años en la carcel por espionaje.* **3** V-I If you **spy on** someone, you watch them secretly. *espiar* ❑ *He spied on her while pretending to work in the yard. La estaba espiando mientras simulaba trabajar en el patio.*

**sq.** **sq.** is used as a written abbreviation for **square** when you are giving the measurement of an area. *cuadrado* ❑ *The building provides about 25,500 sq. ft. of offices. El edificio dispone de aproximadamente 2,370 metros cuadrados para oficinas.*

**squad** /skwɒd/ (**squads**) **1** N-COUNT A **squad** is a section of a police force that is responsible for dealing with a particular type of crime. *brigada* ❑ *Someone called the bomb squad. Alguien llamó a la brigada antiexplosivos.* **2** N-COUNT A **squad** is a group of players from which a sports team will be chosen. *equipo* ❑ *There have been a lot of injuries in the squad. Ha habido muchas lesiones en el equipo.*

**squad|ron** /skwɒdrən/ (**squadrons**) N-COUNT

S

A **squadron** is a section of one of the armed forces, especially the air force. escuadrón ❑ *...a squadron of fighter planes.* *...un escuadrón de aviones de combate.*

**squan|der** /skwɒndər/ (**squanders, squandering, squandered**) V-T If you **squander** money, resources, or opportunities, you waste them. despilfarrar ❑ *He squandered his money on fancy clothes.* *Despilfarró su dinero en ropa elegante.*

**square** /skwɛər/ (**squares, squaring, squared**) **1** N-COUNT A **square** is a shape with four sides that are all the same length and four corners that are all right angles. cuadro ❑ *Cut the cake in squares.* *Corta el pastel en cuadros.* ❑ *There was a calendar on the wall, with squares around some dates.* *Habia un calendario en la pared, con cuadros alrededor de algunas fechas.* **2** N-COUNT In a town or city, a **square** is a flat open place, often in the shape of a square. plaza ❑ *The house is in one of the city's prettiest squares.* *La casa está en una de las plazas más bonitas de la ciudad.* **3** ADJ Something that is **square** has a shape the same as a square or similar to a square. cuadrado ❑ *They sat at a square table.* *Se sentaron a una mesa cuadrada.* **4** ADJ **Square** is used before units of length when referring to the area of something. For example, if something is three feet long and two feet wide, its area is six square feet. cuadrado ❑ *The house covers an area of 3,000 square feet.* *La casa cubre una superficie de 279 metros cuadrados.* **5** V-T To **square** a number means to multiply it by itself. For example, **3 squared** is 3 x 3, or 9. **3 squared** is usually written as $3^2$. elevar al cuadrado ❑ *Find the length of one side and square it.* *Mide el largo de un lado y elévalo al cuadrado.* **6** N-COUNT The **square of** a number is the number produced when you multiply that number by itself. cuadrado ❑ *The square of 25 is 625.* *El cuadrado de 25 es 625.* **7** V-T/V-I If you **square** two different ideas or actions **with** each other or if they **square with** each other, they fit or match each other. concordar ❑ *That explanation doesn't square with the facts.* *Esa explicación no concuerda con los hechos.*
→ see **shape**

▸ **square away** PHR-VERB If you **square** something or someone **away,** you deal with them so that the situation is satisfactory. arreglar ❑ *First we have to square away how much this is going to cost.* *Primero tenemos que arreglar cuánto nos va a costar esto.*

▸ **square off** PHR-VERB If one group or person **squares off against** or **with** another, they prepare to fight or compete against them. alistarse para enfrentarse, alistarse para pelear ❑ *The two politicians squared off against one another in a TV debate.* *Los dos políticos se alistaron para enfrentarse en un debate por televisión.* ❑ *I saw my brother squaring off with another boy.* *Vi a mi hermano alistándose para pelear con otro niño.*

**square root** (**square roots**) N-COUNT The **square root of** a number is another number which produces the first number when it is multiplied by itself. For example, the square root of 16 is 4. raíz cuadrada

**squash** /skwɒʃ/ (**squashes, squashing, squashed**) **1** V-T If someone or something **is squashed,** they are pressed or crushed with such force that they become injured or lose their shape. aplastar, apretujar ❑ *Robert was squashed against a fence by a car.* *Un coche aplastó a Robert contra una cerca.* ❑ *Whole neighborhoods have been squashed flat by bombing.* *Barrios enteros han sido derrumbados por el bombardeo.* **2** ADJ If people or things are **squashed into** a place, they are put or pushed into a place where there is not enough room for them to be. apiñado ❑ *There were 2,000 people squashed into the hall.* *Había 2,000 personas apiñadas en el salón.* **3** N-UNCOUNT **Squash** is a game in which two players hit a small rubber ball against the walls of a court using rackets. squash ❑ *I play squash once a week.* *Juego al squash una vez a la semana.*

**squat** /skwɒt/ (**squats, squatting, squatted**) **1** V-I If you **squat,** you lower yourself toward the ground, balancing on your feet with your legs bent. ponerse en cuclillas ❑ *We squatted beside the pool.* *Nos pusimos en cuclillas junto a la alberca.* ● **Squat down** means the same as **squat.** ponerse en cuclillas ❑ *Albert squatted down to see the bug.* *Albert se puso en cuclillas para ver el insecto.* ● **Squat** is also a noun. cuclillas ❑ *He got down into a squat.* *Se puso en cuclillas.* **2** ADJ If you describe someone or something as **squat,** you mean they are short and thick, usually in an unattractive way. regordete, rechoncho ❑ *Eddie was a short squat fellow.* *Eddie era un tipo chaparro y rechoncho.* **3** V-I People who **squat** occupy an unused building or unused land without having a legal right to do so. ocupar un lugar sin derecho ❑ *Homeless families have been squatting on the land.* *Algunas familias sin hogar han estado ocupando la tierra.*

**squeak** /skwik/ (**squeaks, squeaking, squeaked**) V-I If something or someone **squeaks,** they make a short, high-pitched sound. rechinar, chirriar, crujir ❑ *My boots squeaked as I walked.* *Mis botas rechinaban al caminar.* ❑ *The door squeaked open.* *La puerta chirrió al abrirse.* ● **Squeak** is also a noun. chirrido ❑ *I heard a squeak, like a mouse.* *Oí un chirrido, como de un ratón.*

**squeeze** /skwiz/ (**squeezes, squeezing, squeezed**) **1** V-T If you **squeeze** something, you press it firmly, usually with your hands. apretar ❑ *He squeezed her arm gently.* *Le apretó el brazo suavemente.* ● **Squeeze** is also a noun. apretón ❑ *She took my hand and gave it a squeeze.* *Me dio un apretón de manos.* **2** V-T If you **squeeze** a liquid or a soft substance out of an object, you get the liquid or substance out by pressing the object. apretar ❑ *Joe squeezed some toothpaste out of the tube.* *Joe apretó el tubo de dentífrico para sacar un poco.* **3** V-T/V-I If you **squeeze** a person or thing somewhere or if they **squeeze** there, they manage to get through or into a small space. meter ❑ *Can you squeeze one more box into your car?* *¿Puedes meter una caja más en tu coche?* **4** N-SING If you say that getting a number of people into a small space is **a squeeze,** you mean that it is only just possible for them all to get into it. estar apretado [INFORMAL] ❑ *It was a squeeze with five of us in the car.* *Éramos cinco en el coche y estábamos todos apretados.*

squirrel

**squir|rel** /skwɜrəl/ (**squirrels**) N-COUNT A **squirrel** is a small animal with a long furry tail. Squirrels live mainly in trees. ardilla

S

**squirt** /skwɜrt/ (**squirts, squirting, squirted**) V-T/V-I If you **squirt** a liquid somewhere or if it **squirts** somewhere, the liquid comes out of a narrow opening in a thin fast stream. echar un chorrito, salir a chorros ❑ *Norman squirted tomato sauce onto his plate.* *Norman echó un chorrito de salsa de jitomate en su plato.* ● **Squirt** is also a noun. chorrito ❑ *It needs a little squirt of oil.* *Necesita un chorrito de aceite.*

**stab** /stæb/ (**stabs, stabbing, stabbed**) 1 V-T If someone **stabs** you, they push a knife or sharp object into your body. apuñalar, acuchillar ❑ *Somebody stabbed him in the stomach.* *Alguien lo apuñaló en el estómago.* 2 V-T/V-I If you **stab** something or **stab at** it, you push at it with your finger or with something pointed that you are holding. golpear, agarrar, mover como apuñalando ❑ *Bess stabbed a slice of cucumber.* *Bess picó una rodaja de pepino con el tenedor.* ❑ *Greg stabbed his finger at the photo he wanted to show me.* *Greg le daba con el dedo a la fotografía que quería mostrarme.* 3 N-SING If you have **a stab at** something, you try to do it. intento [INFORMAL] ❑ *Have you ever had a stab at acting?* *¿Alguna vez has hecho el intento de actuar?* 4 N-SING You can refer to a sudden, usually unpleasant feeling as **a stab of** that feeling. punzada [LITERARY] ❑ *He felt a stab of pain above his eye.* *Sintió una punzada de dolor arriba del ojo.*
→ see **carnivore**

**Word Link** *stab ≈ steady : establish, instability, stabilize*

**sta|bi|lize** /steɪbɪlaɪz/ (**stabilizes, stabilizing, stabilized**) V-T/V-I If something **stabilizes**, or **is stabilized**, it becomes stable. estabilizar(se) ❑ *Doctors say her condition has stabilized.* *Los médicos dicen que su condición se ha estabilizado.* ● **sta|bi|li|za|tion** /steɪbɪlɪzeɪʃ^ən/ N-UNCOUNT estabilización ❑ *...the stabilization of house prices.* *...la estabilización de los precios de la vivienda.*

**sta|ble** /steɪb^əl/ (**stabler, stablest, stables**) 1 ADJ If something is **stable**, it is not likely to change or come to an end suddenly. estable ❑ *The price of oil has remained stable this month.* *El precio del petróleo ha permanecido estable este mes.* ● **sta|bil|ity** /stəbɪlɪti/ N-UNCOUNT estabilidad ❑ *It was a time of political stability.* *Fue una época de estabilidad política.* 2 ADJ If an object is **stable**, it is firmly fixed in position and is not likely to move or fall. estable ❑ *Make sure the ladder is stable.* *Asegúrese de que la escalera esté estable.* 3 N-COUNT A **stable** or **stables** is a building in which horses are kept. cuadra, caballeriza

S

**stack** /stæk/ (**stacks, stacking, stacked**) 1 N-COUNT A **stack of** things is a pile of them. montón, pila ❑ *There were stacks of books on the floor.* *Había montones de libros en el piso.* 2 V-T If you **stack** a number of things, you arrange them in neat piles. apilar, colocar ❑ *She was stacking the clean bottles onto the shelf.* *Estaba colocando las botellas limpias en el estante.* ● **Stack up** means the same as **stack**. apilar ❑ *They stacked up pillows behind his back.* *Le pusieron unas almohadas para que apoyara la espalda.* 3 N-PLURAL If you say that someone has **stacks of** something, you mean that they have a lot of it. montón [INFORMAL] ❑ *They have stacks of money.* *Tienen montones de dinero.* 4 PHRASE If you say that **the odds are stacked against** someone, or that particular factors **are stacked against** them, you mean that they are unlikely to succeed in what they want to do because the conditions are not favorable. ser desfavorables las circunstancias para, tener las probabilidades en contra, llevar las de perder ❑ *The odds are stacked against him winning the competition.* *Las probabilidades de ganar la competencia están en su contra.*

**sta|dium** /steɪdiəm/ (**stadiums** or **stadia** /steɪdiə/) N-COUNT A **stadium** is a large sports field with rows of seats all around it. estadio ❑ *...a baseball stadium.* *...un estadio de béisbol.*

**staff** /stæf/ (**staffs, staffing, staffed**)

**Staves** is the usual plural form for meaning 5.

1 N-COUNT The **staff** of an organization are the people who work for it. personal ❑ *The hospital staff were very good.* *El personal del hospital era muy bueno.* ❑ *We have a staff of six people.* *Tenemos seis empleados.* ❑ *...staff members.* *...los empleados.* 2 → see also **chief of staff** 3 N-PLURAL People who are part of a particular staff are often referred to as **staff**. empleados ❑ *10 staff were moved to different departments.* *Diez empleados fueron trasladados a diferentes departamentos.* 4 V-T If an organization **is staffed by** particular people, they are the people who work for it. dotar de personal ❑ *The office is staffed by volunteers.* *El personal de la oficina está compuesto de voluntarios.* ● **staffed** ADJ dotado de personal ❑ *The hotel was pleasant and well staffed.* *El hotel era agradable y estaba bien dotado de personal.* 5 A **staff** is the five lines that music is written on. pentagrama

**staff|er** /stæfər/ (**staffers**) N-COUNT A **staffer** is a member of a staff, especially in political organizations or in journalism. empleado o empleada, funcionario o funcionaria ❑ *...White House staffers.* *...funcionarios de la Casa Blanca.*

**stage** /steɪdʒ/ (**stages, staging, staged**) 1 N-COUNT A **stage of** an activity, process, or period is one part of it. etapa ❑ *...the first stage of the plan to reopen the airport.* *...la primera etapa del plan para reabrir el aeropuerto.* 2 N-COUNT In a theater, the **stage** is an area where actors or other entertainers perform. escenario ❑ *The band walked onto the stage.* *La banda entró al escenario.* 3 N-COUNT The **stage** on a microscope is the place where you put the specimen that you want to look at. platina, portaobjetos 4 V-T If someone **stages** a play or other show, they organize and present a performance of it. poner en escena, montar, representar ❑ *He plans to stage "Hamlet" in Chicago.* *Tiene pensado montar Hamlet en Chicago.* 5 V-T If you **stage** an event or ceremony, you organize it and usually take part in it. hacer ❑ *Workers are planning to stage a strike.* *Los obreros están planeando hacer huelga.*
→ see **concert, drama, theater**

**Word Partnership** Usar *stage* con:

ADJ. **advanced** stage, **critical** stage, **crucial** stage, **early** stage, **final** stage, **late/later** stage 1
N. stage **of development**, stage **of a disease**, stage **of a process** 1
**actors on** stage, **center** stage, **concert** stage, stage **fright**, stage **manager** 2
V. **reach a** stage 1
**leave the** stage, **take the** stage 2

**stage crew** (**stage crews**) N-COUNT A **stage crew** is a team of workers who move the scenery about in a play or other theatrical production. *tramoyistas*

**stage left** ADV **Stage left** is the left side of the stage for an actor who is standing facing the audience. *parte del escenario a la izquierda de un actor de cara al público*

**stage man|ag|er** (**stage managers**) N-COUNT At a theater, a **stage manager** is the person who is responsible for the scenery and lights and for the way that actors or other performers move around and use the stage during a performance. *director de escena*

**stage right** ADV **Stage right** is the right side of the stage for an actor who is standing facing the audience. *parte del escenario a la derecha de un actor de cara al público*

**stag|ger** /stægər/ (**staggers, staggering, staggered**) 1 V-I If you **stagger**, you walk very unsteadily, for example because you are ill. *tambalearse* ❑ *He staggered back and fell over. Retrocedió tambaleándose y cayó.* 2 V-T If something **staggers** you, it surprises you very much. *dejar perplejo, dejar estupefacto* ❑ *Their stupidity staggers me. Su estupidez me asombra.* ● **stag|gered** ADJ *perplejo, estupefacto* ❑ *I felt staggered by how much everything cost. Me dejó perplejo lo mucho que costaba todo.* 3 V-T To **stagger** things means to arrange them so that they do not all happen at the same time. *alternar, escalonar* ❑ *The university staggers the summer vacation periods for students. La universidad alterna los períodos de vacaciones de verano de los estudiantes.*

**stag|ger|ing** /stægərɪŋ/ ADJ Something that is **staggering** is very surprising. *asombroso* ❑ *The cost was a staggering $900 million. El costo era la asombrosa suma de 900 millones de dólares.*

**stain** /steɪn/ (**stains, staining, stained**) 1 N-COUNT A **stain** is a mark on something that is difficult to remove. *mancha* ❑ *How do you remove tea stains? ¿Cómo se quitan las manchas de té?* 2 V-T If a liquid **stains** something, the thing becomes colored or marked by the liquid. *manchar* ❑ *Some foods can stain the teeth. Algunos alimentos pueden manchar los dientes.* ● **stained** ADJ *manchado* ❑ *His clothing was stained with mud. Tenía la ropa manchada de lodo.* ❑ *...ink-stained fingers. ...los dedos manchados de tinta.*

**stain|less steel** /steɪnlɪs stil/ N-UNCOUNT **Stainless steel** is a metal made from steel and chromium which does not rust. *acero inoxidable* ❑ *...a stainless steel sink. ...un fregadero de acero inoxidable.*
→ see **pan**

**stair** /stɛər/ (**stairs**) 1 N-PLURAL **Stairs** are a set of steps inside a building which go from one floor to another. *escalera(s)* ❑ *Nancy began to climb the stairs. Nancy empezó a subir las escaleras.* ❑ *We walked up a flight of stairs. Subimos un tramo de escalera.* 2 N-COUNT A **stair** is one of the steps in a flight of stairs. *escalón, peldaño* ❑ *Terry was sitting on the bottom stair. Terry estaba sentado en el último escalón.*

**stair|case** /stɛərkeɪs/ (**staircases**) N-COUNT A **staircase** is a set of stairs inside a building. *escalinata* ❑ *They walked down the staircase together. Bajaron juntos la escalinata.*
→ see **house**

**stair|lift** /stɛərlɪft/ (**stairlifts**) also **stair lift** N-COUNT A **stairlift** is a device that is attached to a staircase in a house in order to allow an elderly or sick person to go upstairs. *elevador de escalera*

**stair|way** /stɛərweɪ/ (**stairways**) N-COUNT A **stairway** is a staircase or a flight of steps, inside or outside a building. *escalinata* ❑ *...the stairway leading to the top floor. ...la escalinata que lleva al piso superior.*

**stake** /steɪk/ (**stakes, staking, staked**) 1 PHRASE If something is **at stake,** it is being risked and might be lost or damaged if you are not successful. *en juego, en riesgo, comprometido* ❑ *There was so much at stake in this game. Era mucho lo que había en juego en este partido.* 2 N-PLURAL The **stakes** involved in a contest or a risky action are the things that can be gained or lost. *apuesta* ❑ *They play cards, but not for high stakes. Juegan a las cartas, pero las apuestas no son altas.* 3 V-T If you **stake** something such as your money or your reputation **on** the result of something, you risk your money or reputation on it. *apostar, jugar(se), arriesgar* ❑ *She staked her reputation as a writer on this article. Arriesgó su reputación como escritora con este artículo.* 4 N-COUNT If you have a **stake in** something such as a business, it matters to you, for example because you own part of it or because its success or failure will affect you. *tener interés* ❑ *We all have a stake in the success of the next generation of children. Todos tenemos interés en el éxito de la próxima generación de niños.* 5 N-COUNT A **stake** is a pointed wooden post which is pushed into the ground, for example in order to support a young tree. *estaca* ❑ *She hung the clothes on a rope tied between two wooden stakes. Colgó la ropa en una cuerda atada a dos estacas.* 6 PHRASE If you **stake a claim,** you say that something is yours or that you have a right to it. *reivindicar un derecho* ❑ *His children have all staked their claim to his money. Todos sus hijos reivindican el derecho a su dinero.*

**Word Partnership** Usar *stake* con:

N. **interests at** stake, **issues at** stake 1
stake **lives on** ***something*** 3
stake **in a company/firm, majority/minority** stake 4
ADJ. **controlling** stake, **personal** stake 4

**stale** /steɪl/ (**staler, stalest**) 1 ADJ **Stale** food or air is no longer fresh. *rancio, añejo, viejo* ❑ *....stale bread. ...pan rancio.* 2 ADJ If a place, an activity, or an idea is **stale,** it has become boring because it is always the same. *anquilosado* ❑ *Her relationship*

S

with Mark has become stale. Su relación con Mark se ha anquilosado.

**stalk** /stɔk/ (**stalks, stalking, stalked**) 1 N-COUNT The **stalk** of a flower, leaf, or fruit is the thin part that joins it to the plant or tree. tallo ❑ *A single flower grows on each long stalk.* *Brota una sola flor en cada uno de los largos tallos.* 2 V-T If you **stalk** a person or a wild animal, you follow them quietly in order to kill them, catch them, or observe them carefully. acechar ❑ *...a picture of a hunter stalking a deer.* *...un cuadro de un cazador acechando a un ciervo.* 3 V-T If someone **stalks** someone else, they keep following them or contacting them in an annoying and frightening way. acosar, asediar, perseguir ❑ *I see you everywhere I go—are you stalking me?* *—Lo veo dondequiera que voy; ¿por qué me acosa?* ● **stalk|er** N-COUNT (**stalkers**) acosador o acosadora ❑ *She was followed by a stalker.* *La siguió un hombre, acosándola.*

**stall** /stɔl/ (**stalls, stalling, stalled**) 1 V-T/V-I If a process **stalls,** or if someone or something **stalls** it, the process stops but may continue at a later time. estancar, dar largas ❑ *They're trying to stall the meeting.* *Están tratando de darle largas a la reunión.* ❑ *The peace process stalled.* *Se estancó el proceso de paz.* 2 V-I If you **stall,** you try to avoid doing something until later. dar largas ❑ *Thomas spent all week stalling over his decision.* *Thomas se pasó toda la semana dándole largas a su decisión.* 3 V-T/V-I If a vehicle **stalls** or if you accidentally **stall** it, the engine stops suddenly. ahogar(se) ❑ *The engine stalled.* *Se ahogó el motor.* 4 N-COUNT A **stall** is a large table on which you put goods that you want to sell, or information that you want to give people. puesto, tenderete ❑ *...market stalls selling fruit and vegetables.* *...en los puestos del mercado venden frutas y verduras.* 5 N-COUNT A **stall** is a small enclosed area in a room which is used for a particular purpose, for example a shower. cubículo, compartimiento, compartimento ❑ *She went into the shower stall and turned on the water.* *Fue a la regadera y abrió la llave del agua.*
→ see **traffic**

**sta|men** /steɪmən/ (**stamens**) N-COUNT The **stamen** is the male part of a flower, which produces pollen. Compare **pistil.** estambre [TECHNICAL]
→ see **flower**

S

**stam|mer** /stæmər/ (**stammers, stammering, stammered**) 1 V-T/V-I If you **stammer,** you speak with difficulty, hesitating and repeating words or sounds. tartamudear, balbucear ❑ *A lot of children stammer.* *Muchos niños tartamudean.* ❑ *"Forgive me," I stammered.* *—Discúlpame, —balbuceé.* ● **stam|mer|ing** N-UNCOUNT tartamudeo ❑ *Stammering can be embarrassing.* *El tartamudeo puede ser embarazoso.* 2 N-SING Someone who has a **stammer** tends to stammer when they speak. tartamudeo ❑ *She helps children who have stammers.* *Ayuda a los niños que tartamudean.*

**stamp** /stæmp/ (**stamps, stamping, stamped**) 1 N-COUNT A **stamp** or a **postage stamp** is a small piece of paper which you stick on an envelope or package before you mail it to pay for the cost of the postage. estampilla, timbre ❑ *...a book of stamps.* *...un álbum de estampillas.* ❑ *She put a stamp on the corner of the envelope.* *Puso un timbre en una esquina del sobre.* 2 N-COUNT A **stamp** is a small block of wood or metal with words, numbers or a pattern on it. You press it onto an pad of ink and then onto a piece of paper in order to produce a mark on the paper. The mark is also called a **stamp.** sello ❑ *...a date stamp.* *...un sello con la fecha.* 3 V-T If you **stamp** a mark or word on an object, you press the mark or word onto the object using a stamp or other device. troquelar ❑ *They stamp a special number on new cars to help find stolen ones.* *Troquelan un número especial en los automóviles nuevos que ayuda a encontrar los robados.* 4 V-T/V-I If you **stamp** or **stamp** your **foot**, you put your foot down very hard on the ground, for example because you are angry. patear, pisotear ❑ *I stamped my foot in anger.* *Enojado, di una patada en el piso.* ❑ *His foot stamped down on my toe.* *Me pisoteó un dedo del pie.*
▸ **stamp out** PHR-VERB If you **stamp** something **out,** you put an end to it. erradicar ❑ *It's impossible to stamp out crime completely.* *Es imposible erradicar el crimen por completo.*

**stam|pede** /stæmpid/ (**stampedes, stampeding, stampeded**) 1 N-COUNT If there is a **stampede,** a group of people or animals run in a wild, uncontrolled way. estampida, desbandada ❑ *There was a stampede for the door.* *Todos se abalanzaron hacia la puerta.* 2 V-T/V-I If a group of animals or people **stampede** or if something **stampedes** them, they run in a wild, uncontrolled way. salir en desbandada ❑ *The crowd stampeded and many people were injured.* *Hubo una desbandada general de la multitud y muchas personas resultaron heridas.* ❑ *...a herd of stampeding cows.* *...un hato de vacas en estampida.*

**stance** /stæns/ (**stances**) 1 N-COUNT Your **stance** on a particular matter is your attitude to it. postura, posición ❑ *What is your stance on the war?* *¿Cuál es su postura sobre la guerra?* 2 N-COUNT Your **stance** is the way that you are standing. postura, posición [FORMAL] ❑ *Take a wide stance and bend your knees a little.* *Adopte una postura extendida y doble un poco las rodillas.*

**Word Partnership** Usar *stance* con:

| | |
|---|---|
| PREP. | stance **against/on/toward** ***something*** 1 |
| ADJ. | **aggressive** stance, **critical** stance, **hard-line** stance, **tough** stance 1 |
| V. | **adopt a** stance, **take a** stance 1 2 |

**stand**
1 VERB USES
2 NOUN USES
3 PHR-VERBS

1 **stand** /stænd/ (**stands, standing, stood**)
→ Please look at categories 12 to 14 to see if the expression you are looking for is shown under another headword. 1 V-I When you **are standing,** your body is upright, your legs are straight, and your weight is supported by your feet. estar de pie, estar parado ❑ *She was standing beside my bed.* *Estaba de pie junto a mi cama.* ❑ *They told me to stand still and not to turn around.* *Me dijeron que me quedara quieto y no me volviera.* ● **Stand up** means the same as **stand.** estar de pie, estar parado ❑ *We waited, standing up, for an hour.* *Esperamos de pie durante una hora.*

**2** V-I When someone who is sitting **stands,** they change their position so that they are upright and on their feet. *ponerse de pie, pararse* ❑ *Becker stood and shook hands with Ben. Becker se puso de pie y le estrechó la mano a Ben.* ● **Stand up** means the same as **stand.** *ponerse de pie, pararse* ❑ *When I walked in, they all stood up. Cuando entré, todos se pusieron de pie.* **3** V-I If you **stand aside** or **stand back,** you move a short distance sideways or backward, so that you are standing in a different place. *hacerse a un lado, hacerse para atrás* ❑ *I stood aside to let her pass me. Me hice a un lado para dejarla pasar.* **4** V-I If something such as a building or a piece of furniture **stands** somewhere, it is upright in that position. *alzarse* [WRITTEN] ❑ *The house stands alone on top of a hill. La casa se alza solitaria en la cima de una colina.* **5** V-T If you **stand** something somewhere, you put it there in an upright position. *colocar, poner* ❑ *Stand the plant in a sunny place. Ponga la planta en un lugar soleado.* **6** V-I If you ask someone **where** or **how** they **stand on** a particular issue, you are asking them what their attitude or view is. *tener una postura, tener una posición* ❑ *Where do you stand on the issue of private schools? ¿Cuál es su postura respecto del tema de las escuelas privadas?* **7** V-I If a decision, law, or offer **stands,** it still exists and has not been changed or canceled. *seguir en vigor* ❑ *The rule still stands. La regla sigue en vigor.* **8** V-I If something that can be measured **stands at** a particular level, it is at that level. *llegar a* ❑ *The number of missing people now stands at 30. El número de personas perdidas llegó a treinta.* **9** V-T If something can **stand** a situation or a test, it is good enough or strong enough to cope with it. *soportar, resistir, aguantar* ❑ *These shoes can stand a lot of use. Estos zapatos pueden resistir mucho uso.* **10** V-T If you cannot **stand** someone or something, you dislike them very strongly. *soportar* [INFORMAL] ❑ *I can't stand that awful man. No soporto a ese hombre detestable.* **11** V-T If you **stand to gain** something, you are likely to gain it. If you **stand to lose** something, you are likely to lose it. *poder ganar* ❑ *He stands to gain a lot of money if he wins the competition. Puede ganar mucho dinero si vence en la competencia.* **12** to **stand a chance** → see **chance** **13** to **stand** your **ground** → see **ground**

**❷ stand** /stænd/ (**stands**) **1** N-COUNT If you take or make a **stand,** you do something or say something in order to make it clear what your attitude to a particular thing is. *adoptar una actitud firme* ❑ *He made a stand against racism. Adoptó una actitud firme contra el racismo.* **2** N-COUNT A **stand** is a small store or stall, outdoors or in a large public building. *puesto* ❑ *I bought a magazine from a newspaper stand. Compré una revista en un puesto de periódicos.* **3** N-PLURAL The **stands** at a sports stadium or arena are a large structure where people sit or stand to watch what is happening. *tribuna(s)* ❑ *The people in the stands at Candlestick Park stood and cheered. El público en las tribunas del Estadio Candlestick Park se puso de pie y vitoreó.* **4** N-COUNT A **stand** is an object or piece of furniture that is designed for supporting or holding a particular kind of thing. *base, pedestal* ❑ *Take the television set off its stand. Quite el televisor de su base.* **5** N-COUNT A **stand** is an area where taxis or buses can wait to pick up passengers. *sitio, parada* ❑ *There was a taxi stand nearby. Había un sitio de taxis cerca.* **6** N-SING In a law court, **the stand** is the place where a witness sits to answer questions. *estrado* ❑ *When the father took the stand today, he said his son was a good man. Cuando el padre subió al estrado hoy, declaró que su hijo era un buen hombre.*

→ see **laboratory**

**❸ stand** /stænd/ (**stands, standing, stood**)

▸ **stand by** **1** PHR-VERB If you **are standing by,** you are ready and waiting to provide help or to take action. *estar en alerta* ❑ *American ships are standing by to help. Los barcos estadounidenses están en alerta para ayudar.* **2** → see also **standby** **3** PHR-VERB If you **stand by** and let something bad happen, you do not do anything to stop it; used showing disapproval. *mantenerse al margen* ❑ *I will not stand by and let them tells lies about my friend. No voy a mantenerme al margen y dejarlos contar mentiras sobre mi amigo.*

▸ **stand down** PHR-VERB If someone **stands down,** they resign from an important job or position, often in order to let someone else take their place. *retirarse* ❑ *After ten years, the leader stood down. Después de diez años, el dirigente se retiró.*

▸ **stand for** **1** PHR-VERB If you say that a letter **stands for** a particular word, you mean that it is an abbreviation for that word. *significar* ❑ *AIDS stands for Acquired Immune Deficiency Syndrome. SIDA significa síndrome de inmunodeficiencia adquirida.* **2** PHR-VERB The ideas or attitudes that someone or something **stands for** are the ones that they support or represent. *defender* ❑ *What does the Democratic Party stand for? ¿Cuál es la plataforma del Partido Democráta?* **3** PHR-VERB If you will **not stand for** something, you will not allow it to happen or continue. *tolerar* ❑ *We won't stand for this bad behavior anymore. No toleraremos más esa mala conducta.*

▸ **stand in** **1** PHR-VERB If you **stand in for** someone, you take their place or do their job, because they are sick or away. *substituir* ❑ *I had to stand in for her on Tuesday when she was sick. Tuve que substituirla el martes, cuando se enfermó.* **2** → see also **stand-in**

▸ **stand out** PHR-VERB If something **stands out,** it is very noticeable. *resaltar* ❑ *The black necklace stood out against her white dress. El collar negro resaltaba contra su vestido blanco.*

▸ **stand up** **1** → see **stand ❶ 1** → see **stand ❶** **2** **2** PHR-VERB If something such as a claim or a piece of evidence **stands up,** it is accepted as true or satisfactory after being carefully examined. *admitir* ❑ *He gave the police a lot of information, but none of it stood up in court. Le dio mucha información a la policía, pero nada de lo que dijo fue admitido en el juicio.*

▸ **stand up for** PHR-VERB If you **stand up for** someone or something, you defend them and make your feelings or opinions very clear. *defender* ❑ *They stood up for what they believed to be right. Defendieron lo que creían que era justo.*

▸ **stand up to** **1** PHR-VERB If something **stands up to** bad conditions, it is not damaged or harmed by them. *resistir* ❑ *Is this building going to stand up to the strong winds? ¿Resistirá los vientos fuertes el edificio?* **2** PHR-VERB If you **stand up to** someone more powerful than you, you defend yourself against their attacks or demands. *enfrentar, hacer frente* ❑ *He was too afraid to stand up to her. Tenía mucho temor de hacerle frente.*

**stand|ard** /stændərd/ (**standards**) 1 N-COUNT A **standard** is a level of quality or achievement, especially a level that is thought to be acceptable. calidad ❑ *The standard of his work is very low.* *La calidad de su trabajo es muy baja.* 2 N-PLURAL **Standards** are moral principles which affect people's attitudes and behavior. *norma de conducta* ❑ *My father always had high moral standards.* *Las normas de conducta de mi padre siempre fueron estrictas.* 3 ADJ You use **standard** to describe things which are usual and normal. *normal* ❑ *It's just a standard size car.* *Es tan sólo un coche de tamaño normal.*

**Word Partnership** Usar *standard* con:

V. **become a** standard, **maintain a** standard, **meet a** standard, **raise a** standard, **set a** standard, **use a** standard 1 2

N. standard **of excellence, industry** standard 1 2
standard **English**, standard **equipment**, standard **practice**, standard **procedure** 3

**stan|dard Ameri|can Eng|lish** N-UNCOUNT **Standard American English** is the form of English that is spoken by most people in the United States. *inglés estadounidense común*

**stan|dard de|via|tion** (**standard deviations**) N-VAR The **standard deviation** of a set of data is a statistical measure of how much variation there is in the data. *desviación normal*, *desviación tipo*, *desviación estándar* [TECHNICAL]

**stand|ard|ize** /stændərdaɪz/ (**standardizes, standardizing, standardized**) V-T To **standardize** things means to change them so that they all have the same features. *normalizar*, *uniformar* ❑ *They should standardize the parts so they fit any machine.* *Deberían estandarizar las partes para que sirvan para cualquier máquina.* • **stand|ardi|za|tion** /stændərdɪzeɪʃən/ N-UNCOUNT *uniformación*, *estandarización* ❑ *...the standardization of working hours.* *...la uniformación de la jornada de trabajo.*

**stand|ard of liv|ing** (**standards of living**) N-COUNT Your **standard of living** is the level of comfort and wealth which you have. *nivel de vida*, *estándar de vida* ❑ *We're trying to improve their standard of living.* *Estamos tratando de mejorar su nivel de vida.*

**stand|by** /stændbaɪ/ (**standbys**) also **stand-by** 1 N-COUNT A **standby** is something or someone that is always ready to be used if they are needed. *reserva* ❑ *Canned vegetables are a good standby.* *Siempre es bueno tener verduras enlatadas de reserva.* 2 PHRASE If someone or something is **on standby,** they are ready to be used if they are needed. *listo*, *en guardia* ❑ *Five ambulances are on standby.* *Hay cinco ambulancias de guardia.* 3 ADJ A **standby** ticket for something such as the theater or a plane trip is a cheap ticket that you buy just before the performance starts or the plane takes off, if there are still some seats left. *sujeto a disponibilidad*, *de lista de espera* ❑ *He bought a standby ticket to New York and flew to JFK airport six hours later.* *Estaba en lista de espera para volar a Nueva York y tomó el avión al aeropuerto John F. Kennedy seis horas después.* • **Standby** is also an adverb. *en lista de espera* ❑ *Magda was going to fly standby.* *Magda iba a esperar en el aeropuerto hasta que hubiera un boleto disponible.*

**stand-in** (**stand-ins**) N-COUNT A **stand-in** is a person who takes someone else's place or does someone else's job for a while, for example because the other person is sick or away. *substituto o substituta* ❑ *He was a stand-in for my regular doctor.* *Era el substituto del médico que me atendía normalmente.*

**stand|ing wave** (**standing waves**) N-COUNT A **standing wave** is a wave such as a sound wave that appears not to move, because another wave of the same frequency is traveling in the opposite direction. *onda estacionaria* [TECHNICAL]

**stand|off** /stændɔf/ (**standoffs**) N-COUNT A **standoff** is a situation in which neither of two opposing groups or forces will make a move until the other one does something, so nothing can happen until one of them gives way. *callejón sin salida* ❑ *There was a standoff between the crowd and the police.* *El enfrentamiento entre la multitud y la policía estaba en un callejón sin salida.*

**stand|point** /stændpɔɪnt/ (**standpoints**) N-COUNT **From** a particular **standpoint** means looking at an event, situation, or idea in a particular way. *punto de vista*, *perspectiva* ❑ *From a business standpoint, this is a great deal.* *Desde un punto de vista comercial, es un gran negocio.*

**stand|still** /stændstɪl/ N-SING If movement or activity comes **to** or is brought to **a standstill,** it stops completely. *detención*, *paralización* ❑ *The cars came to a standstill.* *Los automóviles se detuvieron por completo.*

**stand-up** also **standup** 1 ADJ A **stand-up** comic or comedian stands alone in front of an audience and tells jokes. *(cómico) de micrófono* ❑ *He can do jokes—he could be a stand-up comic.* *Sabe contar chistes; podría trabajar como cómico de micrófono.* 2 N-UNCOUNT **Stand-up** is stand-up comedy. *comedia* ❑ *It takes a lot of courage to do stand-up.* *Se necesita mucho valor para hacer comedia.*

**sta|ple** /steɪpəl/ (**staples, stapling, stapled**) 1 ADJ A **staple** food, product, or activity is one that is basic and important in people's everyday lives. *básico* ❑ *Rice is the staple food of more than half the world's population.* *El arroz es el alimento básico de más de la mitad de la población mundial.* • **Staple** is also a noun. *alimento básico* ❑ *Fish is a staple in the diet of many Africans.* *El pescado es un alimento básico de la dieta de muchos africanos.* 2 N-COUNT **Staples** are small pieces of bent wire that are used mainly for holding sheets of paper together firmly. You put the staples into the paper using a device called a stapler. *grapa* 3 V-T If you **staple** something, you fasten it to something else or fix it in place using staples. *engrapar* ❑ *Staple some sheets of paper together.* *Engrapa unas hojas de papel.*

**sta|pler** /steɪplər/ (**plural**) N-COUNT A **stapler** is a device used for putting staples into sheets of paper. *engrapadora*
→ see **office**

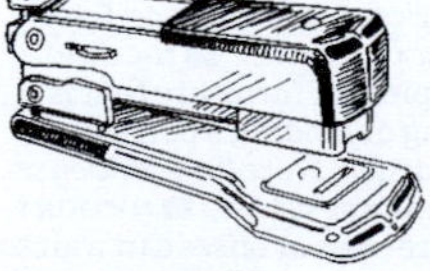

stapler

**star** /stɑr/ (**stars, starring, starred**) 1 N-COUNT A **star** is a large ball of burning gas in

**Word Web** **star**

**Astronomy** is the oldest science. It is the study of **stars** and other objects in the **night sky**. People sometimes confuse astronomy and **astrology**. Astrology is the belief that the stars affect people's lives. Long ago people named groups of stars after gods, heroes, and imaginary animals. One of the most famous of these **constellations** is the Big Dipper. Its original name meant "the big bear." It is easy to find and it points toward the North Star*. For centuries sailors have used the North Star to **navigate**. The best-known star in our **galaxy** is the **sun**.

*North Star: the star that the earth's northern axis points toward.*

space. Stars appear to us as small points of light in the sky on clear nights. *estrella, astro* ❑ *Stars lit the sky. Las estrellas iluminaron el cielo.* 2 N-COUNT You can refer to a shape or an object as a **star** when it has four, five, or more points sticking out of it in a regular pattern. *estrella* ❑ *Children at school receive colored stars for good work. A los niños les dan estrellas de colores en la escuela cuando hacen bien las cosas.* 3 N-COUNT Famous actors, musicians, and sports players are often referred to as **stars**. *estrella* ❑ *...star of the TV series "Friends." ...la estrella de la serie de televisión "Friends".* ❑ *Murphy is Hollywood's top comedy star. Murphy es la estrella más brillante de la comedia en Hollywood.* 4 V-I If an actor or actress **stars in** a play or movie, he or she has one of the most important parts in it. *protagonizar* ❑ *Adolphson starred in a play in which Ingrid had a part. Adolphson protagonizó una obra en la que Ingrid tuvo un papel secundario.* 5 V-T If a play or movie **stars** a famous actor or actress, he or she has one of the most important parts in it. *tener como protagonista* ❑ *...a movie starring Anthony Quinn. ...una película que tiene como protagonista a Anthony Quinn.* 6 N-PLURAL Predictions about people's lives which are based on astrology and appear regularly in a newspaper or magazine are sometimes referred to as **the stars**. *los astros* ❑ *There was nothing in my stars to say I'd have travel problems! ¡Los astros no decían que fuese a tener problemas en el viaje!*
→ see Word Web: **star**
→ see **galaxy, navigation**

**Word Partnership** Usar *star* con:

| | |
|---|---|
| ADJ. | **bright** star 1 |
| | **bronze** star, **gold** star 2 |
| | **big** star, **former** star, **rising** star 3 |
| N. | **all-star cast/game, basketball/football/ tennis** star, **film/movie** star, **guest** star, **pop/rap** star, **TV** star 3 |
| | star **in a film/movie/show** 4 |

**starch** /stɑrtʃ/ (**starches**) 1 N-VAR **Starch** is a substance that is found in foods such as bread, potatoes, pasta, and rice, and that gives you energy. *almidón, fécula* ❑ *You should eat less starch, salt, and fat. Debería comer menos carbohidratos, sal y grasa.* 2 N-UNCOUNT **Starch** is a substance that is used for making cloth stiffer. *almidón* ❑ *He never puts enough starch in my shirts. Nunca almidona lo suficiente mis camisas.*
→ see **rice**

**stare** /stɛər/ (**stares, staring, stared**) V-I If you **stare at** someone or something, you look at them for a long time. *mirar* ❑ *Ben continued to stare out the window. Ben siguió mirando por la ventana.* ● **Stare** is also a noun. *mirada* ❑ *Harry gave him a long stare. Harry se le quedó mirando fijamente.*

**Word Partnership** Usar *stare* con:

| | |
|---|---|
| ADJ. | **blank** stare |
| V. | **continue to** stare, **turn to** stare |

**stark** /stɑrk/ (**starker, starkest**) 1 ADJ **Stark** choices or statements are harsh and unpleasant. *duro* ❑ *Companies face a stark choice if they want to succeed. Las empresas enfrentan una dura decisión si desean triunfar.* ● **stark|ly** ADV *crudamente* ❑ *"She never loved you," he said starkly. —Ella nunca te quiso, —le dijo crudamente.* 2 ADJ If two things are in **stark** contrast to one another, they are very different from each other. *marcado* ❑ *His opinions were in stark contrast to my own. El contraste entre sus opiniones y las mías era muy marcado.*

**Star of David** /stɑr əv deɪvɪd/ (**Stars of David**) N-COUNT The **Star of David** is a six-pointed star that is a symbol of Judaism and the state of Israel. *estrella de David* ❑ *Sarah wears a Star of David around her neck. Sara lleva un collar con la estrella de David.*

**start** /stɑrt/ (**starts, starting, started**) 1 V-T If you **start to** do something, you do something that you were not doing before. *empezar, comenzar* ❑ *I started to follow him up the stairs. Empecé a seguirlo escaleras arriba.* ❑ *Susanna started the work on the garden in 1956. Susanna comenzó a trabajar en el jardín en 1956.* ● **Start** is also a noun. *comienzo, principio* ❑ *After several starts, she read the report properly. Después de empezar varias veces, leyó el informe correctamente.* 2 V-T/V-I When something **starts**, or if someone **starts** it, it takes place from a particular time. *empezar, comenzar, iniciarse* ❑ *The fire started in an upstairs room. El fuego se inició en un cuarto del piso superior.* ❑ *I started the day with a swim. Empecé mi día nadando un poco.* ● **Start** is also a noun. *inicio, comienzo, principio* ❑ *...1918, four years after the start of the Great War. ...en 1918, cuatro años después del inicio de la gran guerra.* 3 V-I You

S

use **start** to say what your first job was. empezar, comenzar ❑ *Betty started as an office girl.* Betty empezó como oficinista. ● **Start off** means the same as **start.** empezar, comenzar ❑ *Mr. Dambar started off as an assistant to Mrs. Spear's husband.* El señor Dambar comenzó como ayudante del esposo de la señora Spear. **4** V-T When someone **starts** something such as a new business, they create it or cause it to begin. abrir, montar ❑ *George Granger has started a health center and he's looking for staff.* George Granger abrió un centro de salud y está buscando personal. ● **Start up** means the same as **start.** abrir, montar ❑ *...the cost of starting up a day-care center for children.* ...el costo de montar una guardería infantil. **5** V-T/V-I If you **start** an engine, car, or machine, or if it **starts,** it begins to work. encender, arrancar, prender ❑ *He started the car, which hummed smoothly.* Encendió el coche y éste ronroneó suavemente. ● **Start up** means the same as **start.** encender, arrancar, prender ❑ *He started up the car and drove off.* Prendió el motor del coche y arrancó. ❑ *Turn the key to start the car up.* Dé vuelta a la llave para prender el motor. **6** V-I If you **start,** your body suddenly moves slightly as a result of surprise or fear. sobresaltarse ❑ *She banged the bottle down on the table. He started at the sound.* Dio un golpe en la mesa con la botella y él se sobresaltó con el ruido. ● **Start** is also a noun. sobresalto ❑ *Sylvia woke with a start.* Sylvia despertó con un sobresalto. **7** PHRASE You use **for a start** or **to start with** to introduce the first of a number of things or reasons that you want to mention or could mention. para empezar ❑ *You need her name and address, and that's a problem for a start.* Necesitas su nombre y dirección; y eso es un problema, para empezar. **8** to **get off to a flying start** → see **flying**

▸ **start off** **1** PHR-VERB If you **start off by** doing something, you do it as the first part of an activity. empezar por, comenzar por ❑ *She started off by clearing some space on the table.* Empezó por hacer un poco de espacio en la mesa. **2** → see **start 3**

▸ **start on** PHR-VERB If you **start on** something that needs to be done, you start dealing with it. empezar con, comenzar con ❑ *Before you start on the cleaning, put on some old clothes.* Antes de que empiece con la limpieza, póngase ropa que sea vieja.

▸ **start out** **1** PHR-VERB If someone or something **starts out as** a particular thing, they are that thing at the beginning although they change later. empezar como, comenzar como ❑ *Daly started out as a salesman.* Daly empezó como vendedor. **2** PHR-VERB If you **start out by** doing something, you do it at the beginning of an activity. empezar por, comenzar por ❑ *I always start out by saying clearly what I want.* Siempre comienzo por decir claramente lo que quiero.

▸ **start over** PHR-VERB If you **start over** or **start** something **over,** you begin something again from the beginning. empezar de nuevo, comenzar de nuevo ❑ *I did it all wrong and had to start over.* Lo hice todo mal y tuve que comenzar de nuevo.

▸ **start up** → see **start 4, 5**

**Thesaurus** *start* Ver también:

V. begin, commence, originate **1** **2**
establish, found, launch **4**
N. beginning, onset **1** **2**
jump, scare, shock **6**

**star|tle** /stɑrtᵊl/ (**startles, startling, startled**) V-T If something sudden and unexpected **startles** you, it surprises and frightens you slightly. sobresaltar ❑ *The telephone startled him.* El teléfono lo sobresaltó. ● **star|tled** ADJ asustado ❑ *Martha gave her a startled look.* Martha le dirigió una mirada asustada.

**star|tling** /stɑrtᵊlɪŋ/ ADJ Something that is **startling** is so different, unexpected, or remarkable that people react to it with surprise. asombroso, sorprendente ❑ *Sometimes the results are startling.* En ocasiones, los resultados son sorprendentes.

**starve** /stɑrv/ (**starves, starving, starved**) **1** V-I If people **starve,** they suffer greatly from lack of food which sometimes leads to their death. pasar hambre, morir(se) de hambre ❑ *A number of the prisoners are starving.* Varios prisioneros están pasando hambre. ❑ *In the 1930s, millions of Ukrainians starved to death.* En los años 30, millones de ukranianos murieron de hambre. ● **star|va|tion** /stɑrveɪʃᵊn/ N-UNCOUNT hambre, inanición ❑ *Over three hundred people died of starvation.* Más de trescientas personas murieron de inanición. **2** V-T To **starve** someone means not to give them any food. privar de comida ❑ *He was starving himself.* No estaba comiendo nada. **3** V-T If a person or thing **is starved of** something that they need, they are suffering because they are not getting enough of it. sufrir por la falta de, morir(se) por la falta de ❑ *She felt awful, starved of his love.* Se sentía terrible, privada de su amor.

**starv|ing** /stɑrvɪŋ/ ADJ If you say that you are **starving,** you mean that you are very hungry. morirse de hambre [INFORMAL] ❑ *Does anyone have any food? I'm starving.* —¿Alguien tiene algo de comer? Me muero de hambre.

**state** /steɪt/ (**states, stating, stated**) **1** N-COUNT You can refer to countries as **states,** particularly when you are discussing politics. estado ❑ *...a socialist state.* ...un estado socialista. **2** N-COUNT Some large countries such as the U.S. are divided into smaller areas called **states.** estado ❑ *Leaders of the Southern states are meeting in Louisville.* Los dirigentes de los estados sureños están reunidos en Louisville. **3** N-PROPER The U.S. is sometimes referred to as **the States.** Estados Unidos [INFORMAL] ❑ *She bought it in the States.* Lo compró en Estados Unidos. **4** N-SING You can refer to the government of a country as **the state.** Estado ❑ *In Sweden, child care is provided by the state.* En Suecia, el cuidado infantil lo proporciona el Estado. **5** ADJ A **state** occasion is a formal one involving the head of a country. de estado ❑ *The president of the Czech Republic is in Washington on a state visit.* El presidente de la República Checa se encuentra en Washington en visita de estado. **6** N-COUNT When you talk about the **state of** someone or something, you are referring to the condition they are in or what they are like at a particular time. estado ❑ *For the first few months after Daniel died, I was in a state of shock.* Los primeros meses después de la muerte de Daniel me los pasé en un estado de shock. **7** V-T If you **state** something, you say or write it in a formal or definite way. exponer, escribir, consignar ❑ *Clearly state your address and telephone number.* Escriba claramente su dirección y número de teléfono. ❑ *The police report stated that he was arrested for stealing a car.* El informe de la policía consignaba que lo arrestaron por robar un automóvil. **8** PHRASE **States of matter** are

S

the different physical forms in which substances can exist. The most common states of matter are solid, liquid, and gas. *estado de la materia* 9 → see also **head of state**
→ see **matter**

**Thesaurus** *state* Ver también:
N. government, land, nation, republic, sovereignty 1
attitude, condition, mood, situation 6
V. articulate, express, narrate, relate, say, tell 7

**state line** (**state lines**) N-COUNT A **state line** is a border between two states within a country. *límite del estado* ❑ *Then they crossed the state line into Mississippi. Luego cruzaron el límite del estado y entraron a Mississippi.*

**state|ment** /steɪtmənt/ (**statements**) 1 N-COUNT A **statement** is something that you say or write which gives information in a formal or definite way. *afirmación, declaración* ❑ *I was very angry when I made that statement. Estaba muy enojado cuando hice esa afirmación.* 2 N-COUNT A printed document showing how much money has been paid into and taken out of a bank or investment account is called a **statement.** *estado de cuenta* ❑ *...the address at the top of your monthly statement. ...la dirección en la parte superior de su estado de cuenta mensual.*

**state of emer|gen|cy** (**states of emergency**) N-COUNT If a government declares a **state of emergency** in an area, it introduces special measures such as increased powers for the police or army, usually because of civil disorder or because of a natural disaster such as an earthquake. *estado de alarma, estado de emergencia* ❑ *The government declared a state of emergency in New Orleans. El gobierno declaró el estado de emergencia en Nueva Orléans.*

**state of mind** (**states of mind**) N-COUNT Your **state of mind** is your mood or mental state at a particular time. *estado de ánimo* ❑ *I want you to get into a whole new state of mind. Quiero que cambies por completo tu estado de ánimo.*

**state-of-the-art** ADJ If you describe something as **state-of-the-art,** you mean that it is the best available because it has been made using the most modern techniques and technology. *con tecnología de punto, último modelo, de vanguardia* ❑ *...a state-of-the-art computer. ...una computadora con tecnología de punto.*
→ see **technology**

**State of the Un|ion** N-UNCOUNT A **State of the Union** speech or address is a speech, given once a year, in which the president of the United States talks about the current political issues that affect the country as a whole and about his plans for the year ahead. *informe sobre el estado de la nación, informe presidencial en los Estados Unidos* ❑ *In his State of the Union message, the president talked about change. En su informe sobre el estado de la nación, el presidente habló sobre el cambio.*

**state school** (**state schools**) N-COUNT In the United States, a **state school** is a college or university that is part of the public education system provided by the state government. *institución escolar o universitaria pública*

**states|man** /steɪtsmən/ (**statesmen**) N-COUNT A **statesman** is an important and experienced politician, especially one who is widely known and respected. *hombre de estado, estadista* ❑ *Hamilton is a great statesman and political thinker. Hamilton es un gran estadista y pensador político.*

**state trooper** (**state troopers**) N-COUNT In the U.S., a **state trooper** is a member of the police force in one of the states. *policía estatal* ❑ *State troopers said the truck driver was going too fast. Los policías estatales afirmaron que el conductor del camión conducía con exceso de velocidad.*

**state uni|ver|sity** (**state universities**) N-COUNT A **state university** is the same as a **state school.** *universidad pública* ❑ *He was a professor at the local state university. Era profesor en la universidad pública del estado.*

**Word Link** *stat* ≈ *standing* : *static, station, stationary*

**stat|ic** /stætɪk/ 1 ADJ Something that is **static** does not move or change. *estático, estacionario, invariable* ❑ *The number of people without work has remained static. El número de personas sin trabajo ha permanecido invariable.* 2 N-UNCOUNT **Static** or **static electricity** is electricity which collects on things such as your body or metal objects. *electricidad estática* ❑ *When the weather turns cold and dry, my clothes develop a static problem. Cuando el clima es frío y seco, mi ropa genera electricidad estática.* 3 N-UNCOUNT If there is **static** on the radio or television, you hear a series of loud noises which spoils the sound. *interferencia* ❑ *A voice came through the static on the radio. Se oyó una voz en medio de la interferencia de la radio.*

**sta|tion** /steɪʃᵊn/ (**stations, stationing, stationed**) 1 N-COUNT A **station** or a train **station** is a building by a railroad track where trains stop so that people can get on or off. *estación del ferrocarril* ❑ *Ingrid went with him to the train station. Ingrid fue con él a la estación del ferrocarril.* 2 N-COUNT A bus **station** is a building, usually in a town or city, where buses stop, usually for a while, so that people can get on or off. *estación de autobuses* ❑ *I walked to the bus station and bought a ticket home. Caminé a la estación de autobuses y compré un boleto para ir a casa.* 3 N-COUNT If you talk about a particular radio or television **station,** you are referring to the company that broadcasts programs. *estación de radio o canal de televisión* ❑ *...a local radio station. ...una estación de radio local.* 4 V-T PASSIVE If soldiers or officials **are stationed** in a place, they are sent there to do a job or to work for a period of time. *destacar, apostar* ❑ *Troops are stationed on the streets. Hay tropas apostadas en las calles.* 5 → see also **gas station, police station, power station, space station**
→ see **cellphone, radio, satellite, television**

**Word Partnership** Usar *station* con:
N. **railroad** station, **subway** station 1
**radio** station, **television/TV** station 3
ADJ. **local** station 3

S

**Word Link** *stat ≈ standing : static, station, stationary*

**sta|tion|ary** /steɪʃənɛri/ ADJ Something that is **stationary** is not moving. *estacionario, inmóvil* ❑ *...a stationary line of vehicles. ...una fila de vehículos inmóviles.*

**sta|tion|ery** /steɪʃənɛri/ N-UNCOUNT **Stationery** is paper, envelopes, and other materials or equipment used for writing. *artículos o útiles de escritorio* ❑ *...paper and other office stationery. ...papel y otros artículos de escritorio.*
→ see **office**

**sta|tion house** (**station houses**) N-COUNT A **station house** is a police station or a fire station, or a building that is attached to a police station or a fire station. *comisaría* ❑ *They were taken in a police van to the station house. Los llevaron a la comisaría en un vehículo de la policía.*

**sta|tion mod|el** (**station models**) N-COUNT A **station model** is a weather map containing symbols that represent the weather conditions around a particular weather station. *modelo climático, modelo meteorológico* [TECHNICAL]

**sta|tion wag|on** (**station wagons**) N-COUNT A **station wagon** is a car with a long body, a door at the rear, and space behind the back seats. *camioneta*
→ see **car**

station wagon

**sta|tis|tic** /stətɪstɪk/ (**statistics**) **1** N-COUNT **Statistics** are facts which are obtained from analyzing information and are expressed in numbers. *estadística(s)* ❑ *Statistics show that wages are rising. Las estadísticas indican que los salarios están aumentando.* ● **sta|tis|ti|cal** ADJ *estadístico* ❑ *The report contains a lot of statistical information. El informe contiene mucha información estadística.* ● **sta|tis|ti|cal|ly** /stətɪstɪkli/ ADV *estadísticamente* ❑ *The results are not statistically correct. Los resultados no son estadísticamente válidos.* **2** N-UNCOUNT **Statistics** is a branch of mathematics concerned with the study of information that is expressed in numbers. *estadística* ❑ *...a professor of mathematical statistics. ...un profesor de estadística matemática.*

**statue** /stætʃu/ (**statues**) N-COUNT A **statue** is a large sculpture of a person or an animal, made of stone or metal. *estatua* ❑ *...a stone statue of a horse. ...una estatua de piedra de un caballo.*

**sta|tus** /steɪtəs, stæt-/ **1** N-UNCOUNT Your **status** is your social or professional position. *categoría* ❑ *...women and men of status. ...mujeres y hombres de categoría.* **2** N-UNCOUNT The **status** of someone or something is the importance that people give them. *categoría* ❑ *Nurses do not have the same status as doctors. Las enfermeras no tienen la misma categoría que los médicos.* **3** N-UNCOUNT **Status** is an official description that gives a person, organization, or place particular rights or advantages. *condición* ❑ *They were proud of their status as guards. Estaban orgullosos de su condición de guardias.*

S

**Word Partnership** Usar *status* con:

| | |
|---|---|
| V. | **achieve** status, **maintain/preserve** *one's* status **1** |
| N. | **celebrity** status, **wealth and** status **1** **2**<br>**change of** status **1** – **3**<br>**marital** status, **tax** status **3** |
| ADJ. | **current** status **1** – **3**<br>**economic** status, **financial** status **3** |

**sta|tus quo** /steɪtəs kwoʊ, stæt-/ N-SING **The status quo** is the state of affairs that exists at a particular time. *statu quo* ❑ *They wanted to keep the status quo. Querían mantener el statu quo.*

**stat|ute** /stætʃut/ (**statutes**) N-VAR A **statute** is a rule or law which has been formally written down. *ley* ❑ *The new statute is about the protection of children. La nueva ley versa sobre la protección del niño.*

**stat|ute of limi|ta|tions** (**statutes of limitations**) N-COUNT If there is a **statute of limitations on** a legal case such as a crime, people can no longer be accused after a certain period of time has passed. *ley de prescripción* ❑ *The statute of limitations on most crimes is five years. La prescripción de la mayoría de los crímenes es de cinco años.*

**statu|tory** /stætʃʊtɔri/ ADJ **Statutory** means relating to rules or laws which have been formally written down. *reglamentario* [FORMAL] ❑ *...statutory law. ...ley reglamentaria.*

**stay** /steɪ/ (**stays, staying, stayed**) **1** V-I If you **stay** where you are, you continue to be there and do not leave. *quedarse* ❑ *"Stay here," Trish said. "I'll bring the car to you." —Quédate ahí —dijo Trish, —voy a traer el coche.* **2** V-T/V-I If you **stay** in a city, or hotel, or at someone's house, you live there for a short time. *alojarse, quedarse* ❑ *Gordon stayed at The Park Hotel, Milan. Gordon se alojó en el hotel El Parque, en Milán.* ❑ *Can't you stay a few more days? ¿Puedes quedarte unos días más?* ● **Stay** is also a noun. *estancia* ❑ *Please contact the hotel reception if you have any problems during your stay. Favor de comunicarse con la recepción del hotel si tiene algún problema durante su estancia.* **3** V-LINK If someone or something **stays** in a particular state or situation, they continue to be in it. *mantenerse* ❑ *If you want to stay ahead you have to work hard. Si quieres mantenerte en la delantera, tienes que trabajar duro.* ❑ *...classes on how to stay healthy. ...clases para mantenerse saludable.* **4** V-I If you **stay away from** a place, you do not go there. *parar* ❑ *Most workers stayed away from work during the strike. La mayoría de los trabajadores dejó de laborar durante la huelga.* **5** V-I If you **stay out of** something, you do not get involved in it. *no intervenir* ❑ *I try to stay out of other people's arguments. Procuro no intervenir en las discusiones de otras personas.* **6** PHRASE If you **stay put,** you remain somewhere. *quedarse* ❑ *I want you to stay put while I go and find out what's happening. Quiero que te quedes aquí mientras voy a ver qué está pasando.*
▸ **stay in** PHR-VERB If you **stay in** during the evening, you remain at home and do not go out. *quedarse* ❑ *We decided to stay in and have dinner at home. Decidimos quedarnos y cenar en casa.*
▸ **stay on** PHR-VERB If you **stay on** somewhere, you remain there after other people have left or after the time when you were going to leave. *permanecer, quedarse* ❑ *He arranged to stay on in*

*Adelaide.* *Hizo arreglos para permanecer en Adelaida.*
▸ **stay out** PHR-VERB If you **stay out** at night, you remain away from home, especially when you are expected to be there. *pasar fuera cierto tiempo* ❑ *That was the first time Elliot stayed out all night.* *Era la primera vez que Elliot pasaba fuera toda la noche.*
▸ **stay up** PHR-VERB If you **stay up**, you remain out of bed at a later time than normal. *quedarse levantado* ❑ *I used to stay up late with my mom and watch movies.* *Solía quedarme levantado hasta tarde y ver películas con mamá.*

**steady** /stɛdi/ (**steadier, steadiest, steadies, steadying, steadied**) **1** ADJ A **steady** situation continues or develops gradually without any interruptions and is not likely to change quickly. *constante* ❑ *...the steady progress of the building work.* *...el avance constante del trabajo de construcción.* ❑ *The improvement in standards has been steady.* *El mejoramiento de las normas ha sido constante.*
● **steadi|ly** /stɛdɪli/ ADV *regularmente* ❑ *Relax and keep breathing steadily.* *Relájese y siga respirando regularmente.* **2** ADJ If an object is **steady,** it is firm and does not shake or move around. *fijo* ❑ *Hold the camera steady.* *Sostén fija la cámara.* **3** ADJ If you look at someone or speak to them in a **steady** way, you look or speak in a calm, controlled way. *firme* ❑ *"Well, go on," said Camilla, her voice steady.* *—Bueno; vamos—dijo Camilla con voz firme.* ● **steadi|ly** ADV *fijamente* ❑ *He stared steadily at Elaine.* *Miró fijamente a Elaine.* **4** V-T/V-I If you **steady** something or if it **steadies,** it stops shaking or moving around. *fijar, sujetar* ❑ *Two men were at the back of the house, steadying a ladder.* *Había dos hombres en la parte trasera de la casa, sujetando una escalera.* **5** V-T If you **steady yourself**, you control your voice or expression, so that people will think that you are calm and not nervous. *tranquilizarse* ❑ *Somehow she steadied herself.* *De alguna manera, logró tranquilizarse.*

**Thesaurus** *steady* Ver también:

ADJ. consistent, continuous, uninterrupted **1**
constant, fixed, stable **2**
calm, cool, reserved, sedate **3**

**Word Partnership** Usar *steady* con:

N. steady **decline/increase**, steady **diet**, steady **growth**, steady **improvement**, steady **income**, steady **progress**, steady **rain**, steady **rate**, steady **supply** **1**
V. **remain** steady **1** **2**
**hold/keep** ***something*** steady **2**

**steak** /steɪk/ (**steaks**) **1** N-VAR A **steak** is a large flat piece of beef without much fat on it. You cook it by grilling or frying it. *filete* ❑ *...a steak cooking on the grill.* *...un filete asándose en la parrilla.* **2** N-COUNT A fish **steak** is a large piece of fish that contains few bones. *filete* ❑ *...fresh salmon steaks.* *...filetes de salmón fresco.*

**steal** /stil/ (**steals, stealing, stole, stolen**) V-T/V-I If you **steal** something **from** someone, you take it away from them without their permission and without intending to return it. *robar(se)* ❑ *They said he stole a small boy's bicycle.* *Dicen que robó la bicicleta de un niño.* ❑ *It's wrong to steal.* *Robar es malo.* ● **steal|ing** N-UNCOUNT *robo, robar* ❑ *She was put in jail for stealing.* *La metieron a la cárcel por robar.*
● **sto|len** /stoʊlən/ ADJ *robado* ❑ *We have now found the stolen car.* *Ya encontramos el automóvil robado.*

**steam** /stim/ (**steams, steaming, steamed**) **1** N-UNCOUNT **Steam** is the hot mist that forms when water boils. **Steam** vehicles and machines are operated using steam as a means of power. *vapor* ❑ *The heat converts water into steam.* *El agua se convierte en vapor con el calor.* **2** V-I If something **steams,** it gives off steam. *arrojar vapor* ❑ *Coffee pots steamed on their burners.* *Las cafeteras en los quemadores arrojaban vapor.* **3** V-T/V-I If you **steam** food or if it **steams,** you cook it in steam rather than in water. *cocinar al vapor, cocer al vapor* ❑ *Steam the carrots until they are slightly soft.* *Cueza las zanahorias al vapor hasta que estén ligeramente suaves.* ❑ *Leave the vegetables to steam over the rice.* *Deje que las verduras se cuezan al vapor sobre el arroz.* **4** PHRASE If you **run out of steam,** you stop doing something because you have no more energy or enthusiasm left. *cansarse* [INFORMAL] ❑ *I decided to paint the bathroom but ran out of steam halfway through.* *Decidí pintar el cuarto de baño, pero me cansé a mitad del camino.*
→ see **cook, train**

**Word Partnership** Usar *steam* con:

N. steam **bath, clouds of** steam, steam **engine**, steam **locomotive**, steam **pipes**, steam **turbine** **1**
ADJ. steam **powered, rising** steam **1**

**steel** /stil/ (**steels, steeling, steeled**) **1** N-UNCOUNT **Steel** is a very strong metal which is made mainly from iron. *acero* ❑ *...steel pipes.* *...tubos de acero.* ❑ *...the iron and steel industry.* *...la industria del hierro y el acero.* **2** → see also **stainless steel** **3** V-T If you **steel yourself**, you prepare to deal with something unpleasant. *armarse de valor* ❑ *They are steeling themselves for the coming battle.* *Están armándose de valor para la próxima batalla.*
→ see **bridge, train**

**steep** /stip/ (**steeper, steepest**) **1** ADJ A **steep** slope rises at a very sharp angle and is difficult to go up. *escarpado, abrupto* ❑ *Some of the hills in San Francisco are very steep.* *Algunas de las colinas de San Francisco son muy escarpadas.* ● **steep|ly** ADV *abruptamente* ❑ *The road climbs steeply.* *La carretera asciende abruptamente.* **2** ADJ A **steep** increase or decrease in something is a very big increase or decrease. *marcado* ❑ *There have been steep price increases.* *Los aumentos de precios han sido muy marcados.* ● **steep|ly** ADV *considerablemente* ❑ *Unemployment is rising steeply.* *El desempleo está aumentando considerablemente.*

**steer** /stɪər/ (**steers, steering, steered**) **1** V-T When you **steer** a car, boat, or plane, you control it so that it goes in the direction that you want. *conducir, dirigir, gobernar* ❑ *What is it like to steer a big ship?* *¿Qué se siente gobernar un gran buque?* **2** V-T If you **steer** someone in a particular direction, you guide them there. *llevar, conducir* ❑ *Nick steered them into the nearest seats.* *Nick los llevó a los asientos más cercanos.* **3** PHRASE If you **steer clear of** someone or something, you deliberately avoid them. *evitar* ❑ *We steered clear of the subject of religion.* *Evitamos el tema de la religión.*

S

**steer|ing wheel** (**steering wheels**) N-COUNT In a car or other vehicle, the **steering wheel** is the wheel which the driver holds when he or she is driving. *volante, timón*

**stem** /stɛm/ (**stems, stemming, stemmed**) **1** V-I If a condition or problem **stems from** something, it was caused originally by that thing. *provenir, ser producto de* ❑ *All my problems stem from my childhood. Todos mis problemas provienen de mi niñez.* **2** V-T If you **stem** something, you stop it from spreading, increasing, or continuing. *contener* [FORMAL] ❑ *She tied some cloth around his arm to try to stem the flow of blood. Se ató un trozo de tela alrededor del brazo para tratar de contener el flujo de sangre.* **3** N-COUNT The **stem** of a plant is the thin, upright part on which the flowers and leaves grow. *tallo* ❑ *He cut the stem and gave her the flower. Cortó el tallo y le dio la flor.*
→ see **flower**

**Word Partnership** Usar *stem* con:

N. **charges** stem **from** ***something***, **problems** stem **from** ***something*** **1**
stem **the flow of** ***something***, stem **losses**, stem **the tide of** ***something*** **2**

**ste|nog|ra|pher** /stənɒgrəfər/ (**stenographers**) N-COUNT A **stenographer** is a person who types and writes shorthand, usually in an office. *taquígrafo o taquígrafa, estenógrafo o estenógrafa*

**step** /stɛp/ (**steps, stepping, stepped**) **1** N-COUNT If you take a **step**, you lift your foot and put it down in a different place, for example when you are walking. *paso* ❑ *I took a step toward him. Di un paso hacia él.* ❑ *She walked on a few steps. Caminó unos cuantos pasos.* **2** V-I If you **step on** something or **step** in a particular direction, you put your foot on the thing or move your foot in that direction. *pisar, dar pasos* ❑ *Neil Armstrong was the first man to step on the Moon. Neil Armstrong fue el primer hombre que pisó la Luna.* ❑ *Doug stepped sideways. Doug dio un paso de lado.* **3** N-COUNT A **step** is a raised flat surface, often one of a series, on which you put your feet in order to walk up or down to a different level. *escalón* ❑ *This little room was along a passage and down some steps. El cuartito estaba a lo largo de un pasillo, unos escalones abajo.* ❑ *A little girl was sitting on the step of the house. Una niña estaba sentada en el escalón de entrada de la casa.* **4** → see also **doorstep** **5** N-COUNT A **step** is one of a series of actions that you take in order to achieve something. *paso* ❑ *The agreement is the first step toward peace. El acuerdo es el primer paso hacia la paz.* **6** PHRASE If you stay **one step ahead of** someone or something, you manage to achieve more than they do or avoid competition or danger from them. *un paso adelante de* ❑ *Teachers should always keep one step ahead of their students. Los maestros siempre deben mantenerse un paso adelante de sus alumnos.* **7** PHRASE If people are **in step with** each other, their ideas or opinions are the same. If they are **out of step with** each other, their ideas or opinions are different. *estar en sintonía* ❑ *Colorado is in step with other states around the country. Colorado está en sintonía con otros estados del país.* **8** PHRASE If you do something **step by step**, you do it by progressing gradually from one stage to the next. *paso a paso* ❑ *I am not rushing things and I'm taking it step by step. No estoy apresurando las cosas; las llevo paso a paso.*
▸ **step aside** → see **step down**
▸ **step back** PHR-VERB If you **step back** and think about a situation, you think about it as if you were not involved in it. *retroceder, distanciarse, tomar distancia* ❑ *I stepped back and thought about the situation. Tomé distancia para reflexionar sobre la situación.*
▸ **step down** or **step aside** PHR-VERB If someone **steps down** or **steps aside**, they resign from an important job or position. *hacerse a un lado, renunciar* ❑ *He stepped down as the trial judge. Renunció a ser el juez en el proceso.*
▸ **step in** PHR-VERB If you **step in**, you get involved in a difficult situation because you think you can or should help with it. *intervenir* ❑ *If no agreement was reached, the army would step in. Si no se llegara a un acuerdo, el ejército intervendría.*
▸ **step up** PHR-VERB If you **step up** something, you increase it or increase its intensity. *aumentar, redoblar* ❑ *We need to step up our efforts to save energy. Necesitamos redoblar nuestros esfuerzos por ahorrar energía.*

**Word Partnership** Usar *step* con:

ADV. step **outside** **2**
step **ahead**, step **backward**, step **closer**, step **forward** **2** **5** **6**
ADJ. **big** step, **bold** step, **critical** step, **giant** step, **important** step, **positive** step, **the right** step **5**
N. step **in a process** **5**

**Word Link** *step* ≈ *related by remarriage* : ***step**family*, ***step**father*, ***step**mother*

**step|family** /stɛpfæmɪli, -fæmli/ (**stepfamilies**) N-COUNT A **stepfamily** is a family that consists of a husband and wife and one or more children from a previous marriage or relationship. *familia con hijastros* ❑ *Stepfamilies are much more common than they used to be. Las familias con hijastros son mucho más comunes que antes.*

**step|father** /stɛpfɑðər/ (**stepfathers**) also **step-father** N-COUNT Someone's **stepfather** is the man who has married their mother after the death or divorce of their father. *padrastro*

**step|mother** /stɛpmʌðər/ (**stepmothers**) also **step-mother** N-COUNT Someone's **stepmother** is the woman who has married their father after the death or divorce of their mother. *madrastra*

**ste|reo** /stɛrioʊ, stɪər-/ (**stereos**) **1** ADJ **Stereo** is used to describe a sound system in which the sound is played through two speakers. Compare **mono**. *estereofónico* ❑ *...equipment that gives stereo sound. ...equipo con sonido estereofónico.* **2** N-COUNT A **stereo** is a CD player with two speakers. *Reproductor estereofónico de discos compactos.*

**ste|reo|type** /stɛriətaɪp, stɪər-/ (**stereotypes, stereotyping, stereotyped**) **1** N-COUNT A **stereotype** is a fixed general image or set of characteristics that a lot of people believe represents a particular type of person or thing. *estereotipo* ❑ *There's always been a stereotype about successful businessmen. Siempre ha existido el estereotipo del hombre de negocios exitoso.* **2** V-T If

S

someone **is stereotyped** as something, people form a fixed general idea or image of them, so that it is assumed that they will behave in a particular way. *catalogar* ❑ *He was stereotyped by some people as a trouble-maker. Algunas personas lo catalogaron como un alborotador.*

**ster|ile** /stɛrəl/ **1** ADJ Something that is **sterile** is completely clean and free from germs. *estéril* ❑ *Cover the cut with a sterile bandage. Cubra la herida con una venda estéril.* ● **ste|ril|ity** /stərɪlɪti/ N-UNCOUNT *esterilidad, asepsia* ❑ *...the sterility of the hospital. ...la asepsia del hospital.* **2** ADJ A person or animal that is **sterile** is unable to have or produce babies. *estéril* ❑ *George was sterile. George era estéril.* ● **ste|ril|ity** N-UNCOUNT *esterilidad* ❑ *This disease causes sterility in both males and females. Esa enfermedad causa esterilidad tanto en los hombres como en las mujeres.*

**steri|lize** /stɛrɪlaɪz/ (**sterilizes, sterilizing, sterilized**) **1** V-T If you **sterilize** a thing or a place, you make it completely clean and free from germs. *esterilizar* ❑ *Sterilize the needle by boiling it. Hierva la aguja para esterilizarla.* ● **steri|li|za|tion** /stɛrɪlɪzeɪʃᵊn/ N-UNCOUNT *esterilización* ❑ *...the sterilization of milk. ...la esterilización de la leche.* **2** V-T If a person or an animal **is sterilized,** they have a medical operation that makes it impossible for them to have babies. *esterilizar* ❑ *My wife was sterilized after the birth of her fourth child. Mi esposa se hizo esterilizar después del nacimiento de nuestro cuarto hijo.* ● **steri|li|za|tion** N-VAR (**sterilizations**) *esterilización* ❑ *Doctors advised her to have a sterilization. Los médicos le aconsejaron hacerse esterilizar.*

**ster|ling** /stɜrlɪŋ/ **1** ADJ If you describe someone's work or character as **sterling,** you mean that it is very good. *excelente* [FORMAL] ❑ *She has some sterling qualities. Tiene algunas cualidades excelentes.* **2** N-UNCOUNT **Sterling** is the British money system. *libra esterlina* ❑ *He paid for the goods in sterling. Pagó los artículos con libras esterlinas.*

**stern** /stɜrn/ (**sterner, sternest**) **1** ADJ **Stern** words or actions are very severe. *severo* ❑ *He gave a stern warning to people who leave garbage in the streets. Hizo una severa advertencia a la gente que arroja basura en las calles.* ● **stern|ly** ADV *severamente* ❑ *"We will punish anyone who breaks the rules," she said sternly. —Castigaremos a todo aquel que infrinja la ley —dijo severamente.* **2** ADJ Someone who is **stern** is very serious and strict. *severo* ❑ *Her father was a stern man. Su padre era un hombre severo.*

**ster|oid** /stɪrɔɪd, stɛr-/ (**steroids**) N-COUNT A **steroid** is a type of chemical substance found in your body. Steroids can also be artificially introduced into your body. *esteroide*

**stew** /stu/ (**stews, stewing, stewed**) **1** N-VAR A **stew** is a meal which you make by cooking meat and vegetables in liquid at a low temperature. *estofado, puchero* ❑ *She gave him a bowl of beef stew. Le sirvió un plato de puchero.* **2** V-T When you **stew** meat, vegetables, or fruit, you cook them slowly in liquid in a covered pot. *guisar a fuego lento, estofar, cocer a fuego lento* ❑ *Stew the apples for half an hour. Cueza las manzanas a fuego lento durante media hora.*

**stew|ard** /stuərd/ (**stewards**) **1** N-COUNT A **steward** is a man who works on a ship, plane, or train, taking care of passengers and serving meals to them. *camarero, sobrecargo, auxiliar de vuelo* **2** N-COUNT A **steward** is a man or woman who helps to organize a race, march, or other public event. *organizador u organizadora* ❑ *The steward at the march was talking to a police officer. El organizador de la marcha estaba hablando con un oficial de la policía.*

**stew|ard|ess** /stuərdɪs/ (**stewardesses**) N-COUNT A **stewardess** is a woman who works on a ship, plane, or train, taking care of passengers and serving meals to them. This term is considered old-fashioned and people generally use **steward** when referring to men and women. *camarera, sobrecargo, auxiliar de vuelo*

**stick**
❶ NOUN USES
❷ VERB USES

❶ **stick** /stɪk/ (**sticks**) **1** N-COUNT A **stick** is a thin branch which has fallen off a tree. *vara, rama* ❑ *He put some dry sticks on the fire. Puso unas ramas secas en el fuego.* **2** N-COUNT A **stick** is a long thin piece of wood which is used for a particular purpose. *palillo, baqueta* ❑ *...drum sticks. ...baquetas de tambor.* **3** N-COUNT Some long thin objects that are used in sports are called **sticks.** *bastón, palo* ❑ *...a hockey stick. ...un bastón de hockey.* **4** N-COUNT A **stick of** something is a long thin piece of it. *rama* ❑ *...a stick of celery. ...una rama de apio.*

❷ **stick** /stɪk/ (**sticks, sticking, stuck**) **1** V-T If you **stick** something somewhere, you put it there in a rather casual way. *meter* [INFORMAL] ❑ *He folded the papers and stuck them in his desk. Dobló los papeles y los metió en su escritorio.* **2** V-T/V-I If you **stick** a pointed object **in** something, or if it **sticks in** something, it goes into it or through it. *clavar* ❑ *The nurse stuck a needle in my back. La enfermera me clavó una aguja en la espalda.* **3** V-T If you **stick** one thing to another, you attach it using glue, tape, or another sticky substance. *pegar* ❑ *Then stick your picture on a piece of paper. Luego pegue su fotografía en una hoja de papel.* **4** V-I If one thing **sticks to** another, it becomes attached to it and is difficult to remove. *adherirse* ❑ *The paper sometimes sticks to the bottom of the cake. El papel se adhiere a veces al fondo del pastel.* **5** → see also **stuck**

**Word Partnership** Usar *stick* con:

ADV. stick together ❷ **3**
PREP. stick to *something* ❷ **4**

▸**stick around** PHR-VERB If you **stick around,** you stay where you are. *quedarse* [INFORMAL] ❑ *Stick around a while and see what happens. Quédate un rato y ve lo que pasa.*

▸**stick by** PHR-VERB If you **stick by** someone, you continue to give them help or support. *no abandonar* ❑ *...friends who stuck by me during the difficult times. ...los amigos que no me abandonaron en los momentos difíciles.*

▸**stick out** **1** PHR-VERB If something **sticks out** or if you **stick** it **out,** it extends beyond something else. *sacar* ❑ *She stuck out her tongue at him. Le sacó la lengua.* **2** PHRASE If someone in an unpleasant or difficult situation **sticks it out,** they do not leave or give up. *soportar* ❑ *I didn't like New York, but I decided* to stick it out a little longer. No me gustó Nueva York, pero decidí soportarlo un tiempo más.

▸ **stick to** 1 PHR-VERB If you **stick to** something, you stay close to it or with it and do not change to something else. *atenerse a* ❑ *Let's stick to the road we know. Vamos a atenernos al camino que conocemos.* 2 PHR-VERB If you **stick to** a promise, agreement, decision, or principle, you do what you said you would do, or do not change your mind. *cumplir con* ❑ *We are waiting to see if he sticks to his promise. Estamos esperando a ver si cumple con su promesa.*

▸ **stick together** PHR-VERB If people **stick together,** they stay with each other and support each other. *mantenerse unidos* ❑ *If we all stick together, we will be okay. Si nos mantenemos unidos, todo saldrá bien.*

▸ **stick up for** PHR-VERB If you **stick up for** a person or a principle, you support or defend them forcefully. *defender* ❑ *My father always sticks up for me. Mi padre siempre me defiende.*

▸ **stick with** PHR-VERB If you **stick with** someone or something, you stay with them and do not change to something else. *perseverar* ❑ *If you're in a job that keeps you busy, stick with it. Si tiene un trabajo que lo mantenga ocupado, persevere en él.*

**stick|er** /stɪkər/ (**stickers**) N-COUNT A **sticker** is a small piece of paper or plastic, with writing or a picture on one side, that you can stick onto a surface. *etiqueta engomada, calcomanía* ❑ *...a sticker that said, "I love Florida." ...una calcomanía que decía: "I love Florida."*

**stick|er price** (**sticker prices**) N-COUNT The **sticker price** of an item, especially a car, is the price at which is it advertised. *precio de lista* ❑ *This car has a sticker price of nearly $27,000. Este coche tiene un precio de lista de casi 27,000 dólares.*

**stick|er shock** N-UNCOUNT **Sticker shock** is the shock you feel when you find out how expensive something is. *sorpresa causada por el precio de algo* ❑ *Get over the sticker shock and buy some good kitchen knives. Olvídate del precio y compra unos buenos cuchillos de cocina.*

**stick fig|ure** (**stick figures**) N-COUNT A **stick figure** is a simple drawing of a person that uses straight lines to show the arms and legs. *figura esquemática* ❑ *Claire drew a stick figure on a sheet of paper. Claire pintó un mono en una hoja de papel.*

**stick shift** (**stick shifts**) N-COUNT A **stick shift** is the lever that you use to change gear in a car or other vehicle. *palanca de velocidades*

**sticky** /stɪki/ (**stickier, stickiest**) 1 ADJ A **sticky** substance is soft, or thick and liquid, and can stick to other things. **Sticky** things are covered with a sticky substance. *pegajoso* ❑ *...sticky toffee. ...chicloso.* ❑ *If the mixture is sticky, add more flour. Si la masa está pegajosa, añada más harina.* 2 ADJ **Sticky** weather is unpleasantly hot and damp. *húmedo, bochornoso* ❑ *...four hot, sticky days in the middle of August. ...cuatro días de calor y bochorno a medio agosto.* 3 ADJ A **sticky** situation involves problems or is embarrassing. *penoso* [INFORMAL] ❑ *There were some sticky moments. Hubo unos momentos penosos.*

**stiff** /stɪf/ (**stiffer, stiffest**) 1 ADJ Something that is **stiff** is firm or does not bend easily. *rígido, tieso* ❑ *The furniture was stiff and uncomfortable. Los muebles eran rígidos e incómodos.* ❑ *His pants were new and stiff. Sus pantalones eran nuevos y estaban tiesos.* ● **stiff|ly** ADV *rígidamente* ❑ *Moira sat stiffly upright in her chair. Moira se sentó toda rígida en la silla.* 2 ADJ Something such as a door or drawer that is **stiff** does not move as easily as it should. *duro, apretado* ❑ *Train doors have stiff handles, so you cannot open them accidentally. Las puertas del tren tienen manijas muy apretadas para que no se pueda abrirlas accidentalmente.* 3 ADJ If you are **stiff,** your muscles or joints hurt when you move. *entumecido* ❑ *A hot bath is good for stiff muscles. Un baño de agua caliente es bueno para los músculos entumecidos.* ● **stiff|ly** ADV *con rigidez* ❑ *He climbed stiffly from the car. Bajar del coche fue un trance doloroso para él.* ● **stiff|ness** N-UNCOUNT *rigidez* ❑ *...stiffness in the neck. ...una tortícolis.* 4 ADJ **Stiff** behavior is rather formal and not very friendly or relaxed. *ceremonioso, afectado* ❑ *They always seemed stiff and formal with each other. Siempre parecían muy ceremoniosos el uno con el otro.* ● **stiff|ly** ADV *ceremoniosamente, de manera poco amistosa* ❑ *"Why don't you borrow your sister's car?" said Cassandra stiffly. —¿Por qué no le pide prestado el auto a su hermana? —preguntó Cassandra de manera poco amistosa.* 5 ADJ **Stiff** means difficult or severe. *tenaz* ❑ *Despite stiff competition, they won the game. A pesar de la tenaz competencia, ganaron el juego.* 6 ADV If you are bored **stiff,** worried **stiff,** or scared **stiff,** you are extremely bored, worried, or scared. *a más no poder* [INFORMAL] ❑ *Anna tried to look interested, but she was bored stiff. Anna trató de aparentar interés, pero se aburría como una ostra.*

**still**

1 ADVERB USES
2 NOT MOVING OR MAKING A NOISE

**1 still** /stɪl/ 1 ADV If a situation that used to exist **still** exists, it has continued and exists now. *todavía, aún* ❑ *I still love Simon. Todavía quiero a Simon.* ❑ *Brian's toe is still badly swollen. Brian tiene el dedo del pie muy hinchado todavía.* 2 ADV If something that has not yet happened could **still** happen, it is possible that it will happen. *todavía, aún* ❑ *They could still win the game. Todavía podrían ganar el juego.* ❑ *We could still get there before dinner. Todavía podríamos llegar antes de la cena.* 3 ADV You use **still** to emphasize that something is true in spite of what you have just said. *todavía, aún* ❑ *My weight is average. But I still feel I'm fatter than I should be. Mi peso es normal, pero todavía siento que estoy más gordo de lo que debería.* 4 ADV You use **still** to indicate that a problem or difficulty is not really worth worrying about. *de todos modos* ❑ *I didn't know where I was. Still, I had a map. No sabía dónde estaba, pero tenía un mapa, de todos modos.* 5 ADV You use **still** in expressions such as **still further, still another,** and **still more** to show that you find the number or quantity of things you are referring to surprising or excessive. *todavía, aún* ❑ *We need to improve still further. Necesitamos mejorar aún más.* 6 ADV You use **still** with comparatives to indicate that something has even more of a quality than something else. *todavía, aún* ❑ *It's good to travel, but it's better still to come home. Es bueno viajar, pero volver a casa es aún mejor.*

**2 still** /stɪl/ (**stiller, stillest**) 1 ADJ If you stay

S

**still,** you stay in the same position and do not move. *quieto* ❑ *He played the tape through once, then stayed very still for several minutes. Oyó el casete completo una vez y luego se quedó muy quieto durante varios minutos.* **2** ADJ If something is **still,** there is no movement or activity there. *tranquilo, quieto* ❑ *Inside the room it was very still. Todo estaba muy tranquilo dentro del cuarto.* • **still|ness** N-UNCOUNT *tranquilidad, quietud* ❑ *...the stillness of the night air. ...la quietud del aire nocturno.*

**still life** (**still lifes**) N-VAR A **still life** is a painting or drawing of an arrangement of objects such as flowers or fruit. **Still life** refers to this type of painting or drawing. *naturaleza muerta, bodegón* ❑ *...a still life by a French artist. ...una naturaleza muerta de un pintor francés.*
→ see **painting**

**stimu|lant** /stɪmyələnt/ (**stimulants**) N-COUNT A **stimulant** is a drug that makes your body work faster, often increasing your heart rate and making you less likely to sleep. *estimulante* ❑ *It is not a good idea to take stimulants when you are tired. No es buena idea tomar estimulantes cuando se está cansado.*

**stimu|late** /stɪmyəleɪt/ (**stimulates, stimulating, stimulated**) **1** V-T To **stimulate** something means to encourage it to begin or develop further. *estimular* ❑ *America is trying to stimulate its economy. Estados Unidos está tratando de estimular su economía.* • **stimu|la|tion** /stɪmyəleɪʃən/ N-UNCOUNT *estímulo, estimulación* ❑ *...an economy in need of stimulation. ...una economía que necesita estímulos.* **2** V-T If you **are stimulated by** something, it makes you feel full of ideas and enthusiasm. *estimular* ❑ *Bill was stimulated by the challenge. El desafío estimuló a Bill.* • **stimu|lat|ing** ADJ *estimulante* ❑ *It is a stimulating book. Es un libro estimulante.* • **stimu|la|tion** N-UNCOUNT *estímulo, estimulación* ❑ *Many people enjoy the stimulation of a difficult job. A muchas personas les gusta el estímulo que brinda un trabajo difícil.* **3** V-T If something **stimulates** a part of a person's body, it causes it to move or start working. *estimular* ❑ *Exercise stimulates your body. El ejercicio estimula el cuerpo.* • **stimu|lat|ing** ADJ *estimulante* ❑ *...the stimulating effect of some drugs. ...el efecto estimulante de algunas drogas.* • **stimu|la|tion** N-UNCOUNT *estímulo, estimulación* ❑ *...physical stimulation. ...estimulación física.*

**stimu|lus** /stɪmyələs/ (**stimuli** /stɪmyəlaɪ/) N-VAR A **stimulus** is something that encourages activity in people or things. *estímulo* ❑ *What was the stimulus that made you take this job? ¿Qué lo impulsó a aceptar este trabajo?*

**sting** /stɪŋ/ (**stings, stinging, stung**) **1** V-T/V-I If a plant, animal, or insect **stings** you, a sharp part of it, usually covered with poison, is pushed into your skin so that you feel a sharp pain. *picar(se)* ❑ *A wasp stung her. La picó una avispa.* ❑ *This type of bee rarely stings. Este tipo de abeja casi nunca pica.* **2** N-COUNT The **sting** of an insect or animal is the part that stings you. *aguijón* ❑ *Remove the bee sting from your body. Quítese el aguijón de la abeja.* **3** N-COUNT If you feel a **sting,** you feel a sharp pain in your skin or other part of your body. *piquete* ❑ *This won't hurt—you will just feel a little sting. —No va a dolerte; sólo sentirás un piquetito.* **4** V-T/V-I If a part of your body **stings,** or if a substance **stings** it, you feel a sharp pain there. *cortar* ❑ *His cheeks were stinging from the cold wind. El frío viento le cortaba las mejillas.* **5** V-T If someone's remarks **sting** you, they make you feel hurt and annoyed. *herir profundamente* ❑ *Some of the criticism stung him. Algunas de sus críticas lo hirieron profundamente.* • **sting|ing** ADJ *hiriente, punzante* ❑ *...a stinging attack on the government. ...un punzante ataque contra el gobierno.*
→ see **insect**

**stink** /stɪŋk/ (**stinks, stinking, stank, stunk**) **1** V-I To **stink** means to smell very bad. *apestar* ❑ *We all stank and nobody cared. Todos apestábamos y a nadie le importó.* ❑ *The kitchen stinks of fried onions. La cocina apesta a cebolla frita.* • **Stink** is also a noun. *mal olor* ❑ *He was aware of the stink of garlic on his breath. Era consciente del olor a ajo de su aliento.* **2** V-I If you say that something **stinks,** you disapprove of it because it involves ideas, feelings, or practices that you do not like. *apestar* [INFORMAL] ❑ *I think their methods stink. Creo que sus métodos apestan.*

**sti|pend** /staɪpɛnd/ (**stipends**) N-COUNT A **stipend** is a sum of money that is paid to a student for their living expenses. *estipendio*

**stir** /stɜr/ (**stirs, stirring, stirred**) **1** V-T If you **stir** a liquid or other substance, you mix it in a container using something such as a spoon. *menear, revolver, remover* ❑ *Stir the soup for a few seconds. Remueva la sopa unos cuantos segundos.* ❑ *Mrs. Bellingham stirred sugar into her tea. La señora Bellingham puso azúcar al té y lo revolvió.* **2** V-I If you **stir,** you move slightly, for example because you are uncomfortable or beginning to wake up. *moverse, agitarse* [WRITTEN] ❑ *Eileen shook him, and he started to stir. Eileen lo sacudió y él comenzó a despertar.* **3** V-T/V-I If a particular memory, feeling, or mood **stirs** or **is stirred in** you, you begin to think about it or feel it. *agitarse, despertar* [WRITTEN] ❑ *Then a memory stirs in you and you start feeling anxious. Entonces un recuerdo viene a la memoria y uno empieza a inquietarse.* ❑ *Amy remembered the anger he stirred in her. Amy recordó la ira que había despertado en ella.* **4** N-SING If an event causes a **stir,** it causes great excitement, shock, or anger among people. *revuelo* ❑ *His movie caused a stir. Su película provocó un revuelo.*
▸ **stir up 1** PHR-VERB If something **stirs up** dust or **stirs up** mud in water, it causes it to rise up and move around. *levantar* ❑ *They saw first a cloud of dust and then the car that was stirring it up. Primero vieron una polvareda y luego el automóvil que la levantaba.* **2** PHR-VERB If someone **stirs up** a particular mood or situation, usually a bad one, they cause it. *provocar* ❑ *As usual, Harriet is trying to stir up trouble. Como siempre, Harriet está tratando de provocar problemas.*
→ see **cook**

**Word Partnership** Usar *stir* con:

| | |
|---|---|
| N. | stir **a mixture**, stir **in sugar** 1 |
| V. | **cause a** stir, **create a** stir 4 |

**stir|rup** /stɜrəp, stɪr-/ (**stirrups**) N-COUNT **Stirrups** are the two metal loops which are attached to a horse's saddle by long pieces of leather. You place your feet in the stirrups when riding a horse. *estribo*
→ see **horse**

S

**stitch** /stɪtʃ/ (**stitches, stitching, stitched**) **1** V-T/V-I If you **stitch** cloth, you use a needle and thread to join two pieces together or to make a decoration. *coser, bordar* ❑ *Stitch the two pieces of fabric together. Una las dos piezas de tela con una costura.* ❑ *We stitched for hours. Nos pasamos horas bordando.* **2** N-COUNT **Stitches** are the short pieces of thread that have been sewn in a piece of cloth. *puntada* ❑ *...a row of straight stitches. ...una hilera de puntadas rectas.* **3** N-COUNT A **stitch** is a loop made by one turn of wool around a knitting needle. *punto* ❑ *Her mother counted the stitches on her knitting needles. Su madre contó los puntos que tenía en las agujas de tejer.* **4** V-T When doctors **stitch** a wound, they use a special needle and thread to sew the skin together. *suturar* ❑ *Jill washed and stitched the wound. Jill limpió y suturó la herida.* **5** N-COUNT A **stitch** is a piece of thread that has been used to sew the skin of a wound together. *punto de sutura* ❑ *He had six stitches in a head wound. Tenía seis puntos en la herida de la cabeza.* **6** N-SING A **stitch** is a sharp pain in your side, usually caused by running or laughing a lot. *punzada* ❑ *He was laughing so much he got a stitch. Se estaba riendo tanto que le dio una punzada.*

**stock** /stɒk/ (**stocks, stocking, stocked**) **1** N-COUNT **Stocks** are shares in the ownership of a company, or investments on which a fixed amount of interest will be paid. *acción* [BUSINESS] ❑ *...the buying and selling of stocks.s ...la compraventa de acciones.* **2** N-UNCOUNT A company's **stock** is the amount of money which the company has made through selling shares. *capital comercial* [BUSINESS] ❑ *The company's stock was valued at $38 million. El capital comercial de la empresa estaba valuado en 38 millones de dólares.* **3** V-T If a store **stocks** particular products, it keeps a supply of them to sell. *tener existencias* ❑ *The store stocks everything from pens to TV sets. La tienda tiene existencias de todo, desde plumas hasta televisores.* **4** N-UNCOUNT A store's **stock** is the total amount of goods which it has available to sell. *existencias* ❑ *Most of the store's stock was destroyed in the fire. Casi todas las existencias de la tienda fueron destruidas por el fuego.* **5** N-COUNT A **stock of** things is a supply of them. *reserva* ❑ *I keep a stock of blank video tapes. Mantengo una reserva de cintas de video vírgenes.* **6** N-VAR **Stock** is a liquid, usually made by boiling meat, bones, or vegetables in water, that is used to give flavor to soups and sauces. *caldo* ❑ *Finally, add the beef stock. Finalmente, añada el caldo de res.* **7** PHRASE If goods are **in stock,** a store has them available to sell. If they are **out of stock,** it does not. *existencias* ❑ *Check that your size is in stock. Compruebe que haya existencias de su talla.* **8** PHRASE If you **take stock,** you pause to think about all the aspects of a situation or event before deciding what to do next. *evaluar, estimar* ❑ *It was time to take stock of the situation. Ya era hora de evaluar la situación.*

S

▶ **stock up** PHR-VERB If you **stock up on** something, you buy a lot of it, in case you cannot get it later. *abastecerse, aprovisionarse* ❑ *We stocked up on food for the weekend. Nos aprovisionamos de alimentos para el fin de semana.*

**stock|broker** /stɒkbroʊkər/ (**stockbrokers**) N-COUNT A **stockbroker** is a person whose job is to buy and sell stocks and shares for people who want to invest money. *corredor de valores o corredora de valores* [BUSINESS]

**stock char|ac|ter** (**stock characters**) N-COUNT A **stock character** is a character in a play or other story who represents a particular type of person, for example the mad scientist or the nosy neighbor, rather than a fully-developed individual. *personaje estereotipado*

**stock ex|change** (**stock exchanges**) N-COUNT A **stock exchange** is a place where people buy and sell stocks and shares. *bolsa (de valores)* [BUSINESS] ❑ *The daily newspapers print a list of stocks trading on the stock exchange. Los diarios publican una lista de las acciones comercializadas en la bolsa.*

**stock|holder** /stɒkhoʊldər/ (**stockholders**) N-COUNT A **stockholder** is a person who owns shares in a company. *accionista* [BUSINESS] ❑ *He was a stockholder in a hotel corporation. Era accionista de un consorcio hotelero.*

**stock|ing** /stɒkɪŋ/ (**stockings**) N-COUNT **Stockings** are items of women's clothing which fit closely over their feet and legs. Stockings are usually made of nylon and are held in place by garters. *media* ❑ *...a pair of silk stockings. ...un par de medias de seda.*

**stock mar|ket** (**stock markets**) N-COUNT **The stock market** consists of the general activity of buying stocks and shares, and the people and institutions that organize it. *mercado de valores, mercado bursátil* [BUSINESS] ❑ *...a practical guide to investing in the stock market. ...una guía práctica para invertir en el mercado de valores.*

**stock op|tion** (**stock options**) N-COUNT A **stock option** is an opportunity for the employees of a company to buy shares at a special price. *opción a la compra de acciones* [BUSINESS] ❑ *He sold shares that he bought under the company's stock option program. Vendió las acciones que había adquirido en el programa de opción de compra de acciones de la empresa.*

**stock|pile** /stɒkpaɪl/ (**stockpiles, stockpiling, stockpiled**) **1** V-T If people **stockpile** things such as food or weapons, they store large quantities of them for future use. *almacenar, hacer acopio* ❑ *People are stockpiling food for winter. La gente está haciendo acopio de alimentos para el invierno.* **2** N-COUNT A **stockpile of** things is a large quantity of them that have been stored for future use. *reservas, acopio* ❑ *...an agreement to cut stockpiles of weapons. ...un acuerdo para reducir el acopio de armas.*

**stocky** /stɒki/ (**stockier, stockiest**) ADJ A **stocky** person has a body that is broad, solid, and often short. *fornido, bajo y fornido* ❑ *...a short stocky man. ...un hombre bajo y fornido.*

**stoked** /stoʊkt/ ADJ If you are **stoked about** something, you are very excited about it. *emocionado, alborotado* [INFORMAL] ❑ *I am so stoked about this trip. Estoy tan alborotado con el viaje.*

**sto|len** /stoʊlən/ **Stolen** is the past participle of **steal**. *participio pasado de **steal***

**sto|ma** (**stomata**) N-COUNT **Stomata** are small holes on the leaves of plants that allow water and air to enter and leave the plant. *estoma* [TECHNICAL]

**stom|ach** /stʌmək/ (**stomachs, stomaching, stomached**) **1** N-COUNT Your **stomach** is the organ inside your body where food is digested. *estómago* ❑ *He has stomach problems. Tiene problemas de estómago.* **2** N-COUNT You can refer to the front part of your body below your waist as your **stomach.** *estómago* ❑ *The children lay down on their stomachs. Los niños se acostaron de panza.* **3** V-T If you cannot **stomach** something, you cannot accept it because you dislike it or disapprove of it. *tolerar* ❑ *I cannot stomach cruelty to animals. No puedo tolerar la crueldad con los animales.*

**stomp** /stɒmp/ (**stomps, stomping, stomped**) V-I If you **stomp** somewhere, you walk there with very heavy steps, often because you are angry. *pisotear, caminar con paso enérgico* ❑ *He stomped off up the hill. Enojado, subió la colina con pasos enérgicos.*

**stomp|ing ground** (**stomping grounds**) N-COUNT Someone's **stomping ground** is a place where they like to go often. *territorio personal, lugar predilecto, guarida*

**stone** /stoʊn/ (**stones**) **1** N-VAR **Stone** is a hard solid substance found in the ground and often used for building. *piedra* ❑ *...a stone floor. ...un piso de piedra.* ❑ *Marble is a natural stone. El mármol es una piedra natural.* **2** N-COUNT A **stone** is a small piece of rock that is found on the ground. *piedra* ❑ *He removed a stone from his shoe. Se sacó una piedra del zapato.* **3** N-COUNT You can refer to a jewel as a **stone.** *piedra (preciosa), gema* ❑ *...a diamond ring with three stones. ...un anillo de diamantes con tres piedras.*

**Stone Age** N-PROPER **The Stone Age** is a very early period of human history, when people used tools and weapons made of stone, not metal. *Edad de Piedra*

**stool** /stul/ (**stools**) N-COUNT A **stool** is a seat with legs but no support for your arms or back. *taburete, banco* ❑ *O'Brien sat on a stool and leaned on the counter. O'Brien se sentó en un banco y se apoyó en la barra.*

**stop** /stɒp/ (**stops, stopping, stopped**) **1** V-T/V-I If you have been doing something and then you **stop** doing it, you no longer do it. *dejar de, detener(se), hacer una pausa* ❑ *Stop throwing those stones! —¡Deja de arrojar piedras!* ❑ *How can we stop the fighting? ¿Cómo podemos detener los combates?* ❑ *She stopped and then continued eating. Hizo una pausa y luego siguió comiendo.* **2** V-T If you **stop** something from happening, or you **stop** something happening, you prevent it from happening or prevent it from continuing. *evitar* ❑ *...a way of stopping the war. ...una manera de evitar la guerra.* ❑ *He must stop her from destroying him. Debe evitar que lo arruine.* **3** V-I If an activity or process **stops,** it is no longer happening. *dejar de, parar* ❑ *The rain has stopped. Ya dejó de llover.* ❑ *It started snowing and building work had to stop. Empezó a nevar y tuvieron que parar la construcción del edificio.* **4** V-T/V-I If something such as a machine **stops** or **is stopped,** it is no longer moving or working. *pararse, detenerse* ❑ *The clock stopped at 11:59 Saturday night. El reloj se paró faltando un minuto para la medianoche del sábado.* ❑ *Arnold stopped the engine and got out of the car. Arnold apagó el motor y bajó del automóvil.* **5** V-T/V-I When a moving person or vehicle **stops** or **is stopped,** they no longer move. *detenerse* ❑ *The car failed to stop at a stoplight. El automóvil no se detuvo en el semáforo.* ❑ *He stopped and waited for her. Se detuvo y la esperó.* **6** N-SING If something that is moving comes **to a stop** or is brought **to a stop,** it slows down and no longer moves. *detenerse* ❑ *Do not open the door before the train comes to a stop. No abra la puerta antes de que el tren se detenga por completo.* **7** N-COUNT A **stop** is a place where buses or trains regularly stop so that people can get on and off. *parada, paradero* ❑ *The closest subway stop is Houston Street. La estación más cercana del metro es la de la calle Houston.* **8** V-I If you **stop** somewhere on a journey, you stay there for a short while. *detenerse* ❑ *We stopped at a small restaurant just outside of Atlanta. Nos detuvimos en un pequeño restaurante de las afueras de Atlanta.* **9** PHRASE If you **put a stop to** something that you do not like or approve of, you prevent it from happening or continuing. *poner fin a* ❑ *I'm going to put a stop to all this talk. Voy a poner fin a todos esos rumores.* **10** to **stop dead** → see **dead**

▸ **stop by** or **stop in** PHR-VERB If you **stop by** somewhere, you make a short visit to a person or place. *pasar a* [INFORMAL] ❑ *Perhaps I'll stop by the hospital. Tal vez pase al hospital.*

▸ **stop off** PHR-VERB If you **stop off** somewhere, you stop for a short time in the middle of a trip. *hacer una parada breve* ❑ *The president stopped off in Poland on his way to Munich. El presidente hizo una breve parada en Polonia de camino a Múnich.*

**stop|light** /stɒplaɪt/ (**stoplights**) also **stop light** N-COUNT A **stoplight** is a set of colored lights which controls the flow of traffic on a road. *semáforo*

**stop|per** /stɒpər/ (**stoppers**) N-COUNT A **stopper** is a piece of glass, plastic, or cork that fits into the top of a bottle or jar to close it. *tapón* ❑ *...a bottle of colorless liquid sealed with a cork stopper. ...una botella con un líquido incoloro, tapada con un corcho.* → see **laboratory**

**stor|age** /stɔrɪdʒ/ N-UNCOUNT **Storage** is the process of keeping something in a special place until it is needed. *almacenaje, almacenamiento, depósito* ❑ *...the storage of fuel. ...el almacenamiento de combustible.* ❑ *Some of the space is used for storage. Parte del espacio se usa para almacenamiento.*

**store** /stɔr/ (**stores, storing, stored**) **1** N-COUNT A **store** is a building or part of a building where things are sold. *tienda* ❑ *They are selling them for $10 each at a few stores in Texas. Las están vendiendo a 10 dólares la pieza en unas cuantas tiendas de Texas.* ❑ *...grocery stores. ...tiendas de comestibles.* **2** V-T When you **store** things, you put them in a container or other place and leave them there until they are needed. *almacenar, guardar* ❑ *Store the cookies in a tin. Guarde las galletas en una lata.*
• **Store away** means the same as **store.** *guardar* ❑ *He stored the tapes away. Guardó las cintas.* **3** N-COUNT A **store of** things is a supply of them that you keep somewhere until you need them. *provisión, reserva* ❑ *I have a secret store of chocolate. Tengo una reserva secreta de chocolate.* **4** N-COUNT A **store** is a place where things are kept while they are not being used. *almacén, depósito, bodega* ❑ *...a store for food supplies. ...una bodega para alimentos.* **5** → see also **department store** **6** PHRASE If something is **in store for** you, it is going to happen at some time in the future. *en reserva* ❑ *Surprises were in store for me. Me esperaba una sorpresa.* → see **city**

S

▸ **store away** → see **store 2**

▸ **store up** PHR-VERB If you **store** something **up**, you keep it until you think that the time is right to use it. *hacer acopio* ❑ *I stored up stories about people to use in my book. Hice acopio de historias personales para usarlas en mi libro.*

| **Thesaurus** | *store* | Ver también: |
|---|---|---|
| N. | business, market, shop 1 | |
| | collection, reserve, stock 3 | |
| V. | accumulate, keep, save 2 | |

**store-bought** ADJ **Store-bought** products are sold in stores, rather than being made at home. *comprado* ❑ *You can use this sauce with store-bought pasta. Puede emplear esta salsa con pasta comprada.*

**store brand** (**store brands**) N-COUNT **Store brands** are products which have the trademark or label of the store which sells them, especially a supermarket chain. *marca libre* ❑ *...a tub of store-brand ice cream. ...un bote de helado de marca libre.*

**stored en|er|gy** N-UNCOUNT **Stored energy** is the same as **potential energy**. *energía acumulada, energía almacenada, energía potencial* [TECHNICAL]

**store|front** /stɔrfrʌnt/ (**storefronts**) 1 N-COUNT A **storefront** is the outside part of a store which faces the street, including the door and windows. *fachada de una tienda* 2 N-COUNT A **storefront** is a small store or office that opens onto the street and is part of a row of stores or offices. *tienda que da a la calle, oficina que da a la calle* ❑ *Main Street has many small storefronts and restaurants. En la calle Main hay muchas tiendas, oficinas y restaurantes.* ❑ *...a tiny storefront office on the main street. ...una pequeña oficina que da a la calle principal.*

**store|keeper** /stɔrkipər/ (**storekeepers**) N-COUNT A **storekeeper** is a person who owns or manages a small store. *tendero o tendera*

**storm** /stɔrm/ (**storms, storming, stormed**) 1 N-COUNT A **storm** is very bad weather, with heavy rain, strong winds, and often thunder and lightning. *tormenta, tempestad* ❑ *...the violent storms along the East Coast. ...las violentas tormentas a lo largo de la costa Este.* 2 N-COUNT If something causes a **storm**, it causes an angry or excited reaction from a large number of people. *tormenta, tempestad, escándalo* ❑ *The photos caused a storm when they were first published. Las fotografías causaron un escándalo cuando fueron publicadas por primera vez.* 3 V-I If you **storm into** or **out of** a place, you enter or leave it quickly and noisily, because you are angry. *salir/entrar bramando de cólera* ❑ *After an argument, he stormed out. Después de una discusión, salió bramando de cólera.* 4 V-T If a place that is being defended **is stormed**, a group of people attack it, usually in order to get inside it. *asaltar, tomar por asalto* ❑ *Government buildings have been stormed. Algunos edificios gubernamentales han sido tomados por asalto.* • **storm|ing** N-UNCOUNT *toma por asalto* ❑ *...the storming of the Bastille. ...la toma de la Bastilla.* 5 PHRASE If someone or something **takes** a place or activity **by storm,** they are extremely successful. *tomar por asalto* ❑ *Kenya's runners have taken the athletics world by storm. Los corredores de Kenya han tomado por asalto el mundo del atletismo.*

→ see Word Web: **storm**

→ see **forecast, hurricane, weather**

| **Word Partnership** | Usar *storm* con: |
|---|---|
| N. | storm **clouds**, storm **damage**, **ice/rain/snow** storm, storm **warning**, storm **winds** 1 |
| | **center of a** storm, **eye of a** storm 1 2 |
| | storm **a building** 4 |
| ADJ. | **tropical** storm 1 |
| | **gathering** storm, **heavy** storm, **severe** storm 1 2 |
| V. | **hit by a** storm, **weather the** storm 1 2 |
| | **cause a** storm 2 |

**storm surge** (**storm surges**) N-COUNT A **storm surge** is an increase in the sea level along a shore that accompanies a hurricane or storm. *aumento del nivel del mar a lo largo de la costa a causa de una tempestad* [TECHNICAL]

**stormy** /stɔrmi/ (**stormier, stormiest**) 1 ADJ If there is **stormy** weather, there are strong winds and heavy rain. *tormentoso, tempestuoso* ❑ *...a night of stormy weather, with heavy rain and strong winds. ...una noche tempestuosa, con fuertes lluvias y vientos.* 2 ADJ If you describe a situation as **stormy,** you mean it involves a lot of angry argument or criticism. *violento, tempestuoso* ❑ *It was a stormy meeting. Fue una reunión tempestuosa.*

**sto|ry** /stɔri/ (**stories**) 1 N-COUNT A **story** is a description of imaginary people and events, which is written or told in order to entertain. *historia, cuento, relato* ❑ *The story is called "The Student." El cuento se titula El estudiante.* ❑ *I shall tell you a story about four little rabbits. Voy a contarte el cuento de los cuatro conejitos.* 2 N-COUNT A **story** is a description or account of something that has happened. *relato, anécdota, historia* ❑ *The parents*

S

**Word Web** storm

Here's how to protect yourself and your property when a severe **storm** hits. Listen for warnings from the **weather** service. Strong **wind** may blow trash cans around and **hail** may damage your car. Both should go into the garage. If you are outdoors when a storm strikes, get under cover. If you are in the open, **lightning** could hit you. Heavy **rainfall** can cause **flooding**. After the **rain** has passed, do not drive on flooded roads. The water may be deeper than you think. Be sure to buy food and batteries before a **blizzard** since **snow** may clog the roads.

*all had interesting stories about their children.* *Todos los padres tenían anécdotas interesantes sobre sus hijos.* ❑ *...the story of the women's movement.* *...la historia del movimiento femenil.* **3** N-COUNT A news **story** is a piece of news in a newspaper or in a news broadcast. *artículo*, *noticia* ❑ *Those are some of the top stories in the news.* *Esas fueron algunas de las noticias principales.* **4** N-COUNT A **story** of a building is one of its different levels, which is situated above or below other levels. *piso* ❑ *...long buildings, two stories high.* *...largos edificios de dos pisos de altura.* **5** PHRASE You use **a different story** to refer to a situation, usually a bad one, which exists in one set of circumstances when you have mentioned that it does not exist in another set of circumstances. *harina de otro costal*, *otro cantar* ❑ *Where Marcella lives, the rents are cheap, but further north it's a different story.* *Donde vive Marcella, las rentas son baratas, pero, más al norte, es harina de otro costal.* **6** PHRASE If you say **it's the same old story** or **it's the old story,** you mean that something unpleasant or undesirable seems to happen again and again. *la historia de siempre* ❑ *It's the same old story. They want one person to do three people's jobs.* *Es la historia de siempre: quieren una persona que haga el trabajo de tres.* **7** PHRASE If you say that something is **only part of the story** or is **not the whole story,** you mean that the explanation or information given is not enough for a situation to be fully understood. *sólo parte de la historia* ❑ *This is true but it is only part of the story.* *Es cierto; pero sólo es parte de la historia.* **8** PHRASE If someone tells you their **side of the story,** they tell you why they behaved in a particular way and why they think they were right, when other people think that person behaved wrongly. *versión de las cosas* ❑ *He had already decided before even hearing her side of the story.* *Él ya lo había decidido incluso antes de oír la versión que ella tenía de las cosas.*
→ see **myth**

**Thesaurus** *story* Ver también:

| | |
|---|---|
| N. | epic, fable, fairy tale, romance, saga, tale **1** |
| | account, report **2** |
| | article, feature **3** |

**Word Partnership** Usar *story* con:

| | |
|---|---|
| N. | **character in a** story, **horror** story, story **hour**, story **line**, **narrator of a** story, **title of a** story, story **writer** **1** |
| | **beginning of a** story, **end of a** story, **version of a** story **1**–**3** |
| | **life** story **2** |
| | **front page** story, **news** story **3** |
| ADJ. | **classic** story, **compelling** story, **familiar** story, **funny** story, **good** story, **interesting** story **1**–**3** |
| | **the full** story, **untold** story **2** **3** |
| | **the whole** story **2** **3** **7** |
| | **big** story, **related** story, **top** story **3** |
| V. | **hear a** story, **publish a** story, **read a** story, **tell a** story, **write a** story **1**–**3** |

**stout** /staut/ (**stouter, stoutest**) **1** ADJ A **stout** person is quite fat. *gordo* ❑ *He was a tall, stout man with gray hair.* *Era un hombre alto, gordo y de cabello cano.* **2** ADJ **Stout** shoes, branches, or other objects are thick and strong. *sólido*, *resistente* ❑ *I hope you have stout shoes.* *Espero que tengas zapatos resistentes.*

**stove** /stouv/ (**stoves**) N-COUNT A **stove** is a piece of equipment which provides heat, either for cooking or for heating a room. *estufa* ❑ *She put the saucepan on the gas stove.* *Puso la cacerola en la estufa de gas.*

**strad|dle** /stræd^əl/ (**straddles, straddling, straddled**) **1** V-T If you **straddle** something, you put or have one leg on either side of it. *ponerse o sentarse a horcajadas* ❑ *He sat down, straddling the chair.* *Se sentó a horcajadas sobre la silla.* **2** V-T If something **straddles** a river, road, border, or other place, it stretches across it or exists on both sides of it. *extenderse sobre*, *unir* ❑ *A wooden bridge straddled the stream.* *Un puente de madera libraba el arroyo.* **3** V-T Someone or something that **straddles** different periods, groups, or fields of activity exists in, belongs to, or takes elements from them all. *tener un pie en un lugar y el otro en otra parte* ❑ *He straddles two cultures, because he grew up in the United States but now lives in India.* *Está a caballo entre dos culturas, porque se crió en Estados Unidos y ahora vive en la India.*

**straight** /streɪt/ (**straighter, straightest**) **1** ADJ If something is **straight,** it continues in one direction or line and does not bend or curve. *recto*, *derecho*, *lacio* ❑ *Keep the boat in a straight line.* *Mantenga el bote en línea recta.* ❑ *Grace had long straight hair.* *El pelo de Grace era largo y lacio.* ● **Straight** is also an adverb. *erguido*, *directamente* ❑ *Stand straight and stretch the left hand to the right foot.* *Póngase erguido y después tóquese el pie derecho con la mano izquierda.* ❑ *He was looking straight at me.* *Estaba mirándome directamente.* **2** ADV If you go **straight** to a place, you go there immediately. *inmediatamente* ❑ *We went straight to Alan for advice.* *Inmediatamente fuimos a pedirle consejo a Alan.* **3** ADJ If you give someone a **straight** answer, you answer them clearly and honestly. *directo* ❑ *Why can't you give a straight answer to a straight question?* *—¿Por qué no puedes dar una respuesta directa a una pregunta directa?* ● **Straight** is also an adverb. *francamente*, *con franqueza* ❑ *I told him straight that I thought he was wrong.* *Le dije francamente que creía que estaba equivocado.* **4** PHRASE If you **get** something **straight,** you make sure that you understand it properly or that someone else does. *asegurarse de* [SPOKEN] ❑ *You need to get your facts straight.* *Necesitas asegurarte de los hechos.* **5** **a straight face** → see **face**
→ see **hair**

**Word Partnership** Usar *straight* con:

| | |
|---|---|
| V. | **drive** straight, **keep going** straight, **look** straight, **point** straight **1** |
| N. | straight **line**, straight **nose** **1** |

**straight ar|row** (**straight arrows**) N-COUNT A **straight arrow** is someone who is very traditional, honest, and moral. *muy convencional y correcto* ❑ *...a straight-arrow group of young people.* *...un grupo de jóvenes muy convencionales y correctos.*

**straight|en** /streɪt^ən/ (**straightens,**

S

**straightening, straightened)** 1 V-T If you **straighten** something, you make it neat or put it in its proper position. *enderezar* ❑ *She straightened a picture on the wall. Enderezó uno de los cuadros del muro.* • **Straighten up** means the same as **straighten.** *ordenar* ❑ *This is my job, to straighten up and keep the offices tidy. Ese es mi trabajo: ordenar y mantener arregladas las oficinas.* 2 V-I If you are standing and you **straighten,** you make your back or body straight and upright. *enderezarse* ❑ *The three men straightened and stood waiting. Los tres hombres se enderezaron y se quedaron aguardando.* • **Straighten up** means the same as **straighten.** *enderezarse* ❑ *He straightened up and put his hands in his pockets. Se enderezó y metió las manos en los bolsillos del pantalón.* 3 V-T/V-I If you **straighten** something, or it **straightens,** it becomes straight. *enderezar* ❑ *Straighten both legs. Enderece las piernas.* • **Straighten out** means the same as **straighten.** *enderezar(se)* ❑ *She straightened out her skirt. Se enderezó la falda.*

▸**straighten out** 1 PHR-VERB If you **straighten out** a confused situation, you succeed in getting it organized and cleaned up. *aclarar* ❑ *We need to straighten out a couple of things. Necesitamos aclarar un par de cosas.* 2 → see **straighten 3**

▸**straighten up** → see **straighten 2**

**straight|forward** /streɪtfɔrwərd/ 1 ADJ If you describe something as **straightforward,** you approve of it because it is easy to do or understand. *fácil, sencillo* ❑ *The computer system is straightforward to use. El sistema de la computadora es de uso sencillo.* ❑ *The question seemed straightforward to me. A mí me pareció fácil la pregunta.* • **straight|forward|ly** ADV *con sencillez* ❑ *He never gives his ideas straightforwardly. Nunca expone sus ideas con sencillez.* 2 ADJ If you describe a person or their behavior as **straightforward,** you approve of them because they are honest and direct, and do not try to hide their feelings. *franco* ❑ *She is straightforward, and very honest. Es franca y muy honesta.* • **straight|forward|ly** ADV *francamente, con franqueza* ❑ *Speak straightforwardly but be careful not to offend anyone. Habla con franqueza, pero cuídate de no ofender a nadie.*

**strain** /streɪn/ **(strains, straining, strained)** 1 N-VAR If **strain** is put **on** a person or organization, they have to do more than they are really able to do. *presión* ❑ *The prison service is under a lot of strain. El servicio de la prisión está sometido a mucha presión.* ❑ *...the stresses and strains of a demanding career. ...las tensiones y presiones de una carrera que exige mucho.* 2 V-T To **strain** something means to make it do more than it is able to do. *ejercer presión* ❑ *The large number of customers is straining our system. El gran número de clientes está ejerciendo demasiada presión sobre nuestro sistema.* 3 N-VAR **Strain** is an injury to a muscle in your body, caused by using the muscle too much or twisting it. *torcedura, esguince* ❑ *Avoid muscle strain by not doing too much exercise. No haga demasiado ejercicio, para evitar las torceduras musculares.* 4 V-T If you **strain** a muscle, you injure it by using it too much or twisting it. *torcerse* ❑ *He strained his back playing tennis. Se torció la espalda jugando al tenis.* 5 V-T If you **strain to** do something, you make a great effort to do it when it is difficult to do. *hacer un gran esfuerzo para* ❑ *I had to strain to hear. Tuve que que hacer un gran esfuerzo para oír.* 6 V-T When you **strain** food, you separate the liquid part of it from the solid parts. *colar, escurrir* ❑ *Strain the soup and put it back into the pan. Escurra la sopa y vuelva a ponerla en la cacerola.*

**Word Partnership** Usar *strain* con:

ADJ. **great** strain 1
N. **stress and** strain 1
**muscle** strain 3
strain **a muscle** 4

**strait** /streɪt/ **(straits)** 1 N-COUNT You can refer to a narrow strip of ocean which joins two large areas of ocean as a **strait** or **the straits.** *estrecho* ❑ *1,600 ships pass through the strait every year. Cada año pasan 1,600 barcos a través del estrecho.* 2 N-PLURAL If someone is **in** dire or desperate **straits,** they are in a very difficult situation. *estar en apuros, pasar apuros* ❑ *Many small businesses are in desperate financial straits. Muchos negocios pequeños están pasando grandes apuros económicos.*

**strand** /strænd/ **(strands, stranding, stranded)** 1 N-COUNT A **strand of** something such as hair, wire, or thread is a thin piece of it. *pelo, alambre, hebra* ❑ *She tried to blow a strand of hair from her eyes. Lanzó un soplido para tratar de quitarse un pelo de los ojos.* 2 V-T If you **are stranded,** you are prevented from leaving a place, for example because of bad weather. *quedarse varado* ❑ *The climbers were stranded by a storm. Los alpinistas se quedaron varados por una tormenta.*

**strange** /streɪndʒ/ **(stranger, strangest)** 1 ADJ Something that is **strange** is unusual or unexpected. *extraño, raro* ❑ *There was something strange about the way she spoke. Había algo raro en su manera de hablar.* • **strange|ly** ADV *de manera rara, de manera extraña* ❑ *She noticed he was acting strangely. Notó que estaba actuando de una manera extraña.* ❑ *Strangely, they didn't invite her to join them. Aunque parezca raro, a ella no la invitaron.* • **strange|ness** N-UNCOUNT *rareza, lo raro* ❑ *...the strangeness of the music. ...lo raro de la música.* 2 ADJ A **strange** place is one that you have never been to before. A **strange** person is someone that you have never met before. *extraño* ❑ *I was alone in a strange city. Me encontraba solo en una ciudad extraña.*

**Thesaurus** *strange* Ver también:

ADJ. bizarre, different, eccentric, odd, peculiar, unusual, weird; (*ant.*) ordinary, usual 1
exotic, foreign, unfamiliar 2

**stran|ger** /streɪndʒər/ **(strangers)** 1 N-COUNT A **stranger** is someone you have never met before. *extraño, extraña* ❑ *Telling a complete stranger about your life is difficult. Es difícil hablarle de tu vida a un completo extraño.* 2 N-PLURAL If two people are **strangers,** they do not know each other. *extraños, extrañas* ❑ *The two women were strangers. Eran extrañas una para la otra.* 3 N-COUNT If you are a **stranger to** something, you have had no experience of it or do not understand it. *no serle desconocido algo a alguien* ❑ *He is no stranger to trouble. Los conflictos no le son desconocidos.*

**stran|gle** /stræŋgᵊl/ **(strangles, strangling,**

S

**strangled)** **1** V-T To **strangle** someone means to kill them by squeezing their throat tightly so that they cannot breathe. *estrangular* ❑ *He tried to strangle a policeman.* *Trató de estrangular a un policía.* **2** V-T To **strangle** something means to prevent it from succeeding or developing. *estrangular* ❑ *The country's economic problems are strangling its development.* *Los problemas económicos del país están estrangulando su desarrollo.*

**strap** /stræp/ (**straps, strapping, strapped**) **1** N-COUNT A **strap** is a narrow piece of leather, cloth, or other material. Straps are used to carry things, fasten things together, or to hold a piece of clothing in place. *correa, tira* ❑ *Nancy held the strap of her bag.* *Nancy sostuvo la correa de su bolsa.* ❑ *Her shoes had elastic ankle straps.* *Sus zapatos tenían tiras elásticas para los tobillos.* **2** V-T If you **strap** something somewhere, you fasten it there with a strap. *sujetar con correa* ❑ *She strapped the baby seat into the car.* *Sujetó al coche el asiento del bebé con las correas.*

**stra|tegic** /strətidʒɪk/ **1** ADJ **Strategic** means relating to the most important, general aspects of something such as a military operation or political policy. *estratégico* ❑ *We need a strategic plan for reducing crime.* *Necesitamos una estrategia para reducir el crimen.* • **stra|tegi|cal|ly** /strətidʒɪkli/ ADV *estratégicamente* ❑ *...strategically important roads.* *...carreteras estratégicamente importantes.* **2** ADJ **Strategic** weapons are very powerful missiles that can be fired only after a decision to use them has been made by a political leader. *estratégico* ❑ *...strategic nuclear weapons.* *...armas nucleares estratégicas.* **3** ADJ If you put something in a **strategic** position, you place it cleverly in a position where it will be most useful or have the most effect. *estratégico* ❑ *Benches are placed at strategic points throughout the gardens.* *Las bancas están colocadas en lugares estratégicos de los jardines.* • **stra|tegi|cal|ly** ADV *estratégicamente* ❑ *We hid behind a strategically placed chair.* *Nos ocultamos tras una silla estratégicamente dispuesta.*

**Word Partnership** Usar *strategic* con:

N. strategic **decisions**, strategic **forces**, strategic **interests**, strategic **planning**, strategic **targets**, strategic **thinking** **1**
strategic **missiles**, strategic **nuclear weapons** **2**
strategic **location**, strategic **position** **3**

**strat|egy** /strætədʒi/ (**strategies**) **1** N-VAR A **strategy** is a general plan or set of plans intended to achieve something, especially over a long period. *estrategia, plan* ❑ *Do you have a strategy for solving this problem?* *¿Tienes algún plan para solucionar el problema?* **2** N-UNCOUNT **Strategy** is the art of planning the best way to gain an advantage or achieve success, especially in war. *estrategia* ❑ *...the basic principles of strategy.* *...los principios fundamentales de la estrategia.*

**Thesaurus** *strategy* Ver también:

N. plan, policy, tactic **1**

**Word Partnership** Usar *strategy* con:

N. **campaign** strategy, **investment** strategy, **marketing** strategy, **part of a** strategy, **pricing** strategy, strategy **shift** **1**
V. **adopt a** strategy, **change a** strategy, **develop a** strategy, **plan a** strategy **1**
**use (a)** strategy **1** **2**
ADJ. **aggressive** strategy, **new** strategy, **political** strategy, **successful** strategy, **winning** strategy **1**
**military** strategy **1** **2**

**strati|fi|ca|tion** /strætɪfɪkeɪʃᵊn/ N-UNCOUNT In geology, **stratification** is the process by which layers of sediment accumulate over time to produce separate layers of rock. *estratificación* [TECHNICAL]

**strati|fied drift** N-UNCOUNT **Stratified drift** is layers of sand and gravel that have been deposited by melted ice from a glacier. *morena estratificada, derrubio estratificado* [TECHNICAL]

**stra|tus** /streɪtəs, stræt-/ (**strati**) N-VAR **Stratus** is a type of thick gray cloud that forms at low altitudes. *estrato* [TECHNICAL]
→ see **cloud**

**straw** /strɔ/ (**straws**) **1** N-UNCOUNT **Straw** consists of the dried, yellowish stalks from crops such as wheat or barley. *paja* ❑ *The floor of the barn was covered with straw.* *El piso del granero estaba cubierto de paja.* **2** N-COUNT A **straw** is a thin tube of paper or plastic, which you use to suck a drink into your mouth. *popote, paja, pajita* ❑ *...a bottle of soda with a straw in it.* *...una botella de refresco con un popote dentro.* **3** PHRASE If an event is **the last straw** or **the straw that broke the camel's back,** it is the latest in a series of unpleasant or undesirable events, and makes you feel that you cannot tolerate a situation any longer. *el colmo, la gota que derrama el vaso* ❑ *When he broke my radio, that was the last straw.* *El colmo fue cuando rompió mi radio.*
→ see **rice**

**straw|berry** /strɔbɛri/ (**strawberries**) N-COUNT A **strawberry** is a small red fruit which is soft and juicy and has tiny yellow seeds on its skin. *fresa* ❑ *...strawberries and cream.* *...fresas con crema.*

strawberries

**stray** /streɪ/ (**strays, straying, strayed**) **1** V-I If someone **strays** somewhere, they wander away from where they are supposed to be. *extraviarse, perderse* ❑ *Be careful not to stray into dangerous parts of the city.* *Tenga cuidado de no extraviarse en algún lugar peligroso de la ciudad.* **2** ADJ A **stray** dog or cat has wandered away from its owner's home. *perdido* ❑ *A stray dog came up to him.* *Se le acercó un perro perdido.* • **Stray** is also a noun. *callejero* ❑ *The dog was a stray.* *El perro era un callejero.* **3** V-I If your mind or your eyes **stray,** you do not concentrate on or look at one particular subject, but start thinking about or looking at other

S

things. *divagar, distraerse* ❑ *My mind keeps straying when I'm trying to work. Siempre comienzo a divagar cuando trato de trabajar.* **4** ADJ **Stray** things have become separated from other similar things. *suelto* ❑ *...a few stray hairs. ...algunos pelos sueltos.*

**streak** /strik/ (**streaks, streaking, streaked**) **1** N-COUNT A **streak** is a long stripe or mark on a surface. *línea* ❑ *There are dark streaks on the surface of the moon. La superficie de la Luna tiene largas líneas oscuras.* **2** V-T If something **streaks** a surface, it makes long stripes or marks on the surface. *vetear, surcar, chorrear* ❑ *Rain began to streak the windows. La lluvia empezó a formar surcos en las ventanas.* **3** N-COUNT If someone has a **streak** of a particular type of behavior, they sometimes behave in that way. *rasgo* ❑ *There is a streak of madness in Christina. Christina tiene un rasgo de locura.* **4** V-I If something or someone **streaks** somewhere, they move there very quickly. *cruzar o pasar velozmente* ❑ *A plane streaked across the sky. Un avión pasó velozmente por el cielo.* **5** N-COUNT In geology, the **streak** of a mineral is the color of the powder that is produced when the mineral is rubbed against a hard, white surface. *veta, filón* [TECHNICAL]

**stream** /strim/ (**streams, streaming, streamed**) **1** N-COUNT A **stream** is a small narrow river. *arroyo, riachuelo* ❑ *There was a small stream at the end of the garden. Había un riachuelo al final del jardín.* **2** N-COUNT A **stream of** things is a large number of them occurring one after another. *torrente, sarta* ❑ *The TV show caused a stream of complaints. El programa de televisión provocó un torrente de quejas.* ❑ *...a stream of jokes. ...una sarta de bromas.* **3** V-I If a mass of people, liquid, or light **streams** somewhere, it enters or moves there in large amounts. *correr, entrar a raudales* ❑ *Tears streamed down their faces. Las lágrimas les corrían por las mejillas.* ❑ *Sunlight was streaming into the room. El sol entraba a raudales en el cuarto.*
→ see **cave, river**

**stream|line** /strimlaɪn/ (**streamlines, streamlining, streamlined**) V-T To **streamline** an organization or process means to make it more efficient by removing unnecessary parts of it. *racionalizar* ❑ *They are streamlining the tax system. Están racionalizando el sistema fiscal.* ● **stream|lined** ADJ *racionalizado* ❑ *...the streamlined organizations of the future. ...las organizaciones racionalizadas del futuro.*

S

**street** /strit/ (**streets**) **1** N-COUNT A **street** is a road in a city, town, or village, usually with houses along it. *calle* ❑ *He lived at 66 Bingfield Street. Vivía en el número 66 de la calle Bingfield.* **2** N-COUNT You can use **street** or **streets** when talking about activities that happen out of doors in a city or town rather than inside a building. *calle* ❑ *You can wear these shoes indoors or outdoors, in the car or on the street. Puede usar estos zapatos bajo techo o al aire libre, en el auto o en la calle.* ❑ *We need to get homeless people off the streets. Necesitamos rescatar de las calles a las personas sin hogar.*

| **Thesaurus** | *street* | Ver también: |
|---|---|---|
| N. | avenue, drive, road **1** | |

**street|car** /stritkɑr/ (**streetcars**) N-COUNT A **streetcar** is an electric vehicle for carrying people which travels on rails in the streets of a city or town. *tranvía*
→ see **transportation**

**street crime** N-UNCOUNT **Street crime** refers to crimes such as vandalism, car theft, and mugging that are usually committed outdoors. *delincuencia callejera*

**street smart** also **street-smart** ADJ Someone who is **street smart** knows how to deal with difficult or dangerous situations, especially in big cities. *experimentado en la vida callejera* [INFORMAL] ❑ *He is street smart and is not afraid of this neighborhood. Conoce bien la vida callejera y no tiene miedo de este barrio.*

**street smarts** N-PLURAL You can use **street smarts** to refer to the skills and intelligence people need to be successful in difficult situations, especially in a city. *experiencia necesaria para vivir en una ciudad difícil* [INFORMAL] ❑ *The boys learned their street smarts early. Los muchachos aprendieron pronto a vivir en la ciudad.*

**strength** /strɛŋkθ, strɛŋθ/ (**strengths**) **1** N-UNCOUNT Your **strength** is the physical energy that you have, which gives you the ability to perform various actions, such as lifting or moving things. *fuerza* ❑ *Swimming builds up the strength of your muscles. La natación fortalece los músculos.* ❑ *He threw the ball forward with all his strength. Lanzó la pelota con todas sus fuerzas.* **2** N-UNCOUNT; N-SING Someone's **strength** in a difficult situation is their confidence or courage. *fuerza, fortaleza* ❑ *Something gave me the strength to overcome the difficulty. Algo me dio la fuerza necesaria para superar la dificultad.* ❑ *He copes with his illness very well. His strength is amazing. Sobrelleva muy bien su enfermedad. Tiene una fortaleza asombrosa.* **3** N-VAR The **strength** of an object or material is its ability to be treated roughly, or to carry heavy weights. *resistencia* ❑ *He checked the strength of the rope. Verificó la resistencia de la cuerda.* **4** N-VAR The **strength** of a person, organization, or country is the power or influence that they have. *potencia* ❑ *...America's military strength. ...la potencia militar de Estados Unidos.* **5** N-UNCOUNT If you refer to the **strength of** a feeling, opinion, or belief, you are talking about how deeply it is felt or believed by people, or how much they are influenced by it. *intensidad* ❑ *He was surprised at the strength of his own feeling. Le sorprendió la intensidad de sus propios sentimientos.* **6** N-VAR Someone's **strengths** are the qualities and abilities that they have which are an advantage to them, or which make them successful. *virtud* ❑ *What are your strengths and weaknesses? ¿Cuáles son sus virtudes y defectos?* **7** N-UNCOUNT The **strength** of a group of people is the total number of people in it. *efectivos* ❑ *These soldiers make up one-tenth of the strength of the army. Estos soldados son la décima parte de los efectivos del ejército.* **8** PHRASE If a person or organization **goes from strength to strength,** they become more and more successful or confident. *tener un éxito tras otro* ❑ *The company has gone from strength to strength. La empresa ha tenido un éxito tras otro.* **9** PHRASE If one thing is done **on the strength of** another, it is done because of the influence of that other thing. *como consecuencia de* ❑ *She got the job on the strength of her*

*interview.* *Le fue muy bien en la entrevista y obtuvo el empleo.*
→ see **muscle**

**strength|en** /strɛŋθᵊn/ (**strengthens, strengthening, strengthened**) V-T/V-I If something **strengthens** or if something **strengthens** it, it becomes stronger. *fortalecer* ❑ *Cycling strengthens all the muscles of the body.* *El ciclismo fortalece todos los músculos del cuerpo.* ❑ *The dollar strengthened against most other currencies.* *El dólar se fortaleció con respecto a la mayoría de las demás monedas.*

**strep** /strɛp/ also **strep throat** N-UNCOUNT **Strep** or **strep throat** is an illness that is caused by bacteria and which gives you a fever and a very sore throat. *inflamación estreptocócica, inflamación de garganta, infección en la garganta* ❑ *Nicola had strep.* *Nicola tenía una infección en la garganta.* ❑ *I have strep throat.* *Tengo una infección en la garganta.*

**stress** /strɛs/ (**stresses, stressing, stressed**) **1** V-T If you **stress** a point in a discussion, you put extra emphasis on it because you think it is important. *hacer hincapié, subrayar* ❑ *He stressed that the problem was not serious.* *Hizo hincapié en que el problema no era grave.* ❑ *Her teachers stressed the need for her to do more work at home.* *Sus maestros subrayaron la necesidad de que hiciera más tarea en casa.* • **Stress** is also a noun. *énfasis* ❑ *Japanese car makers are putting more stress on overseas sales.* *Los fabricantes de automóviles japoneses están poniendo más énfasis en las ventas en el extranjero.* **2** N-VAR If you feel under **stress,** you are worried and tense because of difficulties in your life. *tensión* ❑ *Katy cannot think clearly when she is under stress.* *Katy no puede pensar con claridad cuando está tensa.* **3** V-T If you **stress** a word or part of a word when you say it, you put emphasis on it so that it sounds slightly louder. *poner énfasis, acentuar* ❑ *She stressed the words "very important."* *Puso énfasis en las palabras "muy importante".* • **Stress** is also a noun. *acento* ❑ *The stress is on the first part of this word.* *Esta palabra lleva el acento en la primera sílaba.* **4** N-VAR **Stresses** are strong physical pressures applied to an object. *tensión, esfuerzo*
→ see **emotion**

**Word Partnership** Usar *stress* con:

| | |
|---|---|
| N. | stress **the importance of** *something* **1** **anxiety and** stress, **effects of** stress, **job/work-related** stress, stress **management**, stress **reduction**, **response to** stress, **symptoms of** stress, stress **test** **2** |
| V. | **cause** stress, **cope with** stress, **deal with** stress, **experience** stress, **induce** stress, **reduce** stress, **relieve** stress **2** |
| ADJ. | **emotional** stress, **excessive** stress, **high** stress, **physical** stress, stress **related**, **severe** stress **2** |

**stress frac|ture** (**stress fractures**) N-COUNT A **stress fracture** is a slight break in a bone that is usually caused by using a part of your body too much, for example, as a result of exercise or sport. *fractura por fatiga* ❑ *I had a stress fracture in my left leg.* *La fatiga me provocó una fractura en la pierna izquierda.*

**stress|ful** /strɛsfəl/ ADJ If a situation or experience is **stressful,** it causes the person involved to feel stress. *estresante* ❑ *I've got one of the most stressful jobs there is.* *Tengo uno de los trabajos más estresantes que pueda haber.*

**stretch** /strɛtʃ/ (**stretches, stretching, stretched**) **1** V-I Something that **stretches** over an area or distance covers or exists in the whole of that area or distance. *extenderse, alargarse* ❑ *The line of cars stretched for several miles.* *La fila de automóviles se extendía varios kilómetros.* **2** N-COUNT A **stretch of** road, water, or land is a length or area of it. *tramo, trecho* ❑ *It's a very dangerous stretch of road.* *Es un tramo muy peligroso de la carretera.* **3** V-T/V-I When you **stretch,** you put your arms or legs out straight and tighten your muscles. *estirar(se), desperezarse* ❑ *He yawned and stretched.* *Bostezó y se desperezó.* ❑ *Try stretching your legs and pulling your toes upwards.* *Trate de estirar las piernas y doblar los dedos de los pies hacia arriba.* • **Stretch** is also a noun. *estiramiento* ❑ *At the end of a workout do some slow stretches.* *Al final de los ejercicios, estire lentamente todo el cuerpo varias veces.* **4** N-COUNT A **stretch of** time is a period of time. *período* ❑ *...an 18-month stretch in the army.* *...un período de 18 meses en el ejército.* **5** V-I If something **stretches from** one time **to** another, it begins at the first time and ends at the second, which is longer than expected. *extenderse* ❑ *...a working day that stretches from seven in the morning to eight at night.* *...una jornada de trabajo que se extiende de las siete de la mañana a las ocho de la noche.* **6** V-T/V-I When something soft or elastic **stretches** or **is stretched,** it becomes longer or bigger as well as thinner, usually because it is pulled. *estirar(se)* ❑ *The rope won't stretch.* *La cuerda no se estira.* **7** V-T If something **stretches** your money or resources, it uses them up so you have hardly enough for your needs. *no agotar* ❑ *The war was stretching resources.* *La guerra estaba agotando los recursos.* • **stretched** ADJ *que no da más de sí* ❑ *...our stretched finances.* *...nuestra situación financiera no da más de sí.*

▸ **stretch out** **1** PHR-VERB If you **stretch out** or **stretch yourself out,** you lie with your legs and body in a straight line. *estirarse* ❑ *The bathtub was too small to stretch out in.* *La tina era demasiado pequeña para estirarse en ella.* **2** PHR-VERB If you **stretch out** a part of your body, you hold it out straight. *alargar, extender* ❑ *He stretched out his hand to touch me.* *Alargó la mano y me tocó.*

**Word Partnership** Usar *stretch* con:

| | |
|---|---|
| PREP. | stretch **across** **1** **3** **along a** stretch **of road, down the road a** stretch **2** **during a** stretch **3** **4** **at a** stretch **4** |
| N. | stretch **of highway/road,** stretch **of a river** **2** stretch *your* **legs** **3** |

**S**

**strick|en** /strɪkən/ ADJ If a person or place is **stricken by** something such as an unpleasant feeling, an illness, or a natural disaster, they are severely affected by it. *agobiado* ❑ *He was stricken with illness for several weeks.* *Estuvo agobiado por una enfermedad durante varias semanas.* ❑ *...hunger-stricken parts of Africa.* *...regiones de África agobiadas por el hambre.*

**strict** /strɪkt/ (**stricter, strictest**) **1** ADJ A **strict** rule or order is very clear and precise or severe and must be obeyed completely. *estricto* ❑ *Their leader gave them strict instructions not to get out of the car. Su jefe les dio órdenes estrictas de no bajar del automóvil.* ❑ *The school's rules are very strict. Las reglas de la escuela son muy estrictas.* • **strict|ly** ADV *estrictamente, rigurosamente* ❑ *The acceptance of new members is strictly controlled. La aceptación de nuevos miembros se controla rigurosamente.* **2** ADJ A **strict** person regards many actions as unacceptable and does not allow them. *estricto* ❑ *My parents were very strict. Mis padres eran muy estrictos.* • **strict|ly** ADV *estrictamente, rigurosamente* ❑ *They brought their children up very strictly. Criaron a sus hijos muy estrictamente.* **3** ADJ If you talk about the **strict** meaning of something, you mean the precise meaning of it. *riguroso, estricto* ❑ *She's not Belgian in the strict sense, but she was born in Belgium. Nació en Bélgica, pero en sentido estricto, no es belga.* • **strict|ly** ADV *rigurosamente* ❑ *That is not strictly true. Eso no es rigurosamente cierto.* **4** ADJ You use **strict** to describe someone who never does things that are against their beliefs. *riguroso* ❑ *Millions of Americans are now strict vegetarians. En la actualidad, millones de estadounidenses son vegetarianos rigurosos.*

**strict|ly** /strɪktli/ **1** ADV You use **strictly** to emphasize that something is of one particular type, or intended for one particular thing or person, rather than any other. *estrictamente* ❑ *The trip was strictly business. El viaje fue estrictamente de negocios.* **2** → see also **strict**

**stride** /straɪd/ (**strides, striding, strode**) **1** V-I If you **stride** somewhere, you walk there with quick, long steps. *dar zancadas* ❑ *The farmer came striding across the field. El granjero se acercó cruzando el campo a zancadas.* **2** N-COUNT A **stride** is a long step which you take when you are walking or running. *zancada* ❑ *With every stride, runners hit the ground hard. A cada zancada, los corredores golpean el suelo con fuerza.* **3** N-COUNT If you **make strides** in something that you are doing, you make rapid progress in it. *progreso* ❑ *The country has made big strides politically. El país ha hecho grandes progresos en lo político.* **4** PHRASE If you **take** a problem or difficulty **in stride,** you deal with it calmly and easily. *tomarse las cosas con calma* ❑ *He took the school tests in stride. Se tomó con calma los exámenes de la escuela.*

S

**Word Partnership** Usar *stride* con:

| | |
|---|---|
| V. | **break** *(your)* stride, **lengthen** *your* stride **2** |
| ADJ. | **long** stride **2** |

**strike**
❶ NOUN USES
❷ VERB USES
❸ PHR-VERBS

❶ **strike** /straɪk/ (**strikes**) **1** N-COUNT When there is a **strike,** workers stop doing their work for a period of time, usually in order to try to get better pay or working conditions. *huelga* [BUSINESS] ❑ *Workers began a three-day strike. Los trabajadores iniciaron una huelga de tres días.* ❑ *Staff at the hospital went on strike. El personal del hospital se declaró en huelga.* **2** N-COUNT A military **strike** is a military attack, especially an air attack. *ataque* ❑ *...an air strike. ...un ataque aéreo.* **3** PHRASE If someone has **two strikes against** them, they are in a bad situation or at a disadvantage. *desventaja* [INFORMAL] ❑ *The Hotel has two strikes against it. One, it's an ugly building. Second, it's in an ugly place. El hotel tiene dos desventajas: una, es un edificio horrible; y dos, está en un lugar horrible.*
→ see **union**

❷ **strike** /straɪk/ (**strikes, striking, struck**) **1** V-I When workers **strike,** they go on strike. *hacer huelga* [BUSINESS] ❑ *Workers have the right to strike. Los trabajadores tienen el derecho de hacer huelga.* ❑ *They shouldn't be striking for more money. No deberían estar haciendo huelga para obtener más dinero.* • **strik|er** N-COUNT (**strikers**) *huelguista* ❑ *The strikers want higher wages. Los huelguistas quieren mejores salarios.* **2** V-T If you **strike** someone or something, you deliberately hit them. *golpear, dar golpes* [FORMAL] ❑ *She took two steps forward and struck him across the mouth. Dio dos pasos hacia él y le dio una bofetada.* ❑ *Why did you strike him? —¿Por qué lo golpeó?* **3** V-T If something that is falling or moving **strikes** something, it hits it. *golpear(se)* [FORMAL] ❑ *His head struck the bottom when he dived into the pool. Se golpeó la cabeza contra el fondo de la alberca cuando se zambulló.* **4** V-I To **strike** someone or something means to attack or affect them quickly and violently. *atacar, afectar* ❑ *We hope the killer will not strike again. Esperamos que el asesino no vuelva a atacar.* ❑ *A storm struck the northeastern United States on Saturday. Una tormenta afectó al noreste de Estados Unidos el sábado.* **5** V-T If an idea or thought **strikes** you, it suddenly comes into your mind. *venir a la mente* ❑ *A thought struck her. Was she jealous of her mother? Una idea le vino a la mente: ¿se sentía celosa de su madre?* **6** V-T If something **strikes** you **as** being a particular thing, it gives you the impression of being that thing. *parecer, dar la impresión de* ❑ *He struck me as a very friendly person. Me dio la impresión de que es una persona muy amable.* **7** V-T If you **are struck** by something, you think it is very impressive, noticeable, or interesting. *impresionar* ❑ *She was struck by the kindness in his voice. Se quedó impresionada por la amabilidad de su tono de voz.* **8** V-T If something **strikes** fear **into** people, it makes them very frightened or anxious. *infundir* [LITERARY] ❑ *The Brazilians strike fear into opposing teams. Los brasileños infunden temor a sus contrincantes.* **9** V-T/V-I When a clock **strikes,** its bells make a sound to indicate what the time is. *dar la hora, sonar la hora* ❑ *The clock struck nine. El reloj dio las nueve.* ❑ *I didn't hear the clock strike. No oí sonar el reloj.* **10** V-T When you **strike** a match, you make it produce a flame by moving it quickly against something rough. *encender* ❑ *Robina struck a match and lit the fire. Robina encendió un cerillo y prendió la lumbre.* **11** V-T If someone **strikes** oil or gold, they discover it in the ground as a result of mining or drilling. *encontrar* ❑ *The company has struck oil in Syria. La compañía encontró petróleo en Siria.*

❸ **strike** /straɪk/ (**strikes, striking, struck**)
▸ **strike down** **1** PHR-VERB If someone **is struck down,** especially by an illness, they are killed or severely harmed. *abatir* [WRITTEN] ❑ *Frank has been*

## Picture Dictionary strings

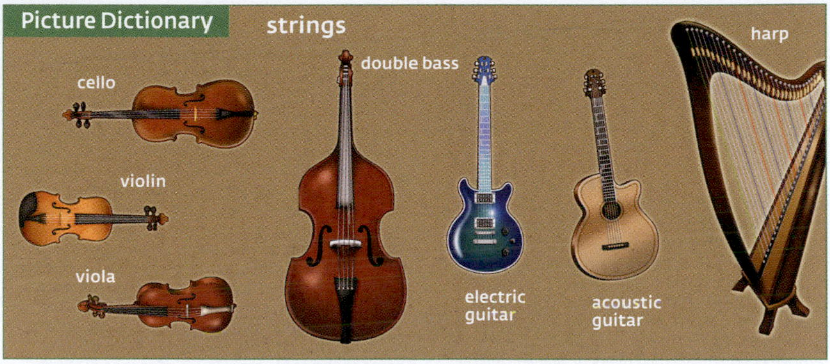


struck down by serious illness. Una grave enfermedad abatió a Frank. 2 PHR-VERB If a judge or court **strikes down** a law or regulation, they say that it is illegal and end it. abolir, derogar, abrogar ❏ *The Court struck down a law that prevents criminals from earning money from books about their crimes.* El tribunal derogó una ley que impedía que los criminales ganaran dinero con libros sobre sus crímenes.

▸ **strike out** 1 PHR-VERB In baseball, if a pitcher **strikes out,** they fail three times to hit the ball and end their turn. If a pitcher **strikes out,** they throw three balls that the batter fails to hit, and end the batter's turn. ponchar(se) ❏ *Trachsel struck Bonds out seven times.* Trachsel ponchó a Bonds siete veces. ❏ *The third baseman struck out four times.* El tercera base se ponchó cuatro veces. 2 PHR-VERB If you **strike out,** you begin to do something different, often because you want to become more independent. actuar por su propia cuenta, hacerse independiente ❏ *She wanted me to strike out on my own and buy a business.* Quería que me hiciera independiente y comprara un negocio. 3 PHR-VERB If someone **strikes out,** they fail. fracasar [INFORMAL] ❏ *His first lawyer struck out completely.* Su primer abogado fracasó por completo.

▸ **strike up** PHR-VERB When you **strike up** a conversation or friendship with someone, you begin one. entablar [WRITTEN] ❏ *I followed her into the store and struck up a conversation.* La seguí al interior de la tienda y entablé conversación con ella.

**strik|er** /straɪkər/ (**strikers**) N-COUNT In soccer and some other team sports, a **striker** is a player who mainly attacks and scores goals, rather than defends. delantero o delantera ❏ *The striker scored a great goal.* El delantero anotó un magnífico gol.

**strik|ing** /straɪkɪŋ/ 1 ADJ Something that is **striking** is very noticeable or unusual. asombroso, sorprendente ❏ *The most striking feature of the garden is the swimming pool.* El detalle más sorprendente del jardín es la alberca. ● **strik|ing|ly** ADV asombrosamente, sorprendentemente ❏ *The two men were strikingly similar.* Ambos eran asombrosamente parecidos. 2 ADJ Someone who is **striking** is very attractive, in a noticeable way. atractivo ❏ *She was a striking woman with long blonde hair.* Era una mujer muy atractiva con largo pelo rubio.

**string** /strɪŋ/ (**strings**) 1 N-VAR **String** is thin rope made of twisted threads, used for tying things together or tying up packages. cordel ❏ *He held out a small bag tied with string.* Le tendió una bolsita atada con un cordel. 2 N-COUNT A **string of** things is a number of them on a piece of string, thread, or wire. collar ❏ *She wore a string of pearls around her neck.* Llevaba un collar de perlas. 3 N-COUNT A **string of** places or objects is a number of them that form a line. sucesión ❏ *We traveled through a string of villages.* Pasamos por una sucesión de pueblos. 4 N-COUNT The **strings** on a musical instrument such as a violin or guitar are the thin pieces of wire or nylon stretched across it that make sounds when the instrument is played. cuerda ❏ *He changed a guitar string.* Le cambió una cuerda a la guitarra. 5 N-PLURAL **The strings** are the section of an orchestra which consists of stringed instruments played with a bow. cuerdas ❏ *The strings play this section of the music.* Esta parte del concierto es para las cuerdas. 6 PHRASE If something is offered to you with **no strings attached** or with **no strings,** it is offered without any special conditions. sin condición, incondicionalmente ❏ *We should help them with no strings attached.* Deberíamos ayudarlos sin condiciones.

→ see Picture Dictionary: **strings**
→ see **orchestra**

**Thesaurus** *string* Ver también:

| | |
|---|---|
| N. | cord, fiber, rope 1 |
| | chain, file, line, row, sequence, series 3 |

**Word Partnership** Usar *string* con:

| | |
|---|---|
| N. | **piece of** string 1 |
| | string **of pearls** 2 |
| | **banjo** string, **guitar** string 4 |
| ADJ. | **long** string 1–3 |

**string bean** (**string beans**) N-COUNT **String beans** are long, narrow green vegetables consisting of the cases and seeds of a climbing plant. ejote

**strip** /strɪp/ (**strips, stripping, stripped**) 1 N-COUNT A **strip of** something such as paper, cloth, or food is a long, narrow piece of it. tira ❏ *They pressed the two strips of wood together.* Prensaron juntas las dos tiras de madera. ❏ *...rugs made from strips of fabric.* ...tapetes hechos con tiras de tela. 2 N-COUNT A **strip of** land or water is a long

S

narrow area of it. *franja* ❑ *He owns a narrow strip of land on the coast. Es dueño de una franja angosta de tierra en la costa.* **3** N-COUNT A **strip** is a long street in a city or town, where there are a lot of stores, restaurants, and hotels. *avenida* ❑ *...a busy shopping strip in North Dallas. ...una concurrida avenida comercial en el norte de Dallas.* **4** V-I If you **strip**, you take off your clothes. *desvestirse, desnudarse* ❑ *They stripped and jumped into the pool. Se desnudaron y se metieron en la alberca de un salto.* ● **Strip off** means the same as **strip**. *desvestirse, desnudarse* ❑ *The children were stripping off and running into the ocean. Los niños se desvestían y corrían al mar.* **5** V-T If someone **is stripped,** their clothes are taken off by another person, for example in order to search for hidden or illegal things. *desnudar* ❑ *He was stripped and searched at the airport. Lo desnudaron y registraron en el aeropuerto.* **6** V-T To **strip** something means to remove everything that covers it. *quitar la ropa de, deshacer (una cama)* ❑ *I stripped the bed, then put on clean sheets. Deshice la cama y puse sábanas limpias.* **7** V-T To **strip** someone **of** their property, rights, or titles means to take those things away from them. *despojar* ❑ *They stripped us of our passports. Nos despojaron de nuestros pasaportes.* **8** N-COUNT In a newspaper or magazine, a **strip** is a series of drawings which tell a story. *tira* ❑ *...a cartoon strip. ...una tira cómica*

▸ **strip away** PHR-VERB To **strip away** something, especially something that hides the true nature of a thing, means to remove it completely. *despojar* ❑ *Altman strips away the glamor of the film industry. Altman despoja de su encanto a la industria fílmica.*

▸ **strip off** PHR-VERB If you **strip off** your clothes, you take them off. *quitarse la ropa* ❑ *He stripped off his wet clothes. Se quitó la ropa mojada.* → see also **strip 4**

**stripe** /straɪp/ (**stripes**) N-COUNT A **stripe** is a long line which is a different color from the areas next to it. *lista, raya* ❑ *...a skirt with a white stripe down the side. ...una falda con una lista blanca en un lado.*
→ see **patterns**

**striped** /straɪpt/ ADJ Something that is **striped** has stripes on it. *listado, rayado* ❑ *...a green and red striped tie. ...una corbata con rayas verdes y rojas.*

**strip mall** (**strip malls**) N-COUNT A **strip mall** is a shopping area consisting of one or more long buildings. *centro comercial* ❑ *...a parking lot outside a strip mall. ...un estacionamiento afuera de un centro comercial.*

**strip mine** (**strip mines**) N-COUNT A **strip mine** is a mine in which the coal, metal, or mineral is near the surface, and so underground passages are not needed. *mina a tajo abierto*

**strip min|ing** also **strip-mining** N-UNCOUNT **Strip mining** is a method of mining that is used when a mineral is near the surface and underground passages are not needed. *explotación a tajo abierto*

**strive** /straɪv/ (**strives, striving**)

> The past tense is either **strove** or **strived**, and the past participle is either **striven** or **strived.**

V-I If you **strive to** do something or **strive for** something, you make a great effort to do it or get it. *esforzarse* ❑ *He strives hard to keep himself fit. Se esfuerza mucho por mantenerse en forma.*

**stroke** /stroʊk/ (**strokes, stroking, stroked**) **1** V-T If you **stroke** someone or something, you move your hand slowly and gently over them. *acariciar* ❑ *Carla was stroking her cat. Carla estaba acariciando a su gato.* **2** N-COUNT If someone has a **stroke,** a blood vessel in their brain bursts or becomes blocked, which may kill them or make them unable to move one side of their body. *ataque de apoplejía, derrame cerebral* ❑ *He had a stroke last year, and now cannot walk. Tuvo un derrame cerebral el año pasado y ya no puede caminar.* **3** N-COUNT The **strokes** of a pen or brush are the movements or marks that you make with it when you are writing or painting. *trazo* ❑ *Use short strokes of the pencil. Haga trazos breves con el lápiz.* **4** N-COUNT When you are swimming or rowing, your **strokes** are the repeated movements that you make with your arms or the oars. *brazada, golpe de remo* ❑ *I turned and swam a few strokes further out to sea. Me volví y di unas cuantas brazadas mar adentro.* **5** N-COUNT A swimming **stroke** is a particular style or method of swimming. *brazada, estilo* ❑ *Which stroke is the fastest for swimming? ¿Cuál estilo es el más rápido para nadar?* **6** N-COUNT The **strokes** of a clock are the sounds that indicate each hour. *campanada* ❑ *On the stroke of 12, they ring a bell. Cuando el reloj da la campanada de las doce, hacen sonar un timbre.* **7** N-COUNT In sports such as tennis, baseball, golf, and cricket, a **stroke** is the action of hitting the ball. *golpe* ❑ *He hit the ball a long way with each stroke. Arrojaba la pelota muy lejos con cada golpe.* **8** N-SING **A stroke of** luck or good fortune is something lucky that happens. *golpe* ❑ *It didn't rain, which was a stroke of luck. No llovió, lo cual fue un golpe de suerte.*

| Word Partnership | Usar *stroke* con: |
|---|---|
| V. | **die from a** stroke, **have a** stroke, **suffer a** stroke **2** |
| N. | **risk of a** stroke **2**<br>stroke **of a pen** **3** |

**stroll** /stroʊl/ (**strolls, strolling, strolled**) V-I If you **stroll** somewhere, you walk there in a slow, relaxed way. *caminar tranquilamente, caminar despreocupadamente* ❑ *He strolled to the kitchen window. Caminó tranquilamente hacia la ventana de la cocina.* ● **Stroll** is also a noun. *paseo, caminata* ❑ *After dinner, I took a stroll round the city. Después de cenar, di un paseo por la ciudad.*
→ see **park**

**strong** /strɔŋ/ (**stronger** /strɔŋgər/ (**strongest** /strɔŋgɪst/) **1** ADJ Someone who is **strong** is healthy with good muscles. *fuerte* ❑ *I'm not strong enough to carry him. No soy lo bastante fuerte para cargarlo.* **2** ADJ Someone who is **strong** is confident and determined. *fuerte, sólido* ❑ *He has a very strong character. Tiene un carácter muy sólido.* ❑ *You have to be strong and do what you believe is right. Tienes que ser fuerte y hacer lo que creas que es lo correcto.* **3** ADJ **Strong** objects or materials are not easily broken. *sólido* ❑ *The strong plastic will not crack. El plástico sólido no se rompe.* ● **strong|ly** ADV *sólidamente* ❑ *The wall was very strongly built. El muro era muy sólido.* **4** ADJ **Strong** means great in degree or intensity. *fuerte, firme, sólido* ❑ *I have very strong feelings for my family. Mis sentimientos por mi familia son* *muy fuertes.* ❑ *She has strong support from her friends. Cuenta con el sólido apoyo de sus amigos.* • **strong|ly** ADV *fuertemente, firmemente, marcadamente* ❑ *He is strongly influenced by Spanish painters. La influencia de los pintores españoles es muy fuerte en él.* **5** ADJ If you have **strong** opinions on something or express them using **strong** words, you have extreme or very definite opinions which you are willing to express or defend. *firme, ardiente* ❑ *She has strong views on Cuba. Tiene opiniones muy firmes sobre Cuba.* ❑ *I am a strong supporter of the president. Soy un ardiente partidario del presidente.* • **strong|ly** ADV *convencido* ❑ *Obviously you feel very strongly about this. Obviamente, estás muy convencido de esto.* **6** ADJ If someone in authority takes **strong** action, they act firmly and severely. *enérgico* ❑ *Congress decided to take strong action. El Congreso decidió emprender una acción enérgica.* **7** ADJ Your **strong** points are your best qualities or talents, or the things you are good at. *fuerte* ❑ *Cooking is not Jeremy's strong point. La cocina no es el punto fuerte de Jeremy.* **8** ADJ A **strong** competitor, candidate, or team is good or likely to succeed. *fuerte* ❑ *This year we have a very strong team. Este año tenemos un equipo muy fuerte.* **9** ADJ You can use **strong** when you are saying how many people there are in a group. For example, if a group is twenty strong, there are twenty people in it. *fuerza* ❑ *The country's army is 400,000 strong. El ejército del país tiene una fuerza de 400,000 hombres.* **10** ADJ A **strong** drink, chemical, or drug contains a lot of the particular substance which makes it effective. *fuerte* ❑ *...a cup of strong coffee. ...una taza de café fuerte.* **11** ADJ A **strong** color, flavor, smell, sound, or light is intense and easily noticed. *penetrante* ❑ *Onions have a strong smell. La cebolla tiene un olor penetrante.* • **strong|ly** ADV *mucho* ❑ *He smelled strongly of sweat. Olía mucho a sudor.* **12** PHRASE If someone or something is still **going strong**, they are still alive, in good condition, or popular after a long time. *marchar bien, funcionar bien* [INFORMAL] ❑ *The old car was still going strong. El viejo coche todavía funcionaba bien.*

**Thesaurus** *strong* Ver también:

ADJ. mighty, powerful, tough; (*ant.*) weak **1**
confident, determined; (*ant.*) cowardly **2**
solid, sturdy **3**

**strong|hold** /strɔŋhoʊld/ (**strongholds**) N-COUNT If a place or region is a **stronghold of** a particular attitude or belief, most people there share this attitude or belief. *plaza fuerte, baluarte, bastión* ❑ *The city is a stronghold of terrorism. La ciudad es una plaza fuerte del terrorismo.*

**struc|tur|al** /strʌktʃərəl/ ADJ **Structural** means relating to or affecting the structure of something. *estructural* ❑ *The bomb caused structural damage to the building. La estructura del edificio resultó dañada por la bomba.* • **struc|tur|al|ly** ADV *estructuralmente* ❑ *When we bought the house, it was structurally in very good condition. Cuando compramos la casa, la estructura estaba en muy buenas condiciones.*

**struc|ture** /strʌktʃər/ (**structures, structuring, structured**) **1** N-VAR The **structure of** something is the way in which it is made, built, or organized. *estructura* ❑ *The typical family structure was two parents and two children. La estructura familiar típica era de dos padres y dos hijos.* **2** N-COUNT A **structure** is something that is built from or consists of parts connected together in an ordered way. *estructura* ❑ *Your feet are structures made up of 26 small bones. Los pies son estructuras formadas por 26 huesos pequeños.* ❑ *...structures such as roads and bridges. ...estructuras como carreteras y puentes.* **3** V-T If you **structure** something, you arrange it in a careful, organized pattern or system. *estructurar* ❑ *We structure the class in two parts. Estructuramos la clase en dos partes.* • **struc|tured** ADJ *estructurado* ❑ *...a more structured training program. ...un programa de adiestramiento más estructurado.*

**strug|gle** /strʌgᵊl/ (**struggles, struggling, struggled**) **1** V-I If you **struggle to** do something difficult, you try hard to do it. *luchar* ❑ *They had to struggle against all kinds of problems. Tuvieron que luchar contra toda clase de problemas.* **2** N-VAR A **struggle** is a long and difficult attempt to achieve something such as freedom or political rights. *lucha* ❑ *...the struggle for power between Nixon and Kennedy. ...la lucha por el poder entre Nixon y Kennedy.* ❑ *...a young boy's struggle to survive. ...la lucha de un niño por sobrevivir.* **3** V-I If you **struggle** when you are being held, you twist, kick, and move violently in order to get free. *forcejear* ❑ *I struggled, but she was too strong for me. Forcejeé, pero ella era demasiado fuerte para mí.* **4** V-RECIP If two people **struggle with** each other, they fight. *luchar* ❑ *They struggled on the ground. Lucharon en el suelo.* • **Struggle** is also a noun. *lucha, refriega* ❑ *He died in a struggle with prison officers. Murió en una refriega con los guardias de la prisión.* **5** V-I If you **struggle to** move yourself or **to** move a heavy object, you try to do it, but it is difficult. *forcejear* ❑ *I could see the young boy struggling to free himself. Podía ver al muchacho forcejeando por liberarse.* **6** N-SING An action or activity that is **a struggle** is very difficult to do. *lucha* ❑ *Losing weight was a terrible struggle. La lucha por bajar de peso fue terrible.*

**Word Partnership** Usar *struggle* con:

N. struggle **for democracy**, struggle **for equality**, struggle **for freedom/independence**, struggle **for survival** **1** **2**
**power** struggle **2**

ADJ. **bitter** struggle, **internal** struggle, **long** struggle, **ongoing** struggle, **political** struggle, **uphill** struggle **2**
**locked in a** struggle **2** **4**

**strut** /strʌt/ (**struts, strutting, strutted**) **1** V-I Someone who **struts** walks in a proud way, with their head held high and their chest out, as if they are very important. *pavonearse, farolear* ❑ *He struts around town as if he's really important. Se pavonea por el pueblo como si fuese realmente importante.* **2** N-COUNT A **strut** is a piece of wood or metal which holds the weight of other pieces in a building or other structure. *puntal* ❑ *...the struts of a bridge. ...los puntales de un puente.*

**stub** /stʌb/ (**stubs, stubbing, stubbed**) **1** N-COUNT The **stub** of a pencil is the last short piece of it which remains when the rest has been used. *cacho* ❑ *He pulled the stub of a pencil from behind his ear. Tomó el cacho de lápiz que traía en la oreja.* **2** N-COUNT A ticket or check **stub** is the

S

part that you keep. talón ❑ *Save the ticket stubs from every game.* *Guarde los talones de los boletos de todos los juegos.* ❑ *I have every check stub we've written since 1990.* *Tengo los talones de todos los cheques que hemos hecho desde 1990.* **3** V-T If you **stub** your **toe**, you hurt it by accidentally kicking something. *golpearse un dedo del pie, tropezar* ❑ *I stubbed my toes against a table leg.* *Me golpeé los dedos del pie contra una pata de la mesa.*

▸ **stub out** PHR-VERB When someone **stubs out** a cigarette, they put it out by pressing it against something hard. *apagar* ❑ *A sign told visitors to stub out their cigarettes.* *Un letrero indicaba a los visitantes que debían apagar sus cigarros.*

**stub|born** /stʌbərn/ **1** ADJ Someone who is **stubborn** or who behaves in a **stubborn** way is determined to do what they want and is very unwilling to change their mind. *obstinado, terco* ❑ *He is a stubborn character and always gets what he wants.* *Es un tipo obstinado y siempre se sale con la suya.* ● **stub|born|ly** ADV *obstinadamente* ❑ *He stubbornly refused to tell her the truth.* *Se rehusó obstinadamente a decir la verdad.* ● **stub|born|ness** N-UNCOUNT *obstinación* ❑ *His refusal to talk was simple stubbornness.* *Su rechazo a hablar era simple obstinación.* **2** ADJ A **stubborn** stain or problem is difficult to remove or to deal with. *persistente* ❑ *This product removes the most stubborn stains.* *Este producto remueve las manchas más persistentes.* ● **stub|born|ly** ADV *persistentemente* ❑ *Prices stayed stubbornly high.* *Los precios se mantuvieron persistentemente altos.*

**stuck** /stʌk/ **1** **Stuck** is the past tense and past participle of **stick**. *pasado y participio pasado de stick* **2** ADJ If something is **stuck** in a particular position, it is fixed tightly in this position and is unable to move. *atascado* ❑ *His car got stuck in the snow.* *Su coche se quedó atascado en la nieve.* **3** ADJ If you are **stuck** in a place or in a boring or unpleasant situation, you want to get away from it, but are unable to. *metido, estancado* ❑ *I was stuck at home sick.* *Estaba enfermo y me quedé metido en casa.* ❑ *I don't want to get stuck in another job like that.* *No quiero quedarme estancado en otro trabajo como ese.* **4** ADJ If you get **stuck** when you are trying to do something, you are unable to continue doing it because it is too difficult. *atorarse* ❑ *They will be there to help if you get stuck.* *Van a estar ahí para ayudarte si te atoras.*

S

**stud** /stʌd/ (**studs**) **1** N-COUNT **Studs** are small pieces of metal which are attached to a surface for decoration. *tachón* ❑ *You see studs on lots of front doors.* *Se ven tachones en muchas puertas de la calle.* **2** N-UNCOUNT Horses or other animals that are kept for **stud** are kept to be used for breeding. *semental* ❑ *Most of the young horses are sold, but a few are kept for stud.* *La mayoría de los potros se vende, pero algunos se dejan para servir como sementales.*

**stu|dent** /stud°nt/ (**students**) **1** N-COUNT A **student** is a person who is studying at an elementary school, secondary school, college, or university. *estudiante, alumno o alumna* ❑ *Warren's eldest son is an art student.* *El hijo mayor de Warren es estudiante de arte.* **2** → see also **graduate student**
→ see **graduation**

**stu|dent body** (**student bodies**) N-COUNT A **student body** is all the students of a particular school, considered as a group. *estudiantado, alumnado* ❑ *Those groups make up a quarter of the student body.* *Esos grupos constituyen la cuarta parte del estudiantado.*

**stu|dent coun|cil** (**student councils**) N-VAR A **student council** is an organization of students within a school that represents the interests of the students who study there. *asociación o federación estudiantil* ❑ *Jim Blaschek is student council president at Sandburg High School.* *Jim Blaschek es el presidente de la federación estudiantil de la Secundaria Sandburg.*

**stu|dent loan** (**student loans**) N-COUNT A **student loan** is a government loan that is available to students at a college or university in order to help them pay their expenses. *préstamo estudiantil* ❑ *...the government's $12 billion student loan program.* *...el programa gubernamental de préstamos estudiantiles de 12,000 millones de dólares.*

**stu|dent un|ion** (**student unions**) N-COUNT **The student union** is the building at a college or university which usually has food services, a bookstore, meeting places for leisure activities, and offices for the student government. *centro estudiantil*

**stu|dio** /studioʊ/ (**studios**) **1** N-COUNT A **studio** is a room where a painter, photographer, or designer works. *estudio* ❑ *She was in her studio painting on a large canvas.* *Estaba en su estudio, pintando un gran lienzo.* **2** N-COUNT A **studio** is a room where radio or television programs are recorded, CDs are produced, or movies are made. *estudio* ❑ *She's much happier performing live than in a recording studio.* *Es mucho más feliz cantando en vivo que en un estudio de grabación.*
→ see **art**

**Word Partnership** Usar *studio* con:

N. studio **album**, studio **audience**, **music** studio, **recording** studio, **television/TV** studio **2**

**study** /stʌdi/ (**studies, studying, studied**) **1** V-T/V-I If you **study**, you spend time learning about a particular subject or subjects. *estudiar* ❑ *She spends most of her time studying.* *Pasa la mayor parte del tiempo estudiando.* ❑ *He studied History and Economics.* *Estudió historia y economía.* **2** N-VAR **Study** is the activity of studying. *estudio* ❑ *...the study of local history.* *...el estudio de la historia local.* **3** N-COUNT A **study** of a subject is a piece of research on it. *estudio* ❑ *Recent studies suggest many new mothers suffer from depression.* *Los estudios recientes sugieren que muchas madres primerizas sufren depresiones.* **4** N-PLURAL You can refer to educational subjects or several related courses as **studies** of a particular kind. *estudios* ❑ *...a center for Islamic studies.* *...un centro de estudios islámicos.* **5** V-T If you **study** something, you look at it or consider it very carefully. *estudiar* ❑ *Debbie studied her friend's face.* *Debbie estudió el rostro de su amigo.* **6** N-COUNT A **study** is a room in a house which is used for reading, writing, and studying. *estudio* ❑ *We sat together in his study.* *Nos sentamos en su estudio.* **7** → see also **case study**
→ see **laboratory**

**study hall** (**study halls**) N-VAR A **study hall** is a room where students can study during free time between classes, or a period of time during which such study takes place. *sala de estudio* ❑ *Children are working hard in the study hall.* *Los niños están trabajando duro en la sala de estudio.*

**stuff** /stʌf/ (**stuffs, stuffing, stuffed**) **1** N-UNCOUNT You can use **stuff** to refer to things in a general way without mentioning the thing itself by name. *cosas* [INFORMAL] ❑ *I like tea, but not that herbal stuff.* *Me gusta el té, pero no esas cosas de hierbas.* ❑ *He pointed to a bag. "That's my stuff." —Esas son mis cosas —dijo señalando una bolsa.* **2** V-T If you **stuff** something somewhere, you push it there quickly and roughly. *meter* ❑ *I stuffed my hands in my pockets.* *Metí las manos en los bolsillos.* **3** V-T If you **stuff** a container or space **with** something, you fill it with something or with a quantity of things until it is full. *atestar* ❑ *He took my purse, stuffed it full, then gave it back to me.* *Tomó mi bolsa, la atestó de cosas y luego me la devolvió.* **4** V-T If you **stuff** a bird such as a chicken or a vegetable such as a pepper, you put a mixture of food inside it before cooking it. *rellenar* ❑ *Will you stuff the turkey and put it in the oven for me?* *¿Quiere hacerme el favor de rellenar el pavo y meterlo al horno?* **5** V-T If a dead animal **is stuffed,** it is filled with a substance so that it can be preserved and displayed. *disecar* ❑ *...his collection of stuffed birds.* *...su colección de aves disecadas.*

| **Thesaurus** | *stuff* | Ver también: |
|---|---|---|
| N. | belongings, goods, material, substance **1** | |
| V. | crowd, fill, jam, squeeze **2** **3** | |

**stuffed ani|mal** (**stuffed animals**) N-COUNT **Stuffed animals** are toys that are made of cloth filled with a soft material and which look like animals. *animal de peluche*

**stuff|ing** /stʌfɪŋ/ (**stuffings**) **1** N-VAR **Stuffing** is a mixture of food that is put inside a bird such as a chicken, or a vegetable such as a pepper, before it is cooked. *relleno* ❑ *...a stuffing for chicken.* *...un relleno para pollo.* **2** N-UNCOUNT **Stuffing** is material that is used to fill things such as cushions or toys in order to make them firm or solid. *relleno* ❑ *...a doll with all the stuffing coming out.* *...una muñeca con todo el relleno de fuera.*

**stuffy** /stʌfi/ (**stuffier, stuffiest**) ADJ If it is **stuffy** in a place, it is unpleasantly warm and there is not enough fresh air. *viciado (aire)* ❑ *It was hot and stuffy in the classroom.* *Hacía calor en el salón de clases y el aire estaba viciado.*

**stum|ble** /stʌmbᵊl/ (**stumbles, stumbling, stumbled**) V-I If you **stumble,** you put your foot down awkwardly while you are walking or running and nearly fall over. *tropezar* ❑ *He stumbled and almost fell.* *Tropezó y estuvo a punto de caer.*

▸ **stumble across** or **stumble on** PHR-VERB If you **stumble across** something or **stumble on** it, you find it or discover it unexpectedly. *tropezar con, dar con, encontrar* ❑ *I stumbled across a good way of saving money.* *Di con una buena manera de ahorrar dinero.*

**stum|bling block** (**stumbling blocks**) N-COUNT A **stumbling block** is a problem which stops you from achieving something. *obstáculo, impedimento, escollo* ❑ *The major stumbling block in the talks was money.* *El mayor escollo de las pláticas fue el dinero.*

**stump** /stʌmp/ (**stumps, stumping, stumped**) **1** N-COUNT A **stump** is a small part of something that remains when the rest of it has been removed or broken off. *tocón* ❑ *...a tree stump.* *...un tocón.* **2** V-T If you **are stumped** by a question or problem, you cannot think of any solution or answer to it. *dejar perplejo* ❑ *He was stumped by an unexpected question.* *Lo dejó perplejo una pregunta inesperada.*

**stun** /stʌn/ (**stuns, stunning, stunned**) **1** V-T If you **are stunned** by something, you are extremely shocked or surprised by it and are therefore unable to speak or do anything. *dejar perplejo* ❑ *He's stunned by today's news.* *Las noticias de hoy lo dejaron con la boca abierta.* • **stunned** ADJ *perplejo* ❑ *When they told me she was missing I was totally stunned.* *Cuando me dijeron que no sabían dónde estaba, me quedé completamente perplejo.* **2** V-T If something such as a blow on the head **stuns** you, it makes you unconscious or confused and unsteady. *conmocionar* ❑ *The blow to his head stunned him.* *El golpe en la cabeza lo conmocionó.* **3** → see also **stunning**

**stung** /stʌŋ/ **Stung** is the past tense and past participle of **sting**. *pasado y participio pasado de* **sting**

**stun gun** (**stun guns**) N-COUNT A **stun gun** is a device that can immobilize a person or animal for a short time without causing them serious injury. *arma para aturdir*

**stun|ning** /stʌnɪŋ/ ADJ A **stunning** person or thing is extremely beautiful or impressive. *despampanante* ❑ *She was 55 and still a stunning woman.* *Tenía 55 años y seguía siendo una mujer despampanante.* • **stun|ning|ly** ADV *asombrosamente* ❑ *...stunningly beautiful countryside.* *...una campiña asombrosamente bella.*

| **Word Partnership** | Usar *stunning* con: |
|---|---|
| N. | stunning **blow**, stunning **defeat/loss**, stunning **images**, stunning **success**, stunning **upset**, stunning **victory**, stunning **views** |

**stu|pid** /stupɪd/ (**stupider, stupidest**) **1** ADJ If you say that someone or something is **stupid,** you mean that they show a lack of good judgment or intelligence and they are not at all sensible. *estúpido, tonto* ❑ *I'll never do anything so stupid again.* *Nunca volveré a hacer algo tan estúpido.* ❑ *I made a stupid mistake.* *Cometí un error estúpido.* • **stu|pid|ly** ADV *tontamente* ❑ *We were stupidly looking at the wrong information.* *Estábamos viendo tontamente la información equivocada.* • **stu|pid|ity** /stupɪdɪti/ N-VAR (**stupidities**) *estupidez* ❑ *I was surprised by his stupidity.* *Me sorprendió su estupidez.* **2** ADJ You say that something is **stupid** to indicate that you do not like it or that it annoys you. *tontería* ❑ *It's not art. It's just stupid and ugly.* *No es arte; es una tontería horrible.*

**Usage** **stupid** and **ignorant**

Be careful not to confuse *stupid* and *ignorant*. A *stupid* person isn't intelligent or sensible; an *ignorant* person doesn't know something but can be both intelligent and sensible nevertheless: *When Dayani first came to the United States, she was ignorant about many ordinary things, such as how to have electricity turned on in her apartment; her neighbors thought she was stupid and were very surprised to find out she was studying to be a doctor.*

**Word Partnership** Usar *stupid* con:

V. **(don't) do anything/*something*** stupid, **feel** stupid, **look** stupid 1
**think *something* is** stupid 1 2
N. stupid **idea**, stupid **man**, stupid **mistake**, stupid **people**, stupid **question** 1
stupid **things** 1 2

**stur|dy** /stɜrdi/ (**sturdier, sturdiest**) ADJ Someone or something that is **sturdy** looks strong and is unlikely to be easily injured or damaged. *robusto* ❑ *She was a short, sturdy woman.* *Era una mujer bajita y robusta.* • **stur|di|ly** ADV *sólidamente* ❑ *The table was strong and sturdily built.* *La mesa era fuerte y sólida.*

**stut|ter** /stʌtər/ (**stutters, stuttering, stuttered**) 1 N-COUNT If someone has a **stutter,** they find it difficult to say the first sound of a word, and so they often hesitate or repeat it two or three times. *tartamudeo* ❑ *He spoke with a stutter.* *Tartamudeó al hablar.* 2 V-I If someone **stutters,** they have difficulty speaking because they find it hard to say the first sound of a word. *tartamudear* ❑ *I thought I would stutter when I spoke.* *Creí que iba a tartamudear al hablar.* • **stut|ter|ing** N-UNCOUNT *tartamudeo* ❑ *Then his stuttering started.* *Entonces empezó a tartamudear.*

**style** /staɪl/ (**styles, styling, styled**) 1 N-COUNT The **style** of something is the general way in which it is done or presented. *estilo, manera* ❑ *Children have different learning styles.* *Los niños tienen diferentes maneras de aprender.* ❑ *I prefer the Indian style of cooking.* *Prefiero el estilo de cocina hindú.* 2 N-UNCOUNT If people or places have **style,** they are fashionable and elegant. *estilo* ❑ *Boston has style.* *Boston tiene estilo.* ❑ *Both women love doing things in style.* *A las dos mujeres les gusta hacer las cosas elegantemente.* 3 N-VAR The **style** of a product is its design. *estilo* ❑ *He has strong feelings about style.* *Tiene opiniones muy firmes sobre el estilo.* 4 V-T If something such as a piece of clothing, a vehicle, or your hair **is styled** in a particular way, it is designed or shaped in that way. *diseñar, peinar* ❑ *His thick blond hair was styled before his trip.* *Se hizo peinar su gruesa cabellera rubia antes del viaje.* 5 N-COUNT The **style** of a writer, painter, or other artist is the particular way that their work is constructed and the way that it differs from the work of other artists. *estilo* 6 N-COUNT A **style** is a set of characteristics which defines a culture, period, or school of art. *estilo*

S

**Word Partnership** Usar *style* con:

N. **leadership** style, **learning** style, style **of life**, **management** style, **music** style, **prose** style, **writing** style 1
**differences in** style 1 – 3
ADJ. **distinctive** style, **particular** style, **personal** style 1 – 3

**styl|ish** /staɪlɪʃ/ ADJ Someone or something that is **stylish** is elegant and fashionable. *elegante* ❑ *...a stylish woman of 27.* *...una elegante mujer de 27 años de edad.* • **styl|ish|ly** ADV *elegantemente* ❑ *...stylishly dressed men.* *...hombres vestidos elegantemente.*

**sty|lis|tic nu|ance** (**stylistic nuances**) N-VAR The **stylistic nuances** of an artistic performance or work are the small details in the way it is performed or constructed that give it a distinctive style. *matiz estilístico*

**sub** /sʌb/ (**subs**) 1 N-COUNT A **sub** is a long soft bread roll filled with a combination of foods such as meat, cheese, and salad. **Sub** is an abbreviation for "submarine sandwich." *sándwich* 2 N-COUNT A **sub** is the same as a **substitute teacher**. *maestro suplente o maestra suplente* 3 N-COUNT In team games such as football, a **sub** is a player who is brought into a game to replace another player. *suplente* [INFORMAL] ❑ *A few kids from the youth team were used as subs.* *Unos cuantos muchachos del equipo juvenil jugaron como suplentes.* 4 N-COUNT A **sub** is the same as a **submarine**. *submarino* [INFORMAL]

**sub|con|scious** /sʌbkɒnʃəs/ 1 N-SING Your **subconscious** is the part of your mind that can influence you or affect your behavior even though you are not aware of it. *subconsciente* ❑ *...the power of the subconscious.* *...el poder del subconsciente.* 2 ADJ A **subconscious** feeling or action exists in or is influenced by your subconscious. *subconsciente, inconsciente* ❑ *He caught her arm in a subconscious attempt to stop her from leaving.* *La tomó del brazo en un intento inconsciente por evitar que lo abandonara.* • **sub|con|scious|ly** ADV *inconscientemente* ❑ *Subconsciously I knew that I wasn't in danger.* *Inconscientemente sabía que no estaba en peligro.*

**sub|cul|ture** /sʌbkʌltʃər/ (**subcultures**) N-COUNT A **subculture** is the ideas, art, and way of life of a group of people within a society, which are different from the ideas, art, and way of life of the rest of the society. *subcultura* ❑ *...the latest American subculture.* *...la última subcultura estadounidense.*
→ see **culture**

**sub|due** /səbdu/ (**subdues, subduing, subdued**) 1 V-T If soldiers or the police **subdue** a group of people, they defeat them or bring them under control by using force. *someter* ❑ *They took control of the land by violently subduing its people.* *Se apoderaron de la tierra sometiendo violentamente a la gente.* 2 V-T To **subdue** feelings means to make them less strong. *mitigar* ❑ *He forced himself to subdue his fears.* *Se obligó a mitigar sus temores.*

**sub|ject** (**subjects, subjecting, subjected**)

The noun and adjective are pronounced /sʌbdʒɪkt/. The verb is pronounced /səbdʒɛkt/.

1 N-COUNT The **subject** of something such as a

conversation, letter, or book is the thing that is being discussed or written about. tema, materia ❑ *I raised the subject of plastic surgery.* *Saqué el tema de la cirugía plástica.* ❑ *...the president's own views on the subject.* *...la opinión del presidente sobre el tema.* **2** N-COUNT A **subject** is an area of knowledge or study, especially one that you study in school, or college. materia ❑ *Math is my favorite subject.* *Mi materia favorita es mate.* **3** N-COUNT In grammar, the **subject** of a clause is the noun group that refers to the person or thing that is doing the action expressed by the verb. For example, in "My cat keeps catching birds," "my cat" is the subject. sujeto **4** ADJ To be **subject to** something means to be affected by it or to be likely to be affected by it. sujeto a ❑ *Prices may be subject to change.* *Los precios están sujetos a cambio.* **5** V-T If you **subject** someone **to** something unpleasant, you make them experience it. someter ❑ *He subjected her to a life of misery.* *La sometió a una vida miserable.* **6** N-COUNT The people who live in or belong to a particular country, usually one ruled by a monarch, are the **subjects** of that monarch or country. súbdito o súbdita ❑ *His subjects thought he was a good king.* *Sus súbditos pensaban que era un buen rey.* **7** PHRASE If an event will take place **subject to** a condition, it will take place only if that thing happens. sujeto a, sujeto de ❑ *They agreed to a meeting, subject to certain conditions.* *Aceptaron la reunión, pero sujeta a ciertas condiciones.*

**Word Partnership** Usar *subject* con:

- ADJ. **controversial** subject, **favorite** subject, **touchy** subject **1**
- V. **change the** subject **1**
  **broach a** subject, **study a** subject **1** **2**
- N. **knowledge of a** subject **1** **2**
  subject **of a debate**, subject **of an investigation** **2**
  subject **of a sentence**, subject **of a verb** **3**
- PREP. subject **to approval**, subject **to availability**, subject **to laws**, subject **to scrutiny**, subject **to a tax** **4**

**sub|jec|tive** /səbdʒɛktɪv/ ADJ Something that is **subjective** is based on personal opinions and feelings rather than on facts. subjetivo ❑ *Art is very subjective.* *El arte es muy subjetivo.* • **sub|jec|tive|ly** ADV subjetivamente, de manera subjetiva ❑ *You are just thinking about this subjectively.* *Nada más lo estás pensando de manera subjetiva.* • **sub|jec|tiv|ity** /sʌbdʒəktɪvɪti/ N-UNCOUNT subjetividad ❑ *They accused her of subjectivity in her reporting of events in their country.* *La acusaron de subjetividad en la forma en que informó de lo sucedido en su país.*

**sub|ject mat|ter** N-UNCOUNT The **subject matter** of something such as a book, lecture, movie, or painting is the thing that is being written about, discussed, or shown. contenido, tema ❑ *Artists can choose any subject matter.* *Los artistas pueden elegir cualquier tema.*

**sub|junc|tive** /səbdʒʌŋktɪv/ N-SING In English, a clause expressing a wish or suggestion can be put in **the subjunctive**, or in the **subjunctive** mood, by using the base form of a verb or "were." Examples are "He asked that they be removed" and "I wish I were somewhere else." These structures are formal. subjuntivo, modo subjuntivo [TECHNICAL]

**sub|li|ma|tion** /sʌblɪmeɪʃᵊn/ (**sublimations**) N-VAR **Sublimation** is the change that occurs when a solid substance becomes a gas without first becoming a liquid. sublimación [TECHNICAL]

**Word Link** *mar ≈ sea : marine, maritime, submarine*

**Word Link** *sub ≈ below : submarine, submerge, subway*

**sub|ma|rine** /sʌbmərin/ (**submarines**) N-COUNT A **submarine** is a type of ship that can travel both above and below the surface of the ocean. The abbreviation **sub** is also used. submarino ❑ *...a nuclear submarine.* *...un submarino nuclear.*

**Word Link** *merg ≈ sinking : emerge, merge, submerge*

**sub|merge** /səbmɜrdʒ/ (**submerges, submerging, submerged**) V-T/V-I If something **submerges** or if you **submerge** it, it goes below the surface of water or another liquid. sumergir(se) ❑ *The frog submerged.* *La rana se sumergió.*

**sub|mis|sion** /səbmɪʃᵊn/ N-UNCOUNT **Submission** is a state in which people can no longer do what they want to do because they have been brought under the control of someone else. sumisión, rendición ❑ *You can't bully me into submission.* *No puedes acosarme y hacer que me rinda.*

**sub|mit** /səbmɪt/ (**submits, submitting, submitted**) **1** V-I If you **submit to** something, you do it unwillingly, for example because you are not powerful enough to resist. someterse ❑ *Mrs. Jones submitted to an operation on her knee to relieve the pain.* *La Sra. Jones se sometió a una operación de la rodilla para aliviar el dolor.* **2** V-T If you **submit** a proposal, report, or request **to** someone, you formally send it to them so that they can consider it or decide about it. presentar, entregar ❑ *They submitted their reports yesterday.* *Ayer entregaron sus informes.*

**sub|or|di|nate** (**subordinates, subordinating, subordinated**)

The noun and adjective are pronounced /səbɔrdᵊnɪt/. The verb is pronounced /səbɔrdᵊneɪt/.

**1** N-COUNT If someone is your **subordinate,** they have a less important position than you in the organization that you both work for. subordinado o subordinada, subalterno o subalterna ❑ *Haig did not ask for advice from subordinates.* *Haig no les pidió consejo a sus subordinados.* **2** ADJ Someone who is **subordinate to** you has a less important position than you and has to obey you. subordinado, subalterno ❑ *Sixty of his subordinate officers were with him.* *Sesenta de los oficiales a su cargo estaban con él.* **3** ADJ Something that is **subordinate to** something else is less important than the other thing. subordinado ❑ *Science became subordinate to technology.* *La ciencia se subordinó a la tecnología.* **4** V-T If you **subordinate** something **to** another thing, you regard it or treat it as less important than the other thing. subordinar ❑ *He subordinated everything to his job.* *Subordinaba todo a su trabajo.* • **sub|or|di|na|tion** /səbɔrdᵊneɪʃᵊn/ N-UNCOUNT *subordinación* ❑ *...the social subordination of women.* *...la subordinación social de la mujer.*

**sub|or|di|nate clause** (**subordinate clauses**) N-COUNT A **subordinate clause** is a clause in a sentence which adds to or completes the information given in the main clause. It cannot usually stand alone as a sentence. Compare **main clause**. *oración subordinada* [TECHNICAL]

**sub|scribe** /səbskraɪb/ (**subscribes, subscribing, subscribed**) **1** V-I If you **subscribe to** an opinion or belief, you are one of a number of people who have this opinion or belief. *suscribir, apoyar, estar de acuerdo* ❑ *I don't subscribe to the view that men are better than women.* *No concuerdo con la idea de que los hombres son mejores que las mujeres.* **2** V-I If you **subscribe to** a magazine, newspaper, or service, you pay money regularly to receive it. *suscribirse* ❑ *Why do you subscribe to "New Scientist"?* *¿Por qué te suscribes a "New Scientist"?* ● **sub|scrib|er** N-COUNT (**subscribers**) *suscriptor o suscriptora* ❑ *I am a subscriber to "Newsweek."* *Soy suscriptor de "Newsweek".* ❑ *China has millions of subscribers to cable television.* *En China hay millones de suscriptores de la televisión por cable.*

**sub|script** /sʌbskrɪpt/ (**subscripts**) N-COUNT In chemistry and mathematics, a **subscript** is a number or symbol that is written below another number or symbol and to the right of it, for example the "2" in $H_2O$. *subíndice*

**sub|scrip|tion** /səbskrɪpʃᵊn/ (**subscriptions**) **1** N-COUNT A **subscription** is an amount of money that you pay regularly in order to belong to or support an organization, to receive copies of a magazine or newspaper, or to receive a service. *suscripción, abono, cuota* ❑ *Members pay a subscription every year.* *Los miembros pagan una cuota anual.* **2** ADJ **Subscription** television is television that you can watch only if you pay a subscription. A **subscription** channel is a channel that you can watch only if you pay a subscription. *de paga* ❑ *Premiere is a subscription channel.* *Premiere es un canal de paga.*

**sub|se|quent** /sʌbsɪkwənt/ ADJ You use **subsequent** to describe something that happened or existed after the time or event that has just been referred to. *subsecuente, subsiguiente* [FORMAL] ❑ *...the increase of prices in subsequent years.* *...el incremento de los precios en años subsiguientes.* ● **sub|se|quent|ly** ADV *posteriormente* ❑ *He subsequently worked in Canada.* *Después trabajó en Canadá.*

S

**sub|sidi|ary** /səbsɪdiɛri/ (**subsidiaries**) **1** N-COUNT A **subsidiary** or a **subsidiary** company is a company which is part of a larger and more important company. *subsidiaria, filial* [BUSINESS] ❑ *WM Financial Services is a subsidiary of Washington Mutual.* *WM Financial Services es filial de Washington Mutual.* **2** ADJ If something is **subsidiary,** it is less important than something else with which it is connected. *subsidiario, secundario, adicional* ❑ *The marketing department plays a subsidiary role to the sales department.* *El departamento de mercadotecnia desempeña un papel secundario al de ventas.*

**sub|si|dize** /sʌbsɪdaɪz/ (**subsidizes, subsidizing, subsidized**) V-T If a government or other authority **subsidizes** something, they pay part of the cost of it. *subsidiar* ❑ *The government subsidizes farming.* *El gobierno subsidia a la agricultura.* ● **sub|si|dized** ADJ *subsidiado* ❑ *...subsidized prices for housing, bread, and meat.* *...precios subsidiados para la vivienda, el pan y la carne.*

**sub|si|dy** /sʌbsɪdi/ (**subsidies**) N-COUNT A **subsidy** is money that is paid by a government or other authority in order to help an industry or business, or to pay for a public service. *subsidio* ❑ *...farm subsidies.* *...subsidios a la agricultura.*

**sub|species** /sʌbspiʃiz/ (**subspecies**) also **sub-species** N-COUNT A **subspecies of** a plant or animal is one of the types that a particular species is divided into. *subespecie*

**sub|stance** /sʌbstəns/ (**substances**) **1** N-COUNT A **substance** is a solid, powder, liquid, or gas. *sustancia, substancia* ❑ *The waste contained several unpleasant substances.* *En los desechos había varias sustancias desagradables.* **2** N-UNCOUNT **Substance** is the quality of being important or significant. *sustancia, lo esencial* [FORMAL] ❑ *Was anything of substance achieved?* *¿Se logró algo importante?* **3** N-SING **The substance of** what someone says or writes is the main thing that they are trying to say. *fundamento, esencia* ❑ *The substance of his discussions doesn't really matter.* *La esencia de sus discusiones realmente no importa.* **4** N-UNCOUNT If you say that something has no **substance,** you mean that it is not true. *sustancia, base* [FORMAL] ❑ *There is no substance to what he says.* *Lo que dice no tiene solidez.*

**Word Partnership** Usar *substance* con:

| | |
|---|---|
| ADJ. | **banned** substance, **chemical** substance, **natural** substance **1** |
| N. | **lack of** substance **2** |

**sub|stance abuse** N-UNCOUNT **Substance abuse** is the use of illegal drugs. *abuso de sustancias, toxicomanía* ❑ *...accidents caused by substance abuse.* *...accidentes causados por el abuso de sustancias.*

**sub|stan|tial** /səbstænʃᵊl/ ADJ **Substantial** means large in amount or degree. *sustancial, considerable, importante* [FORMAL] ❑ *A substantial number of mothers do not go out to work.* *Un número importante de madres no trabaja fuera de casa.* ● **sub|stan|tial|ly** /səbstænʃəli/ ADV *sustancialmente, de modo sustancial* ❑ *The number of women in engineering has increased substantially.* *El número de mujeres que se dedican a la ingeniería se ha incrementado sustancialmente.*

**Word Partnership** Usar *substantial* con:

| | |
|---|---|
| N. | substantial **amount**, substantial **changes**, substantial **difference**, substantial **evidence**, substantial **improvement**, substantial **increase**, substantial **loss**, substantial **number**, substantial **part**, substantial **progress**, substantial **savings**, substantial **support** |
| ADV. | **fairly** substantial, **very** substantial |

**sub|sti|tute** /sʌbstɪtut/ (**substitutes, substituting, substituted**) **1** V-T/V-I If you **substitute** one thing **for** another, or if one thing **substitutes for** another, it takes the place or performs the function of the other thing. *sustituir*

❑ *They were substituting argument for discussion.* *Sustituían pelea por discusión.* ❑ *Will you substitute for me?* *¿Me puedes sustituir?* • **sub|sti|tu|tion** /sʌbstɪtuʃən/ N-VAR (**substitutions**) *sustitución* ❑ *...the substitution of oil for butter.* *...la sustitución de aceite por mantequilla.* **2** N-COUNT A **substitute** is something that you have or use instead of something else. *sustituto o sustituta, suplente o sucedáneo* ❑ *She is seeking a substitute for her father.* *Está buscando un sustituto para su padre.* **3** N-COUNT In team games such as football, a **substitute** is a player who is brought into a game to replace another player. *sustituto o sustituta, suplente* ❑ *Jefferson entered as a substitute in the 60th minute.* *Jefferson entró como sustituto en el minuto 60.*

**sub|sti|tute teach|er** (**substitute teachers**) N-COUNT A **substitute teacher** is a teacher whose job is to take the place of other teachers at different schools when they are unable to be there. *maestro suplente o maestra suplente*

**Word Link** *terr ≈ earth : subterranean, terrace, territory*

**sub|ter|ra|nean** /sʌbtəreɪniən/ ADJ A **subterranean** river or tunnel is under the ground. *subterráneo* [FORMAL] ❑ *The city has 9 miles of subterranean passages.* *La ciudad tiene 9 kilómetros de pasajes subterráneos.*
→ see **cave**

**sub|text** /sʌbtɛkst/ (**subtexts**) N-VAR The **subtext** is the implied message or subject of something that is said or written. *trasfondo, subtexto*

**sub|tle** /sʌtəl/ (**subtler, subtlest**) **1** ADJ Something that is **subtle** is not immediately obvious or noticeable. *sutil, leve, ligero* ❑ *Subtle changes take place in all living things.* *Todas las cosas vivas experimentan cambios sutiles.* • **sub|tly** ADV *sutilmente* ❑ *The truth is subtly different.* *La verdad es levemente diferente.* **2** ADJ **Subtle** smells, tastes, sounds, or colors are pleasantly complex and delicate. *sutil* ❑ *...subtle shades of brown.* *...sutiles matices cafés.* • **sub|tly** ADV *sutilmente, veladamente* ❑ *...subtly colored rugs.* *...alfombras de colores tenues.*

**Word Link** *tract ≈ dragging, drawing : contract, subtract, tractor*

**sub|tract** /səbtrækt/ (**subtracts, subtracting, subtracted**) V-T If you **subtract** one number **from** another, you do a calculation in which you take it away from the other number. For example, if you subtract 3 from 5, you get 2. *restar, sustraer* • **sub|trac|tion** /səbtrækʃən/ (**subtractions**) N-VAR *resta, sustracción* ❑ *She's ready to learn subtraction.* *Está lista para aprender las restas.*
→ see **fractions, mathematics**

**sub|trac|tive sculp|ture** /səbtræktɪv skʌlptʃər/ (**subtractive sculptures**) N-VAR **Subtractive** sculpture is sculpture that is created by removing material such as clay or wax until the sculpture is complete. Compare **additive**. *escultura sustractiva* [TECHNICAL]

**sub|tropical** /sʌbtrɒpɪkəl/ ADJ **Subtropical** places have a climate that is warm and wet, and are often near tropical regions. *subtropical* ❑ *...the subtropical region of the Chapare.* *...la zona subtropical del Chapare.*

**Word Link** *urb ≈ city : suburb, suburban, urban*

**sub|urb** /sʌbɜrb/ (**suburbs**) N-COUNT The **suburbs of** a city or large town are the areas on the edge of it where people live. *suburbio, periferia* ❑ *Anna was born in a suburb of Philadelphia.* *Anna nació en las afueras de Filadelfia.* ❑ *His family lived in the suburbs.* *Su familia vivía en los suburbios.*
→ see **city, transportation**

**sub|ur|ban** /səbɜrbən/ ADJ **Suburban** means relating to a suburb. *suburbano* ❑ *...a comfortable suburban home.* *...una cómoda casa suburbana.*

**Word Link** *sub ≈ below : submarine, submerge, subway*

**sub|way** /sʌbweɪ/ (**subways**) N-COUNT A **subway** is an underground railroad. *metro, ferrocarril subterráneo, subte, ferrocarril metropolitano* ❑ *I don't ride the subway late at night.* *No uso el metro en la noche.*
→ see **transportation**

**suc|ceed** /səksid/ (**succeeds, succeeding, succeeded**) **1** V-I To **succeed** means to achieve the result that you wanted or to perform in a satisfactory way. *tener éxito, lograr, dar resultado* ❑ *We have already succeeded in starting our own company.* *Ya logramos arrancar nuestro propio negocio.* ❑ *Do you think these talks will succeed?* *¿Crees que algo saldrá de esas pláticas?* **2** V-T If you **succeed** another person, you are the next person to have their job or position. *suceder* ❑ *David Rowland will succeed him as chairman.* *David Rowland lo sucederá como presidente.*

**Thesaurus** *succeed* Ver también:
V. accomplish, conquer, master; (*ant.*) fail **1**
displace, replace; (*ant.*) precede **2**

**suc|cess** /səksɛs/ (**successes**) **1** N-UNCOUNT **Success** is the achievement of something that you have been trying to do. *logro, éxito, triunfo* ❑ *It is important for the success of any diet to vary your meals.* *Para que una dieta dé resultado, es importante variar los alimentos.* ❑ *Hard work is the key to success.* *La clave del éxito es trabajar duro.* ❑ *We were surprised by the play's success.* *Nos sorprendió el éxito de la obra.* **2** N-COUNT Someone or something that is a **success** achieves a high position, makes a lot of money, or is admired a great deal. *éxito* ❑ *We hope the movie will be a success.* *Esperamos que la película sea un éxito.*

**Word Partnership** Usar *success* con:
N. success **of a business** **1**
**chance for/of** success, success **or failure**, **key to** success, **lack of** success, **measure of** success **1** **2**
V. **achieve** success, success **depends on** *something*, **enjoy** success **1** **2**
ADJ. **great** success, **huge** success, **recent** success, **tremendous** success **1** **2**

**suc|cess|ful** /səksɛsfəl/ ADJ Someone or something that is **successful** achieves a desired result or performs in a satisfactory way. *exitoso, triunfador, de éxito, próspero* ❑ *How successful will this new treatment be?* *¿Qué tan exitoso será este nuevo tratamiento?* ❑ *Women do not have to be like men to*

S

be successful in business. Las mujeres no tienen que ser como los hombres para triunfar en los negocios.
● **suc|cess|ful|ly** ADV satisfactoriamente ❑ *The disease can be successfully treated with drugs.* La enfermedad puede responder a los fármacos.

**suc|ces|sion** /səksɛʃᵊn/ (**successions**) **1** N-SING A **succession of** things of the same kind is a number of them that exist or happen one after the other. sucesión, secuencia, serie ❑ *Adams took a succession of jobs.* Adams tuvo una serie de empleos. **2** N-UNCOUNT **Succession** is the act or right of being the next person to have an important job or position. sucesión ❑ *He became king in succession to his father.* Fue el sucesor de su padre en el trono.

**suc|ces|sive** /səksɛsɪv/ ADJ **Successive** means happening or existing one after another without a break. sucesivo ❑ *Jackson was the winner for a second successive year.* Jackson fue el ganador por segundo año consecutivo.

**suc|ces|sor** /səksɛsər/ (**successors**) N-COUNT Someone's **successor** is the person who takes their job after they have left. sucesor o sucesora ❑ *His successor is Dr. John Todd.* Su sucesor es el Dr. John Todd.

**suc|cess sto|ry** (**success stories**) N-COUNT Someone or something that is a **success story** is very successful, often unexpectedly or in spite of unfavorable conditions. evento exitoso ❑ *His company is a success story.* Su empresa ha sido una historia de éxitos.

**such** /sʌtʃ/

> When **such** is used as a predeterminer, it is followed by "a" and a count noun in the singular. When it is used as a determiner, it is followed by a count noun in the plural or by an uncountable noun.

**1** DET You use **such** to refer back to the thing or person that you have just mentioned or to something similar. tal ❑ *We each have an account. Such individual accounts are held at the local post office.* Cada quien tiene una cuenta, y tales cuentas individuales están en la oficina local de correos. ● **Such** is also a predeterminer. tal ❑ *If I need more information, how do I make such a request?* ¿Cómo hago tal solicitud si necesito más información? ❑ *Now he's very satisfied. Unfortunately, not every story has such a happy ending.* Ya está muy satisfecho, desafortunadamente no todas las historias tienen tal final feliz. ● **Such** is also a pronoun used before **be**. así ❑ *We are scared to say anything wrong—such is the atmosphere in our house.* Nos da miedo equivocarnos—así es el ambiente de nuestra casa. **2** DET You use **such...as** or **such as** to introduce one or more examples of something. de cierto tipo ❑ *...such careers as teaching and nursing.* ...carreras como la enseñanza y la enfermería. ❑ *...serious offenses, such as assault on a police officer.* ...delitos graves, como atacar a un oficial de la policía. **3** DET You use **such** to emphasize the degree or extent of something. tan, tanto ❑ *Most of us don't want to read what's in the newspaper in such detail.* La mayoría no quiere leer en tanto detalle lo que publican los periódicos. ❑ *Why does he feel such anger?* ¿Por qué está tan enojado? ● **Such** is also a predeterminer. tan ❑ *It was such a pleasant surprise.* Fue una sorpresa tan agradable. **4** DET You use **such...that** or **such that** in order to say what the result or consequence of something is. tal... que ❑ *She looked at him in such distress that he had to look away.* Lo miró con tal angustia, que él tuvo que bajar la mirada. ❑ *His problems are such that he has to go to a special school.* Sus problemas son tales, que tiene que ir a una escuela especial. ● **Such** is also a predeterminer. tal ❑ *He could put an idea in such a way that you would believe it was your own.* Podía expresar una idea de tal manera, que pensarías que era la tuya propia. **5** PHRASE You use **such and such** to refer to a thing or person when you do not want to be exact or precise. tal [SPOKEN] ❑ *They usually say, "Can you come over tomorrow at such and such a time?"* Siempre dicen —¿pueden venir mañana a tal hora?— **6** PHRASE You use **as such** with a negative to indicate that a word or expression is not a very accurate description of the actual situation. como tal ❑ *I am not a learner as such—I used to ride a bike years ago.* No soy un principiante en sí—solía andar en moto hace años. **7** PHRASE You use **as such** after a noun to indicate that you are considering that thing on its own, separately from other things or factors. como tal ❑ *He's not against taxes as such.* No está en contra de los impuestos como tales.

S

**suck** /sʌk/ (**sucks, sucking, sucked**) **1** V-T/V-I If you **suck** something, you hold it in your mouth and pull at it with the muscles in your cheeks and tongue, for example in order to get liquid out of it. chupar, succionar, aspirar, libar ❑ *They sucked their candies.* Chuparon sus caramelos. ❑ *The baby sucked on his bottle of milk.* El bebé succionaba de su biberón. **2** V-T If something **sucks** a liquid, gas, or object in a particular direction, it draws it there with a powerful force. succionar, aspirar ❑ *The pump will suck the water out of the basement.* La bomba succionará el agua del sótano.

**suck|er** /sʌkər/ (**suckers**) **1** N-COUNT; N-VOC If you call someone a **sucker**, you mean that it is very easy to cheat them. imbécil [INFORMAL] ❑ *Poor Lionel! What a sucker.* ¡Pobre del imbécil de Lionel! **2** N-COUNT If you describe someone as a **sucker for** something, you mean that they find it very difficult to resist it. tener debilidad por algo [INFORMAL] ❑ *I'm such a sucker for romance.* Me encantan las novelas de amor. **3** N-COUNT The **suckers** on some animals and insects are the parts on the outside of their body which they use in order to stick to a surface. ventosa

**sud|den** /sʌdᵊn/ **1** ADJ **Sudden** means happening quickly and unexpectedly. repentino, súbito, inesperado ❑ *He was shocked by the sudden death of his father.* Estaba aturdido por la repentina muerte de su padre. ❑ *It was all very sudden.* Todo fue muy inesperado. ● **sud|den|ly** ADV repentinamente, de repente ❑ *Suddenly, she looked ten years older.* De repente, pareció diez años más vieja. ❑ *Her expression suddenly changed.* Su expresión cambió de improviso. ● **sud|den|ness** N-UNCOUNT lo imprevisto ❑ *The enemy seemed surprised by the suddenness of the attack.* El enemigo pareció sorprendido por lo repentino del ataque. **2** PHRASE If something happens **all of a sudden,** it happens quickly and unexpectedly. de pronto, repentinamente ❑ *All of a sudden she didn't look tired anymore.* De repente desapareció su expresión de cansancio.

**sue** /su/ (**sues, suing, sued**) V-T/V-I If you **sue** someone, you start a legal case against them, usually in order to claim money from them because they have harmed you in some way.

**Word Web** sugar

**Sugar cane** was discovered in prehistoric New Guinea*. As people migrated across the Pacific Islands and into India and China, they brought sugar cane with them. At first, people just chewed on the cane. They liked the **sweet taste.** When sugar cane reached the Middle East, people discovered how to **refine** it into **crystals. Brown sugar** is created by stopping the refining process earlier. This leaves some of the molasses syrup in the sugar. Today two-fifths of sugar comes from **beets.** Refined sugar is used in many **foods** and **beverages.** Too much sugar can cause health problems, such as **obesity** and **diabetes.**

*New Guinea: a large island in the southern Pacific Ocean.*

*demandar, entablar una demanda* ❑ *A company that makes toothpaste has been sued for false advertising. Una empresa que fabrica pasta de dientes fue demandada por falsedades en su publicidad.* ❑ *The company could be sued for damages. Podrían demandar a la empresa por daños.*

**suf|fer** /sʌfər/ (**suffers, suffering, suffered**) **1** V-T/V-I If you **suffer** pain, you feel it in your body or in your mind. *sufrir, padecer* ❑ *She was very sick, suffering great pain. Estaba muy enferma y sufría intensos dolores.* ❑ *He suffered terribly the last few days. Sufrió terriblemente en los últimos días.* **2** V-I If you **suffer from** an illness or from some other bad condition, you are badly affected by it. *sufrir de, padecer de* ❑ *He was suffering from cancer. Padecía de cáncer.* ● **suf|fer|er** (**sufferers**) N-COUNT *el que sufre* ❑ *...sufferers of mental health problems. ...quienes sufren problemas de salud mental.* ❑ *...asthma sufferers. ...aquejados de asma* **3** V-T If you **suffer** something bad, you are in a situation in which something painful, harmful, or very unpleasant happens to you. *sufrir* ❑ *They could suffer complete defeat. Podrían sufrir una rotunda derrota.* **4** V-I If you **suffer,** you are badly affected by an event or situation. *sufrir, ser afectado* ❑ *It is the children who suffer. Son los niños quienes resultan afectados.* **5** V-I If something **suffers,** it becomes worse because it has not been given enough attention or is in a bad situation. *resentirse, perjudicarse* ❑ *I'm not surprised that your studies are suffering. No me sorprende que tus estudios resulten perjudicados.*

**suf|fer|ing** /sʌfərɪŋ/ (**sufferings**) **1** N-VAR **Suffering** is serious pain which someone feels in their body or their mind. *sufrimiento, dolor* ❑ *They began to recover from their pain and suffering. Empezaron a recuperarse de su dolor y su sufrimiento.*

**suf|fi|cient** /səfɪʃᵊnt/ ADJ If something is **sufficient for** a particular purpose, there is enough of it for the purpose. *suficiente, bastante* ❑ *The amount of food was sufficient for 12 people. La cantidad de comida era suficiente para 12 personas.* ● **suf|fi|cient|ly** ADV *suficientemente* ❑ *She recovered sufficiently to go on vacation with her family. Se recuperó lo suficiente como para irse de vacaciones con su familia.*

**Word Link** *fix ≈ fastening : fixture, prefix, suffix*

**suf|fix** /sʌfɪks/ (**suffixes**) N-COUNT A **suffix** is a letter or group of letters, for example "-ly" or "-ness," which is added to the end of a word in order to form a different word, often of a different word class. For example, the suffix "-ly" is added to "quick" to form "quickly." Compare **affix** and **prefix.** *sufijo*

**suf|fo|cate** /sʌfəkeɪt/ (**suffocates, suffocating, suffocated**) V-T/V-I If someone **suffocates** or **is suffocated,** they die because there is no air for them to breathe. *sofocarse, asfixiarse, ahogarse* ❑ *He either suffocated, or froze to death. O se asfixió, o murió de frío.* ● **suf|fo|ca|tion** /sʌfəkeɪʃᵊn/ N-UNCOUNT *asfixia, ahogo, sofocación* ❑ *Many of the victims died of suffocation. Muchas de las víctimas murieron de asfixia.*

**suf|fra|gist** /sʌfrədʒɪst/ (**suffragists**) N-COUNT A **suffragist** is a person who is in favor of women having the right to vote, especially in societies where women are not allowed to vote. *sufragista*

**sug|ar** /ʃʊgər/ (**sugars**) **1** N-UNCOUNT **Sugar** is a sweet substance that is used to make food and drinks sweet. It is usually in the form of small white or brown crystals. *azúcar* ❑ *...bags of sugar. ...bolsas de azúcar* **2** N-COUNT If someone has one **sugar** in their tea or coffee, they have one small spoon of sugar or one sugar lump in it. *azúcar* ❑ *How many sugars do you take? ¿Cuánto te pongo de azúcar?* **3** N-COUNT **Sugars** are substances that occur naturally in food. When you eat them, the body converts them into energy. *azúcar*
→ see Word Web: **sugar**
→ see **dish**

**sug|gest** /səgdʒɛst/ (**suggests, suggesting, suggested**) **1** V-T If you **suggest** something, you put forward a plan or idea for someone to think about. *sugerir, proponer, insinuar* ❑ *I suggested a walk in the park. Propuse un paseo por el parque.* ❑ *I suggest you ask him some questions about his past. Te sugiero que le hagas algunas preguntas sobre su pasado.* ❑ *No one has suggested how this might happen. Nadie ha sugerido cómo podría pasar.* **2** V-T If you **suggest that** something is true, you say something which you believe is true. *sugerir* ❑ *I'm not suggesting that is what is happening. No estoy sugiriendo que está pasando eso.* ❑ *It is wrong to suggest that there is an easy solution. No está bien insinuar que la solución es sencilla.* **3** V-T If one thing **suggests** another, it implies it or makes you think that it might be the case. *indicar, sugerir* ❑ *Earlier reports suggested that a meeting would take place on Sunday. Los primeros reportes indican que el domingo podría haber una reunión.*

**Word Partnership** Usar *suggest* con:

N. **analysts** suggest, **experts** suggest, **researchers** suggest 1 2
**data** suggest, **findings** suggest, **results** suggest, **studies** suggest, **surveys** suggest 3

**sug|ges|tion** /səgdʒɛstʃᵊn/ (**suggestions**) 1 N-COUNT If you make a **suggestion**, you put forward an idea or plan for someone to think about. *sugerencia, propuesta, insinuación* ❑ *She made suggestions as to how I could improve my diet. Me hizo algunas sugerencias sobre cómo mejorar mi alimentación.* ❑ *Perhaps he followed her suggestion of a walk to the river. Quizá aceptó su insinuación de ir a caminar por el río.* 2 N-COUNT A **suggestion** is something that a person says which implies that something is true. *insinuación* ❑ *We reject any suggestion that the law needs changing. Rechazamos cualquier insinuación de que es necesario modificar la ley.*

**Word Partnership** Usar *suggestion* con:

V. **follow a** suggestion, **make a** suggestion 1
**reject a** suggestion 1 2

**sug|ges|tive** /səgdʒɛstɪv/ ADJ Something that is **suggestive of** something else is quite like it or may be a sign of it. *indicativo* ❑ *...long nails suggestive of animal claws. ...uñas largas que hacen pensar en garras de animales.*

**sui|cid|al** /suɪsaɪdᵊl/ ADJ People who are **suicidal** want to kill themselves. *suicida* ❑ *I was suicidal and just couldn't stop crying. Tenía ideación suicida y nomás no podía dejar de llorar.*

**Word Link** *cide ≈ killing : genocide, pesticide, suicide*

**sui|cide** /suɪsaɪd/ (**suicides**) N-VAR People who commit **suicide** deliberately kill themselves. *suicidio* ❑ *She tried to commit suicide several times. Varias veces intentó suicidarse.* ❑ *...a case of attempted suicide. ...un caso de intento de suicidio.*

**Word Partnership** Usar *suicide* con:

V. **attempt** suicide, **commit** suicide
N. suicide **bomber**, suicide **prevention**, suicide **rate**, **risk of** suicide

**suit** /sut/ (**suits, suiting, suited**) 1 N-COUNT A man's **suit** consists of a jacket, pants, and sometimes a vest, all made from the same fabric. *traje, terno* ❑ *...a dark business suit. ...un traje oscuro de calle.* 2 N-COUNT A woman's **suit** consists of a jacket and skirt, or sometimes pants, made from the same fabric. *traje, traje sastre* ❑ *I was wearing my yellow suit. Me puse el traje amarillo.* 3 N-COUNT A particular type of **suit** is a piece of clothing that you wear for a particular activity. *traje* ❑ *The divers wore special rubber suits. Los buzos llevaban trajes especiales de látex.* 4 V-T If something **suits** you, it is convenient for you or is the best thing for you in the circumstances. *convenir, venir bien, ser apropiado* ❑ *They will only release information if it suits them. Sólo si les conviene harán pública la información.* 5 V-T If a piece of clothing or a particular style or color **suits** you, it makes you look attractive. *quedar bien algo* ❑ *Green suits you. Te ves bien de verde.* 6 N-COUNT In a court of law, a **suit** is a legal action taken by one person or company against another. *demanda, juicio* ❑ *Many former employees filed personal injury suits against the company. Muchos ex empleados demandaron a la compañía por lesiones.* 7 → see also **pantsuit**
→ see **clothing**

**suit|able** /sutəbᵊl/ ADJ Someone or something that is **suitable for** a particular purpose or occasion is right or acceptable for it. *adecuado, conveniente* ❑ *Employers usually decide within five minutes whether someone is suitable for the job. Los patrones suelen decidir en cinco minutos si alguien es adecuado para el puesto.* ● **suit|abil|ity** /sutəbɪlɪti/ N-UNCOUNT *idoneidad, lo apropiado* ❑ *...information on the suitability of a product for use in the home. ...información sobre la idoneidad de un producto para uso en el hogar.* ● **suit|ably** ADV *adecuadamente, como es debido* ❑ *We need suitably qualified staff. Necesitamos personal adecuadamente capacitado.*

**Word Link** *cas ≈ box, hold : case, casette, suitcase*

**suit|case** /sutkeɪs/ (**suitcases**) N-COUNT A **suitcase** is a case for carrying your clothes when you are traveling. *maleta, petaca, valija* ❑ *It did not take Andrew long to pack a suitcase. A Andrew no le tomó mucho tiempo hacer su maleta.*

suitcase

**suite** /swit/ (**suites**) 1 N-COUNT A **suite** is a set of rooms in a hotel or other building. *suite, piso, departamento, habitaciones* ❑ *They stayed in a suite at the Paris Hilton. Se quedaron en una suite del Paris Hilton.* 2 N-COUNT A **suite** is a set of matching furniture. *juego* ❑ *...a three-piece suite. ...una sala de tres piezas.* 3 N-COUNT A bathroom **suite** is a matching bathtub, sink, and toilet. *juego* ❑ *...the horrible pink suite in the bathroom. ...los horribles muebles rosa del baño.* 4 N-COUNT A **suite** is a piece of instrumental music consisting of several short, related sections. *suite*
→ see **hotel**

**suit|ed** /sutɪd/ ADJ If something or someone is well **suited to** a particular purpose or person, they are right or appropriate for that purpose or person. *apropiado, adecuado* ❑ *Adriana is well suited to caring for children. Adriana es buena para cuidar niños.*

**Word Partnership** Usar *suited* con:

ADV. **ill** suited, **perfectly** suited, **uniquely** suited, **well** suited
PREP. suited **to** ***something***

**sul|fur** /sʌlfər/ N-UNCOUNT **Sulfur** is a yellow chemical which has a strong smell. *azufre* ❑ *Burning sulfur creates an unpleasant smell. Cuando se quema, el azufre produce un olor desagradable.*
→ see **firework**

**sum** /sʌm/ (**sums, summing, summed**)
**1** N-COUNT A **sum of** money is an amount of money. *suma, cantidad, monto* ❑ *Large sums of money were lost. Se perdieron sumas importantes de dinero.*
**2** N-SING In mathematics, **the sum of** two or more numbers is the number that is obtained when they are added together. *suma* ❑ *The sum of all the angles of a triangle is 180 degrees. La suma de los ángulos de un triángulo es 180 grados.*
▸ **sum up** PHR-VERB If you **sum** something **up**, you describe it as briefly as possible. *resumir, sintetizar* ❑ *The story is too complicated to sum up in one or two words. La historia es demasiado complicada como para resumirla en unas cuantas palabras.*

**Word Partnership** Usar *sum* con:
ADJ. **equal** sum, **large** sum, **substantial** sum, **undisclosed** sum **1**
N. sum **of money** **1**

**sum|ma cum lau|de** /sʊmɑ kʊm laʊdeɪ/ ADV If a college student graduates **summa cum laude,** they receive the highest honor that is possible. *summa cum laude, sobresaliente* ❑ *Jeremy Heyl graduated summa cum laude with a degree in modern history. Jeremy Heyl se graduó summa cum laude en historia moderna.* ● **Summa cum laude** is also an adjective. *summa cum laude* ❑ *...a summa cum laude graduate of Princeton. ...un graduado de Princeton summa cum laude.*

**sum|ma|rize** /sʌməraɪz/ (**summarizes, summarizing, summarized**) V-T/V-I If you **summarize** something, you give a summary of it. *resumir, sintetizar, hacer un resumen* ❑ *Table 3.1 summarizes the information given above. En la tabla 3.1 se resume la información anterior.* ❑ *The article can be summarized in three sentences. El artículo puede sintetizarse en tres frases.* ❑ *To summarize, this is a clever solution to the problem. Resumiendo, es una forma inteligente de solucionar el problema.*

**sum|mary** /sʌməri/ (**summaries**) N-COUNT A **summary of** something is a short account of it, which gives the main points but not the details. *resumen, síntesis* ❑ *What follows is a brief summary of the process. A continuación, una breve síntesis del proceso.* PHRASE ● You use **in summary** to indicate that what you are about to say is a summary of what has just been said. *en resumen, en síntesis* ❑ *In summary, I think the meeting was a success. En pocas palabras, considero que la reunión fue un éxito.*

**sum|mer** /sʌmər/ (**summers**) N-VAR **Summer** is the season between spring and fall. In the summer the weather is usually warm or hot. *verano* ❑ *I flew to Maine this summer. Este verano fui a Maine.* ❑ *It was a perfect summer's day. Fue un perfecto día de verano.*

**sum|mer camp** (**summer camps**) N-COUNT A **summer camp** is a place in the country where parents can pay to send their children during the school summer vacation. *campamento de verano*

**sum|mer school** (**summer schools**) N-VAR **Summer school** is a summer term at a school, college, or university, for example for students who need extra teaching or who want to take extra courses. *verano, curso de verano*

**sum|mer squash** (**summer squashes**) N-COUNT A **summer squash** is a type of squash that is used after being picked rather than being stored for the winter. *calabacita fresca*

**sum|mit** /sʌmɪt/ (**summits**) **1** N-COUNT A **summit** is a meeting at which the leaders of two or more countries discuss important matters. *cumbre* ❑ *...next week's Washington summit. ...la cumbre de Washington de la próxima semana.* **2** N-COUNT The **summit** of a mountain is the top of it. *cima, cumbre* ❑ *...the first man to reach the summit of Mount Everest. ...el primer hombre en llegar a la cima del Everest.*
→ see **mountain**

**sum|mon** /sʌmən/ (**summons, summoning, summoned**) **1** V-T If you **summon** someone, you order them to come to you. *llamar, convocar, mandar llamar* [FORMAL] ❑ *Howe summoned a doctor. Howe mandó llamar a un médico.* ❑ *Suddenly we were summoned to his office. Nos llamaron intempestivamente a su oficina.* **2** V-T If you **summon** a quality such as courage or energy, you make a great effort to have it. *reunir* ❑ *It took her a month to summon the courage to tell her mother. Le tomó un mes tener el valor de decirle a su madre.* ● **Summon up** means the same as **summon.** *llamar, convocar, mandar llamar, reunir* ❑ *He finally summoned up courage to ask her to a game. Por fin tuvo el valor de invitarla a jugar.*

**sum|mons** /sʌmənz/ (**summonses**) **1** N-COUNT A **summons** is an order to come and see someone. *citatorio* ❑ *I received a summons to the principal's office. Recibí un citatorio y tuve que ir a la oficina del director.*
**2** N-COUNT A **summons** is an official order to appear in court. *citatorio* ❑ *She received a summons to appear in court. Le llegó un citatorio para que se presentara en la corte.*

**sun** /sʌn/ **1** N-SING **The sun** is the ball of fire in the sky that the Earth goes around, and that gives us heat and light. *sol* ❑ *The sun was now high in the sky. El sol ya estaba alto en el cielo.* ❑ *The sun came out. Salió el sol.* **2** N-UNCOUNT You refer to the light and heat that reach us from the sun as **the sun.** *sol* ❑ *They went outside to sit in the sun. Salieron a sentarse al sol*
→ see Word Web: **sun**
→ see **astronomer, earth, eclipse, navigation, solar, solar system, star**

**sun|burned** /sʌnbɜrnd/ also **sunburnt** ADJ Someone who is **sunburned** has sore bright pink skin because they have spent too much time in hot sunshine. *quemado por el sol, bronceado, asoleado* ❑ *A badly sunburned face is extremely painful. Es muy dolorosa una quemadura de sol en la cara.*
→ see **skin**

**Sun|day** /sʌndeɪ, -di/ (**Sundays**) N-VAR **Sunday** is the day after Saturday and before Monday. *domingo* ❑ *We went for a drive on Sunday. El domingo salimos a pasear.*

**sun|down** /sʌndaʊn/ N-UNCOUNT **Sundown** is the time when the sun sets. *puesta de sol, caída de la tarde, atardecer* ❑ *We got home about two hours after sundown. Llegamos a casa unas dos horas después del atardecer.*

**sun|flower** /sʌnflaʊər/ (**sunflowers**) N-COUNT A **sunflower** is a very tall plant with large yellow flowers. *girasol, maravilla*

**sun|glasses** /sʌnglæsɪz/ N-PLURAL **Sunglasses** are glasses with dark lenses which you wear to

**Word Web** sun

The **sun**'s core contains **hydrogen** atoms. These atoms combine to form helium. This process is called **fusion**. It makes the core very hot. The corona is a layer of hot, glowing gases surrounding the sun. Large flames also burn on the surface of the sun. They are called solar flares. **Infrared** and **ultraviolet** light are **invisible** parts of **sunlight**. Sometimes dark patches called sunspots appear on the sun. They can appear every eleven years. Scientists believe that sunspots affect the growth of plants on Earth. They also affect radio transmissions.

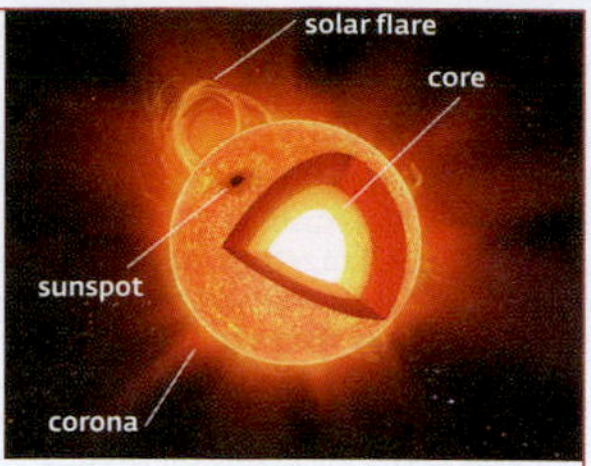


protect your eyes from bright sunlight. *lentes de sol, anteojos de sol* ❑ *She put on a pair of sunglasses. Se puso unos lentes de sol.*

**sun|light** /sʌnlaɪt/ N-UNCOUNT **Sunlight** is the light that comes from the sun during the day. *luz del día, luz del sol, luz solar* ❑ *Sunlight filled the room. El cuarto estaba lleno de luz del sol.*
→ see **habitat, photosynthesis, rainbow, skin, sun**

**Sun|ni** /sʊni/ (**Sunnis**) **1** N-UNCOUNT **Sunni** is the main branch of Islam. *suni, sunita* **2** N-COUNT A **Sunni** is a Muslim who follows the Sunni branch of Islam. *suni, sunita*

**sun|ny** /sʌni/ (**sunnier, sunniest**) **1** ADJ When it is **sunny**, the sun is shining brightly. *soleado* ❑ *The weather was warm and sunny. El tiempo era cálido y soleado.* **2** ADJ **Sunny** places are brightly lit by the sun. *soleado, alegre* ❑ *...a sunny window seat. ...un asiento en el sol junto a la ventana.*

**sun|rise** /sʌnraɪz/ (**sunrises**) **1** N-UNCOUNT **Sunrise** is the time in the morning when the sun first appears in the sky. *salida del sol, amanecer, alba* ❑ *The rain began before sunrise. La lluvia empezó antes del amanecer.* **2** N-COUNT A **sunrise** is the colors and light that you see in the eastern part of the sky when the sun first appears. *amanecer* ❑ *There was a beautiful sunrise yesterday. Ayer estuvo muy lindo el amanecer.*

**sun|screen** /sʌnskrin/ (**sunscreens**) N-VAR A **sunscreen** is a cream that protects your skin from the sun's rays, especially in hot weather. *crema para el sol, protector solar, filtro solar* ❑ *Use a sunscreen when you go outside. No salgas sin ponerte crema para el sol.*
→ see **skin**

**sun|set** /sʌnsɛt/ (**sunsets**) **1** N-UNCOUNT **Sunset** is the time in the evening when the sun disappears out of sight from the sky. *puesta del sol, atardecer, crepúsculo* ❑ *The party ends at sunset. La fiesta termina al ponerse el sol.* **2** N-COUNT A **sunset** is the colors and light that you see in the western part of the sky when the sun disappears in the evening. *atardecer* ❑ *There was a red sunset over Paris. Vimos un rojo atardecer en París.*

**sun|shine** /sʌnʃaɪn/ N-UNCOUNT **Sunshine** is the light and heat that comes from the sun. *luz del sol, rayos del sol, rayos solares, calor del sol* ❑ *She was sitting outside a cafe in bright sunshine. Estaba sentada fuera de un café, en la brillante luz del sol.*

**sun|spot** /sʌnspɒt/ (**sunspots**) N-COUNT **Sunspots** are dark cool patches that appear on the surface of the sun and last for about a week. *peca, mancha solar*

**sun|tan** /sʌntæn/ (**suntans**) **1** N-COUNT If you have a **suntan**, the sun has turned your skin an attractive brown color. *bronceado* ❑ *They want to go to the Bahamas and get a suntan. Quieren ir a las Bahamas para broncearse.* **2** ADJ **Suntan** lotion, oil, or cream protects your skin from the sun. *bronceador* ❑ *She rubbed suntan lotion on his neck. Le puso bronceador en el cuello.*
→ see **skin**

**sun-up** also **sunup** N-UNCOUNT **Sun-up** is the time of day when the sun rises. *amanecer, alba, salida del sol* ❑ *We worked from sunup to sunset. Trabajamos del amanecer al anochecer.*

**su|per** /supər/ **1** ADV **Super** is used before adjectives to indicate that something has a lot of a quality. *súper* ❑ *I want to be super slim. Quiero estar súper delgada.* **2** ADJ **Super** is used before nouns to indicate that something is larger, better, or more advanced than similar things. *súper* ❑ *...a new super plane. ...un nuevo súper avión.* **3** ADJ Some people use **super** to mean very nice or very good. This use can be regarded as old-fashioned. *súper* [INFORMAL] ❑ *We had a super time. Nos la pasamos súper bien.*

**su|perb** /supɜrb/ ADJ If something is **superb**, its quality is very good indeed. *soberbio, magnífico, espléndido, excelente* ❑ *There is a superb golf course 6 miles away. Hay un magnífico campo de golf a 6 kilómetros de aquí.* • **su|perb|ly** ADV *magníficamente* ❑ *The orchestra played superbly. La orquesta tocó espléndidamente.*

**Su|per Bowl** (**Super Bowls**) also **Superbowl** N-COUNT **The Super Bowl** is a football game that is held each year in the United States between the two best professional football teams. *Super Bowl, Super Tazón* ❑ *The Giants won the Super Bowl in 1987. Los Gigantes ganaron el Super Tazón en 1987.*

**super|cell** /supərsɛl/ (**supercells**) N-COUNT A **supercell** is a powerful thunderstorm that often produces tornadoes. *supercelda* [TECHNICAL]

**Word Link** *super ≈ above : superficial, supernatural, superpower*

**super|fi|cial** /supərfɪʃᵊl/ **1** ADJ If you describe someone as **superficial**, you disapprove of them because they do not think deeply, and have little understanding of anything serious or important. *superficial* ❑ *This guy is superficial and stupid. Este*

S

*muchacho es muy tonto y superficial.* • **super|fi|cial|ity** /su̲pərfɪʃiæ̲lɪti/ N-UNCOUNT *superficialidad* ❑ *...the superficiality of Hollywood.* *...la superficialidad de Hollywood.* **2** ADJ If you describe something such as an action, feeling, or relationship as **superficial,** you mean that it includes only the simplest and most obvious aspects of that thing, and not those aspects which require more effort to deal with or understand. *superficial, por encima* ❑ *He gave the newspaper a superficial look.* *Le dio una ojeada al periódico.* • **super|fi|cial|ity** N-UNCOUNT *superficialidad* ❑ *...the superficiality of the music business.* *...la superficialidad del negocio de la música.* • **super|fi|cial|ly** ADV *superficialmente* ❑ *The movie deals with these questions, but only superficially.* *La película toca ese tema, pero sólo superficialmente.* **3** ADJ **Superficial** injuries are not very serious, and affect only the surface of the body. You can also describe damage to an object as **superficial.** *superficial* ❑ *He escaped the crash with superficial injuries.* *De milagro sólo recibió heridas superficiales en el choque.*

**super|gi|ant** /su̲pərdʒaɪənt/ (**supergiants**) N-COUNT A **supergiant** is a very large, bright star. *supergigante* [TECHNICAL]

**super|high|way** /su̲pərhaɪweɪ/ (**superhighways**) **1** N-COUNT A **superhighway** is a large, fast highway or freeway with several lanes. *supercarretera* ❑ *He drove to the city on the superhighway.* *Se fue a la ciudad por la supercarretera* **2** N-COUNT The information **superhighway** is the network of computer links that enables computer users all over the world to communicate with each other. *supercarretera de la información*

| Word Link | *ent ≈ one who does, has : dependent, resident, superintendent* |
|---|---|

**super|in|ten|dent** /su̲pərɪntɛ̲ndənt, su̲prɪn-/ (**superintendents**) **1** N-COUNT A **superintendent** is a person who is responsible for a particular thing or the work done in a particular department. *superintendente, inspector o inspectora, encargado o encargada* ❑ *He became superintendent of the bank's East African branches.* *Llegó a director de las sucursales del banco del este de África.* **2** N-COUNT A **superintendent** is a person whose job is to take care of a large building such as a school or an apartment building and deal with small repairs to it. *conserje, portero o portera* ❑ *The superintendent opened the door with one of his keys.* *El conserje abrió la puerta con una de sus llaves.*

**su|peri|or** /supɪ̲əriər/ (**superiors**) **1** ADJ You use **superior** to describe someone or something that is better than other similar people or things. *superior* ❑ *We have a relationship that is superior to those of our friends.* *Nuestra relación es mucho mejor que las relaciones de nuestros amigos.* ❑ *...superior quality coffee.* *...café de calidad superior.* • **su|peri|or|ity** /supɪ̲əriɔ̲rɪti/ N-UNCOUNT *superioridad* ❑ *...the technical superiority of CDs over tapes.* *...la superioridad técnica del CD respecto de las cintas.* **2** ADJ A **superior** person or thing is more important than another person or thing in the same organization or system. *superior* ❑ *She complained to her superior officers.* *Se quejó con funcionarios de mayor rango que ella.* **3** N-COUNT Your **superior** in an organization that you work for is a person who has a higher rank than you. *superior, jefe o jefa* ❑ *They do not have much communication with their superiors.* *No tienen mucha comunicación con sus superiores.* **4** ADJ If you describe someone as **superior,** you dislike them because they behave as if they are better, more important, or more intelligent than other people. *arrogante* ❑ *Fred gave a superior smile.* *Fred sonrió con suficiencia.* • **su|peri|or|ity** /supɪ̲əriɔ̲rɪti/ N-UNCOUNT *superioridad* ❑ *He had a sense of his own superiority.* *Estaba consciente de su superioridad.*

| Word Partnership | Usar *superior* con: |
|---|---|
| ADV. | **far** superior, **morally** superior, **vastly** superior **1** |
| N. | superior **performance**, superior **quality**, superior **service** **1** |

**su|peri|or court** (**superior courts**) also **Superior Court** N-VAR A **superior court** is a law court that deals with serious or important cases. *corte superior, tribunal superior* ❑ *...a Superior Court of the District of Columbia.* *...una Corte Superior del Distrito de Columbia.* ❑ *...a Los Angeles Superior Court judge.* *...un juez de la Corte Superior de Los Ángeles.*

**super|la|tive** /supɜ̲rlətɪv/ (**superlatives**) ADJ In grammar, the **superlative** form of an adjective or adverb is the form that indicates that something has more of a quality than anything else in a group. For example, "biggest" is the superlative form of "big." Compare **comparative.** *superlativo* • **Superlative** is also a noun. *superlativo* ❑ *His writing contains many superlatives.* *Sus escritos tienen muchos superlativos.*

**super|mar|ket** /su̲pərmɑrkɪt/ (**supermarkets**) N-COUNT A **supermarket** is a large store which sells all kinds of food and some household goods. *supermercado, super* ❑ *Most of us do our food shopping in the supermarket.* *Casi todos compramos los alimentos en el supermercado.*

| Word Link | *super ≈ above : superficial, supernatural, superpower* |
|---|---|

**super|natu|ral** /su̲pərnæ̲tʃərəl, -næ̲tʃrəl/ ADJ **Supernatural** creatures, forces, and events are believed by some people to exist or happen, although they are impossible according to scientific laws. *sobrenatural* ❑ *These evil spirits had supernatural powers.* *Estos espíritus malignos tenían poderes sobrenaturales.* • **The supernatural** is things that are supernatural. *lo sobrenatural* ❑ *He writes stories about the supernatural.* *Escribe historias de lo sobrenatural.*

**super|no|va** /su̲pərno̲ʊvə/ (**supernovas** or **supernovae** /su̲pərno̲ʊvi/) N-COUNT A **supernova** is an exploding star. *supernova*
→ see **telescope**

**super|pow|er** /su̲pərpaʊər/ (**superpowers**) N-COUNT A **superpower** is a very powerful and influential country, usually one that is rich and has nuclear weapons. *superpotencia* ❑ *The United States is a military and economic superpower.* *Los Estados Unidos constituyen una superpotencia militar y económica.*

**super|size** /su̲pərsaɪz/ (**supersizes, supersizing, supersized**) **1** ADJ **Supersize** or **supersized** things are very large. *extragrande* ❑ *...a supersize portion of fries.* *...un paquete extragrande de papas fritas.* ❑ *...a*

S

*supersized mug of coffee.* *...una taza extragrande de café.* **2** V-T If a fast-food restaurant **supersizes** a portion of food, it offers the customer a larger portion. *ofrecer porciones enormes* ❑ *Fast-food restaurants encourage people to supersize their orders.* *Los restaurantes de comida rápida instan a la gente a pedir órdenes enormes.*

**super|son|ic** /su̲pərsɒ̲nɪk/ ADJ **Supersonic** aircraft travel faster than the speed of sound. *supersónico* ❑ *...a supersonic jet.* *...un avión (a reacción) supersónico.*
→ see **sound**

**super|sti|tion** /su̲pərstɪʃᵊn/ (**superstitions**) N-VAR **Superstition** is belief in things that are not real or possible, for example magic. *superstición* ❑ *Many people have superstitions about numbers.* *Muchas personas creen en supersticiones relacionadas con los números.*

**super|sti|tious** /su̲pərstɪʃəs/ ADJ People who are **superstitious** believe in things that are not real or possible, for example magic. *supersticioso* ❑ *Jean was superstitious and believed the color green brought bad luck.* *Jean era supersticiosa y creía que el color verde daba mala suerte.*

**super|vise** /su̲pərvaɪz/ (**supervises, supervising, supervised**) V-T If you **supervise** an activity or a person, you make sure that the activity is done correctly or that the person is doing a task or behaving correctly. *supervisar, vigilar, inspeccionar* ❑ *I supervised the packing of orders.* *Yo supervisé el empacado de las órdenes.* ● **super|vi|sion** /su̲pərvɪʒᵊn/ N-UNCOUNT *supervisión, vigilancia* ❑ *Young children need close supervision.* *Los niños pequeños requieren de mucha supervisión.* ● **super|vi|sor** (**supervisors**) N-COUNT *supervisor, supervisora* ❑ *...a job as a supervisor at a factory.* *...un puesto de supervisor en la fábrica.*

**sup|per** /sʌ̲pər/ (**suppers**) **1** N-VAR Some people refer to the main meal eaten in the early part of the evening as **supper.** *cena* ❑ *Would you like to join us for supper?* *¿Cenas con nosotros?* **2** N-VAR **Supper** is a simple meal eaten just before you go to bed at night. *merienda, cena* ❑ *She gives the children their supper, then puts them to bed.* *Les sirve la cena a los niños y después los acuesta.*

S

**sup|plement** /sʌ̲plɪmənt/ (**supplements, supplementing, supplemented**) V-T If you **supplement** something, you add something to it in order to improve it. *complementar, completar* ❑ *Some people do extra jobs to supplement their incomes.* *Algunas personas hacen trabajos extra para completar sus ingresos.* ● **Supplement** is also a noun. *complemento, suplemento* ❑ *These classes are a supplement to school study.* *Estas clases son el complemento de lo que se estudia en la escuela*

**sup|pli|er** /səplaɪər/ (**suppliers**) N-COUNT A **supplier** is a person, company, or organization that sells or supplies something such as goods or equipment to customers. *proveedor o proveedora, abastecedor o abastecedora* [BUSINESS] ❑ *...one of the country's biggest food suppliers.* *...uno de los proveedores de alimentos más grandes del país.*

**sup|ply** /səplaɪ/ (**supplies, supplying, supplied**) **1** V-T If you **supply** someone with something that they want or need, you give them a quantity of it. *proveer, abastecer, proporcionar, suministrar, aprovisionar* ❑ *...an agreement not to supply chemical weapons.* *...un acuerdo para no suministrar armas químicas.* ❑ *The pipeline will supply Greece with Russian natural gas.* *El gasoducto abastecerá a Grecia de gas natural ruso.* **2** N-PLURAL You can use **supplies** to refer to food, equipment, and other essential things that people need, especially when these are provided in large quantities. *provisiones, víveres, existencias* ❑ *What happens when there are no more food supplies?* *¿Qué pasará cuando se acaben los víveres?* **3** N-VAR A **supply of** something is an amount of it which someone has or which is available for them to use. *surtido, inventario, existencias* ❑ *The brain needs a constant supply of oxygen.* *El cerebro necesita un abasto constante de oxígeno.* **4** N-UNCOUNT **Supply** is the quantity of goods and services that can be made available for people to buy. *surtido, inventario, existencias* [BUSINESS] ❑ *Prices change according to supply and demand.* *Los precios cambian según la oferta y la demanda.* **5** PHRASE If something is **in short supply,** there is very little of it available and it is difficult to find or obtain. *escasear* ❑ *Food is in short supply all over the country.* *Los alimentos están escaseando en todo el país.*

**Word Partnership** Usar *supply* con:

N. supply **electricity**, supply **equipment**, supply **information** **1**
ADJ. **abundant** supply, **large** supply, **limited** supply **3**

**sup|ply chain** (**supply chains**) N-COUNT A **supply chain** is the entire process of making and selling commercial goods, including every stage from the supply of materials and the manufacture of the goods through to their distribution and sale. *cadena de producción y distribución*

**sup|port** /səpɔ̲rt/ (**supports, supporting, supported**) **1** V-T If you **support** someone or their ideas or aims, you agree with them, and perhaps help them because you want them to succeed. *apoyar, ayudar, sostener, soportar* ❑ *The vice president said that he supported the people of New York.* *El vicepresidente dijo que apoyaba al pueblo de Nueva York.* ● **Support** is also a noun. *apoyo, soporte, sostén* ❑ *The president gave his full support to the reforms.* *El presidente dio su apoyo total a las reformas.* ● **sup|port|er** (**supporters**) N-COUNT *defensor o defensora, partidario o partidaria, seguidor o seguidora* ❑ *...the president's supporters.* *...los partidarios del presidente.* **2** N-UNCOUNT If you give **support** to someone during a difficult or unhappy time, you are kind to them and help them. *apoyo, respaldo, ayuda* ❑ *She gave me a lot of support when my husband died.* *Me ayudó mucho cuando murió mi esposo.* **3** N-UNCOUNT Financial **support** is money provided to enable an organization to continue. *apoyo, soporte, ayuda* ❑ *The company gets support from government.* *La compañía recibe apoyo del gobierno.* **4** V-T If you **support** someone, you provide them with money or the things that they need. *sostener* ❑ *I have three children to support.* *Tengo tres hijos que mantener.* **5** V-T If a fact **supports** a statement or a theory, it helps to show that it is true or correct. *apoyar, sustentar* ❑ *A lot of research supports this theory.* *Esta teoría está sustentada por muchas investigaciones.* ● **Support** is also a noun. *soporte,* apoyo ❑ *History offers some support for this view.* *Parte del apoyo de esta opinión proviene de la historia.* **6** V-T If something **supports** an object, it is underneath the object and holding it up. *sostener* ❑ *Thick wooden posts supported the roof.* *Gruesos postes de madera soportaban el techo.* **7** N-COUNT A **support** is a bar or other object that supports something. *soporte* ❑ *Each piece of metal was on wooden supports.* *Cada pieza de metal se apoyaba en soportes de madera.* **8** V-T If you **support yourself**, you prevent yourself from falling by holding onto something or by leaning on something. *sostenerse, apoyarse* ❑ *He supported himself on a nearby wall.* *Se apoyó en un muro cercano.* • **Support** is also a noun. *soporte, apoyo* ❑ *Alice leaned against him for support.* *Alice se apoyó en él.*

**sup|port|ive** /səpɔrtɪv/ ADJ If you are **supportive,** you are kind and helpful to someone at a difficult or unhappy time in their life. *que da apoyo* ❑ *They were always supportive of each other.* *Siempre se apoyaron uno al otro.*

**sup|pose** /səpoʊz/ (**supposes, supposing, supposed**) **1** V-T You can use **suppose** or **supposing** before mentioning a possible situation or action. You usually then go on to consider the effects that this situation or action might have. *suponer, presumir, creer, imaginarse* ❑ *Suppose someone gave you a check for $6 million dollars. What would you do with it?* *Imagínate que alguien te diera un cheque por 6 millones de dólares, ¿qué harías?* **2** V-T If you **suppose that** something is true, you believe that it is probably true. *suponer* ❑ *I suppose you're in high school, too?* *Supongo que tú también estás en prepa.* ❑ *The problem was more complex than he supposed.* *El problema era más complejo de lo que suponía.* **3** PHRASE You can say **"I suppose"** when you want to express slight uncertainty. *creer, suponer* [SPOKEN] ❑ *I suppose I'd better do some homework.* *Creo que mejor hago algo de tarea.* ❑ *"Is that the right way?"— "Yeah. I suppose so."* *—¿Así está bien? —Creo que sí.*

**sup|posed**

> Pronounced /səpoʊzd/ or /səpoʊst/ for meanings **1** and **2**, and /səpoʊzd/ for meaning **3**.

**1** PHRASE If you say that something **is supposed to** happen, you mean that it is planned or expected. Sometimes this use suggests that the thing does not really happen in this way. *se supone* ❑ *This is the girl he is supposed to marry.* *Esta es la chica con quien se supone que se va a casar.* ❑ *He was supposed to go back to Brooklyn on the last bus.* *Se suponía que regresaba a Brooklyn en el último camión.* **2** PHRASE If you say that something **is supposed to** be true, you mean that people say it is true but you do not know for certain that it is true. *se supone* ❑ *"The Whipping Block" is supposed to be a really good poem.* *Se supone que The Whipping Block es realmente un buen poema.* **3** ADJ You can use **supposed** to suggest that something that people talk about or believe in may not in fact exist, happen, or be as it is described. *supuesto, presunto, imaginado* ❑ *...the supposed cause of the accident.* *...la supuesta causa del accidente.* • **sup|pos|ed|ly** /səpoʊzɪdli/ ADV *supuestamente* ❑ *It was supposedly his own work.* *Supuestamente era su propio trabajo.*

**sup|press** /səprɛs/ (**suppresses, suppressing, suppressed**) **1** V-T If someone in authority **suppresses** an activity, they prevent it from continuing, by using force or making it illegal. *suprimir, reprimir, contener* ❑ *As we know, it's difficult to suppress crime.* *Como sabemos, es difícil suprimir a la delincuencia.* • **sup|pres|sion** /səprɛʃ^ən/ N-UNCOUNT *represión* ❑ *...the suppression of protests.* *...la represión de las protestas.* **2** V-T If a natural function or reaction of your body **is suppressed,** it is stopped, for example by drugs or illness. *suprimir, reprimir* ❑ *The growth of cancer cells can be suppressed by various treatments.* *Hay varios tratamientos para inhibir el crecimiento de las células cancerosas.* • **sup|pres|sion** N-UNCOUNT *supresión, inhibición* ❑ *...suppression of the immune system.* *...inhibición del sistema inmunológico.* **3** V-T If you **suppress** your feelings or reactions, you do not express them, even though you might want to. *reprimir* ❑ *Liz thought of Barry and suppressed a smile.* *Liz pensó en Barry y reprimió una sonrisa.* • **sup|pres|sion** N-UNCOUNT *represión, inhibición* ❑ *A mother's suppression of her own feelings can cause problems.* *Que una madre reprima sus sentimientos puede causarle problemas.* **4** V-T If someone **suppresses** a piece of information, they prevent other people from learning it. *ocultar, suprimir* ❑ *They did not try to suppress the information.* *No intentaron ocultar la información.* • **sup|pres|sion** N-UNCOUNT *ocultamiento, supresión* ❑ *...the suppression of official documents.* *...el ocultamiento de documentos oficiales.*

**su|preme** /sʊprim/ **1** ADJ **Supreme** is used in the title of a person or an official group to indicate that they are at the highest level in a particular organization or system. *supremo* ❑ *...the supreme ruler of Eastern Russia.* *...el dirigente supremo de la Rusia oriental.* ❑ *...the Supreme Court.* *...la Suprema Corte.* **2** ADJ You use **supreme** to emphasize that a quality or thing is very great. *supremo* ❑ *Her happiness was of supreme importance.* *Su felicidad era de la mayor importancia.* • **su|preme|ly** ADV *sumamente* ❑ *She does her job supremely well.* *Hace excelentemente su trabajo.*

**sure** /ʃʊ^ər/ (**surer, surest**) **1** ADJ If you are **sure** that something is true, you are certain that it is true. If you are not **sure** about something, you do not know for certain what the true situation is. *seguro* ❑ *He was not sure that he wanted to be a teacher.* *No estaba seguro de querer ser maestro.* ❑ *I'm not sure where he lives.* *No estoy segura de dónde vive.* **2** ADJ If someone is **sure of** getting something, they will definitely get it or they think they will definitely get it. *seguro* ❑ *How can you be sure of getting quality?* *¿Cómo puedes estar seguro de obtener calidad?* **3** PHRASE If you say that something **is sure to** happen, you are emphasizing your belief that it will happen. *seguro* ❑ *With a face like that, she's sure to get a boyfriend.* *Con esa cara, seguro consigue novio.* **4** ADJ **Sure** is used to emphasize that something such as a sign or ability is reliable or accurate. *seguro* ❑ *There were black clouds in the sky, a sure sign of rain.* *Había nubes negras en el cielo, signo seguro de que llovería.* **5** CONVENTION **Sure** is an informal way of saying "yes" or "all right." *sí* ❑ *"Do you know where she lives?"— "Sure."* *—¿Sabes dónde vive? —Claro.* **6** PHRASE You say **sure enough,** especially when telling a story, to confirm that something was really true or was actually happening.

*efectivamente* ❑ *The pie looked good. Sure enough, it tasted great. El pay se veía bueno, y en efecto, estaba delicioso.* **7** PHRASE If you say that something is **for sure** or that you know it **for sure,** you mean that it is definitely true. *seguro* ❑ *One thing's for sure, women still love Barry Manilow. Y no hay duda de que a las mujeres todavía les encanta Barry Manilow.* **8** PHRASE If you **make sure that** something is done, you take action so that it is done. *asegurarse* ❑ *Make sure that you follow the instructions carefully. Asegúrate de seguir las instrucciones al pie de la letra.* **9** PHRASE If you **make sure that** something is the way that you want or expect it to be, you check that it is that way. *asegurarse, checar, verificar* ❑ *He looked in the bathroom to make sure that he was alone. Se asomó al baño para cerciorarse de que estaba solo.* **10** PHRASE If you are **sure of yourself,** you are very confident about your own abilities or opinions. *seguro de uno mismo* ❑ *I've never seen him so sure of himself. Nunca lo había visto tan seguro de sí.* **11** CONVENTION You say **"sure thing"** to show that you agree with someone or will do as they say. *sin duda* [SPOKEN] ❑ *"Be careful!" — "Sure thing, Dad." —¡Ten cuidado!—Claro, pa.*

**sure|ly** /ʃʊərli/ **1** ADV You use **surely** to emphasize that you think something should be true, and you would be surprised if it was not true. *seguramente, con seguridad* ❑ *You're an intelligent woman, surely you realize by now that I'm helping you. Eres una mujer inteligente, con seguridad ya te diste cuenta de que te estoy ayudando.* ❑ *You surely haven't forgotten Dr. Walters? Seguramente reconoces al Dr. Walters.* **2** PHRASE If you say that something is happening **slowly but surely,** you mean that it is happening gradually but it is definitely happening. *lento pero seguro* ❑ *Slowly but surely she was starting to like him. Poco a poco le empezaba a gustar.*

**surf** /sɜrf/ (**surfs, surfing, surfed**) **1** N-UNCOUNT **Surf** is the mass of white bubbles that is formed by waves as they fall upon the shore. *oleaje, espuma, resaca* ❑ *...surf rolling onto white sand beaches. ...olas deslizándose hacia playas de arena blanca.* **2** V-I If you **surf,** you ride on big waves in the ocean on a special board. *surf, surfear* ❑ *I'm going to buy a board and learn to surf. Voy a comprarme una tabla para aprender a surfear.* ● **surf|er** (**surfers**) N-COUNT *el/la que surfea* ❑ *...this small fishing village, which continues to attract surfers. ...esa pequeña aldea de pescadores que sigue atrayendo a los aficionados al surf.* ● **surf|ing** N-UNCOUNT *surfear* ❑ *My favorite sport is surfing. Mi deporte favorito es el surf.* **3** V-T If you **surf** the Internet, you spend time finding and looking at things on the Internet. *navegar* [COMPUTING] ❑ *No one knows how many people currently surf the Net. Nadie sabe cuantas personas navegan en la Red hoy en día.* ● **surf|er** (**surfers**) N-COUNT *quienes navegan en Internet, internauta* ❑ *Net surfers can use their credit cards to pay for goods. Los internautas puede usar su tarjeta de crédito para pagar sus compras.* ● **surf|ing** N-UNCOUNT *navegar* ❑ *...your surfing habits. ...tu forma de navegar.*

→ see **beach**

| Word Link | *sur ≈ above : surface, surpass, surplus* |
|---|---|

**sur|face** /sɜrfɪs/ (**surfaces, surfacing, surfaced**) **1** N-COUNT The **surface** of something is the flat top part of it or the outside of it. *superficie, cara* ❑ *There were pen marks on the table's surface. La superficie de la mesa tenía rayas de pluma.* ❑ *...waves on the surface of the water. ...olas en la superficie del agua.* **2** N-SING When you refer to **the surface** of a situation, you are talking about what can be seen easily rather than what is hidden or not immediately obvious. *superficie, aspecto superficial* ❑ *Back home, things appear, on the surface, simpler. Allá en casa aparentemente las cosas eran más sencillas.* **3** V-I If someone or something under water **surfaces,** they come up to the surface of the water. *salir a la superficie, emerger* ❑ *He surfaced, trying to get air. Salió a la superficie, intentando tomar aire.*

| Word Partnership | Usar *surface* con: |
|---|---|
| N. | surface **area, Earth's** surface, surface **level**, surface **of the water** **1** |
| ADJ. | **flat** surface, **rough** surface, **smooth** surface **1** |
| V. | **break the** surface **1** |
| | **scratch the** surface **1** **2** |

**sur|face cur|rent** (**surface currents**) N-COUNT A **surface current** is a current of water that flows at or near the surface of the sea. Compare **deep current.** *corriente de superficie, corriente superficial*

**sur|face grav|ity** (**surface gravities**) N-VAR The **surface gravity** of a planet is the gravitational force that exists on the surface of the planet. *gravedad superficial* [TECHNICAL]

**sur|face ten|sion** (**surface tensions**) N-VAR **Surface tension** is the force that acts on the surface of a liquid and causes it to form droplets. *tensión superficial* [TECHNICAL]

**surface-to-volume ra|tio** (**surface-to-volume ratios**) N-COUNT The **surface-to-volume ratio** of a cell or organ is the difference between the surface area of the cell or organ and its volume. *relación superficie-volumen* [TECHNICAL]

**sur|face wave** (**surface waves**) N-COUNT In physics, a **surface wave** is a wave that travels along the boundary between two substances with different densities, such as the sea and the air. In geology, a **surface wave** is a vibration from an earthquake that travels close to the Earth's surface. *onda de superficie, onda superficial* [TECHNICAL]

**surge** /sɜrdʒ/ (**surges, surging, surged**) **1** N-COUNT A **surge** is a sudden large increase in something that has previously been steady, or has only increased or developed slowly. *incremento repentino* ❑ *...the recent surge in prices. ...la reciente elevación de los precios.* **2** V-I If something **surges,** it increases suddenly and greatly, after being steady or developing only slowly. *aumentar* ❑ *The Freedom Party's support surged from 10 percent to nearly 17 percent. El apoyo para el Partido de la Libertad se incrementó del 10 a casi el 17 por ciento.* **3** V-I If a crowd of people **surge** forward, they suddenly move forward together. *avanzar violentamente* ❑ *The crowd was getting angry and suddenly surged forward into the store. La multitud empezaba a enojarse y de repente se abalanzó hacia el interior de la tienda.* **4** N-COUNT A **surge** is a sudden powerful movement of a physical force such as wind or water. aumento repentino ❑ *The whole car shook with a surge of power.* *Todo el carro se sacudió con un aumento repentino de potencia.* **5** V-I If a physical force such as water or electricity **surges** through something, it moves through it suddenly and powerfully. penetrar ❑ *The wall fell and water surged into the yard.* *El muro se derrumbó y el agua entró violentamente al patio.*

**sur|geon** /sɜrdʒən/ (**surgeons**) N-COUNT A **surgeon** is a doctor who is specially trained to perform surgery. cirujano o cirujana ❑ *...a heart surgeon.* *...cirujano especializado en corazón.*

**sur|geon gen|er|al** (**surgeons general**) also **Surgeon General** N-COUNT In the United States, the **surgeon general** is the head of the public health service. inspector general de sanidad o inspectora general de sanidad, director general de salud pública o directora general de salud pública

**sur|gery** /sɜrdʒəri/ (**surgeries**) **1** N-UNCOUNT **Surgery** is medical treatment in which your body is cut open so that a doctor can repair, remove, or replace a diseased or damaged part. cirugía, intervención quirúrgica, operación ❑ *His father just had heart surgery.* *Su papá acaba de ser sometido a una operación del corazón.* **2** N-COUNT A **surgery** is the area in a hospital with operating rooms where surgeons operate on their patients. sala de operaciones, quirófano
→ see **cancer, laser**

**sur|gi|cal** /sɜrdʒɪkəl/ **1** ADJ **Surgical** equipment and clothing is used in surgery. quirúrgico ❑ *...a collection of surgical instruments.* *...un juego de instrumentos quirúrgicos.* **2** ADJ **Surgical** treatment involves surgery. quirúrgico ❑ *...a simple surgical operation.* *...una intervención quirúrgica sencilla.* ● **sur|gi|cal|ly** ADV quirúrgicamente, mediante cirugía ❑ *The lump on his arm will be surgically removed.* *Le van a extirpar quirúrgicamente la bola del brazo.*

**sur|name** /sɜrneɪm/ (**surnames**) N-COUNT Your **surname** is the name that you share with other members of your family. In English speaking countries and many other countries it is your last name. apellido ❑ *She didn't know his surname, only his first name.* *No sabía el apellido de él, sólo su nombre.*

| **Word Link** | *sur ≈ above : surface, surpass, surplus* |
|---|---|

**sur|pass** /sərpæs/ (**surpasses, surpassing, surpassed**) V-T If one person or thing **surpasses** another, the first is better than, or has more of a particular quality than, the second. superar, sobrepasar, rebasar ❑ *He wanted to surpass the achievements of his older brothers.* *Quería superar los logros de sus hermanos mayores.*

**sur|plus** /sɜrplʌs, -pləs/ (**surpluses**) **1** N-VAR If there is a **surplus of** something, there is more than is needed. excedente, superávit ❑ *...countries where there is a surplus of labor.* *...países donde hay excedentes de mano de obra.* **2** ADJ **Surplus** is used to describe something that is extra or that is more than is needed. sobrante, excedente ❑ *Few people have large sums of surplus cash.* *Pocas personas tienen excedentes importantes de efectivo.* ❑ *I sell my surplus birds to a local pet shop.* *Vendo mi excedente de aves a una tienda de mascotas local.* **3** N-COUNT If a country has a trade **surplus,** it exports more than it imports. superávit ❑ *Japan's annual trade surplus is around 100 billion dollars.* *El superávit comercial anual de Japón es de unos 100 mil millones de dólares.* **4** N-COUNT If a government has a budget **surplus,** it has spent less than it received in taxes. superávit ❑ *Norway's budget surplus has fallen from 5.9%.* *El superávit presupuestal de Noruega bajó de 5.9 por ciento.*

**sur|prise** /sərpraɪz/ (**surprises, surprising, surprised**) **1** N-COUNT A **surprise** is an unexpected event, fact, or piece of news. sorpresa ❑ *I have a surprise for you: We are moving to Switzerland!* *Te tengo una sorpresa: ¡nos mudamos a Suiza!* ❑ *It may come as a surprise that a child is born with many skills.* *Puede ser una sorpresa que los niños nazcan con muchas habilidades.* ● **Surprise** is also an adjective. sorpresa ❑ *Baxter arrived this afternoon, on a surprise visit.* *Baxter llegó esta tarde en una visita sorpresa.* **2** N-UNCOUNT **Surprise** is the feeling that you have when something unexpected happens. sorpresa ❑ *The Pentagon has expressed surprise at his comments.* *El Pentágono expresó su sorpresa ante los comentarios de él.* ❑ *"You mean he's going to vote against her?" Scobie asked in surprise.* *—¿Me estás diciendo que va a votar en contra de ella? —preguntó Scobie con sorpresa.* **3** V-T If something **surprises** you, it gives you a feeling of surprise. sorprender ❑ *We'll do the job ourselves and surprise everyone.* *Haremos el trabajo nosotros mismos y sorprenderemos a todos.* ❑ *It surprised me that a driver of Alain's experience should make those mistakes.* *Me sorprendió que un chofer con la experiencia de Alain cometiera esos errores.* **4** → see also **surprised, surprising**

| **Word Partnership** | Usar *surprise* con: |
|---|---|
| ADJ. | **big** surprise, **complete** surprise, **great** surprise, **pleasant** surprise **1** |
| N. | surprise **announcement**, surprise **attack**, **a bit of a** surprise, surprise **move**, surprise **visit** **1** **element of** surprise **2** |

**sur|prised** /sərpraɪzd/ **1** ADJ If you are **surprised** at something, you have a feeling of surprise, because it is unexpected or unusual. sorprendido ❑ *I was surprised at how easy it was.* *Estaba sorprendido de lo fácil que era.* **2** → see also **surprise**

**sur|pris|ing** /sərpraɪzɪŋ/ **1** ADJ Something that is **surprising** is unexpected or unusual and makes you feel surprised. sorprendente ❑ *It is not surprising that children learn to read at different rates.* *No es sorprendente que los niños aprendan a leer a diferente ritmo.* ● **sur|pris|ing|ly** ADV sorprendentemente, con sorpresa ❑ *The party was surprisingly good.* *La fiesta estuvo sorprendentemente buena.* **2** → see also **surprise**

S

**sur|ren|der** /sərɛndər/ (**surrenders, surrendering, surrendered**) **1** V-I If you **surrender,** you stop fighting or resisting someone and agree that you have been beaten. rendirse, entregarse, capitular ❑ *The army finally surrendered.* *El ejército acabó por rendirse.* ● **Surrender** is also a noun. rendición, capitulación ❑ *...the government's surrender to demands made by the people.* *...la capitulación del gobierno ante las demandas del pueblo.* **2** V-T If you **surrender** something you would rather keep, you give it up or let someone else have it, for example after a struggle. renunciar ❑ *Nadja had to surrender*

all rights to her house. Nadja tuvo que renunciar a los derechos de su casa. • **Surrender** is also a noun. renuncia, entrega ❑ ...the surrender of weapons. ...la rendición de las armas.
→ see **war**

| **Thesaurus** | *surrender* Ver también: |
|---|---|
| v. | abandon, give in, give up 1 2 |

**sur|ro|gate** /sɜrəgeɪt, -gɪt/ (**surrogates**) ADJ You use **surrogate** to describe a person or thing that is given a particular role because the person or thing that should have the role is not available. suplente, sustituto ❑ *Martin became Howard Cosell's surrogate son.* Martin llegó a ser el hijo sustituto de Howard Cosell. • **Surrogate** is also a noun. sustituto, suplente ❑ *He was using her as a surrogate for someone he loved long ago.* Él la usaba como sustituta de alguien a quien había amado tiempo atrás.

**sur|round** /səraʊnd/ (**surrounds, surrounding, surrounded**) 1 V-T If a person or thing **is surrounded** by something, that thing is situated all around them. rodear ❑ *The church was surrounded by a low wall.* La iglesia estaba rodeada de un bajo muro. ❑ *The shell surrounding the egg has many important functions.* El cascarón en que está encerrado el huevo desempeña muchas funciones importantes. ❑ *...Chicago and the surrounding area.* ...Chicago y el área circundante. 2 V-T If you **are surrounded** by soldiers or police, they spread out so that they are in positions all the way around you. cercar, rodear ❑ *When the car stopped it was surrounded by soldiers.* Cuando el auto se detuvo, fue rodeado por soldados. 3 V-T The circumstances, feelings, or ideas which **surround** something are those that are closely associated with it. rodear ❑ *A lot of the facts surrounding the case are unknown.* Se desconocen muchos de los hechos en torno al caso. 4 V-T If you **surround yourself with** certain people or things, you make sure that you have a lot of them near you all the time. rodearse ❑ *He surrounds himself with intelligent people.* Se rodea de personas inteligentes.

**sur|round|ings** /səraʊndɪŋz/ N-PLURAL When you are describing the place where you are at the moment, or the place where you live, you can refer to it as your **surroundings.** ambiente, entorno ❑ *He soon felt at home in his new surroundings.* Pronto se sintió como en casa en su nuevo ambiente.

S

**sur|veil|lance** /sərveɪləns/ N-UNCOUNT **Surveillance** is the careful watching of someone, especially by an organization such as the police or the army. vigilancia, observación ❑ *They kept him under constant surveillance.* Lo mantuvieron bajo vigilancia constante.

**sur|vey** (**surveys, surveying, surveyed**)

The noun is pronounced /sɜrveɪ/. The verb is pronounced /sərveɪ/, and can also be pronounced /sɜrveɪ/ in meanings 2 and 5.

1 N-COUNT If you carry out a **survey,** you try to find out detailed information about a lot of different people or things, usually by asking people a series of questions. sondeo, encuesta ❑ *They conducted a survey to see how students study.* Llevaron a cabo un sondeo para saber cómo estudian los alumnos. 2 V-T If you **survey** a number of people, companies, or organizations, you try to find out information about their opinions or behavior, usually by asking them a series of questions. sondear, encuestar ❑ *They surveyed 211 companies for the report.* Para el informe, hicieron encuestas en 211 empresas. 3 V-T If you **survey** something, you look at or consider the whole of it carefully. revisar, reconocer ❑ *He stood up and surveyed the room.* Se puso de pie y revisó la habitación. 4 N-COUNT If someone carries out a **survey** of an area of land, they examine it and measure it, usually in order to make a map of it. inspección, peritaje, levantamiento, planimetría ❑ *...a survey of India.* ...una planimetría de la India. 5 V-T If someone **surveys** an area of land, they examine it and measure it, usually in order to make a map of it. deslindar, medir ❑ *The area was surveyed in detail.* Inspeccionaron el área en detalle. • **sur|vey|or** /sərveɪər/ (**surveyors**) N-COUNT topógrafo o topógrafa, perito o perita, deslindador o deslindadora ❑ *...surveyor's maps.* ...mapas de topógrafo.

**sur|viv|al** /sərvaɪvᵊl/ N-UNCOUNT The **survival** of something or someone is the fact that they manage to continue or exist in spite of difficulty or danger. supervivencia, sobrevivencia ❑ *...companies which have been struggling for survival.* ...empresas que han luchado por su supervivencia.

| **Word Link** | *viv ≈ living : revival, survive, vivid* |
|---|---|

**sur|vive** /sərvaɪv/ (**survives, surviving, survived**) 1 V-T/V-I If a person or living thing **survives** in a dangerous situation such as an accident or an illness, they do not die. sobrevivir, salir con vida, salvar la vida ❑ *It's a miracle that anyone survived.* Es un milagro que alguien haya salido con vida. ❑ *He survived heart surgery.* Sobrevivió a la cirugía del corazón. • **sur|vi|vor** (**survivors**) N-COUNT sobreviviente, superviviente ❑ *Officials said there were no survivors of the plane crash.* Los funcionarios dijeron que no hubo sobrevivientes del avión que se estrelló. 2 V-T/V-I If you **survive** in difficult circumstances, you manage to live or continue in spite of them. sobrevivir ❑ *People are struggling to survive without jobs.* La gente lucha por sobrevivir sin un trabajo. ❑ *How do people survive the pressure of working all the time?* ¿Cómo sobrevive la gente a la presión de trabajar todo el tiempo? • **sur|vi|vor** (**survivors**) N-COUNT sobreviviente ❑ *...survivors of abuse.* ...sobrevivientes de maltrato. 3 V-T If you **survive** someone, you continue to live after they have died. sobrevivir a ❑ *Most women will survive their husbands.* La mayoría de las mujeres sobrevivirán a sus esposos. • **sur|vi|vor** (**survivors**) N-COUNT familiar, deudo ❑ *The money will go to him or his survivors.* El dinero será para él o para sus deudos.

**sus|pect** (**suspects, suspecting, suspected**)

The verb is pronounced /səspɛkt/. The noun and adjective are pronounced /sʌspɛkt/.

1 V-T You use **suspect** when you are stating something that you believe is probably true, in order to make it sound less strong or direct. sospechar, recelar, tener sospechas ❑ *I suspect they were right.* Sospecho que tenían razón. ❑ *He is, I suspect, a very kind man.* Sospecho que es un hombre muy amable. 2 V-T If you **suspect** that something dishonest or unpleasant has been done, you believe that it has probably been done. If you **suspect** someone **of** doing an action of this kind, you believe that

they probably did it. sospechar, tener sospechas ❑ *He suspected that she was telling lies.* *Tenía la sospecha de que ella estaba mintiendo.* ❑ *The police did not suspect him of anything.* *La policía no sospechaba de él.* **3** N-COUNT A **suspect** is a person who the police or authorities think may be guilty of a crime. sospechoso o sospechosa ❑ *Police have arrested a suspect.* *La policía arrestó a un sospechoso.* **4** ADJ **Suspect** things or people are ones that you think may be dangerous or may be less good or genuine than they appear. sospechoso ❑ *They had to leave the building when a suspect package was found.* *Tuvieron que evacuar el edificio cuando se encontró un paquete sospechoso.*

**sus|pend** /səspɛnd/ (**suspends, suspending, suspended**) **1** V-T If you **suspend** something, you delay it or stop it from happening for a while or until a decision is made about it. suspender, dejar de hacer algo temporalmente ❑ *The company will suspend production June 1st.* *La empresa suspenderá la producción el 1° de junio.* **2** V-T If someone **is suspended,** they are prevented from holding a particular job or position for a fixed length of time or until a decision is made about them. suspender, expulsar temporalmente ❑ *Julie was suspended from her job.* *A Julie la suspendieron en el trabajo.* **3** V-T If something **is suspended** from a high place, it is hanging from that place. suspender, colgar ❑ *A map was suspended from the ceiling.* *Del techo colgaba un mapa.*

**sus|pend|ers** /səspɛndərz/ N-PLURAL **Suspenders** are a pair of straps that go over someone's shoulders and are fastened to their pants at the front and back to prevent the pants from falling down. tirantes, tiradores

**sus|pense** /səspɛns/ N-UNCOUNT **Suspense** is a state of excitement or anxiety about something that is going to happen very soon, for example about some news that you are waiting to hear. suspenso, suspense, incertidumbre ❑ *The suspense ended when the judges gave their decision.* *El suspenso acabó cuando los jueces anunciaron su decisión.*

**sus|pen|sion** /səspɛnʃᵊn/ (**suspensions**) **1** N-UNCOUNT The **suspension** of something is the act of delaying or stopping it for a while or until a decision is made about it. suspensión ❑ *There was a suspension of flights out of Miami.* *Suspendieron los vuelos que salen de Miami.* **2** N-VAR Someone's **suspension** is their removal from a job or position for a period of time or until a decision is made about them. suspensión ❑ *No one knows the reason for his suspension.* *Nadie sabe el porqué de la suspensión.* **3** N-VAR A vehicle's **suspension** consists of the springs and other devices attached to the wheels, which give a smooth ride over uneven ground. suspensión ❑ *There's a problem with the car's suspension.* *Hay un problema con la suspensión del auto.* **4** N-COUNT In chemistry, a **suspension** is a mixture containing tiny particles floating in a fluid. suspensión [TECHNICAL]

**sus|pi|cion** /səspɪʃᵊn/ (**suspicions**) **1** N-VAR **Suspicion** or a **suspicion** is a belief or feeling that someone has committed a crime or done something wrong. sospecha, recelo, desconfianza ❑ *There was a suspicion that this student was cheating.* *Tenían la sospecha de que ese estudiante hacía trampa.* **2** N-VAR If there is **suspicion of** someone or something, people do not trust them or consider them to be reliable. recelo ❑ *There is suspicion of police among homeless people.* *Las personas sin hogar muestran recelo ante la policía.* **3** N-COUNT A **suspicion** is a feeling that something is probably true or is likely to happen. sospecha ❑ *I have a suspicion that they are going to succeed.* *Tengo la sospecha de que van a tener éxito.*

**sus|pi|cious** /səspɪʃəs/ **1** ADJ If you are **suspicious of** someone or something, you do not trust them. desconfiado, suspicaz ❑ *He was suspicious of me until I told him I was not writing about him.* *Se mostraba desconfiado hasta que le dije que no estaba escribiendo sobre él.* • **sus|pi|cious|ly** ADJ sospechosamente ❑ *"What is it you want me to do?" Adams asked suspiciously.* *—¿Qué quieres que haga? —preguntó sospechosamente Adams.* **2** ADJ If you describe someone or something as **suspicious,** you mean that there is some aspect of them which makes you think that they are involved in a crime or a dishonest activity. sospechoso ❑ *Two suspicious-looking characters approached him.* *Se le acercaron dos tipos de aspecto sospechoso.* • **sus|pi|cious|ly** ADV sospechosamente ❑ *Has anyone been acting suspiciously over the last few days?* *¿Alguien ha actuado de forma sospechosa en los últimos días?*

**sus|tain** /səsteɪn/ (**sustains, sustaining, sustained**) **1** V-T If you **sustain** something, you continue it or maintain it for a period of time. sostener, mantener, apoyar ❑ *He sustained his strong political views throughout his life.* *Mantuvo sus sólidas opiniones políticas durante toda su vida.* **2** V-T If you **sustain** something such as a defeat, loss, or injury, it happens to you. sufrir [FORMAL] ❑ *The aircraft sustained some damage.* *El avion sufrió algunos daños.* **3** V-T If something **sustains** you, it supports you by giving you help, strength, or encouragement. mantener [FORMAL] ❑ *The money his father gave him sustained him for the moment.* *Por el momento se ha sostenido con el dinero que le dio su padre.*

**sus|tain|able** /səsteɪnəbᵊl/ **1** ADJ You use **sustainable** to describe the use of natural resources when this use is kept at a steady level that is not likely to damage the environment. sustentable, sostenible ❑ *...the sustainable development of forests.* *...el desarrollo sustentable de las selvas.* • **sus|tain|abil|ity** /səsteɪnəbɪlɪti/ N-UNCOUNT sustentabilidad ❑ *...environmental sustainability.* *...sustentabilidad ambiental.* **2** ADJ A **sustainable** plan, method, or system is designed to continue at the same rate or level of activity without any problems. sostenible, sustentable ❑ *We need to create a sustainable transport system.* *Necesitamos crear un sistema de transporte sustentable.* • **sus|tain|abil|ity** N-UNCOUNT sustentabilidad ❑ *...the sustainability of the American economic recovery.* *...la sustentabilidad de la recuperación económica estadounidense.*

**SUV** /ɛs yu vi/ (**SUVs**) N-COUNT An **SUV** is a powerful vehicle with four-wheel drive that can be driven over rough ground. **SUV** is an abbreviation for **sport utility vehicle.** vehículo con tracción en las cuatro ruedas, vehículo todo terreno → see **car**

**swal|low** /swɒloʊ/ (**swallows, swallowing, swallowed**) **1** V-T/V-I If you **swallow** something, you cause it to go from your mouth down into your stomach. tragar(se), ingerir, deglutir ❑ *I swallowed my coffee.* *Me tragué el café.* ❑ *Polly took a bite of the apple*

S

and swallowed. *Polly le dio una mordida a la manzana y se la tragó.* • **Swallow** is also a noun. *trago* ❑ *Jane lifted her glass and took a quick swallow. Jane levantó su vaso y le dio un rápido trago.* **2** V-T If someone **swallows** a story or a statement, they believe it completely. *tragar(se), creer* ❑ *They didn't swallow most of what I said. No creyeron casi nada de lo que dije.* **3** N-COUNT A **swallow** is a kind of small bird with pointed wings and a forked tail. *golondrina*

**swamp** /swɒmp/ (**swamps, swamping, swamped**) **1** N-VAR A **swamp** is an area of very wet land with wild plants growing in it. *ciénaga, pantano* ❑ *I spent one night by a swamp listening to frogs. Pasé una noche a la orilla de un pantano, oyendo a las ranas.* **2** V-T If something **swamps** a place or object, it fills it with water. *anegar, inundar, sumergir, hundir* ❑ *A big wave swamped the boat. Una ola enorme inundó el barco.* **3** V-T If you **are swamped** by things or people, you have more of them than you can deal with. *abrumar(se), inundar(se)* ❑ *He is swamped with work. Está abrumado de trabajo.*
→ see **wetland**

**swap** /swɒp/ (**swaps, swapping, swapped**) **1** V-RECIP If you **swap** something with someone, you give it to them and receive a different thing in exchange. *cambiar, intercambiar* ❑ *Next week they will swap places. La próxima semana van a intercambiar lugares.* ❑ *I swapped my shirt for one of Karen's. Cambié mi blusa por una de Karen.* • **Swap** is also a noun. *cambio, intercambio* ❑ *There followed a swap of signed photos. Después hubo un intercambio de fotos autografiadas.* **2** V-T If you **swap** one thing **for** another, you remove the first thing and replace it with the second, or you stop doing the first thing and start doing the second. *cambiar(se)* ❑ *He swapped his overalls for a suit and tie. Se quitó el overol y se puso traje y corbata.*

**swarm** /swɔrm/ (**swarms, swarming, swarmed**) **1** N-COUNT A **swarm of** bees or other insects is a large group of them flying together. *enjambre* ❑ *The bees traveled in a swarm. Todo el enjambre de abejas se desplazaba.* **2** V-I When bees or other insects **swarm,** they move or fly in a large group. *pulular, enjambrar* ❑ *A group of bees came swarming toward me. Se me acercó un enjambre de abejas.* **3** V-I When people **swarm** somewhere, they move there quickly in a large group. *pulular, irrumpir, amontonarse, aglomerarse* ❑ *People swarmed to the stores, buying everything they could. La gente se amontonaba en las tiendas y compraba todo lo que podía.* **4** N-COUNT A **swarm of** people is a large group of them moving about quickly. *multitud, montón* ❑ *A swarm of people came out of the hotel. Un gentío salió del hotel.* **5** V-I If a place **is swarming with** people, it is full of people moving about in a busy way. *hervir, pulular* ❑ *The place was swarming with police officers. El lugar estaba plagado de oficiales de la policía.*

**swathe** /swɑð/ (**swathes, swathing, swathed**)

| The noun is also spelled **swath**. |
|---|

**1** N-COUNT A **swathe of** land is a long strip of land. *franja, faja* ❑ *Great swathes of countryside have disappeared. Han desaparecido franjas considerables de campo.* **2** V-T To **swathe** someone or something **in** cloth means to wrap them in it completely. *envolver, cubrir* ❑ *She swathed her enormous body in black fabrics. Envolvió su enorme cuerpo con telas negras.* ❑ *His head was swathed in bandages. Tenía la cabeza toda vendada.*

**SWAT team** /swɒt tim/ (**SWAT teams**) N-COUNT A **SWAT team** is a group of police officers who have been specially trained to deal with very dangerous or violent situations. **SWAT** is an abbreviation for "Special Weapons and Tactics." *policía de élite, grupo táctico, grupo de ataque y armas especiales*

**S-wave** /ɛs weɪv/ (**S-waves**) N-COUNT **S-waves** are waves of energy that are released in an earthquake, after the release of waves called P-waves. **S-wave** is an abbreviation for "secondary wave." *onda S* [TECHNICAL]

**sway** /sweɪ/ (**sways, swaying, swayed**) **1** V-I When people or things **sway,** they lean or swing slowly from one side to the other. *balancear(se), mecerse* ❑ *The people swayed back and forth singing. La gente se balanceaba cantando.* ❑ *The whole boat swayed and tipped. La embarcación completa se balanceaba e inclinaba.* **2** V-T If you **are swayed by** someone or something, you are influenced by them. *influir, influenciar* ❑ *Don't ever be swayed by fashion. Nunca permitas que la moda te dirija.* **3** PHRASE If someone or something **holds sway,** they have great power or influence over a particular place or activity. *prevalecer, dominar* ❑ *Powerful chiefs hold sway over more than 15 million people. Jefes poderosos se imponen a más de 15 millones de personas.*

**swear** /swɛər/ (**swears, swearing, swore, sworn**) **1** V-I If someone **swears,** they use language that is considered to be vulgar or offensive. *jurar, insultar, maldecir* ❑ *It's wrong to swear and shout. No está bien maldecir ni gritar.* **2** V-T If you **swear to** do something, you promise in a serious way that you will do it. *jurar, prometer* ❑ *Alan swore that he would do everything he could to help us. Alan juró que haría todo lo que estuviera en sus manos para ayudarnos.* ❑ *We have sworn to fight cruelty. Hemos jurado luchar contra la crueldad.* **3** V-T/V-I If you say that you **swear** that something is true or that you can **swear** to it, you are saying very firmly that it is true. *jurar* ❑ *I swear I've told you all I know. Te juro que ya te dije todo lo que sé.* **4** V-T If someone **is sworn to** secrecy or **is sworn to** silence, they promise another person that they will not reveal a secret. *jurar, prometer solemnemente* ❑ *She wanted to tell everyone the news but was sworn to secrecy. Quería darles a todos la noticia, pero había jurado guardar el secreto.*

▸ **swear by** PHR-VERB If you **swear by** something, you believe that it can be relied on to have a particular effect. *tener fe ciega en algo* [INFORMAL] ❑ *Many people swear by vitamin C to prevent colds. Muchas personas juran que la vitamina C previene los resfriados.*

▸ **swear in** PHR-VERB When someone **is sworn in,** they formally promise to fulfill the duties of a new job or appointment. *prestar juramento, juramentar* ❑ *Mary Robinson was sworn in as Ireland's first woman president. Mary Robinson prestó juramento como presidenta de Irlanda, primera mujer en ocupar dicho cargo.*

S

**Word Partnership** Usar *swear* con:

N. swear **words** 1
swear **allegiance,** swear **an oath** 2
ADV. **solemnly** swear 3

**sweat** /swɛt/ (**sweats, sweating, sweated**) 1 N-UNCOUNT **Sweat** is the salty colorless liquid which comes through your skin when you are hot, sick, or afraid. *sudor* ❑ *Both horse and rider were dripping with sweat.* *Tanto el caballo como el jinete chorreaban de sudor.* 2 V-I When you **sweat,** sweat comes through your skin. *sudar, transpirar* ❑ *It's really hot. I'm sweating.* *Hace tanto calor que estoy sudando.* • **sweat|ing** N-UNCOUNT *sudor, sudoración* ❑ *Sweating can be an embarrassing problem.* *La sudoración puede ser un problema incómodo.* 3 N-COUNT If someone is **in a sweat,** they are sweating a lot. *bañado en sudor, empapado en sudor* ❑ *Every morning I break out in a sweat.* *Todas las mañanas amanezco empapado en sudor.* ❑ *Cool down very gradually after working up a sweat.* *Enfríate poco a poco después de ejercitarte y sudar.* 4 N-PLURAL **Sweats** are loose, warm, stretchy pants or pants and top which people wear to relax and do exercise. *pants, conjunto deportivo* [INFORMAL] 5 PHRASE If someone is **in a cold sweat** or **in a sweat,** they feel frightened or embarrassed. *sudar frío* ❑ *The thought of talking to him brought me out in a cold sweat.* *La idea de hablar con él me hizo sudar frío.*

**sweat|er** /swɛtər/ (**sweaters**) N-COUNT A **sweater** is a warm knitted piece of clothing which covers the upper part of your body and your arms. *suéter, jersey, pulóver, chompa*
→ see **clothing, petroleum**

**sweat gland** (**sweat glands**) N-COUNT Your **sweat glands** are the organs in your skin that release sweat. *glándula sudorípara*

**sweat|shirt** /swɛtʃɜrt/ (**sweatshirts**) also **sweat shirt** N-COUNT A **sweatshirt** is a loose warm piece of casual clothing, usually made of thick stretchy cotton, which covers the upper part of your body and your arms. *sudadera*
→ see **clothing**

**sweep** /swip/ (**sweeps, sweeping, swept**) 1 V-T/V-I If you **sweep** an area of floor or ground, you push dirt or garbage off it using a brush with a long handle. *barrer* ❑ *The owner of the store was sweeping his floor.* *El propietario de la tienda estaba barriendo el piso.* ❑ *She was in the kitchen sweeping food off the floor.* *Estaba en la cocina barriendo la comida que había caído al piso.* ❑ *Norma picked up the broom and began sweeping.* *Norma tomó la escoba y se puso a barrer.* 2 V-T If you **sweep** things off something, you push them off with a quick smooth movement of your arm. *empujar, quitar* ❑ *She swept the cards from the table.* *Quitó las cartas de la mesa.* 3 V-T If wind, a stormy sea, or another strong force **sweeps** someone or something somewhere, it moves them there quickly. *aventar* ❑ *The flood swept cars into the sea.* *La inundación aventó los carros al mar.* 4 V-T/V-I If events, ideas, or beliefs **sweep** through a place or **sweep** a place, they spread quickly through it. *extenderse* ❑ *Then war swept through Europe.* *Entonces la guerra se propagó por Europa.* 5 PHRASE If someone **sweeps** something bad or wrong **under the carpet,** or if they **sweep** it **under the rug,** they try to prevent people from hearing about it. *ocultar* ❑ *For a long time this problem has been swept under the carpet.* *El problema ha estado escondido bajo el tapete por mucho tiempo.*
▸ **sweep up** PHR-VERB If you **sweep up** garbage or dirt, you push it together with a brush and then remove it. *barrer* ❑ *Get a broom and sweep up that glass.* *Trae una escoba y barre esos vidrios.*

**sweet** /swit/ (**sweeter, sweetest, sweets**) 1 ADJ **Sweet** food and drink contains a lot of sugar. *dulce, endulzado, azucarado* ❑ *...a cup of sweet tea.* *...una taza de té endulzado.* ❑ *If the sauce is too sweet, add some salt.* *Si la salsa está demasiado dulce, ponle un poco de sal.* • **sweet|ness** N-UNCOUNT *dulzura, dulzor* ❑ *Fruit has a natural sweetness.* *La fruta tiene un dulzor natural.* 2 ADJ A **sweet** smell is a pleasant one, for example the smell of a flower. *dulce* ❑ *...the sweet smell of her soap.* *...el agradable olor del jabón.* 3 ADJ A **sweet** sound is pleasant, smooth, and gentle. *dulce, melodioso* ❑ *The young girl's voice was soft and sweet.* *La voz de la niña era suave y melodiosa.* • **sweet|ly** ADV *dulcemente* ❑ *He sang sweetly.* *Cantó dulcemente.* 4 ADJ If you describe something as **sweet,** you mean that it gives you great pleasure and satisfaction. *dulce, agradable, encantador* [WRITTEN] ❑ *Success is sweet.* *El éxito sabe a gloria.* 5 ADJ If you describe someone as **sweet,** you mean that they are pleasant, kind, and gentle toward other people. *agradable, amable, amoroso, tierno, mono* ❑ *He was a sweet man.* *Era un hombre amoroso.* • **sweet|ly** ADV *dulcemente, con suavidad* ❑ *I just smiled sweetly and said no.* *Sólo sonreí con dulzura y dije no.* 6 ADJ If you describe a small person or thing as **sweet,** you mean that they are attractive in a simple or unsophisticated way. *tierno, lindo, mono* [INFORMAL] ❑ *...a sweet little baby.* *...un bebé monísimo.* 7 N-PLURAL **Sweets** are foods that have a lot of sugar. *dulce, caramelo, postre* ❑ *Eat more fruit and vegetables and less fats and sweets.* *No comas tantas grasas y dulces, come más frutas y verduras.*
→ see **sugar, taste**

**sweet|en|er** /switᵊnər/ (**sweeteners**) N-VAR A **sweetener** is an artificial substance that can be used in drinks instead of sugar. *edulcorante, endulzante artificial*

**sweet|heart** /swithɑrt/ (**sweethearts**) N-VOC You call someone **sweetheart** if you are very fond of them. *querido, amor, vida, cariño* ❑ *Happy birthday, sweetheart.* *Feliz cumpleaños, amor.*

**swell** /swɛl/ (**swells, swelling, swelled, swollen**)

The forms **swelled** and **swollen** are both used as the past participle.

1 V-T/V-I If the amount or size of something **swells** or if something **swells** it, it becomes larger than it was before. *hincharse, inflarse, crecer, aumentar* ❑ *His army swelled to one hundred thousand men.* *Su ejército llegó a tener cien mil hombres.* ❑ *Sales swelled by 50%.* *Las ventas se incrementaron en 50 por ciento.* 2 V-I If something such as a part of your body **swells,** it becomes larger and rounder than normal. *hincharse, inflamarse* ❑ *Do your legs swell at night?* *¿Se le hinchan las piernas por la noche?* • **Swell up** means the same as **swell.** *hincharse, inflamarse* ❑ *His neck swelled up.* *Se le inflamó el cuello.* 3 N-COUNT **Swells** are large, smooth waves on the surface of the sea that are produced by the wind

S

and can travel long distances. *oleaje* **4** → see also **swollen**

**swept** /swɛpt/ **Swept** is the past tense and past participle of **sweep**. *pasado y participio pasado de sweep*

**swerve** /swɜrv/ (**swerves, swerving, swerved**) V-T/V-I If a vehicle or other moving thing **swerves** or if you **swerve** it, it suddenly changes direction, often in order to avoid hitting something. *virar bruscamente, desviarse* ❑ *Drivers swerved to avoid the tree in the road. Los conductores cambiaban bruscamente de dirección para evitar el árbol que estaba en el camino.* ❑ *Her car swerved off the road. Su auto se salió del camino.* ● **Swerve** is also a noun. *viraje brusco, volantazo* ❑ *He swung the car to the left and that swerve saved his life. Desvió el coche a la izquierda y ese volantazo le salvó la vida.*

**swift** /swɪft/ (**swifter, swiftest, swifts**) **1** ADJ A **swift** event or process happens very quickly or without delay. *veloz, rápido* ❑ *We need to make a swift decision. Tenemos que tomar una decisión rápida.* ● **swift|ly** ADV *rápidamente, velozmente* ❑ *We have to act as swiftly as we can. Tenemos que actuar tan rápidamente como podamos.* ● **swift|ness** N-UNCOUNT *rapidez, velocidad* ❑ *...the swiftness of the invasion. ...la rapidez de la invasión.* **2** ADJ Something that is **swift** moves very quickly. *rápido, veloz* ❑ *With a swift movement, Matthew sat up. Matthew se sentó con un movimiento rápido.* ● **swift|ly** ADV *rápidamente, velozmente* ❑ *Lenny moved swiftly and silently across the grass. Lenny se deslizó rápida y silenciosamente por el pasto.*

**swim** /swɪm/ (**swims, swimming, swam, swum**) **1** V-T/V-I When you **swim**, you move through water by making movements with your arms and legs. *nadar, flotar* ❑ *She learned to swim when she was 10. Aprendió a nadar a los 10 años.* ❑ *Let's go to the other side of the pool then swim back. Nademos de ida y vuelta.* ❑ *I swim a mile a day. Nado un kilómetro al día.* ● **Swim** is also a noun. *nado, natación* ❑ *When can we go for a swim? ¿Cuándo podemos ir a nadar?* ● **swim|mer** (**swimmers**) N-COUNT *nadador o nadadora* ❑ *I'm a good swimmer. Soy una buena nadadora.* **2** V-I If your head **is swimming,** you feel unsteady and slightly ill. *dar vueltas, girar* ❑ *The smell made her head swim. El olor hizo que le diera vueltas la cabeza.*

**S**

**swim blad|der** (**swim bladders**) N-COUNT A **swim bladder** is an organ in fish that contains air or gas and allows the fish to rise or sink through the water. *vejiga natatoria*

**swim|ming** /swɪmɪŋ/ N-UNCOUNT **Swimming** is the activity of swimming, especially as a sport or for pleasure. *nado, natación* ❑ *Swimming is a great form of exercise. La natación es un excelente ejercicio.*

**swim|ming pool** (**swimming pools**) N-COUNT A **swimming pool** is a large hole that has been made and filled with water so that people can swim in it. *alberca, piscina, pileta*

**swim|suit** /swɪmsut/ (**swimsuits**) N-COUNT A **swimsuit** is a piece of clothing that is worn for swimming, especially by women and girls. *traje de baño, bañador, vestido de baño, malla de baño* ❑ *...10 different styles of swimsuit for men. ...10 diferentes estilos de trajes de baño para caballero.*

**swin|dle** /swɪnd$^{ə}$l/ (**swindles, swindling, swindled**) V-T If someone **swindles** a person or an organization, they deceive them in order to get money from them. *estafar, timar, transar* ❑ *He swindled people out of millions of dollars. Estafó millones de dólares a varios.* ● **Swindle** is also a noun. *estafa, timo, transa* ❑ *He was involved in a tax swindle. Estuvo involucrado en una estafa fiscal.* ● **swind|ler** (**swindlers**) N-COUNT *estafador o estafadora, timador o timadora* ❑ *...an insurance swindler. ...un estafador de seguros.*

**swing** /swɪŋ/ (**swings, swinging, swung**) **1** V-T/V-I If something **swings** or if you **swing** it, it moves repeatedly backward and forward or from side to side from a fixed point. *balancear(se), columpiar(se)* ❑ *The sign came loose and started to swing from one side to the other. El letrero se soltó y empezó a balancearse de un lado al otro.* ❑ *She was swinging a bottle of soda in her hand. Balanceaba en la mano una botella de refresco.* ● **Swing** is also a noun. *balanceo, vaivén, oscilación* ❑ *She walked with a slight swing to her hips. Caminaba balanceando ligeramente las caderas.* **2** V-T/V-I If a vehicle **swings** in a particular direction, or if the driver **swings** it, it turns suddenly in that direction. *girar, dar(se) vuelta, virar* ❑ *Joanna swung back and headed for the airport. Joanna se dio la vuelta y se encaminó al aeropuerto.* **3** V-I If you **swing at** a person or thing, you try to hit them with your arm or with something that you are holding. *intentar dar un golpe* ❑ *Blanche swung at her but missed. Blanche trató de pegarle, pero no pudo.* ● **Swing** is also a noun. *cambio, viraje, golpe* ❑ *I often want to take a swing at someone to relieve my feelings. A veces me dan ganas de darle a alguien para tranquilizarme.* **4** N-COUNT A **swing** is a seat hanging by two ropes or chains from a metal frame or from the branch of a tree. You can sit on the seat and move forward and backward through the air. *columpio, péndulo, hamaca* ❑ *I took the kids to the park to play on the swings. Llevé a los niños al parque para que jugaran en los columpios.* **5** N-COUNT A **swing** in people's opinions, attitudes, or feelings is a change in them, especially a sudden or big change. *cambio, viraje, vaivén* ❑ *There are a lot of swings and changes in education. En la educación hay muchos cambios y virajes.* ❑ *She suffers from mood swings. Sufre por sus cambios de humor.* **6** V-I If people's opinions, attitudes, or feelings **swing**, they change, especially in a sudden or extreme way. *cambiar, oscilar* ❑ *In the next election the voters could swing again. Los votantes podrían volver a cambiar en las próximas elecciones.* **7** PHRASE If something is **in full swing**, it is operating fully and is no longer in its early stages. *en plena marcha, en pleno desarrollo* ❑ *When we returned, the party was in full swing. Cuando regresamos, la fiesta ya estaba muy animada.*

**Word Partnership** Usar *swing* con:

ADJ. **good** swing, **perfect** swing **1**
**big** swing **1 3 5**
**in full** swing **7**

N. swing **a bat, golf** swing **1**
swing **at a ball 3**
**porch** swing **4**
**voters** swing **6**

**swing vote** (**swing votes**) N-COUNT In a situation when people are about to vote, the **swing vote** is used to talk about the vote of a person or group which is difficult to predict and which will be important in deciding the result. voto indeciso [JOURNALISM] ❑ *...a Democrat who holds the swing vote on the committee.* *...un Demócrata que tiene los votos indecisos del comité.*

**swing vot|er** (**swing voters**) N-COUNT A **swing voter** is a person who is not a firm supporter of any political party, and whose vote in an election is difficult to predict. votante indeciso

**swipe** /swaɪp/ (**swipes, swiping, swiped**) V-I If you **swipe at** a person or thing, you try to hit them with a stick or other object, making a swinging movement with your arm. golpear con algo ❑ *She swiped at Roger as though he was a fly.* *Le dio un manotazo a Roger, como si fuera una mosca.* • **Swipe** is also a noun. manotazo ❑ *He took a swipe at Andrew that made him fall on the floor.* *Le dio tal golpe a Andrew, que lo tumbó.*

**swipe card** (**swipe cards**) also **swipecard** N-COUNT A **swipe card** is a plastic card with a magnetic strip on it which contains information that can be read or transferred by passing the card through a special machine. tarjeta (de banda magnética) ❑ *They use a swipe card to go in and out of their offices.* *Usan una tarjeta para entrar y salir de sus oficinas.*

**switch** /swɪtʃ/ (**switches, switching, switched**) **1** N-COUNT A **switch** is a small control for an electrical device which you use to turn the device on or off. switch, interruptor, apagador, llave de encendido ❑ *She shut the dishwasher and pressed the switch.* *Cerró la lavadora de platos y oprimió el switch.*

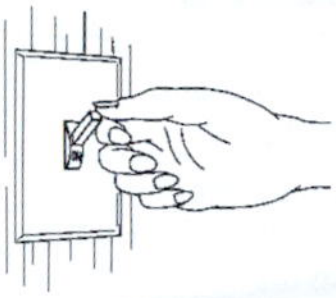

switch

**2** N-PLURAL On a railroad track, the **switches** are the levers and rails at a place where two tracks join or separate. The **switches** enable a train to move from one track to another. aguja ❑ *...a set of railroad tracks—including switches—and a model train.* *...un juego de vías de ferrocarril—incluye agujas—y un tren a escala.* **3** V-T/V-I If you **switch to** something different, for example to a different system, task, or subject of conversation, you change to it from what you were doing or saying before. cambiar ❑ *Maybe you should switch to a different medication.* *Tal vez tengas que cambiar de medicina.* ❑ *The law would help companies to switch from coal to cleaner fuels.* *Las leyes ayudarían a las empresas a cambiar de carbón a combustibles más limpios.* • **Switch** is also a noun. cambio ❑ *She decided on a switch to part-time work.* *Decidió hacer un cambio y trabajar de medio tiempo.* **4** V-T If you **switch** two things, you replace one with the other. cambiar, intercambiar ❑ *They switched the keys, so Karen had the key to my room and I had the key to hers.* *Cambiaron las llaves, así que Karen tenía la de mi habitación y yo la de ella.*

▸ **switch off** **1** PHR-VERB If you **switch off** a light or other electrical device, you stop it from working by operating a switch. apagar ❑ *She switched off the coffee machine.* *Apagó la cafetera.* **2** PHR-VERB If you **switch off,** you stop paying attention or stop thinking or worrying about something. desconectarse, dejar de poner atención [INFORMAL] ❑ *I switch off when he starts complaining.* *Cuando se empieza a quejar, me desconecto.*

▸ **switch on** PHR-VERB If you **switch on** a light or other electrical device, you make it start working by operating a switch. prender, encender ❑ *He switched on the lamp.* *Prendió la lámpara.*

**Word Partnership** Usar *switch* con:

| | |
|---|---|
| V. | **flick a** switch, **flip a** switch, **turn a** switch **1** <br> **make a** switch **3** |
| N. | **ignition** switch, **light** switch, **power** switch **1** <br> switch **sides** **3** |

**swol|len** /swoʊlᵊn/ **1** ADJ If a part of your body is **swollen,** it is larger and rounder than normal, usually as a result of injury or illness. hinchado, inflamado ❑ *My eyes were swollen and I could hardly see.* *Tenía los ojos hinchados y apenas veía.* **2** **Swollen** is the past participle of **swell**. participio pasado de **swell**

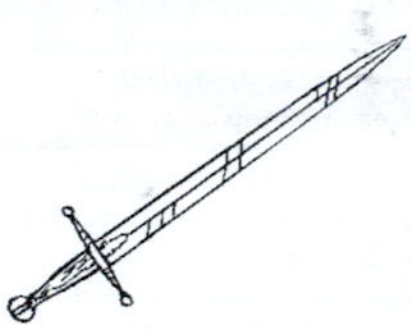

sword

**sword** /sɔrd/ (**swords**) N-COUNT A **sword** is a weapon with a handle and a long sharp blade. espada
→ see **army**

**swum** /swʌm/ **Swum** is the past participle of **swim**. participio pasado de **swim**

**swung** /swʌŋ/ **Swung** is the past tense and past participle of **swing**. pasado y participio pasado de **swing**

**syl|labi|ca|tion** /sɪlæbɪkeɪʃᵊn/ also **syllabification** /sɪlæbɪfɪkeɪʃᵊn/ N-UNCOUNT **Syllabication** or **syllabification** is the division of a word into its separate syllables. silabeo, división en sílabas [TECHNICAL]

**syl|la|ble** /sɪləbᵊl/ (**syllables**) N-COUNT A **syllable** is a part of a word that contains a single vowel sound and that is pronounced as a unit. So, for example, "book" has one syllable, and "reading" has two syllables. sílaba ❑ *We children called her Oma, accenting both syllables.* *De niños le decíamos Oma, acentuando ambas sílabas.*

**Word Link** *osis ≈ state or condition : diagnosis, mitosis, symbiosis*

**sym|bio|sis** /sɪmbioʊsɪs, -baɪ-/ N-UNCOUNT **Symbiosis** is a close relationship between two organisms of different kinds which benefits both organisms. simbiosis [TECHNICAL] ❑ *...the link between bacteria, symbiosis, and the evolution of plants and animals.* *...la relación entre bacterias, simbiosis y la evolución de plantas y animales.*

**sym|bol** /sɪmbᵊl/ (**symbols**) **1** N-COUNT Something that is a **symbol of** a society or an aspect of life seems to represent it because it is very typical of it. símbolo ❑ *For her people, she is a symbol of freedom.* *Para su gente, ella es símbolo de libertad.* **2** N-COUNT A **symbol of** something such as an idea is a shape or design that is used to represent it. símbolo ❑ *The rose is an Irish symbol.* *La rosa es un símbolo irlandés.* **3** N-COUNT A **symbol for**

S

an item in a calculation or scientific formula is a number, letter, or shape that represents that item. *símbolo* ❑ *What's the chemical symbol for oxygen? ¿Cuál es el símbolo químico del oxígeno?*
→ see **myth**

**sym|bol|ic** /sɪmbɒlɪk/ **1** ADJ If you describe an event, action, or procedure as **symbolic,** you mean that it represents an important change, although it has little practical effect. *simbólico* ❑ *The president's trip is of symbolic importance. La importancia del viaje del presidente es simbólica.* ● **sym|boli|cal|ly** /sɪmbɒlɪkli/ ADV *simbólicamente* ❑ *Museums symbolically remove paintings to remember when particular artists died. Los museos quitan simbólicamente las obras de ciertos artistas para recordar la fecha en que murieron.* **2** ADJ **Symbolic** is used to describe things involving or relating to symbols. *simbólico* ❑ *...the symbolic meaning of names. ...el signficado simbólico de los nombres.* ● **sym|bol|ism** /sɪmbəlɪzəm/ N-UNCOUNT *simbolismo* ❑ *...the writer's use of symbolism. ...el uso del simbolismo en sus escritos.*

**Word Link** *sym ≈ together : symmetrical, sympathy, symphony*

**sym|met|ri|cal** /sɪmɛtrɪkᵊl/ ADJ If something is **symmetrical,** it has two halves which are exactly the same, except that one half is the mirror image of the other. *simétrico* ❑ *The rows of windows were perfectly symmetrical. Las hileras de ventanas eran perfectamente simétricas.* ● **sym|met|ri|cal|ly** /sɪmɛtrɪkli/ ADV *de manera simétrica* ❑ *She placed the sandwiches symmetrically on a plate. Acomodó simétricamente los sándwiches en un platón.*

**sym|pa|thet|ic** /sɪmpəθɛtɪk/ **1** ADJ If you are **sympathetic** to someone who is in a bad situation, you are kind to them and show that you understand their feelings. *favorablemente dispuesto* ❑ *She was very sympathetic to the problems of her students. Era muy receptiva a los problemas de sus estudiantes.* ● **sym|pa|theti|cal|ly** /sɪmpəθɛtɪkli/ ADV *con comprensión, con sensibilidad* ❑ *She nodded sympathetically. Asintió comprensivamente.* **2** ADJ If you are **sympathetic to** a proposal or action, you approve of it and are willing to support it. *favorable, receptivo* ❑ *...judges who are more sympathetic to crime control. ...jueces más favorables al control de la criminalidad.*

S

**sym|pa|thize** /sɪmpəθaɪz/ (**sympathizes, sympathizing, sympathized**) **1** V-I If you **sympathize** with someone who is in a bad situation, you show that you are sorry for them. *compadecer(se), comprender* ❑ *I know what it's like when a parent dies, and I sympathize with you. Sé lo que es que muera uno de tus padres, te comprendo.* **2** V-I If you **sympathize with** someone's feelings, you understand them and are not critical of them. *comprender, entender* ❑ *Some Europeans sympathize with the Americans over the issue. Algunos europeos simpatizan al respecto con los estadounidenses.* **3** V-I If you **sympathize with** a person or group, you approve of them and are willing to support them. *simpatizar, aprobar* ❑ *Most of the people living there sympathized with the government. La mayoría de la gente que vivía ahí simpatizaba con el gobierno.* ● **sym|pa|thiz|er** N-COUNT (**sympathizers**) *simpatizante, partidario o partidaria* ❑ *...a Communist sympathizer. ...un partidario de los comunistas.*

**Word Link** *path ≈ feeling : empathy, pathetic, sympathy*

**sym|pa|thy** /sɪmpəθi/ (**sympathies**) **1** N-UNCOUNT If you have **sympathy** for someone who is in a bad situation, you are sorry for them, and show this in the way you behave toward them. *compasión, lástima* ❑ *We expressed our sympathy at the death of her mother. Le expresamos nuestro pésame por la muerte de su madre.* ❑ *I get no sympathy from my family when I'm sick. Mi familia no me comprende cuando estoy enfermo.* **2** N-UNCOUNT If you have **sympathy** with someone's ideas or opinions, you agree with them. *aprobación* ❑ *I have some sympathy with this point of view. Concuerdo en parte con ese punto de vista.* **3** N-UNCOUNT If you take some action **in sympathy with** someone else, you do it in order to show that you support them. *afinidad* ❑ *Several hundred workers went on strike in sympathy with their colleagues. Varios cientos de trabajadores se fueron a huelga para apoyar a sus colegas.*

**Word Partnership** Usar *sympathy* con:

ADJ. **deep** sympathy, **great** sympathy, **public** sympathy **1**
V. **express** sympathy, **feel** sympathy, **gain** sympathy, **have** sympathy **1** **2**

**Word Link** *phon ≈ sound : microphone, symphony, telephone*

**sym|pho|ny** /sɪmfəni/ (**symphonies**) N-COUNT A **symphony** is a piece of music written to be played by an orchestra. Symphonies are usually made up of four separate sections called movements. *sinfonía* ❑ *...Beethoven's Ninth Symphony. ...la Novena Sinfonía de Beethoven.*
→ see **music, orchestra**

**sym|pho|ny or|ches|tra** (**symphony orchestras**) N-COUNT A **symphony orchestra** is a large orchestra that plays classical music. *orquesta sinfónica*

**symp|tom** /sɪmptəm/ (**symptoms**) **1** N-COUNT A **symptom** of an illness is something wrong with your body or mind that is a sign of the illness. *síntoma* ❑ *One symptom of mental illness is hearing imaginary voices. Oír voces imaginarias es síntoma de enfermedad mental.* ❑ *...patients with flu symptoms. ...pacientes con síntomas de gripe.* **2** N-COUNT A **symptom of** a bad situation is something that happens which is considered to be a sign of this situation. *síntoma* ❑ *The food problem is a symptom of a much deeper crisis in the country. El problema de los alimentos en el país es síntoma de una crisis mucho más profunda.*
→ see **diagnosis, illness**

**syna|gogue** /sɪnəgɒg/ (**synagogues**) N-COUNT A **synagogue** is a building where Jewish people meet to worship or to study their religion. *sinagoga*

**syn|cline** /sɪnklaɪn/ (**synclines**) N-COUNT A **syncline** is a rock formation in which layers of rock are folded so that they resemble the shape of a letter U. *sinclinal, pliegue sinclinal* [TECHNICAL]

**Word Link** *syn ≈ together : syncopation, syndicate, synthetic*

**syn|co|pa|tion** /sɪŋkəpeɪʃən/ (**syncopations**) N-VAR **Syncopation** is the quality that music has when the weak beats in a bar are stressed instead of the strong ones. *síncopa*

**syn|di|cate** /sɪndɪkɪt/ (**syndicates**) N-COUNT A **syndicate** is an association of people or organizations that is formed for business purposes or in order to carry out a project. *agrupación, agencia de distribución de publicaciones* ❑ *They formed a syndicate to buy the car. Formaron un grupo para comprar el coche.* ❑ *...a syndicate of 152 banks. ...una organización de 152 bancos.*

**syn|drome** /sɪndroʊm/ (**syndromes**) N-COUNT A **syndrome** is a medical condition that is characterized by a particular group of signs and symptoms. *síndrome* ❑ *No one knows what causes Sudden Infant Death Syndrome. Nadie sabe cuál es la causa del síndrome de muerte infantil súbita.*

**syno|nym** /sɪnənɪm/ (**synonyms**) N-COUNT A **synonym** is a word or expression which means the same as another word or expression. *sinónimo* ❑ *"Afraid" is a synonym for "frightened." Miedo es sinónimo de susto.*

**syn|the|sis re|ac|tion** (**synthesis reactions**) N-COUNT A **synthesis reaction** is a chemical reaction in which two or more substances combine to form a compound. *reacción de síntesis* [TECHNICAL]

**syn|thet|ic** /sɪnθɛtɪk/ ADJ **Synthetic** products are made from chemicals or artificial substances rather than from natural ones. *sintético* ❑ *...synthetic rubber. ...hule sintético.*

**syr|up** /sɪrəp, sɜr-/ (**syrups**) N-VAR **Syrup** is a sweet liquid made by cooking sugar with water or fruit juice. *jarabe, almíbar, sirope* ❑ *...canned fruit with syrup. ...fruta en almíbar enlatada.*

**sys|tem** /sɪstəm/ (**systems**) **1** N-COUNT A **system** is a way of working, organizing, or doing something which follows a fixed plan or set of rules. *sistema, método* ❑ *You need a better system for organizing your CDs. Necesitas un mejor sistema para organizar tus CD.* **2** N-COUNT A **system** is a set of equipment, parts or devices. *sistema* ❑ *There's something wrong with the computer system. Algo está mal en el sistema de la computadora.* ❑ *...a heating system. ...un sistema de calefacción.* **3** N-COUNT A **system** is a network of things that are linked together so that people or things can travel from one place to another or communicate. *sistema* ❑ *...Australia's road and rail system. ...el sistema ferroviario y de carreteras de Australia.* **4** N-COUNT A **system** is a particular set of rules, especially in mathematics or science, which is used to count or measure things. *sistema* ❑ *...the decimal system of weights and measures. ...el sistema decimal de pesas y medidas.* **5** N-SING People sometimes refer to the government or administration of a country as **the system**. *sistema* ❑ *These feelings are likely to make people try to overthrow the system. Probablemente estos sentimientos lleven al pueblo a tratar de derrocar al sistema.* **6** → see also **ecosystem, immune system, nervous system, solar system**

**sys|tem|at|ic** /sɪstəmætɪk/ ADJ Something that is done in a **systematic** way is done according to a fixed plan, in a thorough and efficient way. *sistemático, metódico* ❑ *They searched the area in a systematic way. Hicieron la búsqueda de forma sistemática.* ● **sys|tem|ati|cal|ly** /sɪstəmætɪkli/ ADV *sistemáticamente* ❑ *They have systematically destroyed all our hard work. Destruyeron sistemáticamente lo que hicimos con tanto trabajo.*

**sys|tem|ic** /sɪstɛmɪk/ ADJ **Systemic** means affecting the whole of something. *sistémico* [FORMAL] ❑ *The economy is in a systemic crisis. La economía se encuentra en una crisis sistémica.*
→ see **cardiovascular system**

**sys|tem|ic cir|cu|la|tion** N-UNCOUNT **Systemic circulation** is the flow of blood between the heart and the rest of the body except for the lungs. Compare **pulmonary circulation**. *circulación sistémica, circulación general* [TECHNICAL]

# Tt

**ta|ble** /teɪbᵊl/ (**tables, tabling, tabled**) **1** N-COUNT A **table** is a piece of furniture with a flat top that you put things on or sit at. *mesa* ❑ *She was sitting at the kitchen table. Estaba sentada a la mesa de la cocina* **2** V-T If someone **tables** a proposal or plan, they decide to discuss it at a later date, rather than right away. *posponer, diferir* ❑ *We will table that for later. Dejaremos eso para más adelante.* **3** N-COUNT A **table** is a written set of facts and figures arranged in columns and rows. *tabla* ❑ *See the table on page 104. Véase la tabla de la página 104.*

**tab|leau** /tæbloʊ, tæbloʊ/ (**tableaux**) N-COUNT A **tableau** is a scene, often from a picture, that consists of a group of people in costumes who do not speak or move. *cuadro vivo*

**table|spoon** /teɪbᵊlspun/ (**tablespoons**) N-COUNT A **tablespoon** is a large spoon used for serving food and in cooking. *cuchara para servir*

**tab|let** /tæblɪt/ (**tablets**) N-COUNT A **tablet** is a small solid piece of medicine which you swallow. *tableta, pastilla* ❑ *...a sleeping tablet. ...una pastilla para dormir.*

**tab|loid** /tæblɔɪd/ (**tabloids**) N-COUNT A **tabloid** is a newspaper that has small pages, short articles, and a lot of photographs. *tabloide, periódico sensacionalista, periódico amarillista* ❑ *I sometimes read the tabloids. A veces leo los periódicos sensacionalistas.*

**tack** /tæk/ (**tacks, tacking, tacked**) **1** N-COUNT A **tack** or a **thumbtack** is a short pin with a broad, flat top that you can push with your thumb, used especially for fastening papers to a bulletin board. *chinche, tachuela, chincheta* **2** N-COUNT A **tack** is a short nail with a broad, flat top, especially one that is used for fastening carpets to the floor. *tachuela* ❑ *...a box of carpet tacks. ...una caja de tachuelas para alfombra.* **3** → see also **thumbtack** **4** V-T If you **tack** something to a surface, you pin it there with tacks or thumbtacks. *clavar* ❑ *He tacked a note to her door. Puso una nota en su puerta con una tachuela.* **5** N-SING If you change **tack** or try a different **tack**, you try a different method for dealing with a situation. *enfoque, táctica, estrategia* ❑ *Seeing the puzzled look on his face, she tried a different tack. Viendo el asombro en su cara, intentó un enfoque diferente.*

→ see **office**

▸ **tack on** PHR-VERB If you say that something **is tacked on** to something else, you think that it is added in a hurry and in an unsatisfactory way. *agregar, añadir, pegar* ❑ *A small kitchen is tacked on to the back of the beautiful stone house. En la parte posterior de la hermosa casa de piedra le pegaron una cocinita.*

**tack|le** /tækᵊl/ (**tackles, tackling, tackled**) **1** V-T If you **tackle** a difficult problem or task, you deal with it in a determined way. *atacar, enfrentar, abordar* ❑ *We must tackle these problems in order to save children's lives. Tenemos que enfrentar estos problemas para salvar la vida de los niños.* **2** V-T If you **tackle** someone in a game such as football or rugby, you try to stop them from running or try to take the ball away from them. *taclear* ❑ *Foley tackled the quarterback. Foley tacleó al quarterback.* ● **Tackle** is also a noun. *tacleada* ❑ *Owens ran out of a tackle. Owens se escapó de una tacleada.* **3** V-T If you **tackle** someone about a particular matter, you speak to them honestly about it, usually in order to get something changed or done. *abordar, confrontar* ❑ *I tackled him about his poor work. Me le enfrenté por lo mediocre de su trabajo.* **4** N-UNCOUNT **Tackle** is the equipment that you need for a sport or activity, especially fishing. *aparejos* ❑ *...fishing tackle. ...avíos de pesca.*

**tac|tic** /tæktɪk/ (**tactics**) N-COUNT **Tactics** are the methods that you choose to use in order to achieve what you want in a particular situation. *táctica, estrategia* ❑ *I decided to change my tactics. Decidí cambiar de táctica.*

**tac|ti|cal** /tæktɪkᵊl/ ADJ A **tactical** action or plan is intended to help someone achieve what they want in the future, rather than immediately. *táctico* ❑ *His latest offer may simply be a tactical move. Su último ofrecimiento podría no haber sido más que una movida táctica.* ● **tac|ti|cal|ly** /tæktɪkli/ ADV *tácticamente* ❑ *Many people voted tactically against the government. Mucha gente votó tácticamente contra el gobierno.*

**tad|pole** /tædpoʊl/ (**tadpoles**) N-COUNT **Tadpoles** are small water creatures that look like fish and grow into frogs or toads. *renacuajo*

**taf|fy** /tæfi/ N-VAR **Taffy** is a sticky candy that you chew. It is made by boiling sugar and butter together with water. *chicloso, caramelo masticable*

**tag** /tæg/ (**tags, tagging, tagged**) **1** N-COUNT A **tag** is a small piece of cardboard or cloth which is attached to an object or person and has information about that object or person on it. *etiqueta, gafete, rótulo* ❑ *The staff wore name tags. El personal llevaba etiquetas con su nombre.* **2** V-T If you **tag** something, you attach something to it or mark it so that it can be identified later. *etiquetar, marcar* ❑ *He only has a short time to tag the birds before spring. Tiene poco tiempo para marcar los pájaros antes de la primavera.*

▸ **tag along** PHR-VERB If you **tag along** with someone, you go with them, especially when they have not asked you to. *pegársele a alguien, ir con alguien sin ser invitado* ❑ *I let him tag along. Lo dejé que se nos pegara.*

**tai chi** /taɪ tʃi/ also **Tai Chi** N-UNCOUNT **Tai chi**

is a type of Chinese physical exercise in which you make slow, controlled movements. tai chi

**tai|ga** /taɪgə/ (**taigas**) N-VAR The **taiga** is an area of thick forest in the far north of Europe, Asia, and North America, situated immediately south of the tundra. taiga

**tail** /teɪl/ (**tails, tailing, tailed**) **1** N-COUNT The **tail** of an animal, bird, or fish is the part extending beyond the end of its body. cola ❑ *...a black dog with a long tail.* *...un perro negro de cola larga.* **2** N-COUNT You can use **tail** to refer to the end or back of something, especially something long and thin. cola ❑ *...the plane's tail.* *...la cola del avión.* **3** V-T To **tail** someone means to follow close behind them and watch where they go and what they do. seguir [INFORMAL] ❑ *Officers tailed the gang for weeks.* *La policía siguió a la pandilla durante semanas.*
→ see **fish, horse**

▸ **tail off** PHR-VERB When something **tails off**, it gradually becomes less, often before coming to an end completely. disminuir, mermar ❑ *His voice tailed off in the last part of his speech.* *La voz se le apagó en la última parte de su discurso.*

**tail|gate par|ty** /teɪlgeɪt pɑrti/ (**tailgate parties**) N-COUNT A **tailgate party** is a social gathering at which food is served from or near a vehicle, especially in a parking lot before a sports game. picnic al lado de un coche [INFORMAL]

**tai|lor** /teɪlər/ (**tailors, tailoring, tailored**) **1** N-COUNT A **tailor** is a person whose job is to make and repair clothes. sastre o sastra **2** V-T If you **tailor** something such as a plan or system **to** your needs, you make it suitable by changing the details of it. adaptar ❑ *We can tailor the program to the patient's needs.* *Podemos adaptar el programa a las necesidades del paciente.*

**tail|pipe** /teɪlpaɪp/ (**tailpipes**) N-COUNT A **tailpipe** is the end pipe of a car's exhaust system. tubo de escape, escape

**tail|spin** /teɪlspɪn/ **1** N-SING If something such as an industry or an economy goes into **a tailspin,** it begins to perform very badly or to fail. picada ❑ *The war has thrown the economy into a tailspin.* *La economía va en picada a causa de la guerra.* **2** N-SING If an aircraft goes into **a tailspin,** it falls very rapidly toward the ground in a spiral movement. en picada ❑ *The aircraft went into a tailspin before crashing.* *El avión cayó en picada antes de estrellarse.*

> **take**
> ❶ USED WITH NOUNS DESCRIBING ACTIONS
> ❷ OTHER USES

❶ **take** /teɪk/ (**takes, taking, took, taken**)

> **Take** is used in combination with a wide range of nouns, where the meaning of the combination is mostly given by the noun. Many of these combinations are common idiomatic expressions whose meanings can be found at the appropriate nouns. For example, the expression **take care** is explained at **care**.

**1** V-T You can use **take** to say that someone does something. For example, you can say "**she took a shower**" instead of "she showered." tomar ❑ *She was too tired to take a shower.* *Estaba demasiado cansada como para bañarse.* ❑ *Betty took a photograph of us.* *Betty nos tomó una fotografía.* **2** V-T You can use **take** with a range of nouns instead of using a more specific and often more formal verb. For example, you can say "**he took control**" or "**she took a positive attitude**" instead of "he assumed control" or "she adopted a positive attitude." tomar ❑ *Castro took power in 1959.* *Castro tomó el poder en 1959.* ❑ *Workers should take control of their careers.* *Los trabajadores deben tomar el control de su carrera.*
→ see **photography**

❷ **take** /teɪk/ (**takes, taking, took, taken**) **1** V-T If you **take** something, you reach out for it and hold it. tomar, coger ❑ *Let me take your coat.* *Dame tu abrigo* ❑ *He took a handkerchief from his pocket.* *Sacó un pañuelo del bolsillo.* **2** V-T If you **take** something with you when you go somewhere, you carry it or have it with you. llevar ❑ *Mark often took his books to Bess's house to study.* *Mark solía llevarse sus libros a casa de Bess para estudiar.* ❑ *You should take your passport with you when changing money.* *Debe llevar consigo su pasaporte para cambiar dinero* **3** V-T If a person, vehicle, or path **takes** someone somewhere, they transport or lead them there. llevar, transportar ❑ *She took me to a Mexican restaurant.* *Me llevó a un restaurante mexicano.* **4** V-T If you **take** something from its owner, you steal it. robar, quitar ❑ *He took my money.* *Me robó mi dinero.* **5** V-T To **take** something or someone means to win or capture them from an enemy or opponent. tomar, ocupar, adueñarse ❑ *An army unit took the town.* *Una unidad del ejército ocupó el pueblo.* **6** V-T If you cannot **take** something unpleasant, you cannot tolerate it without becoming upset, ill, or angry. tolerar ❑ *Don't ever ask me to look after those kids again. I just can't take it!* *Nunca más me vuelvas a pedir que cuide a esos niños. ¡Nomás no lo tolero!* **7** V-T If something **takes** a certain amount of time, that amount of time is needed in order to do it. tomar, llevar ❑ *Since the roads are very bad, the trip took us a long time.* *El viaje nos llevó mucho tiempo porque los caminos están muy malos.* ❑ *Your application could take a couple of months.* *Su solicitud podría llevarse un par de meses.* ❑ *The sauce takes 25 minutes to prepare.* *La salsa estará lista en 25 minutos.* **8** V-T If something **takes** a particular quality or thing, it requires it. necesitar ❑ *Walking across the room took all her strength.* *Necesitó toda su fuerza para atravesar el cuarto.* ❑ *It takes courage to say what you think.* *Se necesita valor para decir lo que uno piensa.* **9** V-T If you **take** something that is offered to you, you accept it. aceptar ❑ *When I took the job I thought I could change the system.* *Cuando acepté el puesto, pensé que podría cambiar el sistema.* **10** V-T If you **take** something in a particular way, you react in the way mentioned. tomar ❑ *No one took my opinion seriously.* *Nadie tomó en serio mi opinión.* **11** V-T If you **take** a road or route, you choose to travel along it. tomar, seguir ❑ *Take Old Mill Road to the edge of town.* *Vete por Old Mill Road hasta las orillas del pueblo.* **12** V-T If you **take** a car, train, bus, or plane, you use it to go from one place to another. tomar ❑ *She took the train to New York.* *Tomó el tren a Nueva York.* **13** V-T If you **take** a subject or course at school or college, you choose to study it. tomar, llevar ❑ *Students can take European history and American history.* *Los estudiantes pueden llevar historia europea e historia americana.* **14** V-T If you **take** a test or examination, you do it or take part in it. *hacer* ❑ *She took her driving test yesterday. Ayer hizo su examen de manejo.* **15** V-T If someone **takes** a drug or medicine, they swallow it. *tomar* ❑ *She's been taking sleeping pills. Ha estado tomando pastillas para dormir.* **16** V-T If you **take** a particular size in shoes or clothes, that size fits you. *usar, quedarlo algo* ❑ *"What size do you take?"—"I take a size 7." —¿De qué número calza?—Calzo del 7.* **17** CONVENTION If you say to someone **"take it or leave it,"** you are telling them that they can accept something or not accept it, but that you are not prepared to discuss any other alternatives. *tómelo o déjelo* ❑ *A 72-hour week, 12 hours a day, 6 days a week, take it or leave it. Semana de 72 horas, 12 horas al día, 6 días a la semana, tómelo o déjelo.* **18** to **take the cake** → see **cake**

**Thesaurus** *take* Ver también:

v. grab, grasp, hold **2** **1**
drive, escort, transport **2** **3**
steal **2** **4**
capture, seize **2** **5**

▸ **take after** PHR-VERB If you **take after** a member of your family, you look or behave like them. *heredar, parecerse a* ❑ *She was a smart, brave woman. You take after her. Era una mujer inteligente y valiente, lo heredaste de ella.*

▸ **take apart** PHR-VERB If you **take** something **apart,** you separate it into its different parts. *desarmar, deshacer* ❑ *When the clock stopped, he took it apart. Cuando el reloj se paró, lo desarmó.*

▸ **take away** **1** PHR-VERB If you **take** something **away from** someone, you remove it from them. *llevarse, quitar* ❑ *They're going to take my chickens away because they are too noisy. Se van a llevar mis pollos porque son muy ruidosos.* ❑ *They took everything away from him. Le confiscaron todo.* **2** PHR-VERB If you **take** one number or amount **away from** another, you subtract one number from the other. *restar* ❑ *Add up the bills for each month. Take this away from the income. Suma las cuentas de cada mes y réstalo del ingreso.*

▸ **take back** **1** PHR-VERB If you **take** something **back,** you return it. *regresar, devolver* ❑ *If I buy something he doesn't like, I take it back. Si algo de lo que compro no le gusta, lo devuelvo.* **2** PHR-VERB If you **take** something **back,** you admit that something that you said or thought is wrong. *retractarse* ❑ *Take back what you said about Jeremy! ¡Retira lo que dijiste sobre Jeremy!*

▸ **take down** **1** PHR-VERB If you **take down** a structure, you remove each piece of it. *quitar, desmontar* ❑ *The Canadian army took down the fences. El ejército canadiense desmontó las vallas.* **2** PHR-VERB If you **take down** a piece of information or a statement, you write it down. *anotar, apuntar, escribir* ❑ *I think we took your number down incorrectly. Creo que apuntamos mal tu número.*

▸ **take in** **1** PHR-VERB If you **take** someone **in,** you allow them to stay in your house or your country. *acoger, aceptar* ❑ *He persuaded Jo to take him in. Convenció a Jo de que lo recibiera.* **2** PHR-VERB If you **are taken in by** someone or something, you are deceived or fooled by them. *engañar* ❑ *I was taken in by his charm. Me engañó con su encanto.* **3** PHR-VERB If you **take** something **in,** you pay attention to it and understand it when you hear it or read it. *registrar, asimilar* ❑ *I could tell she wasn't taking it in. Me di cuenta de que no lo estaba asimilando.*

▸ **take off** **1** PHR-VERB When an airplane **takes off,** it leaves the ground and starts flying. *despegar* ❑ *We took off at 11 o'clock. Despegamos a las 11 en punto.* **2** PHR-VERB If you **take** a garment **off,** you remove it. *quitarse* ❑ *He wouldn't take his hat off. No quiso quitarse el sombrero.* **3** PHR-VERB If you **take** time **off,** you obtain permission not to go to work for a short period of time. *pedir un permiso* ❑ *Mitchel's boss did not allow him to take time off. El jefe de Mitchel no le dio permiso de faltar.*

▸ **take on** **1** PHR-VERB If you **take on** a job or responsibility, especially a difficult one, you accept it. *aceptar, hacerse cargo de* ❑ *No other organization was willing to take on the job. Ninguna otra organización quiso encargarse del trabajo.* **2** PHR-VERB If something **takes on** a new appearance or quality, it develops that appearance or quality. *adoptar, adquirir* ❑ *His face took on a look of fear. En la cara se le veía el miedo.* **3** PHR-VERB If you **take** someone **on,** you employ them to do a job. *contratar* ❑ *He spoke to a publishing company. They're going to take him on. Habló a una editorial y lo van a contratar.* **4** PHR-VERB If you **take** someone **on,** you fight them or compete against them, especially when they are more powerful than you are. *enfrentar* ❑ *Democrats were unwilling to take on such a popular president. Los Demócratas no quisieron enfrentar a un presidente tan popular.*

▸ **take out** **1** PHR-VERB If you **take out** something such as a loan or an insurance policy, a company agrees to let you have it. *solicitar* ❑ *I'll have to take out a loan. Voy a tener que pedir un crédito.* **2** PHR-VERB If you **take** someone **out,** you take them somewhere enjoyable, and usually you pay for everything. *llevar, sacar* ❑ *Jessica's grandparents took her out for the day. Jessica se fue de paseo con sus abuelos todo el día.* ❑ *Sophia took me out to lunch. Sophia me invitó a comer.*

▸ **take over** **1** PHR-VERB To **take over** something such as a company or country means to gain control of it. *asumir el control, apoderarse* [BUSINESS] ❑ *I'm going to take over the company one day. Uno de estos días voy a tomar el control de la empresa.* **2** PHR-VERB If you **take over** a job or if you **take over,** you start doing it after someone else has stopped doing it. *hacerse cargo* ❑ *His widow took over the running of the business after he died. Su viuda se encargó del negocio después de que él murió.* ❑ *In 2001, I took over from him as mayor. En 2001 asumí el cargo de alcalde que él dejó.* **3** → see also **takeover**

▸ **take to** **1** PHR-VERB If you **take to** someone or something, you start to like them very quickly. *adaptarse, sentirse a gusto* ❑ *Did the children take to him? ¿Les simpatizó a los niños?* **2** PHR-VERB If you **take to** doing something, you begin to do it as a regular habit. *aficionarse* ❑ *They took to walking through the streets. Les gustó caminar por las calles.*

▸ **take up** **1** PHR-VERB If you **take up** an activity or a job, you start doing it. *empezar, emprender* ❑ *He did not want to take up a competitive sport. No quiso empezar con un deporte de competencia.* **2** PHR-VERB If you **take up** a question, problem, or cause, you act on it or discuss how you are going to act on it. *tratar* ❑ *If you have a problem, take it up with the authorities. Si tienes un problema, trátalo con las autoridades.* ❑ *The issue will be taken up on Monday* *when the Russian president arrives.* *El asunto se discutirá el lunes, cuando llegue el presidente de Rusia.* **3** PHR-VERB If you **take up** an offer or a challenge, you accept it. *asumir* ❑ *Since she offered to babysit, I took her up on it.* *Como ella se ofreció a cuidar a los niños, le tomé la palabra.* **4** PHR-VERB If something **takes up** a particular amount of time, space, or effort, it uses that amount. *tomar, llevar* ❑ *I don't want to take up too much of your time.* *No quiero quitarle demasiado tiempo.*

**tak|en** /teɪkən/ **1** **Taken** is the past participle of **take**. *participio pasado de take* **2** ADJ If you are **taken with** something or someone, you are very interested in them or attracted to them. *entusiasmado* [INFORMAL] ❑ *She was very taken with the idea.* *Le gustaba mucho la idea.*

**take|off** /teɪkɔf/ (**takeoffs**) also **take-off** N-VAR **Takeoff** is the beginning of a flight, when an aircraft leaves the ground. *despegue* ❑ *What time is takeoff?* *¿A que hora es el despegue?*

**take|out** /teɪkaʊt/ (**takeouts**) **1** N-UNCOUNT **Takeout** or **takeout** food is hot cooked food which you buy from a store or restaurant and eat somewhere else. *comida preparada, comida para llevar* ❑ *...a takeout pizza.* *...una pizza para llevar.* **2** N-COUNT A **takeout** is a store or restaurant that sells hot cooked food that you eat somewhere else. *tienda de comida para llevar* ❑ *...a Chinese takeout.* *...un puesto de comida china para llevar.*

**take|over** /teɪkoʊvər/ (**takeovers**) **1** N-COUNT A **takeover** is the act of gaining control of a company by buying more of its shares than anyone else. *adquisición, absorción* [BUSINESS] ❑ *He lost his job after the takeover.* *Después de la adquisición, perdió su empleo.* **2** N-COUNT A **takeover** is the act of taking control of a country, political party, or movement by force. *toma del poder político* ❑ *There was a military takeover.* *Los militares asumieron el poder.*

**tale** /teɪl/ (**tales**) **1** N-COUNT A **tale** is a story, often involving magic or exciting events. *cuento, relato, historia* ❑ *...stories, poems and folk tales.* *...historias, poemas y relatos tradicionales.* **2** N-COUNT You can refer to an interesting, exciting, or dramatic account of a real event as a **tale**. *historia* ❑ *...tales of horror about Monday's earthquake.* *...historias de horror sobre el terremoto del lunes.* **3** → see also **fairy tale**

**tal|ent** /tælənt/ (**talents**) N-VAR **Talent** is the natural ability to do something well. *talento, capacidad* ❑ *Both her children have a talent for music.* *Sus dos hijos tienen talento para la música.* ❑ *He's got lots of talent.* *Tiene muchísimo talento.*

| **Thesaurus** | *talent* | Ver también: |
| --- | --- | --- |
| N. | ability, aptitude, gift | |

| **Word Partnership** | Usar *talent* con: |
| --- | --- |
| ADJ. | **great** talent, **musical** talent, **natural** talent |
| V. | **have (a)** talent, **have got** talent |
| N. | talent **pool**, talent **search** |

**tal|ent|ed** /tæləntɪd/ ADJ Someone who is **talented** has a natural ability to do something well. *talentoso, capaz* ❑ *Howard is a talented pianist.* *Howard es un pianista talentoso.*

**talk** /tɔk/ (**talks, talking, talked**) **1** V-I When you **talk**, you use spoken language to express your thoughts, ideas, or feelings. *hablar, conversar, platicar* ❑ *He was too upset to talk.* *Estaba demasiado molesto como para hablar.* ❑ *They were talking about American food.* *Estaban platicando sobre platillos estadounidenses.* ❑ *I talked to him yesterday.* *Ayer hablé con él.* • **Talk** is also a noun. *plática, conversación* ❑ *We had a long talk about her father.* *Tuvimos una larga plática sobre su padre.* **2** V-I If you **talk on** or **about** something, you make an informal speech about it. *hablar, exponer* ❑ *She will talk on the issues she cares most about.* *Hablará de los problemas que más le preocupan.* • **Talk** is also a noun. *exposición, plática* ❑ *A guide gave a brief talk on the history of the site.* *Un guía nos platicó brevemente sobre la historia del sitio.* **3** N-PLURAL **Talks** are formal discussions intended to produce an agreement, usually between different countries or between employers and employees. *plática, conversación* ❑ *...the next round of Middle East peace talks.* *...la siguiente ronda de conversaciones sobre la paz en el Medio Oriente.* **4** V-RECIP If one group of people **talks to** another, or if two groups **talk**, they have formal discussions in order to do a deal or produce an agreement. *hablar* ❑ *We're talking to some people about opening an office in Boston.* *Estamos hablando con algunas personas sobre la apertura de una oficina en Boston.* ❑ *...the day when the two sides sit down and talk.* *...el día que ambas partes se sienten a hablar.* **5** V-I If someone **talks** when they are being held by police or soldiers, they reveal important or secret information, usually unwillingly. *hablar, cantar, delatar* ❑ *They'll talk, and say I was involved.* *Ellos hablarán, y van a decir que yo estaba implicado.* **6** V-T If you **talk** something such as politics or sports, you discuss it. *hablar de, discutir* ❑ *...middle-aged men talking business.* *...hombres maduros discutiendo de negocios.*

▸ **talk down** PHR-VERB If someone **talks down** a particular thing, they reduce its value or importance by saying bad things about it. *menospreciar, restar importancia a* ❑ *Businessmen are tired of politicians talking the economy down.* *Los hombres de negocios están cansados de que los políticos resten importancia a la economía.*

▸ **talk into** PHR-VERB If you **talk** a person **into** doing something, you persuade them to do it. *persuadir* ❑ *He talked me into marrying him.* *Me convenció de que me casara con él.*

▸ **talk out of** PHR-VERB If you **talk** someone **out of** doing something, you persuade them not to do it. *disuadir* ❑ *My mother tried to talk me out of getting a divorce.* *Mi madre trató de convencerme de que no me divorciara.*

▸ **talk over** PHR-VERB If you **talk** something **over**, you discuss it thoroughly and honestly. *discutir* ❑ *He always talked things over with his friends.* *Siempre discutía las cosas con sus amigos.*

▸ **talk through** PHR-VERB If you **talk** something **through** with someone, you discuss it with them thoroughly. *analizar* ❑ *He and I have talked through the problem.* *Él y yo hemos hablado a fondo del problema.*

▸ **talk up** PHR-VERB If someone **talks up** a particular thing, they increase its value or importance by saying exaggerated things about it. *alabar* ❑ *He talked up the area as a great place to live.* *Habló muy bien de la región y dijo que era un gran lugar para vivir.*

**Thesaurus** *talk* Ver también:

N. argument, conversation, dialogue, discussion, interview, negotiation; (*ant.*) silence 1

V. chat, discuss, gossip, say, share, speak, tell; (*ant.*) listen 1

**talk ra|dio** N-UNCOUNT **Talk radio** is radio broadcasting which consists mainly of discussions with people who call the show rather than, for example, music or drama. *estación radiofónica especializada en comentarios, noticieros* ❑ *...a talk radio station. ...una estación de radio hablada.*

**Word Link** *er ≈ more : bigger, louder, taller*

**tall** /tɔl/ (**taller, tallest**) 1 ADJ Someone or something that is **tall** has a greater height than is normal or average. *alto* ❑ *John was very tall. John era muy alto.* 2 ADJ You use **tall** to ask or talk about the height of someone or something. *alto* ❑ *How tall is the building? ¿Cuánto mide el edificio?* 3 PHRASE If something is **a tall order,** it is very difficult. *empresa difícil* ❑ *Paying for college may seem like a tall order. Pagar estudios universitarios puede parecer difícil.*

**tam|bou|rine** /tæmbərin/ (**tambourines**) N-COUNT A **tambourine** is a musical instrument which you shake or hit with your hand. It consists of a drum skin on a circular frame with pairs of small round pieces of metal all around the edge. *pandero, pandereta*
→ see **percussion**

**tame** /teɪm/ (**tames, taming, tamed, tamer, tamest**) 1 ADJ A **tame** animal or bird is not afraid of humans. *domesticado, domado* ❑ *Deer never become tame; they will run away if you approach them. Los ciervos no se domestican; siempre huirán si te acercas.* 2 ADJ If you say that something or someone is **tame,** you are criticizing them for being weak and uninteresting. *insípido* ❑ *Its programs are tame, even boring. Sus programas no tienen chiste, hasta son aburridos.* 3 V-T If someone **tames** a wild animal or bird, they train it not to be afraid of humans. *domar, domesticar* ❑ *They were the first people to tame horses. Fueron los primeros en domar caballos.*

**tam|per** /tæmpər/ (**tampers, tampering, tampered**) V-I If someone **tampers with** something, they interfere with it or try to change it when they have no right to do so. *manipular indebidamente* ❑ *I don't want to be accused of tampering with the evidence. No quiero que me acusen de haber alterado las pruebas.*

T

**tan** /tæn/ (**tans, tanning, tanned**) 1 N-SING If you have a **tan,** your skin has become darker than usual because you have been in the sun. *bronceado* ❑ *She is tall and blonde, with a tan. Es alta y rubia, y está bronceada.* 2 V-T/V-I If a part of your body **tans** or if you **tan** it, your skin becomes darker than usual because you spend a lot of time in the sun. *broncearse* ❑ *I have very pale skin that never tans. Mi piel es demasiado pálida y no me bronceo.* • **tanned** ADJ *bronceado* ❑ *Her skin was tanned and glowing. Su bronceada piel brillaba.*

**tan|dem** /tændəm/ (**tandems**) 1 N-COUNT A **tandem** is a bicycle designed for two riders. *tándem* 2 PHRASE If one thing happens or is done **in tandem with** another thing, the two things happen at the same time. *en tándem* ❑ *They are working in tandem with local police. Están trabajando en tándem con la policía local.*

**tan|gle** /tæŋgᵊl/ (**tangles, tangling, tangled**) 1 N-COUNT A **tangle of** something is a mass of it twisted together in a messy way. *maraña* ❑ *...a tangle of wires. ...una maraña de cables.* 2 V-T/V-I If something **is tangled** or **tangles,** it becomes twisted together in a messy way. *enredar(se), enmarañar(se)* ❑ *Animals get tangled in fishing nets and drown. Los animales se enredan en las redes de pescar y se ahogan.* ❑ *Her hair tends to tangle. Su cabello tiende a enmarañarse.*

**tank** /tæŋk/ (**tanks**) 1 N-COUNT A **tank** is a large container for holding liquid or gas. *tanque, depósito* ❑ *...an empty fuel tank. ...un tanque de gasolina vacío.* ❑ *Two water tanks have a total capacity of 400 liters. La capacidad total de dos tanques de agua es de 400 litros.* 2 N-COUNT A **tank** is a large military vehicle that is equipped with weapons and moves along on metal tracks that are fitted over the wheels. *tanque*

**tank|er** /tæŋkər/ (**tankers**) N-COUNT A **tanker** is a large ship or truck used for transporting large quantities of gas or liquid, especially oil. *camión cisterna, buque/barco cisterna, (barco) petrolero* ❑ *...a Greek oil tanker. ...un petrolero griego.*
→ see **oil, ship**

**tank top** (**tank tops**) N-COUNT A **tank top** is a soft cotton shirt with no sleeves, collar, or buttons. *camiseta sin mangas*

**tan|ning bed** (**tanning beds**) N-COUNT A **tanning bed** is a piece of equipment with ultraviolet lights. You lie on it to make your skin tan. *instalación para broncearse con rayos ultravioleta*

**tap** /tæp/ (**taps, tapping, tapped**) 1 V-T/V-I If you **tap** something, you hit it with a quick, light blow or a series of quick, light blows. *tamborilear, dar golpecitos* ❑ *He tapped the table nervously with his fingers. Tamborileaba nerviosamente sobre la mesa con los dedos.* ❑ *Grace tapped on the bedroom door and went in. Grace dio unos golpecitos en la puerta de la recámara y entró.* • **Tap** is also a noun. *tamborileo, golpecitos* ❑ *A tap on the door interrupted him. Unos golpecitos en la puerta lo interrumpieron.* 2 V-T If someone **taps** your telephone, they attach a special device to the line so that they can secretly listen to your conversations. *intervenir* ❑ *The government passed laws allowing the police to tap telephones. El gobierno aprobó una ley que permite a la policía intervenir los teléfonos.* • **Tap** is also a noun. *intervención* ❑ *...phone taps. ...intervenciones telefónicas.*

**Word Partnership** Usar *tap* con:

N. tap **on a door,** tap ***someone*** **on the shoulder** 1
tap **a (tele)phone** 2

**tap dance** (**tap dances**) N-VAR A **tap dance** is a dance in which the dancer wears special shoes with pieces of metal on the heels and toes. The shoes make loud sharp sounds when the dancer's feet move. *tap, claqué*
→ see **dance**

**tape** /teɪp/ (**tapes, taping, taped**) 1 N-UNCOUNT

**Tape** is a sticky strip of plastic used for sticking things together. cinta adhesiva ❑ *...a roll of tape.* *...un rollo de cinta adhesiva.* **2** N-UNCOUNT **Tape** is a narrow plastic strip covered with a magnetic substance. It is used to record sounds, pictures, and computer information. cinta ❑ *Tape loses sound quality every time it is copied.* *Cada vez que se copia una cinta, su calidad sonora se reduce.* **3** V-T/V-I If you **tape** music, sounds, or television pictures, you record them using a tape recorder or a video recorder. grabar (en cinta) ❑ *She has just taped an interview.* *Acaba de grabar una entrevista.* ❑ *He shouldn't be taping without the singer's permission.* *No debería estar grabando sin la autorización del cantante.* **4** V-T If you **tape** one thing to another, you stick it on using tape. unir con cinta adhesiva, pegar con cinta adhesiva, sujetar con cinta adhesiva ❑ *I taped the envelope shut.* *Cerré el sobre con cinta adhesiva.* **5** N-COUNT A **tape** is a ribbon that is stretched across the finishing line of a race. cinta de llegada ❑ *...the finishing tape.* *...la cinta de llegada.* **6** → see also **red tape, videotape**
→ see **office**

**Word Partnership** Usar *tape* con:

N. **piece of** tape, **roll of** tape **1**
cassette tape, **music** tape, tape **player**, **reel of** tape **2**
tape **a conversation**, tape **an interview**, tape **a show** **3**
V. **listen to a** tape, **make a** tape, **play a** tape, **watch a** tape **2**

**tape meas|ure** (**tape measures**) N-COUNT A **tape measure** is a strip of metal, plastic, or cloth which has numbers marked on it and is used for measuring. metro, cinta métrica

tape measure

**tape|worm** /teɪpwɜrm/ (**tapeworms**) N-COUNT A **tapeworm** is a long, flat parasite which lives in the stomach and intestines of animals or people. (lombriz) solitaria, tenia

**tap|root** /tæprut/ (**taproots**) also **tap root** N-COUNT Plants that have a **taproot** have one main root that grows straight downward. raíz primaria [TECHNICAL]

**tar|get** /tɑrgɪt/ (**targets, targeting** or **targetting, targeted** or **targetted**) **1** N-COUNT A **target** is something that someone is trying to hit with a weapon or other object. blanco ❑ *The village lies beside a main road, making it an easy target.* *El pueblo está junto a un camino principal, lo cual hace de él un blanco fácil.* **2** N-COUNT A **target** is a result that you are trying to achieve. objetivo ❑ *...her target of 20 goals this season.* *...su objetivo de 20 goles en esta temporada.* **3** V-T To **target** a particular person or thing means to decide to attack or criticize them. dirigir ❑ *The attacks targeted civilians.* *Los ataques iban dirigidos a la población civil.* ● **Target** is also a noun. objeto ❑ *They have been the target of abuse.* *Han sido objeto de abusos.* **4** V-T If you **target** a particular group of people, you try to appeal to those people or affect them. atraer ❑ *The union is eager to target young people.* *El sindicato ansía atraer a los jóvenes.* **5** PHRASE If someone or something is **on target**, they are making good progress and are likely to achieve the result that is wanted. dentro del plazo previsto ❑ *We were still right on target for our deadline.* *Todavía estábamos dentro del plazo previsto.*

**Word Partnership** Usar *target* con:

V. **attack a** target **1**
**hit a** target, **miss a** target **1** **2**
ADJ. **easy** target, **moving** target **1**
**intended** target, **likely** target, **possible** target, **prime** target **1** **3**
N. target **practice** **1**
target **date** **2**
target **of criticism**, target **of an investigation** **3**

**tar|iff** /tærɪf/ (**tariffs**) N-COUNT A **tariff** is a tax on goods coming into a country. arancel [BUSINESS] ❑ *...tariffs on items such as electronics.* *...los aranceles sobre artículos como los productos electrónicos.*

**tarp** /tɑrp/ (**tarps**) N-COUNT A **tarp** is a sheet of heavy waterproof material that is used as a protective cover. lona impermeabilizada

**tar|tar sauce** /tɑrtər sɔs/ also **tartare sauce** N-UNCOUNT **Tartar sauce** is a thick cold sauce made from mayonnaise and chopped pickles, usually eaten with fish. salsa tártara

**task** /tæsk/ (**tasks**) N-COUNT A **task** is an activity or piece of work which you have to do, usually as part of a larger project. tarea, misión ❑ *Walden had the task of breaking the bad news to Mark.* *Walden tenía la misión de darle las malas nuevas a Mark.*

**Thesaurus** *task* Ver también:

N. assignment, job, responsibility

**Word Partnership** Usar *task* con:

V. **accomplish a** task, **assign** *someone* **a** task, **complete a** task, **face a** task, **give** *someone* **a** task, **perform a** task
ADJ. **complex** task, **difficult** task, **easy** task, **enormous** task, **important** task, **impossible** task, **main** task, **simple** task

**task|bar** /tæskbɑr/ (**taskbars**) also **task bar** N-COUNT The **taskbar** on a computer screen is a narrow strip, usually at the bottom of the screen, that shows you which windows are open and that allows you to control functions such as the Start button. barra de trabajo [COMPUTING]

**taste** /teɪst/ (**tastes, tasting, tasted**) **1** N-UNCOUNT Your sense of **taste** is your ability to recognize the flavor of things with your tongue. gusto ❑ *...an excellent sense of taste.* *...un agudo sentido del gusto.* **2** N-COUNT The **taste** of something is the individual quality that it has when you put it in your mouth, for example whether it is sweet or salty. sabor ❑ *I like the taste of chocolate.* *Me gusta el sabor del chocolate.* **3** V-I If food or drink **tastes of** something, it has that particular flavor. saber (a) ❑ *The water tasted of metal.* *El agua sabía a metal.* ❑ *The pizza tastes delicious.* *La pizza sabe*

**Word Web** taste

What we think of as **taste** is mostly **odor.** The sense of **smell** controls about 80% of the experience. We taste only four **sensations: sweet, salty, sour,** and **bitter.** We experience sweetness and saltiness through **taste buds** near the tip of the **tongue.** We sense sourness at the sides and bitterness at the back of the tongue. Some people have more taste buds than others. Scientists have discovered some "supertasters" with 425 taste buds per square centimeter. Most of us have about 184 and some "nontasters" have only about 96.

*delicioso.* **4** V-T If you **taste** some food or drink, you eat or drink a small amount of it in order to see what the flavor is like. *probar* ❑ *Don't add salt until you've tasted the food. No añada sal hasta haber probado la comida.* ● **Taste** is also a noun. *gusto* ❑ *Once you get a taste of the pie, you want more. Una vez que pruebe el pastel, querrá más.* **5** V-T If you can **taste** something that you are eating or drinking, you are aware of its flavor. *saber, distinguir el sabor de* ❑ *You can taste the green chili in the dish. Se puede distinguir el sabor del chile en el platillo.* **6** V-T If you **taste** something such as a way of life or a pleasure, you experience it for a short period of time. *probar, experimentar* ❑ *Once you have tasted the life in southern California, it's hard to return to Montana in winter. Cuando se ha probado la vida del sur de California, es difícil volver a Montana en el invierno.* ● **Taste** is also a noun. *prueba, experiencia* ❑ *This trip was his first taste of freedom. En este viaje experimentó la libertad por primera vez.* **7** N-SING If you have a **taste for** something, you enjoy it. *gusto* ❑ *That gave me a taste for reading. Eso me imbuyó el gusto por la lectura.* **8** N-UNCOUNT A person's **taste** is their choice **in** the things that they like or buy, for example, their clothes, possessions, or music. *gusto* ❑ *His taste in clothes is extremely good. Tiene muy buen gusto para la ropa.* **9** PHRASE If you say that something that is said or done is **in bad taste** or **in poor taste,** you mean that it is offensive. *de mal gusto* ❑ *He rejects the idea that his film is in bad taste. No está de acuerdo con la idea de que su película sea de mal gusto.*
→ see Word Web: **taste**
→ see **sugar**

T

**Word Partnership** Usar *taste* con:

| | |
|---|---|
| N. | **sense of** taste **1** |
| ADJ. | **bitter/salty/sour/sweet** taste **2** |
| | taste **bitter/salty/sour/sweet**, taste **good** **3** |
| | **acquired** taste, **bad/good/poor** taste **8** |
| | **in bad/good/poor** taste **9** |
| V. | **like the** taste **of** ***something*** **2** |
| | **get a** taste **of** ***something*** **6** |
| ADV. | taste **like** ***something*** **3** |

**taste bud** (**taste buds**) also **tastebud** N-COUNT Your **taste buds** are the little points on the surface of your tongue which enable you to recognize the flavor of a food or drink. *papila gustativa*
→ see **taste**

**taste|less** /teɪstlɪs/ **1** ADJ If you describe something as **tasteless,** you consider it to be vulgar and unattractive. *de mal gusto* ❑ *...a house full of tasteless furniture. ...una casa llena de muebles de mal gusto.* **2** ADJ If you describe something such as a remark or joke as **tasteless,** you mean that it is offensive. *de mal gusto, vulgar* ❑ *...the most tasteless remark I have ever heard in my life. ...es el comentario más vulgar que he oído en mi vida.* **3** ADJ If you describe food or drink as **tasteless,** you mean that it has very little or no flavor. *insípido, desabrido* ❑ *The fish was tasteless. El pescado estaba insípido.*

**tasty** /teɪsti/ (**tastier, tastiest**) ADJ If you say that food is **tasty,** you mean that it has a pleasant, fairly strong flavor which makes it good to eat. *sabroso, apetitoso* ❑ *Try this tasty dish for supper. Pruebe este apetitoso platillo en la cena.*

**tat|too** /tætu/ (**tattoos, tattooing, tattooed**) **1** N-COUNT A **tattoo** is a design on a person's skin made using needles to make little holes and filling them with colored dye. *tatuaje* ❑ *He has a tattoo of a heart on his arm. Tiene tatuado un corazón en un brazo.* **2** V-T If someone **tattoos** you, they give you a tattoo. *tatuar* ❑ *They painted and tattooed their bodies. Se pintaban y tatuaban el cuerpo.*

**tax** /tæks/ (**taxes, taxing, taxed**) **1** N-VAR **Tax** is an amount of money that you have to pay to the government so that it can pay for public services such as roads and schools. *impuesto* [BUSINESS] ❑ *No one enjoys paying tax. A nadie le agrada pagar impuestos.* ❑ *...a promise not to raise taxes. ...la promesa de no aumentar los impuestos.* **2** V-T When a person or company **is taxed,** they have to pay a part of their income or profits to the government. When goods **are taxed,** a percentage of their price has to be paid to the government. *imponer contribuciones, gravar* [BUSINESS] ❑ *Husband and wife are now taxed separately. Ahora los esposos deben pagar sus impuestos individualmente.* **3** → see also **income tax**

**tax|able** /tæksəbᵊl/ ADJ **Taxable** income is income on which you have to pay tax. *gravable* [BUSINESS] ❑ *Taxpayers can reduce their taxable income by up to $2,500. Los contribuyentes pueden deducir hasta 2,500 dólares de sus ingresos gravables.*

**taxa|tion** /tækseɪʃᵊn/ **1** N-UNCOUNT **Taxation**

is the system by which a government takes money from people and spends it on things such as education, health, and defense. *tributación, contribución de impuestos, carga fiscal* [BUSINESS] ❑ *...changes in taxation. ...cambios en la tributación.* **2** N-UNCOUNT **Taxation** is the amount of money that people have to pay in taxes. *contribución, carga fiscal* [BUSINESS] ❑ *The result will be higher taxation. El resultado será una mayor carga fiscal.*

**tax break** (**tax breaks**) N-COUNT If the government gives a **tax break** to a particular group of people or type of organization, it reduces the amount of tax they have to pay or changes the tax system in a way that benefits them. *exención fiscal* ❑ *...tax breaks for businesses that create new jobs. ...exenciones fiscales para las empresas que creen puestos de trabajo.*

**tax-deferred** ADJ If you have savings in a **tax-deferred** account, you do not have to pay tax on them until a later time. *de impuestos diferidos*

**tax-exempt** ADJ Income or property that is **tax-exempt** is income or property that you do not have to pay tax on. *exento de impuestos* ❑ *About 15 percent of the town's property is tax-exempt. Aproximadamente el 15 por ciento de los bienes raíces de la ciudad están exentos de impuestos.*

**tax-free** ADJ **Tax-free** is used to describe income on which you do not have to pay tax. *libre de impuestos* [BUSINESS] ❑ *...a tax-free investment plan. ...un plan de inversión libre de impuestos.*

**taxi** /tæksi/ (**taxis, taxiing, taxied**) **1** N-COUNT A **taxi** is a car driven by a person whose job is to take people where they want to go in return for money. *taxi, coche de alquiler* ❑ *The taxi stopped in front of the club. El taxi se detuvo frente al club.* **2** V-T/V-I When an aircraft **taxis** along the ground or when a pilot **taxis** a plane somewhere, it moves slowly along the ground. *rodar* ❑ *The plane taxied into position for takeoff. El avión rodó hasta la posición de despegue.*

taxi

**taxi|cab** /tæksikæb/ (**taxicabs**) also **taxi-cab** N-COUNT A **taxicab** is the same as a **taxi**. *taxi, coche de alquiler*

**tax in|cen|tive** (**tax incentives**) N-COUNT A **tax incentive** is a government measure that is intended to encourage individuals and businesses to spend money or to save money by reducing the amount of tax that they have to pay. *incentivo fiscal* ❑ *...a new tax incentive to encourage investment. ...un nuevo incentivo fiscal para alentar la inversión.*

**taxi stand** (**taxi stands**) N-COUNT A **taxi stand** is a place where taxis wait for passengers, for example at an airport. *parada de taxis, paradero de taxis, sitio de taxis*

**tax|ono|my** /tæksɒnəmi/ (**taxonomies**) N-VAR **Taxonomy** is the process of naming and classifying things such as animals and plants into groups within a larger system, according to their similarities and differences. *taxonomía* [TECHNICAL]

**tax|payer** /tækspeɪər/ (**taxpayers**) N-COUNT **Taxpayers** are people who pay a percentage of their income to the government as tax. *contribuyente* [BUSINESS] ❑ *This is not going to cost the taxpayer anything. Esto no le va a costar nada al contribuyente.*

**TB** /ti bi/ N-UNCOUNT **TB** is an extremely serious infectious disease that affects your lungs and other parts of your body. **TB** is an abbreviation for **tuberculosis**. *tuberculosis*

**TBA** also **tba** **TBA** is sometimes written in announcements to indicate that something such as the place where something will happen or the people who will take part is not yet known and will be announced at a later date. **TBA** is an abbreviation for "to be announced." *será anunciado*

**T-ball** N-UNCOUNT **T-ball** is a game for children, similar to baseball, in which the batter hits a ball that has been placed on top of a post. *juego infantil similar al béisbol en el que la pelota se coloca sobre un poste para que el bateador la golpee*

**TCP/IP** N-UNCOUNT **TCP/IP** is a set of rules for putting data onto the Internet. **TCP/IP** is a written abbreviation for "Transmission Control Protocol/Internet Protocol." *protocolo de control de transmisión, protocolo de internet (TCP/IP)* [COMPUTING]

**tea** /ti/ (**teas**) **1** N-VAR **Tea** is a drink made by pouring boiling water on the chopped dried leaves of a plant called the tea bush. *té* ❑ *...a cup of tea. ...una taza de té.* ❑ *Would you like some tea? ¿Gusta un poco de té?* **2** N-VAR **Tea** is the chopped dried leaves of the plant that tea is made from. *té* ❑ *...a box of tea. ...una caja de té.*
→ see Word Web: **tea**

**teach** /titʃ/ (**teaches, teaching, taught**) **1** V-T If you **teach** someone something, you give them instructions so that they know about it or how to do it. *enseñar* ❑ *She taught me to read. Ella me enseñó a leer.* ❑ *George taught him how to ride a horse. George le enseñó a montar a caballo.* **2** V-T To **teach** someone something means to make them think, feel, or act in a new or different way. *enseñar* ❑ *We have to teach*

**Word Web** tea

Do you want to **brew** a good cup of **tea?** Don't use a **tea bag**. For the best taste, use fresh **tea leaves**. First, boil water in a **teakettle**. Use some of the water to warm the inside of a china **teapot**. Empty the pot, and add the tea leaves. Pour in more boiling water. Let the tea steep for at least five minutes. Serve the tea in thin china **cups**. Add milk and sugar if you wish.

t

drivers to respect pedestrians. *Tenemos que enseñar a los conductores a respetar a los peatones.* **3** V-T/V-I If you **teach** or **teach** a subject, you help students to learn about a subject by explaining it or showing them how to do it. *enseñar* ❑ *Ingrid is currently teaching mathematics at the high school. Actualmente, Ingrid enseña matemáticas en la secundaria.* ❑ *She taught English to Japanese business people. Enseñaba inglés a hombres de negocios japoneses.* ❑ *She has taught for 34 years. Ha enseñado durante 34 años.* • **teach|er** (**teachers**) N-COUNT *maestro o maestra, profesor o profesora* ❑ *I was a teacher for 21 years. Fui maestro durante 21 años.* • **teach|ing** N-UNCOUNT *enseñanza* ❑ *The quality of teaching in the school is excellent. La calidad de la enseñanza es excelente en la escuela.* **4** to **teach** someone **a lesson** → see **lesson**
→ see also **learn**

**Thesaurus** *teach* Ver también:

V. educate, train **1**–**3**

**Word Partnership** Usar *teach* con:

ADV. teach *someone* how **1**
N. teach *someone* a skill, teach students **1**
teach children **1**–**3**
teach classes, teach courses, teach English/history/reading/science, teach school **3**
teach *someone* a lesson **4**
V. try to teach **1**–**3**

**teach|er's aide** (**teacher's aides**) N-COUNT A **teacher's aide** is a person who helps a teacher in a school classroom but who is not a qualified teacher. *ayudante de maestro*

**teach|ing** /titʃɪŋ/ (**teachings**) N-COUNT The **teachings** of a particular person, school of thought, or religion are all the ideas and principles that they teach. *enseñanza* ❑ *...the teachings of Jesus. ...las enseñanzas de Jesús.*

**teach|ing as|sis|tant** (**teaching assistants**) N-COUNT A **teaching assistant** is a graduate student at a college or university who teaches some classes. *maestro auxiliar o maestra auxiliar, pasante de maestro* ❑ *She is working as a teaching assistant. Está trabajando como pasante de maestro.*

**tea|kettle** /tikɛtᵊl/ (**teakettles**) also **tea kettle** N-COUNT A **teakettle** is a kettle that is used for boiling water to make tea. *tetera*
→ see **tea**

T

**team** /tim/ (**teams, teaming, teamed**)
**1** N-COUNT A **team** is a group of people who play a particular sport or game together against other similar groups of people. *equipo* ❑ *...a soccer team. ...un equipo de fútbol.* ❑ *The team is close to the bottom of the league. El equipo está cerca del último lugar en la liga.* **2** N-COUNT You can refer to any group of people who work together as a **team**. *equipo* ❑ *...a team of doctors. ...un equipo de médicos.*

▸ **team up** PHR-VERB If you **team up with** someone, you join them in order to work together for a particular purpose. *asociarse con, unirse con* ❑ *A friend asked me to team up with him for a working holiday in Europe. Un amigo me pidió que me le uniera para ir a trabajar a Europa en las vacaciones.*

**team|mate** /timmeɪt/ (**teammates**) also **team-mate** N-COUNT In a game or sport, your **teammates** are the other members of your team. *compañero de equipo o compañera de equipo* ❑ *He was a great example to his teammates. Era un gran ejemplo para sus compañeros de equipo.*

**team|work** /timwɜrk/ N-UNCOUNT **Teamwork** is the ability a group of people have to work well together. *trabajo en equipo* ❑ *She knows the importance of teamwork. Ella conoce la importancia del trabajo en equipo.*

**tea|pot** /tipɒt/ (**teapots**) also **tea pot** N-COUNT A **teapot** is a container with a lid, a handle, and a spout, used for making and serving tea. *tetera*
→ see **tea**

**tear**
❶ CRYING
❷ DAMAGING OR MOVING

❶ **tear** /tɪər/ (**tears**) **1** N-COUNT **Tears** are the drops of liquid that come out of your eyes when you are crying. *lágrima* ❑ *Her eyes filled with tears. Se le llenaron los ojos de lágrimas.* ❑ *I wept tears of joy. Lloré de alegría.* **2** N-PLURAL You can use **tears** in expressions such as **in tears, burst into tears,** and **close to tears** to indicate that someone is crying or is almost crying. *lágrimas* ❑ *He was in tears. Estaba llorando.* ❑ *She burst into tears and ran from the kitchen. Se le saltaron las lágrimas y salió corriendo de la cocina.*
→ see **cry, cut**

❷ **tear** /tɛər/ (**tears, tearing, tore, torn**) **1** V-T If you **tear** paper, cloth, or another material, you pull it into two pieces or you pull it so that a hole appears in it. *rasgar* ❑ *I tore my coat on a nail. Me rasgué el saco con un clavo.* • **Tear** is also a noun. *desgarradura, rotura* ❑ *I looked through a tear in the curtains. Miré a través de una desgarradura de las cortinas.* **2** V-T To **tear** something from somewhere means to remove it violently. *arrancar* ❑ *She tore the windshield wipers from his car. Arrancó los limpiadores del parabrisas de su coche.* **3** V-I If you **tear** somewhere, you run, drive, or move there very quickly. *andar apresuradamente* ❑ *Miranda tore into the room. Miranda entró apresuradamente al cuarto.*
→ see **cut**

**Usage** **tear** and **break**

The verbs *tear* and *break* both mean "to damage something," but *tear* is used only for paper, cloth, or other thin, flexible materials that you can pull apart: *Phailin fell down the stairs; she not only broke her arm, but she also tore a muscle in her leg. When the window broke, a piece of the glass tore Niran's shirt.*

▸ **tear apart** PHR-VERB If something **tears** people **apart,** it causes them to argue or to leave each other. *separar, desgarrar, destrozar* ❑ *The quarrel was tearing the family apart. La pelea estaba desgarrando a la familia.*

▸ **tear away** PHR-VERB If you **tear** someone **away from** a place or activity, you force them to leave the place or stop doing the activity, even though they want to remain there or continue. *arrancar(se)* ❑ *He finally tore himself away from the TV. Finalmente se arrancó de la televisión.*

▸ **tear down** PHR-VERB If you **tear** something

**Word Web** technology

**Innovative technologies** affect everything in our lives. In new homes, **state-of-the-art** computer systems control heating, lighting, communication, and entertainment systems. **Gadgets** such as **digital** music players are small and easy to carry. But high technology has a serious side, too. **Biotechnology** may help us cure diseases. It also raises many ethical questions. **Cutting-edge** biometric technology is replacing old-fashioned security systems. Soon your ATM will check your identity by scanning the iris of your eye and your laptop will scan your fingerprint.

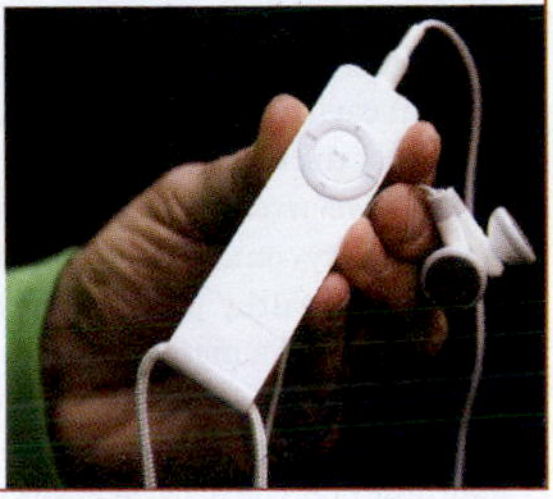

**down,** you destroy it or remove it completely. *destrozar, derribar* ❑ *Angry protesters tore down the statue. Los airados manifestantes derribaron la estatua.*

▸ **tear off** PHR-VERB If you **tear off** your clothes, you take them off in a rough and quick way. *arrancar(se)* ❑ *He tore his clothes off and fell into bed. Se arrancó la ropa y se echó en la cama.*

▸ **tear up** PHR-VERB If you **tear up** a piece of paper, you tear it into a lot of small pieces. *rasgar, romper* ❑ *Don't you dare tear up her ticket. No se atreva a romper su boleto.*

**tease** /tiz/ (**teases, teasing, teased**) V-T To **tease** someone means to laugh at them or make jokes about them in order to embarrass, annoy, or upset them. *burlarse* ❑ *He teased me about my hair. Se burló de mi pelo.*

**Thesaurus** *tease* Ver también:

V. aggravate, bother, provoke

**tea|spoon** /tispun/ (**teaspoons**) N-COUNT A **teaspoon** is a small spoon used for eating, for putting sugar into tea or coffee, or in cooking. *cucharita, cucharilla* ❑ *Drop the dough onto a baking sheet with a teaspoon. Distribuya la masa con una cucharita en una charola para hornear.*

**tech|ni|cal** /tɛknɪkəl/ **1** ADJ **Technical** means involving the sorts of machines, processes, and materials that are used in industry, transportation, and communications. *técnico* ❑ *A number of technical problems will have to be solved. Será necesario resolver varios problemas técnicos.*
● **tech|ni|cal|ly** /tɛknɪkli/ ADV *técnicamente* ❑ *...technically-advanced medical products. ...productos médicos técnicamente avanzados.* **2** ADJ You use **technical** to describe the practical skills and methods used to do an activity such as an art, a craft, or a sport. *técnico* ❑ *Their technical ability is exceptional. Su habilidad técnica es excepcional.*
● **tech|ni|cal|ly** ADV *técnicamente* ❑ *...a technically brilliant movie. ...una película con una técnica magnífica.* **3** ADJ **Technical** language involves using special words to describe the details of a specialized activity. *técnico* ❑ *The technical term for sunburn is "erythema." El término técnico para quemadura de sol es "eritema solar".*

**Word Partnership** Usar *technical* con:

N. technical **knowledge** **1**
technical **assistance**, technical **difficulties**, technical **expertise**, technical **experts**, technical **information**, technical **issues**, technical **problems**, technical **services**, technical **skills**, technical **support**, technical **training** **2**

ADV. **highly** technical **1**–**3**

**tech|ni|cian** /tɛknɪʃən/ (**technicians**) N-COUNT A **technician** is someone whose job involves skilled practical work with scientific or medical equipment, for example, in a laboratory. *técnico o técnica* ❑ *...a laboratory technician. ...un técnico laboratorista.*

**tech|nique** /tɛknik/ (**techniques**) **1** N-COUNT A **technique** is a particular method of doing an activity, usually a method that involves practical skills. *técnica* ❑ *...the techniques of modern agriculture. ...las técnicas de la agricultura moderna.* **2** N-UNCOUNT **Technique** is skill and ability in an artistic, sporting, or other practical activity that you develop through training and practice. *técnica* ❑ *He went to the Amsterdam Academy to improve his technique. Asistió a la Academia Ámsterdam para mejorar su técnica.*

**tech|nol|ogy** /tɛknɒlədʒi/ (**technologies**) N-VAR **Technology** refers to methods, systems, and devices which are the result of scientific knowledge being used for practical purposes. *tecnología* ❑ *Technology is changing fast. La tecnología está cambiando rápidamente.* ● **tech|no|logi|cal** /tɛknəlɒdʒɪkəl/ ADJ *tecnológico* ❑ *...a time of rapid technological change. ...una época de veloz cambio tecnológico.* ● **tech|no|logi|cal|ly** /tɛknəlɒdʒɪkli/ ADV *tecnológicamente* ❑ *...technologically-advanced aircraft. ...aeronaves tecnológicamente avanzadas.*
→ see Word Web: **technology**

**Word Partnership** Usar *technology* con:

ADJ. **advanced** technology, **available** technology, **educational** technology, **high** technology, **latest** technology, **medical** technology, **modern** technology, **new** technology, **sophisticated** technology, **wireless** technology

N. **computer** technology, **information** technology, **science and** technology

**Word Web** teeth

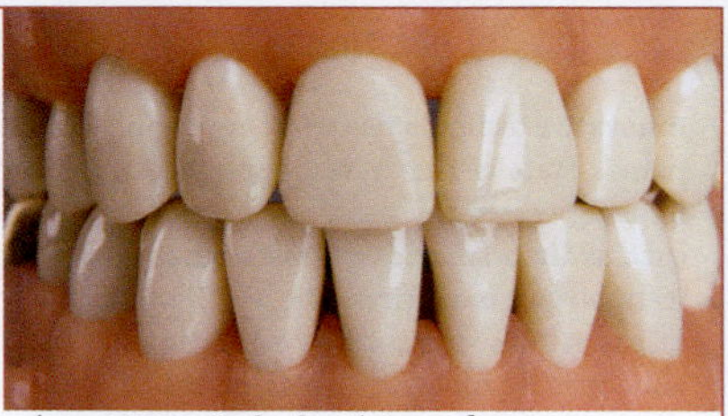

**Dentists** say **brushing** and flossing every day helps prevent **cavities.** Brushing removes food from the surface of the **teeth.** Flossing removes **plaque** from between teeth and **gums.** In many places, the water supply contains fluoride which also helps keep teeth healthy. If **tooth decay** does develop, a dentist can use a metal or plastic **filling** to repair the tooth. A badly damaged or broken tooth may require a **crown.** Orthodontists use **braces** to straighten uneven rows of teeth. Occasionally, a dentist must remove all of a patient's teeth. Then **dentures** take the place of natural teeth.

**tec|ton|ic plate** /tɛktɒnɪk pleɪt/ (**tectonic plates**) N-COUNT **Tectonic plates** are very large pieces of the Earth's surface or crust. *placa tectónica* [TECHNICAL]
→ see **earthquake**

**te|di|ous** /tidiəs/ ADJ If you describe something such as a job, task, or situation as **tedious,** you mean it is boring and frustrating. *tedioso, aburrido* ❑ *The list is long and tedious to read. Es tedioso leer esta lista tan larga.* ● **te|di|ous|ly** ADV *tediosamente, aburridamente* ❑ *Her life was tediously routine. Su vida era una rutina tediosa.*

**tee** /ti/ (**tees, teeing, teed**) **1** N-COUNT In golf, a **tee** is a small piece of wood or plastic which is used to support the ball before it is hit at the start of each hole. *tee, soporte para golpear la pelota de golf* **2** N-COUNT On a golf course, a **tee** is one of the small flat areas of ground from which people hit the ball at the start of each hole. *punto de partida*
▸ **tee off** **1** PHR-VERB If someone or something **tees** you **off,** they make you angry or annoyed. *molestar, hacer enojar* [INFORMAL] ❑ *Something the boy said to him teed him off. El niño dijo algo que lo hizo enojarse.* ❑ *That really teed off the old man. Eso realmente hizo enojar al anciano.* **2** PHR-VERB In golf, when you **tee off,** you hit the ball from a tee at the start of a hole. *dar el primer golpe a la pelota de golf* ❑ *In a few hours most of the world's top golfers tee off in the U.S. Masters. Dentro de unas horas, la mayoría de los mejores golfistas del mundo darán inicio al Torneo de Maestros de Estados Unidos.*

**teen** /tin/ (**teens**) **1** N-PLURAL If you are in your **teens,** you are between thirteen and nineteen years old. *adolescencia* ❑ *I met John when I was in my teens. Conocí a John cuando yo estaba en la adolescencia.* ● A **teen** is a person in his or her teens. *adolescente* **2** ADJ **Teen** is used to describe things such as movies, magazines, bands, or activities that are aimed at or are done by people who are in their teens. *para adolescentes, juvenil* ❑ *...a new teen center. ...un nuevo centro juvenil.*

**T**

**teen|age** /tineɪdʒ/ **1** ADJ **Teenage** children are aged between thirteen and nineteen years old. *adolescente* ❑ *She looked like any other teenage girl. Parecía una adolescente común y corriente.* **2** ADJ **Teenage** is used to describe things such as movies, magazines, or activities that are aimed at or are done by teenage children. *para adolescentes* ❑ *...a teenage magazine. ...una revista para adolescentes.*

**Word Link** *teen ≈ plus ten, from 13-19 : eighteen, seventeen, teenager*

**teen|ager** /tineɪdʒər/ (**teenagers**) N-COUNT A **teenager** is someone who is between thirteen and nineteen years old. *adolescente*
→ see **age, child**

**teeth** /tiθ/ **Teeth** is the plural of **tooth.** *plural de tooth*
→ see Word Web: **teeth**
→ see **face**

**tee|to|tal|er** /titoʊtᵊlər/ (**teetotalers**) N-COUNT A **teetotaler** is someone who does not drink alcohol. *abstemio o abstemia*

**TEFL** /tɛfᵊl/ N-UNCOUNT **TEFL** is the teaching of English to people whose first language is not English, especially people from a country where English is not spoken. **TEFL** is an abbreviation for "teaching English as a foreign language." *enseñanza del inglés como lengua extranjera*

**Te|ja|no** /tɛhɑnoʊ/ (**Tejanos**) N-COUNT A **Tejano** is a person from Mexico, or a person whose family is from Mexico, who lives in Texas. *tejano-mexicano, mexicano o descendiente de mexicanos avecindado en Texas* ● **Tejano** is also an adjective. *tejano-mexicano* ❑ *...the growing popularity of Tejano music. ...la creciente popularidad de la música tejano-mexicana.*

**tele|cast** /tɛlɪkæst/ (**telecasts**) N-COUNT A **telecast** is a program that is broadcast on television, especially a program that is broadcast live. *transmisión por televisión, emisión por televisión*

**tele|com|mu|ni|ca|tions** /tɛlɪkəmyunɪkeɪʃᵊnz/ N-UNCOUNT **Telecommunications** is the technology of sending signals and messages over long distances using electronic equipment, for example, by radio and telephone. *telecomunicación* ❑ *...the telecommunications industry. ...la industria de las telecomunicaciones.*

**tele|mar|ket|ing** /tɛlɪmɑrkɪtɪŋ/ N-UNCOUNT **Telemarketing** is the selling of products or services by telephone. *ventas por teléfono* [BUSINESS]

**Word Link** *phon ≈ sound : microphone, symphony, telephone*

**Word Web** telescope

Once there were only two types of **telescopes**. **Refracting** telescopes had lenses. **Reflecting** telescopes had a **concave mirror**. The lenses and the mirror had the same purpose. They **focused light rays** and made a clear **image**. Today scientists use **radio telescopes** to study the **universe**. These telescopes can detect **X-rays**, **gamma rays**, and other types of invisible light **waves**. But sometimes a person makes important discoveries without fancy tools. Robert Evans is an amateur **astronomer** in Australia. He has discovered more **supernovas** than anyone else in the world. And he uses a very simple 16-inch reflecting telescope set up in his backyard.

**Word Link** *tele ≈ distance : telephone, telescope, television*

**tele|phone** /tɛlɪfoʊn/ (**telephones, telephoning, telephoned**) **1** N-UNCOUNT The **telephone** is an electrical system of communication used to talk directly to someone else in a different place, by dialing a number on a piece of equipment and speaking into it. *teléfono* ❑ *It's easier to reach her by telephone than by e-mail. Es más fácil comunicarse con ella por teléfono que por correo electrónico.* ❑ *I hate to think what our telephone bill is going to be. No quiero ni pensar en lo que vamos a tener que pagar de teléfono.* **2** N-COUNT A **telephone** is the piece of equipment that you use when you talk to someone by telephone. *teléfono* ❑ *He got up and answered the telephone. Se levantó y contestó el teléfono.* **3** V-T/V-I If you **telephone** someone, you dial their telephone number and speak to them by telephone. *telefonear, llamar por teléfono* ❑ *I had to telephone Owen to say I was sorry. Tuve que llamar por teléfono a Owen para pedirle que me disculpara.* ❑ *They usually telephone first to see if she's home. Normalmente llaman por teléfono primero para ver si está en casa.* **4** PHRASE If you are **on the telephone,** you are speaking to someone by telephone. *al teléfono* ❑ *Linda was on the telephone for three hours. Linda estuvo al teléfono durante tres horas.*

**tele|phone pole** (**telephone poles**) N-COUNT A **telephone pole** is a tall wooden pole with telephone wires attached to it, connecting several different buildings to the telephone system. *poste de teléfonos*

**Word Link** *scope ≈ looking : gyroscope, microscope, telescope*

**tele|scope** /tɛlɪskoʊp/ (**telescopes**) N-COUNT A **telescope** is an instrument shaped like a tube. It has lenses inside it that make distant things seem larger and nearer when you look through it. *telescopio*
→ see Word Web: **telescope**

**tele|vise** /tɛlɪvaɪz/ (**televises, televising, televised**) V-T If an event or program **is televised,** it is filmed and shown on television. *televisar* ❑ *The game will be televised. El juego va a ser televisado.*

**Word Link** *vid, vis ≈ seeing : television, videotape, visible*

**tele|vi|sion** /tɛlɪvɪʒᵊn, -vɪʒ-/ (**televisions**) **1** N-COUNT A **television** or **television set** is a piece of electrical equipment consisting of a box with a glass screen on it on which you can watch programs with pictures and sounds. *televisor, televisión* ❑ *She turned the television on. Prendió la televisión.* **2** N-UNCOUNT **Television** is the system of sending pictures and sounds by electrical signals over a distance so that people can receive them on a television in their home. *televisión* ❑ *People will do anything to be on television. La gente hace cualquier cosa por salir en la televisión.*
→ see Word Web: **television**

**tell** /tɛl/ (**tells, telling, told**) **1** V-T If you **tell** someone something, you give them information. *decir, narrar* ❑ *I told Phyllis I got the job. Le dije a Phyllis que me dieron el empleo.* ❑ *I called Andie to tell her how angry I was. Llamé a Andie para decirle que estaba muy enojada.* ❑ *Claire made me promise to tell her the truth. Claire me obligó a prometerle que le diría la verdad.* ❑ *He told his story to The New York Times. Le narró su historia al New York Times.* **2** V-T If you **tell** someone **to** do something, you order or advise them to do it. *decir* ❑ *Officers told him to get out of his car. Los agentes le dijeron que se bajara del coche.* **3** V-T If you can **tell** what is happening or what is true, you are able to judge correctly what is happening or what is true. *saber* ❑ *You can never tell what life is going to bring you. Nunca podemos saber lo que la vida nos tiene reservado.* ❑ *I could tell that he was angry. Se veía que estaba enojado.* **4** V-T If facts or events **tell** you something, they reveal certain information to you through ways other than speech. *indicar, narrar* ❑ *The facts tell us that this is not true. Los hechos nos indican que no es cierto.* ❑ *The photographs tell a different story. Las fotografías narran una historia diferente.* **5** V-I If an unpleasant or tiring experience begins to **tell,** it begins to have a serious effect. *afectar* ❑ *The hot weather was beginning to tell on all of us. El calor estaba empezando a afectarnos a todos.*

▸ **tell apart** PHR-VERB If you can **tell** people or things **apart**, you are able to recognize the differences between them and can therefore identify each of them. *distinguir* ❑ *It's easy to tell the*

## Word Web television

For many years, all **televisions** used cathode ray tubes. These tubes made the picture. They shot a stream of **electrons** at a **screen**. When the electrons hit the screen, they made a tiny lighted area. This area

is called a pixel. The average cathode ray TV screen has about 200,000 pixels. Today, **high definition** TV is very popular. Ground **stations**, **satellites**, and **cables** still supply the TV **signal**. But **high definition** television uses **digital** information. It produces the picture on a flat screen. Digital **receivers** can show two million pixels per square inch. So they produce a much clearer **image**.

*sisters apart. Es fácil distinguir a las hermanas.*
▸**tell off** PHR-VERB If you **tell** someone **off**, you speak to them angrily or seriously because they have done something wrong. *regañar* ❑ *He never listened to us when we told him off. Nunca nos hacía caso cuando lo regañábamos.* ❑ *I'm always being told off for being so clumsy. Siempre me están regañando por ser tan torpe.*

**tell|er** /tɛlər/ (**tellers**) N-COUNT A **teller** is someone who works in a bank and who customers pay money to or get money from. *cajero o cajera* ❑ *Every bank pays close attention to the speed and accuracy of its tellers. Todos los bancos prestan mucha atención a la rapidez y precisión de sus cajeros.*

**telo|phase** /tɛləfeɪz/ (**telophases**) N-VAR **Telophase** is the final stage of cell division, when two completely separate cells are formed. *telofase*

**tem|per** /tɛmpər/ (**tempers**) **1** N-VAR If you say that someone has a **temper**, you mean that they become angry very easily. *humor, carácter, genio* ❑ *He had a temper and could be nasty. Tenía mal genio y podía ser muy desagradable.* **2** N-VAR If you are **in** a particular type of **temper**, that is the way you are feeling. *humor, carácter, genio* ❑ *I was in a bad temper last night. Anoche estaba de mal humor.* **3** PHRASE If you **lose** your **temper**, you become so angry that you shout or lose control of your behavior. *perder la paciencia, perder los estribos* ❑ *I've never seen him lose his temper. Nunca lo he visto perder los estribos.*

**Word Partnership** Usar *temper* con:

N. temper **tantrum** **1**
V. **control your** temper, **have a** temper **1**
**lose your** temper **3**
ADJ. **bad** temper, **violent** temper **1** **2**
**explosive** temper, **quick** temper, **short** temper **1**

**tem|per|ate zone** (**temperate zones**) N-COUNT The Earth's **temperate zones** are the areas where the climate is never extremely hot or extremely cold. The northern temperate zone extends from the Arctic Circle to the Tropic of Cancer, and the southern temperate zone extends from the Tropic of Capricorn to the Antarctic Circle. *zona templada*

**tem|pera|ture** /tɛmprətʃər, -tʃʊər/ (**temperatures**) **1** N-VAR The **temperature** of something is how hot or cold it is. *temperatura* ❑ *The temperature dropped below freezing. La temperatura descendió bajo cero.* **2** N-UNCOUNT Your **temperature** is the temperature of your body, that shows whether you are healthy. *temperatura, fiebre, calentura* ❑ *His temperature continued to rise. La fiebre le siguió aumentando.* **3** PHRASE If you **are running a temperature** or if you **have a temperature,** your temperature is higher than it should be. *tener calentura, tener fiebre, tener temperatura* **4** PHRASE If someone **takes** your **temperature,** they use an instrument called a thermometer to measure the temperature of your body. *tomar la temperatura* ❑ *The doctor will probably take your child's temperature. Es probable que el médico le tome la temperatura a su hijo.*
→ see **calorie, climate, cooking, forecast, greenhouse effect, habitat, wind**

**Word Partnership** Usar *temperature* con:

ADJ. **average** temperature, **high/low** temperature, **normal** temperature **1**
V. **reach a** temperature **1**
N. **changes in/of** temperature, temperature **increase**, **ocean** temperature, **rise in** temperature, **room** temperature, **surface** temperature, **water** temperature **1**
**body** temperature **2**

**tem|ple** /tɛmpᵊl/ (**temples**) **1** N-VAR A **temple** is a building used for the worship of a god or gods, especially in the Buddhist, Jewish, Mormon, and Hindu religions. *templo* ❑ *...a small Hindu temple. ...un pequeño templo hindú.* ❑ *We go to temple on Saturdays. Vamos al templo los sábados.* **2** N-COUNT Your **temples** are the flat parts on each side of the front part of your head, near your forehead. *sien* ❑ *The hair at his temples was gray. Tenía las sienes canosas.*

**tem|po|rary** /tɛmpərɛri/ ADJ Something that is **temporary** lasts for only a limited time. *temporal, provisional* ❑ *His job here is only temporary. Su trabajo aquí es sólo temporal.* ❑ *...a temporary loss of memory. ...una pérdida temporal de la memoria.*
• **tem|po|rari|ly** /tɛmpərɛərɪli/ ADV *temporalmente* ❑ *The peace agreement has temporarily halted the civil war. El acuerdo de paz detuvo temporalmente la guerra civil.*

**tempt** /tɛmpt/ (**tempts, tempting, tempted**) V-T Something that **tempts** you attracts you and makes you want it, even though it may be wrong or harmful. *tentar* ❑ *Cars like that may tempt drivers into driving too fast. Los automóviles como ese pueden* *tentar a los conductores a ir muy rápido.* ❑ *Don't let credit tempt you to buy something you can't afford.* *No permita que el crédito lo tiente a comprar algo que no pueda pagar.* ● **tempt|ing** ADJ *tentador* ❑ *...Raoul's tempting offer of a trip to Palm Beach.* *...la tentadora propuesta de Raoul de hacer un viaje a Palm Beach.*

| Word Link | **tempt ≈ trying : attempt, temptation, tempted** |
|---|---|

**temp|ta|tion** /tɛmpteɪʃᵊn/ (**temptations**) N-VAR **Temptation** is the feeling that you want to do something or have something, even though you know you really should avoid it. *tentación* ❑ *Will they be able to resist the temptation to buy?* *¿Podrán resistir la tentación de comprar?*

**tempt|ed** /tɛmptɪd/ ADJ If you are **tempted to** do something, you would like to do it. *tentado* ❑ *I'm very tempted to sell my car.* *Estoy muy tentado a vender mi coche.*

**ten** /tɛn/ (**tens**) NUM **Ten** is the number 10. *diez* ❑ *Over the past ten years things have changed.* *Las cosas han cambiado en los últimos diez años.*

**ten|ant** /tɛnənt/ (**tenants**) N-COUNT A **tenant** is someone who pays rent for the place they live in, or for land or buildings that they use. *inquilino o inquilina* ❑ *...the obligations of a landlord to the tenant.* *...las obligaciones del casero para con el inquilino.*

**tend** /tɛnd/ (**tends, tending, tended**) **1** V-T If something **tends to** happen, it usually happens or it often happens. *tender a, soler* ❑ *Smaller cars tend to be noisy.* *Los coches pequeños suelen ser ruidosos.* **2** V-I If you **tend toward** a particular characteristic, you often display that characteristic. *tener tendencias* ❑ *Artistic people often tend toward liberal views.* *Los artistas suelen tener tendencias liberales.*

| Word Partnership | Usar *tend* con: |
|---|---|
| V. | tend **to agree**, tend **to avoid**, tend **to become**, tend **to blame**, tend **to develop**, tend **to feel**, tend **to forget**, tend **to happen**, tend **to lose**, tend **to stay**, tend **to think** **1** |
| N. | **Americans** tend, **children/men/women** tend, **people** tend **1** **2** |

**ten|den|cy** /tɛndənsi/ (**tendencies**) N-COUNT A **tendency** is a worrying or unpleasant habit or action that keeps occurring. *tendencia* ❑ *...the government's tendency to secrecy in recent years.* *...la tendencia del gobierno al secreto en los años recientes.*

**tender**
❶ ADJECTIVE USES
❷ NOUN AND VERB USES

❶ **ten|der** /tɛndər/ (**tenderer, tenderest**) **1** ADJ Someone or something that is **tender** expresses gentle and caring feelings. *tierno, cariñoso, cálido* ❑ *Her voice was tender.* *Tenía una voz cálida.* ● **ten|der|ly** ADV *tiernamente* ❑ *Mr. Williams tenderly embraced his wife.* *El señor Williams abrazó tiernamente a su esposa.* ● **ten|der|ness** N-UNCOUNT *ternura, calidez* ❑ *She smiled, politely rather than with tenderness.* *Sonrió cortésmente, antes bien que con calidez.* **2** ADJ If someone does something at a **tender** age, they do it when they are still young and have not had much experience. *tierno* ❑ *He began playing the game at the tender age of seven.* *Empezó a jugar a la tierna edad de siete años.* **3** ADJ Meat or other food that is **tender** is easy to cut or chew. *tierno, blando* ❑ *Cook for a minimum of 2 hours, until the meat is tender.* *Cocine durante al menos 2 horas, hasta que la carne esté tierna.* **4** ADJ If part of your body is **tender,** it is sensitive and painful when it is touched. *sensible* ❑ *My tummy felt very tender.* *Tenía la barriga muy sensible.*
→ see **cooking**

❷ **ten|der** /tɛndər/ (**tenders, tendering, tendered**) V-I If a company **tenders for** something, it makes a formal offer to supply goods or do a job for a particular price. *licitar* [BUSINESS] ❑ *The company tendered for contracts in Spain and Germany.* *La empresa se presentó en licitaciones para obtener contratos en España y Alemania.* ● **Tender** is also a noun. *propuesta* [BUSINESS] ❑ *Builders will be asked to submit a tender for the work.* *Se pedirá a las constructoras que sometan una propuesta para la obra.*

**ten|don** /tɛndən/ (**tendons**) N-COUNT A **tendon** is a strong cord of tissue in your body joining a muscle to a bone. *tendón* ❑ *...a torn tendon in his right shoulder.* *...un tendón desgarrado en el hombro derecho.*

**ten|nis** /tɛnɪs/ N-UNCOUNT **Tennis** is a game played by two or four players on a rectangular court with a net across the middle. The players use rackets to hit a ball over the net. *tenis*
→ see Picture Dictionary: **tennis**
→ see **park**

**tense** /tɛns/ (**tenser, tensest, tenses, tensing, tensed**) **1** ADJ If you are **tense,** you are anxious and nervous and cannot relax. *tenso* ❑ *Mark was very tense at first.* *Mark estaba muy tenso al principio.* **2** ADJ If your body is **tense,** your muscles are tight and not relaxed. *tenso* ❑ *A bath can relax tense muscles.* *Un baño de tina puede relajar los músculos tensos.* **3** V-T/V-I If your muscles **tense,** or if you **tense** them, they become tight and stiff, often because you are anxious or frightened. *tensar(se)* ❑ *Newman's stomach muscles tensed.* *Los músculos estomacales de Newman se tensaron.* ● **Tense up** means the same as **tense.** *tensar(se)* ❑ *When we are under stress our bodies tend to tense up.* *Cuando estamos presionados, nuestro cuerpo se tensa.* **4** N-COUNT The **tense** of a verb is its form, which shows whether you are referring to past, present, or future time. *tiempo verbal* ❑ *They were already speaking of her in the past tense.* *Ya estaban hablando de ella en tiempo pasado.*

| Word Partnership | Usar *tense* con: |
|---|---|
| N. | tense **atmosphere**, tense **moment**, tense **mood**, **muscles** tense, tense **situation** **1** |
| V. | **feel** tense **1** **2** |
| ADV. | **very** tense **1** **2** |
| ADJ. | **future/past/perfect/present** tense **4** |

**ten|sion** /tɛnʃᵊn/ **1** N-UNCOUNT **Tension** is a feeling of worry and anxiety which makes it difficult for you to relax. *tensión* ❑ *Laughing can relieve tension.* *La risa puede aliviar la tensión.* **2** N-UNCOUNT **Tension** is a feeling of anxiety produced by a difficult or dangerous situation, especially one in which there is a possibility of conflict or violence. *tensión* ❑ *The tension between*

t

Picture Dictionary tennis

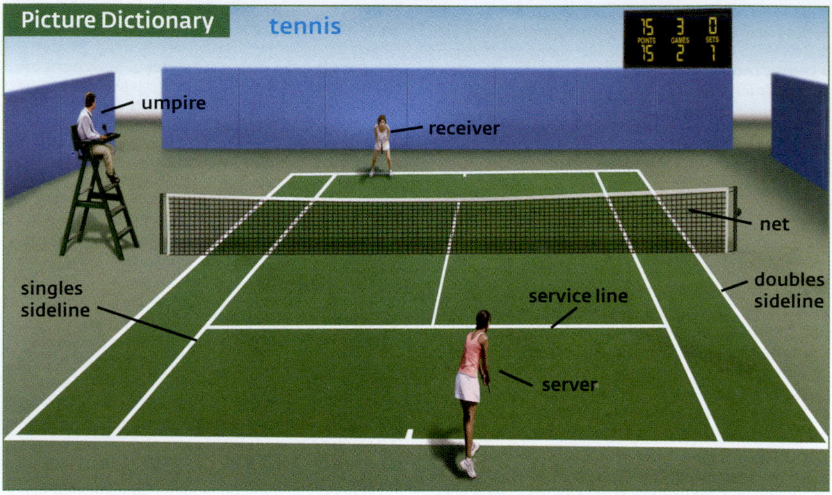


the two countries is likely to remain. Es probable que se mantenga la tensión entre los dos países. **3** N-UNCOUNT The **tension** in a rope or wire is the extent to which it is stretched tight. *tensión* ❑ *It is possible to change the tension of the cable.* *Es posible modificar la tensión del cable.*

→ see **anger**

**Word Partnership** Usar *tension* con:

| | |
|---|---|
| V. | **ease** tension, tension **grows**, tension **mounts**, **relieve** tension **1** **2** |
| N. | **source of** tension **1** – **3** |
| ADJ. | **racial** tension **2** |

tent

**tent** /tɛnt/ (**tents**) N-COUNT A **tent** is a shelter made of canvas or nylon which is held up by poles and ropes, and is used mainly by people who are camping. *tienda*

**ten|ta|tive** /tɛntətɪv/ **1** ADJ **Tentative** agreements or plans are not definite or certain, but have been made as a first step. *provisional* ❑ *...a tentative agreement to hold a conference.* *...un acuerdo provisional para sostener una conferencia.* **2** ADJ If someone is **tentative,** they are cautious and not very confident because they are uncertain or afraid. *vacilante, indeciso* ❑ *My first attempts at complaining were tentative.* *Mis primeros intentos por quejarme fueron vacilantes.* ● **ten|ta|tive|ly** ADV *vacilantemente, indecisamente* ❑ *I tentatively suggested an alternative route.* *Con indecisión, sugerí una ruta alterna.*

**tenth** /tɛnθ/ ORD The **tenth** item in a series is the one that you count as number ten. *décimo* ❑ *...her tenth birthday.* *...su cumpleaños número diez.*

**term** /tɜrm/ (**terms, terming, termed**) **1** PHRASE If you talk about something **in terms of** something or **in** particular **terms,** you are specifying which aspect of it you are considering. *desde el punto de vista de* ❑ *Our goods compete in terms of quality and price.* *Nuestros productos son competitivos desde el punto de vista de calidad y precio.* **2** N-COUNT A **term** is a word or expression with a specific meaning. *término* ❑ *"Myocardial infarction" is the medical term for a heart attack.* *"Infarto de miocardio" es el término médico para ataque al corazón.* **3** V-T If you say that something **is termed** a particular thing, you mean that that is what people call it or consider it to be. *calificar de, llamar* ❑ *He was termed a temporary employee.* *Lo calificaron de empleado temporal.* **4** N-VAR A **term** is one of the periods of time that a school, college, or university divides the year into. *trimestre* ❑ *...the summer term.* *...el tercer trimestre.* **5** N-COUNT A **term** is a period of time that someone spends doing a particular job or in a particular place. *período* ❑ *Nixon never completed his term of office.* *Nixon no terminó su período en el cargo.* ❑ *...a 12-month term of service.* *...un período de servicio de 12 meses.* **6** N-PLURAL The **terms** of an agreement or arrangement are the conditions that must be accepted by the people involved in it. *término* ❑ *...the terms of the Helsinki agreement.* *...los términos del acuerdo de Helsinki.* **7** PHRASE If you **come to terms with** something difficult or unpleasant, you learn to accept and deal with it. *aceptar* ❑ *She has come to terms with her husband's death.* *Ya logró aceptar la muerte de su esposo.* **8** PHRASE If two people or groups compete **on equal terms** or **on the same terms,** neither of them has an advantage over the other. *en igualdad de condiciones* ❑ *I want to compete with men on equal terms.* *Quiero competir con los hombres en igualdad de condiciones.* **9** PHRASE If two people are **on good terms** or **on friendly terms,** they are friendly with each other. *tener buenas relaciones con* ❑ *Madeleine is on good terms with Sarah.* *Madeleine se lleva bien con Sarah.* **10** PHRASE You use the expressions **in the long term, in the short term,** and **in the medium term** to talk about what will happen

T

over a long period of time, over a short period of time, and over a medium period of time. *a corto/mediano/largo plazo* ❑ *In the long term we hope to open an office in Moscow. A largo plazo, esperamos abrir una oficina en Moscú.* **11** PHRASE If you say that you **are thinking in terms of** doing a particular thing, you mean that you are considering it. *pensar en* ❑ *You should be thinking in terms of graduating next year. Deberías estar pensando en graduarte el año que viene.* **12** **in no uncertain terms** → see **uncertain**

| Word Link | *term, termin ≈ limit, end : determine, terminal, terminate* |
|---|---|

**ter|mi|nal** /tɜrmɪnᵊl/ (**terminals**) **1** ADJ A **terminal** illness or disease causes death and cannot be cured. *terminal* ❑ *...terminal cancer. ...cáncer terminal.* ● **ter|mi|nal|ly** ADV *en fase terminal* ❑ *The patient is terminally ill. El paciente está desahuciado.* **2** N-COUNT A **terminal** is a place where vehicles, passengers, or goods begin or end a journey. *terminal* ❑ *...a new terminal at Dulles airport. ...una nueva terminal en el aeropuerto Dulles.* **3** N-COUNT A computer **terminal** is a piece of equipment consisting of a keyboard and a screen connected to a computer. *terminal* [COMPUTING] ❑ *Carl sits at a computer terminal 40 hours a week. Carl se pasa sentado a la computadora 40 horas a la semana.*

**ter|mi|nal ve|loc|ity** (**terminal velocities**) N-VAR The **terminal velocity** of a falling object is the maximum speed it reaches. *velocidad final, velocidad de llegada* [TECHNICAL]

**ter|mi|nate** /tɜrmɪneɪt/ (**terminates, terminating, terminated**) **1** V-T/V-I When you **terminate** something or when it **terminates,** it ends completely. *terminar(se), poner fin a, poner término a, vencer* [FORMAL] ❑ *She suddenly terminated the conversation. Puso fin a la conversación repentinamente.* ❑ *His contract terminates at the season's end. Su contrato vence al final de la temporada.* ● **ter|mi|na|tion** /tɜrmɪneɪʃᵊn/ N-UNCOUNT *terminación, interrupción* ❑ *...the sudden termination of electricity. ...la interrupción repentina de la electricidad.* **2** V-I When a train or bus **terminates** somewhere, it ends its journey there. *llegar al final del recorrido* [FORMAL] ❑ *This train will terminate at Lamy. La última terminal de este tren es en Lamy.*

**ter|mite** /tɜrmaɪt/ (**termites**) N-COUNT **Termites** are small insects that do a lot of damage by eating wood. *termita*

**term pa|per** (**term papers**) N-COUNT A **term paper** is an essay or report which a student writes on a subject that he or she has studied during a term at a school, college, or university. *exposición o ensayo que se presenta en la escuela sobre algún tema estudiado durante un trimestre*

| Word Link | *terr ≈ earth : subterranean, terrace, territory* |
|---|---|

**ter|race** /tɛrɪs/ (**terraces**) **1** N-COUNT A **terrace** is a flat area of stone or grass next to a building, where people can sit. *terraza* ❑ *...a terrace overlooking the sea. ...una terraza con vista al mar.* **2** N-COUNT **Terraces** are a series of flat areas built like steps on the side of a hill so that crops can be grown there. *terraza* ❑ *...terraces on steep mountain slopes. ...terrazas en laderas montañosas abruptas.*

**ter|res|trial plan|et** /tɪrɛstriəl plænɪt/ (**terrestrial planets**) N-COUNT A **terrestrial planet** is a planet with a rocky surface similar to the Earth's. In our solar system the four planets closest to the sun are **terrestrial planets.** *planeta similar a la Tierra, planeta terrestre, telúrico o rocoso* [TECHNICAL]

**ter|ri|ble** /tɛrɪbᵊl/ **1** ADJ **Terrible** means extremely bad. *malísimo, atroz* ❑ *She admits her French is terrible. Ella admite que su francés es malísimo.* ❑ *Thousands suffered terrible injuries. Miles de personas sufrieron heridas atroces.* ● **ter|ri|bly** ADV *muchísimo* ❑ *My son has suffered terribly. Mi hijo ha sufrido muchísimo.* **2** ADJ You use **terrible** to emphasize the great extent or degree of something. *perfecto* ❑ *I was a terrible fool. Fui un perfecto tonto.* ● **ter|ri|bly** ADV *enormemente* ❑ *I'm terribly sorry to bother you at this hour. Estoy enormemente apenado por tener que molestarlo a esta hora.*

**ter|rif|ic** /tərɪfɪk/ **1** ADJ If you describe something or someone as **terrific,** you are very pleased with them or very impressed by them. *estupendo* [INFORMAL] ❑ *What a terrific idea! ¡Que estupenda idea!* **2** ADJ **Terrific** means very great in amount, degree, or intensity. *aterrador* ❑ *There was a terrific bang. Hubo un estallido aterrador.*

**ter|ri|fy** /tɛrɪfaɪ/ (**terrifies, terrifying, terrified**) **1** V-T If something **terrifies** you, it makes you feel extremely frightened. *aterrar, aterrorizar* ❑ *Flying terrifies him. Volar lo aterra.* ● **ter|ri|fied** ADJ *aterrado, aterrorizado* ❑ *He was terrified of heights. La altura lo aterraba.* **2** → see also **terror**

**ter|ri|fy|ing** /tɛrɪfaɪɪŋ/ ADJ If something is **terrifying,** it makes you very frightened. *aterrador, espantoso, horroroso* ❑ *It was a terrifying accident. Fue un accidente espantoso.*

**ter|ri|to|rial** /tɛrɪtɔriəl/ ADJ **Territorial** means concerned with the ownership of a particular area of land or water. *territorial* ❑ *...territorial disputes. ...disputas territoriales.*

| Word Link | *ory ≈ place where something happens : dormitory, factory, territory* |
|---|---|

**ter|ri|tory** /tɛrətɔri/ (**territories**) **1** N-VAR **Territory** is land which is controlled by a particular country or ruler. *territorio* ❑ *...Afghan territory ...territorio afgano.* **2** N-UNCOUNT You can use **territory** to refer to an area of knowledge or experience. *terreno* ❑ *Atwood's latest novel returns to more familiar territory. La última novela de Atwood vuelve a un terreno más familiar.* **3** N-UNCOUNT **Territory** is land with a particular character. *territorio, región* ❑ *...mountainous territory. ...región montañosa.* **4** N-VAR An animal's **territory** is an area which it regards as its own and which it defends when other animals try to enter it. *territorio*

| Word Partnership | Usar **territory** con: |
|---|---|
| N. | **enemy** territory, **part of a** territory **1** |
| ADJ. | **vast** territory **1 3** |
| | **controlled** territory, **disputed** territory, **familiar** territory, **uncharted** territory **3** |

t

**ter|ror** /tɛrər/ **1** N-UNCOUNT **Terror** is very great fear. terror ❑ *I shook with terror.* Temblé de terror. **2** N-UNCOUNT **Terror** is violence or the threat of violence, especially when it is used for political reasons. terror ❑ *...the war on terror.* ...la guerra al terror. ❑ *...a campaign of terror.* ...una campaña de terror.

**Word Partnership** Usar *terror* con:

N. **acts of** terror, terror **alert**, terror **attack**, terror **campaign**, **fight against** terror, **reign of** terror, terror **suspects** **2**

**ter|ror|ist** /tɛrərɪst/ (**terrorists**) N-COUNT A **terrorist** is a person who uses violence, especially murder and bombing, in order to achieve political aims. terrorista ❑ *...terrorist attacks.* ...ataques terroristas. ● **ter|ror|ism** N-UNCOUNT terrorismo ❑ *...the threat of global terrorism.* ...la amenaza del terrorismo mundial.

**ter|ror|ize** /tɛrəraɪz/ (**terrorizes, terrorizing, terrorized**) V-T If someone **terrorizes** you, they keep you in a state of fear by making it seem likely that they will attack you. aterrorizar ❑ *Gangs terrorized the city's inhabitants.* Las pandillas aterrorizaban a los habitantes de la ciudad.

**test** /tɛst/ (**tests, testing, tested**) **1** V-T When you **test** something, you try using it or touching it in order to find out what it is, what condition it is in, or how well it works. probar ❑ *Test the temperature of the water with your wrist.* Pruebe la temperatura del agua en su muñeca. ● **Test** is also a noun. prueba ❑ *...the banning of nuclear tests.* ...la prohibición de las pruebas nucleares. **2** V-T If you **test** someone, you ask them questions in order to find out how much they know about something. examinar ❑ *Each teacher spent an hour testing students.* Cada maestro pasó una hora examinando estudiantes. ● **Test** is also a noun. examen ❑ *Out of 25 students only 15 passed the test.* Sólo 15 de 25 estudiantes aprobaron el examen. **3** → see also **quiz** **4** N-COUNT If an event or situation is a **test of** a person or thing, it reveals their qualities or effectiveness. prueba de ❑ *Vacations are a major test of any relationship.* Las vacaciones son una prueba importante de toda relación. **5** V-T If you **are tested for** a particular disease or medical condition, you are examined or go through various procedures in order to find out whether you have that disease or condition. analizar ❑ *My doctor wants me to be tested for diabetes.* Mi médico quiere que me hagan análisis para ver si padezco diabetes. **6** N-COUNT A medical **test** is an examination of a part of your body in order to check that you are healthy. análisis ❑ *...blood tests.* ...análisis de sangre. **7** PHRASE If you **put** something **to the test,** you find out how useful or effective it is by using it. poner a prueba ❑ *The team is now putting its theory to the test.* Ahora el equipo está poniendo a prueba su teoría.
→ see **experiment**

**Word Partnership** Usar *test* con:

N. test **a drug**, **flight** test, test **a hypothesis** **1**
**achievement** test, **aptitude** test, **crash** test, test **data/results**, **intelligence** test, test **items**, **math/reading** test, test **preparation**, test **scores**, **standardized** test, **stress** test, test **takers** **2**
**blood** test, **drug** test, **HIV** test, **pregnancy** test **5**
ADJ. **nuclear** test **1**
**diagnostic** test **5** **6**
V. **administer a** test, test **drive**, **fail a** test, **give** *someone* **a** test, **pass a** test, **study for a** test, **take a** test **2**

**test drive** (**test drives, test driving, test drove, test driven**) also **test-drive** V-T If you **test drive** a car or other vehicle, you drive it for a short period to help you decide whether to buy it. hacer la prueba de carretera ❑ *...invitations to test drive expensive cars.* ...invitaciones para hacer la prueba de carretera de automóviles lujosos. ● **Test drive** is also a noun. prueba de carretera ❑ *People are buying cars from websites without ever going for a test drive.* La gente está comprando automóviles por Internet sin siquiera ir a hacer la prueba de carretera.

**tes|ti|fy** /tɛstɪfaɪ/ (**testifies, testifying, testified**) V-T/V-I When someone **testifies** in a court of law, they give a statement of what they saw someone do or what they know of a situation, after having promised to tell the truth. testificar, declarar, dar testimonio, prestar testimonio ❑ *He testified that he saw the officers hit Milner.* Testificó que había visto a los policías golpear a Milner. ❑ *Eva testified to seeing Herndon with a gun.* Eva testificó que había visto a Herndon con un arma.

**tes|ti|mo|ny** /tɛstɪmoʊni/ (**testimonies**) **1** N-VAR In a court of law, your **testimony** is a formal statement that you make about what you saw someone do or what you know of a situation, after having promised to tell the truth. testimonio, declaración ❑ *His testimony was an important element of the case.* Su testimonio fue un aspecto importante del caso. **2** N-UNCOUNT; N-SING If one thing is **testimony to** another, it shows clearly that the second thing has a particular quality. prueba de, muestra de ❑ *The environmental movement is testimony to people's love of nature.* El movimiento ecologista es una muestra del amor de la gente por la naturaleza.
→ see **trial**

**tes|tis** /tɛstɪs/ (**testes** /tɛstiz/) N-COUNT A man's **testes** are his **testicles**. testículo [MEDICAL]

**test tube** (**test tubes**) also **test-tube** N-COUNT A **test tube** is a small tube-shaped container made from glass. Test tubes are used in laboratories. probeta, tubo de ensayo
→ see **laboratory equipment**

**Tex-Mex** /tɛksmɛks/ ADJ You use **Tex-Mex** to describe things such as food or music that combine typical elements from Mexico and Texas. Tex-Mex (tejano-mexicano) [INFORMAL] ❑ *...Tex-Mex restaurants.* ...restaurantes Tex-Mex.

**text** /tɛkst/ (**texts, texting, texted**) **1** N-UNCOUNT **Text** is any written material. texto

T

❑ *The machine can turn handwriting into printed text.* *La máquina puede convertir el texto manuscrito en texto impreso.* **2** N-COUNT A **text** is a book or other piece of writing, especially one connected with science or learning. *texto* ❑ *...his study of religious texts.* *...su estudio de textos religiosos.* **3** N-COUNT A **text** is the same as a **text message**. *mensaje de texto* ❑ *The new system can send a text to a cellphone.* *El nuevo sistema puede enviar un mensaje de texto a un celular.* **4** V-T If you **text** someone, you send them a text message on a cellphone. *enviar un mensaje de texto* ❑ *Mary texted me when she got home.* *Mary me envió un mensaje cuando llegó a la casa.* **5** N-COUNT The **text** of a speech, broadcast, or recording is the written version of it. *versión impresa*
→ see **diary**

**text|book** /tɛkstbʊk/ (**textbooks**) also **text book** N-COUNT A **textbook** is a book containing facts about a particular subject that is used by people studying that subject. *libro de texto* ❑ *...a textbook on international law.* *...un libro de texto sobre derecho internacional.*

**tex|tile** /tɛkstaɪl/ (**textiles**) **1** N-COUNT **Textiles** are types of woven cloth. *productos textiles* ❑ *...textiles for the home.* *...productos textiles para el hogar.* **2** N-PLURAL **Textiles** are the industries concerned with the manufacture of cloth. *industria textil* ❑ *75,000 jobs will disappear in textiles.* *Se perderán 75,000 empleos en la industria textil.*
→ see **industry, quilt**

**text|ing** /tɛkstɪŋ/ N-UNCOUNT **Texting** is the same as **text messaging**. *envío de mensajes de texto*

**text mes|sage** (**text messages**) N-COUNT A **text message** is a written message that you send using a cellphone. *mensaje de texto* ❑ *She has sent text messages to her family telling them not to worry.* *Mandó a su familia mensajes de texto en que decía que no se preocuparan.*

**text mes|sag|ing** N-UNCOUNT **Text messaging** is the sending of written messages using a cellphone. *envío de mensajes de texto* ❑ *...the popularity of text messaging.* *...la popularidad de los mensajes de texto.*

**tex|ture** /tɛkstʃər/ (**textures**) **1** N-VAR The **texture** of something is the way that it feels when you touch it. *textura* ❑ *Her skin had a smooth texture.* *Su piel tenía una muy suave textura.* **2** N-VAR The **texture** of a piece of music is the way that the different sounds combine to produce an overall effect. *textura* **3** N-VAR The **texture** of something, especially food or soil, is its structure, for example, whether it is light with lots of holes, or very heavy and solid. *textura*

**than** /ðən, STRONG ðæn/ **1** PREP You use **than** to link two parts of a comparison or contrast. *que, de* ❑ *Children learn faster than adults.* *Los niños aprenden más rápido que los adultos.* ❑ *They talked on the phone for more than an hour.* *Hablaron más de una hora por teléfono.* ❑ *It feels much more like a car than a truck.* *Se siente más como coche que como camión.* ● **Than** is also a conjunction. *que* ❑ *He should have helped her more than he did.* *Debió haberla ayudado más de lo que lo hizo.* **2** **less than** → see **less** **3** **more than** → see **more** **4** **more often than not** → see **often** **5** **other than** → see **other** **6** **rather than** → see **rather**

> **Usage** **than and then**
>
> *Than* and *then* are often confused. Use *than* to make a comparison. *The unemployment rate is lower now than it was last year.* *Then* means "at that time" or "next." *There were a lot more unemployed people then. Slice the skin off the fruit and then cut it into quarters.*

**thank** /θæŋk/ (**thanks, thanking, thanked**) **1** CONVENTION You use **thank you** or, in more informal English, **thanks** to express your gratitude when someone does something for you or gives you what you want. *gracias* ❑ *Thank you very much for your call.* *Muchas gracias por llamar.* ❑ *Thanks for the information.* *Gracias por la información.* ❑ *"Would you like a cup of coffee?"—"Thank you, I'd love one."* *—¿Quiere un café? —Gracias, me encantaría.* ❑ *"Tea?" —"No thanks."* *—¿Té? —No, gracias.* **2** CONVENTION You use **thank you** or **thank you very much** in order to say firmly that you do not want help or to tell someone that you do not like the way that they are behaving toward you. *gracias, muchas gracias* ❑ *I can find my own way home, thank you.* *Sé como irme, gracias.* **3** V-T When you **thank** someone **for** something, you express your gratitude to them for it. *agradecer, dar las gracias* ❑ *I thanked them for their long and loyal service.* *Les di las gracias por sus prolongados y leales servicios.* **4** N-PLURAL When you express your **thanks** to someone, you express your gratitude to them for something. *agradecimiento, gratitud* ❑ *They accepted their certificates with words of thanks.* *Recibieron sus certificados con palabras de agradecimiento.* **5** PHRASE You say **"Thank God," "Thank goodness,"** or **"Thank heavens"** when you are very relieved about something. *gracias a Dios, gracias al cielo* ❑ *I was wrong, thank God.* *A Dios gracias, me había equivocado.* **6** PHRASE If you say that something happens **thanks to** a particular person or thing, you mean that they are responsible for it happening or caused it to happen. *merced a, gracias a* ❑ *Thanks to this committee, many new supporters have come forward.* *Gracias a este comité, se han presentado más personas a ofrecer su apoyo.*

**thank|ful** /θæŋkfəl/ ADJ When you are **thankful**, you are very happy and relieved that something has happened. *agradecido* ❑ *I'm just thankful that I've got a job.* *No puedo más que agradecer por haber conseguido un trabajo.*

> **that**
> 1 DEMONSTRATIVE USES
> 2 CONJUNCTION AND RELATIVE PRONOUN USES

**❶ that** /ðæt/ **1** PRON You use **that** to refer back to an idea, situation, or period of time that you have referred to previously. *eso, aquello* ❑ *They said you wanted to talk to me. Why was that?* *Me dijeron que querías hablarme, ¿y eso?* ❑ *"There's a party tonight."—"Is that why you're phoning?"* *—En la noche hay una fiesta. —¿Por eso me llamas?* ● **That** is also a determiner. *aquel, aquella, ese, esa* ❑ *She's away; for that reason I'm cooking tonight.* *Ella salió. Es por esa razón que estoy cocinando hoy.* ❑ *The story was published later that week.* *El reportaje lo publicaron al final de aquella semana.* **2** DET You use **that** when

t

you are referring to someone or something which is a distance away from you in position or time, especially when you indicate or point to them. When there are two or more things near you, **that** refers to the more distant one. *aquel, aquella, ese, esa* ❑ *Look at that guy over there. Fíjate en aquel muchacho, el que está allá.* ● **That** is also a pronoun. *aquel, aquella, aquello, ese, esa, eso* ❑ *What's that you're writing? ¿Qué es eso que estás escribiendo?* ❑ *"Who's that with you?" — "A friend of mine." —¿Quién es ese que está contigo? —Un amigo.* **3** ADV If something is **not that** bad, funny, or expensive, for example, it is not as bad, funny, or expensive as it might be or as has been suggested. *tan* ❑ *Not even Gary is that stupid. Ni siquiera Gary es tan estúpido.* **4** → see also **those** **5** PHRASE You use **that is** or **that is to say** to indicate that you are about to express the same idea more clearly or precisely. *es decir* ❑ *I am a good student. That is, I do as I'm told. Soy buen estudiante, es decir, hago lo que me dicen.* **6** PHRASE You use **that's that** to say there is nothing more you can do or say about a particular matter. *es todo* [SPOKEN] ❑ *If that's the way you want it, I guess that's that. Si así lo quieres, supongo que no hay más que decir.* **7** **like that** → see **like** **8** **this and that** → see **this**

**❷ that** /ðət, STRONG ðæt/ **1** CONJ You can use **that** after many verbs, adjectives, nouns, and expressions to introduce a clause. *que* ❑ *He said that he and his wife were coming to New York. Dijo que él y su esposa venían a Nueva York.* ❑ *...the news that your contract has ended. ...la noticia de que se acabó su contrato.* ❑ *It's interesting that you like him. Es interesante que te guste.* **2** PRON You use **that** to introduce a clause which gives more information to help identify the person or thing you are talking about. *que* ❑ *...a decision that will make the problem disappear. ...una decisión que acabará con el problema.* **3** CONJ You use **that** after expressions with "so" and "such" in order to introduce the result or effect of something. *que* ❑ *She was so nervous that she started shaking. Estaba tan nerviosa que empezó a temblar.*

**that's** /ðæts/ **That's** is a spoken form of "that is." *forma hablada de* ***that is***

**thaw** /θɔ/ (**thaws, thawing, thawed**) **1** V-T/V-I When ice, snow, or something else that is frozen **thaws**, it melts. *derretir(se), fundir(se), deshacer(se), disolver(se)* ❑ *It's so cold the snow doesn't get a chance to thaw. Hace tanto frío que la nieve ni siquiera se deshace.* ❑ *Always thaw chicken thoroughly. El pollo debe descongelarse perfectamente siempre.* **2** N-COUNT A **thaw** is a period of warmer weather when snow and ice melt. *deshielo* ❑ *...an early spring thaw. ...deshielo de principios de primavera.*

T

**the**

> **The** is the definite article. It is used at the beginning of noun groups. **The** is usually pronounced /ðə/ before a consonant and /ði/ before a vowel, but pronounced /ði:/ when you are emphasizing it.

**1** DET You use **the** at the beginning of noun groups to refer to someone or something when they are generally known about or when it is clear which particular person or thing you are referring to. *el, la* ❑ *Six of the 38 people were U.S. citizens. Seis de las 38 personas eran ciudadanos estadounidenses.* ❑ *It's always hard to think about the future. Siempre es difícil pensar en el futuro.* ❑ *The doctor's on his way. El doctor viene en camino.* **2** DET You use **the** in front of a singular noun when you want to make a general statement about things or people of that type. *el, la* ❑ *The computer has developed very fast in recent years. La computación se ha desarrollado muy rápidamente en los últimos años.* **3** DET You use **the** with adjectives and plural nouns to refer to all people of a particular type or nationality. *los, las* ❑ *...the poor in Los Angeles. ...los pobres de Los Angeles.* ❑ *We must keep the British and the French involved in this. Es importante que los ingleses y los franceses se involucren.* **4** DET You use **the** in front of an adjective when you are referring to a particular thing that is described by that adjective. *lo* ❑ *He knows he's wishing for the impossible. Sabe que está pidiendo lo imposible.* **5** DET You use **the** in front of numbers to refer to days and dates. *el* ❑ *The meeting should take place on the fifth of May. La reunión tiene que hacerse el cinco de mayo.* ❑ *It's hard to imagine how bad things were in the thirties. Es difícil imaginarse lo difícil que era en los años treinta.* **6** DET You use **the** in front of superlative adjectives and adverbs. *el, la* ❑ *Daily walks are the best exercise. El mejor ejercicio es caminar todos los días.* **7** DET You use **the** in front of each of two comparative adjectives or adverbs when you are describing how one amount or quality changes in relation to another. *mientras más ...más* ❑ *The more you learn, the greater your chances of success. Mientras más aprendas, mayores tus oportunidades de éxito.* **8** DET When you express rates, prices, and measurements, you can use **the** to say how many units apply to each of the items being measured. *por* ❑ *...cars that get more miles to the gallon. ...vehículos que dan más kilómetros por litro.*

**thea|ter** /θi̲ətər/ (**theaters**) also **theatre** **1** N-COUNT A **theater** is a building with a stage on which plays and other performances take place. *teatro* ❑ *We went to the theater. Fuimos al teatro.* **2** N-COUNT A **theater** or a **movie theater** is a place where people go to watch movies for entertainment. *cine* ❑ *We're excited about getting a new movie theater. Estamos emocionados porque van a abrir un nuevo cine.* **3** N-UNCOUNT **Theater** is entertainment that involves the performance of plays. *teatro, representación teatral, obra de teatro* ❑ *...American musical theater. ...los musicales estadounidenses.* **4** N-SING You can refer to work in the theater such as acting or writing plays as **the theater.** *teatro, arte dramático*
→ see Word Web: **theater**
→ see **city, drama**

**thea|ter of the ab|surd** N-SING The **theater of the absurd** is a style of theater that began in the 1950s. It represents life as meaningless or irrational. *teatro del absurdo*

**the|at|ri|cal** /θiæ̲trɪkəl/ **1** ADJ **Theatrical** means relating to the theater. *teatral, dramático, escénico* ❑ *...great theatrical performances. ...grandes representaciones teatrales.* **2** ADJ **Theatrical** behavior is deliberately exaggerated and unnatural. *afectado, artificial, artificioso, histriónico* ❑ *...a theatrical gesture. ...un gesto teatral.* ● **the|at|ri|cal|ly** /θiæ̲trɪkli/ ADV *teatralmente, con afectación* ❑ *He*

**Word Web** theater

It only takes two hours to watch a **play**. It takes a lot of time, money, and work before the curtain rises on the **stage**. First, a **playwright** writes an interesting story. Then, a **producer** gets the money for the **production** and finds a **theater**. **Actors audition** for the play. The **director casts** the actors in the **roles**. **Rehearsals** sometimes go on for months. The **set**, **lighting**, and **costumes** all have to be designed and made. Special **props** and **make-up** are usually necessary. A **band** or an **orchestra** is needed if the play is a **musical**. It takes a large **crew** to do all these things.

*A scene from the Broadway play, Les Miserables*

*looked theatrically at his watch.* Miró afectadamente su reloj.

**the|at|ri|cal con|ven|tion** (theatrical conventions) N-VAR A **theatrical convention** is a part of the style or structure of a play which is traditional and therefore familiar to most audiences. convención teatral

**the|at|ri|cal ex|peri|ence** (theatrical experiences) N-COUNT A **theatrical experience** is an occasion when someone attends a play, musical, or other theatrical production. experiencia teatral

**the|at|ri|cal game** (theatrical games) N-COUNT **Theatrical games** are exercises, such as role-playing, that are designed to develop people's acting skills. juego teatral

**theft** /θɛft/ (thefts) N-VAR **Theft** is the crime of stealing. robo, hurto ❑ *Auto theft has increased by over 56 percent.* El robo de autos se ha incrementado más de 56 por ciento.
→ see **crime**

**their** /ðɛər/

**Their** is the third person plural possessive determiner.

**1** DET You use **their** to indicate that something belongs or relates to the group of people, animals, or things that you are talking about. su ❑ *Janis and Kurt have announced their engagement.* Janis y Kurt anunciaron su compromiso ❑ *They took off their coats.* Se quitaron el abrigo. **2** DET You use **their** instead of "his or her" to indicate that something belongs or relates to a person without saying whether that person is a man or a woman. Some people think this use is incorrect. su ❑ *Each student decides their own pace.* Cada estudiante define su ritmo.

**Usage** **their, there, and they're**

*Their, there,* and *they're* sound the same but have very different meanings. *Their* is the possessive form of *they*: *They took off their shoes to avoid getting the floor muddy. There* can be the subject of *be* and can indicate location: *There are two seats here and another two there. They're* is the contraction of *they are*: *They're wondering what time dinner will be ready.*

**theirs** /ðɛərz/

**Theirs** is the third person plural possessive pronoun.

**1** PRON You use **theirs** to indicate that something belongs or relates to the group of people, animals, or things that you are talking about. el suyo ❑ *...the table next to theirs.* ...la mesa cercana a la de ellos. ❑ *Theirs was a happy marriage.* El de ellos fue un matrimonio feliz. **2** PRON You use **theirs** instead of "his or hers" to indicate that something belongs or relates to a person without saying whether that person is a man or a woman. Some people think this use is incorrect. el suyo ❑ *I don't know whose book it is. Somebody must have left theirs.* No sé de quién es este libro, alguien olvidó el suyo.

**them** /ðəm, STRONG ðɛm/

**Them** is a third person plural pronoun. **Them** is used as the object of a verb or preposition.

**1** PRON You use **them** to refer to a group of people, animals, or things. a ellos ❑ *Kids these days have no one to tell them what's right and wrong.* En estos tiempos, los niños no tienen quien les diga que está bien y qué está mal. **2** PRON You use **them** instead of "him or her" to refer to a person without saying whether that person is a man or a woman. Some people think this use is incorrect. a él, a ella ❑ *It takes great courage to face your child and tell them the truth.* Se necesita mucho valor para enfrentar a un hijo y decirle la verdad.

**theme** /θim/ (themes) **1** N-COUNT A **theme** in a piece of writing, a discussion, or a work of art is an important idea or subject that runs through it. tema, asunto, idea principal ❑ *The novel's theme is the conflict between men and women.* El asunto de la novela es el conflicto entre hombres y mujeres. **2** N-COUNT A **theme** in an artist's work or in a work of literature is an idea in it that the artist or writer develops or repeats. tema
→ see **myth**

**Word Partnership** Usar *theme* con:

N. theme **of a book/movie/story** 1 2
ADJ. **central** theme, **common** theme, **dominant** theme, **main** theme, **major** theme, **new** theme, **recurring** theme 1 2

**theme and vari|ation** (themes and variations) N-VAR Music that uses **theme and variation** begins with a particular musical theme and then repeats the theme with small changes. tema y variación

**them|selves** /ðəmsɛlvz/

> **Themselves** is the third person plural reflexive pronoun.

1 PRON You use **themselves** to refer to people, animals, or things when the object of a verb or preposition refers to the same people or things as the subject of the verb. *ellos mismos, ellas mismas, sí mismos, sí mismas, se* ❑ *They all seemed to be enjoying themselves. Todos parecían estarse divirtiendo.* ❑ *The men talked among themselves. Los hombres hablaban entre ellos.* 2 PRON You use **themselves** to emphasize the people or things that you are referring to. **Themselves** is also sometimes used instead of "them" as the object of a verb or preposition. *(ellos) mismos, (ellas) mismas* ❑ *The games themselves are very popular. Los juegos mismos son muy populares.* ❑ *...other people who are in the same position as themselves. ...otras personas que están en la misma posición que ellos.* 3 PRON You use **themselves** instead of "himself or herself" to refer back to the person who is the subject of a sentence without saying whether it is a man or a woman. Some people think this use is incorrect. *a sí mismo, a sí misma* ❑ *What can a patient with heart disease do to help themselves? ¿Qué pueden hacer las personas con males cardiacos para ayudarse?*

**then** /ðɛn/ 1 ADV **Then** means at a particular time in the past or in the future. *entonces, luego, después, antes* ❑ *Since then, house prices have fallen. Los precios de las casas han bajado desde entonces.* ❑ *Until then, he won't need any more money. Hasta entonces, no necesitará más dinero.* 2 ADV You use **then** to say that one thing happens after another, or is after another on a list. *después, luego* ❑ *Add the oil and then the onion. Ponga el aceite y después la cebolla.* 3 ADV You use **then** to signal the end of a topic or the end of a conversation. *pues* ❑ *"I'll talk to you on Friday anyway."—"Yes. Okay then." —De todas formas te llamo el viernes. —Bueno, sí.* 4 ADV You use **then** with words like "now," "well," and "okay," to introduce a new topic or a new point of view. *pues* ❑ *Now then, I'm going to explain everything to you. Muy bien, ahora les explico todo.* 5 ADV You use **then** to introduce the second part of a sentence which begins with "if." The first part of the sentence describes a possible situation, and **then** introduces the result of the situation. *entonces* ❑ *If the answer is "yes," then we need to leave now. Si la respuesta es "sí", entonces ya tenemos que irnos.* 6 ADV You use **then** at the beginning of a sentence or after "and" or "but" to introduce a comment or an extra piece of information to what you have already said. *por otra parte* ❑ *He sounded sincere, but then, he always did. Parecía sincero, pero por otra parte, siempre lo pareció.* 7 **now and then** → see **now** 8 **there and then** → see **there**
→ see also **than**

T

**theo|reti|cal** /θiərɛtɪkᵊl/ ADJ **Theoretical** means based on or using the ideas and abstract principles of a particular subject, rather than its practical aspects. *teórico, hipotético* ❑ *...theoretical physics. ...física teórica*

**theo|rize** /θiəraɪz/ (**theorizes, theorizing, theorized**) V-T/V-I If you **theorize** that something is true or **theorize** about it, you develop an abstract idea or set of ideas about something in order to explain it. *especular, teorizar* ❑ *Police are theorizing that the robbers may be local. La policía especula que podría tratarse de ladrones de la localidad.* ❑ *By studying the way people behave, we can theorize about what they are thinking. Estudiando el comportamiento de las personas, se puede especular sobre lo que están pensando.* ● **theo|rist** /θiərɪst/ (**theorists**) N-COUNT *teórico o teórica* ❑ *...a leading political theorist. ...un importante teórico de la política* ● **theo|riz|ing** N-UNCOUNT *especulación, teoría* ❑ *This is no time for theorizing. No es momento para especulaciones.*

**theo|ry** /θiəri/ (**theories**) 1 N-VAR A **theory** is a formal idea or set of ideas intended to explain something and which is capable of being tested. *teoría* ❑ *...a new theory about historical change. ...una nueva teoría sobre el cambio histórico.* 2 N-COUNT If you have a **theory** about something, you have your own opinion about it which you cannot prove but which you think is true. *teoría* ❑ *There was a theory that he wanted to marry her. Se decía que quería casarse con ella.* 3 N-UNCOUNT The **theory** of a practical subject or skill is the set of rules and principles that form the basis of it. *teoría* ❑ *He taught us music theory. Nos enseñó teoría de la música.* 4 PHRASE You use **in theory** to say that although something is supposed to be true or to happen in the way stated, it may not in fact be true or happen in that way. *teóricamente* ❑ *In theory I'm available day and night. En teoría, estoy disponible día y noche.*
→ see **evolution, experiment, science**

**Word Partnership** Usar *theory* con:

| | |
|---|---|
| N. | theory **and practice** 1<br>**evidence for a** theory, **support for a** theory 1 2<br>**conspiracy** theory 2<br>**learning** theory 3 |
| V. | **advance a** theory, **develop a** theory, **propose a** theory, **test a** theory 1 – 3 |
| ADJ. | **economic** theory, **literary** theory, **scientific** theory 3 |

**thera|pist** /θɛrəpɪst/ (**therapists**) N-COUNT A **therapist** is a person who is skilled in a particular type of therapy, especially psychotherapy. *terapeuta* ❑ *My therapist helped me to deal with my anger. Mi terapeuta me ayudó a manejar mi enojo.*

**the|rap|sid** /θəræpsɪd/ (**therapsids**) N-COUNT **Therapsids** were animals similar to reptiles that lived in prehistoric times and evolved into mammals. *terápsido* [TECHNICAL]

**thera|py** /θɛrəpi/ (**therapies**) 1 N-UNCOUNT **Therapy** is the process of talking to a trained counselor about your emotional problems and your relationships in order to understand and improve the way you feel and behave. *terapia* ❑ *Children may need therapy to help them deal with death. Los niños pueden necesitar terapia para ayudarles a enfrentar la muerte.* 2 N-VAR **Therapy** or a **therapy** is a treatment for a particular illness or condition. *terapia, tratamiento* [MEDICAL] ❑ *...vitamin therapies. ...tratamientos con vitaminas.*
→ see **cancer**

**there**

> Pronounced /ðər, STRONG ðɛr/ for meaning 1, and /ðɛər/ for meanings 2 to 11.

**1** PRON **There** is used as the subject of the verb "be" to say that something exists or does not exist, or to draw attention to it. ❑ *There must be another way of doing this.* *Debe haber otra manera de hacer esto.* ❑ *Are there any cookies left?* *¿Quedaron galletas?* **2** ADV If something is **there,** it exists or is available. *ahí, allí, allá* ❑ *The group of old buildings is still there today.* *El conjunto de viejos edificios sigue allí.* **3** ADV You use **there** to refer to a place which has already been mentioned. *ahí, allí, allá* ❑ *I'm going back to California. My family have lived there for many years.* *Voy a California, mi familia ha vivido ahí por muchos años.* ❑ *"Come on over, if you want."— "How do I get there?"* *—Ven, si quieres. —¿Cómo llego?* **4** ADV You use **there** to indicate a place that you are pointing to or looking at. *ahí, allí, allá* ❑ *There it is, on the corner over there.* *Allá está, en aquella esquina.* ❑ *There she is on the left up there.* *Ahí está ella, a la izquierda, allá.* **5** ADV You use **there** when speaking on the telephone to ask if someone is available to speak to you. *¿se encuentra...?* ❑ *Hello, is Gordon there please?* *Buenas tardes, ¿está Gordon, por favor?* **6** ADV You use **there** to refer to a point that someone has made in a conversation. *en eso* ❑ *I think you're right there, John.* *Creo que tienes razón en eso, John.* **7** ADV You use **there** to refer to a stage that has been reached in an activity or process. *ese punto* ❑ *We are investigating and will take the matter from there.* *Estamos investigando y partiremos de ese punto.* **8** ADV You can use **there** in expressions such as **there you go** or **there we are** when accepting that an unsatisfactory situation cannot be changed. *ahí está* [SPOKEN] ❑ *We've had this argument before, but there we are.* *Ya hemos discutido esto antes, pero seguimos en las mismas.* **9** ADV You can use **there** in expressions such as **there you go** and **there we are** when emphasizing that something proves that you were right. *ahí está* [SPOKEN] ❑ *There you go. I knew you'd be upset.* *¿Ves? Sabía que te iba a molestar.* **10** PHRASE If something happens **there and then** or **then and there,** it happens immediately. *de inmediato* ❑ *Many people thought that he should have resigned there and then.* *Muchos pensaban que debió haber renunciado en ese momento.* **11** CONVENTION You say **"there you are"** or **"there you go"** when you are offering something to someone. *ahí tiene* [SPOKEN] ❑ *"There you go, Mr. Walters," she said, giving him his documents.* *—Listo, Mr. Walters —le dijo al momento de darle sus documentos.*
→ see also **their**

**there|after** /ðɛərǽftər/ ADV **Thereafter** means after the event or date mentioned. *de ahí en adelante* [FORMAL] ❑ *The plan will help you lose 3–4 pounds the first week, and 1–2 pounds the weeks thereafter.* *El plan le ayudará a bajar de un kilo y medio a dos kilos durante la primera semana, y de medio a un kilo las semanas siguientes.*

**there|by** /ðɛərbaɪ/ ADV You use **thereby** to introduce an important result or consequence of the event or action you have just mentioned. *con lo cual* [FORMAL] ❑ *Our bodies sweat, thereby losing heat.* *Nuestro cuerpo suda, y por lo tanto, pierde calor.*

**there|fore** /ðɛərfɔr/ ADV You use **therefore** to introduce a logical result or conclusion. *por lo tanto, por consiguiente, por ende, de modo que* ❑ *The process is much quicker and therefore cheaper.* *El proceso es más rápido y, por lo tanto, menos costoso.*

**ther|mal** /θɜrməl/ **1** ADJ **Thermal** means relating to or caused by heat. *térmico* ❑ *...thermal power stations.* *...centrales de energía térmica.* **2** ADJ **Thermal** clothes are specially designed to keep you warm. *térmico* ❑ *...thermal underwear.* *...ropa interior térmica.*
→ see **solar**

**ther|mal en|er|gy** N-UNCOUNT **Thermal energy** is energy in the form of heat. *energía térmica*

**ther|mal equi|lib|rium** N-UNCOUNT Two or more substances that are in **thermal equilibrium** have the same temperature. *equilibrio térmico* [TECHNICAL]

**ther|mal ex|pan|sion** N-UNCOUNT **Thermal expansion** is the increase in a substance's size or volume that occurs when it is heated. *expansión térmica* [TECHNICAL]

**ther|mal pol|lu|tion** N-UNCOUNT **Thermal pollution** is an increase in the temperature of a river or lake that is harmful to the organisms living there. Thermal pollution often occurs when water that has been used in industrial processes is returned to a river or lake. *contaminación térmica* [TECHNICAL]

**ther|mo|cline** /θɜrməklaɪn/ (**thermoclines**) N-COUNT A **thermocline** is a layer of water in an ocean or lake that separates the warmer water on the surface from the colder water below it. *termoclina* [TECHNICAL]

**ther|mo|cou|ple** /θɜrməkʌpəl/ (**thermocouples**) N-COUNT A **thermocouple** is a kind of thermometer that uses an electric current to measure temperature. *termopar, termocupla* [TECHNICAL]

**ther|mom|eter** /θərmɒmɪtər/ (**thermometers**) N-COUNT A **thermometer** is an instrument for measuring the temperature of a place or of a person's body. *termómetro*
→ see Word Web: **thermometer**

**ther|mo|sphere** /θɜrməsfɪər/ (**thermospheres**) N-COUNT The **thermosphere** is the highest layer of the Earth's atmosphere. *termosfera* [TECHNICAL]

**these**

> The determiner is pronounced /ðiz/. The pronoun is pronounced /ðiz/.

**1** DET You use **these** to refer to someone or something that you have already mentioned or identified. *estos, estas* ❑ *These people can make quick decisions which would take us months.* *Estas personas pueden tomar decisiones rápidas que a nosotros nos llevarían meses.* • **These** is also a pronoun. *estos, estas* ❑ *These are good players.* *Estos son buenos jugadores.* **2** DET You use **these** to introduce people or things that you are going to talk about. *estos, estas* ❑ *If you're looking for a builder, these phone numbers will be useful.* *Si estás buscando constructores, estos números de teléfono te pueden servir.* • **These** is also a pronoun. *estos, estas* ❑ *These are some of the things you can do for yourself.* *Estas son cosas que tú mismo puedes hacer.* **3** DET In spoken English, people use **these** to introduce people or things into a story. *estos, estas* ❑ *I was by myself and these guys suddenly came towards me.* *Yo estaba sola, y de repente se me dejaron venir estos tipos.* **4** PRON You use **these** when you are identifying a group or asking about

**Word Web** thermometer

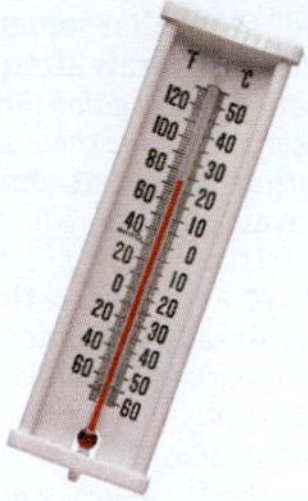


The first scientist to **measure** heat was Galileo. He invented a simple water **thermometer** in 1593. But his thermometer did not have a **scale** to show exact temperatures. In 1714, a German named Daniel Fahrenheit invented a **mercury** thermometer. In 1724, he added the **Fahrenheit scale** of temperatures with 32°F* as the **freezing** temperature of water. On this scale, water **boils** at 212°F. In 1742, **Anders Celsius** invented the **centigrade** scale. Centigrade means "divided into 100 **degrees**." On this scale, water freezes at 0°C* and boils at 100°C.

*32°F=thirty-two degrees Fahrenheit.*
*°C=zero degrees Celsius or zero degrees centigrade.*

their identity. *estos, estas* ❑ *These are my children. Estos son mis hijos* 5 DET You use **these** to refer to people or things that are near you, especially when you touch them or point to them. *estos, estas* ❑ *These scissors are heavy. Estas tijeras pesan.* • **These** is also a pronoun. *estos, estas* ❑ *These are the people who are helping us. Estas son las personas que nos están ayudando.* 6 DET You use **these** in the expression **these days** to mean "at the present time." *en esta época* ❑ *These days, people appreciate a chance to relax. En esta época, la gente agradece la oportunidad de relajarse.*

**the|sis** /θi̲sɪs/ (**theses** /θi̲siz/) 1 N-COUNT A **thesis** is an idea or theory that is expressed as a statement and is discussed in a logical way. *argumento* ❑ *This thesis is only partly true. Esta tesis es válida sólo en parte.* 2 N-COUNT A **thesis** is a long piece of writing based on your own ideas and research that you do as part of a college degree, especially a higher degree such as a Ph.D. *tesis*
→ see **graduation**

**they** /ðeɪ/

**They** is a third person plural pronoun. **They** is used as the subject of a verb.

1 PRON You use **they** to refer to a group of people, animals, or things. *ellos, ellas* ❑ *She said goodbye to the children as they left for school. Se despidió de los niños cuando se iban a la escuela.* ❑ *People matter because of who they are, not what they have. Las personas son importantes por quiénes son, no por lo que tienen.* 2 PRON You use **they** instead of "he or she" to refer to a person without saying whether that person is a man or a woman. Some people think this use is incorrect. *él, ella* ❑ *The teacher is not responsible for the student's success or failure. They are only there to help the student learn. El maestro no es responsable del éxito o el fracaso de los estudiantes, su tarea es ayudarlos a aprender.* 3 PRON You use **they** in expressions such as **they say** or **they call it** to refer to people in general when you are making general statements about what people say, think, or do. *se dice* ❑ *They say there are plenty of opportunities out there. Dicen que allá hay innumerables oportunidades.*

**they'd** /ðeɪd/ 1 **They'd** is a spoken form of "they had," especially when "had" is an auxiliary verb. *forma hablada de **they had*** ❑ *They'd both lived on this road all their lives. Los dos habían vivido en esta calle toda su vida.* 2 **They'd** is a spoken form of "they would." *forma hablada de **they would*** ❑ *He agreed that they'd visit her later. Quedaron de acuerdo en que la visitarían más tarde.*

**they'll** /ðeɪl/ **They'll** is the usual spoken form of "they will." *forma hablada de **they will*** ❑ *They'll probably be here Monday. Quizá estén aquí el lunes.*

**they're** /ðeər/ **They're** is the usual spoken form of "they are." *forma hablada usual de **they are*** ❑ *People eat when they're depressed. Cuando está deprimida, la gente come.*
→ see also **their**

**they've** /ðeɪv/ **They've** is the usual spoken form of "they have," especially when "have" is an auxiliary verb. *forma hablada de **they have*** ❑ *They've gone out. Salieron.*

**thick** /θɪ̲k/ (**thicker, thickest**) 1 ADJ Something that is **thick** has a large distance between its two opposite sides. *grueso* ❑ *...a thick slice of bread and butter. ...una rebanada gruesa de pan con mantequilla.* ❑ *He wore thick glasses. Usaba lentes gruesos.* • **thick|ly** ADV *de forma gruesa* ❑ *Slice the meat thickly. Rebana gruesa la carne.* 2 ADJ You can use **thick** to talk or ask about how wide or deep something is. *grueso, gordo* ❑ *The folder was two inches thick. El fólder tenía cinco centímetros de grueso.* ❑ *How thick are these walls? ¿Qué tan gruesos son estos muros?* • **thick|ness** N-VAR (**thicknesses**) *grosor* ❑ *The cooking time depends on the thickness of the steaks. El tiempo de cocimiento depende del grosor de los bisteces.* 3 ADJ If something that consists of several things is **thick**, it has a large number of them very close together. *espeso* ❑ *...thick, wavy hair. ...cabellera espesa y ondulada.* • **thick|ly** ADV *de forma espesa* ❑ *The trees grew thickly. Los árboles crecían muy juntos.* 4 ADJ **Thick** smoke, fog, or cloud is difficult to see through. *espeso* ❑ *The smoke was thick and black. El humo era espeso y negro.* 5 ADJ **Thick** liquids are fairly stiff and solid and do not flow easily. *espeso* ❑ *It rained last night, so the garden was thick mud. Llovió anoche, así que el jardín estaba lleno de lodo.*

**Word Partnership** Usar *thick* con:

| | |
|---|---|
| N. | thick **glass**, thick **ice**, thick **layer**, thick **lips**, thick **neck**, thick **slice**, thick **wall** 1<br>thick **carpet**, **feet/inches** thick 2<br>thick **beard**, thick **fur**, thick **grass**, thick **hair** 3<br>thick **air**, thick **clouds**, thick **fog**, thick **smoke** 4 |
| ADV. | **so** thick, **too** thick, **very** thick 1–5 |

**thick|en** /θɪ̲kən/ (**thickens, thickening, thickened**) V-T/V-I If something **thickens**, or if you **thicken** it, it becomes more closely grouped together or more solid than it was before. *espesar(se), dar consistencia* ❑ *The dust thickened into a cloud. El polvo se espesó, hasta formar una nube.* ❑ *Thicken the soup with potato. Ponle papa a la sopa para darle consistencia.*

**thief** /θif/ (**thieves** /θivz/) N-COUNT A **thief** is a person who steals something from another person. *ladrón o ladrona, ratero o ratera, caco* ❑ *The thieves took his camera. Los ladrones se llevaron su cámara.*

**thigh** /θaɪ/ (**thighs**) N-COUNT Your **thighs** are the top parts of your legs, between your knees and your hips. *muslo*
→ see **body**

**thin** /θɪn/ (**thinner, thinnest, thins, thinning, thinned**) **1** ADJ If something is **thin,** there is a small distance between its two opposite surfaces. *delgado, fino* ❑ *...a thin cable. ...un cable delgado.* ❑ *...a book printed on thin paper. ...un libro impreso en papel delgado.* ● **thin|ly** ADV *delgadamente* ❑ *Peel and thinly slice the onion. Pela las cebollas y rebánalas finamente.* **2** ADJ A person or animal that is **thin** has no extra fat on their body. *delgado, flaco* ❑ *He was a tall, thin man. Fue un hombre alto y delgado.* **3** ADJ Liquids that are **thin** are weak and watery. *claro, aguado* ❑ *The soup was thin and clear. A la sopa le faltaba consistencia.* **4** V-T/V-I When you **thin** something or when it **thins,** it becomes less crowded because people or things have been removed from it. *escasear(se)* ❑ *By midnight the crowd was thinning. Para medianoche casi no había nadie.* ● **Thin out** means the same as **thin.** *disminuir, hacer menos denso* ❑ *Thin out plants if they become crowded. Entresaca plantas si se tupen demasiado.*

**Thesaurus** *thin* Ver también:

ADJ. flimsy, transparent; (*ant.*) dense, solid, thick **1**
lean, skinny, slender, slim; (*ant.*) fat, heavy **2**
watery, weak; (*ant.*) thick **3**

**Word Partnership** Usar *thin* con:

N. thin **film**, thin **ice**, thin **layer**, thin **line**, **razor** thin, thin **slice**, thin **smile**, thin **strips** **1**
thin **body**, thin **face**, thin **fingers**, thin **legs**, thin **lips**, thin **mouth** **1** **2**
thin **man/woman** **2**
ADJ. **long and** thin **1**
**tall and** thin **2**
ADV. **extremely** thin, **too** thin, **very** thin **1** – **3**

**thing**
❶ NOUN USES
❷ PHRASES

❶ **thing** /θɪŋ/ (**things**) **1** N-COUNT You can use **thing** as a substitute for another word when you cannot, need not, or do not want to be more precise. *cosa, eso* ❑ *What's that thing in the middle of the road? ¿Que es eso, en medio de la calle?* ❑ *She was clearing away the breakfast things. Estaba recogiendo lo del desayuno.* ❑ *They spend their money on things like rent and groceries. Gastan su dinero en cosas como la renta y alimentos.* **2** N-SING **Thing** is often used instead of the pronouns "anything," or "everything" in order to emphasize what you are saying. *nada* ❑ *Don't you worry about a thing. No te preocupes por nada.* ❑ *It isn't going to solve a single thing. No va a resolver nada.* **3** N-COUNT A **thing** is a physical object that is considered as having no life of its own. *cosa* ❑ *It's not a thing. It's a human being! No es una cosa, ¡es un ser humano!* **4** N-COUNT You can call a person or an animal a particular **thing** when you want to mention a particular quality that they have and express your feelings toward them, usually affectionate feelings. *cosita* [INFORMAL] ❑ *She is such a cute little thing. ¡Es una lindura!* **5** N-PLURAL Your **things** are your clothes or possessions. *cosas* ❑ *Sara told him to take all his things and not to return. Sara le dijo que sacara sus cosas y no volviera.* **6** N-PLURAL **Things** can refer to the situation or life in general and the way it is changing or affecting you. *cosa* ❑ *Everyone agrees things are getting better. Todos están de acuerdo en que las cosas van mejorando.*

❷ **thing** /θɪŋ/ (**things**) **1** PHRASE If you do something **first thing,** you do it at the beginning of the day, before you do anything else. If you do it **last thing,** you do it at the end of the day, before you go to bed or go to sleep. *lo primero, lo último* ❑ *I'll go see her, first thing tomorrow. Voy a verla a primera hora.* **2** PHRASE You can say **for one thing** when you are explaining a statement or answering a question, to suggest that you are not giving the whole explanation or answer, and that there are other points that you could add to it. *en primer término* ❑ *She couldn't sell the house because for one thing, it was too big. No pudo vender la casa, pues, para empezar, era demasiado grande.* **3** PHRASE You say **"the thing is"** to introduce an explanation, comment, or opinion that relates to something that has just been said. **"The thing is"** is often used to identify a problem relating to what has just been said. *lo importante es* [SPOKEN] ❑ *I have a place at college. The thing is, I'm not sure I want to go anymore. Me aceptaron en la universidad, pero la verdad, ya no estoy seguro de querer ir.*

**think**
❶ VERB AND NOUN USES
❷ PHRASES
❸ PHRASAL VERBS

t

❶ **think** /θɪŋk/ (**thinks, thinking, thought**) **1** V-T/V-I If you **think** that something is the case, you believe that it is the case. *pensar, creer, considerar* ❑ *I think you will agree I made the right decision. Creo que estarás de acuerdo en que tomé la decisión correcta.* ❑ *What do you think of my idea? ¿Qué te parece mi idea?* ● **think|ing** N-UNCOUNT *idea, opinión, pensamiento* ❑ *...his thinking on education. ...sus ideas sobre la educación.* **2** V-T If you say that you **think** that something is true or will happen, you mean that you have the impression that it is true or will happen, although you are not certain of the facts. *considerar, suponer* ❑ *Nora thought he was seventeen years old. Nora pensó que él tenía diecisiete años.* **3** V-I When you **think** about ideas or problems, you make a mental effort to consider them. *meditar, reflexionar, pensar* ❑ *She closed her eyes* for a moment, trying to think. *Cerró los ojos un momento, tratando de concentrarse.* ❑ *I have often thought about this problem. Muchas veces he reflexionado sobre ese problema.* ● **think|ing** N-UNCOUNT *pensamiento, idea, opinión* ❑ *...quick thinking. ...reacciones rápidas.* **4** V-T/V-I If you **think of** something, it comes into your mind or you remember it. *ocurrirse, imaginar(se)* ❑ *Nobody could think of anything to say. A nadie se le ocurría qué decir.* ❑ *I was trying to think what else we could do. Estaba tratando de pensar qué otra cosa podíamos hacer.* **5** V-T If you **are thinking** something at a particular moment, you have words or ideas in your mind without saying them out loud. *pensar, reflexionar* ❑ *She must be sick, Tatiana thought. Debe estar enferma, pensó Tatiana.* ❑ *I remember thinking how lovely he looked. Recuerdo haber pensado en lo guapo que se veía.* **6** V-T/V-I If you **think** a lot **of** someone or something, you admire them very much or think they are very good. *tener en buen concepto* ❑ *To tell the truth, I don't think much of doctors. La verdad, no tengo muy buena opinión de los médicos.* ❑ *Everyone in my family thought very highly of him. Todos en mi familia lo estimaban mucho.* **7** V-I If you **are thinking of** or **are thinking about** taking a particular course of action, you are considering it as a possible course of action. *pensar, considerar, idear* ❑ *Martin was thinking of taking legal action. Martin estaba pensando en recurrir a las autoridades.* **8** → see also **thinking, thought**

| **Thesaurus** | *think* | Ver también: |
|---|---|---|
| v. | believe, consider, feel, judge, understand ❶ **1** | |
| | analyze, evaluate, meditate, reflect, study ❶ **3** | |
| | recall, remember; (*ant.*) forget ❶ **4** | |

❷ **think** /θɪŋk/ (**thinks, thinking, thought**) **1** PHRASE You use **"I think"** as a way of being polite when you are explaining or suggesting something, giving your opinion, or responding to an offer. *creo, opino* ❑ *I think I'll go home. Creo que me voy a casa.* ❑ *Thanks, but I think I can do it myself. Gracias, pero creo que puedo hacerlo sola.* **2** PHRASE If you **think nothing of** doing something that other people might consider difficult, strange, or wrong, you consider it to be easy or normal. *hacer como si nada* ❑ *I thought nothing of walking 20 miles. No me parecía gran cosa caminar 20 kilómetros.*

T

❸ **think** /θɪŋk/ (**thinks, thinking, thought**) ▸ **think back** PHR-VERB If you **think back**, you make an effort to remember things that happened to you in the past. *recordar, hacer memoria* ❑ *I thought back to the time when my son was very ill. Me remonté a la época en que mi hijo estaba muy enfermo.* ▸ **think over** PHR-VERB If you **think** something **over**, you consider it carefully before making a decision. *pensar, reflexionar* ❑ *She said she needs time to think it over. Dice que necesita tiempo para pensarlo.* ▸ **think through** PHR-VERB If you **think** a situation **through**, you consider it thoroughly, together with all its possible effects or consequences. *pensar detenidamente* ❑ *He went for a long bike ride to think the problem through. Se fue a dar un largo paseo en bici para analizar el problema.* ❑ *The administration has not thought through what it will do once the war ends. El gobierno no sabe todavía qué hará una vez que termine la guerra.* ▸ **think up** PHR-VERB If you **think** something **up**, for example, an idea or plan, you invent it using mental effort. *idear, crear, inventar, imaginar* ❑ *Julian has been thinking up new ways of raising money. Julian ha estado pensando en cómo juntar más dinero.*

**think|ing** /θɪŋkɪŋ/ → see **think**

**third** /θɜrd/ (**thirds**) **1** ORD The **third** item in a series is the one that you count as number three. *tercero* ❑ *The third door on the right. La tercera puerta a la derecha.* **2** ORD A **third** is one of three equal parts of something. *tercio, tercera parte* ❑ *A third of the cost went into machinery. Una tercera parte del costo se fue en maquinaria.*

**Third World** N-PROPER Countries that are poor and do not have much industrial development are sometimes referred to together as **the Third World.** Some people find this term offensive. *Tercer Mundo* ❑ *...development in the Third World. ...el desarrollo del Tercer Mundo.*

**thirst** /θɜrst/ (**thirsts**) **1** N-VAR **Thirst** is the feeling of wanting to drink something. *sed* ❑ *Drink water to quench your thirst. Toma agua para calmar la sed.* **2** N-UNCOUNT **Thirst** is the condition of not having enough to drink. *sed* ❑ *They died of thirst. Murieron de sed.*

**thirsty** /θɜrsti/ (**thirstier, thirstiest**) ADJ If you are **thirsty,** you feel a need to drink something. *sediento* ❑ *Drink whenever you feel thirsty. Bebe cada vez que sientas sed.*

**thir|teen** /θɜrtin/ (**thirteens**) NUM **Thirteen** is the number 13. *trece*

**thir|teenth** /θɜrtinθ/ ORD The **thirteenth** item in a series is the one that you count as number thirteen. *decimotercero, treceavo* ❑ *...his thirteenth birthday. ...su decimotercer cumpleaños.*

**thir|ti|eth** /θɜrtiəθ/ ORD The **thirtieth** item in a series is the one that you count as number thirty. *trigésimo* ❑ *...the thirtieth anniversary of my parents' wedding. ...el treinta aniversario de boda de mis padres.*

**thir|ty** /θɜrti/ (**thirties**) **1** NUM **Thirty** is the number 30. *treinta* **2** N-PLURAL When you talk about the **thirties,** you are referring to numbers between 30 and 39. For example, if you are **in** your **thirties,** you are aged between 30 and 39. If the temperature is **in the thirties,** the temperature is between 30 and 39 degrees. *treinta* ❑ *He lived in Chicago throughout his twenties and early thirties. Vivió en Chicago de los veinte a los treinta y tantos años.* **3** N-PLURAL **The thirties** is the decade between 1930 and 1939. *década de los treinta, los treinta, los años treinta* ❑ *She was well-known in the thirties. Fue muy conocida en la década de los treinta.*

**this**

The determiner is pronounced /ðɪs/. In other cases, **this** is pronounced /ðɪs/.

**1** DET You use **this** to refer back to a particular person or thing that has been mentioned or implied. *este, esta* ❑ *The president is prepared for this challenge. El presidente está preparado para este reto.* ● **This** is also a pronoun. *este, esta, esto* ❑ *I have seen many movies, but never one like this. He visto muchas películas, pero ninguna como esta.* **2** PRON You use **this** to introduce someone or something that you are going to talk about. *este, esta, esto* ❑ *This is* *what I will do. I will telephone Anna and explain.* Esto es lo que voy a hacer, hablarle a Anna y explicarle. ● **This** is also a determiner. este, esta ❑ *This report is from our Science Unit.* Este reporte proviene de nuestra Unidad Científica. **3** DET In spoken English, people use **this** to introduce a person or thing into a story. este, esta ❑ *I was watching what was going on, when this girl came up to me.*, Estaba viendo lo que pasaba, cuando se me acercó esta niña. **4** PRON You use **this** to refer to a person or thing that is near you, especially when you touch them or point to them. When there are two or more people or things near you, **this** refers to the nearest one. este, esta, esto ❑ *Is this what you were looking for?* ¿Es esto lo que busca? ❑ *"If you'd like a different one I'll gladly change it for you." — "No, this is great."* —Si quiere algo diferente, con gusto se lo cambio. —No, este está perfecto. ● **This** is also a determiner. este, esta ❑ *I like this room much better than mine.* Este cuarto me gusta mucho más que el mío. **5** PRON You use **this** when you refer to a general situation, activity, or event which is happening or has just happened and which you feel involved in. esto ❑ *I thought, this is why I traveled thousands of miles.* Esto es por lo que viajé miles de kilómetros, pensé. ❑ *Tim, this is awful.* Tim, es horrible. **6** DET You use **this** to refer to the next occurrence in the future of a particular day, month, season, or festival. este, esta ❑ *...this Sunday's performance.*, ...la función de este domingo. ❑ *We're getting married this June.* Nos casamos este junio. **7** PRON You use **this is** in order to say who you are or what organization you are representing, when you are speaking on the telephone, radio, or television. soy, está usted escuchando ❑ *Hello, this is John Thompson.* Buenas tardes, soy John Thompson. **8** → see also **these** **9** PHRASE If you say that you are doing or talking about **this and that,** or **this, that, and the other** you mean that you are doing or talking about a variety of things that you do not want to specify. esto y aquello ❑ *"And what are you doing now?" — "Oh this and that."* —¿Y qué estás haciendo ahora? —Cosas.

**thong** /θɔŋ/ (**thongs**) **1** N-COUNT A **thong** is a piece of underwear worn on the lower part of your body that has a very narrow piece of cloth at the back. tanga, hilo dental **2** N-COUNT **Thongs** are open shoes which are held on your foot by a V-shaped strap that goes between your big toe and the toe next to it. chancla, chancla de pata de gallo

**thor|ax** /θɔræks/ (**thoraxes** or **thoraces** /θɔrəsiz/) **1** N-COUNT Your **thorax** is the part of your body between your neck and your waist. tórax [MEDICAL] **2** N-COUNT An insect's **thorax** is the central part of its body to which the legs and wings are attached. tórax [TECHNICAL] → see **insect**

**thor|ough** /θɜroʊ/ **1** ADJ A **thorough** action or activity is one that is done very carefully and in a detailed way. completo, cuidadoso, concienzudo, riguroso, minucioso ❑ *We are making a thorough investigation.* Estamos investigando a fondo. ● **thor|ough|ly** ADV completamente, perfectamente ❑ *The food must be thoroughly cooked.* Los alimentos deben estar perfectamente cocidos. ● **thor|ough|ness** N-UNCOUNT esmero, rigor ❑ *...the thoroughness of the work.* ...la minuciosidad del trabajo. **2** ADJ Someone who is **thorough** is always very careful in their work, so that nothing is forgotten. minucioso, riguroso, cuidadoso ❑ *He was calm and thorough.* Era calmado y cuidadoso. ● **thor|ough|ness** N-UNCOUNT meticulosidad, esmero, rigor ❑ *His thoroughness and attention to detail is amazing.* Su rigor y atención a los detalles son impresionantes. **3** ADJ **Thorough** is used to emphasize the large degree or extent of something. completo, perfecto ❑ *This seemed like a thorough waste of time.* Parecía una total pérdida de tiempo. ● **thor|ough|ly** ADV completamente, perfectamente ❑ *I thoroughly enjoy your program.* Verdaderamente disfruto tu programa.

**those**

> The determiner is pronounced /ðoʊz/. The pronoun is pronounced /ðoʊz/.

**1** DET You use **those** to refer to people or things which have already been mentioned. aquellos, aquellas, esos, esas ❑ *I don't know any of those people.* No conozco a ninguna de esas personas. ● **Those** is also a pronoun. aquellos, aquellas, esos, esas ❑ *You had some concerns. Tell me about those.* Algo te preocupaba, dímelo. **2** DET You use **those** when you are referring to people or things that are a distance away from you in position or time, especially when you indicate or point to them. aquellos, aquellas, esos, esas ❑ *What are those buildings?*, ¿Qué son aquellos edificios? ● **Those** is also a pronoun. aquellos, aquellas, esos, esas ❑ *Those are nice shoes.*, Esos son unos zapatos bonitos. **3** PRON You use **those** to mean "people." quien, quienes ❑ *Selfish behavior hurts those around us.* El comportamiento egoísta hiere a quienes nos rodean.

**though** /ðoʊ/ **1** CONJ You use **though** to introduce a statement in a subordinate clause which contrasts with the statement in the main clause, or makes it seem surprising. aunque, si bien, bien que ❑ *Everything I told them was correct, though I forgot a few things.* Todo lo que les dije estaba bien, a pesar de que se me olvidaron algunas cosas. ❑ *I like him. Though he makes me angry sometimes.* Él me agrada, aunque a veces me enoja. **2** **as though** → see **as** **3** **even though** → see **even**

**thought** /θɔt/ (**thoughts**) **1** **Thought** is the past tense and past participle of **think.** pasado y participio pasado de **think** **2** N-COUNT A **thought** is an idea or opinion. pensamiento, idea, opinión ❑ *The thought of Nick made her sad.* Pensar en Nick la ponía triste. ❑ *I just had a thought.* Se me acaba de ocurrir algo. ❑ *Many of you wrote to us to tell us your thoughts.* Muchos de ustedes nos escribieron para expresar sus ideas. **3** N-UNCOUNT **Thought** is the activity of thinking, especially deeply, carefully, or logically. pensamiento, idea, reflexión, opinión ❑ *Alice was deep in thought.* Alice estaba sumida en sus pensamientos. ❑ *He gave some thought to what she told him.* Reflexionó sobre lo que ella le había dicho. **4** N-UNCOUNT **Thought** is the group of ideas and beliefs which belongs, for example, to a particular religion, philosophy, science, or political party. pensamiento ❑ *...the history of Western thought.* ...la historia de las ideas occidentales.

**thought|ful** /θɔtfəl/ **1** ADJ If you are **thoughtful,** you are quiet and serious because you are thinking about something. pensativo, meditabundo ❑ *Nancy was looking thoughtful.* Nancy se veía pensativa. ● **thought|ful|ly** ADV cuidadosamente, a fondo ❑ *Daniel nodded thoughtfully.* Daniel movió la

t

*cabeza pensativo.* **2** ADJ If you describe someone as **thoughtful,** you approve of them because they remember what other people want, need, or feel, and try not to upset them. *atento, considerado* ❑ *...a thoughtful and caring man. ...un hombre considerado y bondadoso.* ● **thought|ful|ly** ADV *consideradamente* ❑ *He thoughtfully brought flowers to the party. Amablemente llevó flores a la fiesta.*

**thou|sand** /θaʊzənd/ (**thousands**)

> The plural form is **thousand** after a number, or after a word or expression referring to a number, such as "several" or "a few."

**1** NUM **A thousand** or **one thousand** is the number 1,000. *mil* ❑ *...five thousand people. ...cinco mil personas.* **2** QUANT If you refer to **thousands of** things or people, you are emphasizing that there are very many of them. *miles, montones* ❑ *I must have driven past that place thousands of times. Debo haber pasado por ese lugar miles de veces.* ● You can also use **thousands** as a pronoun. *miles* ❑ *Thousands came to his funeral. Miles asistieron a su funeral.*

**thread** /θrɛd/ (**threads, threading, threaded**) **1** N-VAR **Thread** or a **thread** is a long very thin piece of a material such as cotton, nylon, or silk, especially one that is used in sewing. *hilo, hebra* ❑ *...a piece of thread. ...un pedazo de hilo.* **2** V-T When you **thread** a needle, you put a piece of thread through the hole in the top of the needle in order to sew with it. *ensartar, enhebrar* ❑ *I sat down and threaded a needle. Me senté a ensartar una aguja.* **3** N-COUNT The **thread** of a story or a situation is an aspect of it that connects all the different parts together. *hilo, secuencia* ❑ *He lost the thread of the story. Perdió el hilo de la historia.* **4** N-COUNT The **thread** on a screw, or on something such as a lid, is the raised spiral line around it which allows it to be fixed in place by twisting. *rosca, filete* **5** V-T/V-I If you **thread** your **way** through a group of people or things, or **thread through** it, you move through it carefully. *abrirse paso, abrirse camino* ❑ *Slowly she threaded her way back through the crowd. Lentamente se abrió camino entre la multitud.* **6** V-T If you **thread** small objects such as beads onto a string or thread, you join them together by pushing the string or thread through them. *ensartar* ❑ *She was threading glass beads on a string. Estaba ensartando cuentas de vidrio en un cordón.* **7** N-COUNT On websites such as newsgroups, a **thread** is one of the subjects that is being written about. *tema* [COMPUTING] ❑ *You can go back to previous threads and read them. Puedes volver a temas anteriores y leerlos.*

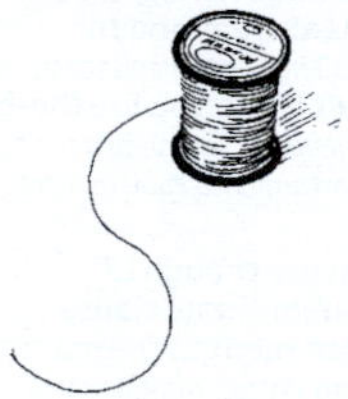

thread

T

**threat** /θrɛt/ (**threats**) **1** N-VAR A **threat to** a person or thing is a danger that something bad might happen to them. A **threat** is also the cause of this danger. *riesgo, peligro, amenaza* ❑ *Stress is a threat to people's health. El estrés es un riesgo para la salud de las personas.* **2** N-COUNT A **threat** is a statement by someone that they will hurt you in some way, especially if you do not do what they want. *amenaza* ❑ *He may carry out his threat to leave. Podría cumplir su amenaza de irse.*

**Word Partnership** Usar *threat* con:

ADJ. **biggest** threat, **greatest** threat, **major** threat **1**
**credible** threat, **potential** threat, **real** threat, **serious** threat, **significant** threat **1** **2**

N. threat **to** ***someone's*** **health** **1**
threat **of attack**, threat **to peace**, threat **to stability**, threat **of a strike**, **terrorist** threat, threat **of violence**, threat **of war** **1** **2**
**death** threat **2**

**threat|en** /θrɛtən/ (**threatens, threatening, threatened**) V-T If a person **threatens to** do something bad to you, or if they **threaten** you, they say or imply that they will hurt you in some way, especially if you do not do what they want. *amenazar* ❑ *Army officers threatened to destroy the town. Los oficiales del ejército amenazaron con destruir la ciudad.* ❑ *If you threaten me I will go to the police. Si me amenazas, recurriré a la policía.*

**threat|en|ing** **1** ADJ ❑ *...threatening behavior. ...comportamiento amenazador.* **2** V-T If something **threatens** people or things, it is likely to harm them. *amenazar, poner en riesgo* ❑ *The fire threatened a street of houses just off the freeway. El fuego puso en riesgo una serie de casas cerca de la carretera.* **3** V-T If something bad **threatens to** happen, it seems likely to happen. *amenazar, amagar* ❑ *It's threatening to rain. Presagia lluvia.*

**three** /θri/ (**threes**) NUM **Three** is the number 3. *tres* ❑ *We waited three months before going back. Esperamos tres meses para volver.*

**three-dimensional** ADJ A **three-dimensional** object is solid rather than flat, because it can be measured in three different directions, usually the height, length, and width. *tridimensional* ❑ *...a three-dimensional model. ...un modelo tridimensional.*

**three-quarters** QUANT **Three-quarters** is an amount that is three out of four equal parts of something. *tres cuartos, tres cuartas partes* ❑ *Three-quarters of the students are African-American. Tres cuartas partes de los estudiantes son afroamericanos.* ● **Three-quarters** is also a pronoun. *tres cuartas partes* ❑ *Applications have increased by three-quarters. Las inscripciones se han incrementado en tres cuartas partes.*

**thresh|old** /θrɛʃhoʊld/ (**thresholds**) **1** N-COUNT The **threshold** of a building or room is the floor in the doorway, or the doorway itself. *umbral, puerta* ❑ *He stopped at the threshold of the bedroom. Se detuvo a la puerta de la recámara.* **2** N-COUNT A **threshold** is an amount, level, or limit on a scale. *umbral* ❑ *Mathers has a high threshold for pain. El umbral del dolor de Mathers es alto.* **3** PHRASE If you are **on the threshold of** something exciting or new, you are about to experience it. *en el umbral de, a las puertas de* ❑ *We are on the threshold of a new age of discovery. Estamos a las puertas de una nueva era de descubrimientos.*

**thrift** /θrɪft/ N-UNCOUNT **Thrift** is the quality and practice of being careful with money and not wasting things. economía, ahorro, frugalidad ❑ *Is thrift a thing of the past? ¿Será el ahorro algo del pasado?*

**thrift shop** (**thrift shops**) N-COUNT A **thrift shop** or **thrift store** is a shop that sells used goods cheaply and gives its profits to a charity. bazar de cosas usadas

**thrill** /θrɪl/ (**thrills, thrilling, thrilled**) **1** N-COUNT If something gives you a **thrill,** it gives you a sudden feeling of great excitement, pleasure, or fear. emoción ❑ *I can remember the thrill of opening my birthday presents. Recuerdo la emoción de abrir mis regalos de cumpleaños.* **2** V-T If something **thrills** you, it gives you a feeling of great pleasure and excitement. emocionar, entusiasmar ❑ *The atmosphere both terrified and thrilled him. El ambiente lo aterrorizó y emocionó al mismo tiempo.*

**thrill|er** /θrɪlər/ (**thrillers**) N-COUNT A **thriller** is a book, movie, or play that tells an exciting fictional story about something such as criminal activities or spying. de suspenso ❑ *...a tense crime thriller. ...una tensa novela negra.*

**thrill|ing** /θrɪlɪŋ/ ADJ Something that is **thrilling** is very exciting and enjoyable. emocionante ❑ *...a thrilling adventure movie. ...una emocionante película de aventuras.*

**thrive** /θraɪv/ (**thrives, thriving, thrived**) V-I If someone or something **thrives,** they do well and are successful, healthy, or strong. prosperar, enriquecerse, tener éxito ❑ *He appears to be thriving. Aparentemente está prosperando.* ❑ *Her company continues to thrive. Su compañía sigue teniendo éxito.* ❑ *Many people thrive on a stressful lifestyle. Muchas personas triunfan en un estilo de vida estresante.*

**throat** /θroʊt/ (**throats**) **1** N-COUNT Your **throat** is the back of your mouth and the top part of the tubes that go down into your stomach and your lungs. garganta ❑ *She had a sore throat. Le dolía la garganta.* **2** N-COUNT Your **throat** is the front part of your neck. cuello ❑ *His tie was loosened at his throat. Tenía floja la corbata.* **3** PHRASE If you **clear** your **throat,** you cough once either to make it easier to speak or to attract people's attention. aclararse la garganta, carraspear ❑ *Crossley cleared his throat and spoke. Crossley carraspeó y habló.*

**throne** /θroʊn/ (**thrones**) **1** N-COUNT A **throne** is a decorative chair used by a king, queen, or emperor on important official occasions. trono **2** N-SING You can talk about **the throne** as a way of referring to the position of being king, queen, or emperor. trono ❑ *...the queen's 50 years on the throne. ...los 50 años de la reina en el trono.*

**through**

1. ADVERBS AND PREPOSITIONS: PHYSICAL MOVEMENTS AND POSITIONS
2. ADVERBS AND PREPOSITIONS, ABSTRACT USES: TIMES, EXPERIENCES, CAUSES
3. ADJECTIVES

**❶ through** **1** PREP To move, cut, or travel **through** something means to move, cut, or travel from one side or end to the other. por, a través de ❑ *Go straight through that door. Entra directamente por esa puerta.* ❑ *We walked through the crowd. Caminamos entre la multitud* ● **Through** is also an adverb. de un lado a otro ❑ *There was a hole in the wall and water was coming through. Había un hoyo en la pared, por donde se metía el agua.* **2** PREP If you see, hear, or feel something **through** a particular thing, that thing is between you and the thing you can see, hear, or feel. a través, por ❑ *Alice looked through the window. Alice se asomó por la ventana.*

**❷ through** **1** PREP If something happens or exists **through** a period of time, it happens or exists from the beginning until the end. durante ❑ *She kept quiet all through breakfast. Estuvo callada durante todo el desayuno.* ● **Through** is also an adverb. continuamente ❑ *We'll be working right through to the summer. Vamos a estar trabajando todo el tiempo hasta el verano.* **2** PREP If something happens from a particular period of time **through** another, it starts at the first period and continues until the end of the second period. de ...a ❑ *The office is open Monday through Friday from 9 to 5. La oficina abre de lunes a viernes, de 9 a 5.* **3** PREP If you go **through** a particular experience or event, you experience it, and if you behave in a particular way **through** it, you behave in that way while it is happening. por ❑ *We have been going through a bad time. Hemos tenido una mala época.* **4** PREP If something happens because of something else, you can say that it happens **through** it. gracias a, merced a ❑ *I only succeeded through hard work. Lo conseguí a fuerza de puro trabajo.* **5** PREP If someone gets **through** an examination or a round of a competition, they succeed or win. de principio a fin ❑ *I got through my exams. Terminé mis exámenes.* ● **Through** is also an adverb. a la siguiente etapa ❑ *Only the top four teams go through. Sólo los cuatro primeros equipos pasan.* **6** PREP If you look or go **through** a lot of things, you look at them or deal with them one after the other. de principio a fin ❑ *Let's go through the numbers together. Vamos a revisar juntos las cifras.*

**❸ through** **1** ADJ If you are **through with** something or if it is **through,** you have finished doing it. terminado ❑ *We're through with dinner. Ya acabamos de cenar.* **2** ADJ If you are **through with** someone, you do not want to have anything to do with them again. no querer nada con ❑ *I'm through with her! ¡Estoy harta de ella!*

In addition to the uses shown here, **through** is used in phrasal verbs such as "follow through," "see through," and "think through."

The preposition is pronounced /θru/. In other cases, **through** is pronounced /θru/.

**through|out** /θruaʊt/ **1** PREP If you say that something happens **throughout** a particular period of time, you mean that it happens during the whole of that period. durante ❑ *The school runs cooking courses throughout the year. En la escuela dan clases de cocina todo el año.* ❑ *The themes are repeated throughout the film. Los temas se repiten a lo largo de la película.* ● **Throughout** is also an adverb. todo el tiempo ❑ *The first song didn't go too badly except that everyone talked throughout. La primera canción no estuvo tan mal, sólo que la gente no dejaba de hablar.* **2** PREP If you say that something happens or exists **throughout** a place, you mean that it happens or exists in all parts of that place. por todo ❑ *They run projects throughout Africa. Ejecutan* *proyectos por toda África.* • **Throughout** is also an adverb. *por todos lados* ❑ *The route is well marked throughout. Todo el camino está bien señalizado.*

**throw** /θroʊ/ (**throws, throwing, threw, thrown**) **1** V-T When you **throw** an object that you are holding, you move your hand or arm quickly and let go of the object, so that it moves through the air. *tirar, lanzar, aventar, arrojar* ❑ *He spent hours throwing a tennis ball against a wall. Se pasó horas aventando una pelota de tenis contra la pared.* ❑ *The crowd began throwing stones. La multitud empezó a lanzar piedras.* • **Throw** is also a noun. *lanzamiento, tiro, tirada* ❑ *I made a good throw. Hice un buen lanzamiento.* **2** V-T If you **throw** your body or part of your body into a particular position or place, you move it there suddenly and with a lot of force. *echar(se), aventar(se)* ❑ *She threw her arms around his shoulders. Le lanzó los brazos al cuello.* ❑ *She threw herself onto her bed. Se echó a la cama.* **3** V-T To **throw** something or someone into a particular place or position means to cause them to fall there. *echar, aventar* ❑ *He threw his jacket onto the back seat. Aventó su saco al asiento de atrás.* ❑ *He threw me to the ground. Me aventó al suelo.* **4** V-T If a horse **throws** its rider, it makes the rider fall off. *tirar* ❑ *The horse stopped suddenly, throwing its rider. El caballo se detuvo súbitamente y tiró al jinete.* **5** V-T If a person or thing **is thrown into** a bad situation or state, something causes them to be in it. *caer, sumir(se)* ❑ *The city was thrown into chaos because of a protest by taxi drivers. La ciudad se sumió en el caos por una manifestación de taxistas.* **6** V-T If you **throw** yourself, your energy, or your money **into** a particular job or activity, you become involved in it very actively or enthusiastically. *dedicarse a algo intensamente* ❑ *She threw herself into a modeling career. Se metió de lleno en su carrera de modelo.* **7** V-T If you **throw** a fit or a tantrum, you suddenly start to behave in an uncontrolled way. *enfurecerse* ❑ *I used to throw tantrums all over the place. Solía hacer berrinches por todos lados.* **8** V-T If something such as a remark or an experience **throws** you, it surprises you or confuses you because it is unexpected. *desconcertar* ❑ *Her sudden change in attitude threw me. Su repentino cambio de actitud me sacó de onda.* **9** V-T When someone **throws** a party, they organize one. *organizar, dar* [INFORMAL] ❑ *Why not throw a party for your friends? ¿Por qué no hacer una fiesta para tus amigos?* **10** to **throw light on** something → see **light** **11** to **throw in the towel** → see **towel**

▸ **throw away** or **throw out** **1** PHR-VERB When you **throw away** or **throw out** something that you do not want, you get rid of it. *tirar, deshacerse de* ❑ *I never throw anything away. Yo nunca tiro nada.* **2** PHR-VERB If you **throw away** an opportunity, advantage, or benefit, you waste it. *desaprovechar, desperdiciar, malgastar* ❑ *Don't throw away your chances of finding happiness. No desperdicies la oportunidad de encontrar la felicidad.*

▸ **throw out** **1** → see **throw away 1** **2** PHR-VERB If a judge **throws out** a case, he or she rejects it and the accused person does not have to stand trial. *rechazar* ❑ *The defense wants the judge to throw out the case. La defensa pretende que el juez rechace el caso.* **3** PHR-VERB If you **throw** someone **out**, you force them to leave a place or group. *echar a alguien de algún lugar, expulsar* ❑ *I threw him out of the house. Lo corrí de la casa.*

▸ **throw up** PHR-VERB When someone **throws up**, they vomit. *vomitar, devolver, guacarearse* ❑ *I went to the rest room and threw up. Fui al baño y vomité.*

**Word Partnership** Usar *throw* con:

N. throw **a ball**, throw **a pass**, throw **a pitch**, throw **a rock/stone**, throw **strikes** **1**

**thrown** /θroʊn/ **Thrown** is the past participle of **throw**. *participio pasado de throw*

**throw rug** (**throw rugs**) N-COUNT A **throw rug** is a rug that covers a small part of the floor. *tapete pequeño*

**thrust** /θrʌst/ (**thrusts, thrusting, thrust**) **1** V-T If you **thrust** something or someone somewhere, you push or move them there quickly with a lot of force. *empujar* ❑ *They thrust him into the back of a car. Por la fuerza lo metieron al asiento posterior de un coche.* • **Thrust** is also a noun. *empujón, embestida* ❑ *...arm thrusts. ...empujones con los brazos.* **2** N-UNCOUNT **Thrust** is the power or force that is required to make a vehicle move in a particular direction. *propulsión*

**thru|way** /θruweɪ/ (**thruways**) also **throughway** N-COUNT A **thruway** is a wide road that is specially designed so that a lot of traffic can move along it very quickly. *autopista*

**thumb** /θʌm/ (**thumbs**) N-COUNT Your hand has four fingers and one **thumb**. *pulgar* ❑ *...the tip of her left thumb. ...la punta de su pulgar izquierdo.*
→ see **hand**

**thumb|tack** /θʌmtæk/ (**thumbtacks**) N-COUNT A **thumbtack** is a short pin with a broad, flat top which is used for fastening papers or pictures to a bulletin board, wall, or other surface. *chinche, chincheta, tachuela*
→ see **office**

**thun|der** /θʌndər/ (**thunders, thundering, thundered**) **1** N-UNCOUNT **Thunder** is the loud noise that you hear from the sky after a flash of lightning, especially during a storm. *trueno, estruendo* ❑ *There was thunder and lightning. Hubo rayos y truenos.* **2** V-I When **it thunders,** a loud noise comes from the sky after a flash of lightning. *tronar* ❑ *It will probably thunder later. Quizá se oigan truenos más tarde.* **3** N-UNCOUNT The **thunder of** something that is moving or making a sound is the loud deep noise it makes. *estruendo, fragor, estrépito* ❑ *...the thunder of the sea on the rocks. ...el fragor del mar contra las rocas.* **4** V-I If something or someone **thunders** somewhere, they move there quickly and with a lot of noise. *pasar haciendo mucho ruido* ❑ *The horses thundered across the valley. Los caballos cruzaron el valle en medio de un gran estruendo.*

**thunder|storm** /θʌndərstɔrm/ (**thunderstorms**) N-COUNT A **thunderstorm** is a storm with thunder and lightning and a lot of heavy rain. *tormenta eléctrica*

**Thurs|day** /θɜrzdeɪ, -di/ (**Thursdays**) N-VAR **Thursday** is the day after Wednesday and before Friday. *jueves* ❑ *On Thursday Barrett invited me for a drink. Barrett me invitó a tomar un trago el jueves.* ❑ *We do the weekly shopping every Thursday morning. Los jueves por la mañana hacemos la compra de la semana.*

T

**thus** /ðʌs/ 1 ADV You use **thus** to show that what you are about to mention is the result of something else that you have just mentioned. *por lo tanto, por consiguiente, por eso* [FORMAL] ❑ *Neither of them turned on the TV. Thus they didn't hear the news. Ninguno prendió la tele, así que no oyeron las noticias.* 2 ADV If you say that something is **thus** or happens **thus** you mean that it is, or happens, as you have just described or as you are just about to describe. *así* [FORMAL] ❑ *Joanna was pouring the tea. While she was thus occupied, Charles sat on an armchair. Joanna estaba sirviendo el té, y mientras tanto, Charles se sentó en un sillón.*

**thy|mine** /θaɪmin, -mɪn/ (**thymines**) N-VAR **Thymine** is one of the four basic components of the DNA molecule. It bonds with adenine. *timina* [TECHNICAL]

**thy|mus** /θaɪməs/ (**thymuses** /θaɪməsɪz/ or **thymi** /θaɪmaɪ/) N-COUNT The **thymus** is an organ in your chest that forms part of the body's immune system. *timo* [TECHNICAL]

**tick** /tɪk/ (**ticks, ticking, ticked**) V-I When a clock or watch **ticks,** it makes a regular series of short sounds as it works. *hacer tictac* ❑ *A clock ticked on the kitchen counter. Un reloj hacía tictac en el mostrador de la cocina.* ● **Tick** is also a noun. *tictac* ❑ *...the tick of the clock. ...el tictac del reloj.* ● **tick|ing** N-UNCOUNT *tictac* ❑ *She could hear the ticking of a clock. Ella podía oír el tictac de un reloj.*

▸ **tick off** PHR-VERB If you say that someone or something **ticks** you **off,** you mean that they annoy you. *fastidiar, molestar* [INFORMAL] ❑ *That ticks me off. Eso me saca de quicio.*

**tick|et** /tɪkɪt/ (**tickets**) 1 N-COUNT A **ticket** is a small, official piece of paper or card which shows that you have paid to enter a place such as a theater or a sports stadium, or shows that you have paid for a trip. *boleto, billete, entrada* ❑ *...two tickets for the game. ...dos boletos para el juego* ❑ *...a plane ticket to Paris. ...un boleto de avión para París.*

ticket

2 N-COUNT A **ticket** is an official piece of paper which orders you to pay a fine or to appear in court because you have committed a driving or parking offense. *multa, boleta, papeleta* ❑ *Slow down or you'll get a ticket. No vayas tan rápido para que no te multen.*

**Word Partnership** Usar *ticket* con:

ADJ. **free** ticket 1
N. ticket **agent**, ticket **booth**, ticket **counter**, ticket **holder**, **plane** ticket, ticket **price** 1
**parking** ticket, **speeding** ticket 2
V. **buy/pay for a** ticket 1
**get a** ticket 1 2

**ticket|less** /tɪkɪtlɪs/ 1 ADJ Someone who is **ticketless** does not have a ticket for a particular event such as a concert or a sports game. *sin boleto* ❑ *The band begged ticketless fans to stay away. La banda pidió a sus simpatizantes que no tenían boleto que no vinieran.* 2 ADJ A **ticketless** system is a way of buying something, such as a seat on an aircraft, without being given a paper ticket. *sin boleto* ❑ *...a ticketless reservation system. ...sistema de reservaciones sin boleto impreso.*

**tick|le** /tɪkᵊl/ (**tickles, tickling, tickled**) 1 V-T When you **tickle** someone, you move your fingers lightly over a sensitive part of their body, often in order to make them laugh. *hacer cosquillas* ❑ *I was tickling him, and he was laughing. Le hacía cosquillas y él se reía.* 2 V-T/V-I If something **tickles** you or **tickles,** it causes an irritating feeling by lightly touching a part of your body. *hormiguear, sentir cosquillas, picar, tener comezón* ❑ *...a hat with a feather that tickled her ear. ...un sombrero con una pluma que le picaba la oreja.*

**tic-tac-toe** /tɪktæktoʊ/ also **tick-tack-toe** N-UNCOUNT **Tic-tac-toe** is a game in which two players take turns in drawing either an "O" or an "X" in one square of a grid consisting of nine squares. The winner is the first player to get three of the same symbols in a row. *gato, tres en línea*

**tid|al bore** (**tidal bores**) N-COUNT A **tidal bore** is a large wave that moves up a river as the tide rises. *macareo*

**tid|al range** (**tidal ranges**) N-COUNT The **tidal range** is the difference in height between the low tide and the high tide at a particular place. *amplitud de la marea*

**tide** /taɪd/ (**tides**) 1 N-COUNT **The tide** is the regular change in the level of the ocean on the beach. *marea, corriente* ❑ *The tide was going out. La marea estaba bajando.* 2 N-SING The **tide of** opinion, for example, is what the majority of people think at a particular time. *corriente* ❑ *The tide of opinion seems to be in his favor. La opinión parece estar de su parte.*
→ see Word Web: **tide**
→ see **ocean**

**tie** /taɪ/ (**ties, tying, tied**) 1 V-T If you **tie** two things **together** or **tie** them, you fasten them together with a knot. *anudar, atar, amarrar* ❑ *He tied the ends of the plastic bag together. Amarró los dos extremos de la bolsa de plástico.* ● **Tie up** means the same as **tie**. *anudar, atar, amarrar* ❑ *She tied up the bag and took it outside. Amarró la bolsa y la llevó afuera.* 2 V-T If you **tie** something or someone in a particular place or position, you put them there and fasten them using rope or string. *amarrar, atar* ❑ *He tied the dog to one of the trees. Ató el perro a uno de los árboles.* ● **Tie up** means the same as **tie**. *amarrar, atar* ❑ *Would you go and tie your horse up please? ¿Puedes ir a amarrar tu caballo, por favor?* 3 V-T If you **tie** a piece of string or cloth around something or **tie** something **with** a piece of string or cloth, you put the piece of string or cloth around it and fasten the ends together. *amarrar, atar, anudar* ❑ *She tied her scarf over her head. Se amarró la mascada alrededor de la cabeza.* ❑ *Roll the meat and tie it with string. Enrolla la carne y amárrala con un cordel.* 4 V-T If you **tie** a knot or bow **in** something or **tie** something **in** a knot or bow, you fasten the ends together. *anudar, hacer un nudo, hacer un moño* ❑ *He took a short piece of rope and tied a knot. Tomó un pedazo pequeño de cuerda e hizo un nudo.* ❑ *...a large red ribbon tied in a bow. ...un ancho listón rojo hecho moño.* 5 N-COUNT A **tie** is a long narrow piece of cloth that is worn around the neck under a shirt

**Word Web** **tide**

The **gravitational** pull of the **moon** on the earth's **oceans** causes **tides.** It moves the water in the earth's oceans. **High tides** occur twice a day at any given point on the earth's surface. Then the water **ebbs** gradually. After six hours **low tide** occurs. In some places tidal energy powers hydroelectric **plants.** Riptides cause the deaths of hundreds of swimmers each year. But a riptide is not really a tide. It is a strong ocean **current.**

collar and tied in a knot at the front. Ties are worn mainly by men. corbata ❑ *Jason took off his jacket and loosened his tie.* *Jason se quitó el saco y se aflojó la corbata.* 6 V-T If one thing **is tied to** another or two things **are tied,** the two things have a close connection or link. conectar, relacionar, vincular ❑ *My social life is closely tied to my work.* *Mi vida social está muy relacionada con mi trabajo.* 7 N-COUNT **Ties** are the connections you have with people or a place. vínculo, relación ❑ *Quebec has close ties to France.* *Quebec tiene estrechos vínculos con Francia.* 8 V-RECIP If two people **tie** in a competition or game or if they **tie with** each other, they have the same number of points or the same degree of success. empatar, igualar ❑ *Ronan Rafferty tied with Frank Nobilo.* *Ronan Rafferty empató con Frank Nobilo.* ● **Tie** is also a noun. empate, igualada ❑ *The first game ended in a tie.* *El primer juego terminó en empate.*
→ see **clothing, jewelry**
▶ **tie up** → see **tie 1 and 2**

**ti|ger** /taɪgər/ (**tigers**) N-COUNT A **tiger** is a large fierce animal belonging to the cat family. Tigers are orange with black stripes. tigre

**tight** /taɪt/ (**tighter, tightest**) 1 ADJ **Tight** clothes or shoes are small and fit closely to your body. pegado, ajustado, apretado, ceñido ❑ *She walked off the plane in a tight black dress.* *Bajó del avión enfundada en un ajustado vestido negro.* ● **tight|ly** ADV apretadamente ❑ *He buttoned his collar tightly round his neck.* *Abrochó el cuello del abrigo para que le quedara apretado.* 2 ADV If you hold someone or something **tight,** you hold them firmly and securely. apretadamente, estrechamente ❑ *She just fell into my arms, holding me tight.* *Apenas cayó en mis brazos, se pegó a mí con fuerza.* ❑ *Just hold tight to my hand and follow me.* *No me sueltes la mano, y sígueme.* ● **Tight** is also an adjective. firme, fuerte, apretado ❑ *He kept a tight hold of her arm.* *Le sostuvo el brazo con firmeza.* ● **tight|ly** ADV apretadamente, firmemente ❑ *He folded his arms tightly across his chest.* *Cruzó los brazos sobre el pecho, con fuerza.* 3 ADJ **Tight** controls or rules are very strict. estricto, riguroso ❑ *The rules include tight control of the media.* *Las reglas incluyen un riguroso control de los medios.* ❑ *The government is keeping a tight hold on inflation.* *El gobierno mantiene un estrecho control de la inflación.* ● **tight|ly** ADV estrictamente ❑ *The media was tightly controlled by the government.* *Los medios eran rigurosamente controlados por el gobierno.* 4 ADJ Skin, cloth, or string that is **tight** is stretched or pulled so that it is smooth or straight. tirante, estirado ❑ *My skin feels tight and dry.* *Siento la piel seca y tirante.* ● **tight|ly** ADV ajustadamente ❑ *Pull the cloth tightly across the wooden frame.* *Estira mucho la tela al montarla en el marco de madera.* 5 ADJ **Tight** is used to describe a group of things or an amount of something that is closely packed together. apretado ❑ *She curled up in a tight ball.* *Se hizo un ovillo apretado.* ● **Tight** is also an adverb. tirante, apretado ❑ *She pulled her hair tight into a bun.* *Se restiró el cabello para hacerse un chongo apretado.* ● **tight|ly** ADV apretadamente ❑ *Many animals travel in tightly-packed trucks.* *Muchos animales son transportados en camiones llenísimos.* 6 ADJ A **tight** schedule or budget allows very little time or money for unexpected events or expenses. apretado ❑ *It's difficult to fit everything into a tight schedule.* *Es difícil acomodar todo en un horario limitado.* ❑ *Emma is on a tight budget for clothes.* *El presupuesto de Emma para ropa es reducido.* 7 → see also **airtight** 8 to **sit tight** → see **sit**

**Word Partnership** Usar *tight* con:

N. tight **dress/jeans/pants** 1
tight **fit** 1 4
tight **grip,** tight **hold** 2
tight **control,** tight **security** 3
ADV. **extremely** tight, **a little** tight, **so** tight, **too** tight, **very** tight 1 – 6

**tight|en** /taɪtᵊn/ (**tightens, tightening, tightened**) 1 V-T/V-I If you **tighten** your grip on something, or if your grip **tightens,** you hold the thing more firmly or securely. apretar ❑ *Luke tightened his hold on her shoulder.* *Luke le apretó el hombro todavía más.* 2 V-T/V-I If you **tighten** something such as a rope, chain, or belt, or if it **tightens,** it is stretched or pulled hard until it is straight. apretar(se) ❑ *The man leaned back, tightening the rope.* *El hombre se inclinó hacia atrás y la cuerda se tensó.* 3 V-T When you **tighten** a screw, nut, or other device, you turn it or move it so that it is more firmly in place or holds something more firmly. apretar ❑ *She tightened one of the screws holding the gas can in place.* *Apretó uno de los tornillos que sostenían el tanque de gas.* ● **Tighten up** means the same as **tighten.** apretar, ajustar, tensar ❑ *It's important to tighten up the wheels properly.* *Es importante apretar muy bien las ruedas.* 4 V-T/V-I To **tighten** rules or controls means to make them stricter. hacer más estricto, restringir ❑ *The United States plans to tighten import controls.* *Los Estados Unidos piensan hacer más estrictos los controles de importación.* ❑ *...an attempt by management to tighten the rules.* *...un intento de la administración por hacer más estrictas las reglas.* ● **Tighten up** means the same as **tighten.** hacer más estricto, restringir ❑ *Every attempt to tighten up the law has failed.* *Todos los intentos* *por hacer más estrictas las leyes han fracasado.* **5** to **tighten** your **belt** → see **belt**

**tile** /taɪl/ (**tiles**) N-VAR **Tiles** are flat, square pieces of baked clay, carpet, cork, or other substance, which are fixed as a covering onto a floor, wall, or roof. *baldosa, loza, azulejo, mosaico, loseta*

**till** /tɪl/ (**tills**) **1** PREP In spoken English and informal written English, **till** is often used instead of **until**. *hasta* ❑ *They had to wait till Monday to phone the bank. Tuvieron que esperar hasta el lunes para telefonear al banco.* ● **Till** is also a conjunction. *hasta* ❑ *I didn't leave home till I was nineteen. Viví con mis padres hasta los diecinueve años.* **2** N-COUNT A **till** is the drawer of a cash register, where the money is kept. *caja registradora* ❑ *There was money in the till. Había dinero en la caja.* **3** N-UNCOUNT **Till** or **glacial till** is the same as **glacial drift**. *depósito glacial, aluvión glaciárico, morrena, acarreo glacial* [TECHNICAL]

**tilt** /tɪlt/ (**tilts, tilting, tilted**) **1** V-T/V-I If you **tilt** an object or if it **tilts**, it moves into a sloping position with one end or side higher than the other. *inclinar(se), ladear(se)* ❑ *She tilted the mirror and combed her hair. Ladeó el espejo para peinarse el cabello.* ❑ *Leonard tilted his chair back and stretched his legs. Leonard inclinó hacia atrás la silla y estiró las piernas.* **2** N-UNCOUNT The **tilt** of something is the fact that it tilts or slopes, or the angle at which it tilts or slopes. *inclinación, declive*

**tim|ber** /tɪmbər/ N-UNCOUNT **Timber** is wood that is used for building houses and making furniture. *madera de construcción* ❑ *...a single-story timber building. ...un edificio de madera de un solo piso.*
→ see **forest**

**tim|bre** /tæmbər/ (**timbres**) N-COUNT The **timbre** of someone's voice or of a musical instrument is the particular quality of sound that it has. *timbre*

**time**
❶ NOUN USES
❷ VERB USES
❸ PHRASES

❶ **time** /taɪm/ (**times**) **1** N-UNCOUNT **Time** is what we measure in minutes, hours, days, and years. *tiempo* ❑ *...a two-week period of time. ...un lapso de dos semanas* ❑ *Time passed, and still Mary did not come back. El tiempo pasaba, y Mary no volvía.* **2** N-SING You use **time** to ask or talk about a specific point in the day, which can be stated in hours and minutes and is shown on clocks. *hora* ❑ *"What time is it?"—"Eight o'clock." —¿Qué hora es?—Las ocho.* ❑ *He asked me the time. Me preguntó la hora.* **3** N-COUNT The **time** when something happens is the point in the day when it happens or is supposed to happen. *hora, momento* ❑ *Departure times are 08:15 from Baltimore, and 10:15 from Newark. La hora de salida de Baltimore son las 8:15, y de Newark, las 10:15.* **4** N-UNCOUNT; N-SING You use **time** to refer to the period that you spend doing something or when something has been happening. *tiempo, rato* ❑ *Adam spent a lot of time in his grandfather's office. Adam pasaba mucho tiempo en la oficina de su abuelo.* ❑ *He wouldn't have the time or money to take care of me. No tendría ni el tiempo ni el dinero para atenderme.* ❑ *Listen to me, I haven't got much time. Escúchame, no tengo mucho tiempo.* **5** N-SING If you say that something has been happening for **a time,** you mean that it has been happening for a fairly long period of time. *tiempo, periodo* ❑ *I lived for a time in Ontario, Canada. Viví un tiempo en Ontario, Canadá.* ❑ *He stayed for quite a time. Se quedó por bastante tiempo.* **6** N-COUNT You use **time** or **times** to talk about a particular period of time. *época* ❑ *We were in the same college, which was male-only at that time. Estábamos en la misma universidad, que en ese tiempo era sólo para hombres.* ❑ *By this time he was thirty. En esa época tenía treinta años.* ❑ *They were hard times and his parents were struggling to raise their family. Eran momentos difíciles y sus padres batallaban para mantener a la familia.* ❑ *It was a time of great uncertainty. Eran tiempos de gran incertidumbre.* **7** N-COUNT When you describe the **time** that you had on a particular occasion or during a particular part of your life, you are describing the sort of experience that you had then. *rato* ❑ *Sarah and I had a great time while the kids were away. Sarah y yo la pasamos muy bien mientras los niños estaban fuera.* **8** N-UNCOUNT If you say it is **time for** something, **time to** do something, or **time** you did something, you mean that this thing ought to happen or be done now. *momento, ocasión* ❑ *...a feeling among the public that it was time for a change. ...el público sentía que era el momento de hacer un cambio.* ❑ *It was time for him to go to work. Era hora de que se fuera al trabajo.* **9** N-COUNT When you talk about a **time** when something happens, you are referring to a specific occasion when it happens. *vez, ocasión* ❑ *Every time she travels on the bus it's late. Cuando se va en camión, es que se le ha hecho tarde.* **10** N-COUNT You use **time** after numbers to say how often something happens. *vez* ❑ *It was her job to make tea three times a day. Era su obligación hacer té tres veces al día.* **11** N-PLURAL You use **times** after numbers when comparing one thing to another and saying, for example, how much bigger, smaller, better, or worse it is. *vez* ❑ *Its profits are rising four times faster than the average company. Sus utilidades se están incrementando cuatro veces más rápido que en la empresa promedio.* **12** CONJ You use **times** to show multiplication. Three **times** five is 3x5. *por* ❑ *Four times six is 24. Cuatro por seis igual a 24.* **13** N-COUNT The **time** of a piece of music is the number of beats that the piece has in each bar. The **time** of a dance measures body rhythms such as breath and heartbeat. *compás*
→ see Picture Dictionary: **time**
→ see **time**

❷ **time** /taɪm/ (**times, timing, timed**) **1** V-T If you **time** something **for** a particular hour, day, or period, you plan or decide to do it or cause it to happen at this time. *programar* ❑ *I timed our visit for March 7. Programé nuestra visita para el 7 de marzo.* **2** V-T If you **time** an action or activity, you measure how long someone takes to do it or how long it lasts. *cronometrar, medir el tiempo* ❑ *He timed the speed of the baseball. Midió la velocidad de la pelota de béisbol.* **3** → see also **timing**

❸ **time** /taɪm/ (**times**) **1** PHRASE If you say it is **about time** that something was done, you are saying in an emphatic way that it should happen or be done now, and really should have

t

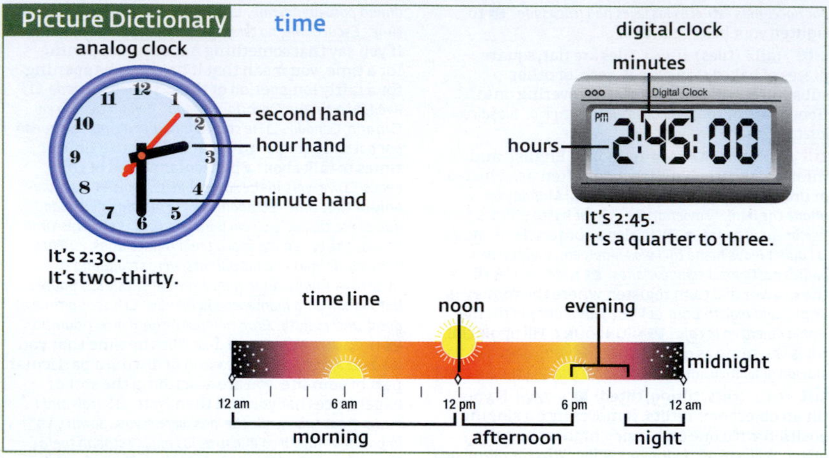


happened or been done sooner. *ser hora de* ❑ *It's about time he learned to behave well.* *Ya es hora de que aprenda a comportarse.* **2** PHRASE If someone is **ahead of** their **time** or **before** their **time,** they have new ideas a long time before other people start to think in the same way. *adelantado* ❑ *He was ahead of his time in employing women.* *Se adelantó a su tiempo empleando a mujeres.* **3** PHRASE If something happens or is done **all the time,** it happens or is done continually. *todo el tiempo, siempre, continuamente* ❑ *We can't be together all the time.* *No podemos estar juntos todo el tiempo.* **4** PHRASE If you say that something was the case **at one time,** you mean that it was the case during a particular period in the past. *anteriormente* ❑ *At one time 400 men, women and children lived in the village.* *En una época, en el pueblo vivían 400 hombres, mujeres y niños.* **5** PHRASE You use **at the same time** to introduce a statement that contrasts with the previous statement. *a la vez* ❑ *I was afraid of her, but at the same time I really liked her.* *Le tenía miedo, pero al mismo tiempo realmente me simpatizaba.* **6** PHRASE If something is the case or will happen **for the time being,** it is the case or will happen now, but only until something else becomes possible or happens. *por el momento, entretanto* ❑ *The situation is calm for the time being.* *Por ahora, la situación está tranquila.* **7** PHRASE If you do something **from time to time,** you do it occasionally. *de tiempo en tiempo, de cuando en cuando, de vez en vez* ❑ *Her daughters visited him from time to time.* *Sus hijas lo visitaban de vez en cuando.* **8** PHRASE If you are **in time for** something, or if you are **on time,** you are not late. *a tiempo* ❑ *I arrived just in time for my flight to Hawaii.* *Llegué puntual para mi vuelo a Hawaii.* **9** PHRASE If something will happen **in time,** it will happen eventually. *con el tiempo* ❑ *He will solve his own problems, in time.* *Con el tiempo resolverá sus propios problemas.* **10** PHRASE If you say that something will happen, for example, **in** a week's **time** or **in** two years' **time,** you mean that it will happen a week from now or two years from now. *lapso, plazo* ❑ *Presidential elections will be held in ten days' time.* *Las elecciones para presidente serán en diez días.* **11** PHRASE If you say that someone or something is, for example, the best writer **of all time,** or the most successful movie **of all time,** you mean that they are the best or most successful that there has ever been. *de todos los tiempos* ❑ *"Monopoly" is one of the best-selling games of all time.* *"Monopolio" es el juego más vendido de todos los tiempos* **12** PHRASE If you say that something will **take time,** you mean that it will take a long time. *llevar tiempo, tomar tiempo* ❑ *Change will come, but it will take time.* *El cambio se dará, pero con el tiempo.* **13** PHRASE If you **take** your **time** doing something, you do it slowly and do not hurry. *tomar(se) su tiempo* ❑ *"Take your time," Ted told him. "I'm in no hurry."* *—No te apresures —le dijo Ted—, no tengo prisa.* **14** **time and again** → see **again**

**time-honored** ADJ A **time-honored** tradition or way of doing something is one that has been used and respected for a very long time. *tradicional, consagrado* ❑ *Their cheese is made in the time-honored way.* *Hacen su queso a la manera tradicional.*

**time|line** /taɪmlaɪn/ (**timelines**) also **time line** **1** N-COUNT A **timeline** is a visual representation of a sequence of events, especially historical events. *cronología, línea cronológica, línea de tiempo* ❑ *The timeline shows important events from the Earth's creation to the present day.* *La línea cronológica muestra los sucesos importantes desde la creación de la Tierra hasta el presente.* **2** N-COUNT A **timeline** is the length of time that a project is expected to take. *calendario, programa* [BUSINESS] ❑ *Use your deadlines to establish the timeline for your research plan.* *Básese en los plazos límite que tiene para establecer el calendario de su proyecto de investigación.*
→ see **time, history**

**time|table** /taɪmteɪbᵊl/ (**timetables**) N-COUNT A **timetable** is a plan of the times when particular events will take place. *horario, itinerario* ❑ *Don't you realize we're working to a timetable?* *¿No te das cuenta de que tenemos que cumplir con un horario?*

**tim|id** /tɪmɪd/ ADJ **Timid** people are shy, nervous, and lack courage or confidence in themselves. *tímido, huraño* ❑ *Isabella was a timid child.* *Isabella era una niña tímida.* • **ti|mid|ity** /tɪmɪdɪti/ N-UNCOUNT timidez ❑ *He tried to overcome his natural timidity.* Trataba de superar su natural timidez. ● **tim|id|ly** ADV tímidamente ❑ *The little boy stepped forward timidly.* El niño dio un paso adelante con timidez.

**tim|ing** /taɪmɪŋ/ **1** N-UNCOUNT **Timing** is the skill or action of judging the right moment in a situation or activity at which to do something. oportunidad, sincronización ❑ *His photo caught the happy moment with perfect timing.* Tomó la foto en el momento oportuno y captó el momento feliz. **2** N-UNCOUNT **Timing** is used to refer to the time at which something happens or is planned to happen, or to the length of time that something takes. oportunidad ❑ *They are worried about the timing of the report.* Les preocupa que el reportaje se publique en el momento oportuno. **3** → see also **time**

**tin** /tɪn/ (**tins**) **1** N-UNCOUNT **Tin** is a soft, silvery-white metal. estaño, hojalata ❑ *...tin cans.* ...latas. **2** N-COUNT A **tin** is a metal container with a lid in which things such as cookies, cakes, or tobacco can be kept. lata, bote ❑ *Store the cookies in an airtight tin.* Guarda las galletas en una lata hermética. ❑ *...a tin of paint.* ...una lata de pintura.
→ see **pan**

**tiny** /taɪni/ (**tinier, tiniest**) ADJ Something or someone that is **tiny** is extremely small. diminuto, chiquito, minúsculo, menudo ❑ *The living room is tiny.* La sala es chiquitita. ❑ *Though she was tiny, she had a very loud voice.* Si bien era muy chiquita, su voz era muy potente.

**tip** /tɪp/ (**tips, tipping, tipped**) **1** N-COUNT The **tip** of something long and narrow is the end of it. punta, extremo ❑ *...the tips of his fingers.* ...las puntas de los dedos. **2** V-T/V-I If you **tip** an object or part of your body or if it **tips**, it moves into a sloping position with one end or side higher than the other. inclinar ❑ *She had to tip her head back to see him.* Tenía que inclinar la cabeza hacia atrás para verlo. **3** V-T If you **tip** something somewhere, you pour it there. verter, vertir, vaciar, servir ❑ *Tip the vegetables into a bowl.* Vacía las verduras en un tazón. **4** V-T If you **tip** someone such as a waiter in a restaurant, you give them some money in order to thank them for their services. dar propina ❑ *We usually tip 18–20%.* En general, damos de 18 a 20% de propina. ● **Tip** is also a noun. propina ❑ *I gave the barber a tip.* Le di propina al peluquero. **5** N-COUNT A **tip** is a useful piece of advice. sugerencia, consejo práctico, tip ❑ *The article gives tips on applying for jobs.* En el artículo sugieren cómo solicitar un empleo.

▸ **tip off** PHR-VERB If someone **tips** you **off**, they give you information about something that has happened or is going to happen. avisar, pasar información, prevenir, poner sobre aviso ❑ *Greg tipped police off about his neighbor.* Greg informó a la policía sobre su vecino. ● **tip-off** N-COUNT (**tip-offs**) pitazo, soplo, chivatazo ❑ *The man was arrested at his home after a tip-off.* Arrestaron al hombre en su casa gracias a un pitazo.

▸ **tip over** PHR-VERB If you **tip** something **over** or if it **tips over**, it falls over or turns over. volcar, caerse ❑ *He tipped the table over in front of him.* Tiró la mesa que tenía enfrente. ❑ *Don't tip over that glass.* No vayas a tirar ese vaso.

**Word Partnership** Usar *tip* con:

| | |
|---|---|
| N. | tip **of your finger/nose** 1 |
| | tip **your hat** 2 |
| ADJ. | **northern/southern** tip **of an island** 1 |
| | **anonymous** tip 5 |

**tire** /taɪər/ (**tires, tiring, tired**) **1** N-COUNT A **tire** is a thick piece of rubber which is fitted onto the wheels of vehicles such as cars, buses, and bicycles. llanta, neumático, goma **2** V-T/V-I If something **tires** you or you **tire**, you feel that you have used a lot of energy and you want to rest or sleep. cansar(se) ❑ *If driving tires you, take the train.* Si manejar te cansa, toma el tren. **3** V-I If you **tire of** something, you no longer wish to do it, because you have become bored of it or unhappy with it. cansarse de algo, aburrirse ❑ *He never tired of listening to her stories.* Nunca se cansaba de oír sus historias.
→ see **bicycle**

**tired** /taɪərd/ **1** ADJ If you are **tired**, you feel that you want to rest or sleep. cansado, fatigado ❑ *Michael is tired and he has to rest after his long trip.* Michael está fatigado y tiene que descansar después de su largo viaje. ● **tired|ness** N-UNCOUNT cansancio ❑ *He left early because of tiredness.* Se fue temprano, por el cansancio. **2** ADJ If you are **tired of** something, you do not want it to continue because you are bored of it or unhappy with it. cansado, aburrido ❑ *I am tired of all the uncertainty.* Estoy cansada de tanta incertidumbre.
→ see **sleep**

**Word Partnership** Usar *tired* con:

| | |
|---|---|
| V. | **look** tired 1 |
| | **be** tired, **feel** tired, **get** tired, **grow** tired 1 2 |
| ADJ. | tired **and hungry** 1 |
| | **sick and** tired **of** ***something*** 2 |
| ADV. | **a little** tired, **(just) too** tired, **very** tired 1 2 |

**tire|some** /taɪərsəm/ ADJ If you describe someone or something as **tiresome,** you mean that you find them irritating or boring. tedioso, pesado, molesto ❑ *...the tiresome old lady next door.* ...la viejita pesada de al lado.

**tir|ing** /taɪərɪŋ/ ADJ If you describe something as **tiring,** you mean that it makes you tired so that you want to rest or sleep. agotador, cansado ❑ *It was a long and tiring day.* Fue un día largo y cansado. ❑ *Traveling is tiring.* Viajar es cansado.

**tis|sue** /tɪʃu/ (**tissues**) **1** N-VAR In animals and plants, **tissue** consists of cells that are similar to each other in appearance and that have the same function. tejido ❑ *...muscle tissue.* ...tejido muscular. **2** N-UNCOUNT **Tissue** or **tissue paper** is thin paper that is used for wrapping things that are easily damaged, such as objects made of glass or china. papel de china, papel de seda ❑ *...a small package wrapped in tissue paper.* ...un paquetito envuelto en papel de china. **3** N-COUNT A **tissue** is a piece of thin, soft paper that you use to blow your nose. pañuelo desechable, kleenex ❑ *...a box of tissues.* ...una caja de kleenex.
→ see **cancer**

**ti|tle** /taɪtᵊl/ (**titles**) **1** N-COUNT The **title** of a book, play, movie, or piece of music is its name. título ❑ *"Patience and Sarah" was first published under the title "A Place for Us."* *La primera vez que publicaron "Patience y Sarah", su título era "Un lugar para nosotros".* **2** N-COUNT Someone's **title** is a word such as "Doctor," "Mr." or "Mrs." that is used before their own name in order to show their status or profession. título, tratamiento ❑ *Please fill in your name and title.* *Escriba su nombre y su título.* **3** N-COUNT A **title** in a sports competition is the position of winner or champion. título, campeonato ❑ *He won the 400-meter title in 1948.* *En 1948 ganó el título de los 400 metros.*
→ see **graph**

**ti|tled** /taɪtᵊld/ ADJ In Britain, someone who is **titled** has a title such as "Lord," "Lady," "Sir," or "Princess" before their name, showing that they have a high rank in society. que tiene un título nobiliario ❑ *Her mother was a titled lady.* *Su madre tenía título de nobleza.*

**TLC** /ti̱ ɛl si̱/ N-UNCOUNT If someone or something needs some **TLC,** they need to be treated in a kind and caring way. **TLC** is an abbreviation for "tender loving care." cariño, cuidado [INFORMAL] ❑ *Plants with small, yellow leaves will need some TLC.* *Las plantas de hojas amarillas y pequeñas necesitan cuidados amorosos.*

**to**

❶ PREPOSITION AND ADVERB USES
❷ USED BEFORE THE BASE FORM OF A VERB

**❶ to**

Usually pronounced /tə/ before a consonant and /tu/ before a vowel, but pronounced /tu/ when you are emphasizing it.

In addition to the uses shown below, **to** is used in phrasal verbs such as "see to" and "come to." It is also used with some verbs that have two objects in order to introduce the second object.

**1** PREP You use **to** when indicating the place that someone or something visits, moves toward, or points at. a ❑ *Two friends and I drove to Florida.* *Dos amigos y yo nos fuimos manejando a Florida.* ❑ *She went to the window and looked out.* *Se dirigió a la ventana y se asomó.* **2** PREP If you go **to** an event, you go where it is taking place. a ❑ *We went to a party at Kurt's house.* *Fuimos a una fiesta a casa de Kurt.* ❑ *He came to dinner.* *Vino a cenar.* **3** PREP If something is attached **to** something larger or fixed **to** it, the two things are joined together. en ❑ *There was a piece of cloth tied to the dog's collar.* *Había una telita en el collar del perro.* **4** PREP You use **to** when indicating the position of something. For example, if something is **to** your left, it is nearer your left side than your right side. a ❑ *The bathroom is to the right.* *El baño está a la derecha* **5** PREP When you give something **to** someone, they receive it. a ❑ *He picked up the knife and gave it to me.* *Tomó el cuchillo y me lo dio.* **6** PREP You use **to** to indicate who or what an action or a feeling is directed toward. con, a ❑ *Marcus has been really mean to me today.* *Marcus se portó muy mal conmigo hoy.* ❑ *...troops loyal to the government.* *...tropas leales al gobierno.* **7** PREP You use **to** when describing someone's reaction to something or someone's feelings about a situation or event. para ❑ *To his surprise, the bedroom door was locked.* *Para su sorpresa, la puerta de la recámara estaba con llave.* **8** PREP **To** can show whose opinion is being stated. para ❑ *It was clear to me that he respected his boss.* *Para mí era obvio que respetaba a su jefe.* **9** PREP You use **to** when indicating what something or someone is becoming, or the state or situation that they are progressing toward. en ❑ *The shouts changed to laughter.* *Los gritos se convirtieron en risas.* ❑ *...an old house that was converted to a nature center.* *...una vieja casa convertida en centro para el estudio de la naturaleza.* **10** PREP **To** can indicate the last thing in a range of things. hasta ❑ *I read everything from fiction to science.* *Leo de todo, desde novelas hasta ciencia.* **11** PREP You use **to** when you are stating a time less than thirty minutes before an hour. For example, if it is "five **to** eight," it is five minutes before eight o'clock. para ❑ *At twenty to six I was waiting by the entrance to the station.* *A los veinte para las seis estaba esperando en la entrada de la estación.* **12** PREP You use **to** when giving ratios and rates. a ❑ *...engines that can run at 60 miles to the gallon.* *...motores que dan 60 millas por galón.* **13** → see also **according to** **14** → see also **too**

**❷ to**

Pronounced /tə/ before a consonant and /tu/ before a vowel.

**1** You use **to** before the base form of a verb to indicate the purpose or intention of an action. para ❑ *...using the experience of big companies to help small businesses.* *...aprovechar la experiencia de las empresas grandes para ayudar a los negocios pequeños.* **2** You use **to** before the base form of a verb when you are expressing your attitude or intention in making a statement. para ❑ *I'm disappointed, to be honest.* *Para ser honesta, estoy desilusionada.* **3** You use **to** before the base form of a verb in many other constructions when talking about an action or state. delante de infinitivo ❑ *The management wanted to know.* *El gobierno quería saber.* ❑ *Nuclear plants are expensive to build.* *Cuesta mucho construir una planta nuclear.* ❑ *...advice about how to do her job.* *...asesoría sobre cómo hacer su trabajo.* ❑ *The president is to visit China.* *El presidente va a ir a China.*

**toast** /to̱ʊst/ (**toasts, toasting, toasted**) **1** N-UNCOUNT **Toast** is slices of bread heated until they are brown and crisp. pan tostado, tostada ❑ *...a piece of toast.* *...una rebanada de pan tostado.* **2** V-T When you **toast** bread, you heat it so that it becomes brown and crisp. tostar ❑ *Toast the bread lightly on both sides.* *Tostar ligeramente el pan de ambos lados.* **3** N-COUNT When you drink a **toast** to someone or something, you drink some wine or another alcoholic drink, in order to show your appreciation of them or to wish them success. brindis ❑ *Eleanor and I drank a toast to the bride and groom.* *Eleanor y yo hicimos un brindis por la novia y el novio.* ● **Toast** is also a verb. brindar ❑ *We all toasted his health.* *Todos brindamos por su salud.*
→ see **cook**

**toast|er** /to̱ʊstər/ (**toasters**) N-COUNT A **toaster**

T

is a piece of electrical equipment used to toast bread. tostador

**to|bac|co** /təbækoʊ/ (**tobaccos**) N-VAR **Tobacco** is the dried leaves of a plant which people smoke in pipes, cigars, and cigarettes. tabaco

**to|day** /tədeɪ/ **1** ADV You use **today** to refer to this day on which you are speaking or writing. *hoy* ❑ *How are you feeling today?* *¿Cómo te sientes hoy?* ● **Today** is also a noun. *hoy* ❑ *Today is Friday, September 14th.* *Hoy es viernes 14 de septiembre.* **2** → see also **tomorrow, yesterday** **3** ADV You can refer to the present period of history as **today.** *actualmente, hoy en día, hoy* ❑ *More and more young people today are working for themselves.* *En la actualidad, cada vez más jóvenes trabajan por su cuenta.* ● **Today** is also a noun. *hoy* ❑ *In today's America, health care is one of the very biggest businesses.* *En los Estados Unidos de hoy, la atención de la salud es uno de los negocios más lucrativos.*

**tod|dler** /tɒdlər/ (**toddlers**) N-COUNT A **toddler** is a young child who has only just learned to walk. *niño que ha empezado a caminar o niña que ha empezado a caminar* ❑ *I had a toddler at home and two other children at school.* *Tenía en casa un hijo que estaba aprendiendo a caminar y otros dos en la escuela.*

**toe** /toʊ/ (**toes**) N-COUNT Your **toes** are the five movable parts at the end of each foot. *dedo del pie* ❑ *She wiggled her toes in the sand.* *Movió los dedos de los pies en la arena.*
→ see **foot**

**to|fu** /toʊfu/ N-UNCOUNT **Tofu** is a soft, white or brown food made from soybeans. *tofu*

**to|geth|er** /təgɛðər/

> In addition to the uses shown below, **together** is used in phrasal verbs such as "piece together," "pull together," and "sleep together."

**1** ADV If people do something **together,** they do it with each other. *juntos, uno con otro* ❑ *We went on long bicycle rides together.* *Juntos dábamos largos paseos en bicicleta.* ❑ *He and I worked together on a book.* *Él y yo trabajamos conjuntamente en un libro.* **2** ADV If things are joined **together,** they are joined with each other so that they touch or form one whole. *junto* ❑ *Mix the ingredients together thoroughly.* *Integra los ingredientes perfectamente.* **3** ADV If things or people are situated **together,** they are in the same place and very near to each other. *juntos* ❑ *The trees grew close together.* *Los árboles crecían muy juntos.* ❑ *Ginette and I gathered our things together.* *Ginette y yo juntamos nuestras cosas.* **4** ADV If two things happen or are done **together,** they happen or are done at the same time. *a un tiempo, simultáneamente* ❑ *Three horses crossed the finish line together.* *Tres caballos cruzaron la meta al mismo tiempo.* **5** ADV You use **together** when you are adding two or more amounts or things to each other in order to consider a total amount or effect. *juntos* ❑ *Together we earn $60,000 per year.* *Juntos ganamos 60,000 dólares al año.* **6** PHRASE You use **together with** to mention someone or something else that is also involved in an action or situation. *junto con* ❑ *Return the completed form, together with your check for $60.* *Devuelva la forma completada con su cheque por 60 dólares.* **7** **put together** → see **put**

**Word Partnership** Usar *together* con:

- V. **live** together, **play** together, **spend time** together, **work** together **1**
  - **come** together **1** – **4**
  - **get** together **1** **3**
  - **act** together, **go** together **1** **6**
  - **fit** together, **glue** together, **join** together, **lump** together, **mix** together, **string** together, **stuck** together, **tied** together **2**
  - **gather** together, **sit** together, **stand** together **3**
- ADJ. **bound** together **2**
  - **close** together **3** **4**

**toi|let** /tɔɪlɪt/ (**toilets**) N-COUNT A **toilet** is a large bowl with a seat, or a platform with a hole, which is connected to a water system and which you use when you want to get rid of urine or feces from your body. *excusado, taza, inodoro, retrete* ❑ *She flushed the toilet and went back into the bedroom.* *Le jaló al baño y volvió a la recámara.*
→ see **bathroom, petroleum**

**toi|let pa|per** also **toilet tissue** N-UNCOUNT **Toilet paper** is thin, soft paper that people use to clean themselves after they have gotten rid of urine or feces from their body. *papel higiénico, papel de baño, papel sanitario, papel confort*
→ see **bathroom**

**toi|let tissue** → see **toilet paper**

**to|ken** /toʊkən/ (**tokens**) **1** ADJ You use **token** to describe things or actions which are meant to show an intention or feeling, but which are small or unimportant and may not be sincere. *simbólico* ❑ *Please accept this gift as a token of our thanks.* *Por favor, acepte este obsequio como símbolo de nuestro agradecimiento.* **2** N-COUNT A **token** is a round, flat piece of metal or plastic that is sometimes used instead of money. *ficha* ❑ *...slot-machine tokens.* *...fichas para las máquinas tragamonedas.* **3** PHRASE You use **by the same token** to introduce a statement that you think is true for the same reasons that were given for a previous statement. *de igual modo, por la misma razón* ❑ *If you give up exercise, your muscles shrink and fat increases. By the same token, if you do more exercise you will lose fat.* *Si se deja de hacer ejercicio, los músculos se encogen y se acumula grasa, de ahí que, si se hace más ejercicio, se pierda grasa.*

**told** /toʊld/ **1** **Told** is the past tense and past participle of **tell.** *pasado y participio pasado de* **tell** **2** PHRASE You can use **all told** to introduce or follow a summary, general statement, or total. *con todo* ❑ *All told, he went to 14 different schools.* *Para acabar pronto, asistió a 14 escuelas diferentes.*

**tol|er|ate** /tɒləreɪt/ (**tolerates, tolerating, tolerated**) **1** V-T If you **tolerate** a situation or person, you accept them although you do not particularly like them. *tolerar, aguantar, soportar* ❑ *She can no longer tolerate the position that she's in.* *Ya no aguanta más la posición en que está.* **2** V-T If you can **tolerate** something bad or painful, you are able to bear it. *tolerar, aguantar, soportar* ❑ *The ability to tolerate pain varies from person to person.* *La capacidad para aguantar el dolor varía de persona a persona.*

**toll** /toʊl/ (**tolls, tolling, tolled**) **1** V-I When a bell **tolls**, it rings slowly and repeatedly, often as a sign that someone has died. *tañer, tocar, doblar* ❑ *Church bells tolled as people arrived for the funeral. Doblaban las campanas de la iglesia mientras iban llegando los asistentes al funeral.* **2** N-COUNT A **toll** is a sum of money that you have to pay in order to use a particular bridge or road. *cuota, peaje, derecho* ❑ *You can pay a toll to drive on Pikes Peak Highway. Puedes pagar el peaje e irte por Pikes Peak Highway.* **3** N-COUNT A **toll** road or **toll** bridge is a road or bridge that you have to pay to use. *de cuota* ❑ *Most people who drive the toll roads don't use them every day. La mayoría de las personas que transitan por las carreteras de cuota no lo hacen todos los días.* **4** N-COUNT A **toll** is a total number of deaths, accidents, or disasters that occur in a particular period of time. *número de víctimas, índice de siniestralidad* ❑ *There are fears that the toll of dead and injured may be higher. Se teme que el número de muertos y heridos sea mayor.* **5** → see also **death toll** **6** PHRASE If you say that something **takes** its **toll** or **takes a heavy toll,** you mean that it has a bad effect or causes a lot of suffering. *cobrar(se)* ❑ *Winter takes its toll on your health. El invierno afecta la salud.*

**Word Link** *free ≈ without : freeway, hands-free, toll-free*

**toll-free** ADJ A **toll-free** telephone number is one which you can dial without having to pay for the call. *gratuito* • **Toll-free** is also an adverb. *gratuitamente* ❑ *Call our customer-service staff toll-free. Contacte sin costo a nuestro personal de atención al cliente.*

**to|ma|to** /təmeɪtoʊ/ (**tomatoes**) N-VAR **Tomatoes** are soft, red fruit that you can eat raw in salads or cooked as a vegetable. *jitomate, tomate* → see **vegetable**

**to|mor|row** /təmɔroʊ/ (**tomorrows**) **1** ADV **Tomorrow** refers to the day after today. *mañana* ❑ *Bye, see you tomorrow. Adiós, nos vemos mañana.* • **Tomorrow** is also a noun. *mañana* ❑ *What's on your schedule for tomorrow? ¿Qué tienes programado para mañana?* **2** ADV You can refer to the future as **tomorrow.** *mañana* ❑ *What is education going to be like tomorrow? ¿Cómo será la educación del futuro?* • **Tomorrow** is also a noun. *mañana* ❑ *...tomorrow's computer industry. ...la industria de la computación del mañana.*

T

**ton** /tʌn/ (**tons**) N-COUNT A **ton** is a unit of weight that is equal to 2,000 pounds. *tonelada* ❑ *Hundreds of tons of oil spilled into the ocean. Cientos de toneladas de petróleo se derramaron en el océano.*

**to|nal|ity** /toʊnælɪti/ (**tonalities**) N-VAR **Tonality** is the presence of a musical key in a piece of music. *tonalidad* [TECHNICAL]

**tone** /toʊn/ (**tones, toning, toned**) **1** N-COUNT The **tone** of a sound is its particular quality. *tono* ❑ *Chris heard him speaking in low tones to Sarah. Chris lo oyó hablar en voz baja a Sarah.* **2** N-COUNT Someone's **tone** is a quality in their voice which shows what they are feeling or thinking. *tono* ❑ *I didn't like his tone of voice; he sounded angry. No me gustó el tono de su voz, parecía enojado.* **3** N-SING The **tone** of a speech or piece of writing is its style and the opinions or ideas expressed in it. *tono* ❑ *The tone of the letter was very friendly. El tono de la carta era muy amistoso.* **4** V-T/V-I Something that **tones** your body makes it firm and strong. *tonificar, dar tono* ❑ *This movement lengthens your spine and tones the back muscles. Con este movimiento se alarga la espina y se tonifican los músculos de la espalda.* • **Tone up** means the same as **tone.** *tonificar, dar tono* ❑ *Exercise tones up your body. El ejercicio tonifica el cuerpo.* **5** N-COUNT In painting, a **tone** is a color that has had gray added to it in order to make it darker. *tono*
▸ **tone down** PHR-VERB If you **tone down** something that you have written or said, you make it less forceful, severe, or offensive. *moderar, atenuar* ❑ *The leader toned down his statements after the meeting. El líder moderó sus declaraciones después de la reunión.*

**Word Partnership** Usar *tone* con:

| | |
|---|---|
| ADJ. | **clear** tone, **low** tone **1** |
| | **different** tone **2** |
| | **serious** tone **2** **3** |
| V. | **change your** tone **2** |
| N. | tone **of voice** **2** |

**tone poem** (**tone poems**) N-COUNT A **tone poem** is a piece of music for an orchestra that is based upon something such as a novel or painting. *poema sinfónico*

**tongue** /tʌŋ/ (**tongues**) **1** N-COUNT Your **tongue** is the soft movable part inside your mouth which you use for tasting, licking, and speaking. *lengua* ❑ *I walked over to the mirror and stuck my tongue out. Me acerqué al espejo y saqué la lengua.* **2** N-COUNT A **tongue** is a language. *lengua, idioma, lenguaje* [LITERARY] ❑ *English is not her native tongue. El inglés no es su lengua materna.* **3** PHRASE A **tongue-in-cheek** remark or attitude is not serious, although it may seem to be. *comentario medio en broma* ❑ *...a lighthearted, tongue-in-cheek approach. ...un enfoque irónico y despreocupado.*
→ see **diagnosis, face, taste**

**to|night** /tənaɪt/ ADV **Tonight** is used to refer to the evening of today or the night that follows today. *esta noche* ❑ *I'm at home tonight. Esta noche no salgo.* ❑ *Tonight he proved what a great player he was. Esta noche demostró qué gran jugador es.* • **Tonight** is also a noun. *esta noche* ❑ *Tonight is the opening night of the opera. Hoy es la noche de estreno de la ópera.*

**ton|sils** /tɒnsəlz/

The form **tonsil** is used as a modifier.

N-PLURAL Your **tonsils** are the two small soft lumps in your throat at the back of your mouth. *amígdala*

**too**
❶ ADDING SOMETHING OR RESPONDING
❷ INDICATING EXCESS

❶ **too** /tu/ **1** ADV You use **too** after mentioning another person, thing, or aspect that a previous statement applies to or includes. *también, asimismo, además* ❑ *"Nice to talk to you." — "Nice to talk to you too." —Qué gusto hablar con usted. —Igualmente.* ❑ *"I've got a great feeling about it." — "Me too." —Me da la impresión de que va a resultar* *muy bien. —A mí también.* **2** ADV You use **too** after adding a piece of information or a comment to a statement, in order to emphasize that it is surprising or important. *de veras* ❑ *We learned to read, and quickly too. Aprendimos a leer, y rápido, también.*

**❷ too** /tu/ **1** ADV You use **too** in order to indicate that there is a greater amount or degree of something than is desirable, necessary, or acceptable. *demasiado* ❑ *Jeans that are too big will make you look larger. Los jeans demasiado grandes te hacen ver gorda.* ❑ *I'm turning up the heat because it's too cold. Voy a prender la calefacción porque hace demasiado frío.* **2** ADV You use **too** with a negative to make what you are saying sound less forceful or more polite or cautious. *muy* ❑ *I'm not too happy with what I've written. No estoy muy contenta con lo que escribí.* **3** PHRASE You use **all too** or **only too** to emphasize that something happens to a greater extent or degree than is good or desirable. *de veras, muy* ❑ *She remembered it all too well. Lo recordaba demasiado bien.* **4** **none too** → see **none**

**Usage** **too, two,** and **to**

*Too, two,* and *to* are frequently confused. Their meanings and uses are very different, but they sound exactly the same. *Too* means "also" or "excessively"; *two* is the number 2; and *to* has many different uses as a preposition and in the *to*-infinitive: *Bahati asked Sekou to sit with her on the swing, but it was too small for the two of them, so they went to the movies instead.*

**took** /tʊk/ **Took** is the past tense of **take**. *pasado de take*

**tool** /tul/ **(tools)** **1** N-COUNT A **tool** is any instrument or simple piece of equipment, for example a hammer or a knife, that you hold in your hands and use to do a particular kind of work. *herramienta, instrumento, utensilio* ❑ *The best tool for the purpose is a hammer. La mejor herramienta para esto es un martillo.* **2** N-COUNT You can refer to anything that you use for a particular purpose as a particular type of **tool**. *herramienta* ❑ *Writing is a good tool for expressing feelings. La escritura es un buen medio para expresar sentimientos.*
→ see Picture Dictionary: **tools**

**Word Partnership** Usar *tool* con:

N. tool **belt** **1**
**communication** tool, **learning** tool, **management** tool, **marketing** tool, **teaching** tool **2**
V. **use a** tool **1** **2**
ADJ. **effective** tool, **important** tool, **valuable** tool **1** **2**
**powerful** tool **2**

**tool|bar** /tulbɑr/ **(toolbars)** N-COUNT A **toolbar** is a narrow strip across a computer screen containing pictures, called icons, which represent different computer functions. *barra de herramientas* [COMPUTING]

**tooth** /tuθ/ **(teeth)** **1** N-COUNT Your **teeth** are the hard white objects in your mouth, which you use for biting and chewing. *diente* ❑ *She had very straight teeth. Tenía los dientes muy parejos.* **2** N-PLURAL The **teeth** of something such as a comb, saw, or zipper are the parts that stick out in a row on its edge. *diente, púa* ❑ *...a comb with most of its teeth missing. ...un peine al que le faltan casi todos los dientes.*
→ see **teeth**

**Word Partnership** Usar *tooth* con:

N. tooth **decay**, tooth **enamel** **1**
V. **lose a** tooth, **pull a** tooth **1**

**tooth|brush** /tuθbrʌʃ/ **(toothbrushes)** N-COUNT A **toothbrush** is a small brush that you use for cleaning your teeth. *cepillo de dientes*

**tooth|paste** /tuθpeɪst/ **(toothpastes)** N-VAR **Toothpaste** is a thick substance which you put on your toothbrush and use to clean your teeth. *pasta de dientes, dentífrico, pasta dentífrica* ❑ *...shaving supplies, toothpaste, and soap. ...cosas de rasurar, pasta de dientes y jabón.*

**top**
❶ NOUN AND ADJECTIVE USES
❷ PHRASAL VERBS
❸ PHRASES

**❶ top** /tɒp/ **(tops)** **1** N-COUNT The **top** of

t

## Picture Dictionary tools

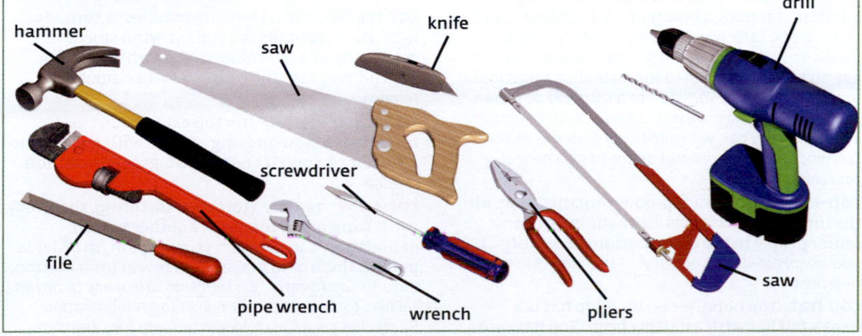

something is its highest point or part. *parte superior, parte de arriba* ❑ *I waited at the top of the stairs. Esperé arriba de las escaleras.* ❑ *Don't fill it up to the top. No lo llenes hasta el tope.* ● **Top** is also an adjective. *parte superior, parte de arriba* ❑ *...the top corner of the newspaper. ...la esquina superior del periódico.* **2** ADJ The **top** thing or layer in a series of things or layers is the highest one. *superior, de arriba* ❑ *I can't reach the top shelf. No alcanzo el último anaquel.* **3** N-COUNT The **top** of a bottle, jar, or tube is its cap or lid. *tapa, tapón* ❑ *...the plastic tops from soda bottles. ...las tapas de plástico de las botellas de refresco.* **4** N-COUNT A **top** is a piece of clothing that you wear on the upper half of your body, for example, a blouse or shirt. *top, blusa, playera* [INFORMAL] ❑ *Look at my new top. Mira mi top nuevo.* **5** ADJ You can use **top** to describe the highest level of a scale or measurement. *máximo, tope* ❑ *The car has a top speed of 100 miles per hour. El máximo de velocidad del coche son 160 kilómetros por hora.* **6** N-SING The **top** of an organization or career structure is the highest level in it. *cúspide, cumbre* ❑ *He joined the company as a salesman and worked his way to the top. Entró a la empresa como vendedor y llegó a ser el número uno.* ● **Top** is also an adjective. *lo mejor, lo más alto* ❑ *...the top people in this company. ...los altos ejecutivos de esta empresa.* **7** N-SING If someone is **at the top of** a class or league or is **the top of** it, their performance is better than that of all the other people involved. *en la cúspide, el primero o la primera* ❑ *She was always top of the class at school. En la escuela siempre era la primera de la clase.* ● **Top** is also an adjective. *mejor* ❑ *He was the top student in physics. Era el mejor estudiante de física.*

| **Thesaurus** | *top* | Ver también: |
|---|---|---|
| N. | peak, summit; (*ant.*) base, bottom ❶ **1** | |
| ADJ. | best ❶ **7** | |

**❷ top** /tɒp/ (**tops, topping, topped**)
▸ **top out** PHR-VERB If something such as a price **tops out at** a particular amount, that is the highest amount that it reaches. *alcanzar* ❑ *The temperature topped out at 99 degrees. La temperatura llegó a los 37 grados.*

**❸ top** /tɒp/ (**tops**) **1** PHRASE If you **are on top of** or **get on top of** something that you are doing, you are dealing with it successfully. *tener el control* ❑ *...the government's inability to get on top of the situation. ...la incapacidad del gobierno para controlar la situación.* **2** PHRASE If one thing is **on top** of another, it is placed over it or on its highest part. *sobre, arriba* ❑ *He was asleep on top of the covers. Estaba dormido sobre las cobijas.* **3** PHRASE You can use **on top** or **on top of** to indicate that a particular problem exists in addition to a number of other problems. *además, encima* ❑ *We have all the problems a normal family has, with additional problems on top. Tenemos todos los problemas de una familia normal, y para colmo, otros.*

**top-down** ADJ In a **top-down** organization, all the important decisions are made by the most senior people in the organization. *verticalista* ❑ *...a traditional top-down company. ...una empresa vertical tradicional.*

**top hat** (**top hats**) N-COUNT A **top hat** is a man's tall hat with a narrow brim. Top hats are considered old-fashioned now, but are sometimes worn by dancers and performers. *sombrero de copa, chistera*

**top|ic** /tɒpɪk/ (**topics**) N-COUNT A **topic** is a particular subject that you discuss or write about. *tema, tópico, materia, asunto* ❑ *The weather is a constant topic of conversation in Alaska. En Alaska, el clima es un tema constante de conversación.*

**topi|cal** /tɒpɪkᵊl/ ADJ **Topical** is used to describe something that concerns or relates to events that are happening at the present time. *de interés actual, del día* ❑ *The newscast covers topical events and entertainment. El noticiero cubre eventos y espectáculos de actualidad.*

**top|ic sen|tence** (**topic sentences**) N-COUNT A **topic sentence** is a statement that expresses the main idea in a short piece of writing such as a paragraph. *tema, idea principal* [TECHNICAL]

**topo|graph|ic map** /tɒpəgræfɪk mæp/ (**topographic maps**) N-COUNT A **topographic map** is a map of an area that shows the height of the land by means of contour lines. *mapa topográfico*

**top|ple** /tɒpᵊl/ (**topples, toppling, toppled**) **1** V-I If someone or something **topples** somewhere, they become unsteady or unstable and fall over. *caerse, tambalearse, perder el equilibrio* ❑ *He toppled slowly backwards. Cayó lentamente hacia atrás.* ● **Topple over** means the same as **topple**. *caerse, tambalearse, perder el equilibrio* ❑ *The tree is so badly damaged they are worried it might topple over. El árbol está tan dañado que les preocupa que se caiga.* **2** V-T To **topple** a government or leader, especially one that is not elected by the people, means to cause them to lose power. *derrocar, derribar* ❑ *...the revolution which toppled the government. ...la revolución que derrocó al gobierno.*

**top-shelf** ADJ **Top-shelf** things or people are of a very high standard or quality. *de primer nivel* ❑ *...top-shelf hotel resorts. ...centros vacacionales de primerísima calidad.*

**To|rah** /tɔrə/ N-PROPER In the Jewish religion, **the Torah** is the first five books of the Old Testament of the Bible. *Torá* ❑ *...the study of the Torah. ...el estudio del Torá.*

**torch** /tɔrtʃ/ (**torches**) N-COUNT A **torch** is a long stick or device with a flame at one end, used to provide light, to set things on fire, or to melt or cut something. *antorcha* ❑ *They carried torches to light their way. Llevaban antorchas para alumbrarse en el camino.*

**tor|na|do** /tɔrneɪdoʊ/ (**tornadoes** or **tornados**) N-COUNT A **tornado** is a violent wind storm consisting of a tall column of air which spins around very fast and causes a lot of damage. *tornado*

**tor|toise** /tɔrtəs/ (**tortoises**) N-COUNT A **tortoise** is a slow-moving animal with a shell into which it can pull its head and legs for protection. *tortuga*

**tor|ture** /tɔrtʃər/ (**tortures, torturing, tortured**) V-T If someone **is tortured,** another person deliberately causes them terrible pain, in order to punish them or to make them reveal information. *torturar, atormentar, dar tormento* ❑ *In many countries soldiers torture captured enemies to get information. En muchos países, los soldados torturan a los enemigos*

T

*capturados para obtener información.* • **Torture** is also a noun. *tortura, tormento, suplicio* ❑ *...cases of torture by the guards. ...casos de tortura a manos de los guardias.*

**toss** /tɔ̲s/ (**tosses, tossing, tossed**) **1** V-T If you **toss** something somewhere, you throw it there lightly, often in a careless way. *tirar, lanzar, aventar, arrojar* ❑ *Just toss it in the trash. Nada más échalo a la basura.* **2** V-T If you **toss** your head, you move it backward, quickly and suddenly, often as a way of expressing anger or contempt. *sacudir* ❑ *"I'm sure I don't know." Debbie tossed her head. —Estoy segura, no lo sé —Debbie movió la cabeza.* **3** V-T In sports and informal situations, if you decide something by **tossing** a coin, you spin a coin into the air and guess which side of the coin will face upward when it lands. *echar un volado, sortear* ❑ *We tossed a coin to decide who would go out and buy the cakes. Echamos un volado para decidir quién iría a comprar los pasteles.* • **Toss** is also a noun. *volado* ❑ *It would be better to decide it on the toss of a coin. Lo mejor sería decidirlo con un volado.*

→ see **sleep**

**to|tal** /to̲ʊtᵊl/ (**totals, totaling** or **totalling, totaled** or **totalled**) **1** N-COUNT A **total** is the number that you get when you add several numbers together or when you count how many things there are in a group. *total* ❑ *The companies have a total of 1,776 employees. Las empresas tienen 1,776 empleados en total.* • **Total** is also an adjective. *total* ❑ *The total cost of the project would be more than $240 million. El costo total del proyecto sería de más de 240 millones de dólares.* **2** PHRASE If there are a number of things **in total**, there are that number when you count or add them all together. *en total* ❑ *The business lasted eight years in total. En total, el negocio duró ocho años.* **3** V-T If several numbers or things **total** a certain figure, that figure is the total of all the numbers or all the things. *sumar, hacer un total de* ❑ *The firm's profits will total $5 million this year. Este año, las utilidades de la empresa ascendieron a 5 millones de dólares.* **4** ADJ **Total** means complete. *total, completo* ❑ *I felt like a total failure. Me sentí como un verdadero fracaso.* • **to|tal|ly** ADV *totalmente* ❑ *...something totally different. ...algo completamente diferente.*

**Word Partnership** Usar *total* con:

N. total **amount**, total **area**, total **cost**, total **expenses**, total **population**, total **sales**, total **savings**, **sum** total, total **value** **1**
ADJ. **grand** total **1** **2**

**to|tal eclipse** (**total eclipses**) N-COUNT A **total eclipse of** the sun is an occasion when the moon is between the Earth and the sun, so that for a short time you cannot see any part of the sun. A **total eclipse of** the moon is an occasion when the Earth is between the sun and the moon, so that for a short time you cannot see any part of the moon. Compare **partial eclipse**. *eclipse total*

**tote bag** (**tote bags**) N-COUNT A **tote bag** is a large strong bag. *bolsón, bolsa grande* ❑ *She was carrying a tote bag. Llevaba una bolsa grande.*

**touch**
❶ VERB AND NOUN USES
❷ PHRASES AND PHRASAL VERBS

**❶ touch** /tʌ̲tʃ/ (**touches, touching, touched**) **1** V-T/V-I If you **touch** something, you put your hand onto it in order to feel it or to make contact with it. *tocar, tentar, sentir* ❑ *Her tiny hands gently touched my face. Tocó suavemente mi cara con sus manitas.* ❑ *Don't touch! ¡No tocar!* • **Touch** is also a noun. *toque, tacto, contacto* ❑ *...a light touch on the face. ...una ligera sensación en el rostro.* **2** V-RECIP If two things **are touching,** or if one thing **touches** another, their surfaces come into contact with each other. *tocar(se), estar en contacto* ❑ *Their knees were touching. Sus rodillas rozaban.* ❑ *Her feet touched the floor. Tocó el piso con los pies.* **3** N-UNCOUNT Your sense of **touch** is your ability to tell what something is like when you feel it with your hands. *tacto* ❑ *Our sense of touch declines with age. Nuestro sentido del tacto declina con la edad.* **4** V-I If you **touch on** a particular subject, you mention it briefly. *tratar por encima, aludir, referirse* ❑ *The film only touches on these issues. En la película apenas tocan esos temas.* **5** V-T If something that someone says or does **touches** you, it affects you emotionally, often because that person is suffering or is being very kind. *afectar, influir* ❑ *Their kindness touched me deeply. Su gentileza me conmovió profundamente.* • **touched** ADJ *conmovido* ❑ *He was touched that we came. Se emocionó de que hayamos venido.* • **touch|ing** ADJ *enternecedor, emocionante* ❑ *...the touching tale of a wife who nursed the husband she loved. ...la conmovedora historia de una mujer que cuidó del esposo al que amaba.* **6** → see also **touch** **7** N-COUNT A **touch** is a detail which is added to something to improve it. *toque, detalle* ❑ *They called the event "a tribute to heroes," which was a nice touch. Llamaron al evento "Tributo a los héroes", que me pareció un buen detalle.*

**Word Partnership** Usar *touch* con:

ADJ. **gentle** touch, **light** touch ❶ **1**
**finishing** touch, **nice** touch, **personal** touch, **soft** touch ❶ **7**

**❷ touch** /tʌ̲tʃ/ (**touches, touching, touched**) **1** PHRASE If you are **in touch with** someone, you write, phone, or visit each other regularly. *en contacto con* ❑ *We have to keep in touch by phone. Tenemos que mantenernos en contacto por teléfono.* ❑ *I will get in touch with my lawyer about this. Tengo que informar a mi abogado de esto.* **2** PHRASE If you are **in touch with** a subject or situation, or if someone keeps you **in touch with** it, you know the latest news or information about it. If you are **out of touch with** it, you do not know the latest news or information about it. *al corriente, informado* ❑ *I try to keep in touch with what's happening. Trato de mantenerme al corriente de lo que está pasando.* **3** PHRASE If you **lose touch with** someone, you gradually stop writing, phoning, or visiting them. *perder contacto con* ❑ *In my job you often lose touch with friends. Con un trabajo como el mío, es frecuente perder de vista a los amigos.* **4** **the finishing touch** → see **finish**

▸ **touch down** PHR-VERB When an aircraft

**touches down,** it lands. *aterrizar* ❑ *The space shuttle touched down yesterday. El transbordador espacial aterrizó ayer.*

**tough** /tʌf/ (**tougher, toughest**) **1** ADJ A **tough** person is strong and determined, and can tolerate difficulty or suffering. *duro, firme, fuerte, estricto, inflexible* ❑ *He built up a reputation as a tough businessman. Se hizo fama de implacable en los negocios.* ● **tough|ness** N-UNCOUNT *dureza, agresividad* ❑ *...a reputation for toughness and determination. ...una reputación de firmeza y determinación.* **2** ADJ A **tough** task or problem is difficult to do or solve. *difícil, duro, peliagudo* ❑ *It was a very tough decision, but we feel we made the right one. Fue una decisión muy difícil, pero creemos haber tomado la correcta.* **3** ADJ A **tough** substance is strong, and difficult to break, cut, or tear. *duro, correoso, resistente* ❑ *The beans have a tough outer skin. La piel de los frijoles es dura.*

**Word Partnership** Usar *tough* con:

N. tough **guy** **1**
tough **choices**, tough **competition**, tough **conditions**, tough **decision**, tough **fight**, tough **going**, tough **job**, tough **luck**, tough **question**, tough **sell**, tough **situation**, tough **time** **2**
V. **get** tough, **talk** tough **1** **2**
**make the** tough **decisions** **2**

**tour** /tʊər/ (**tours, touring, toured**) **1** V-T/V-I When people such as musicians, politicians, or theater companies **tour,** they go to several different places, stopping to perform or to meet people. *hacer una gira, andar de gira* ❑ *A few years ago they toured the country. Hace unos años hicieron una gira por el país.* ● **Tour** is also a noun. *recorrido, gira* ❑ *Their tour was a sell-out. Toda la gira se vendió.* ❑ *The band will be going on tour. La banda se va de gira.* **2** N-COUNT A **tour** is a trip to an interesting place or around several interesting places. *tour, recorrido, viaje* ❑ *...a tour of the major cities of Europe. ...un recorrido por las principales ciudades de Europa.* **3** V-T If you **tour** a place, you go on a trip around it. *recorrer, viajar, visitar* ❑ *You can tour the site on a bicycle. Se puede recorrer el sitio en bicicleta.*

**Word Partnership** Usar *tour* con:

N. **concert** tour, **farewell** tour **1**
tour **bus**, tour **guide**, **museum** tour, **walking** tour, **world** tour **2**
V. **begin a** tour, **finish a** tour **1** **2**
**take a** tour **2**

T

**tour guide** (**tour guides**) N-COUNT A **tour guide** is someone who helps tourists who are on vacation or shows them around a place. *guía de turistas* ❑ *A tour guide will organize activities every day. Un guía organizará las actividades de cada día.*

**Word Link** *ism ≈ action or state : communism, optimism, tourism*

**tour|ism** /tʊərɪzəm/ N-UNCOUNT **Tourism** is the business of providing services for people on vacation, for example, hotels, restaurants, and trips. *turismo* ❑ *Tourism is important economically. El turismo es importante para la economía.*
→ see **industry**

**tour|ist** /tʊərɪst/ (**tourists**) N-COUNT A **tourist** is a person who is visiting a place for pleasure, especially when they are on vacation. *turista, viajero o viajera, visitante* ❑ *...a tourist attraction. ...atractivo turístico.*
→ see **city**

**tour|na|ment** /tʊərnəmənt, tɜr-/ (**tournaments**) N-COUNT A **tournament** is a sports competition in which players who win a game continue to play further games in the competition until just one person or team is left. *torneo, justa, certamen, competencia* ❑ *...the biggest golf tournament in the world. ...el torneo de golf más grande del mundo.*

**tour of duty** (**tours of duty**) N-COUNT A soldier's **tour of duty** is a period of time when he or she is involved in a particular mission or stationed in a particular place. *servicio* ❑ *He served two tours of duty in Vietnam. Estuvo dos veces de servicio en Vietnam.*

**tow** /toʊ/ (**tows, towing, towed**) V-T If one vehicle **tows** another, it pulls it along behind it. *remolcar, arrastrar* ❑ *He uses the truck to tow his work trailer. Utiliza el camión para llevar su remolque de trabajo.* ❑ *They threatened to tow away my car. Amenazaron con llevarse mi coche con grúa.*

**to|ward** /tɔrd/ also **towards**

In addition to the uses shown below, **toward** is used in phrasal verbs such as "count toward" and "lean toward."

**1** PREP If you move, look, or point **toward** something or someone, you move, look, or point in their direction. *en dirección de* ❑ *They were all moving toward him down the stairs. Todos se movían hacia él, escaleras abajo.* ❑ *When he looked toward me, I smiled and waved. Cuando me miró, sonreí y lo saludé con la mano.* **2** PREP If things develop **toward** a particular situation, that situation becomes nearer in time or more likely to happen. *hacia* ❑ *The agreement is a major step toward peace. El acuerdo es un paso importante en pro de la paz.* **3** PREP If you have a particular attitude **toward** something or someone, that is the way you feel about them. *en relación con, para con* ❑ *This man changed my attitude toward religion. Este hombre cambió mi actitud respecto de la religión.* **4** PREP If something happens **toward** a particular time, it happens just before that time. *cercano a, próximo* ❑ *There was a forecast of cooler weather toward the end of the week. Se pronostica más frío alrededor del fin de semana.* **5** PREP If something is **toward** part of a place or thing, it is near that part. *hacia* ❑ *...a small island toward the eastern shore. ...una pequeña isla cerca de la playa este.* **6** PREP If you give money **toward** something, you give it to help pay for that thing. *en favor de* ❑ *He gave them $50,000 toward a house. Les dio 50,000 dólares para una casa.*

**tow|el** /taʊəl/ (**towels, toweling** or **towelling, toweled** or **towelled**) **1** N-COUNT A **towel** is a piece of thick soft cloth that you use to dry yourself. *toalla* ❑ *...a bath towel. ...una toalla de baño.* ❑ *...a beach towel. ...una toalla de playa.* **2** V-T If you **towel** something, you dry it with a towel. *secar con toalla* ❑ *James came out of his bedroom, toweling his wet hair. James salió de su cuarto secándose el cabello con una toalla.* ❑ *I toweled myself dry. Me sequé con una toalla.* **3** PHRASE If you **throw in the**

**towel,** you stop trying to do something because you realize that you cannot succeed. tirar la toalla [INFORMAL] ❑ *The boys only softball league threw in the towel and accepted girls on their teams.* *La liga de softbol sólo para niños se dio por vencida y aceptó a niñas en sus equipos.*
→ see **bathroom**

**tow|er** /taʊər/ (**towers, towering, towered**) **1** N-COUNT A **tower** is a tall, narrow building, that either stands alone or forms part of another building such as a church or castle. torre ❑ *...a castle with high towers.* *...un castillo con altas torres.* **2** V-I Someone or something that **towers over** surrounding people or things is a lot taller than they are. ser mucho más alto que ❑ *He stood up and towered over her.* *Al ponerse de pie, se vio que era mucho más alto que ella.*
→ see **computer**

**town** /taʊn/ (**towns**) **1** N-COUNT A **town** is a place with streets and buildings, smaller than a city, where people live and work. ciudad, pueblo, población ❑ *...the northern California town of Albany.* *...la ciudad de Albany, al norte de California.* **2** N-UNCOUNT You use **town** in order to refer to the town where you live. ciudad ❑ *He doesn't even know when his brother is in town.* *Ni siquiera sabe cuándo está su hermano en la ciudad.*

**town meet|ing** (**town meetings**) N-COUNT A **town meeting** is a meeting held by the residents of a town, or by the people who are eligible to vote in a town. consejo municipal de vecinos

**town|ship** /taʊnʃɪp/ (**townships**) **1** N-COUNT In the United States and Canada, a **township** is an area of land, especially a part of a county which is organized as a unit of local government. municipio, ayuntamiento, municipalidad ❑ *...her 20 years of service with the township and county.* *...sus 20 años de servicio en el municipio y el condado.* **2** N-COUNT In South Africa, a **township** was a town where only black people lived. distrito segregado ❑ *...the South African township of Soweto.* *...el ghetto sudafricano de Soweto.*

**tox|ic** /tɒksɪk/ ADJ A **toxic** substance is poisonous. tóxico ❑ *...the cost of cleaning up toxic waste.* *...el costo de recoger los residuos tóxicos.*
→ see **cancer**

**toy** /tɔɪ/ (**toys, toying, toyed**) N-COUNT A **toy** is an object that children play with, for example, a doll or a model car. juguete ❑ *He was really too old for children's toys.* *En realidad ya no tenía edad para juguetes infantiles.*
▸ **toy with** **1** PHR-VERB If you **toy with** an idea, you consider it casually without making any decisions about it. jugar con, dar(le) vueltas a una idea, considerar ❑ *He toyed with the idea of going to China.* *Jugaba con la idea de ir a China.* **2** PHR-VERB If you **toy with** food or drink, you do not eat or drink it with any enthusiasm, but only take a bite or a little drink from time to time. juguetear ❑ *She had no appetite, and toyed with the bread and cheese.* *No tenía apetito y apenas probó el pan y el queso.*

**trace** /treɪs/ (**traces, tracing, traced**) **1** V-T If you **trace** the origin or development of something, you find out or describe how it started or developed. rastrear, seguir la pista, investigar ❑ *The exhibition traces the history of furniture design in America.* *En la exposición se reconstruye la historia del diseño de muebles en los Estados Unidos.* • **Trace back** means the same as **trace**. rastrear, seguir la pista ❑ *...residents who trace their families back to Dutch settlers.* *...residentes que siguen la huella de su familia hasta los colonizadores holandeses.* **2** V-T If you **trace** someone or something, you find them after looking for them. localizar, ubicar ❑ *Police are trying to trace two men seen leaving the house just before 8 a.m.* *La policía está tratando de encontrar a dos hombres a quienes se vio salir de la casa poco antes de las 8 a.m.* **3** V-T If you **trace** a picture, you copy it by covering it with a piece of transparent paper and drawing over the lines underneath. calcar ❑ *She learned to draw by tracing pictures out of old storybooks.* *Aprendió a dibujar calcando figuras de viejos libros de cuentos.* **4** N-COUNT A **trace of** something is a very small amount of it. vestigio, indicio ❑ *Wash them in cold water to remove all traces of sand.* *Lave con agua fría para eliminar toda la arena.*
→ see **draw, fossil**

**Word Partnership** Usar *trace* con:

N. trace ***your*** **ancestry/origins/roots,** trace **the history of** ***something***, trace **the origins/roots of** ***something*** **1**
trace **of an accent**, trace **amount**, trace **minerals** **4**

**trace gas** (**trace gases**) N-COUNT **Trace gases** are gases that make up less than one percent of the Earth's atmosphere, such as carbon dioxide and methane. oligoelemento, microelemento, elemento menor

**tra|chea** /treɪkiə/ (**tracheas** or **tracheae** /treɪkii/) N-COUNT Your **trachea** is the passage from your **larynx** to your **lungs**. tráquea [MEDICAL]

**track** /træk/ (**tracks, tracking, tracked**) **1** N-COUNT A **track** is a rough, unpaved road or path. camino, sendero ❑ *We set off once more, over a rough mountain track.* *Nos pusimos de nuevo en camino por un sendero montañoso sin pavimentar.* **2** N-COUNT A **track** is a piece of ground that is used for races. pista ❑ *...the running track and the gym.* *...la pista de carreras y el gimnasio.* **3** N-COUNT Railroad **tracks** are the rails that a train travels along. vía, vía férrea, riel ❑ *A cow stood on the tracks.* *Había una vaca en las vías.* **4** N-COUNT A **track** is one of the songs or pieces of music on a CD, record, or tape. tema, pieza ❑ *I only like two of the ten tracks on this CD.* *Sólo me gustan dos de las diez canciones de este disco.* **5** N-PLURAL **Tracks** are marks left in the ground by the feet of animals or people. huella, pisada ❑ *The only evidence of the animals was their tracks in the snow.* *El único rastro de los animales eran sus huellas en la nieve.* **6** V-T If you **track** animals or people, you try to find them by following their footprints or other signs. rastrear, seguir(le) la pista ❑ *He decided to track this wolf and see where it lived.* *Decidió seguirle la pista a ese lobo y ver dónde vivía.* **7** → see also **soundtrack** **8** PHRASE If you **keep track of** a situation or a person, you have accurate information about them all the time. estar al día, mantenerse informado ❑ *With eleven thousand employees, it's very difficult to keep track of them all.* *Con once mil empleados, es muy difícil acordarse de todos.* **9** PHRASE If you **lose track of** someone or something, you no longer know where they are or what is happening.

t

*perder el rastro* ❑ *I'm sorry, I guess I lost track of time. Disculpa, creo que perdí la noción del tiempo.* **10** PHRASE If you are **on the right track,** you are acting or progressing in a way that is likely to result in success. *estar bien encaminado* ❑ *Guests are returning in increasing numbers—a sure sign that we are on the right track. Cada vez son más los huéspedes que vuelven—señal de que vamos por buen camino.*
→ see **fossil, transportation**

▸**track down** PHR-VERB If you **track down** someone or something, you find them after a difficult or long search. *encontrar, localizar, averiguar* ❑ *She spent years trying to track down her parents. Pasó años tratando de dar con sus padres.*

| Word Partnership | Usar *track* con: |
|---|---|
| N. | **dirt** track **1** **2**<br>track **meet**, track **team** **2**<br>**train** track **3** |

**track meet** (**track meets**) N-COUNT A **track meet** is an event in which athletes come to a particular place in order to take part in a race or races. *torneo de atletismo*

**track rec|ord** (**track records**) N-COUNT The **track record** of a person, company, or product is their past performance, achievements, or failures. *historial, antecedentes* ❑ *The job needs someone with a good track record in sales. Para el puesto se necesita alguien con un buen historial en ventas.*

**tract** /trækt/ (**tracts**) **1** N-COUNT A **tract of** land is a very large area of land. *espacio, extensión* ❑ *A vast tract of land is ready for development. Un terreno muy grande ya está listo para urbanizarse.* **2** N-COUNT A **tract** is a system of organs and tubes in an animal's or person's body that has a particular function, especially the function of processing a substance in the body. *sistema (de órganos), tracto* [MEDICAL] ❑ *Foods are broken down in the digestive tract. Los alimentos se descomponen en el sistema digestivo.*

| Word Link | *tract ≈ dragging, drawing : contract, subtract, tractor* |
|---|---|

**trac|tor** /træktər/ (**tractors**) **1** N-COUNT A **tractor** is a farm vehicle that is used to pull farm machinery. *tractor* **2** N-COUNT A **tractor** is a short vehicle with a powerful engine and a driver's cab, used to pull a trailer. *tractor* ❑ *The truck was an 18-wheeler with a white tractor. El camión tenía 18 ruedas y un tractor blanco.*
→ see **barn**

T

**tractor-trailer** (**tractor-trailers**) N-COUNT A **tractor-trailer** is a large truck that is made in two separate sections, a tractor and a trailer, which are joined together by metal bars. *camión con remolque, camión con tráiler*

**trade** /treɪd/ (**trades, trading, traded**) **1** V-RECIP If someone **trades** one thing **for** another or if two people **trade** things, they agree to exchange one thing for the other thing. *comerciar, intercambiar, canjear* ❑ *They traded land for goods and money. Intercambiaron tierras por productos y dinero.* ❑ *Kids used to trade baseball cards. Los niños acostumbraban intercambiar tarjetas de béisbol.* ● **Trade** is also a noun. *comercio, negocio* ❑ *I am willing to make a trade with you. Estoy dispuesto a hacer negocios con usted.* **2** V-RECIP If you **trade** places **with** someone or if the two of you **trade** places, you move into the other person's position or situation, and they move into yours. *cambiar de lugar* ❑ *Mike asked George to trade places with him. Mike le pidió a George que intercambiaran sus lugares.* **3** V-I When people, companies, or countries **trade,** they buy, sell, or exchange goods or services between themselves. *comerciar* [BUSINESS] ❑ *They had years of experience of trading with the West. Tenían años de experiencia comerciando con Occidente.* ● **Trade** is also a noun. *comercio* ❑ *Texas has a long history of trade with Mexico. Es larga la tradición de comercio entre México y Texas.* ❑ *...a new international trade agreement. ...un nuevo tratado comercial internacional.* ● **trad|ing** N-UNCOUNT *comercio, actividad comercial* ❑ *...trading on the stock exchange. ...operaciones bursátiles.* **4** V-T In professional sports, for example football or baseball, if a player **is traded** from one team to another, they leave one team and begin playing for another. *cambiar de equipo, vender* ❑ *He was traded from the Giants to the Yankees. Pasó de los Gigantes a los Yankees.* ❑ *The A's have not won a game since they traded him. Los A's no han ganado un juego desde que lo vendieron.*

| Thesaurus | *trade* Ver también: |
|---|---|
| V. | barter, exchange, swap **1** **3** |

**trade defi|cit** (**trade deficits**) N-COUNT A **trade deficit** is a situation in which a country imports goods worth more than the value of the goods that it exports. *déficit comercial, déficit de la balanza comercial* [BUSINESS]

**trade|mark** /treɪdmɑrk/ (**trademarks**) N-COUNT A **trademark** is a name or symbol that a company uses on its products and that cannot legally be used by another company. *marca de fábrica, marca registrada* [BUSINESS] ❑ *Kodak is a trademark of Eastman Kodak Company. Kodak es una marca registrada de Eastman Kodak Company.*

**trad|er** /treɪdər/ (**traders**) N-COUNT A **trader** is a person whose job is to trade in goods or stocks. *comerciante, vendedor o vendedora, operador de bolsa u operadora de bolsa* [BUSINESS] ❑ *Market traders display a selection of the island's produce. Los comerciantes del mercado exhiben una selección de los productos de la isla.*

**trade show** (**trade shows**) N-COUNT A **trade show** is an exhibition where manufacturers show their products to other people in industry and try to get business. *feria comercial*

**trade wind** (**trade winds**) also **tradewind** N-COUNT The **trade winds** are winds that blow from east to west near the equator. *viento alisio*

**trad|ing card** (**trading cards**) N-COUNT A **trading card** is one of a set of thin pieces of cardboard with a picture relating to a particular theme, such as baseball or football, printed on it, for people to collect and trade with other collectors. *estampa, lámina*

**tra|di|tion** /trədɪʃᵊn/ (**traditions**) N-VAR A **tradition** is a custom or belief that has existed for a long time. *tradición, costumbre* ❑ *...the rich traditions of Afro-Cuban music. ...las ricas tradiciones de la música afrocubana.* ● **tra|di|tion|al**

/trədɪʃən^əl/ ADJ tradicional ❑ *...traditional teaching methods.* *...métodos tradicionales de enseñanza.* ● **tra|di|tion|al|ly** ADV por tradición ❑ *December 26 is traditionally one of the busiest days for malls.* *Tradicionalmente, los centros comerciales tienen mucha actividad el 26 de diciembre.*

| **Thesaurus** | *tradition* Ver también: |
|---|---|
| N. | culture, custom, practice, ritual |

**traf|fic** /træfɪk/ (**traffics, trafficking, trafficked**) **1** N-UNCOUNT **Traffic** refers to all the vehicles that are moving along the roads in a particular area. *tráfico, circulación, tránsito* ❑ *There was heavy traffic on the roads.* *Había mucho tráfico en las calles.* ❑ *Traffic was unusually light for that time of day.* *La circulación era excepcionalmente escasa para esa hora.* **2** N-UNCOUNT **Traffic** refers to the movement of ships, trains, or aircraft between one place and another. *tráfico, movimiento* ❑ *Air traffic has returned to normal.* *El tráfico aéreo ha vuelto a la normalidad.* **3** N-UNCOUNT **Traffic in** something such as stolen goods is an illegal trade in them. *tráfico, movimiento* ❑ *...the traffic in stolen paintings.* *...tráfico de cuadros robados.* **4** V-I Someone who **traffics in** something such as stolen goods buys and sells them even though it is illegal to do so. *traficar con* ❑ *He was accused of trafficking in stolen vehicles.* *Lo acusaban de traficar con vehículos robados.* ● **traf|fick|ing** N-UNCOUNT *tráfico, comercio* ❑ *...charges of gun trafficking.* *...cargos por tráfico de armas.* ● **traf|fick|er** N-COUNT (**traffickers**) *traficante* ❑ *...suspected drug traffickers.* *...supuestos traficantes de drogas.*
→ see Word Web: **traffic**

| **Word Partnership** | Usar *traffic* con: |
|---|---|
| ADJ. | **heavy** traffic, **light** traffic, **oncoming** traffic, **stuck in** traffic **1** |
| N. | traffic **accident**, **city** traffic, traffic **congestion**, traffic **flow**, traffic **pollution**, traffic **problems**, **rush hour** traffic, traffic **safety**, traffic **signals**, traffic **violation** **1** |
| | **air** traffic **2** |
| | **drug** traffic **3** |

**traf|fic jam** (**traffic jams**) N-COUNT A **traffic jam** is a long line of vehicles that cannot move forward because there is too much traffic, or because the road is blocked. *embotellamiento, atascamiento*
→ see **traffic**

**trag|edy** /trædʒɪdi/ (**tragedies**) **1** N-VAR A **tragedy** is an extremely sad event or situation. *tragedia, situación trágica* ❑ *They have suffered an enormous personal tragedy.* *Sufrieron una tragedia personal espantosa.* **2** N-VAR **Tragedy** is a type of serious drama, usually ending in the death of the main character. *tragedia* ❑ *...the tragedies of Shakespeare.* *...las tragedias de Shakespeare.*

**trag|ic** /trædʒɪk/ **1** ADJ A **tragic** event or situation is extremely sad, usually because it involves death or suffering. *trágico, dramático, funesto* ❑ *It was a tragic accident.* *Fue un accidente trágico.* ❑ *...the tragic loss of so many lives.* *...la pérdida dramática de tantas vidas.* ● **tragi|cal|ly** /trædʒɪkli/ ADV *de manera trágica* ❑ *He died tragically young.* *Murió trágicamente joven.* **2** ADJ **Tragic** is used to refer to tragedy as a type of literature. *trágico* ❑ *...Shakespeare's tragic hero, Hamlet.* *...Hamlet, trágico héroe shakesperiano.*

**trail** /treɪl/ (**trails, trailing, trailed**) **1** N-COUNT A **trail** is a rough path across open country or through forests. *sendero, senda, vereda* ❑ *He was walking along a trail through the trees.* *Caminaba por un sendero, entre los árboles.* **2** N-COUNT A **trail** is a series of marks or other signs of movement or other activities left by someone or something. *huella, rastro, estela* ❑ *Everywhere in the house was a sticky trail of orange juice.* *Por toda la casa había un reguero pegajoso de jugo de naranja.* **3** V-T If you **trail** someone or something, you follow them secretly, often by finding the marks or signs that they have left. *rastrear, seguir, seguir la pista* ❑ *Two detectives were trailing him.* *Dos detectives le seguían la pista.* **4** V-T If you **trail** something, it hangs down loosely behind you as you move along. *arrastrar* ❑ *She came down the stairs slowly, trailing the coat behind her.* *Bajó lentamente las escaleras, arrastrando tras ella el abrigo.* **5** PHRASE If you are **on the trail of** a person or thing, you are trying hard to find them or find out about them. *siguiendo la pista* ❑ *The police are already on his trail.* *La policía ya está tras él.*

| **Word Partnership** | Usar *trail* con: |
|---|---|
| N. | **hiking** trail **1** |
| V. | **follow a** trail **1** **2** |
| | **leave a** trail, **pick up a** trail **2** |

t

## Word Web traffic

Boston's Southeast Expressway opened in 1959. It was built to handle 75,000 **vehicles** a day. But it wasn't enough and **commuter traffic** crawled. Sometimes it **stalled** completely. The 27 entrance **ramps** and no **breakdown lanes** caused frequent **gridlock**. By the 1990s, **traffic congestion** was even worse. Nearly 200,000 cars were using the **highway** every day and there were constant **traffic jams**. In 1994, a ten-year **road** construction project called the Big Dig began. The project built underground roadways, six-**lane** bridges, and improved **tunnels**. As a result of the project, traffic **flows** more smoothly through the city.

**Word Web** train

In sixteenth-century Germany, a **railway** was a horse-drawn **wagon** traveling along wooden **rails**. By the 19th century, **steam locomotives** and **steel rails** had replaced the older system. At first, railroads operated only **freight lines**. Later, they began to run **passenger** trains. And soon Pullman cars were added to make overnight trips more comfortable. Today, Japan's bullet trains carry people at speeds up to 300 miles per hour. This type of train doesn't have an engine or use tracks. Instead, an electromagnetic field allows the **cars** to float just above the ground. This electromagnetic field also pushes the train ahead.

*A Japanese Bullet Train.*

**trail|er** /treɪlər/ (**trailers**) **1** N-COUNT A **trailer** is a long narrow house made to be driven to a home site, where it becomes a permanent home. *tráiler, casa rodante, cámper, remolque* **2** N-COUNT A **trailer** is a temporary vacation home that is pulled by a car to each vacation spot. *tráiler, casa rodante, cámper, remolque* **3** N-COUNT A **trailer** is a container on wheels which is pulled by a truck, tractor, or other vehicle and which is used for transporting large or heavy items. *tráiler, remolque* **4** N-COUNT A **trailer** for a movie or television program is a set of very short scenes which are shown to advertise it. *avance publicitario, corto, avances*

**trail|er park** (**trailer parks**) N-COUNT A **trailer park** is an area where people can pay to park their trailers and live in them. *tráiler park, campamento para remolques*

**trail|er truck** (**trailer trucks**) N-COUNT A **trailer truck** is a truck that is made in two or more sections joined together by metal bars, so that the vehicle can turn more easily. *camión con remolque*

**train**
❶ NOUN USES
❷ VERB USES

❶ **train** /treɪn/ (**trains**) **1** N-COUNT A **train** is a number of cars or trucks pulled by an engine along a railroad. *tren, ferrocarril* ❑ *We can catch the early morning train. Podemos tomar el primer tren de la mañana.* ❑ *He arrived in New York by train. Llegó en tren a Nueva York.* **2** N-COUNT A **train of** thought or a **train of** events is a connected series of thoughts or events. *serie, sucesión* ❑ *He lost his train of thought for a moment. Por un momento perdió el hilo de sus pensamientos.*
→ see Word Web: **train**
→ see **transportation**

❷ **train** /treɪn/ (**trains, training, trained**) **1** V-T If you **train to** do something, or if someone **trains** you **to** do it, you learn the skills that you need in order to do it. *capacitar(se), entrenar(se)* ❑ *Stavros was training to be a priest. Stavros se estaba preparando para ser sacerdote.* ● **-trained** ADJ ❑ *...a professionally-trained chef.* ● **train|er** (**trainers**) N-COUNT *entrenador o entrenadora, instructor o instructora, preparador o preparadora* ❑ *...teachers and teacher trainers. ...maestros e instructores para maestros.* ● **train|ing** N-UNCOUNT *capacitación, formación, entrenamiento* ❑ *Kennedy had no formal training. Kennedy no tenía capacitación formal.* **2** V-T/V-I If you **train for** an activity such as a race or if someone **trains** you **for** it, you prepare for it by doing particular physical exercises. *preparar(se)* ❑ *Strachan is training for the new season. Strachan está entrenando para la nueva temporada.* ● **train|er** (**trainers**) N-COUNT *entrenador o entrenadora, preparador físico o preparadora física, instructor o instructora* ❑ *She went to the gym with her trainer. Fue al gimnasio con su entrenadora.* ● **train|ing** N-UNCOUNT *entrenamiento, acondicionamiento físico* ❑ *...keeping fit through exercises and training. ...conservar la condición física con ejercicio y entrenamiento.*

**trait** /treɪt/ (**traits**) N-COUNT A **trait** is a particular characteristic, quality, or tendency that someone or something has and which can be inherited. *rasgo* ❑ *...personality traits. ...rasgos de la personalidad.*

**tram** /træm/ (**trams**) **1** N-COUNT A **tram** is a public transportation vehicle, usually powered by electricity, which travels along rails laid in the surface of a street. *tren, tranvía* ❑ *You can get to the beach by tram. Puedes llegar a la playa en el tranvía.* **2** N-COUNT A **tram** is the same as a **cable car**. *teleférico*
→ see **transportation**

**trans|ac|tion** /trænzækʃᵊn/ (**transactions**) N-COUNT A **transaction** is a piece of business, for example, an act of buying or selling something. *transacción, negocio, operación* [FORMAL, BUSINESS] ❑ *...a cash transaction. ...una operación monetaria.*

**Word Partnership** Usar *transaction* con:

N. **cash** transaction, transaction **costs**, transaction **fee**
V. **complete** a transaction

**Word Link** *script ≈ writing : manuscript, prescription, transcript*

**tran|script** /trænskrɪpt/ (**transcripts**) N-COUNT A **transcript of** a conversation or speech is a written text of it, based on a recording or notes. *transcripción* ❑ *A transcript of this program is available through our website. En nuestro website está disponible una transcripción de este programa.*

T

**Word Link** *trans* ≈ *across* : *transfer, transition, translate*

**trans|fer** (**transfers, transferring, transferred**)

The verb is pronounced /trænsfɜr/. The noun is pronounced /trænsfɜr/.

1 V-T/V-I If you **transfer** something or someone **from** one place **to** another, or they **transfer from** one place **to** another, they go from the first place to the second. *transferir, cambiar de lugar* ❑ *Transfer the meat to a plate and leave in a warm place. Pon la carne en un platón y déjala en un lugar cálido.* ● **Transfer** is also a noun. *transferencia, traspaso* ❑ *Arrange for the transfer of medical records to your new doctor. Prepare la transferencia de su historia clínica a su nuevo médico.* 2 V-T/V-I If you **are transferred,** or if you **transfer, to** a different job or place, you move to a different job or place within the same organization. *trasladar(se), pasar* ❑ *I was transferred to the book department. Me cambiaron al departamento de libros.* ● **Transfer** is also a noun. *traslado, cambio* ❑ *He told me he was unhappy and wanted a transfer. Me dijo que no estaba contento y que quería que lo cambiaran.*

**Word Partnership** Usar *transfer* con:

N. **balance** transfer, transfer **funds**, transfer **money** 1
transfer **schools, students** transfer 2

**trans|form** /trænsfɔrm/ (**transforms, transforming, transformed**) V-T To **transform** someone or something means to change them completely. *transformar, convertir, transfigurar* ❑ *The railroad transformed America. El ferrocarril transformó a los Estados Unidos.* ❑ *Your body transforms food into energy. El organismo transforma los alimentos en energía.* ● **trans|for|ma|tion** /trænsfərmeɪʃ$^{\text{ə}}$n/ (**transformations**) N-VAR *transformación, cambio* ❑ *...the transformation of a bedroom into an office. ...la transformación de una recámara en oficina.*

**trans|form bounda|ry** (**transform boundaries**) N-COUNT A **transform boundary** is a place on the Earth's surface where two tectonic plates meet and slide past each other. Compare **plate boundary.** *límite de transformación* [TECHNICAL]

**trans|it** /trænzɪt/ 1 N-UNCOUNT **Transit** is the carrying of goods or people by vehicle from one place to another. *tránsito, transporte* ❑ *...the transit of goods between the two countries. ...el tránsito de productos entre los dos países.* ❑ *...a transit time of about 42 minutes. ...un tiempo de tránsito de aproximadamente 42 minutos.* 2 PHRASE If people or things are **in transit,** they are traveling or being taken from one place to another. *en tránsito, de tránsito* 3 ADJ A **transit** area is an area where people wait or where goods are kept between different stages of a journey. *tránsito* ❑ *...refugees arriving at the two transit camps. ...refugiados que llegan a los dos campamentos de tránsito.* 4 N-UNCOUNT **Transit** is a system for moving people or goods from one place to another, for example, using buses or trains. *transporte* ❑ *If fuel prices go up, transit prices go up. Si el precio de los combustibles se incrementa, el precio del transporte sube.*
→ see **transportation**

**tran|si|tion** /trænzɪʃ$^{\text{ə}}$n/ (**transitions**) 1 N-VAR **Transition** is the process in which something changes from one state to another. *transición* ❑ *...the transition from dictatorship to democracy. ...la transición de la dictadura a la democracia.* ● **tran|si|tion|al** ADJ *de transición* ❑ *...the transitional stage between the old and new methods. ...la etapa de transición entre los viejos y los nuevos métodos.* 2 N-COUNT In dance and music, a **transition** is a part of a dance or piece of music where one section ends and another section begins. *transición*

**tran|si|tive** /trænzɪtɪv/ ADJ A **transitive** verb has a direct object. *transitivo*

**trans|late** /trænzleɪt/ (**translates, translating, translated**) 1 V-T/V-I If something said or written **is translated,** it is said or written again in the second language. *traducir* ❑ *Only a small number of Kadare's books have been translated into English. Apenas unos cuantos de los libros de Kadare se han traducido al inglés.* ❑ *The Spanish word "acequia" is translated as "irrigation ditch." La palabra española "acequia" se traduce como "irrigation ditch".* ❑ *The girls waited for Mr. Esch to translate. Las chicas esperaron a que el Sr. Esch tradujera.* ● **trans|la|tion** N-UNCOUNT *traducción* ❑ *The papers have been sent for translation. Se enviaron los documentos a traducción.* ● **trans|la|tor** (**translators**) N-COUNT *traductor o traductora* ❑ *She works as a translator. Es traductora.* 2 V-T To **translate** one thing **into** another means to change it into something else. *traducir, convertir* ❑ *Your decision must be translated into action. Tu decisión debe convertirse en acción.*

**trans|la|tion** /trænzleɪʃ$^{\text{ə}}$n/ (**translations**) 1 N-COUNT A **translation** is a piece of writing or speech that has been put into a different language. *traducción* ❑ *...a translation of the Bible. ...una traducción de la Biblia.* 2 → see also **translate** 3 N-VAR In geometry, **translation** is the change of position of a figure such as a triangle in which all the points of the figure are moved the same distance and in the same direction. *traslación* [TECHNICAL]

**trans|lu|cent** /trænzlus$^{\text{ə}}$nt/ ADJ If a material is **translucent,** some light can pass through it. *translúcido* ❑ *The roof is made of translucent plastic. El techo es de plástico translúcido.*

**trans|mis|sion** /trænzmɪʃ$^{\text{ə}}$n/ (**transmissions**) 1 N-UNCOUNT The **transmission** of something is the passing or sending of it to a different person or place. *transmisión* ❑ *...e-mail and other forms of electronic data transmission. ...correo electrónico y otras formas de transmisión electrónica de datos.* 2 N-UNCOUNT The **transmission** of television or radio programs is the broadcasting of them. *transmisión* ❑ *The transmission of the program was canceled. Se canceló la transmisión del programa.* 3 N-COUNT A **transmission** is a broadcast. *transmisión, emisión* ❑ *...foreign television transmissions. ...transmisiones de televisión extranjera.* 4 N-UNCOUNT **Transmission** is the passage of light through matter. *transmisión*

**trans|mit** /trænzmɪt/ (**transmits, transmitting, transmitted**) 1 V-T/V-I When radio and television programs, computer data, or other electronic messages **are transmitted,** they are sent using wires, radio waves, or satellites. *transmitir* ❑ *The game was transmitted live. El juego se transmitió en vivo.* ❑ *...the best way to transmit certain types of data. ...la*

t

**Word Web** transportation

**Mass transportation** began more than 200 years ago. By 1830, there were horse-drawn **streetcars** in New York City and New Orleans. They ran on **rails** built into the **right of way** of city streets. The first electric **tram** opened in Berlin in 1881. Later, **buses** became more popular because they didn't require **tracks**. Today, **commuter trains** link **suburbs** to cities everywhere. Many large cities also have an underground train system. It may be called the **subway**, metro, or tube. In cities with steep hills, cable cars are a popular form of mass **transit**.

*mejor manera de transmitir cierto tipo de datos.* **2** V-T If one person or animal **transmits** a disease to another, they have the disease and cause the other person or animal to have it. *transmitir, contagiar* [FORMAL] ❑ *...insects that transmit disease to humans. ...insectos que transmiten enfermedades al ser humano.*

**trans|mit|ter** /trænzmɪtər/ (**transmitters**) N-COUNT A **transmitter** is a piece of equipment that is used for broadcasting television or radio programs. *transmisor* ❑ *...a homemade radio transmitter. ...un radio transmisor casero.*
→ see **cellphone, radio**

**trans|par|ent** /trænspɛərənt, -pær-/ **1** ADJ If an object or substance is **transparent,** you can see through it. *transparente, translúcido* ❑ *...a sheet of transparent plastic. ...un pliego de plástico transparente.* **2** ADJ If a situation, system, or activity is **transparent,** it is easily understood or recognized. *transparente, claro* ❑ *The company has to make its operations as transparent as possible. La empresa tiene que hacer sus operaciones de la manera más transparente posible.*
→ see **glass**

**tran|spi|ra|tion** /trænspɪreɪʃən/ N-UNCOUNT **Transpiration** is the process by which plants release water vapor into the air through their leaves. *transpiración* [TECHNICAL]

**trans|plant** (**transplants, transplanting, transplanted**)

> The noun is pronounced /trænsplænt/. The verb is pronounced /trænsplænt/.

**1** N-VAR A **transplant** is a medical operation in which a part of a person's body is replaced because it is diseased. *trasplante* ❑ *...a heart transplant. ...un trasplante de corazón.* **2** V-T To **transplant** something or someone means to move them to a different place. *trasplantar, trasladar* ❑ *...an operation to transplant a kidney. ...un trasplante de riñón.*
→ see **donor, hospital**

**tran|spond|er** /trænspɒndər/ (**transponders**) N-COUNT A **transponder** is a type of radio transmitter that transmits signals automatically when it receives particular signals. *radiofaro de respuesta, transpondedor*

**trans|port** (**transports, transporting, transported**)

> The verb is pronounced /trænspɔrt/. The noun is pronounced /trænspɔrt/.

V-T To **transport** people or goods somewhere is to take them from one place to another in a vehicle. *transportar, acarrear* ❑ *Buses transported passengers to the town. Los pasajeros fueron llevados a la ciudad en autobús.*

**trans|por|ta|tion** /trænspərteɪʃən/ **1** N-UNCOUNT **Transportation** refers to any type of vehicle that you can travel in or carry goods in. *transporte* ❑ *The company will provide transportation. La empresa pondrá el transporte.* **2** N-UNCOUNT **Transportation** is a system for taking people or goods from one place to another, for example, using buses or trains. *transporte* ❑ *...public transportation. ...transporte público.* **3** N-UNCOUNT **Transportation** is the activity of taking goods or people from one place to another in a vehicle. *transporte* ❑ *...transportation costs. ...costos del transporte.*
→ see Word Web: **transportation**

**trans|ver|sal** /trænzvɜrsəl/ (**transversals**) N-COUNT A **transversal** is a straight line that crosses two or more other lines. *transversal* [TECHNICAL]

**trans|verse wave** /trænzvɜrs weɪv/ (**transverse waves**) N-COUNT **Transverse waves** are waves, such as those in water, in which the material that the waves are passing through moves at right angles to the waves. Compare **longitudinal wave.** *onda transversa* [TECHNICAL]

**trap** /træp/ (**traps, trapping, trapped**) **1** N-COUNT A **trap** is a device for catching animals. *trampa* ❑ *Nathan's dog got caught in a trap. El perro de Nathan se quedó atrapado en una trampa.* **2** V-T To **trap** animals means to catch them using traps. *atrapar, cazar* ❑ *People were encouraged to trap and kill mice. Se instaba a las personas a que atraparan y mataran ratones.* **3** N-COUNT A **trap** is a trick that is intended to catch or deceive someone. *trampa, artimaña, ardid* ❑ *He suspected a police trap. Sospechaba de una celada de la policía.* **4** V-T If someone **traps** you, they trick you so that you do or say something that you do not want to. *tender una trampa* ❑ *Were you trying to trap her into making an admission? ¿Estabas tratando de acorralarla para que aceptara?* **5** V-T If you **are trapped** somewhere, something falls onto you or blocks your way and

T

prevents you from moving. atrapar ❑ *The train was trapped underground by a fire.* *El tren quedó atrapado bajo tierra por un incendio.* ❑ *The car turned over, trapping both men.* *El carro se volteó y los dos hombres quedaron atrapados.*

**Word Partnership** Usar *trap* con:

V. **avoid a** trap, **caught in a** trap, **fall into a** trap, **set a** trap 1 3

**trash** /træʃ/ 1 N-UNCOUNT **Trash** consists of unwanted things or waste material such as used paper, empty containers and bottles, and waste food. basura, desecho, desperdicio ❑ *The yards are full of trash.* *Los patios están llenos de desperdicios.* 2 N-UNCOUNT If you say that something such as a book, painting, or movie is **trash,** you mean that it is of very bad quality. basura, porquería [INFORMAL] ❑ *Pop music doesn't have to be trash.* *La música pop no tiene que ser de mala calidad.*

**Thesaurus** *trash* Ver también:

N. debris, garbage, junk, litter 1

**trash can** (**trash cans**) N-COUNT A **trash can** is a large round container which people put their trash in and which is usually kept outside their house. bote de basura, cubo de basura, basurero, tacho de basura

**trau|ma** /traʊmə, trɔ-/ (**traumas**) N-VAR **Trauma** is a very severe shock or very upsetting experience, which may cause psychological damage. trauma ❑ *I've been through the trauma of divorce.* *He estado pasando por el trauma del divorcio.*

**trav|el** /træv^əl/ (**travels, traveling** or **travelling, traveled** or **travelled**) 1 V-T/V-I If you **travel,** you go from one place to another, often to a place that is far away. viajar, hacer un viaje ❑ *You could travel to Nova Scotia tomorrow.* *Podrías irte a Nova Scotia mañana.* ❑ *I've been traveling all day.* *He estado viajando todo el día.* ❑ *Students often travel hundreds of miles to get here.* *Los estudiantes suelen viajar cientos de kilómetros para llegar aquí.* 2 N-UNCOUNT **Travel** is the activity of traveling. viaje ❑ *Information on travel in New Zealand is available at the hotel.* *En el hotel tienen información sobre cómo viajar en Nueva Zelanda.* ❑ *He hated air travel.* *Detestaba los viajes por aire.* 3 V-I When light or sound from one place reaches another, you say that it **travels** to the other place. propagarse ❑ *When sound travels through water, strange things can happen.* *Cuando el sonido se propaga por el agua, pueden suceder cosas extrañas.* 4 N-PLURAL Someone's **travels** are the trips that they make to places a long way from their home. viaje ❑ *He collects souvenirs on his travels abroad.* *Colecciona souvenirs de sus viajes al extranjero.*

**Thesaurus** *travel* Ver también:

V. explore, trek, visit 1
N. expedition, journey, trip 2

**Word Partnership** Usar *travel* con:

N. travel **the world** 1
**air** travel, travel **arrangements**, travel **books**, **car** travel, travel **delays**, travel **expenses**, travel **guide**, travel **industry**, travel **insurance**, travel **plans**, travel **reports**, travel **reservations** 2
ADV. travel **abroad**, travel **overseas** 1 2

**trav|el agen|cy** (**travel agencies**) N-COUNT A **travel agency** or **travel agent's** is a business which makes arrangements for people's vacations and trips. agencia de viajes

**trav|el|er** /trævələr/ (**travelers**) also **traveller** N-COUNT A **traveler** is a person who is on a trip or a person who travels a lot. viajero o viajera, viajante, turista ❑ *...airline travelers.* *...pasajeros de las líneas aéreas.*

**trav|el|er's check** (**traveler's checks**) N-COUNT **Traveler's checks** are special checks that you can use as cash or exchange for the currency of the country that you are in when you travel. cheque de viajero, traveler's check

**tray** /treɪ/ (**trays**) N-COUNT A **tray** is a flat piece of wood, plastic, or metal which is used for carrying things, especially food and drinks. charola, bandeja

**tread** /trɛd/ (**treads, treading, trod, trodden**) 1 N-VAR The **tread** of a tire or shoe is the pattern of thin lines cut into its surface that stops it from slipping. dibujo ❑ *The tires had a good depth of tread.* *El dibujo de las llantas tenía buena profundidad.* 2 V-I If you **tread** in a particular way, you walk that way. pisar [LITERARY] ❑ *She trod softly up the stairs.* *Subió suavemente las escaleras.* 3 V-I If you **tread** carefully, you behave in a careful or cautious way. irse con cuidado ❑ *If you are hoping to form a new relationship, tread carefully and slowly to begin with.* *Si esperas formar una nueva relación, al principio, ándate con cuidado.*

**treas|ure** /trɛʒər/ (**treasures, treasuring, treasured**) 1 N-UNCOUNT In stories, **treasure** is a collection of valuable old objects, such as gold coins and jewels. tesoro [LITERARY] ❑ *...buried treasure.* *...tesoro enterrado* 2 N-COUNT **Treasures** are valuable objects, especially works of art and items of historical value. tesoro, riqueza ❑ *The house was large and full of art treasures.* *La casa era grande y estaba llena de tesoros artísticos.* 3 V-T If you **treasure** something that you have, you keep it or care for it carefully because it gives you great pleasure and you think it is very special. atesorar, apreciar mucho ❑ *She treasures her memories of those happy days.* *Atesora sus recuerdos de aquellos días felices.* • **treas|ured** ADJ preciado ❑ *...my most treasured possessions.* *...mis bienes más preciados.*

**treas|ur|er** /trɛʒərər/ (**treasurers**) N-COUNT The **treasurer** of a society or organization is the person in charge of its finances. tesorero o tesorera

**treas|ury bill** /trɛʒəri bɪl/ (**treasury bills**) also **Treasury bill** or **Treasury Bill** N-COUNT A **treasury bill** is a short-term bond that is issued by the United States government in order to raise money. bono del Tesoro

**treat** /trit/ (**treats, treating, treated**) 1 V-T If

t

you **treat** someone or something in a particular way, you behave toward them or deal with them in that way. tratar, considerar ❑ *All faiths should be treated with respect.* *Todas las religiones deben tratarse con respeto.* ❑ *Stop treating me like a child.* *Deja de tratarme como niño.* **2** V-T When a doctor or nurse **treats** a patient or an illness, he or she tries to make the patient well again. tratar, atender, curar ❑ *Doctors treated her with medication.* *Los médicos le dieron medicamentos.* ❑ *The boy was treated for a minor head wound.* *Al niño le atendieron una pequeña herida en la cabeza.* **3** V-T If something **is treated with** a particular substance, the substance is put onto or into it, for example in order to clean or protect it. tratar ❑ *The fields are treated with insecticide.* *Los campos se tratan con insecticida.* **4** V-T If you **treat** someone **to** something special, you buy it or arrange it for them. invitar, convidar, obsequiar ❑ *She was always treating him to ice cream.* *Siempre le estaba invitando helados.* ❑ *Tomorrow I'll treat myself to a day's gardening.* *Mañana me voy a dar el lujo de dedicar el día a la jardinería.* ● **Treat** is also a noun. regalo, obsequio, agasajo, gusto ❑ *Lesley returned from town with a special treat for him.* *Lesley volvió de la ciudad con un regalo especial para él.*

**Word Partnership** Usar *treat* con:

ADV. treat **differently**, treat **equally**, treat **fairly**, treat **well** **1**
PREP. treat **with contempt/dignity/respect** **1**
N. treat **people**, treat **women** **1** **2**
treat **AIDS**, treat **cancer**, treat **a disease**, **doctors** treat **2**

**treat|ment** /tri̲tmənt/ (**treatments**) **1** N-VAR **Treatment** is medical attention given to a sick or injured person or animal. tratamiento, terapia, régimen terapéutico ❑ *Many patients are not getting the medical treatment they need.* *Muchos pacientes no reciben el tratamiento médico que necesitan.* **2** N-UNCOUNT Your **treatment** of someone is the way you behave toward them or deal with them. trato ❑ *We don't want any special treatment.* *No queremos trato especial.*
→ see **cancer, illness**

**Word Partnership** Usar *treatment* con:

V. **get/receive** treatment, **give** treatment, **undergo** treatment **1**
N. treatment **of addiction**, **AIDS** treatment, **cancer** treatment, treatment **center**, treatment **of an illness** **1**
treatment **of prisoners** **2**
ADJ. **effective** treatment, **medical** treatment **1**
**better** treatment, **equal/unequal** treatment, **fair** treatment, **humane** treatment, **special** treatment **2**

**trea|ty** /tri̲ti/ (**treaties**) N-COUNT A **treaty** is a written agreement between countries. tratado, acuerdo, convenio ❑ *...a treaty on global warming.* *...un tratado sobre el calentamiento global.*

**tre|ble clef** (**treble clefs**) N-COUNT A **treble clef** is a symbol that you use when writing music in order to show that the notes on the staff are above middle C. clave de sol

**tree** /tri̲/ (**trees**) N-COUNT A **tree** is a tall plant that has a hard trunk, branches, and leaves. árbol ❑ *I planted those apple trees.* *Yo planté esos manzanos.*
→ see Word Web: **tree**
→ see **forest, location, plant**

**trek** /trɛ̲k/ (**treks, trekking, trekked**) V-I If you **trek** somewhere, you go on a journey across difficult country, usually on foot. caminar fatigosamente, hacer senderismo ❑ *...trekking through the jungle.* *...caminar por la selva.* ● **Trek** is also a noun. caminata ❑ *He is on a trek through the desert.* *Participa en una caminata por el desierto.*

**trem|ble** /trɛ̲mbᵊl/ (**trembles, trembling, trembled**) **1** V-I If you **tremble,** you shake slightly because you are frightened or cold. temblar, estremecerse, vibrar ❑ *He began to tremble all over.* *Empezó a temblar todito.* ❑ *Lisa was white and trembling with anger.* *Lisa palideció y temblaba de ira.* **2** V-I If something **trembles,** it shakes slightly. temblar, estremecer(se) [LITERARY] ❑ *He felt the earth tremble under him.* *Sintió que la tierra se estremecía bajo sus pies.*

**tre|men|dous** /trɪmɛ̲ndəs/ **1** ADJ You use **tremendous** to emphasize how strong a feeling or quality is, or how large an amount is. tremendo, enorme, formidable, extraordinario ❑ *I felt a tremendous pressure on my chest.* *Sentí una presión tremenda en el pecho.* ● **tre|men|dous|ly** ADV tremendamente ❑ *I thought they played tremendously well, didn't you?* *Pensé que jugaban formidablemente bien, ¿tú no?* **2** ADJ You can describe someone or something as **tremendous** when you think they are very good or very impressive. formidable, impresionante, increíble ❑ *I thought her performance was absolutely tremendous.* *Pensé que su interpretación había sido absolutamente formidable.*

**trend** /trɛ̲nd/ (**trends**) N-COUNT A **trend** is a change or development toward something different. tendencia, inclinación ❑ *...a trend toward part-time employment.* *...una tendencia hacia empleos de tiempo parcial.*

**Word Partnership** Usar *trend* con:

V. **continue a** trend, **reverse a** trend, **start a** trend
ADJ. **current** trend, **disturbing** trend, **growing** trend, **latest** trend, **new** trend, **overall** trend, **recent** trend, **upward** trend, **warming** trend

**tri|ad** /tra̲ɪæd/ (**triads**) N-COUNT In music, a **triad** is a chord consisting of three notes. triada, acorde perfecto [TECHNICAL]

**tri|al** /tra̲ɪəl/ (**trials**) **1** N-VAR A **trial** is a formal meeting in a law court, at which a judge and jury listen to evidence and decide whether a person is guilty of a crime. If someone is **on trial,** they are being judged in this way. juicio, proceso ❑ *New evidence showed the witness lied at the trial.* *Con nuevas evidencias se demostró que el testigo había mentido en el juicio.* ❑ *He is currently on trial for burglary.* *Actualmente lo están juzgando por robo con allanamiento.* **2** N-VAR A **trial** is an experiment in which you test something by using it or doing it for a period of time to see how well it works. If something is **on trial,** it is being tested in this way. experimento, prueba ❑ *The drug is being tested in clinical trials.* *El*

T

**Word Web** tree

**Trees** are one of the oldest living things. They are also the largest **plant**. Some scientists believe that the largest living thing on Earth is a coniferous giant redwood tree named General Grant. Other scientists think a huge **grove** of **deciduous** aspen trees known as Pando is larger. This grove is a single plant because all of the trees grow from the root system of just one tree. Pando covers more than 106 acres. Some aspen trees **germinate** from seeds, but most come from natural cloning. In this process the parent tree sends up new **sprouts** from its root system. Fossil records show tree clones may live up to a million years.

*fármaco está siendo sometido a pruebas clínicas.* ❑ *I took the car out for a trial on the roads. Salí a probar el coche en las calles.* **3** PHRASE If you do something **by trial and error,** you try several different methods of doing it until you find the method that works best. *ensayo y error* ❑ *Many life-saving drugs were discovered by trial and error. Muchas sustancias que salvan vidas se descubrieron por ensayo y error.*
→ see Word Web: **trial**

**Word Partnership** Usar *trial* con:

V. **await** trial, **bring** ***someone*** **to** trial, **face** trial, **go on** trial, **put on** trial **1**
ADJ. **civil** trial, **fair** trial, **federal** trial, **speedy** trial, **upcoming** trial **1**
**clinical** trial **2**
N. trial **date**, **jury** trial, **murder** trial, **outcome of a** trial **1**
trial **and error** **3**

**Word Link** *tri ≈ three : triangle, trillion, triple*

**tri|an|gle** /traɪæŋgᵊl/ (**triangles**) N-COUNT A **triangle** is a shape with three straight sides. *triángulo* ❑ *Its outline forms a triangle. Su contorno forma un triángulo.* ● **tri|an|gu|lar** /traɪæŋgyələr/ ADJ *triangular* ❑ *...a triangular roof. ...un techo en forma de triángulo.*
→ see **shape**

**tribe** /traɪb/ (**tribes**) N-COUNT **Tribe** is sometimes used to refer to a group of people of the same race, language, and customs, especially in a developing country. Some people disapprove of this use. *tribu* ❑ *...three hundred members of the Xhosa tribe. ...trescientos miembros de la tribu Xhosa.* ● **trib|al** /traɪbᵊl/ ADJ *tribal* ❑ *...tribal lands. ...tierras de la tribu.*

**tri|bu|nal** /traɪbyunᵊl/ (**tribunals**) N-COUNT A **tribunal** is a special court or committee that is appointed to deal with particular problems. *tribunal, juzgado, comisión investigadora* ❑ *His case comes before an industrial tribunal in March. Su caso se presentará ante un tribunal industrial en marzo.*

**tribu|tary** /trɪbyətɛri/ (**tributaries**) N-COUNT A **tributary** is a stream or river that flows into a larger one. *tributario*

**trib|ute** /trɪbyut/ (**tributes**) **1** N-VAR A **tribute** is something that you say, do, or make to show your admiration and respect for someone. *tributo, homenaje* ❑ *The song is a tribute to Roy Orbison. La canción es un homenaje a Roy Orbison.* **2** N-SING If one thing is **a tribute to** another, the first thing is the result of the second and shows how good it is. *resultado, tributo* ❑ *His success has been a tribute to hard work. Sus éxitos se deben a un intenso trabajo.*

**trick** /trɪk/ (**tricks, tricking, tricked**) **1** V-T If someone **tricks** you, they deceive you, often in order to make you do something. *engañar, embaucar* ❑ *Stephen is going to be very upset when*

**Word Web** trial

Many countries have **trial** by jury. The **judge** begins by explaining the **charges** against the **defendant**. Next the defendant **pleads guilty** or not guilty. Then the **lawyers** for the **plaintiff** and the defendant present **evidence**. Both **attorneys** interview **witnesses**. They can also question each other's **clients**. Sometimes the lawyers **cross-examine** witnesses about their **testimony**. When the lawyers finish, the **jury** meets to **deliberate**. They deliver their **verdict**. If the jury says the defendant is guilty, the judge **pronounces** the **sentence**. Sometimes the defendant may be able to **appeal** the verdict and ask for a new trial.

*he finds out how you tricked him.* *Stephen se va a decepcionar mucho cuando se dé cuenta de cómo lo engañaste.* ❑ *His family tricked him into going camping.* *Su familia lo engatusó para ir de campamento.* ● **Trick** is also a noun. *ardid, treta, jugarreta, broma, truco* ❑ *We are playing a trick on a man who keeps bothering me.* *Vamos a hacerle una jugarreta a un hombre que no deja de molestarme.* **2** N-COUNT A **trick** is a clever or skillful action that someone does in order to entertain people. *truco* ❑ *He shows me card tricks.* *Me enseña trucos con las cartas.* **3** N-COUNT A **trick** is a clever way of doing something. *truco* ❑ *I use a trick of my mother's for perfect mashed potatoes.* *Uso un secreto de mi madre para que el puré de papa me salga perfecto.* **4** PHRASE If something **does the trick,** it achieves what you wanted. *resolver el problema, surtir efecto* [INFORMAL] ❑ *Sometimes a few words will do the trick.* *A veces unas cuantas palabras son suficientes.*

**Word Partnership** Usar trick con:

ADJ. **cheap** trick **1**
**clever** trick, **neat** trick, **old** trick **1**–**3**
V. **play a** trick, **pull a** trick, **try to** trick ***someone*** **1**
**do the** trick **4**
N. **card** trick **2**

**tricky** /trɪki/ (**trickier, trickiest**) ADJ A **tricky** task or problem is difficult to deal with. *difícil, delicado, peliagudo* ❑ *Parking can be tricky downtown.* *Estacionarse en el centro puede ser una lata.*

**tri|col|or** /traɪkʌlər/ (**tricolors**) N-COUNT A **tricolor** is a flag which is made up of blocks of three different colors, such as the Mexican flag. *tricolor*

**tried** /traɪd/ **1** ADJ **Tried** is used in the expressions **tried and tested** and **tried and true,** which describe a product or method that has already been used and has been found to be successful. *de probada calidad* ❑ *...over 1,000 tried-and-tested recipes.* *...más de 1000 recetas comprobadas.* **2** → see also **try**

**trig|ger** /trɪgər/ (**triggers, triggering, triggered**) **1** N-COUNT The **trigger** of a gun is a small lever which you pull to fire it. *gatillo* ❑ *A man pointed a gun at them and pulled the trigger.* *Un hombre les apuntó con un arma y jaló el gatillo.* **2** V-T To **trigger** a bomb or system means to cause it to work. *hacer estallar, disparar* ❑ *The thieves triggered the alarm.* *Los ladrones activaron la alarma.* **3** V-T If something **triggers** an event or situation, it causes it to begin to happen or exist. *desencadenar* ❑ *...the incident which triggered the outbreak of the war.* *...el incidente que desató la guerra.* ● **Trigger off** means the same as **trigger.** *provocar, desatar* ❑ *It is still not clear what triggered off the demonstrations.* *Seguimos sin conocer la causa de las protestas.* **4** N-COUNT If something acts as a **trigger for** another thing such as an illness, event, or situation, the first thing causes the second thing to begin to happen or exist. *disparador* ❑ *Stress may be a trigger for these illnesses.* *El estrés puede desencadenar esas enfermedades.*

**Word Link** *tri ≈ three : triangle, trillion, triple*

**tril|lion** /trɪlyən/ (**trillions**)

The plural form is **trillion** after a number, or after a word or expression referring to a number, such as "several" or "a few."

NUM A **trillion** is 1,000,000,000,000. *billón* ❑ *...a 4 trillion dollar debt.* *una deuda de cuatro billones de dólares.*

**trim** /trɪm/ (**trimmer, trimmest, trims, trimming, trimmed**) **1** ADJ Something that is **trim** is neat and attractive. *bonito, pulcro* ❑ *The neighbors' gardens were trim and neat.* *Los jardines de los vecinos estaban muy bien cuidados.* **2** ADJ If someone has a **trim** figure, they are slim. *esbelto, elegante* ❑ *...a trim young woman.* *...una joven muy estilizada.* **3** V-T If you **trim** something, you cut off small amounts of it in order to make it look neater. *recortar, arreglar* ❑ *My friend trims my hair every eight weeks.* *Mi amigo me despunta el cabello cada ocho semanas.* ● **Trim** is also a noun. *corte, recorte* ❑ *His hair needed a trim.* *Necesitaba un corte de cabello.* **4** V-T If something such as a piece of clothing **is trimmed with** a type of material or design, it is decorated with it, usually along its edges. *adornar con, decorar con* ❑ *...jackets which are trimmed with ribbon.* *...sacos ribeteados con listón.* **5** N-VAR The **trim** on something such as a piece of clothing is a decoration along its edges in a different color or material. *ribete, adorno* ❑ *...a white scarf with black trim.* *...una bufanda blanca con ribete negro.*

**tri|mes|ter** /traɪmɛstər/ (**trimesters**) **1** N-COUNT A **trimester** of a pregnancy is one of the three periods of three months into which it is divided. *trimestre* ❑ *...the end of the first trimester.* *...el final del primer trimestre.* **2** N-COUNT In some colleges and universities, a **trimester** is one of the three main periods into which the year is divided. *trimestre*

**trio** /triοʊ/ (**trios**) N-COUNT A **trio** is a group of three people, especially musicians or singers. *trío, terceto, terna* ❑ *...American songs from a Texas trio.* *...canciones estadounidenses con un trío texano.*

**trip** /trɪp/ (**trips, tripping, tripped**) **1** N-COUNT A **trip** is a journey that you make to a particular place. *viaje, excursión* ❑ *We're taking a trip to Montana.* *Vamos a un recorrido por Montana.* ❑ *On Thursday we went out on a day trip.* *El jueves fuimos a una excursión de un día.* **2** → see also **round trip** **3** V-I If you **trip** when you are walking, you knock your foot against something and fall or nearly fall. *tropezar(se), dar un traspié* ❑ *She tripped and broke her hip.* *Se tropezó y al caer se rompió la cadera.* ● **Trip up** means the same as **trip.** *tropezar(se), dar un traspié* ❑ *I tripped up and hurt my foot.* *Al tropezarme, me lastimé el pie.* **4** V-T If you **trip** someone who is walking or running, you put your foot or something else in front of them, so that they knock their own foot against it and fall or nearly fall. *poner una zancadilla, hacer tropezar* ❑ *One guy stuck his foot out and tried to trip me.* *Un tipo estiró la pierna y trató de ponerme una zancadilla.* ● **Trip up** means the same as **trip.** *poner una zancadilla, hacer tropezar* ❑ *He made a sudden dive for Uncle Jim's legs to try to trip him up.* *Se abalanzó a las piernas del tío Jim para tratar de hacerlo caer.*

T

**Word Partnership** Usar *trip* con:

N. boat trip, bus trip, business trip, camping trip, field trip, trip home, return trip, shopping trip, train trip, vacation trip 1
V. cancel a trip, make a trip, plan a trip, return from a trip, take a trip 1
ADJ. free trip, last trip, long trip, next trip, recent trip, safe trip, short trip 1

**Word Link** *tri ≈ three : triangle, trillion, triple*

**tri|ple** /trɪpᵊl/ (**triples, tripling, tripled**) 1 ADJ **Triple** means consisting of three things or parts. *triple* ❑ *...a triple somersault. ...un mortal triple.* 2 V-T/V-I If something **triples** or if you **triple** it, it becomes three times as large in size or number. *triplicar(se)* ❑ *I got a fantastic new job and my salary tripled. Conseguí un fantástico trabajo y mi salario se triplicó.* ❑ *The exhibition has tripled in size from last year. La exposición es tres veces más grande que la del año pasado.*

**tri|ple me|ter** (**triple meters**) N-VAR Music that is written in **triple meter** has a beat that is repeated in groups of three. Compare **duple meter**. *compás ternario* [TECHNICAL]

**tri|umph** /traɪʌmf/ (**triumphs, triumphing, triumphed**) 1 N-VAR A **triumph** is a great success or achievement. *éxito, triunfo, victoria* ❑ *The championships were a personal triumph for the coach. Los campeonatos fueron un triunfo personal para el entrenador.* 2 N-UNCOUNT **Triumph** is a feeling of great satisfaction and pride resulting from a success or victory. *triunfo* ❑ *...her sense of triumph. ...su sensación de triunfo.* 3 V-I If someone or something **triumphs,** they win a great victory or succeed in overcoming something. *triunfar, obtener una victoria* ❑ *The movie is about good triumphing over evil. La película trata del triunfo del bien sobre el mal.*

**trom|bone** /trɒmboʊn/ (**trombones**) N-VAR A **trombone** is a brass musical instrument which you play by blowing into it and sliding part of it backward and forward. *trombón* ❑ *Her husband played the trombone. Su esposo tocaba el trombón.*
→ see **brass**

**troop** /tru̲p/ (**troops, trooping, trooped**) 1 N-PLURAL **Troops** are soldiers. *tropas, soldados* ❑ *...35,000 troops from a dozen countries. ...35,000 soldados de una docena de países.* 2 N-COUNT A **troop** is a group of soldiers. *tropa, ejército, escuadrón* ❑ *...a troop of American marines. ...una compañía de marines estadounidenses.* 3 V-I If people **troop** somewhere, they walk there in a group. *apiñarse, agruparse, entrar/salir en tropel* [INFORMAL] ❑ *They all trooped back to the house for a rest. Todos volvieron en bola a la casa a descansar.*
→ see **army**

**troop|er** /tru̲pər/ (**troopers**) 1 N-COUNT In the United States, a **trooper** is a police officer in a state police force. *agente de policía* ❑ *He considered becoming a state trooper. Pensó en hacerse policía de la guardia civil.* 2 N-COUNT; N-TITLE A **trooper** is a soldier of low rank in the cavalry or in an armored regiment in the army. *soldado de caballería* ❑ *...a trooper from the 7th Cavalry. ...un soldado del 7° de caballería.*

**tro|phy** /troʊfi/ (**trophies**) N-COUNT A **trophy** is a prize such as a cup, given to the winner of a competition. *trofeo, copa* ❑ *The special trophy for the best rider went to Chris Read. El trofeo especial al mejor jinete lo ganó Chris Read.*

**tropi|cal** /trɒpɪkᵊl/ ADJ **Tropical** means belonging to or typical of the tropics. *tropical* ❑ *...tropical diseases. ...enfermedades tropicales.*
→ see **habitat**

**tropi|cal de|pres|sion** (**tropical depressions**) N-COUNT A **tropical depression** is a system of thunderstorms that begins in the tropics and has relatively low wind speeds. It is the second stage in the development of a hurricane. *depresión tropical*
→ see **hurricane**

**tropi|cal dis|turb|ance** (**tropical disturbances**) N-COUNT A **tropical disturbance** is a system of thunderstorms that begins in the tropics and lasts for more than 24 hours. It is the first stage in the development of a hurricane. *perturbación tropical*

**tropi|cal storm** (**tropical storms**) N-COUNT A **tropical storm** is a system of thunderstorms that begins in the tropics and has relatively high wind speeds. It is the third stage in the development of a hurricane. *tormenta tropical*
→ see **disaster, hurricane**

**tropi|cal zone** (**tropical zones**) N-COUNT The **tropical zone** is the part of the Earth's surface near the equator, where the climate is hot and wet. *zona tropical, región tropical*

**tro|pism** /troʊpɪzəm/ (**tropisms**) N-VAR A **tropism** is the involuntary movement of a plant or other organism in response to an external stimulus such as heat or light. *tropismo* [TECHNICAL]

**tropo|sphere** /trɒpəsfɪər, troʊ-/ N-SING The **troposphere** is the layer of the Earth's atmosphere that is closest to the Earth's surface. *tropósfera, troposfera*

**trou|ble** /trʌbᵊl/ (**troubles, troubling, troubled**) 1 N-VAR You can refer to problems or difficulties as **trouble.** *contratiempo, problema, inconveniencia* ❑ *I had trouble parking. Tuve problemas para estacionarme.* ❑ *You've caused us a lot of trouble. Nos has causado muchos inconvenientes.* 2 N-SING If you say that one aspect of a situation is **the trouble,** you mean that it is the aspect which is causing problems or making the situation unsatisfactory. *problema* ❑ *The trouble is that he's still sick. La cosa es que sigue enfermo.* 3 N-UNCOUNT If you have, for example, kidney **trouble** or back **trouble,** there is something wrong with your kidneys or your back. *problema, trastorno, enfermedad* ❑ *Her husband has never had any heart trouble. Su esposo nunca ha tenido trastornos cardíacos.* 4 N-UNCOUNT If there is **trouble,** people are arguing or fighting. *disturbio, agitación* ❑ *Police were sent to the city to prevent trouble. Mandaron policías a la ciudad para evitar conflictos.* 5 V-T If something **troubles** you, it makes you feel worried. *preocupar, molestar, inquietar, afligir* ❑ *Is anything troubling you? ¿Qué te preocupa?* ● **trou|bling** ADJ *inquietante, perturbador* ❑ *Most troubling of all was the fact that nobody knew what was going on. Lo más preocupante de todo era que nadie sabía qué estaba* pasando. 6 PHRASE If someone is **in trouble,** they have broken a rule or law and are likely to be punished by someone in authority. *en problemas*, *en aprietos* ❑ *He was in trouble with his teachers.* *Estaba en problemas con sus maestros.* 7 PHRASE If you **take the trouble to** do something, you do something which requires some time or effort. *tomarse la molestia* ❑ *He did not take the trouble to see the movie before he criticized it.* *No se preocupó por ver la película antes de criticarla.*

**Word Partnership** Usar *trouble* con:

| | |
|---|---|
| DET. | **no** trouble 1 |
| V. | **cause** trouble, **make** trouble, **run into** trouble, **spell** trouble, **start** trouble 1 |
| | **have** trouble 1 3 |
| | **get in/into** trouble, **get out of** trouble, **stay out of** trouble 6 |
| N. | **engine** trouble 1 |
| | **sign of** trouble 1 3 4 |
| ADJ. | **financial** trouble 1 |
| | **big** trouble, **deep** trouble, **real** trouble, **serious** trouble 1 4 |
| | **heart** trouble 3 |
| PREP. | trouble **with** 1 2 4 |
| | **in** trouble 6 |
| ADV. | trouble **ahead** 1 4 |

**trou|bled** /trʌbᵊld/ ADJ **Troubled** means worried or full of problems. *preocupado*, *atribulado* ❑ *Rose sounded deeply troubled.* *A Rose se le oía muy preocupada.* ❑ *...this troubled country.* *...ese conflictivo país.*

**Word Link** *some ≈ causing : awesome, troublesome, worrisome*

**trou|ble|some** /trʌbᵊlsəm/ ADJ Someone or something that is **troublesome** causes annoying problems or difficulties. *penoso*, *fastidioso*, *problemático* ❑ *...a troublesome back injury.* *...una incómoda lesión de espalda.*

**trough** /trɔf/ (**troughs**) 1 N-COUNT A **trough** is a long narrow container from which farm animals drink or eat. *artesa*, *comedero*, *abrevadero* ❑ *...the old stone cattle trough.* *...la vieja artesa de piedra para el ganado.* 2 N-COUNT A **trough** is a low point in a pattern that has regular high and low points. *depresión* ❑ *The industry's worst trough was in 2001 and 2002.* *La peor depresión de la industria fue en 2001 y 2002.* 3 N-COUNT A **trough** is a low area between two big waves on the sea. *seno*
→ see **sound**

T

**trou|sers** /traʊzərz/

The form **trouser** is used as a modifier.

N-PLURAL **Trousers** are a piece of clothing that cover the body from the waist downward, and that cover each leg separately. *pantalón*, *pantalones* [FORMAL] ❑ *He was dressed in a shirt, dark trousers and boots.* *Llevaba camisa, pantalones oscuros y botas.*

**trow|el** /traʊəl/ (**trowels**) 1 N-COUNT A **trowel** is a small garden tool which you use for digging small holes or removing weeds. *desplantador*, *paleta* 2 N-COUNT A **trowel** is a small tool with a flat blade that you use for spreading things such as cement and plaster onto walls and other surfaces. *llana*
→ see **garden**

**truce** /trus/ (**truces**) N-COUNT A **truce** is an agreement between two people or groups of people to stop fighting or arguing for a short time. *tregua*, *respiro*, *pausa* ❑ *The fighting has given way to an uneasy truce between the two sides.* *La lucha había cedido ante una incómoda tregua entre las partes.*

**truck** /trʌk/ (**trucks, trucking, trucked**) 1 N-COUNT A **truck** is a large vehicle that is used to transport goods by road. *camión de carga* ❑ *They heard the roar of a heavy truck.* *Oyeron el estruendo de un camión pesado.* ❑ *My dad is a truck driver.* *Mi papá es camionero.* 2 N-COUNT A **truck** is a vehicle with a large area in the back for carrying things and with low sides to make it easy to load and unload. *camioneta*, *pick-up* ❑ *There are only two seats in the truck.* *La pick-up sólo tiene dos asientos.*

**truck|er** /trʌkər/ (**truckers**) N-COUNT A **trucker** is someone who drives a truck as their job. *camionero o camionera*, *conductor de camión o conductora de camión*, *transportista*

**truck stop** (**truck stops**) N-COUNT A **truck stop** is a place where drivers, especially truck drivers, can stop to rest or to get something to eat. *paradero de camiones*

**true** /tru/ (**truer, truest**) 1 ADJ If something is **true,** it is accurate and based on facts, and is not invented or imagined. *cierto*, *válido*, *verdadero*, *real* ❑ *Everything she said was true.* *Todo lo que dijo era verídico.* ❑ *The movie is based on a true story.* *La película está basada en una historia real.* 2 ADJ **True** means real, genuine, or typical. *real*, *genuino* ❑ *This country claims to be a true democracy.* *Este país se las da de ser una genuina democracia.* ❑ *Maybe one day you'll find true love.* *Quizá algún día encuentres el verdadero amor.* 3 ADJ **True north** is the same as the **North Pole. True south** is the same as the **South Pole.** *norte/sur geográfico*, *norte/sur verdadero* [TECHNICAL] 4 PHRASE If a dream, wish, or prediction **comes true,** it actually happens. *resultar cierto*, *realizarse* ❑ *When I was 13, my dream came true and I got my first horse.* *Cuando tenía 13 años, mi sueño se hizo realidad y recibí mi primer caballo.* 5 PHRASE If a general statement **holds true** in particular circumstances, or if your previous statement **holds true** in different circumstances, it is true or valid in those circumstances. *seguir siendo cierto* [FORMAL] ❑ *I'm not sure that what you are saying holds true.* *No estoy segura de que lo que dices siga siendo cierto.* 6 **tried and true** → see **tried**

**true-breeding** ADJ A **true-breeding** plant is a plant that fertilizes itself and therefore produces offspring with exactly the same genetic characteristics as itself. *autofertilizante* [TECHNICAL]

**tru|ly** /truli/ 1 ADV **Truly** means completely and genuinely. *sinceramente*, *correctamente* ❑ *...a truly democratic system.* *...un sistema verdaderamente democrático.* ❑ *Believe me, Susan, I am truly sorry.* *Créeme, Susan, lo siento muchísimo.* 2 ADV You can use **truly** in order to emphasize your description of something. *de veras*, *efectivamente* ❑ *...a truly great man.* *...de verdad, un gran hombre.* 3 CONVENTION You can write **Yours truly** before your signature at the end of a letter to someone you do not know very well. *cordiales saludos*, *su seguro servidor* ❑ *Yours* *truly, Phil Turner.* *Atentamente, Phil Turner.*

**trum|pet** /trʌmpɪt/ (**trumpets**) N-VAR A **trumpet** is a brass musical instrument. *trompeta* ❑ *I played the trumpet in the school orchestra.* *Yo tocaba la trompeta en la orquesta de la escuela.*
→ see **brass, orchestra**

**trunk** /trʌŋk/ (**trunks**) 1 N-COUNT The **trunk** of a tree is the large main stem from which the branches grow. *tronco* ❑ *The trunk of the tree was more than five feet across.* *El tronco del árbol tenía más de un metro de diámetro.* 2 N-COUNT The **trunk** of a car is a covered space at the back in which you put luggage or other things. *cajuela, baúl, maletero* ❑ *She opened the trunk of the car and took out a bag of groceries.* *Abrió la cajuela del coche y sacó una bolsa de comestibles.* 3 N-COUNT A **trunk** is a large, strong case or box used for storing things or for taking on a trip. *baúl* ❑ *Maloney unlocked his trunk and took out some clothing.* *Maloney abrió su baúl y sacó algo de ropa.* 4 N-COUNT An elephant's **trunk** is its long nose. *trompa*

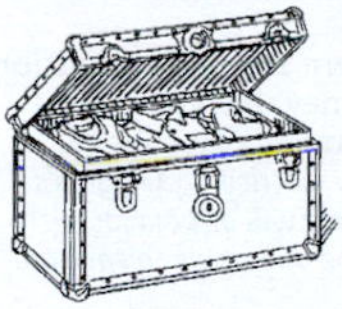
trunk

**trust** /trʌst/ (**trusts, trusting, trusted**) 1 V-T If you **trust** someone, you believe that they are honest and will not deliberately do anything to harm you. *confiar, tener confianza, fiar(se)* ❑ *"I trust you completely," he said.* *—Confío plenamente en ti —le dijo.* ● **Trust** is also a noun. *confianza, fe* ❑ *He destroyed my trust in men.* *Él acabó con mi fe en los hombres.* ❑ *...a shared feeling of trust.* *...una sensación de confianza compartida.* 2 V-T If you **trust** someone **to** do something, you believe that they will do it. *confiar en que alguien hará algo* ❑ *I trust you to keep this secret.* *Confío en que guardarás el secreto.* 3 V-T If you **trust** someone **with** something, you allow them to look after it or deal with it. *confiar(le) a* ❑ *I would trust him with my life.* *A él le confiaría mi vida.* ● **Trust** is also a noun. *confianza, responsabilidad* ❑ *She holds a position of trust.* *Su puesto es de confianza.* 4 V-T If you do not **trust** something, you feel that it is not safe or reliable. *desconfiar* ❑ *She nodded, not trusting her own voice.* *Asintió, pero no confiaba en su propia voz.* ❑ *He didn't trust his legs to hold him up.* *Creía que sus piernas no lo sostendrían.* 5 V-T If you **trust** someone's judgment or advice, you believe that it is good or right. *confiar, tener confianza* ❑ *Jake has raised two kids and I trust his judgment.* *Jake crió a dos hijos y confío en su juicio.* 6 N-COUNT A **trust** is a financial arrangement in which a group of people or an organization keeps and invests money for someone. *fondo de inversiones, fideicomiso* [BUSINESS] ❑ *You could set up a trust for the children.* *Podrías establecer un fideicomiso para los niños.*

**Word Partnership** Usar *trust* con:

V. **build** trust, **create** trust, **learn to** trust, **place** trust **in** *someone* 1
ADJ. **mutual** trust 1
**charitable** trust 6
N. trust *your* **instincts**, trust *someone's* **judgment** 5
**investment** trust 6

**trus|tee** /trʌsti/ (**trustees**) N-COUNT A **trustee** is someone with legal control of money or property that is kept or invested for another person, company, or organization. *fiduciario o fiduciaria, fideicomisario o fideicomisaria, síndico* [BUSINESS]

**truth** /truθ/ (**truths**) 1 N-UNCOUNT **The truth** about something is all the facts about it, rather than things that are imagined or invented. *verdad, veracidad, realidad* ❑ *Is it possible to tell truth from fiction?* *¿Es posible distinguir la realidad de la ficción?* ❑ *I must tell you the truth about this business.* *Tengo que decirte la verdad sobre este negocio.* 2 N-UNCOUNT If you say that there is some **truth in** a statement or story, you mean that it is true, or at least partly true. *verdad* ❑ *There is no truth in this story.* *No hay nada cierto en esa historia.* 3 N-COUNT A **truth** is something that is believed to be true. *verdad* ❑ *...a universal truth.* *...una verdad universal*

**Word Partnership** Usar *truth* con:

V. **accept the** truth, **find the** truth, **know the** truth, **learn the** truth, **search for the** truth, **tell the** truth 1
N. **a grain of** truth, **the** truth **of the matter** 1
ADJ. **the awful** truth, **the plain** truth, **the sad** truth, **the simple** truth, **the whole** truth 1
**absolute** truth 1 3

**try** /traɪ/ (**tries, trying, tried**) 1 V-T/V-I If you **try** to do something, you make an effort to do it. *tratar, intentar, procurar* ❑ *He tried to help her at work.* *Se esforzaba por ayudarle en el trabajo.* ❑ *Does it annoy you if others don't seem to try hard enough?* *¿Te molesta que parezca que los demás no se esfuerzan lo suficiente?* ❑ *I must try and see him.* *Tengo que intentar verlo.* ● **Try** is also a noun. *intento, prueba, tentativa* ❑ *It was worth a try.* *Valía la pena hacer el intento.* 2 V-I If you **try for** something, you make an effort to get it or achieve it. *intentar conseguir* ❑ *I'll just keep trying for a job.* *Voy a seguir buscando empleo.* 3 V-T If you **try** something new or different, you use it or do it in order to discover its qualities or effects. *probar* ❑ *You could try a little cheese melted on the top.* *Podrías probar cubriéndolo con un poco de queso fundido.* ● **Try** is also a noun. *prueba, intento* ❑ *All we're asking is that you give it a try.* *Lo único que te pedimos es que lo intentes.* 4 V-T If you **try** a particular place or person, you go to that place or person because you think that they may be able to provide you with what you want. *intentar, probar* ❑ *Have you tried the local music stores?* *¿Ya buscaste en las tiendas de música de aquí cerca?* 5 V-T When a person **is tried**, he or she appears in a law court and is found innocent or guilty after the judge and jury have heard the evidence. *someter a juicio, juzgar, procesar, juzgar* ❑ *Those responsible should be tried for war crimes.* *Los responsables deberían de ser juzgados por crímenes de guerra.* 6 → see also **tried** 7 to **try** your **hand** → see **hand**

▸**try on** PHR-VERB If you **try on** a piece of clothing, you put it on to see if it fits you or if it looks nice. *probar(se)* ❑ *Try on clothing and shoes to make sure they fit.* *Pruébate la ropa y los zapatos para estar segura de que te quedan.*

▸ **try out** PHR-VERB If you **try** something **out**, you test it in order to find out how useful or effective it is. *probar, poner a prueba* ❑ *I wanted to try the boat out next weekend. Quería probar el bote la próxima semana.*
▸ **try out for** PHR-VERB If you **try out for** a sports team or an acting role, you compete or you perform a test in an attempt to be chosen. *presentarse a una prueba* ❑ *He should have tried out for the Olympic team. Debían de haberlo probado para el equipo olímpico.*

**T-shirt** (**T-shirts**) also **tee-shirt** N-COUNT A **T-shirt** is a cotton shirt with no collar or buttons. T-shirts usually have short sleeves. *t-shirt, camiseta, playera*
→ see **clothing**

**tsu|na|mi** /tsʊnɑmi/ (**tsunamis**) N-COUNT A **tsunami** is a very large wave, often caused by an earthquake, that flows onto the land and can cause widespread death and destruction. *tsunami*

**tub** /tʌb/ (**tubs**) **1** N-COUNT A **tub** is the same as a **bathtub.** *tina, bañera, bañadera* ❑ *She lay back in the tub. Se recostó en la tina.* **2** N-COUNT A **tub** is a deep container of any size. *envase, tarrina* ❑ *...four tubs of ice cream. ...cuatro envases de helado.*
→ see **soap**

**tube** /tub/ (**tubes**) **1** N-COUNT A **tube** is a long hollow object that is usually round, like a pipe. *tubo, conducto* ❑ *He is fed by a tube that enters his nose. Lo alimentan por un tubo que entra por la nariz.* **2** N-COUNT A **tube of** something such as paste is a long, thin container which you squeeze in order to force the substance out. *tubo* ❑ *...a tube of toothpaste. ...un tubo de pasta de dientes.*
→ see **container**

**tube worm** (**tube worms**) also **tubeworm** N-COUNT A **tube worm** is a type of worm that lives in the sea and constructs a tube from sand and other material, which it lives in. *poliqueto tubícola*

**tuck** /tʌk/ (**tucks, tucking, tucked**) V-T If you **tuck** something somewhere, you put it there so that it is safe, comfortable, or neat. *meter, fajar(se)* ❑ *He tried to tuck his shirt inside his pants. Trató de fajarse la camisa dentro de los pantalones.*
▸ **tuck away** **1** PHR-VERB If you **tuck away** something such as money, you store it in a safe place. *guardar* ❑ *The extra income means that Phillippa can tuck away the rent. El ingreso extra significa que Phillippa puede ahorrar el dinero de la renta.* **2** PHR-VERB If someone or something **is tucked away,** they are well hidden in a quiet place where very few people go. *ocultar* ❑ *We were tucked away in a corner of the room. Estábamos escondidos en un rincón de la sala.*
▸ **tuck in** **1** PHR-VERB If you **tuck in** a piece of material, you keep it in position by placing one edge or end of it behind or under something else. *fajar(se), meter(se)* ❑ *Tuck your shirt in. Métete la camisa.* **2** PHR-VERB If you **tuck** a child **in** bed, you make them comfortable in bed by straightening the sheets and blankets and pushing the loose ends under the mattress. *arropar* ❑ *I read Lily a story and tucked her in. Leí a Lily un cuento y la tapé con las cobijas.*

T

**Tues|day** /tuzdeɪ, -di/ (**Tuesdays**) N-VAR **Tuesday** is the day after Monday and before Wednesday. *martes* ❑ *He phoned on Tuesday, just before you came. Llamó el martes, justo antes de que llegaras.* ❑ *Talks will start next Tuesday. Las pláticas empiezan el próximo martes.*

**tug** /tʌg/ (**tugs, tugging, tugged**) **1** V-T/V-I If you **tug** something or **tug at** it, you give it a quick and usually strong pull. *tirar de, jalar, arrastrar* ❑ *A little boy came running up and tugged at his sleeve excitedly. Un niñito llegó corriendo y le jaló la manga, emocionado.* • **Tug** is also a noun. *tirón, jalón* ❑ *I felt a tug at my sleeve. Sentí un tirón en la manga.* **2** N-COUNT A **tug** or a **tug boat** is a small powerful boat which pulls large ships, usually when they come into a port. *remolcador* ❑ *...an oil tanker pulled by five tug boats. ...un buque petrolero del que tiran cinco remolcadores.*

**tui|tion** /tuɪʃᵊn/ N-UNCOUNT You can use **tuition** to refer to the amount of money that you have to pay for being taught in a university, college, or private school. *colegiatura, matrícula* ❑ *Angela's $35,000 tuition at college this year will be paid for with scholarships. Este año, los 35,000 dólares de colegiatura de Angela se pagarán con becas.*

**tum|ble** /tʌmbᵊl/ (**tumbles, tumbling, tumbled**) V-I If someone or something **tumbles,** they fall with a rolling or bouncing movement. *caerse, desplomarse* ❑ *A small boy tumbled off the step. Un niñito se cayó del escalón.* • **Tumble** is also a noun. *caída* ❑ *He broke his leg in a tumble from his horse. Se rompió la pierna en una caída del caballo.*

**tu|mor** /tumər/ (**tumors**) N-COUNT A **tumor** is a mass of diseased or abnormal cells that has grown in a person's or animal's body. *tumor, bulto, masa, bola* ❑ *...a brain tumor. ...un tumor en el cerebro.*
→ see **cancer**

**tun|dra** /tʌndrə/ (**tundras**) N-VAR **Tundra** is one of the large flat areas of land in the north of Europe, Asia, and America. The ground below the top layer of soil is always frozen and no trees grow there. *tundra*

**tune** /tun/ (**tunes, tuning, tuned**) **1** N-COUNT A **tune** is a series of musical notes that is pleasant to listen to. *melodía, canción, aire, tonada* ❑ *She was humming a little tune. Tarareaba una cancioncilla.* **2** V-T When someone **tunes** a musical instrument, they adjust it so that it produces the right notes. *afinar* ❑ *We tune our guitars before we go on stage. Afinamos nuestras guitarras antes de subir al escenario.* • **Tune up** means the same as **tune.** *afinar* ❑ *Others were quietly tuning up their instruments. Otros afinaban tranquilamente sus instrumentos.* **3** V-T If your radio or television **is tuned to** a particular channel or broadcasting station, you are listening to or watching the programs being broadcast by that station. *sintonizar, poner* ❑ *A small color television was tuned to a movie channel. Una pequeña TV de color estaba en un canal de películas.* **4** → see also **fine-tune** **5** PHRASE If you say that someone **has changed** their **tune,** you are criticizing them because they have changed their opinion or way of doing things. *cambiar de parecer, cambiar de idea* ❑ *You've changed your tune since this morning, haven't you? Eso no es lo que pensabas esta mañana, ¿o sí?* **6** PHRASE A person or musical instrument that is **in tune** produces exactly the right notes. A person or musical instrument that is **out of tune** does not produce exactly the right notes. *afinado/desafinado* ❑ *It was just an ordinary voice, but he sang in tune. Su*

**Word Web** **tunnel**

The Egyptians built the first **tunnels** as entrances to tombs. Later the Babylonians* built a tunnel under the Euphrates River*. It connected the royal palace with the Temple of Jupiter*. The Romans **dug** tunnels when **mining** for gold. By the late 1600s, **explosives** had replaced **digging**. Gunpowder was used to build the **underground** section of a canal in France in 1679. Nitroglycerin explosions helped create a railroad tunnel in Massachusetts in 1867. The longest continuous tunnel in the world is the Delaware Aqueduct. It carries water from the Catskill Mountains* to New York City and is 105 miles long.

*Babylonians: people who lived in the ancient city of Babylon.*
*Euphrates River: a large river in the Middle East.*
*Temple of Jupiter: a religious building.*
*Catskill Mountains: a mountain range in the northeastern U.S.*

*voz no era nada especial, pero era afinado.*

▸**tune in** PHR-VERB If you **tune in** to a particular television or radio station or program, you watch or listen to it. *sintonizar, ver, oír* ❑ *All over the country, youngsters tune in to "Sesame Street" every day. En todo el país, los pequeños ven "Plaza Sésamo" todos los días.*

**tun|nel** /tʌnᵊl/ (**tunnels, tunneling** or **tunnelling, tunneled** or **tunnelled**) **1** N-COUNT A **tunnel** is a long passage which has been made under the ground, usually through a hill or under the sea. *túnel* ❑ *Boston drivers love the tunnel. A los conductores de Boston les encanta el túnel.* **2** V-I To **tunnel** somewhere means to make a tunnel there. *abrir un túnel, hacer un túnel* ❑ *The thieves tunneled deep under the walls. Los ladrones excavaron muy profundamente por debajo de los muros.*
→ see Word Web: **tunnel**
→ see **traffic**

**tur|bine** /tɜrbɪn, -baɪn/ (**turbines**) N-COUNT A **turbine** is a machine or engine which uses a stream of air, gas, water, or steam to turn a wheel and produce power. *turbina* ❑ *The ship will be powered by two gas turbines. El barco será impulsado por dos turbinas de gas.*
→ see **electricity, wheel**

turkey

**tur|key** /tɜrki/ (**turkeys**) N-COUNT A **turkey** is a large bird that is kept on a farm for its meat. *pavo, guajolote* ● **Turkey** is the meat of this bird eaten as food. *pavo, guajolote* ❑ *...a traditional turkey dinner. ...la cena tradicional con pavo.*

**tur|moil** /tɜrmɔɪl/ (**turmoils**) N-VAR **Turmoil** is a state of confusion or great anxiety. *agitación, confusión* ❑ *Her feelings were in turmoil. Se sentía muy confundida.*

**turn**
❶ VERB USES
❷ NOUN USES
❸ PHRASAL VERBS

❶ **turn** /tɜrn/ (**turns, turning, turned**) **1** V-T/V-I To **turn** means to move in a different direction or to move into a different position. *volver(se), dar (media) vuelta, dar(se) vuelta* ❑ *He turned and walked away. Dio media vuelta y se alejó caminando.* ❑ *She turned the chair to face the door. Dio vuelta a la silla para quedar frente a la puerta.* ❑ *He sighed, turning away and looking at the sea. Suspiró y apartó la vista para mirar hacia el mar.* ● **Turn around** means the same as **turn.** *volverse* ❑ *I felt a tap on my shoulder and I turned around. Sentí una palmada en la espalda y me di la vuelta.* **2** V-T/V-I When something **turns,** or when you **turn** it, it moves around in a circle. *girar, dar vuelta* ❑ *The wheel turned. La rueda giró.* ❑ *Turn the key three times to the right. Dé vuelta a la derecha a la llave tres veces.* **3** V-T/V-I When you **turn** in a particular direction or **turn** a corner, you change the direction in which you are moving or traveling. *dar vuelta, doblar* ❑ *He turned into the narrow street where he lived. Dio vuelta en la callejuela donde vivía.* ❑ *Now turn right to follow West Ferry Road. Ahora doble a la derecha, para seguir por West Ferry Road.* ● **Turn** is also a noun. *vuelta* ❑ *You can't do a right-hand turn here. No puedes dar vuelta a la derecha aquí.* **4** V-I If you **turn to** a particular page in a book or magazine, you open it at that page. *ir a* ❑ *To order, turn to page 236. Para hacer su pedido, vaya a la página 236.* **5** V-T/V-I If you **turn** your attention or thoughts **to** a particular subject or if you **turn to** it, you start thinking about it or discussing it. *concentrarse en, ir a* ❑ *We turn now to our main question. Vayamos ahora a la cuestión principal.* **6** V-I If you **turn to** someone, you ask for their help or advice. *acudir a, recurrir a* ❑ *For assistance, they turned to one of the city's museums. Recurrieron a uno de los museos de la ciudad en busca de colaboración.* **7** V-T/V-I If something **turns into** something else, or if you **turn** it **into** something else, it becomes something different. *convertir en, ponerse* ❑ *They plan to turn the country into a one-party*

state. Están planeando convertir al país en un estado monopartidista. ❑ *The sky turned pale pink.* El cielo adquirió un color rosa claro. 8 V-T When someone **turns** a particular age, they pass that age. When it **turns** a particular time, it passes that time. *cumplir* ❑ *He made a million dollars before he turned thirty.* Ganó un millón de dólares antes de cumplir los treinta años.
→ see **sleep**

**❷ turn** /tɜrn/ (**turns**) 1 N-COUNT If a situation or trend takes a particular kind of **turn**, it changes so that it starts developing in a different or opposite way. *giro* ❑ *The situation took a new turn over the weekend.* La situación dio un giro durante el fin de semana. 2 N-COUNT If it is your **turn to** do something, you now have the duty, chance, or right to do it, when other people have done it before you or will do it after you. *turno* ❑ *Tonight it's my turn to cook.* Esta noche es mi turno para cocinar. 3 PHRASE You use **in turn** to refer to actions or events that are in a sequence one after the other. *a la vez de* ❑ *He told his girlfriend, who in turn told her father.* Se lo dijo a su novia, quien a su vez se lo dijo a su padre. 4 PHRASE If two or more people **take turns to** do something, they do it one after the other several times, rather than doing it together. *turnarse* ❑ *We took turns driving.* Nos turnamos para manejar.

| **Thesaurus** | *turn* | Ver también: |
|---|---|---|
| V. | bend, pivot, revolve, rotate, spin, twist ❶ 1–3 become ❶ 7 8 | |
| N. | chance, opportunity ❷ 2 | |

**❸ turn** /tɜrn/ (**turns, turning, turned**)

▸ **turn against** PHR-VERB If you **turn against** someone or something, or if you **are turned against** them, you stop supporting them, trusting them, or liking them. *volverse, ponerse* ❑ *One of my friends turned against me.* Uno de mis amigos se volvió en mi contra.

▸ **turn around** 1 → see **turn ❶ 1** 2 PHR-VERB If you **turn** something **around**, or if it **turns around**, it is moved so that it faces the opposite direction. *dar vuelta a* ❑ *Bud turned the truck around, and started back for Dalton Pond.* Bud dio media vuelta al camión y regresó por Dalton Pond.

▸ **turn away** PHR-VERB If you **turn** someone **away**, you do not allow them to enter your country, home, or other place. *rechazar* ❑ *Many colleges are turning away students.* Muchos colegios están rechazando estudiantes.

T

▸ **turn back** PHR-VERB If you **turn back** or if someone **turns** you **back** when you are going somewhere, you change direction and go toward where you started from. *regresar, volver, hacer retroceder* ❑ *She turned back toward home.* Dio media vuelta y regresó hacia su casa. ❑ *Police attempted to turn back protesters.* La policía trató de hacer retroceder a los manifestantes.

▸ **turn down** 1 PHR-VERB If you **turn down** a person or their request or offer, you refuse their request or offer. *rechazar* ❑ *I thanked him for the offer but turned it down.* Le agradecí el ofrecimiento, pero lo rechacé. 2 PHR-VERB When you **turn down** a radio, heater, or other piece of equipment, you reduce the amount of sound or heat being produced, by adjusting the controls. *bajar* ❑ *He turned the heater down.* Le bajó al calefactor.

▸ **turn off** 1 PHR-VERB If you **turn off** the road or path you are going along, you start going along a different road or path which leads away from it. *abandonar, salir, dejar* ❑ *The truck turned off the main road.* El camión abandonó el camino principal. 2 PHR-VERB When you **turn off** a piece of equipment or a supply of something, you stop heat, sound, or water from being produced by adjusting the controls. *apagar* ❑ *The light's a bit bright. Can you turn it off?* La luz deslumbra un poco. ¿Podrías apagarla?

▸ **turn on** 1 PHR-VERB When you **turn on** a piece of equipment or a supply of something, you cause heat, sound, or water to be produced by adjusting the controls. *prender, encender* ❑ *I want to turn on the television.* Quiero encender la televisión. 2 PHR-VERB If someone **turns on** you, they suddenly attack you or speak angrily to you. *volverse contra, emprenderla contra* ❑ *Demonstrators turned on police.* Los manifestantes la emprendieron contra la policía.

▸ **turn out** 1 PHR-VERB If something **turns out** a particular way, it happens in that way or has the result or degree of success indicated. *resultar* ❑ *I didn't know my life was going to turn out like this.* No sabía que mi vida iba a resultar así. ❑ *I was certain things were going to turn out fine.* Estaba seguro de que las cosas iban a resultar bien. 2 PHR-VERB If something **turns out to** be a particular thing, it is discovered to be that thing. *resultar ser/estar* ❑ *The weather forecast turned out to be completely wrong.* Resultó que el pronóstico del tiempo estaba completamente equivocado. 3 PHR-VERB When you **turn out** something such as a light, you move the switch or knob that controls it so that it stops giving out light or heat. *apagar* ❑ *Turn the lights out.* Apaga las luces.

▸ **turn over** 1 PHR-VERB If you **turn** something **over**, or if it **turns over**, it is moved so that the top part is now facing downward. *dar vuelta, volcarse* ❑ *Liz picked up the envelope and turned it over.* Liz recogió el sobre y le dio la vuelta. ❑ *The car turned over and landed in a ditch.* El coche se volcó y terminó en una zanja. 2 PHR-VERB If you **turn** something **over in** your mind, you think carefully about it. *dar vueltas a* ❑ *You could see her turning things over in her mind.* Se podía percibir que estaba dándoles vueltas a las cosas en la cabeza. 3 PHR-VERB If you **turn** something **over to** someone, you give it to them when they ask for it, because they have a right to it. *entregar* ❑ *I turned the evidence over to the police.* Entregué las pruebas a la policía. 4 → see also **turnover**

▸ **turn up** 1 PHR-VERB If you say that someone or something **turns up**, you mean that they arrive unexpectedly or after you have been waiting a long time. *aparecer* ❑ *They finally turned up at nearly midnight.* Finalmente aparecieron cerca de la medianoche. 2 PHR-VERB When you **turn up** a radio, heater, or other piece of equipment, you increase the amount of sound, heat, or power being produced, by adjusting the controls. *subir* ❑ *Can you turn up the TV?* ¿Podría subirle a la televisión? ❑ *I turned the volume up.* Subí el volumen.

> **Turn** is used in a large number of other expressions which are explained under other words in the dictionary. For example, the expression "turn a blind eye" is explained at **blind**.

**turn|over** /tɜrnoʊvər/ (**turnovers**) **1** N-VAR The **turnover** of a company is the value of the goods or services sold during a particular period of time. *facturación* [BUSINESS] ❑ *The company had a turnover of $3.8 million.* *La empresa tuvo una facturación de 3.8 millones de dólares.* **2** N-VAR The **turnover** of people in an organization or place is the rate at which people leave and are replaced. *renovación, movimiento* [BUSINESS] ❑ *Staff turnover is high because they don't pay people very much.* *El movimiento de personal es alto porque no pagan mucho a la gente.*

**turn|pike** /tɜrnpaɪk/ (**turnpikes**) N-COUNT A **turnpike** is a road, especially an expressway, which people have to pay to drive on. *camino de peaje o cuota*

**turn sig|nal** (**turn signals**) N-COUNT A car's **turn signals** are the flashing lights that tell you it is going to turn left or right. *direccional*

turtle

**tur|tle** /tɜrtᵊl/ (**turtles**) N-COUNT A **turtle** is any reptile that has a thick shell around its body, for example a tortoise, and can pull its whole body into its shell. *tortuga*

**turtle|neck** /tɜrtᵊlnɛk/ (**turtlenecks**) N-COUNT A **turtleneck** or **turtleneck sweater** is a sweater with a high neck which folds over. *cuello (de) tortuga, cuello alto*

**tu|tor** /tutər/ (**tutors**) **1** N-COUNT A **tutor** is someone who gives private lessons to one student or a very small group of students. *maestro particular o maestra particular* ❑ *...a Spanish tutor.* *...un maestro particular de español.* **2** N-COUNT In some American universities or colleges, a **tutor** is a teacher of the lowest rank. *maestro/maestra de la categoría inferior en algunas universidades o colegios estadounidenses*

**tu|to|rial** /tutɔriəl/ (**tutorials**) **1** N-COUNT In a university or college, a **tutorial** is a regular meeting between a tutor or professor and one or several students, for discussion of a subject that is being studied. *clase impartida por un maestro encargado de orientar más de cerca a determinado grupo de alumnos* **2** N-COUNT A **tutorial** is part of a book or a computer program which helps you learn something step-by-step without a teacher. *guía práctica sobre algún tema*

**TV** /ti vi/ (**TVs**) N-VAR **TV** means the same as **television**. *tele, televisión* ❑ *The TV was on.* *La tele estaba encendida.* ❑ *What's on TV?* *¿Qué hay en la televisión?* ❑ *They watch too much TV.* *Ven mucha televisión.*

**twelfth** /twɛlfθ/ (**twelfths**) **1** ORD The **twelfth** item in a series is the one that you count as number twelve. *duodécimo, decimosegundo* ❑ *...the twelfth anniversary of the revolution.* *...el duodécimo aniversario de la revolución.* **2** N-COUNT A **twelfth** is one of twelve equal parts of something. *duodécimo, doceavo* ❑ *She will get a twelfth of her father's money.* *Recibirá la doceava parte del dinero de su padre.*

**twelve** /twɛlv/ (**twelves**) NUM **Twelve** is the number 12. *doce*

**twelve-bar blues** N-UNCOUNT **Twelve-bar blues** is a form of blues music based on a system of twelve bars to each verse. *blues de doce compases*

**twelve-tone** ADJ A **twelve-tone** scale is a musical scale consisting of all twelve notes in an octave. **Twelve-tone** music is music that is composed using a twelve-tone scale. *dodecafónico* [TECHNICAL]

**twen|ti|eth** /twɛntiəθ/ (**twentieths**) **1** ORD The **twentieth** item in a series is the one that you count as number twenty. *vigésimo* ❑ *...the twentieth century.* *...el siglo XX.* **2** N-COUNT A **twentieth** is one of twenty equal parts of something. *vigésimo* ❑ *...a few twentieths of a gram.* *...unos vigésimos de gramo.*

**twen|ty** /twɛnti/ (**twenties**) **1** NUM **Twenty** is the number 20. *veinte* **2** N-PLURAL When you talk about the **twenties**, you are referring to numbers between 20 and 29. For example, if you are **in** your **twenties**, you are aged between 20 and 29. If the temperature is **in the twenties**, the temperature is between 20 and 29 degrees. *veinte* ❑ *They're both in their twenties.* *Los dos tienen veintitantos años.* **3** N-PLURAL **The twenties** is the decade between 1920 and 1929. *los años veinte* ❑ *It was written in the twenties.* *Fue escrito en los años veinte.*

**24-7** /twɛntifɔrsɛvᵊn/ also **twenty-four seven** ADV If something happens **24-7**, it happens all the time without ever stopping. **24-7** means twenty-four hours a day, seven days a week. *de día y de noche, toda la semana* [INFORMAL] ❑ *I feel like sleeping 24-7.* *Tengo ganas de dormir sin parar toda una semana.* • **24-7** is also an adjective. *de día y de noche, toda la semana* ❑ *...a 24-7 radio station.* *...una estación de radio que transmite todo el día.*

**twice** /twaɪs/ **1** ADV If something happens **twice**, it happens two times. *dos veces* ❑ *He visited me twice that fall.* *Me visitó dos veces ese otoño.* ❑ *I phoned twice a day.* *Llamé dos veces al día.* **2** ADV If one thing is, for example, **twice as** big or old **as** another, the first thing is double the size or age of the second. *doble* ❑ *The figure of seventy million dollars was twice as big as expected.* *La cifra de setenta millones de dólares fue el doble de lo esperado.* • **Twice** is also a predeterminer. *doble* ❑ *Unemployment here is twice the national average.* *El desempleo aquí es el doble del promedio nacional.*

**twin** /twɪn/ (**twins**) **1** N-COUNT **Twins** are two people who were born at the same time from the same mother. *gemelo o gemela* ❑ *Sarah was looking after the twins.* *Sarah estaba cuidando a los gemelos.* **2** ADJ **Twin** is used to describe a pair of things that look the same and are close together. *doble, bi-* ❑ *...a twin-engined aircraft.* *...un bimotor.*
→ see **clone**

**twist** /twɪst/ (**twists, twisting, twisted**) **1** V-T If you **twist** something, you turn it to make a spiral shape, for example, by turning the two ends of it in opposite directions. *torcer, retorcer* ❑ *She sat twisting the handles of the bag.* *Se sentó, retorciendo las correas de la bolsa.* **2** V-T/V-I If you **twist** something, especially a part of your body, or if it

t

twists, it moves into an unusual, uncomfortable, or bent position. *poner, retorcer* ❑ *Can you twist your arms behind your back? ¿Puedes poner los brazos en la espalda?* ❑ *...the twisted wreckage of a train. ...los restos retorcidos de un tren.* **3** V-T/V-I If you **twist** part of your body such as your head or your shoulders, you turn that part while keeping the rest of your body still. *volver, retorcer* ❑ *She twisted her head sideways. Volvió la cabeza a un lado.* ❑ *Susan twisted around in her seat. Susan se retorció en su asiento.* **4** V-T If you **twist** a part of your body such as your ankle or wrist, you injure it by turning it too sharply, or in an unusual direction. *torcerse* ❑ *He fell and twisted his ankle. Se cayó y se torció un tobillo.* **5** V-T If you **twist** something, you turn it so that it moves around in a circular direction. *dar vuelta* ❑ *She was twisting the ring on her finger. Estaba dándole vueltas al anillo que tenía en un dedo.* **6** V-T If someone **twists** something that you have said, they repeat it in a way that changes its meaning, in order to harm you or benefit themselves. *torcer, tergiversar* ❑ *The media can twist your words. Los medios de comunicación pueden tergiversar lo que se dice.* **7** N-COUNT A **twist** in something is an unexpected and significant development. *giro* ❑ *The battle between them took a new twist. La lucha entre ellos dio un giro.*

**Word Partnership** Usar *twist* con:

ADV. twist **around** 1 5
ADJ. **added** twist, **bizarre** twist, **interesting** twist, **latest** twist, **new** twist, **unexpected** twist 7
V. **plot** twist, **story** twist 7

**twist|ed** /twɪstɪd/ ADJ If you describe a person as **twisted,** you dislike them because you think they are bad or mentally unbalanced. *retorcido* ❑ *He was an evil, twisted man. Era un hombre malvado, retorcido.*

**two** /tu/ (**twos**) NUM **Two** is the number 2. *dos*

**two-dimensional** also **two dimensional** ADJ A **two-dimensional** object or figure is flat rather than solid so that only its length and width can be measured. *bidimensional*

**two-percent milk** N-UNCOUNT **Two-percent milk** is milk from which some of the fat has been removed. *leche descremada*

T

**two-point per|spec|tive** (**two-point perspectives**) N-VAR A **two-point perspective** is a method of representing three-dimensional space on a two-dimensional surface by the use of two vanishing points on the horizon. *perspectiva angular, perspectiva de dos conjuntos* [TECHNICAL]

**two-thirds** also **two thirds** QUANT **Two-thirds of** is an amount that is two out of three equal parts of it. *dos tercios* ❑ *Two-thirds of families own their own homes. Dos tercios de las familias son propietarias de su casa.* ● **Two-thirds** is also a pronoun. *dos terceras partes* ❑ *Sales are down by two-thirds. Las ventas cayeron el 66 por ciento.* ● **Two-thirds** is also an adverb. *dos tercios* ❑ *Do not fill the container more than two-thirds full. No llene el recipiente a más de dos tercios de su capacidad.* ● **Two-thirds** is also an adjective. *dos tercios* ❑ *A two-thirds majority is needed to make changes. Se necesita una mayoría de dos tercios para hacer cambios.*

**two-way** ADJ **Two-way** means moving or working in two opposite directions. *doble sentido, bidireccional* ❑ *The bridge is now open to two-way traffic. El puente ya está abierto al tráfico en ambos sentidos.* ❑ *...a two-way radio. ...un aparato emisor y receptor.*

**type**
❶ SORT OR KIND
❷ WRITING AND PRINTING

**❶ type** /taɪp/ (**types**) **1** N-COUNT A **type of** something is a group of those things that have particular features in common. *tipo* ❑ *...several types of lettuce. ...varios tipos de lechuga.* ❑ *There are various types of the disease. Hay varios tipos de enfermedades.* **2** N-COUNT If you refer to a particular thing or person as a **type of** something more general, you are considering that thing or person as an example of that more general group. *tipo* ❑ *Have you done this type of work before? ¿Ya ha hecho antes este tipo de trabajo?* ❑ *I am a very determined type of person. Soy un tipo de persona muy decidida.* **3** N-COUNT If you refer to a person as a particular **type,** you mean that they have that particular appearance, character, or type of behavior. *tipo* ❑ *I'm an outdoor type. Soy de los que les gusta el aire libre.*

**❷ type** /taɪp/ (**types, typing, typed**) V-T/V-I If you **type** something, you use a typewriter or computer keyboard to write it. *teclear, escribir a máquina, mecanografiar* ❑ *I can type your essays for you. Puedo pasar a máquina sus ensayos por usted.* ❑ *I never really learned to type properly. Realmente nunca aprendí a escribir a máquina como se debe.* ● **typ|ing** N-UNCOUNT *mecanografía* ❑ *I'm taking a typing class. Estoy tomando clases de mecanografía.*

▸ **type in** or **type into** PHR-VERB If you **type** information **into** a computer or **type** it **in,** you press keys on the keyboard so that the computer stores or processes the information. *escribir* ❑ *Officials type each passport number into a computer. Los oficiales escriben el número de cada pasaporte en una computadora.* ❑ *You have to type in commands, such as "help" and "print." Tiene que escribir las órdenes, como "ayuda" e "imprimir".*

▸ **type up** PHR-VERB If you **type up** a text that has been written by hand, you produce a typed copy of it. *pasar a máquina* ❑ *When the first draft was completed, Nichols typed it up. Cuando estuvo terminado el primer borrador, Nichols lo pasó a maquina.*

**type|writ|er** /taɪpraɪtər/ (**typewriters**) N-COUNT A **typewriter** is a machine with keys which are pressed in order to print letters, numbers, or other characters onto paper. *máquina de escribir*

**ty|phoon** /taɪfun/ (**typhoons**) N-COUNT A **typhoon** is a very violent tropical storm. *tifón* → see **disaster**

**typi|cal** /tɪpɪkᵊl/ **1** ADJ You use **typical** to describe someone or something that shows the most usual characteristics of a particular type of person or thing, and is therefore a good example of that type. *típico* ❑ *He is everyone's image of a typical cop. Es la imagen que todo el mundo tiene de un policía* *típico.* **2** ADJ If a particular action or feature is **typical of** someone or something, it shows their usual qualities or characteristics. *característico de, representativo de* ❑ *These boys are typical of children their age. Estos muchachos son representativos de los niños de su edad.*

**typi|cal|ly** /tɪpɪkli/ **1** ADV You use **typically** to say that something usually happens in the way that you are describing. *típicamente, como de costumbre* ❑ *The day typically begins with swimming. Como de costumbre, el día empieza con la natación.* **2** ADV You use **typically** to say that something shows all the most usual characteristics of a particular type of person or thing. *típicamente* ❑ *The food is typically American. La comida es típicamente estadounidense.* **3** ADV You use **typically** to indicate that someone has behaved in the way that they normally do. *como es característico* ❑ *Typically, he took her comments in good humor. Como es característico en él, tomó sus comentarios con buen humor.*

**typ|ist** /taɪpɪst/ (**typists**) N-COUNT A **typist** is someone who works in an office typing letters and other documents. *mecanógrafo o mecanógrafa, dactilógrafo o dactilógrafa*

**ty|po** /taɪpoʊ/ (**typos**) N-COUNT A **typo** is a typographical error. *error de imprenta* [INFORMAL] ❑ *There are no typos or misprints. No hay errores de imprenta ni tipográficos.*

# Uu

**ubiqui|tous** /yubɪkwɪtəs/ ADJ If you describe something or someone as **ubiquitous,** you mean that they seem to be everywhere. *omnipresente* [FORMAL] ❑ *Sugar is ubiquitous in the diet. El azúcar es omnipresente en la dieta.*

**ugly** /ʌgli/ (**uglier, ugliest**) **1** ADJ If you say that someone or something is **ugly,** you mean that they are very unattractive and unpleasant to look at. *feo* ❑ *...an ugly little hat. ...un sombrerito feo.* ● **ug|li|ness** N-UNCOUNT *fealdad* ❑ *...the ugliness of his native city. ...la fealdad de su ciudad natal.* **2** ADJ If you refer to an event or situation as **ugly,** you mean that it is very unpleasant, usually because it involves violence. *desagradable, feo* ❑ *There have been some ugly scenes. Ha habido algunas escenas desagradables.* ❑ *The mood turned ugly. El ambiente se puso feo.*

**ul|ti|mate** /ʌltɪmɪt/ **1** ADJ You use **ultimate** to describe the final result or aim of a long series of events. *último, primordial, fundamental* ❑ *The ultimate aim is to keep kids in school. El fin primordial es mantener a los niños en la escuela.* **2** ADJ You use **ultimate** to describe the most important or extreme thing of a particular kind. *último, fundamental* ❑ *Our ultimate goal is to win. Nuestro objetivo fundamental es ganar.* **3** PHRASE **The ultimate in** something is the best or most advanced example of it. *lo último en* ❑ *This hotel is the ultimate in luxury. Este hotel es lo último en lujo.*

**Word Partnership** Usar *ultimate* con:

N. ultimate **aim/goal/objective**, ultimate **outcome** **1**
ultimate **authority**, ultimate **decision**, ultimate **experience**, ultimate **power**, ultimate **weapon** **2**

**ul|ti|mate|ly** /ʌltɪmɪtli/ **1** ADV **Ultimately** means finally, after a long series of events. *finalmente, en resumidas cuentas* ❑ *Who, ultimately, is going to pay? En resumidas cuentas, ¿quién va a pagar?* **2** ADV You use **ultimately** to indicate that what you are saying is the most important point in a discussion. *en resumidas cuentas, en última instancia* ❑ *Ultimately, the judge has the final decision. En última instancia, el juez tiene la decisión final.*

**ultra|sound** /ʌltrəsaʊnd/ N-UNCOUNT **Ultrasound** is sound waves which travel at such a high frequency that they cannot be heard by humans. Ultrasound is used in medicine to get pictures of the inside of people's bodies. *ecografía* ❑ *...ultrasound photos of his unborn child. ...unas ecografías de su bebé antes de nacer.*

**ultra|vio|let** /ʌltrəvaɪəlɪt/ ADJ **Ultraviolet** light or radiation is what causes your skin to become darker in color after you have been in sunlight. *ultravioleta* ❑ *The sun's ultraviolet rays are responsible for both tanning and burning. Los rayos ultravioleta del sol producen las quemaduras y el bronceado.*
→ see **ozone, skin, sun, wave**

**um|bili|cal cord** /ʌmbɪlɪkəl kɔrd/ (**umbilical cords**) N-COUNT The **umbilical cord** is the tube that connects an unborn baby to its mother, through which it receives oxygen and food. *cordón umbilical*

**um|brel|la** /ʌmbrɛlə/ (**umbrellas**) **1** N-COUNT An **umbrella** is an object which you use to protect yourself from the rain or hot sun. It consists of a long stick with a folding frame covered in plastic or cloth. *paraguas* ❑ *Harry held an umbrella over Denise. Harry cubrió a Denise con un paraguas.* **2** N-SING **Umbrella** is used to refer to a single group or description that includes a lot of different organizations or ideas. *organización que aglutina numerosos grupos* ❑ *...a national umbrella group of thirty-five businesses. ...una organización nacional que aglutina treinta y cinco negocios.*

umbrella

**um|pire** /ʌmpaɪr/ (**umpires, umpiring, umpired**) **1** N-COUNT An **umpire** is a person whose job is to make sure that a sports contest or game is played fairly and that the rules are not broken. *árbitro o árbitra* ❑ *The umpire's decision is final. La decisión del árbitro es definitiva.* **2** V-T/V-I To **umpire** means to be the umpire in a sports contest or game. *arbitrar* ❑ *He umpired baseball games. Solía arbitrar juegos de beisbol.*
→ see **tennis**

**un|able** /ʌneɪbəl/ ADJ If you are **unable to** do something, it is impossible for you to do it. *incapaz* ❑ *He was unable to walk. No podía caminar.*

**Word Partnership** Usar *unable* con:

ADV. **physically** unable
V. unable **to afford**, unable **to agree**, unable **to attend**, unable **to control**, unable **to cope**, unable **to decide**, unable **to explain**, unable **to find**, unable **to hold**, unable **to identify**, unable **to make**, unable **to move**, unable **to pay**, unable **to perform**, unable **to reach**, unable **to speak**, unable **to walk**, unable **to work**

**un|ac|cep|table** /ʌnəksɛptəbəl/ ADJ If you describe something as **unacceptable,** you strongly disapprove of it or object to it and feel that it should not be allowed to continue. *inaceptable* ❑ *It is unacceptable for children to swear. Es inaceptable que* *los niños digan groserías.*

**un-Ameri|can** /ʌnəmɛrɪkən/ **1** ADJ If you describe someone or something as **un-American,** you think that they do not follow or fit in with American ideals and customs. *anti-estadounidense* ❑ *This is a deeply un-American attitude. Esta es una actitud profundamente anti-estadounidense.* **2** ADJ **Un-American** activities are political activities that are considered to be against the interests of the U.S. *anti-estadounidense* ❑ *...the House Un-American Activities Committee. ...la Comisión sobre Actividades Antiestadounidenses de la Cámara.*

**Word Link** ***anim ≈ alive, mind : animal, animation, unanimous***

**unani|mous** /yunænɪməs/ ADJ When a group of people are **unanimous,** they all agree about something. *unánime* ❑ *Their decision was unanimous. Su decisión fue unánime.* • **unani|mous|ly** ADV *por unanimidad* ❑ *They unanimously approved the project last week. Aprobaron el proyecto por unanimidad la semana pasada.*

**un|armed** /ʌnɑrmd/ ADJ If a person or vehicle is **unarmed,** they are not carrying any weapons. *desarmado* ❑ *The soldiers were unarmed. Los soldados estaban desarmados.*

**un|ashamed** /ʌnəʃeɪmd/ ADJ If you describe someone's behavior or attitude as **unashamed,** you mean that they are open and honest about things that other people might find embarrassing or shocking. *sin vergüenza alguna, sin reparo alguno* ❑ *She cried unashamed tears of joy. Lloró de felicidad sin vergüenza alguna.* • **un|asham|ed|ly** /ʌnəʃeɪmɪdli/ ADV *sin reparo alguno* ❑ *Bernstein was unashamedly American. Bernstein no tenía reparo alguno en admitir que era estadounidense.*

**un|avoid|able** /ʌnəvɔɪdəbᵊl/ ADJ If something is **unavoidable,** it cannot be avoided or prevented. *inevitable* ❑ *The delay was unavoidable. El retraso fue inevitable.*

**un|aware** /ʌnəwɛər/ ADJ If you are **unaware of** something, you do not know about it. *sin darse cuenta* ❑ *Many people are unaware of how much they eat. Muchas personas no se dan cuenta de lo mucho que comen.*

**Word Partnership** Usar *unaware* con:

ADV. **apparently** unaware, **blissfully** unaware, **completely** unaware, **totally** unaware

**un|bal|anced forces** N-PLURAL In physics, **unbalanced forces** are forces that are not equal and opposite to each other, so that an object to which the forces are applied moves. *fuerzas desequilibradas*

**un|bear|able** /ʌnbɛərəbᵊl/ ADJ If you describe something as **unbearable,** you mean that it is so unpleasant, painful, or upsetting that you feel unable to accept it or deal with it. *insoportable* ❑ *The pain was unbearable. El dolor era insoportable.* • **un|bear|ably** /ʌnbɛərəbli/ ADV *insoportablemente* ❑ *In the evening it became unbearably hot. La tarde se puso insoportablemente calurosa.*

**un|beat|able** /ʌnbitəbᵊl/ **1** ADJ If you describe something as **unbeatable,** you mean that it is the best thing of its kind. *inmejorable* ❑ *We're making an unbeatable offer. Estamos haciendo una oferta inmejorable.* **2** PHRASE **Unbeatable prices** are the lowest prices you can find. *precios inmejorables* ❑ *Their prices are unbeatable. Tienen precios inmejorabes.*

**un|beat|en** /ʌnbitᵊn/ ADJ In sports, if a person or their performance is **unbeaten,** nobody else has performed well enough to beat them. *invicto* ❑ *He's unbeaten in 20 fights. Se ha mantenido invicto en 20 peleas.*

**un|be|liev|able** /ʌnbɪlivəbᵊl/ **1** ADJ If you say that something is **unbelievable,** you are emphasizing that it is very extreme, impressive, or shocking. *increíble* ❑ *His guitar solos are just unbelievable. Sus solos de guitarra son sencillamente increíbles.* ❑ *It's unbelievable that people can accept this sort of behavior. Es increíble que la gente acepte esta clase de conducta.* • **un|be|liev|ably** /ʌnbɪlivəbli/ ADV *increíblemente* ❑ *What you did was unbelievably stupid. Lo que hiciste fue increíblemente tonto.* **2** ADJ If an idea or statement is **unbelievable,** it seems so unlikely to be true that you cannot believe it. *increíble* ❑ *This story is both fascinating and unbelievable. Esta historia es fascinante e increíble.* • **un|be|liev|ably** ADV *increíblemente* ❑ *Unbelievably, I made it to the final twice. Por increíble que parezca, llegué dos veces a la final.*

**Thesaurus** *unbelievable* Ver también:

ADJ. astounding, incredible, remarkable **1** inconceivable, preposterous, unimaginable **2**

**un|born** /ʌnbɔrn/ ADJ An **unborn** child has not yet been born and is still inside its mother's uterus. *nonato, que aún no nace* ❑ *...her unborn baby. ...su bebé que aún no nace.* • **The unborn** are children who are not born yet. *feto, nonato* ❑ *...a law that protects the lives of pregnant women and the unborn. ...una ley que protege la vida de la mujer embarazada y del feto.*

**un|can|ny** /ʌnkæni/ ADJ If something is **uncanny,** it is strange and difficult to explain. *extraño, asombroso* ❑ *Cathy had an uncanny feeling that she knew this man. Cathy tenía la extraña sensación de que ya conocía a ese hombre.* • **un|can|ni|ly** /ʌnkænɪli/ ADV *asombrosamente* ❑ *They have uncannily similar voices. Tienen voces asombrosamente parecidas.*

**Word Link** ***cert ≈ determined, true : certain, certificate, uncertain***

**un|cer|tain** /ʌnsɜrtᵊn/ **1** ADJ If you are **uncertain about** something, you do not know what you should do, what is going to happen, or what the truth is about something. *inseguro* ❑ *He was uncertain about his future. Se sentía inseguro respecto a su futuro.* ❑ *They were uncertain of the value of the goods. No estaban seguros del valor de los bienes.* • **un|cer|tain|ly** ADV *con aire vacilante* ❑ *He entered the room and stood uncertainly. Entró a la habitación y se paró con aire vacilante.* **2** ADJ If something is **uncertain,** it is not known or definite. *incierto, inseguro* ❑ *The company's future is uncertain. El futuro de la compañía es incierto.* ❑ *It's uncertain whether they will accept the plan. No es seguro que vayan a aceptar el plan.* **3** PHRASE If you say that someone tells a

U

person something **in no uncertain terms,** you are emphasizing that they say it strongly and clearly so that there is no doubt about what they mean. *muy claramente, inequívocamente* ❑ *She told him in no uncertain terms to go away. Le dijo muy claramente que se fuera.*

**Word Partnership** Usar *uncertain* con:

PREP. uncertain **about** *something* 1
V. **be** uncertain, **remain** uncertain 1 2
ADV. **highly** uncertain, **still** uncertain 1 2

**un|cer|tain|ty** /ʌnsɜrtᵊnti/ (**uncertainties**) N-VAR **Uncertainty** is a state of doubt about the future or about what is the right thing to do. *incertidumbre* ❑ *...a time of political uncertainty. ...tiempos de incertidumbre política.*

**un|chal|lenged** /ʌntʃælɪndʒd/ ADJ When something goes **unchallenged** or is **unchallenged,** people accept it without asking questions about whether it is right or wrong. *sin respuesta, indiscutible* ❑ *That kind of statement cannot go unchallenged. Ese tipo de afirmación no puede quedarse sin respuesta.* ❑ *...his unchallenged leadership. ...su indiscutible liderazgo.*

**un|changed** /ʌntʃeɪndʒd/ ADJ If something is **unchanged,** it has stayed the same for a particular period of time. *igual, invariable* ❑ *For many years prices have remained unchanged. Durante muchos años, los precios se han mantenido invariables.*

**un|cle** /ʌŋkᵊl/ (**uncles**) N-COUNT; N-TITLE Your **uncle** is the brother of your mother or father, or the husband of your aunt. *tío* ❑ *My uncle was the mayor of Memphis. Mi tío era el alcalde de Memphis.* ❑ *An e-mail from Uncle Fred arrived. Llegó un correo electrónico del tío Fred.*
→ see **family**

**un|clear** /ʌnklɪər/ 1 ADJ If something is **unclear,** it is not known or not certain. *poco claro* ❑ *It is unclear how much support they have. No está claro cuánto apoyo tienen.* 2 ADJ If you are **unclear** about something, you do not understand it well or are not sure about it. *poco claro* ❑ *He is unclear about his future. No tiene claro su futuro.*

**Uncle Sam** /ʌŋkᵊl sæm/ N-PROPER Some people refer to the United States of America or its government as **Uncle Sam.** *tío Sam* ❑ *...the best education Uncle Sam could provide. ...la mejor educación que podía proporcionar el tío Sam.*

**un|com|fort|able** /ʌnkʌmftəbᵊl, -kʌmfərtə-/ 1 ADJ If you are **uncomfortable,** you are slightly worried or embarrassed, and not relaxed and confident. *incómodo* ❑ *The request for money made them feel uncomfortable. La solicitud de dinero los hizo sentirse incómodos.* ❑ *She was uncomfortable with the situation. Se sentía incómoda con la situación.*
● **un|com|fort|ably** /ʌnkʌmftəbli, -kʌmfərtə-/ ADV *inquietantemente* ❑ *Sam's face was uncomfortably close to Brad's. El rostro de Sam estaba incómodamente cercano al de Brad.* 2 ADJ Something that is **uncomfortable** makes you feel slight pain or physical discomfort when you experience it or use it. *incómodo* ❑ *...an uncomfortable chair. ...una silla incómoda.* ❑ *The ride back to the center of the town was hot and uncomfortable. El viaje de regreso al centro de la ciudad fue caluroso e incómodo.* ● **un|com|fort|ably** ADV *desagradablemente* ❑ *The water was uncomfortably cold. El agua estaba desagradablemente fría.* 3 ADJ If you are **uncomfortable,** you are not physically content and relaxed, and feel slight pain or discomfort. *incómodo* ❑ *I sometimes feel uncomfortable after eating in the evening. A veces me siento incómodo despúes de haber cenado.* ● **un|com|fort|ably** ADV *desagradablemente* ❑ *He felt uncomfortably hot. Se sintió desagradablemente acalorado.*

**Thesaurus** *uncomfortable* Ver también:

ADJ. awkward, embarrassed, troubled; (*ant.*) comfortable 1
irritating, painful 2 3

**un|com|pro|mis|ing** /ʌnkɒmprəmaɪzɪŋ/ ADJ If you describe someone as **uncompromising,** you mean that they are determined not to change their opinions or aims in any way. *inflexible* ❑ *...an uncompromising politician. ...un político inflexible.*

**un|con|di|tion|al** /ʌnkəndɪʃənᵊl/ ADJ Something that is **unconditional** is done or given freely, without anything being required in return. *incondicional* ❑ *Children need unconditional love from their parents. Los niños necesitan que el amor de sus padres sea incondicional.* ● **un|con|di|tion|al|ly** ADV *incondicionalmente* ❑ *They accepted our offer unconditionally. Aceptaron nuestra oferta incondicionalmente.*

**un|con|scious** /ʌnkɒnʃəs/ 1 ADJ Someone who is **unconscious** is in a state similar to sleep, usually as the result of a serious injury or a lack of oxygen. *inconsciente* ❑ *By the time the ambulance arrived he was unconscious. Estaba inconsciente cuando llegó la ambulancia.* ● **un|con|scious|ness** N-UNCOUNT *inconsciencia* ❑ *...a knock to the head which led to unconsciousness. ...un golpe en la cabeza que le produjo un estado de inconsciencia.* 2 ADJ If you are **unconscious of** something, you are unaware of it. *inconsciente* ❑ *He seemed unconscious of his failure. Parecía inconsciente de su fracaso.* ● **un|con|scious|ly** ADV *inconscientemente* ❑ *His hand unconsciously went to the back of his head. Se llevó inconscientemente la mano a la nuca.* 3 ADJ If feelings or attitudes are **unconscious,** you do not know that you have them, but they show in the way that you behave. *inconsciente* ❑ *...my unconscious fear of becoming a mother. ...mi temor inconsciente de ser madre.*
● **un|con|scious|ly** ADV *inconscientemente* ❑ *We unconsciously form opinions about people we meet. Solemos formarnos opiniones inconscientes sobre la gente que conocemos.*

**un|con|sti|tu|tion|al** /ʌnkɒnstɪtuʃənᵊl/ ADJ If something is **unconstitutional,** it breaks the rules of a constitution. *inconstitucional* ❑ *...laws they believe are unconstitutional. ...leyes que ellos creen inconstitucionales.*

**un|con|ven|tion|al** /ʌnkənvɛnʃənᵊl/ ADJ If someone is **unconventional,** they do not behave in the same way as most other people in their society. *poco convencional* ❑ *Linus Pauling was an unconventional genius. Linus Pauling era un genio poco convencional.*

**un|cool** /ʌnkul/ ADJ If you say that a person, thing, or activity is **uncool,** you disapprove of them because they are not fashionable,

U

sophisticated, or attractive. no estar en la onda [INFORMAL] ❑ *He was fat, uncool, and unpopular.* Era gordo, no era popular y no estaba en la onda.

**un|count noun** /ʌnkaʊnt naʊn/ (**uncount nouns**) N-COUNT An **uncount noun** is a noun such as "gold" or "information" which has only one form and can be used without a determiner (e.g. **a**, **the**, **some** or **this**). nombre incontable

**un|cov|er** /ʌnkʌvər/ (**uncovers, uncovering, uncovered**) **1** V-T If you **uncover** something secret, you find out about it. descubrir ❑ *We must uncover every detail.* Debemos descubrir cada detalle. **2** V-T To **uncover** something means to remove something that is covering it. destapar ❑ *Uncover the dish and cook the chicken for about 15 minutes.* Destape el plato y cocine el pollo aproximadamente 15 minutos.

**Word Partnership** Usar *uncover* con:

N. uncover **evidence**, uncover **a plot**, uncover **the truth** **1**
V. **help** uncover *something* **1** **2**

**un|de|ni|able** /ʌndɪnaɪəbəl/ ADJ If you say that something is **undeniable**, you mean that it is definitely true. innegable ❑ *Her charm is undeniable.* Su encanto es innegable. ● **un|de|ni|ably** /ʌndɪnaɪəbli/ ADV innegablemente ❑ *Bringing up a baby is undeniably hard work.* Innegablemente, criar a un bebé implica mucho trabajo.

**un|der** /ʌndər/

In addition to the uses shown below, **under** is also used in phrasal verbs such as "go under" and "knuckle under."

**1** PREP If a person or thing is **under** something, they are directly below or beneath it. debajo, bajo ❑ *...tunnels under the ground.* ...túneles. ❑ *A path runs under the trees.* El sendero corre bajo los árboles. ❑ *She held her breath for three minutes under the water.* Aguantó la respiración bajo el agua durante tres minutos. **2** PREP If something happens **under** particular circumstances or conditions, it happens when those circumstances or conditions exist. en ❑ *Under the circumstances I think we did well.* Dadas las circunstancias, creo que salió bien. ❑ *He was able to work under pressure.* Podía trabajar bajo presión. **3** PREP If something happens **under** a particular person or government, it happens when that person or government is in power. en, bajo ❑ *I hope that there will be a change under this government.* Espero que haya un cambio bajo este gobierno. **4** PREP If you study or work **under** a particular person, that person teaches you or tells you what to do. bajo el mando de, bajo la tutela de ❑ *I have eight hundred people working under me.* Tengo a ochocientas personas trabajando bajo mi mando. ❑ *General Lewis Hyde served under General Mitchell.* El general Lewis Hyde sirvió bajo el mando del general Mitchell. **5** PREP If you do something **under** a particular name, you use that name instead of your real name. con ❑ *Did you write any of your books under the name Amanda Fairchild?* ¿Escribió algún libro con el seudónimo Amanda Fairchild? **6** PREP You use **under** to say which section of a list, book, or system something is in. bajo ❑ *Look on page 164, under the heading "Top Ten Cities."* Busque en la página 164, bajo el título "Las diez mejores ciudades". **7** PREP If something or someone is **under** a particular age or amount, they are less than that age or amount. menor ❑ *...jobs for those under 65.* ...empleos para adultos menores de 65 años. ● **Under** is also an adverb. menor ❑ *...free health insurance for children 13 and under.* ...seguro médico gratuito para niños de 13 años y menores.
→ see **location**

**under|brush** /ʌndərbrʌʃ/ N-UNCOUNT **Underbrush** consists of bushes and plants growing close together under trees in a forest. maleza ❑ *...the cool underbrush of the rain forest.* ...la fresca maleza de la selva tropical. ❑ *The trail was thick with underbrush.* El sendero estaba lleno de maleza.

**under|class** /ʌndərklæs/ (**underclasses**) N-COUNT A country's **underclass** consists of those members of its population who are poor, and who have little chance of improving their situation. clase marginada ❑ *There is a growing underclass of people in poor neighborhoods.* Las clases marginadas están aumentando en los barrios pobres.

**under|cov|er** /ʌndərkʌvər/ ADJ **Undercover** work involves secretly obtaining information for the government or the police. secreto ❑ *...a five-day undercover operation.* ...una operación secreta de cinco días. ❑ *...undercover FBI agents.* ...agentes secretos del FBI.

**under|cur|rent** /ʌndərkɜrənt/ (**undercurrents**) N-COUNT If there is an **undercurrent of** a feeling, you are hardly aware of the feeling, but it influences the way you think or behave. trasfondo ❑ *Most comedy has an undercurrent of truth.* Casi toda la comedia tiene un trasfondo de verdad.

**under|cut** /ʌndərkʌt/ (**undercuts, undercutting**)

The form **undercut** is used in the present tense and is also the past tense and past participle.

V-T If you **undercut** someone or **undercut** their prices, you sell a product more cheaply than they do. vender más barato, rebajar los precios [BUSINESS] ❑ *...promises to undercut air fares on some routes by 40 percent.* ...las promesas de rebajar en un 40 por ciento las tarifas de ciertos vuelos.

**under|dog** /ʌndərdɔg/ (**underdogs**) N-COUNT **The underdog** in a competition or situation is the person who seems least likely to succeed or win. el que tiene menos posibilidades ❑ *Most people were cheering for the underdog to win.* La mayoría apoyaba al que tenía menos posibilidades de ganar.

**under|es|ti|mate** /ʌndərɛstɪmeɪt/ (**underestimates, underestimating, underestimated**) **1** V-T If you **underestimate** something, you do not realize how large or great it is or will be. subestimar ❑ *Never underestimate the power of anger.* Nunca subestimes el poder de la ira. **2** V-T If you **underestimate** someone, you do not realize what they are capable of doing. subestimar ❑ *I think a lot of people still underestimate him.* Creo que muchos aún lo subestiman.

**under|go** /ʌndərgoʊ/ (**undergoes, undergoing, underwent, undergone**) V-T If you **undergo** something necessary or unpleasant, it happens to you. sufrir, someterse ❑ *She is undergoing treatment for cancer.* Se está sometiendo a un tratamiento contra el cáncer.

U

**under|gradu|ate** /ʌndərgrædʒuɪt/ (**undergraduates**) N-COUNT An **undergraduate** is a student at a university or college who is studying for a bachelor's or associate's degree. estudiante universitario o estudiante universitaria ❑ *More than 55 percent of undergraduates are female.* *Más del 55 por ciento de los estudiantes universitarios son mujeres.*

| Word Link | *ground ≈ bottom : background, groundwater, underground* |
|---|---|

**under|ground**

The adverb is pronounced /ʌndərgraʊnd/. The noun and adjective are pronounced /ʌndərgraʊnd/.

**1** ADV Something that is **underground** is below the surface of the ground. subterráneo ❑ *It was unclear whether the water was underground or on the surface.* *No era claro si el agua era subterránea o corría sobre la superficie.* ● **Underground** is also an adjective. subterráneo ❑ *...an underground parking garage for 2,100 vehicles.* *...un estacionamiento subterráneo para 2,100 vehículos.* **2** ADJ **Underground** groups and activities are secret because their purpose is to oppose the government and they are illegal. clandestino ❑ *...an underground terrorist group.* *...un grupo terrorista clandestino.*
→ see **tunnel**

**under|growth** /ʌndərgroʊθ/ also **underbrush** N-UNCOUNT **Undergrowth** consists of bushes and plants growing together under the trees in a forest. maleza ❑ *...hidden by trees and undergrowth.* *...oculto por los árboles y la maleza.*

**under|hand** /ʌndərhænd/ also **underhanded** **1** ADJ If something is done in an **underhand** way, it is done secretly and dishonestly. turbio ❑ *...underhand financial deals.* *...transacciones financieras turbias.* **2** ADJ You use **underhand** or **underhanded** to describe actions, such as throwing a ball, in which you do not raise your arm above your shoulder. sin levantar el brazo por encima del hombro ❑ *...an underhanded pitch.* *...un lanzamiento sin levantar el brazo por encima del hombro.* ● **Underhand** is also an adverb. sin levantar el brazo por encima del hombro ❑ *In softball, pitches are tossed underhand.* *En softbol, los lanzamientos se hacen sin levantar el brazo por encima del hombro.*

**under|line** /ʌndərlaɪn/ (**underlines, underlining, underlined**) **1** V-T If one thing, for example an action or an event, **underlines** another, it draws attention to it and emphasizes its importance. poner de relieve ❑ *This accident underlines the danger of traveling there.* *Este accidente pone de relieve el peligro de viajar a ese lugar.* **2** V-T If you **underline** something such as a word or a sentence, you draw a line underneath it in order to make people notice it or to give it extra importance. subrayar ❑ *She underlined her name.* *Subrayó su nombre.*
→ see **answer**

**Word Partnership** Usar *underline* con:

N. underline **the need for** *something* **1**
underline **passages**, underline **text**, underline **titles**, underline **words** **2**

**un|der|ly|ing** /ʌndərlaɪɪŋ/ **1** ADJ The **underlying** features of an object, event, or situation are not obvious, and it may be difficult to discover or reveal them. oculto ❑ *You have to understand the underlying causes of the problem.* *Debes entender las causas ocultas del problema.*

**under|mine** /ʌndərmaɪn/ (**undermines, undermining, undermined**) V-T If you **undermine** something such as a feeling or a system, you make it less strong or less secure. debilitar, minar ❑ *He undermined my position.* *Debilitó mi posición.*

**Word Partnership** Usar *undermine* con:

N. undermine **authority**, undermine **government**, undermine **peace**, undermine **security**
V. **threaten to** undermine, **try to** undermine

**under|neath** /ʌndərniθ/ **1** PREP If one thing is **underneath** another, it is directly under it. debajo, bajo ❑ *The bomb exploded underneath a van.* *La bomba explotó debajo de una camioneta.* ● **Underneath** is also an adverb. debajo ❑ *He was wearing a long-sleeved blue shirt with a white T-shirt underneath.* *Traía puesto un suéter azul de manga larga con una playera blanca debajo.* **2** ADV The part of something which is **underneath** is the part which normally touches the ground or faces toward the ground. debajo ❑ *The robin is a brown bird with red underneath.* *El petirrojo es un pájaro café con el pecho rojo.* ● **Underneath** is also a noun. parte de abajo ❑ *Now I know what the underneath of a car looks like.* *Ahora ya sé cómo se ve la parte de abajo de un coche.* **3** ADV You use **underneath** when talking about feelings and emotions that people do not show in their behavior. en el fondo ❑ *He was a violent man underneath.* *En el fondo era un hombre violento.* ● **Underneath** is also a preposition. debajo, tras ❑ *Underneath his friendly behavior Luke was shy.* *Tras su fachada amistosa, Luke era tímido.* ❑ *The idea of getting away from home was underneath my mind.* *La idea de irme de casa rondaba mi mente.*
→ see **location**

**under|pants** /ʌndərpænts/ N-PLURAL **Underpants** are a piece of underwear which have two holes to put your legs through and elastic around the top to hold them up around your waist or hips. calzoncillos, calzones ❑ *...white cotton underpants.* *...calzoncillos blancos de algodón.*

**under|per|form** /ʌndərpərfɔrm/ (**underperforms, underperforming, underperformed**) also **under-perform** V-T/V-I If someone **underperforms** in something such as a sports contest, they do not perform as well as they could. If one thing **underperforms** another thing, it performs less well than the other thing. tener un rendimiento bajo ❑ *Our team has underperformed all year.* *El rendimiento de nuestro equipo ha sido bajo todo el año.* ❑ *Smaller companies have underperformed larger ones in the past several years.* *En los últimos años, el rendimiento de las pequeñas empresas ha sido inferior al de las grandes.* ● **under|per|form|er** /ʌndərpərfɔrmər/ N-COUNT (**underperformers**) de bajo rendimiento ❑ *They transformed the bank from an underperformer to one of the best in the world.* *Lograron que el banco pasara de su bajo rendimiento a ser uno de los mejores del mundo.* ● **under|per|for|mance** /ʌndərpərfɔrməns/

U

N-UNCOUNT *bajo rendimiento* ❑ *...the movie's underperformance in theaters.* *...el bajo rendimiento de la película en la taquilla.*

**under|score** /ʌndərskɔr/ (**underscores, underscoring, underscored**) **1** V-T If something such as an action or an event **underscores** another, it draws attention to the other thing and emphasizes its importance. *poner de relieve* ❑ *The report underscores a larger problem.* *El informe pone de relieve un problema mayor.* **2** V-T If you **underscore** something such as a word or a sentence, you draw a line underneath it in order to make people notice it or give it extra importance. *subrayar* ❑ *He heavily underscored his note to Shelley.* *Subrayó con una gruesa línea la nota que le dirigió a Shelley.*

**under|shirt** /ʌndərʃɜrt/ (**undershirts**) N-COUNT An **undershirt** is a piece of clothing that you wear on the top half of your body next to your skin in order to keep warm. *camiseta* ❑ *He put on a pair of short pants and an undershirt.* *Se puso unos pantalones cortos y una camiseta.*

**under|stand** /ʌndərstænd/ (**understands, understanding, understood**) **1** V-T If you **understand** someone or **understand** what they are saying, you know what they mean. *entender, comprender* ❑ *I think you heard and understood me.* *Creo que me escuchaste y me entendiste.* ❑ *I don't understand what you are talking about.* *No entiendo de qué hablas.* **2** V-T To **understand** someone means to know how they feel and why they behave in the way that they do. *entender, comprender* ❑ *I feel she really understands me.* *Siento que ella realmente me comprende.* **3** V-T You say that you **understand** something when you know why or how it happens. *entender, comprender* ❑ *They are too young to understand what is going on.* *Son muy jóvenes para comprender qué está pasando.* **4** V-T If you **understand** that something is true, you think it is true because you have heard or read that it is. *entender* ❑ *We understand that she's going to be here all day.* *Tenemos entendido que estará aquí todo el día.* ❑ *As I understand it, she has a house in the city.* *Según entiendo, tiene una casa en la ciudad.*
→ see **philosophy**

| **Thesaurus** | *understand* | Ver también: |
|---|---|---|
| V. | catch on, comprehend, get, grasp; (*ant.*) misunderstand **1** | |

**under|stand|able** /ʌndərstændəbᵊl/ ADJ If you describe someone's behavior or feelings as **understandable**, you think that they have reacted to a situation in a natural way or in the way you would expect. *comprensible* ❑ *His unhappiness was understandable.* *Su infelicidad era comprensible.*
● **under|stand|ably** /ʌndərstændəbli/ ADV *comprensiblemente* ❑ *They are understandably upset.* *Es comprensible que estén molestos.*

**under|stand|ing** /ʌndərstændɪŋ/ (**understandings**) **1** N-VAR If you have an **understanding of** something, you know how it works or know what it means. *comprensión, entendimiento* ❑ *Children need an understanding of right and wrong.* *Los niños necesitan comprender lo que está bien y lo que está mal.* **2** ADJ If you are **understanding** toward someone, you are kind and forgiving. *comprensivo* ❑ *He was very understanding when we told him about our decision.* *Fue muy comprensivo cuando le comunicamos nuestra decisión.* **3** N-UNCOUNT If there is **understanding between** people, they are friendly toward each other and trust each other. *entendimiento* ❑ *There was complete understanding between Wilson and myself.* *Había un entendimiento absoluto entre Wilson y yo.* **4** N-COUNT An **understanding** is an informal agreement about something. *acuerdo, entendido* ❑ *We have an understanding about the way we work.* *Tenemos un acuerdo sobre nuestra manera de trabajar.* ❑ *He was free to come and go as he wished on the understanding that he would not run away.* *Era libre de ir y venir como quisiera, en el entendido de que no huiría.*

| **Word Partnership** | Usar *understanding* con: |
|---|---|
| V. | **develop an** understanding, **lack an** understanding **1**<br>**lack** understanding **3** |
| ADJ. | **basic** understanding, **clear** understanding, **complete** understanding **1**<br>**deep/deeper** understanding, **greater** understanding **1 3 4**<br>**better** understanding **1 4**<br>**mutual** understanding **3 4** |

**under|state** /ʌndərsteɪt/ (**understates, understating, understated**) V-T If you **understate** something, you describe it in a way that suggests that it is less important or serious than it really is. *subestimar* ❑ *The government understated the increase in prices.* *El gobierno subestimó el alza de precios.*

**under|state|ment** /ʌndərsteɪtmənt/ (**understatements**) N-VAR An **understatement** is a statement that does not say fully how true something is. *declaración exageradamente modesta* ❑ *To say I'm disappointed is an understatement.* *Decir que estoy decepcionado es poco decir.*

**un|der|stood** /ʌndərstʊd/ **Understood** is the past tense and past participle of **understand**. *pasado y participio pasado de* ***understand***

**under|take** /ʌndərteɪk/ (**undertakes, undertaking, undertook, undertaken**) **1** V-T When you **undertake** a task or job, you start doing it and accept responsibility for it. *encargarse* ❑ *A carpenter will usually undertake this kind of work for you.* *Un carpintero es el que suele encargarse de este tipo de trabajos.* ● **under|tak|ing** /ʌndərteɪkɪŋ/ N-COUNT (**undertakings**) *empresa, tarea* ❑ *Organizing the show has been a huge undertaking.* *La organización del espectáculo ha sido una tarea inmensa.* **2** V-T If you **undertake to** do something, you promise that you will do it. *comprometerse* ❑ *He undertook to write the letter himself.* *Se comprometió a escribir la carta él mismo.*

**under|tak|er** /ʌndərteɪkər/ (**undertakers**) N-COUNT An **undertaker** is a person whose job is to care for the bodies of people who have died and to arrange funerals. *director o directora de funeraria, empleado o empleada de funeraria* ❑ *An undertaker had already taken the body away.* *Un empleado de la funeraria ya se había llevado el cuerpo.*

**un|der|took** /ʌndərtʊk/ **Undertook** is the past tense of **undertake**. *pasado de* ***undertake***

**under|way** /ʌndərweɪ/ ADJ If an activity is **underway,** it has already started. If an activity gets underway, it starts. en marcha ❑ *Plans are underway to build more homes.* *Ya están en marcha los planes para construir más casas.*

**under|wear** /ʌndərwɛər/ N-UNCOUNT **Underwear** is items of clothing that you wear next to your skin and under your other clothes. ropa interior ❑ *For Christmas my brother and I got new underwear, a toy, and a book.* *En Navidad, a mi hermano y a mí nos trajeron ropa interior nueva, un juguete y un libro.*

**under|world** /ʌndərwɜrld/ N-SING The **underworld** is organized crime and the people who are involved in it. bajo mundo ❑ *People say that she still has connections to the criminal underworld.* *La gente dice que ella todavía tiene contactos en el bajo mundo.*

**under|write** /ʌndəraɪt/ (**underwrites, underwriting, underwrote, underwritten**) V-T If an institution or company **underwrites** an activity or **underwrites** the cost of it, they agree to provide any money that is needed to cover losses or buy special equipment, often for an agreed-upon fee. asegurar, respaldar [BUSINESS] ❑ *The two firms are likely to underwrite the deal.* *Es probable que las dos compañías respalden el trato.*

**un|dip|lo|mat|ic** /ʌndɪpləmætɪk/ ADJ If someone is described as **undiplomatic,** they say or do things that offend people, usually not on purpose. poco diplomático, descortés ❑ *He's the most undiplomatic man ever to work here.* *Es el hombre más descortés que haya trabajado aquí.* ● **un|dip|lo|mati|cal|ly** ADV con poca diplomacia ❑ *He undiplomatically described his two years in Dublin as "very, very boring."* *Con poca diplomacia, describió los dos años que pasó en Dublín como "muy, muy aburridos".*

**undo** /ʌndu/ (**undoes, undoing, undid, undone**) **1** V-T If you **undo** something, you unfasten, loosen, or untie it. abrir, desabrochar ❑ *I managed to undo a corner of the package.* *Logré abrir una esquina del paquete.* ❑ *I undid the bottom two buttons of my gray shirt.* *Desabroché los dos botones inferiores de mi camisa gris.* **2** V-T To **undo** something that has been done means to reverse its effect. anular, reparar ❑ *A heavy-handed approach from the police could undo that good impression.* *Una actitud autoritaria de la policía podría anular esa buena impresión.* ❑ *She knew it would be difficult to undo the damage.* *Sabía que sería difícil reparar el daño.*

**un|doubt|ed** /ʌndaʊtɪd/ ADJ You can use **undoubted** to emphasize that something exists or is true. indudable ❑ *The event was an undoubted success.* *El acto fue un éxito indudable.* ❑ *...a man of your undoubted ability.* *...un hombre de tu indudable habilidad.* ● **un|doubt|ed|ly** ADV indudablemente ❑ *He was undoubtedly right.* *Indudablemente, él tenía la razón.*

U

**un|dress** /ʌndrɛs/ (**undresses, undressing, undressed**) V-T/V-I When you **undress,** you take off your clothes. If you **undress** someone, you take off their clothes. desvestir(se) ❑ *She went out, leaving Rachel to undress and take a shower.* *Salió, dejando que Rachel se desvistiera y se diera un baño.* ● **un|dressed** ADJ desvestido ❑ *Fifteen minutes later he was undressed and in bed.* *Quince minutos después, ya estaba desvestido y acostado.*

**un|due** /ʌndu/ ADJ If you describe something bad as **undue,** you mean that it is greater or more extreme than you think is reasonable or appropriate. excesivo, demasiado ❑ *I don't want to put any undue pressure on them to win the baseball game.* *No quiero ejercer una presión excesiva sobre ellos para que ganen el juego de beisbol.* ● **un|du|ly** ADV excesivamente ❑ *"But you're not unduly worried about doing this report?"—"No."* *—¿No te preocupas excesivamente por hacer este informe?—No.*

**Word Partnership** Usar *undue* con:

N. undue **attention**, undue **burden**, undue **delay**, undue **emphasis**, undue **hardship**, undue **influence**, undue **interference**, undue **pressure**, undue **risk**

**un|easy** /ʌnizi/ **1** ADJ If you are **uneasy,** you feel that something is wrong and you are anxious or uncomfortable about it. inquieto ❑ *He looked uneasy and refused to answer questions.* *Se veía inquieto y se negaba a responder preguntas.* ❑ *I was uneasy about the time.* *Estaba inquieto por la hora.* ● **un|easi|ly** /ʌnizɪli/ ADV nerviosamente ❑ *Meg moved uneasily on her chair.* *Meg se movía nerviosamente en la silla.* ● **un|easi|ness** N-UNCOUNT inquietud ❑ *Her uneasiness grew as she looked at him.* *Su inquietud aumentó cuando puso la mirada en él.* **2** ADJ If you describe a situation or relationship as **uneasy,** you mean that the situation is not settled and may not last. precario ❑ *An uneasy calm has settled over Los Angeles.* *Una calma precaria se ha asentado sobre Los Ángeles.* ❑ *There is an uneasy relationship between us and the politicians.* *Hay una relación precaria entre los políticos y nosotros.* ● **un|easi|ly** ADV incómodamente ❑ *The boutique sat uneasily between a butcher's and a shoe store.* *La boutique estaba encajada entre una carnicería y una zapatería.*

**un|em|ployed** /ʌnɪmplɔɪd/ ADJ Someone who is **unemployed** does not have a job. desempleado ❑ *The problem is millions of people are unemployed.* *El problema es que millones de personas están desempleadas.* ❑ *This workshop helps young unemployed people.* *Este taller es para ayudar a jóvenes desempleados.* ● **The unemployed** are people who are unemployed. los desempleados ❑ *We want to create jobs for the unemployed.* *Queremos crear puestos de trabajo para los desempleados.*

**un|em|ploy|ment** /ʌnɪmplɔɪmənt/ **1** N-UNCOUNT **Unemployment** is the fact that people who want jobs cannot get them. desempleo ❑ *...periods of high unemployment.* *...épocas de alto desempleo.* **2** N-UNCOUNT **Unemployment** is the same as **unemployment compensation.** subsidio por desempleo ❑ *He's out of work and is getting unemployment.* *Está sin trabajo y recibe el subsidio por desempleo.*

**un|em|ploy|ment com|pen|sa|tion** N-UNCOUNT **Unemployment compensation** is money that some people receive from the state, usually for a limited time after losing a job, when they do not have a job and are unable to find one. subsidio por desempleo, seguro de desempleo ❑ *He has to manage on unemployment compensation.* *Tiene que sobrevivir con el seguro de desempleo.*

**un|em|ploy|ment line** (**unemployment lines**) N-COUNT When people talk about **the**

**unemployment line,** they are talking about the state of being unemployed, especially when saying how many people are unemployed. *filas del desempleo* ❑ *Being without work means standing in the unemployment line. El estar sin trabajo significa pertenecer a las filas del desempleo.*

**un|equaled** /ʌnikwəld/ ADJ If you describe something as **unequaled,** you mean that it is greater, better, or more extreme than anything else of the same kind. *inigualado* ❑ *This record figure was unequaled for 13 years. Este récord permaneció inigualado durante 13 años.*

**un|even** /ʌnivᵊn/ **1** ADJ An **uneven** surface or edge is not smooth, flat, or straight. *disparejo, accidentado* ❑ *He fell on the uneven surface. Cayó en el suelo disparejo.* ❑ *The pathways were uneven, broken, and dangerous. Los senderos eran accidentados, irregulares y peligrosos.* **2** ADJ Something that is **uneven** is not regular or consistent. *entrecortado* ❑ *Her breathing was uneven. Su respiración era entrecortada.*

**Thesaurus** *uneven* Ver también:
ADJ. jagged, rough; (ant.) even **1** inconsistent, irregular **2**

**un|ex|pec|ted** /ʌnɪkspɛktɪd/ ADJ If something is **unexpected,** it surprises you because you did not think that it was likely to happen. *inesperado* ❑ *His death was totally unexpected. Su muerte fue totalmente inesperada.* ● **un|ex|pect|ed|ly** ADV *inesperadamente* ❑ *May was unexpectedly hot. Nadie se esperaba que mayo fuera a ser tan caluroso.*

**Thesaurus** *unexpected* Ver también:
ADJ. startling, surprising

**Word Link** un ≈ not : unfair, unrealistic, unsure

**un|fair** /ʌnfɛər/ ADJ An **unfair** action or situation is not right or fair. *injusto* ❑ *Her position as president gives her an unfair advantage. Su puesto de presidenta le da una ventaja injusta.* ❑ *It was unfair that he should suffer so much. Era injusto que sufriera tanto.* ● **un|fair|ly** ADV *injustamente* ❑ *He unfairly blamed Frances for his failure. Culpó injustamente a Frances de su fracaso.* ● **un|fair|ness** N-UNCOUNT *injusticia* ❑ *...the unfairness of life. ...la injusticia de la vida.*

**un|fit** /ʌnfɪt/ **1** ADJ If someone or something is **unfit** for a particular purpose, they are not suitable or not good enough for that purpose. *no apto, inadecuado* ❑ *The water was unfit for swimming. El agua no era adecuada para nadar.* ❑ *...tunnels filled with air unfit to breathe. ...túneles llenos de aire no apto para respirar.* **2** ADJ If you are **unfit,** your body is not in good condition because you have not been getting regular exercise. *fuera de forma* ❑ *Many children are so unfit they cannot do even basic exercises. Muchos niños están tan fuera de forma que ni siquiera pueden hacer los ejercicios básicos.*

**un|fold** /ʌnfoʊld/ (**unfolds, unfolding, unfolded**) **1** V-I If a situation or story **unfolds,** it develops and becomes known or understood. *desenvolverse* ❑ *We'll see how the situation unfolds in the next 24 hours. Veremos cómo se desenvuelve la situación en las próximas 24 horas.* ❑ *The policeman listened carefully as the story unfolded. El policía escuchaba atentamente mientras la historia se desenvolvía.* **2** V-T/V-I If someone **unfolds** something which has been folded or if it **unfolds,** it is opened out and becomes flat. *desdoblar* ❑ *She unfolded the piece of paper. Desdobló el trozo de papel.*

**un|for|get|table** /ʌnfərgɛtəbᵊl/ ADJ If something is **unforgettable,** it is so beautiful, enjoyable, or unusual that you remember it for a long time. *inolvidable* ❑ *The day was truly unforgettable. El día fue verdaderamente inolvidable.* ❑ *...the outdoor activities that will make your vacation unforgettable. ...las actividades al aire libre que harán de sus vacaciones algo inolvidable.*

**un|for|tu|nate** /ʌnfɔrtʃənɪt/ **1** ADJ If you describe someone as **unfortunate,** you mean that something unpleasant or unlucky has happened to them. *desafortunado* ❑ *I've just been unfortunate to be ill. Sólo he tenido la mala suerte de estar enfermo.* **2** ADJ If you describe something that has happened as **unfortunate,** you think that it is inappropriate, embarrassing, awkward, or undesirable. *inoportuno* ❑ *It is unfortunate that your flight was canceled. Qué inoportuno que tu vuelo haya sido cancelado.*

**un|for|tu|nate|ly** /ʌnfɔrtʃənɪtli/ ADV You can use **unfortunately** to express regret about what you are saying. *desgraciadamente* ❑ *Unfortunately, I don't have time to stay. Desgraciadamente, no tengo tiempo para quedarme.*

**un|friend|ly** /ʌnfrɛndli/ ADJ If you describe someone as **unfriendly,** you mean that they behave in an unkind or hostile way. *hostil, desagradable* ❑ *Some people were unfriendly to her. Algunas personas fueron hostiles con ella.* ❑ *People always complain that banks are unfriendly and unhelpful. La gente siempre se queja de que los empleados de los bancos son desagradables y poco serviciales.*

**un|gram|mati|cal** /ʌngrəmætɪkᵊl/ ADJ If someone's language is **ungrammatical,** it is not considered correct because it does not obey the rules of grammar. *gramaticalmente incorrecto* ❑ *The sentence is unclear but not totally ungrammatical. La oración es poco clara, pero no del todo incorrecta gramaticalmente.* ● **un|gram|mati|cal|ly** ADV *con agramaticalidad* ❑ *She speaks ungrammatically but fluently. Habla con fluidez, pero comete errores gramaticales.*

**un|hap|py** /ʌnhæpi/ (**unhappier, unhappiest**) **1** ADJ If you are **unhappy,** you are sad and depressed. *desdichado* ❑ *He was a shy, sometimes unhappy man. Era un hombre tímido y a veces desdichado.* ● **un|hap|pi|ly** ADV *tristemente* ❑ *"I don't have your imagination," Kevin said unhappily. —No tengo tu imaginación —dijo Kevin tristemente.* ● **un|hap|pi|ness** N-UNCOUNT *infelicidad* ❑ *There was a lot of unhappiness in my childhood. Tuve una infancia muy infeliz.* **2** ADJ If you are **unhappy about** something, you are not pleased about it or not satisfied with it. *descontento* ❑ *College students are unhappy with their school bookstores. Los alumnos universitarios están descontentos con sus librerías escolares.* ● **un|hap|pi|ness** N-UNCOUNT *descontento* ❑ *She spoke about her unhappiness with her job. Habló de su descontento con el trabajo.* **3** ADJ An **unhappy** situation or choice is not satisfactory or desirable. *desafortunado* ❑ *...his unhappy choice of words. ...su desafortunada elección de palabras.*

**Thesaurus** *unhappy* Ver también:

ADJ. depressed, miserable, sad; (*ant.*) happy 1

**un|healthy** /ʌnhɛlθi/ (**unhealthier, unhealthiest**) 1 ADJ Something that is **unhealthy** is likely to cause illness or bad health. *poco saludable* ❑ *Avoid unhealthy foods such as hamburgers and fries. Evite la comida poco saludable, como las hamburguesas y las papas fritas.* 2 ADJ If you are **unhealthy,** you are sick or not in good physical condition. *enfermizo* ❑ *...a pale, unhealthy looking man. ...un hombre de aspecto pálido y enfermizo.*

**un|heard of** /ʌnhɜrd ʌv/ ADJ An event or situation that is **unheard of** never happens. *inexistente* ❑ *Riots are almost unheard of in Japan. Los disturbios son prácticamente inexistentes en Japón.*

**uni|cel|lu|lar** /yunɪsɛlyələr/ ADJ **Unicellular** organisms are organisms that consist of a single cell, such as bacteria. Compare **multicellular.** *unicelular* [TECHNICAL]

**Word Link** *ident ≈ same : identical, identification, unidentified*

**un|iden|ti|fied** /ʌnaɪdɛntɪfaɪd/ ADJ If you describe someone or something as **unidentified,** you mean that nobody knows who or what they are. *desconocido* ❑ *An unidentified woman was in the car. Una mujer desconocida estaba en el auto.*

**uni|fi|ca|tion** /yunɪfɪkeɪʃən/ N-UNCOUNT **Unification** is the process by which two or more countries join together and become one country. *unificación* ❑ *...the unification of East and West Germany in 1990. ...la unificación de Alemania Oriental y Occidental en 1990.*

**Word Link** *uni ≈ one : uniform, unilateral, union*

**uni|form** /yunɪfɔrm/ (**uniforms**) 1 N-VAR A **uniform** is a special set of clothes which some people wear to work in and which some children wear in school. *uniforme* ❑ *The police wear dark blue uniforms. La policía utiliza uniformes azul oscuro.* ❑ *He was dressed in his school uniform. Traía puesto su uniforme escolar.* 2 ADJ If something is **uniform,** it is even and regular. *uniforme* ❑ *Plants do not all grow to uniform size. No todas las plantas alcanzan un tamaño uniforme.*

uniform

• **uni|form|ity** /yunɪfɔrmɪti/ N-UNCOUNT *uniformidad* ❑ *...uniformity of color. ...uniformidad de color.* • **uni|form|ly** ADV *uniformemente* ❑ *Outside, the November day was uniformly gray. Afuera, ese día de noviembre era uniformemente gris.* 3 ADJ If you describe a number of things as **uniform,** you mean that they are all the same. *uniforme* ❑ *Along each wall were uniform green metal filing cabinets. A lo largo de cada pared había archiveros metalicos de un verde uniforme.* • **uni|form|ity** N-UNCOUNT *uniformidad* ❑ *...the dull uniformity of the houses. ...la aburrida uniformidad de las casas.*

→ see **basketball, football, soccer**

**uni|formed** /yunɪfɔrmd/ ADJ **Uniformed** people are wearing a uniform while they do their job. *uniformado* ❑ *...uniformed policemen. ...policías uniformados.*

**uni|fy** /yunɪfaɪ/ (**unifies, unifying, unified**) V-T/V-I If someone **unifies** different things or parts, or if the things or parts **unify,** they are brought together to form one thing. *unificar* ❑ *They are trying to unify boys' and girls' basketball rules in Washington. En Washington están tratando de unificar las reglas del basquetbol varonil y femenil.* • **uni|fied** ADJ *uniforme* ❑ *You are sending a loud and unified message. Estás enviando un mensaje enérgico y uniforme.*

**uni|lat|er|al** /yunɪlætərᵊl/ ADJ A **unilateral** decision is made by only one of the groups, organizations, or countries that are involved in a particular situation, without the agreement of the others. *unilateral* ❑ *...a unilateral decision. ...una decisión unilateral.*

**un|in|forma|tive** /ʌnɪnfɔrmətɪv/ ADJ Something that is **uninformative** does not give you enough useful information. *poco revelador* ❑ *He was polite but uninformative. Fue cortés, pero poco revelador.*

**un|in|stall** /ʌnɪnstɔl/ (**uninstalls, uninstalling, uninstalled**) V-T If you **uninstall** a computer program, you remove it permanently from your computer. *desinstalar* [COMPUTING] ❑ *If you don't like the program, just uninstall it. Si no le gusta el programa, sólo tiene que desinstalarlo.*

**un|ion** /yunyən/ (**unions**) 1 N-COUNT A **union** is a workers' organization which represents its members and which tries to improve things such as their working conditions and pay. *sindicato* ❑ *Ten new members joined the union. Diez trabajadores nuevos se unieron al sindicato.* 2 N-UNCOUNT When the **union** of two or more things occurs, they are joined together and become one thing. *unión* ❑ *...the union of Tanganyika and Zanzibar to form Tanzania. ...la unión de Tanganyika y Zanzíbar para formar Tanzania.*

→ see Word Web: **union**

→ see **factory**

**unique** /yunik/ 1 ADJ Something that is **unique** is the only one of its kind. *único* ❑ *Each person's signature is unique. La firma de cada persona es única.* • **unique|ly** ADV *excepcionalmente* ❑ *She's a dog with uniquely colored eyes; one is brown and one is blue. Es una perra con ojos de color excepcional: uno es café y el otro azul.* • **unique|ness** N-UNCOUNT *singularidad* ❑ *I like the uniqueness of flavors in Australian cooking. Me gusta la singularidad de los sabores de la cocina australiana.* 2 ADJ You can use **unique** to describe things that you admire because they are very unusual and special. *excepcional* ❑ *She was a woman of unique talent. Era una mujer de talento excepcional.* • **unique|ly** ADV *excepcionalmente* ❑ *...a uniquely beautiful city. ...una ciudad excepcionalmente bella.* 3 ADJ If something is **unique to** one thing, person, group, or place, it concerns or belongs only to that thing, person, group, or place. *exclusivo de* ❑ *This animal is unique to Borneo. Este animal es exclusivo de Borneo.* • **unique|ly** ADV *exclusivamente* ❑ *The problem isn't uniquely American. El problema no es exclusivamente estadounidense.*

U

**Word Web** union

In some places, **laborers** work long hours with little chance for a **raise** in **wages**. **Workdays** of 10 to 12 hours are common. Some people work seven days a week. Conditions like this lead to unhappiness among **workers**. At that point, **organizers** can encourage them to join a **union**. Union leaders do **collective bargaining** with business owners. They may ask for a shorter workday or better working conditions. If the **employees** are not satisfied with the results, they may **strike**. In Sweden, 85% of laborers and 75% of **white-collar** employees belong to unions.

**Thesaurus** *unique* Ver también:

ADJ. different, one-of-a-kind, special; (*ant.*) common, standard, usual 1

**uni|son** /yunɪsən, -zən/ 1 PHRASE If two or more people do something **in unison**, they do it together at the same time. *al unísono* ❑ *They were singing in unison. Estaban cantando al unísono.* 2 N-UNCOUNT In dance, **unison** is the performance of a series of movements by two or more dancers at the same time. [TECHNICAL]

**unit** /yunɪt/ (**units**) 1 N-COUNT If you consider something as a **unit**, you consider it as a single, complete thing. *unidad, hablando de familias, se refiere a la familia nuclear (no extendida)* ❑ *...a happy family unit enjoying the day together. ...una familia feliz que disfruta de un día juntos.* 2 N-COUNT A **unit** is a group of people who work together at a specific job, often in a particular place. *unidad* ❑ *...a firefighting unit. ...una unidad de bomberos.* 3 N-COUNT A **unit** is a small machine which has a particular function, often part of a larger machine. *unidad* ❑ *The unit plugs into any TV set. La unidad se conecta a cualquier aparato de televisión.* 4 N-COUNT A **unit** of measurement is a fixed standard quantity, length, or weight that is used for measuring things. The quart, the inch, and the ounce are all units. *unidad*
→ see **graph**

**Uni|tar|ian** /yunɪtɛəriən/ (**Unitarians**) 1 N-COUNT **Unitarians** are Christians who reject the idea of the Trinity and believe that God is a single being. *unitario o unitaria* ❑ *They were Unitarians. Ellos eran unitarios.* 2 ADJ **Unitarian** means relating to the religious beliefs or practices of Unitarians. *unitario* ❑ *...a Unitarian minister. ...un ministro unitario.*

**unite** /yunaɪt/ (**unites, uniting, united**) V-T/V-I If a group of people or things **unite** or if something **unites** them, they join together and act as a group. *unir* ❑ *Only the president can unite the people. Sólo el presidente puede unir al pueblo.*

**unit|ed** /yunaɪtɪd/ 1 ADJ When people are **united** about something, they agree about it and act together. *unido* ❑ *They were united by their love of music. Los unía su amor a la música.* 2 ADJ **United** is used to describe a country which has been formed from two or more states or countries. *unificado* ❑ *...a united Germany. ...una Alemania unificada.*

**Unit|ed Na|tions** N-PROPER **The United Nations** is an organization which most countries belong to. Its role is to encourage international peace, cooperation, and friendship. *Naciones Unidas*

**Unit|ed States of Ameri|ca** N-PROPER **The United States of America** is the official name for the country in North America that consists of fifty states and the District of Columbia. It is bordered by Canada in the north and Mexico in the south. The form **United States** is also used. *Estados Unidos de América*

**unit frac|tion** (**unit fractions**) N-COUNT A **unit fraction** is a fraction in which the top part of the fraction is always the number one, for example ½ or ¼. *fracción unitaria* [TECHNICAL]

**unity** /yunɪti/ 1 N-UNCOUNT **Unity** is the state of different areas or groups being joined together to form a single country or organization. *unidad* ❑ *...the unity of Eastern and Western Europe. ...la unidad de Europa oriental y occidental.* 2 N-UNCOUNT When there is **unity**, people are in agreement and act together for a particular purpose. *unidad* ❑ *The president called for unity between the United States and Europe. El presidente hizo un llamado a la unidad de Estados Unidos y Europa.* 3 N-UNCOUNT The **unity** of a work of art such as a painting or a piece of music is the impression it gives that it is complete and that all the different parts belong together. *unity*

**uni|ver|sal** /yunɪvɜrsᵊl/ ADJ Something that is **universal** relates to everyone in the world or everyone in a particular group or society. *general* ❑ *...universal health care. ...servicios de salud generales.* ● **uni|ver|sal|ly** /yunɪvɜrsəli/ ADV *mundialmente* ❑ *...a universally-accepted point of view. ...un punto de vista mundialmente aceptado.*

**uni|ver|sal gravi|ta|tion** /yunɪvɜrsᵊl grævɪteɪʃᵊn/ N-SING **The law of universal gravitation** is a principle in physics which states that all objects in the universe attract one another because of the force of gravity. *gravitación universal* [TECHNICAL]

**uni|verse** /yunɪvɜrs/ (**universes**) N-COUNT **The universe** is the whole of space and all the stars, planets, and other forms of matter and energy in it. *universo* ❑ *...all the stars and planets in the universe. ...todas las estrellas y los planetas del universo.*
→ see **biosphere, galaxy, telescope**

u

**uni|ver|sity** /yu̲nɪvɜrsɪti/ (**universities**) N-VAR A **university** is an institution where students study for degrees and where academic research is done. *universidad* ❑ *...the University of Washington. ...la Universidad de Washington.* ❑ *She goes to Duke University. Ella va a la Universidad Duke.*

**un|just** /ʌndʒʌ̲st/ ADJ If you describe an action, system, or law as **unjust,** you think that it treats a person or group badly in a way that they do not deserve. *injusto* ❑ *The attack on Charles was unjust. El ataque contra Charles fue injusto.* ● **un|just|ly** ADV *injustamente* ❑ *She was unjustly accused of stealing money. La acusaron injustamente de robar dinero.*

**un|known** /ʌnno̲u̲n/ (**unknowns**) **1** ADJ If something is **unknown** to you, you have no knowledge of it. *desconocido* ❑ *An unknown number of people were killed. Asesinaron a un número desconocido de personas.* ❑ *The child's age is unknown. Se desconoce la edad del niño.* ● An **unknown** is something that is unknown. *incógnita* ❑ *There are still a lot of unknowns about the illness. Aún hay muchas incógnitas sobre la enfermedad.* **2** ADJ An **unknown** person is not famous or publicly recognized. *desconocido* ❑ *He was an unknown writer. Era un escritor desconocido.* ● An **unknown** is a person who is unknown. *desconocido o desconocida* ❑ *...a group of complete unknowns. ...un grupo de completos desconocidos.* **3** N-SING **The unknown** refers generally to things or places that people do not know about or understand. *lo desconocido* ❑ *...fear of the unknown. ...temor a lo desconocido.*

**un|lead|ed** /ʌnlɛ̲dɪd/ ADJ **Unleaded** fuel contains a smaller amount of lead than most fuels so that it produces less harmful substances when it is burned. *sin plomo* ❑ *He filled up his car with regular unleaded gas. Llenó el tanque de su auto con gasolina normal sin plomo.* ● **Unleaded** is also a noun. *combustible sin plomo* ❑ *All its engines will run happily on unleaded. Todos sus motores funcionarán sin problemas con combustible sin plomo.*

**un|leash** /ʌnli̲ʃ/ (**unleashes, unleashing, unleashed**) V-T If someone or something **unleashes** a powerful force, feeling, activity, or group, they suddenly release it. *dar rienda suelta a* ❑ *She unleashed her anger on him during the meeting. Dio rienda suelta a su enojo contra él durante la junta.*

**un|less** /ʌnlɛ̲s/ CONJ You use **unless** to introduce the only circumstances in which an event you are mentioning will not take place or in which a statement you are making is not true. *si no, a menos que* ❑ *I'm not happy unless I drive every day. No me siento contento si no manejo todos los días.*

U

**un|li|censed** /ʌnla̲ɪsᵊnst/ **1** ADJ If you are **unlicensed,** you do not have official permission from the government or from the authorities to do something. *no autorizado, ilegal, tolerado, pirata* ❑ *...unlicensed cab drivers. ...choferes de taxi no autorizados.* **2** ADJ If something that you own or use is **unlicensed,** you do not have official permission to own it or use it. *sin registro* ❑ *Owners of unlicensed cats may face a $250 fine. Los propietarios de gatos sin registro podrían hacerse acreedores a una multa de 250 dólares.*

**Word Link** | like ≈ similar : alike, likewise, unlike

**un|like** /ʌnla̲ɪk/ **1** PREP If one thing is **unlike** another thing, the two things have different qualities or characteristics from each other. *diferente, distinto* ❑ *He's so unlike his father. Es muy diferente a su padre.* **2** PREP You can use **unlike** to contrast two people, things, or situations, and show how they are different. *a diferencia de* ❑ *Unlike most meetings, this one was a lot of fun. A diferencia de la mayoría de las reuniones, esta fue muy divertida.* **3** PREP If you describe something that a particular person has done as being **unlike** them, you mean that you are surprised by it because it is not typical of their character or normal behavior. *no propio de* ❑ *It was unlike him to say something like that. No era propio de él decir cosas así.*

**un|like|ly** /ʌnla̲ɪkli/ (**unlikeliest**) ADJ If you say that something is **unlikely to** happen or **unlikely to** be true, you believe that it will not happen or that it is not true, although you are not completely sure. *improbable, remoto* ❑ *They are unlikely to arrive before nine o'clock. No es probable que lleguen antes de las nueve.*

**Word Partnership** Usar *unlikely* con:

| | |
|---|---|
| N. | unlikely **event** |
| ADV. | **extremely** unlikely, **highly** unlikely, **most** unlikely, **very** unlikely |
| V. | unlikely **to change**, unlikely **to happen**, **seem** unlikely |

**un|load** /ʌnlo̲u̲d/ (**unloads, unloading, unloaded**) V-T If you **unload** goods from a vehicle, or if you **unload** a vehicle, you remove the goods from the vehicle. *descargar* ❑ *We unloaded everything from the car. Descargamos todas las cosas del coche.*

**un|lock** /ʌnlɒ̲k/ (**unlocks, unlocking, unlocked**) V-T If you **unlock** something such as a door, a room, or a container, you open it using a key. *abrir (algo cerrado con llave)* ❑ *He unlocked the car and threw the coat on to the back seat. Abrió el coche y aventó el abrigo al asiento trasero.*

**un|moved** /ʌnmu̲vd/ ADJ If you are **unmoved by** something, you are not emotionally affected by it. *indiferente, impasible* ❑ *He seemed unmoved by the news. Parecía que la noticia lo había dejado indiferente.*

**un|natu|ral** /ʌnnæ̲tʃərᵊl/ **1** ADJ If you describe something as **unnatural,** you mean that it is strange and often frightening, because it is different from what you normally expect. *poco natural, poco normal, artificial* ❑ *His eyes were an almost unnatural shade of blue. Sus ojos eran de un tono de azul que parecía artificial.* ● **un|natu|ral|ly** ADV *extrañamente* ❑ *The house was unnaturally silent. La casa estaba extrañamente silenciosa.* **2** ADJ Behavior that is **unnatural** seems artificial and not normal or genuine. *poco natural, forzado* ❑ *She gave him a smile which seemed unnatural. Le dirigió una sonrisa que pareció forzada.* ● **un|natu|ral|ly** ADV *anormalmente* ❑ *She smiled, showing a row of unnaturally perfect teeth. Sonrió y mostró una hilera de dientes anormalmente perfectos.*

**un|nec|es|sary** /ʌnnɛ̲səsɛri/ ADJ If you describe something as **unnecessary,** you mean that it is not needed or does not have to be done. *innecesario, inútil, superfluo* ❑ *It's unnecessary to go until I'm needed. No es necesario que vaya, hasta que me necesiten.* ● **un|nec|es|sari|ly** /ʌnnɛsəsɛ̲ərɪli/

ADV *innecesariamente* ❑ *I didn't want to upset my husband unnecessarily.* *No quería alterar a mi esposo innecesariamente.*

**un|of|fi|cial** /ʌnəfɪʃᵊl/ ADJ An **unofficial** action or statement is not organized or approved by a person or group in authority. *extraoficial* ❑ *Memorial Day is the unofficial start of summer.* *El verano empieza extraoficialmente el día de los caídos en guerra, o Memorial Day.* • **un|of|fi|cial|ly** ADV *extraoficialmente* ❑ *The park has been unofficially open since September.* *El parque ha estado abierto extraoficialmente desde septiembre.*

**un|ortho|dox** /ʌnɔrθədɒks/ ADJ If you describe someone's behavior, beliefs, or customs as **unorthodox,** you mean that they are different from what is generally accepted. *poco convencional, poco ortodoxo* ❑ *...his unorthodox management style.* *...su poco convencional estilo de administrar.* ❑ *...an unorthodox approach to problems.* *...un enfoque poco ortodoxo de los problemas.*

**un|pack** /ʌnpæk/ (**unpacks, unpacking, unpacked**) V-T/V-I When you **unpack** a suitcase, box, or similar container, or when you **unpack,** you take the things out of the container. *desempacar, deshacer las maletas* ❑ *He unpacked his bag.* *Sacó las cosas de su maleta.*

**un|pal|at|able** /ʌnpælɪtəbᵊl/ ADJ If you describe an idea as **unpalatable,** you mean that you find it unpleasant and difficult to accept. *desagradable* ❑ *I began to learn the unpalatable truth about John.* *Me empecé a enterar de la desagradable verdad sobre John.*

**un|par|al|leled** /ʌnpærəlɛld/ ADJ If you describe something as **unparalleled,** you are emphasizing that it is, for example, bigger, better, or worse than anything else of its kind. *sin par, inigualado* ❑ *...his unparalleled career record.* *...su experiencia profesional sin par.*

**un|pleas|ant** /ʌnplɛzᵊnt/ **1** ADJ If something is **unpleasant,** it gives you bad feelings, for example by making you feel upset or uncomfortable. *desagradable* ❑ *The plant has an unpleasant smell.* *La planta tiene un olor desagradable* • **un|pleas|ant|ly** ADV *desagradablemente* ❑ *We were unpleasantly surprised to hear about the problem.* *Fue una sorpresa desagradable enterarnos del problema.* **2** ADJ An **unpleasant** person is very unfriendly and rude. *antipático* ❑ *She thought he was an unpleasant man.* *Pensó que era un hombre antipático.* • **un|pleas|ant|ly** ADV *desagradablemente* ❑ *Melissa laughed unpleasantly.* *Melissa soltó una risa desagradable.*

**un|plug** /ʌnplʌg/ (**unplugs, unplugging, unplugged**) V-T If you **unplug** an electrical device or telephone, you pull a wire out of an outlet so that it stops working. *desconectar, desenchufar* ❑ *Whenever there's a storm, I unplug my computer.* *Siempre que hay tormenta, desconecto mi computadora.*

| Word Link | *popul ≈ people : popular, population, unpopular* |
|---|---|

**un|popu|lar** /ʌnpɒpyələr/ ADJ If something or someone is **unpopular,** most people do not like them. *impopular* ❑ *It was an unpopular decision.* *Fue una decisión impopular.* ❑ *I was very unpopular in high school.* *Yo no era muy popular en la secundaria.* • **un|popu|lar|ity** /ʌnpɒpyəlærɪti/ N-UNCOUNT *impopularidad* ❑ *...his unpopularity among his colleagues.* *...su impopularidad entre sus colegas.*

**un|prec|edent|ed** /ʌnprɛsɪdɛntɪd/ **1** ADJ If something is **unprecedented,** it has never happened before. *sin precedentes, inaudito* ❑ *Such an action is rare, but not unprecedented.* *Una acción así es rara, pero no inaudita.* **2** ADJ If you describe something as **unprecedented,** you are emphasizing that it is very great in quality or amount. *sin precedentes, inaudito* ❑ *...an unprecedented success.* *...un éxito sin precedentes.*

**un|pre|dict|able** /ʌnprɪdɪktəbᵊl/ ADJ If you describe someone or something as **unpredictable,** you mean that you cannot tell what they are going to do or how they are going to behave. *impredecible* ❑ *He is completely unpredictable.* *Es completamente impredecible.* • **un|pre|dict|abil|ity** /ʌnprɪdɪktəbɪlɪti/ N-UNCOUNT *lo impredecible* ❑ *...the unpredictability of the weather.* *...lo impredecible del clima.*

**un|pro|duc|tive** /ʌnprədʌktɪv/ ADJ Something that is **unproductive** does not produce any good results. *improductivo* ❑ *...a busy but unproductive night.* *...una noche agitada, pero improductiva.*

**un|prof|it|able** /ʌnprɒfɪtəbᵊl/ ADJ An industry, company, or product that is **unprofitable** does not make enough profit. *improductivo* [BUSINESS] ❑ *...unprofitable, badly-run industries.* *...industrias improductivas, mal dirigidas.*

**un|pro|tect|ed** /ʌnprətɛktɪd/ **1** ADJ An **unprotected** person or place is not watched over or defended, and so they may be harmed or attacked. *desprotegido* ❑ *...a 4,800-kilometer unprotected border.* *...una frontera desprotegida de 4,800 kilómetros.* **2** ADJ If something is **unprotected,** it is not covered or treated with anything, and so it may easily be damaged. *desprotegido* ❑ *If we are unprotected from the sun for long enough, our skin will burn.* *Si pasamos largo tiempo al sol sin protección para la piel, nos quemamos.*

**un|pub|lished** /ʌnpʌblɪʃt/ ADJ An **unpublished** book, letter, or report has never been published. *inédito* ❑ *Much of his writing is unpublished.* *Gran parte de sus escritos están inéditos.*

**un|quali|fied** /ʌnkwɒlɪfaɪd/ **1** ADJ If you are **unqualified,** you do not have any qualifications, or you do not have the right qualifications for a particular job. *no calificado* ❑ *She was unqualified for the job.* *No cumplía con los requisitos para el trabajo.* **2** ADJ **Unqualified** means total or unlimited. *rotundo* ❑ *The event was an unqualified success.* *El acto tuvo un éxito rotundo.*

**un|ques|tion|able** /ʌnkwɛstʃənəbᵊl/ ADJ If you describe something as **unquestionable,** you are emphasizing that it is so obviously true or real that nobody can doubt it. *innegable* ❑ *His ability is unquestionable.* *Su capacidad es innegable.* • **un|ques|tion|ably** /ʌnkwɛstʃənəbli/ ADV *indudablemente, sin lugar a dudas* ❑ *The next two years were unquestionably the happiest of his life.* *Indudablemente, los siguientes dos años fueron los más felices de su vida.*

**un|rav|el** /ʌnrævᵊl/ (**unravels, unraveling, unraveled**) **1** V-T/V-I If you **unravel** something that is knotted or knitted, or if it **unravels,** it

u

becomes one straight piece again or separates into different threads. desenmarañar, desenredar ❑ *He could unravel knots others couldn't.* *Podía deshacer nudos como nadie.* **2** V-T/V-I If you **unravel** a mystery or puzzle, or it **unravels,** it gradually becomes clearer until you can work out the answer to it. desentrañar, aclarar, descifrar ❑ *Carter was still trying to unravel the truth of the woman's story.* *Carter todavía estaba tratando de desentrañar la verdad de la historia de la mujer.*

| Word Link | *un ≈ not : unfair, unrealistic, unsure* |
|---|---|

**un|re|al|is|tic** /ʌnriəlɪstɪk/ ADJ If you say that someone is being **unrealistic,** you mean that they do not recognize the truth about a situation, especially about the difficulties involved. poco realista, irreal ❑ *It was unrealistic to expect us to finish this in time.* *No era realista esperar que lo termináramos a tiempo.*

**un|re|lent|ing** /ʌnrɪlɛntɪŋ/ **1** ADJ If you describe someone's behavior as **unrelenting,** you mean that they are continuing to do something in a very determined way. tenaz, riguroso, implacable ❑ *Rosie directed the project, and she was unrelenting.* *Rosie dirigió el proyecto y fue implacable.* **2** ADJ If you describe something unpleasant as **unrelenting,** you mean that it continues without stopping. constante ❑ *...an unrelenting downpour of rain.* *...un aguacero que parecía no terminar nunca.*

**un|re|pent|ant** /ʌnrɪpɛntənt/ ADJ If you are **unrepentant,** you are not ashamed of your beliefs or actions. impenitente ❑ *Pamela was unrepentant about her strong language.* *Pamela no se arrepentía de su lenguaje subido de tono.*

**un|rest** /ʌnrɛst/ N-UNCOUNT If there is **unrest** in a particular place or society, people are expressing anger and dissatisfaction, often by demonstrating or rioting. malestar, descontento, intranquilidad ❑ *There is growing unrest among students in several major cities.* *Cada vez es mayor el descontento entre los estudiantes en varias ciudades importantes.*

**un|ru|ly** /ʌnruli/ **1** ADJ If you describe people, especially children, as **unruly,** you mean that they behave badly and are difficult to control. indisciplinado, ingobernable ❑ *...unruly behavior.* *...comportamiento ingobernable.* **2** ADJ **Unruly** hair is difficult to keep tidy. rebelde ❑ *The man had remarkably black, unruly hair.* *El hombre tenía un cabello increíblemente negro y rebelde.*

| Word Link | *sat, satis ≈ enough : insatiable, satisfy, unsatisfactory* |
|---|---|

U

**un|sat|is|fac|tory** /ʌnsætɪsfæktəri/ ADJ If you describe something as **unsatisfactory,** you mean that it is not as good as it should be, and cannot be considered acceptable. insatisfactorio, deficiente ❑ *He called her answer "unsatisfactory and disappointing."* *Calificó su respuesta de "insatisfactoria y decepcionante".*

**un|satu|rat|ed hydro|car|bon** /ʌnsætʃəreɪtɪd haɪdrəkɑrbən/ (**unsaturated hydrocarbons**) N-VAR An **unsaturated hydrocarbon** is a chemical compound consisting of carbon and hydrogen in which there is less than the maximum amount of hydrogen. hidrocarburo insaturado [TECHNICAL]

**un|scathed** /ʌnskeɪðd/ ADJ If you are **unscathed** after a dangerous experience, you have not been injured or harmed by it. indemne, ileso ❑ *Tony was unscathed apart from a severely-bruised finger.* *Tony resultó ileso, salvo por un dedo que tenía severamente magullado.*

**un|set|tling** /ʌnsɛtəlɪŋ/ ADJ If you describe something as **unsettling,** you mean that it makes you feel worried or uncertain. inquietante, perturbador ❑ *Phil had unsettling dreams every night.* *Phil tenía sueños inquietantes todas las noches.*

**un|sight|ly** /ʌnsaɪtli/ ADJ If you describe something as **unsightly,** you mean that it is ugly. de aspecto feo ❑ *...an unsightly pile of garbage.* *...un montón de basura de aspecto feo.*

**un|sports|man|like** /ʌnspɔrtsmənlaɪk/ ADJ **Unsportsmanlike** behavior is behavior that is rude, aggressive or unfair, especially during a game. antideportivo ❑ *He was sent off for unsportsmanlike conduct.* *Lo expulsaron por su conducta antideportiva.*

**un|suc|cess|ful** /ʌnsəksɛsfəl/ **1** ADJ Something that is **unsuccessful** does not achieve what it was intended to achieve. infructuoso, fallido ❑ *His efforts were unsuccessful.* *Sus esfuerzos fueron infructuosos.* ❑ *...a second unsuccessful operation on his knee.* *...una infructuosa segunda operación de rodilla.* ● **un|suc|cess|ful|ly** ADV en vano, sin resultado alguno ❑ *He tried unsuccessfully to sell the business.* *Trató de vender el negocio, sin resultado alguno.* **2** ADJ Someone who is **unsuccessful** does not achieve what they intended to achieve, especially in their career. sin éxito, infructuoso ❑ *He and his friend Boris were unsuccessful in getting a job.* *Él y su amigo Boris trataron en vano de encontrar trabajo.*

**un|sure** /ʌnʃʊər/ **1** ADJ If you are **unsure of yourself**, you lack confidence. inseguro ❑ *Phyllis was worried and unsure of herself.* *Phyllis estaba preocupada y se sentía insegura.* **2** ADJ If you are **unsure about** something, you feel uncertain about it. indeciso ❑ *Fifty-two percent were unsure about the idea.* *El cincuenta y dos por ciento estaba indeciso sobre la cuestión.*

| Word Link | *un ≈ reversal : untie, unusual, unzip* |
|---|---|

**un|tie** /ʌntaɪ/ (**unties, untying, untied**) **1** V-T If you **untie** something that is tied to another thing or if you **untie** two things that are tied together, you remove the string or rope that holds them or that has been tied around them. desatar, desamarrar ❑ *Please untie my hands.* *Por favor, desáteme las manos.* **2** V-T If you **untie** something such as string or rope, you undo it so that there is no knot in it. desamarrar, desanudar ❑ *She untied the laces on one of her shoes.* *Desamarró la agujeta de uno de sus zapatos.*

**un|til** /ʌntɪl/ **1** PREP If something happens **until** a particular time, it happens during the period before that time and stops at that time. hasta ❑ *Until 2004, she lived in Canada.* *Vivió en Canadá hasta 2004.* ● **Until** is also a conjunction. hasta que ❑ *I waited until it got dark.* *Esperé hasta que oscureció.* **2** PREP If something does not happen **until** a particular time, it does not happen before that time and only starts happening at that time. hasta ❑ *I won't know anything until Saturday.* *No sabré nada* *hasta el sábado.* • **Until** is also a conjunction. *hasta* ❑ *They'll never be safe until they get out of the country. Nunca estarán seguros hasta salir del país.* **3** up

**until** → see **up**

**un|treat|ed** /ʌntrɪtɪd/ **1** ADJ If an injury or illness is left **untreated,** it is not given medical treatment. *sin tratar, no tratado* ❑ *If left untreated, the condition may become serious. Si no se trata, la enfermedad podría agravarse.* **2** ADJ **Untreated** materials, water, or chemicals are harmful and have not been made safe. *no tratado, sin tratar* ❑ *...untreated drinking water. ...agua sin tratar.*

**Word Link** *un ≈ reversal : untie, unusual, unzip*

**un|usual** /ʌnyuʒuəl/ ADJ If something is **unusual,** it does not happen very often or you do not see it or hear it very often. *raro, inusual* ❑ *It's unusual for him to make a mistake. Es raro que cometa errores.* • **un|usu|al|ly** /ʌnyuʒuəli/ ADV *excepcionalmente* ❑ *...an unusually cold winter. ...un invierno excepcionalmente frío.*

**Thesaurus** *unusual* Ver también:

ADJ. abnormal, different, interesting, strange, uncommon, unconventional; *(ant.)* common, conventional, normal, usual

**un|veil** /ʌnveɪl/ **(unveils, unveiling, unveiled)** **1** V-T If someone formally **unveils** something such as a new statue or painting, they open the curtain which is covering it. *develar, descubrir, revelar* ❑ *There is a plan to unveil a statue in front of the building. Se tiene planeado develar una estatua frente al edificio.* **2** V-T If you **unveil** a plan, new product, or some other thing that has been kept secret, you introduce it to the public. *revelar* ❑ *The company unveiled plans to open 100 new stores. La compañía reveló sus planes de abrir 100 nuevas tiendas.*

**un|want|ed** /ʌnwɒntɪd/ ADJ If you say that something or someone is **unwanted,** you mean that you do not want them, or that nobody wants them. *indeseado, no deseado* ❑ *...unwanted calls and e-mails. ...llamadas y correos electrónicos no deseados.* ❑ *She felt unwanted. Se sintió indeseada.*

**un|wieldy** /ʌnwildi/ **1** ADJ An **unwieldy** object is difficult to move or carry because it is so big or heavy. *estorboso* ❑ *They came to the door with their unwieldy baggage. Llegaron a la puerta con su estorboso equipaje.* **2** ADJ An **unwieldy** system does not work very well because it is too large or badly organized. *inmanejable* ❑ *...costly and unwieldy social services. ...servicios sociales costosos e inmanejables.*

**un|will|ing** /ʌnwɪlɪŋ/ ADJ If you are **unwilling** to do something, you do not want to do it. *mal dispuesto, que no está dispuesto a* ❑ *Many people are unwilling to change their e-mail addresses. Muchas personas no están dispuestas a cambiar su dirección de correo electrónico.* • **un|will|ing|ly** ADV *de mala gana, a regañadientes* ❑ *He accepted his orders very unwillingly. Aceptó sus órdenes de muy mala gana.* • **un|will|ing|ness** N-UNCOUNT *renuencia* ❑ *...their unwillingness to listen to good advice. ...su renuencia a oír buenos consejos.*

**un|wind** /ʌnwaɪnd/ **(unwinds, unwinding, unwound)** **1** V-I When you **unwind,** you relax after you have done something that makes you tense or tired. *relajarse* ❑ *It helps them to unwind after a busy day at work. Los ayuda a relajarse después de un día de trabajo intenso.* **2** V-T/V-I If you **unwind** something that is wrapped around something else, you loosen it and make it straight. You can also say that it **unwinds.** *desenrollar, desenredar* ❑ *She unwound the scarf from her neck. Se desenredó la bufanda del cuello.*

**un|wit|ting** /ʌnwɪtɪŋ/ ADJ If you describe a person or their actions as **unwitting,** you mean that the person does something or is involved in something without realizing it. *involuntario, sin querer* ❑ *It had been an unwitting mistake on his part. Había sido un error involuntario de su parte.* • **un|wit|ting|ly** ADV *involuntariamente* ❑ *...people who unwittingly break the law. ...personas que involuntariamente violan la ley.*

**un|zip** /ʌnzɪp/ **(unzips, unzipping, unzipped)** **1** V-T/V-I When you **unzip** something which is fastened by a zipper or when it **unzips,** you open it by pulling open the zipper. *abrir el cierre/la cremallera, bajar el cierre/la cremallera* ❑ *James unzipped his bag. James abrió el cierre de su maleta.* **2** V-T To **unzip** a computer file means to open a file that has been made smaller so that it is quicker and easier to send by e-mail. *descomprimir* [COMPUTING] ❑ *Unzip the file with the password. Use la contraseña para descomprimir el archivo.*

**up**

❶ PREPOSITION, ADVERB, AND ADJECTIVE USES

❷ USED IN COMBINATION AS A PREPOSITION

❸ VERB USES

## ❶ up

The preposition is pronounced /ʌp/. The adverb and adjective are pronounced /ʌp/.

**Up** is often used with verbs of movement such as "jump" and "pull," and also in phrasal verbs such as "give up" and "wash up."

**1** PREP **Up** means toward a higher place or in a higher place. *arriba* ❑ *They were climbing up a mountain road. Trepaban por un camino montañoso.* ❑ *I ran up the stairs. Subí corriendo las escaleras.* ❑ *He was up a ladder. Estaba trepado en una escalera de mano.* • **Up** is also an adverb. *arriba* ❑ *Keep your head up. Mantén erguida la cabeza.* ❑ *I went up to John's room. Subí al cuarto de John.* **2** ADV If someone stands **up,** they move so that they are standing. *(ponerse) de pie* ❑ *He stood up and went to the window. Se puso de pie y fue a la ventana.* **3** PREP If you go or look **up** something such as a road or river, you go or look along it. If you are **up** a road or river, you are somewhere along it. *a lo largo de, por* ❑ *A dark blue truck came up the road. Un camión azul oscuro se acercó por el camino.* ❑ *We stood on the bridge and looked up the river. Nos paramos en el puente y miramos río arriba.* **4** ADV If you go **up** to something or someone, you move to the place where they are and stop there. *hasta* ❑ *The girl ran across the street and up to the car. La niña atravesó corriendo la calle hasta el auto.* **5** ADV If an amount of something goes **up,** it increases. If an amount of something is **up,** it has increased and is at a higher level than it was.

*hacia arriba* ❑ *Gasoline prices went up 1.3 percent in June.* *Los precios de la gasolina subieron 1.3 por ciento en junio.* ❑ *Jobs are up, income is up.* *Hay más trabajo y los ingresos han aumentado.* **6** ADJ If you are **up,** you are not in bed. *levantado* ❑ *They were up very early.* *Ya estaban levantados muy temprano.* **7** ADJ If a period of time is **up,** it has come to an end. *pasado* ❑ *When the half-hour was up, Brooks left.* *Cuando pasó la media hora, Brooks se fue.* **8** PHRASE If you move **up and down** somewhere, you move there repeatedly in one direction and then in the opposite direction. *de arriba abajo, de un lado a otro* ❑ *I used to jump up and down to keep warm.* *Acostumbraba dar saltos para conservar el calor.* ❑ *I walked up and down before calling a taxi.* *Caminé de un lado a otro antes de llamar un taxi.*

**❷ up** /ʌp/ **1** PHRASE If you feel **up to** doing something, you are well enough to do it. *con ánimo para, capaz de* ❑ *You have a visitor if you feel up to seeing him.* *Tienes visita, si te sientes con ánimo para verla.* ❑ *They were not up to running the business without him.* *No eran capaces de dirigir el negocio sin él.* **2** PHRASE If you say that it is **up to** someone to do something, you mean that it is their responsibility to do it. *corresponder a* ❑ *It was up to him to tell her what to do.* *A él le correspondía decirle qué hacer.* **3** PHRASE **Up until** or **up to** are used to indicate the latest time at which something can happen. *hasta* ❑ *Please feel free to call me any time up until 9:30 at night.* *No dude en llamarme en cualquier momento hasta las 9:30 de la noche.* **4** PHRASE You use **up to** to say how large something can be or what level it has reached. *hasta* ❑ *...buildings up to thirty stories high.* *...edificios de hasta 30 pisos de altura.* **5** PHRASE If someone or something is **up for** election, review, or discussion, they are about to be considered. *sujeto a* ❑ *A third of the Senate is up for election every two years.* *La tercera parte del Senado se elige cada dos años.* **6** PHRASE If you are **up against** something, you have a very difficult situation or problem to deal with. *contra* ❑ *They were up against a good team but did very well.* *Iban contra un buen equipo, pero salieron bien.*

**❸ up** /ʌp/ (**ups, upping, upped**) **1** V-T If you **up** something such as the amount of money you are offering for something, you increase it. *subir, aumentar, acelerar* ❑ *He upped his offer for the company.* *Subió su oferta por la compañía.* **2** V-I If you **up** and leave a place, you go away from it, often suddenly or unexpectedly. *decidir abruptamente* ❑ *One day he just upped and left.* *Un buen día se fue, sin decir agua va.*

**up-and-coming** ADJ **Up-and-coming** people are likely to be successful in the future. *ambicioso, emprendedor* ❑ *Their daughter is an up-and-coming tennis player.* *Su hija es una tenista con un gran futuro.*

U

**up|beat** /ʌpbit/ ADJ If people or their opinions are **upbeat,** they are cheerful and hopeful about a situation. *optimista* [INFORMAL] ❑ *Neil was in an upbeat mood in spite of the bad news.* *Neil se mantenía optimista, a pesar de las malas noticias.*

**up|bring|ing** /ʌpbrɪŋɪŋ/ N-UNCOUNT Your **upbringing** is the way that your parents treat you and the things that they teach you when you are growing up. *educación, crianza* ❑ *Her son had a good upbringing.* *Su hijo tuvo una buena educación.*

**up|com|ing** /ʌpkʌmɪŋ/ ADJ **Upcoming** events will happen in the near future. *cercano, próximo* ❑ *She talked about her upcoming birthday party.* *Hablaba de su ya cercana fiesta de cumpleaños.*

**up|date** /ʌpdeɪt/ (**updates, updating, updated**)

> The verb is pronounced /ʌpdeɪt/. The noun is pronounced /ʌpdeɪt/.

**1** V-T/V-I If you **update,** or **update** something, you make it more modern, usually by adding new parts to it or giving new information. *poner al día* ❑ *We update our records regularly.* *Ponemos nuestros archivos al día con frecuencia.* **2** N-COUNT An **update** is a news item containing the latest information about a particular situation. *información reciente* ❑ *...a weather update.* *...la información más reciente sobre el clima.*

**up|draft** /ʌpdræft/ (**updrafts**) N-COUNT An **updraft** is a rising current of air, which often produces a cumulus cloud. *corriente ascendente*

**up front** also **up-front** **1** ADJ If you are **up front about** something, you act openly or publicly so that people know what you are doing or what you believe. *franco* [INFORMAL] ❑ *I wanted to be up front about it.* *Quise ser muy franco al respecto.* **2** ADV If a payment is made **up front,** it is made in advance and openly, so that the person being paid can see that the money is there. *por adelantado* ❑ *She paid about $800 up front.* *Pagó aproximadamente 800 dólares por adelantado.*

**up|grade** /ʌpgreɪd, -greɪd/ (**upgrades, upgrading, upgraded**) V-T If equipment or services **are upgraded,** they are improved or made more efficient. *mejorar* ❑ *The road is being upgraded.* *Están mejorando la carretera.* ● **Upgrade** is also a noun. *actualización* ❑ *...equipment which needs expensive upgrades.* *...equipo que requiere actualizaciones costosas.*
→ see **hotel**

**up|heav|al** /ʌphivᵊl/ (**upheavals**) N-COUNT An **upheaval** is a big change which causes a lot of trouble, confusion, and worry. *agitación* ❑ *...a time of political upheaval.* *...una época de agitación política.*

**up|hill** /ʌphɪl/ **1** ADV If something or someone is **uphill** or is moving **uphill,** they are near the top of a hill or are going up a slope. *cuesta arriba* ❑ *He ran uphill a long way.* *Corrió cuesta arriba un gran trecho.* ● **Uphill** is also an adjective. *cuesta arriba, difícil* ❑ *...a long, uphill journey.* *...un largo viaje cuesta arriba.* **2** ADJ If you refer to something as an **uphill** battle or an **uphill** struggle, you mean that it requires a lot of effort and determination, but it should be possible to achieve it. *arduo* ❑ *It was an uphill battle to get what she wanted.* *Fue una ardua batalla conseguir lo que quería.*

**up|hold** /ʌphoʊld/ (**upholds, upholding, upheld**) V-T If you **uphold** something such as a law, a principle, or a decision, you support and maintain it. *apoyar* ❑ *Our policy is to uphold the law.* *Nuestra política es apoyar la ley.*

**up|hol|stery** /ʌphoʊlstəri, əpoʊl-/ N-UNCOUNT **Upholstery** is the soft covering on chairs and seats that makes them more comfortable to sit on. *tapicería* ❑ *...white leather upholstery.* *...tapicería en piel blanca.*

**up|keep** /ʌpkip/ **1** N-UNCOUNT The **upkeep** of a building or place is the work of keeping it in good condition. *mantenimiento* ❑ *We will use the money for the upkeep of the park.* *Utilizaremos el dinero para el mantenimiento del parque.* **2** N-UNCOUNT

The **upkeep** of a group of people or services is the process of providing them with the things that they need. *mantenimiento* ❑ *He paid $250 a month toward his son's upkeep.* *Pagaba 250 dólares al mes para el mantenimiento de su hijo.*

**up|lift|ing** /ʌplɪftɪŋ/ ADJ You describe something as **uplifting** when it makes you feel very cheerful and happy. *alentador* ❑ *...an uplifting story of hope.* *......una historia esperanzadora que nos alienta.*

**upon** /əpɒn/

In addition to the uses shown below, **upon** is used in phrasal verbs such as "come upon" and "look upon," and after some other verbs such as "decide" and "depend."

**1** PREP If one thing is **upon** another, it is on it. *encima de, sobre* [LITERARY] ❑ *He put the tray upon the table.* *Puso la bandeja sobre la mesa.* **2** PREP You use **upon** when mentioning an event that is followed immediately by another event. *en el momento de, al* [FORMAL] ❑ *She had to give the store her full name upon entering.* *Tuvo que dar su nombre completo al entrar a la tienda.* **3** PREP You use **upon** between two occurrences of the same noun in order to say that there are large numbers of the thing mentioned. *tras, y* ❑ *Row upon row of women moved forwards.* *Una fila tras otra de mujeres avanzó.* **4** PREP If an event is **upon** you, it is just about to happen. *inminente* [LITERARY] ❑ *The storm was upon us.* *La tormenta era inminente*

**up|per** /ʌpər/ **1** ADJ You use **upper** to describe something that is above something else. *de arriba* ❑ *There is a good restaurant on the upper floor.* *Hay un buen restaurante en el piso de arriba.* **2** ADJ The **upper** part of something is the higher part of it. *superior* ❑ *...the upper part of the foot.* *...la parte superior del pie.* ❑ *...the upper back and chest.* *...la parte superior de la espalda y el pecho.* **3** PHRASE If you have **the upper hand** in a situation, you have an advantage over other people involved, for example because you have more power or success. *ventaja* ❑ *The home team had the upper hand.* *El equipo de casa tenía la ventaja.*

**up|per class** (**upper classes**) also **upper-class** N-COUNT The **upper class** or the **upper classes** are the group of people in a society who own the most property and have the highest social status. *clase privilegiada* ❑ *...members of the upper class.* *...miembros de la clase privilegiada.* • **Upper-class** is also an adjective. *privilegiado* ❑ *All of them came from wealthy, upper-class families.* *Todos ellos venían de familias privilegiadas y adineradas.*

**upper|class|man** /ʌpərklæsmən/ (**upperclassmen**) N-COUNT An **upperclassman** is a male junior or senior student in an American high school, college, or university. *varón estudiante de los últimos años de preparatoria o universidad*

**upper|class|woman** /ʌpərclæswʊmən/ (**upperclasswomen**) N-COUNT An **upperclasswoman** is a female junior or senior student in a high school, college, or university. *mujer estudiante de los últimos años de preparatoria o universidad*

**up|per man|tle** N-SING *The* **upper mantle** is the part of the Earth's interior that lies immediately beneath the crust. *manto superior*

**up|right** /ʌpraɪt/ **1** ADJ If you are sitting or standing **upright,** you are sitting or standing with your back straight, rather than bending or lying down. *erguido* ❑ *Helen sat upright in her chair.* *Helen se sentó erguida en su silla.* ❑ *He moved into an upright position.* *Se enderezó.* **2** ADJ You can describe people as **upright** when they are careful to follow acceptable rules of behavior and behave in a moral way. *recto* ❑ *...a very upright, trustworthy man.* *...un hombre muy recto y digno de confianza.*

**up|ris|ing** /ʌpraɪzɪŋ/ (**uprisings**) N-COUNT When there is an **uprising,** a group of people start fighting against the people who are in power in their country, because they want to bring about a political change. *revuelta, revolución, alzamiento* ❑ *...an uprising against the government.* *...un alzamiento en contra del gobierno.*

**up|roar** /ʌprɔr/ **1** N-UNCOUNT; N-SING If there is **uproar,** there is a lot of shouting and noise because people are very angry or upset about something. *alboroto, protesta* ❑ *The uproar was loud and immediate.* *La protesta fue fuerte e inmediata.* **2** N-UNCOUNT; N-SING You can also use **uproar** to refer to a lot of public criticism and debate about something that has made people angry. *escándalo, conmoción* ❑ *The town is in an uproar over the decision.* *La población está escandalizada por la decisión.*

**up|scale** /ʌpskeɪl/ ADJ **Upscale** is used to describe products or services that are expensive, of good quality, and aimed at people in a high social class. *de muy buena calidad, caro* ❑ *...sporting goods with an upscale image.* *...productos deportivos con la imagen de ser costosos.* ❑ *...upscale department-store chains such as Bloomingdale's and Saks Fifth Avenue.* *...cadenas de almacenes costosos, como Bloomingdale's y Saks Fifth Avenue.*

**up|set** (**upsets, upsetting, upset**)

The verb and adjective are pronounced /ʌpsɛt/. The noun is pronounced /ʌpsɛt/.

**1** ADJ If you are **upset,** you are unhappy or disappointed because something bad has happened to you. *trastornado, alterado* ❑ *After she died I was very, very upset.* *Después de que ella murió, me sentí muy, muy alterado.* ❑ *Marta looked upset.* *Marta se veía alterada.* **2** V-T If something **upsets** you, it makes you feel worried or unhappy. *trastornar, molestar* ❑ *Your letter upset me.* *Tu carta me molestó.* • **up|set|ting** ADJ *angustioso* ❑ *Childhood sickness can be upsetting for children and parents alike.* *Las enfermedades infantiles pueden ser angustiosas tanto para los hijos como para los padres.* **3** V-T If events **upset** what normally happens, they make it go wrong. *trastornar* ❑ *Political problems could upset agreements between Moscow and Kabul.* *Los problemas políticos podrían trastornar los acuerdos entre Moscú y Kabul.* **4** ADJ An **upset** stomach is a slight sickness in your stomach caused by an infection or by something you have eaten. *descompuesto* ❑ *Paul was unwell last night with an upset stomach.* *Paul estuvo enfermo anoche con el estómago descompuesto.*

→ see **anger**

| **Thesaurus** | *upset* | Ver también: |
|---|---|---|
| ADJ. | disappointed, hurt, unhappy **1** | |
| | ill, sick, unsettled **4** | |

U

**Word Partnership** Usar *upset* con:

PREP. upset **about/by/over** *something* 1
V. **become** upset, **feel** upset, **get** upset 1
ADV. **so** upset, **very** upset, **visibly** upset 1
**really** upset 1 2
N. **stomach** upset (*or* upset **stomach**) 4

**up|side down** /ʌpsaɪd daʊn/ also **upside-down** ADV If something is or has been turned **upside down,** it has been turned around so that the part that is usually lowest is above the part that is usually highest. *al revés, de cabeza* ❑ *The painting was hung upside down. La pintura estaba colgada de cabeza.* ● **Upside down** is also an adjective. *de cabeza, al revés* ❑ *...an upside-down triangle. ...un triángulo de cabeza.*

**up|stairs** /ʌpstɛərz/ 1 ADV If you go **upstairs** in a building, you go up a staircase toward a higher floor. *hacia arriba, escaleras arriba* ❑ *He went upstairs and changed his clothes. Subió y se cambió la ropa.* 2 ADV If something or someone is **upstairs** in a building, they are on a floor that is higher than the ground floor. *en un piso de arriba* ❑ *The restaurant is upstairs. El restaurante está en un piso de arriba.* 3 ADJ An **upstairs** room or object is on a floor of a building that is higher than the ground floor. *en un piso de arriba* ❑ *Marsani lived in the upstairs apartment. Marsani vivía en el departamento de arriba.* 4 N-SING **The upstairs** of a building is the floor or floors that are higher than the ground floor. *el piso de arriba* ❑ *The upstairs had only two bedrooms. En el piso de arriba había únicamente dos recámaras.*

**up|start** /ʌpstɑrt/ (**upstarts**) N-COUNT You can refer to someone as an **upstart** when they behave as if they are important, but you think that they are too new in a place or job to be treated as important. *advenedizo, arribista* ❑ *A young upstart came to town. Un joven advenedizo llegó a la ciudad.*

**up|state** /ʌpsteɪt/ ADJ **Upstate** means belonging or relating to the parts of a state that are furthest to the north or furthest from the main city. *en el norte, lejos de la ciudad capital* ❑ *...a little village in upstate New York. ...un pueblito en el norte del estado de Nueva York.* ● **Upstate** is also an adverb. *más arriba, más al norte* ❑ *He wants to move upstate to Woodstock. Quiere cambiarse más al norte, a Woodstock.*

**up|stream** /ʌpstrim/ ADV Something that is moving **upstream** is moving toward the source of a river. Something that is **upstream** is toward the source of a river. *río arriba, contra la corriente* ❑ *...fish trying to swim upstream. ...los peces tratando de nadar río arriba.* ● **Upstream** is also an adjective. *río arriba* ❑ *We'll go to the upstream side of that big rock. Iremos al otro lado de esa gran piedra, río arriba.*

U

**up|surge** /ʌpsɜrdʒ/ N-SING If there is an **upsurge in** something, there is a sudden, large increase in it. *aumento repentino* ❑ *...an upsurge in oil prices. ...un aumento repentino de los precios del petróleo.*

**up-to-date** also **up to date** 1 ADJ If something is **up-to-date,** it is the newest thing of its kind. *al día, muy moderno* ❑ *...up-to-date weather information. ...la información más reciente sobre el clima.* 2 ADJ If you are **up-to-date** about something, you have the latest information about it. *al día, bien informado* ❑ *We'll keep you up to date with any news. Los mantendremos bien informados de cualquier noticia que surja.*

**up|town** /ʌptaʊn/ ADV If you go **uptown,** or go to a place **uptown,** you go away from the center of a city or town toward the edge. **Uptown** sometimes refers to a part of the city other than the main business district. *hacia el norte, en el norte* ❑ *He rode uptown and went to Bob's apartment. Manejó hacia el norte para ir al departamento de Bob.* ❑ *Susan lived uptown. Susan vivía en el norte de la ciudad.* ● **Uptown** is also an adjective. *en el norte* ❑ *...a small uptown radio station. ...una pequeña estación de radio en el norte de la ciudad.*

**up|turn** /ʌptɜrn/ (**upturns**) N-COUNT If there is an **upturn** in the economy or in a company or industry, it improves or becomes more successful. *repunte, mejora* [BUSINESS] ❑ *Some companies report an upturn in business. Algunas compañías informan sobre un repunte de los negocios.*

**up|ward** /ʌpwərd/

The form **upwards** is also used for the adverb.

1 ADJ An **upward** movement or look is directed towards a higher place or a higher level. *ascenso, escalada* ❑ *She started on the upward climb. Dio comienzo a la escalada.* ❑ *She gave him a quick, upward look, then lowered her eyes. Le lanzó una rápida mirada ascendente y luego bajó la vista.* 2 ADV If someone moves or looks **upward,** they move or look up toward a higher place. *hacia arriba* ❑ *She turned her face upward. Volteó la cara hacia arriba.* ❑ *"There," said Jack, pointing upwards. —Ahí —dijo Jack, señalando hacia arriba.* 3 ADV If an amount or rate moves **upward,** it increases. *al alza, en aumento* ❑ *...with prices moving upward in stores. ...con los precios al alza en las tiendas.* ❑ *Unemployment will continue upward for much of this year. El desempleo seguirá en aumento la mayor parte de este año.* 4 PHRASE A quantity that is **upwards of** a particular number is more than that number. *más de, mayor que* ❑ *The package costs upwards of $9.99 a month. El paquete cuesta más de 9.99 dólares al mes.*

**up|wards** /ʌpwərdz/ → see **upward**

**up|wel|ling** /ʌpwɛlɪŋ/ (**upwellings**) N-COUNT An **upwelling** is a process in which cold water from deep in the ocean rises to the surface near a shoreline, bringing nutrients with it. *afloramiento, surgencia* [TECHNICAL]

**ura|nium** /yʊreɪniəm/ N-UNCOUNT **Uranium** is a radioactive metal that is used to produce nuclear energy and weapons. *uranio*

**Ura|nus** /yʊərənəs, yʊreɪ-/ N-PROPER **Uranus** is the seventh planet from the sun. *Urano*
→ see **solar system**

**Word Link** *urb ≈ city : suburb, suburban, urban*

**ur|ban** /ɜrbən/ ADJ **Urban** means belonging to, or relating to, a city or town. *urbano* ❑ *Most urban areas are close to a park. La mayoría de las zonas urbanas están cerca de un parque.*
→ see **city**

**urethra** /yʊəriθrə/ (**urethras**) N-COUNT The **urethra** is the narrow tube inside a man's penis that carries urine and semen out of the body. *uretra*

**urge** /ɜrdʒ/ (**urges, urging, urged**) **1** V-T If you **urge** someone **to** do something, you try hard to persuade them to do it. *alentar, instar* ❑ *Doctors urged him to change his diet. Los médicos lo instaron a que cambiara su dieta.* **2** N-COUNT If you have an **urge to** do or have something, you have a strong wish to do or have it. *impulso irrefrenable de hacer algo* ❑ *He had an urge to laugh. Sintió unas ganas enormes de reírse.*

**Word Partnership** Usar *urge* con:

N. **leaders/officials** urge, urge **people**, urge **voters** **1**
ADV. **strongly** urge **1**
V. **feel an** urge, **fight an** urge, **get an** urge, **resist an** urge **2**

**ur|gent** /ɜrdʒᵊnt/ **1** ADJ If something is **urgent,** it needs to be dealt with as soon as possible. *urgente* ❑ *There is an urgent need for food and water. Hay una necesidad urgente de alimentos y agua.* ● **ur|gen|cy** N-UNCOUNT *urgencia* ❑ *...the urgency of the problem. ...la urgencia del problema.* ● **ur|gent|ly** ADV *urgentemente* ❑ *The Red Cross said they urgently needed bread and water. La Cruz Roja dijo que necesitaban pan y agua urgentemente.* **2** ADJ If you speak in an **urgent** way, you show that you are anxious for people to notice something or to do something. *apremiante* ❑ *His voice was low and urgent. Su voz era baja y apremiante.* ● **ur|gen|cy** N-UNCOUNT *apremio* ❑ *She was surprised at the urgency in his voice. Estaba sorprendida por lo apremiante de su tono.* ● **ur|gent|ly** ADV *con tono apremiante* ❑ *"Did you find it?" he asked urgently. —¿Lo encontraste? —preguntó con un tono apremiante.*

**Word Partnership** Usar *urgent* con:

N. urgent **action**, urgent **business**, urgent **care**, urgent **matter**, urgent **meeting**, urgent **mission**, urgent **need**, urgent **problem** **1**
urgent **appeal**, urgent **message** **2**

**uri|nate** /yʊərɪneɪt/ (**urinates, urinating, urinated**) V-I When you **urinate,** you get rid of urine from your body. *orinar*

**urine** /yʊərɪn/ N-UNCOUNT **Urine** is the liquid that you get rid of from your body when you go to the toilet. *orina* ❑ *The doctor took a urine sample and a blood sample. El medico tomó muestras de la orina y la sangre.*

**URL** /yu ɑr ɛl/ (**URLs**) N-COUNT A **URL** is an address that shows where a particular page can be found on the World Wide Web. **URL** is an abbreviation for "Uniform Resource Locator." *URL, localizador uniforme de recursos* [COMPUTING] ❑ *The URL for Collins Dictionaries is http://www.collinslanguage.com. El URL de los Diccionarios Collins es http://www.collinslanguage.com.*

**us** /əs, STRONG ʌs/

**Us** is the first person plural pronoun. **Us** is used as the object of a verb or a preposition.

PRON A speaker or writer uses **us** to refer both to himself or herself and to one or more other people. *nosotros, nos, nuestro* ❑ *Heather went to the kitchen to get drinks for us. Heather fue a la cocina a traernos bebidas.* ❑ *He is one of us. Es uno de los nuestros.*

**us|able** /yuzəbᵊl/ ADJ If something is **usable,** it is in a good enough state or condition to be used. *usable, utilizable* ❑ *The house had eleven usable rooms. La casa tenía once cuartos habitables.*

**us|age** /yusɪdʒ/ **1** N-UNCOUNT **Usage** is the way in which words are actually used in particular contexts, especially with regard to their meanings. *uso, modo de usarse* ❑ *...a book on English usage. ...un libro de uso del inglés.* **2** N-UNCOUNT **Usage** is the degree to which something is used or the way in which it is used. *uso, modo de uso* ❑ *...an increase in computer usage. ...un aumento del uso de computadoras.*

**USB** /yu ɛs bi/ (**USBs**) N-COUNT A **USB** or **USB port** on a computer is a place where you can attach another piece of equipment, for example a printer. **USB** is an abbreviation for "Universal Serial Bus." *USB, bus serial universal* [COMPUTING] ❑ *It plugs into the computer's USB port. Se conecta al puerto USB de la computadora.*

**use**
❶ VERB USES
❷ NOUN USES

❶ **use** /yuz/ (**uses, using, used**) **1** V-T If you **use** something, you do something with it in order to do a job or to achieve a particular result or effect. *usar, utilizar* ❑ *They wouldn't let him use the phone. No le permitían usar el teléfono.* ❑ *She used the money to help her family. Utilizó el dinero para ayudar a su familia.* **2** V-T If you **use** a supply of something, you finish it so that none of it is left. *usar, utilizar* ❑ *She used all the shampoo. Usó todo el champú.* ● **Use up** means the same as **use**. *acabarse* ❑ *Daisy used up all the hot water. Daisy se acabó toda el agua caliente.* **3** V-T If you **use** a particular word or expression, you say or write it, because it has the meaning that you want to express. *utilizar, usar* ❑ *He used the word "sorry" six times. Usó la palabra "perdón" seis veces.* **4** V-T If you say that someone **uses** people, you disapprove of them because they make others do things for them in order to benefit or gain some advantage from it, and not because they care about the other people. *usar, aprovecharse de* ❑ *I felt he was using me. Sentí que estaba aprovechándose de mí.* **5** → see also **used**

❷ **use** /yus/ (**uses**) **1** N-UNCOUNT; N-SING Your **use** of something is the action or fact of your using it. *uso* ❑ *...the use of computers in classrooms. ...el uso de computadoras en la clase.* **2** N-VAR If something has a particular **use,** it is intended for a particular purpose. *uso* ❑ *There are many good uses for e-mail. El e-mail tiene muchos usos buenos.* ❑ *We can always find a use for the money. Siempre podemos encontrarle un uso al dinero.* **3** N-UNCOUNT If you have the **use of** something, you have the permission or ability to use it. *uso* ❑ *She has the use of the car one night a week. Ella dispone del auto una noche a la semana.* ❑ *...people who have lost the use of their legs. ...gente que ha perdido el uso de las piernas.* **4** N-COUNT A **use** of a word is a particular meaning that it has or a particular way in which it can be used. *uso* ❑ *There are new uses of words coming in all the time. Constantemente aparecen nuevos usos de las palabras.* **5** PHRASE If something such as a technique, building, or machine is **in use,** it is used regularly by people. If it has gone **out of use,** it is no longer used regularly by people. *en uso* ❑ *...the number of homes with televisions in use.* *...el número de casas con una televisión en uso.* **6** PHRASE If you **make use of** something, you do something with it in order to do a job or achieve a particular result or effect. *hacer uso de* [WRITTEN] ❑ *We made use of the extra time we had.* *Usamos el tiempo sobrante que teníamos.* **7** PHRASE If you say **it's no use,** you mean that you have failed to do something and realize that it is useless to continue trying because it is impossible. *no tener caso* ❑ *"It's no use talking to him," said Kate.* *—No tiene caso hablar con él —dijo Kate.*

**used**
❶ MODAL USES AND PHRASES
❷ ADJECTIVE USES

❶ **used** /yust/ **1** PHRASE If something **used to** be done or **used to** be true, it was done regularly in the past or was true in the past. *acostumbrar, soler, Su uso en inglés corresponde al pretérito imperfecto (-ía, -aba) del español.* ❑ *People used to come and visit him every day.* *La gente solía venir a visitarlo todos los días.* ❑ *He used to be one of my teachers.* *Era uno de mis maestros.* **2** PHRASE If you **are used to** something, you are familiar with it because you have done it or experienced it many times before. *estar acostumbrado a* ❑ *I'm used to hard work.* *Estoy acostumbrado al trabajo duro.* **3** PHRASE If you **get used to** something or someone, you become familiar with it or get to know them. *acostumbrarse a* ❑ *This is how we do things here. You'll soon get used to it.* *Así hacemos las cosas aquí. Pronto te acostumbrarás.*

**Usage** used to

*Used to* is often confused with *be/get used to.* *Used to* refers to something in the past: *We used to live in an apartment, but we now live in a house.* *Be/get used to* means "be or become accustomed to": *We're used to living in an apartment, but we're getting used to our new house.*

❷ **used** /yuzd/ **1** ADJ A **used** object is dirty or spoiled because it has been used, and usually needs to be thrown away or washed. *usado* ❑ *...a used coffee cup* *...una taza de café ya usada.* **2** ADJ A **used** car has already had one or more owners. *de segunda mano* ❑ *Would you buy a used car from this man?* *¿Le comprarías un carro de segunda mano a este hombre?*

U

**use|ful** /yusfəl/ **1** ADJ If something is **useful,** you can use it to do something or to help you in some way. *útil* ❑ *...pages of useful information.* *...páginas con información útil.* ● **use|ful|ly** ADV *útilmente* ❑ *Adams usefully divides his book into two parts.* *Adams divide su libro en dos partes, lo cual resulta muy útil.* ● **use|ful|ness** N-UNCOUNT *utilidad* ❑ *...the usefulness of his work.* *...la utilidad de su trabajo.* **2** PHRASE If an object or skill **comes in useful,** it can help you achieve something in a particular situation. *ser útil, venir bien* ❑ *Extra paper will probably come in useful.* *Un poco de papel extra nos va a venir bien.*

**Word Partnership** Usar *useful* con:

ADV. **also** useful, **especially** useful, **extremely** useful, **less/more** useful, **particularly** useful, **very** useful **1**
N. useful **information**, useful **knowledge**, useful **life**, useful **purpose**, useful **strategy**, useful **tool** **1**

**use|less** /yuslɪs/ **1** ADJ If something is **useless,** you cannot use it. *inservible* ❑ *Their money was useless in this country.* *Su dinero era inservible en este país.* **2** ADJ If something is **useless,** it does not achieve anything helpful or good. *inútil* ❑ *She knew it was useless to argue.* *Sabía que era inútil discutir.* **3** ADJ If you say that someone or something is **useless,** you mean that they are no good at all. *inútil, negado* ❑ *He was useless at any game with a ball.* *Era negado para todo juego de pelota.*

**user** /yuzər/ (**users**) N-COUNT A **user** is a person or thing that uses something such as a place, facility, product, or machine. *usuario o usuaria* ❑ *...Internet users.* *...los usuarios de Internet.* ❑ *...a regular user of the subway.* *...un usuario normal del metro.*
→ see **Internet**

**U-shaped val|ley** (**U-shaped valleys**) N-COUNT A **U-shaped valley** is a valley with steep sides that forms when a glacier is eroded. *valle en U*

**ush|er** /ʌʃər/ (**ushers, ushering, ushered**) **1** V-T If you **usher** someone somewhere, you show them where they should go by going with them. *hacer pasar a, acompañar* [FORMAL] ❑ *I ushered him into the office.* *Lo hice pasar a la oficina.* **2** N-COUNT An **usher** is a person who shows people where to sit, for example at a wedding or at a concert. *acomodador o acomodadora* ❑ *He did part-time work as an usher in a theater.* *Trabajaba parte del tiempo como acomodador en un teatro.*

**usu|al** /yuʒuəl/ **1** ADJ **Usual** is used to describe what happens or what is done most often in a particular situation. *habitual, común y corriente* ❑ *February was warmer than usual.* *En febrero hizo más calor que lo habitual.* **2** PHRASE You use **as usual** to indicate that you are describing something that normally happens or that is normally true. *como siempre, como es de esperarse* ❑ *As usual, there will be the local and regional elections on June twelfth.* *Como siempre, habrá elecciones locales y regionales el doce de junio.* **3** PHRASE If something happens **as usual,** it happens in the way that it normally does, especially when other things have changed. *como siempre* ❑ *He's late, as usual.* *Llega tarde, como siempre.*

**Word Partnership** Usar *usual* con:

ADV. **less/more than** usual, **longer than** usual **1**
N. usual **place**, usual **routine**, usual **self**, usual **stuff**, usual **suspects**, usual **way** **1**

**usu|al|ly** /yuʒuəli/ ADV If something **usually** happens, it is the thing that most often happens in a particular situation. *generalmente* ❑ *We usually eat in here.* *Generalmente comemos aquí.*

**usurp** /yusɜrp, -zɜrp/ (**usurps, usurping, usurped**) V-T If you say that someone **usurps** a job,

## Picture Dictionary

### kitchen utensils

role, title, or position, they take it from someone when they have no right to do this. usurpar [FORMAL] ❑ *Did she usurp his place in his mother's heart?* *¿Usurpó ella su lugar en el corazón de su madre?*

**uten|sil** /yutɛnsᵊl/ (**utensils**) N-COUNT **Utensils** are tools or objects that you use in order to help you to cook, serve food, or eat. utensilios ❑ *...utensils such as cooking pots or pans.* *...utensilios como ollas y sartenes.*

→ see Picture Dictionary: **kitchen utensils**

**util|ity** /yutɪlɪti/ (**utilities**) N-COUNT A **utility** is an important service such as water, electricity, or gas that is provided for everyone, and that everyone pays for. servicio, empresa de utilidad pública ❑ *...public utilities such as gas and electricity.* *...servicios públicos como el gas y la electricidad.*

**util|ity pole** (**utility poles**) **1** N-COUNT A **utility pole** is a tall pole with telephone or electrical wires attached to it. poste de servicios públicos ❑ *The bus hit a tree and knocked down a utility pole.* *El autobús golpeó un árbol y tiró un poste de servicios públicos.* **2** → see also **telephone pole**

**uti|lize** /yutɪlaɪz/ (**utilizes, utilizing, utilized**) V-T If you **utilize** something, you use it. utilizar [FORMAL] ❑ *...how to utilize the knowledge and talent of everyone in the company.* *...cómo utilizar en la compañía los conocimientos y el talento de todo el mundo.* • **uti|li|za|tion** /yutɪlɪzeɪʃᵊn/ N-UNCOUNT aprovechamiento ❑ *...the best utilization of space.* *...el mejor aprovechamiento del espacio.*

| Word Link | *most ≈ superlative degree : almost, mostly, utmost* |
|---|---|

**ut|most** /ʌtmoʊst/ **1** ADJ You can use **utmost** to emphasize the importance or seriousness of something or to emphasize the way that it is done. máximo, mayor ❑ *The decision is of the utmost importance.* *La decisión es de la mayor importancia.* ❑ *...driving with utmost care.* *...manejar con el máximo cuidado.* **2** N-SING If you say that you are doing your **utmost to** do something, you are emphasizing that you are trying as hard as you can to do it. lo máximo ❑ *He did his utmost to help her.* *Hizo todo lo que pudo para ayudarla.*

**uto|pia** /yutoʊpiə/ (**utopias**) N-VAR If you refer to a real or imaginary situation as a **utopia**, you mean that it is one in which society is perfect and everyone is happy. utopía ❑ *...a relaxing utopia of sea and sand.* *...un sitio utópico de mar y arena para relajarse.*

**ut|ter** /ʌtər/ (**utters, uttering, uttered**) **1** V-T If someone **utters** sounds or words, they say them. articular, pronunciar [LITERARY] ❑ *He uttered the words "I'm sorry."* *Articuló la frase: "Lo siento".* **2** ADJ You use **utter** to emphasize that something is great in extent, degree, or amount. total, absoluto ❑ *This is utter nonsense.* *Esto es una absoluta tontería.*

**ut|ter|ance** /ʌtərəns/ (**utterances**) N-COUNT Someone's **utterances** are the things that they say. expresión, declaración [FORMAL] ❑ *"I'm very happy," was his first utterance.* *—Soy muy feliz —fue lo primero que dijo.*

**ut|ter|ly** /ʌtərli/ ADV You use **utterly** to emphasize that something is very great in extent, degree, or amount. completamente ❑ *He didn't want to appear utterly stupid.* *No quería parecer completamente tonto.* ❑ *He felt completely and utterly alone.* *Se sentía completamente solo.*

**U-turn** (**U-turns**) **1** N-COUNT If you make a **U-turn** when you are driving or riding a bicycle, you turn in a half circle in one movement, so that you are then going in the opposite direction. vuelta en U ❑ *Dave made a U-turn on North Main and drove back to Depot Street.* *Dave dio una vuelta en U en North Main y regresó hacia la calle Depot.* **2** N-COUNT If you describe a change in a someone's policy, plans, or actions as a **U-turn**, you mean that it is a complete change. giro de 180 grados ❑ *He did a U-turn and decided not to retire.* *Dio un giro de 180 grados y decidió no retirarse.*

# Vv

**v.** **v.** is a written abbreviation for **versus.** *versus*

**va|can|cy** /veɪkənsi/ (**vacancies**) **1** N-COUNT A **vacancy** is a job or position that has not been filled. *vacante* ❑ *We have a vacancy for an assistant.* *Tenemos una vacante de ayudante.* **2** N-COUNT If there are **vacancies** at a hotel, some of the rooms are available to stay in. *cuarto disponible* ❑ *The hotel still has a few vacancies.* *El hotel todavía tiene algunos cuartos disponibles.*

**Word Link** *vac ≈ empty : evacuate, vacant, vacuum*

**va|cant** /veɪkənt/ **1** ADJ If something is **vacant,** it is not being used by anyone. *desocupado, vacío* ❑ *...a vacant seat.* *...un asiento desocupado.* **2** ADJ If a job or position is **vacant,** no one is doing it or in it at present, and people can apply for it. *vacante* ❑ *The position of chairman has been vacant for three months.* *El cargo de presidente ha estado vacante durante tres meses.* **3** ADJ A **vacant** look or expression is one that suggests that someone does not understand something or that they are not concentrating. *ausente, distraído* ● **va|cant|ly** ADV *distraídamente* ❑ *He looked vacantly out of the window.* *Miró distraídamente por la ventana.*

**va|cant lot** (**vacant lots**) N-COUNT A **vacant lot** is a small area of land in a city or town that is not occupied or not being used. *baldío* ❑ *There is a vacant lot at the corner of the street.* *Hay un terreno baldío en la esquina de la calle.*

**va|ca|tion** /veɪkeɪʃᵊn/ (**vacations, vacationing, vacationed**) **1** N-COUNT A **vacation** is a period of time during which you relax and enjoy yourself away from home. *vacaciones* ❑ *They planned a vacation in Europe.* *Planearon pasar las vacaciones en Europa.* **2** N-COUNT A **vacation** is a period of the year when schools, universities, and colleges are officially closed. *vacaciones* ❑ *During his summer vacation he visited Russia.* *Durante las vacaciones de verano fue a Rusia.* **3** N-UNCOUNT If you have a particular number of days' or weeks' **vacation,** you do not have to go to work for that number of days or weeks. *vacaciones* ❑ *The French get five to six weeks' vacation a year.* *Los franceses tienen de cinco a seis semanas de vacaciones al año.* **4** V-I If you **are vacationing** in a place away from home, you are on vacation there. *pasar las vacaciones en* ❑ *Mike vacationed in Jamaica.* *Mike pasó sus vacaciones en Jamaica.*

V

**va|ca|tion|er** /veɪkeɪʃənər/ (**vacationers**) N-COUNT **Vacationers** are people who are on vacation in a particular place. *persona que está de vacaciones, vacacionista*

**vac|ci|nate** /væksɪneɪt/ (**vaccinates, vaccinating, vaccinated**) V-T If a person or animal **is vaccinated,** they are given a vaccine, usually by injection, to prevent them from getting a disease. *vacunar* ❑ *Has your child been vaccinated against measles?* *¿Ya están vacunados sus hijos contra el sarampión?* ● **vac|ci|na|tion** /væksɪneɪʃᵊn/ N-VAR (**vaccinations**) *vacunación* ❑ *...a flu vaccination.* *...la vacunación contra la gripe.*

**vac|cine** /væksin/ (**vaccines**) N-VAR A **vaccine** is a substance containing a harmless form of the germs that cause a particular disease. It is given to people to prevent them from getting that disease. *vacuna* ❑ *...flu vaccine.* *...vacuna contra la gripe.*
→ see **hospital**

**vacu|ole** /vækyuoʊl/ (**vacuoles**) N-COUNT A **vacuole** is a space within a plant cell that contains water, waste products, or other substances. *vacuola* [TECHNICAL]

**vacuum** /vækyum, -yuəm/ (**vacuums, vacuuming, vacuumed**) **1** N-COUNT If someone or something creates a **vacuum,** they leave a place or position that then needs to be filled by another person or thing. *vacío* ❑ *When she resigned she left a power vacuum in the company.* *Cuando renunció, dejó un vacío de poder en la compañía.* **2** N-COUNT A **vacuum** is a space that contains no air or other gas. *vacío* ❑ *...a vacuum caused by hot air rising.* *...un vacío provocado por el aire caliente ascendente.* **3** V-T/V-I If you **vacuum,** or **vacuum** something, you clean it using a vacuum cleaner. *pasar la aspiradora, aspirar* ❑ *It's important to vacuum regularly.* *Es importante pasar la aspiradora regularmente.*

**vacuum clean|er** (**vacuum cleaners**) N-COUNT A **vacuum cleaner** or a **vacuum** is an electric machine that sucks up dust and dirt from carpets. *aspiradora*

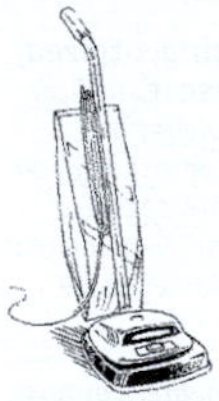

vacuum cleaner

**vague** /veɪg/ (**vaguer, vaguest**) **1** ADJ If something written or spoken is **vague,** it does not explain or express things clearly. *vago* ❑ *The description was pretty vague.* *La descripción era muy vaga.* ● **vague|ly** ADV *vagamente* ❑ *"I'm not sure," Liz said vaguely.* *—No estoy segura —dijo Liz vagamente.* **2** ADJ If you have a **vague** memory or idea of something, the memory or idea is not clear. *vago* ❑ *They have only a vague idea of how much money is left.* *Sólo tienen una idea vaga de la cantidad de dinero que queda.* ● **vague|ly** ADV *vagamente* ❑ *Judith could vaguely remember playing the game as a child.* *Judith recordaba vagamente que había jugado a ese juego de niña.* **3** ADJ A **vague** shape or outline is not clear and is therefore not easy to see. *vago* ❑ *The bus was a vague shape in the distance.* *El autobús era una forma vaga en la distancia.*

**vague|ly** /veɪgli/ ADV **Vaguely** means to a small degree. ligeramente ❑ *The voice on the phone was vaguely familiar.* *La voz al teléfono era ligeramente familiar.*

**vain** /veɪn/ (**vainer, vainest**) 1 ADJ **A vain** attempt or action is one that fails to achieve what was intended. vano, inútil ❑ *We worked through the night in a vain attempt to finish on time.* *Trabajamos toda la noche en un vano intento por terminar a tiempo.* • **vain|ly** ADV en vano, inútilmente ❑ *He looked vainly through his pockets for a piece of paper.* *Buscó en vano en sus bolsillos un trozo de papel.* 2 ADJ If you describe someone as **vain,** you are critical of their extreme pride in their own beauty, intelligence, or other good qualities. vano, vanidoso, presumido ❑ *He was so vain he spent hours in front of the mirror.* *Era tan vanidoso que pasaba horas frente al espejo.* 3 PHRASE If you do something **in vain,** you do not succeed in achieving what you intend. en vano ❑ *She tried in vain to open the door.* *Trató en vano de abrir la puerta.*

**vale|dic|to|ri|an** /vælɪdɪktɔriən/ (**valedictorians**) N-COUNT A **valedictorian** is the student who has the highest grades in their class when they graduate from high school or college, and who gives a speech at their graduation ceremony. alumno que pronuncia el discurso de despedida durante la ceremonia de graduación

**va|lence elec|tron** /veɪləns ɪlɛktrɒn/ (**valence electrons**) N-COUNT **Valence electrons** are the outermost electrons in an atom, which combine with other atoms to form molecules. electrón de valencia [TECHNICAL]

**val|et park|ing** N-UNCOUNT **Valet parking** is a service that operates at places such as hotels and restaurants, in which customers' cars are parked by an attendant. servicio de estacionamiento de autos

**val|id** /vælɪd/ 1 ADJ A **valid** argument, comment, or idea is based on sensible reasoning. válido ❑ *They gave many valid reasons for not signing the contract.* *Dieron muchas razones válidas para no firmar el contrato.* • **va|lid|ity** /vəlɪdɪti/ N-UNCOUNT validez ❑ *I question the validity of this argument.* *Dudo de la validez de este argumento.* 2 ADJ If a ticket or other document is **valid,** it can be used and will be accepted by people in authority. válido ❑ *All tickets are valid for two months.* *Todos los boletos son válidos por dos meses.*

**vali|date** /vælɪdeɪt/ (**validates, validating, validated**) V-T To **validate** something such as a claim or statement means to prove or confirm that it is true or correct. validar [FORMAL] ❑ *This discovery seems to validate his claims.* *Este descubrimiento parece validar sus afirmaciones.* • **vali|da|tion** /vælɪdeɪʃən/ N-VAR (**validations**) validación, ratificación, confirmación ❑ *She saw this as a validation of her decision.* *Lo consideró como una confirmación de su decisión.*

**val|ley** /væli/ (**valleys**) N-COUNT A **valley** is a low stretch of land between hills, especially one that has a river flowing through it. valle ❑ *...a wooded valley.* *...un valle boscoso.*
→ see **landform, river**

**val|or** /vælər/ N-UNCOUNT **Valor** is great bravery, especially in battle. valentía [LITERARY]

**valu|able** /vælyuəbəl/ 1 ADJ If you describe something or someone as **valuable,** you mean that they are very useful and helpful. valioso ❑ *Television can be a valuable tool in the classroom.* *La televisión puede ser una herramienta valiosa en el salón de clases.* 2 ADJ **Valuable** objects are worth a lot of money. de valor ❑ *Do not leave any valuable items in your hotel room.* *No deje ningún objeto de valor en el cuarto del hotel.*

**Thesaurus** *valuable* Ver también:

ADJ. helpful, important, useful; (*ant.*) useless 1
costly, expensive, priceless; (*ant.*) worthless 2

**Word Partnership** Usar *valuable* con:

V. **learn a** valuable **lesson** 1
N. valuable **experience**, valuable **information**, valuable **lesson, time is** valuable 1
valuable **asset**, valuable **resource** 1 2
valuable **property** 2
ADV. **extremely** valuable, **less** valuable, **very** valuable 1 2

**valu|ables** /vælyuəbəlz/ N-PLURAL **Valuables** are things that you own that are worth a lot of money, especially small objects such as jewelry. objetos de valor ❑ *Lock your valuables in the hotel safe.* *Deje sus objetos de valor en la caja fuerte del hotel.*

**value** /vælyu/ (**values, valuing, valued**) 1 N-UNCOUNT; N-SING The **value** of something such as a quality, attitude, or method is its importance or usefulness. valor ❑ *Don't underestimate the value of work experience.* *No subestime el valor de la experiencia en el trabajo.* 2 V-T If you **value** something or someone, you think that they are important and you appreciate them. valuar, apreciar ❑ *I value my husband's opinion.* *Yo aprecio las opiniones de mi esposo.* 3 N-VAR The **value** of something is how much money it is worth. valor ❑ *The value of the house rose by $50,000 in a year.* *El valor de la casa aumentó 50,000 dólares en un año.* ❑ *...jewelry of high value.* *...joyería de gran valor.* 4 V-T When experts **value** something, they decide how much money it is worth. evaluar, valorar, tasar ❑ *He valued the property at $130,000.* *Evaluó la propiedad en 130,000 dólares.* 5 N-PLURAL The **values** of a person or group are their moral principles and beliefs. valores ❑ *The countries of South Asia share many common values.* *Los países del sur de Asia tienen muchos valores en común.* 6 N-VAR In painting, the **value** of a color is how light or dark it is. White is the lightest value and black is the darkest value. valor [TECHNICAL]

**Thesaurus** *value* Ver también:

N. importance, merit, usefulness 1
cost, price, worth 3
V. admire, honor, respect 2
appraise, estimate, price 4

**Word Partnership** Usar *value* con:

ADJ. **artistic** value 1
**actual** value, **equal** value, **great** value 1 3
**estimated** value 3
V. **decline in** value, **increase in** value, **lose** value 1 3
N. **cash** value, **dollar** value, value **of an investment**, **market** value 3

**value scale** (value scales) N-COUNT A **value scale** is an arrangement of all the different colors used in painting, organized according to their lightness or darkness. *escala de valores* [TECHNICAL]

**valve** /vælv/ (valves) N-COUNT A **valve** is a device attached to a pipe or a tube that controls the flow of air or liquid through the pipe or tube. *válvula*
→ see **engine**

**vam|pire** /væmpaɪər/ (vampires) N-COUNT In horror stories, **vampires** are creatures that come out of graves at night and suck the blood of living people. *vampiro*
→ see **bat**

**van** /væn/ (vans) N-COUNT A **van** is a small or medium-sized road vehicle with one row of seats at the front and a space for carrying goods in the back. *camioneta*, *vagoneta*
→ see **car**

**van|dal** /vændᵊl/ (vandals) N-COUNT A **vandal** is someone who deliberately damages things, especially public property. *vándalo* ❑ *The street lights were broken by vandals. Unos vándalos rompieron las lámparas de la calle.*

**van|dal|ism** /vændᵊlɪzəm/ N-UNCOUNT **Vandalism** is the deliberate damaging of things, especially public property. *vandalismo* ❑ *Vandalism, such as breaking windows, is a problem here. El vandalismo, como la rotura de ventanas, es un problema aquí.*

**van|dal|ize** /vændᵊlaɪz/ (**vandalizes, vandalizing, vandalized**) V-T If something such as a building or part of a building **is vandalized** by someone, it is damaged on purpose. *dañar*, *estropear* ❑ *The walls were vandalized with spray paint. Pintarrajearon los muros con pintura en aerosol.*

**va|nil|la** /vənɪlə/ N-UNCOUNT **Vanilla** is a flavoring used in ice cream and other sweet food. *vainilla*

**van|ish** /vænɪʃ/ (**vanishes, vanishing, vanished**) V-I If someone or something **vanishes,** they disappear suddenly or in a way that cannot be explained. *desaparecer* ❑ *He vanished ten years ago and was never seen again. Desapareció hace diez años y nunca se le volvió a ver.* ❑ *The car vanished from outside the house. El automóvil desapareció del frente de la casa.*

V

**van|ish|ing point** (vanishing points) N-COUNT The **vanishing point** is the point in the distance where parallel lines seem to meet. *punto de (la) vista*, *punto de fuga*

**van|ity** /vænɪti/ N-UNCOUNT If you refer to someone's **vanity,** you are critical of them because they are too proud of their appearance or abilities. *vanidad* ❑ *Do you want to lose weight for your health, or out of vanity? ¿Quieres bajar de peso por cuestiones de salud o por vanidad?*

**va|por** /veɪpər/ (vapors) N-VAR **Vapor** consists of tiny drops of water or other liquids in the air, that appear as mist. *vapor* ❑ *...water vapor. ...vapor de agua.*

**va|por|ize** /veɪpəraɪz/ (**vaporizes, vaporizing, vaporized**) V-T/V-I If a liquid or solid **vaporizes** or if you **vaporize** it, it changes into vapor or gas. *evaporar(se)*, *vaporizar(se)* ● **va|pori|za|tion** /veɪpərɪzeɪʃᵊn/ N-UNCOUNT *evaporación*, *vaporización* ❑ *...the energy required to cause vaporization of water. ...la energía requerida para provocar la evaporación del agua.*

**va|por|iz|er** /veɪpəraɪzər/ (vaporizers) N-COUNT A **vaporizer** is a device that produces steam or that converts liquid medicine into vapor so that it can be breathed in. *vaporizador*

**vari|able** /vɛəriəbᵊl/ (variables) 1 ADJ Something that is **variable** changes quite often, and there usually seems to be no fixed pattern to these changes. *variable* ❑ *The quality of his work is very variable. La calidad de su trabajo es muy variable.* ● **vari|abil|ity** /vɛəriəbɪlɪti/ N-UNCOUNT *variabilidad* ❑ *There's a lot of variability between individuals. Hay mucha variabilidad entre los individuos.* 2 N-COUNT A **variable** is a factor in a situation that can change. *variable* ❑ *Consider variables such as price and delivery dates. Tome en consideración las variables como los precios y las fechas de entrega.* 3 N-COUNT A **variable** is a quantity that can have any one of a set of values. *variable* [TECHNICAL]
→ see **experiment**

**vari|ation** /vɛərieɪʃᵊn/ (variations) 1 N-COUNT A **variation on** something is the same thing presented in a slightly different form. *variación* ❑ *...a delicious variation on an omelet. ...una variación deliciosa de la omelet.* 2 N-VAR A **variation** is a change or difference in a level, amount, or quantity. *variación* ❑ *Can you explain the wide variation in your prices? ¿Puede explicar las grandes variaciones de sus precios?*

**var|ied** /vɛərid/ 1 ADJ Something that is **varied** consists of things of different types, sizes, or qualities. *variado* ❑ *Your diet should be varied and balanced. Su dieta debe ser variada y equilibrada.* 2 → see also **vary**

**va|ri|ety** /vəraɪɪti/ (varieties) 1 N-UNCOUNT If something has **variety,** it consists of things that are different from each other. *variedad* ❑ *Susan wanted variety in her lifestyle. Susan quería que hubiera variedad en su forma de vida.* 2 N-SING A **variety of** things is a number of different kinds or examples of the same thing. *variedad* ❑ *The West Village has a variety of good stores. En el barrio West Village hay una variedad de buenas tiendas.* ❑ *The island has a wide variety of plants. La isla tiene una gran variedad de plantas.* 3 N-COUNT A **variety** of something is a type of it. *variedad* ❑ *They make 20 varieties of bread every day. Todos los días hacen 20 variedades de pan.* 4 N-UNCOUNT **Variety** is the quality that something such as a painting or a dance has when it consists of different parts that are combined in an interesting way, for example because some parts contrast with other parts or change them. *variación*

**Word Partnership** Usar *variety* con:

N. variety **of activities**, variety **of colors**, variety **of foods**, variety **of issues**, variety **of problems**, variety **of products**, variety **of reasons**, variety **of sizes**, variety **of styles**, variety **of ways** 2
V. **choose a** variety, **offer a** variety, **provide a** variety 2

**va|ri|ety store** (**variety stores**) N-COUNT A **variety store** is a store that sells a wide range of small, inexpensive items. *bazar*

**vari|ous** /vɛəriəs/ ADJ If you say that there are **various** things, you mean there are several different things of the type mentioned. *vario* ❑ *He spent the day doing various jobs around the house. Pasó el día haciendo varios trabajos en la casa.*

**var|sity** /vɑrsɪti/ (**varsities**) N-COUNT The **varsity** is the main or first team for a particular sport at a high school, college, or university. *equipo titular de una secundaria, colegio o universidad en un deporte en particular* ❑ *...the varsity basketball team. ...el equipo titular de básquetbol.*

**vary** /vɛəri/ (**varies, varying, varied**) 1 V-I If things **vary,** they are different from each other in size, amount, or degree. *variar, diferir* ❑ *The jugs are handmade, so they vary slightly. Las jarras están hechas a mano, por lo que varían ligeramente.* ❑ *Her story varies from her friends' accounts. Su historia difiere de las versiones de sus amigos.* 2 V-T/V-I If something **varies** or if you **vary** it, it becomes different or changed. *variar* ❑ *The cost of coffee varies according to where it comes from. El costo del café varía según su lugar de procedencia.* 3 → see also **varied**

**Word Partnership** Usar *vary* con:

N. **prices** vary, **rates** vary, **styles** vary 1
vary **by location**, vary **by size**, vary **by state**, vary **by store** 1 2
ADV. vary **considerably**, vary **greatly**, vary **slightly**, vary **widely** 1 2

**vas|cu|lar plant** /væskyələr plænt/ (**vascular plants**) N-COUNT **Vascular plants** are plants that have tissues which can carry water and other fluids through the body of the plant. *planta vascular* [TECHNICAL]

**vas de|fe|rens** /væs dɛfərɛnz/ (**vasa deferentia** /veɪzədɛfərɛnʃiə, -ʃə/) N-COUNT The **vas deferens** is the pair of narrow tubes in a man's body that carries sperm from his testicles towards his penis. *conducto deferente* [TECHNICAL]

**vase** /veɪs, vɑz/ (**vases**) N-COUNT A **vase** is a jar, usually made of glass or pottery, used for holding cut flowers or as an ornament. *jarrón, florero* ❑ *...a vase of red roses. ...un jarrón de rosas rojas.*
→ see **glass**

**vast** /væst/ (**vaster, vastest**) ADJ Something that is **vast** is extremely large. *vasto* ❑ *...farmers who own vast stretches of land. ...granjeros que son propietarios de vastas extensiones de tierra.*

**Word Partnership** Usar *vast* con:

N. vast **amounts**, vast **distance**, vast **expanse**, vast **knowledge**, vast **majority**, vast **quantities**

**vau|de|ville** /vɔdvɪl, vɔdə-/ N-UNCOUNT **Vaudeville** is a type of entertainment consisting of short acts of comedy, singing, and dancing, that was popular in the early twentieth century. *vodevil*

**VCR** /vi si ɑr/ (**VCRs**) N-COUNT A **VCR** is a machine that can be used to record television programs or movies onto videotapes. **VCR** is an abbreviation for "video cassette recorder." *grabadora de videocintas*

**vec|tor** /vɛktər/ (**vectors**) N-COUNT A **vector** is a variable quantity, such as force, that has size and direction. *vector* [TECHNICAL]

**veer** /vɪər/ (**veers, veering, veered**) V-I If something **veers** in a certain direction, it suddenly moves in that direction. *virar, dar un viraje* ❑ *The plane veered off the runway. El avión dio un viraje y se salió de la pista.*

**veg|eta|ble** /vɛdʒtəbəl, vɛdʒɪ-/ (**vegetables**) N-COUNT **Vegetables** are plants such as cabbages, potatoes, and onions that you can cook and eat. *verduras*
→ see Picture Dictionary: **vegetables**
→ see **vegetarian**

**Word Link** ***arian*** *≈ believing in, having :* ***humanitarian, sectarian, vegetarian***

**veg|etar|ian** /vɛdʒɪtɛəriən/ (**vegetarians**) ADJ Someone who is **vegetarian** never eats meat or fish. *vegetariano* ❑ *...a strict vegetarian diet. ...una dieta vegetariana estricta.* • A **vegetarian** is someone who is vegetarian. *vegetariano o vegetariana* ❑ *...a special menu for vegetarians. ...un menú especial para vegetarianos.*
→ see Word Web: **vegetarian**

**Word Web** **vegetarian**

The Greek philosopher Pythagoras was a **vegetarian.** He believed that if humans killed animals, they would also kill each other. So he did not eat **meat.** Vegetarians eat many kinds of food, not just **vegetables.** They eat fruits, grains, oils, fats, and sugar. Vegans are vegetarians who don't eat eggs or dairy products. Some people choose this **diet** for health reasons. A well-balanced veggie diet can be healthy. Some people choose this diet for religious reasons. Others want to make the world's **food** supply go further. It takes fifteen pounds of grain to produce one pound of meat.

V

**veg|eta|tion** /vɛdʒɪteɪʃᵊn/ N-UNCOUNT Plants, trees, and flowers can be referred to as **vegetation.** *vegetación* [FORMAL] ❑ *...tropical vegetation. ...vegetación tropical.*
→ see **erosion, habitat, herbivore**

**veg|eta|tive re|pro|duc|tion** /vɛdʒɪteɪtɪv riprədʌkʃᵊn/ also **vegetative propagation** N-UNCOUNT **Vegetative reproduction** is a process by which new plants are produced without using seeds, for example by using cuttings instead. *reproducción asexual, también llamada reproducción vegetativa* [TECHNICAL]

**veg|gie** /vɛdʒi/ (**veggies**) N-COUNT **Veggies** are vegetables. *verduras* [INFORMAL] ❑ *...fresh fruit and veggies. ...frutas y verduras frescas.*

**ve|hi|cle** /viɪkᵊl/ (**vehicles**) **1** N-COUNT A **vehicle** is a machine with an engine, such as a bus, car, or truck, that carries people or things from place to place. *vehículo* ❑ *There are too many vehicles on the road. Hay demasiados vehículos en la carretera.* **2** N-COUNT You can use **vehicle** to refer to something that you use in order to achieve a particular purpose. *vehículo, medio* ❑ *Her art became a vehicle for her political beliefs. Su arte se convirtió en el medio de expresión de sus opiniones políticas.*
→ see **car, traffic**

V

veil

**veil** /veɪl/ (**veils**) **1** N-COUNT A **veil** is a piece of thin soft cloth that women sometimes wear over their heads and that can also cover their face. *velo* ❑ *She wore a veil over her face. Llevaba un velo que le cubría la cara.* **2** N-COUNT You can refer to something that hides or partly hides a situation or activity as a **veil.** *velo* ❑ *It is time for the government to lift the veil of secrecy over this matter. Ya es hora de que el gobierno descorra el velo del secreto sobre esta cuestión.*

**vein** /veɪn/ (**veins**) **1** N-COUNT Your **veins** are the thin tubes in your body through which your blood flows toward your heart. *vena* **2** N-COUNT Something that is written or spoken **in a** particular **vein** is written or spoken in that style or mood. *vena* ❑ *Her next book was in a lighter vein. En su segundo libro echó mano de una vena más ligera.* **3** N-COUNT The **veins** on a leaf are the thin lines on it. *vena*
→ see **cardiovascular system**

**vel|vet** /vɛlvɪt/ (**velvets**) N-VAR **Velvet** is soft material made from cotton, silk, or nylon, that has a thick layer of short cut threads on one side. *terciopelo*

**ven|dor** /vɛndər/ (**vendors**) N-COUNT A **vendor** is someone who sells things such as newspapers, drinks, or food from a small stall or cart. *vendedor ambulante o vendedora ambulante* ❑ *...ice cream vendors. ...vendedores de helados.*

**venge|ance** /vɛndʒᵊns/ **1** N-UNCOUNT **Vengeance** is the act of killing, injuring, or harming someone because they have harmed you. *venganza* ❑ *He swore vengeance on everyone involved in the murder. Juró venganza contra todo el que estuviera implicado en el asesinato.* **2** PHRASE If you say that something happens **with a vengeance,** you are emphasizing that it happens to a great extent. *en sumo grado, de veras, con ganas* ❑ *It began to rain with a vengeance. Empezó a llover con ganas.*

**Venn dia|gram** /vɛn daɪəgræm/ (**Venn diagrams**) N-COUNT A **Venn diagram** is a diagram in mathematics that uses overlapping circles to represent features that are common to, or unique to, two or more sets of data. *diagrama de Venn*

**vent** /vɛnt/ (**vents, venting, vented**) **1** N-COUNT

A **vent** is a hole in something through which air can come in and smoke, gas, or smells can go out. ventilador, ventila, orificio de ventilación ❑ *Steam escaped from the vent at the front of the machine.* *El vapor escapaba por el orificio de ventilación del frente de la máquina.* **2** V-T If you **vent** your feelings, you express your feelings forcefully. ventilar, desahogar ❑ *She telephoned her best friend to vent her frustration.* *Llamó por teléfono a su mejor amiga para desahogar su frustración.* **3** N-COUNT A **vent** is a crack in the Earth's surface through which lava and gas are released. falla volcánica (lava), fumarola (gases o vapores)

**ven|ti|late** /vɛntəleɪt/ (**ventilates, ventilating, ventilated**) V-T If you **ventilate** a room or building, you allow fresh air to get into it. ventilar ❑ *You must ventilate the room well when painting.* *Debe ventilar bien el cuarto cuando esté pintando.* ● **ven|ti|la|tion** /vɛntəleɪʃən/ N-UNCOUNT ventilación ❑ *The only ventilation came from one tiny window.* *Una ventanita era el único medio de ventilación.*

**ven|tri|cle** /vɛntrɪkəl/ (**ventricles**) N-COUNT A **ventricle** is a part of the heart that pumps blood to the arteries. ventrículo [MEDICAL]

**ven|ture** /vɛntʃər/ (**ventures, venturing, ventured**) **1** N-COUNT A **venture** is a project or activity that is new, exciting, and difficult because it involves the risk of failure. empresa ❑ *...a joint venture between two schools.* *...una empresa conjunta entre dos escuelas.* **2** V-I If you **venture** somewhere, you go somewhere that might be dangerous. aventurarse [LITERARY] ❑ *People are afraid to venture out at night.* *La gente tiene miedo de aventurarse a salir por la noche.* **3** V-I If you **venture into** an activity, you do something that involves the risk of failure because it is new and different. aventurarse ❑ *He ventured into business but had no success.* *Se aventuró en los negocios, pero no tuvo éxito.*

**venue** /vɛnyu/ (**venues**) N-COUNT The **venue** for an event or activity is the place where it will happen. lugar ❑ *The Convention Center is the venue for a three-day arts festival.* *El Centro de Convenciones es donde tendrá lugar un festival de las artes de tres días.*
→ see **concert**

**Ve|nus** /vinəs/ N-PROPER **Venus** is the second planet from the sun, situated between Mercury and the Earth. Venus
→ see **solar system**

**verb** /vɜrb/ (**verbs**) **1** N-COUNT A **verb** is a word such as "sing," "feel," or "die" that is used with a subject to say what someone or something does or what happens to them, or to give information about them. verbo **2** → see also **phrasal verb**

| Word Link | *verb ≈ word : adverb, proverb, verbal* |
|---|---|

**ver|bal** /vɜrbəl/ **1** ADJ You use **verbal** to indicate that something is expressed in speech rather than in writing or action. verbal ❑ *We will not tolerate verbal or physical abuse of our employees.* *No toleraremos que se abuse ni verbal ni físicamente de nuestros empleados.* ● **ver|bal|ly** ADV verbalmente ❑ *We complained both verbally and in writing.* *Nos quejamos verbalmente y por escrito.* **2** ADJ You use **verbal** to indicate that something is connected with words and the use of words. verbal, oral ❑ *...verbal skills.* *...capacidad oral.*

**verb phrase** (**verb phrases**) N-COUNT A **verb phrase** or **verbal phrase** consists of a verb, or of a main verb following a modal or one or more auxiliaries. Examples are "walked," "can see," and "has been waiting." perífrasis verbal, frase verbal

| Word Link | *ver ≈ truth : verdict, verify, version* |
|---|---|

**ver|dict** /vɜrdɪkt/ (**verdicts**) **1** N-COUNT In a court of law, the **verdict** is the decision that is given by the jury or judge at the end of a trial. veredicto ❑ *The jury delivered a verdict of not guilty.* *El jurado emitió un veredicto de inocencia.* **2** N-COUNT Someone's **verdict** on something is their opinion of it, after thinking about it or investigating it. opinión ❑ *The doctor's verdict was that he was healthy.* *La opinión del médico fue que estaba sano.*
→ see **trial**

| Word Link | *verg, vert ≈ turning : convert, divert, verge* |
|---|---|

**verge** /vɜrdʒ/ (**verges, verging, verged**) PHRASE If you are **on the verge of** something, you are going to do it very soon or it is likely to happen or begin very soon. al borde de ❑ *Carole was on the verge of tears.* *Carole estaba al borde de las lágrimas.*
▸ **verge on** PHR-VERB If someone or something **verges on** a particular state or quality, they are almost the same as that state or quality. rayar en ❑ *Her anger verged on madness.* *Su ira rayaba en la locura.*

**veri|fy** /vɛrɪfaɪ/ (**verifies, verifying, verified**) **1** V-T If you **verify** something, you check that it is true by careful examination or investigation. verificar ❑ *We haven't yet verified his information.* *Todavía no hemos verificado su información.* ● **veri|fi|ca|tion** /vɛrɪfɪkeɪʃən/ N-UNCOUNT verificación ❑ *...the verification of her story.* *...la verificación de su historia.* **2** V-T If you **verify** something, you state or confirm that it is true. confirmar, corroborar ❑ *The government has not verified any of those reports.* *El gobierno no ha corroborado ninguno de esos informes.*

**ver|sa|tile** /vɜrsətəl/ **1** ADJ If you say that a person is **versatile,** you approve of them because they have many different skills. versátil ❑ *He was one of our most versatile athletes.* *Fue uno de nuestros atletas más versátiles.* ● **ver|sa|til|ity** /vɜrsətɪlɪti/ N-UNCOUNT versatilidad ❑ *...her versatility as an actress.* *...su versatilidad como actriz.* **2** ADJ A tool, machine, or material that is **versatile** can be used for many different purposes. versátil, de usos múltiples ❑ *Computers today are so versatile.* *Hoy en día las computadoras son muy versátiles.* ● **ver|sa|til|ity** N-UNCOUNT versatilidad ❑ *Plastic is known for its versatility.* *El plástico es conocido por la multiplicidad de sus usos.*

**verse** /vɜrs/ (**verses**) **1** N-UNCOUNT **Verse** is writing arranged in lines that have rhythm and that often rhyme at the end. verso ❑ *...a few lines of verse.* *...unas cuantas líneas en verso.* **2** N-COUNT A **verse** is one of the parts into which a poem, a song, or a chapter of the Bible or the Koran is divided. estrofa, versículo

**ver|sion** /vɜrʒən/ (**versions**) **1** N-COUNT A **version of** something is a particular form of it in which some details are different from earlier or later forms. *versión* ❑ *He is bringing out a new version of his book.* *Va a publicar una nueva versión de su libro.* **2** N-COUNT Someone's **version of** an event is their own description of it. *versión* ❑ *...the official version of events.* *...la versión oficial de los sucesos.*

**ver|sus** /vɜrsəs/ **1** PREP You use **versus** to indicate that two figures, ideas, or choices are opposed. *versus, frente a* ❑ *They discussed getting a job after graduation versus going to college.* *Hablaron de los pros y contras entre conseguir empleo después de la graduación o ir a la universidad.* **2** PREP **Versus** is used to indicate that two teams or people are competing against each other in a sports event. *contra* ❑ *It will be the U.S. versus Belgium in tomorrow's game.* *El juego de mañana será de Estados Unidos contra Bélgica.*

**ver|te|brate** /vɜrtɪbrɪt/ (**vertebrates**) N-COUNT A **vertebrate** is a creature that has a skull and a spine. Mammals, birds, reptiles, and fish are vertebrates. *vertebrados*

**ver|ti|cal** /vɜrtɪkᵊl/ ADJ Something that is **vertical** stands or points straight up. *vertical, cortado a pico* ❑ *...a vertical wall of rock.* *...una pared de roca cortada a pico.* ● **ver|ti|cal|ly** ADV *verticalmente* ❑ *Cut each lemon in half vertically.* *Corte los limones en dos verticalmente.*
→ see **graph**

**very** /vɛri/ **1** ADV **Very** is used to give emphasis to an adjective or adverb. *muy* ❑ *The answer is very simple.* *La respuesta es muy simple.* ❑ *I'm very sorry.* *Estoy muy apenado.* **2** PHRASE **Not very** is used with an adjective or adverb to say that something is not at all true, or that it is true only to a small degree. *no muy/mucho* ❑ *She's not very impressed with them.* *No la impresionan mucho.* ❑ *"How well do you know her?"— "Not very."* *—¿Qué tan bien la conoces? —No mucho.* **3** ADJ You use **very** with certain nouns in order to specify an extreme position or extreme point in time. *justo, hasta* ❑ *At the very back of the yard was a tree.* *Justo en el fondo del patio había un árbol.* ❑ *I turned to the very end of the book.* *Fui hasta el final del libro.* **4** ADJ You use **very** with nouns to emphasize that something is exactly the right one or exactly the same one. *precisamente* ❑ *She died in this very house.* *Murió precisamente en esta casa.* **5** PHRASE **Very much so** is an emphatic way of answering "yes" to something or saying that it is true or correct. *muchísimo* ❑ *"Are you enjoying your vacation?"— "Very much so."* *—¿Estás disfrutando tus vacaciones? —¡Muchísimo!* **6** CONVENTION **Very well** is used to say that you agree to do something or you accept someone's answer, even though you might not be completely satisfied with it. *muy bien* ❑ *"Very well," she said, "you may go."* *—Muy bien —le dijo—, puede marcharse.*



| **Thesaurus** | *very* | Ver también: |
|---|---|---|
| ADV. | absolutely, extremely, greatly, highly **1** | |

**vesi|cle** /vɛsɪkᵊl/ (**vesicles**) N-COUNT A **vesicle** is a compartment within a living cell in which substances are carried or stored. *vesícula* [TECHNICAL]

**ves|sel** /vɛsᵊl/ (**vessels**) **1** N-COUNT A **vessel** is a ship or large boat. *navío, nave, buque* [FORMAL] ❑ *...a New Zealand navy vessel.* *...un buque de la marina de Nueva Zelanda.* **2** → see also **blood vessel**
→ see **ship**

**vest** /vɛst/ (**vests**) N-COUNT A **vest** is a sleeveless piece of clothing with buttons that people usually wear over a shirt. *chaleco*

**ves|tig|ial struc|ture** /vɛstɪdʒiəl strʌktʃər, -stɪdʒəl/ (**vestigial structures**) also **vestigial organ** N-COUNT A **vestigial structure** or **vestigial organ** is a part of the body of an animal, such as the appendix in humans, that was useful at an earlier stage of the animal's evolution but no longer has any function. *órgano rudimentario* [TECHNICAL]

**vet** /vɛt/ (**vets, vetting, vetted**) N-COUNT A **vet** is someone who is qualified to treat sick or injured animals. **Vet** is an abbreviation for **veterinarian**. *veterinario o veterinaria* [INFORMAL]

**vet|er|an** /vɛtərən/ (**veterans**) **1** N-COUNT A **veteran** is someone who has served in the armed forces of their country, especially during a war. *veterano o veterana, ex combatiente* ❑ *...veterans of the Vietnam War.* *...veteranos de la guerra de Vietnam.* **2** N-COUNT You use **veteran** to refer to someone who has been involved in a particular activity for a long time. *veterano o veterana* ❑ *...a veteran movie critic.* *...un crítico de cine veterano.*

**vet|eri|nar|ian** /vɛtərɪnɛəriən/ (**veterinarians**) N-COUNT A **veterinarian** is a person who is qualified to treat sick or injured animals. *veterinario o veterinaria*

**veto** /vitoʊ/ (**vetoes, vetoing, vetoed**) **1** V-T If someone in authority **vetoes** something, they forbid it, or stop it from being put into action. *vetar* ❑ *The president vetoed the bill passed by Congress.* *El presidente vetó la ley aprobada por el Congreso.* ● **Veto** is also a noun. *veto* ❑ *The chairperson of the committee used her veto.* *El presidente de la comisión hizo uso de su derecho de veto.* **2** N-UNCOUNT **Veto** is the right that someone in authority has to forbid something. *veto* ❑ *...the president's power of veto.* *...el derecho de veto del presidente.*

**vex** /vɛks/ (**vexes, vexing, vexed**) V-T If someone or something **vexes** you, they make you feel annoyed, puzzled, and frustrated. *irritar, molestar* ❑ *Their attitude vexed him.* *Su actitud lo irritó.* ● **vexed** ADJ *irritado* ❑ *Farmers are vexed and blame the government.* *Los granjeros están irritados y culpan al gobierno.* ● **vex|ing** ADJ *irritante* ❑ *...a vexing problem.* *...un problema irritante.*

**via** /vaɪə, viə/ **1** PREP If you go somewhere **via** a particular place, you go through that place on the way to your destination. *por, vía* ❑ *I'm flying to Sweden via New York.* *El avión vuela a Suecia vía Nueva York.* **2** PREP If you do something **via** a particular means or person, you do it by making use of that means or person. *por, a través de* ❑ *We can continue the discussion via e-mail.* *Podemos continuar la discusión por correo electrónico.*

**vi|able** /vaɪəbᵊl/ ADJ Something that is **viable** is capable of doing what it is intended to do. *viable* ❑ *The business in its current state is not viable.* *En su estado actual, el negocio no es viable.* ● **vi|abil|ity** /vaɪəbɪlɪti/ N-UNCOUNT *viabilidad* ❑ *...worries about the company's long-term viability.* *...preocupación por la viabilidad de la empresa en el largo plazo.*

**vi|brate** /vaɪbreɪt/ (**vibrates, vibrating, vibrated**) V-T/V-I If something **vibrates** or if you **vibrate** it, it shakes with repeated small, quick movements. vibrar ❑ The ground seemed to vibrate. El suelo parecía vibrar. • **vi|bra|tion** /vaɪbreɪʃᵊn/ N-VAR (**vibrations**) vibración ❑ The vibration of the trucks rattled the windows. El ruido de los camiones hizo vibrar las ventanas.

→ see **ear, sound**

**vice** /vaɪs/ (**vices**) **1** N-COUNT A **vice** is a habit that is regarded as a weakness in your character, but not usually as a serious fault. vicio ❑ My only vice is that I spend too much on clothes. Mi único vicio es que gasto demasiado en ropa. **2** N-UNCOUNT **Vice** refers to criminal activities, especially those connected with pornography or prostitution. vicio

**vice ver|sa** /vaɪsəvɛrsə, vaɪs/ PHRASE **Vice versa** is used to indicate that the reverse of what you have said is true. For example, "women may bring their husbands with them, and vice versa" means that men may also bring their wives with them. viceversa

**vi|cin|ity** /vɪsɪnɪti/ N-SING If something is **in the vicinity of** a particular place, it is near it. vecindad, inmediaciones, alrededores [FORMAL] ❑ There were several hotels in the vicinity of the station. Había varios hoteles en las inmediaciones de la estación.

**vi|cious** /vɪʃəs/ **1** ADJ A **vicious** person or a **vicious** blow is violent and cruel. despiadado ❑ ...a cruel and vicious man. ...un hombre cruel y despiadado. • **vi|cious|ly** ADV brutalmente ❑ He was viciously attacked. Fue atacado brutalmente. • **vi|cious|ness** N-UNCOUNT ferocidad ❑ ...the viciousness of his hatred. ...la ferocidad de su odio. **2** ADJ A **vicious** remark is cruel and intended to upset someone. cruel ❑ ...a vicious comment about his appearance. ...un comentario cruel sobre su apariencia. • **vi|cious|ly** ADV cruelmente ❑ "He deserved to die," said Penelope viciously. —Merecía morir—, dijo Penélope cruelmente.

| **Thesaurus** | *vicious* | Ver también: |
|---|---|---|
| ADJ. | brutal, cruel, violent; (*ant.*) nice **1** **2** | |

**vic|tim** /vɪktəm/ (**victims**) N-COUNT A **victim** is someone who has been hurt or killed. víctima ❑ ...the victims of violent crime. ...las víctimas de la violencia criminal.

**vic|tim|ize** /vɪktəmaɪz/ (**victimizes, victimizing, victimized**) V-T If someone **is victimized,** they are deliberately treated unfairly. tratar injustamente ❑ The students were victimized because they opposed the government. Trataron injustamente a los estudiantes porque se oponían al gobierno. • **vic|timi|za|tion** /vɪktəmɪzeɪʃᵊn/ N-UNCOUNT discriminación ❑ ...society's victimization of women. ...la discriminación social de la mujer.

**vic|tor** /vɪktər/ (**victors**) N-COUNT The **victor** in a battle or contest is the person who wins. vencedor o vencedora [LITERARY]

**Vic|to|rian** /vɪktɔriən/ (**Victorians**) **1** ADJ **Victorian** means belonging to, connected with, or typical of Britain in the middle and last parts of the 19th century, when Victoria was Queen. victoriano ❑ ...a lovely old Victorian house. ...una encantadora casa victoriana. **2** ADJ You can use **Victorian** to describe people who have old-fashioned attitudes, especially about good behavior and morals. conservador, decimonónico ❑ Victorian attitudes have no place in modern society. Las actitudes decimonónicas no tienen lugar en la sociedad moderna. **3** N-COUNT The **Victorians** were the British people who lived in the time of Queen Victoria. victoriano o victoriana

**vic|to|ri|ous** /vɪktɔriəs/ ADJ You use **victorious** to describe someone who has won a victory in a struggle, war, or competition. victorioso, vencedor, triunfante ❑ ...the victorious team in the World Cup. ...el equipo vencedor de la Copa Mundial.

| **Word Link** | *vict, vinc ≈ conquering : convict, convince, victory* |
|---|---|

**vic|to|ry** /vɪktəri, vɪktri/ (**victories**) N-VAR A **victory** is a success in a struggle, war, or competition. victoria ❑ The Democrats celebrated their victory. Los demócratas celebraron su victoria.

| **Thesaurus** | *victory* | Ver también: |
|---|---|---|
| N. | conquest, success, win; (*ant.*) defeat | |

**video** /vɪdioʊ/ (**videos, videoing, videoed**) **1** N-COUNT A **video** is a movie or television program recorded on tape. video ❑ ...sports and exercise videos. ...videos de deportes y ejercicios. **2** N-UNCOUNT **Video** is the system of recording movies and events on tape. video ❑ She has watched the show on video. Ya vio el espectáculo en video.

**video ar|cade** (**video arcades**) N-COUNT A **video arcade** is a place where you can play video games on machines which work when you put money in them. sala recreativa (con videojuegos)

**video game** (**video games**) N-COUNT A **video game** is an electronic or computerized game that you play on your television or on a computer screen. videojuego

| **Word Link** | *vid, vis ≈ seeing : television, videotape, visible* |
|---|---|

**video|tape** /vɪdioʊteɪp/ (**videotapes**) also **video tape** N-VAR **Videotape** is magnetic tape that is used to record moving pictures and sounds to be shown on television. cinta de video ❑ ...the use of videotape in court cases. ...la grabación en video de los juicios.

**vie** /vaɪ/ (**vies, vying, vied**) V-RECIP If one person or thing **is vying with** another for something, the people or things are competing for it. rivalizar, competir [FORMAL] ❑ The brothers vied with each other to offer help to their parents. Los hermanos rivalizaban entre sí por ayudar a sus padres.

**view** /vyu/ (**views, viewing, viewed**) **1** N-COUNT Your **views** on something are the beliefs or opinions that you have about it. opinión, punto de vista ❑ We have similar views on politics. Tenemos opiniones similares en política. **2** N-SING Your **view of** a particular subject is the way that you understand and think about it. visión ❑ Something happened to change my view of this place and of my work there. Algo pasó que cambió mi visión de ese lugar y de mi trabajo ahí. **3** V-T If you **view** something in a particular way, you think of it in that way. considerar ❑ Immigrants viewed the United States as a land of opportunity. Los inmigrantes consideraban a Estados Unidos como la tierra de la oportunidad. ❑ Linda views her daughter's talent with pride. Linda se siente orgullosa del talento de su hija. **4** N-COUNT The **view**

from a window or high place is everything that can be seen from that place, especially when it is considered to be beautiful. *vista* ❑ *From our hotel room we had a great view of the ocean. Teníamos una magnífica vista del mar desde nuestro cuarto del hotel.* **5** N-SING If you have a **view of** something, you can see it. *vista* ❑ *He stood up to get a better view of the blackboard. Se puso de pie para ver mejor el pizarrón.* **6** N-UNCOUNT You use **view** in expressions to do with being able to see something. For example, if something is **in view,** you can see it. If something is **in full view of everyone,** everyone can see it. *vista* ❑ *She was lying there in full view of anyone who walked by. Estaba tendida ahí, a plena vista de todo el que pasara por el lugar.* **7** V-T If you **view** something, you look at it for a particular purpose. *ver* [FORMAL] ❑ *They came to view the house again. Vinieron a ver la casa otra vez.* **8** PHRASE You use **in view of** when you are taking into consideration facts that have just been mentioned or are just about to be mentioned. *en vista de* ❑ *In view of the heavy rain we are staying at home. En vista de que llueve muy fuerte, nos quedamos en casa.* **9** PHRASE If something such as a work of art is **on view,** it is shown in public for people to look at. *en exhibición* ❑ *Her paintings are on view at the Portland Gallery. Sus cuadros están en exhibición en la Galería Portland.* **10** PHRASE If you do something **with a view to** doing something else, you do it because you hope it will result in that other thing being done. *con miras a, con el propósito de* ❑ *We called a meeting with a view to resolving the dispute. Convocamos a la reunión con el propósito de resolver la disputa.*

**view|er** /vyuər/ (**viewers**) N-COUNT **Viewers** are people who watch television, or who are watching a particular program on television. *expectador, televidente* ❑ *19 million viewers watch the show every week. Diecinueve millones de televidentes ven el programa cada semana.*

**view|point** /vyupɔɪnt/ (**viewpoints**) N-COUNT Someone's **viewpoint** is the way that they think about things in general, or the way they think about a particular thing. *punto de vista* ❑ *The book is written from the girl's viewpoint. El libro está escrito desde el punto de vista de la niña.*

**vig|or** /vɪgər/ N-UNCOUNT **Vigor** is physical or mental energy and enthusiasm. *vigor, energía, vitalidad* ❑ *He approached his new job with vigor. Emprendió su nuevo empleo con energía.*

**vig|or|ous** /vɪgərəs/ ADJ **Vigorous** physical activities involve using a lot of energy, usually to do short and repeated actions. *vigoroso* ❑ *...vigorous exercise. ...ejercicio vigoroso.* • **vig|or|ous|ly** ADV *vigorosamente, enérgicamente* ❑ *He shook his head vigorously. Negó enérgicamente con la cabeza.*

V

**vil|la** /vɪlə/ (**villas**) N-COUNT A **villa** is a fairly large house, especially one in a hot country or a resort. *villa, casa de campo*

**vil|lage** /vɪlɪdʒ/ (**villages**) N-COUNT A **village** consists of a group of houses, together with other buildings such as a church and a school, in a country area. *pueblo, aldea*

**vil|lag|er** /vɪlɪdʒər/ (**villagers**) N-COUNT You refer to the people who live in a village, especially the people who have lived there for most or all of their lives, as the **villagers.** *vecino o vecina, aldeano o aldeana*

**vil|lain** /vɪlən/ (**villains**) N-COUNT A **villain** is someone who deliberately harms other people or breaks the law in order to get what he or she wants. *villano, villana* ❑ *They called him a villain and a murderer. Lo llamaron villano y asesino.*

**vine** /vaɪn/ (**vines**) N-VAR A **vine** is a plant that grows up or over things, especially one that produces grapes. *vid, parra*

**vin|egar** /vɪnɪgər/ (**vinegars**) N-VAR **Vinegar** is a sharp-tasting liquid, usually made from sour wine or malt, that is used in cooking to make things such as salad dressing. *vinagre*

**vine|yard** /vɪnyərd/ (**vineyards**) N-COUNT A **vineyard** is an area of land where grape vines are grown in order to produce wine. *viñedo, viña*

**vin|tage** /vɪntɪdʒ/ (**vintages**) **1** N-COUNT The **vintage** of a good quality wine is the year and place that it was made. *vendimia, cosecha* ❑ *This wine is from one of the best vintages of the decade. Este vino es de una de las mejores cosechas de la década.* **2** ADJ **Vintage** wine is good quality wine that has been stored for several years in order to improve its quality. *añejo* **3** ADJ **Vintage** cars or airplanes are old but are admired because they are considered to be the best of their kind. *clásico, antiguo*

**vi|nyl** /vaɪnɪl/ N-UNCOUNT **Vinyl** is a strong plastic used for making things such as floor coverings and furniture. *vinilo* ❑ *...vinyl floor covering. ...piso de vinilo.*

**vio|la** /vioʊlə/ (**violas**) N-VAR A **viola** is a musical instrument that is like a violin, but is slightly larger. *viola*

→ see **string**

**vio|late** /vaɪəleɪt/ (**violates, violating, violated**) **1** V-T If someone **violates** an agreement, law, or promise, they break it. *violar* [FORMAL] ❑ *They went to prison because they violated the law. Los enviaron a la cárcel porque violaron la ley.* • **vio|la|tion** /vaɪəleɪʃᵊn/ N-VAR (**violations**) *violación* ❑ *...a violation of state law. ...una violación de la ley del estado.* **2** V-T If you **violate** someone's privacy or peace, you disturb it. *violar* [FORMAL] **3** V-T If someone **violates** a special place such as a grave, they damage it or treat it with disrespect. *profanar* • **vio|la|tion** N-VAR *profanación* ❑ *...the violation of the graves. ...la profanación de las tumbas.*

**vio|lence** /vaɪələns/ **1** N-UNCOUNT **Violence** is behavior that is intended to hurt, injure, or kill people. *violencia* ❑ *Twenty people died in the violence. La violencia causó veinte muertos.* **2** N-UNCOUNT If you do or say something with **violence,** you use a lot of force and energy in doing or saying it, often because you are angry. *violencia* [LITERARY] ❑ *The violence of her behavior shocked him. La violencia de su conducta lo horrorizó.*

**vio|lent** /vaɪələnt/ **1** ADJ If someone is **violent,** or if they do something that is **violent,** they use physical force or weapons to hurt, injure, or kill other people. *violento* ❑ *These men have committed violent crimes. Estos hombres cometieron crímenes violentos.* ❑ *...violent anti-government demonstrations. ...violentas manifestaciones en contra del gobierno.* • **vio|lent|ly** ADV *violentamente* ❑ *Some politicians have been violently attacked. Algunos políticos han sido atacados violentamente.* **2** ADJ A **violent** event happens suddenly and with great force.

*violento* ❑ *A violent explosion shook the city. Una violenta explosión sacudió la ciudad.* • **vio|lent|ly** ADV *violentamente* ❑ *The volcano erupted violently. El volcán hizo erupción violentamente.* **3** ADJ If you describe something as **violent,** you mean that it is said, done, or felt very strongly. *violento, intenso, agudo* ❑ *He had violent stomach pains. Tenía agudos dolores estomacales.* • **vio|lent|ly** ADV *enérgicamente* ❑ *She protested violently. Protestó enérgicamente.*

**vio|let** /vaɪəlɪt/ **(violets)** **1** N-COUNT A **violet** is a small plant that has purple or white flowers in the spring. *violeta* **2** COLOR Something that is **violet** is a bluish-purple color. *violeta, violáceo, violado*
→ see **color, rainbow**

**vio|lin** /vaɪəlɪn/ **(violins)** N-VAR A **violin** is a musical instrument made of wood with four strings. You play the **violin** by holding it under your chin and moving a bow across the strings. *violín* ❑ *Lizzie plays the violin. Lizzie toca el violín.* • **vio|lin|ist** N-COUNT **(violinists)** *violinista* ❑ *Rose's father was a talented violinist. El padre de Rose fue un violinista talentoso.*
→ see **orchestra, string**

**VIP** /vi aɪ pi/ **(VIPs)** N-COUNT A **VIP** is someone who is given better treatment than ordinary people because they are famous, influential, or important. **VIP** is an abbreviation for "very important person." *persona muy importante* ❑ *...VIPs such as Prince Charles and Bill Clinton. ...personas muy importantes, como el príncipe Carlos y Bill Clinton.*

**vir|gin** /vɜrdʒɪn/ **(virgins)** **1** N-COUNT A **virgin** is someone who has never had sex. *virgen* • **vir|gin|ity** /vərdʒɪnɪti/ N-UNCOUNT *virginidad* ❑ *At American weddings, brides often wear white, the color of purity and virginity. En las bodas estadounidenses, las novias suelen vestir de blanco, el color de la pureza y la virginidad.* **2** ADJ You use **virgin** to describe something such as land that has never been used or spoiled. *virgen* ❑ *...virgin forest. ...bosque virgen.*

**vir|tual** /vɜrtʃuəl/ **1** ADJ You can use **virtual** to indicate that something is so nearly true that for most purposes it can be regarded as true. *virtual* ❑ *He was a virtual prisoner in his own home. Prácticamente, era un prisionero en su propia casa.* • **vir|tu|al|ly** /vɜrtʃuəli/ ADV *virtualmente, prácticamente* ❑ *She does virtually all the cooking. Ella hace prácticamente toda la comida.* **2** ADJ **Virtual** objects and activities are generated by a computer to simulate real objects and activities. *virtual* [COMPUTING] ❑ *...a virtual world of role playing. ...un mundo virtual de juegos de papeles.*

**vir|tual re|al|ity** N-UNCOUNT **Virtual reality** is an environment that is produced by a computer and seems very like reality to the person experiencing it. *realidad virtual* [COMPUTING]

**vir|tue** /vɜrtʃu/ **(virtues)** **1** N-UNCOUNT **Virtue** is thinking and doing what is right and avoiding what is wrong. *virtud* ❑ *The priests talked to us about virtue. Los párrocos nos hablaban sobre la virtud.* **2** N-COUNT A **virtue** is a good quality or way of behaving. *virtud* ❑ *His greatest virtue is patience. Su mayor virtud es la paciencia.* **3** N-COUNT The **virtue** of something is an advantage or benefit that it has, especially in comparison with something else. *ventaja* ❑ *The virtue of doing it this way is it's very quick and easy. La ventaja de hacerlo así es que es muy rápido y fácil.* **4** PHRASE You use **by virtue of** to explain why something happens or is true. *en virtud de* [FORMAL] ❑ *We have these rights by virtue of being human. Tenemos estos derechos en virtud de que somos seres humanos.*

**vir|tu|ous** /vɜrtʃuəs/ **1** ADJ A **virtuous** person behaves in a moral and correct way. *virtuoso* ❑ *...a courageous and virtuous man. ...un hombre valiente y virtuoso.* **2** ADJ If you describe someone as **virtuous,** you mean that they have done what they ought to do and feel very pleased with themselves, perhaps too pleased. *orgulloso* ❑ *I cleaned the apartment, which made me feel virtuous. Limpié el departamento y eso me hizo sentir muy orgulloso.* • **vir|tu|ous|ly** ADV *orgullosamente* ❑ *"I've already done that," said Ronnie virtuously. —Ya lo hice —dijo orgullosamente Ronnie.*

**vi|rus** /vaɪrəs/ **(viruses)** **1** N-COUNT A **virus** is a kind of germ that can cause disease. *virus* ❑ *There are many different strains of flu virus. Hay muchas variedades diferentes del virus de la gripe.* **2** N-COUNT In computer technology, a **virus** is a program that introduces itself into a system, altering or destroying the information stored in the system. *virus* [COMPUTING] ❑ *You should protect yourself against computer viruses. Debe protegerse contra los virus informáticos.*
→ see **illness**

**visa** /vizə/ **(visas)** N-COUNT A **visa** is an official document, or a stamp put in your passport, that allows you to enter or leave a particular country. *visa*

**vis|cos|ity** /vɪskɒsɪti/ N-UNCOUNT **Viscosity** is the quality that some liquids have of being thick and sticky. *viscosidad*

**Word Link** *vid, vis ≈ seeing : television, videotape, visible*

**vis|ible** /vɪzɪbᵊl/ **1** ADJ If something is **visible,** it can be seen. *visible* ❑ *The warning lights were clearly visible. Las luces de advertencia eran claramente visibles.* **2** ADJ You use **visible** to describe something or someone that people notice or recognize. *visible, evidente* ❑ *He made a visible effort to control his temper. Hizo un esfuerzo evidente por dominar su mal carácter.* • **vis|ibly** /vɪzɪbli/ ADV *visiblemente* ❑ *She was visibly upset. Estaba visiblemente molesta.*
→ see **wave**

**Word Partnership** Usar *visible* con:

N. visible **to the naked eye** **1**
ADV. **barely** visible, **clearly** visible, **highly** visible, **less** visible, **more** visible, **still** visible, **very** visible **1** **2**
V. **become** visible **1** **2**

**vi|sion** /vɪʒᵊn/ **(visions)** **1** N-COUNT Your **vision of** a future situation or society is what you imagine or hope it would be like if things were very different from the way they are now. *visión* ❑ *I have a vision of world peace. Me imagino que habrá paz en el mundo.* **2** N-UNCOUNT Your **vision** is your ability to see clearly with your eyes. *vista, visión* ❑ *He's suffering from loss of vision. Está perdiendo la vista.*

V

**Word Partnership** Usar *vision* con:

V. **have a** vision, **share a** vision 1
N. vision **of the future**, vision **of peace**, vision **of reality** 1
**color** vision, **field of** vision 2
ADJ. **clear** vision 1 2
**blurred** vision 2

**vis|it** /vɪzɪt/ (**visits, visiting, visited**) 1 V-T/V-I If you **visit** someone, you go to see them and spend time with them. visitar ❑ *He wanted to visit his brother.* *Quería visitar a su hermano.* ❑ *In the evenings, friends often visit.* *Los amigos suelen venir a visitarnos por la noche.* ● **Visit** is also a noun. visita ❑ *Helen recently paid him a visit.* *Helen le hizo una visita recientemente.* 2 V-T/V-I If you **visit** a place, you go there for a short time. visitar ❑ *He'll be visiting four cities including Cagliari.* *Va a visitar cuatro ciudades, entre ellas Cagliari.* ❑ *...a visiting family from Texas.* *...una familia de Texas que está de visita.* ● **Visit** is also a noun. visita ❑ *...the Queen's visit to Canada.* *...la visita de la reina a Canadá.*
▸ **visit with** PHR-VERB If you **visit with** someone, you go to see them and spend time talking with them. visitar ❑ *I visited with him in San Francisco.* *Fui a visitarlo a San Francisco.*

**Thesaurus** *visit* Ver también:

V. call on, go, see, stop by 1

**Word Partnership** Usar *visit* con:

N. visit **family/relatives**, visit **friends**, visit ***your* mother** 1
**weekend** visit 1 2
visit **a museum**, visit **a restaurant** 2
V. **come to** visit, **go to** visit, **invite *someone* to** visit, **plan to** visit 1 2
ADJ. **brief** visit, **last** visit, **next** visit, **recent** visit, **short** visit, **surprise** visit 1 2
**foreign** visit, **official** visit 2

**vis|ita|tion rights** /vɪzɪteɪʃ<sup></sup>ən raɪts/ N-PLURAL If a parent who is divorced and does not live with their child has **visitation rights,** they officially have the right to spend time with their child. derecho de visita ❑ *The divorce court did not give him any visitation rights.* *El tribunal familiar no le otorgó ningún derecho de visita.*

**vis|it|ing hours** N-PLURAL In an institution such as a hospital or prison, **visiting hours** are the times during which people from outside the institution are officially allowed to visit people who are staying at the institution. horario de visitas ❑ *Visiting hours are 3 to 7 p.m.* *El horario de visitas es de las tres a las siete de la tarde.*

**vis|it|ing pro|fes|sor** (**visiting professors**) N-COUNT A **visiting professor** is a professor at a college or university who is invited to teach at another college or university for a short period such as one term or one year. profesor visitante

**visi|tor** /vɪzɪtər/ (**visitors**) N-COUNT A **visitor** is someone who is visiting a person or place. visitante ❑ *We had some visitors from Milwaukee.* *Tuvimos unos visitantes de Milwakee.*

**vis|ual** /vɪʒuəl/ ADJ **Visual** means relating to sight, or to things that you can see. visual ❑ *...careers in the visual arts.* *...carreras en artes plásticas.* ● **visu|al|ly** ADV visualmente ❑ *The movie is visually spectacular.* *La película es espectacular en el plano visual.*

**Word Partnership** Usar *visual* con:

N. visual **arts**, visual **effects**, visual **information**, visual **memory**, visual **perception**

**visu|al|ize** /vɪʒuəlaɪz/ (**visualizes, visualizing, visualized**) V-T If you **visualize** something, you imagine what it is like by forming a mental picture of it. imaginar ❑ *Susan visualized her wedding day.* *Susan se imaginó el día de su boda.* ❑ *He could not visualize her as old.* *No podía imaginarla vieja.*

**vis|ual lit|era|cy** N-UNCOUNT **Visual literacy** is the ability to understand and interpret visual images. alfabetismo visual, comprensión visual [TECHNICAL]

**vis|ual meta|phor** (**visual metaphors**) N-VAR A **visual metaphor** is a way of describing something by referring to another thing that shares similar visual qualities to the thing being described. For example, a family tree is a visual metaphor for the history of a family. metáfora visual [TECHNICAL]

**vi|tal** /vaɪtəl/ ADJ If something is **vital,** it is necessary or very important. vital, esencial, fundamental ❑ *It is vital that children attend school regularly.* *Es fundamental que los niños asistan a la escuela regularmente.* ● **vi|tal|ly** ADV vitalmente ❑ *Lesley's job is vitally important to her.* *El empleo de Lesley es de vital importancia para ella.*

**Thesaurus** *vital* Ver también:

ADJ. crucial, essential, necessary; (*ant.*) unimportant

**Word Partnership** Usar *vital* con:

ADV. **absolutely** vital
N. vital **importance**, vital **information**, vital **interests**, vital **link**, vital **organs**, vital **part**, vital **role**

**vita|min** /vaɪtəmɪn/ (**vitamins**) N-COUNT **Vitamins** are substances in food that you need in order to remain healthy. vitamina ❑ *...problems caused by lack of vitamin D.* *...problemas causados por la falta de vitamina D.* ❑ *...vitamin pills.* *...píldoras vitamínicas.*

**Word Link** *viv ≈ living : revival, survive, vivid*

**viv|id** /vɪvɪd/ 1 ADJ If you describe memories and descriptions as **vivid,** you mean that they are very clear and detailed. vívido ❑ *It was a very vivid dream.* *Fue un sueño muy vívido.* ● **viv|id|ly** ADV vívidamente ❑ *I can vividly remember the first time I saw him.* *Puedo recordar vívidamente la primera vez que lo vi.* 2 ADJ Something that is **vivid** is very bright in color. vivo ❑ *...a vivid blue sky.* *...un cielo de un azul muy vivo.* ● **viv|id|ly** ADV vivamente ❑ *...vividly colored birds.* *...pájaros de colores muy vivos.*

V

**Word Link** *voc ≈ speaking : advocate, vocabulary, vocal*

**vo|cabu|lary** /voʊkæbyəlɛri/ (**vocabularies**) 1 N-VAR Your **vocabulary** is the total number of words you know in a particular language. *vocabulario* ❑ *He has a very wide vocabulary.* *Tiene un vocabulario muy extenso.* 2 N-SING The **vocabulary** of a language is all the words in it. *léxico, vocabulario* ❑ *...a new word in the German vocabulary.* *...una nueva palabra del léxico alemán.*
→ see **English**

**Word Partnership** Usar *vocabulary* con:

| | |
|---|---|
| N. | **part of** ***someone's*** vocabulary 1 |
| | vocabulary **development** 1 2 |
| V. | **learn** vocabulary 2 |

**vo|cal** /voʊkᵊl/ 1 ADJ You say that people are **vocal** when they speak forcefully about something that they feel strongly about. *enérgico* ❑ *Local people were very vocal in their opposition to the plan.* *La gente del lugar se mostró muy enérgica en su oposición al plan.* 2 ADJ **Vocal** means involving the use of the human voice, especially in singing. *vocal, vocálico* ❑ *...a range of vocal styles.* *...una gama de estilos de canto.*

**vo|cal|ist** /voʊkəlɪst/ (**vocalists**) N-COUNT A **vocalist** is a singer who sings with a group. *cantante, vocalista* ❑ *...the band's lead vocalist.* *...el principal vocalista de la banda.*

**vo|cal pro|jec|tion** N-UNCOUNT **Vocal projection** is the same as **projection**. *proyección vocal*

**vo|cal qual|ity** (**vocal qualities**) N-VAR A person's **vocal quality** is the way their voice sounds, for example whether it is deep or loud or high-pitched. *timbre vocálico*

**vo|cals** /voʊkᵊlz/ N-PLURAL In a pop song, the **vocals** are the singing, in contrast to the playing of instruments. *letra, voz* ❑ *Johnson sings backing vocals for Mica Paris.* *Johnson canta la segunda voz con Mica Paris.*

**vogue** /voʊg/ 1 N-SING If there is a **vogue for** something, it is very popular and fashionable. *moda* ❑ *...a vogue for herbal teas.* *...una moda de infusiones.* 2 PHRASE If something is **in vogue,** it is very popular and fashionable. If it comes **into vogue,** it becomes very popular and fashionable. *de moda* ❑ *Pale colors are in vogue.* *Los colores pálidos están de moda.*

**voice** /vɔɪs/ (**voices**) 1 N-COUNT When someone speaks or sings, you hear their **voice.** *voz* ❑ *She spoke in a soft voice.* *Habló con voz suave.* 2 N-COUNT Someone's **voice** is their opinion on a particular topic and what they say about it. *voz* ❑ *The government refuses to listen to the voice of the people.* *El gobierno se rehúsa a escuchar la voz del pueblo.* 3 V-T If you **voice** something such as an opinion or an emotion, you say what you think or feel. *expresar* ❑ *She voiced her opinion about what was going on.* *Expresó su opinión sobre lo que estaba pasando.* 4 N-SING In grammar, if a verb is in **the active voice,** the person who performs the action is the subject of the verb. If a verb is in **the passive voice,** the thing or person affected by the action is the subject of the verb. *voz activa/pasiva*

**void** /vɔɪd/ (**voids**) 1 N-COUNT If you describe a situation or a feeling as a **void,** you mean that it seems empty because there is nothing interesting or worthwhile about it. *vacío* ❑ *His death left a void in her life.* *Su muerte dejó un vacío en su vida.* 2 N-COUNT You can describe a large or frightening space as a **void.** *vacío* ❑ *He looked over the edge of the mountain into the void.* *Miró al vacío que se extendía más allá del borde de la montaña.* 3 ADJ Something that is **void** or **null and void** is officially considered to have no value or authority. *nulo, inválido* ❑ *The elections were declared void.* *Las elecciones fueron declaradas nulas.* 4 ADJ If you are **void of** something, you do not have any of it. *carente, desprovisto* [FORMAL] ❑ *His face was void of emotion.* *Su rostro no mostraba emoción alguna.*

**vola|tile** /vɒlətᵊl/ 1 ADJ A situation that is **volatile** is likely to change suddenly and unexpectedly. *volátil* ❑ *There have been riots and the situation is volatile.* *Ha habido disturbios y la situación es volátil.* 2 ADJ If someone is **volatile,** their mood often changes quickly. *voluble* ❑ *...a volatile, passionate man.* *...un hombre apasionado y voluble.*

**vol|ca|no** /vɒlkeɪnoʊ/ (**volcanoes**) N-COUNT A **volcano** is a mountain from which hot melted rock, gas, steam, and ash from inside the earth sometimes burst. *volcán* ❑ *The volcano erupted last year.* *El volcán hizo erupción el año pasado.*
→ see Word Web: **volcano**
→ see **rock**

**volley|ball** /vɒlibɔl/ N-UNCOUNT **Volleyball** is a game in which two teams hit a large ball with their hands back and forth over a high net. *voleibol, volibol*

**Word Web** volcano

The most famous **volcano** in the world is Mount Vesuvius, near Naples, Italy. This mountain sits in the middle of the much older **volcanic cone** of Mount Somma. In 79 AD the sleeping volcano **erupted**, and **magma** rose to the surface. The people of the nearby city of Pompeii were terrified. Huge black clouds of **ash** and pumice came rushing toward them. The clouds blocked out the sun and smothered thousands of people. Pompeii was buried under hot ash and **molten lava**. Centuries later the remains of the people and town were found. The discovery made this active volcano famous.

**Picture Dictionary** **volume**

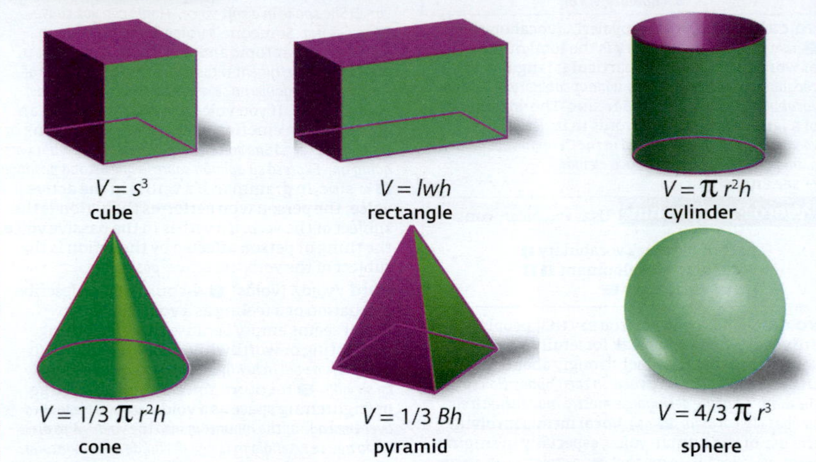


**volt** /voʊlt/ (**volts**) N-COUNT A **volt** is a unit used to measure the force of an electric current. *voltio*

**vol|ume** /vɒlyum/ (**volumes**) **1** N-COUNT The **volume of** something is the amount of it that there is. *volumen* ❑ *The volume of sales has increased. El volumen de ventas aumentó.* **2** N-COUNT The **volume** of an object is the amount of space that it contains or occupies. *volumen* ❑ *The volume of a cube with sides of length 3 cm is 27 cm. El volumen de un cubo de tres centímetros por lado es de 27 centímetros cúbicos.* **3** N-COUNT A **volume** is one book in a series of books. *volumen* ❑ *...the first volume of his autobiography. ...el primer volumen de su autobiograbía.* **4** N-UNCOUNT **The volume** of a radio, television, sound system, or someone's voice is the loudness of the sound it produces. *volumen* ❑ *He turned down the volume. Le bajó al volumen.*
→ see Picture Dictionary: **volume**

**vol|un|tary** /vɒlənteri/ **1** ADJ **Voluntary** actions or activities are done because someone chooses to do them and not because they have been forced to do them. *voluntario, opcional* ❑ *...classes where attendance is voluntary. ...clases opcionales.* ● **vol|un|tar|ily** /vɒləntɛərɪli/ ADV *voluntariamente* ❑ *I would never leave here voluntarily. Nunca me iría de aquí voluntariamente.* **2** ADJ **Voluntary** work is done by people who are not paid for it, but who do it because they want to do it. *voluntario* **3** ADJ A **voluntary** organization is controlled and organized by the people who have chosen to work for it, often without being paid. *de beneficencia* **4** ADJ **Voluntary** movements are movements of your body that you make because you choose to, rather than because they are automatic. *voluntario*
→ see **muscle**

**Word Partnership** Usar *voluntary* con:

Usar *voluntary* con:

N. voluntary **action**, voluntary **basis**, voluntary **compliance**, voluntary **contributions**, voluntary **program**, voluntary **retirement**, voluntary **test** **1**
voluntary **organizations** **3**

**vol|un|teer** /vɒləntɪər/ (**volunteers, volunteering, volunteered**) **1** N-COUNT A **volunteer** is someone who does work without being paid for it, because they want to do it. *voluntario o voluntaria* ❑ *She helps in a local school as a volunteer. Ayuda como voluntaria en una escuela del lugar.* **2** N-COUNT A **volunteer** is someone who offers to do a particular task or job without being forced to do it. *voluntario o voluntaria* ❑ *I need two volunteers to help me move these tables. Necesito dos voluntarios que me ayuden a mover estas mesas.* **3** V-I If you **volunteer** to do something, you offer to do it without being forced to do it. *ofrecerse, alistarse como voluntario* ❑ *Mary volunteered to clean up the kitchen. Mary se ofreció para limpiar la cocina.* ❑ *He volunteered for the army in 1939. Se alistó como voluntario en el ejército en 1939.* **4** V-T If you **volunteer** information, you tell someone something without being asked. *ofrecer información sin que sea solicitada* [FORMAL] ❑ *No one volunteered any information. Nadie ofreció ninguna información.* ❑ *"They were great friends," Ryle volunteered. —Eran grandes amigos—, dijo Ryle, sin que le preguntaran.* **5** N-COUNT A **volunteer** is someone who chooses to join the armed forces, especially during a war, as opposed to someone who is forced to join by law. *voluntario o voluntaria* ❑ *They fought as volunteers. Combatieron como voluntarios.*

**Word Partnership** Usar *volunteer* con:

N. **community** volunteer, **Red Cross** volunteer **1**
volunteer **organization**, volunteer **program**, volunteer **work** **1** **2**
volunteer **for the army**, volunteer **for service** **3**
volunteer **information** **4**

V. **need a** volunteer **1** **2** **5**
volunteer **to help**, volunteer **to work** **3**

**vom|it** /vɒmɪt/ (**vomits, vomiting, vomited**) **1** V-I If you **vomit,** food and drink comes back up from your stomach and out through your mouth. *vomitar* ❑ *Cow's milk made him vomit.* *La leche de vaca lo hacía vomitar.* **2** N-UNCOUNT **Vomit** is partly digested food and drink that comes out of your mouth when you vomit. *vómito*

**vote** /voʊt/ (**votes, voting, voted**) **1** N-COUNT A **vote** is a choice made by a particular person or group in a meeting or an election. *voto* ❑ *He went to the polling place to cast his vote.* *Fue a la casilla electoral a emitir su voto.* **2** N-SING **The vote** is the total number of votes or voters in an election, or the number of votes received or cast by a particular group. *votación* ❑ *The vote was in favour of the Democratic Party.* *La votación fue en favor del Partido Demócrata.* **3** N-SING If you have **the vote** in an election, or have **a vote** in a meeting, you have the legal right to indicate your choice. *derecho de voto* ❑ *At that time, women did not have a vote.* *En esa época, las mujeres no tenían el derecho de voto.* **4** V-T/V-I When you **vote,** you indicate your choice officially at a meeting or in an election, for example, by raising your hand or writing on a piece of paper. *votar* ❑ *Nearly everyone voted for Buchanan.* *Casi todos votaron por Buchanan.* ❑ *The workers voted to strike.* *Los trabajadores votaron por declarar la huelga.* ● **vot|ing** N-UNCOUNT *votación* ❑ *Voting began about two hours ago.* *La votación comenzó hace aproximadamente dos horas.* ● **vot|er** N-COUNT (**voters**) *votante* ❑ *...registered voters.* *...votantes registrados.*
→ see Word Web: **vote**
→ see **election**

**vouch|er** /vaʊtʃər/ (**vouchers**) N-COUNT A **voucher** is a ticket or piece of paper that can be used instead of money to pay for something. *vale* ❑ *...a voucher for two movie tickets.* *...un vale por dos boletos para el cine.*

**vow** /vaʊ/ (**vows, vowing, vowed**) **1** V-T If you **vow** to do something, you make a serious promise or decision that you will do it. *jurar* ❑ *She vowed to get her revenge.* *Juró vengarse.* ❑ *I vowed that someday I would go back to Europe.* *Juré que algún día volvería a Europa.* **2** N-COUNT A **vow** is a serious promise or decision to do a particular thing. *promesa solemne* ❑ *I made a vow to be more careful in the future.* *Hice la promesa solemne de que tendría más cuidado en el futuro.*

**vow|el** /vaʊəl/ (**vowels**) N-COUNT A **vowel** is a sound, such as the ones represented in writing by the letters **a, e, i, o** and **u**, that you pronounce with your mouth open, allowing the air to flow through it. *vocal*

**voy|age** /vɔɪɪdʒ/ (**voyages**) N-COUNT A **voyage** is a long journey on a ship or in a spacecraft. *viaje, travesía* ❑ *...Columbus's voyage to the West Indies.* *...la travesía de Colón a las Indias Occidentales.*

**vs.** **vs.** is a written abbreviation for **versus.** *contra* ❑ *We were watching the Yankees vs. the Red Sox.* *Estábamos viendo a los Yanquis contra los Medias Rojas.*

**vul|ner|able** /vʌlnərəbəl/ **1** ADJ Someone who is **vulnerable** is weak and without protection, with the result that they are easily hurt physically or emotionally. *vulnerable* ❑ *Older people are particularly vulnerable to colds and flu in cold weather.* *Los ancianos son particularmente vulnerables a los resfríos y la gripe en época de frío.* ● **vul|ner|abil|ity** /vʌlnərəbɪlɪti/ N-VAR (**vulnerabilities**) *vulnerabilidad* ❑ *...the vulnerability of children.* *...la vulnerabilidad de los niños.* **2** ADJ If someone or something is **vulnerable to** something, they have some weakness or disadvantage which makes them more likely to be harmed or affected by that thing. *vulnerable* ❑ *Children from 6 to 24 months are most vulnerable to the flu.* *Los niños de seis a 24 meses de edad son muy vulnerables a la gripe.* ● **vul|ner|abil|ity** N-UNCOUNT *vulnerabilidad* ❑ *...vulnerability to infection.* *...vulnerabilidad a las infecciones.*

**Word Partnership** Usar *vulnerable* con:

N. vulnerable **children/people/women** **1**

V. **feel** vulnerable **1**
**become** vulnerable, **remain** vulnerable **1** **2**

ADV. **especially** vulnerable, **extremely** vulnerable, **highly** vulnerable, **particularly** vulnerable, **so** vulnerable, **too** vulnerable, **very** vulnerable **1** **2**

**Word Web** vote

Today in almost all **democracies** any adult can **vote** for the **candidate** of his or her choice. But years ago women could not vote. Not until the suffrage movement revolutionized voting rights did women have the right to vote. In 1893, New Zealand became the first country to give women full voting rights. Women could finally enter a **polling place** and **cast** a **ballot**. Many countries soon followed. They included Canada, Finland, Germany, Sweden, and the U.S. However, China, France, India, Italy, and Japan didn't grant suffrage to women until the mid-1900s.

# Ww

**wage** /weɪdʒ/ (**wages, waging, waged**)
**1** N-COUNT Someone's **wages** are the amount of money that is regularly paid to them for the work that they do. salario ❑ *His wages have gone up.* Su salario aumentó. **2** V-T To **wage** a campaign or a war means to start it and continue it over a period of time. hacer ❑ *New York City officials waged a campaign to host the Olympics.* Los funcionarios de Nueva York hicieron una campaña para lograr que la ciudad sea anfitriona de los Juegos Olímpicos.
→ see **factory, union**

| Thesaurus | *wage* | Ver también: |
|---|---|---|
| N. | earnings, pay, salary **1** | |

| Word Partnership | Usar *wage* con: |
|---|---|
| ADJ. | **average** wage, **high/higher** wage, **hourly** wage, **low/lower** wage **1** |
| V. | **offer a** wage, **pay a** wage, **raise a** wage **1** |
| N. | wage **cuts**, wage **earners**, wage **increases**, wage **rates** **1** |
| | wage **a campaign**, wage **war** **2** |

**wag|on** /wægən/ (**wagons**) N-COUNT A **wagon** is a strong vehicle with four wheels, usually pulled by horses or oxen and used for carrying heavy loads. carro, carromato, carreta
→ see **train**

**waist** /weɪst/ (**waists**) **1** N-COUNT Your **waist** is the middle part of your body where it narrows slightly above your hips. cintura ❑ *Ricky put his arm around her waist.* Ricky la enlazó por la cintura. **2** N-COUNT The **waist** of a dress, coat, or pair of pants is the part of it which covers the middle part of your body. cintura ❑ *The waist of these pants is a little tight.* Estos pantalones me aprietan un poco en la cintura.
→ see **body**

**wait** /weɪt/ (**wait, waiting, waited**) **1** V-T/V-I When you **wait** for something or someone, you spend some time doing very little, before something happens or someone arrives. aguardar, esperar ❑ *I walked to the street corner and waited for the school bus.* Caminé hasta la esquina y esperé el autobús escolar. ❑ *I waited to hear what she said.* Aguardé para oír lo que decía. ❑ *We had to wait a week before we got the results.* Tuvimos que esperar una semana antes de tener los resultados. ● **wait|ing** ADJ que espera ❑ *She walked toward the waiting car.* Caminó hacia el auto que la esperaba. **2** N-COUNT A **wait** is a period of time in which you do very little, before something happens. espera ❑ *There was a four-hour wait at the airport.* Hubo una espera de cuatro horas en el aeropuerto. **3** V-T/V-I If something **is waiting for** you, it is ready for you to use, have, or do. aguardar, esperar ❑ *There'll be a car waiting for you.* La estará esperando un automóvil. ❑ *When we came home we had a meal waiting for us.* Cuando llegamos a casa, la comida ya estaba lista. **4** V-I If you say that something can **wait,** you mean that it is not important or urgent and so you will deal with it or do it later. esperar ❑ *I want to talk to you, but it can wait.* Quiero hablar contigo, pero no hay prisa. **5** V-T **Wait** is used in expressions such as **wait a minute, wait a second,** and **wait a moment** to interrupt someone when they are speaking, for example, because you object to what they are saying or because you want them to repeat something. esperar [SPOKEN] ❑ *"Wait a minute!" he interrupted. "This isn't fair!"* —¡Espérate! —interrumpió—, ¡no es justo! **6** PHRASE If you say that you **can't wait** to do something or **can hardly wait** to do it, you are emphasizing that you are very excited about it and eager to do it. no ver la hora de [SPOKEN] ❑ *We can't wait to get started.* No vemos la hora de empezar.
▸ **wait around** PHR-VERB If you **wait around,** you stay in the same place, usually doing very little, because you cannot act before something happens or before someone arrives. esperar a, esperar para ❑ *I'm tired of waiting around for her to call me.* Ya me cansé de esperar a que me llame. ❑ *I waited around to speak to the doctor.* Esperé para hablar con el médico.

| Thesaurus | *wait* | Ver también: |
|---|---|---|
| V. | anticipate, expect, hold on, stand by; (*ant.*) carry out, go ahead **1** | |
| N. | delay, halt, holdup, pause **2** | |

| Word Partnership | Usar *wait* con: |
|---|---|
| ADV. | wait **forever**, wait **here**, **just** wait, wait **outside**, wait **patiently** **1** |
| N. | wait **for an answer**, wait **days/hours**, wait **a long time**, wait ***your* turn** **1** |
| | wait **a minute**, wait **until tomorrow** **1** **4** |
| V. | **(can't) afford to** wait **1** |
| | **can/can't/couldn't** wait, **have to** wait, **will/won't/wouldn't** wait **1** **4** |
| | wait **to hear**, wait **to say** **1** **4** **6** |
| | **can't** wait, **can hardly** wait **6** |
| ADJ. | **worth the** wait **2** |

**wait|er** /weɪtər/ (**waiters**) N-COUNT A **waiter** is a man whose job is to serve food in a restaurant. mesero o mesera, camarero o camarera

**wait|ress** /weɪtrɪs/ (**waitresses**) N-COUNT A **waitress** is a woman whose job is to serve food in a restaurant. mesera, camarera

**wait|staff** /weɪtstæf/ N-COUNT **Waitstaff** are waiters or waitresses. meseros, camareros ❑ *The* *waitstaff are there when you need them.* *Los meseros están para atenderle.*

**Word Link** *wak ≈ being awake : awake, awaken, wake*

**wake** /weɪk/ (**wakes, waking, woke, woken** or **waked**) **1** V-T/V-I When you **wake** or when someone or something **wakes** you, you become conscious again after being asleep. *despertar(se)* ❑ *It was cold and dark when I woke at 6:30.* *Cuando me desperté a las seis y media, estaba oscuro y frío.* ❑ *She went upstairs to wake Milton.* *Subió a despertar a Milton.* ● **Wake up** means the same as **wake**. *despertar(se)* ❑ *One morning I woke up and felt something was wrong.* *Una mañana desperté y sentí que algo andaba mal.* **2** N-COUNT The **wake** of a boat or other object moving in the water is the track of waves it makes behind it as it moves through the water. *estela* ❑ *The wake of the boats washed against the shore.* *La estela de los botes llegaba a la orilla.* **3** N-COUNT A **wake** is a gathering or social event that is held before a funeral. *velorio* **4** PHRASE If one thing follows **in the wake of** another, it happens after the other thing is over, often as a result of it. *secuela, resultado* ❑ *There are more police on the streets in the wake of last week's attack.* *Hay más policías en las calles como secuela del ataque de la semana pasada.*

**Word Partnership** Usar *wake* con:

PREP. wake **up during the night**, wake **up in the middle of the night**, wake **up in the morning** **1**
ADV. wake ***(someone)*** **up** **1**

**walk** /wɔk/ (**walks, walking, walked**) **1** V-T/V-I When you **walk**, you move forward by putting one foot in front of the other in a regular way. *caminar* ❑ *Rosanna and Forbes walked in silence.* *Rosanna y Forbes caminaron en silencio.* ❑ *We walked into the hall.* *Entramos al salón.* ❑ *I walked a few steps toward the fence.* *Di unos pasos hacia la cerca.* **2** N-COUNT A **walk** is a trip that you make by walking, usually for pleasure. *paseo, caminata* ❑ *I went for a walk.* *Fui a dar un paseo.* **3** N-SING A **walk** of a particular distance is the distance that a person has to walk to get somewhere. *caminata* ❑ *It was only a short walk from there.* *No estaba lejos, se podía ir caminando.* **4** N-SING **A walk** is the action of walking rather than running. *paso, marcha* ❑ *She slowed to a steady walk.* *Aminoró la marcha hasta adoptar un paso regular.* **5** V-T If you **walk** someone somewhere, you walk there with them. *escoltar, acompañar* ❑ *She walked me to my car.* *Me acompañó hasta mi coche.*
▶ **walk off with** PHR-VERB If you **walk off with** something such as a prize, you win it or get it very easily. *llevarse* ❑ *We'd like to see him walk off with the big prize.* *Nos gustaría ver que se llevara el primer premio.*
▶ **walk out** **1** PHR-VERB If you **walk out of** a meeting, a performance, or an unpleasant situation, you leave it suddenly, usually to show that you are angry or bored. *abandonar* ❑ *Several people walked out of the meeting in protest.* *Varias personas abandonaron la reunión en señal de protesta.* ● **walk|out** /wɔkaʊt/ N-COUNT (**walkouts**) *suspensión, paro* ❑ *Hundreds of students held a walkout Thursday.* *Cientos de estudiantes suspendieron las clases el jueves en señal de protesta.* **2** PHR-VERB If someone **walks out on** their family or their partner, they leave them suddenly and go to live somewhere else. *abandonar* ❑ *Her husband walked out on her.* *Su esposo la abandonó.* **3** PHR-VERB If workers **walk out,** they stop doing their work for a period of time, usually in order to try to get better pay or conditions for themselves. *paro de labores* ❑ *Union workers walked out last Thursday.* *Los trabajadores sindicalizados pararon labores el jueves.* ● **walk|out** N-COUNT (**walkouts**) *paro de labores* ❑ *Union leaders are calling for a walkout.* *Los dirigentes del sindicato están convocando a un paro de labores.*

**Thesaurus** *walk* Ver también:

V. amble, hike, stroll **1**
N. hike, march, parade, stroll **1** **2**

**Word Partnership** Usar *walk* con:

ADV. walk **alone**, walk **away**, walk **back**, walk **home**, walk **slowly** **1**
V. **begin to** walk, **start to** walk **1**
**go for a** walk, **take a** walk **2** **3**
ADJ. **(un)able to** walk **1**
**brisk** walk, **long** walk, **short** walk **2** – **4**

**wall** /wɔl/ (**walls**) **1** N-COUNT A **wall** is one of the vertical sides of a building or room. *muro, pared* ❑ *...the bedroom walls.* *...las paredes de la recámara.* **2** N-COUNT A **wall** is a long narrow vertical structure made of stone or brick that surrounds or divides an area of land. *muro, muralla* ❑ *He sat on the wall in the sun.* *Se sentó al sol en el muro.* **3** N-COUNT The **wall** of something hollow is its side. *pared* ❑ *...the stomach wall.* *...la pared del estómago.*

**Word Partnership** Usar *wall* con:

PREP. **against a** wall, **along a** wall, **behind a** wall, **near a** wall, **on a** wall **1** **2**
N. **back to the** wall, **brick** wall, **concrete** wall, **glass** wall, **stone** wall **1** **2**
V. **build a** wall, **climb a** wall, **lean against/on a** wall **1** **2**

**wall cloud** (**wall clouds**) N-COUNT A **wall cloud** is an area of cloud that extends beneath a thunderstorm and sometimes develops into a tornado. *muralla de nubes* [TECHNICAL]

**wal|let** /wɒlɪt/ (**wallets**) N-COUNT A **wallet** is a small, flat folded case, usually made of leather or plastic, in which you can keep money and credit cards. *cartera, billetera*

**wall|paper** /wɔlpeɪpər/ (**wallpapers, wallpapering, wallpapered**) **1** N-VAR **Wallpaper** is thick colored or patterned paper that is used for covering and decorating the walls of rooms. *papel tapiz* **2** V-T If someone **wallpapers** a room, they cover the walls with wallpaper. *empapelar* **3** N-UNCOUNT **Wallpaper** is the background on a computer screen. *imagen de fondo, papel tapiz* [COMPUTING]

**wal|nut** /wɔlnʌt, -nət/ (**walnuts**) N-VAR **Walnuts** are edible nuts that have a wrinkled shape and a hard round shell that is light brown in color. *nuez, nuez de Castilla*

**wan|der** /wɒndər/ (**wanders, wandering, wandered**) **1** V-T/V-I If you **wander** in a place, you walk around there in a casual way, often without intending to go in any particular direction. *deambular, vagar, pasear* ❑ *When he got bored he wandered around the park. Cuando se aburrió, se fue a pasear al parque.* ❑ *People wandered the streets. La gente deambulaba por las calles.* ● **Wander** is also a noun. *paseo* ❑ *A wander around the garden is a relaxing experience. Un paseo por el jardín es una experiencia relajante.* **2** V-I If a person or animal **wanders** from a place where they are supposed to stay, they move away from the place without going in a particular direction. *alejarse* ❑ *We aren't allowed to wander far. No nos está permitido alejarnos mucho.* **3** V-I If your mind **wanders** or your thoughts **wander,** you stop concentrating on something and start thinking about other things. *dejar vagar la imaginación, distraerse, divagar* ❑ *His mind was starting to wander. Estaba empezando a divagar.*

**want** /wɒnt/ (**wants, wanting, wanted**) **1** V-T If you **want** something, you feel a desire or a need for it. *querer* ❑ *I want a drink. Quiero beber algo.* ❑ *People wanted to know who she was. La gente quería saber quién era.* ❑ *They wanted their father to be the same as other dads. Querían que su padre fuese como otros padres.* ❑ *They didn't want people staring at them. No querían que la gente se les quedara mirando.* **2** V-T If you tell someone that they **want to** do a particular thing, you are advising them to do it. *deber* [INFORMAL] ❑ *You want to be very careful what you say. Debes tener mucho cuidado con lo que dices.* **3** V-T If someone **is wanted** by the police, the police are searching for them because they are thought to have committed a crime. *buscar* ❑ *He was wanted for the murder of a judge. Lo buscaban por el asesinato de un juez.* ● **want|ed** ADJ *buscado* ❑ *He is one of the most wanted criminals in Europe. Es uno de los criminales más buscados de Europa.* **4** PHRASE If you do something **for want of** something else, you do it because the other thing is not available or not possible. *a falta de, por falta de* ❑ *When he failed it was not for want of trying. Si fracasó, no fue por falta de ganas.*

| Thesaurus | *want* | Ver también: |
|---|---|---|
| V. | covet, desire, long, need, require, wish **1** | |

**want ad** (**want ads**) N-COUNT The **want ads** in a newspaper or magazine are small advertisements, usually offering things for sale or offering jobs. *anuncio clasificado* ❑ *I saw the address in a want ad. Vi la dirección en un anuncio clasificado.*

**war** /wɔr/ (**wars**) **1** N-VAR A **war** is a period of fighting or conflict between countries. *guerra* ❑ *He spent part of the war in France. Pasó parte de la guerra en Francia.* **2** N-VAR **War** is intense economic competition between countries or organizations. *guerra* ❑ *...a trade war. ...una guerra comercial.* **3** → see also **civil war**
→ see Word Web: **war**
→ see **army, history**

**ward** /wɔrd/ (**wards, warding, warded**) N-COUNT A **ward** is a room in a hospital which has beds for many people, often people who need similar treatment. *sala* ❑ *They took her to the children's ward. La llevaron a la sala de pediatría.*
→ see **hospital**
▸ **ward off** PHR-VERB To **ward off** a danger or illness means to prevent it from affecting you or harming you. *proteger(se)* ❑ *We needed warm coats to ward off the winter cold. Necesitábamos abrigos para protegernos del frío invernal.*

**ward|robe** /wɔrdroʊb/ (**wardrobes**) **1** N-COUNT Someone's **wardrobe** is the total collection of clothes that they have. *guardarropa, vestuario* ❑ *He had no time to think about his wardrobe. No tenía tiempo de pensar en su guardarropa.* **2** N-COUNT A **wardrobe** is a tall closet or cabinet in which you can hang your clothes. *armario, ropero* ❑ *She shut the wardrobe door. Cerró la puerta del ropero.*

**Word Link** *ware ≈ merchandise : hardware, software, warehouse*

**ware|house** /wɛərhaʊs/ (**warehouses**) N-COUNT A **warehouse** is a large building where raw materials or manufactured goods are stored. *depósito, bodega, almacén*

**war|fare** /wɔrfɛər/ N-UNCOUNT **Warfare** is

**Word Web** war

The Hague Conventions* and the Geneva Convention* are rules for **war**. They try to make war more humane. First, they say countries should avoid **armed conflict**. They suggest a **neutral mediator** or a 30-day "time out." A country must **declare** war before **combat** can begin. Sneak **attacks** are forbidden. The rules for **firearms** use are quite simple. One rule states it is illegal to **kill** or **injure** a person who **surrenders**. **Wounded soldiers**, **prisoners**, and **civilians** must get medical care immediately. And countries must not use **biological** and **chemical weapons**.

*Hague Conventions: agreements between many nations on rules to limit warfare and weapons.*
*Geneva Convention: an agreement between most nations on treatment of prisoners of war and the sick, injured, or dead.*

W

the activity of fighting a war. *guerra, contienda, conflicto* ❑ *...desert warfare. ...guerra del desierto.*

**warm** /wɔrm/ (**warmer, warmest, warms, warming, warmed**) **1** ADJ Something that is **warm** has some heat but not enough to be hot. *tibio, templado* ❑ *...places which have cold winters and warm, dry summers. ...lugares en que los inviernos son fríos y los veranos templados y secos.* ❑ *Because it was warm, David wore only a white cotton shirt. Como el tiempo era templado, David se puso únicamente una camisa blanca de algodón.* **2** ADJ **Warm** clothes and blankets are made of a material such as wool that protects you from the cold. *caliente* ● **warm|ly** ADV *calurosamente* ❑ *Remember to dress warmly on cold days. Recuerda abrigarte bien cuando haga frío.* **3** ADJ **Warm** colors have red or yellow in them rather than blue or green, and make you feel comfortable and relaxed. *cálido* **4** ADJ A **warm** person is friendly and shows a lot of affection or enthusiasm in their behavior. *cariñoso, afectuoso* ❑ *She was a warm and loving mother. Era una madre cálida y amorosa.* ● **warm|ly** ADV *cariñosamente, afectuosamente, calurosamente* ❑ *We warmly welcome new members. Damos una bienvenida afectuosa a los nuevos miembros.* **5** V-T If you **warm** a part of your body or if something hot **warms** it, it stops feeling cold and starts to feel hotter. *calentar* ❑ *The sun warmed his back. El sol le calentó la espalda.* **6** V-I If you **warm to** a person or an idea, you become fonder of the person or more interested in the idea. *simpatizar* ❑ *Those who got to know him warmed to him. Aquellos que llegaron a conocerlo simpatizaron con él.*

▸ **warm up** **1** PHR-VERB If you **warm** something **up** or if it **warms up,** it gets hotter. *calentar* ❑ *He blew on his hands to warm them up. Se sopló las manos para calentárselas.* ❑ *She warmed up the pie. Calentó el pastel.* **2** PHR-VERB If you **warm up** for an event such as a race, you prepare yourself for it by doing exercises or by practicing just before it starts. *calentar(se), prepararse* ❑ *In an hour the drivers will be warming up for the main event. Dentro de una hora, los pilotos estarán calentando para la prueba principal.* ● **warm-up** N-COUNT (**warm-ups**) *ejercicio de calentamiento, calentamiento* ❑ *These exercises are a good warm-up. Estos ejercicios son un buen calentamiento.* **3** PHR-VERB When a machine or engine **warms up** or someone **warms** it **up,** it becomes ready for use a little while after being switched on or started. *calentarse* ❑ *He waited for his car to warm up. Aguardó a que su coche se calentara.*

| **Word Partnership** | Usar *warm* con: |
|---|---|
| N. | warm **air**, warm **bath**, warm **breeze**, warm **hands**, warm **water**, warm **weather** 1 |
| | warm **clothes** 2 |
| | warm **smile**, warm **welcome** 4 |
| ADJ. | warm **and sunny** 1 |
| | warm **and cozy**, warm **and dry** 1 2 |
| | **soft and** warm 2 |
| | warm **and friendly** 4 |

**warm-blooded** ADJ A **warm-blooded** animal, such as a bird or a mammal, has a fairly high body temperature that does not change much and is not affected by the surrounding temperature. *de sangre caliente*

→ see **mammal, whale**

**warmth** /wɔrmθ/ **1** N-UNCOUNT The **warmth** of something is the heat that it has or produces. *calor* ❑ *...the warmth of the fire. ...el calor del fuego.* **2** N-UNCOUNT The **warmth** of something such as clothing or a blanket is the protection that it gives you against the cold. *calor* ❑ *The blanket will provide additional warmth and comfort in bed. Con la manta se está más abrigado y cómodo en la cama.*

**warn** /wɔrn/ (**warns, warning, warned**) **1** V-T/V-I If you **warn** someone about something such as a possible danger or problem, you tell them about it so that they are aware of it. *advertir* ❑ *The doctor warned her that too much sugar was bad for her health. El médico le advirtió que el exceso de azúcar era dañino para su salud.* ❑ *They warned him of the dangers of sailing alone. Le advirtieron sobre los peligros de navegar solo.* **2** V-T/V-I If you **warn** someone not to do something, you advise them not to do it so that they can avoid possible danger or punishment. *advertir* ❑ *Mrs. Blount warned me not to interfere. La señora Blount me advirtió que no interfiriera.* ❑ *"Don't do anything yet," he warned. —¡Todavía no hagas nada! —le advirtió.*

| **Thesaurus** | *warn* | Ver también: |
|---|---|---|
| V. | alert, caution, notify 1 2 | |

**Word Link** *war* ≈ *watchful* : *aware, beware, warning*

**warn|ing** /wɔrnɪŋ/ (**warnings**) N-VAR A **warning** is something said or written to tell people of a possible danger, problem, or other unpleasant thing that might happen. *advertencia, aviso* ❑ *It was a warning that we should be careful. Era un aviso de que debíamos tener cuidado.* ❑ *Suddenly and without warning, a car crash changed her life forever. Repentinamente y sin aviso previo, un accidente automovilístico cambió su vida para siempre.*

| **Word Partnership** | Usar *warning* con: |
|---|---|
| ADJ. | **advance** warning, **early** warning, **stern** warning |
| N. | warning **of danger**, **hurricane** warning, warning **labels**, warning **signs**, **storm** warning |
| V. | **give (a)** warning, **ignore a** warning, **receive (a)** warning, **send a** warning |

**war|rant** /wɔrənt/ (**warrants, warranting, warranted**) **1** V-T If something **warrants** a particular action, it makes the action seem necessary or appropriate. *justificar* ❑ *Her illness was serious enough to warrant being in the hospital. La gravedad de su enfermedad justificaba la hospitalización.* **2** N-COUNT A **warrant** is a legal document that allows someone to do something, especially one that gives the police permission to arrest someone or search their house. *orden* ❑ *Police issued a warrant for his arrest. La policía expidió una orden de arresto en su contra.*

**war|ri|or** /wɔriər/ (**warriors**) N-COUNT A **warrior** is a fighter or soldier, especially one in former times who was very brave and experienced in fighting. *guerrero, guerrera* ❑ *...the great warriors* *of the past.* *...los grandes guerreros del pasado.*

**war|ship** /wɔrʃɪp/ (**warships**) N-COUNT A **warship** is a ship with guns that is used for fighting in wars. *buque de guerra*
→ see **ship**

**war|time** /wɔrtaɪm/ N-UNCOUNT **Wartime** is a period of time when a war is being fought. *tiempo de guerra, de la guerra* ❑ *He served his country during wartime. Sirvió a su país durante la guerra.*

**wary** /wɛəri/ (**warier, wariest**) ADJ If you are **wary of** something or someone, you are cautious because you do not know much about them and you believe they may be dangerous or cause problems. *cauteloso, precavido* ❑ *People teach their children to be wary of strangers. La gente enseña a sus hijos a desconfiar de los extraños.* ● **wari|ly** /wɛərɪli/ ADV *cautelosamente* ❑ *She studied me warily, as if I might become violent. Me estudió cautelosamente, como si pudiera volverme violento.*

**was** /wəz, STRONG wʌz, wɒz/ **Was** is the first and third person singular of the past tense of **be**. *primera y tercera persona singular del pasado de **be***

**wash** /wɒʃ/ (**washes, washing, washed**) **1** V-T If you **wash** something, you clean it using water and usually a substance such as soap or detergent. *lavar* ❑ *She finished her dinner and washed the dishes. Terminó de cenar y lavó los platos.* ❑ *It took a long time to wash the dirt out of his hair. Le llevó mucho tiempo quitarse la mugre del pelo.* **2** V-T/V-I If you **wash**, or if you **wash** part of your body, especially your hands and face, you clean part of your body using soap and water. *lavar(se)* ❑ *They look as if they haven't washed in days. Parece que no se han bañado en días.* ❑ *She washed her face with cold water. Se lavó la cara con agua fría.* **3** V-T/V-I If a sea or river **washes** somewhere, it flows there gently. You can also say that something carried by a sea or river **washes** or **is washed** somewhere. *bañar* ❑ *The sea washed against the shore. El mar bañaba la orilla.* **4** PHRASE If something such as an item of clothing **is in the wash**, it is being washed, is waiting to be washed, or has just been washed and should therefore not be worn or used. *estar algo sucio, lavándose o recién lavado* [INFORMAL] ❑ *Your jeans are in the wash. Tus jeans se están lavando.* **5** to **wash** your **hands of** something → see **hand**
→ see **soap**

▶ **wash away** PHR-VERB If rain or floods **wash away** something, they destroy it and carry it away. *arrasar, llevarse* ❑ *Flood waters washed away one of the bridges. La crecida se llevó uno de los puentes.*

▶ **wash down** PHR-VERB If you **wash** something, especially food, **down** with a drink, you drink the drink after eating the food, especially to make the food easier to swallow or digest. *acompañar la comida con un líquido* ❑ *...a sandwich washed down with a bottle of lemonade. ...un sándwich y una botella de limonada.*

**W**

▶ **wash up** **1** PHR-VERB If you **wash up**, you clean part of your body with soap and water, especially your hands and face. *lavarse* ❑ *He went to the bathroom to wash up. Fue al cuarto de baño a lavarse.* **2** PHR-VERB If something **is washed up** on a piece of land, it is carried by a river or sea and left there. *ser traído, llevado o arrastrado por la corriente* ❑ *Thousands of fish were washed up on the beach during the storm. La corriente arrastró miles de peces hasta la playa durante la tormenta.*

**Thesaurus** *wash* Ver también:

| | |
|---|---|
| V. | clean, rinse, scrub **1** |
| | clean, bathe, soap **2** |

**Word Partnership** Usar *wash* con:

| | |
|---|---|
| N. | wash **a car**, wash **clothes**, wash **dishes** **1** |
| | wash ***your* face/hair/hands** **2** |

**wash|cloth** /wɒʃklɔθ/ (**washcloths**) N-COUNT A **washcloth** is a small cloth that you use for washing yourself. *toallita para lavarse, paño para lavarse*
→ see **bathroom**

**wash|er** /wɒʃər/ (**washers**) **1** N-COUNT A **washer** is a thin flat ring of metal or rubber that is placed over a bolt before the nut is screwed on. *arandela, rondana, roldana* **2** N-COUNT A **washer** is the same as a **washing machine**. *lavadora* [INFORMAL]

**wasn't** /wʌzᵊnt, wɒz-/ **Wasn't** is the usual spoken form of "was not." *forma hablada usual de **was not***

**waste** /weɪst/ (**wastes, wasting, wasted**) **1** V-T If you **waste** something such as time, money, or energy, you use too much of it doing something that is not important or necessary, or is unlikely to succeed. *desperdiciar, perder, gastar* ❑ *She didn't want to waste time looking at old cars. No quería perder el tiempo viendo coches viejos.* ❑ *I decided not to waste money on a hotel. Decidí no gastar dinero en un hotel.* ● **Waste** is also a noun. *desperdicio, pérdida* ❑ *It is a waste of time complaining about it. Quejarse por eso es una pérdida de tiempo.* **2** N-UNCOUNT **Waste** is material that has been used and is no longer wanted, for example, because the valuable or useful part of it has been taken out. *desecho* ❑ *Waste materials such as paper and aluminum cans can be recycled. Los materiales de desecho como el papel y las latas de aluminio se pueden reciclar.* **3** V-T If you **waste** an opportunity for something, you do not take advantage of it when it is available. *desperdiciar* ❑ *Let's not waste this opportunity. No desperdiciemos esta oportunidad.*
→ see **dump**

▶ **waste away** PHR-VERB If someone **wastes away**, they become extremely thin or weak because they are ill or worried and they are not eating properly. *consumirse* ❑ *She began to waste away. Cada vez estaba más demacrada.*

**Thesaurus** *waste* Ver también:

| | |
|---|---|
| V. | misuse, squander **1** |
| N. | garbage, junk, trash **2** |

**Word Partnership** Usar *waste* con:

| | |
|---|---|
| N. | waste **energy**, waste **money**, waste **time**, waste **water** **1** |
| V. | **reduce** waste **1** **2** |
| | **recycle** waste **2** |
| ADJ. | **hazardous** waste, **human** waste, **industrial** waste, **nuclear** waste, **toxic** waste **2** |

**waste|basket** /weɪstbæskɪt/ (**wastebaskets**) N-COUNT A **wastebasket** is a container for trash, especially paper. cesto de papeles, papelera, basurero

**watch**
1 LOOKING AND PAYING ATTENTION
2 INSTRUMENT THAT TELLS THE TIME

1 **watch** /wɒtʃ/ (**watches, watching, watched**) 1 V-T/V-I If you **watch** someone or something, you look at them, usually for a period of time, and pay attention to what is happening. observar, mirar ❑ *A man stood in the doorway, watching him.* *Había un hombre en la entrada, observándolo.* ❑ *He seems to enjoy watching me work.* *Parece que disfruta viéndome trabajar.* ❑ *Watch how I do this, OK?* —*Fíjate cómo hago esto, ¿sí?* 2 V-T If you **watch** something on television or an event such as a sports contest, you spend time looking at it, especially when you see it from the beginning to the end. ver ❑ *I stayed up late to watch the movie.* *Me quedé hasta tarde para ver la película.* 3 V-T/V-I If you **watch** a situation or event, you pay attention to it or you are aware of it, but you do not influence it. observar ❑ *Human rights groups are closely watching the situation.* *Los grupos pro derechos humanos están observando de cerca la situación.* 4 V-T If you tell someone to **watch** a particular person or thing, you are warning them to be careful that the person or thing does not get out of control or do something unpleasant. tener cuidado ❑ *You really have to watch him.* *De veras tienes que cuidarte de él.* 5 PHRASE If someone **keeps watch**, they look and listen all the time, while other people are asleep or doing something else, so that they can warn them of danger or an attack. hacer guardia ❑ *Josh climbed a tree to keep watch.* *Josh se trepó a un árbol para hacer guardia.* 6 N-COUNT A hurricane **watch** or a storm **watch** is an official announcement that severe weather conditions may soon develop in a particular area. alerta 7 PHRASE If you **keep watch** on events or a situation, you pay attention to what is happening, so that you can take action at the right moment. vigilar ❑ *U.S. officials are keeping watch on the situation.* *Los funcionarios estadounidenses están vigilando la situación.* 8 PHRASE You say "**watch it**" in order to warn someone to be careful, especially when you want to threaten them about what will happen if they are not careful. tener cuidado ❑ *"Now watch it, Patsy," said John.* —*¡Ten cuidado, Patsy!* —*le dijo John.*

▸ **watch for** or **watch out for** PHR-VERB If you **watch for** something or **watch out for** it, you pay attention so that you notice it, either because you do not want to miss it or because you want to avoid it. estar atento a ❑ *We'll be watching for any developments.* *Estaremos atentos a todo lo que pase.*

▸ **watch out** PHR-VERB If you tell someone to **watch out**, you are warning them to be careful, because something unpleasant might happen to them or they might get into difficulties. tener cuidado ❑ *You have to watch out because this is a dangerous city.* *Se debe tener cuidado, porque esta ciudad es peligrosa.*

▸ **watch out for** → see **watch for**

**Usage** **look, see,** and **watch**

If you *look* at something, you purposely direct your eyes at it: *Daniel kept turning around to look at the big-screen TV—he had never seen one before.* If you *see* something, it is visible to you: *Maria couldn't see the TV because Hector was standing in front of her and watching it.* If you *watch* something, you pay attention to it and keep it in sight: *Everyone was watching TV instead of looking at the photo album.*

**Word Partnership** Usar *watch* con:

ADV. watch **carefully**, watch **closely** 1 1 3 4
N. watch **a DVD**, watch **a film/movie**, watch **fireworks**, watch **a game**, watch **the news**, watch **people**, watch **television/TV**, watch **a video** 1 2
watch **children** 1 4
V. **check** ***your*** watch, **glance at** ***your*** watch, **look at** ***your*** watch 2

2 **watch** /wɒtʃ/ (**watches**) N-COUNT A **watch** is a small clock that you wear on a strap on your wrist, or on a chain. reloj de pulsera, reloj de pulso, reloj de bolsillo
→ see **jewelry**

**wa|ter** /wɔtər/ (**waters, watering, watered**) 1 N-UNCOUNT **Water** is a clear thin liquid that has no color or taste when it is pure. It falls from clouds as rain. agua ❑ *Get me a glass of water, please.* *Tráigame un vaso de agua, por favor.* 2 N-PLURAL You use **waters** to refer to a large area of sea, especially the area of sea that is near to a country and that is regarded as belonging to it. aguas ❑ *The ship will remain outside Australian waters.* *El barco permanecerá fuera de aguas australianas.* 3 V-T If you **water** plants, you pour water over them in order to help them to grow. regar 4 V-I If your eyes **water**, tears build up in them because they are hurting or because you are upset. llenarse los ojos de lágrimas, llorar los ojos 5 V-I If you say that your mouth **is watering**, you mean that you can smell or see some nice food that makes you want to eat it. hacerse agua (la boca) ❑ *...cookies to make your mouth water.* *...galletas para hacerle agua la boca.*
→ see Word Web: **water**
→ see **biosphere, erosion, habitat, lake, photosynthesis**

▸ **water down** PHR-VERB If something such as a proposal, speech, or statement **is watered down**, it is made much weaker and less forceful, or is less likely to make people angry. diluir, suavizar, atenuar

**wa|ter cool|er** (**water coolers**) N-COUNT A **water cooler** is a machine that cools water for people to drink, usually in an office. enfriador de agua, bebedero (de agua refrigerada)

**wa|ter cy|cle** (**water cycles**) N-COUNT The **water cycle** is the continuous process in which water from the surface of the Earth evaporates to form clouds and then returns to the surface as rain or snow. ciclo del agua [TECHNICAL]

**wa|ter pow|er** also **waterpower** N-UNCOUNT **Water power** is the same as **hydropower**. energía

**Word Web** water

**Water** changes its form in the **hydrologic cycle**. The sun warms oceans, lakes, and rivers. Some water **evaporates**. Evaporation creates a gas called **water vapor**. Plants also give off water vapor through transpiration. Water vapor rises into the **atmosphere**. It hits cooler air and **condenses** into drops of water. These drops form **clouds**. When these drops get heavy enough, they begin to fall. They form different types of precipitation. Rain forms in warm air. Cold air creates **freezing rain**, **sleet**, and **snow**.

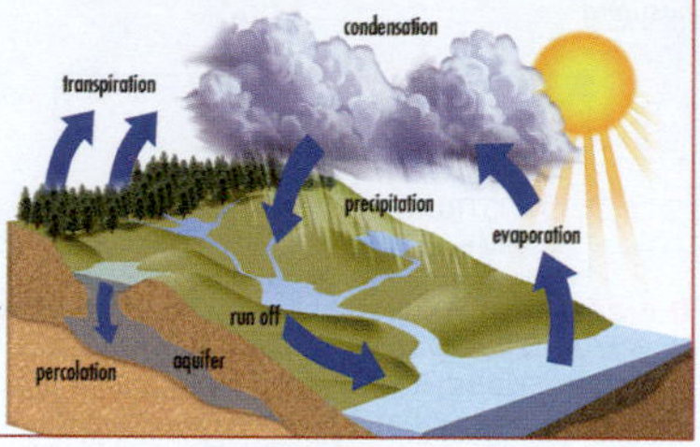


hidráulica, fuerza hidráulica, energía hidroeléctrica

**water|proof** /wɔtərpruf/ ADJ Something that is **waterproof** does not let water pass through it. *impermeable* ❑ *Take waterproof clothing—Oregon weather is unpredictable. Lleve ropa impermeable; el clima de Oregon es impredecible.*

**water|spout** /wɔtərspaʊt/ (**waterspouts**) N-COUNT A **waterspout** is a small tornado that occurs over water. *tromba marina, manga, torbellino*

**wa|ter ta|ble** (**water tables**) N-COUNT **The water table** is the level below the surface of the ground where water can be found. *nivel freático*

**wa|ter va|por** N-UNCOUNT **Water vapor** is water in the form of gas in the air. *vapor de agua*
→ see **greenhouse effect, precipitation, water**

**wa|ter vas|cu|lar sys|tem** (**water vascular systems**) N-COUNT The **water vascular system** is a network of water-filled tubes and pumps in the bodies of animals such as starfish, which helps them to move, eat, and breathe. *sistema acuovascular* [TECHNICAL]

**wa|ter wave** (**water waves**) N-COUNT A **water wave** is a wave that occurs in water, especially in the sea. *ola*

**waterwheel** /wɔtərwil/ (**waterwheels**) also **water wheel** N-COUNT A **waterwheel** is a large wheel that is turned by water flowing through it. Waterwheels are used to provide power to drive machinery. *rueda hidráulica, noria*
→ see **wheel**

**wave** /weɪv/ (**waves, waving, waved**) **1** V-T/V-I If you **wave** or **wave** your hand, you move your hand from side to side in the air, usually in order to say hello or goodbye to someone. *agitar, saludar* ❑ *Jessica saw Lois and waved to her. Jessica vio a Lois y la saludó con la mano.* ❑ *He smiled, waved, and said, "Hi!" Sonrió, saludó con la mano y dijo: "¡Hola!".* ● **Wave** is also a noun. *gesto* ❑ *Steve stopped him with a wave of the hand. Steve lo detuvo con un gesto de la mano.* **2** V-T If you **wave** someone away or **wave** them on, you make a movement with your hand to indicate that they should move in a particular direction. *hacer señas para que alguien se vaya* ❑ *Ben waved her away but smiled. Ben le hizo señas para que se fuera, pero sonrió.* **3** V-T If you **wave** something, you hold it up and move it rapidly from side to side. *ondear* ❑ *More than 4000 people waved flags and sang songs. Más de 4,000 personas ondeaban banderas y cantaban.* **4** N-COUNT A **wave** is a raised mass of water on the surface of water, especially the sea, which is caused by the wind or by tides making the surface of the water rise and fall. *ola* ❑ *...the sound of the waves breaking on the shore. ...el ruido de las olas rompiendo contra la orilla.* **5** N-COUNT **Waves** are the form in which things such as sound, light, and radio signals travel. *onda* ❑ *...sound waves. ...ondas sonoras.* **6** N-COUNT If you refer to a **wave of** a particular feeling, you mean that it increases quickly and becomes very intense, and then often decreases again. *oleada* ❑ *She felt a wave of panic. Sintió una oleada de pánico.* **7** N-COUNT A **wave** is a sudden increase in a particular activity or type of behavior, especially an undesirable or unpleasant one. *oleada* ❑ *...the current wave of violence. ...la actual oleada de violencia.*
→ see Word Web: **wave**
→ see **beach, earthquake, echo, ocean, radio, sound, telescope**

**wave height** (**wave heights**) N-VAR The difference in height between the highest point of

**Word Web** wave

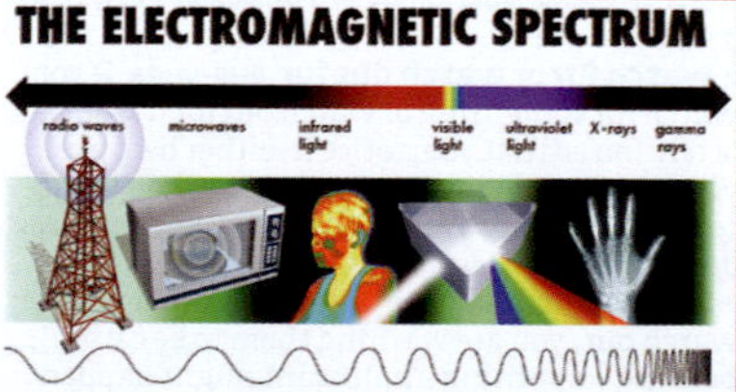


As **wind** blows across water, it makes **waves**. It does this by giving energy to the water. If the waves hit an object, they bounce off it. Light also moves in waves and acts the same way. We can see an object only if light waves bounce off it. Light waves have different **frequencies**. Wave frequency is usually the measure of the number of waves per second. **Radio waves** and **microwaves** are examples of low-frequency light waves. **Visible light** has medium-frequency light waves. **Ultraviolet radiation** and **X-rays** are high-frequency light waves.

W

a water wave and the lowest point of the following wave can be referred to as the **wave height.** altura de las olas

**wave|length** /weɪvlɛŋθ/ (**wavelengths**) **1** N-COUNT A **wavelength** is the distance between a part of a wave of energy such as light or sound and the next similar part. longitud de onda ❑ *Short wavelength X-rays are strong enough to pass through the skin.* *Los rayos X de onda corta poseen la fuerza para atravesar la piel.* **2** N-COUNT A **wavelength** is the size of radio wave that a particular radio station uses to broadcast its programs. longitud de onda, frecuencia ❑ *She found the station's wavelength on her radio.* *Encontró la frecuencia de la estación en su radio.* **3** PHRASE If two people are **on the same wavelength,** they find it easy to understand each other and they tend to agree, because they share similar interests or opinions. estar en sintonía ❑ *We finished each other's sentences because we were on the same wavelength.* *Uno terminaba de decir lo que el otro empezaba porque estábamos en sintonía.*

**wave pe|ri|od** (**wave periods**) N-COUNT The time difference between the passage of two water waves can be referred to as the **wave period.** período de onda

**wave speed** (**wave speeds**) N-VAR **Wave speed** is the speed at which a wave such as a sound wave or a water wave is traveling. velocidad de onda

**wavy** /weɪvi/ (**wavier, waviest**) ADJ **Wavy** hair is not straight or curly, but curves slightly. ondulado ❑ *She had short, wavy brown hair.* *Su pelo era castaño y ondulado, y lo llevaba corto.*
→ see **hair**

**wax** /wæks/ (**waxes**) N-VAR **Wax** is a solid, slightly shiny substance made of fat or oil that is used to make candles and polish. cera ❑ *...candle wax.* *...cera de vela.*

**wax pa|per** N-UNCOUNT **Wax paper** is paper that has been covered with a thin layer of wax. It is used mainly in cooking or to wrap food. papel encerado, papel de cera

**way**
1 NOUN AND ADVERB USES
2 PHRASES: GROUP 1
3 PHRASES: GROUP 2

**1 way** /weɪ/ (**ways**) **1** N-COUNT If you refer to a **way** of doing something, you are referring to how you can do it, for example, the action you can take or the method you can use to achieve it. manera, modo ❑ *One way of making friends is to go to an evening class.* *Una manera de hacer amigos es tomar clases vespertinas.* **2** N-COUNT If you talk about the **way** someone does something, you are talking about the qualities their action has. manera ❑ *She smiled in a friendly way.* *Sonrió amistosamente.* **3** N-COUNT If a general statement or description is true **in** a particular **way,** this is the form of it that is true in a particular case. manera ❑ *Airlines have cut costs in several ways.* *Las aerolíneas han reducido los costos de varias maneras.* ❑ *She was afraid in a way that was quite new to her.* *Sentía miedo de una manera que le era completamente desconocida.* **4** N-COUNT You use **way** in expressions such as **in some ways, in many ways,** and **in every way** to indicate the degree or extent to which a statement is true. sentido ❑ *In some ways, I liked him a lot.* *Me gusta mucho, en ciertos sentidos.* **5** N-PLURAL The **ways** of a particular person or group of people are their customs or their usual behavior. costumbre, hábito ❑ *I'm too old to change my ways.* *Soy muy viejo para cambiar mis hábitos.* **6** N-SING You use **way** in expressions such as **push your way, work your way,** or **eat your way,** followed by a prepositional phrase or adverb, in order to indicate movement, progress, or force as well as the action described by the verb. paso ❑ *She pushed her way into the crowd.* *Se abrió paso entre la multitud.* **7** N-COUNT **The way** somewhere consists of the different places that you go through or the route that you take in order to get there. camino ❑ *Does anybody know the way to the bathroom?* *¿Sabe alguien por dónde está el baño?* ❑ *I'm afraid I can't remember the way.* *Me temo que no recuerdo el camino.* **8** N-SING If you go or look a particular **way,** you go or look in that direction. sentido, dirección ❑ *As he walked into the kitchen, he passed Dad coming the other way.* *Al entrar en la cocina, pasó junto a su papá, que salía en ese momento.* ❑ *They wondered which way to go next.* *Se preguntaban en qué dirección seguir.* **9** N-SING You use **way** in expressions such as **the right way up** and **the other way around** to refer to one of two or more possible positions or arrangements that something can have. boca arriba, por el otro lado ❑ *Hold that bottle the right way up!* *¡Sostén la botella como debe ser!* **10** ADV You can use **way** to emphasize, for example, that something is a great distance away or is very much below or above a particular level or amount. lejos, demasiado ❑ *The town of Freiburg is way down in the valley.* *La ciudad de Freiburg está muy lejos valle adentro.* ❑ *You've waited way too long.* *Aguardaron demasiado tiempo.* **11** N-SING **Way** is used in expressions such as **a long way, a little way,** and **quite a way,** to say how far away something is or how far you have traveled. lejano, alejado, lejos ❑ *...places quite a long way from here.* *...lugares muy lejos de aquí.* ❑ *A little way down the road we passed a house.* *Seguimos avanzando, y un poco más lejos pasamos frente a una casa.* **12** N-SING You use **way** in expressions such as **all the way, most of the way** and **half the way** to refer to the extent to which an action has been completed. todo ❑ *I listened to the story all the way through.* *No me perdí nada de la historia.*

**2 way** /weɪ/ (**ways**) **1** PHRASE You say **by the way** when you add something to what you are saying, especially something that you have just thought of. por cierto [SPOKEN] ❑ *By the way, how is your back?* *Por cierto, ¿cómo sigues de la espalda?* **2** PHRASE If someone says that you **can't have it both ways,** they are telling you that you have to choose between two things and cannot do or have them both. tener que decidirse ❑ *You can't have it both ways: you're either doing it properly or not.* *Tienes que decidirte, o lo estás haciendo bien, o no.* **3** PHRASE **Every which way** and **any which way** are used to emphasize that something happens, or might happen, in a lot of different ways, or using a lot of different methods. en todos sentidos [INFORMAL] ❑ *Her short hair stuck up every which way.* *De tan corto, tenía todo el cabello parado.* **4** PHRASE If someone **gets** their **way** or **has** their **way,** nobody stops them from doing what they want to do. You can also say that someone **gets** their **own** way or **has**

their **own way.** salirse con la suya ❑ *She is very good at getting her own way.* Es muy buena para salirse con la suya. **5** PHRASE If one thing **gives way to** another, the first thing is replaced by the second. dar paso ❑ *First he felt sad. Then the sadness gave way to anger.* Primero se sintió triste; luego, la tristeza dio paso a la rabia. **6** PHRASE If an object that is supporting something **gives way,** it breaks or collapses, so that it can no longer support that thing. ceder ❑ *He fell when the floor gave way beneath him.* El piso cedió bajo él y se cayó.

**❸ way** /weɪ/ (**ways**) **1** PHRASE If you say that something is true **in a way,** you mean that although it is not completely true, it is true to a limited extent or in certain respects. You use **in a way** to reduce the force of a statement. en cierto sentido ❑ *In a way, I guess I'm frightened of failing.* En cierto sentido, supongo que me da miedo fracasar. **2** PHRASE If you say that someone **gets in the way** or **is in the way,** you are annoyed because their presence or their actions stop you from doing something properly. interponerse ❑ *"We won't get in the way," Suzanne promised.* —No nos interpondremos —prometió Suzanne. **3** PHRASE If one person or thing **makes way for** another, the first is replaced by the second. ceder el lugar ❑ *He said he was happy to make way for younger people.* Dijo que le hacía feliz ceder el lugar a los jóvenes. **4** PHRASE If you **go out of** your **way to** do something, for example, to help someone, you make a special effort to do it. hacer todo lo que se puede ❑ *He went out of his way to help me.* Hizo todo lo que pudo por ayudarme. **5** PHRASE If someone **keeps out of** your **way** or **stays out of** your **way,** he or she avoids you or does not get involved with you. no interponerse ❑ *I kept out of his way as much as I could.* Traté hasta donde pude de no interponerme en su camino. **6** PHRASE When something is **out of the way,** it has finished or you have dealt with it, so that it is no longer a problem or needs no more time spent on it. quitarse de encima ❑ *Let's get this out of the way first.* Vamos a quitarnos esto de encima primero. **7** → see also **underway**

**way of life** (**ways of life**) N-COUNT A **way of life** is the behavior and habits that are typical of a particular person or group, or that are chosen by them. estilo de vida ❑ *They're teaching me a lot about their way of life.* Están enseñándome mucho sobre su estilo de vida.

**we** /wɪ, STRONG wi/

> **We** is the first person plural pronoun. **We** is used as the subject of a verb.

PRON A speaker or writer uses **we** to refer both to himself or herself and to one or more other people as a group. nosotros o nosotras, Se expresa con la terminación del verbo, **-mos**. ❑ *We said we'd be friends for ever.* Dijimos que seríamos amigos para siempre. ❑ *We bought a bottle of lemonade.* Compramos una botella de limonada.

W

**weak** /wik/ (**weaker, weakest**) **1** ADJ If someone is **weak,** they are not healthy or do not have good muscles, so that they cannot move quickly or carry heavy things. débil ❑ *I was too weak to move.* Estaba muy débil como para moverme.
• **weak|ly** ADV débilmente ❑ *"I'm all right," Max said weakly.* —Estoy bien—, dijo Max débilmente.
• **weak|ness** N-UNCOUNT debilidad ❑ *The condition can lead to weakness and rash.* Ese estado puede provocar debilidad y sarpullido. **2** ADJ If someone has an organ or sense that is **weak,** it is not very effective or powerful, or is likely to fail. débil ❑ *She had a weak heart.* Tenía problemas de corazón. **3** ADJ If you describe someone as **weak,** you mean that they are not very confident or determined, so that they are often frightened or worried, or easily influenced by other people. débil ❑ *He was a good doctor, but a weak man.* Era buen médico, pero como persona, era débil.
• **weak|ness** N-UNCOUNT debilidad ❑ *Some people see crying as a sign of weakness.* Algunas personas consideran el llanto como muestra de debilidad. **4** ADJ If something such as an argument or case is **weak,** it is not convincing or there is little evidence to support it. pobre, poco convincente ❑ *The argument against him was weak.* La argumentación en su contra fue poco convincente. **5** ADJ A **weak** drink, chemical, or drug contains very little of a particular substance, for example, because a lot of water has been added to it. aguado ❑ *...a cup of weak tea.* ...una taza de té aguado. **6** → see also **weakness**
→ see **muscle**

| **Thesaurus** | *weak* | Ver también: |
|---|---|---|
| ADJ. | feeble, frail; (*ant.*) strong **1** | |
| | cowardly, insecure; (*ant.*) strong **3** | |

| **Word Partnership** | Usar *weak* con: |
|---|---|
| ADV. | **relatively** weak, **still** weak, **too** weak, **very** weak **1** – **5** |

**weak|en** /wikən/ (**weakens, weakening, weakened**) **1** V-T/V-I If you **weaken** something or if it **weakens,** it becomes less strong or less powerful. debilitar(se) ❑ *The illness weakened his heart.* La enfermedad debilitó su corazón. ❑ *Families are weakening and breaking up.* Las familias están debilitándose y deshaciéndose. **2** V-I If you **weaken,** you become less certain about a decision you have made. flaquear ❑ *Jennie weakened, and finally agreed that they could stay another half hour.* Jennie flaqueó y finalmente aceptó que se quedaran otra media hora.

| **Word Link** | *ness ≈ state, condition : consciousness, sickness, weakness* |
|---|---|

**weak|ness** /wiknɪs/ (**weaknesses**) **1** N-COUNT If you have a **weakness for** something, you like it very much. debilidad ❑ *Stephen had a weakness for chocolate.* Stephen tenía debilidad por el chocolate. **2** → see also **weak**

**wealth** /wɛlθ/ **1** N-UNCOUNT **Wealth** is the possession of a large amount of money, property, or other valuable things. You can also refer to a particular person's money or property as their **wealth.** riqueza ❑ *His own wealth grew.* Su riqueza personal aumentó. **2** N-SING **A wealth of** something is a very large amount of it. abundancia [FORMAL] ❑ *The city has a wealth of beautiful churches.* Las iglesias bellas abundan en la ciudad.

| **Thesaurus** | *wealth* | Ver también: |
|---|---|---|
| N. | affluence, funds, money; (*ant.*) poverty **1** | |

**wealthy** /wɛlθi/ (**wealthier, wealthiest**) ADJ

Someone who is **wealthy** has a large amount of money, property, or valuable possessions. rico, acaudalado, adinerado ❑ *...a wealthy businessman. ...un acaudalado hombre de negocios.* ● **The wealthy** are people who are wealthy. los ricos ❑ *Good education should be available to everyone, not just the wealthy. La educación de calidad debe estar al alcance de todos, no sólo de los ricos.*

**weap|on** /wɛpən/ (**weapons**) N-COUNT A **weapon** is an object such as a gun, a knife, or a missile, which is used to kill or hurt people in a fight or a war. arma ❑ *...nuclear weapons. ...armas nucleares.*
→ see **army, war**

**weap|ons of mass de|struc|tion** N-PLURAL **Weapons of mass destruction** are biological, chemical, or nuclear weapons. The abbreviation **WMD** is often used. armas de destrucción masiva

**wear** /wɛər/ (**wears, wearing, wore, worn**) **1** V-T When you **wear** something such as clothes, shoes, or jewelry, you have them on your body or on part of your body. usar, vestir, llevar ❑ *He was wearing a brown shirt. Vestía una camisa café.* **2** V-T If you **wear** your hair or beard in a particular way, you have it cut or styled in that way. llevar ❑ *She wore her hair in a long ponytail. Llevaba el pelo recogido en una larga cola de caballo.* **3** N-UNCOUNT You use **wear** to refer to clothes that are suitable for a certain time or place. ropa ❑ *...a new range of evening wear. ...una nueva gama de ropa de noche.* **4** N-UNCOUNT **Wear** is the amount or type of use that something has over a period of time. uso ❑ *You'll get more wear out of a good quality pair of shoes. Un par de zapatos de buena calidad le durarán mucho más.* **5** N-UNCOUNT **Wear** is the damage or change that is caused by something being used a lot or for a long time. desgaste ❑ *...a large armchair which showed signs of wear. ...un sillón grande que se veía desgastado.* **6** V-I If something **wears,** it becomes thinner or weaker because it is constantly being used over a long period of time. desgastarse ❑ *The stone steps are beginning to wear. Los peldaños de piedra están empezando a desgastarse.*
→ see **makeup**

▸ **wear away** PHR-VERB If you **wear** something **away** or if it **wears away,** it becomes thin and eventually disappears because it is used a lot or rubbed a lot. desgastarse ❑ *The paint has worn away from the edge of the door. Ya se desgastó la pintura del borde de la puerta.*

▸ **wear down** **1** PHR-VERB If you **wear** something **down** or if it **wears down,** it becomes flatter or smoother as a result of constantly rubbing against something else. erosionar, desgastar ❑ *Rivers have worn down the rocks over the years. Con los años, los ríos han erosionado las rocas.* ❑ *The heels on his shoes have worn down. Ya se desgastaron los tacones de sus zapatos.* **2** PHR-VERB If you **wear** someone **down,** you make them gradually weaker or less determined until they eventually do what you want. cansar ❑ *She wore him down until he eventually signed the letter. Lo cansó hasta que finalmente firmó la carta.*

▸ **wear off** PHR-VERB If a sensation, or feeling **wears off,** it disappears slowly. pasar ❑ *Now that the shock was wearing off, he was in pain. Una vez que se le pasó el shock, le empezó a doler.*

▸ **wear out** **1** PHR-VERB When something **wears out** or when you **wear** it **out,** it is used so much that it becomes thin or weak and unable to be used anymore. agotarse, acabarse ❑ *The batteries of her watch were wearing out. Se le estaba acabando la pila a su reloj.* ❑ *He wore out his shoes wandering around Mexico City. Se acabó los zapatos paseando por la ciudad de México.* **2** PHR-VERB If something **wears** you **out,** it makes you feel extremely tired. cansar [INFORMAL] ❑ *The young people wore themselves out playing soccer. Los jóvenes se cansaron jugando futbol.*
**3** → see also **worn out**

**Word Partnership** Usar *wear* con:

| | |
|---|---|
| N. | wear **black/red/white**, wear **clothes**, wear **contact lenses**, wear **glasses**, wear **gloves**, wear **a hat/helmet**, wear **a jacket**, wear **jeans**, wear **makeup**, wear **a mask**, wear **a suit**, wear **a uniform** **1** |
| ADJ. | **casual** wear, **day** wear, **evening** wear **3** |

**wea|ry** /wɪəri/ (**wearier, weariest**) **1** ADJ If you are **weary,** you are very tired. cansado, agotado, exhausto ❑ *Rachel looked pale and weary. Rachel se veía pálida y agotada.* **2** ADJ If you are **weary of** something, you have become tired of it and have lost your enthusiasm for it. cansado ❑ *We're getting very weary of Alan's behavior. La conducta de Alan nos está agotando la paciencia.*

**weath|er** /wɛðər/ (**weathers, weathering, weathered**) **1** N-UNCOUNT The **weather** is the temperature and condition of the air, for example, if it is raining, hot, or windy. clima, tiempo ❑ *The weather was bad. Hacía mal tiempo.* ❑ *I like cold weather. Me gusta el frío.* **2** V-T/V-I If something such as wood or rock **weathers** or **is weathered,** it changes color or shape as a result of the wind, sun, rain, or cold. erosionar(se), desgastar(se) ❑ *Unpainted wood weathers to a gray color. La madera sin pintar adquiere un tono gris.* **3** V-T If you **weather** a difficult time or a difficult situation, you survive it. capear, sobrellevar ❑ *The company has weathered the recent difficulties. La empresa se las ha arreglado para hacer frente a los problemas recientes.*
→ see Word Web: **weather**
→ see **storm**

**Usage** **weather** and **whether**

*Weather* and *whether* sound exactly alike, but are very different. *Weather* refers to the conditions out of doors—hot or cold, wet or dry, cloudy or clear; *whether* refers to alternative situations: *Umar doesn't care whether it's rainy or sunny outside—he likes running through the park in all kinds of weather.*

**Word Partnership** Usar *weather* con:

| | |
|---|---|
| ADJ. | **bad** weather, **clear** weather, **cold** weather, **cool** weather, **dry** weather, **fair** weather, **good** weather, **hot** weather, **inclement** weather, **mild** weather, **nice** weather, **rainy** weather, **rough** weather, **severe** weather, **stormy** weather, **sunny** weather, **warm** weather, **wet** weather **1** |
| N. | weather **conditions**, weather **prediction**, weather **report**, weather **service** **1** |
| V. | weather **permitting** **1** |

## Word Web — weather

Researchers believe the **weather** affects our bodies and minds. The **barometric pressure** drops before a **storm.** The difference in pressure may change the blood flow in the brain. Some people get migraine headaches. In **damp, humid** weather people have problems with arthritis. A sudden **heat wave** can produce heatstroke. Some people get seasonal affective disorder, or SAD, in the winter. They feel depressed during the short, **gloomy** days. As the word "sad" suggests, people with this condition feel depressed. The bitter cold of a **blizzard** can cause frostbite. The **hot, dry** Santa Ana winds* in southern California create confusion and depression in some people.

*Santa Ana winds: strong, hot, dry winds that blow in southern California in fall and early spring.*

**weath|er fore|cast** (**weather forecasts**) N-COUNT A **weather forecast** is a statement saying what the weather will be like the next day or for the next few days. *pronóstico del tiempo*
→ see **forecast**

**weath|er|ing** /wɛðərɪŋ/ **1** N-UNCOUNT **Weathering** is a process in which rocks near the Earth's surface are broken into smaller pieces as a result of exposure to rain, wind, and ice. *erosión* **2** → see also **chemical weathering, mechanical weathering**

**weath|er map** (**weather maps**) N-COUNT A **weather map** is a chart that shows what the weather is like or what it will be like. *mapa climatológico*

**weave** /wiv/ (**weaves, weaving, wove, woven**)

> The form **weaved** is used for the past tense and past participle for meaning **2**.

**1** V-T/V-I If you **weave** cloth or a carpet, you make it by crossing threads over and under each other using a frame or machine called a loom. *tejer* ❑ *We gathered wool and learned how to weave it into cloth. Reunimos lana y aprendimos a tejer telas con ella.* ● **weav|er** N-COUNT (**weavers**) *tejedor, tejedora* ❑ *...a linen weaver from Ireland. ...una tejedora de lino irlandesa.* ● **weav|ing** N-UNCOUNT *tejido, cestería* ❑ *I studied weaving. Aprendí a tejer cestas.* **2** V-T/V-I If you **weave** your way somewhere, you move between and around things as you go there. *zigzaguear* ❑ *He weaved around the tables to where she sat with Bob. Zigzagueó entre las mesas hasta donde estaba sentada con Bob.*
→ see **industry**

**web** /wɛb/ (**webs**) **1** N-PROPER **The Web** is a computer system that links documents and pictures into a database that is stored in computers in many different parts of the world and that people everywhere can use. It is also referred to as the **World Wide Web.** *la red* [COMPUTING] ❑ *The handbook is available on the Web. El manual está disponible en la red.* **2** N-COUNT A **web** is a complicated pattern of connections or relationships, sometimes considered as an obstacle or a danger. *red, maraña* ❑ *...a web of lies. ...una maraña de mentiras.* **3** N-COUNT A **web** is the thin net made by a spider from a sticky substance that it produces in its body. *telaraña* ❑ *There's a spider's web in the window. Hay una telaraña en la ventana.*
→ see **blog**

**web|cam** /wɛbkæm/ (**webcams**) also **Webcam** N-COUNT A **webcam** is a video camera that takes pictures that can be viewed on a website. *cámara* [COMPUTING]

**web|log** /wɛblɔg/ (**weblogs**) N-COUNT A **weblog** is a website containing a diary or journal on a particular subject. *bitácora en la red, blog* [COMPUTING] ❑ *...a weblog for writing about New York. ...un blog sobre Nueva York.* ● **web|log|ger** /wɛblɔgər/ N-COUNT (**webloggers**) *que participa en blogs de internet* ❑ *Many webloggers are getting into blogging for the wrong reasons. Muchos de los que participan en blogs de internet lo hacen por razones erróneas.* ● **web|log|ging** /wɛblɔgɪŋ/ N-UNCOUNT *bitácora en línea, blog* ❑ *...a popular online diary and weblogging site. ...un popular sitio web de diarios y blogs.*

**web|master** /wɛbmæstər/ (**webmasters**) N-COUNT A **webmaster** is someone who is in charge of a website, especially someone who does that as their job. *administrador de un sitio de la red, administradora de un sitio de la red* [COMPUTING]
→ see **Internet**

**web page** (**web pages**) also **Web page** N-COUNT A **web page** is a set of data or information that is designed to be viewed as part of a website. *página (de un sitio de internet), página web* [COMPUTING]
→ see **Internet**

> **Word Link** — *site, situ ≈ position, location : situated, situation, website*

**web|site** /wɛbsaɪt/ (**websites**) also **Web site** or **web site** N-COUNT A **website** is a set of data and information about a particular subject that is available on the Internet. *sitio de internet, sitio web* [COMPUTING]
→ see **blog, Internet**

**wed|ding** /wɛdɪŋ/ (**weddings**) N-COUNT A **wedding** is a marriage ceremony and the party or special meal that often takes place after the

**Word Web** **wedding**

Some **weddings** are fancy, like the one in this picture. Most ceremonies include a similar group of attendants. The **maid of honor** or **matron of honor** helps the **bride** get ready for the ceremony. She also signs the **marriage certificate** as a legal **witness**. The **bridesmaids** plan the bride's wedding **shower**. The best man arranges for the **bachelor party** the night before the wedding. He also helps the groom dress for the wedding. After the **ceremony**, the guests gather for a **reception**. When the party is over, many couples leave on a **honeymoon** trip.

ceremony. *boda* ❑ *Many couples want a big wedding. Muchas parejas desean una gran boda.*
→ see Word Web: **wedding**
→ see **jewelry**

**wedge** /wɛdʒ/ (**wedges, wedging, wedged**) **1** V-T If you **wedge** something, you force it to remain in a particular position by holding it there tightly or by putting something next to it to prevent it from moving. *cuña, calza, calce* ❑ *I shut the door and wedged it with a piece of wood. Cerré la puerta y la calcé con una cuña de madera.* **2** V-T If you **wedge** something somewhere, you fit it there tightly. *calzar, meter, tapar* ❑ *Wedge the plug into the hole. Ponga el tapón en el agujero.* **3** N-COUNT A **wedge** of something such as fruit or cheese is a piece of it that has a thick triangular shape. *rebanada, tajada* ❑ *Serve the fish with a wedge of lemon. Sirva el pescado con una rebanadita de limón.* **4** N-COUNT A **wedge** is an object with one pointed edge and one thick edge, which you put under a door to keep it firmly in position. *cuña, calza, calce* **5** N-COUNT A **wedge** is a piece of metal with a pointed edge which is used for splitting a material such as stone or wood, by being hammered into a crack in the material. *cuña*

**Wednes|day** /wɛnzdeɪ, -di/ (**Wednesdays**) N-VAR **Wednesday** is the day after Tuesday and before Thursday. *miércoles* ❑ *Come and have supper with us on Wednesday, if you're free. Ven a cenar con nosotros el miércoles, si no tienes otro compromiso.*

**weed** /wid/ (**weeds, weeding, weeded**) **1** N-COUNT A **weed** is a wild plant that grows in gardens or fields of crops and prevents the plants that you want from growing properly. *mala hierba, maleza* ❑ *The garden was full of weeds. El jardín estaba lleno de maleza.* **2** V-T/V-I If you **weed** an area, you remove the weeds from it. *escardar, deshierbar* ❑ *Try not to walk on the flowerbeds while weeding. Trata de no pisar los arriates mientras deshierbas.*
→ see **plant**
▸ **weed out** PHR-VERB If you **weed out** things or people that are useless or unwanted in a group, you find them and get rid of them. *eliminar* ❑ *It is difficult to weed out bad employees. Es difícil eliminar a los malos empleados.*

**week** /wik/ (**weeks**) **1** N-COUNT A **week** is a period of seven days. Some people consider that a week starts on Monday and ends on Sunday. *semana* ❑ *I had a letter from my mother last week. Recibí carta de mi madre la semana pasada.* ❑ *I thought about it all week. Pensé en ello toda la semana.* **2** N-COUNT Your working **week** is the hours that you spend at work during a week. *semana laboral* ❑ *Many women work a 40-hour week. Muchas mujeres tienen una semana laboral de 40 horas.* **3** N-SING **The week** is the part of the week that does not include Saturday and Sunday. *entre semana* ❑ *Anna looked after the children during the week. Anna cuidaba a los niños entre semana.*
→ see **year**

**week|day** /wikdeɪ/ (**weekdays**) N-COUNT A **weekday** is any of the days of the week except Saturday and Sunday. *día entre semana*

**week|end** /wikɛnd/ (**weekends**) N-COUNT A **weekend** is Saturday and Sunday. *fin de semana* ❑ *I had dinner with him last weekend. Cenamos juntos el fin de semana pasado.*

**week|ly** /wikli/ (**weeklies**) **1** ADJ A **weekly** event or publication happens or appears once a week or every week. *semanal* ❑ *We do the weekly shopping every Thursday. Hacemos las compras de la semana los jueves.* • **Weekly** is also an adverb. *semanalmente* ❑ *The group meets weekly. El grupo se reúne semanalmente.* **2** N-COUNT A **weekly** is a newspaper or magazine that is published once a week. *semanario* ❑ *Two of the four national daily papers are to become weeklies. Dos de los cuatro diarios nacionales van a convertirse en semanarios.*

**weep** /wip/ (**weeps, weeping, wept**) V-T/V-I If someone **weeps**, they cry. *llorar* [LITERARY] ❑ *She wept tears of joy. Lloró de alegría.*
→ see **cry**

**weigh** /weɪ/ (**weighs, weighing, weighed**) **1** V-T If someone or something **weighs** a particular amount, this amount is how heavy they are. *pesar* ❑ *It weighs nearly 65 pounds. Pesa casi 29 kilos y medio.* **2** V-T If you **weigh** something or someone, you measure how heavy they are. *pesar(se)* ❑ *Lisa weighed the boxes for postage. Lisa pesó las cajas para el franqueo.* **3** V-T If you **weigh** the facts about a situation, you consider them very carefully before you make a decision, especially by comparing the various facts involved. *sopesar* ❑ *She weighed her options. Sopesó sus opciones.*
▸ **weigh down** PHR-VERB If something that you are wearing or carrying **weighs** you **down**, it stops you moving easily by making you heavier. *agobiar* ❑ *I was weighed down by my backpack. El peso de la mochila me agobiaba.*

**Word Partnership** Usar *weigh* con:

ADV. weigh **less**, weigh **more** 1
weigh **carefully** 2 3
N. weigh **10 pounds** 1
weigh **alternatives**, weigh **benefits**, weigh **costs**, weigh **the evidence**, weigh **risks** 3

**weight** /weɪt/ (**weights**) 1 N-VAR The **weight** of a person or thing is how heavy they are, measured in units such as kilograms, pounds, or tons. *peso* ❑ *What is your height and weight? ¿Cuánto mide y cuánto pesa?* PHRASE • If someone **loses weight**, they become lighter. If they **gain weight** or **put on weight**, they become heavier. *bajar/subir de peso* ❑ *I'm lucky because I never put on weight. Tengo suerte, nunca subo de peso.* 2 N-COUNT **Weights** are objects that weigh a known amount and that people lift as a form of exercise. *pesas* ❑ *I was in the gym lifting weights. Estaba en el gimnasio, haciendo pesas.* 3 N-COUNT You can refer to a heavy object as a **weight,** especially when you have to lift it. *peso* ❑ *Lifting heavy weights can hurt your back. Te puedes lastimar la espalda levantando cosas muy pesadas.* 4 N-UNCOUNT The **weight** of something is the vertical force exerted on it as a result of gravitation. Weight is measured in units called "newtons." *peso* 5 PHRASE If you **pull** your **weight,** you work as hard as everyone else who is involved in the same task or activity. *poner de su parte* ❑ *We must make sure that everyone is pulling his or her weight. Debemos asegurarnos de que todos estén poniendo de su parte.*
→ see **diet**

**Word Partnership** Usar *weight* con:

V. **add** weight, **gain/lose** weight, **put on** weight 1
N. **body** weight, weight **gain/loss**, **height and** weight, **size and** weight 1
weight **training** 2
ADJ. **excess** weight, **healthy** weight, **ideal** weight, **normal** weight 1
**heavy** weight, **light** weight 3

**weight train|ing** N-UNCOUNT **Weight training** is a kind of physical exercise in which people lift or push heavy weights with their arms and legs in order to strengthen their muscles. *hacer pesas*

**weird** /wɪərd/ (**weirder, weirdest**) ADJ If you describe something or someone as **weird,** you mean that they are strange. *raro, extraño* [INFORMAL] ❑ *He's a very weird guy. Es un tipo muy raro.*

W

**wel|come** /wɛlkəm/ (**welcomes, welcoming, welcomed**) 1 V-T/V-I If you **welcome** someone, you greet them in a friendly way when they arrive somewhere. *dar la bienvenida, acoger* ❑ *She was there to welcome him home. Estaba ahí para recibirlo cuando volviera a casa.* • **Welcome** is also a noun. *bienvenida* ❑ *They gave him a fantastic welcome. Le dieron una bienvenida fantástica.* 2 CONVENTION You use **welcome** in expressions such as **welcome home, welcome to Boston,** and **welcome back** when you are greeting someone who has just arrived somewhere. *bienvenido* ❑ *Welcome to Washington. Bienvenido a Washington.* 3 V-T If you **welcome** an action, decision, or situation, you approve of it and are pleased that it has occurred. *alegrarse* ❑ *She welcomed the decision but said that the changes didn't go far enough. Se alegró de la decisión, pero dijo que los cambios no eran suficientemente profundos.* 4 ADJ If you describe something as **welcome,** you mean that people wanted it and are happy that it has occurred. *bienvenido* ❑ *"Any improvement is welcome," he said. —Toda mejoría es bienvenida —, dijo.* 5 ADJ If you say that someone is **welcome** in a particular place, you are encouraging them to go there by telling them that they will be liked and accepted. *bienvenido* ❑ *New members are always welcome. Siempre son bienvenidos los nuevos miembros.* 6 ADJ If you tell someone that they are **welcome** to do something, you are encouraging them to do it by telling them that they are allowed to do it. *bienvenido* ❑ *You are welcome to visit the hospital at any time. Puede venir a visitar el hospital cuando quiera.* 7 PHRASE If you **make** someone **welcome** or **make** them **feel welcome,** you make them feel happy and accepted in a new place. *acoger* 8 CONVENTION You say **"You're welcome"** to someone who has thanked you for something in order to acknowledge their thanks in a polite way. *de nada, no hay de qué* ❑ *"Thank you for dinner." — "You're welcome." —Gracias por la cena. —¡No hay de qué!*

**Word Partnership** Usar *welcome* con:

ADJ. **warm** welcome 1
N. welcome **guests**, welcome **visitors** 1 5
ADV. welcome **home** 2
**always** welcome 4 – 6

**wel|fare** /wɛlfɛər/ 1 N-UNCOUNT The **welfare** of a person or group is their health, comfort, and happiness. *bienestar* ❑ *I don't believe he is thinking of Emma's welfare. No creo que esté pensando en el bienestar de Emma.* 2 ADJ **Welfare** services are provided to help with people's living conditions and financial problems. *asistencia social* ❑ *...child welfare services. ...servicios de protección a la infancia.* 3 N-UNCOUNT **Welfare** is money that is paid by the government to people who are unemployed, poor, or sick. *prestaciones sociales* ❑ *Some states are making cuts in welfare. Algunos estados están reduciendo las prestaciones sociales.*

**Word Partnership** Usar *welfare* con:

ADJ. **public** welfare, **social** welfare 1
N. **animal** welfare, **child** welfare, **health and** welfare 1
welfare **programs**, welfare **reform**, welfare **system** 2
welfare **benefits**, welfare **checks** 3

**well**
1 DISCOURSE USES
2 ADVERB USES
3 PHRASES
4 ADJECTIVE USE
5 NOUN USES
6 VERB USES

**1 well** /wɛl/

Well is used mainly in spoken English.

1 ADV You say **well** to indicate that you are about to say something. *bueno, vaya, este* ❑ *Well, it's a pleasure to meet you. Vaya, qué gusto de conocerlo.* 2 ADV You say **well** just before or after you pause, especially to give yourself time to think about what you are going to say. *este* ❑ *I'm sorry I woke you, and, well, I just wanted to tell you I was all right. Discúlpeme que lo haya despertado. Este...sólo quería decirle que estoy bien.* 3 ADV You say **well** when you are correcting something that you have just said. *bueno* ❑ *There was a note. Well, a letter really. Había una nota; bueno, más bien era una carta.* 4 CONVENTION You say **oh well** to indicate that you accept a situation or that someone else should accept it, even though you or they are not very happy about it, because it is not too bad and cannot be changed. *bueno* ❑ *Oh well, it could be worse. Bueno, podía ser peor.* 5 **very well** → see **very**

**2 well** /wɛl/ (**better, best**) 1 ADV If you do something **well,** you do it to a high standard or to a great extent. *bien* ❑ *It's important that we play well at home. Es importante que juguemos bien en nuestro campo.* ❑ *He speaks English well. Habla muy bien el inglés.* 2 ADV If you do something **well,** you do it thoroughly and completely. *bien* ❑ *Mix the butter and sugar well. Mezcle bien la mantequilla y el azúcar.* 3 ADV You use **well** to ask or talk about the extent or standard of something. *bien, mejor* ❑ *How well do you remember your mother? ¿Qué tanto recuerda a su madre?* ❑ *She can speak French much better than me. Ella habla el francés mucho mejor que yo.* 4 ADV You use **well** in front of a prepositional phrase to emphasize it. For example, if you say that one thing happened **well before** another, you mean that it happened a long time before it. *mucho, bastante* ❑ *Frank did not arrive until well after midnight. Frank no llegó hasta mucho después de la medianoche.* ❑ *...well over a million people. ...bastante más de un millón de personas.* 5 ADV You use **well** after verbs such as "may" and "could" when you are saying what you think is likely to happen. *bien* ❑ *That could well be the problem. Ese bien podría ser el problema.*

**3 well** /wɛl/ 1 PHRASE You use **as well** when mentioning something that happens in the same way as something else already mentioned, or that should be considered at the same time as that thing. *también* ❑ *If you work in the garden in spring you'll have less to do in summer—and a more beautiful garden, as well. Si trabaja en su jardín en la primavera, tendrá menos quehacer en el verano, y también un jardín más hermoso.* 2 PHRASE You use **as well as** when you want to mention another item connected with the subject you are discussing. *tanto...como* ❑ *Adults as well as children will enjoy the movie. Niños y adultos disfrutarán la película.* 3 PHRASE If you say that something that has happened **is just as well,** you mean that it is fortunate that it happened in the way it did. *qué mejor* ❑ *From what you've said, it's just as well she wasn't there. Por lo que dices, qué mejor que ella no haya estado ahí.* 4 PHRASE If you say that you **might as well** do something, or that you **may as well** do it, you mean that you will do it although you do not have a strong desire to do it and may even feel slightly unwilling to do it. *bien se podría* ❑ *Anyway, you're here; you might as well stay. Si ya estás aquí, bien podrías quedarte.*

**4 well** /wɛl/ ADJ If you are **well,** you are healthy and not ill. *bien* ❑ *I'm not very well today. No me siento muy bien hoy.*

**5 well** /wɛl/ (**wells**) 1 N-COUNT A **well** is a hole in the ground from which a supply of water is extracted. *pozo* ❑ *I carried the water home from the well. Llevé el agua del pozo a la casa.* 2 N-COUNT A **well** is an oil well. *pozo* ❑ *About 650 wells are on fire. Hay incendios en unos 650 pozos.*
→ see **oil**

**6 well** /wɛl/ (**wells, welling, welled**) V-I If tears **well** in your eyes, they come to the surface. *brotar, manar* • **Well up** means the same as **well.** *brotar, manar* ❑ *Tears welled up in Annie's eyes. A Annie se le llenaron los ojos de lágrimas.*

**well-being** N-UNCOUNT Someone's **well-being** is their health and happiness. *bienestar* ❑ *Singing can create a sense of well-being. El canto puede hacer sentir bien.*

**well-intentioned** also **well intentioned** ADJ If you say that a person or their actions are **well-intentioned,** you mean that they intend to be helpful or kind but they are unsuccessful or cause problems. *bienintencionado, que tiene buenas intenciones* ❑ *He is well-intentioned but disorganized. Tiene buenas intenciones, pero es desorganizado.*

**well-known** ADJ A **well-known** person or thing is known about by a lot of people and is therefore famous or familiar. *bien conocido* ❑ *She was a very well-known author. Era una escritora bien conocida.*

**well-off** ADJ Someone who is **well-off** is rich enough to be able to do and buy most of the things that they want. *adinerado* [INFORMAL]

**well-to-do** ADJ A **well-to-do** person is rich enough to be able to do and buy most of the things that they want. *adinerado* ❑ *...a well-to-do family. ...una familia adinerada.*

**well-traveled** ADJ A **well-traveled** person has traveled a lot in foreign countries. *que ha viajado mucho, que ha visto mucho mundo*

**went** /wɛnt/ **Went** is the past tense of **go.** *pasado de* ***go***

**wept** /wɛpt/ **Wept** is the past tense and past participle of **weep.** *pasado y participio pasado de* ***weep***

**were** /wər, STRONG wɜr/ 1 **Were** is the plural and the second person singular of the past tense of **be.** *plural y segunda persona singular del pasado de* ***be*** 2 **Were** is sometimes used instead of "was" in certain structures, for example, in conditional clauses or after the verb "wish." *forma de subjuntivo de* ***be*** [FORMAL] ❑ *Jerry wished he were back in Washington. Jerry deseaba estar de regreso en Washington.*

**weren't** /wɜrnt, wɜrənt/ **Weren't** is the usual spoken form of "were not." *forma hablada usual de **were not***

**west** /wɛst/ also **West** **1** N-UNCOUNT The **west** is the direction you look toward in the evening in order to see the sun set. *poniente, oeste* ❑ *I drove to Flagstaff, a hundred miles to the west. Manejé hasta Flagstaff, ciento sesenta kilómetros al poniente.* **2** N-SING **The west of** a place, country, or region is the part of it which is in the west. *poniente, oeste* ❑ *Many of the buildings in the west of the city are on fire. Hay incendios en muchos de los edificios del poniente de la ciudad.* **3** ADV **West** means toward the west, or positioned to the west of a place or thing. *poniente, oeste* ❑ *We are going west to California. Vamos al poniente, a California.* ❑ *Penryn is about 60 miles west of Philadelphia. Penryn está a aproximadamente 100 kilómetros al poniente de Filadelfia.* **4** ADJ A **west** wind blows from the west. *viento poniente* **5** N-SING **The West** is used to refer to the United States, Canada, and the countries of Western Europe. *Occidente* ❑ *...relations between Japan and the West. ...las relaciones entre Japón y Occidente.*

**west|ern** /wɛstərn/ (**westerns**) also **Western** **1** ADJ **Western** means in or from the west of a region, state, or country. *occidental* ❑ *Visitors from Western Europe to the United States rose one percent in 2003. El turismo de Europa Occidental a Estados Unidos aumentó el uno por ciento en 2003.* **2** ADJ **Western** is used to describe things, people, ideas, or ways of life that come from or are associated with the United States, Canada, and the countries of Western Europe. *occidental* ❑ *They need billions of dollars from Western governments. Necesitan miles de millones de dólares de los gobiernos de Occidente.* **3** N-COUNT A **western** is a book or movie about life in the western United States and territories in the nineteenth century, especially the lives of cowboys. *novela de vaqueros, novela del oeste, película de vaqueros, película del oeste*
→ see **genre**

**west|ern|er** /wɛstərnər/ (**westerners**) also **Westerner** N-COUNT A **Westerner** is a person who was born in or lives in the United States, Canada, or Western Europe. *occidental* ❑ *There are many Westerners living in China. Hay muchos occidentales viviendo en China.*

**west|ward** /wɛstwərd/

The form **westwards** is also used.

ADV **Westward** or **westwards** means toward the west. *hacia el poniente, hacia el oeste* ❑ *He sailed westward. Navegó al poniente.* ● **Westward** is also an adjective. *poniente, oeste* ❑ *...the one-hour westward flight over the Andes to Lima. ...el vuelo de una hora sobre los Andes para llegar a Lima, al poniente.*

**wet** /wɛt/ (**wetter, wettest, wets, wetting, wet** or **wetted**) **1** ADJ If something is **wet,** it is covered in water or another liquid. *mojado* ❑ *He dried his wet hair with a towel. Se secó el cabello con una toalla.* **2** V-T To **wet** something means to get water or some other liquid over it. *humedecer* ❑ *Wet the shirts before you iron them. Humedezca las camisas antes de plancharlas.* **3** ADJ If the weather is **wet,** it is raining. *lluvioso* ❑ *If the weather is wet or cold, stay indoors. Si llueve o hace frío, quédate en casa.* **4** ADJ If something such as paint, ink, or cement is **wet,** it is not yet dry or solid. *fresco* **5** V-T If people, especially children, **wet** their beds or clothes or **wet** themselves, they urinate in their beds or in their clothes because they cannot stop themselves. *orinarse (en la cama), mojar (la cama)* ❑ *Many children wet the bed. Muchos niños se orinan en la cama.*

**Word Partnership** Usar *wet* con:

| | |
|---|---|
| V. | **get** wet **1** |
| N. | wet **clothes**, wet **feet**, wet **grass**, wet **hair**, wet **sand** **1** |
| | wet **snow**, wet **weather** **3** |
| | wet **the bed** **5** |
| ADJ. | **soaking** wet **1** |
| | **cold and** wet **1** **3** |

**wet|land** /wɛtlænd/ (**wetlands**) N-VAR A **wetland** is an area of very wet, muddy land with wild plants growing in it. You can also refer to an area like this as **wetlands.** *tierra pantanosa, humedal* ❑ *...a plan to protect the wetlands. ...un plan para proteger los humedales.*
→ see Word Web: **wetlands**

**we've** /wɪv, STRONG wiv/ **We've** is the usual spoken form of "we have," especially when "have" is an auxiliary verb. *forma hablada usual de **we have*** ❑ *It's the first time we've been to the cinema together as a family. Es la primera vez que hemos ido al cine en familia.*

**whale** /weɪl/ (**whales**) N-COUNT **Whales** are very large mammals that live in the sea. *ballena*
→ see Word Web: **whale**

**wharf** /wɔrf/ (**wharves** or **wharfs**) N-COUNT A **wharf** is a platform by a river or the sea where

**Word Web** wetlands

Saltwater **wetlands** protect beaches from erosion. These **tidal flats** are homes for shellfish and migrating birds. In some areas, mangrove **swamps** form along the shore. They shelter many kinds of fish. They also filter groundwater before it reaches the ocean. Inland wetlands also form along rivers and streams. They become **marshes** and **freshwater** swamps. A **bog** is an unusual type of freshwater wetland. A layer of **peat** forms on the surface of the water. This layer can support shrubs, trees, and small animals. In some places people dry peat to burn. They use it for cooking and heating.

**Word Web** whale

**Whales** are part of a group of animals called cetaceans. This group also includes **dolphins** and porpoises. Whales live in the water, but they are **mammals**. They breathe air and are warm-blooded. Whales are adapted to life in the **ocean**. They have a 2-inch thick layer of blubber just under their skin. This insulates them from the cold ocean water. They sing beautiful songs that can be heard miles away. Blue whales are the largest animals in the world. They can become almost 100 feet long and weigh up to 145 tons.

ships can be tied up. muelle, embarcadero

**what** /wʌt, wɒt/

Usually pronounced /wɒt/ for meanings 2 and 4.

1 PRON You use **what** in questions when you ask for information. qué ❑ *What do you want?* *¿Qué quieres?* ❑ *"Has something happened?" — "Yes." — "What?"* *—¿Pasó algo? —Sí. —¿Qué?* • **What** is also a determiner. qué ❑ *What time is it?* *¿Qué hora es?* 2 CONJ You use **what** after certain words, especially verbs and adjectives, when you are referring to a situation that is unknown or has not been specified. qué ❑ *I want to know what happened to Norman.* *Quiero saber qué le pasó a Norman.* • **What** is also a determiner. qué ❑ *I didn't know what else to say.* *No supe qué más decir.* 3 CONJ You use **what** at the beginning of a clause in structures where you are changing the order of the information to give special emphasis to something. que ❑ *What I wanted, more than anything, was a few days' rest.* *Lo que quería, más que nada, era unos días de descanso.* 4 CONJ You use **what** to indicate that you are talking about the whole of an amount that is available to you. que ❑ *He drank what was left in his cup.* *Bebió lo que quedaba en la taza.* • **What** is also a determiner. que ❑ *They spent what money they had.* *Gastaron todo el dinero que tenían.* 5 CONVENTION You say **"What?"** when you ask someone to repeat the thing that they have just said because you did not hear or understand it properly. "What?" is more informal and less polite than expressions such as "Pardon?" and "Excuse me?" qué [SPOKEN] ❑ *"We could buy this place," she said. "What?" he asked.* *—Podríamos comprar este lugar —dijo ella. —¿Qué? —preguntó él.* 6 CONVENTION You say **"What"** to express surprise. qué ❑ *"I love you." — "What?"* *—Te quiero. —¡¿Qué?!* 7 PREDET You use **what** in exclamations to emphasize an opinion or reaction. qué ❑ *What a horrible thing to do!* *¡Qué horrible hacer eso!* • **What** is also a determiner. qué ❑ *What pretty hair she has!* *¡Qué bonito pelo tiene!* 8 PHRASE In conversation, you say **or what?** after a question as a way of stating an opinion forcefully and showing that you expect other people to agree. no ❑ *Look at that moon. Is that beautiful or what?* *¡Mira la luna! Es bonita, ¿no?* 9 PHRASE You use **what about** at the beginning of a question when you make a suggestion, offer, or request. qué ❑ *What about going out with me tomorrow?* *¿Qué tal si sales conmigo mañana?* 10 PHRASE You say **what if** at the beginning of a question when you ask about the consequences of something happening, especially something undesirable. y ❑ *What if this doesn't work?* *¿Y si no funciona?* 11 **what's more** → see **more**

**what|ev|er** /wʌtɛvər, wɒt-/ 1 CONJ You use **whatever** to refer to anything or everything of a particular type. lo que ❑ *Frank was free to do whatever he wanted.* *Frank estaba en libertad de hacer lo que quisiera.* • **Whatever** is also a determiner. sin importar, independientemente de ❑ *Whatever their size or shape, the best gardens have beautiful flowers.* *Independientemente de su tamaño o forma, los mejores jardines tienen flores bonitas.* 2 CONJ You use **whatever** to say that something is the case in all circumstances. no importa ❑ *I will always love you, whatever happens.* *Siempre te querré, no importa lo que pase.* 3 CONJ You use **whatever** when you are indicating that you do not know the precise identity, meaning, or value of the thing just mentioned. sea lo que fuere ❑ *I thought that my childhood was "normal," whatever that is.* *Yo creía que mi niñez había sido "normal", sea lo que sea eso.*

**what's** /wʌts, wɒts/ **What's** is the usual spoken form of "what is" or "what has," especially when "has" is an auxiliary verb. forma hablada usual de **what is**, forma hablada usual de **what has**

**what|so|ev|er** /wʌtsoʊɛvər, wɒt-/ ADV You use **whatsoever** to emphasize something negative. en absoluto, absolutamente ❑ *James did nothing whatsoever to help.* *James no hizo absolutamente nada por ayudar.* ❑ *It made no sense to me whatsoever.* *No tenía absolutamente ningún sentido para mí.*

**wheat** /wit/ (**wheats**) N-UNCOUNT **Wheat** is a cereal crop grown for food, which is ground into flour and used to make bread. trigo
→ see **bread, grain**

**wheel** /wil/ (**wheels, wheeling, wheeled**)
1 N-COUNT The **wheels** of a vehicle are the circular objects that are attached underneath it and that enable it to move along the ground. rueda ❑ *The car's wheels slipped on the wet road.* *Las ruedas del coche derraparon en la carretera mojada.* 2 N-COUNT **The wheel** of a car or other vehicle is the circular object that is used to steer it. volante ❑ *Curtis sat behind the wheel and they drove back.* *Curtis se sentó al volante y regresaron.* 3 V-T If you **wheel** an object that has wheels somewhere, you push it along. dirigir, conducir, enfilar ❑ *He wheeled his bike into the alley.* *Enfiló su bicicleta hacia el callejón.* 4 → see also **steering wheel**
→ see Word Web: **wheel**
→ see **bicycle, color**

W

## Word Web **wheel**

In about 5000 BC the **wheel** was invented in Mesopotamia, part of modern-day Iraq. That's when someone first **spun** a **potter's wheel** to make a clay jar. About 1,500 years later, people put wheels on an **axle** and created the **chariot**. These first wheels were solid wood and were very heavy. However, in about 2000 BC the Egyptians invented much lighter wheels with **spokes**. The wheel has driven the development of all kinds of modern technology. The waterwheel, **spinning wheel,** and **turbine** were important to the Industrial Revolution. Even the propeller and jet engine are based on the wheel.

**Word Partnership** Usar *wheel* con:

N. wheel **of a car/truck/vehicle** 1 2
V. **grip the** wheel, **slide behind the** wheel, **spin the** wheel, **turn the** wheel 2

**wheel|barrow** /wi̲lbæroʊ/ (**wheelbarrows**) N-COUNT A **wheelbarrow** is a small open cart with one wheel and handles that is used for carrying things, for example, in the garden. *carretilla* ❑ *Next to her is a wheelbarrow full of flowers for planting. Junto a ella hay una carretilla llena de flores para plantar.*
→ see **garden**

**wheel|chair** /wi̲ltʃɛər/ (**wheelchairs**) N-COUNT A **wheelchair** is a chair with wheels that you use in order to move around in if you cannot walk properly, for example, because you are disabled or sick. *silla de ruedas*
→ see **disability**

**when** /wɛ̲n/ 1 PRON You use **when** to ask questions about the time at which things happen. *cuándo* ❑ *When are you going home? ¿Cuándo te vas a tu casa?* ❑ *When did you get married? ¿Cuándo te casaste?* 2 CONJ You use **when** to introduce a clause in which you mention something that happens at some point during an activity, event, or situation. *cuando* ❑ *When I met Jill, I was living on my own. Cuando conocí a Jill, yo estaba viviendo solo.* 3 CONJ You use **when** to introduce a clause where you mention the circumstances under which the event in the main clause happened or will happen. *cuando* ❑ *When he brought Jane her drink she gave him a smile. Cuando le llevó la bebida a Jane, ella le sonrió.* 4 CONJ You use **when** after certain words, especially verbs and adjectives, to introduce a clause where you mention the time at which something happens. *cuándo* ❑ *I asked him when he was coming back. Le pregunté cuándo iba a volver.* 5 CONJ You use **when** to introduce the reason for an opinion, comment, or question. *cuando, si* ❑ *How can you understand when you don't have kids? ¿Cómo vas a entender, si no tienes hijos?* 6 CONJ You use **when** in order to introduce a fact or comment which makes the other part of the sentence rather surprising or unlikely. *cuando* ❑ *Our mothers made us read, when all we really wanted to do was play. Nuestras madres nos ponían a leer, y nosotros lo único que queríamos era jugar.*

**when|ever** /wɛnɛ̲vər/ CONJ You use **whenever** to refer to any time or every time that something happens or is true. *siempre que, cuando* ❑ *Whenever I talked to him, he seemed like a pretty regular guy. Siempre que hablé con él, me pareció alguien muy normal.* ❑ *You can stay at my house whenever you like. Puedes quedarte en mi casa cuando quieras.*

**where** /wɛ̲ər/

Usually pronounced /wɛər/ for meanings 2 and 3.

1 PRON You use **where** to ask questions about the place something is in, or is coming from or going to. *dónde* ❑ *Where did you meet him? ¿Dónde lo conociste?* ❑ *Where's Anna? ¿Dónde está Anna?* 2 CONJ You use **where** to specify or refer to the place in which something is situated or happens. *dónde* ❑ *People were looking to see where the noise was coming from. La gente trataba de ver de dónde venía el ruido.* ❑ *He knew where Henry Carter was. Él sabía dónde estaba Henry Carter.* ● **Where** is also a relative pronoun. *donde* ❑ *The police closed off the area where the accident occurred. La policía cercó el lugar donde ocurrió el accidente.* 3 ADV You use **where** when you are referring to or asking questions about a situation, a stage in something, or an aspect of something. *dónde* ❑ *Where will it all end? ¿Dónde acabará todo?* ● **Where** is also a relative pronoun. *en que* ❑ *I've got to the point where I'll talk to almost anyone. He llegado a un punto en que puedo hablar con casi todo el mundo.*

**where|as** /wɛəræ̲z/ CONJ You use **whereas** to introduce a comment that contrasts with what is said in the main clause. *mientras que* ❑ *She knows her feelings, whereas I don't. Ella sabe lo que siente, pero yo, no.*

**where|by** /wɛərba̲ɪ/ PRON A system or action **whereby** something happens is one that makes that thing happen. *conforme a* [FORMAL] ❑ *...an arrangement whereby employees may choose when to start work. ...un convenio conforme al cual los empleados pueden decidir cuándo empezar a trabajar.*

**wher|ever** /wɛərɛ̲vər/ 1 CONJ You use **wherever** to indicate that something happens or is true in any place or situation. *dondequiera, en cualquier parte* ❑ *Some people enjoy themselves wherever they are. Algunas personas se divierten dondequiera.* 2 CONJ You use **wherever** when you indicate that you do not know where a person or place is. *dondequiera* ❑ *I'd like to join my children, wherever they are. Quisiera reunirme con mis hijos, dondequiera que estén.*

**wheth|er** /wɛ̲ðər/ 1 CONJ You use **whether** when you are talking about a choice or doubt between two or more alternatives. *si* ❑ *They now have two weeks to decide whether or not to buy. Ahora tienen dos semanas para decidir si compran o no.* 2 CONJ You use **whether** to say that something is true in any of the circumstances that you mention. *ya sea*

W

que ❑ *We're in this together, whether we like it or not.* *Estamos juntos en esto, nos guste o no.*

**Usage** **whether and if**

*Whether* and *if* are often interchangeable: *Jorge wondered whether/if Sania really liked the cake—he wasn't sure whether/if she was being sincere or just polite.* Only *whether* can be used after a preposition: *Sania didn't like the cake, but she wanted Jorge to like her—she was uncertain about whether to be honest.*

**which** /wɪtʃ/

Usually pronounced /wɪtʃ/ for meanings **2**, **3** and **4**.

**1** PRON You use **which** in questions when there are two or more possible answers or alternatives. *cuál, qué* ❑ *"You go down that road."— "Which one?" —Tomas por ese camino. —¿Cuál?* ❑ *Which man or woman do you like best? ¿Qué hombre o mujer te gusta más?* **2** DET You use **which** to refer to a choice between two or more possible answers or alternatives. *cuál, qué* ❑ *I want to know which school you went to. Quiero saber a qué escuela fuiste.* ❑ *I can't remember which teachers I had. No puedo acordarme qué maestros tuve.* **3** PRON You use **which** at the beginning of a relative clause when specifying the thing that you are talking about. In such clauses, **which** has the same meaning as **that**. *que* ❑ *Police stopped a car which didn't stop at a red light. La policía detuvo un coche que no se detuvo en la luz roja.* **4** PRON You use **which** to refer back to what has just been said. *lo que* ❑ *They ran out of milk, which didn't bother me because I don't drink milk. Se les acabó la leche; no me molestó, porque yo no tomo leche.* ● **Which** is also a determiner. *cuyo* ❑ *She may be ill, in which case she needs to see a doctor. Puede estar enferma, en cuyo caso, necesita ver a un médico.*

**while**
❶ CONJUNCTION USES
❷ NOUN AND VERB USES

❶ **while** /waɪl/ **1** CONJ If something happens **while** something else is happening, the two things are happening at the same time. *mientras* ❑ *I sat on the chair to unwrap the package while he stood behind me. Me senté en la silla para desenvolver el paquete, en tanto que él se paró atrás de mí.* **2** CONJ You use **while** at the beginning of a clause to introduce information that contrasts with information in the main clause. *mientras que* ❑ *The first two services are free, while the third costs $35. Los primeros dos servicios son gratuitos, mientras que el tercero cuesta 35 dólares.* **3** CONJ You use **while** before making a statement in order to introduce information that partly conflicts with your statement. *aunque* ❑ *While the weather is good today, it may be bad tomorrow. Aunque hoy hace buen tiempo, mañana podría descomponerse.*

**Usage** **while**

*While* is used to join two verb phrases. *I listen to music while I exercise.*

❷ **while** /waɪl/ (**whiles, whiling, whiled**) **1** N-SING A **while** is a period of time. *rato, poco (tiempo)* ❑ *They walked on in silence for a while. Caminaron un rato en silencio.* ❑ *He got married a little while ago. Se casó hace poco.* **2** **once in a while** → see **once** **3** **worth** your **while** → see **worth**

▸ **while away** PHR-VERB If you **while away** the time in a particular way, you spend time in that way, because you are waiting for something else to happen, or because you have nothing else to do. *matar el tiempo, pasar el rato, entretenerse* ❑ *They whiled away the hours telling stories. Se entretuvieron horas contando cuentos.*

**whip** /wɪp/ (**whips, whipping, whipped**) **1** N-COUNT A **whip** is a long thin piece of material such as leather or rope, fastened to a stiff handle. It is used for hitting people or animals. *látigo* **2** V-T If someone **whips** a person or animal, they beat them or hit them with a whip or something like a whip. *azotar, fustigar* ❑ *Mr. Melton whipped the horse several times. El señor Melton fustigó el caballo repetidas veces.* ● **whip\|ping** N-COUNT (**whippings**) *tunda, paliza, zurra* ❑ *His father threatened to give him a whipping. Su padre lo amenazó con darle una zurra.* **3** V-T If someone **whips** something out or **whips** it off, they take it out or take it off very quickly and suddenly. *a todo prisa, rápidamente* ❑ *Bob whipped out his notebook. Bob sacó rápidamente su cuaderno.* ❑ *She whipped off her skis and ran up the hill. Se quitó los esquís a toda prisa y corrió colina arriba.* **4** V-T When you **whip** something liquid such as cream or an egg, you stir it very fast until it is thick or stiff. *batir* ❑ *Whip the cream until it is thick. Bata la crema hasta que espese.*

▸ **whip up** PHR-VERB If someone **whips up** an emotion such as hatred, they deliberately cause and encourage people to feel that emotion. *excitar* ❑ *He blamed politicians for whipping up fear. Culpó a los políticos de provocar miedo.*

**whisk** /wɪsk/ (**whisks, whisking, whisked**) **1** V-T If you **whisk** someone or something somewhere, you take them or move them there quickly. *rápidamente* ❑ *He whisked her across the dance floor. La llevó rápidamente al otro lado de la pista de baile.* **2** V-T If you **whisk** eggs or cream, you stir them very fast, often with an electric device, so that they become full of small bubbles. *batir* **3** N-COUNT A **whisk** is a kitchen tool used for whisking eggs or cream. *batidor, batidora* → see **utensil**

**whis\|key** /wɪski/ (**whiskeys**) N-VAR **Whiskey** is a strong alcoholic drink made, especially in the United States and Ireland, from grain such as barley or rye. *whisky* ● A **whiskey** is a glass of whiskey. *whisky* ❑ *Beattie took two whiskeys from a tray. Beattie cogió dos vasos de whisky de una charola.*

**whis\|ky** /wɪski/ (**whiskies**) N-VAR **Whisky** is whiskey that is made in Scotland and Canada. *whisky* ● A **whisky** is a glass of whisky. *whisky*

**whis\|per** /wɪspər/ (**whispers, whispering, whispered**) V-T/V-I When you **whisper,** you say something very quietly, using your breath rather than your throat, so that only one person can hear you. *susurrar, murmurar* ❑ *"Be quiet," I whispered. —Cállate—, le susurré.* ❑ *She sat on Ross's knee as he whispered in her ear. Se sentó en una rodilla de Ross mientras le susurraba al oído.* ❑ *He whispered the message to David. Le susurró el mensaje a David.* ● **Whisper** is also a noun. *susurro, murmullo* ❑ *Men*

W

*were talking in whispers in every office.* En todas las oficinas los hombres habalaban en susurros.

**whis|tle** /wɪsᵊl/ (**whistles, whistling, whistled**) **1** V-T/V-I When you **whistle,** you make sounds by forcing your breath out between your lips or teeth. silbar, chiflar ❑ *He was whistling softly to himself.* Silbaba suavemente para él mismo. **2** V-I If something such as a train or a kettle **whistles,** it makes a loud, high sound. silbar, pitar ❑ *Somewhere a train whistled.* En algún lugar, un tren pitó. **3** V-I If something such as the wind or a bullet **whistles** somewhere, it moves there, making a loud, high sound. silbar, aullar ❑ *The wind whistled through the building.* El viento aulló por entre el edificio. **4** N-COUNT A **whistle** is a small metal or plastic tube that you blow in order to produce a loud sound and attract someone's attention. silbato ❑ *The guard blew his whistle and the train started to move.* El guardia sopló su silbato y el tren empezó a moverse.

**whistle-blowing** also **whistleblowing** N-UNCOUNT **Whistle-blowing** is the act of telling the authorities or the public that the organization you work for is doing something immoral or illegal. denuncia

**white** /waɪt/ (**whiter, whitest, whites**) **1** COLOR Something that is **white** is the color of snow or milk. blanco ❑ *He had nice white teeth.* Tenía unos hermosos dientes blancos. **2** ADJ A **white** person has a pale skin and belongs to a race of European origin. blanco ❑ *A family of white people moved into a house up the street.* Una familia de blancos se mudó a una casa calle arriba. ● **Whites** are white people. blancos ❑ *The school has brought blacks and whites and Hispanics together.* La escuela ha unido a los negros, los blancos y los latinoamericanos. **3** ADJ **White** wine is pale yellow in color. blanco **4** N-VAR The **white** of an egg is the transparent liquid that surrounds the yellow part called the yolk. clara (de huevo) **5** N-COUNT The **white** of your eye is the white part that surrounds the colored part called the iris. blanco (del ojo)
→ see **color**

**white blood cell** (**white blood cells**) N-COUNT **White blood cells** are the cells in your blood which your body uses to fight infection. Compare **red blood cell.** glóbulo blanco
→ see **cardiovascular system**

**white|cap** /waɪtkæp/ (**whitecaps**) N-COUNT A **whitecap** is a wave in the ocean that is blown by the wind so that the top of the wave appears white. cabrilla, borrego

**white-collar** also **white collar** ADJ **White-collar** workers work in offices rather than doing physical work such as making things in factories or building things. oficinista, empleado de oficina ❑ *White-collar workers now work longer hours.* Los empleados de oficina trabajan más horas hoy en día.
→ see **union**

W

**white dwarf** (**white dwarfs** or **white dwarves**) N-COUNT A **white dwarf** is a very small, dense star that has collapsed. enana blanca

**White House** N-PROPER **The White House** is the official home in Washington DC of the president of the United States. You can also use **the White House** to refer to the president of the United States and his or her officials. Casa Blanca ❑ *He drove to the White House.* Se dirigió a la Casa Blanca. ❑ *The White House has not yet commented publicly.* La Casa Blanca todavía no ha hecho públicos sus comentarios.

**white light** N-UNCOUNT **White light** is light such as sunlight that contains all the colors of the visible spectrum in roughly equal amounts. luz blanca [TECHNICAL]

**White Pages** N-PLURAL **White Pages** is used to refer to the section of a telephone directory which lists names and telephone numbers in alphabetical order. sección blanca

**whiz** /wɪz/ (**whizzes, whizzing, whizzed**) also **whizz** V-I If something **whizzes** somewhere, it moves there very fast. zumbar [INFORMAL] ❑ *Stewart felt a bottle whiz past his head.* Stewart sintió que una botella le pasaba zumbando junto a cabeza.

**whiz kid** (**whiz kids**) N-COUNT If you refer to a young person as a **whiz kid,** you mean that they have achieved success at a young age because they are very clever and very good at something. fenómeno, prodigio, niño prodigio [INFORMAL] ❑ *...a computer whiz kid.* ...un prodigio para las computadoras.

**who** /hu/

| |
|---|
| Usually pronounced /hu/ for meanings **2** and **3**. |

| |
|---|
| **Who** is used as the subject or object of a verb. See entries at **whom** and **whose**. |

**1** PRON You use **who** in questions when you ask about the name or identity of a person or group of people. quién ❑ *Who's there?* ¿Quién está ahí? ❑ *Who is the least popular man around here?* ¿Quién es el hombre más impopular aquí? ❑ *"You remind me of somebody." —"Who?"* —Me recuerdas a alguien. —¿A quién? **2** CONJ You use **who** to introduce a clause where you talk about the identity of a person or a group of people. quién ❑ *Police have not found out who did it.* La policía no ha descubierto quién lo hizo. **3** PRON You use **who** at the beginning of a relative clause when specifying the person or group of people you are talking about or when giving more information about them. que ❑ *...a woman who is 23 years old and has two children.* ...una mujer que tiene 23 años de edad y dos hijos.

**WHO** /dʌbᵊlyu eɪtʃoʊ/ N-PROPER **WHO** is an abbreviation for **World Health Organization.** abreviatura de World Health Organization

**who'd** /hud, hud/ **1** **Who'd** is the usual spoken form of "who had," especially when "had" is an auxiliary verb. forma hablada usual de **who had** **2** **Who'd** is a spoken form of "who would." forma hablada usual de **who would**

**who|ever** /huɛvər/ **1** CONJ You use **whoever** to refer to someone when their identity is not yet known. quienquiera ❑ *Whoever did this will sooner or later be caught.* Quienquiera que lo haya hecho, será atrapado tarde o temprano. ❑ *Whoever wins the prize is going to be famous for life.* Quienquiera que gane el premio será famoso de por vida. **2** CONJ You use **whoever** to indicate that the actual identity of the person who does something will not affect a situation. quien uno quiera ❑ *You can have whoever you like visit you.* Puede visitarte quien tú quieras.

**whole** /hoʊl/ (**wholes**) **1** QUANT If you refer to **the whole of** something, you mean all of it. todo

❑ *This is a problem for the whole of the western world.* *Es un problema para de el mundo occidental.* • **Whole** is also an adjective. *todo* ❑ *We spent the whole summer in Italy that year.* *Ese año pasamos todo el verano en Italia.* **2** N-COUNT A **whole** is a single thing that contains several different parts. *totalidad* ❑ *We should look at the writer's work as a whole, not just in parts.* *Debemos examinar la obra del autor en su totalidad, no sólo en partes.* **3** ADJ If something is **whole,** it is in one piece and is not broken or damaged. *entero* ❑ *He took an ice cube from the glass and swallowed it whole.* *Tomó un cubito de hielo del vaso y se lo tragó entero.* **4** ADV You use **whole** to emphasize what you are saying. *totalmente* [INFORMAL] ❑ *It was like seeing a whole different side of somebody.* *Era como ver un aspecto totalmente diferente de alguien.* • **Whole** is also an adjective. *todo* ❑ *That saved me a whole bunch of money.* *Con eso me ahorré un montón de dinero.* **5** PHRASE If you refer to something **as a whole,** you are referring to it generally and as a single unit. *en conjunto, en general* ❑ *He said it was a victory for the people of South Africa as a whole.* *Dijo que era una victoria para el pueblo de Sudáfrica en general.* **6** PHRASE You use **on the whole** to indicate that what you are saying is true in general but may not be true in every case, or that you are giving a general opinion or summary of something. *en general* ❑ *On the whole I agree with him.* *En general, estoy de acuerdo con él.*

**whole note** (**whole notes**) N-COUNT A **whole note** is a musical note that has a time value equal to two half notes. *redonda, semibreve*

**whole|sale** /hoʊlseɪl/ **1** N-UNCOUNT **Wholesale** is the activity of buying and selling goods in large quantities and therefore at cheaper prices, usually to stores who then sell them to the public. Compare **retail**. *al por mayor, al mayoreo* [BUSINESS] ❑ *Members can buy goods at wholesale prices.* *Los miembros pueden comprar mercancías a precios de mayoreo.* **2** ADV If something is sold **wholesale,** it is sold in large quantities and at cheaper prices, usually to stores. *al por mayor, al mayoreo* [BUSINESS] ❑ *The goods are sold wholesale.* *Los artículos se venden al por mayor.* **3** ADJ You use **wholesale** to describe the destruction, removal, or changing of something when it affects a very large number of things or people. *general* ❑ *...the company's wholesale reorganization.* *...la reorganización general de la empresa.*

**whole|wheat** /hoʊlwit/ also **whole wheat** **1** ADJ **Wholewheat** flour is made from the complete grain of the wheat plant, including the outer part. **Wholewheat** bread or pasta is made from wholewheat flour. *de trigo entero, integral* ❑ *...vegetables with wholewheat noodles.* *...verduras con fideos de trigo entero.* **2** N-UNCOUNT **Wholewheat** means wholewheat bread or wholewheat flour. *pan integral, harina de trigo entero, harina de trigo integral* ❑ *...a chicken salad sandwich on whole wheat.* *...un sándwich de ensalada de pollo en pan integral.*

**who'll** /hul, hul/ **Who'll** is a spoken form of "who will" or "who shall." *forma hablada usual de **who will**, forma hablada usual de **who shall***

**whol|ly** /hoʊlli/ ADV **Wholly** means completely. *totalmente, completamente* ❑ *This is a wholly new approach.* *Es un enfoque completamente nuevo.*

**whom** /hum/

> **Whom** is used in formal or written English instead of "who" when it is the object of a verb or preposition.

**1** PRON You use **whom** in questions when you ask about the name or identity of a person or group of people. *a quién* ❑ *"I want to send a telegram."—"Fine, to whom?"* *—Quiero enviar un telegrama. —Perfecto, ¿a quién?* ❑ *Whom did he expect to answer his phone?* *¿Quién esperaba que contestara su teléfono?* **2** CONJ You use **whom** to introduce a clause where you talk about the name or identity of a person or a group of people. *quién* ❑ *He asked whom I'd told.* *Me preguntó a quién le había dicho.* **3** PRON You use **whom** at the beginning of a relative clause when specifying the person or group of people you are talking about or when giving more information about them. *quien* ❑ *One writer in whom I took an interest was John Grisham.* *Un escritor en quien me interesé fue John Grisham.*

**whoop|ing crane** (**whooping cranes**) N-COUNT A **whooping crane** is a rare bird belonging to the crane family that lives only in North America. *grulla americana*

**who's** /huz, huz/ **Who's** is the usual spoken form of "who is" or "who has," especially when "has" is an auxiliary verb. *forma hablada usual de **who is**, forma hablada usual de **who has*** ❑ *Who's going to argue with that?* *¿Quién va a discutir eso?*

**whose** /huz/

> Usually pronounced /huz/ for meanings **2** and **3**.

**1** PRON You use **whose** at the beginning of a relative clause where you mention something that belongs to or is associated with the person or thing mentioned in the previous clause. *cuyo* ❑ *...a driver whose car was blocking the street.* *...un chofer cuyo coche estaba bloqueando la calle.* **2** PRON You use **whose** in questions to ask about the person or thing that something belongs to or is associated with. *de quién* ❑ *"Whose is this?"—"It's mine."* *—¿De quién es esto? —Es mío.* • **Whose** is also a determiner. *de quién* ❑ *Whose daughter is she?* *¿De quién es hija?* **3** DET You use **whose** after certain words, especially verbs and adjectives, to introduce a clause where you talk about the person or thing that something belongs to or is associated with. *de quién* ❑ *I'm wondering whose mother she is.* *Me pregunto de quién es madre.* ❑ *I can't remember whose idea it was.* *No recuerdo de quién fue la idea.*

> **Usage** **whose**
>
> *Whose* and *who's* are often confused. *Whose* expresses possession: *Are you the one whose cell phone kept ringing during class today? Who's* means *who is* or *who has*: *Who's calling you at this hour? Who's been calling you all night?*

**who've** /huv, huv/ **Who've** is the usual spoken form of "who have," especially when "have" is an auxiliary verb. *forma hablada usual de **who have*** ❑ *These are people who've never used a computer before.* *Es gente que nunca antes ha usado una computadora.*

**why** /waɪ/

> The conjunction and the pronoun are usually pronounced /waɪ/.

**1** PRON You use **why** in questions when you ask about the reasons for something. *por qué* ❑ *Why hasn't he brought the money? ¿Por qué no ha traído el dinero?* ❑ *Why didn't he stop me? ¿Por qué no me detuvo?* **2** CONJ You use **why** at the beginning of a clause in which you talk about the reasons for something. *por qué* ❑ *He couldn't say why the elevator was stuck. No sabía por qué se había atorado el ascensor.* ● **Why** is also an adverb. *por qué* ❑ *I don't know why. No sé por qué.* **3** ADV You use **why** with "not" in questions in order to introduce a suggestion. *por qué* ❑ *Why not give Charmaine a call? ¿Por qué no llamar a Charmaine?* **4** CONVENTION You say **why not** in order to agree with what someone has suggested. *porqué no* ❑ *"Would you like to spend the afternoon with me?"— "Why not?" —¿Te gustaría pasar la tarde conmigo?—¿Porqué no?* **5** EXCLAM People say **"Why!"** at the beginning of a sentence when they are surprised, shocked, or angry. *vaya* ❑ *Why hello, Tom! ¡Vaya! ¡¿Qué tal, Tom?!*

**wick|ed** /wɪkɪd/ ADJ You use **wicked** to describe someone or something that is very bad and deliberately harmful to people. *malvado, perverso, vil* ❑ *She described the shooting as a wicked attack. Describió el tiroteo como un ataque vil.* ● **wickedness** N-UNCOUNT *iniquidad* ❑ *...the wickedness of war. ...la iniquidad de la guerra.*

**wide** /waɪd/ (**wider, widest**) **1** ADJ Something that is **wide** measures a large distance from one side or edge to the other. *ancho, amplio* ❑ *The sidewalk was only wide enough for two people. En la banqueta sólo cabían dos personas.* ❑ *...a shirt with wide sleeves. ...una camisa con mangas anchas.* **2** ADJ If you open or spread something **wide,** you open or spread it as far as possible or to the fullest extent. *ampliamente* ❑ *"It was huge," he announced, spreading his arms wide. —¡Era enorme! —dijo, abriendo los brazos lo más que daban.* **3** ADJ You use **wide** to talk or ask about how much something measures from one side or edge to the other. *ancho* ❑ *...a strip of land four miles wide. ...una franja de tierra de seis kilómetros y medio de ancho.* ❑ *The road is only one lane wide. El camino sólo tiene el ancho de un carril.* **4** ADJ You use **wide** to describe something that includes a large number of different things or people. *amplio* ❑ *The brochure offers a wide choice of hotels. El folleto presenta una amplia selección de hoteles.* ● **wide|ly** ADV *ampliamente* ❑ *...the most widely read newspaper in Hungary. ...el periódico que más se lee en Hungría.* **5** ADJ **Wider** is used to describe something that relates to the most important or general parts of a situation, rather than to the smaller parts or to details. *más importante* ❑ *He spoke about the wider issues. Habló de las cuestiones más importantes.* **6** **wide awake** → see **awake** **7** **wide of the mark** → see **mark**

> **Thesaurus** *wide* Ver también:
>
> ADJ. broad, large; (*ant.*) narrow **1 3 4**

> **Word Partnership** Usar *wide* con:
>
> N. wide **grin/smile**, wide **margin**, wide **shoulders** **1**
> **arms/eyes/mouth open** wide **2**
> wide **array**, wide **audience**, wide **selection**, wide **variety** **4**

**wid|en** /waɪdᵊn/ (**widens, widening, widened**) **1** V-T/V-I If you **widen** something or if it **widens,** it becomes greater in measurement from one side or edge to the other. *ampliar, ensanchar* ❑ *They are planning to widen the road. Están planeando ensanchar la carretera.* **2** V-T/V-I If you **widen** something or if it **widens,** it becomes greater in range or it affects a larger number of people or things. *ampliar, extender* ❑ *The search for the missing boy widened. Se extendió la búsqueda del niño desaparecido.*

**wide|screen** /waɪdskrin/ ADJ A **widescreen** television has a screen that is wide in relation to its height. *de pantalla ancha*

**wide|spread** /waɪdsprɛd/ ADJ Something that is **widespread** exists or happens over a large area, or to a great extent. *generalizado* ❑ *Food shortages are widespread. La escasez de alimentos es generalizada.*

**wid|ow** /wɪdoʊ/ (**widows**) N-COUNT A **widow** is a woman whose husband has died and who has not married again. *viuda* ❑ *She became a widow a year ago. Se quedó viuda hace un año.*

**width** /wɪdθ, wɪtθ/ (**widths**) N-VAR The **width** of something is the distance it measures from one side or edge to the other. *ancho, anchura* ❑ *Measure the full width of the window. Mida el ancho total de la ventana.*

**wie|ner** /winər/ (**wieners**) also **weenie** or **wienie** N-COUNT **Wieners** are sausages made from smoked beef or pork. *salchicha de Viena, salchicha de Frankfurt*

**wife** /waɪf/ (**wives**) N-COUNT A man's **wife** is the woman he is married to. *esposa* ❑ *He married his wife Jane 37 years ago. Se casó con su esposa Jane hace 37 años.*
→ see **family, love**

**wig** /wɪg/ (**wigs**) N-COUNT A **wig** is a covering of false hair that you wear on your head. *peluca*

**wild** /waɪld/ (**wilds, wilder, wildest**) **1** ADJ **Wild** animals or plants live or grow in natural surroundings and are not taken care of by people. *salvaje, silvestre, montés* ❑ *...wild cats. ...gatos monteses.* **2** ADJ **Wild** land is natural and is not used by people. *silvestre* ❑ *...a wild area of woods and lakes. ...una región silvestre de bosques y lagos.* **3** N-PLURAL **The wilds** of a place are the natural areas that are far away from cities and towns. *región silvestre* ❑ *...the wilds of Canada. ...las regiones silvestres del Canadá.* **4** ADJ **Wild** behavior is uncontrolled, excited, or energetic. *loco* ❑ *The crowds went wild when they saw him. La multitud se volvió loca cuando apareció él.* ● **wild|ly** ADV *a rabiar* ❑ *As she finished each song, the crowd clapped wildly. Cada vez que terminaba una canción, la multitud le aplaudía a rabiar.* **5** ADJ A **wild** idea is unusual or extreme. A **wild** guess is one that you make without much thought. *suposición aventurada* ❑ *Go on, take a wild guess. Anda, di lo primero que se te ocurra.* ● **wild|ly** ADV *aventuradamente* ❑ *"Thirteen?"*

W

*he guessed wildly.* *—¿Trece? —aventuró.* 6 → see also **wildly**
→ see **carnivore, fire**

| **Thesaurus** | *wild* | Ver también: |
|---|---|---|
| ADJ. | desolate, natural, overgrown 2<br>excited, rowdy, uncontrolled 4 | |

| **Word Partnership** | Usar *wild* con: |
|---|---|
| N. | wild **animal**, wild **beasts/creatures**, wild **game**, wild **horse**, wild **mushrooms** 1<br>wild **pitch**, wild **swing** 4 |
| V. | **go** wild, **run** wild 4 |

**wil|der|ness** /wɪldərnɛs/ (**wildernesses**) N-COUNT A **wilderness** is a desert or other area of natural land which is not used by people. *desierto, páramo, soledad* ❑ *...the icy Canadian wilderness.* *...las heladas soledades canadienses.*

**wild|life** /waɪldlaɪf/ N-UNCOUNT You can use **wildlife** to refer to the animals and other living things that live in the wild. *vida silvestre* ❑ *The area is rich in wildlife.* *La región es rica en vida silvestre.*
→ see **zoo**

**wild|ly** /waɪldli/ 1 ADV You use **wildly** to emphasize the degree, amount, or intensity of something. *disparatadamente* ❑ *Milk costs twice what it should and meat is also wildly over-priced.* *La leche cuesta lo doble de lo que debería y el precio de la carne también es exageradísimo.* 2 → see also **wild**

**will**
1 MODAL VERB USES
2 WANTING SOMETHING TO HAPPEN

❶ **will** /wɪl/

> **Will** is a modal verb. It is used with the base form of a verb. In spoken English and informal written English, the form **won't** is often used in negative statements.

1 MODAL You use **will** to indicate that you hope, think, or have evidence that something is going to happen or be the case in the future. *auxiliar de futuro* ❑ *Will you ever be happy here?* *¿Alguna vez serás feliz aquí?* ❑ *The ship will not be ready for a month.* *El barco no va a estar listo antes de un mes.* 2 MODAL You use **will** to indicate your intention to do something. *auxiliar de futuro* ❑ *Will you be staying?* *¿Vas a quedarte?* ❑ *What will you do next?* *¿Qué vas a hacer después?* 3 MODAL You use **will** in questions in order to make polite invitations or offers. *querer* ❑ *Will you stay for supper?* *¿Quiere quedarse a cenar?* ❑ *Will you have dinner with me?* *¿Quieres cenar conmigo?* 4 MODAL You use **will** to say that someone is willing to do something. You use **will not** or **won't** to indicate that someone refuses to do something. *auxiliar de futuro* ❑ *I'll answer the phone.* *Yo contesto el teléfono.* 5 → see also **willing**

❷ **will** /wɪl/ (**wills, willing, willed**) 1 N-VAR **Will** is the determination to do something. *voluntad, deseo, intención* ❑ *He has lost his will to live.* *Ya no tiene ganas de vivir.* 2 N-SING If something is **the will of** a person or group of people with authority, they want it to happen. *voluntad* ❑ *...the will of God.* *...la voluntad de Dios.* 3 V-T If you **will** something **to** happen, you try to make it happen by using mental effort rather than physical effort. *desear* ❑ *I looked at the telephone, willing it to ring.* *Me quedé mirando el teléfono, deseando que sonara.* 4 N-COUNT A **will** is a document in which you say what you want to happen to your money and property when you die. *testamento*

**will|ing** /wɪlɪŋ/ 1 ADJ If someone is **willing to** do something, they are fairly happy about doing it and will do it if they are asked or required to do it. *dispuesto a* ❑ *She's willing to answer questions.* *Está dispuesta a responder preguntas.* • **willingly** ADV *con gusto, de buen grado, por voluntad propia* ❑ *Bryant talked willingly to the police.* *Bryant habló voluntariamente con la policía.* • **willingness** N-UNCOUNT *disposición, buena voluntad* ❑ *She showed her willingness to work hard.* *Mostró su disposición a trabajar con empeño.* 2 ADJ **Willing** is used to describe someone who does something fairly enthusiastically and because they want to do it rather than because they are forced to do it. *dispuesto* ❑ *He was a natural and willing learner.* *Era un aprendiz natural y con buena disposición.*

**win** /wɪn/ (**wins, winning, won**) 1 V-T/V-I If you **win** something such as a competition, battle, or argument, you defeat those people you are competing or fighting against, or you do better than everyone else involved. *ganar* ❑ *He does not have a chance of winning the fight.* *No tiene ninguna probabilidad de ganar la pelea.* ❑ *The top four teams all won.* *Ganaron los cuatro equipos mejor clasificados.* • **Win** is also a noun. *triunfo* ❑ *They played eight games without a win.* *Jugaron ocho partidos sin un solo triunfo.* 2 V-T If you **win** something such as a prize or medal, you get it because you have defeated everyone else in something such as an election, competition, battle, or argument, or have done very well in it. *ganar* ❑ *The first correct entry wins the prize.* *La primera respuesta correcta gana el premio.* 3 V-T If you **win** something that you want or need, you succeed in getting it. *lograr* ❑ *...moves to win the support of the poor.* *...medidas para lograr el apoyo de los pobres.* 4 → see also **winning**

▶ **win over** PHR-VERB If you **win** someone **over**, you persuade them to support you or agree with you. *convencer* ❑ *Not everyone agrees but I am winning them over.* *No todos están de acuerdo, pero ya estoy convenciéndolos.*

| **Thesaurus** | *win* | Ver también: |
|---|---|---|
| V. | conquer, succeed, triumph; (*ant.*) lose 1 | |
| N. | conquest, success, victory; (*ant.*) defeat 1 | |

**wind**
1 AIR
2 TURNING OR WRAPPING

❶ **wind** /wɪnd/ (**winds, winding, winded**) 1 N-VAR A **wind** is a current of air that is moving across the Earth's surface. *viento* ❑ *A strong wind was blowing.* *Estaba soplando un fuerte viento.* 2 V-T If you **are winded** by something such as a blow, the air is suddenly knocked out of your lungs so that you have difficulty breathing for a short time. *dejar sin aliento, cortar la respiración* ❑ *He was winded*

**Word Web** **wind**

The earth's surface **temperature** isn't the same everywhere. This temperature difference causes **air** to move from one area to another. We call this airflow **wind**. As warm air expands and rises, air pressure goes down. Then denser cool air **blows** in. The amount of difference in air pressure determines how strong the wind will be. It can be anything from a **breeze** to a **gale**. The earth's geography creates prevailing winds. For example, air in the warmer areas near the Equator is always rising, and cooler air from polar regions is always flowing in to take its place.

*by the fall.* *La caída lo dejó sin aliento.* 3 N-UNCOUNT **Wind** energy or **wind** power is energy or power that is obtained from the wind, for example by the use of a turbine. *energía eólica*
→ see Word Web: **wind**
→ see **beach, electricity, erosion, hurricane, storm, wave**

**Word Partnership** Usar *wind* con:

V. **blown/driven by the** wind, wind **blows**, wind **whips** ❶ 1
ADJ. **cold** wind, **hot** wind, **howling** wind, **icy** wind, **warm** wind ❶ 1
N. **desert** wind, **gust of** wind, **wind** power, **winter** wind ❶ 1

❷ **wind** /waɪnd/ (**winds, winding, wound**) 1 V-T/V-I If a road, river, or line of people **winds** in a particular direction, it goes in that direction with a lot of bends or twists in it. *serpentear* ❑ *The road winds along by the river.* *El camino serpentea paralelo al río.* 2 V-T When you **wind** something flexible around something else, you wrap it around it several times. *enrollar* ❑ *She wound the rope around her waist.* *Se enrolló la soga alrededor de la cintura.* 3 V-T When you **wind** a mechanical device, for example, a watch or a clock, you turn a knob, key, or handle on it several times in order to make it operate. *dar cuerda*

**Thesaurus** *wind* Ver también:

N. air, current, gust ❶ 1
V. bend, loop, twist; (*ant.*) straighten ❷ 2

▸ **wind down** PHR-VERB If someone **winds down** a business or activity, they gradually reduce the amount of work that is done or the number of people that are involved, usually before closing or stopping it completely. *reducir paulatinamente* ❑ *Aid workers have begun winding down their operation.* *Los voluntarios han empezado a reducir paulatinamente sus operaciones.*

▸ **wind up** 1 PHR-VERB When you **wind up** an activity, you finish it or stop doing it. *poner fin a, concluir* ❑ *The president is winding up his visit to Somalia.* *El presidente está dando por concluida su visita a Somalia.*

W

**wind chill fac|tor** also **wind-chill factor** or **windchill factor** N-SING A **wind chill factor** is a measure of the cooling effect of the wind on the temperature of the air. *factor de sensación térmica* ❑ *...a wind chill factor of 80 degrees below zero.* *...un factor de sensación térmica de 62 grados bajo cero.*

**win|dow** /wɪndoʊ/ (**windows**) 1 N-COUNT A **window** is a space in the wall of a building or in the side of a vehicle, which has glass in it so that light can come in and you can see out. *ventana* ❑ *He looked out of the window.* *Miró por la ventana.* 2 N-COUNT On a computer screen, a **window** is one of the work areas that the screen can be divided into. *recuadro, ventana* [COMPUTING] ❑ *Open the document in a new window.* *Abra el documento en una nueva ventana.*

**Word Partnership** Usar *window* con:

N. **car** window, window **curtains**, window **display**, **kitchen** window, window **screen**, **shop** window, **store** window, window **treatment** 1
ADJ. **broken** window, **dark** window, **large/small** window, **narrow** window 1 **open** window 1 2
V. **look in/out a** window, **peer in/into/out/through a** window, **watch through a** window 1 **close/open a** window 1 2

**win|dow shade** (**window shades**) N-COUNT A **window shade** is a piece of stiff cloth or heavy paper that you can pull down over a window as a covering. *visillo, cortinilla*

**wind|shield** /wɪndʃild/ (**windshields**) N-COUNT The **windshield** of a car or other vehicle is the glass window at the front through which the driver looks. *parabrisas*

**wind|shield wip|er** (**windshield wipers**) N-COUNT A **windshield wiper** is a device that wipes rain from a vehicle's windshield. *limpiaparabrisas*

**wind|sock** /wɪndsɒk/ (**windsocks**) also **wind sock** N-COUNT A **windsock** is a device, consisting of a tube of cloth mounted on a pole, that is used at airports and airfields to indicate the direction and force of the wind. *manga catavientos, manga de viento, cono de viento*

**wind vane** (**wind vanes**) N-COUNT A **wind vane** is a metal object on the roof of a building that turns around as the wind blows. It is used to show the direction of the wind. *veleta*

**windy** /wɪndi/ (**windier, windiest**) ADJ If it is **windy**, the wind is blowing a lot. *ventoso* ❑ *The sun was setting after a day of windy weather.* *El sol estaba poniéndose después de un día ventoso.*

**wine** /waɪn/ (**wines**) N-VAR **Wine** is an alcoholic drink made from grapes. *vino* ❑ *...a bottle of white wine.* *...una botella de vino blanco.*

**Word Link** *ery ≈ place where something happens : bakery, cemetery, winery*

**win|ery** /waɪnəri/ (**wineries**) N-COUNT A **winery** is a place where wine is made. *bodega, vinería*

**wing** /wɪŋ/ (**wings**) **1** N-COUNT The **wings** of a bird or insect are the two parts of its body that it uses for flying. *ala* ❑ *The bird flapped its wings. El pájaro batió las alas.* **2** N-COUNT The **wings** of an airplane are the long flat parts sticking out of its side which support it while it is flying. *ala, alerón* ❑ *The plane dipped its wings, then circled back. El avión bajó los alerones, dio media vuelta y regresó.* **3** N-COUNT A **wing** of a building is a part of it that sticks out from the main part. *ala* ❑ *Her office was in the west wing of the building. Su oficina estaba en el ala oeste del edificio.* **4** N-COUNT A **wing** of an organization, especially a political organization, is a group within it which has a particular function or particular beliefs. *ala* ❑ *...the military wing of the African National Congress. ...el ala militar del Congreso Nacional Africano.* **5** → see also **left-wing, right-wing** **6** N-PLURAL In a theater, **the wings** are the sides of the stage that are hidden from the audience by curtains or scenery. *bastidores* ❑ *I watched the start of the play from the wings. Vi el inicio de la obra entre bastidores.*
→ see **bird, insect**

**Word Partnership** Usar *wing* con:

| | |
|---|---|
| N. | **aircraft** wing **2** |
| ADJ. | **military/political** wing **4** |

**wink** /wɪŋk/ (**winks, winking, winked**) V-I When you **wink at** someone, you look toward them and close one eye very briefly, usually as a signal that something is a joke or a secret. *parpadear, guiñar el ojo* ● **Wink** is also a noun. *guiño* ❑ *I gave her a wink. Le hice un guiño.*

**win|ner** /wɪnər/ (**winners**) N-COUNT The **winner** of a prize, race, or competition is the person, animal, or thing that wins it. *ganador, ganadora* ❑ *She will present the prizes to the winners. Ella va a entregar los premios a los ganadores.*

**win|ning** /wɪnɪŋ/ **1** ADJ You can use **winning** to describe a person or thing that wins something such as a competition, game, or election. *ganador* ❑ *...the winning ticket. ...el boleto ganador.* **2** ADJ You can use **winning** to describe actions or qualities that please other people and make them feel friendly toward you. *encantador* ❑ *She gave him a winning smile. Le dirigió una sonrisa encantadora.* **3** → see also **win**

**win|ter** /wɪntər/ (**winters**) N-VAR **Winter** is the season between fall and spring. In the winter the weather is usually cold. *invierno* ❑ *In winter the nights are long and cold. En invierno, las noches son largas y frías.*

**wipe** /waɪp/ (**wipes, wiping, wiped**) **1** V-T If you **wipe** something, you rub its surface to remove dirt or liquid from it. *limpiar* ❑ *I'll just wipe my hands. Nada más me lavo las manos.* ● **Wipe** is also a noun. *limpieza, limpiada* ❑ *I'm going to give the table a good wipe. Voy a darle a la mesa una buena limpiada.* **2** V-T If you **wipe** dirt or liquid from something, you remove it by using a cloth or your hand. *limpiar(se)* ❑ *Gary wiped the sweat from his face. Gary se limpió el sudor del rostro.*
▶ **wipe out** PHR-VERB To **wipe out** something such as a place or a group of people or animals means to destroy them completely. *exterminar, aniquilar* ❑ *The disease wiped out thousands of birds. La enfermedad exterminó miles de aves.*

**Word Partnership** Usar *wipe* con:

| | |
|---|---|
| ADJ. | wipe *something* **clean** **1** |
| N. | wipe **blood**, wipe **your eyes**, wipe **someone's face**, wipe **tears** **2** |

**wire** /waɪər/ (**wires**) **1** N-VAR A **wire** is a long thin piece of metal that is used to fasten things or to carry electric current. *alambre* ❑ *...fine copper wire. ...alambre de cobre delgado.* **2** → see also **barbed wire**
→ see **metal**

**wired** /waɪərd/ ADJ If someone is **wired,** they are tense, nervous, and unable to relax. *nervioso* [INFORMAL] ❑ *They were so wired with fear that they could not sleep. El miedo los tenía tan tensos que no pudieron dormir.*

**Word Link** *less ≈ without : endless, hopeless, wireless*

**wire|less** /waɪərlɪs/ ADJ **Wireless** technology uses radio waves rather than electricity and therefore does not require any wires. *inalámbrico* ❑ *...the fast-growing wireless communication market. ...el mercado de la comunicación inalámbrica en rápido crecimiento.*
→ see **cellphone**

**Word Link** *dom ≈ state of being : boredom, freedom, wisdom*

**wis|dom** /wɪzdəm/ **1** N-UNCOUNT **Wisdom** is the ability to use your experience and knowledge in order to make sensible decisions or judgments. *sabiduría* ❑ *...the wisdom that comes from old age. ...la sabiduría de la vejez.* **2** N-SING If you talk about **the wisdom of** a particular decision or action, you are talking about how sensible it is. *prudencia* ❑ *They are questioning the wisdom of the plan. Están dudando de que el plan sea acertado.*

**wise** /waɪz/ (**wiser, wisest**) ADJ A **wise** person is able to use their experience and knowledge in order to make sensible decisions and judgments. *sabio, prudente* ❑ *She's a wise woman. Es una mujer prudente.* ● **wise|ly** ADV *prudentemente* ❑ *They spent their money wisely. Gastaron su dinero prudentemente.*

**wish** /wɪʃ/ (**wishes, wishing, wished**) **1** N-COUNT A **wish** is a desire for something. *deseo* ❑ *Her wish is to become a doctor. Su deseo es llegar a ser médico.* **2** V-T/V-I If you **wish** to do something, you want to do it. *desear, querer* [FORMAL] ❑ *I wish to leave a message. Quisiera dejar un mensaje.* ❑ *We can do as we wish now. Ya podemos hacer lo que queramos.* **3** V-T If you **wish** something were true, you would like it to be true, even though you know that it is impossible or unlikely. *desear* ❑ *I wish I could do that. Quisiera poder hacer eso.* **4** V-I If you **wish for** something, you express the desire for that thing silently to yourself. In fairy tales, when a person wishes for something, the thing they wish for often happens by magic. desear ❑ *Be careful what you wish for. You might get it! ¡Cuidado con lo que deseas, podría hacerse realidad!* ● **Wish** is also a noun. deseo ❑ *Did you make a wish? ¿Pediste un deseo?* **5** V-T If you **wish** someone something such as luck or happiness, you express the hope that they will be lucky or happy. desear ❑ *I wish you both a good trip. Les deseo un buen viaje.* **6** N-PLURAL If you express your good **wishes** toward someone, you are politely expressing your friendly feelings toward them and your hope that they will be successful or happy. saludo ❑ *Please give him my best wishes. Salúdalo de mi parte.*

**Word Partnership** Usar *wish* con:

V. wish **come true**, **get** ***your*** wish, **grant a** wish, **have a** wish, **make a** wish **1** **4**
N. wish ***someone*** **the best**, wish ***someone*** **luck** **5**

**wit** /wɪt/ (**wits**) **1** N-UNCOUNT **Wit** is the ability to use words or ideas in an amusing, clever, and imaginative way. ingenio, agudeza ❑ *He writes with great wit. Escribe con mucho ingenio.* **2** N-PLURAL You can refer to your ability to think quickly and effectively in a difficult situation as your **wits.** ingenio ❑ *She has used her wits to get to where she is today. Se ha valido de su ingenio para llegar hasta donde está hoy.*

**witch** /wɪtʃ/ (**witches**) N-COUNT In fairy tales, a **witch** is a woman, usually an old woman, who has evil magic powers. bruja, brujo

**witch hunt** (**witch hunts**) N-COUNT A **witch hunt** is an attempt to find and punish a particular group of people who are being blamed for something, often simply because of their opinions and not because they have actually done anything wrong. caza de brujas ❑ *...a political witch hunt. ...políticos a la caza de brujas.*

**with** /wɪð, wɪθ/

In addition to the uses shown below, **with** is used after some verbs, nouns and adjectives in order to introduce extra information. **With** is also used in most reciprocal verbs, such as "agree" or "fight," and in some phrasal verbs, such as "deal with" and "go along with."

**1** PREP If one person is **with** another, they are together in one place. con ❑ *Her son and daughter were with her. Sus hijos estaban con ella.* **2** PREP If you discuss something **with** someone, or if you fight or argue **with** someone, you are both involved in a discussion, fight, or argument. con ❑ *We didn't discuss it with each other. No lo discutimos entre nosotros.* ❑ *About a thousand students fought with police. Unos mil estudiantes lucharon con la policía.* **3** PREP If you do something **with** a particular tool, object, or substance, you do it using that tool, object, or substance. con ❑ *Turn the meat over with a fork. Voltee la carne con un tenedor.* ❑ *I don't allow my children to eat with their fingers. Yo no permito que mis hijos coman con los dedos.* **4** PREP If someone stands or goes somewhere **with** something, they are carrying it. con ❑ *A woman came in with a cup of coffee. Entró una mujer con una taza de café.* **5** PREP Someone or something **with** a particular feature or possession has that feature or possession. de ❑ *He was tall, with blue eyes. Era alto, de ojos azules.* **6** PREP If something is filled or covered **with** a substance or **with** things, it has that substance or those things in it or on it. de ❑ *His legs were covered with dirt. Tenía las piernas llenas de mugre.* **7** PREP You use **with** to indicate what a state, quality, or action relates to, involves, or affects. con ❑ *He has a problem with money. Tiene un problema con el dinero.* ❑ *I'm familiar with the neighborhood. Estoy familiarizado con el vecindario.* **8** PREP You use **with** when indicating the way that something is done or the feeling that a person has when they do something. con ❑ *He listened with great care. Escuchó con mucho cuidado.* **9** PREP You use **with** when indicating a sound or gesture that is made when something is done, or an expression that a person has on their face when they do something. con ❑ *"It's still early," he said with a smile. —Todavía es temprano—, dijo con una sonrisa.* ❑ *The front door closed with a crash. La puerta del frente se cerró con estrépito.* **10** PREP You use **with** to indicate the feeling that makes someone have a particular appearance or type of behavior. de ❑ *Gil was white and shaking with anger. Gil estaba pálido y temblaba de ira.* **11** PREP You use **with** when mentioning the position or appearance of a person or thing at the time that they do something, or what someone else is doing at that time. con ❑ *Joanne stood with her hands on the sink, staring out the window. Joanne se quedó con las manos en el fregadero, mirando por la ventana.* **12** PREP You use **with** to introduce a current situation that is a factor affecting another situation. con ❑ *With all the bad things that have happened, he's had a difficult year. Con todo lo malo que ha pasado, ha tenido un año difícil.*

**Word Link** ***with*** ***≈ against, away : withdraw, withhold, without***

**with|draw** /wɪðdrɔ, wɪθ-/ (**withdraws, withdrawing, withdrew, withdrawn**) **1** V-T If you **withdraw** something from a place, you remove it or take it away. retirar, sacar [FORMAL] ❑ *He reached into his pocket and withdrew a sheet of paper. Metió la mano en el bolsillo y sacó una hoja de papel.* **2** V-T/V-I When groups of people such as troops **withdraw** or when someone **withdraws** them, they leave the place where they are fighting or where they are based and return nearer home. retirar(se) ❑ *The army will withdraw as soon as the war ends. El ejército se retirará tan pronto termine la guerra.* **3** V-T If you **withdraw** money from a bank account, you take it out of that account. retirar, sacar ❑ *He withdrew $750 from his account. Retiró 750 dólares de su cuenta.* **4** V-I If you **withdraw from** an activity or organization, you stop taking part in it. retirarse ❑ *...the second tennis player to withdraw from the games. ...el segundo tenista que se retira del torneo.*

**Word Partnership** Usar *withdraw* con:

N. withdraw **an offer**, withdraw **support** **1**
**decision to** withdraw **1** – **4**
**deadline to** withdraw, **forces/troops** withdraw **2**
withdraw **money** **3**

**with|draw|al** /wɪðdrɔəl, wɪθ-/ (**withdrawals**) **1** N-VAR The **withdrawal** of something is the

W

act or process of removing it, or ending it. *retiro, abandono* [FORMAL] ❑ *...the withdrawal of food and medical treatment. ...abandonar el tratamiento dietético y médico.* **2** N-UNCOUNT Someone's **withdrawal from** an activity or an organization is their decision to stop taking part in it. *retiro* ❑ *...his withdrawal from government in 1946. ...su retiro del gobierno en 1946.* **3** N-COUNT A **withdrawal** is an amount of money that you take from your bank account. *retiro* ❑ *I went to the cash machine to make a withdrawal. Fui al cajero automático a hacer un retiro.*

**with|drew** /wɪðdru, wɪθ-/ **Withdrew** is the past tense of **withdraw**. *pasado de* ***withdraw***

| Word Link | *with ≈ against, away : withdraw, withhold, without* |
|---|---|

**with|hold** /wɪðhoʊld, wɪθ-/ (**withholds, withholding, withheld** /wɪðhɛld, wɪθ-/) V-T If you **withhold** something that someone wants, you do not let them have it. *retener, ocultar* [FORMAL] ❑ *Police withheld the man's name until they could tell his family about the accident. La policía no reveló la identidad del hombre hasta no informar a su familia sobre el accidente.*

**with|in** /wɪðɪn, wɪθ-/ **1** PREP If something is **within** a place, area, or object, it is inside it or surrounded by it. *dentro, en* [FORMAL] ❑ *The sports fields must be within the city. Los campos deportivos deben estar en la ciudad.* ● **Within** is also an adverb. *adentro* ❑ *A small voice called from within. "Yes, I'm just coming." Desde adentro se oyó una vocecita: —Sí, ya voy.* **2** PREP Something that happens or exists **within** a society, organization, or system, happens or exists inside it. *en* ❑ *He is working within a system that doesn't allow him to make many changes. Trabaja en una institución que no le permite hacer muchos cambios.* ● **Within** is also an adverb. *adentro* ❑ *The real dangers came from within. El verdadero riesgo venía del interior.* **3** PREP If something is **within** a particular limit or set of rules, it does not go beyond it or is not more than what is allowed. *dentro* ❑ *He had to stay within a range of five miles. No podía alejarse más de ocho kilómetros.* **4** PREP If you are **within** a particular distance of a place, you are less than that distance from it. *a* ❑ *The man was within a few feet of him. El hombre estaba a unos pasos de él.* **5** PREP **Within** a particular length of time means before that length of time has passed. *antes de* ❑ *Within twenty-four hours I had the money. Antes de veinticuatro horas, ya tenía el dinero.* **6** PREP If something is **within sight, within earshot,** or **within reach,** you can see it, hear it, or reach it. *a la vista* ❑ *He parked the car within sight of Sandra's house. Estacionó el coche a la vista de la casa de Sandra.*

**with|out** /wɪðaʊt, wɪθ-/

| In addition to the uses shown below, **without** is used in the phrasal verbs "do without" and "go without". |
|---|

**1** PREP You use **without** to indicate that someone or something does not have or use the thing mentioned. *sin* ❑ *I don't like him without a beard. No me gusta sin barba.* ❑ *You shouldn't drive without a seat belt. No deberías manejar sin el cinturón de seguridad.* **2** PREP If one thing happens **without** another thing, or if you do something **without** doing something else, the second thing does not happen or occur. *sin* ❑ *He left without speaking to me. Se fue sin decirme nada.* ❑ *They worked without stopping until about eight in the evening. Trabajaron sin parar hasta cerca de las ocho de la noche.* **3** PREP If you do something **without** a particular feeling, you do not have that feeling when you do it. *sin* ❑ *"Hello, David," he said without surprise. —Hola, David—, dijo sin mostrarse sorprendido.* **4** PREP If you do something **without** someone else, they are not in the same place as you are or are not involved in the same action as you. *sin* ❑ *I told Frank to start dinner without me. Le dije a Frank que empezara a cenar sin mí.*

**wit|ness** /wɪtnɪs/ (**witnesses, witnessing, witnessed**) **1** N-COUNT A **witness** to an event such as an accident or crime is a person who saw it. *testigo* ❑ *Witnesses say they saw an explosion. Los testigos dicen que vieron una explosión.* **2** V-T If you **witness** something, you see it happen. *presenciar* ❑ *Anyone who witnessed the attack should call the police. Quienes presenciaron el asalto deben comunicarse con la policía.* **3** N-COUNT A **witness** is someone who appears in a court of law to say what they know about a crime or other event. *testigo* ❑ *Eleven witnesses appeared in court. Se presentaron once testigos ante el tribunal.* **4** N-COUNT A **witness** is someone who writes their name on a document that you have signed, to confirm that it really is your signature. *testigo* ❑ *You must sign the document in front of two witnesses. Debe firmar el documento ante dos testigos.* **5** V-T If someone **witnesses** your signature on a document, they write their name after it, to confirm that it really is your signature. *atestiguar*
→ see **trial, wedding**

**wit|ness stand** N-SING **The witness stand** in a court of law is the place where people stand or sit when they are giving evidence. *estrado de los testigos* ❑ *O'Donnell took the witness stand Thursday. O'Donnell rindió testimonio el jueves.*

**wit|ty** /wɪti/ (**wittier, wittiest**) ADJ Someone or something that is **witty** is amusing in a clever way. *ingenioso* ❑ *His books were very witty. Sus libros eran muy ingeniosos.*

**wives** /waɪvz/ **Wives** is the plural of **wife**. *plural de* ***wife***

**wiz|ard** /wɪzərd/ (**wizards**) **1** N-COUNT In legends and fairy tales, a **wizard** is a man who has magic powers. *mago, brujo* **2** N-COUNT If you admire someone because they are very good at doing a particular thing, you can say that they are a **wizard**. ❑ *...a financial wizard. ...un genio de las finanzas.* **3** N-COUNT A **wizard** is a computer program that guides you through the stages of a particular task. *programa guía de computadora* [COMPUTING]

**WMD** /dʌbᵊlyu ɛm di/ N-PLURAL **WMD** is an abbreviation for **weapons of mass destruction**. *abreviatura de* ***weapons of mass destruction***

wolf

**wolf** /wʊlf/ (**wolves, wolfs, wolfing, wolfed**) **1** N-COUNT A **wolf** is a wild animal that looks like a large dog. *lobo, loba* **2** V-T If someone **wolfs** their food, they eat it all very quickly and greedily. *devorar,*

engullir(se) [INFORMAL] ❑ *He wolfed doughnuts and pastries.* *Se devoró las donas y las pastitas.* ● **Wolf down** means the same as **wolf.** devorar, engullir(se) ❑ *He wolfed down the rest of the sandwich.* *Devoró el resto del sándwich.*
→ see **carnivore**

**Word Link** *man ≈ human being : foreman, humanity, woman*

**wom|an** /wʊmən/ (**women**) N-COUNT A **woman** is an adult female human being. *mujer* ❑ *My favorite woman is my mother.* *Mi mujer preferida es mi madre.*
→ see **age**

**wom|en's room** (**women's rooms**) N-COUNT **The women's room** is a toilet for women in a public building. *baño de damas, baño de mujeres*

**wom|en's shel|ter** (**women's shelters**) N-COUNT A **women's shelter** is a place where women can go for safety and protection, for example, if they feel threatened by violence. *refugio para mujeres maltratadas*

**won** /wʌn/ **Won** is the past tense and past participle of **win.** *pasado y participio pasado de* ***win***
→ see **election**

**won|der** /wʌndər/ (**wonders, wondering, wondered**) **1** V-T/V-I If you **wonder** about something, you think about it, and try to guess or understand more about it. *preguntarse* ❑ *I wondered what the noise was.* *Me pregunté qué era ese ruido.* ❑ *"We've been wondering about him," said Max.* *—Hemos estado preguntándonos qué habrá sido de él—, dijo Max.* **2** V-T/V-I If you **wonder at** something, you are very surprised about it or think about it in a very surprised way. *asombrarse* ❑ *Angie wondered at her calmness.* *Angie se asombró de su calma.* **3** N-SING If you say that it is a **wonder that** something happened, you mean that it is very surprising and unexpected. *milagro* ❑ *It's a wonder that we're still friends.* *Es un milagro que sigamos siendo amigos.* **4** N-UNCOUNT **Wonder** is a feeling of great surprise and pleasure that you have, for example, when you see something that is very beautiful, or when something happens that you thought was impossible. *maravilla* ❑ *"That's right!" Bobby shouted in wonder.* *—¡Es cierto!—, gritó Bobby maravillado.* **5** N-COUNT A **wonder** is something that causes people to feel great surprise or admiration. *maravilla* ❑ *...the wonders of nature.* *...las maravillas de la naturaleza.* **6** PHRASE If you say **"no wonder," "little wonder,"** or **"small wonder,"** you mean that something is not surprising. *no ser de extrañar* ❑ *No wonder my brother wasn't feeling well.* *No es de extrañar que mi hermano no se sintiera bien.* **7** PHRASE If you say that a person or thing **works wonders** or **does wonders,** you mean that they have a very good effect on something. *hacer maravillas* ❑ *A few hours' sleep can work wonders.* *Una cuantas horas de sueño pueden hacer maravillas.*

W

**won|der|ful** /wʌndərfəl/ ADJ If you describe something or someone as **wonderful,** you think they are extremely good. *maravilloso, estupendo* ❑ *The cold air felt wonderful on his face.* *El aire frío en la cara le cayó de perlas.* ❑ *It's wonderful to see you.* *Es estupendo verte.* ● **won|der|ful|ly** ADV *de maravilla, riquísimo* ❑ *The vegetables are wonderfully tasty.* *Las verduras saben riquísimo.*

**won't** /woʊnt/ **Won't** is the usual spoken form of "will not." *forma hablada usual de* ***will not*** ❑ *I won't hurt you.* *No voy a lastimarte.*

**woo** /wu/ (**woos, wooing, wooed**) V-T If you **woo** people, you try to encourage them to help you, support you, or vote for you, for example, by promising them things which they would like. *atraer* ❑ *They wooed customers with low prices.* *Atraían a los clientes con precios bajos.*
→ see **love**

**wood** /wʊd/ (**woods**) **1** N-VAR **Wood** is the material that forms the trunks and branches of trees. *madera* ❑ *Some houses are made of wood.* *Algunas casas son de madera.* **2** N-COUNT A **wood** or **woods** is a fairly large area of trees growing near each other. *bosque* ❑ *We went for a walk in the woods.* *Fuimos a dar una caminata por el bosque.*
→ see **energy, fire, forest, percussion**

**wood|en** /wʊdᵊn/ ADJ **Wooden** objects are made of wood. *de madera* ❑ *...wooden chair.* *...una silla de madera.*
→ see **utensil**

**wood|land** /wʊdlənd/ (**woodlands**) N-VAR **Woodland** is land with a lot of trees. *bosque* ❑ *...an area of dense woodland.* *...una zona de bosques densos.*

**woods|man** /wʊdzmən/ (**woodsmen**) also **woodman** N-COUNT A **woodsman** is a person who cuts down trees for timber, or a person who lives in a wood. *leñador*

**wool** /wʊl/ (**wools**) **1** N-UNCOUNT **Wool** is the hair that grows on sheep and on some other animals. *lana* **2** N-VAR **Wool** is a material made from animal's wool that is used to make things such as clothes, blankets, and carpets. *lana* ❑ *...a wool coat.* *...un abrigo de lana.*

**word**
❶ NOUN AND VERB USES
❷ PHRASES

❶ **word** /wɜrd/ (**words, wording, worded**) **1** N-COUNT A **word** is a single unit of language that can be represented in writing or speech. In English, a word has a space on either side of it when it is written. *palabra* ❑ *How many words do you see on this page?* *¿Cuántas palabras ve en esta página?* **2** N-SING If you have **a word** with someone, you have a short conversation with them, usually in private. *hablar con, tener una conversación con* [SPOKEN] ❑ *I think you should have a word with him.* *Creo que deberías hablar con él.* **3** N-COUNT If you offer someone **a word of** something such as warning, advice, or praise, you warn, advise, or praise them. *tener algo importante que decir* ❑ *I'd like to say a word of thanks to all the people who helped me.* *Quisiera decir unas palabras de agradecimiento a todos los que me ayudaron.* **4** N-SING If you say that someone does **not** hear, understand, or say **a word,** you are emphasizing that they hear, understand, or say nothing at all. *nada* ❑ *I can't understand a word she says.* *No entiendo una palabra de lo que dice.* **5** N-UNCOUNT If there is **word** of something, people receive news or information about it. *información, noticia* ❑ *Is there any word on Joyce's husband?* *¿Hay noticias del esposo de Joyce?* **6** N-SING If you give your **word,** you make a sincere promise to someone. prometer ❑ *He gave his word the boy would be safe.* *Dio su palabra de que el niño estaría a salvo.* **7** V-T To **word** something in a particular way means to choose or use particular words to express it. expresar(se) ❑ *He worded his letter carefully.* *Redactó su carta cuidadosamente.* ● **-worded** ADJ redactado ❑ *...a strongly-worded speech.* *...un discurso muy duro.* → see **English**

❷ **word** /wɜrd/ (**words**) **1** PHRASE If someone has **the last word** or **the final word** in a discussion, argument, or disagreement, they are the one who wins it or who makes the final decision. decir la última palabra ❑ *She likes to have the last word in any discussion.* *Siempre quiere ganar las discusiones.* **2** PHRASE You say **in other words** in order to introduce a different, and usually simpler, explanation or interpretation of something that has just been said. en otras palabras ❑ *Ray is in charge of the office. In other words, he's my boss.* *Ray está a cargo de la oficina; en otras palabras, es mi jefe.* **3** PHRASE If you repeat something **word for word**, you repeat it exactly as it was originally said or written. palabra por palabra ❑ *I learned the song word for word.* *Me aprendí de memoria la canción.* **4** **the operative word** → see **operative**

**word pro|cess|ing** also **word-processing** N-UNCOUNT **Word processing** is the work or skill of producing printed documents using a computer. tratamiento de textos, procesamiento de textos [COMPUTING]

**word rec|og|ni|tion** N-UNCOUNT **Word recognition** is the ability to recognize a written word and to know how it is pronounced and what it means. reconocimiento de palabras

**work**

❶ VERB USES AND PHRASES
❷ NOUN USES AND PHRASES
❸ PHRASAL VERBS

❶ **work** /wɜrk/ (**works, working, worked**) **1** V-I People who **work** have a job, usually one which they are paid to do. trabajar ❑ *He worked as a teacher for 40 years.* *Trabajó como maestro durante 40 años.* ❑ *I want to work, I don't want to be on welfare.* *Quiero trabajar, no depender de la seguridad social.* **2** V-T/V-I When you **work**, you do the things that you are paid or required to do in your job. trabajar ❑ *I can't talk to you right now—I'm working.* *No puedo hablar contigo ahora, estoy trabajando.* ❑ *They work forty hours a week.* *Trabajan cuarenta horas a la semana.* **3** V-I If a machine or piece of equipment **works**, it operates and performs a particular function. funcionar ❑ *"The phone doesn't work," he said.* *—El teléfono no funciona—, dijo.* **4** V-I If an idea, system, or way of doing something **works**, it is successful, effective, or satisfactory. surtir efecto ❑ *95 percent of diets do not work.* *El 95 por ciento de las dietas no surte efecto.* **5** V-T If you **work** a machine or piece of equipment, you use or control it. operar, manejar, manipular ❑ *Do you know how to work the DVD player?* *¿Sabe cómo funciona un reproductor de discos de video?* **6** → see also **working** **7** PHRASE If you **work** your **way** somewhere, you move or progress there slowly, and with a lot of effort or work. abrirse camino ❑ *Many managers started as assistants and worked their way up.* *Muchos gerentes empezaron como dependientes y se abrieron camino hasta la cima.* → see **factory**

❷ **work** /wɜrk/ (**works**) **1** N-UNCOUNT Your **work** consists of the things you are paid or required to do in your job. trabajo ❑ *I've got work to do.* *Tengo trabajo.* ❑ *I sometimes take work home.* *A veces me llevo trabajo a la casa.* **2** N-UNCOUNT **Work** is the place where you do your job. trabajo ❑ *Many people travel to work by car.* *Mucha gente va a su trabajo en coche.* **3** N-COUNT A **work** is something such as a painting, book, or piece of music produced by an artist, writer, or composer. obra ❑ *I think this is his greatest work.* *Creo que esta es su mejor obra.* **4** N-UNCOUNT In physics, **work** is the energy that is transferred to a moving object as the result of a force acting upon the object. trabajo

**Thesaurus** *work* Ver también:

| | |
|---|---|
| V. | labor ❶ **1** **2** function, go, operate, perform, run ❶ **3** **4** |
| N. | business, craft, job, occupation, profession, trade, vocation; (ant.) entertainment, fun, pastime ❷ **1** **2** |

❸ **work** /wɜrk/ (**works, working, worked**)

▸ **work off** PHR-VERB If you **work off** energy, stress, or anger, you get rid of it by doing something that requires a lot of physical effort. desahogarse ❑ *If I've had a bad day I work it off by cooking.* *Cuando tengo un mal día, me desahogo cocinando.*

▸ **work out** **1** PHR-VERB If you **work out** a solution to a problem or mystery, you manage to find the solution by thinking or talking about it. encontrar ❑ *It took me some time to work out the answer.* *Me llevó algún tiempo encontrar la respuesta.* **2** PHR-VERB If something **works out** at a particular amount, it is calculated to be that amount after all the facts and figures have been considered. salir ❑ *The price per pound works out to be $3.20.* *El precio por kilo resulta en 3.20 dólares.* **3** PHR-VERB If a situation **works out** well or **works out,** it happens or progresses in a satisfactory way. resultar, salir ❑ *Things didn't work out as planned.* *Las cosas no resultaron como se planearon.* **4** PHR-VERB If a process **works** itself **out,** it reaches a conclusion or satisfactory end. resultar, salir ❑ *I'm sure it will all work itself out.* *Estoy seguro de que todo saldrá bien.* **5** PHR-VERB If you **work out,** you do physical exercises in order to make your body fit and strong. hacer ejercicio, entrenar ❑ *I work out at a gym twice a week.* *Hago ejercicio en un gimnasio dos veces a la semana.* **6** → see also **workout**

▸ **work up** **1** PHR-VERB If you **work** yourself **up,** you make yourself feel very upset or angry about something. ponerse ❑ *She worked herself up into a rage.* *Se puso furiosa.* ● **worked up** ADJ furioso ❑ *Steve shouted at her. He was really worked up now.* *Steve le gritó, ya estaba verdaderamente furioso.* **2** PHR-VERB If you **work up** the enthusiasm or courage to do something, you succeed in making yourself feel it. reunir ❑ *We could go for a swim, if you can work up the energy.* *Podríamos ir a nadar, si logras reunir fuerzas.*

**work|day** (**work days**) also **work day** N-COUNT A **workday** is the amount of time during a day which you spend doing your job. jornada ❑ *His*

*workday starts at 3:30 a.m. and lasts 12 hours.* *Su jornada empieza a las tres y media de la mañana y dura doce horas.*
→ see **union**

**work|er** /wɜrkər/ (**workers**) **1** N-COUNT **Workers** are people who are employed in industry or business and who are not managers. *trabajador o trabajadora, obrero u obrera, operador u operadora* ❑ *...factory workers.* *...trabajadores fabriles.* **2** N-COUNT You can use **worker** to say how well or badly someone works. *trabajador o trabajadora* ❑ *He is a hard worker.* *Es muy trabajador.* **3** → see also **social worker**
→ see **factory, union**

| **Thesaurus** | *worker* Ver también: |
|---|---|
| N. | employee, help, laborer **1** |

**work|force** /wɜrkfɔrs/ (**workforces**) **1** N-COUNT The **workforce** is the total number of people in a country or region who are physically able to do a job and are available for work. *fuerza laboral, potencial de mano de obra* ❑ *Half the workforce is unemployed.* *La mitad de la fuerza laboral está desempleada.* **2** N-COUNT The **workforce** is the total number of people who are employed by a particular company. *personal, planta laboral* ❑ *...an employer of a very large workforce.* *...empleador de una planta importante.*

**work|ing** /wɜrkɪŋ/ (**workings**) **1** ADJ **Working** people have jobs that they are paid to do. *que trabaja, empleado* ❑ *Working women and men come to the evening classes.* *A las clases vespertinas vienen hombres y mujeres que trabajan.* **2** ADJ Your **working** life is the period of your life in which you have a job or are the right age to have a job. *vida activa, vida laboral, vida de trabajo* ❑ *He started his working life as a truck driver.* *Empezó su vida de trabajo como conductor de camiones.* **3** N-PLURAL **The workings of** a piece of equipment, an organization, or a system are the ways in which it operates and the processes which are involved in it. *funcionamiento* ❑ *...computer systems which copy the workings of the brain.* *...sistemas informáticos que imitan el funcionamiento del cerebro.* **4** **in working order** → see **order**

**work|ing class** (**working classes**) N-COUNT **The working class** or **the working classes** are the group of people in a society who do not own much property, who have low social status, and who often do jobs that involve using physical skills. *clase obrera, clase trabajadora* • **Working class** is also an adjective. *de clase obrera* ❑ *...a man from a working class background.* *...un hombre de clase obrera.*

**work in|put** (**work inputs**) N-VAR In physics, **work input** is the amount of effort that is applied to a machine in order to do work. Compare **work output**. *carga de trabajo*

W

**work|out** /wɜrkaʊt/ (**workouts**) N-COUNT A **workout** is a period of physical exercise or training. *sesión de ejercicio* ❑ *...a 35-minute workout.* *...un entrenamiento de 35 minutos.*
→ see **muscle**

**work out|put** (**work outputs**) N-VAR In physics, **work output** is the amount of work that is done by a machine. Compare **work input**. *rendimiento*

**work|place** /wɜrkpleɪs/ (**workplaces**) also **work place** N-COUNT Your **workplace** is the place where you work. *lugar de trabajo* ❑ *This decision will make the workplace safer for everyone.* *Esta decisión hará que el lugar de trabajo sea más seguro para todos.*

**work|shop** /wɜrkʃɒp/ (**workshops**) **1** N-COUNT A **workshop** is a period of discussion or practical work on a particular subject in which a group of people share their knowledge or experience. *taller* ❑ *...a jazz workshop.* *...un taller de jazz.* **2** N-COUNT A **workshop** is a building that contains tools or machinery for making or repairing things, especially using wood or metal. *taller*

**work|station** /wɜrksteɪʃən/ (**workstations**) also **work station** **1** N-COUNT Your **workstation** is the desk and computer that you sit at when you are at work. *lugar de trabajo* **2** N-COUNT A **workstation** is a screen and keyboard that are part of an office computer system. *estación de trabajo*

**work week** (**work weeks**) N-COUNT A **work week** is the amount of time during a normal week which you spend doing your job. *semana laboral* ❑ *The union wants a shorter work week.* *El sindicato quiere una semana laboral más corta.*

**world** /wɜrld/ (**worlds**) **1** N-SING **The world** is the planet that we live on. *mundo* ❑ *It's a beautiful part of the world.* *Es una parte muy bella del mundo.* **2** ADJ You can use **world** to describe someone or something that is one of the most important or significant of its kind on earth. *mundial* ❑ *He's a world expert on heart disease.* *Es un experto mundial en enfermedades cardiacas.* **3** N-COUNT Someone's **world** is the life they lead, the people they have contact with, and the things they experience. *mundo* ❑ *His world was very different from mine.* *Su mundo era muy diferente al mío.* **4** N-SING You can use **world** to refer to a particular field of activity, and the people involved in it. *mundo* ❑ *...the latest news from the movie world.* *...las últimas noticias del mundo del cine.* **5** N-SING You can use **world** to refer to a particular group of living things, for example, **the animal world, the plant world,** and **the insect world.** *mundo* **6** → see also **real world, Third World** **7** PHRASE If you say that someone has **the best of both worlds,** you mean that they have only the benefits of two things and none of the disadvantages. *tener todas las ventajas* ❑ *I have a lot of friends but I also have my career, so I have the best of both worlds.* *Tengo muchos amigos, pero también tengo mi carrera, así que soy muy afortunado.* **8** PHRASE You can use **the outside world** to refer to all the people who do not live in a particular place or who are not involved in a particular situation. *el mundo exterior* ❑ *I was his only link with the outside world.* *Yo era su único vínculo con el mundo exterior.*

| **Word Partnership** | Usar *world* con: |
|---|---|
| PREP. | **all over the** world, **anywhere in the** world, **around the** world **1** |
| V. | **travel the** world **1** |
| N. | world **history**, world **peace**, world **premiere** **1**<br>world **record** **2**<br>world **of** ***something*** **3** **5** |

**World Health Or|gani|za|tion** N-PROPER **The**

**World Health Organization** is an organization within the United Nations that is responsible for helping governments to improve their health services. The abbreviation **WHO** is also used. *OMS, Organización Mundial de la Salud*

**world war** (**world wars**) N-VAR A **world war** is a war that involves countries all over the world. *guerra mundial* ❑ *...the second world war. ...la segunda guerra mundial.*

| Word Link | *wide ≈ extending throughout : citywide, nationwide, worldwide* |
|---|---|

**world|wide** /wɜrldwaɪd/ ADV If something exists or happens **worldwide,** it exists or happens throughout the world. *en todo el mundo* ❑ *His books have sold more than 20 million copies worldwide. Se han vendido más de 20 millones de ejemplares de sus libros en todo el mundo.* ● **Worldwide** is also an adjective. *en todo el mundo* ❑ *...$20 billion in worldwide sales. ...20 mil millones de dólares en ventas en todo el mundo.*

**World Wide Web** N-PROPER **The World Wide Web** is a computer system that links documents and pictures into a database that is stored in computers in many different parts of the world and that people everywhere can use. The abbreviations **WWW** and the **Web** are often used. *la red mundial, Internet, WWW* [COMPUTING]
→ see **Internet**

**worm** /wɜrm/ (**worms**) N-COUNT A **worm** is a small animal with a long thin body, no bones, and no legs. *gusano*

**worn** /wɔrn/ **1** **Worn** is the past participle of **wear**. *participio pasado de* **wear** **2** ADJ **Worn** is used to describe something that is damaged or thin because it is old and has been used a lot. *desgastado* ❑ *...a worn blue carpet. ...una alfombra azul desgastada.*

**worn out** also **worn-out** **1** ADJ Something that is **worn out** is so old, damaged, or thin from use that it cannot be used anymore. *desgastado* ❑ *We need to replace the worn out tires on the car. Necesitamos remplazar las llantas desgastadas del carro.* **2** ADJ Someone who is **worn out** is very tired after hard work or a difficult or unpleasant experience. *agotado, exhausto* ❑ *Before the race, he was fine. After the race, he was worn out. Antes de la carrera, estaba bien; después, estaba exhausto.*

| Word Link | *some ≈ causing : awesome, troublesome, worrisome* |
|---|---|

**wor|ri|some** /wɜrisəm/ ADJ Something that is **worrisome** causes people to worry. *preocupante* ❑ *It's Johnson's injury that is the most worrisome. Lo más preocupante es la herida de Johnson.*

**wor|ry** /wɜri, wʌri/ (**worries, worrying, worried**) **1** V-T/V-I If you **worry,** you keep thinking about problems that you have or about unpleasant things that might happen. *preocuparse* ❑ *Don't worry, I'm sure he'll be fine. No te preocupes; estoy seguro de que va a estar bien.* ❑ *I worry about her all the time. Me preocupo por ella todo el tiempo.* ❑ *They worry that he works too hard. Se preocupan porque trabaja muy duro.* ● **wor|ried** ADJ *preocupado* ❑ *He seemed very worried. Parecía muy preocupado.* **2** V-T If someone or something **worries** you, they make you anxious because you keep thinking about problems or unpleasant things that might be connected with them. *preocupar* ❑ *"Why didn't you tell us?" — "I didn't want to worry you." —¿Por qué no nos dijiste? —No quería preocuparlos.* **3** N-UNCOUNT **Worry** is the state or feeling of anxiety and unhappiness caused by the problems that you have or by thinking about unpleasant things that might happen. *preocupación* ❑ *Modern life is full of worry. La vida moderna está llena de preocupaciones.* **4** N-COUNT A **worry** is a problem that you keep thinking about and that makes you unhappy. *preocupación* ❑ *My parents had a lot of worries. Mis padres tenían muchas preocupaciones.*

**Word Partnership** Usar *worry* con:

N. **analysts** worry, **experts** worry, **people** worry **1**
V. **begin to** worry, **don't** worry, **have things/nothing to** worry **about, not going to** worry **1**

**worse** /wɜrs/ **1** **Worse** is the comparative of **bad**. *peor* **2** **Worse** is the comparative of **badly**. *peor* **3** PHRASE If a situation changes **for the worse,** it becomes more unpleasant or more difficult. *empeorar, para mal* ❑ *Jackson's life took a turn for the worse. La vida de Jackson cambió para mal.*

**wors|en** /wɜrsən/ (**worsens, worsening, worsened**) V-T/V-I If a bad situation **worsens** or if something **worsens** it, it becomes more difficult, unpleasant, or unacceptable. *empeorar* ❑ *The weather was worsening. El tiempo estaba empeorando.*

**wor|ship** /wɜrʃɪp/ (**worships, worshiping, worshiped**) **1** V-T/V-I If you **worship** a god, you show your respect to the god, for example, by saying prayers. *adorar, venerar, rendir culto* ❑ *...different ways of worshiping God. ...diferentes maneras de rendir culto a Dios.* ❑ *He likes to worship in his own home. Le gusta rendir culto en su propia casa.* ● **Worship** is also a noun. *culto* ❑ *...places of worship. ...lugares de culto.* ● **wor|ship|er** N-COUNT (**worshipers**) *adorador o adoradora, devoto o devota* ❑ *The mosque holds 1000 worshipers. En la mezquita caben 1,000 fieles.* **2** V-T If you **worship** someone or something, you love them or admire them very much. *adorar, venerar* ❑ *She worshiped him for many years. Lo veneró durante muchos años.*

**worst** /wɜrst/ **1** **Worst** is the superlative of **bad**. *peor* **2** **Worst** is the superlative of **badly**. *peor* **3** N-SING **The worst** is the most unpleasant or unfavorable thing that could happen or does happen. *lo peor* ❑ *Many people still fear the worst. Muchas personas siguen temiendo lo peor.* **4** PHRASE You use **at worst** or **at the worst** to indicate that you are mentioning the worst thing that might happen in a situation. *en el peor de los casos* ❑ *At best she will be sick for months; at worst she could die. En el mejor de los casos, estará enferma durante meses; en el peor, podría morir.* **5** PHRASE When someone is **at their worst,** they are as unpleasant, bad, or unsuccessful as it is possible for them to be. *en su peor momento* ❑ *He was at his worst when work wasn't going well. Se sentía peor que nunca cuando el trabajo no iba bien.*

**Usage** **worst** and **worse**

*Worst* and *worse* sound very similar. You should avoid substituting one for the other in various expressions: *Emily's condition has changed for the worse; at the worst, she'll have to go to the hospital.*

**worst-case** ADJ The **worst-case** scenario is the worst possible thing that could happen in a particular situation. *el peor de los casos* ❑ *The worst-case scenario is that the aircraft could crash.* *En el peor de los casos, el avión podría estrellarse.*

**worth** /wɜrθ/ **1** V-T If something is **worth** a particular amount of money, it can be sold for that amount or is considered to have that value. *valer* ❑ *The picture is worth $500.* *El cuadro vale 500 dólares.* **2** **Worth** combines with amounts of money, so that when you talk about a particular amount of money**'s worth of** something, you mean the quantity of it that you can buy for that amount of money. *por un valor de* ❑ *I went and bought six dollars' worth of potato chips.* *Fui y compré seis dólares de papas fritas.* **3** V-T If you say that something is **worth** having, you mean that it is pleasant or useful, and therefore a good thing to have. *valer la pena* ❑ *He decided to see if the house was worth buying.* *Decidió ver si valía la pena comprar la casa.* **4** V-T If something is **worth** a particular action, or if an action is **worth** doing, it is considered to be important enough for that action. *valer* ❑ *This restaurant is well worth a visit.* *Este restaurante bien vale una visita.* **5** PHRASE If an action or activity is **worth** your **while,** it will be helpful, useful, or enjoyable for you if you do it, even though it requires some effort. *valer la pena* ❑ *It might be worth your while to look at their website.* *Podría valer la pena que vieras su sitio en Internet.*

**Word Partnership** Usar *worth* con:

N. worth **five dollars**, worth **a fortune**, worth **money**, worth **the price** **1** worth **the effort**, worth **the risk**, worth **the trouble**, worth **a try** **4**
V. worth **buying**, worth **having** **3** worth **fighting for**, worth **remembering**, worth **saving**, worth **watching** **4**

**worth|less** /wɜrθlɪs/ ADJ Something that is **worthless** is of no real value or use. *sin (ningún) valor* ❑ *...a worthless piece of paper.* *...un trozo de papel sin valor.*

**worth|while** /wɜrθwaɪl/ ADJ If something is **worthwhile,** it is enjoyable or useful, and worth the time, money, or effort that is spent on it. *que vale la pena* ❑ *The president's trip was worthwhile.* *El viaje del presidente valió la pena.*

**Thesaurus** *worthwhile* Ver también:

ADJ. beneficial, helpful, useful; (*ant.*) worthless

W

**wor|thy** /wɜrði/ (**worthier, worthiest**) ADJ If a person or thing is **worthy of** something, they deserve it because they have the qualities or abilities required. *digno* [FORMAL] ❑ *She was a worthy winner.* *Fue una digna ganadora.*

**would** /wəd, STRONG wʊd/

**Would** is a modal verb. It is usually used with the base form of a verb. In spoken English, **would** is often abbreviated to **'d**.

**1** MODAL You use **would** when you are saying what someone believed, hoped, or expected to happen or be the case. *forma modal para formar el potencial de los verbos* ❑ *No one believed there would actually be a war.* *Nadie creía que realmente habría guerra.* ❑ *Would he always be like this?* *¿Será siempre así?* **2** MODAL You use **would** when you are referring to the result or effect of a possible situation. *forma modal para formar el potencial de los verbos* ❑ *It would be fun to learn to ski.* *Sería divertido aprender a esquiar.* **3** MODAL You use **would** to say that someone was willing to do something. You use **would not** to indicate that they refused to do something. *forma modal para formar el potencial de los verbos* ❑ *He said he would help her.* *Dijo que la ayudaría.* ❑ *She wouldn't say where she bought her shoes.* *No quiso decir dónde compró sus zapatos.* **4** MODAL You use **would,** especially with "like," "love," and "wish," when saying that someone wants to do or have a particular thing or wants a particular thing to happen. *forma modal para formar el potencial de los verbos* ❑ *She asked me what I would like to do.* *Me preguntó qué me gustaría hacer.* ❑ *I'd love to have another baby.* *Me encantaría tener otro hijo.* **5** **would rather** → see **rather** **6** MODAL You use **would** with "if" clauses in questions when you are asking for permission to do something. *forma modal para formar el potencial de los verbos* ❑ *Would it be all right if I opened a window?* *¿Le molestaría si abro una ventana?* **7** MODAL You use **would,** usually in questions with "like," when you are making a polite offer or invitation. *forma modal para formar el potencial de los verbos* ❑ *Would you like a drink?* *¿Quieres algo de tomar?* **8** MODAL You say that someone **would** do something when it is typical of them and you are critical of it. You emphasize the word **would** when you use it in this way. *forma modal para formar el potencial de los verbos* ❑ *Well, you would say that: you're a man.* *Bueno, ¿qué otra cosa podrías decir? Tú eres hombre.* **9** MODAL You use **would** or **would have** to express your opinion about something that you think is true. *forma modal para formar el potencial de los verbos* ❑ *I think you'd agree he's a very good singer.* *Estarás de acuerdo en que es un cantante muy bueno, ¿no?* ❑ *I would have thought he was too old to do that job.* *Yo habría pensado que era demasiado viejo para hacer ese trabajo.* **10** MODAL You use **would have** with a past participle when you are referring to the result or effect of a possible event in the past. *forma modal para formar el potencial de los verbos* ❑ *I would have written to you if I had known your address.* *Te habría escrito, si hubiera tenido tu dirección.* **11** MODAL If you say that someone **would have** liked or preferred something, you mean that they wanted to do or have it but were unable to. *forma modal para formar el potencial de los verbos* ❑ *I would have liked a little more time.* *Me habría gustado tener un poco más de tiempo.*

**would-be** ADJ You can use **would-be** to describe someone who wants or attempts to do a particular thing. For example, a **would-be** writer is someone who wants to be a writer. *supuesto, pretendido, aspirante*

**wouldn't** /wʊdᵊnt/ **Wouldn't** is the usual

spoken form of "would not." *forma hablada usual de* ***would not*** ❑ *My parents wouldn't allow me to stay up late. Mis padres no me permitían quedarme levantado hasta tarde.*

**would've** /wʊdəv/ **Would've** is a spoken form of "would have," when "have" is an auxiliary verb. *forma hablada usual de* ***would have*** ❑ *My mom would've loved one of us to go to college. A mamá le habría gustado que uno de nosotros hubiese ido a la universidad.*

**wound** (**wounds, wounding, wounded**)

> Pronounced /waʊnd/ for meaning **1**, and /wund/ for meanings **2**, **3** and **4**.

**1** **Wound** is the past tense and past participle of **wind**. *pasado y participio pasado de* ***wind*** → see **wind②** **2** N-COUNT A **wound** is damage to part of your body, especially a cut or a hole in your flesh, which is caused by a gun, knife, or other weapon. *herida* ❑ *The wound is healing nicely. La herida está sanando bien.* **3** V-T If a weapon or something sharp **wounds** you, it damages your body. *herir* ❑ *He killed one man with a knife and wounded five other people. Mató a un hombre con un cuchillo e hirió a otras cinco personas.* **4** V-T If you **are wounded** by what someone says or does, your feelings are deeply hurt. *herir* ❑ *He was deeply wounded by his son's comments. Los comentarios de su hijo lo hirieron profundamente., Se sintió profundamente herido por los comentarios de su hijo.*
→ see **war**

| Word Partnership | Usar *wound* con: |
|---|---|
| N. | **bullet** wound, **chest** wound, **gunshot** wound, **head** wound **2** |
| V. | **die from a** wound, wound **heals**, **inflict a** wound **2** |
| ADJ. | **fatal** wound, **open** wound **2** |

**wrap** /ræp/ (**wraps, wrapping, wrapped**) **1** V-T When you **wrap** something, you fold paper or cloth tightly around it to cover it. *envolver* • **Wrap up** means the same as **wrap**. *envolver* ❑ *Diana is wrapping up the presents. Diana está envolviendo los regalos.* **2** V-T When you **wrap** something such as a piece of paper or cloth around another thing, you put it around it. *envolver(se)* ❑ *She wrapped a cloth around her hand. Se envolvió la mano con un trapo.*
▸ **wrap up** **1** PHR-VERB If you **wrap up**, you put warm clothes on. *abrigarse* ❑ *She wrapped up in her warmest clothes. Se puso su ropa más abrigadora.* ❑ *It'll be cold, so wrap up well. Va a hacer frío, así que abrígate bien.* **2** PHR-VERB If you **wrap up** something such as a job or an agreement, you finish it in a satisfactory way. *dar por terminado* ❑ *The president wrapped up the meeting earlier today. El presidente dio por terminada la reunión más temprano hoy.* **3** → see also **wrap 1**

**wrap|per** /ræpər/ (**wrappers**) N-COUNT A **wrapper** is a piece of paper, plastic, or thin metal that covers and protects something that you buy, especially food. *envoltura* ❑ *...candy wrappers. ...envolturas de dulces.*

**wreck** /rɛk/ (**wrecks, wrecking, wrecked**) **1** V-T To **wreck** something means to completely destroy or ruin it. *destrozar* ❑ *The storm wrecked the garden. La tormenta destrozó el jardín.* **2** N-COUNT A **wreck** is something such as a ship, car, plane, or building that has been destroyed, usually in an accident. *naufragio* ❑ *...the wreck of a sailing ship. ...el naufragio de un velero.*

**wrench** /rɛntʃ/ (**wrenches, wrenching, wrenched**) **1** V-T If you **wrench** something that is fixed in a particular position, you pull or twist it violently, in order to move or remove it. *arrebatar* ❑ *Two men wrenched the suitcase from his hand. Dos hombres le arrebataron la petaca de la mano.* **2** N-COUNT A **wrench** is an adjustable metal tool used for tightening or loosening metal nuts of different sizes. *llave, llave de tuercas* **3** V-T If you **wrench** your neck, you hurt it by pulling or twisting it in an unusual way. *torcer(se), dislocar(se)*
→ see **tool**

**wres|tle** /rɛsᵊl/ (**wrestles, wrestling, wrestled**) **1** V-I When you **wrestle with** a difficult problem, you try to deal with it. *batallar, lidiar* ❑ *They wrestled with the problem for hours. Lidiaron con el problema durante horas.* **2** V-I If you **wrestle** with someone, you fight them by forcing them into painful positions or throwing them to the ground, rather than by hitting them. Some people wrestle as a sport. *luchar* ❑ *My father taught me to wrestle. Mi padre me enseñó a luchar.*

**wrin|kle** /rɪŋkᵊl/ (**wrinkles, wrinkling, wrinkled**) **1** N-COUNT **Wrinkles** are lines that form on your face as you grow old. *arruga* **2** V-T/V-I If cloth **wrinkles**, or if someone or something **wrinkles** it, it gets folds or lines in it. *arrugar(se)* ❑ *Her stockings wrinkled at the ankles. Se le arrugaron las medias en los tobillos.* • **wrin|kled** ADJ *arrugado* ❑ *His suit was wrinkled and he looked very tired. Su traje estaba arrugado y él se veía muy cansado.* **3** V-T/V-I When you **wrinkle** your nose or forehead, or when it **wrinkles**, you tighten the muscles in your face so that the skin folds. *arrugar, fruncir*
→ see **skin**

**wrist** /rɪst/ (**wrists**) N-COUNT Your **wrist** is the part of your body between your hand and your arm that bends when you move your hand. *muñeca*
→ see **body, hand**

**write** /raɪt/ (**writes, writing, wrote, written**) **1** V-T/V-I When you **write**, you use something such as a pen or pencil to produce words, letters, or numbers. *escribir* ❑ *Write your name and address on a postcard and send it to us. Escriba su nombre y dirección en una tarjeta postal y envíenosla.* ❑ *I'm teaching her to read and write. Estoy enseñándole a leer y escribir.* **2** V-T If you **write** something such as a book, a poem, or a piece of music, you create it and record it on paper, on a computer or on a recording device. *escribir* ❑ *She wrote articles for French newspapers. Escribía artículos para periódicos franceses.* **3** V-T/V-I When you **write** someone or **to** someone or **write** them a letter, you give them information, ask them something, or express your feelings in a letter. You can also **write** someone a note or an e-mail. *escribir a* ❑ *She wrote to her aunt asking for help. Le escribió a su tía para pedirle ayuda.* ❑ *I wrote a letter to the manager. Escribí una carta al gerente.* **4** V-T When someone **writes** something such as a check, receipt, or prescription, they put the necessary information on it and usually sign it. *escribir, hacer, llenar* ❑ *She got out her checkbook and wrote a check. Sacó su chequera y llenó un cheque.* **5** → see also **writing, written**

▸ **write down** PHR-VERB When you **write** something **down,** you record it on a piece of paper using a pen or pencil. *anotar* ❑ *I wrote down what I thought was good about the training course. Anoté lo que me pareció bueno sobre el curso de capacitación.*

▸ **write in** PHR-VERB If you **write in** to an organization, you send them a letter. *escribir* ❑ *What's the point in writing in when you only print half the letter anyway? ¿De qué sirve escribirles, si sólo imprimes la mitad de la carta de todos modos?*

▸ **write into** PHR-VERB If a rule or detail **is written into** a contract, law, or agreement, it is included in it when the contract, law, or agreement is made. *incluir*

▸ **write off** **1** PHR-VERB If someone **writes off** a debt or an amount of money that has been spent on a project, they accept that they are never going to get the money back. *dar por perdido* [BUSINESS] ❑ *He wrote off the money years ago. Dio por perdido el dinero hace años.* **2** PHR-VERB If you **write** someone or something **off,** you decide that they are unimportant or useless and that they are not worth further serious attention. *descartar* ❑ *He gets angry when people write him off because of his age. Se enoja cuando la gente no lo toma en cuenta debido a su edad.*

▸ **write up** PHR-VERB If you **write up** something that has been done or said, you record it on paper in a neat and complete form, usually using notes that you have made. *describir, redactar un informe* ❑ *He wrote up his visit in a report. Describió su visita en un informe.*

| Word Link | ***er, or** ≈ one who does, that which does : auth**or**, paint**er**, writ**er*** |
|---|---|

**writ|er** /raɪtər/ (**writers**) **1** N-COUNT A **writer** is a person who writes books, stories, or articles as a job. *escritor, escritora* ❑ *...detective stories by American writers. ...novelas policiacas de escritores estadounidenses.* **2** N-COUNT The **writer** of a particular article, report, letter, or story is the person who wrote it. *autor, autora* ❑ *Callie Khouri is the writer of "Thelma and Louise." Callie Khouri es la autora de "Thelma y Louise".*

**writ|ing** /raɪtɪŋ/ **1** N-UNCOUNT **Writing** is something that has been written or printed. *escrito* ❑ *Joe tried to read the writing on the next page. Joe trató de leer el escrito de la página siguiente.* **2** N-UNCOUNT You can refer to any piece of written work as **writing,** especially when you are considering the style of language used in it. *estilo* ❑ *The writing is very funny. El estilo es muy divertido.* **3** N-UNCOUNT **Writing** is the activity of writing, especially of writing books for money. *escribir* ❑ *She was bored with writing books about the same thing. Estaba aburrida de escribir libros sobre lo mismo.* **4** N-UNCOUNT Your **writing** is the way that you write with a pen or pencil, which can usually be recognized as belonging to you. *escritura, letra* ❑ *It's difficult to read your writing. Es difícil entender tu letra.*

**writ|ten** /rɪtən/ **1** **Written** is the past participle of **write**. *participio pasado de write* **2** ADJ A **written** test or piece of work is one that involves writing rather than doing something practical or giving spoken answers. *escrito* ❑ *...a short written test. ...un breve examen escrito.* **3** ADJ A **written** agreement, rule, or law has been officially written down. *tácito* ❑ *The newspaper broke a written agreement not to sell the photographs. El periódico violó un acuerdo tácito de no vender las fotografías.*

**wrong** /rɔŋ/ (**wrongs**) **1** ADJ If you say there is something **wrong,** you mean there is something unsatisfactory about the situation, person, or thing you are talking about. *mal, malo* ❑ *Pain is the body's way of telling us that something is wrong. El dolor es la manera que tiene el cuerpo de decirnos que algo anda mal.* ❑ *What's wrong with him? ¿Qué le pasa?* **2** ADJ If you choose the **wrong** thing, person, or method, you make a mistake and do not choose the one that you really want. *equivocado* ❑ *He went to the wrong house. Fue a la casa equivocada.* ● **Wrong** is also an adverb. *mal* ❑ *You've done it wrong. Lo hiciste mal.* **3** ADJ If something such as a decision, choice, or action is **the wrong** one, it is not the best or most suitable one. *malo* ❑ *I made the wrong decision. Tomé una decisión equivocada.* **4** ADJ If something is **wrong,** it is incorrect. *incorrecto* ❑ *I did not know if Mark's answer was right or wrong. No sabía si la respuesta de Mark era correcta o incorrecta.* ● **Wrong** is also an adverb. *mal* ❑ *I must have added it up wrong. Debo de haberlo sumado mal.* ● **wrong|ly** ADV *equivocadamente, injustamente* ❑ *She was wrongly accused of stealing. La acusaron injustamente de robar.* **5** ADJ If you are **wrong** about something, what you say or think about it is not correct. *equivocado* ❑ *I was wrong about the time of the meeting. Estaba equivocado sobre la hora de la reunión.* **6** ADJ If you say that something someone does is **wrong,** you mean that it is bad or immoral. *mal* ❑ *She was wrong to leave her child alone. Hizo mal en dejar solo a su hijo.* ● **Wrong** is also a noun. *mal* ❑ *I did him a great wrong. Le hice mucho mal.* **7** N-UNCOUNT **Wrong** is used to refer to activities or actions that are considered to be morally bad and unacceptable. *mal* ❑ *He can't tell the difference between right and wrong. No conoce la diferencia entre el bien y el mal.* **8** PHRASE If a situation **goes wrong,** it stops progressing in the way that you expected or intended, and becomes much worse. *ir mal* ❑ *My marriage started to go wrong after six months. Mi matrimonio empezó a ir mal después de seis meses.* **9** PHRASE If someone who is involved in an argument or dispute is **in the wrong,** they have behaved in a way that is morally or legally wrong. *obrar mal* ❑ *You were completely in the wrong. Obraste muy mal.*

| Thesaurus | *wrong* | Ver también: |
|---|---|---|
| ADJ. | incorrect; (*ant.*) right **4** | |
| | corrupt, immoral, unjust **6** | |
| N. | abuse, offense, sin **7** | |

**wrote** /roʊt/ **Wrote** is the past tense of **write**. *pasado de* ***write***

**WWW** /dʌbəlyu dʌbəlyu dʌbəlyu/ **WWW** is an abbreviation for **World Wide Web.** It appears at the beginning of website addresses in the form **www.** *WWW, World Wide Web, red de redes* [COMPUTING] ❑ *Check our website at www.collinslanguage.com. Consulte nuestro sitio de Internet en www.collinslanguage.com.*

# Xx

**X-rated** ADJ An **X-rated** movie or video contains sexual scenes that are considered suitable only for adults. *sólo para adultos*

**X-ray** (**X-rays, X-raying, X-rayed**) also **x-ray**
**1** N-COUNT **X-rays** are a type of radiation that can pass through most solid materials. X-rays are used by doctors to examine the bones or organs inside your body and are also used at airports to see inside people's bags. *rayos X* **2** N-COUNT An **X-ray** is a picture made by sending X-rays through something, usually someone's body. *radiografía* ❑ *She had to have a chest X-ray. Tuvieron que hacerle una radiografía del tórax.* **3** V-T If someone or something **is X-rayed,** an X-ray picture is taken of them. *hacer una radiografía, radiografiar* ❑ *All bags were x-rayed. Pasaron todas las maletas por la máquina de rayos X.*
→ see **telescope, wave**

**xy|lem** /zaɪləm, -lɛm/ (**xylems**) N-VAR **Xylem** is the layer of material in plants that carries water and nutrients from the roots to the leaves. Compare **phloem.** *xilema* [TECHNICAL]

# Yy

**yad|da** /yɑdə/ also **yada** CONVENTION You use **yadda yadda yadda** or **yadda, yadda, yadda** to refer to something that is said or written without giving the actual words, because you think that they are boring or unimportant. *bla-bla-bla* [INFORMAL] ❑ *Oh, I know, I know, it's meant to be so sad, yadda yadda yadda. Sí, ya sé, ya sé, se supone que es muy triste, bla-bla-bla.*

**y'all** /yɔl/ In the Southern United States, people use **y'all** when addressing a two or more people. **Y'all** is an informal way of saying "you all." *contracción de* ***you all*** [INFORMAL] ❑ *Y'all just talk amongst yourselves. Nada más platiquen entre ustedes.*

**yam** /yæm/ (**yams**) **1** N-VAR A **yam** is a root vegetable which is like a potato, and grows in tropical regions. *ñame, camote* **2** N-VAR **Yams** are the same as **sweet potatoes.** *camote*

**yang** /yæŋ/ N-UNCOUNT In Chinese philosophy, **yang** is one of the two opposing principles whose interaction is believed to influence everything in the universe. **Yang** is positive, bright, and masculine while **yin** is negative, dark, and feminine. *yang* ❑ *...a perfect balance of yin and yang. ...un equilibrio perfecto entre el yin y el yang.*

**Yan|kee** /yæŋki/ (**Yankees**) **1** N-COUNT A **Yankee** is a person from a northern or north-eastern state of the United States. *yanqui* **2** N-COUNT Some speakers of British English refer to anyone from the United States as a **Yankee.** This use could cause offence. *yanqui* [INFORMAL]

**yard** /yɑrd/ (**yards**) **1** N-COUNT A **yard** is a unit of length equal to thirty-six inches or approximately 91.4 centimeters. *yarda* ❑ *...500 yards from where he was standing. ...a 400 metros de donde estaba parado.* **2** N-COUNT A **yard** is a flat area of concrete or stone that is next to a building and often has a wall around it. *patio* ❑ *I saw him standing in the yard. Lo vi en el patio.* **3** N-COUNT You can refer to a large open area where a particular type of work is done as a **yard.** *patio (ferrocarriles), taller (industrial), astillero (naval)* ❑ *...a rail yard. ...patio de ferrocarriles.* **4** N-COUNT A **yard** is a piece of land next to a house, with grass and plants growing in it. *jardín*
→ see **football, measurement**

**yard|age** /yɑrdɪdʒ/ **1** N-UNCOUNT **Yardage** is a measurement of the length or distance of something, expressed in yards. *medida en yardas* ❑ *Where are you taking the yardage from—the front or the back? ¿Desde dónde estás midiendo, del frente o de atrás?* **2** N-UNCOUNT In a game of football, **yardage** is the number of yards that a team or player manages to move the ball forward toward their opponent's end zone. **Yardage** is measured by lines that cross the field every five yards. *longitud en yardas* ❑ *He made huge yardage every time he got the ball. Corrió muchas yardas cada vez que le dieron el balón.*

**yard sale** (**yard sales**) N-COUNT A **yard sale** is a sale where people sell things they no longer want from a table outside their house. *bazar casero, venta de garaje* ❑ *...clothes he'd picked up at yard sales. ...ropa que conseguía en bazares caseros.*

**yarn** /yɑrn/ (**yarns**) N-VAR **Yarn** is thread used for knitting or making cloth. *hilo, estambre* ❑ *She brought me a bag of wool yarn and knitting needles. Me trajo una bolsa de estambre y agujas de tejer.*

**yawn** /yɔn/ (**yawns, yawning, yawned**) V-I If you **yawn,** you open your mouth very wide and breathe in more air than usual, often when you are tired or when you are not interested in something. *bostezar* ❑ *She yawned, and stretched lazily. Bostezó y se estiró perezosamente.* ● **Yawn** is also a noun. *bostezo* ❑ *She woke and gave a huge yawn. Despertó y dio un gran bostezo.*
→ see **sleep**

**yeah** /yɛə/ **1** CONVENTION **Yeah** means yes. *sí* [INFORMAL, SPOKEN] ❑ *"Bring us something to drink." — "Yeah, yeah." —Traenos algo de beber. —Sí, sí.*
**2** → see also **yes**

**year** /yɪər/ (**years**) **1** N-COUNT A **year** is a period of twelve months or 365 or 366 days, beginning on the first of January and ending on the thirty-first of December. *año* ❑ *The year was 1840. El año era 1840.* ❑ *We had an election last year. Tuvimos elecciones el año pasado.* **2** N-COUNT A **year** is any period of twelve months. *año* ❑ *Graceland has more than 650,000 visitors a year. Graceland recibe más de 650,000 visitantes al año.* **3** N-COUNT A school **year** or academic **year** is the period of time in each twelve months when schools or colleges are open and students are studying there. The school year starts in August or September. *año escolar, año académico*
**4** N-COUNT A financial or business **year** is an exact period of twelve months which businesses or institutions use as a basis for organizing their finances. *año fiscal* [BUSINESS] **5** N-PLURAL You can use **years** to emphasize that you are referring to a long time. *años* ❑ *I haven't laughed so much in years. No me había reído tanto en años.* **6** PHRASE If you say something happens **all year round** or **all the year round,** it happens continually throughout the year. *todo el año* ❑ *The gardens produce flowers nearly all year round. Los jardines tienen flores casi todo el año.*
→ see Word Web: **year**

**yeast** /yist/ (**yeasts**) N-VAR **Yeast** is a kind of fungus which is used to make bread rise, and in making alcoholic drinks such as beer. *levadura*
→ see **fungus**

## Word Web year

The earth takes a **year** to orbit the sun. It is about 365 **days**. The exact time is 365.242199 days. To make the years come out even, every four years there is a leap year. It has 366 days. The **months** on a **calendar** are based on the phases of the moon. The Greeks had a 10-month calendar. About about 60 days were left over. So the Romans added two months. The idea of seven-day **weeks** came from the Bible. The Romans named the days. We still use three of these names: Sunday (sun day), Monday (moon day), and Saturday (Saturn day).

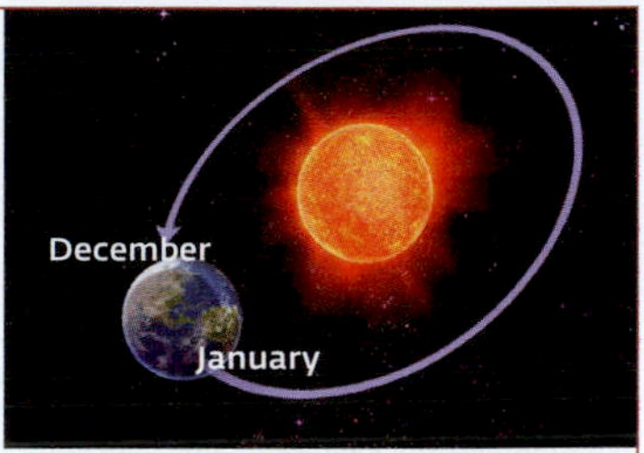


**yell** /yɛl/ (**yells, yelling, yelled**) V-T/V-I If you **yell,** you shout loudly, usually because you are excited, angry, or in pain. *gritar* ❑ *"Eva!" he yelled.* *—¡Eva!—, gritó.* ❑ *I'm sorry I yelled at you last night.* *Discúlpame por haberte gritado anoche.* ● **Yell out** means the same as **yell.** *gritar* ❑ *"Are you coming or not?" they yelled out after him.* *—¿Vienes o no?—, le gritaron.* N-COUNT A **yell** is a loud shout given by someone who is afraid or in pain. *grito* ❑ *Bob let out a yell.* *Bob profirió un grito.*

**Thesaurus** *yell* Ver también:

v. cry, scream, shout; (*ant.*) whisper 1

**yel|low** /yɛloʊ/ COLOR Something that is **yellow** is the color of lemons, butter, or the middle part of an egg. *amarillo* ❑ *The walls were painted bright yellow.* *Las paredes estaban pintadas de amarillo brillante.* ❑ *She was wearing a yellow dress.* *Llevaba un vestido amarillo.*
→ **see color, rainbow**

**yel|low card** (**yellow cards**) N-COUNT In soccer, if a player is shown the **yellow card,** the referee holds up a yellow card to indicate that the player has broken the rules, and that if they do so again, they will be ordered to leave the field. *tarjeta amarilla, tarjeta de amonestación*

**yen** /yɛn/ (**yen**) N-COUNT The **yen** is the unit of currency used in Japan. *yen* ❑ *...2,000 yen.* *...2,000 yenes.*

**yes** /yɛs/

In informal English, **yes** is often pronounced in a casual way that is usually written as **yeah.**

1 CONVENTION You use **yes** to give a positive response to a question. *sí* ❑ *"Are you a friend of Nick's?"—"Yes."* *—¿Eres amigo de Nick?—Sí.* 2 CONVENTION You use **yes** to accept an offer or request, or to give permission. *sí* ❑ *"More coffee?"—"Yes please."* *—¿Más café?—Sí, por favor.* 3 CONVENTION You use **yes** to tell someone that what they have said is correct. *sí* ❑ *"Well I suppose it's based on fact, isn't it?"—"Yes, that's right."* *—Bueno, supongo que se basa en los hechos, ¿verdad?—Sí, así es.* 4 CONVENTION You use **yes** to say that a negative statement or question that the previous speaker has made is wrong or untrue. *sí* ❑ *"That is not possible," she said.—"Oh, yes, it is!" Mrs. Gruen insisted.* *—No es posible—dijo.—¡Claro que sí!—insistió la señora Gruen.*

**yes|ter|day** /yɛstərdeɪ, -di/ 1 ADV You use **yesterday** to refer to the day before today. *ayer* ❑ *She left yesterday.* *Se fue ayer.* ● **Yesterday** is also a noun. *ayer* ❑ *In yesterday's games, Switzerland were the winners.* *En los juegos de ayer, el ganador fue Suiza.* 2 N-UNCOUNT You can refer to the past, especially the recent past, as **yesterday.** *ayer* ❑ *The worker of today is different from the worker of yesterday.* *El obrero de hoy es diferente al de ayer.*

**yet** /yɛt/ 1 ADV You use **yet** in negative statements to indicate that something has not happened up to the present time, although it probably will happen. You can also use **yet** in questions to ask if something has happened up to the present time. *todavía, aún* ❑ *They haven't finished yet.* *Todavía no han terminado.* ❑ *No decision has yet been made.* *Aún no se llega a una decisión.* ❑ *She hasn't yet set a date for her marriage.* *Todavía no ha fijado la fecha para su matrimonio.* 2 ADV If you say that something should not or cannot be done **yet,** you mean that it should not or cannot be done now, although it will have to be done at a later time. *todavía, aún* ❑ *Don't get up yet.* *No te levantes todavía.* ❑ *You can't go home just yet.* *Todavía no puedes irte a casa.* 3 ADV You can use **yet** to say that there is still a possibility that something will happen. *todavía, aún* ❑ *This story may yet have a happy ending.* *Esta historia aún puede tener un final feliz.* 4 ADV You can use **yet** after expressions that refer to a period of time, when you want to say how much longer a situation will continue for. *todavía, aún* ❑ *Unemployment will go on rising for some time yet.* *El desempleo seguirá aumentando todavía por algún tiempo.* 5 ADV If you say that you have **yet to** do something, you mean that you have never done it, especially when this is surprising or bad. *todavía, aún* ❑ *She has yet to spend a Christmas with her husband.* *Aún le falta pasar una Navidad con su esposo.* 6 CONJ You can use **yet** to introduce a fact that is rather surprising after the previous fact you have just mentioned. *sin embargo* ❑ *I don't eat much, yet I am a size 16.* *No como mucho; sin embargo, soy talla 46.* 7 ADV You can use **yet** to emphasize a word, especially when something is surprising because it is more extreme than previous things of its kind, or a further case of them. *todavía* ❑ *I saw yet another doctor.* *Todavía fui a ver a otro médico.*
→ see also **but**

**yield** /yild/ (**yields, yielding, yielded**) 1 V-I If you **yield to** someone or something, you stop resisting them. *ceder* [FORMAL] ❑ *Carmen yielded to pressure and took the child to the doctor.* *Carmen cedió a la presión y llevó al niño con el médico.* 2 V-T If you **yield** something that you have control of or responsibility for, you allow someone else to have control or responsibility for it. *ceder* [FORMAL] ❑ *He may yield control. Es probable que ceda el control.* **3** V-I If a moving person or a vehicle **yields,** they slow down in order to allow other people or vehicles to pass in front of them. *ceder el paso* ❑ *Motorists must yield to buses. Los automovilistas deben ceder el paso a los autobuses.* ❑ *...examples of common signs like No Smoking and Yield. ...ejemplos de señales comunes, como "Prohibido fumar" y "Ceda el paso".* **4** V-I If something **yields,** it breaks or moves position because force or pressure has been put on it. *ceder* ❑ *He pushed the door and it yielded. Empujó la puerta y ésta cedió.* **5** V-T When something **yields** an amount of something such as food or money, it produces that amount. *producir* ❑ *400,000 acres of land yielded a crop worth $1.75 billion. 162,000 hectáreas de tierra produjeron una cosecha con valor de 1,750 millones de dólares.*

**Word Partnership** Usar *yield* con:

N. yield **to pressure**, yield **to temptation** **1**
yield **information**, yield **a profit**, yield **results** **5**
V. **refuse to** yield **1**–**4**
ADJ. **annual** yield, **expected** yield, **high/higher** yield **5**

**yin** /yɪn/ also **ying** /yɪŋ/ N-UNCOUNT In Chinese philosophy, **yin** is one of the two opposing principles whose interaction is believed to influence everything in the universe. **Yin** is negative, dark, and feminine, while **yang** is positive, bright, and masculine. *yin* ❑ *...a perfect balance of yin and yang. ...un equilibrio perfecto entre el yin y el yang.*

**yip** /yɪp/ (**yips, yipping, yipped**) V-I If a dog or other animal **yips,** it gives a sudden short cry, often because of fear or pain. *aullar* ❑ *Coyotes yipped in the distance. Los coyotes aullaron en la distancia.* ● **Yip** is also a noun. *aullido* ❑ *...a yip of pain. ...un aullido de dolor.*

**yo|gurt** /yoʊgərt/ (**yogurts**) also **yoghurt** N-VAR **Yogurt** is a food in the form of a thick, slightly sour liquid that is made by adding bacteria to milk. A **yogurt** is a small container of yogurt. *yogur, yogurt*

**yolk** /yoʊk/ (**yolks**) N-VAR The **yolk** of an egg is the yellow part in the middle. *yema* ❑ *Only the yolk contains cholesterol. Sólo la yema contiene colesterol.*

**you** /yu/

**You** is the second person pronoun. **You** can refer to one or more people and is used as the subject of a verb or the object of a verb or preposition.

**1** PRON A speaker or writer uses **you** to refer to the person or people that they are talking or writing to. *pronombre sujeto y objeto, segunda persona, singular y plural* ❑ *When I saw you across the room I knew I'd met you before. Cuando te vi al otro lado del cuarto, sabía que te había visto antes.* ❑ *You two seem very different to me. Ustedes dos me parecen muy diferentes.* **2** PRON In spoken English and informal written English, **you** is sometimes used to refer to people in general. *pronombre sujeto y objeto, segunda persona singular y plural* ❑ *Getting good results gives you confidence. Los buenos resultados dan confianza.* ❑ *In those days you did what you were told. En aquella época hacías lo que te decían.*
→ see also **one**

**Y**

**young** /yʌŋ/ (**younger** /yʌŋgər/ (**youngest** /yʌŋgɪst/) **1** ADJ A **young** person, animal, or plant has not lived or existed for very long and is not yet mature. *joven, tierno* ❑ *...information written for young people. ...información escrita para jóvenes.* ❑ *...a field of young barley. ...un campo de cebada tierna.* ● **The young** are people who are young. *los jóvenes* ❑ *Everyone from the young to the elderly can enjoy yoga. Todos, desde los jóvenes hasta los ancianos, pueden disfrutar el yoga.* **2** N-PLURAL The **young** of an animal are its babies. *cría, hijuelo* ❑ *The hen may not be able to feed its young. Tal vez la gallina no pueda alimentar a sus polluelos.*
→ see **age, mammal**

**Thesaurus** *young* Ver también:

ADJ. childish, immature, youthful; (*ant.*) mature, old **1**
N. family, litter **2**

**young|ster** /yʌŋstər/ (**youngsters**) N-COUNT Young people, especially children, are sometimes referred to as **youngsters.** *joven, niño o niña, chico o chica, muchacho o muchacha*

**your** /yɔr, yʊər/

**Your** is the second person possessive determiner. **Your** can refer to one or more people.

**1** DET A speaker or writer uses **your** to indicate that something belongs or relates to the person or people that they are talking or writing to. *tu, su* ❑ *I trust your opinion. Confío en su opinión.* ❑ *I left all of your messages on your desk. Dejé todos tus mensajes en tu escritorio.* **2** DET In spoken English and informal written English, **your** is sometimes used to indicate that something belongs to or relates to people in general. *tu, tus, su, sus* ❑ *Painkillers are very useful to bring your temperature down. Los analgésicos son muy útiles para bajar la temperatura.*

**Usage** **your** and **you're**

Be careful not to confuse *your* and *you're*, which are pronounced the same. *Your* is the possessive form of *you*, while *you're* is the contraction of *you are*: *Be careful! You're going to spill your coffee!*

**yours** /yɔrz, yʊərz/

**Yours** is the second person possessive pronoun. **Yours** can refer to one or more people.

**1** PRON A speaker or writer uses **yours** to refer to something that belongs or relates to the person or people that they are talking or writing to. *tuyo, tuya, tuyos, tuyas, suyo, suyos, suya, suyas, de usted, de ustedes* ❑ *I believe Paul is a friend of yours. Creo que Paul es amigo tuyo.* **2** CONVENTION People write **yours, yours sincerely, sincerely yours,** or **yours truly** at the end of a letter before they sign their name. *atentamente* ❑ *With best regards, Yours, George. Saludos. George*

**your|self** /yɔrsɛlf, yʊər-, yər-/ (**yourselves**)

**Yourself** is the second person reflexive pronoun.

**1** PRON A speaker or writer uses **yourself** to refer to the person that they are talking or writing to. **Yourself** is used when the object of a verb or preposition refers to the same person as the subject of the verb. *tú mismo o tú misma, usted mismo* *o usted misma, ustedes mismos* ❑ *Look after yourself. Cuídate.* **2** PRON You use **yourself** to emphasize the person that you are referring to. *tú mismo* ❑ *Don't do that yourself—get someone else to do it. No lo hagas tú mismo; busca alguien que lo haga.* **3** **by yourself** → see **by**

**youth** /yu̲θ/ (**youths** /yu̲ðz/) **1** N-UNCOUNT Someone's **youth** is the period of their life during which they are a child, before they are a fully mature adult. *juventud* ❑ *In my youth my ambition was to be a dancer. En mi juventud, mi anhelo era ser bailarín.* **2** N-UNCOUNT **Youth** is the quality or state of being young. *juventud* ❑ *The team is now a good mixture of experience and youth. El equipo es ahora una buena mezcla de experiencia y juventud.* **3** N-COUNT Journalists often refer to young men as **youths,** especially when they are reporting that the young men have caused trouble. *joven* ❑ *A 17-year-old youth was arrested yesterday. Un joven de 17 años de edad fue arrestado ayer.* **4** N-PLURAL **The youth** are young people considered as a group. *juventud* ❑ *Tell that to the youth of today and they won't believe you. Dile eso a la juventud de hoy y no va a creerte.*

**Word Partnership** Usar *youth* con:

N. youth **center**, youth **culture**, youth **groups**, youth **organizations**, youth **programs**, youth **services** **4**

**yuck** /yʌ̲k/ also **yuk** EXCLAM Some people say "**yuck**" when they think something is very unpleasant or disgusting. *fuchi, guácala, guácatelas* [INFORMAL] ❑ *"It's corned beef and cabbage," said Malone. "Yuck," said Maureen. —Es cecina con col —dijo Malone. —¡Fuchi!—dijo Maureen.*

**yucky** /yʌ̲ki/ ADJ If you describe a food or other substance as **yucky,** you mean that it disgusts you. *asqueroso* [INFORMAL] ❑ *It tastes yucky, so Mom adds sugar to make it go down easier. Sabe horrible, así que mamá le pone azúcar para que pase más fácilmente.*

# Zz

**zero** /zɪəroʊ/ (**zeros** or **zeroes**) **1** NUM **Zero** is the number 0. *cero* **2** N-UNCOUNT **Zero** is a temperature of 0°. It is freezing point on the Celsius scale, and 32° below freezing point on the Fahrenheit scale. *cero* ❑ *...a few degrees above zero.* *...unos cuantos grados sobre cero.* **3** ADJ You can use **zero** to say that there is none at all of the thing mentioned. *cero, nada, nulo* ❑ *He has zero personality.* *Su personalidad es nula.*
→ see Word Web: **zero**

| **Thesaurus** | *zero* | Ver también: |
|---|---|---|
| NUM. | none, nothing | |

**zeros of a func|tion** also **zeroes of a function** N-PLURAL The **zeros of a function** are the points on a graph or in an algebraic expression at which the value of a mathematical function is zero. *raíz de una función, cero de una función* [TECHNICAL]

**zig|zag** /zɪgzæg/ (**zigzags, zigzagging, zigzagged**) also **zig-zag** **1** N-COUNT A **zigzag** is a line that has a series of angles in it like a continuous series of Ws. *zigzag* **2** V-T/V-I If you **zigzag,** you move forward by going at an angle first to one side then to the other. *zigzaguear* ❑ *He zigzagged his way across the field.* *Caminó zigzagueando por el campo.*

**zinc** /zɪŋk/ N-UNCOUNT **Zinc** is a bluish-white metal which is used to make other metals such as brass, or to cover other metals such as iron to stop rust from forming. *zinc, cinc*

**zip code** (**zip codes**) N-COUNT Your **zip code** is a short sequence of numbers at the end of your address, which helps the post office to sort the mail. *código postal*

**zip|per** /zɪpər/ (**zippers**) N-COUNT A **zipper** is a device used to open and close parts of clothes and bags. It consists of two rows of metal or plastic teeth which separate or fasten together as you pull a small handle along them. *cierre (de cremallera), zíper*
→ see **button**

**zone** /zoʊn/ (**zones, zoning, zoned**) **1** N-COUNT A **zone** is an area that has particular features or characteristics. *zona* ❑ *The area is a disaster zone.* *El lugar es una zona de desastre.* **2** V-T If an area of land **is zoned,** it is formally set aside for a particular purpose. *dividir en zonas, zonificar* ❑ *The land was not zoned for commercial use.* *La tierra no fue dividida en zonas para uso comercial.* ● **zon|ing** N-UNCOUNT *zonificación* ❑ *...city zoning regulations.* *...reglamento de zonificación urbana.*
→ see **football**

| **Thesaurus** | *zone* | Ver también: |
|---|---|---|
| N. | area, region, section **1** | |

**zoo** /zu/ (**zoos**) N-COUNT A **zoo** is a park where live animals are kept so that people can look at them. *zoológico* ❑ *He took his son to the zoo.* *Llevó a su hijo al zoológico.*
→ see Word Web: **zoo**
→ see **park**

**zoom** /zum/ (**zooms, zooming, zoomed**) V-I If you **zoom** somewhere, you go there very quickly. *ir como bólido, pasar volando* [INFORMAL] ❑ *We zoomed through the gallery.* *Pasamos volando por la galería.*
▸ **zoom in** PHR-VERB If a camera **zooms in on** something that is being filmed or photographed, it gives a close-up picture of it. *acercar* ❑ *The television cameras zoomed in on me.* *Las cámaras de televisión me tomaron un primer plano.*

**zoo|plank|ton** /zoʊəplæŋktən/ N-UNCOUNT **Zooplankton** are tiny animals that live in water and are found in plankton. Compare **phytoplankton**. *zooplancton* [TECHNICAL]

**zuc|chi|ni** /zukini/ (**zucchini** or **zucchinis**)

**Word Web** **zero**

The **number zero** developed after the other numbers. At first, ancient peoples used numbers for real objects. They **counted** two children or four sheep. Over time they moved from "four sheep" to "four things" to the concept of "four." The idea of a **place** holder like zero came from the Babylonians*. Originally, they wrote numbers like 23 and 203 the same way. The reader had to figure out the difference based on the context. Later they used zero to represent the idea of **null** value. It shows that there is no amount of something. For example, the number 203 shows that there are 2 hundreds, no tens, and 3 ones.

*Babylonians: people who lived in the ancient city of Babylon.*

**Word Web** zoo

In **zoos** people enjoy looking at animals. But zoos are important for another reason, too. More and more species are becoming extinct. Zoos help preserve **biological diversity**. They do this through educational programs, **breeding** programs, and **research** studies. One example is the Smithsonian National Zoological Park in Washington, DC. It trains **wildlife** managers from 80 countries. The Wolong Reserve in China has a breeding program. It has produced 38 **pandas** since 1991. And the Tama Zoo in Hino, Japan, does research. It studies **chimpanzee** behavior. One chimp has even learned to use a vending machine.

N-VAR **Zucchini** are long thin vegetables with a dark green skin. *calabacita, calabacín*

**zy|gote** /zaɪgoʊt/ (**zygotes**) N-COUNT A **zygote** is an egg that has been fertilized by sperm, and which could develop into an embryo. *zigoto*
→ see **reproduction**

# Index

This is an alphabetical index of the translations found in this dictionary. English references in the text are given in alphabetical order following the Spanish word or phrase. The order of the English words does not imply any order of importance and words with similar senses are not grouped together.

The index directs you to the relevant English entry in the dictionary through the medium of Spanish. The Index is ***not*** a dictionary as such, although the English words to which you are referred can function as translations of the Spanish in many cases. For example, the English word *date* appears in the index against the Spanish phrase *hasta el momento*. To find *hasta el momento* look up date in the dictionary and you will find that *hasta el momento* relates to the phrase *to date*.

*acallar:* crush
*acalorado:* heated
*acampar:* camp
*acantilado:* cliff
*acaparar:* corner, hog
*acariciar:* pet, stroke
*acarrear:* incur, transport
*acarreo glacial:* till
*acaso:* maybe
*acatar:* conform
*acaudalado:* wealthy
*acceder:* give
*acceder a:* access
*accesible:* accessible
*accesible (económicamente):* affordable
*acceso:* access, approach, entry
*accesorio:* accessory, attachment, auxiliary, fitting
*accesorios:* accessory, fitting
*accidentado:* hilly, uneven
*accidental:* accidental
*accidentalmente:* accident
*accidente:* accident
*accidente automovilístico:* crack-up
*accidente en el que el conductor se da a la fuga:* hit-and-run
*accidente geográfico:* landform
*acción:* act, action, deed, share, stock
*acción afirmativa:* affirmative action
*acción creciente:* rising action
*acción refleja:* reflex
*acciones ordinarias:* common stock
*accionista:* shareholder, stockholder
*acechar:* stalk
*acedo:* sour
*aceitar:* oil
*aceite:* oil
*aceite de oliva:* olive oil
*aceituna:* olive
*aceitunado:* olive
*aceleración:* acceleration
*aceleración centrípeta:* centripetal acceleration
*aceleración negativa:* negative acceleration
*aceleración positiva:* positive acceleration
*acelerador:* accelerator, gas pedal
*acelerar:* accelerate, gas, rush, up
*acento:* accent, emphasis
*acentuar:* stress
*acepción:* meaning
*aceptable:* acceptable, reasonable, respectable
*aceptación:* recognition
*aceptado:* accepted
*aceptar:* accept, come, consent, embrace, meet, take, term
*aceptar el reto:* challenge
*aceptar inmediatemente:* jump
*acequible:* accessible
*acera:* curb, sidewalk
*acerca de:* about, concerning
*acercar:* approach, come, draw, edge
*acercarse a:* approach, close, come
*acería/fundición (acero):* mill
*acero:* iron, steel
*acero inoxidable:* stainless steel
*acertijo:* puzzle, riddle
*achicar:* bail, cut, reduce
*achú:* achoo
*acicatear:* spur
*ácido:* acid, sharp, sour
*ácido desoxirribonucleico:* DNA
*ácido nucleico:* nucleic acid
*aclamación:* acclaim
*aclamar:* acclaim, cheer
*aclarar:* clarify, clear, illustrate, light, place, sort, straighten, unravel
*aclimatar:* acclimate
*acné:* acne
*acogedor:* cozy, homey
*acoger:* foster, greet, receive, take, welcome
*acogida:* reception
*acolchado:* padded
*acolchar:* quilting
*acomodador:* usher
*acomodadora:* usher
*acomodar:* fit, put
*acomodar en capas:* layer
*acompañamiento:* side
*acompañante:* escort
*acompañar:* accompany, company, escort, go, join, show, usher, walk
*acondicionamiento del aire:* air-conditioning
*aconsejar:* advise, counsel, preach, recommend
*acontecimiento:* development
*acontecimiento importante:* landmark
*acopio:* stockpile
*acoplarse:* dock
*acorazado:* battleship
*acordar:* set
*acordar de:* remind
*acordarse de:* remember
*acorde:* chord
*acorde perfecto:* triad
*acorralar:* bay, corner, corral, pen
*acortar:* cut, shorten
*acosador:* bully
*acosadora:* bully
*acosar:* bully, hound, pester, stalk
*acostarse:* lie, sleep
*acostumbrarse a:* used
*acotamiento:* shoulder
*acre:* acre
*acrecentar:* heighten
*acreditación:* proof
*acreedor:* creditor
*acreedora:* creditor
*acribillar:* pepper
*acribillar a preguntas:* grill
*acrónimo:* acronym
*acta:* certificate, minute
*actitud:* attitude, manner, outlook
*activar:* activate, go
*actividad:* activity, movement, pursuit
*actividad suplementaria:* sideline
*activista:* activist
*activo:* active, alive, asset
*acto:* act, deed
*acto reflejo:* reflex
*acto sexual:* intercourse
*actor:* actor
*actriz:* actor, actress
*actuación:* acting
*actual:* contemporary, current, going, present
*actualmente:* nowadays, today
*actuar:* act, behave, feature, perform, play
*actuar como mediador:* mediate
*actuar de manera distinta:* react
*actuar por su propia cuenta:* strike
*acuchillar:* slash, stab
*acuchillar.:* knife
*acuclillarse:* crouch
*acudir a:* turn
*acudir en tropel:* flock
*acuerdo:* accord, agreement, deal, settlement, treaty, understanding
*acuerdo prenupcial:* prenup, prenuptial agreement
*acuífero:* aquifer
*acumulación:* build-up
*acumular:* accumulate, add, collect, gather, heap, mount, pile
*acunar:* cradle
*acuñar:* coin, mint
*acurrucarse:* curl
*acusación:* accusation, allegation, charge
*acusada:* accused, defendant
*acusado:* accused, defendant
*acusar:* accuse, finger, level
*acusar recibo de:* acknowledge
*acústica:* acoustic
*acústico:* acoustic
*ad hominem:* ad hominem
*adaptación:* adaptation
*adaptar:* acclimate, adapt, adjust, tailor, take
*adecuado:* adequate, all right, appropriate, apt, fit, fitting, proper, right, suitable, suited

*adecuado para:* equal
*adelantado:* ahead, fast, time
*adelantar:* advance, further, somewhere
*adelante:* after, ahead, forward, front
*adelante de:* ahead of
*adelgazar:* lose, slim
*ademán:* gesture, motion
*además:* addition, besides, furthermore, moreover, too, top
*además de:* apart, aside, else
*adenina:* adenine
*adenosín trifosfato:* ATP
*adentrarse:* inroads
*adentro:* in, indoor, indoors, inside
*aderezar:* season
*aderezo:* dressing
*adeudar:* owe
*adherirse:* bond, stick
*adhesivo:* adhesive
*adicción:* addiction
*adición:* addition
*adicional:* auxiliary, extra, fresh, further, spare, subsidiary
*adictivo:* addictive
*adicto:* addict, addicted
*adinerado:* wealthy, well-off, well-to-do
*adiós:* bye, goodbye
*aditamentos:* fitting, fixture
*aditivo:* additive
*adivinanza:* puzzle, riddle
*adivinar:* guess
*adjetivo:* adjective
*adjetivo o pronombre posesivo:* possessive
*adjuntar:* attach, enclose
*administración:* administration, management
*Administración de la Seguridad y Salud Ocupacionales:* OSHA
*administración pública:* civil service
*administrador:* administrator, manager
*administrador de un sitio de la red:* webmaster
*administrador financiero:* fund manager
*administradora:* administrator, manager, manageress
*administradora de un sitio de la red:* webmaster
*administradora financiera:* fund manager
*administrar:* administer, manage
*administrativo:* administrative, ministerial
*admirable:* impressive, remarkable
*admiración:* admiration
*admirador:* fan, following
*admiradora:* fan, following
*admiradoras:* fan base
*admiradores:* fan base
*admirar:* admire
*admisible:* acceptable
*admisión:* admission
*admitir:* acknowledge, admit, own, stand
*ADN:* DNA
*ADN recombinante:* recombinant DNA
*adobo:* pickle
*adolescencia:* teen
*adolescente:* adolescent, teenage, teenager
*adolorido:* painful, sore
*adoptar:* adopt, assimilate, assume, cultivate, embrace, take
*adoptar una actitud firme:* stand
*adorable:* lovely
*adorar:* adore, worship
*adormecido:* numb
*adormilado:* sleepy
*adornar:* decorate, grace
*adornar con:* trim
*adorno:* decoration, trim
*adquirir:* acquire, gain, pick, purchase, take
*adquisición:* acquisition, purchase, takeover
*adrede:* deliberate
*aduana:* customs
*aducir:* plead
*adueñarse:* take
*adular:* flatter
*adulterar:* doctor
*adulto:* adult, grown, grown-up, mature
*advenedizo:* upstart
*adverbio:* adverb
*adversario:* opponent
*adverso:* adverse, ill
*advertencia:* advisory, warning
*advertir:* caution, detect, warn
*aéreo:* aerial, airborne
*aerobics:* aerobics
*aerófono:* aerophone
*aerolínea:* airline
*aeronave:* aircraft
*aeroplano:* airplane
*aeropuerto:* airport
*aerosol:* spray
*aerotransportado:* airborne
*afanador:* cleaner
*afanadora:* cleaner
*afección:* complaint, condition, disorder
*afectado:* artificial, stiff, theatrical
*afectar:* affect, bite, disrupt, erode, get, hit, impact, inroads, interfere, shake, strike, tell, touch
*afecto:* affection
*afectuoso:* caring, loving, warm
*afelio:* aphelion
*aferrar:* claw, hold
*aferrarse a:* cling, hang
*afianzar:* clamp
*aficionada:* amateur, enthusiast, fan, fanatic, lover
*aficionado:* amateur, enthusiast, fan, fanatic, lover
*aficionado de:* fond
*aficionarse:* take
*afídido:* aphid
*áfido:* aphid
*afijo:* affix
*afilado:* sharp
*afilar:* sharpen
*afiliación:* membership
*afiliarse a:* join
*afiliarse con:* affiliate
*afinado/desafinado:* tune
*afinar:* fine-tune, tune
*afinidad:* sympathy
*afirmación:* claim, statement
*afirmar:* affirm, assert, claim, contend, maintain
*aflicción:* distress
*afligir:* distress, trouble
*aflojar:* ease, loosen, relax
*afloramiento:* upwelling
*aflujo:* runoff
*afortunadamente:* fortunately, happily
*afortunado:* fortunate, lucky
*afrenta:* offense
*africano:* African
*afroamericana:* African-American
*afroamericano:* African-American
*afrocaribeño:* African-Caribbean
*afrontar:* brave, cope
*afuera:* back, outdoors
*agachar:* bend, duck, flatten, get, hunker
*agallas:* gut
*agarrado:* cheap
*agarrar:* grab, grasp, grip, hold, seize, stab
*agarrar con fuerza:* clutch
*agarrarla con:* pick
*agarrarle la onda (a algo):* hang
*agasajar:* entertain, feast
*agazaparse:* crouch
*agencia:* agency, branch
*agencia de cobro:* collection agency
*agencia de distribución de publicaciones:* syndicate
*agencia de noticias:* news agency
*agencia de publicidad:* ad agency
*agencia de viajes:* travel agency

jolly, joyful, joyous, merry, sunny
*alegría:* joy
*alejado:* apart, away, far off, lonesome, remote, way
*alejamiento:* departure
*alejándose:* off
*alejar:* alienate, drive, frighten
*alejarse:* back, draw, get, pull, recede, wander
*alelo:* allele
*alentador:* encouraging, refreshing, uplifting
*alentar:* cheer, encourage, urge
*alergia:* allergy
*alérgico:* allergic
*alerón:* fin, wing
*alerta:* alert, watch
*alertar:* alert
*aleta:* fin
*aletear:* flap
*alfabético:* alphabetical
*alfabetismo visual:* visual literacy
*alfabeto:* alphabet
*alfarería:* pottery
*alféizar:* sill
*alfil:* bishop
*alfiler:* pin
*alfombra:* carpet, rug
*alga:* algae, seaweed
*alga marina:* seaweed
*álgebra:* algebra
*algo:* anything, element, kind, little, something
*algodón:* cotton, cotton wool, pad
*algodón de azúcar:* cotton candy
*algoritmo:* algorithm
*alguacil:* constable, sheriff
*alguien:* anyone, somebody, someone
*alguno:* any, certain, some
*aliado:* allied, ally
*aliados:* friend
*alianza:* alliance, ring
*alianza estratégica:* joint venture
*aliarse:* ally
*alicate(s):* pliers
*alienígena:* alien
*aliento:* breath, encourage, encouragement
*alimentado:* fueled
*alimentar:* feed, raise
*alimentarse de:* prey
*alimento:* food
*alimento virgen:* natural food
*alimentos:* board
*alineación:* alignment
*aliño:* dressing
*alisar:* brush, smooth
*alistarse:* enlist
*alistarse como voluntario:* volunteer
*alistarse en:* join
*alita:* brownie
*alitas:* brownie
*aliteración:* alliteration
*aliviado:* relieved
*aliviar:* ease, release, relieve, soothe
*alivio:* relief
*allá:* over, there
*allanar:* raid
*allegado:* close
*allí:* over, there
*alma:* soul
*almacén:* repository, store, warehouse
*almacenaje:* storage
*almacenamiento:* storage
*almacenar:* stockpile, store
*almeja:* clam
*almíbar:* syrup
*almidón:* starch
*almirante:* admiral
*almohada:* pillow
*almohadilla:* pad
*almuerzo:* box lunch, lunch
*alocado:* mad
*alojamiento:* accommodation
*alojar:* accommodate, house, lodge, put, sleep, stay
*alpinismo:* climbing
*alpiste:* birdseed
*alquilado:* charter
*alquilar:* charter, lease, rent
*alquiler:* lease, rent, rental
*alrededor:* around
*alrededor de:* about, circa, region, some, somewhere
*alrededores:* outskirts, scenery, vicinity
*alta fidelidad:* high fidelity
*alta presión:* H
*alta tecnología:* high technology
*altanero:* proud
*altavoz:* bullhorn
*alteración del orden público:* disorderly conduct
*alterado:* upset
*alterar:* alter, doctor
*alternar:* alternate, socialize, stagger
*alternar (el trabajo):* job share
*alternativa:* alternative, choice
*alternativamente:* alternatively
*alternativo:* alternate, alternative
*alterno:* alternate
*altiplanicie:* highlands
*altitud:* altitude, elevation, height
*alto:* aloud, high, highly, hold, tall
*alto horno:* furnace
*alto mando:* brass
*altoestrato:* altostratus
*altricial:* altricial
*altura:* height, level
*altura de las olas:* wave height
*alud de lodo:* mudflow
*alud de lodo.:* mudslide
*alud de rocas:* rock fall
*aludir:* touch
*alumbramiento:* delivery
*alumbrar:* shine
*aluminio:* aluminum
*alumna:* alum, schoolgirl, student
*alumnado:* student body
*alumno:* alum, alumnus, pupil, schoolboy, student
*aluvión:* alluvium
*aluvión glaciárico:* till
*alveolo:* alveolus
*alvéolo:* socket
*alza:* upward
*alzamiento:* uprising
*alzar:* lift, raise, revolt, stand
*ama de casa:* homemaker, housewife
*amable:* friendly, kind, kindly, neighborly, nice, sweet
*amado:* beloved
*amagar:* threatening
*amainar:* die
*amalgamar:* fuse
*amamantar:* feed
*amañar:* fix, rig
*amanecer:* break, dawn, sunrise, sun-up
*amante:* lover
*amar:* love
*amargado:* bitter, cynical, sour
*amargar:* sour
*amargo:* bitter
*amarillo:* yellow
*amarrar:* bind, lace, lash, moor, rope, tie
*amasar:* knead
*amazona:* rider
*ambición:* ambition
*ambicioso:* ambitious, up-and-coming
*ambientalista:* environmentalist
*ambiente:* atmosphere, background, environment, surroundings
*ambiguo:* ambiguous
*ámbito:* scene, scope, sphere
*ambivalente:* mixed
*ambos:* both
*ambulancia:* ambulance
*ambulante:* mobile
*amenaza:* threat
*amenaza de bomba:* scare
*amenazar:* hang, loom, threaten, threatening
*americano:* American
*ameritar:* merit
*ametralladora:* machine gun

*amiba:* amoeba
*amiga:* girlfriend
*amigable con el ambiente:* eco-friendly
*amígdala:* tonsils
*amigo:* bud, friend, kiddo
*aminorar:* ease, slow
*amish:* Amish
*amistoso:* friendly, good-humored
*amnios:* amnion
*amnistía:* amnesty
*amo:* master
*amoblar:* furnish
*amonestar:* scold
*amontonar:* accumulate, heap, pile, crowd, scramble, swarm
*amor:* darling, love, sweetheart
*amor propio:* self-esteem
*amorío:* affair
*amoroso:* loving, sweet
*amortiguar:* cushion, soften
*amotinarse:* riot
*ampliación:* extension
*ampliamente:* wide
*ampliar:* elaborate, enlarge, extend, widen
*amplificar:* magnify
*amplio:* broad, generous, large, spacious, wide
*amplitud:* amplitude
*amplitud de la marea:* tidal range
*amueblar:* furnish
*amuleto:* charm
*añadir:* add, insert
*anaeróbico:* anaerobic
*anafase:* anaphase
*analfabeto:* illiterate
*analgésico:* painkiller
*análisis:* analysis, exam, test
*análisis de muestras de ADN:* DNA fingerprinting
*análisis detallado:* breakdown
*análisis dimensional:* dimensional analysis
*análisis literario:* literary analysis
*analista:* analyst
*analizar:* analyze, consider, look, test
*análogo:* analog
*anaranjado:* ginger, orange
*anatomía:* anatomy
*ancho:* broad, wide, width
*ancho (amplitud anchura) de banda:* bandwidth
*anchura:* width
*anciano:* aged, elderly, old
*ancla:* anchor
*anclar:* anchor
*ándale:* come
*andamiaje:* scaffolding
*andamio:* scaffolding
*andar:* go, run
*andar a la caza de:* chase
*andar a la rebatiña:* scramble
*andar apresuradamente:* tear
*andar de gira:* tour
*andar de un lugar a otro:* schlep
*andar detrás de:* chase
*andar en:* ride
*andar en bici:* cycle
*andar en bicicleta:* cycle
*andar en busca:* chase
*andar errado:* base
*andén:* platform
*andrajos:* rag
*andrajoso:* ratty
*anécdota:* anecdote, story
*anegar:* flood, swamp
*añejo:* stale, vintage
*anemia:* anemia
*anémico:* anemic
*anemómetro:* anemometer
*anestesia:* anesthetic
*anestesióloga:* anesthesiologist
*anestesiólogo:* anesthesiologist
*anestesista:* anesthesiologist
*anexar:* attach, enclose
*anexo:* addition, attachment, extension
*anfibio:* amphibian
*anfiteatro:* amphitheater, balcony
*anfitrión:* host
*anfitriona:* host, hostess
*ángel:* angel
*angiosperma:* angiosperm
*anglófona:* anglophone
*anglófono:* anglophone
*anglohablante:* anglophone
*angostarse:* narrow
*angosto:* narrow
*anguila:* eel
*angula:* eel
*ángulo:* angle
*ángulo recto:* right angle
*angustia:* anguish, distress
*angustiar:* distress
*anhelar:* desire, hunger, pine
*anhelo:* desire
*añicos:* dash, smash
*anidar:* nest
*anillo:* ring
*anillo anual:* annual ring
*animación:* animation
*animado:* alive, bright, high, lively
*animador:* animator, entertainer
*animadora:* animator, entertainer
*animal:* animal
*animal de caza:* game
*animal de peluche:* stuffed animal
*animar:* cheer, encourage
*animarse (una persona):* brighten
*ánimo:* encouragement, morale
*aniquilador:* devastating
*aniquilar:* knee
*aniversario:* anniversary
*año:* year
*año académico:* year
*año bisiesto:* leap year
*año escolar:* year
*año fiscal:* year
*año luz:* light year
*Año Nuevo:* New Year's
*anoche:* night
*anochecer:* dusk
*anomalía:* irregular
*anómalo:* abnormal
*anonadar:* overwhelm
*anónimo:* anonymous
*añorar:* homesick, long
*años cuarenta:* forty
*años luz:* light year
*anotación:* entry
*anotado:* down
*anotar:* jot, log, mark, note, put, score, take, write
*anquilosado:* stale
*ansiar:* hunger
*ansias:* hunger
*ansiedad:* anxiety
*ansioso:* anxious, eager, hungry, impatient, itch
*antagonista:* antagonist
*ante:* before, face
*ante todo:* all
*antebrazo:* forearm
*antecedente:* antecedent, background
*antecedentes:* history, track record
*antecedentes penales:* rap sheet
*antecesor:* predecessor
*antena:* antenna, mast
*antena de satélite:* satellite dish
*antena parabólica:* dish
*anteojera:* blinders
*anteojos:* eyeglasses, glass
*anteojos de sol:* sunglasses
*antepasada:* ancestor
*antepasado:* ancestor
*antepasado común:* common ancestor
*antepecho:* sill
*antera:* anther
*anterior:* former, last, past, previous, prior
*anteriormente:* formerly, time
*antes:* before, earlier, formerly, once, previously, then
*antes de:* ahead of, by, prior, within
*antes de Jesucristo:* BC
*antes de nuestra era:* BCE
*antes que:* rather
*antes que nada:* all, first
*antibiótico:* antibiotic
*anticipado:* advance
*anticipar:* advance, anticipate,

further, predecir
*anticipo:* advance
*anticlinal:* anticline
*anticoncepción:* contraception
*anticonceptivo:* contraceptive
*anticuado:* old-fashioned, outdated
*anticuerpo:* antibody
*antideportivo:* unsportsmanlike
*anti-estadounidense:* un-American
*antifaz:* mask
*antigüedad:* antique
*antiguo:* ancient, former, old, one-time, vintage
*antipático:* unpleasant
*antiséptico:* antiseptic
*antitranspirante:* antiperspirant
*antivirus:* anti-virus
*antojar:* feel
*antorcha:* torch
*antropóloga:* anthropology
*antropología:* anthropology
*antropólogo:* anthropology
*anual:* annual
*anudar:* knot, tie
*anulación:* override
*anular:* override, overturn, undo
*anular (legal):* reverse
*anunciar:* advertise, announce, declare, herald, here
*anunciar algo:* here
*anuncio:* ad, advertisement, announcement
*anuncio clasificado:* want ad
*anuncios clasificados:* personals
*apachurrar:* crush
*apagado:* dull, off, out
*apagador:* switch
*apagar:* cut, die, fade, go, peter, put, switch, turn
*apagón:* outage
*apalear:* batter
*aparador:* cupboard
*aparato:* appliance, device, gadget
*aparato de Golgi:* Golgi complex
*aparato ortopédico:* brace
*aparato respiratorio:* respiratory system
*aparear:* mate
*aparecer:* appear, break, emerge, feature, figure, show, turn
*aparejo de poleas:* block and tackle
*aparejos:* tackle
*aparentar:* present, pretend
*aparente:* apparent, outward
*aparentemente:* apparently
*aparición:* appearance
*apariencia:* appearance, exterior, look
*apartado:* isolated
*apartamento:* flat
*apartar:* avert, back, dodge, isolate, set
*aparte:* aside, separate
*aparte de:* aside, else
*apartheid:* apartheid
*apasionado:* intense, passionate
*apatía:* inertia
*apegado:* attached
*apego:* attachment
*apelación:* appeal
*apelar:* appeal
*apellido:* surname
*apenado:* embarrassed
*apenar:* sorry
*apenas:* barely, few, hardly, just, mere, merely, only, scarcely
*apéndice:* appendix
*aperitivo:* cocktail, starter
*apestar:* reek, smell, stink
*apetecer:* feel
*apetito:* appetite
*apetitoso:* tasty
*apilar:* heap, pile, stack
*apiñado:* squash
*apiñar:* pack, troop
*apio:* celery
*aplanar:* flatten
*aplastar:* crush, flatten, put, squash
*aplaudir:* acclaim, applaud, clap
*aplauso:* acclaim, applause
*aplazar:* postpone
*aplicación:* application
*aplicación de la ley:* law enforcement
*aplicar:* apply, deal
*apodar:* hold, dub, nickname, take
*apodo:* nickname
*apogeo:* peak
*apología:* eulogy
*apoquinar:* pony
*aporrear:* bash, batter
*aportación:* contribution, input
*aportar:* contribute, kick
*aposición:* appositive
*apósito:* dressing
*apostar:* bet, gamble, stake, station
*apostar a que:* bet
*apóstrofo:* apostrophe
*apoyar:* aid, back, behind, brace, lean, lend, prop, recline, rest, second, sponsor, subscribe, support, sustain, uphold
*apoyo:* aid, backing, backup, support
*apoyo fraterno:* fraternity
*apoyo moral:* moral
*apreciar:* appreciate, prize, recognize, value
*apreciar mucho:* treasure
*aprecio:* esteem, favor
*apremiante:* urgent
*apremiar:* hurry
*aprender:* learn, pick
*apresurado:* hasty
*apresurar:* hurry, rush, scramble
*apretadamente:* tight
*apretado:* stiff, tight
*apretar:* clutch, press, screw, squeeze, tighten
*apretón:* grasp
*apretón de manos:* handshake
*apretujar:* crush, squash
*aprieto:* plight
*aprobación:* approve, approval, sympathy
*aprobado:* pass
*aprobar:* approve, carry, enact, endorse, sanction, sympathize
*apropiado:* apt, clean, decent, proper, suited
*aprovechar:* advantage, seize
*aprovecharse de:* advantage, exploit, milk, use
*aprovisionamiento:* provision
*aprovisionar:* supply
*aproximadamente:* around, order, somewhere
*aproximado:* approximate, like, rough
*aproximar:* approximate
*aptitud:* bent
*apuesta:* gamble, stake
*apuñalar:* stab
*apuntar:* aim, mark, point, put, take
*apurar:* hurry
*apuro:* hardship, plight
*aquel:* that
*aquellos:* anyone, those
*aquí:* here, over
*arácnido:* arachnid
*arado:* plow
*araña:* spider
*arañar:* claw, graze, scratch
*arañazo:* scratch
*arancel:* tariff
*arandela:* washer
*arar:* plow
*árbitra:* referee, umpire
*arbitrar:* judge, mediate, referee, umpire
*arbitrariedad:* injustice
*arbitrario:* arbitrary
*árbitro:* referee, umpire
*árbol:* shaft, tree
*árbol de Navidad:* Christmas tree
*árbol de Pascua:* Christmas tree
*arboleda:* grove
*arbusto:* bush, shrub
*arce:* maple
*archivar:* file
*archivo:* archive, file
*archivo de audio:* podcast
*arcilla:* clay

*arco:* arch, bow
*arco del proscenio:* proscenium
*arco iris:* rainbow
*arder:* blaze, burn, itch, smart, smolder
*arder (sin llamas):* smolder
*ardid:* trap
*ardiente:* burning, strong
*ardilla:* squirrel
*arduo:* uphill
*área:* area, ground, region
*área de descanso:* rest area
*área de reposo:* rest area
*área silvestre:* bush
*arena:* sand
*arenas:* sand
*arenero:* sandbox
*arenoso:* sandy
*arete:* earring
*argot:* slang
*argüir:* contend
*argumentar:* argue, contend
*argumento:* argument, contention, plot, plotline, point, proposition, thesis
*argumento de autoridad:* appeal to authority
*argumento emocional:* appeal to emotion, appeal to pathos
*argumento racional:* appeal to reason
*árido:* dry
*arista:* arête
*aristócrata:* noble
*aritmética:* arithmetic
*arma:* ammunition, gun, weapon
*arma biológica:* bioweapon
*arma para aturdir:* stun gun
*armada:* navy
*armado:* armed
*armadura:* armor
*armar:* arm, assemble, put, set
*armar caballero:* knight
*armario:* closet, cupboard, wardrobe
*armarse de valor:* steel
*armas:* arm
*armas de destrucción masiva:* weapons of mass destruction
*armas de fuego:* firearm
*armazón:* frame, framework
*armonía:* harmony
*armonizar:* blend
*ARN (ácido ribonucleico):* RNA
*aro:* ring
*aroma:* fragrance, scent
*arpa:* harp
*arpón:* spear
*arponear:* spear
*arqueado:* bowed
*arquear:* arch
*arquebacteria:* Archaebacteria
*arqueología:* archeology
*arqueológico:* archeology
*arquetipo:* archetype
*arquitecta:* architect
*arquitecto:* architect
*arquitectura:* architecture
*arraigado:* ingrained
*arrancar:* boot, kick-start, pull, rip, start, tear
*arrancar bien:* flying
*arrancar de/a:* drag
*arrancar el alma:* heart
*arranque:* burst, impulse
*arrasar:* level, wash
*arrastrar:* drag, haul, pull, tow, trail, tug
*arrastrar los pies:* drag, shuffle
*arrastrar y soltar:* drag and drop
*arrastrarse:* crawl
*arrear (animales):* drive
*arrebatar:* snatch, wrench
*arreglado:* settle
*arreglar:* adjust, arrange, fix, patch, rig, settle, sort, square, trim
*arreglar un jardín:* landscape
*arreglárselas:* cope, get, manage
*arreglárselas solo:* fend
*arreglo:* accord, arrangement, compromise, deal, setup
*arremeter contra:* lash
*arremolinarse:* roil
*arrendador:* landlord
*arrendamiento:* lease
*arrendar:* lease
*arrepentimiento:* regret
*arrepentir:* regret
*arrestar:* arrest
*arriar:* herd
*arriate:* bed
*arriba:* high, top, up
*arriba de:* above
*arriba de ochenta:* eighty
*arribista:* upstart
*arriesgar:* chance, plunge, risk, stake
*arrimar:* draw
*arrodillado:* knee
*arrodillar:* kneel
*arrogante:* arrogant, proud, superior
*arrojar:* dive, fling, hurl, pitch, throw, toss
*arrojar chorros de agua:* spray
*arrojar con violencia:* slap
*arrojar luz:* light
*arrojar vapor:* steam
*arrojar violentamente:* slap
*arrojo:* daring
*arrollador:* runaway
*arrollar:* overwhelm
*arropar:* tuck
*arrostrar:* brave
*arroyo:* stream
*arroz:* rice
*arruga:* line, wrinkle
*arrugar:* wrinkle
*arruinar:* bankrupt, destroy, mess, ruin
*arte:* art
*arte de acción:* performance art
*arte dramático:* creative drama, theater
*arte marcial:* martial art
*artefacto:* device, gadget
*arteria:* artery
*artesa:* trough
*artesanía:* craft
*articulación:* articulation, joint
*articular:* utter
*artículo:* article, commodity, feature, item, paper, piece, story
*artículo de exportación:* export
*artículo definido:* definite article
*artículo determinado:* definite article
*artículo indefinido:* indefinite article
*artículos de confección:* dry goods
*artículos de opinión:* op-ed
*artículos o útiles de escritorio:* stationery
*artífice:* architect
*artificial:* man-made, theatrical, unnatural
*artificioso:* theatrical
*artillería:* artillery
*artilugio:* gadget
*artimaña:* trap
*artista:* artist, entertainer
*artístico:* artistic
*artritis:* arthritis
*arveja:* snow pea
*as:* ace
*asa:* handle
*asado:* barbecue, cookout, roast
*asador:* barbecue
*asaltar:* attack, hold, mug, raid, rob, storm
*asalto:* assault, raid, robbery, round
*asamblea:* assembly, gathering
*asar:* barbecue, roast
*asar a la parrilla:* grill
*ascender:* climb, graduate, promote, rise, spiral
*ascendiente:* influence
*ascensión:* rise
*ascenso:* upward
*ascensor:* elevator
*asediar:* besiege, mob, stalk
*asegurado:* secure
*aseguradora:* insurer
*asegurar:* assure, ensure, fasten, insure, lock, secure, sure, underwrite

*atraer:* appeal, attract, court, draw, engage, invite, lure, seduce, target, woo
*atraer la atención de:* eye
*atragantar:* choke
*atrapado:* grip
*atrapar:* catch, trap
*atrás:* back, behind
*atrasado:* backward, behind, overdue, slow
*atrasarse:* lag, run
*atravesar:* cross, go, pass, span
*atrayente:* attractive
*atreverse:* dare
*atreverse a:* presume
*atrevido:* daring, off-color, snippy
*atribuir:* attribute, pin
*atribuir el crédito:* credit
*atribulado:* troubled
*atributo:* attribute, complement
*atrincherarse:* barricade
*atrocidad:* atrocity
*atropellar:* run
*atroz:* miserable, terrible
*aturdido:* giddy
*aturdirse:* reel
*AU:* AU
*audacia:* daring
*audaz:* bold, daring
*audible:* audible
*audición:* audition, hearing
*audicionar:* audition
*audiencia:* audience, court, hearing
*audífonos:* earphone, headphones
*audio:* audio
*auditar:* audit
*auditorio:* audience, auditorium
*auge:* boom
*aula del curso:* homeroom
*aullar:* howl, whistle, yip
*aumentar:* escalate, expand, gain, grow, heighten, increase, magnify, mount, raise, rise, surge, swell, up
*aumentar de volumen:* rise
*aumentar rápidamente:* balloon, snowball
*aumento:* increase, raise, rise
*aumento dramático:* explosion
*aumento repentino:* surge, upsurge
*aun:* even
*aún:* even, still, yet
*aun así:* equally, even
*aun cuando:* even
*aún más:* further, furthest
*aun si:* even
*aunque:* albeit, although, if, though, while
*aurícula:* atrium
*auricular:* receiver
*auriculares:* headphones
*aurora:* dawn
*ausencia:* absence
*ausente:* absent, absentee, distant, gone, vacant
*ausente por enfermedad:* sick
*australopithecine:* Australopithecine
*auténtico:* authentic, full-blown, genuine, legitimate
*auto:* automobile
*auto deportivo:* sports car
*autobiografía:* autobiography
*autobús:* bus, coach
*autóctono:* indigenous
*autodeterminación:* self-determination
*autódromo:* racecourse, raceway
*autoestudio:* self-study
*autofecundado:* self-pollinating
*autofertilizante:* true-breeding
*autografiar:* autograph
*autógrafo:* autograph
*automático:* automatic, mechanical
*automatizar:* mechanize
*automóvil:* automobile
*automovilista:* motorist
*autonomía:* autonomy
*autopista:* freeway, motorway, thruway
*autopolinizado:* self-pollinating
*autopsia:* postmortem
*autor:* author, playwright, writer
*autor intelectual:* brain
*autora:* author, playwright, writer
*autora intelectual:* brain
*autoridad:* authority, influence, leadership
*autoritario:* authoritative
*autorización:* authority, clearance, license
*autorizado:* authoritative, licensed
*autorizar:* authorize, clear, license
*autosuficiente:* self-sufficient
*auxiliar:* aid, auxiliary
*auxiliar de vuelo:* steward, stewardess
*auxilio:* aid, help, relief
*avalancha:* avalanche
*avalúo:* appraisal
*avance:* advance, development, march, movement, preview, progress
*avance espectacular:* quantum
*avance publicitario:* trailer
*avances:* trailer
*avanzada:* scout
*avanzado:* advanced
*avanzar:* advance, along, come, go, move, progress, somewhere
*avanzar pesadamente:* lumber
*avanzar violentamente:* surge
*ave:* bird
*ave de corral:* fowl
*avecinarse:* brew, loom
*avena:* oatmeal, oats, porridge
*avenida:* avenue, parkway, strip
*avenirse a algo:* conform
*aventar:* bundle, fling, plunk, sweep, throw, toss
*aventón:* ride
*aventura:* adventure, fling
*aventurado:* risky
*aventurar:* hazard, limb, venture
*avergonzado:* ashamed, embarrassed
*avergonzar:* embarrass, shame, shy
*avería:* breakdown
*averiar:* break
*averiguación:* inquiry
*averiguar:* find, inquire
*aversión:* dislike
*aves de corral:* poultry
*aviación:* aviation
*aviario:* aviary
*avinagrado:* sour
*avión:* aircraft, airplane, plane, shuttle
*avión a reacción:* jet
*avión de combate:* fighter
*avión de pasajeros:* jetliner
*avíos:* gear
*avisar:* notice, tip
*aviso:* heads-up, notice, warning
*aviso de despido:* pink slip
*avispero:* nest
*axila:* armpit
*axioma:* axiom
*axón:* axon
*ayer:* yesterday
*ayuda:* aid, assistance, relief, support
*ayudante:* helper
*ayudante (de la policía):* deputy
*ayudante de enfermera:* LPN
*ayudante de enfermería:* LPN
*ayudante de maestro:* teacher's aide
*ayudante de mesero:* bus boy
*ayudar:* aid, assist, help, lend, support
*ayudar a recordar:* refresh
*ayudar en el parto:* deliver
*ayunar:* fast
*ayuno:* fast
*ayuntamiento:* civic, council, township
*azadón:* hoe
*azar:* random
*azotar:* batter, lash, slam, whip

*azote*: lash
*azúcar*: sugar
*azúcar glas(é)*: confectioners' sugar
*azúcar morena*: brown sugar
*azucarado*: sweet
*azucena*: lily
*azufre*: sulfur
*azul*: blue
*azul marino*: navy
*azulejo*: tile

**B**
*babor*: port
*bacalao*: cod
*bachillerato*: high school
*bacteria*: bacteria
*bacterias productoras de metano*: methanogen
*bádminton*: badminton
*bafle*: speaker
*bagatelas*: small potatoes
*baguette*: loaf
*bahía*: bay
*bailar*: dance
*bailarín*: dancer
*bailarina*: dancer
*baile*: ball, dance
*baile de graduación*: prom
*baile de la escuela*: prom
*baile de salón*: ballroom dancing
*baile social*: social dance
*baja*: casualty
*baja presión*: L
*bajar*: come, dim, down, drop, duck, ebb, fall, go, lower, mark, turn
*bajar de las nubes*: earth
*bajar de peso*: lose
*bajar el cierre/la cremallera*: unzip
*bajar el ritmo*: ease
*bajar el sonido o el volumen*: mute
*bajo*: bass, beneath, flat, gentle, low, low-rise, poor, short, under, underneath
*bajo control*: control, hand
*bajo el mando de*: under
*bajo en*: poor
*bajo impacto*: low-impact
*bajo la tutela de*: under
*bajo los reflectores*: glare
*bajo mundo*: underworld
*bajo órdenes de*: order
*bajo techo*: indoor, indoors
*bajo y fornido*: stocky
*bala*: bullet
*balancear*: bounce, juggle, sway, swing
*balanza*: balance
*balazo*: shot
*balbucear*: babble, stammer
*balcón*: balcony
*baldaquín*: canopy
*balde*: pail
*baldío*: vacant lot
*baldosa*: tile
*ballena*: whale
*ballena jorobada*: humpback whale
*ballet*: ballet
*balneario*: seaside
*balneario de aguas termales*: spa
*balón de futbol*: football
*balsa*: raft
*baluarte*: stronghold
*bambú*: bamboo
*bañadera*: tub
*bañado en sudor*: sweat
*bañador*: swimsuit
*banana*: banana
*bañar*: bathe, dip, lap, smother, shower, wash
*bañarse con agua caliente*: soak
*banca*: banking, bench
*bancarrota*: bankruptcy
*banco*: bank, stool
*banco de alimentos*: food bank
*banco de esperma*: sperm bank
*banco de semen*: sperm bank
*banda*: band, belt, boy band, gang, ring
*banda ancha*: broadband
*banda ciudadana*: citizens band
*banda elástica*: rubber band
*banda sonora*: soundtrack
*bandada*: flock
*bandeja*: platter, tray
*bandeja de entrada*: inbox
*bandeja de salida*: outbox
*bandera*: flag
*bandera de Estados Unidos*: Old Glory
*banderín*: flag
*báner*: banner ad
*bañera*: bathtub, tub
*baño*: bath, bathroom, lavatory, shower
*baño (de tina)*: bath
*baño de damas*: women's room
*baño de hombres*: men's room
*baño de mujeres*: women's room
*baño(s) (edificio público)*: bathroom
*baños*: restroom
*banquera*: banker
*banquero*: banker
*banqueta*: curb, sidewalk
*banquete*: feast
*banquillo de los acusados*: dock
*banquina*: shoulder
*baqueta*: stick
*bar*: pub
*baraja*: deck, playing card
*barajar*: shuffle
*barata*: sale
*barato*: cheap, downscale, inexpensive
*barba*: beard
*barbero*: barber
*barbilla*: chin
*barbiquejo*: guard
*barboquejo*: guard
*barcaza*: barge
*barco*: boat, ship
*barco de pasajeros*: liner
*barco petrolero*: tanker
*barman*: bartender
*barométrico*: barometric
*barómetro*: barometer, bellwether
*barra*: bar, cash bar, loaf, rail, rod
*barra de herramientas*: toolbar
*barra de labios*: lipstick
*barra de pesas*: barbell
*barra de trabajo*: taskbar
*barra deslizable*: scroll bar
*barra diagonal*: forward slash
*barra oblicua*: forward slash
*barranco*: gulch, gully
*barrer*: sweep
*barrera*: barrier
*barriada*: slum
*barricada*: barricade
*barriga*: belly, pot
*barril*: barrel, drum
*barrio*: neighborhood, quarter
*barrio bajo*: slum
*barro*: clay
*barros*: acne
*basalto*: basalt
*basar*: base
*basarse en*: build
*báscula*: scale
*base*: basis, footing, foundation, fundamentals, stand, substance
*base de datos*: database
*base de los dedos del pie*: ball
*base del bateador*: home plate
*base del pulgar*: ball
*bases*: grassroots
*básicamente*: essentially
*básico*: basic, elementary, skeleton, staple
*básquetbol*: basketball
*bastante*: bit, enough, fairly, pretty, quite, reasonable, sufficient, well
*bastar*: do
*bastardilla*: italic
*bastidores*: wing
*bastilla*: cuff
*bastión*: stronghold
*basto*: club
*bastón*: cane, stick
*bastón de caramelo*: candy cane
*bastoncillo*: rod
*bastonera*: drum majorette
*basura*: garbage, litter, refuse, trash

*basurero:* dump, garbage can, garbage collector, garbage dump, garbage man, trash can, wastebasket
*bata:* robe, scrub
*bata de laboratorio:* lab apron
*batalla:* battle
*batallar:* wrestle
*batallón:* battalion
*bate:* bat
*bateador:* batsman, batter, slugger
*bateadora:* batsman, batter, slugger
*batear:* bat
*batear de emergencia:* pinch-hit
*batería:* battery
*baterista:* drum
*batidor:* whisk
*batidora:* whisk
*batir:* beat, scramble, whip, whisk
*batir las alas:* flap
*baúl:* footlocker, trunk
*baya:* berry
*bazar:* fair, variety store
*bazar casero:* yard sale
*bazar de cosas usadas:* thrift shop
*bebé:* baby, infant
*bebedero (de agua refrigerada):* water cooler
*beber:* booze, drink
*beberse:* consume
*bebida:* beverage, booze, liquor
*bebida alcohólica:* liquor
*bebida alcóholica:* alcohol
*bebida espirituosa:* liquor
*bebidas alcohólicas:* spirit
*beca:* grant, scholarship
*beige:* ocre, beige
*béisbol:* baseball
*beisbolista:* ballplayer
*bella:* beauty
*belleza:* beauty
*bello:* beautiful, beauty
*bemol:* flat
*bencina:* petrol
*bendecir:* bless
*bendición:* blessing
*beneficiar:* benefit
*beneficiarse con algo:* profit
*beneficio:* benefit, payoff, profit
*beneficio indirecto:* spinoff
*beneficioso:* beneficial, helpful
*benéfico:* charitable
*benevolente:* charitable
*bengala:* flare
*benigno:* mild
*bentos:* benthos
*berenjena:* eggplant
*berrear:* scream
*besar:* kiss
*besos:* love
*bestia:* animal
*betabel:* beet
*betún:* frosting, icing, polish
*bi-:* twin
*Biblia:* Bible
*bíblico:* Bible
*bibliografía:* bibliography
*bibliografía anotada:* annotated bibliography
*biblioteca:* library
*bibliotecaria:* librarian
*bibliotecario:* librarian
*bicentenario:* bicentennial
*bicho:* bug
*bicho raro:* freak
*bici:* bike, cycle
*bicicleta:* bicycle, cycle
*bicicleta de montaña:* mountain bike
*bicimoto:* moped
*bicla:* bike, cycle
*bidimensional:* two-dimensional
*bidireccional:* two-way
*bidón:* drum
*bien:* all right, asset, fine, good, okay, okey dokey, right, well
*bien conocido:* well-known
*bien informado:* up-to-date
*bien que:* albeit, though
*bien raíz:* real estate, real property
*bien se podría:* well
*bienes:* goods
*bienestar:* health, welfare, well-being
*bienintencionado:* well-intentioned
*bienvenido:* welcome
*bifurcación:* fork
*bifurcarse:* fork
*bigote:* mustache
*bilé:* lipstick
*bilingüe:* bilingual
*billar:* pool, pool hall
*billete:* fare, ticket
*billete (de banco):* bill
*billetera:* billfold, wallet
*billón:* trillion
*bingo:* bingo
*binoculares:* binoculars
*binomio:* binomial
*biodegradable:* biodegradable
*biodiversidad:* biodiversity
*biógrafa:* biographer
*biografía:* biography
*biógrafo:* biographer
*bióloga:* biology
*biología:* biology
*biológicamente:* organic
*biológico:* biological
*biólogo:* biology
*bioma:* biome
*biomasa:* biomass
*biombo:* screen
*bioquímica:* biochemistry
*bioquímico:* biochemical, biochemistry
*biosfera:* biosphere
*biotecnología:* biotechnology
*biótico:* biotic
*bióxido de carbono:* carbon dioxide
*birlar:* pinch
*birrete:* mortarboard
*bisoño:* raw
*bisutería:* bling
*bit:* bit
*bitácora:* log
*bitácora en la red:* weblog
*bizcocho:* pound cake
*bla-bla-bla:* yadda
*blackjack:* blackjack
*blanca:* half note
*blanco:* butt, fair, target, white
*blanco (del ojo):* white
*blanco y negro:* black and white
*blando:* floppy, soft, tender
*blanquear:* bleach
*blindado:* armored
*blindaje:* armor
*bloc de notas:* pad
*blog:* weblog
*blogósfera:* blogosphere
*bloque:* bloc, block
*bloque de concreto de cenizas:* cinder block
*bloque de falla:* fault-block mountain
*bloque fallado:* fault-block mountain
*bloquear:* bar, block, blockade, jam, lock
*bloqueo:* blockade
*blues:* blue
*blues de doce compases:* twelve-bar blues
*bluetooth:* Bluetooth
*blusa:* blouse, shirt, top
*bobo:* dumb, sappy
*boca:* mouth, muzzle
*boca arriba:* way
*bocado:* bit, nosh
*bocanada:* puff
*bochorno:* flush
*bochornoso:* close, sticky
*bocina:* earphone, speaker
*boda:* marriage, wedding
*bodega:* hold, store, warehouse, winery
*bodegón:* still life
*bogar:* row
*boicotear:* boycott
*boina:* beret
*bol:* basin
*bola:* ball, tumor
*bola de nieve:* snowball
*boleta:* ticket

*boleta de calificaciones:* report card
*boletería:* box office
*boletín:* bulletin
*boletín general:* all-points bulletin
*boleto:* fare, ticket
*boliche:* bowling
*bolillo:* roll
*bolita de chicle:* gumball
*bolitas:* marble
*bollo:* bun
*bollo inglés:* English muffin
*bolos:* bowl, bowling
*bolsa:* bag, pocket, pocketbook, pouch, purse
*bolsa (de mano):* handbag
*bolsa (de valores):* stock exchange
*bolsa de aire:* air sac
*bolsa de dormir:* sleeping bag
*bolsa de sorpresas:* grab bag
*bolsa grande:* tote bag
*bolsa pequeña:* pouch
*bolsas de mano:* carry-on
*bolsillo:* pocket
*bolsita de dulces:* goody bag
*bolso:* purse
*bolsón:* tote bag
*bomba:* bomb, pump
*bomba (de excusado):* plunger
*bombardear:* bomb, shell
*bombardero:* bomber
*bombear:* pump
*bombera:* firefighter
*bombero:* firefighter
*bombilla:* light bulb
*bombín:* derby
*bonche de:* bunch
*bondad:* goodness
*bondadoso:* caring
*bonificación:* bonus
*bonito:* lovely, pretty, trim
*bono:* bond
*bono del Tesoro:* treasury bill
*boquera:* fever blister
*bordado:* embroidery
*bordar:* stitch
*borde:* border, edge, rim
*borde de:* verge
*borde de la acera:* curbstone
*borde de la banqueta:* curbstone
*borde del camino:* roadside
*bordear:* border, skirt
*borona:* crumb
*borracha:* drunk
*borracho:* drunk
*borrador:* draft, eraser
*borrar:* blur, delete, erase, rub
*borrego:* lamb, sheep, whitecap
*borroso:* dim, fuzzy
*bosque:* forest, wood, woodland
*bosque (ecuatorial o pluvial):* rain forest
*bosquejar:* outline, sketch
*bosquejo:* outline, sketch
*bostezar:* yawn
*bota:* boot
*bota de goma:* rubber boot
*bota de hule:* rubber boot
*botánica:* botany
*botánico:* botany
*botar:* bounce, chuck, ditch, dump, launch
*botas vaqueras:* cowboy boots
*bote:* boat, jar, tin
*bote de basura:* garbage can, trash can
*bote de remos:* rowboat
*botella:* bottle
*botica:* drugstore, pharmacy
*botín:* boot
*botiquín:* first aid kit
*botón:* button, pin
*botón regulador:* dial
*botones:* bellhop
*boulevard:* avenue
*box:* boxing, box spring
*box lunch:* box lunch
*box plot:* box plot
*box spring:* box spring
*boxeador:* fighter
*boxeadora:* fighter
*boxear:* box
*boxeo:* boxing
*bóxer:* short
*boy band:* boy band
*boya:* buoy
*bozal:* muzzle
*bra:* bra
*bracera:* field hand
*bracero:* field hand
*brackets:* brace
*bragueta:* fly
*bramar:* roar
*branquia:* gill
*brasier:* bra
*brassiere:* bra
*bravo:* brave
*bravucón:* bully
*bravucona:* bully
*bravuconería:* saber-rattling
*brazada:* stroke
*brazalete:* band, bracelet
*brazo:* arm
*brazo de gitano:* jelly roll
*break:* break
*breakdown:* breakdown
*brecha:* gap
*breve:* brief
*bridge:* bridge
*brigada:* brigade, gang, squad
*brillante:* bright, brilliant, shiny
*brillar:* flash, shine, sparkle
*brillar con luz tenue:* glow
*brillo:* glitter, luster, polish, shine
*brincar:* bounce, jump, leap, skip, spring
*brincar de cojito:* hop
*brindis:* toast
*brisa:* breeze
*británica:* Briton
*británico:* British, Briton
*brocha:* brush, paintbrush
*broche:* barrette, brooch, button, clip, pin
*brócoli:* broccoli
*bromear:* joke, kid
*bronce:* bronze
*bronceado:* sunburned, suntan, tan
*bronceador:* suntan
*broncearse:* tan
*bronces:* brass
*bronquios:* bronchi
*brotar:* pour, well
*brote:* outbreak, shoot
*bruja:* witch
*brujo:* witch, wizard
*brújula:* compass, orientation
*bruma:* mist
*brumoso:* foggy, hazy
*brusco:* abrupt, rough
*brutal:* brutal
*bruto:* gross
*bucal:* oral
*bucear:* dive
*bucle:* curl
*bucodental:* oral
*budín:* pudding
*budismo:* Buddhism
*budista:* Buddhist
*buen:* fond
*buen juicio:* judgment
*buen/mal tirador:* shot
*buena suerte:* luck
*buena voluntad:* goodwill
*buena/mala tiradora:* shot
*buenas tardes:* good afternoon
*buenas/malas nuevas:* news
*bueno:* fair, fine, fond, good, good guy, handsome, hello, nice, now, solid, well
*buenos modales:* manner
*buey:* ox
*búfalo:* buffalo
*bufanda:* scarf
*buffet:* buffet
*búho:* owl
*bujía:* spark plug
*bulbo:* bulb
*bulbo raquídeo:* medulla
*bulla:* racket
*bullicio de rumores:* buzz
*bullicioso:* lively
*bullir:* buzz
*bullpen:* bullpen
*bulto:* lump, tumor
*búnker:* bunker
*buque:* ship, vessel
*buque de guerra:* warship

*callar*: quiet, shut, silence
*callarse algo*: keep
*calle*: avenue, road, street
*calle lateral*: side street
*calle mayor*: main street
*calle principal*: main drag
*callejón*: alley
*callejón sin salida*: dead end, no-win situation, standoff
*callo de hacha*: scallop
*calma*: calm
*calmar*: calm, cool, ease, quiet, quieten, soothe
*calmarse*: cool, ease, pull, settle
*calor*: heat, warmth
*calor del sol*: sunshine
*calor específico*: specific heat capacity
*caloría*: calorie
*calorímetro*: calorimeter
*calumnia*: smear
*calumniar*: libel
*calurosamente*: warm
*caluroso*: hot
*calvo*: bald
*calza*: wedge
*calzar*: wedge
*calzoncillos*: short, underpants
*calzones*: brief, panties, underpants
*cama*: bed, box spring
*cámara*: camera, chamber, house, webcam
*cámara de seguridad*: security camera
*cámara digital*: digital camera
*cámara lenta*: slow motion
*camarera*: bartender, stewardess, waiter, waitress
*camarero*: bartender, steward, waiter
*camareros*: waitstaff
*camarón*: shrimp
*camarote*: cabin
*cambiar*: barter, break, change, move, remold, replace, reverse, revise, shift, swap, swing, switch
*cambio*: change, swing
*cambio físico*: physical change
*cambio químico*: chemical change
*camello*: camel
*camellón*: median strip
*camilla*: gurney
*caminando*: foot
*caminar*: get, walk
*caminar con dificultad*: limp
*caminar con paso enérgico*: stomp
*caminar despreocupadamente*: stroll
*caminar fatigosamente*: trek
*caminar tranquilamente*: stroll
*caminata*: hike, walk
*caminata rápida*: power walking
*camino*: approach, course, lane, path, pathway, road, route, track, way
*camino de entrada*: drive, driveway
*camino de peaje o cuota*: turnpike
*camino del éxito*: high road
*camino secundario*: side road
*camión*: lorry
*camión cisterna*: tanker
*camión con remolque*: tractor-trailer, trailer truck
*camión con tráiler*: tractor-trailer
*camión de bomberos*: fire engine, fire truck
*camión de carga*: truck
*camión de la basura*: garbage truck
*camión de remolque*: rig
*camionera*: trucker
*camionero*: trucker
*camioneta*: pickup, station wagon, truck, van
*camioneta de reparto*: panel truck
*camisa*: shirt
*camiseta*: T-shirt, undershirt
*camiseta sin mangas*: tank top
*camisón*: nightgown
*camote*: yam
*campamento*: camp, campsite
*campamento de verano*: summer camp
*campamento para remolques*: trailer park
*campana*: bell
*campaña*: campaign
*campaña publicitaria*: ad campaign
*campanada*: chime, stroke
*campeón*: champion
*campeona*: champion
*campeonato*: championship, title
*cámper*: recreational vehicle, RV, trailer
*campesino*: peasant
*campestre*: rural
*campiña*: countryside
*camping*: campground
*camping para casas rodantes*: caravan site
*campo*: country, course, domain, field, front, land, park, realm, rural, scope
*campo de batalla*: battlefield
*campo de fuerza*: force field
*campo de fútbol*: football field
*campo de tiro*: range
*campo de trabajos forzados*: labor camp
*campo local*: home field
*campo magnético*: magnetic field
*campo traviesa*: cross-country
*campo visual*: field
*caña*: cane
*canal*: channel
*canal de televisión*: channel
*canalizar*: channel
*canasta*: basket, hamper
*canasto*: basket
*cancelado*: off
*cancelar*: cancel, plug
*cáncer*: cancer
*cancha*: course, court, field
*cancha de futbol*: football field
*cancha de fútbol*: football field
*canciller*: chancellor
*canción*: song, tune
*canción infantil*: nursery rhyme
*canción publicitaria*: jingle
*cancionero*: songbook
*candidata*: candidate
*candidato*: candidate, nominee
*canela*: cinnamon
*cañería*: plumbing
*cañería principal*: main
*cangrejo*: crab
*cangrejo de río*: crawfish
*cangurera*: fanny pack
*canguro*: kangaroo
*canica*: marble
*canicas*: marble
*canícula*: dog days
*canilla*: faucet, spigot
*canjeable*: convertible
*canjear*: exchange, trade
*canoa*: canoe
*canola*: canola
*canon*: canon
*cañón*: barrel, cannon, canyon
*cañón (de un arma)*: muzzle
*cañón de órgano*: pipe
*cansado*: tired, tiring, weary
*cansancio*: fatigue
*cansar*: tire, wear
*cansarse*: steam
*cansarse de algo*: tire
*cantante*: singer, vocalist
*cantar*: chant, crow, sing, talk
*cántico*: chant
*cantidad*: amount, pool, quantity, sum
*cantidad sustancial*: lot
*cantinera*: bartender
*cantinero*: bartender
*canto*: chant, song
*caos*: chaos, mess
*capa*: cape, coat, covering, film, layer
*capa de ozono*: ozone layer
*capacidad*: capacity, competence, power, talent
*capacidad de persistencia*: carrying capacity
*capacitado*: fit
*capacitar*: qualify, train
*capataz*: foreman
*capaz*: capable, talented
*capaz de*: equal, up

*ciclo del agua:* hydrologic cycle, water cycle
*ciclo hidrológico:* hydrologic cycle
*ciclón:* cyclone
*ciclopista:* bike path
*ciego:* blind, mindless
*cielo:* heaven, sky
*ciempiés:* centipede
*cien:* hundred
*cien por ciento:* hundred
*ciénaga:* bog, marsh, swamp
*ciencia:* science
*ciencia ficción:* science fiction, sci-fi
*ciencias biológicas:* life science
*ciencias de la tierra:* earth science
*ciencias de la vida:* life science
*ciencias físicas:* physical science
*ciencias sociales:* social science
*ciénega:* marsh
*cieno:* silt
*científica:* scientist
*científico:* scientific, scientist
*cientos:* hundred
*cierre:* catch, closure, shutdown
*cierre (de cremallera):* zipper
*cierta cantidad:* so
*cierto:* certain, positive, some, true
*ciervo:* deer
*cifra:* figure
*cifrar:* pin
*cigarrillo:* cigarette
*cigarro:* cigarette
*cilantro:* cilantro
*cilindro:* cylinder
*cilio:* cilia
*cima:* crest, peak, summit
*cimientos:* foundation
*cinc:* zinc
*cinco:* five
*cincuenta:* fifty
*cincuentavo:* fiftieth
*cine:* cinema, motion picture, movie, movie theater, theater
*cínico:* cynical
*cinta:* band, ribbon, tape
*cinta adhesiva:* duct tape, tape
*cinta de llegada:* tape
*cinta de video:* videotape
*cinta métrica:* tape measure
*cintura:* waist
*cinturón:* belt
*cinturón de asteroides:* asteroid belt
*cinturón de Kuiper:* Kuiper belt
*cinturón de seguridad:* seat belt
*circo:* circus
*circo mediático:* media circus
*circuito:* circuit
*circuito cerrado:* closed-circuit
*circuito en paralelo:* parallel circuit
*circuito en serie:* series circuit
*circuito integrado:* chip
*circulación:* circulation, traffic
*circulación general:* systemic circulation
*circulación pulmonar:* pulmonary circulation
*circulación sistémica:* systemic circulation
*circular:* circulate, cruise, form letter, get, memo
*circulatorio:* circulatory
*círculo:* circle
*circuncidar:* circumcise
*circunferencia:* circumference
*circunspección:* restraint
*circunstancia:* circumstance, matter, picture
*cirro:* cirrus
*ciruela:* plum
*ciruela pasa:* prune
*cirugía:* surgery
*cirugía de puente coronario:* bypass
*cirujana:* surgeon
*cirujano:* surgeon
*cisma:* split
*cita:* date, engagement, quotation, quote
*cita con:* appointment
*citar:* cite, quote
*citatorio:* summons
*citocinesis:* cytokinesis
*citoplasma:* cytoplasm
*citosina:* cytosine
*cítrico:* citrus
*ciudad:* city, town
*ciudad dormitorio:* bedroom
*ciudad pequeña:* Main Street
*ciudad universitaria:* campus
*ciudadana:* citizen, national
*ciudadanía:* citizenship
*ciudadano:* citizen, national
*cívico:* civic
*civil:* civilian
*civilización:* civilization
*civilizado:* civilized
*civismo:* civics
*clamar:* bay, cry
*clamar por:* clamor
*clan:* clan
*clandestino:* underground
*claqué:* tap dance
*clara (de huevo):* white
*claridad:* clarity, definition, light
*clarificar:* clarify
*clarinete:* clarinet
*claro:* anyway, clear, clearing, course, distinct, explicit, light, marked, obviously, of course, opening, pale, plain, sharp, thin, transparent
*claro está:* indeed
*claro que no:* not, of course
*clase:* breed, class, lesson, sort
*clase dirigente:* establishment
*clase marginada:* underclass
*clase media:* middle class
*clase obrera:* working class
*clase privilegiada:* upper class
*clase trabajadora:* working class
*clásico:* classic, classical, derby, vintage
*clasificar:* class, classify, fall, file, place, qualify, rank, rate, sort
*cláusula:* clause
*clavada:* slam dunk
*clavar:* dig, drive, hammer, nail, plunge, stick, tack
*clave:* central, clef, code, crucial, key, password
*clave contextual:* context clue
*clave de fa:* bass clef
*clave de sol:* treble clef
*clave dicotómica:* dichotomous key
*clavija:* plug
*clavo:* clove, nail, pin
*claxon:* horn
*clerecía:* ministry
*clérigo:* Reverend
*clero:* clergy, ministry
*click:* click
*cliente:* client, customer, patron
*clientela:* practice
*clima:* climate, weather
*clímax:* climax
*clínica:* clinic
*clínico:* clinical
*clip:* paper clip
*clon:* clone
*clonar:* clone
*cloro:* bleach
*clorofila:* chlorophyll
*clorofluorocarbono:* CFC
*cloroplasto:* chloroplast
*clóset:* closet, cupboard
*club:* club
*club de golf:* golf club
*club estudiantil masculino:* fraternity
*club nocturno:* nightclub
*clutch:* clutch
*cm:* cm
*coacción:* constraint
*coalición:* coalition
*cobarde:* coward
*cobertizo:* shed
*cobertura:* coverage, reporting
*cobijas:* cover
*cobrador:* collector, conductor
*cobradora:* collector, conductor
*cobrar:* cash, charge, claim, gain, gather, toll
*cobrar vida:* alive
*cobre:* copper
*coca:* coke
*cocaína:* cocaine
*cocer:* boil

merchant, shopkeeper, trader
*comerciar:* trade
*comerciar en:* deal
*comercio:* commerce
*comestible:* edible
*comestibles:* grocery
*comestibles no perecederos:* dry goods
*cometa:* comet, kite
*cometa Halley:* Halley's comet
*cometer:* commit
*cometer un error:* err
*comezón:* itch
*cómic:* comic book
*cómica:* comedian, comic
*cómico:* comedian, comic, comical, funny
*comida:* cooking, dinner, food, lunch, meal
*comida en el campo:* picnic
*comida para llevar:* takeaway, takeout
*comida preparada:* takeaway, takeout
*comida rápida:* fast food
*comienzo:* beginning, outset
*comillas:* inverted commas, quotation mark, quote
*comiquísimo:* hilarious
*comisaría:* police station, station house
*comisión:* commission
*Comisión Controladora de Acciones y Valores:* SEC
*comisión investigadora:* tribunal
*comisionada:* commissioner
*comisionado:* commissioner
*comisionar:* commission
*comité:* committee
*comité de acción política:* political action committee
*como:* as, instance, like
*cómo:* how, however
*cómo (estás):* how
*como consecuencia de:* strength
*como de costumbre:* typically
*como es de esperarse:* usual
*como estarlo viendo:* mind
*como guste:* please
*como loco:* mad
*como más:* most
*como pez en el agua:* element
*como rayo:* lightning
*como sea:* however
*como si:* as, if
*como siempre:* ever, usual
*como sigue:* follow
*como tal:* such
*cómo te atreves/se atreve/se atreven:* dare
*como último recurso:* resort
*cómoda:* bureau
*comodidad:* comfort, convenience
*comodidades:* comfort, convenience
*comodín:* joker
*comodino:* NIMBY
*cómodo:* comfortable, convenient, ease, snug
*compactado:* compacted
*compacto:* compact, dense
*compadecer:* feel, pity, sympathize
*compaginar:* gel
*compañera:* companion, date, peer
*compañera de candidatura:* running mate
*compañera de clase:* classmate
*compañera de equipo:* teammate
*compañera de trabajo:* colleague
*compañero:* companion, date, fellow, peer
*compañero de candidatura:* running mate
*compañero de clase:* classmate
*compañero de cuarto:* roommate
*compañero de equipo:* teammate
*compañero de trabajo:* colleague
*compañía:* company, corporation, firm, operation
*compañía afiliada:* affiliate
*compañía de seguros:* insurer
*compañía de telecomunicaciones:* carrier
*compañía multinacional:* multinational
*comparable:* matched
*comparación:* comparison
*comparado con:* compared, proportion
*comparar:* compare, contrast, match
*comparar notas:* note
*comparativo:* comparative
*comparativo de late:* later
*comparecer:* appear
*compartimento:* compartment, stall
*compartimiento:* stall
*compartir:* share
*compartir archivos:* file-sharing
*compás:* bar, measure, meter, time
*compás binario:* duple meter
*compás compuesto:* compound meter
*compás mixto:* mixed meter
*compás ternario:* triple meter
*compasión:* compassion, sympathy
*compatible:* compatible
*compensación:* comp, compensation
*compensar:* balance, compensate, offset
*competencia:* competence, competition, contest, derby, tournament
*competente:* capable, competent
*competidor:* competitor, contestant
*competidora:* contestant
*competir:* compete, contend, vie
*competir (con alguien por algo):* compete
*competitivo:* competitive
*compilar:* compile
*complacer:* oblige, please
*complacido:* pleased
*complaciente:* fond, indulgent
*complejidad:* complexity
*complejo:* complex, compound, elaborate, intricate, involved, sophisticated
*complejo de viviendas:* housing project
*complementar:* complement, supplement
*complemento:* complement
*complemento directo:* direct object
*completamente:* entirely, full, fully, utterly, wholly
*completamente despierto:* awake
*completar:* complete, supplement
*completo:* all, all-around, book, complete, full, full-length, thorough, total
*complexión:* build, constitution
*complicación:* complication
*complicado:* complicated, elaborate
*complicar:* complicate, confuse
*complicarla existencia:* fuss
*cómplice:* accessory
*componente:* component, constituent
*componer:* compose, heal
*comportamiento:* behavior
*comportamiento aprendido:* learned behavior
*comportarse:* act, behave, sound
*composición:* composition, essay, makeup
*compositor:* composer
*compositora:* composer
*composta:* compost
*compostura:* restraint
*compra:* acquisition, buy, purchase
*comprado:* store-bought
*comprar:* buy, fix, purchase, shop
*comprar acciones de socios:* buy
*comprar todo lo posible:* buy
*comprar un seguro:* insure
*compras:* shopping
*compraventa por correo:* mail order
*comprender:* embrace, grasp, make, realize, sink,

sympathize, understand
*comprender mal:* misunderstand
*comprensible:* understandable
*comprensión:* comprehension, grasp, understanding
*comprensión visual:* visual literacy
*comprensivo:* understanding
*comprimido:* caplet
*comprobar:* check
*comprometer:* bind, compromise, pin, pledge, undertake
*comprometerse a:* commit
*comprometido:* engaged, involved, on board, stake
*compromiso:* commitment, engagement
*compuesto:* composite, compound, double-barreled
*compuesto covalente:* covalent compound
*compuesto iónico:* ionic compound
*compuesto orgánico:* organic compound
*computación:* computing
*computadora:* computer
*computadora central:* mainframe
*computadora personal:* personal computer
*computadora portátil:* laptop, notebook
*computarizar:* computerize
*común:* common, crude, ordinary, popular, regular
*común y corriente:* garden-variety, usual
*comunicación:* communication
*comunicaciones:* communication
*comunicado de prensa:* news release
*comunicar:* communicate, inform, let, put, reach
*comunicarse con:* communicate
*comunicativo:* forthcoming
*comunidad:* community
*comunismo:* communism
*comunitario:* communal
*con:* in, of, on, to, under, with
*cóncavo:* concave
*concebir:* conceive, devise, formulate
*conceder:* accord
*concentración:* concentration, rally
*concentrado:* concentrated, full
*concentrar:* center, cluster, concentrate, focus, mass, mind
*concentrarse en:* concentrate, turn
*concepto:* concept, idea
*concernir:* concern
*concertar:* arrange, broker
*concesión:* concession, franchise
*concesiones mutuas:* give
*concha:* shell
*conchita:* shell
*conciencia:* conscience, consciousness
*conciencia fonémica:* phonemic awareness
*concientizar:* educate
*concienzudo:* thorough
*concierto:* concert, concerto
*conciso:* brief
*concluido:* complete
*concluir:* close, conclude, finalize, finish, wind
*conclusión:* conclusion, ending
*conclusiones finales:* closing argument
*concordar:* agree, match, square
*concretamente:* specifically
*concretar:* fix, nail
*concreto:* concrete, hard, particular
*concreto asfáltico:* blacktop
*concurrencia:* attendance
*concursante:* competitor, contestant
*concurso:* quiz
*concurso de belleza:* beauty pageant
*concurso de horneado:* bake-off
*concurso de ortografía:* spelling bee
*condado:* county, parish
*conde:* count
*condecoración:* medal
*condena:* conviction
*condenado:* doomed
*condenar:* condemn, convict
*condensación:* condensation
*condensar:* condense
*condescendiente:* indulgent
*condición:* condition, qualification, status
*condicional:* conditional
*condicionar:* condition
*condiciones:* condition
*condimentar:* season
*condimento:* flavoring
*condominio:* condominium
*condón:* condom
*conducción:* conduct, conduction, leadership
*conducir:* conduct, drive, guide, lead, navigate, shepherd, steer, wheel
*conducir a:* lead
*conducir bajo la influencia del alcohol:* DUI, DWI
*conducta:* behavior, conduct
*conducta social:* social behavior
*conductismo:* behaviorism
*conductista:* behaviorism
*conducto:* duct, pipeline, tube
*conducto deferente:* vas deferens
*conductor:* broadcaster, conductor
*conductor de camión:* trucker
*conductor ebrio:* drunk driver
*conductora (de televisión):* broadcaster
*conductora de camión:* trucker
*conductora ebria:* drunk driver
*conectar:* connect, hook, link, tie
*conectar con:* connect
*conejo:* rabbit
*conejo de cola de algodón:* cottontail
*conexión:* connection, link
*conexiones:* connection
*confabulado con:* league
*confederación:* confederation
*conferencia:* lecture
*conferencia de prensa:* news conference, press conference
*conferenciante:* lecturer
*conferencista:* lecturer
*conferir:* accord
*conferir poder:* empower
*confesar:* confess, own
*confesarse (culpable):* plead
*confesión:* confession
*confesional:* sectarian
*confiable:* reliable, solid, sound
*confiado:* assertive, assured
*confianza:* confidence, faith
*confianza del consumidor:* consumer confidence
*confiar:* trust
*confiar en:* confident, rely
*confiar en que alguien hará algo:* trust
*confiar(le) a:* trust
*confidencial:* classified, confidential, inside
*confinado:* confined
*confinar:* confine
*confirmar:* bear, confirm, verify
*conflicto:* conflict, warfare
*confluir:* merge
*conformación:* shape
*conformarse:* make
*conforme:* content
*conforme a:* according to, whereby
*confort:* comfort
*confrontación:* confrontation
*confrontar:* tackle
*confrontar con:* confront
*confundido:* confused, lost, mixed up, muddled
*confundir:* cloud, confuse, mistake, mix, muddle, puzzle
*confusión:* confusion, turmoil
*confuso:* confused, confusing, fuzzy, mixed up
*congelado:* freezing, frozen
*congelador:* freezer
*congeladora:* freezer

rely, spare
*contemplar:* contemplate, entertain, eye
*contemporáneo:* contemporary
*contender:* run
*contendiente:* challenger
*contenedor:* container, holder
*contener:* check, contain, curb, hold, include, restrain, stem, suppress
*contenerse:* hold
*contenido:* content, subject matter
*contenido emocional:* expressive content
*contentar:* please
*contento:* content, glad, happy, high, pleased
*contento de:* happy
*contestador automático:* answering machine
*contestar:* answer, back, reply
*contexto:* context
*contienda:* contest, race, warfare
*continental:* continental
*continente:* continent, mainland
*Continente Americano:* Americas
*contingente:* contingent
*continuación:* follow-up
*continuamente:* time
*continuar:* carry, continue, follow, go
*continuar con:* pursue
*continuar haciendo algo:* keep
*continuo:* continual, continuous
*contra:* against, into, minus, up, versus, vs.
*contra la corriente:* upstream
*contra la ley:* illegal
*contra las reglas:* illegal
*contra reembolso:* C.O.D.
*contraatacar:* counter
*contrabajo:* double bass
*contrabandear:* smuggle
*contracepción:* contraception
*contradecir:* contradict
*contradicción:* contradiction
*contradictorio:* contradictory
*contraer:* catch, contract, get
*contraer matrimonio:* marry
*contraer nupcias:* marry
*contraerse:* contract
*contrainterrogar:* cross-examine
*contraoferta:* counteroffer
*contraparte:* counterpart
*contrapeso:* counterbalance
*contrapunto:* descant
*contrario:* contrary, counter, far, opposite, reverse
*contrastar:* contrast
*contraste:* contrast
*contratar:* contract, employ, engage, hire, sign, take
*contratiempo:* setback, trouble
*contratista:* contractor
*contrato:* contract
*contravención:* breach
*contraventana:* shutter
*contribución:* contribution, taxation
*contribución de impuestos:* taxation
*contribuir:* contribute
*contribuir a:* contribute
*contribuyente:* taxpayer
*contrincante:* opponent
*control:* grip, hold
*control de crucero:* cruise control
*control de la ira:* anger management
*control de la natalidad:* birth control
*control de retroalimentación:* feedback control
*control remoto:* remote control
*controlado:* control
*controlador:* driver
*controlarse:* ahold, control
*controversia:* controversy
*controvertido:* controversial
*contundente:* decisive, emphatic
*convección:* convection
*convencer:* convince, get, induce, into, satisfy, win
*convencer de:* persuade
*convención:* convention
*convención teatral:* theatrical convention
*convencional:* conventional
*convencionalismo:* convention
*conveniencia:* convenience
*conveniente:* convenient, desirable, helpful, suitable
*convenio:* accord, agreement, deal, settlement, treaty
*convenir:* pay, suit
*convenir algo:* interest
*convenir en:* agree
*conversa:* convert
*conversación:* conversation, talk
*conversar:* chat, talk
*conversión:* metamorphosis
*conversión de energía:* energy conversion
*converso:* convert
*convertible:* convertible
*convertir:* change, convert, make, transform, translate
*convertir en:* turn
*convertirse en:* become, evolve
*convertirse en realidad:* realize
*convicción:* conviction, persuasion
*convidar:* treat
*convincente:* compelling, convincing, plausible
*convocar:* call, convene, summon
*convoy:* convoy
*conyugal:* marital
*cónyuge:* spouse
*cookie:* cookie
*cool:* cool
*cooperar:* cooperate
*cooperativa:* collective
*coordenadas:* coordinate
*coordenadas polares:* polar coordinate
*coordinar:* conjunction, coordinate
*copa:* cup, drink, trophy
*copia:* copy
*copiadora:* copier, copy machine
*copiar:* copy, duplicate, imitate
*copo de nieve:* snowflake
*coprotagonizar:* costar
*copyright:* copyright
*coque:* coke
*coqueta:* flirt
*coquetear:* flirt
*coqueto:* flirt
*coraje:* backbone, bravery, nerve
*coral:* chorale
*Corán:* Koran
*corazón:* core, heart
*corbata:* tie
*corcovear:* buck
*cordel:* string
*cordero:* lamb
*cordial:* friendly, hearty
*cordiales saludos:* truly
*cordillera:* range
*cordillera oceánica central:* mid-ocean ridge
*cordón:* lace, shoestring
*cordón umbilical:* umbilical cord
*cordura:* sanity
*corer:* get
*córnea:* cornea
*cornear:* gore
*coro:* choir, chorale, chorus
*corona:* crown
*coronar:* cap, crown
*coronel:* colonel
*coronilla:* crown
*corporación privada:* privately held corporation
*corporativo:* corporate
*corpúsculo (del espacio):* planetesimal
*corral:* barnyard, bay, corral, pen
*correa:* belt, strap
*correcaminos:* roadrunner
*corrección:* correction
*correctamente:* truly
*correctivo:* correction
*correcto:* correct, grammatical, proper, right
*corrector:* editor
*corrector ortográfico:* spell-checker

*correctora:* editor
*corredor:* aisle, broker, corridor, hall, runner
*corredor de valores:* stockbroker
*corredora:* runner
*corredora de valores:* stockbroker
*corregir:* correct, edit, heal, reform
*corregir la ortografía:* spell-check
*correligionario:* fellow
*correo:* e-mail, mail, post office
*correo certificado:* certified mail
*correo electrónico:* e-mail
*correoso:* tough
*correr:* circulate, draw, fire, flow, race, run, rush, stream
*correr (lentamente):* jog
*correr con:* meet
*correr con suerte:* lucky
*correr el riesgo:* chance, risk
*correr rápidamente:* sprint
*correr riesgos:* risk
*correspondencia:* correspondence, mail
*correspondencia electrónica no deseada:* spam
*correspondencia entre:* correspondence
*corresponder:* correspond, equate, go, repay, return
*corresponder a:* up
*corresponsal:* correspondent
*corriente:* cheap, current, draft, informed, tide, touch
*corriente (oceánica) de aguas profundas:* deep current
*corriente ascendente:* updraft
*corriente costera longitudinal:* longshore current
*corriente de convección:* convection current
*corriente de superficie:* surface current
*corriente descendente:* downdraft
*corriente en chorro:* jet stream
*corriente litoral:* longshore current
*corriente longitudinal de la costa:* longshore current
*corriente principal:* mainstream
*corriente superficial:* surface current
*corroborar:* verify
*corroer:* eat
*corromper:* corrupt
*corrupción:* corruption
*corrupto:* corrupt
*cortado:* dead, sour
*cortado a pico:* vertical
*cortadora de pasto:* lawnmower
*cortante:* abrupt, cutting
*cortar:* carve, chop, clip, cut, hack, nick, pick, ring, shred, slit, split, sting
*cortar al ras:* crop
*cortar en cubitos:* dice
*cortar la respiración:* wind
*cortar por:* cut
*cortar por lo sano:* bud
*cortarse la comunicación:* cut
*cortarse la línea:* cut
*corte:* court, cutoff, nick, slit
*corte (de pelo):* haircut
*corte de apelaciones:* appeals court
*corte de luz:* outage
*corte de pelo:* haircut
*corte de pelo estilo militar:* buzz cut
*corte superior:* superior court
*cortés:* civil, courteous, gentle, polite
*cortesía:* courtesy
*corteza:* bark, crust
*corteza inferior:* lower mantle
*corteza terrestre:* crust
*cortinas:* curtain
*cortinero:* curtain rod, rail
*cortinilla:* window shade
*corto:* short, trailer
*corto de:* short
*corto de dinero:* pocket
*corto de vista:* near-sighted
*corto plazo:* short-term
*cortos:* short
*corva (de la rodila):* crook
*cosa:* matter, thing
*cosa imprescindible:* must
*cosa segura:* certainty
*cosas:* matter, stuff, thing
*cosas que están cerca o junto a otra:* neighbor
*cosas usadas:* secondhand
*cosecha:* crop, harvest, vintage
*cosechar:* harvest
*coseno:* cosine
*coser:* sew, stitch
*cosido:* sewn
*cosita:* thing
*cosmético:* cosmetic
*cosmología:* cosmology
*cosquillas:* tickle
*costa:* coast, coastline, seaside, shore
*costado:* flank, side
*costal:* punching bag, sack
*costal de boxeo:* punching bag
*costar:* cost, price, set
*costear:* finance
*costilla:* chop, rib
*costo:* cost, price
*costoso:* big-ticket, costly
*costra:* crust
*costumbre:* custom, ritual, tradition, way
*costura:* seam
*cota:* contour line
*cotidiano:* day-to-day
*cotiledón:* cotyledon
*cotización:* quotation, quote
*cotizar:* quote
*cotizar en bolsa:* float
*cotonete:* cotton swab
*cotorrear:* chatter, schmooze
*country:* country
*coyuntura feliz:* break
*CPT:* certified public accountant
*crack:* crack
*cráneo:* skull
*cráter:* crater
*crayón:* crayon
*creación:* construction, creation, formation
*creador:* author
*creadora:* author
*crear:* build, create, establish, form, found, set
*creativo:* creative
*crecer:* build, grow, increase, mature, swell
*crecer bien:* flourish
*crecer como hongo:* mushroom
*crecer rápidamente:* snowball
*creciente:* crescent
*crecimiento:* development, growth
*credencial:* card, ID card, identification card
*credencial de identificación:* identity card
*crédito:* credit, credit hour, loan
*créditos:* credit
*credo:* persuasion
*creencia:* belief, faith, persuasion
*creer:* believe, feel, fool, give, suppose, swallow, think
*creíble:* credible, plausible
*creído:* grand
*crema:* cream
*crema ligera:* light cream
*crema para el sol:* sunscreen
*cremera:* creamer
*creo:* think
*crepúsculo:* dawn, sunset
*cresa:* maggot
*crespo:* fuzzy
*cresta:* arête, crest, ridge
*cría:* young
*cría selectiva:* selective breeding
*criadero:* kennel
*crianza:* upbringing
*crianza de animales:* farming
*criar:* breed, bring, grow, nurture, raise, rear
*criar animales:* farm
*criatura:* creature, infant
*cricket:* cricket
*crimen:* crime, offense
*criminal:* criminal
*crin:* mane
*crioclastia:* ice wedging

*críptico:* obscure
*críquet:* cricket
*crisálida:* chrysalis
*crisis:* depression, head
*crisis de identidad:* identity crisis
*crisis nerviosa:* breakdown
*crispar (los nervios):* jar, nerve
*cristal:* crystal
*cristal cortado:* crystal
*cristalino:* lens
*cristiana:* Christian
*cristianismo:* Christianity
*cristiano:* Christian
*criterio:* criterion, judgment
*criterios estéticos:* aesthetic criteria
*crítica:* critic, criticism, review
*crítica arquetípica:* archetypal criticism
*crítica de arte:* art criticism
*crítica literaria:* literary criticism
*criticar:* attack, criticize, exception, fault, level
*criticar severamente:* damn
*crítico:* critic, critical
*croissant:* croissant
*crol:* crawl
*Cro-Magnon:* Cro-Magnon
*Cromañón:* Cro-Magnon
*cromátide:* chromatid
*cromosfera:* chromosphere
*cromosoma sexual:* sex chromosome
*crónica:* chronicle, commentary
*crónico:* chronic
*cronología:* timeline
*cronometrar:* time
*cross-country:* cross-country
*cruce:* crossing, crossroads
*cruce de peatones:* crosswalk
*crucero:* crossing, cruise, railroad crossing
*crucial:* crucial
*crucigrama:* crossword
*crudo:* bleak, brutal, crude, raw
*cruel:* inhuman, mean, nasty, ruthless, vicious
*crujiente:* crisp
*crujir:* crunch, squeak
*cruz:* cross
*cruza:* cross
*cruzamiento:* crossing over
*cruzar:* cross, fold
*cruzar los dedos:* finger
*cruzar o pasar velozmente:* streak
CST: CST
*cuaderno (de notas):* notebook
*cuaderno para colorear:* coloring book
*cuadra:* block, stable
*cuadrado:* sq., square
*cuadragésimo:* fortieth
*cuadrante:* dial
*cuadrar:* add, fit
*cuadrilátero:* ring
*cuadrilla:* gang
*cuadro:* frame, painting, picture, piece, plaid, square
*cuadro al óleo:* oil painting
*cuadro de diálogo:* dialog box
*cuadro de honor:* honor roll
*cuadro vivo:* tableau
*cuádruple:* quadruple, quadruplet
*cuadruplicar:* quadruple
*cuaga (mamífero africano extinto):* quagga
*cuajar:* gel, jell, set
*cuál:* which
*cualidad:* attribute, quality
*cualitativo:* qualitative
*cualquier:* any, anything, old
*cualquiera:* anybody, anyone
*cuan largo es:* full-length
*cuando:* as, when, whenever
*cuándo:* when
*cuando menos:* least
*cuando mucho:* best, latest, maximum
*cuando pasa la tormenta:* dust
*cuando se tiene tiempo:* leisure
*cuando uno quiere:* leisure
*cuánta:* many
*cuántas:* many
*cuantioso:* massive
*cuánto:* how, long, many
*cuántos:* many
*cuarenta:* forty
*cuarentavo:* fortieth
*cuarentena:* quarantine
*cuarta parte:* fourth, quarter
*cuartel:* barracks
*cuartel general:* headquarters
*cuarteto:* quartet
*cuarto:* bedroom, fourth, quarter, room
*cuarto (de galón):* quart
*cuarto [un cuarto de kilo/libra]:* quarter
*cuarto de baño:* bathroom
*cuarto de final:* quarterfinal
*cuarto de la tele:* family room
*cuarto de televisión:* family room
*cuarto disponible:* vacancy
*cuarto oscuro:* darkroom
*cuata:* friend
*cuate:* buddy, dude, friend, pal
*cuatrera:* rustler
*cuatrero:* rustler
*cuatro:* four
*cubeta:* bucket, pail
*cúbico:* cubic
*cubículo:* carrel, cubicle, stall
*cubierta:* binding, cover, deck, hood, jacket
*cubierta de cocina:* countertop
*cubierta de vuelo:* flight deck
*cubierto:* plastered
*cubiertos:* cutlery, flatware
*cubito para caldo:* bouillon cube
*cubo:* bucket, cube
*cubo de basura:* trash can
*cubrir:* blanket, bury, coat, cover, fall, fill, hedge, mask, span, swathe
*cubrir con azúcar glaseada:* frost
*cubrir de:* shower
*cucaracha:* cockroach, roach
*cuchara:* scoop, spoon
*cuchara para servir:* tablespoon
*cucharear:* spoon
*cucharilla:* teaspoon
*cucharita:* teaspoon
*cucharón:* ladle, scoop
*cuchilla:* blade
*cuchillo:* knife
*cuello:* collar, neck, throat
*cuello (de) tortuga:* turtleneck
*cuello alto:* turtleneck
*cuello azul:* blue-collar
*cuenca:* basin, socket
*cuenca (fluvial):* drainage basin
*cuenca abisal (océanica):* deep ocean basin
*Cuenca del Pacífico:* Pacific Rim
*cuenco:* basin
*cuenta:* account, bead, bill, check, count
*cuenta corriente:* checking account, current account
*cuenta de cheques:* checking account
*cuenta regresiva:* countdown
*cuentas:* account
*cuento:* story, tale
*cuento de hadas:* fairy tale
*cuerda:* cord, line, rope, string, wind
*cuerda de saltar:* jump rope
*cuerda para/de saltar:* skip rope
*cuerdo:* sane
*cuerno:* croissant, horn
*cuero crudo o sin curtir:* rawhide
*cuerpo:* body, corps, flesh, frame
*cuerpo de abogados:* bar
*cuerpo docente:* faculty
*cuerpo legislativo:* legislature
*cuerpo que entra en una reacción química:* reactant
*cuervo:* crow
*cuesta:* incline
*cuesta arriba:* uphill
*cuesta continental:* continental rise
*cuestión:* issue, matter, question
*cuestión de:* case
*cuestionar:* challenge
*cuestionario:* questionnaire
*cueva:* cave
*cuidado:* beware, look, watch, TLC

*delincuente sexual:* sex offender
*delineador (de ojos):* eyeliner
*delinquir:* offend
*delito:* crime, offense
*delito grave:* felony
*delta:* delta
*demacrado:* drawn
*demanda:* demand, suit
*demandada:* defendant
*demandado:* defendant
*demandante:* plaintiff, prosecutor
*demandar:* sue
*demasiado:* much, too, undue, way
*demasiado tarde:* late
*demente:* insane
*democracia:* democracy
*demócrata:* democrat
*democrático:* democratic
*demoler:* bulldoze
*demolir:* demolish
*demonios:* earth
*demora:* lag
*demorar:* delay, detain
*demostración:* show
*demostrar:* demonstrate, establish, illustrate, prove, register, show
*demostrar la propia valía:* prove
*demostrar poder:* muscle
*dendrita:* dendrite
*denegación:* denial
*denegar:* deny
*denotar:* indicate
*densidad:* density
*denso:* dense
*dentado:* jagged
*dentadura (postiza):* dentures
*dental:* dental
*dentífrico:* toothpaste
*dentista:* dentist, doctor
*dentro:* in, indoor, indoors, inside, into, within
*dentro de poco:* long, shortly
*dentro de una tienda:* in-store
*dentro del plazo previsto:* target
*denuncia:* whistle-blowing
*denunciar:* denounce, lodge, report
*departamento:* apartment, department, flat, office, suite
*departamento de bomberos:* fire department
*departamento de emergencias:* ER
*departamento de policía:* police department
*Departamento de Salud y Seguridad en el Trabajo:* OSHA
*depender:* depend, rest
*depender de:* depend, hang, rely
*dependienta:* clerk, shop assistant
*dependiente:* assistant, clerk, dependent, shop assistant
*deportar:* deport
*deporte:* game, sport
*deportes:* athletics, phys ed, physical education
*deportista:* sportsman, sportswoman
*deportivo:* sporting
*depositar:* deposit, down, lay, put
*depósito:* deposit, deposition, repository, storage, store, tank, warehouse
*depósito de madera:* lumberyard
*depósito glacial:* till
*depósito para combustibles:* bunker
*depredador:* consumer, predator
*depresión:* depression, slump, trough
*depresión posparto:* postpartum depression
*depresión tropical:* tropical depression
*deprimente:* depressing
*deprimido:* depressed, down, low
*deprimir:* depress, get
*depurador de gases:* scrubber
*derby:* derby
*derecha:* right
*derechista:* right-wing
*derecho:* erect, law, right, right-handed, straight, toll
*derecho de aduana:* duty
*derecho de paso:* right of way
*derecho de visita:* visitation rights
*derecho de voto:* franchise, vote
*derechos:* copyright, fee
*derechos civiles:* civil rights
*derechos de autor:* copyright
*derechos humanos:* human rights
*deriva de los continentes:* continental drift
*derivar:* derive, divert
*dermatóloga:* dermatologist
*dermatología:* dermatologist
*dermatólogo:* dermatologist
*dermis:* dermis
*derogar:* strike
*derramar:* overflow, shed, spill
*derrame cerebral:* stroke
*derrame de petróleo:* slick
*derrapar:* skid
*derretido:* melt
*derretir:* melt, thaw
*derribar:* break, demolish, fell, shoot, topple
*derribar:* demoler, destruir, knock
*derrocar:* overthrow, topple
*derrochador:* lavish
*derrochar:* lavish
*derrota:* defeat
*derrota en cero:* shutout
*derrotar:* beat, defeat, knock
*derrubio estratificado:* stratified drift
*derrumbamiento:* landslide
*derrumbarse:* cave, collapse, crash, crumble
*derrumbe:* landslide
*desabotonar:* open
*desabrido:* tasteless
*desabrochar:* open, undo
*desacatar:* defy
*desaceleración:* negative acceleration
*desacreditar:* discredit
*desacuerdo:* disagreement, dissent
*desafiante:* challenging, defiant
*desafiar:* challenge, dare, defy
*desafilado:* blunt
*desafinado:* flat
*desafío:* challenge, dare, defiance
*desafortunado:* unfortunate, unhappy
*desagradable:* messy, rude, sour, ugly, unfriendly, unpalatable, unpleasant
*desaguar:* drain
*desahogar:* vent, work
*desairar:* slight, snub
*desaire:* snub
*desalentado:* dismay, gloomy
*desalentador:* gloomy, grim, negative
*desalentar:* discourage, put
*desaliento:* dismay, gloom
*desalinización:* desalination
*desamarrar:* untie
*desanimado:* dismay, low
*desanimar:* discourage
*desánimo:* dismay
*desanudar:* untie
*desaparecer:* disappear, melt, vanish
*desaparecido:* missing
*desaparecido en acción:* MIA
*desaprobar:* disapprove, fault
*desaprovechar:* miss, throw
*desarmado:* unarmed
*desarmador:* screwdriver
*desarmar:* apart, dismantle
*desarreglado:* disheveled
*desarreglar:* mess
*desarrollado:* advanced, mature
*desarrollar:* break, develop, mature, move, evolve, progress, set
*desarrollo:* evolution, progress
*desarrollo habitacional:* apartment complex
*desasosiego:* discomfort
*desastre:* disaster, mess
*desastroso:* disastrous, fatal
*desatar:* spark, untie
*desatascador:* plunger
*desatender:* neglect
*desatino:* nonsense

*desmayar:* black, faint
*desmedido:* excessive
*desmelenado:* disheveled
*desmentido:* denial
*desmentir:* disprove
*desmenuzar:* shred
*desmerecer:* eclipse
*desmontar:* dismantle, take
*desmonte:* clearance
*desmoronar:* crumble, fall
*desnudar:* strip
*desnudo:* bare, naked
*desobedecer:* defy, disobey
*desobediencia:* disobedience
*desocupado:* empty, free, idle, vacant
*desodorante:* antiperspirant, deodorant
*desolado:* bleak
*desolador:* bleak
*desollar:* skin
*desorden:* disorder, mess
*desorden alimenticio:* eating disorder
*desorden bipolar:* bipolar disorder
*desordenado:* messy
*desordenar:* mess, muss
*desorientado:* lost, mixed up
*desovar:* lay
*despachador:* dispatcher
*despachadora:* dispatcher
*despachar:* dispatch
*despacho:* firm, practice
*despampanante:* stunning
*desparramado:* scattered
*despatarrarse:* sprawl
*despedida:* goodbye
*despedida de soltera:* bachelorette party
*despedida de soltero:* bachelor party
*despedir:* dismiss, excuse, fire, notice, release, send
*despedir a un empleado:* lay
*despegar:* ground, peel, take
*despegue:* cleavage, takeoff
*despeinar:* muss
*despejado:* clear, crisp, fair
*despejar el ambiente:* air
*despeje:* clearance
*despellejar:* skin
*desperdiciar:* throw, waste
*desperdicio:* refuse, scrap, trash
*desperdigado:* scattered
*desperezarse:* stretch
*despertado:* awoken
*despertador:* alarm, alarm clock
*despertar:* arouse, awaken, excite, stir, wake
*despiadado:* ruthless, vicious
*despido:* dismissal
*despierto:* awake
*despilfarrar:* squander
*desplantador:* trowel
*desplazamiento:* movement
*desplazar:* displace
*desplazarse:* cruise, get
*desplegable:* drop-down menu
*desplegar:* deploy
*despliegue:* array, blaze, display, show
*desplomarse:* collapse, drop, flop, plunge, slump, tumble
*despojar:* strip
*despojarse de:* shed
*despostillar:* chip
*despotricar:* rave
*desprecio:* contempt, dismissal
*desprender:* break
*desprendido:* selfless
*desprendimiento de rocas:* rock fall
*despreocupado:* carefree, casual
*desprestigiar:* discredit
*desproporción:* imbalance
*desproporcionado:* proportion
*desprotegido:* unprotected
*desprovisto:* void
*después:* after, afterward, beyond, following, later, since, then
*después de todo:* all, mean
*desquitarse:* retaliate
*destacado:* leading, outstanding, prominent
*destacar:* excel, feature, highlight, shine, station
*destapador:* opener, plunger
*destapar:* uncover
*destellar:* flash, glitter, sparkle
*destello:* flash
*desternillarse (de risa):* double
*destinado:* destined
*destinar:* devote, earmark
*destinar a:* intend
*destinataria:* recipient
*destinatario:* recipient
*destino:* destination, destiny, fate
*destreza:* skill
*destripar:* gut
*destrozar:* blow, shatter, tear, wreck
*destructivo:* destructive
*destruir:* destroy, knee, shred
*destruir el interior de un edificio:* gut
*desvalido:* helpless, impotent
*desván:* attic
*desvanecerse:* disappear, fade, melt, recede
*desvariar:* rave
*desvelado:* sleepless
*desventaja:* disadvantage, drawback, handicap, liability, minus, strike
*desvergüenza:* nerve
*desvestir:* undress
*desvestirse:* strip
*desviación:* departure, detour
*desviación estándar:* standard deviation
*desviación normal:* standard deviation
*desviación tipo:* standard deviation
*desviar:* avert, divert
*desviarse:* curve, swerve
*desvivirse:* lavish
*detalladamente:* length
*detallado:* close, detailed
*detallar:* detail
*detalle:* detail, touch
*detalles:* particulars
*detalles (específicos):* specifics
*detección a distancia:* remote sensing
*detectar:* detect
*detective:* investigator
*detector de humo:* smoke detector
*detención:* detention, standstill
*detención o aprehensión llevada a cabo por un ciudadano común:* citizen's arrest
*detener:* arrest, check, contain, detain, halt, inhibit, keep, stop
*detener en tierra:* ground
*detenerse:* pause, rest, stop
*detenerse con gran chirrido de frenos.:* grind
*detenido:* close, custody, detainee
*detergente:* detergent
*detergente para lavaplatos/ lavavajillas:* dishwashing liquid
*deteriorar:* deteriorate
*determinación:* decision, determination
*determinado:* determined, given
*determinante:* determiner
*determinar:* decide, determine, dictate, plot
*determinar la antigüedad de:* date
*detestable:* nasty
*detonación:* bang
*deuda:* debt, liability
*deuda nacional:* national debt
*devaluar:* devalue
*devastado:* shattered
*devastador:* devastating
*devastar:* devastate
*develar:* unveil
*devengar:* earn
*devoción:* devotion
*devolución:* refund
*devolver:* back, bounce, refund, restore, return, take
*devorar:* wolf
*devoto:* devoted
*día:* day, daytime, topical, up-to-date
*día de fiesta nacional:* national holiday

*discrepar*: conflict, differ, disagree, dissent
*discrepar de*: disagree
*discreto*: discreet, gentle
*discriminación*: discrimination
*discriminar*: discriminate
*disculpa*: apology
*disculpar*: apologize, excuse, sorry
*Disculpe*: pardon
*disculpe*: excuse
*discurso*: speech
*discurso indirecto*: reported speech
*discusión*: argument, contention, debate, discussion
*discusión larga*: bull session
*discutible*: questionable
*discutir*: argue, debate, discuss, fight, talk
*disecar*: stuff
*diseminar*: disperse, spread
*diseñador*: designer
*diseñadora*: designer
*diseñar*: design, style
*diseño*: design
*diseño correlacionado*: correlational design
*diseño descriptivo*: descriptive design
*diseño experimental*: experimental design
*diseño gráfico*: graphic
*disensión*: dissent
*disentir*: dissent
*disertación*: dissertation, lecture
*disfraces*: dress-up
*disfraz*: mask
*disfrazado*: disguise, masked
*disfrazar*: disguise, mask
*disfrutar*: delight, enjoy, indulge
*disfrutar de*: enjoy
*disgustado*: sore
*disgustar*: dislike
*disidente*: dissident
*disimular*: disguise, mask
*disimulo*: sneak
*disiparse*: melt
*dislexia*: dyslexia
*dislocar*: wrench
*disminución*: decline, decrease, drop-off, reduction
*disminuir*: break, cut, decline, decrease, diminish, ease, ebb, fall, flag, mute
*disolver*: break, disband, dissolve, thaw
*disparador*: trigger
*disparar*: blast, fire, let, rocket, shoot, soar, spiral, trigger
*disparatadamente*: wildly
*disparatar*: rave
*disparate*: nonsense
*disparejo*: uneven
*disparo*: fire, shot
*disparo (uno)*: round
*disparos*: gunfire
*dispersar*: disband, disperse, split, spread
*dispersión*: scattering
*disperso*: scattered
*disponer*: lay, provide
*disponible*: available, grab
*disposición*: directive, disposal, provision
*dispositivo*: device
*dispuesto*: inclined, poised, ready, willing
*dispuesto a*: willing
*disputa*: contention, dispute
*disputar*: dispute
*disquet*: floppy disk
*disquete*: floppy disk
*distancia*: distance, span
*distancia vertical*: contour interval
*distanciado*: estranged
*distanciamiento*: distance
*distanciar*: alienate, distance, drive, grow
*distante*: distant, far off, remote, removed
*distinción*: distinction
*distinguido*: distinguished, select
*distinguir*: differentiate, discriminate, distinguish, make, pick, separate, single, tell
*distinguir el sabor de*: taste
*distinto*: different, distinct, unlike
*distorsionar*: distort
*distraer*: divert, mind, put, stray, wander
*distraídamente*: vacant
*distraído*: absent-minded, vacant
*distribución*: distribution
*distribución binómica*: binomial distribution
*distribuir*: distribute, market, spread
*distrito*: borough, district
*distrito electoral*: constituency
*distrito escolar*: school district
*distrito segregado*: township
*disturbio*: disorder, disturbance, riot, trouble
*disuadir*: deter, discourage
*divagar*: stray, wander
*diván*: ottoman
*divergir*: diverge
*diversidad*: diversity
*diversificar*: diversify
*diversión*: amusement, fun, pleasure, recreation
*diverso*: broad, diverse, mixed
*divertido*: amused, amusing, fun, funny, humorous
*divertir*: amuse, entertain
*divertirse mucho*: ball
*dividendo*: dividend
*dividir*: break, divide, fork, sort, split
*dividir en dos*: halve
*dividir en zonas*: zone
*dividir por partes iguales*: share
*divino*: divine
*divisa*: crest
*divisar*: glimpse
*divisas*: currency
*división*: divide, division, split
*división celular*: cell division
*división en sílabas*: syllabication
*divorciada*: divorcée
*divorciado*: divorcé, divorced
*divorciar*: divorce
*divorcio*: divorce
*divulgar*: publicize, release
*dobladillo*: cuff
*doblar*: bend, dub, fold, give, lean, round, toll, turn
*doblarse (de dolor)*: double
*doblarse las piernas o las rodillas*: buckle
*doble*: double, dual, twice, twin
*doble consonante*: consonant doubling
*doble crema*: heavy cream
*doble espacio*: double-space
*doble hélice*: double helix
*doble sentido*: two-way
*dobles*: double
*doblez*: fold
*doce*: twelve
*doceavo*: twelfth
*docena*: dozen
*doctor*: professor
*doctor en filosofía*: doctor of philosophy
*doctora*: professor
*doctorado*: doctorate, Ph.D.
*doctrina*: doctrine
*documentación*: documentation
*documental*: documentary
*documentar*: document
*documento*: document
*documento de identificación*: ID card
*documentos*: paper
*dodecafónico*: twelve-tone
*dodo*: dodo
*dólar*: buck, dollar
*doler*: ache, hurt, pain
*dolor*: ache, grief, pain, suffering
*dolor de cabeza*: headache
*doloroso*: painful
*domado*: tame
*domar*: tame
*domesticado*: tame
*domesticar*: tame
*doméstico*: domestic
*domicilio principal*: base

*empeine:* liverwort
*empeñado en:* bent
*empeñar:* pawn
*empeorar:* escalate, worse, worsen
*empequeñecer:* dwarf
*emperador:* emperor
*emperatriz:* empress
*empezar:* begin, break, go, initiate, start, take
*empezar a:* become, get
*empezar como:* start
*empezar con:* start
*empezar con el pie derecho:* flying
*empezar por:* start
*empinar el codo:* booze
*empinarse:* rear
*empírico:* empirical
*emplazar:* cite, site
*empleada:* clerk, employee, shop assistant, staffer
*empleada de funeraria:* undertaker
*empleado:* clerk, employee, shop assistant, staffer, undertaker, working
*empleado de oficina:* white-collar
*empleador:* employer
*empleadora:* employer
*empleados:* staff
*emplear:* employ
*empleo:* employment, job
*empoderar:* empower
*empotrar:* build
*emprendedor:* entrepreneur, go-ahead, up-and-coming
*emprender:* embark, go, launch, take
*emprender una guerra:* fight
*emprenderla contra:* turn
*empresa:* business, enterprise, firm, operation, operator, venture
*empresa conjunta:* joint venture
*empresa de utilidad pública:* utility
*empresa difícil:* tall
*empresa punto com:* dot-com
*empresa que ofrece las mismas oportunidades:* equal opportunity employer
*empresaria:* entrepreneur
*empresarial:* entrepreneur
*empresario:* entrepreneur
*empréstito:* loan
*empujar:* press, push, shove, sweep, thrust
*empujar con los codos:* elbow
*empuje:* drive
*empujones:* shove
*emsombrecer:* shadow
*en:* about, against, at, by, for, in, inside, into, on, to, under, within
*enamoramiento:* crush
*enamorarse:* fall, love
*enana blanca:* white dwarf
*enano:* dwarf
*enardecer:* flare
*encabezado:* headline
*encabezamiento:* headline
*encabezar:* head, lead
*encabritarse:* rear
*encajar:* fit
*encaje:* lace
*encaminar:* route
*encantado:* delighted
*encantado de conocerlo/conocerla:* pleased
*encantador:* charming, delightful, lovely, sweet, winning
*encantamiento:* spell
*encantar:* charm, fancy
*encanto:* appeal, charm, spell
*encaramar:* perch
*encarar:* brave, confront
*encarcelar:* imprison, lock
*encargada:* attendant, groundskeeper, superintendent
*encargado:* attendant, groundskeeper, superintendent
*encargarle (algo a alguien):* commission
*encargarse:* undertake
*encargarse (de algo):* handle
*encargarse de:* arrange, see
*encargo:* commission
*encariñado con:* fond
*encarnizado:* bitter
*encéfalo:* brain
*encefalopatía espongiforme bovina:* BSE
*encender:* boot, come, fire, flare, go, light, put, start, strike, turn
*encenderse la luz:* light
*encendido:* on
*encerrar:* imprison, lock, pen, put
*enchapado en oro:* gilt
*enchinar:* curl
*enchufe:* outlet, plug, socket
*encía:* gum
*enciclopedia:* encyclopedia
*encima:* bargain, on, top
*encima de:* over, upon
*encogerse:* shrink
*encogerse de hombros:* shrug
*encontrado:* mixed
*encontrar:* come, find, hold, encounter, lie, link, meet, strike, work
*encontrar a:* ahold
*encontrar defectos a alguien:* fault
*encontrar el camino:* find
*encontrar una mina de oro:* paydirt
*encontrarse con:* encounter, run
*encorvado:* bowed
*encorvarse:* lean
*encrespado:* ruffled
*encrucijada:* crossroads
*encuadernación:* binding
*encuadernado:* bind
*encubierto:* masked
*encuentro:* meeting
*encuesta:* poll, survey
*encuesta de opinión:* opinion poll
*encuesta de salida:* exit poll
*encuestar:* survey
*encurtido:* pickle
*enderezar:* right, sit, straighten
*endibia:* endive
*endocitosis:* endocytosis
*endocrino:* endocrine
*endoesqueleto:* endoskeleton
*endotérmico:* endothermic
*endotermo:* endotherm
*endulzado:* sweet
*endulzante artificial:* sweetener
*endurecer:* harden
*enemigo:* enemy
*energía:* energy, power, vigor
*energía acumulada:* stored energy
*energía almacenada:* stored energy
*energía de activación:* activation energy
*energía de luz:* light energy
*energía eléctrica:* electrical energy, electricity, electric power
*energía eólica:* wind
*energía hidráulica:* water power
*energía hidroeléctrica:* hydropower, water power
*energía mecánica:* mechanical energy
*energía nuclear:* nuclear energy
*energía potencial:* potential energy, stored energy
*energía potencial gravitacional:* gravitational potential energy
*energía química:* chemical energy
*energía sonora:* sound energy
*energía térmica:* thermal energy
*enérgico:* alive, emphatic, firm, hearty, strong, vocal
*enero:* January
*enfadado:* cross
*enfado:* anger, irritation
*énfasis:* all, emphasis
*énfasis negativo:* like
*énfasis superlativo:* all
*enfático:* emphatic
*enferma alcohólica:* alcoholic
*enfermar:* sick
*enfermedad:* disease, illness, infection, sickness, trouble
*enfermedad de las vacas locas:* BSE
*enfermedad de transimisión sexual:* sexually transmitted disease
*enfermedad del beso:* mono, mononucleosis

*entrometerse:* interfere
*entronque:* junction
*entumecer:* numb
*entumecido:* numb, stiff
*entusiasmado:* enthusiastic, excited, taken
*entusiasmar:* encourage, thrill
*entusiasmo:* enthusiasm, excitement
*entusiasta:* enthusiast, enthusiastic
*enumerar:* list, recite
*enunciativo:* declarative
*envasar:* enclose, pack, package
*envase:* packaging, tub
*envejecer:* age
*envenenar:* poison
*envergadura:* span
*enviada plenipotenciaria:* envoy
*enviado:* envoy
*enviado plenipotenciario:* envoy
*enviar:* dispatch, forward, route, send
*enviar mensajes electrónicos:* message
*enviar por barco:* ship
*enviar por correo:* mail
*enviar por fax:* fax
*enviar un mensaje de texto:* text
*enviar/mandar por correo electrónico:* mail
*envidia:* jealousy
*envidiar:* envy
*envidioso:* envious, jealous
*envío:* shipment, shipping
*envío de mensajes de texto:* texting, text messaging
*envoltura:* wrapper
*envolver:* enclose, envelop, swathe, wrap
*enzima:* enzyme
*epicentro:* epicenter, focus
*épico:* epic
*epidemia:* epidemic
*epidermis:* epidermis
*epidídimo:* epididymis
*episodio:* episode
*época:* age, day, era, time
*epopeya:* epic
*equilátero:* equilateral
*equilibrado:* balanced
*equilibrar:* balance
*equilibrio:* balance, footing
*equilibrio térmico:* thermal equilibrium
*equipaje:* baggage, luggage
*equipar:* equip, outfit
*equiparable:* comparable
*equiparar:* equate, match
*equipo:* crew, equipment, gear, kit, outfit, squad, team
*equipo de primeros auxilios:* first aid kit
*equipo para mantener la vida:* life support
*equipo titular de una secundaria:* colegio o universidad en un deporte en particular, varsity
*equitación:* horseback riding, riding
*equivalente:* equivalent
*equivaler:* equate
*equivocación:* error, mistake
*equivocado:* erroneous, incorrect, mark, misplaced, mistaken, wrong
*equivocarse:* err
*era:* age, era
*era cenozoica:* Cenozoic era
*era paleozoica:* Paleozoic era
*erecto:* erect
*erguido:* erect, upright
*erigir:* erect
*erizado:* ruffled
*erosión:* weathering
*erosionar:* erode, wear, weather
*erótico:* erotic, steamy
*erradicar:* eradicate, root, stamp
*errado:* mark
*errar:* err, miss
*erróneo:* erroneous, improper, inaccurate, incorrect
*error:* blooper, bug, error, flub, misperception, mistake
*error de imprenta:* typo
*erudición:* scholarship
*erudita:* scholar
*erudito:* learned, scholar
*erupción:* rash
*eruptivo:* extrusive
*es decir:* mean, namely, say, short, that
*es el colmo (algo):* cake
*es evidente:* say
*es mejor que:* better
*es posible:* possibly
*esa:* that
*esas:* those
*esbelto:* slim, trim
*esbozar:* sketch
*esbozar con los labios:* mouth
*esbozo:* sketch
*escabeche:* pickle
*escabullirse:* scuttle, sneak
*escala:* layover, range, scale
*escala de cinco notas:* pentatonic scale
*escala de valores:* value scale
*escala del tiempo geológico:* geological time scale
*escala diatónica:* diatonic scale
*escala pentatónica:* pentatonic scale
*escalada:* upward
*escalar:* climb, scale
*escalera:* ladder
*escalera de mano:* ladder
*escalera eléctrica:* escalator
*escalera(s):* stair
*escaleras abajo:* downstairs
*escaleras arriba:* upstairs
*escalinata:* staircase, stairway
*escalofriante:* creepy, hairy
*escalofrío:* chill
*escalón:* stair, step
*escalonar:* stagger
*escama:* scale
*escandalizar:* outrage, shock
*escándalo:* fuss, outrage, scandal, storm, uproar
*escandaloso:* loud, outrageous, shocking
*escáner:* scanner
*escaño:* seat
*escapar:* break, escape, flee, get, run
*escapársele a uno algo:* miss
*escape:* exhaust pipe, tailpipe
*escarabajo:* beetle
*escarbar:* dig
*escarcha:* frost
*escardar:* weed
*escarpado:* jagged, sheer, steep
*escasea:* premium
*escasear:* supply, thin
*escasez:* shortage
*escaso:* insufficient, light, little, narrow, scarce, short, slim
*escena:* scene, sketch
*escenario:* scenario, scene, setting, stage
*escénico:* theatrical
*escenografía:* scenery
*escepticismo:* disbelief
*escéptico:* cynical, skeptical
*escindir:* split
*escisión:* fragmentation, split
*esclava:* slave
*esclavitud:* slavery
*esclavo:* slave
*esclerosis múltiple (EM):* MS
*esclusa:* lock
*escoba:* broom
*escocer:* smart
*escoger:* choose, pick, select
*escogido:* select
*escollo:* stumbling block
*escolta:* escort
*escoltar:* escort, walk
*escombros:* debris
*esconder:* hide
*escondido:* hidden, hiding
*escopeta:* shotgun
*escopeta de aire comprimido:* BB gun
*escotilla:* hatch
*escribir:* make, mark, pen, put, state, take, write, writing
*escribir a:* write

*escribir a doble espacio:* double-space
*escribir a la carrera:* dash
*escribir a máquina:* type
*escribir con letra de molde:* print
*escribir un prefacio:* preface
*escrito:* writing, written
*escrito a mano:* handwritten
*escrito difamatorio:* libel
*escritor:* author, writer
*escritor mercenario:* hack
*escritora:* author, writer
*escritorio:* desk, desktop
*escritura:* deed, script, writing
*escritura creativa:* creative writing
*escritura emocional:* expressive writing
*escroto:* scrotum
*escrúpulo (de conciencia):* qualm
*escrutar:* scan
*escuadrón:* squadron, troop
*escuchar:* catch, hear, listen
*escuchar a escondidas:* eavesdrop
*escuchar con imparcialidad:* hearing
*escudo:* shield
*escudriñar:* peer, probe, scan
*escuela:* college, school
*escuela (edificio):* schoolhouse
*escuela comunitaria:* community college
*escuela de gobierno:* public school
*escuela elemental:* elementary school
*escuela oficial:* public school
*escuela primaria:* elementary school
*escuela pública:* public school
*escuela religiosa:* parochial school
*escuela secundaria:* junior high school
*escuela semisuperior:* junior college
*escuela técnica:* junior college
*escueto:* bare
*escuincle:* boy
*escultura:* sculpture
*escultura aditiva:* additive
*escultura sustractiva:* subtractive sculpture
*escupir:* spit
*escurridor:* colander
*escurridora:* colander
*escurrimiento:* runoff
*escurrir:* drain, drip, sneak, strain
*ese:* that
*ese punto:* there
*esencia:* essence, substance
*esencial:* bare-bones, essential, indispensable, vital
*esencialmente:* essentially
*esfera:* dial, realm, sphere
*esforzarse:* endeavor, labor, strive
*esfuerzo:* effort, endeavor, stress
*esfumarse:* drain
*esgrima:* fencing
*esguince:* strain
*eslabón:* link
*eslogan:* catchword
*esmalte:* enamel
*esmerarse:* pain
*esmog:* smog
*esnob:* snob
*eso:* so, that, thing
*esos:* those
*espacial:* spatial
*espaciar:* space
*espacio:* gap, room, space, tract
*espacio aéreo:* airspace
*espacio estrecho bajo el techo o piso que permite el acceso a la plomería o a los cables.:* crawl space
*espacio exterior:* outer space
*espacio sideral:* outer space
*espacioso:* spacious
*espada:* spade, sword
*espadón:* brass
*espagueti:* spaghetti
*espalda:* back
*espaldas:* shoulder
*espantar:* appall, frighten
*espantoso:* appalling, dreadful, fearful, frightening, hideous, terrifying
*esparcido:* dotted, scattered
*esparcimiento:* recreation
*esparcir:* diffuse, filter, scatter, spray
*espárrago:* asparagus
*espátula:* palette knife
*especia:* spice
*especiación:* speciation
*especial:* particular, special
*especialidad:* field, speciality, specialty
*especialista:* consultant, specialist
*especializado:* skilled, specialized
*especializarse:* major, specialize
*especialmente:* especially, notably, specially
*especie:* breed, species
*específicamente:* specifically
*especificar:* specify
*específico:* particular, special, specific
*espécimen:* specimen
*espectacular:* dramatic, spectacular
*espectáculo:* entertainment, exhibition, show, spectacle
*espectáculo cómico en que actores blancos representaban a personajes negros:* minstrel show
*espectáculo realista:* reality show
*espectador:* spectator
*espectadora:* spectator
*espectro:* spectrum
*espectro electromagnético:* electromagnetic spectrum
*especular:* speculate, theorize
*espejo:* mirror
*espeleóloga aficionada:* spelunker
*espeleólogo aficionado:* spelunker
*espeluznante:* harrowing, shocking
*espera:* wait
*esperanza:* hope
*esperanzado:* hopeful
*esperanzador:* encouraging, hopeful
*esperar:* await, expect, hang, hold, hope, wait
*esperar (un bebé):* expect
*esperar algo:* in
*esperar que (alguien) tenga suerte:* hope
*esperma:* sperm
*espermatozoide:* sperm
*espesar:* thicken
*espeso:* thick
*espía:* agent, spy
*espiar:* eavesdrop, spy
*espiga:* ear, peg
*espina dorsal (de todos los vertebrados menos del hombre):* backbone
*espinaca:* spinach
*espinal:* spinal
*espinilla:* shin
*espiral:* curl, spiral
*espíritu:* heart, soul, spirit
*espiritual:* spiritual
*espita:* spigot
*espléndidamente:* brilliant
*espléndido:* glorious, lavish, magnificent, marvelous, splendid, superb
*espolvorear:* sprinkle
*esponja:* sponge
*esponja (euplectella aspergillus):* basket sponge
*espontáneo:* hearty, spontaneous
*esporofito:* sporophyte
*esporófito:* sporophyte
*esposa:* spouse, wife
*esposo:* husband, spouse
*espuma:* surf
*esqueje:* cutting
*esqueleto:* skeleton
*esquema:* scheme
*esquí:* ski
*esquiar:* ski
*esquina:* corner, turning
*esquivar:* avoid, dodge, duck, fend
*esta:* this
*esta noche:* tonight
*estabilidad:* keel
*estabilizar:* level, stabilize

*familia:* family, household
*familia con hijastros:* stepfamily
*familia política:* in-laws
*familiar:* flesh
*familiarizado con:* familiar
*famoso:* celebrated, famous, renowned
*fanática:* fan, fanatic, nut
*fanático:* fan, fanatic, nut
*fanfarronada:* saber-rattling
*fango:* mud
*fantasear:* daydream, fantasize
*fantasía:* daydream, fantasy, imagination
*fantasma:* ghost
*fantástico:* fantastic
*farándula:* show business
*faringe:* pharynx
*farmacéutico:* pharmaceutical
*farmacia:* drugstore, pharmacy
*faro:* headlight
*farol:* lantern
*farolear:* strut
*farsante:* phony
*fascículo:* installment
*fascinante:* fascinating, intriguing
*fascinar:* entrance, fancy, fascinate
*fascista:* fascist
*fase:* phase
*fastidiar:* bug, tick
*fastidio:* peeve, pest
*fastidioso:* troublesome
*fatal:* fatal
*fatalidad:* fatality
*fatiga:* fatigue
*fatigado:* tired
*fatigoso:* labored
*fauces:* jaw
*faul:* foul
*favor:* favor
*favorable:* sympathetic
*favorablemente dispuesto:* sympathetic
*favorecedores:* friend
*favorecer:* favor, further, help, second
*favorita:* favorite
*favoritismo:* favoritism
*favorito:* bookmark, favorite, pet
*fax:* fax
*fe:* faith
*febrero:* February
*febril:* furious
*fecha:* date
*fecha de caducidad:* expiration date
*fecha de nacimiento:* DOB
*fecha límite:* closing date, deadline
*fecha tope:* closing date
*fechamiento relativo:* relative dating
*fechar:* date
*fécula:* starch
*fecundo:* fertile
*federación:* federation, league
*federal:* federal
*feldespato:* feldspar
*felicidades:* congratulations
*felicitaciones:* congratulations
*felicitar:* congratulate
*feligreses:* congregation
*felino:* cat
*feliz:* content, happy, joyful, merry
*felizmente:* mercifully
*felpudo:* mat
*félsico:* felsic
*femenino:* female, feminine
*fémico (máfico):* mafic
*feminista:* feminist
*fenómeno:* freak, phenomenon, whiz kid
*fenómeno de circo:* freak
*fenotipo:* phenotype
*feo:* ugly
*féretro:* coffin
*feria:* carnival, fair
*feria comercial:* trade show
*fermentar:* ferment
*feromona:* pheromone
*feroz:* fierce, furious
*ferretería:* hardware
*ferrocarril:* railroad, train
*ferrocarril metropolitano:* subway
*ferrocarril subterráneo:* subway
*ferry:* ferry
*fértil:* fertile
*fertilidad:* fertile
*fertilización externa:* external fertilization
*fertilización interna:* internal fertilization
*fertilizante:* fertilizer
*fertilizar:* fertilize
*festejar:* feast
*festín:* feast
*festival:* festival
*fétido:* foul
*feto:* fetus
*fiambre:* lunch meat
*fiambres:* cold cuts
*fianza:* bail
*fiar:* trust
*fiasco:* flop
*fibra:* backbone, fiber, pad
*fibra de vidrio:* fiberglass
*fibra óptica:* optical fiber
*ficción:* fiction
*ficha:* counter, token
*fichar:* sign
*ficticio:* fiction
*fidedigno:* authentic, authoritative, reliable
*fideicomisaria:* trustee
*fideicomisario:* trustee
*fideicomiso:* endowment, trust
*fidelidad:* allegiance, loyalty
*fideo:* noodle
*fiduciaria:* trustee
*fiduciario:* trustee
*fiebre:* fever, temperature
*fiebre glandular:* mono, mononucleosis
*fiel:* accurate, faithful, loyal
*fieles:* congregation
*fieltro:* felt
*fiera:* beast
*fiero:* fierce
*fiesta:* festival, party
*fiesta callejera:* street party
*fiesta de disfraces:* costume party
*fiesta del barrio:* block party
*fiesta patria:* national holiday
*fiestear:* party
*figura:* face card, figure, force, shape
*figura esquemática:* stick figure
*figura pública:* public
*figurado:* figurative
*figurar:* figure, imagine
*figurativo:* figurative
*fijar:* anchor, fasten, fix, look, post, set, steady
*fijar la mirada:* gaze
*fijarse en:* look
*fijo:* fixed, flat, secure, set, steady
*fila:* line, row
*filas:* rank
*filas del desempleo:* unemployment line
*fildeador:* field
*fildeadora:* field
*fildear:* field
*filete:* filet, steak, thread
*filial:* affiliate, subsidiary
*film:* film
*filmar:* film, shoot
*filme:* film
*filo:* edge, phylum
*filón:* seam, streak
*filosofía:* philosophy
*filosófico:* philosophical
*filósofo:* philosopher
*filtrar:* filter, leak, soak
*filtro:* filter
*filtro solar:* sunscreen
*filum:* phylum
*fin:* last
*fin:* end, extreme, finish, passing, purpose
*fin de semana:* weekend
*final:* finally
*final:* bottom, end, ending, eventual, extreme, final, finish, playoff
*finalizar:* finalize

*fracción:* fraction
*fracción unitaria:* unit fraction
*fraccionamiento cerrado:* gated community
*fractura:* fracture
*fractura por fatiga:* stress fracture
*fracturar:* break, fracture
*fragancia:* fragrance, scent
*fragante:* fragrant
*frágil:* delicate, fragile
*fragmentación:* fragmentation
*fragmentar:* fragment
*fragmento:* extract, fragment, snatch
*fragor:* thunder
*fraguar:* forge, set
*frambuesa:* raspberry
*francamente:* frankly, openly
*franco:* blunt, direct, duty, frank, open, straightforward, up front
*franja:* belt, strip, swathe
*franqueo:* postage
*franquicia:* concession, franchise
*frasco:* flask, jar
*frasco para conservas:* mason jar
*frase:* expression, phrase
*frase adjetival:* adjective phrase
*frase adverbial:* adverb phrase
*frase hecha:* phrase
*frase verbal:* phrasal verb, verb phrase
*fraseo:* phrasing
*fraternidad:* fraternity
*fraude:* fraud
*fraude organizado:* racket
*fraudulento:* dishonest, fraudulent
*freak:* freak
*frecuencia:* frequency, wavelength
*frecuente:* frequent
*frecuentemente:* often, oftentimes
*fregadero (cocina):* sink
*fregador:* dishrag
*fregar:* scrub
*fregón:* dishrag
*freír:* fry
*frenar:* brake, check, curb
*frenético:* frantic, furious
*freno:* brake
*freno de emergencia:* emergency brake
*freno de mano:* emergency brake
*frenos:* brace
*frente:* front
*frente:* forehead, front
*frente a:* before, front, off, opposite, versus
*frente a la costa:* offshore
*frente de batalla:* front
*frente interno:* home front
*fresa:* preppy, strawberry
*fresca:* fresh
*fresco:* cool, fresh, sassy, wet
*frescura:* nerve
*fresno:* ash
*fricción:* friction, rubdown
*friega:* rubdown
*frijol:* bean, kidney bean
*frijol carita:* black-eyed pea
*frijol de soya:* soybean
*frijol pinto:* pinto bean
*frijoles refritos:* refried beans
*frío:* brisk, chilly, clinical, cold, cool, crisp
*frito de los dos lados:* over easy
*frívolo:* light
*frontal:* head-on
*frontera:* border, boundary, frontier
*frontera de placas tectónicas:* plate boundary
*frotar:* rub
*frotar contra:* rub
*fructífero:* productive
*fructificar:* fruit
*frugalidad:* thrift
*fruncir:* purse, wrinkle
*fruncir el ceño:* frown
*fruncir el entrecejo:* frown
*fruslería:* small potatoes
*frustrar:* defeat, foil, frustrate
*fruta:* fruit
*fruto:* fruit
*fruto:* fruit
*fuchi:* yuck
*fuego:* fever blister, fire
*fuego amigo:* friendly fire
*fuegos artificiales:* firework
*fuegos de artificio:* firework
*fuegos pirotécnicos:* firework
*fuente:* fountain, platter, source, spring
*fuente de energía:* energy source
*fuente de los medios:* media source
*fuente energética:* energy source
*fuente luminosa:* light source
*fuente mediática:* media source
*fuente puntual de la contaminación:* point-source pollution
*fuera:* away, out, outside
*fuera de:* beyond, off, out, outside, outta
*fuera de circulación:* action
*fuera de condición:* shape
*fuera de control:* control, hand
*fuera de duda:* doubt
*fuera de foco:* focus
*fuera de forma:* unfit
*fuera de las horas pico:* off-peak
*fuera de línea:* offline
*fuera de lo normal:* ordinary
*fuera de sí:* beside
*fuereño:* out-of-state
*fuerte:* firm, fort, heavy, high, loud, powerful, strong, tough
*fuerza:* force, intensity, power, pull, strength, strong
*fuerza aérea:* air force
*fuerza ascensional:* lift
*fuerza de esfuerzo:* effort force
*fuerza de flotación:* buoyant force
*fuerza eléctrica:* electric force
*fuerza hidráulica:* water power
*fuerza hidroeléctrica:* hydropower
*fuerza laboral:* labor, labor force, workforce
*fuerza neta:* net force
*fuerzas armadas:* armed forces, service
*fuerzas del orden:* police force
*fuerzas desequilibradas:* unbalanced forces
*fuerzas equilibradas:* balanced forces
*fuga:* flight, fugue, leak
*fugado:* run
*fugarse:* escape, run
*fugaz:* brief
*fugazmente:* briefly
*fugitiva:* fugitive
*fugitivo:* fugitive, runaway
*fulcro:* fulcrum
*fulgor:* luster
*fumar:* puff, smoke
*fumarola (gases o vapores):* vent
*fumigar:* crop dusting
*función:* function, performance, role
*función cuadrática:* quadratic function
*función exponencial:* exponential function
*funcional:* functional
*funcionamiento:* behavior, operation, working
*funcionar:* function, operate, run, work
*funcionar bien:* order, strong
*funcionar con:* run
*funcionar también como:* double
*funcionaria:* incumbent, official, staffer
*funcionaria pública:* civil servant
*funcionario:* incumbent, official, staffer
*funcionario público:* civil servant
*funda:* slipcover
*fundación:* foundation
*fundamentado:* informed
*fundamental:* basic, cardinal, fundamental, ultimate, vital
*fundamentalismo:* fundamentalism
*fundamentalmente:* basically
*fundamentar:* ground
*fundamento:* footing, foundation, fundamentals, substance

*global:* overall
*globo:* balloon, fly ball, globe
*globo aerostático:* balloon
*globo ocular:* eyeball
*globo terráqueo:* globe
*glóbulo blanco:* white blood cell
*glóbulo rojo:* red blood cell
*gloria:* glory
*glorias:* glory
*glorioso:* glorious
*glosa:* anecdotal scripting
*glucosa:* glucose
*gnomo:* leprechaun
*go kart:* go-cart
*gobernador:* governor
*gobernadora:* governor
*gobernante:* ruler
*gobernar:* govern, rule, steer
*gobierno:* government
*gobierno local:* local government
*gogles:* goggles
*gol:* goal
*gol de campo:* field goal
*golf:* golf
*golfo:* gulf
*golondrina:* swallow
*golpe:* bang, strike
*golpe:* blow, stroke
*golpe de estado:* coup
*golpe de nocaut:* knockout
*golpe de remo:* stroke
*golpe maestro:* coup
*golpear:* bang, bash, beat, hammer, hit, knock, pound, slam, smash, stab, strike
*golpear (la pelota):* putt
*golpear con:* bump
*golpear con algo:* swipe
*golpearse un dedo del pie:* stub
*golpecito:* tap
*golpetear:* drum, rap
*goma:* eraser, rubber, tire
*goma de borrar:* eraser
*gong:* gong
*gorda:* fatso
*gordinflón:* fatso, pudgy
*gordinflona:* fatso
*gordo:* fat, fatso, stout, thick
*gorila:* gorilla
*gorila de montaña:* mountain gorilla
*gorra:* cap
*gorra de béisbol:* baseball cap
*gorrión:* sparrow
*gorro:* bonnet
*gospel:* gospel
*gota:* bead, drip, drop
*gota de lluvia:* raindrop
*gotear:* drip, leak
*gotero:* drip
*gotita:* droplet
*gozar:* enjoy
*GPS:* GPS
*grabación:* recording
*grabadora de discos de video:* DVD burner
*grabadora de videocintas:* VCR
*grabadora portátil:* boom box
*grabar:* carve, printmaking, record
*grabar (en cinta):* tape
*gracia:* grace, spark
*gracias:* thank
*gracias a:* thank, through
*gracias a Dios:* thank
*gracias al cielo:* thank
*gracioso:* funny, humorous
*gradería:* bleachers
*grado:* degree, grade, pitch
*grado (militar):* rank
*grados Celsius:* Celsius
*grados centígrados:* Celsius
*graduación:* graduation
*graduada:* grad, graduate
*graduado:* grad, graduate, graduated
*gradual:* gradual
*graduarse:* graduate
*gráfica:* chart, graph
*gráfica circular:* pie chart
*gráfica de barras:* bar graph, histogram
*gráfica de caja:* box plot
*gráfica de datos:* data table
*gráfica de dispersión:* scatterplot
*gráfica lineal:* line graph
*gráficas:* graphic
*gráfico:* chart, graphic
*gráfico circular:* pie chart
*grafiti:* graffiti
*gramática:* grammar
*gramatical:* grammatical
*gramaticalmente incorrecto:* ungrammatical
*gramo:* gram
*gramófono:* record player
*gran:* grand, high, keen
*gran almacén:* department store
*gran avance:* breakthrough
*gran cantidad:* host, mass, score
*gran esfuerzo:* labor
*gran espectáculo:* spectacular
*gran liga:* major league
*gran número:* load
*gran preocupación:* alarm
*gran slam:* grand slam
*grande:* big, enormous, grand, great, large, long
*grandísimo:* immense, massive
*granero:* barn
*granizo:* hail
*granja:* farm
*granjera:* farmer
*granjero:* farmer
*grano:* bean, grain
*granola:* granola
*grapa:* staple
*grasa:* fat, grease
*graso:* fatty
*grasoso:* fatty, rich
*gratificante:* rewarding
*gratis:* charge, free
*gratitud:* gratitude, thank
*gratuitamente:* charge, toll-free
*gratuito:* toll-free
*gravable:* taxable
*gravamen:* levy
*gravar:* tax
*grave:* deep, grave, large, severe
*gravedad:* gravity
*gravedad específica:* specific gravity
*gravedad superficial:* surface gravity
*gravemente:* badly
*gravitación universal:* universal gravitation
*gravitacional:* gravitational
*gravitropismo:* gravitropism
*gremio:* guild, labor union
*grieta:* crevasse, rift
*grifo:* faucet
*grillo:* cricket
*gripa:* flu
*gripe:* flu
*gripe aviar:* bird flu
*gris:* gray
*gritar:* call, cry, scream, shout, yell
*grito:* cry, yell
*grosero:* abusive, coarse, rude
*grúa:* crane
*grueso:* coarse, fat, thick
*grulla:* crane
*grulla americana:* whooping crane
*grunge:* grunge
*gruñir:* babble
*grupito:* gang
*grupo:* batch, cluster, crowd, gang, group, lot, network, party, pool
*grupo de ataque y armas especiales:* SWAT team
*grupo de control:* control
*grupo de pesión:* lobby
*grupo de reseña literaria:* book group
*grupo de sondeo:* focus group
*grupo de votantes:* constituency
*grupo táctico:* SWAT team
*guácala:* yuck
*guácatelas:* yuck
*guajolote:* turkey
*guanina:* guanine
*guante:* glove
*guapísimo:* gorgeous
*guapo:* good-looking, handsome
*guardacostas:* Coast Guard
*guardaespaldas:* bodyguard,

*inmune:* immune
*inmunidad:* freedom
*inmunizar:* immunize
*inmunodeficiencia:* immunodeficiency
*inn:* inn
*innato:* born, natural
*innecesario:* unnecessary
*innegable:* undeniable, unquestionable
*innovación:* innovation
*innovador:* innovative
*inocencia:* innocence
*inocente:* innocent
*inocuo para el ambiente:* eco-friendly
*inocuo para la capa de ozono:* ozone-friendly
*inodoro:* bowl, odorless, toilet
*inofensivo:* harmless
*inolvidable:* unforgettable
*inoportuno:* inappropriate, inconvenient, unfortunate
*inorgánico:* nonliving
*input:* input
*inquietante:* disturbing, unsettling
*inquietar:* concern, fuss, rattle, trouble
*inquieto:* restless, uneasy
*inquietud:* concern, discomfort
*inquilina:* occupant, tenant
*inquilino:* occupant, tenant
*inquirir:* inquire, query
*inquisitivo:* inquisitive
*insaciable:* insatiable
*insatisfactorio:* unsatisfactory
*inscribir:* enroll, enter
*inscripción:* inscription
*insecticida:* insecticide
*insecto:* insect
*insecto nocivo:* pest
*inseguro:* insecure, uncertain, unsure
*insensato:* foolish, insane, mindless
*insensible:* indifferent, insensitive
*inseparable:* inseparable
*insertar:* insert, sandwich
*inservible:* useless
*insignificante:* insignificant, little, petty, small
*insinuación:* hint, suggestion
*insinuar:* hint, imply, intimate, suggest
*insípido:* bland, flavorless, tame, tasteless
*insistencia:* persuasion
*insistente:* insistent
*insistir:* insist, persist, press
*insistir en:* harp
*insólito:* freak
*insomnio:* insomnia
*insoportable:* impossible, unbearable
*inspección:* survey
*inspeccionar:* inspect, supervise
*inspector:* superintendent
*inspector general de sanidad:* surgeon general
*inspectora:* inspector, superintendent
*inspectora general de sanidad:* surgeon general
*inspiración:* inspiration
*inspiración súbita:* brainstorm
*inspirar:* command, inspire, model
*instalación:* facility, installation art
*instalaciones:* accommodation
*instalar:* fit, fix, install, lay
*instalar con tornillos:* screw
*instantánea:* snap, snapshot
*instantáneo:* instant
*instante:* instant, minute, moment
*instar:* urge
*instintivo:* instinctive
*instinto:* instinct
*institución:* institution
*institución de beneficencia:* charity
*institución escolar o universitaria pública:* state school
*instituir:* institute
*instituto:* bureau, institute
*instrucción:* instruction, mandate
*instrucciones:* instruction
*instructivo:* informative, instructive
*instructor:* instructor
*instructora:* instructor
*instruir:* instruct, learn
*instrumental:* instrumental
*instrumentar:* implement
*instrumento:* gadget, implement, instrument, means, medium, puppet, tool
*instrumento de cuerda:* chordophone
*instrumento musical:* musical instrument
*insuficiente:* inadequate, insufficient
*insulina:* insulin
*insulso:* bland
*insultar:* curse, insult, name, swear
*insulto:* insult, offense
*insultos:* abuse
*insurrección:* insurrection
*intacto:* intact
*integral:* brown, wholewheat
*íntegramente:* full
*integrantes:* lineup
*integrar:* absorb, assimilate, integrate, join
*integridad:* integrity
*íntegro:* intact
*intelecto:* brain, intellect
*intelectual:* intellectual
*inteligencia:* brain, intellect, intelligence
*inteligente:* bright, clever, intelligent, perceptive, rational
*intención:* intent, intention, meaning, will
*intencional:* deliberate
*intencionalmente:* purpose
*intensidad:* intensity, strength
*intensificar:* escalate, intensify
*intensivo:* intensive
*intensivo en mano de obra:* labor-intensive
*intenso:* concentrated, deep, full, heavy, high, intense, intensive, loud, profound, violent
*intentar:* attempt, endeavor, seek, try
*intentar conseguir:* try
*intentar dar un golpe:* swing
*intento:* attempt, bid, endeavor, go, intent, stab
*interactivo:* interactive
*interactuar:* interact
*intercalar:* sandwich
*intercambiar:* exchange, swap, switch, trade
*intercambio:* exchange
*intercambio de gases:* gas exchange
*interceptar:* intercept
*intercolegial:* intercollegiate
*interés:* concern, focus, interest
*interés propio:* self-interest
*interesado:* interested
*interesante:* attractive, colorful, interesting
*interesar:* interest
*interesarse por algo:* follow
*intereses:* interest
*interestatal:* interstate
*interfase:* interface
*interfaz:* interface
*Interfaz Gráfica de Usuario (GUI por sus siglas en inglés):* GUI
*interferencia:* interference, static
*interferir:* interfere
*interino:* acting, interim
*interior:* inner, inside, interior, overhead
*interior de un país:* inland
*intermediario:* middleman
*intermedio:* break, interlude, intermediate, medium
*interminable:* drawn-out, endless, running

*legislativo:* legislative
*legislatura:* legislature
*legítima defensa:* self-defense
*legitimidad:* justice
*legítimo:* authentic, genuine, legitimate, rightful
*lego:* lay
*lejano:* distant, far, faraway, far off, way
*Lejano Oriente:* Far East
*lejísimos:* farthest, mile
*lejos:* away, far, way
*lejos de:* away, far
*lejos de la ciudad capital:* upstate
*lema:* slogan
*leña:* log
*leñador:* logger, lumberman, woodsman
*lengua:* language, tongue
*lengua persa:* Farsi
*lenguaje:* language, tongue
*lenguaje hablado:* speech
*lenguaje obsceno:* foul
*lengüetazo:* lap
*lentamente:* inch
*lente:* lens
*lente cóncavo:* concave lens
*lente convexa:* convex lens
*lente de contacto:* contact lens
*lenteja:* lentil
*lentes:* eyeglasses, glass
*lentes de sol:* sunglasses
*lento:* slow
*lento pero seguro:* surely
*león:* lion
*león de montaña:* mountain lion
*leotardos:* leggings
*lesbiana:* lesbian
*lesión:* battery, injury
*lesionado:* injured
*lesionar:* injure
*letal:* deadly, lethal
*letargo estival:* estivation
*letra:* handwriting, letter, lyric, script, vocals, writing
*letras:* art
*letrero:* inscription, notice, sign
*levadura:* yeast
*levantado:* up
*levantamiento:* insurrection, revolt, survey
*levantar:* clear, elevate, erect, foot, get, lift, pick, put, raise, rise, scoop, stir
*levantar cargos:* press
*levantar el ánimo:* cheer
*levantar la ceja/las cejas:* eyebrow
*leve:* subtle
*lexema:* base word
*léxico:* vocabulary
*ley:* act, law, statute
*ley de Boyle:* Boyle's law
*ley de Gay-Lussac:* Charles's law
*ley de la reflexión de la luz:* reflection
*ley de Pascal:* Pascal's principle
*ley de periodicidad:* periodic law
*ley de prescripción:* statute of limitations
*ley mordaza:* gag rule
*leyenda:* legend
*leyes:* law
*liado:* mixed up
*libar:* suck
*libelo:* libel
*libélula:* dragonfly
*liberado:* liberated
*liberal:* liberal
*liberalizar:* liberalize
*liberar:* free, let, liberate, release
*liberar (prisión):* discharge
*libertad:* freedom, latitude, liberty
*libertad de expresión:* free speech
*libertad de expresión.:* freedom of speech
*libertar:* liberate
*libra:* pound
*libra esterlina:* pound, sterling
*libramiento:* bypass
*librar:* get, hook
*librar de:* rid
*libre:* free, grab, off
*libre comercio:* free trade
*libre de:* free
*libre de impuestos:* tax-free
*libre de servicio:* duty
*libremente:* freely
*librería:* bookstore
*librero:* bookcase
*libreta:* book
*libro:* book
*libro (de contabilidad):* book
*libro de cocina:* cookbook
*libro de pasta dura:* hardcover
*libro de recetas:* cookbook
*libro de texto:* textbook
*libro para colorear:* coloring book
*licencia:* authority, leave, license
*licencia de manejo:* driver's license
*licencia de matrimonio:* marriage license
*licencia matrimonial:* marriage license
*licencia para casarse:* marriage license
*licencia poética:* poetic license
*licenciada:* grad, graduate, lawyer
*licenciado:* grad, graduate, lawyer
*liceo:* high school
*licitar:* tender
*lícito:* permissible
*licorería:* liquor store, off-licence
*líder:* leader
*liderazgo:* leadership
*lidiar:* wrestle
*lidiar con:* contend
*lienzo:* canvas
*liga:* elastic, league, rubber band, scrunchie
*liga mayor:* major
*liga menor:* minor league
*Liga Nacional de Fútbol:* NFL
*Liga Nacional de Hockey sobre hielo:* NHL
*ligar:* hook
*ligeramente:* slightly, vaguely
*ligero:* faint, light, lightweight, mild, short, slight, subtle
*liguero:* garter belt
*lijar:* sand
*lima:* file
*limar:* file
*limitación:* constraint, limitation, qualification, restraint
*limitaciones:* limitation
*limitado:* confined, limited
*limitar:* confine, keep, limit, restrict
*limitar con:* border
*limitarse a:* limit
*límite:* bound, boundary, breaking point, ceiling, cutoff, frontier, limit, line
*límite convergente:* convergent boundary
*límite de crédito:* credit limit
*límite de transformación:* transform boundary
*límite de velocidad:* speed limit
*límite del estado:* state line
*límite divergente:* divergent boundary
*limo:* silt
*limón:* lemon
*limón (verde):* lime
*limonada:* lemonade
*limosnera:* beggar
*limosnero:* beggar
*limpiador:* cleaner
*limpiadora:* cleaner
*limpianieve:* snowplow
*limpiaparabrisas:* windshield wiper
*limpiar:* bus, clean, cleanse, clear, gut, wipe
*limpiar con una esponja:* sponge
*limpiar en seco:* dry-clean
*limpiar y arreglar:* preen
*limpiar y ordenar:* clear
*limpieza completa:* spring-cleaning
*limpieza y arreglado:* preen
*limpio:* clean, clear
*linchar:* lynch
*lindar con:* border
*linde:* boundary
*lindero:* boundary
*lindo:* beautiful, cute, lovely,

*lubricante*: lubricant
*luces altas*: bright, high beams
*lucha*: battle, struggle
*luchador*: fighter
*luchadora*: fighter
*luchar*: battle, fight, struggle, wrestle
*luchar por*: fight, pursue, push
*luchar por algo*: labor
*luchar por la vida*: life
*lucrativo*: for-profit, lucrative, profitable
*luego*: then
*lugar*: ground, place, point, room, site, somewhere, space, spot, venue
*lugar alguno*: anyplace
*lugar común*: garden-variety, platitude
*lugar de interés*: sight
*lugar de nacimiento*: birthplace
*lugar de trabajo*: workplace, workstation
*lugar favorito*: haunt
*lugar predilecto*: stomping ground
*lugarteniente de la gobernadora*: lieutenant governor
*lugarteniente del gobernador*: lieutenant governor
*lúgubre*: grim
*lujo*: luxury
*lujoso*: fancy, luxury
*lumbre*: fire
*luminoso*: bright
*luna*: moon
*luna de miel*: honeymoon
*lunar*: beauty mark, lunar
*lunares*: polka dots
*lunch*: box lunch, brown-bag
*lunes*: Monday
*lustrar*: polish
*lustre*: luster
*luterana*: Lutheran
*luterano*: Lutheran
*luz*: light
*luz artificial*: artificial light
*luz blanca*: white light
*luz de (la) luna*: moonlight
*luz de día*: daylight
*luz del día*: sunlight
*luz del sol*: sunlight, sunshine
*luz natural*: daylight, natural light
*luz solar*: sunlight
*luz verde*: go-ahead

**M**
*ma*: mamá, mom
*macana*: nightstick
*macareo*: tidal bore
*macarrones con queso*: macaroni and cheese
*machacar acerca de*: harp
*machaqueo*: drumbeat
*macho*: buck, bull, macho, male
*machucón*: boo-boo
*macroeconomía*: macroeconomics
*madera*: lumber, smarts, wood
*madera de construcción*: timber
*maderería*: lumberyard
*maderero*: logger
*madrastra*: stepmother
*madre*: mother, parent
*madre patria*: mother country
*madre soltera*: single parent
*madrina*: attendant
*madrina de boda*: matron of honor
*madurar*: grow, mature, ripen
*madurez*: manhood, mature, middle age
*maduro*: mature, middle-aged, ripe
*maestra auxiliar*: teaching assistant
*maestra de ceremonias*: emcee
*maestra particular*: tutor
*maestra suplente*: sub, substitute teacher
*maestro*: master
*maestro auxiliar*: teaching assistant
*maestro de ceremonias*: emcee
*maestro particular*: tutor
*maestro suplente*: sub, substitute teacher
*mafia*: Mafia
*maga*: magician
*magia*: magic
*mágico*: magic, magical
*magma (m.)*: magma
*magnético*: magnetic
*magnetizar*: magnetize
*magnifíco*: glorious
*magnífico*: beautiful, fine, glorious, gorgeous, magnificent, shining, splendid, superb
*magnitud*: magnitude, size
*magnitud absoluta*: absolute magnitude
*magnitud aparente*: apparent magnitude
*mago*: magician, wizard
*magro*: lean
*maicena*: cornstarch
*maíz*: corn, maize
*majestad*: majesty
*majestuosidad*: majesty
*majestuoso*: grand, majestic
*mal*: bad, badly, bad off, foul, ill, illness, poor, wrong
*mal comportamiento*: misbehavior
*mal dispuesto*: unwilling
*mal momento*: senior moment
*mal necesario*: necessary
*mal rato*: ride
*mala conducta*: misbehavior, misconduct
*mala hierba*: weed
*mala pasada*: raw
*mala suerte*: luck
*malabares*: juggle
*malagua*: medusa
*maldad*: mischief, spite
*maldecir*: curse, swear
*maldición*: curse
*maldito*: doggone
*maleable*: malleable
*malecón*: boardwalk, jetty
*maleducado*: ignorant, rude
*malestar*: discomfort, unrest
*maleta*: baggage, suitcase
*maletas*: luggage
*maletero*: porter, trunk
*maleza*: scrub, underbrush, undergrowth, weed
*malgastar*: throw
*malhumorado*: bad-tempered
*maligno*: malignant
*malinterpretar*: misread
*malísimo*: terrible
*malla de baño*: swimsuit
*mallas*: leggings
*mallones*: leggings
*malo*: bad, foul, ill, lame, low, mean, wrong
*malvado*: evil, wicked
*mama*: breast
*mamá*: mama, momma, mum
*mamario*: mammary
*mambo*: mambo
*mameluco*: overall
*mami*: mommy
*mamífera*: mammal
*mamífero*: mammal
*mamífero placentado*: placental mammal
*mamífero placentario*: placental mammal
*mamografía*: mammography
*mampara*: screen
*manada*: herd
*mañana*: morning, tomorrow
*manantial*: fountain, spring
*manar*: flow, well
*manatí*: manatee
*mancha*: mark, smear, spot, stain
*mancha solar*: sunspot
*manchar*: stain
*mandado*: errand
*mandar*: command, dispatch, forward, instruct, send
*mandar a la cárcel*: jail
*mandar de acá para allá*: order
*mandar en avión*: fly
*mandar hacer*: have
*mandar llamar*: summon
*mandar mensajes instantáneos*: instant messaging

*más bien*: instead, rather
*más bien que*: rather
*más de*: more, over, plus, upward
*más importante*: wide
*más lejano*: furthest
*más lejos*: farther, further
*más o menos*: fairly, give, like, so
*más que*: better, else, excess, more, only
*más reciente*: latest
*más tarde*: later
*más temprano*: earlier
*más vale que*: better
*más y más*: more
*masa*: bank, batter, bulk, dough, mass, pastry, tumor
*masa atómica*: atomic mass
*masa continental*: land mass
*masa de aire*: air mass
*masa fermentada*: sourdough
*masacrar*: massacre, slaughter
*masacre*: massacre
*masaje*: massage, rubdown
*masajear*: massage
*masas*: mass
*mascada*: scarf
*máscara*: face mask, mascara, mask
*mascarilla*: face mask, mask
*mascota*: pet
*masculino*: male, masculine
*mascullar*: mutter
*masivo*: mass, massive
*masticar*: chew
*masticar haciendo ruido*: crunch
*mástil*: mast
*mata*: shrub
*matanza*: massacre
*matar*: kill, put, slaughter
*matar el tiempo*: while
*matar en la cámara de gases*: gas
*matar en masa*: massacre
*mate*: dull, maths, matte
*matemática*: mathematician
*matemáticas*: math, mathematics, maths
*matemático*: mathematical, mathematician
*materia*: credit hour, material, matter, subject, topic
*materia gris*: gray matter
*materia principal*: major
*material*: material
*material impreso*: matter
*material para cercas*: fencing
*material piroclástico*: pyroclastic material
*materiales*: material
*maternal*: maternal
*maternidad*: maternity
*materno*: maternal, native
*matiné*: matinee
*matiz*: shade
*matiz estilístico*: stylistic nuance
*matorral*: scrub
*matrícula*: tuition
*matrimonial*: double
*matrimonio*: marriage
*matriz escalar*: scalar matrix
*máximo*: full
*máximo*: maximum, most, top, utmost
*mayo*: May
*mayonesa*: mayonnaise
*mayor*: elder, eldest, grown-up, major, senior, utmost
*mayor parte*: bulk
*mayor que*: upward
*mayoreo*: bulk, wholesale
*mayoría*: majority
*mayormente*: largely
*mayúscula*: capital
*mazo*: deck
*mazorca*: ear
*me*: me
*me temo*: afraid
*mecánica*: mechanic
*mecánico*: mechanic, mechanical, mindless
*mecanismo*: mechanic, mechanism
*mecanismo de defensa*: defense mechanism
*mecanismo elemental*: simple machine
*mecanizar*: mechanize
*mecanógrafa*: typist
*mecanografiar*: type
*mecanógrafo*: typist
*mecenas*: patron
*mecer*: rock, sway
*mechar*: slash
*mechón*: lock
*medalla*: medal
*Medalla de Honor*: Medal of Honor
*medalla de oro*: gold medal
*medallista*: medalist
*médano*: sand dune
*media*: mean, sock, stocking
*media hora*: half-hour
*media luna*: crescent
*medialuna*: croissant
*mediana*: median, median strip
*mediana edad*: middle age
*mediano*: medium, moderate
*medianoche*: midnight
*mediante*: means
*mediar*: mediate
*medias*: pantyhose
*médica*: medic, physician, practitioner
*médica de cabecera*: GP
*médica familiar*: GP
*médica forense*: medical examiner
*médica interna*: resident
*medicación*: medication, medicine
*Medicaid*: Medicaid
*medicamento*: drug, medication, medicine
*Medicare*: Medicare
*medicina*: medication, medicine
*médico*: doctor, medic, medical, medical examiner, physician, practitioner
*médico de cabecera*: GP
*médico familiar*: GP
*médico interno*: resident
*medida*: action, measurement
*medida en yardas*: yardage
*medidas*: provision
*medidas enérgicas*: crackdown
*medidor*: gauge, meter
*medieval*: medieval
*medio*: half, means, medium, middle, midfielder, vehicle
*medio*: sistema, facility
*medio ambiente*: environment
*medio ambiente béntico*: benthic environment
*medio litro*: pint
*medio mal*: funny
*Medio Oriente*: Middle East
*medio plano*: ground
*medio tiempo*: part-time
*medio tiempo.*: halftime
*medio/mediocampista*: midfield
*mediocre*: indifferent, inferior, mediocre
*mediodía*: noon, noontime
*medios*: means
*medios de comunicación*: media
*medios de comunicación (de masas)*: mass media
*medios de vida*: living
*medios electrónicos*: electronic media
*medir*: gauge, measure, survey
*medir el tiempo*: time
*meditabundo*: thoughtful
*meditar*: deliberate, meditate, think
*médula*: medulla
*médula espinal*: spinal cord
*médula oblonga*: medulla
*medusa*: jellyfish, medusa
*megabyte*: megabyte
*megatienda*: big-box
*meiosis*: meiosis
*mejilla*: cheek
*mejillón*: mussel
*mejor*: best, better, prime, well
*mejor momento*: best
*mejora*: pickup, upturn
*mejorar*: enhance, improve, mend, raise, refine, upgrade
*melanina*: melanin
*melena*: mane
*melodía*: melody, ringtone, tune

*melodioso:* sweet
*melón:* melon
*membrana celular:* cell membrane
*membranófono:* membranophone
*memorable:* memorable
*memorándum:* memo
*memoria:* memory
*memoria sensorial:* sense memory
*memorias:* memoirs
*memorizar:* learn, memorize
*mención honorífica:* honorable mention
*mencionar:* cite, mention
*mendiga:* beggar
*mendigar:* beg, panhandle
*mendigo:* beggar
*menear:* bob, stir
*menisco:* meniscus
*menonita:* Mennonite
*menopausia:* menopause
*menopáusico:* menopause
*menor:* junior, least, lesser, minor, minor league, petty, under
*menor de edad:* minor
*menorá:* menorah
*menos:* least
*menos:* but, least, less, minus
*menos aún:* let
*menos de:* less
*menos importante:* minor
*menos que:* less
*menospreciar:* devalue, talk
*mensaje:* mail, message
*mensaje de texto:* text, text message
*mensaje instantáneo:* IM, instant message
*mensajera:* page
*mensajería instantánea.:* instant messaging
*mensajero:* courier, messenger, page
*menso:* dingbat
*menstruar:* menstruate
*mensual:* monthly
*mensualidad:* allowance
*menta:* mint
*mental:* mental
*mente:* head, mind
*mente en blanco:* blank
*mentir:* lie
*mentira:* lie
*mentón:* chin
*mentor:* mentor
*mentora:* mentor
*menú:* menu
*menudo:* petite, tiny
*mercadería:* merchandise
*mercado:* market
*mercado bursátil:* stock market
*mercado de divisas:* foreign exchange
*mercado de valores:* stock market
*mercado laboral:* labor market
*mercancía:* commodity, merchandise
*mercante:* merchant
*merced a:* thank, through
*Mercurio:* Mercury
*mercurio:* mercury
*merecer:* deserve, merit
*meridional:* southern
*merienda:* supper
*merienda campestre:* especialmente en la playa, donde se sirven almejas y otros alimentos, clambake
*mérito:* credit, merit
*mermelada:* jam, jelly
*mero:* mere
*mes:* month
*mesa:* table
*mesa de trabajo:* bench
*mesada:* allowance
*mescolanza:* mixture
*mesera:* server, waiter, waitress
*mesero:* server, waiter
*meseros:* waitstaff
*meseta:* mesa
*Mesías:* Messiah
*mesosfera:* mesosphere
*mesozoico:* Mesozoic era
*meta:* aim, finish line, goal, mark
*metabolismo:* metabolism
*metadona:* methadone
*metafase:* metaphase
*metáfora:* metaphor
*metáfora visual:* visual metaphor
*metafórico:* figurative
*metal:* metal
*metal alcalino:* alkali metal
*metal de tierra alcalina:* alkaline-earth metal
*metales:* brass
*metaloide:* metalloid
*metamórfico:* metamorphic
*metamorfosis:* metamorphosis
*metanol:* methanol
*metedura de pata:* snafu
*meteoroide:* meteoroid
*meteorología:* meteorology
*meter:* break, dig, dip, drop, get, go, grind, insert, place, poke, score, slot, squeeze, stick, stuff, tuck, wedge
*meter a fuerza:* force
*meter a la cárcel:* imprison
*meter a presión:* jam
*meter de contrabando:* smuggle
*meter en la cárcel:* imprison
*meter en líos:* land
*meter en problemas:* land
*meter la mano:* reach
*meter la pata:* flub
*meterse algo en la cabeza:* head
*meterse con:* mess, pick
*metida de pata:* boo-boo, flub
*metido:* stuck
*metódico:* methodical, systematic
*método:* method, system
*método científico:* scientific method
*metraje:* footage
*métrico:* metric
*metro:* meter, metro, subway, tape measure
*metropolitano:* metro, metropolitan
*metros por segundo:* meter
*mezcla:* blend, composition, cross, meld, mix, mixture
*mezcla heterogénea:* heterogeneous mixture
*mezcla homogénea:* homogeneous mixture
*mezclado:* mixed up
*mezclar:* blend, combine, integrate, meld, mix
*mezclilla:* denim
*mezcolanza:* jumble
*mezquino:* petty, sleazy
*mezquita:* mosque
*mezzanine:* mezzanine
*mi:* my
*mí:* me
*mí/mío:* mine
*micótico:* fungus
*microbio:* germ
*microcircuito:* microchip
*microclima:* microclimate
*microeconomía:* microeconomics
*microelemento:* trace gas
*microfibra:* microfiber
*micrófono:* microphone
*microorganismo:* microorganism
*microscópico:* microscopic
*microscopio:* microscope
*microscopio compuesto:* compound light microscope
*microscopio de electrones:* electron microscope
*microscopio electrónico:* electron microscope
*miedo:* fear, fright
*miedoso:* fearful
*miel:* honey
*miembro:* fellow, limb, member
*miembro de la Cámara de Representantes de Estados Unidos:* Rep.
*miembro de un grupo:* insider
*miembro del jurado:* juror
*miembro del parlamento:* Member of Parliament
*miembro fundador:* founding member

*miembro veterano:* holdover
*miembros de la iglesia:* congregation
*mientras:* meantime, process, while, whilst
*mientras más ... más:* the
*mientras que:* whereas, while
*mientras tanto:* meantime, meanwhile
*miércoles:* Wednesday
*miga:* crumb
*migaja:* crumb
*migración:* immigration
*migraña:* migraine
*migrar/emigrar:* migrate
*mil:* thousand
*mil dólares o mil libras.:* grand
*mil millones:* billion
*milagro:* miracle, wonder
*milagroso:* miracle
*miles:* thousand
*miles de años:* light year
*miles de millones:* billion
*milicia:* militia
*miligramo:* milligram
*miligramo (mg):* mg
*mililitro:* ml
*milímetro:* millimeter, mm
*militante:* militant
*militar:* military, serviceman
*milla terrestre inglesa = 1.609 kilómetros:* mile
*millón:* million
*millonaria:* millionaire
*millonario:* millionaire
*millones de años:* light year
*millonésimo:* millionth
*mimar:* fuss, indulge
*mimbre:* cane
*mina:* lead, mine, pit
*mina a tajo abierto:* strip mine
*minar:* undermine
*mineral:* ore
*mineral sin silicatos:* nonsilicate mineral
*miniatura:* miniature
*minibús:* minibus
*minimalismo:* minimalism
*mínimo:* low, marginal, minimal, minimum, skeleton, slight
*ministerial:* ministerial
*ministerio:* department, ministry, office
*ministra:* minister, secretary
*ministra de hacienda/economía:* chancellor
*Ministra de Relaciones Exteriores:* Secretary of State
*ministro:* chancellor, minister, secretary
*Ministro de Relaciones Exteriores:* Secretary of State
*minivan:* minivan
*minoría:* minority
*minorista:* merchandiser, retail, retailer
*minstrel show:* minstrel show
*minucioso:* thorough
*minúsculo:* tiny
*minusválido:* disabled
*minuta:* minute
*minuto:* minute
*minuto luz:* light minute
*miocardio:* heart
*miope:* far-sighted, near-sighted
*mira:* look
*mirada:* eye, glance
*mirada fija:* gaze
*mirada furiosa:* glare
*mirada penetrante:* gaze
*mirar:* look, stare, watch
*mirar a hurtadillas:* peek
*mirar con:* regard
*mirar detenidamente:* peer
*mirar fijamente:* gaze
*mirar furiosamente:* glare
*mirar los toros desde la barrera:* fence
*misa:* mass
*miscelánea:* general store
*miseria:* misery
*misil:* missile, rocket
*misión:* mission, task
*misionera:* missionary
*misionero:* missionary
*mismo:* equal, identical, itself, same
*mismo nivel:* level
*mismo tiempo:* once, process
*misterio:* mystery, puzzle, riddle
*misterioso:* mysterious, mystery
*mitad:* half, half note
*mitad de un período:* midterm
*mitades:* half
*mitigar:* subdue
*mito:* legend, myth
*mitocondria:* mitochondrion
*mitología:* mythology
*mitosis:* mitosis
*mixto:* coed, heterogeneous, miscellaneous, mixed
*mixtura:* mix, mixture
*mL:* ml
*ml:* ml
*mm:* mm
*mmm:* er
*mochila:* rucksack
*moción:* motion
*moda:* fashion, vogue
*moda pasajera:* fad
*modelar:* model, mold
*modelo:* model
*modelo a escala:* scale
*modelo climático:* station model
*modelo de conducta:* role model
*modelo meteorológico:* station model
*moderado:* gentle, moderate, modest
*moderar:* moderate, qualify, restrain, soften, tone
*modernizar:* modernize
*moderno:* cool, modern
*modestia:* modesty
*modesto:* humble, modest
*modificado genéticamente:* genetically-modified
*modificador:* modifier
*modificar:* modify, reform
*modismo:* idiom
*modo:* manner, mode, way
*modo de usarse:* usage
*modo de uso:* usage
*modo de vida:* mode
*modo subjuntivo:* subjunctive
*modulación:* inflection
*módulo de maniobra y mando:* command module
*módulo lunar:* lunar module
*mofle:* exhaust pipe
*moho:* mold
*mojado:* wet
*mojar:* dip
*mojar (la cama):* wet
*molde:* mold
*molde para galletas:* cookie cutter
*molde para pastel:* cake pan
*moldear:* mold, shape
*molécula:* molecule
*moler:* grind
*molestar:* annoy, bother, disturb, irritate, pester, spite, tee, tick, trouble, upset, vex
*molestia:* annoyance, bother, irritation
*molesto:* tiresome
*molido:* ground
*molino:* mill
*momento:* instant, minute, moment, momentum, point, time
*momentum:* momentum
*monarca:* monarch
*monarquía:* monarchy
*monasterio:* monastery
*moneda:* coin, currency
*moneda de veinticinco centavos:* quarter
*monedas:* change
*monedas de plata:* silver
*monedero:* pocketbook
*monetario:* monetary
*monitor:* monitor
*monja:* nun
*monje:* monk
*mono:* ape, cute, monkey, sweet
*moño:* bow
*monocromático:* monochromatic
*monolítico:* monolithic

*nevera:* refrigerator
*newton:* newton
*ni:* neither, nor
*ni con mucho:* nearly, nowhere
*ni en sueños:* dream
*ni falta hace decirlo:* say
*ni hablar de:* mind
*ni mucho menos:* far
*ni por asomo:* nowhere
*ni siquiera cerca:* near
*ni uno ni otro:* neither
*ni...ni:* either
*nicho:* niche
*nido:* nest
*niebla:* fog
*nieta:* grandchild, granddaughter
*nieto:* grandchild, grandson
*nieve:* ice cream, sherbet, snow
*nimbo:* nimbus
*nimio:* petty
*niña:* child, girl, kid, youngster
*niña guía exploradora:* brownie
*niña que ha empezado a caminar:* toddler
*niñas guías exploradoras:* brownie
*niñera:* nanny
*niñez:* childhood, infancy
*ningún lugar:* anywhere
*ninguno:* any, neither
*ninguno:* ninguna, none
*niño:* boy, child, kid, youngster
*niño en edad preescolar:* preschooler
*niño prodigio:* whiz kid
*niño que ha empezado a caminar:* toddler
*níquel:* nickel
*nítido:* sharp
*nitrato:* nitrate
*nitrógeno:* nitrogen
*nivel:* league, level
*nivel de vida:* standard of living
*nivel del mar:* sea level
*nivel freático:* water table
*nivelador:* leveler
*nivelarse:* level
*no:* not, what
*No.:* No
*noble:* lord, noble
*nocaut:* knockout
*noche:* night, nite
*noche de brujas:* Halloween
*noche y día:* night
*Nochebuena:* Christmas Eve
*noción:* conception, idea
*noctívago:* nocturnal
*nocturno:* nocturnal
*nódulo linfático:* lymph node
*nogal americano:* hickory
*nómada:* nomad
*nómade:* nomad
*nombramiento:* appointment, commission, nomination
*nombrar:* appoint, call, elect, name, nominate
*nombre:* first name, name, noun
*nombre contable:* countable noun, count noun
*nombre de pila:* Christian name, first name
*nombre del archivo:* filename
*nombre incontable:* uncount noun
*nombre propio:* proper noun
*nomenclatura binómica:* binomial nomenclature
*nómina:* payroll
*nómina de socios:* membership
*nominación:* nomination
*nominal:* nominal
*nominar:* nominate
*non:* odd
*nonagésimo:* ninetieth
*nonato:* unborn
*noquear:* knock
*noreste/nordeste:* northeast, northeastern
*noria:* waterwheel
*norma:* norm, rule
*norma de conducta:* standard
*normal:* ordinary, regular, standard
*normalizar:* standardize
*normalmente:* normally
*norte:* north
*norte/sur geográfico:* true
*norte/sur verdadero:* true
*norteño:* northerner
*nos:* ourselves, us
*nos vemos:* see
*nosotras:* we
*nosotros:* ourselves, us, we
*nosotros mismos:* ourselves
*nota:* mark, note
*nota a pie de página:* footnote
*nota al margen:* anecdotal scripting
*nota al pie:* footnote
*nota de pie de página:* footnote
*nota necrológica:* obituary
*notable:* impressive, marked, notable, note, outstanding
*notación:* notation
*notación científica:* scientific notation
*notar:* detect, note, notice, spot
*notas:* handout
*noticia:* news, report, story, word
*noticiario:* newscast
*noticias:* news
*noticiero:* newscast
*notificar:* notify
*notorio:* notorious
*novata:* freshman, novice, rookie
*novatada:* hazing
*novato:* freshman, inexperienced, novice, raw, rookie
*novedad:* innovation, release
*novedoso:* novel
*novela:* novel
*novela de misterio/suspenso:* mystery
*novela de vaqueros:* western
*novela del oeste:* western
*novela romántica:* romance
*novela rosa:* romance
*novelista:* novelist
*noveno:* ninth
*noventa:* ninety
*novia:* bride, fiancée, girlfriend
*noviembre:* November
*novio:* boyfriend, bridegroom, fiancé, groom, lover
*nube:* cloud, puff
*nube de electrones:* electron cloud
*Nube de Oort:* Oort cloud
*nublado:* cloudy
*nublar:* cloud
*nuclear:* nuclear
*núcleo:* core, heart
*núcleo externo:* outer core
*nucleótido:* nucleotide
*nudillo de la mano:* knuckle
*nudo:* knot
*nuera:* daughter-in-law
*nuestro:* our, ours, us
*nueva:* news
*nueve:* nine
*nuevo:* brand-new, fresh, new
*nuez:* nut, walnut
*nuez de Castilla:* walnut
*nulo:* nil, null, void, zero
*numerar:* number
*número:* figure, issue, number, schtick, size
*número atómico:* atomic number
*número de la Seguridad Social:* Social Security number
*número de masa:* mass number
*número de muertos:* death toll
*número de placa:* license number
*número de víctimas:* death toll, toll
*número entero:* integer
*número irracional:* irrational number
*número másico:* mass number
*número primo:* prime
*número racional:* rational number
*número real:* real number
*números complejos:* complex number
*numeroso:* numerous
*nunca:* ever, never
*nunca jamás:* never
*nunca sabes:* know
*nupcial:* marital
*nupcias:* marriage
*nutrición:* nutrition

*nutriente:* nutrient
*nutritivo:* nutritious

**O**

*o:* either, else, or
*o...o:* either, else
*oasis:* oasis
*obedecer:* obey
*obertura:* opening
*obeso:* fat, obese
*obispo:* bishop
*obituario:* obituary
*objeción:* objection
*objetar:* exception, object
*objetivamente:* perspective
*objetivo:* end, idea, objective, objective lens, purpose, target
*objeto:* aim, artifact, item, object
*objeto curioso:* curiosity
*objeto de oro:* gold
*objeto directo:* direct object
*objeto indirecto:* indirect object
*objeto perdido:* lost and found
*objetos de cerámica:* ceramic
*objetos de valor:* valuables
*objetos de vidrio:* glass
*objetos perdidos:* lost and found
*objetos salvados:* salvage
*obligación:* duty, obligation
*obligado:* bind
*obligar:* bind, force, make, oblige, push, require
*obligar a:* compel, drive
*obligar a alguien a hacer algo:* bully
*obligatorio:* binding, compulsory
*obra:* making, piece, play, work
*obra de teatro:* theater
*obra dramática:* drama
*obra en construcción:* site
*obra maestra:* masterpiece
*obrar mal:* wrong
*obras viales:* roadwork
*obrera:* laborer, worker
*obrero:* laborer, worker
*obsceno:* filthy, indecent
*obscuro:* black
*obsequiar:* treat
*obsequio:* gift
*observación:* observation, point, remark, scrutiny, surveillance
*observador:* observer
*observadora:* observer
*observar:* eye, look, monitor, observe, remark, watch
*obsesión:* obsession
*obsesionar:* obsess
*obstaculizar:* impede
*obstáculo:* bar, hurdle, obstacle, speed bump, stumbling block
*obstinado:* insistent, stubborn
*obstinarse:* insist
*obstruccionismo:* filibuster
*obstruido:* plugged
*obstruir:* clog
*obtener:* acquire, derive, elicit, obtain, score
*obtener una victoria:* triumph
*obturador:* shutter
*obviamente:* obviously
*obvio:* distinct, obvious
*ocasión:* occasion, time
*ocasional:* casual, occasional, odd
*ocasionar:* produce, rise
*occidental:* western, westerner
*Occidente:* west
*océano:* ocean, sea
*oceanografía:* oceanography
*ochenta:* eighty
*ochentavo:* eightieth
*ocho:* eight, figure eight
*ocio:* pleasure
*ocioso:* idle
*octagésimo:* eightieth
*octava:* eighth note
*octava parte:* eighth
*octavo:* eighth
*octubre:* October
*ocular:* eyepiece
*ocultar:* conceal, cover, disguise, hide, hold, keep, mask, occupy, screen, suppress, sweep, tuck, withhold
*ocultar micrófonos:* bug
*oculto:* hidden, underlying
*ocupación:* occupation
*ocupado:* busy, busy signal
*ocupante:* occupant, occupier
*ocupar:* fill, line, occupy, take
*ocupar un lugar sin derecho:* squat
*ocuparse (de algo):* handle
*ocuparse de:* deal, look, man, see
*ocuparse de algo:* see
*ocurrente:* funny
*ocurrir:* come, happen, mind, occur, think
*odiar:* hate
*odio:* hatred
*odisea:* odyssey
*odómetro:* odometer
*oeste:* west
*ofender:* injured, insult, offend, offense
*ofendido:* hurt
*ofensa:* insult, offense
*ofensiva:* offense, offensive
*ofensivo:* offensive
*oferta:* bid, offer, offering, proposal, proposition
*oficial:* officer, official
*oficial de policía:* police officer
*oficina:* bureau, office
*oficina central:* headquarters, HQ
*oficina de atención al público:* front office
*oficina que da a la calle:* storefront
*oficinista:* clerk, white-collar
*oficio religioso:* service
*ofrecer:* bid, host, offer, volunteer
*ofrecer información sin que sea solicitada:* volunteer
*ofrecer servicios:* cater
*ofrecer un servicio:* hire
*ofrecer una disculpa:* apologize
*ofrecimiento:* offer
*ofrezca:* obo
*ofuscar:* cloud
*ofuscar ante:* blind
*oh:* aw
*oído:* ear, hearing
*oír:* hear, listen, sound
*oír de:* hear
*oir razones:* listen
*oír razones:* listen
*ojal:* buttonhole, eye
*ojear:* glance
*ojera:* bag
*ojo:* eye
*ojo compuesto:* compound eye
*ojo morado:* black eye
*ojo para:* eye
*ola:* water wave, wave
*oleada:* glow, wave
*oleaje:* surf, swell
*óleo:* oil paint, oil painting
*oler:* reek, scent, smell, sniff
*oler a:* smack
*oler a algo:* reek
*olfatear:* scent, sniff
*olfato:* smell
*oligoelemento:* trace gas
*olimpiadas:* Olympic, Olympic Games
*olímpico:* Olympic
*olivo:* olive
*olla:* kettle, pot
*olor:* odor, scent, smell
*olor corporal:* body odor
*olvidadizo:* forgetful
*olvidar:* forget, leave, mind, omit
*omelet:* omelet
*omitir:* cut, miss, omit, skip
*omnipresente:* ubiquitous
*omnívora:* omnivore
*omnívoro:* omnivore, omnivorous
*OMS:* World Health Organization
*once:* eleven
*once de septiembre:* nine-eleven
*onceavo:* eleventh
*onda:* wave
*onda (primaria):* P wave
*onda de radio:* radio wave
*onda de superficie:* surface wave
*onda electromagnética:* electromagnetic wave
*onda estacionaria:* standing wave
*onda expansiva:* shock wave
*onda longitudinal:* longitudinal wave

*oxígeno:* oxygen
*oye:* say
*oyente:* listener
*ozono:* ozone

**P**

*pa:* pop
*pabellón de los condenados a muerte:* death row
*PAC:* PAC
*paciencia:* patience
*paciente:* patient
*pacífico:* peaceful
*pacto:* pact
*padecer:* suffer
*padecer de:* suffer
*padecimiento:* illness
*padrastro:* stepfather
*padre:* father, parent
*padre soltero:* single parent
*padres:* folk
*padrino:* attendant
*padrino de bodas:* best man
*padrón:* register, registration, roll
*pagano:* pagan
*pagar:* pay, pony, repay, settle
*pagar a plazos:* spread
*pagar dividendos:* dividend
*pagar la cuenta:* check
*pagar la fianza:* bail
*pagar por adelantado:* pre-pay
*pagaré:* promissory note
*página:* page
*página (de un sitio de internet):* web page
*página web:* web page
*páginas:* page
*pago:* payment, repayment
*pago contra entrega:* C.O.D.
*pago en especie:* kind
*país:* country, land, nation
*paisaje:* landscape, scenery
*Paisley:* paisley
*paja:* straw
*pajarera:* aviary
*pájaro:* bird
*pajita:* straw
*pala:* scoop, shovel, spade
*palabra:* language, word
*palabra clave:* keyword
*palabra de fácil reconocimiento para un lector sin análisis de sus partes:* sight word
*palabra de uso frecuente:* high-frequency word
*palabra por palabra:* word
*palacio:* palace
*paladar:* roof
*paladín:* champion
*palanca de velocidades:* gearshift, stick shift
*palangana:* basin
*palco:* box
*palco de platea:* orchestra
*palear:* shovel
*paleontóloga:* paleontology
*paleontología:* paleontology
*paleontólogo:* paleontology
*palestra:* arena
*paleta:* paddle, palette knife, trowel
*pálido:* dull, light, pale
*palillo:* stick
*palito de pescado:* fish stick
*palma:* palm
*palmada:* smack
*palmaditas:* pat
*palmearse:* smack
*palmera:* palm
*palo:* stick
*palo de golf:* club, golf club
*paloma:* pigeon
*palomita:* check mark
*palomitas:* popcorn
*palote:* rolling pin
*palpar:* feel, finger
*palpitar:* beat
*pan:* bread
*pan comido:* cakewalk
*pan de centeno:* rye
*pan francés:* French toast
*pan integral:* wholewheat
*pan tostado:* toast
*panadera:* baker
*panadería:* bakery
*panadero:* baker
*pañal:* diaper, nappy
*pancarta:* banner
*panceta:* bacon
*pancito:* roll
*panda:* giant panda, panda
*panda gigante:* giant panda
*pandereta:* tambourine
*pandero:* tambourine
*pandilla:* band, gang
*pandillera:* gangster
*pandillero:* gangster
*panecillo:* popover
*panel:* panel
*panel solar:* solar collector
*panelista:* panelist
*Pangaea:* Pangaea
*pánico:* panic
*paño para lavarse:* washcloth
*panorama:* landscape, outlook, scenery
*panquecito:* muffin
*panqueque:* muffin
*pantalla:* desktop, front, screen
*pantalla de plasma:* plasma screen
*pantalón:* trousers
*pantalones:* pants, trousers
*pantalones cargo:* cargo pants
*pantalones cortos:* short
*pantalones de peto:* overall
*pantano:* bog, marsh, swamp
*panteón:* cemetery
*pantomima:* pantomime
*pants:* sweat
*pantufla:* slipper
*pañuelo:* handkerchief
*pañuelo desechable:* tissue
*panza:* belly
*papa:* potato, potato chip
*papá:* dad, father
*papalote:* kite
*paparazzi:* paparazzi
*papás:* folk
*papas a la francesa:* French fries, fries, fry
*papas fritas:* chip, French fries, fries, fry
*papel:* cast
*papel:* line, paper, part, role
*papel aluminio:* foil
*papel confort:* toilet paper
*papel de baño:* toilet paper
*papel de cera:* wax paper
*papel de china:* tissue
*papel de seda:* tissue
*papel destacado:* profile
*papel encerado:* wax paper
*papel higiénico:* toilet paper
*papel periódico:* newspaper
*papel principal:* lead
*papel sanitario:* toilet paper
*papel tapiz:* wallpaper
*papeleo:* red tape
*papeleo burocrático:* paperwork
*papelera:* wastebasket
*papeleta:* ticket
*papi:* daddy
*papila gustativa:* taste bud
*papito:* daddy
*paquete:* bundle, mailer, pack, package, packet, parcel, pkg.
*paquete postal:* parcel post
*par:* couple, even, pair, peer
*para:* for, of, order, to
*para acabarla de amolar:* insult
*para adolescentes:* teen, teenage
*para bien:* better
*para colmo:* insult
*para colmo de males:* insult
*para con:* toward
*para decir lo menos:* least
*para efectos prácticos:* intent
*para el provecho de uno:* advantage
*para empezar:* begin, first, start
*para llevar:* go
*para mal:* worse
*para mayor seguridad:* safe
*para nada:* near
*para presupuestos reducidos:* budget
*para que:* so
*para siempre:* forever, good
*para su información:* FYI
*para todos:* board

*pase*: pass
*pase de abordar*: boarding pass
*pase usted*: after
*pasear*: pace, wander
*paseo*: drive, ride, walk
*pasillo*: aisle, corridor, hall, hallway, landing, passage
*pasión*: passion
*pasiva*: passive
*pasivo*: debit, liability, passive
*paso*: access, footstep, move, pace, pass, passage, step, walk, way
*paso a desnivel*: overpass
*paso a nivel*: railroad crossing
*paso a paso*: inch, step
*paso elevado*: overpass
*paso en falso*: misstep
*paso superior*: overpass
*pasta*: paste
*pasta blanda*: softcover
*pasta de dientes*: toothpaste
*pasta dentífrica*: toothpaste
*pastar*: graze
*pastel*: cake, pie
*pastel de chocolate y nueces*: brownie
*pastel de frutas*: shortcake
*pastel de queso*: cheesecake
*pastelera*: baker
*pastelería*: bakery
*pastelero*: baker
*pastilla*: tablet
*pastilla de menta*: mint
*pastizal*: grassland
*pasto*: grass, lawn
*pastor*: minister, shepherd
*pastor alemán*: German shepherd
*pastora*: minister, shepherd
*pastura*: pasture
*pata*: leg, paw
*patada*: kickoff, shot
*patada a bote pronto*: drop kick
*patada inicial*: kickoff
*patalear*: kick
*pateador*: kicker
*pateadora*: kicker
*patear*: kick, shoot, stamp
*patentar*: patent
*patente*: apparent, manifest, patent
*paternal*: paternal
*paternidad*: parenthood
*patético*: pathetic
*patillas*: sideburns
*patín*: runner
*patines de hielo*: skate
*patines de ruedas*: skate
*patines en línea*: in-line skate
*patio*: barnyard, courtyard, yard
*patio (ferrocarriles)*: yard
*patio de recreo*: playground
*patio trasero*: backyard
*pato*: duck
*patria*: homeland
*patriarca*: elder
*patrimonio*: heritage
*patriota*: patriot, patriotic
*patrocinador*: backer, patron, sponsor
*patrocinadora*: backer, patron, sponsor
*patrocinar*: sponsor
*patrocinio*: sponsorship
*patrón*: employer, master, pattern, skipper
*patrón de movimiento*: movement pattern
*patrona*: employer, skipper
*patrulla*: patrol
*patrulla de reconocimiento*: scout
*patrullar*: patrol, police
*patrullero*: patrolman
*pausa*: break, pause, truce
*pauta*: guideline, indication
*pava*: kettle
*pavimentar*: pave
*pavimento*: pavement
*pavo*: turkey
*pavonearse*: strut
*pay*: pie
*payasa*: clown
*payasear*: clown
*payaso*: clown
*paz*: peace
*PBS*: PBS
*PC*: BTW
*PC (computadora personal)*: PC
*PDF*: archivos de computadora, PDF
*peaje*: toll
*peatón*: pedestrian
*peatona*: pedestrian
*peca*: sunspot
*pecado*: sin
*pecar*: sin
*pecar de*: err
*pecera*: fishbowl
*pecho*: breast, chest
*pechuga*: breast
*pectoral*: pectoral
*peculiar*: peculiar
*pedacito*: chip, scrap
*pedagoga*: educator
*pedagogo*: educator
*pedal*: pedal
*pedalear*: pedal
*pedazo*: chunk, gob, length, piece
*pedestal*: stand
*pedestre*: pedestrian
*pediatra*: pediatrician
*pedido*: order
*pedir*: ask, order, press, seek, send
*pedir a gritos*: cry
*pedir prestado*: borrow
*pedir un permiso*: take
*pegado*: form-fitting, plastered, tight
*pegajoso*: icky, sticky
*pegamento*: adhesive, glue
*pegar*: attach, bash, catch, cement, fasten, glue, knock, paste, stick
*pegar con cinta adhesiva*: tape
*pegar contra*: flatten
*peinar*: comb, style
*peine*: comb
*pelaje*: coat, fur
*pelar*: peel, shell
*pelar (verduras)*: shuck
*peldaño*: stair
*pelea*: quarrel
*pelea a puñetazos*: fistfight
*peleador*: fighter
*peleadora*: fighter
*pelear*: battle, fall, fight, quarrel
*pelear por algo*: scramble
*pelearse con*: fight
*peliagudo*: nasty, tough, tricky
*película*: feature, film, motion picture, movie, picture
*película adherente*: plastic wrap
*película de vaqueros*: western
*película del oeste*: western
*película para mujeres*: chick flick
*peligro*: danger, distress, hazard, threat
*peligroso*: dangerous, risky, rough
*pelirrojo*: ginger, red
*pellejo*: hide
*pellizcar*: pinch
*pellizco*: pinch
*pelo*: coat, fur, hair, pile, strand
*pelo absorbente o radical*: root hair
*pelota*: ball
*pelota de futbol*: football
*peluca*: wig
*peludo*: hairy
*peluquera*: barber
*peluquero*: barber
*pelusa*: lint
*pena*: embarrassment, grief, penalty, pity, shame
*pena capital*: capital punishment
*pena por*: sorry
*penal*: criminal, penalty
*penalti*: penalty
*penalty*: penalty
*peñasco*: rock
*pendiente*: earring, grade, gradient, incline, outstanding, pending, slope
*pendiente resbaladiza*: slippery
*péndulo*: swing
*pene*: penis
*penetrante*: strong
*penetrar*: break, penetrate, surge
*península*: peninsula

*revoltijo:* mess
*revoltoso:* rambunctious
*revoltura:* jumble
*revolución:* revolution, uprising
*revolucionaria:* revolutionary
*revolucionario:* revolutionary
*revolver:* jumble, mix, roil, scramble, shuffle, stir
*revólver:* revolver
*revuelo:* stir
*revuelta:* revolt, uprising
*rey:* king, ruler
*rezagarse:* lag, leave
*rezar:* pray
*rezos:* prayer
*riachuelo:* stream
*ribera:* bank, shore
*ribera del lago:* lakefront
*ribete:* trim
*ribosoma:* ribosome
*rico:* flavorful, nice, rich, wealthy
*rico en:* high, rich
*ridículo:* ridiculous
*riel:* rail, runner, track
*rienda:* rein
*riesgo:* danger, gamble, liability, risk, threat
*riesgoso:* risky
*rifarse:* lot
*rifle:* rifle
*rígido:* rigid, stiff
*riguroso:* rigid, rigorous, strict, thorough, tight, unrelenting
*rima:* rhyme
*rimar:* rhyme
*rímel:* mascara
*riña:* quarrel
*rincón:* corner
*ring:* ring
*rinoceronte negro:* black rhino
*riñón:* kidney
*río:* river
*río arriba:* upstream
*riqueza:* rich, treasure, wealth
*risotada:* laughter
*ritmo:* beat, pace, pacing, rate, rhythm
*ritmo circadiano:* circadian rhythm
*ritmo propio:* pace
*rito:* rite
*ritual:* ritual
*rival:* challenger, opponent, rival
*rivalidad:* rivalry
*rivalizar:* rival, vie
*rizado:* curly, fuzzy
*rizar:* curl
*rizarse:* curl
*rizo:* curl
*rizoide:* rhizoid, root hair
*rizoma:* rhizome, root hair
*robar:* burglarize, loot, rob, steal, take
*robar en tiendas:* shoplift
*roble:* oak
*robo:* break-in, burglary, robbery, theft
*robo de identidad:* identity theft
*robot:* robot
*robusto:* healthy, robust, sturdy
*roca:* boulder, rock
*roca de dislocación:* fault block
*roca lamelar:* foliated
*roce:* run-in
*rociador:* sprinkler
*rociar:* lace, spray, sprinkle
*rocío:* spray
*rock:* rock
*rodar:* film, roll, shoot, taxi
*rodear:* envelop, ring, round, surround
*rodeo:* detour, roundup
*rodilla:* knee
*rodillas:* knee
*rodillo:* roller, rolling pin
*roedor:* rodent
*roer:* eat
*rogar:* beg
*rojo:* red
*rojo (vivo):* red-hot
*roldana:* washer
*rollo:* reel, roll
*ROM (memoria de lectura únicamente):* ROM
*romance:* romance
*romano:* Roman
*romanticismo:* romance
*romántico:* romantic
*rombo:* diamond, rhombus
*rompeolas:* breaker zone
*romper:* breach, break, bust, rip, rupture, smash, snap, split
*romper (las olas):* break
*romper con:* break
*romper el corazón:* heart
*romper el hervor:* boil
*romper el hielo:* ice
*romper filas:* rank
*romperse (el cascarón):* hatch
*rompimiento:* breach, breakdown, breakup
*roncar:* snore
*roncha:* rash
*ronco:* hoarse
*ronda:* round
*ronda eliminatoria:* round
*rondana:* washer
*rondar:* haunt
*rondó:* rondo
*ropa:* clothes, clothing, garment, gear, wear
*ropa de cama:* bedding
*ropa heredada:* hand-me-down
*ropa interior:* underwear
*ropa lavada:* laundry
*ropa para lavar:* laundry
*ropa vistosa:* bling
*ropero:* wardrobe
*rosa:* pink, rose
*rosado:* pink
*rosca:* thread
*rosquilla:* doughnut
*rostizar:* broil
*rostro:* face
*rotación:* rotation
*rotación prógrada:* prograde rotation
*rotación retrógrada:* retrograde rotation
*rotar:* rotate
*rottweiler (raza de perros):* rottweiler
*rotular:* label
*rótulo:* label, tag
*rotundo:* emphatic, flat, outright, unqualified
*rotura:* rupture
*round:* round
*rozar:* brush, graze, scrape
*RR.PP.:* PR
*rubia:* blonde
*rubio:* blonde, fair
*rubor:* flush, glow
*ruborizarse:* flush
*rúbrica:* rubric
*rudimentario:* crude, primitive
*rueca:* spinning wheel
*rueda:* wheel
*rueda de la fortuna:* Ferris wheel
*rueda de prensa:* news conference
*rueda de recambio:* spare tire
*rueda de repuesto:* spare tire
*rueda hidráulica:* waterwheel
*rugby:* rugby
*rugido:* roar
*rugir:* rage, roar
*ruido:* noise, sound
*ruidoso:* noisy
*ruin:* sleazy
*ruina:* downfall, ruin
*ruinas:* ruin
*rumbo:* course
*rumor:* rumor
*ruptura:* breakup, rupture
*rural:* rural
*rústica:* softcover
*ruta:* route
*ruta de navegación:* lane
*rutabaga:* rutabaga
*rutina:* routine
*rutinario:* routine

**S**

*sábado:* Saturday
*sabana:* savanna
*sábana:* sheet
*sabedor:* informed
*sabelotodo:* know-it-all

*sarta:* stream
*sartén:* frying pan, pan
*sasafrás:* sassafras
*sastra:* tailor
*sastre:* tailor
*satélite:* satellite
*satélites meteorológicos geoestacionarios:* GOES
*satín:* satin
*sátira:* satire
*satisfacción:* satisfaction
*satisfacción con el empleo:* job satisfaction
*satisfacer:* fulfill, gratify, meet, satisfy
*satisfactorio:* satisfactory, satisfying
*satisfecho:* content, full, proud, satisfied
*saturar:* flood
*Saturno:* Saturn
*sazonado:* flavored
*sazonador:* flavoring
*sazonar:* flavor, season
*scatterplot:* scatterplot
*sci-fi:* sci-fi
*score:* score
*scroll bar:* scroll bar
SEC: SEC
*secadora:* dryer
*secar:* dry
*secar con toalla:* towel
*secarse la frente:* mop
*sección:* section, segment
*sección blanca:* White Pages
*seco:* dried, dry
*secoya:* sequoia
*secreción:* discharge
*secretamente:* secret
*secretaria:* minister, secretary
*secretaría:* department, ministry
*secretaria de admisiones:* registrar
*Secretaria de Estado:* Secretary of State
*secretaria de hacienda/economía:* chancellor
*secretario:* chancellor, minister, secretary
*secretario de admisiones:* registrar
*Secretario de Estado:* Secretary of State
*secreto:* classified, hidden, secrecy, secret, undercover
*secta:* cult, sect
*sectario:* sectarian
*sector:* industry, section, sector, segment
*sector público:* public sector
*secuela:* aftermath, sequel, wake
*secuencia:* footage, sequence, succession, thread
*secuencia de pasos de baile:* dance sequence
*secuencia geométrica:* geometric sequence
*secuestrar:* kidnap, seize
*secuestro:* kidnap
*secular:* secular
*secundar:* second
*secundaria:* secondary
*secundario:* incidental, marginal, secondary, subsidiary
*sed:* thirst
*seda:* silk
*sedán:* sedan
*sede:* host
*sediento:* thirsty
*sedimentario:* sedimentary
*sedimento:* deposit, deposition, sediment
*seducir:* lure, seduce
*seductor:* seductive
*seglar:* lay, secular
*segmento:* segment
*segmento (de baile/danza):* dance phrase
*segregación racial:* apartheid
*seguido:* running, solid
*seguido de:* follow
*seguidor:* follower, following
*seguidora:* follower, following
*seguidos:* row
*seguimiento:* follow-up
*seguir:* continue, follow, go, keep, tail, take, trail
*seguir adelante:* go, going, proceed
*seguir adelante con:* push
*seguir adelante con algo:* follow
*seguir con:* follow
*seguir de cerca:* monitor, shadow
*seguir el ejemplo:* example
*seguir en vigor:* stand
*seguir la corriente:* humor
*seguir la pista:* trace, trail
*seguir los pasos:* footstep
*seguir siendo cierto:* true
*seguir(le) la pista:* track
*según:* according to
*según parece:* look
*según se dice:* reportedly
*según se informa:* reportedly
*segunda enseñanza:* secondary
*segundas:* second
*segundo:* deputy, latter, second
*seguramente:* surely
*seguridad:* certainty, reassure, safety, security
*seguridad nacional:* national security
*seguridad social:* Social Security
*seguro:* certain, certainly, insurance, positive, safe, secure, sure
*seguro de desempleo:* unemployment compensation
*seguro de sí mismo:* self-confident
*seguro de uno mismo:* sure
*seguro y fácil ganador:* shoo-in
*seis:* six
*selección:* array, choice, extract, selection
*selección natural:* natural selection
*seleccionar:* pick, select
*selectivo:* selective
*selecto:* choice, select
*sellar:* seal
*sello:* seal, stamp
*sello hermético:* seal
*selva:* forest, jungle
*selva (tropical):* rain forest
*semáforo:* stoplight
*semana:* week
*semana laboral:* week, work week
*semanal:* weekly
*semanario:* weekly
*sembradío:* field
*sembrar:* farm, plant, sow
*semejante:* alike, analogous, similar
*semejanza:* similarity
*semen:* sperm
*semental:* stud
*semestral:* semiannual
*semestre:* semester
*semibreve:* whole note
*semiconductor:* semiconductor
*semifinal:* semifinal
*semilla:* seed
*semillero:* nursery
*seminario:* seminar
*semínima:* quarter note
*semítico:* Semitic
*seña:* gesture
*senado:* Senate
*senador:* senator
*senadora:* senator
*señal:* cue, impression, mark, sign, signal
*señalador:* bookmark
*señalar:* gesture, indicate, mark, point, single
*señalar (con el dedo):* point
*señalar con el dedo:* finger
*señalar con la cabeza:* nod
*sencillo:* one-way, plain, single, straightforward
*senda:* trail
*sendero:* lane, path, pathway, track, trail
*senil:* senile
*seno:* breast, sine, trough
*Señor:* lord
*señor:* gentleman, lord, master, mister, sir
*señor (Sr.):* Mr.
*señora:* lady, ma'am, madam
*señora (Sra.):* Mrs.
*señorita:* Miss

*silabeo:* syllabication
*silbar:* whistle
*silbato:* whistle
*silenciar:* silence
*silencio:* silence
*silencioso:* silent
*silicato:* silicate mineral
*sílice:* silica
*silicio:* silicon
*silicona:* silicone
*silla:* chair
*silla de montar:* saddle
*silla de playa:* beach chair
*silla de ruedas:* wheelchair
*silla para jardín:* lawn chair
*sillar de clave:* keystone
*sillón:* armchair, sofa
*sillón reclinable:* recliner
*silueta:* figure
*silvestre:* wild
*silvicultura:* forestry
*simbiosis:* symbiosis
*simbólico:* symbolic, token
*símbolo:* symbol
*símbolo de radioactividad:* radioactive symbol
*simetría:* symmetry
*simetría bilateral:* bilateral symmetry
*simetría radial:* radial symmetry
*simétrico:* symmetrical
*simiente:* seed
*similar:* like, similar
*similitud:* similarity
*simio:* ape
*simpático:* friendly
*simpatizar:* sympathize, warm
*simple:* mere, plain, simple
*simple decoración:* eye candy
*simplemente:* just, merely, simply
*simplificar:* simplify
*simulacro:* drill, dry run
*simulado:* mock
*simulador:* fraud
*simuladora:* fraud
*simular:* fake
*simultáneamente:* together
*simultáneo:* simultaneous
*sin:* free, minus, without
*sin duda:* certainly, doubt, sure
*sin duda alguna:* definitely, doubt
*sin embargo:* hand, however, nevertheless, nonetheless, yet
*sin falta:* fail
*sin importar:* however, matter
*sin par:* second, unparalleled
*sin parar:* end
*sin pensarlo:* spur
*sin plomo:* unleaded
*sin problema:* ease
*sin querer:* accident, unwitting
*sin sentido:* meaningless, mindless, pointless, senseless
*sinagoga:* synagogue
*sinceramente:* sincerely, truly
*sincero:* frank, genuine, hearty, open, sincere
*sinclinal:* syncline
*síncopa:* syncopation
*sincronización:* timing
*sindicato:* labor union, union
*síndico:* receiver, trustee
*síndrome:* syndrome
*síndrome de Down:* Down's syndrome
*síndrome de inmunodeficiencia adquirida:* AIDS
*sinfonía:* symphony
*singular:* singular
*siniestro:* sinister
*sinónimo:* synonym
*síntesis:* summary
*sintético:* man-made, synthetic
*sintetizar:* sum, summarize
*síntoma:* symptom
*sintonizador:* dial
*sintonizar:* tune
*sinvergüenza:* crook
*síquico:* psychic
*Sir:* sir
*sirena:* siren
*sirope:* syrup
*sirvienta:* maid, servant
*sirviente:* servant
*sísmico:* seismic
*sismo:* quake
*sismógrafo:* seismograph
*sismograma:* seismogram
*sismóloga:* seismology
*sismología:* seismology
*sismólogo:* seismology
*sistema:* order, regime, setup, system
*sistema (de órganos):* tract
*sistema acuovascular:* water vascular system
*sistema británico de pesos y medidas:* imperial
*sistema cardiovascular:* cardiovascular system
*sistema cerrado:* closed system
*sistema circulatorio abierto:* open circulatory system
*sistema circulatorio cerrado:* closed circulatory system
*sistema de coordenadas.:* coordinate system
*sistema de órganos:* organ system
*sistema de posicionamiento global:* global positioning system
*sistema inmune:* immune system
*sistema inmunitario:* immune system
*sistema integumentario:* integumentary system
*sistema intravenoso:* IV
*sistema linfático:* lymphatic system
*sistema métrico decimal:* metric system
*sistema muscular:* muscular system
*sistema nervioso:* nervous system
*sistema nervioso central:* central nervous system
*sistema nervioso periférico:* peripheral nervous system
*sistema operativo:* OS
*sistema periódico de los elementos:* periodic table
*sistema respiratorio:* respiratory system
*sistema solar:* solar system
*sistema tegumentario:* integumentary system
*sistemático:* regular, systematic
*sistémico:* systemic
*sitiar:* besiege
*sitio:* siege, site, space, stand
*sitio de internet:* website
*sitio de taxis:* taxi stand
*sitio web:* website
*situación:* business, matter, picture, scene, situation
*situación peligrosa:* plight
*situación trágica:* tragedy
*situado:* situated
*situar:* locate, put
*situar la escena:* set
*situarse:* lie, locate
*sketch:* schtick
*smartphone:* smart phone
*snowboard:* snowboard
*sobaco:* armpit
*sobajar:* run
*soberana:* ruler, sovereign
*soberanía:* sovereignty
*soberano:* ruler, sovereign
*soberbio:* glorious, superb
*sobornar:* bribe
*soborno:* bribe, payoff
*sobrante:* surplus
*sobrar:* spare
*sobras:* scrap
*sobre:* about, above, against, envelope, into, mailer, on, over, top, upon
*sobre aviso:* alert
*sobre franqueado con los datos del destinatario:* stamped addressed envelope
*sobre la pista de:* onto
*sobre pedido:* made to order
*sobre todo:* especially, largely
*sobrecargo:* steward, stewardess
*sobrecoger:* overtake
*sobredosis:* overdose
*sobrellevar:* cope, weather
*sobrenatural:* supernatural

*tarjeta amarilla:* yellow card
*tarjeta bancaria:* bank card
*tarjeta de amonestación:* yellow card
*tarjeta de crédito:* bank card, charge card, credit card
*tarjeta de débito:* debit card
*tarjeta de embarque:* boarding pass
*tarjeta de felicitación:* greeting card
*tarjeta de memoria:* memory card
*tarjeta de red:* network card
*tarjeta para raspar:* scratch card
*tarjeta que funciona como llave electrónica:* key card
*tarjeta roja:* red card
*tarjeta sim (módulo de identificación del suscriptor):* SIM card
*tarjeta telefónica:* phonecard
*tarrina:* tub
*tarro:* mug
*tarta de queso:* cheesecake
*tartamudear:* stammer, stutter
*tartamudeo:* stammer, stutter
*tasa:* rate
*tasa de natalidad:* birth rate
*tasar:* value
*tatuaje:* tattoo
*tatuar:* tattoo
*taxi:* cab, taxi, taxicab
*taxonomía:* taxonomy
*taza:* bowl, cup, toilet
*tazón:* bowl
*té:* tea
*te lo juro:* honest
*té verde:* green tea
*teatral:* theatrical
*teatro:* creative drama, theater
*teatro convencional:* formal theater
*teatro de lectura:* reader's theater
*teatro de marionetas:* puppetry
*teatro de títeres:* puppetry
*teatro del absurdo:* theater of the absurd
*teatro épico:* epic theater
*teatro griego:* Greek theater
*teatro informal:* informal theater
*teatro isabelino:* Elizabethan theater
*teatro musical:* musical theater
*teatro no/nō:* Noh
*techo:* ceiling, roof
*tecla:* key
*teclado:* keyboard
*teclear:* type
*técnica:* technician, technique
*técnica mixta:* mixed media
*técnico:* technical, technician
*tecnología:* technology
*tecnología de la información:* information technology
*tecolote:* owl
*tectónica de placas:* plate tectonics
*tedioso:* tedious, tiresome
*tee:* tee
*teja de pizarra:* slate
*tejado:* roof
*tejemanejes:* goings-on
*tejer:* knit, spin, weave
*tejido:* tissue
*tejido conjuntivo:* connective tissue
*tejido de punto:* jersey
*tejido epitelial:* epithelial tissue
*tejido muscular:* muscle tissue
*tejido nervioso:* nervous tissue
*tela:* cloth, fabric, material
*tela de algodón especial para camisas:* oxford
*tela vaquera:* denim
*telar:* loom
*telaraña:* web
*tele:* telly, TV
*telecomunicación:* telecommunications
*teleférico:* cable car, tram
*telefonear:* phone, telephone
*teléfono:* phone, telephone
*teléfono:* phone, telephone
*teléfono celular:* cellphone, cellular phone, mobile phone
*teléfono celular versátil:* smart phone
*teléfono móvil:* cellphone, cellular phone
*telenovela:* soap, soap opera
*telescopio:* telescope
*telescopio de refracción:* refracting telescope
*televidente:* viewer
*televisar:* televise
*televisión:* set, television, TV
*televisión de circuito cerrado:* CCTV
*televisión digital:* digital television
*televisión oficial:* public television
*televisión realista:* reality TV
*televisor:* television
*televisor digital:* digital television
*telofase:* telophase
*telón:* curtain
*tema:* issue, item, subject, subject matter, theme, thread, topic, topic sentence, track
*tema y variación:* theme and variation
*temblar:* jar, quake, shiver, tremble
*temblor:* earthquake
*temblor (de tierra):* quake
*tembloroso:* shaky
*temer:* dread, fear, scared
*temerario:* daring
*temeroso:* fearful
*temor:* fear, scare
*témpano de hielo:* iceberg
*temperamental:* moody
*temperatura:* fever, temperature
*tempestad:* storm
*tempestuoso:* stormy
*templado:* warm
*temple:* spirit
*templo:* temple
*temporada:* run, season
*temporada de rebajas:* sale
*temporal:* temporary
*temprano:* early
*tenaz:* persistent, stiff, unrelenting
*tendencia:* orientation, tendency, trend
*tendencioso:* biased, loaded
*tender:* hang
*tender a:* tend
*tender la mano:* hold
*tender un puente:* bridge
*tender una trampa:* trap
*tendera:* grocer, shopkeeper, storekeeper
*tenderete:* stall
*tendero:* grocer, shopkeeper, storekeeper
*tendido del sol:* bleachers
*tendón:* tendon
*tenedor:* fork
*tener:* contain, got, have, hold, own
*tenia:* tapeworm
*teniente:* lieutenant
*teñir:* color, dye
*tenis:* sneaker, tennis, trainer
*tensar:* tense
*tensión:* stress, tension
*tensión arterial:* blood pressure
*tensión superficial:* surface tension
*tenso:* tense
*tentación:* lure, temptation
*tentado:* tempted
*tentar:* finger, lure, tempt, touch
*tentativa:* attempt, endeavor
*tentempié:* snack
*tentenpié:* nosh
*tenue:* dim, faint
*teorema binomio:* binomial theorem
*teoría:* theory
*teoría celular:* cell theory
*teoría de la gran explosión:* big bang theory
*teoría de los colores:* color theory
*teoría del big bang:* big bang theory
*teóricamente:* theory
*teórico:* theoretical
*teorizar:* theorize
*terapeuta:* therapist
*terapia:* therapy, treatment
*terapia física:* physical therapy, physiotherapy

*tocar la bola:* bunt
*tocino:* bacon
*tocón:* stump
*todavía:* even, on, still, yet
*todavía más:* further, furthest
*todo:* all, entire, every, everything, full, full-blown, way, whole
*Todo:* completo, integral, all-over
*todo el año:* round, year
*todo el mundo:* everyone
*todo el tiempo:* along, time
*todo en uno:* all-in-one, roll
*todo un:* quite
*todos:* everybody, everyone
*todos los días:* daily
*tofu:* tofu
*toga:* gown, robe
*toldo:* marquee
*tolerado:* unlicensed
*tolerante:* liberal
*tolerar:* endure, stand, stomach, take, tolerate
*toma:* shot
*toma de conciencia:* reality check
*toma del poder político:* takeover
*toma y daca:* give
*tomacorriente:* outlet, socket
*tomando:* on
*tomar:* arrive, catch, cup, drink, get, have, hold, seize, snatch, take
*tomar el pelo:* razz
*tomar en consideración:* account, allowance, consider, consideration
*tomar en cuenta:* assuming, consideration, factor
*tomar en serio:* seriously
*tomar forma:* germinate
*tomar la iniciativa:* initiative
*tomar la ofensiva:* offensive
*tomar la temperatura:* temperature
*tomar las cosas con calma:* easy
*tomar medidas:* act, measure
*tomar nota:* log, note
*tomar parte:* part
*tomar partido por:* side
*tomar por asalto:* storm
*tomar posesión:* install
*tomar prestado:* borrow
*tomar prisionero:* captive
*tomar represalias:* retaliate
*tomar su tiempo:* time
*tomar tiempo:* time
*tomar un atajo:* cut
*tomar una sobredosis de:* overdose
*tomarse la molestia:* trouble
*tomarse las cosas con calma:* slow, stride
*tomárselo con calma:* easy
*tomate:* tomato
*tómelo o déjelo:* take
*tonada:* tune
*tonalidad:* tonality
*tonel:* barrel
*tonelada:* ton
*tonelada (métrica):* metric ton, tonne
*tonificar:* tone
*tono:* key, pitch, shade, tone
*tono de discado:* dial tone
*tono de marcar:* dial tone
*tono menor:* minor key
*tonta:* fool
*tontería:* moonshine, nonsense, stupid
*tonterías:* baloney
*tonto:* dingbat, dumb, fool, foolish, silly, stupid
*top:* top
*toparse con:* encounter, run
*tope:* ceiling, speed bump, top
*tópico:* platitude, ready-made, topic
*toque:* electric shock, finish, touch
*toque de bola:* bunt
*toque de queda:* curfew
*toque final:* finish
*Torá:* Torah
*tórax:* breast, chest, thorax
*torbellino:* rush, waterspout
*torcedura:* strain
*torcer:* bend, buckle, curve, strain, twist, wrench
*torcer el gesto:* screw
*torcerse en espiral:* spiral
*torcido:* crooked
*tordo norteamericano:* robin
*tormenta:* firestorm, storm
*tormenta de nieve:* blizzard
*tormenta eléctrica:* thunderstorm
*tormenta tropical:* tropical storm
*tormentoso:* stormy
*tornado:* tornado
*torneo:* tournament
*torneo de atletismo:* track meet
*tornillo:* bolt, screw
*toro:* bull
*toronja:* grapefruit
*torpe:* awkward, clumsy, geek, klutz, labored, slowpoke
*torre:* tower
*torreja:* French toast
*torrente:* flash flood, rush, stream
*tortilla de huevo:* omelet
*tortitas:* cake
*tortuga:* tortoise, turtle
*tortuga boba:* loggerhead turtle
*tortuga marina:* sea turtle
*tortuga mordedora:* loggerhead turtle
*torturar:* torture
*tos:* cough
*toser:* cough
*tostada:* toast
*tostador:* toaster
*tostar:* brown, toast
*total:* complete, dead, full, implicit, total, utter
*totalidad:* whole
*totalmente:* altogether, entirely, fully, hundred, quite, whole, wholly
*totopos:* nacho
*tour:* tour
*tóxico:* toxic
*toxicómana:* drug addict
*toxicomanía:* substance abuse
*toxicómano:* drug addict
*TQM:* love
*trabajador:* hobo, laborer, worker
*trabajador agrícola:* laborer
*trabajador de la industria automotriz:* autoworker
*trabajador extranjero:* migrant
*trabajador social:* social worker
*trabajadora:* laborer, worker
*trabajadora agrícola:* laborer
*trabajadora de la industria automotriz:* autoworker
*trabajadora extranjera:* migrant
*trabajadora itinerante:* hobo
*trabajadora social:* social worker
*trabajadores:* labor, labor force
*trabajar:* work
*trabajar (de empleado:* oficinista, dependiente o vendedor), clerk
*trabajar con las manos:* labor
*trabajar de/como disc-jockey:* deejay
*trabajar en conjunto:* pull
*trabajar en el jardín:* garden
*trabajar incansablemente:* labor
*trabajar la tierra:* farm
*trabajitos:* odd jobs
*trabajo:* assignment, duty, employment, essay, job, occupation, project, work
*trabajo comunitario:* community service
*trabajo de campo:* legwork
*trabajo de esclavos:* slave labor
*trabajo duro:* labor
*trabajo en equipo:* teamwork
*trabajo innecesario para mantenerse ocupado:* busywork
*trabajo pesado:* grunt work
*trabajo preliminar:* legwork
*trabajo social:* social work
*trabajos forzados:* hard labor
*trabajoso:* labored
*trabar:* jam
*trabar amistad:* friend
*tracción integral:* four-wheel drive
*tracto:* tract

*tribunal de distrito:* district court
*tribunal superior:* superior court
*tributación:* taxation
*tributario:* tributary
*tributo:* tribute
*tricolor:* tricolor
*tridimensional:* three-dimensional
*trifosfato de adenosina:* ATP
*trigésimo:* thirtieth
*trigo:* wheat
*trimestral:* quarterly
*trimestre:* quarter, term, trimester
*trineo:* bobsled, sled
*trino:* song
*trío:* trio
*tripas:* gut
*triple:* triple
*triplicar:* triple
*tripulación:* crew
*tripulado:* manned
*triste:* bleak, lonely, lonesome, sad
*triturador:* garbage disposal
*trituradora:* garbage disposal
*triturar:* crunch, crush
*triunfador:* successful
*triunfante:* victorious
*triunfar:* triumph
*triunfo:* achievement, success, triumph
*triunfo o partido en el que el equipo perdedor no marca tantos:* shutout
*trivial:* petty
*trocito:* chip
*trofeo:* cup, trophy
*tromba:* funnel
*tromba marina:* waterspout
*trombón:* trombone
*trompa:* trunk
*trompa de Falopio:* fallopian tube
*trompeta:* trumpet
*tronar:* flunk, thunder
*tronco:* body, log, trunk
*trono:* throne
*tropa:* troop
*tropas:* troop
*tropel:* flock
*tropezar:* stub, stumble, trip
*tropezar con:* run
*tropezarse con:* run
*tropical:* tropical
*tropismo:* tropism
*troposfera:* troposphere
*tropósfera:* troposphere
*troquelar:* stamp
*trozo:* chunk, fragment, lump, piece, slip
*truco:* trick
*trueno:* clap, thunder
*t-shirt:* T-shirt
*tsunami:* tsunami
*tu:* your
*tú misma:* yourself
*tú mismo:* yourself
*tuberculosis:* TB
*tubería:* pipe, plumbing
*tubería principal:* main
*tubo:* pipe, tube
*tubo de ensayo:* test tube
*tubo de escape:* tailpipe
*tubo de órgano:* pipe
*tubo fluorescente:* fluorescent
*túbulo seminífero:* seminiferous tubule
*tuerca:* nut
*tumba:* grave
*tumbar:* break
*tumbona:* beach chair
*tumbos:* bump, flounder
*tumor:* growth, tumor
*tumulto:* crush
*tundra:* tundra
*túnel:* tunnel
*túnica:* burqa
*turba:* mob, peat
*turbina:* turbine
*turbio:* cloudy, underhand
*turismo:* tourism
*turista:* tourist, traveler
*turnar:* rotate, turn
*turno:* go, shift, turn
*turno de noche:* graveyard shift
*turno nocturno:* graveyard shift
*tus:* your
*tutor:* guardian
*tutora:* guardian
*tuya:* yours
*tuyas:* yours
*tuyo:* yours
*tuyos:* yours

**U**

*ubicación:* location
*ubicado:* set
*ubicar:* locate, trace
*UE:* EU
*ufano:* proud
*úlcera (por decúbito):* bedsore
*últimamente:* lately
*último:* bottom, final, last, later, latest, latter, ultimate
*último modelo:* state-of-the-art
*último suspiro:* gasp
*último toque:* finish
*últimos momentos:* gasp
*ultrajar:* outrage
*ultraje:* outrage
*ultravioleta:* ultraviolet
*umbral:* doorstep, threshold
*un:* a, an, one, some
*un cachito:* bit
*un desastre:* hopeless
*un dineral:* big bucks
*un exceso:* bit
*un gran negocio:* big business
*un momento:* minute
*un paso adelante de:* step
*un pedacito:* bit
*un poco:* bit, little, some
*un poco de:* some
*un poquito:* bit
*un tanto:* somewhat
*un volado:* hit-and-miss
*uña:* fingernail, nail
*una carrera contra el tiempo:* race
*una cosa tras otra:* another
*una especie de:* sort
*una lotería:* hit-and-miss
*una mala racha:* patch
*una persona que hace una llamada telefónica:* caller
*una vez:* once
*una vez que:* once
*una y otra vez:* again
*unánime:* unanimous
*undécimo:* eleventh
*únicamente:* purely
*unicelular:* unicellular
*único:* isolated, one-of-a-kind, one-time, only, sole, unique
*unidad:* unit, unity
*unidad astronómica:* astronomical unit, AU
*unidad de disco:* disk drive, drive
*unidad de disco portátil:* flash drive
*unidad de masa atómica:* atomic mass unit
*unidad de masa atómica.:* amu
*unidad no normalizada:* nonstandard unit
*unido:* united
*unificación:* unification
*unificado:* united
*unificar:* unify
*uniformado:* uniformed
*uniformar:* standardize
*uniforme:* even, gear, uniform
*uniforme de faena:* fatigue
*unilateral:* unilateral
*unión:* link, union
*unión de crédito:* credit union
*Unión Europea:* European Union
*unir:* bind, hook, join, meld, merge, pull, straddle, unite
*unir con cinta adhesiva:* tape
*unir en matrimonio:* marry
*unir fuerzas:* force
*unir los pedazos de:* piece
*unirse a:* join
*unirse en apoyo de:* rally
*unísono:* unison
*unitaria:* Unitarian
*unitario:* Unitarian
*universidad:* college, school, university
*universidad pública:* state university

*universitario:* collegiate
*universo:* universe
*uno a otro:* each
*uno al otro:* another
*uno con otro:* together
*uno de los dos:* one
*uno mismo:* oneself
*uno o dos:* one
*uno que otro:* odd
*uno u otro:* one
*uno y otro:* either
*unos:* some
*unos cuantos:* few
*untar:* spread
*untar mantequilla:* butter
*uranio:* uranium
*Urano:* Uranus
*urbanismo:* city planning, planning
*urbanismo funcional:* smart growth
*urbanismo orgánico:* smart growth
*urbanizado:* built-up
*urbanizar:* develop
*urbano:* urban
*uretra:* urethra
*urgente:* immediate, urgent
*URL:* localizador uniforme de recursos, URL
*urna:* poll
*usable:* usable
*usado:* pre-owned, secondhand, used
*usar:* employ, run, take, use, wear
*usb:* flash drive
*USB:* bus serial universal, USB
*uso:* usage, use, wear
*usted misma:* yourself
*usted mismo:* yourself
*ustedes mismos:* yourself
*usuaria:* user
*usuario:* user
*usuario final:* end user
*usurpar:* usurp
*utensilio:* implement, instrument, tool
*utensilio para hacer palomitas:* popper
*utensilios:* utensil
*útil:* helpful, useful
*utilería:* prop
*utilidad:* profit
*utilizable:* usable
*utilizar:* employ, use, utilize
*utopía:* utopia
*uva:* grape

**V**

*vaca:* cow, pot
*vacaciones:* vacation
*vacacionista:* vacationer
*vacante:* opening, vacancy, vacant
*vaciar:* discharge, empty, pour, tip
*vaciar un lugar y limpiarlo:* clean
*vacilante:* tentative
*vacilar:* hesitate, hover
*vacilar a:* razz
*vacío:* bare, blank, empty, vacant, vacuum, void
*vacuna:* vaccine
*vacunar:* immunize, vaccinate
*vacuno:* dairy
*vacuola:* vacuole
*vagabunda:* hobo
*vagabundo:* hobo
*vagar:* roam, wander
*vago:* dim, hazy, indefinite, vague
*vagón:* car, carriage, coach
*vagón de carga:* freight car
*vagón de equipaje:* baggage car
*vagoneta:* van
*vainilla:* vanilla
*vaivén:* backward, swing
*vajilla:* crockery
*vale:* coupon, voucher
*vale por suspensión o cancelación de un espectáculo:* rain check
*valenciana:* cuff
*valentía:* bravery, valor
*valer:* worth
*valer la pena:* pay, worth
*valeroso:* brave
*valerse por sí mismo:* fend
*Valgame Dios:* goodness
*validar:* validate
*válido:* legitimate, true, valid
*valiente:* brave, courageous, nervy
*valija:* suitcase
*valioso:* important, valuable
*valla:* barrier, fence
*vallas:* hurdle
*valle:* valley
*valle en U:* U-shaped valley
*valle pendiente:* hanging valley
*valor:* backbone, bravery, courage, nerve, value
*valor absoluto:* absolute value
*valor medio:* median
*valor nominal:* face value
*valor pH:* pH
*valoración:* estimate
*valorar:* gauge, value
*valores:* value
*valores de producción:* production values
*valores familiares:* family values
*valores tradicionales:* family values
*valuar:* value
*válvula:* valve
*válvula de escape:* outlet
*vamos:* come, now
*vamos a ver:* see
*vampiro:* vampire
*vandalismo:* vandalism
*vándalo:* punk, vandal
*vanidad:* vanity
*vanidoso:* vain
*vano:* hollow, pointless, vain
*vapor:* steam, vapor
*vapor de agua:* water vapor
*vaporización:* vaporize
*vaporizador:* vaporizer
*vaporizar:* vaporize
*vaquero:* cowboy
*vara:* stick
*variable:* variable
*variable aleatoria:* random variable
*variación:* variation, variety
*variado:* diverse, miscellaneous, varied
*variante:* permutation
*variar:* vary
*variar de... a:* range
*variedad:* brew, choice, range, variety
*varilla:* rod
*vario:* number, various
*varios:* several
*varón:* male
*varonil:* masculine
*vaso:* drink, glass
*vaso (de precipitados):* beaker
*vaso capilar:* lymphatic vessel
*vasto:* large, vast
*vaya:* oh, well, why
*vecina:* neighbor, villager
*vecindad:* vicinity
*vecindario:* neighborhood
*vecino:* neighbor, neighboring, resident, villager
*vector:* vector
*vedar:* ban
*vegetación:* vegetation
*vegetal:* plant
*vegetales:* Plantae
*vegetariano:* vegetarian
*vehemente:* intense
*vehículo:* vehicle
*vehículo con tracción en las cuatro ruedas:* SUV
*vehículo de recreo:* recreational vehicle, RV
*vehículo todo terreno:* SUV
*veinte:* twenty
*vejiga natatoria:* swim bladder
*vela:* candle, sail
*velar:* sit
*velear:* sail
*veleo:* sailing
*velero:* sailboat
*veleta:* wind vane
*vello:* hair

*velo:* veil
*velocidad:* rate, speed
*velocidad de llegada:* terminal velocity
*velocidad de onda:* wave speed
*velocidad final:* terminal velocity
*velocidad promedio:* average speed
*velocidad resultante:* resultant velocity
*velocidades:* gear
*velorio:* wake
*veloz:* fast, quick, rapid-fire, swift
*vena:* vein
*venado:* deer
*vencedor:* victor, victorious
*vencedora:* victor
*vencer:* beat, conquer, defeat, overcome, run, terminate
*vencido:* due, overdue
*venda:* bandage
*vendaje:* bandage, dressing
*vendar:* bandage
*vendaval:* gale
*vendedor:* clerk, sales clerk, salesman, seller, shop assistant, trader
*vendedor ambulante:* vendor
*vendedora:* clerk, seller, shop assistant, trader
*vendedora ambulante:* vendor
*vender:* fetch, get, market, sell, trade
*vender al por menor:* retail
*vender ilegalmente:* push
*vender más barato:* undercut
*venderse todo:* sell
*vendimia:* vintage
*veneno:* poison
*venenoso:* poisonous
*venerar:* worship
*venganza:* in, revenge, vengeance
*vengar:* avenge, retaliate
*venidero:* ahead
*venir:* come
*venir a la mente:* strike
*venir bien:* suit, useful
*venir de:* come
*venir de lo profundo de uno:* deep
*venir desde:* carryover
*venirse abajo:* fall
*venta:* sale
*venta de artículos donados con fines caritativos:* rummage sale
*venta de garage:* garage sale
*venta de garaje:* yard sale
*ventaja:* advantage, edge, merit, plus, upper, virtue
*ventana:* window
*ventas:* business, sale
*ventas por teléfono:* telemarketing
*ventila:* vent
*ventilador:* fan, vent
*ventilar:* air, vent, ventilate
*ventisquero:* drift
*ventosa:* sucker
*ventoso:* windy
*ventrículo:* ventricle
*Venus:* Venus
*ver:* sight
*ver:* hear, look, meet, reflect, see, show, sight, view, watch
*ver hacia un lugar:* look
*ver las cosas color de rosa:* rose-colored
*ver venir:* sight
*veracidad:* truth
*verano:* summer, summer school
*verbal:* verbal
*verbo:* verb
*verbo auxiliar:* auxiliary
*verbo reflexivo:* reflexive verb
*verdad:* truth
*verdaderamente:* real
*verdadero:* full-blown, genuine, proper, real, something, true
*verde:* green
*verduras:* vegetable, veggie
*vereda:* trail
*veredicto:* verdict
*vergonzoso:* disgusting, dishonorable, guilty
*vergüenza:* disgrace, embarrassment, shame
*verificar:* check, sure, verify
*verosímil:* authentic, credible, plausible
*versátil:* versatile
*verse envuelto en:* catch
*verse recompensado:* money
*vérselas con:* reckon
*versículo:* verse
*versión:* version
*versión de las cosas:* story
*versión del director:* director's cut
*versión impresa:* text
*verso:* verse
*versus:* v., versus
*vertebrados:* vertebrate
*vertedero:* dump, landfill
*verter:* pour, tip
*vertical:* sheer, vertical
*verticalista:* top-down
*vertiginoso:* dizzying
*vertir:* tip
*vesícula:* vesicle
*vestíbulo:* hall, lobby
*vestido:* clothed, dress, dressed
*vestido (de):* dressed
*vestido de baño:* swimsuit
*vestido de gala:* gown
*vestigio:* holdover, trace
*vestir:* dress, wear
*vestir informalmente:* dress
*vestuario:* wardrobe
*veta:* grain, streak
*vetar:* veto
*vetear:* streak
*veterana:* veteran
*veterano:* veteran
*veterinaria:* doctor, vet, veterinarian
*veterinario:* doctor, vet, veterinarian
*veto:* veto
*vez:* time
*vía:* rail, railroad, route, track, via
*vía de acceso:* on-ramp
*vía de salida:* off-ramp
*vía férrea:* track
*vía intravenosa:* IV
*Vía Láctea:* Milky Way
*viable:* credible, viable
*viajante:* traveler
*viajar:* get, journey, ride, tour, travel
*viajar en avión:* fly
*viajar en jet:* jet
*viajar todos los días (de la casa al trabajo):* commute
*viaje:* journey, tour, travel, trip, voyage
*viaje de estudio:* field trip
*viaje de ida y vuelta:* round trip
*viaje largo y cansado:* haul
*viaje redondo:* round trip
*viajera:* tourist, traveler
*viajero:* tourist, traveler
*vías respiratorias:* respiratory system
*vibrar:* tremble, vibrate
*vice-:* deputy
*vicegobernador:* lieutenant governor
*vicegobernadora:* lieutenant governor
*viceversa:* vice versa
*viciado (aire):* stuffy
*vicio:* vice
*vicisitudes:* fortune
*víctima:* casualty, victim
*víctima mortal:* fatality
*victoria:* triumph, victory
*victoria arrolladora:* landslide
*victoriana:* Victorian
*victoriano:* Victorian
*victorioso:* victorious
*vid:* vine
*vida:* being, life, lifetime, sweetheart
*vida activa:* working
*vida al aire libre:* outdoors
*vida cotidiana:* daily
*vida de casado:* marriage
*vida de trabajo:* working
*vida laboral:* working
*vida media.:* half-life
*vida o muerte:* death

## SIMPLE PRESENT TENSE

**A. With states, feelings, and perceptions**

The simple present tense describes states, feelings, and perceptions that are true at the moment of speaking.

- The box *contains* six cans. (state)
- Jenny *feels* tired. (feeling)
- I *see* three stars in the sky. (perception)

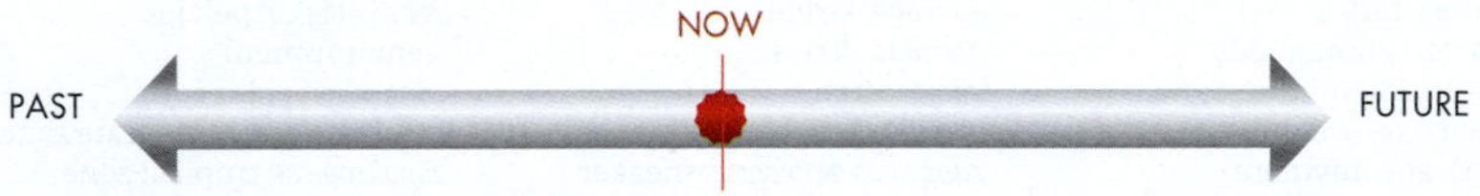


**B. With situations that extend before and after the present moment**

The simple present tense can also describe ongoing activities, or things that happen all the time.

- Tina *works* for a large corporation.
- She *lives* in California.
- Jim *goes* to San Francisco State College.

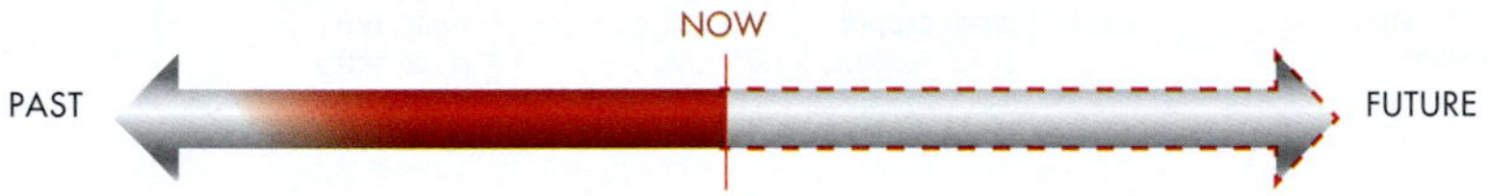


The simple present tense can also describe repeated activities that occur at regular intervals, including people's habits or customs.

- I *exercise* every morning.
- Peter usually *walks* to work.
- Anna often *cooks* dinner.

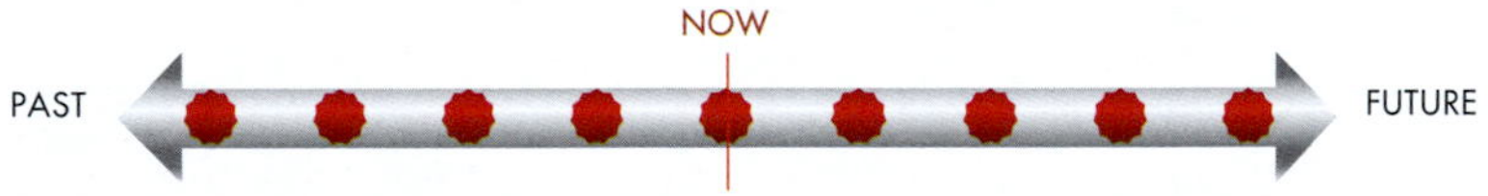


**NOTE:** Notice the adverbs of frequency *every morning*, *usually*, and *often* in these sentences. Other adverbs of frequency used this way include *always*, *sometimes*, *rarely*, and *never*.

**C. With general facts**

The simple present tense describes things that are always true.

- The Empire State Building *is* in New York City.
- The heart *pumps* blood throughout the body.
- Water *boils* at 100° Celsius.

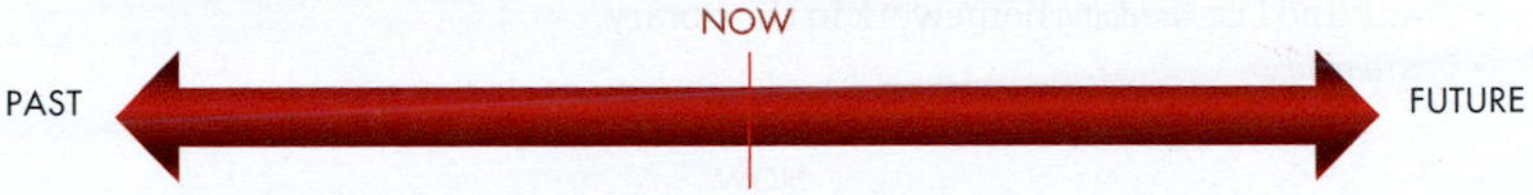


**D. With future activities**

The simple present tense is sometimes used to talk about scheduled events in the future.

- The train *arrives* at 8:00 tonight.
- We *leave* at 10:00 tomorrow morning.
- The new semester *begins* in September.

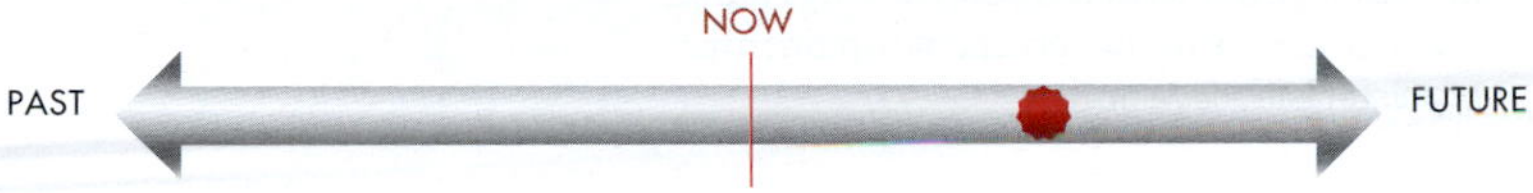

# PRESENT CONTINUOUS TENSE

**A. For actions that are happening right now**

The present continuous tense describes an action that is happening at the moment of speaking. These activities started a short time before and will probably end in the near future.

- Ali *is watching* television right now.
- Frank and Lisa *are doing* homework in the library.
- It *is raining*.

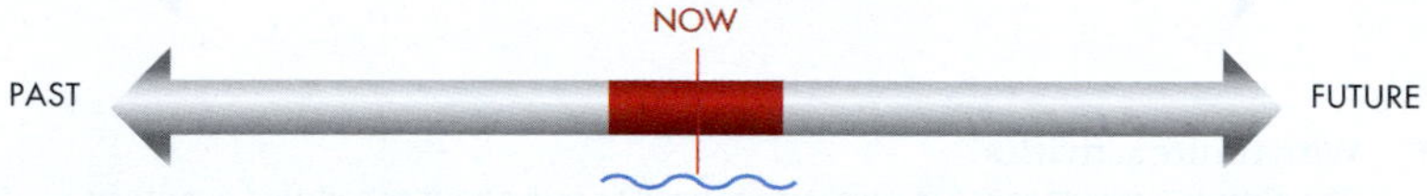


**B. For ongoing activities that aren't necessarily happening at this moment**

The present continuous tense can describe a continuing action that started in the past and will probably continue into the future. However, the action may not be taking place at the exact moment of speaking.

- Mr. Chong *is teaching* a Chinese cooking course.
- We *are practicing* for the soccer championships.
- My sister *is making* a quilt.

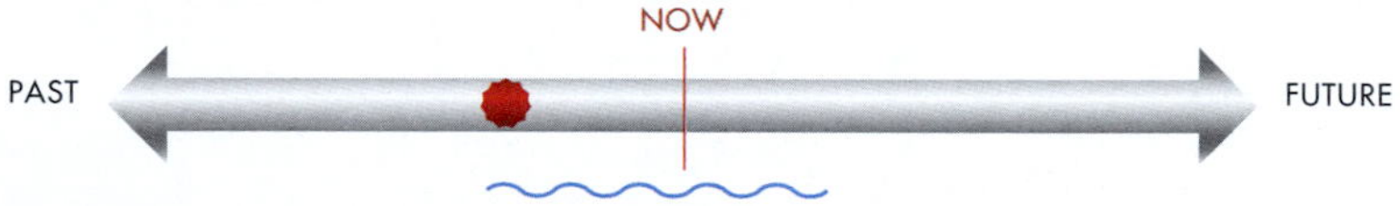


**C. With situations that will happen in the future**

The present continuous tense can also describe planned activities that will happen in the future.

- I *am studying* French next semester.
- We *are having* a party Friday night.
- Raquel *is taking* her driver's test on Saturday.

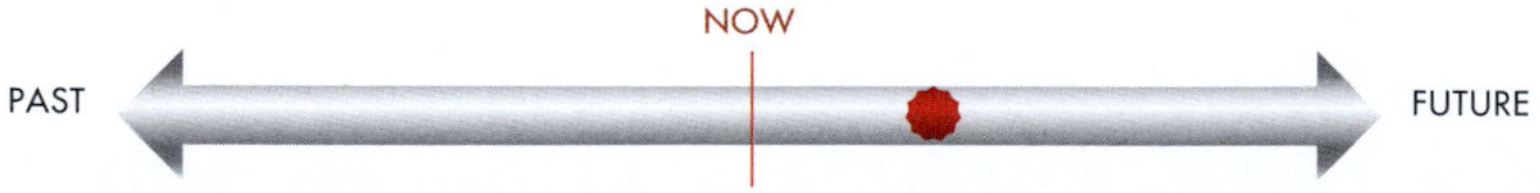


**NOTE:** The use of expressions like *next semester*, *Friday night*, and *on Saturday* help make it clear that the activity is planned and is not happening at the present moment, but will happen in the future.

# Simple past and past continuous

**A. Simple past for one-time and repeated activities that happened in the past**

The simple past tense can describe single or repeated occurrences in the past.

- I *saw* Linda at the post office yesterday.
- Alex *visited* Paris last year.
- We *played* tennis every day last summer. (repeated activity)

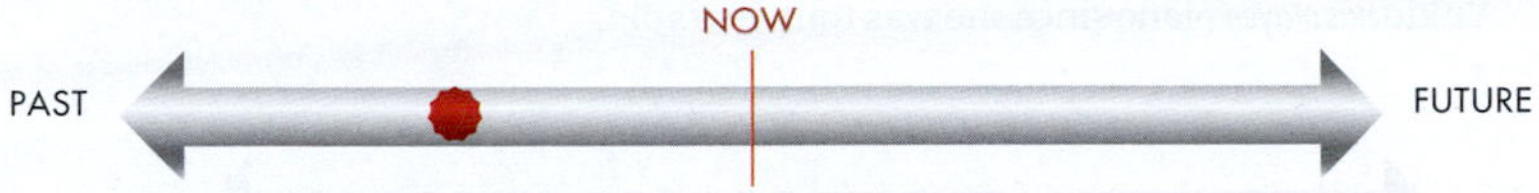


**B. Past continuous for continuous actions in the past**

The past continuous tense can describe ongoing activities that went on for a period of time in the past.

- Anna *was living* in Mexico.
- The baby *was sleeping*.
- Snow *was falling*.

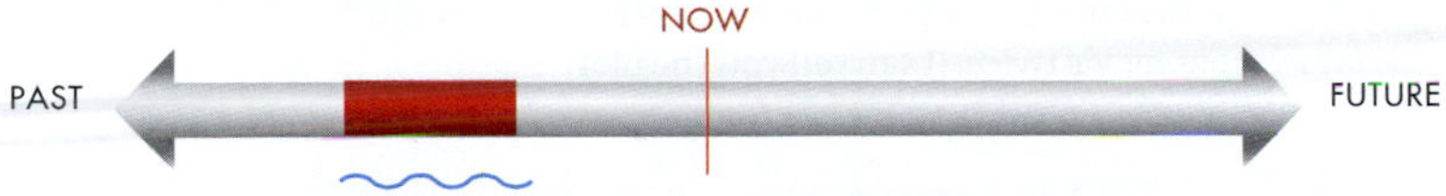


**C. Simple past and past continuous to show a past action that was interrupted**

The simple past tense can describe an action that interrupted an ongoing (past continuous) activity.

- I *met* Alice while I *was living* in New York.
- I *dropped* my purse while I *was crossing* the street.
- The phone *rang* while I *was studying*.

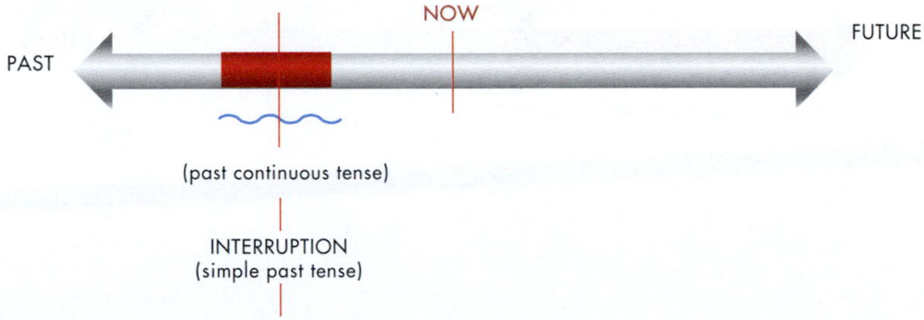

# Present perfect and present perfect continuous

**A. Present perfect for actions or situations that started in the past and continue in the present and possibly the future**

The present perfect tense describes an action that started in the past, continues up to the present, and may continue into the future.

- Lee *has collected* stamps for ten years.
- Carmen *has lived* in this country since 1995.
- Yukio *has played* piano since she was four years old.

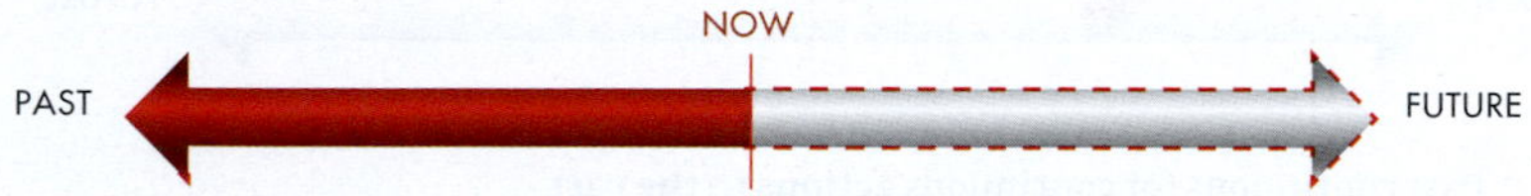


**B. Present perfect for experience in general, without mentioning when something occurred**

The present perfect tense can show that something happened in the past and the results can be seen in the present.

- We *have caught* several big fish. (they are on the table/in the boat)
- Larry *has met* my family. (they know each other)
- I *have seen* that movie twice. (I can tell you the plot)

**C. Present perfect continuous for ongoing actions that started in the past and continue in the present**

The present perfect continuous tense describes an ongoing activity that went on for a period of time in the past and is still going on.

- It *has been raining* for three days. (it's raining now)
- The baby *has been crying* for ten minutes. (she is still crying)
- We *have been waiting* for the bus since 9:00. (we're still waiting)

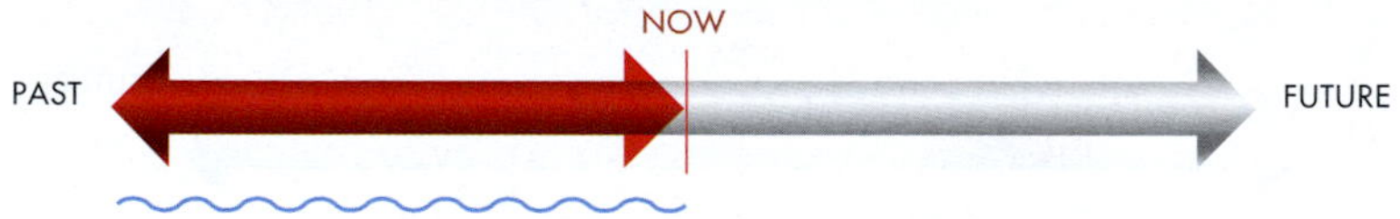

# Simple past vs. present perfect

**A. Simple past for situations that started and ended in the past vs. present perfect for things that started in the past but continue in the moment**

The simple past tense describes an action that started and ended in the past, while the present perfect tense describes situations that started in the past but continue up to the present and maybe into the future.

**Past:** John *worked* as a waiter for two years when he was in college.

**Present perfect:** Carol *has worked* as an engineer since 1998.

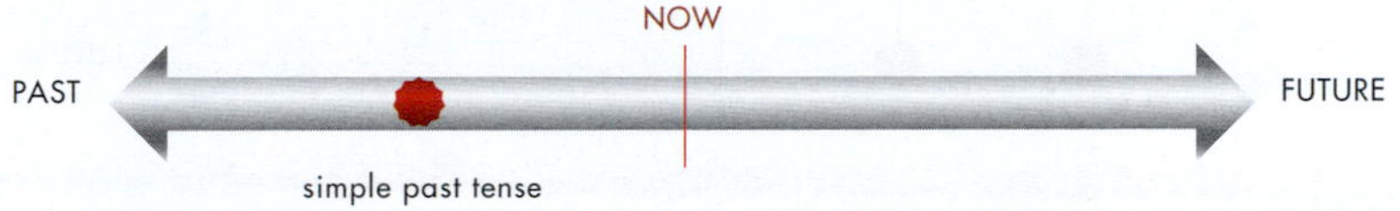


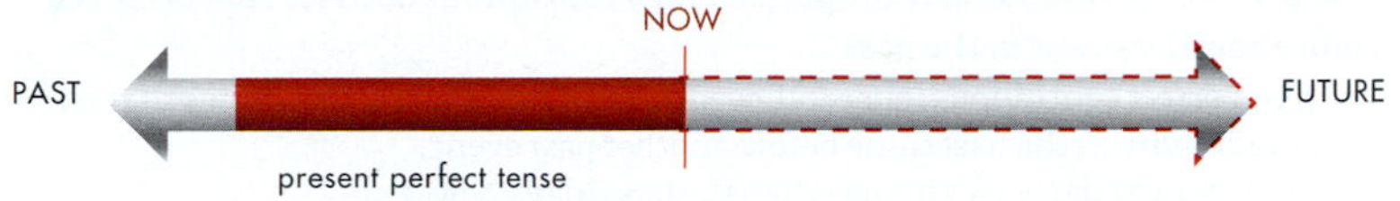


**B. Simple past to emphasize when something happened vs. present perfect to emphasize that something happened, without indicating when**

The simple past emphasizes when something happened, and the present perfect emphasizes its impact on the present.

**Past:** Peter *graduated* from college in 2007. (at a known point in the past: 2007)

**Present perfect:** Alice *has graduated* from college, and is working in the city. (exactly when is unknown)

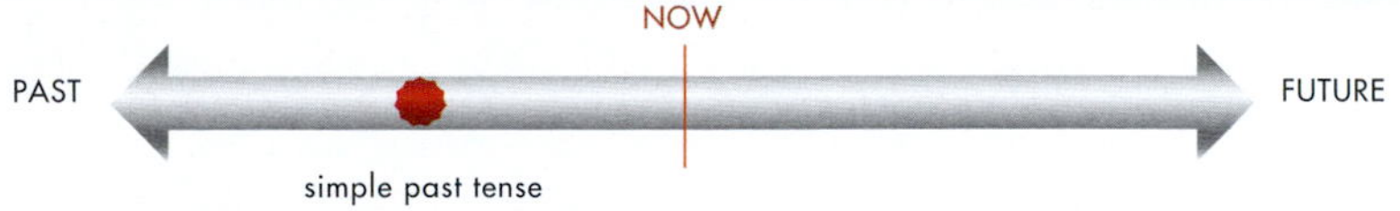

# Simple past, past perfect, and past perfect continuous

**A. Past and past perfect tenses with an activity that occurred before another activity in the past**

Two simple past tenses are used to show a sequence of events in the past.

**Simple past + simple past:** Ali *said* goodbye before he *left*.
I *closed* the door and then *locked* it.

**B. Past perfect continuous and simple past for a continuous activity that occurred before another event in the past**

The past perfect continuous tense followed by the simple past tense shows that an ongoing activity in the past came before another past event.

- We *had been waiting* for two hours when the bus finally *arrived*.
- I *had been thinking* about the problem for days when the answer suddenly *occurred* to me.
- Terry *had been hoping* for the answer that he *got*.

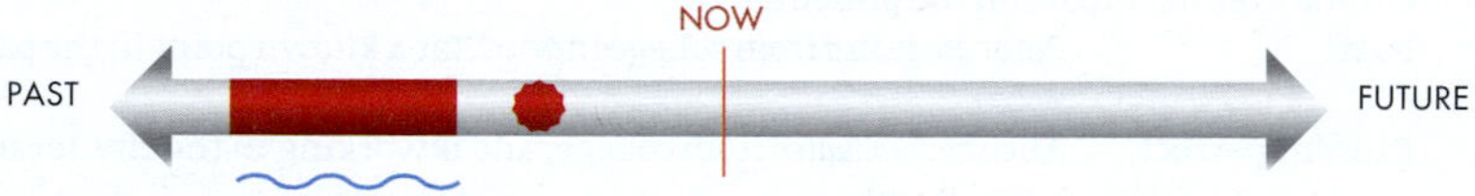

# FUTURE WITH *will* AND *going to*

**A. *Will* or *going to* for simple facts**

Either *will* or *going to* can be used to give information about the future. *Will* is used to give definite information.

- Class *will start* in ten minutes.
- The class *is going* to use a new textbook.
- Your teacher *will be* Mr. Ellis.
- There *is going to be* a final exam.

**B. *Will* or *going to* for prediction**

Either *will* or *going to* can be used to describe things that are likely to happen in the future. *Will* is used when there is evidence that things are likely to happen.

- It *will rain* this afternoon.
- You *are going to love* that movie!
- They *are going to study* a lot the night before the exam.
- They *will* probably *stay up* all night.

**C. *Will* for promises**

*Will* is used to give a guarantee concerning a future action.

- I *will be there* on time.
- Your father and I *will pay for* your college education.
- I *won't tell* anyone.
- I *will save* you a seat.

**D. *Will* for decisions made at the time of speaking**

*Will* is used for decisions made at the time of speaking.

- I *will help* you with your homework.
- We're out of milk. I*'ll go* to the store on my way home.
- I can't talk right now, but I*'ll call* you later.
- Danny *will be* happy to wash your car.

## GRAMMAR

# MODALS *can*, *should/ought to*, *must*, AND *have to*

**A. *Can* and *can't* for ability, permission, and requests**

*Can* and *can't* are used to:

- make statements about things people are and are not able to do.
- describe what people are allowed or not allowed to do.
- make requests.

| | |
|---|---|
| ***Can/can't* for ability:** | Alan *can swim* very well.<br>I *can't run* very fast. |
| ***Can/can't* for permission:** | You *can leave* whenever you want.<br>We *can't use* our dictionaries during the test. |
| ***Can/can't* for requests:** | *Can I* borrow your laptop?<br>*Can't you* turn down the TV? |

**B. *Should* and *ought to* for advice and warnings**

*Should* and *ought to* are used to tell people what to do or what to avoid doing.

| | |
|---|---|
| ***Should/shouldn't* for advice/warnings:** | What *should* I *do*?<br>You *should ask* questions in class.<br>You *shouldn't drive* so fast. |
| ***Ought to* for advice/warnings:** | You *ought to save* more money.<br>He *ought to buy* some new clothes. |

**NOTE:** *Ought to* is almost never used in questions or negative statements.

~~Ought I to go?~~ ~~You ought not see that movie.~~

**C. *Must* and *mustn't* for rules and laws**

*Must* and *mustn't* are used in formal situations to show that something is necessary or prohibited.

| | |
|---|---|
| ***Must* for necessity:** | My doctor told me that I *must lose* weight. |
| ***Must* for obligation:** | Swimmers *must shower* before entering the pool. |
| ***Mustn't* for prohibition:** | You *mustn't be* late to class. |

*Must* and *mustn't* are not always opposites. *Needn't (need not)* expresses a lack of obligation to do something, whereas *mustn't* expresses an obligation not to do something.

**D. *Have to* and *don't have to* for personal obligations**

*Have to* and *don't have to* are used in informal or personal situations to show that something is necessary or not necessary.

| | |
|---|---|
| ***Have to* for necessity:** | I *have to call* my mother tonight.<br>We *have to remember* to buy Jimmy a birthday present. |
| ***Don't/doesn't have to* for lack of necessity:** | You *don't have to return* the pen. You can keep it.<br>Grandpa *doesn't have to comb* his hair. He doesn't have any. |

## Modals *may*, *might*, *could*, and *would*

**A. *May* and *might* to discuss possibility and permission**

*May* and *might* are used to describe future possibilities. *May* is used to give permission in formal situations.

| | |
|---|---|
| ***May* for possibility:** | We're not sure yet, but we *may leave* tomorrow.<br>The weather *may not be* good this weekend. |
| ***Might* for possibility:** | I *might fly* to Florida this weekend, but I probably won't.<br>We both *might get* 100 on the test. |

**NOTE:** Sentences with *might* are less definite than sentences with *may*.

| | |
|---|---|
| ***May* for permission:** | *May I call* you Jimmy?<br>You *may turn in* your paper Monday if it's not ready today.<br>No, you *may not have* my telephone number. |
| ***Might* for permission:** | I wonder if I *might leave* early.<br>When *might* I *need* to see the doctor again? |

**NOTE:** *Can* also works in these sentences, but *may* is more polite and formal. Sentences with *might* are often indirect questions.

**B. *Could* to show possibility, past ability, and to make requests**

*Could* is used to indicate future possibilities, past abilities, and to ask for things.

| | |
|---|---|
| ***Could* for future possibilities:** | The dog *could have* six or seven puppies.<br>The movie *could make* a million dollars if it's really popular. |
| ***Could* for past ability:** | When I was six, I *could* already *speak* two languages.<br>Tina *could walk* when she was only eight months old. |
| ***Could* for requests:** | *Could* you *give* me the remote control?<br>*Could* I *have* another cookie? |

**C. *Would* to ask permission and to make requests**

*Would* is used to request permission and to ask for things.

| | |
|---|---|
| ***Would* to ask permission:** | *Would* you *mind* if I asked your age?<br>*Would* he *mind* if I borrowed his book? |
| ***Would* to make requests:** | *Would* you *give* me a ride home?<br>I *would like* two tickets for the 7:00 show. |

## GRAMMAR

# *Used to*

**A.** ***Used to*** **for statements and questions about past habits or customs**

*Used to* shows that something that was true in the past is no longer true.

- Years ago, children *used to be* more polite.
- I *used to hate* broccoli, but now I like it.
- Children *didn't use to have* TVs in their bedrooms.
- Did girls *use to play* on high school football teams?

**NOTE:** When using the negative and question forms with *used to*, drop the past tense *-d* from the word *used*.

**B.** ***Used to*** **for repeated past events**

*Used to* also shows that something that happened regularly in the past no longer does.

- We *used to go* to the movies every Friday night.
- Taylor *used to visit* his grandmother every Sunday.
- I didn't *use to sleep* late on Saturday, but now I do.
- Did you *use to walk* home every day?

**C.** ***Be used to*** **for statements and questions about things people have become accustomed to**

*Be used to* statements and questions discuss how strange or normal something feels.

- Gail has lived in Chicago and New York. She *is used to living* in big cities.
- I have six brothers and sisters. I *am used to sharing* everything with them.
- Pete *isn't used to doing* homework every night.
- *Are* you *used to* drinking black coffee yet?

**NOTE:** When using the negative and question forms with *be used to*, don't drop the past tense *-d* from the word *used*.

**D.** ***Get used to*** **for statements and questions about becoming accustomed to something new**

*Get used to* statements and questions focus on the process of becoming accustomed to something.

- After three weeks, I *got used to* the noise outside my apartment.
- I *am getting used to* living with three roommates.

**NOTE:** The negative form of *get used to* usually employs the modal *can't* or *couldn't*.

I *can't get used to* getting up at 6:00 AM.

Ellen *couldn't get used to* the cold weather in Chicago.

# Conditionals

## A. Unreal conditions in the present

To describe a conditional situation that is unlikely to happen, use a past form in the conditional clause and the modal *would* or *could* in the main clause.

| Conditional clause | Main clause |
|---|---|
| If I *had* enough money, | I *would buy* a boat. |
| If we *went* to Paris, | we *could visit* the Eiffel Tower. |
| If the traffic *got* any worse, | I *wouldn't drive* my car every day. |
| If Shelia *knew* the answer, | she *would tell* us. |

## B. Possible conditions in the future

To describe a conditional situation that is likely to happen, use a present form in the conditional clause and the future with *will* or the modal *can* in the main clause.

| Conditional clause | Main clause |
|---|---|
| If I *have* enough money, | I *will buy* a boat. |
| If we *go* to Paris, | we *can visit* the Eiffel Tower. |
| If the traffic *gets* any worse, | I *won't drive* my car every day. |
| If Shelia *knows* the answer, | she *will tell* us. |

## C. Unreal conditions in the past

To describe a situation from a future point of view, use the past perfect in the conditional clause and *would have* + the past participle in the main clause.

| Conditional clause | Main clause |
|---|---|
| If we *had known* it was raining, | we *would have taken* our umbrellas. |
| If Roberto *had been* home, | he *would have answered* the phone. |
| If you *had known* my grandmother, | you *would have loved* her. |
| If the movie *hadn't been* boring, | I *wouldn't have fallen* asleep. |

## D. Unreal conditions in the present

When discussing unreal conditions, the *if* clause is sometimes not stated; it is implied.

| Conditional statement or question | Implied statement |
|---|---|
| I *would* never *borrow* money from a friend. | (if I had the opportunity) |
| *Would* you *want* to visit the moon? | (if you had the chance) |
| That *wouldn't work*. | (if you tried it) |
| *Would* he *borrow* your car without telling you? | (if he had the opportunity) |

# Passive voice

## A. Passive statements and questions with *be* + past participle

The passive voice is used when it is not important (or we don't know) who performs the action. The passive can be used with any tense as well as with modals.

| Sentence with passive voice | Verb form |
|---|---|
| The winner *was chosen* last night. | past tense |
| New cures *are being discovered* every day. | present continuous |
| *Will* the renovations *be finished* by next week? | future |
| Aspirin *should be taken* with a full glass of water. | modal *should* |

## B. Passives with an agent

To put the emphasis on the subject of the sentence and also tell who performed the action, use *by* followed by the agent at the end of the sentence.

- The missing girl was finally found *by her older brother.*
- The theory of relativity was discovered *by Albert Einstein.*
- The modern movie camera was invented *by Thomas Edison.*

## C. Passives with *get*

In everyday speech, *get* instead of *be* is often used to form the passive. The verb *do* (instead of the verb *be*) is used for questions and negatives with the *get* passive.

- Most hourly workers *get paid* on Thursday or Friday.
- I *got caught* going 40 miles per hour in a 25 mile per hour zone.
- *Did* anyone *get killed* in the accident?
- Roger *didn't get hired* for the job.

# Reported speech

## A. Shifting verb tenses in reported speech

When reporting someone's exact words, the verb in the noun clause usually moves back one tense. Only the past perfect tense remains the same in reported speech.

| Exact quote | Reported speech | Change in verb tense |
|---|---|---|
| I *am* tired. | He said that he *was* tired. | Simple present to simple past |
| We *are waiting.* | They told me that they *were waiting*. | Present continuous to past continuous |
| I *finished* the book last night. | She said that she *had finished* the book the night before. | Simple past to past perfect |
| We *are enjoying* the good weather. | They reported that they *were enjoying* the good weather. | Past continuous to past perfect continuous |
| I *have lived* here for two years. | He added that he *had lived* here for two years. | Present perfect to past perfect |
| We *had eaten* breakfast before we left the house. | They said that they *had eaten* breakfast before they left the house. | Past perfect remains the same |

## B. Shifting modals in reported speech

Many modals change form in reported speech.

| Exact quote | Reported speech | Change in modal form |
|---|---|---|
| I *can speak* French. | She said that she *could speak* French. | *Can* to *could* |
| We *may need* help. | They said that they *might need* help. | *May* (for possibility) to *might* |
| You *may use* my pencil. | She said that I *could use* her pencil. | *May* (for permission) to *could* |
| I *must make* a phone call. | He said that he *had to make* a phone call. | *Must* to *had to* |
| We *will help* you. | They said that they *would help* me. | *Will* to *would* |
| I *should stop* smoking. | He said that he *should stop* smoking. | *Should* (no change) |
| We *should have left* at 9:00. | They said that they *should have left* at 9:00. | *Should have* (no change) |
| I *could have saved* money with a coupon. | She said that she *could have saved* money with a coupon. | *Could have* (no change) |
| She *must have gone* to bed early. | He said that she *must have gone* to bed early. | *Must have* (no change) |

**C. *Say* vs. *tell* in reported speech**

The passive voice is used when it is not important (or we don't know) who performs the action. The passive can be used with any tense as well as with modals.

- When using *say* with reported speech, an object is not required. (Other verbs that work this way are *add*, *answer*, *explain*, and *reply*.)
- When using *tell* with reported speech, there is always a direct object. (Other verbs that work this way are *inform*, *notify*, *remind*, and *promise*.)

| Exact quote | Reported speech | Direct object |
|---|---|---|
| It is raining. | He *said* that it was raining. | No |
| I was late to class. | She *explained* that she had been late to class. | No |
| I bought a camera at the mall. | He *told me* that he had bought a camera at the mall. | Yes |
| There is a test on Friday. | She *informed the students* that there was a test on Friday. | Yes |

## Comparatives and superlatives

Comparatives and superlatives have several different forms.

**A. With one-syllable adjectives and adverbs**

Add *-er* or *-est*.

| Adjective / Adverb | Comparative / superlative form | Example |
|---|---|---|
| cold | colder | December is *colder* than November. |
| hard | harder | The wind blows *harder* in winter than in summer. |
| short | shortest | December 21 is *the shortest* day of the year. |
| fast | fastest | Summer passes *the fastest* of any season. |

**B. With two-syllable adjectives ending in *-y***

Change the *-y* to *-i* and add *-er* or *-est*.

| Adjective / Adverb | Comparative / superlative form | Example |
|---|---|---|
| easy | easier | Yesterday's assignment was *easier* than today's. |
| busy | busiest | This is the *busiest* shopping day of the year. |

**C. With most adjectives of two or more syllables not ending in *-y***

Use *more* + adjective for comparatives and *the most* + adjective for superlatives.

| Adjective / Adverb | Comparative / superlative form | Example |
|---|---|---|
| famous | more famous | Amy's Pizza is *more famous* than Bennie's Pizza. |
| frequent | most frequent | Amy's has the *most frequent* specials of any pizzeria. |
| expensive | more expensive | Bennie's Pizza is *more expensive* than Amy's. |
| delicious | most delicious | Bennie's makes the *most delicious* pizza in town. |

**D. Irregular comparatives and superlatives**

Some adjectives and superlatives have irregular forms.

| Adjective / Adverb | Comparative / superlative form | Example |
|---|---|---|
| bad | worse, worst | SUVs have *worse* safety records than sedans. |
| good | better, best | Sedans drive *better* than SUVs. |
| much | more, most | An SUV can carry *the most* people. |
| far | farther, farthest | A sedan can go *the farthest* on a tank of gas. |

**E. Comparisons with *as...as***

Use *as . . . as* + adjective or adverb to describe things that are equal, and *not as . . . as* + adjective or adverb to describe inequalities.

| | |
|---|---|
| Adjective | Algebra was *as difficult as* geometry for me. |
| Adjective with negative | However, geometry was*n't as interesting as* algebra. |
| Adverb | I worked *as hard as* anyone else, but I got a C in algebra. |
| Adverb with negative | I did*n't* do *as well as* many other students. |

# Infinitives and Gerunds

A verb (or sometimes an adjective) near the beginning of a sentence determines whether a second verb form should be an infinitive or a gerund. Below are lists of some common main verbs (and adjectives) and the type of verb form that follows each.

**NOTE:** Each list contains several high-frequency items, but the lists are not comprehensive.

**A. Verb + infinitive**

These verbs are followed by an infinitive, not a gerund: *ask, attempt, begin, decide, expect, hope, like, plan, promise, start.*

I *attempted* to start the car.
They *decided* to stay home last night.
We *hope* to save at least $1000 by the end of the year.

**WRONG:** She plans ~~giving~~ a party this weekend.

**B. Causatives + infinitives**

When a person causes something to happen, the causative verb is followed by a direct object plus an infinitive, not a gerund. These causative verbs are followed by an infinitive: *allow, convince, encourage, get, force, persuade, require.*

We *convinced* the teacher to postpone the test until Monday.
The teacher *encouraged* us to study over the weekend.
I *got* my brother to help me with the grammar.

**WRONG:** The teacher required us ~~leaving~~ our dictionaries at home.

**C. Verb + gerund**

These verbs are followed by a gerund, not an infinitive: *avoid, discuss, dislike, enjoy, finish, imagine, practice, quit, recommend, suggest.*

The couple *discussed* having another child.
The children *enjoy* going to the park.
The couple *can't imagine* having four children.

**WRONG:** They avoided ~~to talk~~ about it for a few days.

**D. Preposition + infinitive and preposition + gerund**

An infinitive is the preposition *to* and the base of a verb: *to speak*. Gerunds can be used with other prepositions such as *about*, *at*, *for*, *in*, *of*, and *on*.

I want *to go* on vacation in August.
I never even think *about swimming* in the winter.
This organization plans *on having* a fundraising drive.

**WRONG:** They are responsible for ~~help~~ thousands of animals.
The guests are sorry to ~~leaving~~ the party so early.

## PUNCTUATION

### Apostrophe

- The apostrophe + *s* is used with singular and plural nouns to show possession.

    Jim**'s** computer          the children**'s** toys

    my boss**'** file          the Smiths**'** house [Only the apostrophe is needed when
                               a word ends in *s*.]

- The apostrophe + *s* is used to show ownership.

    Pedro and Ana**'s** CDs [The *'s* on the second name shows they own the CDs together.]

    Pedro**'s** and Ana**'s** hats [The *'s* on both names shows they each own different hats.]

- The apostrophe is used in contractions.

    I**'**m (= I am)          they**'**ll (= they will)

### Brackets

- Brackets are used to add your own information in quoted material.

    Jason said, "This is a good time [meaning today] for us to start looking for a new apartment."

- Brackets with three dots are used when you omit words from a quotation.

    Jason said, "This is a good time [. . .] for a new apartment."

### Colon

- The colon is used with clock time.

    11:30          9:45

- The colon is used to introduce a list.

    Jean enjoys all kinds of physical activity: hiking, playing tennis, and even cleaning house.

- The colon is used in the salutation of a business letter.

    Dear Ms. Mansfield:

### Comma

- Commas are used with dates and addresses.

    Monday, December 1, 1964    16 Terhune Street, Teaneck, NJ 07666

- Commas are used after introductory phrases or clauses.

    After finishing school, she joined the Navy.

- Commas are used to set off items in a series.

    They served pizza, pasta, lasagna, and salad at the party.

- Commas are used to set off added information in nonrestrictive phrases or clauses.

    Mr. Karas, my sister's teacher, comes from Greece.

    Rita, who almost never misses class, is absent today.

- Commas are used in the salutation in informal correspondence and at the close of a letter.

    Dear Grace,          Sincerely yours,

### Dash

- Dashes are used instead of commas when the added information contains commas.

  The school offers several math courses—algebra, geometry, and trigonometry—as well as a wide variety of science classes.

### Exclamation Point

- An exclamation point is used after a word or group of words to show strong feeling.

  Stop! Don't run over that cat!

### Hyphen

- Hyphens appear in compound words or numbers.

  mother-in-law twenty-one
- Hyphens are used to divide words at the end of a line.

  After Mrs. Leander finished exploring all her options, she decided the best plan was to return home and start out tomorrow.

### Parentheses

- Parentheses are used with nonessential information and with numbers and letters in lists.

  We left the party (which started at 7:00 P.M.) sometime after midnight.

  My requirements are (1) a room with a view and (2) a working air conditioner.

### Period

- A period is used at the end of any sentence that is not a question or an exclamation.

  Rutgers University offers a wide variety of social science courses.
- A period is used after many abbreviations.

  Mr. etc. P.M. Jr. i.e.

### Question Mark

- A question mark is used after a word or sentence that asks a question.

  What? Did you say you don't have a ride home?

### Quotation Marks

- Quotation marks are used to set off a direct quotation but not an indirect quotation.

  Smithers said, "Homer, you must go home now."

  Smithers said Homer must go home.
- Quotation marks are used with the titles of short written material such as poems, short stories, chapters in books, songs, and magazine articles.

  My favorite poem is "A Spider Sewed at Night" by Emily Dickinson.

### Semicolon

- The semicolon is used to link independent clauses when there is no coordinating conjunction (such as *and, but, or, nor,* or *for*) between them.

  Some people like country music; some people don't.

- The semicolon is also used to link independent clauses before a conjunctive adverb (such as *however, furthermore*).

  Some people like country music; however, other people dislike it intensely.

### Slash

- The slash separates alternatives.

  and/or
- The slash divides numbers in dates, and divides numerators and denominators in fractions.

  the memorable date 9/11/01 Ten and 50/100 dollars
- The slash is used when quoting lines of poetry to show where each line ends.

  My favorite lines from this poem are, "She slept beneath a tree / remembered but by me."

## CAPITALIZATION

### Capitalize proper nouns and proper adjectives.

- Main words in titles: **G**one with the **W**ind
- People: **J**ohn **L**ennon, **P**élé
- Cities, nations, states, nationalities, and languages: **I**stanbul, **T**urkey, **C**alifornia, **B**razil, **A**merican, **S**panish
- Geographical items: **M**ekong **R**iver, **M**ount **O**lympus, **C**entral **P**ark
- Companies and organizations: **F**ord **M**otor **C**ompany, **H**arvard **U**niversity, **N**ational **O**rganization for **W**omen
- Departments and government offices: **E**nglish **D**epartment, **I**nternal **R**evenue **S**ervice
- Buildings: the **E**mpire **S**tate **B**uilding
- Trademarked products: **K**leenex tissue, **S**cotch tape
- Days, months, and holidays: **T**uesday, **J**anuary, **R**amadan
- Some abbreviations without periods: **AT&T, UN, YMCA**
- Religions and related words: **H**indu, **B**ible, **M**uslim
- Historical periods, events, and documents: **C**ivil **W**ar, **D**eclaration of **I**ndependence
- Titles of people: **S**enator Clinton, **P**resident Lincoln, **M**s. Tanaka, **D**r. Lee
- Titles of printed matter: *Collins COBUILD Inglés/Español Diccionario para Estudiantes Latinoamericanos: Collins COBUILD Student's Dictionary of American English, English/Spanish*

## ITALICIZATION

### In handwritten or typed copy, italics are shown by underlining.

**Use italics for the following types of material.**

- Words or phrases you wish to emphasize.

  Is this *really* your first time in an airplane?

  She feeds her dog *T-bone steak.* [It's best not to use italics for emphasis very often.]

- A publication that is not part of a larger publication.

  *The Daily News* (newspaper)

  *The Sun Also Rises* (book)

  *Newsweek* (magazine)

  *Titanic* (movie)

- Foreign words in an English sentence.

  The first four numbers in Turkish are *bir, iki, üc, dört.*

  The French have a saying: *Plus ça change . . .*

- Letters used in algebraic equations.

  $E = mc^2$

## SPELLING

### Frequently Misspelled Words

**People sometimes confuse the spelling of the following words:**

accept, except
access, excess
advice, advise
affect, effect
aisles, isles
alley, ally
already, all ready
altar, alter
altogether, all together
always, all ways
amoral, immoral
angel, angle
ask, ax
assistance, assistants
baring, barring, bearing
began, begin
believe, belief
board, bored
break, brake
breath, breathe
buy, by, bye
capital, capitol
censor, censure, sensor
choose, chose
cite, site, sight
clothes, cloths
coarse, course
complement, compliment
conscience, conscious
council, counsel
diary, dairy
decent, descent, dissent
desert, dessert
device, devise
discreet, discrete
dyeing, dying
elicit, illicit
emigrate, immigrate
envelop, envelope
fair, fare
faze, phase
fine, find
formerly, formally
forth, fourth
forward, foreword
gorilla, guerrilla
have, of
hear, here
heard, herd
heroin, heroine
hole, whole
holy, wholly
horse, hoarse
human, humane
its, it's
later, latter
lay, lie
lead, led
lessen, lesson
lightning, lightening
lose, loose
marital, martial
maybe, may be
miner, minor
moral, morale
of, off
passed, past
patience, patients
peace, piece
personal, personnel
plain, plane
pray, prey
precede, proceed
presence, presents
principle, principal
prophecy, prophesy
purpose, propose
quiet, quit, quite
raise, rise
respectfully, respectively
right, rite, write
road, rode
sat, set
sense, since

| | | |
|---|---|---|
| shown, shone | throne, thrown | were, wear, where, we're |
| stationary, stationery | to, too, two | which, witch |
| straight, strait | tract, track | who's, whose |
| than, then | waist, waste | your, you're |
| their, there, they're, there're | weak, week | |
| threw, through, thorough | weather, whether | |

**NOTE:** The following summary will answer many spelling questions. However, there are many more rules and also many exceptions. Always check your dictionary if in doubt.

### *Ei* and *ie*

There is an old saying that says: "I before *e*, except after *c*, or when pronounced like *ay* as in *neighbor* and *weigh*."

- *I* before *e*: br**ie**f, n**ie**ce, f**ie**rce
- *E* before *i* after the letter *c*: rec**ei**ve, conc**ei**t, **cei**ling
- *E* before *i* when pronounced like *ay*: **ei**ght, w**ei**ght, th**ei**r

### Prefixes

A prefix changes the meaning of a word but no letters are added or dropped.

- usual, **un**usual
- interested, **dis**interested
- use, **re**use

### Suffixes

- Drop the final *e* on the base word when a suffix beginning with a vowel is added.
  drive, driv**ing**   combine, combin**ation**
- Keep the silent *e* on the base word when a suffix beginning with a consonant is added.
  live, live**ly**   safe, safe**ly** [Exceptions: truly, ninth]
- If the base word (1) ends in a final consonant, (2) is a one-syllable word or a stressed syllable, and (3) the final consonant is preceded by a vowel, double the final consonant.
  hit, hi**tt**ing   drop, dro**pp**ing
- Change a final *y* on a base word to *i* when adding any suffix except *-ing*.
  day, da**i**ly   try, tr**i**ed   BUT: play, pla**ying**

## GRAMMAR

### Conjunctions

Conjunctions are words that connect words, phrases, or clauses.

### Coordinating Conjunctions

The coordinating conjunctions are: *and, but, for, nor, or, so, yet*

- Sarah **and** Michael
- on vacation **for** three weeks
- You can borrow the book from a library **or** you can buy it at a bookstore.

### Correlative Conjunctions

Correlative conjunctions are used in pairs.

The correlative conjunctions are: *both . . . and, either . . . or, neither . . . nor, not only . . . but also, whether . . . or*

- **Neither** Sam **nor** Madeleine could attend the party.
- The singer was **both** out of tune **and** too loud.
- Oscar **not only** ate too much, **but also** fell asleep at the table.

### Subordinating Conjunctions

Subordinating conjunctions are used to connect a subordinate clause to a main clause.

- Antonia sighed loudly **as if** she were really exhausted.
- Uri arrived late **because** his car broke down.

**Here is a list of subordinating conjunctions:**

| | | | | |
|---|---|---|---|---|
| after | before | no matter how | than | where |
| although | even if | now that | though | wherever |
| as far as | even though | once | till | whether |
| as if | how | provided that | unless | while |
| as soon as | if | since | until | why |
| as though | in as much as | so that | when | |
| because | in case | supposing that | whenever | |

### Conjunctive Adverbs

Two independent clauses can be connected using a semicolon, plus a conjunctive adverb and a comma. The conjunctive adverb often comes right after the semicolon.

- Kham wanted to buy a car**; however,** he hadn't saved up enough money.
- Larry didn't go right home**; instead,** he stopped at the health club.

Some conjunctive adverbs can appear in different positions in the second clause.

- Kham wanted to buy a car; he hadn't, **however,** saved up enough money.
- Larry didn't go right home; he stopped at the health club **instead.**

**Here is a list of conjunctive adverbs:**

| | | | | |
|---|---|---|---|---|
| also | finally | indeed | nevertheless | then |
| anyhow | furthermore | instead | next | therefore |
| anyway | hence | likewise | otherwise | thus |
| besides | however | meanwhile | similarly | |
| consequently | incidentally | moreover | still | |

### Transitional Phrases

If all the sentences in a passage begin with subject + verb, the effect can be boring. To add variety, use a transitional phrase, followed by a comma, at the beginning of some sentences.

- Rita needed to study for the test. **On the other hand,** she didn't want to miss the party.
- Yuki stayed up all night studying. **As a result,** he overslept and missed the test.

**Here is a list of transitional phrases:**

| | | |
|---|---|---|
| after all | by the way | in fact |
| as a result | even so | in other words |
| at any rate | for example | on the contrary |
| at the same time | in addition | on the other hand |

### Common Prepositions

A preposition describes a relationship to another part of speech; it is usually used before a noun or pronoun.

- Sancho was waiting **outside** the club.
- I gave the money **to** him.

**Here is a list of common prepositions:**

| | | | | | |
|---|---|---|---|---|---|
| about | at | by | in | out | to |
| above | before | concerning | inside | outside | toward |
| across | behind | despite | into | over | under |
| after | below | during | lie | past | unlike |
| against | beneath | down | near | regarding | until |
| among | beside | except | of | round | up |
| around | between | for | off | since | upon |
| as | beyond | from | on | through | with |

### Phrasal Prepositions

**Here is a list of phrasal prepositions:**

| | | | |
|---|---|---|---|
| according to | by means of | in front of | out of |
| along with | by reason of | in lieu of | up to |
| apart from | by way of | in place of | with reference to |
| as for | due to | in regard to | with regard to |
| as regards | except for | in spite of | with respect to |
| as to | in addition to | instead of | with the exception of |
| because of | in case of | on account of | |

## DOCUMENTATION

Some high school teachers and most college instructors require one of three formats (APA, Chicago, or MLA) to document the information you use in research papers and essays. The following pages compare and contrast the highlights of these three styles.

### APA Style (American Psychological Association style)

1. General Endnote Format

   Title the page "References." Double-space the page and arrange the names alphabetically by authors' last names, the date in parentheses, followed by the rest of the information about the publication.

2. Citation for a Single Author

   Moore, (1992). *The care of the soul*. New York: HarperPerennial.

3. Citation for Multiple Authors

   List the last names first followed by initials and use the "&" sign before the last author.

   Spinosa, C., Flores, F., & Dreyfus, H.L. (1997). *Disclosing new worlds: Entrepreneurship, democratic action, and the cultivation of solidarity*. Cambridge, MA: MIT Press.

4. Citation for an Editor as Author

   Wellwood, J. (Ed.). (1992). *Ordinary magic: Everyday life as a spiritual path*. Boston: Shambhala Publications.

5. Citation for an Article in a Periodical

   List the author, last name first, the year and month (and day if applicable) of the publication. Then list the title of the article (not underlined), the name of the publication (followed by the volume number if there is one) and the page number or numbers.
   Gibson, S. (2001, November). Hanging wallpaper. *This Old House*, 77.

6. Citation of Online Materials

   Provide enough information so that readers can find the information you refer to. Try to include the date on the posting, the title, the original print source (if any), a description of where you found the information, and the date you found the material.

   Arnold, W. (April 26, 2002). "State senate announces new tax relief." *Seattle Post-Intelligencer*. Retrieved May 1, 2002, from http://seattle.pi.nwsource.com/printer2/index.asp?ploc=b

7. General In-text Citation Format

   Include two pieces of information: the last name of the author or authors of the work cited in the References and the year of publication.
   (Moore, 1992).

**Chicago Style** (from *The Chicago Manual of Style*)

1. General Endnote Format

   Title the page "Notes." Double-space the page. Number and indent the first line of each entry. Use full authors names, not initials. Include page references at the end of the entry.

2. Citation for a Single Author

   Thomas Moore, *The Care of the Soul* (New York: HarperPerennial, 1992), 7–9.

3. Citation for Multiple Authors

   Charles Spinosa, Ferdinand Flores, and Hubert L. Dreyfus, *Disclosing New Worlds: Entrepreneurship, Democratic Action, and the Cultivation of Solidarity* (Cambridge: MIT Press, 1997), 66.

4. Citation for an Editor as Author

   John Wellwood, ed. 1992. *Ordinary Magic: Everyday Life as Spiritual Path* (Boston: Shambhala Publications).

5. Citation for an Article in a Periodical

   List the author, last name first. Then put the title of the article in quotation marks, the name of the publication, the volume number (if one is given), the month, and the page number or numbers.

   Gibson, Stephen, "Hanging Wallpaper," *This Old House* 53 (2001): 77.

6. Citation of Online Materials

   Number and indent each entry and provide enough information so that readers can find the information you refer to. Try to include the author (first name first), the date on the posting (in parentheses), the title, the original print source (if any), a description of where you found the information, the URL, and the date you found the material (in parentheses).

   1. William Arnold, "State Senate Announces New Tax Relief," *Seattle Post-Intelligencer*, April 26, 2002, http://seattle.pi.nwsource.com/printer2/index.asp?ploc=b

7. General In-text Citation Format

   Number all in-text notes. The first time you cite a work within the text, use all the information as shown in 2. above. When citing the same work again, include only the last name of the author or authors and the page or pages you refer to.

   (Moore, 8)

## MLA Style (Modern Language Association style)

1. General Endnote Format

   Title the page "Works Cited." Double-space the page and arrange the names alphabetically by authors' last names, followed by the rest of the information about the publication as shown below.

2. Citation for a Single Author

   Moore, Thomas. *The Care of the Soul*. New York: HarperPerennial, 1992.

3. Citation for Multiple Authors

   List the first author's names in the same order as on the title page. List only the first author's last name first.

   Spinosa, Charles, Ferdinand Flores, and Hubert L. Dreyfus. *Disclosing New Worlds: Entrepreneurship, Democratic Action, and the Cultivation of Solidarity.* Cambridge: MIT, 1997.

4. Citation for an Editor as Author

   Wellwood, John, ed. *Ordinary Magic: Everyday Life as Spiritual Path*. Boston; Shambhala, 1992.

5. Citation for an Article in a Periodical

   List the author (last name first), the title of the article (using quotation marks), the title of the magazine (with no period), the volume number, the date (followed by a colon), and the page number.

   Gibson, Stephen. "Hanging Wallpaper." *This Old House* 53 (2001): 77.

6. Citation of On-line Materials

   Provide enough information so that readers can find the information you refer to. Try to include the date on the information, the title, the original print source (if any), the date you found the material, and the URL (if possible).

   Arnold, William. "State Senate Announces New Tax Relief." *Seattle Post-Intelligencer* 26 Apr. 2002 http://seattle.pi.nwsource.com/printer2/index.asp?ploc=b

7. General In-text Citation Format

   Do not number entries. When citing a work listed in the "Works Cited" section, include only the last name of the author or authors and the page or pages you refer to. (Moore 7-8)

## BLOCK LETTER FORMAT

Using the block letter format, there are no indented lines.

| | |
|---|---|
| **Return address** | 77 Lincoln Avenue<br>Wellesley, MA 02480 |
| **Date** | May 10, 2009 |
| **Inside address** | Dr. Rita Bennett<br>Midland Hospital Senior Care Center<br>5000 Poe Avenue<br>Dayton, OH 45414 |
| **Salutation** | Dear Dr. Bennett: |
| **Body of the letter** | I am responding to your advertisement for a dietitian in the May 5 edition of the *New York Times*. I graduated from Boston University two years ago. Since graduation, I have been working at Brigham and Women's Hospital and have also earned additional certificates in nutritional support and diabetes education.<br><br>I am interested in locating to the Midwest and will be happy to arrange for an interview at your convenience. |
| **Complimentary close** | Sincerely, |
| **Signature** | *Daniel Chin* |
| **Typed name** | Daniel Chin |

## INDENTED LETTER FORMAT

Using the indented format, the return address, the date, and the closing appear at the far right side of the paper. The first line of each paragraph is also indented.

| | |
|---|---|
| **Return address** | 77 Lincoln Avenue<br>Wellesley, MA 02480 |
| **Date** | May 15, 2009 |
| **Inside address** | Dr. Rita Bennett<br>Senior Care Center<br>5000 Poe Avenue<br>Dayton, OH 45414 |
| **Salutation** | Dear Dr. Bennett: |
| **Body of the letter** | It was a pleasure to meet you and learn more about the programs offered at the Senior Care Center. I appreciate your taking time out to show me around and introduce me to the staff.<br>I am excited about the possibility of working at the Senior Care Center and I look forward to talking with you again soon. |
| **Complimentary close** | Sincerely, |
| **Signature** | *Daniel Chin* |
| **Typed name** | Daniel Chin |

## RESUMES

### Successful resume strategies

- **Length:** One page
- **Honesty:** Never say something that is untrue
- **Inclusiveness:** Include information about your experience and qualifications. You do not have to include your age, religion, marital status, race, or citizenship. It is not necessary to include a photo.

### Heading

Include name, address, e-mail, and phone number.

### Objective

Include your goals or skills or both.

### Skills

Include any skills that you have that may be helpful in the job that you are applying for.

### Experience

Describe the jobs you've held. Include your accomplishments and awards. Use positive, action-oriented words with strong verbs. Use present-tense verbs for your current job and past-tense verbs for jobs you've had in the past. Include the job titles that you've held.

### Education

Include schools attended. If you are a college graduate, don't include high school. List degrees with most recent first.

### Interests

This is not required, but can help a potential employer see you as a well-rounded person.

### Sample Resume

There are several different acceptable resume formats. Here is one example.

**Maria Gonzales**
9166 Main Street, Apartment 3G
Los Angeles, CA 93001
gonzales@email.com
213-555-9878

| | |
|---|---|
| **OBJECTIVE:** | Experienced manager seeks a management position in retail sales |
| **EXPERIENCE:** | |
| **Assistant Director of Retail** | |
| 2005 – Present | Shopmart, Los Angeles, CA<br>Manage relationships with vendors to complete orders, create accounts, and resolve issues. Maintain inventory and generate monthly inventory reports. Plan weekly promotions. Communicate with all retail employees to improve product knowledge and selling techniques. Implemented new customer service procedures. |
| **Server** | |
| 2005 – Present | Chuy's Grill, Santa Monica, CA<br>Greet and seat guests. Bus tables. Answer phones and take and prepare in-house, phone, or fax orders. Train new and existing employees. Awarded Employee of the Month five times for exceeding company expectations for quality and service. |
| **Store Supervisor** | |
| 1999 – 2005 | Impact Photography Systems, Waco, TX<br>Oversaw daily operations, including customer and employee relations, counter sales, inventory management, maintaining store appearance, banking transactions, and equipment maintenance. Managed, trained, and scheduled staff of 35. |
| **SKILLS:** | Fluent in English and Spanish. Expert in MS Word and Excel. |
| **EDUCATION:** | |
| **Associate of Arts Degree** | |
| 1997 – 2000 | Los Angeles Community College, Los Angeles, CA<br>Coursework in business management, marketing, studio art, communication, psychology, and sociology. |
| **Study Abroad** | |
| 2000 – 2001 | University of Valencia, Valencia, Spain<br>Coursework in Spanish and international business. |
| **INTERESTS:** | Backpacking, playing softball, and volunteering as a tutor for Literacy First. |

## PROOFREADING MARKS

Teachers often use the following correction abbreviations and symbols on students' papers.

| Problem area | Symbol | Example |
|---|---|---|
| agreement | **agr** | He **go** to work at 8:00. |
| capital letters | **cap** | the United states |
| word division or hyphenation | **div** **hy** | disorienta**ti** **-on** |
| sentence fragment | **frag** | **Where she found the book.** |
| grammar | **gr** | It's the **bigger** house on the street. |
| need italics | **ital** | I read it in **The Daily News.** |
| need lower case | **lc** | I don't like **P**eanut **B**utter. |
| punctuation error | **p** | Where did you find that coat. |
| plural needed | **pl** | I bought the **grocery** on my way home. |
| spelling error | **sp** | Did you rec**ie**ve my letter yet? |
| wrong tense | **t** | I **see** her yesterday. |
| wrong word | **ww** | My family used to **rise** corn and wheat. |
| need an apostrophe | ⋎ | I **don't** know her name. |
| need a comma | ‸ | However, we will probably arrive on time. |
| delete something | ⌇ | We had the most best meal of our lives. |
| start a new paragraph | ¶ | . . . since last Friday. ¶ Oh, by the way . . . |
| transpose words | ∽ | They live on the floor first. |

## 1. Greetings, Introductions, and Leave-taking

### Greeting someone you know
Hello.
Hi.
Hey.
Morning.
How's it going? [Informal]
What's up? [Informal]

### Greeting someone you haven't seen for a while
It's good to see you again.
It's been a long time.
How long has it been?
Long time no see! [Informal]
You look great! [Informal]
So what have you been up to? [Informal]

### Greeting someone you don't know
Hello.
Good morning.
Good afternoon.
Good evening.
Hi, there! [Informal]

### Saying goodbye
Goodbye.
Bye.
Bye-bye.
See you.
See you later.
Have a good day.
Take care.
Good night. [Only when saying goodbye]

### Introducing yourself
Hi, I'm Tom.
Hello, my name is Tom.
Excuse me.
We haven't met.
My name is Tom. [Formal]
I saw you in (science) class.
I met you at Jane's party.

### Introducing other people
Have you two met?
Have you met Maria?
I'd like you to meet Maria.
There's someone I'd like you to meet.
Let me introduce you to Maria.

**You:** This is my friend Maria.
**Ali:** Glad to meet you, Maria.
**You:** Maria, this is Ali.
**Maria:** Nice to meet you, Ali.

I've been wanting to meet you.
Tom has told me a lot about you.

### Greeting guests
Welcome.
Oh, hi.
How are you?
Please come in.
Glad you could make it.
Did you have any trouble finding us?
Can I take your coat?
Have a seat.
Please make yourself at home.

**You:** Can I get you something to drink?
**Guest:** Yes, please.
**You:** What would you like?
**Guest:** I'll have some orange juice.

What can I get you to drink?
Would you like some . . . ?

### Saying goodbye to guests
Thanks for coming.
Thanks for joining us.
I'm so glad you could come.
It wouldn't have been the same without you.
Let me get your things.
Stop by anytime.

## 2. Having a Conversation

### Starting a conversation
Nice weather, huh?
Aren't you a friend of Jim's?
Did you see last night's game?
What's your favorite TV show?
So, what do you think about (the situation in Europe)?
So how do you like (your new car)?
Guess what I did last night.

### Showing that you are listening
Uh-huh.
Right.
Exactly.
Yeah.
OK . . .
I know what you mean.

### Giving yourself time to think
Well . . .
Um . . .
Uh . . .
Let me think.
Just a minute.

**Other:** We should ride our bikes.
**You:** It's too far. And, I mean . . ., it's raining and we're already late.

### Checking for comprehension
Do you see what I mean?
Are you with me?
Does that make sense?

### Checking for agreement
Don't you agree?
So what do you think?
We have to (act fast), you know?

### Expressing agreement
You're right.
I couldn't agree with you more.
Good thinking! [Informal]
You said it! [Informal]
You're absolutely right.
Absolutely! [Informal]

### Expressing disagreement
I'm afraid I disagree.
Yeah, but . . .
I see your point, but . . .
That's not true.
You must be joking! [Informal]
No way! [Informal]

### Asking someone to repeat something
Excuse me?
Sorry?
I didn't quite get that.
Could you repeat that?
Could you say that again?
Say again? [Informal]

### Interrupting someone
Excuse me.
Yes, but (we don't have enough time).
I know, but (that will take hours).
Wait a minute. [Informal]
Just hold it right there! [Impolite]

### Changing the topic
By the way, what do you think about (the new teacher)?
Before I forget, (there's a free concert on Friday night).
Whatever . . . (Did you see David's new car?)
Enough about me. Let's talk about you.

### Ending a conversation
It was nice talking with you.
Good seeing you.
Sorry, I have to go now.

## 3. Using the Telephone

### Making personal calls
Hi, this is David.
Is this Alice?
Is Alice there?
May I speak with Alice, please? [Formal]
I work with her.
We're in the same science class.
Could you tell her I called?
Would you ask her to call me?

### Answering personal calls
Hello?
Who's calling, please?
Oh, hi David. How are you?
I can't hear you.
Sorry, we got cut off.
I'm in the middle of something.
Can I call you back?
What's your number again?
Listen. I have to go now.
It was nice talking to you.

### Answering machine greetings
You've reached 212-555-6701.
Please leave a message after the beep.
Hi, this is Carlos.
I can't take your call right now.
Sorry I missed your call.
Please leave your name and number.
I'll call you back as soon as I can.

### Answering machine messages
This is Magda. Call me back when you get a chance. [Informal]
Call me back on my cell.
I'll call you back later.
Talk to you later.
If you get this message before 11:00, please call me back.

### Making business calls
Hello. This is Andy Larson.
I'm calling about . . .
Is this an OK time?

### Answering business calls
Apex Electronics. Rosa Baker speaking. [Formal]
Hello, Rosa Baker.
May I help you?
Who's calling, please?

**Caller:** May I speak with Mr. Hafner, please?
**Businessperson:** This is he.

**Caller:** Mr. Hafner, please.
**Businessperson:** Speaking.

### Talking to an office assistant
Extension 716, please.
Customer Service, please.
May I speak with Sheila Spink, please?
She's expecting my call.
I'm returning her call.
I'd like to leave a message for Ms. Spink.

### Making appointments on the phone
**You:** I'd like to make an appointment to see Ms. Spink.
**Assistant:** How's 11:00 on Wednesday?
**You:** Wednesday is really bad for me.
**Assistant:** Can you make it Thursday at 9:00?
**You:** That would be perfect!
**Assistant:** OK. I have you down for Thursday at 9:00.

### Special explanations
I'm sorry. She's not available.
Is there something I can help you with?
Can I put you on hold?
I'll transfer you to that extension.
If you'll leave your number, I'll have Ms. Spink call you back.
I'll tell her you called.

## 4. Interviewing for a Job

### Small talk by the interviewer
Thanks for coming in today.
Did you have any trouble finding us?
How was the drive?
Would you like a cup of coffee?
Do you happen to know (Terry Mendham)?

### Small talk by the candidate
What a great view!
Thanks for arranging to see me.
I've been looking forward to meeting you.
I spent some time exploring the company's web site.
My friend, Dale, has worked here for several years.

### Getting serious
OK, shall we get started?
So, anyway . . .
Let's get down to business.

### General questions for a candidate
Tell me a little about yourself.
How did you get into this line of work?
How long have you been in this country?
How did you learn about the opening?
What do you know about this company?
Why are you interested in working for us?

### General answers to an interviewer
I've always been interested in (finance).
I enjoy (working with numbers).
My (uncle) was (an accountant) and encouraged me to try it.
I saw your ad in the paper.
This company has a great reputation in the field.

### Job-related questions for a candidate
What are your qualifications for this job?
Describe your work experience.
What were your responsibilities on your last job?
I'd like to hear more about (your supervisory experience).

**Interviewer:** Have you taken any courses in (bookkeeping)?
**You:** Yes, I took two courses in business school and another online course last year.

What interests you about this particular job?
Why do you think it's a good fit?
Why did you leave your last job?
Do you have any experience with (HTML)?
Would you be willing to (travel eight weeks a year)?
What sort of salary are you looking for?

### Describing job qualifications to an interviewer
In (2000), I started working for (Booker's) as a (sales rep).
After (two years), I was promoted to (sales manager).
You'll notice on my resume that (I supervised six people).
I was responsible for (three territories).
I was in charge of (planning sales meetings).
I have experience in all areas of (sales).
I helped implement (online sales reports).
I had to (contact my reps) on a daily basis.
I speak (Spanish) fluently.
I think my strong points are (organization and punctuality).

### Ending the interview
I'm impressed with your experience.
I'd like to arrange a second interview.
When would you be able to start?
You'll hear from us by (next Wednesday).
We'll be in touch.

## 5. Presentations

### Introducing yourself

Hello, everyone. I'd like to thank you all for coming.
Let me tell you a little bit about myself.
My name is (Rita Nazario).
I am president of (Catco International).
Hi. I'm (Ivan Wolf) from (Peekskill Incorporated).
Two years ago (I started out as a salesperson at Peekskill).
Today (I supervise the West Coast sales team).

### Introducing someone else

This is (Tina Gorman), a (woman) who needs no introduction.
(Tina) is one of America's best-known (lawyers).
(She) is going to talk to us about (car insurance).
Let's give (her) a warm welcome.
We are lucky to have with us today (Barry Rogers).
As you know, (he) is (the president of Ranger Incorporated).
It gives me great pleasure to present (Barry Rogers).
And so without further ado, I'd like to present (Barry Rogers).

### Stating the purpose

Today I'd like to talk to you about (managing your money).
Today I'm going to show you how to (save a lot of money).
I'll begin by (outlining the basics).
Then I'll (go into more detail).
I'll tell you (everything you need to know about savings accounts).
I'll provide an overview of (different types of investments).
I also hope to interest you in (some safe investments).
I'll list (the three biggest mistakes people make).
By the end, you'll (feel like an expert).

### Relating to the audience

Can everyone hear me?
Raise your hand if you need me to repeat anything.
Please stop me at any point if you have a question.
How many people here (plan to continue their education)?
If you're like me, (you haven't saved up enough money).
We all know what that's like, don't we?
Does this ring a bell?
Don't you hate it when (people tell you what you should do)?

### Citing sources

According to the *New York Times*, . . .
A study conducted by Harvard University showed that . . .
Recent research shows that . . .
Medical researchers have discovered that . . .
Peter Butler said, and I quote, ". . ."
I read somewhere that . . .
(The federal government) released a report stating that . . .

### Making transitions

I'd like to expand on that before we move on.
The next thing I'd like to talk about is . . .
Now let's take a look at . . .
Moving right along . . .
To sum up what I've said so far, . . .
Now let's move on to the question of . . .
Now that you have an overview, let's look at some of the specifics.
Recapping the main points, . . .
I'm afraid we have to move on.

### Emphasizing important points

I'd like to emphasize that . . .
Never forget that . . .
This is a key concept.
The bottom line is . . .
If you remember only one thing I've said today, . . .
I can't stress enough the importance of . . .

### Using visuals

Take a look at (the chart on the screen).
I'd like to draw your attention to (the poster over there).
You'll notice that . . .
Pay special attention to the . . .
If you look closely, you'll see that . . .
So what does this tell us?

### Closing

And in conclusion, . . .
Let's open the floor to questions.
It's been a pleasure being with you today.

## 6. Agreeing and Disagreeing

### Agreeing
Yeah, that's right.
I know it.
I agree with you.
You're right.
That's true.
I think so, too.
That's what I think.
Me, too.
Me neither.

### Agreeing strongly
You're absolutely right!
Definitely!
Certainly!
Exactly!
Absolutely!
Of course!
I couldn't agree more.
You're telling me! [Informal]
You said it! [Informal]

### Agreeing weakly
I suppose so.
Yeah, I guess so.
It would seem that way.

### Remaining neutral
I see your point.
You have a point there.
I understand what you're saying.
I see what you mean.
I'd have to think about that.
I've never thought about it that way before.
Maybe yes, maybe no.
Could be.

### Disagreeing
No, I don't think so.
I agree up to a point.
I really don't see it that way.
That's not what I think.
I agree that (going by car is faster), but . . .
But what about (the expense involved)?
Yes, but . . .
I know, but . . .
No, it wasn't. / No, they don't. / etc.

**Other person:** We could save a lot of money by taking the bus.
**You:** <u>Not really</u>. It would cost almost the same as driving.

### Disagreeing strongly
I disagree completely.
That's not true.
That is not an option.
Definitely not!
Absolutely not!
You've made your point, but . . .
No way! [Informal]
You can't be serious. [Informal]
You've got to be kidding! [Informal]
Where did you get that idea? [Impolite]
Are you out of your mind! [Impolite]

### Disagreeing politely
I'm afraid I have to disagree with you.
I'm not so sure.
I'm not sure that's such a good idea.
I see what you're saying, but . . .
I'm sure many people feel that way, but . . .
But don't you think we should consider (other alternatives)?

## 7. Interrupting, Clarifying, Checking for Understanding

### Informal interruptions
Ummm.
Sir? / Ma'am?
Just a minute.
Can I stop you for a minute?
Wait a minute! [Impolite]
Hold it right there! [Impolite]

### Formal interruptions
Excuse me, sir / ma'am.
Excuse me for interrupting.
Forgive me for interrupting you, but . . .
I'm sorry to break in like this, but . . .
Could I interrupt you for a minute?
Could I ask a question, please?

### Asking for clarification—Informal
What did you say?
I didn't catch that.
Sorry, I didn't get that.
I missed that.
Could you repeat that?
Could you say that again?
Say again?
I'm lost.
Could you run that by me one more time?
Did you say . . . ?
Do you mean . . . ?

### Asking for clarification—Formal
I beg your pardon?
I'm not sure I understand what you're saying.
I can't make sense of what you just said.
Could you explain that in different words?
Could you please repeat that?
Could you go over that again?

### Giving clarification—Informal
I'll go over it again.
I'll take it step by step.
I'll take a different tack this time.
Stop me if you get lost.
OK, here's a recap.
Maybe this will clarify things.
To put it another way, . . .
In other words, . . .

### Giving clarification—Formal
Let me put it another way.
Let me give you some examples.
Here are the main points again.
I'm afraid you didn't understand what I said.
I'm afraid you've missed the point.
What I meant was . . .
I hope you didn't think that . . .
I didn't mean to imply that . . .
I hope that clears things up.

### Checking for understanding
Do you understand now?
Is it clearer now?
Do you see what I'm getting at?
Does that help?
Is there anything that still isn't clear?
What other questions do you have?

**Speaker:** What else?
**Listener:** I'm still not clear on the difference between a preposition and a conjunction.

Now explain it to me in your own words.

## 8. Apologizing

### Apologizing for a small accident or mistake

Sorry.
I'm sorry.
Excuse me.
It was an accident.
Pardon me. [Formal]
Oops! [Informal]
My mistake. [Informal]
I'm terrible with (names).
I've never been good with (numbers).
I can't believe I (did) that.

### Apologizing for a serious accident or mistake

I'm so sorry.
I am really sorry that I (damaged your car).
I am so sorry about (damaging your car).
I feel terrible about (the accident).
I'm really sorry but (I was being very careful).
I'm sorry for (causing you a problem).
Please accept my apologies for . . . [Formal]
I sincerely apologize for . . . [Formal]

### Apologizing for upsetting someone

I'm sorry I upset you.
I didn't mean to make you feel bad.
Please forgive me. [Formal]
I just wasn't thinking straight.
That's not what I meant to say.
I didn't mean it personally.
I'm sorry. I'm having a rough day.

### Apologizing for having to say *no*

I'm sorry. I can't.
Sorry, I never (lend anyone my car).
I wish I could say *yes*.
I'm going to have to say *no*.
I can't. I have to (work that evening).
Maybe some other time.

### Responding to an apology

Don't worry about it.
Oh, that's OK.
Think nothing of it. [Formal]
Don't mention it. [Formal]

**Other person:** I'm afraid I lost the pen you lent me.
**You:** No big thing.

It doesn't matter.
It's not important.
Never mind.
No problem.
It happens.
Forget it.
Don't sweat it. [Informal]
Apology accepted. [Formal]

### Showing regret

I feel really bad.
It won't happen again.
I wish I could go back and start all over again.
I don't know what came over me.
I don't know what to say.
Now I know better.
Too bad I didn't . . .
It was inexcusable of me. [Formal]
It's not like me to . . .
I hope I can make it up to you.
That didn't come out right.
I didn't mean to take it out on you.

### Sympathizing

This must be very difficult for you.
I know what you mean.
I know how you're feeling.
I know how upset you must be.
I can imagine how difficult this is for you.

## 9. Suggestions, Advice, Insistence

### Making informal suggestions
Here's what I suggest.
I know what you should do.
Why don't you (go to the movies with Jane)?
What about (having lunch with Bob)?
Try (the French fries next time).
Have you thought about (riding your bike to work)?

### Accepting suggestions
Thanks, I'll do that.
Good idea!
That's a great idea.
Sounds good to me.
That's a plan.
I'll give it a try.
Guess it's worth a try.

### Refusing suggestions
No. I don't like (French fries).
That's not for me.
I don't think so.
That might work for some people, but . . .
Nawww. [Informal]
I don't feel like it. [Impolite]

### Giving serious advice—Informal
Listen!
Here's the plan.
Take my advice.
Take it from one who knows.
Take it from someone who's been there.
Here's what I think you should do.
Hey! Here's an idea.
How about (waiting until you're 30 to get married)?
Don't (settle down too quickly).
Why don't you (see the world while you're young)?
You can always (settle down later).
Don't forget—(you only live once).

### Giving serious advice—formal
Have you ever thought about (becoming a doctor)?
Maybe it would be a good idea if you (went back to school).
It looks to me like (Harvard) would be your best choice.
If I were you, I'd study (medicine).
In my opinion, you should (consider it seriously).
Be sure to (get your application in early).
I always advise people to (check that it was received).
The best idea is (to study hard).
If you're really smart, you'll (start right away).

### Accepting advice
You're right.
Thanks for the advice.
That makes a lot of sense.
I see what you mean.
That sounds like good advice.
I'll give it a try.
I'll do my best.
You've given me something to think about.
I'll try it and get back to you.

### Refusing advice
I don't think that would work for me.
That doesn't make sense to me.
I'm not sure that would be such a good idea.
I could never (become a doctor).
Thanks for the input.
Thanks, but no thanks. [Informal]
You don't know what you're talking about. [Impolite]
I think I know what's best for myself. [Impolite]
Back off! [Impolite]

### Insisting
You have to (become a doctor).
Try to see it my way.
I know what I'm talking about.
If you don't (go to medical school), I won't (pay for your college).
I don't care what you think. [Impolite]

## 10. Describing Feelings

### Happiness
I'm doing great.
This is the best day of my life.
I've never been so happy in my life.
I'm so pleased for you.
Aren't you thrilled?
What could be better?
Life is good.

### Sadness
Are you OK?
Why the long face?
I'm not doing so well.
I feel awful.
I'm devastated.
I'm depressed.
I'm feeling kind of blue.
I just want to crawl in a hole.
Oh, what's the use?

### Fear
I'm worried about (money).
He dreads (going to the dentist).
I'm afraid to (drive over bridges).
She can't stand (snakes).
This anxiety is killing me.
He's scared of (big dogs).
How will I ever (pass Friday's test)?
I have a phobia about (germs).

### Anger
I'm really mad at (you).
They resent (such high taxes).
How could she (do) that?
I'm annoyed with (the neighbors).
(The noise of car alarms) infuriates her.
He was furious with (the children).

### Boredom
I'm so bored.
There's nothing to do around here.
What a bore!
Nothing ever happens.
She was bored to tears.
They were bored to death.
I was bored stiff.
It was such a monotonous (movie).
(That TV show) was so dull.

### Disgust
That's disgusting.
Eeew! Yuck! [Informal]
I hate (raw fish).
How can you stand it?
I almost vomited.
I thought I'd puke. [Impolite]
I don't even like to think about it.
How can you say something like that?
I wouldn't be caught dead (wearing that dirty old coat).

### Compassion
I'm sorry.
I understand what you're going through.
Tell me about it.
How can I help?
Is there anything I can do?
She is concerned about him.
He worries about the children.
He cares for her deeply.
My heart goes out to them. [Old-fashioned]

### Guilt
I feel terrible that I (lost your mother's necklace).
I never should have (borrowed it).
I feel so guilty!
It's all my fault.
I blame myself.
I make a mess of everything.
I'll never forgive myself.

## TEXTING ABBREVIATIONS

| | |
|---|---|
| 1 | used to replace "*-one*": *NE1* = anyone |
| 2 | **to** or **too**: *it's up 2 U* = it's up to you; *me 2* = me too<br>used to replace "**to-**": *2day* = today |
| 2DAY | **today** |
| 2MORO | **tomorrow** |
| 2NITE | **tonight** |
| 4 | **for**: *4 U* = for you<br>used to replace "**-fore**": *B4* = before |
| 411 | **information**: *TNX 4 the 411* |
| 8 | used to replace "**-ate**" or "**-eat**": *GR8* = great; *C U L8R* = see you later |
| 86 | discard, get rid of |
| AFAIK | **as far as I know** |
| B | **be**: used to replace "**be-**" in other words: *B4* = before |
| B4 | **before** |
| B4N | **bye for now** |
| BRB | **be right back** |
| BTW | **by the way** |
| C | **see**: *C U 2moro* = see you tomorrow |
| CID | **consider it done** |
| CU | **see you** |
| CUL8R | **call you later** |
| D8 | **date** |
| EZ | **easy** |
| FWIW | **for what it's worth**: used for saying that someone may or may not be interested in what you have to say |
| FYI | **for your information**: used as a way of introducing useful information |
| GR8 | **great** |
| G2G | **got to go** |
| HHIS | **hanging head in shame**: used for showing that you are embarassed |

| | |
|---|---|
| IB | **I'm back** |
| IYSS | **if you say so** |
| K | **OK** |
| L8 | **late** |
| L8R | **later**: *CUL8R* =see you later |
| LOL | **laughing out loud**: used for showing that you think something is funny |
| MSG | **message** |
| MYOB | **mind your own business**: for telling people not to ask questions about something that you do not want them to know about |
| NE | **any** |
| NE1 | **anyone** |
| NO1 | **no one** |
| NETHING | **anything** |
| OIC | **Oh, I see** |
| OTOH | **on the other hand** |
| PCM | **please call me** |
| PLS | **please** |
| prolly | **probably** |
| R | **are**: *RU free 2nite* = Are you free tonight? |
| RUCMNG | **Are you coming?** |
| RUOK? | **Are you OK?** |
| SPK | **speak** |
| SRY | **sorry** |
| THNQ | **thank you**: *THNQ for visiting my home page.* |
| THX/TX | **thanks**: *THX 4 the info.* |
| TTUL/TTYL | **talk to you later** |
| U | **you**: *CUL8R* = see you later |
| URW | **You're welcome.** |
| W8 | **wait** |
| WAN2 | **want to** |
| WRK | **work** |
| XLNT | **excellent** |
| YR | **your** |
| ZZZZ | **sleeping** |

## Emoticons Horizontal →

<table>
<tr><td>:-)</td><td>smiling; agreeing</td></tr>
<tr><td>:-D</td><td>laughing</td></tr>
<tr><td>|-)</td><td>hee hee</td></tr>
<tr><td>|-D</td><td>ho ho</td></tr>
<tr><td>‘-) or ;-)</td><td>winking; just kidding</td></tr>
<tr><td>:*)</td><td>clowning</td></tr>
<tr><td>:-(</td><td>frowning; sad</td></tr>
<tr><td>:(</td><td>sad</td></tr>
<tr><td>:’-(</td><td>crying and really sad</td></tr>
<tr><td>>:-< or :-||</td><td>angry</td></tr>
<tr><td>:-@</td><td>screaming</td></tr>
<tr><td>:-V</td><td>shouting</td></tr>
<tr><td>:-p or :-r</td><td>sticking tongue out</td></tr>
<tr><td>|-O</td><td>yawning</td></tr>
<tr><td>: *</td><td>kiss</td></tr>
<tr><td>((((name))))</td><td>hug</td></tr>
<tr><td>@-{----</td><td>rose</td></tr>
<tr><td><3</td><td>heart</td></tr>
<tr><td></3</td><td>broken heart</td></tr>
</table>

## Emoticons Vertical ↓

<table>
<tr><td>(^_^)</td><td>smiling</td></tr>
<tr><td>(`_^) or (^_~)</td><td>winking</td></tr>
<tr><td>(>_<)</td><td>angry, or ouch</td></tr>
<tr><td>(-_-)zzz</td><td>sleeping</td></tr>
<tr><td>\(^o^)/</td><td>very excited (raising hands)</td></tr>
<tr><td>(-_-;) or (^_^’)</td><td>nervous, or sweatdrop (embarrassed; semicolon can be repeated)</td></tr>
<tr><td>d-_-b title.mp3</td><td>listening to music, labelling title afterwards</td></tr>
<tr><td>\m/</td><td>rocker fingers</td></tr>
<tr><td>\m/(>_<)\m/</td><td>rocker dude</td></tr>
</table>

# Defining Vocabulary

a
abandon
ability
able
abortion
about
above
abroad
absence
absolute
absolutely
abuse
academic
accept
acceptable
accepted
access
accident
accompany
accord
according to
account
accurate
accuse
achieve
achievement
acid
acknowledge
acquire
acquisition
acre
across
act
action
active
activist
activity
actor
actress
actual
actually
ad
add
addition
address
adequate
adjust
administration
admire
admit
adopt
adult
advance
advanced
advantage
advertise
advice
advise
adviser
advocate
affair
affect
afford
afraid
after
afternoon
afterward
again
against
age
agency
agenda
agent
aggressive
ago
agree
agreement
agriculture
ahead
ahead of
aid
AIDS
aim
air
aircraft
air force
airline
airport
alarm
album
alcohol
alert
alive
all
allegation
alliance
allied
allow
all right
ally
almost
alone
along
alongside
already
also
alter
alternative
although
altogether
always
amateur
amazing
ambassador
ambition
amendment
among
amount
analysis
analyst
ancient
and
anger
angle
angry
animal
anniversary
announce
announcement
annual
another
answer
antique
anxiety
anxious
any
anybody
anymore
anyone
anything
anyway
anywhere
apart
apartment
apparent
apparently
appeal
appear
appearance
apple
application
apply
appoint
appointment
appreciate
approach
appropriate
approval
approve
April
area
aren't
argue
argument
arise
arm
armed
armed forces
army
around
arrange
arrangement
arrest
arrival
arrive
art
article
artist
as
Asian
aside
ask
aspect
assault
assembly
assess
asset
assist
assistance
assistant
associate
association
assume
assumption
assured
at
athlete
atmosphere
attach
attack
attempt
attend
attention
attitude
attorney
attract
attractive
auction
audience
audio
August
aunt
author
authority
automatic

autumn
available
avenue
average
avoid
await
award
aware
away
awful
baby
back
background
backing
bad
badly
bag
bake
balance
ball
ballot
ban
band
bank
banker
banking
bar
bare
barely
bargain
barrel
barrier
base
baseball
basic
basically
basis
basketball
bass
bat
bath
bathroom
battle
bay
be
beach
bean
bear
bearing
beat
beautiful
beauty
because
become
bed
bedroom
beer
before
begin
beginning
behalf
behave
behavior
behind
being
belief
believe
bell
belong
below
belt
bend
beneath
benefit
beside
besides
best
bet
better
between
beyond
bid
big
bike
bill
billion
bird
birth
birthday
bit
bite
bitter
black
blame
blast
blind
block
blood
bloody
blow
blue
board
boat
body
boil
bomb
bond
bone
book
boom
boost
boot
border
bore
born
borrow
boss
both
bother
bottle
bottom
bound
bowl
box
boy
brain
branch
brand
brave
bread
break
breakfast
breast
breath
breathe
breed
bridge
brief
bright
brilliant
bring
broad
broadcast
broker
brother
brown
brush
budget
build
building
bunch
burden
burn
burst
bury
bus
business
businessman
busy
but
butter
button
buy
by
bye
cabinet
cable
cake
call
calm
camera
camp
campaign
can
cancel
cancer
candidate
cap
capable
capacity
capital
captain
caption
capture
car
carbon
card
care
career
careful
caring
carrier
carry
case
cash
cast
castle
casualty
cat
catch
category
Catholic
cause
cautious
cave
CD
cease
ceasefire
celebrate
cell
center
central
century
ceremony
certain

certainly
chain
chair
chairman
challenge
chamber
champion
championship
chance
chancellor
change
channel
chaos
chapter
character
characteristic
charge
charity
chart
charter
chase
chat
cheap
check
cheer
cheese
chemical
chest
chicken
chief
child
childhood
chip
chocolate
choice
choose
chop
Christian
Christmas
church
cigarette
cinema
circle
circuit
circumstance
cite
citizen
city
civil
civilian
civil war
claim
clash
class
classic
classical
clean
clear
clever
client
climate
climb
clinic
clock
close
clothes
clothing
cloud
club
coach
coal
coalition
coast
coat
code
coffee
cold
collapse
colleague
collect
collection
collective
college
colonel
color
colored
column
combat
combination
combine
come
comedy
comfort
comfortable
coming
command
commander
comment
commentator
commerce
commercial
commission
commissioner
commit
commitment
committee
common
communicate
communication
communism
community
company
compare
compared
comparison
compensation
compete
competition
competitive
competitor
complain
complaint
complete
complex
complicated
component
comprehensive
compromise
computer
concede
concentrate
concentration
concept
concern
concert
concession
conclude
conclusion
concrete
condemn
condition
conduct
conference
confidence
confident
confirm
conflict
confront
confrontation
Congress
connection
conscious
consciousness
consequence
conservative
consider
considerable
consideration
considering
consist
consistent
constant
constitution
construction
consult
consultant
consumer
contact
contain
contemporary
content
contest
context
continent
continue
contract
contrast
contribute
contribution
control
controversial
controversy
convention
conventional
conversation
convert
convict
conviction
convince
cook
cooking
cool
cooperate
cope
copy
core
corner
corporate
corporation
correct
correspondent
corruption
cost
cottage
cotton
cough
could
council
counsel
count
counter
counterpart
country
countryside
county

coup
couple
courage
course
court
cousin
cover
coverage
cow
crack
craft
crash
crazy
cream
create
creative
credit
crew
cricket
crime
criminal
crisis
critic
critical
criticism
criticize
crop
cross
crowd
crown
crucial
cruise
cry
crystal
cue
cultural
culture
cup
cure
curious
currency
current
curtain
customer
cut
cutting
cycle
dad
daily
damage
dance
danger
dangerous
dare
dark
data
date
daughter
day
dead
deadline
deal
dear
death
debate
debt
debut
decade
December
decide
decision
deck
declaration
declare
decline
decorate
deep
defeat
defend
defense
deficit
define
definitely
definition
degree
delay
delegate
delegation
deliberate
delight
delighted
deliver
delivery
demand
democracy
democrat
democratic
demonstrate
deny
department
departure
depend
deposit
depression
depth
deputy
describe
description
desert
deserve
design
designer
desire
desk
desperate
despite
destroy
detail
detailed
detective
determine
determined
develop
development
device
dialogue
diary
didn't
die
diet
difference
different
difficult
difficulty
dig
digital
dinner
diplomat
diplomatic
direct
direction
director
dirty
disappear
disappointed
disaster
discipline
discount
discover
discovery
discuss
discussion
disease
dish
dismiss
display
dispute
distance
distribution
district
divide
dividend
division
divorce
do
doctor
document
doesn't
dog
dollar
domestic
dominate
done
door
double
doubt
down
downtown
dozen
Dr.
draft
drag
drain
drama
dramatic
draw
dream
dress
dressed
drift
drink
drive
driver
drop
drug
drum
dry
due
dump
during
dust
duty
each
eager
ear
earlier
early
earn
earnings
earth
ease
easily
east
eastern
easy

eat
echo
economic
economics
economist
economy
edge
edit
edition
editor
editorial
education
effect
effective
efficient
effort
egg
eight
eighteen
eighteenth
eighth
eightieth
eighty
either
elderly
elect
election
electoral
electric
electricity
electronic
elegant
element
eleven
eleventh
eliminate
else
elsewhere
e-mail
embassy
emerge
emergency
emotion
emotional
emphasis
emphasize
empire
employ
employee
employer
employment
empty
enable
encounter
encourage
end
enemy
energy
engage
engine
engineer
engineering
English
enhance
enjoy
enormous
enough
ensure
enter
enterprise
entertain
entertainment
enthusiasm
entire
entirely
entitle
entrance
entry
environment
equal
equally
equipment
equivalent
era
error
escape
especially
essential
essentially
establish
establishment
estate
estimate
etc.
ethnic
European
even
evening
event
eventually
ever
every
everybody
everyone
everything
everywhere
evidence
evil
exact
exactly
examination
examine
example
excellent
except
exception
excerpt
excess
exchange
exchange rate
exciting
excuse
execute
executive
exercise
exhaust
exhibition
exile
exist
existence
existing
expand
expect
expectation
expense
expensive
experience
experiment
expert
explain
explanation
explode
exploit
explore
explosion
export
expose
exposure
express
expression
extend
extensive
extent
extra
extraordinary
extreme
eye
fabric
face
facility
fact
faction
factor
factory
fade
fail
failure
fair
fairly
faith
fall
false
familiar
family
famous
fan
fancy
fantasy
far
fare
farm
farmer
fashion
fast
fat
fate
father
fault
favor
favorite
fear
feature
February
federal
federation
fee
feed
feel
feeling
fellow
female
fence
festival
few
field
fierce
fifteen
fifteenth
fifth
fiftieth
fifty
fight
fighter
figure
file

fill
film
final
finally
finance
financial
find
fine
finger
finish
fire
firm
first
fiscal
fish
fishing
fit
five
fix
fixed
flag
flash
flat
flavor
flee
fleet
flexible
flight
float
flood
floor
flow
flower
fly
focus
fold
folk
follow
following
food
fool
foot
football
for
force
forecast
foreign
foreigner
forest
forget
form
formal
former
formula
forth
fortieth
fortune
forty
forward
found
foundation
founder
four
fourteen
fourteenth
fourth
frame
fraud
free
freedom
freeze
frequent
fresh
Friday
friend
friendly
friendship
from
front
fruit
frustrate
fry
fuel
fulfill
full
fully
fun
function
fund
fundamental
funding
funny
furniture
further
future
gain
gallery
game
gang
gap
garden
gas
gate
gather
gay
gear
gene
general
general election
generally
generate
generation
generous
gentle
gentleman
genuine
gesture
get
giant
gift
girl
give
given
glad
glance
glass
global
go
goal
god
going
gold
golden
golf
gone
good
goods
got
govern
government
governor
grab
grade
graduate
grain
grand
grant
grass
grave
gray
great
green
grip
gross
ground
group
grow
growth
guarantee
guard
guerrilla
guess
guest
guide
guilty
guitar
gun
guy
habit
hair
half
hall
halt
hand
handle
hang
happen
happy
harbor
hard
hardly
harm
hat
hate
have
he
head
headline
headquarters
heal
health
health care
healthy
hear
hearing
heart
heat
heaven
heavy
height
helicopter
hell
hello
help
her
here
hero
herself
hi
hide
high
highlight
highly
high school
highway

hill
him
himself
hint
hip
hire
his
historic
historical
history
hit
HIV
hold
holder
hole
holiday
holy
home
homeless
homosexual
honest
honor
hook
hope
horror
horse
hospital
host
hostage
hot
hotel
hour
house
household
housing
how
however
huge
human
human rights
humor
hundred
hundredth
hunt
hunter
hurt
husband
I
ice
idea
ideal
identify
identity
if
ignore
ill
illegal
illness
illustrate
image
imagination
imagine
immediate
immediately
immigrant
immigration
immune
impact
implement
implication
imply
import
important
impose
impossible
impress
impression
impressive
improve
in
Inc.
inch
incident
include
including
income
increase
increasingly
incredible
indeed
independent
index
indicate
indication
individual
industrial
industry
inevitable
infect
infection
inflation
influence
inform
information
ingredient
initial
initially
initiative
injured
injury
inner
innocent
inquiry
inside
insist
inspect
inspector
install
instance
instant
instead
institute
institution
instruction
instrument
insurance
integrate
intellectual
intelligence
intelligent
intend
intense
intention
interest
interested
interesting
interim
interior
internal
international
Internet
interview
into
introduce
invasion
invest
investigate
investment
invitation
invite
involve
involved
involvement
iron
Islam
island
issue
it
item
its
itself
jacket
jail
January
jazz
jersey
Jesus
jet
Jew
Jewish
job
join
joint
joke
journal
journalist
journey
joy
judge
judgment
juice
July
jump
June
junior
jury
just
justice
justify
keen
keep
key
kick
kid
kill
killer
kilometer
kind
king
kiss
kitchen
knee
knife
knock
know
know-how
knowledge
label
labor
laboratory
lack
lady
lake
land
land mass

lane
language
lap
large
largely
last
late
later
latest
latter
laugh
laughter
launch
law
lawsuit
lawyer
lay
layer
lead
leader
leadership
leading
leaf
league
leak
lean
leap
learn
lease
least
leather
leave
lecture
left
leg
legal
legislation
lend
length
lens
lesbian
less
lesson
let
let's
letter
level
liberal
liberate
liberty
library
license
lie
life
lift
light
like
likely
limit
limited
line
link
lip
list
listen
literary
literature
little
live
living
load
loan
lobby
local
location
lock
long
long-time
look
loose
lord
lose
loss
lost
lot
loud
love
lovely
lover
low
lower
luck
lucky
lunch
luxury
machine
mad
magazine
magic
mail
main
mainly
maintain
major
majority
make
maker
makeup
male
man
manage
management
manager
manner
manufacture
manufacturer
many
map
march
March
margin
marine
mark
marked
market
marriage
married
marry
mask
mass
massive
master
match
mate
material
matter
maximum
may
May
maybe
mayor
me
meal
mean
meaning
means
meanwhile
measure
meat
mechanism
medal
media
medical
medicine
medium
meet
meeting
member
membership
memory
mental
mention
merchant
mere
merely
merger
mess
message
metal
method
middle
middle class
Middle East
midnight
might
mild
mile
militant
military
milk
mill
million
millionth
mind
mine
minimum
minister
ministry
minor
minority
minute
mirror
Miss
miss
missile
missing
mission
mistake
mix
mixed
mixture
mm
mobile
model
moderate
modern
modest
mom
moment
Monday
monetary
money
monitor
month
monthly

mood
moon
moral
more
moreover
morning
mortgage
most
mostly
mother
motion
motivate
motor
mount
mountain
mouth
move
movement
movie
Mr.
Mrs.
Ms.
much
murder
muscle
museum
music
musical
musician
Muslim
must
mutual
my
myself
mystery
myth
name
narrow
nation
national
nationalist
native
natural
naturally
nature
naval
navy
near
nearby
nearly
neat
necessarily
necessary
neck
need
negative
negotiate
negotiation
neighbor
neighborhood
neither
nerve
nervous
net
network
never
nevertheless
new
newly
news
news agency
newscaster
newspaper
next
nice
night
nightmare
nine
nineteen
nineteenth
ninetieth
ninety
ninth
no
nobody
nod
noise
none
no one
nor
normal
normally
north
northeast
northern
nose
not
note
noted
nothing
notice
notion
novel
November
now
nowhere
nuclear
number
numerous
nurse
object
objective
observe
observer
obtain
obvious
obviously
occasion
occasional
occupation
occupy
occur
ocean
o'clock
October
odd
of course
off
offense
offensive
offer
offering
office
officer
official
often
oh
oil
okay
old
Olympic
on
once
one
one's
online
only
onto
open
opening
opera
operate
operation
operator
opinion
opponent
opportunity
oppose
opposed
opposite
opposition
opt
optimistic
option
or
orange
order
ordinary
organization
organize
organized
origin
original
other
otherwise
ought
our
ourselves
out
outcome
outline
output
outside
outstanding
over
overall
overcome
overnight
overseas
overwhelming
owe
own
owner
ownership
pace
pack
package
pact
page
pain
painful
paint
painting
pair
palace
pale
pan
panel
panic
paper
parent
park
parliament
parliamentary
part

participate
particular
particularly
partly
partner
partnership
party
pass
passage
passenger
passion
past
path
patient
pattern
pause
pay
payment
peace
peaceful
peak
peer
peg
pen
penalty
penny
pension
people
pepper
per
percent
percentage
perfect
perform
performance
perhaps
period
permanent
permission
permit
person
personal
personality
personally
personnel
perspective
persuade
pet
phase
philosophy
phone
photo
photograph
photographer
phrase
physical
pick
pickup
picture
piece
pile
pill
pilot
pin
pink
pipe
pit
pitch
place
plain
plan
plane
planet
planning
plant
plastic
plate
platform
play
player
playoff
pleasant
please
pleased
pleasure
pledge
plenty
plot
plunge
plus
pocket
poem
poet
poetry
point
point of view
pole
police
policeman
police officer
policy
political
politician
politics
poll
pollution
pool
poor
pop
popular
population
port
portrait
pose
position
positive
possibility
possible
possibly
post
pot
potato
potential
pound
pour
poverty
power
powerful
practical
practice
praise
precisely
predict
prefer
pregnant
premier
premium
preparation
prepare
prepared
presence
present
preserve
presidency
president
presidential
press
pressure
presumably
pretty
prevent
previous
previously
price
pride
priest
primary
prime
prime minister
prince
princess
principal
principle
print
prior
priority
prison
prisoner
private
privatize
prize
probably
problem
procedure
proceed
process
produce
product
production
profession
professional
professor
profile
profit
program
progress
project
prominent
promise
promote
prompt
proof
proper
property
proportion
proposal
propose
prosecution
prospect
protect
protection
protein
protest
proud
prove
provide
province
provision
provoke
psychological
public
publication
publicity
publish
publisher

publishing
pull
pump
punch
pupil
purchase
pure
purple
purpose
pursue
push
put
qualified
qualify
quality
quantity
quarter
quarterback
queen
question
quick
quiet
quite
quote
race
racial
racing
radical
radio
rage
raid
rail
rain
raise
rally
range
rank
rape
rapid
rare
rarely
rate
rather
rating
raw
ray
reach
react
reaction
read
reader
reading
ready
real
real estate
reality
realize
really
rear
reason
reasonable
rebel
recall
receive
recent
recently
recession
reckon
recognition
recognize
recommend
record
recording
recover
recovery
recruit
red
reduce
reduction
reel
refer
reference
referendum
reflect
reform
refugee
refuse
regard
regime
region
register
regret
regular
regulation
regulator
reject
relate
related
relation
relationship
relative
relax
release
reliable
relief
religion
religious
reluctant
rely
remain
remaining
remark
remarkable
remember
remind
remote
remove
renew
rent
repair
repeat
replace
replacement
reply
report
reporter
reporting
represent
representative
republic
republican
reputation
request
require
requirement
rescue
research
reserve
resident
resign
resignation
resist
resistance
resolution
resolve
resort
resource
respect
respond
response
responsibility
responsible
rest
restaurant
restore
result
resume
retail
retain
retire
retirement
retreat
return
reveal
revenue
reverse
review
revolution
revolutionary
reward
rhythm
rice
rich
rid
ride
rider
right
right-wing
ring
riot
rise
risk
rival
river
road
rock
rocket
role
roll
Roman
romantic
roof
room
root
rose
rough
round
route
routine
row
royal
rugby
ruin
rule
ruling
rumor
run
runner
running
rural
rush
sack
sacrifice
sad
safe

safety
sail
saint
sake
salary
sale
salt
same
sample
sanction
sand
satellite
satisfied
Saturday
sauce
save
savings
say
scale
scandal
scene
schedule
scheme
school
science
scientific
scientist
score
scream
screen
script
sea
seal
search
season
seat
second
secret
secretary
Secretary of State
section
sector
secure
security
see
seed
seek
seem
segment
seize
select
selection
self
sell
Senate
senator
send
senior
sense
sensible
sensitive
sentence
separate
September
series
serious
seriously
servant
serve
service
session
set
settle
settlement
setup
seven
seventeen
seventeenth
seventh
seventieth
seventy
several
severe
sex
sexual
shade
shadow
shake
shall
shame
shape
shaped
share
shareholder
sharp
she
shed
sheet
shell
shelter
shift
ship
shirt
shock
shoe
shoot
shop
shopping
shore
short
shortage
shortly
short-term
shot
should
shoulder
shout
show
shut
sick
side
sigh
sight
sign
signal
significant
silence
silent
silver
similar
simple
simply
since
sing
singer
single
sink
sir
sister
sit
site
situation
six
sixteen
sixteenth
sixth
sixtieth
sixty
size
ski
skill
skin
sky
sleep
slice
slide
slight
slightly
slim
slip
slow
small
smart
smash
smell
smile
smoke
smooth
snap
snow
so
so-called
soccer
social
socialist
society
soft
software
soil
soldier
solicitor
solid
solution
solve
some
somebody
somehow
someone
something
sometimes
somewhat
somewhere
son
song
soon
sophisticated
sorry
sort
soul
sound
source
south
southeast
southern
southwest
space
spare
spark
speak
speaker
special
specialist
specialize
species
specific

specifically
spectacular
speculate
speech
speed
spell
spend
spin
spirit
spiritual
spite
split
spokesman
spokeswoman
sponsor
sport
spot
spray
spread
spring
spur
squad
square
squeeze
stable
stadium
staff
stage
stake
stamp
stand
standard
star
stare
start
state
statement
station
statistic
status
stay
steady
steal
steam
steel
stem
step
sterling
stick
still
stimulate
stir
stock
stock exchange
stock market
stomach
stone
stop
store
storm
story
straight
strain
strange
strategic
strategy
stream
street
strength
strengthen
stress
stretch
strict
strike
striking
string
strip
stroke
strong
structure
struggle
student
studio
study
stuff
stupid
style
subject
subsequent
subsidy
substance
substantial
substitute
succeed
success
successful
such
sudden
suffer
sufficient
sugar
suggest
suggestion
suicide
suit
suitable
sum
summer
summit
sun
Sunday
super
superb
superior
supply
support
suppose
supposed
supreme
sure
surely
surface
surgery
surplus
surprise
surprised
surprising
surrender
surround
survey
survival
survive
suspect
suspend
suspicion
sustain
sweep
sweet
swim
swing
switch
symbol
sympathy
symptom
system
table
tackle
tactic
tail
take
takeover
tale
talent
talk
tall
tank
tap
tape
target
task
taste
tax
tea
teach
teaching
team
tear
technical
technique
technology
teenager
telephone
television
tell
temperature
temple
temporary
ten
tend
tendency
tennis
tension
tenth
term
terrible
territory
terror
terrorist
test
text
than
thank
that
the
theater
their
them
theme
themselves
then
theory
therapy
there
therefore
these
they
thick
thin
thing
think
thinking
third
Third World
thirteen
thirteenth

thirtieth
thirty
this
thorough
those
though
thought
thousand
threat
threaten
three
throat
through
throughout
throw
Thursday
thus
ticket
tide
tie
tight
till
time
tiny
tip
tired
tissue
title
titled
to
today
together
tomorrow
ton
tone
tonight
too
tool
tooth
top
torture
total
touch
tough
tour
tourist
tournament
toward
tower
town
toy
trace
track
trade
trader
tradition
traffic
tragedy
trail
train
transaction
transfer
transform
transition
transport
transportation
trap
travel
traveler
treat
treatment
treaty
tree
tremendous
trend
trial
trick
trigger
trip
triumph
troop
trouble
truck
true
truly
trust
truth
try
tube
Tuesday
tune
tunnel
turn
TV
twelfth
twelve
twentieth
twenty
twice
twin
twist
two
type
typical
ultimate
ultimately
unable
uncle
under
underground
undermine
understand
understanding
unemployment
unexpected
unfair
unfortunately
unhappy
unidentified
uniform
union
unique
unit
united
United Nations
unity
universe
university
unknown
unless
unlike
unlikely
until
unusual
up
upon
upper
upset
urban
urge
urgent
us
use
used
useful
user
usual
usually
valley
valuable
value
van
variety
various
vary
vast
vegetable
vehicle
venture
venue
verdict
version
very
vessel
veteran
via
vice
victim
victimize
victory
video
view
village
violate
violence
violent
virus
visible
vision
visit
visitor
vital
vitamin
voice
volume
voluntary
volunteer
vote
vulnerable
wage
wait
wake
walk
wall
want
war
warm
warn
warning
wash
waste
watch
water
wave
way
we
weak
weaken
wealth
weapon
wear
weather
web
website
wedding

Wednesday
week
weekend
weekly
weigh
weight
welcome
welfare
well
well-known
west
western
wet
what
whatever
wheel
when
whenever
where
whereas
whether
which
while
whip
whisper
white
White House
who
whole
whom
whose
why
wide
widespread
wife
wild
will
willing
win
wind
window
wine
wing
winner
winning
winter
wipe
wire
wireless
wise
wish
with
withdraw
withdrawal
within
without
witness
woman
wonder
wonderful
wood
wooden
word
work
worker
working
world
world war
worldwide
worry
worth
would
wound
wrap
write
writer
writing
written
wrong
yard
yeah
year
yellow
yen
yes
yesterday
yet
yield
you
young
youngster
your
yours
yourself
youth
zone

# Academic Word List

This list contains the head words of the families in the Academic Word List. The numbers indicate the sublist of the Academic Word List, with Sublist 1 containing the most frequent words, Sublist 2 the next most frequent and so on. For example, *abandon* and its family members are in Sublist 8 of the Academic Word List.

| | | | | | | | |
|---|---|---|---|---|---|---|---|
| abandon | 8 | assist | 2 | communicate | 4 | converse | 9 |
| abstract | 6 | assume | 1 | community | 2 | convert | 7 |
| academy | 5 | assure | 9 | compatible | 9 | convince | 10 |
| access | 4 | attach | 6 | compensate | 3 | cooperate | 6 |
| accommodate | 9 | attain | 9 | compile | 10 | coordinate | 3 |
| accompany | 8 | attitude | 4 | complement | 8 | core | 3 |
| accumulate | 8 | attribute | 4 | complex | 2 | corporate | 3 |
| accurate | 6 | author | 6 | component | 3 | correspond | 3 |
| achieve | 2 | authority | 1 | compound | 5 | couple | 7 |
| acknowledge | 6 | automate | 8 | comprehensive | 7 | create | 1 |
| acquire | 2 | available | 1 | comprise | 7 | credit | 2 |
| adapt | 7 | aware | 5 | compute | 2 | criteria | 3 |
| adequate | 4 | behalf | 9 | conceive | 10 | crucial | 8 |
| adjacent | 10 | benefit | 1 | concentrate | 4 | culture | 2 |
| adjust | 5 | bias | 8 | concept | 1 | currency | 8 |
| administrate | 2 | bond | 6 | conclude | 2 | cycle | 4 |
| adult | 7 | brief | 6 | concurrent | 9 | data | 1 |
| advocate | 7 | bulk | 9 | conduct | 2 | debate | 4 |
| affect | 2 | capable | 6 | confer | 4 | decade | 7 |
| aggregate | 6 | capacity | 5 | confine | 9 | decline | 5 |
| aid | 7 | category | 2 | confirm | 7 | deduce | 3 |
| albeit | 10 | cease | 9 | conflict | 5 | define | 1 |
| allocate | 6 | challenge | 5 | conform | 8 | definite | 7 |
| alter | 5 | channel | 7 | consent | 3 | demonstrate | 3 |
| alternative | 3 | chapter | 2 | consequent | 2 | denote | 8 |
| ambiguous | 8 | chart | 8 | considerable | 3 | deny | 7 |
| amend | 5 | chemical | 7 | consist | 1 | depress | 10 |
| analogy | 9 | circumstance | 3 | constant | 3 | derive | 1 |
| analyze | 1 | cite | 6 | constitute | 1 | design | 2 |
| annual | 4 | civil | 4 | constrain | 3 | despite | 4 |
| anticipate | 9 | clarify | 8 | construct | 2 | detect | 8 |
| apparent | 4 | classic | 7 | consult | 5 | deviate | 8 |
| append | 8 | clause | 5 | consume | 2 | device | 9 |
| appreciate | 8 | code | 4 | contact | 5 | devote | 9 |
| approach | 1 | coherent | 9 | contemporary | 8 | differentiate | 7 |
| appropriate | 2 | coincide | 9 | context | 1 | dimension | 4 |
| approximate | 4 | collapse | 10 | contract | 1 | diminish | 9 |
| arbitrary | 8 | colleague | 10 | contradict | 8 | discrete | 5 |
| area | 1 | commence | 9 | contrary | 7 | discriminate | 6 |
| aspect | 2 | comment | 3 | contrast | 4 | displace | 8 |
| assemble | 10 | commission | 2 | contribute | 3 | display | 6 |
| assess | 1 | commit | 4 | controversy | 9 | dispose | 7 |
| assign | 6 | commodity | 8 | convene | 3 | distinct | 2 |

| | |
|---|---|
| distort | 9 |
| distribute | 1 |
| diverse | 6 |
| document | 3 |
| domain | 6 |
| domestic | 4 |
| dominate | 3 |
| draft | 5 |
| drama | 8 |
| duration | 9 |
| dynamic | 7 |
| economy | 1 |
| edit | 6 |
| element | 2 |
| eliminate | 7 |
| emerge | 4 |
| emphasis | 3 |
| empirical | 7 |
| enable | 5 |
| encounter | 10 |
| energy | 5 |
| enforce | 5 |
| enhance | 6 |
| enormous | 10 |
| ensure | 3 |
| entity | 5 |
| environment | 1 |
| equate | 2 |
| equip | 7 |
| equivalent | 5 |
| erode | 9 |
| error | 4 |
| establish | 1 |
| estate | 6 |
| estimate | 1 |
| ethic | 9 |
| ethnic | 4 |
| evaluate | 2 |
| eventual | 8 |
| evident | 1 |
| evolve | 5 |
| exceed | 6 |
| exclude | 3 |
| exhibit | 8 |
| expand | 5 |
| expert | 6 |
| explicit | 6 |
| exploit | 8 |
| export | 1 |
| expose | 5 |
| external | 5 |
| extract | 7 |
| facilitate | 5 |
| factor | 1 |
| feature | 2 |
| federal | 6 |
| fee | 6 |
| file | 7 |
| final | 2 |
| finance | 1 |
| finite | 7 |
| flexible | 6 |
| fluctuate | 8 |
| focus | 2 |
| format | 9 |
| formula | 1 |
| forthcoming | 10 |
| foundation | 7 |
| found | 9 |
| framework | 3 |
| function | 1 |
| fund | 3 |
| fundamental | 5 |
| furthermore | 6 |
| gender | 6 |
| generate | 5 |
| generation | 5 |
| globe | 7 |
| goal | 4 |
| grade | 7 |
| grant | 4 |
| guarantee | 7 |
| guideline | 8 |
| hence | 4 |
| hierarchy | 7 |
| highlight | 8 |
| hypothesis | 4 |
| identical | 7 |
| identify | 1 |
| ideology | 7 |
| ignorance | 6 |
| illustrate | 3 |
| image | 5 |
| immigrate | 3 |
| impact | 2 |
| implement | 4 |
| implicate | 4 |
| implicit | 8 |
| imply | 3 |
| impose | 4 |
| incentive | 6 |
| incidence | 6 |
| incline | 10 |
| income | 1 |
| incorporate | 6 |
| index | 6 |
| indicate | 1 |
| individual | 1 |
| induce | 8 |
| inevitable | 8 |
| infer | 7 |
| infrastructure | 8 |
| inherent | 9 |
| inhibit | 6 |
| initial | 3 |
| initiate | 6 |
| injure | 2 |
| innovate | 7 |
| input | 6 |
| insert | 7 |
| insight | 9 |
| inspect | 8 |
| instance | 3 |
| institute | 2 |
| instruct | 6 |
| integral | 9 |
| integrate | 4 |
| integrity | 10 |
| intelligence | 6 |
| intense | 8 |
| interact | 3 |
| intermediate | 9 |
| internal | 4 |
| interpret | 1 |
| interval | 6 |
| intervene | 7 |
| intrinsic | 10 |
| invest | 2 |
| investigate | 4 |
| invoke | 10 |
| involve | 1 |
| isolate | 7 |
| issue | 1 |
| item | 2 |
| job | 4 |
| journal | 2 |
| justify | 3 |
| label | 4 |
| labor | 1 |
| layer | 3 |
| lecture | 6 |
| legal | 1 |
| legislate | 1 |
| levy | 10 |
| liberal | 5 |
| license | 5 |
| likewise | 10 |
| link | 3 |
| locate | 3 |
| logic | 5 |
| maintain | 2 |
| major | 1 |
| manipulate | 8 |
| manual | 9 |
| margin | 5 |
| mature | 9 |
| maximize | 3 |
| mechanism | 4 |
| media | 7 |
| mediate | 9 |
| medical | 5 |
| medium | 9 |
| mental | 5 |
| method | 1 |
| migrate | 6 |
| military | 9 |
| minimal | 9 |
| minimize | 8 |
| minimum | 6 |
| ministry | 6 |
| minor | 3 |
| mode | 7 |
| modify | 5 |
| monitor | 5 |
| motive | 6 |
| mutual | 9 |
| negate | 3 |
| network | 5 |
| neutral | 6 |
| nevertheless | 6 |
| nonetheless | 10 |
| norm | 9 |
| normal | 2 |
| notion | 5 |
| notwithstanding | 10 |
| nuclear | 8 |
| objective | 5 |
| obtain | 2 |
| obvious | 4 |
| occupy | 4 |

| | | | | | | | |
|---|---|---|---|---|---|---|---|
| occur | 1 | professional | 4 | role | 1 | target | 5 |
| odd | 10 | prohibit | 7 | route | 9 | task | 3 |
| offset | 8 | project | 4 | scenario | 9 | team | 9 |
| ongoing | 10 | promote | 4 | schedule | 8 | technical | 3 |
| option | 4 | proportion | 3 | scheme | 3 | technique | 3 |
| orient | 5 | prospect | 8 | scope | 6 | technology | 3 |
| outcome | 3 | protocol | 9 | section | 1 | temporary | 9 |
| output | 4 | psychology | 5 | sector | 1 | tense | 8 |
| overall | 4 | publication | 7 | secure | 2 | terminate | 8 |
| overlap | 9 | publish | 3 | seek | 2 | text | 2 |
| overseas | 6 | purchase | 2 | select | 2 | theme | 8 |
| panel | 10 | pursue | 5 | sequence | 3 | theory | 1 |
| paradigm | 7 | qualitative | 9 | series | 4 | thereby | 8 |
| paragraph | 8 | quote | 7 | sex | 3 | thesis | 7 |
| parallel | 4 | radical | 8 | shift | 3 | topic | 7 |
| parameter | 4 | random | 8 | significant | 1 | trace | 6 |
| participate | 2 | range | 2 | similar | 1 | tradition | 2 |
| partner | 3 | ratio | 5 | simulate | 7 | transfer | 2 |
| passive | 9 | rational | 6 | site | 2 | transform | 6 |
| perceive | 2 | react | 3 | so-called | 10 | transit | 5 |
| percent | 1 | recover | 6 | sole | 7 | transmit | 7 |
| period | 1 | refine | 9 | somewhat | 7 | transport | 6 |
| persist | 10 | regime | 4 | source | 1 | trend | 5 |
| perspective | 5 | region | 2 | specific | 1 | trigger | 9 |
| phase | 4 | register | 3 | specify | 3 | ultimate | 7 |
| phenomenon | 7 | regulate | 2 | sphere | 9 | undergo | 10 |
| philosophy | 3 | reinforce | 8 | stable | 5 | underlie | 6 |
| physical | 3 | reject | 5 | statistic | 4 | undertake | 4 |
| plus | 8 | relax | 9 | status | 4 | uniform | 8 |
| policy | 1 | release | 7 | straightforward | 10 | unify | 9 |
| portion | 9 | relevant | 2 | strategy | 2 | unique | 7 |
| pose | 10 | reluctance | 10 | stress | 4 | utilize | 6 |
| positive | 2 | rely | 3 | structure | 1 | valid | 3 |
| potential | 2 | remove | 3 | style | 5 | vary | 1 |
| practitioner | 8 | require | 1 | submit | 7 | vehicle | 8 |
| precede | 6 | research | 1 | subordinate | 9 | version | 5 |
| precise | 5 | reside | 2 | subsequent | 4 | via | 8 |
| predict | 4 | resolve | 4 | subsidy | 6 | violate | 9 |
| predominant | 8 | resource | 2 | substitute | 5 | virtual | 8 |
| preliminary | 9 | respond | 1 | successor | 7 | visible | 7 |
| presume | 6 | restore | 8 | sufficient | 3 | vision | 9 |
| previous | 2 | restrain | 9 | sum | 4 | visual | 8 |
| primary | 2 | restrict | 2 | summary | 4 | volume | 3 |
| prime | 5 | retain | 4 | supplement | 9 | voluntary | 7 |
| principal | 4 | reveal | 6 | survey | 2 | welfare | 5 |
| principle | 1 | revenue | 5 | survive | 7 | whereas | 5 |
| prior | 4 | reverse | 7 | suspend | 9 | whereby | 10 |
| priority | 7 | revise | 8 | sustain | 5 | widespread | 8 |
| proceed | 1 | revolution | 9 | symbol | 5 | | |
| process | 1 | rigid | 9 | tape | 6 | | |

# USA States, Abbreviations, and Capitals

| State | Capital |
|---|---|
| Alabama (AL) | Montgomery |
| Alaska (AK) | Juneau |
| Arizona (AZ) | Phoenix |
| Arkansas (AR) | Little Rock |
| California (CA) | Sacramento |
| Colorado (CO) | Denver |
| Connecticut (CT) | Hartford |
| Delaware (DE) | Dover |
| Florida (FL) | Tallahassee |
| Georgia (GA) | Atlanta |
| Hawaii (HI) | Honolulu |
| Idaho (ID) | Boise |
| Illinois (IL) | Springfield |
| Indiana (IN) | Indianapolis |
| Iowa (IA) | Des Moines |
| Kansas (KS) | Topeka |
| Kentucky (KY) | Frankfort |
| Louisiana (LA) | Baton Rouge |
| Maine (ME) | Augusta |
| Maryland (MD) | Annapolis |
| Massachusetts (MA) | Boston |
| Michigan (MI) | Lansing |
| Minnesota (MN) | Saint Paul |
| Mississippi (MS) | Jackson |
| Missouri (MO) | Jefferson City |
| Montana (MT) | Helena |
| Nebraska (NE) | Lincoln |
| Nevada (NV) | Carson City |
| New Hampshire (NH) | Concord |
| New Jersey (NJ) | Trenton |
| New Mexico (NM) | Santa Fe |
| New York (NY) | Albany |
| North Carolina (NC) | Raleigh |
| North Dakota (ND) | Bismarck |
| Ohio (OH) | Columbus |
| Oklahoma (OK) | Oklahoma City |
| Oregon (OR) | Salem |
| Pennsylvania (PA) | Harrisburg |
| Rhode Island (RI) | Providence |
| South Carolina (SC) | Columbia |
| South Dakota (SD) | Pierre |
| Tennessee (TN) | Nashville |
| Texas (TX) | Austin |
| Utah (UT) | Salt Lake City |
| Vermont (VT) | Montpelier |
| Virginia (VA) | Richmond |
| Washington (WA) | Olympia |
| West Virginia (WV) | Charleston |
| Wisconsin (WI) | Madison |
| Wyoming (WY) | Cheyenne |
| **Capital of the United States of America (USA)** | |
| District of Columbia (DC) | Washingon (commonly abbreviated: Washington, D.C.) |

# Geographical Places and Nationalities

This list shows the spelling and pronunciation of geographical names. If a country has different words for the country, adjective, and person, these are all shown. Inclusion in this list does not imply status as a sovereign nation.

**Af|ghan|i|stan** /æfgænıstæn/; Af|ghan, Af|ghani /æfgæn/, /æfgæni, -gɑni/

**Af|ri|ca** /æfrıkə/; Af|ri|can /æfrıkən/

**Al|ba|nia** /ælbeıniə/; Al|ba|ni|an /ælbeıniən/

**Al|ge|ria** /ældʒıəriə/; Al|ge|ri|an /ældʒıəriən/

**An|dor|ra** /ændɔrə/; An|dor|ran /ændɔrən/

**An|go|la** /æŋgoʊlə/; An|go|lan /æŋgoʊlən/

**Ant|arc|ti|ca** /æntɑrktıkə, -ɑrtı-/; Ant|arc|tic /æntɑrktık, -ɑrtık/

**An|ti|gua and Bar|bu|da** /æntigə ən bɑrbudə/; An|ti|guan, Bar|bu|dan /æntigən/, /bɑrbudən/

**(the) Arc|tic Ocean** /(ði) ɑrktık oʊʃən, ɑrtık/; Arc|tic /ɑrktık, ɑrtık/

**Ar|gen|ti|na** /ɑrdʒəntinə/; Ar|gen|tine, Ar|gen|tin|ian, or Ar|gen|tin|ean /ɑrdʒəntin, -taın/, /ɑrdʒəntıniən/

**Ar|me|nia** /ɑrminiə/; Ar|me|nian /ɑrminiən/

**A|sia** /eıʒə/; A|sian /eıʒən/

**(the) At|lan|tic Ocean** /(ði) ætlæntık oʊʃən/

**Aus|tra|lia** /ɔstreılyə/; Aus|tra|lian /ɔstreılyən/

**Aus|tria** /ɔstriə/; Aus|tri|an /ɔstriən/

**Azer|bai|jan** /æzərbaıdʒɑn, ɑzər-/; Azer|bai|ja|ni, Azeri /æzərbaıdʒɑni, ɑzər-/, /əzɛri/

**(the) Ba|ha|mas** /(ðə) bəhɑməz/; Ba|ha|mian /bəheımiən, -hɑ-/

**Bah|rain** /bɑreın/; Bah|raini /bɑreıni/

**Ban|gla|desh** /bɑŋglədɛʃ, bæŋ-/; Ban|gla|deshi/bɑŋglədɛʃi, bæŋ-/

**Bar|ba|dos** /bɑrbeıdoʊs/; Bar|ba|di|an /bɑrbeıdiən/

**Be|la|rus** /bɛlərus, byɛl-/; Be|la|ru|si|an /bɛlərʌʃən, byɛl-/

**Bel|gium** /bɛldʒəm/; Bel|gian /bɛldʒən/

**Be|lize** /bəliz/; Be|liz|ean /bəliziən/

**Be|nin** /bənin/; Be|ni|nese /bɛnıniz/

**Bhu|tan** /butɑn, -tæn/; Bhu|tani, Bhu|ta|nese /butɑni, -tæni/, /butᵊniz/

**Bo|liv|ia** /bəlıviə/; Bo|liv|i|an /bəlıviən/

**Bos|nia and Her|ze|go|vi|na** /bɒzniə ən hɛrtsəgoʊvinə/; Bos|ni|an, Her|ze|go|vi|ni|an /bɒzniən/, /hɛrtsəgoʊviniən/

**Bo|tswa|na** /bɒtswɑnə/; Ba|tswa|nan/ bɒtswɑnən/; Mo|tswan|a (person), Ba|tswa|na (people) /mɒtswɑnə/, /bɑtswɑnə/

**Bra|zil** /brəzıl/; Bra|zil|ian /brəzılyən/

**Bru|nei Da|rus|sa|lam** /brunaı dɑrusaləm/; Bru|nei, Bru|nei|an /brunaı/, /brunaıən/

**Bul|gar|ia** /bʌlgɛəriə/; Bul|gar|i|an /bʌlgeəriən/

**Bur|ki|na Fa|so** /bərkinə fɑsoʊ/; Bur|kin|abe, Bur|kin|ese /bɜrkınɑbeı/, /bɜrkıniz/

**Bur|ma—See Myanmar** /bɜrmə/; Bur|mese—/bɜrmiz/

**Bu|run|di** /bʊrʊndi/; Bu|run|di|an /bʊrʊndiən/

**Cam|bo|dia** /kæmboʊdiə/; Cam|bo|di|an /kæmboʊdiən

**Cam|er|oon** /kæmərun/; Cam|er|oo|ni|an /kæməruniən/

**Can|a|da** /kænədə/; Ca|na|di|an /kəneıdiən/

**Cape Verde** /keıp vɜrd/; Cape Verd|ean /keıp vɜrdiən/

**Cen|tral Af|ri|can Re|pub|lic** /sɛntrəl æfrıkən rıpʌblık/; Cen|tral Af|ri|can /sentrəl æfrıkən/

**Chad** /tʃæd/; Chad|ian /tʃædiən/

**Chi|le** /tʃıli, -leı/; Chil|ean /tʃıliən, tʃıleı-/

**Chi|na** /tʃaınə/; Chi|nese /tʃaıniz/

**Co|lom|bia** /kəlʌmbiə/; Co|lom|bi|an /kəlʌmbiən/

**Com|o|ros** /kɒmərouz/; Com|or|an /kəmɔrən/

**Cos|ta Ri|ca** /kɒstə rikə/; Cos|ta Ri|can /kɒstə rikən/

**Côte d'Ivoire** /kout divwar/; Ivoir|i|an /ivwariən/

**Cro|a|tia** /krouei∫ə/; Cro|a|tian /krouei∫ən/

**Cu|ba** /kyubə/; Cu|ban /kyubən/

**Cy|prus** /saɪprəs/; Cyp|riot /sɪpriət/

**(the) Czech Re|pub|lic** /(ðə) t∫ɛk rɪpʌblɪk/; Czech /t∫ɛk/

**Dem|o|crat|ic Re|pub|lic of the Con|go, or (the) Con|go** /dɛməkrætɪk rɪpʌblɪk əv ðə kɒŋgou/, /(ðə) kɒŋgou/; Con|go|lese /kɒŋgəliz, -lis/

**Den|mark** /dɛnmark/; Dan|ish, Dane /deɪnɪ∫/, /deɪn/

**Dji|bou|ti** /dʒɪbuti/; Dji|bou|tian /dʒɪbutiən/

**Dom|i|ni|ca** /dɒmɪnikə, dəmɪnɪkə/; Do|mi|ni|can /dɒmɪnikən/

**(the) Do|min|i|can Re|pub|lic** /(ðə) dəmɪnɪkən rɪpʌblɪk; Do|mi|ni|can /dəmɪnɪkən/

**East Ti|mor** /ist timɔr/; East Ti|mor|ese /ist timɔriz/

**Ec|ua|dor** /ɛkwədɔr/; Ec|ua|dor|ian / ɛkwədɔriən/

**Egypt** /idʒɪpt/; Egyp|tian /ɪdʒɪp∫ən/

**El Sal|va|dor** /ɛl sælvədɔr/; Sal|va|do|ran, Sal|va|do|rean /sælvədɔrən/, /sælvədɔriən/

**Eng|land** /ɪŋglənd/; Eng|lish /ɪŋglɪ∫/

**Equi|to|ri|al Guinea** /ɛkwɪtɔriəl gɪni/; Equi|to|ri|al Guin|ean, Equi|to|guinean /ɛkwɪtɔriəl gɪniən/, /ɛkwɪtougɪniən/

**Er|i|trea** /ɛrɪtriə/; Er|i|tre|an /ɛrɪtriən/

**Es|to|nia** /ɛstouniə/; Es|to|ni|an /ɛstouniən/

**Ethi|o|pia** /iθioupiə/; Ethi|o|pi|an /iθioupiən/

**Eu|rope** /yuərəp/; Eu|ro|pe|an /yuərəpiən/

**Fi|ji** /fidʒi/; Fi|ji|an /fidʒiən, fiji-/

**Fin|land** /fɪnlənd/; Fin|nish, Finn, Fin|land|er /fɪnɪ∫/, /fɪn/, /fɪnləndər, -lændər/

**France** /fræns/; French /frɛnt∫/

**Ga|bon** /gaboun/; Gab|o|nese /gæbəniz/

**(the) Gam|bia** /(ðə) gæmbiə/; Gam|bi|an /gæmbiən/

**Geor|gia** /dʒɔrdʒə/; Geor|gian /dʒɔrdʒən/

**Ger|ma|ny** /dʒɜrməni/; Ger|man /dʒɜrmən/

**Gha|na** /ganə/; Gha|na|ian /ganiən, gəneɪən/

**Greece** /gris/; Greek /grik/

**Gre|na|da** /grɪneɪdə/; Gre|na|di|an /grɪneɪdiən/

**Gua|te|ma|la** /gwatəmalə/; Gua|te|ma|lan /gwatəmalən/

**Guin|ea** /gɪni/; Guin|ean /gɪniən/

**Guin|ea-Bis|sau** /gɪni bɪsau/; Guin|ean /gɪniən/

**Guy|ana** /gaɪænə, -anə/; Guy|a|nese /gaɪəniz/

**Hai|ti** /heɪti/; Hai|tian /heɪ∫ən/

**Hon|du|ras** /hɒnduərəs/; Hon|du|ran /hɒnduərən/

**Hun|ga|ry** /hʌŋgəri/; Hun|gar|i|an /hʌŋgɛəriən/

**Ice|land** /aɪslənd/; Ice|lan|dic, Ice|land|er /aɪslændɪk/, /aɪsləndər, -lændər/

**In|dia** /ɪndiə/; In|di|an /ɪndiən/

**(the) In|di|an Ocean** /(ði) ɪndiən ou∫ən/

**In|do|ne|sia** /ɪndəniʒə/; In|do|ne|sian /ɪndəniʒən/

**Iran** /ɪran, ɪræn, aɪræn/; Ira|ni|an, Iran|i /ɪreɪniən, ɪra-, aɪreɪ-/, /ɪrani/

**I|raq** /ɪræk, ɪrak/; I|raq|i /ɪræki, ɪraki/

**Ire|land** /aɪərlənd/; Ir|ish /aɪrɪ∫/

**Is|ra|el** /ɪzriəl, -reɪəl/; Is|rae|li /ɪzreɪli/

**It|a|ly** /ɪtəli/; Ital|ian /ɪtælyən/

**Ja|mai|ca** /dʒəmeɪkə/; Ja|mai|can /dʒəmeɪkən/

**Ja|pan** /dʒəpæn/; Jap|a|nese /dʒæpəniz/

**Jor|dan** /dʒɔrdən/; Jor|da|ni|an /dʒɔrdeɪniən/

**Ka|zakh|stan** /kazakstan, -stæn/; Ka|zakh|stan|i, Ka|zakh /kazakstani, -stæni/, /kazak, kəzæk/

**Ken|ya** /kɛnyə, kin-/; Ken|yan /kɛnyən, kin-/

**Ki|ri|bati** /kɪərəbati, -bæs/; I-Ki|ri|bati /i kɪərəbati, -bæs/

**Ko|rea, South Ko|rea, North Ko|rea** /kəriə, kɔ-/, /souθ kəriə, kɔ-/, /nɔrθ kəriə, kɔ-/; Ko|rean /kəriən, kɔ-/, /souθ kəriən, kɔ-/, /nɔrθ kəriən, kɔ/

**Ku|wait** /kuweɪt/; Ku|wai|ti /kuweɪti/

**Kyr|gyz|stan** /kɪərgɪstan, -stæn/; Kyr|gyz|sta|ni /kɪərgɪstani, -stæni/

**Laos** /laous, laus/; Lao, Lao|tian /laou, lau/, /leɪouʃən/

**Lat|via** /lætviə, lat-/; Lat|vi|an /lætviən, lat-/

**Leb|a|non** /lɛbənən, -nɒn/; Leb|a|nese /lɛbəniz/

**Le|so|tho** /ləsoutou, -sutu/ So|tho, Mo|so|tho (person), Ba|so|tho (people) /soutou, sutu/, /məsoutou, -sutu/, /basoutou, -sutu/

**Li|be|ria** /laɪbɪəriə/; Li|be|ri|an /laɪbɪəriən/

**Lib|ya** /lɪbiə/; Lib|y|an /lɪbiən/

**Liech|ten|stein** /lɪktənstaɪn/; Liech|ten|stein, Liech|ten|stein|er /lɪktənstaɪn/, /lɪktənstaɪnər/

**Lith|u|a|nia** /lɪθueɪniə/; Lith|u|a|ni|an /lɪθueɪniən/

**Lux|em|bourg** /lʌksəmbɜrg/; Lux|em|bourger, /lʌksəmbɜrgər/

**Mac|e|do|nia** /mæsɪdouniə/; Mac|e|do|ni|an /mæsɪdouniən/

**Mad|a|gas|car** /mædəgæskər/; Mad|a|gas|can, Mala|gasy /mædəgæskən/, /mæləgæsi/

**Ma|la|wi** /məlawi/; Ma|la|wi|an /məlawiən/

**Ma|lay|sia** /məleɪʒə/; Ma|lay|sian /məleɪʒən/

**Mal|dives** /mɔldivz, -daɪvz/; Mal|div|ian /mɔldɪviən/

**Ma|li** /mali/; Ma|lian /maliən/

**Mal|ta** /mɔltə/; Mal|tese /mɔltiz/

**(the) Mar|shall Is|lands** /(ðə) marʃəl aɪləndz/; Mar|shall|ese /marʃəliz/

**Mau|ri|ta|nia** /mɔrɪteɪniə/; Mau|ri|ta|ni|an /mɔrɪteɪniən/

**Mau|ri|ti|us** /mɔrɪʃəs/; Mau|ri|tian /mɔrɪʃən/

**Mex|i|co** /mɛksɪkou/; Mex|i|can /mɛksɪkən/

**Mi|cro|ne|sia** /maɪkrəniʒə/; Mi|cro|ne|sian /maɪkrəniʒən/

**Mol|do|va** /mɔldouvə/; Mol|do|van / mɔldouvən/

**Mo|na|co** /mɒnəkou/; Mo|na|can, Mon|e|gasque /mɒnəkən/, /mɒnɪgæsk/

**Mon|go|lia** /mɒŋgouliə/; Mon|go|li|an /mɒŋgouliən/

**Mo|roc|co** /mərɒkou/; Mo|roc|can /mərɒkən/

**Mo|zam|bique** /mouzæmbik, -zəm-/; Mo|zam|bi|can /mouzæmbikən, -zəm-/

**Myan|mar** (Burma) /myanmar (bɜrmə)/; Bur|mese /bərmiz/

**Na|mib|ia** /nəmɪbiə/; Na|mib|ian /nəmɪbiən/

**Na|u|ru** /nauru/; Na|u|ru|an /nauruən/

**Ne|pal** /nəpɔl/; Nep|a|lese /nɛpəliz/

**(the) Neth|er|lands** /(ðə) nɛðərləndz/; Dutch /dʌtʃ/

**New Zea|land** /nu zilənd/; New Zea|land, New Zea|land|er /nu zilənd/, /nu ziləndər/

**Nic|a|ra|gua** /nɪkəragwə/; Nic|a|ra|guan /nɪkəragwən/

**Ni|ger** /naɪdʒər, niʒɛər/; Ni|ge|rien, Ni|ger|ois /naɪdʒɪəriən, niʒeryɛn/, /niʒɛrwa/

**Ni|ge|ria** /naɪdʒɪəriə/; Ni|ge|ri|an /naɪdʒɪəriən/

**Nor|way** /nɔrweɪ/; Nor|we|gian /nɔrwidʒən/

**Oman** /ouman/; Omani /oumani/

**(the) Pa|cif|ic Ocean** /(ðə) pəsɪfɪk ouʃən/

**Pa|ki|stan** /pækɪstæn, pakɪstan/; Pa|ki|sta|ni /pækɪstæni, pakɪstani/

**Pa|lau** /palau, pə-/; Pa|lau|an /palauən, pə-/

**Pan|a|ma** /pænəma, -mɔ/; Pan|a|ma|ni|an /pænəmeɪniən/

**Pap|ua New Guin|ea** /pæpyuə nu gɪni, papua/; Pa|p|ua New Guin|ean, Pap|uan /pæpyuə nu gɪniən, papua/, pæpyuən, papuən/

**Par|a|guay** /pærəgwaɪ, -gweɪ/; Par|a|guay|an /pærəgwaɪən, -gweɪən/

**Pe|ru** /pəru/; Pe|ru|vi|an /pəruviən/

**(the) Phil|ip|pines** /(ðə) fɪlɪpinz/; Phil|ip|pine, Fi|li|pi|no, Fi|li|pi|na /fɪlɪpin/, /fɪlɪpinou/, /fɪlɪpinə/

**Po|land** /pouland/; Po|lish, Pole /poulɪʃ/, /poul/

**Por|tu|gal** /pɔrchəgəl/; Por|tu|guese / pɔrchəgiz/

**Qa|tar** /kətar/; Qa|tari /kətari/

**Ro|ma|nia** /roumeɪniə/; Ro|ma|nian / roumeɪniən/

**Rus|sia** /rʌʃə/; Rus|sian /rʌʃən/

**Rwan|da** /ruandə/; Rwan|dan /ruandən/

**Saint Kitts–Ne|vis** /seɪnt kɪts nivɪs/; Kit|ti|tian, Ne|vis|ian /kɪtɪʃən/, /nɪvɪʒən/

**Saint Lu|cia** /seɪnt luʃə/; Saint Lu|cian /seɪnt luʃən/

**Saint Vin|cent and the Gren|a|dines** /seɪnt vɪnsənt ən ðə grenədinz/; Saint Vin|cen|tian, Vin|cen|tian /seɪnt vɪnsɛnʃən/, /vɪnsɛnʃən/

**Sa|moa** /səmouə/; Sa|mo|an /səmouən/

**San Ma|ri|no** /sæn mərinou/; Sam|ma|ri|nese, San Ma|ri|nese /sæmmærɪniz/, /sæn mærɪniz/

**São To|mé and Prin|ci|pe** /soun tɔmeɪ ən prɪnsɪpi/; Sao To|me|an /soun tɔmeɪən/

**Sau|di Ara|bia** /soudi əreɪbiə/; Sau|di Ara|bi|an /soudi əreɪbiən/

**Scot|land** /skɒtlənd/; Scot|tish, Scot(s) /skɒtɪʃ/, /skɒts/

**Sen|egal** /sɛnɪgɔl, -gal/; Sen|e|gal|ese /sɛnɪgəliz/

**Ser|bia and Mon|te|negro** /sɜrbiə ən mɒntɪnɛgrou/ Ser|bi|an, Serb, Mon|te|ne|grin /sɜrbiən/, /sɜrb/, /mɒntɪnɛgrɪn/

**(the) Sey|chelles** /(ðə) seɪʃɛlz/; Sey|chel|lois /seɪʃɛlwa/

**Sier|ra Le|one** /siɛrə lioun/; Sier|ra Le|on|ean /siɛrə liouniən/

**Sin|ga|pore** /sɪŋəpɔr, sɪŋgə-/; Sin|ga|por|ean /sɪŋəpɔriən, sɪŋgə-/

**Slo|va|kia** /slouvakiə, -vækiə/; Slo|vak, Slo|va|ki|an /slouvæk/, /slouvakiən, -væk-/

**Slo|ve|nia** /slouviniə/; Slo|vene /slouvin/; Slo|ve|nian /slouviniən/

**Sol|o|mon Is|lands** /sɒləmən aɪləndz/; Sol|o|mon Is|land|er /sɒləmən aɪləndər/

**So|ma|lia** /səmaliə, sou-/; So|ma|li, So|ma|lian /səmali, sou-/, /səmaliən, sou-/

**South Af|rica** /souθ æfrɪkə/; South Af|ri|can /souθ æfrɪkən/

**(the Re|pub|lic of) Spain** (ðə rɪpʌblɪk əv) speɪn/; Span|ish, Span|iard /spænɪʃ/, /spænyərd/

**Sri Lan|ka** /sri laŋkə, ʃri/; Sri Lan|kan /sri laŋkən, ʃri/

**Su|dan** /sudæn, -dan/; Su|da|nese /sudəniz/

**Su|ri|na|me** /suərɪnam/; Su|ri|na|mer, Su|ri|na|mese /suərɪnamər/, /suərɪnəmiz/

**Swa|zi|land** /swazilænd/; Swazi /swazi/

**Swe|den** /swidən/; Swe|dish, Swede /swidɪʃ/, /swid/

**Swit|zer|land** /swɪtsərlənd/; Swiss /swɪs/

**Syr|ia** /sɪəriə/; Syr|ian /sɪəriən/

**Tai|wan** /taɪwan/; Tai|wan|ese /taɪwaniz/

**Ta|jik|i|stan** /tadʒɪkɪstæn, -stan/; Ta|jik|i|stan|i, Ta|jik /tadʒɪkɪstæni, -stani/, /tadʒɪk, -dʒik/

**Tan|za|nia** /tænzəniə/; Tan|za|nian / tænzəniən/

**Thai|land** /taɪlænd, -lənd/; Thai /taɪ/

**To|go** /tougou/; To|go|lese /tougəliz/

**Ton|ga** /tɒŋgə/; Ton|gan /tɒŋgən/

**Trin|i|dad and To|ba|go** /trɪnɪdæd ən təbeɪgou/; Trin|i|da|di|an, To|ba|go|ni|an /trɪnɪdeɪdiən/, /toubəgouniən/

**Tu|ni|sia** /tuniʒə/; Tu|ni|sian /tuniʒən/

**Tur|key** /tɜrki/; Turk|ish, Turk /tɜrkɪʃ/, /tɜrk/

**Turk|men|i|stan** /tərkmɛnɪstæn, -stan/; Turk|men /tərkmɛn, -mən/

**Tu|va|lu** /tuvalu, tuvəlu/; Tu|va|luan /tuvəluən/

**Ugan|da** /yugændə, ugan-/; Ugan|dan /yugændən, ugan-/

**Ukraine** /yukreɪn/; Ukrai|ni|an /yukreɪniən/

**(the) Unit|ed Ar|ab Emir|ates** /(ðə) yunaɪtɪd ærəb ɛmərɪts, -əreɪts/; Emir|ati /ɛmərati/

**(the) Unit|ed King|dom of Great Brit|ain and North|ern Ire|land** /(ðə) yunaɪtɪd kɪŋdəm əv greɪt brɪtᵊn ən nɔrðərn aɪərlənd/; Brit|ish /brɪtɪʃ/

**(the) Unit|ed States of Amer|i|ca** /(ðə) yunaɪtɪd steɪts əv əmɛrɪkə/; Amer|i|can /əmɛrɪkən/

**Uru|guay** /yʊərəgweɪ, -gwaɪ/; Uru|guay|an /yʊərəgweɪən, -gwaɪən/

**Uz|bek|i|stan** /ʊzbɛkɪstæn, -stan, uz-/; Uz|bek|i|stani,

**Uz|bek** /ʊzbɛkɪstæni, -stani, uz-/, /ʊzbɛk, uz-/

**Va|nua|tu** /vænwatu/; Ni-Va|nua|tu /ni vænwatu/

**Vat|i|can City** /vætɪkən sɪti/

**Ven|e|zue|la** /vɛnɪzweɪlə/; Ven|e|zue|lan /vɛnɪzweɪlən/

**Vi|et|nam** /viɛtnam, vyɛt-/; Vi|et|nam|ese /viɛtnəmiz, vyɛt-/

**Wales** /weɪlz/; Welsh /wɛlʃ/

**Ye|men** /yɛmən/; Ye|meni, Ye|men|ite /yɛməni/, /yɛmənaɪt/

**Zam|bia** /zæmbiə/; Zam|bi|an /zæmbiən/

**Zim|ba|bwe** /zɪmbabweɪ, -wi/; Zim|ba|bwe|an /zɪmbabweɪən, -wiən/

# Credits

## Illustrations:

**Higgins Bond**: pp. 199, 329, 373, 402, 445, 500, 569, 704, 875, 1059, 1064; © Higgins Bond/ Anita Grien

**Richard Carbajal**: pp. 35, 176, 296, 367, 596, 635, 694, 887, 964, 1072; © Richard Carbajal/ illustrationOnLine.com

**Ron Carboni**: pp. 127, 152, 189, 285, 387, 600, 690, 878, 910 (top), 1012; © Ron Carboni/ Anita Grien

**Todd Daman**: pp. 23, 81; © Todd Daman/illustrationOnLine.com

**Dick Gage**: pp. 109, 136, 300 (top); © Dick Gage/illustrationOnLine.com

**Patrick Gnan**: pp. 32, 171, 316, 520, 630, 668 (right), 718 (bottom), 824, 1017; © Patrick Gnan/ illustrationOnLine.com

**Sharon and Joel Harris**: pp. 100, 101, 230, 258, 379 (top), 440, 647, 808 (fetus), 812, 895; © Sharon and Joel Harris/illustrationOnLine.com

**Philip Howe**: pp. 131, 168, 344, 638, 695, 848, 1096; © Philip Howe/illustrationOnLine.com

**Robert Kayganich**: pp. 72, 75, 91, 92, 110, 255, 300 (bottom), 307, 400, 412, 459, 539, 935, 966, 1110; © Robert Kayganich/illustrationOnLine.com

**Robert Kemp**: pp. 201, 214, 312, 425, 665; © Robert Kemp/illustrationOnLine.com

**Stephen Peringer**: pp. 170, 206, 253, 304, 378, 406, 387; © Stephen Peringer/ illustrationOnLine.com

**Alan Reingold**: pp. 221, 437; © Alan Reingold/Anita Grien

**Mark Ryan**: pp. 872 (top), 911, 1071; © Mark Ryan/illustrationOnLine.com

**Simon Shaw**: pp. 89, 97, 308, 560 (top), 712, 780; © Simon Shaw/illustrationOnLine.com

**Daniel M. Short**: pp. 317; © Daniel M. Short

**Gerard Taylor**: pp. 20, 79, 144, 349, 508, 915, 1080 (top and bottom); © Gerard Taylor/ illustrationOnLine.com

**Ralph Voltz**: pp. 46, 74, 350, 379 (bottom), 419, 470, 597, 603, 679, 907 (bottom), 994; © Ralph Voltz/illustrationOnLine.com

**Cam Wilson**: pp. 110 (top), 209, 270, 315, 375, 386, 428, 527, 541, 588, 710, 910 (bottom), 953; © Cam Wilson/illustrationOnLine.com

**Photos:**

**48:** (right) © Burstein Collection/CORBIS, (left) © Archivo Iconografico, S.A./CORBIS
**54:** © Louie Psihoyos/CORBIS
**114:** AM Corporation / Alamy
**133:** Craig Lovell / Eagle Visions Photography / Alamy
**135:** (left) Phil Talbot / Alamy
**138:** Robert E Barber / Alamy
**161:** (bottom) © William Manning/Corbis
**166:** © Jonathan Blair/CORBIS
**190:** Redferns Music Picture Library / Alamy;
**207:** Imageshop / Alamy
**218:** © Tim Wright/CORBIS
**225** (top): Blend Images / Alamy
**226:** (right) BananaStock / Alamy, (center) Kimball Hall / Alamy, (left) Digital Archive Japan / Alamy
**232:** © Bettmann/CORBIS
**234:** (top left) © Comstock/Corbis, (top middle) © Gail Mooney/CORBIS, (top right) © Robbie Jack/Corbis, (bottom left) © Mario Tama/Getty Images, (bottom middle) © Masterfile Royalty Free (RF), (bottom right) © Julie Lemberger/Corbis
**259:** Dinodia Images / Alamy
**261:** BananaStock / Alamy
**263:** Frances Roberts / Alamy
**266:** Dinodia Images / Alamy
**280:** Owe Andersson /Alamy
**298:** (bottom) David Butow/CORBIS SABA
**306:** David Turnley / Corbis
**322:** © Herbert Spichtinger/zefa/Corbis
**385:** © CORBIS
**345:** © CORBIS
**381:** Dennis MacDonald/ Alamy
**382:** Bill Marsh Royalty Free Photography / Alamy
**394:** (apple) © age fotostock / SuperStock, (orange segment) © Envision/Corbis, (pear, fig) © Getty Royalty Free, (pineapple, lemon, grapes, banana, kiwi, watermelon, orange) © PhotoObjects
**397:** nagelestock.com / Alamy
**413:** Janine Wiedel Photolibrary / Alamy
**424:** Medioimages / Alamy
**426:** David Noton Photography / Alamy
**436:** (far left) © Don Mason/Corbis, (left) © Bert Leidmann/zefa/Corbis, (right) © J. A. Kraulis/Masterfile, (far right) © Frans Lanting/Corbis
**454:** (top) James Cadwell / Alamy, (bottom) © Alexander Burkatovski/ CORBIS
**468:** BananaStock / Alamy
**469:** Jeff Greenberg / Alamy
**493:** (left) image100 / Alamy, (right top) Trevor Smithers ARPS / Alamy
**530:** © CORBIS
**537:** © Bettmann/CORBIS
**538:** MONSERRATE J. SCHWARTZ / Alamy;
**557:** Dynamic Graphics Group / IT Stock Free / Alamy
**576:** © Royalty-Free/Corbis
**583:** ImageState / Alamy
**624:** (right) Craig Lovell / Eagle Visions Photography / Alamy
**626:** © NASA/Roger Ressmeyer/CORBIS

**629**: numb / Alamy
**634**: BananaStock / Alamy
**643**: (right) Comstock Images / Alamy
**707**: Nikreates / Alamy
**715**: (top left) Food folio / Alamy
**715**: (bottom) © Bill Ross/CORBIS
**716**: (left) © Araldo de Luca/CORBIS, (center) © The Art Archive/Corbis
(right) © Bettmann/CORBIS
**718**: (top) Stockbyte Platinum / Alamy
**726**: Wildscape / Alamy
**735**: oote boe / Alamy
**744**: Westend61 / Alamy
**751**: © Betmann / CORBIS
**753**: © Bettmann/CORBIS
**777**: © Bohemian Nomad Picturemakers/CORBIS
**781**: AM Corporation / Alamy
**808**: (far left) © Matthias Kulka/zefa/Corbis, (left) © Yorgos Nikas/ Getty Images, (right) © Neil Harding/ Getty Images, (far right) © Thinkstock/Corbis
**819**: Food Features / Alamy
**872**: (bottom) ImageState / Alamy
**877**: Stock Connection Distribution / Alamy
**889**: © Mark Peterson/CORBIS
**898**: Blend Images / Alamy
**905**: © Freeman Patterson/ Masterfile
**946**: Jon Arnold Images / Alamy
**986**: STOCK IMAGE/PIXLAND / Alamy
**989**: © Kim Kulish/Corbis
**991**: Mark Hamilton / Alamy
**992**: (right) Rex Argent / Alamy, (left) Leslie Garland Picture Library / Alamy
**999**: North Wind Picture Archives / Alamy
**999**: © Susanna Raab/Sygma/Corbis
**1002**: © Masterfile Royalty Free (RF)
**1010**: © Richard T. Nowitz/CORBIS
**1024**: © HASHIMOTO NOBORU/CORBIS SYGMA
**1026**: © Bettmann/CORBIS
**1029**: (bottom) Comstock Images / Alamy
**1035**: Digital Archive Japan / Alamy
**1049**: © Robert Galbraith / Reuters / Corbis
**1063**: Alamy
**1073**: © Betmann / Corbis
**1076**: © Stapleton Collection/CORBIS
**1085**: Purestock / Alamy
**1089**: Stephen Frink Collection / Alamy
**1114**: John Sturrock / Alamy

Photos on the following pages are from JUPITER IMAGES. © 2006 Jupiterimages Corporation: 34, 76, 156, 225 (bottom), 233, 311, 366, 475, 544, 560 (bottom), 587, 598, 601, 608, 624 (left), 643 (left, center), 668 (left), 669, 693, 698, 715 (top right), 741, 842, 902, 907 (top), 909, 923, 987, 1023

Photos on the following pages are from IndexOpen. © 2006 IndexOpen: 44, 45, 135 (right), 145, 155, 188, 365, 601, 614, 1084, 1090